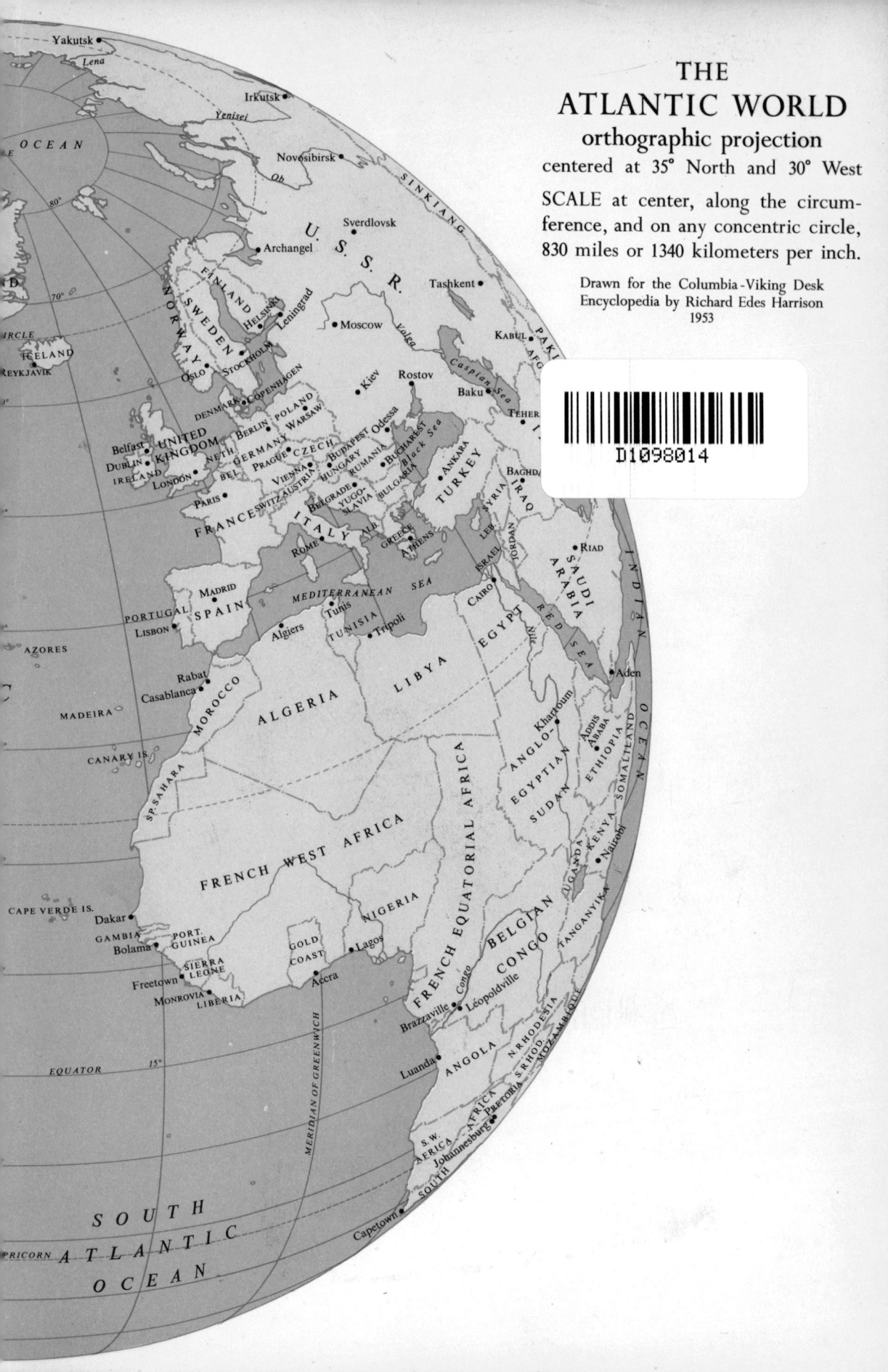

THE
ATLANTIC WORLD
orthographic projection
centered at 35° North and 30° West

SCALE at center, along the circumference, and on any concentric circle,
830 miles or 1340 kilometers per inch.

Drawn for the Columbia-Viking Desk
Encyclopedia by Richard Edes Harrison
1953

D1098014

PRONUNCIATION KEY

ā fate (fāt), fail (fāl),
   vacation (vākā'shùn)
â care (kâr), Mary (mâ'rē)
ă bat (băt), add (ăd),
   marry (mă'rē)
ä father (fä'dhùr),
   marble (mär'bul)
ã French tant (tã), Rouen
   (rōoã'), and similar
   sounds in some other
   languages
b back (băk), cab (kăb)
ch chap (chăp)
d dock (dŏk), cod (kŏd)
dh father (fä'dhùr), then
   (dhĕn). Compare with
   th.
ē even (ē'vùn), clearing
   (klēr'ĭng), obvious
   (ŏb'vēùs)
ĕ end (ĕnd), met (mĕt),
   merry (mĕ'rē)
ẽ French vin (vẽ), bien
   (byẽ), and similar
   sounds in some other
   languages
f fat (făt), Philip (fĭ'lĭp)
g get (gĕt), tag (tăg)
h hat (hăt). See also ch,
   dh, kh, sh, th, zh, and
   hw
hw where (hwâr), what
   (hwŏt)
ī fine (fīn), buyer (bī'ùr)
ĭ pin (pĭn), pit (pĭt), spirit
   (spĭ'rĭt), fated (fā'tĭd)
j jam (jăm), edge (ĕj),
   ginger (jĭn'jùr)
k cook (kŏok), tackle
   (tă'kùl)
kh loch (lŏkh), German
   Aachen (ä'khùn), Licht
   (lĭkht), and similar
   sounds in some other
   languages
l peal (pēl), pull (pŏol)
m hammer (hă'mùr)
n dinner (dĭ'nùr)
ng singing (sĭng'ĭng),
   finger (fĭng'gùr), sang
   (săng), sank (săngk)
ō hope (hōp), potato
   (pùtā'tō)
ô orbit (ôr'bĭt), fall (fôl)
ŏ hot (hŏt), toddy (tŏ'dē),
   borrow (bŏ'rō)
õ French dont (dō),
   chanson (shăsō'), and
   similar sounds in some
   other languages
oi boil (boil), royal (roi'ùl)
ŏŏ boot (bŏot), lose (lŏoz)
ŏŏ foot (fŏot), purely
   (pyŏŏr'lē), manipulate
   (mùnĭ'pyŏŏlāt)
ou scout (skout), crowd
   (kroud)

p pipe (pīp), happy
   (hă'pē)
r road (rōd), appeared
   (ùpērd'), carpenter
   (kär'pùntùr)
s saw (sô), case (kās)
sh shall (shăl), nation
   (nā'shùn)
t tight (tīt), rating
   (rā'tĭng)
th thin (thĭn), myth (mĭth).
   Compare with dh.
ū fume (fūm),
   euphemism (ū'fùmĭzm)
û curl (kûrl), Hamburg
   (hăm'bûrg), French
   œuvre (û'vrù), peu (pû),
   German schön (shûn),
   Goethe (gû'tù), and
   similar sounds in some
   other languages
ŭ butter (bŭ'tùr), suds
   (sŭdz), hurry (hŭ'rē)
ù affair (ùfâr'), sofa
   (sō'fù), contravene
   (kŏntrùvēn'), monopoly
   (mùnŏ'pùlē), suburban
   (sùbûr'bùn), callous
   (kă'lùs), rather (ră'dhùr)
ü French Cluny (klünē'),
   German Lübeck
   (lü'bĕk), and similar
   sounds in some other
   languages
ũ French Melun (mùlũ'),
   Chambrun (shăbrũ'),
   and similar sounds in
   some other languages
v vest (vĕst), trivial
   (trĭ'vēùl)
w wax (wăks)
y you (yŏo), bunion
   (bŭ'nyùn)
z zipper (zĭ'pùr), ease
   (ēz), treads (trĕdz)
zh pleasure (plĕ'zhùr),
   rouge (rŏozh)
' main accent, written
   after accented vowel or
   syllable: Nebraska
   (nùbrăs'kù), James
   Buchanan (jămz'
   bŭkă'nùn)
" secondary accent: Mis-
   sissippi (mĭ"sùsĭ'pē)
— dash, replacing obvious
   portion of pronuncia-
   tion: hegemony
   (hĭjĕ'mùnē, hē—,
   hĕ'jùmō"nē, hĕ'gù—)
- hyphen, to prevent
   ambiguity: Erlanger
   (ûr'lăng-ùr), dishearten
   dĭs-här'tùn)

NOTES

The purpose of the pronunciation symbols is to give at least one serviceable way in which the word in question may be pronounced when used by careful speakers of English.

In this work a pronunciation is ordinarily indicated for words printed in boldface when this pronunciation is not obvious to the English-speaking reader. Of two or more words or names in succession spelled and pronounced alike, a pronunciation is frequently indicated for the first occurrence only.

For names of localities in English-speaking areas the local pronunciation is preferred, provided it is acceptable to careful speakers.

For foreign words and names the speaker of English desires to use a pronunciation that will be acceptable to other speakers of English (unless he is speaking in a foreign language). In many cases (e.g., Paris) there is a traditional pronunciation that resembles little the current native pronunciation, and attempts to introduce into English conversation an approximation of the native form (something like pärē') are regarded as an affectation. It is customary with foreign names that have no conventional English form to pronounce them with English sounds approximating the foreign ones. Such an approximation is indicated in this work, whenever there is no established usage to follow.

Actual good foreign-language pronunciations can be acquired only through imitation and study. Nevertheless, Englishmen and Americans have for many years made a practice of imitating roughly five French sounds: ã, ẽ, õ, ũ, and ü. A speaker of English can attain ã by saying äng without the closure at the back of the mouth necessary to make ng, breathing through nose and mouth as well: ẽ is similarly like the beginning of äng, õ like that of ông, and ũ like that of ûng. To approximate ü say ŏo with vigor, then, keeping the lips rounded, change the sound quickly to ē.

For Latin words the venerable English tradition is followed [e.g., Caesar (sē'zùr)], except where some other pronunciation is well established, as in ecclesiastical names [e.g., Salve Regina (säl'vä räjē'nù)]. The so-called classical pronunciation, which approximates the pronunciation Caesar used [e.g., Caesar (kī'sär)], is not given, as being not usual in English conversation.

THE COLUMBIA-
VIKING DESK
ENCYCLOPEDIA

H. Ben Schmid
722 Harter Rd
Dallas 18

Tex R. M.

THE COLUMBIA-VIKING DESK ENCYCLOPEDIA

Compiled and edited at Columbia University

by the staff of The Columbia Encyclopedia

WILLIAM BRIDGWATER, Editor-in-chief

PUBLISHED BY THE VIKING PRESS

NEW YORK

PREFACE

The Columbia-Viking Desk Encyclopedia is a compact volume presenting ready-to-use information in brief and portable form. It is derived from *The Columbia Encyclopedia,* specifically from the second edition of that standard reference book, published in 1950. Every effort has been made to keep the spirit of *The Columbia Encyclopedia* through careful pruning of the articles and elimination of headings. The present work has some 31,000 entries covered in about a million and a quarter words.

Like the parent volume, this book is an encyclopedia and makes no attempt to be a dictionary. Entries that would supply no more than dictionary information are excluded. The limited space has been given to specific headings that seem most useful to the ordinary reader. Articles on general topics, such as American literature, which could be covered only inadequately, have been disregarded, while articles giving directly useful facts, such as those on important figures in American literature, have been scrupulously retained. The book is not what is called in English an encyclopedic dictionary. It is rather a parallel in English to the compact hand encyclopedias issued on the Continent. It is designed to give as much finger-tip knowledge as can be offered in brief scope.

This is an American encyclopedia, and therefore stress has been laid on places and persons in the United States, Canada, and Latin America. The European tradition in Western culture has not been ignored. There are thousands of articles on European places, persons, and history, but the accent is American. This desk encyclopedia belongs primarily to the New World.

In preparing this much reduced form of an encyclopedia, the writers have used as many abbreviations as seemed feasible for the convenience of the ordinary reader. Similarly, wherever the subject of a sentence is clear, that word has been omitted. These practices, however, have been limited to sentences where no ambiguity could occur. When full sentences are required for the ease of the reader, all the words appear. The seeming inconsistency has been adopted to save as much space as possible without cost to the reader's understanding. Shorter and more rapidly comprehensible articles are more abbreviated than the longer articles, which require longer concentration of the reader's attention.

In this book even more than in *The Columbia Encyclopedia* the cross references are of the utmost importance. To save space, the writers have avoided repeating the same information under different headings. The cross references within articles are indicated by the use of SMALL CAPITALS. These appear only when the reader will find under the other heading further information on the heading he is consulting. Learning to follow out such cross references will benefit the reader immeasurably.

This volume contains a number of illustrations and maps for the convenience of the reader. The maps on the end papers and in the text are not intended to replace an atlas but may, like the articles, give information rapidly to the busy reader. The illustrations also present knowledge in brief compass.

Since *The Columbia Encyclopedia* appeared in 1950 the world has seen many events, and many new faces have appeared. *The Columbia-Viking Desk Encyclopedia* has taken these happenings and persons into account so far as the allowance of space would permit.

Figures for populations, for areas of countries, and for altitudes of mountains have also been brought up to date according to the latest official data available from various parts of the world. The populations given for places in the United States are those listed in the 1950 census. Elsewhere the latest complete census figures or official estimates have been inserted.

The articles are written for English-speaking readers, and English forms have been used throughout. The pronunciations given are those that are current among educated Americans. Wherever a foreign spelling, differing from the English form, would seem of use to the reader, that spelling is given in italics after the ordinary form.

The articles are capsules of information, too small to contain extended discussion. Therefore it has seemed to the editors of this work of the utmost importance to examine every line with the intention of eliminating any possible bias. Where it has proved misleading to avoid controversy, extra space has been taken to offer brief statements of both sides of the disagreement.

The spirit that has breathed life into the making of this work has come ultimately from the late Clarke Fisher Ansley, who planned and edited the first edition of *The Columbia Encyclopedia.* More directly the makers of this volume are indebted to Elizabeth J. Sherwood, who was one of the two editors of the second edition and a shaper of the ideals that have guided the workers on *The Columbia-Viking Desk Encyclopedia.*

Though the publication of this book is an undertaking of The Viking Press, the work itself owes much to Columbia University. It would be impossible to list all those at the University who contributed to the creation of *The Columbia Encyclopedia* and to the abridged version.

The chief burden of creating this volume fell upon the assistant editors whose names appear in small capitals in the staff list. They gave generously of their own time and vigor to make this book as useful as possible.

The staff of The Viking Press, having undertaken the hardships of producing a reference book, have borne with fortitude and patience the mishaps and delays that seem inevitable in such projects. Thanks are particularly due to Harold K. Guinzburg for his constructive thinking about all aspects of the problem; to Milton B. Glick, who gave the project its first impetus at The Viking Press and was responsible for

design and production; and to Marshall A. Best, who undertook the task of reading all the copy and suggested many changes, always for the betterment of the book.

The book also owes much to Charles G. Proffitt, Director of Columbia University Press, and Henry H. Wiggins, Manager of the Publication Department.

WILLIAM BRIDGWATER
EDITOR-IN-CHIEF

April 20, 1953

EDITORIAL STAFF

WILLIAM BRIDGWATER, Editor-in-chief

ELIZABETH E. ADAMS		J. CHRISTOPHER HEROLD
BEATRICE ALDRICH		SONO ROSENBERG
GWENDOLYN JONES		MILDRED M. MALKIN

| William F. Bernhardt | Ida T. Hopper | Arthur J. Moore |
| James T. Burns, Jr. | Joan McQuary | Barbara Melissa Voorhis |

George L. Groman, Evelyn Merrin, Warren William Paul, Philip L. Perl, Walter L. Sherry, Jr.

CONTRIBUTORS

Philip M. Bergovoy	Marjorie P. Johnson	Hans R. Reinhardt
Nelda Cassuto	Annie Kessler	Henry B. Reuben
Rollin P. Dickerson	Matthew Lipman	Maureen Rosenhaupt
Lily Edelman	Helene K. Marer	David G. Rubin
Alida Fortier Gaewsky	Dorothée Nolan	Jean Rubin
Natalie Gurney	Henry Paolucci	Marie-Anne Phelps Seabury
V. J. Harward	Geraldine Pelles	Ann Smith
Glenn Hasselrooth	Esther I. Persson	Helen E. Stroop
Elva D. Hoover	Julius Rabin	Elizabeth K. Valkenier
George M. Johnson		Peter Welgos

ILLUSTRATIONS

All illustrations especially designed for this volume

Research Editor: NATALIE RAYMOND; Technical drawings by I. N. STEINBERG and Associates

Continental maps drawn by JACK LUBOFF (*New York Herald Tribune*)
Consultant: GERARD L. ALEXANDER (*Map Division, New York Public Library*)

World maps by RICHARD EDES HARRISON

The following were among the advisers and contributors

to *The Columbia Encyclopedia, Second Edition,* of which this book is a condensed version

EVELYN B. BOYCE	LEON E. SELTZER	RAYMOND J. DIXON
Adriaan J. Barnouw	William M. Mitchell	William B. S. Smith
Chung-Yuan Chang	Robert Molloy	Peter Stern
Elliott Van Kirk Dobbie	José Ferrater Mora	Emerson H. Swift
Mary K. Dobbie	H. C. Nixon	William York Tindall
Clarissa P. Farrar	Norma Pfeiffer	George L. Trager
James Gilbert	Bernard K. Sandwell	James G. Van Derpool
Talbot Hamlin	Carl T. Schmidt	Isabella Wakeham, M.D.
William Robert Irwin	Theodore Shabad	Ralph F. Weld
John Kepke		Henry H. Wiggins

MAPS, ILLUSTRATIONS, TABLES, LISTS

MAPS

As a rule the articles on places do not give cross references to maps; but countries, principal cities, large rivers, and many other geographic features may be located on the maps of their respective continents

WORLD MAPS

THE ATLANTIC WORLD   *Front end paper*   THE PACIFIC WORLD   *Back end paper*

CONTINENT MAPS

AFRICA	15	EUROPE	313
ASIA	57	NORTH AMERICA	703
AUSTRALIA	67	SOUTH AMERICA	933

ILLUSTRATIONS

Grouped under subject headings for convenient comparison of related material. A number of subjects have been included in the illustrations, though not in the text, when it was felt that a picture served the purpose better than words

AIRCRAFT   19
Diagram of atmospheric layers; diagrams of airplane, liquid-fuel rocket, helicopter, and turbojet engine.

ELEMENTS OF ARCHITECTURE   47
The five classic orders; types of arches; floor plans of basilica and cathedral; groined and ribbed vaulting; flying buttress.

DEVELOPMENT OF ARMOR   53
Greek, Roman, 12th century, 13th century, 14th century, 15th century, 16th century, and 17th-century pikeman.

BIRDS   105
Labeled drawing of a bird; some types of bills, feet, and nests.

TYPES OF BRIDGES   131
Footbridge, pontoon, Roman arch, steel arch, steel truss, cantilever, suspension, swing, bascule, and vertical-lift bridges.

WESTERN COSTUME   229
Greek, Roman, Medieval, early Renaissance, early Tudor, Elizabethan, Louis XIV, Louis XVI, Empire, time of George IV, early Victorian, and mid-Victorian.

ELECTRICITY AND ELECTRONICS   293
Electrical and radio symbols; diagrams of series and parallel wiring; diagrams of triode, transistor, photoelectric tube, and simple radio circuit.

ENGINE PRINCIPLES   303
Diagrams of reciprocating steam engine, water turbines and steam turbine, four-cycle internal-combustion engine, and Diesel engine.

FURNITURE STYLES: The Chair through the Ages   356
Egyptian; Greek; Etruscan; Roman; central European; 15th-century Italian; 15th- and 16th-century Spanish; 18th-century Chinese; English Tudor, Queen Anne, Hepplewhite, Adam, Chippendale, and Sheraton; French Louis XV, Louis XVI, Directoire, and Empire; American Pennsylvania, New England Windsor, Duncan Phyfe, Hitchcock, and modern.

HOUSE-BUILDING TERMS   447
Labeled skeleton diagram of house construction; diagram of stairs; types of joints, windows, and roofs.

INSECTS   469
External features of grasshopper and beetle; life cycles of mosquito and silkworm; examples of fifteen insect orders.

ANATOMY OF MAN   595
  Labeled skeleton; bones of the foot; diagrams of circulatory system and viscera; distribution of spinal nerves; cross-section diagrams of brain and eyeball.

SIMPLE MECHANICS   619
  The six basic machines (lever, pulley, wheel and axle, inclined plane, wedge, and screw), with illustrations of each principle.

MICROORGANIC LIFE   633
  Diagrams of animal and plant cells and of mitotic cell division; representative types of bacteria (round, spiral, and rod forms); simple animals (protozoa: amoeba and paramecium) and plants (algae and fungi); types of blood cells; malarial invasion of blood cell.

MUSICAL INSTRUMENTS   667
  Strings: Greek lyre, rebec, lute, guitar, violin, viola, and cello; *woodwinds:* flute, recorder, oboe, clarinet, bass clarinet, English horn, and bassoon; *brasses:* trumpet, hunting horn, trombone, French horn, and tuba.

NUCLEAR PHYSICS   773
  Diagrams of simple nuclei; spontaneous disintegration of radioactive elements; nuclear fission of uranium-235; diagram of cyclotron; diagram of proton-proton cycle taking place in the sun.

PLANT FORMS   783
  Labeled simple flower and composite flower; diagram of pollination; labeled bean seedling; types of leaves, roots, and fruits.

SAILING CRAFT   865
  Labeled full-rigged ship (clipper); types of fore-and-aft sails; Egyptian pleasure craft; Phoenician vessel; Norse ship; Spanish galleon; brig, brigantine, bark; labeled schooner; cutter, ketch, and sloop.

THE EARTH AND THE SOLAR SYSTEM   927
  Relative sizes and positions of planets; phases of the moon; diagram of solar and lunar eclipses; diagram showing the earth's revolution around the sun.

VEHICLES   1029
  Egyptian, Assyrian, Greek, and Cambodian chariots; Norse sledge; horse litter; chaise or shay; sedan chair; coach; barouche; spring victoria; brougham; surrey; full-top cabriolet; landau; hansom cab; gig; jinrikisha.

TABLES

The following data are arranged in tabular form

ELEMENTS	295	NATIONAL PARKS AND MONUMENTS	676
GEOLOGIC ERAS	370	NOBEL PRIZES	699
LANGUAGE: LINGUISTIC FAMILIES	535	WEIGHTS AND MEASURES	1055

LISTS

Some of the ready-reference material in the text is located as follows

ABBREVIATIONS	2	STAIN REMOVAL	943
FORMS OF ADDRESS	10	STATE FLOWERS	947
AREA COMPUTATION	48	TITLES OF SOVEREIGNTY, NOBILITY, AND HONOR	992
59 IMPORTANT BATTLES	85		
The PROVINCES OF CANADA	156	The 16 REPUBLICS OF THE USSR	1015
The COUNTIES OF ENGLAND	302	The MEMBER COUNTRIES OF THE UNITED NATIONS	1016
The RULERS OF ENGLAND	302		
FIRST-AID MEASURES	330	The 48 UNITED STATES	1017
The RULERS OF THE HOLY ROMAN EMPIRE	440	The PRESIDENTS OF THE UNITED STATES	1018
		VOLUME COMPUTATION	1042
The POPES OF THE ROMAN CATHOLIC CHURCH	740	SIGNS OF THE ZODIAC	1090

THE COLUMBIA-
VIKING DESK
ENCYCLOPEDIA

A

A, chemical symbol of element ARGON.

Aa (ä), name of many small streams of N Europe and Switzerland. The word is derived from an Indo-European root meaning "water."

Aachen (ä'khùn) or **Aix-la-Chapelle** (āks'-lä-shùpĕl'), city (pop. 129,967), North Rhine-Westphalia, W Germany, near Dutch and Belgian borders, in a brown-coal dist. Machinery, rubber, textile mfg. Hot mineral baths in use since Roman times. Charlemagne built splendid palace, and founded cathedral (rebuilt 10th cent.; partly Byzantine, partly Gothic), which contains his tomb. German kings were crowned at Aachen until 1531. Free imperial city until annexed by France (1801); awarded to Prussia 1814. Except for cathedral, most of historic buildings were devastated in World War II, when U.S. troops captured Aachen after bitter fighting (Oct. 21, 1944). For treaties signed here 1668 and 1748, see AIX-LA-CHAPELLE, TREATY OF.

Aakjaer, Jeppe (yĕp'ù ôk'yâr), 1866–1930, Danish poet, author of *Songs of the Rye* (1906) and *Heimdal's Wanderings* (1924). Also wrote novels.

Aaland Islands, Finland: see ALAND ISLANDS.

Aalborg, Dan. *Ålborg* or *Aalborg* (all: ôl'bôrg), city (pop. 79,806), Denmark, in N Jutland; a port on S shore of Lim Fjord.

Aalesund, Norway: see ALESUND.

Aalst, Belgium: see ALOST.

Aalto, Alvar (ôl'vär äl'tō), 1899–, Finnish architect and furniture designer. Pioneered in evolving functional plywood furniture.

Aanrud, Hans (häns' ôn'rōōd), 1863–, Norwegian writer of stories, plays, and books for children. Portrayed life in his home valley, Gudbrandsdal.

Aar (är), river, 183 mi. long, Switzerland, rising in Bernese Alps and flowing through L. Brienz and L. Thun, past Bern, Solothurn, and Aarau, into the Rhine.

Aarau (ä'rou), town (pop. 14,295), cap. of Aargau canton, N Switzerland, on the Aar. Mfg. shoes, scientific instruments.

aardvark (ärd'värk), nocturnal mammal, order Tubulidentata. Two species (genus *Orycteropus*), one in central, one in S Africa. Long snout, erect ears; naked or sparse hair on body; c.6 ft. long; long tail. Also called ant bear and earth pig.

Aargau (är'gou), canton (542 sq. mi.; pop. 300,442), N Switzerland; cap. Aarau. Traversed by fertile Aar valley. Swiss possession since 1415; canton since 1803. Pop. is Protestant, German-speaking.

Aarhus, Dan. *Århus* or *Aarhus* (all: ôr'hōos), city (pop. 116,167), Denmark, in E Jutland, on Aarhus Bay, which opens on the Kattegat. Second largest Danish city; commercial and industrial center. An episcopal see since 13th cent., it has a medieval cathedral and many fine Renaissance houses.

Aaron (â'rùn), in Bible, first high priest, brother of Moses and his spokesman in Egypt. Descendants were high priests and priests. Jehovah performed miracles through him (e.g., blossoming of Aaron's rod). Aaron made the golden calf and led worship of it. Ex. 4.14–16; 6.20; 7.1–12; 28–32; Num. 12; 17; 18; 20; 33.38, 39; Deut. 10.6.

Aasen, Ivar Andreas (ē'vär ändrā'äs ô'sùn), 1813–96, Norwegian lexicographer. By standardizing the dialects of his people he created a speech (i.e., Landsmaal) which became the national language.

abacus, in mathematics, simple calculating device. One type is frame with movable counters on parallel rods or in grooves.

Abadan (äbädän'), city (pop. 39,739), E Iran, on Abadan isl., in delta of the Shatt-el-Arab at head of Persian Gulf. Site of huge oil refinery.

Abaddon (ùbăd'ùn) [Heb.,= destruction], Hebrew name of the destroying angel. See SATAN.

abalone (ăbùlō'nē), popular name in America of univalve mollusk, genus *Haliotis,* also called ear shell or sea ear. Common food on California coast.

Abana (ùbā'nù), river of Damascus. 2 Kings 5.12. It is probably the Barada, flowing near Damascus.

abandonment, in law, absolute relinquishment of property rights, accomplished in such a manner that another person may acquire them in an original (not derived) form. See also DESERTION.

Abano, Pietro d' (pyā'trō dä'bänō), 1250?–1316?, Italian physician and philosopher, chief founder of Paduan school of medical learning.

Abarbanel, Isaac: see ABRAVANEL, ISAAC.

A battery: see BATTERY, ELECTRIC.

Abbadides (ă'bùdīdz), Arabian dynasty in Spain; ruled emirate of SEVILLE 1023–91. Succeeding the caliphs of Córdoba as chief Moorish power in Spain, they were replaced in turn by the ALMORAVIDES.

Abbas (ă'bùs, äbäs'), d. 652, uncle of Mohammed; ancestor of Abbasid caliphs.

Abbas I (Abbas the Great), 1557–1628, shah of Persia (1587–1628), of Safavid dynasty. Took large area from the Turks 1603–23; estab. order.

Abbas II (Abbas Hilmi), 1874–1944, khedive of Egypt (1892–1914), deposed by the British.

Abbasid (ùbā'sĭd, ă'bùsĭd) or **Abbaside** (–sīd, –sĭd), Arabic family, descended from Abbas (uncle of Mohammed), which held caliphate 749–1258. First caliph was ABU-L-ABBAS AS-SAFFAH; second was MANSUR. Early years of Abbasid rule were brilliant, especially under HARUN-AL-RASHID and MAMUN. Rival caliphs (see CALIPHATE) helped to weaken power of the Abbasid, who were finally overthrown 1258 by Hulagu Khan (grandson of Jenghiz Khan).

Abbe, Cleveland (ăb'ē), 1838–1916, American meteorologist. As Cincinnati Observatory director, he inaugurated daily weather forecasting based on telegraph reports. Influenced establishment of, and served in, government weather service.

Abbe, Ernst (ĕrnst ä'bù), 1840–1905, German physicist; owner of Zeiss optical works. Invented Abbe refractometer.

Abbeville (äbvēl'), city (pop. 16,098), Somme dept., N France, on Somme R. Textile mfg., especially linen. Here Louis IX made advantageous treaty with Henry III of England (1259). Gothic Church of St. Wolfram damaged in World War II.

Abbeville (ăb'ēvĭl). **1** Town (pop. 9,338), S La., N of Vermilion Bay of Gulf of Mexico, in a rice-growing area. Grew around Roman Catholic chapel (1845). **2** City (pop. 5,395), NW S.C., near Savannah R. WNW of Columbia. Mfg. of textiles.

Abbey, Edwin Austin, 1852–1911, American artist, noted for book illustrations. Official painter of coronation of Edward VII.

abbey, autonomous monastic community, especially among Benedictine, Cistercian, Carthusian, and Clu-

SMALL CAPITALS = cross references. Pronunciation key on inside end pages. Abbreviations: p. 2.

1

niac orders. Generally a courtyard (ecclesiastical atrium) is surrounded by cloister; buildings center about church, and all are enclosed by a wall. In Benedictine expansion after 8th cent., abbeys were centers of peaceful arts in chaotic Europe.

Abbey Theatre, Irish theatrical group. Experiments with an Irish theater resulted in forming (1902) of Irish Natl. Theatre Society, whose playwright-directors included Yeats, A.E., Lady Gregory, Synge. The Abbey Theatre (donated for free use by Miss A. E. F. Horniman 1904) was purchased 1910. Building burned down 1951. First to present plays of such writers as Sean O'Casey and Paul Vincent Carroll.

Abbot, Charles Greeley, 1872–, American astrophysicist, authority on solar radiation. Associated with Smithsonian Institution from 1896.

Abbotsford, estate (1811–32) of Sir Walter Scott, Roxburghshire, Scotland. Contains relics of Scott.

Abbott, Grace, 1878–1939, American social worker, director of Child Labor Division of U.S. Children's Bureau. Her sister, **Edith Abbott,** 1876–, became (1924)

dean of School of Social Service Administration, Univ. of Chicago.

Abbott, Jacob, 1803–79, American writer of over 180 books, including the *Rollo* series for boys. His son was **Lyman Abbott,** 1835–1922, American clergyman. Edited *Christian Union* (later *Outlook*) with Henry Ward Beecher. Succeeded him at Plymouth Church, Brooklyn, 1888; resigned 1899 for editorial duties. Leader in "social gospel" movement.

abbreviation, in writing, arbitrary shortening of a word, usually by cutting off letters from the end, e.g., U.S.A., Geo. (George). Contraction serves the same purpose but is understood strictly to be the shortening of a word by cutting out letters in the middle, the omission sometimes being indicated by an apostrophe. Many writers hold that a contraction (in which last letter of the word appears) should not be followed by a point, though an abbreviation should. Usage, however, differs widely. A period is never used when apostrophes appear. A select list of widely used abbreviations, including all used in this volume, follows:

LIST OF ABBREVIATIONS

a = are [100 sq. meters]
a.= acre, acres
AAA = Agricultural Adjustment Administration
A.A.A.= American Automobile Association
A.B.= Able-bodied Seaman; *Artium Baccalaureus* [Bachelor of Arts]
abbr. (*or* abbrev.) = abbreviation
Abp.= Archbishop
abr.= abridged
AC = alternating current
Acad.= Academy
acct.= account
A.D.= *anno Domini* [in the year of the Lord] (often small capitals)
ad fin.= *ad finem* [to the end, at the end]
adj.= adjective
Adjt.= Adjutant
ad lib.= *ad libitum* [at pleasure]
Adm.= Admiral, Admiralty
adv.= adverb
ad val. (*or* adv.)= *ad valorem* [on the value]
advt. (*or* adv.)= advertisement
AEC = Atomic Energy Commission
A.E.F.= American Expeditionary Force
aet. (*or* aetat.)= *aetatis* [of age]
A.F. of L. (*or* A.F.L.)= American Federation of Labor
Afr.= Africa
agr.= agriculture, agricultural
agt.= agent
A.H.= *anno Hegirae* [in the year of the Hegira] (often small capitals)
A.I.A.= American Institute of Architects
A.L.A.=American Library Association
Ala.= Alabama
alt.= altitude
Alta.= Alberta
A.M.= *ante meridiem* [before noon] (often small capitals); *anno mundi* [in the year of

the world] (often small capitals); *Artium Magister* [Master of Arts]
A.M.A.= American Medical Association
A.M.D.G.= *ad majorem Dei gloriam* [to the greater glory of God]
Amer. (*or* Am.) = America, American
amp.= ampere, amperes
amt.= amount
anc.= ancient
ann.= annual, annals
anon.= anonymous
AP = Associated Press
A.P.A.= American Protective Association
app.= appendix, appointed
apt.= apartment
Ariz.= Arizona
Ark.= Arkansas
art.= article
A.S. (*or* AS) = Anglo-Saxon
ASCAP = American Society of Composers, Authors, and Publishers
assn.= association
ASSR=Autonomous Soviet Socialist Republic
asst.= assistant
atty.= attorney
at. wt.= atomic weight
A.U.C.=*ab urbe condita* [from the founding of the city] or *anno urbis canditae* [in the year of the founding of the city] (often small capitals)
Aug.= August
AUS = Army of the United States
AV = Authorized Version
Av. (*or* Ave.)=Avenue
av.= average, avoirdupois
AVC= American Veterans Committee
avdp. (*or* av.)= avoirdupois
Ave. (*or* Av.)=Avenue
AWOL = absent without leave
b.= born, born in
B.A.= Bachelor of Arts
bal.= balance
Bapt.= Baptist

B.Arch.= Bachelor of Architecture
Bart.= Baronet
B.B.C.= British Broadcasting Corporation
bbl.= barrel
B.C.=before Christ (often small capitals); British Columbia
B.D.= Bachelor of Divinity
bd.= board
bf = boldface
Bl.= Blessed
Bldg.= Building
B.Lit.= Bachelor of Literature
Blvd.= Boulevard
B.Mus.= Bachelor of Music
bor.= borough
Bp.= Bishop
B.P.O.E.= Benevolent Protective Order of Elks
Br. (*or* Brit.)=British
Brig. Gen.= Brigadier General
Brit. (*or* Br.)=British
bro.= brother
B.S.= Bachelor of Science
B.Sc.= Bachelor of Science
B.T.U.= British thermal unit
bu.= bushel, bushels
bul.= bulletin
Bulg.= Bulgarian
bur.= bureau
B.V.M.= Blessed Virgin Mary
C.= centigrade, Caius
c.= copyright
c. (*or* ca.) = *circa* [about]
ca = centare
cal.= calorie
Calif.= California
Can.= Canadian
can.= canon, canto
Cant.= Canticles (Song of Solomon)
Cantab.= *Cantabrigiensis* [of Cambridge]
cap.= capital, capital letter, *capitulum* [chapter]
Capt.= Captain
car. (*or* k.)=carat
CARE=Cooperative for American Remittances to Everywhere, Inc.
Cath.= Catholic
C.B.= Companion of the Order of the Bath

C.C.= Chamber of Commerce
c.c. (*or* cc.)=cubic centimeter
CCC = Civilian Conservation Corps, Commodity Credit Corporation
C.E.= Civil Engineer
cen.= central
cent.= century, centuries
cf.= *confer* [compare]
cgs = centimeter-gram-second
chap.= chapter
Chem.E.= Chemical Engineer
Chron.= Chronicles
Cia = *Compañia* [Company]
C.I.D.= Criminal Investigation Department
Cie=*Compagnie* [Company]
CINC=Commander in Chief
C.I.O.= Congress of Industrial Organizations
C.J.= Chief Justice
cm = centimeter, centimeters
Cn.= Cneius
Co.= Company
co.= county
C.O.D.= cash (also collect) on delivery
coed.= coeducational
Col.= College, Colonel, Colossians
col.= collector, column
Coll.= Collection
Colo.= Colorado
Comdr.= Commander
comp.= compiled, compiler
Cong.= Congregational, Congressional
conj.= conjunction
Conn.= Connecticut
cont.= continued
Cor.= Corinthians
cor.= corrected
Corp.= Corporal
corp.= corporation
CP = Communist party
c.p.= candle power
C.P.A.= Certified Public Accountant
CPO = Chief Petty Officer
Cr.= credit, creditor
C.S.= Christian Science
C.S.A.= Confederate States of America
cu.= cubic

SMALL CAPITALS = cross references. Pronunciation key on inside end pages. Abbreviations: **p. 2.**

CVA = Columbia Valley Authority

cwt.= hundredweight

C.Z.= Canal Zone

D.= Don or Doña (Span. address), Dom or Dona (Port. address); Decimus

d.= daughter; *denarius* [penny], *denarii* [pence]; died, died in

Dan.= Daniel, Danish

D.A.R.= Daughters of the American Revolution

DC = direct current

D.C.= District of Columbia

D.C.L.= Doctor of Civil Law

D.D.= Doctor of Divinity

D.D.S.= Doctor of Dental Surgery

DDT = Dichlorodiphenyltrichloroethane

Dec.= December

deg.= degree, degrees

Del.= Delaware

Dem.= Democrat, Democratic

dept.= department

Deut.= Deuteronomy

diam.= diameter

dict.= dictionary

dist.= district

div.= division

DM = Deutschemark

do.= ditto [the same]

doz.= dozen, dozens

DP = displaced person

Dr.= debtor, Doctor

dr.= dram, drams

D.S.C.= Distinguished Service Cross

D.Sc.= Doctor of Science

D.S.M.= Distinguished Service Medal

D.S.O.=Companion of the Distinguished Service Order

Du.= Dutch

D.V.= *Deo volente* [God willing]

dwt.= pennyweight

E = east

ECA = Economic Cooperation Administration

Eccles.= Ecclesiastes

Ecclus.= Ecclesiasticus

ed.= edited, edition, editor, educated

E.E.= Electrical Engineer

e.g.= *exempli gratia* [for example]

E.M.= Engineer of Mines

emf = electromotive force

ency. (*or* encyc.) = encyclopedia

ENE = east-northeast

Eng.= English

engr.= engraved

enl.= enlarged

Eph.= Ephesians

Epis. (*or* Episc.) = Episcopal

ERP = European Recovery Program

ESE = east-southeast

esp.= especially

Esq.= Esquire

est.= estimated

estab.= establish, established

et al.= *et alibi* [and elsewhere]; *et alii* [and others]

etc.= *et cetera* [and others, and so forth]

et seq.= *et sequens* [and the following]

et sqq.= *et sequentes, et sequentia* [and those following]

Eur.= Europe

Ex.= Exodus

ex.= example, except

Ezek.= Ezekiel

F.= Fahrenheit, Fellow

F. (*or* Fri.) = Friday

f.= and the following page

f. (*or* fem.) = feminine

fac.= facsimile

F.A.G.S.= Fellow of the American Geographical Society

F. and A.M.= Free and Accepted Masons

FAO = Food and Agriculture Organization of the United Nations

FBI = Federal Bureau of Investigation

FCC = Federal Communications Commission

Feb.= February

fed.= federated, federation

fem. (*or* f.)=feminine

FEPC=Fair Employment Practices Committee

ff.= and the following pages

fig.= figure

fl.= *floruit* [flourished]

Fla.= Florida

fl. oz.= fluid ounce

fo.= folio

f.o.b.= free on board

Fr.= French, Father, Friar

fr.= franc

F.R.A.S.= Fellow of the Royal Astronomical Society

F.R.C.P.= Fellow of the Royal College of Physicians

F.R.C.S.= Fellow of the Royal College of Surgeons

F.R.G.S.= Fellow of the Royal Geographical Society

Fri. (*or* F.) = Friday

front.= frontispiece

F.R.S.= Fellow of the Royal Society

FSA = Federal Security Agency

ft.= foot, feet, fort

FTC = Federal Trade Commission

g = gram, grams

Ga.= Georgia

Gal.= Galatians

gal.= galley, gallon, gallons

Gall.= Gallery

G.A.R.= Grand Army of the Republic

G.C.= Knight Grand Cross; Knight Grand Commander (of various British orders, when followed by abbreviation designating the order)

G.C.B.= Knight Grand Cross of the Order of the Bath

Gen.= General, Genesis

Ger.= German

GHQ = General Headquarters

G.I.= general issue (term for common soldier); gastro-intestinal

gloss.= glossary

G.O.P.=Grand Old Party (Republican Party)

Gov.= Governor

govt.= government

Gr.= Greek

gr.= grain, grains

grad.= graduate, graduated, graduated at

ha = hectare

Hab.= Habakkuk

Hag.= Haggai

Heb.= Hebrew, Hebrews (NT)

hhd.= hogshead

H.M.S.= His (Her) Majesty's Ship; His (Her) Majesty's Service

Hon.= the Honorable

hp = horsepower

hq.= headquarters

H.R.= House of Representatives

hr.= hour, hours

H.R.H.= His (Her) Royal Highness

ht.= height

Hung.= Hungarian

ib. (*or* ibid.) = *ibidem* [in the same place]

ICAO = International Civil Aviation Organization

ICC=Interstate Commerce Commission

I.E. (*or* I-E *or* IE) = Indo-European

i.e.= *id est* [that is]

IHS = *Iesus Hominum Salvator* [Jesus, the Savior of Men]; *in hoc signo* [in this sign] (originally three letters of the Greek for Jesus)

Ill.= Illinois

ill. (*or* illus.) = illustrated, illustration

ILO = International Labor Organization

in.= inch, inches

inc.= incorporated

incl.= including, inclusive

incog.= incognito [unknown, unrecognized]

Ind.= Indiana

ind.= index

inf.= infinitive, *infra* [below]

I.N.R.I.= *Iesus Nazarenus, Rex Iudaeorum* [Jesus of Nazareth, King of the Jews]

Inst.= Institute, Institution

inst.= instant [the present month]

int.= interest

internatl.= international

introd.= introduction

I.O.F.= Independent Order of Foresters

I.O.O.F.= Independent Order of Odd Fellows

I O U = I owe you

I.Q. (*or* IQ) = intelligence quotient

Ir.= Irish

IRO = International Refugee Organization

Isa.= Isaiah

isl.= island

Ital. (*or* It.) = Italian

ital = italic type

ITO = International Trade Organization

I.W.W.=Industrial Workers of the World

JAG = Judge Advocate General

Jap.= Japanese

Jan.= January

J.D.= *Juris Doctor* [Doctor of Laws]

Jer.= Jeremiah

jg = junior grade (in U.S. Navy)

jour.= journal

J.P.= Justice of the Peace

Jr.= Junior

J.U.D.= *Juris Utriusque Doctor* [Doctor of Both Civil and Canon Laws]

k. (*or* car.) = carat

K.C.= King's Counsel; Knight Commander (of various British orders, when followed by abbreviation designating the order)

K.C. (*or* K. of C.)=Knights of Columbus

kc = kilocycle, kilocycles

K.G.= Knight of the Order of the Garter

kg = kilogram, kilograms

K.K.K.= Ku Klux Klan

kl = kiloliter, kiloliters

km=kilometer, kilometers

K. of C. (*or* K.C.)=Knights of Columbus

K.P.= Knights of Pythias

K.T.= Knight Templar

Kt.= Knight

kw = kilowatt, kilowatts

kwh = kilowatt hour, kilowatt hours

Ky.= Kentucky

L.= Lake; Left (in stage directions); Lucius

£ = *libra* [pound]

l = liter, liters

l.= line

La.= Louisiana

Lab.= Labrador

Lam.= Lamentations

Lat.= Latin

lat.= latitude

lb.= *libra* [pound], *librae* [pounds]

l.c.= lower case [not capitalized]

Lev.= Leviticus

L.H.D.= *Litterarum Humaniorum Doctor* [Doctor of Humane Letters]

L.I.= Long Island

Lieut.= Lieutenant

Litt.B.= *Litterarum Baccalaureus* [Bachelor of Literature]

Litt.D.= *Litterarum Doctor* [Doctor of Literature]

ll.= lines

LL.B.= *Legum Baccalaureus* [Bachelor of Laws]

LL.D.= *Legum Doctor* [Doctor of Laws]

loc. cit.= *loco citato* [in the place cited]

log.= logarithm

long.= longitude

Lt.= Lieutenant

Ltd.= Limited

Luth.= Lutheran

M.= mark [German coin]; *meridies* [noon] (often small capitals); Monsieur [Mr., Sir]; Marcus

m = meter, meters

m.= married

m. (*or* masc.) = masculine

M.A.= Master of Arts

Mac.= Maccabees

Maj.= Major

Mal.= Malachi

Man.= Manitoba

masc. (*or* m.) = masculine

Mass.= Massachusetts

Mat.= Matthew

max.= maximum

M.D.=*Medicinae Doctor* [Doctor of Medicine]

Md.= Maryland

mdse.= merchandise

M.E.= Mechanical Engineer, Methodist Episcopal

M.E. (*or* ME *or* Mid. Eng.)= Middle English

memo.= memorandum

Messrs.= Messieurs [Gentlemen] (plural of Mr.)

Met. E.= Metallurgical Engineer

Meth.= Methodist

Mex.= Mexican

mfg.= manufacturing

M.F.H.= Master of Foxhounds

mg = milligram, milligrams

Mgr = Monsignor

mgr.= manager

M.H.G. (*or* MHG) = Middle High German

mi.= mile, miles

Mich.= Michigan

Mid. Eng. (*or* M.E. *or* ME)= Middle English

min.=minimum, minute, minutes

Minn.= Minnesota

misc.= miscellaneous

Miss.= Mississippi

ml = milliliter, milliliters

Mlle = Mademoiselle [Miss]

MM.= Messieurs [Gentlemen] (plural of M.)

mm = millimeter, millimeters

Mme = Madame

Mo.= Missouri

mo.= month

Mon.= Monday

Mont.= Montana

M.P.= Member of Parliament

mph = miles per hour

Mr.= Mister (always abbreviated)

Mrs.= Mistress (always abbreviated)

MS = manuscript

M.S. (*or* M.Sc.) = Master of Science

Msgr = Monsignor

MSS = manuscripts

mt.= mount, mountain

mus.= museum, music

Mus.B.= *Musicae Baccalaureus* [Bachelor of Music]

Mus.D.=*Musicae Doctor* [Doctor of Music]

MVA = Missouri Valley Authority

N = north

n.= *natus* [born], neuter, noun

n. (*or* nom.)=nominative

N.A.=National Academy, North America

N.A.M.= National Association of Manufacturers

natl.= national

NATO=North Atlantic Treaty Organization

N.B.= New Brunswick; *nota bene* [note well]

N.C.= North Carolina

NCO = Noncommissioned Officer

n.d.= no date

N.Dak.= North Dakota

NE = northeast

N.E.A. National Educational Association

Nebr.= Nebraska

Neh.= Nehemiah

neut. (*or* n.)=neuter

Nev.= Nevada

N.F.= Newfoundland

N.H.= New Hampshire

N.J.= New Jersey

NLRB = National Labor Relations Board

N.Mex.= New Mexico

NNE = north-northeast

NNW = north-northwest

No., no.= *numero* [number]

Nor.= Norwegian

Nov.= November

N.P.= Notary Public

NRA = National Recovery Administration

NROTC = Naval Reserve Officers' Training Corps

N.S.= New Style, Nova Scotia

NT = New Testament

Num.= Numbers

NW = northwest

N.Y.= New York

NYA = National Youth Administration

ob.= *obiit* [died]

Obad.= Obadiah

obs.= obsolete

Oct.= October

O.E. (*or* OE)= Old English

O.F.M.= *Ordo Fratrum Minorum* [Order of Friars Minor] (Franciscan)

O.Fr (*or* O.F. *or* OF)= Old French

O.H.G. (*or* OHG)= Old High German

O.Ir.= Old Irish

O.K. (*or* OK) = correct

Okla.= Oklahoma

O.M.= Order of Merit

O.N. (*or* ON) = Old Norse

Ont.= Ontario

O.P.=Order of Preachers (Dominicans)

op.= *opus* [work]

OPA = Office of Price Administration

op. cit.= *opere citato* [in the work cited]

opp.= opposite

O.S.= Old Style

O.S.B.= *Ordo Sancti Benedicti* [Order of St. Benedict] (Benedictines)

OSS = Office of Strategic Services

OT = Old Testament

Oxon.= *Oxoniensis* [of Oxford]

oz.= ounce, ounces

P.= Publius

p.= page

Pa.= Pennsylvania

Pat. Off.= Patent Office

p.c.= per cent

pd.= paid

Pd. D.= *Pedagogiae Doctor* [Doctor of Pedagogy]

P.E.= Protestant Episcopal

P.E.I.= Prince Edward Island

PFC (*or* Pfc) = Private First Class

Pg. (*or* Port.) = Portuguese

Ph.B.= *Philosophiae Baccalaureus* [Bachelor of Philosophy]

Ph.D.= *Philosophiae Doctor* [Doctor of Philosophy]

Philip.= Philippians

P.I.= Philippine Islands

pinx.= *pinxit* [he painted]

pk.= peck

pl.= plate

pl. (*or* plur.) = plural

plur. (*or* pl.) = plural

P.M.= Postmaster; *post meridiem* [afternoon] (often small capitals)

PO = Petty Officer

P.O.= post office

Pol.= Polish

pop.= population

Port. (*or* Pg.) = Portuguese

POW = prisoner of war

pp.= pages

P.R.= Puerto Rico

pref.= preface

prep.= preparatory, preposition

Pres.= President

Presb.= Presbyterian

pron.= pronoun, pronounced

Prot.= Protestant

pro tem.= *pro tempore* [temporarily]

Prov.= Proverbs

prov.= province

prox.= *proximo* [of the next month]

P.S.= *post scriptum* [postscript]

Ps.= Psalm

pseud.= pseudonym

Pss.= Psalms

pt.= part, pint, pints, point

pub.= published, publisher

Pvt.= Private

PWA = Public Works Administration

Q.= Quintus

Q.C.= Queen's Counsel

Q.E.D.=*quod erat demonstrandum* [which was to be demonstrated]

Q.E.F.= *quod erat faciendum* [which was to be done]

QM = Quartermaster

qq.v.= *quae vide* [which see] (plural)

qt.= quart, quarts

Que.= Quebec

q.v.= *quod vide* [which see]

R.= River; Réaumur; *Rex*

[King]; *Regina* [Queen]; Right (stage direction)

R.A.= Royal Academician

RAF = Royal Air Force

R.C.=Red Cross, Roman Catholic

Rd.= Road

REA = Rural Electrification Administration

recd.= received

rect. (*or* rept.) = receipt

reestab.= reestablish, reestablished

Regt.= Regiment

Rep.= Republican, Representative

rept.= report

rept. (*or* rect.) = receipt

Ret.= Retired

Rev.= Revelations, the Reverend

rev.= revised

RFC = Reconstruction Finance Corporation

R.F.D.= rural free delivery

R.I.= Rhode Island

R.I.P.=*requiescat in pace* [may he rest in peace]

RM.= Reichsmark

R.N.= Registered Nurse, Royal Navy

Rom.= Romans

rom = roman type

ROTC = Reserve Officers' Training Corps

rpm.= revolutions per minute

RR = railroad

RSFSR=Russian Socialist Federated Soviet Republic

R.S.V.P.= *Répondez, s'il vous plaît* [An answer is requested]

Rt. Rev.= the Right Reverend

Rus.= Russian

RV = Revised Version

Ry.= railway

S = south

S.= *San, Santa, Santo,* or *São* [Saint]

S. (*or* Sun.)=Sunday

s.= *solidus* [shilling], *solidi* [shillings]

S.A.= Salvation Army; South America; *Sociedad Anónima, Société Anonyme* [Limited]

Sam.= Samuel

S.A.R.= Sons of the American Revolution

Sask.= Saskatchewan

Sat.= Saturday

S.C.= South Carolina

s.c.= small capitals

sc.= *scilicet* [namely]

Sc.D.= *Scientiae Doctor* [Doctor of Science]

S.Dak.= South Dakota

SE = southeast

SEC = Securities and Exchange Commission

sec.= second, seconds, section, sections

secy.= secretary

Sen.= Senator

Sept.= September

ser.= series

Sex.= Sextus

Sgt.= Sergeant

SHAEF = Supreme Headquarters, Allied Expeditionary Force

SHAPE=Supreme Headquarters, Allied Powers in Europe

sing.= singular

S.J.= *Societas Jesu* [Society of Jesus]

Skt.= Sanskrit

Soc.= society

SOS = distress signal (not a true abbreviation)

Span. (*or* Sp.) = Spanish

S.P.C.A.= Society for the Prevention of Cruelty to Animals

S.P.C.C.= Society for the Prevention of Cruelty to Children

sp. gr.= specific gravity

S.P.Q.R.= *Senatus Populusque Romanus* [the Senate and People of Rome]

sq.= *sequens* [the following]; square

sqq.= *sequentes, sequentia* [those following]

Sr.= Senior

SS.= Saints

S.S.=Steamship, Sunday School

SSE = south-southeast

SSR = Soviet Socialist Republic

SSW = south-southwest

St.= Saint, Street

S.T.D.= *Sacrae Theologiae Doctor* [Doctor of Sacred Theology]

Ste = *Sainte* [Saint, feminine]

Sun. (*or* S.) = Sunday

sup.= supplement, *supra* [above]

Supt.= Superintendent

s.v.= *sub verbo* (under the entry)

SW = southwest

Swed. (*or* Sw.) = Swedish

T.= Titus

Tenn.= Tennessee

T.H.= Territory of Hawaii

Th. (*or* Thurs.) = Thursday

Thess.= Thessalonians

Thurs. (*or* Th.) = Thursday

Ti.= Tiberius

Tim.= Timothy

TNEC = Temporary National Economic Committee

T.N.T. (*or* TNT)=trinitrotoluene, trinitrotoluol

tp.= township

t.p. (*or* t.-p.) = title page

tr.=transitive, translated, translation, translator, transpose

treas.= treasurer

Tu. (*or* Tues.) = Tuesday

TVA = Tennessee Valley Authority

U.C.V.= United Confederate Veterans

U.D.C.= United Daughters of the Confederacy

ult.=*ultimo* [of the last month]

UN = United Nations

UNESCO = United Nations Educational, Scientific, and Cultural Organization

uninc.= unincorporated

Unit.= Unitarian

Univ.= Universalist, University

UNRRA = United Nations Relief and Rehabilitation Administration

UP = United Press

U.S.= United States

USA = United States Army

U.S.A.= United States of America

USBGN = United States Board on Geographic Names

USCG = United States Coast Guard

USMC = United States Marine Corps

USN = United States Navy

USO = United Service Organizations

U.S.S.= United States Ship

USSR = Union of Soviet Socialist Republics

v.= *vide* [see]

v. (*or* vb.)= verb

v. (*or* vs.)= *versus* [against]

VA=Veterans' Administration

Va.= Virginia

V.C.= Victoria Cross

Ved.= Vedic

Ven.= the Venerable

V.I.= Virgin Islands

viz.= *videlicet* [namely]

vol.= volume, volunteer

vs.= verse, versus

Vt.= Vermont

W = west

W. (*or* Wed.) = Wednesday

WAC = Women's Army Corps

Wash.= Washington

WAVES = Women Accepted for Voluntary Emergency Service (United States Women's Naval Reserve)

W.C.T.U.= Woman's Christian Temperance Union

Wed. (*or* W.) = Wednesday

WHO = World Health Organization

W.I.= West Indies

Wis.= Wisconsin

wk.= week

WNW = west-northwest

WO = Warrant Officer

WPA=Work Projects Administration

WSW = west-southwest

wt.= weight

W.Va.= West Virginia

Wyo.= Wyoming

yd.= yard, yards

Y.M.C.A.=Young Men's Christian Association

Y.M.H.A.= Young Men's Hebrew Association

yr.= year

Y.W.C.A.= Young Women's Christian Association

Y.W.H.A.= Young Women's Hebrew Association

Zech.= Zechariah

Zeph.= Zephaniah

A.B.C. Powers, term applied to Argentina, Brazil, and Chile when acting in unison.

Abd al-Rahman. For Moslem rulers thus named, see ABDU-R-RAHMAN.

Abd-el-Krim (äb″dĕl-krĭm′), 1882?–, leader of the Riffian tribes of Morocco. Defeated 1925 by a joint Franco-Spanish army and deported to Réunion isl. Escaped 1947 to Egypt, where he became a leader of the N African independence movement.

Abdera (ăbdēr′ù), Gr. *Avdera,* town (pop. 2,821), Greece, in SW Thrace. Agr. market. Founded c.650 B.C. Protagoras and Democritus lived here.

Abderhalden, Emil (ā′mĕl äp′dürhäl″dùn), 1877–, Swiss physiologist and biochemist. Worked on enzymes and food metabolism. Devised pregnancy test.

Abdias: see OBADIAH.

abdication, renunciation of high public office, usually by a monarch. Known from antiquity and in many lands, act may be voluntary (e.g., Emperor Charles V) or forced (many cases in China, including Hsüan T'ung in 1912). Forbidden in Great Britain since 1688 unless with consent of Parliament, as in the case of Edward VIII (1936).

abdomen, portion of trunk below diaphragm. Cavity, lined by membrane (peritoneum), contains stomach, intestines, liver, pancreas, spleen, kidneys; in lower part (called pelvis) are bladder, rectum, some of reproductive organs. See *ill.,* p. 595.

abduction, unlawful taking away of a person, especially of a woman under an age prescribed by law or of a married woman without consent of husband.

Abdu-l-Aziz IV (äb″dōol-äzēz′), 1881?–1943, sultan of Morocco (1894–1908). French influence in Morocco was strengthened during his weak and unpopular reign. Deposed by his brother Abdu-l-Hafid.

Abdu-l-Aziz, 1830–76, Ottoman sultan (1861–76). During his reign Turkey became financially dependent on the West; Rumania, Serbia, Egypt gained virtual independence. Overthrown by MIDHAT PASHA, he died

a few days later (probably, but not certainly, murdered).

Abdu-l-Hamid (–hämēd′), Ottoman sultans. **Abdu-l-Hamid I,** 1725–89, reigned 1774–89. Made peace with Russia in Treaty of KUCHUK-KAINARJI (1774); renewed war 1787. **Abdu-l-Hamid II,** 1842–1918, reigned 1876–1909. He suspended the constitution; disposed of MIDHAT PASHA. After Congress of BERLIN (1878), he began a pro-German policy. Called Red Sultan for his part in Armenian massacres (1894–96). Deposed by Young Turks 1909.

Abdu-l-Kadir (–kädēr′), 1808–83, Algerian leader, of Arab descent. As emir of Mascara, he extended his power over much of N Algeria (1832–39). In 1839 declared a holy war against the French. Driven by Gen. Bugeaud into Morocco, where he won the sultan's support. Defeated 1844 at Isly, surrendered 1847, imprisoned in France until 1852.

Abdullah (äbdŭ′lù, äbdōōlä′), d. c.570, father of Mohammed.

Abdullah, 1882–1951, king of JORDAN (1946–51), b Mecca. Lost Hejaz to Ibn Saud. Led British-trained Arab Legion against Israel in 1948. Assassinated 1951.

Abdu-l-Malik (äb″dōol-mùlĭk′), c.646–705, the 5th OMAYYAD caliph (685–705). Overthrew rival caliphs and united Islam.

Abdu-l-Mejid (–mĕjēd′), 1823–61, Ottoman sultan (1839–61). Promoted reform. Revolt of MOHAMMED ALI was checked by Great Powers. CRIMEAN WAR and Congress of PARIS (1856) brought Turkey no gain. Decline of sultanate began.

Abdu-l-Mumin (–mōō′mĭn), 1094–1163, founder of the ALMOHADES. Conquered Morocco in the 1140s, became dominant in Spain in 1151, and extended his African domain as far east as Tripoli, 1158–59.

Abdu-r-Rahman (äb″dōor-rä′män, –rämän′) *or* **Abd al-Rahman** (äb″dōol–), OMAYYAD rulers of Córdoba. **Abdu-r-Rahman I,** d. 788, fled Damascus, seized power in Córdoba (756), ruled as emir till his death. **Abdu-r-Rahman III,** 891–961, ruled as emir from

912, as caliph from 929. Under him Moslem Spain reached height of glory. Also ruled Moslem part of N Africa 939–47.

Abdu-r-Rahman or **Abd al-Rahman,** d. 732, Moslem governor in Spain. Defeated in battle of Tours or Poitiers by CHARLES MARTEL (732).

à Becket, Thomas: see THOMAS À BECKET, SAINT.

Abed-nego (ŭbĕd′nēgō), one of THREE HOLY CHILDREN.

Abel, shepherd son of Adam and Eve, killed by Cain, his brother. Gen. 4.1–8.

Abel, Sir Frederick Augustus, 1826–1902, English chemist. Improved guncotton manufacture. Invented cordite (with Dewar) and Abel test for flash point of petroleum.

Abel, John Jacob, 1857–1938, American pharmacologist, associated with Johns Hopkins from 1893. He isolated epinephrine (adrenaline), crystalline form of insulin, and amino acids from blood.

Abel, Niels Henrik (nēls′ hĕn′rĕk″ ä′bùl), 1802–29, Norwegian mathematician.

Abelard, Peter (ă′bùlärd), Fr. *Pierre Abélard,* 1079–1142, French scholastic. Regarded as founder of Univ. of Paris. His romance and secret marriage with his pupil Heloise, niece of Fulbert, a canon of Notre Dame, ended when Fulbert had him emasculated by hired ruffians. Abelard became monk at Saint-Denis; left in 1120 to teach. Hostility of St. Bernard of Clairvaux caused condemnation of certain of his doctrines at Council of Soissons (1121). Abelard built a hermitage near Troyes, adding a monastery, the Paraclete, to house students; later he gave it to Heloise, who became abbess of a sisterhood there. To avoid condemnation at Council of Sens (1141), he made submission and retired to Cluny. Abelard applied logical methods to truths of faith; considered universals as existing only in thought but with basis in particulars (see SCHOLASTICISM). Chief work: *Sic et non* (collection of contradictory statements of Church Fathers). *Historia calamitatum* is autobiographical. Letters of Abelard and Heloise belong to world literature.

Abell, Kjeld (kyĕl′ ä′bĕl), 1901–, Danish dramatist, an innovator in stage techniques. Among his plays on social problems are *Anna Sophie Hedvig* (1939) and *The Queen Walks Again* (1943).

Abercrombie, Lascelles (lăs′ùls ăb′ùrkrŏmbĭ), 1881–1938, English poet and critic. Wrote long blank-verse poems.

Abercromby, Sir Ralph, 1734–1801, British general. Won major military reputation for campaigns against the French, especially in Flanders (1794–95) and W Indies. Killed in successful battle at Aboukir.

Aberdeen, George Hamilton-Gordon, 4th earl of (ăbùr-dēn′), 1784–1860, British statesman. By Treaty of Töplitz (1813) cemented Austria to anti-Napoleonic coalition. By Webster-Ashburton Treaty (1842) settled Northeast Boundary Dispute with U.S. Prime Minister (1852–55), he resigned after failure to stop British involvement in unpopular Crimean War.

Aberdeen, independent burgh (pop. 182,714), Aberdeenshire and Kincardine, Scotland, on North Sea at mouth of the Dee; chief port and largest city of NE Scotland. Called the Granite City. Univ. of Aberdeen includes King's Col. (1494) and Marischal Col. (1593).

Aberdeen. 1 Town (pop. 2,944), N Md., NE of Baltimore. Near by are Aberdeen Proving Ground and Army Chemical Center. **2** Cotton city (pop. 5,290), NE Miss., on Tombigbee R. and N of Columbus. **3** City (pop. 21,051), NE S.Dak., NW of Watertown; platted 1881. Rail and distribution center for agr. area. Has mfg. of farm machinery. **4** City (pop. 19,653), W Wash., port on Grays Harbor adjoining Hoquiam; settled c.1865. Has lumbering, mfg. of wood products, fishing, and canning.

Aberdeenshire, maritime county (1,971 sq. mi.; pop. 308,055), NE Scotland; cap. Aberdeen. Chief occupations agr., fishing, and cattle breeding. At Braemar is British royal residence, Balmoral Castle.

Aberhart, William (ä′bùrhärt), 1878–1943, Canadian statesman. Organizer of Social Credit party of Alberta; premier of Alberta (1935–43).

aberration, optics, blurring or loss of clearness in images produced by lenses or mirrors. It is spherical when rays of light from a point are not brought to a single focus, chromatic when image is blurred and fringes of color appear at its edges.

Abertawe, Glamorganshire, Wales: see SWANSEA.

Aberystwyth (ăbŭrĭst′wĭth), municipal borough (pop. 9,323), Cardiganshire, Wales; summer resort on Cardigan Bay. Has a constituent college of Univ. of Wales and Natl. Library of Wales.

Abgar, Epistles of: see PSEUDEPIGRAPHA.

Abiathar (ŭbī′–), priest, son of Ahimelech. Escaped massacre by Doeg. 1 Sam. 22.9–23; 2 Sam. 15.17,29; 1 Kings 1.7; 2.27; Mark 2.26. Name sometimes exchanged with his father's.

Abigail (ăb′ùgāl) [Heb.,= my father is joy]. **1** Wife of Nabal. After his death, she married David. 1 Sam. 25; 2 Sam. 3.13; 1 Chron. 3.1. **2** David's stepsister. 2 Sam. 17.25; 1 Chron. 2.16,17.

Abihu (ŭbī′hū), son of Aaron, destroyed for offering "strange" fire. Ex. 6.23; 24.1,9; 28.1; Lev. 10.1; Num. 3.2,4; 26.60,61; 1 Chron. 6.3; 24.1,21.

Abijah (ŭbī′jù), died c.911 B.C., king of Judah (c.914–c.911 B.C.); successor of Rehoboam. Jeroboam warred against him. 2 Chron. 13. Abijam: 1 Kings 15.1–8.

Abilene. 1 City (pop. 5,775), central Kansas, on Smoky Hill R. and W of Topeka; laid out 1860; wheat-shipping point. Was cow town and railhead for CHISHOLM TRAIL. Early home of Eisenhower. **2** City (pop. 45,570), W central Texas, WSW of Fort Worth; founded 1881. Distributing center for livestock, cotton, wheat, and dairy region. Refines oil. Seat of Hardin-Simmons Univ. (Baptist; 1891), Abilene Christian Col., and McMurry Col. (Methodist; 1923), all located.

Abimelech (ŭbĭm′ùlĕk). **1** See AHIMELECH. **2** Son of Gideon. Slew his 70 brothers, except Jotham, and became "king." Judges 9.1–57; 2 Sam. 11.21.

Abinadab (ŭbĭn′ùdäb). **1** Son of King Saul, killed at battle of Mt. Gilboa. 1 Sam. 31.2; 1 Chron. 10.2. **2** Keeper of ark for 20 years. 1 Sam. 7.1,2; 2 Sam. 6.3,4; 1 Chron. 13.7.

Abington, town (pop. 7,152), SE Mass., SSE of Boston. Mfg. of shoes.

Abiram (ŭbī′rùm), rebel (with KORAH) against Moses.

Abishag (ăb′–), handmaid to David in his old age. Adonijah wanted to marry her after David's death, and thus incurred Solomon's wrath. 1 Kings 1; 2.

Abitibi, Fort (ăbùtĭb′ē), important Canadian fur-trading post, on Abitibi L., built 1686.

Abkhaz Autonomous Soviet Socialist Republic (ăbkăz′, Rus. ŭpkhäs′) or **Abkhasia,** autonomous state (3,300 sq. mi.; pop. c.300,000) NW Georgian SSR; cap. Sukhum. Annexed by Russia from Turkey 1810. Abkhasians (30% of pop.) are largely Mohammedans.

ablative: see CASE.

ablaut (äp′lout), in inflection, the variation between vowels in related words (e.g., English, *ring, rang, rung*) indicating a corresponding modification of meaning. At an earlier unknown period the corresponding forms of the language had differences in accent, not differences in vowel.

Abner, head of Saul's army. Killed by Joab. 1 Sam. 9.1; 14.50,51; 17.55; 2 Sam. 2; 3.

Abo, Finland: see TURKU.

abolitionists, in U.S. history, especially 1830–60, advocates of compulsory freeing of Negro slaves, as distinguished from free-soilers, opposed only to extension of slavery. Active campaign had mainspring in religious revival in 1820s and reached crusading stage in 1830s led by T. D. Weld, Tappan brothers, and W. L. GARRISON. American Anti-Slavery Society, estab. 1833, flooded slave states with literature and lobbied in Washington. Writers such as J. G. Whittier and orators such as Wendell Phillips lent strength to cause. Despite unanimity on goal, there was division over methods, Garrison advocating moral suasion, others direct political action. Stringent fugitive slave laws in 1850 increased activity on UNDERGROUND RAILROAD. Harriet B. Stowe's *Uncle Tom's Cabin* and the Kansas question aroused both North and South, culminating in John Brown's raid on Harpers Ferry. Uncompromising temper of movement made war the only solution. See also SLAVERY.

abortion, expulsion of product of conception before fetus can survive. Spontaneous abortion popularly called miscarriage. Induced abortion criminal offense in U.S. except to save mother's life.

abortion, contagious: see BRUCELLOSIS.

Aboukir or **Abukir** (both: ä″bōōkēr′), village, Egypt, on Aboukir Bay, SW of Rosetta mouth of the Nile. Nelson's victory here over the French fleet in 1798 restored British prestige in the Mediterranean. The battle is sometimes called the battle of the Nile.

abracadabra (ăb′rŭkŭdăb′rŭ), magic formula used by Gnostics in 2d cent. to invoke aid of benevolent spirits to ward off affliction; usually engraved on amulets as protective charm. The word gradually lost occult significance; now means any hocus-pocus.

Abraham [according to Gen. 17.5 = father of many] or **Abram** [Heb.,= the father is high], forefather of the Hebrews through his son Isaac and of the Arabs through his son Ishmael. Chiefly important as the founder of Judaism. He instituted circumcision and received God's word that his people would gain the promised land of Canaan. Revered by many faiths as a symbol of devotion to, and trust in, God (as shown in willingness to sacrifice Isaac, kindliness to his wayward nephew Lot). Gen. 11–25.

Abraham, Plains of, field adjoining upper part of Quebec city. Here the English under Wolfe defeated French under Montcalm (1759), ending FRENCH AND INDIAN WARS and deciding fate of Canada.

Abraham Lincoln National Historical Park: see NATIONAL PARKS AND MONUMENTS (table).

Abram: see ABRAHAM.

Abramovich, Sholem (or **Solomon**) **Yakob:** see MENDELE MOCHER SFORIM.

abrasive, material used in grinding, cutting, polishing. Natural forms include DIAMOND, CORUNDUM, emery, SAND, PUMICE, chalk. Alundum (see ALUMINA) and Carborundum (see SILICON CARBIDE) are artificial. For special purposes powdered abrasives are often mixed with oil or water, molded with cement into wheels or sticks, or glued on cloth or paper.

Abravanel or **Abarbanel, Isaac** (übrä′vŭnĕl, –bärbŭ–), 1437–1508, Jewish theologian, a Portuguese government official. His writings upheld miracles against the rationalism of Maimonides.

Abruzzi, Luigi Amedeo, duca degli (äbrōōt′tsē), 1873–1933, Italian naval officer, mountain climber, and arctic explorer, b. Madrid. Duke of the Abruzzi was cousin of Victor Emmanuel III.

Abruzzi e Molise (–ā môlē′zĕ), region (5,883 sq. mi.; pop. 1,589,804), central Italy, in most rugged part of Apennines (Gran Sasso d'Italia); cap. Aquila. Vineyards, olives, sheep raising. Shared history of kingdom of NAPLES.

Absalom (ăb′sŭlŏm), beloved but treacherous son of David. He fled after murdering his brother Amnon. Forgiven by David but led abortive revolt and was slain. 2 Sam. 3.3; 13–19; 2 Chron. 11.20,21.

Absalon (äp′sälôn) or **Axel** (äk′sŭl), c.1128–1201, Danish churchman, archbishop of Lund. Held great political influence, warred against Wends, defeated Duke Bogislav of Pomerania in naval battle (1184). Patron of Saxo Grammaticus.

Absaroka Indians: see CROW INDIANS.

Absaroka Range (äbsŭrō′kŭ), part of Rocky Mts., c.150 mi. long; in Yellowstone Natl. Park, NW Wyo., and S Mont.

absenteeism, originally system under which a person controls, and derives income from, land or capital in a region in which he does not live. Notable abuse in

Ireland in 18th and 19th cent. and in E Europe until 20th cent. Recently term applied to concentrated control of wealth through corporate devices, shutting investor from conduct of business.

absinthe (ăb′sĭnth), a toxic green LIQUEUR distilled from wormwood and other aromatics. Excessive use may cause delirium and idiocy. Switzerland and France have banned manufacture and sale; importation forbidden by U.S. in 1912.

absolute, the (often with capital letter), in metaphysics, the unknowable, all-comprehensive principle underlying all reality; the opposite of relative. In various philosophic systems variously defined. In theology identified with God. See also HEGEL.

absolute zero: see TEMPERATURE.

absolutism, system of government with SOVEREIGNTY highly concentrated and in theory unchecked by portions of the body politic or by the people as a whole. In practice limited by existing law and custom, by danger of war and revolution. Tyrants of Greek cities were absolute. In Hellenic and Roman periods, some of the rulers were regarded as gods. In Renaissance, absolutism triumphed over feudalism in West. Absolute rule of Louis XIV of France was a standard example. In 20th cent. absolutism of DICTATOR or party rose with Fascism and Communism. See also DIVINE RIGHT.

absorption: see GAS; OSMOSIS; SPECTRUM.

abstract art, 20th-cent. painting style stressing basic formalized structures and ignoring representation of objects. Cézanne is an example of the initial period; cubism and expressionism thrived later. Abstract art may be "pure" (e.g., geometric) or mixed with other styles. Also used in other arts.

Abu Bakr (ä′bŏŏ bä′kŭr), 573–634, 1st caliph, father of AYESHA, Mohammed's wife; most zealous convert, first outside Prophet's family. Mohammed's only companion on the Hegira. During his critical two-year caliphate Arabian opposition was crushed; extension of Islam as world religion began.

Abu Hanifa (–hänē′fü), 699–767, Moslem jurist, founder of a system of Islamic jurisprudence.

Abu Khasim, Arabian physician: see ABULCASIS.

Abukir, Egypt: see ABOUKIR.

Abu-l-Abbas as-Saffah (ä′bŏŏl-äbäs′äs-säfä′), d. 754, 1st ABBASID caliph (749–54). Took caliphate from the Omayyad with help of Abu Muslim.

Abu-l-Ala al-Maarri (–äl-mä-är-rē′), 973–1057, blind Arabic poet, a fatalistic freethinker. Discarded classicism for intellectual urbanity.

Abulcasis (ä′bŏŏlkä′sĭs) or **Abu Khasim** (ä′bŏŏ kä′-sĭm), fl. 11th cent., Arabian physician, author of influential text, *Tasrif*, on medicine and surgery.

Abu-l-Faraj Ali of Isfahan (ä′bŏŏlfä′räj), 897–967, Arabic scholar. His *Book of Songs* is an annotated compilation of Arabic poems set to music.

Abu Muslim (ä′bŏŏ mŏŏ′slĭm), c.728–755, Persian revolutionist. Won the caliphate for the Abbasid, who later killed him.

Abu Nuwas (–nŏŏwäs′), d. c.810, Arabic poet. His poetry echoes extravagance of Baghdad court.

Abu Said ibn Abi-l-Khair (sä′ĭd ä′bĕl-khīr′), 967–1049, Persian poet, a Sufi dervish. First to write rubaiyat in Sufistic strain.

abutilon (ŭbū′tĭlŭn) or **flowering maple,** tropical shrubs (*Abutilon*), with yellow, white, or pink bell-shaped flowers, lobed leaves. House plant in North.

Abydos (ŭbī′dŭs), city of anc. Egypt, NW of Thebes; center of worship of Osiris.

Abydos, anc. Greek town, on the Hellespont. Near by Athenian fleet defeated Sparta (411 B.C.). Abydos was the scene of the story of Hero and Leander.

Abyssinia: see ETHIOPIA.

Ac, chemical symbol of the element ACTINIUM.

acacia (ŭkā′shŭ), leguminous, tropical or subtropical trees or shrubs of genus *Acacia*, with fluffy clusters of yellow or white flowers. Known as wattle in Australia. Yield GUM arabic, dyes, tanning aids, furniture wood,

CATECHU, and SHITTIM WOOD mentioned in the Bible.

academic costume, dress required on stated occasions by educational institutions for faculty, students, degree candidates, degree holders. In U.S. style adopted 1895, revised 1932, accepted by over 700 institutions. Includes gown, showing academic rank (see DEGREE, ACADEMIC); hood, lined with color of institution giving degree; mortarboard, a skullcap supporting stiff square top with tassel.

academic freedom, right of scholars to teach, pursue research, and publish unrestrained by employing institution. A civil right in democratic countries, it usually includes right of tenure. Academic freedom is based on beliefs that open investigation best reveals truth and that scholars ought to pursue research regardless of personal opinion. The idea of completely free inquiry, evolving in the period of Enlightenment, was first accepted in Prussia and other German states. In England, Jeremy Bentham, Herbert Spencer, Charles Darwin, and Thomas Huxley showed value of free investigation. In U.S. the Association of University Professors maintains standards of academic freedom and obligation.

Académie française: see FRENCH ACADEMY.

Academy, garden near Athens where PLATO taught (c.387 B.C.), and his followers met until banned by Justinian (A.D. 529).

Acadia (ùkā'dēù), region and former French colony, E Canada, centered on Nova Scotia but including Prince Edward Isl. and mainland coast from Gulf of St. Lawrence S into Maine. First and chief town, Port Royal, was founded 1605. Attacked and taken by British 1710. In 1755 French settlers who refused to swear allegiance to Great Britain were deported. Exiles found refuge in many places. Longfellow's *Evangeline* tells of those in St. Martinville, La., where the Cajuns—as they are popularly called—maintain a separate folk culture. In 1762 a new mass deportation was thwarted, and gradually some exiles returned. Today in Canada, Acadian (French *Acadien*) means a French-speaking inhabitant of Maritime Provs.

Acadia National Park: see NATIONAL PARKS AND MONUMENTS (table).

Acadia University: see WOLFVILLE, N.S.

acanthus (ùkăn'–), perennial herbs (*Acanthus*), with deeply cut leaves often copied in architectural motif (see CORINTHIAN ORDER).

Acapulco (äkäpōōl'kō), city (pop. 9,993), Guerrero, SW Mexico; Pacific port. Winter resort.

Acarya: see BHASCARA.

Accad: see AKKAD.

Accault, Michel, French explorer: see ACO.

accent, in language, emphasis given a particular sound. In English each independently spoken form has an accented vowel. The English accent is phonemic (or significant), for there are words different from each other only in their accent, e.g., *contract*, verb and noun. The so-called accents in French, acute ('), grave (`), and circumflex (ˆ), are borrowed from Greek writing, where they probably showed differences in pitch. Some languages have significant variations of both pitch and loudness.

accessory, person somehow connected with a crime other than the principal perpetrator. The law usually distinguishes between one who in some way abets the committing of crime (before the fact) and who aids the criminal after the crime is committed (after the fact).

accordion, small portable musical instrument, consisting of rectangular bellows expanded and contracted between the hands. Buttons or keys operated by the player determine tones. Introduced in 1822; keyboard added in 1852. Similar to the concertina, which is smaller and has bellows attached to hexagonal blocks that have handles and buttons.

accounting, classifying, analyzing, interpreting of BOOKKEEPING records intended to show business operation in light of profit and loss. AUDITING is branch of accounting.

Accra (ùkrä'), city (pop. 135,456), cap. of the Gold Coast, a port on Gulf of Guinea.

accusative: see CASE.

Aceldama (ùsĕl'dùmù), "field of blood," apparently place where Judas died. Money given him for betraying Jesus was used to buy this place for burial of strangers. Earlier it had been called "potter's field," hence term for paupers' burying ground. Mat. 27.3–10; Acts 1.16–19.

acetaldehyde: see ALDEHYDE.

acetic acid (ùsē'tĭk), weak organic acid (constituent of vinegar), a colorless liquid with pungent odor; boils at 118.5°C. Miscible with water; heat evolved. Pure (99.5%) acid called glacial acetic acid. Its compounds used in plastics, medicines, lacquers, and as mordants.

acetone (ăs'ĭtōn), colorless, inflammable liquid with minty taste and odor; boils at 56.1°C. Used as a solvent for organic substances and in making celluloid, smokeless powders, and chloroform.

acetylene (ùsĕt'ĭlēn), colorless gas, boiling at −84°C., with ethereal odor when pure. Forms explosive mixture with air; explosive when liquefied. Used as illuminant and for cutting and welding metals (see OXYACETYLENE FLAME).

Achaea (ùkē'ù), region of anc. Greece, in N Peloponnesus, on Gulf of Corinth; the home of the **Achaeans,** powerful in Greece by 1300 B.C. Their cities were formed before 5th cent. B.C. in the first **Achaean League,** which lasted until it opposed Philip II of Macedon (338 B.C.) and was then dissolved. The second Achaean League was formed in 3d cent. B.C. and tried to liberate Greece from Macedonian rule but ran into opposition of Sparta. In 198 B.C. the league got Roman help and gained power. Later suspected by Rome of sympathy for Macedon, many Achaeans were deported (168 B.C.) to Italy. In 146 B.C. Achaeans waged suicidal war against Rome.

Achaemenidae (ăkĭmē'nĭdē) or **Achaemenids** (ăkĭmē'nĭdz), dynasty of ancient Persia, c.550–330 B.C., founded by CYRUS THE GREAT.

Ache, Caran d': see CARAN D'ACHE.

Achelous (ăkĭlō'ùs), in Greek religion, river-god. The son of Oceanus and Tethys, he was father of the Sirens and other nymphs.

Achelous (ăkĕlō'ŏs), river, 137 mi. long, NW Greece, flowing from Pindus mts. S to the Ionian Sea. Also known as Aspropotamos.

Acheron (ă'kùrŏn), in Greek religion, river of Hades.

Acheson, Dean (Gooderham) (ăch'ĭsùn), 1893–, U.S. Secretary of State (1949–53). He was Asst. Secretary of State 1941–45, Undersecretary 1945–47.

Acheson, Edward Goodrich, 1856–1931, American inventor. Discovered carborundum; developed processes for producing silicon, aluminum, synthetic graphite.

Acheulian (ùshōō'lēun), phase of Paleolithic period named for Saint-Acheul, France, where typical implements were found.

Achilles (ùkĭ'lēz), in Greek legend, hero of the *Iliad*, prominent Greek warrior in TROJAN WAR; son of Peleus and Thetis. His mother, hearing prophecy of his death at Troy, dipped him in river Styx to make him invulnerable, but the water did not touch the heel she held. She disguised him as a girl and hid him at Skyros. Odysseus persuaded him to join expedition against Troy. He quarreled with AGAMEMNON and sulked in his tent, but to avenge the death of his friend PATROCLUS, he fought again and slew Hector. He was killed by Paris, who wounded his heel.

Achitophel, variant of AHITHOPHEL.

acid, according to ionization theory (see ION), compound yielding hydrogen ions when dissolved in water. Properties result from presence of hydrogen ion: in aqueous solution acids taste sour, turn blue litmus red, react with bases and basic oxides (see NEUTRALIZATION) to form salts and water. Can conduct electricity. Most acids are solids, few are liquids, and very few are gases. Strong acids (e.g., nitric) are largely ionized in solution; weak acids (e.g., acetic) are little ionized.

Classified also by number of replaceable hydrogen ions in molecule as monobasic (e.g., nitric), dibasic (e.g., sulphuric), tribasic (e.g., phosphoric). Carboxyl group (–COOH) characteristic of organic acids.

acidosis, reduction of the body's alkali reserve resulting from starvation, diabetes, nephritis, infectious diseases. It does not imply real acidity of the blood. Alkalosis is abnormal increase in alkali reserve.

Ackia Battleground National Monument: see NATIONAL PARKS AND MONUMENTS (table).

Acmeists (ăk'mēĭsts), school of Russian poets, started 1912 in reaction against symbolists. Strove after concreteness of image, clarity of expression. Leading Acmeists: Akhmatova, Gumilev, Mandelstam.

acne (ăk'nē), disease of sebaceous glands common during adolescence. Characterized by pink pimples (papules) surrounding blackheads, especially on face, back, and chest. Sometimes chronic.

Aco or **Accault, Michel** (äkō'), fl. 1680–1702, French explorer of region of upper Mississippi R.; lieutenant of La Salle.

Acoma or **Ácoma** (both: ä'kŭmù), Indian pueblo village (1948 pop. 1,482), W central N.Mex., W of Albuquerque, on mesa above reservation villages of Santa María de Ácoma and Acomita. Visited by Coronado's men (1540), Juan de Onate (1598), and Fray Juan Ramírez (1629). Scene of revolts against Spanish in 1599 and late 1600s. Language is Western Keresan. Farming and pottery-making. Holds festival to St. Stephen, Sept. 2.

Aconcagua (äkōnkä'gwä), peak, 22,835 ft. high, W Argentina, in Andes; considered highest peak in W Hemisphere.

aconite (ăk'–), **monkshood,** or **wolfsbane** (*Aconitum*), hardy plant with blue, purple, yellow, or white hooded flowers. Drug aconite, a sedative, contains poisonous alkaloid aconitine. Winter aconite (*Eranthis*) has small, yellow flowers in spring.

Açores: see AZORES.

acorn: see OAK.

Acosta, Joaquín (hwäkēn' äkō'stä), 1799?–1852, Colombian scientist. Fought in revolution. Wrote on Colombian geography, history, meteorology.

acoustics (ùkoō'stĭks), science of sound, its production, transmission, and effects. Acoustical problems in buildings include reverberation (repeated reflection of sound waves from smooth surface in enclosed space) and interference (from reflection of sound waves of different frequencies). Some reverberation avoids sound deadening; interference either reinforces or destroys sound.

acquittal, discharge of an indicted person. An acquittal-in-fact follows on a verdict of not guilty on the basis of facts and cannot be appealed. An acquittal-in-law results from the operation of the rules of law.

Acre (ä'kùr, ä'kùr), Arabic *Acca*, Heb. *Acco*, city (pop. 8,000), N Palestine, a port on Bay of Acre opposite Haifa. Biblical names are Accho and Ptolemais. Taken by Arabs 638, held by Crusaders 1104–87 and by Knights Hospitalers 1190–1291. Surrender to Saracens in 1291 marked decline of Latin Kingdom of Jerusalem and the Crusades. Held by Turkey 1517–1832, 1840–1918, by Egypt 1832–40, and by Great Britain 1918–48. Partition of Palestine in 1948 assigned Acre to Arabs, but Israeli forces captured it.

Acre (ä'krä), river rising at border of Peru and Brazil and flowing NE. Treaty of Petrópolis (1903) gave Brazil most of territory surrounding river, with large indemnity to Bolivia.

acre, land measure used by English-speaking peoples, now set at 160 sq. rods (4,840 sq. yd.; 43,560 sq. ft.; 1/640 sq. mi.). Local variations survive.

Acrocorinthus (ä"krōkùrĭn'thùs), rock, 1,886 ft. high, site of the Acropolis of Old CORINTH, Greece. On its summit stood temple of Aphrodite; below was fountain of Pirene, from which Pegasus drank.

Acropolis (ùkrŏp'ùlĭs), elevated, fortified section of ancient Greek cities. Athenian Acropolis, a hill c.260

ft. high, was adorned, chiefly during time of Cimon and Pericles, with some of world's greatest architectural works (PROPYLAEA, PARTHENON, ERECHTHEUM). See ELGIN MARBLES.

Actaeon (ăk-tē'ùn), in Greek legend, a hunter. Because he saw Artemis bathing, she changed him into a stag, and his own dogs killed him.

actinic ray: see RAY; SPECTRUM; SUNLIGHT.

actinium (ăktĭn'ēùm), radioactive element of actinide series (symbol = Ac; see also ELEMENT, table). Occurs in minerals containing uranium; is disintegration product of protactinium; emits beta rays.

Actium (ăk'tēùm, ăk'shēùm), Gr. *Aktion*, promontory NW Greece. Here forces of Octavian (later AUGUSTUS) defeated Antony and Cleopatra (31 B.C.).

active: see VOICE.

act of God, accident caused by an extraordinary, unforeseeable, and unavoidable natural force. The injured party has in general no right to damages.

Acton, John Emerich Edward Dalberg Acton, 1st Baron, 1834–1902, English historian. Taught at Cambridge from 1895. Planned *Cambridge Modern History*. Notable as a liberal and a Roman Catholic. Wrote *History of Freedom* (1907), essays.

Acton, Sir John Francis Edward, 1736?–1811, Neapolitan statesman of British origin. Favorite of Marie Caroline. Chief minister 1779–1804.

Acts of the Apostles, book of Bible between Gospels and Epistles, only contemporary historical account of early expansion of Christianity. Written in Greek A.D. c.60–80. Traditional author is St. Luke. Three critical events are: descent of the Holy Ghost, martyrdom of St. Stephen, conversion of St. Paul.

actuary, originally, in England, registrar recording court acts or managing a joint stock company. Later managers of insurance companies only, now especially insurance statisticians who calculate probabilities (e.g., length of life, accident rate) to determine premium rates.

Acuña, Cristóbal de (krēstō'bäl dā äkoō'nyä), 1597–1676?, Spanish Jesuit missionary and explorer. Accompanied Teixeira on journey down Amazon (1638), wrote earliest firsthand description of river (1639).

Ada, city (pop. 15,995), S central Okla., near Canadian R. SE of Oklahoma City; settled 1889. Industrial center for oil and agr. area with mfg. of cement, machinery, and glass.

Adak (ā'dăk), off W Alaska, one of ALEUTIAN ISLANDS. U.S. base in World War II, important in Aleutian campaign.

Adalbert, d. 1072, archbishop of Hamburg-Bremen, a diocese which included Scandinavia. Favorite of Emperor Henry III; guardian of Henry IV. Relentlessly ambitious, he helped to consolidate imperial authority despite opposition of nobles and clergy.

Adalia, Turkey: see ANTALYA.

Adam [Heb.,= mankind], in Bible, the first man. His story from creation to expulsion from Garden of Eden (with his wife EVE) is told in Gen. 1.26–5.5. To St. Paul, Adam represented earthly side of man (1 Cor. 15.20–22,42–58). Higher criticism compares Adam's story with Babylonian myths of creation. For examples of Judaic and Islamic legends stemming from biblical account, see LILITH; PSEUDEPIGRAPHA.

Adam, Adolphe (ädōlf' ädä'), 1803–56, French composer of comic opera and other stage works, known for his ballet *Giselle* and the popular *Cantique de Noël*.

Adam, Robert (ăd'ùm), 1728–92, and **James Adam,** 1730–94, Scottish architects, brothers. Chiefly inspired by classic architecture, they created a style of great elegance. Designed important buildings in England and Scotland. Also furniture (see *ill.*, p. 356).

Adam de la Halle (ädä' dù lä äl'), 1237?–c.1285, French dramatist. Author of *Le Jeu de Robin et de Marion,* sometimes called earliest comic opera.

Adamic, Louis (ăd'ùmĭk), 1899–1951, American author, b. Slovenia; in U.S. after 1913. Wrote on immigrants, racial tolerance; *The Native's Return* (1934)

was popular. He died in mysterious circumstances.
Adams, family of distinguished Americans from Mass.
John Adams, 1735–1826, was 2d President of the
United States (1797–1801). A patriot leader who opposed British measures leading to American Revolution, he later served in both Continental Congresses
and argued eloquently for the Declaration of Independence, which he signed. Served as Washington's
Vice President (1789–97). His administration as President revealed his honest and stubborn integrity; though
allied with the conservative Federalists, he was not
dominated by them in their struggle against the Jeffersonians. By conciliation he prevented war with France;
he had reservatïons about the ALIEN AND SEDITION
ACTS. His wife, **Abigail (Smith) Adams,** 1744–1818,
was one of the most distinguished and influential first
ladies in U.S. history. Their son, **John Quincy Adams,**
1767–1848, was 6th President of the United States
(1825–29). As U.S. Senator from Mass. (1803–8), he
outraged his fellow Federalists by supporting Jeffersonian policies. Served in several ministerial positions.
Best-known achievement as U.S. Secretary of State
(1817–25) was MONROE DOCTRINE. Elected President
in House of Representatives through support of Henry
Clay, Adams had an unhappy, ineffective administration. Won new renown as U.S. Representative from
Mass. (1831–48); eloquently attacked all measures expanding slavery. Promoted Smithsonian Inst. His diary is a valuable historical document. His son, **Charles
Francis Adams,** 1807–86, was minister to Great Britain (1861–68). He won British respect for wisdom in
upholding Northern cause, especially in *Trent* and
Alabama incidents. Later represented U.S. in settlement of Alabama claims. His son, **Charles Francis Adams,** 1835–1915, American historian and railroad expert, was president of the Union Pacific (1884–90).
Author of *Three Episodes of Massachusetts History*
(1892). His brother, **Brooks Adams,** 1848–1927, was
also an historian. He developed theory that civilization rose and fell according to growth and decline of
commerce in *The Law of Civilization and Decay*
(1895). His ideas influenced another brother, **Henry
(Brooks) Adams,** 1838–1918, also an historian. In developing a basic philosophy of history he found a unifying principle in force or energy. Applied this theory
in two books, *Mont-Saint-Michel and Chartres* (privately printed 1904, pub. 1913), and *The Education of
Henry Adams* (privately printed 1906, pub. 1918). Also wrote study of administrations of Jefferson and
Madison. **Charles Francis Adams,** 1866–, grandson of
Charles Francis Adams (1807–86), was U.S. Secretary
of the Navy (1929–33).
Adams, Franklin Pierce, pseud. **F. P. A.,** 1881–, American columnist ("The Conning Tower"). Humorous
verse and light essays. Became member of "Information Please" radio program in 1938.
Adams, Henry (Brooks): see ADAMS, family.
Adams, Herbert, 1858–1945, American sculptor, a
founder of the Natl. Sculpture Society.
Adams, James Truslow, 1878–1949, American histo-
rian. His books on the American scene include *The
Epic of America* (1931), *The Adams Family* (1930),
and *Henry Adams* (1933). Editor in chief of *Dictionary of American History, Atlas of American History,*
and *Album of American History.*
Adams, John: see ADAMS, family.
Adams, John Couch, 1819–92, English astronomer.
Calculated position of then unknown planet NEPTUNE.
Adams, John Quincy: see ADAMS, family.
Adams, Maude, 1872–, American actress, whose real
name is Kiskadden. Famous in Barrie plays, she
starred in his *Little Minister* (1897), *Quality Street*
(1901), *What Every Woman Knows* (1908), and *Peter
Pan* (1905), role for which she is best known.
Adams, Roger, 1889–, American chemist. Developed
methods of identification, preparation, and synthesis.
Among first to synthesize the local anesthetics butyn
and procaine.

Adams, Samuel, 1722–1803, American Revolutionary
patriot, signer of Declaration of Independence; second
cousin of John Adams. Leader of extremists in colonial resistance to British.
Adams, Walter Sydney, 1876–, American astronomer,
authority on motions and spectroscopy of stars. Director (1923–46) of Mt. Wilson Observatory.
Adams, Will(iam), 1564?–1620, first Englishman to
visit Japan. Settled there permanently as successful
shipbuilder and trader.
Adams, town (pop. 12,034), NW Mass., in the Berkshires and on Hoosic R. Mfg. of textiles, paper. Calcium quarried. Birthplace of Susan B. Anthony.
Adams, Mount. 1 Peak, N.H.: see PRESIDENTIAL
RANGE. **2** Peak (12,307 ft.), SW Wash., in Cascade
Range.
Adana (ä′dänä), city (pop. 117,799), S Turkey, on
Seyhan R. Once a Roman colony, it is now a commercial center.
Addams, Jane, 1860–1935, American social worker.
Founded (1899, with Ellen G. Starr) noted social
settlement, Hull House, in Chicago. Leader in woman-
suffrage and peace movements. Awarded 1931 Nobel
Peace Prize. Wrote *Twenty Years at Hull-House*
(1910).
adder, poisonous snake of European viper family. Species also found in Asia, Africa, Australia. In U.S.
name is applied to various harmless snakes.
adding machine: see CALCULATING MACHINE.
Addington, Henry: see SIDMOUTH, HENRY ADDINGTON,
VISCOUNT.
Addis Ababa (ä′dïs ä′bùbù), city (pop. c.300,000), cap.
of Ethiopia. Founded 1887 by Menelik II, who made
it his cap. in 1889. It was cap. of Italian East Africa,
1936–41. Imperial palace is near by.
Addison, Joseph, 1672–1719, English essayist. First
achieved notice with epic poem *The Campaign* (1704)
and later wrote poems, dramas (e.g., tragedy, *Cato,*
1713) and criticism (notably on *Paradise Lost,* praising Milton), but he is best remembered for witty, urbane essays, some of the finest in English. He began in
1710 to contribute to Richard Steele's *Tatler* and later
continued his essays in the *Spectator* (1711–12). His
most popular papers were on the imaginary squire, Sir
Roger de Coverley (invented by Steele), and his co-
terie. Addison held a seat in Parliament and government posts.
Addison, Thomas: see ADDISON'S DISEASE.
Addison, W.Va.: see WEBSTER SPRINGS.
Addison's disease, serious malady resulting from destruction of cortex of adrenal glands. First described
by **Thomas Addison,** 1793–1860, English pathologist.
addition, a basic arithmetical operation using the symbol +. Properties important in higher algebra include
associativity (of three numbers, sum of two may be
added to third without affecting final sum), commutivity (of two numbers, either may be added to other without affecting sum), distributivity (result of multiplying sum of two numbers by third number same as multiplying each number alone and adding products). To
add numerical quantities all must be converted to
same denomination.
address, forms of. Both spoken and written salutations
differ widely even in English-speaking countries. Mo-
narchical traditions and hereditary titles give rise to
great complexity; England has a multiplicity of forms
and a strict code of address. The U.S. has fewer and
simpler forms, which have grown out of custom and
convenience rather than inheritance and are indicative,
not of a man's birth or family, but of his professional
or political position. However, in all official and diplomatic correspondence and in formal social intercourse,
modes of addressing letters and invitations, as well as
the manner of personal address, are of great importance. The President of the U.S. is addressed in speech
as *Mr. President,* in writing as *The President, The
White House, Washington.* The formal opening of a
letter may be *Sir,* the informal opening *My Dear Mr.*

SMALL CAPITALS = cross references. Pronunciation key on inside end pages. Abbreviations: p. 2.

President. Ambassadors, in speech, are *Your Excellency,* in writing *His Excellency the Ambassador of Great Britain.* A governor of a state is spoken of formally as *His Excellency the Governor of Ohio.* An invitation would read *The Honorable the Governor of New York.* The Vice President, heads of executive departments (cabinet members), justices of the higher courts, mayors of cities, American ministers, Senators and Representatives, and ex-Presidents are addressed as *The Honorable,* e.g., *The Honorable the Vice President of the United States, The Honorable the Secretary of State.* The secretary to the President, heads of independent boards and commissions, assistant secretaries of executive departments, are also addressed as *Honorable. Esquire* is used after the names of chief clerks and chiefs of the bureaus of executive departments, diplomatic officers below the rank of minister, consular officers, clerk of the Supreme Court and officers of other courts. *Reverend* or *Honorable* should be preceded by the word *the* and should not be abbreviated; letters after the heading should begin (this is known as the salutation) *Dear Mr.* ———. Professional titles precede the name, and professional abbreviations follow. Church dignitaries are addressed in writing thus: the pope, *His Holiness Pope Pius XII,* in the salutation *Your Holiness* or *Most Holy Father;* cardinals, *His Eminence the Cardinal Archbishop of New York* or (when not an archbishop) *His Eminence Cardinal* ———, salutation *Your Eminence;* archbishops, *His Grace the Archbishop of* ———, salutation *My Lord Archbishop* or *Your Grace;* bishops, *The Right Reverend Bishop* ——— or *The Right Reverend Bishop of* ———, salutation *Dear Sir* or *My Lord;* Methodist Episcopal bishops, *The Reverend Bishop* ——— ———, salutation *Dear Sir;* deans, *The Very Reverend* ——— ———, salutation *Very Reverend Sir.* English titles are numerous and complex. The king and the queen, in speech with intimates, are *Sir* and *Ma'am.* Addressed by letter, the king is *His Most Gracious Majesty the King;* the salutation of the letter is *Sire* or *Your Majesty.* The queen in writing is *Her Most Gracious Majesty the Queen,* salutation *Madame* or *Your Majesty.* A prince is in writing *His Royal Highness the Prince of* ———, a princess *Her Royal Highness the Princess Margaret Rose.* A duke is in writing *His Grace the Duke of* ———, salutation *My Lord Duke* or *Your Grace.* A countess is in writing *The Right Honourable the Countess of* ———, salutation *Madame* or *Your Ladyship.* An earl is in writing *The Right Honourable the Earl of* ———, salutation *My Lord* or *Your Lordship.* Members of Parliament add the letters M.P. to their address. A privy councilor is *The Right Honourable* ——— ———. In addressing invitations the full title is used except in the case of barons. The title *Right Honourable* belongs to all peers and is the right of members of the privy council and of cabinet ministers. Professional titles precede titles of rank as *Captain the Honourable John Blank.* The use of *Esquire,* formerly limited to lawyers, country gentlemen, and eldest sons of knights, is now more general. The title *Honourable* is ignored in conversation and is never used on visiting cards.

Ade, George, 1866–1944, American journalist, humorist, dramatist, satirist of the Midwest. Notable book is *Fables in Slang* (1900). Also wrote comedies, comic operas, musical-comedy librettos.

Adelaide, empress: see OTTO I, emperor.

Adelaide, city (pop. 34,990; metropolitan pop. 382,454), cap. of South Australia, near Gulf St. Vincent. Founded 1836, it is the state's oldest city. Seat of Univ. of Adelaide. Has knitting mills and state-owned munitions plants.

Adelard of Bath (ă′dùlärd), fl. 12th cent., English scholastic philosopher, noted for Arabic studies.

Adelheid, empress: see OTTO I, emperor.

Adélie Coast, region, Antarctica, in Australian quadrant, W of George V Coast and E of Wilkes Land. Heavily glaciated, has strongest winds in world. Discovered 1840.

Adelphi, the (ùdĕl′fē), area in central London, developed by Adam brothers. Here many literary and theatrical great lived.

Adelphi College: see GARDEN CITY, N.Y.

Adelsberg, Yugoslavia: see POSTOJNA.

Aden (ā′dùn, ä′–), British crown colony (80 sq. mi.; pop. 81,236, including PERIM), SW Arabia, on Gulf of Aden. Captured by Moslems 636; occupied by Turks almost continuously 1538–1630; under British administration as part of India 1839–1937. Town of Aden is a free port; important air base in World War II. British protectorate of Aden (c.112,000 sq. mi.; pop. c.630,000) is bordered by Yemen and Saudi Arabia. Mostly mountainous or desert.

Aden, Gulf of, W arm of Arabian Sea, between Aden protectorate and Somaliland. On trade route from Mediterranean Sea to Indian Ocean via Suez Canal.

adenoids, pharyngeal tonsils, masses of lymphoid tissue in upper part of throat. When unusually large, may interfere with normal breathing.

Adeste Fideles (ädĕs′tä fēdā′lĕs), Christian hymn, written in Latin in 17th or 18th cent. Best-known English version, beginning "O come, all ye faithful," by Frederick Oakely (1802–80). Usual tune, *Portuguese Hymn,* is from collection of hymns called *Cantus Diversi;* author and composer are unknown.

adhesive, substance used for bonding surfaces. Animal glue, made from hides, hoofs, bones, probably was known to prehistoric man. In 19th cent. appeared many vegetable adhesives including gums, resins, mucilage, and starch. Other adhesives are made from casein, soybeans, rubber, cellulose, and synthetic substances.

Adige (ä′dējĕ), Ger. *Etsch,* river, 225 mi. long, N Italy. Flows from Alps, past Verona, to Adriatic.

Adighe, Caucasian people: see CIRCASSIA.

Adirondack Mountains (ădīrŏn′dăk), NE N.Y., sometimes mistakenly included in Appalachian system; geologically a S extension of Laurentian Plateau. Its preCambrian metamorphic rock with intruded igneous rock has been uplifted and eroded through countless years. Group, bounded E by L. Champlain and L. George region, extends from foothills near St. Lawrence R. (N) to Mohawk valley (S). Rises to 5,344 ft. in Mt. Marcy, highest point in N.Y., where L. Tear of the Clouds is source of chief headstream of the Hudson. Another well-known peak is Whiteface (4,872 ft.), ski center with meteorological station on summit. Both are near L. Placid and Saranac Lakes. Much of region —noted for wild scenery, beautiful forests, many lakes —is in Adirondack Forest Preserve (2,177,701 acres) and includes many summer and winter resorts. Iron mining revived c.1938; much ore produced in World War II.

Adlai (ăd′lī, ăd′lā), father of Shaphat, one of David's officers. 1 Chron. 27.29.

Adler, Alfred (äd′lùr), 1870–1937, Austrian psychiatrist, founder of school of individual psychology. He rejected Freudian emphasis on sex and maintained that all personality difficulties or behavior disorders are overcompensation for deficiencies, environmental repressions, or feelings of inferiority. Later Adler lectured and practiced in U.S.

Adler, Cyrus, 1863–1940, founder of American Jewish Historical Society; an editor of the *Jewish Encyclopedia* and of the *American-Jewish Year Book.*

Adler, Denkmar, 1844–1900, American architect, b. Germany; associate of Louis SULLIVAN.

Adler, Felix, 1851–1933, American educator and founder of ETHICAL CULTURE MOVEMENT, b. Germany. Was professor of ethics, Columbia Univ., after 1902 and leader in social welfare activities.

Adler, Viktor, 1852–1918, Austrian politician, founder of Austrian Social Democratic party. His son, **Friedrich Adler,** 1879–, Socialist leader, shot Count STÜRGKH (1916); amnestied 1918.

Admetus (ădmē′tùs), in Greek legend, Thessalian king, whom Apollo served. On condition that his life be spared, his wife, ALCESTIS, gave her life, but Hercules rescued her from Hades.

Admiralty Island (1,164 sq. mi.), off SE Alaska, in ALEXANDER ARCHIPELAGO and SW of Juneau. Separated from mainland by Stephens Passage. Has fish canning and lumbering.

Admiralty Islands, small volcanic group, area 800 sq. mi., SW Pacific, W of New Ireland, in BISMARCK ARCHIPELAGO. Japanese air base on Manus (main island) was taken 1944 by Allied forces.

Admiralty Range, N part of great mountain range in Victoria Land, W of Ross Sea, Antarctica. Its peaks reach 10,000 ft.

adolescence (ă"dŭlĕ'sŭns), physical stage between puberty and maturity lasting generally from ages of 12 to 21. Adolescent physiological changes strengthen heterosexual drives and strivings for independence. Typical emotional difficulties arise from conflicting biological changes and inability to express new needs in socially acceptable form.

Adolf of Nassau, d. 1298, German king (1292–98). Deposed by diet; defeated and slain by army of Albert I.

Adonai, another name for GOD.

Adonijah (ăd"nījŭ, ŭdŏn'ŭjŭ), son of David. He schemed for the throne, but David gave it to Solomon. 2 Sam. 3.4; 1 Kings 1; 2.1–25.

Adonis (ŭdō'nĭs), in Greek religion, young man loved by APHRODITE. When he was killed by a wild boar, Aphrodite persuaded the gods to let him live for six months of each year. Hence his death and resurrection were celebrated in midsummer festival Adonia, symbolizing yearly growth and decay.

adoptionism, heresy in Spain in 8th and 9th cent., holding old belief that Christ is a man adopted as Son of God by baptism.

Adour (ädoor'), river, 210 mi. long, SW France. Rises in Pyrenees, enters Bay of Biscay near Bayonne. Forms N limit of Basque country.

Adowa, Ethiopia: see ADUWA.

Adrammelech (ŭdrăm'–), in Bible, one of two men named as murderers of their father, Sennacherib; Sharezer was the other. 2 Kings 19.37 (= Isa. 37.38).

adrenal gland (ădrē'nŭl) or **suprarenal gland** (sōōprŭrē'nŭl), one of two small, endocrine glands, one resting on upper part of each kidney. Outer layer (cortex) secretes hormone (cortin) influencing metabolism and sex function; inner portion (medulla) secretes hormone adrenaline.

adrenaline (ŭdrĕn'ŭlĭn) or **epinephrine** (ĕpĭnĕf'rĭn), hormone secreted by medulla of adrenal gland. Helps to maintain normal blood pressure. Takamine obtained it in pure form (1901). Synthesized 1904. Injections are used to cause contraction of capillaries.

Adria (ā'drēŭ), ancient name of the Adriatic, extended to mean central Mediterranean in Acts 27.27.

Adrian I, d. 795, pope (772–95). Called on CHARLEMAGNE to repulse Lombard king, Desiderius. Increased papal lands through Donation of Charlemagne. Supported Empress IRENE against ICONOCLASM.

Adrian IV, d. 1159, pope (1154–59), an Englishman named Nicholas Breakspear. Driven from Rome by ARNOLD OF BRESCIA, he returned by 1155 and put down rebels with help of FREDERICK I, whom he crowned. Adrian had difficulties with William I of Sicily and Frederick. His donation of Ireland as fief to Henry II of England much disputed.

Adrian, emperor: see HADRIAN.

Adrian, Edgar Douglas, 1889–, English physiologist, authority on nervous system. Shared 1932 Nobel Prize in Physiology and Medicine for work on function of neuron.

Adrian, city (pop. 18,393), S Mich., SW of Detroit; settled 1835. Farm trade center with chrysanthemum culture and mfg. of metal and paper products.

Adrianople (ā"drēŭnō'pŭl) or **Edirne** (ĕdēr'nĕ), city (pop. 30,245), European Turkey, in Thrace. Commercial center; silk and cotton mfg. Founded by Emperor Hadrian A.D. c.125, it was the scene of a fateful Visi-

gothic victory over Emperor VALENS in 378. Passed to the Turks 1361; residence of the sultans 1361–1453. Briefly held by Bulgaria in the Balkan Wars (1913), it was given to Greece in 1920 and restored to Turkey in 1923. Chief among landmarks is the Mosque of Selim I, built by Sinan.

Adrianople, Treaty of, 1829, ended Russo-Turkish War of 1828–29. Turkey ceded some territories on Black Sea to Russia, allowed Russian occupation of Moldavia and Walachia, and granted Russia exclusive protective rights over Palestinian holy places and over Christian subjects of sultan. Dardanelles opened to all commercial vessels; autonomy given to Serbia, and promised to Greece.

Adriatic Sea (ādrēă'tĭk), arm of the Mediterranean, between Italy and Balkan Peninsula; 500 mi. long, 60–140 mi. wide, max. depth 4,035 ft. Low W and N shores belong to Italy, rugged E shore to Yugoslavia and Albania. Chief ports: Trieste, Venice, Bari, Fiume.

adsorption, attraction and adhesion of molecules of one substance to surface of another; no chemical change. Certain solids (e.g., charcoal) readily adsorb gases. Particles in colloidal solution may adsorb much of the solvent. Adsorption used in removing colors from solutions, in photography, in hydrogenation of oils, and in gas analysis.

Adullam (ŭdŭl'–), town of Judah, SW of Jerusalem. David hid in Cave of Adullam when fleeing from Saul. 1 Sam. 22; 2 Sam. 23.13–17; 1 Chron. 11.15–19.

adult education, training of adults beyond school age. Usual forms are lecture, reading, discussion groups. Formal attempts to organize adult education in 19th-cent. Europe gave rise to continuation schools in Switzerland and Germany, the FOLK SCHOOL in Denmark. In U.S. lectures of the LYCEUM and of the Lowell Institute of Boston long preceded the Chautauqua movement. Lectures supplemented by extension and correspondence courses offered by many colleges in 20th cent. Political and labor organs have promoted adult education, including VOCATIONAL TRAINING. Libraries have also advanced adult education groups, as has the Federal government. A separate program is that of the "great books" groups, which began meeting in 1947; the "great books" were published in a set in 1952. American Association for Adult Education was estab. (1926) to systematize philosophy and methods. In U.S., USSR, Mexico, and elsewhere adult-education schemes have successfully combated illiteracy.

Aduwa or **Adowa** (both: ä'dŭwä), town (pop. 6,000), N Ethiopia. Scene in 1896 of Menelik II's decisive victory over the Italian invaders.

Advent, four-week penitential season. In West, from Sunday nearest Nov. 30 (St. Andrew's) to Christmas. First season of church year.

Adventists, religious groups centering belief on second coming of Christ. William MILLER led Millerites or Second Adventists; Advent Christian Church (1861) was a branch. Seventh-Day Adventists adopted (1846) Saturday as Sabbath; divided on Ellen Gould White's prophecies. Church of God (organized c.1866) became (1888) Churches of God in Jesus Christ. There are other Adventist groups.

advertising, public notices, especially those designed to influence sales or use of the product made by the announcer (the advertiser). Major media are magazines, newspapers, television and radio, and such outdoor advertising as billboards and posters. Advertising agencies (becoming prominent in 1860s) have done much to put "salesmanship" into what had previously been merely "offers for sale."

Ady, Andrew (ŏ'dē), Hung. *Ady Endre,* 1877–1919, Hungarian modernist poet.

Adyge, Caucasian people: see CIRCASSIA.

Adzhar Autonomous Soviet Socialist Republic (ŭjär', ä'jär) or **Adzharistan** (ŭjä'rĭstän"), autonomous state (1,100 sq. mi.; pop. c.200,000, largely Mohammedan), SW Georgian SSR; cap. BATUM. Annexed by Russia from Turkey 1829 and 1878.

A. E., poet: see RUSSELL, GEORGE WILLIAM.

Aeëtes, king of Colchis: see JASON; MEDEA.

Aegadian Isles (ēgă'dēŭn), Latin *Aegates,* small archipelago, Italy, in Mediterranean off W Sicily. Here Roman naval victory (241 B.C.) ended First Punic War.

Aegean civilization (ējē'ŭn), general term for cultures of pre-Hellenic Greece. MINOAN CIVILIZATION was a rich culture of Crete (late 4th millennium B.C.). MYCENAEAN CIVILIZATION occupied mainland of Greece later. Other centers at Troy and in Cyclades.

Aegean Sea, arm of Mediterranean, c.400 mi. long and c.200 mi. wide, between Greece and Asia Minor; connected by Dardanelles with the Sea of Marmara. Its ancient name, Archipelago, now applies to its numerous islands, which include EUBOEA, N and S SPORADES, CYCLADES, and DODECANESE.

Aegeus (ē'jēŭs, ē'jōŏs), legendary king of Athens. Believing his son, Theseus, killed by the Minotaur, drowned himself in the sea (hence called Aegean).

Aegina (ējī'nŭ), Gr. *Aigina,* island (32 sq. mi.; pop. 10,-052), off SE Greece, in the Gulf of Aegina (Saronic Gulf), an arm of the Aegean, near Athens; chief town Aegina (pop. 5,820), on NW shore. Agr.; sulphur springs. Influenced by MINOAN CIVILIZATION, island was conquered c.1000 B.C. by Dorian Greeks. It struck first Greek coins and rose to great commercial importance. Was sacked by Athens against whom it sided in Peloponnesian War (431 B.C.). AEGINETAN MARBLES discovered near by (1811).

Aegineta, Paulus: see PAUL OF AEGINA.

Aeginetan marbles (ē"jĭnē'tŭn), Greek sculptures, probably of the 5th cent. B.C., discovered 1811 in Aegina. Depict story of Troy.

Aegisthus (ējĭs'thŭs), in Greek legend, lover of Clytemnestra. The lovers killed her husband, Agamemnon. In revenge her son, ORESTES, killed both.

Aegospotamos (ē"gŭspŏ'tŭmŭs), river of anc. Thrace. At its mouth occurred the final battle of the PELOPONNESIAN WAR (405 B.C.) when Lysander of Sparta destroyed the Athenian fleet.

Ælfric (ăl'frĭk), c.955–1020, English churchman, author of homilies, saints' lives, free version of first seven books of the Bible.

Aemilian Way: see ROMAN ROADS.

Aeneas (ĭnē'ŭs), Trojan prince who escaped from Troy to Carthage (where he met Dido) and finally went to Italy, where his descendants founded Rome. The *Aeneid* (ĭnē'ĭd), a 12-book Latin epic by VERGIL, tells of his adventures.

Aeolia, ancient Greek region: see AEOLIS.

Aeolian Islands: see LIPARI ISLANDS.

Aeolis (ē'ŭlĭs) or **Aeolia** (ēō'lēŭ), collective term for cities on W coast of Asia Minor planted by the Aeolians, a branch of the Hellenic peoples.

Aeolus (ē'ŭlŭs), in Greek mythology. **1** Wind-god, who kept winds in cave on Aeolia. **2** Son of Hellen and ancestor of Aeolian branch of Hellenic race.

aerial: see ANTENNA.

aerial photography, taking of still or moving-picture photographs from flying aircraft. Top military intelligence source in World War II. Photogrammetry is a map-making development.

aerodynamics: see FLIGHT.

aeroplane: see AIRPLANE.

Aeschines (ē'skĭnēs), c.389–314? B.C., Athenian orator, rival of Demosthenes.

Aeschylus (ēs'kĭlŭs, ēs–), 525–456 B.C., first of three great Greek poets of TRAGEDY. Added an actor and increased possibilities of the drama; won 13 first prizes. Author of perhaps 90 plays, seven in full extant: *The Suppliants, The Persians, The Seven against Thebes, Prometheus Bound,* and only extant ancient trilogy; the *Oresteia,* which contains the plays *Agamemnon, The Choëphoroe,* and *The Eumenides.*

Aesculapius: see ASCLEPIUS.

Aesir, Norse Olympian gods: see ASGARD.

Aesop (ē'sŭp, –sŏp), 6th cent. B.C., Greek fabulist, a slave of Samos (existence is doubtful). See FABLE.

aesthetics, philosophy of beauty and art. It studies the nature of beauty and laws governing its expression, as in the fine arts, as well as principles of artistic criticism. Some philosophers stress objectivity of nature of beauty, others claim that it is purely subjective.

Æthelbald (ĕ'thŭlbôld, ă'–), Anglo-Saxon kings. **Æthelbald,** d. 757, king of Mercia (716–57). A strong ruler, by 731 he controlled all England S of the Humber. Murdered by his bodyguard. **Æthelbald,** d. 860, king of Wessex, son of ÆTHELWULF and brother of ALFRED. Refused to allow his father to return to the kingdom after a pilgrimage to Rome. Married his father's widow, Judith of France, 858.

Æthelbert (–bŭrt, –bûrt), Anglo-Saxon kings. **Æthelbert,** d. 616, king of Kent (560?–616), was strongest ruler S of the Humber. St. Augustine converted him to Christianity and made his cap., Canterbury, a great Christian center. His laws are earliest extant body of laws in any Germanic language. **Æthelbert,** d. 866, king of Wessex (860–66), was son of Æthelwulf and brother of Alfred.

Æthelflæd (–flĕd) or **Ethelfleda** (ēthŭlflē'dŭ), d. 918, daughter of ALFRED. Reigned over Mercia alone from 911; was known as Lady of the Mercians. Her wise government made her known as one of English history's outstanding women.

Æthelfrith (–frĭth), d. 617, king of Northumbria; first great leader of N Angles. He forced his brother-in-law EDWIN (who pretended to throne) into exile. Killed in battle with Edwin's supporters near Nottingham.

Æthelred (–rĕd), Anglo-Saxon kings. **Æthelred,** d. 871, king of Wessex (866–71), son of ÆTHELWULF and brother of ALFRED. **Æthelred,** 965?–1016, king of England (978–1016), called Æthelred the Unready (Old Eng.= without counsel), son of Edgar and brother of EDWARD THE MARTYR. A weak king, he reigned at height of Danish power. He first levied DANEGELD 991. Danes returned in 997; stayed to plunder until 1000. He married (1002) Emma, sister of duke of Normandy, possibly to gain an ally. National navy built by 1009 was rendered useless by treason of its commanders. Danish king SWEYN was received by the DANELAW in 1013; London capitulated; Æthelred fled to Normandy. Restored on Sweyn's death (1014). Æthelred's son EDMUND IRONSIDE succeeded him (1016) and made treaty with CANUTE, son of Sweyn, who ruled England and married Æthelred's widow.

Æthelstan, English king: see ATHELSTAN.

Æthelwulf (–wŏŏlf), d. 858, king of Wessex (839–56), son of EGBERT and father of ÆTHELBALD, ÆTHELBERT, ÆTHELRED, and ALFRED. With Æthelbald won notable victory over Danes at Aclea (851). Married Judith of France in 856. A man of great piety, he learned while on pilgrimage in Rome that Æthelbald would resist his return; he left his son as king of Wessex and ruled in Kent and dependencies.

Aetius (āē'shēŭs), c.396–454, Roman general. Defeated the Germans in Gaul. Repulsed Attila and the Huns at Châlons (451). Murdered by Valentinian III.

Aetna: see ETNA.

Aetolia (ētōl'yŭ), region of anc. Greece, N of Gulf of Corinth and Gulf of Calydon. Its people, the Aetolians, were farmers and shepherds. Cities of Aetolia joined in **Aetolian League** in 4th cent. B.C. to oppose Achaean League and the Macedonians. With Roman help it defeated Philip V of Macedon in 200 B.C. but then joined Antiochus III and went down with his defeat (189 B.C.).

Afanasyev, Aleksandr Nikolayevich (ŭlyĭksän'dŭr nyĭkŭlī'ŭvĭch ŭfŭnä'syŭf), 1826–71, Russian folklorist. His collections of popular tales introduced Russian folklore to world literature.

affidavit, written statement sworn to by a person making it and signed by him and by officer administering the oath. It is used whenever written attestation of facts is needed, but in court only when cross-examination is not necessary.

Afghan hound: see HOUND.

Afghanistan (ăfgă'nĭstăn"), kingdom (253,000 sq. mi.; pop. 12,000,000), SW Asia; cap. Kabul. Bounded on N by USSR, on W by Iran, and on S and E by Pakistan. Mostly mountainous, with ranges fanning out from the Hindu Kush. Wheat, rice, and fruits are grown in fertile valleys; chief export is karakul. Helmand is longest river, with Amu Darya R. marking part of boundary with USSR. To the N are Afghan Turkistan and highlands of Badakshan (noted for lapis lazuli). Communications are poor (there are no railroads), and industry is in stage of infancy. Diversified population comprises Afghans, Tazhiks, Hazaras, Turkmen, and Uzbeks; unifying factor is religion, for almost all are Moslem. Chief languages are Afghan or Pushtu and Iranian. Area was annexed 516 B.C. by Darius I and conquered 326 B.C. by Alexander the Great on his way to India. Kingdom of BACTRIA (fl. 3d cent.–2d cent. B.C.) fell to Parthians and rebellious tribes. Buddhism spread from the E but had brief survival; stable religion was provided by Moslem conquest, begun in 7th cent. Greatest of many Moslem states was that of Mahmud of Ghazni, who in 11th cent. conquered parts of Persia and India. Area was later conquered by Jenghiz Khan and Tamerlane, and in 16th cent. Baber used Kabul as base for conquest of India. Unified state covering most of present Afghanistan was estab. in 18th cent. by AHMED SHAH. Reigns of DOST MOHAMMED and SHERE ALI saw Afghan Wars (1839–42, 1878–81), resulting from rivalry between Britain and Russia for Afghan buffer state. Anglo-Russian agreement (1907) guaranteeing country's independence under British influence roused anti-British feeling and led to short war in 1919. Emirate was changed to a kingdom in 1926 under Amanullah, who was deposed in 1929 by fanatical Moslem subjects who resented his radical reforms. His successor, Mohammed Nadir Shah, was assassinated in 1933 for continuing the program of modernization. He was succeeded by his son, Mohammed Zahir Shah. Despite Afghan opposition, Pakistan in 1950 took over the vaguely defined lands of Pathan tribes within Durand line (boundary estab. 1893 by Sir Mortimer Durand between North-West Frontier Prov., India, and Afghanistan). In 1953 Afghanistan was still supporting Pathans' desire for independent state of Pushtunistan.

Afghan language (ăf'găn"), Iranian language of Indo-European family, also called Pushtu. See LANGUAGE (table).

A.F. of L.: see AMERICAN FEDERATION OF LABOR.

Afonso. For rulers thus named, see ALFONSO.

Africa, continent (with adjacent islands c.11,500,000 sq. mi.; pop. c.200,000,000), joined to Asia by Sinai peninsula and facing Europe across Strait of Gibraltar. Mainly a plateau with its highest point at Mt. Kilimanjaro (19,565 ft.). In east is L. Victoria, its greatest lake. Vast river systems include the Nile, Niger, Congo, and Zambezi. The deserts, notably the Sahara, are edged by savannas. Jungles cover W equatorial Africa. In the civilization of Egypt (dating from before 3,000 B.C.) Africa may claim one of the world's most ancient settled cultures. The N African coast was colonized by Rome after the defeat of Carthage (149 B.C.). Islam was brought by the Arab invasion, 7th–11th cent. Moslem peoples (chiefly Moors) from N Africa launched a series of European invasions which ended in 15th cent. European exploration of the coast began in 15th cent. with Diaz's voyage around the Cape of Good Hope in 1488. The Portuguese were followed by Dutch, British, and French traders, 16th–17th cent. Explorations of interior revealed Africa's great wealth and led to large-scale colonization. By 1912 the European powers had partitioned Africa, with only Egypt, Ethiopia, and Liberia retaining a measure of independence. After World War I Germany lost her colonies to France and England (see BRITISH EMPIRE; FRENCH UNION). Other powers with lesser interests in Africa are Belgium, Portugal, and Spain. Italy after World War II was shorn by the UN of virtually all her African holdings. In World War II a series of major campaigns in NORTH AFRICA ended in 1943 with Axis defeat.

African Methodist Episcopal Church, American Negro denomination, founded (1794) by Richard ALLEN.

African Negro art, primarily the art of equatorial Africa. Known examples are mostly of recent origin, due to ravages of tropical climate. Style ranges from extreme naturalism to extreme formalism, from crudity to greatest refinement. Animism led to creation of ritual masks and fetishes. Highly prized ivories and bronzes of Benin, Nigeria, were produced 16th–17th cent. White domination brought rapid decline in production. Popular in Europe since 1905; vastly influenced abstract modern art.

African Negro music is highly rhythmic and polyphonic. Instruments are mainly percussive and wind. It was little studied until after invention of the phonograph. Extent of its influence on American Negro spirituals and jazz is subject of much debate.

Afrikaans (ä"frĭkäns', –känz'), standard language of the South African Dutch, a Germanic language of Indo-European family. See LANGUAGE (table).

afterbirth: see PLACENTA.

Afton, river of Ayrshire, Scotland. It is the "sweet Afton" of Burns's poem.

Ag, chemical symbol of the element SILVER.

Agade, ancient Mesopotamian city: see AKKAD.

Agadir (ägädēr'), town (pop. 12,438), French Morocco, a port on the Atlantic. Occupied and fortified by the Portuguese 1505–41. In 1911 when French troops were intervening in a Moroccan revolt, the German cruiser *Panther* appeared here, ostensibly to protect German property. The incident created a tense situation, later eased by agreements.

Agag (ā'găg), king of the Amalekites. Defeated and spared by Saul, he was killed by Samuel. I Sam. 15.

Aga Khan (ä'gä khän'), 1877–, Indian leader, the hereditary head of Mohammedan Ismaili sect. Sought Moslem support of British rule in India by founding All-India Moslem League in 1906. Represented India at League of Nations in 1930s. Famous for his wealth and for interest in horse racing.

Agamemnon (ä"gümĕm'nŏn), in Greek legend, leader of Greek armies in TROJAN WAR; brother of Menelaus. Quarrel with Achilles is a main theme of the *Iliad*. He married CLYTEMNESTRA, who bore him ELECTRA, ORESTES, and IPHIGENIA. Murdered by his wife and Aegisthus, he was avenged by his son, Orestes.

Agana (ägä'nyä), municipality, on Guam, near naval base at Apra Harbor. Before its destruction by the Japanese in 1945, it was Guam's largest town (1940 pop. 10,004; 1950 pop. 1,330).

Aganippe (ăg"ünĭp'ē), in Greek legend, nymph whose fountain on HELICON gives poetic inspiration to all who drink from it. Muses are often called Aganippides [Gr.,= daughters of Aganippe].

agar (ä'gär), or **agar-agar,** gelatinous product from red algae or seaweed, used as a laxative, sizing, food thickening, and culture medium for bacteria.

Agasias (ägä'shēäs), name of two Greek sculptors of the 1st cent. B.C. The creator of the Borghese Warrior (Louvre) was the son of Dositheus; the other was the son of Menophilus.

Agassiz, (Jean) Louis (Rodolphe) (zhä' lwē rōdôlf' ăg'üsē), 1807–73, Swiss-American zoologist, geologist. His research on fossil fish, exposition of glacial movement and deposit, and his teaching made Univ. of Neuchâtel a center of scientific study. As professor of zoology and geology at Lawrence Scientific School at Harvard he stimulated scientific study of nature in U.S. Agassiz's first wife died in Germany in 1848. His second wife **Elizabeth Cary Agassiz,** 1822–1907, was an author and educator. She accompanied her husband on expeditions to Brazil (1865–66) and along the E and W coasts of the Americas (1871–72). Influential in the founding of Radcliffe College, she

SMALL CAPITALS = cross references. Pronunciation key on inside end pages. Abbreviations: p. 2.

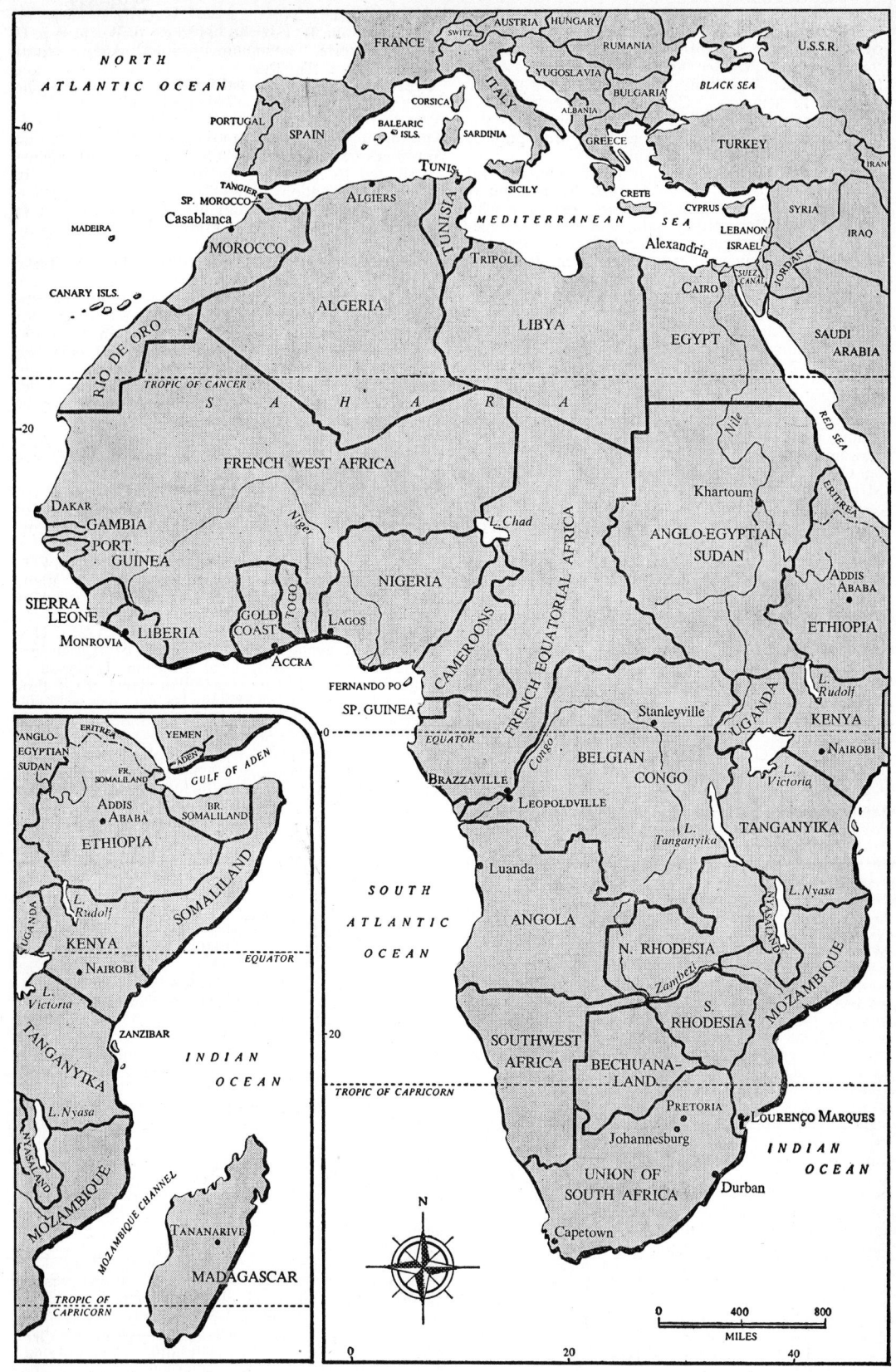

CAPITAL CITIES are designated by CAPITAL AND SMALL CAPITAL type

served to 1903 as its first president. With her husband she wrote *A Journey in Brazil* (1868) and with her stepson Alexander, *Seaside Studies in Natural History* (1885). **Alexander Agassiz**, 1835–1910, son of Louis Agassiz, was from 1862 connected with Harvard and its Museum of Comparative Zoology. Much of the wealth he acquired from copper mines was used for scientific expeditions and research publication. Noted also as oceanographer.

Agassiz, Lake, former lake, c.700 mi. long, 250 mi. wide, of Pleistocene epoch, formed by melting of continental ice sheet c.10,000 years ago over what are now NW Minn., NE N.Dak., S Manitoba. Named in 1879 for Louis Agassiz. Water drained N into Hudson Bay, left many smaller lakes and rich, deep soils.

agate, variety of QUARTZ banded in two or more colors. Used as semiprecious gem. Found in Brazil, India, Uruguay, and U.S.

Agatharchus (ăg″ŭthär′kŭs), 5th cent. B.C., Greek painter, credited with discoveries in perspective.

agave (ŭgā′vē, -gā′–), plant of genus *Agave* with long, stiff, fleshy leaves. Important in tropical America for fibers (e.g., SISAL HEMP), soap (see SOAP PLANT), food, and beverages (e.g., PULQUE and mescal). One species, century plant, used as house plant in North.

Agawam (ă′gŭwäm). **1** Town (pop. 10,166), SW Mass., on Connecticut R. below Springfield; settled 1635. Mfg. of woolens. **2** Former name of IPSWICH, Mass.

Ageladas (ăj″ŭlā′dŭs), c.540–c.460 B.C., Greek sculptor, famous for his statues of gods and athletes. Possibly taught Phidias and Myron.

Agen (äzhĕ′), city (pop. 26,051), cap. of Lot-et-Garonne dept., SW France, on the Garonne. Vineyards and orchards. Romanesque cathedral.

Agenor (ŭjē′–), Phoenician king; father of CADMUS and EUROPA.

ageratum (ăj″ŭrā′tŭm), popular annual (*Ageratum*), also called flossflower, with clustered lavender flowers. It is grown in borders and pots.

Agesander: see LAOCOÖN.

Agesilaus II (ŭjē″sīlā′ŭs), c.444–360 B.C., king of Sparta; successor of Agis I. Though admired by Xenophon, he gave Greek cities to Persia by King's Peace (386) and, having excluded Thebes from a peace treaty, was defeated by Epaminondas at Leuctra (371 B.C.).

Agincourt (ă′jĭnkôrt), modern Fr. *Azincourt* (äzĕkōōr′), village, Pas-de-Calais dept., N France. Here Henry V of England routed French Oct. 25, 1415.

Agis I (ā′jĭs), d. 398? B.C., king of Sparta, victor at Mantinea (418 B.C.).

Aglaia, one of the GRACES.

Agnes, Saint, 4th cent., noble Roman virgin martyred at 13 for rejecting pagan suitor. Feast: Jan. 21.

Agnes Scott College: see EMORY UNIVERSITY.

agnosticism, form of skepticism holding that reason cannot go beyond experience and that metaphysical beliefs (notably belief in God) cannot be definitely proved. Broadly, agnosticism includes teaching that metaphysical belief rests on faith alone (e.g., Kant) as well as materialistic systems (e.g., Comte, T. H. Huxley, Spencer).

Agnus Dei (än′yōōs dā′ē) [Latin,= Lamb of God, i.e., Jesus Christ], precommunion hymn in the Mass, so called from opening words; final number of sung Masses. The figure is of crucified Christ as sacrifice for mankind (sacrificial lamb).

Agoracritus (ăg″ōrăk′rĭtŭs), fl. 5th cent. B.C., Greek sculptor, said to have been a pupil of Phidias. Fragments of his colossal *Nemesis* survive.

Agoult, Marie (de Flavigny), comtesse d' (märē′ dŭ flävēnyē′ kōtĕs′ dägoō′), pseud. **Daniel Stern**, 1805–76, French author of autobiographical romances and social and political writings. Mistress of Liszt; mother of Cosima WAGNER.

agouti (ŭgoō′tē), rodents of genera *Dasyprocta* and *Myoprocta* of Central and South America, West Indies. Length c.1½ ft.; coat speckled reddish to black; legs long, slender.

Agra (ä′grŭ), city (pop. 284,149), W Uttar Pradesh, India, on Jumna R. Founded 1566 by Akbar as cap. of Mogul empire. Outstanding among many splendid buildings are the TAJ MAHAL, Pearl Mosque, and Great Mosque. Important rail junction. Cotton spinning and carpet mfg. Seat of Agra Col.

Agra and Oudh, India: see UTTAR PRADESH.

Agram, Yugoslavia: see ZAGREB.

Agrapha of Jesus (ăg′rŭfŭ) [Gr.,= not written], sayings attributed to Jesus not found in the four Gospels. There are quotations in the New Testament (e.g., Acts 20.35), and Agrapha from oral tradition appear in early Christian literature. Many are probably pseudepigrapha.

agrarian laws, in ancient Rome, regulated disposition of public lands. Patricians tended to gain (and hold) large areas, nominally as state tenants. Poorer classes' land hunger gave rise to laws, mostly ineffectual, beginning in 5th cent. B.C. Despite Licinian Rogations (367 B.C.), Sempronian Law (133 B.C.) and its revival (123 B.C.), and later large-scale reassignments, Domitian's edict (1st cent. A.D.) giving lands to their holders only confirmed long trend toward dependency of the poor upon the powerful.

Agricola (Cneius Julius Agricola) (ŭgrĭ′kŭlŭ), A.D. c.37–A.D. 93, Roman general, governor and pacifier of Britain; father-in-law of Tacitus.

Agricola, Georg (gā′ôrk), 1490?–1555, German physician and scientist, pioneer in scientific classification of minerals, and author of *De re metallica* (1556; Eng. tr. 1912).

Agricola, Johann or **Johannes** (yō′hän, yōhän′ŭs), 1492–1566, German Protestant minister (family name Schnitter, originally Schneider). Broke with Luther by upholding antinomianism.

Agricultural Adjustment Administration (AAA), U.S. government agency estab. in Dept. of Agriculture (1933) as part of New Deal program. Designed to help farmers by cutting supplies of staple crops, thus raising farm prices and changing agr. pattern from overproduction of staple crops to more diversified farming. In 1936 Supreme Court declared important sections of act invalid for infringing on powers of the states. Soil Conservation and Domestic Allotment Act (1936) subsidized conservation. Agricultural Adjustment Act of 1938 estab. "ever-normal granary"; empowered AAA to store surplus crops and maintain balance of prices between years of low yield and years of high yield. Functions of AAA taken over in 1946 by Production and Marketing Administration.

agriculture, in its narrow sense, is tilling the soil; more broadly, it includes stock raising, forestry, some mfg. (e.g., buttermaking). In prehistory, the change from hunting economy to tillage and domestication of beasts marked beginning of settlement, hence beginning of civilization. European agr. has long been mixed farming, much of it on subsistence level; in U.S., because of conquest of vast frontiers, increased growth of cities, and mechanization, farming tends to be on larger scale. Agr. colleges and government bureaus seek to increase productivity, improve depleted soil, and develop new plant and animal breeds.

Agriculture, United States Department of, division of U.S. government. Federal aid to agr. began modestly in 1839; Dept. of Agriculture, under a commissioner, was created 1862; Secretary of Agriculture became Cabinet member 1889. One of chief research, planning, service, and regulatory agencies of government; helps farmers with production, marketing, farm organization, land tenure, and land utilization problems, conducts huge research program, serves urban consumers, and issues many valuable publications.

Agrigento (ägrējĕn′tō), city (pop. 27,785), S Sicily, Italy, on a height 2 mi. from sea; called Girgenti before 1927. Founded as Acragas c.580 B.C. by Greek colonists from Gela; one of most splendid cities of anc. Grecian world. Remains of Doric temples (6th–5th cent. B.C.). Birthplace of the Greek philosopher, Empedocles, for whom near-by Porto Empedocle is named.

agrimony (ăg′rĭmō″nē), perennial plant of genus *Agrimonia*. Grows wild in N temperate zone and is cultivated in herb gardens. It has aromatic leaves and yellow flowers, followed by top-shaped burs.

Agrippa, in Palestinian history: see HEROD.

Agrippa, Marcus Vipsanius (mär′kŭs vĭpsā′nēŭs ŭgrĭ′pŭ), c.63 B.C.–c.12 B.C., Roman general, lieutenant and son-in-law of Augustus. Fought against Sextus Pompeius and against Antony at Actium.

Agrippina I (ă″grĭpī′nŭ), d. A.D. 33, Roman matron, daughter of Agrippa, granddaughter of Augustus, mother of Caligula. She accused Tiberius of having her husband Germanicus poisoned. Her daughter, **Agrippina II,** d. A.D. 59, was mother of NERO by her first marriage; after marriage to her uncle CLAUDIUS I she persuaded him to adopt Nero, then probably poisoned him to advance Nero, who had her murdered.

Agua (ä′gwä), inactive volcano, 12,310 ft. high, S Guatemala. In 1541 a flood from the mountain destroyed Ciudad Vieja, then cap. of Guatemala.

Aguascalientes (ä″gwäskälyän′tās), state (2,499 sq. mi.; pop. 188,104), N central Mexico, on central plateau; cap. Aguascalientes (pop. 82,234), founded 1575. State is rich in agr. produce and cattle; has mineral resources (largely unexploited) and warm mineral springs.

Aguinaldo, Emilio (ägwĭnäl′dō; āmē′lyō ägēnäl′dō), 1869?–, Philippine leader. Led insurrection in Spanish-American War; headed rebellion (1899–1901) against U.S. occupying forces until captured.

Aguirre, Lope de (lō′pä dä ägē′rä), c.1510–1561, Spanish rebel in colonial South America, noted for violence and cruelty. On expedition down Marañón and Amazon (1560), he killed Ursúa, the leader, laid waste Indian villages; held Margarita Isl. in terror (1561); and proclaimed rebellion against Spain. Surrounded at Barquisimeto, before he surrendered and was shot, he had his own daughter murdered.

Agulhas, Cape (ŭgŭ′lŭs), W Cape Prov., South Africa; most southerly point of Africa. On dividing line between Atlantic and Indian oceans.

Ahab (ā′hăb), d. c.853 B.C., king of Israel (c.874–c.853 B.C.), politically one of its greatest kings, religiously one of its wickedest; successor of Omri. He consolidated foreign relations by strategic marriages: his own to JEZEBEL of Tyre, his daughter Athaliah's to son of king of Judah. Bible account concerned chiefly with religious aspects of his reign. His foreign wife, with her Tyrian cults, led him into constant clashes with ELIJAH. He died in battle against Benhadad of Syria. 1 Kings 16.28–22.40.

Ahasuerus (ŭhăs″ūē′rŭs), Hebrew form of Xerxes used in Bible. In Esther probably Xerxes I; in Tobit 14.15 may be Cyaxares I, destroyer of Nineveh. Father of DARIUS THE MEDE given as Ahasuerus.

Ahaz (ā′hăz), d. c.727 B.C., king of Judah (c.731–727 B.C.). His reign marks end of Judah's real independence. Coalition of Israel and Syria attacked him and nearly took Jerusalem. He appealed to Assyrians, who defeated his enemies but demanded tribute, which he paid with Temple gold. Succeeded by Hezekiah. Isaiah was a contemporary of Ahaz. 2 Kings 16; 2 Chron. 28; Isa. 7; 38. Achaz: Mat. 1.9.

Ahaziah (āhŭzī′ŭ). **1** Died c.852 B.C., king of Israel (c.853–852 B.C.), son of Ahab. 1 Kings 22.51–53; 2 Kings 1; 2 Chron. 20.35–37. **2** Died c.846 B.C., king of Judah (c.846 B.C.), son of Jehoram 2 and Athaliah. Killed in Jehu's coup d'état. His mother succeeded him. 2 Kings 8.25–29; 9; 2 Chron. 22.

Ahijah (ŭhī′jŭ) [Heb.,= brother of God], priest in Saul's time. May be same as AHIMELECH. 1 Sam. 14.3.

Ahimelech (ŭhĭm′ŭlĕk), priest, brother of (or perhaps same as) Ahijah. Saul had him killed for helping David. 1 Sam. 22.9–19. Abimelech: 1 Chron. 18.16.

Ahithophel (ŭhĭth′ŭfĕl), David's counselor. Plotted with Absalom; facing ruin, he killed himself. 2 Sam. 15.12; 16:20–17.23; 11.3; 23.34. Dryden's satire, *Absalom*

and Achitophel, uses instead the Vulgate form of name.

Ahmadabad, India: see AHMEDABAD.

Ahmed IV (ä′mĕd), d. 1603, sultan of Morocco (1578–1603). Defeated the Portuguese at Alcazarquivir in 1578. Morocco prospered under his reign.

Ahmed, Ottoman sultans. **Ahmed I,** 1589–1617, reigned 1603–17. Made peace with Austria (1606), recognizing Transylvanian independence. Lost Tabriz to ABBAS I. **Ahmed III,** 1673–1736, reigned 1703–30. Harbored CHARLES XII of Sweden. In war with Russia (1710–11) he recovered Azov. Defeated by the Austrians, he signed Treaty of PASSAROWITZ (1718). He was overthrown by the Janizaries.

Ahmed, 1898–1930, shah of Persia (1909–25), last of Kajar dynasty; deposed by Reza Shah Pahlevi.

Ahmedabad or **Ahmadabad** (both: äm″ŭdŭbäd′), city, (pop. 595,210), NW Bombay, India. Sacred to Gujarat sect of Jains. Cotton textile mills.

Ahmed Shah (ä′mĕd shä′), c.1723–1773, Afghan ruler, founder of Durani dynasty. Won Afghan rule by supporting Nadir Shah of Iran.

Ahriman: see ZOROASTRIANISM.

Ahura Mazdah: see ZOROASTRIANISM.

Ahvenanmaa, Finland: see ALAND ISLANDS.

aids, in feudalism, type of feudal due paid by a vassal to his suzerain or lord. Their exact nature is subject to controversy. In English-speaking countries, as specified in MAGNA CARTA of 1215, aids were due on knighting of lord's eldest son, on marriage of his eldest daughter, for ransom when lord was in captivity. In France aids were converted into a form of royal tax and continued to 1789. See also SCUTAGE; TALLAGE.

Aigues-Mortes (ĕg-môrt′), town (pop. 3,320), Gard dept., S France, near Mediterranean. Louis IX built port (now silted up). Medieval towers, ramparts.

Aijalon (ă′jŭ–, ī′jŭ–, ā′jŭ–), valley over which Joshua commanded moon to stand still. Joshua 10.12.

Aiken, Conrad (ā′kĭn), 1889–, American poet, novelist. Poems (e.g., *The Jig of Forslin*, 1916; *Preludes for Memnon*, 1931) show preoccupation with music. Novels (e.g., *Blue Voyage*, 1927) are psychological. Also wrote short stories, criticism, autobiography.

Aiken, city (pop. 7,083), W S.C., NE of Augusta, Ga. Resort, trade, and industrial center for farming and forest area.

ailanthus (ālăn′–) or **tree of heaven,** hardy deciduous tree (*Ailanthus*), with large compound leaves. Native to China, common in European and American cities. Is tolerant of smoke and other handicaps.

Ailly, Pierre d' (pyĕr′dāyē′), 1350–1420, French cardinal. Favored calling of general council to end Great Schism and was prominent in Council of Constance. His astronomical work, *Imago mundi,* studied by Columbus.

Ailsa Craig (āl′sŭ), conspicuous rocky island (1,114 ft. high) off SW Scotland, in Ayrshire.

Ain (ē), department (2,249 sq. mi.; pop. 306,778), E France, in Bresse; cap. Bourg-en-Bresse.

Aintab, Turkey: see GAZIANTEP.

Aintree, difficult and dangerous racecourse, Lancashire, England. The Grand National is run here.

Ainu (ī′nōō), aborigines of Japan. Forced by Japanese to retreat to N islands where they now live as hunters and food gatherers. Short, stocky, and hairy, they resemble Europeans more than Mongoloids. Their language is unrelated to any known speech.

air: see ATMOSPHERE; LIQUID AIR; VENTILATION.

air, law of the, law, both national and international, regulating civil aviation. Generally national legislation has been modeled in most countries on rules adopted in international conventions. The Paris meeting in 1919 drew up Paris Convention. In 1944 conference of 52 nations (not including the USSR) led to agreements and to founding of Internatl. Civil Aviation Organization. Question of national rights *vs.* freedom of the air not settled.

aircraft carrier, ship designed to store, launch, and land aircraft. Used experimentally in World War I; most important of capital ships in World War II battles.

Airedale terrier: see TERRIER.

airfoil, surface designed to react in particular way to moving air stream. Thus aircraft wing surfaces produce lift, movable aileron surfaces make possible rotation around longitudinal axis, and variable pitch propeller blades produce change in thrust. Autogiro rotor blades with suddenly changed pitch can jump craft into air.

air mail. Demonstrated in U.S. and England in 1911. Army pilots and aircraft began regular U.S. civilian service with New York-to-Washington flight May 15, 1918; continued by Post Office Dept. 1920–21. Coast-to-coast service (all by air) operated by Post Office Dept. 1924–27. Commercial contracts authorized in 1925. Service extends to most of world.

airplane or **aeroplane,** heavier-than-air craft developing propulsive power and sustained by air action on external surfaces. First man-carrying, power-driven, heavier-than-air flight was that of Wright brothers' biplane (Kitty Hawk, N.C., Dec. 17, 1903). Airplanes are usually monoplane (one wing). Main structures: fuselage (main body); one or more power plants (engines), each with propeller; landing gear; and movable control surfaces (ailerons for longitudinal control; rudder for vertical control; and elevator for horizontal control). See also JET PROPULSION. See *ill.,* p. 19.

air plant or **epiphyte,** plant, such as orchid and Spanish moss, not normally rooted in soil, but unlike PARASITE, able to make its food by PHOTOSYNTHESIS. Grows on another plant or other support and gets water from atmosphere.

airport, land area with runways suitable for heavier aircraft. Provides taxiing and parking strips; hangars; repair and fueling facilities; traffic tower; radio and meteorological apparatus; passenger and cargo stations; beacons, floodlights, obstacle lights, other illumination. See also AIRWAY.

air power. Use of aircraft in World War I led some theorists (notably the American William Mitchell and the Italian Giulio Douhet) to develop the idea of predominance of air power—victory by aircraft alone. In World War II airplanes were used extensively, and Germans and Italians used aircraft effectively (as in capture of Crete). Similarly, loss of air supremacy locally (as in attacks on Britain, 1940–41) and generally in 1944–45 played a large part in defeat of the Axis. Aircraft carriers were prominent in the Pacific warfare. Yet the question of victory by air alone was not settled, and was complicated by introduction of atomic bombs and jet propulsion.

airship, self-propelled, steerable (dirigible) balloon. Internal gas pressure shapes nonrigid (e.g., blimp) and semirigid types. Rigid airships (largest type) are elongated, have rigid frame or latticework of aluminum or duralumin compartmented for gas cells and covered by fabric. Engines inside drive propellers outside. Lift is provided by hydrogen gas (most buoyant) or helium (noninflammable).

airsickness, any disorder arising from flight at high altitudes or great speed. Similar to seasickness but caused by aircraft motion. Rapid ascent causes aeroembolism (circulation blocked by nitrogen bubbles released in blood by sudden change of atmospheric pressure). Anoxia (insufficient oxygen in cells), a form of altitude sickness induced by decrease of pressure and oxygen, may result in loss of muscular control and unconsciousness.

airway, air route between air traffic centers over terrain most suitable for emergency landings, spaced with landing fields equipped with air navigation and radio facilities. Civil Aeronautics Authority supervises U.S. airway traffic and facilities and enforces flight rules.

Airy, Sir George Biddell, 1801–92, English astronomer, authority on magnetism and on meteorology, astronomer royal (1835–81).

Aisha: see AYESHA.

Aisne (ān, Fr. ěn), department (2,868 sq. mi.; pop. 453,-

411), NE France; cap. Laon. Towns: Soissons, Château-Thierry, Saint-Quentin. Aisne R., tributary of Oise, was important battle line in World War I.

Aitken, Robert Grant (āt′kǐn), 1864–1951, American astronomer, authority on double stars. Director (1930–35) Lick Observatory.

Aix-en-Provence (ěks′-ä-prŏvãs′, ěk″sä-), city (pop. 32,076), Bouches-du-Rhône dept., SE France. Founded c.122 B.C. by Romans as Aquae Sextiae; scene of Marius' victory over Teutons (102 B.C.); cap. of Provence before 1789; center of medieval Provençal culture. University founded 1409, now partly in Marseilles.

Aix-la-Chapelle, Germany: see AACHEN.

Aix-la-Chapelle, Treaty of. 1 Compact of May 2, 1668, which ended War of DEVOLUTION. France kept most of its conquests in Flanders but returned Franche-Comté to Spain. Spanish possessions in Low Countries were guaranteed by TRIPLE ALLIANCE. **2** Treaty of 1748, ending War of the AUSTRIAN SUCCESSION. It generally restored the prewar map, but awarded Silesia to Prussia and conferred Parma, Piacenza, and Guastalla on the Spanish infante, Philip. PRAGMATIC SANCTION was confirmed.

Aix-les-Bains (ěks′-lä-bě′), town (pop. 10,720), Savoie dept., E France, on Lake Bourget; spa.

Ajaccio (Fr. äzhäksyō′, It. äyät′chô), city (pop. 27,536), cap. of Corsica, France; seaport. Birthplace of Napoleon I.

Ajanta (ùjŭn′tù), village, NW Hyderabad, India. Has cave dwellings and shrines decorated with Buddhist art (200 B.C.–A.D. 600).

Ajax (ā′jăks), Gr. *Aias,* in Greek legend. **1** Hero of Trojan War, called Telemonian Ajax. A giant, slow of mind and speech. Rescued body of Achilles. When Achilles' armor was given to Odysseus, he committed suicide. **2** Leader of Locrian forces in Trojan War, called the Locrian Ajax. Violated Cassandra. Rescued from shipwreck by Poseidon, he defied the lightning and was struck dead.

Ajmer (ăjmēr′), state (2,400 sq. mi., pop. 583,693), NW India. Comprises two detached areas surrounded by Rajasthan. **Ajmer,** city (pop. 147,258), state cap. was founded c.1100. Cotton mills, railroad shops.

Ajo (ä′hō), village (pop. 5,817), SW Ariz., SW of Phoenix. Health resort and smelting center in mining area. Organ Pipe Cactus Natl. Monument is S.

Ajodhya, India: see FYZABAD.

Akbar (ăk′bär), 1542–1605, Mogul emperor of India (1556–1605), grandson of Baber. Enlarged his original domain in N central India to include Afghanistan and all of N India. Known for administrative reforms and religious tolerance.

Akeley, Carl Ethan (āk′lē), 1864–1926, American naturalist, sculptor. Noted for improved methods of mounting habitat groups, invention of cement gun and Akeley camera, and bronze works of sculpture of African wildlife and natives. Made numerous African expeditions for American museums. Author of *In Brightest Africa* (1923).

Akhenaton: see IKHNATON.

Akhmatova, Anna (ùkhmä′tùvù), pseud. of Anna Andreyevna Gorenko, 1888–, Russian poet, a leading Acmeist. Her poems of love and tragedy are sculptured in their simplicity yet rhythmic in the tradition of Pushkin. Long very popular in Soviet Russia, she was criticized in 1948 by the Communist party for "bourgeois aristocratic aestheticism."

Akiba ben Joseph (ùkī′bù), A.D. c.50–c.132, Palestinian rabbi, one of first to systematize Hebrew oral laws. Aided revolt of Simon Bar Kochba against Rome.

Akihito (äkē′hētō), 1933–, Japanese prince, son of Emperor Hirohito. Officially named heir apparent to Japanese throne in Nov., 1952.

Akkad (ă′kăd, ä′käd), northern part of Babylonia, in Mesopotamia; the southern part was Sumer. From the 4th millennium B.C. a Semitic people flourished and under Sargon (c.2800) became an imperial power. Un-

---

SMALL CAPITALS = cross references. Pronunciation key on inside end pages. Abbreviations: p. 2.

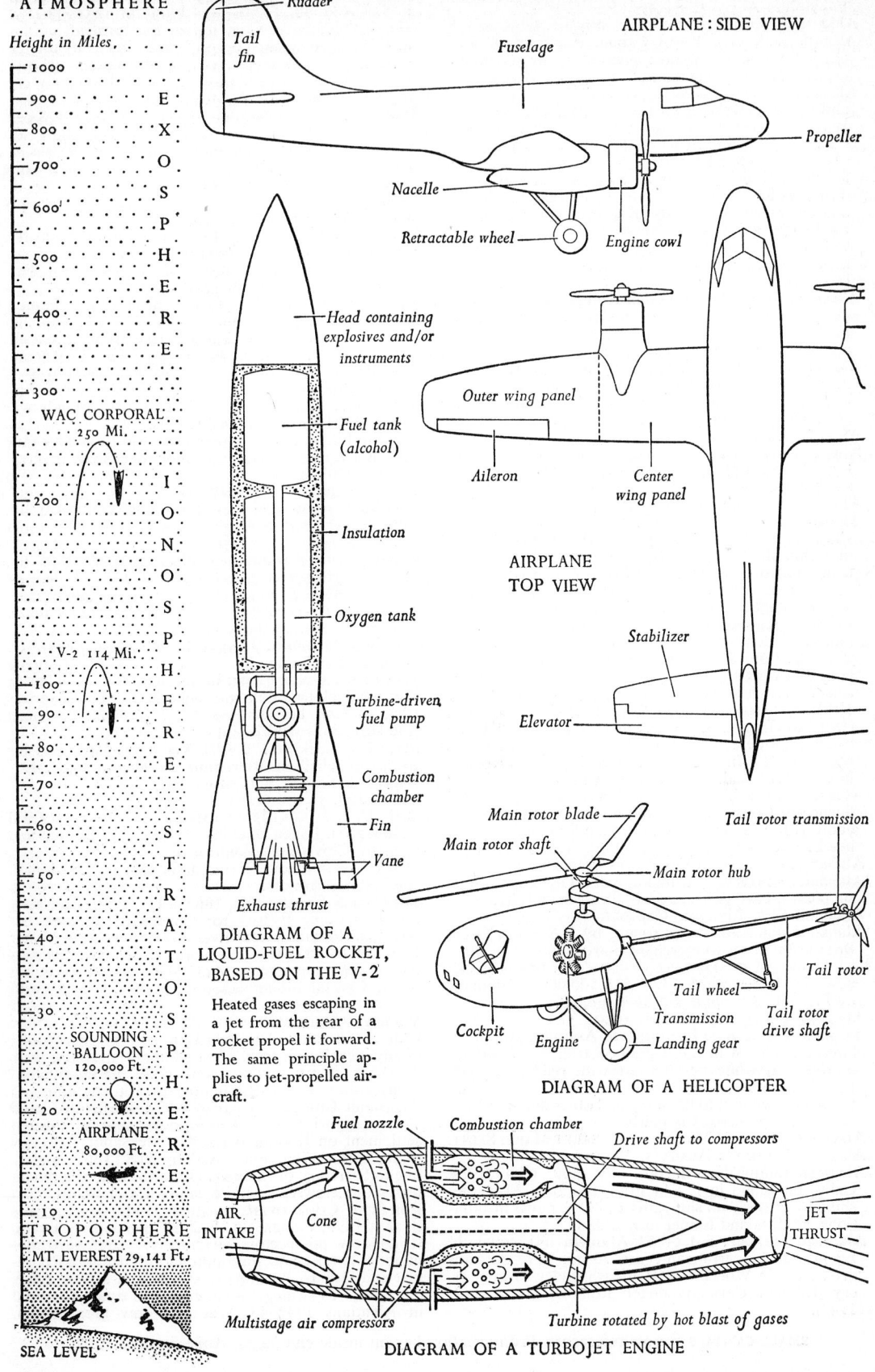

ATMOSPHERE

Height in Miles

1000

900 — E
800 — X
700 — O
600 — S
— P
500 — H
— E
400 — R
— E
300

WAC CORPORAL
250 Mi.

200 — I
— O
— N
— O
— S
V-2 114 Mi. — P
100 — H
90 — E
80 — R
70 — E
60 — S
50 — T
40 — R
— A
30 — T
— O
SOUNDING — S
BALLOON — P
120,000 Ft. — H
20 — E
AIRPLANE — R
80,000 Ft. — E
10

TROPOSPHERE

MT. EVEREST 29,141 Ft.

SEA LEVEL

Rudder

Tail fin

AIRPLANE : SIDE VIEW

Fuselage

Propeller

Nacelle

Retractable wheel

Engine cowl

Head containing explosives and/or instruments

Fuel tank (alcohol)

Outer wing panel

Insulation

Aileron

Center wing panel

AIRPLANE TOP VIEW

Oxygen tank

Stabilizer

Turbine-driven fuel pump

Elevator

Combustion chamber

Fin

Vane

Main rotor blade

Tail rotor transmission

Main rotor shaft

Main rotor hub

Exhaust thrust

DIAGRAM OF A LIQUID-FUEL ROCKET, BASED ON THE V-2

Heated gases escaping in a jet from the rear of a rocket propel it forward. The same principle applies to jet-propelled aircraft.

Cockpit

Engine

Tail wheel

Tail rotor

Transmission

Landing gear

Tail rotor drive shaft

DIAGRAM OF A HELICOPTER

Fuel nozzle

Combustion chamber

Drive shaft to compressors

AIR INTAKE

Cone

JET THRUST

Multistage air compressors

Turbine rotated by hot blast of gases

DIAGRAM OF A TURBOJET ENGINE

der Hammurabi Akkad and Sumer were united as Babylonia. Also spelled Accad.

Akkerman: see BELGOROD-DNESTROVSKY, Ukraine.

Aklavik (äklä'vĭk), Royal Canadian Mounted Police post and public seaplane anchorage in Mackenzie dist., Northwest Territories, Canada, on Peel R.

Akron, city (pop. 274,605), NE Ohio, on Cuyahoga R. and SE of Cleveland; settled 1807. Its site was in the WESTERN RESERVE. Growth was spurred by opening (1827) of Ohio and Erie Canal. Hub of U.S. rubber industry and U.S. center for lighter-than-air craft, it has airport stadium, Zeppelin airdock (*Akron* and *Macon* dirigibles built here), and mfg. of cereals, machinery, and chemicals. **University of Akron** (city supported; coed.) was chartered 1870, opened 1872 as Buchtel Col., became (1913) Municipal Univ., renamed 1926; includes Guggenheim Airship Inst. and city testing laboratory.

Aksakov, Sergei Timofeyevich (syĭrgä' tyĭmùfyä'ùvĭch ŭksä'kùf), 1791–1859, Russian writer. Author of *The Family Chronicle* (1856; Eng. tr., 1916–24), a remarkable picture of life of landed gentry.

Aksum or **Axum** (both: äksōōm'), town (pop. 10,000), N Ethiopia. Was cap. of dynasty (1st–6th cent.) which ruled over parts of modern Ethiopia and the Sudan. A major center of Coptic Christianity.

Akte, Greek peninsula: see ATHOS.

Akureyri (ä'kürä''rē), port (pop. 7,017), N Iceland, on Eyja Fjord. Exports train oil, fish products, wool, sheepskins.

Al, chemical symbol of the element ALUMINUM.

Alabama (ălùbă'mù), state (51,609 sq. mi.; pop. 3,061,- 743), SE U.S.; admitted 1819 as 22d state (slaveholding); cap. MONTGOMERY. N part is on Cumberland Plateau; mineral-rich highlands; BIRMINGHAM is iron and steel center. Alluvial plains in S drained by Alabama and Tombigbee rivers. Extreme SW touches Gulf of Mexico; great port is MOBILE. Around Tennessee R. is industrial development of TENNESSEE VALLEY AUTHORITY. Long a "cotton" state, Ala. has usual problems following one-crop culture. Agr. now much diversified. Area first explored by Spanish (esp. De Soto 1540), first settled (1702) by French under BIENVILLE. Ceded to Great Britain 1763, to U.S. 1783. Settlement heavy after defeat (1814) of Creek Indians. Made territory in 1817. In Confederacy (seceded Jan. 11, 1861) in Civil War. Industrial development later.

Alabama, navigable river formed in central Ala. by confluence of Coosa and Tallapoosa rivers above Montgomery. Flows 318 mi. W, SW, then S to join Tombigbee R. and form Mobile R. c.30 mi. N of Mobile.

Alabama, ship: see CONFEDERATE CRUISERS.

Alabama, University of, mainly near Tuscaloosa; state supported, coed.; chartered 1820, opened 1831.

Alabama City, Ala.: see GADSDEN.

Alabama claims, damages sought by U.S. from Great Britain for losses to merchant marine caused by British-financed CONFEDERATE CRUISERS. Tribunal at Geneva (1871–72) awarded U.S. $15,500,000 for damage by *Florida, Alabama,* and *Shenandoah.*

Alabama College: see MONTEVALLO.

Alabama Polytechnic Institute: see AUBURN, Ala.

alabaster, (ăl'ùbăs''tùr), fine-grained, translucent variety of GYPSUM, white or streaked with reddish brown. Used for statues, decorations. Very soft, hence easily worked but subject to breaking and other damage. Alabaster of the ancients is marble.

Alacoque, Margaret Mary: see MARGARET MARY, SAINT.

Alagez, Mount: see ARAGATS, MOUNT.

Alameda (ălùmē'dù, –mä'dù), city (pop. 64,430), W Calif., on island in E San Francisco Bay. Mfg. and shipping center with shipyards and U.S. naval installations. Bridges and tunnel to mainland.

Alamein (ălùmān', ä–) or **El Alamein** (ĕl), town, N Egypt, on Mediterranean coast, 70 mi. W of Alexandria. Here in World War II British under Montgomery defeated Germans under Rommel (Nov. 1–2, 1942).

Alamo, the (ăl'ùmō) [Spanish,= cottonwood], building in San Antonio, Texas, "the cradle of Texas liberty." Heroic but hopeless defense of the fortified building in Feb., 1836, against Santa Anna's demands for surrender, roused fighting anger among Texans, who six weeks later defeated the Mexicans at San Jacinto, crying, "Remember the Alamo!"

Alamogordo (ăl'ùmùgôr'dō), town (pop. 6,783), S central N.Mex. Trade center in farm, timber, and resort area. First atomic bomb, made at Los Alamos, was exploded in desert region NW on July 16, 1945. White Sands Natl. Monument is near.

Alamo Heights, city (pop. 8,000), S central Texas, N suburb of San Antonio.

Alamosa (ălùmō'sù), city (pop. 5,354; alt. c.7,500 ft.), S Colo., on Rio Grande; founded 1878. Processing and shipping center for farm and ranch area. Great Sand Dunes Natl. Monument is NE.

Aland Islands (ä'lùnd, ô'–), Finnish *Ahvenanmaa,* Swed. *Ålandsöerna,* archipelago (572 sq. mi.; pop. 22,- 569), Finland, in Baltic Sea, strategically placed at entrance to Gulf of Bothnia; chief town Mariehamn. Pop. largely Swedish. Fishing, farming. Ceded by Sweden to Russia 1809; became part of independent Finland 1917. Finnish-Swedish dispute over islands was settled 1921 by League of Nations, which awarded islands to Finland (with autonomous status) and forbade remilitarization. Russo-Finnish demilitarization agreement (1940) was renewed after World War II. Also spelled Aaland.

Alarcón, Hernando de (ĕrnän'dō dä älärkōn'), fl. 1540, Spanish explorer in American Southwest, discovered Colorado R.

Alarcón, Pedro Antonio de (pād'rō äntō'nyō), 1833–91, Spanish writer. His short novels, such as *El final de Norma* (1855), *El sombrero de tres picos* (1874, Eng. tr. *The Three-cornered Hat,* 1891), and *El capitán Veneno* (1881), are popular.

Alarcón y Mendoza, Juan Ruiz de (hwän' rōōĕth' dä älärkōn' ē mändō'thä), d. 1639, Spanish dramatic poet of the Golden Age, b. Mexico. His comedies in the classical tradition are notable for characterization; perhaps best known is *La verdad sospechosa* [the suspicious truth].

Alaric I (ä' lùrĭk), c.370–410, Visigothic king. Led his troops in rebellion after death of Theodosius I, devastated S Balkans until stopped by Stilicho. Invaded Italy (408); sacked Rome (410).

Alaric II, d. 507, Visigothic king of Spain and S Gaul (c.484–507). Issued BREVIARY OF ALARIC. Routed and slain by Clovis I at Vouillé.

Alaska, U.S. territory (571,065 sq. mi.: pop. 128,643), NW North America; admitted 1912; cap. JUNEAU. Bounded N by Arctic Ocean; W by Bering Sea; S by Pacific Ocean; E by Canada. Includes ALEUTIAN ISLANDS, PRIBILOF ISLANDS, KODIAK ISLAND, SAINT LAWRENCE ISLAND; other coastal islands. BROOKS RANGE separates interior lands from Barren Grounds of N. Coastal mountains and ALASKA RANGE (with Mt. McKinley) rim valleys in S (esp. the MATANUSKA VALLEY, with its metropolis, ANCHORAGE). Panhandle, with ALEXANDER ARCHIPELAGO, is most accessible, highly developed area. Fishing main industry (esp. Alaska salmon); mining (gold, coal, platinum, antimony, tin). Fur trade still important. Vitus BERING and Aleksandr Chirikov first reached Alaska from Russia 1741. Grigori SHELEKHOV founded first permanent settlement on Kodiak Isl. 1784; Aleksandr BARANOV estab. SITKA 1799. Purchased by U.S. 1867, mostly due to Secretary of State W. H. Seward. Development proceeded slowly. Boundaries set 1903; BERING SEA FUR-SEAL CONTROVERSY settled 1911. Gold strikes (NOME 1899; FAIRBANKS 1902) followed 1896 Yukon strike, drew prospectors, adventurers. Attempt of monopolies to take over was opposed by Theodore Roosevelt and Gifford Pinchot. World War II saw Alaska's emergence as strategic area. Japanese estab. foothold in Aleutians 1942–43. War also saw great boom, which has continued with present military, economic concern over area. Hopes for statehood shared by many in U.S.

Alaska, University of, at College, near Fairbanks; land grant and territorial, coed.; chartered 1917. Opened 1922 as Alaska Agricultural Col. and School of Mines; became university 1935. Has school of mines, geophysical observatory, and a seismograph. Cooperates in research with government and private institutions.

Alaska Highway, 1,527 mi. long, from Dawson Creek, B.C., Canada, to Fairbanks, Alaska, formerly called Alaska Military Highway, Alaska International Highway, and Alcan Highway. Noted engineering feat, built March–Oct., 1942, by U.S. troops to supply Alaskan forces. Haines Cutoff connects it with Alaska's Panhandle. Last stretch to Fairbanks uses previously built Richardson Highway. Canadian part of road transferred 1946 to Canadian control.

Alaska Range, S central Alaska, rising to 20,270 ft. in Mt. McKinley, highest point in North America. Range divides S central Alaska from great interior plateau.

Alastor (ùlä'stùr), in Greek mythology, the spirit of vengeance.

Ala-Tau (ä'lä-tou'), six lofty mountain ranges of central Asia. Four of them rise to more than 16,000 ft. In general they are near L. Issyk Kul and belong to Tien Shan system.

Álava, Spain: see BASQUE PROVINCES.

Alba or **Alva, Fernando Álvarez de Toledo, duque de** (fĕrnän'dō äl'värāth dä tōlä'dhō dōō'kä dä äl'vä), 1508–1582, duke of Alba, Spanish general. Succeeded (1567) Margaret of Parma as regent in Netherlands for Philip II. To suppress rebellion set up "Court of Blood" (18,000 executed, including EGMONT). Resigned 1573. Conquered Portugal (1580); seized Lisbon, permitted massacre there.

Albacete (älbäthä'tä), city (pop. 50,567), cap. of Albacete prov., SE Spain, in Murcia; agr. center.

Alba-Iulia (äl'bä-yōō'lyä), Hung. *Gyulafehérvár,* Ger. *Karlsburg,* city (pop. 14,420), central Rumania, in a wine-growing region. Former seat of Transylvanian princes. Fortress built by Emperor Charles VI.

Alba Longa (äl'bù lông'gù), city of anc. Latium. In legend founded by son of Aeneas; birthplace of Romulus and Remus; destroyed by Roman king, Tullus Hostilius (c.600 B.C.?).

Albania (älbä'nyù), Albanian *Shqipnija* or *Shqiperia,* republic (10,629 sq. mi.; pop. 1,122,044), SE Europe, on Adriatic coast of Balkan Peninsula, between Yugoslavia and Greece; cap. Tirana. A rugged mountain country (except for a fertile coastal strip, with ports of DURAZZO and VALONA), it has rich copper and coal deposits but is economically underdeveloped. The people are mainly hill tribes of very ancient stock; c.60% are Moslem, 20% Greek Orthodox, 10% Roman Catholic. Large Albanian minorities live in Yugoslavia and Greece. Including parts of ancient ILLYRIA and EPIRUS, Albania has known many masters (notably Macedon, Rome, Byzantium, and Turkey), but their domination was never effective among the inland mountain clans. Italian penetration began with ROBERT GUISCARD (11th cent.). It was continued by Naples and Venice, which held Durazzo until 1501, when the Turkish conquest, long delayed by SCANDERBEG, became final. Independence from Turkey was proclaimed 1912 during the first Balkan War. An international commission assigned large areas claimed by Albania to Montenegro, Serbia, and Greece (1913). A battleground and the scene of political chaos during and after the second Balkan War and World War I, Albania passed in turn under the kingship of WILLIAM, PRINCE OF WIED, the dictatorship of ESSAD PASHA, and the dictatorship (after 1928 kingship) of ZOG. It soon became a virtual Italian protectorate. In April, 1939, Italy occupied the country, set up a puppet government, and proclaimed Victor Emmanuel III king of Albania. The base for Italy's attack on Greece (1940), Albania again became a battleground in World War

II. After the Allied landing (1944), the antifascist guerrilla leader Enver Hoxha seized control, and in 1946 set up a Communist dictatorship.

Albano, Lake (älbä'nô), crater lake, central Italy, in Alban Hills, SE of Rome; circumference 6 mi. Underground tunnel, built 4th cent. B.C., is still its only outlet. Alba Longa was near by.

Albany, dukes of: see STUART OR STEWART, family.

Albany, Louisa, countess of, 1752–1824, wife of Charles Edward STUART. Married in 1772, she left her dissolute husband after eight years. Was mistress of poet Vittorio Alfieri until his death (1803) and then mistress of French artist François Fabre.

Albany, ancient and literary name of Scotland.

Albany. 1 Residential city (pop. 17,590), W Calif., on San Francisco Bay adjoining Berkeley. **2** City (pop. 31,155), SW Ga., on Flint R.; founded 1836. Pecan and peanut market. Meat packing; mfg. of farm machinery and hosiery. Tourist center for near-by Radium Springs resort. **3** City (pop. 134,995), state cap. (since 1797), E N.Y., on W bank of the Hudson. Site visited by Henry Hudson, 1609; Dutch estab. Fort Nassau near by, 1614; Walloons began permanent settlement at Fort Orange (Albany after 1664) in 1623; chartered as city 1686. Was fur-trading center. Commerce grew after Erie Canal opened (1820s). A major shipping point, it has oil refineries, railroad shops, and mfg. of machinery, chemicals, and paper. Seat of N.Y. State Col. for Teachers and parts of Union Univ. **4** City (pop. 10,115), NW Oregon, on Willamette R. and S of Salem; founded 1848. Farm trade center.

Albany, river rising in W central Ont., Canada, and flowing c.610 mi. E and NE to James Bay.

Albany, Fort, fur-trading post, at mouth of Albany R. on James Bay, Ont., Canada. One of earliest Hudson's Bay Co. forts (before 1682). From 1697 to 1713 was only post in region in possession of British company.

Albany Congress, 1754, meeting at Albany, N.Y., in which treaty was concluded between seven British colonies and the Iroquois. Benjamin Franklin's Plan of Union for the colonies, though accepted favorably, was later rejected by colonial legislatures and the crown.

Albany Regency, informal group of leaders of Democratic party in N.Y. after 1820. Enforced party regularity and controlled elections, partly through SPOILS SYSTEM. Martin Van Buren was member. Slavery issue and quarrel between BARNBURNERS and HUNKERS led to decay; prestige dwindled after 1848.

albatross (äl'bùtrôs), sea bird, order of tube-nosed swimmers (includes petrels, shearwaters, fulmars), found chiefly in S Pacific. Wandering albatross (of Coleridge's *Rime of the Ancient Mariner*) has wingspread 10–12 ft.

Albemarle, George Monck or Monk, 1st duke of: see MONCK OR MONK, GEORGE.

Albemarle, town (pop. 11,798), central N.C., ENE of Charlotte. Textile, lumber, cotton, hosiery, and flour mills.

Albemarle Sound, Atlantic Ocean arm, 5–15 mi. wide, NE N.C., extending inland c.50 mi. Fishing and boating resort. Bridged near Edenton.

Albéniz, Isaac (ēsäk' älbä'nĕth), 1860–1909, Spanish pianist and composer; used Spanish folk themes in his music. Best known is his piano suite, *Iberia.*

Alberdi, Juan Bautista (hwän' boutē'stä älbĕr'dē), 1810–84, Argentine publicist, diplomat. Suggestions in his *Bases y puntos de partida para la organización política de la república argentina* were incorporated into 1853 constitution.

Alberni, city (pop. 3,323), on S central Vancouver Isl., B.C., Canada, adjoining PORT ALBERNI.

Alberoni, Giulio (jōō'lyō älbärō'nē), 1664–1752, Italian cardinal, chief minister to Philip V of Spain. His efforts to nullify Peace of Utrecht were stopped by Quadruple Alliance. Dismissed 1719.

Albert, rulers of Holy Roman Empire. **Albert I,** c.1250–1308, son of Rudolf I, was elected German king after his victory over ADOLF OF NASSAU (1298). Put down rebellion of Rhenish archbishops and of elector palatine (1300); secured crowns of Hungary and Bohemia for his son Rudolf (1306). Assassinated by conspirators. **Albert II,** 1397–1439, German king and king of Bohemia and Hungary (1438–39); son-in-law of Emperor Sigismund. Was unable to suppress revolt of Bohemia. With him began continuous HAPSBURG rule over empire.

Albert I, 1875–1934, king of the Belgians (1909–34). Led Belgian resistance to German invasion in World War I; improved social conditions in Belgium and Belgian Congo; won great popularity through his democratic ways. Died in rock-climbing accident. Married Queen ELIZABETH 1900.

Albert (Prince Albert), 1819–61, royal consort of VICTORIA of Great Britain; son of Ernest I of Saxe-Coburg-Gotha. Initial unpopularity was modified through his devotion to queen and responsible concern with public affairs. His insistence on moderate approach to Trent affair may have averted war with the U.S.

Albert, Eugen Francis Charles d' (däl′běr), 1864–1932, pianist and composer, b. Glasgow, of German-French origins. Known for operas *Tiefland* (1903) and *Die toten Augen* (1916).

Albert, Lake: see ALBERT NYANZA.

Alberta, province (c.248,800 sq. mi.; with water surface 255,285 sq. mi.; pop. 939,501), W Canada; cap. EDMONTON. Other cities are CALGARY, LETHBRIDGE, MEDICINE HAT, and RED DEER. Westernmost of the Prairie Provs., it has grass-covered plains to S and woodlands to N. W in the Rockies are Banff, Jasper, and Waterton Lakes national parks. Drained by Peace, Athabaska, Red Deer, St. Mary, and Milk rivers, and north and south branches of the Saskatchewan. Largest lakes are ATHABASKA and LESSER SLAVE. Population is centered in S and in wheatlands of Peace R. valley. Farming, supplemented by ranching and dairying, is basic industry. Province produces much of Canada's domestic supply of crude oil, natural gas, and coal. After exploration by fur traders in mid-18th cent., North West and Hudson's Bay companies estab. trading posts. Area ceded to Canada by Hudson's Bay Co. 1869 and incorporated into Northwest Territories. Became a district 1882, a province 1905. Canadian Pacific RR arrived 1883. During World War II Edmonton was important as S focal point of Alaska Highway traffic.

Alberta, University of, at Edmonton; provincially supported, coed.; chartered 1906, opened 1908. Affiliated are two men's colleges, St. Joseph's (R.C.) and St. Stephen's (United Church).

Albert Canal, waterway, 81 mi. long, Belgium, from Meuse R. at Liége to Scheldt R. at Antwerp. Inaugurated 1939. Its fortifications were quickly overrun by German forces in May, 1940.

Alberti, Domenico (älběr′tē), c.1710–c.1740, Venetian composer. Developed a type of broken-chord bass accompaniment, now called Alberti bass.

Alberti, Leone Battista (lāo′nä bät-tēs′tä), 1404–72, Italian architect. Wrote the first printed book on architecture; it helped spread appreciation for the classical Roman style.

Albertinelli, Mariotto (märyôt′tō älběr″tēnēl′lē), 1474–1515, Florentine painter, pupil of Piero di Cosimo. His masterpiece is the *Visitation* (Uffizi).

Albert Lea (lē), city (pop. 13,545), S Minn., near Iowa line S of Minneapolis; settled 1855. In a farm area, it has mfg. of oil burners and clothing.

Albert Nyanza (nīăn′zù), lake, area 2,064 sq. mi., central Africa, on Belgian Congo-Uganda border; alt. 2,018 ft. Also called L. Albert.

Albert of Brandenburg, 1490–1568, grand master of TEUTONIC KNIGHTS (1511–25), first duke of PRUSSIA (1525–68). Turned to Protestantism 1525 and transformed dominions of his order into hereditary duchy, under Polish suzerainty.

Albert the Bear, c.1100–1170, first margrave of Bran-

denburg (1150?–1170). A loyal follower of Lothair II and Conrad III, he temporarily held Austria and Saxony, but is most notable for obtaining, partly by peaceful methods, the Wendish territory of BRANDENBURG. He helped to Christianize NE Germany.

Albertus Magnus, Saint (Albert the Great) (ălbûr′tùs măg′nùs), b. 1193 or 1206, d. 1280, scholastic philosopher, called the Universal Doctor, a Dominican, b. Swabia. Taught in Germany (esp. at Cologne) and in Paris. Tried in *Summa theologiae* to reconcile Aristotelianism and Christianity and to oppose the attempt of Averroës to reconcile them. Had great influence on his pupil, St. Thomas Aquinas. Interested, like Roger Bacon, in natural science, wrote on botany and metals. Feast: Nov. 15.

Albertville, city (pop. 5,397), NE Ala., NNW of Gadsden, in cotton and corn area. Lumber milling.

Albi (älbē′), city (pop. 27,185), cap. of Tarn dept., S France. Famous as former center of the ALBIGENSES and for well-preserved medieval architecture (mostly in red brick), including Gothic cathedral, episcopal palace, 11th-cent. bridge.

Albigenses (ălbĭjĕn′sēz), religious group of S France, strong in 12th and 13th cent. Officially called heretics, they were actually non-Christian Cathari who believed in absolute Manichaean dualism of good and evil and held that Jesus lived only in semblance. An ascetic, enthusiastic sect, the Albigenses had powerful preachers and gained protectors—notably RAYMOND VI of Toulouse (backed by the Catholic Peter II of Aragon). St. Bernard of Clairvaux tried to convert them, as did the Dominicans. Murder of a Cistercian set off the **Albigensian Crusade,** proclaimed by Pope Innocent III (1208). Troops led by Simon de Montfort in interests of France turned this into a political affair and victory at Muret (1213) paved the way for Louis IX of France to get Toulouse (1229) from Raymond VII, son of Raymond VI. Use of the Inquisition and ardent preaching converted Albigensians slowly.

albino (ălbī′nō), animal or plant lacking normal pigmentation. In animals the absence of pigment is observed in the body covering (skin, hair, and feathers) and in the iris of the eye. Blood vessels of the iris show through, giving it a pinkish color, and eyes are very sensitive to light. Albinism is inherited as a Mendelian recessive character.

Albion, ancient and literary name of Britain.

Albion (ăl′bēùn). **1** City (pop. 2,287), SE Ill., W of Mt. Carmel; founded 1818 by Englishmen led by Morris Birkbeck, George Flower. **2** City (pop. 10,-406), S Mich., on Kalamazoo R. and S of Lansing; settled 1833. Mfg. of trucks. Seat of Albion Col. (Methodist; coed.; 1835).

Alboin (ăl′boin), d. 572?, Lombard chieftain. Conquered most of N and central Italy (568–72); crowned first Lombard king 569. See also ROSAMOND.

Alborg, Denmark: see AALBORG.

Albornoz, Gil Álvarez Carrillo de (hēl′ äl′väräth kärē′lyō dä älbôrnōth′), 1310?–1367, cardinal, Spanish and papal statesman and general. Sent (1353) by pope (then at Avignon) as legate to Papal States and entered Rome with RIENZI. Temporarily restored papal authority in Marches and Romagna.

Albrecht. For rulers thus named, see ALBERT.

Albret, Jeanne d': see JEANNE D'ALBRET.

Albret (älbrä′), former fief, SW France, in the Landes of Gascony. By his marriage (1494) with the heiress of FOIX, Lord Jean d'Albret acquired Navarre, Foix, and Béarn. His son, Henri d'Albret, married (1527) Margaret of Navarre, who had inherited Armagnac from her first husband. In 1550 Albret was made a duchy. Henry IV of France, son of JEANNE D'ALBRET, added duchy to royal domain (1607).

Albright, Ivan Le Lorraine, 1897–, American painter. His paintings, meticulously executed, are macabre and symbolic. His twin brother, **Malvin Albright,** also a painter, is called Zsissly.

Albuquerque, Afonso de (äfō′zō dù äl″bùkěr′kù), 1453–

1515, Portuguese admiral, founder of Portuguese Empire in East. Succeeded Almeida in India; took Goa (1510), Malacca (1511), also Socotra Isl. and Hormuz. Died off Goa after his dismissal.

Albuquerque (ăl′bŭkûr″kē), city (pop. 96,815), W central N.Mex., on upper Rio Grande and SW of Santa Fe, in mountain region. State's largest city, it is a commercial, industrial, rail, and air center. Area is rich in timber, mineral (coal), farm, and livestock area. Health resort. Has rail shops, lumber mills, wool warehouses, metal works, food-processing plants (meat, dairy products, fruit), and Indian handicraft. Old town was founded 1706, new town platted 1880. Here are Church of San Felipe de Neri (1706), old-town plaza, U.S. school for Indians, near-by Indian pueblos, United Pueblos Agency, Kirtland Air Force Base, and Sandia Base (guided-missiles experiment station). Seat of Univ. of New Mexico (state supported; coed.; chartered 1889, opened 1892).

Alcaeus (ălsē′ŭs), d. c.580 B.C., Greek lyric poet, associate of Sappho. His Alcaic strophe (ălkā′ĭk) was widely imitated by the Greeks and by Horace.

Alcalá de Henares (älkälä′ dā ānä′räs), city (pop. 18,-013), central Spain, in New Castile. Great univ. (1508–1836). Birthplace of Cervantes.

Alcalá Zamora, Niceto (nēthä′tō älkälä′ thämō′rä), 1877–1949, president of Spain (1931–36), a liberal.

Alcamenes (ăl″kŭmē′nēz), 5th cent. B.C., Athenian sculptor. His *Aphrodite of the Gardens* was one of the great masterpieces of antiquity.

Alcántara (älkän′tärä), town (pop. 4,404), W Spain, in Estremadura. Military religious Order of Alcántara founded here in 13th cent. Roman bridge (see *ill.,* p. 131) and ruins of order's church and convent.

Alcatraz (ăl′kŭtrăz″), island in San Francisco Bay, W Calif. Fortified by Spanish and used after 1859 as U.S. military prison and after 1933 as Federal prison.

Alcazarquivir (älkäsär′kēvēr′), city (pop. 35,786), W Spanish Morocco. Here in 1578 Ahmed IV's Moroccan army decisively defeated the Portuguese forces led by King Sebastian, who was killed.

Alcestis (ălsē′stĭs), in Greek mythology, daughter of Pelias. She married ADMETUS, who met her father's demand that suitor come for her in chariot drawn by wild animals. Her wifely devotion led her to sacrifice herself in place of her husband.

alchemy (ăl′kŭmē), learning, originating either in anc. Egypt or China, and dealing with attempts to change one substance into another (notably to turn base metals into gold). The alchemical belief in a miraculous philosopher's stone may have originated in Alexandria. Alchemy was influenced by Hellenistic philosophy, later (probably after 8th cent.) by Moslems. In 12th cent. it reached Europe through the Arabs. There the art, though symbolic and cryptic, gave rise gradually to modern chemistry. The TRANSMUTATION OF ELEMENTS has now been accomplished. Alchemy long a sister science of astrology.

Alcibiades (ălsĭbī′ŭdēz), c.450–404 B.C., Athenian statesman. Leader in the struggle against Sparta in the PELOPONNESIAN WAR, he was defeated at Mantinea (418 B.C.). Promoted Sicilian campaign (415), but was accused (probably falsely) of sacrilege and was called home for trial. Instead he fled to Sparta (where he counseled Agis I), then to Persian lands. Back in Athens after 411, he won a naval victory (410), but Athenian forces were defeated at Notium (406) by Lysander, who procured the murder of Alcibiades (then in exile).

Alcinoüs (ălsĭ′nōŭs), in Greek legend, father of Nausicaä, host to Odysseus and to Jason and Medea.

Alciphron (ăl′sĭfrŏn), fl. A.D. c.200?, Greek satirist. Wrote imaginary letters, supposedly by Athenians of 4th cent. B.C.

Alcmaeon (ălkmē′ŭn), in Greek legend, one of the EPIGONI. Having killed his mother, Eriphyle, for the murder of his father, he was pursued by the Furies. Later, for his wife Callirrhoë, he tried to get the robe

and necklace of Harmonia from his former wife, Arsinoë, but was killed.

Alcmaeonidae (ălk″mēō′nĭdē), powerful Athenian family, 7th–5th cent. B.C. Members were CLEISTHENES, PERICLES, and ALCIBIADES.

Alcmene (ălkmē′nē), in Greek legend, wife of AMPHITRYON; mother of Hercules by Zeus.

Alcoa (ălkō′ŭ), city (pop. 6,355), E Tenn., S of Knoxville. Aluminum reduction plants.

Alcobaça (älkōōbä′sù), town (pop. 4,016), Estremadura, W central Portugal, near Leiria. Cistercian abbey (building begun 1152), greatest of medieval Portugal, is burial place of early kings.

alcohol, organic compound of carbon and hydrogen with one or more hydroxyl radicals (see HYDROXIDE) on each molecule. Alcohol popularly used to mean ETHYL ALCOHOL. Classes (by number of hydroxyl groups in molecule): monohydric (one group), e.g., methyl; dihydric (two groups), e.g., glycol; trihydric (three groups), e.g., glycerin.

alcoholism, abnormal and persistent desire to drink excessive amounts of ethyl alcohol; also, the condition resulting from that drinking. Acute form connected with action of alcohol on central nervous system. Chronic alcoholism is generally considered a symptom of psychic instability. It may produce psychological and structural changes. Problem attacked through scientific studies, clinics for inebriates, organizations such as Alcoholics Anonymous (founded 1934), and Research Council on Problems of Alcohol (organized 1937).

Alcott, (Amos) Bronson (ôl′kùt), 1799–1888, American educational reformer, transcendentalist philosopher; father of Louisa May Alcott. Founded Temple School (Boston, 1834), "Fruitlands" community (1843). Both failed, but ideas gained notice.

Alcott, Louisa May, 1832–88, American writer of juvenile stories; daughter of Bronson Alcott. *Little Women* (1868–69) is her beloved classic of girls' literature. Among other works (many in series) are *Little Men* (1871), *Eight Cousins* (1875), *Rose in Bloom* (1876), *Under the Lilacs* (1878), *Jo's Boys* (1886).

Alcuin (ăl′kwĭn), 735?–804, English churchman, scholar at court of Charlemagne, center of Carolingian renaissance; founder of schools at Tours and Aix-la-Chapelle.

Aldan (ŭldän′), city (1939 pop. over 10,000), Yakut ASSR, RSFSR, in E Siberia. Gold mining.

Aldanov, Mark (ŭldä′nùf), pseud. of Mark Aleksandrovich Landau, 1886–, Russian novelist. Emigrated to France after 1917, to America in 1941; became U.S. citizen. Among his works are the tetralogy *The Thinker* (4 vols., 1921–1927; on the Napoleonic era), *The Fifth Seal* (1939), and *The Escape* (1950; both on Bolshevism).

Aldegrever, Heinrich (hīn′rĭkh äl′dùgrävùr), b. 1502, d. after 1555, painter and engraver, one of German Little Masters.

aldehyde (ăl′dĭhīd), organic compound with a carbon-hydrogen-oxygen (CHO) group. Used in synthetic resins and dyestuffs. Aldehyde is often used to mean acetaldehyde, prepared from oxidation of ethyl alcohol; oxidizes to acetic acid. FORMALDEHYDE is simplest aldehyde. See also FURFURAL.

Alden, John, c.1599–1687, Puritan settler in Plymouth Colony. Legendary romance with Priscilla Mullens made familiar by Longfellow's poem, *The Courtship of Miles Standish.*

Alder, Kurt (äl′dùr), 1902–, German chemist. Shared 1950 Nobel Prize for work on methods of synthesizing complex compounds.

alder, deciduous tree and shrub of genus *Alnus,* with conelike fruits, widely found in N Hemisphere. Bark of black alder is used for dyes and tanning, wood of Western red alder for furniture.

Alderney: see CHANNEL ISLANDS.

Aldershot, municipal borough (pop. 36,184), Hampshire, England; site of largest and most complete military training center (estab. 1854) in United Kingdom.

Aldington, Richard (ôl'–), 1892–, English poet. Once a leader of IMAGISTS, he later opposed them. Also a novelist, biographer (e.g., of Wellington), critic, editor, translator.

Aldrich, Nelson Wilmarth, 1841–1915, U.S. Senator from R.I. (1881–1911). Spokesman of big business in Republican party. Co-author of Payne-Aldrich Tariff Act (1909). Concerned with monetary problems.

Aldrich, Thomas Bailey, 1836–1907, American author, editor. His *Story of a Bad Boy* (1870) is based on his Portsmouth (N.H.) boyhood. Wrote poems, short stories (*Marjorie Daw and Other People,* 1873), edited (1881–90) *Atlantic Monthly.*

Aldus Manutius (mùnū'shùs), 1450–1515, Venetian printer, humanist. Through Aldine Press (with dolphin and anchor mark), made classical manuscripts available to scholars. Had *italic* type designed (1501).

ale: see BEER.

Alegría, Ciro (sē'rō älägrē'ä), 1909–, Peruvian novelist, Wrote novels of social protest, e.g., *El mundo es ancho y ajeno* (Latin American Novel Prize, 1941; Eng. tr., *Broad and Alien Is the World,* 1941).

Aleichem, Sholom (shō'lùm älä'khùm) [Heb.,= Peace be upon you! (a Yiddish greeting)], 1859–1916, author of tragicomic Yiddish tales about late 19th-cent. Russian Jewry. Real name Rabinowitz.

Aleijadinho (ùlä"zhùdē'nyō), 1730–1814, Brazilian sculptor, b. Minas Gerais. Though crippled, he created fine Churrigueresque church sculpture.

Alekhine, Alexander (ùlyĕkh'ēn), 1892–1946, Russian-French chess player. He was world champion 1927–35, 1937–46.

Aleksandrovsk-Sakhalinski (ùlyĭksän'drùfsk-sùkhùlyēn'skē), city (pop., with environs, c.100,000), Far Eastern RSFSR, on N Sakhalin; a port on Tatar Strait. Coal mining.

Alemán, Mateo (mätä'ō älämän'), 1547–1614?, Spanish novelist, author of picaresque *Guzmán de Alfarache* (two parts, 1599, 1604).

Alemán, Miguel (mēgĕl' älämän'), 1902–, president of Mexico (1946–52).

Alemanni (älĭmä'nĭ), Germanic tribe which occupied territories along the Rhine (present Alsace, Baden, and NE Switzerland) in 5th cent. A.D. Defeated by Franks under Clovis I in 496, they retired into Rhaetia, and in 536 passed under Frankish rule. High German dialects of SW Germany and Switzerland are called Alemannic. See also GERMANS.

Alembert, Jean le Rond d' (zhä' lù rō' dälãbär'), 1717–83, French mathematician and philosopher. As coeditor of Diderot's ENCYCLOPÉDIE he wrote its remarkable "Preliminary discourse." For his work in dynamics, see D'ALEMBERT'S PRINCIPLE.

Alemtejo, Portugal: see ALENTEJO.

Alençon, François, duc d': see FRANCIS, duke of Alençon and Anjou.

Alençon (äläsō'), town (pop. 16,692), cap. of Orne dept., N France, on Sarthe R.; famous for its lace.

Alentejo (äläntä'zhō), historic province, SE Portugal, now divided into Upper Alentejo (4,888 sq. mi.; pop. 375,511; cap. Évora) and Lower Alentejo (5,318 sq. mi.; pop. 355,771; cap. Beja). "Granary of Portugal." Also livestock, wine, olives, fruit. Formerly spelled Alemtejo.

Alep (ùlĕp') or **Aleppo** (ùlĕ'pō), city (pop. c.320,000), NW Syria. Was the Greek and biblical Beroea or Berea. Ancient city on main caravan route across Syria to Baghdad, center of a Hittite kingdom before 1000 B.C. Flourished as city of Byzantine Empire. Taken by Arabs in 7th cent. and by Seljuk Turks in 11th cent. Crusaders besieged it unsuccessfully 1124, Saladin took it 1183. Mongols seized Alep in 1260 and 1401. Held by the Turks (1517–1832, 1840–1920) and by Egypt (1832–40). Produces silk and cotton textiles; trades in wool, hides, and fruit.

Alesia (ùlē'zhù), town in anc. Gaul, held by Vercingetorix, besieged by Caesar (52 B.C.). Its surrender because of starvation marked the end of Gallic resistance.

Alesius, Alexander (ù-lē'shùs), 1500–1565, Scottish Protestant theologian, early preacher of Lutheranism in England and Germany.

Alessandria (äles-sän'drēä), city (pop. 51,949), Piedmont, N Italy. Felt hats, commerce. Founded 1168 by Pope Alexander III.

Alesund or **Aalesund,** Nor. *Ålesund* (all: ô'lùsöōn), city (pop. 18,143), W Norway, on three small islands at mouth of Stor Fjord. Largest Norwegian fishing harbor; whaling base.

Aletsch (ä'lĕch), largest glacier (66 sq. mi.) of Swiss Alps, between Jungfrau and Aletschhorn, in Bernese Alps.

Aleutian Islands (ùlōō'shùn), chain of volcanic islands SW from tip of Alaska Peninsula and approaching Russian Komandorski Isls. Partially submerged, they are a continuation of Aleutian Range dividing the Bering Sea from the Pacific. There are four main groups. Fox Isls. nearest Alaska include Unimak, Unalaska (with Dutch Harbor on small Amaknak Isl.) and Umnak. Andreanof Isls. are many, including Adak. Important in Rat Isls. are Amchitka and Kiska. Near Isls., farthest W and smallest group of all, include Attu. Islands are generally rugged, of volcanic action, and have few good harbors, owing to reefs. Temperature is relatively moderate, but fog is constant. They are almost completely treeless with dense vegetation. Vitus BERING discovered islands 1741. Russian fur traders exploited native Aleuts. Fishing and fur hunting are now state controlled. Dutch Harbor became transshipping point for Nome 1900, and U.S. Naval Base 1940. Japanese occupied Attu and Kiska 1942–43; withdrawal forced by bitter U.S. fighting.

Aleutian Range, mountain chain, SW Alaska, extending along entire Alaska Peninsula and continuing, partly submerged, in Aleutian Isls. Recent volcanic activity was notable at Katmai (Valley of Ten Thousand Smokes), one of world's largest volcanoes.

Alexander III, d. 1181, pope (1159–81), a Sienese named Rolando Bandinelli. A learned canon lawyer, he issued many legal rules for governing church. Backed Lombard League in opposing Emperor Frederick I, who exiled him to France. His rule contested by antipopes until 1178. Convened Third LATERAN COUNCIL.

Alexander VI, 1431–1503, pope (1492–1503), a Spaniard named Rodrigo de Borja (of BORGIA family). Notorious in following centuries as corrupt and worldly Renaissance pope, he showered money and favors on his children by a Roman woman, Cesare and Lucrezia Borgia. Opposed Charles VIII of France, who invaded Italy. Proclaimed the line of demarcation between Spanish and Portuguese colonial spheres (1494).

Alexander, emperors of Russia. **Alexander I,** 1777–1825? (reigned 1801–25), succeeded his father, PAUL I, in whose murder he may have had indirect part. His early liberalism did not lead to internal reform. Alexander joined coalition against NAPOLEON I (1805); was defeated at Austerlitz, Friedland; made peace at TILSIT 1807. After repulsing French invasion (1812), led allies into Paris (1814) and attended Congress of VIENNA. Under influence of Metternich and Julie de KRÜDENER he turned to extreme reaction and promoted HOLY ALLIANCE. Officially, he died at Taganrog; according to popular belief—shared by some historians—he retired to live in penitence as a hermit. His tomb, opened 1926, was empty. His brother, Nicholas I, succeeded him. **Alexander II,** 1818–81, son of Nicholas I, reigned 1855–81. A liberal reformer, he abolished serfdom (1861; see EMANCIPATION, EDICT OF), introduced ZEMSTVO system of local government and new judicial system (1864). Reforms did not satisfy the radicals. Terrorism and NIHILISM increased; led to Alexander's assassination. Other events of reign: end of CRIMEAN WAR; Russian expansion in Asia; and Russo-Turkish War of 1877–78. Succeeded by his son, **Alexander III,** 1845–94 (reigned 1881–94), a fanatic reactionary. Fostered persecution of Jews and forcible Russification of minorities. Suppressed liberal thought, but promoted peace policy and industrial development. Nicholas II succeeded him.

Alexander, 1893–1920, king of the Hellenes (1917–20). Succeeded his deposed father, Constantine, with aid of Allies, who favored him over his elder brother (later King George II).

Alexander, kings of Scotland. **Alexander I,** 1078?–1124, ruled 1107–24. He opposed English efforts to rule church in Scotland. Estab. abbeys at Inchcolm and Scone. **Alexander II,** 1198–1249, ruled 1214–49. **Alexander III,** 1241–86, ruled 1249–86. Acquired for Scotland Western Isles and Isle of Man, already claimed from Norway. After his death struggle between ROBERT I and John de BALIOL (1249–1315) began.

Alexander, rulers of Serbia and Yugoslavia. **Alexander** (Alexander Karageorgevich), 1806–85, prince of Serbia (1842–58); son of KARAGEORGE. Deposed. **Alexander** (Alexander Obrenovich), 1876–1903, king of Serbia (1889–1903); son and successor of MILAN. Abolished liberal constitution 1894. His marriage in 1900 to Draga Mashin, a lady of scandalous past, aggravated the opposition. Royal couple was assassinated by an army clique, the Obrenovich dynasty deposed, and Peter I made king. **Alexander,** 1888–1934, king of Yugoslavia (1921–34); son and successor of Peter I. Became regent of kingdom of Serbs, Croats, and Slovenes 1918; ruled dictatorially 1929–31 to unify kingdom, which he renamed Yugoslavia. Antagonized Croatian and Macedonian separatists. In foreign policy he was loyal to French alliance and LITTLE ENTENTE. Assassinated, with Louis BARTHOU, by Yugoslav terrorist at Marseilles, France.

Alexander (Alexander of BATTENBERG), 1857–93, prince of Bulgaria (1879–86). He was elected with Russian support and ruled under Turkish overlordship. His annexation of E RUMELIA (1885) antagonized Russia and caused Serbia to declare war. Though victorious, he was deposed by a pro-Russian faction.

Alexander, in Greek legend, another name for PARIS.

Alexander, Harold Rupert Leofric George, Earl Alexander of Tunis, 1891–, British field marshal. In World War II commanded retreats of Dunkirk and Burma and triumphs in N Africa and Sicily. Governor general of Canada 1945–52. Made defense minister in Churchill cabinet 1952.

Alexander, John White, 1856–1915, American painter, best remembered for his graceful studies of women.

Alexander, Samuel, 1859–1938, British naturalist philosopher. He held that space-time was ultimate principle of all existence.

Alexander, Sir William, d. 1640: see STIRLING, WILLIAM ALEXANDER, EARL OF.

Alexander Archipelago, just off SE Alaska. It and mountainous coast make up Panhandle of Alaska, Territory's most populous area. A submerged mountain system, the islands rise steeply from sea. Deep channels separate them, cut them from the mainland, making part of the Inside Passage from Seattle to Alaska. Included are CHICHAGOF ISLAND, ADMIRALTY ISLAND, BARANOF ISLAND (with Sitka), WRANGEL ISLAND (with Wrangel), REVILLAGIGEDO ISLAND (with Ketchikan), and PRINCE OF WALES ISLAND.

Alexander Balas (bā′–), d. 145 B.C., ruler of Syria. Seized power from his uncle Demetrius I. Jonathan the Maccabee supported him. Eventually defeated by Ptolemy Philometor. 1 Mac. 10–11.

Alexander City, city (pop. 6,430), E central Ala., SE of Birmingham, near Martin L. Textiles.

Alexander Nevski, Saint (něv′skē), 1220?–1263, grand duke of Vladimir-Suzdal; Russian national hero. Defeated Swedes on the Neva (1240) and Livonian Knights near Lake Peipus (1242).

Alexander of Hales (hālz), d. 1245, English scholastic philosopher, called the Unanswerable Doctor, a Fran-

ciscan who taught at Univ. of Paris. Introduced Aristotle as authority in systematic exposition of Christian doctrine.

Alexander Severus (Marcus Aurelius Alexander Severus) (sĭvēr′ŭs), d. 235, Roman emperor (222–35).

Alexander the Great (Alexander III), 356–323 B.C., king of Macedon (336–323); son of PHILIP II. He put down rebellion in Greece, and in 334 he undertook what was to be the widest conquest of ancient times. Victories at the Granicus (334), the Issus (333), and Gaugamela (or Arbela, 331) punctuated his seizure of Asia Minor, peaceful occupation of Egypt, and overthrow of the Persian Empire of Darius III. He pushed on through Bactria and into India. There his men refused to go farther. A fleet was sent back under Nearchus, but Alexander led his men back across deserts, reaching Susa in 324. Married Roxana, a Bactrian princess, and adopted Persian ways. Died of a fever at 33. One of the greatest generals of all time, he was also one of the most romantic figures of antiquity. His great empire was broken by wars of the DIADOCHI.

Alexandra, 1844–1925, queen consort of Edward VII of Great Britain; daughter of Christian IX of Denmark. Married Edward 1863.

Alexandra, Mount: see RUWENZORI.

Alexandra Feodorovna (fĕô″dŭrŏv′nŭ), 1872–1918, Russian empress, consort of NICHOLAS II; a Hessian princess, granddaughter of Queen Victoria. Under influence of RASPUTIN, she encouraged tsar's reactionary policies. Shot by Bolsheviks 1918.

Alexandretta or **Alexandrette,** Turkish seaport: see ISKENDERUN.

Alexandretta, sanjak of (sän″jăk′, ä″lĭgzăndrě′tŭ), former name of Hatay prov. (2,141 sq. mi.; pop. 245,141), S Turkey, comprising cities of Antioch and its port Alexandretta (now Iskenderun). Awarded 1920 to Syria, given autonomous status 1937. Turkish-Arab riots resulted 1938 in joint military control by France and Turkey. Transferred to Turkey 1939.

Alexandria, Arabic *Al Iskandariya,* city (pop. 928,237), N Egypt, port on Mediterranean. Founded 332 B.C. by Alexander the Great. Cap. of the Ptolemies (304–30 B.C.), it received much Mediterranean trade and soon outgrew Carthage to become largest city in West. The great center of Hellenistic and Jewish culture. Became part of Roman Empire (30 B.C.) and was greatest provincial cap. with free population of 300,000. In 642 fell to the Arabs who moved the cap. to modern Cairo. Today handles most of Egypt's foreign trade.

Alexandria. 1 City (pop. 5,147), E central Ind., NE of Indianapolis. Produces rock wool and limestone. **2** City (pop. 34,913), central La., on Red R. opposite PINEVILLE; laid out 1810. Processes cotton, foodstuffs, and lumber, and has chemical and metal works. Has cathedral (R.C.; 1898). **3** City (pop. 6,319), W Minn., SE of Fergus Falls, in resort and agr. region. KENSINGTON RUNE STONE is here. **4** City (pop. 61,787), N Va., S of Washington, D.C., port on Potomac R. Permanently settled in early 18th cent., it was once a part of D.C. (1789–1847). A rail center, it has mfg. of fertilizers, concrete and metal products. Points of interest (many associated with George Washington) include Gadsby's Tavern (1752), Carlyle House (1752), Christ Church (1767–73), and Ramsay House (1749–51). George Washington Natl. Memorial Temple houses Washington mementoes. Near-by Woodlawn, Washington family estate, was made national shrine in 1949.

Alexandria Bay, resort village (pop. 1,688), N N.Y., on the St. Lawrence and N of Watertown. Near by are Thousand Isls. Internatl. Bridge to Canada.

alexandrine, in poetry, a line of 12 or 13 syllables. Considered an iambic hexameter, the last foot has a final unstressed syllable if the line has 13 syllables. Name probably derives from a medieval romance on Alexander. Rhyming alexandrine couplets are the classic form for French serious poetry (works of Ronsard, Racine, Corneille). The Spenserian stanza ends with an alexandrine.

Alexis, 1629–76, tsar of Russia (1645–76), successor of Michael Romanov. He acquired part of Ukraine, began a schism by deposing Patriarch NIKON, suppressed Stenka RAZIN rebellion, and promulgated law code of 1648, which favored middle class, but tied peasants to soil. His son Feodor III succeeded him. Peter the Great was his son by a second marriage.

Alexishafen, (ûlĕk'sĭs-hä"fûn), harbor, E New Guinea, in Territory of New Guinea. Japanese air base here was taken 1944 by Allied forces.

Alexius (ûlĕk'sēûs), Byzantine emperors. **Alexius I** (Comnenus), 1048–1118; nephew of Isaac I. Gained throne by overthrowing Nicephorus III (1081). Withstood Norman invasions under ROBERT GUISCARD and BOHEMOND; defeated Petchenegs (1091) and Cumans (1095). In the First Crusade he persuaded leaders to pledge their conquests to him, later forced Bohemond to recognize his suzerainty over Antioch. His last years brought struggle with the Turks and intrigues of his daughter ANNA COMNENA against his son John II. Restored Byzantine prestige. **Alexius III** (Angelus), d. after 1210. Gained throne by deposing his brother ISAAC II (1195). This gave the leaders of the Fourth Crusade a pretext for attacking Constantinople (1203). Alexius III fled; Isaac was restored, with his son **Alexius IV** (d. 1204) as joint emperor. In 1204 **Alexius V** (Ducas Mourtzouphlos), son-in-law of Alexius III, led the Byzantine national party in the overthrow of Isaac and Alexius IV. This act brought the sack of Constantinople by the Crusaders, who had Alexius V executed (1204) and set up the Latin Empire of Constantinople.

alfalfa (ălfăl'fŭ), a perennial (*Medicago sativa*), also called lucerne, native to Europe, with usually blue or purple flowers; North America's chief leguminous forage plant. Adaptable to diverse conditions, it can be mowed two to six times yearly, enriches soil, and is high in protein. See *ill.,* p. 783.

Alfieri, Vittorio, Conte (vēt-tō'rēō kōn'tä älfyä'rē), 1749–1803, Italian tragic poet, b. Piedmont. After a dissipated youth, he became a poet and poured his hatred of tyranny into tragedies, intentionally harsh and unornamented—*Saul* (1782), *Antigone* (1783), *Maria Stuart* (1804). Also wrote comedies, satires, political tracts, autobiography. Allied with Louisa, countess of Albany.

Alfonsine tables, improved revision of Ptolemaic planetary tables, made at Toledo by astronomers assembled by Alfonso X of Spain. Completed c.1252; printed 1483 in Venice.

Alfonso, kings of Aragon. **Alfonso I,** d. 1134, king of Aragon and Navarre (1104–34), husband of URRACA of Castile. Took Saragossa and Calatayud from Moors. **Alfonso II,** 1152–96, king of Aragon (1164–96), count of Barcelona (1162–96). Inherited Provence (1166); Roussillon (1172). Wrote Provençal poetry. **Alfonso V** (the Magnanimous), 1396–1458, king of Aragon and Sicily (1416–58), became king of Naples (1443–58) after defeating René of Anjou. His splendid court at Naples was center of arts and letters.

Alfonso, kings of Portugal. **Alfonso I** (Port. *Afonso Henriques*), 1111?–1185, became first king of Portugal (1139), took Santarém and Lisbon (1147). **Alfonso II** (the Fat), 1185–1223, reigned 1211–23. **Alfonso III** (Port. *Afonso o Bolonhez*), 1210–79, reigned 1248–79. Completed reconquest of Portugal from Moors; quarreled with Alfonso X of Castile over Algarve, and with Church; and called Cortes of Leiria (1254; first to include commoners). Fostered commerce and cultural revival. **Alfonso IV,** 1291–1357, reigned 1325–57. Approved murder of Inés de CASTRO. **Alfonso V** (the African), 1432–81, reigned 1438–81. Took Tangier (1471). His marriage with Juana la Beltraneja led to unsuccessful war with Ferdinand and Isabella. **Alfonso VI** (the Victorious), 1643–83, reigned 1656–67. Physically and mentally defective, he yet ousted his mother from regency with aid of count of Castelho Melhor, who took over the government and repulsed

the Spanish in 1663. Alfonso's wife, Marie Françoise of Savoy, and his brother (later Peter II) forced him to abdicate. After having her marriage annulled, the queen married Peter, who ruled as regent.

Alfonso, Spanish kings. **Alfonso I** (the Catholic), 693?–757, king of Asturias (739–57), conquered parts of Galicia, Leon, and Santander from Moors. **Alfonso III** (the Great), 838?–910?, king of Asturias (866–909), consolidated kingdom. **Alfonso V** (the Noble), 994?–1027, king of Asturias and Leon (999–1027), gave Leon its *fuero* [code of laws]. **Alfonso VI,** 1030–1109, king of Leon (1065–1109) and Castile (1072–1109), took Galicia from his brother García (1073), and Toledo from Moors (1085). His court at Toledo was meeting place of Christian and Moorish cultures. **Alfonso VII** (the Emperor), 1104–57, king of Castile and Leon (1126–57. Recovered places lost by his mother, URRACA, to her second husband; had himself crowned emperor in Leon (1135); and took Almería from Moors. **Alfonso VIII** (the Noble), 1155–1214, king of Castile (1158–1214), won great victory of Navas de Tolosa (1212) over Moors. **Alfonso X** (the Wise), 1221–84, king of Castile and Leon (1252–84), grandson of Emperor Philip of Swabia, was elected German king (1256) by faction of German princes, but renounced claim in 1275. Took Cádiz from Moors (1262). Patron of learning; largely responsible for great legal compilation, *Siete partidas,* and ALFONSINE TABLES. **Alfonso XI,** 1311–50, king of Castile and Leon (1312–50), defeated Moors at Tarifa (1340), took Algeciras (1344), died in siege of Gibraltar. **Alfonso XII,** 1857–85, king of Spain (1870–85), son of Isabella II, lived in exile (1868–75) during Carlist revolt. Proclaimed king 1874; returned to Madrid 1875 and restored order. **Alfonso XIII,** 1886–1941, king of Spain (1886–1931), supported dictatorship of Primo de Rivera (1923–30). Went into exile when republicans won election (1931).

Alfred [Old Eng. Ælfred], 849–899?, overking of England; one of best-loved figures of English history. Victory over Danes at Ashdown being followed by defeats, he decided, in face of their threat to overrun England, to make them payments. His flight to fens of Somerset (878) gave basis for legend of Alfred and the cakes. Victory over Danes at Ethandun (Edington) led to program of reform and to code of laws combining Christian doctrine with strong centralized monarchy. His greatest achievements were creation of a navy, revival of learning among the clergy, education for youths and nobles at court, the establishment of old English literary prose, his own English translation of Latin works, and his influence on extant form of ANGLO-SAXON CHRONICLE. Many heroic legends later embroidered his career. See editions of his own works and contemporary biography by Bishop Asser, *Life of King Alfred* (1906).

Alfred University, at Alfred village (pop. 2,053), N.Y., SW of Hornell; nonsectarian, with state and private support, coed.; opened as school 1836, chartered as univ. 1857. Includes state college of ceramics.

Alfsborg, county, Sweden: see ALVSBORG.

algae (ăl'jē), primitive plants lacking true roots, stems, leaves, and flowers, but having chlorophyll. Chief aquatic plants in fresh and salt water (including pond scum and SEAWEED) are algae, ranging from microscopic size to 100 ft. long (e.g., kelp). See also DIATOM; GULFWEED; IRISH MOSS. See *ill.,* p. 633.

Algardi, Alessandro (älĕs-sän'drō älgär'dē), 1602–54, Italian architect and sculptor, pupil of Lodovico Carracci. Designed the Villa Doria Pamphili.

Algarve (älgär'vù), southernmost province (1,958 sq. mi.; pop. 317,628), Portugal; cap. Faro.

Al-Gazel (ăl-gùzĕl') or **Al-Ghazali** (gäzä'lē), 1058–1111, Arabian mystical philosopher.

algebra, branch of mathematics which generalizes arithmetic operations. Elementary algebra achieves this by use of letters to represent numbers. Product of several numbers and letters, e.g., a term such as $6xy^3$ depends on values of unknowns x and y; number 6 is a coefficient; number ^{3} (written above, to right of y) is an exponent. There are rules for addition, subtraction, multiplication, and division of such expressions and for simplifying resulting expressions, often involving factoring, combining like terms, canceling, removing parentheses (grouping symbols). Algebra is used in most mathematics branches (geometry, trigonometry, calculus) and in other fields, e.g., physics, statistics; in these it is usually needed to solve equations expressing the relation of unknown to known quantities. Modern abstract algebra generalizes not only numbers but also operations.

Algeciras (äljüsēr'ùs, Span. älhäthē'räs), city (pop. 20,-226), S Spain, in Andalusia; Mediterranean port on Bay of Algeciras opposite Gibraltar. British victory (1801) over French-Spanish fleet.

Algeciras Conference: see MOROCCO.

Alger, Horatio (ăl'jür), 1834–99, American writer of boys' stories. His more than 100 books show success gained by exemplary living, heroic deeds, struggle against odds.

Algeria (äljēr'ēù), French government general (847,-552 sq. mi.; pop. 7,234,684) of the FRENCH UNION, N Africa; cap. ALGIERS. The Atlas Mts. are between the long Mediterranean coastal strip and the grain-producing TELL. In interior are semiarid plateaus and the great Sahara. Natives are of mixed Berber and Arab stock. Carthage was the first to dominate area. The richness of the Tell attracted the Roman conquerors, who subjugated NUMIDIA and MAURETANIA. In the Christian days of the empire, St. Augustine was bishop at Hippo Regius (now Bône). The declining civilization was conquered by Vandals (430–31) and by Byzantines (534). Arab invasion (7th cent.) brought Islam, which profoundly affected Algerian culture. In the 16th cent. the Turks estab. their control over the coast, which became a stronghold for pirates (see BARBARY STATES). In 1847 France won complete control over Algeria, except for the Saharan area (subdued 1900–1909). New crops (esp. grapes and tobacco) were introduced, and the exploitation of mineral resources was begun. Algeria played a vital part in World War II (see NORTH AFRICA, CAMPAIGNS IN).

Algerine War: see DECATUR, STEPHEN; TRIPOLITAN WAR.

Algiers (äljērz'), Fr. *Alger*, city (pop. 266,165), N Algeria, cap. of Algeria; a major port of N Africa. Founded in late 10th cent. by the Berbers on site of the Roman Icosium. Became important after establishment of Turkish rule by Barbarossa in 1518. A base for Barbary pirates, it was visited by several European punitive expeditions. Occupied in 1830 by the French, who later built modern city along the harbor. The 16th-cent. Casbah (fortress), surmounting a height, gives its name to whole of old quarter. In World War II, after capture by Allies in Nov., 1942, it became hq. of Gen. de Gaulle's government.

Algona (älgō'nù), city (pop. 5,415), N Iowa, N of Fort Dodge on Des Moines R., in farm area.

Algonquian (älgŏng'kwēùn, –kēun), linguistic family of North America, a widespread stock of Canadian and U.S. Indians. See LANGUAGE, table.

Algonquin Indians (älgŏng'kwĭn, –kŭn), North American Indian people in Canada, of Algonquian linguistic stock. Friendly to the French, they were dispersed by Iroquois in 17th cent.

Algonquin Provincial Park, 2,741 sq. mi., S Ont., Canada; estab. 1893 as game preserve and recreation area.

algum: see ALMUG.

Alhambra (älhăm'brù), city (pop. 51,359), S Calif., NE of Los Angeles; founded 1881. Mfg. of aircraft and oil-refining machinery.

Alhambra [Arabic,= the red], group of Moorish buildings on a hill overlooking Granada, Spain. Comprises citadel remains, palace of kings, and quarters of nobles and officials. Halls and chambers, with intricate geometric ornament and honeycomb vaulting, surrounded a series of open courts with fountains and gardens. Built 1248–1354, it was mutilated after expulsion of the Moors in 1492 and extensively restored after 1828.

Ali (ä'lē, älē'), 602?–661, 4th caliph (656–61); first cousin and faithful follower of Mohammed, husband of Fatima. Caliphate opposed by Ayesha and Muawiya. Shiite-Sunnite division in Islam stems from this period. Ali and his son HUSEIN major Shiite saints.

Alicante (älēkän'tä), city (pop. 83,140), cap. of Alicante prov., SE Spain, in Valencia; Mediterranean port.

Alice, city (pop. 16,449), S Texas, W of Corpus Christi. Cattle and oil center with mfg. of dairy and cotton products.

Alice in Wonderland: see CARROLL, LEWIS.

Alice Springs, town (pop. 1,871), Northern Territory, Australia, at terminus of Central Australian RR. Formerly called Stuart, it was cap. of Central Australia 1926–31. Opal mining.

Alien and Sedition Acts, 1798, passed by U.S. Congress when warfare with France threatened (see XYZ AFFAIR). Empowered President to expel "dangerous" aliens; provided for indictment of those who should "unlawfully combine or conspire" against the administration or should write or speak "with intent to defame" the government, the Congress, or the President. Acts provoked KENTUCKY AND VIRGINIA RESOLUTIONS.

Aligarh (ùlēgùr'), city (pop. 112,655) W Uttar Pradesh, India; trade center. Moslem university.

alimentary canal, tubular passage (c.30 ft. long) from mouth to anus functioning in DIGESTION and absorption of food. Includes pharynx, esophagus, STOMACH, INTESTINE, and rectum. See *ill.,* p. 595.

alimony, allowance which by court order a husband pays to wife not living with him. Temporary alimony is allowed pending a suit for separation, divorce, or nullity of marriage; permanent alimony, only after a decree has been rendered.

Ali Pasha (ä'lē päshä'), 1741?–1822, Turkish governor of Yannina (1787–1820); called the Lion of Yannina. Originally an Albanian brigand chief, he ruled as quasi-independent despot over most of Albania and Epirus. Ordered deposed for his ambitious plans (1820), he rebelled and resisted Turkish troops (badly needed in fight against Greek insurrection) until his assassination by a Turkish agent. Byron described his rugged court in *Childe Harold.*

Aliquippa (älĭkwĭp'ù), borough (pop. 26,132), W Pa., on Ohio R. and NW of Pittsburgh. Has steel mills.

Alisal, village (pop. 16,714), W Calif., near Salinas.

Aljubarrota (älzhōobùrô'tù), village, Estremadura, W central Portugal. Here Portuguese, aided by English, defeated Spanish, kept independence (1385).

alkali (ăl'kùlī), in chemistry, a strong BASE, e.g., sodium hydroxide (see LYE). Has properties of bases: soluble in water, and neutralizes acids. Strongly CAUSTIC. Used to make soap, cotton goods, paper. **Alkali metals** are cesium, rubidium, potassium, sodium, and lithium. Oxides of barium, strontium, calcium, and sometimes magnesium called **alkaline earths** because they act like alkalis.

alkali soils contain an excess of soluble salts: in white alkali soils, chiefly sulphates of sodium, magnesium, potassium; in black alkali soils, sodium carbonate. Such soils may be improved by adding lime or gypsum, cultivating thoroughly, and growing alkali-tolerant plants; flooding and then underdraining actually removes some alkali.

alkaloid, organic compound composed of carbon, hydrogen, nitrogen, and usually oxygen. Derived from plants; name indicates properties of a BASE. Examples: ATROPINE, CAFFEINE, COCAINE, MORPHINE, NICOTINE, QUININE, STRYCHNINE, codeine.

Al-Khowarizmi (äl-khōwärēz'mē), fl. 820, Arabian mathematician, noted for treatises on Hindu arithmetic and algebra. He is said to have given algebra its name. Latin translations of his works were a major source of knowledge in medieval Europe.

SMALL CAPITALS = cross references. Pronunciation key on inside end pages. Abbreviations: p. 2.

Al-Kindi, Arabian philosopher: see KINDI.

Alkmaar (älk'mär), municipality (pop. 37,837) and town, North Holland prov., NW Netherlands. Market center; iron foundries. Weekly cheese market in front of ancient weighhouse is famous.

Allah (ä'lù, ä'lù), Arabic name for God, used in Islam and Arabic-speaking Christian countries.

Allahabad (äl"ühübäd'), city (pop. 260,630), S Uttar Pradesh, India. On site of Prayag, ancient Aryan holy city, at junction of the sacred Jumna and Ganges rivers. Trade center.

All-American Canal, SE Calif., largest irrigation canal in U.S.; built 1934–40 by Bureau of Reclamation. Taps Colorado R. at Imperial Dam, N of Yuma, Ariz., and runs 80 mi. W, past Calexico, Calif. Serves IMPERIAL VALLEY and Coachella Valley.

Allan, Sir Hugh, 1810–82, Canadian financier and shipowner, b. Scotland. Involved in PACIFIC SCANDAL over construction of Canadian Pacific Ry.

Allbutt, Sir Thomas Clifford (ôl'bŭt), 1836–1925, English physician, authority on diseases of circulatory and nervous systems. Wrote on history of medicine.

Allegany (äl'ügä"nē), village (pop. 1,738), W N.Y., on Allegheny R. and W of Olean. Near by is St. Bonaventure Univ. (Catholic; for men; 1859).

Alleghany, variant spelling: see ALLEGHENY.

Allegheny (ä'lùgä"nē), river rising in N Pa., and flowing NW to N.Y., then SW into Pa., joining the Monongahela at Pittsburgh to form the Ohio; 325 mi. long. Transports some freight.

Allegheny College: see MEADVILLE, Pa.

Allegheny Mountains, a W part of Appalachian Mts., extending SW from N Pa. through Md., W.Va., and Va., and rising to 4,860 ft. in Spruce Knob, W.Va. E portion has Allegheny Front, a steep escarpment; W portion is plateau reaching into E Ohio and Ky. Allegheny upland largely formed by folding of sedimentary rock. Much erosion and leveling followed. Range is rich in coal and contains iron, oil, and gas.

allegory (äl'ĭgôr"ē), literary work expressing through elaborate symbols a commentary or account of social, political, or artistic ideas. Characters are types or personifications. Spenser's *Faerie Queene* and Bunyan's *Pilgrim's Progress* are famous examples.

Allegri, Gregorio (grägō'rēō äl-lā'grē), 1582–1652, Italian composer of a nine-part *Miserere* sung annually during Holy Week in the Sistine Chapel.

Alleluia, Latin form of HALLELUJAH.

Allen, Ethan, 1738–89, hero of American Revolution, leader of GREEN MOUNTAIN BOYS. Helped capture Ticonderoga (1775). Captured by British on expedition against Canada (1775). Promoted independence and statehood of Vt. His brother, **Ira Allen,** 1751–1814, was a political leader in early Vt.

Allen, Hervey, 1889–1949, American author. After World War I he taught at Charleston, S.C., where with DuBose Heyward he wrote poems in *Carolina Chansons* (1922). He is best known for his historical novels, which include *Anthony Adverse* (1933) and three volumes of an unfinished series (begun with *The Forest and the Fort*, 1943).

Allen, Horatio, 1802–90, American civil and mechanical engineer. Operated first steam locomotive (English-built) to run on rails in U.S.; designed steamboats.

Allen, Ira: see ALLEN, ETHAN.

Allen, James Lane, 1849–1925, American novelist. Wrote stories, poems on Ky. Novels include *A Kentucky Cardinal* (1894), *The Choir Invisible* (1897).

Allen, Richard, 1760–1831, founder of the African Methodist Episcopal Church (1794). He was born a slave in Philadelphia.

Allenby, Edmund Henry Hynman Allenby, 1st Viscount (ä'lùnbē), 1861–1936, British field marshal. Invaded Palestine and ended Turkish resistance (1918). British high commissioner for Egypt 1919–25.

Allen Park, village (pop. 12,329), SE Mich., W suburb of Detroit; settled 1776.

Allenstein (ä'lünshtīn), Pol. *Olsztyn,* city (pop. 29,053), S East Prussia; under Polish administration since 1945. Trade and railroad center. Founded 1348 by Teutonic Knights, who built its impressive castle. Resettled by Poles after World War II.

Allentown, industrial city (pop. 106,756), E Pa., on Lehigh R. and NNW of Philadelphia, in Pennsylvania Dutch region; settled by German religious groups, laid out c. 1752. Has metal and textile industries. Liberty Bell brought here (1777) for safekeeping; munitions center for Continental Army. Seat of Cedar Crest Col. and Muhlenberg Col. (Lutheran; for men; 1848).

allergy, excessive sensitivity to a usually harmless substance. Agents (known as allergens) include air-borne substances, vegetable oils, bacteria, various proteins, and physical agents, e.g., light, cold. Allergens produce antibodies in blood stream; said to cause tissues to produce histamine.

Allia (ä'lēù), river, Latium, Italy, tributary of Tiber. Gauls defeated Romans on Allia 390 B.C.

Alliance. 1 City (pop. 7,891), NW Nebr., in Great Plains region. Ships grain, seed potatoes, and livestock. Has railroad repair shops. **2** City (pop. 26,161), NE Ohio, NE of Canton and SE of Akron, on Mahoning R.; laid out 1838. Mfg. (esp. steel, aircraft, machinery), distributing, and rail center. Seat of Mt. Union Col. (Methodist; coed.; 1846), with Clarke Observatory.

Allier (älyā'), department (2,850 sq. mi.; pop. 373,381), central France, in Bourbonnais; cap. Moulins. Traversed by Allier R. (tributary of Loire).

alligator, large reptile (order Crocodilia) similar to CROCODILE. American alligator, c.12 to 14 ft. long, ranges N Carolina to Florida, Gulf states. Adults black, young dark brown or black with yellow bands. Eats water life.

alligator pear: see AVOCADO.

Allori, Alessandro (äles-sän'drō äl-lō'rē), 1535–1607, Florentine painter, pupil and foster son of Il Bronzino; known also as Alessandro Bronzino. Many portraits in the Uffizzi, Florence. His son and pupil, **Cristofano Allori** (krēstōfä'nō), 1577–1621, was also a portraitist.

allotropy (ùlŏt'rùpē), occurrence of chemical element in two or more forms differing in atomic arrangement and physical properties but alike in chemical properties. Among elements showing allotropy: arsenic, carbon, oxygen, phosphorus, sulphur.

Allouez, Claude Jean (klōd' zhä' älwä'), 1622–89, French Jesuit missionary in Canada and Old Northwest. Founded missions in present Wis.

Alloway (äl'–), hamlet, Ayrshire, Scotland; birthplace of Robert Burns.

alloy (äl'oi), combination of metal with metallic or nonmetallic elements to form mixture or compound having metallic properties suitable for special purposes. May be heterogeneous (composed of crystals embedded in a matrix or of interlocking crystals of several types) or homogeneous (solid solution with uniform physical properties). See also BRASS; BRONZE; GOLD; STEEL.

All Souls College: see OXFORD UNIVERSITY.

allspice, dried green berry from tropical pimento or allspice tree (*Pimenta officinalis*), used in medicine and food seasoning. Carolina allspice is *Calycanthus.*

Allston, Washington, 1779–1843, American painter, a pupil of Benjamin West. His work is usually biblical or classical in subject.

alluvium (ùlōo'vēŭm), land built up of sediments deposited by running water. Common forms are alluvial fans and cones, river deltas, and flood plains.

Alma, city (pop. 8,341), S Mich., N of Lansing. Beet-sugar and oil refineries. Seat of Alma Col.

Alma-Ata (äl'mù-ä'tä, Rus. ŭlmä"-ŭtä'), city (pop. 230,-528), cap. of Kazakh SSR, on Turk-Sib RR. Processes cotton, fruit, meat, tobacco.

Almadén (älmädhän'), city (pop. 12,468), central Spain, in New Castile. Center of rich mercury mines exploited since Roman times.

Almagest: see PTOLEMY (Claudius).

Almagro, Diego de (dyä'gō dä älmä'grō), c.1475–1538,

Spanish conquistador, a leader with Pizarros in conquest of Peru. Led expedition into Chile 1535.

Al-Mansur: see MANSUR.

Almeida, Francisco de (fränsĕsh'kō dù älmä'dù), c.1450–1510, Portuguese admiral. Became (1505) viceroy of Portuguese India and fortified E coast of Africa. Routed Egyptians and their Indian allies off Diu (1509). Sought Portuguese supremacy on seas. Killed by Hottentots on way home.

Almeida Garrett, João Batista de (zhwãō' bùtĕsh'tù dù älmä'dù gùrĕt'), 1799–1854, Portuguese romantic dramatist and poet. Notable are plays *Alfageme de Santarém* and *Frei Luis de Sousa,* and long poems *Camões* and *Dona Branca.*

Almería (älmärē'ä), city (pop. 69,824), cap of Almería prov., S Spain, in Andalusia; Mediterranean port. Ships fruits, esparto, minerals. Probably founded by Phoenicians. Flourished (13th–15th cent.) under Moors. Gothic cathedral.

Almohades (ăl'mŭhădz, –hădz) or **Almohads** (–hădz), Berber Moslem dynasty, 12th–13th cent. of Morocco and Spain. Puritanical anti-ALMORAVIDES sect founded by Mohammed ibn Tumart c.1120. His successors conquered Morocco, Moslem Spain, displacing Almoravides by 1174. Defeated by Spanish and Portuguese 1212; by Merenide dynasty in Morocco 1269.

almond, fruit kernel of an orchard tree (*Prunus amygdalus*), resembling the peach and bearing single or double spring blossoms, pink in sweet, white in bitter. Both yield almond oil, and the bitter yields also amygdalin, which on decomposing gives prussic acid. Sweet almond nut used in confections. Flowering almonds are ornamental shrubs of other *Prunus* species.

Almoravides (älmô' rùvīdz, –vĭdz) or **Almoravids** (–vĭdz), Berber Moslem dynasty, 11th–12th cent., of Morocco and Spain; militant puritanical reform sect founded by Abdullah ibn Yasin (d. 1059). His successors founded Marrakesh (1062), helped Spanish Moors stem Christian reconquest (1086), then took over Moslem Spain. Overthrown by ALMOHADES by 1174.

Almquist, Carl Jonas Love (kärl' yōō'näs lōō'vù älm'kvĭst), 1793–1866, Swedish writer. Novels, plays, poems, and short stories are in *The Book of the Thorn Rose* (14 vols., 1832–51).

almug or **algum,** precious wood, mentioned in Bible, used in the Temple and Solomon's palace. 2 Chron. 2.8; 9.10, 11. Perhaps a red sandalwood.

aloe (ăl'ō), perennial of genus *Aloe* (ăl'ōē), with stiff, fleshy leaf clusters, red or yellow flowers. Some are a few inches high, others tree size. Native to South Africa; tub plant elsewhere. Yields drugs and fibers (for cords and nets).

Alost (älôst'), Flemish *Aalst,* town (pop. 42,193), East Flanders, Belgium. Textile mfg.

alpaca (ălpăk'ù), partially domesticated South American hoofed mammal of camel family. Of same genus (*Lama*) as wild guanaco (probably descended from it) and vicuña. Bred chiefly for long, lustrous wool (black through shades of brown to white) by Indians in highlands of Peru, Chile, Bolivia.

Alp Arslan (älp ärslän'), 1029–72, Seljuk sultan of Persia (1063–72). Vigorous conqueror of Christians; victor of MANZIKERT.

Alpena, resort city (pop. 13,135), N Mich., on Thunder Bay of L. Huron; laid out 1856. Has fisheries, limestone quarries, and cement and paper plants.

Alpes-Maritimes (älp'-märētēm'), department (1,644 sq. mi.; pop. c.453,000—incl. BRIGUE AND TENDE), SE France, on French RIVIERA; cap. Nice.

alphabet, type of writing, theoretically having a one-for-one relation between character (or letter) and phoneme (see PHONETICS). Few alphabets have achieved the ideal exactness. An alphabet is called a syllabary when one character represents a syllable rather than a phoneme (e.g., kana of Japan). The modern Western European alphabet is that of Rome (developed from Greek), the base of most alphabets used for newly written languages of Africa and Amer-

ica. The Cyrillic alphabet, an augmented Greek alphabet, is used for Russian, Serbian, Bulgarian, and many languages of the USSR. Greek (developed from Phoenician), Hebrew, Arabic, and Devanagari of India (with syllabic features) all have their own alphabets, based ultimately on Egyptian HIEROGLYPHIC writing. This, though not alphabetic, bore the germ of phonemic writing in the phonogram. A similar development created Persian CUNEIFORM syllabary.

alpha particle and **alpha ray:** see RADIOACTIVITY; RADIUM; RAY.

Alpheus (älfē'ùs), Gr. *Alpheios,* river, 69 mi. long, S Greece, flowing from Taygetus mts. NW through Peloponnesus to the Ionian Sea. In mythology its waters were said to pass under the sea and emerge as fountain of Arethusa at Syracuse. Hercules turned the river through Augeas' stables to clean them. It is the river Alph of Coleridge's *Kubla Khan.*

Alphonso. For rulers thus named, see ALFONSO.

Alphonsus Liguori, Saint (älfŏn'sùs līgwō'rē), 1696–1787, Italian Catholic churchman, Doctor of the Church, founder of Redemptorist order. Wrote many hymns. Original name Alfonso Maria de' Liguori. Feast: Aug. 2.

Alpine (ăl'pīn), resort town (pop. 5,261), W Texas, in mountains N of Big Bend of Rio Grande. Rail junction, it ships cattle and sheep. Big Bend Natl. Park is near by.

Alps, mountain system, S central Europe, forming great arc from Mediterranean coast between France and Italy to Adriatic coast of Yugoslavia. Covering most of Switzerland and Austria, the Alps separate Po plain (N Italy) from France (W), Germany (N), and Danubian plain (E). Many rivers (Rhine, Rhone, Po) originate in the Alpine watershed. Cattle raising, dairying are common in high Alps; agr., orchards, vineyards in valleys. Hydroelectric plants. Beautiful, varied scenery attracts many tourists. Towering peaks, covered by glaciers and perpetual snow, rise above the relatively low base level (3,000–4,000 ft.) and the many fine lakes, e.g., Geneva, Lucerne, Como, Garda, Maggiore. Best-known peaks include Mont Blanc (15,-781 ft.; highest of chain), Monte Rosa, Matterhorn (all in W Alps); Jungfrau, Finsteraarhorn, Piz Bernina (Central Alps, in Bernese Oberland and Engadine); Ortles, Grossglockner, Zugspitze (E Alps, including Dolomites, Hohe Tauern, Bavarian Alps). Principal tunnels and highway passes: Mont CENIS, SIMPLON, SAINT GOTTHARD, ARLBERG, BRENNER PASS, Great and Little SAINT BERNARD, FURKA, MALOJA, STELVIO PASS.

Als (äls), Ger. *Alsen,* island (121 sq. mi.; pop. 34,294), Denmark, in the Little Belt, separated from S Jutland by narrow Als Sound; chief city Sonderborg. Agr., fruitgrowing. Held by Prussia 1864–1920.

Alsace (ăl'säs, äl'säs, Fr. älzäs'), Ger. *Elsass* (ĕl'zäs), region and former province, E France, along Rhine border with Germany; crossed by Vosges mts. Comprises Bas-Rhin, Haut-Rhin, and Territory of Belfort depts. Chief cities: Strasbourg, Colmar, Mulhouse. Bilingual (French, German), 25% of pop. is Protestant. Agr., vineyards, cotton mfg., and potash mines. Included in East Frankish (later German) kingdom (870); Peace of Westphalia (1648) and annexations by Louis XIV (1680–97) gave most of Alsace to France; rest annexed in French Revolution. Ceded (except Belfort) to Germany with part of Lorraine (1871), but recovered by France (1918). Occupied by Germany (1939–44).

alsike: see CLOVER.

Altai or **Altay** (ăl'tī, ältī'), mountain system of SW Siberia, RSFSR and Kazakh SSR, and of W Mongolia. Highest peak (15,266 ft.) is in Mongolia. Forests, meadows, rich mineral deposits (lead, zinc, silver, wolfram, copper, mercury, gold). Larger part of mountains is administratively included in **Altai Territory** (101,000 sq. mi.; pop. c.2,400,000), RSFSR, which also has some of richest black-earth area of Siberia; cap. Barnaul. Drained by Ob R. Population is largely Russian; in mountains Altai-speaking Oirats or Oirots predominate. Oirats were seminomadic until recent settlement on collective farms.

Altamira (äl″tämē′rä) site of the caverns in N Spain, near Santander, where famous examples of CAVE ART were discovered in 1879.

Altamirano, Ignacio Manuel (ēgnä′syō mänwĕl′ ältämērä′nō), 1834–93, Mexican novelist, of pure Indian blood. Key figure in reconstruction of republic after collapse of Maximilian's empire. Wrote novels *Clemencia* and *La navidad en las montañas*.

Altay: see ALTAI.

Altdorf (ält′dôrf), town (pop. 5,692), cap. of Uri, Switzerland. Scene of William Tell's exploits.

Altdorfer, Albrecht (äl′brĕkht ältdôr′fŭr), 1480–1538, German painter and engraver, follower of Dürer. Painted landscapes in a romantic vein.

Altenburg, Germany: see SAXE-ALTENBURG.

alternating current: see ELECTRICITY; GENERATOR.

Altgeld, John Peter (ält′gĕlt), 1847–1902, governor of Ill. (1892–96), b. Germany. A Democrat and sturdy champion of human rights, he pardoned the men convicted for Haymarket riots and opposed sending of Federal troops when there was a strike at PULLMAN (1894).

Althing (äl′thĭng), parliament of Iceland. Oldest assembly in Europe, first convened 930. Dissolved 1800, revived as advisory body 1843, restored 1874.

Altichiero da Zevio (ältēkyä′rō dä tsäv′yō), c.1330–c.1395, Italian painter, follower of Giotto, founder of school of Verona.

altimeter (ältĭm′ĭtŭr, äl′tĭmē″tŭr), altitude-measuring device for aircraft, usually a BAROMETER indicating altitude above sea level only. Newer type uses radio waves and shows actual distance.

altitude sickness: see AIRSICKNESS.

Alto Adige, Italy: see TRENTINO-ALTO ADIGE.

Alton (âl′tŭn), city (pop. 32,550), SW Ill., on the Mississippi and N of St. Louis; laid out 1817. Shipping center with mfg. of flour, metal products, and glass. Has monument to E. P. LOVEJOY, and tablet marking scene of a Lincoln-Douglas debate (1858). The Principia (coed. college; Christian Scientist; chartered 1921) is near by.

Altona, Germany: see HAMBURG.

Altoona, industrial city (pop. 77,177), central Pa., E of Pittsburgh, in bituminous coal region; settled c.1769. Has railroad shops and mfg. of textiles, automobile parts, and metal products. Horseshoe Curve of Pennsylvania RR is W.

Altus (äl′tŭs), city (pop. 9,735), SW Okla., between Wichita Mts. and Red R. Produces cotton and food products. Main city of W. C. Austin (formerly Altus) project (1941; irrigation).

alum (äl′ŭm), double crystalline salt, a sulphate of a univalent and a trivalent cation (positively charged atom or radical). Alum in popular use means double sulphate of potassium and aluminum, i.e., potassium alum or potash alum.

alumina (ŭloo′mĭnŭ) or **aluminum oxide,** occurs nearly pure as CORUNDUM and is combined with silica in clay. Corundum and emery (an impure form) are among the hardest of abrasives. Alundum is an artificial form used as an abrasive. Alumina from BAUXITE is important source of metallic aluminum.

aluminum, silvery-white metallic element (symbol = Al; see also ELEMENT, table). Ductile and malleable; resists corrosion; excellent conductor of heat and electricity; very light. Used in dirigibles, airplanes, autos, kitchen utensils, wrapping foil, paints, high-tension wires. Main source is BAUXITE.

alundum: see ALUMINA.

Alva, Fernando de: see ALBA.

Alva, city (pop. 6,505), NW Okla., on Salt Lake Fork of Arkansas R. Center of wheat-growing area.

Alvarado, Juan Bautista (hwän′ boutēs′tä älvärä′dhō), 1809–82, governor of Alta California (present California) 1836–42. Local rivalries and immigration of

U.S. citizens brought about recurrent disturbances.

Alvarado, Pedro de (pä′dhrō dä), 1485?–1541, Spanish conquistador. Served under Hernán Cortés in conquest of Mexico. Sent out by Cortés, he conquered Guatemala and Salvador (1523). Governor of Guatemala until his death; his wife, Beatriz de la Cueva, succeeded him. Led expedition to Ecuador (1534–35) but was defeated. Killed in Mixtón War.

Álvarez Quintero, Serafín (säräfēn′ äl′väräth kēntä′ro), 1871–1938, and **Joaquín Álvarez Quintero** (hwäkēn′), 1873–1944, Spanish dramatists; brothers. Collaborated on plays, notably comedies of Andalusian middleclass life.

Alvsborg, Swed. *Älvsborgs län* (ĕlfs′bôr″yùs lĕn′), county (4,919 sq. mi.; pop. 358,506), SW Sweden; cap. Vanersborg. N section, W of Vanern lake, is agr. and lumbering district; important textile plants in S; large power works at TROLLHATTAN. Alfsborg and Elfsborg are former spellings.

alyssum (–lĭs′–), plant of genus *Alyssum,* low perennials with yellow flowers, used in borders and rock gardens. **Sweet alyssum** is an annual species of *Lobularia* with fragrant white or lavender flowers.

Am, chemical symbol of the element AMERICIUM.

Amadeus VIII (ămŭdē′ùs), 1383–1451, duke of Savoy, antipope (1439–49), as Felix V. Had few supporters and yielded to Nicholas V.

Amadeus, 1845–90, king of Spain (1870–73), duke of Aosta, son of Victor Emmanuel II of Italy. Elected king after expulsion of Isabella II. His difficulties with his own government, and with the rebel CARLISTS, compelled him to abdicate.

Amadis of Gaul (ă′mŭdĭs), romance of chivalry, first composed in Spain or Portugal (13th or 14th cent.), probably based on French sources. Often rewritten and translated, it gives ideal of perfect knight.

Amado, Jorge (zhôr′zhù ùmä′dō), 1912–, Brazilian novelist. Wrote with grim realism of Brazilian life, especially of the economically oppressed.

Amagasaki (ä′mägäsä′kē), industrial city (pop. 233,183), S Honshu, Japan; a port on Osaka Bay.

Amager (ä′mägùr), island (25 sq. mi.; pop. 150,775), Denmark, in the Oresund. N end is occupied by part of Copenhagen.

Amalasuntha (ä″mùlùsùn′thù), d. 535, Ostrogothic queen in Italy, daughter of Theodoric the Great. Regent for son Athalaric (526–34); ruled after his death till murdered by order of her husband.

Amalek (ăm′ŭlĕk), people of Canaan, descendants of Esau, hereditary enemies of Hebrews until dispersed by Saul. Gen. 14.7; Ex. 17.8–16; Gen. 36.12,16; Num. 13.29; 14.25,45; 24.20; Judges 3.13; 6.3,33; 7.12; 1 Sam. 15.5–8; 30.1–20; 1 Chron. 1.36; 4.43.

Amalfi (ämäl′fē), town (pop. 4,259), Campania, S Italy, on Gulf of Salerno. First Italian maritime republic (9th cent.); duchy from 953 until fall to Normans (1131). Cathedral in Sicilian-Arabic style was begun in the 10th cent.

amalgam, ALLOY of mercury with any metal except platinum or iron. Most are made artificially. Amalgamation process extracts gold and silver, which are dissolved from ores.

Amalric (ùmăl′rĭk) or **Amaury** (ùmô′rē), Latin kings of Jerusalem. **Amalric I,** c.1135–74, reigned 1163–74. Lost suzerainty of Egypt to NUREDDIN. **Amalric II,** d. 1205, gained the title in 1197 through marriage to Isabella, eldest daughter of Amalric I. Succeeded his brother Guy of Lusignan as king of Cyprus in 1194.

Amalthaea (ămŭlthē′ù), nurse of Zeus, often represented as a goat with wonderful horns; one horn became the CORNUCOPIA.

Amana Society (ùmän′ù), corporate name of seven villages, E central Iowa, grouped around Iowa R. WNW of Iowa City; settled 1855 by members of Community of True Inspiration. Community originated in 17th-cent. German religious sect. Fled to U.S. 1843 under Christian Metz to escape persecution. Settled first near Buffalo, N.Y. One of most successful U.S. communal communities. Made cooperative corporation with separation of religious and economic administration, 1932. Wool and wood handicrafts prominent.

amaranth (ăm'–), coarse annual plant (*Amaranthus*), with colorful foliage and chaffy flower spikes. Garden kinds include love-lies-bleeding or tassel flower, Joseph's coat. Some species are weeds, e.g., pigweed, TUMBLEWEED.

Amarapura (ŭ"mŭrăpōō'rä), town, Upper Burma, on Irrawaddy R. Was cap. of Burma 1783–1823, 1837–60.

Amarillo (ămŭrĭl'ō), city (pop. 74,246), N Texas; settled c.1887 (though spot known to Indians, hunters, and cowboys before). A former cow town, it now processes meat, zinc, oil, and flour and produces machinery and farm and dairy products. Main city of Panhandle, it has VA hospital, symphony orchestra, and annual music festival.

amaryllis (ăm"ŭrĭl'ĭs), South African bulbous plant (*Amaryllis belladonna*), the belladonna lily, often cultivated for its rose-red, fragrant flowers. Name used for related plants, especially for those of the genus *Hippeastrum*, whose heavy stalks bear clusters of vivid lilylike flowers.

Amasa (ăm'ŭsŭ), cousin of Absalom with whom he revolted. 2 Sam. 17.25; 19.13; 20.4–13; 1 Kings 2.5.

Amasis I (ŭmā'sĭs) (Ahmose), d. c.1557 B.C., king of Egypt. Founded XVIII dynasty and drove out HYKSOS.

Amati (ämä'tē), family of violinmakers of Cremona, beginning with Andrea Amati (fl. 1535–80). Niccolò Amati (1596–1684) brought the Amati violin to its peak. Antonio Stradivari was his pupil.

Amaury. For persons thus named, see AMALRIC.

Amaziah (ăm"ŭzī'ŭ), died c.775 B.C., king of Judah c.802–c.775 B.C.), successor of Jehoash of Judah. Two events of reign were conquest of Edom and unprovoked attack on King Jehoash of Israel. Jehoash took Amaziah prisoner, entered Jerusalem, sacked the Temple. Amaziah was killed. 2 Kings 14; 2 Chron. 25.

Amazon (ă'mŭzŏn), in Greek legend, one of tribe of women who spent time in hunting and warfare. One of Hercules' 12 labors was to steal girdle of Queen Hippolyte. In Trojan War they fought against Greeks, and their leader, Penthesilea, was slain by Achilles.

Amazon, Port. *Amazonas.* (ämŭzō'nŭsh), river rising in Peruvian Andes in two major headstreams, MARAÑÓN and Ucayali, and flowing across Brazil to Atlantic. Carries more water than any other river. Length is 3,000 mi. with Marañón or 4,000 with Ucayali. Extremely low gradient and enormous drainage basin. In lowlands E of Andes is world's largest rain forest. Principal tributaries from N are NEGRO, NAPO, PUTUMAYO, Caquetá; from S are JURUÁ, PURUS, MADEIRA, XINGÚ, TAPAJÓS, TOCANTINS. Below Xingú, Amazon reaches delta and divides around MARAJÓ isl.; S stream called Pará. Basin sparsely peopled, mostly by Indians. Early explorers include Vicente Ýañez Pinzón (lower part, 1500), ORELLANA (from Napo, 1540–41; his fanciful story of female warriors gave Amazon its name), Pedro de Ursúa (1559), TEIXEIRA (1637–39). Resources of basin are principally wild rubber (important in early 20th cent.), cacao, woods, jute. Brazilian government in 1940s undertook development of area and estab. health service.

ambassador: see DIPLOMATIC SERVICE.

Ambato (ämbä'tō), city (pop. 33,908), central Ecuador, a commercial town in high Andean basin.

amber, fossil resin exuded as gum by coniferous trees in past geologic time. It is either transparent or cloudy and is used in making beads, mouthpieces, and small ornaments. Ancient Greeks knew that rubbing it with fur produced static electricity.

ambergris (ăm'bŭrgrēs), waxlike substance produced by abnormal conditions in sperm whale's digestive tract. Floats in tropical seas as yellow, gray, black, or variegated mass. Perfume fixative.

Ambiorix (ămbī'ŭrĭks), fl. 54 B.C., Gallic chieftain. Though earlier in Roman favor, he joined in attacking Caesar's legates. When Caesar approached, he

fled across the Rhine and disappeared from history.

Ambleside, village, Westmorland, England; Lake District tourist center. Church has stained glass window given by admirers of Wordsworth.

Amboina (ămboi'nŭ), island (314 sq. mi.; pop. 66,821), Moluccas, Indonesia. Produces nutmeg, cloves, rice, and sugar. Discovered 1512 by the Portuguese, taken 1600 by the Dutch. Port town of Amboina (pop. 17,-334) was allied naval base in early phase of World War II.

Amboise, Georges d' (zhôrzh' däbwäz'), 1460–1510, cardinal, French statesman. Chief minister of Louis XII; patron of arts and letters.

Amboise (äbwäz'), town (pop. 4,224), Indre-et-Loire dept., central France, on the Loire. Famous castle was royal residence 15th–16th cent.

Amboise, conspiracy of, 1560, unsuccessful plot of French Huguenots and others to abduct Francis II from Amboise and to arrest Charles and François de Guise. The rebels were massacred.

Ambridge, borough (pop. 16,429), W Pa., on Ohio R. and NW of Pittsburgh: HARMONY SOCIETY estab. communistic settlement Economy here 1825–1906. Mfg. of steel, metal products, and electrical machinery.

Ambrose, Saint, 339?–397, bishop of Milan, Doctor of the Church, b. Trier. As governor in NW Italy, he won much esteem; the people insisted on his being made bishop (371). He administered the diocese ably, refusing to bow to the emperors: he opposed the Arianism favored by Valentinian II, persuaded Gratian to outlaw heresy, and made Theodosius I do penance for a massacre of rebellious citizens of Salonica. His brilliant religious writing molded classic learning in a Christian context. His name is also associated with the type of plain song called Ambrosian chant, and he wrote hymns (many ascribed to him are spurious). He was one of the chief "founders" of the Middle Ages. Feast: Dec. 7.

Ambrosian Library, public library (founded c.1609), Milan, rich in Greek and Latin texts and incunabula.

Amchitka (ămchĭt'kŭ), island, 40 mi. long, off W Alaska, one of ALEUTIAN ISLANDS. Had U.S. air base in World War II.

amendment, in law, alteration of provisions of legal document (STATUTE or CONSTITUTION). In parliamentary law also, proposed changes of bill or motion. In judicial procedure, correction of errors. Amendment to Constitution of the United States requires approval of two thirds of each house of Congress, ratification by three quarters of states.

Amenemhet (ä"mĕnĕm'hĕt, ä"–), kings of anc. Egypt of the XII dynasty. **Amenemhet I,** d. 1970 B.C., seized throne, centralized government, and humbled nobles. **Amenemhet III,** d. 1801 B.C., son and successor of Sesostris III, reclaimed the Fayum.

Amenhotep (ä"mĕnhō'tĕp, ä"–), or **Amenophis** (ä"mĕnō'fĭs), kings of anc. Egypt of the XVIII dynasty. **Amenhotep I,** fl. 1557 B.C., successor to his father, Amasis I, pushed S boundary to second Nile cataract and invaded Syria. **Amenhotep II** succeeded his father, Thutmose III (1448 B.C.), kept conquests already made. **Amenhotep III** succeeded his father, Thutmose IV (c.1411 B.C.). His was an age of splendor and comparative peace. His son and successor was IKHNATON.

America [for Amerigo VESPUCCI], the lands of the Western Hemisphere—North America, Central America (sometimes Middle America), and South America. In English, America and American are often used to refer only to U.S. Martin WALDSEEMÜLLER first used the name.

America, patriotic hymn of the U.S., beginning, "My country, 'tis of thee." Words written in 1832 by Samuel F. Smith to a tune found in book of German school songs. Only later did he discover he had used tune of *God Save the King.*

American, river rising in N central Calif. and flowing W and SW to Sacramento R. at Sacramento. Gold dis-

SMALL CAPITALS = cross references. Pronunciation key on inside end pages. Abbreviations: p. 2.

covered along its banks (1848) brought great gold rush.

Americana, all that has been printed in and about the Americas or written by Americans; usually restricted to formative period in history of the two continents. Earliest-known example is Columbus letter (1493), on discovery of West Indies. Some early American books were printed by Juan Pablos, Stephen Daye and William Bradford.

American Academy in Rome, founded 1894 as the American School of Architecture in Rome, chartered by New York state 1897, inc. under its present name by act of Congress 1905. Comprises schools of fine arts and classical studies. Annual awards include residence in Rome, travel allowance, and yearly stipend for U.S. citizens under 30. Only men are eligible for the fine arts fellowships.

American Colonization Society, organized Dec., 1816–Jan., 1817, at Washington, D.C., to transport free Negroes from U.S. and settle them in Africa. Purchase of land in Africa in 1822 led to foundation of LIBERIA. Colonization movement attacked by abolitionists, who charged that removal of free Negroes strengthened slavery in the South. Society declined after 1840.

American Expeditionary Force: see WORLD WAR I.

American Falls, city (pop. 1,874), SE Idaho, on Snake R. and SW of Pocatello. Oregon Trail camps were near actual falls. City moved ½ mi. after dam was built (1925–27) on former site; 25-mi. reservoir serves MINIDOKA PROJECT. Wheat center.

American Federation of Labor (A.F. of L.), federation of trade unions in the U.S. and Canada; formed 1881, present name adopted 1886. A fairly loose combination of craft unions, the A.F. of L. opposes organization by industry. Under leadership of Samuel Gompers and, after 1924, of William Green, the A.F. of L. has become the largest American labor federation. The CONGRESS OF INDUSTRIAL ORGANIZATIONS and the UNITED MINE WORKERS OF AMERICA split with the A.F. of L.

American Fork, city (pop. 5,126), N central Utah, S of Salt Lake City. Resort and poultry-raising center served by Provo river project.

American Fur Company, chartered 1808 by John Jacob Astor (1763–1848) as rival to companies in Canada. Company maintained virtual monopoly, expanded from Lakes region W to Rocky Mts.

Americanization, term used to describe cultural process by which the immigrant to U.S. assimilates American speech, ideals, traditions, ways of life. Name also given to the movement fostering assimilation, which grew to crusading proportions in first quarter of 20th cent. as result of great immigration from E and S Europe from 1880 to World War I (see IMMIGRATION). Federal bureaus of education and of naturalization joined crusade and aided private Americanization groups. Passage of immigrant education legislation by states plus return of "normalcy" after World War I and, more especially, coming of the quota system of immigration caused Americanization move to subside.

American Labor party, organized in N.Y. by labor leaders and liberals in 1936, primarily to support the New Deal. Pro-Soviet faction caused internal strife after 1939. Right-wing dissenters formed Liberal party 1944.

American Legion, national association of veterans of First and Second World Wars, founded in Paris in 1919. Largest of veterans' associations, it exerts considerable influence on national life. Has done much work in social welfare, particularly child care; obtained benefits for veterans; attacked "subversive" or "anti-American" teachings and organizations.

American Museum of Natural History, incorporated (1869) in New York city to promote study of natural science and related subjects. Buildings on present site opened 1877; Hayden Planetarium (1935) and Roosevelt Memorial building (1936) added since.

American party: see KNOW-NOTHING MOVEMENT.

American Red Cross: see RED CROSS.

American Revolution, 1775–83, struggle by which the THIRTEEN COLONIES on Atlantic seaboard of North America won independence from Great Britain. By middle of 18th cent., differences in thought and interests had developed between colonies and mother country. STAMP ACT (1765) aroused colonial resistance as act of taxation without representation. TOWNSHEND ACTS (1767) led to such incidents as BOSTON MASSACRE (1770), burning of the GASPEE (1772), and BOSTON TEA PARTY (1773). Parliament replied with the INTOLERABLE ACTS. At CONTINENTAL CONGRESS (1774) grievances were listed in petitions to the king. Fighting began at Lexington and Concord on April 19, 1775, followed by capture of Ticonderoga from British and battle of Bunker Hill. QUEBEC CAMPAIGN (1775–76) was disastrous. DECLARATION OF INDEPENDENCE was adopted on July 4, 1776, but many colonists remained pro-British LOYALISTS. SARATOGA CAMPAIGN (1777), successful for colonists, was followed by harsh winter at Valley Forge. Aid from France helped patriot cause. In West, George Rogers CLARK estab. patriot hold on frontier. CAROLINA CAMPAIGN (1780–81) led into YORKTOWN CAMPAIGN. Surrender of Cornwallis at Yorktown in Oct., 1781, ended fighting. Treaty of Paris (1783) formally recognized U.S. as nation.

American Samoa: see SAMOA.

American University: see WASHINGTON, D.C.

American Veterans Committee (AVC), organization of veterans of World War II, founded Jan., 1943. Opposed special privileges for veterans.

American Veterans of World War II (Amvets), organization of veterans of World War II, founded Dec., 1944; chartered 1947.

americium (ămŭrĭ'shēŭm), radioactive element (symbol = Am; atomic no.= 95) of the actinide series. Was first produced from plutonium in cyclotron.

Americus (ùmĕr'ĭkùs), city (pop. 11,389), SW Ga., SE of Columbus, in farm and lumber area. Food canning, peanut processing, and clothing mfg. Near-by national cemetery contains graves of over 13,000 Union soldiers, most of whom died (1864–65) in Andersonville Prison.

Ames, Fisher, 1758–1808, American political leader from Mass. U.S. Congressman (1789–97), a staunch Federalist and violent attacker of Jefferson.

Ames, James Barr, 1846–1910, American jurist, dean of Harvard Law School after 1895. Helped make case method popular in law study.

Ames, Joseph, 1689–1759, English bibliographer. Compiled list of English books printed before 1600.

Ames, Oakes, 1804–73, American manufacturer, railroad promoter, and politician. U.S. Congressman (1863–73). Involved in CRÉDIT MOBILIER scandal.

Ames, Winthrop, 1871–1937, American theatrical producer. Encouraged noncommercial experimentation.

Ames, city (pop. 22,898), central Iowa, N of Des Moines; laid out 1864. Mfg. of apparel and metal products. Has atomic-energy laboratory. IOWA STATE COLLEGE OF AGRICULTURE AND MECHANIC ARTS is near by.

Amesbury, town (pop. 10,851), including Amesbury village (pop. 9,711), NE Mass., on Merrimack R.; settled 1654. Mfg. of metal goods, hats, and boats. Whittier lived here.

amethyst (ăm'ŭthĭst), variety of QUARTZ, violet to purple in color. Valued as a semiprecious gem.

Amharic (ămhä'rĭk), standard language of Ethiopia, belonging to Ethiopic group of Semitic languages. See LANGUAGE (table).

Amherst, Jeffrey Amherst, Baron (ăm'ŭrst), 1717–97, British army officer. Commanded British forces in French and Indian War; captured Louisburg (1758) and Montreal (1760). Amherst, Mass., named for him.

Amherst, town (pop. 9,870), N N.S., Canada, NW of Truro. Has iron foundries, woolen mills, and mfg. of railroad cars and machinery. Near by are ruins of Fort Lawrence and Fort Beausejour.

Amherst, town (pop. 10,856), including Amherst village (pop. 7,900), W Mass., NE of Northampton; settled

1703; named for Lord Amherst. Emily Dickinson and Noah Webster lived here. Seat of Univ. of Massachusetts (land-grant, state supported; coed.; chartered 1863, opened 1867; called Massachusetts Agr. Col. to 1931, Massachusetts State Col. to 1947) and Amherst Col. (nonsectarian; for men; opened 1821, chartered 1825 by Congregationalists), which holds in trust Folger Shakespeare Memorial Library.

Amherstburg, town (pop. 3,638), S Ont., Canada, on Detroit R. at entrance to L. Erie. Fort Malden built here 1796. Was British garrison town and naval station in War of 1812. Held by Americans at end of war.

Amherst College: see AMHERST, Mass.

Amicis, Edmondo de: see DE AMICIS, EDMONDO.

Amiel, Henri Frédéric (ărē′ frădārēk′ ämyĕl′), 1821–81, Swiss critic. His introspective *Journal intime,* published posthumously, reveals a personality seeking to explain and justify his lifelong inactivity (partial Eng. tr., 1936).

Amiens (ämyē′), city (pop. 79,807), cap. of Somme dept., N France, on Somme R.; historic cap. of Picardy. Old textile industry. Fought over in World War I, half destroyed in World War II. Cathedral (begun 1220), largest and among finest French Gothic cathedrals, escaped damage.

Amiens, Treaty of, 1802, made by England with France, Spain, Batavian Republic. France agreed to evacuate Naples; England to give up most conquests made in French Revolutionary Wars.

Amiot, Joseph: see AMYOT, JOSEPH.

Amish Church: see MENNONITES.

Amityville, residential and resort village (pop. 6,164) SE N.Y., on S shore of Long Isl.; settled 1780.

Amman, Jost (yōst′ äm′än), 1539–91, Swiss engraver, noted for Bible illustrations.

Amman (ämän′), city (pop. c.90,000), N Jordan, cap. and royal residence, on Wadi Zerka (Jabbok R.), on Hejaz RR, and ENE of Jerusalem. Industrial and commercial center. Was biblical Rabbah (răb′ŭ) or Rabbath, cap. of Ammonites. Rebuilt as Philadelphia; has noted Roman ruins.

Ammanati, Bartolomeo (bärtōlōmä′ō äm-mänä′tē), 1511–92, Italian architect and sculptor. Collaborated with Vignola and Vasari on villa of Pope Julius III. As architect to Cosimo de' Medici, he designed court façade of Pitti Palace (Florence).

Ammann, Othmar Hermann (ôt′mär, ŏ′mŏn), 1879–, American civil engineer. Engaged in major bridge-building projects in New York city and San Francisco (Golden Gate Bridge).

ammeter: see GALVANOMETER.

Ammi (ăm′ī) [Heb.,= my people], figurative name of Israel after reconciliation with God. Hosea 2.1. Cf. LOAMMI.

Ammon (ăm′ŭn), in Bible, marauding, nomadic people living E of Dead Sea, relentlessly hostile to Hebrews. Gen. 19.38; Deut. 2.19,20,37; 23.3,4; Judges 3.13; 1 Sam. 11; 2 Sam. 10–12; 2 Chron. 20; Neh. 2.10; 4.7; Jer. 49.1–6.

Ammon, Egyptian god: see AMON.

ammonia, compound of nitrogen and hydrogen in proportion of one to three. Colorless gas with penetrating odor. Very soluble in water (household ammonia is aqueous solution); solution basic. Easily liquefied with pressure. Forms salts with acids. Used to make SAL AMMONIAC, nitric acid, soda; in REFRIGERATION; in medicine. Prepared by destructive distillation of coal, by HABER PROCESS, by treating calcium carbide with nitrogen. Occurs in air, in plant and animal decomposition products, in animal excretions. Amides are derivatives formed by replacing one or more hydrogen atoms of ammonia by organic acid radicals; amines by replacing them with alkyl groups (chains of carbon and hydrogen atoms) or aryl groups (rings of the same).

amnesia, temporary or prolonged loss of memory of events before or after the causative shock, injury, illness, or mental disease. It is usually cured by establishment of associations with the past by suggestion or hypnotism. It is distinct from aphasia, the loss of verbal usages.

Amnon [Heb.,= faithful], David's eldest son. He ravished his half sister Tamar and was killed by her brother Absalom in revenge. 2 Sam. 3.2; 13.

amoeba (ŭmē′bŭ), member of genus (*Amoeba*) of PROTOZOA. *A. proteus* (common species) of fresh waters is c.1/100 in. long. Amoeba, a single cell, has oval nucleus surrounded by granular mass, in turn surrounded by outer clear layer. Locomotion is by false feet or pseudopods formed by outpushing of clear layer with granular mass flowing into outpushings. Pseudopods also engulf food (minute animals, plants) in water; food circulates through protoplasm until digested. Sensitive to light, heat, food. See *ill.,* p. 633.

Amon (ā′mŏn), d. c.641 B.C., idolatrous king of Judah (c.643–c.641 B.C.). He was murdered by servants and succeeded by Josiah. Jeremiah was a contemporary. 2 Kings 21.19–26; 2 Chron. 33.20–25.

Amon (ā′mŭn, ä′–) or **Ammon** (ă′mŭn), ancient Egyptian deity, originally local god of Thebes. He was early represented as a ram or as a man with ram's head. The principal temple to him was in Libyan desert. Identified by Greeks with Zeus and by Romans with Jupiter. See EGYPTIAN RELIGION.

amontillado (ŭmŏn″tĭlä′dō), dry sherry noted for delicate bouquet. It resembles the wine produced in Montilla, Spain, from which it derives its name.

Amor, Roman god of love: see CUPID; EROS.

amortization, reduction, liquidation, or satisfaction of a debt or the sum used for this purpose. In security investment, amortization is charging off premium or discount to bring value of security to par at maturity. Other forms of amortization: paying off mortgage, paying off debt by sinking fund, and paying off public corporation bonds annually.

Amos (ā′mŭs), book of Old Testament, written by a shepherd-prophet in time of Jeroboam II. The book falls into 3 parts: God's judgment on Gentile nations, finally on Israel; three sermons on doom of Israel; five visions of destruction, the last promising redemption.

Amoskeag Falls: see MANCHESTER, N.H.

Amoy (ùmoi′), commercial city (pop. 158,271), Fukien prov., China; port on Amoy Isl. in inlet of Formosa Strait. Treaty port, opened 1842. Exports sugar, tobacco, and tea. Seat of a university.

ampelopsis (ăm″pĭlŏp′–), woody vines of genus *Ampelopsis,* including pepper vine of S U.S. Berries are blue, purple, yellow, or orange in various species.

Ampère, André Marie (ăm′pēr; ädrā′ märē äpēr′), 1775–1836, French physicist, mathematician, natural philosopher. Worked in electrodynamics, derived Ampère's law, studied relationship of electricity and magnetism.

ampere [for A. M. Ampère], electrical unit of current strength and measurement unit of rate of current flow. Current intensity (in amperes) determined by dividing volts (electromotive force) by ohms (resistance).

amphibian (ămfĭ′bēŭn), cold-blooded vertebrate animal of class Amphibia, intermediate between fish and reptiles. Characteristic metamorphosis is from aquatic to partially terrestrial form. See FROG; NEWT; SALAMANDER; TOAD.

amphibious warfare (ămfĭ′bēŭs), the combined use of land and sea forces in warfare. Known from the time of the ancient Greeks, it is in modern war also supported by air power. In World War II, many special vessels were made for landing tanks, supplies, and men in shallow water. Warfare in the Pacific and the invasion of Europe used amphibious warfare extensively.

Amphilochus (ămfĭ′lŭkŭs), in Greek legend, son of Amphiaraüs and Eriphyle. He was one of the EPIGONI, and fought in Trojan War.

Amphitheater, suburb (pop. 12,664) of Tucson, Ariz.

Amphitrite (ămfītrī′tē), in Greek religion, queen of the sea; wife of Poseidon and mother of Triton.

Amphitryon (ămfĭ'trēŭn, –ŏn"), in Greek legend, husband of Alcmene. In Amphitryon's absence, Zeus assumed his form and visited Alcmene; she bore him Hercules, whom Amphitryon accepted as his son.

Amram ben Scheschna (shĕsh'nä) or **Amram Gaon** (gä'ŏn), d. 875, author of *Siddur Rab Amram,* a prayer book, the basis for Orthodox Jewish religious rites.

Amritsar (ŭmrĭt'sŭr), city (pop. 391,010), NW Punjab, India. Founded 1577 by Ram Das, 4th guru [Hindustani = teacher], it is center of Sikh religion. Mfg. of silks and carpets. At open-air meeting, April 13, 1919, many Gandhi followers were killed or wounded by British forces.

Amru-l-Kais (kīs'), 6th cent., Arabian poet. Subjective, formally perfect verse is esteemed by Arabs as model for erotic poetry. Included in MUALLAQAT.

Amsterdam (ăm'stŭrdăm", Dutch ämstŭrdäm'), municipality (pop. 803,847), and city, constitutional cap. and largest city of the Netherlands, in North Holland. Situated mainly on S bank of the Ij and connected by canals with the North Sea and the Rhine delta, it is a major port and a great commercial, intellectual, and artistic center. Stock exchange and diamond-cutting industry are important. Amsterdam is built on wooden piles; some 400 bridges cross numerous concentric and radial canals. Chartered in 1300, it joined the Hanseatic League in 1369 and the United Provs. in 1578. Large influx of refugees from all nations (notably French Protestants and Spanish and Portuguese Jews) contributed to rapid growth after late 16th cent. Birthplace of Spinoza and residence of Rembrandt, Amsterdam reached apex as cultural center in 17th cent. It was taken by the French in 1795; served as cap. of kingdom of Netherlands under Louis Bonaparte; was declared cap. under 1814 constitution. Actually, the government is at The Hague; sovereigns are merely sworn in at Amsterdam. German occupation (1940–45) in World War II brought severe hardship. Of the large Jewish population only a few survived. Points of interest include Oude Kerk [old church], built c.1300; weighhouse (15th cent.); city hall (16th cent.); Rijks Mus. (has Dutch masters); Univ. of Amsterdam (1632; reorganized 1876).

Amsterdam, industrial city (pop. 32,240), E central N.Y., on Mohawk R. and NW of Albany. Center for rug and carpet mfg. Fort Johnson, home of Sir William Johnson, is near.

Amu Darya (ä'moo där'yŭ), river, 1,577 mi. long, central Asia. Ancient name is Oxus.

amulet, object worn as charm to ward off evil influences. Reliance on such devices is common to many cultures. Egyptians wore many amulets; Hebrews wore phylacteries containing scriptural texts; Christians of 4th cent. wore crosses and amulets enclosing sacred objects and scriptural verses. Materials of amulets vary from teeth of animals to precious stones and may bear engravings of symbols, such as wheel of sun-god or a swastika.

Amundsen, Roald (rō'äl ä'moͦonsŭn), 1872–1928, Norwegian polar explorer. Commanded first negotiation of Northwest Passage (1903–6). First to reach South Pole (1911). Flew over North Pole with Lincoln Ellsworth (1926). Died in attempt to rescue a former associate, Umberto Nobile.

Amur (ämoͦor'), Chinese *Hei-lung-kiang* (hā'-loͦong'jēäng'), river, 1,767 mi. long, NE Asia. Formed by junction of Shilka and Argun at Russo-Manchurian border; follows border for 1,100 mi.; turns NE near Khabarovsk and empties into Tatar Strait opposite Sakhalin isl. Important transport artery during ice-free summer months.

Amurath: see MURAD.

amylase: see DIASTASE.

Amyot, Jacques (zhäk' ämyō'), 1513–93, French humanist, translator of Plutarch's *Lives* (1559).

Amyot or **Amiot, Joseph** (zhôzĕf' ämyō'), 1718–1794?, French Jesuit missionary in China. He was one of first Europeans to make Chinese literature, antiquities, and

customs known to Europe and also was an early authority on Manchu language.

Anabaptists [from Gr.,= rebaptizers], Protestant sects insisting on rebaptism for believers only. Persecuted for preaching separation of Church and state, they were disunited. Luther opposed them. Chief leaders were Thomas Münzer and John of Leiden. Group under Menno Simons became MENNONITES. Descendants of Jacob Hutter estab. HUTTERISCHE COMMUNITY (1874) in S.Dak.

Anabasis (ŭnă'bŭsĭs) [Gr.,= going up, i.e., to the sea], famed Greek prose history by XENOPHON of retreat of the Ten Thousand from Persia (c.399 B.C.)

Anacharsis (ănŭkär'sĭs), 6th cent. B.C., Scythian prince supposed to have toured Greece; in legend a very witty, wise man.

Anacletus, Saint: see CLETUS, SAINT.

Anaconda (ănŭkŏn'dŭ), city (pop. 11,254), SW Mont., NW of Butte; laid out 1883. Chosen by Marcus DALY for smelter of Anaconda Copper Mining Co. City, dominated by smelter, also has by-product plants (arsenic, sulphuric acid, phosphate fertilizer).

anaconda, nonvenomous South American snake, mostly aquatic, partially arboreal, related to boa constrictor, python. Largest is water boa (to 30 ft.).

Anacortes (ănŭkôr'tĕz), port city (pop. 6,919), NW Wash., S of Bellingham. Processes and ships lumber, fish, and food.

Anacostia (ănŭkŏs'tēŭ), river rising near Bladensburg, Md., and flowing into Potomac R. at Washington, D.C. Naval installations on shores.

Anacreon (ŭnăk'rēŭn, –ŏn), fl. c.521 B.C., Greek lyric poet, author of drinking and love songs.

Anadarko (ănŭdär'kō), city (pop. 6,184), SW Okla., on Washita R. and SW of Oklahoma City. Center of cotton, grain, livestock, and oil area. Has remnants of Delaware Indians. Annual Indian exposition.

Anadyr (ŭnŭdír'), river, 700 mi. long, RSFSR. Flows from extreme NE Siberia into Bering Sea. Coal and gold deposits along shores.

anae-, for words beginning thus: see ANE-.

Anaheim (ăn'ŭhīm), city (pop. 14,556), S Calif., SE of Los Angeles; founded 1857. Has mfg. of canning equipment and plants to pack and process food.

Anáhuac (änä'wäk) [Aztec,= near the water], geographical term in Mexico, today referring specifically to part of central plateau comprising Pánuco and Lerma river systems and lake basin of Valley of Mexico.

Anakim (ăn'ŭkĭm) or **Anakims,** in Bible, a race of giants inhabiting Hebron at time of conquest of Canaan. Practically extirpated by Joshua and Caleb. Num. 13.22,28,33; Deut. 1.28; 9.2; Joshua 11.21; 14.15; 15.13,14; 21.11; Judges 1.20.

Anamosa (ănŭmō'sŭ), city (pop. 3,910), E central Iowa, NE of Cedar Rapids. Birthplace of Grant Wood is near by.

Ananias (ăn'ŭnī'ŭs). **1** Man who, with his wife Sapphira, kept back part of gift to church and lied about it. He was rebuked by Peter and fell dead. Acts 5.1–11. Name became term for a liar. **2** High priest at Jerusalem, Roman sympathizer. Acts 23.2–5. **3** Christian who took care of the newly converted Paul. Acts 19.10–22. **4** One of THREE HOLY CHILDREN.

anarchism (ăn'ŭrkĭzŭm), theory that the state should be abolished and replaced by free association of groups (no private property). Differs from SOCIALISM in considering the state an intrinsic evil. Philosophic and literary anarchy appeared early (e.g., Zeno of Citium, medieval religious groups), political later (e.g., Anabaptists, Levelers). Modern anarchism outlined by William GODWIN and P. J. PROUDHON. Violent tone introduced by BAKUNIN, resisted by KROPOTKIN. Anarchism suppressed in Russia by Soviets. Violent doctrines brought from Europe to U.S. The Haymarket riot and the assassination of McKinley brought a law to keep anarchists from country. The Sacco and Vanzetti Case was linked to fear of anarchism.

Anatolia, the Asiatic part of TURKEY. A mountainous

peninsula between the Black Sea (N), Aegean Sea (W), and Mediterranean (S), it comprises 97% (287,-117 sq. mi.; pop. 12,308,441) of all Turkey. The name sometimes designates all ASIA MINOR.

anatomy, study of body structure and structural relationships. Includes study of body tissues (histology), of structure of various animal forms (comparative anatomy), and of prenatal development (embryology). International nomenclature estab. 1895. See *ill.,* p. 595.

Anaxagoras (ăn″ŭksă′gŭrus), c.500–c.428 B.C., Greek philosopher. Held that an all-pervading mind (*nous*) initiated motion and order by combining mass of particles into actual objects.

Anaximander (ŭnăk″sĭmăn′dŭr), c.611–c.547 B.C., Greek philosopher. Thought that the primary source of all things was "the boundless," which by constant motion caused the physical world to emerge. He had a crude theory of evolution.

Anaximenes (ăn″ŭksĭm′ĭnēz), 6th cent. B.C., Greek philosopher, who taught that air was basic universal substance.

Anchieta, José de (zhōōzā′ dù ānshēā′tù), 1530–97, Portuguese missionary in Brazil, a Jesuit, called first Brazilian writer.

Anchises (ăn-kī′sēz, ăngkī′sēz), in Greek Legend, Trojan hero; father of Aeneas by Aphrodite.

Anchorage (ăng′kŭrĭj), city (pop. 11,254), S central Alaska, at head of Cook Inlet; founded 1915 as hq. of Alaska RR. Alaska's largest city, it is important in defense and as a commercial, communications, and distribution center for agr., mining, and lumbering area. It has fisheries, sawmills, and railroad shops. Connected with Alaska Highway.

anchovy (ăn′chōvē), small fish of herring family. Spanish and Italian anchovies (*Engraulis encrasicholus*) cured by using fermentation; Norwegian or Swedish sprats or brislings (genus *Clupea*) without it.

Ancon (ăng′kŏn, Span. ängkōn′), town (pop. 1,695), Panama Canal Zone, near Pacific end of canal and just NW of Panama city. Residential and medical center on transisthmian railroad.

Ancona (ängkô′nä), city (pop. 57,100), cap. of the Marches, central Italy; Adriatic port. Settled by Syracusan Greeks 4th cent. B.C.; medieval maritime republic; passed under direct papal rule 1532. Byzantine-Romanesque cathedral (11th–13th cent.; damaged in World War II); Arch of Trajan.

Ancren Riwle (äng′krŭn rē′ōōlù, rōōl′, äng′krŭn) [Mid. Eng.,= anchoresses' rule], anonymous tract written (c.1200) for three ladies about to enter hermitage. Rare example of Middle English prose.

Ancyra: see ANKARA, Turkey.

Andalusia (ăndùlōō′zhù, –shù), Span. *Andalucía,* southernmost region (33,675 sq. mi.; pop. 5,219,362), Spain, crossed by Sierra Nevada and Sierra Morena and by Guadalquivir R. Cities: Seville, Granada, Córdoba, Cádiz, Málaga, Huelva. The climate is subtropical, the soil partly very fertile, producing cereals, fruit, olives. Cattle and horse raising. Copper, iron, zinc, and lead mines have been exploited since anc. times. Settled by Phoenicians (11th cent. B.C.), then by Greeks, Carthaginians, Romans, Andalusia was conquered by the Moors (A.D. 711), under whom it reached greatest prosperity. It was reconquered by Castile in 13th cent., except GRANADA, which fell in 1492.

Andalusia (ăn″dùlōō′zhù), city (pop. 9,162), S Ala., S of Montgomery, near Fla. line. Processing center in area yielding cotton, peanuts, cattle, pine.

Andaman and Nicobar Islands (ăn′dùmùn, nĭkōbär′), state (3,143 sq. mi.; pop. 30,963), India, in Bay of Bengal; cap. Port Blair. Lumber and copra.

Andersen, Hans Christian, 1805–75, Danish writer of fairy tales. After poverty-ridden, unhappy early years and failure of early writings, he gained success with a novel *Improvisatoren* (1835). In same year appeared *Eventyr,* first of many volumes of fairy tales that were to make him revered and beloved all over the world. Among stories are "The Ugly Duckling," "The Brave

Tin Soldier," "The Little Mermaid," "The Red Shoes."

Andersen Nexo, Martin, Dan. *Nexø,* 1869–, Danish novelist. His proletarian novels (e.g., *Pelle the Conqueror,* 4 vols., 1906–10) did much to improve social conditions in Denmark. In his later years lived much in Russia.

Anderson, Alexander, 1775–1870, American engraver, first successful wood engraver in America.

Anderson, Carl David, 1905–, American physicist. Shared 1936 Nobel Prize for discovery of POSITRON. Co-discoverer of MESON.

Anderson, Elizabeth Garrett, 1836–1917, English physician. Opened hospital, first in England to be staffed by women physicians. Her efforts led to opening of British medical examinations to women.

Anderson, Marian, 1907?–, American Negro contralto. Her first great successes were in Europe. After her return to the U.S. in 1935 she became one of the best loved of American concert singers.

Anderson, Mary Antoinette, later **Madame de Navarro,** 1859–1940, American actress, popular in U.S. and England as Desdemona, Rosalind, and Lady Macbeth. Married and retired to England 1890.

Anderson, Maxwell, 1888–, American dramatist. Was a journalist until the success of play written with Lawrence Stallings, *What Price Glory* (1924). Among plays (some in blank verse): *Saturday's Children* (1927), *Elizabeth the Queen* (1930), *Both Your Houses* (1933), *Winterset* (1935), *High Tor* (1937), *Joan of Lorraine* (1946).

Anderson, Robert, 1805–71, American army officer, defender of Fort SUMTER.

Anderson, Sherwood, 1876–1941, American author, b. Ohio. Starting work at 12, he had varied experience in advertising and commerce. His novels—e.g., *Windy McPherson's Son* (1916), *Poor White* (1920), *Dark Laughter* (1925), *Kit Brandon* (1936)—and short stories (e.g., in *Winesburg, Ohio,* 1919) are strongly American and Midwest in subject and feeling.

Anderson. 1 Industrial city (pop. 46,820), E central Ind., on White R. and NE of Indianapolis; platted 1823. Mfg. of machinery, metal and glass products. Mounds State Park has Indian mounds and museum. Moravian Indian mission was near by (1801–6). **2** City (pop. 19,770), NW S.C., SW of Greenville; laid out 1827. Has textile mills, foundries, and beverage plants.

Andersonville Prison: see AMERICUS, Ga.

Andes (ăn′dēz), mountain system, over 4,000 mi. long, South America, paralleling Pacific coast. Stretching from Tierra del Fuego N to VENEZUELA, Andes form one of world's great mountain masses, only Himalayas exceeding them in height. On border between ARGENTINA and CHILE, in Patagonia, are high glacier-fed lakes with noted resorts. Farther N lies highest range, with ACONCAGUA and Tupungato separated by USPALLATA PASS. Central Andes broaden in BOLIVIA and PERU, and on plateau and in valleys Inca civilization had its home. Lake Titicaca and volcanoes here. Ranges narrow again in ECUADOR, then divide in COLOMBIA—W range running along coast, E range into Venezuela. Andes influence communication, climate, weather, and life of all South America. Copper, silver, tin are mined in several areas.

Andorra (ändô′rù), small state (191 sq. mi.; pop. 5,231), SW Europe, in E Pyrenees between France and Spain; cap. Andorra la Vella. Catalan-speaking population engages in sheep raising and smuggling. Nominally, Andorra has been under the joint suzerainty of the Spanish bishops of Urgel and the rulers of France since the Middle Ages, but actually it is governed by a council and a syndic.

Andover, town (pop. 12,437), NE Mass., S of Lawrence; settled 1643. Mfg. of woolens, soap, and rubber goods. Harriet Beecher Stowe buried here. Seat of Phillips Acad. (nonsectarian, for boys; opened 1778, chartered 1780 by Samuel Phillips); often called Andover or Phillips Andover.

Andrade, Olegario Víctor (ōlägä'ryō vēk'tōr ändrä'dhä), 1839?–1882, Argentine romantic poet, journalist, called national poet because of patriotism.

Andrassy, Julius, Count (ŏn'dräsh-shē), Hung. *Andrássy Gyula,* 1823–90, Hungarian statesman. Leading figure in revolution of 1848–49; returned from exile 1858; negotiated creation of AUSTRO-HUNGARIAN MONARCHY 1867. As prime minister of Hungary he fostered Magyar supremacy over Slavic and other minorities. As foreign minister of Austria-Hungary (1871–79) he signed alliance with Germany (1879). His son, **Count Julius Andrassy,** 1860–1929, Austro-Hungarian foreign minister in 1918, tried unsuccessfully to secure separate peace with Allies. Later led Hungarian royalists.

André, John (än'drē), 1751–80, British spy in American Revolution. Hanged after negotiating with Benedict ARNOLD for betrayal of West Point.

Andrea del Sarto: see SARTO, ANDREA DEL.

Andreanof Islands: see ALEUTIAN ISLANDS.

Andree, Salomon August (ändra'), 1854–97, Swedish polar explorer. Aeronautical engineer, first to attempt arctic exploration by balloon. Entire expedition lost.

Andreev, Leonid Nikolayevich: see ANDREYEV.

Andreini (ändrā̃e'nē), family of Italian actors, celebrated in COMMEDIA DELL' ARTE. **Francesco Andreini,** 1548–1624, was less famous than his celebrated wife, **Isabella Andreini,** 1562–1604, player in his troupe, the Gelosi, and author of poems and a pastoral. Her son, **Giovanni Battista** or **Giambattista Andreini** (jämbättēs'tä), 1579?–1654, managed the Fidele troupe. **Virginia Andreini,** 1583–c.1628, his wife, was noted both for acting and beauty.

Andrew, Saint [Gr.,= manly], one of Twelve Disciples; brother of Peter. Mat. 4.18; 10.2; Mark 3.16; 13.3; Luke 6.14; John 1.40–42; 6.8,9; 12.22; Acts 1.13. Traditionally a missionary in Asia Minor, Macedonia, S Russia. When martyred, he is said to have died on X-shaped cross (St. Andrew's cross). Andrew is patron of Russia and of Scotland (Union Jack has white St. Andrew's cross on blue field). Feast day Nov. 30.

Andrew II, d. 1235, king of Hungary (1205–35). Signed Golden Bull, the "Magna Carta of Hungary" (1222; expanded 1231). Father of St. Elizabeth of Hungary and of Bela IV.

Andrewes, Lancelot, 1555–1626, Anglican bishop of Chichester, Ely, and Winchester. A learned preacher, he helped translate Authorized version of Bible and led High Church party opposed to Puritanism.

Andrew Johnson National Monument: see NATIONAL PARKS AND MONUMENTS (table).

Andrews, Roy Chapman, 1884–, American naturalist and explorer, director of American Mus. of Natural History (1935–41). Specialist in water mammals of Alaska, Malayan seas, and Asiatic coast, he also led expeditions to study fossil and living animals and plants in central Asia.

Andreyev or **Andreev, Leonid Nikolayevich** (lyĭunyĕt' nyĭkŭlī'uvĭch ŭndrā'ŭf), 1871–1919, Russian author. A revolutionist and friend of Gorki, he turned against Bolshevism in 1917 and died in Finland. *The Seven Who Were Hanged* (1908; Eng. tr., 1909) is a story of idealistic revolutionists. Other works reflect a morbid, negative view of society, as the short novel *The Red Laugh* (1905; Eng. tr., 1905) and the dramas *King Hunger* (1907; Eng. tr., 1911) and *He Who Gets Slapped* (1916; Eng. tr., 1921).

Andromache (ändrŏ'mùkē), in Greek legend, Trojan wife of Hector and mother of Astyanax. After Trojan War she was abducted by Neoptolemus and later married Hector's brother Helenus.

Andromeda (ändrŏ'mùdù), in Greek religion, Ethiopian princess; daughter of Cepheus and Cassiopeia. Poseidon, angered by claim that she was more beautiful than Nereids, sent sea monster appeasable only by sacrifice of king's daughter. She was rescued by Perseus, who married her.

Andronicus, Livius: see LIVIUS ANDRONICUS.

Andros, Sir Edmund, 1637–1714, British colonial governor in America. Bitterly criticized as governor of N.Y. (1674–81) for highhanded methods. Deposed as governor of Dominion of New England in 1689. Governor of Va. (1692–97).

Andros (än'drŏs), Aegean island (145 sq. mi.; pop. 17,-926), off Greece, second largest and northernmost of CYCLADES, chief town and port Andros (pop. 3,028). Silk, fruits, wine; manganese.

Androscoggin (ändrŭskŏg'ĭn), river formed in NE N.H. Flows E and S through W Maine to join Kennebec R. near Bath. Used for power and logging.

Androuet du Cerceau (ädrōō-ā' dü sĕrsō'), family of French architects. Founded by **Jacques Androuet** (zhäk) c.1510–c.1584, a leader in introducing Italian Renaissance style into France. His son **Baptiste Androuet du Cerceau** (bätēst'), c.1544–1602, designed Pont-Neuf (Paris). Another son **Jacques Androuet du Cerceau,** d. 1614, worked on Tuileries. Both worked on Louvre.

Andrusov, Treaty of, 1667, peace treaty between Russia and Poland. Smolensk and Ukraine E of Dnieper (incl. Kiev) passed to Russia.

anemia, condition resulting from reduction in number or in hemoglobin content of red blood corpuscles. Causes include loss of blood, excessive destruction of red corpuscles, or inadequate blood formation owing to deficiency of iron or of antianemic factor of liver or to bone marrow malfunction.

anemometer: see WIND.

anemone (ŭnĕm'ŭnē) or **windflower,** perennial plant of genus *Anemone.* Some have showy flowers, e.g., the poppy anemone of florists, and the PASQUEFLOWER and fall Japanese anemone of gardens. Among wild kinds is spring-flowering wood anemone. Rue anemone is *Anemonella thalictroides.*

aneroid barometer: see BAROMETER.

anesthesia (änĭsthē'zhù), loss of sensation induced by drugs. General anesthesia causes unconsciousness; produced by inhalation of anesthetic. Local anesthesia affects area about site of application. Spinal anesthesia produced by injection beneath spinal cord membranes; caudal, by injection into caudal canal. Anesthesia pioneers include Horace WELLS, C. W. LONG, W. T. G. MORTON, Sir J. Y. SIMPSON.

Aneto, Pico de (pē'kō dä änä'tō), Fr. *Pic de Néthou* or *Pic d'Anethou,* peak, 11,168 ft. high, NE Spain, near French border; highest of Pyrenees.

angel [Gr.,= messenger], bodiless, immortal spirit, limited in knowledge and power. In traditional belief of Judaism, Christianity, and Islam, good angels are accepted as intermediate beings between God and man, living in heaven, able to visit earth in visible or invisible form—sometimes depicted with wings. Hierarchy given in three choirs in descending order: seraphim, cherubim, thrones; dominions, virtues, powers; principalities, archangels, angels. The Bible tells of guardian angels protecting nations or individuals (Dan. 10.13,20; Mat. 18.10), a concept popular in Western Christendom. Angels of hell, dark angels, or devils, are the evil counterpart of heavenly host; they lead man into evil ways and are headed by SATAN (or Lucifer). Famous literary depictions are in Milton's *Paradise Lost* and Dante's *Divine Comedy.* See also ARCHANGEL; CHERUB; SERAPH.

angelica (änjĕl'ĭkù), perennial herb (*Angelica*). Compound leaves effective in herb gardens. Roots and fruits yield oil used in perfume and liqueurs.

Angelico, Fra (frä änjĕl'ĭkō), 1387–1455, Florentine painter of religious subjects, b. Tuscany. In 1407 entered Dominican convent at Fiesole where he executed some of his best work. Lovely color and gentleness of spirit mark his 200 to 300 extant works, which include frescoes in convent of St. Mark's (Florence) and scenes from lives of St. Stephen and St. Lawrence in Vatican.

Angel Island, W Calif., largest island in San Francisco Bay. U.S. army base, 1863–1946.

Angell, James Burrill, 1829–1916, American educator,

editor, and diplomat. Left teaching in 1860 to edit Providence *Journal*, but returned to education to be president of the Univ. of Vermont (1866–71) and the Univ. of Michigan (1871–1909). Minister to China (1880–81) and to Turkey (1897–98). His son, **James Rowland Angell**, 1869–1949, was educator and psychologist. Taught psychology at Univ. of Chicago (1894–1920) and was dean (1911–18) and acting president (1918–19). President of Yale Univ. 1921–37. After 1937 he was educational counselor to the National Broadcasting Company.

Angell, Sir Norman, 1874–, British internationalist, valiant fighter for peace. Gained fame with *The Great Illusion* (1910), arguing futility of war because of economic interests of nations. Many later books. Received 1933 Nobel Peace Prize. Original name was Ralph Norman Angell Lane.

Angels Camp, city (pop. 1,147), central Calif., E of Stockton; founded 1848 after gold discovery. Annual Jumping Frog Jubilee honors Mark Twain's story.

Angelus (ăn′jŭlŭs), family name of ISAAC II, ALEXIUS III, and ALEXIUS IV, Byzantine emperors.

Angelus Silesius (ăn′jŭlŭs sĭlē′zhŭs), pseud. of **Johannes Scheffler** (yōhän′ŭs), 1624–77, German poet. After conversion to Catholicism he wrote deeply mystical poems, the best of their period.

Angerman, Swed. *Ångermanälven* (ông′ŭrmänĕl′vŭn), river, 280 mi. long, rising in N central Sweden and flowing into Gulf of Bothnia at Harnosand. It is a main logging artery.

Angermanland, Swed. *Ångermanland,* historic province, NE Sweden. Now divided between Vasternorrland and Vasterbotten counties.

Angers (äzhā′), city (pop. 86,083), cap. of Maine-et-Loire dept., W France, on Maine R., historic cap. of Anjou. Dates from pre-Roman times. Cathedral 12th–13th cent.), medieval castle, museum.

Angevin (ăn′jŭvĭn), name of two medieval dynasties and their several branches.

First Angevin dynasty, originated 10th cent. with counts of ANJOU. Geoffrey Plantagenet (see GEOFFREY) conquered NORMANDY 1144. His son became king of England as Henry II and founded Angevin or Plantagenet dynasty of English kings (see list of kings at end of article ENGLAND). Count Fulk V of Anjou (see FULK) also became king of Jerusalem, which passed to his younger son, Baldwin III, and to Baldwin's heirs (see JERUSALEM, LATIN KINGDOM OF).

Second Angevin dynasty, main line, collateral branch of Capetian dynasty; originated 1246 when Louis IX granted Anjou in appanage to younger brother Charles (see CHARLES I of Naples); ruled PROVENCE from 1246 and kingdom of NAPLES from 1266 until deposition of JOANNA I (1381).

Second Angevin dynasty, collateral lines. In Naples: CHARLES III, LANCELOT, and JOANNA II, lineal descendants of Charles II of Naples through a younger son, ruled 1381–1435. Succession was contested by Duke Louis of Anjou and his heirs (see LOUIS, kings of Naples; RENÉ). They made good their claim to Provence but not to Naples, which eventually was seized by Alfonso V of Aragon (1442). Their extinction (1486) left the French crown their heir. In Hungary and Poland: see CHARLES I of Hungary; LOUIS I of Hungary and Poland.

Anghiera, Pietro Martire d' (märtē′rä däng-gyä′rä), 1457?–1526, Italian geographer and historian. Moved to Spain in 1487. From explorers and navigators (esp. Columbus, Vespucci, Magellan) he learned latest information about explorations in his time. Wrote *De orbe decades octo* (1530).

angina pectoris (ănjī′nŭ pĕk′tŭrĭs), disease marked by chest pain. Caused by obstruction of coronary arteries, resulting in lack of oxygen to heart muscle.

Angkor Thom (äng′kôr tôm′), ruined cap. of KHMER EMPIRE, W Cambodia, Indo-China. Among ruins of temples and royal palace are rows of huge seated stone figures. Most ornate carvings are those on the Bayon,

temple of Siva or, more probably, of Lokesvara.

Angkor Wat, great temple of anc. Khmer Empire, Cambodia. Comparable as architectural entity to Taj Mahal. The moat-surrounded, richly carved temple contains a shrine of Vishnu.

angle, in plane geometry, figure formed by meeting of two straight lines. Meeting point called vertex; lines called sides. In solid geometry, two or more planes meeting form angle; two-plane-intersection line forms dihedral angle; three-plane-intersection angle called trihedral. In trigonometry the plane angle is defined as the degree one (initial) side must rotate about its vertex to reach the position of the other (terminal) side.

Angles: see ANGLO-SAXONS; EAST ANGLIA; MERCIA; NORTHUMBRIA.

Anglesey or **Anglesea** (both: ăng′gŭlsē), island county (276 sq. mi.; pop. 50,637), NW Wales. Shows traces of prehistoric occupation. Chief occupations are agr., sheep-raising, and fishing. Holyhead is terminus of packet service to Dublin.

Anglican Communion, body of churches in communion with Church of England, including Protestant Episcopal Church of America, Scottish Episcopal Church, and Church of Ireland.

Anglin, Margaret (Mary), 1876–, American actress, b. Canada. Won fame (1898) as Roxane in *Cyrano de Bergerac* and appeared (1903–4) with Henry Miller in *Camille* and *The Devil's Disciple*. Especially noted in *Antigone, Electra,* and *Medea.*

Anglo-Egyptian Sudan (sōōdän′), condominium (967,-500 sq. mi.; est. pop. 8,053,669), NE Africa, on Red Sea; cap. Khartoum. Comprises most of the SUDAN. E section is watered by the Nile; Nubia (N half) is mainly desert, inhabited by pastoral nomads. Negroes inhabit the south, which is largely jungle. Ancient Egypt colonized Nubia before 1,500 B.C. In 6th cent. the Nubians embraced Coptic Christianity but were converted to Islam in 15th cent. by Arab conquerors. Unification of area began in early 19th cent. with conquest by Mohammed Ali. In 1870s Anglo-Egyptian armies under Sir Samuel Baker and Gen. Charles Gordon suppressed the slave trade and set up military posts on the upper Nile. MAHDISTS, who began their revolt in 1881, were defeated in 1898 by Lord Kitchener's Anglo-Egyptian army. Anglo-Egyptian condominium set up by 1899 convention was reaffirmed by treaty in 1936, but in 1951 Egypt declared full sovereignty over area. Anglo-Egyptian agreement of 1953 provided for Sudanese freedom within three years.

Anglo-Saxon Chronicle, annals of the English until 1154. Extant form probably begun c.892 by Winchester monks under supervision of Alfred the Great.

Anglo-Saxon literature, literary writings in Old English. Many early poems, though recorded after English conversion to Christianity, retain paganism, materials, or somber tone of old Germanic tradition (e.g., the epic BEOWULF; WIDSITH; and *Deor,* earliest English lyric). Hymn of CÆDMON first religious poem; later poets often paraphrased parts of Bible to produce stirring poems like epic fragment *Judith.* CYNEWULF and his school adapted saints' lives and homilies. "The Dream of the Rood" notable for vividness and religious intensity. Usual metrical form is alliterative, four-stress line broken into two half-lines and end-stopped. Literary prose began with translations from Latin by King ALFRED, who probably also directed ANGLO-SAXON CHRONICLE. Finest original prose in homilies of ÆLFRIC. Much contemporary writing was in Latin.

Anglo-Saxons, name given Germanic-speaking people who settled in England at end of Roman rule. Angles probably came from Schleswig late 5th cent. and formed foundations for kingdoms of East Anglia, Mercia, and Northumbria. Saxons, a Germanic tribe, settled in England at same time; kingdoms of Sussex, Wessex, and Essex were outgrowths of their settlements. Jutes, probably from area at mouth of the

Rhine, settled in Kent and Isle of Wight. Term "Anglo-Saxons," denoting non-Celtic settlers of England, dates from 16th cent. Now more loosely used to denote any people (or their descendants) of British Isles, including Danes and Normans.

Angmagsalik (ängmäg′sälĭk), trading post, E Greenland coast, S of Arctic Circle. Strategic radio meteorological station estab. 1925.

Angola (ăng-gō′lù) or **Portuguese West Africa,** colony (with CABINDA 481,351 sq. mi.; pop. 3,378,010), W Africa, on Atlantic Ocean; cap. Luanda. Mostly desert or savanna land, except for narrow coastal strip and jungle in NE. Sugar, coffee, and palm oil are main exports. The Portuguese first settled here in 15th cent. Angola supplied most of the slaves sent to Brazil in 19th cent.

Angola (ăng″gō′lù), resort city (pop. 5,081), NE Ind., NE of Fort Wayne, in hilly lake region.

Angora, Turkey: see ANKARA.

Angostura, Venezuela: see CIUDAD BOLÍVAR.

angostura bark (ăng″gùstū′rù), bitter bark of a South American tree, *Cusparia.* It is used in **angostura bitters** to flavor cocktails.

Angoulême, Louis Antoine de Bourbon, duc d' (lwē′ ätwän′ dù bŏŏrbŏ′ dük′ dägōōlěm′), 1775–1844, last dauphin of France, son of Charles X. Renounced his claim in favor of Henri, comte de Chambord (1830).

Angoulême, Margaret of or **Marguerite d':** see MARGARET OF NAVARRE.

Angoulême (ägōōlěm′), city (pop. 39,987), cap. of Charente dept., W France, on Charente R. Brandy distilleries. Seat of counts of Angoulême, 9th–16th cent.; cap. of Angoumois prov. till 1789.

Angstrom, Anders Jons (än′dùrs yûns′ ōng′strûm), 1814–74, Swedish physicist. Studied light, spectrum analysis. His son **Knut Johan Angstrom** (knūt yōō′hän), 1857–1910, worked on solar radiation.

angstrom unit (ăng′strŭm) [for A. J. Angstrom], length unit ($\frac{1}{100,000,000}$ cm) for wave lengths of light.

Anguier, François (fräswä′ ägyä′), 1604–69, French sculptor. With his brother, **Michel Anguier** (mēshěl′), 1614–86, considered among best sculptors of 17th cent. Another brother, **Guillaume Anguier** (gēyōm′), 1628–1708, was a painter.

Angus, earls of: see DOUGLAS, ARCHIBALD.

Angus, maritime county (874 sq. mi.; pop. 274,870), E Scotland; co. town Forfar. Mainly agr., also has jute and linen milling. Historic remains include Glamis Castle. Formerly called Forfarshire.

Anhalt (än′hält), former German state (898 sq. mi.; 1939 pop. 432,289), central Germany, included since 1949 in state of Saxony-Anhalt, [East] German Democratic Republic; cap. Dessau. Minerals (salt, lignite, copper, zinc); chemical and textile industries; agr. (sugar beets, grain, cattle). Ruled until 1918 by princely house descended from Albert the Bear. Joined German Empire 1871.

Anhwei or **An-hui** (both: än′hwā′), province (54,000 sq. mi.; pop. 25,000,000), E China. Since 1949 divided into North Anhwei (cap. Hofei) and South Anhwei (cap. Wuhu). Zone of transition between S Yangtze hills and N China plain. Produces c.60% of China's tea. Coal, iron, and copper mines. Occupied by the Japanese 1938–45.

anhydride (ănhī′drīd), nonmetallic oxide which forms acid with water. Also refers to metallic oxide which forms base with water.

Aniakchak (ănēăk′chăk), volcano, W Alaska, in Aleutian Range, on Alaska Peninsula; crater 6 mi. in diameter. Erupted 1931.

aniline (ăn′ùlēn), colorless, oily liquid, compound of carbon, hydrogen, nitrogen; a basic amine. Used as starting substance and aid in making dyes. Prepared by reduction of nitrobenzene.

animal, member of animal (as distinct from plant) kingdom. Animals require organized food; green plants can manufacture food from inorganic substances (see PHOTOSYNTHESIS). Animals have more highly developed nervous systems, sense organs, locomotion; adapted for securing, ingesting, digesting food. Classification of some microscopic forms disputed. See also INVERTEBRATE; VERTEBRATE; ZOOLOGY.

animated cartoon, form of moving picture in which a series of static drawings are photographed and synchronized with sound. Emile Cohl pioneered with animated puppets 1905, was first to use animated drawings 1907. Paper cut-outs also were used. Walt DISNEY has been a notable figure in the field.

animism, belief that all objects in world have consciousness and some personality. These "spirits" must be propitiated or outwitted. They may include spirits of the dead, leading to ancestor worship; or there may be a general, nonpersonalized spirit akin to the manito of the American Indian. Animism, prevalent in early cultures, has tended to disappear with growth of organized religions, but remains part of Japanese Shinto. See IDOL; SHAMAN.

anise (ăn′ĭs), annual plant, *Pimpinella anisum.* Flower clusters yield aniseed of commerce. Oil from leaves and seeds used as perfume and flavoring. **Anisette** is anise-flavored liqueur.

Anjou (ăn′jōō, Fr. äzhōō′), region and former duchy, W France, roughly coextensive with Maine-et-Loire dept.; historic cap. Angers. Drained by Loire, it is fertile and has excellent vineyards. Early counts of Anjou (see ANGEVIN dynasty) acquired Saumur, Touraine, Maine, Normandy and acceded to English throne with Henry II (1154). Anjou was confiscated (1204) by Philip II of France; became appanage of royal house; was raised to duchy 1360.

Ankara (ăng′kärä), city (pop. 286,781), cap. of Turkey, central Anatolia; known anciently as Ancyra, later as Angora. An important town from Hittite times and a provincial cap. under the Romans, it later sank into insignificance until it replaced Constantinople as Turkish cap. in 1923. Except for its old citadel it is a completely modern city. Its university was founded 1925. Ankara was the scene of Tamerlane's victory over BAJAZET I (1402). The region is famed for its longhaired goats and the production of Angora wool or mohair.

Anking (än′chĭng), commercial city (pop. 121,379), S Anhwei prov., China, on Yangtze R. Became treaty port 1902. Called Hwaining from 1912 to 1949.

Ann, Cape, NE Mass., N of Mass. Bay. Noted for old fishing villages, resorts, and artists' colonies (esp. GLOUCESTER and ROCKPORT).

Anna (Anna Ivanovna), 1693–1740, empress of Russia (1730–40), cousin and successor of Peter II. Ruled autocratically through her German favorites. Intervened in War of the POLISH SUCCESSION; campaigned against Turkey (1736–39). Ivan VI succeeded her.

Anna [Gr.,= Heb. HANNAH]. 1 Aged prophetess who hailed Jesus' presentation at the Temple. Luke 2.36–38. 2 In Tobit, the mother of young Tobias.

Anna Comnena (kŏmnē′nù), b. 1083, d. after 1148, Byzantine princess and historian; daughter of Alexius I. Plotted against her brother JOHN II, seeking to put her husband on the throne. Discovered, she was pardoned and retired to a convent to write the *Alexiad,* a history covering the reign of Alexius I and the First Crusade.

Anna Ivanovna: see ANNA, empress of Russia.

Annam (ùnăm′), state (c.57,000 sq. mi.; pop. c.7,200,000), E. Indo-China; cap. Hué. Between Tonkin (N) and Cochin China (S). Its 800-mi. coast is on China Sea. Crops include rice (insufficient for Annam's needs), cinnamon, cocoa, and cotton. Even before Chinese invasion of Annam (c.214 B.C.), the Annamese had been under influence of Chinese culture for c.2000 years. Chinese rule lasted until 1428, when the Annamese estab. independent kingdom. After 1558 Annam was split between two dynasties of Hué and Tonkin; united again 1802 under the Hué. Maltreatment of French missionaries by native officials led to France's military campaigns (begun 1858), resulting in establishment of French protectorate over Annam in

1884. Under regime of Bao Dai, Annam forms part of VIET NAM.

Annandale-on-Hudson (ăn'ŭndāl–), village, SE N.Y., on E bank of the Hudson S of Hudson. Seat of Bard Col. (coed.; 1860; affiliated 1928–44 with Columbia Univ.).

Annapolis (ŭnăp'ŭlĭs), city (pop. 10,047), state cap., central Md., on Severn R. near its mouth on Chesapeake Bay S of Baltimore. Trade center of agr. area, it has boatyards and seafood industry. Settled c.1648 as Providence by Va. Puritans, and later called Anne Arundel, it became provincial cap. in 1694 and was named Annapolis. Was social and commercial center in colonial days. Annapolis convention (1786) led to Federal Constitutional Convention. Seat of UNITED STATES NAVAL ACADEMY and of Saint John's Col. (nonsectarian, for men; opened 1789 as successor to King William's School, estab. 1696), which since 1937 has had nonelective curriculum based on "great books" plan. Points of interest are statehouse (1772), meeting place of Congress (1783) where Washington resigned as commander in chief of Continental army; Old Treasury (c.1695); and library (1737).

Annapolis, river, N.S., Canada, rising NE of Annapolis Royal in a valley noted for apple orchards. Flows c.75 mi. into **Annapolis Basin,** tidal arm of Bay of Fundy (c.10 mi. long, 3–5 mi. wide).

Annapolis Royal, town (pop. 784), W N.S., Canada, on Annapolis R. Founded as Port Royal by de Monts (1605), it was destroyed by Samuel Argall in 1614 and later rebuilt by the French. Changed hands between French and English until 1710, when it was captured by New Englanders under Francis Nicholson. Cap. of N.S. to 1749. Ruins of fort in Fort Anne Natl. Park (c.31 acres; estab. 1917).

Annapurna (ŭn-nŭpŏŏr'nŭ), mountain, Nepal, in Himalayas; highest mountain climbed by man. Annapurna I (26,502 ft.), the higher of its two peaks, was climbed 1950 by French expedition led by Maurice Herzog. Annapurna II is 26,041 ft. high.

Ann Arbor, city (pop. 48,251), S Mich., on Huron R. and W of Detroit, in fruitgrowing area; laid out 1824. Mfg. of tools and metal products. Here are famous Nichols Arboretum, hq. of Michigan Municipal League, and Univ. of MICHIGAN.

Annas, Jewish high priest, who questioned Jesus. Non-Bible sources call him retired high priest. Was Caiaphas' father-in-law. John 18.13,24; Acts 4.6–22.

Anne, Saint [from Heb. Hannah], in tradition, mother of the Virgin, wife of St. Joachim. She is not mentioned in Scripture. Patroness of Quebec (Ste Anne de Beaupré) and Brittany (Sainte-Anne-d'Auray). Feast: July 26.

Anne, 1665–1714, queen of England, Scotland, and Ireland (1702–7), later first queen of Great Britain (1707–14); last Stuart ruler. Her reign, one of transition to parliamentary government, dominated by War of SPANISH SUCCESSION (1702–13). Many victories won by duke of MARLBOROUGH (whose wife was long favorite of the queen), but high cost of war source of friction between Tories and Whigs. None of Anne's children survived her and, by Act of Settlement (1701), George I succeeded to the throne. Despite personal mediocrity, her reign was marked by intellectual awakening, popularization of Palladian architecture, and by growth of empire and constitution and of the political power of the press.

Annecy (änsē'), city (pop. 24,414), cap. of Haute-Savoie dept., E France, on scenic Lake Annecy. Seat of bishops of Geneva after 1535; birthplace of St. Francis of Sales. Picturesque old city crossed by canals; medieval castle of counts of Geneva.

Anne de Beaujeu (dù bōzhû'), c.1460–1522, regent of France for her brother, Charles VIII, after death of Louis XI (1483). Arranged Charles's marriage with Anne of Brittany.

Anne of Austria, 1601–66, queen of France, daughter of Philip III of Spain; married Louis XIII (1615). Neg-

lected by husband; persecuted by Richelieu. Her regency (1643–61) for her son, Louis XIV, was dominated by MAZARIN, disturbed by Fronde.

Anne of Brittany, 1477–1514, queen of France as wife of Charles VIII (1491–98) and of Louis XII (1499–1514); duchess of Brittany (1488–1514). Struggling to keep Brittany independent from invading French, she married by proxy (1490) Maximilian of Austria (later Emperor Maximilian I). Maximilian's dilatoriness and the use of force by France forced her to annul marriage. Her two subsequent marriages led to union of France and Brittany.

Anne of Cleves (klēvz), 1515–57, queen of England, fourth wife of Henry VIII. Henry married her (1540) for political purposes under influence of Thomas CROMWELL, but had marriage nullified same year.

Anne of Denmark, 1574–1619, queen consort of James I of England.

annexation, formal act asserting a state's sovereignty over newly incorporated territory (generally areas not inhabited by civilized peoples, areas settled by nationals of annexing power, areas already under protectorates, or conquered territory). The governing body of annexing power must ratify the act. Consent of all interested powers necessary for recognition in international law.

Anniston, city (pop. 31,066), NE Ala., ENE of Birmingham, in mining region of Appalachian foothills; founded 1872. Mfg. of iron, steel, textile, chemical products. U.S. Fort McClellan is near.

annual, plant which germinates, flowers, seeds, and dies within one year (e.g., marigold and zinnia), as distinguished from BIENNIAL and PERENNIAL plants.

Annunzio, Gabriele D': see D'ANNUNZIO, GABRIELE.

anode: see ELECTRODE and ELECTROLYSIS.

Anoka (ùnō'kù), city (pop. 7,396), E Minn., on the Mississippi at junction with Rum R. and NW of Minneapolis. Farm trade center and resort.

Ansbach (äns'bäkh), city (pop. 33,134), cap. of Middle Franconia, W Bavaria. Produces cars, motors, chemicals. Grew around 8th-cent. abbey; residence from 1331 of Franconian branch of the HOHENZOLLERN dynasty. To Prussia 1791; to Bavaria 1806. Has Romanesque church (12th–15th cent.).

Anschluss (än'shlōōs) [Ger.,= junction], term applied to the project of union between Austria and Germany. Though forbidden by the peace treaties of 1919, it was advocated in Austria by both Socialists and National Socialists and became a reality when Hitler annexed Austria to Germany (1938–45).

Anselm, Saint (än'sĕlm), 1034?–1109, archbishop of Canterbury (1093–1109), Doctor of the Church, b. Italy. As abbot of Bec in Normandy, he gained wide reputation before succeeding his friend and master Lanfranc as archbishop. He stoutly upheld the papal claims in the quarrel over power to appoint bishops (see INVESTITURE) and had long quarrels with Kings William II and Henry I. His theological writings (e.g., *Monologium* and *Cur Deus homo?*) were influential. Offered ontological proof of existence of God—that the fact that the human mind can conceive of an Infinite Being necessarily means that such a Being must exist. Feast: April 21.

Anshan (än'shän'), city (pop. 219,715), Manchuria, on branch of South Manchurian RR; major steel center.

Anson, Adrian Constantine (Cap Anson), 1852–1922, American baseball player-manager. Four times National League batting champion.

Anson, George Anson, Baron, 1697–1762, British admiral. Sailed around world to attack Spanish possessions in South America. As first lord of the admiralty he estab. corps of marines (1755).

Anson, city (pop. 2,708), W central Texas, NW of Abilene. Has annual Cowboy's Christmas Ball.

Ansonia, city (pop. 18,706), SW Conn., on Naugatuck R. and NW of New Haven; settled 1651. Metals center.

ant, cosmopolitan social insect, order Hymenoptera. Three body sections; narrow constriction between thorax and abdomen; usually black or various shades of brown, red, yellow. Majority nest underground, others in decaying trees or plants; some make paper nests. Colonies (dozens to hundred thousands) usually include one or more queens (egg-laying, usually winged females); female wingless workers, usually sterile; and fertile males, usually winged. Males and females swarm in nuptial flight; males die; female sheds wings, and for rest of life (up to 15 years) can lay fertilized eggs. Workers live 4 to 7 years. Adult ants eat chiefly liquids of plants and animals; colonies often have parasites, sometimes enslave other species. TERMITE is miscalled white ant. See *ill.,* p. 469.

Antaeus (ăntē'ûs), in Greek mythology, giant; son of Poseidon. He became stronger when touching earth (his mother, Gaea). Hercules overcame him by lifting him into the air.

Antakya, Turkey: see ANTIOCH.

Antalya (äntälyä'), city (pop. 27,478), SW Turkey; a Mediterranean seaport. Silk mfg.; chrome and manganese deposits near by. Known anciently as Attaleia or Attalia; in Middle Ages as Satalia or Satalieh; more recently as Adalia.

Antar (äntär'), fl. 600, Arabian warrior and poet. Rose from slave to tribal chief. Represented in MUALLAQAT. Hero of popular Arabic romance *Antar.*

Antarctica, continent of 5,000,000–6,000,000 sq. mi. surrounding South Pole. Encircling waters, sometimes called Antarctic Ocean, challenge navigation. Roughly circular outline broken by Ross and Weddell seas and Palmer Peninsula, c.600 mi. from South America, the only relatively near land. Coasts circled by pack ice hundreds of miles wide ending in sheer ice cliffs. Giant mountain ranges (peaks over 15,000 ft.) surround perpetually ice-capped central plateau. Highest average altitude and severest climate of any continent. Discovered by whalers, explored by 19th-cent. voyages of Palmer, Biscoe, Weddell, Ross, and others. Exploration impeded until 20th cent. technology made possible Amundsen, Scott, and U.S. naval expeditions (led by Byrd). Conflicting national claims nullified by impossibility of colonization. **Antarctic regions,** extending beyond Antarctic Circle (lat. 23° 30'S to lat. 50°S), are inimical to human life; have only mosses, lichens, algae, and support no year-round animal life except small wingless insects, microscopic organisms, and penguins. In summer, whales, seals, birds, and other penguins inhabit coast and sea. Once temperate or tropical, continent may again be habitable in millions of years, say some scientists.

anteater, name for sundry insect-eating animals; more accurately applied to a toothless group, order Edentata, of Central and South America. Great anteater or ant bear (*Myrmecophaga*) has long, nearly round head and snout, sticky tongue, coarse-haired body (c.4 ft. long), sharp claws, and long broad tail. Collared or lesser anteater (*Tamandua*) is half as large, short-haired, yellowish and black, and arboreal. Two-toed (*Cyclopes*) is squirrel-sized with silky yellow fur. See also PANGOLIN.

antelope, hoofed ruminant mammal, order Artiodactyla, family Bovidae or, in some classifications, family Antilopidae. True antelopes confined to Asia and Africa. African include bushbuck, waterbuck, lechwe, marshbuck, impala or palla, kudu, nyala, springbuck, bongo, dik-dik, klipspringer, ELAND, GNU. Nilgai or blue bull, four-horned antelope, and black buck in India. See also GAZELLE; PRONGHORN; ROCKY MOUNTAIN GOAT.

antenna (ăntĕn'ù) or **aerial** (âr'ēûl), in radio, system of wires or metal bars to project or intercept radio waves. Frequency characteristic is based on wire length which is inherently tuned to radio wave of same length or simple fraction of it. Because of property of directivity of antenna arrays (except vertical conductors), more efficient transmission obtained by concentrating signal in desired area. Specially built antenna are needed for specific circuit requirements of television.

Antenor (ăntē'nùr), fl. last half of 6th cent. B.C., Greek sculptor. Did bronze statues of Harmodius and Aristogiton.

anthem, short sacred choral composition. Arose in the Anglican church as English counterpart of the Latin motet. Important names in its history are Thomas Tallis, William Byrd, Henry Purcell, Handel, and Mendelssohn. Term also used for any hymn of praise or jubilation; hence, "national anthem."

Anthemius of Tralles (ănthē'mēùs, trăl'ēz), 6th cent., Greek architect and mathematician. With Isidorus of Miletus he built the church of HAGIA SOPHIA in Constantinople, A.D. 532–37.

Anthony, Saint (ăn'tùnē, –thùnē), 251?–c.350, Egyptian hermit. In the desert he resisted temptations of devil. Colony of hermits grew about his retreat. Feast: Jan. 17.

Anthony, Marc, Roman soldier: see ANTONY.

Anthony, Susan B(rownell) (ăn'thùnē), 1820–1906, American reformer, leader of woman-suffrage movement. Founder of Daughters of Temperance. Coorganizer (1863) of Women's Loyal League to support Lincoln's government, especially emancipation policy. With Elizabeth Cady Stanton she secured first laws in N.Y. giving women rights over their children and property, and with Mrs. Stanton organized Natl. Woman Suffrage Association. She helped compile a history of the woman-suffrage movement and was president (1892–1900) of the Natl. American Woman Suffrage Association.

Anthony of Padua, Saint, 1195–1231, Portuguese Franciscan. In a vision he received the child Jesus in his arms, and is usually so depicted in art. Canonized 1232. Invoked to find lost articles. Feast: June 13.

anthracene (ăn'thrùsēn), colorless, crystalline solid with blue fluorescence, melting at 217°C. and boiling at c.350°C. Molecule has 14 carbon and 10 hydrogen atoms; carbons are arranged in three benzene rings set side by side and interlocking, with hydrogen atoms attached at each corner. It is obtained from coal tar and its derivatives are used in producing certain dyes. It is first member of **anthracene series** of aromatic hydrocarbons.

anthrax, infectious bacterial disease of animals transmissible to man by contact. Causative bacillus may exist as spore for years. Koch proved relation of bacillus to the disease; Pasteur developed method of vaccinating sheep and cattle against it. See *ill.,* p. 633.

anthropology (ănthrùpŏl'ùjē), science of man and his works. Concerned with the origin, development, and varieties of mankind and CULTURE, emphasizing data from nonliterate peoples. Physical and cultural anthropology are the two major divisions. Cultural anthropology includes ARCHAEOLOGY, the study of extinct cultures; ethnology, the study of living cultures; and linguistics.

anthropometry (ănthrùpŏm'ùtrē), measurement of human body and its parts for studies in race classification, growth, and human paleontology.

Antibes (ātēb'), town (pop. 13,778), Alpes-Maritime dept., SE France; a Mediterranean port. Near-by Cap d'Antibes is a fashionable resort.

antibiotic substances (ăn"tēbīō'tĭk), substances obtained from living organisms and inhibiting growth of or destroying certain microorganisms. Used in treatment of human diseases are PENICILLIN; streptomycin, discovered by S. A. Waksman and associate (1943); chloromycetin; and aureomycin. R. J. Dubos isolated (1939) first antibiotic substance (composed of gramicidin and tyrocidine) from soil bacteria.

antibody, specific substance produced by tissues when stimulated by an antigen (e.g., bacteria, toxins, foreign proteins) and capable of neutralizing or giving immunity against a specific antigen.

Antichrist, in Christian belief, person who will lead forces of evil on earth against ultimately victorious forces of good. 1 John 2.18–22; 4.3; 2 John 7. Often identified with Beast of Revelation; wrongly linked to

Satan. Christians have tended to call opponents of their particular beliefs the Antichrist.

Anti-Comintern Pact: see COMINTERN and AXIS.

Anti-Corn-Law League, organization formed 1839 to work for repeal of English CORN LAWS. Its leading figures were Richard COBDEN and John BRIGHT.

Anticosti, island (pop. 424), 140 mi. long, 30 mi. wide, E Que., Canada, at mouth of St. Lawrence R. Lumbering is main industry. Discovered by Cartier 1534. Granted to Jolliet and long held by his heirs. Now belongs to paper interests.

Antietam campaign (ăntē'tùm), Sept., 1862, of Civil War. In invasion of Md. and Pa., R. E. Lee sent Stonewall Jackson to take Harpers Ferry and moved toward Hagerstown. Harpers Ferry taken Sept. 15, but Gen. G. B. McClellan on Sept. 14 stopped Lee, who fell back to Sharpsburg (c.9 mi. W of South Mt.), behind Antietam Creek. Sept. 17 was bloodiest day of war, a Union victory only in that Lee was stopped.

antifreezing solution, aqueous solution with freezing point below that of water used in automobile cooling systems. Solutions include alcohol (evaporates rapidly); salt (formerly used; highly corrosive); glycerin or glycerol (sluggish at low temperatures); and ethylene glycol (acts upon rubber).

antifriction metal, ALLOY used to line machinery bearings when ball bearings are not used. Consists of soft matrix in which hard particles are embedded. See also BABBITT METAL.

antigen: see ANTIBODY.

Antigo (ăn'tĭgō), city (pop. 9,902), NE Wis., NE of Wausau. Produces dairy and wood products.

Antigone (ăntĭ'gùnē), in Greek legend, daughter of Oedipus. When CREON forbade burial of her brother POLYNICES, she defied him and performed the funeral rites. Creon buried her alive.

Antigonish (ăn"tĭgōnĭsh'), town (pop. 3,196), NE N.S., Canada, on West R. and NE of Truro. Seat of St. Francis Xavier Univ. (R.C.; for men and women; 1853) which has promoted a noted cooperative here.

Antigonus (ăntĭ'gùnùs), rulers of anc. Macedon. **Antigonus I** (Cyclops), 382?–301 B.C., general of Alexander the Great and ruler in Asia. He tried to rebuild the entire empire, but in the wars of the DIADOCHI he was defeated and killed at Ipsus (301). His son, Demetrius I, conquered Macedonia. Demetrius' son, **Antigonus II** (Gonatas), c.320–239 B.C., took Macedon 276, rebuilt the state and amid much warfare briefly united Greece. Succeeded by Demetrius II. **Antigonus III** (Doson), d. 221 B.C., was regent for Demetrius' son, PHILIP V, but proclaimed himself king (227). Aided the Achaean League against Cleomenes and rebuilt power in Greece.

Antigua (ăntē'gwù), city (pop. 10,691), S central Guatemala, a commercial and tourist center. Founded 1542 to succeed Ciudad Vieja as cap. In 18th cent. had much splendor. Earthquakes caused removal of cap. to Guatemala City (1776).

Antigua (ăntē'gwù), island, area 108 sq. mi., British West Indies, chief island of Antigua presidency (pop. 40,778) in LEEWARD ISLANDS; cap. SAINT JOHN'S. Discovered by Columbus 1493, settled by British 1632.

Anti-Lebanon, mountain range between Syria and Lebanon, rising to Mt. HERMON.

Antilles: see WEST INDIES.

Anti-Masonic party, American political organization which rose after the disappearance in W N.Y. in 1826 of William Morgan. The Masons were said, without proof, to have murdered him, and in reaction local organizations arose to refuse support to Masons for public office. At Baltimore, in 1831, Anti-Masons held first national nominating convention of any party and issued first written party platform. Helped in 1834 to form Whig party.

antimony (ăn'tĭmō"nē), silver-white crystalline element (symbol = Sb [L. *stibium*]; see also ELEMENT, table), with properties of metal and nonmetal. Forms stibine, a poison gas, with hydrogen; combines readily with oxygen, sulphur, phosphorus, and the halogens. Used in making BABBITT METAL, BRITANNIA METAL, TYPE METAL, castings, batteries, and medicines. Chief ore is STIBNITE. Detected by MARSH'S TEST.

antinomianism (ăntĭnō'mēŭnĭzŭm) [Gr.,= against law], belief in Christianity that Christians, redeemed by Christ and justified by faith, need not follow the moral law (esp. that of the Old Testament). Considered heretical by majority from early Christian days to accusation of Anne Hutchinson in colonial Mass. Only large sect to hold the doctrine was that of ANABAPTISTS.

Antinoüs (ăntĭ'nōŭs), c.110–130, favorite of Emperor Hadrian, b. Bithynia. Notable for his youthful beauty, he was drowned in the Nile. Hadrian honored his memory by naming cities after him and having him deified.

Antioch or **Antakya** (äntäkyä'), town (pop. 30,385), S Turkey, on Orontes R., at foot of Mt. Silpius. Founded c.300 B.C. by Seleucus I. At crossing of routes from the Euphrates to the sea and from El Bika to Asia Minor, it soon became one of world's largest trade centers. Here followers of Jesus were first called Christians. City is one of three ancient patriarchates: seat of a Melchite, a Maronite, and a Jacobite patriarch. Fell to Persians 538 and to Arabs 637. Was under Byzantine Empire 969–1085 and under Seljuk Turks 1085–98. Taken 1098 by Crusaders, it became virtually independent fief of Latin Kingdom of Jerusalem under BOHEMOND I and successors. Fell to Mamelukes of Egypt 1268 and to Ottoman Turks 1516. Transferred to Syria 1920 but restored to Turkey 1939. Modern Antioch occupies mere fraction of ancient city, remains of whose walls, aqueduct, theater, and castle survive. Excavations here and at near-by Daphne have yielded splendid mosaics. An early find was Great Chalice of Antioch, held by many to be Holy Grail.

Antioch, town (pop. 11,051), W Calif., on San Joaquin R.; founded 1849–50. Central Valley project power plant is here.

Antioch College, at Yellow Springs, Ohio; nonsectarian, coed.; opened 1853, with Horace Mann as president. Pioneered in plan by which students alternate study with full-time work.

Antiochus (ăntĭ'ŭkŭs), kings of anc. Syria. **Antiochus I** (Soter), d. c.261 B.C. (reigned 280–c.261 B.C.), was son of Seleucus I. **Antiochus II** (Theos), d. 247 B.C. (reigned c.261–247 B.C.). Rivalry with PTOLEMY II ended with marriage to Ptolemy's daughter Berenice, but warfare followed his death. **Antiochus III** (the Great), d. 187 B.C. (reigned 223–187 B.C.), son of Seleucus II, tried to restore crumbling Seleucid empire. An ally of Philip V, he won much territory, but was crushed by the Romans at Thermopylae (191) and Magnesia (190). **Antiochus IV** (Epiphanes), d. 163 B.C. (reigned 175–163 B.C.), son of Antiochus III, successor of his brother, Seleucus IV. Attempted to Hellenize Judaea, arousing MACCABEES. His invasion of Egypt was thwarted by the Romans.

Antiope (ăntĭ'ùpē), in Greek legend. **1** Daughter of king of Boeotia. Visited by Zeus in form of satyr, she bore him Amphion and Zethus. **2** Sister of Hippolyte, queen of the Amazons. In one legend, she is mother of Hippolytus by Theseus.

Antipas: see HEROD.

Antipater (ăntĭ'pùtùr), d. 319 B.C., Macedonian general under Alexander the Great, regent in Macedon (334–323 B.C.). Opposed PERDICCAS and later held the kingdom together. After his death came wars of the DIADOCHI.

Antipater, in Bible: see HEROD.

Antiphilus (ăntĭ'ĭlŭs), fl. 4th cent. B.C., Greek artist, of Egyptian origin. Painted portraits of Philip of Macedon and Alexander the Great.

antipope, one supposed to be pope but not subsequently recognized by Holy See. See, e.g., GUIBERT OF RAVENNA; LUNA, PEDRO DE; COSSA, BALDASSARRE.

Anti-Saloon League, U.S. organization working for prohibition of sale of alcoholic liquors. Founded in Ohio 1893. Wielded great political influence.

anti-Semitism, sentiment against the JEWS. Pre-19th-cent. anti-Semitism, largely religious, was expressed in persecutions, expulsions, and restrictions (see GHETTO). The Jews were limited to such means of living as usury, and anti-Semitism became economic. After the 19th-cent. emancipation of Jews, "race" feeling, allied with rising nationalism, developed. All evils were blamed on the Jews, either by demagogues or by governments (as in Russia) to divert popular discontent. The "Protocols of the Wise Men of Zion," a spurious document purporting to outline a Jewish plan for world domination, appeared in early 20th-cent. Russia. The teachings of Gobineau and Houston Stewart Chamberlain were climaxed by pseudoscientific doctrine of "Aryan" superiority in NATIONAL SOCIALISM. Hitler exterminated an estimated 6,000,000 European Jews between 1939 and 1945.

antiseptic, agent inhibiting growth of or destroying microorganisms. Influenced by Pasteur's theory that microorganisms cause infection, LISTER was first to use antiseptic in surgery. Modern techniques founded on asepsis (absence of pathogenic organisms).

antislavery movement: see SLAVERY; ABOLITIONISTS.

Anti-Taurus, Turkish mountain range: see TAURUS.

antitoxin: see TOXIN.

Anti-Trust Act: see CLAYTON ANTI-TRUST ACT; SHERMAN ANTI-TRUST ACT.

Antium, Italy: see ANZIO.

Antofagasta (äntōfägä'stä), city (pop. 43,318), N Chile; a Pacific port. Its founding by Chileans (1870) in Bolivian territory was a cause of war (see PACIFIC, WAR OF THE). Nitrates and copper are chief exports.

Antoine, André (ädrä' ätwän'), 1858–1943, French theatrical manager. Formed Théâtre Libre company 1887 and presented works of naturalist school. His work became a model for European and American experimental theaters.

Antonello da Messina (äntōněl'lō dä mäs-sē'nä), c.1430–c.1479, one of the first Italian painters to utilize Flemish technique of oil painting.

Antonescu, Ion (yôn äntôně'skoo), 1882–1946, Rumanian marshal and dictator. Appointed premier 1940; forced abdication of Carol II in favor of King MICHAEL; brought Rumania into AXIS camp; gave Hitler virtual control of country. Arrested 1944; executed.

Antonines (än'tūnīnz), name used for several 2d-cent. Roman emperors including Antoninus Pius, Marcus Aurelius, and Commodus.

Antoninus, Wall of, ancient Roman wall built across N Britain in reign of Antoninus Pius—probably A.D. 140–42. It was 37 mi. long.

Antoninus Pius (äntōnī'nŭs pī'ŭs), A.D. 86–A.D. 161, Roman emperor (138–161). Adopted by HADRIAN, he succeeded and administered the empire well. Succeeded by his adopted son, MARCUS AURELIUS.

Antony or **Marc Antony,** Latin *Marcus Antonius,* c.83 B.C.–30 B.C., Roman political leader and general. A dashing young soldier of good family, he became a protégé of Julius Caesar, and as tribune he (with Cassius) vetoed the bill to strip Caesar of his army. After serving as Caesar's lieutenant in the Civil War against Pompey, he gained power from the victory. Caesar was assassinated in 44 B.C., and Antony roused the people against the conspirators responsible. He formed an uneasy alliance with Octavian (later AUGUSTUS), was embroiled in trouble trying to gain the province of Gaul assigned to him, and was a member of the Second Triumvirate (Octavian, Lepidus, Antony). He and Octavian defeated the republicans at Philippi (42 B.C.), and in the proscription that followed Antony brought about the death of his enemy Cicero. Antony undertook to rule Asia. In Rome his wife, Fulvia, intrigued against Octavian, but she died, and Antony married Octavian's sister, Octavia. The alliance went on. Antony had, however, already met Cleopatra and fallen under her sway; he ruled from Alexandria in great luxury. Octavian grew impatient, and Antony was deprived of power. Civil war followed. Antony and Cleopatra were defeated in the naval battle at Actium (31 B.C.) and fled to Alexandria. When Octavian approached, Antony committed suicide. He is known to English-speaking people largely through Shakspere's *Julius Caesar* and *Antony and Cleopatra.* Also Marc or Mark Anthony.

Antrim, maritime county (1,098 sq. mi.; pop. 231,099, excluding Belfast), Ulster prov., Northern Ireland. County town is BELFAST, a major British port and chief industrial center of Ireland. Region mainly agr. with fishing and cattle breeding. E part of county mountainous. N coast has formation known as GIANT'S CAUSEWAY.

Antung (än'tŏong), industrial city (pop. 271,115), cap. Liaotung prov., Manchuria; port at mouth of Yalu R. Opened to foreign trade 1907.

Antwerp (än'twûrp), Flemish *Antwerpen,* Fr. *Anvers,* province (1,104 sq. mi.; pop. 1,296,687), N Belgium. It is a cultivated plain drained by Scheldt R. and Albert Canal. Population is largely Flemish-speaking. The province was part of the duchy of BRABANT. Its cap. is **Antwerp** (pop. 266,636; with suburbs 599,240), on the Scheldt. Rivaled only by Rotterdam as largest sea and transit port of continental Europe, Antwerp is also a world center of the diamond trade and industry and the seat of the oldest stock exchange (founded 1460). It has oil refineries, automobile plants, flourmills. Its churches and museums contain treasures of Flemish art. Rising into prominence with the decline of Bruges and Ghent, Antwerp was by the 16th cent. the commercial and financial hub of Europe. Its prosperity suffered a fatal blow when it was sacked by mutinous Spanish troops (the "Spanish Fury," 1576), but it resisted for 14 months before surrendering to the Spanish under Alexander Farnese (1584–85). The Peace of Westphalia (1648) closed the Scheldt to navigation. Antwerp was reduced to insignificance until 1863, when Belgium redeemed from the Dutch the right to collect a toll on Scheldt shipping. The city suffered in both world wars. Captured by British troops in Aug., 1944, it became a vital Allied supply base and was heavily damaged by German rocket weapons. Antwerp was the home of Rubens and the birthplace of Sir Anthony Van Dyck. Among its many splendid buildings are the Gothic Cathedral of Notre Dame and the old guild houses on the Groote Markt [market place]. The zoological garden has long been world famous.

Anuradhapura (ùnoo'rädùpoo'rù), town (pop. 12,287), N Ceylon. On the site of an ancient cap. (4th cent. B.C.–8th cent. A.D.) of Ceylon. A great Buddhist center, it has ruins of large stupas and the Brazen Palace. Buddhist pilgrims visit bo tree, grown from slip of tree at Buddh Gaya.

Anville, Jean Baptiste Bourguignon d' (boorgēnyō' dävēl'), 1697–1782, French geographer and cartographer. Noted for accurate maps of ancient geography; had largest collection of maps, atlases, and geographic material in France.

Anyox (ä'něŏks"), village, W B.C., Canada, NNE of Prince Rupert. Center for copper mining and smelting, with large pyrite smelter.

Anza, Juan Bautista de (hwän'boutēs'tä dä än'sä), 1735–88, Spanish explorer and official in Southwest and Far West, founder of San Francisco, b. Mexico. Governor of New Mexico 1777–88.

Anzengruber, Ludwig (loot'vĭkh än'tsùngroo"bùr), 1839–89, Austrian author of successful folk plays. *Das vierte Gebot* [the fourth commandment] is considered one of first naturalistic plays.

Anzio (än'tsyō), Latin *Antium,* town (pop. 5,989), Latium, central Italy, on Tyrrhenian Sea. Bathing resort since Roman times; important Roman ruins. Scene of fierce fighting between Allied beachhead forces and Germans, Jan.–May, 1944.

Aomori (äōmō'rē), city (pop. 90,828), extreme N Honshu, Japan; chief port of N Honshu.

Aosta, Val d' (väldäö'stä), autonomous region (1,260 sq. mi.; pop. 83,455), NW Italy, on French and Swiss borders. Includes Gran Paradiso and Italian slopes of Mont Blanc, Matterhorn, Monte Rosa; many resorts. Most of pop. speaks French dialect. The capital is Aosta (pop. 13,466), near junction of Great and Little St. Bernard roads.

Apache Indians (ŭpăch'ē), Indian people of U.S. Southwest, speaking Athapascan languages (see LANGUAGE, table). Divided into many groups. Chiefly known for fierce opposition (late 19th cent.) to white intrusion into N.Mex. and Ariz. Notable leaders were Geronimo and Cochise.

Apalachee Bay (ăpŭlăch'ē), a Gulf of Mexico arm (c.30 mi. wide), NW Fla., S of Tallahassee.

Apalachicola (ăp″ŭlăchĭkō'lŭ), city (pop. 3,222), NW Fla., SW of Tallahassee, on Apalachicola Bay (bridged 1935); founded c.1820. Seafood (oysters, shrimp). Its important cotton-shipping activities (after 1830) were adversely affected by Civil War blockade. City is at mouth of the **Apalachicola**, navigable river formed by junction of Chattahoochee and Flint rivers at Ga. line and flowing 112 mi. S to the bay.

apatite (ăp'ŭtīt), calcium phosphate mineral containing fluorine, chlorine, or both. Colorless when pure; impure colored types sometimes cut as gem stones. Used in making phosphorus fertilizers.

ape, usually name for primates most closely resembling man (GORILLA, CHIMPANZEE, ORANGUTAN, GIBBON). These lack external tails, cheek pouches, ischial callosities (except gibbon); stand semierectly. Brain structure similar to man. Name was once used for tailless monkeys or as synonym for monkey.

Apeldoorn (ä'pŭldōrn), municipality (pop. 62,876), and town, Gelderland prov., E central Netherlands. Produces pharmaceuticals, refrigerators, papers. Royal summer palace of Het Loo is near by.

Apelles (ŭpĕl'ēz), fl. 4th cent. B.C., Greek painter, the most celebrated of antiquity, but now known only through descriptions of his works. Court painter to Philip and Alexander.

Apennines (ă'pŭnīnz), mountain system traversing entire Italian peninsula. Mts. of Sicily are a continuation. Highest peak (9,560 ft.) in Gran Sasso d'Italia group. Extensive pastures. Forests (chestnut, birch, oak, pine) much reduced by erosion.

aphid (ā'fĭd, ăf'ĭd) or **plant louse,** parasitic insect, also called green fly and blight. Injures vegetation. Species seen on field plants is soft-bodied, green, with long legs, antennae, two pairs membranous wings (some wingless). Reproductive cycle varies with species; many lay fertilized eggs in fall which hatch in spring or summer into stem mothers. These produce several generations by PARTHENOGENESIS. Winged descendants migrate to other host plants to continue cycle. Numbers reduced by other insects, fungi, damp weather. See also GALL.

Aphrodite (ăfrŭdī'tē), in Greek religion, Olympian goddess of love, beauty, and fertility; wife of Hephaestus. Daughter of Zeus and Dione or of the sea into which blood of Uranus fell. Mother of Eros by Ares, of Aeneas by Anchises, and of Priapus by Dionysus. As goddess of fertility she is closely linked with ADONIS. Known also as Aphrodite Urania; her worship may have been imported from Orient, and she is akin to Astarte or Ishtar. Identified with Roman Venus. By awarding Aphrodite APPLE OF DISCORD, Paris won Helen and thus caused Trojan War.

Apo, Mount (ä'pō), active volcano, 9,690 ft. high, on S Mindanao; highest peak of the Philippines.

apocalypse (ŭpŏk'ŭlĭps) [Gr.,= uncovering], type of ancient Hebrew and Christian prophetic literature, usually written in veiled symbolism and inspired by visions (e.g., FOUR HORSEMEN OF THE APOCALYPSE). The biblical REVELATION is often called simply the Apocalypse.

Apocrypha (ŭpŏk'rĭfŭ) [Gr.,= hidden things], appendix to Authorized Version of Old Testament containing following books or parts of books: 1 and 2 ESDRAS; TOBIT; JUDITH; ESTHER 10.4–16; WISDOM; ECCLESIASTICUS; BARUCH; Dan. 3.24–90 (see DANIEL and THREE HOLY CHILDREN); Dan. 13 (see SUSANNA); Dan. 14 (see BEL AND THE DRAGON); Prayer of Manasses (see MANASSEH 2); 1 and 2 MACCABEES. All but Prayer of Manasses, 1 and 2 Esdras considered canonical by Roman Catholics (Council of Trent, 1546). Protestants regard Apocrypha valuable for instruction but not canonical (see OLD TESTAMENT). For Jewish and Christian works resembling biblical books but not included in Western or Hebrew canon, see PSEUDEPIGRAPHA.

Apodaca, Juan Ruiz de (hwän' rōōēth' dä äpōdhä'kä), 1754–1835, last viceroy of New Spain (1816–21).

Apollinaire, Guillaume (gēyōm' äpōlēnâr'), 1880–1918, French poet, b. Rome. Of illegitimate birth, he was christened Wilhelm Apollinaris de Kostrowitzky. His bizarre, exquisite poems (*Alcools,* 1913; *Calligrammes,* 1918) and his surrealist drama, *Les Mamelles de Tirésias* (1918), were influential experiments. His art criticism promoted cubism.

Apollinarianism (ŭpŏlĭnâ'rēŭnĭzŭm), popular heretical doctrine of Apollinaris or Apollinarius (c.315–c.390) of Laodicea. Taught Christ possessed Logos in place of human mind. Anticipated MONOPHYSITISM.

Apollo (ŭpŏ'lō) or **Phoebus Apollo** (fē'bŭs), in Greek religion, Olympian god of light, music, poetry, pastoral pursuits, and prophecy. As god of music, the lyre was sacred to him (he was father of ORPHEUS). He was also god of healing and father of Asclepius. Identified with Helios as the sun-god. Son of Zeus and Leto, he (with twin sister ARTEMIS) was born in DELOS. At his temple in DELPHI, he was god of prophecy. Later he was best known as god of music and poetry, attended by MUSES. The **Apollo Belvedere** (bĕl″vĭdēr'), a marble figure in the Vatican, Roman copy of Greek original in bronze, is best-known statue of him.

Apollodorus (ŭpŏl″ōdôr'ŭs), fl. c.415 B.C., Athenian painter, reputedly first to use light and shadow.

Apollonius of Perga, fl. 247–205 B.C., Greek mathematician of Alexandrian school. Treatise on conic sections included work of Euclid and others.

Apollonius of Tralles: see FARNESE BULL.

Apollonius Rhodius (rō'dēŭs), 3d cent. B.C., epic poet, librarian at Alexandria, author of *Argonautica.*

Apollyon (ŭpŏl'yŭn), Greek name of the destroying angel. Rev. 9.11. See SATAN and HELL.

Apopka, Lake (ŭpŏp'kŭ), central Fla.; fishing. Winter Garden is on S shore.

apoplexy or **stroke,** result of cerebral hemorrhage. Often accompanied by coma and followed by partial paralysis abating as blood clot is resorbed.

apostle (ŭpŏs'ŭl) [Gr.,= envoy], one of prime missionaries of Christendom. The chief 12: PETER, ANDREW, JAMES (the Greater), JOHN, THOMAS, JAMES (the Less), JUDE (or Thaddeus), PHILIP, BARTHOLOMEW (may be same as Nathanael), MATTHEW, SIMON, and MATTHIAS (replacing JUDAS ISCARIOT). Traditional list of Twelve Disciples includes Judas and not Matthias, list of Twelve Apostles includes Matthias and not Judas. Number originally symbolic of 12 tribes of Israel. St. PAUL is always classed a chief apostle though not of the 12. Name also given to others such as St. BARNABAS. For Apostles' Creed, see CREED; see also DIDACHE.

Apostle Islands, group of over 20 islands, off N Wis., in SW L. Superior. Connected with Wis. mainland by boat. Have noted wave-eroded cliffs. Madeline, the largest, includes LA POINTE town.

Apostolic Constitutions: see CONSTITUTIONS, APOSTOLIC.

apostolic succession, in some Christian churches, belief that the position of the apostles of Christ has been transmitted from generation to generation in unbroken succession so that the bishops of today are the true inheritors of the power of the apostles. This is stoutly denied in churches that do not recognize any episcopacy. The apostolic succession is to be distinguished from the doctrine of Petrine supremacy (see PAPACY).

Apoxyomenus (ŭpŏk″sēŏm′ĭnŭs) [Gr.,= scraping one's self], Roman copy in marble of a bronze statue by LYSIPPUS. Represents an athlete.

Appalachian Mountains (ăpŭlā′chŭn), great mountain system of E North America, extending SW from St. Lawrence valley in Quebec prov., Canada, to Gulf Coast plain in Ala., and rising to 6,684 ft. in Mt. MITCHELL. They include WHITE MOUNTAINS, GREEN MOUNTAINS, CATSKILL MOUNTAINS, ALLEGHENY MOUNTAINS, BLUE RIDGE, GREAT SMOKY MOUNTAINS, and other ranges. Mainly formed by folding (see MOUNTAIN), they consist largely of sedimentary rocks and are much eroded. W portions, less rugged than E portions, are largely plateau formations of horizontal rock structure. System has deposits of coal, iron, oil, and gas. With few passes, they barred early expansion W. Remote settlements in mountain valleys have preserved old ways of life more than any other U.S. region. Beautiful scenery and many resorts line system.

Appalachian Trail, for hikers, extending 2,050 mi. along ridges of Appalachian Mt. system from Mt. Katahdin, Maine, to Mt. Oglethorpe, N Ga.

appeal, process by which a superior court reviews errors allegedly committed by a lower court. If case had a jury trial only errors of law (i.e., in legal rules) may be reviewed; if trial had no jury, errors both of law and of fact (erroneous interpretation of evidence) may be reviewed.

appendix, vermiform, tubular outgrowth (c.3 in. long) of large intestine, in lower right abdomen, probably vestigial remnant. Infection may result in **appendicitis,** usually making imperative the removal of appendix; use of cathartics entails risk of rupture of appendix and spread of infection (see PERITONITIS).

Appenzell (ä′pùntsĕl), canton, E Switzerland. Mostly meadowland; textile mfg. Ruled by abbots of St. Gall after 11th cent.; rebelled 1403; joined Swiss Confederation 1513. In 1597 Appenzell split into two independent half-cantons. Ausser-Rhoden (94 sq. mi.; pop. 48,026; cap. Herisau) accepted Reformation. Inner-Rhoden (67 sq. mi.; pop. 13,448) remained Catholic; its cap., Appenzell (pop. 4,983), has noted embroidery mfg.

Appian (ă′pēùn), fl. 2d cent., Roman historian. His history of Roman conquests reproduces documents and sources otherwise lost. Of 24 books, in Greek, only VI–VII and XI–XVII are fully preserved.

Appian Way, Latin *Via Appia,* road built under Appius Claudius Caecus (312 B.C.). Connecting Rome with Brundisium, it was chief highway to Greece and the provinces in Asia.

apple, best known and commercially most important fruit of temperate zones and its tree, *Malus sylvestris,* member of rose family. Cultivated from prehistoric times. Long lived and easy to grow. North America leads in apple production. See also CRAB APPLE.

Appleby, county town (pop. 1,704), Westmoreland, England; site of historic Appleby Castle.

applejack, brandy made from hard cider or fermented apple pomace, the residue from cider making.

apple of discord, in Greek mythology, a golden apple inscribed "for the fairest," thrown by uninvited ERIS among guests at wedding of Peleus and Thetis. It was claimed by Aphrodite, Athena, and Hera. Paris, selected to decide, chose Aphrodite, who offered him the fairest of women, Helen. His abduction of Helen caused TROJAN WAR.

Appleseed, Johnny: see CHAPMAN, JOHN.

Appleton, Daniel, 1785–1849, American publisher, founder of a large publishing house.

Appleton, Sir Edward Victor, 1892–, English physicist. Won 1947 Nobel Prize for studies of ionosphere which led to development of radar.

Appleton, city (pop. 34,010), E Wis., on Fox R., near its exit from L. Winnebago, in dairying and stock-raising region; settled before 1850. Mfg. of paper, wool, and wood products. Had first U.S. hydroelectric

plant. Seat of Lawrence Col. of Wisconsin (nonsectarian, coed. [pioneer]; chartered 1847, opened 1849 with grant from A. A. Lawrence), with affiliated Inst. of Paper Chemistry.

Appomattox (ăpùmă′tùks), town (pop. 1,094) central Va., E of Lynchburg, near source of Appomattox R. R. E. Lee surrendered to U. S. Grant at near-by **Appomattox Courthouse,** April 9, 1865. Retreating from Petersburg and Richmond, Lee was cut off here by P. H. Sheridan and yielded. This was end of war, as other Southern armies followed suit.

apprenticeship, system of learning a trade by paying with years of work for instruction from one skilled in the trade. Known in ancient world, the system was also part of medieval guild system. Apprenticeship less widespread after Industrial Revolution, but it survives in highly skilled trades. Typically apprentice becomes journeyman (working for master for wages), finally master.

APRA: see HAYA DE LA TORRE, VÍCTOR RAÚL; PERU.

Apra Harbor (ä′prä) or **Port Apra,** in Sumay town, W Guam; U.S. naval base. Port is closed to foreign vessels except by permit.

apricot, a tree, *Prunus armeniaca,* and its orange-colored fruit. It is a commercial crop in California.

Apries (ā′prē-ēz), king of anc. Egypt (588–569 B.C.), of the XXVI dynasty. Succeeded Psamtik II and sought to recover Syria and Palestine from NEBUCHADNEZZAR. Murdered by Amasis II.

April: see MONTH.

Apsheron, Azerbaijan SSR: see BAKU.

Apuleius, Lucius (ä″pyōōlē′ùs), fl. 2d cent., Latin writer. His novel, *Golden Ass* or *Metamorphoses,* strongly influenced the later novel.

Apulia (ùpū′lēù), Ital. *Puglia* (pōō′lyä), region (7,469 sq. mi.; pop. 2,642,076), S Italy, occupying southernmost third of Italian E coast; cap. Bari. In anc. times only N part of region was called Apulia. Cities: Bari, Brindisi, Foggia, Taranto, Lecce. Wine, olives, almonds, corn are grown despite scarcity of water. Sheep and goat raising. Conquered (11th–12th cent.) from Byzantines by Normans, who made it a powerful duchy, it later became part of kingdom of Naples.

Aquae Sextiae: see AIX-EN-PROVENCE.

aquamarine, transparent BERYL with blue to blue-green tint. Found in Brazil, Ceylon, Germany, Siberia, and U.S. Similar to emerald save for color.

aquarium, tank, bowl, artificial pond, or museum for aquatic animals and plants, preferably rectangular, with no copper, brass, zinc, or galvanized iron in contact with water. Tanks with new wood or concrete should be filled with water and changed at intervals for several weeks before putting in fish. Green aquarium plants are valuable oxygenators. A properly set up and unpolluted aquarium rarely needs complete change of water, only replacement of loss by evaporation.

Aquarius [Lat.,= water bearer], 11th sign of ZODIAC.

aqueduct (ä′kwùdùkt), channel or trough conveying water, usually fresh water to a city. First used probably in Mesopotamia; greatly developed later by Romans. Aqueduct to present Mexico city built by Mayas before Spanish Conquest. Aqueducts carry water to many large U.S. cities from great distances.

Aquidneck (ùkwĭd′nĭk), Indian and early colonial name of Rhode Island, isl. in Narragansett Bay.

Aquila or **Aquila degli Abruzzi** (ä′kwēlä dā′lyē äbrōōt′sē), city (pop. 20,573), cap. of Abruzzi e Molise region, S central Italy, below Gran Sasso d'Italia; medieval architecture.

Aquila Ponticus (pŏn′tĭkùs), 2d cent., Jewish translator of Old Testament from Hebrew into Greek. Much used by Jews. No complete specimen exists.

Aquilegia: see COLUMBINE.

Aquileia (äkwēlā′yä), town (pop. 1,116), Friuli-Venezia Giulia, NE Italy, near Adriatic. Founded 181 B.C.; important Roman stronghold; see of patriarchate, 6th–18th cent. Early Romanesque basilica has splendid mosaic floor. Grado, on near-by island, is a bathing resort.

Aquinas, Saint Thomas: see THOMAS AQUINAS, SAINT.

Aquitaine (ăk'wĭtān), former duchy, SW France; historic cap., Bordeaux. Frontiers shifted often. A Roman prov., it passed to Visigoths (5th cent.), then to Franks (507), and was a kingdom (781–838) under Charlemagne's son Louis, and grandson Pepin. Late in 9th cent. it emerged as duchy, enfeoffed to French crown. It grew powerful and came to include most of SW and S central France. Second marriage (1152) of ELEANOR OF AQUITAINE started French-English struggle over duchy; Hundred Years War gave France victory. See also GUIENNE; GASCONY.

Arabia, peninsula (c.1,000,000 sq. mi.; pop. 12,000,-000), SW Asia, between Red Sea and Gulf of Aqaba on W and Persian Gulf and Gulf of Oman on E. Bounded on S by Arabian Sea and Gulf of Aden. Occupied by SAUDI ARABIA, YEMEN, British protectorates of Aden, Bahrein, Kuwait, Oman, Qatar, and Trucial Oman, and British colony of Aden. Mainly desert; more habitable areas in HEJAZ, NEJD, and the SW (only section fit for extensive agriculture). Pastoral nomads raise goats and sheep. Rich oil fields (exploited by European and American firms) are in E. Much of ancient Arabia was divided between domains of Ma'in and SHEBA. Ethiopia twice held S coast (HADRAMAUT) and Yemen (300–378, 525–70). In 7th cent. dynamic faith of MOHAMMED the Prophet unified Arab tribes, inspiring them to conquer neighboring states. OMAYYAD caliphate conquered Persia but was checked in E by Byzantines and in W by defeat in battle of Tours, France (732). After removal of seat of caliphate from Medina to Damascus, Arabia again lost political cohesion. Nominally ruled after 1517 by Ottoman Turks, harassed 18th–19th cent. by WAHABI movement. Turkish rule was broken during World War I by IBN SAUD and HUSEIN IBN ALI.

Arabian art and architecture: see MOSLEM ART AND ARCHITECTURE.

Arabian music, term used popularly to include the music of all Islamic peoples. It is related to Greek, Hebrew, and Hindu music. Present-day scale has 17 notes. Rhythms are provided by the meters of poetry. Its principal form is the *nuba,* which is a sort of cantata, in nine parts, some of which are instrumental, some vocal. Chief instruments are a long lute and a short lute; influence of Arabian music on that of Europe lies mainly in the introduction of the lute by the Moors in Spain.

Arabian Nights: see THOUSAND AND ONE NIGHTS.

Arabian Sea, NW part of Indian Ocean, lying between Arabia and India.

Arabic language, Semitic language, one of most widely spoken languages in the world. See LANGUAGE (table).

Arabic literature. Golden age of lyric poets (Amru-l-Kais, Antar, Zuhair) lasted from 4th to 7th cent. It was marked by personal odes about love, fighting, and hunting, with references to power of God. These survive only in the collections MUALLAQAT, HAMASA, and MOFADDALIYAT. KORAN supplanted poetry (decried by Mohammed) until Arabic-Persian cultural renascence under Abbasids at Baghdad (8th–9th cent). New court poetry of Abu-l-Atahiya and Abu Nuwas soon became precious, as in poetry of Hariri (11th cent.). Prose romances, notably THOUSAND AND ONE NIGHTS, superseded poetry. They show Hindu and Persian influence but are essentially Arabic in form. Bukhari, Tabari, Masudi, Ibn Khaldun, and Ibn Batuta are noted for historical and geographical writing. Omayyad Spain fostered vigorous Arabic literature; its great philosophers were Avempace, Averroës, and Ibn Tufail. Since 1300 there has been little Arabic literature of wide interest.

Arab League, association of countries predominantly Arabic in descent. Protocol calling for it was signed 1944 at Alexandria. Constitution drafted 1945 at Cairo was accepted by Egypt, Syria, Lebanon, Trans-Jordan, Iraq, Saudi Arabia, and Yemen. A representative of Palestinian Arabs also has a vote in the League. Charter provides for coordination on domestic and foreign policies and forbids use of force to settle disputes among members. League countries joined in unsuccessful attack on new state of Israel in 1948.

Arachne (ŭrăk'nē) [Gr.,= spider], in Greek legend, girl who challenged Athena to a trial of skill in weaving. The goddess changed her into a spider.

Arad (ärăd'), city (pop. 87,291), W Rumania, on Mures R. and near Hungarian border. Commercial and mfg. center (flour, leather, machinery). Population c.40% Hungarian.

Aradus (ăr'ŭdŭs), islet and town of anc. Phoenicia, the modern Ruad, N of Tripoli off Syrian coast, most important of N Phoenician centers. Called Arvad in Old Testament.

Arafat (äräfät'), granite hill, Saudi Arabia, near Mecca. Mohammed's stop here on his flight from Mecca to Medina is commemorated by pilgrims.

Arafura Sea (ärüfōō'rŭ), part of the Pacific between Australia and New Guinea.

Aragats, Mount (ărŭgăts'), or **Mount Alagez** (ŭlŭgyôs'), extinct volcano, 13,435 ft. high, Armenian SSR. Astrophysical research center.

Aragon, Louis (lwē' ärägŏ') 1897–, French poet and novelist. Onetime Dadaist and surrealist and later a Communist and leader of wartime resistance. *Le Crève-Cœur* (1941) is among his best poetry.

Aragon (ă'rŭgŏn), Span. *Aragón* (ärägōn'), region (18,-382 sq. mi.; pop. 1,058,806) and former kingdom, NE Spain, in E Pyrenees and Ebro plain; historic cap. Saragossa. Other cities: Huesca, Teruel. Region is arid and sparsely populated, but irrigated areas yield cereals, wine, olives, sugar beets. Sheep and cattle raising. Kingdom was created (1035) out of W part of Navarre for Ramiro I. It grew at expense of emirate of SARAGOSSA and was united, by personal union, with Catalonia after 1137. Union of Aragon with Castile began in 1469 through marriage of Ferdinand and Isabella.

Aragon, house of, family which ruled in Aragon, CATALONIA, MAJORCA, SICILY, the kingdom of NAPLES, SARDINIA, ROUSSILLON, ATHENS, and other lands in Middle Ages; founded by RAMIRO I. Aragon and Catalonia were in personal union after 1137, but the other territories were generally ruled separately by branches of the house. Alfonso V, who conquered Naples in 1442, temporarily united all Aragonese dominions. The marriage of Ferdinand II of Aragon with Isabella of Castile led to union of the two kingdoms. In their grandson, Emperor CHARLES V, the houses of Aragon and Castile were merged with that of Hapsburg.

Arakan (ärŭkän'), division (14,194 sq. mi.; pop. 1,152,-733) of Lower Burma, on Bay of Bengal; cap. Akyab. Area was annexed 1784 by Burma, ceded 1826 to the British.

Arakcheyev, Aleksey Andreyevich (ŭlyĭksyä' ŭndrā'yĭvĭch äräkchä'ĕf), 1769–1834, Russian general, minister of war under Alexander I. An extreme reactionary who greatly influenced his period.

Aral Sea (ä'rŭl, Rus. ŭräl'), inland sea (24,635 sq. mi.), USSR, in Kazakh SSR and Kara-Kalpak ASSR. Fed by Amu Darya and Syr Darya rivers, it has no outlet, and is shallow, slightly saline. Fisheries.

Aram (ä'răm), an anc. people and their country, roughly identified with Syria. Their language a form of Aramaic. Bible records constant contacts between Hebrews and Aram.

Aram, Eugene, 1704–59, English philologist, hanged after discovery that he had murdered (1745) his friend Daniel Clark. This story was used for a poem by Thomas Hood, a novel by Bulwer-Lytton.

Aramaic (ărŭmā'ĭk), Semitic languages of Syria, flourishing in the centuries before and after Christ. See LANGUAGE (table).

Aranha, Oswaldo (ŭzhväl'dō ŭrä'nyŭ), 1894–, Brazilian statesman, ambassador to U.S. (1934–38), foreign minister (1938–44), president of General Assembly, United Nations (1947).

Aran Islands or **Arran Islands** (both: är'ün), in Galway Bay, Co. Galway, Ireland. The three islands are Inishmore, Inisheer, and Inishmaan. They are barren, and living conditions are primitive.

Aranjuez (äränghwäth') town (pop. 21,771), central Spain, in New Castile, near the Tagus. Its palace, a royal residence since 16th cent., rebuilt 1727.

Aransas Pass (ürän'zús), city (pop. 5,396), S Texas, on Aransas Bay and NE of Corpus Christi. Port on deep-water ship channel passing through Harbor Isl., between St. Joseph and Mustang islands (Port Aransas) and emptying into Gulf of Mexico. Ships oil. Has carbon-black plant and fisheries.

Arany, John (ö'rönyü), Hung. *Arany János,* 1817–82, Hungarian epic poet, author of *Toldi* (1846).

Arapaho Peak: see FRONT RANGE.

Arapaho Indians (üräp'ühō), North American people, of Algonquian linguistic stock. Three main divisions are Gros Ventre (allied with Blackfoot), Southern Arapaho (allied with Cheyenne), and Northern Arapaho (considered the parent group). Ceremonial societies for different age groups are notable.

Ararat (ä'rürăt), region, W Turkey and E Armenian SSR, called Massis in Armenian, Aghri (or Egri) Dagh in Turkish, Koh-i-nuh in Persian. Identical with Armenia in many ancient records; Assyrians called it Urartu. Mt. Ararat (16,946 ft.) highest peak in Turkey; in the Bible, the landing place of Noah's ark.

Araucanian Indians (ä"rôkä'nēŭn, ä"rü), South American people occupying much of present Chile at time of Spanish Conquest (1540). Opposition to Spanish under Pedro de VALDIVIA gave Araucanian leaders, Lautaro and CAUPOLICÁN, fame immortalized in epic of ERCILLA Y ZÚÑIGA. Resistance to whites ended in Chile in war of 1880–81. Araucanians who fled earlier to Argentina were subjugated 1883. Chief language: Mapuche.

Araunah (ärō'nü), man who sold his threshing floor to David who erected altar there. Site, on Mt. Moriah, later used for Temple. 2 Sam. 24.15–25. Ornan: 1 Chron. 21.14–30; 2 Chron. 3.1.

Arbela (ärbē'lü), town, anc. Assyria (modern Erbil). Near here (at Gaugamela) Alexander the Great defeated Darius III (331 B.C.).

Arblay, Madame d': see BURNEY, FRANCES.

Arbogast (är'bügäst), d. 394, Frankish general in Roman service. After murder of VALENTINIAN II (392), he set up puppet emperor, Eugenius, but both were defeated by THEODOSIUS (394).

arborvitae (är"bürvī'tē), evergreen tree or shrub (*Thuja*), with scalelike leaves, fanlike branchlets, and small cones. There are many garden forms of American arborvitae or northern white cedar (*Thuja occidentalis*), and less hardy Oriental species (*T. orientalis*). Wood of western red cedar (*T. plicata*) used in interiors and to make shingles and doors.

Arbuckle Mountains, low range, S Okla., average height 700 ft. Have geological formations. Platt Natl. Park is near.

Arbuthnot, John (ärbŭth'–, är'–), 1667–1735, English satirical writer, court physician to Queen Anne; a friend of Swift, Pope, and Gay.

Arc, Joan of: see JOAN OF ARC.

arc, in electricity, highly luminous, intensely hot path formed when two charcoal rods, originally touching and transmitting electric current, are pulled a short distance apart and current still flows between them. Formerly used for LIGHTING. Principle is used in WELDING and to generate heat in electric furnaces. For mercury-arc lamp see MERCURY; for oscillating arc, see OSCILLATOR.

arc, in geometry, a curved line or any part of it, in particular a portion of the circumference of a circle.

Arcadia (ärkä'dēü), region of anc. Greece in mid-Peloponnesus, inhabited by a pastoral people.

Arcadia, city (pop. 28,733), S Calif., E of Pasadena, in

agr. (oranges, walnuts, truck) and poultry area. Santa Anita race track is here.

Arcadius (ärkä'dēŭs), c.377–408, Roman emperor of the East (395–408), son and successor of Theodosius I. His brother Honorius inherited the West. During his reign ALARIC I invaded Greece and was expelled (395–96) by Stilicho.

Arcagnolo: see ORCAGNA.

Arc de Triomphe de l'Étoile (ärk' dù trēōf' dù lätwäl'), triumphal arch in Paris at end of the Avenue des Champs Élysées and in center of the Place de l'Étoile. Commemorates Napoleon's victories. Built 1806–36 mainly on designs by J. F. Chalgrin, it is 160 ft. high, c.150 ft. wide, and 72 ft. deep, with colossal groups flanking the arch. In 1920 a French unknown soldier was buried beneath it.

Arce, Manuel José (mänwěl' hōsä' är'sä), d. 1847, first president of Central American Federation (1825–29). Ruled arbitrarily.

archaeology (ärkēō'lüje), scientific study of the relics of man found in deposits and ruins. To find, interpret, and preserve materials which delineate prehistoric life and supplement the documentary material of historic eras, modern archaeologists work with various experts and technicians and are often sponsored by museums, organizations, and societies which publish and maintain collections of their findings. Such materials had long been collected, but excavations at HERCULANEUM and POMPEII in the 18th cent., and the discovery of the ROSETTA STONE, inspired systematic research into the historic past. In 1832 C. J. Thomsen showed that cultural stages may be defined according to principal materials used for weapons and implements. These stages, the PALEOLITHIC PERIOD, NEOLITHIC PERIOD, BRONZE AGE, and IRON AGE, indicate the condition of a people, rather than divisions of time. Study of such prehistoric finds as at LA TÈNE and of remains of barrow, KITCHEN MIDDEN, LAKE DWELLING, various mounds, and MEGALITHIC MONUMENTS, have been enhanced by the study of existent aboriginal groups. See GEOLOGY, table.

archaeopteryx (är"kēŏp'türiks), ancient bird. Fossil remains indicate it to be link between reptiles and birds.

Archaeozoic era: see ARCHEOZOIC ERA.

Archangel (ärk'–), Rus. *Arkhangelsk* (ŭrkhän'gĭlsk), city (pop. 281,091), RSFSR, on mouth of Northern Dvina; major White Sea port (ice-free July–Sept.). Chief sawmilling center of USSR. Founded 1583 as Novo-Kholmogory after CHANCELLOR had landed here; renamed 1716. Major supply port in both World Wars; occupied 1918–20 by Allies and White Army.

archangel (ärk'–), chief ANGEL, differing from other angels only in importance. Best known are MICHAEL, GABRIEL, RAPHAEL.

Archbald, mining and industrial borough (pop. 6,304), NE Pa., on Lackawanna R. and NE of Scranton.

Archeozoic era (är"kēŭzō'ĭk), first grand division of geologic time, marked by formation of oldest rocks. One large exposed area is the Canadian Shield (see LAURENTIAN PLATEAU), mainly of gneiss, granite, and schist. Earliest named rock system is the Keewatin, consisting of intermingled lava layers and sediments. No fossils yet discovered have been definitely proved of Archeozoic origin. See GEOLOGY, table.

Archer, William, 1856–1924, English critic. Translated Ibsen; helped G. B. Shaw; wrote popular play *The Green Goddess* (1921); was influential as London *World* dramatic critic.

Archer, the, in astronomy: see ZODIAC.

archery. An important military skill in ancient and medieval times, shooting with bow and arrow was revived as sport (c.1675) by Charles II of England. Archers try to hit inner circle (or "bull's eye") of target composed of concentric circles.

Arches National Monument: see NATIONAL PARKS AND MONUMENTS (table).

Archimedes (ärkĭmē'dēz), 287–212 B.C., Greek mathematician, physicist, inventor. Nine of his famous trea-

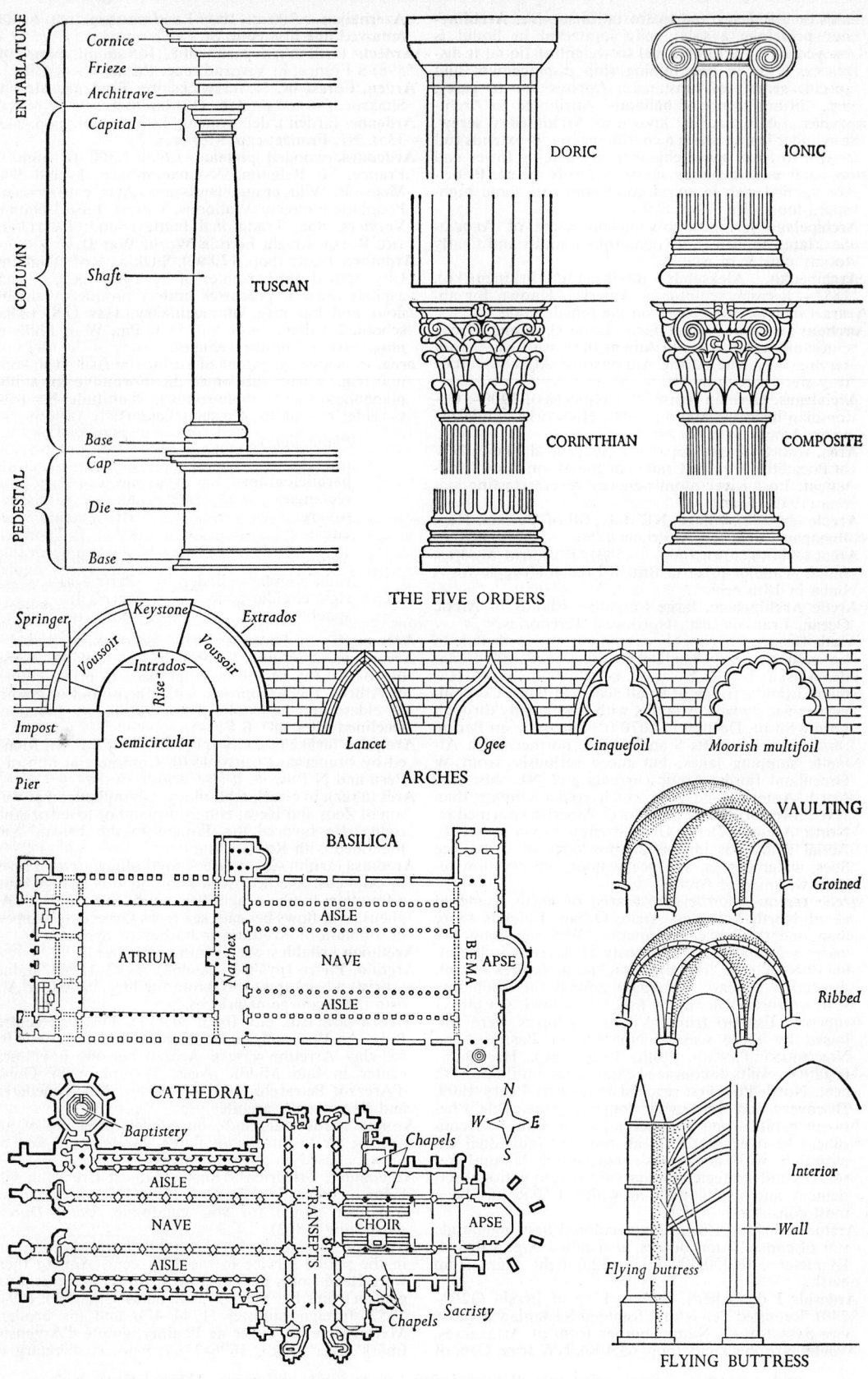

THE FIVE ORDERS

ARCHES

VAULTING

FLYING BUTTRESS

tises on geometry and hydrostatics survive. **Archimedes' principle:** a solid body immersed in liquid is buoyed up by a force equal to weight of liquid it displaces. Used in determining ship displacement and specific gravity of substances. Applies also to gases, e.g., "lifting" force of balloons. Attributed to Archimedes also is machine known as **Archimedes' screw,** a cylinder inside which a continuous screw extends full length to form spiral chamber. By placing lower end in water and revolving screw, water is raised. Principle applied also in spiral conveyors and some high-speed tools. See *ill.*, p. 619.

Archipelago (ärkĭpē′lŭgō), ancient name of AEGEAN SEA, later applied to its numerous islands, and finally to any cluster of islands.

Archipenko, Aleksandr (ŭlyĭksändr′ ärkĭpĕng′kō), 1887–, Russian sculptor in America. Known for abstract figures, often based on the female nude.

archons (är′kŏnz, –kŭnz) [Gr.,= leaders], in anc. Greek cities; officers of state. In Athens there were nine; after serving they entered the AREOPAGUS. After 487 B.C. they were chosen by lot.

Arciniegas, Germán (hĕrmän′ ärsēnyä′gäs), 1900–, Colombian historian and diplomat. His works publicized Latin American history in U.S.

Arco, resort village (pop. 961), SE central Idaho, NW of Pocatello. Hq. for Craters of the Moon Natl. Monument. Lost River atomic-energy reactor testing station (1949) near.

Arcole (är′kōlä), village, NE Italy, SE of Verona. Here Bonaparte defeated Austrians 1796.

Arcot (ärkŏt′), town (pop. 16,583), E central Madras, India. A major prize in British-French struggle for S India in 18th cent.

Arctic Archipelago, large Canadian islands in Arctic Ocean, Franklin dist., Northwest Territories.

Arctic Ocean, sea, roughly circular, from North Pole to lat. c.70°N, nearly landlocked (by Greenland, Canada, Alaska, USSR, Norway), c.5,400,000 sq. mi. Has many islands, fringe of small seas and bays. Communicates widely with Atlantic, with Pacific only through Bering Strait. Deepest (14,070 ft.) near pole on Bering Strait side. Ice drifts S and W into northernmost Atlantic shipping lanes, but more seriously from W Greenland fjords. Arctic currents give NE shores of North America and Asia much colder climate than NW shores of Europe and North America (warmed by North Atlantic Drift, Gulf Stream, Japan Current). Aerial study has increased knowledge of drifts, ice floes, water depths, and ocean floor. Observation reveals warming of Arctic.

arctic regions, northernmost area of earth, centered about North Pole and Arctic Ocean. Extends more than one third way to equator. Weather boundary varies seasonally, set arbitrarily at Arctic Circle (lat. 66°17′N). Under "midnight sun" temperatures mount, vegetation appears. Abundant animal life (including seal, walrus, whale, many fish, water fowl, sea birds) supports ESKIMO tribes. Viking explorers were followed by those seeking NORTHWEST PASSAGE and NORTHEAST PASSAGE (16th, 17th cent.). Hardships, negative results discouraged exploration until late 18th cent. North Pole first reached by Robert Peary 1909. Discovery that shortest air routes ("great circle") between capitals and commercial centers of N Hemisphere lie over Arctic Ocean replaced individual exploration with cooperative enterprise. Natural resources and strategic military value led to national settlement and exploitation in which USSR has been most consistently active.

Arcturus (ärktyŏŏr′ŭs), orange-colored first magnitude star of constellation Boötes, also called Alpha Boötis. Diameter c.18,000,000 mi.; c.32.6 light years from earth.

Ardashir I (ärdäshēr′), d. 240, king of Persia (226?–240). Reunited Persia and founded Sassanian dynasty (see SASSANIDAE). Name another form of Artaxerxes.

Ardebil (ärdŭbēl′), city (pop. 63,406), NW Iran. Cap. of

Azerbaijan c.700–c.1100. Russians took city 1828; removed fine library to St. Petersburg.

Ardèche (ärdĕsh′), department (2,145 sq. mi.; pop. 254,-598) S France, in Vivarais; cap. Privas.

Arden, Forest of, N Warwickshire, England. Most of Shakspere's *As You Like It* is laid here.

Ardennes (ärden′), department (2,078 sq. mi.; pop. 245,-335), NE France; cap. Mézières.

Ardennes, wooded plateau, 1,600–2,300 ft. high, N France, SE Belgium, N Luxembourg, E and S of Meuse R. Wild, craggy landscape. Agr., cattle raising. Population mostly Walloons. Cities: Liége, Namur, Verviers, Spa. Traditional battleground; BATTLE OF THE BULGE fought here in World War II.

Ardmore. 1 City (pop. 17,890), S Okla., S of Oklahoma City; settled 1887. Center of agr., livestock, oil, and asphalt area, it processes cotton products, oil, and flour and has mfg. of machinery. Has U.S. Indian school. **2** Village (pop. 9,015), E Pa., W of Philadelphia. Mfg. of motor vehicles.

area, in geometry, extent of surface measured in some unit (e.g., square feet or acres). Formulae for simple plane figures and simple solids (a = altitude; b = base; s = side; r = radius; l = slant height):

Plane figures	Area
triangle	$ab/2$
parallelogram	ab
rectangle	ab
square	s^2
circle	πr^2

Solids	Total area
right circular cylinder	$2\pi r(r + a)$
right circular cone	$\pi r(r + l)$
sphere	$4\pi r^2$

Areopagite: see DIONYSIUS THE AREOPAGITE, SAINT.

Areopagus (ărēŏ′pŭgŭs), rocky hill NW of the Acropolis of Athens, sacred meeting place of prime council of Athens, the **Areopagus,** which arose out of council of elders and had judicial and legislative functions. Declined after 487 B.C.

Arequipa (äräkē′pä), city (pop. 79,185), S Peru; founded by Francisco Pizarro 1540. Commercial hub of S Peru and N Bolivia, it also draws tourists.

Ares (â′rēz), in Greek mythology, Olympian god of war; son of Zeus and Hera; either husband or lover of Aphrodite. He favored the Trojans in the Trojan War. Identified with Roman Mars.

Arethusa (ărĭthū′sŭ), in Greek mythology, nymph loved by Alpheus. She fled from him and was changed into a fountain, but he caught her; hence the story that Alpheus river flows beneath sea from Greece to reappear in fountain of Arethusa in harbor of Syracuse.

Aretinian syllables: see GUIDO D'AREZZO.

Aretino, Pietro (pyä′trō ärätē′nō), 1492–1556?, Italian satirist, adventurer who wrote for hire, called by Ariosto the "scourge of princes."

Arezzo (ärät′tsō), city (pop. 24,411), Tuscany, central Italy. An Etruscan, later a Roman, town (famous for red-clay Arretine vases), Arezzo became a cultural center in late Middle Ages. Birthplace of Guido d'Arezzo, Petrarch, Aretino, Vasari. Much medieval and Renaissance architecture.

Argand burner (är′gănd), introduced principle of admitting air to interior of flame. Modern gas and oil burners based on this principle.

Argelander, Friedrich Wilhelm August (frē′drĭkh vĭl′-hĕlm ou′gŏŏst är′gŭländŭr), 1799–1875, German astronomer, noted for star catalogue, *Bonn Durchmusterung* (1862).

Argenson (ärzhäsō′), French noble family, prominent in the public service in the 18th cent. Among them were **René Louis de Voyer de Paulmy, marquis d'Argenson** (rŭnä′ lwē dù vwäyä′ dù pōlmē′, märkē′), 1694–1757, foreign minister (1744–47), and his brother, **Marc Pierre de Voyer de Paulmy, comte d'Argenson** (märk′ pyĕr′, kŏt′), 1696–1764, who as secretary of war (1743–57) reformed the army and founded the École militaire. Both brothers were friends of Voltaire and the Encyclopedists.

Argenteuil (ärzhätû'ē), town (pop. 53,513), Seine-et-Oise dept., N France, on the Seine; industrial suburb of Paris. Convent where Heloise was prioress destroyed in French Revolution.

Argentia, N.F.: see PLACENTIA BAY.

Argentina, La, d. 1936, Spanish dancer, whose real name was Antonia Mercé. Revived interest in Spanish classical dance by performances in U.S. 1928.

Argentina (ärjüntē'nù), republic (1,073,699 sq. mi.; pop. 15,893,827), S South America, between Andes and Atlantic; cap. BUENOS AIRES. Second largest South American nation, stretches from subtropics 2,000 mi. S to TIERRA DEL FUEGO. Argentina claims FALKLAND ISLANDS, which are held by British. Towering Andes (crossed by TRANSANDINE RAILWAY; highest peak ACONCAGUA; snow-topped volcanoes) are W border with Chile. Arid Andean highlands and CHACO border Bolivia in NW. Rivers of Río de la PLATA system form boundaries across N: Pilcomayo, Paraguay, Paraná, with Paraguay; Uruguay, with Uruguay and Brazil. In extreme NE, Argentina meets Brazil and Paraguay in Brazilian highlands at IGUASSÚ FALLS. N Argentina, mostly plain, yields QUEBRACHO, MATE, agr. produce. To the S, vast plain of the PAMPA (once the wild home of the GAUCHO; tamed in 19th cent. by Italian immigrants) provides from farms and ranches the basic wealth of Argentina. Chief cities here are Buenos Aires, on Río de la Plata estuary, one of great ports of world; LA PLATA; ROSARIO; SANTA FE; MAR DEL PLATA; BAHÍA BLANCA. On W edge of Pampa is CÓRDOBA. MENDOZA, SAN JUAN, TUCUMÁN, and SALTA are productive oases in arid Andean foothills. In S is PATAGONIA (with COMODORO RIVADAVIA and other oil fields), producing 70% of nation's oil. Argentine pop. is overwhelmingly of European descent (with native Indians in far N and Andean areas only). First European explorers: VESPUCCI (1502), Juan Díaz de SOLÍS (1516), MAGELLAN (1520), Sebastian CABOT. Buenos Aires first founded (1536) by Pedro de MENDOZA, abandoned after Indian attacks, refounded (1580) from Asunción by GARAY. It was finally (1776) made cap. of Spanish vice-royalty. From 1810 to 1816, successful struggle for Argentine independence led by patriot generals BELGRANO, MORENO, PUEYRREDÓN, and (most distinguished) SAN MARTÍN. Civil war lasted until harsh dictatorship (1829–32, 1835–52) of Juan Manuel de ROSAS, who was opposed by intellectuals (e.g., SARMIENTO, ALBERDI), defeated by URQUIZA. New constitution in 1853. Under MITRE, Sarmiento, and Nicolás Avellaneda schools were built, liberal reforms started. In 1880 long struggle between centralism and federalism settled in favor of federal system. Conquest (1878–79) of Indians by Roca opened S and SW to European immigration. Argentina became one of world's granaries, and industry developed, aided by British. Refrigerating plants for meat forwarded commerce. Argentine-Chilean boundary dispute settled 1902; perpetual peace symbolized by CHRIST OF THE ANDES. Politics showed military tradition and conflict. In 1946 Juan D. PERÓN established a new type of Latin American dictatorship, supported by workers, nationalists, reactionaries, clericals, army. Argentina remained neutral in World War I, belatedly entered World War II on side of Allies, and became (1945) member of UN.

Arginusae, battle of (ärjĭnū'sē), 406 B.C., last Athenian naval victory in the PELOPONNESIAN WAR, off the Arginusae Isls., near Asia Minor. A storm caused six Athenian ships to founder. The commanders' failure to rescue the crews was used as a pretext by their political enemies to have them executed. A son of Pericles was among the victims.

Argo (är'gō), in Greek mythology, ship in which the Argonauts sailed to find the GOLDEN FLEECE.

argol: see TARTAR.

Argolis (är'gùlĭs), region of anc. Greece, in NE Peloponnesus, around Argive plain; dominated by city of Argos.

argon (är'gŏn), colorless, odorless, tasteless, inert gaseous element (symbol = A; see also ELEMENT, table). Occurs in air and some volcanic gases. Used in electric-light bulbs, electric signs.

Argonaut (är'gùnôt'') [Gr.,= sailor on Argo], in Greek mythology, one of band led by JASON who went to Colchis in quest of GOLDEN FLEECE. Among the voyagers were Argus, Orpheus, Hercules, and the huntress Atalanta. Voyage was interrupted for a year while they tarried on Lemnos. The ship safely passed the Symplegades (floating cliffs) and also SCYLLA and CHARYBDIS, and the mariners escaped the wiles of the Sirens' singing.

Argonne (är'gŏn, Fr. ärgôn'), hilly and wooded region, NE France, in Champagne and Lorraine. French repulsed Prussians here at Valmy 1792. In World War I, the Meuse-Argonne sector was carried by U.S. troops Sept.–Nov., 1918.

Argos, in Greek legend: see ARGUS.

Argos (är'gŏs, –gùs), city of anc. Greece, NE Peloponnesus, near modern Nauplia. Center of Argolis, it struggled with Sparta and rivaled Athens and Corinth. Taken by Sparta (c.494 B.C.). Flourished under Rome after 146 B.C.

Arguedas, Alcides (älsē'däs ärgä'däs), 1879–, Bolivian novelist. Deep interest in Bolivian social ills expressed in *Un pueblo enfermo* (1910).

Argun (ärgōōn'), river, 980 mi. long, NE Asia, a headstream of the Amur. Forms part of border between USSR and Manchuria.

Argus (är'gùs) or **Argos** (är'gŏs, –gùs), in Greek myth. **1** The hundred-eyed guardian of Io, ancestor of people of Argos. **2** Son of Phrixus. Builder of the ARGO and an Argonaut. **3** Dog of Odysseus, first creature to welcome him home.

Argyll, dukes of, earls of, and **marquesses of,** Scottish nobles: see the family name, CAMPBELL.

Argyllshire (ärgīl'shĭr) or **Argyll,** maritime county (3,110 sq. mi.; pop. 63,270), W Scotland; co. town Inverary. Includes numerous islands of Inner Hebrides. Wild and mountainous, has agr. on coast only. One of chief sheep-raising areas of British Isles. Iona has remains of ancient monastic center.

Argyrokastron (äryērō'kästrôn), Albanian *Argirokastra,* city (pop. 10,910), S Albania, above Drin R. Its old castle was rebuilt (19th cent.) by Ali Pasha. Held by Greeks 1940–41 during World War II.

Arhus, Denmark: see AARHUS.

aria, air or melody, especially an accompanied solo in an opera, oratorio, or cantata. The *aria da capo* has a contrasting, usually shorter, middle section followed by a repetition of the first section.

Ariadne (ăreăd'nē), in Greek legend, Cretan princess, daughter of Minos and Pasiphaë. Gave THESEUS thread to guide him out of Labyrinth after he slew Minotaur. He took her away with him but deserted her.

Arianism, heretical movement arising from teaching of Arius (c.256–336), a Libyan theologian, priest in Alexandria. He advanced the doctrine that before the general creation God had created and begotten a Son, the first creature, but neither eternal nor equal with the Father. This idea spread, and the unity of Christendom was threatened by the resultant conflict. Emperor Constantine called the First Council of NICAEA, where ATHANASIUS vigorously opposed Arius and won a victory. Arianism was condemned, but the matter had become political as well as religious. Arius, condemned locally in 321 and anathematized by the council, was brought back from exile (335). The conflict went on, with whole groups of bishops being exiled by emperors favoring one or the other party. The Arians split into three groups, mutually antagonistic. Finally the doctrines favored by Athanasius and Rome triumphed. Theodosius made Catholicism the state religion. Arianism had, however, been carried to the

Goths and Vandals, and it survived in Africa until the 6th cent., in Visigothic Spain until the 7th. Contrary to popular belief, Arianism had nothing to do with the split between Eastern and Western Churches or with Protestantism.

Arias de Ávila, Pedro (pä′dhrō ä′ryäs dä ä′vēlä), known as **Pedrarias** (pädhrä′ryäs), c.1440–1531?, Spanish colonial administrator. Sent (1514) as governor of Darien, he had BALBOA executed, was notoriously cruel. Extended Spanish dominions; founded Panama city (1519). Went to Nicaragua (1526) and held power until death.

Arias de Saavedra, Hernando (ĕrnän′dō ä′ryäs dä sävä′drä), known as **Hernandarias** (ĕrnändä′ryäs), 1561–1634, b. Asunción. First American-born governor of Río de la Plata prov., he was able administrator.

Arica (ärē′kä), city (pop. 14,064), N Chile, Pacific port won from Peru in War of the Pacific (1879–84). In settlement of Tacna-Arica controversy (1929), Chile was required to furnish port facilities to Peru. Subject to earthquake.

Ariège (äryĕzh′), department (1,893 sq. mi.; pop. 145,956), SW France, in Pyrenees; cap. Foix.

Aries [Lat.,= ram], first sign of ZODIAC.

Arikara Indians (ürĭ′kürü), North American tribe, formerly on Missouri R., of Caddoan linguistic stock. Semisedentary, they hunted buffalo and grew maize.

Ariminium: see RIMINI, Italy.

Arion (ürĭ′ŭn), legendary Greek poet, inventor of the DITHYRAMB (supposedly 7th cent. B.C.).

Ariosto, Ludovico (loōodōvĕ′kō äryōs′tō), 1474–1533, Italian epic and lyric poet, famous for his *Orlando Furioso* (1532), epic treatment of the Roland story, a sequel to the unfinished poem of BOIARDO. Written for his patrons, the Este family, *Orlando Furioso* combines irony and grandeur and is called the greatest Renaissance poem.

Ariovistus (â″rēōvĭ′stŭs), fl. 58 B.C., Germanic chieftain, leader of the Suebi. Came to dominate much of GAUL, and in 60 B.C. became a friend and ally of Rome, but his power threatened Roman rule in Gaul, and Caesar defeated and drove him out (58).

Aristarchus of Samos (ăr″ĭstär′kŭs, sā′mŏs), 3d cent. B.C. Greek astronomer of Alexandrian school. One of first to conclude that earth moves around sun and to state causes of day and night and of change of seasons.

Aristides (ărĭstī′dēz), d. c.468 B.C., Athenian statesman and general. Ostracized by Themistocles, he was recalled and commanded the fleet in victory over the Persians at Plataea (479 B.C.). Later organized Delian League. Called Aristides the Just.

Aristides, probably two Greek painters, often confused. One was of the 5th cent. B.C., the other of the 4th cent. B.C.

aristocracy (ăr″ĭstŏk′rŭsē), in political science, government by best in interest of all. All governments contain an aristocratic element since rulers are thought best fitted for rule. Aristocracy usually based on landed possessions (flourishing chiefly within monarchy), sometimes on wealth (e.g., medieval Venice).

Aristogiton: see HARMODIUS AND ARISTOGITON.

Aristophanes (ăr″ĭstŏf′ŭnēz), b. c.448, d. after 388 B.C., greatest Greek poet of COMEDY. His plays, only full samples of the Greek Old Comedy, mix political, social, and literary satire. Among surviving eleven plays are: *The Clouds, The Wasps, The Birds, Lysistrata,* and *The Frogs.*

Aristotle (ăr″ĭstŏt′ŭl), 384–322 B.C., Greek philosopher, b. Stagira (hence the Stagirite). Studied under Plato (366–347 B.C.), later tutored Alexander the Great (343–336 B.C.), and finally founded Peripatetic school in the Lyceum at Athens. His extant works are *Organon* (six treatises on logic), *Metaphysics, Physics, On the Heavens, History of Animals, On the Parts of Animals, On the Soul, Politics, Nichomachean Ethics, Rhetoric,* and *Poetics.* Like Plato, Aristotle saw the universe as an ideal world, but they differed as to the relation of form and matter, Aristotle arguing that

these were inseparable. This union became a principle by which he explained all growth, all movement. Motion and change are the realization of form in matter. In scientific works he differed from Plato in using close observation and accurate classification of nature. His analysis of nature into four elements, earth, air, fire, and water, perpetuated a common Greek error. His ethics argue that the goodness of a thing lies in realization of its specific nature, and for man this consisted of the exercise of man's rational faculty through agency of the golden mean. The *Poetics* (which, like all his works, was revered by many later generations) explained the imitative and cathartic nature of tragic poetry and set the unities as formal elements of tragedy.

arithmetic, elementary and anc. branch of mathematics. Includes calculation (concrete, practical, or elementary arithmetic) and theory of numbers (abstract, theoretical, or higher arithmetic). Both deal with number behavior in four basic operations: ADDITION, SUBTRACTION, MULTIPLICATION, DIVISION; and operations of involution, evolution. Higher arithmetic generalizes number concept to include complex numbers, quaternions, tensors, abstract entities.

Arius, theologian: see ARIANISM.

Arizona, state (113,580 sq. mi.; pop. 749,587), SW U.S.; admitted 1912 as 48th state; cap. PHOENIX. TUCSON other main city. In COLORADO R. drainage basin; river forms most of W boundary. Has mountains, plateaus, chasms (GRAND CANYON), deserts (PAINTED DESERT), scenic wonders (Petrified Forest), Indian ruins. Mining (copper, gold, silver, lead, zinc), farming, cattle raising. Lack of rainfall necessitates irrigation projects. Main industry is mining and processing of copper. Spanish first came 1539–40. Missions founded by Eusebio KINO in 1690s. Became part of U.S. by Treaty of GUADALUPE HIDALGO (1848) and GADSDEN PURCHASE (1853); made a territory in 1863. Warfare with the Apache troubled region (1861–86). Tourist trade has become quite important.

Arizona, University of: see TUCSON.

ark, in Bible. **1** Boat built by NOAH to save his family and some animals from Deluge. Gen. 6–9; Luke 17.27; Heb. 11.7; 1 Peter 3.20. **2** Wooden chest, overlaid with gold, known as Ark of the Covenant, sacred symbol of early Hebrews, representative of God. Touching it was a desecration punishable by death. Its presence implied victory, so was carried into battle by poles thrust through rings on its sides. Taken by Philistines, it brought them disaster and was sent back to Israel. Brought by David to Jerusalem, placed in Temple by Solomon. Since lost from view. Possibly held tables of Ten Commandments. Ex. 25.10–21; Num. 10.33–36; Deut. 10.1–5; Joshua 3–6; 1 Sam. 4–7; 2 Sam. 6; 15.24,29; 1 Kings 8.3,9; 1 Chron. 13; 15–16.6; 2 Chron. 5; Jer. 3.16; Heb. 9.4.

Arkadelphia (ärkŭdĕl′fĕu), city (pop. 6,819), SW Ark., on Ouachita R., in timber and agr. area. Seat of Ouachita Col.

Arkansas (är′kŭnsô″), state (52,725 sq. mi.; pop. 1,909,511), S central U.S., admitted 1836 as 25th state (slaveholding); cap. LITTLE ROCK. Other major cities are FORT SMITH, PINE BLUFF, HOT SPRINGS, TEXARKANA. Bounded on E by Mississippi R. Mississippi alluvial plains S and E; OZARK MOUNTAINS in NW. Has ARKANSAS R., SAINT FRANCIS R., WHITE RIVER, OUACHITA R., RED RIVER. Produces cotton, corn, rice, grains, truck, livestock, timber, petroleum, bauxite, coal. Industries based on processing of raw materials. QUAPAW INDIANS lived here. Hernando De Soto led first white men into region in 1541–42. Trading center at Arkansas Post estab. by French 1686. Part of French territory, region was ceded to Spain (1762) and back to France before going to U.S. in Louisiana Purchase. 1818 cotton boom brought many settlers. Became territory 1819. Joined Confederacy 1861. State not readmitted to Union until 1868. Reconstruction turbulent. Depression of 1930s hit cotton economy hard, causing much migration (esp. to Calif.). World War II caused further population loss, also boomed new industries (esp. aluminum). Has growing tourist trade.

Arkansas (ärkăn'zŭs, är'kŭnsô"), river rising in the Rockies of central Colo. and flowing c.1,500 mi. SE, across Colo., Kansas, Okla., and Ark., to the Mississippi between Memphis, Tenn., and Vicksburg, Miss. Bridged at Royal Gorge canyon (granite walls rise sharply to over 1,000 ft.), Colo. Receives Cimarron and Canadian rivers in Okla. Passes through Wichita (Kansas), Tulsa (Okla.), and Little Rock (Ark.). Flood-control, irrigation, and power project on river and its tributaries includes John Martin Dam (153 ft. high, 13,946 ft. long, completed 1948), Colo., and others. Cotton, rice, wheat, sugar beets, and fruit are grown in river's valley. There are also oil refining and coal mining.

Arkansas, University of: see FAYETTEVILLE.

Arkansas City, city (pop. 12,903), S Kansas, SSE of Wichita at junction of Arkansas and Walnut rivers; laid out 1870. Refines and ships oil.

Arkansas Post, community, SE Ark., on Arkansas R. and SE of Little Rock; founded 1686 by French; oldest white settlement in state. Confederate stronghold until captured by Gen. McClernand (1863).

Arkhangelsk, RSFSR: see ARCHANGEL.

Ark of the Covenant: see ARK.

Arkwright, Sir Richard, 1732–92, English inventor. His construction of a spinning machine (patented 1769) an early step in the INDUSTRIAL REVOLUTION.

Arlberg (ärl'bĕrk), pass, 5,910 ft. high, W Austria, near Arlberg peak. Arlberg Tunnel is 6½ mi. long.

Arles (ärl), city (pop. 20,138), Bouches-du-Rhône dept., SE France, in Provence, on Rhone delta. Silk mfg., wine trade. A flourishing Roman town (Arelas) and the metropolis of Gaul under late empire, it became the cap. of medieval kingdom of Arles and was the site of many Church councils and a center of Provençal culture. Roman remains include huge arena, theater. Church of St. Trophime was begun 11th cent. Arles was damaged in World War II.

Arles, kingdom of, formed 933 when Rudolph II united his kingdom of Transjurane BURGUNDY with the kingdom of PROVENCE or Cisjurane Burgundy. Emperor Conrad II joined it to Holy Roman Empire in 1033. Government by imperial vicars was nominal; France, Savoy, Switzerland, and Burgundy held actual control over component territories. After the dauphin (later Charles VI of France) was made vicar in 1378, the kingdom survived only in theory.

Arlington, Henry Bennet, 1st earl of, 1618–85, English courtier. Under Charles II was a secretary of state and member of unscrupulous CABAL ministry.

Arlington. 1 Residential town (pop. 44,353), E Mass., NW suburb of Boston; settled c.1630. **2** See POUGHKEEPSIE, N.Y. **3** Village (pop. 5,085), S N.C., W of Gastonia. **4** City (pop. 7,692), N Texas, E of Fort Worth. Market and industrial center of agr. area. Seat of North Texas Agricultural Col. (branch of Agricultural and Mechanical Col. of Texas). **5** Uninc. town, N Va., on Potomac R. (bridged) opposite Washington, D.C. Here are government offices, ARLINGTON NATIONAL CEMETERY, and Lee Mansion National Memorial.

Arlington Heights, residential village (pop. 8,768), NE Ill., just NW of Chicago. Has race track.

Arlington National Cemetery, 408 acres, N Va., on Potomac R. opposite Washington, D.C.; estab. 1864, extended 1889 and 1897. Here are graves of c.60,000 war dead, tomb of Unknown Soldier, and marble amphitheatre. Cemetery is part of "Arlington," former estate of Custis and Lee families.

Arliss, George, 1868–1946, English stage and film actor. Had his first great success (1911) in the title role of *Disraeli*. Later appeared in such plays as *The Green Goddess* and *Old English*. Repeated many of his stage triumphs in moving pictures.

Armada, Spanish (ärmä'dŭ), 1588, fleet launched by Philip II of Spain against England; called also Invincible Armada. Consisting of c.130 ships and 30,000 men, and commanded by duke of Medina Sidonia, it was to go to Flanders and from there convoy the army of Alessandro Farnese to invade England and seize the throne for Philip. The Armada set out from Lisbon in May, was delayed at Coruña, and in July, at Plymouth, found the English fleet, under Charles Howard (later earl of Nottingham). Among the English captains were Sir Francis Drake, Sir John Hawkins, and Sir Martin Frobisher. Forced up the English Channel, the Armada suffered losses in several engagements, but escaped north with favorable wind. Only half the fleet reached home; the rest was dispersed by storms off Ireland and its crews killed or captured by the Irish.

armadillo (ärmŭdĭl'ō), mammal of order Edentata, found from Patagonia northward to parts of S and SW U.S. Armor of bone and horny material almost covers head and body; tail has bony rings. Is omnivorous but eats chiefly insects. Nine-banded armadillo (*Dasypus*), only U.S. species. Flesh palatable.

Armageddon (–gĕd'ŭn), great battlefield, to be site of final conflict between powers of good and evil. Rev. 16.16. Name may come from MEGIDDO.

Armagh (ärmä'), inland county (449 sq. mi.; pop. 114,-226), N. Ireland. Mainly a farming region, also noted for its linen. County town is **Armagh,** urban district (pop. 9,279), religious center of Ireland. St. Patrick was bishop here 5th cent. Seat of Roman Catholic and Protestant archbishoprics.

Armagnac (ärmänyäk'), region and former county, SW France, in Gascony; historic cap. Auch. Produces brandy. Added to royal domain 1607.

Armagnacs and Burgundians, opposing factions in 15th-cent. France. Their struggle arose out of rivalry of Louis d'ORLÉANS and JOHN THE FEARLESS of Burgundy. After Louis's murder (1407) his followers were led by BERNARD VII, count of Armagnac—hence their nickname. The Burgundians—followers of John the Fearless—were strong in Paris, where the radical CABOCHIENS supported them. Civil war broke out (1411) and merged after 1415 with the HUNDRED YEARS WAR. In 1418 the Burgundians seized Paris and massacred the Armagnacs; in 1419 the Armagnacs murdered John the Fearless. The Burgundians now became full allies of England, while the Armagnacs, led by the dauphin (later Charles VII), represented the national party.

armature. 1 Part of electric GENERATOR and MOTOR. Coil of wire that rotates in magnetic field between opposite magnetic poles and cuts magnetic lines of force between them, generating current in coil. **2** Piece of iron or steel, called a keeper, placed between or across poles of magnet to prevent decrease in magnetic property.

Armenia (ärmē'nèù), region and former kingdom of Asia Minor. Roughly includes E Turkey and ARMENIAN SOVIET SOCIALIST REPUBLIC. Tradition says kingdom was founded in region of Lake Van by Haig or Haik, descendant of Noah. A battleground of Assyrians, Medes, and Persians, it became a Persian satrapy c.6th cent. B.C. Conquered 4th cent. B.C. by Alexander the Great; later ruled by Seleucus I. Was independent kingdom from 189 B.C. to 69 B.C., when it fell to Rome. Armenia is oldest Christian state. After 3d cent., when region was under Persian rule, Armenian Christians suffered much persecution. Enjoyed autonomy 885–1046 under the native Bagratids. Reconquered 1046 by the Byzantines, who were ousted by Seljuk Turks. Pushed westward, an Armenian group estab. kingdom of Little Armenia in CILICIA. Greater Armenia was occupied 1386–94 by Tamerlane. All Armenia was under Turkish rule by 16th cent., but E Armenia was claimed also by Persia, who lost it to Russia in 1828. Congress of Berlin (1878) gave some Armenian territory to Russia, but much of it was restored 1921 to Turkey. Armenians were sporadically massacred by the Turks 1894–1915. Treaty of Brest-Litovsk (1918), which made Russian Armenia independent under German auspices, was superseded by Treaty of Sèvres (1920) which created independent Greater Armenia (comprising Turkish and Russian parts), but in same year Communists proclaimed Russian Armenia a Soviet Republic. With Russo-Turkish treaty (1921) marking present boundaries Armenian independence was ended.

Armenian Church, group that split from the orthodox Christians in 4th cent. and accepted (5th cent.) some doctrines of MONOPHYSITISM. Liturgical language is Classical Armenian. In 1198 the Cilician Armenians reunited with the Holy See but have kept close relations with Armenian Church to the present.

Armenian language, subfamily of Indo-European languages. See LANGUAGE (table).

Armenian literature. First work (c.5th cent.), a translation of Bible, became standard of Classical Armenian. Armenian Church fostered literature, mostly saints' lives and histories. Among secular works were translations of Aristotle and the romance of Alexander. History of Moses of Khorni is main source on pre-Christain Armenia. Catholicos Narses IV, 12th cent. prelate and poet, had unexcelled literary style. In 12th cent. vernacular came into use for contemporary topics. In 18th cent. Mechitar, Catholic Armenian monk, founded monastic literary community at Constantinople. The Mechitarists, now centered at Venice, publish works in Armenian.

Armenian Soviet Socialist Republic, constituent republic (11,500 sq. mi.; pop. c.1,345,000), USSR, in S Transcaucasia, bordering on Turkey and Iran; cap. Erivan. Mountainous (Mt. Aragats, 13,435 ft., is highest peak), it has good pastures. Valleys are artificially irrigated. Main products are wine, cotton, wool, copper. Hydroelectric power from L. Sevan. A part of ancient ARMENIA, territory was taken by Russia from Persia in 1828.

Armentières (ärmŭntērz´, Fr. ärmätyēr´), town (pop. 18,691), Nord dept., N France, on Lys R. Famous for World War I song, *Mademoiselle from Armentières*.

Arminius (ärmĭ´nēŭs), d. A.D. 21?, leader of the Germans. When Romans pushed E from the Rhine, Arminius, ex-Roman citizen and soldier, gathered a great force and destroyed the army of P. Quintilius VARUS. Rome never again tried to conquer E of Rhine. In German he is Hermann.

Arminius, Jacobus, 1560–1609, Dutch Reformed theologian (originally Jacob Harmensen), professor at Leiden after 1603. Arminianism, as fully formulated later by Simon Episcopius, opposed predestination and was in favor of election and doctrine of the Wesleys and Methodist Church.

Armitage, Edward, 1817–96, English historical and religious painter.

armor, protective covering in warfare for persons, horses, vehicles, naval vessels, and aircraft. Body armor was known to many peoples, and metal armor became elaborate in the Middle Ages. Increased emphasis on mobile warfare and introduction of firearms (16th cent.) reduced importance of armor almost to zero, but in 20th cent. steel helmet was reintroduced, and the TANK and armor plate for ships and aircraft became important. Many experiments were made in World War II in personal armor. See *ill.,* p. 53.

Armorica: see BRITTANY.

Armour Institute of Technology: see CHICAGO, Ill.

Arms, John Taylor, 1887–, American etcher, noted for studies of medieval architecture.

Armstrong, Edwin Howard, 1890–, American engineer. Radio contributions include regenerative circuit; superheterodyne circuit (basis for design of most receivers); super-regenerative circuit; development of "wide-swing" frequency modulation.

Armstrong, John, 1758–1843, American army officer, U.S. Secretary of War (1813–14). Held responsible for disasters in War of 1812; resigned in disfavor.

Armstrong, Samuel Chapman, 1839–93, American educator and philanthropist. A major general of the Union army, he later helped found (1868) and was head of Hampton Normal and Agricultural Inst. (now Hampton Inst.).

Armstrong, William George, 1810–1900, English inventor of a breech-loading gun with rifle-bored barrel. His firm became Vickers, Armstrong, Ltd.

army worm, striped green, brown, and yellow larva of a noctuid moth; in North America, found E of Rocky Mts. Moving in hordes, they ravage crops; controlled by poisoning and trapping in ditches.

Arnaud, Henri (ārē´ ärnō´), 1641–1721, Savoyard pastor, leader of WALDENSES at home and in exile.

Arnauld (ärnō´), French family involved in JANSENISM. Also Arnaut, Arnault. **(Marie) Angélique (de Sainte Madeleine)** (äzhälēk´), 1591–1661, was abbess of PORT-ROYAL. Under the influence of St. Francis de Sales, she reformed her abbey. Later DUVERGIER DE HAURANNE led her to adopt Jansenist ideas. Her younger brother, **Antoine Arnauld** (ätwän´), 1612–94, was a Jansenist controversialist, author of *De la fréquente communion* (1643), collaborator in famous Port-Royal textbooks. His older brother, **Robert Arnauld d'Andilly** (rōbĕr´, dädēyē´), 1588–1674, translated religious writings and wrote poetry.

Arnhem (är´nùm), municipality (pop. 97,350) and city, cap. of Gelderland prov., E Netherlands; a port on the Lower Rhine. Industrial center. In Sept., 1944, British troops landed here in a huge Allied airborne operation; isolated, they made a heroic stand and lost two thirds of their strength before they were evacuated.

Arnhem Land, aboriginal reservation, area 31,200 sq. mi., Northern Territory, Australia, on a peninsula W of Gulf of Carpentaria.

Arnim, Achim von (äkh´ĭm fŭn är´nĭm), 1781–1831, German romantic writer. Published, with brother-in-law Clemens BRENTANO, collection of folk songs, *Des Knaben Wunderhorn* [the boy's magic horn] (1806–8). *Isabella von Ägypten* (1812; Eng. tr., 1927), a short novel, is his best-known work. His wife, **Bettina von Arnim** (bĕtē´nä), 1785–1859, is also known under her maiden name, Elisabeth Brentano. A friend of Beethoven and, supposedly, of Goethe, she wrote the unreliable *Goethe's Correspondence with a Child* (1835; Eng. tr., 1837).

Arno (är´nō), river, 150 mi. long, central Italy. Flows past Florence, Pisa into Tyrrhenian Sea.

Arnold, Benedict, 1741–1801, American Revolutionary general and traitor. Took part in QUEBEC CAMPAIGN and SARATOGA CAMPAIGN. Plot to betray West Point to British failed with capture of John ANDRÉ. Arnold escaped and fought for British.

Arnold, Sir Edwin, 1832–1904, English poet, author of a long blank-verse epic on Buddha, *The Light of Asia* (1879).

Arnold, H(enry) H(arley), 1886–1950, American general, chief of Army Air Forces (1941–46). Called Hap or Happy Arnold.

Arnold, Matthew, 1822–88, English poet and critic; son of Thomas Arnold. Inspector of elementary schools 1851–86, he became (1857) professor of poetry at Oxford. Believed poetry should be objective, but his own poetry showed romantic pessimism (e.g., "Dover Beach"; elegy for A. H. Clough, "Thyrsis"; "The Scholar Gypsy"). Also wrote "Rugby Chapel" (on his father), long narratives (e.g., "Sohrab and Rustum"), and many lyrics. His criticism, based on classical standards, was mostly directed against "Barbarians" (the aristocracy) and "Philistines" (the bourgeoisie); he was the apostle of "culture."

Arnold, Thomas, 1795–1842, English educator; father of Matthew Arnold, grandfather of Mrs. Humphry Ward. As headmaster at Rugby (1827–42) he gave new life to whole English public school system by reforms (adding mathematics, modern languages to course of study; introducing monitorial system; encouraging independent thought). Also classical schol-

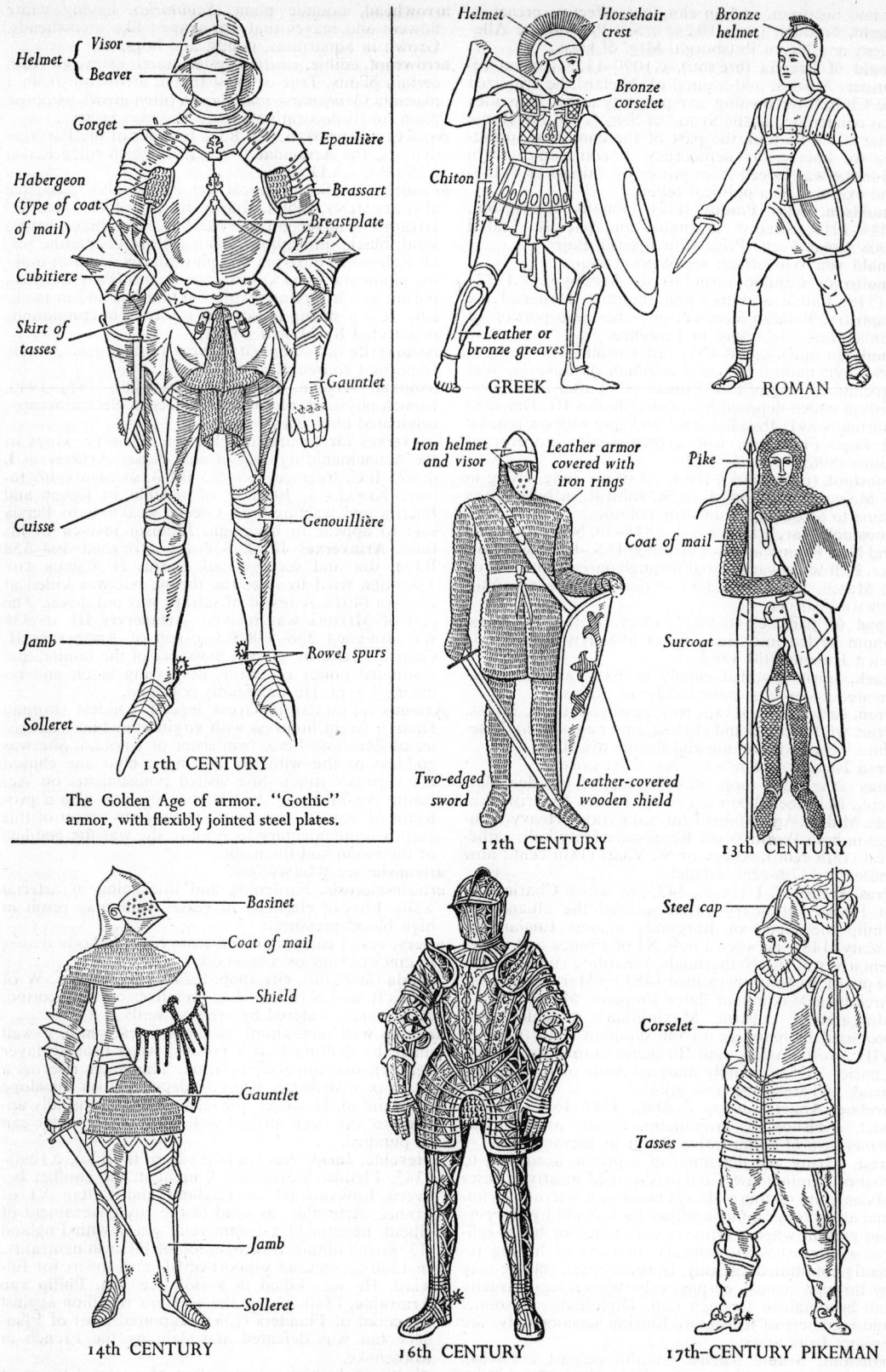

15th CENTURY

Helmet { Visor, Beaver }
Gorget
Epaulière
Habergeon (type of coat of mail)
Brassart
Breastplate
Cubitiere
Skirt of tasses
Gauntlet
Cuisse
Genouillière
Jamb
Rowel spurs
Solleret

The Golden Age of armor. "Gothic" armor, with flexibly jointed steel plates.

GREEK

Helmet
Horsehair crest
Bronze corselet
Chiton
Leather or bronze greaves

ROMAN

Bronze helmet

12th CENTURY

Iron helmet and visor
Leather armor covered with iron rings
Two-edged sword
Leather-covered wooden shield

13th CENTURY

Pike
Coat of mail
Surcoat

14th CENTURY

Basinet
Coat of mail
Shield
Gauntlet
Jamb
Solleret

Metal plates were added for protection at vital spots.

16th CENTURY

Gunpowder, introduced in the 14th century, outdated armor, which became increasingly elaborate, decorative, and nonfunctional.

17th-CENTURY PIKEMAN

Steel cap
Corselet
Tasses

Even these remnants of steel plate disappeared by the end of the century.

ar and historian, and an eloquent, effective preacher.

Arnold, borough (pop. 10,263), SW Pa., on the Allegheny and NE of Pittsburgh. Mfg. of glass.

Arnold of Brescia (brĕ'shü), c.1090–1155, Italian reformer. A priest and a pupil of Abelard, he criticized the Church for owning any property at all. This idea was condemned at the Synod of Sens (1140). In Rome after 1145, he took the part of the commune, pleading for liberty and democracy. Excommunicated in 1148, he was forced from power by Adrian IV (1155) and executed as a political rebel.

Arnoldson, Klas Pontus (kläs' pôn'tùs är'nôldsōn), 1844–1916, Swedish journalist and pacifist. Shared 1908 Nobel Peace Prize with Fredrik Bajer.

Arnold von Winkelried: see WINKELRIED.

Arnolfo di Cambio (ärnōl'fō dē käm'byō), c.1232–c.1310, Italian architect and sculptor. Designed the Baptistry, Palazzo Vecchio, and the basic portion of Santa Maria del Fiore in Florence.

Arnulf (är'nŭlf), c.850–899, last Carolingian emperor (896–99); natural son of Carloman of Bavaria. Was proclaimed king of East Franks (887) after leading rebellion which deposed his uncle Charles III. Defeated Normans 891. Invaded Italy 894 and 895 on request of Pope Formosus, who crowned him emperor at Rome (896).

Aroostook (ùrōōs'tŏŏk), river, c.140 mi. long, rising in N Maine and winding E to St. John R. in N.B. Gives name to a county famous for potatoes.

Aroostook War, brief conflict, 1838–39, between Maine and New Brunswick over disputed U.S.–Canadian border. Full-scale war averted through agreement reached in March, 1839. Boundary settled by WEBSTER-ASHBURTON TREATY.

Arpad (ŏr'päd), c.840–907?, chief of the MAGYARS, whom he led into Hungary in 895. His descendants ruled Hungary till 1301.

arrack, spirits distilled chiefly in Far East from fermented juices (e.g., palm toddy) or grains.

Arran, earls of: see HAMILTON, JAMES; STUART, JAMES.

Arran, wild rocky island (165 sq. mi.; pop. 4,506), Buteshire, Scotland; hunting and fishing resort.

Arran Islands, Ireland: see ARAN ISLANDS.

Arras (äräs'), city (pop. 30,065), cap. of Pas-de-Calais dept., N France; historic cap. of Artois. Flourished in late Middle Ages (famed for TAPESTRY). Heavy damage in both World Wars. Renaissance city hall; cathedral (18th cent.); Abbey of St. Vaast (18th cent.; now museum); 17th-cent. citadel.

Arras, Treaty of. 1 Treaty, 1435, by which Charles VII of France, at heavy costs, secured the alliance of Philip the Good of Burgundy against England. **2** Treaty, 1482, between Louis XI of France and representatives of the Netherlands, regarding succession to MARY OF BURGUNDY; ratified 1483 by Mary's widower, Archduke Maximilian (later Emperor Maximilian I). Margaret of Austria, Maximilian's daughter, was promised in marriage to the dauphin (later Charles VIII), with Artois and Franche-Comté as dowry. Charles VIII eventually married Anne of Brittany instead, and treaty became void.

Arreboe, Anders (än'ùrs ä'rùbō), 1587–1637, Danish poet, a bishop of Trondheim, author of the *Hexaemeron* (1661), narrative poem in alexandrines.

arrest, seizure and detention of a person according to civil or criminal law. Civil arrest, used mostly in cases of contempt of court, always requires a warrant. Criminal arrest may be made without a warrant by any person present when a crime is committed or by an officer who reasonably suspects someone of having recently committed a felony. In some cases, release may be through habeas corpus; otherwise release usually can be obtained through bail. Diplomatic personnel and members of legislature (during sessions only) are exempt from arrest.

Arrhenius, Svante August (sfän'tù ou'gŭst ärä'nēŭs), 1859–1927, Swedish chemist. Won 1903 Nobel Prize for ionization theory; worked on osmosis, toxins.

arrowhead, aquatic plant (*Sagittaria*), having white flowers and leaves that are shaped like arrowheads. Grown in aquariums, ponds, and bogs.

arrowroot, edible, easily digested starch extracted from certain plants. True or West Indian arrowroot from a maranta (*Maranta arundinacea*), often grown as house plant for its decorative foliage. See also TAPIOCA.

Arsaces (är'sùsēz), fl. 250 B.C., founder of the Parthian dynasty, the **Arsacidae** (–sä'sĭdē"), which ruled Persia c.250 B.C.–A.D. 226.

arsenic (är'sùnĭk), chemical element (symbol = As; see also ELEMENT, table). Known in three forms (see ALLOTROPY): silver-gray crystalline, metallike, brittle solid; black, amorphous form; yellow, crystalline solid. Related to nitrogen and phosphorus. Used in making pigments, weed killers, insecticides (PARIS GREEN), poison gas; in dyeing textiles, in tanning, and in medicine. It is a strong poison. Its presence in compounds is detected by MARSH'S TEST.

arsenopyrite (är"sĭnōpī'rīt), silvery to steel-gray PYRITE. Important source of arsenic.

Arsonval, Arsène d' (ärsĕn' därsōväl'), 1851–1940, French physicist, physician. Pioneer in electrotherapy; originated term *diathermy*.

Artaxerxes (är"tùzûrk'sēz), Persian *Ardashir*, kings of the Achaemenid dynasty of anc. Persia. **Artaxerxes I,** d. 425 B.C. (reigned 465–425 B.C.), succeeded his father, XERXES I. Because of trouble in Egypt and Bactria and warfare with Greeks weakness of Persia said to appear in his reign. Judaism revived in his time. **Artaxerxes II,** d. 358 B.C. (reigned 404–358 B.C.), son and successor of Darius II. CYRUS THE YOUNGER tried to seize the throne but was killed at Cunaxa (401). A revolt of satraps was put down. The cult of MITHRA was revived. **Artaxerxes III,** d. 338 B.C. (reigned 358–338 B.C.), son of Artaxerxes II. Gained throne by general massacre of the family, and continued policy of terror, destroying Sidon and reducing Egypt. He was finally poisoned.

Artemis (är'tùmĭs), in Greek legend, goddess (Roman Diana), virgin huntress with virgin attendants; daughter of Zeus and Leto, twin sister of APOLLO. She was goddess of the wild. By loosing a boar she caused CALYDONIAN HUNT. She visited punishments on Actaeon, Agamemnon, and Niobe. She was also a protector of women (temple at Ephesus was center of this cult). Complementary to Apollo, she was the goddess of the moon and the night.

artemisia: see WORMWOOD.

arteriosclerosis, hardening and thickening of arterial walls. Loss of elasticity of vessel walls may result in high blood pressure.

artery, vessel carrying blood from heart to body tissues in CIRCULATION OF THE BLOOD.

Artesia (ärtē'zhù), city (pop. 8,244), SE N.Mex., W of Pecos R. and N of Carlsbad, in a livestock, oil, cotton, alfalfa area, watered by artesian wells.

artesian well (ärtē'zhùn), in the strictest sense, a well made by drilling into a porous, water-bearing layer between two impervious strata. The water rises as a result of hydrostatic pressure dependent on the slope and rainfall. However, the term artesian is usually applied to any deep, drilled well from which water can be pumped.

Artevelde, Jacob van (yä'kôp vän är'tùvĕldù), c.1290–1345, Flemish statesman. Caught in the conflict between EDWARD III of England and PHILIP VI of France, Artevelde, as head of the city government of Ghent, negotiated a commercial treaty with England (1338) and obtained recognition of Flemish neutrality. In 1340 he secured support of Flemish towns for Edward. He was killed in a riot. His son, **Philip van Artevelde,** 1340–82, led the weavers' rebellion against the count of Flanders (1381), captured most of Flanders, but was defeated and slain by the French at Roosebeke.

arthritis (ärthrī'tĭs), inflammation of a joint. Classes of chronic arthritis: atrophic, marked by degenerative changes in joint structure; hypertrophic, marked also by bony spicules in joint.

arthropod (är'thrŭpŏd"), member of phylum of invertebrate animals called Arthropoda (more species than all other animal groups combined). Includes CRUSTACEAN; SPIDER and relatives; CENTIPEDE; MILLIPEDE; INSECT; and extinct TRILOBITE. They have segmented bodies, jointed appendages, horny outer skeleton. Respiratory organs are gills or trachea.

Arthur: see ARTHURIAN LEGEND.

Arthur, dukes of Brittany. **Arthur I,** 1187–1203, posthumous son of Geoffrey, second son of Henry II of England. Succeeded his mother, duchess Constance, 1196. His claim to England was passed over (1199) in favor of his uncle JOHN, but he was invested by Philip II of France with all the French fiefs of the deceased Richard Cœur de Lion. In the ensuing warfare with John, Arthur was captured (1202), imprisoned at Rouen, and probably murdered. His brother-in-law succeeded him in Brittany as Peter I. **Arthur III,** 1393–1458, was known as comte de Richemont before his accession in 1457. As constable of France in the Hundred Years War, he captured Paris from the English (1436); led in reconquest of Normandy.

Arthur, Chester Alan, 1830–86, 21st President of the United States (1881–85). Collector of the port of New York (1871–78); his removal by Pres. Hayes defied the Conkling machine. His nomination for Vice President placated that group. Succeeding to the presidency after Garfield's assassination, Arthur had an honest, efficient, dignified administration. Supported civil service reform act of 1883; vetoed Chinese exclusion bill violating a treaty with China; prosecuted STAR ROUTE trials.

Arthurian legend, vast body of medieval story centering about King Arthur of Britain. First references to him, early as c.600, indicate that Arthur was historically a British leader in the Anglo-Saxon invasion, but *Historia* (1137) of GEOFFREY OF MONMOUTH makes him head of magnificent court and master of Europe. Meanwhile the legend had developed, with traditional Irish hero stories joining those of Welsh (see MABINOGION), Cornish, and North Britons. The expanded stories of Arthur were transmitted (before the year 1000) to the Bretons, who spread the tales over Western Europe. After Geoffrey came the chronicles of WACE, then of English LAYAMON. More important, the romances *Perceval* by CHRESTIEN DE TROYES and *Parzifal* by WOLFRAM VON ESCHENBACH became sources of PARSIFAL story. Early in the 13th cent. GOTTFRIED VON STRASSBURG composed his *Tristan,* first great version of TRISTRAM AND ISOLDE romance, which became attached to Arthurian legend. The third main theme, the knightly quest for Holy GRAIL, also developed. In England, Arthurian legend flourished in *Sir Gawain and the Green Knight* (see PEARL, THE) and the *Morte d'Arthur* of Sir Thomas MALORY. The full, later legend has Arthur, King Uther Pendragon's illegitimate son, show his royal blood by drawing a sword from a stone. His own sword, Excalibur, is given him by the Lady of the Lake; he keeps grand court with knights around honored Round Table at Camelot. When fatally wounded by his treacherous nephew (or son) Sir Mordred, Arthur is taken by three queens to the isle Avalon, whence he will return to save his people. Other characters in the legends are: Sir Launcelot of the Lake, gallant but faithless knight, lover of Arthur's queen; Elaine of Astolat, hopelessly in love with Launcelot; Elaine, daughter of Pelles, mother (by Launcelot) of the pure Sir Galahad, leader of Grail quest; Sir Gawain, Arthur's nephew, an ideal knight; Guinevere, Arthur's faithless queen, mistress of Launcelot; Sir Kay, churlish foster brother of Arthur; Merlin, great court magician; Morgan le Fay, Arthur's sister, an enchantress; and Sir Percivale (Parsifal).

artichoke, name for two different edible plants. Fleshy base of flower head and scales of the globe (or French) artichoke (*Cynara scolymus*) are eaten as salad or veg-

etable. It is a commercial crop in California. **Jerusalem artichoke** (*Helianthus tuberosus*) is a perennial sunflower with tuberous roots, potatolike but starchless, and grown for human food, stock feed, and as a source of inulin which yields levulose sugar.

artificial respiration, maintenance of breathing by artificial means. Mechanical devices are iron lung, respirator, pulmotor. Common hand method is Schafer (Schäfer, Schaefer) prone pressure method in which victim lies on stomach and operator presses and releases pressure on back 12–14 times per minute. More recently introduced is the back pressure arm lift method.

Artigas, José Gervasio (hōsā' hĕrvä'syō ärtē'gäs), 1764–1850, national hero of Uruguay. Typical gaucho of BANDA ORIENTAL, he championed Uruguayan independence from Spain, from Buenos Aires, and from Brazil. Exiled after annexation by Brazil (1820).

artillery, term originally applied to all projectiles employed in war, but later limited to certain types of heavy guns and the troops serving them. Small guns are said to have been used at Crécy (1346). The use of artillery against fortifications put an end to the security of the medieval castle. Artillery may be fixed or mobile. Artillery is now almost entirely mechanized (i.e., drawn by tractors or mounted on self-propelled trucks).

Art Institute of Chicago, museum and art school, inc. 1879 as Chicago Acad. of Fine Arts. It has galleries of paintings and sculpture; departments of textiles, prints, furniture, and Oriental art; the Ryerson Library; and a school of drama.

Artois (ärtwä'), region and former province, N France, in Pas-de-Calais dept.; historic cap., Arras. Agr., coal mines, and textile mfg. Annexed from Flanders to France (12th cent.), it passed to Burgundy (14th cent.) and to Hapsburgs (1493). It was conquered by France in 1640 and formally ceded by Spain to France in 1659. A battleground in many wars, particularly World War I.

Art Students League of New York, art school, founded 1875 in New York city by a group of students; self-governing. A board of control elected annually by members selects noted artists to serve as teachers.

Artzybashev, Mikhail Petrovich (mēkhüyĕl' pĕtrô'vĭch ärtsĭbä'shĕf), 1878–1927, Russian author. He leaped into fame with the sensational novel *Sanine* (1903; Eng. tr., 1914). Emigrated after October Revolution. Father of **Boris Artzybasheff,** 1899–, American illustrator of books and periodicals.

Aruba, Dutch West Indies: see CURAÇAO.

Arundel, Henry Fitzalan, 12th **earl of** (ä'rŭndŭl), c.1518–80, English statesman. Powerful Catholic noble, he helped bring Mary to the throne.

Arundel, Thomas Howard, 2d **earl of,** c.1586–1646, first great English art collector. First a privy councilor, later earl marshal of England. **Arundel Marbles** are his collection of ancient sculptures donated 1667 to Oxford Univ. **Arundel Collection** of manuscripts are in British Mus. **Arundel Society** (1849–97) reproduced works of famous artists. **Arundel Club,** founded 1904, reproduces in photogravure privately owned art works.

Arundel (ä'rŭndŭl), municipal borough (pop. 2,680), Sussex W, England. Arundel Castle (12th cent.), seat of dukes of Norfolk, overlooks town.

Arval Brothers (är'vŭl), in Roman religion, organization of 12 priests, with the emperor always a member. Their festival in May was a blessing of fields.

Arvida (ärvē'dŭ), city (pop. 11,078), S Que., Canada, on Saguenay R. and W of Chicoutimi. Has large aluminum and bauxite-reduction plants.

Aryabhatta (är"yŭbhŭt'ŭ), fl. 5th cent., Hindu mathematician, astronomer. One of first known users of algebra. Writings include rules of arithmetic, plane and spherical trigonometry; solutions of quadratic equations.

Aryan, name used by Hindus to designate themselves and other speakers of Indo-Iranian languages. Came to be used also for other Indo-European languages. Was favorite term of unscientific racism.

As, chemical symbol of the element ARSENIC.

Asa (ā'sù) [Heb.,= physician], d. c.870 B.C., king of Judah (c.911–c.870 B.C.); a "good" king, zealous in abolishing idols. Succeeded by Jehoshaphat. 1 Kings 15.8–24; 2 Chron. 14–16.

Asama, Mount (äsä'mä), active volcano, c.8,200 ft. high, central Honshu, Japan.

Asbestos, town (pop. 8,190), SE Que., Canada, NNW of Sherbrooke. Asbestos mining and mfg. center.

asbestos, any magnesium silicate mineral fibrous in structure and resistant to acid and fire. Often forms veins in other rock; probably results from metamorphism. Found in Canada, South Africa, U.S. It can be ground to make cement, woven into cloth, pressed into plasterboard. Used in pipe covering, fire-fighting equipment, shingles, etc.

Asbjørnsen, Peter Christian (äs'byûrnsùn), Nor. *Asbjørnsen,* 1812–85, Norwegian folklorist.

Asbury, Francis, 1745–1816, American Methodist bishop, b. England. As missionary (1771) he promoted circuit rider system. Became bishop 1784.

Asbury Park, Atlantic resort city (pop. 17,094), E N.J., SE of New Brunswick; founded 1869.

Ascalon (ăs'kù–), variant of ASHKELON.

Ascension, island in the S Atlantic, part of the British St. Helena Colony. A small island with few inhabitants, it is a naval station and had U.S. airfield World War II.

Asch, Sholem or **Shalom** (shō'lùm ăsh', shä'lùm), 1880–, Yiddish novelist and playwright, b. Poland, naturalized in U.S. 1920. Among novels are *The Nazarene* (1939), *The Apostle* (1943), *Mary* (1949).

Aschaffenburg (äshä'fùnbŏŏrk), city (pop. 44,919), Lower Franconia, NW Bavaria, on Main R. Textile and paper mfg. Anc. Roman garrison city; summer residence of archbishops of Mainz after 9th cent. Heavily damaged in World War II.

Ascham, Roger (ăs'kùm), 1515–68, English humanist, an outstanding scholar in Latin and Greek. Served as tutor (1548–50) to Princess Elizabeth and Latin secretary to Queen Mary (1553–58). Wrote *Toxophilus* (1545; on archery) and *The Scholemaster* (1570; a treatise on teaching Latin).

Asclepiades of Bithynia (ùsklēpēăd'ēz, bĭthĭn'ēù), c.124 B.C.–40 B.C., Greek founder of influential school of medicine in Rome.

Asclepius (ăsklē'pēùs), Latin *Aesculapius,* legendary Greek physician and god of medicine; son of Apollo and Coronis. Sick treated at his temples. Serpent and cock sacred to him.

Ascot, village, Berkshire, England. Nearby Ascot Heath has annual horse races held since 1711.

Asenath (ăs'ùnăth), Egyptian wife of Joseph. Gen. 41.45, 50–52; 46.20. Their marriage is subject of story of Joseph and Asenath, one of PSEUDEPIGRAPHA.

Asgard (ăs'gärd) [Norse,= home of gods], Norse Olympus, home of 12 chief gods (Aesir).

ash, any tree or shrub of genus *Fraxinus,* e.g., white ash (*Fraxinus americana*), a valuable American timber tree with strong wood, black ash (*F. nigra*), and blue ash (*F. quadrangulata*). Mountain ash and prickly ash are not true ashes.

Ashanti (ùshăn'tē), British protectorate (24,560 sq. mi.; pop. 823,672), Gold Coast, W Africa; cap. Kumasi. Formerly a strong native kingdom, founded 1697. Under British protection since 1896.

Ashby-de-la-Zouch (–zōōch', –zōōsh'), urban district (pop. 6,406), Leicestershire, England. Figures in Scott's *Ivanhoe.* Mary Queen of Scots held in Ashby Castle 1569.

Ashdod, ancient city of Philistines, between Jaffa and Gaza, of military importance in wars between Egypt and countries to N. Seat of the worship of Dagon, it was destroyed by the Maccabees. Now a village called Esdud. 1 Sam. 5.1; Joshua 15.47; 2 Chron. 26.6; Neh. 4.7; 13.23; Isa. 20.1; Jer. 25.20.

Asheboro (ăsh'bùrù), town (pop. 7,701), central N.C., in piedmont S of Greensboro. Produces hosiery, textiles, furniture, and flour. Near-by prehistoric Keyauwee Indian burial ground excavated 1936.

Asher (ăsh'ùr), son of Jacob, ancestor of one (Asher) of 12 tribes of Israel. Tribe occupied NW Palestinc. Gen. 30; Deut. 33.24; Joshua 19.24–31; Judges 5.17, 18. Aser: Luke 2.36; Rev. 7.6.

Asheville, city (pop. 53,000), W N.C., on French Broad R., on plateau in Blue Ridge; founded after 1791. Resort and financial, transportation, and commercial center of W N.C., it is near Great Smoky Mountains Natl. Park, Pisgah Natl. Forest, and Mt. Mitchell (6,684 ft.). Mfg. of textiles, leather goods, and furniture. Birthplace of Thomas Wolfe. "Biltmore," the Vanderbilt estate, is showplace.

Ashkelon (ăsh'kù–) or **Ascalon** (ăs'–), ancient city of Philistines on Mediterranean coast, between Jaffa and Gaza; center of worship of goddess Astarte. Played important role in Crusades. Also in Bible, Askelon, Eshkalon.

Ashkenazim (–năz'–), term referring to the German Jews as distinguished from Sephardim, the Jews of Spain and Portugal.

Ashkhabad (ùshkhùbăt'), city (pop. 126,580), cap. of Turkmen SSR, on Trans-Caspian RR, near Iranian border. Cotton and silk mills.

Ashland. 1 City (pop. 31,131), E Ky., on Ohio R. near influx of Big Sandy R. and NW of Huntington, W. Va.; settled 1815. Air, rail, and river shipping center in coal, oil, gas, and lumber region, it processes iron, steel, coke, oil, chemicals, leather, and brick. "Traipsin' Woman's Cabin," scene of annual American Folk Song Festival, is near by. **2** City (pop. 14,287), N Ohio, NE of Mansfield; laid out 1815. Mfg. of machinery, hardware, and rubber goods. Seat of Ashland Col. **3** City (pop. 7,739), SW Oregon, W of Klamath Falls, near Calif. line. Lumber, fruit, grain center. Resort near mountains. Holds annual Shakspere festival. **4** Borough (pop. 6,192), E Pa., near Pottsville. Produces coal, metal products, textiles. **5** Town (pop. 2,610), central Va., N of Richmond. Seat of RANDOLPH-MACON COLLEGE. Birthplaces of Patrick Henry and Henry Clay and girlhood home of Dolly Madison are near by. **6** City (pop. 10,640), N Wis., port on Chequamegon Bay of L. Superior; settled 1854 near site of Father Allouez's mission (1665). Industrial and shipping center with woodworking and paper plants and ironworks. Apostle Isls. to N.

Ashley, Anthony Ashley Cooper, Baron: see SHAFTESBURY, ANTHONY ASHLEY COOPER, 1st EARL OF.

Ashley, William Henry, c.1778–1838, American fur trader, U.S. Representative from Mo. (1831–37). After 1821 he sent expeditions to upper Missouri R. region and into Green R. valley.

Ashley, borough (pop. 5,243), NE Pa., near Wilkes-Barre. Produces anthracite and metal products.

Ashley, river: see CHARLESTON, S.C.

Ashmead, William Harris, 1855–1908, American entomologist who described 607 new genera and 3,100 new species.

Ashokan Reservoir, N.Y.: see CATSKILL AQUEDUCT.

Ashtabula (ăsh"tùbū'lù), city (pop. 23,696), NE Ohio, on L. Erie; settled c.1801. Receiving port for ore. Mfg. of metal products, leather goods, and chemicals. Hothouse vegetables grown.

Ashtaroth (ăsh'tùrŏth), Hebrew form of ASTARTE. A city of Bashan was named Ashtaroth. Joshua 9.10; 12, 4; 13.12, 31; 1 Chron. 6.71.

Ashtoreth (ăsh'tŏrĕth), Hebrew form of ASTARTE.

Ashur, anc. Assyrian city: see ASSYRIA.

Ashur-bani-pal, Assyrian king: see ASSUR-BANI-PAL.

Ashurnasirpal III (ä"shŏŏrnä'zĭrpäl), d. 860? B.C., king of anc. Assyria (884–860? B.C.). Conquered westward to the Mediterranean and estab. administration of empire.

Ash Wednesday: see LENT.

Asia, world's largest continent. Forms with Europe the

CAPITAL CITIES are designated by CAPITAL AND SMALL CAPITAL type

Eurasian land mass. Its boundary with Europe lies along Ural Mts., Ural R., and Greater Caucasus. Thus defined, Asia has area of c.16,000,000 sq. mi. and pop. of c.1,050,000,000. In W separated from Europe by the Bosporus, Dardanelles, and Aegean Sea, in NE separated from N America by Bering Strait. Suez Canal (between Mediterranean and Red Sea) breaks Asia's connection with Africa. Washed on S by Arabian Sea, on E by China Sea, Yellow Sea, Sea of Japan, Sea of Okhotsk, and Bering Sea, and on N by Arctic Ocean. Westernmost part of Asia is ASIA MINOR (major part of Turkey). To SE is peninsula of Arabia, N of which are Syria, Lebanon, Israel, Jordan, Iraq. Farther E are Iran, Afghanistan, India, and Pakistan. On SE peninsula are Burma, Malaya, Thailand, and Indo-China. Much of SE and central Asia belongs to China, bordered by Mongolian People's Republic, Tibet, and Korea. A major part of Asia is occupied by USSR.

Asia Minor, peninsula, extreme W Asia; called also Anatolia. It is bounded by the Black Sea, the Bosporus, the Sea of Marmara, and the Dardanelles (N); the Mediterranean (S); and the Aegean Sea (W). A high plateau, it is crossed by mountains, notably the TAURUS near the S coast, and is roughly identical with Asiatic TURKEY. Asia Minor, in close touch with Greece and Mesopotamia, was the chief meeting place of the ancient Orient and Occident. After the decline of the Hittites, the Greeks colonized coastal Ionia, coming in contact with Lydia, Phrygia, and more especially Troy. Conquest of Asia Minor by the Persians led to the Persian Wars. Divided into several small rival states in Hellenistic times, it was reintegrated by the Romans, but was subject to almost constant invasions under the Byzantine Empire and finally fell to the Ottomans in the 13th–15th cent.

Asiatic cholera: see CHOLERA.

Aske, Robert (äsk), d. 1537, English revolutionist, leader of PILGRIMAGE OF GRACE. He was executed.

Askelon (ăs'kŭ-), variant of ASHKELON.

Asmara (äsmä'rä), city (pop. c.95,000), cap. of Eritrea; alt. c.7,700 ft. In 1897 it succeeded Massawa as cap. of Eritrea.

Asmodeus (ăs″mōdē'ŭs), demon of Hebrew story, important in book of Tobit (3.6; 8).

Asmoneans: see MACCABEES.

Asoka (ŭsō'kŭ), d. c.237 B.C., emperor (c.255–c.237 B.C.) of MAURYA empire. Domain included most of India and Afghanistan. Converted to Buddhism c.257. Pillars inscribed with his pious sayings survive.

Aso-san (ä'sō-sän), group of five volcanic cones, central Kyushu, Japan. Only the central cone is active. Crater floor is 37.2 mi. in circumference.

asp, popular name of poisonous snake (probably either Egyptian cobra or horned viper), known as instrument in story of Cleopatra's suicide.

Aspadana: see ISFAHAN, Iran.

asparagus (ŭspăr'ŭ–), perennial garden vegetable (*Asparagus officinalis*). Its tender shoots are eaten in spring. Feathery foliage sometimes used by florists but more popular decorative species include SMILAX and asparagus fern.

Aspasia (ăspā'zhŭ), 5th cent. B.C., Greek courtesan; beautiful, learned mistress of Pericles.

Aspen, city (pop. 916; alt. 7,850 ft.), W central Colo., W of Leadville. Once a rich silver camp, it is now a resort. Had Goethe festival, 1949.

aspen, name for several species of POPLAR, e.g., quaking aspen (*Populus tremuloides*) and large-toothed aspen (*P. grandidentata*). The long leafstalks cause their broad leaves to tremble in even the faintest breeze.

Aspern (äs'pŭrn), eastern suburb of Vienna, Austria. Scene of Austrian victory over Napoleon I (1809).

asphalt (ăs'fôlt), brownish-black natural mixture of hydrocarbons used in road making, roofing, waterproofing, in making paints and varnishes. Varies from solid to semisolid, has great tenacity, melts when heated.

asphodel (ăs'fŭdĕl″), hardy stemless plant (*Asphodelus*) with showy flower spikes. The ancient asphodel sacred to Persephone belongs to the genus *Asphodeline*.

Aspropotamos, Greek river: see ACHELOUS.

Asquith, Herbert Henry: see OXFORD AND ASQUITH, HERBERT HENRY ASQUITH, 1ST EARL OF.

ass, smaller animal of HORSE genus, known in domesticated state as the donkey; male is called a jack or jackass, female a jennet or jenny. Hardy and surefooted, it has large head, small hoofs, short mane and tail, long ears. The diminutive burro is common pack animal in W U.S., Mexico. Ass was probably domesticated by c.4000 B.C. in Mesopotamia and Egypt. Several breeds have been used to breed the MULE.

Assam (ăsăm'), state (54,084 sq. mi.; pop. 9,129,442), NE India; cap. Shillong. Rugged terrain with fertile valleys of the Brahmaputra and Surma. Cherrapunji village in SW reputedly has world's heaviest rainfall (c.500 in. annually). Crops include rice, citrus fruits, sugar cane, tea, cotton, and jute. Lumbering is important. Suffered Burmese invasions from 13th to early 19th cent. Became part of British India in 1826. Japan held S area in 1944. A SW section was included 1947 in E Pakistan.

Assandun, battle of (ä'sŭndŭn), victory (1016) of the Danes under CANUTE over the English.

Assassin (ŭsă'sĭn) [Arabic,= under the influence of hashish], European name for member of secret order of SHIITES, which ruthlessly murdered enemies. Founded c.1090, flourished in Syria and Persia. Grand master, Sheikh al Jabal, known in W Europe as Old Man of the Mountain, was absolute ruler.

assault, any unlawful attempt to use violence to cause bodily harm. If successful, the offense becomes BATTERY. Every criminal assault entitles the victim to sue for damages. Simple assault is a misdemeanor; aggravated assault (e.g., with intent to kill) a felony.

assaying, in metallurgy, process of determining content of a specific metal in an ore or alloy. To obtain representative sample, often several samples are crushed and mixed. "Wet" assay (using liquid reagents) determines weight of metal; "dry" or fire assay yields metal in pure state.

Asser, Tobias Michael Carel (tōbē'äs mē'khäl kä'rŭl äs'ŭr), 1838–1913, Dutch statesman and jurist. For his work in international arbitration, he shared 1911 Nobel Peace Prize with Alfred Fried.

Assideans: see HASIDIM.

Assiniboine (ŭsĭn'ŭboin), river, c.600 mi. long, rising in E. Sask., Canada, and flowing SE into SW Man. to join Qu'Appelle R., then SE and E to Red R. at Winnipeg. Valley is a leading wheat area. Discovered 1736 by the Vérendryes, it became route of fur traders and settlers westward.

Assiniboine, Mount, 11,870 ft. high, on Alta.–B.C. line, Canada, in Rocky Mts. and S of Banff.

Assisi (äs-sē'zē), town (pop. 4,686), Umbria, central Italy; birthplace of St. Francis. Above saint's tomb are two superimposed Gothic churches, with frescoes by Cimabue and Giotto. Medieval in atmosphere, Assisi has many churches, including cathedral and (outside town) Santa Maria degli Angeli, built around Porziuncola chapel.

association, psychological tendency to link words and ideas consciously or unconsciously. In free association, a basic psychoanalytic technique, the patient voices all thoughts, however apparently trivial or disconnected, to reveal conflict areas, repressed desires, traumatic events; psychoanalyst observes manifest content and accompanying somatic reactions which expose attempted suppression of material.

Assuan, Egypt: see ASWAN.

Assur, anc. Assyrian city: see ASSYRIA.

Assur-bani-pal (ä″sōōr-bä'-nē-päl) or **Ashur-bani-pal** (ä″shōōr–), d. 626 B.C.?, king of anc. Assyria (669?–626? B.C.), son and successor of Esar-Haddon. Under him Assyria reached height of glory in riches, art, and learning (his library was famous). He conquered

SMALL CAPITALS = cross references. Pronunciation key on inside end pages. Abbreviations: p. 2.

Egypt and set Necho in power but later lost power there to Necho's son, Psamtik I. Put down revolt led by his brother, but power of empire was fading. Identified with Osnapper or Asnappar of Bible, Sardanapalus of Greeks.

Assyria (ŭsĭ'rēŭ), anc. empire of W Asia, originating around city of Ashur or Assur on upper Tigris R., with cap. later at Calah and resplendent Nineveh. Nucleus of a struggling Semitic city-state, it was overshadowed by Babylonia, but in 12th cent. B.C. rose to transitory greatness under TIGLATH-PILESER I. Real importance began in 9th cent. with conquests of ASHURNASIRPAL III, who set up an imperial administration. Later kings (SHALMANESER III, TIGLATH-PILESER III, and SARGON) gained hegemony in the Middle East. SENNACHERIB consolidated the holdings, and ESAR-HADDON (reigned 681–668 B.C.) defeated the Chaldaeans and won power in Egypt. Under his successor, ASSUR-BANI-PAL (reigned 669?–626? B.C.), Assyria reached its height of learning, art, and splendor. Yet Egypt broke away, and decline was rapid. Soon after his death Nineveh was sacked (612 B.C.). The Babylonian empire returned briefly to power, and the Persian Empire was founded.

Assyrian language, Semitic language of anc. times, in Akkadian group. See LANGUAGE (table).

Astaroth (ăs'tŭrŏth), Hebrew form of Astarte.

Astarte (ăstär'tē), Semitic goddess of fertility, beauty, and love. She was the most important Phoenician goddess, corresponding to Ishtar (also to APHRODITE), and was sometimes regarded as goddess of moon. The Bible refers to her as Ashtaroth or Ashtoreth.

astatine (ăs'tŭtēn), chemical element (symbol = At; atomic no.= 85). Discovery was announced in 1931; was at first called alabamine. In 1940 was produced in cyclotron at Univ. of California.

Astell, Mary (ăs'tŭl), 1666–1731, English author and feminist. Advocated a woman's college in *Serious Proposal to the Ladies* (1694–97).

aster, perennial plant (often called wild aster) of genus *Aster,* with small daisylike flowers. Most important garden varieties derived from North American fall-blooming species and grown in Europe as Michaelmas daisies. China aster (*Callistephus*) is a popular garden annual with larger heads of ray flowers, ranging from white and pink to purple.

asteroid or **planetoid,** minor planet revolving around sun. Over 1,500 recognized; orbits of most lie between Mars and Jupiter. Ceres (diameter c.480 mi.), largest and first known, discovered Jan. 1, 1801, by Piazzi.

asthma, condition marked by labored breathing. Allergy probable cause; specific agent determinable by skin tests.

Asti (ăs'tē), city (pop. 26,476), Piedmont, NW Italy; famous sparkling wine.

Astolat, in ARTHURIAN LEGEND: see GUILDFORD.

Aston, Francis William, 1877–1945, English chemist. Won 1922 Nobel Prize for discovery of a number of isotopes in nonradioactive elements.

Astor, John Jacob, 1763–1848, American merchant, b. Germany. Chartered AMERICAN FUR COMPANY. Richest man in U.S. at death; left fortune that has kept family name prominent. His great-grandson, **William Waldorf Astor, 1st Viscount Astor,** 1848–1919, American-British capitalist, moved to England in 1890. Contributed huge sums to public causes. His elder son, Waldorf Astor, married **Nancy Witcher (Langhorne) Astor, Viscountess Astor,** 1879–, British political leader, b. Va. As Conservative, the first woman to sit in Parliament. In late 1930s began with her husband to take a large part in politics through the "Cliveden set"—named after Astor country home.

Astoria (ăstôr'ēŭ), city (pop. 12,331), NW Oregon, on S bank of Columbia R. near its mouth. American fur-trading post estab. here in 1811 under John Jacob Astor. Trade in British hands after 1813. Refounded 1843 by overlanders; grew as port of entry.

Astrakhan (ă'strŭkăn"), city (pop. 253,655), SE European RSFSR; Caspian port on Volga delta. Fishing, caviar processing; transshipment point for Baku oil. Cap. of a Tatar khanate until 1557, when Ivan IV conquered it. Oriental in character, city has kept old kremlin, with cathedral, monastery, and palace.

astrolabe (ăs'trŭlāb), instrument formerly used to determine positions of heavenly bodies. Simple astrolabe had suspended disk with degrees marked on circumference and movable pointer at center. In navigation superseded by sextant (18th cent.).

astrology [Gr.,= science of stars], method of DIVINATION based on theory that stars influence human affairs. Its lore is very old and was basis for ancient knowledge of astronomy. In Middle Ages it was associated with alchemy and occult sciences. After Copernicus, astrology and astronomy diverged. In astrology a horoscope is a map of the heavens at time of birth, using chart of the zodiac; the "house" or sign in the ascendant at time of one's birth is said to determine his temperament, tendencies to disease, and liability to certain fortunes or calamities.

astronomy, scientific study of the heavenly bodies. Arose from need for designating time intervals; was early associated with astrology. Theoretical contributions stem from Greeks including Thales, Pythagoras, Eratosthenes, and Aristarchus of Samos. Earth-centered view of HIPPARCHUS and other Alexandrian Greeks, preserved in *Almagest* of Claudius PTOLEMY, was displaced in 16th cent. by sun-centered view of COPERNICUS, which was supported by observations of GALILEO, Tycho BRAHE, and KEPLER. Astronomical knowledge was advanced by scientists including Edmund Halley, Sir William and Sir J. F. W. Herschel, C. G. Abbot, Einstein, G. E. Hale, Sir James Jeans, Sir A. S. Eddington, Harlow Shapley, and Otto Struve and also by application of physics (astrophysics) in studies of radiation, light, and composition of heavenly bodies. See also ASTEROID; COMET; COSMOGONY; METEOR; MOON; PLANET; STAR; SUN. See *ill.,* p. 927.

Asturias (ăstoo'ryäs), region (4,207 sq. mi.; pop. 836,-642), NW Spain, on Bay of Biscay, crossed by Cantabrian Mts.: historic cap. Oviedo. Coal, iron, zinc mines, steel mills; cattle raising; fishing. Chief port: Gijón. Reconquest of Spain from Moors was begun by Christian nobles who had held out in Asturian mountains. Kingdom of Asturias was joined with Leon in 10th cent.

Astyages (ăstī'ŭjēz), 6th cent. B.C., semilegendary king of the Medes. His grandson, CYRUS THE GREAT, is supposed to have overthrown him to found greatness of Persian Empire.

Astyanax (ŭstī'ŭnăks), in Greek legend, son of Hector and Andromache. Slain by Greeks at Troy.

Asunción (äsōōnsyōn'), city (pop. 113,598; with suburbs, 144,327), cap. of Paraguay, on Paraguay R.; port and commercial center. Has many small industries. Founded in 1536 or 1537, Asunción was most important town in Río de la Plata region until rise of Buenos Aires.

Aswan or **Assuan** (both: äswän'), city (pop. 25,397), Upper Egypt, at First Cataract of the Nile. Near by is the great **Aswan Dam** (built 1902), 1¼ mi. long, 176½ ft. high.

Asyut (äsūt'), anc. *Lycopolis,* largest city (pop. 88,730) of Upper Egypt; trade center in Nile valley. Near by is Asyut barrage (for irrigation).

At, chemical symbol of the element ASTATINE.

Atacama, Desert of (ätäkä'mä), arid region, c.600 mi. long, N Chile, c.2,000 ft. above sea level, between Pacific coastal range and Andes. Has no vegetation, but is rich in nitrate and copper. ALMAGRO was first European to cross it (1537). Passed from Bolivia to Chile in War of the Pacific.

Atahualpa (ätäwäl'pä), d. 1533, last Inca of Peru. Successfully rebelled against HUÁSCAR (who shared rule with him), took whole empire. Francisco Pizarro imprisoned Atahualpa (1532) and in spite of offer of a roomful of gold as ransom had him put to death.

Atalanta (ătùlăn'tù), in Greek legend, huntress who joined Calydonian hunt and Argonaut voyage. She ran a race with each suitor, on condition that winner should marry her but loser should die. Hippomenes (hǐpŏ'mǐnēz) won by dropping three apples; Atalanta paused to pick them up.

Ataturk, Kemal (kĕmäl' ätätürk'), 1880–1938, Turkish leader, founder of Modern Turkey; known before 1934 as Mustafa Kemal or Kemal Pasha. An army officer, he took part in the Young Turk revolution of 1908, distinguished himself in World War I, and after Turkey's collapse organized the Nationalist party and army in E Anatolia. After the Greek landing at SMYRNA (1919), he convoked Nationalist congresses at Erzerum and Sivas, was outlawed by the Allied-controlled government at Constantinople, and set up a rival government at Ankara. The signing of the Treaty of SÈVRES by the Constantinople government made the split with Ankara final. Kemal expelled the Greeks from Anatolia in a brilliant campaign (1921–22), which earned him the title Ghazi [victorious]; abolished the sultanate (1922); secured honorable peace at the LAUSANNE CONFERENCE (1923); and served as president of the Turkish republic for five terms (1927–35). Ruling dictatorially, he carried out a drastic program of Westernization and reform which changed the face of TURKEY.

Ataulf (ä'taülf), d. 415, Visigothic king (410–15). Led VISIGOTHS from Italy into S Gaul (412), later into N Spain. Married GALLA PLACIDIA.

Atchafalaya (ùchä'fùlī"ù), river branching in E La. from Red R. near its junction with the Mississippi, and flowing c.170 mi. S through several lakes to Atchafalaya Bay of Gulf of Mexico. Navigable.

Atchison, city (pop. 12,792), NE Kansas, on the Missouri; settled 1854. Grew as river port, rail terminus, and supply point for westward travel. Trade center for grain, livestock, and apple area, it mills flour and has mfg. of steel products. Seat of Mt. St. Scholastica Col. (R.C.; for women; 1863).

Ate (ā'tē) [Gr.,= folly], in Greek religion, personification of rash impulse leading to folly.

Athabaska, Lake, 3,058 sq. mi., c.200 mi. long, 5–35 mi. wide, NE Alta. and NW Sask., Canada. Receives Athabaska and Peace rivers in SW, drains NW into Great Slave R., thence via Mackenzie R. into Arctic Ocean. On edge of Laurentian Plateau, it is connected to Churchill R. by canoe route. Fort Chipewyan, at W end of lake, built 1788. Lake surveyed and mapped by Philip Turnor 1790–92.

Athabaska, Mount, 11,452 ft. high, W Alta., Canada, on edge of Columbia Icefield and surrounded by Athabaska and Saskatchewan glaciers.

Athabaska Pass, 5,736 ft. high, W Alta. and E B.C., Canada, from headwaters of Athabaska R. across Continental Divide to Columbia R. Discovered c.1811, it became route to Columbia R. country.

Athaliah (ăth"ùlī'ù), died c.841 B.C., queen of Judah (c.846–c.841 B.C.); daughter of Ahab and Jezebel, wife of Jehoram of Judah. She succeeded her murdered son, Ahaziah of Judah. Killed in coup d'état in favor of JEHOASH **2.** She is subject of Racine's ATHALIE. 2 Kings 11; 2 Chron. 22–23.

Athanagild (ùthä'nùgĭld), d. 567, Visigothic king of Spain (554–67). Helped into power by Byzantines, to whom he ceded part of S Spain. Later fought Byzantines, Franks, Basques. Held splendid court at Toledo. Father of Brunhilda and Galswintha.

Athanasius, Saint (ăthùnä'zhùs), 295–373, patriarch of Alexandria, Doctor of the Church. Distinguished himself at First Council of NICAEA by eloquent opposition to ARIANISM and fought it later steadfastly. He was exiled five times. When he fled to Rome, he gained the aid of Pope Julius I. A vigorous administrator in his patriarchate, he was also a gifted writer against Arianism and helped to shape the statement of Catholic doctrine. Feast: May 2. The **Athanasian**

Creed was not by him but by a Western writer of the 6th cent. It is an exact statement of Catholic belief on the Trinity and the Incarnation. Sometimes called QUICUNQUE VULT.

Athapascan (ăthùpăs'kùn), linguistic stock of North America, widely distributed among Indian tribes of W Canada and W U.S. See LANGUAGE, table.

atheism, doctrine that there is no supernatural being. Through history many nonatheists have been accused of atheism because they held unorthodox views (e.g., Socrates, Spinoza, the deists). Atheism is related to, and often confused with, AGNOSTICISM.

Athelstan or **Æthelstan** (both: ăth'ùlstùn, –stăn"), d. 940, king of the English (924–40). Grandchild of ALFRED, built up state on foundations laid by him. Issued laws that attempted to impose royal authority on customary law.

Athena (ùthē'nù) or **Pallas Athena** (pă'lùs), Olympian goddess of wisdom, patron of arts of peace and war, ruler of storms, and guardian of Athens, a virgin goddess, sprung from the forehead of Zeus. She is usually shown wearing helmet and aegis with head of MEDUSA. Parthenon was her temple, Panathenaea her festival. Identified with Roman Minerva.

Athena Parthenos, a gold and ivory statue by PHIDIAS, dedicated c.438 B.C. in the Parthenon. It was the chief treasure of Athens.

Athenodorus: see LAOCOÖN.

Athens (ăth'ĭnz), Gr. *Athenai,* city (pop. 559,250; greater Athens, with port PIRAEUS and other cities, 1,368,142), cap. of Greece, on the plain of Attica. It is cultural, religious (focus of Greek Orthodox Church), and industrial (textiles, machine-tool plants, utilities) center of country. Many tourists come to view remains in city that was fountainhead of Western civilization. Early history is mixed with legend (e.g., story of Theseus as consolidator of cities of Attica, account of early kings). Aristocratic archons held power when Solon presumably began reforms in 594 B.C. A period of tyrants under Pisistratus and his sons Hippias and Hipparchus lasted until 510 B.C., when CLEISTHENES founded the democracy that was to persist in the period of greatness. In the period of the PERSIAN WARS (500–449 B.C.) small Athens emerged, under hero leaders such as MILTIADES, THEMISTOCLES, and CIMON, as a great naval power, and the DELIAN LEAGUE became practically an Athenian empire. Architecture, art, and literature rose to astonishing height in the Golden Age under Pericles (5th cent. B.C.). The Parthenon was built; SOCRATES spoke his philosophy; Greek drama was founded with AESCHYLUS, SOPHOCLES, and EURIPIDES. In later decline this glory went on with PLATO and ARISTOTLE, ARISTOPHANES and the orator DEMOSTHENES. In the long-drawn PELOPONNESIAN WAR Athens was finally conquered by SPARTA. Recovery after defeat in 404 B.C. was rapid but transitory, and in the 4th cent. Athens was subjected by PHILIP II of Macedon and his son, ALEXANDER THE GREAT. When Roman greatness grew Athens became a provincial cap., and attempts to regain power resulted in humiliation (notably the sack by Sulla, 86 B.C.). Yet the tradition of Athens affected Rome and even more affected the Byzantine Empire, under which it fell. With the fall of that empire Athens passed (1205) to a French nobleman and became a duchy, later prosperous in Catalan hands (under house of Aragon). A brief renascence under the rule of Florentine nobles, the Acciajuoli, in the late 14th and early 15th cent. was followed by decline under Ottoman rule after 1458. When Greece was freed, Athens became the cap. of independent Greece and gradually grew to its present position. It retains relics of the past. On the ACROPOLIS are the Parthenon, the Propylaea, and the Erechtheum. Elsewhere about the city are fine Greek and Roman remains.

Athens. 1 City (pop. 6,309), N Ala., near Tenn. line, N of Birmingham, in cotton area. Hosiery and lumber mills. Sacked and occupied by Federals (1862), recaptured by N. B. Forrest (1864). **2** City (pop. 28,180), NE Ga., on Oconee R. and ENE of Atlanta. Founded 1801 as site of Univ. of GEORGIA. Cotton market and mfg. center (textiles, tire cord, cottonseed oil). Has many fine classic revival homes. **3** City (pop. 11,660), SE Ohio, W of Marietta. Surveyed 1795–96 by Ohio Co. of Associates as university site, its settlement soon followed. Has printing and mfg. of meat products and machinery. Seat of Ohio Univ. (state controlled; coed.; chartered 1804, opened 1809, oldest college in the Old Northwest). **4** City (pop. 8,618), E Tenn., NE of Chattanooga. Trade center of agr. and timber area with mfg. of clothing and furniture. **5** City (pop. 5,194), E Texas, WSW of Tyler. Shipping center of oil and agr. area with mfg. of clay products.

athlete's foot: see RINGWORM.

Athlone, Godart van Ginkel, 1st earl of: see GINKEL.

Athlone (ăthlōn′), urban district (pop. 8,379), Co. Westmeath, Ireland, on Shannon R. Athlone Castle was of strategic value in early Irish history.

Athol (ă′thŏl), town (pop. 11,554), including Athol village (pop. 9,708), N Mass., W of Fitchburg. Mfg. of machinery and tools.

Atholl or **Athole** (both: ăth′ŭl), mountainous district, 450 sq. mi., N Perthshire, Scotland.

Athos (ăth′ŏs, ā′thŏs) or **Akte** (äk′tā), easternmost peninsula of CHALCIDICE, NE Greece; c.30 mi. long, 1½–7 mi. wide. It forms the autonomous state of the Greek Orthodox monks of **Mount Athos,** or Hagion Oros [Holy Mountain], rising c.6,000 ft. at S tip of peninsula. The community, founded 10th cent., consists of 20 convents. Under direct rule of the patriarch of Constantinople, it has always enjoyed virtual independence. No female, human or animal, is admitted. Libraries contain a wealth of Byzantine manuscripts.

Atkinson, Henry, 1782–1842, American army officer, general commander in BLACK HAWK WAR.

Atlanta, city (pop. 331,314), state cap. (since 1868), NW Ga., near Chattahoochee R. Largest city in state. Chief rail center of the South and one of its principal distributing, industrial, commercial, and cultural centers. Mfg. of textiles, furniture, cottonseed oil, machinery, electrical goods, shoes, and pharmaceuticals. Hardy Ivy settled here in 1833. Town founded 1837 as Terminus (end of a rail line) and renamed 1845. Important as a Confederate supply and communications center, it fell to W. T. SHERMAN on Sept. 2, 1864 (see ATLANTA CAMPAIGN). He burned it (Nov. 15) before his march to the sea. Conventions and expositions in 19th and 20th cent. drew attention to city's strategic distributory position. Federal penitentiary (1899) here is widely known. Here are High Mus. of Art, state archives building, co-cathedral of Christ the King (R.C.), building with *Cyclorama of the Battle of Atlanta*, stockyards, farmers' market, and Fort McPherson. Seat of GEORGIA INSTITUTE OF TECHNOLOGY, Oglethorpe Univ. (coed.; 1916), and Morris Brown Col. (Negro; Methodist; coed.; 1885). EMORY UNIVERSITY is near. Atlanta Univ. System (Negro; 1929) has four affiliated schools with adjacent campuses and some common facilities: Atlanta Univ. (coed.; grad.; opened 1865), Atlanta Univ. School of Social Work (coed.; 1920; joined 1938), Morehouse Col. (for men; 1867), Spelman Col. (for women; 1881). Clark Col. (Negro; Methodist; coed.; opened 1870) cooperates with Atlanta Univ. System.

Atlanta campaign, May–Sept., 1864, of Civil War. W. T. Sherman gathered Union armies near Chattanooga with two aims—to destroy J. E. Johnston's army and to capture Atlanta. By flanking actions he forced Johnston from successive positions to Chattahoochee R. Here J. B. Hood counterattacked but failed to stop advance, and retired to Atlanta. After Union army cut communications, Confederates abandoned city Sept. 1. Sherman occupied it Sept. 2.

Atlanta University System: see ATLANTA, Ga.

Atlantic, city (pop. 6,840), SW Iowa, ENE of Council Bluffs. Trade and processing center in a farming area.

Atlantic Charter, program of peace aims, jointly enunciated by Prime Minister Winston Churchill of Great Britain and Pres. F. D. Roosevelt of U.S. on Aug. 14, 1941. Aims incorporated in UN declaration of 1942.

Atlantic City, seaside resort and convention city (pop. 61,657), SE N.J., c.60 mi. SE of Philadelphia, c.100 mi. SW of New York. Boardwalk built 1870; present boardwalk lined with shops and hotels. Has large municipal auditorium, six amusement piers.

Atlantic Highlands, resort borough (pop. 3,083), NE N.J., on Sandy Hook Bay near Navesink Highlands, one of highest (c.276 ft.) U.S. Atlantic coastal ridges.

Atlantic Ocean, second largest ocean, est. area 31,830,-000 sq. mi., extends in S-shape from arctic to antarctic regions between the Americas, Europe, and Africa. Connected with the Pacific by Panama Canal, and (through Mediterranean) with Red Sea by Suez Canal. Chief western arms: Hudson and Baffin bays, Gulf of Mexico, Caribbean Sea. Chief eastern arms: Baltic and North seas, Bay of Biscay, the Mediterranean, Gulf of Guinea. Shortest trans-Atlantic distance is between Dakar, Africa, and bulge of Brazil. More large rivers drain into it than into any other ocean. Surface waters of trade-wind belts attain highest oceanic salinity known. Chief currents: North and South Equatorial, Brazil, Guinea, and GULF STREAM, which meets Labrador Current in Grand Banks off Newfoundland, forming heavy fogs. Gulf Stream then bends eastward to form part of NORTH ATLANTIC DRIFT. This area, part of busiest shipping lane in world, is patrolled for icebergs by U.S. coast guard. A submarine ridge extends from E Greenland to N Scotland, bearing telegraph cable network. Mid-Atlantic ridge, 300–600 mi. wide, from Iceland almost to Antarctic Circle, rises to average height of c.10,-000 ft. It is center of volcanic activity and earthquakes; a few of its peaks emerge as islands. Chief Atlantic deeps are Milwaukee Depth (30,246 ft.) near the Bahamas and Nares Deep (27,972 ft.) near Puerto Rico. Discovery of an 800-mile canyon in floor of the Atlantic midway between Bermuda and the Azores was reported in 1952.

Atlantis, in Greek legend, large island in western sea. Plato, who describes it as a Utopia, tells of high civilization there until its destruction by earthquake. Question of its actual existence has provoked much speculation.

Atlas (ăt′lùs), in Greek religion, Titan. After the downfall of the Titans he was condemned to hold up the sky on his head and hands.

Atlas Mountains, mountain system of NW Africa, extending c.1500 mi. NE from Morocco through Algeria to Cape Bon in Tunisia.

Atlin Lake, 308 sq. mi., 66 mi. long, 2–6 mi. wide, NW B.C. and S Yukon, Canada. On E shore is Atlin village, hq. of gold-mining region.

atmosphere, gaseous envelope around earth, probably extending at least 600 mi. Lower layer (troposphere) extends to limiting boundary (tropopause) and decreases in height from c.10 mi. at equator to c.5 mi. at poles; above lies stratosphere, first reached by Auguste Piccard in balloon ascent (1931). Within troposphere, air is mixed by ascending and descending currents; temperature decreases c.1°C. per 500-ft. altitude increase; air is composed of nitrogen (78.09%), oxygen (20.95%), and small amounts of argon, carbon dioxide, and other gases, and also containing water vapor and dusts. Air pressure decreases with altitude (see BAROMETER); standard pressure at sea level is 14.7 lb. per sq. in. (called an atmosphere); $c.\frac{9}{10}$ of mass of atmosphere is within 10 mi. above sea level. See also IONOSPHERE. See *ill.,* p. 19.

atoll: see CORAL.

atom, according to atomic theory, minute particle of matter. Formerly considered indivisible unit of matter. Now believed to consist of protons (positively charged [+] particles), electrons (negatively charged

[−] particles), and neutrons (neutral particles). Central nucleus contains protons and neutrons, has + charge. Because extranuclear electrons are equal in number to nuclear protons, atom is neutral. Ions are atoms or groups of atoms with electrical charge. Atoms of different elements differ in weight (ATOMIC WEIGHT) and in number of protons and electrons (this number indicated by atomic number; see PERIODIC LAW). Electron arrangement varies in different elements. Chemically, atoms of an element react the same; sometimes differ in mass (see ISOTOPE). Atoms of elements joined in MOLECULE. Discovery of ELECTRON and RADIOACTIVITY essential to modern concept of atom. Among contributors to knowledge of atom: N. H. D. BOHR, Sir W. H. BRAGG, W. L. BRAGG, James CHADWICK, John DALTON, Albert EINSTEIN, Enrico FERMI, Otto HAHN, Werner HEISENBERG, Irving LANGMUIR, Max von LAUE, Lise MEITNER, R. A. MILLIKAN, H. G. MOSELEY, Max PLANCK, 1st Baron RUTHERFORD. See also ATOMIC BOMB; ATOMIC ENERGY. See ill., p. 773.

atomic bomb, weapon deriving explosive force from release of atomic energy. Reported splitting of uranium nucleus in Germany led in 1940 to organized research in U.S. First bombs produced at Los Alamos, used on HIROSHIMA and NAGASAKI in World War II.

atomic energy is derived from fission (splitting) of nucleus of atom. Experimenting with CYCLOTRON, U.S. scientists (1939) confirmed the splitting of uranium nucleus by Germany. Roosevelt named committee to investigate military uses of atomic energy. In 1942, a group under Fermi achieved, in a "pile" of graphite and uranium, first nuclear chain reaction (uranium nucleus splits as result of capture of a bombarding neutron, releases other neutrons causing more nuclear fissions). U-235 (uranium isotope, atomic wt. 235) by capturing a neutron becomes unstable and splits in two. When nucleus of U-238, the most abundant isotope in uranium ore, captures a neutron, neptunium (atomic no. 93) is produced. Neptunium yields plutonium (new element; atomic no. 94). Plutonium and U-235 both yield some 200,000,000 electron volts during fission. To produce explosion must set up chain reaction that results in many fissions; such a chain-reacting system later called a reactor. Use of atomic energy as power source and in biology and medicine among peacetime research projects. UN devised plan for international control of research and production independent of Security Council. This was favored by Western powers; opposed by USSR, which wanted prohibition and destruction of existing bombs, then control by group with limited powers, regulated by Security Council. Negotiations became deadlocked. See ill., p. 773.

atomic number: see PERIODIC LAW.

atomic theory, holds that matter is made up of minute particles, atoms. John Dalton (19th cent.) revived ancient (5th cent. B.C.) theory of atom, accepted early idea of indivisibility (no longer held), and believed that atoms of any element are same in size and weight and unite chemically in simple numerical ratios to form compounds. Mendelejeff and Arrhenius contributed to theory. Modern theory based on discovery of ELECTRON and RADIOACTIVITY.

atomic weight, ratio of weight of atom of element to weight of atom of standard element. Hydrogen once used as standard. Later oxygen (O = 16) used, since it forms more compounds than hydrogen. Atomic weight determined by quantitative analysis of compounds; specific-heat method used to determine that of elements forming no stable gaseous compounds. Atomic weight of elements having atoms of different weights (see ISOTOPE) is an average.

atonality, in music, the absence of TONALITY. Term often applied to any 20th-cent. music which does not observe the principles of harmonic relationship of the 18th or 19th cent. From time of Rameau the seven tones of the diatonic scale were felt to bear certain definite relations to one another. The five additional chromatic tones were available as auxiliary tones. Increased use of auxiliary tones by 19th-cent. composers reached a peak in the chromaticism of Wagner. In his and in Debussy's music the feeling of tonality began to break down. Polytonality, in which several different keys were used simultaneously, contributed to the process. Finally all 12 tones were regarded as equal, bearing no fixed relations to one another. The 12-tone technique, which Schönberg arrived at in 1914, is a specific system to give form to this new concept. The composer arranges the 12 chromatic tones into a tone row, in which the tones may be used in any order but none may be repeated until all 12 have been used. This tone row is the basis of the composition. It may be transposed, inverted, used backward, used to form chords, or used in counterpoint with itself—transformations which the uninitiated ear finds difficult to follow. System yet in its infancy; its significance yet to be determined. Among Schönberg's disciples were Alban Berg and Ernst KRENEK.

Atonement, Day of, Heb. *Yom Kippur,* the most sacred Hebrew holy day, in late September or early October (the 10th day of the 7th month), a day of fasting and prayer for forgiveness of sins.

Atreus (ā'trēus), in Greek legend, king of Mycenae; father of Agamemnon and Menelaus. He slew three sons of his brother Thyestes and served them to him at a feast. The fourth son of Thyestes killed him.

atropine (ăt'rŭpēn, –pĭn), poisonous alkaloid discovered in belladonna (deadly nightshade) by P. L. Geiger (1833). Used to dilate pupil of eye and as antispasmodic, narcotic, and pain reliever.

Atropos, one of the FATES.

Attalla (ŭtăl'ŭ), railroad city (pop. 7,537), NE Ala., W of Gadsden, in iron, cotton area. Foundries.

Attica (ăt'ĭkŭ), region of E central anc. Greece, around ATHENS. According to legend its four tribes founded by Ion and combined as a state by Theseus.

Attila (ăt'ĭlŭ), d. 453, king of the HUNS (c.433–53), called the Scourge of God. He extorted tribute from Rome, but in 450 emperors Marcian and Valentinian III refused to pay. In the same year Valentinian's sister Grata secretly offered herself in marriage to Attila, who demanded half the Western Empire as dowry. Turned down, he invaded Gaul but was defeated by AETIUS at Chalons (451). In 452 he invaded N Italy but abandoned his plan to take Rome, according to some because of the plea of Pope LEO I, but more probably because of a shortage of supplies. Accounts of his savagery, though based on fact, are probably exaggerated.

Attis (ă'tĭs) or **Atys** (ā'tĭs), Phrygian fertility god. Like Adonis, he died and was resurrected yearly.

Attleboro, city (pop. 23,809), SE Mass., NE of Providence, R.I.; settled 1634. Mfg. of jewelry, tools, and paper and metal specialties.

Attlee, Clement R(ichard) (ăt'lē), 1883–, British statesman and LABOUR PARTY leader. A former social service worker, held posts in 1924 and 1929 Labour governments. Became party leader 1935. Was deputy prime minister (1942–45) in Churchill's wartime coalition cabinet. Made prime minister (1945) while attending POTSDAM CONFERENCE. His government nationalized much industry, began national health service, ended Palestine mandate and control of India, and strengthened ties with U.S. Stress on rearmament caused opposition, headed by Aneurin BEVAN, within Labour party. After loss to Conservatives in 1951 elections Attlee became opposition leader.

Attu (ă'tōō), island, 30 mi. long, off W Alaska, westernmost of ALEUTIAN ISLANDS. Very rugged, it rises above 4,000 ft. Japanese occupied it 1942 and removed inhabitants to Japan. U.S. forces landed May 11, 1943, retook island in three weeks of bloody fighting, and estab. air base.

Atys: see ATTIS.

Au, chemical symbol of the element GOLD.

Aube (ōb), department (2,327 sq. mi.; pop. 235,237),

NE France, in arid part of Champagne; cap. Troyes.

Auber, Daniel François (fräswä' ōbĕr'), 1782–1871, French composer, known chiefly for his comic opera. Among his works are *Fra Diavolo, Le Domino Noir,* and *La Muette de Portici* (also called *Masaniello*).

Aubigné, Théodore Agrippa d' (tāŏdôr' ägrēpä' dōbēnyä'), 1552–1630, French poet and Huguenot soldier. His reputation rests on *Les Tragiques,* a powerful, partly satirical, partly epical poem.

Aubrey, John, 1626–97, English biographer, author of *Lives of Eminent Men* (pub. 1813; later called *Brief Lives*).

Auburn or **Lissoy,** village, Co. Westmeath, Ireland; scene of Goldsmith's *Deserted Village.*

Auburn. 1 City (pop. 12,939), E Ala., ENE of Montgomery. Seat of Alabama Polytechnic Inst. (landgrant, state supported; coed.; chartered and opened 1872 as Alabama Agricultural and Mechanical Col., renamed 1899). **2** Resort city (pop. 4,653), N central Calif., NE of Sacramento; settled 1848 after gold discovery. *Placer Herald* published here since 1852. Old New Orleans Hotel was chronicled by Bret Harte. **3** City (pop. 5,879), NE Ind., N of Fort Wayne. Mfg. of metal products. **4** City (pop. 23,134), SW Maine, on Androscoggin R. (bridged) opposite Lewiston; settled c.1786. Mfg. of shoes (since c.1835). **5** Town (pop. 8,840), S central Mass., S of Worcester; settled 1714. Concrete and metal products. **6** City (pop. 36,-722), W central N.Y., in Finger Lakes region, on outlet of Owasco L. and SW of Syracuse; settled 1793. Mfg. of metal and food products and clothing. Here are Auburn State Prison and home and grave of W. H. Seward. **7** City (pop. 6,497), W Wash., between Seattle and Tacoma. Agr. center and rail junction.

Aubusson, Pierre d' (pyĕr' dōbüsō'), 1423–1503, French cardinal, grand master of Knights Hospitalers. Defended Rhodes heroically against Turks (1480).

Aubusson (ōbüsō'), town (pop. 4,935), Creuse dept., central France. Famous tapestry and carpet manufacture dates from 15th cent.

Aucassin et Nicolette (ōkäsĕ' ĕ nēkōlĕt') medieval French love story in prose and verse (probably 13th cent.). The original music, to which verses were to be sung, has been preserved. The simplicity of the story is its charm. Many English translations.

Auch (ōsh), city (pop. 11,489), cap. of Gers dept., S France; wine, brandy trade. Archiepiscopal see from 9th cent.; was cap. of Armagnac and of Gascony. Cathedral contains magnificent stained glass.

Auckland (ôk'lŭnd), city (pop. 123,457, metropolitan pop. 263,370), N North Isl., New Zealand, in hotsprings area; founded 1841. Former cap. (1841–65) and chief port of dominion. Exports dairy products, hides, and timber. Has shipyards, ammunition plants, and canneries. Seat of Auckland Univ. Col., and museum with collection of Maori art.

Aude (ōd), department (2,449 sq. mi.; pop. 268,889), SE France, in Languedoc; cap. Carcassonne.

Auden, W(ystan) H(ugh) (ô'dŭn), 1907–, Anglo-American poet, b. England. Leader of left-wing literary group at Oxford, he wrote (with Isherwood) verse plays: *The Dog beneath the Skin* (1935), *The Ascent of F 6* (1936), *On the Frontier* (1938). Perhaps better known are lyrics such as those in *Collected Poetry* (1945).

Audenarde, Belgium: see OUDENARDE.

audio frequency: see VIBRATION.

auditing, examination and checking of accounts and related documents by persons unconnected with their preparation. System became common in 19th cent. as increasingly complex businesses required licensed experts to conduct annual audits. The accountant records the facts of a business; the auditor determines whether such recording has been accurately done.

Audubon, John James (ô'dùbŏn), d. 1851, American ornithologist. Birth date and place disputed (New Orleans, 1780, or Aux Cayes, Haiti, 1785). Came to U.S. in 1803. His bird-banding experiments near Philadel-

phia (c.1803) were first in America. Married Lucy Bakewell (1808); lived mostly in Henderson, Ky., during 1808–20, changing occupation frequently, observing birds. Taught drawing in New Orleans. On 1826 trip to England he secured publication of *The Birds of America* and *Ornithological Biography* (with William MacGillivray). Later, in New York he began with John Bachman *The Viviparous Quadrupeds of North America,* completed by his sons, Victor Gifford Audubon and John Woodhouse Audubon. National Association of Audubon Societies devoted to preserving and studying American wildlife publishes *Audubon Magazine.*

Aue, Hartmann von: see HARTMANN VON AUE.

Auenbrugger, Leopold (lä'ōpôlt ou'ùnbrŏŏg"ùr), 1722–1809, Viennese physician, pioneer in use of percussion in diagnosing chest diseases.

Auerbach, Berthold (bĕrt'hōlt ou'ùrbäkh), 1812–82, German novelist. Virtual founder of peasant-story genre in German. *Village Tales from the Black Forest* (1843; Eng. tr., 1846–47), somewhat stylized pictures of peasant life, were much imitated.

Auerstedt (ou'ùrshtĕt), village, central Germany, NE of Weimar. Here the French Marshal Davout defeated Prussians on same day that Napoleon I triumphed at Jena (Oct. 14, 1806).

Augeas (ôjē'ùs), in Greek legend, king who owned 3,000 oxen. Hercules, commanded to clean in one day the Augean stables, untouched for 30 years, did so by turning rivers Peneus and Alpheus through them.

Augier, Émile (āmēl' ōzhyä'), 1820–89, French dramatist and satirist. Best-known comedy is *Le Gendre de M. Poirier* (1854), written with J. Sandeau.

Augsburg (ouks'bŏŏrk), city (pop. 184,712), cap. of Swabia, W Bavaria, on Lech R. Textile center of S Germany. Founded by Augustus 15 B.C. as Augusta Vindelicorum; free imperial city 1276; prominent member of Swabian League (1488–1534). Home of Fugger family and birthplace of Holbein, it was a major commercial, banking, and cultural center in 15th–16th cent. Its architectural treasures were heavily damaged in World War II.

Augsburg, League of, defensive alliance formed 1686 against Louis XIV of France by Emperor Leopold I with Sweden, Spain, Bavaria, Palatinate, and other German states. Transformed into GRAND ALLIANCE (1689) after adherence of Holland, England, Savoy.

Augsburg, Peace of, 1555, temporary settlement within Holy Roman Empire of conflicts arising from the Reformation. Chief principle: *Cuius regio, eius religio*—i.e., each prince was to determine whether Lutheranism or Catholicism was to prevail in his lands. All Church property held by abbots or bishops who had changed their faith after 1552 was to be forfeited by them.

Augsburg Confession: see CREED.

Augsburg Interim: see REFORMATION.

August: see MONTH.

Augusta. 1 City (pop. 71,508), E Ga., at head of navigation on Savannah R. (levees). Cotton market, it has mfg. of cotton products, brick, tile, fertilizer, lumber, and chemicals and food processing. Winter resort with mild climate. Laid out 1735 as trading post by Oglethorpe. Finally fell in 1781 to Continentals under Andrew Pickens and Light-Horse Harry Lee. Cap. of Ga. 1785–95. Site of largest Confederate powder works in Civil War. Here are Paine Col. (Negro; Methodist; coed.; 1883), Univ. of Ga. School of Medicine, a U.S. arsenal (1819), boyhood home of Woodrow Wilson, and many old Georgian and classic revival homes. **2** City (pop. 20,913), state cap., SW Maine, at head of navigation on Kennebec R. and NE of Portland. Trading post estab. here by Plymouth Co. in 1628. After founding of Fort Western (1754) the town grew as a river port. A dam (1837) stimulated industry. Mfg. of wood products, shoes, paper, and textiles. James G. Blaine's home is now governor's mansion. Has airport and U.S. arsenal.

Augustana College and Theological Seminary: see ROCK ISLAND, Ill.

Augustine, Saint (ô'gŭstēn, –tĭn; ôgŭ'stĭn), 354–430, Doctor of the Church, b. Tagaste, N Africa. Though reared as a Christian by his mother, St. Monica, he became a Manichaean. In Milan as a teacher of rhetoric, he was attracted by the teachings of St. Ambrose and again became a Christian (387). Returned to Tagaste, became a hermit, was later (396) made bishop of Hippo. Brought immense learning to bear on exposition of Christian doctrine and in arguments against Manichaeism, Donatism, and Pelagianism. Theologians, both Catholic and Protestant, have drawn on his works heavily and considered him master of theology. Among lay readers his autobiographical *Confessions* and his *City of God* (a profound view of the actual and the ideal in Christian society) are still very popular. Feast: Aug. 28.

Augustine of Canterbury, Saint, d. c.605, first archbishop of Canterbury. A Roman Benedictine sent with some monks to England by Pope Gregory I, he gained the favor of King Æthelbert of Kent. Introduced to England Roman rites and calendar which later triumphed over Celtic forms introduced in the N. The "apostle of England." Feast: May 28 or (in England) May 26.

Augustinians, Roman Catholic religious orders. The canons regular (Augustinians, or Austin canons) use an old rule of St. Augustine. Austin friars are a different group dating from 13th cent.

Augustus, 63 B.C.–A.D. 14, first Roman emperor. Grandnephew of Julius CAESAR, he was adopted and made heir by Caesar, without his knowledge. Originally Octavius (Caius Octavius), he became on adoption Octavian (Caius Julius Caesar Octavianus). After Caesar was assassinated he gained power in Rome and allied himself with Antony and Lepidus in the Second Triumvirate. He and Antony defeated the republicans under Brutus and Cassius at Philippi (42 B.C.). He and his lieutenant, Agrippa, drove the pirate forces of Sextus Pompeius from the sea, then after differences with Antony (see ANTONY) defeated that general and Cleopatra at Actium (31 B.C.). Augustus then was master of the Roman world. The senate showered titles on him, including *imperator* [general; from it comes word *emperor*] and *augustus* [revered]. He reformed administration, solidified Roman holdings (his only reverse was defeat of his general Varus by German leader Arminius), and beautified the city (he is said to have claimed that he found Rome of brick and left it of marble). Roman roads were extended and improved. Architecture flourished, and he was a patron of Vergil, Ovid, Livy, and Horace in the age of literature called Augustan. He imposed the Pax Romana [Roman peace] on the known civilized world. His stepson, Tiberius, succeeded him.

Augustus, kings of Poland. **Augustus I:** see SIGISMUND II (Sigismund Augustus). **Augustus II** (the Strong), 1670–1733, as Frederick Augustus I, elector of Saxony (1694–1733), was elected to succeed John III on the Polish throne (1697). Opportunistic, he became a Catholic, granted the Polish nobility unprecedented privileges, and allied himself with Russia and Denmark against CHARLES XII of Sweden (see NORTHERN WAR). Charles forced him to renounce the Polish crown in favor of STANISLAUS I (1706), but after Charles's defeat at Poltava (1709) Augustus recovered Poland (1716). Among his innumerable mistresses and illegitimate offspring were Maria Aurora von KÖNIGSMARK and her son, Maurice de Saxe. His son **Augustus III,** 1696–1763, succeeded him as elector of Saxony as Frederick Augustus II and claimed Poland from Stanislaus I, who had been reelected on Augustus II's death. After The War of the POLISH SUCCESSION he was elected Polish king (1736). As son-in-law of Emperor Joseph I, he claimed the Hapsburg lands in the War of the AUSTRIAN SUCCESSION, but he changed sides in 1742. In the SEVEN YEARS WAR

(1756–63) he fled Saxony and took residence in Poland. Indolent, he left the government to Count BRÜHL.

auk (ôk), swimming, diving bird of N Atlantic, Pacific; related to puffin. Legs set far back on body. Auk is clumsy on land, where it nests. Flightless great auks, largest species, once abundant in N Atlantic, were killed off (c.1844) for flesh, feathers, oil. Least auklet (c.6½ in.), common in Bering Sea, is smallest. Largest surviving (16–18 in.) is razor-billed auk.

Aulis (ô'lĭs), small port of ancient Greece, in Boeotia. Here Greek fleet was becalmed on way to Troy; resumed sail after sacrifice of IPHIGENIA.

Aurangzeb (ôr'ŭngzĕb"), 1618–1707, Mogul emperor (1658–1707), son of Shah Jehan. Won throne by defeating his brothers and imprisoning his father. Brought empire to greatest extent by military conquests. Intensely devoted to Islam.

Auray (ôrā'), town (pop. 8,038), Morbihan dept., NW France, in Brittany. Famous pilgrimage shrine of Sainte-Anne-d'Auray is 4 mi. N.

Aurelian (ôrē'lĕŭn), c.212–275, Roman emperor (270–75). After succeeding Claudius II, he defended the empire vigorously against barbarians and ambitious rulers (notably Zenobia of Palmyra); consolidated rule once again in Britain, Gaul, Spain, Egypt, Syria, and Mesopotamia; and revived the glory of Rome.

aureomycin: see ANTIBIOTIC SUBSTANCES.

Auriesville, village, E central N.Y., near Amsterdam. Site of Roman Catholic shrine to St. Isaac Jogues and other Jesuit Martyrs of North America, killed by Iroquois.

Aurignac (ôrēnyäk'), village, S France, SW of Toulouse. Its caves contain relics of prehistoric man (Aurignacian period; see PALEOLITHIC PERIOD.)

Auriol, Vincent (vēsā' ôryôl'), 1884–, president of French republic (1947–); a moderate Socialist.

aurochs (ôr'ŏks), name for now extinct European wild ox or urus (*Bos primigenius*), large, blackish-brown, and believed ancestor of European domestic cattle. European bison often called aurochs.

Aurora (ùrô'rù, ôrō'–), in Roman religion, goddess of dawn, identified with Greek Eos.

Aurora. 1 Residential city (pop. 11,421), N central Colo., just E of Denver, in metropolitan area. **2** City (pop. 50,576), NE Ill., W of Chicago and on Fox R. Has railroad shops and mfg. of metal products, textiles, and office supplies. **3** Village (pop. 711), W central N.Y., on Cayuga L. Seat of Wells Col. (for women; 1868).

aurora borealis (bō"rēā'lĭs, –ā'lĭs) and **aurora australis** (ôstrā'lĭs), luminous displays of N and S Hemispheres respectively, called also northern and southern lights. Visible in a variety of colors and forms over areas near geomagnetic poles, they extend to altitudes from c.35 to c.600 mi. Believed to result from collisions of charged particles from sun with gases of upper atmosphere. Occurrence correlated with sunspot activity and magnetic storms.

Au Sable (ôsä'bŭl –sā'–), river rising in several branches in N Mich. and flowing swiftly c.80 mi. SE to L. Huron N of mouth of Saginaw Bay. Once important for log driving.

Ausable, river, NE N.Y., formed by E and W branches (rise in the Adirondacks) at Au Sable Forks village and flowing c.20 mi. NE to L. Champlain S of Plattsburg. Above Keeseville (1842 bridge) is **Ausable Chasm,** with waterfalls, rapids, odd rock formations.

Auschwitz, Poland: see OSWIECIM.

Ausonius (Decimus Magnus Ausonius) (ŏsō'nēŭs dĕs'-ĭmŭs), c.310–c.393, Latin poet, a prefect of Gaul and consul (379). He pictures contemporary society.

Aussig, Czechoslovakia: see USTI NAD LABEM.

Austen, Jane, 1775–1817, English novelist. A clergyman's daughter, she lived a quiet life, and her novels of social comedy have a small stage, though they are made masterpieces by her observation, witty characterization, and sparkling, polished style. Published in her lifetime were *Sense and Sensibility* (1811), *Pride and Prejudice* (1813), *Mansfield Park* (1814), *Emma* (1816). *Northanger Abbey* (satire on the romances of Mrs. Radcliffe), written early, appeared with *Persuasion* in 1818. Little known in her day, Jane Austen later became one of the best-known and best-loved English novelists.

Austerlitz (ô'stŭrlĭts, ou'-), Czech *Slavkov u Brna*, small town, Czechoslovakia, E of Brno. Here, on Dec. 2, 1805, Napoleon I won the most brilliant victory of his career over the Russians and Austrians under emperors Alexander I and Francis I ("battle of the three emperors"), thus forcing Austria out of the war.

Austin, John, 1790–1859, English jurist, who argued that will of authority, not ethics, was basis of law.

Austin, Mary (Hunter), 1868–1934, American author. Long lived in Calif. and N. Mex.; did much to introduce Indian and Spanish elements of U.S. culture into American literature.

Austin, Moses, 1761–1821, American pioneer. Secured grant from Spanish to settle 300 families in Texas. His son, **Stephen Fuller Austin,** 1793–1836, took up plans when his father died and estab. settlements between Brazos and Colorado rivers. Opposed SANTA ANNA and thus forwarded Texas Revolution.

Austin, Warren R(obinson), 1877–, U.S. representative at the United Nations (1946–52).

Austin. 1 City (pop. 23,100), SE Minn., on Cedar R. near Iowa line; settled 1853. Rail center of agr. area with meat packing plants and railroad shops. **2** City [named for S. F. Austin] (pop. 132,459), state cap., S central Texas, on Colorado R. Laid out 1838, voted cap. 1839. Temporary cap. after annexation to U.S.; made permanent 1870. Grew to industrial city through power and flood-control projects on Colorado R. and urgencies of World War II. Mfg. of clay and food products, metalwork, and machinery. Has capitol (1885) and other state buildings. Seat of Univ. of TEXAS, Samuel Huston and Tillotson Cols. (Negro), and Texas Southern Univ. (Negro). Has O. Henry's house, Elizabeth Ney's studio (both museums), and old French embassy. Near pleasure spots (esp. Barton Springs).

Austin canons: see AUGUSTINIANS.

Australia, island continent between Indian and Pacific oceans. Nearly as large as continental U.S., it spans c.2,400 mi. from E to W and c.2,000 mi. from N to S. With the island state of TASMANIA, it forms the Commonwealth of Australia, a British dominion (2,-974,581 sq. mi.; pop. 7,580,820, excluding aboriginals). The five continental states are QUEENSLAND, NEW SOUTH WALES, VICTORIA, SOUTH AUSTRALIA, and WESTERN AUSTRALIA. NORTHERN TERRITORY and AUSTRALIAN CAPITAL TERRITORY (containing Canberra, the federal cap.) are areas under direct federal control. Australia owns Territory of Papua (see PAPUA, TERRITORY OF), Norfolk Isl., and Australian Antarctic Territory; holds under UN trusteeship the Territory of New Guinea (see NEW GUINEA, TERRITORY OF) and NAURU (jointly with the United Kingdom and New Zealand). The W half of the Australian continent is an arid plateau (important mainly for large gold fields) while the extreme N areas are wet jungle. In the east are the Great Dividing Range and the Murray R. The main coal-mining state is New South Wales. Staple products are wool and grain. Australia is noted for its distinctive animal life which includes the kangaroo and the platypus. The continent was first sighted in the early 17th cent. by the Portuguese and the Spaniards. In 1770 Capt. James Cook claimed the E coast for Great Britain, and in 1829 the whole continent was brought under British rule. Federation of the former Australian colonies was achieved in 1901. Executive power is vested in a governor-general (representing the British crown) and a cabinet headed by a prime minister. Parliament consists of a Senate and a House of Representatives. See map, p. 67.

Australian Alps, mountain ranges, SE Australia, comprising S part of Great Dividing Range. Mt. Kosciusko (7,305 ft.) is highest peak in Australia.

Australian Antarctic Territory, comprising the islands and territory (except Adélie Land) between long. 45°E and 160°E and below lat. 60°S. Claimed in 1933 by Australia.

Australian Capital Territory (911 sq. mi.; pop. 16,905), SE Australia, within New South Wales; contains Canberra, cap. of Commonwealth of Australia. Ceded 1911 by state to commonwealth. Area was called Federal Capital Territory until 1938.

Austral Islands: see TUBUAI ISLANDS.

Austrasia (ôstrā'zhǔ), Frankish kingdom (6th–8th cent.), comprising E France, W Germany, Netherlands; cap. Metz. For history, see MEROVINGIANS.

Austria, Ger. *Österreich,* federal republic (32,375 sq. mi.; pop. 6,918,959), central Europe, traversed by the Danube, bounded by Yugoslavia and Italy (S), Switzerland and Liechtenstein (W), Bavaria and Czechoslovakia (N), and Hungary (E); cap. Vienna. Its nine provinces—VORARLBERG, TYROL, SALZBURG, CARINTHIA, STYRIA, UPPER AUSTRIA, LOWER AUSTRIA, BURGENLAND, and VIENNA—are largely self-governing and are represented in the upper chamber of the federal bicameral parliament. Population is predominantly Roman Catholic and German-speaking. The ALPS, covering three quarters of the country, rise to 12,460 ft. in the HOHE TAUERN. Largely agricultural—yet not self-sufficient in major food staples—Austria also has industries (metallurgy, machinery, chemicals, textiles), concentrated mainly in the Vienna basin and at LINZ, STEYR, and GRAZ. Mineral resources include iron, manganese, copper, lead, zinc, petroleum (at Zistersdorf), and salt. The area of present Austria was inhabited by Celts when it was conquered by Rome (15 B.C.–10 A.D.). It was overrun after the 5th cent. by Huns, Goths, Lombards, and Bavarians; conquered 788 by Charlemagne; reconquered 955 from the Magyars by Otto I; and attached as Eastern March to Bavaria 955–76. In subsequent history, the word *Austria* has four distinct meanings: (1) Austria proper, i.e., Upper and Lower Austria, including Vienna. This was ruled from 976 as margraviate (after 1156, duchy) by the house of Babenberg, and acquired in 1251 by OTTOCAR II of Bohemia. In 1276 Ottocar had to cede Austria, along with Styria, Carinthia, and CARNIOLA, to RUDOLF I of Hapsburg, in whose family it remained until 1918 (raised to archduchy 1453). (2) With the rise of Hapsburg greatness, the term *Austria* came to designate the house of Hapsburg or Austria, which ruled the HOLY ROMAN EMPIRE from 1438 to 1806 and at one time held an hereditary empire which embraced the world (see HAPSBURG). The chief historic importance of Austria proper in that period was as bulwark against Turkish onslaughts, which culminated and ended with the siege of Vienna in 1683. The house of Austria lost its primacy in German affairs in the THIRTY YEARS WAR and the wars of the 18th cent. As a result, it concentrated, especially under MARIA THERESA and JOSEPH II, on internal consolidation of its hereditary lands and on eastward expansion (esp. in POLAND and Balkans). Thrice defeated in the French Revolutionary and Napoleonic Wars (see FRANCIS II, emperor), it nevertheless emerged in 1815 from the CONGRESS OF VIENNA as leader of the GERMAN CONFEDERATION. (3) Shortly before the dissolution of the Holy Roman Empire, Francis II assumed the title "Francis I, emperor of Austria." The Austrian Empire, which is the third meaning of the term, consisted after 1815 of, roughly, German-speaking Austria, Bohemia, Moravia, S Poland, Lombardy, Venetia, Carniola, Istria, Dalmatia, and the separate kingdom of Hungary, with Croatia and Slavonia. The Revolution of 1848 drove METTERNICH from power but Emperor FRANCIS JOSEPH soon restored absolutism. In the Italian War of 1859 Austria lost Lombardy; the AUSTRO-PRUSSIAN WAR of 1866 cost it Venetia and eliminated it from German affairs. In 1867 a general reorganization of the empire resulted in the creation of the AUSTRO-HUNGARIAN MONARCHY, which collapsed at the end of World War I. (4) In Nov., 1918, German Austria was proclaimed a republic. The Treaty of SAINT-GERMAIN (1919) fixed the boundaries of present Austria—i.e., the German-speaking remnant of the Austrian Empire—a small country of 6,000,000 people (a third of whom lived in the capital), stripped of its former raw materials, food, and markets. Chronic bankruptcy, unemployment, and political unrest resulted. The three-cornered struggle among Socialists, clerico-fascists, and National Socialists led to the establishment in 1934 of a corporative, authoritarian regime under Chancellor DOLLFUSS and his successor, SCHUSCHNIGG. The growth of local Nazism, German pressure, and Western appeasement resulted in the occupation of Austria by Germany in 1938. It was fully incorporated into the Reich in 1940. Conquered in 1945 by American and Russian troops, Austria was restored as a republic and divided into five zones of occupation—Vorarlberg and Tyrol (French); Salzburg and W Upper Austria (U.S.); E Upper Austria, Lower Austria, and Burgenland (Russian); Carinthia and Styria (British); and Vienna (joint four-power occupation). Though Austria was formally recognized in 1946, no peace treaty was signed, largely because of basic disagreements between Russia and the West on the reparations question. As of 1952, a Catholic-Socialist coalition cabinet is in power.

Austrian Succession, War of the, 1740–48, European war precipitated by succession of MARIA THERESA of Austria to the Hapsburg lands by virtue of PRAGMATIC SANCTION. Her succession was challenged by the elector of Bavaria (later Emperor CHARLES VII), PHILIP V of Spain, and AUGUSTUS III of Poland and Saxony, while FREDERICK II of Prussia claimed part of SILESIA. Prussia opened war by invading Silesia, was joined (1741) by France, Spain, Bavaria, Saxony; made separate peace 1742; reentered war 1744; made final separate peace 1745 (Treaty of Dresden). England, then at war with Spain (see JENKINS'S EAR, WAR OF) supported Austria, as did Holland and Sardinia. Saxony went over to Austrian side 1743. Bavaria withdrew from war at death of Charles VII (1745). Notable military events up to 1745: Prussian victory at MOLLWITZ (1741); capture of Prague by Franco-Bavarians (1742); occupation of Bavaria and recapture of Prague by Austrians (1742); English victory at DETTINGEN (1743); French victory at FONTENOY (1745); Prussian victory at HOHENFRIEDBERG (1745). By Treaty of Dresden Prussia obtained most of Silesia but promised to support election of Maria Theresa's husband as emperor (Francis I). The remaining belligerents fought on inconclusively in N Italy, Low Countries, America (see FRENCH AND INDIAN WARS), and India until Treaty of AIX-LA-CHAPELLE of 1748.

Austro-Hungarian Monarchy or Dual Monarchy, the Hapsburg empire from the constitutional compromise (*Ausgleich*) of 1867 between AUSTRIA and HUNGARY until its fall in 1918. Rulers: FRANCIS JOSEPH (1867–1916), CHARLES I (1916–18). Empire was divided into Cisleithania (lands W of Leitha R.), including Austria proper, Bohemia, Moravia, Austrian Silesia, and Austrian Poland; and Transleithania, including Hungary, Transylvania, CROATIA, Slovenia, and part of Dalmatia. Cisleithania was ruled by emperor of Austria, Transleithania by king of Hungary (both dignities being united in the same monarch); each elected its own parliament and had its own cabinet and customs regime. A three-man common cabinet governed foreign policy, defense, imperial finances. Economically an organic whole, empire was torn and eventually broken up by nationalist aspirations of its many minorities, notably Czechs, Poles, Serbs, Italians, Rumanians. Threatened by pan-Slavism (spearheaded by Serbia and supported by Russia), Austria-Hungary concluded

alliance with Germany (1879), joined also by Italy (1882; see TRIPLE ALLIANCE and TRIPLE ENTENTE). The annexation of BOSNIA AND HERCEGOVINA (1908) envenomed relations with Serbia and Russia. The assassination of Archduke FRANCIS FERDINAND precipitated WORLD WAR I (1914), Austria-Hungary surrendered Nov. 3, 1918. The Treaties of Versailles, Trianon, and Saint-Germain fixed boundaries of successor states.

Austro-Prussian War or Seven Weeks War, June 15–Aug. 23, 1866, between Prussia, allied with Italy, and Austria, seconded by Bavaria, Württemberg, Saxony, Hanover, Baden, and several smaller German states. Provoked by BISMARCK with object of expelling Austria from GERMAN CONFEDERATION. Austro-Prussian dispute over administration of SCHLESWIG-HOLSTEIN served as pretext. Prussia quickly overran German states, crushed Austrians at SADOWA. Austrian victories over Italians at Custozza and Lissa proved useless at Peace of Prague (Aug. 23, 1866): Austria had to cede Venetia to Italy. Prussia demanded no territory from Austria but annexed Hesse-Kassel, Hanover, Frankfurt. New NORTH GERMAN CONFEDERATION was estab. under Prussian leadership. War paved way for founding of German Empire in 1871.

Auteuil (ōtû′ē), section of Paris, France, near Bois de Boulogne. Famous racecourse.

authentic modes, in music: see MODE.

autogiro (ô′tōjī′rō) or **gyroplane** (jī′rŭplān), first aircraft to depart from Wright brothers type. Overhead airfoils, rotated by aerodynamic forces arising from craft's propulsion by ordinary engine and propeller, provide principal lift; wing area much reduced. Inventor, Juan de la CIERVA. Generally superseded by HELICOPTER.

automaton: see ROBOT.

automobile. Probably the first self-propelled vehicle was a steam-driven, three-wheeled carriage introduced 1769 in Paris by Nicolas Joseph Cugnot. In early 19th cent. attempts to operate steam road carriages failed in England because of excessive tolls and restrictive legislation (e.g., the Red Flag Act). In Germany, INTERNAL-COMBUSTION ENGINE was used in 1885 by Karl Benz to operate vehicle; improved engine built by Gottlieb Daimler c.1885. Internal-combustion models manufactured in U.S. during 1890s by Charles Duryea, J. Frank Duryea, Elwood Haynes, Henry Ford, Ransom E. Olds, and Alexander Winton. By 1903 Detroit was becoming U.S. automotive center. Free growth of the industry was threatened by patent granted (1895) to George Selden for gasoline car. Manufacturers licensed by Selden formed association (1903) to control manufacture. Independents, led by Henry Ford, opposed this; U.S. Circuit Court of Appeals ruled (1911) Selden's patent valid but applicable to two-cycle engines only. Steam-driven cars thereafter were rapidly displaced by gasoline models; electric models retain limited use for local delivery trucks.

automobile racing, sport in which specially constructed, high-speed automobiles race on outdoor or indoor tracks. Started 1894 in France, 1895 in U.S. Indianapolis Speedway meet first held 1911. Famous drivers include William K. Vanderbilt, Barney Oldfield, Edward V. Rickenbacker, Wilbur Shaw.

autonomy (ôtŏn′ŭmē), in political sense, limited self-government, short of independence. The objective test of autonomy is recognition that the group may legislate for itself. The right may be delegated or permitted by the state. Situation of the autonomous border regions of USSR today is peculiar because one object of autonomy is to attract others into the Russian orbit.

Autun (ōtû′), city (pop. 11,767), Saône-et-Loire dept., E central France. Early medieval center of learning. Roman ruins; 12th-cent. cathedral.

Auvergne (ōvĕr′nyù), region and former province, central France, in the Massif Central, in Cantal, Puy-de-Dôme, Haute-Loire depts.; historic cap., Clermont

CHINA
Canton
TROPIC OF CANCER
Hanoi
FORMOSA
HONG KONG
HAINAN
PACIFIC
THAILAND
OCEAN
MARIANAS
LUZON
INDO-CHINA
Manila
GUAM
Saigon
PHILIPPINES
SOUTH CHINA SEA
PALAWAN
YAP
MALAYA
MINDANAO
PALAU
TRUK
CELEBES SEA
CAROLINE ISLS.
Singapore
BORNEO
HALMAHERA
MOLUCCA SEA
EQUATOR
SUMATRA
CELEBES
NEW GUINEA
BISMARCK ARCHIPELAGO
JAKARTA
CERAM
I N D O N E S I A
JAVA SEA
BANDA SEA
SOLOMON ISLS.
BALI
JAVA
TIMOR
ARAFURA SEA
Port Moresby
TIMOR SEA
Darwin
GULF OF CARPENTARIA
CORAL SEA
NORTHERN TERRITORY
GREAT SANDY DESERT
AUSTRALIA
QUEENSLAND
20
WESTERN
TROPIC OF CAPRICORN
GIBSON DESERT
Alice Springs
AUSTRALIA
Brisbane
L. Eyre
SOUTH AUSTRALIA
GREAT VICTORIA DESERT
L. Torrens
NEW SOUTH WALES
Perth
Newcastle
Fremantle
Sydney
GREAT AUSTRALIAN BIGHT
Adelaide
CANBERRA
Melbourne
VICTORIA
TASMAN SEA
INDIAN
40
OCEAN
TASMANIA
Hobart
Auckland
N
NORTH ISL.
40
WELLINGTON
Christchurch
0   400   800
MILES
SOUTH ISL.
NEW ZEALAND
110
130
170

CAPITAL CITIES are designated by CAPITAL AND SMALL CAPITAL type

(now Clermont-Ferrand). Auvergne mts. culminate in Mont-Dore and Puy de Dôme. Stock raising, dairying in mountains; agr. in valleys. Mineral springs and spas. Auvergnats descend from Celtic Arverni, whose leader Vercingetorix led Gallic revolt against Caesar. Region passed to English (1154) as part of Aquitaine; later was incorporated in several stages into French royal domain.

Auxerre (ōsĕr′), town (pop. 20,809), cap. of Yonne dept., E central France; trading center for Chablis wines. Fine medieval architecture: Church and Abbey of St. Germain; Gothic cathedral.

AV, the Authorized Version or King James Version of the Bible. See also OLD TESTAMENT.

Avalon (ăv′ŭlŏn), in Celtic mythology, island of the happy otherworld. See ARTHURIAN LEGEND.

Avalon. 1 See SANTA BARBARA ISLANDS, Calif. **2** Residential borough (pop. 6,463), SW Pa., NW suburb of Pittsburgh.

Avalon Peninsula, 3,579 sq. mi., SE N.F., Canada, most densely populated part of the province. Deeply indented at center by Conception Bay (N) and St. Mary's Bay (S).

Aveiro (ävä′rō), city (pop. 11,247), Beira Litoral, NW Portugal. Notable fishing port since 16th cent. Partially built over water: "Portuguese Venice."

Avellaneda (äväyänä′dhä), city (pop. 278,621), Buenos Aires prov., Argentina; industrial city, usually considered part of greater Buenos Aires.

Ave Maria (ä′vä märē′ä) [Latin,= hail, Mary], Roman Catholic prayer in Latin to the Virgin. Much set to music (notably by Schubert, Gounod). The English version, *Hail, Mary,* one of the most common of Catholic prayers.

Avempace (ä′vŭmpäs, ä″vĕmpä′thä), Arabic *Ibn Bajja,* d. 1138, Spanish-Arabian Aristotelian philosopher.

Avenches (äväsh′), Latin *Aventicum,* small town, Vaud canton, W Switzerland. Flourished 1st cent. B.C.–2d cent. A.D. as chief town (pop. c.80,000) of Helvetia. Numerous Roman remains.

Avenzoar (ăv′ŭnzō′ur, –zōär′) or **Ibn Zohr** (ĭb′n zōr′), c.1090?–1162, Arabian physician, pioneer in experimental medicine.

average, statistical measure expressing numerically the characteristics of a group of figures. See MEAN; MEDIAN; MODE.

Avernus (ŭvûr′nŭs), Ital. *Averno,* small crater lake, Campania, S Italy, near Cuma. For its sulphuric vapors and gloomy aspect, it was regarded by Romans as entrance to hell; later the name was used for hell itself.

Averroës (ŭvĕr′ōēz), 1126–98, Moorish philosopher. In his study of Aristotle, he sought to reconcile philosophy with religion, holding religion to be a symbolic expression of philosophical truth.

Avery Island, S La., in sea marshes and swamps, SW of New Iberia. Has bird (esp. egret) sanctuary and Jungle Gardens (rare plants). Rock salt has been mined since 1791. Has yielded prehistoric relics.

Aveyron (ävärō′), department (3,386 sq. mi.; pop. 307,-717), S central France, in Rouergue; cap. Rodez.

aviation, term applied broadly to all activities, facilities, and enterprises related to flying. Leonardo da Vinci first studied flight scientifically. Flight first achieved (1783) in lighter-than-air craft (see BALLOON). Among pioneers in heavier-than-air flight: Sir George Cayley (mechanics-of-flight analysis, 1809–10); W. S. Henson (foreshadowed modern monoplane, 1842); John Stringfellow (power-driven model plane, said to be first to fly); F. H. Wenham (devised wind tunnel, 1866); Alphonse Penaud (with Paul Gauchot designed amphibian monoplane, 1878); Clément Ader (his bat-fashioned monoplane flew, 1890); Sir Hiram S. Maxim (steam-driven plane with crew rose into air, 1894); and Americans, S. P. LANGLEY, Octave CHANUTE, and Otto LILIENTHAL. First man-carrying, motor-driven airplane flight was by Orville Wright, repeated by Wilbur Wright (Dec. 17, 1903, Kitty Hawk,

N.C.). Louis BLÉRIOT flew English Channel (1909). Glenn Curtis built first flying boat (1912). After World War I, aviation grew in importance. First N Atlantic crossing was by A. C. Read in U.S. Navy flying boat (May, 1919). John Alcock and A. W. Brown flew Newfoundland–Ireland (1919); Ross Smith London–Australia (1919). Richard E. Byrd and Floyd Bennett flew Spitsbergen–North Pole (1926). Charles A. Lindbergh flew the Atlantic solo (1927). Hermann Köhl, J. C. Fitzmaurice, and G. von Hünefeld flew Ireland–Newfoundland (1928). Charles Kingsford-Smith was first to fly Pacific (1928), San Francisco–Australia with two stops. Clyde E. Pangborn and Hugh Herndon flew from Japan to Washington state nonstop (1931). Wiley Post and Harold Gatty flew round the world (1931). Post circled world solo (1933). Howard Hughes and four companions circled world (1938). Amelia Earhart Putnam was first woman to fly Atlantic as passenger (1928) and solo (1932). U.S. air transport chiefly of mail until, after 1930, passenger carrying became profitable. Pan American Airways (later Pan American World Airways) began transpacific air-mail service in 1934; added passenger service with San Francisco-to-Manila China Clipper. World War II saw Army Air Transport Command and Navy Air Transport Service pioneer in global air routes. See also AERIAL PHOTOGRAPHY; AIR, LAW OF THE; AIRPLANE; AIR POWER; AIRSHIP. See *ill.,* p. 19.

Avicebron: see IBN GABIROL, SOLOMON BEN JUDAH.

Avicenna (ăvĭsĕn′ŭ), Arabic *Ibn Sina,* 980–1037, Arabian philosopher. Interpreted Aristotle in Neoplatonic fashion, but was known in West chiefly as a writer on medicine and other sciences.

Avignon (ävēnyō′), city (pop. 47,040), cap. of Vaucluse dept., SE France, in Provence. Wine trade, silk mfg. See of popes during "Babylonian captivity," 1309–78, and of several antipopes during Great Schism, 1378–1408. City was bought (1348) by Clement VI from countess of Provence; remained papal property until annexed by France (1791). Landmarks: 14th-cent. papal palace, Basilica of St. Peter, fragment of 12th-cent. bridge.

Ávila. Gil González de: see GONZÁLEZ DE ÁVILA.

Ávila (ä′vēlä), city (pop. 19,590), cap of Ávila prov., central Spain, in Old Castile; birthplace of St. Theresa. Medieval walls; cathedral.

Ávila Camacho, Manuel (mänwĕl′ ä′vēlä kämä′chō), 1897–, president of Mexico (1940–46).

Aviz, Port. *Avis* (both: ŭvēsh′), village, central Portugal. Granted (c.1162) to branch of Knights of Calatrava, which became the separate Order of Aviz. Master of order became King John I of Portugal, establishing dynasty of Aviz (1383–1580).

Avoca or **Ovoca** (both: ŭvō′kŭ), river of Co. Wicklow, Ireland, formed by union of Avonmore R. and Avonbeg R. (Thomas Moore's "Meeting of the Waters").

avocado (ăv″ŭkä′dō), broad-leaved evergreen tree (*Persea*), grown in Calif. and Fla. for pear-shaped, oil-rich fruit (alligator pear) often used in salads.

avocet (ăv′ŭsĕt) wading bird (c.15–18 in. long) related to snipe and stilt. North and South America, Europe, and Australia each have one species. North American "blue shanks," hunted for food, are rare E of Mississippi. See *ill.,* p. 105.

Avogadro, Amadeo (ämädä′ō ävōgä′drō), 1776–1856, Italian physicist, a count. Avogadro's law: equal volumes of gases under same pressure and temperature have same number of molecules. Avogadro's number (6.02 x 10²³): number of molecules in gram molecular volume of gas.

Avon (ā′vŭn, ăv′ŭn) [Celtic,= river], name of several rivers in England. **1 Bristol Avon** or **Lower Avon** rises in Gloucestershire and flows 75 mi. through Wiltshire and Somerset, past Bath and Bristol, to the Severn. **2 East Avon,** in Wiltshire and Hampshire, flows 48 mi. past Salisbury to the English Channel. **3 Upper Avon,** in Northamptonshire, Leicestershire, Warwickshire, and Worcestershire is most famous. Flows 96 mi. past Rugby, Warwick, and Stratford-on-Avon to the Severn.

ax or **axe,** tool used since prehistoric times for felling trees, working wood, preparing soil, and as a weapon. It was a major item in equipment of American pioneers. Related tools are hatchet (short-handled ax with hammer head) and hammer. Double-bitted ax was religious emblem in Crete and elsewhere.

Axel: see ABSALON.

Axis, coalition of states headed by Germany, Italy, and Japan, 1936–45 (see WORLD WAR II). Original Italo-German accord of 1936 became full alliance 1939 and was acceded to by Japan in Berlin Pact of 1940, to which Hungary, Rumania, Bulgaria, Slovakia, and Croatia adhered later. The related Anti-Comintern Pact of 1936 (see COMINTERN), between Germany and Japan, later included Berlin Pact nations, Spain, Finland, and others.

Axminster, urban district (pop. 2,673), Devonshire, England. Its famous carpets now made at Wilton.

Axum, Ethiopia: see AKSUM.

Ayacucho (äyäkōō′chō), city (pop. 18,275), S Peru. Defeat of Spanish by Sucre here (1824) secured Peruvian independence, marked triumph of revolution in South America and guaranteed independence from Spain.

Ayala, Ramón Pérez de: see PÉREZ DE AYALA.

Ayer (âr), town (pop. 5,740), N Mass., ESE of Fitchburg. U.S. Fort Devens is near by.

Ayesha (Aisha) (ī′shù, ä′īshä″), d. 678, Mohammed's favorite wife; Abu Bakr's daughter. Fomented unsuccessful revolt during caliphate of ALI.

Aylesbury (ālz′bùrē), county town (pop. 21,054) of Buckinghamshire, England; agr. market for upper Thames valley famed for its ducks.

Aymara (īmärä′), South American Indians inhabiting L. Titicaca basin. Although subjugated by the Inca in 15th cent. and by Pizarro brothers (1538), they continue to dominate region.

Aymer of Valence (ā′mùr, vùlĕns′, väläs′), d. 1260, bishop of Winchester. Half brother of King Henry III of England, he was elected at the king's order. Hostility towards him important factor in BARONS' WAR.

Ayodhya, India: see FYZABAD.

Ayolas, Juan de (hwän′dä äyō′läs), d. 1537?, Spanish conquistador, explorer of Río de la Plata region (esp. Paraguay); lieutenant of Pedro de MENDOZA.

Ayrshire (âr′shĭr) or **Ayr,** maritime county (1,132 sq. mi.; pop. 321,184), SW Scotland. Has pleasant terrain and is primarily agr. and pastoral. Ayr cows are famous. Country of Robert Bruce, Burns, and Boswell. The county town, **Ayr** (âr), burgh (pop. 43,011), on the Firth of Clyde, is heart of the Burns country and has Burns memorials. Alloway, his birthplace, is a suburb.

Ayuthia or **Ayutthaya** (both: äyōōt′hīä), town (pop. 15,-821), S Thailand, on Menam R.; trade center. Was Siamese cap. (c.1350–1767).

azalea: see RHODODENDRON.

Azaña, Manuel (mänwäl′ äthä′nyä), 1880–1940, Spanish republican statesman. As premier (1931–33, 1936), he pressed for social reforms. President of Spain 1936–39. Fled to France near end of Civil War.

Azariah (ăzùrī′ù). **1** One of THREE HOLY CHILDREN. Greek form is Azarias.

Azerbaijan (ä″zùrbījän′), region (41,160 sq. mi.; pop. 2,734,973), extreme NW Iran. Aras R. in N separates it from Azerbaijan SSR. Mainly mountainous with fertile lowlands yielding grain and fruit. Chief city is

TABRIZ. In remote times region was dominated by kings of Van and Urartu (in Armenia). Settled by Medes before 8th cent. B.C.; became a province in Persian empire. Supposedly birthplace of Zoroaster. Persian Atropates estab. himself as independent king here after 328 B.C. Region again became part of Persia in 3d cent. A.D. Converted to Islam in 7th cent. by Arabs, who brought it under caliphate. Dominated by Seljuk Turks 11th–12th cent., conquered in 14th cent. by Tamerlane. Ruled by shahs from early 17th to early 19th cent., when N part was ceded to Russia. Remainder was organized as a Persian province, which was divided 1938 into Third and Fourth provs.

Azerbaijan (ä″sùrbījän′), constituent republic (33,100 sq. mi.; pop. c.3,100,000), USSR, bordering Iranian Azerbaijan in E; cap. BAKU. Includes E ranges of Greater and Lesser Caucasus; hot, arid Kura valley; subtropical Lenkoran lowland and oil-rich Apsheron peninsula on Caspian coast. Chief products: oil, cotton, grapes, tea, fruit, tobacco. Sheep raising in mountains. Population largely Turkic Azers or Azerbaijani—Shiite Moslems of Persian culture. Region ceded by Persia to Russia (1813, 1828). For earlier history, see preceding article.

Azores (ùzôrz′, ā′zôrz), Port. *Açores* (ùsô′rĭsh), islands (888 sq. mi.; pop. 318,686), in N Atlantic, administratively part of Portugal. São Miguel is largest island. Chief cities: Ponta Delgada (on São Miguel), Angra do Heroísmo (Terceira isl.), Horta (Fayal isl.). Products: grain, fruit, wine. Islands were known by 1351; colonized by Portuguese in 1445.

Azorín: see MARTÍNEZ RUIZ, JOSÉ.

Azov (ā′zŏv, Rus. ŭzôf′), city (pop. 17,545), S European RSFSR; fishing port near mouth of Don and Sea of Azov. Strategic fortress until late 18th cent. Peter the Great took it from khan of Crimea 1696, had to return it 1711. Definitively secured by Russia 1774. Ancient Greek colony of Tanais was near by. The **Sea of Azov,** Latin *Palus Maeotis,* is a N arm (c.14,-000 sq. mi.) of the Black Sea, with which it is connected by the Kerch Strait. Fed by the Don and Kuban, it has important fisheries. Rostov-on-Don, Taganrog, Kerch are chief ports. SIVASH SEA is a W branch.

Aztec (ăz′tĕk″), Indian people dominating central Mexico at time of Spanish Conquest. Arrived in Valley of Mexico from N in 12th cent.; nomadic until founding of their cap., TENOCHTITLÁN (c.1325; present Mexico city). Created a composite civilization based on TOLTEC and Mixteca-Puebla heritage. Among their accomplishments were a stone wheel or calendar stone, weaving, sculpture, engineering, metalwork, music, picture writing. Agr. well advanced; education almost universal. Political and social life based on caste system (nobility; priesthood; military and merchant). Civilization fell before Spanish under Hernán CORTÉS. See also MONTEZUMA; CUAHTEMOC.

Aztec Ruins National Monument: see NATIONAL PARKS AND MONUMENTS (table).

Azuela, Mariano (märyä′nō äswä′lä), 1873–1952, Mexican novelist. Experiences with Villa's revolutionary forces gave material for *Los de abajo* (1915).

azurite (ăzh′ùrīt), mineral, the blue basic carbonate of copper, an important copper ore. Occurs in monoclinic crystals and in masses. Crystals used for ornament are found in SW U.S. and in France.

Azusa (ùzōō′sù), city (pop. 11,042), S Calif., E of Pasadena; founded 1887. Ships citrus fruit.

B

B, chemical symbol of element BORON.

Ba, chemical symbol of element BARIUM.

Baal (bā'ŭl), plural **Baalim** (bā'ŭlĭm) [Semitic,= possessor], term used in Old Testament for the gods of Canaan. Each locality had its own Baal who either had his own name, as Melkart of Tyre, or a name formed by adding the name of a place or special attribute to the word Baal, e.g., Baal-peor [Heb.,= Baal of Peor] or Baal-hanan [Heb.,= Baal is gracious]. Baal worship was usually characterized by fertility rites and human sacrifice. At first Hebrews adopted the term for their God, but as struggle between Canaanite polytheism and Hebrew monotheism grew, name became synonymous with evil—hence Beelzebub (see SATAN), probably from Baal-zebub, god of Ekron. Other forms of Baal: Bel (in Babylonian religion); endings in Tyrian names (e.g., Jezebel, Hannibal).

Baalbek (bäl'bĕk), town, Lebanon, N of Damascus. Has ruins of great ancient city devoted to worship of Baal or Bel, the sun-god, hence called in Greek Heliopolis [city of the sun]; notable in Roman days.

Baal-peor (-pē'ôr), local god of Peor. Practices of his worship were especially abominable to the Hebrews, hence his name became a symbol of all shameful cults. Num. 25; Deut. 4.3; Ps. 106.28; Hosea 9.10. Under form of Belphegor, this was name of a devil in Middle Ages; Machiavelli used it in his *Belfagor*.

Baal-Schem-Tov (bäl-shĕm'-tōv') [Heb.,= the man with a reputation], 1700–1760, first leader of the modern Hasidim, b. Russia; real name Israel ben Eliezer. Gained fame as a miracle worker. Taught that man reaches God through joy rather than sorrow, that learning is not necessary for prayer, and that repentance is always possible.

Baal-zebub: see BAAL and SATAN.

Baasha (bā'āshù), d. c.886 B.C., king of Israel (c.909–c.886 B.C.). Murdered Nadab and royal family to make himself king. 1 Kings 15.27–16.7; 2 Chron. 16.

Babar: see BABER.

Babbitt, Irving, 1865–1933, American teacher, humanist, vigorous critic of romanticism.

Babbitt metal, silver-white ANTIFRICTION METAL alloy, originally of tin, antimony, and copper, later also of varying composition. Developed by Isaac Babbitt (1799–1862), American inventor.

Babcock, Stephen Moulton, 1843–1931, American agr. chemist. Babcock test (1890) for percentage of butterfat in milk advanced the dairy industry.

Babel, Isaac Emmanuelovich (ē'säk ūmänōōā'lùvĭch bä'bùl), 1894–, Russian author. One of the "fellow travelers," he won fame with his concise, realistic stories of the ghetto and the revolution, notably *Odessa Tales* (1923–24), *Red Cavalry* (1926; Eng. tr., 1929), *Benia Krik* (1927; Eng. tr., 1935).

Babel (bā'bùl), city where Noah's descendants (who spoke one language) tried to build tower to heaven. For this presumption they lost ability to speak intelligibly to each other. Gen. 11.1–9. Some see in this an explanation of world's many languages.

Baber or **Babar** (both: bä'bùr), popular name of Zahir-ud-din Mohammed, 1480–1530, founder of Mogul empire of India; descendant of Tamerlane. Invaded India from Afghanistan, conquering nearly all N India (1525–26). Autobiography is greatest of his literary works. Was also an excellent musician.

Babeuf, François Noël (fräswä' nôĕl' bäbûf'), 1760–97, French revolutionist. Argued for economic and social as well as political equality. After brief imprisonment he formed a group to forward economic equality and communism. After the Directory banned the group, a plot (the Conspiracy of the Equals) was made to overthrow the government. It was betrayed, and Babeuf was executed.

Babington, Anthony (bā'bĭngtùn), 1561–86, English conspirator. Plotted murder of Queen Elizabeth and freeing of MARY QUEEN OF SCOTS. Proof against him was used to bring about Mary's execution.

Babism (bä'bĭzùm), religion of 19th-cent. Persian sect, founded 1843, when Mirza Ali Mohammed of Shiraz proclaimed himself Bab ed-Din [gate of faith], successor to Moses, Christ, and Mohammed. Doctrines from Sufism, Gnosticism, Shiite Islam. The sect rebelled unsuccessfully 1848; the Bab was executed 1850. Babism supplanted by Bahaism.

baboon, large, chiefly terrestrial monkey (genus *Papio*) of Africa, Arabia. Face doglike, canine teeth large, limbs powerful; medium tail is carried arched. Travels in packs; eats scorpions, insects, other animals, plant food. Most are yellowish or brown. MANDRILL and chacma are large baboons.

Babson, Roger Ward, 1875–, American statistician. Founded Babson Statistical Organization (1904), which publishes business statistics. Founded Babson Institute (1919) to train business executives.

baby: see INFANT.

Babylon (bā'bĭlùn), city of anc. Mesopotamia, on the Euphrates; center of Babylonia. HAMMURABI founded its greatness, which was destroyed by SENNACHERIB but revived in later period. Under NEBUCHADNEZZAR (d. 562 B.C.) it reached a height of luxury that made it fabulous; its Hanging Gardens were considered one of the wonders of the world. After capture by Persians (538 B.C.) it declined.

Babylon, residential and resort village (pop. 6,015), SE N.Y., on S shore (Great South Bay) of Long Isl.

Babylonia (bäbĭlō'nēù), anc. Mesopotamian empire, centered on Babylon. Name sometimes used to include all S Mesopotamia with city-states (Lagash, Akkad, Erech, Ur) that flourished 3d millennium B.C., but more often limited to Semitic civilization founded by SARGON and brought to a peak by HAMMURABI (c.2100 B.C.). Learning (with cuneiform writing), commerce, and architecture flourished. Attacks by Hittites and nomadic Kassites (18th cent. B.C.) caused decline, but Babylonia again flowered under the Assyrian empire. A revolt was put down by SENNACHERIB (late 8th cent. B.C.), but later Nabopolassar estab. (625 B.C.) Babylonian independence, and the empire grew to new and greater splendor under NEBUCHADNEZZAR. After conquest by Persians under Cyrus the Great (538 B.C.) Babylonia declined. Its contributions to art, science, and other aspects of civilization were incalculable.

Babylonian captivity: see CAPTIVITY and PAPACY.

Babylonian religion. The religion of the whole Tigris-Euphrates valley was really one, with many local gods. Dominant gods were determined by dominant cities (e.g., when Babylon was paramount, Marduk, or Bel or BAAL, was king of gods). Priests were very powerful. The rich mythology of Babylon, further elaborated by Assyria, was preserved in cuneiform writing on clay tablets. It included stories of creation of world, of flood covering whole world, journey of Ishtar to underworld, and legends of gods and heroes. Babylon was indebted to Sumerian culture for its religion, and its great towers (suggesting BABEL) were reminiscent of Sumerian worship of high places.

baby's-breath, garden perennial, *Gypsophila panicu-*

SMALL CAPITALS = cross references. Pronunciation key on inside end pages. Abbreviations: p. 2.

70

lata, marked by delicate panicles of small white blooms.

Bacchae (băk'kē) or **Bacchantes** (bŭkăn'tēz, bŭkănts', bă'kŭnts), in Greek and Roman religion, female worshipers of DIONYSUS or BACCHUS. Their secret rites, performed in frenzied ecstasy, involved the thyrsus, the myrtle, drinking, and sweet wild music. Also called Maenads.

Bacchanalia (băkŭnā'lēŭ) [Latin], in Roman religion, festival in honor of BACCHUS. Originally religious, it became a drunken orgy and was outlawed.

Bacchantes: see BACCHAE.

Bacchus (băk'ŭs), in Greek and Roman mythology, god of wine, identified with DIONYSUS; also god of vegetation and fertility. His rites were orgiastic.

Bacchylides (băkĭ'lĭdēz), fl. c.470 B.C., Greek lyric poet, b. Ceos; contemporary of Pindar.

Bach (bäkh), German family of distinguished musicians beginning with **Hans Bach,** c.1580–1626, a Thuringian violinist who was called The Player. Two of his grandsons were **Johann Christoph Bach,** 1642–1703, a composer and organist at Eisenach, and **Johann Ambrosius Bach,** 1645–95, a violinist at Eisenach and father of Johann Sebastian Bach (see separate article). The eldest son of Johann Ambrosius was **Johann Christoph Bach,** 1671–1721, an organist. When his parents died he took his younger brother, Johann Sebastian, into his home and became his teacher. Of Johann Sebastian's 20 children, several became outstanding musicians. **Wilhelm Friedeman Bach** (frē'dümän), 1710–84, was an organist, composer, and musical director at Halle. **Carl Philipp Emanuel Bach,** 1714–88, wrote cantatas, oratorios, symphonies, Passion music, and two volumes of sonatas; also a treatise on clavier playing. **Johann Christian Bach,** 1735–82, lived in Italy and England. He became a Roman Catholic and wrote Masses and church music, operas, and sonatas and concertos for clavier.

Bach, Alexander, 1813–93, Austrian statesman; created baron 1854. Minister of interior 1849–59. Instituted reactionary "Bach system" of bureaucratic control, centralization, and Germanization of Hapsburg empire, along with beneficial reforms, e.g., abolition of internal tariff barriers.

Bach, Johann Sebastian, 1685–1750, German composer, b. Eisenach. Became organist at Arnstadt (1703) and at Mülhausen (1707); court organist and chamber musician at Weimar (1708), musical director (1714); musical director at Cöthen (1717); cantor at Leipzig (1723) until his death. Few of Bach's works were published during his lifetime, hence exact dates cannot be fixed for all of them, but most of them can be placed in their proper period. At Arnstadt and Mülhausen he began a series of organ works which culminated in the great works of Weimar period—the Passacaglia and Fugue in C minor, most of the noted preludes and fugues, the 45 chorale-preludes of *Das Orgelbüchlein*. At Cöthen he produced instrumental works, e.g., the English and French Suites, the Two-Part and Three-Part Inventions, *The Well-Tempered Clavier,* Book I, the unaccompanied violin sonatas, and the Brandenburg concertos. Great works of the Leipzig period include the St. John Passion, the Magnificat, the St. Matthew Passion, the Mass in B-Minor, *The Well-Tempered Clavier,* Book II, and the *Clavierübung* (including the Six Partitas, the Italian Concerto, and the Goldberg variations). His last work was *The Art of the Fugue* (1749). Despite his many secular compositions, Bach is regarded primarily as a church composer.

Bach Choir, name of choral organizations producing music of J. S. Bach. Outstanding are the Bach Choir of London, founded 1875, and the Bach Choir of Bethlehem, Pa., founded 1900.

Bache, Benjamin Franklin (bāch), 1769–98, American journalist; grandson of Benjamin Franklin. Founded Philadelphia *General Advertiser* (later the *Aurora*) in 1790. Denounced Federalists; arrested under Sedition Act; released on parole. His son, **Franklin Bache,**

1792–1864, physician and chemist, prepared (with G. B. Wood) the first 11 editions of *The Dispensatory of the United States* (1st ed., 1833). His cousin, **Alexander Dallas Bache,** 1806–67, was an educator and physicist. He influenced development of free education in Philadelphia. Estab. (1839) first magnetic observatory in North America; reorganized U.S. Coast Survey; founded Natl. Acad. of Sciences.

Bache, Jules Semon, 1861–1944, American financier and art collector. His collection, which includes works by Raphael and Titian, is in the Metropolitan Mus.

bachelor's button: see CORNFLOWER.

bacillus: see BACTERIA.

Back, Sir George, 1796–1878, British explorer in N Canada. Explored Great Fish R. (now Back R.) in Northwest Territories (1833–35). Explored the arctic coast of Canada (1836–37).

backbone: see SPINAL COLUMN.

Backbone Mountain, ridge of the Alleghenies, NW Md., rises to 3,360 ft., highest elevation in state.

Bacon, Delia Salter: see BACON, LEONARD.

Bacon, Francis, 1561–1626, English philosopher and statesman. Advanced slowly under Elizabeth but swiftly under James I from knight (1603) to lord chancellor (1621). Pleaded guilty 1621 to accepting bribes, was barred from office, and spent the rest of his life in retirement. His shrewd, concentrated *Essays* (1597) are his most popular works. Inductive method of modern experimental science was his tremendous contribution to philosophy. Of his projected reorganization of all human knowledge, *Instauratio Magna,* he completed two parts, *The Advancement'of Learning* (1605) and *Novum Organum* (1620). *The New Atlantis* (1627) describes a utopia established on scientific principles.

Bacon, Henry, 1866–1924, American architect. Designed Lincoln Memorial, Washington, D.C.

Bacon, Leonard, 1802–81, American Congregational minister, pastor for 41 years of First Church of New Haven, and noted antislavery leader. His sister, **Delia Salter Bacon,** 1811–59, was an author. She held that Shakspere's plays were written by group including Francis Bacon.

Bacon, Nathaniel, 1647–76, leader of Bacon's Rebellion, 1676, popular revolt in colonial Va. Uprising precipitated by failure of governor, Sir William BERKELEY, to defend frontier against Indian attacks. Underlying cause was economic exploitation of small farmers by England and tidewater aristocracy. Rebellion collapsed after Bacon's death.

Bacon, Peggy, 1895–, American illustrator and etcher, best known for satirical etchings and dry points.

Bacon, Roger, c.1214–1294?, English scholastic philosopher, a Franciscan, called the Admirable Doctor. A learned teacher at Oxford, he pugnaciously entered into many quarrels with other learned men and was in constant trouble. In modern times Friar Bacon has been celebrated chiefly for his interest in natural science, experiments, and direct observation. He considered science as complementary to, not opposed to, faith. His best-known works are the *Opus majus,* *Opus minor,* and *Opus tertium.* Because he wrote works on alchemy, many others on alchemy and magic have been attributed to him. The claim that he invented gunpowder is false, and the idea that he had a telescope or microscope is highly improbable.

Bacon's Rebellion: see BACON, NATHANIEL.

bacteria, minute unicellular organisms, usually classified as plants (class Schizomycetes) of division of thallophytes called fungi. Sometimes classified with blue-green algae as separate division of plant kingdom. Rod-shaped (bacillus), round (coccus), spiral (spirillum) are typical forms; range from c.$\frac{1}{250,000}$ in. to $\frac{1}{250}$ in. long; reproduce chiefly by transverse fission. Parasitic (or pathogenic) bacteria cause such diseases as tuberculosis, diphtheria, cholera, typhoid fever, pneumonia, tetanus, gangrene, anthrax, tularemia. Some bacteria attack tissues directly; some produce poisonous toxins. Vaccination induces immunity to some diseases. Useful bacteria outnumber harmful; NITROGEN-FIXING BACTERIA and NITRIFYING BACTERIA help enrich soil, as do decay bacteria. See *ill.,* p. 633.

bacteriophage (băktēr'ēufāj). Believed to be composed of ultramicroscopic particles destructive to bacteria. F. H. d'Herelle and followers believe it resembles virus, acts as parasite; others think it similar to enzyme. Several bacteriophages recognized; each acts only on specific bacteria.

Bactria (băk'trēu), ancient Greek kingdom of central Asia (now N Afghanistan and E Iran); cap. was Bactra (modern BALKH). As satrapy of Persian Empire, it was taken 328 B.C. by Alexander the Great. Later under Seleucidae. Declared independence in 240 B.C. and became powerful Greco-Bactrian state. Fell c.130 B.C. to nomadic Sakas.

Badajoz (bädhähōth'), city (pop. 32,604), cap. of Badajoz prov., W Spain, in Estremadura, on Guadiana R. Seat of a Moorish emirate (1022–94), reconquered by the Christians 1228. In Peninsular War it resisted French siege (1808–9), fell to French 1811, was liberated by Wellington 1812. Large 13th-cent. cathedral; ruins of Moorish citadel.

Badakhshan, USSR: see MOUNTAIN-BADAKHSHAN.

Bad Ems, Germany: see EMS.

Baden (bä'dùn), former German state, SW Germany, on right bank of the Rhine from the Main to Lake Constance; former cap. Karlsruhe. After World War II its S part became the French-occupied state of Baden (3,842 sq. mi.; pop. 1,335,458; cap. Freiburg); N part (1,984 sq. mi.; pop. 1,467,316), including Karlsruhe, Mannheim, and Heidelberg, was incorporated into American-occupied state of WÜRTTEMBERG-BADEN. Landscape, notably NECKAR valley and BLACK FOREST, is famed for its beauty. Agr., wine growing; industries in N. Until French Revolution Baden had no political unity, consisting of several petty margraviates; the bishoprics of Mainz, Speyer, Strasbourg, and Constance; the Mannheim-Heidelberg dists. of Rhenish PALATINATE; and the BREISGAU, under Hapsburg rule. In 1771 the margraviates of Baden-Baden and Baden-Durlach were united under the same branch of the old house of ZÄHRINGEN. Margrave Charles Frederick, an ally of Napoleon, was raised to grand duke (1806) and by 1810 had acquired the entire state. Prussian troops helped to suppress Revolution of 1848. Baden sided with Austria in Austro-Prussian War (1866); joined German Empire 1871; became republic 1918.

Baden or **Baden-bei-Wien** (-bī-vēn'), city (pop. 20,528), Lower Austria. Hot sulphur springs; resort.

Baden, town (pop. 11,595), Aargau, N Switzerland, on the Limmat. Noted for sulphur baths since antiquity. Meeting place of Swiss diet 1424–1712. For treaty signed here 1714, see UTRECHT, PEACE OF.

Baden-Baden, city (pop. 37,007), S Baden, SW Germany, in Black Forest. Fashionable spa.

Baden-bei-Wien: see BADEN, Lower Austria.

Baden-Powell of Gilwell, Robert Stephenson Smyth Baden-Powell, 1st **Baron** (bā'dùn-pōul), 1857–1941, British soldier, founder (1908) of the Boy Scouts.

badger, carnivorous mammal of family Mustelidae. Broad, heavy body; rather long snout; sharp claws; shaggy fur, usually gray and brownish with black and white markings. Include *Meles* of Europe and Asia; *Taxidea* of America; ferret badger (*Helictis*) and sand or hog badger (*Arctonyx*) of Asia.

Bad Godesberg (bät' gō'dùsbĕrk), town (pop. 44,536), North Rhine-Westphalia, NW Germany, idyllically situated on a height above Bonn on the Rhine. Radioactive spa. Ruined castle (built 1210). Scene of meeting between Hitler and Neville Chamberlain in 1938 (see MUNICH PACT).

Bad Ischl, Austria: see ISCHL.

Badlands, arid plateau, c.120 mi. long and 30–50 mi. wide, SW S.Dak., E of the Black Hills. Has fantastic scenery and deposits of prehistoric fossils. The Bad-

lands Natl. Monument occupies part of region.

badminton (băd'mĭntùn), game played by two or four persons, in which a shuttlecock—small, cork hemisphere with feathers attached—is volleyed over a net. Light, gut-string rackets are used. Probably originated in India. Popular in England in 1870s, taking name from seat of duke of Beaufort.

Bad Nauheim (bät' nou'hīm), town (pop. 11,896), Hesse, W Germany, in Taunus Mts. World-famous health resort for heart diseases.

Badoglio, Pietro (pyā'trō bädō'lyō), 1871–, Italian field marshal. Completed conquest of Ethiopia (1936); succeeded Mussolini as premier (1943–44); signed armistice with Allies (1943).

Bad Pyrmont, Germany: see PYRMONT.

Baduila, king of Ostrogoths: see TOTILA.

Baeda: see BEDE.

Baedeker, Karl (bā'dùkùr), 1801–59, German publisher, founder of Baedeker guidebooks.

Baer, Karl Ernst von, 1792–1876, Estonian biologist. Considered a founder of modern embryology. He discovered mammalian ovum in 1827 and originated theory of embryonic germ layers.

Baeyer, Adolf von (ä'dôlf fũn bā'yùr), 1835–1917, German chemist. Won 1905 Nobel Prize for work on organic dyes and hydroaromatic compounds. Discovered molecular structure of indigo, cerulein, eosin.

Baffin, William, c.1584–1622, British arctic explorer. Failed to find Northwest Passage but discovered Baffin Bay and Baffin Isl.

Baffin Bay, arm of Arctic Ocean between Greenland and Arctic Archipelago. Connects with the Arctic by Smith Sound and with the Atlantic by Davis Strait. Labrador Current brings many icebergs, making navigation hazardous.

Baffin Island, 197,754 sq. mi., largest and most easterly of the Arctic Archipelago, in Arctic Ocean. Formerly considered Baffin Land, it is geographically a N continuation of Labrador, separated from mainland by Hudson Strait. Interior has fresh-water lakes; mountains in E. Population largely Eskimo. Trading posts generally have Royal Canadian Police posts and mission schools. First visited by Frobisher 1576–78.

Bagdad, Iraq: see BAGHDAD.

Bagehot, Walter (băj'ùt), 1826–77, English social scientist and critic. Among his books are *The English Constitution* (1867), *Lombard Street* (1873; on banking), *Physics and Politics* (1875; pioneer analysis of relations of natural and social sciences), and *Literary Studies* (1879).

Baghdad or **Bagdad** (both: băg'dăd, bägdäd'), city (pop. 364,049), cap. of Iraq, on the Tigris and 25 mi. N of the Euphrates. From Sumerian times site was center for desert travel and trade. Founded A.D. 762 by MANSUR, city became great commercial center, reaching its height under HARUN-AL-RASHID. Its glory is reflected in many tales of *Thousand and One Nights.* City declined after Harun's death and temporary removal of caliphate to Samarra. Sacked by Mongols (1258) and destroyed by Tamerlane (1400) and by Ismail (1524). Later fell prey to warring Turks and Persians. By 1638, when it became part of Ottoman Empire, city had only c.14,000 people. Few antiquities remain, but city is still partly enclosed by ancient wall. Captured 1917 by British forces. Became cap. of Iraq 1920. City is major rail and air terminus.

Baghdad Railway, connecting Haidarpasha (opposite Istanbul), Turkey, with Basra, Iraq. Branch lines to N Iran, USSR, and Palestine. Begun with German capital (1896), it aroused protests of England (which saw in it a threat to its Indian Empire) and others. Work was suspended and then resumed (1911) when the line became a factor leading to World War I. Last link between Mosul and Samarra completed 1940 with British funds.

Bagnell Dam, central Mo., in Osage R.; built 1929–31. State's largest power dam (2,543 ft. long, 148 ft. high), it forms L. of the OZARKS.

bagpipe, musical instrument of anc. origin. Called the musette in 18th-cent. France. Now chiefly associated with Scotland. Consists of a leathern bag with either bellows or tube to inflate it: chanters or chaunters (melody pipes having finger holes); and drones, each of which produces one sustained tone.

Bagration, Piotr Ivanovich, Prince (pyô′tŭr ēvä′nŭvĭch bägrätēōn′), 1765–1812, Russian general. Commanded an army at BORODINO; mortally wounded.

Baguio (bä′gēō), city (pop. 29,262; alt. c.5,000 ft.), on W Luzon, Philippines; summer cap. of the republic. A resort and gold-mining center. Severely damaged in World War II.

bagworm, larva of moth family including species destructive to forest and shade trees in E U.S. Growing larva travels in silken covering; passes pupa stage in this bag (sometimes leaf-covered) fastened to twig. Adult female emerges partly, male fertilizes eggs. Female lays eggs inside; dies.

Bahaism (bä′häïzùm bùhä′–), religion founded 1862, when Baha Ullah (a Persian originally named Mirza Hussein Ali), announced himself prophet succeeding the Bab (see BABISM). Bahaists believe in simple living, universal education, unity of all religions, world peace, equality of men and women. Religion spread in 20th cent. (U.S. center Wilmette, Ill.).

Bahama Islands or **Bahamas** (bùhä′mùz), archipelago (4,403 sq. mi.; pop. 68,846) c.700 islands and islets, beginning c.50 mi. off SE Florida and extending c.750 mi. SE almost to Haiti. Governed as British crown colony; cap. NASSAU on New Providence Isl. Winter resort. Spanish visited islands, but English settled them in 17th cent. and imported Negroes. Islands were haunt of pirates (17th–18th cents.), notably Blackbeard; of blockade runners in Civil War; of rum runners during prohibition era in U.S. Used as U.S. military bases in World War II.

Bahawalpur (bùhä′wùlpoōr″), princely state (17,494 sq. mi.; pop. 1,341,209), W Pakistan; cap. Bahawalpur (pop. 40,015). Mostly a sandy waste. Grain, dates, and cotton are grown in irrigated area.

Bahia or **Baía** (both: bäē′ä), state (217,688 sq. mi.; pop. 4,900,419), E Brazil; cap. SALVADOR, port on Todos os Santos Bay, once chief city of Brazil. SE Bahia is one of great cacao-growing regions of world. State formerly sugar-growing.

Bahía Blanca (bäē′ä bläng′kä), city (pop. 122,059), SE Argentina, Atlantic port. Offers access to S Pampa, oilfields of Neuquén, Patagonian lakes.

Bahrein Islands (bärän′), archipelago (c.200 sq. mi.; pop. c.120,000), off Arabia, in Persian Gulf. Ruled by Arab sheik; under British protection since 1861. Chief port and cap. is Manamah on Bahrein or Aval isl. Oil discovered here 1932.

Bahr el-Huleh (bär′ ĕl-hoō′lä), lake, NE Palestine. Jordan R. headwaters flow through it. May be same as Waters of Merom (site of great victory). Joshua 11.

Baía, Brazil: see BAHIA.

Baia (bī′ä), Latin *Baiae*, village, Campania, S Italy, on Bay of Naples. Celebrated resort in ancient times. Remains of Roman baths.

Baïf, Antoine de (ätwän′ dù bäēf′), 1532–89, French poet; one of the PLÉIADE.

Baikal (bīkäl′), lake, area 13,180 sq. mi.; RSFSR, in SE Siberia; largest fresh-water lake of Asia, deepest lake in world (5,710 ft.).

Baikie, William Balfour (bä′kē), 1825–64, Scottish explorer in W Africa, a philologist. Opened Niger R. to trade and translated Scriptures into Hausa.

bail, release from prison of a person awaiting trial, on the deposit of a security, which is to be forfeited in case of failure of the accused to surrender at an appointed time. Bail is usually granted in all civil arrests, but is sometimes refused in criminal cases (e.g., that of a murder charge).

Baile Átha Cliath, Ireland: see DUBLIN.

Bailén (bīlän′), city (pop. 9,727), S Spain, in Andalusia; scene of French defeat (1808) by Spanish.

Bailey, Liberty Hyde, 1858–, American botanist and horticulturist, noted for clarifying plant classifications. He edited cyclopedias of agr. and horticulture, compiled *Hortus* and *Hortus Second* (1941).

Baillie, Matthew, 1761–1823, English physician, an authority on pathology and morbid anatomy.

Bailly, Jean Sylvain (zhä′ sēlvē′ bäyē′), 1736–93, French astronomer and politician. Won distinction as scientist before his election as president of National Assembly (1789); mayor of Paris 1789–91. Permitted National Guard to fire upon demonstrators (July 17, 1791). Arrested 1793; guillotined.

Bain, Alexander, 1818–1903, Scottish philosopher. Helped to found modern psychology by eliminating metaphysics and stressing physiology. Long associated with the Univ. of Aberdeen.

Bainbridge, William, 1774–1833, American naval officer. As commander of U.S. vessel, insult offered him by dey of Algiers contributed greatly to American declaration of war against BARBARY STATES.

Bainbridge, city (pop. 7,562), SW Ga., on Flint R. Trade center for farm and timber area. Mfg. of wood products and peanut shelling.

Baird, John Logie, 1888–1946, Scottish inventor. First to demonstrate true television (1926), and, in 1928, transatlantic and color television.

Baird, Spencer Fullerton, 1823–87, American zoologist known for pioneer studies of North American fauna. Secretary of Smithsonian Institution (from 1878); influenced establishing of U.S. Bureau of Fisheries and marine biological station (Woods Hole, Mass.)

Bairnsfather, Bruce, 1888–, English illustrator and author. Created the character "Old Bill," who typified the British infantryman in World War I.

Baja California: see LOWER CALIFORNIA.

Bajazet (bäjŭzĕt′), Ottoman sultans; also spelled Bayazit, Bayazid. **Bajazet I,** 1347–1403, reigned 1389–1402. Conquered E Anatolia; defeated Christian army at NIKOPOL (1396). His siege of Constantinople (1402) was interrupted by the invasion of TAMERLANE, who defeated him at Ankara (1402) and reputedly carried him in an iron cage (really a palanquin). **Bajazet II,** 1447–1513, reigned 1481–1512; put down the revolt of his brother Djem, who fled and eventually died in custody of Charles VIII of France (1495). The sultan lost Cilicia to the Egyptian Mamelukes (1491) and warred unsuccessfully against Venice (1499–1503), but he furthered Ottoman culture and rebuilt Constantinople after an earthquake (1509).

Bajer, Fredrik (frädh′rĭk bī′ùr), 1837–1922, Danish pacifist and writer. Helped to found Internatl. Peace Bureau at Berne (1891). Shared 1908 Nobel Peace Prize with K. P. Arnoldson.

Bakacs, Thomas: see BAKOCZ, THOMAS.

Bakelite (bä′kŭlīt), trade name for synthetic resin (amber or colorless unless dyed) made by heating under pressure the product of reaction between phenol and formaldehyde. Used in making many small molded articles (e.g., drinking glasses) and for many purposes. Invented by Leo Hendrik Baekeland (1863–1944).

Baker, Sir Benjamin, 1840–1907, English civil engineer of metropolitan railway systems.

Baker, George Pierce, 1866–1935, American educator (Harvard, 1888–1924; Yale, 1925–33). At Harvard instituted the 47 Workshop, a laboratory of the drama. O'Neill, Sidney Howard, R. E. Jones, and others studied there. Works include *Dramatic Technique.*

Baker, Newton D(iehl), 1871–1937, U.S. Secretary of War (1916–21). Much criticized at first, he was later praised for his direction of World War I.

Baker, Ray Stannard, pseud. **David Grayson,** 1870–1946, American author. A Chicago journalist, he became a muckraker for *McClure's.* As "David Grayson" he wrote gentle essays (e.g., *Adventures in Contentment,* 1907). Intimate of Pres. Wilson, Baker went to Europe (1918) as his special agent. Wrote *Woodrow Wilson and World Settlement* (3 vols., 1922), edited Wilson's papers, and wrote a biography.

Baker, city (pop. 9,471), NE Oregon, SE of Pendleton and on Powder R.; laid out 1865. Trade center in farm, stock, lumber, and mine region.

Baker Island, coral islet, area 1 sq. mi., central Pacific near the equator. Claimed 1857 by U.S., colonized 1935 by Americans from Hawaii, placed under Dept. of the Interior 1936. Held by the Japanese 1942–44. Now a naval station.

Baker Lake, 1,029 sq. mi., Keewatin dist., Northwest Territories, Canada, near Chesterfield Inlet. At W end is Royal Canadian Mounted Police post.

Bakersfield, city (pop. 34,784), S central Calif., on Kern R. and N of Los Angeles; laid out 1869. Center for oil area with refineries and mfg. of oil tools. Paint and chemical plants.

Baker University: see BALDWIN CITY, Kansas.

Bakhchisarai (bäkh″chĕsŭrī′), city (pop. c.10,000), RSFSR, in S Crimea; historic cap. of khanate of Crimea (15th cent.–1783). Celebrated for palace of khans, built 16th cent.

Bakhtiari (bäkh″tēä′rē), mountainous region of SW Iran. Chief home of nomadic Bakhtiari tribe, famed for warlike behavior. Region became important with discovery of oil in late 19th cent. Tribe played decisive part in revolution of 1908–9.

baking powder, mixture containing baking soda (sodium bicarbonate) and one or more acid-producing ingredients and used in making quick breads, cakes, and pastry. Acted upon by moisture (and by oven heat if "double-acting" type), produces carbon dioxide, thus leavening dough more rapidly than yeast.

baking soda: see SODA.

Bakocz or **Bakacs, Thomas** (bŏ′kôts, bŏ′kŏch), Hung. *Bakócz* or *Bakács Tamás,* c.1442–1521, Hungarian statesman and cardinal. Of unbounded ambition, he rose from servile origin to chancellor and archprimate of Hungary. In 1514 he suppressed, with help of John Zapolya, a peasant rebellion; peasants were reduced to serfdom. He died enormously rich.

Bakst, Lev Nikolayevich (lyĕf′ nyĭkùlī′ùvĭch bäkst′), 1866?–1924, Russian painter. Created settings and costumes for Diaghilev's ballet company.

Baku (bäkōō′), cap. of Azerbaijan, USSR, on Caspian Sea. Greater Baku (pop. 809,347) includes entire Apsheron peninsula, which extends c.40 mi. into Caspian Sea and contains 15% of world's petroleum reserves. The chief oil center of USSR, Baku also has a large port and many cultural institutions. First mentioned 5th cent. A.D., it had Zoroastrian shrines of constantly burning fires (from oil and gas wells). Ceded by Persia to Russia 1813. Oil industry began late 19th cent.

Bakunin, Mikhail (mēkhŭyĕl′ bŭkōō′nyĭn), 1814–76, Russian anarchist. Young aristocrat turned revolutionist, he was exiled (1849) to Siberia, but escaped. In First International after 1868 he was opposed by Marxists, who expelled him (1872). He believed "anarchism, collectivism, and atheism" would give man complete freedom and advocated violent revolution.

Balaam (bā′lùm), prophet hired by King of Moab to curse the Hebrews. By order of God he was forced to bless them instead. Num. 22–24; 31.8, 16; Micah 6.5; 2 Peter 2.15,16; Jude 11; Rev. 2.14.

Balak (bā′lăk), king of Moab who hired Balaam to curse the Hebrews. Num. 22–24.

Balakirev, Mili (Alekseyevich) (mē′lyĭ bŭlä′kyĭrĭf), 1837–1910, Russian composer and conductor. With Borodin, Moussorgsky, Rimsky-Korsakov, and Cui he formed a group of highly nationalistic composers known as the Russian Five. Best-known works are piano fantasy *Islamey* and the incidental music for *King Lear.*

Balaklava (bä″lùklä′vù), city (pop. 2,323), RSFSR, in S Crimea, near Sevastopol; fishing port and resort on Black Sea. Famous for allied victory (1854) in Crimean War and for suicidal charge of an English light-cavalry brigade, celebrated by Tennyson.

balalaika: see STRINGED INSTRUMENTS.

Balance, the, in astronomy: see ZODIAC.

balance, instrument to measure MASS or weight. Equal-arm (beam) balance simplest; based on LEVER principle. Beam is suspended at its center on knife-edge at right angles to it; pans of equal weight are suspended at each end, equidistant from fulcrum (point of support). Pointer is at zero when beam is in equilibrium. Object to be weighed is put in one pan, standard weights in other until balanced. Platform balances may be equal- or unequal-arm types. Spring balance (from which object is suspended) measures force of gravity at certain point on earth's surface. TORSION BALANCE not strictly a balance. See also SCALES.

balance of trade, difference between exports and imports of a country. Mercantilists believed that a country should have a "favorable" balance of trade—an excess of exports over imports; though refuted by Adam Smith and David Hume, this idea is still widely held, notably in nations seeking "autarchy."

Balanchine, George, 1904–, Russian-American choreographer and ballet dancer. Performed in Russia 1921–24 and with Diaghilev troupe in Paris 1924–28. In U.S. since 1933; founded School of American Ballet 1934. Directed Metropolitan Opera ballet 1934–37 and New York City ballet 1948–.

Balard, Antoine Jérôme (ätwän′ zhärōm′ bälär′), 1802–76, French chemist. Discovered bromine; extracted sodium sulphate from sea water.

Balassa, Baron Balint (bä′lĭnt bùläs′ù, bŏ′lōsh-shŏ), 1551–94, Hungarian poet, regarded as the creator of Hungarian lyric poetry.

Balaton (bä′lùtŏn, Hung. bŏ′lŏtôn), Ger. *Plattensee,* lake (231 sq. mi.), W Hungary, largest in Central Europe. Fisheries; vineyards; resorts.

Balbo, Italo (ē′tälō bäl′bō), 1896–1940, Italian Fascist leader and aviator. Took part in March on Rome (1922); became minister of aviation 1929, governor of Libya 1933. Died in plane accident.

Balboa, Vasco Núñez de (vä′skō nōō′nyäth dā bälbō′ä) c.1475–1519?, Spanish conquistador, discoverer of Pacific. After reaching DARIEN (1510), he won friendship of Indians, who accompanied him on epic march across isthmus (1513). Claimed Pacific and all shores washed by it for Spain. Pedrarias had him beheaded for treason.

Balboa, town (pop. 4,168), Panama Canal Zone, Pacific port. Has administration hq. of Zone and canal. Balboa dist. comprises Pacific half of Zone.

Balch, Emily Greene, 1867–, American economist and sociologist. She shared the 1946 Nobel Peace Prize with John R. Mott.

Balchen, Bernt (bäl′kùn), 1899–, Norwegian-American aviator. Headed arctic search for Amundsen and Ellsworth (1925) and joined their 1926 expedition. Chief pilot of Byrd's antarctic expedition, 1928–30. World War II colonel in U.S. Army Air Forces, recalled (1948) to active service.

Balder (bôl′dùr), Norse god of light; son of Odin and Frigg. One legend says that, invulnerable to everything but mistletoe, he was killed by a mistletoe dart made by Loki.

Baldoon, locality, S Ont., Canada, near Chatham. Failure of settlement here led Lord Selkirk to sponsor Red River Settlement.

Baldovinetti, Alessio (äläs′syō bäldō vēnĕt′tē), c.1425–1499, Italian painter, one of the first Florentine artists to experiment with oil painting. Taught Ghirlandaio.

Baldung, Hans (häns′ bäl′dōong), c.1480–1545, German religious and mythological painter, surnamed Grien or Grün because of his predilection for green.

Baldwin, Latin emperors of Constantinople (see CONSTANTINOPLE, LATIN EMPIRE OF). **Baldwin I,** 1171–1205, count of Flanders and a leader of the Fourth Crusade, was elected emperor in 1204. Captured in battle with the Bulgarians (1205), he died in captivity. Succeeded by his brother, Henry of Flanders. **Baldwin II,** 1217–73, succeeded his brother ROBERT OF COURTENAY (1228). JOHN OF BRIENNE was regent till 1237.

SMALL CAPITALS = cross references. Pronunciation key on inside end pages. Abbreviations: p. 2.

He sold part of the True Cross to Louis IX of France and pawned his son with the Venetians to get funds for his tottering throne, but in 1261 MICHAEL VIII stormed Constantinople and Baldwin fled.

Baldwin, kings of Jerusalem. **Baldwin I,** 1058?–1118, brother of GODFREY OF BOUILLON, whom he accompanied on First Crusade. Took title king 1100; consolidated the Latin states; gained the chief ports of Palestine. His cousin and successor, **Baldwin II** (Baldwin du Bourg), d. 1131, fought the Turks in N Syria and made Tyre and Antioch dependent on his crown. **Baldwin III,** 1130–63, son of FULK of Anjou, reigned 1143–63. The decay of Latin power in the East had begun. Edessa fell to the Moslems (1144); the Second Crusade failed; and Sultan NUREDDIN seized N Syria (1154). His nephew, **Baldwin IV** (the Leper), c.1161–85, spent his whole reign (1174–85) defending the kingdom against SALADIN. Disabled by leprosy, he made Guy of LUSIGNAN his lieutenant, but withdrew the commission and had his five-year-old nephew crowned (1183) as **Baldwin V** (d. 1186), with RAYMOND, count of Tripoli, as regent.

Baldwin, Abraham, 1754–1807, American statesman. U.S. Representative from Ga. (1789–99); U.S. Senator (1799–1807). A founder of present Univ. of Georgia.

Baldwin, Loammi (lŏä′mĭ), 1740–1807, American civil engineer, builder of Middlesex Canal. Developed Baldwin apple. His son, **Loammi Baldwin,** 1780–1838, engineer of Union Canal and dry-dock builder.

Baldwin, Matthias William, 1795–1866, American industrialist, founder of Baldwin Locomotive Works.

Baldwin, Robert, 1804–58, Canadian statesman, leader of movement for representative government in Canada. In the assembly he led opposition group and effected alliance with French in Lower Canada. In 1842 he joined with Louis H. LaFONTAINE to form a coalition government. Second Baldwin-LaFontaine ministry (1848–51), often called the "great ministry," accomplished reform of local government in Ontario, promoted judicial and educational reforms.

Baldwin, Stanley, 1867–1947, British statesman. Conservative party leader 1923–37, he was three times prime minister. Broke 1926 general strike. League of Nations declined, Fascist powers rose, and Edward VIII abdicated during his third government (1935–37).

Baldwin City, city (pop. 1,741), NE Kansas, SE of Topeka. Seat of Baker Univ. (Methodist; coed.; 1858).

Baldwyn, town (pop. 1,567), NE Miss., N of Tupelo. Brices Cross Roads Natl. Battlefield Site, where Gen. N. B. Forrest routed Union force June 10, 1864, is near by.

Bâle, Switzerland: see BASEL.

Balearic Islands (bălēă′rĭk, Span. *Baleares,* archipelago in W Mediterranean, forming a province (1,936 sq. mi.; pop. 407,497) of Spain; cap. Palma. Chief islands: Majorca, Minorca, Iviza. Agr., fishing, tourist trade. Export of majolica ware, silver filigree. Inhabited since prehistoric times, the islands were occupied by Iberians, Phoenicians, Greeks, Carthaginians, Romans, Byzantines; conquered by Moors 8th cent. A.D.; made a kingdom 11th cent.; conquered by Aragonese 13th cent. See also MAJORCA.

Balfour, Arthur James (băl′fŏŏr), 1848–1930, British statesman. Held many posts. As foreign secretary, issued (1917) Balfour Declaration pledging British support for a Jewish national home in Palestine. Devoted to cause of international peace.

Bali (bä′lē), island (2,533 sq. mi.; pop. 1,074,925), Lesser Sundas, Indonesia, separated from Java by Bali Strait. Culturally and economically one of the most important islands of Indonesia. Chief products are copra, rice, coffee, and teakwood. Hinduism has been dominant here since 7th cent. The Dutch first landed here in 1597.

Balieff, Nikita (bä′lyĕf), 1877–1936, Russian impresario. Founded and acted as master of ceremonies in the *Chauve-Souris* revue.

Balikesir (bä″lĭkĕsĕr′), city (pop. 36,001), NW Turkey.

Rail junction; agr. center. Has a large annual fair.

Balinese music, chiefly a survival of pre-Islamic music of Java, using the tonal systems of JAVANESE MUSIC. The orchestra of tuned percussion instruments is called a *gamelan.* Each type of dance or drama has its own *gamelan.* Basic instruments include bronze or bamboo xylophones, gongs, flutes, fiddles, rattles, and cymbals. Little use is made of notation; compositions are learned by rote.

Baliol, John de (bā′lēul), d. 1269, English baron, founder of Balliol Col., Oxford. A regent for Alexander III of Scotland, he was removed from office for treason. His third son, **John de Baliol,** 1249–1315, king of Scotland (1292–96), claimed the throne at the death of MARGARET MAID OF NORWAY. EDWARD I of England supported him, over ROBERT I, in return for feudal overlordship and he was crowned. Renounced (1296) his oath of fealty, was defeated, and surrendered to Edward. Retired to France 1299. His son, **Edward de Baliol,** d. 1363, king of Scotland, invaded Scotland (1332) with aid of Edward III and defeated supporters of DAVID II. After David's return from France (1341), he never held power.

Balkan Peninsula, SE Europe, extending S from Danube and Sava rivers. Bounded by Black Sea (E); Bosporus, Sea of Marmara, Dardanelles, Aegean Sea (S); Ionian and Adriatic seas (W). Comprises ALBANIA, BULGARIA, continental GREECE, SE RUMANIA, European TURKEY, most of YUGOSLAVIA. Very mountainous, it contains the DINARIC ALPS, the RHODOPE mts., and the **Balkans,** a range of N Bulgaria, culminating at 7,785 ft. in Yumrukchal and crossed by Shipka Pass.

Balkan Wars, 1912–13, two short wars for possession of European Turkey. In the first war Serbia, Bulgaria, Greece, and Montenegro expelled the Turks from all their European holdings except Constantinople (1912). The territorial settlement made by the Great Powers in 1913 disappointed Serbia, which was cut off from the Adriatic by the creation of independent Albania. Serbia now demanded Bulgaria cede the larger part of Macedonia, thus precipitating the Second Balkan War. Rumania, Greece, and Turkey joined Serbia against Bulgaria, which was defeated and lost territory to all its enemies in the Treaty of Bucharest (1913). Balkan Wars heightened nationalism and prepared way for World War I.

Balkh (bälkh), town (pop. 10,000), N Afghanistan. Was cap. of ancient BACTRIA. Taken 653 by Arabs, sacked 1221 by Jenghiz Khan.

Balkhash (bŭl-khäsh′), city (pop. c.70,000), SE Kazakh SSR, on N shore of Lake Balkhash; founded 1929. Railroad terminus; port; copper smelting. The saline **Lake Balkhash** (6,680 sq. mi.) stretches for 375 mi. between Kazakh Hills (N) and desert (S). Fed by Ili R., has no outlet.

Balkis, name given in Koran to the queen of Sheba.

Ball, John, d. 1381, English priest; an instigator of the Peasants' Revolt under Wat TYLER.

ballad (bă′lŭd), narrative poem of unknown authorship, intended to be sung, preserved by oral tradition among people culturally homogeneous. Objective, impersonal, abounding in set phrases. Francis Child made definitive collection, *English and Scottish Popular Ballads* (5 vols., 1883–98). Word *ballad* popularly used for any narrative poem. In music *ballad* refers to simple, often sentimental type of song (not folk song).

Ballarat (băl′ŭrăt′), city (pop. 38,140; metropolitan pop. 40,181), Victoria, Australia; founded 1851. Once a noted mining center. Woolen mills.

ball bearings: see BEARINGS.

ballet (bă′lā, bălā′), solo or ensemble dancing of drama set to music. First appeared as part of opera. Ballet, though known in 15th-cent. Italy, was first seen as a coordinated whole in the Ballet comique de la Reine (Paris, 1581). The five absolute ballet positions were set down by Rameau (1725). Ballet flourished in early 19th-cent. Italy and reached a zenith in mid-19th-cent. Russia. Such Russians as FOKINE and DIAGHILEV (aided by such dancers as Nijinsky and Pavlova) extended Russian influence to Europe in early 20th cent. The dawning of a non-Russian ballet followed, aided by such groups as Jooss Ballet (Germany), Sadler's Wells (England), Ballet Theatre (U.S.), and such artists as Anthony Tudor (England) and Agnes de Mille (U.S.).

Ballinger, Richard Achilles (băl′ĭnjùr), 1858–1922, U.S. Secretary of the Interior (1909–11). Center of controversy over handling of natural resources.

Ballinger, city (pop. 5,302), W central Texas, on Colorado R. at mouth of Elm Creek and SSW of Abilene. Processing center in livestock and agr. area. Reservoir on Elm Creek is unit of Colorado River project.

Balliol College: see OXFORD UNIVERSITY.

ballistics (băl′ĭ′stĭks), science of projectile propulsion and motion. Includes interior ballistics (processes and motion of projectile within gun) and exterior ballistics (projectile's motion outside gun, or its trajectory).

balloon, aircraft lacking propulsive system, obtaining lift from lighter-than-air gas in containers. J. M. and J. É. Montgolfier of France credited with invention (1783). Pilâtre de Rozier, using hot-air-filled balloon attached to ground, first man to make balloon ascent (1783). Also in 1783 Robert brothers and J. A. C. Charles ascended and traveled 27 mi. in hydrogen-filled balloon. Balloons carried messages in siege of Paris (1870). Observation balloons used in World War I; in World War II balloons held by cables used in air defense. In sport, James Gordon Bennett Cup prize for international race. Altitude record 72,395 ft. by A. W. Stevens and O. A. Anderson in 1935.

balm: see LEMON BALM; for bee balm, see OSWEGO TEA.

balm of Gilead, name for several unrelated plants: historic Old World *Commiphora meccanensis,* a small evergreen tree (referred to in Jer. 8.22), and the source of commercial balm of Gilead; American balm of Gilead, a poplar (*Populus candicans*); and Canary balm, *Cedronella canariensis,* a small shrub.

Balmoral Castle (băl′mŏr′ùl), royal residence in Braemar, Aberdeenshire, Scotland. Built by Queen Victoria 1854.

balsa, deciduous tree (*Ochroma*), native to tropical America. Its very light wood (also called corkwood) is used in airplane construction, in life preservers and floats, and for insulating purposes.

balsam, resin of various trees, including commercial and tolu balsam of South America, Mecca balsam or BALM OF GILEAD, copaiba, and CANADA BALSAM. For the herbaceous balsam plant, see IMPATIENS.

balsam fir or **balsam,** a fir (*Abies balsamea*) of Canada and NE U.S. Valuable for CANADA BALSAM contained in its bark. Much used as a Christmas tree.

Balthazar: see WISE MEN OF THE EAST.

Baltic provinces and **Baltic states,** countries bordering on extreme E coast of Baltic Sea. See COURLAND; LIVONIA; ESTONIA; LATVIA; LITHUANIA.

Baltic Sea, arm of Atlantic Ocean, indenting N Europe, surrounded by Sweden, Finland, USSR (incl. Baltic states), Poland, Germany, and Denmark. Area c.160,000 sq. mi. (incl. gulfs of Bothnia, Finland, and Riga). Many islands (see DENMARK). Connected with North Sea by ORESUND and Great and Little BELT (by way of Kattegat and Skagerrak); KIEL CANAL is a more direct connection. Other canal systems link it with White Sea and Volga R. Generally shallow; important fisheries. Chief ports: Copenhagen, Stettin, Gdynia, Danzig, Leningrad, Helsinki, Stockholm.

Baltimore, Charles Calvert, 3d **Baron:** see CALVERT, GEORGE.

Baltimore, George Calvert, 1st **Baron:** see CALVERT, George.

Baltimore (bôl′tĭmôr) city (pop. 949,708), N Md., on Patapsco R. near Chesapeake Bay. State's largest city and sixth largest in U.S., it is cultural, commercial, and industrial center and main port for importing iron and other ores. Among diverse industries are shipbuilding, meat packing, food processing, sugar,

petroleum, and copper refining, printing and publishing, and mfg. of tin cans, machinery, autos, and tractors. Area settled in early 17th cent.; royal governor authorized building of Baltimore 1729. Fine harbor encouraged shipping; extensive rail lines, beginning with Baltimore & Ohio RR (1830), later fed town. Shipbuilding thrived and brought fame with clippe: ships of early 1800s. Continental Congress met here in 1776–77. In 1814 F. S. Key wrote STAR-SPANGLED BANNER during defense of Fort McHENRY here. Although a Union supply base during the Civil War, city held divided loyalties. Was shipbuilding and supply point in both World Wars. Seat of JOHNS HOPKINS UNIVERSITY, Loyola Col., Morgan State Col., and Col. of Notre Dame of Maryland. Points of interest include Washington Monument, first Roman Catholic cathedral in U.S. (built 1806–21), Walters Art Gall., Enoch Pratt Free Library, Maryland Inst. of Art, Peabody Inst., Westminster Churchyard (with grave of E. A. Poe), Baltimore Mus. of Art, and Pimlico race track.

Baltimore & Ohio Railroad, first railroad in U.S. open for public traffic (1830). Rapid decline of Baltimore after trans-Allegheny traffic had gravitated toward Erie Canal in N.Y. led to its construction. Successful trial in 1830 of the *Tom Thumb,* built by Peter Cooper, brought introduction of steam locomotives. Railroad was important life line in Civil War. Centrally located route maintains prominence of railroad.

Baltimore oriole: see ORIOLE.

Baluchi (bùlōō′chē), Eastern Iranian language of Indo-Iranian subfamily of Indo-European languages. See LANGUAGE (table).

Baluchistan (bùlōō′chĭstăn), arid region in SE Iran and W Pakistan. Iranian section was formerly a separate province; since 1938 a part of Kerman Prov. Pakistani region (134,139 sq. mi.; pop. 1,178,000) was added 1946–47 to Pakistan. Comprises Baluchistan proper and several princely states.

baluchitherium (bùlōōchĭthēr′ēùm), extinct primitive, rhinoceros of Miocene period. Fossilized bones found in central Asia. Believed largest of land mammals; estimated height 18 ft., weight 10 tons.

Balue, Jean (zhä′bälü′), c.1421–1491, French cardinal and statesman, adviser to Louis XI. Conspired with Charles the Bold of Burgundy against Louis, who had him imprisoned in an iron cage (1469–80). Freed by papal intervention.

Balzac, Honoré de (ōnôrä′ dù bälzäk′), 1799–1850, French novelist. His greatest work, "La Comédie humaine," is a vast edifice of partly interconnected novels and short novels, recreating French society of his time and picturing in precise detail individuals of every class and profession. Among best-known novels are *Eugénie Grandet* (1833), *Le Père Goriot* (1835), *La Cousine Bette* (1847), *Le Cousin Pons* (1847). Balzac wrote some masterly short stories but failed in his attempts at drama.

Balzac, Jean Louis Guez de (zhä′ lwē′ gä′), 1597?–1654, French writer, influential in reforming French prose style.

Bamberg (bäm′bĕrk), city (pop. 75,830), Upper Franconia, NE Bavaria, on Regnitz R. Cotton mfg. Now an archiepiscopal see, it was the cap. of a powerful prince-bishopric until 1802. Splendid 13th-cent. cathedral contains tombs of Emperor Henry VI, his wife St. Kunigunde, and Pope Clement II. Episcopal palaces date from 16th and 18th cent.

bamboo, a woody perennial grass of warm and tropical regions. It has rounded, hollow, jointed stalks, is usually treelike but occasionally low or climbing. Wood used for construction, furniture, utensils, and paper. Chief commercial species is *Bambusa arundinacea.* A few species are native to the S U.S., e.g., cane or cane reed, *Arundinaria gigantea.*

banana, tropical palmlike plant (*Musa*) and its long, fleshy fruit, usually yellow or red skinned. An important commercial crop. Fruit is edible raw or cooked and is rich in carbohydrates. Other banana species are plantain, the fruit of which is cooked as a vegetable in the tropics, and MANILA HEMP.

Banat (bä′nät′), term originally used for several military frontier provs. of Hungary and Croatia; governors had title *ban*. The former **Banat of Temesvar** (tĕ′mĕshvär), a fertile plain between Danube, Theiss, and Mures rivers, was an integral part of Hungary; chief city Temesvar (see TIMISOARA). Partitioned 1920 between Yugoslavia and Rumania.

Banbury, municipal borough (pop. 18,917), Oxfordshire, England. Still produces famous cakes. Banbury Cross of the nursery rhyme destroyed in 1602; new one built in 19th cent.

Bancroft, Edward, 1744–1821, American Revolutionary spy. Operated as secret agent to American commissioners in France, but also reported their movements to British.

Bancroft, George, 1800–1891, American historian and statesman, author of monumental *History of the United States* (10 vols., 1834–74). As Secretary of the Navy, he estab. U.S. Naval Academy at Annapolis. Minister to Britain 1846–49. An antislavery Democrat, he supported Lincoln in Civil War. Minister to Prussia 1867–74. Revised and extended editions of the *History* (6 vols.; 1876, 1883–85) won high praise.

Bancroft, Hubert Howe, 1832–1918, American publisher and historian. Collected materials on all W America, culminating in Bancroft Library of Univ. of California. Collection has some 60,000 volumes of books, manuscripts, transcripts, and personal narratives. He edited and published a history (39 vols., 1874–90), reissued (1882–90) as *The Works of Hubert Howe Bancroft.*

band, in music, a group of musicians playing chiefly upon wind instruments. Present-day band originated from military ensembles used for marches. First significant band in America was the U.S. Marine Band, founded 1798. In 1854 the concert band developed. The bands and band music of Sousa and Franko Goldman have been most important in the U.S. Modern bands usually include the chief brass, wood-wind, and percussion instruments, while concert bands and jazz bands may employ strings and harp.

Banda Oriental (bän′dä ōryäntäl′) [Span.,= eastern shore, i.e., of the Río de la Plata], region, S Uruguay. Term applied to Uruguay in Spanish colonial period. Most of Uruguayan population concentrated here.

Bandar, India: see MASULIPATAM.

Banda Sea (bän′dä), part of Pacific Ocean, bounded by S Moluccan isls. of Indonesia.

Bandelier, Adolph Francis Alphonse, 1840–1914, American archaeologist, b. Switzerland. Carried on field researches in N.Mex. (1880–89) and explored Peru and Bolivia (1892–1902).

Bandelier National Monument: see NATIONAL PARKS AND MONUMENTS (table).

Bandello, Matteo (mät-tä′ō bändĕl′lō), c.1480–1562, Italian novelist, a priest, author of *novelle.*

Bandera (bändâ′rŭ), village (pop. 1,036), SW Texas, on Medina R. and SW of San Antonio; founded 1854 by Mormons (later Polish settlement). Tourist trade.

Bandung (bän′dŏong), town (pop. 166,815), W Java, Indonesia. Produces textiles and quinine.

baneberry, perennial plant (*Actaea*), with compound leaves, clusters of small white flowers, and poisonous but handsome white, red, or black berrylike fruits. Also called cohosh.

Banér, Johan (yōō′hän bänâr′), 1596–1641, Swedish general in Thirty Years War. Succeeded Gustavus Adolphus in command of Swedish forces in Germany (1632). Routed at Nördlingen 1634. Restored Swedish prestige by victory at Wittstock (1636) and reconquest of Pomerania and Mecklenburg (1638).

Banff (bämf), famous summer and winter resort town (1946 pop. 2,081), SW Alta., Canada, on Bow R. in the Rocky Mts. Here is Canadian Pacific RR station for Banff Natl. Park (2,564 sq. mi.; estab. 1887). Has annual winter carnival. Park has hot sulphur springs.

Banffshire or Banff, county (630 sq. mi.; pop. 50,135), NE Scotland; co. town Banff. Largely agr., it has fishing villages along the rolling fertile coast. Fine whisky distilled. Scene of many battles between Scots and Norse invaders, it was later torn by religious strife after the Reformation.

Bangalore (băn-gŭlôr′), city (pop. 406,760), SE Mysore, India; cap. and commercial center of Mysore. Has remains of Tippoo Sahib's palace. Rail hub and textile center. Seat of Mysore Univ.

Bangka (bäng′kä), island (4,611 sq. mi.; pop. 205,363), Indonesia, in Java Sea SE of Sumatra. Major tin producer since c.1710.

Bangkok (băng′kŏk″), city (pop. 688,832), cap. of Thailand, on Menam R., near Gulf of Siam. Industrial center, chief port of Thailand. Exports rice, tin, teak, and rubber. Rice mills, oil refineries, sawmills. In 1782 succeeded Ayuthia as Thai cap.

Bangor (băng′gùr), municipal borough (pop. 20,615), Co. Down, N. Ireland. Scene of annual yachting regatta. Has remains of an abbey founded c.555.

Bangor (băng′gôr). **1** City (pop. 31,558), S Maine, at head of navigation on Penobscot R. opposite Brewer; settled 1769. Commercial center and gateway to resort area. Once-dominant lumbering and paper milling industries are now supplemented by mfg. of shoes, dental supplies, and machinery. **2** Borough (pop. 6,050), E Pa., N of Easton. Has slate quarrying and mfg. of textiles.

Bangor (băng′gôr), municipal borough (pop. 12,822), Caernarvonshire, Wales. Seat of Univ. Col. of North Wales. Cathedral dates from 15th–16th cent.

Bangorian Controversy, in Church of England. Bishop Benjamin Hoadly, of Bangor, Wales, denied (1717) that Christ delegated authority to church. Opposed by William Law and some 50 writers in 200 pamphlets.

Bang's disease: see BRUCELLOSIS.

Bangweulu (bängwāōō′lōō), lake, 60 mi. long, 25 mi. wide, in Northern Rhodesia. Discovered 1868 by David Livingstone.

Banja Luka (bän′jä lōō′kä), city (pop. 33,191), Bosnia, N Yugoslavia; seat of pashas 1580–1640. Orthodox cathedral, 16th-cent. mosque, ruins of Roman baths.

banjo: see STRINGED INSTRUMENTS.

Bankhead, Tallulah (Brockman), 1903–, American actress. Since her debut in 1918, her flamboyant personality has won her fame in England and U.S. in plays (e.g., *The Little Foxes*), films (e.g., *Lifeboat*), and on radio and television.

banking, financial transactions through institutions primarily devoted to accepting deposits and making loans. Practiced in ancient Egypt and Greece and developed by the Romans, banking during the Middle Ages came to be largely dominated by Jews because of Christian prejudice against interest. Modern banking developed in 18th and 19th cent. In U.S. first bank was founded at Philadelphia 1781. The BANK OF THE UNITED STATES was the subject of political controversy. An act in 1863 set up the national banks, but banks of deposit continued under state charters and grew in number. In 1913 the FEDERAL RESERVE SYSTEM was set up.

Bank of England, popularly known as the Old Lady of Threadneedle Street, founded (1694) by William Paterson as commercial bank. Bank Charter Act of 1842 set up present system. Issue department issues bank notes; banking department handles other functions (e.g., national debt). Nationalized 1945.

Bank of the United States. Against opposition of the Jeffersonian party the Federalists under Alexander HAMILTON estab. a central bank, the Bank of the United States (1791–1811). Its conservative policies were unpopular, and it was not rechartered, but after financial difficulties in the War of 1812, the second Bank of the United States was given (1816) a 20-year charter. Under Nicholas BIDDLE it prospered, but was viewed as a tool of Eastern moneyed interests by the followers of Andrew JACKSON. It was a chief issue of the 1832 election and Jackson, successful, took government deposits from it in 1833.

bankruptcy, settlement of liabilities of a debtor wholly or partially unable to meet his obligations. Bankruptcy laws intended to distribute the bankrupt's assets equitably among his creditors and to discharge him from liability. Present U.S. bankruptcy act that of 1898, with amendments.

Banks, Sir Joseph, 1743–1820, British naturalist. Collected (on round-the-world voyage with Capt. Cook and other travels) many previously unknown plants. Long influential in activities of Kew Gardens and Royal Society.

Banks, Nathaniel Prentiss, 1816–94, American politician and Union general in Civil War. U.S. Congressman before and after war. Governor of Mass. 1858–60. Helped Grant open the Mississippi by capture of PORT HUDSON, July, 1863.

Banksia [for Sir Joseph Banks], genus of Australian trees and shrubs with yellow, honey-bearing blooms.

Bankside, locality by the Thames, in Southwark metropolitan borough, London, England. Amusement center 16th–17th cent.; Globe Theatre and other places associated with Shakspere were here. Palace of bishop of Winchester and the CLINK were also here.

Bannack, ghost town, SW Mont., SW of Butte; founded 1862 with discovery of gold. First town in Mont., it was territorial cap. 1864–65. Declined when richer Virginia City fields attracted miners.

Banning, city (pop. 7,034), S Calif., E of Riverside; laid out 1883. Health resort.

Bannockburn, field on Bannock R., Stirlingshire, Scotland. Site of Battle of Bannockburn June 23–24, 1314, in which Robert the Bruce defeated the English under Edward II and estab. himself on the Scottish throne.

Bantam fowl: see POULTRY.

Banting, Sir Frederick Grant, 1891–1941, Canadian physician, noted for research. Shared 1923 Nobel Prize in Physiology and Medicine for isolating INSULIN.

Bantry Bay, inlet of the Atlantic, 21 mi. long and 4 mi. wide, in Co. Cork, Ireland; one of Europe's best natural anchorages.

Bantu (băn'tōō"), ethnic and (principally) linguistic group of Africa, numbering c.40,000,000. They are a Negro people inhabiting all the continent S of the Congo except extreme SW. There are several hundred Bantu languages and dialects, including Kafir, Zulu, and Swahili. Highly developed Bantu states included Buganda. In 19th cent. several additional confederations developed, e.g., Zulu and Basuto. Matabele is also a well-known Bantu tribe.

Banville, Théodore de (täõdôr' dü bävēl'), 1823–91, French poet; one of PARNASSIANS. His volumes of verse include *Odes funambulesques* (1857) and *Occidentales* (1869).

banyan (băn'yùn), tree (*Ficus benghalensis*) of fig genus, native to India. Its branches put forth numerous aerial roots, which on reaching the ground, enlarge to form many trunks.

baobab (bā'ō–), gigantic tree (*Adansonia digitata*) of Senegal. Its fruit is edible and the bark yields rope and cloth.

baptism: see SACRAMENT.

Baptists, denomination of Christians who hold that baptism is only for believers and only by immersion. Separatists under John Smyth formed (c.1608) in Amsterdam first English Baptist congregation. First group in London estab. 1611. First American church founded (1639) by Roger Williams in Providence, R.I. Baptist churches are congregational, with nongoverning general associations—American Baptist Convention, Southern Baptist Convention, Natl. Baptist Convention, U.S.A., and many other associations and independent bodies.

bar, the, court or system of courts. Persons authorized to conduct court trials also known collectively as the bar; hence lawyers collectively. The distinction between the pleader before the court (barrister, advocate, counselor at law) and the agent merely advising the client (solicitor, attorney) has disappeared in U.S., while it is retained in England.

Barabbas (bùrăb'ùs), notorious bandit whom mob demanded be released from punishment, demanding instead the death of Jesus. Mat. 27.15–18; Mark 15.6–14; Luke 23.13–25; John 18.39,40.

Baraboo (băr'ùbōō), city (pop. 7,264), central Wis., on Baraboo R. and NW of Madison. Farm trade center. Ringling Brothers' circus began here. Dells of the Wisconsin near by.

Barak (bā'răk) [Heb.,= lightning], leader who joined Deborah in fighting Jabin and Sisera. Judges 4–5.

Baranof Island (bă'rùnôf), off SE Alaska, in ALEXANDER ARCHIPELAGO; over 100 mi. long, 1,607 sq. mi. in area. Was named for Aleksandr Baranov. On it is SITKA, center of fur trade and administration during Russian ownership.

Baranov, Aleksandr Andreyevich (bŭră'nôf), 1746–1819, Russian trader, chief figure during Russian control in Alaska. Virtual governor of Russian activities in North America (1799–1817).

Barany, Robert (rō'bert bä'ränē), 1876–1936, Austrian physician. Won 1914 Nobel Prize in Physiology and Medicine for work on vestibular apparatus of ear.

Barataria Bay (bărùtär'ēù), SE La., S of New Orleans, cut off from Gulf of Mexico by islands. Was base of pirates under Jean LAFITTE.

Barbados (bärbā'dōz), island (166 sq. mi.; pop. 192,-841) British West Indies, and colony; cap. Bridgetown. Winter resort. Claimed by British from 1605. Produces sugar, rum, cotton.

Barbara, Saint, 3d or 4th cent., virgin martyr, supposed to have been killed by her father for being a Christian. Feast: Dec. 4.

Barbarossa (bärbùrŏs'ù), surname of Algerian corsair Khair ad-Din (c.1483–1546). His brother, Koruk, or Aruj (c.1474–1518), seized Algiers from the Spanish (1518), and Barbarossa put Algeria under Turkish suzerainty. As admiral of the Turkish fleet, he twice defeated Andrea Doria and ravaged the coast of S Europe (1533–44).

Barbarossa, Frederick: see FREDERICK I, emperor.

Barbary Coast, former (till 1917) waterfront area of San Francisco, Calif. After 1849 gold rush its open gambling, prostitution, and gangsterism had world notoriety.

Barbary States, term used for the N African states of TRIPOLITANIA, TUNISIA, and ALGERIA (and usually also MOROCCO), which were semi-independent under Turkish rule from 16th cent. onward. Rulers derived revenue from large-scale piracy on Mediterranean shipping. European powers launched punitive expeditions against them but generally relied on payment of tribute as a means of protection. The U.S. joined in this system. The insult offered by the dey of Algiers to William BAINBRIDGE, taking U.S. tribute to Algiers, led to the TRIPOLITAN WAR. French capture of Algiers (1830) marked the end of piracy in the region.

Barbauld, Anna Laetitia (Aikin) (bär'bôld), 1743–1825, English author of didactic works for children, *Hymns in Prose* and *Early Lessons* (both 1781).

barbecue (bär'bùkū), in U.S., open-air political or social gathering, where carcass or large joints of meat are roasted whole. Barbecued meat may also be smaller cuts, basted with spicy sauce.

Barber, Samuel, 1910–, American composer. Despite experimentation with modern techniques, his music is conservative. Among his works are a setting for Matthew Arnold's "Dover Beach"; two *Essays for Orchestra; Adagio for Strings;* a ballet, *Medea;* two symphonies.

Barberini vase: see PORTLAND VASE.

barberry, spiny shrub (*Berberis*), used for hedges. Some have bright autumn foliage; others, less hardy, are evergreen. Berries are red or black. Common barberry (*Berberis vulgaris*) is a wheat rust host.

Barberton, city (pop. 27,820), NE Ohio, SW of Akron; laid out 1891. Mfg. of metal and rubber products and chemicals.

Barbey d'Aurevilly, Jules (zhül' bärbä' dōrvēyē'), 1809–89, French author. His novels and short novels (notably *Les Diaboliques,* 1874), laid in his native Normandy, are remarkable for vigorous style, psychological realism, and morbid imagination. He also was an intransigeant critic and polemicist.

Barbizon school, informal school of French landscape painting which flourished c.1830–1870. Barbizon village, near the forest of Fontainebleau, was a favorite resort of a group of painters who, by painting from nature in rebellion against the prevalent classical tradition, helped pave the way for the later realists and impressionists. The group (called the "Men of Thirty") included Theodore Rousseau, Corot, and Millet.

Barbon, Praise-God: see BAREBONE, PRAISE-GOD.

Barbosa, Ruy or **Rui** (both: rōō'ē bûrbô'sù), 1849–1923, Brazilian philosopher of law, noted jurist, member of World Court.

Barbour, John, c. 1320–1395, Scottish poet and churchman. *The Bruce* (1375) chronicles deeds of ROBERT I.

Barbourville, city (pop. 2,926), S Ky., in Cumberland R. valley NW of Middlesboro. Seat of Union Col. (Methodist; coed.; 1880). Near state park with cabin of first white people in Ky. (replica).

Barbusse, Henri (ärē' bärbüs'), 1873–1935, French author. Best known for *Under Fire* (1916; Eng. tr., 1917), a realistic story of World War I.

Barca, surname of Carthaginian family, which included HANNIBAL.

Barcelona (bärthälō'nä), city (pop. 1,076,601), cap. of Barcelona prov. and of Catalonia, NE Spain, on Mediterranean. Second-largest city, largest port, chief commercial and industrial center of Spain. Machinery mfg. Flourished under Romans and Visigoths, fell to Moors (8th cent.) and to Charlemagne (801). Counts of Barcelona acquired all CATALONIA and parts of S France. Marriage of Count Raymond Berengar IV with heiress of Aragon united Catalonia and Aragon (1137). Barcelona became royal residence, powerful trade and banking center. Univ. founded 1450. City declined after unification of Spain, was center of Catalan separatism and various radical movements. A modern city, Barcelona also has medieval landmarks: Gothic cathedral, city hall, exchange, Church of Santa María del Mar.

Barclay de Tolly, Mikhail, Prince (mēkhüyēl', bûrklī' dù tô'lyē), 1761–1818, Russian field marshal, of Scottish descent. Commanded Russian forces against Napoleon (1812), adopted strategy of retreat into heart of Russia. Replaced by Kutuzov after defeat at Smolensk (August) but resumed command 1813.

Bar Cochba, Simon: see BAR KOKBA, SIMON.

Bard, Samuel, 1742–1821, American physician, active in developing institution which became medical school of Columbia Univ. Writings include midwifery text, works on pathology and medical education.

bard, in Wales, a minstrel and poet who served as a national chronicler and enjoyed many noble privileges, regardless of birth. The order (estab. 940) became hereditary. After their power was broken by Edward I, they became professional poets and singers. The poets in Ireland are similar.

Bard College: see ANNANDALE-ON-HUDSON, N.Y.

Bardstown, city (pop. 4,154), central Ky., SSE of Louisville in farm area; settled 1778. Center of early missionary work in Mississippi valley and of institutions founded by Bishop J. B. M. David. Taken in Civil War (Sept., 1862) by Bragg's Confederates. Has several old structures (Foster may have written *My Old Kentucky Home* in one house).

Barebone or **Barbon, Praise-God** (both: bär'bŏn), 1596?–1679, English lay preacher, member of Cromwell's nominated parliament (1653). This called Barebone's Parliament, though his part was insignificant.

Bareilly (bùrā'lē), city (pop. 192,688), N central Uttar Pradesh, India; founded 1537; a commercial center.

Barents Island: see SPITSBERGEN.

Barents Sea, arm of Arctic Ocean, N of Norway and European RSFSR. Shallow, it is warmed by remnants of North Atlantic Drift.

Barentz or **Barents, Willem,** d. 1597, Dutch navigator. Noted for extent of exploration and accuracy of charts in search for Northwest Passage.

Barge Canal: see NEW YORK STATE BARGE CANAL.

Bargello (bärjĕl'lō), 13th-cent. palace in Florence, Italy, which houses the national museum. Once used by the chief of police (*bargello*). Its treasures include Giotto's frescoes and Michelangelo's *David.*

Barham, Richard Harris (bär'm), pseud. **Thomas Ingoldsby** (ĭn'glùlzbē), 1788–1845, English humorist, a clergyman, author of *The Ingoldsby Legends* (prose tales, verse, modern satire).

Bar Harbor, town (pop. 3,864), on Mt. Desert Isl., S Maine, SE of Bangor. A famous summer resort of New England coast, it developed in mid-1800s.

Bar-Hebraeus, Gregorius (bär-hēbrē'ùs), 1226–86, Syrian scholar, catholicos of Jacobite church. Noted for Syriac chronicle of the world since Adam and for commentaries on Aristotle.

Bari or **Bari delle Puglie** (bä'rē dĕl'lē pōō'lyĕ), city (pop. 162,238), cap. of Apulia, S Italy; Adriatic seaport. Center of fertile agr. area. Founded by Romans; conquered from Byzantines by Normans 1071; port of embarkation during Crusades. Has Romanesque Basilica of St. NICHOLAS of Bari (shrine of pilgrimage), cathedral, medieval castle. University founded 1924. Port bombarded in World War II.

Baring-Gould, S(abine) (bā'rĭng-gōōld'), 1834–1924, English novelist, folklorist, hymn writer, a clergyman, best known for words of hymn *Onward, Christian Soldiers* (1865).

barite (bā'rīt), **barytes** (bùrī'tēz), or **heavy spar,** natural mineral, barium sulphate. Almost insoluble. Used to test for SULPHATE, as source of barium, and to make paint and lithopone (white pigment).

Barito (bärē'tō), river, c.550 mi. long, in S Borneo; flows to Java Sea.

barium (bâ'–), silvery-white active, poisonous metallic element (symbol = Ba; see also ELEMENT, table). Divalent, alkaline earth; resembles calcium. Oxidizes in air; ionizes in solution; with water, forms hydroxide, liberates hydrogen. Forms many compounds used in ceramic industry, medicine, etc. Barium carbonate and sulphate found in nature; metal obtained by hydrolysis of chloride. Gives green FLAME test in Bunsen burner.

barium sulphate: see BARITE.

Bar-jesus or **Elymas** (ĕl'ĭmăs), sorcerer who tried to mislead a prospective Christian. Acts 13.4–12.

Bar-jona (-jō'–) [Aramaic,= son of Jonah], patronymic of St. Peter. Mat. 16.17.

bark, covering of stems and roots, best developed in woody plants. Outer portion is cork layer and inner (see BAST) is separated from wood by cambium. Bark yields TANNIN, latex (a source of rubber), dyes, and cork (see CORK OAK).

bark (bärk), three-masted sailing vessel with fore- and mainmasts square-rigged and mizzenmast fore-and-aft-rigged. Modern bark may be as large as 6,000 tons. A four-master bark has its aftermast fore-and-aft-rigged. A barkentine has three masts, with foremast square-rigged, others fore-and-aft-rigged.

bark cloth, primitive fabric made by many peoples from soft inner bark of certain tropical and subtropical trees. It is often elaborately decorated. Tapa cloth is a fine kind made in Pacific isls.

Barker, Harley Granville-: see GRANVILLE-BARKER.

Barkla, Charles Glover (bär'klù), 1877–1944, English physicist. Won 1917 Nobel Prize for discovery of characteristic X rays of elements.

Barkley, Alben W(illiam), 1877–, Vice President of the United States (1949–53). Earlier was Democratic Representative (1913–27) and Senator (1927–49) from Ky.

Bar Kokba, Simon, or **Simon Bar Cochba** (kŏk'bù) [Heb.,= son of the stars], d. 135, Hebrew leader of revolt against Rome (131–135), a self-proclaimed Messiah. The revolt failed disastrously.

Barlaam and Josaphat (bär'lȧum, jō'sùfȧt), popular romance found in many languages. A Christianized version of the Buddha legend (c.980) by Euthymius, a Georgian monk, and later elaborated, it tells of the conversion to Christianity of a young Indian prince, Barlaam, by the hermit Josaphat.

Barlach, Ernst (ĕrnst' bär'läkh), 1870–1938, German sculptor. Illustrated his own poems and plays.

Bar-le-Duc (bär-lù-dük'), town (pop. 14,015), cap. of Meuse dept., NE France; historic cap. of county (later duchy) of Bar (united with Lorraine in 15th cent.). Exports famed preserves, jellies.

barley, cereal grass (*Hordeum vulgare*), probably one of earliest cereals cultivated by man. Matures quickly, hence has a wide range, including high altitudes. Used for stock feed, malting, flour; until 16th cent., was chief breadstuff of Europe.

Barlow, Joel, 1754–1812, American poet and diplomat, one of the Connecticut Wits. His best-known poetic works are the epic *The Vision of Columbus* (1787; rev. ed., *The Columbiad,* 1807) and the mock eulogy *The Hasty-Pudding* (written 1793). Wrote *Advice to the Privileged Orders* (1792), a prose tract for democracy, and also an able critique of the French constitution of 1791. Sent to Europe as agent for an ill-fated Ohio land company, he remained abroad 17 years and was for a time U.S. consul in Algiers. Died of exposure on a diplomatic mission to Napoleon at time of retreat from Moscow.

Barmecides: see HARUN-AL-RASHID.

Barmen, Germany: see WUPPERTAL.

Barnabas, Saint (bär'nùbùs), apostle, missionary, companion of Paul and Mark. Acts 4.36,37; 9.27; 11.22–15.41; 1 Cor. 9.6; Gal. 2.1,9,13; Col. 4.10. Among Christian PSEUDEPIGRAPHA is an epistle attributed to him. Named in Canon of Mass. Feast: June 11.

barnacle, marine crustacean usually attached to rocks, stones, seaweed, wharf piles, ships, and marine animals. Shell-like plates cover adult's body. Usually has six pairs of plumelike legs, which are plied to draw food to mouth.

Barnard, Edward Emerson (bär'nùrd), 1857–1923, American astronomer, pioneer in astronomical photography. Discoverer of Jupiter's fifth satellite and 16 comets.

Barnard, Frederick Augustus Porter, 1809–89, American educator, a mathematician. Professor, Univ. of Alabama (1837–54); professor, Univ. of Mississippi (1854–61), president (1856–58), chancellor (1858–61). As president of Columbia Col. (1864–89) he expanded the curriculum, supported sciences, extended elective system, fostered School of Mines. Advocated equal educational privileges for men and women; Barnard Col. named for him.

Barnard, George Grey, 1863–1938, American sculptor. His realistic statue of Lincoln caused heated controversy in 1917. His collection of Gothic art is in the CLOISTERS in New York city.

Barnard, Henry, 1811–1900, American educator, a leader in reform of common schools in Conn. and R.I. Chancellor of the Univ. of Wisconsin (1858–60), president of St. John's Col., Annapolis (1866–67), and first U.S. commissioner of education (1867–70).

Barnard College: see COLUMBIA UNIVERSITY.

Barnato, Barnett (bärnä'tō), 1852–97, South African financier, b. London; originally named Barney Isaacs. Made a fortune by buying up and exploiting worked-out Kimberley diamond mines. Later combined his interests with those of Cecil Rhodes.

Barnave, Joseph (zhōzĕf' bärnäv'), 1761–93, French revolutionist. An extremist, he was sent in 1791 to bring fugitive royal family back from Varennes and turned monarchist. He supported Mirabeau, led FEUILLANTS, and was guillotined.

Barnburners, radical element of Democratic party in N.Y. (1843–48), opposed to HUNKERS. Name arose from story of Dutchman who burned his barn to get rid of rats, implying that Barnburners would destroy corporations and public works to do away with their abuses. Group also opposed extension of slavery. United with FREE-SOIL PARTY in 1848.

Barnegat Bay (bär'nùgăt), Atlantic arm, c.30 mi. long, E N.J., entered via inlet between Long Beach isl. and Island Beach peninsula. Lighthouse built 1858; replaced 1930 by lightship.

Barnes, Juliana: see BERNERS, JULIANA.

Barnes, William, 1801–86, English writer, author of poems in Dorset dialect.

Barneveldt, Jan van Olden: see OLDENBARNEVELDT.

Barnstable (bärn'stùbùl), resort town (pop. 10,480), SE Mass., on Cape Cod; settled 1639. Includes Hyannis resort (pop. 4,235), with Massachusetts Maritime Acad., and Cotuit village, noted for oysters.

Barnum, Phineas Taylor, 1810–91, American showman. Gained fame (1842) with his American Museum in N.Y., publicized by extravagant advertising and exhibits such as a bearded lady. Major attractions included "Gen. TOM THUMB." Managed U.S. tour of singer Jenny LIND. His circus ("The Greatest Show on Earth"), soon an American institution, opened 1871. Merged (1881) with J. A. Bailey's, circus continued under name Barnum and Bailey.

Baroda (bùrō'dù), former princely state; since 1949 part of Bombay state, India. Became independent Mahratta kingdom in 18th cent. under the Gaekwars. Its former cap. Baroda (pop. 153,301) has a palace and several colleges; cotton-milling center.

Baroja (y Nessi), Pío (pē'ō bärō'hä ē nĕ'sē), 1879–, Spanish novelist of Basque origin, prominent in the literary group, Generation of 1898. Best known of his trilogies is *La lucha por la vida* [the struggle for existence] (1904). *Memorias de un hombre de acción* [memoirs of a man of action] is cycle of historical novels.

barometer (bùrŏm'ùtùr), instrument for measuring atmospheric pressure. Torricelli mercurial barometer uses 3-ft. mercury-filled glass tube (sealed at one end) supported vertically with open end under surface of mercury in container exposed to atmospheric pressure. Standard pressure at sea level holds mercury in tube to height of 29.92 in., 76 cm., or 1013.2 millibars (space above mercury is vacuum). Height of column varies with changes in air pressure; slight changes occur continually. Air pressure diminishes with altitude, the barometer reading dropping roughly one inch per 1,000 ft. until at c.3.5 mi. above earth's surface air pressure is about one half that at sea level; at c.10 mi. above earth pressure is c.10% that at sea level and it diminishes ultimately to zero. **Aneroid barometer** is metal box partially exhausted of air, its surface reacting to outside air pressure which registers on dial face.

Baronius, Caesar (bùrō'nēùs), 1538–1607, Italian cardinal, author of an erudite history of the Roman Catholic Church to 1198. A librarian of the Vatican, he was largely responsible for the Roman Martyrology.

Barons' War, 1263–67, phase of the English struggle between king and barons. Henry III reasserted his power in 1261. Barons led by Simon de MONTFORT resorted to arms. Failed to estab. power of the nobles but helped prepare for constitutional developments of reign of EDWARD I.

baroque (bùrōk'), in architecture and decoration, a grandiose, richly ornamented, often extravagant style which originated in Italy in late 16th cent. as reaction against classicism. Reaching its height throughout Europe a century later, it was dethroned by 18th-cent. classic revival. Epitomized in Rome in Bernini's colonnades in St. Peter's Square and in works by Borromini and Vignola. In France the style culminated under Louis XIV and gave way to ROCOCO under

Louis XV. It flourished in Germany and Austria, and reached extremes in Spain in work of Churriguera.

baroque, in music, a style which extends from 1600, the date of production of the first extant opera music, to 1750, the year of Bach's death. It grew from the late 16th-cent. revolt against POLYPHONY. Baroque music is romantic with emotional extremes. Major and minor scales replaced church modes (see MODE). The individual character and capacities of instruments and voices were now considered. Principal forms: vocal —opera, oratorio, and cantata; instrumental—fugue, sonata, concerto, and overture.

Barotseland: see NORTHERN RHODESIA.

Barquisimeto (bärkēsēmä'tō), city (pop. 105,080) NW Venezuela; founded 1552. A commercial center on Pan American Highway, it ships cattle.

barracuda (bărŭkōo'dŭ), elongated fish of tropical and subtropical seas. It has a long snout, large sharp-edged teeth, projecting lower jaw. Swift and voracious, it kills other fish and is often a hazard to human bathers.

Barranquilla (bärängkē'yä), city (pop. 150,395), N Colombia, Caribbean port, near mouth of Magdalena; founded 1629. It has small industries.

Barras, Paul, vicomte de (pōl' vēkōt' dü bäräs'), 1755–1829, French revolutionist. At first a Jacobin, he turned against Robespierre on 9 THERMIDOR; led in Thermidorian reaction. Was chief member of DIRECTORY; supported Bonaparte on 18 Brumaire (1799). Notoriously corrupt and immoral.

Barre, city (pop. 10,922), central Vt., surrounded by Barre town and near Montpelier. Granite quarries were developed after War of 1812. Goddard Col. is at near-by Plainfield.

Barre des Écrins (bär' dāzäkrē'), peak, 13,461 ft. high, SE France; highest of Dauphiné Alps.

barren grounds, arctic prairie region of NW Canada, NW of Hudson Bay and E of the Mackenzie basin. Geologically part of the LAURENTIAN PLATEAU, it has large areas of bare rock, few trees, and limited vegetation. The many lakes and streams contain fish, and musk oxen are found in the N. Vast herds of caribou cross the area seasonally. Barren grounds first crossed by Samuel Hearne 1770–71.

Barrès, Maurice (mōrēs' bärēs'), 1862–1923, French novelist. From his early advocacy of egoism, expressed in the trilogy *Le Culte du moi* (1888–91), he turned to ardent nationalism and royalism. *Les Déracinés* [the uprooted] (1897), his best-known work, is typical of his lucid, powerful style.

Barrett, Elizabeth: see BROWNING, ELIZABETH.

Barrie, Sir J(ames) M(atthew) (bă'rē), 1860–1927, British novelist and playwright. Novels laid in his native Scotland (e.g., *The Little Minister,* 1891; *Sentimental Tommy,* 1896) were followed by whimsical, sentimental plays (e.g., *Quality Street,* 1901; *The Admirable Crichton,* 1902; *Peter Pan,* 1904; *What Every Woman Knows,* 1908; *Dear Brutus,* 1917).

Barrie, town (pop. 12,514), S Ont., Canada, on arm of L. Simcoe. Resort in farming and dairying region. Has meat packing and flour milling.

Barrier Reef, Australia: see GREAT BARRIER REEF.

Barrington, residential and resort town (pop. 8,246), E R.I., SE of Providence; settled c.1670. Mfg. of brick and textiles; shipbuilding; shellfishing.

Barron, James, 1769–1851, U.S. naval officer. Court-martialed as commander of CHESAPEAKE, frigate involved in famous incident in 1807. Mortally wounded Stephen Decatur in duel in 1820.

Barrow, Sir John, 1764–1848, British geographer, promoter of arctic exploration. Founder of Royal Geographical Society (1830).

Barrow, river of Ireland, rising in the Slieve Bloom mts. and flowing 119 mi. to Waterford Harbour.

Barrow, Point, Alaska: see POINT BARROW.

Barrow-in-Furness (-fûr'nŭs), county borough (pop. 67,473), on SW coast of FURNESS peninsula, Lancashire, England; one of Britain's chief steel producing

cities. Also has shipbuilding and armaments mfg. Near-by Walney Isl. connected by bridge.

Barry, Sir Charles, 1795–1860, English architect, best known for Westminster Palace, London.

Barry, John, 1745–1803, U.S. naval officer and hero in American Revolution, b. Ireland.

Barry, Philip, 1896–1949, American dramatist. Studied under George Pierce Baker. His gently satirical comedies of manners were popular, notably *Paris Bound* (1927), *Holiday* (1928), and *The Philadelphia Story* (1939). Also wrote symbolic philosophical dramas such as *White Wings* (1926), *Hotel Universe* (1930), and *Here Come the Clowns* (1938).

Barry, municipal borough (pop. 40,979), Glamorganshire, Wales; a great coal exporting port of Britain.

Barrymore, family of actors. The first, **Maurice Barrymore** (real name Herbert Blythe), 1847–1905, was English. In U.S. (1875), joined Augustin Daly's stock company. Acted in Modjeska's company with his wife, **Georgiana Drew Barrymore,** 1856–93, American actress, one of the great comediennes of her day. Her oldest son, **Lionel Barrymore,** 1878–, appeared in such plays as *Peter Ibbetson;* won acclaim in *Macbeth.* Among first distinguished actors to star in films, he is also famed for radio appearances in Dickens's *Christmas Carol.* His sister, **Ethel Barrymore,** 1879–, actress of great depth, has been on stage since 1894 (e.g., in *The Silver Box, The Corn Is Green*) and also in films. Her brother, **John Barrymore,** 1882–1942, attempted painting, but turned to stage to give distinguished performances, e.g., in *Peter Ibbetson, Richard III,* and as a notable Hamlet. Films include *Grand Hotel* and *Dinner at Eight.*

Barsabas: see JOSEPH BARSABAS.

Barsetshire: see TROLLOPE, ANTHONY.

Barstow, city (pop. 6,135), SE Calif., on dry Mojave R. Railroad division point. Outfitting point for Death Valley expeditions.

Bart, Jean (zhä' bär'), 1650–1702, French naval hero. A privateer from 1672, he was ennobled and created rear admiral (1696) by Louis XIV, as reward for spectacular exploits in War of the Grand Alliance. Noted for his naive bluntness.

Bartas, Guillaume de Salluste du: see DU BARTAS.

Barth, Karl, 1886–, Swiss Protestant Reformed theologian. Argues for revelation by faith—a return to doctrine of predestination.

Bartholdi, Frédéric Auguste (frädärēk' ōgüst' bärtōldē'), 1834–1904, French sculptor. Best-known works are *Lion of Belfort* and Statue of LIBERTY.

Bartholomew, Saint (–thŏl'ŭmū), one of the Twelve Apostles. May be same as Nathanael (Nathanael given name, Bartholomew patronymic). Mat. 10.3; Mark 3.18; Luke 6.14; Acts 1.13. Feast: Aug. 24.

Barthou, Louis (lwē' bärtōō'), 1862–1934, French foreign minister (1934). Assassinated with King ALEXANDER of Yugoslavia.

Bartimaeus (–mē'ŭs), blind man cured by Jesus. Mat. 22.29–34; Mark 10.46–52; Luke 18.35–43.

Bartlesville city (pop. 19,228), NE Okla., on Caney R. and N of Tulsa; founded c.1877 on trading-post site. Distributes food stuffs, oil. Has hq. for oil firms and a U.S. Bureau of Mines experiment station. Oil refining and zinc smelting.

Bartlett, John, 1820–1905, American compiler of *Familiar Quotations,* first published in 1855. Also compiled a Shakspere concordance.

Bartlett, Robert Abram (Captain Bob), 1875–1946, American arctic explorer, b. Newfoundland. Noted especially for exploring and scientific work in Greenland. Made annual arctic cruises from 1925 to 1941.

Bartok, Bela (bä'lŭ bär'tôk), 1881–1945, Hungarian composer, pianist, collector of folk music (which greatly influenced his own compositions). He played and lectured in Europe and America. Among his principal works: six string quartets; three orchestral suites; a set of progressive piano studies, *Mikrokosmos;* Music for Two Pianos and Percussion; and concertos and rhapsodies for violin and for piano. His music, harsh and vigorous, sometimes combines four melodies in different keys.

Bartolomeo, Fra (frä′ bärtōlōmä′ō), 1472?–1517, Florentine painter of religious subjects; also called Baccio della Porta. Became a Dominican in 1500. Influenced by Raphael, Bellini, and Giorgione; collaborated on several pictures with Albertinelli.

Barton, Clara, 1821–1912, American humanitarian. Nurse to Civil War soldiers. Organized American Natl. Committee (1877), which later became American Red Cross; served as its president until 1904.

Barton, Elizabeth, 1506?–1534, English prophetess, called the Maid of Kent or the Nun of Kent. After prophecies against Henry VIII's divorce, she was tried, induced to confess, and executed for treason.

Bartow, city (pop. 8,694), central Fla., E of Tampa and W of L. Kissimmee. Processes and ships phosphates, citrus fruit, and truck.

Bartram, John, 1699–1777, pioneer American botanist. In 1728, in Philadelphia, he established the first botanical garden in U.S. His son, **William Bartram,** 1739–1823, was a naturalist. His *Travels* (1791) written after he explored SE U.S. served Wordsworth, Coleridge, and others as a source of descriptions of the American wilderness.

Baruch (bā′rŭk) [Heb.,= blessed], Jeremiah's scribe for whom book of Baruch is named.

Baruch, Bernard M(annes) (bùrŏok′), 1870–, U.S. government adviser on economics.

Baruch, in Western canon, book of Old Testament; placed in Apocrypha in AV. Named for Jewish prince Baruch (fl. 600 B.C.), faithful scribe of Jeremiah. Jer. 32.12–16; 36; 43.3,6; 45. Book contains: message from exiled Jews to those at home; well-known Messianic allusion (3.37); words of consolation; letter of Jeremiah (sometimes called Epistle of Jeremy). For Apocalypse of Baruch, see PSEUDEPIGRAPHA.

Barye, Antoine Louis (ätwän′ lwē′ bärē′), 1796–1875, French animal sculptor, popular for his small studies designed for commercial reproduction.

barytes: see BARITE.

Barzun, Jacques (zhäk′ bär′zùn), 1907–, American historian and teacher, b. France. He began (1928) teaching history in Columbia Col., becoming professor of history in 1945. He is also known as a critic of literature and the arts (esp. music).

basalt (bùsôlt′), common fine-grained extrusive lava, dark gray to black. The Deccan trap, Columbia R. plateau, and Iceland flows are of basalt.

base, chemical compound that, by theory of ION, yields hydroxyl (OH) ions in aqueous solution. Described also as HYDROXIDE of metal or of positive RADICAL. OH ion has a negative charge, tastes bitter, feels soapy, turns red litmus blue. In solution bases conduct electricity, react with acids (NEUTRALIZATION); strong bases (alkalis) ionize freely.

baseball, "national game" of U.S. Derived from English cricket and rounders. Commission headed by A. G. Mills reported (1907) that Abner Doubleday created the modern game at Cooperstown, N.Y., in 1839, though the question has been hotly disputed. Professional baseball's two major leagues (eight teams each) are the National (organized 1876) and the American (organized 1901). Since 1903, winners of these leagues have met in the World Series. The sport's greatest stars have been elected to Natl. Baseball Hall of Fame and Mus., built at Cooperstown 1939.

Basedow, Johann Bernhard (yōhän′ bĕrn′härt bä′zùdō), 1723–90, German educator. Emphasized realistic teaching, including physical education, manual training, nature study.

Basel (bä′zùl), Fr. *Bâle,* canton, N Switzerland, bordering on France and Germany; in English also spelled Basle. Crossed by Rhine R. (navigable from here) and by Jura mts. Population is Protestant, German-speaking. Canton has been divided since 1833 into two independent half cantons—Basel-Land (165 sq. mi.; pop.

107,393), with cap. at Liestal, and Basel-Stadt, coextensive with city of **Basel** and suburbs (14 sq. mi.; pop. 196,658), on the Rhine. A commercial, industrial, and intellectual center, it is the seat of the Bank for International Settlements, the Swiss Industries Fair, and of important chemical and other industries. Univ. was founded 1460. A Roman colony, Basel became a bishopric in 7th cent. A free imperial city from 11th cent., it joined the Swiss Confederation in 1501 and in 1523 accepted the Reformation. (The prince-bishops of Basel, expelled from the city, continued to rule their vast territory from DELÉMONT until 1792.) The oppressive regime of the city patriciate led to civil troubles (1831–33) and the secession of Basel-Land. Among notable buildings are the cathedral (founded 1019) and the 16th-cent. city hall, with a Holbein collection. Erasmus and Holbein the Younger lived here; Euler and the Bernoulli family were born here.

Basel, Council of, 1431–49, council of Roman Catholic Church. A primary reason for its being summoned was trouble with the Hussites, and an agreement called the Compactata was drawn up (1433) and later split the Hussites (with the Utraquists rejoining the Church). The council is, however, remarkable chiefly for trying to put in practice the conciliar theory already advanced at the Council of Constance—the theory that ultimate authority resides in the general council, not the pope. Pope EUGENE IV early ordered it dissolved, but tried to compromise with the council, which instituted a process against the pope. He denounced the council in a bull (*Doctoris gentium,* 1437). The council deposed him and elected AMADEUS VIII of Savoy (antipope Felix V). Eugene, who summoned the Council of FERRARA-FLORENCE, had the support of most rulers. Though the French adopted many ideas of the council and many reforms proposed were adopted by the Church, the council failed. Felix V resigned in favor of Eugene's successor, Nicholas V, and the conciliar theory died with the council.

Bashan (bā′–), in Bible, region E of Jordan R., known for cattle and sheep. Num. 21.33; Deut. 3; 2 Kings 10.33; Ps. 22.12; 68.15; Amos 4.1.

Bashkir Autonomous Soviet Socialist Republic (bŭshkēr′), autonomous state (55,400 sq. mi.; pop. 3,144,-713), E European RSFSR, partly in S Urals; cap. Ufa. Agr., timber, minerals (iron, copper, manganese, gold, chromium, lead, bauxite, petroleum). Bashkirs (24% of pop.) are Moslem, Turkic-speaking people, tributary to Russia since 1556; rest of population mainly Russians (40%) and Turko-Tatars.

Bashkirtsev, Marie (bäsh′kùrtsĕf), 1860–84, French diarist and painter, b. Russia. Famous for her journal (published posthumously), a frank record of a precocious child avid for fame.

Basil, Saint: see BASIL THE GREAT, SAINT.

Basil, Byzantine emperors. **Basil I** (the Macedonian), c.813–86. Boon companion of Emperor MICHAEL III, whom he persuaded to make him coemperor (866) and whom he ordered slain (867). Capable, he reformed finances and the law code, and restored Byzantine military prestige. He strove vainly to prevent a schism of E and W churches and restored IGNATIUS OF CONSTANTINOPLE to the patriarchate (867). **Basil II,** c.958–1025, was co-ruler with his brother Constantine VIII after the reigns of usurpers NICEPHORUS II (963–67) and JOHN I (967–76). He suppressed the revolts of the landowners, revived laws of ROMANUS I, annexed Bulgaria (1018), and extended his empire to Caucasus. Called Bulgaroktonos, "Bulgar slayer."

Basil III, grand duke of Moscow: see VASILY III.

basil (băz′ùl), tender herb or shrub of genus *Ocimum.* Cultivated for aromatic leaves used as seasoning.

Basilian monks (bùzĭ′lēùn), monks of the Eastern Church, following the rule of St. BASIL THE GREAT. They live in collections of small cells without central government. The reformation by St. THEODORE OF STUDIUM (9th cent.) revitalized the order. Noted monasteries (hermitages) are at Mt. Athos and Mt. Sinai.

Basilicata (bäzēlēkä′tä), region (3,856 sq. mi.; pop. 543,-262), S Italy; cap. Potenza. Other cities: MELFI, Matera. Poor, arid soil. Sheep and goat raising. Comprising parts of anc. Lucania and Samnium, region fell to Lombards, Byzantines; annexed (11th cent.) to Norman duchy of Apulia.

Basilius Valentinus (bùsīl′ēùs văl′ùntī′nùs), believed pseudonym of Johannes Thölde. Wrote on chemistry, use of antimony in fevers (1604).

Basil the Great, Saint (bä′zīl, bä′-), c.330–379, Greek churchman, one of the Greek Fathers, Doctor of the Church, bishop of Caesarea in Cappadocia; brother of St. Gregory of Nyssa. He wrote most of the two rules for the Basilian monks. As aid and successor to Eusebius, he helped estab. orthodoxy over ARIANISM.

Baskerville, John, 1706–75, English type designer, printer for Cambridge Univ. after 1758. Introduced influential "modern" type faces. His books are large, with wide margins and excellent paper and ink.

basketball. Played by two opposing teams of five players each on regulation court 94 ft. long, 50 ft. wide. Originated (1891) in U.S. by James Naismith, physical director of Y.M.C.A. college, Springfield, Mass.

Basket Makers, early Indian people of U.S. Southwest, dating possibly from c.1500 B.C. Had great skill in making baskets; developed from nomadic hunters to farmers; lived in pit houses. Succeeded by ancestors of Pueblo Indians.

Basle, Switzerland: see BASEL.

Basque Provinces (băsk), Basque *Euzkadi,* Span. *Vascongadas,* region (2,803 sq. mi.; pop. 955,764), N Spain, S of Bay of Biscay, consisting of Álava, Guipúzcoa, and Vizcaya provs. Chief cities: Bilbao, Vitoria, San Sebastián. Iron, lead, copper mines; shipyards; fisheries. Majority of pop. are **Basques,** a stoutly Catholic people of peasants, shepherds, and fishermen. There are c.1,550,000 Basques in Spanish Navarre and Basque Provs.; c.200,000 in SW France (Labourd, Soule, and Lower Navarre dists.); c.250,-000 in S America and rest of world. Possibly descended from Cro-Magnon man, they antedate anc. Iberian tribes of Spain. Their language is related to no other. Before Roman conquest of Spain and Gaul, Basque pop. extended further N and S than now. Core of Basque country fought off Romans, Visigoths, Moors, and Franks. Basque victory at RONCESVALLES threw off short-lived overlordship of Charlemagne (778). In GASCONY the duchy set up by Basques in 601 fell apart in 9th cent., but in 824 the Basque kingdom of NAVARRE was founded; under SANCHO III it united nearly all Basques (1000–1035). Basques lost independence as Castile acquired Guipúzcoa (1200), Álava (1332), Vizcaya (1370), and most of Navarre (1512), but they retained their old democratic rights. Their assemblies at GUERNICA remain famous. In 1873 Basque privileges were abolished after Basques' pro-Carlist stand in Carlist wars. The three Basque Provs. were granted autonomy in 1936. They stoutly resisted Franco, who revoked autonomy after conquering them in 1937.

Basra (bùs′rù), city (pop. 206,302), SE Iraq, port on the Shatt el Arab, 75 mi. from Persian Gulf. Founded A.D. 636 by Caliph Omar, declined during Abbasid caliphate. Railroad link to Baghdad revived its importance. Exports dates, barley, and wool.

Bas-Rhin (bä-rĕ′), department (1,848 sq. mi.; pop. 673,-281), E France, in Alsace; cap. Strasbourg.

Bass, Sam, 1851–78, American desperado. Train robber in S.Dak. and Texas. Career provided material for frontier ballads.

bass, name for various food and game fish, chiefly seabass family (Serranidae) and sunfish family (Centrarchidae). Common sea bass (*Centropristes striatus*) along U.S. coast from Massachusetts to N Florida. Sometimes classed as sea bass and sometimes as separate family (Moronidae) are striped bass or rockfish (*Roccus saxatilis* or *R. lineatus*); white bass (*R. chrysops*); yellow bass (*Morone interrupta*); white or silver

perch (*M. americana*). *M. labrax* found on coast SW Europe and Mediterranean.

Bassano, Jacopo (yäkō′pō bäs-sä′nō), 1510–92, Venetian painter, b. Bassano. His real name was Da Ponte. Perhaps the first Italian genre artist. His son and follower was **Leandro Bassano** (lään′drō), 1558–1623.

Bassano, town (pop. 624), E Alta., Canada, ESE of Calgary. Bassano or Horseshoe Bend Dam near by on Bow R. is one of world's longest.

Bassano (bäs-sä′nō), city (pop. 11,774), Venetia, NE Italy, on Brenta R. Free commune in Middle Ages; under Venice 1402–1797. Home of Da Ponte family of painters (surnamed BASSANO) and of famous Remondini printing plant (17th–18th cent.). Palaces and churches recall past glory. Scene of Bonaparte's victory over Austrians 1796.

Basses-Alpes (bäs-zälp′), department (2,698 sq. mi.; pop. 83,354), SE France, in Provence; cap. Digne.

Basses-Pyrénées (bäs″-pērānä′), department (2,978 sq. mi.; pop. 415,797), SW France; cap. Pau.

Basse-Terre (bästĕr′), port (pop. 10,086), cap. of Guadeloupe dept., French West Indies.

Basseterre, town (pop. 12,194), SAINT KITTS, cap. of St. Kitts-Nevis presidency, British West Indies.

Bassett, John Spencer, 1867–1928, American historian. Founder (1902) of *South Atlantic Quarterly.* His many works on American history include *The Federalist System, 1789–1801* (1906) and *The Life of Andrew Jackson* (1911).

Bassompierre, François, baron de (fräswä′ bärō′ dù bäsōpyĕr′), 1579–1646, marshal of France. Served under Henry IV; later fought Huguenots (1621–22, 1627–28). His opposition to Richelieu caused his imprisonment in Bastille (1631–43). Wrote memoirs.

bassoon: see WIND INSTRUMENTS.

Bass Strait (băs), channel, 80–150 mi. wide, between Tasmania and Victoria, Australia. Its discovery by George Bass in 1798 destroyed belief that Tasmania was part of Australian continent.

basswood: see LINDEN.

bast, inner bark of plant stems which is phloem or food-conducting tissue. Source of valuable fibers in such plants as hemp, flax, jute, ramie, sunn hemp.

bastard, person born out of wedlock, illegitimate child. It is legally presumed that any child born to a married woman is the child of her husband. The latter has the burden of proof if he contests his paternity on the ground of physical impossibility. Attitudes toward illegitimacy have varied greatly under different social conditions. Under English common law illegitimate children had few rights. Rights now given by statutes. In U.S. state laws on illegitimacy vary greatly; generally subsequent marriage of parents legitimizes child, and some states provide special judicial proceedings for legitimation.

Bastard of Orléans, French general: see DUNOIS, JEAN, COMTE DE.

Bastia (bästē′ä), town (pop. 37,122), NE Corsica, France; seaport. The chief commercial center of Corsica, Bastia was its cap. till 1791. Citadel.

Bastian, Adolf (ä′dôlf bäs′tyän), 1826–1905, German anthropologist. His concept of "elemental ideas" as common to all mankind, foreshadowed culture-area theory.

Bastidas, Rodrigo de (rôdhrē′gō dä bästē′dhäs), c.1460–1526, Spanish conquistador in Colombia. Discovered mouth of Magdalena (1501), founded Santa Marta (1525).

Bastien-Lepage, Jules (zhül′ bästyē′-lùpäzh′), 1848–84, French painter of figures in the open air.

Bastille (băstēl′), former state prison in Paris, France. Begun as fortress c.1369; demolished 1789. Fouquet, Man with the Iron Mask, and Voltaire were imprisoned here. Despite horror stories, most political prisoners were treated mildly. On July 14, 1789, a Parisian mob, protesting Necker's dismissal, stormed Bastille. The date, marking outbreak of French Revolution, became national holiday of republican France.

Bastogne (bästô'nyù), town (pop. 4,717), Luxembourg prov., SE Belgium, in Ardennes. During BATTLE OF THE BULGE, U.S. troops under Gen. Anthony McAuliffe held encircled town until relieved by U.S. 3d Army (Dec. 20–26, 1944). McAuliffe's supposed reply when invited to surrender: "Nuts!"

Bastrop, town (pop. 12,769), NE La., NNE of Monroe; founded c.1845. Processes paper, carbon, and brick.

Basutoland (bùsōō'tōländ"), British territory (11,716 sq. mi.; pop. 624,605), enclave in Union of South Africa, administered directly by the crown; cap. Maseru. Basuto nation was formed (1815–31) from tribal remnants left in the wake of Zulu and Matabele raids. Under British rule since 1868.

bat, mammal of order Chiroptera. Found in most temperate and tropical regions, it is only mammal with power of true flight. Wing is membrane stretched between elongated bones of four fingers, extending in most bats along body from forelimbs to hind limbs to tail. Thumb is small, clawed, free of membrane. Chiefly nocturnal, they have some sight; avoid collision in flight mostly by keen senses of hearing, touch. In temperate climates, some bats hibernate in caves in winter; some migrate.

Bataan (bätăn', bätä-än'), peninsula and province (157 sq. mi.; pop. 92,901), W Luzon, Philippines. Forms W shore of Manila Bay. After fall of Manila in World War II, U.S. troops (first led by Gen. MacArthur and later by Lt. Gen. Wainwright) made a gallant stand here Jan.–April, 1942.

Bataille, Henry (ärē' bätä'yù'), 1872–1922, French dramatist. His plays are based on morbid psychology. *Maman Colibri* (1904) and *La Vierge folle* [the foolish virgin] (1910) were most successful.

Batalha (bùtä'lyù), town, Estremadura, W central Portugal, S of Leiria. John I built its famous Dominican monastery and church to commemorate victory of Aljubarrota (1385).

Batavia, Indonesia: see JAKARTA.

Batavia. 1 City (pop. 5,838), NE Ill., W of Chicago. Mfg. of machines and cosmetics. **2** City (17,799), W N.Y., SW of Rochester. Settled 1801 by a HOLLAND LAND COMPANY agent. Mfg. of shoes, paper and metal products. Has U.S. veterans' hospital.

Batavian Republic, 1795–1806. The United Provs. of the Netherlands, occupied by French in the French Revolutionary Wars, were reconstituted as the Batavian Republic in 1795, remaining under French tutelage. In 1806 Napoleon made it into kingdom of Holland for his brother Louis.

Bates, Henry Walter, 1825–92, English naturalist, explorer of upper Amazon with A. R. Wallace. In 1859 returned with 8,000 new species of animals. First to state plausible theory of mimicry.

Bates College: see LEWISTON, Maine.

Batesville, city (pop. 6,414), N central Ark., on White R. in the Ozarks. Processing center of area yielding cotton, fruit, poultry, milk, corn, lumber, manganese, and marble.

Bath, county borough (pop. 79,275) and city, Somerset, England, on the Avon. Romans discovered warm springs here 1st cent. A.D.; built elaborate walls and baths. In Chaucer's time, it had become wool and cloth town. Became famous spa in 18th cent., with Beau Nash as social arbiter. John WOOD and his son planned streets and buildings such as the Royal Crescent, Assembly Rooms (destroyed in 1942 air raid), and Circus. Now residential and resort town with mfg. and quarrying. Has 17th-cent. abbey.

Bath. 1 City (pop. 10,644), SW Maine, on lower Kennebec R. (bridged 1927); settled c.1670. Longtime shipbuilding center. Has Davenport Memorial, with marine exhibits. **2** Village (pop. 5,416), S N.Y., NW of Elmira, in farm area; settled 1793. Has U.S. veterans' administration center (1878). **3** Town, E N.C., on Pamlico R. and SE of Washington; settled 1690 on Indian village site. State's oldest town, was cap. of province of N.C. **4** See BERKELEY SPRINGS, W.Va.

Bath, Order of the, British order of knighthood. Estab. 1725 as military order, in 1847 opened also to civilians. Ranks second to Order of the Garter.

Bathory (bä'tôrē), Hung. *Báthory*, Pol. *Batory*, Hungarian noble family. **Stephen Bathory**, 1477–1534, voivode of Transylvania (1529–34) was the father of STEPHEN BATHORY, king of Poland, and of **Christopher Bathory**, 1530–81, prince of Transylvania (1575–81). Christopher's son **Sigismund Bathory**, 1572–1613, was recognized as hereditary prince of Transylvania by Rudolf II (1594). Probably insane, he abdicated 1596, but soon afterward returned to power, with Bocskay's help, as vassal of the sultan. He briefly abdicated again in 1599, and definitively in 1601 (in favor of Rudolf). Other members of the family include **Elizabeth Bathory**, d. 1614, celebrated as a werewolf (she is said to have slaughtered 600 virgins to renew her youth by bathing in their blood), who died in prison, and **Gabriel Bathory**, 1589–1613, prince of Transylvania (1608–13), murdered by rebellious nobles.

Bath-sheba (băth-shē'bù), wife of Uriah the Hittite. David caused Uriah's death and married her. She bore him Solomon. 2 Sam. 11; 12; 1 Kings 1; 2; Mat. 1.6.

Bathurst, town (pop. 4,453), NE N.B., Canada, on arm of Chaleur Bay; fishing and resort center.

bathysphere: see DIVING.

Batista (y Zaldívar), Fulgencio (fōōlhĕn'sēō bätē'stä ē sôldē'vär), 1901–, president of Cuba (1940–44), "strong man" (1933–44). After exile in U.S. (1945–49), led successful coup in Cuba 1952.

Batoche (bätôsh'), village, central Sask., Canada, S of Prince Albert. Hq. of Louis RIEL in Riel's Rebellion.

Baton Rouge (băt'ùn rōōzh"), city (pop. 125,629), state cap., SE La., NW of New Orleans, on E bank of Mississippi R.; settled 1719 by French. Taken by Farragut in Civil War (May, 1862). Major distributing and commercial center, it has one of world's largest oil refineries; also food-processing, woodworking, chemical plants. Seat of LOUISIANA STATE UNIVERSITY AND AGRICULTURAL AND MECHANICAL COLLEGE. Southern Univ. and Agricultural and Mechanical Col. (Negro; land grant; coed.; 1880) is near.

Batory: see BATHORY.

Battenberg (bä'tünbûrg), princely family issued from morganatic marriage of Alexander, younger son of Louis II of Hesse-Darmstadt, and countess Julia von Hauke, created princess of Battenberg 1858. Their oldest son, Louis, an admiral in British service, was created marquess of Milford Haven, married a granddaughter of Queen Victoria, changed his name to Mountbatten in World War I; father of Earl MOUNTBATTEN and grandfather of duke of EDINBURGH. Alexander's second son was Prince ALEXANDER of Bulgaria. A third son, Henry, married Beatrice, daughter of Queen Victoria; their daughter, Victoria Eugenie, married Alfonso XIII of Spain.

Battersea, metropolitan borough (pop. 117,130) of SW London, England, on S bank of the Thames. Chiefly workingmen's residences, suffered much air raid damage 1940–41. Has 200 acre Battersea Park.

Battery, the, park at S tip of Manhattan isl., New York city. Castle Clinton fort (built here c.1807, razed 1941) later became, in turn, Castle Garden amusement hall (scene of Jenny Lind's American debut 1850), immigration station (1855–92), and municipal aquarium (1896–1941); it was designated a national monument in 1950.

battery, unlawful touching by an aggressor—directly or indirectly, intentionally or negligently—of any part of another person. Intentional battery justifies a claim for damages regardless of physical injury. "Assault and battery" presupposes such injury, however slight.

battery, electric, commonly describes electric CELL; more correctly means group of cells used as source of electric current. A or **filament battery** provides current to heat FILAMENT in vacuum tube of radio. **B battery** is the source of current in plate circuit; produces needed voltage on plates of vacuum tubes. Usually consists of small dry cells connected in series; also may be of storage type. **C battery** is used in grid circuit of tube (see TUBE, VACUUM) to create bias (usually negative) on grid of tube. **Storage battery** is a much used current source, e.g., in automobile; has electric cells in series (see ELECTRIC CIRCUIT; *ill.,* p. 293).

Battle, former urban district (pop. 3,491), Sussex E., England, NW of Hastings. Scene of 1066 battle which resulted in death of Harold and elevation of Norman conqueror as WILLIAM I of England. Has ruins of **Battle Abbey,** founded by William after his victory. **Battle Abbey Roll,** which was kept here, supposedly listed William's noble battle companions. Its authenticity is doubtful.

battle, in war, single conflict or, more broadly, prolonged combat over extended area. Sir E. S. Creasy's list of 15 decisive battles of the world, 490 B.C.–1815, nominates Marathon (490 B.C.), Syracuse (413 B.C.), Arbela (331 B.C.), Metaurus (207 B.C.), the Teutoburg Forest (A.D. 9), Chalons-sur-Marne or Catalaunian Fields (451), Tour or Poitiers (732), Hastings or Senlac (1066), Orléans (1429), victory over Spanish Armada (1588), Blenheim (1704), Poltava (1709), Saratoga (1777), Valmy (1792), and Waterloo (1815). Others are Salamis (480 B.C.), Issus (333 B.C.), Cannae (216 B.C.), Zama (202 B.C.), Pharsala (48 B.C.), Philippi (42 B.C.), Actium (31 B.C.), Adrianople (A.D. 378), Lechfeld (955), Bouvines (1214), Sluis (1340), Crécy (1346), Nikopol (1396), Agincourt (1415), Constantinople (1453), Pavia (1525), Mohacs (1526), Mühlberg (1547), Lepanto (1571), White Mt. (1620), Lützen (1632), Rossbach (1757), Plassey (1757), Kings Mt. (1780), Yorktown (1781), Aboukir Bay or battle of the Nile (1798), Austerlitz (1805), Trafalgar (1805), Leipzig (1813), Ayacucho (1824), Solferino (1859), Vicksburg (1863), Gettysburg (1863), Sedan (1870), Manila Bay (1898), Tsushima (1905), two battles of the Marne (1914, 1918), Jutland (1916), Verdun (1916), Coral Sea and Midway (1942), Alamein (1942), and Stalingrad (1942–43).

Battle Abbey and **Battle Abbey Roll:** see BATTLE.

Battle above the Clouds: see CHATTANOOGA CAMPAIGN.

Battle Creek, city (pop. 48,666), S Mich., SW of Lansing, at junction of Kalamazoo R. and the Battle Creek; settled 1831. Farm trade center and health resort, known for mfg. of cereal foods, it also has mfg. of auto parts, farm equipment, and ink. Here are Battle Creek Sanitarium, hq. of W. K. Kellogg Foundation (child welfare), and an army hospital. U.S. VA center is at near-by Fort Custer.

Battleford, town (pop. 1,319), W Sask., Canada, on North Saskatchewan R. at mouth of Battle R. NW of Saskatoon. Cap. of Northwest Territories 1876–83. Prominent in Riel's Rebellion.

Battle Hymn of the Republic, The: see HOWE, JULIA WARD.

Battle of the Bulge, popular name given in World War II to last German offensive on Western Front (Dec., 1944–Jan., 1945). On Dec. 16 Germans under von Rundstedt in surprise attack broke through American front in Belgian Ardennes, creating a "bulge" in Allied lines. Allied counterthrusts turned German offensive into rout by mid-January. U.S. troops suffered heavy casualties. Defense of BASTOGNE was a notable episode.

Battle of the Spurs. 1 Victory, 1302, near Courtrai, Belgium, of Flemish towns over French army sent by Philip IV; so called for trophy formed by spurs of fallen French. **2** Victory, 1513, at GUINEGATE, of Henry VIII of England over French; possibly so-called for speedy flight of French cavalry.

Batu Khan (bä'tŏō kän'), d. 1255, Mongol commander of GOLDEN HORDE; grandson of Jenghiz Khan. Conquered Russia, Hungary, and Poland.

Batum (bŭtŏōm'), city (pop. 70,807), cap. of Adzhar ASSR, Georgian SSR, on Black Sea. Connected by pipe lines with Baku; major oil-refining and -shipping center. Ceded by Turkey to Russia 1878.

Baucis: see PHILEMON AND BAUCIS.

Baudelaire, Charles (shärl' bōdlâr'), 1821–67, French poet. His neurotic, eccentric personality led him along a road of poverty, misunderstanding, excesses, and disease. A perfectionist, he labored for years on his one volume of verse, *Les Fleurs du Mal* [flowers of evil] (1857), six poems of which were condemned as obscene by a court. Baudelaire never recovered fully from that blow. His other work includes remarkable literary and art criticism and exceptionally fine translations of Poe, to whom he felt great affinity. His influence on all subsequent poetry is immeasurable. There are several English translations of his poems.

Baudouin (bōdōōĕ'), 1930–, king of the Belgians (1951–); son and successor of LEOPOLD III.

Bauer, Louis Agricola, 1865–1932, American magnetician. Influential in international coordination of work in terrestrial magnetism. Founded and edited *Terrestrial Magnetism and Atmospheric Electricity*.

Bauhaus (bou'hous), art school in Germany. It revolutionized art training by combining the teaching of pure arts with the study of crafts. Founded in 1919 at Weimar with Walter GROPIUS as director, it stressed functional craftsmanship in every field with a realization of the industrial problems of mass production. Bauhaus met vigorous opposition which forced its removal to Dessau and later to Berlin. Finally closed in 1933 by the German government, but Bauhaus ideas concerning architecture and many industrial fields found wide acclaim. The Chicago Inst. of Design carried on its teaching plan.

Bauhin, Gaspard (gäspär' bŏē'), 1560–1624, Swiss botanist. He classified plants by genus and species, anticipating the binomial system of Linnaeus.

Baum, L(yman) Frank (bôm), 1856–1919, American author of juvenile books laid in imaginary magic land of Oz (e.g., *The Wonderful Wizard of Oz,* 1900).

Baumé, Antoine (ātwän' bōmā'), 1728–1804, French chemist. Invented a graduated hydrometer, discovered various important industrial processes.

Bausch, Edward (boush), 1854–1944, American inventor. Worked on kinetoscope, camera, microscope.

Bautzen (bou'tsùn), city (pop. 38,524), Saxony, SE Germany, in Upper Lusatia, on the Spree. Machine and textile mfg. Napoleon I defeated Russo-Prussian forces near by (1813).

Baux, Les (lä bō'), ruined medieval town near Arles, SE France. Was seat of powerful feudal family. Impressive ruins. Bauxite, first discovered here, is named for Les Baux.

bauxite, hydrate of ALUMINA, with other oxides. A claylike, earthy mineral, white to red or brown. Chief source of aluminum and its compounds.

Bavaria, Ger. *Bayern,* state (27,119 sq. mi.; pop. 9,118,-635), S Germany; cap. MUNICH. Rises in S to Bavarian Alps (highest peak ZUGSPITZE) along Austrian frontier; BOHEMIAN FOREST forms E frontier with Czechoslovakia. Danube and Main are chief rivers. State consists of Bavaria proper, i.e. Upper Bavaria (cap. Munich) and Lower Bavaria (cap. Landshut) in S; of Upper, Middle, and Lower FRANCONIA (with BAYREUTH, BAMBERG, NUREMBERG, WÜRZBURG) in N; of SWABIA (cap. AUGSBURG) in W; and of the Upper PALATINATE (cap. REGENSBURG) in NE. Rich in agr. and forests, Bavaria also has mfg. (machinery, textiles, beer, toys), resorts and spas for tourists. Roman Catholicism is predominant except in N. Until early 19th cent. Bavaria did not include Franconia and Swabia, which have separate histories. Conquered by Romans 15 B.C., the region was made a duchy 6th cent. A.D. by an invading Germanic tribe (Baiuoarii). Under Carolingians 788–911; under GUELPHS 1070–1180 (with interruptions); under WITTELSBACH dynasty 1180–1918. Austria, Carinthia, and Upper Palatinate were detached (976) from original duchy to curb power of dukes. Wittelsbach fiefs (incl. Rhenish PALATINATE) were long united among various branches of family, fully united only in 1799. Duke MAXIMILIAN I received Upper Palatinate and electoral rank (1623; see ELECTORS). Enlarged and raised to kingdom (1806), Bavaria emerged from Congress of Vienna with present territory and Rhenish Palatinate (1815). Sided with Austria in Austro-Prussian War (1866), with Prussia in Franco-Prussian War (1870–71); joined German Empire 1871. As chief German state after Prussia, it retained special position and separatist tendencies. Republic set up Nov., 1918; joined Weimar Republic after unsuccessful Communist revolution (1919). All Bavaria under U.S. occupation after 1945, except for Rhenish Palatinate and LINDAU dist., which were detached and occupied by France. New constitution adopted 1946. Joined Federal Republic of [Western] Germany 1949. Kings of Bavaria: MAXIMILIAN I, LOUIS I, MAXIMILIAN II, LOUIS II, OTTO I, LOUIS III.

Bavarian Succession, War of the, 1778–79. Elector Maximilian III having died childless in 1777, Bavaria passed to the elector palatine, Charles Theodore, who in return for certain concessions ceded Bavaria to Austria. Prussia protested the transfer. The ensuing campaign, spent entirely in provisioning the armies, has been called the Potato War. At the Congress of Teschen (1779) Austria renounced its claims.

Bax, Sir Arnold, 1883–, English composer. His works, which reflect Wagner and Debussy, include several tone poems, e.g., *The Garden of Fand;* seven symphonies; instrumental and vocal compositions.

Baxter, Richard, 1615–91, English nonconformist clergyman. A supporter of Cromwell, yet a moderate, he sought under Charles II to keep dissenters in Church; after Act of Uniformity (1662) withdrew from Church of England, but continued preaching despite persecution. Wrote *The Saints' Everlasting Rest* (1650).

bay or **sweet bay:** see LAUREL.

Bayard, Pierre du Terrail, seigneur de (bä′ùrd, Fr. pyĕr′ dü tĕrī′yù sänyûr′ dü bäyär′), c.1474–1524, French hero, *le chevalier sans peur et sans reproche* [the knight without fear or blame]. Fought in Italian Wars; fell in battle.

Bayazid or **Bayazit:** see BAJAZET.

bayberry, American shrub (*Myrica pennsylvanica*), native to the eastern seacoast of U.S. It is often cultivated for its handsome aromatic foliage. Its gray, waxy berries are used in winter bouquets and in making candles. California bayberry (*Myrica californica*) is evergreen and treelike.

Bay City. 1 City (pop. 52,523), S Mich., on Saginaw R. near its mouth on Saginaw Bay; settled c.1831. Port for Great Lakes and ocean shipping, it has shipbuilding and fishing. Mfg. of auto parts, machinery, and metal and chemical products. Coal mines in area. **2** Town (pop. 9,427), S Texas, SW of Houston near Colorado R. Shipping and industrial center for oil and farm area.

Bayer, Johann (yō′hän bī′ùr), 1572–1625, German astronomer, known for system of designating stars of a CONSTELLATION (using Greek letters with constellation names) and for star chart, *Uranometria* (1603).

Bayeux (bäyû′), town (pop. 8,744), Calvados dept., N France, in Normandy. First French town liberated (June 8, 1944) by Allies in World War II. Fine Gothic cathedral. In Bayeux Mus. is the **Bayeux tapestry,** an embroidery chronicling the Norman conquest of England in 1066; it is worked on coarse linen, 230 ft. by 20 in. Its date is disputed.

Bay Islands, archipelago, off N coast of Honduras, in Caribbean. Held by British for years after 1848.

Bayle, Pierre (bäl), 1647–1706, French rationalist philosopher. Through his works (among them *Dictionnaire historique et critique,* 1697) he influenced the philosophers of the Enlightenment in France and the deists in England.

Bayley, Richard, 1745–1801, American physician, known for scientific account of yellow fever epidemic of 1795 in New York city.

Bayliss, Sir William Maddock (bā′lĭs), 1860–1924, English physiologist, pioneer (with Starling) in evolving theory of hormone action after discovering secretion.

Baylor University, mainly at Waco, Texas; chartered, opened 1845 by Baptists at Independence; moved and absorbed Waco Univ. 1886. Medical college at Houston, dental college and nursing school at Dallas. Fine Robert Browning collection. Connected with Mary Hardin-Baylor Col. at BELTON.

Bayonne (bäyôn′), city (pop. 28,110), Basses-Pyrénées dept., SW France, in Basque country, on Adour R. near Bay of Biscay; fortified seaport. Bayonet invented here in 17th cent. Gothic cathedral; museums of fine arts and of Basque folklore.

Bayonne (bāyōn′), city (pop. 77,203), NE N.J. on peninsula S of Jersey City, between New York harbor (bridged 1931 to Staten Isl.) and Newark Bay; settled by Dutch c.1650, taken by British 1664. Oil refineries (receives pipe line from SW), U.S. naval dry dock. Mfg. of chemicals, clothing, machinery.

Bay Psalm Book, hymnal used in Mass. Bay colony, appearing as *The Whole Book of Psalms Faithfully Translated into English,* first book published (1640) in Thirteen Colonies.

Bayreuth (bīroit′), city (pop. 58,630), cap. of Upper Franconia, NE Bavaria. Textile, metal, and food mfg. Founded 1194; under HOHENZOLLERN family 1248–1807. Residence of Richard WAGNER 1872–83; celebrated for annual music festivals. Wagner and Liszt are buried here. Wagner's house, "Villa Wahnfried," destroyed in World War II.

Bay Shore, village (pop. 9,665), SE N.Y., on S shore (Great South Bay) of Long Isl. Center for fishing and duck hunting. Ferry to Fire Isl.

Baytown, city (pop. 22,983), S Texas, on Galveston Bay SE of Houston. Formed 1947 by combining Goose Creek, Pelly, and Baytown. Oil port, it has refineries and chemical plants.

Bay Village, city (pop. 6,917) NE Ohio, W suburb of Cleveland.

Bazaine, Achille (äshēl′ bäzĕn′), 1811–88, marshal of France. In Franco-Prussian War he allowed Germans to lock up his army at Metz and eventually capitulated (1870). MacMahon's attempt to relieve Metz led to disaster of Sedan. Condemned for treason (1873), Bazaine escaped abroad.

Bazán, Emilia Pardo: see PARDO BAZÁN.

Bazargic, Bulgaria: see TOLBUKHIN.

B battery: see BATTERY, ELECTRIC.

Be, chemical symbol of the element BERYLLIUM.

Beach, Chester, 1881–, American sculptor, b. San Francisco. Works include many portrait busts.

Beach, Moses Yale, 1800–1868, American journalist. After buying the New York *Sun* (1838) from his brother-in-law, Benjamin Day, he rivaled James Gordon Bennett in hustling for news, speeding transmission, widening coverage. Helped found the New York Associated Press and was first to have European edition of a U.S. paper and to syndicate articles.

beach grass or **marram grass,** perennial grass of genus *Ammophila.* Helps to control shifting sands.

Beacon, city (pop. 14,012), SE N.Y., on E bank of the Hudson opposite Newburgh; formed (1913) with union of Fishkill Landing and Matteawan. Has Matteawan State Hospital for insane criminals.

Beaconsfield, Benjamin Disraeli, 1st earl of: see DISRAELI, BENJAMIN.

beagle: see HOUND.

Bean, Roy, c.1825–1903, American frontiersman. Justice of the peace—self-styled "law west of the Pecos" —at Vinegaroon (later renamed Langtry), Texas. Meted out justice in his saloon, the "Jersey Lily," named for actress Lillie Langtry.

Bean, Tarleton Hoffman, 1846–1916, American ichthyologist. His fish-propagation methods widely used.

bean, name for various genera and species of the legume family. Prolific, adaptable, and easily grown, beans have been from prehistoric times an important food crop for humans and cattle. Some are grown for forage and cover crops. Both pods and seeds of snap or string beans are edible while only seeds of kidney and lima beans are eaten. Scarlet runner bean is an ornamental. See also CAROB; FRIJOLE; SOYBEAN.

Bear, river rising in NE Utah in Uinta Mts., flowing 350 mi. in long loop N, NW through Wyo., around Bear L. in Idaho, S into Utah to Great Salt L.

bear, mammal of family Ursidae of order Carnivora, found almost exclusively in N Hemisphere. Feet are plantigrade, claws nonretractile, fur thick and shaggy, tail very short, and body clumsy appearing. Some run at 25–30 mi. an hour speed; excepting heavy grizzly bears, most climb trees. Bears eat fruits, roots, honey, insects, fish, carrion, and infrequently mammals. Where winters are cold they hibernate. Young, usually twins, are born during winter in undeveloped state.

bear, in speculative markets: see BULLS AND BEARS.

bearberry, trailing woody plant (*Arctostaphylos uva-ursi*) of N Hemisphere. Evergreen, astringent leaves and red berries. Often used as ground cover.

Beard, Charles A(ustin), 1874–1948, American historian. As professor (1904–17) at Columbia Univ., he broadened history teaching to embrace civilization. Helped found New School for Social Research. Widely known for *The Rise of American Civilization* (2 vols., 1927), *America in Midpassage* (1939), and *The American Spirit* (1943). These were written in collaboration with his wife, **Mary (Ritter) Beard,** 1876–.

Beard, Daniel Carter, 1850–1941, American illustrator and naturalist, a founder of the Boy Scouts of America (1910).

Beardsley, Aubrey (Vincent), 1872–98, celebrated English black-and-white illustrator. Art editor of the *Yellow Book,* 1894–96.

Beardstown, city (pop. 6,080), W central Ill., WNW of Springfield and on Illinois R., in agr. area. Has rail shops and commercial fisheries.

beardtongue or **penstemon,** any herb or shrub of genus *Penstemon* with showy tubular flowers. Most species native to W U.S. and Canada.

bearings, in general, machine parts supporting a shaft, and intended to minimize FRICTION. Generally made of ANTIFRICTION METAL, such as BABBITT METAL. Since friction generates heat, bearing efficiency depends largely upon lubrication. High-speed machinery usually fitted with ball bearings (these and roller bearings known as antifriction bearings). Bearings should fit so shaft turns freely but cannot otherwise move to set up vibration. Thrust bearings designed to resist forces in shaft along direction of its length, as in a ship's propeller shaft.

Bear Island: see SPITSBERGEN.

Bear Lake, c.20 mi. long, N Utah and SE Idaho.

Bear Mountain, peak, 1,314 ft. high, SE N.Y., in Palisades Interstate Park, overlooking the Hudson (bridged 1924) S of Newburgh.

Béarn (bäärn´), region and former province, SW France, in Basses-Pyrénées dept.; historic cap. Orthez, later Pau. Agr., cattle breeding. Viscounty of Béarn passed (13th cent.) to counts of FOIX, thence, along with Navarre, to houses of Albret (1494) and Bourbon (1572); inc. into France 1620.

beatification: see CANONIZATION.

Beatitudes (bēăt´–) [Latin,= blessing], blessings spoken by Jesus at opening of Sermon on Mount. Mat. 5.3–12. Luke 6.20–26.

Beaton, Cecil (Walter Hardy), 1904–, English photographer and stage designer.

Beaton or **Bethune, David** (both: bē´tùn), 1494–1546, Scottish churchman, cardinal of the Roman Church. Arranged marriage of James V and Mary of Guise. Failed to gain regency for Mary Queen of Scots. Murdered for execution of George WISHART.

Beatrice (bēăt´rĭs), city (pop. 11,813), SE Nebr., on Big Blue R. and S of Lincoln; founded 1857 on old Oregon Trail. Trade center for grain, dairy, and livestock area. Mfg. of farm equipment. Homestead Natl. Monument of America is near.

Beatrice Portinari (bē´ùtrĭs; bäätrē´chä pōrtēnä´rē), 1266–90, Florentine lady believed to be the Beatrice named in the writings of Dante.

Beatty, David Beatty, 1st Earl (bē´tē), 1871–1936, British admiral. Aided in defeat of German fleet at Jutland 1916. Commanded British fleet 1916–19 and was first sea lord 1919–27.

Beauce (bōs), flat region, N France, SW of Paris; chief city Chartres. The "granary of France," it is covered with wheat fields.

Beauchamp, English noble family: see WARWICK, GUY DE BEAUCHAMP, EARL OF.

Beaufort, Edmund: see SOMERSET, EDMUND BEAUFORT, 2D DUKE OF.

Beaufort, Henry (bō´fùrt), c.1377–1447, English prelate and statesman; half brother of Henry IV. Chancellor 1403–4; fell when Prince Henry lost power. Again made chancellor when prince became Henry V. Swung English influence (1417) to elect Pope Martin V. Was chancellor (1424–26) in regency for Henry VI. Became a cardinal in 1426 and was a papal legate. Crowned Henry VI in Paris, 1431.

Beaufort, Margaret, countess of Richmond and Derby, 1443–1509, English noblewoman; mother of Henry VII. Founded Christ's Col. and St. John's Col., Cambridge. Patron of Caxton.

Beaufort (bū´fùrt), resort city (pop. 5,081), on Port Royal Isl., S S.C., SW of Charleston; founded 1711. State's second oldest town, it has old buildings, national cemetery, and arsenal. Has good harbor. Shipping and canneries for agr. and fishing area. Held by North in most of Civil War.

Beaufort Sea (bō´fùrt), part of Arctic Ocean, between N Alaska and Arctic Archipelago of Canada.

Beauharnais Alexandre, vicomte de (älĕksä´drù vēkŏt´ dù bōärnä´), 1760–94, French general in American Revolution and in French Revolutionary Wars. Guillotined in Reign of Terror. His widow, **Josephine de Beauharnais,** married Napoleon I (see JOSEPHINE). Alexandre's and Josephine's son, **Eugène de Beauharnais** (ûzhĕn´), 1781–1824, served as general under Napoleon, who made him viceroy of Italy in 1805. Capable administrator. Retired to Munich after Napoleon's downfall. His sister, **Hortense de Beauharnais** (ôrtäs´), 1783–1837, married Louis BONAPARTE, whom Napoleon made king of Holland (1806–10); mother of Napoleon III and the duc de Morny.

Beauharnois (bōhär´nwä), town (pop. 5,694), S Que., Canada, on S shore of L. St. Louis, SW of Montreal. **Beauharnois Canal,** opened 1843 on S side of St. Lawrence R. to bypass rapids, was superseded by Soulange Canal on N side in 1899. New Beauharnois Canal, begun 1930 for power development, was subject of political scandal. Province bought plant as public-ownership enterprise in 1945.

Beaujeu, Anne de: see ANNE DE BEAUJEU.

Beaujolais (bōjōlā´), hilly region, Rhône dept., E central France; famous for light red wine. Once the fief of lords of Beaujeu.

Beaumarchais, Pierre Augustin Caron de (pyĕr´ ōgüstē´ kärō´ dù bōmärshä´), 1732–99, French dramatist, at first a watchmaker by trade. His sparkling comedies, *Le Barbier de Séville* (1775) and *Le Mariage de Figaro* (1784) are famous in their own right and as sources for operas by Rossini and Mozart. Beaumarchais was chronically engaged in litigation, about which he wrote many witty pamphlets, and also was in the secret service of the monarchy. His dealings with Silas DEANE and Arthur LEE led to the estab. of his mock firm, Hortalès & Cie, which furnished arms to the American revolutionists (1776–77). Repayment was delayed until 1835, when the U.S. Congress made a grant to his heirs. Another costly venture was a 70-vol. edition of Voltaire (1784–90).

Beaumont, Francis (bō´mŏnt), 1584?–1616, English dramatist. *The Woman Hater* (1606) and *The Knight of the Burning Pestle* (c.1608) show traces of John FLETCHER, with whom he began collaborating by 1610 to produce *Philaster* (1608?–1610?), *A King and No King* (1611), and other romantic tragicomedies.

Beaumont, William, 1785–1853, American physician, author of work (1833) which revolutionized knowledge of digestive process. Observations based on case of Alexis St. Martin, victim of stomach wound leaving an opening to exterior of body.

Beaumont, city (pop. 94,014), SE Texas, on Neches R. (arm of Sabine-Neches Waterway) and ENE of Houston; settled before 1835. Industrial and transportation center of oil and agr. area, it has refineries, rice mills, mfg. of paper, synthetic rubber, and metal products, and shipbuilding. Deepwater channel to city completed 1916.

Beaune (bōn), town (pop. 11,022), Côte-d'Or dept., E France, in Burgundy. Wine center. Once a residence of dukes of Burgundy. The Hôtel Dieu hospital (founded 1443) contains Roger van der Weyden's *Last Judgment.* Romanesque church with Flemish tapestries; Hôtel de la Rochepot (c.1501).

Beauport, town (pop. 5,390), S Que., Canada, on St. Lawrence R. and NE of Quebec. One of oldest communities in Canada, settled 1634. French repulsed Wolfe's attacks here (1759) in Quebec campaign.

Beauregard, Pierre Gustave Toutant, 1818–93, Confederate general. Commander in NE Va., second in command at first battle of Bull Run. Defended coast of S.C. and Ga., and supported R. E. Lee in Va., especially at Petersburg. Stronger as engineer than as field commander.

Beauséjour, Fort, national park in SE N.B., Canada, (81 acres; estab. 1926), WNW of Amherst, N.S. Built 1751–55 by French; captured in 1755 by British and American troops under Gen. Monckton.

Beauvais (bōvā'), city (pop. 20,910), cap. of Oise dept., N France. Famous until World War II as tapestry mfg. center. War damage virtually wiped out center of city, a gem of medieval architecture. Famous cathedral (partly damaged) was begun 1227 as highest building in Christendom; choir vault (154 ft.; highest of Gothic vaults) fell 1284 but was reinforced; nave uncompleted.

Beaux-Arts, École des: see ÉCOLE DES BEAUX-ARTS.

Beaver. 1 Town (pop. 1,495), NW Okla., on North Canadian R. in Panhandle. Was cap. (1887) of Territory of CIMARRON. **2** Residential borough (pop. 6,360), W Pa., NW of Pittsburgh. Site of Fort McIntosh (1778), first U.S. military post N of the Ohio.

beaver, rodent, family Castoridae, of Europe, North America. Has thick fur, round head, small ears, scaly, flattened tail (c.10 in. long, c.6 in. wide), webbed hind feet, and body c.30 in. long. Weighs 40–50 lb. Tail is used as rudder when swimming, for support while gnawing tree, or to slap water to warn other beavers of danger. American beaver *Castor canadensis* usually builds twig and mud "lodges" with underwater entrances. If water is too shallow, makes dam of tree trunks or mud. *C. fiber* found in small numbers in parts of Europe.

Beaverbrook, William Maxwell Aitken, 1st Baron, 1879–, British statesman and newspaper owner. A Canadian, he amassed a fortune before going to England. Since 1917 his newspapers (*Daily Express, Sunday Express,* and *Evening Standard*) have thundered out his Imperialist views. Held several posts in Churchill's wartime cabinet 1940–45.

Beaver Dam, locality, S Ont., Canada, S of St. Catherines. Scene of a British victory, June 24, 1813, in War of 1812.

Beaver Dam, city (pop. 11,867), central Wis., SW of Fond du Lac and on Beaverdam L.; settled 1841. Mfg. of shoes and stoves.

Beaver Falls, city (pop. 17,375), W Pa., on Beaver R. and NW of Pittsburgh; settled c.1793. Chinaware and metal and cork products. Seat of Geneva Col. (Reformed Presbyterian; coed.; 1848).

Beaver Island, 13 mi. long, c.3–6 mi. wide, off N Mich., in L. Michigan NNW of Charlevoix (connected by ferry and plane). Largest of Beaver Archipelago; has lakes, beaches, and a harbor at St. James village. Inhabitants mainly fishermen. J. STRANG had Mormon settlement here 1847–56.

Bebel, August (ou'gŏost bā'bùl), 1840–1913, German Socialist. Helped found German Social Democratic party (1869); promoted its union with Lassallean socialists (1875).

Bec (bĕk), former Benedictine abbey, N France, in Normandy, S of Rouen. Founded 11th cent. Lanfranc taught here, Anselm was abbot. Fell into ruin after suppression in French Revolution.

Beccafumi, Domenico di Pace (dōmā'nēkō dē pä'chä bĕk-käfōo'mē), 1486–1551, Italian artist. Designed famous pavement of Siena cathedral 1517–46.

Beccaria, Cesare Bonesana, marchese di (chä'zärä bōnäzä'nä märkā'zä dē bĕk-kärē'ä), 1738–94, Italian economist, jurist, and criminologist. Brought about local economic reforms, but his notable contribution was bringing about penal reform throughout Europe. Also applied mathematics to economics.

Béchamp, Pierre Jacques Antoine (pyĕr' zhäk' ätwän' bāshä'), 1816–1908, French chemist, first to prepare aniline from nitrobenzene.

Becher, Johann Joachim (yō'hän yō'äkhĭm bā'khùr), 1635–82, German chemist, cofounder of PHLOGISTON THEORY.

Bechuanaland (bĕchōoä'nùländ"), British protectorate (c.275,000 sq. mi.; pop. 296,883), S Africa; administered from Mafeking. Bounded on S by South Africa. Stock raising is main occupation. Nearly whole area is a native reservation. Under British protection since 1885.

Beck, Theodric (or **Theodoric**) **Romeyn,** 1791–1855, American physician, author of standard work (1823) on medical jurisprudence.

Becker, Carl Lotus, 1873–1945, American historian. Professor (1917–41) at Cornell Univ. Books include *The Eve of the Revolution* (1918) and *The Heavenly City of the Eighteenth-Century Philosophers* (1932).

Becket, Thomas: see THOMAS À BECKET, SAINT.

Beckford, William, 1760–1844, English author of an Oriental romance, *Vathek* (written in French; pub. in English, 1784). His spendthrift, dissolute life caused much scandal.

Beckley, city (pop. 19,397), W.Va., N of Bluefield, in coal area; chartered 1838.

Becknell, William: see SANTA FE TRAIL.

Beckwith, James Carroll, 1852–1917, American painter, best known for portraits.

Becque, Henry (ārē' bĕk'), 1837–99, French dramatist. *The Vultures* (1882; Eng. tr., 1913) and *The Woman of Paris* (1885; Eng. tr., 1913) are mordant portraits of French bourgeois life.

Bécquer, Gustavo Adolfo (gōostä'vō ädôl'fō bā'kĕr), 1836–70, Spanish lyric poet. Wrote subtle, dreamlike *Rimas.* Also prose *leyendas.*

Becquerel, Antoine César (ätwän' säzär' bĕkùrĕl'), 1788–1878, French physicist. Pioneer in electrochemistry; studied telegraphy, magnetism. His son Alexandre Edmond Becquerel (älĕksä'drù ĕdmō'), 1820–91, also a physicist, professor at the Muséum d'Histoire naturelle, studied light, photochemistry, phosphorescence; invented phosphoroscope. Antoine Henri Becquerel, 1852–1908, son of Alexandre Edmond, discovered radioactivity in uranium and shared with the Curies the 1903 Nobel Prize in Physics.

bedbug, bug of order Hemiptera found over most of world. Common species *Cimex lectularius* is flat, reddish-brown, c.⅕ in. long; unpleasant odor; eats only blood. Attacks man, other mammals, poultry.

Beddoes, Thomas Lovell, 1803–49, English poet. Grotesque contrasted with delicate lyricism in poems (*The Improvisatore,* 1821; *The Bride's Tragedy,* 1822), play (*Death's Jest-Book; or, The Fool's Tragedy,* 1850).

Bede (bēd) or **Baeda** (bē'dù), 673?–735, English historian; Benedictine monk called Venerable Bede and St. Bede. Writings are summary of learning of his time.

Best known for *Ecclesiastical History of the English Nation,* in Latin, often translated.

Bedford, dukes and earls of: see RUSSELL, family; JOHN OF LANCASTER.

Bedford, England: see BEDFORDSHIRE.

Bedford. 1 City (pop. 12,562), S Ind., near East Fork of White R. SSE of Bloomington; laid out 1826. Limestone-quarrying center. **2** Town (pop. 5,234), E Mass., NW of Boston. **3** Residential city (pop. 9,105), NE Ohio, SE of Cleveland. **4** Borough (pop. 3,521), S Pa., SE of Johnstown. Colonial fort (built c.1757) was Washington's hq. (1794) in Whisky Rebellion. Some colonial buildings remain.

Bedfordshire or **Bedford,** county (473 sq. mi.; pop. 311,-844), S central England. More than four fifths of flat fertile area cultivated, mainly in market gardening. Luton, largest town, known for lace and straw plait mfg. Part of ancient kingdom of Mercia, region laid waste by King Canute. County town is **Bedford,** municipal borough (pop. 53,065), a market center on Ouse R. Has memorial chapel to John Bunyan, who preached here. Bedford School (estab. 1552) one of England's largest public schools.

Bédier, Joseph (zhōsĕf′ bādyä′), 1864–1938, French authority on medieval literature. *Les Légendes épiques* (4 vols., 1908–13) developed a new theory of the origin of the great medieval romances.

Bedlam [i.e., Bethlehem], oldest English insane asylum, estab. c.1400 in Lambeth borough (London); after 1930 near Croydon.

Bedlington terrier: see TERRIER.

Bedloe's Island, N.Y.: see LIBERTY, STATUE OF.

Bedouin (bĕ′dōōĭn) nomad peoples of interior Arabia of Semitic stock. Devout believers in Islam. Economy based on cattle breeding.

bee, insect of the order Hymenoptera. There are several kinds of solitary bees. Best known of the social bees are the honeybee, especially *Apis mellifera* (or *mellifica*), of Old World origin, and the bumblebee, of the genus *Bombus.* Honeybees are invaluable agents of pollination and producers of HONEY and beeswax. Honeybee colony has a single queen (who mates once in her lifetime and lays countless eggs), thousands of sexually undeveloped workers, and a few hundred males (drones). Workers build wax cells, make honey, clean and defend hive, feed queen and larvae; life span is only about six weeks during active season. Use of bee's lancet (sting) on a human or animal usually kills insect. Stingless bees live in tropics. See *ill.,* p. 469.

bee balm: see OSWEGO TEA and LEMON BALM.

Beebe, William (bē′bē), 1877–, American scientist, explorer, author. Noted as curator of ornithology at New York Zoological Society and for underwater explorations in a bathysphere.

beech, large, deciduous tree (*Fagus*) of N Hemisphere. Edible nuts and smooth gray bark. Valued for timber and for landscaping (especially copper and purple varieties of European beech). American and European beeches are dominant forest trees.

Beecham, Sir Thomas, 1879–, English conductor. He introduced the operas of Richard Strauss into England and was a champion of the music of Delius.

Beecher, Lyman, 1775–1863, American Protestant minister in N.Y., Conn., and Mass. President (1832–52) of Lane Theological Seminary, Cincinnati. A founder (1816) of the American Bible Society and preacher of temperance. One daughter was Harriet Beecher STOWE. Another was **Catharine Esther Beecher,** 1800–1878, who promoted liberal education for women. One of Lyman's sons was **Henry Ward Beecher,** 1813–87, American Congregational minister, one of the great speakers of his time; pastor after 1847 of Plymouth Church, Brooklyn. Championed reforms (antislavery, woman suffrage). He was the center of a trial resulting from Theodore Tilton's accusing Beecher of adultery; the jury disagreed.

Beech Grove, suburban town (pop. 5,685), central Ind., near Indianapolis. Has railroad shops.

beef, flesh of CATTLE, prepared for food. In U.S. a chief product of MEAT PACKING industry. It is sold fresh (chilled), frozen, or cured. Finest carcasses go to retail butchers for cutting into consumers' portions; others yield such products as sausage, beef extract, pickled or corned beef, and potted and canned products.

Beefeaters, popular name for YEOMEN OF THE GUARD and for Tower of London warders. They both wear colorful Elizabethan uniforms.

Beelzebub (bēĕl′zĭbŭb), in Bible: see SATAN.

beer, one of oldest known alcoholic beverages. Brewing processes are similar in various countries but beer varies in color, flavor, alcoholic content (usually 3–6%). Mash of crushed malt (usually barley) and cereal adjuncts is heated and agitated, then the liquid is boiled with hops, cooled, liquid yeast is added, and fermentation is allowed to take place. Ale, in England, means any light-colored beer; in U.S. it is a pale, strongly hopped beverage. Porter is a strong, dark ale; stout is darker, stronger, and maltier than porter.

Beerbohm, Sir Max, 1872–, English satirist, caricaturist. Contributed to *Yellow Book,* was dramatic critic of the *Saturday Review.* Mordant satire shown in caricatures, in novel *Zuleika Dobson* (1911), and in sketches, literary and graphic.

Beer-Hofmann, Richard (rikh′ärt bär′-hôf′män), 1866–1945, Austrian poet and dramatist. Among his poems is *Schlaflied für Mirjam* [cradle song for Miriam] (1898). *Der Graf von Charolais* (1904) is his first and best-known play. Lived in U.S. after 1939.

Beernaert, Auguste (ōgüst′ bârnärt′, bâr′närt), 1829–1912, Belgian statesman, prominent in Hague Peace Conferences of 1899 and 1907. Shared 1909 Nobel Peace Prize with Estournelles de Constant.

Beers, Clifford W(hittingham), 1876–1943, American founder of mental hygiene movement. Wrote autobiographical *A Mind That Found Itself* (1908).

Beersheba (bērshē′bù), town, S Israel, SW of Jerusalem. In Bible times Beersheba was S extremity of Palestine, Dan was N extremity; hence expression "from Dan to Beersheba." Especially associated with Abraham, Hagar, Isaac, and Elijah. Gen. 21.31; 26.33; Joshua 19.-1,2; Judges 20.1; 1 Chron. 21.2; 2 Kings 23.8; 2 Chron. 19.4; Neh. 11.30.

beet, vegetable (*Beta vulgaris*), cultivated for its edible roots. Other varieties grown for edible leaves (e.g., Swiss chard), for cattle feed (e.g., mangelwurzel), and one, sugar beet, for beet sugar.

Beethoven, Ludwig van (bā′tōvùn), 1770–1827, German composer, b. Bonn. Among his teachers were Mozart and Haydn. He appeared as a solo pianist, but his growing deafness made a career as a virtuoso impossible. Most critics divide his compositions into three periods: the early years, lasting until 1801, when he was still mostly writing in the classic tradition; the middle period, lasting until 1814, when, although already beset with deafness, he wrote some of his greatest music, e.g., the Third (or Eroica) Symphony, the Fifth Symphony, the Sixth (or Pastoral) Symphony, the Fifth (or Emperor) Piano Concerto, and his one opera *Fidelio;* and the last years, beginning in 1817, when most of his music was composed in total deafness. Belonging to this final period are the Ninth Symphony, the *Missa Solemnis,* and the last five string quartets. Beethoven wrote much chamber music—16 string quartets; 10 sonatas for violin and piano, including the Ninth (or Kreutzer) Sonata; and 32 sonatas for piano. His orchestral compositions include a violin concerto, five piano concertos, and nine symphonies. The "Jena" symphony, attributed to him, is an early work and not counted among the nine. Beethoven is regarded as the last of the classic and the first of the romantic composers.

beetle, insect of order Coleoptera (includes c.180,000 species). North America has c.22,000 species. Most have two pairs of wings; modified front wings form thickened wing covers protecting body and membranous hind wings. Metamorphosis is complete; larva usually called a grub. Majority are terrestrial; few families aquatic. See BOLL WEEVIL; COLORADO POTATO BEETLE; FIREFLY; JAPANESE BEETLE; JUNE BEETLE; LADYBIRD; SCARAB; TUMBLEBUG; WIREWORM; WEEVIL. See also ill., p. 469.

Beeville, city (pop. 9,348), S Texas, NW of Corpus Christi. Former cowtown, it is center of oil, cattle, and agr. area.

Begas, Karl Joseph (kärl′ yō′zĕf bā′gäs), 1794–1854, German historical and portrait painter.

Beggars of the Sea: see GUEUX.

Beggar's Opera, The: see GAY, JOHN.

beggarweed, leguminous plant (*Desmodium purpureum*), grown in S U.S. for forage and for green manure.

Beghards (bĕg′ŭrdz), religious associations of men, first known (1220) at Louvain, later widespread in Netherlands, Germany, France, and Italy. Organization was like that of BEGUINES. Charged by Council of Vienne (1311) with teaching that a man may attain such perfection that no later action of his may be considered sinful. Beghards lasted until 15th cent.

begonia, tropical perennial of genus *Begonia*. Showy single or double flowers (e.g., wax and tuberous types), succulent stems and leaves, often richly colored (e.g., rex begonias). Grown in beds and pots.

Beguines (bāgēn′), religious associations of women estab. in the Low Countries in 12th cent. They took no vows and lived by no rule, but did charitable work. In 13th and 14th cent. their communities (beguinages) came into disrepute and most were dissolved. Those remaining are almshouses (esp. for spinsters). See also BEGHARDS.

Beham (bā′häm), **Behem** (–hĕm), or **Peham** (pā′–), name of two engravers, among most famous of German Little Masters. Both banished 1525 from Nuremberg for freethinking. **Hans Sebald Beham** (sä′bält), 1500–1550, was a pupil of Dürer. Best work depicted daily life. His brother, **Barthel Beham** (bär′tùl), 1502–40, was painter to Duke William of Bavaria.

behaviorism, explanation of human behavior entirely as physiological response to environmental stimuli. Introduced by J. B. Watson, 1912; based on mechanistic concepts of Democritus, Epicurus, and Thomas Hobbes; supported by conditioned-reflex experiments of Pavlov and Bekhterev. Watson denied value of introspection and consciousness as unscientific concepts, saw all mental processes as bodily movements. Influential in U.S. between World Wars.

Behem, artists: see BEHAM.

behemoth (bē′hĭmŏth) [Heb.,= plural of *beast*], animal mentioned in Job 40.15–24, possibly the hippopotamus (there are various theories).

Behistun (bāhĭstōōn′) or **Bisutun** (bēsōōtōōn′), village, W Iran, E of Kermanshah. Near by is mountainous rock with cuneiform inscriptions and bas-relief depicting Darius I. In 1835 Sir Henry Rawlinson scaled rock and copied writings, thus making it possible to decipher the Assyrian text and provide key for study of ancient Mesopotamia.

Behm, Ernst (bām′), 1830–84, German geographer and statistician of *Almanach de Gotha* (1876–84).

Behn, Aphra (bān, bēn), 1640–89, English writer, supposedly b. Surinam. Her works, witty, coarse, and vigorous, include comedy *The Lucky Chance* (1686) and novel *Oroonoko* (1688).

Behrens, Peter (pā′tùr bā′rùns), 1868–1940, German architect, influential in the evolution of modern architectural style. Emphasized utilitarian aspect of design in his buildings in Vienna. Taught Le Corbusier and Walter Gropius.

Behring, Emil Adolph von (ā′mĭl ä′dôlf fùn bâr′ĭng), 1854–1917, German physician, pioneer in serum therapy. Won 1901 Nobel Prize in Physiology and Medicine for demonstrating immunization against diphtheria (1890) and tetanus (1892) by antitoxin injections.

Behrman, S(amuel) N(athaniel) (bâr′mùn), 1893–, American dramatist. Studied with George Pierce

Baker. Among his plays, notable for literate and subtle dialogue, are *The Second Man* (1927), *Biography* (1932), and *No Time for Comedy* (1939).

Beira (bā′rù, bā′ĭrù), historic province, N central Portugal, S of the Douro; cap. Coimbra. It is now occupied by the provinces of Beira Alta (3,682 sq. mi.; pop. 662,616; cap. Viseu), Beira Baixa (2,897 sq. mi.; pop. 334,788; cap. Castelo Branco), and part of Beira Litoral (2,908 sq. mi.; pop. 896,719; cap. Coimbra). Largely mountainous, it has agr., vineyards, and olive groves. Was long contested between Portugal and Castile.

Beirut or **Beyrouth** (both: bāroōt′), anc. *Berytus,* city (pop. 181,271), cap. of Lebanon; port on Mediterranean at foot of Lebanon range. Ancient Phoenician trade center. Flourished under Seleucids, Romans, and Byzantines. Captured 635 by Arabs. Taken 1110 by Crusaders, it remained part of Latin Kingdom of Jerusalem until 1291. Controlled by Druses under Ottoman Empire. In 19th cent. it was a storm center of revolt of Mohammed Ali of Egypt. Seat of important American university.

Beisan (bāsän′), village, NE Israel, in Jordan valley, 322 ft. below sea level. Site of biblical BETH-SHAN. Has ruins dating from c.1500 B.C.

Bejapur, India: see BIJAPUR.

Béjart or **Béjard** (both: bāzhär′), French family of actors, a successful troupe associated (after 1643) with MOLIÈRE. Included Joseph (c.1616–1659), sisters Madeleine (1618–72; Molière's mistress) and Geneviève (1624–75), brother Louis (1630–78), and Madeleine's sister or daughter, Armande Grésinde (Molière's wife 1662; d. 1700). Absorption of two rival troupes resulted (1680) in COMÉDIE FRANÇAISE.

Beke, Charles Tilstone (bēk), 1800–1874, English traveler and author. Mapped much of Ethiopia, compiled vocabularies of 14 languages or dialects.

Bekescsaba or **Csaba,** Hung. *Békéscsaba* (bā′kĕshchō′bō), city (pop. 52,404), SE Hungary, in a silk-raising and tobacco-growing dist. Textile mfg.

Bekhterev, Vladimir Mikhailovich (vlŭdyē′mĭr mēkhī′lùvĭch byĕkh′ tyĭrĭf), 1857–1927, Russian neurologist, psychologist. He studied localization of functions in brain areas and applied his study of conditioned reflexes in dogs to interpretation of human behavior. His emphasis on physiological nature of psychic phenomena influenced behaviorists.

Bel, deity of BABYLONIAN RELIGION; a form of BAAL. For Bel in Bible, see BEL AND THE DRAGON.

Bela IV (bē′lù, bā′lù), 1206–70, king of Hungary (1235–70). Defeated by Mongols at Mohi 1241; invited foreigners to settle depopulated country after Mongols withdrew. His last years disturbed by rebellion of son, later King Stephen V.

Bel and the Dragon, name given to Daniel 14 in Western canon, a chapter placed in the Apocrypha in AV. Verses 1–22 tell how Daniel brilliantly outwitted the priests of the idol Bel. Verses 23–42 tell of a dragon or great beast who was worshiped as a god. Daniel killed the dragon and was thrown into the lions' den but was protected by God.

Belasco, David, 1853–1931, American actor, playwright, manager. Acted in plays ranging from *Hamlet* to *Uncle Tom's Cabin*. Prolific playwright, he excelled in collaboration with James HERNE, J. L. Long, W. C. De Mille, and others. As independent producer was famous for lighting and scenic effects. Built Stuyvesant, later Belasco, Theatre 1907.

Belém (bùlān′), city (pop. 230,181), cap. of Pará state, NE Brazil, on the Pará, chief port and metropolis of Amazon basin. Founded in 17th cent., city reached peak of prosperity in wild-rubber boom of early 20th cent. Sometimes called Pará.

Belfast, county borough (pop. 443,670), cap. of N. Ireland, in Co. Antrim and Co. Down. Has 8½-mi.-long harbor navigable to largest ships and great shipyards. Center of Irish linen industry, stimulated by French Huguenots. Had heavy air raids 1941. Seat of Queen's

SMALL CAPITALS = cross references. Pronunciation key on inside end pages. Abbreviations: p. 2.

Univ. and Protestant cathedral. Parliament House at Stormont, a suburb.

Belfast, resort city (pop. 5,960), S Maine, on Penobscot Bay opposite Castine; settled 1770. Sacked by British, 1779 and 1814. Shipping center in 19th cent. Now has mfg. of marine supplies and shoes.

Belfort (bůfôr', bĕ-, bĕl-), town (pop. 35,952), cap. of Territory of Belfort (235 sq. mi.; pop. 86,648), E France. Strategic fortress commanding Belfort Gap between Vosges and Jura mts. Huge statue, *Lion of Belfort,* by Bartholdi, commemorates resistance to siege (1870–71) in Franco-Prussian War. Belfort remained French when rest of Alsace went to Germany (1871).

Belgae: see GAUL.

Belgian Congo, colony (904,754 sq. mi.; pop. 10,962,-799), equatorial Africa; cap. Leopoldville. Belgium's only colony, it includes the UN trust territory RU-ANDA-URUNDI. Bordered on W by French Equatorial Africa along CONGO R. and on E by Tanganyika. Exportable wealth includes copper, uranium ore, diamonds, gold, and tin, with Katanga prov. as leading mining area. Main centers include Leopoldville, Stanleyville, and Elizabethville. Population consists mainly of Bantu tribes and Pygmies. In 1878 Henry STANLEY was commissioned by Leopold II of Belgium to make surveys of the area and conclude treaties with native rulers. Congo Free State was organized in 1885 (with Leopold as monarch). International protest against harsh treatment of natives led to area's annexation by Belgium in 1908.

Belgium (bĕl'jŭm), Flemish *België,* Fr. *Belgique,* kingdom (11,779 sq. mi.; pop. 8,512,195), NW Europe, bounded by North Sea and Netherlands (N), Germany and grand duchy of Luxembourg (E); and France (W); cap. Brussels. Constitutional monarchy; bicameral legislature. Its nine provinces—Antwerp, Brabant, East Flanders, West Flanders, Hainaut, Liége, Limburg, Luxembourg, Namur—are partly selfgoverning. BELGIAN CONGO is a valuable colony. Lowlying, except for ARDENNES plateau in S, Belgium is crossed by the MEUSE and SCHELDT rivers and by a dense network of canals and railroads. Truck farming and cattle raising are important, but Belgium is one of the world's most intensely industrialized countries. Mining (coal, zinc, iron) and steel and chemical industries are concentrated in Sambre and Meuse valleys, at MONS, CHARLEROI, NAMUR, and LIÉGE. West Flanders and Hainaut have a huge textile industry, notably at Courtrai and Tournai. BRUSSELS, BRUGES, and MALINES are famed for their lace. ANTWERP and GHENT are major ports. Belgium is a leading nation in shipping and transit trade. Despite industrialization, the old cities of Belgium have retained many treasures of medieval architecture and art. A language border running, roughly, E-W through Brussels divides the Flemish-speaking north from the French-speaking south (see also WALLOONS); German is spoken in EUPEN and MALMÉDY dists. The Church, with the archbishop of Malines as primate, plays a leading role in overwhelmingly Catholic Belgium. As sovereign state, Belgium dates only from 1831. It is named after the Belgae, a people of ancient GAUL. The cradle of the Carolingian dynasty, the region (except Flanders) was comprised in LOTHARINGIA and later in the duchy of Lower Lorraine, which by the 12th cent. had broken up into the duchies of BRABANT and LUXEMBOURG, the county of HAINAUT, and lesser feudal states. The history of these and of FLANDERS constitute the medieval history of Belgium. By the 15th cent. all of present Belgium had passed to the dukes of BURGUNDY. The death of MARY OF BURGUNDY (1482) opened three centuries of Hapsburg rule (see NETHERLANDS, AUSTRIAN AND SPANISH). In 1797 the area was annexed by France. The Treaty of Paris (1815) gave it to the Netherlands, but in 1830 Belgium rose against WILLIAM I and proclaimed its independence. LEOPOLD I, of the house of Saxe-Coburg-Gotha, was chosen king (1831); Anglo-French inter-

vention stopped warfare with the Dutch (1832); peace was signed in 1839. Rapid industrialization under LEOPOLD II brought grave social problems. Belgian neutrality was violated by Germany in both world wars. In World War I Belgian forces under ALBERT I fought alongside the Allies even though Belgium was occupied by the Germans (1914–18). In World War II LEOPOLD III surrendered Belgium on May 28, 1940, after a disastrous two-week campaign; the Belgian government continued the fight from London as one of United Nations. German occupation brought a reign of terror. Liberated by the Allies and by Belgian underground fighters (Sept., 1944), war-scarred Belgium recovered quickly. The king's fitness to govern was a burning issue until Leopold abdicated in favor of his son BAUDOUIN (1951). In 1947 Belgium, the Netherlands, and Luxembourg joined to form a customs union, the "Benelux" bloc, which entered a Five-Power-Pact with England and France (1948), took part in the European Recovery Program, and joined in the North Atlantic Treaty (1949).

Belgorod-Dnestrovsky (byĕl'gůrŭd-důnyĕstrôf'skē), Rumanian *Cetatea-Alba,* Turkish *Akkerman,* city (1930 pop. 20,907), S Ukraine, in Bessarabia. Port on mouth of Dniester. Founded as Tyras by Greek colonists 7th cent. B.C. Under Turks 1484–1812.

Belgrade, town (pop. 1,099), SW Maine, SW of Waterville. Hq. for Belgrade Lakes resort area.

Belgrade (bĕl'grâd), Serbo-Croatian *Beograd,* city (pop. 388,246), cap. of Yugoslavia and of Serbia, on the Danube and the Sava. Seat of univ. (founded 1863), of Orthodox patriarch, and of archbishop (R.C.). The "key to the Balkans," it has been a strategic fortress since Roman times. Became cap. of Serbia in 12th cent.; repulsed Turks 1456; fell to Turks 1521; was stormed 1688, 1717, and 1789 by Austrians, who held it briefly (1717–39). Turkish garrison withdrew 1867. Occupied by Austrians in World War I, by Germans in World War II, when it was heavily damaged and suffered great hardship.

Belgrano, Manuel (mänwäl' bĕlgrä'nō), 1770–1820, Argentine revolutionist, member of first patriot governing junta (1810). Commander of Army of the North (1812–14; 1816–19), he was succeeded by San Martín.

Belgravia, fashionable section of London. Touches Buckingham Palace gardens and Hyde Park.

Belial (bē'lēŭl), name applied to SATAN.

Belinsky, Vissarion Grigoryevich (vĭsŭryôn' grĭgôr'yŭvĭch byĭlyĭn'skē), 1810–48, Russian writer. The founder of modern Russian literary criticism and a liberal, he championed Dostoyevsky and Turgeniev.

Belisarius (bĕlĭsâr'ēŭs), c.505–565, Byzantine general under Justinian I. Suppressed *Nika* rebellion (532). Defeated Vandals of Africa (533–34). Led expedition to recover Italy from Ostrogoths (535–40; 544–48); took Naples, Rome, Milan, Ravenna. Handicapped by political intrigue; replaced by NARSES 548. Drove Bulgarians from Constantinople (559). Briefly disgraced and imprisoned (562).

Belize (bůlēz'), city (pop. 21,884), cap. and chief port of British Honduras, at mouth of Belize R.

Belknap, William Worth, 1829–90, U.S. Secretary of War (1869–76). Evidence that he had indirectly taken bribes led to his resignation; impeachment attempt failed.

Bell, Alexander Graham, 1847–1922, American scientist, inventor of telephone. Improved education for deaf, carrying forward the work of his father, Alexander Melville Bell. In 1865 conceived idea of transmitting speech by electric waves; developed principle in 1875 and transmitted first sentence 1876. Organized Bell Telephone Co. in 1877. Estab. Volta Laboratory, where first successful phonograph record was produced. Invented photophone to transmit speech by light waves, audiometer, induction balance to locate metallic objects in body, wax recorders for phonographs, and tetrahedral kite. Influenced founding of *Science* (1880). Estab. Astrophysical Observatory at

Smithsonian Institution and founded Aerial Experiment Association.

Bell, Andrew, 1753–1832, British educator. In Madras, India, he devised MONITORIAL SYSTEM.

Bell, Sir Charles, 1774–1842, Scottish anatomist and surgeon, first to distinguish between motor and sensory functions of nerves. His brother **John Bell,** 1763–1820, was a founder of modern blood vessel surgery.

Bell, Gertrude Margaret Lowthian, 1868–1926, English expert on Near East, traveler, author. Invaluable as liaison officer of Arab Bureau in Iraq and assistant political officer, largely responsible for selection of Feisal I as king.

Bell, Henry, 1767–1830, British ship designer, pioneer steamship builder. Introduced practical steam river navigation in Europe (1812).

Bell, John, surgeon: see BELL, SIR CHARLES.

Bell, John, 1797–1869, American statesman. U.S. Representative from Tenn. (1827–41); U.S. Senator (1847–59). Leader of conservative Southern element. Presidential candidate of CONSTITUTIONAL UNION PARTY 1860, he unintentionally helped elect Lincoln.

Bell, city (pop. 15,430), S Calif., near Los Angeles. Mfg. of steel and iron products.

bell, in music, a percussion instrument consisting of a hollow vessel usually cup-shaped, set into vibration by a blow from a clapper within or from a hammer without. A set of bells tuned to the intervals of the major scale is called a chime. A set with chromatic intervals is called a carillon. The bells of a carillon are stationary, are struck from without by a hammer, and are played from a keyboard. Carillon making developed in the Low Countries, reached its peak in the 18th cent., declined, revived at end of 19th cent., when English bellmakers rediscovered the tuning secrets used by 17th cent. craftsmen. In England, carillon playing was less popular than change ringing. In this practice a group of ringers, using a set of bells tuned to the diatonic scale, ring the bells by swinging them in full circle in various stated orders. Bells are of ancient origin and have been used in all major religions except Islam.

belladonna, Old World perennial (*Atropa belladonna*), in NIGHTSHADE family. Grown for narcotic poison (ATROPINE) used medicinally. See *ill.,* p. 783.

Bellaire. 1 City (pop. 12,573), E Ohio, on Ohio R. below Wheeling, W.Va.; settled c.1802. Has coal mining and mfg. of enamelware and glass products. **2** Suburb, S Texas, SW residential section (pop. 10,173) of Houston, absorbed 1948.

Bellamy, Edward (bĕ′lŭmĭ), 1850–98, American writer of novels and short stories, now known chiefly for *Looking Backward, 2000–1887* (1888). This utopian romance, representing the triumphantly socialistic state of A.D. 2000, had great influence immediately and later. "Nationalist" clubs, a monthly (1889–91) and a weekly periodical (1891–94) forwarded his socialist ideas.

Bellarmine (bĕlär′mĭn), 1542–1621, Italian cardinal, originally named Roberto Francesco Romolo Bellarmino; a Jesuit. His polemical works setting forth Catholic views against the Protestants and popular devotional works made him widely known. He greatly influenced the Catholic Reform.

Bellay, Joachim du: see DU BELLAY, JOACHIM.

Belle-Alliance (bĕl′-älyäs′), village near Waterloo, Belgium: see WATERLOO CAMPAIGN.

Belleau, Remy (rŭmē′ bĕlō′), 1528–77, French poet; one of the PLÉIADE.

Belleau Wood (bĕ′lō, bĕlō′), forested area, N France, E of Château-Thierry. Here U.S. troops stopped German advance in World War I (June, 1918).

Bellefontaine (bĕlfoun′tĭn), city (pop. 10,232), W central Ohio, N of Springfield; laid out 1820. Trade and rail center for farm area.

Bellefonte, borough (pop. 5,651), central Pa., NE of Altoona. Resort and farm trade town.

Belle Fourche, river, rising in NE Wyo., flowing N of Black Hills to Cheyenne R. in W central S.Dak. U.S.

project uses Belle Fourche Dam and Keyhole Dam.

Belle Glade, town (pop. 7,219), S central Fla., W of Palm Beach near S tip of L. Okeechobee; founded c.1925. Trade center for truck area. Devastated by hurricane in 1928.

Belle-Isle, Charles Fouquet, duc de (shärl′ fŏŏkā′ dük′ dü bĕl-ēl′), 1684–1761, marshal of France. Noted for epic retreat from Prague (1742) in War of the Austrian Succession.

Belle Isle, Strait of, 10–15 mi. wide, 60 mi. long, between N.F. and Lab., Canada, N entrance to Gulf of St. Lawrence.

Bellerophon (bŭlĕ′rŭfŏn″, –fŭn), in Greek legend, hero who slew the CHIMERA. He accomplished this task with aid of winged horse Pegasus. Grown proud, he tried to fly to heaven on Pegasus, but was thrown and blinded—according to one legend, killed.

Belleville, city (pop. 19,519), S Ont., Canada, on Bay of Quinte. Port with mfg. of machinery and optical equipment. Seat of Albert Col.

Belleville. 1 City (pop. 32,721), SW Ill., adjoining East St. Louis, in coal, clay, sand area; platted 1815. Mfg. of stoves, clay products, and clothing. Scott Air Force Base near by. **2** Town (pop. 32,019), NE N.J., on Passaic R. just N of Newark; settled c.1680. Mfg. of machinery, chemicals, and leather.

Bellevue. 1 City (pop. 9,040), N Ky., near Ohio R., suburb of Covington and Cincinnati. **2** Village (pop. 3,858), E Nebr., on the Missouri and S of Omaha. Oldest town in state, it was estab. c.1823 as trading post. Site of a Presbyterian Indian mission (1848). **3** City (pop. 6,906), N Ohio, SW of Sandusky. Rail center in farm area. **4** Residential borough (pop. 11,604), SW Pa., near Pittsburgh; settled 1802.

bellflower or **campanula** (kămpăn′ŭlù), plant of genus *Campanula* with bell- or star-shaped flowers, often blue. Species for rock gardens and borders include Canterbury bells, a biennial; HAREBELL; and the edible rampion.

Bellingham, port city (pop. 34,112), NW Wash., on Bellingham Bay, near Canada; settled 1852. Shipping and processing center for truck, fruit, salmon, coal, lumber, dairy products, and poultry. Gateway to recreational area.

Bellini (bĕl-lē′nē), family of Venetian painters of the Early Renaissance. **Jacopo Bellini** (yä′kōpō), c.1400–c.1464, was father and teacher of Giovanni and Gentile. **Giovanni Bellini** (jōvän′nē), c.1426–1516, became teacher of Giorgione and Titian. Serenity, majesty, and luminous color characterize his works, which include altarpieces in the Frari and San Zaccaría, Venice; *Feast of the Gods* (Natl. Gall., Washington, D.C.); *St. Francis* (Frick Coll., New York). **Gentile Bellini** (jäntē′lä), c.1427–c.1507, painted contemporary Venetian life and used Turkish subjects after visit to Constantinople.

Bellini, Vincenzo (vēnchän′tsō bĕl-lē′nē), 1801–35, Italian operatic composer. Among his operas are *Norma* and *La sonnambula* (both 1831).

Bellinzona (bĕl-lēntsō′nä), town (pop. 12,073), cap. of Ticino, S Switzerland, on Ticino R. Has several churches and castles dating from 15th–16th cent.

Bell Island (11 sq. mi.; pop. c.8,167), SE N.F., Canada, in Conception Bay. Bell Island town is oldest industrial center in N.F.

Bellman, Carl Michael, 1740–95, Swedish writer of drinking songs, pastorals, and comic songs.

Bellmawr (bĕl″mär′), residential borough (pop. 5,213), SW N.J., near Camden.

bell metal: see BRONZE.

Bello, Andrés (ändrās′ bā′yō), 1781–1865, South American intellectual leader, b. Venezuela. After 19 years in London (1810–29), he went to Chile, became leader in education. Wrote poems, works on grammar and law; forwarded American intellectual freedom.

Belloc, Hilaire (bĕl′ŏk), 1870–, British author, b. France. A poet, essayist, and biographer, he wrote many works, some of Roman Catholic apologetics.

Bellona (bùlō'nù), in Roman religion, goddess of war. She was associated with Mars, and her temple stood in Campus Martius.

Bellows, George (Wesley), 1882–1925, American painter and lithographer. His work is marked by a direct, unself-conscious realism.

Bellows Falls, Vt.: see ROCKINGHAM.

Bellwood, residential village (pop. 8,746), NE Ill., near Chicago. Metal products plants.

Belmar, resort borough (pop. 4,636), E N.J., on the Atlantic S of Asbury Park.

Belmont. 1 City (pop. 5,567), W Calif., SE of San Francisco. Ships flowers. **2** Residential town (pop. 27,381), E Mass., NW suburb of Boston; settled 1636. **3** Town (pop. 5,330), W central N.C., on Catawba R. and W of Charlotte. In agr. piedmont region, it has textile mills and dye works.

Belmonte, Juan (hwän' bĕlmōn'tä), 1892–, Spanish bullfighter.

Belo Horizonte (bĕl' ōrēzõnt'), city (pop. 346,207), cap. of Minas Gerais, E Brazil. A planned city built to replace Ouro Prêto as state cap. (1895), it handles minerals, cattle, agr. produce. Opening of hydroelectric plant (1946) speeded growth of industries.

Beloit (bīloit'), city (pop. 29,590), S Wis., on Rock R. at Ill. line; founded c.1837. Mfg. of paper and metal products. Winter sports. Seat of **Beloit College** (nonsectarian; coed.), chartered 1846, organized 1847 by Congregationalists and Presbyterians; noted for anthropology courses.

Belorussia (bye"lùrōō'sĕù) or **White Russia,** constituent republic (80,150 sq. mi.; pop. c.7,220,000), W European USSR; cap. Minsk. Largely a lowland, drained by Dnieper, Western Dvina, Niemen. PRIPET MARSHES in S. Agr., with chemical, textile, machinery industries. Population is 80% Belorussian, a Slavic group influenced by Polish culture, partly Roman Catholic, partly Russian Orthodox. Region was part of Kievan Russia from 9th cent.; conquered by LITHUANIA 14th cent.; passed to Russia through Polish partitions of 1772–95. Treaty of Riga (1921) gave part to Poland. Belorussian SSR, founded 1919, joined USSR 1922, was nearly doubled in Polish partition of 1939. Joined U.N. 1945. Devastated in World War II. Also spelled Bielorussia, Byelorussia.

Belsen (bĕl'zùn), village, Lower Saxony, NW Germany, near Celle. Site of notorious concentration camp during Hitler regime.

Belshazzar (bĕlshäz'ùr), in Bible, son of Nebuchadnezzar, last king of Babylon. At his riotous feast, handwriting appeared on the wall and was interpreted by Daniel as sign of doom. That night Babylon fell to Cyrus. Dan. 5. Identity of Belshazzar uncertain. May be same as Nabonidus (last king of Babylon but unrelated to Nebuchadnezzar) or possibly Belshar-uzur (royal governor but not a king).

Belt, Great, and **Little Belt,** shallow straits connecting Kattegat with Baltic Sea. Great Belt, c.10 mi. wide, separates Zealand and Fyn isls., Denmark. Little Belt, ½–c.20 mi. wide, between Fyn and Jutland, is crossed by railroad and road bridge.

Belteshazzar (–shäz'–), Babylonian name of DANIEL.

Belton, city (pop. 6,246), central Texas, W of Temple. Farming market center. Seat of Mary Hardin–Baylor Col. (Baptist; women; 1845; connected with Baylor Univ.). Prehistoric skeletons and artifacts have been found near by.

Belvedere (bĕl'vùdēr), a gallery and court of the Vatican, Rome, containing the *Apollo Belvedere* and the *Laocoön;* built 1490. A palace by this name in Vienna houses the Mus. of History and Art.

Belvidere, city (pop. 9,422), N Ill., E of Rockford. Trade center of agr. area, it has mfg. of food and metal products.

Bely, Andrei (ùndrä' byĕ'lē), pseud. of Boris Nikolayevich Bugayev, 1880–1934, Russian poet, a leading symbolist. Besides poetry (collected in *Symphonies,* 4 vols., 1901–8), he wrote rich, masterful novels, nota-

bly *The Silver Dove* (1910) and *Petersburg* (1912).

Bembo, Pietro (pyä'trō bĕm'bō), 1470–1547, Italian humanist, cardinal of the Roman Church, secretary of Leo X. Arbiter of literary taste, he insisted on preserving classic traditions.

Bemidji (bùmĭj'ē), city (pop. 10,001), N central Minn., on Bemidji L.; settled c.1892. The Mississippi flows through lake. Resort and farm trade center in lake and forest region.

Bemis Heights, battle of: see SARATOGA CAMPAIGN.

Benaiah (bēnā'yù), heroic warrior, loyal follower of David and Solomon. 2 Sam. 8.18; 20.23; 23.20–23; 1 Kings 1; 2; 1 Chron. 11.22–25; 18.17; 27.5, 6.

Benalcázar, Sebastián de (sävästyän' dä bänälkä'thär), c.1479–1551, Spanish conquistador. Accompanied Columbus on third voyage (1498), served in Darien and Nicaragua, then joined Pizarros in conquest of Peru (1532). From 1533 to 1550 was active in conquest of present Ecuador and Colombia.

Benares (bùnä'rīz), city (pop. 263,100), SE Uttar Pradesh, India, on Ganges R. Great Hindu center since 6th cent. B.C. Also sacred to Buddhists and Jains. Annually c.1,000,000 pilgrims visit numerous ghats and shrines stretching 4 mi. along Ganges R. Site of Golden Temple (1777) and Aurangzeb's mosque. Rail and trade center. Textiles, brassware, jewelry industries. Hindu university.

Benavente (y Martínez), Jacinto (häthĕn'tō bä"nävän'tä ē märtē'nĕth), 1866–, Spanish dramatist. Notable works are the farce *Los intereses creados* (1907; Eng. tr., *Bonds of Interest,* 1917) and the rural drama *La malquerida* (1913). Awarded 1922 Nobel Prize in Literature.

Benbow, William, fl. 1825–40, English pamphleteer. Introduced theory of the general strike.

Benchley, Robert (Charles), 1889–1945, American humorist. Long the dramatic critic of *Life* (1920–29) and the *New Yorker* (1929–40), he is better known for gently sardonic short pieces, collected in such volumes as *Of All Things* (1921) and *My Ten Years in a Quandary* (1936). He wrote, directed, and acted in humorous film shorts.

Bend, city (pop. 11,409), W central Oregon, on Deschutes R. just E of Cascade Range. Trade center for lumber, irrigated-farm, and resort area.

Benda, Julien (zhülyĕ' bädä'), 1867–, French novelist and critic. A humanist, he attacked the aesthetic philosophy of Bergson. *The Yoke of Pity* (1912; Eng. tr., 1913), a novel, won immediate recognition. *The Treason of the Intellectuals* (1927; Eng. tr., 1928) stated the theory that the thinker in pursuit of truth should disregard practical consequences.

Bendemann, Eduard Julius Friedrich (ā'dōōärd" yōō'lyōōs frēd'rĭkh bĕn'dùmän), 1811–89, German Jewish historical and portrait painter.

Bender (bĕn'dùr) Rumanian *Tighina,* Rus. *Bendery,* city (1930 pop. 31,384), S Moldavian SSR, in Bessarabia. Conquered by Turks 1538. Residence of CHARLES XII of Sweden 1709–13.

Bendigo (bĕn'dĭgō), municipality (pop. 26,739; metropolitan pop. 30,779), Victoria, Australia; founded 1851. Formerly an important mining town, now a wheat-trading center.

Bendix, N.J.: see TETERBORO.

bends: see CAISSON DISEASE.

Benedetti, Vincent, Comte (vēsā' kōt' bänädĕt'tē), 1817–1900, French ambassador to Prussia (1864–70). His interview with William I at Ems was published by Bismarck in an altered version (see EMS DISPATCH) which precipitated Franco-Prussian War.

Benedetto da Majano (bänädĕt'tō dä mäyä'nō), 1442–97, Florentine sculptor. Chief work is altarpiece in Church of Monte Oliveto at Naples.

Benedict, Saint, d. c.547, Italian monk, founder of the Benedictines, b. Norcia (or Nursia). Became a hermit at Subiaco, where monks gathered around him. Later founded first Benedictine monastery, at MONTE CASSINO, and created the Rule of St. Benedict, the chief rule of Western monasticism. Feast: March 21.

Benedict XIII, antipope: see LUNA, PEDRO DE.

Benedict XIV, 1675–1758, pope (1740–58), b. Bologna; originally named Prospero Lambertini. He was renowned for learning, for patronizing art, and for protecting Eastern Catholic rites from Latinization.

Benedict XV, 1854–1922, pope (1914–22), b. Genoa; originally named Giacomo della Chiesa. In World War I, he kept the Vatican neutral and strenuously tried to restore peace.

Benedict, Ruth (Fulton), 1887–1948, American anthropologist. Student and colleague of Franz Boas at Columbia Univ. Contributed to enlarging scope of anthropology through work on concept of culture motif and relation of personality to culture. Her works include *Patterns of Culture* (1934).

benedictine (bĕnŭdĭk'tēn), sweet, brown LIQUEUR originated in 1510 by Benedictine monks in France.

Benedictines, monks of the Roman Catholic Church, estab. at MONTE CASSINO by St. BENEDICT, whose rule they follow. Unlike earlier groups they stress communal living, and their abbeys are like homes of Christian families with abbots as fathers. Their waking hours are devoted principally to worship and work—chiefly manual work, though the Benedictines did much to preserve learning through the early Middle Ages. Many notable missionaries were Benedictines (e.g., St. Augustine of Canterbury, St. Boniface), and with urging of Pope Gregory I (a Benedictine himself) and others, the abbeys were spread across Europe as outposts of civilization. Among these were St. Gall, Fulda, Solesmes, Monserrat, and St. Albans. Later reforms created new orders within the general Benedictine family—the CLUNIAC ORDER, the CISTERCIANS, and the TRAPPISTS (Cistercians of the Stricter Observance).

benefice, in feudal law, an estate held for life, a nonhereditary fief. The term early became restricted to ecclesiastical holdings—usually an income attached to an office or a position or to a particular parish or cure. Since the benefice was usually granted by a layman, it posed serious problems of lay control in the Church and led to many abuses in the late Middle Ages. The Council of Trent disestablished them in the Roman Catholic Church. Benefices continue in England for the holding of rectories, vicarages, and the like (not for simple offices).

Bene Israel or **Beni Israel** (both: bā'nē) [Heb.,= sons of Israel], Jewish community (c.15,000) of Bombay, India, possibly dating from 2d cent. A.D. In the last 200 years, a program of Jewish education has greatly changed the once Hindulike customs of this group.

Benelux, name of the customs union of Belgium, the Netherlands, and Luxembourg, estab. 1947 and in force after 1948.

Benes, Eduard, Czech *Beneš* (bĕ'nĕsh), 1887–1948, Czech statesman. Chief collaborator of T. G. Masaryk, he was foreign minister (1918–35), premier (1921–22), president of the republic (1935–38; 1945–48), and leader of the National Socialist (i.e., liberal) party. The Franco-Czech alliance and LITTLE ENTENTE were mainly his work. Exiled after the MUNICH PACT, he headed the Czech provisional government at London during World War II; was reelected president of liberated Czechoslovakia; resigned after Communist coup d'état of 1948.

Benét, Stephen Vincent (bĕnā'), 1898–1943, American poet, novelist, and short-story writer. He is especially noted for his vigorous use of American historical and folk materials as in his long Civil War poem, *John Brown's Body* (1928); poems for children in *A Book of Americans* (1933 with his wife, Rosemary Benét); his unfinished epic *Western Star* (1943); and notable short stories such as "Johnny Pye and the Fool-Killer" and "The Devil and Daniel Webster." His brother, **William Rose Benét,** 1886–1950, was also a poet, author of many romantic lyrics and ballads and other narrative poems. He was an editor of

Century Magazine, the *Saturday Review of Literature* (which he helped found 1924), and a volume called *The Reader's Encyclopedia* (1948). *The Dust Which Is God* (1941) is verse autobiography. Also wrote essays and novels. Elinor Wylie was his second wife.

Benevento (bĕnŭvĕn'tō), city (pop. 26,692), Campania, S Italy. Was important Roman town on Appian Way; cap. of powerful Lombard duchy (6th–11th cent.); later under papal rule. Many Roman remains. Church of Santa Sofia (8th cent.). Heavy damage in World War II.

Ben Ezra: see IBN EZRA, ABRAHAM BEN MEIR.

Bengal (bĕng-gôl'), region in NE India and E Pakistan, on Bay of Bengal. Mostly in Ganges-Brahmaputra delta between Bihar and Assam. Himalayan forests in N, Sundarban jungles in S. The British took Bengal from Mogul empire in 1764. Divided 1947 between India and Pakistan. **East Bengal,** province (54,501 sq. mi.; pop. 42,119,000), is coextensive with E Pakistan; cap. Dacca. Includes large jute-growing area. **West Bengal,** state (29,476 sq. mi.; pop. 24,786,683) of India; cap. Calcutta. Includes former native state of Cooch Behar. Contains industrial area and large coal fields.

Bengal, Bay of, arm, c.1,300 mi. long and c.1,000 mi. wide, of Indian Ocean, with India on W and Burma and Malaya on E.

Bengali (bĕngäl'ē), Indo-European language. See LANGUAGE (table).

Bengasi or **Benghazi** (both: bĕngä'zē), city (pop. 56,325), Cyrenaica, Libya; Mediterranean port. In World War II it was captured and held by the British in Dec., 1942.

Ben-Gurion, David (bĕn-gōō'rĭŏn), 1886–, Israeli statesman, prime minister of Israel (1948–), b. Poland. Fled to Palestine after pogroms of 1905. Exiled by Turks for Zionist and pro-British activity in World War I. Helped organize Jewish Legion which fought on British side in Palestine and was later a Jewish leader there. First prime minister of Israel (1948), he again won the post in 1952.

Benhadad (-hā'dăd), kings of Damascus. **1** Fl. 890 B.C., ally of Asa of Judah against Baasha of Israel. 1 Kings 15.17–20. **2** Fl. 854 B.C., continued traditional enmity with Israel and defeated Ahab and Jehoshaphat. Murdered and succeeded by Hazael. 1 Kings 20; 22; 2 Kings 8.15. **3** Fl. 800 B.C., son of Hazael. Defeated Jehoash of Israel. 2 Kings 13.25; Amos 1.4.

Benicia (bŭnĭ'shŭ), city (pop. 7,284), W Calif., port on Carquinez Strait NE of Oakland. U.S. army ordnance depot and arsenal are here.

Beni Hassan (bĕ'nē hä'sän), village, central Egypt, on the Nile. Has 39 rock-cut tombs of XII dynasty of ancient Egypt.

Beni Israel: see BENE ISRAEL.

Benjamin, youngest son of Jacob and Rachel, eponymous ancestor of one of 12 tribes of Israel. Tribe occupied E central Palestine. Tribesmen were noted archers. Famous son of House of Benjamin was Saul. Gen. 35.18; 42–46; 49.27; Num. 1.36; 13.9; 26.38–41; 34.21; Deut. 33.12; Joshua 18.11–28; Judges 3.15; 20–21; 1 Chron. 8.40; 12.2; 2 Chron. 14.8; 17.17.

Benjamin, Asher, 1773–1845, American architect. Books popularized details of Late Colonial style.

Benjamin, Judah Philip, 1811–84, Confederate statesman and British barrister, b. Virgin Isls. Ably defended Southern policy as U.S. Senator (1853–61). In Southern government he was successively attorney general, secretary of war, and secretary of state. Known in North as "the brains of the Confederacy." On its collapse in 1865, he escaped to England, where he became prominent lawyer.

Benjamin of Tudela (tōōdā'lä), d. 1173, Spanish rabbi, author of an account of a journey to China (Eng. tr., *Itinerary of Benjamin of Tudela*).

Ben Macdhui or **Ben Muich-Dhui** (măkdōō'ē), peak, 4,296 ft. high, Aberdeenshire, Scotland; second highest peak in Scotland.

Bennet, Henry: see ARLINGTON, HENRY BENNET, 1ST EARL OF.

Bennett, (Enoch) Arnold, 1867–1931, English naturalistic novelist. Among his many novels, *The Old Wives' Tale* (1908), and a trilogy of life in the "Five Towns."

Bennett, Floyd, 1890–1928, American aviator. In 1926, with Byrd, flew nonstop Spitsbergen to North Pole and return, first flight over either pole. Appointed second in command of Byrd's antarctic expedition, but died of pneumonia contracted on *Bremen* rescue flight.

Bennett, James Gordon, 1795–1872, American journalist, b. Scotland. Coming to the U.S. in 1819, he won fame as a reporter. He founded (1835) the New York *Herald,* which he made a phenomenal popular success, increasing the field of news (e.g., with financial news, with reports of foreign correspondents, with accent on detailed accounts of crimes and sensations), using the telegraph and other means to speed reporting, and employing illustrations. In 1867 he relinquished control of the *Herald* to his son, **James Gordon Bennett,** 1841–1918, who also founded the *Evening Telegram* and London and Paris daily editions of the *Herald.* He stressed international news and attention-getting "stunts" (e.g., financing Stanley's expedition to Africa in order to find David Livingstone and G. W. De Long's Arctic expedition). He helped found Commercial Cable Co. Was also a yachtsman and gave a trophy for international yacht races.

Bennett, Richard Bedford, 1870–1947, Canadian prime minister (1930–35), leader of Conservative party. Urged preferential tariff for the empire, and saw policy adopted 1932.

Bennettsville, town (pop. 5,140), NE S.C., NE of Columbia. Trade and processing center in agr. area. Mfg. of aircraft parts.

Ben Nevis (nĕ'vĭs, nĕv'ĭs), peak, 4,406 ft. high, Inverness-shire, Scotland; highest peak in Great Britain. NE side has precipice of more than 1,450 ft.

Bennington, town (pop. 12,411), SW Vt., NE of Albany, N.Y.; chartered 1749 as a N.H. town (first W of Connecticut R.); settled 1761. Includes industrial Bennington village (pop. 8,002; textiles, paper); North Bennington village (pop. 1,327), seat of **Bennington College** (nonsectarian; for women; chartered 1925, opened 1932), a leading experimental col. with program of self-dependent education and a noted summer school of modern dance; and historic Old Bennington village (pop. 198), now a resort. Has shaft commemorating battle of Bennington (see SARATOGA CAMPAIGN); marked site of Catamount Tavern, rendezvous of Green Mountain Boys; and Old First Church (1806; restored 1937 as state monument). Prized stoneware was made at Bennington from late 18th to late 19th cent.

Benois, Aleksandr Nikolayevich, (bĕnōōä'), 1870–, Russian painter. Did scenery for Diaghilev's ballet productions, notably *Petrouchka.*

Benoît de Sainte-More or **Benoît de Sainte-Maure** (bûnwä' dù sĕt-môr'), fl. 1175, French TROUVÈRE. His *Roman de Troie,* a romance based on Dares and Dictys, became source of medieval version of the Trojan legend, notably of TROILUS AND CRESSIDA.

Benson, Ezra Taft, 1899–, U.S. Secretary of Agriculture (1953–). Marketing specialist; executive secretary of Natl. Council of Farmer Cooperatives (1939–44). Official in Mormon Church.

Bent, Charles, 1799–1847, American frontiersman. Led expeditions on Santa Fe Trail. Member of famous trading firm. His brother, **William Bent,** 1809–69, also a trader and frontiersman, was long the manager of BENT'S FORT.

bent grass, any species of genus *Agrostis,* slender, delicate grasses. Grown for pasture, hay, lawn (e.g., creeping bent, established by planting stolons).

Bentham, George (bĕn' thŭm), 1800–1884, English botanist, a great systematist.

Bentham, Jeremy, 1748–1832, English philosopher, founder of utilitarianism, which holds that the goal of social ethics is to achieve the greatest good (i.e., pleasure) of the greatest number. In his influential studies of political theory he urged that political institutions and laws should serve social ethics. He argued for political democracy but not for the economic equality of all. Wrote *Principles of Morals and Legislation* (1789; second part, *The Limits of Jurisprudence Defined,* pub. 1945).

Bentinck, William: see PORTLAND, WILLIAM BENTINCK, 1ST EARL OF.

Bentley, Richard, 1662–1742, English philologist, generally considered greatest of English classical scholars. His exposure of a 2d-cent. forgery, *The Epistles of Phalaris,* gained notice.

Benton, Thomas Hart, 1782–1858, American statesman. U.S. Senator from Mo. (1821–51) and U.S. Representative (1853–55). Supported currency measures to benefit common man; drew up Pres. Jackson's Specie Circular (1836). Supported all legislation favoring Western development and aiding settlers. Opposed extension of slavery. His grandnephew is **Thomas Hart Benton,** 1889–, American painter. Dramatized American themes (notably in his murals) with characterizations of popular types.

Benton. 1 City (pop. 6,277), central Ark., SW of Little Rock. Mfg. of furniture and pottery. Bauxite mines. **2** City (pop. 7,848), S Ill. S of Mount Vernon. Agr. and coal-mining center. **3** Town (pop. 1,980), SW Ky., SE of Paducah. Has annual Southern Harmony Singing Festival (since 1884) and "Tater Day" (potatoes).

Benton Harbor, city (pop. 18,769), SW Mich., on L. Michigan at mouth of St. Joseph R. opposite St. Joseph city; settled c.1840. In rich fruitgrowing area, it is a resort with mineral springs. Municipal fruit market here said to be nation's largest. Has mfg. of metal products. Religious colony, House of David (founded 1903), has business and farm holdings here; its rival, Israelite City of David, is near by. Annual Blossom Festival held with St. Joseph.

bentonite: see CLAY.

Bent's Fort, noted trading post of the American West, on Arkansas R. in present SE Colo., E of La Junta. The successful trading company headed by Charles Bent and Ceran St. Vrain estab. post here in 1828 after founding it near by in 1826. Fort (often called Bent's Old Fort) completed 1832. On the mountain branch of Santa Fe Trail, it dominated trade with Indians, Mexicans, Americans. Kit Carson hunted here 1831–42. American troops used it briefly in Mexican War. Tradition says that manager William Bent blew it up. He built Bent's New Fort further downstream in 1852 or 1853, leased it to U.S. in 1859. Fort destroyed by flood shortly thereafter and replaced by new army fort.

Benzedrine, drug used to stimulate higher nerve centers. Should be used only on prescription.

benzene (bĕn'zēn) or **benzol** (bĕn'zōl), colorless liquid, aromatic odor, boils at 80.1°C., solidifies at 5.48°C. Molecule has six carbons arranged in ring, with one hydrogen attached to each. First in series of aromatic hydrocarbons, **benzene series;** all from coal tar. Used to make dyes, explosives, synthetic drugs, perfumes, lacquers, and as organic solvent. Derivatives are carbolic acid, picric acid, nitrobenzene, and aniline.

benzine (bĕn'zēn), colorless inflammable liquid mixture of hydrocarbons chiefly of methane (not benzene) series; obtained from petroleum by fractional distillation. Used as cleaning agent, organic solvent; used in some dyes and paints.

benzoate of soda: see SODIUM BENZOATE.

benzoic acid (bĕnzō'ĭk), solid, crystalline, organic acid. Used as antiseptic, as starting point for organic syntheses, in making dyes.

benzoin (bĕn'zoin), balsamic RESIN, dried exudate from pierced bark of benzoin tree (*Styrax*). Used in perfumery, incense, and in medicine.

benzol: see BENZENE.

Ben-Zvi, Itzhak (yĭts′häk bĕn-tsvē′), 1884–, Israeli statesman and Orientalist, second president of Israel, b. Russia. An active Zionist, he emigrated 1907 to Palestine, where he worked closely with Ben-Gurion. Succeeded Chaim Weizman as president of Israel, 1952.

Beograd, Yugoslavia: see BELGRADE.

Beowulf (bā′uwōŏlf), oldest English epic, probably composed early 8th cent. by Anglian bard in the vicinity of Northumbria. Materials for the poem mainly from Scandinavian history, folk tale, mythology, and the events take place in Denmark and Sweden. In the first part the young hero kills water monster Grendel and Grendel's mother; in second, at end of long life of honor, he conquers a dragon and dies. Written in strongly accentual, alliterative verse.

Béranger, Pierre Jean de (pyĕr′ zhä′ dü bāräzhä′), 1780–1857, French poet, author of many popular songs. Like Burns he fitted his verse to existing melodies. Many of his songs helped to further the Napoleonic legend.

Berar, India: see MADHYA PRADESH.

Berat (bĕrät′), town (pop. 11,872), S central Albania, probably on site of anc. Antipatrea. Has 13th-cent. Byzantine citadel, 15th-cent. mosque.

Berbers, aboriginal peoples of N Africa. Moslems, they speak Arabic and Hamitic tongues. Economy is based on agr.

Berceo, Gonzalo de (gônthä′lō dā bĕrthā′ō), 1180?–1247?, Spanish poet, Benedictine monk. His are the earliest-known poems in vernacular.

Berchtesgaden (bĕrkh′tüsgä″dün), winter and summer resort, S Bavaria, in Bavarian Alps. Favorite residence of Hitler, who built a retreat on the Obersalzberg.

Berchtold, Leopold, Graf von (lā′ōpôlt gräf fün bĕrkh′tôlt), 1863–1942, Austro-Hungarian foreign minister (1912–15). Directed the policy which precipitated WORLD WAR I after assassination of Archduke FRANCIS FERDINAND.

Berdyaev, Nicholas (bĕrdyī′üf), 1874–1948, Russian Orthodox religious philosopher, in exile from Russia after 1922. Early a Marxist, he later stressed the need for spiritual meaning and direction in individual life and in history.

Berea or **Beroea** (both: bērēŭ′), Greek name of three places in Bible. **1** Syrian camp. **2** Mac. 9.4. **2** See VEROIA, Macedonia. **3** See ALEP, Syria.

Berea (bŭrē′ŭ). **1** Town (pop. 3,372), central Ky., SSE of Lexington. Seat of Berea Col. (nonsectarian; coed.); opened 1855 by J. G. FEE, chartered 1866, became college 1869. Town utilities and other businesses are owned by school and operated by students. Products of crafts classes are sold. Has extension services, schools for mountain people, and land holdings. **2** City (pop. 12,051), NE Ohio, SW of Cleveland; settled 1809. Seat of Baldwin-Wallace Col.

Berengar II (bē′rĭng-gŭr), d. 966, marquis of Ivrea. Made himself king of Italy in 950. His designs on Adelaide led to intervention of Emperor OTTO I. He swore fealty to Otto (952) but continued his intrigues until Otto imprisoned him (963).

Berengar of Tours, c.1000–1088, French theologian, head of the cathedral school at Tours. He was widely known as a dialectician, but his views on the Eucharist were considered radical and suspect by some theologians though approved by others (Leo IX and Gregory VII early defended him). A very bitter quarrel with LANFRANC led Berengar to an angry reply rejecting authority. This was condemned, and Berengar was declared a heretic. Also Bérenger, Berengarius.

Berenice (bĕrŭnī′sē), members of royal family of Egypt. **1** Born c.340 B.C., consort and half sister of Ptolemy I. **2** Died 246 B.C., daughter of Ptolemy II, wife of ANTIOCHUS II. After the death of her husband, she and her infant son were murdered by Seleucus II before her brother, Ptolemy III, arrived with aid. **3** Died 221? B.C., a Cyrenian, wife of Ptolemy III; joint ruler with her son Ptolemy IV, who had her murdered. The constellation Berenice's Hair is named for her.

Berenice, Jewish princesses. **1** Late 1st cent. B.C., sister of Herod the Great, wife of her nephew Aristobulus, whom she supposedly had killed. Her second husband was put to death for a plot against Herod. She married a third time and settled in Rome. **2** Born A.D. c.28, granddaughter of Berenice **1**. Her devotion to her brother, Herod Agrippa II, was greater than her love of her husbands. Titus apparently planned to marry her but could not because of unpopularity of Jews in Rome.

Berenson, Bernard (bĕ′rŭnsŭn), 1865–, American art critic, b. Lithuania, grad. Harvard, 1887. Authority on Italian art, especially of the Renaissance.

Berezina (bĕrĕzē′nŭ), river, 365 mi. long, Belorussia; tributary of Dnieper. Scene of heroic, costly crossing of Napoleon's fleeing army (Nov., 1812).

Berg, Alban (bĕrk), 1885–1936, Austrian composer. He used the 12-tone technique invented by his teacher, Arnold Schönberg. Although he met violent opposition, his opera *Wozzeck* (1925) attained considerable success. Among other compositions are a *Lyric Suite* (1926) for string quartet; a violin concerto (1936); an unfinished opera, *Lulu*.

Berg, former duchy (before 1380, county), NW Germany; chief city Düsseldorf. Under dukes of JÜLICH 1348–1524; under dukes of CLEVES 1524–1609; under Wittelsbachs (Palatinate line) 1666–1806. Raised to grand duchy (1806) by Napoleon I in favor of Joachim Murat. To Prussia 1815.

Bergamo (bĕr′gämō), city (pop. 73,534), Lombardy, N Italy. Textile mfg. Ruled by Venice 1427–1797. Romanesque cathedral; baptistery; Renaissance Colleoni chapel. Birthplace of Donizetti.

bergamot (bûr′gŭmŏt), citrus tree (*Citrus bergamia*). Fruit, an orange, yields oil for perfumes and eau de Cologne. Wild bergamot is related to OSWEGO TEA.

Bergen (bûr′gŭn, Nor. bĕr′gŭn), city (pop. 110,424), SW Norway, on the Vagen and the Pudde Fjord–both inlets of North Sea. Main shipping center and second largest city of Norway. Founded c.1070, it was the chief city and royal residence of medieval Norway, an episcopal see, and a cultural center. HANSEATIC LEAGUE created c.1350 one of its four great foreign establishments here and dominated the city until 1560. In World War II the German naval installations were heavily bombed. Ancient buildings (mostly restorations) include Haakon's Hall, a 12th-century palace; cathedral (13th cent.); Rosenkrantz Tower (16th cent.). Bergen has a university. Its theater gained international importance in 19th cent. through association with Ibsen and Bjornson.

Bergen, N.J.: see JERSEY CITY.

Bergenfield, residential borough (pop. 17,647), NE N.J., NE of Hackensack. Mfg. of machinery, cutlery, knitwear, and wood products.

Bergen op Zoom (bĕr′gŭn ôp zōm′), municipality (pop. 26,642) and town, North Brabant prov., SW Netherlands; a North Sea port on the Eastern Scheldt. Once strongly fortified, it was often besieged in the wars of the 16th–18th cent.

Berger, Victor Louis, 1860–1929, American Socialist leader and Congressman, b. Austria-Hungary. First Socialist member of Congress (1911–13). Sentenced to 20-year prison term for sedition; decision reversed by U.S. Supreme Court in 1921.

Bergerac, Cyrano de: see CYRANO DE BERGERAC.

Bergh, Henry, 1811–88, American philanthropist. Founded American Society for the Prevention of Cruelty to Animals (1866) and helped Elbridge T. Gerry estab. Society for the Prevention of Cruelty to Children (1875).

Bergius, Friedrich (frēd′rĭkh bĕr′gēŏŏs), 1884–1949, German chemist. Transformed coal into liquid fuel, wood into sugar. Shared 1931 Nobel Prize.

Bergman, Torbern Olof (tōōr'bùrn ōō'lôv bĕr'yùmän), 1735–84, Swedish chemist, physicist, naturalist. Developed theory of chemical affinity, improved chemical analysis and rock classification, worked in crystallography.

Bergmann, Ernst von (ērnst fùn bĕrg'män), 1836–1907, German surgeon, introducer (1886) of steam sterilization of instruments and dressings.

Bergson, Henri (ärĕ' bĕrgsō'), 1859–1941, French philosopher, long a professor at the Collège de France. He opposed prevailing positivistic thought by accenting the dualism between the dynamic *élan vital* [life force] and resistant matter. Man knows matter through intellect, but, more important, knows through intuition how the *élan vital* operates and also discovers the true nature of time, which is duration in terms of life experience, not a mathematically clocked measurement.

Berhampore (bûr'ùmpôr'), town (pop. 41,558), N West Bengal, India. Scene of first uprising of Sepoy Rebellion (1857).

Beria, Lavrenti Pavlovich (bĕ'ryä), 1899?–, Russian Communist leader. Head of the NKVD (Russian secret police; now MVD) from 1938; deputy premier in charge of ministries of state control and interior.

beriberi (bĕ'rēbĕ'rē), disease affecting nervous system and resulting from unbalanced diet low in vitamin B. Common among Orientals subsisting on polished rice.

Bering, Vitus Jonassen (vē'tōōs yō'näsùn bā'rĭng), 1681–1741. Danish explorer in Russian employ. Planned and carried out with government support notable expedition to map Siberian arctic regions. Died on Bering Isl. after leading expedition to Alaska.

Bering Island, off Kamchatka, extreme NE Asiatic RSFSR, in Bering Sea, largest of KOMANDORSKI ISLANDS. Here Vitus Bering was wrecked and died.

Bering Sea, northward extension of Pacific between Siberia and Alaska, c.878,000 sq. mi. Screened from Pacific by Aleutian Isls., navigable only after late May; connected with Arctic Ocean by Bering Strait, navigable only after late June. Contains several islands owned by U.S. and USSR. Bering voyages revealed fur-seal wealth, and from mid-18th cent. unregulated slaughter threatened their extinction. Protection of seals became subject of **Bering Sea Fur-Seal Controversy** (1886), international dispute over pelagic (open sea) sealing. Court of arbitration in 1893 declared against U.S. claim to control all of Bering Sea, and damages were paid to seized Canadian vessels. In 1911 international agreement gave U.S. supervision of seal summering places in Pribilof Isls., prohibited pelagic sealing, and forbade altogether the killing of sea otters.

Bering Strait, waterway between NE Asia and NW North America. Connects Arctic Ocean and Bering Sea. Narrowness (c.50 mi.) makes it plausible place of American Indian entry into America.

Berkeley, George (bär'klē), 1685–1753, British philosopher, b. Ireland; bishop of Cloyne after 1734. Going beyond the teachings of Locke, he argued for what has been called subjective idealism—the theory that all qualities are known only in the mind, that matter does not exist apart from its being perceived, and that the observing mind of God makes possible the continued apparent existence of material objects. Tried unsuccessfully to found a college for converting American Indians to Christianity. Among his works are his *New Theory of Vision* (1709), *Treatise concerning the Principles of Human Knowledge* (1710), *Dialogues* (1713).

Berkeley, Sir William, 1606–77, British colonial governor of Va. A tyrant, his negligence brought on rebellion led by Nathaniel BACON. Removed from office after exacting bloody vengeance.

Berkeley (bûrk'lē). **1** City (pop. 113,805), W Calif., on E shore of San Francisco Bay. Originally part of Peralta family's Rancho San Antonio (granted 1820); bought 1853 by Americans. Suburban and educational center, it is seat of Univ. of CALIFORNIA. Has aquatic park and yacht harbor. **2** City (pop. 5,268), E Mo., W suburb of St. Louis.

Berkeley Springs, town (pop. 1,213), W.Va., in E Panhandle, NW of Martinsburg; chartered 1776 as Bath, still its official name. Warm springs have made town a health resort from colonial days.

Berkhampstead or **Berkhamstead**, Hertfordshire, England: see GREAT BERKHAMPSTEAD.

Berkley, city (pop. 17,931), SE Mich., NW suburb of Detroit.

Berkman, Alexander, 1870?–1936, anarchist, b. Vilna, came to U.S. c.1887. Unsuccessful attempt to kill Henry Clay Frick (1892) caused 14 years of imprisonment. He and Emma GOLDMAN long associated, were arrested for obstructing the draft (1917) and deported to Russia (1919). Disappointed with USSR, he left and later committed suicide.

Berkshire (bärk'shĭr, –shùr, bûrk'–) or **Berks**, inland county (725 sq. mi.; pop. 402,939) in Thames R. basin, England; co. town Reading. Largely agr., has dairying and hog raising. At Windsor is famous royal castle.

Berkshire Hills (bûrk'shēr), W Mass., region of wooded hills with many streams, small lakes, resorts, and country homes. Name is sometimes restricted to Mass. part of TACONIC MOUNTAINS, but is generally applied to all highlands in W Mass. Rise to 3,491 ft. in Mt. Greylock, highest point in state, SW of North Adams. Pittsfield, Great Barrington, Lenox, and Stockbridge are here. Chief rivers: Housatonic, Westfield.

Berkshire Symphonic Festival, summer music festival, featuring the Boston Symphony Orchestra, held since 1937 at "Tanglewood" near Lenox, Mass., but mostly in adjoining Stockbridge town. In 1940 a summer school, the Berkshire Music Center, was begun in combination with the festival.

Berle, Adolf A(ugustus), Jr. (bûr'lē), 1895–, U.S. Assistant Secretary of State (1938–44).

Berlichingen, Götz von (gùts fùn bĕr'lĭkhĭng-ùn), c.1480–1562, German knight, adventurer. Led rebellious peasants in PEASANTS' WAR. His memoirs inspired Goethe's drama, *Götz von Berlichingen* (1773).

Berlin, Irving, 1888–, American composer of over 1,000 popular songs, b. Russia. His songs are of many types, e.g., the jazzy *Alexander's Ragtime Band* (his first great success, 1911); the nostalgic *White Christmas*; the patriotic *God Bless America*. He has written music for many musical comedies and films.

Berlin, Ont.: see KITCHENER.

Berlin (bûr'līn', Ger. bĕrlēn'), city (pop. c.3,336,000), former cap. of Germany and of Prussia; N Germany, in Brandenburg (from which it is administratively separate), on the Spree and Havel rivers. City area (344 sq. mi.) includes large forests and lakes. Until its virtual destruction in World War II Berlin was second largest city of Europe; political, economic, cultural center of Germany. It remains a major inland port and communications center (six railroad stations; several airfields, notably Tempelhof) and has much mfg. (textiles, chemicals, electrical machinery). Originating in two Wendish villages, Berlin and Kölln (merged 1307), city rose as member of Hanseatic League; became cap. of Brandenburg (15th cent.) and of Prussia (1701); underwent phenomenal growth after becoming cap. of Germany (1871). Has been occupied by Russo-Austrian forces (1760); by the French (1805); and by the Allies (1945–). Much bombed in World War II, it was most severely damaged by artillery during capture by Russians under Marshal Zhukov (April 28, 1945). Berlin was divided at POTSDAM CONFERENCE into four occupation zones, under joint Allied *Kommandatura*. Mounting friction between Russia and Western Allies resulted in 1948 in withdrawal of Russians from *Kommandatura* and in split of Berlin into two separate cities: "West Berlin," i.e., the combined American, English, and French sectors (188 sq. mi.; pop. c.2,142,000), which in 1949 became a member state of the Federal Republic of Germany; and the "Soviet sector" (pop. c.1,194,000), which in 1949 became the cap. of the [East] German Democratic Republic. Introduction of West German currency into Berlin was the ostensible cause of Russian blockade of West Berlin (June, 1948–May, 1949), during which Allies supplied the city by a constant stream of aircraft—the historic "airlift." Though Russia lifted the blockade, lesser incidents continued. Despite physical destruction and constant tension, Berlin experienced a vigorous intellectual and artistic revival in postwar period. Beside Humboldt Univ. (founded 1810), there is the Free Univ. (founded 1948), in Western sector.

Berlin (bûr'lĭn). **1** Town (pop. 7,470), central Conn., SSW of Hartford; settled 1686. Metal goods. **2** Town (pop. 2,001), Eastern Shore, Md., SE of Salisbury. The racehorse War Admiral was trained on near-by training grounds. Birthplace of Stephen Decatur. **3** City (pop. 16,615), NE N.H., at N edge of White Mts. at falls of Androscoggin R.; settled 1821. Pulp and paper mills. Winter sports center, with first ski club organized in U.S.

Berlin, Congress of, 1878, called by signatories of Treaty of Paris of 1856 to revise Treaty of SAN STEFANO, which Russia had forced on Turkey. Bismarck, acting as "honest broker," was chairman. Other outstanding figures were Disraeli, A. M. Gorchakov, Andrassy. Principal decisions included recognition of Serbia, Montenegro, and Rumania as independent states; threefold division of BULGARIA; assignment of BOSNIA AND HERCEGOVINA to Austro-Hungarian administration; revision of Greco-Turkish boundary.

Berlin Decree, issued in Berlin, Nov. 21, 1806, by Napoleon I in answer to British blockade of commercial ports. Declared British Isles under blockade; initiated CONTINENTAL SYSTEM.

Berliner, Emile (bûr'lĭnùr), 1851–1929, American inventor of loose-contact telephone transmitter, disk record, method for quantity duplication of records. Worked on helicopter. Started program to publicize dangers of raw milk.

Berlin Pact: see AXIS.

Berlioz, Hector (bĕrlēōs'), 1803–69, French romantic composer, whose ideas of orchestral coloring influenced many later composers. His first important work was the *Symphonie fantastique* (1830). In next decade he wrote the symphonies *Harold in Italy* and *Romeo and Juliet.* His outstanding dramatic works are *The Damnation of Faust, The Trojans.*

Bermuda (bùrmū'dù), British crown colony (21 sq. mi.; pop. 35,560), comprising some 300 coral islands (c.20 inhabited), c.650 mi. SE of N. Carolina; cap. HAMILTON, on largest island, Bermuda. Year-round resort. Discovered by Spaniard, Juan de Bermúdez (1515), it was uninhabited until colonists under Sir George Somers were wrecked there (1609).

Bermuda grass, a grass (*Cynodon dactylon*) used for pasture and lawn in the S US. It is resistant to heat and drought.

Bern (bûrn, Ger. bĕrn) or **Berne** (Fr. bĕrn), most populous canton (2,658 sq. mi.; pop. 798,264) of Switzerland. Comprises Bernese Alps or Oberland, with JUNGFRAU and other peaks; Mittelland [midlands], in N foothills of Alps; and Seeland [lake country], in the NW, including Biel and Bernese Jura. Agr., dairying, tourist trade in Oberland and Mittelland; watchmaking in Seeland. Pop. mostly Protestant and—except in Jura—German-speaking. History of canton is largely that of its cap., **Bern** or **Berne** (pop. 145,740), since 1848 also the cap. of Switzerland, on Aar R. Founded 1191; became free imperial city 1218; joined Swiss Confederation 1353; soon became its leading member; conquered AARGAU (1415) and VAUD (1536); accepted the Reformation (1528). Autocratic urban aristocracy governed until 1798, when French revolutionary armies sacked city and dismembered Bernese state. At Congress of Vienna (1815) Berne did not recover Aargau and Vaud but received Bernese Jura

(former bishopric of Basel). Liberal cantonal constitution adopted 1831. Largely medieval in architecture, Bern has 15th-cent. cathedral, quaint arcaded streets, fountains. Modern buildings include federal palace, museums, univ. (founded 1834). Seat of Universal Postal Union, International Copyright Union, and other international agencies.

Bernadette, Saint (bûrnŭdĕt'), 1843–79, French saint, whose visions of the Virgin in a grotto caused Lourdes to become a major Roman Catholic shrine. A poor and unlettered girl (Bernadette Soubirous), she was severely challenged by the skeptical both within the Church and outside before she was allowed to retreat to a quiet convent at Nevers. Canonized 1933. Feast: April 16.

Bernadotte, Count Folke (fôl'kù bĕrnädôt'), 1895–1948, Swedish internationalist; nephew of King Gustavus V. Appointed UN mediator in Palestine (1948), he was assassinated by a Jewish extremist in Jerusalem. Ralph Bunche succeeded him.

Bernadotte, Jean Baptiste Jules: see CHARLES XIV, king of Sweden.

Bernanos, Georges (zhôrzh' bĕrnänōs'), 1888–1948, French author. His novels, such as *Sous le soleil de Satan* (1926; Eng. tr., *The Star of Satan*) and *Journal d'un curé de campagne* (1936; Eng. tr., *The Diary of a Country Priest*), reflect deep mysticism. Though a monarchist and Catholic, Bernanos wrote eloquently against the Insurgents of the Spanish civil war in *Les Grands Cimetières sous la lune* (1938; Eng. tr., *A Diary of My Times*).

Bernard, Saint: see BERNARD OF CLAIRVAUX, SAINT, and BERNARD OF MENTHON, SAINT. For the two Alpine passes, see SAINT BERNARD.

Bernard VII, d. 1418, count of Armagnac, constable of France; father-in-law of Charles d'ORLÉANS. Led Armagnac faction (named for him) after Charles's capture in 1415. Killed in Paris massacre (see ARMAGNACS AND BURGUNDIANS).

Bernard, Claude (klōd bĕrnär'), 1813–78, French physiologist, a founder of experimental medicine through work on digestive process and vasomotor mechanism.

Bernard, Joseph Antoine (zhôzĕf' ätwän' bĕrnär'), 1866–1931, French sculptor, b. Vienna.

Bernardin de Saint-Pierre, Jacques Henri (zhäk' ärĕ' bĕrnärdĕ' dù sĕ-pyĕr'), 1737–1814, French author. Strongly influenced by Rousseau, he is best known for the charming prose idyl *Paul et Virginie* (1788).

Bernardo del Carpio (bĕrnär'dō dĕl kär'pyō), hero of medieval Spanish legend, counterpart of French Roland; supposedly nephew of Alfonso II.

Bernard of Clairvaux, Saint (bûr'nùrd, bûrnärd', klârvō'), 1090?–1153, French churchman, Doctor of the Church. In 1115 he founded a Cistercian monastery at CLAIRVAUX, where he remained as abbot the rest of his life, refusing high church offices. Nevertheless, holiness of life, immense capacity of mind, force of character, and burning eloquence made him the most powerful figure of his day. He sought peace among the rulers of Western Europe and had a hand in many political affairs. He led the successful fight to seat Pope INNOCENT II and was the adviser of Pope Eugene III. His vigorous attacks brought condemnations of ABELARD and ARNOLD OF BRESCIA. His preaching launched the Second Crusade. Bernard was notable also for his charity and his protection of the weak (e.g., the Jews of the Rhineland) from the powerful. Today his greatest importance lies perhaps in his writings, which include many superb sermons and profound and well-written treatises on the Christian life, theology, and mysticism (e.g., *On the Steps of Humility and Pride; On the Love of God; On Grace and Free Will; On Conversion; On Consideration;* and a life of St. Malachy). He probably did not write the hymn, *Jesu, dulcis memoriae,* sometimes attributed to him. Feast: Aug. 20.

Bernard of Menthon, Saint (mätō'), 11th cent., Savoyard churchman, founder of the Alpine hospices in both of the SAINT BERNARD passes. Feast: May 28.

Bern Convention: see COPYRIGHT.

Berne, Switzerland: see BERN.

Berners or **Barnes, Juliana** (bûr'nùrz, bärnz), fl. early 15th cent.?, supposed English author of treatise on hunting in *The Book of St. Albans.*

Bernese Alps, Switzerland: see BERN, canton.

Bernhard of Saxe-Weimar, 1604–39, Protestant general in THIRTY YEARS WAR. Captured Regensburg 1633; was routed at Nördlingen 1634; entered French pay 1635; defeated imperials at Breisach (1638).

Bernhardt, Sarah (bûrn'härt, Fr. bĕrnär'), 1844–1923, stage name of Rosine Bernard, French actress. Superb portrayals, e.g., in *King Lear* (1867), *Ruy Blas* (1867), *Phèdre* (1874), *Hernani* (1877), earned her the title "divine Sarah." She appeared also in Sardou and Rostand plays, toured Europe and U.S. (after 1880), and managed the Théâtre Sarah Bernhardt (1895) where she did *L'Aiglon* and played Hamlet. She made two silent films (1912) and continued acting even after a leg amputation in 1915.

Berni, Francesco (fränchä'skō bĕr'nē), 1497?–1535, Italian humorous poet, a priest, author of revision of the *Orlando Innamorato* of Boiardo.

Bernina (bĕrnē'nä), Alpine mountain group on Swiss-Italian border, culminating in the Piz Bernina at 13,304 ft. The Bernina pass, 7,645 ft. high, is crossed by a road and a railroad.

Bernini, Giovanni Lorenzo (jōvän'nē lōrĕn'tsō bĕrnē'nē), 1598–1680, Italian baroque sculptor and architect. Carved the graceful Apollo and Daphne (Borghese Gall., Rome). Other works include royal staircase in Vatican, colonnades of elliptical plaza before St. Peter's Church, and the bronze baldachin beneath its dome.

Bernoulli or **Bernouilli** (both: bĕrnōoyē'), name of family distinguished in mathematics and other sciences. After leaving Antwerp the family settled in Basel, Switzerland. **Jacob, Jacques,** or **James Bernoulli** (zhäk), 1654–1705, wrote treatise on theory of probability (1713), discovered Bernoulli's numbers. A professor at Basel, he was succeeded by his brother **Jean, Johann,** or **John Bernoulli** (zhä, yō'hän), 1667–1748, known for work in integral and exponential calculus. His son **Daniel Bernoulli** (dänyel'), 1700–1782, a mathematician and physician, solved equation known as Bernoulli's equation and advanced the kinetic theory of gases and fluids.

Bernstein, Eduard (ā'dōoärt bĕrn'shtīn), 1850–1932, German socialist. In Social Democratic party after 1872, he was exiled in 1878 (returned to Germany 1901). Criticized Marxist theories, denying inevitability of world revolution, and became leader of "revisionism."

Bernstein, Henri (ärē' bĕrnstīn'), 1876–, French dramatist, author of many sophisticated comedies. *The Thief* (1906; Eng. tr., 1907) was most successful among his plays performed in America.

Bernstorff, Johann Hartwig Ernst (yohän' härt'vīkh, bĕrns'tôrff), 1712–72, Danish statesman, of German origin. As foreign minister (1751–70) he kept Denmark at peace, negotiated exchange of Oldenburg for ducal Holstein with Russia. Dismissed through influence of STRUENSEE. His nephew, **Andreas Peter Bernstorff,** 1735–97, was Danish foreign minister (1773–80) and chief minister (1784–97). Kept Denmark neutral in French Revolutionary Wars; undertook social, economic, and educational reforms.

Beroea (bērē'ù), the same as BEREA.

Berruguete, Alonso (älōn'sō bĕr-rōogä'tä), c.1480–1561, Spanish court artist to Charles V. Studied with Michelangelo. Known for carved altar screens and other church furniture.

Berry, Charles, duc de (shärl' dük' dù bĕrē'), 1778–1820, younger son of Charles X of France. Fought with Condé against French Revolution. His assassination caused reaction against liberals. His wife, **Caroline Fernande Louise, duchesse de Berry** (kärōlēn'

fĕrnäd' lwēz' düshĕs'), 1798–1870, attempted in 1832 to win French throne for her son, later known as Henri, comte de Chambord. Temporarily imprisoned.

Berry, Martha McChesney, 1866–1942, American educator, founder of school for underprivileged mountain children at Mt. Berry, Ga., in 1902.

Berry (bĕrē'), region and former province, central France; historic cap. Bourges. Dry plateau (cattle raising), except fertile Indre and Cher valleys. Bought by French crown c.1100; duchy-appanage of various princes of the blood 1360–1601.

Bertha of the Big Foot, d. 783, Frankish queen, mother of Charlemagne.

Berthelot, Pierre Eugène Marcelin (pyĕr' ûzhĕn' märsùlĕ' bĕrtùlō'), 1827–1907, French chemist. A founder of modern organic chemistry, he pioneered in producing synthetic organic compounds; also worked in thermochemistry and explosives.

Berthier, Louis Alexandre (lwē' älĕksä'drù bĕrtyä'), 1753–1815, marshal of France. Served in American Revolution and as chief of staff under Napoleon I. Was created prince of Neuchâtel and Wagram. Welcomed return of Bourbons. Committed suicide (or was killed) when Napoleon debarked from Elba.

Berthollet, Claude Louis, Comte (klōd lwē, kôt bĕrtōlä'), 1748–1822, French chemist. Stated theories of chemical equilibrium and of double decomposition of salts; analyzed ammonia. Discovered that chlorine is a bleach, carbon purifies water, and potassium chlorate has detonating properties.

Bertillon system (bûrtĭl'yùn), first scientific method of criminal identification, developed by Alphonse Bertillon (1853–1914), based on classification of body measurements.

Bertrand, Henri Gratien, Comte (ärē' gräsyē' kôt' bĕrträ'), 1773–1844, French general. Followed Napoleon I to St. Helena. His memoirs, *Napoleon at St. Helena,* appeared in English 1952.

Bertrand de Born or **Bertran de Born,** c.1140–c.1214, French troubadour of Limousin. Some of his 40 surviving poems commemorate his part in the struggles between Henry II of England and his sons.

Berwick, James Fitz-James, duke of (bĕr'ĭk), 1670–1734, marshal of France; illegitimate son of James II of England and Arabella Churchill (Marlborough's sister). Fought at the BOYNE and in War of Spanish Succession (took Barcelona 1714). Killed in War of Polish Succession. Author of memoirs.

Berwick (bĕr'ĭk) or **Berwickshire** (bĕr'ĭkshĭr), agr. maritime county (457 sq. mi.; pop. 25,060), SE Scotland; co. town Duns. Separated from England by the Tweed, was long scene of border strife.

Berwick (bûr'wĭk), borough (pop. 14,010), E Pa., on the Susquehanna and SW of Wilkes-Barre; settled 1783. Mfg. of silk, railway cars, and clothing. Site of Fort Jenkins (1777).

Berwick-on-Tweed (bĕr'ĭk) or **Berwick-upon-Tweed,** municipal borough (pop. 12,550), Northumberland, England, on N side of mouth of Tweed R. As leading border town, contested by England and Scotland until made part of Northumberland 1885.

Berwyn, city (pop. 51,280), NE Ill., W suburb of Chicago; founded 1890.

beryl (bĕr'ĭl), very hard silicate of beryllium and aluminum. Most valued variety is emerald.

beryllium (bùrĭl'lēùm) or **glucinum** (glōosī'nùm), rare, steel-white, metallic element (symbol = Be, sometimes G1; see also ELEMENT, table). Resembles magnesium; forms some compounds. Cost of extraction from ore limits use; alloyed with other metals to add hardness, strength, and lightness.

Berzelius, Jons Jakob, Baron (bùrzē'lēùs), 1779–1848, Swedish chemist. Developed modern chemical symbols; prepared table of atomic weights; analyzed many compounds; discovered selenium, thorium, cerium.

Besançon (bùzäsō'), city (pop. 51,939), cap. of Doubs dept., E France, in Franche-Comté. Watch mfg. Archiepiscopal see. Free imperial city until incorporation (1648) into Franche-Comté (then Spanish). After French annexation the cap. of Franche-Comté and a university were transferred from DôLE to Besançon (1676). Medieval and Renaissance architecture. Birthplace of Victor Hugo.

Besant, Annie (Wood) (bĕ'zŭnt), 1847–1933, English theosophist and social reformer. Advocated free thought, Socialism. She and Charles Bradlaugh edited the *National Reformer* and for publishing a pamphlet on birth control (1877) were tried on charges of immorality and acquitted. In 1889 she became a disciple of Mme Blavatsky. She lived in India and furthered the Indian nationalist cause. President of the Theosophical Society after 1907, she wrote much on religion. In 1926–27 she introduced her protégé, Jiddu Krishnamurti, in England and America as the new Messiah (he later declined the honor).

Besant, Sir Walter (bĭzănt'), 1836–1901, English writer and reformer, author of novels on social problems, criticism, biographies, works on London.

Beskids, range of Carpathians, along Polish-Czech border. Highest peak at 5,658 ft.

Besnard, Paul Albert (pôl' älbĕr' bänär'), 1849–1934, French academic painter, known for his murals.

Bessarabia (bĕsŭrä'bēù), region of SE Europe, bounded by the Dniester, Danube and Pruth rivers and the Black Sea. Cities: Kichenev, Izmail, Belgorod-Dnestrovsky. Largely a fertile agr. steppe and grazing land (grain, tobacco, fruit, wool). Always a border country, it was part of Roman Dacia; was invaded by Goths, Petchenegs, Cumans, Mongols; fell to Moldavia 14th cent.; to Turks 15th cent.; to Russia 1812. Congress of Paris (1856) gave S Bessarabia to Moldavia; Congress of Berlin (1878) restored it to Russia. Rumania annexed the entire prov. 1918, was forced to return it to Russia 1940, reoccupied it 1941–44, ceded it formally 1947. Larger part now incorporated with Moldavian SSR, except for S part, which was added to Ukraine.

Bessarion (bĕsä'rēùn), 1395?–1472, Byzantine humanist in Renaissance Italy; made a cardinal 1439, patriarch of Constantinople 1463. Notable for his learning, he translated many Greek works into Latin.

Bessel, Friedrich Wilhelm (frēd'rĭkh vĭl'hĕlm bĕs'ùl), 1784–1846, German astronomer. Made first authenticated measurement of distance of a star (1841).

Bessemer, Sir Henry: see BESSEMER PROCESS.

Bessemer, industrial city (pop. 28,445), central Ala., near Birmingham; founded 1887. Processes iron, steel, chemicals.

Bessemer process (bĕs'ùmùr), industrial process for making steel from cast iron (pig iron). Oxygen of air blown through molten iron oxidizes impurities in it, oxidation heat raising temperature of mass and keeping it molten during operation. Efficiency of process depends upon large steel container (Bessemer converter) lined with silica and clay or with dolomite. To make steel of desired properties, another substance, often spiegeleisen, is usually added to molten metal once oxidation is complete. Basic principle of process invented by **Sir Henry Bessemer,** 1813–98, who erected Bessemer Steel Works at Sheffield, England.

Bessenyei, George (bĕ'shĕnyā), 1747–1811, Hungarian dramatist and writer. Helped make Hungarian a modern literary language.

Best, Charles Herbert, 1899–, Canadian physiologist, developer with Banting of insulin treatment of diabetes. Author of works on physiology.

betatron (bā'tùtrŏn), electron-accelerating machine first developed by D. W. Kerst in 1941. The accelerated electrons are either released as a beam or are directed at a metal target to generate X rays; mesons and other subatomic particles can be produced from the X rays. Betatron is used in study of cosmic rays and in medical and industrial research.

betel nut (bē'–), fruit of a palm (*Areca catechu*). Chewed with leaf of betel pepper smeared with lime, it is narcotic stimulant for many Eastern peoples.

Bethabara (–ăb'ùrù), place on Jordan R., near Dead Sea, where John was baptizing when Jesus came to him. Called Bethany in RV. John 1.28.

Bethany (bĕth'ùnē). **1** Village at SW foot of Mt. Olivet, E of Jerusalem. Home of Lazarus, Martha, and Mary, and often visited by Jesus. Ascension took place near by. Mark 11.1, 11; John 11; Mat. 21.17; 26.6; Mark 14.3; Luke 19.29; 24.50. **2** See BETHABARA.

Bethany. 1 City (pop. 5,705), central Okla., near Oklahoma City. Members of Nazarene sect, who predominate, have college. **2** Town (pop. 1,063), W.Va., NNE of Wheeling near Pa. line. Seat of **Bethany College** (coed.; chartered 1840, opened 1841 by Alexander Campbell).

Bethe, Hans Albrecht (bā'tù), 1906–, American physicist. Developed theories on atomic properties and on origin of solar and stellar energy. Directed theoretical physics division, Los Alamos Atomic Bomb Project, 1943–46.

Bethel (bĕth'ùl) [Heb.,= house of God], ancient city, N of Jerusalem. Here Abraham built altar, Jacob had vision of ladder reaching to heaven, and Samuel often visited. Jeroboam tried to make it a religious capital to rival Jerusalem and set up a golden calf for worship. Bethel became associated with idolatry and was denounced by later prophets. Gen. 12.8; 35.1–15; Judges 20.26, 27; 1 Kings 12.26–33; Amos 3.14. Bible says name originally Luz; modern town called Beitin.

Bethel, town (pop. 5,104), SW Conn., near Danbury. Hat mfg. since c.1800.

Bethesda (–thĕz'–), pool in Jerusalem said to have miraculous healing powers. John 5.2–9. May be same as pool recently discovered in NE corner of city.

Bethesda (bĭthĕz'dù), uninc. town, central Md., NW suburb of Washington, D.C. Here are Natl. Cancer Inst. research center, Naval Medical Center, and Natl. Institutes of Health.

Beth-horon (–hō'–), name of two neighboring towns between Lydda and Jerusalem. Scene of 2 historic victories—one by Joshua and one by Judas Maccabaeus.

Bethlehem (bĕth'lēùm) [Heb.,= house of bread or house of Lahmu, a goddess], Arabic *Beit Lahm,* town (pop. 6,814), S central Palestine, just S of Jerusalem, birthplace of Jesus and one of world's great shrines, now in republic of Israel. Inhabitants, largely Christian, depend on pilgrims for livelihood. In Old Testament, scene of book of Ruth and home of David. In A.D. 330 Constantine erected basilica on traditional site of the Nativity. Church standing there today is shared by monks of Greek, Latin, and Armenian rites. Manger where Jesus was born is said to have been in grotto under church. Bethelehem's older name was Ephrath or Ephratah. Gen. 35.16–20; 48.7; 1 Sam. 16; 17; 2 Sam. 23.13–17; 1 Chron. 15–19.

Bethlehem. 1 Town (pop. 882), NW N.H., in White Mts. and SW of Whitefield. Health resort. **2** City (pop. 66,340), E Pa., on Lehigh R. and N of Philadelphia; settled 1787 by Moravians. Steel products, site of Bethlehem Steel Corp. Seat of LEHIGH UNIVERSITY, Moravian Col. (for men; 1807), and Moravian Col. for Women (1742). Has annual music festival in May with Bach Choir.

Bethlen, Gabriel (bĕth'lùn, bĕt'lĕn), Hung. *Bethlen Gábor,* 1580–1629, prince of Transylvania (1613–29). A Protestant, he allied himself with FREDERICK THE WINTER KING and invaded Hungary, of which he was elected king (1620). After Frederick's defeat he made peace with Emperor Ferdinand II and renounced the royal title (1621). He ruled Transylvania wisely, encouraged law and learning.

Bethlen, Count Stephen, Hung. *Bethlen István,* 1874–1950?, Hungarian premier (1921–31). Though a royalist, he prevented the return of King Charles (Emperor CHARLES I) to avoid military intervention of Little Entente. Sought revision of Treaty of Trianon. His death in a Russian prison was reported but not confirmed.

Bethmann-Hollweg, Theobald von (tā'ōbält fün bāt'–

män-hôl'vāk), 1856–1921, chancellor of Germany (1909–17). Famed for calling guarantee of Belgian neutrality a "scrap of paper" (1914). Overthrown in 1917 for his efforts to negotiate peace.

Bethsaida (–sā'ĭdủ) [Heb.,= house of fish], birthplace of Peter, Andrew, and John. Near, or on, Sea of Galilee, exact location uncertain. Mat. 11.21; Mark 6.45; 8.22; Luke 10.13; John 1.44; 12.21.

Beth-shan (–shän') or **Beth-shean** (–shē'ŭn), anc. fortress in Jordan valley, principal strategic point of E Palestine. Modern name: Beisan.

Bethulia (bĕthū'lēủ), city, Palestine, apparently NE of Samaria. Scene of book of JUDITH. Sometimes identified with Jerusalem.

Bethune, David: see BEATON, DAVID.

Bethune, Mary McLeod (mŭkloud' bủthūn'), 1875–, American Negro educator. Founded (1904) Daytona Normal and Industrial Inst. for Negro Girls (now Bethune-Cookman Col.) and was president 1904–42.

Bethune-Cookman College: see DAYTONA BEACH, Fla.

Bettendorf, city (pop. 5,132), E Iowa, suburb of Davenport, on Mississippi R. Mfg. of industrial gases and machinery.

Betterton, Thomas, 1635?–1710, English actor, manager. In William D'Avenant's company (1661–68) became leading actor of his day. A great Hamlet, Mercutio, and Macbeth, he played many roles in Shakspere adaptations by Dryden, Shadwell, and himself. As actor-manager, opened Haymarket Theatre 1705.

Beulah, allegorical name for Israel. Isa. 62.4, 5.

Beuthen (boi'tủn), Pol. *Bytom,* city (pop. 93,179), Upper Silesia; since 1945 under Polish administration. Mfg. center in Katowice mining region.

Bevan, Aneurin (ủnī'rĭn bĕ'vủn), 1897–, British political leader. Former coal miner and a trade unionist, became minister of health (1945) for Labour government's system of socialized medicine. On return of Churchill government (1951) became chief left-wing opponent of ATTLEE within LABOUR PARTY.

Beveland, North, and **South Beveland** (bā'vủlänt), two islands (combined area 170 sq. mi.), Zeeland prov., SW Netherlands, in the Scheldt estuary. Connected by railroad with mainland and with Walcheren. Agr., livestock raising. British dislodged Germans from islands after heavy fighting late in 1944.

Beveridge, Albert J(eremiah), 1862–1927, U.S. Senator (1899–1911) and historian. Supported policies of Theodore Roosevelt. Wrote biographies of John Marshall and Lincoln.

Beveridge, William Henry, 1879–, British economist. In government service 1908–19, set up labor exchanges and devised wartime food rationing. Was director of London School of Economics 1919–37 and master of Univ. Col., Oxford, 1937–45. In noted government reports, proposed full social security system for all citizens (1942) and planned spending to insure full employment (1944).

Beverley, municipal borough (pop. 15,499), cap. of E. Riding of Yorkshire, England. Famous 13th-cent. minster contains "chair of peace" which gave right of sanctuary.

Beverly. 1 City (pop. 28,884), NE Mass., on coast just N of Salem; settled before 1630. Mfg. of shoes and clothing. Had New England's first successful cotton-weaving mill (1789). O. W. Holmes and his son had summer home here. **2** City (pop. 3,084), SW N.J., on Delaware R. below Burlington. Has natl. cemetery.

Beverly Hills, city (pop. 29,032), S Calif.; planned 1906. A Los Angeles suburb, it is the home of many screen stars.

Bevin, Ernest (bĕ'vủn), 1881–1951, British trade-union and political leader. Merged unions to make powerful Transport and General Workers' Union. Was minister of labor in wartime cabinet 1940–45. As Labour government foreign minister (1945 until his death) his policy toward USSR was uncompromising. His Palestine policy criticized by Arabs and Jews.

Bewick, Thomas (bū'ĭk), 1753–1828, English wood engraver, noted for illustrations of Beilby's *History of British Birds.*

Bexley, residential city (pop. 12,378), central Ohio, near Columbus. Capital Univ. is here.

Beyle, Henri: see STENDHAL.

Beyrouth: see BEIRUT.

Beza, Theodore (bē'zủ), Fr. *Théodore de Bèze* (tāō-dôr' dủ bĕz'), 1519–1605, French reformer and Calvinist theologian, friend and aid of Calvin.

Bezer (bē'zủr), town, E of the Jordan. One of the cities of refuge. Deut. 4.43; Joshua 20.8; 21.36.

Béziers (bāzyā'), city (pop. 59,894), Hérault dept., S France. Wine and spirits trade. Population was massacred (1209) after Simon de Montfort captured city in Albigensian Crusade.

Bezruc, Petr, Czech *Bezruč* (pĕt'ủr bĕz'rōōch), pseud. of Vladimir Vasek, 1867–, Czech poet, author of nationalistic *Silesian Songs* (1903; latest ed., 1944).

Bezwada (bāzwä'dủ), officially *Vizayawada,* city (pop. 86,184), NE Madras, India, on Kistna R. Trade center. Headworks of irrigation-canal system.

Bhagavad-Gita (bŭg'ủvủd-gē'tủ), Sanskrit philosophical poem in MAHABHARATA. Important, widely translated expression of Hinduism.

Bhascara (bŭs'kủrủ), called **Acarya** (ủchär'yủ), b. 1114, Hindu mathematician, astronomer, first to give systematic exposition of decimal system.

Bhatpara (bŭtpä'rủ), city (pop. 117,044), S West Bengal, India; anc. seat of Sanskrit learning.

Bhils (bēlz), people (more than 1,000,000) who inhabit parts of W central India, esp. S Rajputana and N Bombay state. Speak Bhili, an Indo-European language (see LANGUAGE, table); their culture is affected by, but not absorbed into, Hinduism.

Bhopal (bō'päl), state (6,921 sq. mi.; pop. 838,107), central India. At Sanchi is a 54-ft.-high Buddhist stupa (c.300 B.C.). Bhopal (pop. 75,228) is state cap.; trade center with textile mfg.

Bhubaneswar, India: see BHUVANESWAR.

Bhutan (bōōtän'), Indian protectorate (c.18,000 sq. mi.; pop. c.300,000), in E Himalayas, between India and Tibet; cap. Punaka. Formerly under dual control of a spiritual and a temporal ruler; since 1907 under a maharaja. Lamaism is main religion. Largely mountainous and forested. In 1949 India assumed Britain's former role in subsidizing Bhutan and directing its foreign affairs.

Bhuvaneswar (bōōvänĕ'swär) or **Bhubaneswar** (bōōbä–), cap. of Orissa, India. Was center of Sivaism and cap. of Kesaris dynasty from 5th to 10th cent. Has remains of c.500 shrines.

Bi, chemical symbol of the element BISMUTH.

Bialik, Hayyim Nahman (byä'lēk), 1873–1934, Hebrew poet and translator, b. Russia.

Bialowieza, Pol. *Białowieza,* large forest, E Poland. Favorite royal hunting preserve; national park since 1921. Has aurochs, boar, deer.

Bialystok, Pol. *Białystok* (byäwĭs'tôk), city (pop. 65,800), NE Poland. Textile center.

Biard, Pierre (byär), c.1567–1622, French Jesuit missionary in North America. Headed first Jesuit mission to Canada (1611). His *Relation de la Nouvelle France* (1616) has much historical value.

Biarritz (bē'ủrĭts, Fr. byärēts') town (pop. 20,447), Basses-Pyrénées dept., SW France, on Bay of Biscay near Spanish border. Fashionable resort.

Bibiena or **Bibbiena, Galli da** (gäl'lē dä bēbyä'nä), family of Italian artists of 17th and 18th cent. Founder, **Giovanni Maria Galli da Bibiena** (jōvän'nē), 1625–65, painted altarpieces for churches in Bologna. A son, **Ferdinando Galli Bibiena** (fĕrdēnän'dō), 1657–1743, most famous of family, was known throughout Europe for architectural views, theatrical designs, and decorations for court festivities. Rest of family noted also as decorative artists.

Bible [Gr.,= the books], name used by Christians for their Scriptures, for them a holy guide of faith and conduct. For composition and canon of the Bible, see

OLD TESTAMENT; NEW TESTAMENT; APOCRYPHA; PSEUDEPIGRAPHA; articles on individual books. Traditional Christian view is that the Bible was written under the guidance of God and is, therefore, all true, literally or under the veil of allegory. Interpretation of the Bible is one of the chief points of difference between Protestantism, which believes that individuals have the right to interpret the Bible for themselves, and Roman Catholicism, which teaches that individuals may read the Bible only in accord with interpretation of the Church. Among extant manuscripts of the Bible are the Codex Vaticanus (Greek, 4th cent.), at the Vatican; Codex Sinaiticus (Greek, 4th cent.) and Codex Alexandrinus (Greek, 5th cent.), at the British Mus.; and Codex Bezae (Greek and Latin, 6th cent.) at Cambridge, England. First great translation of the whole Bible into Latin was the Vulgate of St. Jerome. The Bible, with Latin text, was the first book to be printed on the press of Johann GUTENBERG. In England there were from Anglo-Saxon times vernacular versions of parts of the Bible, mostly the four Gospels and the Psalms. Great names in the history of the English Bible are: John Wyclif (d. 1384), whose name is borne by two translated versions; William Tyndale (d. 1536), whose New Testament (1525–26) was the first English translation to be printed; Miles Coverdale (d. 1569), who was responsible for the Great Bible (1539), the first to be issued by the crown (in the name of Henry VIII). Greatest of all English translations was the Authorized (AV) or King James Version (1611), made by a committee of churchmen led by Lancelot Andrewes. The Douay, or Rheims-Douay, Version was published by Roman Catholic scholars at Rheims (New Testament, 1582) and Douai, France (Old Testament, 1610), since extensively revised. In the 19th cent., the Authorized Version was revised from the original tongues by the Church of England and appeared as the English Revised Version and American Revised Version (both: RV). English translations begun in the 20th cent. include the Revised Standard Version (Protestant; pub. 1952) and the American Roman Catholic Confraternity of Christian Doctrine (New Testament pub. 1941). Translations have been important in the histories of other literature besides English (e.g., Luther's translation, which had much to do with shaping the modern German language).

Bible school, usual term for nondenominational institution giving daily vacation Bible study to children. First founded (1901) in New York city.

Bible societies, nonsectarian Protestant groups for printing and dissemination of Scriptures. Canstein Bible Society estab. 1710 in Germany. In England societies formed 1780 and 1804. In U.S., American Bible Society estab. 1816. Group called Gideons, International (estab. 1898) places Bibles in hotel rooms. In 1946 United Bible Societies united more than 20 national groups.

Biblical Antiquities, Book of: see PSEUDEPIGRAPHA.

bibliography. The listing of books is of ancient origin. Lists of clay tablets have been found at Nineveh. Library at Alexandria had subject lists of its books. Modern bibliography began with invention of printing. Efforts at universal bibliography resulted in Konrad von Gesner's *Bibliotheca universalis* in 1545. There are lists of publications of publishing houses (e.g., *Trade List Annual,* British *Reference Catalogue of Current Literature*); subject bibliographies (e.g., Sabin's *Dictionary of Books Relating to America*); lists of works of individual authors; monthly lists of books in English (*The Cumulative Book Index*); and many special bibliographies (e.g., *The Cambridge Bibliography of English Literature* and *Literary History of the United States*).

Bibliothèque nationale (bēblēōtĕk′ näsyônäl′), national library of France (with c.5,000,000 books), in Paris. Originated when early French kings made collections of writings. Building erected 1854–75 under direction

of Henri Labrouste; remodeling was done 1932–39.

Bibracte (bĭbrăk′tē), town in Gaul, cap. of the Aedui. Here Caesar defeated the Helvetii (58 B.C.). Autun was built not far away to replace it.

bicarbonate: see CARBONATE.

bicarbonate of soda: see SODA.

Bichat, Marie François (märē′ fräswä′ bēshä′), 1771–1802, French anatomist and physiologist. His study of tissues was basis of modern histology.

Bickerstaff, Isaac, pseudonym used by Jonathan Swift, and later by Richard Steele in the *Tatler.*

bicycle, two-wheeled vehicle propelled by pedals. Developed in Scotland c.1839 from earlier machines operated by thrust of rider's feet upon ground. By the 1880s developments included larger front wheel, hollow-steel frame, ball bearings, tangential metal spokes. Safety bicycle, with equal-sized wheels and sprocket chain drive, was first manufactured c.1885 in England; it displaced other models following introduction of pneumatic tire (c.1888). Later improvements include freewheel, coaster brake, and hand brake. Cycling fad in '80s and '90s stimulated road construction.

Biddeford (bĭd′ĭfŭrd), city (pop. 20,836), SW Maine, at Saco R. falls (water power) opposite Saco. Mfg. of textiles, textile machinery, lumber products.

Biddle, well-known family of Philadelphia. **James Biddle,** 1783–1848, U.S. naval officer, was commander of *Ontario* and took formal possession of Oregon country for U.S. in 1818. **Nicholas Biddle,** 1786–1844, as president of BANK OF THE UNITED STATES (1822–36), was a chief target of Jacksonians. **George Biddle,** 1885–, American painter, did notable frescoes in Dept. of Justice Building, Washington, D.C.

Biddle, John, 1615–62, founder of English Unitarianism. Persecuted for his *Twelve Arguments Drawn Out of Scripture* (c.1645) and *Two-fold Catechism* (1654).

Biedermeier (bē′dùrmīùr), a style of furniture and decorations originating in Germany in the early 19th cent.; named for a humorous character in verses by Ludwig Eichrodt. A simplified and less expensive form of French Empire, Directoire, and 18th-cent. English styles. Cabinets are severe in line and surface, while chairs and sofas have curved lines.

Biel (bēl) or **Bienne** (byĕn), town (pop. 48,401), Bern canton, W Switzerland, on L. of Biel. Watchmaking center. Museum has relics of lake dwellings found in **Lake of Biel,** at foot of Jura mts. Contains Isle of St. Pierre (now a peninsula), made famous because of association with J. J. Rousseau.

Biel-. For Russian names beginning thus, see BEL-.

Bielefeld (bē′lùfĕlt), city (pop. 153,111), North Rhine-Westphalia, NW Germany. Mfg. of linen, silk, glassware, sewing machines. Damaged in World War II.

Bien, Jules (bēn), 1826–1909, American map engraver, b. Germany. Engraved maps for many official publications.

Bienne, Switzerland: see BIEL.

biennial, plant normally living but two years. Produces leaves and roots first year, flowers and seeds second. Some ANNUAL and PERENNIAL plants behave as biennials, while certain biennials act as perennials. Canterbury bells, hollyhock, and foxglove are biennials.

Bienville, Jean Baptiste le Moyne, sieur de (zhä′ bätēst′ lù mwän′ syùr′ dù byēvēl′), 1680–1768, colonizer and governor of Louisiana for France, b. Canada. Aided colonizing plans of brother, sieur d'IBERVILLE. Founded Mobile in 1710 and New Orleans in 1718.

Bierce, Ambrose (Gwinett), 1842–1914?, American author, b. Ohio. After service in the Union army in the Civil War, he settled in San Francisco where he was a journalist (except for years of intense literary productivity in London, 1872–76) until 1896, becoming the literary arbiter of the West Coast. Later he was a Washington correspondent. He was a strong advocate of "pure" and correct (i.e., long-established) usages in English, and his own work is notable for its terse and brilliant vigor, whether in short stories (as in collections *Tales of Soldiers and Civilians*, 1891, and *Can Such Things Be?*, 1893), literary essays, or bitter satires (as in *Fantastic Fables*, 1899). Fascinated by the macabre, he wrote some of the finest of horror stories. In 1913 he went to Mexico, where he disappeared without trace.

Bierstadt, Albert (bēr'stät), 1830–1902, American painter of Western scenes, b. Germany.

Big Ben, bell in Parliament tower (Westminster Palace), London. Name also given huge tower clock.

Big Bend National Park: see NATIONAL PARKS AND MONUMENTS (table).

Big Bethel, locality near Fort Monroe, Va., scene of early battle of Civil War, June 10, 1861. E. W. Pierce led Union brigade against J. B. Magruder's Confederate encampment and was repulsed.

Big Black Mountain, 4,150 ft. high, E Ky., in Cumberlands near Lynch. State's highest peak.

Bigelow, John, 1817–1911, American author and diplomat. Noted for diplomatic service in France during Civil War, preventing her recognition of Confederacy. Author of life of Benjamin Franklin.

Biggs, E(dward) Power, 1906–, English-American organist. Through recitals, broadcasts, and recordings, he has done much to make great organ music familiar to the American public.

Biggs, Hermann Michael, 1859–1923, American physician, noted as public health administrator.

Big Hole Battlefield National Monument: see NATIONAL PARKS AND MONUMENTS (table).

Bighorn, river, 461 mi. long, formed at Riverton, W central Wyo., by confluence of Wind and Popo Agie rivers. Flows N between Absaroka Range and Bighorn Mts. into Mont., where it receives Little Bighorn R. and flows NE to Yellowstone R. MISSOURI RIVER BASIN PROJECT plans provide for Hardin and Boysen projects on Bighorn R. In Bighorn basin are Riverton project and SHOSHONE PROJECT.

bighorn or **Rocky Mountain sheep,** wild sheep (*Ovis canadensis*) of W North America, once plentiful. Grayish-brown, with whitish patch on hind quarters, it is a heavy animal, with curling horns on male, short spikes on female. Alaskan forms are Dall's or white sheep (*O. dalli*) and Stone's or black sheep.

Bighorn Mountains, range of Rocky Mts., c.120 mi. long, in N Wyo. and S Mont., E of Bighorn R. Rises to 13,165 ft. in Cloud Peak, Wyo.

Big Manitou Falls (măn'ĭtoo), 165 ft. high, NW Wis., in Black R. Highest falls in Wis.

Bignonia (bĭgnō'nēŭ), genus of woody vines, especially cross vine or trumpet flower (*Bignonia capreolata*), which has orange-red trumpet-shaped blossoms and compound leaves. Native to the S U.S., it is grown in greenhouses in the North and in milder areas out-of-doors.

Bigod, Hugh: see NORFOLK, HUGH BIGOD, 1ST EARL OF.

Bigot, François (bēgō'), d. after 1760, intendant of New France (1748–59), b. France. His corrupt administration paved way for English conquest.

Big Rapids, resort city (pop. 6,736), N Mich., at falls of Muskegon R. NE of Grand Rapids. Has large gas field and mfg. of machinery and tools.

Big River: see FORT GEORGE, river, Que.

Big Sandy, river rising in W Tenn., N of Lexington, and flowing c.65 mi. NNE to Kentucky Reservoir of Tennessee R.

Big Sandy River, formed by junction of Tug and Levisa forks at Louisa, Ky., and flowing 27 mi. N to the Ohio, forming part of Ky.–W.Va. line.

Big Sioux (soo), river rising in NE S. Dak. and flowing 420 mi. S to Missouri R. at Sioux City, Iowa.

Big Spring, city (pop. 17,286), W Texas, SW of Sweetwater; founded 1881. Spring, now dry, long known. Industrial center of oil and agr. area with rail shops and mfg. of cottonseed, food, and clay products.

Big Stone Gap, town (pop. 5,173), SW Va., near Ky. line. Mountain resort with coal mining and mfg. of dairy products. Southwest Virginia Mus. has regional

collections. Natl. Tunnel, which is c.900 ft. long, is to S.

Big Stone Lake, long narrow lake, W Minn. and NE S. Dak., once a S outlet of glacial L. AGASSIZ.

Bihar (bēhär'), state (70,368 sq. mi.; pop. 36,545,575), NE India; cap. Patna. Agr. area in N is drained by the Ganges. Chief crops are rice, maize, wheat, sugar cane, jute, and tobacco. Major source of India's mineral wealth (mica, copper, coal, iron). In 6th cent. B.C. Bihar was heart of Magadha empire and scene of early development of Buddhism and Jainism. Its history after 17th cent. is linked with that of Bengal.

Bihari (bēhär'ē), Indo-European language. See LANGUAGE (table).

Bijapur or **Bejapur** (both: bĭjä'poor), town (pop. 48,968) SE Bombay, India. Cap. of Deccan kingdom of Bijapur (1490–1686). Cotton ginning.

Bijns, Anna (bīns), c.1494–1575?, Flemish religious poet. Also wrote robust satires.

Bika, El: see LEBANON.

Bikaner: see RAJASTHAN.

Bikini (bēkē'nē), uninhabited atoll comprising 36 islets, central Pacific, one of the Marshall Isls. U.S. atom-bomb tests were made here in 1946.

Bilaspur (bēläs"poor), state (453 sq. mi.; pop. 127,566), NW India, in W Himalayas; cap. Bilaspur. Site of projected dam across Sutlej R.

Bilbao (bēlbä'ō), city (pop. 183,200), cap. of Vizcaya prov., N Spain, near Bay of Biscay. Chief city of Basque Provinces, second-largest port of Spain. Steel mills, shipyards. Iron mines near by.

Bildad, second and least consoling of Job's comforters. Job 8; 18; 25; 42.9.

Bilderdijk, Willem (bĭl'dùrdīk), 1756–1831, Dutch poet. In exile (1795–1806), he returned to the Netherlands under Louis Bonaparte (whom he tutored in Dutch). His poetry is uneven but at its best of a high order.

bile, alkaline fluid formed in liver. In man, stored in gall bladder (pear-shaped sac under liver), then passes through bile ducts into small intestine. Aids in emulsification, digestion, and absorption of fats and in carrying off bile pigments and other excretions. Obstruction of flow may result in digestive disturbances and JAUNDICE.

Bilhah (bĭl'hù), Rachel's maid, Jacob's concubine, mother of Dan and Naphtali. Gen. 29.29; 30.1–8; 35. 22,25; 46.25; 49.4; 1 Chron. 7.13.

Billaud-Varenne, Jean Nicolas (zhä' nēkōlä' bēyō'-värĕn'), 1756–1819, French revolutionist, member of Committee of Public Safety. Deported to French Guiana after Robespierre's fall; refused amnesty from Napoleon. Fled to Haiti 1816.

Billerica (bĭl'rĭkù), town (pop. 11,101), NE Mass., S of Lowell; settled 1637. Mfg. of woolen and asbestos products.

billiards, game played with tapered, leather-tipped stick (cue) and usually three ivory balls on oblong, cloth-covered slate table with raised and cushioned edges. In England table is 6 ft. by 12 ft. with six pockets; in U.S. table is 5 ft. by 10 ft., pocketless. Pool is played on a table with pockets (usually six), and with 15 balls and a cue ball. Variants of billiards were popular in France in 16th cent., similar game played earlier. Willie Hoppe considered world's greatest player.

Billings, John Shaw, 1838–1913, American surgeon and librarian. Medical inspector in Civil War. Began *Index Catalogue* and *Index Medicus.* Helped to create New York Public Library.

Billings, Josh, pseud. of Henry Wheeler Shaw, 1818–85, American author of humorous sketches in exaggerated New England and N.Y. rural dialect; also a popular lecturer.

Billings, William, 1746–1800, American composer, first American professional musician, b. Boston. He chiefly composed hymns and other church music.

Billings, city (pop. 31,834), S Mont., on Yellowstone R. Founded 1882 by Northern Pacific RR, it is a shipping center with oil and sugar refineries and meat processing. Served by Huntley irrigation project. Seat of Rocky Mountain Col. (interdenominational; coed.; formed 1947 by merger of Billings Polytechnic Inst. and Intermountain Union Col.).

Billingsgate, wharf and fish market district of central London, named for old city gate. Also name given coarse language used here and in similar districts.

Bill of Rights, 1689, in British history, a great instrument of the constitution. Accepted by William and Mary, it recognized results of struggle against Stuart kings. Gave inviolable civil and political rights to people and political supremacy to Parliament. Act of SETTLEMENT supplemented it 1701.

Bill of Rights, in U.S. history: see CONSTITUTION.

Billy the Kid, 1859–81, American outlaw, cattle rustler in N. Mex. Real name was William H. Bonney. Shot by a sheriff.

Biloxi (bĭlŭk'sē), city (pop. 37,425), SE Miss., on peninsula between Mississippi Sound and Biloxi Bay. First white settlement in lower Mississippi valley, estab. 1699 by French under IBERVILLE across bay at Old Biloxi (now Ocean Springs). Present city, founded 1719, was cap. of La. until 1722. Resort with fishing, boatbuilding, and seafood processing. Has several U.S. military installations. Near by is "Beauvoir," Jefferson Davis's last home, now state Confederate veterans' home. Ship Isl. is sandy bar off coast.

Biloxi Bay, arm of Mississippi Sound, c.17 mi. long, 1–3 mi. wide, SE Miss. Receives Biloxi R. Bridged from Biloxi to Ocean Springs.

bimetallism, monetary system in which gold and silver are used as a standard and coined at a fixed ratio (as 16 to 1, meaning that 16 oz. of silver = 1 oz. of gold). Bimetallism usual in Western countries until Britain adopted gold standard by acts of 1798 and 1816; new German Empire adopted it 1873. In U.S. political battle on question strong from Civil War to 1910. Gold standard triumphed in most countries, but was dropped in many in 1930s.

Biminis (bĭ'mĭnēz), island group, part of Bahama Isls. Good fishing in near-by waters.

Binet, Alfred (älfrĕd' bēnā'), 1857–1911, French psychologist. With Théodore Simon, he devised (1905–11) tests for human intelligence, revised by others and widely used.

Bingen (bĭng'ùn), city (pop. 16,727), Rhineland-Palatinate, W Germany, on the Rhine. Center of famous wine district. Fortified by Romans 1st cent. B.C. Member of Hanseatic League from 1254. Near by, on rock in the Rhine, is the Mäuseturm, where according to legend Archbishop Hatto of Mainz was devoured by mice for his evil deeds.

Bingham, George Caleb, 1811–79, American genre painter. Active in Missouri politics.

Bingham, Hiram, 1789–1869, American Congregational missionary, b. Vt. Went (1819) to Hawaiian Isls. Developed writing from Hawaiian language. His son, **Hiram Bingham,** 1831–1908, b. Honolulu, was missionary (1857–64) in Gilbert Isls. His son, **Hiram Bingham,** 1875–, became an archaeologist and statesman. U.S. Senator from Conn. 1925–33. Discovered "lost" Inca cities of Vitcos and Machu Picchu.

Bingham Canyon or **Bingham,** mining town (pop. 2,569; alt. 6,100 ft.), N central Utah, SW of Salt Lake City. A Mormon farm (1848) became boom town (gold, silver, lead) in 1860s. Open-pit copper mine is an attraction for tourists.

Binghamton, industrial city (pop. 80,674), S N.Y., at junction of Chenango and Susquehanna rivers; laid out 1800. Largest of the Triple Cities (others are Endicott and Johnson City), which are famous for shoes. Also has mfg. of books, metal products, and textiles.

Binyon, Laurence, 1869–1943, English poet and authority on Oriental art.

Bío-Bío (bē'ō-bē'ō), river, c.240 mi. long, rising in Andes of central Chile and flowing NW to Pacific.

biochemistry, science concerned with chemical processes in living organisms and with their organic products, also called biological or physiological chemistry.

Includes studies of photosynthesis, metabolism, digestion, absorption, biological oxidation. Deals also with chemistry of proteins, carbohydrates, fats, vitamins, hormones, enzymes, blood.

biology, science of living things. Broadly divided into BOTANY and ZOOLOGY, it includes plant and animal cytology (cell study), histology (tissue study), anatomy or morphology, physiology, embryology, ecology, genetics, evolution, paleontology, and systematics. Microbiology is the scientific study of microscopic forms of life, including protozoa, bacteria, algae, fungi, and viruses.

Bion (bī'ŭn), fl. 2d cent.? B.C., Greek bucolic poet, an imitator of Theocritus.

biophysics: see PHYSICS.

Birch, Reginald (Bathurst), 1856–1943, American illustrator of children's books, notably *Little Lord Fauntleroy.*

birch, deciduous tree or shrub of genus *Betula,* widely found in N Hemisphere. Paper or canoe birch (*Betula papyrifera*) and gray birch (*B. populifolia*) are native American trees with white bark. Yellow birch (*B. lutea*) important for timber in NE U.S. Others yield oil of wintergreen, birch beer extract.

Bird, Robert Montgomery, 1806–54, American romantic playwright and novelist. His verse plays for Edwin Forrest (including *The Gladiator* and *The Broker of Bogota*) won a success halted by a quarrel with Forrest. Bird turned to prose romances. Notable are two novels with a Mexico scene (*Calavar,* 1834; *The Infidel,* 1835) and two laid in the U.S. (*The Hawks of Hawk-Hollow,* 1835; *Nick of the Woods,* 1837, which was a tremendous popular success).

Bird, William: see BYRD, WILLIAM (b. 1542 or 1543).

bird, warm-blooded, egg-laying, vertebrate animal covered with FEATHERS, forelimbs modified into WINGS. Four-chambered heart like mammals; body temperature 2° to 14° higher; relatively large brain; keen sight; acute hearing; little sense of smell; believed evolved from reptiles. Adapted for FLIGHT–body weight reduced by horny bill instead of jaws and air sacs in hollow bones; heavy parts located for balanced flight. Feathers renewed in MOLTING; males more vividly colored, aggressor in courtship, superior singer. Most birds build NEST for eggs. Birds valued for insect, weed seed destruction; many scavenge. Bills adapted to food habits. See also MIGRATION OF ANIMALS. See *ill.,* p. 105.

bird of paradise, any of several birds of New Guinea and adjacent islands. Male has bright plumage, elongated tail feathers, ruffs on wings and neck.

bird sanctuary: see WILDLIFE REFUGE.

Bird Woman: see SACAJAWEA.

Birkbeck, Morris, 1764–1825, English pioneer in U.S. Undertook, with George Flower, scheme to create a settlement in Ill. which led to founding of Albion.

Birkeland, Olaf Christian (ō'läv krĭs'tyän bēr'kŭlän), 1867–1917, Norwegian physicist. Developed (with Samuel Eyde) electric-arc process for nitrogen fixation; worked on magnetics.

Birkenhead, county borough (pop. 142,392), Cheshire, England; port opposite Liverpool at mouth of the Mersey. Has grain milling, steel mfg., and shipbuilding. Heavily bombed 1941.

Birkhoff, George David (bûrk'hôf), 1884–1944, American mathematician. Research in dynamics and relativity; conceptual theory of atomic structure.

Birmingham (bûr'mĭng-ùm), second largest English city (pop. 1,112,340), Warwickshire; a great industrial center. Covers 80 sq. mi. Has iron and coal near by and is noted for metal mfg. Most of Britain's brass and bronze coins minted here. Utilities and a bank are city owned. Has noted city orchestra. Site of Anglican and Roman Catholic cathedrals and Univ. of Birmingham. Heavily bombed World War II.

Birmingham. 1 City (pop. 326,037), N central Ala., near S tip of Appalachian system; founded 1871. Largest city in state, leading iron and steel center of

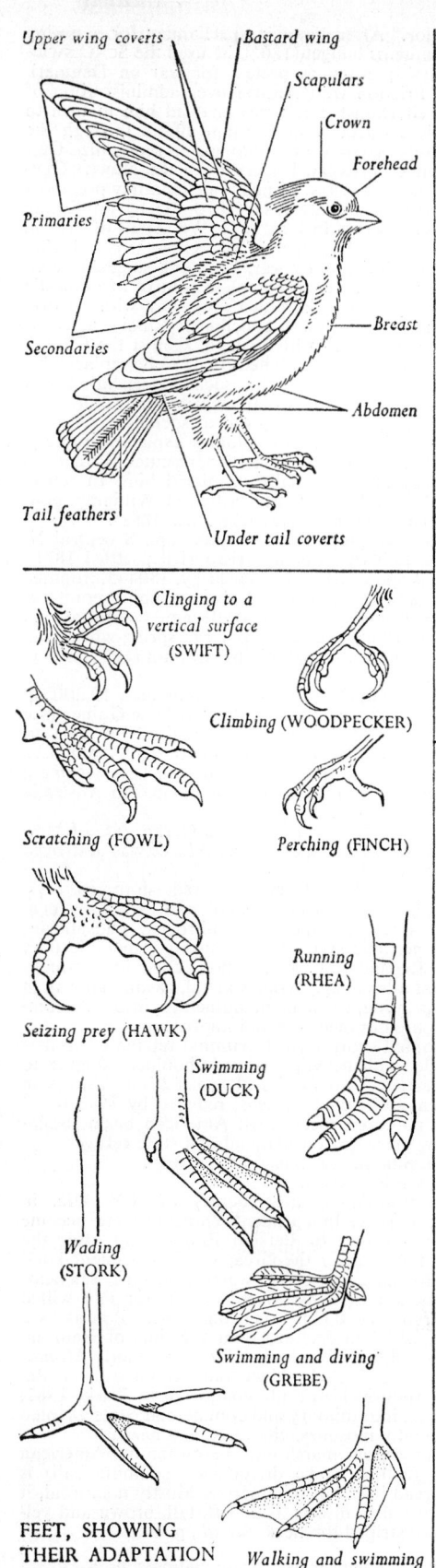

Upper wing coverts

Bastard wing

Scapulars

Crown

Forehead

Primaries

Secondaries

Breast

Abdomen

Tail feathers

Under tail coverts

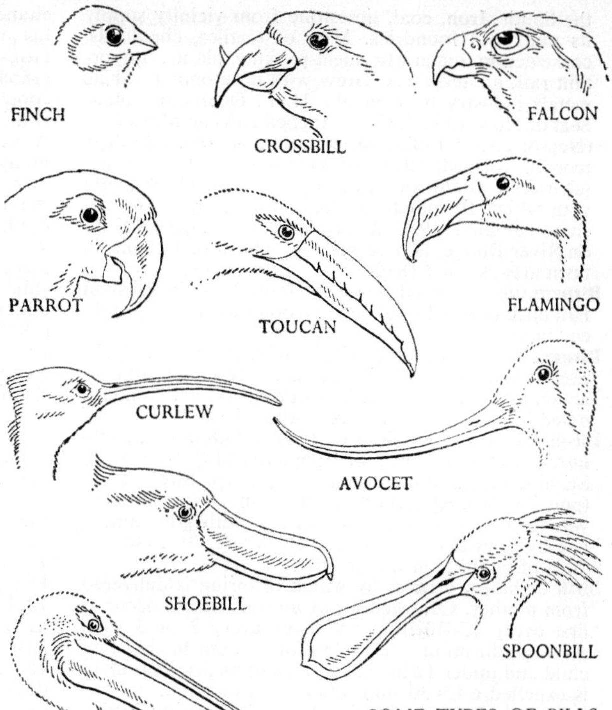

FINCH

CROSSBILL

FALCON

PARROT

TOUCAN

FLAMINGO

CURLEW

AVOCET

SHOEBILL

SPOONBILL

PELICAN

SOME TYPES OF BILLS

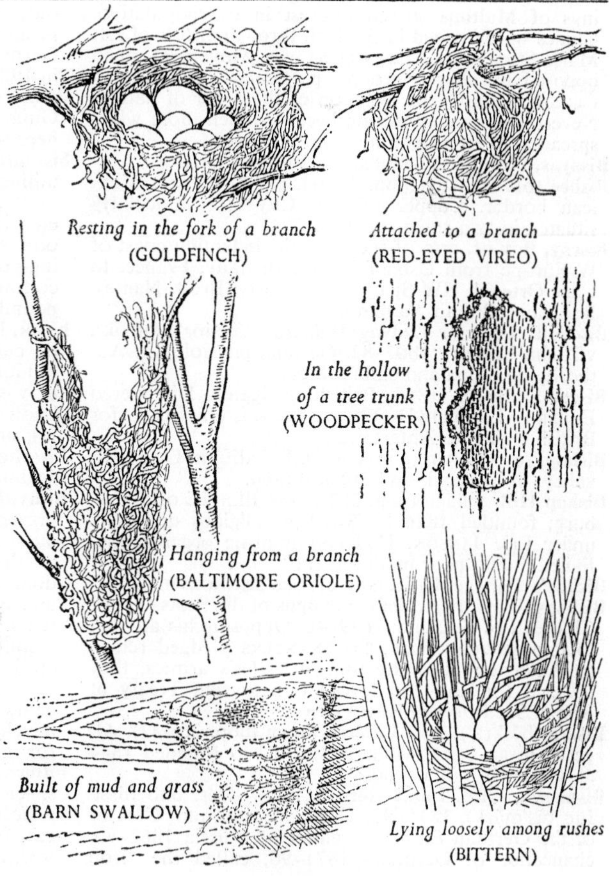

Clinging to a vertical surface (SWIFT)

Climbing (WOODPECKER)

Scratching (FOWL)

Perching (FINCH)

Seizing prey (HAWK)

Running (RHEA)

Swimming (DUCK)

Wading (STORK)

Swimming and diving (GREBE)

Walking and swimming (PELICAN)

FEET, SHOWING THEIR ADAPTATION TO BIRDS' HABITS

Resting in the fork of a branch (GOLDFINCH)

Attached to a branch (RED-EYED VIREO)

In the hollow of a tree trunk (WOODPECKER)

Hanging from a branch (BALTIMORE ORIOLE)

Built of mud and grass (BARN SWALLOW)

Lying loosely among rushes (BITTERN)

SOME TYPES OF NESTS

the South. Iron, coal, limestone from vicinity supply its mills and foundries. Mfg. of textiles, chemicals, construction materials; meat-packing plants. Important rail, air terminus. Grew with development of its metals industry by men like H. F. DE BARDELEBEN. Seat of Howard Col. (Baptist; coed.; 1841); Miles Col. (Negro; coed.; 1907); **Birmingham–Southern College** (coed.), formed 1918 by merging Southern Univ. (chartered 1856) and Birmingham Col. (1898), and with which Birmingham Conservatory of Music became affiliated, 1940. **2** City (pop. 15,467), SE Mich., on River Rouge, NW residential suburb of Detroit, in farm area; settled 1819.

Birnam, village, Perthshire, Scotland. Near by Birnam Hill once covered by Birnam Wood of witches' prophecy in *Macbeth*.

Birney, James Gillespie, 1792–1857, American abolitionist. Edited the *Philanthropist*. Advocated political action and was leader in LIBERTY PARTY, which nominated him for presidency in 1840 and 1844.

Birobidzhan (bē″rŭbējän′) or **Jewish Autonomous Oblast,** district (13,820 sq. mi.; pop. 108,419), RSFSR, in SE Siberia, on Manchurian border; cap. Birobidzhan (pop. 29,654). Agr., timber, gold, iron. *Oblast* [district] was formed 1934 for colonization, with government aid, by Jews from Russia and elsewhere. By 1948 25–50% of population was Jewish.

birth or **labor,** process by which offspring is delivered from mother. Contractions of uterine muscle occur at first every 15–30 min. and later every 2 or 3 min. Average duration is c.18 hr. for woman having first child and under 12 hr. in subsequent births. PLACENTA is expelled c.15–30 min. after birth of child.

birth control, methods of voluntarily limiting births. Limitation of sexual intercourse and mechanical and chemical contraceptives are included. Organized birth-control movement began in England where the writings of Malthus stirred interest in overpopulation. Clinics were opened in the U.S. through efforts of Dr. Marie Stopes and Margaret Sanger. Movement much opposed by church groups, particularly the Roman Catholic Church, as violation of the order of nature. Nevertheless contraception became much more widespread in Western countries in 20th cent.

Bisayas, Philippine Islands: see VISAYAN ISLANDS.

Bisbee (biz′bē), city (pop. 3,801), SE Ariz., near Mexican border. Copper mining. City is spectacularly situated in two steep canyons.

Biscay, Bay of, arm of the Atlantic, indenting coast of W Europe from Ushant isl., off Brittany, France, to Cape Ortegal, NW Spain. Chief ports: Brest, Nantes, Bordeaux, Bilbao, Santander.

Bischoff, Theodor Ludwig Wilhelm (tä′ōdōr lōōt′vĭkh vĭl′hĕlm bĭ′shôf), 1807–82, German physiologist. Authority on blood and embryology.

Biscoe, John, d. 1848, British navigator. Discovered ENDERBY LAND (1831–32); voyage was chief basis for British claims to Antarctica.

Bishop, resort town (pop. 2,891), E Calif., in Owens R. valley, in livestock and mineral area.

Bishop Hill, village (pop. 202), NW Ill., NE of Galesburg; founded 1846 by Swedish religious dissenters under Eric JANSON. Had communistic organization. Failed due to poor management.

Bishop's College, University of: see LENNOXVILLE.

Bishops' Wars, two brief campaigns of the Scots against Charles I of England, 1639–40. Opposing his attempt to impose episcopacy, COVENANTERS pledged return to Presbyterianism. Resisting Charles's armies, they invaded England and forced him to sign Treaty of Ripon. See PURITAN REVOLUTION.

Biskra (bēskrä′), anc. *Vescera,* town (pop. 36,347), Algeria, in an oasis. Modern Biskra was founded 1844 as a French military post.

Bismarck, Otto, Fürst von (biz′märk, Ger. ô′tō fürst′ fün bĭs′märk), 1815–98, German statesman. Creator of the German Empire; premier of Prussia 1862–90; chancellor of Germany 1871–90; called the "iron

chancellor." After dissolving parliament for opposing his armaments budget (1862), he used the SCHLESWIG-HOLSTEIN question as pretext for war on Denmark (1864). Friction with Austria over administration of conquered Danish territories enabled him in turn to eliminate Austria from German affairs through the AUSTRO-PRUSSIAN WAR (1866) and to reorganize Germany under Prussian leadership in the NORTH GERMAN CONFEDERATION. Bismarck deliberately provoked the FRANCO-PRUSSIAN WAR (1870–71) by publishing the EMS DISPATCH. In Jan., 1871, WILLIAM I of Prussia was proclaimed emperor of GERMANY. Having achieved unification by war, Bismarck sought to consolidate it by peace. In complete control of domestic and foreign policy, he allied Germany with Austria (1879) and Italy (1882), conciliated Russia, acted as arbiter of Europe. In his struggle against the Church (see KULTURKAMPF) he failed. In 1883 he replaced his stringent but unsuccessful antisocialist legislation with a series of pioneering social security and labor laws, designed to weaken the appeal of socialism. German commerce, industry, and colonies expanded rapidly. WILLIAM II, who acceded in 1888, resented Bismarck's supremacy and eventually dismissed him. In retirement, Bismarck vigorously criticized William's policies. Wrote reminiscences (Eng. tr., 1898).

Bismarck, city (pop. 18,640), state cap., S central N. Dak., on hills overlooking Missouri R.; settled 1871–72. Lewis and Clark camped near by, 1804–5. Boomed as river and rail center and also as supply point for Black Hills gold mines (1874). Became territorial cap. 1883. Distributing center for large spring-wheat and dairying area, with coal mining. Capitol (1932) is skyscraper.

Bismarck Archipelago, volcanic group, area 19,200 sq. mi., SW Pacific, part of Territory of New Guinea (see NEW GUINEA, TERRITORY OF). Includes NEW BRITAIN (largest island), NEW IRELAND, Lavongai, ADMIRALTY ISLANDS, Duke of York Isls., and Vitu Isls. Became a German protectorate in 1884, mandated to Australia in 1920.

Bismarck Sea, SW arm of Pacific Ocean, NE of New Guinea. In 1943 a Japanese naval force was destroyed here by U.S. aircraft.

bismuth (biz′mŭth), silvery-white, reddish-tinged, crystalline, brittle element (symbol = Bi; see also ELEMENT, table). Grouped with nitrogen, phosphorus, etc., in periodic system; more strongly metallic than others. Expands on solidification. Used in low-melting-point alloys (e.g., Wood's metal, casting alloys), in cotton printing, cosmetic manufacture; insoluble compounds used in medicine and fluoroscopy.

bison, hoofed short-horned mammal related to domestic cattle, with heavily mantled shoulders sloping to hindquarters. Two species of genus *Bison*: European or wisent (miscalled aurochs; reduced by 1948 to 97 known purebred specimens); American bison (buffalo), now protected on national and state refuges.

Bisschop, Simon: see EPISCOPIUS, SIMON.

Bisutun: see BEHISTUN.

Bithynia (bĭthĭ′nĕù), anc. country of NW Asia, in present Turkey. Independent Thracian state became autonomous part of Persian Empire and after the death of Alexander the Great was independent kingdom (3d–1st cent. B.C.), warring against Seleucids and others until King Nicomedus III (or IV) willed it to Rome (74 B.C.). Long joined with Pontus as a colony, Bithynia declined after the time of Hadrian.

Bitolj (bē′tôlyù), Macedonian *Bitola,* formerly *Monastir,* city (pop. 31,131), Macedonia, S Yugoslavia. Became bishopric 11th cent.; conquered by Turks 1382; developed into military and commercial center. Noted for its many mosques, churches, and bazaar.

bittern, migratory marsh bird, heron family. American species (called "stake driver" for booming call) is widespread in E North America. Mostly nocturnal, it eats frogs, fish, insects. Is 2–3 ft. tall, brown and yellow, with striped foreneck. See *ill.,* p. 105.

SMALL CAPITALS = cross references. Pronunciation key on inside end pages. Abbreviations: p. 2.

bitterroot, low perennial (*Lewisia rediviva*), native to W North America. Its large pink or white blossom is Montana state flower. Rock garden plant.

Bitterroot Range, part of Rocky Mts., on Idaho-Mont. line, running NW-SE. Highest peak is Mt. Garfield (10,961 ft.) in range's SE spur, Beaverhead Mts.

bitters, spirituous liquor (to 40% alcohol) containing bitter principles, e.g., angostura bark; used as flavoring (as in cocktails), and as appetizers and digestives.

bittersweet, name for two vines: *Celastrus scandens,* native to North America, which bears clusters of orange-red fruits; and bitter or woody nightshade (*Solanum dulcamara*), a native of the Old World, which has scarlet berries.

Bitzius, Albert: see GOTTHELF, JEREMIAS.

Biwa (bē'wä), lake, c.40 mi. long, 2–12 mi. wide, largest in Japan, in S Honshu.

Bizerta (bizûr'tù), Fr. *Bizerte,* city (pop. 39,327), Tunisia. Its port and naval base are on the Mediterranean and on the lagoon Lake of Bizerte (42 sq. mi.). Anciently a colony of Tyre, it was successively held by the Romans, Vandals, Arabs, Moors, Spaniards, and Barbary pirates. In 1881 occupied by the French who improved and fortified the harbor. A German base in World War II, it was heavily damaged by bombs in 1943 by the Allies.

Bizet, Georges (zhôrzh' bēzā'), 1838–75, French composer. His opera, *Carmen* (based on a story by Mérimée), became immensely popular though not successful when first performed. He also composed other operas: *Les Pêcheurs de perles* and *La Jolie Fille de Perth.* Among non-operatic compositions are suites for Daudet's *Arlesienne,* a Symphony in C.

Bjerknes, Vilhelm Friman Koren (byĕrk'nĕs), 1862–1951, Norwegian physicist. His work in meteorology and on electric waves helped develop wireless telegraphy. Evolved polar-front theory of cyclones with his son, **Jakob Aall Bonnevie Bjerknes** (ôl' bô'nùvē), 1897–, U.S. citizen in 1946. Professor of meteorology, Univ. of California (1940–).

Bjornson, Bjornstjerne (byûrn'styĕrnù byûrn'sōn), Nor. *Bjørnstjerne Bjørnson,* 1832–1910, Norwegian writer. His dramas, novels (many of peasant life), and epic poetry won him repute as foremost Norwegian poet and novelist, second as dramatist only to Ibsen. Among his novels are *Arne* (1859) and *The Fisher Girl* (1868). Among his dramas are *Sigurd Slembe* (1862) and *The Bankrupt* (1875). Awarded 1903 Nobel Prize in Literature.

Black, Greene Vardiman, 1836–1915, American dentist, noted as teacher, author, and originator of methods and instruments.

Black, Hugo LaFayette, 1886–, Associate Justice of U.S. Supreme Court (1937–).

Black, Jeremiah Sullivan, 1810–83, U.S. Attorney General (1857–60) and U.S. Secretary of State (1860–61). Persuaded Pres. Buchanan to send supplies to Fort Sumter.

Black, Joseph, 1728–99, Scottish chemist, physician. Discovered carbon dioxide, studied latent heat. Taught medicine at Glasgow (1756–66) and Edinburgh (from 1766).

black Angus: see CATTLE.

Blackbeard, d. 1718, English pirate whose real name was probably Edward Teach or Thatch. Probably originally a privateer, preyed on West Indies and Atlantic coast 1716–18. Killed by British.

Black Belt, term loosely applied to belt across central S.C. and Ga., and also to black-soil areas in Ala., Miss., and other states.

blackberry, thorny plant (*Rubus*) with juicy, black fruits, eaten raw or used in jams or preserves.

blackbird, in North America a perching bird allied to bobolink, meadow lark, grackle, oriole. Red-winged blackbird common in E U.S.; yellow-headed, tricolored red-winged, Brewer's blackbird known to West; rusty blackbird winters in U.S. European blackbird is a thrush.

Blackburn, Joseph, b. c.1700, d. after 1765, American artist. Painted portraits of members of distinguished New England families.

Blackburn, county borough (pop. 111,217), Lancashire, England; a cotton-weaving center. James Hargreaves invented the spinning jenny here (1764).

Black Canyon of the Gunnison National Monument: see NATIONAL PARKS AND MONUMENTS (table).

black codes: see RECONSTRUCTION.

Black Country, highly industrialized region, mostly in Staffordshire, but also in Worcestershire and Warwickshire, England. Produces coal, iron, and steel. Birmingham is the principal city.

Black Death: see PLAGUE.

Blackett, Patrick Maynard Stuart (blă'kĭt), 1897–, English physicist. Won 1948 Nobel Prize for work in improving and extending use of Wilson cloud chamber and for discoveries concerning cosmic rays.

black-eyed Susan, North American wild herb (*Rudbeckia hirta*), having yellow daisylike blossoms with dark brown centers. Maryland state flower.

Blackfeet Indians: see BLACKFOOT INDIANS.

black fly, small vicious-biting fly with gauzy wings, short legs, humped back. Most attach eggs to underwater plants or rocks; larvae live in flowing water; adult emerges from water in air bubble.

Blackfoot, city (pop. 5,180), SE Idaho, N of Pocatello, between Blackfoot R. and Snake R. near their confluence; founded 1878. Irrigated area produces sugar beets, dairy products, and grain.

Blackfoot Indians, tribes formerly around upper Missouri and Saskatchewan rivers and W to the Rockies, of Algonquian linguistic stock. Three main branches (Siksika or Blackfoot proper, Piegan, and Blood) were united only by sense of being one people. Allied with Gros Ventre and Sarsi Indians, hostile to other groups and whites. They gained wealth from fur trade, but their nomadic Plains culture was destroyed with disappearance of buffalo. Elaborate rituals include the sun dance and the vision quest. Also called Blackfeet.

Black Forest, Ger. *Schwarzwald,* mountain range in S Baden and Württemberg, SW Germany. Covered by dark pine forests; rises to 4,903 ft. in Feldberg. Chief resorts: Baden-Baden and Wildbad. Clock and toy industries.

Black Friday. In 1868 a small group of American financial speculators, including Jay GOULD and James FISK, sought support of Federal officials in drive to corner gold market. Attempt failed when government gold was released for sale. Drive culminated in day of panic when thousands were ruined—Friday, Sept. 24, 1869, popularly called Black Friday.

black gum, sour gum, or **pepperidge,** ornamental tree (*Nyssa sylvatica*), of E North America. In autumn the foliage is bright red. This and other *Nyssa* species are also called tupelo.

Black Hand, name and symbol used by criminal or terrorist groups. Flourished in Sicily in late 19th cent.; carried to U.S. See also CAMORRA.

black haw, a VIBURNUM (*Viburnum prunifolium*), native to E North America. Bluish-black, edible berries.

Black Hawk War. 1 Conflict between Sac and Fox Indians and U.S. in 1832. Treaty imposed on Indians in 1831 compelled removal from Ill. Return in April, 1832, of an Indian group under Black Hawk (1767–1838) resulted in armed conflict; most of Black Hawk's party destroyed by force under command of Henry Atkinson. **2** Conflict between Indians and whites in Utah 1865–68. Treaty signers in 1868 included Black Hawk (d. 1870), Ute chief.

Black Hills, mountains, SW S.Dak. and NE Wyo. They cover c.6,000 sq. mi. between Belle Fourche R. and Cheyenne R., rising amid semiarid plains to altitudes of 5,000 ft. and over. Forests of yellow pine, black from a distance, gave hills their name. Preserved features include Wind Cave, Jewel Cave, Fossil Cycad, and Mt. Rushmore. White settlement and mining were vigorous after 1874 gold discovery. Found here also are silver, tungsten, mica, coal, and oil. Harney Peak (7,242 ft.) is the highest point.

Black Hole of Calcutta: see CALCUTTA.

Blackmore, Richard Doddridge, 1825–1900, English novelist, author of *Lorna Doone* (1869).

Black Mountain, resort town (pop. 1,174), W N.C., in Blue Ridge E of Asheville. Near by are Y.M.C.A. and Presbyterian assembly areas and **Black Mountain College** (nonsectarian; coed.; 1933), experimental school, integrating college-community life with student needs. Students are self-responsible.

Black Mountains, part of Appalachian system, W N.C., rising to 6,684 ft. in Mt. MITCHELL.

Blackmur, R(ichard) P., 1904–, American critic and poet. His critical writings include *The Double Agent* (1935) and *Language as Gesture* (1952).

Blackpool, county borough (pop. 147,131), Lancashire, England; resort on the Irish Sea.

Black Prince: see EDWARD THE BLACK PRINCE.

Black River. 1 Tributary of White R. (Ark.), rising in SE Mo. and flowing c.300 mi. SW to White R. near Newport, Ark. Partly navigable. Clearwater Dam (flood control) completed 1948. **2** River, NE La., formed after Tensas R. joins Ouachita R. Flows 57 mi. into Red R. **3** River, N N.Y., rising in the Adirondacks and flowing c.120 mi. SW, NNW, and WSW to an inlet of L. Ontario W of Watertown. Falls provide power (esp. for paper mills).

Blacksburg, town (pop. 3,358), SW Va., W of Roanoke. Seat of Virginia Polytechnic Inst. (land-grant and state supported; coed.; opened 1872; woman's division at Radford consolidated with V.P.I. in 1944). Mountain Lake, a resort village, is near.

Black Sea, anc. *Pontus Euxinus,* inland sea (c.160,000 sq. mi.; max. depth c.7,360 ft.), connected with Mediterranean by Bosporus, Sea of Marmara, and DARDANELLES. Enclosed by Bulgaria, Rumania, USSR, Turkey. Chief ports: Odessa, Batum, Constanta. Receives Danube, Dnieper, Don rivers. The Sea of Azov is one of its arms.

black snake, nonpoisonous snake of E U.S. Adults dull black, 5–6 ft. long. Seizes prey (small animals) in mouth, pressing it to ground to kill. Pilot black snake of NE U.S. has shiny black scales.

Blackstone, Sir William, 1723–80, English jurist. His *Commentaries on the Law of England* (1765–69) influential in England and the U.S.; long used as authority.

Blackstone, river rising in central Mass. and flowing c.50 mi. SSE, past Worcester, Mass., Woonsocket and Pawtucket, R.I. (below which it is now called Seekonk R.), to Providence R. at Providence.

blackthorn or **sloe,** thorny plum tree (*Prunus spinosa*), of Europe, Asia, N. Africa. Blue fruits used in brandy, sloe gin. Limbs used for canes in Ireland.

Black Tom, part of Jersey City, N.J., called also Black Tom Isl. Here, in Aug., 1916, German saboteurs demolished a munitions plant.

Black Warrior, navigable river, W Ala., formed by forks W of Birmingham and flowing 178 mi. SW to Tombigbee R. at Demopolis.

Black Watch or **Royal Highlanders,** Scottish infantry regiment. Name comes from their dark kilts. Formed 1735 to watch Scottish rebels and keep peace.

Blackwell, Elizabeth, 1821–1910, American physician, b. England; first woman in U.S. to be granted medical degree (1849). Helped to found (1857) New York Infirmary and Col. for Women, first nurses' school in U.S., and London School of Medicine for Women. Her brother, **Henry Brown Blackwell,** 1825–1909, was an abolitionist and, with his wife, Lucy STONE, worked for woman suffrage. Their daughter, **Alice Stone Blackwell,** 1857–1950, edited (1881–1917) the *Woman's Journal,* suffrage organ. **Antoinette Louisa (Brown) Blackwell,** 1825–1921, sister-in-law of Elizabeth Blackwell and H. B. Blackwell, was a Unitarian minister and a worker for woman suffrage.

Blackwell, city (pop. 9,199), N Okla., NE of Enid, in

wheat and oil area. Has oil refineries, zinc smelters, and glass plants.

bladder, urinary, muscular sac in pelvis. Urine secreted by kidneys enters bladder by two tubes (ureters) and is conveyed out of body by another tube (urethra).

bladderwort, carnivorous aquatic or bog plant (*Utricularia* and related genera), equipped with small bladderlike organs to trap minute animal life.

Bladensburg, town (pop. 2,899), W central Md., on Anacostia R., near Washington, D.C. Here British defeated Americans (Aug. 24, 1814) before entering Washington. Stephen Decatur was mortally wounded in duel here.

Blaeu, Willem Janszoon (vĭ'lùm yän'sōn blou'), 1571–1638, Dutch cartographer, printer. Founded unusually fine printing establishment in Amsterdam.

Blagoveshchensk (blŭgùvyĕsh'chĭnsk), city (pop. 58,-761), RSFSR, in extreme E Siberia, on Amur R. and on spur of Trans-Siberian RR. Agr. center.

Blaine, James G(illespie), 1830–93, American politician. U.S. Representative from Maine (1863–76); speaker of House (1869–75). U.S. Senator (1876–81). U.S. Secretary of State (1881, 1889–92). First called "plumed knight" in 1876 Republican convention, where improper influence he had used in case of a railroad in Ark. prevented his nomination. Nominated in 1884, he was largely defeated for President by "rum, Romanism, and rebellion" epithet used to characterize Democrats by New York minister supporting him. As Secretary of State, he fostered closer U.S.-Latin American relations, brought about first Pan American Congress (see PAN-AMERICANISM).

Blaine, tourist city (pop. 1,693), NW Wash. Site of Peace Arch on Canadian border.

Blair, Francis Preston, 1791–1876, American journalist and politician. Founder (1830) of Washington *Globe.* A leader in KITCHEN CABINET. Helped found Republican party; adviser to Pres. Lincoln. Blair House, his Washington residence, is now government property. His son, **Francis Preston Blair,** 1821–75, was a political leader in Mo. and a Union general in Civil War. His regiment of "Wide Awakes" helped keep Mo. loyal to Union. Served with distinction in Vicksburg, Chattanooga, and Atlanta campaigns. U.S. Senator (1871–73). An older brother, **Montgomery Blair,** 1813–83, was U.S. Postmaster General (1861–64). As first U.S. solicitor in Court of Claims (1855–57) he was counsel for Scott in Dred Scott Case.

Blair, James, 1656–1743, Church of England clergyman in Va., b. Scotland, founder (1693) of College of William and Mary.

Blair, Montgomery: see BLAIR, FRANCIS PRESTON.

Blairsville, borough (pop. 5,000), SW Pa., on Conemaugh R. and E of Pittsburgh, in coal and clay area.

Blake, Robert, 1599–1657, English admiral. Without naval training, had brilliant career after 1649. Estab. British power in Mediterranean 1654. Helped develop Commonwealth Navy.

Blake, William, 1757–1827, English artist and poet. An engraver, he (with the assistance of his wife, Catherine Boucher) engraved powerful illustrations for editions of various authors (Edward Young, Cowper, Dante, Thomas Gray, the book of Job) and for all his own volumes of poetry except *Poetical Sketches* (1783). His poems show the same fusing of metaphysical vision and strong, simple lines as his engravings. *Songs of Innocence* (1789) and *Songs of Experience* (1794) have many haunting and familiar short poems (e.g., "Piping down the Valleys Wild," "The Tiger"). Except for lyric bits, the "Prophetic Books" (*The Book of Thel,* 1789; *America,* 1793; *The Book of Urizen,* 1794; *The Book of Los,* 1795; *Milton,* 1804; *Jerusalem,* 1804) are less familiar to ordinary readers; in them he developed his own mythology and religion.

Blakelock, Ralph Albert, 1847–1919, American landscape painter, known for melancholy effects.

Blakely, residential borough (pop. 6,828), NE Pa., near Scranton.

Blakeslee, Albert Francis, 1874–, American botanist. Discovered sexual reproduction in bread molds. Work on inheritance and geographic distribution of Jimson weed (*Datura*) yielded information on chromosome action, genic balance, evolution. Used colchicine, an alkaloid, to produce polyploid plants.

Blanc, Louis (lwĕ′ blä′), 1811–82, French socialist. His *Organisation du travail* (1840) outlined social order based on principle, "From each according to his abilities, to each according to his needs." Leader in the revolution of 1848, he was disappointed when his plan for social workshops was sabotaged; fomented unsuccessful workers' uprising; fled to England, staying until 1871.

Blanc, Mont: see MONT BLANC.

Blanca Peak: see SANGRE DE CRISTO MOUNTAINS.

Blanchard, Jean Pierre (zhä′ pyĕr′ bläshär′), or **François Blanchard** (fräswä′), 1753–1809, French balloonist. Reputed inventor of parachute (1785). With Dr. John Jeffries, he made (1785) first English Channel crossing by air.

Blanche of Castile (kăstēl′), 1185?–1252, queen of Louis VIII of France, regent during minority of her son Louis IX and after his departure on Crusade (1248). Capable and authoritarian.

Blanco Fombona, Rufino (rōͦfē′nō bläng′kō fōmbō′nä), 1874–1944, Venezuelan poet, essayist, novelist, a leader of *modernismo,* active in political affairs.

Bland-Allison Act, 1878, passed by U.S. Congress to provide for freer coinage of silver. Original bill offered by Rep. Richard P. Bland met Western demands for free, unlimited coinage of silver. Sen. William B. Allison offered amended version. Act required U.S. treasury to purchase $2,000,000–$4,000,000 worth of silver bullion each month at market prices for coinage into silver dollars, which were made legal tender for all debts. Neither free-silver nor gold-standard forces were satisfied, but act remained law until passage of SHERMAN SILVER PURCHASE ACT of 1890.

Blanding, town (pop. 1,177), SE Utah, N of San Juan R. Natural Bridges and Hovenweep national monuments are near.

Blane, Sir Gilbert, 1749–1834, Scottish physician, known for introducing lime juice to prevent scurvy and advancing sanitary measures in British navy.

blank verse: see PENTAMETER.

Blanqui, Louis Auguste (lwĕ′ ōgüst′ blākē′), 1805–81, French revolutionist and radical thinker. A leader in February Revolution of 1848. Exiled (1864–70) in Brussels, he opposed Napoleon III, and was instrumental in his deposition. The Commune of Paris of 1871 was largely his creation, though Thiers had him arrested shortly before its proclamation. Freed in 1879. His social theories influenced Marx. Chief work: *Critique sociale* (1869).

Blarney, village, Co. Cork, Ireland. Castle (15th-cent.) contains Blarney stone, supposed to bestow persuasive powers on those who kiss it.

Blasco Ibáñez, Vicente (vēthän′tä blä′skō ēbä′nyäth), 1867–1928, Spanish novelist, b. Valencia, best known for *The Four Horsemen of the Apocalypse* (1916), a novel of World War I.

Blashfield, Edwin Howland, 1848–1936, American mural and genre painter.

Blasket Islands, group of rocky islets off Co. Kerry, SW Ireland. Only one is inhabited. Stronghold of last Irish chieftain to surrender to Cromwell.

blast furnace, structure for smelting, i.e., for extracting metals from ores. Principle involves removing oxygen from metal oxide to obtain metal. Furnace for iron is chimneylike, narrowing at top and bottom. Ore, coke, and flux are fed into top; hot air piped into bottom passes up through the mass. Coke oxidizes to carbon dioxide, which great heat changes to carbon monoxide; this reduces the ore, taking on oxygen and forming carbon dioxide, which is piped off. Molten iron descends to crucible at bottom of furnace and is separated from slag.

blasting, fragmentizing of rock or other material by explosive discharged within it or against it. Four steps in modern blasting: drilling holes to receive charge, placing charge, tamping hole, and igniting or detonating charge. Explosives used include black powder, dynamite, and ammonium nitrate.

Blavatsky, Helena Petrovna (blŭvăt′skē), 1831–91, Russian theosophist and occultist. After traveling widely, she went (1873) to New York where she founded (1875) the Theosophical Society and wrote (1877) *Isis Unveiled.* After 1879 she made her hq. at Madras, India. She was the chief founder of theosophy.

blazing star or **gay-feather,** a North American perennial (*Liatris* or *Lacinaria*), with racemes of purple or white feathery flowers.

bleaching, process of whitening by chemicals or sunlight, commonly applied to textiles, paper pulp, flour, fats, hair, feathers, wood, and other materials. Chemical methods include oxidation, reduction, and adsorption; textiles have long been sun bleached. Chloride of lime, invented 1799, was first of modern chemical bleaches. Javelle water and other chlorine mixtures are common domestic bleaches.

Bled, resort town, Slovenia, N Yugoslavia, in the Julian Alps. Former royal castle is near by.

bleeding: see HEMOPHILIA; HEMORRHAGE.

bleeding heart, perennial (*Dicentra spectabilis*), native to Japan. A spring-flowering garden plant with drooping, deep pink heart-shaped blooms.

Blekinge, Swed. *Blekinge län* (blā′kĭng-ù lĕn′), county (1,173 sq. mi.; pop. 145,909) and historic province, SE Sweden, on the Baltic coast; cap. Karlskrona. Cultivated valleys make it "the garden of Sweden." Conquered from Denmark in 1658.

Blenheim (blĕn′ŭm), Ger. *Blindheim,* village, W Bavaria, on the Danube E of Ulm. Between Blenheim and near-by Höchstädt Marlborough and Prince Eugene defeated French and Bavarians under Tallard in major battle of War of Spanish Succession (1704).

Blenheim Park, estate, Oxfordshire, England; seat of duke of Marlborough. Government provided estate and castle for victor of the battle of Blenheim.

Blennerhassett, Harman, 1765–1831, Anglo-Irish pioneer in America, an associate of Aaron Burr. Advanced money to Burr for Western schemes. Taken into custody after Burr's arrest, but released. In 1798 he bought part of **Blennerhassett Island,** in the Ohio, near Parkersburg, W.Va., and Belpre, Ohio. Here he built mansion and laboratory.

Blériot, Louis (lwĕ′ blärēō′), 1872–1936, French aviator and inventor. First to fly English Channel in heavier-than-air machine (July 25, 1909).

Blessington, Marguerite, countess of, 1789–1849, Irish beauty and intellectual who set up a brilliant salon in Kensington (1822). Wrote novels.

Blest Gana, Alberto (älbĕr′tō blĕst′ gä′nä), 1830–1920, Chilean novelist, generally considered greatest of 19th-cent. Spanish American realists. His masterpiece is *Martín Rivas* (1862).

Blicher, Steen Steensen (stän′ stän′sùn blē′kùr), 1782–1848, Danish realistic novelist, author of *The Diary of a Parish Clerk* (1824). Also wrote poetry.

Bligh, William, 1754–1817, British admiral. Chiefly remembered for mutiny on his ship, the BOUNTY, 1789. Was governor of New South Wales 1805–8.

blindness, lack or loss of sight. May result from injury or certain diseases including cataract, glaucoma. See also COLOR BLINDNESS; BRAILLE SYSTEM.

Bliss, Eleanor Albert, 1899–, American bacteriologist, authority on sulfa drugs.

Bliss, Philip Paul, 1838–76, American evangelist and writer of gospel songs. Among his songs are *Let the Lower Lights Be Burning* and *Jesus Loves Me.*

Bliss, Porter Cornelius, 1833–85, American explorer and adventurer. Explored Gran Chaco for Argentine government. Imprisoned as suspected spy in Paraguay, released on demand of U.S.

Bliss, Tasker Howard, 1853–1930, American army officer and statesman. Appointed chief of staff of U.S. army (1917), he helped work out mobilization plans. Delegate to Paris Peace Conference.

blister rust or **white-pine blister rust,** European disease of white pine, now common in North America. Currant and gooseberry are alternate hosts.

Blixen, Karen, Baroness: see DINESEN, ISAK.

Bloch, Ernest (blök), 1880–, Swiss-American composer. Most work filled with intense Hebraic feeling, (e.g., the Hebrew rhapsody *Schelomo,* 1916). Among other works are an opera, *Macbeth;* a *concerto grosso* for string orchestra and piano.

Bloch, Felix, 1905–, American physicist, b. Switzerland. Shared 1952 Nobel Prize for developing method of measuring magnetic fields in atomic nuclei.

blockade, use of naval vessels to cut off access to a coast, usually to prevent neutral shipping from trade with the enemy. The Declaration of Paris (1856) provided that blockades be announced to all affected parties and be legal only if effective and enforced against all neutrals.

block book, book with each page printed from a separate wood block. European examples (after middle of 15th cent.) were crude, inexpensive (e.g., *Biblia pauperum*). Chinese examples (earliest in 8th cent.) often beautiful.

blockhouse, small fortification, usually temporary, serving as a post for a small garrison. Its use dates probably from the 15th cent. Typical structure in U.S. came to be one of two stories, the second story overhanging.

Block Island, 7 mi. long and 3½ mi. wide, off S R.I., at E entrance to Long Isl. Sound between Point Judith, R.I., and Montauk Point, N.Y.; coextensive with New Shoreham town (pop. 732). Visited by Adriaen Block in 1614, settled 1661. Glaciated surface has low hills, many ponds, peat deposits. Has two lighthouses. Popular summer resort.

Blocksberg, Germany: see BROCKEN.

Blodgett, Katharine Burr, 1898–, American chemist. Worked on tungsten filaments, monomolecular layers. Made nonreflecting glass by coating glass with layers of barium stearate.

Bloemfontein (bloōm'föntän"), city (pop. 67,196), cap. of Orange Free State, South Africa. Seat of Appellate Division of Supreme Court.

Blois (blwä), city (pop. 21,666), cap. of Loir-et-Cher dept., central France, on the Loire. Thibaut the Cheat, 1st count of Blois, acquired Chartres and Touraine (10th cent.); successors added Champagne and Brie. Blois itself was assigned to cadet branch of family, sold to duke of Orleans 1397, incorporated into royal domain 1498. Famous Renaissance château was residence of Francis I, Mary Queen of Scots, Catherine de' Medici; scene of murder of Henri de Guise 1588. The Treaties of Blois (1504–5) were a temporary settlement of the ITALIAN WARS.

Blok, Aleksandr Aleksandrovich (ülyĭksän'dŭr ülyĭksän'drŭvĭch blôk'), 1880–1921, greatest of Russian symbolist poets. He achieved fame through the cycle *Beautiful Lady* (1904). Embracing the Revolution of 1917, he wrote *The Twelve* (1918; Eng. tr., 1920), a powerful epic.

Blomfield, Sir Reginald, 1856–1942, English architect who specialized in Renaissance and Georgian styles. His books are standard reference works.

Blondel, François (fräswä' blŏdĕl'), 1617–86, French architect. Designed triumphal arch, Porte Saint-Denis, Paris. His nephew, **Jacques François Blondel,** 1705–74, was also an eminent architect.

Blondel de Nesle (Fr. blŏdĕl' dü nĕl'), fl. late 12th cent., French troubadour, a favorite of Richard I. According to legend, found Richard in prison by singing song known only to two of them and was able to effect his rescue.

blood, circulating fluid which brings food and oxygen to body tissues and carries off carbon dioxide and other wastes. In man, consists of fluid plasma containing substances essential for CLOTTING OF BLOOD, hormones, and several types of cells including red and white CORPUSCLES. Recognition of four blood groups and RH FACTOR important in BLOOD TRANSFUSION. See also CIRCULATION OF THE BLOOD. See *ills.,* pp. 595, 633.

blood clotting: see CLOTTING OF BLOOD.

bloodhound: see HOUND.

blood poisoning: see SEPTICEMIA.

blood pressure, pressure of blood on walls of blood vessels, especially arteries. Depends on heart action, arterial elasticity, capillary resistance, and volume and viscous quality of blood. Max. pressure during contraction of heart (systole); min. during relaxation (diastole). Normal systolic range 100–140. Persistent high pressure (hypertension) is often associated with obesity, arteriosclerosis, and kidney inflammations.

bloodroot, North American woodland wild flower (*Sanguinaria canadensis*). White blossoms (1–3 in. across, usually borne singly), open in early spring.

blood transfusion, transfer of blood from one person or animal to another. For safe transfusion blood of donor and recipient must belong to groups which when mixed do not cause clumping or agglutination of red blood cells. Classification of human blood based on agglutinating substances present. Four major groups designated by Karl LANDSTEINER as O, A, B, AB; in Jansky system as I, II, III, IV. In Moss system group IV corresponds to O, group I to AB. People in O group called universal donors, in AB group, universal recipients. Blood should be tested also for RH FACTOR.

Bloody Assizes: see JEFFREYS, GEORGE, 1ST BARON JEFFREYS OF WEM.

Bloomer, Amelia Jenks, 1818–94, American reformer. Edited (1848–54) *Lily,* a reform organ. In 1851 adopted dress now known as Bloomer costume.

Bloomfield, Leonard, 1887–1949, American linguist. His masterpiece, *Language* (1933), a standard text, is a clear statement of linguistic principles which are now axiomatic, notably that language study must always be centered in the spoken language, that definitions used in grammar should be based on forms of the language, and that a given language at a given time is a complete system of sounds and forms which exist independently of the past.

Bloomfield. 1 Town (pop. 5,746), N Conn., near Hartford. **2** Town (pop. 49,307), NE N.J., adjoining NW Newark. Mfg. of metal products and chemicals.

Bloomgarden or **Blumengarten, Solomon,** pseud. **Yehoash** (yĕhō'äsh), 1870–1927, American writer of Yiddish poetry. Translated Old Testament from Hebrew into Yiddish.

Bloomington. 1 City (pop. 34,163), central Ill., SE of Peoria; settled 1822. Rail, commercial, industrial center in agr. area; coal fields near. Lincoln made famous "lost speech" to first Republican state convention here 1856. Seat of Illinois Wesleyan Univ. (1854). Annual Passion play. **2** City (pop. 28,163), S central Ind., SW of Indianapolis; settled 1818. Mfg. of wood, limestone (quarries near), and glass products. Seat of INDIANA UNIVERSITY.

Bloomsburg, town (pop. 10,633), E Pa., on Susquehanna R. and SW of Wilkes-Barre; settled 1772. Mfg. of carpets, clothing, and rayon.

Bloomsbury, residential district, central London, England. Has British Mus., Univ. of London, and many squares (e.g., Bedford, Russell, Bloomsbury). Many artists, writers, and students live here.

Blount, William, 1749–1800, American statesman. Governor of Territory South of the River Ohio (present Tenn.) 1790–96. Involved in plan to help British conquer West Florida.

Blow, John, c.1648–1708, English composer, organist at Westminster Abbey, chiefly remembered for his church music and for his masque *Venus and Adonis.* Henry Purcell was his pupil.

Blow, Susan Elizabeth, 1843–1916, American educator,

follower of Froebel. Opened first successful public kindergarten (1873) in U.S.

Bloy, Léon (lǟ' blwä'), 1846–1917, French author. A Roman Catholic and social reformer, he savagely attacked existing society. His novels *Le Désespéré* [the hopeless one] (1886) and *The Woman Who Was Poor* (1897; Eng. tr., 1939) are autobiographical. His correspondence forms a major part of his work.

Blücher, Gebhard Leberecht (blōō'kŭr, Ger. gĕp'härt lā'bŭrĕkht fŭn blü'khŭr), 1742–1819, Prussian general in Napoleonic Wars. Played crucial part in allied victory at Leipzig (1813) and in WATERLOO CAMPAIGN. Created prince of Wahlstatt 1814.

Bluebeard, nickname of the chevalier Raoul in a story by Charles Perrault. Bluebeard's seventh wife opens a locked door and finds the bodies of his former wives. She is saved from death at Bluebeard's hands by the arrival of her brothers.

bluebell: see HAREBELL; VIRGINIA COWSLIP; SQUILL.

blueberry, hardy shrub of genus *Vaccinium*. Varieties of low-bush blueberry (*Vaccinium angustifolium*) cultivated commercially for blue or black edible berries. High-bush blueberry or whortleberry (*V. corymbosum*) valued for brilliant autumn foliage. Blueberries need acid soil.

bluebird, migratory bird of North America, a thrush. In East male is c.7 in. long; blue upper plumage, cinnamon-red breast, white underneath. Related are mountain, Western, azure, and chestnut-backed bluebirds. Symbol of elusive happiness in Maeterlinck's *Blue Bird*.

bluebonnet, spring-blooming LUPINE (*Lupinus subcarnosus*), with blue flowers. State flower of Texas.

Blue Cross plans: see HEALTH INSURANCE.

Bluefield, city (pop. 21,506), S W.Va., and adjoining town (pop. 4,212) in Va., settled 1777. Shipping point for coal area with textile and flour milling and mfg. of mining supplies and equipment.

Bluefields, Caribbean port (pop. 7,463), SE Nicaragua, on Bluefields Bay. An early pirate resort, it became cap. of British protectorate over MOSQUITO COAST (1678). Nominally returned to Nicaragua (1850), it was finally annexed (1894) by Zelaya.

bluefish, stout-bodied, delicately flavored food fish (*Pomatomus saltatrix*), of warm waters of Atlantic and Indian oceans. Adults weigh 10 to 25 lb. Deep bluish, tinged with green above, silver below.

bluegrass, a grass species of genus *Poa* with bluish-green leaves. Used for pasture, hay, and lawns. Best known is Kentucky bluegrass (*Poa pratensis*), in region noted for racehorses.

Blue Island, city (pop. 17,622), NE Ill., just S of Chicago; settled 1835. Has railroad shops. Mfg. of clay and metal products.

blue jay, bird of central and E North America, allied to crow, raven, magpie. Grayish violet-blue upper parts and crest; blue wings and tail, black and white markings; black-collared neck; gray to white under parts; raucous cry, also musical notes.

blue laws, legislation aimed at rigid, minute control of public and private morals. Term originated with Loyalist clergyman, Samuel A. Peters, who in 1781 described "Blue Laws" of Conn. with exaggeration but some truth. Strict laws against Sabbath breaking, drunkenness, sex misconduct common in American colonies. Many blue laws revived in 19th and 20th cent.; now generally disregarded.

Blue Nile, river, c.950 mi. long, in the Anglo-Egyptian Sudan. Rises in L. Tana in NW Ethiopia, joins the White Nile at Khartoum to form the NILE.

Blue Point, village (pop. 1,613), SE N.Y., on S shore of Long Isl. Gives name to blue-point oysters.

blueprint. Plans drawn to scale on translucent material, then placed on paper treated with mixture of ferric salts and exposed to strong light. Ferric salts unprotected by drawing react to give blue color; salts under drawing wash away in water, leaving white lines.

Blue Ridge, range of Appalachian system, W of the piedmont, extending from NW Md. just above Harpers Ferry, W.Va., SW through Va. and N.C. into N Ga. Rises to c.5,000 ft. in S. Famous for scenery. Remote valleys (esp. to S) shelter people who preserve old ways of life and speech.

blues, type of song with melancholy text set to mournful tune. Grew from Negro work songs and spirituals. Typical blues song is W. C. Handy's *St. Louis Blues* (1914).

Blues and Greens [names derived from colors of circus charioteers], political factions in the Byzantine Empire in 6th cent. The Greens usually upheld MONOPHYSITISM; the Blues, orthodoxy. Both joined in the *Nika* sedition against Justinian I and Theodora (532). The empress saved the day by ordering Belisarius to put the rebels down by force; 30,000 were killed.

bluestocking [said by Samuel Johnson to have come from blue rather than formal stockings worn by a man at meetings], member of 18th-cent. English "conversation groups" of intellectuals; later only a woman of the groups, hence an intellectual woman. Famous early bluestockings were Elizabeth Montagu, Elizabeth Carter, Hannah More.

bluestone: see BLUE VITRIOL.

bluet or **quaker-ladies,** small North American wild flower (*Houstonia caerulea*), with blue, yellow-eyed blooms.

blue vitriol or **bluestone,** common blue crystalline hydrous copper salt (cupric sulphate or copper sulphate). Produced when white anhydrous salt crystallizes from aqueous solution. Occurs in nature in chalcanthite. Used in copperplating; as dye mordant.

Bluffton. 1 City (pop. 6,076), NE Ind., on Wabash R. and S of Fort Wayne. Dairying center. **2** Village (pop. 2,423), NW Ohio, NE of Lima. Has large Mennonite population and a Mennonite school.

Blum, Léon (lǟ' blōōm'), 1872–1950, French Socialist statesman. Headed first Popular Front government (1936–37; coalition of Socialists, Radical Socialists, Communists); passed important labor reforms. Arrested by Vichy govt. 1940; defended himself courageously at RIOM trial; held prisoner by Germans until 1945. Briefly headed Socialist cabinet 1946–47. A moderate in his later years.

Blume, Peter (blōōm), 1906–, American painter, b. Russia. Variously classified as expressionist or surrealist.

Blumenbach, Johann Friedrich (yōhän' frē'drĭkh blōō'münbäkh), 1752–1840, German comparative anatomist and physical anthropologist. Notable craniometric studies. Proposed fivefold scheme of race classification.

Blumengarten, Solomon: see BLOOMGARDEN, SOLOMON.

Blunden, Edmund (Charles), 1896–, English poet and critic. Author of poetry of rural England. He is also a scholarly critic, biographer, and editor.

Blunt, Wilfrid Scawen (skō'ĭn), 1840–1922, English poet, author of *The Love Sonnets of Proteus* (1881). Advocated Irish, Indian, and Egyptian home rule.

Blytheville, city (pop. 16,234), NE Ark., near Mississippi R.; settled c.1853. Market and industrial center for state's richest cotton area, where soybeans and feed crops are also produced.

Boabdil (bōūbdēl'), d. 1538, last Moorish king of Granada in Spain (1482–92). Defeated by Ferdinand and Isabella; fled to Morocco.

boa constrictor (bō'ŭ kŭnstrĭk'tŭr), nonpoisonous constrictor snake in South America; of anaconda and python family. Rarely over 12 ft. long. Agile climber.

Boadicea (bō"ŭdĭsē'ŭ), d. A.D. 62, British queen of the Iceni (of Norfolk). Led revolt against the Romans. On defeat she took poison.

Boanerges (bō'ŭnûr'jēz) [Gr.,= sons of thunder], name given by Jesus to James and John. Mark 3.17.

Boardman, Thomas Danforth, 1784–1873, American maker of pewter ware, now prized by collectors.

Boas, Franz (bō'ăz), 1858–1942, American anthropologist. Taught at Columbia Univ. (1896–1936). His approach was independent of theoretical preconceptions and was marked by a rigorous methodology. He did significant work in physical and cultural anthropology and in linguistics. His teachings had lasting influence on other anthropologists.

Boaz (bō'ăz), Ruth's husband, ancestor of David. Ruth 2; 3; 4; Booz: Mat. 1.5; Luke 3.32.

Bobbio (bôb'bēō), small town, Emilia e Romagna, N central Italy, SW of Piacenza. Monastery founded here by St. Columban in 612 was oldest in N Italy, flourished as cultural center 9th–12th cent.

bobcat, small lynx (*Lynx rufus*) of U.S., S Canada, parts of Mexico. Powerful, usually nocturnal hunter. Known also as bay lynx, red lynx, wildcat.

bobolink, in N U.S. and Canada name of American songbird related to blackbird, oriole. Called reed bird and rice bird in South. In autumn, male spring plumage (black with shoulders and lower back white, buff nape) is yellowish-brown, dark stripes on upper parts. Winters in South America.

bobwhite, American game bird of same family as pheasant and partridge. Eastern bobwhite c.10 in. long; male plumage brown, black, white; female brown, buff. Eats insects, weed seeds. Male whistles "bob-white" to attract female.

Boccaccio, Giovanni (jōvän'nē bōk-kät'chō), 1313–75, Italian poet and novelist, b. Paris. He spent his youth at Certaldo, near Florence, went to Naples (c.1330), where he won Petrarch's friendship, and returned to Tuscany 1341, spending his last years in Florence. His chief work is the DECAMERON, one of the world's great books. Other works include a biography of Dante; *Filocolo* (c.1340) and *La Fiammetta* (c.1344), prose romances; *Filostrato*, upon which Chaucer drew for his *Troilus and Criseyde;* and the *Corbaccio*, a verse satire on women.

Boccherini, Luigi (bōk-kērē'nē), 1743–1805, Italian composer. Perhaps most popular of his works is the *Minuet* from his String Quintet in E Minor.

Bochum (bō'khŏŏm), city (pop. 290,406), North Rhine-Westphalia, NW Germany; a center of RUHR dist.

Bocskay, Stephen (bôch'kī), Hung. *Bocskay István,* 1557?–1606, Hungarian noble, prince of Transylvania (1604–6). His chief aim was to secure Transylvanian independence from both Austria and Turkey. In 1604 he led a revolt, supported by Turkey, against Emperor Rudolf II's attempt to reimpose Catholicism on Hungary. The Treaty of Vienna (1606), which he negotiated, guaranteed religious freedom and legalized the threefold partition of HUNGARY (confirmed by Treaty of Szitvatorok between Austria and Turkey).

Bode, Johann Elert (yō'hän ā'lĕrt bō'dŭ), 1747–1826, German astronomer. Compiler of *Uranographia* (1801; star maps and catalogue of stars and nebulae).

Bodel, Jehan (zhä' bōdĕl'), b. c.1165, French trouvère. *Le Jeu de Saint-Nicolas,* a mystery, is first long play entirely in French. He died a leper.

Bodensee: see CONSTANCE, LAKE OF.

Bodenstein, Andreas Rudolf: see CARLSTADT.

Bodh Gaya, India: see BUDDH GAYA.

Bodin, Jean (zhä' bōdē'), 1530–96, French social and political philosopher. His *Les Six Livres de la république* (1576; Eng. tr., 1606) was first attempt to formulate scientific philosophy of history.

Bodleian Library (bŏd'lēŭn), at Oxford Univ. Original library destroyed; replaced in 17th cent. through efforts of Sir Thomas Bodley, who left a fund for its maintenance. Receives a copy of every book published in Great Britain.

Bodley, George Frederick (bŏd'lē), 1827–1907, English architect of ecclesiastical buildings, an adherent of the Victorian Gothic revival.

Bodley, Sir Thomas, 1545–1613, English scholar and diplomat, organizer of the BODLEIAN LIBRARY.

Bodmer, Johann Jakob (yō'hän yä'kôp bōd'mŭr), 1698–1783, Swiss critic. Founded with Johann Jakob Breitinger the critical journal *Diskurse der Mahlern,*

which attacked French classicism and paved the way for Klopstock, Goethe, and Schiller. Translated *Paradise Lost;* edited *Nibelungenlied.*

Bodoni, Giambattista (jämbät-tē'stä bōdō'nē), 1740–1813, Italian printer. Like Baskerville and Didot a leader in producing "modern" type faces. Indifferent to quality of text, editing, and proofreading, Bodoni produced stately quartos and folios of impressive appearance.

body snatching, stealing dead bodies. Before legal provision for supplying needs of medical schools, traffic in cadavers was profitable. Snatchers known as resurrectionists; their activities in 18th and early 19th cent. increased public opposition to dissection and led to violence.

Boehler, Peter (bû'lŭr), 1712–75, German-born missionary of the Moravian Church in America (1738–42, 1753–64). Worked in Ga.; later founded Nazareth and Bethlehem, Pa., and other settlements. In England (1747–53) he was made bishop.

Boehm, Sir Joseph Edgar (bām), 1834–90, English portrait sculptor, b. Vienna.

Boehm, Martin (bām), 1725–1812, American evangelical preacher, b. Pa. Became (1759) Mennonite bishop, but later with P. W. OTTERBEIN founded United Brethren in Christ and was elected bishop (1800).

Boehme or Böhme Jakob (bē'mŭ, Ger. bû'mû), 1575–1624, German mystic. His religious teaching, based on the belief that God is manifest in all aspects of creation and that evil results when one aspect (e.g., man) attempts to become the whole, was highly influential in England and the Continent.

Boeotia (bēō'shŭ), region of anc. Greece, N of the Gulf of Corinth; cap. THEBES. A confederacy of cities was cemented in the Boeotian League (7th cent. B.C.), dominated by Thebes until Athens after many battles broke up the confederacy in 457 B.C. Shortly afterward Thebes returned to power with Epaminondas' victory over Sparta at Leuctra (371 B.C.), and all Boeotia shared with Thebes the defeats by Philip II and Alexander the Great. Athenians generally considered Boeotians dull-witted clods, though Hesiod and Pindar belonged to the region.

Boer (bôr, boor) [Dutch,= farmer], inhabitant of South Africa of Dutch descent. The Boer language is Afrikaans (see LANGUAGE, table).

Boerhaave, Hermann (boor'hävŭ), 1668–1738, Dutch physician and chemist, introducer of clinical teaching at Univ. of Leiden.

Boer War: see SOUTH AFRICAN WAR.

Boethius, Anicius Manlius Severinus (bōē'thēŭs), c.475–525, Roman philosopher. A consul and a minister of Theodoric, he was accused of treason. While in prison awaiting death he wrote *De consolatione philosophiae* [the consolation of philosophy], which has been highly regarded by thoughtful readers from his time to this. Also wrote an influential treatise on music.

Boethus (bōē'thŭs), fl. 1st half of 2d cent. B.C., Greek sculptor, believed to have been the creator of the original SPINARIO.

bog, very old lake without inlet or outlet which becomes overgrown with vegetation. SPHAGNUM and PEAT obtained from bogs. Acid medium of bogs forms natural preservative for remains of animals and plants of earlier times. Typical bog plants are orchids, cranberry, pitcher plant, and sun dew.

Bogalusa (bōgŭloo'sŭ), city (pop. 17,798), SE La., near Pearl R., in lumbering area; founded 1906. Mfg. of paper, furniture, and tung oil products.

Bogdanov, A. (bŭgdä'nŭf), pseud. of **Aleksandr Aleksandrovich Malinovski,** 1873–1928, Russian social philosopher, an active revolutionist after 1905. Led "proletarian culture" movement under Soviet regime.

Bogert, Marston Taylor, 1868–, American chemist. Synthesized aromatic organic compounds.

Boghazkeui (bō"gäzkû'ē), village, N central Asiatic Turkey, where Hugo Winckler discovered (1906–7)

Hittite inscriptions. Name also spelled Boghazkoy.

bog iron ore: see LIMONITE.

Bogomils (bō′gōmĭlz), earliest (10th cent.) group of the CATHARI. Flourishing in Bulgaria and the Balkans, they were distinguished not only by dualistic religious beliefs but also by political nationalism and resentment of Byzantine culture. Various subgroups were called Babuns, Phundaits, and Patarenes. They spread to Italy and converted the ALBIGENSES. Opposition of Christian churches weakened the Bogomils, who were wiped out by the triumph of Islam (15th cent.).

Bogotá (bōgōtä′), city (pop. 325,658; alt. 8,660 ft.) central Colombia; cap. and largest city of country. Founded (1538) by Jiménez de Quesada to succeed center of Chibcha culture. In a broad valley of E Andes, it was difficult of access before air transportation. Called by Alexander von Humboldt (1801) the Athens of America. After independence from Spain, Bogotá was cap. of Greater Colombia until dissolution of union (1830). Organization of American States founded here 1948.

Bogota (būgō′tŭ), borough (pop. 7,662), NE N.J., on Hackensack R. Mfg. of paper and metal products.

Bohemia, Czech *Čechy,* historic province (20,102 sq. mi.; pop. 5,490,000), W Czechoslovakia; cap. PRAGUE. Separated from Bavaria by the BOHEMIAN FOREST, from Saxony by the ERZGEBIRGE, and from Silesia by the SUDETES, it is a fertile, hilly region, drained by the Elbe and Moldau rivers. Industries include mining (coal, silver, copper, lead, radium, uranium), especially in the Erzgebirge; textile and glass mfg.; heavy industries (centered in Prague region); brewing (notably at Pilsen). Many resorts (e.g., Carlsbad, Marienbad). Since the expulsion, after 1945, of most of German-speaking minority, population is overwhelmingly Czech. Bohemia takes its name from the probably Celtic Boii, whom Czech settlers displaced during 1st–5th cent. A.D. Temporarily subjugated by the Avars and later by MORAVIA, and Christianized by SS. CYRIL AND METHODIUS, it became a duchy of the Holy Roman Empire under St. WENCESLAUS (d. 935). Later dukes of the PREMYSL dynasty acquired Moravia and most of SILESIA, and in 1198 OTTOCAR I took the title king. The vast conquests of OTTOCAR II proved ephemeral, and in 1306 the Premyslide line became extinct. Under the Luxembourg dynasty, particularly under Emperor CHARLES IV, Bohemia had its golden age. Charles's Golden Bull (1356) gave the kings of Bohemia the rank of ELECTORS. In the 15th cent. the HUSSITE WARS brought Bohemia into chaos. GEORGE OF PODEBRAD (d. 1471) restored peace, but he was the last native ruler. The crown passed first to the kings of Hungary (see JAGIELLO), and in 1526 to the house of HAPSBURG, which ruled it until 1918. Religious tension continued. When in 1618 Emperor Matthias abrogated religious freedom (granted 1609), the Bohemian diet in defiance deposed their Hapsburg king (later Emperor FERDINAND II) and elected FREDERICK THE WINTER KING. These events led directly to the THIRTY YEARS WAR (1618–48). The Protestant defeat at the WHITE MOUNTAIN (1620) ended Czech freedom. Bohemia became a Hapsburg crownland (1627) and was subjected to rigorous Germanization. Czech nationalism flared up in the Revolution of 1848, but was crushed in 1849. Later concessions to Czech demands for equal status in the AUSTRO-HUNGARIAN MONARCHY were insufficient, and Czech disaffection was one of the causes of Austria's defeat in World War I. With the realization of Czech independence in 1918, the history of Bohemia became that of CZECHOSLOVAKIA.

Bohemian Forest, Czech *Český Les,* Ger. *Böhmerwald,* thickly wooded mountain range along border of Bohemia, Czechoslovakia, and Bavaria, Germany. S section called *Šumava* in Czech. Highest point, Arber (4,780 ft.), is in Bavaria.

Bohemond I (bō′hŭmŏnd), c.1056–1111, prince of Antioch (1099–1111), a leader in First Crusade; son of ROBERT GUISCARD. Swore fealty to ALEXIUS I but, upon capturing Antioch, made himself prince (1098). Defeated by Alexius (1108), he acknowledged him as overlord but retired and made TANCRED regent.

Bohm, Max (bōm), 1868–1923, American marine, figure, and mural painter.

Böhme, Jakob: see BOEHME, JAKOB.

Böhmerwald: see BOHEMIAN FOREST.

Bohol (bôhôl′), island (1,491 sq. mi.; pop. 449,549), Philippines, N of Mindanao and between Cebu and Leyte. Produces rice, hemp, and manganese.

Bohr, Niels Henrik David (nēls′ hăn′rĕk dä′vĕdh bōr), 1885–, Danish physicist. Won 1922 Nobel Prize for concept of structure of atom; reconciled this with quantum theory. Assisted in atomic-bomb research in U.S. (1938–39; 1943–45). Instrumental in founding Inst. of Theoretical Physics, Copenhagen.

Bohun (boōn), English noblemen of Norman descent. **Henry de Bohun,** 1st earl of Hereford, 1176–1220, was one of barons who forced King John to accept Magna Carta (1215). **Humphrey V de Bohun,** 2d earl of Hereford and 1st earl of Essex, d. 1274, led barons of Welsh Marches who returned (1263) to side of Henry III in BARONS' WAR. **Humphrey VII de Bohun,** 3d earl of Hereford and 2d earl of Essex, d. 1298, was constable of England and a leader of barons who forced Edward I to sign confirmation of the charters 1297. **Humphrey VIII de Bohun,** 4th earl of Hereford and 3d earl of Essex, 1276–1322, was one of lord ordainers attempting to curb Edward II in 1310. Aided in execution of Piers GAVESTON.

Bohuslan, Swed. *Bohuslän* (boō′hüslĕn), historic province, SW Sweden, conquered from Denmark 1658.

Boiardo or **Bojardo, Matteo Maria** (mät-tā′ō mä-rē′ä bōyär′dō), c.1434–1494, Italian poet, count of Scandiano. Wrote the unfinished *Orlando Innamorato,* based on the Roland story. The poem was revised satirically by Francesco Berni, and the story was continued by ARIOSTO in *Orlando Furioso.*

Boieldieu, François Adrien (bwäldyû′), 1775–1834, French composer, master of *opéra comique,* composer of *Le Calife de Bagdad, La Dame blanche.*

Boileau Nicolas (nēkôlä′ bwälō), 1636–1711, French critic and poet. His verse treatise on poetics (1674) made him foremost spokesman of CLASSICISM. His poetic repute rests on *Le Lutrin* (1683), a mock epic, and on his *Satires* and *Épîtres.* Full surname Boileau-Despréaux.

boiler, steam-generating device consisting of fire box (furnace to burn fuel) and boiler proper (enclosed vessel where heated water becomes steam). Common types: fire-tube boiler (hot gases in tubes heat outside water) and water-tube boiler (water in tubes heated by outside gases). Safety valve prevents explosions.

boiling point, temperature at which substance changes from liquid to gas with bubbling called "boiling." Under constant pressure each substance has specific boiling point; lowering pressure lowers boiling point, and vice versa. When substance is at boiling point, there is no increase in temperature until VAPORIZATION is complete.

Boisbrûlés (bwäbrülä′) [from Fr.= burnt wood], name given part-Indian descendants of fur traders in W Canada. Important group in Red River Settlement and in Riel's Rebellion.

Boise (boi′sē, –zē), city (pop. 34,393), state cap., SW Idaho, largest city of state, on Boise R.; founded 1863 near gold fields and military post. Became territorial cap. 1864. Grew as mining center, but with building of near-by Arrowrock Dam (1911–15), became trade and processing center for orchards, grain and potato fields, and dairies in BOISE PROJECT. Mineral springs near.

Boise, river, SW Idaho, rising in three forks in mountains E of Boise. Flows NW, past Boise and Caldwell, to Snake R. at Oregon line. First explored by W. P. Hunt in 1811; called Reed's R. in early days for John Reed, fur trader from Astoria, who, near river's mouth, estab. post where he was killed, 1814. Used today in BOISE PROJECT.

Boise, Fort, fur-trading post, SW Idaho. Founded 1834 on Boise R. by Hudson's Bay Co. to rival Fort HALL. Moved 1838 to Snake R. near Boise R. mouth. Abandoned 1855.

Boise project, SW Idaho and E Oregon, in the Boise, Payette, and Snake river valleys, irrigating c.400,000 acres. Arrowrock division, between Boise and Snake rivers, is served by Arrowrock Dam in Boise R., three Deer Flat Dams that create L. Lowell with canal from Boise R., and Anderson Ranch Dam in South Fork of Boise R. Notus division is N of Boise R., between Caldwell and Notus. Payette division, between Boise and Payette rivers and E of Snake R., is served by Black Canyon Diversion Dam in Payette R., Deadwood Dam in Deadwood R., and Cascade Dam in North Fork of Payette R. Some of Black Canyon power goes to MINIDOKA PROJECT and OWYHEE project.

Boisguilbert, Pierre le Pesant, sieur de (pyĕr' lù pùzä' syûr' dù bwägĕlbĕr'), 1646–1714, French economist. Argued that mass consumption was as important as mass production, and urged income tax.

Bois-le-Duc, Netherlands: see 's HERTOGENBOSCH.

Boito, Arrigo (är'rēgō bō'ētō), 1842–1918, Italian composer and librettist. His only significant opera is *Mefistofele.* More important are his librettos for Verdi's *Otello* and *Falstaff.*

Bojardo, Matteo Maria: see BOIARDO.

Bojer, Johan (yō'hän boi'ùr), 1872–, Norwegian novelist and dramatist, noted for portrayal of Norwegian contemporary life, as in *The Power of a Lie* (1896), *The Great Hunger* (1903), *The Last of the Vikings* (1921).

Bok, Edward (William), 1863–1930, American writer, b. Netherlands; editor of the *Ladies' Home Journal* (1889–1919). His limpid style is at its best in autobiography, *The Americanization of Edward Bok* (1920). He financed the Singing Tower at Iron Mt., Fla. He is buried at its base.

Bokhara, Uzbek SSR: see BUKHARA.

Bolan Pass (bōlän'), NE central Baluchistan, W Pakistan; rises to c.5,580 ft. Used by railroad and highway. Historical route for invading India.

Boldini, Giovanni (jōvän'nē bōldē'nē), 1845–1931, Italian painter, known for portraits of women.

Boleslaus (bō'lùslôs), kings of Poland. **Boleslaus I** (the Brave), Pol. *Bolesław Chrobry,* c.966–1025 (reigned 992–1025), was the first Polish ruler to call himself king. He campaigned successfully against Germany, Bohemia, and Kiev but failed to unite all N Slavs under Polish rule. **Boleslaus III,** 1085–1138 (reigned 1102–38), reunited Poland by conquering his brother's share. By a treaty with Emperor Lothair II he was invested with Pomerania and Rügen as fiefs of Holy Roman Empire (1135).

Boleyn, Anne, 1507?–1536, queen consort of Henry VIII; his second wife and mother of Elizabeth. Henry divorced Katharine of Aragon to marry her. The marriage was generally unpopular; his ardor cooled; and she was executed for alleged adultery.

Bolgari: see BULGARS, EASTERN.

Bolingbroke, Henry of: see HENRY IV (England).

Bolingbroke, Henry St. John, Viscount: see ST. JOHN, HENRY.

Bolívar, Simón (sēmōn' bōlē'vär), 1783–1830, South American revolutionist, called the Liberator, b. Caracas. Participating in revolution against Spain from 1810, he was defeated (1812, 1815) but had liberated the N (Colombia, Venezuela, Ecuador, Panama) by 1822. Met in secret with SAN MARTÍN at Guayaquil (1822); San Martín withdrew from W campaign leaving Bolívar in command of army that won final triumph over royalist forces at Ayacucho (1824). Elected president of Venezuela (1819), he became (1919) president of Greater Colombia (present Colombia, Venezuela, Ecuador, Panama). He also organized government for liberated Peru and Bolivia. At the meeting he called at Panama (1826) to promote a united Spanish America, little was accomplished, but the meet-

ing was beginning of Pan-Americanism. He resigned the presidency in 1830 and died of tuberculosis shortly thereafter. Hated by many during his lifetime for his tyrannical dictatorship, he is today revered as greatest of Latin American heroes.

Bolivia (bōlĭ'vēù, Span. bōlē'vyä), republic (412,777 sq. mi.; pop. c.3,990,200), W South America, an inland country. Legal cap. is SUCRE, but LA PAZ is political, financial and commercial center. The E section is tropical, N portion lying in rain forests drained by rivers of Amazon basin, S part merging into the CHACO. The W section is Andean; one cordillera traces border of Chile, the other runs N-S through the center of Bolivia. In the SW is an extensive salt plain, and in the NW the great basin of L. Titicaca. On the high windswept plateau (Altiplano) between mountain ranges and in mountain valleys are the chief centers of population, industries, and transportation. Bolivia has some of the richest mines in the world—tin, silver, copper, wolframite, bismuth, antimony, zinc, lead, gold. Important mining towns are POTOSI and ORURIO, and COCHABAMBA and TARIJA are agr. and commercial centers. There were Indian civilizations on the plateau long before the Inca became dominant, and today a large percentage of the Bolivian people are pure Indian. Spanish conquest began in 1538, when Gonzalo and Hernando Pizarro came in successful search for mineral wealth. Spanish poured in and developed mines, textile mills, and great landed estates, all with Indian labor. As part of the *audiencia* of Charcas, it was attached to viceroyalty of Peru until 1776, then to that of La Plata. Revolution against Spain began in 1809, but independence was gained only by victory of Sucre at Ayacucho (1824). Bolívar drew up a constitution; Upper Peru became Bolivia, Chuquisaca became Sucre. Because the boundaries of the *audiencia* of Charcas were vague and because all the republics were ambitious, Bolivian history has been plagued by disastrous border wars; a Bolivian attempt to reunite Peru and Bolivia failed in 1839; war with Chile (1879–84; see PACIFIC, WAR OF THE) cost Bolivia the nitrate-rich coastal province of Atacama; trouble with Brazil over the Acre region led to Brazil's getting valuable wild-rubber forests (1903); a long-drawn-out dispute over the Chaco led to war (1932–35), in which Paraguay was the victor and Bolivia had to give up large claims. Minerals continued to be the chief basis of Bolivia's international trade, and petroleum found in SE Bolivia brought new railroad development. Demand for tin and wolfram made World War II a boon. Bolivia declared war on the Axis (1943) and became a member of the UN (1945). Recently efforts have been made to improve the lot of the Indians and increase agr. production.

Bollandists (bōl'ùndĭsts), group of Jesuits in Belgium, formed by Jean Bolland (17th cent.) and famous for compiling the *Acta sanctorum,* still being brought up to date.

Bolley, Henry Luke, 1865–, American plant pathologist. He discovered cause of potato scab, methods of preventing oak smut, bunt of wheat, and other diseases, and developed rust-resistant wheat and wilt-resistant flax.

boll weevil, snout beetle whose fiber-eating larvae cause losses up to $200,000,000 yearly to U.S. cotton crop. Combated by dusting with chemicals, early planting, and destroying infected plants in the autumn.

bollworm, name for two cotton pests, both larvae of noctuid moths: pink bollworm, a feeder on blossoms, fiber, and seeds; and cotton bollworm (corn-ear worm), which burrows in the bolls and also attacks corn, tomatoes, and tobacco.

Bologna, Giovanni da (jōvän'nē dä bōlō'nyä), 1524–1608, Flemish sculptor whose real name was Jean Bologne or Boulogne. Identified chiefly with the Italian Renaissance. Famous for his *Flying Mercury* and *The Rape of the Sabines* (Florence).

Bologna (bōlō′nyä), city (pop. 226,771), cap. of Emilia-Romagna, N central Italy. Cultural and commercial center. Of pre-Roman origin, city passed (8th cent.) under papal rule, but a strong free commune was estab. in 12th cent. Guelph-Ghibelline strife enabled several families to seize power over city in 14th–15th cent., Bentivoglio family being most notable. Papal rule, restored 1506, lasted (except during 1797–1815) until unification of Italy (1860). The famous Univ. of Bologna originated (11th cent.) with Roman law school and made city into one of main centers of medieval learning. Painting flourished 15th–17th cent. with Francia, the Carracci, Guido Reni. Seriously damaged in World War II, Bologna retains many fine medieval palaces and churches. Its two leaning towers and its arcaded streets are characteristic.

Bolsena (bôlsā′nä), village, Latium, central Italy, near site of second VOLSINII, on a crater lake. Here occurred c.1265 a famous reputed miracle: a doubting priest saw blood flow from Host at Mass.

Bolshevism and Menshevism (bōl′shùvĭzùm, bŏl′–, mĕn′–shùvĭzùm), the two main branches of Marxist SOCIALISM in Russia from 1903 to 1918. In 1903 the Russian Social Democratic party split into two wings. The *Bolsheviki* [majority members], led by LENIN, advocated immediate revolution and establishment of dictatorship of the proletariat. The *Mensheviki* [minority members], led by PLEKHANOV, held that before reaching socialism Russia must pass through an intermediary democratic or bourgeois regime, like the rest of Europe. Bolsheviks favored a small, disciplined party; Mensheviks sought to appeal to masses and to cooperate with "bourgeois" parties. Within the Social Democratic party, which in theory remained united, the Bolsheviks soon lost their numerical superiority. In the RUSSIAN REVOLUTION of 1917 the Mensheviks cooperated with the Kerensky regime, which the Bolsheviks overthrew in Nov., 1917. The Communist party, formed 1918, absorbed or "liquidated" the remaining Mensheviks.

Bolton or **Bolton-le-Moors** (-lù-mŏŏrz′), county borough (pop. 167,162), Lancashire, England; textile center. Connected with Manchester by canal.

Boltwood, Bertram Borden, 1870–1927, American chemist, physicist. Discovered that radium is disintegration product of uranium, intermediate is ionium, and ultimate product is lead. Developed theories that led to discovery of isotopes and had bearings on origin of elements. Taught at Yale.

Bolzano (bôltsä′nō), Ger. *Bozen* (bō′tsùn), city (pop. 41,722), Trentino-Alto Adige, N Italy, in S Tyrol. Tourist and health resort. Its position on Brenner road made it important medieval trade center. Pop. largely German-speaking.

Bombay, state (115,570 sq. mi.; pop. 35,943,-559) W India, on Arabian Sea. India's leading commercial and industrial area. Fertile coastal strip (edged by W Ghats) is major rice belt. In 3d cent. B.C. Bombay was part of Maurya empire. Akbar annexed N section, but after 17th cent. Mahrattas were dominant until defeated by the British in 19th cent. Baroda and Kolhapur were largest of several former native states absorbed 1947. Its cap. **Bombay** (pop. 1,489,883) is a major port and mfg. center. Was hq. of British East India Co. 1668–1858. Cotton-textile industry.

Bomoseen, Lake (bŏ″mùzēn′), 7½ mi. long and 1½ mi. wide, W Vt., W of Rutland; resort.

Bon, Cape (bŏn), headland, NE Tunisia, jutting into the Mediterranean. German forces in N Africa surrendered here to Allies in May, 1943.

Bona Dea (bō′nù dē′ù) [Latin,= good goddess], Roman earth and mother goddess.

Bonanza Creek, stream of the Yukon flowing into Klondike R. at Dawson. Famous in gold-rush days.

Bonaparte (bō′nùpärt), Ital. *Buonaparte* (bwōnäpär′tä), family name of NAPOLEON I. His father, **Carlo Buonaparte**, 1746–85, a lawyer in Ajaccio, led pro-French party in Corsica. His mother, **Letizia** or **Laetitia Ramolino Bonaparte**, 1750–1836, "Madame Mère," was noted for her stoic virtues. She retired to Rome after Napoleon's fall. Their eldest son, **Joseph Bonaparte**, 1768–1844, was king of Naples (1806–8) and of Spain (1808–13); inefficient on both thrones. Lived mainly at Bordentown, N.J., from 1815–1841; died in Italy. His brother **Lucien Bonaparte**, 1775–1840, helped Napoleon in coup d'état of 18 BRUMAIRE but opposed establishment of empire. Retired to Rome; created prince of Canino by pope. His sister **Elisa Bonaparte**, 1777–1820, married Felice Bacciochi (an infantry captain). Napoleon made her princess of Lucca (1805), grand duchess of Tuscany (1809). Intelligent administrator. Another brother, **Louis Bonaparte**, 1778–1846, king of Holland (1806–10), married Hortense de BEAUHARNAIS. Deposed by Napoleon for defying Continental System. Died in Italy. **Pauline Bonaparte**, 1780–1825, Napoleon's favorite sister, was beautiful but frivolous. Accompanied her first husband, Gen. Leclerc, to Haiti; married Camillo Borghese, a Roman noble, 1803; was made princess of Guastalla 1806. Another sister, **Caroline Bonaparte**, 1782–1839, married Joachim MURAT, was queen of Naples (1808–14), intrigued against Napoleon. Fled to Austria after Murat's execution. Youngest brother, **Jérôme Bonaparte**, 1784–1860, king of Westphalia (1807–13), was extravagant and irresponsible. Early marriage (1803) with Elizabeth PATTERSON, on a visit to U.S., was annulled on pressure by Napoleon. Later married a princess of Württemberg. Returned to France 1847, lived at court of Napoleon III. Among second generation of family, NAPOLEON II (duke of Reichstadt) and NAPOLEON III were most important. Other members also gained prominence. **Charles Lucien Bonaparte**, 1803–57, prince of Canino, son of Lucien, noted ornithologist, lived in U.S. 1824–33, wrote *American Ornithology* (4 vols., 1825–33). **Pierre Napoléon Bonaparte**, 1815–81, another son of Lucien, entered French politics, supported Napoleon III, and killed a journalist during a quarrel (1870) but was acquitted of murder. Notoriously immoral. **Napoléon Joseph Charles Paul Bonaparte**, 1822–91, son of Jérôme, was known as Prince Napoleon or, familiarly, Plon-Plon. At the court of Napoleon III he advocated a liberal policy. His sister, **Mathilde Bonaparte**, 1820–1904, was prominent at Napoleon III's court. Napoleon III's only son, **Napoléon Eugène Louis Jean Joseph Bonaparte**, 1856–79, the Prince Imperial, was killed fighting the Zulus as a member of the British army. The claim to the Bonapartist succession passed to the descendants of Jérôme by his second marriage. From Jérôme's marriage with Elizabeth Patterson the American branch of the family is issued: **Jerome Napoleon Bonaparte**, 1805–70, and his son, **Charles Joseph Bonaparte**, 1851–1921, U.S. Secretary of the Navy (1905–6) and Attorney General (1906–9). He was active in antitrust suits and was among founders of National Municipal League.

Bonar Law, Andrew: see LAW, ANDREW BONAR.

Bonaventure (bŏnùvĕn′chùr) or **Bonaventura, Saint**, bōnäväntōō′rä), 1221–74, Italian-French scholastic theologian, a cardinal, Doctor of the Church, called the Seraphic Doctor, b. near Viterbo. At Univ. of Paris he studied under Alexander of Hales, then taught until he was made general of the Franciscans (1257) and archbishop of Paris (1265). Early works in theology and philosophy were largely devoted to reconciling Aristotelian learning with Augustinian Christianity. Later writings are guides to mysticism, bringing the mystical tradition of St. Bernard of Clairvaux to full flower. Feast: July 14.

Bonaventure Island, 2½ mi. long and ¾ mi. wide, E Que., Canada, in Gulf of St. Lawrence N of Percé Rock. Largest bird sanctuary on N Atlantic coast.

Bonavista Bay, NE N.F., Canada. Irregular bay filled with islands; has many fishing villages on its shores. Bonavista Peninsula (S) ends in Cape Bonavista (S entrance to bay), reputed landfall of Cabot in 1497. Bonavista town is on S shore.

Bond, Carrie Jacobs, 1862–1946, American song writer. The popularity of such songs as *I Love You Truly, Just a-Wearyin' for You,* and *A Perfect Day* earned her a fortune.

Bond, William Cranch, 1789–1859, and a son **George Phillips Bond,** 1825–65, American astronomers, pioneers in celestial photography. Both were associated with Harvard Observatory.

Bond Street, street in London noted for elegant shops. Fashionable residential street 18th–early 19th cent.

Bone, Henry, 1755–1834, English enamel painter.

Bône (bōn), city (pop. 77,675), NE Algeria, a Mediterranean port. Exports iron and phosphates. Once a Carthaginian colony and cap. of Numidian kings. Flourished as Hippo Regius in Roman times and was episcopal see of St. Augustine.

bone, hard tissue composing SKELETON of most adult vertebrates. Permeated with microscopic canals and sheathed by fibrous membrane. Long bones contain marrow, important in forming blood corpuscles.

bone black: see CHARCOAL.

bone implements, first found in Aurignacian phase of Paleolithic. Making of bone awls, needles, fishhooks, knives, dart points, etc., presupposed advanced stone tools. Modern Eskimos work in bone.

bone meal, ground bone used (because of phosphorus and nitrogen content) as fertilizer and feed.

boneset or **thoroughwort,** perennial North American herb (*Eupatorium perfoliatum*), with terminal clusters of small, white flowers in late summer.

Bonham (bŏn′ùm), city (pop. 7,049), E Texas, NE of Dallas. Processes and ships cheese, cotton, and truck. Replica of Fort Inglish near by.

Bonheur, Rosa (bùnûr′), 1822–99, French painter of animals.

Bon Homme Richard: see JONES, JOHN PAUL.

Boniface, Saint (bŏn′ĭfùs, –fās), c.675–754? English missionary called the Apostle of Germany, a monk originally named Winfrid. Leaving England in 718, he soon devoted himself to the task of converting pagan Germany, which he and his companions almost completed in his lifetime. He founded many bishoprics and many abbeys (including Fulda). He was made bishop (722), missionary archbishop (732), and archbishop of Mainz (745). He was killed by pagans in Friesland. Feast: June 5.

Boniface VIII, 1235–1303, pope (1294–1303); originally named Benedetto Caetani; successor of Celestine V. Boniface tried to assert papal authority but was not successful. He interfered unsuccessfully in Sicily, further muddied the waters of the quarrel of GUELPHS AND GHIBELLINES, and was involved in a bitter struggle with PHILIP IV of France. Boniface tried to stop Philip from collecting illegal taxes from the clergy, issuing the bull *Clericis laicos* (1296), but he was forced to agree with Philip. New trouble caused the pope to thunder forth in the bulls *Ausculta fili* (1301) and *Unam sanctam* (1302; the most extreme statement ever made of the duty of princes to be subject to the pope), but the king sent a deputation to depose Boniface. After Sciarra Colonna, one of the deputies, struck Boniface, the enraged people of Anagni drove the French out. Boniface died soon afterward. Philip forced Pope CLEMENT V to repudiate the acts of Boniface. Boniface, an able canon lawyer, issued a code called the *Sext.*

Boniface (bŏn′ùfäs), d. 432, Roman general, governor and count of Africa. His refusal to obey his recall (427) led to warfare with imperial government. Made truce with Rome when Vandals under Gaiseric invaded Africa. Defeated by Vandals at Hippo (430), he was recalled to Italy by Galla Placidia to help her against AETIUS. Boniface defeated Aetius but died of wounds.

Bonifacio, José (zhōōzā′ bōnĭfä′tsēō), 1763?–1838, Brazilian statesman, scientist, author, whose full name was José Bonifacio de Andrade e Silva. Returning to Brazil in 1819 after studying in Europe, he became leader of the movement for the independence of Brazil from Portugal.

Bonington, Richard Parks (bŏn′–), 1801–28, English painter. Helped to bring influence of Constable and Turner to new school of French romanticists.

Bonin Islands (bō′nĭn), Jap. *Ogasawara-gunto,* volcanic island group (40 sq. mi.; 1940 pop. 7,361), N Pacific, c.600 mi. S of Tokyo. Largest is Chichi-jima. Discovered 1543 by Spaniards, claimed 1875 by Japan. Under U.S. control since 1945.

Bonivard, François de: see BONNIVARD, FRANÇOIS DE.

Bonn (bŏn), city (pop. 111,287), North Rhine-Westphalia, NW Germany, on the Rhine; since 1949 temporary cap. of Federal Republic of Germany. Dates from Roman times. Residence of electors of Cologne 1263–1794. Passed to France 1801, to Prussia 1815. Univ. founded 1784. The minster (11th–13th cent.) and electoral palace were gutted in World War II; house where Beethoven was born still stands.

Bonnard, Pierre (pyĕr bônär′), 1867–1947, French painter and lithographer, a postimpressionist known for his luminous and decorative use of color. Notable are his intimate interiors in oil.

Bonneville, Benjamin Louis Eulalie de (bŏn′vĭl), 1796–1878, American army officer, trader in Far West, b. France. Colorful figure who failed as fur trader but helped open Rocky Mt. country.

Bonneville Dam, NW Oregon and SW Wash., in Columbia R., c.40 mi. E of Portland; built 1933–37 for power, flood control, navigation. Bradford Isl. divides river. Spillway in N channel is 1,450 ft. long, averages 170 ft. high; ladders aid fish migration. In S channel are powerhouse and lock.

Bonnie Prince Charlie: see STUART, CHARLES EDWARD.

Bonnivard or **Bonivard, François de** (fräswä′ dù bônĕvär′), c.1493–1570, Swiss hero of Byron's "The Prisoner of Chillon." Supported Geneva's revolt against Charles III of Savoy, who imprisoned him twice (1519–21, 1530–36). Freed when Bernese stormed CHILLON castle. Wrote chronicle of Geneva (published 1831).

Bonpland, Aimé Jacques Alexandre (āmā′ zhäk′ älĕksä′drù bōplä′), 1773–1858, French naturalist and author of works on Mexican and South American plants collected on travels with Humboldt.

Bonsels, Waldemar (väl′dùmär bōn′zĕls), 1881–, German author. *The Adventures of Maya, the Bee* (1912) is a juvenile classic, and a novel *The Adventures of Mario* (1927) was popular.

book, collection of written material, usually considered to have some sort of unity of thought in the contents (e.g., the divisions of anc. manuscripts); primarily today a written work of substantial proportions, printed and bound in a unit of one or more volumes. Volumes are still commonly graded by sizes with names derived from the number of times the original sheet on which the type is printed has been folded–folio, quarto, octavo (very popular modern size) and duodecimo. Papyrus fragments in Egypt preceded the regular organized manuscript book. The Greeks and Romans wrote books mainly on large papyrus rolls of varying size, though in the later period parchment was also used. The method of making books by binding collections of leaves came in the 2d cent. A.D. Vellum, a type of parchment, was popular with the monks who copied and produced the medieval books (some of these made very beautiful by illumination). Many manuscript books were made, but it was the introduction to Europe of PRINTING in the 15th cent. that made large-scale production possible. The development of books and printing thereafter was rapid and diverse. The book has been the primary dispenser of human knowledge. Making and selling of books today involves many specialized skills (editing, designing, printing, selling).

bookbinding, the art and skill of encasing a book

(either manuscript or printed) in protective covering. The protective covering of ancient parchment rolls, unattached to the rolls, is not considered as bookbinding, which first arose in the Middle Ages, when boards were used to protect vellum sheets. Some medieval bindings are exquisite. After the coming of printing to Europe and adoption of the practice of folding printed sheets and sewing pages in small groups, the basic skills of bookbinding developed rapidly. They remain the same today, although machine binding has replaced hand binding to a large degree. The sheets are normally sewed together, and the covering is fastened on. In fine hand binding, the covering is made partly on the book itself; in machine binding it is completed separately and glued on. Popular covering materials are heavy paper, boards covered with cloth or paper, vellum, leather (esp. morocco and calfskin), and imitation leather. With the development of mass-production processes and new materials, new methods of binding have recently become popular. "Perfect" binding uses glue without sewing. In other cases holes are punched through the pages and plastic fasteners (usually hinged) or spiral wire bindings are inserted.

bookkeeping, the keeping of systematic records of money transactions. Proper records reveal losses and profits, assets and liabilities, and the net worth of the business. Commonly two sets of columns are used on a page—one for assets, the other for liabilities; this is double-entry method as opposed to single-entry method, in which debits and credits are entered in one set of columns. "Tabular" bookkeeping uses many columns for entries.

Book of Common Prayer, service book of Church of England and other Anglican churches. Derived from breviary and missal, the first was published 1549; Thomas Cranmer's revision incorporated 1552. Suppressed under Queen Mary, restored under Elizabeth, suppressed (1645–60) under Commonwealth and Protectorate, it was again made official and compulsory by Act of Uniformity (1662). Protestant Episcopal Church adopted first U.S. revised version in 1789.

Book of Concord, collection of authoritative confessions of faith of Lutheran Church, published 1580.

Book of the Dead, Egyptian religious text, probably estab. in final form in 7th-6th cent. B.C., though charms, formulas, and other parts may be found in inscriptions as early as 16th cent. B.C.

boomerang (boo'mürăng), missile in the form of a curved club used as a weapon. The small boomerang (1½ to 2 ft. long), used only for sport, describes a circle of c.50 ft. diameter and returns to the thrower. The larger or war boomerang does not return. Though best known as an Australian implement, the boomerang has been used, in various forms, in numerous civilizations.

Boone, Daniel, 1734–1820, American frontiersman, b. near Reading, Pa. In March, 1775, as advance agent for Transylvania Co., he blazed WILDERNESS ROAD and founded Boonesboro (or Boonesborough) on Kentucky R. Captured by Indians in 1778 but escaped. Moved to Missouri after land titles in Ky. were invalidated. His adventures became well known through so-called autobiographical account by John FILSON.

Boone, city (pop. 12,164), central Iowa, N of Des Moines and on Des Moines R.; laid out 1865. Rail and mining center; coal, clay, and gravel deposits.

Boonesboro, locality, central Ky., on Kentucky R. and SE of Lexington. Named for Daniel BOONE who built fort here 1775 for TRANSYLVANIA COMPANY. Was Transylvania cap. for time; had Indian attacks.

Boonton, town (pop. 7,163), N N.J., NNE of Morristown. Mfg. of radio equipment and plastics.

Boonville. 1 City (pop. 5,092), SW Ind., NE of Evansville. Trade center for coal-mining and agr. area. Has mfg. of underwear and food products. **2** City (pop. 6,686), central Mo., on Missouri R. and W of Columbia, in agr. area. Mfg. of corncob pipes. Civil War

battle near here won by Union troops, June 17, 1861.

Booth, name of English family prominent in SALVATION ARMY. **William Booth,** 1829–1912, was an evangelist in London. There he and his wife, Catherine Mumford Booth (1829–90), estab. the Christian Mission which became (1878) the Salvation Army. A son, **Bramwell Booth,** 1856–1929, succeeded his father as general in 1912. Another son, **Ballington Booth,** 1859–1940, was commander in Australia and then in U.S. (1887–96). In 1896 with his wife he withdrew to found VOLUNTEERS OF AMERICA. A daughter of William Booth, **Emma Moss Booth-Tucker,** 1860–1903, with her husband jointly commanded the Army in U.S. (1896–1903). Another daughter, **Evangeline Cory Booth,** 1865–1950, was commander in Canada (1895–1904), commander in U.S. (1904–34), and general (1934–39).

Booth, Charles, 1840–1916, English social investigator, pioneer in social survey method. Headed group making exhaustive statistical study of London poverty (*Life and Labour of the People in London,* 17 vols., 1891–1903).

Booth, Edwin: see BOOTH, JUNIUS BRUTUS.

Booth, Evangeline Cory: see BOOTH, family.

Booth, Junius Brutus, 1796–1852, English actor of Shaksperian roles; one of the great figures of 19th-cent. theater. After 1821 he was in U.S. He was surpassed by his son, **Edwin Booth,** 1833–93, first great American tragedian. Gentle actor of grace and rare restraint, his roles included Richard III, Lear, Richelieu, Shylock. Toured extensively and built the Booth Theatre (N.Y., 1869), presenting Shakspere there until his bankruptcy in 1873. Also founded the Players Club. Appeared last as Hamlet in 1891. His career temporarily ceased (1865) when his brother, **John Wilkes Booth,** 1838–65, assassinated Abraham LINCOLN. A Confederate sympathizer, unlike his family, Booth first plotted to abduct Lincoln, a plan which failed. On Good Friday, April 14, 1865, learning Lincoln would attend that evening's performance of *Our American Cousin* in Washington, he plotted (with accomplices) simultaneous assassination of Lincoln, Vice Pres. Johnson, and Secretary of State Seward. Seward was seriously wounded, while Johnson was spared. Booth entered the presidential box in Ford's Theater, shot Lincoln, vaulted to the stage (breaking his leg), and escaped on horseback. Found in a barn after two weeks' hysterical searching, Booth was shot (either by himself or his pursuers) and the barn was burned. See also M. E. SURRATT.

Booth, Shirley, 1907–, American actress, whose real name is Thelma Booth Ford. An actress of great range, since her New York debut in 1925 she has been notable in such varied plays as *My Sister Eileen, Come Back, Little Sheba,* and *The Time of the Cuckoo.*

Booth, William: see BOOTH, family.

Boothbay, town (pop. 1,559), S Maine, S of Wiscasset; settled 1630. Resort and artists' colony; boatbuilding and fishing center. Adjacent **Boothbay Harbor,** resort town (pop. 2,290), has summer theater.

Boothia Peninsula, northernmost tip of N Canada, Franklin dist., Northwest Territories, connected with mainland by Isthmus of Boothia. Discovered and explored by Sir John Ross (1829–33) who estab. N magnetic pole here 1831. Later explored by Sir John Franklin (1847–48) and Roald Amundsen (1903–05).

Booth-Tucker, Emma Moss: see BOOTH, family.

Bootle, county borough (pop. 74,302), Lancashire, England; port adjacent to Liverpool. Has tanning, engineering, and flour milling.

Booz (bō'ŏz), same as BOAZ.

Bopp, Franz (fränts' bôp') 1791–1867, German philologist, who demonstrated relationship of Indo-European languages in his *Vergleichende Grammatik* [comparative grammar] (1833–52).

Bora, Katharina von: see LUTHER, MARTIN.

boracic acid: see BORIC ACID.

Borah, William Edgar, 1865–1940, U.S. Senator from Idaho (1907–40), Republican. Notable for independent stands; major interest in foreign policy. Opposed League of Nations, but advocated disarmament. Opposed both economic monopoly and extension of governmental powers.

Borah, Mount, or **Borah Peak** [for W. E. Borah], 12,-655 ft. high, central Idaho, in Lost River Mts. Highest point in state.

borax, hydrated crystalline salt of sodium, boron, oxygen. Used as antiseptic, for cleaning textiles and metal surfaces, and in making glass, enamels, shellacs, ceramic glazes. In large doses it is toxic. In **borax bead test,** borax heated on loop to form "bead," then dipped in substance to be analyzed and reheated. Metals give bead different colors, e.g., cobalt, blue; copper, blue or green.

Bordeaux, Henri, duc de: see CHAMBORD, HENRI, COMTE DE.

Bordeaux, Henry (ärē' bôrdō'), 1870–, French novelist. Wrote witty, popular stories propagating virtues of family life. *Les Rocquevillard* (1902; Eng. tr., *The Will to Live*) is typical.

Bordeaux (bôrdō'), city (pop. 238,653), cap. of Gironde dept., SW France, on the Garonne; historic cap. of Aquitaine and Guienne. Seaport (accessible from Atlantic through the Gironde); export center for wines from Bordeaux region. University founded 1441. As Burdigala, was provincial cap. under Romans; became archiepiscopal see in 4th cent. Under English rule 1152–1453. Temporary cap. of France 1914, 1940. Handsome 18th-cent. architecture partly damaged in World War II. Montaigne and Montesquieu were magistrates in Bordeaux.

Bordeaux mixture, a FUNGICIDE, containing copper sulphate and lime and used as a spray or as a dust.

Borden, Gail, 1801–74, American inventor and surveyor. He patented (1856) a process for evaporating milk. Superintended Texas land surveys before 1851.

Borden, Lizzie Andrew, 1860–1927, New England spinster, accused of killing father and stepmother (1892). Trial ended with verdict of not guilty.

Borden, Sir Robert Laird, 1854–1937, Canadian prime minister (1911–20). Led Canada through World War I. Helped define new status of self-governing dominions in British Empire.

Bordentown, city (pop. 5,497), W N.J., on Delaware R. below Trenton, and at W end of old Delaware and Raritan Canal; settled 1682. Partly destroyed by British 1778. Clara Barton's school (1739) is Red Cross memorial.

Border, the, in British history, region about the boundary between England and Scotland, former scene of much strife. The wild country figures in legends, folklore, and the Border ballads.

Bordet, Jules (zhül bôrdä'), 1870–, Belgian serologist and immunologist. Shared in devising complement fixation technique (1900) later used in Wassermann test and discovered whooping cough bacillus (1906). Won 1919 Nobel Prize in Physiology and Medicine for work in immunity.

Bordone, Paris (pä'rēs bôrdō'nä), 1500–1571?, Venetian painter of portraits and of religious and mythological scenes; pupil of Titian.

Boreas (bō'rēŭs), in Greek legend, north wind; son of Astraeus and Eos.

Borel, Félix Édouard Émile (fäleks' ädwär' ämēl' bôrĕl'), 1871–, French mathematician. Noted for work in infinitesimal calculus, calculus of probabilities.

Borger, city (pop. 18,059), N Texas, NE of Amarillo near Canadian R., in Panhandle. Has oil refineries and carbon-black, synthetic rubber, and metal products plants.

Borgese, Giuseppe Antonio (jōōzĕp'pä äntō'nyō bôrjä'zä), 1882–1952, Italian-American author, b. near Palermo. Opponent of Fascism, he came to U.S. in 1931, taught at Smith College (1932–35) and the Univ. of Chicago (from 1936). One of his political works is *Goliath: the March of Fascism* (1937).

Borghese (bôrgā'zä), Roman noble family. Among its members were Pope PAUL V, several cardinals, and many prominent citizens.

Borghese, Villa (vĕl'lä bôrgā'zä), summer palace in Rome, built by Scipione Cardinal Borghese. Now a repository for paintings.

Borghese Warrior, Greek statue of the 1st cent. B.C. by Agasias. Represents warrior attacking mounted foe. Formerly in Villa Borghese, now in Louvre.

Borgia (bôr'jä), Span. *Borja* (bôr'hä), Spanish-Italian noble family. Among members were Pope CALIXTUS III, Pope ALEXANDER VI, and St. FRANCIS BORGIA. **Cesare Borgia** (chä'zärä), c.1476–1507, younger son of Alexander VI, was an outstanding figure of Renaissance. Cardinal at 17, he resigned after murder of his elder brother (in which he probably took part); entered politics. Allied himself with Louis XII of France, who created him duke of Valentinois, and with his father's encouragement made himself master of Romagna, duchy of Urbino, and other places (1499–1502). He then lured his chief enemies to castle of Sinigaglia, where he had them strangled (1502). His father's death (1503) and Julius II's election to papacy ruined his ambitions. Julius forced him to restore his possessions to the Papal States, and Louis XII turned against him. He found asylum with his brother-in-law, the king of Navarre, in whose service he died fighting. Vicious, ruthless, but of superior intelligence and vision, he was the model for Machiavelli's *Prince.* His sister was **Lucrezia Borgia** (lōōkrä'tsyä), 1480–1519. Her first marriage (1492–97) ended in annulment; her second husband, Alfonso of Aragon (a natural son of Alfonso II of Naples) was murdered by her brother Cesare in 1500. In 1501 she was married to Alfonso d'Este, who became duke of Ferrara in 1505. Once removed from family influence, Lucrezia won wide esteem through her beauty, kindness, piety, despite unfounded rumors of her crimes and vices. Her brilliant court included Ariosto.

Borglum, Gutzon (John Gutzon de la Mothe Borglum) (bôr'glŭm), 1867–1941, American sculptor. The gigantic Mt. Rushmore Natl. Memorial in S.Dak. is his best-known work.

boric acid or **boracic acid,** white, crystalline, weakly acidic compound of boron, hydrogen, oxygen. Used as antiseptic (in solution), in pottery glazing, as fireproofing agent, and in making enamels. Poisonous if taken internally.

Borinage (bôrēnäzh'), region, S Hainaut, Belgium, surrounding Mons and extending W to French border. Important coal-mining district.

Boris, rulers of Bulgaria. **Boris I,** d. 903, ruled as khan 853–88. Baptized 865, he introduced Christianity of Greek rite among Bulgarians. **Boris III,** 1894–1943, tsar (1918–43), son and successor of Tsar FERDINAND. Set up royal dictatorship (1935); forced Rumania to restore S DOBRUJA (1940); joined Berlin Pact (1941; see AXIS). Died mysteriously soon after visiting Hitler. Succeeded by small son, Simeon II.

Boris Godunov: see GODUNOV, BORIS.

Born, Bertrand de: see BERTRAND DE BORN.

Börne, Ludwig (lōōd'vĭkh bûr'nù), 1786–1837, German journalist whose real name was Löb Baruch. With a generally satirical tone, he attacked censorship and encouraged liberalism. He and Heine are considered initiators of the Young Germany movement.

Borneo, island (286,969 sq. mi.; pop. c.3,080,000), SW of the Philippines; largest of Malay Archipelago and third largest in world. Largely jungle and mountainous. Iron, copper, and coal are mined, and there are great oil fields. Interior is inhabited mainly by Dyaks; the coastal areas by Malays, Javanese, and Chinese. The Portuguese visited Borneo in 1521, preceding the Dutch and the English. In 19th cent. the Dutch established their control over W, S, and E Borneo. These Dutch territories (208,285 sq. mi.; pop. 2,168,-661), comprising over two thirds of Borneo, became part of Indonesia in 1949. The British still control the N and NW in BRUNEI, SARAWAK, and NORTH BORNEO.

Bornholm (bôrn'hôlm), island (227 sq. mi.; pop. 48,-134), Denmark, in Baltic Sea, 24 mi. off Swedish coast. Low tableland, rocky and steep on N and W coasts. Agr., fishing; granite, kaolin. Chief town and port is Ronne.

Borobudur or **Boroboedoer** (both: bō'rōbŏŏdōōr'), ruins of a Buddhist monument, Java, Indonesia. Within intricately carved truncated pyramid is a seated Buddha. Dates from 8th and 9th cent.

Borodin, Aleksandr (Porfirevich) (ŭlyĭksän'dŭr bôrô-dēn'), 1833–87, Russian composer. A member of the Russian Five (see BALAKIREV). His chief works are two symphonies; a tone poem, *In the Steppes of Central Asia;* an opera, *Prince Igor.*

Borodino (bŭrŭdyĭnô'), village, RSFSR, W of Mozhaisk. Here in 1812 Russians under Kutuzov made heroic stand against Napoleon's advance on Moscow. Battle cost c.80,000 casualties.

Boroimhe, Brian: see BRIAN BORU.

boron (bō'rŏn), chemical element (symbol = B; see also ELEMENT, table), a brownish to yellow crystalline solid or an amorphous powder. Forms organic and inorganic compounds. Not found free in nature.

Borotra, Jean (zhä' bôrôträ'), 1898–, French tennis player. Member French Davis Cup team that defeated U.S. in 1927 and held the cup until 1933.

Borough, Stephen, 1525–84, English navigator. Master of first ship to round North Cape (1553) and reach Russia by arctic route. Thus direct trade relations became possible.

borough-English, a rule or custom in parts of England whereby land descended to the youngest son in preference to his older brothers. Abolished 1925.

Borromean Islands, Italy: see MAGGIORE, LAGO.

Borromeo, Charles: see CHARLES BORROMEO, SAINT.

Borromini, Francesco (fränchä'skō bōr-rōmē'nē), 1599–1667, Italian baroque architect. Official architect of Rome 1644–55. Collaborated in decoration of St. Peter's; designed façade of Sant' Agnese.

Borrow, George Henry, 1803–81, English writer. A wide wanderer, he distributed Bibles on the Continent and became a friend of the gypsies. Among his extraordinary books are *The Bible in Spain* (1843), *Lavengro* (1851), and *The Romany Rye* (1857).

Borstal system, method intended to rehabilitate delinquents (between ages of 16 and 21) by stressing good conditions, physical and vocational training. Originated 1902 at Borstal Prison, Kent, England.

Boru, Brian: see BRIAN BORU.

Borysthenes: see DNIEPER, river of USSR.

borzoi: see HOUND.

Bos, Jerom: see BOSCH, HIERONYMUS.

Bosanquet, Bernard (bō'zŭnkĭt), 1848–1923, British idealistic philosopher.

Bosch, Carl (bôsh), 1874–1940, German chemist. Shared 1931 Nobel Prize for adapting HABER PROCESS to achieve mass production.

Bosch, Hieronymus (hērôn'ĭmŭs bôs') or **Jerom Bos** (yä'rôm bôs'), c.1460–1516, Flemish painter. Treated such themes as the temptation of St. Anthony and the Last Judgment as fantasies peopled with diabolical little figures. A favorite with Philip II of Spain, some of best work is still in Madrid and the Escorial.

Boscoreale (bôs'kōrä-älä), small town, Campania, S Italy, at foot of Vesuvius. Celebrated collection of silverwork (1st cent. A.D.) unearthed here in 1895; now in Louvre, Paris.

Bose, Sir Jagadis Chandra (jŭgä'dēs chŭn'drŭ bōs), 1858–1937, Indian physicist noted for research in plant life. He invented the crescograph, a device for measuring plant growth.

Bosio, François Joseph, Baron (fräswä' zhôzěf' bärō' bôsyō'), 1769?–1845, French sculptor, imperial portraitist to Napoleon I.

Bosnia and Hercegovina (bŏz'něŭ, hěrtsùgōvē'nù), autonomous republic (19,909 sq. mi.; pop. 2,561,961),

N Yugoslavia; cap. Sarajevo. Consists of Bosnia (N), with Sarajevo, and Hercegovina (S), with Mostar. Crossed by Dinaric Alps and Sava R., it is largely forested and agr. Inhabitants are Serbs and Croats of Catholic, Moslem, and Orthodox faiths. Settled by Serbs in 7th cent., Bosnia appeared as kingdom in 12th cent.; occasionally acknowledged kings of Hungary as overlords; annexed Hercegovina from Serbia late 14th cent.; fell to Turkey 1463. Peasants, held in serfdom by Moslem landlords, rebelled 1875. Serbia and Russia intervened in their favor (see RUSSO-TURKISH WARS). Congress of Berlin (1878) placed Bosnia and Hercegovina under Austro-Hungarian administration but left it, in theory, under Turkish overlordship. Full annexation by Austria-Hungary (1908) nearly brought war with Serbia and Russia, but German mediation in 1909 ended the crisis to Austria's satisfaction. Archduke Francis Ferdinand's assassination at Sarajevo precipitated World War I. Annexed by Serbia 1918, region became one of Yugoslavia's constituent republics 1946.

Bosporus (bŏs'pùrùs), strait, 20 mi. long, 1,800 ft. wide at its narrowest, separating European and Asiatic Turkey and joining Black Sea with Sea of Marmara. Istanbul lies on both shores. See also DARDANELLES.

Bossier City (bō'zhùr), town (pop. 15,470), NW La., on Red R. opposite Shreveport. Processes oil, cotton, and chemicals; railroad shops. Has ruins of Confederate Fort Smith.

Bossuet, Jacques Bénigne (bôsüä'), 1627–1704, French preacher and writer. A canon at Metz, then long tutor to the son of Louis XIV at court (1670–81), and finally bishop of Meaux, he was one of the most celebrated of all French preachers, his panegyric sermons and his funeral orations for the great being particularly notable. He wrote religious polemics in favor of Gallicanism, against the Protestants, and against the quietism of Fénelon. His *Discourse on Universal History* (1681) is a study of the hand of God in human history. His literary style is noted for vigorous purity, simplicity, and flashing eloquence.

Boston, municipal borough (pop. 24,453), Lincolnshire, England. Once an important port, now fishing center. John COTTON and other founders of Massachusetts Bay Colony sailed from here 1633.

Boston, city (pop. 801,444), state cap., E Mass., on Boston Bay; settled 1630 as main colony of MASSACHUSETTS BAY COMPANY. Largest city of New England and 10th largest of U.S., it is a major commercial, financial, industrial, and cultural center and a leading U.S. port. Important market for fish and wool, it has mfg. (textiles, leather and rubber goods, machinery, food products, chemicals), shipbuilding, and publishing. Early center of Puritanism, with vigorous intellectual life, it printed first newspaper in the colonies, *News-Letter* (1704). Important in prelude to Revolution (see BOSTON MASSACRE; BOSTON TEA PARTY; FANEUIL HALL; ADAMS, SAMUEL; REVERE, PAUL). Battle of BUNKER HILL was fought here, June 17, 1775, and city was besieged until March, 1776. After Revolution Boston prospered through world shipping and textile and shoe mfg. on New England rivers. Influence of rich and conservative Beacon Hill and Back Bay (patronized arts and letters, backed reformers) persisted long after industrial growth brought many immigrants (mostly Irish at first). City annexed adjacent towns, e.g., West Roxbury (with BROOK FARM) and CHARLESTOWN. Landmarks of the past include Old North Church, old statehouse (now museum), and Boston Common. Has Boston Symphony Orchestra (1881) and Mus. of Fine Arts. Seat of Simmons Col. (nonsectarian; for women; chartered 1899, opened 1902; first to combine liberal and professional instruction for women), Boston Univ. (nonsectarian; private; coed.; chartered 1869, opened 1871), Boston Public Latin School for boys (opened 1635; one of oldest free public schools in U.S.), New England Conservatory of Music (1867), New England Medical Center, and Harvard Medical School. HARVARD UNIVERSITY is at near-by Cambridge and Boston Col. mainly at CHESTNUT HILL.

Boston fern, house FERN (*Nephrolepis exaltata bostoniensis*), with graceful, drooping fronds.

Boston ivy or **Japanese ivy,** woody vine (*Parthenocissus tricuspidata*), popular for wall coverings. Its three-lobed leaves turn vivid red in the autumn.

Boston Massacre, 1770, pre-Revolutionary incident in which five members of rioting crowd were killed by British soldiers sent to Boston to maintain order and enforce TOWNSHEND ACTS.

Boston Mountains, E Okla. and NW Ark., most rugged section of the Ozarks, rising to c.2,345 ft. White R. rises here.

Boston Museum of Fine Arts: see MUSEUM OF FINE ARTS, at Boston, Mass.

Boston Public Latin School: see BOSTON.

Boston Public Library, founded 1852, chiefly through gift of Joshua Bates. Present building (1895) on Copley Square has murals by Puvis de Chavannes, Edwin Abbey, and John S. Sargent; libraries of John Adams and Nathaniel Bowditch; special collections.

Boston Symphony Orchestra, founded 1881 by Henry Lee Higginson. Among its outstanding conductors have been Pierre Monteux (1919–24), Serge Koussevitsky (1924–49), and Charles Münch (1949–).

Boston Tea Party, 1773, caused by retention of tea tax after repeal of TOWNSHEND ACTS. Group of indignant colonists, disguised as Indians, threw tea from three ships into Boston harbor.

Boston terrier, small, smooth-haired, nonsporting dog, developed in Boston, Mass., from crosses between bull terrier and bulldog. Usually brindle with white markings; body weight 15–25 lb.; erect ears; short tail.

Boston University: see BOSTON.

Bostwick, Arthur Elmore, 1860–1942, American librarian. Wrote *The American Public Library.*

Boswell, James (bŏz'wŭl), 1740–95, British biographer, b. Scotland, author of *The Life of Samuel Johnson, LL.D.* (1791), one of the most celebrated biographies of all time. A Scottish lawyer, he traveled widely on the Continent and spent much time in London. He met Johnson in 1763, became a member of the Johnson circle, and in his biography noted minutely all the doings and sayings of the literary dictator. Among Boswell's other works are his *Account of Corsica* (1768) and *The Journal of a Tour in the Hebrides with Samuel Johnson, LL.D.* (1785; complete ed., 1936). His papers, recovered in 20th cent. by Col. Ralph H. Isham, have yielded in published form *Private Papers* (18 vols., 1928–34), *Boswell's London Journal, 1762–1763* (1950), *Boswell in Holland, 1763–1764* (1952), and other volumes.

Bosworth Field, Leicestershire, England. Scene of battle (1485) in which Richard III was killed and the crown passed to his victor, Henry VII.

botanic garden, place in which plants are grown for display and scientific study. Performs diversified functions, e.g., plant breeding, maintenance of libraries and herbariums, administration of educational programs. Botanic gardens are found in or near most large cities.

botany, scientific study of plant life. Botany and zoology together comprise science of BIOLOGY. Beginnings of plant classification found in work of Aristotle but system of binomial nomenclature established by Linnaeus marked greatest progress in systematics. Among those who contributed to the growth of botany: Robert Brown, A. P. de Candolle, Hugo de Vries, Asa Gray, Nehemiah Grew, John Ray, Lamarck, Mendel, Hugo von Mohl, Julius von Sachs. See *ill.,* plant forms, p. 783.

Botany Bay, inlet, New South Wales, Australia, just S of Sydney. Named by Capt. Cook and the botanist Sir Joseph Banks. Though Australia's first penal colony was often called Botany Bay, its actual site was Sydney.

Botev, Khristo (khrĭ'stō bô'tĕf), 1848–76, Bulgarian poet and patriot, a leader of the revolution against Turkey (in which he was killed).

botfly, hairy fly with parasitic larvae. Horse botfly eggs, laid on horse, mule, donkey hair, are carried by tongue or lips, to mouth, and migrate to stomach, attaching to lining. Ox warble flies (heel fly; bomb fly) lay eggs on cattle, other animals; larvae migrate through skin, cause swellings (warbles). Sheep botfly or gadfly attacks sheep, goats, deer, sometimes man. Mosquitoes and other insects carry eggs of one species to humans.

Both, Andries (än'drēēs bōt'), c.1608–c.1640, and **Jan Both** (yän), c.1618–1652, Flemish painters and etchers; brothers. Jan painted Italian landscapes; Andries did animals and figures.

Botha, Louis (bō'tù), 1862–1919, South African soldier and statesman. Led Boers in South African War, but after 1902 favored working with the British. Premier of the Transvaal, 1907–10, and of Union of South Africa, 1910–19. In World War I he led forces which took German South-West Africa.

Bothnia, Gulf of, northernmost portion of Baltic Sea, between Finland and Sweden.

Bothwell, James Hepburn, 4th **earl of,** c.1536–1578, Scottish nobleman; third husband of MARY QUEEN OF SCOTS. After murder of RIZZIO (1566), Mary trusted only Bothwell. Accused of murdering her husband, Lord DARNLEY, Bothwell was acquitted in rigged trial and married Mary, 1567. Scottish aristocracy attacked him and forced Mary to give him up. Fled to Denmark, was imprisoned, and died insane.

bo tree or **pipal,** fig tree (*Ficus religiosa*) of India, sacred to Buddhists. An ancient specimen grows at Anuradhapura.

Böttger, Johann Friedrich (yō'hän frē'drĭckh bûtkhùr), 1682–1719, German chemist, originator of Dresden china. Developed various glazes and perfected white porcelain.

Botticelli, Sandro (sän'drō bôt"tĭchĕl'lē), c.1444–1510, Florentine painter of the Renaissance; a pupil of Fra Filippo Lippi. A master of color and rhythmic line. Famous for such paintings as *Spring, Venus,* and *Allegory of Calumny* and for illustrations (in silverpoint and pen) of *Divine Comedy.* Painted religious themes in his last years.

botulism (bŏt'ūlĭzùm), food poisoning caused by toxin produced by a bacillus (*Clostridium botulinum*). Toxin attacks nervous system; fatal respiratory paralysis common sequel unless antitoxin serum is given.

Botwood, town (pop. c.2,744), NE central N.F., Canada, at mouth of Exploits R. Final refueling base for planes on N route to Ireland. Site of seaplane base. In World War II was base of North Atlantic air patrol. Airport estab. 1939.

Bouchard, Henry (ärе' bōōshär'), 1875–, French sculptor. His work often represents workers, in action or at rest.

Bouché, Louis (bōōshā'), 1896–, American painter of realistic and abstract pictures. Noted for murals.

Boucher, François (fräswä' bōōshā'), 1703–70, French painter. Famous for boudoir decorations, he was the most fashionable painter of his day. Became director of Gobelins factory.

Bouches-du-Rhône (bōōsh'-dü-rōn'), department (2,026 sq. mi.; pop. 976,241), SE France, in Provence; cap. Marseilles. Includes Rhone delta, CAMARGUE.

Boucicault, Dion (bōō'sĭkôlt), 1822?–1890, British playwright, actor; in U.S. after 1853. Among his more than 300 plays and adaptations (in many of which he acted) are *The Octoroon* (1859), *The Colleen Bawn* (1860), and *Rip van Winkle* (1865).

Boucicaut (bōōsēkō'), c.1366–1421, marshal of France; real name: Jean Le Meingre. Captured by Turks at NIKOPOL 1396. Ransomed, he helped in defense of Constantinople 1399. Governor of Genoa 1401–7. Died in England after capture at Agincourt (1415). Wrote ballads, other poems.

Boudin, Eugène Louis (ûzhĕn' lwĕ' boŏdĕ'), 1824–98, French landscape and marine painter.

Boudinot, Elias (boŏ'dĭnŏt), 1740–1821, American Revolutionary statesman. Member of Continental Congress (1777–78, 1781–84). Supported the Constitution. Director, U.S. mint (1795–1805).

Bougainville, Louis Antoine de (lwĕ' ätwän' dù boŏgĕvĕl'), 1729–1811, French navigator. Made voyage around the world (1767–69), rediscovering Solomon Isls., largest of which is named for him. In American Revolution fought Hood at Martinique. Wrote *Description d'un voyage autour du monde*.

Bougainville (boŏ'gŭnvĭl), volcanic island (3,880 sq. mi.; pop. 50,000), S Pacific, largest of SOLOMON ISLANDS. Visited 1768 by Bougainville. Became a German possession in 1884. Governed since 1920 as part of Territory of New Guinea (see NEW GUINEA, TERRITORY OF). In World War II it was last major Japanese stronghold in Solomons.

bougainvillea (boŏ"gŭnvĭl'ēù), woody vine (*Bougainvillea*) of tropical America, cultivated in U.S. for showy red or purple bracts that enclose flowers.

Bouguereau, Adolphe William (ädôlf' boŏgùrō'), 1825–1905, French academic and sentimental painter.

Bouillon, Godfrey of: see GODFREY OF BOUILLON.

Bouillon, Henri de la Tour d'Auvergne, vicomte de Turenne, duc de (ärĕ' dù lä toŏr' dōvĕr'nyù, vēkôt' dù türĕn' dük dù boŏyō'), 1555–1623, marshal of France and Protestant leader; a grandson of Anne de Montmorency. Acquired duchy of Bouillon by marriage. Briefly a member of regency council under Marie de' Medici, he retired to his duchy after quarrel with queen. His older son, **Frédéric Maurice de la Tour d'Auvergne, duc de Bouillon** (frädärĕk' mōrēs'), c.1605–1652, French general, took part in the CINQ MARS conspiracy but was pardoned. He espoused Catholicism, sided with the princes during Fronde, lost his principality of Sedan to France. TURENNE was his brother.

Bouillon, town (pop. 2,830), Luxembourg prov., S Belgium, in the Ardennes. Its ancient castle belonged to Godfrey of Bouillon, who sold it to bishop of Liége 1095. In 15th cent. town and environs passed to William de la Marck, whose heirs assumed titles duke of Bouillon and prince of Sedan. Bouillon was annexed to France 1678–1815.

Boulanger, Georges (zhôrzh' boŏläzhä'), 1837–91, French general, "the man on horseback." Minister of war, 1886–87; leader of nationalist reactionary movement—Boulangism—which foreshadowed fascism. Won overwhelming victory at polls 1889. A military coup d'état seemed imminent, but Boulanger lost his nerve, fled to Belgium, and killed himself.

Boulanger, Gustave Rodolphe Clarence (güstäv' rôdôlf' kläräs'), 1824–88, French painter of Oriental scenes.

Boulanger, Nadia, 1887–, French teacher of composition, professor at the Paris Conservatoire after 1945. Many American composers studied under her (e.g., Aaron Copland, Virgil Thomson).

Boulder, city (pop. 19,999; alt. c.5,350 ft.), N central Colo., NW of Denver; laid out 1859. Health resort, with mild, dry climate and mineral springs. Rail and trade center for mines and farms. Seat of Univ. of COLORADO. U.S. atomic energy plant begun near by in 1951.

boulder, any large rock fragment, either formed from bedrock below or transported by water or ice.

Boulder City, town (pop. 3,903), S Nev., just W of Hoover Dam. Year-round tourist center.

boulder clay, unstratified mixture of clay, sand, gravel, and boulders left by retreating glacier.

Boulder Dam: see HOOVER DAM.

Boulle or **Buhl, André Charles** (both: ädrä' shärl' boŏl'), 1642–1732, French cabinetmaker who created a distinctive furniture style roughly similar to Louis XIV and Regence design. Excelled in marquetry.

Boulogne-sur-Mer (boŏlô'nyù-sür-mĕr'), city (pop. 34,-389), Pas-de-Calais dept., N France; port on English Channel. From here the Romans sailed A.D. 43 to conquer Britain. Heavily damaged in World War II. Statue of Our Lady of Boulogne, in cathedral, is object of pilgrimages.

Boulton, Matthew (bōl'tùn), 1728–1809, English engineer and manufacturer, partner from 1775 of James Watt in production of steam engines. New British copper coinage estab. 1797 by Boulton.

bouncing Bet: see SOAPWORT.

Boundary Peak, 13,145 ft. high, SW Nev., in White Mts. near Calif. line. Highest point in Nev.

Bound Brook, borough (pop. 8,374), N central N.J., on Raritan R. and NW of New Brunswick; settled 1681. Mfg. of chemicals and textiles. Has flower nurseries. Site of a Cornwallis victory (1777).

Bountiful, city (pop. 6,004), N central Utah; N of Salt Lake City. Early Mormon chapel survives.

Bounty, British naval ship, scene of noted mutiny (1789) while on long trading voyage in the Pacific. Capt. William BLIGH and 18 of crew were set adrift in small boat; sailed c.4,000 mi. to Timor. Some mutineers settled on PITCAIRN ISLAND.

bounty, premium paid by the state for the production or export of certain goods. Unlike SUBSIDY, it involves payment per unit of the product. Used to encourage production or export of favored goods and as substitute for protective tariff. Money payments formerly made to induce army enlistment and rewards for killing destructive animals also called bounty.

Bourassa, Henri (boŏräsä'), 1868–1952, Canadian political leader; grandson of Louis Joseph Papineau. Led powerful opposition (Nationalist) party in Quebec. Opposed diplomatic entanglements with U.S. and Great Britain; also against participation in World War I.

Bourbon (boŏrbō'), royal family which ruled in France, Spain, the Two Sicilies, and Parma; a cadet branch of the Capetians. Takes its name from castle in Bourbonnais (now Allier dept.), whose first lord was Adhémar, a 9th-cent. noble. In 1272 Robert of Clermont, sixth son of Louis IX of France, married the heiress of Bourbon. His son Louis was 1st duke of Bourbon. His descendant, **Charles, duc de Bourbon** (shärl', dük' dù), 1490–1527, constable of France, treacherously went over to Emperor Charles V (1523); was killed while leading imperial troops in sack of Rome. His lands were confiscated; his title discontinued. A younger son of the 1st duke founded line of Bourbon-Vendôme. **Antoine de Bourbon** (ätwän'), 1518–62, duke of Vendôme, became king of Navarre by marrying JEANNE D'ALBRET. From his brother Louis descend the houses of CONDÉ and CONTI. Antoine's son became (1589) the first Bourbon king of France as HENRY IV. His direct descendants ruled FRANCE (except from 1792 to 1814) until 1830, when Charles X was deposed, and died out in 1883 with Henri, comte de CHAMBORD. The younger branch of Bourbon-Orléans (see ORLÉANS, family) gave France King Louis Philippe and inherited Bourbon claim to throne. The house of **Bourbon-Spain,** Span. *Borbón*, began in 1700 with accession of Louis XIV's grandson, PHILIP V, on Spanish throne. The succession in SPAIN was contested (19th cent.) by CARLISTS against ISABELLA II. Alfonso XIII was deposed in 1931. The house of **Bourbon-Sicily,** sprung from the Spanish line, was founded (1759) by FERDINAND I of the TWO SICILIES and ceased to rule when Francis II abdicated (1861). The house of **Bourbon-Parma** was founded (1748) by a younger son of Philip V of Spain. Robert (1848–1907), 5th duke of PARMA and Piacenza, was deposed in 1860. He had 18 children, among them Empress ZITA of Austria and SIXTUS OF BOURBON-PARMA.

Bourbonnais (boŏrbônä'), region and former province, central France, in Allier and Cher depts.; historic cap. Moulins. Other towns: Vichy, Montluçon. Appanage of dukes of BOURBON until 1527.

Bourbon-Parma, Bourbon-Sicily, and **Bourbon-Spain:** see BOURBON, family.

Bourdelle, Émile Antoine (āmēl' ätwän' boõrdĕl'), 1861–1929, French sculptor. Studied under Rodin. Recognized as one of the greatest modern sculptors, he achieved his greatest success in heroic and monumental works.

Bourg-en-Bresse or **Bourg** (boõrk-ä-brĕs'), town (pop. 21,169), cap. of Ain dept., E France, chief town of Bresse; a gastronomic mecca.

Bourgeois, Léon (lāō' boõrzhwä'), 1851–1925, French statesman, social philosopher. Premier 1895–96. Early advocate of League of Nations; won 1920 Nobel Peace Prize. Chief work: *Solidarité* (1896).

bourgeoisie (boõrshwäzē'), name applied to citizens of French towns and subsequently to middle class in all nations. Known in feudal times as Third Estate. If defined as mercantile or trading class, bourgeoisie has existed since earliest history and was powerful in ancient Rome. In eclipse in early Middle Ages, merchants later won contest with nobles. They turned increasingly to principles of constitutionality and natural rights against claims of divine right and promoted English, French, and American revolutions. In 19th cent. position of the bourgeoisie became more insecure due to wars, economic crises, and rising socialist and communist criticism. While concept of bourgeoisie has less relevance to U.S. than to Europe, the influence of the middle class in American affairs has usually predominated.

Bourges (boõrzh), city (pop. 41,597), cap. of Cher dept., central France; historic cap. of Berry. Arms and clothes mfg. Important in Roman times; early archiepiscopal see. University founded 1463, abolished in French Revolution. Cathedral and house of Jacques Cœur are glorious examples of French Gothic. See also PRAGMATIC SANCTION OF BOURGES.

Bourget, Paul (pôl' boõrzhä'), 1852–1935, French novelist. Catholic and conservative, he is noted for works of psychological analysis, as *Le Disciple* (1889), *Le Démon de midi* [the noonday demon] (1914).

Bourget, Le (lù), suburb of Paris, France; one of city's airports. Lindbergh landed here 1927.

Bourget, lake, c.11 mi. long, Savoie dept., E France. Aix-les-Bains is on its scenic shore.

Bourinot, Sir John George (boõ'rīnō''), 1837–1902, Canadian historian, known for standard works on the Canadian government.

Bourne, Francis (bôrn), 1861–1935, English Roman Catholic churchman, archbishop of Westminster (1903–35); made a cardinal 1911.

Bourne, Hugh (boõrn), 1772–1852, English evangelist. Held outdoor revivals despite ban by Wesleyan Conference. Estab. Primitive Methodists 1810.

Bourne, Randolph (Silliman) (bôrn), 1886–1918, American writer. His liberal interests led to vigorous advocacy of many causes, notably progressive education, pacifism, and political and social reform. His ideas, though adopted only in a small group in his life, have had great influence. Crippled and frail, he succumbed to the 1918 influenza epidemic.

Bourne, resort town (pop. 4,720), SE Mass., crossed by Cape Cod Canal. Includes BUZZARDS BAY resort.

Bournemouth (bôrn'mùth), county borough (pop. 144,-276), Hampshire, England; fashionable resort and art center on Poole Bay.

Boutens, Pieter Cornelis (bou'tùns), 1870–1943, Dutch lyric poet.

Bouts, Dierick or **Thierry** (dē'rĭk bouts', tyĕ'rĕ), c.1410–1475, Netherlands painter, famous for landscape backgrounds of his altarpiece panels.

Boutwell, George Sewall (bout'–), 1818–1905, U.S. Secretary of the Treasury (1869–73). His preoccupation with reduction of the national debt led to neglect of more important problems.

Bouvier, John (boõvēr') 1787–1851, American jurist, b. France. His *Law Dictionary* (1839), often revised, is still standard in U.S.

Bouvines (boõvĕn'), village, Nord dept., N France, near Lille. Scene of victory (1214) of Philip II of France over King John of England, Emperor Otto IV, and count of Flanders.

Bow (bō), river of S Alta., Canada. Rises on E slope of the Rockies and flows 315 mi. SE through superb mountain scenery of Banff Natl. Park, past Calgary, to join Oldman R., forming South Saskatchewan R.

Bow Bells (bō), in church of St. Mary-le-Bow in mid London. Traditionally only a person born in sound of Bow Bells is a true Londoner, a "cockney."

Bowditch, Nathaniel, 1773–1838, American navigator, mathematician. Corrected some 8,000 errors in Moore's *Practical Navigator;* new edition (*The New American Practical Navigator*) appeared under his name. His son **Henry Ingersoll Bowditch,** 1808–92, was a physician noted as authority on public health and on chest diseases. **Henry Pickering Bowditch,** 1840–1911, grandson of Nathaniel Bowditch, was known for work at Harvard Univ. in experimental physiology and medical education.

Bowdler, Thomas (boud'lùr, bŏd'–), 1754–1825, English editor. His prudish textual expurgations (especially of Shakspere) gave rise to term *bowdlerize.*

Bowdoin College: see BRUNSWICK, Maine.

Bowen, Elizabeth, 1899–, Anglo-Irish writer, author of novels of upper-class life (e.g., *The Hotel,* 1927; *The Death of the Heart,* 1938) and short stories (e.g., collection *Look at All These Roses,* 1941).

bower bird, any of several species of birds native to Australia and New Guinea. Build stick-grass bower or arbor for play, courtship display. Gardener bower bird makes lawn around bower and decorates with bright objects. Nests are outside bowers.

Bowery, the (bou'ùrē), section and street of lower Manhattan, New York city, between Chatham Square and Astor Place E of Broadway. Street was once a road to farm of Gov. Stuyvesant (buried at St. Mark's-in-the-Bouwerie). By 1860s section had many fine theatres; later became notorious for saloons and dives, and finally for derelicts.

Bowie, James (boõ'ē), 1799–1836, hero of Texas revolution who died at the ALAMO. Legend says bowie knife was named after him or brother, Rezin Bowie.

bowlegs (*genu varum*), deforming curvature of legs, generally the result of rickets in early life.

Bowles, Samuel, 1797–1851, American newspaper proprietor; founded Springfield (Mass.) weekly *Republican.* His son, **Samuel Bowles,** 1826–78, who joined paper at 17 and took control at 25, made it (1845) a morning daily. He and an exceptional staff made the *Republican* one of the country's most influential newspapers. His son, **Samuel Bowles,** 1851–1915, gave close editorial direction to the paper, but wrote little himself. **Chester B(liss) Bowles,** 1901–, grandson of Samuel Bowles (1826–78), was governor of Conn. (1949–51), U.S. ambassador to India (1951–53).

bowling, sport played by rolling heavy ball to knockdown bottle-like pin on indoor alley. Originated in Germany, probably as Christian rite. Dutch introduced game in America, where it became popular in 19th cent. Standardized as 10-pin game in 1895, when American Bowling Congress was founded.

Bowling Green. 1 City (pop. 18,347), S Ky., on Barren R. and SSW of Louisville; founded 1780. Shipping and marketing center of agr. area, it handles tobacco, oil, and livestock and has mfg. of metal and food products. Taken by Federals under Grant and Buell 1862. Near by are Lost River Cave, reputed hideout of James brothers and Gen. J. H. Morgan, and ruins of a Shaker settlement (1800). **2** City (pop. 12,005), NW Ohio, S of Toledo, in farm area; settled 1833. Seat of **Bowling Green State University** (state supported; coed.); chartered 1910, opened 1914 as normal school; became college 1929 and university 1935.

Bowman, Isaiah, 1878–1950, American geographer, b. Ontario. Led expeditions to South America. Territorial adviser to Pres. Wilson at Versailles conference, to Dept. of State in World War II. President of Johns Hopkins Univ. 1935–48.

Bowmanville, town (pop. 5,430), S Ont., Canada, on L. Ontario NE of Toronto. Port and mfg. center.

Bowne, Borden Parker (boun), 1847–1910, American philosopher, exponent of personalism, which emphasizes freedom and importance of the self.

Bowring, Sir John, 1792–1872, British statesman and linguist. Governor of Hong Kong (1854), where he precipitated war with China. Known for translations from many languages.

box, evergreen shrub of genus *Buxus* of Asia and Europe. Common box (*Buxus sempervirens*), slow growing, prized for clipped hedges in S U.S.

boxer: see BULLDOG.

Boxer Rebellion, Chinese revolt (1899–1900), caused by resentment against widening interests of the Western powers and Japan in China. Staged by military group called I Ho Ch'üan [righteous, harmonious fists] or the Boxers, with encouragement of dowager empress Tz'u Hsi. Revolt was crushed by composite force of British, French, Italian, German, Austrian, Russian, American, and Japanese troops. China was forced in 1901 to agree to payment of huge indemnity and to permit stationing of foreign troops in Peking and approach to it from the sea. Also called Boxer Rising or Uprising.

boxing, sport of fighting with the fists, an ancient sport, included in original Olympic games. Marquess of Queensberry's rules (introduced 1865) became standard by 1889. Boxers today fight in a ring, a roped-off area about 20 ft. square. Professional boxing in U.S. largely controlled by rulings of National Boxing Association and N.Y. State Athletic Commission.

Boyacá (bōyäkä'), locality, N central Colombia, where Bolívar defeated the Spanish (1819).

Boyce, William, 1710–79, English organist, composer. Compiled *Cathedral Music* (3 vols., 1760–78).

Boyce Thompson Institute for Plant Research, estab. 1924 at Yonkers, N.Y. through gifts of William Boyce Thompson. Institute is known for research in many branches of botany; fine library; arboretum.

boycott [from Irish land agent, Capt. Charles C. Boycott], concerted economic or social ostracism of an offender (individual, group, nation, or product) to express disapproval or effect coercion. Used in labor disputes and as a weapon in political and racial issues.

Boyd, Belle, 1843–1900, Confederate spy in Civil War. Operated in Shenandoah Valley (1862).

Boyd, Ernest, 1887–1946, American writer and critic, b. Ireland; in New York after 1920. His criticism of German, French, Irish, English, and American authors widened the American literary horizon. Translated the works of Maupassant and others.

Boyd, James, 1888–1944, American author. After World War I service, he lived in N.C. Among his novels of American history are *Drums* (1925), *Long Hunt* (1930), *Roll River* (1935), *Bitter Creek* (1939).

Boyd, Louise Arner, 1887–, American arctic explorer. She led series of explorations for scientific study of E coast of Greenland.

Boyden, Seth, 1788–1870, American inventor. Built locomotives and steam engines incorporating first automatic "cut-off" governor. Initiated U.S. manufacture of patent leather and malleable cast iron.

Boyle, Richard, 1st earl of Cork, 1566–1643, Irish statesman. Improved land, estab. ironworks, founded towns, created trade. As lord high treasurer of Ireland (1631) his opposition to Irish program of earl of STRAFFORD was a major cause of latter's downfall. His son, **Roger Boyle, 1st earl of Orrery,** 1621–79, was a statesman and writer who attempted to keep peace by supporting regime able to govern. Royalist until 1647, served Puritans until restoration of Charles II. Author of rhymed-verse tragedies. His brother **Robert Boyle,** 1627–91, a British chemist, was the first to distinguish between element and compound. He defined chemical reaction and analysis. Boyle's law: at constant temperature, volume of confined gas decreases in proportion to increase in pressure.

Boylston, Zabdiel, 1679–1766, American physician. He introduced in U.S. inoculation against smallpox during Boston epidemic of 1721.

Boyne, river of Ireland, flows 70 mi. NE through Co. Kildare and Co. Meath to the Irish Sea near Drogheda. William III defeated James II in the battle of the Boyne, July 1, 1690.

Boy Scouts, world-wide, nonmilitary organization of boys over 11 years old; founded 1908 by Sir Robert Baden-Powell; inc. in U.S. 1910. Similar movements in U.S. led by Dan Beard and Ernest Thompson Seton. Program designed to better mental, moral, physical development, increase knowledge of outdoors, train for citizenship.

Boys Town, village (pop. 975), E Nebr., founded by Mgr Edward J. Flanagan as community for homeless and abandoned boys.

Bozeman, John M. (bōz'mùn), 1835–67, American pioneer. Found short route in 1862–63 from Bannack, Mont., to Colo., lying E of Bighorn Mts., known as **Bozeman Trail.** In 1865–66 U.S. government estab. forts to guard it; after FETTERMAN MASSACRE part of trail was abandoned.

Bozeman, city (pop. 11,325), SW Mont., SE of Butte and in Gallatin valley; founded 1864 by J. M. Bozeman. Farm and livestock center, it is also a gateway to Yellowstone Natl. Park. Seat of Montana State Col., a part of Univ. of MONTANA.

Bozeman Trail: see BOZEMAN, JOHN M.

Bozen, Italy: see BOLZANO.

Bozzaris, Marco or **Markos** (bôt'särēs), c.1788–1823, Greek hero in War of Independence. Defended Missolonghi against Turks (1822–23); defeated superior Turkish army at Karpenisi but fell in battle.

Br, chemical symbol of the element BROMINE.

Brabant (brùbănt'), former duchy, now divided among the Belgian provs. of ANTWERP and of Brabant (1,268 sq. mi.; pop. 1,811,330; cap. Brussels) and the Dutch prov. of NORTH BRABANT. The duchy emerged from the duchy of Lower Lorraine (12th cent.). Louvain was its cap. until Brussels superseded it (15th cent.). The textile industries and commercial enterprise of its cities gave medieval Brabant extraordinary prosperity. The cities were granted virtual self-government by the dukes, who in 1356 granted a charter, known as *Joyeuse Entrée,* which forbade the dukes to declare war, conclude alliances, or coin money without consent of an assembly or estates (in force until 1789). Brabant passed to the dukes of Burgundy in 1430. For its history after 1477, see NETHERLANDS, AUSTRIAN AND SPANISH.

Brac, Serbo-Croatian *Brač* (bräch), Ital. *Brazza,* Adriatic island (152 sq. mi.), Croatia, NW Yugoslavia; chief town Supetar (San Pietro).

bracken or **brake,** tall, coarse FERN (*Pteridium*) of wide distribution. Often becomes weedy.

Brackenridge, Hugh Henry, 1748–1816, American author, b. Scotland. His satirical and picaresque novel, *Modern Chivalry* (1792–97; with additions, 1813) pictures backwoods life and expresses moderate democratic views.

Brackenridge, borough (pop. 6,178), SW Pa., on the Allegheny and NE of Pittsburgh. Produces coal, coke, stainless steel, and glass.

Bracquemond, Felix (bräkmō'), 1833–1914, French engraver, painter, and decorator of ceramics.

Bracton, Henry de, d. 1268, English jurist, author of *De legibus et consuetudinibus Angliae* [on the laws and customs of England].

Braddock, Edward, 1695–1755, British general in French and Indian Wars. Mortally wounded in disastrous expedition to capture Fort Duquesne from French; more than half his force was lost.

Braddock, borough (pop. 16,488), W Pa. on Monongahela R. and SE of Pittsburgh; settled 1742. Gen. Edward Braddock was defeated here 1775. Was (1794) a center of Whisky Rebellion. Mfg. of machinery and steel (Carnegie Steel Co.).

Bradenton (bră'dŭntŭn), city (pop. 13,604), SW Fla., fishing port on Manatee R. near its mouth on Tampa Bay; founded 1878. Resort. Processes and ships truck and fruit. Dolomite and limestone quarries. Gamble Mansion, post-war refuge of J. P. Benjamin, Confederate Secretary of State, is near.

Bradford, Andrew: see BRADFORD, WILLIAM (1663–1752).

Bradford, Gamaliel (gŭmā'lĕŭl), 1863–1932, American biographer, noted for "psychographs" (short psychological portraits), collected in volumes such as *Confederate Portraits* (1914), *Union Portraits* (1916), and *Damaged Souls* (1923). His autobiography is *Life and I* (1928).

Bradford, John, 1749–1830, pioneer printer of Ky. Founded *Kentucky Gazette* (1787), first Ky. newspaper. Helped found Transylvania Univ.

Bradford, Roark, 1896–1948, American writer, b. Tenn. Biblical stories seen through Negro eyes in *Ol' Man Adam an' His Chillun* (1928) were the source of Marc Connelly's play *The Green Pastures* (1930).

Bradford, William, 1590–1657, governor of Plymouth Colony, b. England. Reelected governor 30 times, he struggled hard to establish colony and discharge debts to London backers.

Bradford, William, 1663–1752, British printer in the American colonies. Set up the first press in Philadelphia and helped found first colonial paper mill (1690). Estab. first New York city newspaper, The *Gazette* (1725). His son, **Andrew Bradford,** 1686–1742, founded the *American Weekly Mercury,* first Pa. newspaper (1719). Imprisoned for criticism of council and assembly, he creditably defended own case for freedom of press. His nephew, **William Bradford,** 1722–91, estab. the Philadelphia *Weekly Advertiser.* A patriot in the American Revolution, he was printer to First Continental Congress and as a major was so badly wounded at Princeton that he did not regain health.

Bradford, county borough (pop. 292,394), Yorkshire, England. A center of the worsted-milling industry, it also has varied mfg.

Bradford, city (pop. 17,354), NW Pa., SE of Jamestown, N.Y. settled c.1823. Oil discovered 1871. Has refineries and mfg. of metal and clay products and chemicals.

Bradlaugh, Charles (brăd'lō), 1833–91, English social reformer, champion of woman suffrage, birth control, and trade unionism.

Bradley, Francis Herbert, 1846–1924, English philosopher, a fellow at Merton Col., Oxford. An absolute idealist, he challenged contemporary metaphysical theories with the assertion that true reality is perfect and changeless (as in *Appearance and Reality,* 1893).

Bradley, James, 1693–1762, English astronomer. Discovered aberration of light and nutation (nodding) of earth's axis. Astronomer royal from 1742.

Bradley, Omar (Nelson), 1893–, U.S. general. Led U.S. 1st Army in invasion of Normandy (1944); vastly aided defeat of Germany in World War II. Chairman of joint chiefs of staff (1949–).

Bradley, village (pop. 5,699), E Ill., just N of Kankakee, in agr. area. Mfg. of wood products.

Bradley University: see PEORIA, Ill.

Bradshaw, George, 1801–53, English map engraver and the originator of railway guides.

Bradstreet, Anne (Dudley), c.1612–1672, American poet, b. England; daughter of Thomas Dudley. First American woman to devote herself to writing. Early poems in *The Tenth Muse Lately Sprung up in America* (1650). Her husband, **Simon Bradstreet,** 1603–97, b. England, was colonial governor of Mass. (1679–86, 1689–92).

Brady, James Buchanan, 1856–1917, American financier and philanthropist, called "Diamond Jim" Brady. Had massive collection of jewelry. Funds he gave founded Urological Institute at Johns Hopkins Hospital, Baltimore.

Brady, Mathew B., 1823–96, American pioneer photographer. Known for his many photographs of Lincoln and for his photographic record of the Civil War. *Gallery of Illustrious Americans* published 1850.

Brady, city (pop. 5,944), central Texas, ESE of San Angelo. Ships turkeys, cotton, wool, and mohair, and has dairying.

Braga, Teófilo (tēô'fĭlō brä'gŭ), 1843–1924, Portuguese intellectual and political leader, influential through his literary criticism and his teaching. A republican and anticlericalist, he served as first president of Portuguese republic (1910–11).

Braga, city (pop. 29,875), Minho prov., NW Portugal. Flourished in Middle Ages as see of powerful bishops. Old cathedral.

Bragança or **Braganza** (both: brŭgän'zŭ), town (pop. 6,977), Tras-os-Montes prov., NE Portugal. Castle was seat of royal family of Braganza.

Braganza (brŭgän'zŭ), royal house that ruled PORTUGAL from 1640 to 1910 and BRAZIL (as independent empire) from 1822 to 1889. Line founded by 1st duke of Braganza, a natural son of John I of Portugal. In 1640 his descendant expelled Spanish and became king as John IV.

Bragg, Braxton, 1817–76, Confederate general. Led A. S. Johnston's 2d Corps in battle of Shiloh. Unsuccessfully invaded Ky. (1862). In CHATTANOOGA CAMPAIGN he won at Chickamauga, but was thoroughly defeated by Grant in Nov., 1863.

Bragg, Sir William Henry, 1862–1942, English physicist. For studies, using X-ray spectrometer, of X-ray spectra and crystal structure, he shared 1915 Nobel Prize with his son, **Sir William Lawrence Bragg,** 1890–, who in 1938 became director of Cavendish Laboratory, Cambridge.

Bragg, Fort: see FAYETTEVILLE, N.C.

Brahe, Tycho (tī'kō brä), 1546–1601, Danish astronomer. By improving instruments and making exact observations of planets and stars, he paved way for discoveries of Kepler and other astronomers. On island of Ven built famed castle, Uranienborg, and observatory, Stjarneborg.

Brahma, supreme deity: see HINDUISM.

Brahman or **Brahmin:** see HINDUISM.

Brahmaputra (brämŭpōō'trŭ), sacred river, c.1,800 mi. long, rising in SW Tibet and flowing through India and Pakistan. Lower course called Jamuna.

Brahms, Johannes (yōhän'ŭs brämz'), 1833–97, German composer, b. Hamburg. Among his closest friends were Robert and Clara Schumann. By 1863 he was earning his living as a composer and settled in Vienna. He wrote in every form except opera. Among his works are: sonatas and short pieces for the piano; the popular Hungarian Dances; chamber music; many lieder; the *Academic Festival Overture; the German Requiem;* and four concertos—two for piano, one for violin, and a double concerto for violin and cello. Brahms's profound admiration of Beethoven made him hesitate to attempt a symphony, but he finally produced his first symphony—the C minor—in 1876. The others soon followed: the Second (1877), the Third (1883), and the Fourth (1884–85). Much of his music, which is increasingly popular, is highly romantic in content.

Braila (brŭē'lä), city (pop. 95,514), SE Rumania, in Walachia, on lower Danube. Exports grain.

Braille, Louis (brāl', Fr. lwĕ' brī'yŭ), 1809?–1852, French inventor of printing and writing system for the blind. Blinded after he was three, he studied and taught at the Institution nationale des Jeunes Aveugles, Paris. The **Braille system,** evolved from Charles Barbier's method, has 63 combinations of six raised points.

brain, mass of nerve tissue in skull. In man, includes cerebrum, the center of consciousness, sensation, and voluntary actions; cerebellum, important in coordination and regulation of muscles; medulla oblongata, pathway from brain to spinal cord. See *ill.,* p. 595.

Brainerd, Ezra, 1844–1924, American botanist, known for work in plant hybridization (esp. violets).

Brainerd, city (pop. 12,637), central Minn., on the Mississippi near Cuyuna iron range; settled 1870. Shipping and industrial center in lumbering and lake resort area.

Braintree, town (pop. 23,161), E Mass., SSE of Boston; settled 1634. Shoes, rubber and petroleum products. Holdup and murders of April 15, 1920, for which Sacco and Vanzetti were executed, occurred here.

Brain Trust, designation for academic group, advisers to F. D. Roosevelt as governor of N.Y. and in first years as President.

brake, in botany: see BRACKEN.

brake, device to retard or stop motion of mechanical body. Friction used to resist motion, changing kinetic to heat energy. Simple types are wood or shoe pressed against wheel rim with force applied through pedal and multiplied by levers; rope wound around axle and pulled taut to brake; metal bands fitted around drum attached to wheel and controlled by levers. Mechanical automobile foot brake regulates bands of metal around outside of drum attached to axle; emergency brake attached to shoes that press outward from inside of drum. Force applied to pedals transmitted by levers, cables, or hydraulic cylinder and piston arrangement. Hydraulic brakes generally used on automobiles; air brakes on railroad cars, buses, and trucks. Electric motor often used to brake electric machines.

Brakelond, Jocelin de: see JOCELIN DE BRAKELOND.

Bramah, Joseph (bräm'ù, brä'–), 1748–1814, English mechanician and inventor, who patented a safety lock (1784) and the HYDRAULIC PRESS (1795).

Bramante, Donato d'Agnolo (dōnä'tō dä'nyōlō brämän'-tä), 1444?–1514, Italian architect of the High Renaissance. Cancelleria Palace and circular Tempietto in courtyard of San Pietro in Montorio, both in Rome, reflect his study of classical remains. His original plans for the new St. Peter's were altered by later architects who worked on church.

Bramantino (brämäntē'nō), c.1455–c.1535, Lombard painter, architect; pupil and imitator of Bramante.

Brampton, town (pop. 8,389), S Ont., Canada, NW of Toronto. Flower-growing center with tanneries.

bran: see GRAIN.

Branch, Anna Hempstead, 1875–1934, American lyric poet, a social worker associated with Christodora House, New York.

Brancusi, Constantin (brän'kōosh), 1876–, Rumanian sculptor. His abstract and frequently symbolic work has led to much controversy. Won lawsuit 1927 against U.S. customs authorities of Port of New York which led to lifting of duty on abstract art.

Brand, Sebastian: see BRANT, SEBASTIAN.

Brandeis, Louis Dembitz (brän'dīs), 1856–1941, Associate Justice of U.S. Supreme Court (1916–39), known for judicial liberalism.

Brandeis University: see WALTHAM, Mass.

Brandenburg (Ger. brän'dùnbŏŏrk), former province (14,779 sq. mi.; 1939 pop. 3,007,933) of Prussia, N Germany; since 1949 a member state (10,415 sq. mi.; pop. 2,527,492) of [East] German Democratic Republic; cap. Potsdam. Flat, sandy region, drained by Havel, Spree, and Oder rivers. Berlin is geographically but not administratively part of Brandenburg. Other cities: Frankfurt-an-der Oder, Brandenburg, Cottbus. SPREE FOREST, in Lower LUSATIA, is inhabited by WENDS, remnants of Slavic people which held the region until its colonization and Christianization by Germans. ALBERT THE BEAR, made first margrave in 1134, became effective ruler after last Wendish prince made him his heir. His descendants (the Ascanians) ruled until 1320; various princes succeeded them until in 1415 the margraviate was given to the house of HOHENZOLLERN. Margraves also held rank of ELECTORS. Reformation was introduced in 1539. In the 17th cent. Brandenburg gained much territory (notably CLEVES, duchy of PRUSSIA, E POMERANIA) and rose in prestige under FREDERICK WILLIAM, the Great Elector, whose son in 1701 took the title king of Prussia as FREDERICK I. Brandenburg shared the history of Prussia until the Potsdam Conference of 1945, when all territory E of the Oder was placed under Polish administration pending final peace settlement.

Brandenburg, city (pop. 70,632), Brandenburg, N Germany, on Havel R. Has mfg. (trucks, textiles, machinery). The Slavic Brennabor, it was conquered 12th cent. by Albert the Bear and gave its name to his margraviate.

Brandes, Georg (Morris Cohen) (brän'dùs), 1842–1927, Danish literary critic. Exerted an invigorating influence on Danish thought. Wrote widely on various literatures. His brother **Carl (Edvard Cohen) Brandes,** 1847–1931, was also a vigorous critic and an able dramatist.

Brandon, Charles: see SUFFOLK, CHARLES BRANDON, 1ST DUKE OF.

Brandon, city (pop. 20,598), SW Man., Canada, on Assiniboine R. and W of Winnipeg. Center of wheat-raising area, it has oil refining, meat packing, and mfg. of metal products. Here are dominion experimental farm and Brandon Col. (Baptist; 1899).

Brandt, Sebastian: see BRANT, SEBASTIAN.

brandy, strong alcoholic spirit distilled from wine or from marc, the residue of the wine press, which yields strong but inferior product. Made in many lands; most noted, called cognac, made from white grapes in Charente district of France. Brandy is also made from fruits (e.g., peach brandy), grains, and fermented sugar cane.

Brandy Station, trading center, NE of Culpeper, Va., scene of greatest cavalry battle in Civil War, June 9, 1863. First clash of Gettysburg campaign.

Brandywine, battle of, in American Revolution, fought Sept. 11, 1777, along Brandywine Creek, near Chadds Ford, SE Pa. British under Sir William Howe defeated Washington and continued advance on Philadelphia.

Branford, borough (pop. 2,552) in Branford town (pop. 10,944), S Conn., on Long Isl. Sound E of New Haven; settled 1644. Metal goods.

Brangwyn, Sir Frank (bräng'wïn), 1867–, British painter. Decorative murals and etchings.

Brannan, Sam(uel), 1819–89, pioneer in Calif. Founded first Calif. newspaper (1847). Organizer and first president (1851) of Committee of Vigilance.

Branner, John Casper, 1850–1922, American geologist. Created model department of geology for Ark. Long associated with Stanford Univ. as professor, vice president, president.

Brant, Joseph, 1742–1807, war chief of Mohawk Indians. Aided British in American Revolution. Led Indian forces in Cherry Valley massacre (1778).

Brant, Brandt, or **Brand, Sebastian** (säbäs'tyän bränt'), 1458–1521, German poet. His chief work is *Das Narrenschiff* [the ship of fools], a series of satirical and moralizing poems (Eng. tr., 1944).

brant or **brant goose,** wild sea goose. American brant breeds in arctic regions, winters along Atlantic coast, rarely inland; black head, neck, tail; brownish gray back; grayish white under parts; eats eelgrass. Black brant migrates to Pacific coast. White brant is snow goose; prairie brant is American white-fronted goose.

Brantford, city (pop. 36,727), S Ont., Canada, on Grand R., WSW of Hamilton. Has mfg. of farm and electrical equipment, machinery, furniture, and paper. Named for Joseph Brant. Hq. of the Six Nations and seat of Indian Inst.

Branting, Hjalmar (yäl'mär brän'tïng), 1860–1925, Swedish statesman and Social Democratic leader, three times premier (1920, 1921–23, 1924–25). Shared 1921 Nobel Peace Prize with C. L. Lange.

Brantôme, Pierre de Bourdeilles, seigneur de (pyèr' dù bōōrdä'yù sänyûr' dù brätôm'), 1535?–1614, French author, a courtier and soldier of fortune. His *Vies des* *hommes illustres et grands capitaines* and *Livre des dames* (Eng. tr., *Lives of Fair & Gallant Ladies,* 1933) form a racy account of his time.

Braque, Georges (zhôrzh' bräk'), 1881–, French painter. In 1905 joined the fauvists, in 1908 with Picasso launched cubism. His painting since has been consistently abstract, restrained and subtle in color and design. Best known for still lifes.

Bras d'Or Lakes (brä dôr'), arm of the Atlantic (360 sq. mi.; 44 mi. long, up to 20 mi. wide), extending into Cape Breton Isl., N.S., Canada. Area was scene of early aviation experiments.

Brasenose College: see OXFORD UNIVERSITY.

Brasidas (brä'sĭdŭs), d. 422 B.C., Spartan general. Won victories over Athens in Peloponnesian War, including that at Amphipolis, in which he was killed.

Brasov (bräshôv'), Ger. *Kronstadt,* Hung. *Brassó,* city (pop. 82,984; c.30% Hungarian and German), central Rumania, in Transylvania. Food, textile, machinery mfg.; lumber. Founded 13th cent. by Teutonic Knights. Has Gothic cathedral (14th cent.), remains of medieval city wall, 17th-cent. citadel.

brass, name for various alloys of copper (60%–90%) and zinc (10%–40%). Properties vary with proportion of two metals; hardness varies with amount of zinc. Can be beaten, rolled into sheets, drawn into wires, machined, cast.

Brasso, Rumania: see BRASOV.

Brasstown Bald, peak, 4,784 ft. high, N Ga., in the Blue Ridge of the Appalachians near N.C. line; highest point in Ga.

brass wind instruments: see WIND INSTRUMENTS.

Bratianu, John (brŭtiä'nŏŏ), 1864–1927, Rumanian premier (1909–11, 1914–18, 1922–27). Governed dictatorially; prevented accession of Carol II (1927).

Bratislava (brä'tēslä'vä), Ger. *Pressburg,* Hung. *Pozsony,* city (pop. 132,509), cap. of Slovakia, Czechoslovakia, on the Danube, near Austrian and Hungarian borders. Large river port; varied industries; univ. (founded 1919). Dates from Roman times; chartered 1291. Usual meeting place of Hungarian diet 1526–1848. To Czechoslovakia 1918. Rich in historical buildings, notably 13th-cent. castle and cathedral, 18th-cent. palace of archbishops (now city hall). Diversified pop. (Slovaks, Magyars, Jews, Czechs, Austrians). Treaty of PRESSBURG signed here 1805.

Brattleboro, town (pop. 11,522), including Brattleboro village (pop. 9,606), SE Vt., on Connecticut R. and E of Bennington; chartered 1753. Winter sports center. Mfg. of pipe organs (Estey's organ works date from c.1850), wood products, and textiles. Hq. of Holstein-Friesian cattle breeders' association. "Naulahka," N of village, was home of Rudyard Kipling.

Braun, Carl Ferdinand (kärl fĕr'dēnänt broun), 1850–1918, German physicist. Shared with Marconi the 1909 Nobel Prize for work on wireless telegraphy.

Braunschweig, Germany: see BRUNSWICK.

Brauwer, Adriaen: see BROUWER, ADRIAEN.

Brawley, city (pop. 11,922), SE Calif. Largest city in IMPERIAL VALLEY.

Bray, Thomas, 1656–1730, English clergyman. He founded Anglican church in Md. and served there and in England. Founded (1701) Society for the Propagation of the Gospel in Foreign Parts.

Bray, parish, Berkshire, England, on Thames R. Ballad about the vicar of Bray often supposed to describe Simon Aleyn, vicar of Bray 1540 to 1588.

Brazil (brŭzĭl'), Port. *Brasil* (bräzēl'), republic (3,287,-842 sq. mi.; pop. 52,645,479), E South America; full name the United States of Brazil; cap. RIO DE JANEIRO. By far the largest of South American countries, it occupies nearly half of the continent. In the N is the enormous basin of the AMAZON (mostly in States of Amazonas and PARÁ), with vast tropical rain forests, once famous for wild rubber, now yielding other forest products. The great inland port is MANAUS. The river near its mouth divides around MARAJÓ isl. On S arm (the Pará) is part of BELÉM. To the E Brazil

thrusts far out toward Africa. This section, the Northeast, includes states of MARANHÃO, PIAUÍ, CEARÁ, RIO GRANDE DO NORTE, PARAÍBA, and Alagoas, with neighboring Sergipe and BAHIA. This area was the center of sugar plantations that for centuries produced great wealth and dominated the country. Many Negroes were imported to work as slaves here. Today on the coastal plains sugar, cotton, rice, and tobacco are raised, while drought-ridden interior regions (*sertões*) have been largely abandoned by farmers to ranchers. Important cities are: PARNAÍBA, TERESINA, FORTALEZA, NATAL, JOÃO PESSOA, RECIFE, MACEIÓ, and SALVADOR. The FERNANDO DA NORONHA isls. lie far out in the Atlantic. S of the "bulge" an irregular coastal plain, bordered on the W by an escarpment marking the edge of the great plateau of Brazil, has good harbors—VITÓRIA, NITERÓI, FLORIANOPOLIS, and PORTO ALEGRE, besides Rio de Janeiro and SANTOS. In the SE and E sections of Brazil stretching far to the N on the plateau and to the S border with Argentina and Paraguay, population, agr., and industry are concentrated. The states on the S coast and inland are Espirito Santo, MINAS GERAIS, RIO DE JANEIRO, SÃO PAULO, PARANÁ, SANTA CATARINA, and RIO GRANDE DO SUL (where plateau ends in Río de la Plata plains). Great influx of Europeans in late 19th and 20th cent. helped build the coffee economy of São Paulo (Brazil is world's largest coffee producer) and later diverse industries especially around the cities of SÃO PAULO and Rio. On the plateau in the center of Brazil is the largely undeveloped state of GOIAS, and in the NW is the developing frontier of MATO GROSSO. Brazilians are proud of their "race" (an amalgamation of Indian, Negro, and various white strains). Portuguese is the official language, and although Vicente Yáñez PINZÓN and possibly others had visited the coast earlier, the Portuguese CABRAL is usually considered the "discoverer" (1500). The first permanent settlement was at São Vicente in São Paulo state (1532). Portuguese settlement was slow even after the coming of Martin Alfonso de SOUSA as governor. French Huguenots had to be driven from Rio de Janeiro harbor (1567), and the Dutch held the Northeast for years before they were driven out in 1654. Portuguese tried unsuccessfully to press claims in the S to present Uruguay and Paraguay. With the Napoleonic invasion of Portugal, king John VI fled (1807–8) to Rio de Janeiro, which became the cap. of the Portuguese Empire. After Napoleon's defeat, John returned to Portugal, leaving his son as regent in Brazil. In 1822 that son proclaimed Brazil independent (at Ipiranga) and became Emperor Pedro I. He had to abdicate in favor of his son, PEDRO II, who reigned 1831–89. Brazil grew as a modern nation, though wars with Argentina and with Paraguay (see TRIPLE ALLIANCE, WAR OF THE) brought little benefit to Brazil. The abolition of slavery (1888) helped bring on the bloodless revolution that made Brazil a republic (1889). Immigration, the expanding coffee market, and the short wild-rubber boom (which caused trouble with neighbors, e.g., in ACRE) brought wealth to Brazil in late 19th and early 20th cent. Later, particularly under the presidency of Getulio VARGAS (1930–45, 1952–), great stress was laid on industrial expansion. The republic joined the Allies in World War I and World War II and became a member of the UN (1945).

Brazil, city (pop. 8,434), W Ind., near Terre Haute. Rail center in coal and agr. region.

Brazil nut, seed of a tall tree (*Bertholletia excelsa*) of tropical America. Borne in large pod, the nuts have a hard brown shell and sweet white meat.

brazilwood, bright red wood of tropical trees of genus *Caesalpinia.* It is used for cabinetwork.

brazing: see SOLDER.

Brazoria (brŭzôr'ĕŭ), town (pop. 776), S Texas, on Brazos R. and SSW of Houston. Founded in 1820s, it was a thriving port in S. P. Austin's colony, then a center for plantations. Town was ruined by time and a hurricane; new town built near by.

Brazos (brăz'ùs), river, formed in NW Texas by union of Double Mountain and Salt forks, joined by Clear Fork, and flowing more than 800 mi. SE through Waco to Freeport on Gulf of Mexico. Brazos water is used for city reservoirs, irrigation, flood control, and power, notably from Possum Kingdom Dam near Graham and Whitney Dam near Hillsboro.

Brazza, Pierre Paul François Camille Savorgnan de (sävôrnyä' dù bräzä'), 1852–1905, Franco-Italian explorer. Naturalized in France (1875) and sent by foreign office to establish French influence in Equatoria. Founded Brazzaville (1880). Estab. French protectorate over Bateke territory.

Brazza, Adriatic island: see BRAC, Yugoslavia.

Brazzaville (brä'zùvĭl), city (pop. 83,400), cap. of French Equatorial Africa, opposite Leopoldville on Stanley Pool of Congo R. Founded 1880 by the French explorer Brazza.

bread, universal article of food made by mixing crushed or ground grain or other seeds with liquids, then baking. Known in both leavened and unleavened forms since earliest history. In Western countries staple product contains white or whole-grain wheat flour, liquid, yeast, shortening, sugar, salt. Other flours may be partly or entirely used: rye, barley, maize, buckwheat, sorghum, millet, potato, soybean, cassava, or rice. Quick breads (e.g., hot biscuits) generally leavened by BAKING POWDER.

Breadalbane, John Campbell, 1st earl of: see CAMPBELL, JOHN, 1ST EARL OF BREADALBANE.

breadfruit, tropical tree (*Artocarpis communis*) and its fruit, a staple food in tropics. When baked, the fruit resembles bread.

Bread Loaf Mountain, 3,823 ft. high, W Vt., E of Middlebury. Middlebury Col. holds summer session in writing and languages near by.

breadroot or **Indian breadroot**, perennial pealike plant (*Psoralea esculenta*), of North American prairies. Valued by Indians for edible, starchy roots.

Breakspear, Nicholas: see ADRIAN IV.

breakwater, structure protecting harbor from full force of waves and providing quieter ship anchorage. Artificial breakwaters may be rock or concrete-block mound, rock foundation and masonry superstructure, or superstructure from sea floor.

breast, frontal portion of chest in which mammary glands exist in most mammals. Gland tissue develops at onset of puberty; composed of lobes, each resembling grape cluster, from which ducts lead to nipple. In females, milk secretion follows birth of young.

Breasted, James Henry, 1865–1935, American Egyptologist. Taught (1894–1933) at Univ. of Chicago; director Haskell Oriental Mus. and Oriental Inst. of Univ. of Chicago. His important archaeological research in Egypt and Mesopotamia was basis for many publications.

breathing: see RESPIRATION.

Brébeuf, Jean de (zhä' dù bräbûf'), 1593–1649, French Jesuit missionary and martyr in North America. Canonized in 1930.

Brecht, Bert (Bertold Brecht) (bĕrt' brĕkht'), 1898–, German author, a leading Communist propagandist. His *Dreigroschenoper* (with music by Kurt Weill, 1928), an adaptation of *The Beggars' Opera*, was an immediate success and was in turn adapted into English (*The Three-Penny Opera*, 1933). Among his books of ballads is *Hauspostille* (1927).

Breckenridge, Hugh Henry, 1870–1937, American painter, a noted teacher of art.

Breckenridge, city (pop. 6,610), N Texas, W of Fort Worth. Processing center for ranch and farm area with oil and gas industries.

Breckinridge, John, 1760–1806, American statesman. Advised Pres. Jefferson on KENTUCKY AND VIRGINIA RESOLUTIONS. Spokesman of Western interests in Senate (1801–5). His grandson, **John Cabell Breck-**

inridge, 1821–75, was Vice President of the United States (1857–61). Presidential candidate of Southern Democratic faction (1860) and a Confederate general in Civil War.

Brecknockshire (brĕk'nôkshĭr) or **Brecon** (brĕk'ùn), inland county (733 sq. mi.; pop. 56,484), S Wales. Mountainous region, rising to 2,910 ft. in Brecon Beacons. Chief occupations are sheep grazing and dairy farming; there is also coal and iron mining, and woolen mfg. County town, **Brecknock** (pop. 6,466), has cathedral dating from 11th cent.

Breda (brädä'), municipality (pop. 81,873) and town, North Brabant prov., SW Netherlands. Machine plants; rayon mfg. Surrender of Breda's heroic garrison to Spanish under Spinola (1625) was painted by Velázquez.

Breda, Compromise of, 1566: see GUEUX.

Breda, Declaration of, 1660: see CHARLES II, king of England.

Breda, Treaty of, 1667: see DUTCH WARS.

breeding of plants and animals to improve the breed, variety, or strain probably began soon after start of DOMESTICATION, as selective breeding—propagation of specimens with desirable qualities. Scientific breeding arose after Gregor Mendel's promulgation of laws of inheritance. Pure lines (in plants) and pure-bred animals show virtual uniformity. Plant hybrids—e.g., hybrid corn—are products of crosses between two strains of a pure line. Vigor of animal breeds is maintained by crossing strains and sometimes by crossing certain breeds. New breeds and varieties are chiefly hybrids and the product of breeding individuals in which mutations have occurred. See also GENETICS; HEREDITY.

Breed's Hill: see BUNKER HILL, BATTLE OF.

Breisgau (brīs'gou), region, S Baden, SW Germany; chief city Freiburg. Held by Hapsburgs 1368–1805.

Breitenfeld (brī'tùnfĕlt"), village, Saxony, SE Germany, near Leipzig. Scene of victory of imperials over Swedes (1631) and of Swedes over imperials (1642) in Thirty Years War.

Breitmann, Hans (brīt'män), pseud. of Charles Godfrey Leland, 1824–1903, American author of poems in German dialect, originally in magazines (collected first in *Hans Breitmann's Ballads*, 1869). Leland edited *Graham's Magazine* and the *Continental Monthly* and wrote many works under his own name.

Bremen (brĕ'mùn, Ger. brä'mùn), state (156 sq. mi.; pop. 568,335), N Germany, on North Sea about the mouth of Weser R. Its fortunes are those of its cap., the free Hansa city of **Bremen** (pop. 444,196), second largest German port and an industrial and commercial center. Created in 845, the archdiocese of Bremen originally included all Scandinavia, Iceland, Greenland. City of Bremen itself was virtually independent from archbishops as its importance grew. Entered HANSEATIC LEAGUE 1358; accepted the Reformation; became free imperial city 1646. Trade was spurred by founding of BREMERHAVEN (1827). "Republic and Hansa city" of Bremen joined German Empire (1871), Weimar Republic (1919), and Federal Republic of [Western] Germany (1949). Heavily damaged by air raids in World War II; under U.S. occupation from 1945. Gothic city hall, with statue of Roland (erected 1404 as symbol of city's freedom) and Cathedral of Sankt Petri (begun 1043) still stand.

Bremer, Fredrika, 1801–65, Swedish writer and feminist, b. Finland, author of *Homes in the New World* (1853; impressions of travel in America).

Bremerhaven (brä'mùrhä"fùn), city (pop. 113,925) Bremen, N Germany; North Sea port on mouth of Weser R. Founded 1827 as transatlantic port.

Bremerton (brĕm'ùrtùn), port city (pop. 27,678), NW Wash., on arm of Puget Sound; founded 1891. Seat of Puget Sound navy yard.

Brenham (brĕn'ùm), city (pop. 6,941), S central Texas, NW of Houston, center of agr. area. Processes cotton and cotton products. Oil fields near.

SMALL CAPITALS = cross references. Pronunciation key on inside end pages. Abbreviations: p. 2.

Brenner Pass (brĕ′nŭr), Ital. *Brennero* (brĕn′nārō), in Tyrolean Alps, 4,495 ft. high, on Austro-Italian border. Highway built 1772; railroad 1867.

Brent, Margaret, 1600–1671?, American feminist. First woman in Maryland to hold land in her own right, she was executrix of Gov. Calvert's estates and acted as attorney for Lord Baltimore.

Brentano, Clemens (brĕntä′nō), 1778–1842, German romantic poet; brother of Bettina von Arnim. Author of fairy tales and stories such as *Geschichte vom bravem Kasperl und dem schönen Annerl* (1817; Eng. tr., *Honor,* 1847), but best-known for collaboration with Achim von ARNIM on folk-song collection *Des Knaben Wunderhorn* (1806–8).

Brentano, Elisabeth: see ARNIM, BETTINA VON.

Brentano, Franz, 1838–1917, German psychologist, professor of philosophy at Vienna (1874–1880). Set out to estab. psychology as a distinct science based on empirical findings.

Brentford and Chiswick (chĭz′ĭk), municipal borough (pop. 59,354), Middlesex, England, a suburb of London at terminus of Grand Junction Canal. Has mfg. of electrical equipment, pharmaceuticals, and tires. Grave of Hogarth at Chiswick.

Brentwood. 1 City (pop. 7,504), E Mo., W suburb of St. Louis. **2** Residential borough (pop. 12,535), W Pa., S of, and near, Pittsburgh.

Brescia (brä′shä), city (pop. 92,583), Lombardy, N Italy. Industrial center (steel, machinery). Of pre-Roman origin; independent commune in Middle Ages. Had flourishing school of painters in 16th cent. (G. B. Moroni, Moretto). Roman remains; medieval, Renaissance, and baroque churches and palaces.

Breslau (brĕs′lou), Pol. *Wrocław,* city (1950 pop. c.340,000), former cap. of Lower Silesia, on Oder; under Polish administration since 1945. Became episcopal see in 1000; cap. of duchy of SILESIA, under Piast dynasty, in 1163. Sacked by Mongols 1241. To Bohemia 1335; under Hapsburgs 1526–1742. Grew into major commercial and industrial center in 19th cent., with metal, textile, and food industries. Had two large annual fairs. Heavily damaged in World War II. City very large (pre-war pop. 615,000) until expulsion of Germans and resettlement by Poles after 1945. Has univ. (founded 1702); archiepiscopal see.

Bresse (brĕs), region, E France, between Saône and Ain, in Ain dept.; chief town Bourg-en-Bresse. Agr., poultry, wine. Pond-dotted Dombes dist. is being drained. Ceded to France by Savoy (1601) and incorporated into Burgundy prov.

Brest, town (pop. 62,707), Finistère dept., NW France, on an inlet of Atlantic into tip of Brittany. Chief French naval station. Harbor created 1631 by Richelieu. German submarine base in World War II, heavily bombed by Allies.

Brest, formerly **Brest-Litovsk** (brĕst′-lĭtôfsk′), city (1931 pop. 48,435), Belorussia, on Western Bug R. Rail and water transportation center; strategic fortress. Passed to Russia in third Polish partition (1795); fortified 1831; held by Germans in both World Wars; to Poland 1921; to USSR 1945. Union of Polish Orthodox and Roman Catholic churches (1596) and Treaty of BREST-LITOVSK (1918) were signed here.

Brest-Litovsk, Treaty of (-lĭtôfsk′), March 1918, separate peace treaty signed by Soviet Russia and the Central Powers at BREST, USSR, following armistice of Dec., 1917. Trotsky was chief Russian negotiator. Russia recognized independence of Poland, Baltic states, Georgia, Ukraine; permitted German occupation of Belorussia; ceded Kars, Ardahan, Batum to Turkey; promised large indemnity. General armistice of Nov., 1918, nullified this treaty.

Brétigny, Treaty of (brātēnyē′), 1360, short-lived truce between England and France in HUNDRED YEARS WAR; signed at Brétigny near Chartres. John II of France paid English 3,000,000 gold crowns for his ransom and ceded nearly half of France.

Breton, André (ädrā′ brŭtō), 1896–, French poet, novelist, critic. First a Dadaist, he was later a leading surrealist.

Breton, Nicholas (brĕt′ŭn), 1551?–c.1623, prolific English poet and miscellaneous writer. *The Passionate Shepherd* (1604) his best-known work.

Bretón de los Herreros, Manuel (mänwäl′ brätôn′ dä lōs ĕr-rä′rôs), 1796–1873, Spanish author of satiric and lyric poems and plays.

Breton literature (brĕ′tŭn), in the Celtic language of Brittany, until the 19th cent. consisted mainly of popular plays (some dating back to c.1500), songs, and stories. Collection of these, as well as a cultivated literature, began mid-19th cent. Outstanding Breton poets include Auguste Brizeux (1803–58), author of collection *Telen Arvor* [the harp of Armorica] (1844), and Jean Pierre Calloc'h (1888–1917), whose poems show piety, love of the sea, and fascination with death. The 20th cent. has seen a revival and expansion of the Breton language.

Bretonneau, Pierre (pyĕr′ brŭtônō), 1778–1862, French physician. His treatise on diphtheria established its identity; he performed first successful tracheotomy for diphtheria 1825. Stated germ theory of disease later established by Pasteur.

Breton Succession, War of the, 1341–64. Duke John III of Brittany having died childless, the succession was contested by his brother, Jean de Montfort, who was backed by England, and by CHARLES OF BLOIS, who had married a niece of the late duke and was backed by France. Charles's death at the battle of Auray (1364) decided the issue, which had merged with the Hundred Years War.

Bretton Woods Conference, name commonly given to United Nations Monetary and Financial Conference, held in July, 1944, at Bretton Woods, N.H. Conference resulted in creation of International Monetary Fund, to promote monetary cooperation, and of International Bank for Reconstruction and Development.

Breuer, Josef (yō′zĕf broi′ŭr), 1842–1925, Austrian physician, whose therapy and theory, developed by Freud, became psychoanalysis.

Breuer, Marcel Lajos (broi′ŭr), 1902–, architect, b. Hungary. Associated with Bauhaus group. Partner of Walter Gropius 1937–42.

Breughel, family of painters: see BRUEGEL.

Breviary of Alaric (ä′lŭrĭk), Visigothic code of Roman law issued (506) by Alaric II for his Roman subjects in Spain and S Gaul.

Brewer, city (pop. 6,862), S Maine, on Penobscot R. opposite Bangor. Pulp and paper mills.

Brewster, Sir David, 1781–1868, Scottish physicist. Notable research on polarization of light. Invented dioptric system of improved lighthouse illumination; said to have invented kaleidoscope.

Brewster, William, 1567–1644, English separatist and religious leader of Plymouth Colony.

Brewton, city (pop. 5,146), S Ala., near Fla. line, NE of Mobile, in cotton, livestock, lumber area.

Brian Boru or **Brian Boroimhe** (both: brī′ŭn or brĕn′, bŭrōō′ or bŭrō′), 962?–1014, high king of Ireland. A local king, he subjugated all Ireland. Annihilated coalition of Norse and his Irish enemies at Clontarf in 1014, but was murdered soon after. His victory broke Norse power in Ireland, but destroyed unity he had achieved.

Briand, Aristide (ärēstēd′ brēä′), 1862–1932, French statesman, 11 times premier between 1909 and 1921. Originally a Socialist, he later was attacked by left and right for his liberalism. As foreign minister (1925–32) he was chief architect of LOCARNO PACT and KELLOGG-BRIAND PACT. Advocated international cooperation and United States of Europe. Shared 1926 Nobel Peace Prize with Stresemann.

Briareus (brīä′rēŭs), in Greek religion, hundred-handed monster, who warred against the gods.

bribery, corrupt tendering or receiving of anything of value in return for official action. At common law a misdemeanor, but made a felony in many U.S. jurisdictions. More loosely bribery includes corrupt influencing of nonofficials (e.g., voters).

bridal wreath: see SPIRAEA.

Bride, Saint: see BRIDGET, SAINT.

Bridewell, parish of central London, England. Bridewell house of correction here until 1864.

bridge, roadway spanning body of water. Developed from primitive log or vine across stream to arched stone structures of 2000 to 4000 B.C., the longer Roman arches, and modern steel bridges. Beginning in mid-19th cent., wooden bridges of early U.S. were largely superseded by cast and wrought iron bridges. Development of Bessemer process of converting cast iron into steel revolutionized bridgebuilding. Use of TRUSS led to vast modern structures including panel-truss bridge (braced parallel trusses supporting road on transverse beams); center-swing bridge (revolves on pier midstream to permit passage of tall ships); cantilever (long spans, usually supported by two piers and two abutments); suspension bridge (a roadway suspended by cables anchored to piers on each bank); vertical lift (truss-type span suspended between steel towers by wire ropes); and bascule or quadrant bridge (rigid, truss-type bridge resting free on one bank and mounted on heavy quadrant on other, to permit lifting clear of water). See also DRAWBRIDGE; PONTOON; VIADUCT. See *ill.*, p. 131.

bridge, card game, developed from whist, played with 52 cards by four players paired as partners. An old form of bridge was played in Middle East in 19th cent. The term *bridge* now usually means contract bridge, a form developed by Harold S. Vanderbilt of New York in 1925.

Bridgeburg, Ont.: see FORT ERIE.

Bridge of Sighs, covered stone bridge in Venice, Italy, built in 16th cent. to connect ducal palace with prison. Prisoners were led over bridge after trial in palace.

Bridgeport. 1 City (pop. 158,709), SW Conn., on harbor on Long Isl. Sound at Poquonock R. mouth; settled 1639. State's chief industrial city (metal goods, machinery). Seaside Park and Barnum Inst. of Science and History commemorate the showman who lived here. "Gen. Tom Thumb" born here. Has Univ. of Bridgeport. Socialist city government since 1933. **2** Borough (pop. 5,827), SE Pa., NW of Philadelphia. Produces coke, iron, and textiles. Dolomite is mined.

Bridger, James, 1804–81, American fur trader, one of most famous of MOUNTAIN MEN. Guided many expeditions in Northwest. Founded Fort Bridger on Oregon Trail in 1843.

Bridger, Fort: see FORT BRIDGER STATE PARK.

Bridges, Calvin Blackman, 1889–1938, American geneticist. Proved chromosome theory of heredity; formulated theory of genic balance; studied gene positions in salivary chromosomes of *Drosophila* (fruit fly or vinegar fly).

Bridges, Harry (Alfred Renton Bridges), 1900–, American labor leader in maritime industry, b. Australia. Sentenced 1950 to five-year prison term for swearing falsely in 1945 that he had never been Communist party member.

Bridges, Robert (Seymour), 1844–1930, English poet laureate after 1913. Wrote lyrics, long poems (e.g., *The Testament of Beauty*, 1929), verse dramas, criticism; published poetry of Gerard Manley Hopkins.

Bridget, Saint, 453?–523?, Irish holy woman. Little is known of her except that she founded a monastery at Kildare and that she is buried at Downpatrick with fellow patrons of Ireland, Patrick and Columba. Also Brigid and Bride. Feast: Feb. 1.

Bridget of Sweden, Saint, c.1300–1375, Swedish nun. A noblewoman and a mother of eight children, she retired to become a nun after the death of her husband. She had celebrated visions, and as a result of one of them founded a new order (the Bridgettines). She lived her last years in Rome (except for pilgrimage to Palestine) and was adviser to popes. Also Birgitta. Feast: Oct. 8.

Bridgeton, city (pop. 18,378), S N.J., S of Philadelphia; settled 1686. Shipping center for agr. region. Has canneries and glassworks.

Bridgetown, city (pop. 68,924), cap. of Barbados, British West Indies. Tourist resort.

Bridgeville, borough (pop. 5,650), SW Pa., SW of Pittsburgh. Mfg. of chemicals and metal products.

Bridgewater, town (pop. 9,512), SE Mass., S of Boston. Shoes, metal products, grain feed.

Bridgman, Laura, 1829–89, New England teacher of sewing, first blind deaf-mute to be successfully educated (by Dr. S. G. Howe of Perkins Inst.)

Bridgman, Percy Williams, 1882–, American physicist. Won 1946 Nobel Prize for work in high pressures.

Brie (brē), region, Marne and Seine-et-Marne depts., N France, E of Paris; chief city Meaux. Rich farm district, famous for cheese.

Brieg (brēk), Pol. *Brzeg,* city (pop. 7,744; 1939 pop. 31,419), Lower Silesia; under Polish administration since 1945. Seat of a principality under PIAST dynasty 1311–1675. Old castle and Renaissance city hall damaged in World War II.

Brienne, Étienne Charles Loménie de: see LOMÉNIE DE BRIENNE, ÉTIENNE CHARLES.

Brienz (brēĕnts'), village, Bern canton, Switzerland, on L. of Brienz. Woodcarving industry.

Brieux, Eugène (ûzhĕn' brēû'), 1858–1932, French dramatist. Wrote on family life and social themes. Well-known plays are *La Robe rouge* (1900) and *Les Avariés* (1901; produced in U.S. as *Damaged Goods*).

Briey (brēā'), town (pop. 2,539), Meurthe-et-Moselle dept., NE France. Center of Lorraine iron-ore basin.

brig, two-masted, square-rigged, sailing vessel, once popular in coastal trade. Length varies from 100 to 115 ft.; tonnages go up to 350. Smaller brigantine has a fore-and-aft mainsail and square topsail on the mainmast. See *ill.*, sailing craft, p. 865.

Briga: see BRIGUE AND TENDE.

brigandage, robbery, blackmail, kidnaping, and plundering by armed bands. Arises from bad economic, political, or social conditions or in a chaotic society as after war or in frontier settlements. Many brigands are romantic figures, as Dick Turpin, Robin Hood, Hereward the Wake, Stenka Razin, Fra Diavolo, and Jesse James of U.S.

Briggs, Le Baron Russell, 1855–1934, American educator. A professor of English at Harvard, he was later dean of Harvard Col. (1891–1902) and president of Radcliffe Col. (1902–23).

Brigham, Albert Perry, 1855–1932, American geographer. Became professor of geology, Colgate Univ., in 1892. His *Geographic Influences in American History* (1903) had wide influence.

Brigham City, city (pop. 6,790), N Utah, N of Ogden; founded 1851. Food-processing center for area (extensive peach culture) served by Ogden R. project.

Brigham Young University, at Provo, Utah; Latter-Day Saints, coed.; opened 1875 as academy, renamed 1903.

Bright, Sir Charles Tilston, 1832–88, English engineer. Among cables he laid were first from Ireland to Scotland (1853) and Ireland to Newfoundland (1858).

Bright, John, 1811–89, English statesman and orator; son of Quaker cotton miller. He and Richard COBDEN were greatest 19-cent. champions of the middle class. Noted for laissez-faire views, support of FREE TRADE, and fight for repeal of CORN LAWS.

Bright, Richard: see BRIGHT'S DISEASE.

Brighton, county borough (pop. 156,440), Sussex East, England, on English Channel. Became fashionable resort under patronage of prince of Wales (later George IV), who built the Royal Pavilion.

Bright's disease, any of several forms of kidney inflammation. Symptoms include albumin in urine, dropsy, high blood pressure. Described 1827 by **Richard Bright,** 1789–1858, English physician noted for clinical observations.

Brigue and Tende (brēg, täd), Ital. *Briga* and *Tenda,* small districts (202 sq. mi.; 1936 pop. 4,274), Alpes-Maritimes dept., SE France. Ceded to France by Italy in Treaty of Paris of 1947.

Brill or **Bril,** two Flemish artists, brothers. **Mattys Brill** (mä′tĭs), 1550–83, and **Paul Brill,** 1554–1626, both worked in Rome. The latter was important in the development of landscape painting.

Brill, A(braham) A(rden), 1874–1948, American psychiatrist, b. Austria. One of the earliest, most active exponents of psychoanalysis in practice, teaching, and writing, he was first translator of many major works of Freud and Jung.

Brillat-Savarin, Anthelme (ätĕlm′ brēyä′-sävärē′), 1755–1826, French lawyer, economist, and gastronomist, famous for *La Physiologie du goût* (1825), published in English as *The Physiology of Taste.*

Brill's disease, mild type of typhus fever. First described, though not identified, by Nathan Edwin Brill, 1860–1925, American physician.

Brindaban (brĭn″dŭbŭn′), town (pop. 20,718), W Uttar Pradesh, India. Traditionally associated with the youth of the Hindu god Krishna.

Brindisi (brēn′dēzē), Latin *Brundisium,* city (pop. 35,-984), Apulia, S Italy; Adriatic port. Important Roman naval station; embarkation port for Crusaders. One of two columns marking end of Appian Way still stands. Vergil died here.

Brinton, Daniel Garrison, 1837–99, American anthropologist, authority on American Indians.

Brinvilliers, Marie Madeleine d'Aubray, marquise de: see POISON AFFAIR.

Brion, Admiral de: see CHABOT, PHILIPPE DE.

Brisbane, Albert (brĭz′bän), 1809–90, American social theorist. An advocate of the ideas of Charles FOURIER, he was instrumental in founding of Fourierist communities at BROOK FARM and Red Bank, N.J.

Brisbane (brĭz′bŭn), city (pop. 21,391; metropolitan pop. 402,030), cap. of Queensland, Australia; port on Brisbane R. above its mouth on Moreton Bay. Area was settled 1824 as a penal colony. Seat of Univ. of Queensland (1909). Exports textiles, wool, meat, gold, and sugar.

Briseis (brīsē′ĭs), maiden in the *Iliad* captured by Achilles, whose wrath was aroused when Agamemnon took her. See also CHRYSEIS.

Brissot de Warville, Jacques Pierre (zhäk′ pyĕr′ brēsō′ dü värvēl′), 1754–93, French revolutionist and pamphleteer, leader of the GIRONDISTS. Also wrote on French-U.S. relations, founded abolitionist society, and originated phrase later made famous by Proudhon: "Property is theft." Guillotined.

Bristol, John Digby, 1st earl of, 1580–1653, English diplomat. Ambassador to Spain 1611–24; offended Charles I and was imprisoned 1626–28. Released by Parliament, he became a moderate leader. As such, was increasingly unpopular and again jailed, 1642. Was royalist in civil war and died in exile. His son, **George Digby, 2d earl of Bristol,** 1612–77, was secretary of state to Charles I in exile and returned to England after Restoration.

Bristol, county borough (pop. 442,281), Gloucestershire, England, on the Avon near mouth of the Severn. A major world port, with extensive trade with North America and Ireland, it is also an industrial center (mfg. of flour, chemicals, paper, biscuits, tiles, and leather goods, and notably of airplanes since 1910). Railroad tunnel under Severn leads to Wales. Early transatlantic steamship built here 1838. The Cabots sailed (1497) from Bristol for American discoveries. Birthplace of Thomas Chatterton and Robert Southey.

Bristol. 1 City (pop. 35,961), central Conn., SW of Hartford; settled 1727. Mfg. of clocks (since 1790) and metal goods. **2** Fishing and resort town (pop. 1,476), S Maine, E of Bath. Includes Pemaquid peninsula, with reproduction of tower of Fort William Henry (built here 1692). MONHEGAN island is near. **3** Borough (pop. 12,710), SE Pa., on Delaware, NE of Philadelphia; settled c.1681. Mfg. of paper, machinery, and textiles. Has old Friends Meetinghouse (c.1710). **4** Town (pop. 12,320), including Bristol village (pop. 10,335), E R.I., on Narragansett Bay SE of Providence; connected with Portsmouth by Mt. Hope Bridge; passed to R.I. from Plymouth Colony, 1746. Yachts, coastwise fishing boats use Bristol Harbor. Boat works (estab. 1863); textile mills. Near-by monument marks place where King Philip fell. **5** City (Tenn. pop., 16,771; Va. pop., 15,954), on Tenn.-Va. line in mountains; settled 1749. Separate municipalities united economically; rail and industrial center in timber, farm, coal, and iron region with mfg. of textiles.

Bristol Avon: see AVON 1, river, England.

Bristol Channel, inlet (length 85 mi.; max. width 43 mi.) of the Atlantic separating Wales and SW England. It is approach, via the Severn, to Bristol.

Bristow, city (pop. 5,400), E central Okla., SW of Tulsa, in oil and farm region.

Britain, conventional name of Great Britain before Germanic invasions of 5th–6th cent. It then became ENGLAND, WALES, and SCOTLAND. Successive waves of migration or invasion were mainly from S and E to N and W. Before 6th cent. B.C. Celtic invasions from continent brought Iron Age culture to British Bronze Age settlements. Brisk trade with Continent developed. Last Celtic invaders (c.75 B.C.) introduced the deep plough and coining of money. First Roman invaders under Julius CAESAR (55 B.C.) found Celtic tribal organization as in Gaul, including DRUIDS. By A.D. 85 Emperor Claudius and his successors had conquered Britain S of the Clyde despite such resistance as revolt of BOADICEA. Risings in N caused building of HADRIAN'S WALL (122 A.D.) and Wall of ANTONINUS (142 A.D.). Former became N frontier. First half of 3d cent. was Roman heyday in Britain, with number of towns whose gridiron plan and architecture were Roman and whose language was probably Latin. ROMAN ROADS, mainly military, radiated from Londinium (London). Decline of Rome and three-sided invasions by Saxons and Irish progressively weakened defense until Honorius supposedly gave Romano-Britons self-rule c.410. A final appeal to Rome for help failed 446 and warring tribal kings gradually took over. Christianization lessened invasion pressure in N and W, but Saxon raids in E were heavier. ANGLO-SAXONS and Jutes began to settle in England and Celtic tribal culture revived. Residue of Roman influence remained in place names, architectural ruins, and in force of tradition.

britannia metal, silvery-white alloy of tin, copper, antimony; sometimes also with bismuth, lead, zinc.

Britannicus (brĭtă′nĭkŭs), A.D. 41?–A.D. 55, Roman prince, son of Claudius I and Messalina. Set aside in favor of Nero, son of his stepmother, Agrippina, he was apparently poisoned later.

British Cameroons: see NIGERIA and CAMEROONS.

British Columbia, province (359,279 sq. mi.; with water surface 366,255 sq. mi.; pop. 1,165,210), W Canada; cap. VICTORIA. Many islands (e.g. Vancouver and Queen Charlotte) lie off the indented W Pacific coastline. VANCOUVER is largest city and chief port. Other cities are NEW WESTMINSTER, NORTH VANCOUVER, and TRAIL. Province is mountainous with interior broken by numerous lakes and rivers. Drained by FRASER, COLUMBIA, KOOTENAY, PEACE, and SKEENA rivers. Population is centered in S and on Vancouver Isl. Lumbering is major industry, supplemented by truck and poultry farming and mining (copper, lead, zinc, silver). Tourist trade is growing. Area first explored by white men (Pérez, Heceta and Quadra, Cook, Meares) in late 18th cent. England gained control when Spanish claims were relinquished in Nootka Convention (1790). Capt. George Vancouver charted coast 1792–94, and Sir Alexander Mackenzie reached Pacific coast by land 1793. Trading posts estab. by North West Co. and Hudson's Bay Co. Boundaries defined with Alaska (1825, 1903) and the

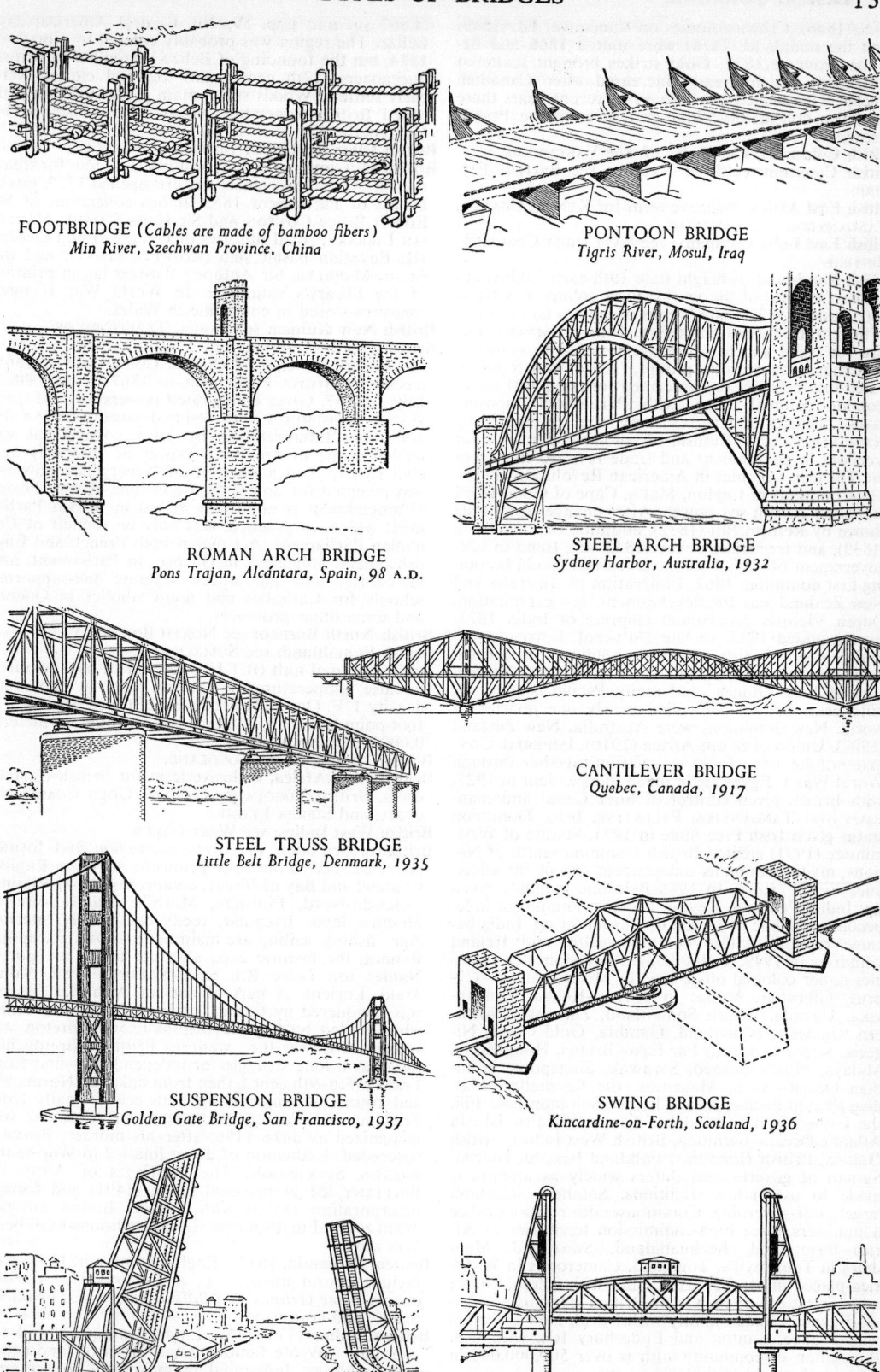

FOOTBRIDGE (*Cables are made of bamboo fibers*)
Min River, Szechwan Province, China

PONTOON BRIDGE
Tigris River, Mosul, Iraq

ROMAN ARCH BRIDGE
Pons Trajan, Alcántara, Spain, 98 A.D.

STEEL ARCH BRIDGE
Sydney Harbor, Australia, 1932

STEEL TRUSS BRIDGE
Little Belt Bridge, Denmark, 1935

CANTILEVER BRIDGE
Quebec, Canada, 1917

SUSPENSION BRIDGE
Golden Gate Bridge, San Francisco, 1937

SWING BRIDGE
Kincardine-on-Forth, Scotland, 1936

BASCULE: ROLLING LIFT BRIDGE
Terminal Railway, Chicago, 1901

VERTICAL-LIFT BRIDGE
Hawthorne Avenue, Portland, Oregon, 1911

U.S. (1846). Crown colonies on Vancouver Isl. (1849) and the mainland (1858) were united 1866 and became province 1871. Gold strikes brought scattered settlement which greatly increased after Canadian Pacific RR reached Vancouver. In recent years there has been considerable immigration from the Prairie Provs.

British Columbia, University of: see VANCOUVER.

British Commonwealth of Nations: see BRITISH EMPIRE.

British East Africa, inclusive term for KENYA, UGANDA, TANGANYIKA, and ZANZIBAR.

British East India Company: see EAST INDIA COMPANY, BRITISH.

British Empire, at its height (late 19th-early 20th cent.) greatest empire of the world. First colony was Newfoundland (1583). Foundations of empire laid in early 17th cent. by formation of EAST INDIA COMPANY. Desire for trade and to settle overseas led to scattered settlements by various groups. These were consolidated into colonies (by agreement or conquest) under London colonial office, with Parliament imposing taxes. Theories of MERCANTILISM were implanted by NAVIGATION ACTS. Refusal of colonists' demands for freedom in government and trade resulted in loss of the Thirteen Colonies in American Revolution (1775–83). Conquests of Ceylon, Malta, Cape of Good Hope increased British sea power. After change in attitude shown by Reform Bill (1832), abolition of slave trade (1833), and free trade policy (1842–46), trend to self-government of settled colonists led to Canada becoming first dominion, 1867. Emigration to Australia and New Zealand was for development, not exploitation. Queen Victoria proclaimed empress of India 1877; Burma added 1885. In late 19th-cent. European colonial race, British enlarged holdings in Africa, gained power in Egypt, and acquired Malaya, Borneo, part of New Guinea, and many Pacific islands. By 20th cent. Britain controlled nearly one quarter of world. New dominions were Australia, New Zealand (1907), Union of South Africa (1910). IMPERIAL CONFERENCE held this loose association together through World War I. Egypt again made independent in 1923, with British given control of Suez Canal and mandates over TANGANYIKA, PALESTINE, IRAQ. Dominion status given Irish Free State in 1921. Statute of Westminster (1931) created British Commonwealth of Nations; made dominions independent except for allegiance to the crown. In 1948 Palestine mandate given up; India, Pakistan, Ceylon became dominions; independent republic of Union of Burma set up. India became republic within commonwealth, and Ireland withdrew in 1949. Today United Kingdom dependencies under colonial office are: in Mediterranean—Cyprus, Gibraltar, Malta; in Africa—Kenya, Tanganyika, Uganda, British Somaliland, Zanzibar, Northern Rhodesia, Nyasaland, Gambia, Gold Coast, Nigeria, Sierra Leone; in Far East—Brunei, Hong Kong, Malaya, North Borneo, Sarawak, Singapore; in Indian Ocean—Aden, Mauritius, the Seychelles, Maldive Isls.; in Pacific Ocean—British Solomon Isls., Fiji, the Gilbert and Ellice Isls., Tonga, Pitcairn Isl.; in Atlantic Ocean—Bermuda, British West Indies, British Guiana, British Honduras, Falkland Isls., St. Helena. System of governments differs widely as attempt is made to use native traditions. Southern Rhodesia largely self-governing. Commonwealth relations office administers three high-commission territories in Africa—Basutoland, Bechuanaland, Swaziland. Mandates in Tanganyika, Togoland, Cameroons in W Africa placed under UN trusteeship with colonial office administration, 1946. Great Britain administers Anglo-Egyptian Sudan jointly with Egypt, New Hebrides with France, Canton and Enderbury Isls. with U.S. Population of commonwealth is over 500,000,000 in an area of nearly 16,000,000 sq. mi.

British Guiana: see GUIANA.

British Honduras (hŏndoō′rŭs), British crown colony (8,867 sq. mi.; pop. 59,220), Central America; cap. Belize. The region was probably entered by Cortés in 1524, but the founding of Belize is credited to British buccaneers (17th cent.), and logwood cutters were early settlers. Woods still a main product. Spain contested British ownership, which is now disputed by Guatemala.

British Isles: see GREAT BRITAIN and IRELAND.

British Museum, national repository, London, for treasures in literature, science, and art; opened 1759, estab. by act of Parliament 1853. It has collections of Sir Robert Bruce COTTON and Sir Hans SLOANE; HARLEIAN LIBRARY; royal libraries of George II and George III; Egyptian basalt slab (ROSETTA STONE); and the ELGIN MARBLES. Sir Anthony PANIZZI began printing of the library's catalogue. In World War II most treasures stored in coal mine in Wales.

British New Guinea: see PAPUA, TERRITORY OF.

British North America Act, constitution of dominion of Canada, sketched at Quebec Conference of 1864, passed by British Parliament in 1867 to take effect July 1, 1867. Gives enumerated powers to local (provincial) legislatures with residual powers left to the dominion. Interpretation by privy council has extended scope of provincial power of "property and civil rights," and a doctrine of "emergency powers" was invented for dominion use in time of war. Power of amendment is nominally vested in British Parliament which, in practice, acts only on request of Canadian Parliament. Act makes both French and English official languages in Quebec, in Parliament, and in courts; and guarantees separate tax-supported schools for Catholics and non-Catholics in Quebec and some other provinces.

British North Borneo: see NORTH BORNEO.

British Somaliland: see SOMALILAND.

British thermal unit (B.T.U.), amount of heat required to raise temperature of 1 lb. of water at maximum density $1°F$. One B.T.U. equals: 251.9 calories; 777.9 foot-pounds; 1055 joules; 107.5 kilogram-meters; 0.0002928 kilowatt-hours.

British Togoland: see TOGOLAND.

British West Africa, inclusive term for British CAMEROONS, British TOGOLAND, GAMBIA, GOLD COAST, NIGERIA, and SIERRA LEONE.

British West Indies: see WEST INDIES.

Brittany (brĭt′ŭnē), Fr. *Bretagne,* region and former province, NW France, a peninsula between English Channel and Bay of Biscay, comprising Ille-et-Vilaine, Côtes-du-Nord, Finistère, Morbihan, and Loire-Inférieure depts. Irregular, rocky coast; hilly interior. Agr., fishing, sailing are main occupations. Excepting Rennes, the historic cap., all chief towns are ports: Nantes (on Loire R.), Saint-Nazaire, Brest, Saint-Malo, Lorient. A part of ancient Armorica, region was conquered by Caesar, received its modern name when settled by fugitive Britons (c.500). Breton still spoken in Lower (i.e., western) Brittany. Breton history was a long struggle for independence—first from Franks (5th–9th cent.), then from dukes of Normandy and counts of Anjou (10th–12th cent.), finally from England and France. ARTHUR I, an ANGEVIN, was recognized as duke 1196; after his murder, PETER I succeeded. Extinction of direct line led to War of the BRETON SUCCESSION. The marriages of ANNE OF BRITTANY led to personal union (1491) and formal incorporation (1532) with France. Breton autonomism revived in 19th cent. Local traditions have been kept alive.

Britten, Benjamin, 1913–, English composer. His works include choral music, e.g., *A Ceremony of Carols;* operas *Peter Grimes* and *Billy Budd;* songs; chamber music; and concertos.

Britton, John, 1771–1857, English antiquary and topographer. Wrote famous descriptions of landscapes and buildings. Influential in movement to preserve ancient monuments.

Britton, Nathaniel Lord, 1859–1934, American botanist, was first director of New York Botanical Garden.

Brixham (brĭk'sùm), urban district (pop. 8,761), Devonshire, England; seaport. William III landed here 1688.

Brizeux, Auguste: see BRETON LITERATURE.

Brno (bŭr'nô), Ger. *Brünn*, city (pop. 133,637), cap. of Moravia, Czechoslovakia. Major mfg. center (textiles, machinery, arms). Seat of Czechoslovak supreme court and of univ. (founded 1919). Large German-speaking pop. expelled 1945. Brno's charter, granted 1229, was a model of medieval liberal town government. Battle of AUSTERLITZ fought near by 1805. Old city includes cathedral (15th cent.), Spielberg fortress (long a celebrated political prison), many fine Gothic and baroque churches and public buildings. Heavily damaged in World War II.

broadcasting, public transmission by radio and television of sound and pictures. Radio broadcasting dates in U.S. from 1920; advertising "time" first sold in 1922; tentative network coast-to-coast hookup in 1924. By 1927 the two major networks had stations so numerous as to cause traffic problems and need for legislation (see FEDERAL COMMUNICATIONS COMMISSION). See also FREQUENCY MODULATION; TELEVISION.

Broad River, rising in W N.C., S of Asheville, and flowing 143 mi. SE, then S through S.C. to the Saluda, forming the Congaree near Columbia.

Broads, the, region of lakes and lagoons connected by rivers, in Suffolk and Norfolk, England; notable as yachting center.

Broadview, village (pop. 5,196), NE Ill., residential suburb of Chicago.

Broadway, famous street (longest in the world), extending 150 mi. N from Bowling Green near foot of Manhattan isl. to Albany, N.Y. Chiefly commercial in New York city where it is a main traffic artery: runs through nation's financial center at Wall St.; enters theater district at Times Square (42d St.) where it becomes the "Great White Way," illuminated by garish electric signs. Points of interest along it include Trinity Church, St. Paul's Chapel, Woolworth and Flatiron buildings, Columbia Univ., and Columbia-Presbyterian Medical Center.

Broca, Paul (pôl brôkä'), 1824–80, French pathologist, anthropologist, and neurosurgeon. Localized center for articulate speech in left frontal lobe of brain. Originated methods of classifying hair and skin color and establishing ratio of brain to skull.

brocade, decorative fabric whose embossed patterns give effect of embroidery. Ground fabric usually silk; design may be of silk, silver, or gold thread. Made since antiquity in Orient; art came to Europe with Moors. Jacquard loom, perfected c.1804, improved modern weaving of intricate designs.

broccoli (brŏk'ŭlē), garden vegetable with loose, green, leafy, edible flower panicles.

Brocéliande, Forest of (brôsālēäd'), in Arthurian legend, the home of Merlin in Brittany, France. Forest of Paimpont, SW of Rennes, is a remnant.

Brock, Sir Isaac, 1769–1812, British general, Canadian hero of War of 1812. Upon outbreak of war joined forces with Tecumseh, captured post at Detroit and gained control of upper lakes, thereby earning name of "hero of Upper Canada." Successfully defended Queenston Heights, where he was mortally wounded.

Brocken (brŏk'ŭn) or **Blocksberg** (blôks'bĕrk), peak, 3,747 ft. high, Saxony-Anhalt, central Germany; highest peak of Harz mts. Legend makes it meeting place of Walpurgis Night or Witches' Sabbath.

Brockton, city (pop. 62,860), SE Mass., S of Boston; settled c.1700. Mfg. of shoes.

Brockville, city (pop. 12,301), S Ont., Canada, on St. Lawrence R. and S of Ottawa, in dairy region. River port and summer resort, with mfg. of electrical equipment and hardware.

Brockway, Zebulon Reed, 1827–1920, American penologist, advocate of prison reforms, superintendent (1876–1900) of pioneer reformatory at Elmira, N.Y.

Broderick, David Colbreth, 1820–59, American politician. Fought with William M. GWINN for Democratic party control in Calif. Killed in famous duel.

Brodie, Sir Benjamin Collins (brō'dē), 1783–1862, English surgeon, authority on joint diseases.

Broglie (broi), French noble family of Piedmontese origin. **François Marie, duc de Broglie** (frãswä' märē', dük dù), 1671–1745, marshal of France, received ducal title from Louis XV. His son, **Victor François, duc de Broglie** (vĕktôr'), 1718–1804, marshal of France, distinguished himself in Seven Years War; was created a prince of Holy Roman Empire. In 1792 he commanded émigré forces against revolutionary France. His great-grandson, **Albert, duc de Broglie** (älbĕr'), 1821–1901, was French premier (1873–74; 1877); wrote important historical works on 18th cent. Two of his grandsons became distinguished physicists: **Maurice, duc de Broglie** (mōrēs'), 1875–, noted for work on X rays and atomic physics; and **Louis Victor, prince de Broglie** (lwē', prēs'), 1892–, who won the 1929 Nobel Prize for his theory of the wave character of electrons.

Broken Hill, municipality (pop. 27,054), New South Wales, Australia; since 1884 the chief silver-lead mining center in Australia.

Bromberg, Poland: see BYDGOSZCZ.

brome grass, large, coarse grass of genus *Bromus*. Smooth brome (also called Hungarian or awnless brome) and rescue grass are used for forage and pasture. Many species have barbed fruits.

bromide (brō'mīd), compound of bromine and another element (except oxygen), salt of hydrobromic acid. Widely distributed in nature. Sodium and potassium bromides used as sedatives; silver bromide used in photography. In aqueous solution, hydrogen bromide is hydrobromic acid.

bromine (brō'mēn), active, nonmetallic element (symbol = Br; see also ELEMENT, table). Brownish-red liquid; vapor has suffocating odor. Member of HALOGEN family; less active than fluorine or chlorine, more active than iodine. Corrosive. Compounds occur in sea water, mineral springs, common salt deposits. Solidifies at −7°C.; boils at 58.8°C.

bronchitis (brŏng-kī'tĭs), inflammation in a bronchus (one of two air passages from windpipe to lung) or its branches caused by bacterial infection or by irritation.

bronco: see MUSTANG.

Brontë, Charlotte (brŏn'tē), 1816–55, **Emily Jane Brontë,** 1818–48, and **Anne Brontë,** 1820–49, English novelists and poets. Life in the parsonage in Haworth, Yorks., caused them to live in an imaginary world and write imaginative literature as children. Later the three sisters produced *Poems* (1846) under pseudonyms of Currer, Ellis, and Acton Bell. Emily's poems were particularly notable, as was her novel, *Wuthering Heights* (1847). Anne wrote novels *Agnes Gray* (1847), *The Tenant of Wildfell Hall* (1848). Generally best known was Charlotte, whose novels—*Jane Eyre* (1847), *Shirley* (1849), *Villette* (1853) and *The Professor* (1857, but earliest written) won her fame that gladdened last year of her life as wife of Arthur Bell Nicholls.

Brontosaurus (brŏntŭsô'rŭs), largest vegetarian dinosaur, probably semiaquatic, length c.70 ft., weight over 30 tons; long neck and tail.

Bronx, the, northernmost borough (land area 41 sq. mi.; pop. 1,451,277) of NEW YORK city, SE N.Y. Settled 1641 under Dutch West India Co., became a New York city borough in 1898 and a co. of N.Y. state in 1914. On peninsula NE of Manhattan and S of Westchester co.; bounded on W by Hudson R., SW by Spuyten Duyvil Creek and Harlem R., S by East R., and E by Long Isl. Sound. Many bridge and tunnel connections to Manhattan and Queens. Mainly residential, though industrialized along Harlem R. Numerous parks include Bronx (zoo, botanic gardens), Van Cortlandt, and Pelham Bay. Seat of FORDHAM UNIVERSITY, Manhattan Col. (R.C., Christian Brothers; for men; opened as academy 1849, chartered as college 1863); parts of NEW YORK UNIVERSITY, and Hunter Col. (see NEW YORK, COLLEGE OF THE CITY OF). Has Yankee Stadium and Poe cottage.

Bronxville, N.Y.: see EASTCHESTER.

bronze, alloy of copper and tin or copper and certain other metals. Sometimes silver, aluminum, zinc, or lead added for brilliance or hardness. Harder and more resistant than brass, zinc, and copper. Used for gun metal and bell metal; also for machine bearings, valves, roofs, cornices, ornaments, and funerary urns and caskets. Ideal for casting art works, engraving, and repoussé work. Used by Egyptians, Greeks, Etruscans, Romans. Renaissance Italy noted for bronze doors of Ghiberti and others; 18th-cent. France for furniture mounts.

Bronze Age, prehistoric period, characterized by use of bronze for tools and artifacts. It followed the Neolithic and preceded the Iron Age, but did not reach all places at the same time. Egypt and SW Asia were in the Bronze Age by 2500 B.C.; Britain c.2000 B.C. The W Hemisphere had no true Bronze Age. Copper was known before bronze, and that period is sometimes termed the Copper Age. Horses and cattle were first used as draft animals in the Bronze Age. Important inventions—arch, wheel, potter's wheel.

Bronzino, Il (ēl brōntsē'nō), 1502?–1572, Florentine painter, whose real name was Agnolo di Cosimo Allori. Portraitist of many celebrated figures, including Cosimo I de' Medici, Dante, Boccaccio, Petrarch.

Bronzino, Alessandro: see ALLORI, ALESSANDRO.

Brook, Alexander, 1898–, American painter. His realistic style is marked by subtle color.

Brooke, Alan Francis, 1st Viscount Alanbrooke, 1883–, British field marshal. Was commander-in-chief of British Home Forces 1940–41 and chief of imperial general staff 1941–46.

Brooke, Sir Charles Johnson: see BROOKE, SIR JAMES.

Brooke, Sir Charles Vyner: see BROOKE, SIR JAMES.

Brooke, Fulke Greville, 1st Baron, 1554–1628, English poet, patron of letters, and statesman, author (as Fulke Greville) of philosophical poems and *Life of the Renowned Sir Philip Sidney* (1652).

Brooke, Sir James, 1803–68, English rajah of Sarawak on Borneo. After aiding local sultan to suppress rebel tribes he was made rajah (1841). Succeeded by his nephew, **Sir Charles Johnson Brooke,** 1829–1917, who abolished slavery and aided prosperity. His son, **Sir Charles Vyner Brooke,** 1874–, ceded Sarawak to Great Britain as a crown colony 1946.

Brooke, Rupert, 1887–1915, English poet. His poetry, *Poems* (1911) and *1914 and Other Poems* (1915), shows the dashing romanticism that made Brooke a legendary figure. Died of blood poisoning on Skyros in World War I.

Brook Farm, experimental community on a 192-acre farm at West Roxbury, Mass. Founded 1841 by transcendentalists George and Sophia Ripley to combine "plain living and high thinking." The members shared manual labor and intellectual life. Nathaniel Hawthorne was a member, R. W. Emerson and Margaret Fuller visitors. Brook Farm was made into a Fourierist community under the aegis of Albert Brisbane in 1845, disbanded 1847.

Brookfield. 1 Village (pop. 15,472), NE Ill., W suburb of Chicago. **2** City (pop. 5,810), N central Mo., SW of Kirksville. Rail shipping point in farm and coal area. Gen. Pershing's boyhood home is near.

Brookhaven. 1 City (pop. 7,801), SW Miss., SSW of Jackson; center of dairy and timber area. **2** Resort village, SE N.Y., on S shore of Long Isl. E of Patchogue. Brookhaven Natl. Laboratory for atomic research is near by.

Brookings, city (pop. 7,764), E S.Dak., N of Sioux Falls and near Big Sioux R. Farm trade center. Seat of South Dakota State Col. of Agriculture and Mechanic Arts (land-grant support; coed.; chartered 1881, opened 1884).

Brookings Institution, at Washington, D.C.; founded by Robert S. Brookings for research and education in social sciences; chartered 1927.

Brookline (brook'lin), beautiful suburban town (pop. 57,589), E Mass., just W of Boston.

Brooklyn. 1 Village (pop. 2,568), SW Ill., on the Mississippi above East St. Louis. An all-Negro town. Post office is Lovejoy. **2** Borough (land area 71 sq. mi.; pop. 2,738,175), of NEW YORK city, SE N.Y., on SW end of Long Isl. adjoining Queens borough. Settled 1636–37 by Walloons and Hollanders; hamlet of Breuckelen estab. c.1645; absorbed various settlements (e.g., Flatbush, a 17th-cent. Dutch village, now a residential section) until it became coextensive with Kings co. (estab. 1683); became a New York city borough 1898. Separated from downtown Manhattan by East R. (many bridges, e.g., BROOKLYN BRIDGE, and tunnels), from Staten Isl. by the Narrows of New York Bay. Though largely residential, borough has important port facilities—New York Naval Shipyard (commonly Brooklyn Navy Yard), Bush Terminal—and industrial establishments (machinery, textiles, paper, chemicals, shoes, processed foods). Seat of Brooklyn Col. (see NEW YORK, COLLEGE OF THE CITY OF); PRATT INSTITUTE; Long Isl. Univ. (nonsectarian; coed.; chartered 1926, opened 1927); St. John's Univ. (R.C., Vincentian; partly coed.; opened 1870, chartered 1871); BROOKLYN INSTITUTE OF ARTS AND SCIENCES; and Long Isl. Historical Society. Here are Prospect Park (see LONG ISLAND, BATTLE OF); Ebbets Field (home of Brooklyn Dodgers); Coney Isl., famed beach resort and amusement center; and many noted churches. **3** City (pop. 6,317), NE Ohio, a S suburb of Cleveland.

Brooklyn Bridge, SE N.Y., bridge (1,595 ft.; suspension) across East R. between Manhattan and Brooklyn. Built (1869–83) by Roebling and son.

Brooklyn College: see NEW YORK, COLLEGE OF THE CITY OF.

Brooklyn Institute of Arts and Sciences, founded 1824. Includes Brooklyn Mus., Children's Mus., Brooklyn Acad. of Music, and a 42-acre botanical garden. The museum collections include water colors by Sargent and sculptures by Barye. Courses in the arts and the physical and social sciences are given.

Brooks, Phillips, 1835–93, American Episcopalian clergyman. Influential as preacher at Trinity Church, Boston, 1869–91. Made bishop of Mass. 1891. Wrote *O Little Town of Bethlehem.*

Brooks, Van Wyck (wīk), 1886–, American critic. Wrote critical biographies (e.g., *The Ordeal of Mark Twain,* 1920) and works on the force of Puritanism in American thought. His series "Makers and Finders: a History of the Writer in America, 1800–1915," begun with *The Flowering of New England* (1936), stressed need for finding a "usable past."

Brooks Range, N Alaska, separating Yukon R. basin from watershed of Arctic Ocean. Embraces many mountain chains; height averages 5,500–6,500 ft. Area thinly settled. Transportation mainly by air.

Brooksville, city (pop. 1,818), W central Fla., N of Tampa. Near by are Devil's Punch Bowl, an arid sink, and Weekiwachee Spring, emptying 100,000 gal. a minute to form river flowing to Gulf of Mexico.

broom, shrubs of two related genera, *Cytisus* and *Genista.* Yellow or white (in *Cytisus,* purple also), pealike flowers. Common or Scotch broom is *Cytisus scoparius.* Florists' genista is *C. canariensis.*

broomcorn: see SORGHUM.

Brosse, Salomon de (sälōmō' dü brôs'), 1565–1626, French architect of Luxembourg Palace. Built hunting chateau which was later to become nucleus of Versailles palace.

Broun, Heywood (Campbell) (broon), 1888–1939, American newspaper columnist. Wrote for several New York papers, attacking social injustices and championing the weak. Founded American Newspaper Guild. Column ("It Seems to Me") syndicated.

Broussais, François Joseph Victor (fränswä′ zhôzĕf′ vĕktôr′ brŏŏsä′), 1772–1838, French physician. Advocate of treatment by starvation and use of leeches.

Brouwer or **Brauwer, Adriaen** (äd″rēän′ brou′wŭr), c.1605–1638, Flemish painter of spirited genre and rustic scenes. Studied with Frans Hals.

Browder, Earl Russell, 1891–, American Communist leader. Opposition to his policies resulted in his removal from Communist party (1946).

Brown, family of bankers in U.S. **Alexander Brown,** 1764–1834, b. Ireland, became wealthy in Baltimore as an international banker. Took sons into partnership. Firm was for a generation leading institution of its kind in U.S. One son, **George Brown,** 1787–1859, helped found Baltimore & Ohio RR.

Brown, Alice, 1857–1948, American author of New England short stories (e.g., *Meadow-Grass,* 1895; *Tiverton Tales,* 1899). Also wrote novels and a play *Children of Earth* (1915).

Brown, Charles Brockden, 1771–1810, first professional American novelist. His interest in character development and abnormal behavior foreshadowed the psychological novel. *Wieland* (1798) was his most popular novel. Others were *Edgar Huntly* (1799), *Arthur Mervyn* (1799–1800), and *Ormond* (1799).

Brown, Elmer Ellsworth, 1861–1934, American educator. A teacher of education in Mich. and Calif., he became U.S. commissioner of education (1906–11). Chancellor of New York Univ. (1911–33).

Brown, Ford Madox, 1821–93, English historical painter, closely affiliated with the Pre-Raphaelites.

Brown, George, U.S. banker: see BROWN, family.

Brown, George, 1818–80, Canadian journalist and statesman, b. Scotland. Founded Toronto *Globe* (1844) which became most powerful political journal in Upper Canada. Elected to the assembly (1851), he led "Clear Grits" faction, which opposed influence of French Canadians in that body. Played important role in movement for confederation.

Brown, John, 1800–1859, American abolitionist. Following sack of LAWRENCE, Kansas (1856), he led retaliatory slaughter of five proslavery men on banks of Pottawatamie R. As step preliminary to liberating Southern slaves he captured U.S. arsenal at Harpers Ferry, Va. (now W.Va.) on Oct. 16, 1859. Arsenal was retaken and Brown was hanged.

Brown, John Carter, 1797–1874, American book collector and philanthropist. Donated library of early Americana to Brown Univ. (named for his father).

Brown, Lancelot, 1715–83, English landscape gardener and architect. Founder of English naturalistic school of landscape design.

Brown, Mather, 1761–1831, American portrait and historical painter, pupil of Benjamin West.

Brown, Moses, 1738–1836, American manufacturer. Estab. first water-powered cotton mill in America (1790) with Samuel Slater.

Brown, Robert, 1773–1858, Scottish botanist and botanical explorer. He collected plants in Australia. In 1827 he observed BROWNIAN MOVEMENT and in 1831 he discovered the cell nucleus.

Brown, William Hill, 1765–93, American writer, probable author of a novel, *The Power of Sympathy* (1789), long ascribed to Sarah Wentworth Morton.

brown coal: see LIGNITE.

Browne, Hablot Knight, pseud. **Phiz,** 1815–82, English illustrator of many of the novels of Charles Dickens.

Browne, Robert, c.1550–c.1633, English clergyman, leader of separatists called Brownists. He preached nonconformity, and his treatises are regarded as first expression of CONGREGATIONALISM.

Browne, Sir Thomas, 1605–82, English author, a physician. His *Religio Medici* (written c.1635), a private confession of faith, and *Hydrotaphia, Urne-Buriall* (1658), reflections on death and immortality, show his convolute, inimitably fine prose style.

Brownell, Herbert, Jr., 1904–, U.S. Attorney General (1953–). Chairman of Republican Natl. Committee

(1944–46). Managed Thomas E. Dewey's 1948 presidential campaign.

Brownell, W(illiam) C(rary), 1851–1928, American literary critic, long a literary adviser to Charles Scribner's Sons, advocate of modern humanism, author of books of art, literary, and social criticism.

Brownfield, town (pop. 6,161), NW Texas, SW of Lubbock on Llano Estacado. Trading, processing center in cattle and agr. region. Has chemical plants.

brown hematite: see LIMONITE.

Brownian movement, irregular movement shown by minute solid particles suspended in fluid; continuous, vibratory, unrelated to outside disturbances. Estab. by Robert Brown. Upholds kinetic molecular theory that matter is composed of particles (see MOLECULE) in constant vibratory motion. Suspended particles are buffeted by molecules of liquid.

Browning, Elizabeth Barrett, 1806–61, English poet, wife of Robert BROWNING. She defied her own invalidism and her tyrannical father to marry him (1846) and go to Italy. Already known as a poet, she later produced *Sonnets from the Portuguese* (1850); *Casa Guidi Windows* (1851), and *Aurora Leigh* (novel in verse, 1856).

Browning, John Moses, 1855–1926, American inventor of an automatic pistol, a machine gun, and an automatic rifle.

Browning, Robert, 1812–89, English poet. His many long narrative poems (*Pauline,* 1833; *Sordello,* 1840, and his masterpiece, *The Ring and the Book,* 1868–69) show the same psychological insight apparent in his dramatic monologues, "Fra Lippo Lippi," "Andrea del Sarto," "The Bishop Orders His Tomb at St. Praxed's Church," "My Last Duchess," and "Soliloquy of the Spanish Cloister." The long poems include lyrics, and he wrote many others. Also wrote poetic dramas (*Strafford,* 1837, *A Blot in the 'Scutcheon,* 1843). His romance with Elizabeth Barrett ended in marriage and happy life in Italy.

Browning, town (pop. 1,691), NW Mont., near Glacier Natl. Park. Hq. of Blackfeet Indian Reservation.

Brownists, followers of Robert BROWNE.

Brownlow, William Gannaway (broun′lō), 1805–77, itinerant Methodist preacher, known as the "fighting parson," governor of Tenn. (1865–69), a union sympathizer. His harsh Reconstruction program left Tenn. broken and impoverished.

Brown-Séquard, Charles Édouard (broun′-säkär′), 1817–94, Franco-American physiologist, pioneer in study of internal secretions and rejuvenation.

Brownson, Orestes (Augustus), 1803–76, American reformer, b. Vt. A vigorous writer on social and religious questions, he went through several phases of religion. At first a Presbyterian, he later became a Universalist, a Unitarian minister, head of a church he founded, finally a Roman Catholic. He agitated for the rights of workingmen and fought social evils. Wrote many works (including novels) and edited magazines to promote these causes.

Browns Valley, village (pop. 1,117), W Minn., on S.Dak. line. Controversial skeleton ("Browns Valley man") discovered near by, 1934.

Brownsville. 1 Borough (pop. 7,643), SW Pa., on the Monongahela and SSE of Pittsburgh. Has distilleries and railroad shops. **2** City (pop. 36,066), S Texas, on Rio Grande. Fort Taylor founded here 1846 by Gen. Zachary Taylor, who fought battles of Palo Alto and Resaca de la Palma coming to its aid. Renamed (1846) for defender, Major Jacob Brown. Fort Brown, held briefly by Union in Civil War and prominent in Mexican border disturbances, was active until 1944. Brownsville, laid out 1848, is an important port of entry across river from Matamoras, Mex. Center of rich region, it is ocean port (channel finished 1936) with oil and natural gas industries.

brown thrush: see THRASHER.

Brown University, at Providence, R.I.; nonsectarian, for men; chartered 1764 as Rhode Island Col. by Baptists at Warren, opened 1765, moved to Providence in 1770, renamed for Nicholas Brown, 1804. John Carter BROWN Library has notable collection of Americana. Brown Univ. has long led in academic freedom and curriculum reform. Pembroke Col. for women undergraduates, organized 1891, has own campus.

Brownwood, city (pop. 20,181), central Texas, WNW of Waco; settled 1856. Industrial and distribution center of agr. area with oil and gas wells. Mfg. of petroleum products, cottonseed oil, bricks, and clothing. Near-by L. Brownwood used for irrigation and recreation.

Bruce, celebrated Scottish family. Descended from 11th-cent. Norman duke, Robert de Brus, who aided William I in conquest of England. In struggle following death of MARGARET MAID OF NORWAY, Bruces claimed succession to the throne. Robert the Bruce was claimant to throne in 1290, rivaled by John de BALIOL. His grandson was famous Robert the Bruce, ROBERT I of Scotland. Edward Bruce, brother of Robert I, was crowned king of Ireland in 1316. Youngest son of Robert I succeeded him as DAVID II. Succeeded by his nephew ROBERT II, first STUART king.

Bruce, earls of Elgin: see ELGIN, THOMAS BRUCE, 7TH EARL OF.

Bruce, Sir David, 1855–1931, British bacteriologist, authority on cause of undulant fever and African sleeping sickness.

Bruce, Stanley Melbourne, 1st **Viscount Bruce of Melbourne,** 1883–, Australian statesman. As prime minister (1923–29) promoted relations with the empire. Was Australian delegate to League of Nations. High commissioner for Australia in London 1933–45.

Bruce, William Speirs, 1867–1921, Scottish explorer, authority on polar regions. Led Scottish Natl. Antarctic Expedition (1902–4); discovered Coats Land.

brucellosis (broosilō′sĭs), **undulant fever,** or **Malta fever,** disease caused by bacteria (certain brucella organisms). It is transmitted to man by infected food or fluids (esp. milk), or by contact with infected animals or tissues; may cause long disability from remittent fever. In animals it is known as contagious abortion (Bang's disease); it spreads through intake of feed or water containing the germs.

Bruch, Max (brookh′), 1838–1920, German composer, known for his Violin Concerto in G Minor and his variations on *Kol Nidre* for cello and orchestra.

Bruckner, Anton (brook′nùr), 1824–96, Austrian romantic composer. He wrote nine symphonies, several Masses and a *Te Deum*, and one string quartet.

Brudenell, James Thomas: see CARDIGAN.

Bruegel, Brueghel, or **Breughel** (all: brû′gùl), family of Flemish genre and landscape painters. The foremost, **Pieter Bruegel** (pē′tùr), c.1525–69, portrayed in vibrant colors the whole living world of field and forest in which gay, robust peasants are at work and play, as in *The Harvesters* (Metropolitan Mus.). In his *Carrying the Cross* (Vienna) and *Massacre of the Innocents* (Brussels) he showed horrors of the Inquisition in a Flemish village. A son, **Pieter Bruegel,** the younger, 1564–1637, was known as Hell Bruegel for his pictures of the infernal regions. His brother, **Jan Bruegel** (yän), 1568–1625, called Velvet Bruegel, painted landscapes and flowers. Shared his father's popularity.

Bruges (broozh, Fr. brüzh), Flemish *Brugge,* city (pop. 52,984), cap. of West Flanders, NW Belgium; connected by canal with ZEEBRUGGE. Once the greatest port of N Europe, it is now a quiet city, famed for its medieval architecture, quaint canals, bridges, convents, and churches. It has lace and beer mfg. and a printing industry. An early and typical Flemish commune, Bruges became (late 12th cent.) the chief port and a major wool-mfg. center of Flanders. It held extensive political privileges, and its government passed gradually from the patricians to the chief guilds—weavers, fullers, shearers, dyers. Leading the

Flemish rebellion against Philip IV of France, Bruges defeated the French in the BATTLE OF THE SPURS (1302). It became the chief warehouse of the HANSEATIC LEAGUE, reached its height as international port in the 14th cent., but foreign competition to the Flemish wool industry and the rise of Antwerp soon caused its decline (15th cent.), and its ports silted up. Bruges was the cradle and remains a treasure house of Flemish art. Among its many Gothic buildings are the Cloth Hall, with a famous belfry and carillon; the city hall; the cathedral; the Church of Notre Dame, with the tomb of Charles the Bold; and the Chapel of the Precious Blood, a major place of pilgrimage. The Hospital of St. John (12th cent.) contains masterpieces of Hans Memling.

Brugsch, Heinrich Karl (hīn′rĭkh kärl′ brooksh′), 1827–94, German Egyptologist. Deciphered demotic and compiled a demotic-hieroglyphic dictionary.

Brühl, Heinrich, Graf von (hīn′rĭkh gräf′ fŭn brül′), 1700–1763, Saxon statesman; chief minister to AUGUSTUS III of Poland and Saxony. Dictated disastrous policy in Seven Years War; amassed huge fortune through fraud.

Brumaire (brümâr′), second month of FRENCH REVOLUTIONARY CALENDAR. Coup d'état of 18 Brumaire (Nov. 9–10, 1799), overthrew DIRECTORY and established CONSULATE under Napoleon.

Brummagem (brŭ′mùjùm) [colloquial form of Birmingham, England], name given counterfeit coin first made in Birmingham 17th cent. Applied to anything not genuine, as "sham Protestants" supporting Exclusion Bill of 1680.

Brummell, George Bryan (Beau Brummell), 1778–1840, wealthy Englishman; noted for fine clothes. Intimate of the prince regent (later George IV).

Brundisium: see BRINDISI.

Brunehaut, Frankish queen: see BRUNHILDA.

Brunei (brooni′), sultanate (c.2,225 sq. mi.; pop. 40,670), NW BORNEO, under British protection since 1888. Bordered by Sarawak.

Brunel, Sir Marc Isambard (broonĕl′), 1769–1849, English engineer and inventor of machinery. Constructed Thames tunnel, assisted by his son, **Isambard Kingdom Brunel,** 1806–59, English engineer and authority on railway traction and steam navigation, and designer and constructor of ocean steamships.

Brunelleschi, Filippo (fēlēp′pō broonĕl-lĕs′kē), 1377–1446, first great architect of the Italian Renaissance, a Florentine. In competition (1401) for bronze doors for Florence baptistry his design placed second to that of Ghiberti. Most famous work is octagonal ribbed dome of Florence cathedral. Other works include Pazzi chapel, churches of San Lorenzo and Santo Spirito, and Pitti Palace (all: Florence).

Brunetière, Ferdinand (fĕrdēnä′ brünütyĕr′), 1849–1906, French literary critic, opponent of naturalism. His *Manuel de l'histoire de la littérature française* (1897) is his masterpiece.

Brunhild (broon′hĭld), **Brünnehilde** (brün″ühĭl′dù), or **Brynhild** (brĭn′hĭld), in Germanic mythology, mighty female warrior. In the NIBELUNGENLIED, as queen of Iceland, she is defeated by SIEGFRIED, whose death she contrives. In the VOLSUNGASAGA, as Brynhild, chief of the Valkyries, she is loved by Sigurd, but when he deserts her, she contrives his death and destroys herself on his funeral pyre. In Wagner's *Ring of the Nibelungs,* she is Brünnehilde, a Valkyrie (see NIBELUNGEN).

Brunhilda (brŭnhĭl′dù) or **Brunehaut** (brünō′), 534?–613, Frankish queen, wife of SIGEBERT I of Austrasia. Played leading part in the bloody war (567–613) against Neustria following the murder of her sister Galswintha by CHILPERIC I of Neustria. Put to horrible death by Clotaire II of Neustria.

Brüning, Heinrich (hīn′rĭkh brü′nĭng), 1885–, German chancellor (1930–32), leader of Catholic Center party. Passed drastic, unpopular financial decrees; dissolved Hitler's storm troops (1932). Pres. Hindenburg dismissed him abruptly and appointed Papen his successor. Brüning left Germany 1934, became professor at Harvard Univ. 1937.

Brünn, Czechoslovakia: see BRNO.

Brünnehilde, another spelling for BRUNHILD.

Brunner, Emil (ä′mēl broōn′ür), 1889–, Swiss Protestant theologian, professor of theology at Univ. of Zurich. His theological position is associated with that of Karl BARTH, with some disagreement.

Bruno, Saint (broō′nō), c.1030–1101, German monk; founder (1084) of CARTHUSIANS at Grande Chartreuse. Feast: Oct. 6.

Bruno, Giordano (jōrdä′nō broō′nō), 1548–1600, Italian philosopher. A Dominican, he was accused of heresy and left the order to become a wandering scholar and teacher. In his metaphysical works he challenged all dogmatic authority, maintaining that each man's view of the world is relative to his position, that any absolute truth is beyond statement, and that possible knowledge is unlimited. He believed that the world is composed of irreducible elements (monads), which operate under laws of relationship governed by a pantheistic principle. He returned to Venice, where he was convicted of heresy and burned at the stake—a martyr for freedom of thought.

Brunswick, dukes of: see CHARLES WILLIAM FERDINAND; FREDERICK WILLIAM.

Brunswick (brŭnz′wĭk), Ger. *Braunschweig,* former state (1,379 sq. mi.; 1939 pop. 602,873), central Germany. It consisted of several enclaves surrounded by Prussian territory. After World War II the larger part (1,182 sq. mi.; pop. 870,291) was incorporated into British-occupied LOWER SAXONY; the rest, into Russian-occupied Saxony-Anhalt. Agr.; mining in N foothills of Harz (silver, copper, lead, iron). Duchy of Brunswick emerged 12th cent. from remnants of domains of HENRY THE LION, who retained only the territories of Brunswick and Lüneburg (roughly, modern Brunswick and Hanover). The Guelphic house repeatedly divided into several branches, notably those of Brunswick-Lüneburg (after 1692 electors of HANOVER) and of Brunswick-Wolffenbüttel, or Brunswick proper. Duchy was part of the kingdom of Westphalia under Jérôme Bonaparte (1807–13); joined German Empire 1871; became republic 1918; joined Weimar Republic 1919. Its early cap., Wolfenbüttel, was replaced in 1753 by **Brunswick** city (pop. 223,263), now in Lower Saxony, on the Oker, a commercial and mfg. center (machinery, beer). Chartered 12th cent., it later joined the Hanseatic League. The picturesque old city suffered severely in World War II. Notable landmarks (all more or less damaged) include the 12th-cent. cathedral, with Henry the Lion's tomb, and the famous 15th-cent. fountain named for Till Eulenspiegel, who lived here. Former Richmond Palace has fine art museum.

Brunswick. 1 City (pop. 17,954), SE Ga., on the Atlantic; founded 1771–72. Shipping center, with shrimp and crab processing plants, shipyards, creosoting works. Mfg. of lumber, naval stores, clothing, paint. National quarantine station. Sea Islands are offshore. Fort Frederica Natl. Monument is near. **2** Town (pop. 10,996), including Brunswick village (pop. 7,342), S Maine, on Androscoggin R. and W of Bath; settled 1628. Has canneries, textile and paper mills. Trade center for resort area. Harriet Beecher Stowe wrote *Uncle Tom's Cabin* here. Seat of Bowdoin Col. (nonsectarian; for men; opened 1802); Hawthorne and Longfellow were alumni.

Brusa, Turkey: see BURSA.

Brush, George de Forest, 1855–1941, American painter, known for paintings of American Indians.

Brussa, Turkey: see BURSA.

Brussels (brŭ′sŭlz), Flemish *Brussel,* Fr. *Bruxelles,* city (centered about Brussels commune, pop. 185,112; pop. of greater Brussels 960,740), cap. of Belgium and of Brabant prov. It is a major commercial, industrial, and cultural center. Lace is its oldest and best-known industry. Dating from 10th cent., Brussels replaced Louvain as cap. of Brabant in 15th cent. and was the seat of the Spanish, later Austrian, governors of the Netherlands (16th–18th cent.). Frequently besieged in the wars of that period, Brussels twice fell to the French in the French Revolutionary Wars (1792, 1794), was Wellington's hq. in the Waterloo campaign (1815), and became the cap. of independent Belgium in 1830. It was occupied by the Germans in both world wars (1914–18, 1940–44) but suffered no physical damage. On its historic center, the Grand' Place, are the city hall (14th–17th cent.); the Renaissance Maison du Roi or Broodhuis, meeting place of the old States-General; and the 18th-cent. royal palace and parliament building. Other notable buildings include the Gothic Church of St. Gudule. The general aspect, however, is modern. The Univ. of Brussels was founded 1834.

Brussels sprouts, variety of CABBAGE with small, edible heads or sprouts along the stem.

Brut, Brute, or **Brutus,** a Trojan, legendary first king of Britain, descendant of Aeneas. His name gave title to long poems by Wace and Layamon.

Bruttium (brŭ′tēŭm), anc. region of S Italy, roughly present Calabria (the "toe" of the "boot"), inhabited in 8th cent. B.C. by native Brutii and Lucani and by Greek colonists. Sybaris and Crotona became important cities of Magna Graecia. After Roman conquest (3d cent. B.C.), Rhegium was favored.

Brutus, surname of anc. Roman family. The semi-legendary **Lucius Junius Brutus,** fl. 510 B.C., was the brother of Lucrece and helped to end the TARQUIN dynasty. He is said to have killed his sons for plotting a restoration of the Tarquins and was honored as founder of the republic. Centuries later **Marcus Junius Brutus,** 85 B.C.–42 B.C., was the principal assassin of Julius Caesar. A partisan of Pompey, he was pardoned by Caesar after the battle of Pharsala and held high office, but joined Cassius in the successful plot to murder Caesar (44 B.C.). Antony fulminated against him and, with Octavian (later Augustus), defeated him at Philippi (42 B.C.). Brutus committed suicide. His character has been much disputed from that day to this. A kinsman, **Decimus Junius Brutus,** d. 43 B.C., also a member of the conspiracy, was besieged and killed by Antony.

Bry, Théodore de (tāōdôr′ dü brē′, brī′), 1528–98, Flemish engraver and publisher. His son, **John Théodore de Bry,** 1561–1623, assisted him.

Bryan, William Jennings, 1860–1925, American political leader. U.S. Representative from Nebr. (1891–95). Advocated free coinage of silver. Famous "Cross of Gold" speech led to Democratic presidential nomination in 1896. Nominee again in 1900 and 1908. As Secretary of State under Pres. Wilson (1913–15), he aided in passing reform measures. In later years Bryan diligently defended religious FUNDAMENTALISM, especially in famous SCOPES TRIAL. A man of integrity, a masterful orator of imposing appearance, he was idolized by the masses (esp. in West).

Bryan. 1 City (pop. 6,365), NW Ohio, NNW of Defiance. Mfg. of metal and wood products. **2** City (pop. 18,102), E central Texas, NW of Houston; founded 1865. Center of farm district, it processes cotton and lumber and makes insecticides. Agricultural and Mechanical Col. of Texas near by.

Bryansk (brēänsk′), city (pop. 87,473), W European RSFSR, on Desna R. Transportation center; ironworks; sawmills. In World War II Bryansk and Vyazma were anchor points of huge German "pincer movement" (Oct., 1941); retaken by Russians 1943.

Bryant, William Cullen, 1794–1878, American romantic poet, b. Mass. Famed when he was a youth for poetry (e.g., "Thanatopsis" and "To a Waterfowl"), he was a lawyer until he became after 1825 a journalist in New York—associate editor, later editor and part owner of free-trade, antislavery *Evening Post.* Among later nature poems are such familiar and widely loved verses as "The Death of the Flowers" and "To the Fringed Gentian." He also translated the *Iliad* and the *Odyssey* in blank verse.

Bryaxis (brĭăk'sĭs), 4th cent. B.C., Greek sculptor. Helped decorate the Mausoleum at Halicarnassus.

Bryce, David, 1803–76, Scottish architect. Used a modified Gothic style, named Scottish Baronial.

Bryce, James Bryce, Viscount, 1838–1922, English historian, statesman, diplomat, and jurist. Noted for wide knowledge and ability to combine deeply scholarly writing with full, active life. In 1888 he issued two monumental works, *History of the Holy Roman Empire* and *The American Commonwealth* (2 vols.), a classic interpretation of American way of life. Ambassador to U.S. 1907–13. In law, his *Studies in History and Jurisprudence* (1901) is major work because of its wide view of liberal principle.

Bryce Canyon National Park: see NATIONAL PARKS AND MONUMENTS (table).

Brynhild, another spelling for BRUNHILD.

Bryn Mawr (brĭnmär'), uninc. village, SE Pa., residential suburb of Philadelphia. Seat of **Bryn Mawr College** (nonsectarian; for women; chartered 1880) opened by Friends 1885. Has group curriculum plan modeled on Johns Hopkins, and pioneer graduate school for women. Social studies are stressed.

Bryson, Lyman, 1888–, American educator, leader in adult education, professor at Teachers College, Columbia Univ. after 1934.

Brythonic (brĭthŏ'nĭk), group of Celtic languages of Indo-European family, including Welsh, Breton, and Cornish (now extinct). See LANGUAGE (table).

Buber, Martin (bōō'bĕr), 1878–, Jewish philosopher, b. Vienna. His mystic and theological writings, many of them on the teachings of the Hasidim, have had influence in and outside Judaism. A militant Zionist, he became a professor at the Hebrew Univ. in Jerusalem in 1938.

bubonic plague: see PLAGUE.

Bucaramanga (bōō"kärämän'gä), city (pop. 41,714), N central Colombia, in E Andes; founded 1622. Became after 1880 a coffee center.

buccaneer: see PIRACY.

Bucephalus (būsĕ'fŭlŭs), horse of Alexander the Great, hence, any horse noted for fire and speed.

Bucer or **Butzer, Martin** (bū'sŭr, bōōt'sŭr), 1491–1551, German Protestant reformer. Influenced by Luther's preaching, he joined (1523) Reformation movement at Strasbourg. Promoted Protestant education, brought about (1536) Wittenberg Concord on doctrine of the Eucharist.

Buchan, Alexander (bŭ'kŭn, –khŭn), 1829–1907, Scottish meteorologist. Curator, Royal Society of Edinburgh library and museum. Responsible for founding Ben Nevis observatory (1883).

Buchan, John, 1st Baron Tweedsmuir (twēdz-mūr), 1875–1940, Scottish author and statesman. Wrote many adventure novels (e.g., *The Thirty-nine Steps,* 1915; *Greenmantle,* 1916; *The Three Hostages,* 1924). Was governor general of Canada 1935–40.

Buchanan, Franklin (bŭkă'nŭn), 1800–1874, American naval officer. First superintendent (1845–47) U.S. Naval Academy. Joined Confederate navy; became ranking officer. Defeated by David G. FARRAGUT at Mobile Bay (Aug. 5, 1864).

Buchanan, George, 1506–82, Scottish humanist.

Buchanan, James, 1791–1868, 15th President of the United States (1857–61), b. Pa. Only bachelor to be President. U.S. Congressman from Pa. (1821–31); U.S. Senator (1834–45); Secretary of State (1845–49). As minister to Great Britain (1853–56) he helped draw up OSTEND MANIFESTO. As President (Democrat), he attempted to keep proslavery and antislavery factions in balance, was opposed by extremists on both sides. In 1860 he maintained that no state had the right to secede, but that he had no power to coerce seceding states; his view that the Federal government could use force in protecting Federal property

made Federal forts in Southern states of paramount importance. Many recent historians consider Buchanan's constitutional views sound; all admire his valiant efforts for peace.

Buchanan, city (pop. 5,224), SW Mich., near Ind. line. Mfg. of auto parts. Indian village sites and mounds near by.

Bucharest (bōō'kŭrĕst) or **Bucuresti** (bōōkōōrĕsht'), city (pop. 886,110), cap. and chief commercial and mfg. center of Rumania, in Walachia. Seat of patriarch of Rumanian Orthodox Church. Univ. (founded 1864). Became residence of Walachian princes 14th cent. Famous until World War II for contrast between palatial buildings and hovels.

Buchenwald (bōō'khŭnvält"), forest near Weimar, Thuringia, central Germany. Site of notorious concentration camp during Hitler regime.

Buchman, Frank (Nathan Daniel) (bŏŏk'mŭn), 1878–, American evangelist, leader of Oxford Group (Buchmanites). In 1921 he preached "world-changing through life-changing" at Oxford Univ. Initiated (1938) Moral Re-Armament (MRA) movement.

Buchner, Eduard (ä'dōōärt bŏŏkh'nŭr), 1860–1917, German chemist. Won 1907 Nobel Prize for establishing yeast enzymes as cause of alcoholic fermentation and discovering zymase (part of yeast enzyme system).

Büchner, Georg (gä'ŏrk bükh'nŭr), 1813–37, German author, a medical student and radical agitator. In his brief life he produced several bold, powerful works —a drama, *Danton's Death* (1835; Eng. tr., 1928); a comedy, *Leonce and Lena* (1879; Eng. tr., 1928); the fragments of a tragedy, *Wozzeck* (1879; Eng. tr., 1928), from which Alban Berg derived his opera; and a short novel, *Lenz.* His brother was **Ludwig Büchner** (lōōt'vĭkh), 1824–99, German philosopher. He protested against idealist metaphysics with a philosophy of extreme materialism.

Buck, Leffert Lefferts, 1837–1909, American civil engineer. Designed Williamsburg Bridge (New York city), Columbia river railroad bridge (Pasco, Wash.), and many others.

Buck, Pearl S(ydenstricker), 1892–, American novelist. Like her parents and her first husband (John Lossing Buck, from whom she was divorced) she was long a missionary in China. She devoted her great talents to promoting understanding between the East and the West. Most of her novels picture Chinese life, notably *The Good Earth* (1931). Awarded the 1938 Nobel Prize in Literature.

buckeye, tree or shrub of genus *Aesculus* of N Hemisphere. It bears clusters of red, white, or yellow flowers in late spring and large spiny fruits. Ohio is called Buckeye State after Ohio buckeye.

Buckhannon, city (pop. 6,016), N W.Va., on Buckhannon R. and S of Clarksburg. Seat of West Virginia Wesleyan Col. Trade center for agr. area.

Buckingham, dukes of (Stafford line): see STAFFORD.

Buckingham, George Nugent Temple Grenville, 1st marquess of: see GRENVILLE.

Buckingham, George Villiers, 1st duke of (vĭl'yŭrz), 1592–1628, English nobleman, a royal favorite. Arrived at English court in 1614 as James I was tiring of Robert Carr. Rose rapidly and by 1620 was dispensing king's patronage. Received credit for preventing unpopular marriage of Charles I to Spanish Infanta. Urged war with Spain and promoted Charles's marriage to Henrietta Maria of France. Remained favorite after Charles came to throne. After failure of several expeditions, he was increasingly unpopular. King dissolved Parliament to prevent action against duke. Killed by a discontented naval officer. His son, **George Villiers, 2d duke of Buckingham,** 1628–87, was strong royalist in civil war. Served Charles II in exile but intrigues and his marriage to Mary Fairfax, daughter of Puritan lord, caused estrangement. Regained favor after Restoration and became one of most powerful courtiers. His temper, recklessness, and dissoluteness kept his career stormy. Was member of the cabal. Dismissed 1674, regained favor 1684 in spite of earlier opposition to James II. Patronized science and learning and had refined taste. Wrote poetry, religious tracts, and plays (including *The Rehearsal*, 1671).

Buckingham, town (pop. 6,129), SW Que., Canada, E of Ottawa. Has lumber and paper mills.

Buckingham Palace, London residence of British sovereigns since 1837. It was originally built by the duke of Buckingham in 1703. Damaged by air raids in World War II.

Buckinghamshire (bŭ'kĭng-ùmshĭr), **Buckingham,** or **Bucks,** inland county (749 sq. mi.; pop. 386,164), S central England; co. town, Aylesbury. Region includes chalky Chiltern Hills and richly agr. Vale of Aylesbury. Southern boundary is the Thames. County has Roman and pre-Roman remains.

Buckle, Henry Thomas, 1821–62, English historian. Projected panoramic history of civilization. Two volumes, *History of Civilization in England* (1857–61), caused sensation. His scientific method and broad approach influenced later historiography.

Bucknell University: see LEWISBURG, Pa.

Buckner, Simon Bolivar, 1823–1914, Confederate general. Surrendered Fort Donelson to Grant (1862). Later commanded in Ky., Tenn., and La.

Bucks, England: see BUCKINGHAMSHIRE.

buckthorn, thorny shrub or small tree (*Rhamnus*). Common buckthorn (*Rhamnus cathartica*) used for hedges. Cascara sagrada comes from *R. purshiana*.

buckwheat, annual plant (*Fagopyrum sagittatum*), widely grown for its three-cornered fruit, valued for buckwheat flour. Also used as poultry and stock feed.

Bucuresti, Rumania: see BUCHAREST.

Bucyrus (būsī'rùs), city (pop. 10,327), N central Ohio, on Sandusky R. and NE of Marion; settled 1819. Has mfg. of metal and rubber products.

bud, in lower plants and animals a protuberance from which a new organism develops. In seed plants, a growing point containing rudiments of flowers, leaves, and shoots. See also BUDDING and CUTTING.

Budaeus: see BUDÉ, GUILLAUME.

Budapest (boō'dùpĕst"), city (pop. 1,164,963), cap. of Hungary, on both banks of the Danube; formed 1873 by union of Buda and Obuda (right bank) with Pest (left bank). Obuda and Pest stand near site of two Roman towns, destroyed by Mongols 1241. Buda was founded as a fortress (13th cent.), became a royal residence (14th cent.), flourished as intellectual center under Matthias Corvinus. All three cities declined under Turkish occupation (1541–1686), but Buda revived through royal favors in 18th cent. The univ. founded 1635 at Trnava by Peter Pazmany was transferred to Buda 1777, to Pest 1784. Pest, rebuilt along modern lines in 19th cent., became a leading commercial and artistic center and was, until World War I, the leading grain market of Europe. Machine, textile, and chemical mfg. developed after World War I. One of the finest cities of Europe, Budapest was 70% destroyed during a 14-week siege by the Russians in World War II (1944–45).

Buddha (boō'dù) [Sanskrit,= the enlightened one], title of Siddhartha Gautama, c.563–483 B.C., Indian religious leader, founder of Buddhism. Son of a ruler of area N of Benares, he at the age of 29 renounced luxury, became an ascetic. "The great enlightenment" gave him principles of religion. He and disciples spread the faith.

Buddh Gaya or **Bodh Gaya** (both: boōd' gä'yä), village, Bihar, India. Here Buddha achieved enlightenment under a bo tree. Relics of Buddhist art.

Buddhism (boōd'ĭzùm), system of philosophy and ethics founded by Buddha; one of the great religions of the world. Its beliefs were in origin closely related to Brahmanism (see HINDUISM), but had less formalism and a greater emphasis on self-denial and compassion. The "four noble truths" of Buddha are: existence is suffering; the origin of suffering is desire; suffering ceases when desire ceases; the way to reach the end of desire is by following the "noble eightfold path." This path comprises right belief, right resolve (to renounce carnal pleasure, harm no living creature, and the like), right speech, right conduct, right occupation or living, right effort, right contemplation or right mindedness, and right ecstasy. The final goal of the religious man is to escape from existence into blissful nonexistence—nirvana [Sanskrit,= annihilation]. Individual man is made up of elements that existed before him, that separate at his death, and that may be recombined in a somewhat similar fashion. It is from this chain of being that man seeks to escape by religious living. These "salvation" doctrines were spread rapidly by Buddhist monks and for a short time Buddhism reached a great height in India under Asoka (3d cent. B.C.). It later died out in India, but persisted in Ceylon and in Burma in its simpler, "purer" form (Hinayana). It entered China in the 1st cent. A.D. and later spread from China to Japan through Korea. Here it developed into Mahayana, which accepts a number of divine beings and has incorporated many aspects of local religion. In Tibet Buddhism became LAMAISM. Various sects and movements have arisen in Buddhism, one being ZEN BUDDHISM, which grew very strong in Japan.

budding, a form of GRAFTING in which scion is a bud. Used chiefly for roses and some fruits.

Budé, Guillaume (gēyōm' büdä'), 1467–1540, French scholar, known also as Budaeus. One of greatest French humanists and scholars, he was a towering figure of the Renaissance. He persuaded Francis I to found Collège de France, used textual criticism in study of Roman law, and helped to establish philology. He fostered Greek learning in France and wrote on various classical subjects.

Budejovice, Czechoslovakia: see BUDWEIS.

Budge, (John) Don(ald), 1915–, American tennis player. In 1938 won American, Australian, French, British singles championships.

Budge, Sir Ernest Alfred Wallis, 1857–1934, English archaeologist, an authority on ancient Egypt and Assyria.

Budweis (Ger. boōt'vīs), Czech *České Budějovice*, city (pop. 38,194), SW Bohemia, Czechoslovakia, on the Moldau. Produces beer, pencils, enamelware. Has fine medieval and baroque architecture.

Buell, Abel (bū'ùl), 1742–1822, American silversmith and engraver of maps; cast first font of native-made American type (1769).

Buell, Don Carlos, 1818–98, Union general in Civil War. Supported Grant in Tenn.; saved the day at Shiloh. Forced Braxton Bragg to leave Ky. Criticized and removed from command, he withdrew entirely from the war.

Buena Park (bwā'nù), village (pop. 5,483), S Calif., just W of Fullerton, in oil, citrus, truck area.

Buenaventura (bwā"nävántoō'rä), city (pop. 14,515), W Colombia, Pacific port; founded c.1540. Original town was burned by Indians and resettled on island in bay. Exports coffee, platinum, gold, and hides.

Buena Vista (bū'nù vīs'tù), city (pop. 5,214), western Va., E of Lexington. Mfg. of paper and textiles.

Buenos Aires (bwā'nùs ī'rēz), city (pop. 2,982,580); cap. of Argentina, in federal district, N Argentina, on right bank of Río de la Plata. A metropolis of Latin America, Buenos Aires is the chief port and financial, industrial, and social center of Argentina. Founded by Pedro de Mendoza (1536), it was abandoned (1541) because of hostility of Indians and resettled (1580) by Juan de Garay. It became cap. of viceroyalty of Río de la Plata in 1776. British invasions in 1806–7 were repulsed by LINIERS. The cabildo deposed the viceroy and established junta (1810). Centralist-federalist struggle in Argentina ended by making Buenos Aires paramount. The city was detached from its province and was federalized (1880). Near-by Buenos Aires prov. (cap. LA PLATA) is rich in cattle and grain.

Buffalo. 1 City (pop. 580,132), W N.Y., on L. Erie and Niagara R.; laid out 1803 under HOLLAND LAND COMPANY. State's second largest city. It is a major Great Lakes port, industrial center, and rail hub. Products are iron, steel, flour, rubber, linseed oil, gypsum and wood products, airplanes, autos, machinery, and packed meat. Burned by British in War of 1812. Commercial and industrial growth was rapid after completion of Erie Canal (1825). Pres. McKinley was assassinated and Theodore Roosevelt took presidential oath here in 1901 during Pan-American Exposition. Presidents Cleveland (became mayor 1881) and Fillmore lived here. Seat of Univ. of Buffalo (nonsectarian; private; coed.; 1846) and Canisius Col. (Jesuit; mainly for men; 1870). Has buildings by Louis Sullivan and F. L. Wright. **2** City (pop. 2,674), N Wyo., SSE of Sheridan. Trade center in resort area. L. De Smet is N.

buffalo, common name for American bison, but accurately applied only to certain related oxlike mammals of Asia, Africa. Asiatic water buffalo (*Bubalis*) or Indian buffalo stands c.5 ft. at shoulder, with spreading, backward-curving horns. Pygmy buffalo (*Anoa*) is wild ox of Celebes. Cape buffalo (*Syncerus*) is in S Africa.

Buffalo, University of: see BUFFALO, N.Y.

buffalo berry, hardy North American shrub (*Shepherdia argentea*). Silvery foliage; female plant bears edible, yellow or scarlet berries.

Buffalo Bill, 1846–1917, American plainsman, scout, and showman; real name William Frederick Cody. Organized Buffalo Bill's Wild West Show in 1883; toured with it for many years.

buffalo fish, name for several fish of sucker family, chiefly in Mississippi valley rivers and lakes. Flesh bony and coarse, but commercially important as food.

buffalo grass, important range grass (*Buchloe dactyloides*) of plains regions. It is sod forming.

Buffon, Georges Louis Leclerc, comte de (zhôrzh' lwĕ' lüklĕrk' kŏt' dü büfô'), 1707–88, French naturalist, author. Devoted life to *Histoire naturelle* (44 vols., 1749–1804).

Bug (bōog), river, 487 mi. long, E Europe. Rises E of Lvov, flows N along Polish-Ukrainian border, then NW into the Narew. Canal connection with Dnieper. Also called Western Bug.

Bug or Southern Bug, Rus. *Yuzhny Bug,* river, 520 mi. long, Ukraine. Flows SE into Black Sea. Used for grain transport March-Dec.

bug, accurately only insect of order Hemiptera. Head has structure for piercing and sucking. Those with wings have two pairs. See *ill.,* p. 469.

Buganda: see UGANDA.

Bugayev, Boris Nikolayevich: see BELY, ANDREI.

Bugge, Sophus (sō'fōōs bōō'gù), 1833–1907, Norwegian philologist. Edited Norse runes and poems of the *Eddas* (1881–89; 2d series, 1896).

bugle, brass wind musical instrument, consisting of a conical tube coiled once upon itself. Chiefly used for military bugle calls, such as taps or reveille. Key and valve bugles developed in 19th cent.

Buhl, André Charles: see BOULLE, ANDRÉ CHARLES.

Buisson, Ferdinand Édouard (fĕrdēnä' ädwär' büĕsō'), 1841–1932, French educator. He became professor of pedagogy at the Sorbonne in 1886 and was a member of chamber of deputies 1902–14 and 1919–24. An ardent pacifist, he attended (1867) first congress of International Peace League. With Ludwig Quidde he received 1927 Nobel Peace Prize.

Buitenzorg (boi'tùnzôrkh), Malay *Bogor,* town (pop. 65,431), W Java, Indonesia. Summer resort at foot of two volcanoes. Notable botanical gardens.

Bukhara (bùkä'rù), city (pop. 50,382), W Uzbek SSR; also spelled Bokhara. Karakul and silk processing. Bokhara rugs originally named after city. One of oldest cities of TURKISTAN and long a center of Islamic culture, it was the cap. of the emirate of Bukhara, which comprised parts of Uzbekistan, Tadzhiki-

stan, and Turkmenistan. Ruled by despotic Uzbek princes after 16th cent., emirate was forced to accept Russian suzerainty in 1868. Last emir deposed 1920. City has splendid mosques and palaces (9th–17th cent.).

Bukhari (bōōkhärē'), d. 870, Arabic scholar and Moslem saint, whose collection of traditional sayings of Mohammed is highly respected in Islam.

Bukharin, Nikolai Ivanovich (nyĭkŭlī' ēvä'nùvĭch bōōkhä'rēn), 1888–1938, Russian Communist. Chief party theoretician after Lenin's death. Purged and executed in treason trials of 1936–38.

Bukovina (bōōkùvē'nù), region, E Europe, in W Ukraine and NE Rumania; chief town Chernovtsy (Ukraine). Traversed by Carpathians and by upper Pruth R., it produces timber, grain, livestock. Mixed pop. includes Rumanians, Ukrainians, Russians, Jews, Magyars. Region was the nucleus of the old principality of Moldavia. Ceded by Turkey to Austria 1775; to Rumania 1919. N part (c.2,000 sq. mi.; pop. c.460,000) ceded to USSR 1940; reoccupied by Rumania 1941–44; formally ceded to USSR 1947. S part (c.2,000 sq. mi.; pop. c.300,000) forms a historic prov. of Rumania.

bulb, thickened fleshy plant bud, usually formed under soil. Carries plant over from one season to another. Examples are tulip, hyacinth, lily. The CORM, TUBER, and RHIZOME are not true bulbs. See *ill.,* p. 783.

bulbul (bōōl'bōōl), name for a number of species of thrushlike birds of Africa and Asia. The bulbul of Persian poetry was probably a nightingale.

Bulfinch, Charles, 1763–1844, American architect. Elegance of his structures in Boston places them among best of early American architecture. Designed Boston statehouse (1799); University Hall, Harvard Univ. (1815); First Church of Christ, Lancaster, Mass. (1816–17); and Mass. General Hospital (1820). Worked on Capitol at Washington, 1818–30.

Bulfinch, Thomas, 1796–1867, American author, popularizer of mythology in *The Age of Fable* (1855).

Bulganin, Nikolai Aleksandrovich (nyĭkŭlī' ùlyĭksän'drùvĭch bōōlgä'nĭn), 1895?–, Russian Communist leader. Helped plan defense of Moscow 1941; later was given rank of marshal; minister of armed forces 1947–49; vice premier of USSR from 1949.

Bulgari: see BULGARS, EASTERN.

Bulgaria (bŭlgâ'rĕù), republic (42,796 sq. mi.; pop. 7,022,206), SE Europe, on Balkan Peninsula, bounded by the Black Sea (E), European Turkey and Greece (S), Yugoslavia (W), and Rumania (N); cap. Sofia. Stalin (formerly Varna) is chief port. Crossed by Balkan mts. and drained by Danube, Struma, and Maritsa rivers, Bulgaria is largely agr. Chief products: cotton textiles, tobacco, attar of roses. Population is mainly Greek Orthodox, with some Moslems. Expulsion of Turkish minority (c.250,000) began 1950. Occupying ancient THRACE and MOESIA, country was conquered A.D. 660 by a group of Eastern BULGARS, who later merged with older Slavic settlers and adopted their language. Their khan Krum exacted tribute from Byzantine Empire (9th cent.); BORIS I introduced Christianity; SIMEON I enlarged territory, took title tsar. Subjugated by Byzantium 1018–1186, Bulgaria again became an empire (with cap. at Trnovo) under Ivan I; reached its height under IVAN II; became tributary to Serbia 1330; was annexed by Turkey after defeats at Kossovo (1389) and Nikopol (1396). Cruel repression of revolt under Stefan STAMBULOV (1875; "Bulgarian atrocities") gave Russia an excuse for war on Turkey (1877–78). Greater Bulgaria, set up by Treaty of SAN STEFANO, was reduced by Congress of BERLIN and divided into three parts: N Bulgaria, as principality under nominal Turkish overlordship; E RUMELIA, as Turkish province with autonomous rights; and MACEDONIA, under direct Turkish rule. ALEXANDER of Battenberg, first prince of Bulgaria, annexed E Rumelia 1885; his successor, FERDINAND of Saxe-Coburg-Gotha, proclaimed full independence 1908, took title tsar. Bulgarian claims to Macedonia led to Balkan Wars of 1912–13, in which Bulgaria first won, then lost, much territory. One of Central Powers in World War I, it lost S Dobruja and outlet to Aegean Sea by Treaty of Neuilly. The regime of Premier Stambuliski was followed by two military dictatorships (1923–26, 1934–35) and a royal dictatorship under Boris III (1935–43). In World War II, Bulgaria joined the Axis (1941) and occupied parts of Yugoslavia and Greece. In Sept., 1944, Russia declared war and invaded Bulgaria. A pro-Russian coalition cabinet took power but was soon replaced by a Communist regime. The monarchy was abolished, Tsar Simeon II deposed (1946). By 1948 all opposition was suppressed. Bulgarian peace treaty (ratified 1947) allowed Bulgaria to keep S Dobruja (ceded by Rumania 1940).

Bulgarian, language of Slavic subfamily of Indo-European languages. See Language (table).

Bulgars, Eastern, people, probably speaking a Finnic language, who had a powerful state in E European Russia, along Middle Volga (8th–13th cent.). Their cap., Bulgari or Bolgari, was near Kazan. Conquered by Mongols 1236. A branch of the people moved west and merged with Slavs in Bulgaria.

Bulge, Battle of the: see Battle of the Bulge.

Bull, Ole (ō′lù), 1810–80, Norwegian violinist. He toured Europe and America, playing mostly his own compositions and Norwegian folk music.

Bull, the, in astronomy: see Zodiac.

bull [Latin *bulla* = leaden seal], solemn official pronouncement of the pope, more solemn than an encyclical (letter to all the bishops) and a brief (short letter). Among well-known bulls are *Clericis laicos* (1296) and *Unam sanctam* (1302; both by Boniface VIII); the bull of demarcation for discoveries (1493, by Alexander VI); *Exsurge Domine* (1520, by Leo X); *Unigenitus* (1713, by Clement XI); *Mirari vos* (1832, by Gregory XVI); *Quanta cura* (1864, by Pius IX); *Pastor aeternus* (1871, of Pius IX); *Aeterni patris* (1879) and *Rerum novarum* (1891; both by Leo XIII); *Quadragesimo anno* (1931, by Pius XI). Pius XI issued two bulls not in Latin—*Non abbiamo bisogno* (1931, against Fascism) and *Mit brennender Sorge* (1937, against Nazism). In recent years the encyclical has been employed much more than the bull. The term *bull* was formerly used for some non-papal documents (e.g., Golden Bull).

bull bat: see Nighthawk.

bulldog, smooth-haired dog. The English bulldog has a heavy, low-slung body, broad chest, undershot jaw, and wrinkled face, with front legs (appearing bowed) shorter than the hind legs. Once bred for bullbaiting, it is now generally good-natured and courageous. The French bulldog is smaller and usually darker. Outstanding are its "bat ears"—wide at the base, tapering to a rounded point, and held erect. Descended from numerous breeds of bulldogs is the boxer, a sleek, muscular, and rather stocky dog developed chiefly in Germany in the 19th cent. It is usually some shade of fawn or brindle; small erect ears and a protruding lower jaw are other characteristics. See also Boston Terrier.

bullfighting, national sport of Spain, also popular in Latin America. Conducted in arena, or *plaza de toros.* The matador, who kills the bull, is assisted by *banderilleros,* who enrage bulls by stabbing them with darts, *picadores,* who jab bulls with lances, and *toreros,* who distract bulls by waving red flags.

bullfinch, any of several European songbirds of finch family, often caged. Common species is woodland bird; blue-gray upper plumage, tile red below.

bullfrog, largest North American frog; aquatic with fully webbed toes. Common bullfrog (*Rana catesbiana*) E of Rocky Mts. Deep bass cry or croaking.

bullhead, name for several species of genus *Ameiurus* of catfish family, found in sluggish waters. Commonest is brown bullhead or horned pout (12 to 18 in.

long); others are black and yellow bullheads. Name also for some species of sculpin family (large-headed, toothed fish).

Bullitt, William C(hristian) (boõl′ĭt), 1891–, American diplomat; first U.S. ambassador to USSR (1933–36); ambassador to France (1936–41).

Bull Moose party: see Progressive party.

Bull Run, small stream, NE Va., c.30 mi. SW of Washington, D.C., scene of two important Civil War battles, July 21, 1861, and Aug. 29–30, 1862. In **first battle of Bull Run,** first major clash of war, Federals under Irvin McDowell attacked Confederates under P. G. T. Beauregard. They met resistance of T. J. Jackson standing "like a stone wall," and were forced into retreat, a rout ending only at defenses of Washington. Victory cheered South, and spurred North to greater efforts. **Second battle of Bull Run,** also a victory for Confederates, was culmination of R. E. Lee's strategy to prevent reinforcement of John Pope's army by G. B. McClellan along Rappahannock R., where Stonewall Jackson had driven it. James Longstreet, after attack by Pope, counterattacked and drove Federals back across Bull Run. In pursuit Jackson was stopped at Chantilly, Sept. 1, 1862, and Pope withdrew to Washington.

bulls and bears. In speculative markets, a "bear" is a speculator who sells what he does not own in the hope that, before he has to deliver, he will be able to buy back at a lower price. A "bull" is the opposite of a bear; he tries to force prices up rather than down.

bull terrier: see Terrier.

Bülow, Bernhard, Fürst von (bĕrn′härt fürst′ fŭn bü′lō), 1849–1929, chancellor of Germany (1900–1909). His aggressive policies (notably in Morocco) isolated Germany and paved way for World War I.

Bülow, Hans von, 1830–94, German pianist, first of modern virtuoso conductors. In 1857 he married Liszt's daughter Cosima, who left him in 1869 and later married Wagner. He was the first to call Bach, Beethoven, and Brahms the three B's of music.

bulrush, sedge of genus *Scirpus,* often with grasslike leaves. Grown in aquatic or bog gardens. Bulrush in which Moses was hidden (Ex. 2.3) was papyrus.

Bulwer-Lytton, Edward George Earle Lytton, 1st Baron Lytton, 1803–73, English novelist and playwright. Among his many popular novels (some historical) are *Eugene Aram* (1832), *The Last Days of Pompeii* (1834), *Rienzi* (1835). Particularly well known among his plays are *The Lady of Lyons* (1838), *Richelieu* (1838). The son born to his unhappy marriage was **Edward Robert Bulwer-Lytton, 1st earl of Lytton,** 1831–91, who wrote under the pseud. **Owen Meredith.** A diplomat and statesman, viceroy of India, he is best remembered for his verse, notably *Lucile* (1880).

Buna rubber: see Rubber, Synthetic.

Bunau-Varilla, Philippe Jean (fēlēp′ zhä′ bünō-värēyä′), 1859–1940, French engineer, prominent in Panama Canal controversy. Organized second French canal-building company; sold it to U.S.; then engineered Panama revolution of 1903. As minister of Panama to U.S. negotiated Hay-Bunau-Varilla Treaty, which gave control of Canal Zone to U.S.

bunchberry or **dwarf cornel,** low North American and Asiatic perennial (*Cornus canadensis*), related to dogwood. White-bracted flowers and red berries.

Bunche, Ralph (Johnson), 1904–, American internationalist, a Negro. Director, UN Trusteeship Division (1946–). Awarded 1950 Nobel Peace Prize.

Bunin, Ivan Alekseyevich (ēvän′ ŭlyĭksyä′yĭvĭch boõ′nyĭn), 1870–, Russian author. A poet of distinction, he is best known for his short stories, especially *The Man* (or *The Gentleman*) *from San Francisco* (1916), and the autobiographical novel *The Well of Days* (1930; Eng. tr., 1933). Resided abroad after 1919. Awarded 1933 Nobel Prize in Literature.

Bunker Hill, battle of, in American Revolution, June 17, 1775, actually fought on neighboring Breed's Hill, Charlestown, Mass. British victory failed to break the triumphant ring of patriots besieging Boston.

Bunner, H(enry) C(uyler), 1855–96, American journalist; author of light verse (as in *Airs from Arcady and Elsewhere,* 1884) and humorous stories (as in *Short Sixes,* 1891); editor of *Puck,* 1877–96.

Bunsen, Robert Wilhelm (bŭn′sùn), 1811–99, German scientist. Studied organic arsenic compounds, photochemistry. Evolved method of gas analysis; with Kirchhoff discovered cesium and rubidium, using spectroscope; invented Bunsen electric cell. Known for **Bunsen burner:** hollow tube fitted around flame, with base opening to admit air; próduces smokeless, nonluminous, high-temperature flame.

bunting, small, plump bird of finch family. American buntings include INDIGO BUNTING; painted bunting or nonpareil; snow bunting; dickcissel. Baywinged bunting is really vesper sparrow.

Buntline, Ned, pseud. of **Edward Zane Carroll Judson,** b. 1822 or 1823, d. 1886, American adventurer, editor of sensational magazine (*Ned Buntline's Own*), author of trashy novels that preceded dime novel. Lynched for murder (1846), he was cut down alive. Introduced Buffalo Bill to the stage.

bunya-bunya (bŭn′yù), large Australian tree (*Araucaria bidwillii*). Its seeds provide a staple food of native tribes.

Bunyan, John, 1628–88, English author, notable for his *Pilgrim's Progress from This World to That Which Is to Come* (1678). A Baptist lay preacher, he wrote many spiritual works, including *Grace Abounding to the Chief of Sinners* (1666; a spiritual autobiography) and *The Life and Death of Mr. Badman* (1680), but it was his allegory of Christian life, *Pilgrim's Progress,* that held the imagination of many generations.

Bunyan, Paul, Gargantuan hero of "tall tales" of American lumber camps from Mich. to the West Coast. He was aided in his feats by Babe, the Blue Ox.

Buonaparte: see BONAPARTE and NAPOLEON I.

Buoninsegna, Duccio di: see DUCCIO.

Burbage, James (bûr′bĭj), d. 1597, English actor. Built London's first permanent theater 1576; moved to Bankside (c.1598), it became the GLOBE THEATRE. Built Blackfriars Theatre also. His son, **Richard Burbage,** 1567?–1619, was leading actor of his day. Appeared in original productions of many plays by Shakspere and Ben Jonson. Noted as Hamlet, Lear, Othello, and Richard III.

Burbank, Luther, 1849–1926, American plant breeder. He developed the Burbank potato, Shasta daisy, and many other new plant varieties.

Burbank, city (pop. 78,577), S Calif., N of Los Angeles; laid out 1887. Industries include moving-picture and aircraft production.

Burchell, William John (bûr′chùl), 1782?–1863, English explorer and scientist. Made vast collections in Africa of natural and meteorological objects. Discovered many animal and plant species.

Burchfield, Charles, 1893–, American painter, widely known as a painter of Victorian mansions, false-front stores, and other relics of the late 19th cent. His work is marked by subtlety of color and a slightly ironic realism.

Burckhardt, Jacob Christoph (yä′kôp krĭs′tôf bŏŏrk′-härt), 1818–97, Swiss historian, a founder of cultural history. His works include the classic *Die Kultur der Renaissance in Italien* (1860).

Burckhardt, John Lewis (bûrk′härt), 1784–1817, explorer, b. Switzerland. Sponsored by English association promoting African discovery. Posing as learned Moslem, was first Christian to reach Medina.

burdock, coarse, weedy biennial (*Arctium*), naturalized in North America. Rounded, many-seeded burs.

Burdwan (bùrdwän′), city (pop. 62,910) S West Bengal, India. A group of 108 Siva linga temples (1788) is near by. Cutlery mfg.

Burgas (bŏŏr′gäs), city (pop. 43,684), E Bulgaria; a Black Sea port.

Burgenland (Ger. bŏŏr′gùnlänt), province (1,576 sq.

mi.; pop. 275,911), E Austria, bordering on Hungary; cap. Eisenstadt. Hilly region, indented by Neusiedler L. Wine growing. Territory transferred from Hungary to Austria by treaties of 1919 and 1920. SOPRON, its leading town, was returned to Hungary by plebiscite (1921).

Bürger, Gottfried August (gôt′frĕt ou′gŏŏst bür′gùr), 1747–94, German poet. Credited with reviving the German ballad, he is best known for "Lenore" (1773), widely translated and highly influential.

Burgess, (Frank) Gelett, 1866–1951, American humorist, illustrator of his own stories and articles; best known for quatrain "The Purple Cow" and for originating the terms *goop* and *bromide.*

Burgess, John William, 1844–1931, American political scientist; educ. at Amherst and in Germany. Helped create faculty of political science at Columbia Univ. Wrote much on political science and U.S. history.

Burgh, Hubert de: see HUBERT DE BURGH.

Burghley or **Burleigh, William Cecil, 1st Baron,** 1520–98, English statesman, chief adviser of Queen Elizabeth. Rose to power 1548, but was not in favor with Mary I. Reappointed by Elizabeth; served her for 40 years. Responsible for execution of Mary Queen of Scots and solidification of Protestantism. His policy helped growing industry and commerce.

burglary, at common law, breaking and entering a dwelling house at night with intent to commit a felony; by statutes in many states of U.S. extended to mean all breaking and entering. Breaking involves only a slight use of force (e.g., turning a key) or by entry through fraud, threat, or conspiracy.

Bürglen (bürk′lùn), village, Uri canton, Switzerland. Alleged birthplace of William Tell.

Burgos (bŏŏr′gōs), city (pop. 51,177), cap. of Burgos prov., N Spain, in Old Castile. Cap. of Castile until 1087, when Toledo replaced it. Gothic cathedral, founded 1221, among finest in S Europe.

Burgoyne, John (bùrgoin′), 1722–92, British general. Helped plan SARATOGA CAMPAIGN, but led poorly equipped army, untrained for frontier fighting. Surrendered at Saratoga, Oct. 17, 1777.

Burgundians, in French medieval history: see ARMAGNACS AND BURGUNDIANS.

Burgundy (bûr′gùndē), Fr. *Bourgogne,* region and former province, E France, in Yonne, Côte-d'Or, Saône-et-Loire, and Ain depts.; historic cap., Dijon. Agr.; wine growing (particularly in Chablis region and Côte-d'Or). Cities: Dijon, Beaune, Auxerre, Chalon-sur-Saône, Mâcon. In history, the term "Burgundy" often designated much wider areas. A part of Roman Gaul, it was peacefully settled (5th cent. A.D.) by the Germanic Burgundii, who founded the **First Kingdom of Burgundy.** This comprised SE France and W Switzerland. Conquered by the Franks (534), it was repeatedly partitioned under the Merovingians and Carolingians, though it survived in name. Two kingdoms emerged in the 9th cent.: Cisjurane Burgundy or PROVENCE in the south; Transjurane Burgundy in the north. These were united (933) in the kingdom of Arles or **Second Kingdom of Burgundy** (see ARLES, KINGDOM OF). A smaller area (roughly, present Burgundy) was created (877) as the **duchy of Burgundy,** which from the 11th cent. was ruled mostly by princes of the French royal house. In the 14th and 15th cent., Burgundy had its golden age under dukes PHILIP THE BOLD, JOHN THE FEARLESS, PHILIP THE GOOD, and CHARLES THE BOLD, who acquired the Low Countries, FRANCHE-COMTÉ, and other territories. The wealthiest state of W Europe and one of the great powers, Burgundy also was a center of art and culture. In the Hundred Years War Burgundy sided with England against France from 1415 until 1435, when its alliance with France turned the tide. (See also ARMAGNACS AND BURGUNDIANS.) The defeat and death (1477) of Charles the Bold left MARY OF BURGUNDY the heir. Through her, the Low Countries passed to the Hapsburgs (see NETHERLANDS, AUSTRIAN AND SPANISH), but the duchy itself was seized by Louis XI, who made it into a French prov.

Buriat-Mongolia, RSFSR: see BURYAT-MONGOL AUTONOMOUS SOVIET SOCIALIST REPUBLIC.

Buridan, Jean (byōō´rĭdŭn, Fr. bürēdä´), fl. 1328, French scholastic philosopher, rector of the Univ. of Paris. A follower of William of Occam, he held man's will enables him to choose the greater good and to suspend choice in order to reconsider. He is credited (probably falsely) with using the figure of "Buridan's ass"—an unfortunate animal midway between identical bundles of hay and starving to death because he cannot decide which bundle to eat.

Burke, Edmund, 1729–97, British statesman and political writer, b. Dublin. Was a member of Dr. Johnson's circle. Strong Whig opponent of William Pitt, in famous speeches he advocated wiser policy in America. Exposed injustices in India by instigating long trial of Warren HASTINGS 1785–94. His opposition to French Revolution led to break with Whigs 1791. Advocate of many practical reforms, he feared political reform.

Burke, John, 1787–1848, Irish genealogist. Issued a publication which became British annual, *Burke's Peerage,* edited by his son, **Sir John Bernard Burke,** 1814–92, also publisher of *Burke's Landed Gentry.*

Burke, Robert O'Hara, 1820–61, Irish explorer of Australia. Crossed continent from Menindee to Gulf of Carpentaria; died from famine on return.

Burleigh, Harry T(hacker) (bûr´lē), 1866–1949, American Negro baritone and composer; soloist at St. George's Church, New York, 1894–1946, and at Temple Emanu-El for 25 years. His concert arrangements of Negro spirituals, such as *Deep River,* are well known.

Burleigh, William Cecil, 1st Baron: see BURGHLEY.

Burleson, Albert Sidney (bûr´lŭsŭn), 1863–1937, U.S. Postmaster General (1913–21). His strict control of communications in World War I aroused the ire of businessmen, labor unions, liberals.

Burley, city (pop. 5,924), S Idaho, on Snake R. It is a MINIDOKA PROJECT farm center, with beet-sugar, alfalfa-meal, and potato-flour mills.

Burlingame, Anson (bûr´lĭng-găm), 1820–70, American diplomat who contracted **Burlingame Treaty** (1868), a pact of friendship between China and U.S. based on Western principles of international law. One clause encouraged Chinese immigration; resulting friction led to policy of CHINESE EXCLUSION.

Burlingame, residential city (pop. 19,886), W Calif., on San Francisco Bay; founded 1868.

Burlingame Treaty: see BURLINGAME, ANSON.

Burlington, town (pop. 6,017), S Ont., Canada, on L. Ontario NE of Hamilton, in fruit-growing area. .

Burlington. 1 City (pop. 30,613), SE Iowa, on four hills overlooking the Mississippi; platted 1833 on sites of Indian village and trading post. Temporary cap. of Wisconsin Territory (1837) and Iowa Territory (1838–40). With railroad shops and docks, it has mfg. of metal and wood products, fertilizer, and clothing. Munitions plant built in World War II. **2** City (pop. 12,051), W N.J., on Delaware R. between Trenton and Camden; settled 1677 by Friends. Early important port, now shipping center for agr. area, it makes textiles. Cap. of West Jersey 1681–1702, alternate cap. with Perth Amboy of united Jerseys 1702–90. Franklin printed first colonial money here 1726; first N.J. newspaper printed here 1777. Has Friends' school (1792) and meetinghouse (1784). **3** City (pop. 24,560), N N.C., E of Greensboro, near Haw R. Mfg. of hosiery, textiles, and wood products. Tobacco warehouses. **4** City (pop. 33,155), NW Vt., overlooking L. Champlain just below Winooski R. mouth; chartered by N.H. 1763, settled 1773. Largest Vt. city. Became important lake port (lumber, potash) after Revolution. Now has mfg. of textiles, wood and metal products; processing of maple syrup, and other food products. State's first Unitarian church organ-

ized here 1810; first Roman Catholic church built here 1831. Has birthplace of John Dewey and grave of Ethan Allen. Seat of Trinity Col. (R.C.; for women) and Univ. of Vermont and State Agricultural Col. (land-grant, state, and private support; coed.); founded by Ira ALLEN, chartered 1791, opened 1800; col. of agr. (chartered 1864) joined the univ. 1865; library, designed by H. H. Richardson, holds state's largest book collection.

Burma, Union of, republic (261,757 sq. mi.; pop. 16,-823,798), SE Asia, on Indo-Chinese peninsula; cap. RANGOON. Densely populated valley of Irrawaddy R. is surrounded by mountains stemming from E Himalayas; its delta forms a great rice-growing area. Rich mineral resources include oil, tungsten, tin, silver, lead, and jade. Rice, teak, and oil are chief exports. Population comprises various Mongoloid groups, including the KARENS, Chins, Shans, and Mons. The Burmese proper, who live mainly in region around MANDALAY, moved down from Tibet before 9th cent. and were unified in 11th cent. by Anawratha, who estab. his cap. at Pagan. He introduced Buddhism, today the main religion. After his successors were crushed by Kublai Khan in 1287, Burma split into petty states ruled by Shan chieftains until 16th cent., when a Burmese dynasty, the Toungoo, became dominant. In 18th cent. the rising Mons were crushed by the Burmese under Alaungpaya, who later raided India and greatly enlarged his domain. European trade had been initiated by the Portuguese in 16th cent., but there were no clashes with Europeans until the Anglo-Burmese wars (1824–26, 1852, 1885), which resulted in annexation of Burma to British India. In 1937 Burma was given quasi-dominion status. In World War II Burma was occupied early 1942–1945 by the Japanese. After the war it became a sovereign republic (Jan. 4, 1948). However, it was soon beset by internal strife, aggravated by presence of many Chinese Nationalist troops who had moved into the area in 1949. Country is divided into Lower Burma, with divisions of ARAKAN, PEGU, TENASSERIM, and Irrawaddy, and Upper Burma, including semi-autonomous CHIN HILLS, constituent units of SHAN, KACHIN, and KARENNI states.

Burman or **Burmese,** Indo-Chinese language. See LANGUAGE (table).

bur marigold, weedy plant (*Bidens*), of daisy family. Burlike fruits. Also called tickseed, beggar-ticks.

Burma Road, from Lashio, Burma, to Kunming, Yunnan prov., China; c.700 mi. long. Construction began 1937, completed 1938. Until Japanese occupation of Burma in 1942, it carried war supplies landed at Rangoon and shipped by rail to Lashio. In Jan., 1945 it was joined to Ledo (Stilwell) Road from Ledo, India, to Myitkyina, and was again a vital supply route. War's end reduced its importance.

Burmese or **Burman,** Indo-Chinese language. See LANGUAGE (table).

Burne-Jones, Sir Edward, 1833–98, English painter and decorator, an eminent exponent of Pre-Raphaelitism. Drew his material from the medieval period. His designs for stained glass were executed by the firm of William Morris.

Burnet, David Gouverneur (bûr´nĭt, bùrnĕt´), 1788–1870, provisional president of Texas (1836). Drew up Texas declaration of independence from Mexico.

burnet (bûr´nĭt), hardy perennial herb (*Sanguisorba*). White or greenish flowers. Leaves used in salads.

Burnett, Frances (Eliza) Hodgson, 1849–1924, American author, b. England, in U.S. after 1865. Among her children's books are *Little Lord Fauntleroy* (1886), *Sara Crewe* (1888), *The Secret Garden* (1909).

Burney, Frances (Fanny), later **Madame D'Arblay,** 1752–1840, English novelist, daughter of Dr. Charles Burney, member of the Samuel Johnson circle. Her acute novels of society include *Evelina; or, The History of a Young Lady's Entrance into the World* (1778), *Cecilia* (1782), and *Camilla* (1796).

SMALL CAPITALS = cross references. Pronunciation key on inside end pages. Abbreviations: p. 2.

Burnham, Daniel Hudson, 1846–1912, American architect and city planner. With his partner John W. Root he designed the 20-story Masonic Temple Building (first important skeleton skyscraper) in Chicago. Their general plan for the Columbia Exposition at Chicago (1893) had an enormous influence on contemporary civic design. Planned Baguio in the Philippines.

Burnham, Sherburne Wesley, 1838–1921, American astronomer, authority on double stars.

burning bush or **wahoo,** handsome North American deciduous shrub (*Euonymus atropurpureus*). Yellow autumn foliage and purple pods with scarlet seeds. Scriptural burning bush (Ex. 3.2) was a thorn.

Burns, John, 1858–1943, British socialist. With Ben Tillett and Tom Mann, led 1889 London dock strike.

Burns, Robert, 1759–96, Scottish lyric, descriptive, and narrative poet, one of the greatest of the romantics. Son of a poor farmer, he gained some education. The jaunty gaiety of some poems reflects his dissolute life, but his love poems have a simple sweetness that make them live. Some songs (e.g., "Flow Gently, Sweet Afton," "John Anderson My Jo," "Auld Lang Syne," "Coming thro' the Rye") are beloved in all English-speaking lands. He first published *Poems, Chiefly in the Scottish Dialect* (1786; 2d ed., 1787) to finance emigration to Jamaica after projected marriage to Mary Campbell. She died, and plan fell through; he later married Jean Armour (who had borne him four children). Briefly lionized in Edinburgh, he died poor. Faithful pictures of Scottish life (e.g., "The Cotter's Saturday Night"), boisterous humor, sincere sentiment, the use of dialect—all contributed to make his poetry distinctive.

burns and scalds. Classified according to depth of tissue damage as first-, second-, third-degree (most severe). Systemic reactions include shock, flow of fluid from blood into injured area, loss of body heat. Scalds are burns caused by moist heat.

Burnside, Ambrose Everett, 1824–81, Union general in Civil War. Won prestige by N.C. coastal campaign. Commanded Army of Potomac until defeat at Fredericksburg. Transferred to Dept. of the Ohio (1863); in 1864 commanded under Meade and Grant in Va.

Burr, Aaron, 1756–1836, American political leader. U.S. Senator (1791–97). Tied with Thomas Jefferson in election of 1800 for presidency; elected Vice President by House of Representatives. Killed Alexander HAMILTON in duel in 1804. Burr's plan for colonization in the Southwest led to his trial for treason in 1807; acquitted, he left for England, but after 1812 practiced law in N.Y.

Burr, William Hubert, 1851–1934, American civil engineer. Served on engineering commissions, e.g., Panama Canal and Port of New York Authority.

Burrillville, town (pop. 8,774), NW R.I., NW of Providence. Mfg. of woolens (since c.1800).

Burritt, Elihu, 1810–79, American worker for world peace, "the learned blacksmith." Supported William LADD in plans for international organization.

burro: see ASS.

Burroughs, John, 1837–1921, American naturalist. He ranged far from his farm at Esopus, N.Y. (from which he was called the Sage of Slabsides) to Alaska and the West Indies to gather material for his smooth philosophic nature essays (as in the books *Wake Robin,* 1871; *Locusts and Wild Honey,* 1879). Later books (e.g., *Time and Change,* 1912; *The Breath of Life,* 1915) are more weightily philosophical. Also wrote poems and early work (1867) on his friend Walt Whitman.

Bursa (bŏŏr'sä), city (pop. 100,007) NW Turkey, near the Sea of Marmara; also known as Brusa or Brussa. Silk and carpet mfg. Ancient Prusa was a flourishing city of Bithynia. Captured by Orkhan 1326; cap. of Ottoman Turks 1326–1423; sacked by Tamerlane 1402. Has fine mosques, tombs of early sultans.

Burton, Sir Richard Francis, 1821–90, English explorer, writer, linguist. Journeyed in various Moslem disguises to Mecca and Medina (1853), in Arabic guise to Harar, Ethiopia (1856). Explored in Africa and Brazil. Wrote accounts of his travels, translated *Arabian Nights* (16 vols., 1885–88).

Burton, Robert, 1577–1640, English clergyman, author of *The Anatomy of Melancholy* (1621; several times enlarged), a vast, wide-ranging treatise.

Burton-Opitz, Russell (–ō'pĭts), 1875–, American physiologist, authority on blood and circulatory system.

Bury, John Bagnell (byŏŏ'rē), 1861–1927, Irish historian, authority on East Roman Empire. His chief works treat Greek, late Roman, and Byzantine history. He also edited Gibbon's *Decline and Fall.*

Bury, Richard de: see RICHARD DE BURY.

Buryat-Mongol Autonomous Soviet Socialist Republic (bŏŏryät'-mŏng'gŏl), autonomous state (135,700 sq. mi.; pop. 542,170), RSFSR, in S Siberia; cap. ULAN-UDE. Mountainous, heavily forested, rich in metals (tungsten, molybdenum, gold, tin, mercury, iron). Population is c.50% Buryat-Mongols (see MONGOLS), mostly herdsmen. Annexed by Russia 17th cent. Also known as Buriat-Mongolia.

bus, public road conveyance. Horse-drawn type introduced 1662 in Paris was operated for a few years. It was reintroduced in Bordeaux (c.1812), Paris (c.1827), London (1829), New York (1830). Buses were motorized in early 20th cent. First motorbus service from Los Angeles to New York estab. 1928.

Busch, Adolf (bŏŏsh'), 1891–1952, German-Swiss violinist. He organized the Busch string quartet and the Busch Chamber Players, both outstanding in the performance of chamber music. His brother, **Fritz Busch,** 1890–1951, was a conductor of opera and symphony and led the Glyndebourne Festivals in England.

Busch, Wilhelm (vĭl'hĕlm bŏŏsh'), 1832–1908, German cartoonist, author of humorous, illustrated poems for children.

Büsching, Anton Friedrich (büsh'ĭng), 1724–93, German geographer, educator. Noted for *Neue Erdbeschreibung* (10 vols., 1754–92); six volumes translated into English as *A New System of Geography* (1762).

Bush, Vannevar, 1890–, American electrical engineer, physicist, and administrator. In 1939 he became president of Carnegie Institution and in 1941 director of the wartime Office of Scientific Research and Development. He designed calculating devices including a differential analyzer. He is author of works on technical subjects and on the significance of research.

bushido (bŏŏshēdō') [way of the warrior], code of honor of feudal Japan which governed the general conduct of the SAMURAI. Codified in 17th–18th cent.; stresses loyalty and self-sacrifice for one's superior and one's honor.

bushmaster, largest New World venomous snake, of pit viper family. Found in Central and South America.

Bushmen, a people of southern Africa related to Pygmies. Nomadic hunters and cave dwellers. Their complex language resembles that of Hottentots.

Bushnell, Horace, 1802–76, American Congregational minister. Minister at North Church, Hartford, Conn., 1833–59. His works helped shape modern religious thought.

Bushrangers, gangs of escaped convicts and adventurers who terrorized rural areas of Australia in 19th cent. Later groups attacked gold convoys.

Busoni, Feruccio (fär-rŏŏt'chō bŏŏzō'nē), 1866–1924, Italian pianist and composer. He transcribed for piano much of Bach's organ music.

Bustamante, Antonio Sánchez de (äntō'nyō sän'chäs dä), 1865–1951, Cuban authority on international law. Drew up a code of international private law.

Butades of Sicyon (bū'tŭdēz, sĭ'shēŏn), c.600 B.C., Greek sculptor, reputedly first to model in clay.

butcher bird: see SHRIKE.

Bute, John Stuart, 3d earl of, 1713–92, English Tory prime minister (1761–63). Confidant of George III, endorsed his aims of supremacy of monarchy, destruction of Whig monopoly, end of war with France. Unpopular Treaty of Paris after declaration of war on Spain (1762) led to his resignation.

Bute, island and county, Scotland: see BUTESHIRE.

Butenandt, Adolf (ä'dȯlf boo'tünänt), 1903–, German biochemist. Determined structure of progestin, female sex hormone; isolated and named androsterone, male sex hormone. Declined 1939 Nobel Prize because of Nazi doctrines.

Buteshire (būt'shĭr) or **Bute,** insular county (218 sq. mi.; pop. 19,285), in the Firth of Clyde, W Scotland; co. town Rothesay. ARRAN and Bute largest islands. Agr. chief occupation; cattle and sheep raised; fishing. Scenery attracts tourists.

Butler, Irish noble family. **Thomas Butler, 10th earl of Ormonde,** 1532–1614, was first of family to become Protestant. Supported movement against Shane O'Neill and had bitter quarrel with earl of Desmond. Made lieutenant governor of Ireland 1597. **James Butler, 12th earl and 1st duke of Ormonde,** 1610–88, was most powerful royalist influence in Ireland during Puritan Revolution. Succeeded earl of Strafford in command of army in Ireland and defeated rebels. Made lord lieutenant 1643. Gave up office after concluding peace with Parliament 1647. Proclaimed Charles II as king of Ireland 1649. After 1660 was again lord lieutenant. Attacked by duke of Buckingham and then earl of Shaftesbury, he was removed from office by intrigue 1684. His son, **Thomas Butler, earl of Ossory,** 1634–80, distinguished himself in naval battles with the Dutch 1665, 1672. Was lieutenant general in Ireland after 1665. His son, **James Butler, 2d duke of Ormonde,** 1665–1745, supported William III and fought at battle of the Boyne. Was lord lieutenant of Ireland (1703–06, 1710–13) and commander in chief of army. Involved in plot to prevent accession of George I, he was impeached 1715. Fled to France, took part in Jacobite rising 1715, and spent rest of his life in exile.

Butler, Benjamin Franklin, 1818–93, American politician and Union general in Civil War. Commander in capture of New Orleans and military governor of city (1862), unpopular with Southerners. In U.S. Congress (1867–75), as radical Republican, was supporter of Reconstruction policy and a leader in impeachment of Pres. Johnson.

Butler, Ellis Parker, 1869–1937, American humorist, best known for sketch *Pigs Is Pigs* (1906).

Butler, Howard Crosby, 1872–1922, American archaeologist. Engaged in excavations at Sardis, in archaeological investigations in Syria.

Butler, James: see BUTLER, family.

Butler, John, 1728–96, Loyalist commander in American Revolution. Organized troop called Butler's Rangers. Defeated Zebulon Butler in Wyoming Valley (1778); Indian allies perpetrated Wyoming Valley massacre. His son, **Walter Butler,** 1752?–1781, also a Loyalist officer, fought with his father and led Cherry Valley massacre (1778).

Butler, Joseph, 1692–1752, English theologian, bishop of Bristol and later of Durham. His *Analogy of Religion, Natural and Revealed, to the Constitution and Course of Nature* (1736) was written to combat deism in England.

Butler, Nicholas Murray, 1862–1947, American educator, president of COLUMBIA UNIVERSITY (1902–45). Largely responsible for expansion of Columbia Col. into Columbia Univ. His efforts in behalf of international peace won him world-wide prestige.

Butler, Samuel, 1612–80, English satiric poet, author of mock romance *Hudibras* (1663–78; against Puritan hypocrisy).

Butler, Samuel, 1835–1902, English author. Spent some years in New Zealand, and New Zealand scenery appears in his utopian *Erewhon; or, Over the Range* (1872) and *Erewhon Revisited* (1901) [anagram of Nowhere]. His novel, *The Way of All Flesh* (1903), is an astringent attack on Victorian family life. His notebooks, bitter and overfrank notations, have been

until the present time only partially published.

Butler, Thomas: see BUTLER, family.

Butler, Walter: see BUTLER, JOHN.

Butler, Zebulon, 1731–95, American colonial leader. Military leader of Conn. settlers in Wyoming Valley. Defeated by Loyalists under John Butler in 1778.

Butler, city (pop. 23,482), W Pa., N of Pittsburgh, in coal, oil, and limestone area; settled c.1800. Makes glass and metal products and auto trailers.

Butler University: see INDIANAPOLIS, Ind.

Butte (būt), city (pop. 33,251; alt. 5,775 ft.), SW Mont., SSW of Helena; founded 1864. First a gold, then a silver town, it developed further with copper discovery (c.1880) and paralleled growth of Anaconda Copper Mining Co. Now state's second largest city and a leading U.S. copper center, with by-product (lead, arsenic, fertilizer) and smelting plants, it also mines zinc and manganese. Seat of Montana School of Mines (see Univ. of MONTANA).

butte, isolated hill, steep-sided and flat-topped, a remnant of erosion. Common in W U.S., Badlands.

butter, nourishing dairy product made by agitating cream or milk to unite the fat globules. Cows' milk is generally the basis, but that of goats, sheep, and mares has been used. Exclusively farm made until c.1850, it has become increasingly a factory product. The use of a starter culture of bacteria has generally replaced natural fermentation of cream; sweet (unsalted) butter is made of sweet cream. Clarified butter (called ghee in India) is much used in Eastern lands.

butter-and-eggs or **toadflax,** weedy perennial (*Linaria vulgaris*) introduced to U.S. from Eurasia. Yellow and orange flowers resemble small snapdragons.

buttercup or **crowfoot,** any *Ranunculus* species with yellow flowers and deeply cut foliage. Often weedy, but a few, e.g., florists' ranunculus and creeping buttercup, are grown for cutting and in gardens.

butterfly, insect of group comprising, with moths, order Lepidoptera. Broad membranous scaled wings. Four-stage life cycle: egg, larva, pupa, adult. Bodies more slender and smoother than in moths, antennae enlarged at tip (in moths, often feathery, rarely knobbed), when at rest wings held vertically (in moths horizontally), chiefly diurnal (moth largely nocturnal).

butterfly flower or **poor-man's-orchid,** showy annual (*Schizanthus*). Grown in greenhouse or garden.

butterfly weed or **pleurisy root,** handsome MILKWEED (*Asclepias tuberosa*) of U.S. Often cultivated for its terminal clusters of bright orange flowers.

butternut, deciduous North American tree (*Juglans cinerea*), also called white walnut, and its fruit, an edible nut. Dye from nut husks used by early settlers.

Butterworth, Hezekiah, 1839–1905, American author of juvenile stories, editor (1870–94) of the *Youth's Companion.*

buttons, knoblike appendages on clothing, either for ornament or fastening. First became important in 10th cent., though used occasionally in Greece and Rome. In 16th cent. their increasing magnificence led many Puritans to use hook-and-eye fastenings in protest. Innumerable materials, from wood, metal, shell, and bone to gems and coins, have been used.

buttonwood: see PLANE TREE.

Butyl rubber: see RUBBER, SYNTHETIC.

Butzer, Martin: see BUCER, MARTIN.

Buxar (bŭksär'), village, N Bihar, India. British won Bengal by defeat of Nawab of Oudh here (1764).

Buxtehude, Dietrich (dē'trĭkh books"tühoo'dù), 1637–1707, Swedish organist at Lübeck. Chiefly composed choral preludes, passacaglias, and fugues for organ.

Buxton, Sir Thomas Fowell, 1786–1845, English reformer. As member of Parliament led in abolishing (1833) slavery in British colonies.

Buys-Ballot, Christoph Heinrich Diedrich (bois'-bälō'), 1817–90, Dutch meteorologist. Strove to organize standard system for representing meteorological findings. Formulated Buys-Ballot's law: if one stands with his back to wind, low pressure area is to his left. Reverse is true in S Hemisphere.

Buzau (boozû'oo), town (pop. 43,365), SE Rumania. Oil refineries, foundries, flour mills.

buzzard, name for certain hawks and vultures. In S U.S. are turkey VULTURE or turkey buzzard, black vulture or black buzzard. Red-tailed, red-shouldered, broad-wing hawks called buzzards.

Buzzards Bay, inlet of the Atlantic, 30 mi. long and 5–10 mi. wide, SE Mass., connected with Cape Cod Bay by Cape Cod Canal and bounded on SE by Elizabeth Isls. **Buzzards Bay,** village (pop. 1,459), seat of Cape Cod Canal Administration, is in Bourne town.

Byblos (bĭb'lŭs), city of anc. Phoenicia, a port near present Beyrouth, Lebanon; biblical Gebal (modern Jebail). It was a center for worship of Adonis. Because of its papyri, it was the source of the Greek word for book (and English words such as Bible, bibliography).

Bydgoszcz (bĭd'gôshch), Ger. *Bromberg,* city (pop. 134,614), NW Poland, on Bydgoszcz Canal (part of Oder-Vistula waterway). Trade center. Passed to Prussia 1772; restored to Poland 1919. Lignite and salt deposits near by.

Byel-. For Russian names beginning thus, see BEL-.

bylini (bĭlē'nē), Russian narrative and heroic poems which were handed down by word of mouth from 11th cent. and began to be collected and studied in 18th cent. The largest cycle has Prince Vladimir of Kiev and the fabulous warrior Ilya of Murom as central figures. Among other cycles, that of Novgorod is most important.

Byng, George: see TORRINGTON, GEORGE BYNG, VISCOUNT.

Byng, John, 1704–57, British admiral; son of Viscount Torrington. Was shot for abandoning his task after defeat by French while attempting to relieve Minorca (1756). Sentence caused much indignation.

Byng, Julian Hedworth George, 1st Viscount Byng of Vimy, 1862–1935, British general. In World War I Canadian troops under his command stormed (1917) Vimy Ridge. He served as governor general of Canada 1921–26.

Byrd, Richard Evelyn (bûrd), 1888–, American aviator and polar explorer. Took part in notable polar and transatlantic flights from 1925. Led expeditions to Antarctica (1929, 1933). From base at LITTLE AMERICA he moved 123 mi. closer to South Pole to spend several winter months alone making observations (1933). Led government expeditions to Antarctic (1939–40, 1946–47). He has published records of his various experiences. His brother, **Harry Flood Byrd,** 1887–, is U.S. Senator from Va. (1933–). A conservative Democrat, he opposed New Deal and Truman administration.

Byrd, William, b. 1542 or 1543, d. 1623, English composer and organist. He composed both Anglican and Roman Catholic church music; also music for the virginal and other instruments. Also Bird, Byrde.

Byrd, William, 1674–1744, American colonial writer, planter, government official in Va. Owned extensive lands. Such writings as *A History of the Dividing Line* and *A Journey to the Land of Eden* are much admired for style and wit.

Byrne, Donn (bûrn), 1889–1928, Irish-American author, b. Brooklyn, N.Y., studied in Ireland. Among his tales are *Messer Marco Polo* (1921), *Blind Raftery* (1924). Full real name Brian Oswald Donn-Byrne.

Byrnes, James F(rancis), 1879–, U.S. Secretary of State (1945–47). Governor of S.C. (1951–).

Byron, George Gordon Noel Byron, 6th **Baron** (bī'rŭn), 1788–1824, English romantic poet, epitome of the romantic in his irregular life and his emotion-charged poetry. Lame from birth, left fatherless in 1791, he grew to be a dark, handsome man, beloved by and contemptuous of women. Lord Byron's name was linked with those of various women before and after his ill-fated marriage (1815–16) to Anne Isabella Mil-

banke. In 1819 he formed a liaison with Countess Teresa Guiccioli. Restlessly wandering about the Continent, he was fired by various causes and died while working for Greek independence. He wrote long romances and stories in verse such as *Childe Harold* (1812–18), *The Giaour* (1813), *The Bride of Abydos* (1813), *Manfred* (1817), *Mazeppa* (1819), and *Cain* (1821; much criticized for skepticism toward religion). He was also a master of satire, as in *English Bards and Scotch Reviewers* (1809), *The Vision of Judgment* (1822), and his masterpiece, *Don Juan* (1819–24). Shorter pieces (e.g., *The Prisoner of Chillon*) and lyrics are familiar works today.

Bytom, Upper Silesia: see BEUTHEN.

Bytown, Ont.: see OTTAWA.

Byzantine architecture (bĭ'zŭntēn, –tīn, bĭzăn'tĭn), style of building which developed after Byzantium (Constantinople) had been made cap. of the Roman Empire (A.D. 330). It crystallized in Ravenna and Constantinople and spread through Greece and the Balkans to Asia Minor, and ultimately to Russia. The style was the product of Roman methods of construction modified by the use of colorful materials and adornments. Under Justinian (527–65) it achieved its first definitive expression in the Church of San Vitale at Ravenna and the renowned HAGIA SOPHIA. The second phase of the style, in which Eastern influences became apparent, is represented by SAINT MARK'S CHURCH at Venice. In its later phases, Byzantine architecture became more ornate in design and decoration, as in Moscow cathedral.

Byzantine art, an art blended of Hellenistic and Oriental traditions which flourished under the Byzantine Empire. It began to develop in the 2d cent. A.D., reaching its first Golden Age c.330. Except for the interruption caused by iconoclasm, the style persisted until the fall of Constantinople in 1453. It emphasized decorativeness, neglecting plasticity in favor of flat-line harmony. Sculpture was characterized by flat, even relief, with delicate, lacy designs. Mosaics reached a high point in the 6th-cent. cathedrals at Ravenna.

Byzantine Empire, successor state to the Roman Empire (see ROME), also called Eastern or East Roman Empire; named for its cap., CONSTANTINOPLE, the anc. Byzantium. The division of the Roman Empire into East and West became permanent in 395, although after the fall of West Rome (476) the Eastern emperors claimed succession to the entire Roman world. The core of the Byzantine Empire was Asia Minor and the S Balkan Peninsula. Throughout its 1,000 years of existence, the empire was beset by foreign invaders—Goths, Huns, Avars, Persians, Bulgars, Slavs, Arabs, Normans, Seljuk Turks, Serbs, the French, Italians, and Ottoman Turks. Its boundaries shifted according to military fortunes and to the vigor of central authority. Religious controversy played a major part in Byzantine history and was frequently interwoven with party strife (see BLUES AND GREENS; NESTORIANISM; MONOPHYSITISM; MONOTHELETISM; ICONOCLASM; PHOTIUS; ORTHODOX EASTERN CHURCH). With all its weaknesses, dissensions, court intrigues, and corruption, the empire possessed astonishing powers of recuperation and survival; it carried on the Graeco-Roman civilization, blended with Oriental influences, at a time when the West was in chaos. The first era of recuperation came under JUSTINIAN I, who recovered Italy and Africa, codified ROMAN LAW, and encouraged Hellenism. Byzantine art and architecture entered their most glorious period (6th cent.). His successors lost most of ITALY to the Lombards, and Syria, Palestine, Egypt, Africa, and Sicily to the Arabs. The reign of IRENE saw the coronation of Charlemagne as emperor of the West (800), and the schism between the Roman and the Eastern Church followed soon afterward, effectually destroying Roman universality. A new period of splendor and vigorous government was inaugurated by BASIL I (9th cent.)

but ended with the Turkish victory at MANZIKERT (1071). After a brief resurgence under ALEXIUS I, a century of decay ended with the breakup of the empire under the impact of the Fourth Crusade (1204; see CRUSADES). However, the Latin Empire of CONSTANTINOPLE proved even less stable than the surviving Byzantine splinter states of NICAEA, TREBIZOND, and EPIRUS; in 1261 MICHAEL VIII of Nicaea recaptured Constantinople and restored the empire. For two centuries the ever-shrinking state held out against the Ottoman Turks, vainly begging the West for aid. At last, after a desperate defense under CONSTANTINE XI, Constantinople fell to Mohammed II (1453), and Turkey fell heir to Byzantium. The modern era is generally reckoned from that day.

Byzantine music, now regarded as an independent musical culture that flourished between the 4th and 15th cent., reached its golden age in the 7th cent. Although some Greek instruments were used, the organ was most important. Almost all extant Byzantine music is liturgical. Its principal form was the hymn; texts were usually biblical. Byzantine chant attempted to depict melodical meaning of the words. Notation was originally only a series of symbols serving to remind the singer of a melody he already knew. Later a staffless notation indicating starting note and subsequent intervals of a melody was used.

Byzantium (bǐzǎn'shēum), anc. city, on site of present Istanbul; trade center founded by Greeks 658 B.C. Taken by Rome (A.D. 196), it was chosen by Constantine I (330) as site for CONSTANTINOPLE, later cap. of Byzantine Empire.

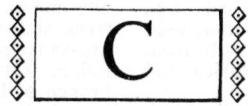

C, chemical symbol of the element CARBON.
Ca, chemical symbol of the element CALCIUM.
Caaba: see KAABA.
Cabal (kŭbǎl'), secret group of advisers of Charles II of England (hence, any secret, conniving clique). Their initials form the word—Clifford of Chudleigh, Ashley (Lord Shaftesbury), Buckingham (George Villiers), Arlington (Henry Bennet), and Lauderdale (John Maitland).
cabala or **cabbala** (both: kǎ'bŭlù) [Heb.,= the received], a system of interpretation of the Scriptures based on the assumption that every word and letter in them has an occult meaning. It arose in the 7th cent. and lasted into the 18th. This attempt to spiritualize formal Judaism grew in an era of severe persecution. It held that all originates in God, that evil is the result of distance from God, that man's soul exists from eternity, and that if pure, the soul overcomes evil. The names of God were thought to have magical powers. Cabala supposedly contained Christian doctrines, and was taken up by Christians at various times. The principal sources of cabala are the *Sefer Yezirah* (Eng. tr., *Book of Creation*), which sets forth a system of numerical interpretation and the doctrine of emanation, and the *Zohar* [Heb.,= splendor], which develops these ideas further. Written by Moses de Leon (13th cent.), the *Zohar* is attributed by him to Simon ben Yohai (2d cent.).
cabbage, leafy garden vegetable (*Brassica oleracea capitata*) with white, green, or red leaves. It is derived from wild cabbage and allied to KALE, BRUSSELS SPROUTS, CAULIFLOWER, and BROCCOLI.
cabbage palm, popular name for several palm species with central edible buds (see PALMETTO PALM).
cabbala: see CABALA.
Cabell, James Branch (kǎ'bùl), 1879–, American novelist. Some novels (notably *Jurgen,* 1919) are set in imaginary medieval land (Poictesme). Also author of critical essays. Wrote both as Branch Cabell and James Branch Cabell.
Cabet, Étienne (ätyěn' käbä'), 1788–1856, French utopian socialist and reformer. In exile (1834–39) in England, he wrote description of ideal society, *Voyage en Icarie* (1840). Urged state control of all economy and social life. Founded several communistic settlements in U.S. Settlers called Icarians.
Cabeza de Vaca, Álvar Núñez (äl'vär nōō'nyäth käbä'thä dä vä'kä), c.1490–c.1557, Spanish explorer. Wandered through American Southwest (1534–36) after shipwreck off Texas coast. Deposed as governor of colony in Paraguay (1544).
Cabinda (kŭbĭn'dù), autonomous district (c.2,800 sq. mi.; pop. 46,277) of ANGOLA, separated from Angola proper by a strip belonging to Belgian Congo.
Cabiri (kŭbī'rī), Greek fertility gods, worshiped with mysteries at Samothrace.
Cable, George Washington, 1844–1925, American author of romantic novels, stories of La. (as in collection, *Old Creole Days,* 1879); novel (*The Grandissimes,* 1880).
cable. Once a term for fibrous rope and now applied to transoceanic telegraph message; to telephone-telegraph line of intertwisted strands in insulating sheath; to chain, heavy rope, or plaited wire used to anchor, moor, or tow ships; to twisted wire rope with many engineering uses; to wire conveying electricity from source to consumer; and to intercity coaxial telephone, telegraph, and television line. The coaxial cable (which permits simultaneous transmission of many signals) consists of a copper tube through the center of which extends a copper wire held in place by insulating disks; a number of such units are enclosed in insulating material.
Cabochiens (käbōshyě'), popular faction in Paris in early 15th cent. Mostly tradespeople chafing at heavy taxation, they sided with Burgundians in civil war between ARMAGNACS AND BURGUNDIANS, seized control of Paris in 1413, passed radical reforms (*ordonnance cabochienne*). Suppressed by Armagnacs 1413.
Cabot, John, fl. 1461–98, English explorer, probably b. Genoa, Italy. Under patent granted by Henry VII, he sailed W from Bristol (1497), presumably seeking access to riches of Far East, and reached North American coast. He set out on second exploratory expedition (1498) whose fate is unknown. English claims in North America were based on his discovery. His son, **Sebastian Cabot,** b. 1483–86?, d. 1557?, was explorer in Spanish service (1512–48). Explored (1526–30) Río

de la Plata country; later reentered English service; as governor of Muscovy Co. was responsible for commercial treaty with Russia.

Cabral, Pedro Alvares (äl'vurĭsh käbräl'), c.1460–1526?, Portuguese navigator. Commanded fleet destined for India (1500), went far west of his course, reached coast of Brazil which he claimed for Portugal. Finally reached Calicut but roused native ire by highhanded practices in trade and religion. His landing in Brazil, accidental or prearranged, was not the first European visit to Brazil, though the question of discovery is still argued.

Cabrillo, Juan Rodríguez (hwän rōdhrē'gäth käbrē'lyō), d. 1543, Spanish conquistador, discoverer of California (1542), b. Portugal.

Cabrillo National Monument: see NATIONAL PARKS AND MONUMENTS (table).

Cabrini, Saint Frances Xavier (kŭbrē'nē), 1850–1917, American nun, b. Italy; first U.S. citizen to be canonized (1946). Founded Missionary Sisters of the Sacred Heart of Jesus, and after coming to the U.S. (1889) worked with the poor and the sick. Feast: Dec. 22.

cacao (kŭkā'ō), tropical American tree (*Theobroma cacao*), bearing pods containing cocoa beans of commerce. After drying, the seeds are screened, roasted, and skinned, resulting in clean kernels known as cocoa nibs, which are made into various products, e.g., edible CHOCOLATE and cocoa, and cocoa butter, used medicinally and in cosmetics. Exported mainly from South and Central America, British West Africa, and West Indies.

Caccini, Giulio (jōō'lyō kät-chē'nē), c.1558–c.1618, Italian composer. With Peri, he composed *Dafne* (c.1597), the first actual opera on record.

Cáceres (kä'thäräs), city (27,463), cap. of Cáceres prov., W Spain, in Estremadura. Cork mfg. Roman and Moorish walls and towers.

cactus, succulent plant, either small or treelike, of family Cactaceae, native to New World. It is characterized by fleshy green stem (leaves inconspicuous or absent), showy flowers, and colorful fruit, often edible (e.g., PRICKLY PEAR) and is adapted to high temperatures and arid regions. Among the cacti are NIGHT-BLOOMING CEREUS, cholla, PEYOTE, and Christmas cactus.

Cadamosto or **Cada Mosto, Luigi da** (lwē'jē dä kädämō'stō), 1432?–1480?, Venetian navigator in Portuguese service, from about 1454. Left a valuable record of Portuguese activity in Canary Isls., and may have been discoverer of Cape Verde Isls. (1456 or 1457).

Caddoan (kä'dōun), linguistic family of North America, embracing many Indian tribes in the West and the South. See LANGUAGE, table.

Cade, Jack, d. 1450, English rebel, leader of uprising in S England in 1450. Grievances were mainly political. Rebels defeated royal army and entered London. Government pardoned (and so dispersed) Cade's men, but executed him.

Cadillac, Antoine de la Mothe (kä'dĭlăk, Fr. ătwän' dù lä môt' kädēyäk'), c.1658–1730, French colonial governor of territory of Louisiana (1713–16), founder of Detroit (1701).

Cadillac, resort city (pop. 10,425), N Mich., SE of Traverse City and on L. Cadillac, in agr. area; settled c.1871. Trading post was estab. by Cadillac. Mfg. of vehicle parts. Indian mounds and winter sports area near by.

Cádiz (Sp. kä'dēth), city (pop. 87,630), cap. of Cádiz prov., SW Spain, in Andalusia; Atlantic port and fortified naval base. Founded c.1100 B.C. by Phoenicians as Gadir, taken by Carthage c.500 B.C. Continued to flourish under Romans, who took it 3d cent. B.C. and called it Gades. Reconquered from Moors by Castile (1262), it prospered again after discovery of America. In 1587 Drake burned Spanish fleet in Cádiz harbor; in 1596 Essex devastated the city. During Peninsular War Cádiz successfully resisted French siege 1810–1812, was seat of Spanish Cortes.

Cadman, Charles Wakefield, 1881–1946, American composer, best known for the songs *From the Land of the Sky-blue Water* and *At Dawning*. Among his other works are the operas *Shanewis* and *A Witch of Salem.*

cadmium (kăd'mēum), metallic element (symbol = Cd; see also ELEMENT, table). White, lustrous, very malleable and ductile; like tin in physical properties, zinc in chemical. Forms oxide, hydroxide, carbonate, chloride, sulphide. Occurs in nature in compounds. Used to make low-melting-point alloys.

Cadmus, in Greek legend, son of Agenor and founder of Thebes; honored as inventor of alphabet.

Cadogan, William Cadogan, 1st Earl, 1675–1726, British general, diplomat. Friend of duke of MARLBOROUGH, aided him in War of the SPANISH SUCCESSION.

Cadorna, Luigi (lwē'jē kädōr'nä), 1850–1928, Italian field marshal in World War I. Took Gorizia 1916. Routed at Caporetto 1917.

Cadoudal, Georges (zhôrzh' kädōōdäl'), 1771–1804, French royalist conspirator. Leader of counterrevolutionists in Vendée and of plot (1803) to oust Bonaparte. Cadoudal was executed, as was the duc d'ENGHIEN, who was unjustly linked to the plot.

caduceus (kŭdū'sēŭs), wing-topped staff, with two snakes winding about it, carried by Hermes. As symbol of fertility, wisdom, and healing, it appeared early in Babylonia. Hermes' staff was carried by Greek heralds and ambassadors and became a Roman symbol of truce and neutrality. Since 16th cent. it has replaced one-snake symbol of Asclepius for medicine. By regulation, it has since 1902 been insignia of medical branch of U.S. Army.

Cadwaladr or **Cadwallader** (both: kädwä'lŭdŭr), semi-legendary British king, leader against Anglo-Saxons in 7th cent.

Cædmon (kăd'mùn), fl. 670, first English Christian poet and first English poet known by name. BEDE, *Ecclesiastical History,* tells how Cædmon, lay brother in abbey of Whitby, was divinely inspired to compose his first work, a brief hymn, and gives Latin version. Other poems described by Bede not extant.

Caen (kä), town (pop. 47,835), cap of Calvados dept., N France, in Normandy. Textile and lace mfg. Favorite residence of William the Conqueror. Center of heavy fighting (June–July, 1944) in World War II. William's castle and the university (founded 1432) were destroyed, but the famous Abbaye aux Hommes [men's abbey], with William's tomb, the Abbaye aux Dames [ladies' abbey], and the Church of St. Nicholas were preserved. All three are gems of 11th-cent. Norman architecture.

Caerleon (kärlē'ùn), urban district (pop. 4,711), Monmouthshire, England. Has extensive remains of Roman fortress Isca. Village often identified with Camelot of Arthurian legend.

Caermarthenshire or **Carmarthenshire** (both: kŭrmär'dhŭnshĭr), maritime county (920 sq. mi.; pop. 171,742), S Wales. Largest of Welsh counties, it is mostly hilly. Chief occupations agr. and grazing, but industrial S Wales coal fields extend into SE corner. Iron, copper, and lead also mined. The county town, **Caermarthen** or **Carmarthen** (pop. 12,121), has castle once headquarters of Welsh chieftains.

Caernarvonshire or **Carnarvonshire** (both: kŭrnär'vŭnshĭr, kär–), maritime county (569 sq. mi.; pop. 124,074), NW Wales. Region is largely mountainous; Snowdon (3,560 ft.) highest peak in England and Wales. Sheep farming, quarrying, and mining (lead, zinc, and manganese) are the chief industries. County town is **Caernarvon** or **Carnarvon** (pop. 9,255), where the prince of Wales is invested. Its castle is fine example of a medieval fortress.

Caesalpinus, Andreas (ăn'drēus sēsälpī'nùs), Latinized from **Andrea Cesalpino,** 1519–1603, Italian botanist and physiologist. He described in part the circulation of blood and developed the first classification of plants according to their fruits.

Caesar (sē'zùr), name used by a patrician family of Rome. The careers of Julius Caesar and the adopted

SMALL CAPITALS = cross references. Pronunciation key on inside end pages. Abbreviations: p. 2.

Augustus led to giving the name an imperial character. It was in the later Roman empire the title given to the subemperor, who would presumably later become the emperor. The title reappeared later as the German *Kaiser* and the Russian *Czar* or *Tsar*.

Caesar, (Caius) Julius, 102? B.C.–44 B.C., Roman statesman, one of the most renowned military commanders in world history. He came of a noble family and married Cornelia, the daughter of Cinna, colleague of Caesar's uncle by marriage, MARIUS, whose party he joined. In the hour of Sulla's triumph Caesar was proscribed. On Sulla's death he began his political career in earnest, becoming the champion of the people against the senate. As pontifex maximus he instituted important reforms in the calendar, creating the Julian calendar. He divorced his second wife, Pompeia, who was involved in a scandal with Clodius, and said "Caesar's wife must be above suspicion." He later married Calpurnia. After service in Spain he returned to Rome (60 B.C.) and organized the First Triumvirate, with POMPEY and CRASSUS. He mediated between his colleagues and himself took command in Gaul, where his prosecution of the GALLIC WARS (58 B.C.–49 B.C.) estab. his reputation as one of the great military commanders of all time. He ended by a journey of conquest in Britain, where he planted Roman power. Again in Gaul, he put down the uprising led by Vercingetorix and made Roman power secure. In 54 B.C. his daughter Julia, wife of Pompey, died, and from that time on rivalry between Pompey, who became the champion of the senatorial party, and Caesar, the popular leader, grew. The death of Crassus set the two face to face (53 B.C.). The senate, fearing Caesar's power, moved to take away his army command. He agreed to submit if Pompey would surrender his. This reply caused the senate to demand (quite illegally) that he disband his army immediately. Two tribunes, Marc ANTONY and CASSIUS, vetoed the bill and fled to Caesar. He made the fateful decision to defy the senate and signalized it by leading his army across the small river Rubicon (49 B.C.). Civil war began. Caesar marched triumphantly to Rome, then pursued Pompey until he conquered him on the plain of Pharsala in Greece (48 B.C.). He followed the defeated Pompey to Egypt and there had a love affair with Cleopatra. From Egypt he went to Pontus and defeated Pharnaces II with an easy victory recorded in his words "Veni, vidi, vici" [I came, I saw, I conquered]. Returning to Rome, he exercised the dictatorial powers granted him, though he refused the title of king, preferring to remain only consul, dictator, and general (44 B.C.). His social reforms won popular support, but his enemies and some of his followers resented his autocratic rule. A conspiracy was formed against him, largely by men he had befriended, most notably M. Junius BRUTUS, Cassius, Casca, and Cimber. Just as he was preparing to leave to conduct war against Parthia, he was stabbed to death in the senate on the Ides of March (March 15), 44 B.C. His will left his money and power to his grandnephew Octavius, who was to become Emperor Augustus after he and Marc Antony had avenged Caesar's murder. The character and achievements of Julius Caesar are still hotly debated by scholars. His military and literary gifts (his *Gallic Wars* and *Civil War* are masterpieces) are unquestioned, but whether he was a purely self-seeking opportunist lover of power, a man dedicated to the redemption of the poor and rejected, the patriot restoring the glory of Rome, or something else is still an open question.

Caesarea (sēsùrē'ù), name given to various anc. cities to honor the Roman Caesars. Among the most important were: Caesarea in Mauretania, a flourishing trade center (on the site of present Cherchel, Algeria) until sacked by the Vandals in the 5th cent.; Caesarea Mazaca or Caesarea of Cappadocia (on the site of present Kayseri, Turkey), a trade center and residence of Cappadocian kings; Caesarea Palestinae, in S Palestine, the capital of Herod the Great and scene of massacre of Jewish citizens by Romans (A.D. 66); and Caesarea Philippi, in N Palestine, at foot of Mt. Hermon, built by Philip the Tetrarch, visited by Jesus.

Caesarean section or **Cesarean section** (both: sēzâ'-rēùn), removal of child from uterus through abdominal incision; so named because of legend that Julius Caesar was delivered thus. Can be performed more than once.

Caesarion: see PTOLEMY XIV.

Caffa, RSFSR: see FEODOSIYA.

caffeine, alkaloid in coffee, tea, kola nut, cocoa. Acts as a stimulant and diuretic. In tea, known as theine. Can be synthesized from uric acid.

Cagayan (kägī'ùn) or **Rio Grande de Cagayan,** river, 220 mi. long, in central Luzon, Philippines.

Cagliari (kä'lyärē), city (pop. 78,632), cap. of Sardinia, Italy; Mediterranean port. Roman remains; medieval castle.

Cagliostro, Alessandro, Conte (älĕs-sän'drō kōn'tä kälyō'strō), 1743–95, Italian adventurer; real name Giuseppe Balsamo. Traveled all over Europe posing as physician, magician, alchemist. Popular at Louis XVI's court. Implicated in Affair of the DIAMOND NECKLACE; acquitted but banished from France. Condemned by Roman Inquisition as heretic and sorcerer (1789); died in prison.

Cahaba (kùhô'bù), deserted village, SW central Ala., SW of Selma. State cap. 1819–26.

Cahaba, river flowing from mountains NE of Birmingham c.200 mi. SW and S to Alabama R. near Selma.

Cahan, Abraham (kän), 1860–1951, Jewish-American journalist and socialist leader, b. Vilna, a founder and editor in chief of the Jewish *Daily Forward.*

Cahokia (kùhō'kēù), village (pop. 794), SW Ill., on the Mississippi just below East St. Louis. First permanent settlement in Ill., it was named for a tribe of ILLINOIS INDIANS served by French mission estab. here 1699. Became one of chief French centers in upper Mississippi valley; taken by British 1765 and by Americans under Clark 1778. Has several 18th cent. buildings.

Cahors (käôr'), city (pop. 12,706), cap. of Lot dept., S central France, on Lot R.; historic cap. of Quercy. Major medieval banking center; Cahorsin moneylenders rivaled Lombards and Jews. Old town contains medieval cathedral, palaces, and fortifications.

Caiaphas (kā'yùfùs), high priest who presided at council that condemned Jesus to death. Also at trial of Peter and John. Mat. 26.57–68; John 11.47–54; 18.24; Acts 4.6; Mark 14.53–65; Luke 22.66–71.

Caicos Islands: see TURKS AND CAICOS ISLANDS.

Caillaux, Joseph (zhôzĕf' kāyō'), 1863–1944, French minister of finance (1899, 1906, 1913–14, 1925, 1926) and premier (1911–12). Introduced income tax (1906); reached peaceful settlement of Morocco crisis with Germany (1911), unpopular with nationalists; resigned 1914 after his wife murdered Gaston Calmette, a journalist who had attacked his private life. (She was acquitted.) Caillaux's pacifist sentiments led to his arrest (1917) and imprisonment (1920) for correspondence with the enemy. Restored to citizenship 1924; later served as senator.

Cain, farmer son of Adam and Eve. Known as world's first murderer for killing of brother Abel. Gen. 4.

Cairngorm, group of mountains (includes Ben Macdhui, Braeriach, and Cairngorm, peaks all over 4,000 ft.), forming part of the Grampians, Scotland. Name also given yellow or brown quartz found here.

Cairns, city (pop. 16,644), Queensland, Australia, on Trinity Bay. Chief sugar port of Australia.

Cairo (kī'rō), Arabic *El Kahirah* [the victorious], city (pop. 2,100,486), cap. of Egypt and largest city of Africa, at head of Nile delta. Commercial and mfg. center of Egypt. Near its site was the ancient Roman city of Babylon, and across the river was Memphis, cap. of ancient Egypt. Founded 969 by the Fatimite general

Jauhar. Unsuccessfully attacked by Crusaders in 12th cent. Ruled by the Mamelukes from the 13th to early 16th cent. and by the Ottoman Turks, 1517–1798. Occupied by Napoleon, 1798–1801, and by the British, 1882–1936. Mosque of El Azhar houses world's most important Moslem university, founded 972. Seat of Mus. of Antiquities and Royal Library. The great citadel was built c.1179 by Saladin.

Cairo (kā′rō, kâ′rō). **1** City (pop. 5,577), SW Ga., W of Thomasville. Ships sugar cane and syrup. Processes pecans, peanuts, and lumber. **2** City (pop. 12,123), extreme S Ill., on levee-protected tongue of land between Mississippi R. (bridged to Mo.) and Ohio R. (bridged to Ky.). Shipping center for agr. area (esp. cotton), it has mfg. of cottonseed, soybean, and lumber products. Federal depot in Civil War; MOUND CITY, 5 mi. N, was naval base.

Cairo Conference, Nov. 22–25, 1943, meeting of U.S. Pres. Roosevelt, British Prime Minister Churchill, and Chinese Generalissimo Chiang Kai-shek at Cairo, Egypt. They pledged war against Japan until her unconditional surrender, foreswore territorial gains, and promised freedom of territory gained by her since 1895, notably Korea.

caisson (kā′sŭn, –sŏn), in engineering, a chamber of steel, wood, or concrete used in constructing foundations or piers in or near water. Types of caissons include open (sunk, and then filled with concrete), pneumatic (air pressure prevents entry of water at cutting edge below, and airtight deck of chamber above is high enough to permit workers under it), and camel (water-filled chamber attached to sunken ship and emptied by compressed air or pump).

caisson disease, disturbances (also known as the bends), owing to tissue injury by nitrogen gas bubbles released from solution by rapid change from high to low pressure. Attacks men who work underwater or in underground chambers.

Caithness (kāth′nĕs), county (686 sq. mi.; pop. 22,705), N Scotland. Coastline is rocky, and much of the county treeless moorland. The county town, Wick, an important herring fishing center.

Caius, John (kēz), 1510–73, English physician who endowed Gonville Hall, renaming it Gonville and Caius College, Cambridge.

Cajal, Santiago Ramón y: see RAMÓN Y CAJAL.

Cajamarca (kähämär′kä), city (pop. 15,553; alt. 9,022 ft.), N Peru. Here Francisco Pizarro captured Atahualpa.

Cajetan (kă′jŭtăn) [Latin,= from Gaeta], 1470–1534, Italian churchman; originally named Giacomo de Vio. Made the general of the Dominicans (1508), he became a cardinal (1517). He tried to keep Luther in the Church and opposed the divorce of Henry VIII from Katharine of Aragon. Noted as a scholar.

Cajuns: see ACADIA.

Calabria (kälä′brēä), region (5,828 sq. mi.; pop. 1,771,-651), S Italy, forming "toe" of Italian boot; cap. Reggio di Calabria. Mountainous, arid, economically backward. Agr., grazing, fruit growing, sericulture. Anc. BRUTTIUM, the region was renamed Calabria in Middle Ages. Conquered by Normans in 11th cent.; later shared history of kingdom of NAPLES.

caladium (kŭlā′dĕŭm), tropical American plant (*Caladium*). Colorful foliage marked with white, purple, or rose. Popular summer bedding and pot plant.

Calais (Fr. kälä′), city (pop. 41,536), Pas-de-Calais dept., N France; a Channel port on Strait of Dover. Held by England 1347–1558. Edward III, who captured it in 1347, promised to spare the town if six prominent citizens offered their lives. The mayor and five others volunteered; the king relented. Monument by Rodin commemorates the event. City partly destroyed in World War II.

Calais (kăl′ĭs), city (pop. 4,589), SE Maine, on St. Croix R. opposite St. Stephen, N.B.. On St. Croix Isl. in the river below Calais the sieur de Monts and Champlain planted a settlement, 1604.

calamander wood: see EBONY.

Calamatta, Luigi (lwē′jē kälämät′tä), 1802–69, Italian engraver. A pupil of Ingres, he became one of the leading engravers in France.

Calamian Islands (kälämyän′), group (c.600 sq. mi.; pop. 16,445), between Mindoro and Palawan. Produces rice and manganese.

Calamis (kă′lŭmĭs), 5th cent. B.C., Greek sculptor.

Calamity Jane, c.1852–1903, American frontier character. Maiden name was Martha Jane Canary; origin of nickname is obscure. Lived in Deadwood, S.Dak. Went into show business.

Calamy, Edmund, 1600–1666, English Presbyterian preacher, a leader of Puritan thought. Ejected from ministry by Act of Uniformity (1662).

Calatrava (käläträ′vä), ruined village, central Spain, near Ciudad Real. Original seat of powerful military religious order of **Knights of Calatrava,** founded 1158 by Cistercians as defense against Moors. Order declined after 13th cent.

Calcasieu (kăl′kŭsoō″), river rising in W central La. and flowing c.215 mi. S through L. Charles and Calcasieu L. (20 mi. long) to Gulf of Mexico. Partly navigable; connects with Intracoastal Waterway.

calceolaria (kăl″sēōlâr′ĕŭ) or **slipperwort,** herbaceous or shrubby plant (*Calceolaria*), with showy pouch-shaped flowers. Most species South American.

calcite (kăl′sīt), common mineral (calcium carbonate), usually white; its hexagonal crystals show perfect cleavage. Some forms of calcite are CHALK, LIMESTONE, MARBLE, MARL, and STALACTITE.

calcium (kăl′sēŭm), silvery-white, relatively soft, active metallic element (symbol = Ca; see also ELEMENT, table). Classed with strontium and barium as metal of alkaline earths. Reacts with water and several elements, forming many compounds. Occurs in nature in widely distributed compounds. Is constituent of most plant and animal matter. Essential for strong bones and teeth; functions in regulation of heart beat and in blood clotting.

calculating machine, device to perform mathematical processes. Simple calculators include SLIDE RULE, ABACUS, and counting rods of John NAPIER. Probably the first adding machine using geared wheels was made by Blaise Pascal 1642. G. W. von Leibniz mechanism multiplied by repeated addition, using stepped wheel (c.1672); commercial version to add, subtract, multiply, and divide, was devised by C. X. Thomas 1820. Later in 19th cent. F. S. Baldwin in U.S. patented type more compact than stepped drum; later it was redesigned by W. J. R. Monroe. Key-driven machine was patented in 1850. D. E. Felt patented key-driven calculator (later developed into comptometer) in 1887. W. S. Burroughs patented key-set adding machine with crank 1888. Charles Babbage designed calculating machine in 1830s, but skills and materials to complete it were unavailable until 20th cent. Vannevar Bush completed mechanical differential analyzer in 1930; later one (1942) operated mechanically or electrically. Complex Computer (1940) embodied telephone-switchboard principle, a prototype of others for government in World War II. Many complex electronic computers developed in subsequent years.

calculus (kăl′kyŭlŭs), in higher mathematics, any advanced method, using a notation system peculiar to itself, to solve problems. Familiar calculi are the differential and integral, which together are often called infinitesimal calculus. Differential provides a means of computing the rate of change of a function relative to its independent variable; the difference between two succeeding values is called the increment. When the increment of the variable approaches zero, the ratio of the increment of the function to the increment of the variable approaches a constant figure, called the derivative of the function; the process is called differentiation. Integral calculus starts with given derivative and finds its function (integral).

calculus or **stone,** in medicine, deposit of mineral salts as a hard concretion of stone in body. Common sites are gall and urinary bladders, kidney, joints, and salivary ducts.

Calcutta (kălkŭ'tù), city (pop. 2,070,619), cap. of West Bengal, India. India's largest city and chief commercial port. Founded by the British in 1690, it was captured 1756 by nawab of Bengal, who killed most of garrison by imprisoning it overnight in a small, stifling room, the notorious "black hole." Retaken 1757 by Clive. Cap. of India, 1833–1912. Industrial center with jute and textile mills. Exports include jute, tea, and mica. Seat of Univ. of Calcutta and Indian Mus.

Calder, Alexander Stirling (kôl'dùr), 1870–1945, American sculptor. His son, **Alexander Calder,** 1898–, is an abstract sculptor, best known for his "mobiles" and "stabiles."

Calderón Bridge (kăldārōn'), over Lerma R., E of Guadalajara, Mexico, scene of battle (1811) in Mexican revolution against Spain.

Calderón (de la Barca), Pedro (pā'dhrō kăldārōn' dä lä bär'kä), 1600–1681, Spanish dramatist, last great figure of the Golden Age. Wrote cape-and-sword plays, one-act religious plays, and philosophical dramas including the masterpiece, *La vida es sueño* [life is a dream]. Became a priest 1651.

Caldwell, Erskine, 1903–, American author of realistic stories and novels, especially about the rural South as in *Tobacco Road* (1932; successfully dramatized) and *God's Little Acre* (1933).

Caldwell. 1 City (pop. 10,487), SW Idaho, on Boise R. and W of Boise; founded 1883 on Oregon Trail. Ships farm, dairy, livestock products of BOISE PROJECT. Has noted cooperatives. Seat of Col. of Idaho (1891). **2** Borough (pop. 6,270), NE N.J., near Montclair. Mfg. of airplane propellers, clothing, and plastics. Birthplace of Grover Cleveland.

Caleb, warrior-champion of Israel's God and chief spy sent into Canaan. When given his choice of land, Caleb, though past 80, chose region still strongly fortified by Canaanites and drove them out. Num. 13.6; 14; 32.12; Joshua 14.6–14. Name associated with tribe in S Palestine. 1 Sam. 30.14; 1 Chron. 2.18,19,42,46, 48,49.

Caledonia (kă"lĭdō'nèù), Roman name for part of Britain lying N of the Firths of Clyde and Forth. Modern rhetorical use usually refers to all Scotland.

Caledonian Canal, waterway (length 60½ mi.), running from Moray Firth to Loch Linnhe, Scotland. Opened in 1847, it is little used now.

calendar, system of reckoning time, usually based on recurrent natural cycle, e.g., seasons and moon's phases. Since length of solar year is 365 days 5 hr. 48 min. 46 sec. and of lunar year (12 months of 29½ days) is 354 days 8 hr. 48 min., solar and lunar reckonings must be harmonized. Because the year is not exactly divisible by months and days, practice arose of making arbitrary divisions and inserting (intercalating) extra days or months. Gregorian calendar widely used today evolved from Roman calendar as reformed (45 B.C.) by Julius Caesar. In Julian calendar April, June, September, and November had 30 days; February, 28 days (29 days every fourth year, leap year); and other months, 31 days. In computation of month, days were counted backward from the Kalends (first day), the Ides (fifteenth day of March, May, July, October and thirteenth day of other months), and the Nones (eighth day before the Ides); hence Jan. 10 was fourth of Ides of January. Since Julian year of 365 days 6 hr. was too long, by the 16th cent. the vernal equinox was displaced from March 21 to March 11. Gregory XIII ordained that 10 days be dropped in 1582 and years ending in hundreds be leap years only if divisible by 400. The non-Roman Catholic countries were slow in accepting the Gregorian (New Style) calendar; it was adopted in England in 1752 and by the Eastern Church in the 20th cent. Christian ecclesiastical calendar was based on the belief that Jesus' resurrection was on a Sunday, hence Easter

should fall on Sunday. First Council of Nicaea (325) decreed that Easter be the Sunday following the first full moon after the vernal equinox; today date varies from astronomical reckoning because certain factors of lunar period were not considered. Chronology is a major problem in ancient and medieval history because years were commonly identified by rulers. Era system of computing years from fixed date, e.g., birth of Christ, simplifies chronology. Calendars used today include Jewish calendar (12 months plus intercalary month seven times in 19 years) and Moslem lunar calendar with c.33 years to every 32 in Gregorian calendar. See also FRENCH REVOLUTIONARY CALENDAR.

calendula (kùlĕn'dùlù), annual plant (*Calendula*), also called pot marigold. Has yellow to orange flower heads. The marigold of Shakspere's time.

Calexico (kùlĕk'sĭkō), city (pop. 6,433), SE Calif., in Imperial Valley and opposite Mexicali, Mexico.

calf, golden, idol erected by Israelites on several occasions (e.g., Aaron made one during absence of Moses); Jeroboam placed one at Bethel and one at Dan. Ex. 32; 1 Kings 12.26–32. Calf (or bull) worship recalls cults of Apis in Egypt, Minotaur in Crete.

Calgary (kăl'gùrē), city (pop. 129,060), S Alta., Canada, on Bow R. near foothills of Rocky Mts. A trade, rail, and industrial center of S Alta., it has oil refineries, meat-packing plants, and grain elevators. The city began 1875 as a fort of the Northwest Mounted Police.

Calhoun, John Caldwell (kăl"hōōn'), 1782–1850, American statesman and political philosopher. A "war hawk" as U.S. Representative from S.C. (1811–17). U.S. Secretary of War (1817–25); Vice President of U.S. (1825–32). Directed passage of S.C. ordinance of nullification (1832). U.S. Senator (1832–43, 1845–50); U.S. Secretary of State (1844–45). Leading defender of minority Southern cause against commercial, industrial North. Calhoun held that the Constitution estab. a government of concurrent majorities composed of the state governments and the Federal government, with states enjoying rights of veto (or nullification) and secession.

Calhoun, city (pop. 3,231), NW Ga., NNW of Atlanta. New Echota Marker Natl. Memorial, site of Cherokee's last cap. in Ga., is near.

Cali (kä'lē), city (pop. 88,366), W Colombia; founded 1536 by Benalcázar; important commercial center.

calico, name for plain-weave, cheap cotton cloth, usually printed; derived from Calicut cloth, fabric first imported into England from India, c.1830.

Calicut (kă'lĭkŭt"), city (pop. 126,352), SW Madras, India; port on Arabian Sea. Visited 1498 by Vasco da Gama. Once famed for calico.

California, state (156,803 sq. mi.; pop. 10,586,223), W U.S.; admitted 1850 as 31st state (free under COMPROMISE OF 1850); cap. SACRAMENTO. Second largest state in area and population. Bordered on S by Mexico, W by the Pacific (1,200-mi. coast), SE by Colorado R. Major ports (largest cities) are LOS ÁNGELES, SAN FRANCISCO, OAKLAND, SAN DIEGO, LONG BEACH. Calif. has amazing topographical, climatic contrasts. Central Valley is walled on W by COAST RANGES, E by SIERRA NEVADA (highest U.S. elevation is Mt. Whitney; lowest is near in Death Valley). In E and SE are vast wastes (e.g., MOJAVE DESERT), with, in contrast, reclaimed IMPERIAL VALLEY. Water supply and control are acute problems (extensive irrigation). Chief industries: petroleum, natural gas, food processing, aircraft, metalworking, textile, movie, fishing, resort. Agr. highly diversified (e.g., fruit, truck, hardy grains). Many minerals produced commercially (e.g., gold, copper). State has several national parks and monuments. Early exploration included voyages of Juan R. CABRILLO (1542), Sir Francis DRAKE (1579), Sebastián VIZCAÍNO (1602). Spanish colonizing began 1769. Control passed to Mexico in 1822. Gradually outsiders such as J. A. SUTTER came by sea and across mountains. Calif. briefly asserted independence in 1836; republic set up at Sonoma under influence of J. C. Frémont (1846). Area finally ceded to U.S. by Treaty of Guadalupe Hidalgo (1848). Gold strike of 1848 and completion of first transcontinental railroad (1869) brought settlers. Population increased sevenfold in 20th cent. due largely to industrial development of S Calif., real-estate boom in 1920s, exodus from Dust Bowl (1936–38), and influx of workers and service personnel in World War II.

California, Gulf of, arm of Pacific, c.700 mi. long, c.100 mi. wide, NW Mexico. Separates peninsula of Lower California from Sonora and Sinaloa. Pearl diving and deep-sea fishing are important.

California, University of, mainly at Berkeley and Los Angeles, with branches at San Francisco and elsewhere; land-grant and state supported, coed. Chartered 1868 and opened 1869 to succeed private Col. of California. Univ. of California at Los Angeles (UCLA), founded 1881 as normal school, was incorporated 1919. California School of Fine Arts at San Francisco is affiliated. Operates Lick Observatory and Scripps Inst. of Oceanography. Library has Western American history collection of H. H. BANCROFT.

California Institute of Technology: see PASADENA.

California laurel, beautiful evergreen tree (*Umbellularia californica*), native to California and Oregon and known also as Oregon myrtle, pepperwood, and California bay. It has fragrant flowers and aromatic foliage. It yields a volatile oil and the wood is used in boat building.

California poppy, annual or perennial wild flower (*Eschscholtzia californica*) with finely cut gray-green foliage and bright yellow blossoms. Native to the W Coast, it is the state flower of California.

californium, highly radioactive chemical element (symbol = Cf; atomic no.= 98), first produced (1950) in the cyclotron at the Univ. of California.

Caligula (kŭlĭg'yŏōlŭ) [little boots], nickname of Caius Caesar Germanicus, A.D. 12–A.D. 41, Roman emperor (A.D. 37–A.D. 41). The son of Germanicus, he got his name from wearing military boots when he was a small boy with his father on the Rhine. He succeeded Tiberius as emperor. An illness had apparently affected his mind, and his rule was one of senseless cruelty and despotism. He is reputed to have expressed regret that all the people did not have a single neck, to be severed with one blow. Also said to have made his horse a consul. He was finally assassinated, and Claudius I succeeded him.

caliphate (kă'lĭfăt), in Islam the office of the caliph (kă'lĭf), head of the theocratic organization as the agent of God. When Mohammed the Prophet died, Abu Bakr was chosen as first caliph. He was succeeded by Omar, Othman, and Ali (the Orthodox caliphs). After Ali's death, Islam split. The Omayyad family became caliphs at Damascus, but were not recognized by the Shiites, who in 750 won the caliphate for the descendants of Ali (the Abbasid family), who ruled from Baghdad. One Omayyad escaped to Spain, where later the Western Caliphate or Caliphate of Córdoba was set up, to last until 1031. A third rival line was supported by the Fatimites in Africa from 909 to 1171. When the Mongols took Baghdad (1258), the Abbasids fled to Egypt, where they nominally continued the caliphate until the Ottomans took Egypt (1517) and Selim I appropriated the title of caliph. This title was used by the Ottoman rulers of Turkey until it was abolished in 1924. See also IMAM.

Calixtines, another name for UTRAQUISTS.

Calixtus I, Saint (kŭlĭk'stŭs), c.160–c.222, pope (c.217–222). Rejected Montanism. Supposedly martyred. Also Callixtus, Callistus. Feast: Oct. 14.

Calixtus II, d. 1124, pope (1119–24). As archbishop of Vienne, he convened a synod (1112) to excommunicate Emperor Henry V. Calixtus triumphed over Henry's antipope Gregory VIII, came to an agreement with Henry in the Concordat of Worms (1122), and called the First Lateran Council.

Calixtus III, 1378–1458, pope (1455–58), a Spaniard named Alonso de Borja. Aided John Hunyadi in his fight against the Turks and tried to organize a crusade against them. He struggled with Alfonso V of Aragon. Estab. Borgia family in power in Italy.

Call, Richard Keith, 1791–1862, territorial governor of Fla. (1836–39, 1841–44). Led campaign against SEMINOLE INDIANS.

calla (kăl'ŭ), South African fleshy-rooted perennial (*Zantedeschia*). It has small flowers in a showy spathe; white in common calla lily, yellow or pink in others. Wild calla (*Calla palustris*) is bog plant of N Temperate Zone.

Callao (käyou'), port (pop. 71,217), W Peru, just W of Lima; notable Pacific port.

Calleja del Rey, Félix María (fä'lĕks märē'ä kälyä'hä dĕl rä'), 1750–1828?, Spanish general, viceroy of New Spain (1813–16), conde de Calderón. Successfully repressed beginning of revolution against Spain led by Hidalgo y Costilla.

Calles, Plutarco Elías (plōōtär'kō ālē'äs kä'yäs), 1877–1945, Mexican statesman, president (1924–28). Many objectives of revolution of 1910 were consolidated in his administration—agrarian and educational reforms, public works, army reorganization. Later became a conservative and opposed reforms of Lázaro Cárdenas.

Callias (kă'lēŭs), fl. 449 B.C., Athenian statesman. Supposed to have negotiated the Peace of Callias, an agreement which set up "spheres of influence" for Persia and Athens. Peace between the two lasted a half century.

Callicrates (kŭlĭ'krŭtēz), 5th cent. B.C., Greek architect. Helped build Parthenon (447–432 B.C.).

Callimachus (kŭlĭm'ŭkŭs), 2d half of 5th cent. B.C., Greek sculptor who reputedly originated the Corinthian capital.

Callimachus, b. 330? B.C., Hellenistic poet, critic. Among his more than 800 works are a literary catalogue and *Actia*, a collection of legends.

Calliope (kŭlī'ōpē) [Gr.,= beautiful of voice], in Greek mythology, greatest of MUSES, patron of epic poetry and eloquence; mother of ORPHEUS by Apollo.

calliopsis: see COREOPSIS.

Callirrhoë (kŭlĭr'ōē), wife of ALCMAEON.

Callisto (kŭlĭ'stō), in Greek legend, virgin attendant of Artemis. She bore a son, Arcas, to Zeus. As punishment she was transformed into a bear. Zeus later transferred them both to heaven, where she became Ursa Major and Arcas became Arcturus.

Calloc'h, Jean Pierre: see BRETON LITERATURE.

Callot, Jacques (zhäk' kälō'), 1592–1635, French engraver and etcher. Studied in Rome. Famous for ability to group crowds in a small space, as in the splendid series *Miseries of War*.

Calmar, Sweden: see KALMAR.

Calonne, Charles Alexandre de (shärl' älĕksä'drŭ dŭ kälōn'), 1734–1802, French statesman; controller general of finances (1783–87). His spending policy, designed to restore public credit, ended in disaster and hastened FRENCH REVOLUTION.

calorie, metric unit of heat measurement. Small calorie (gram-calorie or therm): heat required to raise temperature of 1 gm. of water at maximum density 1°C. Large or kilogram-calorie: heat required to raise temperature of 1 kg. of water at maximum density 1°C. Specific heat is number of calories needed to raise temperature of 1 gm. of any substance 1°C. In physics and chemistry term *calorie* usually means small calorie; in dietetics large calorie used to indicate amount of heat energy food can yield. **Calorimeter** determines number of calories given off by substance in combustion or other chemical reaction, measured by rise in temperature of given quantity of water.

Calpurnia (kălpûr'nēŭ), d. after 44 B.C., third wife of Julius Caesar, to whom she was married in 59 B.C. In story she is the model of the faithful, long-suffering wife.

Calumet, resort village (pop. 1,256), on Keweenaw Peninsula, extreme N Mich. Grew mainly after development of Calumet and Hecla copper mine.

Calumet City, city (pop. 15,799), NE Ill., S suburb of Chicago near Ind. line, in industrial area. Name changed from West Hammond 1924. L. Calumet, just N, connects with L. Michigan.

Calvados (kälvädôs'), department (2,198 sq. mi.; pop. 400,026), N France, in Normandy; cap. Caen. Gives name to strong apple brandy.

Calvary (kăl'vŭrē) [Latin,= a skull] or **Golgotha** (gŏl'-gŭthù) [Heb.,= a skull], place outside wall of Jerusalem where Jesus was crucified. Mat. 27.33; Mark 15.-22; Luke 23.33; John 19.17–20. Church of the Holy Sepulchre now stands on traditional site, but scholars disagree as to exact location.

Calvé, Emma (kälvā'), 1866–1942, French operatic soprano. Sang at the Metropolitan Opera, New York, 1893–1904. Carmen was one of her famous roles.

Calvert, George, 1st **Baron Baltimore,** c.1580–1632, British colonizer. In 1632 he was granted territory N of Potomac R. which became province of MARYLAND. His grandson, **Charles Calvert,** 3d **Baron Baltimore,** 1637–1715, succeeded to proprietorship in 1675. His arbitrary rule was overthrown by revolt in 1689.

Calvin, John, 1509–64, French Protestant theologian of Reformation, b. Noyon. A man learned in theology and law, he experienced (1533) "sudden conversion"; leaving Catholicism, he became a hunted Protestant leader. In 1536 began work at Geneva. Banished in 1538, he preached at Basel and Strasbourg until welcomed back to Geneva in 1541. His monumental *Institutes of the Christian Religion* (written after 1531) sets forth basic Calvinist theology. This diverged from Catholic doctrine in such fundamental ways as rejecting papal authority, accepting justification by faith alone, and systematizing the doctrine of predestination. Calvin held that the Bible is sole source of God's law, and man's duty is to interpret it and preserve order in the world: this aim he set out to realize in Geneva by founding the government solely on religious law. From his teachings grew one of the most important of Christian religious systems, **Calvinism.** Broadly, Calvinism is the system in the Protestant "Reformed churches" (see PRESBYTERIANISM) as distinct from those professing Lutheran doctrines; the chief distinction is in the doctrine of predestination. Calvinism differs from Catholicism fundamentally in holding that redemption is for elect alone, the free gift of God not to be won by good works. Calvinism characterized the Covenanters in Scotland, the Puritans in England and in New England, and the Huguenots in France.

Calvinistic Methodist Church, Protestant denomination. Originated (1735–36) in Wales, where it kept strong as a movement. Separated from Established Church 1811; adopted confession of faith 1823. In U.S. united (1920) with Presbyterian Church.

Calvo, Carlos (kär'lōs käl'vō), 1824–1906, Argentine diplomat and historian, writer on international law. Principle known as **Calvo Doctrine** would prohibit diplomatic intervention to enforce private claims before local remedies have been exhausted. **Calvo Clause,** found in constitutions, treaties, statutes, and contracts, is concrete application of his doctrine.

Calydon (kăl'ĭdùn), ancient city of S Aetolia, Greece. It was scene of legendary **Calydonian hunt,** successfully led by Meleager, prince of Calydon, against a wild boar loosed by Artemis to destroy city for neglect of a sacrifice. Among the hunters were Jason, Castor and Pollux, Theseus, and Atalanta.

Calymna, Greek island: see DODECANESE.

Calypso (kùlĭp'sō), nymph in the *Odyssey*. Lived on isl. of Ogygia, where Odysseus stayed seven years.

calyx (kā'lĭks), outer ring of typical FLOWER parts, made up of sepals which are usually green and leaf-like or united into a tube. Often colored if COROLLA is absent (e.g., buttercup). See *ill.,* p. 783.

Cam or **Granta,** river of England rising in Essex and flowing NE past Cambridge to the Ouse.

Camacho, Manuel Ávila: see ÁVILA CAMACHO.

Camagüey (kämägwä'), city (pop. 80,509), E central Cuba; commercial center of agricultural region producing cattle and sugar.

Camargue (kämärg'), island, SE France, in the Rhone delta. Intensive cattle ranching.

camass or **camas** (kăm'ùs), hardy bulbous plant (*Camassia*), with spikes of dark blue or white flowers. Native to W North America, found in moist soils. Some species grown in gardens.

Cambacérès, Jean Jacques de (zhä' zhäk' dù kōbäsärēs'), 1753–1824, French revolutionist and legislator. Second consul (1799–1804); archchancellor of the empire under Napoleon I. Created duke of Parma 1808. Prepared CODE NAPOLÉON.

Cambay, Gulf of, inlet of the Arabian Sea, between Bombay and Saurashtra states.

Camberwell, metropolitan borough (pop. 179,729), S London, England; residential and park section.

Cambio, Arnolfo di: see ARNOLFO DI CAMBIO.

cambium (kăm'bēùm), thin layer of tissue between bark and wood of stem, most developed in trees. It is the growth area that causes increase in diameter of stems.

Cambodia (kămbō'dēù), state (c.69,900 sq. mi.; pop. c.3,700,000), Indo-China; cap. Pnom Penh. On saucer-shaped plain drained by Mekong R. and surrounded by mountain ranges. Climate is tropical. TONLE SAP is important for fisheries. Rice-growing area in S. Sericulture and weaving are only industries. Prominent during era of KHMER EMPIRE, Cambodia became prey of Siam and Annam 15th–19th cent. King of Cambodia appealed 1854 for French intervention; French protectorate estab. 1863. French-Siamese treaty (1907) restored Cambodia's W provinces. After World War II France gave Cambodia more self-government within French Union.

Cambodian art. Pre-Khmer (pre-7th cent.) art, such as the *Harihara* of Andet and shrines at Sambor and Kornpong Thom, was influenced by Indian Gupta art. Classical period (8th–13th cent.) of Cambodian art of Khmer Empire evolved from Hindu and Buddhist iconography. Step-pyramid plan and profuse sculpture of great temple complexes at Angkor Wat and Angkor Thom were involved in symbolization of "world mountain." Modeled with sensuous subtlety, cult images had closed or half-closed eyes, full lips set in sweet smile. Cambodian culture merged with that of Siam after 14th cent., but distinctive forms survived in music and dance.

Cambon, Paul (pôl' käbō'), 1843–1924, French ambassador to England (1898–1920). One of chief framers of Triple Entente. His brother, **Jules Cambon** (zhül), 1845–1935, was made ambassador to U.S. 1897; mediated peace preliminaries of Spanish-American War. Ambassador to Germany 1907–14.

Cambrai (kābrā'), city (pop. 24,558), Nord dept., N France, on Escaut (Scheldt) R. Old textile center; cambric first manufactured here. Ruled by bishops until seized by Spain (1595); to France 1677. Damaged in both world wars.

Cambrai, League of, 1508–10, alliance of Emperor Maximilian I, Pope Julius II, Louis XII of France, Ferdinand V of Aragon, and several Italian states against Venice. French routed Venetians at Agnadello (1509), but in 1510 Julius II made peace with Venice and formed HOLY LEAGUE against France.

Cambrai, Treaty of, called the **Ladies' Peace,** treaty signed 1529 by Louise of Savoy and Margaret of Austria, representing FRANCIS I of France and Emperor Charles V respectively. It renewed Treaty of Madrid but left Burgundy to France.

Cambria (kăm'brēù) [from Welsh *Cymry* = Welshmen], ancient name of Wales.

Cambrian Mountains, a name for mountains of Wales.

Cambrian period (kăm'brēun, kām'-), first period of PALEOZOIC ERA. Large continental areas lay under shallow seas; thus Cambrian rocks are mostly sedimentary with thickness up to 13,000 ft. in Appalachian region. For the first time fossils of marine invertebrates were abundant—TRILOBITE, brachiopods, snails, sponges. No vertebrate fossils yet discovered, but possibility is not excluded. See GEOLOGY, table.

Cambridge (kām'–), municipal borough (pop. 81,463), co. town of Cambridgeshire, England, on Cam R. The seat of CAMBRIDGE UNIVERSITY, it is an ancient market town retaining much medieval atmosphere. Has many old churches, including St. Benedict's (10th cent.), St. Edward's (13th cent.), and Church of the Holy Sepulchre, one of four Norman round churches in England.

Cambridge. 1 Town (pop. 10,351), Eastern Shore, Md., on Choptank R., SE of Annapolis; founded 1684. Fishing and yachting port, it has seafood industry and processing of foodstuffs. **2** City (pop. 120,740), E Mass., on Charles R. and NW of Boston; settled 1630. Seat of HARVARD UNIVERSITY, Radcliffe Col., MASSACHUSETTS INSTITUTE OF TECHNOLOGY. Washington took command of troops here, July 3, 1775. Stephen Daye estab. first printing press in America here. Longfellow's home is memorial. He and J. R. Lowell are buried in Mt. Auburn Cemetery. Mfg. of metal products, rubber goods, clothing, building supplies, and soap. **3** City (pop. 14,739), E Ohio, NE of Zanesville; settled 1798. Center of agr. and coal area with mfg. of glass, furniture, and pottery.

Cambridge Bay, government post and U.S.–Canadian weather station, SE shore of Victoria Isl., Northwest Territories, Canada.

Cambridge Platform, constitution for government and discipline in Congregational churches; adopted (1648) by synod at Cambridge, Mass. Group in Conn. adopted (1708) new centralizing Saybrook Platform. See also CONGREGATIONALISM.

Cambridge Platonists, school of philosophy at Cambridge Univ. in the late 17th cent. Reacting to mechanism of Thomas Hobbes, the Platonists revived idealism. Among them were Robert Grenville, Ralph Cudworth, Henry More, and John Norris.

Cambridgeshire or **Cambridge,** inland county (864 sq. mi.; pop. 255,901), E England; co. town Cambridge. Isle of Ely, northern section of county, is separate administrative unit. Area is mostly fenland, with chalky East Anglian range (including Gogmagog Hills) in south. Efforts to reclaim the fens, dating back to Romans, completed by vast drainage project 1653. Region has since been agr. Ely, with its famous cathedral, has been an important ecclesiastical center since Anglo-Saxon days.

Cambridge University, Cambridge, England, one of two anc. English universities. Probably had beginnings in 12th cent. Residences or colleges, estab. by end of 13th cent., named for church to which they were attached or for saint to whom dedicated. They are Peterhouse or St. Peter's (1284), Clare (1326), Pembroke (1347), Gonville and Caius (1348), Trinity Hall (1350), Corpus Christi (1352), King's (1441), Queens' (1448), St. Catharine's (1473), Jesus (1496), Christ's (1505), St. John's (1511), Magdalene (1542; pronounced môd'lĭn), Trinity (1546), Emmanuel (1584), Sidney Sussex (1596), and modern colleges, Downing (1800) and Selwyn (1882). Girton (1869) and Newnham (1873) are women's colleges; women admitted to full degree only in 1948. University, which has 19 faculties, has led in science and modern literature. James Chadwick discovered the neutron at famed Cavendish Laboratory here. Univ. Library, Fitzwilliam Mus., and botanic gardens are noteworthy. Cambridge Univ. Press dates from 16th cent. As at OXFORD UNIVERSITY, instruction is by lecturers and tutors (called supervisors). B.A. degree is awarded on passing tripos exam (honors exam at Oxford) after nine terms of continuous residence. Initials of a degree usually followed by Cantab. from Cantabrigia, Latin name of Cambridge.

Cambronne, Pierre (pyĕr' kăbrôn'), 1770–1842, French

general. Commanded Old Guard at Waterloo. Replied to British invitation to surrender with a brisk vulgarism, thus gaining immortality.

Cambyses (kămbī'sēz), d. 521 B.C., king of Persia, son and successor of Cyrus the Great. He disposed of his brother Smerdis, but later a false Smerdis rose to haunt him just after an excursion to pacify Egypt. He died, possibly by suicide.

Camden, Charles Pratt, 1st Earl: see PRATT, CHARLES.

Camden. 1 City (pop. 11,372), S Ark., on Ouachita R.; settled 1824. Shipping point for cotton, corn, and poultry. Mfg. of furniture, paper, and pottery. **2** City (pop. 124,555), W N.J. on Delaware R. (bridged 1926 to Philadelphia); settled 1681. City grew as commercial and mfg. center after coming of railroad 1834. Mfg. of textiles, chemicals, electronic and television products, phonographs, radios, and pens. Has canneries, oil refineries, railroad shops, and marine terminals. Here are home and grave of Walt Whitman. **3** City (pop. 6,986), N central S.C., near Wateree R. NE of Columbia. Trade and processing center in pine and farm area with textile and lumber mills. Winter resort. Battles of Camden (Aug. 16, 1780) and Hobkirks Hill (April 25, 1781) fought near by in CAROLINA CAMPAIGN of American Revolution. Fired in British evacuation of May 8, 1781. Taken and partly burned (Feb. 24, 1865) by part of Sherman's army in Civil War.

camel, hoofed mammal of family Camelidae, which includes true camels (Asian genus *Camelus*) and South American genus *Lama* (wild guanaco, vicuña, domesticated alpaca, llama). Arabian camel or dromedary (*Camelus dromedarius*) has one hump; Bactrian camel (*C. bactrianus*) of central Asia has two humps. Fat is stored in humps. Color varies from dirty white to dark brown; the neck is long; the ears are small, and the teeth strong. Can carry heavy loads (500–600 lb., more for Bactrian camel) and survive without water for several days (longer if juicy plants are available).

camellia (–mēl'–, –mē'–), Asiatic evergreen tree or shrub (*Camellia*), allied to the tea plant. Grown under glass or outdoors in warm regions for its beautiful flowers, single or double, in white or red shades. Leaves are glossy dark green.

Camelot (kăm'ŭlŏt), the seat of King Arthur's court in the ARTHURIAN LEGEND.

Camembert cheese (kă'mǔmbâr), a mold-ripened CHEESE.

camera, light-proof container with lens that focuses image of object on photographic plate or film (see PHOTOGRAPHY). When shutter is open, film is exposed. Many variations in parts and attachments. **Camera lucida** (lōō'sĭdǔ), optical instrument that extends virtual image of object on plane surface so outline can be traced; usually attached to eyepiece of microscope. **Camera obscura** (ŏbskyōō'rǔ), light-tight box with convex lens at one end and screen for image at other; used to make drawings.

Camerarius, Rudolph Jacob (kămǔrâ'rēǔs), 1665–1721, German physician and botanist, first to present definite facts concerning sex in plants.

Cameron, Richard, d. 1680, Scottish leader of Covenanters. Opposed reestablishment of episcopacy in Scotland after Restoration. He was killed by royal troops, but Cameronian sect grew strong, forming a presbytery (1743) as Reformed Presbyterians. Most joined Free Church of Scotland (1876).

Cameron, Simon, 1799–1889, American politician. U.S. Senator from Pa. (1845–49, 1857–61, 1867–77). Notoriously corrupt U.S. Secretary of War (1861–62). Machine he created so dominated Pa. that it was not until 1936 that Democrats carried state in a national election. Definition of an "honest politician" as one who "when bought, stays bought" is attributed to Cameron.

Cameron, city (pop. 5,052), E central Texas, S of Waco, in farm area.

Cameroons, former German colony, W Africa, between Gulf of Guinea and L. Chad. German possession of area was recognized in 1902. In 1911 parts of French Equatorial Africa were added, but these were restored in 1919, when original colony was divided into French and British mandates under League of Nations. In 1946 they became UN trust territories. **British Cameroons** (34,081 sq. mi.; pop. 1,027,500) comprises two detached sections on E border of Nigeria; governed with NIGERIA. **French Cameroons** (166,489 sq. mi.; pop. 3,003,200) fronts on Gulf of Guinea; governed as separate territory by a high commissioner at Yaoundé.

Camille: see DUMAS, ALEXANDRE (fils).

Camillus (Marcus Furius Camillus) (kŭmǐ′lŭs), d. 365? B.C., Roman hero. Elected dictator five times (396–67 B.C.), he each time won a signal victory.

Camisards (kämēsär′), Protestant peasants of the Cévennes, France, who rebelled against religious persecution (1702–10). Successfully used guerrilla methods against superior forces. After defection of their leader Jean CAVALIER they fought on under Roland Laporte but were slowly forced into submission.

Cammaerts, Émile (ämēl′ kä′märts), 1878–, Belgian poet and dramatist, noted for poems of World War I.

Camões or **Camoens, Luís de** (both: lōoēsh′ dù kumō′ĭsh), 1524?–1580, Portuguese epic poet, greatest figure of Portuguese literature. Vasco da Gama's voyage is the main theme of his epic *The Lusiads* (Port. *Os Lusíadas* = sons of Lusus, i.e., the Portuguese), which is modeled on Vergil and influenced by Ariosto, but is an original epic of world literature. Also wrote sonnets and other lyrics.

camomile or **chamomile** (kăm′ùmīl), perennial plant (*Anthemis nobilis*), with daisylike white or yellow flowers and aromatic, finely cut foliage. Dried flowers are source of camomile tea.

Camorra (kùmô′rù), Italian criminal association in Naples and Sicily. First appeared c.1830, grew all-powerful through intimidation, blackmail, bribery; extended terror to Italian immigrants in U.S. Action by citizens of Naples secured its dissolution (1911).

camouflage (kă′mùfläzh), in warfare, disguising of objects to deceive the observer as to their location and so protect them from attack. The principle is very old, a simple form being the wearing of white or light-colored clothing by warriors crossing a snowy waste or a sandy desert. Development of large-scale scientific camouflage came with World War I, when ships were dazzle-painted and false landscapes were created to conceal forts and factories. With the heavy air bombardments of World War II, the use of camouflage to deceive air observers grew very elaborate with the construction of dummy towns and factories to lure bombers as well as with concealing devices for real strategic points.

Camp, Walter (Chauncey), 1859–1925, American football expert, long coach at Yale.

Campagna di Roma (kämpä′nyä dē rō′mä), plain surrounding Rome, Italy. Malarial and arid until reclamation work of 19th and 20th cent. Flocks of grazing sheep and ruins of Roman aqueducts and tombs give landscape a special charm.

Campanella, Tommaso (tōm-mä′zō kämpänĕl′lä), 1568–1639, Italian Renaissance philosopher and poet, a Dominican. *The City of the Sun* is an account of a utopian society, recalling Plato's *Republic*. Insisted on the preeminence of faith, but foreshadowed scientific empiricism.

Campania (kämpä′nyä), region (5,250 sq. mi.; pop. 3,696,632), S Italy, between Apennines and Tyrrhenian Sea; cap. Naples. Other cities: Benevento, Salerno, Caserta. Fertile plains and hills covered with vineyards, orchards, olive groves. Conquered by Rome 4th–2d cent. B.C. In Middle Ages it was held, successively, by Goths, Byzantines, Lombards, Normans. From 1282 it shared history of kingdom of NAPLES.

campanula: see BELLFLOWER.

Campbell, Scottish noble family. Archibald Campbell, 5th earl of Argyll, 1530–73, fluctuated in support of Elizabeth and Mary Queen of Scots. Was lord chancellor under James VI. **Archibald Campbell, 8th earl of Argyll** and **1st marquess of Argyll,** 1607–61, was a powerful Presbyterian statesman. After surrender of Charles I to Scots, he tried to secure Presbyterian settlement in England; crowned Charles II in Scotland. Executed for treason at Restoration. His son, **Archibald Campbell, 9th earl of Argyll,** 1629?–1685, both royalist and Protestant, opposed extreme measures against the COVENANTERS. Was beheaded after leading rebellion in aid of duke of MONMOUTH. His son, **Archibald Campbell, 1st duke of Argyll,** d. 1703, was partly responsible for massacre of the Macdonalds at Glencoe (1692). **John Campbell, 2d duke of Argyll** and **duke of Greenwich,** 1678–1743, Scottish general, supported union with England. Put down rebellion of JACOBITES 1715. His brother, **Archibald Campbell, 3d duke of Argyll,** 1682–1761, commissioner for the union (1706), served as Scottish peer in the united Parliament. Supported Robert Walpole.

Campbell, Alexander, 1788–1866, American clergyman, b. Ireland. His father, **Thomas Campbell,** 1763–1854, settled in W Pa., where he and his congregation withdrew from Presbyterian Church. Alexander came to U.S. in 1809. Became leader of group, for a time (1813–20) joined to Baptists, later to be DISCIPLES OF CHRIST. Advocated return to early Christian simplicity. Founded (1840) Bethany Col. (W.Va.).

Campbell, John, 1st earl of Breadalbane, c.1635–1717, Scottish chieftain. Aided the Restoration. Brutally massacred Macdonald clan at Glencoe (1692) for unavoidable delay in taking oath of submission to William III. Joined in Jacobite rebellion (1715).

Campbell, John Archibald, 1811–89, American jurist. Associate Justice of U.S. Supreme Court (1853–62). Sought to avoid war by mediation.

Campbell, Sir Malcolm, 1885–1949, English racing enthusiast. Set speed records driving motorcycles, airplanes, automobiles, speedboats.

Campbell, Mrs. Patrick, 1865–1940, English actress, whose maiden name was Beatrice Stella Tanner. Won fame in Pinero's *Second Mrs. Tanqueray* 1893. A friend of Shaw's, she created part of Eliza Doolittle in his *Pygmalion* in 1912.

Campbell, Robert: see ROB ROY.

Campbell, Robert, 1808–94, Canadian fur trader and explorer, b. Scotland. Discovered Pelly R. 1840. Descended it in 1843 to its confluence with Lewes R. and here estab. Fort Selkirk.

Campbell, Thomas, 1763–1854: see CAMPBELL, ALEXANDER.

Campbell, Thomas, 1777–1844, Scottish narrative and lyric poet. Wrote long didactic (*The Pleasures of Hope,* 1799) and narrative (*Gertrude of Wyoming,* 1809; *Theodric,* 1824) poems, but is best remembered for patriotic verses, "Hohenlinden," "Ye Mariners of England" and particular lines (e.g., "Coming events cast their shadows before," in "Lochiel's Warning").

Campbell, (William) Wilfred, 1861?–1918, Canadian author. Known for *Lake Lyrics* (1889), volume of nature poetry. *Collected Poems* appeared 1905.

Campbell, city (pop. 12,882), NE Ohio, near Youngstown, on Mahoning R.; called East Youngstown until 1926. Has steel mills.

Campbell-Bannerman, Sir Henry, 1836–1908, British statesman. As prime minister (1905–08), furthered Liberal measures and autonomy for Transvaal and Orange Free State.

Campbellites: see DISCIPLES OF CHRIST.

Campbellton, town (pop. 7,754), N N.B., Canada, on Restigouche R. and W of Dalhousie; a port. Lumbering center and outfitting point for sportsmen.

Camp Borden (20,000 acres), largest military training center in Canada, S Ont., NNW of Toronto.

Campeche (kämpā′chā), state (19,672 sq. mi.; pop. 121,411), SE Mexico, on Gulf of Campeche. Comprises most of W half of Yucatan peninsula. Principal ports Carmen (pop. 7,687) and Campeche (pop. 23,277; also cap.).

Camperdown (kăm'pùrdoun"), Dutch *Kamperduin,* locality near village of Kamp, NW Netherlands, on North Sea. Scene of British naval victory over Dutch (1797).

Camp Fire Girls, American organization for girls 7 to 18 years old; founded 1910 by Luther H. Gulick and others. Object is "to perpetuate the spiritual ideals of the home" and to develop health and character.

Camp Hill, residential borough (pop. 5,934), S Pa., across Susquehanna R. from Harrisburg.

camphor, volatile oil, solid at ordinary temperatures. Commercial camphor, or camphor gum, is white, crystalline, and translucent, and has a penetrating odor. Natural camphor is obtained by steam distillation of wood of the camphor tree (*Cinnamomum camphora*) native to China, Japan, and Formosa, but introduced elsewhere. Much camphor is made synthetically from a turpentine derivative. It is used especially in making celluloid, explosives, and moth preventives, and in medicine and perfumery.

Camphuysen, Dirk Rafelszoon (dĭrk' rä'fĕlsōn kämphoi'zùn), 1586–1627, Dutch painter, author of short religious poems. Most of small interiors and landscapes once ascribed to him are now attributed to his nephew, **Raphael Camphuysen** (rä'fäĕl), 1598–1657, and his son, **Govert Camphuysen** (gō'vùrt), 1624–c.1674.

Campi, Giulio (jōō'lyō käm'pē), c.1500–c.1572, Italian painter and architect, founder of school of painters at Cremona. Did altarpieces and frescoes. His pupils included his brothers, **Cavaliere Antonio Campi** (kävälyä'rä), b. before 1536, d. 1591, and **Vincenzo Campi** (vĕnchän'tsō), 1532–91, portrait and still-life painter. Another brother, **Bernardino Campi,** 1522–c.1590, did colossal biblical frescoes in cupola of San Sigismundo (Cremona).

Campian, Thomas: see CAMPION, THOMAS.

Campin, Robert (käm'pĭn), 1375–1444, Flemish artist, identified with the Master of Flémalle who did *Annunciation* (Brussels). Taught Roger van der Weyden.

Campinas (kämpē'nùsh), city (pop. 101,746), E São Paulo, Brazil. Once a coffee-growing area, it suffered from depletion of soil and falling price of coffee. Now has diversified farming.

Campion, Edmund, c.1540–1581, English Jesuit martyr. At Oxford he was a favorite of Queen Elizabeth I, but in 1571 he fled to the Continent and later became a Jesuit. In 1580 he and Robert Persons came as missionaries to England. He converted many but was taken, tortured, and executed.

Campion or **Campian, Thomas,** 1567–1620, English poet, composer, and lutanist. He wrote Latin poetry and masques, but is most important for his lute songs.

camp meeting, outdoor religious gathering, held in summer over period of days, typical of frontier U.S. Originated c.1800 in Ky. under preaching of James McGready and spread rapidly with revival movement. Camp meetings were held by evangelical sects and were characterized by emotional fervor attendant upon "conversion."

Campoamor, Ramón de (rämōn' dā kämpōämōr'), 1817–1901, Spanish lyric poet.

Campobello, island (pop. 1,181), 9 mi. long, 3 mi. wide, in Passamaquoddy Bay, between Maine and N.B., Canada. Campobello village is on W coast. Summer resort and fishing base. Passed to Canada in Convention of 1817. Summer home of Pres. F. D. Roosevelt was here.

Campo Formio, Treaty of (käm'pō fōr'myō), Oct., 1797, French-Austrian peace treaty at end of Bonaparte's Italian campaign. Austria ceded Austrian Netherlands to France, secretly promised France left bank of Rhine. Venetian republic, despite neutrality, was dissolved: most of it (including Dalmatia) went to Austria; the Ionian Isls. to France; the rest to CISALPINE REPUBLIC.

Campos, Arsenio Martínez de: see MARTÍNEZ DE CAMPOS, ARSENIO.

Campos (kăm'pôsh), city (pop. 63,384), NE Rio de Janeiro state, Brazil, on the Paraíba near mouth; commercial center of rich agr. region.

Camrose, town (pop. 4,131), central Alta., Canada, SE of Edmonton. Has Scandinavian Lutheran college.

Camulodunum: see COLCHESTER, England.

Camus, Albert (älbĕr' kämü'), 1913–, French author. Close in mood to existentialism, he stresses the gloomy absurdity of life in such novels as *The Stranger* (1942; Eng. tr., 1946) and *The Plague* (1947; Eng. tr., 1948).

Cana (kā'nù), ancient town of Galilee where Jesus performed His first miracle by turning water into wine at a wedding. John 2.1,11; 4.46,54; 21.2.

Canaan (kā'nùn). **1** Son of Ham, ancestor of the Canaanites. Gen. 9.20–27; 10.6,15,19. **2** Name given by Israelites to Palestine before they occupied it. To them it was the land promised them by God and goal of their wanderings after leaving Egypt. Gen. 12.5; Ex. 3.8; Num. 13.17,29; 14.45; 21.3; Joshua 22.11,32; Judges 1.

Canachus (kā'nùkùs), fl. 6th cent. B.C., Greek sculptor, known for his great statues of Apollo.

Canada, nation (3,847,597 sq. mi. including inland waters; pop. 14,009,429), N North America, N of U.S.; member of British Commonwealth of Nations; cap. OTTAWA. Consists of ten provinces (NEWFOUNDLAND, NOVA SCOTIA, NEW BRUNSWICK, PRINCE EDWARD ISLAND, QUEBEC, ONTARIO, MANITOBA, SASKATCHEWAN, ALBERTA, BRITISH COLUMBIA), the NORTHWEST TERRITORIES, and YUKON territory. Separated from U.S. by a 3,986.9 mi. land border and the Great Lakes. N it fronts on Arctic Ocean where Boothia Peninsula and ARCTIC ARCHIPELAGO thrust far into the Arctic. Hudson and James bays cut deeply into NE coast. Atlantic coast, broken by Gulf of St. Lawrence, is swept by Labrador Current from N and Gulf Stream from S. Pacific coast is deeply indented with many islands offshore. The LAURENTIAN PLATEAU, a rolling wooded area rich in minerals, covers c.50% of the nation. Major mountains are Canadian Rockies between Alta. and B.C. and Coast Mts. of W B.C. River and lake country is general in N Que. and Ont., the N Prairie Provs., and the N.W.T. Fertile lowlands adjoin Great Lakes and highly productive plains cover S Prairie Provs. Agr. is major industry, followed by ranching, dairying, and lumbering. Although extensive mineral resources remain untouched, there is important mining of gold, copper, coal, nickel, pitchblende, petroleum, and uranium. Fishing and trapping are traditionally important occupations. Water resources have been developed to power Canadian industries. Ont. and Que. are leading industrial provinces. In general population is centered in Maritime Provs. and the S areas of Que., Ont., the Prairie Provs., and B.C. Many groups are represented, notably French (esp. in Que., where French is accepted language), English, Scottish, Irish, and German. John Cabot explored E Canadian coast 1497 and estab. English claims. In 1534 the Frenchman, Jacques Cartier, planted a cross on Gaspé Peninsula. Quebec was estab. 1608 by CHAMPLAIN. The St. Lawrence became gateway to new French empire. Settlements were bases for fur traders, explorers, missionaries, and empire builders, among them LA SALLE, LAVAL, FRONTENAC, MARQUETTE, JOLLIET, and VÉRENDRYE. British opposition to New France centered in ACADIA. Meanwhile HUDSON's BAY COMPANY was building fur-trading empire in NW. Imperial contest closed with defeat of French under MONTCALM on Plains of Abraham (1759); British gained Canada by Treaty of Paris (1763). Exploration opened up land in W. UNITED EMPIRE LOYALISTS advanced Canada. Fight for responsible government, including separate futile rebellions in 1837–38 led by W. L. MACKENZIE in Upper Canada and Louis PAPINEAU in Lower Canada, resulted in victory for democratic groups over entrenched FAMILY COMPACT. Movement for confederation resulted in the BRITISH NORTH AMERICA ACT. Territory was added as Ru-

PERT'S LAND was purchased from Hudson's Bay Co. (1869) and B.C. joined the Union in 1871, P.E.I. in 1873, and Newfoundland in 1949. Man. became a province in 1870, and Sask. and Alta. in 1905. Mining operations developed rapidly after KLONDIKE gold rush in 1896. Organization of cooperatives (in N.S. and Prairie Provs.) and of SOCIAL CREDIT and CO-OPERATIVE COMMONWEALTH FEDERATION originated new forms to meet economic and political problems. Canada made valuable contributions to both World Wars in man power, goods, and in providing air and naval bases.

Canada, Lower: see QUEBEC, province.

Canada balsam, yellow, oily turpentine from BALSAM FIR. Used in preparation of slides for microscopic work, and in paints and polishes.

Canada Company, founded by John GALT, chartered in England 1826 for purpose of making settlements. Held lands on L. Huron side of S Ont., Canada, with hq. at GUELPH. Built first road from L. Ontario to L. Huron. Successful colonizing venture.

Canada First movement, party in Canada formed soon after confederation (1867) to encourage growth of nonpartisan loyalty to new dominion. Although short-lived, its ideals influenced Canadian writers and older political parties.

Canada jay: see JAY.

Canadian, river rising in E N.Mex. and flowing 906 mi. E across Texas Panhandle and most of Okla. Here, joined by North Canadian R., it enters Arkansas R. SE of Muskogee.

Canadian literature, English. Until after 1800 only notable works were recorded travels of explorers. First novelist was John Richardson, whose *Wacousta* (1832) popularized genre of national historical novel. In *The Clockmaker* (1836) T. C. Haliburton began humorous series on Sam Slick, Yankee peddler. Important novelists writing c.1900 include William Kirby, Sir Gilbert Parker, and L. M. Montgomery. Since 1900 Canadian novels have tended toward stricter realism but have remained predominantly regional. Well-known authors are Mazo de la Roche and Hugh MacLennan. Humorous essays of Stephen Leacock remain perennial favorites. Canadian poetry was late in developing. The long poetic drama, *Saul* (1857), by Charles Heavysege, achieved recognition. Beginning c.1880 the "Confederation school"—C. G. D. Roberts, Archibald Lampman, Bliss Carman, and Duncan Campbell Scott—began producing large body of romantic poetry. After her death Isabella V. Crawford was recognized as a genuine poet. Other poets of early 20th cent. include W. H. Drummond, John McCrae, and Robert W. Service. Well-known modern poet is Edwin J. Pratt, who began writing his imaginative, heroic poems in 1926.

Canadian literature, French. The inspiration of almost all Canadian writing in French has been the passionate concern of French Canadians to preserve their identity. Its themes have been found in nationalism, simple lives and folkways of the habitants (French Canadian farmers), devotion to the Catholic Church, and the tie to mother France. First artistic expression of this "racial" impulse was F. X. Garneau's *Histoire du Canada* (1845–48). This classic of French Canadian nationalism inspired first nationalist poet, Octave Crémazie, and the Quebec school of writers—among them L. H. Fréchette, H. R. Casgrain, and Antoine Gérin-Lajoie. Louis Hémon's *Maria Chapdelaine* (1913) gave impetus to more realistic fiction, and there has followed a stream of works on habitant life of backwoods, farms, and villages.

Canadian Mounted Police: see ROYAL CANADIAN MOUNTED POLICE.

Canadian National Railways, government owned and operated transportation system in Canada extending from coast to coast with many branch lines in each province; unified 1923. Amalgamation of several separate private and government lines.

Canadian Pacific Railway, transcontinental transportation system in Canada, extending into U.S., privately owned and operated in competition with Canadian National Railways. Line completed to Pacific coast 1885, after PACIFIC SCANDAL.

canal. Irrigation canals are extremely ancient. Transportation canals (level or with inclines for hauling vessels to each level) came later. Modern canals use locks (see LOCK, CANAL). Canals connect inland waterways and seas to great economic advantage. Used also to avoid falls and shoals, to reclaim land (drainage canals).

Canaletto (känälät'tō), 1697–1768, Venetian painter, whose real name was Antonio Canale or Canal. Known for his Venetian scenes. His nephew and pupil, Bernardo Bellotto (c.1724–80), architectural and landscape painter, was also called Canaletto.

Canal Zone: see PANAMA CANAL ZONE.

Canandaigua (känündä'gwù), city (pop. 8,332), W central N.Y., at N end of Canandaigua L. and SE of Rochester; settled 1789. FINGER LAKES resort and farm trade center. Pickering treaty with the Six Nations signed here, 1794. Courthouse was scene of Susan B. Anthony's trial for voting, 1873.

canary, bird of finch family, a descendant either of wild serin finch or similar wild canary of Canary Isls., Madeira, Azores. Wild birds mostly gray or green; breeders developed both plain and variegated birds of yellow, buff, or greenish. Breed readily in captivity. Finest singers (Harz mt. and St. Andreasberg canaries) originated in Germany.

Canary Islands, group of seven islands (2,912 sq. mi.; pop. 680, 294), off NW Africa, in the Atlantic. Comprise two provinces of Spain: Santa Cruz de Tenerife (including Tenerife, largest island) and Las Palmas (including Grand Canary, most important and populous). Conquered in 15th cent. by Spain. In French Revolutionary Wars, Nelson was repulsed in 1797 at Santa Cruz. Produce tropical fruit and canned fish.

canasta: see RUMMY.

Canaveral, Cape (kùnăv'ùrùl), E Fla., on Atlantic coast, SE of Titusville. Has lighthouse. It is a guided missiles proving ground.

Canberra (kăn'bùrù), city (pop. 15,156), cap. of Commonwealth of Australia, in Australian Capital Territory. Site chosen 1908, city founded 1913. Succeeded Melbourne as federal cap. in 1927. Seat of Duntroon Military Col., Canberra Univ. Col. (1929), and Natl. Mus. of Australian Zoology.

Cancer [Lat.,= crab], in astronomy, fourth sign of ZODIAC.

cancer or **carcinoma** (kärsĭnō'mù), malignant growth or tumor of unknown cause. Wildly growing epithelial cells invade surrounding tissues. Characteristic of malignancy is metastasis, the separation of malignant cells from the original growth and their distribution by way of lymphatics and blood to other parts of body. Any lump, ulcer, or unusual bleeding from body orifice warrants examination by physician. Information offered by American Society for the Prevention of Cancer.

Candia (kăn'dēù), Gr. *Herakleion,* largest city (pop. 53,541) of Crete, Greece; a port on the Gulf of Candia. Heavily damaged in World War II. Has unique museum of Minoan antiquities discovered at ancient Cnossus near by.

Candish, Thomas: see CAVENDISH, THOMAS.

candle, mass of wax, tallow, paraffin, spermaceti or similar material surrounding a wick. Date of origin uncertain; in ancient writings words translated as "candle" may have meant torch or lamp. Formerly made by repeated dipping in melted material or by pouring material into molds; now are usually machine-molded. Used symbolically especially in Roman Catholic rites; blessed on Candlemas Day.

candlefish, fish of smelt family of Pacific coast from Oregon to Alaska. Flesh delicately flavored. Its oily body, if dried and supplied with a wick, will burn, hence its name. An alternative name is eulachon.

Candlemas, Feb. 2, the feast of the Purification of the Blessed Virgin. There is a procession of candles to celebrate the day, and in the Roman Catholic Church candles are blessed. In America this is "groundhog day" (see WOODCHUCK).

candle power: see PHOTOMETRY.

Candlewood, Lake, reservoir, W Conn., N of Danbury. Made (1926) by power dam in tributary of Housatonic R., it is 15 mi. long and covers 6,000 acres.

Candolle, Augustin Pyramus de (ōgüsté' pērämüs' dù kädôl'), 1778–1841, Swiss botanist who advanced the natural system of plant classification.

Candy, Ceylon: see KANDY.

candytuft, low-growing annual or shrubby perennial plant (*Iberis*), with flower clusters of various colors. It is used in borders and rock gardens.

cane: see BAMBOO; RATTAN; SUGAR CANE.

Canea (kùnē'ù), anc. Gr. *Cydonia,* modern Gr. *Khania,* city (pop. 33,837), cap. of Crete, Greece, on the Gulf of Canea. Suffered air and naval attacks in World War II. Landmarks are cathedral, mosques, and old Venetian arsenal.

canella (kùnĕl'ù), small evergreen tree (*Canella winterana*) of S Florida and West Indies; it is also known as wild cinnamon. Its dried inner bark is the canella of commerce which has stimulant qualities.

cane sugar: see SUCROSE.

Canfield, Dorothy: see FISHER, DOROTHY CANFIELD.

Canfield, Richard Albert, 1855–1914, American gambler. His famous gambling house in New York city was closed in 1904. Solitaire game named for him.

Can Grande della Scala: see SCALA, CAN FRANCESCO DELLA.

Canisius College: see BUFFALO, N.Y.

cankerworm, name for destructive larvae (also called measuring worms) of two geometrid moths. Both fall and spring species pupate in ground. Wingless females lay eggs on bark of trees; larvae feed on leaves.

Canlaon, Mount (känläōn'), or **Malaspina** (mäläspē'nä), active volcano, 8,088 ft. high, on Negros isl., Philippines.

canna, tropical perennial (*Canna*) with large leaves and spikes of red or yellow flowers. Planted in parks and formal beds in temperate regions.

cannabis: see HEMP; MARIJUANA.

Cannae (kăn'ē), anc. village, Apulia, S Italy. Hannibal defeated the Romans here in 216 B.C.

Cannes (kän), town (pop. 36,647), Alpes-Maritimes dept., SE France. Fashionable resort on Riviera.

cannibalism, human consumption of human flesh. Practice, known since dawn of history and in many lands (e.g., among Negroes in Africa, Indians of Pacific coast) has been primarily ritual, intended as sympathetic magic. In Western civilization cannibalism considered peculiarly horrible even in time of starvation (e.g., Donner party).

Canning, Elizabeth, 1734–73, London servant girl, subject of a famous mystery. Disappeared for 28 days in 1753. Claimed to have been held in a garret. A gypsy woman was arrested and sentenced to hang but at second trial Elizabeth was accused of perjury and banished to America.

Canning, George, 1770–1827, English Tory statesman. As foreign minister (1807–9) planned seizure of Danish fleet (1807). After suicide of CASTLEREAGH (1822) was again foreign minister. Opposed decisions of Congress of Verona. Aided MONROE DOCTRINE by recognizing independence of Spanish colonies in America. Arranged French-Russian-British agreement resulting in Greek independence. Favored Catholic Emancipation, free trade. Prime minister 1827. His third son, **Charles John Canning, Earl Canning,** 1812–62, was noted for clemency as governor general of India in SEPOY REBELLION. Was first viceroy of India 1858–62.

Canning, Stratford: see STRATFORD DE REDCLIFFE, STRATFORD CANNING, VISCOUNT.

canning, the process of hermetically sealing cooked food for future use, was put into use in France at beginning of 19th cent. and first patented in U.S. c.1815. Glass jars were largely supplanted (except in home canning) by tin cans, patented 1810 in England, 1825 in U.S.; tin-plated steel cans have been mass produced in U.S. since 1847 and are today the basis of a huge industry. Home and commercial processes alike depend on rapid handling of sound raw materials to prevent vitamin loss, bacterial spoilage, and enzyme changes, and on sealing and cooking in containers to kill microorganisms.

Cannizzaro, Stanislao (stänēslä'ō kän-nēt-tsä'rō), 1826–1910, Italian chemist. He discovered cyanamide, worked to differentiate molecular from atomic weights, and obtained alcohols from aldehydes (Cannizzaro's reaction).

Cannon, Annie Jump, 1863–1941, American astronomer, especially noted for her work on Harvard College Observatory's catalogue of stellar spectra.

Cannon, Joseph G(urney), 1836–1926, speaker of U.S. House of Representatives (1903–11). "Uncle Joe" ruled House dictatorially in interest of "Old Guard" Republicans until bill reforming House rules broke his power.

Cannon, Walter Bradford, 1871–1945, American professor of physiology and author of works in the field. He was an authority on digestion and hormones.

Cano, Alonso (älōn'sō kä'nō), 1601–67, Spanish artist. Carved and painted monumental altarpieces; designed façade of Granada cathedral.

Cano, Juan Sebastián del, d. 1526, Spanish navigator, first to circumnavigate the globe. Set out under Magellan, but at Magellan's death took command of the expedition.

canoe (kùnōō'), simple type of watercraft, long and narrow, shaped into sharp ends for guiding and propelled by a paddle or paddles. Known among peoples of low material culture all over the world, the canoe has been made of various materials and in various forms. Among North American Indians, the hollowed-out log or dugout was highly developed on the N Pacific coast, the birchbark canoe was much used in the N woods, and the skin or hide canoe was known in the Plains. The Eskimo developed the kayak, made of sealskin stretched over a driftwood or whalebone frame; the paddler sits in the "manhole" and wears a waterproof skin shirt that fits down over the "manhole" making the whole craft waterproof. In the S Pacific natives developed large, seagoing canoes for interisland journeys; some were elaborately carved. In many parts of the world the canoe survives as a working craft. In the U.S. it is primarily used for sport. Canoeing clubs were popular in the late 19th and early 20th cent., and summer campers use canoes extensively.

canon (kă'nùn), in Christendom, term with several meanings: decree of church council (hence body of such decrees, when ratified, contribute to canon law); official list of saints (hence canonization); list of books recognized or accepted in the Bible (the canonical books, as in the Western canon); the principal part of the MASS; one of certain church officials (canons regular, uncloistered monks; canons attached to a cathedral).

canon, in music, a type of counterpoint in which all voices have the same melody but begin at different times. In the crab canon, the second voice consists of the melody turned backwards. In mensuration canons, each voice has the same melodic patterns but written in different note values. A simple, popular type of canon is the round.

Canon City (kăn'yùn) city (pop. 6,345), S central Colo., on ARKANSAS R. at end of Royal Gorge and WNW of Pueblo. Laid out 1859 on site of Z. M. Pike blockhouse (1807). Trade center for fruitgrowing and mining area.

canonization, in the Roman Catholic Church, process by which a person is officially enrolled among the saints. The method of canonization was set by Urban VIII in acts that came in force in 1634. At a "trial" in Rome, a prosecutor (popularly called *advocatus diaboli* or devil's advocate) attacks the claims proposed by his opponent (*advocatus Dei* or God's advocate) that the proposed saint had lived a holy life and was responsible for at least four miracles. To secure beatification (frequently a step toward canonization) proof of two miracles is offered. The miracles are considered pious belief, but a Catholic is not required to believe in them. A holy person may be considered a saint without formal canonization, as indeed many of the earliest and greatest saints are.

canon law, in the Roman Catholic Church, law of the church courts, based on legislation of councils, popes, and bishops (in local matters). The present great code was promulgated in 1917. It is the culmination of long development, begun with early letters of the bishops of Rome. These and later letters and pronouncements are the decretals, gathered into collections (sometimes spurious, as in the False Decretals). The greatest figure in canon law was GRATIAN, whose compilation was the basis of all later collections. Gregory IX, Boniface VIII, and John XXII issued further collections of decretals (later gathered in *Extravagantes communes*). The Council of Trent (1545–63) added much to canon law, which deals primarily with governance of the clergy and the Church, including administration of the sacraments (notably holy orders and matrimony).

Canonsburg, borough (pop. 12,072), SW Pa., SW of Pittsburgh; settled 1773. Has coal mining and mfg. of metal products. Whisky Rebellion began here 1794. Seat of Log Academy, oldest school building (1780) W of Alleghenies.

Canossa (känôs′sä), hamlet, N central Italy, near Reggio nell' Emilia. The lords of its castle (now in ruins) ruled much of Tuscany and Emilia in 10th–11th cent. Countess MATILDA was last of line. In Jan., 1077, castle was scene of penance by Emperor HENRY IV, who supposedly waited barefoot in the snow for three days before Pope Gregory VII, who was Matilda's guest, lifted excommunication.

Canova, Antonio (äntō′nyō känō′vä), 1775–1822, Italian sculptor, leader of the classical revival in Italy. Did statues of Napoleon and his family.

Cantabrian Mountains (känta′breùn), N Spain, along Bay of Biscay from Pyrenees to Cape Finisterre. Highest peak is Peña de Cerredo (8,687 ft.). Rich in coal and iron.

Cantabrigia: see CAMBRIDGE UNIVERSITY.

Cantacuzene, John: see JOHN VI, emperor.

Cantal (kätäl′), department (2,231 sq. mi.; pop. 186,-843). S central France, in Auvergne; cap. Aurillac. Plomb du Cantal (plô″dü), 6,096 ft. high, an extinct volcano, is highest peak of Cantal mts.

cantaloupe: see MELON.

cantata, musical form developed in Italy in the baroque era. It was a short dramatic piece which in the 17th cent. took on the form of recitative and aria. In France and Italy the secular cantata prevailed; in Germany the church cantata, with choral and instrumental parts, was adopted by J. S. Bach.

Canterbury, county borough (pop. 27,778), on Stour R. at foot of N Downs, Kent, England; spiritual center of England. St. Augustine came from Rome 597 to convert English to Christianity, founded abbey here, and became first archbishop of Canterbury. Town famous in Europe as object of pilgrimage after murder of THOMAS À BECKET. Chaucer's *Canterbury Tales* based upon stories of these travelers. Magnificent cathedral embodies work of several periods and various men (notably Lanfranc and Anselm). Bombed 1942, but cathedral not directly hit. City also site of St. Martin's (Mother Church of England), St. Augustine's Abbey, and other old buildings.

Canterbury bells: see BELLFLOWER.

cantharides (känthä′rŭdēz) or **Spanish fly,** bright green

or bluish beetle, *Lytta* (formerly *Cantharis*) *vesicatoria,* chiefly of S Europe. This and others of same family often called blister beetles because of irritating effect on skin. Poisonous drug **cantharidin** obtained from dried crushed bodies.

Canticles, another name for the SONG OF SOLOMON.

cantilever (kän′tŭlēvŭr), beam supported rigidly at one end to carry load along free arm or at free end. Principle used widely in construction. See *ill.,* p. 131.

Cantire, Argyllshire, Scotland: see KINTYRE.

Canton (kän″tön′), Mandarin *Kuang-chou,* city (pop. 1,413,460), cap. of Kwangtung prov., China; port on Canton R. Major commercial center at terminus of Canton-Hankow RR. Visited by Arab traders in 10th cent. In 1511 Portugal won trade monopoly, which made her first European power to have commercial contact with China. Treaty ending Opium War (1839–42) made Canton a treaty port. After occupation by British and French forces in 1856, Shameen Isl. was made a foreign concession (restored 1946 to China). City was seat of revolutionary movement in 1911. Held 1938–45 by Japan, fell 1949 to Communists.

Canton. 1 City (pop. 11,927), W central Ill., SW of Peoria; founded 1825. Trade and industrial center for agr. (esp. corn) and coal area. 2 Town (pop. 7,465), E Mass., SSW of Boston. Mfg. of textiles. Paul Revere had foundry here. 3 City (pop. 7,048), W central Miss., NNE of Jackson. Trade and processing center of cotton, truck, and timber area. 4 City (pop. 2,490), NE Mo., on the Mississippi above Hannibal. Seat of CULVER-STOCKTON COLLEGE. 5 Village (pop. 4,379), N N.Y., SE of Ogdensburg. Seat of St. Lawrence Univ. (coed.; 1856) and of a state agr. school. 6 City (pop. 116,912), NE Ohio, SE of Akron; laid out 1806. Has important iron and steel works, an oil refinery, and mfg. of roller bearings and engines. William McKinley lived and was buried here.

Canton or Pearl, river, 110 mi. long, Kwangtung prov., S China; main navigation channel linking Canton to Hong Kong. Mouth of river channel called Boca Tigris. Chinese names: Yueh Kiang, Chu Kiang.

Canton Island, atoll (3.5 sq. mi.; pop. 81), central Pacific, one of Phoenix Isls. Important transoceanic air base. Claimed in 1856 by U.S. and in 1937 by Great Britain; agreement was made 1939 for joint control of Canton and near-by ENDERBURY ISLAND for 50 years.

Cantor, Georg (gä′ôrk kän′tôr), 1845–1918, German mathematician known for work on theory of numbers and for introducing term "transfinite numbers."

Canute (kŭnōot′, kŭnūt′), c.995–1035, king of England, Norway, and Denmark, younger son of SWEYN of Denmark. Invaded England with his father in 1013. On Sweyn's death he withdrew to Denmark. Invaded England 1015. Divided country with EDMUND IRONSIDE after battle of Assandun. On death of Edmund (1016), Canute was accepted as sole king. Gave England peace, restored Church to high place, and codified English law. Married Emma, widow of Æthelred. Succeeded to throne of Denmark 1018. After several expeditions to Norway drove out Olaf II in 1028, thus becoming ruler of three kingdoms. He made his son Harthacanute king of Denmark, and his son Sweyn king of Norway. Canute estab. friendly relations with the Holy Roman Empire.

Canute the Saint, d. 1086, king (1080–86) and patron saint of Denmark. Feast Day: Jan. 19.

canvasback: see DUCK.

Canyon, city (pop. 4,364), N Texas, S of Amarillo in Panhandle. Prairie Dog Fork of Red R. is formed near by above Palo Duro Canyon, which draws many visitors. Buffalo L. (SW) is recreational.

Canyon de Chelly National Monument: see NATIONAL PARKS AND MONUMENTS (table).

Capablanca, José Raoul (hōsä′ räōōl′ käpäbläng′kä), 1888–1942, Cuban chess player, world champion 1921–27.

Cap de la Madeleine (käp′ dü lä mädlĕn′), city (pop. 18,-667), S Que., Canada, on St. Lawrence R. opposite

Trois Rivières. Has paper and silk mills and mfg. of aluminum foil.

Cape Breton Island, 3,975 sq. mi., forming NE part of N.S., Canada, bounded by the Atlantic (S and E) and the Gulf of St. Lawrence (W). BRAS D'OR salt lakes occupy center of island. There are many summer lake resorts and coastal fishing villages. SYDNEY and GLACE BAY coal fields feed important steelworks. Cabot Trail is a motor road which circles the center and W part of island, commemorating its discovery by John Cabot (1497). By Peace of Utrecht (1713–14) French retained island (named Île Royale with cap. at LOUISBURG) and some Acadians migrated here. Cape Breton was attached to N.S. in 1763. Was independent with cap. at Sydney 1784–1820.

Cape Charles, town (pop. 2,427), E Va., port on Chesapeake Bay near tip of Eastern Shore peninsula. Has ferries to Old Point Comfort and Norfolk. Occupied by Union forces in Civil War.

Cape Coast, town (pop. 23,061), cap. of the Gold Coast colony, a port on Gulf of Guinea.

Cape Cod, low sandy peninsula of glacial origin, 65 mi. long and 1–20 mi. wide, SE Mass.; bounded by Cape Cod Bay (N and W), the Atlantic (E), Nantucket and Vineyard sounds (S), and Buzzards Bay (SW). Name attributed to Gosnold, who visited here 1602. Known for its summer resorts and fishing towns, e.g., Provincetown (on site where Pilgrims put in, 1620), Barnstable, and Falmouth. Has large cranberry production. Cape Cod Canal (built 1909–14, improved 1927), c.8 mi. long, connects Cape Cod and Buzzards bays, crossing Bourne town.

Cape Colony: see CAPE PROVINCE.

Cape Fear River, formed in central N.C., flows c.200 mi. SE across piedmont and coastal plains to Atlantic Ocean just N of Cape Fear. Wilmington is at head of estuary, Southport at mouth; Elizabethtown and Fayetteville on banks.

Cape Girardeau (jĭrär'dō), city (pop. 21,578), SE Mo., SSE of St. Louis and on the Mississippi; founded 1793 as trading post. Important as a port, it was later a fort in Civil War. Produces shoes, cement, and wood and tobacco products.

Cape jasmine: see GARDENIA.

Capek, Josef, Czech *Čapek* (chä'pěk), 1887–1945, Czech author and primitivist painter. With his brother Karel he collaborated on *The Insect Play* (1921; Eng. tr., 1923), a satire produced in U.S. as *The World We Live In. Poems from a Concentration Camp* (1946) appeared after his death at Belsen. His brother **Karel Capek,** 1890–1938, won international fame with his satirical play *R.U.R.* (*Rossum's Universal Robots,* 1921; Eng. tr., 1923), which introduced the word *robot* into English. Among other works are the play *The Makropoulos Secret* (1923; Eng. tr., 1925), a novel *Krakatit* (1924; Eng. tr., 1925), and three vols. of conversations with T. G. Masaryk.

Capella, Martianus (märshēā'nŭs kŭpĕ'lŭ), fl. 5th cent.?, Latin writer. Long allegory, *The Marriage of Mercury and Philology,* popular in Middle Ages.

Capello, Bianca (byäng'kä käpĕ'lō), 1548–87, Italian adventuress. Became grand duchess of Tuscany by marrying Francesco de' Medici (1579). Died suddenly with her husband; presumably poisoned.

Cape May, Atlantic resort city (pop. 3,607), at end of Cape May peninsula, S extremity of N.J. Peninsula has lighthouse at Delaware Bay entrance. Canal (built by Federal government 1942–43; part of N.J. section of Intracoastal Waterway) bisects the cape c.3 mi. above its S point. **Cape May Court House** (pop. 1,093) is NNE of Cape May city.

Cape Province, officially **Cape of Good Hope Province** (277,169 sq. mi.; pop. 4,053,848), South Africa, on Atlantic and Indian oceans; cap. Capetown. Occupies S tip of Africa. Crops include grains, tobacco, citrus fruit, and grapes (for wine). Diamonds, copper, and coal are mined. The 15th-cent. Portuguese navigator Diaz was first to round Cape of Good Hope, but

the Dutch were first to settle the area, founding Capetown in 1652. The late 17th cent. saw influx of French Huguenots. In 1806 the British annexed area as Cape Colony, and British settlers arrived in 1820. Opposition to British rule led many of the Boer farmers to migrate north (see TREK). In South African War fierce battles were fought at Mafeking and Kimberley. With founding of Union of South Africa in 1910, the colony became a province.

caper, white-flowered shrub (*Capparis spinosa*) of Mediterranean region. Its pickled buds, called capers, are used for flavoring.

Capernaum (kŭpûr'nāŭm) or **Capharnaum** (kŭfär'–), town, NE Palestine, associated with Jesus' ministry. John 2.12; 6.59; Mat. 11.23; 8; 9; Mark 1; 2; Luke 4; 5.

Capetians (kŭpē'shŭnz), royal house of FRANCE, named for HUGH CAPET, who became king in 987. His direct descendants ruled until death of Charles IV (1328), when throne passed to collateral branch of VALOIS.

Capetown or **Cape Town,** city (pop. 383,891), cap. of Cape Prov., legislative cap. of Union of South Africa; a large port on the Atlantic. Scenically located at foot of Table Mt. and overlooking Table Bay. Here are Houses of Parliament (1886) and Univ. of Cape Town (1916). Founded 1652 by the Dutch, taken 1806 by the British.

Cape Verde Islands (vûrd), archipelago and Portuguese colony (1,557 sq. mi.; pop. 147,097), in the Atlantic, c.375 mi. W of Dakar; cap. Praia (on São Tiago Isl.). Under Portuguese rule since late 15th cent. Important stopover point on transatlantic route between Africa and South America.

Cape Vincent, village (pop. 812), N N.Y., on St. Lawrence R. and NW of Watertown; a center for Thousand Isls. resort area.

Cape York Peninsula, N Queensland, Australia, between Gulf of Carpentaria and Coral Sea.

Cap-Haïtien (käp"-hä'shŭn), city (pop. 24,957), N Haiti. Founded by French 1670, it was cap. of colonial Haiti until 1770.

Capharnaum, same as CAPERNAUM.

capillarity causes part of surface of liquid in contact with solid (e.g., a glass jar) to be elevated above or depressed below rest of surface. Named for behavior of liquids in capillary tube placed perpendicularly in liquid: water rises in tube to level above that outside; mercury is depressed. Forces operating are adhesion, cohesion, surface tension.

capillary, minute vessel connecting arterial and venous systems in CIRCULATION OF THE BLOOD.

Capistrano, John of: see JOHN CAPISTRAN, SAINT.

capitalism, economic system characterized by private ownership of property, production of goods for profit, and the institution of bank credit. Its modern importance dates from Industrial Revolution. Capitalism stresses freedom of individual economic enterprise, although ultimate right of state to regulate industry has seldom been questioned. In the 20th cent. the capitalist structure, grown to enormous proportions through quest for profits, has been restricted by social reforms and by totalitarianism.

capital punishment, putting to death by the state. Once imposed even for petty crimes, its use has decreased since 18th cent., because of efforts of such men as Beccaria. Modern methods include hanging, electrocution, gassing, shooting, and guillotining.

Capitol, building, Washington, D.C., over 725 ft. long and c.185 ft. wide; seat of U.S. government. Elevated site chosen by George Washington in consultation with Major L'ENFANT. Building begun in 1793; first architect was William THORNTON. Burned by British in 1814. Charles BULFINCH brought design to completion in 1830. T. U. Walter added extensive wings and dome (c.288 ft. in height) during period 1851–65.

Capitoline Hill or **Capitol,** highest of the seven hills of anc. Rome, historic and religious center of the city. On it were the great temple of Jupiter Capitolinus, the citadel (arx), and the senatorial palace. The temple, twice destroyed by fire, was last rebuilt by Domitian.

Capitol Reef National Monument: see NATIONAL PARKS AND MONUMENTS (table).

capitularies, decrees and written commands of the Merovingian and Carolingian kings of the Franks. Most important were those addressed by Charlemagne to his officers, the *missi dominici,* for administration of the empire and carrying out reforms.

Capiz (kä'pēs), municipality (pop. 32,353), N Panay isl., Philippines. Has rice and sugar mills.

Capo d'Istria, Giovanni Antonio, Count (kä"pō dē'strēä), 1776–1831, Greek and Russian statesman, b. Corfu. Entered Russian service 1809; as Russian foreign minister (1820–22) he helped Greek uprising in 1821. Elected president of Greece 1827, but was unpopular because of aristocratic and pro-Russian leanings. Assassinated.

Capone, Al(fonso) (kŭpō'nē), 1899–1947, American gang leader, b. Italy. His crime syndicate terrorized Chicago in 1920s.

Caporetto (käpōrāt'tō), village of Slovenia, NW Yugoslavia, on Isonzo R; in Italy until 1945. Scene of Italian rout by Austrians in 1917.

Capote, Truman (käpō'tē), 1924–, American author. His works combine a delicate style with bizarre subject matter and Southern scenes. Among his novels are *Other Voices, Other Rooms* (1948) and *The Grass Harp* (1951; he later made this into a play). Some short stories are in *Tree of Night and Other Stories* (1949).

Cappadocia (käpŭdō'shù), anc. region of Asia Minor, now in Turkey; term is used for varying territory. The inhabitants kept some independence even under Alexander the Great, and it became a kingdom in the 3d cent. B.C. Pontus split off from it. Cappadocia became a prosperous Roman province, and the name appears in the Bible.

Cappel, Switzerland: see KAPPEL.

Capper, Arthur, 1865–1951, American journalist and political leader. Published Topeka *Daily Capital* and several farm journals. U.S. Senator from Kansas (1919–49); led farm bloc, staunch isolationist.

Capri (kä'prē), small rocky island (pop. 7,984), S Italy, near entrance to Bay of Naples. Striking scenery, pleasant climate make it a tourist center. Two small towns: Capri, Anacapri. Ruins of villas of emperors Augustus and Tiberius.

Capricornus [Lat.,= goat horn], 10th sign of ZODIAC.

Caprivi, Leo, Graf von (lā'ō gräf fŭn käprē'vē), 1831–99, chancellor of Germany (1890–94). Succeeded Bismarck. Favored industrial interests.

Captivity, Exile, or Babylonian captivity, in history of Israel, period from fall of Jerusalem (586 B.C.) to rebuilding of Temple (516 B.C.) thus lasting the 70 years prophesied for captivity. Jer. 25.11; Dan. 9.2; Zech. 7.5. After capture of city, thousands were deported to Mesopotamia; exiles kept close contact with kinsmen at home. In 538 B.C., Cyrus decreed that worship be restored at Jerusalem and that Jews might return home. The following century was a period of reintegration into a national and religious unit. See books of Ezekiel, Ezra, and Nehemiah. For "Babylonian captivity" of popes, see PAPACY.

Capua (kä'pū̇ä), ancient city, Campania, S Italy, strategically situated on Appian Way. Opened its gates to Hannibal 216 B.C. Retaken by Romans, it became chief center of S Italy. After its destruction by the Arabs (A.D. 841), the inhabitants fled to near-by Casilinum and founded modern Capua (pop. 10,218).

Capuchins (kä'pūchĭnz) [Ital.,= hooded ones], independent order of the Franciscans, officially Friars Minor Capuchin; founded 1525–28. Devoted to preaching and missions, they did much to forward the Catholic Reform.

Capulin Mountain National Monument: see NATIONAL PARKS AND MONUMENTS (table).

capybara (käpĭbä'rù), mammal (*Hydrochoerus capy-*

bara) of Central and much of South America. Also called water hog and carpincho. Largest living rodent (up to 4 ft. long, 75–100 lb.), it has brownish, yellow-flecked hair, no tail, partially webbed feet, and is semi-aquatic. It eats vegetation. Is a source of food, glove leather, and bristles.

caracal (kä'rùkùl) or **Persian lynx,** mammal of cat family, native to Asia, Africa. It is reddish brown with black-tufted ears, and c.3¼ ft. from nose to tip of tail. Preys on small deer, hares, birds.

Caracalla (kärùkä'lù), 188–217, Roman emperor (211–17), son of Septimius SEVERUS. Called Caracalla after his Gallic tunic; real name Marcus Aurelius Antoninus. Had to share rule with his brother Geta, but murdered him and his followers (212). Extended citizenship to all free inhabitants of the empire, presumably to increase his income. He was murdered by Macrinus, who took the imperial rule, only to be replaced by Heliogabalus.

Caracas (kùrà'kùs), city (pop. 376,111; alt. c.3,100 ft.), N Venezuela, cap. and largest city of country. Independence declared here 1811. Earthquake of 1812 hurt patriot cause.

Caracci, family of Italian painters: see CARRACCI.

Caracciolo, Francesco (fränchä'skô kärät'chôlô), 1752–99, Neapolitan admiral. Commanded fleet of PARTHENOPEAN REPUBLIC (1799). Summarily executed by order of Lord Nelson.

Caractacus (kùräk'tùkùs) or **Caradoc** (kùrà'dùk), fl. A.D. 50, British chieftain, son of Cymbeline. Fought for nine years against Romans, was captured and taken to Rome. Claudius spared his life.

Caraman, Turkey: see KARAMAN.

Caran d'Ache (kärà' däsh'), pseud. of **Emmanuel Poiré** (ēmänüël' pwärà'), 1858–1909, French caricaturist and illustrator.

Carausius (kùrô'shēùs), d. 293, Gallo-Roman commander. Condemned by Maximian, he fled to Britain and estab. rule. Diocletian and Maximian recognized him as coemperor. Defeated by Constantius and murdered.

Caravaggio, Michelangelo Amerighi da (mēkälän'jälô ämärē'gē dä käräväd'jō), 1565–1609, Italian painter; founder of naturalist school in Rome. One of earliest masters of dramatic light and shade. In genre and religious pictures he abandoned idealization for emphasis on the character of his lowly models.

caravan, group of travelers or merchants united for mutual assistance and defense on long journeys through dangerous country. Caravan trade preceded sea commerce in Near East, existing from earliest recorded history, since fertile regions were divided by deserts and marauding tribes were a menace. Camels were chief beasts of burden but donkeys were used in Asia Minor. Caravan routes caused ancient wars. Cities rose and fell with trade volume on near-by routes; empires estab. caravansaries to accommodate travelers along the way. Trade continued in this fashion until use of motor trucks and planes. Advent of Islam led to pilgrim caravans to Mecca. Wagon-train commerce over Santa Fe Trail in New World was not unlike caravan trade.

caravel (kä'rùvĕl"), three-masted, usually square-rigged, sailing ship. It had a roundish hull with high bow and stern and was a light ship with small displacement. Its advantage over bulkier ships was important in enabling the Portuguese to open the African coast in the 15th cent. Columbus' flagship, the *Santa María,* was a typical caravel.

caraway, biennial herb (*Carum carvi*) native to Europe. Small seeds are used medicinally and for seasoning pastries and liqueurs (e.g., kümmel).

carbide, compound of carbon and one other element, not hydrogen or oxygen. Generally produced in electric furnace. Many carbides are decomposed by water to yield a gas.

carbohydrate, any organic compound of carbon, hydrogen, oxygen (with hydrogen and oxygen in ratio of

2:1). Important group of heat-energy supplying foods, involved in fat production. Three groups are monosaccharides, e.g., GLUCOSE; disaccharides, e.g., LACTOSE; polysaccharides, e.g., CELLULOSE, STARCH.

carbolic acid or **phenol** (fē′–), colorless, crystalline solid compound of carbon, hydrogen, and hydroxyl radical (OH). Like alcohols in structure; has properties of weak acid. Corrosive and poisonous. Used as antiseptic, disinfectant, and to make resins, explosives, and dyes.

carboloy (kär′buloi), alloy of cobalt, tungsten, carbon. Harder than steel; used for cutting.

carbon, abundant, nonmetallic element (symbol = C; see also ELEMENT, table), found in all organic matter. Forms HYDROCARBON and CARBOHYDRATE compounds. Carbon is in perfumes, drugs, animal and plant secretions, foods, textiles, wood, paper, coal, gaseous fuels, etc. Carbonates are important (e.g., limestone). DIAMOND and GRAPHITE are crystalline forms. Steel contains iron and carbon.

Carbon, Mount: see ELK MOUNTAINS.

Carbonari (kärbōnä′rē), secret revolutionary society in SW Europe in early 19th cent. Active in revolts in Spain, Naples, Piedmont (1820–21).

carbonate, a salt or an ester (in the case of organic carbonates) of carbonic acid. Carbonate RADICAL is –CO₃. Carbonates, except for ammonium, potassium, and sodium, are insoluble in water. Most decompose with heat, yielding carbon dioxide and metallic oxide. Form bicarbonates with carbonic acid. Calcium carbonate occurs in animal shells and as ICELAND SPAR, LIMESTONE, MARBLE, and STALACTITE and STALAGMITE formations. Iron carbonate (siderite) is important iron source. Potassium carbonate is POTASH; sodium, SODA. Calcium bicarbonate causes "hardness" in water.

Carbondale. 1 City (pop. 10,921), S Ill., N of Cairo, in coal and agr. area; founded 1852. Has railroad shops. **2** City (pop. 16,296), NE Pa., on Lackawanna R., NE of Scranton. Anthracite mining and mfg. of textile and metal products.

carbon dioxide, colorless, almost odorless, gaseous compound of carbon and oxygen; formula CO₂. Heavier than air; neither burns nor supports combustion; soluble in water; can be liquefied under pressure. Occurs in ATMOSPHERE. Results from burning of carbon, hydrocarbons, and from decomposition of carbonate. Product of respiration; given off in FERMENTATION, used in photosynthesis. Causes dough to rise when formed by BAKING POWDER; gives effervescence to water when dissolved under pressure; used in fire extinguishers. Also called carbonic acid gas because aqueous solution is weak acid. Dry ice is solid CO₂.

carbonic acid, weak acid known only in solution; formed when carbon dioxide is dissolved in water. Used in carbonated beverages.

carbonic acid gas: see CARBON DIOXIDE.

Carboniferous period (kärbŭnĭ′fŭrŭs), fifth period of PALEOZOIC ERA, marked by COAL formation. In North America it is divided into Lower Carboniferous or Mississippian and Upper Carboniferous or Pennsylvanian. The Mississippian was a period of repeated submergence and rising, with vast sediment deposits, mountain making, and volcanic activity. During the Pennsylvanian warm humid climate and extensive marshes favored rapid growth of the vegetation which later became coal. As in the Mississippian crustal disturbances took place on a huge scale. Land animals included primitive amphibians and reptiles, spiders, snails, scorpions, huge dragonflies. See GEOLOGY, table.

carbon monoxide, colorless, odorless, tasteless gaseous compound of carbon and oxygen; formula CO. May cause fatal poisoning if inhaled. Lighter than air; almost insoluble in water. Used as fuel (in PRODUCER GAS, WATER GAS), and as reducing agent (oxygen remover) in obtaining certain metals from ores. Formed by incomplete combustion of carbon. Present in exhaust of gasoline engines, in illuminating gas, in furnaces when there is insufficient air.

Carborundum: see SILICON CARBIDE.

carburetor (kär′byŭrātŭr). **1** Gasoline-engine device for vaporizing liquid fuel before combustion. Spray type has float chamber (regulates gasoline entry) and mixing chamber (vaporizes fuel spray), with vapor and air passing over throttle valve into cylinder intake manifold. **2** Device to enrich coal or water gas, increasing illuminative power.

Carcassonne (kärkäsôn′), city (pop. 31,752), cap. of Aude dept., S France, on Aude R. Medieval walled city was entirely restored by Viollet-le-Duc (19th cent.). "New city" (13th cent.) lies across Aude.

Carchemish (kär′kĭmĭsh, kärkē′mĭsh), city of anc. Syria; southern city of the HITTITES, taken by Egypt (15th cent. B.C.). Also Charchemish.

carcinoma: see CANCER.

cardamom (kär′dŭmŏm″), plant (*Elettaria cardamomum*), native to India and Ceylon, grown for its aromatic seeds which are used medicinally and in spices.

Cardano, Geronimo (järō′nēmō kärdä′nō), 1501–76, Italian mathematician and physician. Works include treatises on arithmetic and algebra.

Cárdenas, García López de (gärthē′ä lō′pĕth dä kär′dänäs), fl. 1540, Spanish explorer in American Southwest, discoverer of Grand Canyon.

Cárdenas, Lázaro (lä′särō kär′dänäs), 1895–, president of Mexico (1934–40). His reform program included redistribution of land on EJIDO system; expropriation of foreign-owned properties; modernization of Mexico.

Cardiff (kär′dĭf), county borough (pop. 243,627), co. seat of Glamorganshire, Wales, on the Taff near its mouth on Bristol Channel; one of world's great coal shipping ports. There are also large iron and steel works, flour mills, and a fishing industry. Cardiff Castle built 1090 on site of a Roman fort. Welsh Natl. Mus. and University Col. of S Wales and Monmouthshire are in Cathays Park. City and suburbs suffered severe air raid damage in 1941.

Cardigan, James Thomas Brudenell, 7th earl of (kär′dĭgŭn), 1797–1868, British general. In Crimean War led disastrous cavalry charge (1854) immortalized by Tennyson in *The Charge of the Light Brigade.* Cardigan jacket named for him.

Cardiganshire (kär′dĭgŭnshŭr) or **Cardigan,** maritime county (677 sq. mi.; pop. 53,267), on Cardigan Bay, S Wales; co. town Cardigan. Region is largely hilly, with fertile agr. valleys. Chief industries mfg. of woolen goods and lead mining. Welsh language and customs preserved here to a large degree.

cardinal, member of the highest body of the ROMAN CATHOLIC CHURCH below the pope—the college of cardinals, having (since 1059) the duty of electing the pope and all the duties of a privy council to him. The institution grew out of the council of clerics in and around Rome who advised the pope, and the titles of cardinals still reflect this: cardinal bishops (of the sees immediately around Rome), cardinal priests and cardinal deacons (with titles from the church in Rome itself; hence the title "Cardinal of the Roman Church"). The dignity of being a cardinal is quite separate from offices in the Church hierarchy; thus the term *cardinal archbishop* means only that a man is both a cardinal and an archbishop. The rarely attained maximum number of cardinals is 70 (set by Sixtus V). After the death (or in very rare instances resignation) of the pontiff, the cardinals must meet in not less than 15 nor more than 18 days to elect a new pope; they remain closeted until a candidate has been chosen and has accepted the office. Most of the cardinals have separate church offices over the world (usually archbishoprics; the remainder direct the affairs of the papal administration, the Curia Romana. Groups of them (with staffs) constitute the congregations for management of specific affairs—e.g., the Congregation of the Holy Office (see INQUISITION **3**) and Congregation of the Propagation of the Faith (the Propaganda; in charge of missions). A cardinal heads each of the tribunals, the highest ecclesiastic courts. The secretariats, for handling of papal affairs, are also headed by cardinals (e.g., the papal secretary of state). The distinctive badge of a cardinal is a red hat, given him by the pope but never worn thereafter. Cardinals are styled "Eminence." See also PAPACY.

cardinal or **redbird**, North American songbird of finch family. The male eastern cardinal is scarlet with black throat and face, the female brown with red patches. Southern forms are the Arizona, gray-tailed, Louisiana, and San Lucas cardinals.

cardinal flower: see LOBELIA.

Cardozo, Benjamin Nathan (kärdō′zō), 1870–1938, Associate Justice of U.S. Supreme Court (1932–38). Interpreted law according to effects on society.

cards, playing: see PLAYING CARDS.

Cardston, town (pop. 2,487), SW Alta., Canada, SW of Lethbridge. Founded in mid-19th cent. by Mormons. Chief Mormon temple in Canada is here.

Carducci, Giosuè (jōzōōä′ kärdōōt′chē), 1835–1907, Italian poet, professor at Bologna (1860–1904). Works include rebellious *Inno a Satana* [hymn to Satan] (1865), *Rime nuove,* and *Odi Barbare* (1877, 1882, 1889). Critical writings helped form literary taste of his age.

Carew, Thomas (kûrōō′), 1595?–1639?, English lyric poet, one of the Cavalier poets, now best remembered for courtly verses on love (e.g., "Ask me no more where Jove bestows," "He that loves a rosy cheek").

Carey, Henry, c.1690–1743, English poet, musician, author-composer of song *Sally in Our Alley.*

Carey, Mathew, 1760–1839, American publisher, bookseller, economist, b. Dublin; in U.S. after 1784. Edited magazines (notably *American Museum*), stimulated American letters. Argued for protective tariffs. His son, **Henry Charles Carey,** 1783–1879, was a leader in developing economic nationalism. He opposed "pessimism" of Ricardo and Malthus.

Carey Land Act, written by Sen. Joseph M. Carey, passed by U.S. Congress in 1894. Provided for donation of U.S.-owned desert lands to Western states on condition they be irrigated.

Caribbean Sea (kă″rĭbē′ŭn, kŭrĭ′bēŭn), part of Atlantic. Central and South America lie to W and S; Yucatan peninsula and West Indies to N and E.

Carib Indians (kă′rĭb), native people originally inhabiting Lesser Antilles.

Cariboo Mountains (kă′rĭbōō), range, 200 mi. long, S central and E B.C., Canada. It is roughly parallel to the Rockies, extending between upper North Thompson R. and N apex of Fraser R. Mt. Titan is believed to be highest peak (c.11,750 ft.). In W foothills is Cariboo dist., scene of 1860 gold rush. Cariboo Road (built 1862–65) aided settlement of region. After extensive development, gold mining declined and was superseded by ranching and farming.

Caribou, town (pop. 9,923), NE Maine, on Aroostook R. and N of Presque Isle. A center for winter sports. Ships potatoes.

caribou (kă′rĭbōō), American name for mammal of deer family in arctic and subarctic regions. It is of same genus (*Rangifer*) as Old World REINDEER. Two main North American types: barren-ground caribou of Alaska, N Canada; woodland caribou in coniferous forests and bogs in parts of Canada.

Carignan-Salières regiment (kärēnyä-sälyěr′), largest body of French troops ever sent to New France. Arrived in Canada 1665, over 1,000 strong, to render lower St. Lawrence valley safe from Indian raids. About half the regiment remained as settlers near Montreal.

carillon: see BELL.

Carinthia (kŭrĭn′thēŭ), Ger. *Kärnten* (3,681 sq. mi.; pop. 482,886), S Austria; cap. Klagenfurt. Predominantly mountainous; the GROSSGLOCKNER is Austria's highest point. Mining (lead, iron, zinc); agr. in fertile Drava Valley. Tourist trade. In 976 Carinthia (which then included ISTRIA, CARNIOLA, and STYRIA) was detached from Bavaria and created an independent duchy. It was acquired by Ottocar II of Bohemia

1269; fell to Rudolf I of Hapsburg 1276; became Austrian crownland. After 1919 it lost minor territories to Italy and Yugoslavia.

Carleton, Guy, 1st **Baron Dorchester,** 1724–1808, governor of Quebec and British commander in American Revolution. Repulsed attack on Quebec in 1775; captured Crown Point in 1776.

Carleton College: see NORTHFIELD, Minn.

Carlinville, city (pop. 5,116), S central Ill., SW of Springfield, in coal, natural-gas, agr. area.

Carlisle, earls of: see HOWARD, family.

Carlisle, John Griffin (kärlīl′), 1835–1910, American statesman. U.S. Representative from Ky. (1877–90), speaker of House (1883–89). U.S. Senator (1890–93). U.S. Secretary of the Treasury (1893–97).

Carlisle (kärlīl′), county borough (pop. 67,894), Cumberland, England, near Scottish border; an important rail center. Carlisle Castle, built by William Rufus in 1092, withstood many sieges, is now used as barracks. There is a 12th-cent. cathedral.

Carlisle, borough (pop. 16,812), S Pa., SW of Harrisburg; laid out c.1751. Has mfg. of textiles, clothing, and leather goods. French and Indian War expeditions (1758, 1763) were organized here. Was munitions depot in Revolution and Washington's hq. in Whisky Rebellion. Was on Underground Railroad and attacked by Confederates 1863. Seat of Dickinson Col. (coed., opened 1773). From 1879 to 1918 Carlisle Indian School (Federal) was here.

Carlists, partisans of Don Carlos (1788–1855), second son of Charles IV of Spain, and of his successors, who claimed the Spanish throne under the SALIC LAW. Carlos's brother, Ferdinand VII, had abrogated the law of male succession in favor of his daughter, ISABELLA II. In the bloody civil war of 1836–39 Isabella's forces defeated the Carlists. Carlos's son, Don Carlos, conde de Montemolín (1818–61), and the latter's nephew, Don Carlos, duque de Madrid (1848–1909), led unsuccessful uprisings in 1860, 1869, and 1872. In 1873 full-scale civil war broke out again. The Carlists held the Basque Provinces, Catalonia, and other parts of Spain but were completely defeated by 1876. Ultrareactionaries, the Carlists supported Franco in the civil war of 1936–39.

Carloman, 751–71, younger brother of CHARLEMAGNE.

Carloman, d. 880, German king of Bavaria, Pannonia, and Moravia (876–79), king of Italy (877–79); son of Louis the German and father of Arnulf.

Carloman, d. 884, French king (879–84). Ruled jointly with his brother Louis III till 882. Checked Norman invasion at Aisne R.

Carlos. For kings thus named, see CHARLES.

Carlos, 1545–68, Spanish prince; son of Philip II by Maria of Portugal. Mentally unbalanced. Arrested by Philip's order on eve of projected flight to Netherlands; died in prison soon afterward. Hero of Schiller's tragedy *Don Carlos.*

Carlos, name of three Spanish pretenders: see CARLISTS.

Carlotta (kärlō′tü), 1840–1927, empress of Mexico, daughter of Leopold I of Belgium. See MAXIMILIAN.

Carlow (kär′lō), inland county (346 sq. mi.; pop. 34,081), Leinster province, Ireland; co. town Carlow. A mostly fertile region, cattle raising, farming, and dairying are chief occupations.

Carlsbad or **Karlsbad** (kärlz′bäd), Czech *Karlovy Vary,* city (pop. 17,187), NW Bohemia, Czechoslovakia; famous spa. Hot mineral water taken for digestive diseases.

Carlsbad, city (pop. 17,975), SE N.Mex., on Pecos R.; settled 1888. Grazing lands and irrigated farms (cotton, alfalfa) in region. Mining and refining of potash. Served by Carlsbad project. Carlsbad Caverns Natl. Park is near.

Carlsbad Caverns National Park: see NATIONAL PARKS AND MONUMENTS (table).

Carlsbad Decrees, 1819, resolutions of a conference of ministers of German states, convened by Metternich after murder of KOTZEBUE. Provided for press censorship, supervision of universities, suppression of liberal agitation. In force until 1848.

Carlsruhe, Germany: see KARLSRUHE.

Carlstadt or **Karlstadt** (both: kärl'shtät), c.1480–1541, German Protestant reformer, whose original name was Andreas Rudolf Bodenstein. Fervent reformer and follower of Luther, he led in Wittenberg in Luther's retirement but was criticized for abolishing old church practices.

Carlstadt (kärl'stät), borough (pop. 5,591), NE N.J., NE of Newark. Chemicals, clothing, textiles.

Carlyle, Thomas, 1795–1851, British man of letters, b. Ecclefechan, Scotland. After earning a precarious living chiefly as teacher and tutor he became the interpreter of German romanticism in his *Life of Schiller* (in *London Magazine,* 1823–24) and translation of Goethe's *Wilhelm Meister* (1824). A trenchant critic of British society, he expressed his views in a sort of spiritual autobiography, *Sartor Resartus* (in *Frazer's Magazine,* 1833–34), and in his interpretative rather than historical *French Revolution* (1837). His belief that the people could be saved from their woes by great men ("heroes") was put forth in *On Heroes, Hero-Worship, and the Heroic in History* (1841), an edition of the letters and speeches of Oliver Cromwell (1845), and a massive biography of Frederick the Great. *Past and Present* (1843) contrasts 12th-cent. England of Jocelyn de Brakelond with modern chaos. Had great influence on the literary world of his day. That influence was shared by his wife, **Jane (Baillie) Welsh Carlyle,** 1801–66, who was also notable as a letter writer.

Carman, Bliss, 1861–1929, Canadian poet. Friend of Richard Hovey, with whom he published the series *Songs from Vagabondia* (1894, 1896, 1901). Reputation rests on melodic quality of his verse and his sensuous pleasure in nature.

Carmarthen, Wales: see CAERMARTHEN.

Carmathians: see KARMATHIANS.

Carmel, Mount [Heb.,= garden land], mountain, NW Israel. Extends c.12 mi. NW from plain of Esdraelon to Mediterranean Sea, ending in promontory marking S limit of Bay of Acre. Associated with prophets Elijah and Elisha. On slopes are vineyards, a Carmelite monastery, and a Bahaist garden shrine.

Carmel-by-the-Sea or **Carmel** (kärmĕl'), city (pop. 4,351), W Calif., on Carmel Bay and S of Monterey. Art, literary, and recreation center. Father Junípero SERRA is buried at near-by mission.

Carmelites (kär'mŭlĭts), Roman Catholic order of mendicant friars, originating apparently as hermits on Mt. Carmel, Palestine, made into a Western European order by St. Simon Stock (d. 1265). An enclosed order of Carmelite nuns was also estab. and became particularly important after the Carmelites were reformed by the Spanish mystics St. THERESA (of Ávila) and St. JOHN OF THE CROSS.

Carmen Sylva: see ELIZABETH, queen of Rumania.

Carmi (kär'mī), city (pop. 5,574), SE Ill., NE of Harrisburg. Rail and trade center in agr. area.

Carmona, Antonio Oscar de Fragoso (äntô'nyō ûshkär' dù frägō'sō kärmō'nù), 1868–1951, Portuguese general and statesman. Interim president (1926–28) and president (1928–51) of Portugal. His regime was dictatorial, dominated after 1928 by SALAZAR.

Carnac (kärnäk'), village, NW France, near Auray, in Brittany. Site of remarkable MEGALITHIC MONUMENTS, especially menhirs.

Carnarvon, George Edward Stanhope Molyneux Herbert, 5th **earl of** (kärnär'vùn), 1866–1923, English Egyptologist. His most famous discovery in excavating in the Valley of the Kings from 1906 to 1923 (with Howard Carter) was tomb of Tut-ankh-amen.

Carnarvon, Wales: see CAERNARVON.

Carnatic (kärnä'tĭk), region, SE Madras, India. In 18th cent. it was arena of British–French struggle for supremacy in India.

carnation, perennial PINK (*Dianthus caryophyllus*), with double spice-scented flowers in white or shades of red. It is an important greenhouse crop in cold regions and a garden flower where winters are mild.

Carnegie, Andrew (kärnä'gē), 1835–1919, American industrialist, philanthropist, b. Scotland. Concentrated on steel production after 1873; by 1900 the Carnegie Steel Co. produced one quarter of all U.S. steel. His benefactions, totaling about $350,000,000, include Carnegie Hall (1891) in New York city, and over 2,800 libraries.

Carnegie, industrial borough (pop. 12,105), SW Pa., SW of Pittsburgh. Mfg. of steel and metal products. Named for Andrew Carnegie.

Carnegie Corporation, foundation making grants to educational institutions and libraries, and occasionally to other worthy causes; estab. 1911 as chief repository of Andrew Carnegie's wealth.

Carnegie Endowment for International Peace, foundation to promote peace by publicity, support of organizations, and the like; estab. 1910 by gift of $10,000,000 from Andrew Carnegie.

Carnegie Foundation for the Advancement of Teaching, estab. 1905 by gift of $10,000,000; chartered by Congress 1905; further endowed with $17,000,000.

Carnegie Institute of Technology, at Pittsburgh; nonsectarian, partly coed.; opened 1905 with funds from Andrew Carnegie, chartered 1912. Had first collegiate department of drama (1914).

Carnegie Institution of Washington, D.C., chartered 1902 and 1904, organized 1904, endowed by Andrew Carnegie and Carnegie Corp. Projects include astronomy, terrestrial and biological sciences, historical research.

Carniola (kärnēō'lù), Croatian *Kranj,* Ger. *Krain,* mountainous region, Slovenia, NW Yugoslavia; historic cap. Ljubljana. Passed to Hapsburgs 13th cent.; Austrian crownland until 1918. Divided between Italy and Yugoslavia after World War I; to Yugoslavia 1947. Population mostly Slovenian.

carnivorous plants: see BLADDERWORT; PITCHER PLANT; VENUS'S-FLYTRAP.

Carnot, Lazare (läzär' kärnō'), 1753–1823, French revolutionist, the "architect of victory." Trained as military engineer. Organized the republican armies and masterminded strategy in French Revolutionary Wars. Member of Directory. Later held high posts under Napoleon. Exiled 1815. His son, **Nicolas Léonard Sadi Carnot** (nēkôlä' läônär' sädē'), 1796–1832, a physicist, was a founder of modern thermodynamics. His work on relation between heat and mechanical energy anticipated that of Joule, Kelvin, and others. Another son, **Hippolyte Carnot** (ēpôlēt'), 1801–88, took part in Revolution of 1848, was minister of education in provisional government. His son, **Sadi Carnot,** 1837–94, president of France (1887–94), was assassinated by an Italian anarchist.

Caro or **Karo, Joseph ben Ephraim,** 1488–1575, Jewish legist, b. Toledo, Spain, d. Safed, Palestine, compiler of *Shulhan Aruk* [the table set], a basic legal and religious code of orthodox Judaism.

carob (kä'rŭb), leguminous evergreen tree (*Ceratonia siliqua*) native to Mediterranean region, cultivated in other warm areas. It has edible red pods. Called St.-John's-bread from belief it was "locust" eaten by St. John in the wilderness (Mark 1.6).

Carol, kings of Rumania. **Carol I,** 1839–1914, a prince of the house of Hohenzollern-Sigmaringen, was elected prince of Rumania 1866, took title king 1881. Siding with Russia in war against Turkey (1877–78), he obtained at Congress of BERLIN full independence for Rumania. Married Elizabeth of Wied (Carmen Sylva). **Carol II,** 1893–1953, had to renounce right to succession (1925). In 1930 he proclaimed himself king, dethroning his son MICHAEL. Instituted personal dictatorship 1938. Was deposed in 1940 by Ion ANTONESCU and fled abroad with Magda Lupescu, whom he married in 1947.

carol, popular hymn, of joyful nature, especially associated with Christmas. The earliest date from the 15th cent.; many may be from pagan sources. Oldest printed carol is *Boar's Head Carol* (1521). Carols of French origin are also called noels.

Carolina campaign, 1780–81, of American Revolution. After capture of Charleston, British force under Cornwallis swept N, capping success at battle of Camden, Aug. 16, 1780. Patriot defense was broken in Carolinas except for guerrilla bands. American victory at Kings Mt., Oct. 7, 1780, prefaced campaign led by Gen. Nathanael Greene which freed both Carolinas of British and set stage for YORKTOWN CAMPAIGN.

Caroline Affair. In 1837 a small steamer, the *Caroline,* owned by U.S. citizens, carried men and supplies to Canadian rebels under W. L. MACKENZIE on Navy Isl. just above Niagara Falls. On Dec. 29, 1837, British and Canadian loyalists set fire to the ship and sent her over the falls. One American was killed. Affair caused tension in U.S.–British relations but was smoothed over.

Caroline Islands, group (525 sq. mi.; pop. 35,190), W Pacific; included 1947 in U.S. Trust Territory of the Pacific Isls. under UN trusteeship. Group includes two volcanic islands (Kusaie and Ponape), three major island groups (PALAU, TRUK, YAP), and many atolls and islets. Coconuts and sugar cane are produced. Discovered 1526 by Spaniards; was under Spanish rule 1886–99. Sold 1899 to Germany, occupied 1914 by Japan who received mandate over group in 1922. In World War II Palau and Ulithi were taken 1944 by U.S. forces.

Caroline of Anspach, 1683–1737, queen consort of George II of England. Supported Robert Walpole.

Caroline of Brunswick, 1768–1821, consort of George IV of England. Their marriage (1795) forced George, then prince of Wales, to put away his first wife, Mrs. Fitzherbert. Caroline was separated from George in 1796 but in 1820 refused to give up rights as queen. King instituted divorce proceedings, but these were later dropped.

Carolingians, dynasty of Frankish rulers, founded 7th cent. by PEPIN OF LANDEN. Ruled as mayors of the palace under MEROVINGIANS until PEPIN THE SHORT made himself king (751). His son, CHARLEMAGNE, crowned emperor in 800, brought dynasty to its zenith. After death of his son, LOUIS I, Carolingian empire was split by Treaty of VERDUN (843) among Louis's sons: LOTHARINGIA to LOTHAIR I; Germany to LOUIS THE GERMAN; France to CHARLES II. In 870 Lotharingia was divided between Louis and Charles. Arnulf was the last Carolingian emperor (d. 899); Louis the Child, the last Carolingian king in Germany (d. 911); Louis V, the last Carolingian king in France (d. 987).

Carolus-Duran (kärôlüs′-dürä′), 1838?–1917, French portrait and genre painter, teacher of many famous painters.

Carondelet, Francisco Luis Hector, barón de (kŭrŏndŭlĕt′), c.1748–1807, governor of Louisiana and West Florida (1791–97), b. Flanders. Severely taxed relations between Spain and U.S. by intriguing with Indians and Ky. frontiersmen.

carp, fresh-water fish native to Asia, introduced into Europe and America. *Cyprinus carpio,* common in America, is European carp of varied form and color. It has four barbels around the mouth and a greenish or brown thick-scaled body (sometimes yellowish or silvery) with red on fins. Sometimes grows to 3 ft., 25 lb. Raised in ponds in Europe.

Carpaccio, Vittore (vēt-tō′rā kärpät′chō), c.1450–c.1522, Venetian painter, follower of Giovanni Bellini. Depicted pageantry of 15th-cent. Venice.

Carpathian Russia: see RUTHENIA.

Carpathians (kärpā′thēŭnz) or **Carpathian Mountains,** chain of Central Europe, in E Czechoslovakia, S Poland, W Ukraine, and N Rumania. Forming an arc c.900 mi. long, they enclose the Danubian plain in N and E. The TATRA group in the N and the Transyl-

vanian Alps (see TRANSYLVANIA) in the S rise to 8,737 ft. and 8,361 ft. respectively. Rich in timber, minerals, mineral spas.

Carpathian Ukraine: see RUTHENIA.

Carpathus, Greek island: see DODECANESE.

Carpeaux, Jean Baptiste (zhä′ bätēst′ kärpō′), 1827–75, French sculptor, a favorite of the Second Empire.

Carpentaria, Gulf of (kärpŭntâ′rĕu), arm of Arafura Sea, indenting the N coast of Australia.

Carpenter, John Alden, 1876–1951, American composer. His music often depicts scenes of American life (e.g., orchestral suite *Adventures in a Perambulator,* ballet, *Skyscrapers*). He also wrote songs, symphonies, and chamber music.

carpet and **rugs** were used in anc. Nineveh, and in Egypt by c.2500 B.C. Today, types include antique Orientals, European hand-woven (e.g., Aubusson, Savonnerie), Brussels, Wilton, velvet, Axminster (Oriental type), chenille or chenille Axminster, ingrain carpeting (now little used), rag and hooked rugs (often made in households), many kinds of straw and fiber mattings. Handmade Orientals have wool pile knotted by hand (up to 1,000 knots per sq. in.). European industry depended on hand looms until Erastus Bigelow's introduction of power loom, 1841. U.S. rugmaking began in colonial days.

carpetbaggers, epithet used in the South after Civil War to describe Northern adventurers who flocked S to make money and seize political power in RECONSTRUCTION period. Carpetbags held their possessions. Some came as agents of the FREEDMEN'S BUREAU. Most engaged in large-scale political corruption.

Carpini, Giovanni de Piano, (jōvän′nē dā pyä′nō kärpē′nē), 13th cent., Italian traveler, Franciscan monk. Sent in 1245 by Pope Innocent IV to the Tartary court, he crossed Russia and central Asia to Karakorum, Mongolia, on horseback in c.100 days. Brought back important accounts of peoples and places.

Carpocrates (kärpŏk′rŭtēz), fl. c.130–c.150, Alexandrian philosopher. He and his son Epiphanes created a sect that advocated communal ownership of property, including women. The Carpocratians, related to the Gnostics, believed that corrupt man could be restored to union with the Absolute (God) by despising all created things.

Carr, Robert: see SOMERSET, ROBERT CARR, EARL OF.

Carracci or **Caracci** (kärät′chē), family of Italian painters of Bolognese school, founders of Eclectic school. **Lodovico Carracci** (lōdōvē′kō), 1555–1619, was influenced by the Venetians. With his nephews, Agostino and Annibale, and with Anthony de la Tour, he established in Bologna an academy which tried to unite in one system the best characteristics of each of the great masters. Noted pupils included Guido Reni and Domenichino.

Carrantuohill (kä″rŭntōō′ŭl), mountain (height, 3,414 ft.), Co. Kerry; highest peak in Ireland.

Carranza, Venustiano (vānōōstyä′nō kärän′sä), 1859–1920, Mexican statesman. Active in political life of Mexico after overthrow of Díaz (1911), he acted as president (1914–20) and contested leadership of nation with Huerta, Villa, Zapata, and Obregón. Dominant features of his reform program were incorporated in constitution of 1917: national ownership of subsoil deposits, restoration of EJIDO system, church and labor reforms. Constitution was never actually in force.

Carrara (kär-rä′rä), city (pop. 25,259), Tuscany, central Italy. Center of Italian marble industry; over 400 quarries. Constituted a duchy with MASSA. Cathedral (12th cent.); ducal palace.

Carrel, Alexis (kä′rŭl), 1873–1944, American surgeon and experimental biologist, b. France. Won 1912 Nobel Prize in Physiology and Medicine for work in suturing blood vessels, transfusion, and transplantation of organs. With Charles A. Lindbergh invented mechanical heart. Carrel devised methods of keeping tissues and organs alive in nutritive solutions. Wrote *Man, the Unknown* (1935).

Carrera, Rafael (räfäël' kärä'rä), 1814–65, president of Guatemala, a *caudillo*. Led revolt against anticlerical liberal government (1840), restored power of Church in Guatemala. Helped destroy Central American Federation and aided conservative governments in other Central American countries.

Carrera Andrade, Jorge (hôr'hä kärä'rä ändrä'dhä), 1903–, Ecuadorian lyric poet.

carriage, wheeled vehicle, usually horse-drawn, dating from Bronze Age. Early forms include CHARIOT and four-wheel goods wagon. During Middle Ages in Europe wheeled vehicles were largely superseded by litters because of poor roads. Cart and wagon introduced anew c.12th cent. Use of coach spread among nobility in 16th cent. Forms developed in 18th cent. include landau, barouche, phaeton; in 19th cent., hansom cab, brougham, victoria. U.S. carriage-building trade well estab. after 1812; four-wheel buggy with open sides and folding top was popular. See *ill.*, vehicles.

Carriera, Rosalba (rōzäl'bä kär-rēä'rä), 1675–1757, Italian portrait and miniature painter. Her works are delicate in color and vivacious.

Carroll, Charles, 1737–1832, American Revolutionary patriot, signer of Declaration of Independence. Known as Charles Carroll of Carrollton.

Carroll, John, 1735–1815, American Roman Catholic churchman, a Jesuit, b. Md.; educ. in Europe. A friend of Benjamin Franklin and an ardent patriot in the American Revolution, he is notable for his successful efforts to gain toleration for Catholics in the U.S. and to assure Catholicism a place in the republic. He was bishop (1790–1808) and archbishop (1808–15) of Baltimore.

Carroll, Lewis, pseud. of **Charles Lutwidge Dodgson,** 1832–98, English writer. An able mathematician, he developed from stories told to children of Dean Liddell (one of them named Alice) *Alice's Adventures in Wonderland* (1865) and *Through the Looking-Glass and What Alice Found There* (1872). Mingling of fantastic absurdity and shrewd observation has given delight to generations of children and adults. Also wrote humorous verse (e.g., *The Hunting of the Snark*, 1876).

Carroll. 1 City (pop. 6,231), W Iowa, W of Boone. Mfg. of farm equipment. **2** Town (pop. 359), N central N.H., NW of Crawford Notch in White Mts. Includes Twin Mountain, Fabyan House, and Bretton Woods resorts.

Carrollton, city (pop. 7,753), NW Ga., WSW of Atlanta. Farm trade center, with textile mills.

carrot, biennial plant (*Daucus carota*) with edible thickened root, rich in sugar, mineral salts, and vitamins. Cultivated for over 2,000 years.

Carryl, Guy Wetmore, 1873–1904, American humorist. His volumes of light verse include *Fables for the Frivolous* (1898) and *Mother Goose for Grown-Ups* (1900).

Carso, Yugoslavia: see KARST.

Carson, Edward Henry Carson, Baron, 1854–1935, North Irish politician. Opponent of Irish home rule, he denounced creation of Irish Free State (1921) but approved new government of N. Ireland.

Carson, Kit, 1809–68, American frontiersman and guide. Acted as guide for J. C. Frémont's Western expeditions of 1842, 1843–44, 1845; led Gen. Stephen Kearny's troops in trek from N.Mex. to Calif. in 1846. Noted Indian fighter.

Carson City [for Kit Carson], mining and resort city (pop. 3,082), state cap., W Nev., in Carson valley S of Reno. Laid out 1858 on site of a trading post (1851), it grew with discovery in 1859 of COMSTOCK LODE. Later it was a rail shipping point for ore. Became territorial cap. 1861.

Carson-Newman College: see JEFFERSON CITY, Tenn.

Carson Sink, swampy area, c.100 sq. mi., W Nev., NE of Fallon. Remnant of old L. Lahontan. Carson R. disperses here. Lahontan Dam, completed 1915, saves most of river's flow for NEWLANDS PROJECT.

Carstares or **Carstairs, William,** 1649–1715, Scottish statesman and divine. Friend and chaplain of WILLIAM III, powerful in efforts to reconcile him with Scottish church. Under Queen Anne promoted union with England.

Carstensz, Mount (kär'stünz), group of peaks, W central New Guinea, in Netherlands New Guinea. Highest peak, c.16,400 ft., is highest on island.

Cartagena (kärtähä'nä), city (pop. 73,190), N Colombia, Caribbean port; founded 1533. A treasure city of Spanish Main, it was attacked by buccaneers. Declared independence from Spain 1811. Now oil port.

Cartagena, city (pop. 43,104), Murcia prov., SE Spain; Mediterranean port and naval base. Lead, iron, zinc mines near by. Founded c.225 B.C. by Hasdrubal; chief Carthaginian base in Spain; taken by Romans 209 B.C.; sacked by Drake 1585.

Cartago (kärtä'gō), city (pop. 100,725), central Costa Rica; founded 1563. Was political center of country until SAN JOSÉ was made cap. (1821).

Carte, Richard D'Oyly (doi'lē kärt'), 1844–1901, English impresario of Gilbert and Sullivan operas.

cartel, national or international organization of manufacturers or traders allied by agreement to fix prices, limit supply, or divide markets among the member firms. Since it may have international scope, it is broader than the TRUST. Cartels arose in Germany in 1870s. Classic theories of economic competition oppose them, and they are outlawed in some countries.

Carter, Howard, 1873–1939, English Egyptologist. Associate of 5th earl of CARNARVON.

Carter, Mrs. Leslie, 1862–1937, American actress, whose maiden name was Caroline Louise Dudley. Associated with Belasco, she starred in several of his plays 1890–1906.

Carter, Nick, fictional detective character in 19th-cent. melodramatic fiction, probably created by J. R. Coryell, used by F. V. R. Dey and others. Also used as pseudonym.

Carteret, Sir George (kär'tŭrĭt, –rĕt), c.1610–1680, British proprietor of East Jersey, part of present NEW JERSEY. His cousin, **Philip Carteret,** 1639–82, was first governor of the colony.

Carteret, John: see GRANVILLE, JOHN CARTERET, 1st EARL OF.

Carteret, Philip: see CARTERET, SIR GEORGE.

Carteret, borough (pop. 13,030), NE N.J., on Arthur Kill opposite Staten Isl. Mfg of machinery, metal products, chemicals, and textiles.

Cartersville, city (pop. 7,270), NW Ga., NW of Atlanta and on Etowah R. near Allatoona Dam. Mines barite, ochre, manganese, limestone, and marble. Mfg. of textile goods.

Cartesian coordinates (kärtē'zhŭn) [for René Descartes], values representing the location of a point in relation to two straight lines (called axes). One axis is horizontal, the other vertical; the point is located by measuring its distance from each line along a parallel to the other line. Descartes advanced generality in mathematics by showing that an infinite number of curves are referable to one system of coordinates.

Carthage (kär'thĭj), anc. city of N Africa, on the Bay of Tunis; founded (traditionally by DIDO) by Phoenicians from Tyre in 9th cent. B.C. Grew to be a mercantile city-state under an oligarchy, with explorers (e.g., Hanno) going far and wide to gather trade. Leading families contended for control. The attempt to conquer Sicily in the 5th cent. was set back by the victory of Gelon of Syracuse at Himera (480 B.C.). Later Carthaginian excursions into Sicily led to the PUNIC WARS [from Poeni, the Roman name for Carthaginians, i.e., Phoenicians]. The contest between Rome and Carthage was hotly pursued, and the greatest general involved was a Carthaginian, HANNIBAL. Nevertheless, Carthage was finally defeated in the battle of Zama (202 B.C.), and the Carthaginian commercial empire fell. The city itself was destroyed by Scipio Africanus Minor (146 B.C.). A new city was later built and was the Vandal capital (A.D. 439–533), but it was virtually destroyed by the Arabs in 698. Louis IX of France died here on crusade.

Carthage. 1 City (pop. 3,214), W Ill., near the Mississippi and E of Keokuk, Iowa. Joseph Smith, Mormon leader, and brother killed in city jail (now Mormon shrine) by mob 1844. **2** City (pop. 11,188), SW Mo., NE of Joplin; founded 1842. Trade and mfg. center for farms, quarries, and mines (lead, zinc). Scene of a Confederate victory (1861) in Civil War. G. W. Carver was born near by.

Carthusians (kärthū′zhŭnz), Roman Catholic order of monks, noted for austerity, contemplation, and hermit life, founded by St. Bruno at La Grande CHARTREUSE. The Charterhouse in London and the Certosa at Pavia were Carthusian foundations, and their manufacture gave the name to the liqueur chartreuse.

Cartier, Sir Georges Étienne (kärtyā′), 1814–73, Canadian statesman. Elected to legislative assembly in 1848, he became leader of the French Canadians. Joined John A. Macdonald to form Macdonald-Cartier ministry (1857–62). Leading French Canadian advocate of confederation.

Cartier, Jacques, 1491–1557, French navigator, first explorer of Gulf of St. Lawrence and discoverer of St. Lawrence R.

Cartwright, John, 1740–1824, English reformer and pamphleteer. Had early naval career. Refused to fight American colonists; wrote *American Independence: the Glory and Interest of Great Britain* (1774). Called father of reform for advocacy of vote by ballot, abolition of slavery, and other reforms. His brother, **Edmund Cartwright,** 1743–1823, was the inventor of the power loom (1785) and other machines. Cooperated with Fulton in steam navigation experiments.

Caruso, Enrico (kŭrōō′sō), 1873–1921, Italian operatic tenor, considered by many the greatest of all time. Made his New York debut in 1903 as the duke in *Rigoletto.* He also appeared in *La Bohème, Pagliacci,* and in many roles.

Caruthersville, city (pop. 8,614), extreme SE Mo., on the Mississippi. Has cotton ginning and mfg. of shoes.

Carvajal, Francisco de (fränthē′skō dä kärvähäl′), 1464?–1548, Spanish conquistador in Mexico and Peru. Executed for opposing New Laws.

Carver, George Washington, 1864?–1943, American Negro agricultural chemist. Worked to improve economy of South; taught soil improvement, crop diversity; discovered many uses for peanuts, sweet potatoes, soybeans; devised products from cotton wastes.

Carver, John, c.1576–1621, first governor of Plymouth Colony (1620–21), b. England.

Carver, Jonathan, 1710–80, American explorer of the upper Great Lakes and Mississippi region. Hired by Robert ROGERS to seek "Western Ocean."

Carville, town, SE La., on Mississippi R. SSE of Baton Rouge. Has Natl. Leprosarium.

Cary, Alice, 1820–71, and **Phoebe Cary,** 1824–71, American poets, sisters. Phoebe wrote the hymn "One Sweetly Solemn Thought."

Cary, (Arthur) Joyce (Lunel), 1888–, English author. His novels, notable for brilliant characterization, include the comic trilogy made up of *Herself Surprised* (1941), *To Be a Pilgrim* (1942), and *The Horse's Mouth* (1944).

Cary, Phoebe: see CARY, ALICE.

Casa, Giovanni della (dĕl′lä kä′zä), 1503–56, Italian author of *Galateo* (1560), a treatise on manners.

Casabianca, Louis (kä″sùbēäng′kù), d. 1798, French naval officer, b. Corsica. At Aboukir Bay he commanded the *Orient,* which caught fire. He refused to quit his ship, and his young son refused to desert him. Their heroic death is subject of poem by Felicia Hemans.

Casablanca (kä″sùbläng′kù), city (pop. 551,322), French Morocco, a port on the Atlantic. On site of ancient Anfa. Destroyed 1468 and resettled 1515 by the Portuguese. Rebuilt by Mohammed XVI after 1755 earthquake. Under French rule since 1907, it is Morocco's

chief commercial and industrial center and has large exports of phosphates. In World War II it was scene of major Allied landing (Nov., 1942) and of Roosevelt-Churchill meeting (Jan., 1943).

Casablanca Conference, Jan. 14–26, 1943, meeting of U.S. Pres. Roosevelt and British Prime Minister Churchill at Casablanca, French Morocco. War pledged against Axis states until their unconditional surrender. Mediation united rival French forces.

Casadesus, Robert (käsädäsüs′), 1899–, French pianist, known especially for his playing of French music. He has frequently toured the U.S., often playing his own compositions.

Casa Grande National Monument: see NATIONAL PARKS AND MONUMENTS (table).

Casale or **Casale Monferrato** (käzä′lä mōnfär-rä′tō), city (pop. 25,485), Piedmont, NW Italy, on the Po. Cap. of MONTFERRAT from 1435; to Savoy 1703. Long an important fortress.

Casals, Pablo (pä′blō käsäls′), 1876–, Spanish cellist and conductor. He played many concerts in the U.S. In 1950 he emerged from retirement to play and direct at the Prades Music Festivals in S France.

Casanova de Seingalt, Giovanni Giacomo (jōvän′nē jä′kōmō käzänō′vä dä sängält′), 1725–98, Venetian adventurer and author, an international gambler and spy. Imprisoned in Venice (1755–56), escaped and lived in Paris till 1774; became librarian to Count Waldstein at Dux, Bohemia. Wrote brilliantly on subjects ranging from poetry to theology. His remarkable memoirs (in French) stress his innumerable, perhaps partly mythical, feminine conquests.

Casas, Bartolomé de las: see LAS CASAS.

Casca (Publius Servilius Casca Longus) (kăs′kù), d. c.42 B.C., one of the conspirators against Julius Caesar, first to stab him. Said to have committed suicide after defeat at Philippi.

Cascade, village (pop. 943), W Idaho, on North Fork of Payette R., near Cascade Dam in BOISE PROJECT.

Cascade Range, N continuation of the Sierra Nevada extending over 700 mi. through N Calif., Oregon, and Wash. into British Columbia. Parallels Pacific coast c.100–150 mi. inland. Snow covers highest summits and much glaciation is present. Chief peaks are Mt. Shasta (Calif.), Mt. Hood (Oregon), and Mt. Rainier (highest, 14,408 ft., Wash.). Fir, pine, and cedar forests occur (many in national reserves). Klamath and Columbia rivers cut E–W through range.

Casco Bay, inlet of the Atlantic, SW Maine, with principal harbor at Portland. Wooded shores and islands have many summer estates and resorts.

case, in Latin INFLECTION, one of several possible forms of a given noun or adjective, the form being essential to the meaning of the word in context. In the theory of some grammarians case forms represent a fixed relationship of the word to other words in a sentence or to the speaker. The cases (in conventional order with conventional significance) are: nominative [Latin,= for naming], referring to a person performing an action; genitive [Latin,= genetic], indicating a possessor (commonly equated with English possessive); dative [Latin,= for giving], indicating the secondary recipient of an action (indirect object); accusative [Latin,= for accusing], direct recipient of an action (equated with English objective); and ablative [Latin, = for carrying off], indicating separation, cause, instrument, and location of place and time. All these have both singular and plural forms (see NUMBER); adjectives agree in case with corresponding nouns. A sixth case, the vocative [Latin,= for calling], occurs only in singular to refer to a person addressed. In many usages cases do not adhere to these conventional references (e.g., some verbs take genitive instead of accusative). The term *case* is used for noun, pronoun, and adjective inflections in other languages, some having many more cases (e.g., locative [Latin, = for placing], as in Sanskrit; instrumental, in many early and some present Indo-European languages including Russian). Cases called in English by the same name do not necessarily correspond in different languages. The case system in English is simple and shows best in personal pronouns (e.g., *he*, nominative; *his*, possessive; *him*, objective).

casein (kā'sēin), complex PROTEIN and phosphorus compound. Forms c.80% of total protein in milk; enzyme rennin turns it to curds. Important in cheese making. Used in making paints, glues, plastics, and wool.

Case Institute of Technology: see CLEVELAND, Ohio.

Casella, Alfredo (käsĕl'lä), 1883–1947, Italian composer, pianist, conductor, and writer on music. His best-known compositions are the ballets *Il convento veneziano* and *La Giara*. Did much to promote the recognition of contemporary music.

Casement, Roger David, 1864–1916, Irish rebel. Knighted for work in British consular service. Attempted to obtain German aid for 1916 Irish rebellion. Returned in German submarine, captured, and hanged for treason. Irish regard him as martyr patriot.

Caserta (käzĕr'tä), city (pop. 30,910), Campania, S Italy. Sumptuous 18th-cent. palace was residence of kings of Naples. Surrender of German forces in Italy to Allies signed here April 29, 1945.

Casgrain, Henri Raymond (käzgrē'), 1831–1904, French Canadian historian. His writings were inspired by French Canadian nationalism and by French romanticism.

cashew (kushōō', kash'ōō), tropical American tree (*Anacardium occidentale*), valued for kidney-shaped cashew nut of commerce. Nuts are borne on end of fleshy stalk called cashew apple.

Cashmere, India: see KASHMIR.

cashmere, soft under wool of Tibetan or Kashmir goat, used for fine sweaters and cloth.

Casilear, John William (käs"ïlēr'), 1811–93, American engraver and landscape painter.

Casimir (kă'sùmĕr), Polish rulers. **Casimir II,** 1138–94, duke of Cracow (1177–94). Granted privileges to nobles, who in return vested hereditary rights as rulers of Cracow in his descendants (see PIAST). **Casimir III** (the Great), 1310–70, king of Poland (1333–70). During his relatively peaceful reign he acquired most of duchy of GALICH; codified Polish law; improved the lot of the peasants and the Jews; strengthened royal power at expense of nobles; founded Univ. of Cracow. Last Polish king of Piast dynasty, he recognized overlordship of Bohemia over Silesian branch of Piasts (1335). **Casimir IV,** 1427–92, ruled Poland and Lithuania 1447–92. Placed the two nations on equal footing; successfully ended war with Teutonic Knights by Second Peace of TORUN (1466).

Casimir-Perier, Jean Paul Pierre (zhä' pôl' pyĕr' käzēmēr'-pĕryä'), 1847–1907, president of France (1894–95); grandson of Casimir Périer.

Caslon, William, 1692–1766, English type founder. His "old-style" types combine well into legible words and pages without distracting details or "color" variations. Hence printers' maxim, "When in doubt, use Caslon."

Caspar: see WISE MEN OF THE EAST.

Casper, city (pop. 23,673), E central Wyo., on North Platte R.; founded 1888 on site of Oregon Trail ferry crossing (1847). Rail, distributing, processing center in an oil, livestock, and wool area. A city of oil booms, it taps Salty Creek (1890), Big Muddy, Teapot Dome, and Lost Soldier (1948) fields. Near by are Hell's Half Acre, Independence Rock, site of Fort Caspar, and Casper Mt. (recreation area). Region served by Kendrick project (Seminoe and Alcova dams), NORTH PLATTE PROJECT, and MISSOURI RIVER BASIN PROJECT (Kortes Dam).

Caspian dialects, related Western Iranian dialects of Indo-Iranian subfamily of Indo-European languages. See LANGUAGE (table).

Caspian Gates: see DERBENT, RSFSR.

Caspian Sea, salt lake (c.163,800 sq. mi.), USSR and Iran, between Europe and Asia, at 92 ft. below ocean level; world's largest inland body of water. Max. depth c.3,200 ft.; in S. Elburz mts. rise from S (Iranian) coast; Caucasus from SW coast. Fed by Volga, Ural, Kura, Terek rivers, sea has no outlet but a high evaporation rate. Large salt deposits. Fisheries, sealeries. Chief source of black caviar. BAKU and ASTRAKHAN are main ports. Project is under way to raise sea level, which has sunk 7 ft. since 1936.

Cass, Lewis, 1782–1866, American statesman. Governor of Michigan Territory (1813–31); U.S. Senator from Mich. (1845–48, 1849–57). Resigned in 1860 as Pres. Buchanan's Secretary of State, protesting decision not to reinforce Charleston, S.C., forts.

Cassaba, Turkey: see KASSABA.

Cassander (kùsän'dùr), 354?–297 B.C., king of Macedon, one of the DIADOCHI; son of Antipater. He managed to defeat Alexander the Great's mother, Olympias (316 B.C.), and murdered Alexander's widow, Roxana, and infant son. Cassander became the ruler in Macedonia and Greece and helped defeat Antigonus I at Ipsus (301 B.C.).

Cassandra, in Greek legend, Trojan princess; daughter of Priam and Hecuba. She learned art of prophecy from Apollo, but was never believed. As Agamemnon's slave, she was slain by Clytemnestra.

Cassano d'Adda (käs-sä'nō däd'dä), village near Milan, N Italy. Scene of two French victories: 1705, of Vendôme over Eugene of Savoy; 1799, of Moreau over Suvarov.

Cassatt, Mary (kùsăt'), 1845–1926, American painter and etcher. Spent most of her life in France. Greatly influenced by Manet and Degas; early allied herself with the impressionists.

cassava (kùsä'vù) or **manioc** (mă'nēŏk), tropical American plant (*Manihot esculenta*). Its roots yield cassava starch, a staple food in South America, used elsewhere in the form of TAPIOCA.

Cassel (käsĕl'), small town, N France, near Dunkirk. Scene of French victories over Flemings (1328; see PHILIP VI) and over Dutch (1677; see DUTCH WARS).

Cassel, Germany: see KASSEL.

cassia: see CINNAMON.

Cassini (käs-sē'nē), family of French astronomers and topographers, of Italian origin. Four generations successively headed observatory at Paris. **Giovanni Domenico Cassini** (jōvän'nē dōmā'nēkō), 1625–1712, organized the observatory. He discovered four satellites of Saturn and division in its ring, and determined Mars' rotation period. His son, **Jacques Cassini** (zhäk), 1677–1756, continued his work and advanced the science of earth measurement. His son, **César François Cassini** (sāzär' fräswä'), 1714–84, and grandson, **Jacques Dominique, comte de Cassini** (dōmēnēk' kōt' dù), 1748–1845, constructed a great topographical map of France.

Cassino (käs-sē'nō), town (pop. 9,208), Latium, central Italy, in Apennines, on Rapido R. In World War II Germans blocked Allied advance to Rome at Cassino and near-by abbey of MONTE CASSINO, resisting concentrated air and ground attacks (late 1943 to May 18, 1944). Town was virtually destroyed.

Cassiodorus (kăshōdō'rùs), c.480–c.575, Roman statesman and author. Held high office under Theodoric the Great. Made a collection of state papers (*Variae epistolae*); wrote *History of the Goths.*

Cassiopeia (kă"sēōpē'ù), in Greek legend, mother of ANDROMEDA. She was transferred to heaven, becoming the constellation Cassiopeia (five stars in it form a rough W, called Cassiopeia's Chair).

Cassirer, Ernst (käsēr'ùr), 1874–1945, German philosopher, professor at Hamburg (1919–33), later lecturer at Oxford. His profound studies in the relationship of science and philosophy had a stimulating effect over the Western world, and his writings on the nature of the state, on aesthetics, and on the nature of meaning are influential today.

Cassius (kă'shùs), Roman family. One member, **Quintus Cassius Longinus,** d. 45 B.C., won a reputation for greed and corruption when quaestor in Spain. He and Marc Antony vetoed the rule of the senate intended to compel Julius Caesar to surrender his army. Made an official in Spain after Caesar's triumph, he was faced with a rebellion that Caesar had to quell. Another member was **Caius Cassius Longinus**, d. 42 B.C., the Cassius of Shakspere's *Julius Caesar*. A supporter of Pompey, he was pardoned by Caesar but was a chief figure in the successful plot to assassinate Caesar. When Antony roused the people against the conspirators, he took part with Brutus in the battle of Philippi and there committed suicide.

Cassivellaunus (kǎ″sǐvǐlô′nùs), fl. 54 B.C., British chief, leader against invasion of Julius Caesar, 54 B.C. Defeated, he sued for peace.

cassowary (kǎs′ûwâr″ē), flightless, swift-running, pugnacious forest bird of Australia and Malay Archipelago. Smaller than the related ostrich and emu, it has dark, glossy plumage and vivid-colored, wattled neck.

Castagno, Andrea del (ändrā′ä dĕl kästä′nyō), d. c.1457, Florentine painter, a master of realism. Frescoes in Sant' Apollonia monastery, Florence.

Castaigne, André (ädrā′ kästän′), 1861–, French illustrator and painter.

Castalia (kăstä′lyù), spring near Delphi, Greece, on Mt. Parnassus, sacred to Apollo and the Muses.

Castalion or **Castellio, Sébastien** (kästāl′yùn, kästĕl′yō), 1515–63, French Protestant theologian, known for his defense of religious toleration in preface to his Latin translation of Bible (1551). His name also appears as Castellion and Châtillon.

caste, hereditary social class. Members restricted in choice of occupation and range of social participation. Marriage outside the caste prohibited. Social status determined by caste of one's birth. In India, four chief castes (with many subdivisions): Brahmans (priests), Kshatriyas (the military), Vaisyas (farmers and merchants), Sudras (laborers). Lowest social group, the pariahs or "untouchables" are outside caste system.

Castel Gandolfo (kästĕl′ gändōl′fō), village, Latium, central Italy, near Rome; possibly on site of anc. Alba Longa. Summer residence of pope.

Castellammare di Stabia (kästĕl″lämä′rä dē stä′byä), city (pop. 36,469), Campania, S Italy, on Bay of Naples. Navy yards. Anc. Stabiae, near here, was Roman resort; buried A.D. 79 in eruption of Vesuvius.

Castellani, Aldo, 1877–, British-Italian bacteriologist, authority on tropical medicine, and known in this field for research (esp. on sleeping sickness), writing, and organization of schools.

Castellio or **Castellion, Sébastien:** see CASTALION, SÉBASTIEN.

Castello or **Castelli, Bernardo** (bĕrnär′dō kästĕl′lō, –tĕl′lē), 1557–1629, Italian painter of Genoese school. Made the designs for Tasso's *Jerusalem Delivered*. His son, **Valerio Castello,** 1625–69, was a historical painter, whose best-known work is *The Rape of the Sabines* (Palazzo Brignole, Genoa).

Castellón de la Plana (kästĕlyōn′ dä lä plä′nä), city (pop. 42,324), cap of Castellón de la Plana prov., E Spain, in Valencia, near Mediterranean. Its port, Grao, ships oranges, lemons, wine.

Castel Sant' Angelo (kästĕl′ säntän′jälō) or **Hadrian's Mole,** landmark of Rome, on right bank of Tiber. Built A.D. 135–39 by Hadrian as imperial mausoleum; later converted into fortress; used as prison till 1870. Connected by secret passage with Vatican.

Castiglione, Baldassare, Conte (bäldäs-sä′rä kōn′tä kästēlyō′nä), 1478–1529, Italian author of *Libro del Cortegiano* (1518; Eng. tr., *The Courtier,* 1561), lively dialogues on Renassiance courtly ideals.

Castiglione, Giovanni Benedetto (jōvän′nē bänädĕt′-tō), 1616–70, Italian painter and engraver of Genoese school. Excelled at painting animals.

Castiglione delle Stiviere (dĕl′lä stēvyä′rä), small town, N Italy, NW of Mantua. Scene of Bonaparte's victory over Austrians 1796.

Castile (kästēl′), Span. *Castilla,* former kingdom, central and N Spain. Traditionally divided into two re-

gions: Old Castile (19,390 sq. mi.; pop. 1,577,135), in the north, with cities of Burgos, Santander, Segovia; and New Castile (27,933 sq. mi.; pop. 3,129,170), in the south, with Madrid, Toledo, Cuenca. Castile contains most of the high, arid plateau of central Spain. The upper Duero, Tagus, and Guadiana rivers form the chief basins. Agr., sheep grazing; much erosion. Mineral resources include mercury at Almadén. Few industries. Old Castile, at first a county of kingdom of LEON, became virtually independent by 10th cent. Sancho III of Navarre acquired it 1028, made it into separate kingdom for his son FERDINAND I. Later kings expanded territory at expense of Moors (New Castile); achieved permanent union with Leon (1230); estab. authority over rebellious nobles. Marriage of ISABELLA I of Castile with Ferdinand II of Aragon (Ferdinand V of Castile) resulted in personal union of the two kingdoms (1479). Union made permanent 1516 through accession of Charles I (later Emperor CHARLES V), who suppressed *comunidades* uprisings of 1519–21. Later history is that of Spain.

Castillo de San Marcos National Monument: see NATIONAL PARKS AND MONUMENTS (table).

Castine (kästēn′), town (pop. 793), S Maine, on peninsula in Penobscot Bay. Plymouth Colony estab. trading post near by, 1626. Town later changed hands several times among French, British, Dutch, Americans. Baron J. V. St. Castin began his "rule" 1667. British held it in Revolution and War of 1812. Has Fort George (1779; British-built) and Fort Madison (1811; rebuilt in Civil War).

casting: see FOUNDING.

cast iron: see IRON.

Castle, Vernon, 1887–1918, English dancer and aviator, whose real name was Vernon Castle Blythe. Introduced many dances (e.g., "Castle walk") with his wife, **Irene (Foote) Castle,** 1893–. She popularized bobbed hair and boyish figure. He was killed in an airplane accident in World War I.

Castle Garden: see BATTERY, THE, New York city.

Castle Peak: see ELK MOUNTAINS.

Castle Pinckney National Monument: see NATIONAL PARKS AND MONUMENTS (table).

Castlereagh, Robert Stewart, 2d Viscount (kä′sùlrā), 1769–1822, British statesman, b. Dublin. As chief secretary for Ireland, was responsible for suppressing French-aided rebellion in 1798. Secretary of war (1805, 1807–9) during struggle with Napoleon I; planned Peninsular War, coordinated land and sea power, and backed duke of Wellington. Resigned after political betrayal by George CANNING (with whom he fought a duel). As foreign secretary (1812–22), helped organize "concert of Europe" against Napoleon, later confirmed by QUADRUPLE ALLIANCE (1815). Advocate of moderate terms for France at Paris peace conference and Congress of VIENNA, favored policy of balance of power and ascendancy of conservative governments. Committed suicide.

Castle Shannon, borough (pop. 5,459), SW Pa., S suburb of Pittsburgh.

Castor and Pollux, in Greek and Roman religion, twin heroes called Dioscuri [Gr.,= youths of Zeus]. Sons of Leda by Zeus or by Tyndareus. They were giants, gifted in battle, and joined Calydonian hunt and Argonaut expedition. When Castor was slain, Zeus made the brothers into the constellation GEMINI. They were highly honored in Rome. Castor was notable as a horse trainer, Pollux as a boxer. Together they were patrons of sailors. Phenomenon of St. Elmo's fire is still called Castor and Pollux.

castor oil, oil extracted from seed of castor-bean or castor-oil plant (*Ricinus communis*). Used as purgative, lubricant, leather-softener, and in brake fluids, paints, and other materials.

Castracani, Castruccio (kästrōōt′chō kästräkä′nē), 1281–1328, Italian Ghibelline leader. Made duke of Lucca (1327) by Emperor Louis IV, he sought hegemony over Tuscany and was about to conquer Florence when he died and his principality went to pieces.

Castries (kä'strēz), town (pop. c.16,579), cap. of Saint Lucia, British West Indies. Has fine harbor.

Castriota, George: see SCANDERBEG.

Castro, Inés de (ī'nĕz dù kä'strō), d. 1355, Galician noblewoman, mistress of Dom Pedro of Portugal (later PETER I), to whom she probably was secretly married. Pedro's father, Alfonso IV, feared her influence and had her murdered. When Pedro became king he had two of her murderers put to cruel death. The tradition that he had Inés disinterred and crowned is probably untrue. Name is also spelled Inez.

Castrogiovanni, Italy: see ENNA.

Castro y Bellvís, Guillén de (gēlyän' dä käs'trō ē bĕl-vēs'), 1569–1631, Spanish dramatist, author of *Las mocedades del Cid,* which inspired Corneille's *Le Cid.*

cat, small domestic carnivorous mammal related to lion, tiger, leopard, jaguar, puma. It has retractile claws and acute senses (good eyesight in dim light). Longhaired breeds include Persian (now generally includes Angora because of interbreeding), the sacred cat of Burma, and the Tibetan temple cat. Among shorthaired cats are the common short-haired, Manx (tailless), Siamese, and Abyssinian. All are genus *Felis.*

catacombs, burial places of the early Christians, arranged in extensive subterranean vaults and galleries; also used incidentally for refuge from persecution and for religious services. Those at Rome lie outside the city gates, are 22 to 65 ft. below the ground, cover an area of c.600 acres, and were built in the first five centuries. Tombs were cut into walls of narrow plastered passages, which were covered with frescoes. Most bodies were removed to churches by 8th cent. Other catacombs were in Naples, Syracuse, Paris, Alexandria, and Sousse.

Catalan art. Although Catalonia still produces many fine artists, Catalan art as such (the religious art of Middle Ages and Renaissance) ended with 15th cent. Elaborately painted churches, architectural sculpture, and illuminated manuscripts (notably the Bible from Farfa abbey) were in international Romanesque style. Works of more distinctly regional character culminated in gorgeous 15th-cent. religious painting (esp. of Jaime Huguet and of Jaime, Rafael, and Pablo Vergós).

Catalan language, Romanic language of Italic subfamily of Indo-European languages. See LANGUAGE (table).

catalepsy (kä'tùlĕpsē), psychogenic fit, neurotically or hypnotically induced. Voluntary motion and sensibility are suspended, muscles are rigid, body is cold and pale, and pulse and respiration are slow. Duration varies from minutes to days.

Catalina Island: see SANTA BARBARA ISLANDS.

catalogue, descriptive list of names or items, such as an alphabetical list on cards or in a book of the books in a library. Assur-bani-pal's library at Nineveh was catalogued on shelves of slate. First known subject catalogue compiled by Callimachus at the Alexandrian Library in 3d cent. B.C. Sir Anthony PANIZZI began printing of British Museum catalogue of printed books, and Charles A. CUTTER devised modern dictionary catalogue (author, title, and subject in one alphabet). In 1901 Library of Congress began printing catalogue on 3"x5" cards.

Catalonia (kătùlō'nēù), Span. *Cataluña,* region (12,332 sq. mi.; pop. 2,890,974), NE Spain, stretching from Pyrenees southward along Mediterranean; historic cap. Barcelona. Other cities: Gerona, Lérida, Tarragona. Agr.; wine; olive oil. Hydroelectric power furnished by Ebro, Segre, and Cinca rivers has favored industries (textiles, machinery). Both Spanish and Catalan (akin to Provençal) are spoken. Part of the Spanish March founded by Charlemagne, medieval Catalonia was ruled by the counts of BARCELONA. Despite its dynastic union with Aragon from 1137 and with Castile from 1479, it kept its own laws and cortes until 18th cent. Peak of commercial prosperity came in

13th–15th cent., when Catalan merchants and adventurers helped the expansion of the house of ARAGON throughout the Mediterranean. Traditionally rebellious against central government, Catalonia obtained self-government in 1932–34 and in 1936–39; in the civil war it resisted Franco, who abolished its autonomy.

catalpa (kùtăl'pù), ornamental tree of genus *Catalpa,* with large, heart-shaped leaves, large clusters of white flowers, and long beanlike pods. Species in North America, India, and Asia.

catalysis (kùtă'lùsĭs), changing speed of chemical reaction by introducing a **catalyst.** Positive catalysts increase speed of reaction; negative, decrease. Catalyst takes some part in reaction, but can be recovered unchanged chemically. Water acts as catalyst since many compounds react only in solution. Enzymes act as catalysts in metabolic processes.

Catania (kätä'nyä), city (pop. 241,462) and seaport, E Sicily, Italy, in fertile plain at foot of Mt. Etna. Founded 8th cent. B.C. by Greek colonists; flourishing commercial center ever since. Suffered from repeated earthquakes, volcanic eruptions. Damaged in World War II. Cathedral dates partly from 12th cent. Univ. founded 1444.

catapult (kä'tùpŭlt), machine commonly used in medieval warfare; in effect, a giant crossbow operated by a windlass and designed to throw large stones (also arrows and other objects). Used in siege warfare from the 5th cent. B.C. to the 15th cent. A.D., when gunpowder and artillery grew common.

cataract, in medicine, opacity of lens of eye or its capsule. Causes include faulty development, injuries, infections, toxic states, and senility.

catastrophism (kùtäs'trùfĭzùm), doctrine that at intervals all living things have been destroyed by cataclysms and replaced by forms wholly different. This theory was attacked in 18th cent. by James Hutton, precursor of doctrine of UNIFORMISM.

Catawba, river: see WATEREE, river.

catbird, North American songbird and mimic related to mockingbird. It is slate gray, with black on the crown and tail and chestnut under tail coverts. It eats fruits and insects.

catchment area or **drainage basin,** area drained by a stream or other water body. Amount of water reaching stream or reservoir depends on size of catchment area, precipitation, and loss from evaporation and through absorption by soil and vegetation.

Cateau, Le (lù kätō'), town (pop. 7,682), Nord dept., N France; formerly Le Cateau-Cambrésis. Scene of heavy fighting (1914, 1918) in World War I.

Cateau-Cambrésis, Treaty of (käbräzē'), 1559, peace treaty among Spain, France, and England, signed at Le Cateau. From its 60-year struggle with France over hegemony in Italy, Spain emerged triumphant, winning Naples, Sicily, Milan. France restored Savoy to its duke. England, though technically allied with Spain, confirmed Calais in French possession.

catechism [Gr.,= oral instruction], series of questions and answers used in teaching a religious system. Martin Luther's date from 1520 and 1529. Reformed Churches revere Heidelberg Catechism (1563). Presbyterians adopted Longer and Shorter Catechisms (1647, 1648). A section in Book of Common Prayer is an Anglican catechism. Peter Canisius drew up a famous Catholic catechism (1556).

catechu (kä'tùchōō), extract, also called cutch and black catechu, from *Acacia catechu,* tree of India and Burma. It and pale catechu, obtained from Malayan plant (*Uncaria gambier*), are used in dyeing, tanning, and medically as an astringent.

categorical imperative: see KANT, IMMANUEL.

Catena, Vincenzo di Biagio (vēnchän'tsō dē byä'jō kätä'nä), c.1470–1531, Venetian painter. With Giorgione and Titian, ranked by contemporaries as one of three great painters of the day.

catfish, scavenger fish with barbels about mouth, adipose fin, tough scaleless skin (some South American forms contain bony plates). Most larger species are palatable. The blue or Mississippi catfish weighs c.20–150 lb. The mad tom and stone catfishes have pectoral spine with poison gland.

Cathari (kă'thŭrī), name given to various groups of a religious movement that began with the Bogomils in the Balkans (10th cent.) and included the ALBIGENSES. The fundamental ideas of the Cathari were belief in a dualism (God versus Satan, good versus evil) and practice of extreme asceticism. They did not accept the Christian idea of God and rejected sacraments and the priestly hierarchy. There were two classes: the Perfect and the believers. Doctrines apparently descended from Gnosticism and Manichaeism to the Cathari through the Paulicians.

Cathay (kăthā'), medieval European name for China, popularized by Marco Polo.

Cather, Willa (Sibert), 1876–1947, American novelist. Wrote novels and short stories of the Midwest (*O Pioneers!*, 1913; *My Ántonia*, 1918; *A Lost Lady*, 1923) and of historic past (*Death Comes for the Archbishop*, 1927; *Shadows on the Rock*, 1931).

Catherine: see also KATHARINE. Other spellings include Catharine, Katherine, and Kathryn.

Catherine, Saint, 4th cent.?, Alexandrian virgin martyr, traditionally supposed to have miraculously escaped dying on the wheel, only to be beheaded later. Her principal shrine is on Mt. Sinai, her attributes sword, crown, palm, wheel, and book. Her mystical marriage with Christ was popular as a subject of Renaissance art. Feast: Nov. 25.

Catherine, empresses of Russia. Catherine I (Martha Skavronskaya), 1684?–1727, a Livonian servant girl, was a mistress of Peter the Great before he took her as second wife (1711). Chosen his successor (1725), she ruled ably. **Catherine II** or **Catherine the Great** (Princess Sophie of Anhalt-Zerbst), 1729–96, of German birth, married the future PETER III in 1744. His worthlessness soon estranged her. She became thoroughly Russian and very popular. In June, 1762, a group of conspirators, headed by her lover Grigori ORLOV, deposed Peter and proclaimed her empress. Influenced by the Enlightenment, she planned vast reforms, but the PUGACHEV rebellion and the French Revolution drove her into reaction. A liberal law code remained a project; her charter to the nobility (1785) completed the enslavement of the serfs. Her foreign policy was imperialistic. Through her favorite, STANISLAUS II, she made Poland a Russian protectorate, then secured the major share in the Polish partitions of 1772, 1793, and 1795. She annexed the Crimea (1783) and in two wars against Turkey (1768–74, 1787–92) made Russia dominant in Near East. She began the colonization of Alaska. With her main interests in the East, she remained neutral in American and French revolutionary wars. Of versatile gifts, she wrote memoirs, comedies, stories, in French and in Russian, and encouraged birth of modern Russian literature. Among her many lovers, only Orlov and POTEMKIN were of consequence. Her son, Paul I, succeeded her.

Catherine de' Medici (dī mĕd'ĭchē), 1519–89, queen of Henry II of France; daughter of Lorenzo II de' Medici. Regent for her son CHARLES IX (1560–63). Sought to conciliate Protestants but later sided with Catholics. Plotted massacre of SAINT BARTHOLOMEW'S DAY (1572).

Catherine of Braganza, 1638–1705, queen consort of Charles II of England, daughter of John IV of Portugal. Dowry included Bombay and Tangier. Lived apart from court. Accused by Titus OATES of plot to poison the king (1678), but Charles protected her.

Catherine of Siena, Saint (sēē'nù), 1347–80, Italian Dominican nun. She early began to have visions that were to result in her *Dialogue* and *A Treatise of Divine Providence* and make her one of the greatest of Catholic mystics. Her life was one of great pain cheerfully borne, and her charitable love of mankind matched her love of God. In response to a vision, she

went to Avignon and persuaded Gregory XI to end the "Babylonian Captivity" of the papacy, and later her influence was great in supporting the Roman claimant in the Great Schism. Her works were dictated for she never learned to write. Feast: April 30.

Catherine of Valois (văl'wä), 1401–37, queen consort of Henry V of England, daughter of Charles VI of France. Later married Owen TUDOR. Tudor kings descended from them.

Catherine Tekakwitha (tĕk"äkwĭth'ù), 1656–80, American Indian girl of the Mohawk tribe, a Roman Catholic noted for her austere piety.

Catherine the Great: see CATHERINE II, empress.

cathode: see ELECTRODE.

cathode ray: see ELECTRON and X RAY.

Catholic Apostolic Church, religious community founded in England (c.1831) under Edward IRVING (hence its members are called Irvingites). Symbolism, mystery, and stress on second coming of Christ characterize the church.

Catholic Church, term meaning the universal church, adopted by many Christian sects. Generally in English when referring to the time before the Reformation it means the orthodox faith as opposed to movements pronounced heretical; when referring to the time since the Reformation, it usually means the Roman Catholic Church (sometimes also the Orthodox Eastern Church).

Catholic Emancipation, term applied to process by which Roman Catholics in the British Isles were relieved of civil disabilities dating back to Henry VIII. First concessions produced Gordon riots (1780). Most disabilities removed in 1791 for those in Great Britain who took a loyalty oath. Attempts of William Pitt and Pope Pius VII to get general repeal of the PENAL LAWS failed. In Ireland (see IRISH LAND QUESTION) agitation which forced repeal of restrictions (e.g., POYNINGS'S LAW) seemed a threat to Protestant domination. Act of Union (1800) destroyed Irish Parliament; gave Ireland representation in English Parliament. After repeal of the TEST ACT (1828), growing agitation in Ireland, headed by Daniel O'CONNELL, led to Catholic Emancipation Bill (1829) sponsored by Sir Robert PEEL. Most remaining restrictions removed in 1866, 1891, and 1926. Act of SETTLEMENT still excludes Catholics from the throne, from certain civil and religious offices, and from a few university places.

Catholic League, in French history: see LEAGUE.

Catholic University of America, at Washington, D.C.; controlled by Catholic hierarchy, the only U.S. pontifical university; for men and women; chartered 1887, opened 1889. Supported by contributions from all parishes.

Catiline (Lucius Sergius Catilina) (kă'tĭlīn), c.108 B.C.–62 B.C., Roman politician. A partisan of Sulla, he was made praetor and governor of Africa. In 66 B.C. he was barred from candidacy for the consulship because he was accused of misconduct (falsely, as it turned out). Disgruntled he got up an abortive plot to murder the consuls; he and his confederates were acquitted. Running for consul in 63 B.C. he was opposed by Cicero and the conservatives and was defeated. Thereupon he concocted a conspiracy to gain power. Cicero, acting on information from Catiline's mistress, exposed the conspiracy in the first of perhaps the most famous series of orations ever delivered—the orations against Catiline. The conspirators, who even approached the ambassadors of the Allobroges, were arrested and condemned to death, though Julius Caesar urged moderation. Catiline did not surrender and was killed in battle. The question of Catiline's character and guilt is unsettled, since the only sources on him—Cicero and Sallust—are hostile.

Catlettsburg, city (pop. 4,750), E Ky., on Ohio R. at mouth of Big Sandy R. near Ashland. Scene of American Folk Song Festival near by.

Catlin, George, 1796–1872, American artist and traveler. Went over the West and later through Central and South America to paint Indian portraits and scenes. Many pictures in National Mus. Wrote *Manners, Customs, and Condition of the North American Indians* (2 vols., 1841) and other works.

catlinite: see PIPESTONE.

catnip or **catmint,** perennial mint (*Nepeta cataria*), with aromatic leaves often made into tea. Catnip is attractive to cats.

Catoctin Mountain, E prong of the Blue Ridge in Md., extending SSW from just S of Pa. line. "Shangri-La," President Roosevelt's retreat and scene of important World War II conferences, is here.

Cato Street Conspiracy: see THISTLEWOOD, ARTHUR.

Cato the Elder or **Cato the Censor** (Marcus Porcius Cato) (kā′tō), 234–149 B.C., Roman statesman. He spoke much of the austere virtues of old Rome and decried luxury, extravagance, and innovations. He had fought in the Second Punic War, and, when sent in old age to Carthage, returned to insist sternly, "Carthage must be destroyed!" He thus helped to bring on the Third Punic War, in which Carthage was destroyed. A man of great wealth, he was noted for cruelty to his servants and for niggardliness. His history of Rome is now lost, and of his extant works a treatise on farming is the best known. Also Cato Major. His great-grandson, **Cato the Younger** or **Cato Minor,** 95 B.C.–46 B.C., was also named Marcus Porcius Cato. He was known particularly for incorruptible honesty, supported by Stoicism. He opposed Julius Caesar and denounced Catiline. A supporter of Pompey, he continued the struggle against Caesar after the defeat at Pharsala and held Utica. After the crushing defeat at Thapsus, he committed suicide. Also Cato of Utica.

cat's-eye, name for two green gems which show a line of light caused by reflection from parallel fibers. The more valuable is a form of chrysoberyl; the less valuable is a variety of quartz.

Catskill, village (pop. 5,392), SE N.Y., on Hudson R. (Rip Van Winkle Bridge) and S of Albany. Gateway to resorts in Catskill Mts. Farm (dairy, fruit, truck) trade center.

Catskill Aqueduct, SE N.Y., a main unit of New York city water-supply system; planned 1905. Schoharie Reservoir water sent via 18-mi. Shandaken tunnel (opened 1924) to Esopus Creek, which is dammed c.15 mi. downstream to form Ashokan Reservoir (area c.13 sq. mi.; 1916) W of Kingston. After aeration here, Catskill Aqueduct carries the water 92 mi. S, passing for 1,114 ft. under the Hudson at Storm King, to Kensico Reservoir in Bronx R. near White Plains, thence to Hillview Reservoir in Yonkers. (Kensico and Hillview reservoirs also receive water from Delaware R. project, begun 1937 and placed in partial emergency use in 1944.) From Hillview Reservoir tunnels take water to New York city (steel pipe across the Narrows to Staten Isl.)

Catskill Mountains, range of the Appalachians, SE N.Y., W of the Hudson and S of Mohawk Valley, rising to 4,204 ft. in Slide Mt. They are a dissected and glaciated part of the Allegheny Plateau, well wooded and rolling, with deep gorges and many waterfalls. Popular summer and winter resort. Delaware R. headstreams and Esopus, Schoharie, and Catskill creeks are a source of New York city water supply through Catskill and Delaware aqueducts. Catskill Forest Preserve includes region of the Rip Van Winkle legend.

Catt, Carrie (Lane) Chapman, 1859–1947, American suffragist. President of Natl. American Woman Suffrage Association. Led campaign for Federal suffrage amendment. Organized League of Women Voters. After 1923 she devoted efforts to peace movement.

cattail or **reed mace,** marsh perennial of genus *Typha,* with long, narrow leaves and a brown cylindrical spike of flowers used in winter bouquets.

Cattaro, Yugoslavia: see KOTOR.

Cattell, James McKeen (kǔtěl′), 1860–1944, American psychologist, pioneer in psychological research. His dismissal from Columbia Univ. teaching staff (1917) for alleged unpatriotic statements was widely protested. A prolific author, he also established and edited several scientific periodicals.

cattle, domestic animals of bovine genus, probably descended from the AUROCHS; closely related to the buffalo, bison, and yak. First cattle came to W Hemisphere on Columbus' second voyage. Since mid-18th cent., have been improved by selective and scientific breeding. Chief beef breeds are the Aberdeen Angus (black Angus) and Hereford (red, with white face); for dairying, Ayrshire (red and white or brown and white), brown Swiss, Dutch Belted (black, with white midriff), Guernsey (fawn and white), Holstein-Friesian (black and white), Jersey (tan, brown, gray, or cream; sometimes varicolored); for both purposes, Devon (red to chestnut), red polled (cherry red), and shorthorn (or Durham) and the related polled (hornless) shorthorn (red, red and white, or white and roan).

cattle plague: see RINDERPEST.

Catullus (Caius Valerius Catullus) (kŭtŭ′lŭs), 84?–54? B.C., Latin poet, one of greatest lyricists. Poems ascribed to him (116 extant) include many satires and epigrams as well as exquisite lyrics on his beloved (probably Clodia), called Lesbia.

Catulus (kă′chōolŭs), family of anc. Rome. An early member was **Caius Lutatius Catulus,** consul in 242 B.C., victor in the naval engagement with Carthage off the Aegates that ended the First Punic War. Another was **Quintus Lutatius Catulus,** d. 87 B.C., consul in 102 B.C. with Marius. Helped defeat the Cimbri, later opposed Marius, favoring Sulla. In the hour of Marius' triumph he committed suicide or was killed. His son, **Quintus Lutatius Catulus,** d. c.60 B.C., was consul 78 B.C. and leader of archconservatives. He and Claudius put down the revolt of Lepidus. Later he violently opposed Julius Caesar.

Cauca (kou′kä), river, c.600 mi. long, rising in W Colombia and flowing N through Andes to the Magdalena.

Caucasian Gates: see DARYAL, Georgian SSR.

Caucasus (kô′kŭsŭs), mountain system, USSR, between Europe and Asia, extending c.750 mi. from Black Sea SE to Caspian Sea. Main range, the Greater Caucasus, is a majestic chain of snow-capped peaks, culminating in Mt. ELBRUS at 18,481 ft. Pierced by MAMISON, DARYAL, and other passes, it divides N Caucasia, which slopes down to Kuban steppe, from Transcaucasia. The Lesser Caucasus, S of KURA R., is extension of Iranian plateau. Pastures, forests in uplands; agr., orchards, vineyards in valleys. Many health resorts (e.g., Pyatigorsk, Kizlovodsk). Mineral resources include rich oil fields at BAKU, GROZNY, MAIKOP, manganese at Chiatura. Caucasus was known to ancient Greeks: here Prometheus was chained, Jason sought Golden Fleece. Centuries of invasions and migrations left complex ethnical structure. N Caucasia, including historic CIRCASSIA, is part of RSFSR. Transcaucasia is divided into GEORGIAN SSR, AZERBAIJAN SSR, ARMENIAN SSR. Russian penetration in 19th cent. was resisted by Moslem elements until collapse of SHAMYL uprising (1859).

Cauchon, Pierre (pyěr′ kōshō′), d. 1442, bishop of Beauvais, France. President of court that convicted JOAN OF ARC.

Cauchy, Augustin Louis, Baron (ōgüstě′ lwě′ bärō′ kōshē′), 1789–1857, French mathematician, influential in every mathematics branch (especially theory of functions, integral and differential calculus, algebraic analysis) and also in astronomy, optics, and other fields.

caucus, political party gathering or standing party organization. In the U.S., legislative caucuses once nominated presidential candidates, and are still used in Congress to aid in party policy formation. In Great Britain the term usually used to condemn groups.

caudillo (koudhě′yō), type of Hispanic American political leader who arose with wars of independence.

Typical caudillo is usually mestizo with strong appeal to Indian and mestizo masses; has military ability; begins by championing rights of masses against wealthy white classes; later becomes oligarch himself. Famous caudillos: Rosas of Argentina, Carrera of Guatemala, Díaz of Mexico, Juan Vicente Gómez of Venezuela.

Caudine Forks (kô'dīn), narrow passes in Apennines, S Italy. Here in 321 B.C. Samnites routed Roman army, forced it to pass under yoke.

Caughnawaga (kä'näwä"gŭ), village, S Que., Canada, on St. Lawrence R. opposite Lachine. Founded 1667 as refuge for Iroquois Christian converts.

Caulaincourt, Louis, marquis de (lwĕ' märkĕ' dù kōlēkōōr'), b. 1772 or 1773, d. 1827, French general. Ambassador to Russia (1807–11); aide-de-camp to Napoleon on Russian campaign; foreign minister during Hundred Days. Left remarkable memoirs of years 1812–15, first published 1933 (Eng. tr., 1935–36).

cauliflower (kô'lĭ–), variety of cabbage, with edible white head of flowers and flower stems.

Caupolicán (koupōlēkän'), d. 1558, leader of ARAUCANIAN INDIANS who fiercely resisted Spanish Conquest of Chile.

caustic, substance that burns or corrodes organic matter. Caustic SODA is an alkali.

Cauvery or **Kaveri** (kô'vùrē), river, S India; flows c.475 mi. from W Ghats to Bay of Bengal. Sacred to Hindus. Irrigation-canal system at delta.

Cavaignac, Louis Eugène (lwĕ' ûzhĕn' kävänyäk'), 1802–57, French general. Fought in Algeria. As minister of war suppressed workingmen's rising in JUNE DAYS of 1848.

Cavalier, Jean (zhä' kävälyä'), 1679?–1740, French Protestant leader. Led uprising of CAMISARDS but made separate peace with government in 1704.

cavalier, in general, an armed horseman. In English civil war, Cavaliers were followers of Charles I, as against Roundheads, supporters of Parliament. Term for royalists until it was replaced by Tory.

Cavalier poets, literary group at court of Charles I of England, notable for the grace and wit of polished lyrics on love, fleeting youth and beauty. Included Herrick, Lovelace, Suckling, Carew.

Cavallini, Pietro (pyä'trō kävәl-lē'nē), c.1250–c.1330, Italian painter and mosaicist, who influenced Cimabue and Giotto.

cavalry, mounted troops trained to fight from horseback. Used among the anc. Egyptians, cavalry groups were much more commonly used by the Assyrians and the Persians. Speed gave them an advantage, but this was offset by the lack of saddles (until the time of Constantine I), and Greek and Roman victories were won by well-disciplined foot troops. Cavalry was first triumphant when used by Huns, Avars, Magyars, and Mongols in invading Europe. The typical soldierly figure of the Middle Ages was the mounted, armored knight. Reintroduction of mass warfare (e.g., the companies of English bowmen at Crécy, 1346) and the use of gunpowder made the infantry prominent again, but cavalry was extensively used, particularly for mobile striking forces and for scouting. Wherever warfare was open the cavalry shone, and cavalrymen were the elite of soldiery through the time of the American Civil War. In World War I and much more in World War II development of mechanized, motorized, and armored vehicles made horse cavalry obsolete except for very special missions (as in rough mountain terrain). In 1946 the U.S. army abolished cavalry as a separate army.

Cavan (kä'vùn), inland county (730 sq. mi.; pop. 70,-355), Ulster prov., Ireland; co. town Cavan. It is a hilly region of lakes and bogs with cool damp climate. Agr. chief occupation, but only a third of area is cultivated.

cave, a hollow in earth or rock. Formed usually by chemical or mechanical action of water. Ground water dissolves or wears rock; dashing waves cut into rocky shores. Most caves are in limestone, owing to its solubility; many are famous for STALACTITE AND STALAGMITE formations. Caves of Iceland and Hawaii were caused by volcanic action.

cave art, paintings and engravings found on interior cave walls. Earliest examples date from Paleolithic times, the Magdalenian phase showing most highly developed technique. Subject matter of paintings suggests they had magical intent. Famous examples are those of lower Italy, ALTAMIRA (Spain), the Dordogne, and the central Pyrenees.

Cave City, town (pop. 1,119), S Ky., NE of Bowling Green. Center of cave region (Mammoth Cave, Diamond Caverns, and others); tourist center.

Cavell, Edith (kä'vùl), 1865–1915, British nurse. Matron at Brussels hospital in World War I, she was shot by the Germans for aid to Allied prisoners.

Cavendish, Henry, 1731–1810, English physicist, chemist. Determined specific heats for certain substances. Did research on properties of "inflammable air" (hydrogen) that he isolated and described, on composition of air, electricity, density of earth.

Cavendish or **Candish, Thomas,** 1555?–1592, English navigator. Commanded third voyage around the world (1586–88), ravaging Spanish towns and shipping on W coast of South America. Died during disastrous second attempt at circumnavigation.

Cavendish, William: see NEWCASTLE, WILLIAM CAVENDISH, DUKE OF.

Cavendish Laboratory: see CAMBRIDGE UNIVERSITY.

caviar or **caviare** (kä'vēär), roe (eggs) of sturgeon prepared, mainly in Russia, as table delicacy. The eggs are black, green, brown, or yellow ("gray"), and vary in size from tiny grains to pea size.

Cavite (kävē'tā), city (pop. 35,052), SW Luzon, Philippines, on small peninsula in Manila Bay. Naval base (1898) at Sangley Point (opposite city proper) is held by U.S. as limited operational area.

Cavour, Camillo Benso, conte di (kämēl'lō bän'sō kōn'tä dē kävōōr'), 1810–61, Italian statesman, premier of Sardinia (1852–59, 1860–61). Chief architect of Italian unification under Victor Emmanuel II (see RISORGIMENTO).

cavy (kä'vē), name of GUINEA PIG and number of related South American rodents. Wild cavy is usually brown and has no tail. Forms include Patagonian cavy, Bolivian cavy, Peruvian cavy, restless cavy of Brazil, and CAPYBARA.

Cawdor (kô'dùr), parish, Nairnshire, Scotland. Cawdor Castle represented by Shakspere as scene of the slaying of Duncan by Macbeth 1040.

Cawnpore or **Kanpur** (both: kôn'pôr"), city (pop. 487,-324), S Uttar Pradesh, India, on Ganges R. Nana Sahib wiped out British garrison here in Sepoy Rebellion of 1857. Major trade and mfg. center.

Caxton, William, c.1421–1491, English printer. A mercer, he learned printing at Cologne. With Colard Mansion printed first book in English, *The Recuyell of the Historyes of Troye* (Bruges, 1475). He also issued first dated book printed in England, *Dictes or Sayengis of the Philosophres* (Westminster, 1477). He translated works and wrote prologues, epilogues, and additions.

Cayenne (kīĕn'), city (pop. 10,961), cap. of French Guiana, on island at mouth of Cayenne R. Cayenne pepper originally came from here.

Cayman Islands (kā'mùn), archipelago (c.92 sq. mi.; pop. 9,625), dependency in British West Indies, NW of Jamaica.

Cayuga Indians: see IROQUOIS CONFEDERACY.

Cayuga Lake, N.Y.: see FINGER LAKES.

Cazin, Jean Charles (zhä' shärl' käzē'), 1841–1901, French painter of figure compositions in landscape.

Cb, symbol of columbium (see NIOBIUM).

C battery: see BATTERY, ELECTRIC.

Cd, chemical symbol of the element CADMIUM.

Ce, chemical symbol of the element CERIUM.

Ceará (sēừrä'), state (59,168 sq. mi.; pop. 2,735,702), NE Brazil; cap. FORTALEZA. Atlantic coastal plain produces cotton, sugar, coffee. Semiarid uplands are used for cattle and goat raising. Suffered severely from droughts.

Cebu (sāboo'), island (1,702 sq. mi.; pop. 947,309), one of Visayan Isls., Philippines. Cap. and chief port is **Cebu** (pop. 167,503) on E coast, with harbor sheltered by Mactan isl. Founded 1565 by López de Legaspi; cap. of Philippine Isls. until 1571. Exports hemp and copra.

Cech, Svatopluk, Czech *Čech* (svä'tôplook chĕkh'), 1846–1908, Czech poet and novelist. An ardent pan-Slavist, he wrote lyrics and epics based on Czech history (*Zizka*, 1879; *Vaclav of Michalovce*, 1880) and country life (*The Smith of Lesetin*, 1889).

Cecil, Edgar Algernon Robert, 1st **Viscount Cecil of Chelwood** (sĭ'sŭl), 1864–, British statesman. Collaborated in draft of League of Nations Covenant. Won 1937 Nobel Peace Prize.

Cecil, Robert: see SALISBURY, ROBERT CECIL, 1ST EARL OF.

Cecil, Robert Arthur Talbot Gascoyne-: see SALISBURY, ROBERT ARTHUR TALBOT GASCOYNE-CECIL, 3D MARQUESS OF.

Cecil, William: see BURGHLEY, WILLIAM CECIL, 1ST BARON.

Cecilia, Saint, 2d or 3d cent., Roman virgin martyr, patroness of music, whose name is known in English literature through Chaucer, Dryden, and Pope. Also Cecily. Feast: Nov. 22.

Cecrops (sē'krŏps), in Greek mythology, first king of Athens, half man and half serpent. Established monogamy and first principles of law and religion.

Cedar, river rising in SE Minn., and flowing c.300 mi. SE across Iowa to Iowa R. at Columbus Junction.

cedar, name for certain trees, mostly coniferous evergreens, including northern white cedar and western red cedar (ARBORVITAE); red cedar (JUNIPER); southern white cedar (*Chamaecyparis thyoides*). Cedar of Lebanon (*Cedrus libani*) is native to Asia and Africa. Deodar cedar (*C. deodara*) possibly used in building Temple and house of Solomon (1 Kings 5–7).

Cedar Breaks National Monument: see NATIONAL PARKS AND MONUMENTS (table).

Cedar City, town (pop. 6,106; alt. 5,805 ft.), SW Utah, on Dry Coal Creek near Iron Mts.; founded 1851 by Mormon "iron mission" sent to develop coal and iron deposits. Ranch and tourist center near Zion and Bryce Canyon national parks and Cedar Breaks Natl. Monument.

Cedar Falls, city (pop. 14,334), NE Iowa, on Cedar R. just above Waterloo; settled 1845. Mfg. of farm equipment and pumps.

Cedar Grove. 1 Township (pop. 8,022), NE N.J., in Watchung Mts. N of Montclair. **2** Town (pop. 1,738), S W.Va., on Kanawha R. and SE of Charleston. Site of Booker T. Washington's boyhood home is near by.

Cedarhurst, residential village (pop. 6,051), on SW Long Isl., SE N.Y., SE of Jamaica.

Cedar Rapids, city (pop. 72,296), E Iowa, on Cedar R. and NW of Davenport; settled 1838. Railroad shops. Has cereal mills and mfg. of meat, metal, paper and food products. Seat of Coe Col. (coed.; 1881). Czechs settled here early (1852; now c.30% of pop.).

Cedartown, city (pop. 9,470), NW Ga., WNW of Atlanta near Ala. line. Textile goods and chemicals.

cedar waxwing: see WAXWING.

Cedron (sē'–), same as KIDRON.

Cefalù (chäfäloo'), port (pop. 9,654), N Sicily, Italy. Cathedral (12th cent.) is splendid example of Norman-Sicilian architecture.

celandine (sĕl'ŭndīn), Old World biennial plant (*Chelidonium majus*), naturalized in E North America. Its small yellow flowers are borne in loose clusters and the compound leaves are rounded or lobed. Alkaloids are found in the yellow juice and other parts of the plant.

Celebes (sē'lŭbēz), island (69,277 sq. mi.; pop. 3,781,-554), INDONESIA, E of Borneo. Comprises four moun-

tainous peninsulas. Natural resources include gold, silver, coal, nickel, and iron. Coffee, copra, and sago are grown; timber is exported. The Portuguese first came here in 1512 and in 1625 settled in Macassar. They were ousted 1660 by the Dutch. The **Celebes Sea** lies between Celebes and the S Philippines.

celery, biennial plant (*Apium graveolens*) with fleshy stalks, grown largely for use in salads. Celeriac is variety grown for edible, thickened crown.

celesta: see PERCUSSION INSTRUMENTS.

Celestina, La (lä thälästē'nä), Spanish novel in dramatic form attributed to Fernando de ROJAS. Published as *Comedia de Calisto y Melibea* (1499), it came to be called after the principal character, La Celestina, a cunning and kindly old woman.

Celestine I, Saint (sĕ'lŭstīn), d. 432, pope (422–32). Asserted power of the papacy by issuing a judgment against the heresy of Nestorius and instructing his delegates to the Council of Ephesus to judge, not to discuss. Suppressed semi-Pelagianism. Feast: July 27.

Celestine V, Saint, 1215–96, pope (1294), an Italian named Pietro del Murrone. A hermit noted for ascetic holiness, he gathered followers about him (core of the later Celestines). Disagreement among the cardinals led to his being called from his mountain retreat to be made pope. Charles II of Naples took control of affairs, and the impractical pope, realizing that he was a puppet, resigned. Boniface VIII succeeded him. Canonized 1313 at instance of French king Philip IV. Feast: May 19.

Celina (sŭlī'nŭ), resort village (pop. 5,703), W Ohio, SW of Lima, on Grand L. Mfg. of furniture.

Céline, Louis Ferdinand (lwē' fĕrdēnä' sälĕn'), 1894–, French author, whose real name is Louis Ferdinand Destouches. His misanthropic novels, *Journey to the End of Night* (1932; Eng. tr., 1934) and *Death on the Installment Plan* (1936; Eng. tr., 1938), created a sensation. His misanthropy drove him to fascism.

cell, in biology, unit (usually microscopic) of structure and function of which animals and plants are composed. Protoplasm, the living matter of the cell, consists of the nucleus and cytoplasm; in most cells the nucleus contains a nucleolus (small, round, dense mass); delicate plasma membrane develops on outer boundary of cytoplasm. Both plant and animal nuclei have major role in process of cell division; cytoplasm, controlled by nucleus, performs other cell functions. Cytology is the science of cell study. See also MITOSIS. See *ill.*, p. 633.

cell, in electricity, a source of electric current in which current flow is the result of chemical action. Cell consists of a positive ELECTRODE and a negative electrode, which conduct electricity, and an electrolyte which acts chemically upon one of the electrodes. A simple cell form is glass jar with dilute solution of sulphuric acid holding zinc and copper electrodes which are connected externally by a conductor (such as wire). Chemical action causes electrons to flow through wire from negative (zinc) plate to positive (copper) plate; this is opposite to conventional direction of flow of "electric current." Other cells are the Bunsen, Daniell, and Leclanché cells. Voltage depends on activity of substances used. Common dry cell consists of zinc cylinder enclosed at one end and lined with absorbent material, a central core of carbon, and a paste (serving as the electrolyte) of carbon granules and manganese dioxide saturated with a solution of ammonium chloride.

Celle (tsē'lŭ), city (pop. 59,254), Lower Saxony, N Germany, on Aller R. Oil refineries; machinery and soap mfg. Chartered 1294; residence of dukes of Brunswick-Lüneburg until 1705.

Cellini, Benvenuto (chēlē'nē, Ital. bănvānoo'tō chällē'nē), 1500–1571, Italian sculptor, b. Florence. As a metalworker he enjoyed the patronage of Pope Clement VII and later of Francis I of France. Famous for *Perseus with the Head of Medusa* (Florence) and for intricate metalwork, such as the gold and enamel salt-cellar of Francis I. Autobiography describes escapades, enmities, and banishments.

cello or **'cello:** see VIOLIN.

Cellophane (sĕ'lūfān), trade name for thin, transparent, flexible, nonpoisonous, moistureproof sheeting, a cellulose product made by viscose process.

celluloid, transparent, colorless substance made by treating cellulose nitrates with camphor and alcohol to form paste which can be rolled or molded.

cellulose, carbohydrate produced by cytoplasm of plant cells and forming bulk of cell wall. Absorbent cotton, jute, linen are almost pure cellulose; it forms bulk of paper, wood, wood pulp. Inert, insoluble in water, very absorbent. Used to make guncotton, pyroxylin, celluloid, collodion, cellulose acetate, RAYON, and CELLOPHANE.

Celsius, Anders (än'dùrs sĕl'sēŭs), 1701–44, Swedish astronomer, inventor (1742) of centigrade (or Celsius) thermometer. Made studies of aurora borealis.

Celsus, Aulus Cornelius, fl. A.D. 14?, Latin encyclopedist; his extant work, eight books on medicine.

Celt (sĕlt) or **Kelt** (kĕlt). **1** One who speaks a Celtic language or descends from an area where Celtic is or recently was spoken. **2** Member of a group of peoples known from the early 2d millennium B.C., who advanced to political and cultural leadership in W and Central Europe between 1200 and 400 B.C.

Celtic languages, subfamily of Indo-European languages, spoken in British Isles and in Brittany. See LANGUAGE (table).

Cenci, Beatrice (bäätrē'chä chän'chē), 1577–99, Italian noblewoman. Imprisoned by a vicious father, she procured his murder with complicity of her stepmother, brothers, and lover. Executed after a famous trial. Subject of tragedy by Shelley.

Cenis, Mont (mō' sŭnē'), Alpine pass, 6,835 ft. high, on French-Italian border. New road built 1810. Railroad tunnel, 8 mi. long, built 1871, connects Turin with Chambéry.

Cennini, Cennino (chän-nē'nō chän-nē'nē), c.1365–1440, Florentine painter. *Treatise on Painting* describes technical processes of Giotto's followers.

Cenozoic era, fifth grand division of geologic time, covering c.60–75 million years. It has witnessed the shaping of our present landscape. Mammals replaced reptiles as dominant life, and finally man appeared. See also QUATERNARY; TERTIARY; GEOLOGY, table.

censorship, official restriction of any public expression believed to threaten the governing authority or the moral order. There are two types, preventive (before material is issued) and punitive (after material is issued). Practice known in ancient Greece and Rome, was very common in religious troubles of Reformation. Censorship of press, usual in totalitarian countries, is frowned upon in democracies except in wartime. In U.S. most censorship of movies by authorities is on grounds of obscenity.

centaur (sĕn'tôr), in Greek religion, descendant of Ixion, a creature half man and half horse. Centaurs lived in Thessaly. Though generally savage, some, like CHIRON, were friends and teachers of men.

Centennial Exposition, International, held in Philadelphia from May to Nov., 1876, to celebrate 100th anniversary of Declaration of Independence. Fairmount Park was site. First U.S. world's fair, it particularly exhibited U.S. technical advance and industrial growth.

Center Line, residential city (pop. 7,659), SE Mich., near Detroit.

Centerville. 1 City (pop. 7,625), S Iowa, SW of Ottumwa, in coal area. Mfg. of castings and bricks. **2** Borough (pop. 5,845), SW Pa., on Monongahela R., S of Pittsburgh, in agr. and coal area.

centigrade scale: see TEMPERATURE.

centipede (sĕn'tŭpēd), flattened, segmented, wormlike, chiefly nocturnal animal of phylum Arthropoda; related to insects. It has numerous jointed legs, the first pair bearing poison claws to paralyze prey (insects, worms). Centipedes are usually 1–8 in. long. Unlike the MILLIPEDE, the centipede does not eat plants.

Central America, term applied to republics of Costa Rica, Guatemala, Honduras, Nicaragua, Salvador, and one colony, British Honduras. Panama is often included. See map, p. 703.

Central American Federation or **Central American Union,** political confederation of republics of Central America (1825–38). Presidents were Manuel José Arce and Francisco Morazán.

Central Australia: see NORTHERN TERRITORY.

Central City, town (pop. 371; alt. 8,560 ft.), N central Colo., in Clear Creek Canyon W of Denver. Boomed with gold discovery 1859. This "ghost town" revives in July with drama, music festival in opera house (1878). Mines reactivated in World War II.

Central Falls, industrial city (pop. 23,550), NE R.I., on Blackstone R. and adjoining Pawtucket. Mfg. of glass, textiles, leather and wood products, plastics, chemicals, and machinery.

Centralia (sĕntrā'lĕù). **1** City (pop. 13,863), S Ill., E of St. Louis; platted 1853. Shipping center of agr., coal, and oil area with railroad shops and metal and food products. Tragic mine explosion of 1947 led to investigations in which certain mines were declared unsafe. **2** City (pop. 8,657), SW Wash., S of Olympia. Grain, dairy, and lumber center.

Central Park, 840 acres, largest park on Manhattan isl., New York city, between 59th and 110th streets and Fifth and Eighth avenues. Land was acquired by city in 1856 and improved after the plans of F. L. Olmstead and Calvert Vaux. Here are Metropolitan Mus. of Art, a formal conservatory garden, a zoo, an Egyptian obelisk known as "Cleopatra's Needle," the Mall, and recreational facilities.

Central Powers, in WORLD WAR I, the coalition of Germany, Austria-Hungary, Bulgaria, and Turkey.

Central Provinces and Berar: see MADHYA PRADESH.

Central Valley, trough c.450 mi. long, 50 mi. wide, central Calif., between the Sierra Nevada (E) and Coast Ranges; composed of Sacramento (N) and San Joaquin valleys. Project for redistribution and use of region's water resources was begun 1935. Abundant Sacramento R. waters are to benefit San Joaquin Valley. Project now includes Shasta Dam (hydroelectric) and Keswick Dam (both in Sacramento R.); Delta Cross Channel, which fights soil salinity in delta and conducts Sacramento R. water to Delta-Mendota Canal, leading to San Joaquin R. (irrigation); and Contra Costa Canal (48 mi.), which supplies Sacramento water to farms and cities in Contra Costa co. From Friant Canal in San Joaquin R., Madera Canal goes 36 mi. N, and Friant-Kern Canal c.150 mi. S. Steam power plant at Antioch. Many other dams, reservoirs, canals, and powerhouses are planned.

Centre College of Kentucky: see DANVILLE.

centrifugal force and **centripetal force:** see FORCE.

centrifuge (sĕn'trùfūj), device using centrifugal force to separate substances of different density, e.g., liquid and solid portions of blood. Has base (or frame), motor, and rotating part which holds mixture. Cream separator is common type.

century plant: see AGAVE.

Ceos, Greek island: see CYCLADES.

cephalic index (sùfă'lĭk), ratio of breadth of head to its length. Used in anthropological studies.

Cephalonia (sĕfŭlō'nyù), Gr. *Kephallenia,* island (289 sq. mi.; pop. 57,384), Greece, largest of IONIAN ISLANDS. Irregular and mountainous, it rises to 5,314 ft. in Mt. Aenos, formerly crowned with a temple to Zeus. Argostoli, port and chief town, exports currants, wine, and olive oil. Sheep raising; fishing. A member of Aetolian League, Cephalonia was ruled by Rome after 189 B.C. and by Byzantium until its occupation by Venice (1126). In 1797 it was ceded to France, and its later history is that of Ionian Isls.

Cephas (sē'fùs), Jesus' nickname for St. PETER.

Cephisodotus (sĕfĭsŏ'dŭtùs), fl. 4th cent. B.C., two Greek sculptors. The elder was the master of Praxiteles; the younger was probably the son of Praxiteles.

Cephissus (sĭf'ĭ·sŭs), Gr. *Kephisos,* name of Greek rivers. **1** Rising in Parnassus and flowing 75 mi. ESE into N Euboic Gulf. **2** Rising in Mt. Pentelikon and flowing S past Athens into Saronic Gulf.

Ceram (sērăm'), island (7,191 sq. mi.; pop. 100,029), one of the Moluccas, Indonesia. Central mountains rise to over 10,000 ft. Copra, resin, sago.

Ceramic Gulf (sùrà'mĭk), ancient name of Gulf of Kos or Kerme, SW Turkey, an inlet of the Aegean Sea. On it was Halicarnassus.

Cerberus (sûr'bùrùs), in Greek religion, many-headed dog with a mane and a tail of snakes. He watched gate of Hades. The honey cake buried by the Greeks with the dead was to quiet him. His capture was one of 12 labors of HERCULES.

cerebellum: see BRAIN.

cerebrospinal meningitis: see MENINGITIS.

cerebrum: see BRAIN.

Ceres (sēr'ēz), in Roman religion, goddess of agriculture; daughter of Saturn and Ops. Identified with Greek DEMETER. Her worship included fertility rites and rites for the dead. Her most famous temple was on Aventine Hill; her chief festival was Cerealia.

Cerignola (chārēnyō'lä), town (pop. 37,163), Apulia, S Italy. Scene of major Spanish victory (1503) over French in ITALIAN WARS.

cerium (sēr'ēùm), metallic element of RARE EARTHS (symbol = Ce; see also ELEMENT, table). Ductile, malleable, tarnishes in moisture. Forms oxide when heated; alloys. Compounds used to make lamp mantles, and in medicine.

Cernauti: see CHERNOVTSY, Ukraine.

Cerro de Pasco (sĕ'rō dā pä'skō), city (pop. 19,187), central Peru. It is 13,973 ft. high (one of highest cities in world), bleak and barren, but its fabulous silver mines, discovered 1630, have made it world renowned. Copper and vanadium also mined here.

Certosa di Pavia (chārtō'zä dē pävē'ä), former Carthusian abbey in Pavia, Italy; a national monument since 1866. Built between 14th and early 16th cent., it is a masterpiece of the Renaissance, with rich marbles and profuse sculptural decorations.

cerussite (sēr'ùsĭt), colorless, white, or gray brittle carbonate of lead, an important ore of lead.

Cervantes (Saavedra), Miguel de (sùrvän'tēz, Span. mē·gĕl' dä thĕrvän'täs sä"ävä'dhrä), 1547–1616, Spanish novelist, generally regarded as the greatest figure of Spanish literature, author of DON QUIXOTE DE LA MANCHA. As a soldier Cervantes had a highly adventurous life: a wound at the battle of Lepanto cost him his left arm; five years of captivity as a slave in Algiers ended when he was ransomed by his family. After retiring from the army (1582) he was poor and often in debt. Besides *Don Quixote,* one of the masterpieces of world literature, he wrote other fiction (e.g., *Novelas ejemplares,* 1613), a pastoral romance, and plays.

Cervera y Topete, Pascual (päskwäl' thĕrvä'rä ē tōpä'tä), 1839–1909, Spanish admiral, commander of Atlantic fleet in SPANISH-AMERICAN WAR. Blockaded (1898) by U.S. fleet at Santiago de Cuba; tried to run blockade but was utterly defeated and captured.

Cesalpino, Andrea: see CAESALPINUS, ANDREAS.

Cesarean section: see CAESAREAN SECTION.

Cesis (tsā'zēz), Ger. *Wenden,* town (pop. 8,748), N Latvia. Agr. center; paper mills. Former seat of Livonian Knights, who built its ancient castle. Also spelled Tsesis, Zehsis.

cesium (sē'zēùm), rare, silver-white, soft, metallic element (symbol = Cs; see also ELEMENT, table). It is the most active metal, a member of ALKALI METALS, never found free in nature; cesium chloride is widely distributed in minute quantities.

Ceske Budejovice, Czechoslovakia: see BUDWEIS.

cesspool, cistern made to receive sewage. Types include watertight (should be 150 ft. from surface water and 60 ft. from cistern or drinking water source), and leach-

ing (built to allow liquid sewage to soak through). Some have drains to carry liquid sewage to adjoining ground.

Cetinje (tsĕ'tĭnyĕ), small town, Montenegro, Yugoslavia, near Adriatic. Grew around monastery, founded 1485; cap. of Montenegro until 1916.

Cette, France: see SÈTE.

Ceuta (syōō'tù), city (pop. c.67,790), Spanish Morocco, a Mediterranean port, opposite Gibraltar. Built on site of a Phoenician colony. Portugal took it in 1415, making the first permanent European conquest in Africa. Under Spanish rule since 1580.

Cévennes (sāvĕn'), mountain range, S France, limiting the Massif Central toward S and E. Mont Lozère (5,584 ft.) is highest peak. Sheep grazing, sericulture, coal mining. Much erosion.

Ceylon (sēlŏn'), Sanskrit *Lanka,* island (25,332 sq. mi.; pop. 6,657,339), in Indian Ocean, SE of India; since 1948 a dominion of British Commonwealth of Nations; chief port and cap. Colombo. Mainly mountainous with broad coastal plain. Chief crops are rice, coconuts, rubber, and tea. Original inhabitants were conquered in 6th cent. B.C. by Vijaya, Aryan prince of India, who estab. first Singhalese kingdom. Buddhism was introduced in 3d cent. B.C., and ANURADHAPURA became a great Buddhist center. Visited by Arab traders 12th–13th cent. The Portuguese won control over much of the coast in 16th cent. but were ousted by the Dutch in 1658. The British seized Dutch settlements 1795–96 and won control over kingdom of KANDY in 1815.

Cézanne, Paul (pôl' sāzän'), 1839–1906, French painter, an outstanding figure in modern French art. Studied under Pissarro and exhibited at the impressionist show of 1874. He developed a highly original style which has had a profound influence on later artists. The main characteristics of his painting are the use of vivid color, but with a striving for depth in shadows and outlines, and an attempt to unite the best elements of impressionism with the art of the past. He worked in oil and water color and excelled in landscapes (esp. of his native Provence) and still lifes.

Cf, chemical symbol of the element CALIFORNIUM.

Chabas, Paul Émile (pôl' āmēl' shäbäs'), 1869–1937, French painter. Created sensation with exhibition (1912) of his nude, *September Morn.*

Chablis (shäblē'), village, Yonne dept., N central France, in wine-growing region (white Burgundy).

Chabot, Philippe de (fēlēp' dù shäbō'), also known as **Admiral de Brion** (brēō'), 1480–1543, admiral of France. Credited with originating project of a French colony in Canada.

Chabrier, Alexis Emmanuel (shäbrēä'), 1841–94, French composer. Among his works are *Joyeuse marche; Bourrée fantasque;* an opera, *Le Roi malgré lui; España.*

Chaco (chä'kō), extensive, sparsely populated lowland plain, central S America, divided among Paraguay, Bolivia, and Argentina. After Chaco War (1932–35) between Paraguay and Bolivia, treaty was signed giving Paraguay three quarters of disputed N area of Chaco and Bolivia a corridor to Paraguay R. and certain port privileges there.

Chaco Canyon National Monument: see NATIONAL PARKS AND MONUMENTS (table).

Chad, Lake (chăd), central Africa. Bordered mainly by French Equatorial Africa and Nigeria. Its area (4,000–8,000 sq. mi.) varies with seasons.

Chadds Ford: see BRANDYWINE, BATTLE OF.

Chadwick, French Ensor, 1844–1919, U.S. naval officer. Cited for conduct at battle of Santiago in Spanish-American War.

Chadwick, George Whitefield, 1854–1931, American composer, director of the New England Conservatory of Music (1897–1931). Composer of overtures, symphonies, chamber music, and operas (e.g., *Judith*).

Chadwick, Sir James, 1891–, English physicist. Won 1935 Nobel Prize for discovery of NEUTRON.

Chaeronea (kĕrŭnē'ŭ), anc. town, Boeotia, Greece. Birthplace of Plutarch. Here Philip of Macedon defeated Athenians and Boeotians (338 B.C.), Sulla defeated Mithridates VI of Pontus (86 B.C.)

Chaffee, Adna Romanza (chä'fē), 1842–1914, U.S. army officer. Led American contingent in Boxer Rebellion. Army chief of staff 1904–6.

Chagall, Marc (märk shŭgäl'), 1889–, Russian painter, b. Vitebsk. Since 1910 he has lived mainly in France. Considered a forerunner of surrealism. He uses flower and animal symbols and draws his main subject matter from Jewish folklore.

Chagres (chä'grās), small river of Panama used for making Gatun Lake for Panama Canal.

Chahar (chä'här'), province (45,000 sq. mi.; pop. 3,500,-000), N China; cap. Kalgan. Lies mainly between two sections of Great Wall. One of China's main producers of iron ore. Stock raising is important. Originally formed 1914 as Mongol administrative area. Occupied 1937–45 by Japan.

Chaillé-Long, Charles (shäyä'-lông'), 1842–1917, American soldier and African explorer. Served in Civil War and Egyptian army. Explored Nile area.

Chaillu, Paul Belloni du: see DU CHAILLU.

Chain, Ernst Boris, 1906–, English biochemist. Shared 1945 Nobel Prize in Physiology and Medicine for work on PENICILLIN.

Chalcedon (kăl'sĭdŏn, kălsē'dŭn), anc. Greek city of Asia Minor, on Bosporus, facing Byzantium.

Chalcedon, Council of, 451, fourth ecumenical council. It disposed of the heresy of EUTYCHES (which had been advanced by the scandalous Robber Synod) with the final Catholic pronouncement of the nature of Christ in the *Definition*. This, reflecting the *Tome* of Leo I, says that divine nature and human nature of Christ are distinct but inseparably united—Christ is both true man and true God. The decree of the Council that the patriarch of Constantinople should be the single head of the Eastern Church has never been accepted by the Roman Catholic Church.

chalcedony (kălsē'dŭnē), variety of quartz, transparent to translucent, with minute crystals, waxy luster. Agate, carnelian, jasper, and onyx are forms of chalcedony colored by impurities.

Chalcidice (kălsĭ'dĭsē), Gr. *Chalkidike* or *Khalkidiki*, peninsula, NE Greece, projecting into Aegean Sea from SE Macedonia; chief town Polygyros. S coast forms three peninsulas: Kassandra (anc. Gr. *Pallene*), Sithonia, ATHOS. A dry, mountainous region, it produces olive oil, wine, wheat, tobacco. Anciently famous for its timber. Named for Chalcis, which estab. colonies here (7th–6th cent. B.C.). POTIDAEA was an important city. Region was conquered by Macedon (4th cent. B.C.) and by Rome (2d cent. B.C.). Later history follows that of SALONICA.

Chalcis (kăl'sĭs), Gr. *Khalkis,* city (pop. 26,097), Greece; a port on EUBOEA. The chief city of ancient Euboea, it estab. colonies in Sicily and Chalcidice (8th–7th cent. B.C.), led revolt of Euboea against Athens (446 B.C.), and was made tributary to her (411). In 338 B.C. it came under Macedon. Aristotle died here. Called Negropont in Middle Ages.

chalcopyrite (kăl"kŭpī'rīt) or **copper pyrites,** brass-yellow mineral with iridescent and black streaks. A sulphide of iron and copper, it sometimes contains other metals. It is an important and widely distributed copper ore.

Chaldaea or **Chaldea** (both: kăldē'ŭ), S portion of Tigris-Euphrates valley (Mesopotamia), but sometimes loosely used to include all Babylonia. The restored Babylonian kingdom is frequently called the Chaldaean Empire. Chaldaean or Chaldee came to be loosely used to mean astrologer or magician (e.g., Dan. 1.4) because of the astronomical knowledge in Babylonia.

Chaleur Bay (shŭloor'), inlet of Gulf of St. Lawrence, c.85 mi. long, 15–25 mi. wide, between N.B. and Gaspé Peninsula, Canada. Is submerged valley of Resti-

gouche R., which enters at its head. Has famous fishing grounds. Discovered and named by Cartier 1534.

Chalfont (chä'fŭnt, chăl'fŭnt), borough (pop. 828), SE Pa., near Doylestown. Traditional burial place of Delaware Indian chief Tamanend or Tammany.

Chalgrin, Jean François (zhä' fräswä' shälgrē'), 1739–1811, French architect. Chiefly responsible for scheme of Arc de Triomphe de l'Étoile, commissioned by Napoleon.

Chaliapin, Feodor (Ivanovich) (fyô'dùr shŭlyä'pēn), 1873–1938, Russian bass. Appeared at the Metropolitan Opera, New York in 1907 and 1921–29. An excellent actor, he was particularly known for title role in Moussorgsky's *Boris Godunov.*

chalk, a calcium carbonate mineral softer than limestone, consisting of minute marine shells. Chalk cliffs of Dover, England, date from Cretaceous period.

Chalk River, government research establishment, S Ont., Canada, on S shore of Ottawa R., W of Ottawa. Operated by National Research Council of Canada for Atomic Energy Control Board. Has large heavy-water atomic pile (1947).

Challenger expedition, 1872–76, British scientific expedition which cruised in corvette *Challenger* making physical and biological surveys of Atlantic and Pacific oceans.

Challoner, Richard (chä'lùnùr), 1691–1781, English Roman Catholic bishop. Converted as a boy, he was ordained in 1716 and in 1730 returned to England, where he met many difficulties in trying to win toleration for Catholics. He was beset by anti-Catholic movements culminating in the Gordon riots (1780). A notable scholar, he revised the Douay version of the Bible and wrote and translated devotional works.

Chalmers, Thomas, 1780–1847, Scottish theologian, leader of Free Church of SCOTLAND.

Chalmette National Historical Park: see NATIONAL PARKS AND MONUMENTS (table).

Châlons-sur-Marne (shälô'-sür-märn'), town (pop. 28,-251), cap. of Marne dept., NE France, on Marne R. Wool mfg., brewing, wine processing.

Chalon-sur-Saône (–sōn'), town (pop. 29,851), Saône-et-Loire dept., E central France; inland port on Saône and Canal Central. Ships wine and grain. Cap. of Burgundy in 6th cent.

Cham (käm), pseud. of **Amédée, comte de Noé** (ämädä' kôt dù nōä'), 1819–79, French caricaturist and lithographer. Did sketches of French and Algerian life.

Chamberlain, Sir Austen: see CHAMBERLAIN, JOSEPH.

Chamberlain, Houston Stewart, 1855–1927, Anglo-German writer; son-in-law of Richard Wagner. His *Foundations of the Nineteenth Century* (1899; Eng. tr., 1910) was an important forerunner of National Socialist racist doctrines.

Chamberlain, Joseph, 1836–1914, British imperialist statesman. Resigned from Gladstone government (1886), opposing Irish Home Rule. Became Liberal-Unionist leader in House of Commons in 1891. As colonial secretary (1895–1903) advocated social reforms at home and empire expansion and consolidation. Unjustly blamed for acts leading to South African War (1899–1902); led in reconciling Boers after war. Favored tariff giving preference to empire; resigned to advocate policy. This proposal split Liberal-Unionist-Conservative bloc and caused 1906 fall of government but was adopted in lifetime of his sons. His eldest son, **Sir (Joseph) Austen Chamberlain,** 1863–1937, began 45-year parliamentary career in 1892. Twice chancellor of exchequer (1903–6, 1919–21), he carried out in latter term his father's tariff policy. Became Conservative leader in 1921. Helped negotiate Irish Free State treaty. As foreign secretary (1924–29), his most important post, largely responsible for 1925 LoCARNO PACT. Awarded Nobel Peace Prize. His half-brother, **(Arthur) Neville Chamberlain,** 1869–1940, was chancellor of exchequer (1923, 1931–37) and succeeded Baldwin as prime minister (1937). Became symbol of appeasement of Axis powers; signed Mu-

NICH PACT (1938). Remained in office after outbreak of World War II but increasing opposition forced him to resign after British debacle in Norway (1940).

Chamberlin, Thomas Chrowder, 1843–1928, American geologist, founder of *Journal of Geology.* Formulated PLANETESIMAL HYPOTHESIS with F. R. Moulton.

chamber music, ensemble music for small groups of instruments. Originally performed by amateurs in court or aristocratic circles. With Haydn and Mozart the string quartet became the chief chamber form. In this form Beethoven wrote some of his greatest music.

Chambers, Robert: see CHAMBERS, WILLIAM.

Chambers, Sir William, 1726–96, English architect, foremost in his day. Proponent of Inigo Jones traditions of Palladian design, he published standard work on classic style. Chief work is Somerset House.

Chambers, William, 1800–1883, and **Robert Chambers,** 1802–71, Scottish authors, publishers. Their firm best known for *Chambers's Edinburgh Journal, Chambers's Encyclopaedia.*

Chambersburg, borough (pop. 17,212), S Pa., SW of Harrisburg; settled 1730. Trading center in agr. area with fruit growing and mfg. of metal and paper products. Was hq. of John Brown 1859; burned by Confederates 1864. Seat of Wilson Col. (Presbyterian; for women; 1869).

Chambéry (shäbärē'), city (pop. 26,641), cap. of Savoie dept., E France. Historical cap. of Savoy; archiepiscopal see.

Chambiges (shäbëzh'), family of French architects. **Martin Chambiges** (märtē'), d. 1532, helped design cathedrals of Sens, Troyes, and Beauvais. Assisted by son, **Pierre Chambiges** (pyēr'), d. 1544, who also worked on the Hôtel de Ville, Paris.

Chambly (shäblē'), group of villages, S Que., Canada, on Richelieu R. and E of Montreal. Includes Chambly Bassin (pop. 2,160) and Chambly Canton (pop. 1,636). Fort Chambly, built 1665, was captured and burned by Americans 1775–76; restored 1880.

Chambord, Henri, comte de (ärē' kōt' dù shäbôr'), 1820–83, French pretender, known to legitimists as Henry V; posthumous son of duc de Berry. Accompanied his grandfather, Charles X, into exile (1830). Actively claimed throne 1871–73, but lost his prospects through insistence on restoring Bourbon flag. Died childless. Claim passed to Orléans family.

Chambord, village, Loir-et-Cher dept., N central France, between Blois and Orléans. Famous for huge Renaissance château built by Francis I.

chameleon (kùmē'lyùn), small, slow-moving arboreal lizard of Africa and S Asia. Its skin color changes with feelings, varying light intensity, and temperature. The American chameleon is a small lizard of another family.

Chamfort, Sébastien Roch Nicholas (säbästyē' rōk' nēkōlä' shäfôr'), 1740–94, French writer of maxims and epigrams. Though a savage critic of society and a republican, he was favored by the court, persecuted under the Revolution. Commited suicide to escape the guillotine.

Chaminade, Cecile (säsēl' shämēnäd'), 1857?–1944, French composer and pianist. She chiefly wrote songs and piano pieces (e.g., the *Scarf Dance*).

Chamisso, Adelbert von (Chamisso de Boncourt) (ä'dùlbĕrt fùn shùmĭ'sō), 1781–1838, German poet, b. France; son of émigré nobles. His lyric cycle *Frauenliebe und Leben* was set to music by Schumann. His tale of the man who sold his shadow, *Peter Schlemihls wunderbare Geschichte* (1814), has virtually passed into legend.

chamois (shä'mē), hollow-horned hoofed mammal (*Rupicapra*) related to antelope, found in Europe and E Mediterranean lands. It is about the size of a goat, light brown with black tail, and has erect hooked horns. It was the original source of chamois leather; other skins now are so named.

chamomile: see CAMOMILE.

Chamonix (shämônē'), Alpine resort, Haute-Savoie dept., E France, base for the ascent of Mont Blanc.

Champagne, Philippe de: see CHAMPAIGNE.

Champagne (shămpăn', Fr. shäpä'nyù), region, NE France, in Aube, Marne, Haute-Marne, Ardennes, and Yonne depts., roughly coextensive with former Champagne prov.; historic cap. Troyes. Mostly an arid plateau; agr., sheep grazing. Small fertile dist. around RHEIMS and Épernay produces nearly all French champagne wine. Acquired by house of BLOIS (11th cent.), Champagne was among most powerful fiefs of medieval France. Its counts also ruled Navarre from 1234. Louis X of France, inheriting Champagne from his mother, incorporated it with the royal domain (1314). The medieval Fairs of Champagne, particularly those of Troyes and Provins, brought together merchants from all Europe and were of immense economic importance. Large parts of Champagne were devastated in World War I.

champagne, celebrated sparkling white wine. The best is made from grapes grown around Rheims, France. After two fermentations and blending, it is again fermented in bottles and has some sugar (and usually cognac) added, according to desired degree of dryness (from *brut* to sweet).

Champaign (shămpān'), city (pop. 39,563), E central Ill., ENE of Springfield and adjoining URBANA; founded 1854. Rail (has repair shops), commercial, and industrial center in agr. area. Univ. of ILLINOIS lies between Champaign and Urbana.

Champaigne or Champagne, Philippe de (both: fēlēp' dù shäpä'nyù), 1602–74, French painter. Did religious paintings for Marie de' Medici and Richelieu.

Champlain, Samuel de (Fr. sämüēl' dù shäplē'), 1567–1635, French explorer, chief founder of New France. Estab. colony at Quebec, discovered L. Champlain, extended French claims W to Wis.

Champlain, Lake, 107 mi. long, ½–14 mi. wide, forming N.Y.–Vt. state line for c.100 mi. and extending into Que. Lies in broad valley between the Adirondacks (W) and Green Mts. (E). Connected with the Hudson by part of the Barge Canal, with the St. Lawrence by Richelieu R., with L. George by short channel. Plattsburg, N.Y., Burlington, Vt., and many resorts are on its shores. ISLE LA MOTTE and VALCOUR ISLAND are in it. Named for Champlain, who discovered it, 1609. Scene of battles in French and Indian War and in Revolution at CROWN POINT and Ticonderoga and of victory of MACDONOUGH in 1814.

Champollion, Jean François (zhä' fräswä' shäpôlyō'), 1790–1832, French Egyptologist. Considered the founder of Egyptology, he set (1821) the principles for deciphering Egyptian hieroglyphics by using ROSETTA STONE.

Champs Élysées (shä zälēzā'), avenue of Paris, from Place de la Concorde to Arc de Triomphe, famous for its beauty and elegance.

chance, in mathematics: see PROBABILITY.

Chancellor, Richard, d. 1556, English navigator. Sent out by English group in 1553 to seek Northeast Passage. With Stephen Borough, reached White Sea; traveled overland to Moscow to prepare way for trade. Perished on return voyage.

Chancellorsville, battle of, in Civil War, May 2–4, 1863. R. E. Lee attacked Joseph Hooker's Federals, entrenched near Chancellorsville, Va. In brilliant flank attack, Stonewall Jackson surprised and routed Federals, but was mortally wounded. On May 3–4 J. A. Early and J. E. B. Stuart drove Hooker and John Sedgwick across Rappahannock R. in defeat. This was Lee's last great victory.

chancery: see EQUITY.

Chandernagor (chŭn"dùrnùgôr'), town (pop. 44,786), W Bengal, India; port on Hooghly R. Belonged to the French from late 17th cent. to 1949.

Chandler, Raymond (Thornton), 1888–, American writer of "tough" detective fiction (e.g., *The Big Sleep* 1939, *Farewell, My Lovely*, 1940).

Chandler, Zachariah, 1813–79, U.S. Senator from

Mich. (1857–75), and Secretary of the Interior (1875–77). A leading advocate of radical Reconstruction. As cabinet member, a typical Grant appointee.

Chandragupta: see SANDRACOTTUS.

Changchun (chäng'-choōn'), industrial city (pop. 630,-049), central Manchuria, on South Manchurian RR. As Hsinking it was cap. of MANCHUKUO.

change of life: see MENOPAUSE.

change ringing: see BELL.

Chang Hsueh-liang (chäng' shüĕ-lyäng'), 1898–, Chinese general, called the Young Marshal. Succeeded his father Chang Tso-lin as military governor of Manchuria. Ousted 1931 by the Japanese. Kidnaped Chiang Kai-shek at Sian in 1936, allegedly to force him to work with the Communists against Japan. Held prisoner by Chiang Kai-shek since 1937.

Changkiakow (jäng'jyä'kō') or **Kalgan** (kälgän'), city (pop. 151,234), cap. Chahar prov., N China. Leading trade center of Inner Mongolia. Under Communist control since 1948. Formerly called Wanchüan.

Changsha (chäng'shä'), city (pop. 421,616), S central Manchuria; port on Siang R. Major trade and industrial center on Peiping-Canton RR.

Chang Tso-lin (chäng' tsō'-lĭn', jäng'), 1873–1928, Chinese general. Appointed inspector general of Manchuria in 1918; constantly warred to expand personal control of N China. Killed by bombing of train in which he was retreating before Kuomintang army.

Chankiang (chän'jyäng'), municipality (325 sq. mi.; pop. 268,416), SW Kwangtung prov., China. Until 1945 it was French territory of Kwangchowan, leased by China in 1898 for 99 years.

Channel Islands, Fr. *Îles Normandes,* archipelago (75 sq. mi.; pop. 102,770), off Normandy coast, France, in English Channel. Main isles are Jersey, Guernsey, Alderney, Sark, Jethou; all (but a few French owned) have belonged to Great Britain since Norman Conquest. Divided into two administrative areas: Jersey, with half the total population and chief town, St. Helier; and Guernsey, which includes all other islands. English replacing French as official language. Chiefly agr. and pastoral, isles send quantities of produce to English markets. Famous for cattle. Occupied by Germans in World War II.

Channel Islands National Monument, Calif.: see NATIONAL PARKS AND MONUMENTS (table).

Channing, William Ellery, 1780–1842, American author, Unitarian minister in Boston, great preacher, lucid writer on labor problems, education, slavery, religious tolerance, and humanitarianism. His nephew and biographer, **William Henry Channing,** 1810–84, was an author and Unitarian minister, interested in the Brook Farm experiment. His brother, **William Ellery Channing,** 1818–1901, an author, contributed verse to *Dial.* His son was **Edward Channing,** 1856–1931, historian, Harvard professor. Several lesser works preceded his masterpiece, *A History of the United States* (6 vols., 1905–25).

chansons de geste (shäsō' dù zhĕst'), epic poems of medieval France (11th–13th cent.), composed by trouvères in cycles grouped around a great central figure, such as Charlemagne. Oldest and most famous is *Chanson de Roland* (c.1098–1100; see ROLAND).

chant, sacred song in which several syllables of text may be sung to one sustained tone. Chant of Roman Catholic and Orthodox Christianity is called PLAIN SONG. Anglican chant, developed during the Reformation, uses harmonized melodies, English texts.

chantey or **shanty,** work song with marked rhythm, particularly one sung by sailors at work. Often has stanzas sung by leader, each followed with chorus sung by group. Similar songs also sung by shore gangs and lumbermen.

Chantilly (shätēyē'), town (pop. 5,105), Oise dept., N France, NE of Paris. Famous lace mfg.; race course. Château contains art museum.

Chantrey, Sir Francis Legatt, 1781–1841, English sculptor, known for portrait statues and busts.

Chanukah: see HANUKKAH.

Chanute, Octave (shùnoōt'), 1832–1910, American civil engineer, pioneer glider experimenter, b. Paris. Noted iron-bridge builder. Retired 1889 to study gliding. Studies and personal help aided Wright brothers.

Chanute, city (pop. 10,109), SE Kansas, on Neosho R. and WNW of Pittsburg; settled c.1870. Trade center for agr. and oil area, it has railway shops and oil refineries. Site of first mission (1824–29) in state is near.

Chaos (kā'ŏs), in Greek religion, unfathomable space whence arose everything, earthly and divine. From it came Gaea, Tartarus, and Eros.

Chapala (chäpä'lä), lake, c.50 mi. long and 8 mi. wide, W Mexico, in Jalisco and Michoacán; largest in country; popular scenic resort. Fishing is important native occupation.

chaparral (chäpürăl'), plant community of shrubs, both evergreen and deciduous, usually in regions with 10 to 20 in. annual rainfall. It is drier than forest regions but less arid than deserts. Chaparral growth exists in W and SW U.S. and may include scrub oaks, squawbush, western serviceberry, mesquite, buckthorn, and manzanita.

Chapel Hill, town (pop. 9,177), N central N.C., SW of Durham. Seat of Univ. of NORTH CAROLINA.

Chaplin, Charles Spencer, 1889–, Anglo-American film actor who writes, directs, and produces his own pictures. Discovered by Mack Sennet c.1913, Charlie Chaplin soon was famous for his baggy trousers and little mustache. Among his many films are *Easy Street, Shoulder Arms, The Kid, The Gold Rush, City Lights, Modern Times, The Great Dictator, Monsieur Verdoux,* and *Limelight.* His art is the most universal yet to appear on film.

Chapman, George, 1559?–1634, English dramatist and poet. Notable for translations of *Iliad* (1612) and *Odyssey* (1614–15). Among best plays, tragedy *Bussy d'Ambois* (1607) and comedy *All Fools* (1605).

Chapman, John, 1774–1847, American pioneer, more familiarly known as Johnny Appleseed. Wandering cultivator and promoter of apple orchards in Ohio, Ind., and Ill.

Chapman, John Jay, 1862–1933, American essayist, author of fiery works such as *Emerson and Other Essays* (1898), *New Horizons in American Life* (1932).

Chapultepec (chäpool'täpĕk") [Aztec,= grasshopper hill], rocky eminence in SW section of Mexico city. Occupied successively by Aztec emperors, Spanish viceroys, and later rulers of Mexico (including Emperor Maximilian). Pres. Cárdenas decreed (1937) that castle become museum and grounds a public park. For Chapultepec Conference see PAN-AMERICANISM.

Charcas (chär'käs), Spanish colonial *audiencia* and presidency in S America, known also as Upper Peru and Chuquisaca; established 1559 and attached to viceroyalty of Peru. Transferred to viceroyalty of La Plata (1776). Roughly same as modern Bolivia.

Charchemish, anc. city: see CARCHEMISH.

charcoal, substance, mostly pure carbon, from destructive DISTILLATION of wood, animal matter (e.g., bone black from bones), or sugar. A smokeless fuel, it yields a large amount of heat. It is an efficient agent in ADSORPTION of solids from solution and is used in making gunpowder, in sugar refining, in purification of water and air, and in gas masks.

Charcot, Jean Martin (zhä' märtē' shärkō'), 1825–93, French neurologist, organizer of noted Paris clinic for nervous system diseases. He studied the treatment of hysteria by hypnosis.

Chardin, Jean Baptiste (zhä' bätēst' shärdē'), 1699–1779, French painter, famous for still lifes and domestic interiors. One of greatest French colorists.

Charente (shärät'), department (2,306 sq. mi.; pop. 311,137), W France; cap. Angoulême. The **Charente** river, 220 mi. long, flows from central France past Augoulême, Cognac, and Rochefort into Atlantic.

Charente-Maritime (-märētēm'), department (2,792 sq. mi.; pop. 416,187), W France, on Atlantic coast;

cap. La Rochelle. Formerly called Charente-Inférieure.

Chares (kâ′rēz, kā′–), 3d cent. B.C., Greek worker in bronze; sculptor of the COLOSSUS OF RHODES.

chargé d'affaires: see DIPLOMATIC SERVICE.

Charing Cross (chăr′ĭng), open space at W end of Strand, London. One of Eleanor Crosses (see ELEANOR OF CASTILE) erected here. Charing Cross station is busy rail terminal.

chariot (chă′rĕŭt), earliest type of carriage. Ancient form had two wheels; car usually consisted of floor and waist-high semicircular guard in front. Wheels of war chariot sometimes mounted with scythes as weapons. In Greece and Rome chariots were used primarily to carry passengers and were featured in races and processions. See *ill.*, vehicles.

Chariton (shă′rĭtŭn), city (pop. 5,320), S Iowa, W of Ottumwa. Center of farm and coal area.

Charlemagne (shär′lŭmān) (Charles the Great or Charles I), 742–814, emperor of the West (800–814), king of the Franks (768–814); son of Pepin the Short. Shared kingdom with his younger brother Carloman until Carloman's death (771). Invaded Italy to support pope against DESIDERIUS; crowned king of Lombards at Pavia (774). Conquered NE Spain ("Spanish March") from Moors (778); subjugated and Christianized Saxons after long struggle (772–804); defeated Avars and Wends. In 800 he restored LEO III to papal see and was crowned emperor by him in Rome on Christmas Day, thus laying basis for HOLY ROMAN EMPIRE. To assure his succession he had his son, LOUIS I, crowned joint emperor (813). To defend and control his immense empire, Charlemagne created military frontier marches and an administrative system by which his personal representatives (*missi dominici*) made his power felt in regular inspection tours. His CAPITULARIES testify to his concern with general welfare and justice for the poor. He frequently held consultative assemblies and took personal interest in Church reform. His palace school at Aachen, founded by ALCUIN, became the cradle of the "Carolingian renaissance" of learning. He was beatified by the Church and is locally honored as a saint. Legend soon enhanced and distorted his actual achievements. Surrounded by his 12 legendary peers, he became the central figure of a cycle of medieval romances (see CHANSONS DE GESTE).

Charleroi (shärlŭrwä′), town (pop. 26,262), Hainaut prov., S central Belgium, on Sambre R. and on Charleroi-Brussels Canal. Coal-mining and steel-milling center. Important fortress 17th–18th cent.

Charleroi (shär′lŭroi), borough (pop. 9,872), SW Pa., S of Pittsburgh and on Monongahela R. Has glass and iron works and coal mines.

Charles, emperors (see HOLY ROMAN EMPIRE). **Charles I:** see CHARLEMAGNE. **Charles II** (the Bald), 823–77, son of Louis, joined with his brother LOUIS THE GERMAN against his brother LOTHAIR I, whom they defeated at Fontenoy (841). Became king of West Franks (France) by Treaty of VERDUN (843); partitioned Lotharingia with Louis in Treaty of MERSEN (870). Crowned emperor 875. **Charles III** (the Fat), 839–88, inherited Swabia from his father, Louis the German. Crowned king of Italy (879), emperor (881), king of France (885). Deposed 887 after he failed to stop Norman inroads in France. **Charles IV,** 1316–78, succeeded his father JOHN OF LUXEMBURG as king of Bohemia (1346), was elected in the same year antiking to Emperor Louis IV, after whose death he made good his claim. Crowned emperor in 1355, he promulgated in 1356 the Golden Bull (see ELECTORS); added Silesia and Lusatia to his family territories; had his son WENCESLAUS elected German king (1376). His chief interest lay in Bohemia. He embellished Prague and founded Charles Univ. (1348). **Charles V,** 1500–1558, emperor (1519–58) and, as Charles I, king of Spain (1516–56); son of PHILIP I and JOANNA of Castile; grandson of Ferdinand V of Aragon, Isabella of Castile, Emperor Maximilian I, and Mary of Burgundy. The greatest of all Hapsburg emperors, he inherited

an empire on which "the sun never set"—the Spanish kingdoms, Spanish America, Naples, Sicily, the Low Countries, and the Austrian hereditary lands. Born and raised at Ghent, he at first antagonized his Spanish subjects but later espoused their national traits and religious zeal and earned their loyalty. His reign was crucial in every way. A series of social uprisings ended with the victory of central authority in Spain and of the great princes in Germany (1520–25; see Juan de PADILLA; SICKINGEN, FRANZ VON; PEASANTS' WAR). The imperialist struggle with France was a Pyrrhic triumph for Spain (1521–59; see FRANCIS I and HENRY II of France; ITALIAN WARS). In his fight against Protestantism, announced at the Diet of WORMS (1521) but long delayed by war with France and Algiers, Charles seemed triumphant when he defeated the Protestant princes at Mühlberg (1547; see SCHMALKALDIC LEAGUE), but in 1555 he was forced to accept the compromise Peace of AUGSBURG and left Germany forever. He was more successful in his promotion of the Catholic REFORM, and he brought the Spanish empire to its height by the conquest of MEXICO and PERU. After his imperial coronation at Bologna (1530; he was the last German emperor crowned by a pope), Charles increasingly delegated his authority in Germany to his brother Ferdinand. In 1554–58 he abdicated all his titles: his son Philip II received Spain, America, Sicily, Naples, and the Netherlands; his brother became emperor as FERDINAND I. Charles himself retired in 1556 to the monastery of Yuste. **Charles VI,** 1685–1740, emperor (1711–40) and, as Charles III, king of Hungary. Before his accession he claimed the succession to Charles II of Spain (see SPANISH SUCCESSION, WAR OF THE) and in 1733 he became involved in the War of the POLISH SUCCESSION. These dynastic struggles left him with the Spanish Netherlands and Milan. Without male issue, he had a succession problem of his own. The PRAGMATIC SANCTION, by which he settled the Hapsburg lands on his daughter Maria Theresa, was challenged after his death. In his campaigns against Turkey he secured the favorable Treaty of PASSAROWITZ (1718), largely offset by the Treaty of Belgrade (1739). He was a patron of learning and of music. **Charles VII,** 1697–1745, emperor (1742–45) and, as Charles Albert, elector of Bavaria (1726–45), married a niece of Charles VI. He refused to recognize the Pragmatic Sanction, joined the coalition against Maria Theresa in the War of the AUSTRIAN SUCCESSION, and was elected emperor but lost his own Bavaria to Austrian occupation.

Charles I, 1887–1922, last emperor of Austria and, as Charles IV, king of Hungary (1916–18); grandnephew of Francis Joseph. Married Zita of Bourbon-Parma. Failed in attempt to secure separate peace. Abdicated Nov., 1918, but twice sought, without success, to regain Hungarian throne by coup d'état. Died in exile on Madeira. His son Otto succeeded to his claims.

Charles, kings of England, Scotland, and Ireland, of the Stuart house. **Charles I,** 1600–1649, reigned 1625–49. Took little part in politics while his father, James I, ruled except for trip to Spain in abortive negotiations for his marriage. Upon accession, offended English opinion by his marriage to Catholic Henrietta Maria of France, sister of Louis XIII. Foreign ventures of king's favorite, duke of BUCKINGHAM, were unsuccessful. Bitter struggle between king and Parliament known as PURITAN REVOLUTION soon developed. Parliament, largely Puritan, controlled money. Charles supported bishops under William LAUD. Forced to agree to PETITION OF RIGHT 1628, Charles governed without Parliament 1629–40. Civil and religious liberties were at low point and large emigrations to America took place. Attempt to impose episcopacy in Scotland caused Bishops' Wars and king was forced to call Parliament. Long Parliament of 1640, led by John HAMPDEN, PYM, and VANE, secured itself against dissolution and brought about death of earl of STRAFFORD, abolition of Star Chamber courts, and end of

SMALL CAPITALS = cross references. Pronunciation key on inside end pages. Abbreviations: p. 2.

arbitrary taxation. Fear of king and Catholics mounted and civil war broke out. Defeated at Marston Moor (1644) and Naseby (1645), Charles surrendered to Scottish army in 1646 and finally fell into hands of English army. Tried by a high court of justice controlled by enemies, he was convicted of treason and beheaded. His son, **Charles II,** 1630–85, reigned 1660–85. Fled to France 1646. At his father's death, was proclaimed king in Scotland and, accepting terms of Covenanters, was crowned there (1651). After defeat by Cromwell, escaped to Europe and lived in comparative poverty. Issued conciliatory Declaration of Breda. Aided by General MONCK, was restored 1660. Earl of CLARENDON made chief minister. Episcopacy was restored and nonconformity weakened by Clarendon Code although king favored toleration. Great London plague (1665) and fire (1666) took place during second DUTCH WAR (1664–67). CABAL ministry replaced Clarendon (1667). As result of secret Treaty of Dover (1670) with Louis XIV, Charles entered third Dutch War in 1672. It was unpopular and he was forced to approve Test Act (1672) and make peace (1674). Alliance with Louis broken by marriage of king's niece, Mary, to William of Orange. Intervened in Titus OATES affair to protect queen. Dissolved Parliament in 1681 to block passage of Exclusion Act against duke of York and ruled absolutely thereafter. Although father of children by several mistresses (e.g., Nell GWYN), he had no legitimate children and was succeeded by his brother, JAMES II. Reign was marked by gradual increase in power of Parliament, rise of political parties, advance in colonization and trade, and progress of England as a sea power. His pleasure-loving and immoral character set tone of brilliant Restoration period.

Charles, kings of France. **Charles I:** see CHARLEMAGNE. **Charles II** and **Charles III** (the Fat): see CHARLES II and CHARLES III, emperors. **Charles III** (the Simple), 879–929, son of Louis II, joint king with Eudes from 893, sole king 898–923. Ceded Normandy to ROLLO (911). Deposed and imprisoned by rebellious nobles, who made RAOUL king. **Charles IV** (the Fair), 1294–1328, succeeded his brother Philip V in 1322; last of direct Capetians. **Charles V** (the Wise), 1337–80, son of JOHN II, was regent during John's captivity (1356–60), succeeded him in 1364. As regent, dealt with JACQUERIE and reformist movement of Étienne MARCEL. During his reign, DU GUESCLIN drove English out of France (except Guienne). With his ministers, the MARMOUSETS, he strengthened royal power, founded standing army, reformed taxation. Patron of learning. His son, **Charles VI** (the Mad, or the Well Beloved), 1368–1422, reigned 1380–1422. Intermittently insane after 1392. France was ruled and plundered by his uncles; by his brother, Louis d'ORLÉANS; by his wife, ISABEAU OF BAVARIA. Their rivalries led to civil war between ARMAGNACS AND BURGUNDIANS; laid France open to invasion by HENRY V of England (1415). By Treaty of TROYES (1420) he named Henry his successor. His disinherited son, **Charles VII** (the Victorious, or the Well Served), 1403–61, repudiated the treaty. Still called dauphin (or, in derision, "king of Bourges"), he ruled indolently over what parts of France remained to him S of the Loire, but in 1429 JOAN OF ARC spurred him to action and had him crowned king at Rheims. In 1435 he won the alliance of Burgundy against England, and in 1453 he ended the HUNDRED YEARS WAR by expelling the last English from France. He reorganized the army and, with the help of Jacques CŒUR, restored the finances. The PRAGMATIC SANCTION OF BOURGES (1438) and the suppression of the PRAGUERIE (1440) strengthened royal authority against Church and nobles. His last years were troubled by rebellions of his son, Louis XI. **Charles VIII,** 1470–98, son of Louis XI, reigned 1483–98. His sister, Anne de Beaujeu, regent during his minority, arranged his marriage with ANNE OF BRITTANY. In 1495 Charles began the ITALIAN WARS with the short-lived conquest of Naples.

Charles IX, 1550–74, reigned 1560–74, at first under the regency of his mother, CATHERINE DE' MEDICI. Later chose COLIGNY as chief adviser, but was swayed to take part in massacre of SAINT BARTHOLOMEW'S DAY (1572). **Charles X,** 1757–1836, was known as count of Artois before he succeeded his brother, LOUIS XVIII, in 1824. Led powerful ultraroyalist group before his accession; appointed such reactionaries as VILLÈLE, J. A. de POLIGNAC as premiers. Liberal and capitalist forces joined to bring about JULY REVOLUTION of 1830. Charles abdicated and died in exile.

Charles, kings of Hungary. **Charles I** (Charles Robert of Anjou), 1288–1342, grandson of Charles II of Naples; son-in-law of Stephen V of Hungary. Elected king 1308; crowned 1310; founder of Hungarian branch of ANGEVIN dynasty. Reorganized army on feudal basis; increased city privileges. Followed dynastic foreign policy, securing succession to Poland for his oldest son, LOUIS I of Hungary. **Charles II:** see CHARLES III, king of Naples. **Charles III:** see CHARLES VI, emperor. **Charles IV:** see CHARLES I, emperor of Austria.

Charles, kings of Naples. **Charles I,** 1226–85, count of Anjou and Provence, youngest brother of Louis IX of France, championed the papal cause against MANFRED, was crowned king of Naples and Sicily by Pope Clement IV in 1266. Had his rival CONRADIN executed (1268). Won hegemony over Italy as leader of Guelphs; conquered Albania from Byzantium. In 1282 Sicily rebelled (see SICILIAN VESPERS) and chose PETER III of Aragon as king. War against Aragonese continued until 1302 under his son, **Charles II,** 1248–1309, king of Naples and count of Provence (1285–1309). **Charles III** (Charles of Durazzo), 1345–86, king of Naples (1381–86), was a great-grandson of Charles II. JOANNA I adopted him as heir but later repudiated him in favor of Louis of Anjou (LOUIS I of Naples). Charles invaded Naples, was crowned by the pope (1381), and imprisoned Joanna (and probably killed her). Elected king of Hungary as Charles II (1385), he was murdered soon afterward.

Charles II or **Charles the Bad,** 1332–87, king of Navarre (1349–87). Carried on long feud with his father-in-law, John II of France. Helped suppress JACQUERIE (1358). Chosen by Étienne MARCEL to defend Paris against dauphin, he betrayed his trust.

Charles I, 1863–1908, king of Portugal (1889–1908). Yielded to British "ultimatum" (1890) which demanded cessation of Portuguese colonial expansion. His attempt to foster dictatorship under João Franco caused violent reaction. Charles and the heir apparent were shot. Manuel II succeeded him.

Charles, kings of Spain. **Charles I:** see CHARLES V, emperor. **Charles II,** 1661–1700, king of Spain, Naples, and Sicily (1665–1700), last of the Spanish Hapsburgs, saw his country weakened by wars with Louis XIV. Died childless. War of the SPANISH SUCCESSION broke out on his death. **Charles III,** 1716–88, son of Philip V by Elizabeth Farnese, was duke of Parma and Piacenza (1731–35) and king of Naples and Sicily (1735–59) before succeeding his half-brother Ferdinand VI as king of Spain (1759–88). Entered Seven Years War after signing FAMILY COMPACT of 1761 with France; intervened (1779) in American Revolution on American side (for territorial changes, see PARIS, TREATY OF, 1763 and 1783). With his minister FLORIDABLANCA he restored some prosperity in Spain. His son, **Charles IV,** 1748–1819, king of Spain (1788–1808) was dominated by Queen MARÍA LUISA and his minister GODOY. Withdrew from French Revolutionary Wars 1795, entered disastrous alliance with France (1796), which led in 1807 to PENINSULAR WAR. Palace revolution of 1808 forced him to abdicate in favor of his son, FERDINAND VII, but Napoleon I soon afterward enticed both Charles and Ferdinand to Bayonne, forced both to abdicate, and held them captive until 1814.

Charles, kings of Sweden. **Charles IX,** 1550–1611, youngest son of Gustavus I. Acted as regent from

1592; established Lutheranism as state religion; had his nephew, SIGISMUND III of Poland, deposed as king of Sweden (1599); accepted crown 1604. His expansionist policy involved him in wars with Poland and Denmark, which continued after his death under his son, Gustavus II. **Charles X** (Charles Gustavus), 1622–60, succeeded on the abdication of his cousin Christina (1654). Invaded Poland, took Warsaw and Cracow (1655), but was expelled after miracle of CZESTOCHOWA. Russia and Denmark having declared war, he threatened Copenhagen and forced Denmark to accept Treaty of ROSKILDE (1658), but war was resumed in same year. His son, **Charles XI**, 1655–97, ended the war upon his accession (1660) by the Peace of OLIVA and the Treaty of Copenhagen (confirming that of Roskilde). Siding with France in last of DUTCH WARS, he was defeated at Fehrbellin by Frederick William of Brandenburg (1675) but retained Pomerania at Treaty of Saint-Germain (1679). In 1682 he received absolute powers from the Riksdag. His son and successor, **Charles XII**, 1682–1718, was faced in 1699 by a Russo-Polish-Danish alliance which precipitated the NORTHERN WAR (1700–1721). An extraordinarily brilliant but foolhardy strategist, Charles quickly crushed Denmark, routed Peter the Great, and overran Poland, but his Russian campaign of 1708–9 ended disastrously at Poltava. Charles fled to Turkey and persuaded Sultan Ahmed III to declare war on Russia, but after the Russo-Turkish peace of 1711 he was requested to leave Turkey. Charles, residing at Bender, flatly refused and ultimately defended his house with only a handful of men against a whole Turkish army (1713). Taken a prisoner to Adrianople, he finally left in 1714. He invaded Norway in 1716 and was killed by stray bullet while besieging the fortress of Fredrikssten. His heroic failure cost Sweden its rank as a great power. **Charles XIII**, 1748–1818, king of Sweden (1809–18) and of Norway (1814–18) succeeded his nephew GUSTAVUS IV. He accepted a constitution, made peace with Russia (to which he ceded Finland), France, and Denmark, and adopted as heir the French Napoleonic marshal Jean Baptiste Jules Bernadotte (1764–1844; b. Pau, France), who later succeeded him as king of Sweden and Norway styled **Charles XIV**. With the consent of Napoleon, he had agreed to his adoption by Charles XIII (1810) and actually governed in the name of the infirm king. He joined the allies against Napoleon I, played an important part in the battle of Leipzig (1813), and secured the union of NORWAY with Sweden (1814). His reign was an era of economic progress, but his hostility to the liberals made him unpopular. **Charles XV**, 1826–72, king of Sweden and Norway (1859–72), Bernadotte's grandson, was a liberal and popular ruler. He consented to the creation of a bicameral parliament.

Charles, dukes of Lorraine. **Charles IV**, 1604–75, succeeded to duchy in 1624 but lost it repeatedly to Louis XIV because of his anti-French policy. He fought as a general in the imperial service. His son, **Charles V** (Charles Leopold), 1643–90, fought successfully against the Turks at Vienna and in Hungary but never recovered Lorraine.

Charles, Jacques Alexandre César (zhäk' ălĕksä'drü säzär' shärl'), 1746–1823, French physicist. Worked in electricity and aeronautics; ascended in hydrogen balloon (1783). **Charles's law:** at constant pressure, volume of a gas is directly proportional to temperature.

Charles, river in E Mass., winding past Cambridge and Boston to Boston Bay. Harvard boat races.

Charles, Cape, E Va., S point of Eastern Shore opposite Cape Henry; separates Chesapeake Bay from Atlantic Ocean. Ferries connect to Va. mainland.

Charles, Lake, SW La. Calcasieu R. is its inlet and outlet and connects it with Intracoastal Waterway and Gulf of Mexico. Lake Charles city on shores.

Charles Albert, 1798–1849, king of Sardinia (1831–49). To forestall revolution he granted constitution of 1848 (in force until 1947). Fought two compaigns

(1848,1849) of RISORGIMENTO against Austria. Routed at Novara, he abdicated in favor of his son, Victor Emmanuel II.

Charles Augustus, 1757–1828, duke and, after 1815, grand duke of Saxe-Weimar. Friend and patron of GOETHE. Played influential role in German politics.

Charles Borromeo, Saint (bŏrōmā'ō), 1538–84, Italian churchman; nephew of Pius IV. Made a cardinal and papal secretary of state, he brought about reopening of the Council of Trent and pushed the Catholic Reform. As bishop of Milan, he rigorously reformed clerical life and education. Feast: Nov. 4.

Charlesbourg, village (pop. 5,734), S Que., Canada, on St. Charles R. just N of Quebec. One of oldest parishes in Que., settled 1659 as Bourg Royal.

Charles City, city (pop. 10,309), NE Iowa, on Cedar R. and NNW of Waterloo; settled 1850. Mfg. of farm machinery.

Charles Edward Stuart: see STUART or STEWART, JAMES FRANCIS EDWARD.

Charles Martel (märtĕl'), 688?–741, Frankish mayor of the palace (714–41). United all Merovingian kingdoms under his rule. Halted Moslem invasion of Europe in battle of Tours or Poitiers (732), one of decisive battles in history. Father of Pepin the Short; grandfather of Charlemagne.

Charles of Blois (blwä), c.1319–1364, French prince; nephew of Philip VI. One of claimants in War of the BRETON SUCCESSION; killed at Auray. Beatified.

Charles of Valois (välwä'), 1270–1325, French prince; third son of Philip III; father of Philip VI. Sought thrones of Sicily, Byzantium, Rome, and Arles—all without success—and campaigned for Pope Boniface VIII in Italy. Took Florence 1301 and exiled Dante, who in *The Divine Comedy* placed him in Purgatory.

Charles of Viana (vēä'nä), 1421–61, Spanish prince; son of Queen Blanche of Navarre (d. 1442) and John II of Aragon. Ruled Navarre after 1442, but became involved in civil war with his father. Died soon after John had recognized him as heir.

Charles Robert of Anjou: see CHARLES I, king of Hungary.

Charles's law: see CHARLES, JACQUES ALEXANDRE CÉSAR.

Charles the Bad: see CHARLES II, king of Navarre.

Charles the Bold, 1433–77, duke of Burgundy (1467–77). Joined League of the Public Weal (1465) against LOUIS XI of France, whose lifelong adversary he remained. Master of Burgundy, Franche-Comté, and Low Countries, he dreamed of restoring kingdom of Lotharingia. His annexation of Lorraine and several Alsatian towns aroused the Swiss, who defeated him at Grandson and Morat (1476) and at Nancy, where he was killed. His empire fell apart after the accession of his daughter, MARY OF BURGUNDY.

Charles the Great, emperor: see CHARLEMAGNE.

Charleston. 1 City (pop. 9,164), E Ill., SE of Decatur. Mfg. of shoes, brooms. Lincoln Log Cabin State Park (site of Thomas Lincoln's farmhouse) is S. **2** City (pop. 5,501), SE Mo., SW of Cairo, Ill. A cotton center, it also has mfg. of shoes and lumber products. **3** City (pop. 70,174), SE S.C., state's oldest (1670) and largest city, on peninsula between Ashley and Cooper rivers at head of bay formed by them. On or in bay are Fort MOULTRIE, James Isl. (U.S. quarantine station), Morris Isl. (lighthouse), Fort SUMTER, and Castle Pinckney. Center for coastwise and foreign shipping and of a truck and seafood area, it has mfg. of fertilizer, wood products, paper and pulp, chemicals, and steel. Hq. of sixth naval district and SE division of U.S. Corps of Engineers. In Revolution, it was in British hands 1780–82. Convention of secession met here 1860. Fort Sumter was fired on by Confederates April 12, 1861. Charleston, besieged by Union forces, finally fell in 1865. Many old buildings and landmarks remain. Seat of The Citadel (Military Col. of South Carolina; state supported; for men; 1842) and Medical Col. of State of South Carolina. **4** City (pop. 73,-501), state cap., W W.Va., on Kanawha R. at mouth of Elk R., E of Huntington. State's second largest city and industrial, shipping, and wholesale-distribution center of Kanawha valley, it has oil refining and mfg. of ordnance, implements, and glass. Large chemical plants are in outskirts. Near by is West Virginia State Col. City chartered as Charles Town 1794; was cap. 1870–75, became permanent cap. 1885. New capitol (1932) designed by Cass Gilbert.

Charles Town, city (pop. 3,035), W.Va., in E Panhandle SW of Harpers Ferry; laid out 1786 by George Washington's brother Charles, whose home still stands. John Brown was tried (1859) and hanged here. Near by is "Harewood," where Dolly Madison was married. Racing meets held here.

Charlestown, part of Boston, Mass., on Charles R.; settled 1629, included in Boston 1874. Scene of battle of Bunker Hill, June 17, 1775.

Charles William Ferdinand, 1735–1806, duke of Brunswick (1780–1806). Prussian field marshal in Seven Years War; commander (1792–94) of Austro-Prussian armies in the FRENCH REVOLUTIONARY WARS. His son was FREDERICK WILLIAM, duke of Brunswick.

Charlet, Nicolas Toussaint (nēkôlä′ tōōsĕ′ shärlä′), 1792–1845, French lithographer, best known for scenes of the Napoleonic Wars. Also worked in oil and water color.

Charlevoix, Pierre François Xavier de (pyĕr′ fräswä′ zävyä′ dù shärlùvwä′), 1682–1761, French Jesuit traveler and historian. Traveled in New France 1705–9 and 1720. His *Histoire de la Nouvelle France* (1744; Eng. tr., 6 vols., 1900) is only full account of interior America in early 18th cent.

Charlevoix (shär′lùvoi), resort city (pop. 2,695), N Mich., between L. Michigan and L. Charlevoix (fishing). Area has Indian remains.

Charlot, Jean (zhä′ shärlō′), 1898–, American painter, b. France. A favorite subject is the Mexican Indian. Wrote *Art from the Mayans to Disney* (1939).

Charlotte (Sophia), 1744–1818, queen consort of George III of England. During king's mental illness, she was given charge of his person and household.

Charlotte. 1 (shùrlŏt′, shärlŏt′) City (pop. 6,606), S Mich., SW of Lansing, in agr. area. Mfg. of electronic equipment and radios. **2** (shär′lùt) City (pop. 134,042), S N.C., near S.C. line; settled c.1750. State's largest city, it is textile center and rail hub with mfg. of cotton and wool goods, hosiery, and machinery. MECKLENBURG DECLARATION OF INDEPENDENCE signed here May, 1775. Occupied by Cornwallis, Sept.–Oct., 1780. Seat of Queens Col. (Presbyterian; for women; 1857) and Johnson C. Smith Univ. (Negro; Presbyterian; coed.; 1867).

Charlotte Amalie (ùmäl′yù), town (pop. 10,399), cap. of VIRGIN ISLANDS (U.S.), on St. Thomas, founded 1673.

Charlotte Harbor, SW Fla., inlet of Gulf of Mexico, c.25 mi. long and 5 mi. wide.

Charlottesville, city (pop. 25,969), central Va., on Rivanna R. and NW of Richmond; founded 1762. Mfg. of textiles and machinery. Near by are MONTICELLO, home of Jefferson; "Ash Lawn," home of James Monroe; and birthplaces of Meriwether Lewis and G. R. Clark. Seat of Univ. of VIRGINIA. Burgoyne's captured army quartered here 1799–80; Tarleton raided town in 1781. Taken by Federals in Civil War.

Charlottetown, provincial cap. and only city (pop. 15,-887) of Prince Edward Isl., Canada, on S coast. Chief port, with steamship lines and shipbuilding. Seat of Prince of Wales Col. (1860; affiliated with Dalhousie Univ.) and St. Dunstan Univ. (affiliated with Laval Univ.). Founded as French trading post in early 18th cent. Town laid out 1768. Scene of **Charlottetown Conference** of Maritime Provs. (1864), which began Canadian confederation.

Charnwood, Godfrey Rathbone Benson, 1st Baron, 1864–1945, English author of a well-known biography of Abraham Lincoln (1916).

Charolais (shärôlä′), small region and former county, E central France, named for Charolles, a town in

Saône-et-Loire dept. Cattle breeding. Under dukes of Burgundy 1390–1477; then under Hapsburg (Spanish) rule until annexation by Louis XIV, who incorporated it into Burgundy prov. after 1674.

Charon (kā′rŏn), in Greek mythology, ferryman of Hades, who bore newly arrived dead across the STYX.

Charpentier, Gustave (gùstäv′ shärpätyä′), 1860–, French composer. His opera *Louise,* reflecting Parisian bourgeois life, has been very popular.

chartered companies, associations for foreign trade or colonization that appeared with expansion of European national states. Chartered by the state, they had trade or settlement monopolies in specific colonial areas. Foreshadowed by English Merchants Adventurers. Notable companies were British and Dutch East India companies (1600) and Hudson's Bay Co. (1670).

Charterhouse (chär′tùrhous) [Fr.,= Chartreuse], in London, founded as Carthusian monastery 1371; became a boys' school 1611. Now a noted public school. Removed 1872 to Godalming, Surrey. Thackeray describes it in *The Newcomes.*

Charter Oak: see HARTFORD, Conn.

Chartier, Alain (älĕ′ shärtyä′), c.1385–c.1433, French poet, secretary to Charles VII. Wrote *Le Quadrilogue invectif* (1422), anti-English prose pamphlet, and the poem *La Belle Dame sans mercy* (1424).

Chartism, workingmen's reform movement in Great Britain, 1838–48. "People's Charter," drafted by William Lovett and Francis Place, advocated universal manhood suffrage and other reforms.

Chartres (shär′trù), city (pop. 23,509), cap. of Eure-et-Loire dept., N France; chief center of BEAUCE. The magnificent Cathedral of Notre Dame epitomizes the spirit of French Gothic; its stained glass windows and sculpture are particularly famous. City damaged in World War II.

chartreuse (shärtrûz′), a LIQUEUR originated and long made exclusively by Carthusian monks at La Grande Chartreuse, France. Green chartreuse has c.57% alcohol; the sweeter yellow kind, c.43%.

Chartreuse, Grande (gräd′ shärtrûz′), mountain group (highest point 6,487 ft.), SE France, in Dauphiné Alps. The monastery, founded 1084 by St. Bruno in a high valley, was main seat of CARTHUSIANS until expulsion of order from France (1903). The monks were allowed to return in 1940. The present monastery was built in the 17th cent.

Charybdis (kùrĭb′dĭs), in Greek legend, whirlpool near rock of SCYLLA; home of a greedy monster.

Chase, Pliny Earle, 1820–86, American scientist and writer on meteorology, mathematics, philosophy.

Chase, Salmon P(ortland), 1803–73, American statesman. U.S. Senator from Ohio (1849–55, 1861); antislavery leader. U.S. Secretary of the Treasury (1861–64); responsible for national bank system (estab. 1863). Chief Justice of U.S. Supreme Court after 1864. His dissenting opinion in SLAUGHTERHOUSE CASES subsequently became accepted position of the courts as to restrictive force of Fourteenth Amendment. Presided fairly over impeachment trial of Pres. Johnson. Chase earnestly sought the presidency four times, but was never nominated.

Chase, Samuel, 1741–1811, American Revolutionary patriot, signer of Declaration of Independence, Associate Justice of U.S. Supreme Court (1796–1811). Impeached in 1804 on charge of political partiality, but acquitted.

Chase, Stuart, 1888–, American writer. Investigated meat-packing industry (1917–22), and was long with Labor Bureau, Inc. Among his books are *Men and Machines* (1929), *The Economy of Abundance* (1934), *Rich Land, Poor Land* (1936), and *The Tyranny of Words* (1938).

Chase, William Merritt, 1849–1916, American painter and teacher. Known for portraits and still lifes.

Chassériau, Théodore (täōdôr′ shäsärēō′), 1819–56, French painter; a pupil of Ingres. Murals for the

Church of St. Méry, Paris, and for the Palais d'Orsay.

Chassidim: see HASIDIM.

chat, largest American warbler. Yellow-breasted chat is shy; nests in E U.S. in thickets and winters in Mexico and Central America. Long-tailed chat is in W North America. In Europe are found the wheatear, the whinchat, and the stonechat.

Chateaubriand, François René, vicomte de (frȧswä′rŭnä′ věkôt′ dü shätôbrēä′), 1768–1848, French author. Visited U.S. 1791; émigré in England until 1800. A royalist, he was foreign minister (1823–24) and active in politics until 1830. Wrote *The Genius of Christianity* (1802; Eng. tr., 1856), including the famous extracts *Atala* and *René.* Last work was *Mémoires d'outre-tombe* [memoirs from beyond the tomb] (1849–50). A founder of French romanticism, he is noted for his rich, noble, and poetic style.

Château d'If (dēf′), castle on small If isl. off Marseilles, SE France. Built 1524; long a state prison. Scene of Dumas's *Count of Monte Cristo.*

Château Gaillard (gīär′), castle, N France, on the Seine near Les Andelys, SE of Rouen. Built 1196 by Richard I of England to protect Normandy from French; taken 1204 by Philip II. Ruins are splendid example of medieval military architecture.

Chateaugay (shȧ′tügē, shä″tügä′), Fr. *Chateauguay,* river rising in Chateaugay L. in the Adirondacks, NE N.Y., and flowing N through Quebec to empty into St. Lawrence R. Strong American troops under Wade Hampton were defeated (1813) by a small Canadian-Indian force on its Quebec shores.

Château-Thierry (shätō-tyěrē′), town (pop. 7,283), Aisne dept., N France, on Marne R. Focal point in second Marne battle (1918), in which last German offensive was stopped largely by U.S. troops.

Chatham, William Pitt, 1st earl of: see PITT, WILLIAM.

Chatham. 1 Town (pop. 5,223), E N.B., Canada, on Miramichi R. Shipping center with lumber, pulp, and paper mills, shipyards, and fish-processing plants. **2** City (pop. 21,218), S Ont., Canada, E of Detroit, Mich., at head of navigation on Thames R. Industrial center in farming and fruit-raising region. Mfg. of tractors and auto parts.

Chatham, municipal borough (pop. 46,940), Kent, England, on Medway R.; a major naval station. First dockyard estab. by Elizabeth 1588.

Chatham. 1 Resort and fishing town (pop. 2,457), SE Mass., on S Cape Cod; settled 1665. **2** Suburban borough (pop. 7,391), NE N.J., on Passaic R. and W of Newark; settled 1749.

Châtillon, Sébastien: see CASTALION, SÉBASTIEN.

Chatrian, Alexandre: see ERCKMANN-CHATRIAN.

Chattahoochee (chătühoō′chē), river rising in N Ga. and flowing S 436 mi. to Flint R. at Fla. line, forming Apalachicola R. Navigable to Columbus. Forms part of Ga.-Ala. and Ga.-Fla. lines.

Chattahoochee or **River Junction,** town (pop. 8,473), NW Fla., on Apalachicola R. at Ga. line and NW of Tallahassee, in tobacco area. Lumber and furniture.

Chattanooga (chătúnoō′gú), city (pop. 131,041), E Tenn., on Tennessee R. near Ga. line; settled 1815, laid out as Chattanooga 1837. Almost surrounded by mountains, including Missionary Ridge, Signal Mt., and Lookout Mt. First a river port, it grew with coming of railroads in 1840s and 1850s. Strategically important in Civil War (see CHATTANOOGA CAMPAIGN). Near-by Chickamauga and Chattanooga Natl. Military Park, on site of campaign, adjoins Fort Oglethorpe, Ga. Industrial, transportation, market, and resort center for agr. and mining area, and hq. for TVA power system (Chickamauga Dam near); it has mfg. of metal products, farm machinery, textiles, furniture, and hosiery.

Chattanooga campaign, Aug.–Nov., 1863, in Civil War. Chattanooga, as center of communications, was important Union objective. In 1863 Federals under W. S. Rosecrans drove Braxton Bragg from area. Bragg attacked at Chickamauga Sept. 19–20, but G. H. Thom-

as held line until ordered by Rosecrans to Chattanooga. When Bragg besieged town, U. S. Grant opposed him; with Joseph Hooker and Thomas Grant drove Confederates from Lookout Mt. in Battle above the Clouds, and then from Missionary Ridge.

Chatterton, Thomas, 1752–70, English poet. At 12 he was composing his "Rowley Poems," claiming that they were copies of 15th-cent. manuscripts. Came to London in 1770, failed to sell his poems, poisoned himself. His genius was recognized later.

Chaucer, Geoffrey (jěf′rē), c.1340–1400, English poet. The few facts known of his life based mainly on official records. Page in Prince Lionel's household (1357–58), later probably in service of John of Gaunt. Captured while with Edward III's army in France (1359–60), but ransomed. By 1366 married to Philippa (de Roet?), lady-in-waiting to queen. By 1367 valet in king's household. Among frequent diplomatic missions to Continent (1370–78) were trips to Italy (1372–73, 1378). From 1374 held several official posts: comptroller of customs on wool and hides at London (1374–86) and of petty customs (1382–86), knight of the shire for Kent (1386), clerk of the king's works (1389–91). First important poems, *Book of the Duchess* (1369) and partial translation of the ROMAN DE LA ROSE, draw on French sources. From his visits to Italy until c.1385, strongly influenced by Italian literature, especially by Dante in the *House of Fame* and the *Parliament of Fowls.* At height of powers produced *Troilus and Criseyde* (c.1385–86) based on Boccaccio's *Filostrato* (see TROILUS AND CRESSIDA) and began the *Canterbury Tales* (c.1387), richly varied collection of stories represented as told by pilgrims travelling together from London to shrine of St. Thomas at Canterbury. This narrative frame and the characterization of pilgrims vividly presented in Prologue and links between tales. Chaucer is most important figure in English literature before Shakspere. Helped to reestablish English language as vehicle for literature and introduced iambic PENTAMETER into English verse. Always acknowledged great narrative poet, he has recently been recognized as one of greatest English metrists.

Chaudière (shōdyěr′), river rising in SE Que., Canada, N of Maine-Que. line, and flowing 120 mi. NW to St. Lawrence R. above Quebec.

Chaudière Falls (shōdyěr′), 50-ft. drop in Ottawa R., SE Ont., Canada, within city of Ottawa.

Chauliac, Guy de (gē′ dü shōlyäk′) c.1300–c.1370, French surgeon, author of noted work on surgery.

Chaumette, Pierre Gaspard (pyěr′ gäspär′ shōmět′), 1763–94, French revolutionist. Leader of Paris commune; extremist member of CORDELIERS, after whose downfall he was guillotined.

Chaumont (shōmō′), town (pop. 15,068), cap. of Haute-Marne dept., NE France. Linen and cutlery mfg. U.S. field hq. in World War I. For treaty signed here 1814, see QUADRUPLE ALLIANCE.

Chausson, Ernest (shōsō′), 1855–1899, French composer of chamber, orchestral, and operatic music. His work combines elements of romanticism and impressionism. Best known for his Symphony in B Flat and the *Poème* for violin and orchestra.

Chautauqua (shùtôk′wù), resort village, W N.Y., on W shore of **Chautauqua Lake,** 18 mi. long and 1–3 mi. wide, near L. Erie, in resort and fruit-growing region. Chautauqua Inst. (1874) offers popular summer lectures and concerts.

Chautauqua movement, adult education similar to lyceum movement. First institute estab. 1874 at Chautauqua, N.Y., as development of Methodist Episcopal summer Sunday-school institute. Developed into eight-week program of courses and lectures in arts, science, humanities, and religion. Chautauquas were formed in other communities and continued until c.1924. Assembly at Chautauqua still draws thousands each year.

chauvinism (shō′vùnĭzùm) [after Nicolas Chauvin, Napoleonic soldier], aggressive and exaggerated nationalism. Exalts national consciousness and spreads hatred of other peoples.

Chaux-de-Fonds, La (lä shō-dü-fō'), town (pop. 33,154), Neuchâtel canton, W Switzerland; a center for making of watches.

Chavannes, Puvis de: see PUVIS DE CHAVANNES.

Chávez, Carlos (chä'väs), 1899–, Mexican composer and conductor. He has done extensive research in native Indian music, which has influenced his own writing. His works include ballets, symphonies, a piano concerto, and choral works.

Chaykovsky, Nikolai Vasilyevich (nyĭkŭlī' vŭsē'lyŭvĭch chĭkôf'skē), 1850–1926, Russian revolutionist, a leader of People's Socialist party. Headed anti-Bolshevik government at Archangel (1917–19).

Chazars: see KHAZARS.

Cheaha (chē'hô), peak, 2,407 ft. high, in Talladega Mts., E Ala.; highest point in Ala.

Cheapside, street in the City of London, most important market center of medieval London. Tournaments and some executions were held here. Mermaid Tavern was in district.

Cheb, Czechoslovakia: see EGER.

Cheboygan (shĕboi'gŭn), city (pop. 5,687), N Mich., on S channel of Straits of Mackinac at mouth of Cheboygan R. Resort and farm trade center, with mfg. of metal and wood products. Exports fish.

Chechen (chĭchĕn'), Moslem people native to N slopes of central Greater Caucasus, RSFSR. Fought Russian conquest in 19th cent., particularly during SHAMYL rebellion. With closely related Ingush, they formed (1936–44) an autonomous soviet socialist republic (6,100 sq. mi.; pop. 697,408); this was dissolved by USSR government because of their collaboration with Germans in World War II. Population was resettled elsewhere in Russia.

Che-chiang, province, China: see CHEKIANG.

checkers, game for two players, played with 24 counters on board with 64 squares; known in England as draughts. Played in Europe since 16th cent.; similar game known to ancients.

cheese, known as food since antiquity, is today made mainly from milk of cows, sheep, or goats. The making of all the varied kinds begins with coagulation of casein, the chief milk protein, by enzyme action or by lactic acid, or a combination. Hard cheeses include Cheddar (originally from England), Edam and Gouda (Holland), Emmental or Gruyère (Switzerland), and Parmesan (Italy). Stilton, Roquefort, Gorgonzola, and American brick are semihard. Soft cheeses may be either fresh (unripened), e.g., cream cheese and cottage cheese, or softened by microorganisms (which also develop flavor) in ripening: Camembert, Brie, and Limburger.

cheetah (chē'tŭ) or **hunting leopard,** member of cat family, native to Asia and Africa. From early times it was trained to hunt game. *Acinonyx jubatus* of Africa is about the size of a leopard and has long legs and a tawny black-spotted coat.

Chefoo (chē'foō') or **Yentai** (yĕn'tī'), city (pop. 227,-000), E China, on Shantung peninsula and on Yellow Sea. Treaty port, opened 1858.

Chehalis (chĭhā'lĭs), city (pop. 5,639), SW Wash., on Chehalis R. Lumber, coal, and food products.

Cheka: see SECRET POLICE.

Chekhov, Anton Pavlovich (chē'kôf), 1860–1904, Russian author. His prevailing themes are man's essential loneliness and frustration and the dullness and stagnation of Russian life in his day. Sympathetic yet realistic toward his characters, he varied these themes in hundreds of masterful short stories and in the dramas *The Sea Gull* (1898), *Uncle Vanya* (1899), *The Three Sisters* (1901), and *The Cherry Orchard* (1904). Widely translated, Chekhov had immense influence on contemporary literature.

Chekiang or **Che-chiang** (both: chē'kyăng', jŭ'-jyäng'), province (40,000 sq. mi.; pop. 20,000,000), E China, on East China Sea; cap. Hangchow. Includes many islands, notably Chusan Archipelago. Most fertile area is Yangtze delta where rice, cotton, tobacco, and hemp are grown. Also produces tea and silk.

Chelan, Lake (chĭlăn'), c.50 mi. long and ½–1½ mi. wide, N central Wash., in Cascade Range. Resort area.

Chelmno, Pol. *Chełmno* (khĕ'ōōmnô), Ger. *Kulm,* town (pop. 11,634), W Poland, near the Vistula. Dates from 10th cent. Under Teutonic Knights 1226–1466; under Prussia 1772–1919. Napoleon defeated near by, 1813.

Chelmsford (chĕmz'fŭrd), town (pop. 9,407), NE Mass., SW of Lowell; settled 1633. Processes wool.

Chelsea, metropolitan borough (pop. 50,912), W London, England; a literary and artistic quarter. Much damaged by air raids 1940–41.

Chelsea, city (pop. 38,912), E Mass., NE industrial and residential suburb of Boston; settled 1624. Mfg. of rubber goods, shoes, and chemicals.

Cheltenham (chĕlt'nŭm), municipal borough (pop. 62,-823), Gloucestershire, England. A resort near the Cotswolds, it is a hunting center.

Chelyabinsk (chĭlyä'bĭnsk), city (pop. c.450,000), RS-FSR, in W Ural foothills and on Trans-Siberian RR. A major metallurgical center of USSR, it nearly doubled in population after World War II, when many industries were transferred here.

Chelyuskin, Cape (chĭlyōō'skĭn), northernmost point (lat. 77°41'N) of Asiatic continent, on Taimyr peninsula, RSFSR. Named after 18th-cent. Russian navigator. Airfield; observation post.

chemical affinity, attractive force between atoms, i.e., tendency of one element to react with another.

chemical reaction, action taking place during change in internal molecular structure of substance, which loses characteristic properties. In some reactions, heat given off (exothermic); in some, heat absorbed (endothermic). When compound substance is broken down into constituents, it is simple decomposition. When two compounds react to form two new compounds, it is double decomposition. In replacement reactions, place of element in compound is taken by another element. In chemical combination (SYNTHESIS), elements combine to form compounds. OXIDATION and REDUCTION are important reactions. Reaction rate depends on temperature, pressure, concentration, CATALYST, etc. EQUATION represents change.

chemical warfare, in its widest sense, the application of chemical knowledge for offensive or defensive purposes in hostilities. An early example was the use of Greek fire. In World War I poison gas was used extensively. Chlorine was first used April 22, 1915, by the Germans. In World War II preparations for various sorts of chemical warfare were made by all major countries, but little resulted—partly because of mutual fear of retaliation. Chemistry did, however, contribute greatly to the fashioning of new types of airborne bombs and to such implements as flame throwers. It also contributed to the knowledge of nuclear fission that made possible the atomic bomb.

Chemin des Dames (shmĕ dä däm'), road along crest between Aisne and Ailette rivers, N France. Held by Germans in World War I until they were dislodged in bitter fighting (1917–18).

chemistry, science of nature and composition of matter and changes it undergoes. Appearance and behavior of substances are described in physical and chemical properties; changes during reactions are shown by equations. Two categories of matter are elements, represented by symbols; and compounds, represented by formulas. Composition of compounds determined by analysis: qualitative, for elements present, and quantitative, for their proportion. Organic chemistry is study of carbon compounds, and inorganic is study of other elements and compounds plus simple oxides of carbon and metallic carbonates. See also ALCHEMY; BIOCHEMISTRY.

Chemnitz (kĕm'nĭts), city (pop. 250,188), Saxony, SE Germany, on Chemnitz R., near one of world's largest open-pit lignite mines. Leading industrial center, mfg. of machine tools, machinery, chemicals, textiles. Chartered 1143. Suffered greatly in Thirty Years War and World War II.

Chemulpo (chä'mōōl'pô') or **Inchon** (ĭn'chŏn'), city (pop. 265,767), E central Korea; port on Yellow Sea. UN forces landed here 1950. Mfg. center.

Chemung (shĭmŭng'), river formed near Corning, S N.Y., and flowing c.45 mi. SE, past Elmira, to Susquehanna R. near Sayre, Pa. Valley was scene of fighting in Revolutionary campaign of JOHN SULLIVAN.

chemurgy (kĕ'mûrjē), branch of chemistry applied to preparation of industrial materials from agricultural products.

Chenab, India: see PUNJAB.

Chengteh (chŭng'dŭ'), commercial city (pop. 60,000), cap. Jehol prov., Manchuria. Wool trading and weaving. Was summer cap. of Ch'ing dynasty. Formerly called Jehol.

Chengtu or **Ch'eng-tu** (both: chŭng'dōō), commercial city (pop. 647,877), cap. Szechwan prov., S China; port on Min R. Seat of three universities.

Chénier, André (ädrä' shänyā'), 1762–94, French poet. His pamphlets against the excesses of the French Revolutionists led to his execution. His poems range from classical lyrics, such as *La Jeune Captive, Élégies,* and *Bucoliques,* to political satires.

Chennault, Claire Lee (shĕ'nôlt"), 1890–, American general. Formed American Volunteer Group ("Flying Tigers") in China (1941). Headed U.S. air task force in China (1942–45).

Cheops, anc. Egyptian king: see KHUFU.

Chephren: see KHAFRE.

Chequamegon Bay (shĭkwä'mŭgŭn), arm of L. Superior, N Wis. Visited by French explorers in 17th cent. Father Allouez founded mission on its shore 1665. Forms harbor for Ashland.

Cher (shĕr), department (2,820 sq. mi.; pop. 286,070), central France, in Berry; cap. Bourges. It is traversed by the **Cher** river, 200 mi. long, which flows from Massif Central NW to join Loire near Tours.

Cherbourg (shĕrbōōr'), town (pop. 34,034), Manche dept., NW France, on English Channel at tip of Cotentin peninsula. Fortified naval station since 17th cent.; transatlantic port since World War I. Further fortified by Germans in World War II; capitulated to U.S. troops June, 1944.

Cherchel (shĕrshĕl'), town (pop. 7,263), Algeria; a Mediterranean port. As Caesarea it was cap. of Mauretania. Has many relics of Roman period.

Cheremiss, RSFSR: see MARI AUTONOMOUS SOVIET SOCIALIST REPUBLIC.

Cheribon (chĕrĭbŏn'), town (pop. 54,079), N Java, Indonesia; port on Java Sea. Exports sugar, copra, and rice. At near-by village of Linggajati was drafted the agreement mapping eventual formation of United States of Indonesia under Dutch crown.

Cherkess, people of USSR: see CIRCASSIA.

Chernigov (chĭrnyē'gŭf), city (pop. 67,356), N Ukraine; agr. center and port on Desna R. The Spaski Sobor (Byzantine cathedral, built 1024), oldest building in Russia, was destroyed in World War II.

Chernovtsy (chĭrnôf'tsē), Ger. *Czernowitz,* Rumanian *Cernauti,* city (1930 pop. 112,427), W Ukraine, on Pruth R., former cap. of BUKOVINA. Pop. was largely German and Jewish until World War II.

Cherokee (chĕr'ŭkē), city (pop. 7,705), NW Iowa, on Little Sioux R. and ENE of Sioux City. Center for farm, dairy, and livestock area. Near-by Pilot Rock was landmark for early settlers.

Cherokee Indians (chĕr'ŭkē), largest and most important single tribe in SE U.S. Language is of the Iroquoian family. Cherokee Nation (estab. 1827) had a constitution providing for elected chief, senate, and house of representatives. The syllabic alphabet invented by Sequoyah gave them writing, and their material culture was high. In 1838 they were brutally removed from their homes and moved to the Indian Territory. Tribe split by differing sympathies in U.S. Civil War. In

1906 tribe disbanded, and Cherokee became U.S. citizens.

Cherrapunji: see ASSAM.

cherry, name for several trees or shrubs of genus *Prunus* and their fruits, grown in home and commercial orchards. There are many varieties derived from two Old World species—*Prunus avium* (sweet cherry) and *P. cerasus* (sour cherry). Fruit is eaten raw and used in preserves, pies, and liqueurs (see MARASCHINO). Flowering cherry is derived from other species and there are many varieties with showy single or double flowers. Species of American wild cherry include chokecherry, pin cherry, and wild black cherry.

Cherry Valley, village (pop. 760), E central N.Y., W of Albany. Tories and Indians led by Walter Butler and Joseph Brant burned most of the village and massacred over 40 people on Nov. 11, 1778.

Chersiphron (kûr'sĭfrŭn), Cretan architect. Traditional builder of the original Ionic temple of Artemis at Ephesus in 550 B.C.

Cherso (kĕr'sō), Serbo-Croatian *Cres* (tsŭrĕs'), Adriatic island (c.150 sq. mi.), off Croatia, Yugoslavia. Ceded by Italy 1947.

cherub (chĕr'ŭb), plural **cherubim** (–ŭbĭm), kind of angel, with seraphim attendant upon God. In old Jewish tradition described as winged creatures with human, or often, animal faces; late Christian art pictures them as plump children. Gen. 3.24; Ex. 25.18–22; 37.6–9; 1 Kings 6.23–28; Pss. 18.10; 80.1; Ezek. 10.

Cherubini, Maria Luigi (märē'ä lwē'jē kārōōbē'nē), 1760–1842, Italian composer; lived in Paris after 1788. Composed operas (e.g., *Les Deux Journées, Anacreon, Médée*) and church music.

Chesapeake, U.S. frigate, famous for her role in *Chesapeake* affair (June 22, 1807) and for her battle with British ship *Shannon* (June 1, 1813). In *Chesapeake* affair ship was fired on by British ship *Leopard* when James BARRON refused demand to search *Chesapeake* for British deserters. During battle with the *Shannon* James Lawrence reportedly issued famous last command, "Don't give up the ship!" She was, however, captured.

Chesapeake and Delaware Canal, 19 mi. long, connecting head of Chesapeake Bay near Chesapeake City, Md., with Delaware R. below Delaware City, Del. Built 1824–29; bought by U.S. 1919 and enlarged 1935–39.

Chesapeake and Ohio Canal, former waterway, c.185 mi. long, from Washington, D.C., to Cumberland, Md., running along left bank of Potomac R. Built 1828–50. Had busiest days in 1860s. Now included in Natl. Capital Parks.

Chesapeake & Ohio Railway, U.S. transportation company, with 5,062 mi. of lines in six states, Washington, D.C., and Ont., Canada. Incorporated 1878. Merged 1947 with Pere Marquette Railway Co.

Chesapeake Bay, inlet of the Atlantic (c.200 mi. long N–S, 3–30 mi. wide), between Delmarva Peninsula (called Eastern Shore of Md. and Va.) and the major parts of Va. and Md. Enters between Cape Charles and Cape Henry, Va. Receives Susquehanna, Patuxent, Potomac, Rappahannock, York, and James rivers. Important ports on shores are Baltimore, Norfolk, and Hampton Roads area. Has well-known fishing grounds. New bridge connects Kent Isl. of Eastern Shore with main part of Md.

Chesapeake City, town (pop. 1,154), NE Md., S of Elkton. W end of Chesapeake and Delaware Canal.

Cheselden, William (chē'zŭldŭn), 1688–1752, English surgeon who improved the kidney-stone operation and was author of works on bones and on general anatomy.

Cheshire (chĕ'shŭr) or **Chester,** maritime county (1,014 sq. mi.; pop. 1,258,050), W central England, co. town Chester. A low, flat, and fertile region; dairy farming extensive and Cheshire cheese famous. Estuaries of chief rivers, Mersey and Dee, form Wirral peninsula in Irish Sea. Chief industries are salt and coal mining, shipbuilding, and mfg. of railroad cars, textiles, and chemicals. Communications include Manchester Ship Canal.

Cheshire, town (pop. 6,295), S central Conn., N of New Haven; settled before 1700. Metal goods.

Chesney, Francis Rawdon, 1789–1872, British soldier and explorer in Asia. Demonstrated feasibility of Suez Canal route (1829) and surveyed the Tigris and Euphrates (1835), proving their navigability.

chess [from Persian *shah* = king], game for two players each using 16 counters (a king, a queen, two rooks or castles, two bishops, two knights, and 8 pawns) on board of 64 squares. Probably originated in India. By 13th cent. chess was played all over Western Europe. Modern chess dates from 15th cent.

Chester, county borough (pop. 48,229), co. town of Cheshire, England. Site of important Roman camp, it later was last place in England to surrender to William the Conqueror (1070). Many medieval buildings survive, including cathedral with architecture from Norman to Late Perpendicular. Chester Miracle Plays originated here.

Chester. 1 City (pop. 5,389), S Ill., on the Mississippi below St. Louis. Shipping center of agr., coal, and quarry area. Park with site of old KASKASKIA is near by. **2** Village (pop. 1,215), SE N.Y., SW of Newburgh. Trotting horse HAMBLETONIAN was foaled and buried here. **3** City (pop. 66,039), SE Pa., on Delaware R. and SW of Philadelphia; settled c.1644 by Swedes as Uppland. Renamed by William Penn whose house (1683) still stands. One of oldest cities in state, it has shipbuilding and mfg. of steel, paper, and glass products, and chemicals. First provincial assembly met here 1682. **4** City (pop. 6,893), N S.C., NNW of Columbia. Mfg. of textiles, fertilizer, cottonseed oil, and foundry products.

Chesterfield, Philip Dormer Stanhope, 4th earl of, 1694–1773, English statesman, author of worldly-wise *Letters to His Son* (1774; addressed to his natural son). Lord Chesterfield was rebuked in a famous letter by Samuel Johnson for belated tribute to the *Dictionary*.

Chesterton, G(ilbert) K(eith), 1874–1936, English essayist, convert to Roman Catholicism and apologist for Catholicism in many essays and books. His novels include *The Man Who Was Thursday* (1908) and detective fiction, featuring Father Brown. Writings—as in *Tremendous Trifles* (1909)—cover a wide range of literary, social, moral criticism. Associated with Hilaire Belloc. Also wrote poetry (notably narrative *Lepanto*).

Chestertown, town (pop. 3,143), Eastern Shore, Md., on Chester R., NE of Annapolis. Trade center of resort area. Seat of Washington Col.

chestnut, deciduous tree of genus *Castanea* of N Hemisphere and its edible nuts borne in burs. American chestnut (*Castanea dentata*), native E of the Mississippi now nearly extinct because of chestnut blight, a fungus disease. See also CHINQUAPIN. See *ill.,* p. 783.

Chestnut Hill, suburb of Boston, Mass., in Brookline and Newton towns. Main seat of Boston Col. (R.C., Jesuit; partly coed.; 1863).

Chesuncook Lake (chĭsŭn′kook), 22 mi. long and 1–4 mi. wide, N central Maine, in wilderness region noted for hunting and fishing.

Chevalier, Guillaume Sulpice: see GAVARNI.

Chevalier, Michel (mĕshĕl′ shüvälyä′) 1806–79, French economist, an influential advocate of industrialization and free trade.

Cheviot (shĭv′eŭt, shĕv′–), city (pop. 9,944), SW Ohio, W of Cincinnati. Mfg. of boxes and clothes.

Cheviot Hills (chĕv′eŭt), 35 mi. range on Scotland-England border; once scene of much border strife.

Chevreuse, Marie de Rohan-Montbazon, duchesse de (märē′ dü rōä′-mōbäzō′ düshĕs′ dü shüvrûz′), 1600–1679, French beauty, intimate of Anne of Austria. Intrigued against Richelieu; twice exiled. During Fronde she first opposed, then supported, Mazarin.

chewing gum is usually made from chicle, which is melted, sterilized, sweetened, flavored, and shaped into sticks or candy-coated pellets. Insoluble plastics may be mixed with, or substituted for, chicle.

Cheyenne (shīăn′), city (pop. 31,935; alt. c.6,000 ft.), state cap., SE Wyo., near Colo. and Nebr. lines. Selected as Union Pacific RR division point 1867. Became territorial cap. 1869. Cattle ranching and Black Hills gold stimulated growth in 1870s. State's largest city, it is a sheep and cattle market and center for transportation (air, highway, rail) and shipping. Annual Frontier Days celebration (since 1897).

Cheyenne, river, 527 mi. long, rising in E Wyo. and flowing NE to Missouri R. in central S.Dak., above Pierre. Has U.S. projects on river and tributaries (see BELLE FOURCHE R.). River's basin is in MISSOURI RIVER BASIN PROJECT.

Cheyenne Indians, North American tribe of Algonquian linguistic family. Divided (c.1830) at headwaters of Platte river into northern band (now in Mont.) and southern band (now in Okla.); both had typical Plains culture. Southern band had severe war (1861–68) with whites, marked by massacre of Indians by U.S. soldiers at Sandy Creek (1864).

Chiang Kai-shek (chēäng″ kī″-shĕk′, jyäng″), 1886–, Chinese generalissimo and statesman. Chief aide of Sun Yat-sen in revolution of 1911. Became prominent in Kuomintang party in 1923; led army N from Canton. Originally worked with the Communists but broke with them in 1927. Held enormous power as Nationalist leader from 1928 to 1948. With his wife Mei-ling SOONG he attended Cairo Conference (1943) with Roosevelt and Churchill. After World War II unsuccessfully opposed Communist drive into S China; by April, 1950, retained only Formosa.

Chianti, Monti (mōn′tē kyän′tē), small range of Apennines, Tuscany, central Italy. Chianti wine comes from vineyards on its slopes.

Chiapas (chēä′päs), state (28,732 sq. mi.; pop. 903,200), S Mexico, on Pacific, between Isthmus of Tehuantepec and Guatemala; cap. TUXTLA. Exploitation of state's natural resources retarded by its inaccessibility. Recently airlines and Inter-American Highway have been opening country. Notable source of hardwoods.

Chiatura (chēŭtoo′rŭ), city (pop. c.10,000), W central Georgian SSR. Large manganese production.

Chibcha (chĭb′chŭ), group of Indian tribes in E Colombian Andes, with a highly developed material culture (agr., mining of emeralds, making of gold- and copperwork, fine textiles). Two chief tribes, headed by Zaque at Tunja and Zipa at Bogotá, were conquered by Jiménez de Quesada (1536–41). Chibchan languages were probably spoken as far N as Nicaragua. Chibchan custom of gilding new rulers probably gave rise to the legend of El Dorado.

Chicago (shĭkä′gō), city (pop. 3,620,962), NE Ill., on L. Michigan. Second U.S. city in size and importance, it is world's greatest rail and meat-packing center and a highway hub and Great Lakes port. Seat of world's largest grain and livestock markets and of Midwest stock exchange, it has mfg. of iron and steel, machinery, electrical equipment, railroad cars and equipment, chemicals, and textiles. Marquette and Joliet came here 1673 and trading post was founded c.100 years later. Fort DEARBORN was estab. 1803. Erie Canal speeded settling of Midwest, and Chicago was platted 1803. Town grew with lake traffic and coming of railroads. From the ashes of the great fire of 1871 grew a city of stone and steel. With growing industries came labor troubles, notably HAYMARKET SQUARE RIOT of 1886 and Pullman strike of 1894 (see DEBS, E. V., and ALTGELD, J. P.). There was considerable growth in both World Wars. From World War I to 1933, Chicago was known as a resort of gangsters and racketeers. The city's material progress was evidenced in the World's Columbian Exposition of 1893 and Century of Progress Exposition of 1933–34. Notable highlights of this cultural center are Chicago Symphony, ART INSTITUTE OF CHICAGO, CHICAGO NATURAL HISTORY MUSEUM, Hull House, and Chicago Civic

Opera. It is the seat of Univ. of CHICAGO, De Paul Univ. (R.C.; coed.; 1898), Illinois Inst. of Technology (nonsectarian; coed.; since 1940 consists of Armour Col. of Engineering, opened 1893 by P. D. Armour as Inst. of Technology, and Lewis Inst. of Arts and Sciences), LOYOLA UNIVERSITY, Mundelein Col., and parts of Northwestern Univ. and Univ. of Illinois.

Chicago, river, NE Ill., formed in Chicago by junction of two branches. Formerly flowed E to L. Michigan; flow was reversed into South Branch and Sanitary and Ship Canal (1900), carrying Chicago's wastes to Mississippi R. via Illinois Waterway system. Now part of Great Lakes to Gulf of Mexico waterway.

Chicago, Art Institute of: see ART INSTITUTE OF CHICAGO.

Chicago, University of, in Chicago; nonsectarian, private, coed.; chartered 1891 (Baptist), opened 1892 with gifts from J. D. Rockefeller. R. M. HUTCHINS inaugurated "Chicago plan," i.e., a four-year junior college and a liberal arts university divorced from professional schools. University is notable for research and graduate work. Seat of Hutchins' "great books" program. Maintains two observatories (Yerkes, at Williams Bay, Wis., and McDonald, with Univ. of Texas, at Mt. Locke, Texas). Has Oriental Inst. and Inst. for Nuclear Research. Library is rich in Lincolniana and Americana. Includes pioneer Univ. of Chicago Press (1891).

Chicago Heights, industrial city (pop. 24,551), NE Ill., S of Chicago; settled in 1830s. Mfg. of metal products, glass, and chemicals.

Chicago Natural History Museum, founded at Chicago, Ill. 1893, through gifts of Marshall Field and others. Chartered as Columbian Mus. of Chicago, name later became Field Columbian Mus., then Field Mus. of Natural History, and (1943) Chicago Natural History Mus. Known for habitat groups (largely prepared by methods of Carl Akeley), botanical, anthropological, and geological collections, and works of sculpture. Sponsors many expeditions.

Chichagof Island (chĭ'chŭgŏf), off SE Alaska, in ALEXANDER ARCHIPELAGO, N of Baranof Isl. Has fish canning, gold mining, and wolfram deposits.

Chichén Itzá (chěchän' ētsä'), anc. Mayan city, occupied by the Itzá group (according to one system of dating c.514–692 and late 10th cent.–1194). Ruins, showing Old Empire and New Empire architectural styles, have been much studied by archaeologists.

Chicherin, Georgi Vasilyevich (gēôr'gē vŭsē'lyŭvĭch chěchâ'rĭn), 1872–1936, Russian foreign commissar (1918–30). Prepared recognition of USSR by Great Powers at Conference of GENOA and through Treaty of RAPALLO (1922).

Chichester (chĭ'chĭstŭr), municipal borough (pop. 19,-110), Sussex West, England. Once a Roman town; an amphitheater was discovered here 1935. Cathedral (12th–13th cent.) has detached bell tower.

Chichi-jima: see BONIN ISLANDS.

chickadee (chĭk'ŭdē"), small North American bird related to titmouse. Black-capped chickadee is a permanent resident in much of E North America; several species are in W U.S., one in S U.S.

Chickahominy (chĭkŭhŏ'mĭnē), river of E Va., rising NW of Richmond and flowing SE c.90 mi. to the James. In Civil War there was heavy fighting along its banks (see PENINSULAR CAMPAIGN).

Chickamauga (chĭkŭmô'gŭ), city (pop. 1,747), NW Ga., S of CHATTANOOGA, Tenn. Scene of a Civil War battle in CHATTANOOGA CAMPAIGN. Chickamauga and Chattanooga Natl. Military Park is near.

Chickasaw Indians (chĭk'ŭsô), tribe of Natchez-Muskogean linguistic stock, once occupying N Miss. One of FIVE CIVILIZED TRIBES.

Chickasha (chĭk'ŭshä), city (pop. 15,842), SW central Okla., on Washita R. and SW of Oklahoma City. Market and processing center for agr. and oil area, it has cotton gins, cottonseed-oil mills, and oil refineries.

chicken: see POULTRY.

chicken pox (varicella), contagious, infectious childhood disease caused by a filterable virus. Red spots becoming blisters appear on trunk two to three weeks after exposure.

chick-pea, annual plant (*Cicer arietinum*) grown since antiquity for its edible pealike seeds in Asia, S Europe, Mexico, and South America. It is also called *garbanzo* and gram.

chickweed, low-growing weed (*Stellaria media*) of temperate regions. Mouse-ear chickweeds are rock garden perennials of genus *Cerastium*.

chicle (chĭ'kŭl), name for gum obtained from latex of sapodilla tree, a tropical American evergreen (*Achras zapota*) also grown for edible fruit. Chicle exported to U.S. for making chewing gum.

Chico (chē'kō), city (pop. 12,272), N Calif., N of Sacramento, in agr. area (fruit, almonds, alfalfa, grain); laid out 1860. Flour milling, canning, and fruit processing.

Chicopee (chĭ'kŭpē), city (pop. 49,211), SW Mass., on Connecticut R. near Springfield; settled 1652. Mfg. of electrical apparatus, tires, firearms, textiles, sporting goods. U.S. air base is here.

chicory or **succory,** blue-flowered herb (*Cichorium intybus*) of Europe, naturalized in North America. Root used as coffee substitute and adulterant. When blanched for winter salads, known as witloof or French endive. True endive is in same genus.

Chicoutimi (shĭkōō'tĭmē"), city (pop. 23,216), S Que., Canada, on Saguenay R. at mouth of Chicoutimi R. Has pulp, lumber, and woolen mills. Has many Roman Catholic institutions.

Chidambaram (chĭdŭm'bŭrŭm'), town (pop. 26,212), SE Madras, India. Has remains of Dravidian art, including a statue of the dancing Siva.

Chidon (kī'dōn): see PEREZ-UZZA.

chief, a leader of a clan or tribe. Hereditary succession is most common, though special qualities may aid in attainment of this status. Functions of chief may be shared by two or more persons.

Chiemsee (kēm'zä), lake, area 31 sq. mi., Bavaria, SE of Munich. An island has palace built by Louis II in imitation of Versailles.

Ch'ien Lung: see CH'ING, dynasty.

chigger, minute, six-legged, reddish larva of harvest mite or red bug commoner in S U.S. than in N U.S. Related to the spider, the adult has eight legs. Attacks warm-blooded mammals, including man, by attaching to the skin and gorging with blood.

Chignecto (shĭgnĕk'tō), isthmus connecting N.S., Canada, with the Canadian mainland.

chigoe (chĭ'gō) or **jigger,** small flea of tropical America and S U.S. Female bores into flesh of humans and animals; flea's abdomen swells forming sack wherein eggs develop; this irritation gives rise to sores and danger of infection.

Chihli, Gulf of (chē'lē', jû'lē'), Chinese *Po Hai*, arm of Yellow Sea, NE China. Bounded on S by Shantung peninsula and on NE by Liaotung peninsula.

Chihuahua (chēwä'wä), state (94,831 sq. mi.; pop. 841,-077), N Mexico; cap. Chihuahua (pop. 56,805). Largest Mexican state, it is divided into two regions with mountains in W and desert basin in N and E. Chief occupations: mining (silver, gold, copper, manganese), cattle raising, and agr. (by irrigation). First known to Spanish through Cabeza de Vaca; became state after independence from Spain. JUÁREZ, a border city, is commercial link with U.S.

Chihuahua dog: see TOY DOGS.

Chikamatsu, Monzaemon (mōnzä'ämō chĭkä'mätsōō), 1653–1724, great Japanese dramatist, who wrote primarily for puppet stage. Influenced development of modern Japanese theater.

Child, Francis James, 1825–96, American scholar. Compiled *English and Scottish Popular Ballads* (5 vols., 1883–98).

childbirth: see BIRTH.

Childebert (chĭl'dŭbŭrt), Frankish kings. **Childebert I,**

d. 558, king of Paris (511–58). Partitioned his brother Clodomer's kingdom of Orléans with his brothers Clotaire I and Theodoric I (524), and Burgundy and Provence with Clotaire (534). **Childebert II,** 570–96, king of Austrasia (575–96) and Burgundy (593–96). Dominated by his mother, BRUNHILDA.

Childeric I (chĭl'dûrĭk), c.436–481, Merovingian king of Salian Franks; father of Clovis I.

child labor was recognized as a social problem in late 18th-cent. England, where employment in factories became virtual slavery for the children. Factory acts of 1802 and later bettered conditions. Today almost all European countries limit the working day for children to 6–8 hr. In U.S. problem became acute after the Civil War. All but two states forbid full-time employment of children under 14 in industry; 14 states forbid employment of children under 16 in school hours. Congressional laws against child labor were declared invalid 1918 and 1922; attempts to secure a constitutional amendment have failed.

Children's Crusade: see CRUSADES.

Childress (chĭl'drĭs), city (pop. 7,619), N Texas, SE of Amarillo in Pandhandle. Rail hub and center of agr. area in old ranch country.

child welfare. When the effects of the Industrial Revolution in exploiting CHILD LABOR were being recognized in the late 18th and early 19th cent., educators such as Rousseau, Pestalozzi, and Froebel called attention to children's special needs. The 19th cent. saw the organization of charitable institutions for orphaned, destitute, and handicapped children, and the 20th cent. saw the expansion of child welfare agencies and services (private, municipal, state, national, and international). The British Children's Charter Act (1908), the Ohio Children's Code Commission (1911), and the founding of the U.S. Children's Bureau (1912) were early landmarks.

Chile (chĭ'lē, Span. chē'lä), republic (286,396 sq. mi.; pop. 5,760,571), S South America; cap. SANTIAGO. A long (c.2,600 mi.) narrow (never more than 250 mi. wide) strip between the rugged Andes (lofty ACONCAGUA is just over the Argentine border) and the Pacific, Chile also includes outlying EASTER ISLAND and JUAN FERNÁNDEZ isls. The mainland has deserts in the N producing nitrates (see ATACAMA) and copper, exported through ANTOFAGASTA and ARICA. In the center is a long rich valley, the "garden" of Chile, where the population is concentrated (65% mestizo, 30% white, 5% Indian). Here are the cap. and other large cities (notably the port VALPARAISO and near-by VIÑA DEL MAR). Where the Andes approach the sea in the S there is a resort area of alpine lakes near PUERTO MONTT, and further S is a region of wet, wooded islands and the southerly city, PUNTA ARENAS. Chile's S tip is in the frigid TIERRA DEL FUEGO. The predominant language is Spanish, the predominant religion Roman Catholicism—both brought by Spanish conquerors. First of these was Almagro, who in an expedition from Peru (1536) was defeated by the deserts and by fierce Araucanian Indians. Valdivia after 1540 founded Spanish cities, but resistance of the Indians was not really broken until late in the 19th cent. Chile, developed as an area of large pastoral landholdings, was a captaincy general, dependent until 1778 on the viceroyalty of Peru. The first move for independence, led by Juan Martínez de Rosas, Bernardo O'Higgins, and José Miguel Carrera, failed in the battle of Rancagua (1814), but José de San Martín led a force from Argentina through high USPALLATA PASS, and a victory at Maipu (1818) assured Chilean independence. Since the colonial aristocracy and royalist clergy were discredited the revolutionary, the army, the intellectuals, and some creole landholders framed the new government, first crystallized in the constitution of 1830, which gave a base for later emergence of parliamentary government. Longstanding border disputes with Bolivia and Peru were climaxed by the War of the PACIFIC (1879–84), which gave Chile rich nitrate deposits and other minerals but left the TACNA-ARICA CONTROVERSY long unsettled; the end of a border dispute with Argentina was marked by erection of the CHRIST OF THE ANDES. Exploitation of mineral resources brought wealth and growth in commerce and transportation (e.g., the TRANSANDINE RAILWAY) but left Chile vulnerable to changes in world markets and to depressions. This has been met by industrialization (largely with hydroelectric power), mfg., and intensive use of agr. products. Chile, neutral in World War II, is a member of the United Nations.

Chilkoot Pass, c.3,500 ft. high, in Coast Mts. on British Columbia–Alaska boundary. Route through pass between Yukon R. valley and coast was long a monopoly of Chilkoot Indians; first white man passed through 1878. Route to the Klondike from Skagway in gold rush of 1890s with WHITE PASS as alternate.

Chillán (chēyän'), city (pop. 31,280), S central Chile; founded c.1580; agr. and commercial center.

Chillicothe (chĭl'lĭkō'thē). **1** City (pop. 8,694), N Mo., NE of Kansas City near Grand R. A grain trade center, it has mfg. of wood, steel, dairy products. **2** City (pop. 20,133), S central Ohio, on Scioto R. and Paint Creek and S of Columbus; settled 1796. Trade and shipping center with mfg. of shoes, paper and food products, and furniture. Cap. of Northwest Territory 1800; cap. of Ohio 1803–10 and 1812–16.

Chillingworth, William, 1602–44, English theologian. Converted to Catholicism, he left that faith and took orders (1638) in the Church of England. Known for *The Religion of Protestants a Safe Way to Salvation* (1638), arguing the right of the individual to personal interpretation of the Bible, the sole source of religion.

Chilliwack (chĭl'lĭwăk), city (pop. 5,663), SW B.C., Canada, on Fraser R. and E of New Westminster, in agr. and lumbering area.

Chillon (shĭlôn', shĭ'lùn, Fr. shēyô'), castle at E end of L. Geneva, Switzerland, built 9th–13th cent. Prison of François BONNIVARD. Now a museum.

Chiloé (chēlōä'), island (3,241 sq. mi.) off S Chile, largest island of Chile.

Chilperic I (chĭl'pûrĭk), d. 584, Frankish king of Neustria (561–84). With his mistress and future wife, FREDEGUNDE, he murdered his wife Galswintha (567), thus precipitating a savage feud with BRUNHILDA (Galswintha's sister) and his brother Sigebert I of Austrasia (Brunhilda's husband). The feud was inherited by his son, CLOTAIRE II.

Chiltern Hills, chalk hill range (width, 15–20 mi.; length, 45 mi.), NW of London, England.

Chiltern Hundreds, administrative districts in Buckinghamshire, England, known for the phrase "applying for the Chiltern Hundreds" (used by member of Parliament in giving up seat, since he may not resign). Reference is to stewardship of districts (now obsolete but still profitable), which no M.P. may hold.

Chimay, princesse de: see TALLIEN, THÉRÉSA.

Chimayó (chĭmīō'), village (pop. c.2,000), N N.Mex., N of Santa Fe. Spanish frontier post 1598–1695. Famous for blanket weaving in early 19th cent. Has El Santuario shrine (1816). Tsimajó pueblo was here or near by.

Chimborazo (chĕmbōrä'sō), inactive volcano, 20,577 ft. high, central Ecuador.

chime: see BELL.

Chimera (kĭmēr'ù), in Greek legend, monster, part lion, part goat, and part dragon. It was slain by BELLEROPHON.

Chimkent (chĭmkyĕnt'), city (pop. 74,185), S Kazakh SSR, on Turksib RR. Lead refinery, chemical plant, textile mills. Once important caravan center. Citadel stormed by Russians 1864.

chimpanzee, anthropoid ape (*Pan* or *Anthropopithecus*) of central and W Africa. Like the gorilla it is more manlike than other apes; considered the most intelligent and teachable. Adult is 4–5 ft. tall, 150–200 lb. In captivity sometimes turns savage.

Chimu (chē'mōō), ancient Indian civilization on desert coast of N Peru, flourished probably 500–1500 A.D.

Ch'in (chĭn), dynasty of China, which ruled from 221 to 207 B.C. Founder was Shih Hwang-ti [first emperor]. He devised centralized system of government and decreed use of standard style of writing. Built original Great Wall.

Chin, dynasty of China (265–420): see TSIN.

China, republic (3,800,000 sq. mi.; est. pop. 475,000,-000), E Asia. Bounded on NE by USSR and Korea, on N by USSR and Mongolian People's Republic, on SW by India, and on S by Burma and Indo-China. MANCHURIA in N is historically distinctive area. Off shore are HAINAN and FORMOSA. Hsia is traditionally first dynasty, but Shang (c.1523–c.1027 B.C.) is first in documented history. Great cultural and imperialist periods were CHOU, HAN, T'ANG, SUNG, YÜAN, and MING dynasties. Portuguese settled Macao in 1557, but foreign trade was unimportant until 1842, when defeat of CH'ING dynasty by the British in Opium War forced China to make major concessions. Regime was further weakened by Japan's success in First CHINO-JAPANESE WAR (1894–95). U.S. promotion of OPEN DOOR policy failed to prevent BOXER REBELLION, a last effort to expel foreigners. Success of republican revolution, led by SUN YAT-SEN, forced emperor's abdication 1912. Sun's successor Yüan Shih-kai used repressive tactics which led to formation of rival government at Canton. China's entry into World War I on Allied side helped to thwart early expansionist designs of Japan. Washington Conference (1921–22) guaranteed China's territorial integrity. After 1919 civil war raged between Kuomintang and N government (supported by war lords, notably Chang Tso-lin). Winning foreign recognition, Kuomintang government was estab. 1928 at Nanking. The 1927 purge of Communist wing of party had forced Communists, led by Mao Tse-tung and Chu Teh, to retreat to north, which became their center of power. Disunity aided Japan's drive for conquest. Second CHINO-JAPANESE WAR began 1931 with Japanese occupation of Manchuria. Chinese resistance steadily weakened despite Allied aid after Dec., 1941, when Japan's attack on U.S. and British bases merged Chinese war in World War II. At war's end China regained sovereignty over all areas (except Hong Kong and Macao) from foreign powers. Civil war, partly interrupted by World War II, flared anew. In late 1946 natl. assembly (boycotted by Communists) adopted democratic constitution; in 1948 CHIANG KAI-SHEK became first constitutional president. In Sept., 1949, Communists proclaimed rule over all China, setting up Chinese People's Republic, with cap. at Peking (called Peiping by Nationalists) and Chou En-lai as premier. By Jan., 1950, Communist regime was recognized by USSR, Great Britain, and India, but not by U.S. In late April, 1950, Chiang controlled only Formosa. Communists officially entered Korean War in Nov., 1950. Soviet-Chinese pact (Sept., 1952) reaffirmed friendship between two Communist governments. In 1949 the Communists divided China (including Tibet and Inner Mongolia) into six regional districts. These grouped for administrative purposes the existing provinces, which include (besides those in Manchuria) N and S Anhwei, Chahar, Chekiang, Fukien, Honan, Hopeh, Hunan, Hupeh, Kansu, Kiangsi, N and S Kiangsu, Kwangsi, Kwangtung, Kweichow, Ningsia, Pingyuan, Shansi, Shantung, Shensi, Sikang, Sinkiang, Suiyuan, Szechwan, Tsinghai, and Yunnan. For geographical information see under these headings.

China, Great Wall of, fortifications, c.1,500 mi. long, winding across N China, from Kansu prov. to Hopeh prov., mostly along edge of Mongolian plateau. First built in early Ch'in dynasty; present form dates mainly from Ming dynasty.

china clay, a fine-textured, pure clay, consisting chiefly of the mineral kaolinite, and often called kaolin. Easily molded, it turns white when fired and is used in mak-ing fine porcelains. Sometimes used in paper making.

China Sea, western part of Pacific Ocean. Divided by Formosa into East China Sea and South China Sea.

chinch bug, small hemipterous insect. *Blissus leucopterus,* feeding on sap of grains and grasses, causes huge U.S. crop losses (esp. in Mississippi, Missouri, Ohio valleys). *Blissus hirtus* is lawn pest in NE U.S.

chinchilla (chĭnchĭ'lù), small rodent (*Chinchilla*) of South America, living in rocky burrows in Andes of Bolivia, Chile, and Peru. Its soft gray pelt is one of costliest furs.

Chincoteague (chĭng'kùtēg), town (pop. 2,724), E Va., on Chincoteague Isl.; connected to Eastern Shore by causeway and bridge. Hunting and fishing resort. Has annual wild pony roundup and auction. Chincoteague Bay, inlet of the Atlantic, extends N from island.

Chindaswinth (chĭn'dùswĭnth), d. 653, Visigothic king of Spain (642–53). Began compilation of *Forum judicum,* completed by his son RECESWINTH.

Chinese architecture. The classical period of Chinese building was T'ang dynasty (A.D. 618–906), but there are few surviving buildings dated before the Ming dynasty (1368–1644). Major achievement of Ming period is Forbidden City in Peking with its intricate plan and decorations of exceptional richness. Notable is the Temple of Heaven, circular structure on triple platform. Both religious and secular architecture follow one basic type, involving one-story rectangular chamber on stone platform and covered by single or several superimposed roofs of richly colored glazed tiles. The roof, which projects on brackets in upward curve beyond eaves, is supported by interior columns; walls serve merely as screens. Ancient regulations govern dimensions and number of columns. Typical temple has three parallel buildings approached by monumental steps, gateways, and buildings. A main architectural principle is harmonizing of structure with natural settings. Distinctive Chinese structures are PAGODA and pailou (memorial arch with upturned tile roof).

Chinese art. Founding of Shang dynasty (c.1523 B.C.) possibly marks transition from Stone Age to Bronze Age. Cast bronze ritual vessels (with decoration varying from meager to ornate, from abstract to naturalistic) are clearest extant record of Shang, Chou, and Early Han stylistic development. Advent of Buddhism gave new impetus to sculpture; representation of Buddha and bodhisattvas focused interest on human figure. Buddhist sculpture (marked by precise modeling and linear rhythms) reached its height in early T'ang dynasty (618–906) and flourished for c.300 more years. Ancient Chinese art of painting can be traced clearly only from 5th cent. Painters used basic technique of calligraphy, relying mainly on line and silhouette. Little survives of works of T'ang dynasty, classic period of figure painting. Landscape painting reached peak in Sung dynasty. Masterpieces were done in ink (colors or monochrome) on absorbent silk or paper. Though secular in subject, they were Buddhist or Taoist in spirit. After 12th cent. more intimate subjects appeared. Ming period produced paintings of highly decorative quality. Development of Chinese pottery roughly paralleled that of painting; perfected in Sung dynasty, it became technically elaborate in Ming. Chinese art has deeply influenced Western artists since 18th cent.

Chinese Eastern Railroad: see SOUTH MANCHURIAN RAILROAD.

Chinese exclusion. After U.S. acquired Calif., large inflow of Chinese into state was welcomed at first because of need of cheap labor. Treaty Anson Burlingame signed with China in 1868 guaranteed right of Chinese immigration, but did not guarantee right of naturalization. In following decades much anti-Chinese feeling arose in Calif. and complete ban on Chinese immigration was urged. In a treaty of 1880 China allowed U.S. some right to restrict, but not to prohibit, Chinese immigration. Chinese exclusion act of

1882 did, however, ban immigration of Chinese laborers for ten years. Later acts flatly violated 1880 treaty. In a treaty of 1894 China agreed to exclusion of Chinese laborers for ten years. When that period was up, Congress continued exclusion unilaterally until immigration arrangements of 1924 made control automatic.

Chinese language, most important and most widely spoken of Sino-Tibetan or Indo-Chinese languages. See LANGUAGE (table).

Chinese literature. Oldest records date from Shang dynasty (c.1523–c.1027 B.C.). Oldest surviving literature, probably dating from late CHOU dynasty: *Shih Shu* [four books], containing early statements of Confucianism, notably *Book of Mencius; Wu Ching* [five classics], traditionally attributed to Confucius, including records of ancient traditions, chronology of Lu (Confucius's native state), system of divination, description of ceremonials and utopian state, and a collection of 305 poems in simple rhyming stanzas about peasant life and feudal wars. Other important early books include Lao-tze's *Tao-teh-king* (mid-3d cent. B.C.) and works of Chuang-tze. Early Chinese wrote on strips of bamboo and later on silk. Invention of paper (A.D. 105) and wood block printing (8th cent.) stimulated book production. Poetic freedom of Chou period was supplanted by minutely prescribed forms. Prosodic rules of greatest poetic era, T'ang dynasty (618–906), continued to be observed later despite pronunciation changes. Great T'ang poets, notably Li Po, Tu Fu, and Wang Wei, and the later Sung poet Su Tung-po have strongly influenced modern English imagist poets. Chinese poems tend to be brief, suggestive, and nonintellectual. Earliest dynastic history dates from 1st cent. B.C. Popular romances in jingling couplets or easy prose appeared continuously, but few prior to 10th cent. survive. Drama was estab. by Yüan dynasty (1260–1368). Plays have sentimental plots and stylized performances with symbolic props. Trend toward practicality, since 1918 revolution, led to writing in the vernacular, notably by Hu Shih, but use of complex ideographs instead of an alphabet has persisted.

Chinese music can be traced back to very ancient times, but little is known about it, since in 212 B.C., all musical books and instruments were ordered destroyed. However, certain outlines of ancient Chinese music can be ascertained. The single tone was most important and considered an attribute of the substance which produced it. Hence musical instruments were classified according to the material from which they were made—gourd (*sheng*, a free-reed instrument); bamboo (panpipes); wood (*chu*, a kind of percussion instrument); silk (various types of zither with silk strings); clay (flute); metal (bell); stone (sonorous stone); and skin (drum). Music was believed to have power over the elements and had ethical connotations. Scale of Chinese music was five-toned, roughly represented by the black keys on a piano. The various types of notation did not indicate rhythm. Ancient musical practice has given way to folk song, religious music, Western jazz, and classical music in modern China.

Chinese Turkistan: see SINKIANG.

Ch'ing (chǐng) or **Manchu** (măn″chōō), last dynasty of China, which ruled from 1644 to 1912. Estab. by the Manchu, a people of N China. Under Emperor Ch'ien Lung (reigned 1736–96) China reached maximum size, extending in N beyond Amur R. and in S through Indo-China. The Ch'ing strongly opposed sea-borne foreign trade but were forced by series of wars in 19th cent. to open China's ports and to give extraterritorial rights to European powers. Efforts of Emperor Kwang Hsü to promote reforms for strengthening China were blocked by dowager empress Tz'u Hsi. Revolution of 1911 forced abdication of HENRY PU YI.

Chinghai, province: see TSINGHAI.

Chin Hills (chĭn), mountain range, W Burma, bordering Assam. Chin Hills division (13,903 sq. mi.; pop. 220,410) of Upper Burma is semi-autonomous.

Chinnereth or **Chinneroth** (both: kĭn′–; –rŏth): see GALILEE, SEA OF.

Chino (chē′nō), city (pop. 5,784), S Calif., E of Los Angeles. Processing center for walnuts, citrus fruits, and truck.

Chino-Japanese War, First, 1894–95. Caused by rivalry for control of Korea. In 1885 Japan had agreed to Chinese overlordship over Korea, but in 1894 induced Korean king to reject it when a revolt broke out. In ensuing war the Japanese won a quick victory over the Chinese. Treaty of Shimonoseki gave Korea nominal independence and provided for cession of Formosa, Pescadores Isls., and Liaotung peninsula by China to Japan. Also called First Sino-Japanese War.

Chino-Japanese War, Second, 1931–45. Caused by long-standing desire of Japan to dominate E Asia. In 1931 Japan reinforced her garrison in Manchuria, ostensibly to protect Japanese property there. After bombing of Japanese troop train near Mukden the Japanese took over all Manchuria. By 1935 much of NE China had been captured. Peking, Shanghai, and Nanking (national cap.) fell 1937; by 1940 the Japanese had taken all major cities on E coast. The Chinese, based at Chungking (temporary cap.) fought on. Japan's attack on Pearl Harbor merged the war in World War II as China declared war on Axis powers. Despite Allied aid and diversion of Japanese armies, China's military position failed to improve until April, 1945. Japan capitulated Aug., 1945, formally surrendered Sept. 9, 1945. Also called Second Sino-Japanese War.

Chinon (shēnō′), town (pop. 4,312), Indre-et-Loire dept., central France, on Vienne R. Its imposing castle (actually a complex of three castles, built 12th–15th cent.) was a royal residence in Middle Ages. Here Joan of Arc first met the dauphin. Rabelais was born near by.

Chinook Indians (shĭnŏŏk′, chĭ′), tribe in the Columbia valley, of Chinook linguistic stock (as were nearby tribes). Had plank houses in settled villages; were skilled with canoes; traded much; and had the custom of potlatch. **Chinook jargon** was the lingua franca of early trade on the Northwest Coast; had Chinook, Nootka, English, and French words.

chinquapin (chĭng′kŭpĭn), chestnut species (*Castanea pumila*) of E U.S. Golden-leaved chestnut or giant chinquapin (*Castanopsis chrysophylla*) is evergreen tree of W U.S.

Chioggia (kyôd′jä), city (pop. 23,577), Venetia, NE Italy; major fishing port on islet in Adriatic near Venice. Bridge joins it to mainland. Picturesque old houses, canals. Several naval battles were fought here in "Chioggia War" between Venice and Genoa (1378–80), which ended with Venetian victory.

Chios or **Khios** (kī′ŏs), Aegean island (321 sq. mi.; pop. 72,777), Greece, 5 mi. W of Asia Minor; chief town and port Chios (pop. 26,617). Mountainous, it rises to 4,157 ft. in Mt. Elias. Famed for scenic beauty and good climate. Produces wine, fruits, wheat, mastic. Marble, lignite; sulphur springs. Colonized by the Ionians; held by Persia 494–479 B.C.; later under Athenian influence; free city of Roman Empire until Vespasian's reign. From the Byzantines, it passed to the Latin Empire of Constantinople (1204), to Genoa (1261), to Turkey (1566) and to Greece (1912). Anti-Turkish revolt of 1822 ended in massacre of Chian Christians. Chios claims to be Homer's birthplace.

Chipewyan (chĭpŭwī′ŭn), trading post, NE Alta., Canada, on NW shore of L. Athabaska. Old Fort Chipewyan (built 1788), on S shore, was base for Alexander Mackenzie's expeditions in 1789 and 1793. Present post was fur trade center.

chipmunk, rodent of squirrel family. Chipmunk of E U.S. and SE Canada is of genus *Tamias*. Common Eastern chipmunk (*Tamias striatus*) is 5–6 in. long, reddish or grayish brown on top, black and white on sides, with 4–5 in. hairy, flattened tail. It eats nuts, seeds, berries, and insects; carries food in expansible cheek pouches. Winters in underground burrow provided with stores of food. Chipmunks of W North America are of genus *Eutamias*.

Chippawa (chĭ'pŭwô), village (pop. 1,762), S Ont., Canada, just above Niagara Falls. Scene of battle in War of 1812.

Chippendale, Thomas, 1718–79, English cabinetmaker. A whole general category of 18th-cent. English furniture is grouped under his name. His style is based on Queen Anne and Georgian design, but with Chinese, Gothic, and French rococo elaborations. His favorite material was dark mahogany, always without inlays. Influenced American cabinetmakers. See *ill.,* p. 356.

Chippewa (chĭ'pŭwû), river rising in lake region of N Wisconsin, and flowing c.200 mi. S and SW to the Mississippi at foot of L. Pepin. Has three dams.

Chippewa Falls, city (pop. 11,088), W central Wis., on Chippewa R. just NE of Eau Claire, in lake region; settled 1837. Center of dairy and farm area with mfg. of clothing and meat and wood products. Has important hydroelectric plant.

Chippewa Indians: see OJIBWA INDIANS.

Chiputneticook Lakes (chĭpōōtnĕ'tēkŏok), chain on Maine-N.B. border, forming international boundary for 28 mi. Source of St. Croix R.

Chiricahua National Monument: see NATIONAL PARKS AND MONUMENTS (table).

Chirico, Giorgio de (jōr'jō dā kē'rēkō), 1888–, Italian painter, b. Greece. Known mainly for his earlier works (characterized by an atmosphere of mystery) which greatly influenced early surrealist painting. Broke with surrealism in late 1920s.

Chirikov, Aleksei Ilich (ŭlyĭksyä' ĭlyĕch' chē'rĭkŭf), d. 1748, Russian explorer. Lieutenant of Vitus Bering on voyage leading to discovery of Alaska.

Chiron (kī'rŏn), in Greek religion, CENTAUR; son of Cronus, ancestor of Achilles and Ajax. A famous teacher, he taught Jason, Asclepius, Hercules, and Achilles. He gave his immortality to Prometheus.

chiropractic (kī"rŭprăk'tĭk), system of treatment by manipulation, especially of spinal column. Its purpose is to restore normal nerve function. It was originated 1895 by Daniel D. Palmer.

Chisholm (chĭz'ŭm), city (pop. 6,861), NE Minn., on Mesabi iron range and NE of Hibbing.

Chisholm Trail, route over which vast herds of cattle were driven from Texas to railheads in Kansas after Civil War. Took name from Jesse Chisholm, who, in 1866, drove his wagon, heavily loaded with buffalo hides, through Indian Territory which is now Okla. to his trading post near Wichita, Kansas. Wheels cut deeply into prairie; marked route used for almost two decades by traders and drovers.

Chisinau: see KISHINEV, Moldavian SSR.

Chiswick, England: see BRENTFORD AND CHISWICK.

Chita (chētä'), city (pop. 102,555), RSFSR, in SE Siberia, on Trans-Siberian RR; founded 1653. Center of a region rich in tungsten, molybdenum, gold, tin, iron, coal, lumber, cattle.

Chittagong (chĭ'tùgŏng) city (pop. 269,000), SE East Bengal, Pakistan, on Bay of Bengal. E Pakistan's main port, it exports jute, tea, and hides.

Chiusi (kyōō'sē), Latin *Clusium*, Etruscan *Chamars*, town (pop. 2,534), Tuscany, central Italy. Cap. of ancient Etruria under Lars Porsena. Etruscan tombs (5th cent. B.C.); museum.

chivalry: see KNIGHTHOOD AND CHIVALRY.

chive, herb (*Allium schoenoprasum*) with globular lavender flower heads and slender tubular leaves which are used in seasoning.

Chkalov (chkä'lŭf), formerly **Orenburg** (ō'rŭnbōōrg), city (pop. 172,925), E European RSFSR, on Ural R. Agr. processing. Founded 1735 as fortress; resisted (1773–74) siege by Pugachev. Renamed 1938.

Chloë, Greek shepherdess: see DAPHNIS AND CHLOË.

chloral, oily, colorless liquid from treating absolute ethyl alcohol with chlorine. With water it forms

chloral hydrate, used in medicine to produce sleep.

chlorate, salt of chloric acid, compound of metal and chlorate radical. Potassium chlorate is a colorless, crystalline oxidizing agent. Used to make matches, fireworks, and explosives, and as oxygen source. Explosive when mixed with certain chemicals.

chloric acid, compound of hydrogen and chlorate radical (–ClO₃), appears only as colorless solution. It is moderately stable and a strong oxidizing agent. Salts are chlorates.

chloride, compound of chlorine and other element or radical. It is a salt formed by direct union of elements or by reaction of hydrochloric acid with base, metal, or oxide. Most form aqueous solution, conduct electricity, and are decomposed (see ELECTROLYSIS). Among uses: calcium chloride as drying agent and in refrigeration; silver chloride in photography; chloride of sulphur in vulcanizing rubber. In aqueous solution hydrogen chloride (colorless, irritating gas) is called HYDROCHLORIC ACID.

chloride of lime, white powder, a disinfectant and bleach, made by treating slaked lime with chlorine.

chlorine (klô'rīn), active, nonmetallic element (symbol = Cl; see also ELEMENT, table), in HALOGEN family. Greenish-yellow, poisonous gas with suffocating odor, heavier than air. Forms many compounds that occur abundantly in nature. Prepared by electrolysis of sodium chloride. Used in water purification; as disinfectant, antiseptic; to make bleaching powder, dyes, fire extinguishers, explosives; in many poison gases; in medicine.

chloroform (klô'rŭfôrm), volatile liquid, compound of carbon, hydrogen, and chlorine. Discovered 1831, it was first used as anesthetic by Sir J. Y. Simpson (1847). Solvent for fats and other organic compounds.

chlorophyll (klô'rŭfĭl"), substance that gives plants their green color and enables them to carry on PHOTOSYNTHESIS. It is contained in chloroplasts (small, oval bodies in plant cells) and chemically is similar to blood. Sunlight appears to be essential to chlorophyll formation. Certain plants lacking chlorophyll, e.g., yeasts and bacteria, live as parasites or saprophytes. Chlorophyll is used in drugs and as food coloring.

Chmielnicki or **Khmelnitsky, Bohdan** (bŭkhdän' khmĕlnĕt'skē), 1593–1657, hetman of the Ukraine. Stirred Cossack revolt against Polish overlordship (1648). United Ukraine with Russia (1654).

Choate, Joseph Hodges (chōt), 1832–1917, American lawyer and diplomat. Handled many famous cases in New York city. Distinguished himself as U.S. ambassador to Great Britain (1899–1905).

Chocano, José Santos (hōsā' sän'tōs chōkä'nō), 1875–1934, Peruvian poet, a leader of *modernismo*.

chocolate is extracted from seeds of CACAO tree by complex process of grinding, heating, and blending, without removal of fat. Chocolate liquor is used in confectionery, powdered or molded chocolate in chocolate beverage, in confectionery, and cookery.

Choctaw Indians (chŏk'tô), tribe of SE U.S., of Natchez-Muskogean linguistic stock. Culture similar to that of Creek Indians. Were removed to the Indian Territory in 1832. One of FIVE CIVILIZED TRIBES.

Choderlos de Laclos: see LACLOS.

choir. 1 See CHORUS. **2** Instruments of any one type in the orchestra, as brass choir, wood wind choir. **3** That part of a church reserved for the singers and officiating clergy.

Choiseul, Étienne François, duc de (ātyēn' fräswä' dük' dü shwäzûl'), 1719–85, French foreign minister (1758–70). Negotiated FAMILY COMPACT; annexed Lorraine, Corsica. Protégé of Mme de Pompadour.

cholera (kŏ'lŭrŭ) or **Asiatic cholera,** acute infectious disease caused by bacterium (*Vibrio cholerae* or *V. comma*). Transmitted by polluted food or water. Symptoms include watery diarrhea, vomiting, collapse. Death rate high. Preventable by vaccination.

cholera infantum (ĭnfăn'tŭm), condition in infants

probably resulting from severe intestinal infection by various bacteria. Symptoms resemble those of true cholera.

Cholula (chōlōō'lä), town (pop. 8,424), Puebla, E central Mexico. An old Toltec city, it was Aztec sacred city when Spanish came. Cortés destroyed city, built church over pyramid. Has numerous churches and is place of pilgrimage.

Chopin, Frédéric (frädärēk' shōpē'), 1810–49, composer and pianist, b. Poland of French and Polish parents, lived in Paris after 1831. Almost all his music is for solo piano. Even in his two piano concertos, the orchestra is dominated by the piano. Polish nationalism is evident in the sets of mazurkas and polonaises, while the nocturnes, waltzes, and preludes are more often elegiac. He also wrote a series of etudes, scherzos, ballades, and sonatas. His music, highly romantic, is important in the development of piano techniques. He had a notable love affair with George Sand.

Chopin, Kate O'Flaherty (shō'pǎn'), 1851–1904, American author of stories of La., b. St. Louis.

chorale or **choral,** term originally used to denote part of the Roman Mass, usually sung in unison; now, more often, a Protestant hymn of stately tempo. During the Reformation, German composers used the traditional tunes of chorales in writing contrapuntal works with organ accompaniment.

chorea (kōrē'ù) or **Saint Vitus's dance,** nervous disorder accompanied by involuntary jerking and emotional instability. Rarely occurs after puberty.

chorus. 1 In music, group of singers, usually divided into four sections—soprano, alto, tenor, and bass. A chorus performing only sacred music is called a choir. **2** In drama of ancient Greece, the group that speaks to accent the action. They spoke in dithyrambs without action until Thespis in the 6th cent. B.C., introduced the actor, and made it a dramatic chorus. In the 2d cent. B.C. it ceased completely to have anything to do with the action and later disappeared.

Chorzow, Pol. *Chorzów* (hô'zhŏōf), Ger. *Königshütte,* city (pop. c.142,000), SW Poland, in Silesia. Center of KATOWICE mining and industrial region. Passed from Germany to Poland 1921.

Chosroes: see KHOSRU.

Chou (chou), dynasty of China. According to tradition ruled from 1122 to c.256 B.C., but according to some modern scholars from c.1027 to 256 B.C. Confucius, Mencius, and Lao-tze lived in Chou era.

Chouans (shōō'ùnz, shwä), peasants of NW France who rose against French revolutionary government in 1793. Movement merged with royalist risings in VENDÉE, continued sporadically till 1815.

Chou En-lai (jō' ĕn'-lī', chou'), 1898–, Chinese Communist leader. Active Communist since student days in France. Became first premier and foreign minister of People's Republic of China (estab. 1949).

Chouteau, René Auguste (rùnä' ōgüst' shōōtō', shōtō'), 1749–1829, American fur trader and a founder of St. Louis (1763–64) with Pierre LACLEDE. Developed business with brother, **Jean Pierre Chouteau,** 1758–1849, fur trader and U.S. Indian agent. His son, **Auguste Pierre Chouteau,** 1786–1838, aided in the family fur trade. Another son, **Pierre Chouteau,** 1789–1865, bought interest in old American Fur Co. and expanded his business activities.

chow or **chowchow,** dog known from antiquity in the Orient, where it was a hunting dog. It has a massive head, ruffed neck, broad short muzzle, and small pointed ears. The tongue and inside of mouth are blue-black. The dense coat is of solid color, usually reddish brown, black, or slaty blue. The chow, Spitz, and Eskimo or husky dogs probably have a common origin. The Spitz weighs 25–30 lb., is of solid color (usually white or black). The Eskimo dog has long been used in arctic regions for pulling sleds. There are several types, and the colors vary greatly; most Eskimo dogs weigh 70–100 lb. The coat is double with long guard hairs overlying a dense woolly undercoat. Most dogs of this group have tails which curl up over the body.

Chrestien de Troyes or **Chrétien de Troyes** (both: krätyē' dù trwä'), fl. 1164, French poet, author of first great literary treatments of ARTHURIAN LEGEND. Among surviving works are *Érec et Énide; Cligès; Lancelot ou Le Chevalier de la charette; Yvain ou Le Chevalier au lion;* and *Perceval ou Le Conte del Graal* (unfinished; see PARSIFAL). All but the last appear in tr. of W. W. Comfort, *Arthurian Romances* (1913).

Christ: see JESUS.

Christadelphians [Ger.,= brothers of Christ], religious sect founded in U.S. in 1840s by John Thomas. They show simple, early Christian faith and expect second coming of Christ to set up theocracy in Jerusalem.

Christchurch, city (pop. 112,681; metropolitan pop. 150,047), E South Isl., New Zealand; founded 1850. Canterbury Col. (1873) and School of Arts (1882) are here. Has tanneries and meat-packing plants.

Christ Church College: see OXFORD UNIVERSITY.

Christian, Danish kings. **Christian I,** 1426–81, king of Denmark (1448–81), Norway (1450–81), and Sweden (1457–64), count of Oldenburg; founder of Oldenburg dynasty of Danish kings. Also inherited Schleswig and Holstein (1460). His defeat at Brunkeberg by Sten STURE (the elder) ended his attempt to subdue Sweden (1471; see KALMAR UNION). **Christian II,** 1481–1559, king of Denmark and Norway (1513–23), king of Sweden (1520–23). His wholesale massacre of Swedish nobles at Stockholm (1520) led to rebellion. GUSTAVUS I was raised to the Swedish throne, the Kalmar Union terminated. In Denmark Christian alienated the Church and nobility by his high-handed reforms. Deposed 1523, he died a prisoner. **Christian III,** 1503–59, king of Denmark and Norway (1534–59). Broke power of Hanseatic League; established Lutheranism; declared Norway a Danish dependency. **Christian IV,** 1577–1648, king of Denmark and Norway (1588–1648). Playing a major part in THIRTY YEARS WAR, he invaded Germany as champion of Protestants (1625); was defeated by Tilly at Lutter (1626); relieved STRALSUND with Swedish help (1628). He signed a separate peace (1629) but in 1643–45 reentered the war, siding against Sweden, and lost two Norwegian provinces. **Christian V,** 1646–99, king of Denmark and Norway (1670–99). His minister GRIFFENFELD dominated his reign until 1676, made the monarchy absolute. **Christian VII,** 1749–1808, king of Denmark and Norway (1766–1808), was insane. His physician STRUENSEE held power until 1772; A. P. BERNSTORFF was chief minister from 1773. **Christian VIII,** 1786–1848, king of Denmark (1839–48). Proclaimed SCHLESWIG-HOLSTEIN part of Denmark (1846), thus precipitating war of 1848. **Christian IX,** 1818–1906, king of Denmark (1863–1906). Issued from cadet line of Sonderburg-Glücksburg. Annexed Schleswig to Danish crown (1863; see SCHLESWIG-HOLSTEIN). In the resulting war of 1864 with Prussia and Austria he lost Schleswig, Holstein, and Lauenburg. **Christian X,** 1870–1947, king of Denmark (1912–47) and of ICELAND (1912–44). His self-imposed seclusion during the German occupation of Denmark in World War II made him a symbol of national resistance.

Christian Catholic Apostolic Church in Zion, sect founded (1896) by J. A. DOWIE (hq. Zion, Ill.). Members are popularly known as Zionites.

Christian Church: see CHRISTIANS; CHURCHES OF CHRIST; CONGREGATIONALISM; DISCIPLES OF CHRIST.

Christian Endeavor, Protestant interdenominational, international young people's association for encouraging spiritual life and Christian activities; founded 1881 by Dr. F. E. Clark.

Christiania, Norway: see OSLO.

Christianity, all doctrines and religious groups based on the teachings of Jesus Christ. Those who subscribe to any such group are called Christians. Little is definitely known of the years of early spread and nature of the teachings or of the forms of worship, and different interpretations of the known facts give one of the chief bases for the fundamental difference between "traditionalist" churches (e.g., ROMAN CATHOLIC CHURCH, ORTHODOX EASTERN CHURCH), which claim to maintain an elaborated and developed version of early doctrines and rites, and the "reformed" churches (see PROTESTANTISM), which claim to restore pristine doctrines and forms, cleansing them of false additions and developments. From the start Christianity tended to be highly organizational (in contrast to Islam and most other major religions), a tendency that developed in sporadic persecutions by Roman emperors (until toleration was proclaimed by CONSTANTINE I) and in the struggle over differences within the Church. These differences in early times centered on arguments as to the nature of Christ in relationship to the other members of the Christian Trinity. Councils were called to settle these questions, the accepted answers being deemed orthodox, the rejected ones heretical. Among the early heresies were Arianism, Nestorianism, and Monophysitism. Perhaps the most celebrated of the early councils was First Council of Nicaea (325). In the East the Byzantine emperors exercised much control over the Church, in the West the power of the papacy grew. From both centers Christianity was extended until it embraced all Europe, monks playing a large part in the missionary work of converting pagans. Until the rise of Islam, Christianity was also dominant in Asia Minor and N Africa. The break between the Eastern and Western churches was gradual but was more or less permanent after 1054. A main current of development in both areas was conflict between secular and church authorities. When the REFORMATION came as the most important single movement in Christian history since early days, it added a new element in the diversity of sects. Strife between the various groups, attempts at union, and various struggles to establish sound and enduring relationships between religion and the state have characterized modern Christianity.

Christian Reformed Church. Protestant church formed 1857 by Dutch immigrants dissenting from Reformed Church in America. Name adopted 1890.

Christians, name given followers of evangelical, antisectarian preachers on American frontier. Some joined Disciples of Christ; others formed Christian Church, finally merged (1931) with Congregational Churches. See also CHRISTIANITY.

Christian Science, religion based on principles and divine laws formulated from acts and sayings of Jesus Christ by Mary Baker Eddy for Church of Christ, Scientist. Mrs. Eddy's teachings developed after her recovery of health in 1866 through reading in New Testament of healing by Jesus. Her *Science and Health* (1875) is textbook of doctrine. Church founded 1879; Mother Church, the First Church of Christ, Scientist, set up in Boston, 1892.

Christian socialism, movement begun in England in 1848 intended to advance Christian ideals in economic life in opposition to ruthless practices of industrialists. Led by Frederick Denison Maurice and Charles Kingsley, it was very active among workingmen. Its anti-Marxist tradition passed to the Fabian Society, guild socialists, and Catholic groups. In U.S., Society of Christian Socialists (estab. 1889) took up the movement, as did various church groups preaching the "social gospel." On the Continent the term Christian Socialist was given to varied groups, usually connected with particular religious leaders.

Christiansted (krĭs'chŭnstĕd"), town (pop. 4,126), on St. Croix isl.; port of Virgin Islands (U.S.).

Christie, Agatha, English detective-story writer. Her many volumes, extremely popular, often feature the detective Hercule Poirot. They include *The Murder of Roger Ackroyd* (1926), *Murder in the Calais Coach* (1934), and *And Then There Were None* (1940).

Christie's, English firm of art auctioneers and appraisers, founded 1766. One of world's largest clearinghouses for art objects.

Christina, 1626–89, queen of Sweden (1632–54); daughter and successor of Gustavus II. OXENSTIERNA headed a regency until 1644. She ruled irresponsibly and eccentrically, devoting her time to the study of philosophy. Descartes lived at her court. Her refusal to marry was chiefly responsible for her abdication in favor of her cousin, Charles X (1654). She left Sweden in men's clothes, entered the Catholic Church (1655), and settled at Rome. Later attempts to regain the Swedish throne failed.

Christine de Pisan: see PISAN, CHRISTINE DE.

Christmas [Christ's Mass], feast day celebrating the birth of Jesus Christ (the Nativity), in the Western churches Dec. 25, a date almost certainly chosen for its nearness to the Epiphany (Jan. 6). Not observed earlier than A.D. 200, it grew popular in the Middle Ages, and many customs clustered about the feast, especially in English-speaking countries: the Yule log (the Yule season is simply Christmastide), gathering decorations of holly and mistletoe, the singing of carols, giving of gifts, and sending of greeting cards. The Christmas tree is a German contribution to the season; the American Santa Claus is derived from the Dutch customs in N.Y. (see NICHOLAS, SAINT).

Christmasberry or **toyon** (tō'yŭn), western evergreen shrub (*Photinia arbutifolia*), with red berries.

Christmas Island (60 sq. mi.; pop. 866), of Singapore crown colony, in Indian Ocean. Has large deposits of phosphate of lime. Leased to phosphate company.

Christmas Island, largest atoll in the Pacific, area 95 sq. mi., near equator, one of Line Isls. Discovered 1777 by Capt. James Cook, added 1919 to British colony of Gilbert and Ellice Isls.

Christmas rose: see HELLEBORE.

Christ of the Andes, statue built (1904) in Uspallata Pass on Argentine-Chilean boundary to commemorate peace and boundary treaties. Dispute had arisen because crest of Andes and continental watershed did not coincide.

Christophe, Henri (ärē' krēstôf'), 1767–1820, Negro king of Haiti. A freed slave, he aided Toussaint L'Ouverture in liberation of Haiti; was army chief under Dessalines. Elected president of Haiti (1806), he disputed control of island with Pétion. Declared himself king 1811; committed suicide 1820 when revolts broke out.

Christopher, Saint [Gr.,= Christ bearer], 3d cent.?, martyr of Asia Minor. Chief legend is that when he was charitably carrying a child across a river, he felt the weight on his shoulders grow almost too great to bear and discovered that he was carrying Jesus, who carried the world in His hands. He is patron of travelers; hence St. Christopher medals for automobiles. Feast: July 25.

Christophsen, Pieter: see CHRISTUS, PETRUS.

Christ's College: see CAMBRIDGE UNIVERSITY.

Christ's Hospital, once a hospital (founded 1533) in London, it became a school, known as "bluecoat school" from the boys' habit. Now includes school for girls. Has been at Horsham, Sussex, since 1902.

Christ's-thorn, name for several thorny plants, especially a spiny shrub (*Paliurus spina-christi*) with hat-shaped fruit. Also called Jerusalem thorn.

Christus or **Cristus, Petrus** (both: pē'trŭs krĭ'stŭs), c.1400–1473, Flemish painter, also called Pieter Christophsen; a follower of the Van Eycks.

Christy, Edwin P., 1815–62, American showman. Estab. c.1842 a company of Negro minstrels known as Christy's Minstrels, which became the typical minstrel show with interlocutor, end men, and performers in blackface.

Christy, Howard Chandler, 1873–1952, American illustrator. Known for the "Christy girl" of posters and magazine illustrations. Also did portraits.

chromatic scale, in music: see SCALE.

chromium (krō'mēŭm), gray-white, crystalline, hard, nontarnishing metallic element (symbol = Cr; see also ELEMENT, table). Forms chromates and dichromates used as paint pigments, in dyeing, in leather tanning. Metal comparatively rare, always occurs in compounds. Used for PLATING and in several alloy steels, e.g., chromium steel, stainless steel.

chromosome (krō'mŭsōm"), form assumed by chromatin material of cell nucleus during stages of MITOSIS and meiosis. The form and number of chromosomes depend upon the species. They contain genes, which determine hereditary characteristics, and are thus important in heredity, evolution, mutation of plants and animals, and determination of SEX. For process of mitosis, see *ill.,* p. 633.

chromosphere (krō'mŏ–), rarefied layer of gases surrounding sun and lying outside photosphere. It consists chiefly of hydrogen (radiating scarlet light), helium, and calcium and extends 5,000–7,500 mi.; layer 100 to 200 mi. thick at the base is known as reversing layer. Moving gases form projections (prominences) observable during eclipses or through spectroscope. Eruptive prominences burst forth in jets; cloudlike quiescent prominences extend from pole to pole.

Chronicles or **Paralipomenon** (păr"ŭlĭpŏm'ĭnŏn) [Gr., = things left out], books of Old Testament, called 1 and 2 Chronicles in AV, 1 and 2 Paralipomenon in Greek Bible and Western canon. Books contain; genealogies; history of reigns of David and Solomon; history of kingdom of Judah. Historical material parallels (and supplements) parts of Samuel and Kings.

chrysanthemum (krĭsăn'thŭmŭm), annual or perennial plant of genus *Chrysanthemum.* Late-blooming flowers, of various colors except blue or purple, range from single daisylike to large, rounded shaggy forms. Cultivated in Orient for at least 2,000 years.

Chryseis (krīsē'ĭs), in the *Iliad,* girl captured by Agamemnon. Forced by Apollo to return Chryseis, Agamemnon took Briseis from Achilles to replace her and thus aroused the wrath of Achilles.

chrysoberyl (krĭ'sŭbĕ"rĭl), a beryllium aluminate used as a gem. It is transparent to translucent and has a vitreous luster. One variety, alexandrite, is green by daylight and red under artificial light. Chrysolite is a yellow-green chrysoberyl.

Chrysoloras, Manuel (krĭsŭlô'rŭs), c.1355–1415, Greek teacher who helped introduce Greek into Italy.

Chrysostom: see JOHN CHRYSOSTOM, SAINT.

Chuang-tze (chōōäng'-tsä'), fl. 4th cent. B.C., Chinese philosopher, a follower of Lao-tze, whose doctrines he interpreted with great skill and charm.

chuck-will's-widow, bird of S U.S. allied to nighthawk and whippoorwill. Its call has the sound of its name.

Chukchi Peninsula (chōōk'chē), NE extremity of Asia and Siberia, RSFSR, terminating in EAST CAPE. Population largely Chukchis, of Hyperborean language family; subsist on reindeer raising, fishing, fur trapping. Coal mines on Anadyr Gulf. Chukchi Natl. *Okrug* [area] (274,520 sq. mi.; pop. c.20,000) was formed 1930.

Chula Vista (chōō'lŭ), city (pop. 21,578), S Calif., S of San Diego, in agr. area. Aircraft mfg.

Chungking (chōong"kǐng'), commercial city (pop. 1,-000,101), Szechwan prov., SW China; port at junction of Kialing and Yangtze rivers. Opened 1891 to foreign trade. War-time cap. of China (1937–46).

Chuquisaca: see SUCRE, Bolivia.

Chur (kōōr), Fr. *Coire,* town (pop. 19,256), cap. of Grisons canton, E Switzerland, on Plessur R. Roman settlement; early episcopal see. Temporal power of prince-bishops was ended by Reformation (1524–26). Has 8th-cent. church (restored), cathedral (12th–13th cent.), episcopal pa'ace.

Church, Frederick Edwin, 1826–1900, American landscape painter of the Hudson River School.

Church, aggregation of Christian believers; in its widest sense embracing all believers, living and dead, headed by Jesus Christ, who founded the community through his apostles. An early traditionalist division distinguishes the church militant (living Christians) from the church suffering (the dead in Purgatory) and the church triumphant (the saints in Heaven). In more usual parlance the church is the organized aspect of any sect or group of believers (e.g., the Lutheran Church, the Church of England, the Church of the Brethren, the Roman Catholic Church), but in most cases each group conceives itself to be the one true Christian body. See CHRISTIANITY.

Churches of Christ, conservative body of Protestant Christians, formerly united with Disciples of Christ.

Churchill, Charles, 1731–64, English satirical poet, author of *The Rosciad* (1761), satire on actors.

Churchill, John: see MARLBOROUGH, JOHN CHURCHILL, 1ST DUKE OF.

Churchill, Lord Randolph Henry Spencer, 1849–95, British statesman. Sought to create a democratic Tory party. Resigned as chancellor of exchequer 1886 to oppose high military spending. Father of Winston Churchill.

Churchill, Winston, 1871–1947, American author of historical novels (*Richard Carvel,* 1899, *The Crisis,* 1900) and novels on political problems (*The Inside of the Cup,* 1913).

Churchill, Winston (Leonard Spencer), 1874–, British statesman, soldier, and author. Fought in India, the Sudan, and South Africa. Elected to Parliament 1900. First lord of the admiralty in World War I (1911–15) until discredited by failure of Dardanelles campaign. Returned to office in Lloyd George Liberal government 1917–21. Conservative chancellor of exchequer 1924–29; subsequent influence as opponent of "appeasement" of Germany led to his replacing (1940) Neville CHAMBERLAIN as prime minister of coalition government seven months after outbreak of World War II. Became symbol of British resistance. Before the entry of U.S. into war he met President Roosevelt at sea (see ATLANTIC CHARTER). Twice addressed U.S. Congress. Attended series of international conferences—CASABLANCA; QUEBEC; CAIRO; YALTA; TEHERAN; POTSDAM. After Labour Party victory 1945 became leader of the opposition. Conservative victory in 1951 brought him back as prime minister. Author of several histories, biographies, memoirs.

Churchill, river, N Sask. and N Man., Canada, issuing from Methy L. and flowing c.1,000 mi. SE, E, and NE to Hudson Bay at Churchill. Traverses many lakes and was famous fur-trading route. Mouth of river discovered 1619 by Scandinavian Jens Munck. Hudson's Bay Co. estab. trading post (1689) which was later abandoned and then refounded at Fort Churchill (later known as Fort Prince of Wales). Superseded c.1732 when heavy stone fort was built on W side of river's mouth. Remains of this fort now in national park. **Churchill,** port on Hudson Bay at mouth of Churchill R., was selected 1927 as terminus of Hudson Bay RR (completed 1929). Serves N Man. as grain-shipping port from mid-Aug. to mid-Oct.

Churchill Downs: see LOUISVILLE, Ky.

Church of Christ, Scientist: see CHRISTIAN SCIENCE.

Church of England: see ENGLAND, CHURCH OF.

Church of God: see ADVENTISTS.

Church of the Brethren: see DUNKARDS.

Churriguera, José (chŭr"ĭgär'ŭ; hōsā' chōōr-rēgä'rä), 1650–1725, Spanish baroque artist and sculptor, b. Salamanca. Went to Madrid 1688 where he designed the catafalque for Queen María Luisa. Works include palace of Don Juan de Goyeneche. Extravagant design and capricious use of Renaissance motives led to the use of the term **Churrigueresque** (chŭr"ēgŭrĕsk') for Spanish architecture of the late 17th and early 18th cent. The style influenced Spanish colonial work in Mexico and SW U.S.

Churubusco, battle: see CONTRERAS.

Chu Teh (jōō'dŭ'), 1886?–, Chinese Communist leader. Trained at Yünnan military academy and in Germany. Commander in chief of all Chinese Communist forces in World War II; retained that post after founding of People's Republic of China in 1949.

Chuvash Autonomous Soviet Socialist Republic (chōo-väsh'), autonomous state (7,100 sq. mi.; pop. 1,077,-614), E European RSFSR, in middle Volga valley; cap. Cheboksary. Agr., forests. Population 80% Chuvash, a people of Finnic language.

Ciano, Galeazzo (gäläät'tsō chä'nō), 1903–44, Italian Fascist leader, count of Cortellazzo. Married Mussolini's daughter Edda. Foreign minister 1936–43. Helped to bring about Mussolini's fall in 1943. Arrested by Germans; executed by Fascist republic in N Italy. His diaries are a remarkable document.

Cibber, Colley, 1671–1757, English actor and playwright. Successful in comic roles (1692–94), later was a leading actor of eccentric characters (1697–1732). His play, *Love's Last Shift* (1696), regarded as first sentimental comedy. Poet laureate 1730–57, attacked by Pope in *The Dunciad*. His son, **Theophilus Cibber,** 1703–58, acted in Colley's plays. Theophilus's wife, **Susannah Maria (Arne) Cibber,** 1714–66, sang in operas and acted tragic roles (e.g., Lady Macbeth and Desdemona). Handel wrote contralto arias in his *Messiah* for her.

Cibola: see MARCOS DE NIZA; CORONADO, FRANCISCO VÁSQUEZ DE.

cicada (sĭkā'dù), name for homopterous insect with wide, blunt head, prominent eyes, two pairs of membranous wings. Periodical or 17-year (13-year in U.S.) cicada is miscalled locust. Shrill song of males caused by vibrating membranes near abdomen. See *ill.,* p. 469.

Cicero, Marcus Tullius (sĭ'sùrō), or **Tully,** 106–43 B.C., Roman orator, politician, philosopher. Consul from 63 B.C. Prosecuted Cataline. Exiled by Clodius and recalled by Pompey (58–57 B.C.). A republican, he opposed Caesar; attacked Antony in the *Philippics.* Under Augustus he was put to death. His letters reveal Roman life. His philosophical works (*On Ends, On the Nature of the Gods,* etc.) express his mild Stoicism and, together with his rhetorical works, reveal him as the great master of Latin prose.

Cicero, industrial town (pop. 67,544), NE Ill., adjoining Chicago; founded 1857. Electrical equipment, metal products, and building materials.

Cid or **Cid Campeador** (sĭd' kăm'pēûdôr), d. 1099, Spanish national hero; real name Rodrigo (or Ruy) Díaz de Vivar. Served under Castilian kings, emir of Saragossa, fighting Moors and Christians. Conquered Valencia (1094), where he ruled until death. For his chivalry, generosity, became prototype of noble Castilian warrior. Hero of *The Song of the Cid* (12th-cent. anonymous epic) and dramas by Guillén de Castro and Corneille.

cider, in Europe, is fermented juice of apples, often aged in casks; in U.S., unless qualified as "hard" cider, it is unfermented apple juice, usually pasteurized and often blended to balance the flavor.

Ciego de Ávila (syä'gō dä ä'vēlä), city (pop. 23,802), central Cuba; a commercial center halfway between Santiago de Cuba and Havana.

Cienfuegos (syĕnfwä'gōs), city (pop. 52,910), central Cuba, port on Caribbean. Has large and beautiful harbor. Sugar is chief product.

Cierva, Juan de la (hwän' dä lä thyĕr'vä), 1895–1936, Spanish aeronautical engineer. Inventor of autogiro, first flown in 1923.

Cieszyn: see TESCHEN.

cigar and cigarette. Habit of smoking rolls of tobacco was acquired by Spanish conquistadors from Indians of W Hemisphere and it spread into Europe. Cigars consist typically of filler leaves held by binder leaves and wrapped spirally with wrapper leaves; largely machine-made after c.1902. Cigarettes consist of shredded tobacco (usually blended and often sprayed with flavorings) rolled in paper.

Cilicia (sĭlĭ'shù), anc. region of SE Asia Minor, between the Mediterranean and the Taurus range. Divided into unproductive plateau (Cilicia Trachia) and fertile plain (Cilicia Pedias). Part of the Assyrian Empire and the Persian Empire, it was later Hellenized. The cities of Tarsus and Seleucia throve under Roman and Byzantine rule. Cilicia, invaded by Arabs in the 8th cent., and in 1080 an Armenian state was set up here (later Little Armenia), to last until conquered by the Turks in 1375.

Cilician Gates (sĭlĭ'shùn), mountain pass, S Turkey, across Taurus mts., known anciently as Pylae Ciliciae, now as Gulek Bogaz. Crossed by an ancient highway from Cappadocia to Cilicia.

Cimabue, Giovanni (jōvän'nē chēmäbōo'ä), d. c.1302, Florentine painter, reputedly the teacher of Giotto. Frescoes in Church of St. Francis, Assisi, are attributed to him. His work is a transition from the formalized Byzantine style to the more naturalistic 14th-cent. manner.

Cimarosa, Domenico (dōmā'nēkō chēmärō'zä), 1749–1801, Italian composer. *Il matrimonio segreto* is the best of his *opera buffa.* He also wrote serious operas, church music, and instrumental music.

Cimarron (sĭm"ùrōn'), river, 692 mi. long, rising in NE N.Mex. and flowing E, barely touching Okla. Panhandle and SE Colo., to enter Kansas. Crosses and recrosses Okla. line, then swings SE and E across Okla. to Arkansas R. just W of Tulsa.

Cimarron, Territory of, now the Panhandle of Okla. Settled by cattle ranchers. Efforts to estab. separate territory failed, and in 1890 area became part of Oklahoma Territory.

Cimber, Lucius Tillius, d. after 44 B.C., one of the conspirators against Julius Caesar. On the pretext of presenting a petition he approached Caesar, then held him as Casca stabbed him.

Cimbri: see GERMANS.

Cimmerians (sĭmēr'ēunz), anc. people who in 8th cent. B.C. moved from the Crimea to the region of Lake Van. In the early 7th cent. B.C. they swept across Asia Minor. Traditionally considered as fierce barbarians, they are actually little known in history.

Cimon (sĭ'mùn) d. 449 B.C., Athenian general and statesman; son of Miltiades. In the Persian Wars he fought at Salamis and commanded in the defeat of the Persians on the Eurymedon (468 B.C.). The leader of the aristocratic party after the death of Aristides, he was exiled but later recalled.

cinchona (sĭngkō'nù), evergreen tree (*Cinchona*), native to Andes of South America. Its bark is source of QUININE. Before World War II, Java and India grew commercial supply; later South America cultivated wild trees.

Cincinnati (sĭnsĭnă'tē, –nā'tù), city (pop. 503,998), SW Ohio, port on Ohio R. opposite Covington, Ky., at mouth of Licking R.; laid out 1788. State's second largest city and commercial and cultural center for a large area. Meat packing and mfg. of alcoholic beverages, soap, machine tools, steel products, chemicals, and clothing. A busy shipping point for early settlers, it was aided by opening of Miami and Erie Canal. Received settlers from Germany and Ireland. Was early abolitionist center and Underground Railroad station. Survived disastrous floods, notably in 1884 and 1937. Adoption of city-manager government in 1924 ended long period of political misrule. Seat of Univ. of CINCINNATI and Xavier Univ. Points of interest include Music Hall and Exposition Building (houses Cincinnati Symphony and May Music Festival), Taft House Mus., and Eden Park, with city art museum and art academy.

Cincinnati, Society of the [Latin plural of *Cincinnatus*], formed in 1783 by officers of Continental army after American Revolution. Founded for fraternal, patriotic, and allegedly nonpolitical aims.

Cincinnati, University of, at Cincinnati; municipal, coed.; chartered 1870, opened 1873. Col. of Engineering and Commerce, with Inst. of Scientific Research, pioneered in a work and study plan. School has made archaeological excavations at Troy. Library has collection of Historical and Philosophical Society of Ohio. Col. of Music of Cincinnati and Cincinnati Conservatory of Music are allied.

Cincinnatus (sĭnsĭnā'tŭs, –nā'tŭs), fl. 5th cent. B.C., semilegendary Roman hero. Consul in 460, he in 458 left his farm to become dictator, defeated the Aequi and the Volsci, and immediately returned to his farm. He repeated this performance to put down a plebeian revolt in 439.

cinema: see MOVING PICTURES.

cineraria (sĭn"ûrâr'–), pot plant of genus *Senecio,* with daisylike flower clusters above big leaves.

Cinna, Lucius Cornelius (sĭ'nù), d. 84 B.C., Roman statesman, leader of the popular party, consul (87 B.C.–84 B.C.). When Sulla left Italy, Cinna undertook anti-Sullan electoral reforms, and the conservatives drove him from power. He gathered an army, recalled MARIUS from Africa and took Rome, where he slaughtered Sulla's followers. Cinna was murdered in a mutiny as the civil war began. His daughter Cornelia was married to Julius Caesar.

cinnabar (sĭ'nùbär), mineral, sulphide of mercury, used chiefly as a source of mercury.

cinnamon, tropical evergreen tree (*Cinnamomum zeylanicum*) of Ceylon, and its aromatic bark. Cut-back plants produce many shoots from which commercial stick cinnamon, a flavoring, is obtained. Bark of another species, cassia bark tree, is considered inferior substitute. *C. camphora* yields camphor.

cinnamon vine: see YAM.

Cinq Mars, Henri Coëffier, marquis de (ärē' kŏĕfyä' märkē' dù sēmär'), 1620–42, French conspirator. Favorite of Louis XIII; plotted with Spain against Richelieu. Was executed.

cinquefoil (sĭngk'–), plant of widely distributed genus *Potentilla,* bearing yellow flowers and foliage with five leaflets. Some species are grown in rock gardens and some are used for home remedies.

Cinque Ports (sĭngk) (Fr.,= five ports), group of maritime towns in Sussex and Kent, England. Originally five, other places later added. Chartered by Edward the Confessor, they provided ships and men against invasion before English navy estab. Walmar Castle, Deal, is official residence of Lord Warden. This post, now honorary, held by Churchill.

Cintra, Port. *Sintra* (sēn'trù), town (pop. 6,307), Portugal, near Lisbon. Beautiful situation made it favorite residence of Portuguese kings. Has ruins of Moorish castle, old royal palace and monastery. By Convention of Cintra (1808) French troops under Junot were permitted to leave Portugal.

C.I.O.: see CONGRESS OF INDUSTRIAL ORGANIZATIONS.

cipher: see CRYPTOGRAPHY.

Circassia (sùrkă'shù), historic region, SE European RSFSR, between Black Sea, Kuban R., and Greater Caucasus, now in Krasnodar and Stavropol Territories. The Circassians (also known as Cherkess, Adyge, Adighe), a people of the N Caucasian language family, abandoned Christianity for Islam in 17th cent. Circassian women, famed for beauty, were prized as slaves in Turkey. Ceded by Turkey to Russia in 1829, Circassia resisted Russian conquest until 1864. About 400,000 Circassians now live in the Adyge and Cherkess autonomous *oblasts* [regions].

Circe (sûr'sē), in Greek legend, celebrated enchantress; daughter of Helios. She changed companions of Odysseus into swine, but he made her break the spell.

circle, closed plane curve each point of which is equidistant from point within called the center. Also defined as a CONIC SECTION cut by plane perpendicular to cone axis. Surface within curve also called circle; curve itself called circumference; line with each end on circumference called chord; chord through center called diameter; any line joining center with circumference called radius. For formula for area of a circle see AREA.

Circleville, city (pop. 8,723), S central Ohio, on Scioto R., S of Columbus. Laid out 1810 within remains of circular fort erected by mound builders.

circuit, electric: see ELECTRIC CIRCUIT.

circuit rider, itinerant preacher of Methodist denomination, who served "circuit" of 20 to 40 "appointments." System, devised by John Wesley for his scattered English groups and adapted in America by Francis Asbury, greatly aided spread of Methodism.

circulation of the blood, continuous passage of blood through heart and blood vessels. Oxygenated blood is forced into general systemic circulation from left ventricle of heart through arteries into network of capillaries through whose thin walls oxygen and nutriment pass into tissues and carbon dioxide and other wastes enter blood. Deoxygenated blood returns through veins to right auricle of heart, then passes through right ventricle into pulmonary circulation. After interchange of carbon dioxide and oxygen in lungs, oxygenated blood passes through pulmonary veins and left auricle into left ventricle where cycle begins anew. See *ill.,* p. 595.

circus [Latin,= circle], associated historically with horse and chariot races and contests known in anc. Rome as Circensian games. Roman circus was a round or elliptical structure with tiers of spectators' seats enclosing the space in which races, brutal and bloody games, and gladiatorial combats took place. Modern circus (a tent show with wild animals, acrobats, freaks, and clowns) dates from close of 18th cent. Outstanding American circus was that of P. T. BARNUM.

Cirencester (sĭs'ĭtŭr, sĭ'rùnsēstŭr), urban district (pop. 11,188), Gloucestershire, England. Site of Roman settlement Corinium. Royal Agricultural Col. here.

Cirta: see CONSTANTINE, Algeria.

Cisalpine Republic (sĭsăl'pīn), N Italian state created 1797 by Bonaparte through union of Cispadane and Transpadane republics, which he had set up 1796 N and S of Po R. In practice a French protectorate. Renamed Italian Republic 1802. Merged with Venetia in Napoleonic kingdom of Italy 1805.

Cisco (sĭs'kō), city (pop. 5,230), N central Texas, E of Abilene. Shipping and processing center of agr. and oil area. Artificial L. Cisco near by.

Cisleithania: see AUSTRO-HUNGARIAN MONARCHY.

Cisneros, Francisco Jiménez de: see JIMÉNEZ DE CISNEROS, FRANCISCO.

Cispadane Republic: see CISALPINE REPUBLIC.

Cistercians (sĭstûr'shŭnz), order of Roman Catholic monks founded (1098) by St. Stephen Harding in Cîteaux, France (hence the name); the white Monks (from their white habit). The greatness of the order came with their second founder, St. Bernard of Clairvaux, under whom it expanded phenomenally. In attempting to restore the early simplicity of the Benedictines, they stressed love of God, cheerful practice of austerities, and practice of manual labor, especially farming. The order became less prominent after 1400. Of later Cistercian reforms most important was that of the TRAPPISTS. The center of Cistercian communal life is the abbey. Cistercian nuns (order founded 12th cent.) lead contemplative lives, secluded from the world; a 17th-cent. reform of this order gave rise to the remarkable development of Port-Royal.

Citadel, The—The Military College of South Carolina: see CHARLESTON.

Cîteaux, Côte-d'Or dept., France: see CISTERCIANS.

Cithaeron (sĭthē'rùn), Gr. *Kythairon,* mountain ridge, c.10 mi. long, central Greece, between Boeotia (N) and Attica and Megaris (S). Rises to 4,623 ft. Scene of many mythical events; sacred to Dionysus.

citrange, citrus-fruit hybrid from cross between sweet and trifoliate oranges. Hardier than orange.

citric acid (sĭ'trĭk), white, crystalline organic acid with tart taste, found in fruits. With alkaline earths and metals, it forms citrates used as laxatives. Acid used as antalkali, in calico printing, in soft drinks (as lemon juice substitute). May be prepared by fermenting sugar.

citron, small evergreen tree (*Citrus medica*), native to tropical Asia and related to other citrus fruit trees. Rind of its large lemon-shaped fruit, when candied and preserved, is used in confectionery and cookery.

citrus fruits: see CITRANGE; CITRON; GRAPEFRUIT; KUMQUAT; LEMON; LIME; ORANGE; TANGERINE.

Città Vecchia (chĕt-tä' vĕk'kyä), **Città Notabile** (nōtä'bēlä), or **Mdina** (ûmdē'nä), town (pop. 1,384), central Malta. Former cap. of Malta, has old palace of grand masters of Knights Hospitalers.

City College: see NEW YORK, COLLEGE OF THE CITY OF.

city government, political administration of urban areas. In U.S. generally, incorporated urban areas were given freedom in local matters, with a mayor and council as administrators. In 20th cent., complexity increased, efficiency waned, and reform movements (e.g., for commission form or for city manager) developed.

City of David, epithet of BETHLEHEM, the birthplace of David, and of JERUSALEM, his capital.

City Point, Va.: see HOPEWELL.

city-state, autonomous neighborhood as a political and social unity, normally a single city or town with the surrounding countryside. At the dawn of history in Mesopotamia it was the normal type of organized life, and the Babylonian and Assyrian empires grew out of the cities. City-states have been known at various times and in various lands, but the most celebrated were those of ancient Greece, which cradled Western civilization. Though the modern idea of democracy stems from them (particularly from Athens) they were by no means all democracies; more commonly they were monarchies or oligarchies. Other famous examples of the city-state were the free imperial cities of the Holy Roman Empire and many of the Italian states in the Renaissance.

Ciudad (syōodhädh') [Span.,= city]. For cities beginning thus but not so listed, see under following name; e.g., for Ciudad Juárez, see JUÁREZ.

Ciudad Bolívar (syōodhädh' bōlē'vär), city (pop. 31,-009), E Venezuela, port on Orinoco; founded 1764 as Angostura.

Ciudad Real (thyōodhädh' rääl'), city (pop. 30,015), cap. of Ciudad Real prov., central Spain, in New Castile. Medieval walls; Gothic cathedral.

civet (sĭ'vĭt) or **civet cat,** mammal of family Viverridae, related to cats. Both sexes have scent pouch (near anus) which yields fatty secretion used in Orient as perfume base; much of commercial supply comes from African civet (*Civettictis*). Oriental civet (*Viverra*) found in India and SE Asia.

Civilian Conservation Corps (CCC), organization (estab. 1933; abolished 1942) to provide useful work and vocational training for unemployed young men. Aided nation by conservation of natural resources.

civil law, the law governing private affairs in contrast to public law and criminal law. In a restricted sense, signifies a modern legal system (see CODE) based on Roman law, especially as formulated in *Corpus Juris Civilis* and revived by law scholars in 11th and 12th cents. Civil law prevails on Continent, Latin America, and Westernized countries of Asia. Contrasts with COMMON LAW, usual in English-speaking countries (only La. and Quebec have civil law).

civil rights, the rights which a state's inhabitants enjoy by law. They have a legal as well as a philosophical basis. All bars to discrimination because of creed, origin, or color go to estab. civil rights. The **Civil Rights Acts** were passed after the U.S. Civil War to give Negroes legal and political status equal to that of whites. The act of 1875 was largely voided by Supreme Court in 1883.

civil service, body of persons employed in the civil administration of a government (not including the military or elected officials). Term first used for British administrators in India, later for British home officials. It became popular in U.S. with rising demand for reforming the system after the Civil War. A Civil Service Commission was set up (1871) but was allowed to lapse and was restored by Pendleton Act (1883) only after Pres. Garfield was killed by a disappointed office seeker. Commission draws up rules to give positions on merit in certain classifications; the number of classified posts has constantly been increased. The British tradition of separation of civil service from politics has been adopted in U.S., notably by the Hatch Act (1940) forbidding officeholders to contribute to political campaigns. Similar reform movements have advanced in state and local service.

civil war, in English history: see PURITAN REVOLUTION; ROSES, WARS OF THE.

civil war, in Roman history: see MARIUS and SULLA; POMPEY and CAESAR, JULIUS.

Civil War, in U.S. history (1861–65), conflict between Northern states (Union) and Southern states in secession (see CONFEDERACY), also called the War between the States or the War of the Rebellion. Many contributing causes included sectional rivalry, moral campaign of ABOLITIONISTS, and especially quarrel concerning Federal control *vs.* STATES' RIGHTS. When compromise failed, conflict loomed. Election of Abraham Lincoln as President, and secession of Southern states (1860–61), precipitated war. When on April 12, 1861, P. G. T. Beauregard ordered Confederates to fire on Fort Sumter, hostilities began. In 1861 opening battles were Confederate victories. Irvin McDowell was defeated by Beauregard at first battle of BULL RUN, July 21. In 1862 G. B. McClellan's PENINSULAR CAMPAIGN was foiled by R. E. Lee. However, Lee's ANTIETAM CAMPAIGN was checked by McClellan in September. Lincoln then issued EMANCIPATION PROCLAMATION. Year closed with Union defeat at Fredericksburg, Dec. 13. The next year saw Confederate victory over Joseph Hooker at Chancellorsville, May 2–4, marred by death of Stonewall Jackson. Then Lee undertook the GETTYSBURG CAMPAIGN, that marked the down turn of Confederate fortunes. Meanwhile Northern navy had successfully blockaded Southern coast, under D. G. Farragut captured New Orleans (April 28, 1862), and ended day of wooden battleships (see MONITOR AND MERRIMAC). CONFEDERATE CRUISERS, built or bought in England, in turn caused great loss to Northern shipping. In West, U. S. Grant won great victory at Fort DONELSON (Feb., 1862), followed by drawn battle at Shiloh on April 6–7. Union gunboats on the Mississippi opened way for Grant's successful VICKSBURG CAMPAIGN. The Confederate general Braxton Bragg, checked by G. H. Thomas at Chickamauga in CHATTANOOGA CAMPAIGN (1863), was driven back to Ga. Grant moved against Lee in WILDERNESS CAMPAIGN (May–June, 1864), forcing him toward Richmond, and laying siege to PETERSBURG. W. T. Sherman won ATLANTA CAMPAIGN (May–Sept., 1864), and made his march to the sea. After victory of P. H. Sheridan at FIVE FORKS, April 1, 1865, Confederates evacuated Richmond on April 3. His retreat blocked, Lee surrendered to Grant at Appomattox Courthouse, April 9, 1865. Victory was marred by assassination of Pres. Lincoln. But seceding states, after trials of RECONSTRUCTION, were readmitted, and Union was saved, with slavery abolished.

Civitavecchia (chē'vētä-vĕk'kēä), city (pop. 24,822), Latium, central Italy, on Tyrrhenian Sea; port of Rome. Arsenal built by Bernini; citadel by Bramante and Michelangelo.

Cl, chemical symbol of the element CHLORINE.

Clackmannanshire (klăkmă'nünshĭr), smallest county (55 sq. mi.; pop. 37,528) of Scotland, at head of Firth of Forth; co. town Clackmannan. Oats are chief crop. Mfg. includes textiles, ale, and whisky.

Claflin, Tennessee, 1845–1923, lecturer on woman suffrage; sister of Victoria WOODHULL.

Clair, René (klâr'), 1898–, French film director. His

films, filled with sophisticated wit and fantastic satire, include *Sous les toits de Paris*, *A nous la liberté*, *Le Million*, *The Ghost Goes West*, and *Beauty and the Devil*.

Clairaut, Alexis Claude (äleksēs' klōd' klērō'), 1713–65, French mathematician, noted for work on differential equations and curves. He formulated Clairaut's theorem dealing with geodesic lines on ellipsoidal surface.

Clairton, city (pop. 19,652), SW Pa., on Monongahela R. and SE of Pittsburgh. Produces coal and steel and coke by-products.

Clairvaux (klârvô'), former abbey, NE France, SE of Troyes. Founded 1115 by St. BERNARD OF CLAIRVAUX; became center of CISTERCIANS; suppressed in French Revolution.

clam, bivalve mollusk with muscular foot for burrowing in sand or mud. Shell valves are hinged, movable; the mantle, a skin fold of body, secretes shell and with gills carries on respiration; cilia of gills cause water current (bearing food and oxygen) to enter one siphon and exit (with wastes) through other. The hard or round clam (adult of little neck or cherry stone) is widely eaten.

clambake, a form of picnic peculiar to U.S., adopted from New England Indians. Clams (and often lobsters, fish, potatoes, corn, etc.) are steamed on bed of hot stones, under layer of wet seaweed.

clan, social grouping based on common, unilateral descent of its members. Includes number of families and is included in larger tribal organization. Unlike family, descent is traced through one parent. Within clan, family relations are extended beyond biological lines, and in some clans marriage to fellow member is prohibited or discouraged.

Clapham, residential district, SW London, England.

Clare or Clara, Saint, 1193?–1253, Italian nun, founder of the Franciscan nuns or Poor Clares. Feast: Aug. 12.

Clare, John, 1793–1864, English bucolic poet, called the English Burns.

Clare, John Fitzgibbon, 1st earl of, 1749–1802, Irish statesman; lord chancellor of Ireland. Hated by the Irish for advocating union with Britain.

Clare, Richard de: see PEMBROKE, RICHARD DE CLARE, 2D EARL OF.

Clare, maritime county (1,231 sq. mi.; pop. 85,064), Munster prov., Ireland; co. town Ennis. Broken, hilly region, with bogs and lakes and rugged coastline. Fishing and farming chief occupations; much of land barren. Pop. has declined in last cent.

Clare College: see CAMBRIDGE UNIVERSITY.

Claremont. 1 City (pop. 6,327), S Calif., E of Los Angeles. Ships citrus fruits. Seat of Claremont Col. (nonsectarian; coed.; chartered 1925 as Claremont Colleges, renamed 1944) and associated colleges: Claremont Men's Col. (1946), Pomona Col. (coed.; opened 1888 by Congregationalists), and Scripps Col. (for women; opened 1927). **2** Town (pop. 12,811), SW N.H., on Sugar R., near its junction with Connecticut R. and S of Lebanon; settled 1762. Machinery, textiles, shoes, and paper. Has oldest churches in state (R.C., begun 1823; Episcopal, begun 1773).

Claremont College: see CLAREMONT, Calif.

Claremore, city (pop. 5,494), NE Okla., NE of Tulsa. Site of Indian battle near by. Has U.S. Indian hospital and memorial to native son Will Rogers.

Clarence, George, duke of, 1449–78, son of Richard, duke of York. Joined Richard, earl of WARWICK, in rebellions against his brother Edward IV, 1469–70. Arrested for treason and thrown into the Tower (1478); allegedly drowned in a butt of malmsey wine. Prominent character in Shakspere's *Richard III*.

Clarence, Lionel, duke of, 1338–68, third son of Edward III of England. Governor of Ireland 1361–67; presided at assembly adopting notorious Statute of Kilkenny, forbidding all dealings between the English in Ireland and the Irish.

Clarendon, Edward Hyde, 1st earl of, 1609–74, English statesman and historian. A monarchist, he aided Charles I and went into exile with Charles II, whose chief adviser he became. At Restoration became lord chancellor. Favored religious toleration. Unsuccessful in diplomacy and disliked at court, he was removed from office (1667), fled England, and died in exile. Wrote *History of the Rebellion*. His daughter, Anne, married James II.

Clarendon, George William Frederick Villiers, 4th earl of, 1800–1870, English statesman. Three times foreign secretary, in CRIMEAN WAR kept together French alliance with England.

Clarendon, Constitutions of, 16 articles signed in 1164 by Great Council of HENRY II. Important in development of English law; extended jurisdiction of civil over church courts. THOMAS À BECKET later repudiated them, and his quarrel with Henry ended with his murder (1170).

Clarendon Code, English statutes adopted by Cavalier Parliament 1661–65 to strengthen Established Church. Laws, four in number, decreased following of dissenting sects (esp. Presbyterians). Named for earl of Clarendon who opposed enactment but enforced them. Charles II unsuccessfully tried to interfere by Declaration of Indulgences, 1662 and 1672. They were largely superseded by Test Act (1673).

Clarens (klärä'), resort village, Vaud canton, SW Switzerland, on L. Geneva near Montreux. Residence of Byron. Scene of Rousseau's *Nouvelle Héloïse*.

Clarinda (klûrin'dû), city (pop. 5,086), SW Iowa, near Mo. line. Mfg. of dairy products.

clarinet: see WIND INSTRUMENTS.

Clark, Alvan, 1804–87, and his son, **Alvan Graham Clark**, 1832–97, American manufacturers of astronomical lenses, noted also for discoveries of celestial bodies.

Clark, Champ, 1850–1921, American legislator. U.S. Representative from Mo. (1893–95, 1897–1921); speaker of House (1911–19). Led successful fight in 1910 to curtail powers of J. G. CANNON as speaker.

Clark, George Rogers, 1752–1818, American Revolutionary general, conqueror of Old Northwest. Captured Vincennes from British in 1779. Led expeditions against Indians in present Ohio. His brother, **William Clark**, 1770–1838, was a leader of the LEWIS AND CLARK EXPEDITION and later served as governor of Missouri Territory (1813–21).

Clark, John Bates, 1847–1938, American economist, teacher at Columbia (1895–1923). Was chief exponent of theory of marginal utility. His son, **John Maurice Clark**, 1884–, also an economist and Columbia professor, argued for including psychological, sociological, and institutional factors in study of economics.

Clark, Jonas Gilman, 1815–1900, American philanthropist, founder of Clark Univ.

Clark, Mark (Wayne), 1896–, American general. Commanded in N Africa and Italy in World War II. Appointed UN Supreme Commander in Korea (1952).

Clark, Tom (Campbell), 1899–, Associate Justice of U.S. Supreme Court (1949–). He was Attorney General of U.S. 1945–49.

Clark, William: see CLARK, GEORGE ROGERS.

Clark, William Andrews, 1839–1925, U.S. Senator and copper magnate. Struggled with Marcus DALY for control of copper and of political forces in Mont. Elected Senator in 1901 after his election in 1899 had been challenged.

Clark College: see ATLANTA, Ga.

Clarkdale, village (pop. 1,609), central Ariz., on Verde R. and NE of Prescott. Tuzigoot Natl. Monument, with Indian ruins, is near.

Clarke, James Freeman, 1810–88, American religious writer, a Unitarian minister, associated with Transcendentalists. One of his books is *Ten Great Religions* (1871–83).

Clarke, John, 1609–76, one of founders of R.I., b. England. Founded Portsmouth (1638) with Anne HUTCH-

INSON and William CODDINGTON. Chief figure in obtaining R.I. charter of 1663.

Clark Fork, river, c.360 mi. long, part of Columbia R. system, rising in SW Mont. near Butte and flowing N, NW past Missoula to Pend Oreille L. in Idaho Panhandle. PEND OREILLE R., flowing W from lake, is sometimes called part of Clark Fork.

Clarksburg, city (pop. 32,014), N W.Va., SSE of Wheeling and on West Fork of Monongahela R.; chartered 1785. Trade center of mining area with mfg. of stone, clay, carbon, and glass products. Important Union supply base in Civil War. Birthplace of Stonewall Jackson.

Clarksdale, city (pop. 16,539), NW Miss., on Sunflower R. and SSE of Memphis, Tenn., in rich cotton area; settled 1848 on site of Indian fortification.

Clarkson, Thomas, 1760–1846, English abolitionist. Helped Wilberforce abolish British slave trade (1807).

Clarkson College of Technology: see POTSDAM, N.Y.

Clarkston, city (pop. 5,617), SE Wash., on Snake R. at Idaho line. Ships grain, fruit, livestock.

Clarksville, city (pop. 16,246), N Tenn., on Cumberland R. at mouth of Red R. and NW of Nashville; platted 1784. Produces tobacco, flour, and rubber products. Dunbar Cave near by.

Clark University: see WORCESTER, Mass.

clary: see SAGE.

classicism, in literature and art, attention to traditional and recognized forms, producing clearness, elegance, symmetry, and repose. In music it is objectivity of conception, emphasis on balance of structure, and absence of violent passions. To be contrasted with ROMANTICISM.

classic revival, widely diffused phase of taste (known as neoclassic) which influenced architecture and the arts in Europe and the U.S. during the late 18th and first half of the 19th cent. Interest in antiquity was stimulated by excavations at Pompeii and by *Antiquities of Athens* by James Stuart and Nicholas Revett. Stuart's garden temple at Hagley, England, was first example in Europe of Greek design, and the Madeleine in Paris first of Roman temple reproductions. In France, interest in ancient Rome led to the Empire style sponsored by Napoleon. In the U.S. the Greek revival achieved first expression in 1799 in the Bank of Pennsylvania, Philadelphia, by Benjamin H. Latrobe. Fusion of Greek and Roman forms brought movement to its height in c.1820. It was the dominant influence in the U.S. until it gave way to romanticist styles of Victorian period.

Claudel, Paul (pōl' klōděl'), 1868–, French poet, dramatist, diplomat. Ambassador to Japan 1921–26; to U.S. 1927–33. His poetry is influenced by Rimbaud, deeply imbued with Catholic symbolism. Best-known are *Corona Benignitatis Anni Dei* (1914; Eng. tr., *Coronal*) and the plays *Le Partage de midi* (1906), *L'Annonce faite à Marie* (1912; Eng. tr., *Tidings Brought to Mary*), and *Le Soulier de satin* (1928–29; Eng. tr., *The Satin Slipper*).

Claude Lorrain (klōd' lōrě'), 1600–1682, French painter of expansive, luminous landscapes. His real name was Claude Gelée or Gellée. Settled in Rome in 1627 under the patronage of Pope Urban VIII.

Claudian (Claudius Claudianus) (klô'děŭn), d. 408?, last Latin classic poet. Author of minor poems and epics, including the *Rape of Proserpine.*

Claudius (klô'děŭs), Roman emperors. **Claudius I,** 10 B.C.–A.D. 54, reigned A.D. 4–54; son of the elder Drusus and thus nephew of TIBERIUS. When Caligula was murdered, the soldiers found Claudius hiding behind a curtain, hauled him out, and made him emperor. His reign was one of consolidation and renewing of the empire. He landed in Britain and made it a Roman province. He brought about the execution of his third wife, Messalina, and his fourth wife, Agrippina II (his niece), after persuading him to name her son Nero as heir instead of his own son Britannicus, is said to have poisoned him. **Claudius II,**

d. 270, reigned 268–70. Notable chiefly for defeating the Goths at Naissus (Nis) in 269, he was called Gothicus.

Clausel or **Clauzel, Bertrand** (bĕrträ' klōzĕl'), 1772–1842, marshal of France. Commander in chief in Algeria (1830–31; 1835–37).

Clausewitz, Karl von (klou'zŭvĭts), 1780–1831, Prussian general and writer on military strategy, of Polish descent. Saw much active service before he was appointed (1818) director of the German War School. His masterpiece, *On War,* expounded the doctrine of total war, i.e., war against the citizens, territory, and property of the enemy nation in every possible way. The effect of this theory on military science was enormous.

Clausius, Rudolf Julius Emanuel (rōō'dôlf yōō'lyŏŏs ämä'nōōĕl klou'zyŏŏs), 1822–88, German mathematical physicist. Introduced concept of entropy; restated second law of thermodynamics. Developed a kinetic theory of gases and a theory of electrolysis.

Clauzel, Bertrand: see CLAUSEL, BERTRAND.

Claverhouse, John Graham of: see DUNDEE, JOHN GRAHAM OF CLAVERHOUSE, 1ST VISCOUNT.

clavichord: see PIANO.

Clavijero, Francisco Javier (fränsě'skō hävyĕr' klävehä'rō), 1731–87, Mexican scholar and historian, author of *The History of Mexico* (Eng. tr., 1787).

Clavijo y Fajardo, José (hōsä' klävě'hō ē fähär'dhō), 1730?–1806, Spanish journalist. In newspaper *Pensador* forwarded ideas of the Enlightenment. His duel with Beaumarchais inspired a play by Goethe.

Clawson, city (pop. 5,196), SE Mich., near Detroit. Has machine shops.

Clay, Clement Claiborne, 1816–82, U.S. Senator (1853–61). Member of Confederate diplomatic mission to Canada (1864) in abortive plan for peace negotiations with U.S. government. After war, imprisoned for conspiracy, but freed.

Clay, Henry, 1777–1852, American statesman. U.S. Senator from Ky. (1806–7, 1810–11, 1831–42, 1849–52). U.S. Representative (1811–14, 1815–21, 1823–25). Leader of "war hawks" prior to War of 1812. Formulated national program for internal improvement, tariff protection, and rechartering of Bank of the United States. Pushed MISSOURI COMPROMISE through the House. U.S. Secretary of State (1825–29). Opposed Jackson regime, particularly on the bank issue. NATIONAL REPUBLICAN PARTY candidate for President 1832; WHIG PARTY candidate 1844. Denouncing extremists in both North and South, asserting superior claims of the Union, Clay sponsored the COMPROMISE OF 1850. Called the Great Pacificator and the Great Compromiser.

Clay, Lucius D(uBignon), 1897–, American general. As U.S. military governor of Germany (1947–49), directed operations to overcome Berlin blockade.

clay, fine-grained aluminum silicate mixed with other substances. Classed as residual if left by decay of limestone and shale or rocks containing feldspar (see KAOLINITE), or transported if moved by agent of erosion. Bentonites are very fine clays derived usually from volcanic ash. Clays are plastic when wet (hence easily shaped) and become hard when dry or fired. Important uses: making brick, tile, porcelain, china, earthenware, drainage pipes; for filtering and purifying liquids. Some clay is desirable in soil since it helps retain moisture, but an excess has many disadvantages. See also CHINA CLAY.

Clay, Mount: see PRESIDENTIAL RANGE.

Clayton. 1 Suburban city (pop. 16,035), E Mo., just W of St. Louis. **2** Resort village (pop. 1,981), N N.Y., on the St. Lawrence (sailing races) and NW of Watertown, in Thousand Isls. region.

Clayton Anti-Trust Act, 1914, passed by U.S. Congress as amendment to clarify and supplement SHERMAN ANTI-TRUST ACT of 1890. Drafted by Henry De Lamar Clayton. Prohibited exclusive sales contracts, local price cuttings to freeze out competitors, rebates, interlocking directorates in corporations capitalized at $1,000,000 or more in the same field of business, and intercorporate stock holdings. Labor unions and agricultural cooperatives were excluded from the forbidden combinations. Act restricted use of injunction against labor; legalized peaceful strikes, picketing, boycotts. Act was basis for numerous suits against large corporations.

Clayton-Bulwer Treaty (–bōol'wûr), concluded at Washington, D.C., on April 19, 1850, between U.S., represented by Secretary of State John M. Clayton, and Great Britain, represented by Sir Henry Bulwer. U.S.–British rivalries in Central America, particularly over a proposed isthmian canal, led to treaty, which checked British expansion in Central America but prevented U.S. from building its own canal and exercising political control over it. Very unpopular, treaty remained effective until 1901 (see HAY-PAUNCEFOTE TREATY).

Clearchus (klēär'kŭs), d. 401 B.C., Spartan officer. Governor of Byzantium, he recruited the Greek troops who supported CYRUS THE YOUNGER and after the defeat at Cunaxa he led the retreat of the Ten Thousand (as told by XENOPHON) until he was treacherously murdered.

Clearfield, borough (pop. 9,357), W central Pa., on W branch of Susquehanna R. and N of Altoona. Has railroad shops, coal mining, and mfg. of leather and clay products.

Clear Lake, c.21 mi. long, W Calif., NNW of San Francisco. Fishing resort in wooded hills.

Clearwater, city (pop. 15,581), W Fla., on Clearwater Bay (causeway to Clearwater Beach resort) and W of Tampa; settled after Fort Harrison estab. here 1841. Fruit packing and canning.

Cleaveland, Moses, 1754–1806, American pioneer. Led party to settlement in Western Reserve region of Ohio (1796), site of present Cleveland.

Cleburne, Patrick Ronayne, 1828–64, Confederate general, b. Ireland. One of ablest division commanders. Distinguished himself at Murfreesboro.

Cleburne, city (pop. 12,905), N Texas, S of Fort Worth; founded 1867. Shipping and processing center of agr. area, it has cotton gins, cottonseed-oil mills, and creameries.

Cleef or Cleve, Joos van (yōs' vän klāf', klä'vŭ), c.1485–1540, Flemish portrait painter. His son **Cornelis van Cleef** (kŏr'nä'lĭs), c.1520–1567?, painted Italianate religious pictures as well as portraits; called Zotte van Cleef because he went mad.

Cleisthenes (klīs'thĭnēz, klīs'–), fl. 510 B.C., Athenian statesman, head of the family of Alcmaeonidae. Ruler of Athens after the exile of Hippias, he instituted democratic reforms that ended civil strife in Athens.

clematis (klĕm'–), vine or nonclimbing perennial of genus *Clematis*. Flowers are either small and clustered, bell-shaped, or anemonelike; fruits have feathery appendage. Purple-flowered Jackman clematis and white-flowered Japanese clematis are vines widely grown in North America.

Clemenceau, Georges (zhôrzh' klämäsō'), 1841–1929, French premier (1906–9, 1917–19), called "the Tiger." His "Sacred Union" cabinet was instrumental in achieving Allied victory in World War I. Opposed Pres. Wilson at Peace Conference. Though he regarded Versailles Treaty as too lenient, he was defeated in 1919 elections because of his moderate attitude toward Germany.

Clemens, Samuel L(anghorne): see TWAIN, MARK.

Clement I, Saint, pope (A.D. 88?–A.D. 97?). Highly revered in his day, he wrote the *Epistle of St. Clement to the Corinthians* (A.D. 96?), admonishing Corinthians to stop quarreling; the tone of authority indicates the power of the bishop of Rome in the early church. This was in the 4th cent. considered as part of the Scriptures (see NEW TESTAMENT). It and other writings wrongly attributed to him are now classed as PSEUDEPIGRAPHA. Also known as Clemens

Romanus or Clement of Rome. Feast: Nov. 23.

Clement III, antipope: see GUIBERT OF RAVENNA.

Clement V, 1264–1314, pope (1305–14), a Frenchman named Bertrand de Got. Appointed archbishop of Bordeaux by Pope BONIFACE VIII, he gained the favor of the French king Philip IV, who engineered his election as pope. He set up residence in Avignon, thus beginning the long "captivity" of the PAPACY. Completely under the domination of Philip, he did resist attempts to condemn Boniface VIII posthumously but he meekly did the king's bidding in dissolving the Knights Templars on unproved charges. He issued an important collection of canon law.

Clement VI, 1291–1352, pope (1342–52), a Frenchman named Pierre Roger. Kept a splendid court at Avignon. When the Black Death struck Europe he helped sufferers and tried to stem subsequent wave of anti-Semitism. He at first favored then opposed RIENZI.

Clement VII, antipope: see ROBERT OF GENEVA.

Clement VII, 1478–1534, pope (1523–34), originally Giulio de' Medici, a member of the MEDICI family. Was archbishop of Florence and a cardinal before becoming pope. Vacillating and timorous, he seemed unaware of the problems the Reformation posed for the church. He disagreed with Emperor Charles V, who sent troops to sack Rome (1527) and take the pope prisoner. A peace was patched up in 1529, and Clement crowned Charles. The struggle with Henry VIII of England over the king's divorce was vigorously pursued by Clement.

Clement VIII, 1536–1605, pope (1592–1605), an Italian named Ippolito Aldobrandini. He abandoned the traditional papal alliance with Spain and was friendly with Henry IV of France. Clement was noted for piety and charity.

Clement XI, 1649–1721, pope (1700–1721), an Italian named Giovanni Francesco Albani. Known for great learning. As pope, he first favored Philip V as candidate for the Spanish throne, but later was forced to recognize Philip's rival, Charles of Hapsburg. Clement sought to stamp out JANSENISM in the church, and in his bull *Unigenitus* (1713) he condemned several Jansenist doctrines.

Clement XIV, 1705–74, pope (1769–74), an Italian named Lorenzo Ganganelli, a Conventual Franciscan. Much pressure from European monarchies (esp. France and Spain) was being exerted against the Jesuits (see JESUS, SOCIETY OF). In 1773 Clement issued a brief suppressing the order.

Clement, coworker of Paul. Philip. 4.3. Traditionally identified with St. Clement.

Clément, Jacques (zhäk' klämä'), 1567–89, French fanatic, a Dominican monk; assassin of Henry III.

Clementi, Muzio (mōō'tsēō klämĕn'tē), 1752–1832, Italian virtuoso pianist and composer. He was the first to compose in a style for piano rather than harpsichord. His studies, *Gradus ad Parnassum*, and his many sonatas are widely used.

Clement of Alexandria, d. c.215, Greek theologian, b. Athens. After conversion to Christianity he taught at Alexandria and was the first to attempt reconciling Platonic and Christian teachings. Defended orthodoxy against Gnosticism, though he apparently held that intellectual knowledge set the holder of it above other Christians (a Gnostic notion). Fragments of his work survive. Origen was his pupil.

Clemson, town (pop. 1,204), NW S.C., WSW of Greenville. Seat of **Clemson Agricultural College** (landgrant, state supported; for men; chartered 1889, opened 1893 with bequest from T. G. Clemson). Campus formerly J. C. Calhoun's plantation.

Cleomenes (klēŏ'mĭnēz), kings of Sparta, **Cleomenes I,** d. c.489 B.C., helped the Athenians to oust Hippias only to find Cleisthenes an anti-Spartan leader. He is said to have killed 6,000 Argives. **Cleomenes III,** d. 219 B.C., was an energetic ruler who defeated the Achaean League, but was overcome when Antigonus III allied himself with the League (c.222 B.C.).

Cleon (klē′ŏn), d. 422 B.C., Athenian statesman. A relentless enemy of Sparta, he won a victory at Sphacteria, but was killed in the defeat at Amphipolis. He is pictured by his enemies Thucydides and Aristophanes as an unprincipled demagogue.

Cleopatra (klēŭpă′trŭ, –pā′trŭ, –pä′trŭ), 69 B.C.–30 B.C., queen of Egypt, one of the great romantic figures of history; daughter of Ptolemy XI. Married according to family custom to her brother, Ptolemy XII, she led a revolt supported by Julius Caesar. Her husband was accidentally drowned in the Nile, and she was married to her younger brother Ptolemy XIII but was the mistress of Caesar, to whom she bore a son Caesarion (Ptolemy XIV). After Caesar's death she was visited by Marc Antony, who fell in love with her. Their love affair, which for a time threatened the Roman Empire, was ended when Octavian (later Augustus) defeated their forces at Actium (31 B.C.) and later at Alexandria. Antony committed suicide, and Cleopatra, unable to move the cool Octavian, went to her death by having an asp bite her. Apparently not beautiful, she was still a fabulously alluring woman. Shakspere's *Antony and Cleopatra* deals with her later story, G. B. Shaw's *Caesar and Cleopatra* with earlier events.

Cleopatra's Needles, popular name for two Egyptian obelisks, c.69 ft. high, originally erected at Heliopolis in c.1475 B.C. One is now in London, the other in New York.

Clergy Reserves, lands in Upper and Lower Canada set apart under Constitutional Act of 1791 "for the support and maintenance of a Protestant clergy." "Protestant clergy" was interpreted to mean clergy of Church of England. This interpretation, opposed by other Protestant denominations, became an issue in the Rebellion of 1837. In 1854 a law was passed providing for secularization of the reserves, but Anglican and Presbyterian churches retained endowments that had been granted them.

Clerk, Sir Dugald (klärk), 1854–1932, British engineer and inventor of gas engines.

Clerk-Maxwell, James: see MAXWELL, JAMES CLERK.

Clermont-Ferrand (klĕrmō′-fĕrä′), city (pop. 93,695), cap. of Puy-de-Dôme dept., SE France; historic cap. of Auvergne. Formed 1731 by merger of Clermont and Montferrand. Rubber industry (automobile tires). Clermont dates from Roman times. At Church council held here in 1095 Pope Urban II preached First Crusade. Has Gothic cathedral (12th–15th cent.); Romanesque Church of Notre Dame (12th cent.); university (founded 1854).

Cletus (klē′tŭs) or **Anacletus, Saint** (ănŭklē′tŭs), pope (A.D. 76?–A.D. 88?), a martyr. Feast: April 26.

Cleve, Joos van: see CLEEF, JOOS VAN.

Cleve, Germany: see CLEVES.

Cleveland, (Stephen) Grover, 1837–1908, 22d President of the United States (two terms, 1885–89, 1893–97). Mayor of Buffalo (1881–82). Governor of N.Y. (1883–85). Cleveland as President continued his independent, reformist, but conservative course. Argued for lower tariff. Panic of 1893 struck hard blow at his second administration. He secured repeal of SHERMAN SILVER PURCHASE ACT. His tariff measures altered by Senator A. P. GORMAN, he allowed Wilson-Gorman Tariff Act to become law without his signature. Opposed by radical Democrats, especially over gold standard, which he upheld. On grounds that movement of U.S. mail was being halted by the strikers, he sent troops to PULLMAN in 1894. In foreign affairs he took a strong stand on the VENEZUELA BOUNDARY DISPUTE; refused recognition to Hawaiian government set up by Americans.

Cleveland. 1 City (pop. 6,747), NW Miss., NE of Greenville, in cotton-growing area. **2** City (pop. 914,808), NE Ohio, port on L. Erie at mouth of Cuyahoga R. Largest city in state, it was seventh in U.S. in 1950. Great ore port and center of iron and steel production, it has mfg. of chemicals, cement, machinery, and electrical apparatus and oil refineries, lumberyards, and meat-packing plants. Laid out 1796 by Moses CLEAVELAND. Developed rapidly after completion of Ohio and Erie Canal (1832) and arrival of railroad (1851). Iron production began in 1850s and oil refining (including Rockefeller operations) soon became a major industry. Later electrical plants boomed when research hq. of General Electric were located at near-by Nela Park. Seat of Case Inst. of Technology (nonsectarian; for men; chartered 1880; science and engineering school of university grade), WESTERN RESERVE UNIVERSITY, and Fenn Col. (Y.M.C.A.; coed.; 1881). John Carroll Univ. is at near-by UNIVERSITY HEIGHTS. City has Western Reserve Historical Society Mus., Cleveland Mus. of Art, Rockefeller Park, and Cleveland Symphony. **3** City (pop. 12,605), E Tenn., ENE of Chattanooga. Woodworking. Cherokee Natl. Forest hq. **4** City (pop. 5,183), E Texas, near San Jacinto R. and NNE of Houston, in lumber and oil area.

Cleveland Heights, City (pop. 59,141), NE Ohio, E residential suburb of Cleveland.

Cleves (klēvz), Ger. *Kleve* or *Cleve*, former duchy, NW Germany, on both sides of the Rhine; historic cap. Kleve (pop. 28,704), North Rhine-Westphalia. Originally a county; united with county of Mark 1368; raised to duchy 1417. Duke John III inherited JÜLICH, BERG, and RAVENSBURG 1524; his daughter Anne married Henry VIII of England. Extinction of male line (1609) led to complicated dynastic quarrel over succession. Treaties of 1614 and 1666 settled Cleves, Mark, and Ravensburg on Brandenburg; Jülich and Berg on Palatinate branch of Wittelsbachs.

cliff dwellers. Buildings perched on mesas and on ledges of canyon walls in the U.S. Southwest were once thought to be the work of an extinct people, but now it is known that they were built by the ancestors of the Pueblo Indians as defense against nomadic tribes. The cliff dwellers were skilled farmers, employing irrigation. Many of the buildings are now in national parks and monuments.

Clifford of Chudleigh, Thomas Clifford, 1st Baron, 1630–73, English Catholic statesman, member of Cabal ministry of Charles II. Knew of secret passages in Treaty of Dover pledging reestablishment of Catholicism in England. Forced to resign by passage of Test Act (1673) and committed suicide.

Cliffside Park, suburban borough (pop. 17,116), NE N.J., NE of Jersey City and near the Hudson.

Clifton, industrial city (pop. 64,511), NE N.J., adjoining Passaic. Mfg. of airplane propellers, rubber and metal goods, clothing, and chemicals.

Clifton Forge, city (pop. 5,795), western Va., N of Roanoke, in coal area. Railroad shops.

Clifton Heights, borough (pop. 7,549), SE Pa., W of Philadelphia. Has textile mills.

climacteric: see MENOPAUSE.

climate, sum total of weather elements over long period. Elements include temperature, precipitation (see RAIN), HUMIDITY, WIND, barometric pressure. Latitude is primary factor, modified by secondary influences (e.g., relation to water and land; altitude; topography; prevailing winds; OCEAN CURRENTS; cyclonic-storm prevalence). Climatic zones include equatorial zone (see DOLDRUMS); subtropical (trade-wind belts; horse latitudes); intermediate, prevailing-westerlies region; and polar zone. Subtropical-intermediate transition belt (Mediterranean type) found on continental west coasts. Climatic types combining latitude and secondary items: continental (sunny with low humidity, except at equator; temperature extremes), marine (slight temperature changes; much rain on windward side of mountainous islands); coastal or littoral; and mountain or plateau. Climatology is study of climate and its relation to plant and animal life.

climbing perch, spiny-finned, perchlike, fresh-water, walking fish (genus *Anabas*), of India and SE Asia.

Adult is c.10 in. long, dark brown, with a blunt, hard head, thick skin, and scales. It walks and climbs by using its tail, fins, and spines on fins. It can breathe atmospheric oxygen.

Clinch, river formed by juncture of two forks in SW Va. and flowing c.300 mi. SW across E Tenn. to Tennessee R. Impounded by Norris Dam, it flows into Watts Bar Reservoir. Important in TENNESSEE VALLEY AUTHORITY.

clinic, institution providing medical diagnosis and treatment for ambulatory patients. Clinics are maintained by hospitals, public and private organizations, or groups of physicians. They evolved from dispensaries which supplied free drugs to the poor; in England these date from late 17th cent., in U.S. first estab. 1786 in Philadelphia by Benjamin Rush.

Clink, former district on the Bankside in Southwark, London, England; site of the famous prison.

Clinton, George, 1739–1812, American statesman. First governor of N.Y. (1777–95) under new state constitution; managed trade and public welfare problems ably. Opposed Federal Constitution. Was Vice President of United States 1805–12. His nephew, **De Witt Clinton,** 1769–1828, was mayor of New York city for ten annual terms between 1803 and 1815; promoted public education and city planning. Sponsored Erie Canal. Unsuccessful presidential candidate 1812. Governor of N.Y. (1817–21, 1825–28).

Clinton, Sir Henry, 1738?–1795, British general in American Revolution. In supreme command in America 1778–81. Captured Charleston, S.C., 1780.

Clinton. 1 City (pop. 5,945), central Ill., N of Decatur. Farm trade center. Has railroad shops. **2** City (pop. 6,462), W Ind., on Wabash R. and N of Terre Haute. Bituminous coal is mined. Site of Fort William Henry Harrison near by. **3** City (pop. 30,379), E Iowa, on the Mississippi and NE of Davenport; laid out 1838. Industrial and rail center in agr. area with mfg. of metal, wood, grain, and dairy products. **4** Town (pop. 12,287), central Mass., near Wachusett Reservoir; settled 1654. Mfg. of steel goods and chemicals. **5** Town (pop. 2,255), W central Miss., W of Jackson. Seat of Mississippi Col. **6** City (pop. 6,075), W Mo., SE of Kansas City, in farm and coal area. **7** Village (pop. 1,630), central N.Y., SW of Utica. Seat of Hamilton Col. (nonsectarian; for men; chartered 1812, originating from an academy founded by Samuel KIRKLAND). **8** City (pop. 7,555), W Okla., on Washita R. Shipping and mfg. center for wheat, cotton, and livestock area. **9** Town (pop. 7,168), NW S.C., S of Spartanburg, in cotton and grain area. **10** Town (pop. 3,712), E Tenn., NW of Knoxville. OAK RIDGE and Norris Dam are near by.

Clio, Muse of history: see MUSES.

clipper, fastest type of sailing ship. Long and narrow, it had the greatest beam aft of center and carried, besides topgallant and royal sails, skysails and moonrakers. Originated in the U.S., the Baltimore clippers were but forerunners of the real clipper begun with the *Ann McKim* (completed Baltimore 1832). This type was perfected by Donald McKAY of Boston who built the *Flying Cloud,* the *Glory of the Seas,* and the *Lightning.* The clippers dominated long-distance commerce, cutting time and vying in famous races. The clipper at first outran the rival steamship, but in the 1860s the improved steamship began to win out over all sailing ships.

Clisson, Olivier de (ōlēvyä′ dü klēsō′), 1336–1407, constable of France. Defeated Ghent insurgents at Roosebeke (1382). One of MARMOUSETS, he used his position to amass a huge fortune.

Clive, Robert, Baron Clive of Plassey, 1725–74, British of Irish descent. Notable in comedies by Cibber, Gay (*Beggar's Opera*), and Coffey. Kitty Clive also sang in Handel's *Sampson* 1742. Was a friend of Johnson, Fielding, and Horace Walpole.

Clive, Robert, Baron Clive of Plassey, 1725–74, British soldier and statesman. In service of East India Com-

pany he won victories against the French (culminating in Plassey 1757), whose power in India he destroyed by his military genius. Twice governor of Bengal, he brought Behar and Orissa under British control as well as CALCUTTA. Fought corruption and promoted reform. On return to England (1767) was charged with acceptance of large gifts in India; finally acquitted but committed suicide. See *Essay on Clive* by T. B. Macaulay.

clock, instrument for measuring and indicating time. First wheel clock is believed to date from 6th cent., first weight-driven clock from 9th cent. Until 17th cent. there were few mechanical clocks except in cathedral towers, monasteries, and public squares. Smaller, lighter types constructed after coiled spring came into use c.1500. Invention of pendulum clock (c.1656) attributed to Christiaan Huygens. Clocks with long cases to conceal pendulums or weights date from mid-17th cent.; forerunners of grandfather clocks. Electric clocks, first made in 19th cent., extensively used after c.1930. Until 19th cent. clockmaking industry centered chiefly in France and England; later Germany and U.S. became leading producers. Among well-known clocks are astronomical clock with elaborate mechanical devices in cathedral of Strasbourg; clock in tower of British Houses of Parliament, with 13½ ton bell known as Big Ben; and clock in Metropolitan Life Insurance Building, New York city, with four dials, each 26½ ft. in diameter.

Clodia (klō′dēu), fl. 1st cent. B.C., Roman beauty; sister of Publius Clodius. As notable for her immorality as for her appearance, she is supposed to have murdered her husband. The poet Catullus was one of her many lovers.

Clodius (Publius Clodius Pulcher) (klō′dēus), d. 52 B.C., Roman politician. In 62 B.C., disguised as a woman, he took part in the Bona Dea mysteries in the house of Julius Caesar, thus causing Caesar to divorce his wife. Made tribune of the people in 58 B.C., he proved to be a demagogue. His gang of hired ruffians changed the complexion of Roman politics, and he was killed by a rival gang hired by Milo.

Cloisters, the, museum of medieval art, Fort Tryon Park, New York city; a branch of Metropolitan Mus. of Art, opened May, 1938. Five French cloisters, 12th-cent. Romanesque chapel, and chapter house contain 600–700 examples of medieval art. Collection (gathered by George Grey Barnard) was given to the Metropolitan by John D. Rockefeller, Jr.

Clonmacnoise (klŏnmäknoiz′), historic religious center, Co. Offaly, Ireland. Has interesting ruins, including abbey founded by St. Kieran 541.

Cloquet (klōkā′), city (pop. 7,685), NE Minn., on St. Louis R. and W of Duluth, in agr. area. Mfg. of wood products.

closed shop and open shop. A closed shop (or "union shop") is an establishment employing only members of a labor union. An open shop is not restricted to unionized employees. In U.S., since 1840, the closed-shop policy has been adopted by most labor unions. Until 1935, judicial decisions usually went against the closed shop, and many states have banned it. Collective bargaining under the Wagner Act (1935) tended to promote closed-shop policy; the Taft-Hartley (1947) Act, to discourage it.

Clotaire (klōtâr′), Frankish kings. **Clotaire I,** d. 561, became king of Soissons at the death of his father, Clovis I (511). With his brothers THEODORIC I and CHILDEBERT I he conquered Thuringia and Burgundy. Their deaths left him sole king of the Franks by 558. His grandson, **Clotaire II,** 584–629?, succeeded his father CHILPERIC I as king of Neustria (584), his mother FREDEGUNDE acting as regent. In 1613 he put BRUNHILDA to death, became king of all Franks.

clothes moth, name for several moths of family Tineidae; adults of commonest ones are yellowish or buff, c.½ in. long. Larvae feed on wool, furs, other animal products. Fumigation, spraying fabrics with chemicals, cleaning, airing, and cold storage of garments help prevent damage.

Clotho, one of the FATES.

cloth of gold has been made since anc. times, esp. in the East; in medieval Europe, it was much used ceremonially. Gold thread for weaving and embroidery is prepared either as very fine wire or by wrapping a core yarn with thin metal (lamé).

Clotilda, Saint, Frankish queen: see CLOVIS I.

clotting of blood, process of blood coagulation in which red and white corpuscles and blood platelets are caught in network of fibrils consisting of fibrin. Fibrin forms when skin is broken. Normal clotting time about four minutes; prolonged in HEMOPHILIA.

cloud, dense suspension in air of water droplets or ice particles condensed (from water vapor in air cooled below dew point) around nuclei of microscopic atmospheric dust particles. Usually air is cooled by upward movement and expansion; sometimes by reduced air pressure aloft, or mixing of warmer and cooler air currents. Air may rise by convection (from intense ground heat); by cold-air wedge at ground forcing warm air aloft; or by mountain range deflecting air flow upward. Classification of clouds (based on Luke Howard's work, 1803, and proposed by International Meteorological Commission in 1929): high clouds, 20,000 ft. or over (cirrus, cirrocumulus, cirrostratus); middle clouds, 6,500–20,000 ft. (altocumulus, altostratus); low clouds, 6,500 ft. or below (stratocumulus, stratus, nimbostratus); vertical-development clouds, 1,600–20,000 ft. (cumulus, cumulonimbus).

cloud chamber: see WILSON CLOUD CHAMBER.

Cloud Peak: see BIGHORN MOUNTAINS.

Clouet, Jean (zhä′ klōōä′), called **Janet** or **Jehannet,** c.1485–c.1541, court painter to Francis I of France. Probably of Flemish origin. His son **François Clouet** (fräswä′), c.1516–c.1572, was court painter to Francis I, Henry II, Francis II, and Charles IX. Both excelled in precision of draughtsmanship.

Clough, Arthur Hugh (klŭf), 1819–61, English poet, friend of literary figures of his day, best remembered for narrative poem *The Bothie of Toper-na-Fuosich* (1848), for lyric, "Say not the struggle naught availeth"; and for Matthew Arnold's monody on his death, *Thyrsis.* His sister, **Anne Jemima Clough,** 1820–92, was first principal of Newnham College, Cambridge.

clove, evergreen tree (*Syzygium aromaticum* or *Eugenia aromatica*) of the Moluccas, and its unopened flower bud, an important spice. The dried nail-shaped buds are used whole or ground to flavor confections and ham. They yield a volatile oil used medicinally and in perfumes.

Clover, town (pop. 3,276), N S.C., near N.C. line. Kings Mountain Natl. Military Park near by.

clover, leguminous forage and hay plant and cover crop, of genus *Trifolium,* native to northern regions. Common species are red, crimson, and white or Dutch clovers, and alsike (*Trifolium hybridum*). Characterized by three-lobed leaves, clover was emblem of Ireland from which shamrock was derived. Four-leaved clover is symbol of good luck.

Clovis I (klō′vĭs), c.466–511, Frankish king (481–511), founder of Frankish monarchy (see MEROVINGIANS). Rose from tribal chieftain to sole leadership of Salian Franks by dint of patience and murder; conquered most of Gaul and SW Germany by defeating Romans (486, at Soissons), Alemanni (496), Burgundians (500), Visigoths (507, at Vouillé). His wife, St. Clotilda, a Burgundian princess, encouraged his conversion to Christianity, but he was baptized only after 496, in fulfillment of a vow made in battle against Alemanni.

Clovis, city (pop. 17,318), E N.Mex., on the Llano Estacado near Texas line; settled 1907. Rail division point and trade center in farm and cattle area. Artifacts of Folsom culture found near by.

clown, jester in circus or pantomime: see FOOL.

clubfoot (talipes), foot deformity resulting from changes in joints of ankle and foot which arise from muscle defect. A notable sufferer was Lord Byron.

club moss, low evergreen plant, of the genera *Lycopodium* and *Selaginella,* related to ferns but with small needlelike or scalelike leaves. Species of *Lycopodium,* also called ground pine and ground cedar, grow in moist, shaded places. Yellow spores of running pine, *Lycopodium clavatum,* sold as lycopodium powder or vegetable sulphur for medicinal uses. Most *Selaginella* species are tropical but some are found in temperate regions.

clubroot, slime mold disease of cabbage and other plants of mustard family. Attacks roots, causing malformation and preventing normal plant growth.

Cluj (klōōzh), Ger. *Klausenburg,* Hung. *Kolozsvár,* city (pop. 117,915), W Rumania. Chief commercial and cultural center of Transylvania; metallurgical industry. Univ. founded as Jesuit academy by Stephen Bathory (1581). Dating perhaps from Roman times and a free city from 1405, Cluj has kept many historical buildings of 14th–18th cent. Population over 50% Hungarian.

Cluniac order, medieval group of Benedictines, centering in the abbey of Cluny, France; founded 910. In the 10th, 11th, and early 12th cent. the Cluniac monks were a potent force, greatly forwarding the reforms in the church that were to reach a climax with Gregory VII; working for reforms in general Christian life; and promoting independence of the church from lay control. Their centralized organization increased their power, and they were criticized as rich and arrogant; in the 12th cent. they lost in rivalry with the Cistercians.

Cluny (Fr. klüně′), former abbey, E France, NW of Mâcon. Founded 910; center of Cluniac order. Abbey church dates partly from 10th cent.

Cluny Museum, 14th- and 15th-cent. structure in Paris, housing collection of medieval and Renaissance art objects. State-owned since 1842.

Clusium: see CHIUSI, Italy.

cluster, in astronomy, group of stars, probably of common origin, moving at same rate in same direction. More than 300 open, or galactic, clusters are catalogued. About 100 globular clusters are known, the nearest being over 20,000 light years away; in them the stars, numbering many thousands, appear to be densely massed.

clutch, device for controlling power transmission from the drive shaft to another working part, usually without interrupting the rotation of the drive shaft. Commonly consists of friction plates pushed together by springs. Less common are cone clutch, with cone fitting into end of flywheel; band clutch, with expanding segments; and magnetic fluid clutch.

Clyde, river of SW Scotland rising in S Lanarkshire and flowing N and NW for 106 mi. Near Lanark are four series of falls. Below these is Scotland's greatest industrial area, with Glasgow as head of navigation for large vessels. Shipyards here bombed 1940–41. At Dumbarton, river widens into the **Firth of Clyde** (length, 64 mi.; width, 1–37 mi.) with many commercial and industrial ports on its banks.

Clydebank, shipbuilding burgh (pop. 44,625), Dumbartonshire, Scotland, on the Clyde below Glasgow. *Queen Mary* and *Queen Elizabeth* built here. Suffered severe air raid damage 1940–41.

Clymene (klī′mŭnē), in Greek mythology. **1** Daughter of the Titan Oceanus, wife of Iapetus, and mother of Atlas, Prometheus, and Epimetheus. **2** Nymph, wife of Helios and mother of Phaëthon.

Clytemnestra (klī′tŭmně′strŭ), in Greek legend, daughter of Leda and Tyndareus, half sister of Helen. Wife of AGAMEMNON, she was mother of Orestes, Electra, and Iphigenia. When she and her lover Aegisthus slew Agamemnon, Orestes in revenge slew both lovers.

Cm, chemical symbol of the element CURIUM.

Cnidus or **Cnidos** (both: nī′dŭs), anc. Greek city of

Asia Minor, in present SW Asiatic Turkey. The town had the famous statue by Praxiteles, the Aphrodite of Cnidus.

Cnossus or **Knossos** (both: nŏ′sŭs), anc. city near the N coast of Crete. Occupied long before 3000 B.C., it was center of the MINOAN CIVILIZATION, which is known chiefly through excavations of the Cnossus palace. In legend Cnossus was the home of Minos.

Co, chemical symbol of the element COBALT.

coach: see CARRIAGE; STAGECOACH.

Coachella Valley (kō″üchĕl′ŭ), arid region, SE Calif., N of Salton Sea. Irrigated by artesian wells and Coachella Main Canal (123 mi. long; completed 1948), a branch of ALL-AMERICAN CANAL. Produces dates, citrus, truck, alfalfa, and cotton. Indio and Palm Springs resort are here.

coagulation, collection into a mass and precipitation of minute particles of a substance that was dispersed through another substance. In a colloidal solution it results from neutralization of charges on colloidal particles; they remain together on collision and form a precipitate.

Coahuila (kōäwē′lä), state (58,067 sq. mi.; pop. 720,-145), N Mexico, on N bulge of Rio Grande, S of Texas; cap. SALTILLO. Mountains in E Coahuila have quantities of largely unexploited mineral resources. Lumbering and coal mining are important. Cattle raising is chief occupation in NE. Border city, PIEDRAS NEGRAS, is across Rio Grande from Eagle Pass, Texas. LAGUNA DISTRICT lies in S part with TORREÓN its chief city. Exploration of territory began in middle of 16th cent. Joining of Texas and Coahuila (1830) was contributing factor to Texas Revolution (1835–36). Joined to Nuevo León in 1857, Coahuila became independent state in 1868.

coal, fuel of plant origin composed of carbon with varying amounts of mineral matter. There is a complete series, differing in content of carbon, moisture, and volatile substances: peat is lowest in carbon, and it is followed by lignite or brown coal, bituminous, semibituminous, and anthracite (nearly pure carbon). Coal beds or seams occur in sedimentary rocks, having originated from vegetation growing in slowly submerging swampland. Weight of overlying deposits helped the conversion into coal, the greater the pressure the higher the grade of coal produced. Most coal was formed during the Carboniferous period.

Coaldale, borough (pop. 5,318), E central Pa., NE of Pottsville. Has coal mining and mfg. of clothing.

coal gas is obtained in destructive distillation of soft coal as by-product from coke preparation. Composition varies. Used as fuel, illuminant.

Coalinga (kōlǐng′gǔ), city (pop. 5,539), S central Calif., SW of Fresno. Processes oil and dairy products.

coal tar, product of destructive DISTILLATION of coal. Upon distillation it yields coal-tar crudes that form starting point for syntheses of dyes, drugs, explosives, flavoring, perfumes, paints, etc.

coast guard, special U.S. naval force assigned to seaboard duties such as suppressing smuggling, assisting vessels in distress, and providing protection and aid for maritime commerce and air commerce over the sea. Formed in 1915 by the union of the Revenue Cutter Service (estab. 1790) and the Life Saving Service. In 1939 the Lighthouse Service was merged with the coast guard, and the Bureau of Marine Inspection and Navigation was added in 1942. The coast guard is under the Treasury Dept. but comes under the navy in wartime or for such periods as the President directs. The motto is *Semper Paratus* [Latin,= always ready], and the women's reserve created in World War II is called the SPARS.

coast protection. Means of protection against encroachment of sea include dikes, levees, sea walls (of masonry, extending below low-water mark, most effective with slanted or concave front, often with front apron to prevent undermining), and groins (low walls, usually of wood, extending at right angles

from shore into water, and from low-water to high-water level).

Coast Ranges, mountain belt of W North America extending S along the Pacific from St. Elias Mts. in Alaska, through B.C. and U.S., into Mexico c.800 mi. S of the border. Represented by islands in S Alaska and B.C. where they are separated from Coast Mts. by Inside Passage. In U.S. they include Olympic Mts. in Wash., Coast Range in Oregon, and, in Calif., Diablo, Santa Lucia, and San Rafael ranges, all between narrow coastal strip and Central Valley. Connected on S with Sierra Nevada by transverse belt. Coast Ranges are sometimes considered to include broken ranges of S Calif.–e.g., San Gabriel Mts., San Bernardino Mts., San Jacinto Mts., and N part of Peninsular Range—and uplands of Lower Calif. They are geologically young (formed by upheaval), rugged, and well wooded.

Coatesville, city (pop. 13,826), SE Pa., W of Philadelphia; settled c.1717. Steel center with mfg. of textiles, paper, and metal products.

Coaticook (kōä′tǐkōōk), town (pop. 6,341), SE Que., Canada, on Coaticook R. and S of Sherbrooke. Has textile and lumber mills and mfg. of toys.

coaxial cable: see CABLE.

Cobalt, town (pop. 2,230), E Ont., Canada, NE of Sudbury. Center of rich silver district, discovered 1903. Valuable cobalt ores also mined.

cobalt, silvery-white, lustrous, magnetic metallic element (symbol = Co; see also ELEMENT, table). Chemically active, it forms many compounds. Used in pigments. Occurs alone rarely; found in meteoric metal, in ores with other metals. Used in steel alloys and in carboloy.

cobaltite (kō′bôltīt), opaque, silver-white mineral of pyrite group, an important ore of cobalt.

Cobb, Howell, 1815–68, American statesman. U.S. Congressman from Ga. (1843–51, 1855–57); Secretary of the Treasury (1857–60). Chairman of convention in Montgomery which organized Confederacy.

Cobb, Irvin S(hrewsbury), 1876–1944, American humorist, b. Paducah, Ky.

Cobb, Tyrus Raymond (Ty Cobb), 1886–, American baseball outfielder. Had .367 lifetime batting average, made 4,191 hits, stole 892 bases.

Cobbett, William, 1763?–1835, British journalist and reformer. After resigning from army went to U.S. (1792); in effective pamphlets championed Federalists against pro-French Republicans. On return to England became radical working class leader and apostle of agrarianism. After flight to U.S. due to the Gagging Bills (1817), returned to become central figure in English agitation for parliamentary reform. After Reform Bill of 1832, he was elected to Parliament. *Rural Rides* (1829) most famous of his many books.

Cobden, Richard, 1804–65, English statesman, a major influence in repeal of CORN LAWS. Guided policy of Anti-Corn Law League with John BRIGHT, Sir Robert PEEL, Lord John RUSSELL. Helped keep England out of Schleswig-Holstein affair (1864). Negotiated "Cobden Treaty" for reciprocal tariffs with France (1859–60). Favored Union in U.S. Civil War.

Cobequid: see TRURO, N.S.

Cóbh (kōv) [Irish,= cove], seaport (pop. 5,619), Co. Cork, Ireland, on Great Isl. in Cork Harbour. An important transatlantic port, it is also a resort and home of oldest yacht club in the world. Called Queenstown after Queen Victoria's visit (1849), it was renamed Cóbh 1922.

Coblenz or **Koblenz** (both: kō′blĕnts), city (pop. 64,-961), former cap. of Prussian Rhine Prov., W Germany, at confluence of Rhine and Moselle rivers; since 1945 provisional cap. of Rhineland-Palatinate. Important wine trade; mfg. of machinery, furniture, pianos. Founded 1st cent. B.C. by Drusus as Confluentes. Under archbishops of Trier from 11th cent. until capture by French in 1794. Passed to Prussia 1815. Occupied by U.S. troops 1919–23; by French

1923–29; heavily damaged in World War II. Among ancient buildings is Church of St. Castor, founded 9th cent. Ehrenbreitstein fortress, across the Rhine, became part of Coblenz 1937.

Cobleskill, village (pop. 3,208), E central N.Y., W of Albany. Howe Caverns are near by.

Cobourg, town (pop. 7,470), S Ont., Canada, E of Toronto; a port on L. Ontario; summer resort.

cobra, poisonous snake of Africa and Asia. Common cobra of India and Egypt, often used by snake charmers, and Asiatic king cobra or hamadryad (14–18 ft. long) spread their hoods when angered. Some African forms spit poison.

Coburg (kō′bûrg, Ger. kō′bŏŏrk), city (pop. 44,789), Upper Franconia, N Bavaria, on Itz R. Precision instruments, ceramics. First mentioned 1056. For history, see SAXE-COBURG; SAXE-COBURG-GOTHA.

coca, South American shrub, *Erythroxylon* (or *Erythroxylum*) *coca*. Leaves yield COCAINE.

cocaine (kōkān′), alkaloid prepared from leaves of coca shrub. It is a habit-forming drug used as local anesthetic and illegally as narcotic.

Cochabamba (kōchäbäm′bä), city (pop. 80,300; alt. c.8,400 ft.), cap. of Cochabamba dept., W central Bolivia, in agr. area.

Cochet, Henri (ārē′ kôshā′), 1901–, French tennis player. Member French Davis Cup team that defeated U.S. in 1927 and held the cup until 1933.

Cochin (kō′chĭn′), city (pop. 26,320), SW Madras, India; forms enclave within TRAVANCORE-COCHIN state; major port on Malabar Coast. Exports coconut products, tea, and rubber. Visited 1502 by Vasco da Gama. Portuguese post built here by Afonso de Albuquerque in 1503.

Cochin China (kō′chĭn), southernmost state (25,000 sq. mi.; pop. c.5,000,000) of INDO-CHINA; cap. Saigon. Bounded by Cambodia on N, by Annam on NE. One of world's great rice-growing regions. Population is largely Annamese but includes Cambodian, Cham, and Chinese groups. Area was part of ancient Khmer Empire. Conquered by Annam 17th–18th cent., ceded to France mid-19th cent. In 1949 Cochin China joined Annam and Tonkin in state of VIET NAM.

cochineal (kŏchĭnēl′), scarlet dye from extract of bodies of female scale insect found on some cacti.

Cochrane, Thomas: see DUNDONALD, THOMAS COCHRANE, 10TH EARL OF.

Cochrane, town (pop. 3,401), NE Ont., Canada, NNE of Timmins. Commercial center in mining and hunting region of NE Ont. and W Que.

Cockaigne or **Cockayne, Land of** (both: kŏkān′), in medieval tales a legendary country where finest food and drink are to be had for the taking.

cockatoo, name for various crested woodland parrots of Australia. Among them are the pink cockatoo, some white birds with yellow or scarlet on crests, and some with dark plumage.

Cockcroft, Sir John Douglas, 1897–, English physicist. He shared the 1951 Nobel Prize in Physics for pioneer work in transmutation of nuclei of atoms by means of atomic particles accelerated artificially and used as projectiles.

Cockerel, Charles Robert (kŏk′ûrŭl), 1788–1863, English architect, exponent of the classic revival.

cockfighting, sport of pitting gamecocks against each other. Popular in ancient Persia, Greece, and Rome. Jousts usually held on small circular stage. Gamecocks placed beak to beak, then released. Cock is defeated when he refuses to fight or is unable to fight.

cockle, marine bivalve mollusk. Shell is marked by ridges radiating from the hinge. It lives in sand or mud and eats microscopic sea life. Some species move about in water; others dig into bottom. Majority of species are in tropical and subtropical waters; one (*Cardium edule*) eaten in Europe.

cocklebur, coarse annual plant of genus *Xanthium*, a persistent weed with oval burs, also called clotbur.

cock of the plains: see SAGE GROUSE.

Cockran, W(illiam) Bourke, 1854–1923, American politician, b. Ireland. U.S. Representative from N.Y. (1887–89, 1891–95, 1904–9, 1921–23); supported organized labor, opposed restrictions on immigration.

cockroach, orthopterous insect of world-wide distribution (c.1,200 species), abundant in tropics. Omnivorous and mainly nocturnal, it has a flat, oval, usually brownish body, long antennae, large eyes, unpleasant odor (glandular secretion). Croton bug found in NE U.S., wood cockroach in E U.S.

cockscomb, annual plant (*Celosia argentea cristata*), with showy red or gold, rounded, ruffled, or feathery flower spikes, used as an EVERLASTING.

cocktail, short mixed drink of spirituous liquor blended with vermouth, fruit juices, or other ingredients, chilled and served as appetizer. Name also given to fruit juices, mixture of cut-up fruit, and seafood served at start of meal.

cocoa, cocoa butter, and cocoa nibs: see CACAO.

coconut, fruit of coco palm (*Cocos nucifera*), a tree widely scattered through tropical regions. Mature trees may yield 75–200 nuts a year. The nut, encased in a thick fibrous husk, has a hard shell surrounding its white, edible meat, and contains a nutritious milk. Shredded kernels of nuts are used in confectionery. Of world value in commerce is oil extracted from dried fruit kernels (known as copra). A sweet liquid, obtained from flower buds, is distilled to make arrack or boiled down for its sugar. Coir (coarse fibers from nut husks) is made into brushes, matting, and ropes.

Cocteau, Jean (zhä′ kôktō′), 1891–, French author. A versatile spokesman for modernism in all arts, he has written poetry, fiction, dramas, operatic librettos; directed moving pictures; and excelled as draftsman. His best-known works are the novel *Les Enfants terribles* (1929; Eng. tr., 1930) and the drama *La Machine infernale* (1934; Eng. tr., 1936).

cod, food fish abundant in N Pacific and N Atlantic. It lays eggs in mid-ocean, feeds on marine life, and weighs 10–35 (rarely 75) lb. Chief fisheries are in Norway, Newfoundland, and Mass.

Cod, Cape: see CAPE COD.

Coddington, William, 1601–78, one of founders of R.I., b. England. Founded Portsmouth (1638) with Anne HUTCHINSON. Founded Newport (1639) with John CLARKE. Governor of united towns (1640).

code, in communication: see CRYPTOGRAPHY; MORSE CODE.

code, body of legal rules expressed in fixed and written authoritative form as contrasted with customary law (including common law). Corpus Juris Civilis gave term meaning of an entire legal system. *Code Napoléon* outstanding example of such codes. Official collections of statutes also called codes (e.g., the criminal code).

codeine: see OPIUM.

Code Napoléon or **Code Civil,** first modern law CODE, compiled by a commission 1800–1804, promulgated by Napoleon I; a milestone in development of civil law (modern Roman law).

codling moth (kŏd′–) or **codlin moth,** small moth with larva (called apple worm) enormously damaging to apple crop. It also attacks other fruits. Often it has two or three generations a year; eggs are laid on developing fruit. Larva eats into apple and remains there until mature.

Codrington, Sir Edward, 1770–1851, British admiral. Commanded combined British, French, and Russian fleets in victory at Navarino (1827) which made possible the success of Greek war of independence.

Cody, William Frederick: see BUFFALO BILL.

Cody, town (pop. 3,872), NW Wyo., on Shoshone R., in dude-ranch area. Named for W. F. Cody (Buffalo Bill); has museum, statue, birthday fete in his honor. Gateway to Yellowstone Natl. Park (W), Shoshone Cavern Natl. Monument. SHOSHONE PROJECT is NE.

Coe College: see CEDAR RAPIDS, Iowa.

coeducation, teaching of both sexes in same classes;

long opposed as distracting factor, now general in public schools of the U.S. Important growth came with expansion of public education in Western states 1830–45. Girls first admitted to scattered elementary schools, after Civil War to secondary schools. Though Oberlin Col. gave degrees to women in 1837, it was rise of state universities that standardized coeducational higher education.

coefficient, in algebra, a number, letter, letter group, or combination of numbers and letters, preceding another letter and by which it is to be multiplied. Thus in $2xy$, 2 is coefficient of x; $2x$ coefficient of y. For other coefficients see EXPANSION and FRICTION.

Coello, Alonso Sánchez (älōn'thō sän'chäth kōĕl'yō), c.1531–c.1588, Spanish court painter to Philip II.

Coello, Claudio (klou'dyō), c.1630–1693, Spanish baroque painter, famous for the monumental altarpiece for the sacristy of the Escorial.

coercion, unlawful act of compelling a person to do, or to abstain from doing, something by depriving him of the exercise of his free will, particularly by use or threat of physical or moral force. Important in questions of labor-management relations. See also DURESS.

Cœur, Jacques (zhäk' kûr'), c.1395–1456, French merchant prince. Chief adviser to Charles VII, founder of French trade in Levant. Amassed fabulous fortune; financed final campaigns of Hundred Years War. Imprisoned and fined millions of dollars on concocted charge of poisoning Agnès SOREL (1453). Escaped to Rome; died campaigning against Turks.

Coeur d'Alene city (pop. 12,198), N Idaho. Founded in late 1870s in region of gold (1860) and silver and lead (1882) discoveries; mining boom in 1884. Center for mining, lumbering, farming, and dairying area. Summer and winter sports near by.

Coeur d'Alene Lake (kûrdùlän'), N Idaho, E of Spokane, Wash.; 24 mi. long and 1–3 mi. wide. Fed by Coeur d'Alene and St. Joe rivers and drained by Spokane R.

Cœur de Lion: see RICHARD I, king of England.

coffee, beverage made from seeds of a small evergreen tree, the Arabian coffee tree (*Coffea arabica*), native to tropical Africa and from certain other species of *Coffea*. After roasting to develop flavor and aroma, the "beans" are ground. Exhilarating effects result from CAFFEINE content. Coffee was known in Ethiopia before A.D. 1000, in Arabia (whence it spread to Egypt and Turkey) by the 15th cent.; it had reached most of Europe by mid-17th cent. In North America coffee became a staple beverage after the Boston Tea Party.

cofferdam, temporary barrier (wood or steel), a protection against water, used in construction of dams, bridges, etc. In water deeper than 30 ft. CAISSON is generally used instead.

Coffeyville, city (pop. 17,113), SE Kansas, on Verdigris R. near Okla. line; settled 1869. Ships cattle, processes food, and refines oil; has railroad shops. Dalton gang was shot down here, 1892.

Cognac (kônyäk'), town (pop. 16,106), Charente dept., W France, on Charente R. Export center for French brandy (named for town). FRANCIS I of France formed here alliance against Charles V (1526).

Cogswell, Joseph Green, 1786–1871, American librarian and bibliographer. Helped found Astor Library in New York city. Prepared alphabetical and analytic catalogue.

Cohan, George M(ichael), 1878–1942, American playwright, actor. Began in vaudeville with his family. Wrote plays (e.g., *Forty-five Minutes from Broadway,* 1906) and songs (e.g., *Over There; It's a Grand Old Flag*) exemplifying his favorite themes—Broadway and patriotism. Dramatized mystery novel *Seven Keys to Baldpate* (1913). Acted in *Ah, Wilderness!* (1933), *I'd Rather Be Right* (1937).

Cohasset (kōhăs'ĭt), resort town (pop. 3,731), E Mass., on Mass. Bay. Had first U.S. lifeboat service. Lighthouse here since 1850.

Cohn, Ferdinand (fĕr'dēnänt kōn'), 1828–98, German botanist, known as a founder of science of bacteriology.

Cohoes (kùhōz'), industrial city (pop. 21,272), E N.Y., N of Albany at junction of Mohawk and Hudson rivers and on the Barge Canal. Mfg. of knit goods, clothing, paper, machinery; boatbuilding.

coil: see INDUCTION.

Coimbatore (kwĭmbùtôr'), city (pop. 130,348), SW Madras, India. Important in 18th-cent. wars between the British and Mysore sultans.

Coimbra (kwēm'brù), city (pop. 35,437), Beira Litoral, W central Portugal; historic cap. of Beira. Important in Roman days; continued to flourish through Moorish times and after its conquest by Ferdinand I of Leon (1047). Cap. of Portugal until 13th cent. Has fine 12th-cent. cathedral. Famous univ., founded by King Diniz, was moved from Lisbon to Coimbra in 1306.

coin, a piece of metal stamped by authority of a government as a guaranty of its value and used as money. Coinage probably originated in the West in Lydia or the Aegean Isls. (first known coin is Lydian, c.700 B.C.), and in the East in China before 700 B.C. Early coins, die-struck by hand, show many variations. Standardized coins date from use (17th cent.) of a mill and screw machine.

Coire, Switzerland: see CHUR.

Coke, Sir Edward (kōk), 1552–1634, English jurist, greatest of all English common lawyers. Solicitor general and speaker of House of Commons before becoming attorney general 1593. Was severe prosecutor. Made chief justice of common pleas 1606; became champion of Parliament against king. Upheld supremacy of common law and enunciated doctrines of personal liberty. Enmity of James I, Baron Ellesmere, and Francis Bacon caused his dismissal in 1616. Elected to Parliament 1620; was leader of popular party and important in drafting Petition of Right (1628). Writings include *Institutes.*

Coke, Richard (kōk), 1829–97, governor of Texas 1874–77), U.S. Senator (1877–95). Coke, as Democratic governor, restored frontier order, generally rehabilitated state after Reconstruction period.

Coke, Thomas William: see LEICESTER OF HOLKAM, THOMAS WILLIAM COKE, EARL OF.

coke, fuel made by destructive DISTILLATION of soft coal. Its by-products are ammonia, coal tar, and illuminating gas. Used in blast furnace and to make WATER GAS.

Colbert, Jean Baptiste (zhä' bätēst' kōlbĕr'), 1619–83, French statesman, chief adviser to Louis XIV after 1661. Procured conviction of Nicolas FOUQUET. The greatest exponent of MERCANTILISM, he protected industries by subsidies and tariffs, regulated prices and quality of goods, built modern road and canal network, and developed navy and colonization.

Colby College: see WATERVILLE, Maine.

Colchester (kōl'chĭstŭr), municipal borough (pop. 57,436), Essex, England, on Colne R. Once a great pre-Roman city, it has a Norman castle housing Roman antiquities. Colne oyster fisheries important.

colchicine (kōl'chĭsēn), plant alkaloid used chiefly in genetics experiments. It interferes with the separation of nuclei in cell division, and the resulting cells have chromosome numbers that are multiples of species number.

Colchis (kōl'kĭs), anc. country on the Black Sea and in the Caucasus, noted for forest products. In Greek legend it was the home of Medea and the land where Jason sought the Golden Fleece.

Colden, Cadwallader (kōl'dùn), 1688–1776, colonial scholar and political leader of N.Y., b. Ireland, of Scottish parents. Lieutenant governor of N.Y. after 1761. He was botanist of the Linnaean system, which was mastered also by his daughter, **Jane Colden,** 1724–66, who prepared a scientific illustrated work on flora of New York state. In 1759 she married William Farquhar.

cold frame, low, sun-heated structure with transparent cover, sunk into ground. Used for early seed sowing, to propagate cuttings, and to winter nonhardy plants. Hotbed is similar but soil is heated by stable manure, steam, hot air or water, or electricity; used for starting plants early and for growing plants out of season.

colds, infections involving mucous membrane of nose, throat, or larynx. Common cold usually caused by bacteria or virus; lasts 3 to 10 days.

Cold Spring Harbor, resort village, SE N.Y., on N shore of Long Isl., in Huntington town. Former whaling port. Site of a marine biological station and of department of genetics of Carnegie Inst.

Coldstream, burgh (pop. 1,294), Berwickshire, Scotland. Troops raised here (1659–60) to restore Charles II were later called Coldstream Guards, one of guards regiments of the royal household.

Coldwater, city (pop. 8,594), S Mich., SSE of Battle Creek and on Coldwater R. Farm trade center in lake region, it has mfg. of cement, furnaces, and metal products.

Coldwell, Major James, 1888–, Canadian political leader, b. England. Became national leader of CO-OPERATIVE COMMONWEALTH FEDERATION in 1942.

Cole, Charles Woolsey, 1906–, American historian and educator. President of Amherst (1946–). Wrote *Colbert and a Century of French Mercantilism* (1939); *Economic History of Europe* (with S. B. Clough, 1941; rev. ed., 1946).

Cole, G(eorge) D(ouglas) H(oward), 1889–, English economist, a reader at Oxford. Long an exponent of guild socialism, he later returned to his original Fabianism, and headed (1939–46) Fabian Society. Has written books on economic planning. His wife **Margaret (Isabel Postgate) Cole,** 1893–, collaborated with him, notably on many detective stories.

Cole, Thomas, 1801–48, American landscape painter, b. England; a pioneer of the Hudson River school.

Cole, Timothy, 1852–1931, American wood engraver, b. London. Became known for fine reproductions of great European paintings which appeared for many years in *Scribner's* (later the *Century*) magazine.

Coleman, Glenn, 1887–1932, American painter and lithographer of New York street scenes.

Coleman, city (pop. 6,530), W central Texas, NW of Brownwood. Processing and shipping center of agr., livestock, and oil area. Lake Scarborough (city) and Hords Creek (begun 1947) reservoirs are near.

Colepeper: see CULPEPER.

Coleridge, Samuel Taylor, 1772–1834, English poet, critic, and philosopher, a leader of the romantics. With his friend Robert Southey he planned a utopian settlement in America ("pantisocracy"), which failed. His *Poems on Various Occasions* appeared in 1796. In 1798 he and William Wordsworth published *Lyrical Ballads*, the most important single work of the romantic movement; it included Coleridge's "Rime of the Ancient Mariner." Other poems with haunting, musical, fantastic touch are "Christabel," "Kubla Khan," "Dejection: an Ode." Unstable, addicted to drugs, he retained his brilliance in later poetry (*Sybilline Leaves,* 1817), literary criticism, and romantic philosophy (as in *Biographia Literaria,* 1817). Scraps of his conversations and writings, collected later, influenced greatly the writing of next generations. His eldest son, **Hartley Coleridge,** 1796–1849, wrote poetry and critical biographies (*Biographia Borealis,* 1833). S. T. Coleridge's daughter, **Sara Coleridge,** 1802–52, edited some of her father's works, wrote *Phantasmion* (1837; a fairy tale).

Colet, John (kŏ'lĭt), 1467?–1519, English humanist, friend of Erasmus, associate of Sir Thomas More, Grocyn, and Linacre. After years at Oxford was dean of St. Paul's, London (1505–19), and planned St. Paul's school. With Erasmus and William Lily wrote Eton Latin grammar. Urged Church reform but died in the Church before the Reformation.

Colette (kôlĕt'), pen name of Sidonie Gabrielle Claudine Colette de Jouvenel, 1873–, French novelist. Famous for analytical studies of women, such as *Chéri*

(1920; Eng. tr., 1929) and *La Chatte* (1933; Eng. tr., 1936). With her first husband, Willy (pseud. of Henri Gauthier-Villars), she collaborated on the famous *Claudine* stories.

Colfax, town (pop. 1,651), central La., on Red R. Had race riot (April, 1873) in Reconstruction era.

Colgate University: see HAMILTON, N.Y.

colic (kŏ'lĭk), intense pain caused by spasmodic contraction of a hollow organ, especially stomach or intestine. In infants it may follow a large or improper feeding or constipation.

Coligny, Gaspard de (gäspär' dù kōlēnyē'), 1519–72, French Protestant leader, admiral of France; nephew of Anne de Montmorency. With Louis I de Condé, commanded Huguenots in Wars of RELIGION; negotiated peace in 1570. Became favorite adviser to Charles IX, thus arousing enmity of Catherine de' Medici. Was first victim in the celebrated massacre of SAINT BARTHOLOMEW'S DAY.

Colima (kōlē'mä), state (2,010 sq. mi.; pop. 112,292), W Mexico, on Pacific; cap. Colima (pop. 22,601; founded 1523). State includes Revilla Gigedo isls.

Coliseum: see COLOSSEUM.

collective bargaining, in labor relations, negotiating procedure between two parties—union and management—for determining working conditions without dealings with individual workers. Employer's refusal to bargain collectively was made illegal by 1935 National Labor Relations Act. Unions were similarly restrained by 1947 TAFT-HARTLEY Act.

Collège de France (kôlĕzh' dù fräs'), founded in Paris c.1530 by Francis I. Has always been independent and free from supervision. Lectures are open to the public without fee, no examinations are given, and no degrees are granted.

College of Physicians and Surgeons: see COLUMBIA UNIVERSITY.

College of the City of New York: see NEW YORK, COLLEGE OF THE CITY OF.

College Park. 1 City (pop. 14,535), NW Ga., S suburb of Atlanta. **2** Town (pop. 11,170), W central Md., NE of Washington, D.C. Seat of main campus of Univ. of MARYLAND.

Colleges of the Seneca, The: see GENEVA, N. Y.

College Station, city (pop. 7,925), E central Texas, near Bryan. Seat of Agricultural and Mechanical Col. of TEXAS.

Colleoni, Bartolomeo (bärtōlōmä'ō kôl-lāō'nē), 1400–1475, Italian condottiere, generalissimo of Venetian forces from 1454. Equestrian statue by VERROCCHIO.

collie: see SHEEP DOGS.

Collier, Jeremy, 1650–1726, English clergyman, nonjuring bishop (1713), best known for his *Short View of the Immorality and Profaneness of the English Stage* (1698).

Collier, John, 1884–, American social worker and author, commissioner of Indian Affairs (1933–45). Wrote on the American Indian.

Collingdale, borough (pop. 8,443), SE Pa., SW suburb of Philadelphia.

Collingswood, residential borough (pop. 15,800), SW N.J., near Camden; settled 1682.

Collingwood, town (pop. 7,413), S Ont., Canada, at S end of Georgian Bay. Lake port with large shipyards, grain elevators, and dry docks.

Collins, Edward Trowbridge, 1887–1951, American baseball infielder. Had .333 lifetime batting average, made 3,313 base hits, stole more than 740 bases.

Collins, Michael, 1890–1922, Irish leader of the SINN FEIN. Organized guerrilla warfare which forced British to sue for peace. Joined Arthur GRIFFITH in setting up the Free State (1921). He was assassinated.

Collins, (William) Wilkie, 1824–89, English novelist, best known today for two mystery stories, *The Woman in White* (1860) and *The Moonstone* (1868). Friend of Dickens.

Collins, William, 1721–59, English lyric poet, an early romantic. Wrote odes, notably "Ode to Evening,"

"Ode Written in 1746" (beginning "How sleep the brave").

Collinsville, city (pop. 11,862), SW Ill., NE of St. Louis, in coal and agr. area; settled 1817. Mfg. of chemicals and food products.

Collodi, Carlo (kär'lō kōl-lō'dē), pseud. of **Carlo Lorenzini** (lōräntsē'nē), 1826–90, Italian writer, author of *Pinocchio: the Story of a Puppet* (1880, 1883), a children's classic, widely translated.

collodion (kŭlō'dēŭn), alcohol-ether solution of PY-ROXYLIN. When exposed to air, liquid evaporates, leaving thin, colorless, elastic film.

colloid (kŏ'loid), substance dispersed in solvent as particles too small to be seen but larger than molecules. It is not a true SOLUTION for the particles are not of molecular size, do not pass through certain membranes, have only slight effects on freezing and boiling points, and are observable with ultramicroscope; not SUSPENSION, for particles are invisible and do not settle on standing. Milk is an example. COAGULATION and ADSORPTION are characteristic of colloids.

collusion, conspiracy to defraud a person of his legal rights or to obtain some objective by misusing the forms of law. Collusion between husband and wife, or between either and a third party, is a bar to DIVORCE.

Colmar or **Kolmar** (kôl'mär), city (pop. 43,514), cap. of Haut-Rhin dept., E France, in Alsace. Textile mfg. Made free imperial city 13th cent.; annexed by Louis XIV 1673. Old section keeps medieval architecture. St. Martin's Church (13th cent.) contains painting by SCHONGAUER. Museum, in 13th-cent. convent, has Isenheim altarpiece by GRÜNEWALD.

Cologne (kŭlōn'), Ger. *Köln* or *Köln am Rhein,* city (pop. 590,825; 1939 pop. 772,221), North Rhine-Westphalia, NW Germany, on the Rhine. Though largely destroyed in World War II, it remains a major rail junction and river port. Metallurgy; chemical and textile mfg.; EAU DE COLOGNE. Founded A.D. 50 by Romans as Colonia Agrippinensis. Episcopal see from 4th cent.; archbishopric since time of Charlemagne. As princes of Holy Roman Empire, archbishops ruled strip of land on W bank of the Rhine; ranked third among ELECTORS. Their constant feud with citizens of Cologne led to transfer of electoral residence to nearby Brühl and later (1263) to Bonn. A free imperial city from 1474 and a member of Hanseatic League, Cologne flourished as commercial center until 16th cent. It was seized by the French 1794. Archbishopric was secularized 1801. Annexed to Prussia as part of Rhine Province (1814), Cologne developed into largest transit port and depot of NW Germany. Industrial Deutz, on right river bank, was united with Old Cologne, on left bank. Among buildings that escaped major damage in Allied air raids of World War II are the famous cathedral (begun c.1248; completed 1880, after original plans), containing relics of the WISE MEN OF THE EAST, and the Church of St. URSULA. Cologne is the center of N German Catholicism. The university was founded 1388.

Coloma (kŭlō'mù), town, E Calif., on American R. and NE of Sacramento. Has monument to 1848 gold discovery at Sutter's Mill here.

Colomb or **Colombe, Michel** (both: mēshĕl' kôlō'), c.1430–1512, French sculptor, a master of the early French Renaissance.

Colombia (kōlōm'byä), republic (439,828 sq. mi.; pop. 11,259,730), NW South America; cap. BOGOTÁ. The only nation on the continent with both Pacific and Atlantic coasts, Colombia is split by ranges of the Andes that fan out N from the S border with Ecuador. More than half of the land is E of the Andes; there in the S are jungle rain forests of the Amazon basin, threaded with tributaries of the Amazon; in the N are vast plains (llanos), crossed by tributaries of the Orinoco and given over mainly to cattle breeding—Colombia's developing frontier. W of the Andes is the relatively small Pacific area, which produces platinum and gold and (in the N) tropical forest products. The

chief Pacific port is BUENAVENTURA. It is less important than the Atlantic ports in the extreme N of the country, notably BARRANQUILLA, CARTAGENA, and SANTA MARTA. Petroleum from rich Colombian fields is shipped from the N ports, as are the products (notably coffee) from the valleys and plateaus of the mountain region. In the uplands where two great rivers, the MAGDALENA and the CAUCA, run between the ranges, the population has concentrated since the days of the CHIBCHA. Here are the cap. and other cities: TUNJA, BUCARAMANGA and CÚCUTA in the E; industrial centers MEDELLÍN and MANIZALES in the center; and CALI in the W. Besides growing of coffee, the area has mines and industries (with hydroelectric power). Conquered by JIMÉNEZ DE QUESADA and others, the region was the core of the Spanish colony and viceroyalty of New Granada, which included Panama and most of Venezuela. Revolution against Spain began in 1810 (see NARINO, ANTONIO) and ended with the victory of Bolívar at Boyacá (1819). Bolívar set up the republic of Greater Colombia (including Venezuela and Ecuador), but separatist movements broke it, and after 1830 Colombia (sometimes called New Granada) was a reduced nation. It was subject to political quarrels (particularly between federalists and centralists), and strong men (*caudillos*) arose. In the late 19th and early 20th cent. industries grew. A major political problem was that of the PANAMA CANAL, which resulted in 1903 in the independence of PANAMA from Colombia. In World War II Colombia joined the Allied side in 1943 and became a member of the United Nations. The Quito Charter in 1948 promised cooperation among the nations once joined in Greater Colombia.

Colombo (kŭlŭm'bō), commercial city (pop. 355,374), cap. of Ceylon, on Indian Ocean. Ceylon's main port, it ships tea, rubber, and copra. Successively the center of Portuguese, Dutch, and British rule in Ceylon from 1565 to 1948.

Colón (kōlōn'), city (pop. 52,035), Panama, at Caribbean end of Panama Canal; thriving commercial center exporting tropical fruits and woods. Cristobal, within zone, is American residential district.

colon, in anatomy: see INTESTINE.

Colonia (kōlō'nyä), city (pop. 8,000), cap. of Colonia dept., S Uruguay, on Río de la Plata; resort and small port in agr. district. Founded by Portuguese (1680), it was secured by Spanish after bitter fighting.

Colonial Conference, British: see IMPERIAL CONFERENCE.

Colonial Heights, city (pop. 6,077), SE Va., on Appomattox R.; a suburb of Petersburg.

Colonial National Historical Park: see NATIONAL PARKS AND MONUMENTS (table).

Colonna (kōlōn'nä), noble Roman family, prominent 12th–16th cent. Though traditionally Ghibelline and antipapal, produced one of most successful advocates of papal authority in Pope MARTIN V. **Sciarra Colonna** (shär'rä), d. 1329, helped French capture Pope Boniface VIII, whose face he slapped. **Vittoria Colonna, marchesa di Pescara** (vēt-tō'rēä, dē päskä'rä), 1492–1547, Italian poet, was a friend of Michelangelo. Much of her verse was inspired by the death of her husband (1525) and by religious themes.

color, property of light that depends on wave length. Apparent color of object depends on wave length of light it reflects. Object that reflects all wave lengths appears white; one that reflects none, black. Dispersion occurs when sunlight passes through glass prism, producing solar spectrum. Speed at which color travels depends on wave length. Primary colors of light or spectrum are red, green, and blue; they can produce, in combination, all colors. Primary pigments are red, yellow, and blue. Any two colors that produce white when mixed are complementary colors. Light causes different color cones in human retina to react, making color perception possible. See also, LIGHT; PROTECTIVE COLORATION; SPECTRUM; VISION.

Colorado, state (104,247 sq. mi.; pop. 1,325,089), W U.S.; admitted 1876 as 38th state; cap. DENVER. PUEBLO, COLORADO SPRINGS, BOULDER other main cities. Mountain state (Rockies), crossed by Continental Divide. Plains in E section. Agr. (sugar beets, potatoes, fruits, feed crops); mining (coal, uranium, radium, molybdenum, vanadium, gold, silver, zinc); livestock. Processes agr., mining products. Tourist trade important (points of interest are PIKES PEAK, Rocky Mountain Natl. Park, Mesa Verde Natl. Park, 14 national monuments, CENTRAL CITY). COLORADO, Platte, ARKANSAS rivers rise in mountains, as does RIO GRANDE. Area N of Arkansas R. and E of Rockies came to U.S. in Louisiana Purchase, remainder from Mexico (1848), Texas (1850). Penetrated by French, Spanish, and mountain men, but became known mainly through explorations of Z. M. PIKE, S. H. LONG, J. C. FRÉMONT. Boomed with discovery of gold (1859), declined, boomed again with silver (1875). Irrigation, power development extended to aid agr., utilize natural resources.

Colorado. 1 River, rising in N Colo. at Continental Divide and flowing SW through Colo., Utah, and Ariz. (including GRAND CANYON), then between Nev. and Ariz., between Ariz. and Calif., thence to Mexico and into Gulf of California. Great river of SW U.S., c.1,400 mi. long, it drains c.8% of U.S. area aided by the rivers Gunnison (in Colo.), Green (Utah), San Juan, Little Colorado, and Gila (Ariz.). Mouth seen by Francisco de Ulloa 1539, lower part explored by Hernando de Alarcón 1540. Sometimes called Grand R. above entrance of the Green. HOOVER DAM, Davis Dam, ALL-AMERICAN CANAL, and PARKER DAM promote power and irrigation. **2** (kŭlŭrä′dŭ) River rising in NW Texas in Llano Estacado, fed by "draws" in E N.Mex. Flows 970 mi. SE through Austin to Matagorda Bay. Floods caused legislation on flood control, power, and irrigation. Of three boards, Lower Colorado River Authority (1934) is most active, with Buchanan, Roy Inks, Marshall Ford or Mansfield, and Tom Miller dams. Upper and Middle Colorado River Authorities have undertaken reservoir and power plant projects. All uses are coordinated in over-all plan.

Colorado, University of, mainly at Boulder; state supported; coed.; chartered 1861, opened 1877. Has medical school (with hospitals) at Denver.

Colorado Agricultural and Mechanical College: see FORT COLLINS.

Colorado-Big Thompson project, N Colo., planned by U.S. to divert headstreams of Colorado R., W of Continental Divide, to irrigate and provide power for NE Colo. Water blocked by Granby Dam in Colorado R. and by Green Mountain Dam in Blue R. is pumped through Alva B. Adams Tunnel to E slope and Big Thompson R., tributary of South Platte R. Diversion dams near Fort Collins and Estes Park; power plants at Green Mountain Dam and Estes Park.

Colorado City (kŭlŭrä′dŭ), city (pop. 6,774), W Texas, on Colorado R. and S of Snyder. Center of cattle, agr. (cotton, grains, peanuts), and dairying area. Has refineries.

Colorado College: see COLORADO SPRINGS.

Colorado National Monument: see NATIONAL PARKS AND MONUMENTS (table).

Colorado potato beetle or **potato bug,** black-and-yellow-striped beetle, destructive both as adult and larva chiefly to potato plant. Adults winter underground and emerge in spring to lay orange-yellow eggs on underside of leaves. Discovered in 1824 in E Rocky Mt. region, it later spread eastward. See *ill.,* p. 469.

Colorado School of Mines, at Golden; state supported; mainly for men; chartered 1874. Pioneer mining and engineering school of university grade.

Colorado Springs, city (pop. 45,472; alt. c.6,000 ft.), central Colo., S of Denver, at foot of Pikes Peak; founded 1871. Residential city and health resort near Manitou Springs (pop. 2,580; alt. c.6,300), with mineral springs. Garden of the Gods, area of curiously eroded rock formations, is just NW; Cave of the Winds and Will Rogers Shrine near. Here are fine arts center, Colorado Col. (nonsectarian; coed.; 1874), and Ent Air Force Base (hq., since 1951, of Air Defense Command).

color blindness (Daltonism), inability to recognize colors, especially red and green. It is usually a congenital defect occurring in 5% to 10% of men, less than 1% of women.

color photography: see PHOTOGRAPHY.

Colosseum or **Coliseum** (both: kŏlŭse′ŭm), common name of Flavian Amphitheater in Rome, near SE end of Forum. Built A.D. 72–80; largely preserved; most imposing of existing Roman antiquities. Huge four-storied oval held c.50,000 spectators. Arena was scene of gladiatorial combats.

Colossians (–lŏsh′–), epistle of New Testament written to Christians of Colossae and Laodicea by St. Paul. Emphasizes union of all Christians in mystical body of Christ. Among well-known passages are 1.24–29; 2.12–15; 2.20–3.4.

Colossus of Rhodes (kŭlŏ′sŭs), large bronze statue of the sun god, Helios, in Rhodes harbor; one of the seven wonders of the anc. world. Built by Chares, 292–280 B.C., it fell in an earthquake in 224 B.C.

Colt, Samuel, 1814–62, American inventor of a breechloading pistol (patented 1835), which became so popular that Colt grew to be a generic term.

Colton, city (pop. 14,465), S Calif., SW of San Bernardino. Processes and ships citrus fruit. Has mfg. of cement, furniture, and mattresses.

coltsfoot, Eurasian perennial plant (*Tussilago farfara*), naturalized in North America. Has yellow flowers, later downy fruits and large leaves.

Colum, Padraic (pä′drĭk kŏ′lŭm), 1881–, Irish-American poet, dramatist, b. Ireland; in U.S. after 1914. His wife is Mary (Maguire) Colum, Irish-American critic.

Columba or **Columcille, Saint** (kŏlŭmkĭl′ě), 521–97, Irish churchman. Founded monastery schools at Derry (545), Durrow (553), and Kells (c.554). Went with companions in 563 to Iona and later converted N Scots to Christianity. Buried with St. Patrick and St. Bridget at Downpatrick. Feast: June 9.

Columban, Saint (kŭlŭm′bŭn), c.540–615, Irish missionary to the Continent. Founded many notable abbeys, including Luxeuil and Bobbio. His followers founded others, all notable for learning. Feast: Nov. 21 (in Ireland Nov. 24).

Columbia. 1 City (pop. 6,124), S Miss., W of Hattiesburg and on Pearl R., in agr. area. Mfg. of clothing and naval stores. **2** City (pop. 31,974), central Mo., NNW of Jefferson City; laid out 1821. Center of a farm and coal area. Seat of Univ. of MISSOURI and Stephens Col. (Baptist; for women; 1833). **3** Borough (pop. 11,993), SE Pa., on Susquehanna R. and W of Lancaster; settled 1730. Produces textiles, metal products, and tobacco. **4** City (pop. 86,914), state cap. (since 1786), central S.C., at head of navigation on Congaree R. Center of farm area, it has textile, fertilizer, cottonseed-oil, printing, and farm-produce plants. Trading post was near in 18th cent. Burned by Sherman on night of Feb. 17, 1865. Seat of Univ. of South Carolina (state supported; coed.; chartered 1801, opened 1805), Allen Univ., and Benedict Col. Has VA hospital and Woodrow Wilson's boyhood home. Near by are U.S. Fort Jackson and L. Murray. Holds annual music festival. **5** City (pop. 10,911), central Tenn., on Duck R. and SSW of Nashville; settled 1807. Mule market and trade center for agr. and phosphate mining area. Has J. K. Polk home. Race riot and trials of 1946 drew wide interest.

Columbia, river, NW U.S. and SW Canada, c.1,210 mi. long, rising in Rocky Mts. of British Columbia (receives Kootenai R. here). Flows 460 mi. NW and S to enter U.S. in NE Wash.; continues S, W, SE, and W (forming Wash.-Oregon line) to the Pacific near Astoria, Oregon. Cuts through Cascade and Coast ranges, forming beautiful gorges (esp. E of Portland,

Oregon, where a scenic highway parallels it). Commands one of the great U.S. drainage basins (in Idaho, Oregon, Wash., Mont., Wyo., Nev., Utah). Discovered 1792 by Robert GRAY and named for his ship. LEWIS AND CLARK EXPEDITION reached it by land, 1805. Headwaters discovered and entire course explored by David THOMPSON, 1807–11. River was focus of American settlement that created Oregon. Has long supported extensive fisheries (mainly salmon). Irrigation began early (esp. for orchards) and gained great significance with plans beginning in 1932. Goals are flood control, navigation improvement, irrigation, and power. Among first big dams were BONNEVILLE DAM and GRAND COULEE DAM. Contemplated projects now number 238. Included are those in SNAKE (its greatest tributary), WILLAMETTE, John Day, Deschutes, and Yakima rivers and at Vale, Oregon.

Columbia, District of: see DISTRICT OF COLUMBIA.

Columbia College: see COLUMBIA UNIVERSITY.

Columbia Heights, city (pop. 8,175), E Minn., N suburb of Minneapolis.

Columbia University, in Manhattan borough of New York city; founded 1754 as King's Col. by grant of George II. First president was Samuel JOHNSON; succeeded by Myles COOPER and W. S. JOHNSON. Closed during Revolution and reopened 1784 as Columbia Col. It moved to Morningside Heights under Seth Low, and greatly expanded under Pres. N. M. BUTLER (1902–45). Gen. Eisenhower president 1948–53. Named Columbia Univ. 1896 and Columbia Univ. in the City of New York 1912. Columbia Col. remains as undergraduate school for men. Other divisions: Faculty of Medicine (estab. 1767; became responsible in 1945 for programs of schools of Dental and Oral Surgery, Public Health, Nursing); schools of Law (1858), Engineering (estab. 1864 as School of Mines); Architecture (separate status, 1914), Library Service (1926), International Affairs (1946), General Studies (1910; present name 1947), Dramatic Arts (1948), and Painting and Sculpture (1948); graduate schools of Journalism (1912; endowed by PULITZER) and Business (1916; reorganized 1949); faculties of Political Science (1880), Philosophy (1890), and Pure Science (1892); and Russian (1946) and East Asian (1948) institutes. Independent corporations, but parts of Columbia educational system, include Barnard Col. (undergrad.; for women; 1889); Teachers Col. (1888); Col. of Pharmacy (1829); and New York School of Social Work (1898; part of Columbia since 1940, but administered by Community Service Society of New York since 1939). Reciprocal relationship with UNION THEOLOGICAL SEMINARY. Columbia maintains "Nevis," estate (with cyclotron) near Irvington; Lamont Geological Observatory at Palisades; and Yale-Columbia Southern Station in Union of South Africa. Columbia Univ. Press was organized 1893.

Columbine, stock PANTOMIME character, forerunner of the soubrette. Usually Harlequin's beloved.

columbine, perennial plant of genus *Aquilegia,* with spurred blossoms and delicate foliage. Wild red and yellow *Aquilegia canadensis* native to E North America; blue and white *A. coerulea* to W U.S. Garden sorts are evolved from European species.

columbium: see NIOBIUM.

Columbus, Christopher, 1451?–1506, discoverer of America, b. (almost certainly) Genoa, Italy. After much supplication he gained royal support and sailed from Spain in three ships, *Santa María, Pinta,* and *Niña.* He landed on San Salvador Isl., Oct. 12, 1492. His reception in Spain was enthusiastic. On a second expedition (1493), his discoveries included Puerto Rico, Virgin Isls., Jamaica. Upon a third voyage (1498), he discovered the mouth of the Orinoco in Venezuela. His administration of a colony in Haiti resulted in his return to Spain in chains. A fourth expedition (1502), an attempt to regain prestige, reached the coast of Honduras but was forced back by hardships. He died in neglect.

Columbus. 1 City (pop. 79,611), W Ga., at head of navigation on Chattahoochee R. and WSW of Macon. Cotton market and shipping center, it has textile mills (since 1838), foundries, and food-processing plants. Founded 1828 as trading post. Busy river port before railroads came in 1850s. Supply point in Indian war of 1836, Mexican War, and Civil War. Taken by Federals in April, 1865. Hydroelectric plants of 20th cent. have stimulated industrial growth. U.S. Fort Benning is near. **2** City (pop. 18,370), SE Ind., on East Fork of White R. and SE of Indianapolis; settled c.1819. Mfg. of wood and metal products. Large prehistoric Indian mound is here. **3** Town (pop. 482), SW Ky., near Mississippi R. SW of Paducah. Early site (now Clinton) was Confederate stronghold early in Civil War. **4** City (pop. 17,172), NE Miss., on Tombigbee R. near Ala. line; settled 1817. Shipping and processing center for cotton, livestock, and timber area. Seat of Mississippi State Col. for Women (first state-supported woman's college; chartered 1884, opened 1885). **5** City (pop. 8,884), E Nebr., in prairie region, at junction of Loup and Platte rivers W of Omaha. Rail and mfg. center for livestock, dairy, and grain area. Hq. for Loup R. power project. **6** City (pop. 375,901), state cap. (since 1816), central Ohio, on Scioto R. at mouth of Olentangy R.; laid out as state cap. 1812. Coming of feeder canal (1831) to Ohio and Erie Canal, National Road (1833), and first railroad (1850) stimulated growth. Transportation and distribution center of rich farm area, its industries include meat packing, printing and publishing, paper milling, and mfg. of foundry products, aircraft, auto parts, electrical equipment, and glass. Here are OHIO STATE UNIVERSITY, Columbus Gall. of Fine Arts, Batelle Memorial Inst. (industrial research), and U.S. Fort Hayes. Has Confederate cemetery adjoining site of Civil War Camp Chase.

Columbus Day, commemoration of discovery of America. Celebrated Oct. 12 in 34 U.S. states and in Puerto Rico. Observed also in some Latin American nations and in certain Spanish and Italian cities.

Columcille, Saint: see COLUMBA, SAINT.

coma (kō'mù), deep insensibility from which person cannot be roused. It may be caused by brain injury, toxic conditions, shock, sunstroke, hemorrhage, or epilepsy.

Comanche Indians, tribe in N and W Texas and W Okla. after 17th cent., of Shoshonean group of Uto-Aztecan linguistic stock. Nomads with a typical Plains culture, they were fiercely hostile to whites.

Combaconum, India: see KUMBAKONAM.

Combe, William, 1741–1823, English satirist, author of doggerel verse for "Dr. Syntax" series illustrated by Thomas Rowlandson (1812–21).

Combes, Émile (ämēl' cōb'), 1835–1921, French premier (1902–5). Initiated separation of Church and state; abolished religious education.

combine: see REAPER.

combining weight, of an element, is computed by dividing atomic weight by its valence.

combustion, burning or rapid oxidation of a substance, liberating heat and light. Kindling temperature must be reached before substance will burn. In **spontaneous combustion,** substance bursts into flame without apparent cause; usually because there is slow oxidation, without heat loss, until kindling temperature is reached. **Heat of combustion** of a fuel is total amount of heat evolved from burning a given amount of it.

Comédie Française (kōmādĕ' frāsäz') or **Théâtre Français** (tāā'trù frāsä'), state theater of France. Estab. 1680 by royal decree (see BÉJART), company was given an annual grant and a theater. Closed during the Revolution; Napoleon revived it 1803. Has no stars; roles assigned by agreement.

comedy, a light and amusing play or any literary work so presented as to leave a pleasant or happy impression. European comedy originated in ancient boisterous choruses and dialogue of fertility rites at feasts of Dionysus in Greece. These celebrations developed into drama. Plays of Aristophanes are greatest examples of Old Comedy in Greece. Menander was writer of New Comedy, imitated by Plautus and Terence. In England the tradition of the interlude blended with that of Latin classic comedies in 16th cent. Romantic comedy of Elizabethans culminated in plays of Shakspere. In France, Molière combined classical influence with COMMEDIA DELL' ARTE. Reaction against English Restoration comedy of Congreve, Wycherley, and others resulted in sentimental comedy. Later 18th cent. produced brilliant satirical character comedies of Goldsmith and Sheridan. Oscar Wilde carried on comedy of manners in 19th cent. Modern social comedy written by Pinero, G. B. Shaw, Maugham, and Noel Coward.

Comenius, John Amos (kōmē′nēŭs), Czech *Jan Amos Komenský*, 1592–1670, Czech educator, a Moravian churchman. Advocated relating education to everyday life, a universal system with equal opportunities for women, and teaching in vernacular.

comet, heavenly body traveling in orbit around sun. Usually consists of head of cloudy brightness within which lie one or more bright nuclei from which materials, driven away from sun by radiation pressure of sun's light, form a sweeping tail, sometimes over 100,-000,000 mi. long. Periods for covering known orbits range from 3.3 to several thousand years. Periodic comets are officially designated by year of closest approach to sun, followed by Roman numeral indicating order of passage.

comic strip, combination of caricature with a story line, laid out in a series of pictures across a page and concerning the same character or set of characters. The first advance toward the present form was made by R. F. Outcault in 1896 with a single cartoon *The Yellow Kid* (New York *World*) which became very popular. In 1897 Rudolph Dirks, creator of *The Katzenjammer Kids* (New York *American*), developed a four-panel square describing consequent actions and using balloons as frames for dialogue. Bud Fisher with his *Mutt and Jeff* (1907) was the first to lay out the panels in a line. The comic strip rapidly became a regular syndicated feature of most newspapers.

Comines, Commines, or **Commynes, Philippe de** (fēlēp′ dü kōmēn′), c.1447–c.1511, French historian and diplomat. Served Charles the Bold of Burgundy and, after 1472, Louis XI and Charles VIII of France. His *Mémoires* (many translations) are outstanding for penetrating analysis of men and motives.

Cominform (kŏ′mĭnfôrm), Communist Information Bureau, estab. 1947 by Communist parties of USSR, satellite countries, and Italy. Purpose is exchange of experience. Membership is voluntary, and its decisions are not binding, though influence is great. Hq. at Belgrade until expulsion of Yugoslavia in 1948, thereafter at Bucharest, Rumania.

Comintern (kŏ′mĭntûrn) [from Communist International] or **Third International,** estab. 1919 at Moscow to spread Marxian socialism in world. From original core of Russian and German Communists it grew to include Communist parties from many countries. In 1936 Germany and Japan formed Anti-Comintern Pact, renewed 1941 with enlarged membership. In 1943 USSR dissolved Comintern to reassure its allies in World War II.

Commager, Henry Steele (kŏ′mĭjŭr), 1902–, American historian, professor at Columbia Univ. His writings, often in collaboration, are extensive. Probably best-known is *The Growth of the American Republic* (with S. E. Morison).

Commandments, Ten: see TEN COMMANDMENTS.

commando, small military raiding unit organized (1940) by the British in World War II; akin to U.S. army ranger units. First used by Boers in South African War.

commedia dell' arte (kōm-mä′dēä dĕl-lär′tä), form of comedy in 16th-cent. Italy. Using improvised dialogue and masked characters in satiric song, dance, farce, it gave rise to traditional pantomime characters (e.g.,

Harlequin, Columbine). Admitted female performers; helped free Italian theater from artificiality.

Commerce, city (pop. 5,889), E Texas, NE of Dallas. Center of cotton shipping and seat of East Texas State Teachers Col.

Commerce, United States Department of, organized 1903 as Dept. of Commerce and Labor; separated from Dept. of Labor in 1913. Includes Bureau of the Census, Coast and Geodetic Survey, Bureau of Foreign and Domestic Commerce, Weather Bureau, Patent Office, and Civil Aeronautics Administration.

commercial law, body of laws governing business transactions. Beginnings of modern commercial law coincide with opening of large-scale commerce in the late Middle Ages. Strongly influenced by Roman law. Estab. in England in the mid-16th cent. as "law merchant" and was administered by special courts; later under royal courts but in the 18th cent. made a part of the common law and in this form adopted in the U.S., while on the Continent commercial law remains separate with special courts.

Commines, Philippe de: see COMINES.

commissar (kŏ′mĭsär), in the USSR, head of an administration or commissariat, similar to a minister in Western Europe.

Committee for Industrial Organization: see CONGRESS OF INDUSTRIAL ORGANIZATIONS.

Commodus (kŏ′mŭdŭs), 161–92, Roman emperor (180–92), son and successor of Marcus Aurelius. Licentious, vulgar, vain, proud of his physique, he was well hated, finally murdered.

common, formerly in agr., unenclosed tract of land used by community. Old common lands are preserved in some parks in England and also in U.S., e.g., Boston Common, village greens.

common law, legal system of England, originally (13th cent.) so called because common to all England, not limited to a locality; more precisely, that part of the English legal system not reduced to statutes and not arising from EQUITY, maritime law, or other special branches. It is law arising from customs and created by judges to meet problems, unlike modern CIVIL LAW (based upon the code and the STATUTE). Common law followed in British Empire (except Quebec) and the U.S. (except La., Puerto Rico, Virgin Isls.).

Commons, House of: see PARLIAMENT.

Commonwealth of Australia, British dominion including continental AUSTRALIA and TASMANIA.

Commune of Paris, March–May, 1871, government set up in Paris at end of FRANCO-PRUSSIAN WAR, in opposition to government of Adolphe THIERS at Versailles. (Paris had had communal government earlier, a notable occasion being in French Revolution.) Original issue was the Parisians' refusal to accept humiliating peace terms from Prussia. When *Versaillais* troops began siege of Paris (while the Prussians stood by as neutrals), the Commune fell under the sway of leftist extremists, who shot hostages (including archbishop of Paris), burned Tuileries, city hall, palace of justice. On May 28 the *Versaillais* entered Paris. In subsequent reprisals more than 17,000 people, including women and children, were executed.

communicable diseases, diseases caused by microorganisms and transmissible from an infected person or animal to another. They are known also as infectious diseases. Commonly they are called contagious if transmissible by contact with victim of disease or infected objects or secretions. They may be spread also by substances taken into body, e.g., cholera; by bite or sting of infected animal or disease carrier, e.g., rabies, malaria; by contamination of wound, e.g., tetanus. Preventive measures include vaccination, inoculation, quarantine, disinfection. An endemic disease is one always present in a given locality. Disease may become epidemic if many persons lack immunity or if infectious agent is unusually virulent.

communication, transmission and reception of message between two persons or more. Basic forms: signs (sight), sound (hearing; see LANGUAGE). Reduction of message to WRITING was a fundamental step in social evolution, the beginning of recorded history. Save for limited devices (carrier pigeons, smoke signals, heliograph, etc.) speed of early communication was only as fast as man could travel. Invention of TELEGRAPH divorced transportation from communication; RADIO and TELEPHONE extended sphere of nearly instantaneous electrical communication, working profound revolution in society. Made greater centralization in industry and government possible; widened horizon of every community; tends to amalgamate cultures, arts, techniques, languages. FEDERAL COMMUNICATIONS COMMISSION controls radio and television in U.S.; international phases are directed by Office of Transport and Communications, Dept. of State.

communion: see EUCHARIST.

communism, often a vague and misused term, fundamentally is a social system in which property (esp. real property and means of production) is held in common, i.e., by whole group. Communism in this sense is age-old. Many primitive societies, e.g., Mexican, Inca, early German, were communistic. Plato's *Republic* outlined a communal society. Jewish Essenes and some early Christian sects were communal. Medieval feudalism had communal aspects. Peasants' rebellion under Wat Tyler in 14th-cent. England and Peasants' War in 16th-cent. Germany were communistic. Thinkers of the Enlightenment, Jean Jacques Rousseau, and Immanuel Kant attacked institution of private property and prepared the way for the French Revolution, in which BABEUF preached against private property. So-called utopian communism had been advocated in Sir Thomas More's *Utopia,* Tommaso Campanella's *City of the Sun,* and James Harrington's *Oceana.* Cults arose in 19th cent., and communistic settlements were set up, especially in U.S. Leaders of time were Étienne CABET, Charles FOURIER, and Louis BLANC. In same cent. the rise of capitalism and Industrial Revolution produced social and economic conditions that fostered communism. But Communism as we know it today arose in 1848 with *The Communist Manifesto* of Karl MARX and Friedrich ENGELS (see MARXISM). Marxian communism spread with founding of First INTERNATIONAL and rise of Social Democratic parties on Continent. It took more radical form in 1903, in Russia, when Bolsheviks, led by LENIN, urged immediate and violent revolution to crush capitalism and estab. world socialistic state (see BOLSHEVISM AND MENSHEVISM). Triumph of Bolsheviks in RUSSIAN REVOLUTION OF 1917 made them leaders. Leninism was strengthened by World War I and by Third International or COMINTERN, which now became supreme. Leninists urged uniting of all workers for coming world revolution, to be followed by dictatorship of proletariat and state socialism, which would theoretically wither away leaving classless and stateless universal Communism. Antipathy to these ideas has led occasionally in the democracies to "Red hunts" which have sometimes struck against non-Communist liberals as well as actual Reds. Communism now centered in USSR. Death of Lenin (1924) left STALIN and TROTSKY as rivals. Exile and death of Trotsky gave Stalin triumph, and he built up Russia as model and base of world Communism. Victory in World War II added Baltic States to Soviet Union; Stalin later added as satellites Poland, Czechoslovakia, Hungary, Rumania, Bulgaria, and, with reservations, Yugoslavia. Addition of Communist China in 1950 joined two of most heavily populated states. World in 1952 was sharply divided between Communist East and democratic West. See also COMMUNIST PARTY.

communistic settlements, communities practicing common ownership of goods. Existed in ancient and medieval times, and flourished again in 19th-cent. America. Some were religious (e.g., Amana Society, Shaker communities, Oneida Community); others nonreligious and utopian (e.g., New Harmony, Brook Farm, several Fourierist communities, and settlements by Cabet).

Communist party, in U.S., part of world-wide political movement of Communism. First organized 1919. With decline of I.W.W., party became leading revolutionary organization in U.S., having as its avowed aim the overthrow of capitalism and establishment of a dictatorship of the proletariat. Communists led many industrial strikes in 1920s and exploited weaknesses of American democracy. In 1935, following Comintern's new line, party began "cooperating" with liberal groups, and, boring from within, gained control of many organizations (e.g., many trade unions). With the Nazi attack on Russia in June, 1941, party turned overnight from condemnation of World War II as "imperialist" to support of war as "democratic." Following the war cooperation with "progressive" capitalism ended. With the onset of the "cold war," Pres. Truman and Congress took steps to keep Communists out of U.S. government employment and to eliminate their influence in union activity. The Alger Hiss trials (1949, 1950) and the trials and convictions of top Communists served more widely to publicize conspiratorial and subversive nature of U.S. Communism. Party membership, always small, has been drawn mainly from groups that are discriminated against in U.S. society, idealists, and direct-action trade unionists. Political influence has extended into AMERICAN LABOR PARTY and into present PROGRESSIVE PARTY.

community chest, cooperative organization of citizens and social welfare agencies in a city for the purpose of raising and allocating funds for charity.

Commynes, Philippe de: see COMINES.

Comnenus (kŏmnē'nùs), dynasty of Byzantine emperors (reigned 1057–59, 1081–1185): ISAAC I, ALEXIUS I, JOHN II, MANUEL I, Alexius II, Andronicus I. Branch of family founded empire of TREBIZOND (1204–1461).

Como (kō'mō), city (pop. 42,569), Lombardy, N Italy, at SW end of Lake Como. Silk mfg. Founded as Roman colony; independent commune by 11th cent.; conquered 1335 by Milan, after long struggle. Cathedral (14th–18th cent.); town hall (1215). **Lake Como,** Ital. *Lago di Como* or *Lario,* c.30 mi. long, ½–2½ mi. wide, is formed by Adda R. in foothills of Alps. Celebrated scenery; many resorts (Bellagio, Cadenabbia, Cernobbio, Menaggio, Tremezzo).

Comodoro Rivadavia (kōmōdhō'rō rēvädhä'vyä), town (pop. 25,651), SE Argentina; important center of oil production.

Comoro Islands (kŏ'mùrō), French overseas territory (830 sq. mi.; pop. c.152,000), in Indian Ocean, near Mozambique Channel; cap. Dzaoudzi.

Compactata: see UTRAQUISTS.

compass. 1 In mathematics, an instrument for making circles and measuring distances; usually it consists of a pivot leg and a pencil or pen leg or of two pointed legs. **2** In navigation, an instrument for determining direction. Mariner's compass consists of freely suspended magnetic needle which in earth's magnetic field indicates N and S poles. "Boxing the compass" is naming in order the 32 points starting from north (N, N by E, NNE, etc.). Flux-gate or gyro flux-gate compass contains gyroscopic stabilizer and is useful in airplanes.

Compiègne (kôpēā'nyù), town (pop. 15,392), Oise dept., N France, NE of Paris. Château; rebuilt 18th cent., often a royal residence. Joan of Arc was captured (1430) while defending the town. In a railroad car in near-by Forest of Compiègne were signed the armistice of Nov. 11, 1918, which ended World War I, and the French-German armistice of June 22, 1940.

complex, term indicating group or system of ideas originating in a mind as a result of an experience or set of experiences of high emotional content. Although repressed from consciousness, it affects subsequent mental activity and behavior. Undue dominance of a complex over an individual causes psychopathic condition.

composition, in primitive and medieval law, prevention of retribution for acts of violence by payment of money to injured person or his family. Marks transition from vendetta system to system of criminal law where socially dangerous acts are concern of the state rather than of family unit. A well-known instance of composition is the Old English wergild, payment made by a murderer to the victim's family.

compost (kŏm′pōst), decayed organic material, rich in HUMUS, used to improve texture of soil. Made of vegetable wastes (e.g., lawn clippings, leaves), some soil, and sometimes manure, mixed and allowed to decay.

Compostela, Santiago de, Spain: see SANTIAGO DE COMPOSTELA.

compound, homogeneous chemical combination of two or more elements in definite proportion by weight. Has properties distinct from those of its constituents. Can be decomposed by heat and CHEMICAL REACTION. A compound is indicated by a formula showing symbols of constituent elements in proper proportion.

Compromise of 1850. Annexation of Texas to U.S. and addition of new territory at close of Mexican War aggravated North-South tension over extension of SLAVERY into territories. WILMOT PROVISO was source of contention. Compromise measures, largely originating with Stephen A. DOUGLAS, were sponsored in U.S. Senate by Henry CLAY. Measures proposed admission of Calif. as free state; organization of New Mexico and Utah territories without mention of slavery, but with provisions for SQUATTER SOVEREIGNTY; settlement of Texas boundary claims; prohibition of slave trade in D.C.; a more stringent fugitive slave law. Daniel WEBSTER, through speech on March 7, 1850, virtually assured acceptance of proposals. They were passed as separate bills in Sept., 1850. Compromise was hailed as a final solution to slavery question in territories, but issue arose again in 1854 (see KANSAS-NEBRASKA BILL).

Compton, Arthur Holly, 1892–, American physicist. Shared 1927 Nobel Prize for discovering **Compton effect:** increase in wave lengths of X rays on collision with electrons of atoms of low atomic weights. His brother **Karl Taylor Compton,** 1887–, a physicist, is known especially for work on radar, photoelectricity, ionization of gases, ultraviolet spectroscopy, and electric arcs.

Compton, city (pop. 47,991), S Calif., S of Los Angeles, in industrial and farm (truck, dairy) area; settled 1867. Oil refining, with mfg. of oil-well equipment and steel products.

Compton effect: see COMPTON, ARTHUR HOLLY.

compurgation, in medieval law, legal defense by oath of the accused, supported by oaths of other persons that they believed that he swore truthfully. Found in early Germanic law and in English church law.

Comstock, Anthony, 1844–1915, American moral crusader. Secured New York state and Federal legislation against obscene matter. Organized New York Society for the Suppression of Vice.

Comstock Lode, richest known silver deposit, W Nev., on Mt. Davidson in the Virginia Range. Discovered in 1857 by Ethan Allen Grosh and Hosea Ballou Grosh, who died before recording claims. In 1859 Henry Tomkins Paige Comstock laid claim to lode; later disposed of holdings for insignificant sums. Lode became scene of feverish activity, with VIRGINIA CITY its "capital." Great fortunes were made. By 1898 lode was virtually abandoned.

Comtat Venaissin: see VENAISSIN.

Comte, Auguste (ōgüst′ kōt′), 1798–1857, French philosopher, apostle of positivism, a philosophical system completely rejecting metaphysics and relying instead on the findings of modern positive sciences. This he first began to develop when contributing (1818–24) to the publications of Saint-Simon. His final aim was to so reform society that all men might live in harmony and comfort. He ranked sociology (a term he invented) as greatest of the sciences. His *Course of Positive Philosophy* (1830–42) set forth the system later elaborated in other of his works and developed to a

more inclusive scale by followers all over the world in the late 19th cent.

Comus (kō′mŭs), Greek god of mirth, shown as a winged youth bearing torch and drinking cup. Lover of song, dance, and wine, a follower of Dionysus.

Comyn, John (kŭ′mĭn), d. c.1300, Scottish noble. Known as Black Comyn, he became (1286) one of six guardians of realm. Signed treaty by which MARGARET MAID OF NORWAY was to marry eldest son of Edward I of England. On Margaret's death claimed throne, but submitted to Edward. Meanwhile pushed claim of John de BALIOL, who was crowned in 1292. His son, **John Comyn,** d. 1306, aided de Baliol against Edward I. Murdered by Robert Bruce or his followers.

Conanicut Island: see JAMESTOWN, R.I.

Conant, James Bryant, 1893–, American educator, a chemist. Professor of organic chemistry at Harvard (1929–33). President of Harvard after 1933, he encouraged expansion and trend to general education for democracy. In World War II chairman of National Defense Research Committee. Made U.S. High Commissioner for Germany 1953.

concentration camp. In 1933 National Socialist Germany set up forced-labor camps where political undesirables (mainly Jews and Communists) were held without legal procedure. In World War II concentration camps existed throughout German-held Europe. Some (e.g., Majdanek and Oswiecim in Poland) had gas chambers where 6,000,000 (mostly Jews and Poles) were exterminated. Countless others died of mistreatment. Among largest camps in Germany were Buchenwald, Dachau, Belsen.

Concepción (kōnsĕpsēōn′), city (pop. 87,620), cap. of Concepción prov., S central Chile, near mouth of the Bío-Bío. Founded by Valdivia in 1550, it is now one of Chile's largest cities and a major shipping center through its port, Talcahuano. Attacks by Araucanian Indians in first years and recurrent earthquakes (1570, 1730, 1751, 1939) have plagued city.

Concepción del Uruguay (dĕl ōōrōōgwī′), city (pop. 30,-939), NE Argentina, on Uruguay R., one of commercial centers of the Argentine Mesopotamia.

concert, the public performance of music. Earliest recorded public concerts were in London in 1672. Concert life developed greatly in the 18th and 19th cent.; solo recitals were popularized by such artists as Liszt, Clara Schumann, and Paganini.

concertina: see ACCORDION.

concerto, musical form dating from early baroque period. The *concerto grosso,* in which a group of solo instruments alternated with a larger ensemble, was standardized by Corelli and Vivaldi. The form of the classical concerto—three movements, for solo instrument and orchestra—was developed by Mozart.

conch (kŏngk), name for certain marine mollusks with spiral univalve shells, especially those of families Strombidae and Cassididae. Some are called cameo or helmet shells. Conches eat live animal food and also scavenge. Shells, ranging from white to red, are often made into ornaments.

Concini, Concino (kōnchē′nō kōnchē′nē), d. 1617, Florentine adventurer, favorite of MARIE DE′ MEDICI, who made him marshal of France and marquis d'Ancre. Succeeded Sully as chief minister (1611). Notorious for his greed and his spy system. Assassinated by order of Louis XIII. His wife, Leonora Galigaï, was beheaded and burned for sorcery (1617).

Concord. 1 (kŏng′kŭrd) Town (pop. 6,953), W Calif., NE of San Francisco, in agr. (grapes), dairy, and livestock area. **2** Town (pop. 8,623), E Mass., on Concord R. and NW of Boston; settled 1635. Scene of Revolutionary battle on April 19, 1775 (see LEXINGTON AND CONCORD, BATTLES OF) is marked by D. C. French's *Minuteman.* Houses where Emerson, the Alcotts, Hawthorne, and Thoreau lived are preserved. The Old Manse (1765) is public shrine (since 1939). S of the village is Walden Pond, Thoreau's retreat. **3** City (pop. 27,988), state cap. (since 1808), S N.H., on Merrimack R. above Manchester; settled 1725–27, inc. as Rumford in 1733 (Count RUMFORD took his title from this name), renamed 1765. Transportation and trade center for agr. area. Has Rumford Press, famous granite quarries, and factories (wood, metal, leather products). State historical society occupies Franklin Pierce home and office (remodeled 1923). Capitol (1819) is made of granite and marble. Seat of St. Paul's school (prep.; Episcopal; for boys; chartered 1855, opened 1856). Mary Baker Eddy was born at near-by Bow. **4** (kŏn'kôrd'') City (pop. 16,486), W central N.C., in piedmont NE of Charlotte; settled 1796. Center of textile mfg.

Concord, short river, E Mass., joining Merrimack R. at Lowell. Setting for Thoreau's first book.

concordat (kŏnkôr'dăt), contractual agreement between pope, in his spiritual capacity, and temporal authority of a state, regulating points of conflict between Church and state. The earliest concordat (see WORMS, CONCORDAT OF) was concluded in 1122. The Concordat of 1516, with France, abolished the PRAGMATIC SANCTION OF BOURGES but was revoked in 1561. Concordats, common since 19th cent., determine method of appointing bishops and define status of religious schools, orders, and property. Best-known are the LATERAN TREATY with Italy (1929) and the **Concordat of 1801** between Pius VII and Bonaparte, which restored the Roman Church in France. In 1905 France repudiated it and separated Church and state.

Concordia (kŏngkôr'dhyä), city (pop. 52,213), NE Argentina, port on Uruguay R. opposite Salto, Uruguay. One of chief towns of the Argentine Mesopotamia, it exports meat, mate, quebracho, and grain.

Concordia, city (pop. 7,175), N Kansas, on Republic R. and N of Salina. Trade center for wheat, livestock, and poultry area.

concretion (kŏnkrē'shŭn), rounded mass occurring in sedimentary rock and differing from it in composition (e.g., flint nodules in chalk).

Condé (kōdā'), French princely family, cadet branch of house of BOURBON. It originated with **Louis I de Bourbon, prince de Condé** (lwē' dù bōōrbō'), 1530–69, Protestant leader and general. He took part in conspiracy of AMBOISE (1560), commanded Huguenots in Wars of Religion, fell at Jarnac. His great-grandson **Louis II de Bourbon, prince de Condé,** known as **the Great Condé,** 1621–86, won major victories in the Thirty Years War at Rocroi (1643), Freiburg (1644), Nördlingen (1645), Lens (1648). In the FRONDE he turned against his government, taking command of the army of princes in 1651 and of the Spanish army in 1653. Defeated by Turenne, notably in Battle of the Dunes (1658), he was pardoned in 1659 by Louis XIV, for whom he fought successfully in the Dutch War. He was the brother of Armand de CONTI and of Mme de LONGUEVILLE. His great-grandson, **Louis Joseph de Bourbon, prince de Condé** (zhōzĕf'), 1736–1818, formed the "army of Condé" against the French revolutionary forces (dissolved 1801). He was the grandfather of the duc d'ENGHIEN.

condensation, in physics, change in state of substance from gas to liquid. Velocity and distance between molecules of gas are so decreased by heat withdrawal that substance condenses. Dew, fog, and clouds are formed as a result of condensation of water vapor in atmosphere.

condenser, device to increase capacity of conductor for receiving and holding greater electrical charge. LEYDEN JAR is a simple type. Principle is induction. Used in telephone, radio, and ignition system of automobile. Apparatus causing condensation of gas is also called a condenser.

Condillac, Étienne Bonnot de (kōdēyäk'), 1715–80, French philosopher, a priest. He started from Locke's ideas and stressed that all psychological processes in an individual are derived from sensations, and that general ideas are built by experience through the medium of language. This sensationalism, expounded in his *Traité des sensations* (1754), was much discussed and influenced later psychologists. His attempts to arrive at exact terms for social and economic concepts had a clarifying effect in French thought.

condor (kŏn'dŭr), South American vulture which nests on Andean peaks. California condor or vulture (now rare) lives in North American coastal ranges; it is one of largest birds of prey, with wingspread of 9–10 ft.

Condorcet, Antoine Nicolas, marquis de (kōdôrsā'), 1743–94, French philosopher, mathematician, and revolutionist. He was a friend of most of the leading intellectuals of his day. He made valuable contributions to the mathematical theory of probabilities. An enthusiastic supporter of the revolution, he was active politically until he protested the persecution of the Girondists. He was denounced and went into hiding. There he completed his great philosophical work, a historical sketch outlining the progress of man to the French Revolution, which he thought would usher in perfection of human state. Captured by his enemies, he died mysteriously and immediately.

condottiere (kōndôt-tyä'rä), leader of mercenary soldiers in Renaissance Italy. Condottieri hired their own bands, fought for highest bidder, often changed allegiance. Well-known condottieri were Muzio Attendolo Sforza, Colleoni, Sir John de Hawkwood.

conducting, in music, art of unifying the efforts of a number of musicians playing ensemble. Until c.1600 the conductor was primarily a time-beater, using a roll of music as a baton. In the baroque era the group was at first led by the harpsichordist, later by the first violinist, even today called the concertmaster. The nonplaying conductor, using a baton, appeared in the 19th cent. Beethoven, Mendelssohn, and Wagner often conducted; Hans von Bülow was the first of the modern virtuoso conductors.

conduction. 1 Transfer of heat energy from one part of substance to adjoining part, from molecule to molecule. Substances that readily transfer heat are conductors, e.g., metals; those that do so slowly are insulators, e.g., nonmetals, fluids. **2** Transfer of charge of electricity from one point to another. Metals are good conductors; nonmetals are insulators. Electric wires are insulated to prevent escape of charge during conduction.

cone, the fruit of most conifers. Staminate (male) and ovulate (female) cones are borne on same tree, but hard, woody ovulate cones are ones commonly seen. Among largest are the 10–20 in. cones of sugar pine of W U.S.; most are 1–6 in. long.

cone, in mathematics, a surface (called a conical surface), generated by a moving line (generator) which passes through a given point (vertex) and continually intersects a given fixed curve (directrix). A cone is also the solid bounded by such a surface.

Conecuh, river: see ESCAMBIA, river.

Conemaugh (kŏn'ùmô''), river of SW Pa. rising in Alleghenies, and flowing c.70 mi. NW to branch of Allegheny R. Flood control projects are on river.

Conestoga wagon, freight-carrying vehicle originated in Conestoga region of Pennsylvania c.1725. Used by farmers and later in commerce with frontier settlements until c.1850. Large wagons, drawn by six horses, carried up to eight tons. Bottom of the wagon box curved upward at both ends; white hood over wagon was protection against elements.

coney: see CONY.

Coney Island, Atlantic beach resort, N.Y.: see BROOKLYN, New York city.

Confederacy or **Confederate States of America** (1861–65), government estab. by Southern states of U.S. which seceded from Union. When Pres. Lincoln was elected, seven states seceded—S.C., Ga., La., Miss., Fla., Ala., and Texas. Provisional government was set up at Montgomery, Ala., and a constitution drafted. After firing on Fort Sumter and Lincoln's call for troops, four more states joined—Ark., N.C., Va., and Tenn. Richmond, Va., became capital, and Jefferson DAVIS and Alexander H. Stephens were elected president and vice president. Judah P. Benjamin was outstanding member of cabinet. Story of Confederacy was story of loss of Civil War. Its citizens bore privations and invasion with bravery and courage, loyal to end. Refused recognition by England and France, which did recognize Northern blockade of Southern ports. Volunteers were insufficient; conscription used but opposed. Financial troubles were heavy from start, and paper money became worthless. Mounting Union victories made end inevitable. Confederacy fell after Lee's surrender in April, 1865.

Confederate cruisers. In Civil War, Confederacy set out to destroy North's merchant marine. Of some 18 cruisers *Florida, Alabama,* and *Shenandoah* were outstanding. *Florida* took some 60 prizes before her capture in 1864. *Alabama* took almost 70, causing over $6,000,-000 damage as settled in Alabama claims. She was sunk by U.S.S. *Kearsarge,* July, 1864. *Shenandoah* took 38 prizes; she reverted to U.S. Raids caused decline of nation's merchant marine.

Confederate States of America: see Confederacy.

Confederation, Articles of, in U.S. history, ratified in 1781 and superseded by Constitution of U.S. in 1789. Proved unsatisfactory because of subordinate position occupied by central government; Congress was dependent upon states for funds and execution of its decrees. Government commanded little respect because of weaknesses. Most significant achievement was Ordinance of 1787.

confederation, Canadian: see British North America Act.

Confederation of the Rhine, league of German princes, formed 1806 under protection of Napoleon I. Members included Bavaria, Württemberg, Saxony, Westphalia, Baden. Confederation broke apart in 1813.

confession, formal admission of criminal guilt, usually made in the course of examination by the police or by the prosecutor or at the trial. To be admissible must be made voluntarily—not induced by torture, threat, or promises.

confession, in religion: see Penance.

Confession of Augsburg: see Creed.

confirmation: see Sacrament.

conflict of laws, situation arising when the law of more than one territorial unit may be applied to a case; also the legal rules governing such conflicts. In Europe this branch of law is frequently called private international law. In the U.S. the variance of laws from state to state makes the subject of conflict of laws urgent. Certain provisions of the U.S. Constitution—notably the "full faith and credit" clause of Article 4, Section 1—limit the freedom of the states in deciding cases and in certain cases compel one state to treat as valid a judgment rendered in another state which had proper jurisdiction.

Confucius (kŭnfū'shŭs), Chinese *K'ung Fu-tse,* 551–479 B.C., Chinese ethical teacher. Though his life is surrounded by later legend, it is known that he was born in the feudal state of Lu, that he was a public official, and that he and his followers urged social reform. In the midst of warfare, corruption and tyranny, he urged a system of morality and statecraft to bring about peace, justice, and universal order. His teachings became the basis of the moral system of **Confucianism** (kŭnfū'shŭnĭzŭm), which was of course based on earlier ideas and was developed in some of the most important works of Chinese literature, including the *Analects* (sayings of Confucius and his disciples), classic works supposedly edited by Confucius, and the writings of Mencius. The basic moral principle of the system is the maintenance of *jen* (roughly, sympathy) between men by keeping right relationships: treat those who are subordinate to you as you would be treated by those in positions superior to yours. This is the Confucian Golden Rule. Filial piety is heavily stressed and became more dominant as the system endured, but Confucianism created a

universal pattern for government, with emphasis on the middle way, avoidance of extreme. Originally atheistic, Confucianism was later colored by religious elements from earlier beliefs, and the hierarchy of relationships was capped by Shang-Ti [ruler of heaven], the superior of earthly rulers. Confucius was himself deified. Confucianism was triumphant by the 1st cent. A.D. Though it had to contend with Taoism and Buddhism and was often eclipsed by them, the actual system of government continued with Confucian principles. In the Sung dynasty (960–1279), the system was revised as Neo-Confucianism, opposing the meditation and quietism of the other religions by stress on improvement through acquiring knowledge. This remained dominant until the 20th cent. though it gradually rigidified the system of respectful relationship into a conservative approval of the existing social order.

Congaree (kŏng'gŭrē), river, central S.C., formed by junction of Broad and Saluda rivers at Columbia. Flows 52 mi. SE to Wateree R., forming Suntee R.

Congo (kŏng'gō), river, c.2,900 mi. long, 2d longest in Africa. Drainage basin (c.1,450,000 sq. mi.) includes Belgian Congo and much of S French Equatorial Africa and N Angola. Its upper course, from its rise in SE Belgian Congo to Stanley Falls, is called the Lualaba. Forms border of French Equatorial Africa and broadens into Stanley Pool, beyond which begin Livingstone Falls in which the river drops 852 ft. in 220 mi. Its estuary forms Angola border. Its mouth was discovered 1482 by the Portuguese navigator Diogo Cão. Livingstone explored area around upper course 1867–73, Sir Henry Stanley made first known descent to the mouth 1874–77.

Congo, Belgian: see Belgian Congo.

Congo Free State: see Belgian Congo.

Congregationalism, type of Protestant organization in which each local church has free control of its own affairs. It has no bishops or presbyteries. Movement arose in 16th and 17th cent. in England in revolt of Separatists against formalized worship and state control of Established Church. Robert Browne published in 1582 first exposition of Congregational principles. Pilgrims brought Congregationalism to America in 1620. Cambridge Platform was adopted (1648), and Congregationalists took leading part in Great Awakening. Natl. Council of Congregational Churches of the U.S. formed 1871; in 1931 it merged with Christian Church to form General Council of the Congregational and Christian Churches of the U.S.

Congress, Library of: see Library of Congress.

Congress of Industrial Organizations (C.I.O.), originally Committee for Industrial Organization, formed 1935 by affiliates of the A.F. of L. to unionize mass-production workers by industries rather than by crafts. First leader was John L. Lewis. The A.F. of L. expelled (1937) the C.I.O. unions. Powerful in C.I.O. are United Steel Workers and the United Automobile Workers. Lewis and his United Mine Workers left C.I.O. in 1942. Philip Murray, president (1940–52), was succeeded by Walter Reuther. C.I.O. noted for vigorous organizational drives and political activity.

Congress of the United States, legislative branch of Federal government, instituted in 1789 by Article 1 of U.S. Constitution, which prescribes its membership and defines its powers. Congress is composed of two houses, the Senate and the House of Representatives. The Senators, two from each state, have six-year terms and were chosen by the state legislatures until 1913, when the Seventeenth Amendment, providing for their direct popular election, went into force. The terms of one third of the Senators expire every two years. A Senator must be at least 30 years old, not less than nine years a U.S. citizen, and a resident of the state in which he is elected. The Vice President of the United States presides over the Senate, voting only in case of a tie. Representatives are apportioned to the states according to their populations in the Federal census, every state being entitled to at least one Representative. Representatives are chosen for two-year terms, and the entire body comes up for reelection every two years. A Representative must be 25 or older, at least seven years a U.S. citizen, and an inhabitant of the state in which he is elected. The presiding officer of the House, the speaker, is elected by the members of the House. The two houses have an equal voice in legislation, though revenue bills must originate in the House of Representatives. The Senate, regarded as the more powerful body, must ratify all treaties and confirm important presidential appointments.

Congreve, William, 1670–1729, English Restoration dramatist, known for cynical, witty comedies. Among them are *The Old Bachelor* (1693), *The Double Dealer* (1693), *Love for Love* (1695), and his masterpiece *The Way of the World* (1700). His tragedy, *The Mourning Bride* (1697), popular in his day, is now best remembered for lyrics, "Music hath charms" and "Hell hath no fury." Congreve, Vanbrugh, and others attacked for immorality by Jeremy Collier.

conic section (kŏ′nĭk), any curve made by intersection of a right circular conical surface and a plane. These curves are the CIRCLE, ELLIPSE, PARABOLA, HYPERBOLA. If plane passes through vertex, result is a point, straight line, or pair of intersecting lines; these are called degenerate conic sections.

conifer (kŏ′nĭfûr), tree or shrub of order Coniferales, usually evergreen and cone-bearing, e.g., PINE, SPRUCE, CYPRESS, SEQUOIA.

Conjeeveram (kŭnjē′vŭrŭm), city (pop. 74,635), E Madras, India. Sacred to Hindus; known as Benares of the South. As cap. of Pallava empire (c.300–c.750), it was a Brahmanical and Buddhist center. Officially called Kanchipuram.

conjunctivitis, inflammation of membrane covering eyelids and front of eyeball. Infectious forms caused by microorganisms include gonococcal conjunctivitis (see GONORRHEA) and pinkeye.

Conkling, Roscoe, 1829–88, American politician. U.S. Representative from N.Y. (1859–63, 1865–67); U.S. Senator (1867–81). When Pres. James A. GARFIELD ignored him in appointing a collector of the port of New York, this Old Guard leader and Republican state "boss" resigned from the Senate in protest.

Connaught (kŏ′nôt), province (6,611 sq. mi.; pop. 492,-797), W Ireland; comprises counties MAYO, SLIGO, LEITRIM, ROSCOMMON, and GALWAY. Was an ancient kingdom of Ireland. Has some agr., but poor soil.

Conneaut (kŏ′nēŏt″), city (pop. 10,230), NE Ohio, on L. Erie near Pa. line; settled 1799. Lake and rail shipping (iron, coal, steel) center with mfg. of tin cans and communication equipment.

Conneaut Lake, NW Pa., S of L. Erie. Largest natural lake in state.

Connecticut, state (4,899 sq. mi.; pop. 2,007,280), NE U.S.; one of Thirteen Colonies; cap. HARTFORD. NEW HAVEN, BRIDGEPORT, WATERBURY important cities. Bordered S by Long Isl. Sound. Highlands rise gently from coastal plains of Sound, divided by CONNECTICUT R. and its valley, drained E by THAMES R., W by HOUSATONIC R. Mainly industrial, mfg. of metal products (machinery, firearms, clocks, typewriters, hardware), textiles, rubber products; printing, publishing. Farming yields dairy and poultry products, broadleaf tobacco, truck. Fishing, some mining. Connecticut R. discovered 1614 by Adriaen Block (Dutch). Pilgrims of Plymouth Colony estab. trading post 1633, were joined by Puritans from Mass. Bay. FUNDAMENTAL ORDERS adopted 1639. New Haven colony was included under 1662 royal charter. Had semi-liberal religious system, with Congregationalism as official faith. Contributed men, supplies to American Revolution. Oliver ELLSWORTH helped frame U.S. Constitution; Conn. one of first to ratify it. Settled WYOMING VALLEY dispute 1782. Gave up W land claims (1786), except WESTERN RESERVE. Hurt by Embargo Act of 1807, War of 1812; resentment led to HARTFORD CON-

VENTION. Congregational church disestablished by new state constitution (1818). Mfg. grew steadily after decline of shipping. Conn. inventors include Eli WHITNEY. Two world wars greatly expanded industries. SW Conn. has suburbs of New York city.

Connecticut, largest river in New England, c.350 mi. long, rising in lakes in extreme N N.H. and flowing S along Vt.-N.H. line, then across Mass. (past Springfield) and Conn. (past Hartford) to Long Isl. Sound at Old Saybrook. Upper course used for power. Lower valley is good farm land. Great damage done by 1936 flood and 1938 hurricane. Congress authorized flood-control project 1936.

Connecticut, University of: see MANSFIELD, Conn.

Connecticut College: see NEW LONDON, Conn.

Connecticut Lakes, three lakes, N N.H.; source of Connecticut R.

Connecticut Reserve: see WESTERN RESERVE.

Connecticut Wits or **Hartford Wits,** literary group (late 18th–early 19th cent.), mostly Yale men. Attacked anti-Federalists. Representative were Joel BARLOW, Timothy DWIGHT, Theodore DWIGHT, John TRUMBULL.

Connellsville, city (pop. 13,293), SW Pa., on Youghiogheny R. and SE of Pittsburgh; settled c.1770. Mfg. of coke, metal products, and glass. H. C. Frick was attacked here during Homestead strike (1892).

Connelly, Marc(us Cook), 1890–, American dramatist. His Pulitzer Prize play, *The Green Pastures* (1930) is based on Roark Bradford's *Ol' Man Adam an' His Chillun*.

Connemara (kŏnŭmä′rù), wild, mountainous region, W Co. Galway, Ireland. Has many lakes and streams.

Connersville, city (pop. 15,550), E Ind., on Whitewater R. and E of Indianapolis; laid out 1817. Rail center. Mfg. of metal and enamel products.

Connolly, James, 1870–1916, Irish republican leader and socialist. In U.S. (1903–10) helped to organize the I.W.W., but for Ireland believed that the nationalist cause came before socialism.

Conolly, John, 1794–1866, English physician, who introduced humane treatment of insane at Hanwell Asylum, where he abolished mechanical restraints.

Conon (kŏ′nŏn), d. after 392 B.C., Athenian commander in the Peloponnesian War. The fleet under his command was defeated at Aegospotamos (405 B.C.), but later with Persian help he defeated the Spartans off Cnidus (394 B.C.). When Persian favor turned toward Sparta, Conon's fortune fell.

Conon, 3d cent. B.C., Greek astronomer.

Conowingo Dam, NE Md., on Susquehanna R., 4,648 ft. long and 105 ft. high, completed 1927. Here is Conowingo village. Conowingo L. extends 14 mi. N.

Conrad, rulers of Holy Roman Empire. **Conrad I,** d. 918, duke of Franconia, elected German king 911. Unable to impose his authority on great feudal dukes. Designated his ablest foe, Henry the Fowler (Henry I), as successor. **Conrad II,** c.990–1039, duke of Franconia, elected German king 1024, crowned emperor 1027. Suppressed several revolts of his vassals; annexed kingdom of ARLES or Burgundy (1033); intervened energetically in Italian troubles (1026–27, 1035–37); promoted lesser nobility and officials of low birth to affirm his authority in Germany and Italy. **Conrad III,** c.1093–1152, German king (1138–52); nephew of Henry V and founder of the HOHENSTAUFEN dynasty. Antiking to LOTHAIR II from 1127. Warred against Guelphs (see GUELPHS AND GHIBELLINES). Took part in Second Crusade. **Conrad IV,** 1228–54, German king (1237–54), king of Sicily and Jerusalem (1250–54); son of Emperor FREDERICK II. Several antikings challenged his rule in Germany after 1246 and in Italy after 1251, in both cases at the behest of Pope INNOCENT IV, his implacable enemy, who excommunicated him in 1254. His son CONRADIN was the last of the Hohenstaufen to rule.

Conrad, d. 1192, king of Jerusalem (1192), marquis of Montferrat, leader in Third Crusade. Saved Tyre from

the Saracens and became its lord (1187). Sought to displace Guy of LUSIGNAN as king by marrying Isabella, daughter of Amalric I. Acknowledged king, he was mysteriously assassinated. Title passed to two later husbands of Isabella—Henry, count of Champagne (reigned 1192–97), and Amalric II.

Conrad, Joseph, 1857–1924, Polish-born English novelist, originally Teodor Jozef Konrad Korzeniowski. A sailor, he became an officer in the British merchant fleet and a British citizen; after retirement in 1894 wrote novels and short stories in English, with notable, fluid style. Among his novels (laid mostly in South Seas, Malaya, and Indonesia) are *Almayer's Folly* (1895), *An Outcast of the Islands* (1896), *The Nigger of the "Narcissus"* (pub., 1897, as *The Children of the Sea*), *Lord Jim* (1900), *Typhoon* (1903), *Victory* (1915), *The Arrow of Gold* (1919). Most celebrated short story "Youth." His chief theme is demoralizing effect of isolation.

Conradi, Hermann (hĕr′män kônrä′dē), 1862–90, German author, leading exponent of naturalist school. Best known for *Lieder eines Sünders* [songs of a sinner] (1887) and *Adam Mensch* (1889).

Conradin (kŏn′rŭdĭn), 1252–68, duke of Swabia, last legitimate Hohenstaufen; son of Conrad IV. Claimed Sicily after death of his uncle MANFRED. Defeated by Charles of Anjou (Charles I of NAPLES) at Tagliacozzo; beheaded at Naples.

Conrad the Red, d. 955, duke of Lorraine (944–53). Conspired against his father-in-law, Otto I, allied himself with invading Magyars (954), but later submitted and died fighting Magyars on Lechfeld.

Conrad von Hötzendorf, Franz, Graf (fränts′ gräf′ kôn′rät fŭn hût′sŭndôrf), 1852–1925, Austro-Hungarian field marshal. Chief of staff 1906–11, 1912–17. Fanatic promoter of war on Serbia.

Conroe (kŏn′rō), city (pop. 7,298), S Texas, NNW of Houston. Center of oil and timber area, it has recycling and carbon-black plants.

Conscience, Hendrik (kōsēäs′), 1812–83, Flemish novelist, a founder of modern Flemish literature. His works include historical novels (e.g., *The Lion of Flanders*, 1838) and stories of village life (e.g., *Ricke ticke tack*, 1851).

conscientious objector, person who, on grounds of membership in a pacific sect or personal ethical views, passively resists military service. Democracies in world wars faced problem concerning them: how to uphold both personal freedom and authority of the state. U.S. and Great Britain allowed objectors of recognized sects to enter noncombat service, but segregated or imprisoned others.

consciousness, in general a person's awareness of the environment; more specifically, the manner in which he is aware. Freudian psychology distinguishes the conscious (actual awareness) from unconscious (store of experience not recognized by individual). Sometimes consciousness is used to mean the sum of self-understood activities that constitute individual personality.

conscription, compulsory enrollment of personnel for service in the armed forces, as opposed to voluntary service. Enforced service was known from the earliest days of history and was customary in Greece and Rome. The first modern national law conscripting soldiers was, however, that adopted in the French Revolution. In the course of the 19th cent. the practice was adopted in most major European nations. Great Britain accepted conscription in World War I. In the U.S., conscription was practiced on a large scale in the Civil War (see SELECTIVE SERVICE; UNIVERSAL MILITARY TRAINING).

conservation of energy: see ENERGY.

conservation of natural resources, prevention of waste of man's physical environment, including wildlife, timber, fertile topsoil, and pasture. Conservation long practiced in Europe, was forwarded in U.S. by creation of a U.S. commissioner of fish and fisheries

(1871), a forestry bureau (1891), the National Conservation Commission (1909), and the National Park Service (1916). Theodore Roosevelt and Gifford Pinchot outstanding leaders. New Deal forwarded conservation with CCC, TVA, and water-control programs.

Conservative party, British political party, continuation of TORY group which began at end of 17th cent. Name first popularized in 1830. Tory reformers George Canning and Robert PEEL killed old reactionary Tory party by Reform Bill of 1832. Party split over corn laws issue, 1846. Returned to power 1874–80, revitalized by "Tory democracy" and imperialism program of DISRAELI. In office 1885–1905 (with two brief intervals), it split over tariff reforms of Joseph CHAMBERLAIN, with consequent Liberal ascendancy until World War I coalition. Aside from Labour victories in 1924 and 1929 party maintained leadership (1922–40) despite appeasement policies. World War II brought new coalition under Conservative Winston Churchill. After 1945–51 Labour government, Conservatives returned to power under Churchill.

Conshohocken, borough (pop. 10,922), SE Pa., on Schuylkill R. and NW of Philadelphia; settled 1831. Mfg. of steel, automobile tires, and metal products.

Considérant, Victor Prosper (vĕktôr′ prōspâr′ kōsēdärä′), 1808–93, French social theorist and reformer, follower of Fourier.

conspiracy, agreement of two or more persons to commit a criminal or unlawful act, with some overt words or acts to that end. In medieval England conspiracy was only a combination to abuse judicial procedure; later meaning was broader. Some acts lawful when done by an individual are illegal if the aim of a conspiracy. Under this doctrine labor unions were long prosecuted for strikes but later legislation in Great Britain (1875) and U.S. (Norris-LaGuardia Act, 1932) halted this practice.

Constable, John, 1776–1837, English painter, famous for landscapes. *The Hay Wain* created sensation 1824 at Louvre and is said to have profoundly impressed Delacroix. Used broken color with freedom extraordinary in his day. Admired classical painting but worked directly from nature.

Constance, 1152–98, consort of Emperor HENRY VI; mother of Emperor FREDERICK II. Her nephew, William II of Sicily, named her as his successor, but the Sicilians crowned TANCRED instead. Warfare resulted between Tancred and Henry, who was crowned at Palermo after Tancred's death (1194).

Constance, Ger. *Konstanz*, city (pop. 42,209), S Baden, SW Germany, at W end of L. of Constance. Textile and clothing mfg. Founded as Roman fort 4th cent. A.D.; episcopal see from c.580; made free imperial city 1192. Here in 1183 Emperor Frederick I recognized LOMBARD LEAGUE. At Council of Constance John Huss was burned (1415). In 1548 Charles V punished Constance for joining SCHMALKALDIC LEAGUE by abrogating its freedom and awarding it to Austria. City passed to Baden 1805; bishopric was secularized 1802–3; diocese was abolished 1827. Among many historical buildings are the 11th-cent. minster and the Dominican convent where the council was held (now a hotel).

Constance, Council of, 1414–18, council of the Roman Catholic Church, in part considered ecumenical. It was called to end the Great SCHISM, which had produced three rival popes: GREGORY XII (since considered canonical, i.e., legal), John XXIII (see COSSA, BALDASSARRE), and Benedict XIII (see LUNA, PEDRO DE). It also was intended to reform the Church and end heresy. The conciliar theory (that councils are superior to the pope) was actively advanced, and the council was organized on national lines. Gregory resigned, John and Benedict were deposed, and MARTIN V was named pope. Measures of reform were adopted but were rather inconsequential. John HUSS, who had come to the council with a safe-conduct of

Emperor SIGISMUND, was nevertheless burned at the stake for heresy (1415), as was JEROME OF PRAGUE the next year. The rulings on the power of councils were never effective.

Constance, Lake of, Ger. *Bodensee,* lake, 208 sq. mi., bordered by Switzerland, Germany, and Austria. Formed by the Rhine, it divides near Constance into two arms. Remains of lake dwellings have been found.

Constans (kŏn'stănz), Roman and Byzantine emperors. **Constans I,** b. 320 or 323, d. 350; youngest son of Constantine I. Shared empire with his brothers CONSTANTINE II and CONSTANTIUS II upon his father's death (337). His vices and extortions led to his murder. **Constans II,** 630–68, Byzantine emperor (642–68). Forbade discussion of MONOTHELETISM; arrested and banished Pope Martin I. Fought Moslems successfully; reorganized imperial administration. Was assassinated.

Constant (de Rebecque), Benjamin (bĕzhämē' kôstä' dù rübĕk'), 1767–1830, French author and political theorist, b. Switzerland. His liaison with Mme de STAËL (1794–1809) was a tempestuous one. An advocate of constitutional monarchy, he generally opposed but occasionally supported both Napoleon and the Bourbons. His reputation as a writer rests on the introspective and quasi-autobiographical short novel *Adolphe* (1816; Eng. tr., 1908). A similar novel, *Cécile,* was first published 1951.

Constant, (Jean Joseph) Benjamin (bĕzhämē' kôstä'), 1845–1902, French painter. His Oriental scenes, influenced by a journey to Morocco, are remarkable in color, drama, and technique. Did portraits (e.g., Queen Victoria, Queen Alexandra).

Constant, Paul Henri Benjamin, baron d'Estournelles de: see ESTOURNELLES DE CONSTANT.

Constanta (kônstän'tsä), city (pop. 78,586), SE Rumania, in Dobruja; chief Rumanian Black Sea port. Oil pipeline to Ploesti. Founded 4th cent. A.D. by Constantine I.

Constantine (kŏn'stŭntēn, –tīn), Roman and Byzantine emperors. **Constantine I** (the Great), 288?–337, son of CONSTANTIUS I and St. HELENA. Though proclaimed emperor on his father's death at York (306), he was content with the title Caesar until the death of GALERIUS (310), which left four contestants for the imperial office. In the ensuing struggle, Constantine and LICINIUS joined against MAXENTIUS and MAXIMIN, whom they overwhelmed in 312. They then ruled as co-emperors (Constantine in the West, Licinius in the East) until they fell out in 324; Licinius lost his life in the struggle, leaving Constantine sole emperor. Constantine, already attracted by Christianity, had allegedly seen a flaming cross in the sky as the sign by which he would conquer just before his crucial victory at the MILVIAN BRIDGE (312). In 313 he and Licinius established toleration for Christianity by the Edict of Milan. His interest in Christianity continued, though he was baptized only on his deathbed, and in 325 he convened the epoch-making Council of NICAEA. In a reign of peace he rebuilt the empire on a basis of absolutism. He shifted his cap. to CONSTANTINOPLE (330), which he dedicated to the Virgin. At his death he divided the empire among his sons CONSTANS I, CONSTANTIUS II, and **Constantine II,** 316–40, who received Britain, Gaul, and Spain. Feeling cheated in the division, he warred with Constans I, but was killed while invading Italy. **Constantine IV** (Pogonatus), d. 685; Byzantine emperor (668–85). Answered annual naval attacks of Moslems with GREEK FIRE; ceded land S of the Danube to Bulgars after being defeated by them (679); called Third Council of CONSTANTINOPLE (680). **Constantine V** (Copronymus), 718–75, Byzantine emperor (740–75). Able administrator. His rigorous support of ICONOCLASM caused Pope Stephen III to transfer Rome to protection of Pepin the Short. **Constantine VI,** b. c.770, Byzantine emperor (780–97). His mother IRENE was regent, then co-empress (792). In

797 she took advantage of his unpopularity to have him deposed and blinded. **Constantine VII** (Porphyrogenitus), 905–59, Byzantine emperor. His reign (912–59) was interrupted by usurpation of ROMANUS I (919–44). Fostered learning and legal reform. Was a scholar and assiduous writer. **Constantine XI** (Paleologus), d. 1453, last Byzantine emperor (1448–53). Proclaimed union of E and W churches to secure aid from West against Turks (1452). No help came. In 1453 he defended Constantinople for two months against the 20 times superior army of Mohammed II. Died fighting when Turks stormed city.

Constantine, 1868–1923, king of the Hellenes (1913–17, 1920–22). Opposed Premier VENIZELOS in World War I; was forced to abdicate by Allied pressure (1917). Recalled in 1920, he was again deposed after the Turks defeated the Greeks at Smyrna.

Constantine, fortified city (pop. 80,233), E Algeria; a major trade center. Originally a Carthaginian settlement. As Cirta it was cap. of Numidia and vital shipping point in Roman grain supply. Destroyed A.D. 311 in civil war; rebuilt by Constantine I. Taken 1837 by the French.

Constantine, Donation of, document supposed to be a grant by Constantine I of great temporal authority in Italy to the pope. It actually was forged, presumably to enhance papal claims to territory to build what became the Papal States. In practice it had no great effect, but it was important in giving Lorenzo Valla the chance to demonstrate critical methods in proving it false, and his firm, clear argument is called the beginning of modern textual criticism.

Constantine the African, c.1020–c.1087, translator of Arabic works (esp. on medicine) into Latin.

Constantinople, former capital of the Byzantine and Ottoman empires (for modern city, see ISTANBUL). Founded by and named for CONSTANTINE I at ancient BYZANTIUM as new cap. of Roman Empire (A.D. 330), it shared the glory and vicissitudes of the Byzantine Empire, which was finally nearly identical with the city and environs. Only three of many sieges were successful: by the army of the Fourth Crusade (1204), by MICHAEL VIII (1261), and by Sultan MOHAMMED II (1453). Built upon seven hills on the Bosporus and surrounded by a triple wall of fortifications, it was the largest city of medieval Europe, a barbed fortress enclosing a sea of magnificent palaces and gilded domes and towers. At its greatest period (10th cent.) it had c.1,000,000 inhabitants. The Church of HAGIA SOPHIA, the sacred palace of the emperors, the huge hippodrome, and the Golden Gate were its best-known monuments. Its artistic and literary wealth before it was sacked (1204; 1453) was almost inconceivable. Nearly depopulated when it fell to the Turks, it soon revived under the Sultans (whose court was called the Sublime Porte) as a great European center. After World War I it was occupied by the Allies (1918–23). Ankara replaced it as Turkish cap. in 1923.

Constantinople, Councils of, 2d, 5th, 6th, and 8th ecumenical councils of the Roman Catholic Church. **1** Convened (381) by Emperor Theodosius I to confirm the acts of the First Council of Nicaea, it is said to have composed the final Nicene Creed. Declared St. Gregory Nazianzen bishop of Constantinople and appointed his successor when he died. On death of St. Meletius made Flavian of Antioch president, thus prolonging Antiochene schism. Declared against various heresies, and made bishop of Constantinople second only to the pope. **2** Convened (553) by Emperor Justinian I and dominated by him, it condemned the Nestorian writings called the Three Chapters and seems also to have declared Pope Vigilius deposed. Its canons are lost. **3** Convened (680) by Emperor Constantine IV, it condemned the heresy of MONOTHELETISM and condemned several churchmen as Monothelites (including HONORIUS I—a point much discussed). The Oriental Council of 692, called by

Justinian II, is considered in the East a continuation of this council, but is called in the West the Trullan Synod [from Trullo, the dome of the palace]. It made the Apostolic Constitutions binding. **4** Convened (869) at the suggestion of Emperor Basil I, it confirmed the condemnation of PHOTIUS and the restoration of St. IGNATIUS OF CONSTANTINOPLE. It is not recognized by the Orthodox Church, which recognizes instead the council of 880 that supported Photius. The two councils mark the bitter division of Eastern and Western churches.

Constantinople, Latin Empire of, 1204–61, feudal empire established in S Balkans and Greek archipelago by leaders of Fourth Crusade (see CRUSADES). It was modeled on Latin Kingdom of JERUSALEM. BALDWIN I, HENRY OF FLANDERS, ROBERT OF COURTENAY, JOHN OF BRIENNE, and BALDWIN II were rulers. It deteriorated at once after its creation, beset by Greek rulers of NICAEA and EPIRUS, by the Bulgars under IVAN II, by the Turks, and by internal discord. Constantinople was taken by MICHAEL VIII, who restored the Byzantine Empire (1261), but Venice retained most of Greek isles; ATHENS passed to Catalans; Achaia was kept by VILLEHARDOUIN family.

Constantius (kŭnstăn'shŭs), name of several Roman emperors. **Constantius I,** c.250–306, was a general who put away St. Helena (mother of CONSTANTINE I) to marry the daughter of Maximian and become (293) subemperor under Maximian. He was successful as commander in Gaul and Britain. When Diocletian and Maximian abdicated (305), he and Galerius became emperors, but the next year he died at York. Constantine took up his claim. **Constantius II,** 317–61, was son of Constantine I. After 337 he shared the empire with his brothers, CONSTANS I and CONSTANTINE II. Constantine was killed in 340, Constans I murdered in 350. Constantius put down revolt and held sole rule. He advocated ARIANISM. Trouble in Gaul and in Persia caused Constantius to rely on his cousin and general Julian (JULIAN THE APOSTATE), but Julian's men revolted against Constantius, who died on the journey to quell them. **Constantius III,** d. 421, was a general of Honorius. After the murder of his rival ATAULF, he married Ataulf's widow and the emperor's sister, GALLA PLACIDIA. In 421 he became joint emperor but died in a few months.

Constellation, U.S. frigate, launched in 1797. Won victories over French frigates *Insurgente* (Feb., 1799) and VENGEANCE (Feb., 1800). Made a stationary ship at Newport, R.I. (1894).

constellation (kŏnstĭlā'shŭn), originally a configuration formed by a group of stars. The meaning was later extended to refer to 88 areas (boundaries officially estab. 1928) filling sky, in terms of which heavenly bodies are located. Brighter stars are designated (according to Bayer's system), usually in order of brightness, by Greek letters and Latin genitive of constellation in which they lie, e.g., Alpha Tauri, brightest star in Taurus. See also ZODIAC.

Constitution, U.S. 44-gun frigate, nicknamed *Old Ironsides,* launched 1797; perhaps the most famous U.S. naval vessel. Won great sea battle with British vessel *Guerrière* on Aug. 19, 1812. Rebuilt by public subscription in 1925; maintained at Boston navy yard.

constitution, the fundamental principles of government in a nation, either implied in its laws, institutions, and customs or embodied in one document or in several. In the first category is the British constitution; it is termed *flexible,* for it may be modified by an ordinary act of Parliament or by judicial decisions. The **Constitution of the United States** is classified as *rigid*—one that has superior sanction to ordinary laws of the land and that is subject to a gradual process of AMENDMENT. Statutory elaboration and judicial construction (see SUPREME COURT, UNITED STATES, and MARSHALL, JOHN) have been erected on the base of the written document drawn up at the FEDERAL CONSTITUTIONAL CONVENTION (1787). The Constitution (see FEDERALIST PAPERS; MADISON, JAMES), signed on Sept. 17, 1787, and ratified by the required number of states (nine) by June 21, 1788, superseded original charter of U.S. in force since 1781 (see CONFEDERATION, ARTICLES OF) and estab. system of Federal government which began to function in 1789. The Constitution's brevity and its general statement of principles have, by accident more than by design, made possible the extension of meaning that has fostered growth. There are but seven articles and a Preamble; 22 amendments have been adopted. The Preamble's first words, "We the People of the United States," have been used against STATES' RIGHTS advocates. Another phrase of the Preamble, "to . . . promote the general Welfare," has been used to uphold much recent social legislation. The articles set up the legislative, executive, and judicial branches of government and provide for their powers; they also handle problems of the relationships of the states to the Federal government. The first nine amendments, which constitute the Bill of Rights (Tenth Amendment generally considered a part), were added within two years as a result of widespread feeling that Constitution insufficiently guaranteed individual liberties. Remaining amendments provide for matters ranging from income tax to woman suffrage.

Constitutional Convention: see FEDERAL CONSTITUTIONAL CONVENTION.

Constitutional Union party, in U.S. history, organized just before election of 1860. Recognized "no political principle but the Constitution of the country, the union of the states and the enforcement of laws." Ticket of John Bell and Edward Everett carried Ky., Tenn., and Va. in the election.

Constitution Island, N.Y.: see WEST POINT.

Constitution of the United States: see CONSTITUTION.

Constitutions, Apostolic, late 4th-cent. compilation of rules for clergy and laity in the Church, supposedly by the Apostles, but actually apocryphal letters and most of the Didache. Declared binding by the continuation of the Third Council of CONSTANTINOPLE.

consubstantiation: see LORD'S SUPPER.

consul, title of two chief magistrates of anc. Rome. Office supposed to have originated 510 B.C. and was the supreme office in the republic, with control over the army and the treasury as well as civil affairs. Consular elections were the crucial points of political life. At first only patricians could be consuls, but after 367 B.C. plebeians were eligible. Normally a man served as quaestor, aedile, and praetor before running for the consulate. The Roman years were identified by the names of the consuls. Office became nominal under the Roman Empire.

consular service, organized body of agents maintained by a government at foreign ports and trade centers to protect its nationals and their interests, especially in commercial affairs. In U.S., Rogers Act of 1924 united consular and diplomatic services in Foreign Service of Dept. of State. Consuls and consulates enjoy immunity and EXTERRITORIALITY.

Consulate, 1799–1804, French government established after coup d'état of 18 BRUMAIRE. The three consuls were Bonaparte (see NAPOLEON I), Cambacérès, and C. F. Lebrun. Bonaparte, the actual ruler, was made First Consul for life in 1802, emperor in 1804.

Consumers' League, National, estab. in U.S. (1899) to forward movement begun (1890) in England to educate consumers to buy only goods made under good working conditions.

consumption, in economics, use of wealth to satisfy needs or destruction to create new wealth. Production and consumption, closely linked, form the foundation of modern capitalist economy.

consumption, in medicine: see TUBERCULOSIS.

contagious abortion: see BRUCELLOSIS.

contagious diseases: see COMMUNICABLE DISEASES.

contempt of court, in basic meaning interference with the functioning of a court. Criminal contempts are those that lessen the dignity of a court or tend to limit a judge's freedom of action (e.g., defying a judge or creating disorder in courtroom). Indirect criminal contempts are acts prejudicial to justice committed outside court. Civil contempts are primarily injuries to private parties occasioned by disobeying a DECREE or court order.

Conti (kôtē'), French princely family, cadet branch of house of Bourbon. Founded by **Armand de Bourbon, prince de Conti** (ärmä' dü bōōrbō'), 1629–66, brother of the Great CONDÉ, whom he at first assisted during the FRONDE. Reconciled with the court (1653), he married a niece of Mazarin and held a command in war against Spain. A protector of Molière. Later turned to mysticism, lived in retirement. His great-grandson, **Louis François de Bourbon, prince de Conti** (lwē' fräswä'), 1717–76, fought with distinction in War of the Austrian Succession but displeased Mme de Pompadour and lost favor at court. Sided with parlement against Maupeou. Friend of Rousseau.

continent, largest unit of land mass. The continents are Eurasia (Europe and Asia), Africa, North America, South America, Australia, and Antarctica. Including fringe islands, they comprise c.29% of the total surface of the earth. Average land height in all is c.2,700 ft. above sea level, with highest known point Mt. Everest, over 29,000 ft. According to isostatic theory the floor under the oceans and extending under continents is composed of heavy basaltic rock and the continents are of lighter granitic rock; the balance between continent heights and ocean depths is called *isostasy*.

Continental Congress, 1774–89, Federal legislature of Thirteen Colonies and later of U.S. in American Revolution and under Articles of Confederation. First Continental Congress (Sept. 5–Oct. 26, 1774) sent petitions of colonial grievances to the king. Second Continental Congress, meeting May 10, 1775, created Continental Army and adopted Declaration of Independence on July 4, 1776. Though Congress under Articles of Confederation was shackled by weaknesses of Federal structure, it passed Ordinance of 1787.

Continental Divide, "backbone" of a continent. In North America the great ridge of the Rocky Mts. separates streams flowing W from those flowing E. Sometimes called Great Divide, a name occasionally used for the whole Rocky Mt. system.

Continental System, scheme of economic warfare adopted by Napoleon I against England. Began with BERLIN DECREE (1806); intensified by Milan Decree (1807) and other measures. All trade with Britain was forbidden, even to neutrals. Britain replied with ORDERS IN COUNCIL, seizure of neutral Danish fleet, and bombardment of Copenhagen. English naval supremacy made enforcement of system impossible. Russian refusal to abide by system led to Napoleon's disastrous 1812 campaign.

contrabassoon: see WIND INSTRUMENTS.

contract, agreement binding parties to it to perform, or to refrain from, some specific act or acts. Form usually an offer submitted by one party and accepted by the other in a reasonable time or in a stipulated period by word or act, explicitly or implicitly. To make a valid contract the parties must be mentally sound and of legal age and must be acting with free will. It must also comply with the Statute of Frauds; certain classes of contracts must be in writing and signed. In some American states all contracts must involve a consideration (something of value, however slight, even a promise to do something) given by one party to induce the other to perform something. In modern industrial society contract law has been of ever-increasing importance.

contract bridge: see BRIDGE.

contraction, in physics: see EXPANSION.

contraction, in writing: see ABBREVIATION.

Contreras (kōnträ'räs), village, central Mexico, near Mexico city. On Aug. 19–20, 1847, American forces under Gen. Winfield Scott fought Mexican forces under Santa Anna here and at Churubusco in one of most important battles of Mexican War.

convection, form of heat transmission in liquids and gases. It depends on decrease of density with rise in temperature. Hotter parts of fluid move through rest. When liquid is heated in a container, the hotter part rises to the surface and its place is taken by cooler part. Thus convection current is started. Heat is transferred from point to point in fluids by this current. Convection currents that are set up when the earth's atmosphere is heated by warm land areas cause cloud formation and rain.

convulsion, spasmodic muscular contraction. May accompany toxic conditions and nervous disorders. In young children it may result from tetany or sudden high fever. Stimulating mechanism is obscure.

Conway, Sir Martin (Baron Conway of Allington), 1856–1937, English mountain climber, an art critic. Led exploring expeditions to Spitsbergen (1896–97) and the Bolivian Andes (1898).

Conway, Thomas, 1733–c.1800?, Irish soldier of fortune, general in Continental Army in American Revolution. Gave name to Conway Cabal (1777), intrigue to remove Washington as army commander in favor of Horatio Gates. Letter by Conway criticizing Washington was basis of abortive and cloudy scheme.

Conway. 1 City (pop. 8,610), central Ark., NW of Little Rock. Trade center for cotton, livestock, and poultry area. Seat of Hendrix Col. (Methodist; coed.; 1876). **2** Winter resort town (pop. 4,109), E N.H., at junction of Swift and Saco rivers. Includes Conway village (pop. 1,238) and North Conway, resort and art colony. **3** Town (pop. 6,073), E S.C., on Waccamaw R. and SE of Florence, in agr. area. Tourist center with hunting and fishing.

Conway Cabal: see CONWAY, THOMAS.

cony or **coney,** name for rabbit (*Oryctolagus*) and its fur; for pika (*Ochotona*), small high-altitude rodent of both hemispheres; and for hyrax (*Procavia*), herbivorous, hoofed animal of Arabia, Syria, Africa.

Cooch Behar, India: see BENGAL.

Cook, Frederick Albert, 1865–1940, American explorer. Accompanied various polar expeditions. Claimed scaling of Mt. McKinley (1906) and reaching of North Pole (1908). Accused of fraud by Robert E. Peary, deprived of honors, but remained controversial figure. Later he was involved in oilfield swindle; was imprisoned (1925–30).

Cook, James, 1728–79, English explorer and navigator. Circumnavigated globe (1768–71) while charting transit of Venus; also explored New Zealand and E Australian coasts. On expedition to S Pacific (1772–75), he disproved rumor of great southern continent and prevented scurvy by dietary and hygienic measures. Led futile search for Pacific-Atlantic passage through North America. Rediscovered Sandwich Isls. (1778). Killed by Hawaiian natives.

Cook, Thomas, 1808–92, English founder of travel agency which bears his name. His most spectacular achievement was transport of 18,000 men up the Nile in 1884 for attempted relief of Gen. Gordon.

Cook, Mount, 12,349 ft. high, on W South Isl., New Zealand; highest in New Zealand.

Cooke, Jay, 1821–1905, American financier. Marketed Civil War loans of Federal government. Failure in financing of Northern Pacific Railway helped precipitate panic of 1873.

Cooke, John Esten, 1830–86, American novelist, author of novels on Va. and the Civil War (notably *Surry of Eagle's Nest,* 1866).

cookery, developed at early stage of history; making of bread, butter, cheese, wine came close upon start of agr. and herding. Ancient Greeks made art of gastronomy; Rome under the empire saw epicurean banquets and, later, was influenced by the Goths' simple tastes. Finest cooking in Middle Ages arose from need of monasteries to prepare ingenious dishes for fast days. Modern cookery derives from Renaissance Italy.

SMALL CAPITALS = cross references. Pronunciation key on inside end pages. Abbreviations: p. 2.

French cuisine is characterized by finesse and the use of sauces, English by general simplicity; the U.S. cuisine includes borrowings from many lands as well as such native American foods as turkey, clam chowder, corn bread, pumpkin pie, gumbo. The findings obtained by research in chemistry, biology, nutrition, and other sciences contribute to modern cookery.

Cookeville, town (pop. 6,924), central Tenn., E of Nashville. Trade and industrial center in farm, timber, and coal area. Mfg. of clothing.

Cook Islands, formerly **Hervey Islands,** group (84 sq. mi.; pop. 12,380); with MANIHIKI group (pop. 14,519), S Pacific, SE of Samoa. Comprises volcanic islands of Rarotonga and Mangaia and six coral islets. Some were discovered 1773 by Capt. James Cook, others by John Williams in 1823. Made a British protectorate in 1888. Governed since 1901 by New Zealand. Export copra.

Cookworthy, William, 1705–80, English porcelain maker, first to make English porcelain similar to Chinese. In c.1755 discovered Cornish china clay near St. Austell, Cornwall.

Coolidge, Calvin, 1872–1933, 29th President of the United States (1923–29). Governor of Mass. (1919–20). Decision to use militia in a Boston police strike in 1919 brought national prominence. Vice President of U.S. (1921–23); became President after death of Warren G. Harding. Known for his New England simplicity and personal honesty; had strong popular backing. Opposed agr. price-fixing and strongly favored laissez-faire policy toward business, economy in government, and tax cuts.

Coolidge, town (pop. 4,306), E Ariz., near Casa Grande Natl. Monument, SW of Florence, in cotton and alfalfa area. **Coolidge Dam** (built 1927–28) in Gila R., SE of Globe, c.250 ft. high and c.900 ft. long, is used for power. It forms San Carlos Reservoir irrigating 100,000 acres (half are Indian lands) around Florence, Casa Grande, and Coolidge.

coolie labor, unskilled Asiatic laborers. In 1830s and 1840s many Indian and Chinese laborers were taken to British and French colonies on five-year contracts. Practice continued, and coolies were taken to Latin America, U.S., and Canada. Conditions of contract and of work were bad. Chinese labor, much used in building railroads in U.S., shut out by Chinese Exclusion Act of 1888.

cooling system. Many processes and engines while operating require cooling. Cylinder heat generated by internal-combustion engines damages parts if not counteracted, usually by circulating water or air. Blast furnaces, cupolas, gas generators, casting molds, etc., are cooled by water. Rapidly moving machinery is often cooled and lubricated by oil bath. Radial airplane engines expose maximum cylinder surface to cooling effect of air flow. Air-conditioning systems maintain desirable conditions of temperature, humidity, and cleanliness of the air indoors.

Coomaraswamy, Ananda Kentish (ä"nùndä' kĕn'tĭsh kōomä"rùswä'mē), 1877–1947, art historian, b. Ceylon. Largely responsible for great Far Eastern collection of Boston Mus. of Fine Arts.

Cooper, (Alfred) Duff, 1890–, British statesman. A Conservative, he served after 1935 as secretary of state for war and then first lord of the admiralty in the coalition cabinet, resigning in 1938 to protest the Munich Pact. Was later minister of information under Churchill and ambassador to France (1944–47). Author of distinguished biographies. Created Viscount Norwich of Aldwick in 1952.

Cooper, Anthony Ashley: see SHAFTESBURY.

Cooper, Sir Astley Paston, 1768–1841, English surgeon, noted for operations on hernia and aneurysms, and for anatomy lectures and surgical treatises.

Cooper, Hugh Lincoln, 1865–1937, American hydraulic engineer for Dneproges power plant, Ukraine, plants at Keokuk, Iowa, and Niagara Falls, and Wilson Dam project.

Cooper, James Fenimore, 1789–1851, American novelist, the first to gain world reputation. Son of a wealthy landowner, who founded Cooperstown on Otsego L. on the N.Y. frontier, he spent five years in naval service, then became a country gentleman. Entering on a literary career when he was 30, he was a highly prolific writer. Of his many novels best known and best loved are his adventure stories of frontiersmen and Indians, notably the *Leatherstocking Tales* (in order of the narrative: *The Deerslayer,* 1841; *The Last of the Mohicans,* 1826; *The Pathfinder,* 1840; *The Pioneers,* 1823; *The Prairie,* 1827); his sea stories (e.g., *The Pilot,* 1823; *The Red Rover,* 1828); and his historical novels, especially on the American Revolution (e.g., *The Spy,* 1821; his first success). He was an apologist for American democracy, but after several years (1826–33) in Europe he returned to the U.S. and became a mordant critic of the shortcomings of U.S. democracy in action—in satires, polemical works, and novels. His last years were embittered by an excessive number of lawsuits, which he launched to protect himself from his detractors and his lands from invading settlers. Among his works of history is a controversial but excellent history of the U.S. navy (1839).

Cooper, Myles, c.1735–1785, second president of King's College (now Columbia Univ.), b. England. A Loyalist, he fled to England in 1775.

Cooper, Peter, 1791–1883, American inventor, industrialist, and philanthropist. Built the *Tom Thumb,* first railway locomotive to be used successfully on an American railroad (1830). Helped develop national and international telegraph. Led in securing public school system in New York city. COOPER UNION was built to provide education for working classes. Cooper was GREENBACK PARTY presidential candidate 1876.

Cooper, Thomas, 1759–1839, American scientist, b. London, an associate of Joseph Priestley. Also was a Jeffersonian in politics; convicted of violating Alien and Sedition Acts. Taught at Dickinson Col. and Univ. of Pennsylvania. President of South Carolina Col. 1820–34.

Cooper, river: see CHARLESTON, S.C.

cooperative, voluntary association of people for self-management of economic enterprises. Consumers' cooperatives are organized for distribution of products cheaply, with no or few middlemen and little or no advertising. Cooperatives have operated in many fields —banking, housing, insurance, medicine, and marketing of agr. produce. Producer cooperatives, in which workers own the enterprise, are relatively few. Robert Owen in 19th cent. advocated cooperation, which became a movement in Britain with founding (1844) of the Rochdale Society. Cooperatives are numerous and highly successful in Scandinavian countries. Movement slow in U.S. until after World War I.

Co-operative Commonwealth Federation, Canadian political party, popularly known as CCF. Founded (1932) at Calgary, Alta., by representatives from farmer, labor, and socialist parties (largely of the W provinces) with aim of establishing a planned cooperative commonwealth in Canada. Regina Manifesto, issued at the party's first annual convention, outlines aims which include socialization of finance, social ownership of public utilities, and various welfare measures. J. S. Woodsworth was its first leader. M. J. Coldwell succeeded him. In 1944 the party secured a majority in Saskatchewan legislature and estab. first CCF government in Canada. CCF is represented in other provincial legislatures and in Canadian House.

Cooperstown, village (pop. 2,727), E central N.Y., W of Albany and on Susquehanna R. and Otsego L. James Fenimore Cooper lived here and described the region in *Leatherstocking Tales.* Tradition says that Abner DOUBLEDAY invented baseball here. Has Natl. Baseball Hall of Fame and Mus.

Cooper Union, in Manhattan borough of New York

city; nonsectarian, coed.; opened 1859. Founded by Peter Cooper. Pioneered with evening art and engineering schools; day schools added in 1900. Abraham Lincoln made famous speech here in 1860.

Coorg (kōōrg), state (1,593 sq. mi.; pop. 229,255), SW India, in W Ghats; cap. Macara.

Coos (kō'ŏs), island, the modern Kos. Acts 21.1.

Coosa (kōō'sù), navigable river, NW Ga. and E Ala. Formed by headstreams at Rome, Ga.; winds 286 mi. W and S to join Tallapoosa R. and form Alabama R. above Montgomery. Three power dams in lower course.

Coos Bay (kōōs), city (pop. 6,223), SW Oregon, on Coos Bay of the Pacific; founded 1854 as Marshfield, renamed 1944. Ships lumber, fish (esp. salmon).

coot, marsh bird of North America and Europe, related to the rail and crane. American coot or mud hen or marsh hen is slaty gray with black head and neck and white-marked wings. It swims and dives well; the feet are partially webbed.

copal (kō'pùl), resin from certain tropical trees, a source of hard-surfaced lacquers and varnishes.

Copeau, Jacques (zhäk' kôpō'), 1879–, French theatrical producer. Director of influential Théâtre du Vieux-Colombier, in Paris, 1913–24.

Copenhagen (kō'pùnhā"gùn), Dan. *København*, city (pop. 765,580), with suburbs 1,166,204), cap. of Denmark, on E Zealand and N Amager isls. and on the Oresund. Major fishing and naval port; commercial, industrial, cultural center. Shipyards; metallurgy; mfg. of COPENHAGEN WARE. First fortified 12th cent. and chartered 1254, Copenhagen became Danish cap. 1443. It resisted a long Swedish siege (1558–59). Treaty of Copenhagen (1660) confirmed Treaty of ROSKILDE. In 1807 the city was bombarded and nearly destroyed by the British, neutral Denmark having refused to surrender its fleet. Occupied 1940–45 by the Germans in World War II, Copenhagen was bombed by the Allies, but only the shipyards suffered damage. One of the handsomest cities of Europe, it has many famous landmarks, including the picturesque houses along the Nyhavn arm of the harbor; Kongens Nytorv, the central square, with the 17th-cent. Charlottenborg palace; Amalienborg Square, enclosed by four palaces—the present royal residence; the Cathedral Church of Our Lady; and Christiansborg palace (18th cent.), housing the Rigsdag, on moated Slotsholm isl. Most of the historic buildings were restored after 1807. University was founded 1479.

Copenhagen, battle of, 1801, naval engagement of the French Revolutionary Wars. Neutral Denmark having refused to comply with British rules on neutral navigation, an English fleet was sent into the Baltic under admirals Sir Hyde PARKER and Horatio NELSON. The Danish fleet, caught at the roadsteads of Copenhagen, was defeated after a hard battle.

Copenhagen ware, underglaze and overglaze pottery produced in Copenhagen since c.1760. Fine tableware and fluted porcelain of blue Danish pattern (derived from Chinese) are produced by Royal Porcelain works. Animal and figure sculptures (in white underglaze porcelain) are distinctive products.

Copernicus, Nicholas (kōpûr'nĭkùs), 1473–1543, Polish astronomer, founder of Copernican system on which modern astronomy is based. In his famed treatise *De revolutionibus orbium coelestium* (published 1543), he described the sun as the center of great system, with earth revolving around it.

Cophetua (kōfĕ'chōōù), legendary African king who wooed and won a beggar maid. Legend appears in a ballad in Thomas Percy's *Reliques of Ancient English Poetry* (3 vols., 1765).

Copland, Aaron, 1900–, American composer. His music has been influenced by jazz and other American types. He has written concert music in all forms and music for the films and radio. His ballets include *Billy the Kid* (1938), *Rodeo* (1942), and *Appalachian Spring* (1944). Among his important orchestral works are El

Salón México (1936) and *A Lincoln Portrait* (1942).

Copley, John Singleton (kŏp'lē), 1738?–1815, American portrait painter, b. Boston. Settled c.1774 in London, where he enjoyed many honors. His reputation today rests mainly on his early American portraits, rather than on the more polished works of his English period.

Coppard, A(lfred) E(dgar), 1878–, English short-story writer and lyric poet. Both his stories (as in *Adam and Eve and Pinch Me*, 1921; *Selected Tales*, 1946) and his poems (as in *Collected Poems*, 1928; *Cherry Ripe*, 1935) are distinguished by fantasy, wit, and precise word choice.

Coppée, François (fräswä' kôpā'), 1842–1908, French Parnassian poet, noted for poems of sympathy for the underprivileged, as *Les Humbles* (1872).

Copper, river rising in Wrangell Mts., SE Alaska, and flowing c.300 mi. S through the Chugach Mts. to Gulf of Alaska. Copper taken by Indians from deposits near upper river attracted Russians and Americans. Copper River and Northwestern RR (built 1908–11) from Cordova to great Kennecott mine partly followed lower river; was abandoned 1938.

copper, common, malleable, ductile, relatively soft metallic element (symbol = Cu; see also ELEMENT, table). It is a good conductor, changes slowly in air, and resists dilute acids. Salt water causes it to corrode. Used in roofing; for utensils, coins, metalwork; in making electrical apparatus and wires; in alloys. Occurs free and in combination; refined by electrolysis. It was one of first metals known to man. See also BRONZE AGE.

Copper Age: see BRONZE AGE.

copperas (kŏ'pùrùs) or **green vitriol,** ferrous sulphate, a hydrous compound of iron, sulphur, and oxygen. It is a green, crystalline, water-soluble salt.

Copper Cliff, town (pop. 3,974), S Ont., Canada, SW of Sudbury. Has one of largest copper refineries in British Commonwealth. Adjoins smelters of International Nickel Co.

copperhead, poisonous snake of E U.S. It is 2–3 ft. long; has coppery head; body is brown with hourglass-shaped chestnut markings above, pinkish white with dark spots below. Bite is not often fatal.

Copperheads, in Civil War, reproachful term for Northerners sympathetic to South. Especially active in Ill., Ind., and Ohio. KNIGHTS OF THE GOLDEN CIRCLE was Copperhead secret society.

Coppermine, river, Mackenzie dist., Northwest Territories, Canada. Rises N of Great Slave L. and flows 525 mi. NW to Coronation Gulf in Arctic Ocean.

copper pyrites: see CHALCOPYRITE.

Coppet (kôpā'), village, Vaud canton, SW Switzerland, on L. Geneva. Château was residence of Mme de Staël.

copra: see COCONUT.

Copt (kŏpt), member of native Christian group in Egypt that resisted conversion to Islam through the centuries. The **Coptic language** (now extinct) was the form of Egyptian spoken in early Christian times (see LANGUAGE, table). The **Coptic Church** officially holds to MONOPHYSITISM, which was declared a heresy by Orthodox and Roman Catholics in 451. It is in communion with the Church of Ethiopia, and its head, the patriarch of Alexandria, names the head of the Ethiopian church (the abuna). The ritual languages are Greek, Coptic, and Arabic. A few "Catholic Copts" are in communion with the pope.

copyright, property right in works of literature, art, and the like, comprising exclusive right of owner to dispose of his property as he wishes and forbid unauthorized use. Specific protection of literary property was very slow in development. The Bern Convention (1887) was adopted by many countries (not including U.S.) for mutual copyright recognition. A conference of 45 nations at Geneva in 1952 adopted a new Universal Copyright Convention, to come in force after 12 nations ratify it. Copyright in U.S. is under an act

SMALL CAPITALS = cross references. Pronunciation key on inside end pages. Abbreviations: p. 2.

of 1909, with amendments; requires manufacture in U.S., is valid for 28 years, and may be renewed once.

Coquelin, Benoît Constant (bùnwä' kōstä' kôklē'), 1841–1909, French actor. Acted for Comédie Française, his greatest role being Cyrano de Bergerac. Played with Bernhardt in *L'Aiglon.*

coquilla nut (kōkē'yù), hard fruit of Brazilian palm (*Attalea funifera*), used in cabinet work, etc. Tree yields stiff fiber used in brooms and ropes.

coral, small marine invertebrate usually living in a colony. The individuals, known as polyps, each consist of a jellylike body surrounded by a skeleton. They live only in warm seas, and exist in great variety. As a colony produces new polyps, the older members die and new layers build up on the dead skeletons. Wave action may pile up the coral material, helping to form **coral reefs.** A fringing reef is separated from the shore by a narrow lagoon; a barrier reef is farther out, enclosing a wide, deep lagoon; an atoll is a ring-shaped reef surrounding a circular lagoon. Coral (many colored) is much used in jewelry and bric-a-brac.

Coral Gables, residential and resort city (pop. 19,837), SE Fla., part of Greater Miami, on Biscayne Bay; planned and built during Fla. land boom of 1920s. Seat of Univ. of Miami (nonsectarian; coed.; chartered 1925, opened 1926), with Hispanic-American Inst. Tropical Park race track is near.

coral reefs: see CORAL.

Coral Sea, SW arm of the Pacific, E of Australia and SE of New Guinea, W of New Hebrides and New Caledonia. Battle of aircraft carriers here in 1942 ended by checking S expansion of the Japanese.

coral snake, poisonous snake of W Hemisphere, related to cobra. Found chiefly in Mexico, Central and South America. Two species in U.S.: coral or harlequin snake (*Micrurus fulvius*) of SE U.S. is c.2½ ft. long, with small blunt head, body ringed with bands of black and of red, with narrow yellow bands on either side of black; Sonoran coral snake (*M. euryxanthus*) found from Arizona to N Mexico.

Coraopolis (kō"rēō'pùlĭs), borough (pop. 10,498), SW Pa., on Ohio R. and NW of Pittsburgh. Mfg. of metal products and glass.

Corbett, Harvey Wiley (kôr'bĭt), 1873–, American architect. With F. J. Helmle he designed the Bush Terminal Building (1920) in New York, one of the first impressive solutions in skyscraper design.

Corbett, James J(ohn), 1866–1933, American boxer. "Gentleman Jim" won heavyweight championship (1892) by knocking out John L. Sullivan, lost title (1897) to Robert Fitzsimmons.

Corbin, city (pop. 7,744), S Ky., NW of Middlesboro on old Wilderness Road. Shipping center of agr., timber, and coal area with mining and mfg. of clothing and food products.

Corbulo (kôr'byōōlù), d. A.D. 67, Roman general. Under Claudius, Corbulo as legate in Germany built a still-used Meuse-Rhine canal. Later in Asia he defeated the Parthians at Artaxata and Tigranocerta. Still later his successes in Asia caused the jealousy of Nero, who forced him to commit suicide.

Corcoran, William Wilson, 1798–1888, American financier and art collector. Donor of Corcoran Gall. of Art, Washington, D.C., opened 1897.

Corcyra, Greek Ionian Island: see CORFU.

Corday, Charlotte (shärlôt' kôrdä'), 1768–93, French assassin. A sympathizer of GIRONDISTS, she gained admission to MARAT on false pretext, stabbed him in his bath. She was guillotined.

Cordele (kôrdēl'), city (pop. 9,462), S central Ga., SSW of Macon. Market and processing center for farm and timber area.

Cordeliers (kôrdùlyā'), French revolutionary club. Instrumental in destruction of GIRONDISTS (1793). Its early leaders, DANTON and DESMOULINS, were displaced by extreme leftists MARAT and HÉBERT. Suppressed by Robespierre 1794.

Cordilleras (kôrdĭ'lùrùz), general name for mountain

systems of W North America, from N Alaska through Canada, U.S., Mexico, and Panama. In U.S. they include Rocky Mts., ranges of Great Basin, Sierra Nevada, and Coast Ranges. In South America the range from Panama to Cape Horn is known locally as Cordillera de Los Andes.

cordite: see POWDER.

Córdoba, Francisco Fernández de: see FERNÁNDEZ DE CÓRDOBA, FRANCISCO.

Córdoba, Gonzalo Fernández de: see FERNÁNDEZ DE CÓRDOBA, GONZALO.

Córdoba (kôr'dōvä), city (pop. 369,886), cap. of Córdoba prov., central Argentina; cultural and commercial center on E flank of Sierra de Córdoba at W margin of Pampa; founded 1573. Dam on Río Primero furnishes hydroelectric power for industries. Popular tourist and health resort. University founded 1613.

Córdoba, city (pop. 17,865), Vera Cruz, E Mexico; founded 1618. Agr. area produces coffee, sugar, cotton, tropical fruits. Treaty establishing independence of Mexico was signed here (1821).

Córdoba or **Cordova,** city (pop. 351,644), cap. of Córdoba prov., S Spain, in Andalusia, on Guadalquivir R. Flourished under Romans; reached zenith as seat of Moorish emirate (later caliphate) under OMAYYAD dynasty (756–1031). Fell to emir of Seville 1078; to Ferdinand III of Castile 1236. Never regained its former glory but remained famous for its gold, silver, leather crafts. From Omayyad period, when Córdoba was a center of Moslem and Jewish cultures, date the cathedral (built as mosque in 8th cent.) and ruins of alcazar. Birthplace of Seneca, Lucan, Averroës, Maimonides.

Cordova (kôrdō'vù), town (pop. 1,165), S Alaska, port on Prince William Sound. Founded as terminus of Copper River and Northwestern RR to Kennecott copper mine, it declined with closing of mine and railroad (1938). Has fish cannery and cold storage plant.

Cordova, Spain: see CÓRDOBA.

Corelli, Arcangelo (ärkän'jälō kōrĕl'lē), 1653–1713, Italian composer and violinist. He developed the *concerto grosso.* Best known of his many sonatas are his variations on an air, *Folies d'Espagne.*

Corelli, Marie (kùrĕl'ē), 1855–1924, English novelist of Italian-Scottish parentage, educated in France. Her melodramatic novels in lush prose (e.g., *Thelma,* 1887; *Ardath,* 1889; *The Sorrows of Satan,* 1895) suited the popular taste of her day.

coreopsis (–ŏp'–) or **tickseed,** annual or perennial of genus *Coreopsis,* with yellow or yellow-red daisylike flowers. Some forms called calliopsis.

Corfu (kôr'fōō, –fū), Gr. *Kerkyra,* Latin *Corcyra,* island (229 sq. mi.; pop. 106,593), Greece, second largest of Ionian Islands, separated by a narrow channel from Greek and Albanian coast. Rises to c.3,000 ft. at Mt. Pantokrator, but is largely a fertile agr. lowland. Livestock raising; fishing. Corfu has been identified with Scheria, home of Phaeacians in Homer's *Odyssey.* It was colonized by Corinth (8th cent. B.C.), and with Corinth helped found Epidamnus (see DURAZZO). Rivalry with Corinth over its control led to an alliance with Athens and helped precipitate PELOPONNESIAN WAR (431–404 B.C.). In 229 B.C. Corfu passed to Rome. It was seized repeatedly from the Byzantines by ROBERT GUISCARD and his successors; was held by Venice 1386–1797; shared later history of IONIAN ISLANDS. In 1923 Italy bombarded and occupied Corfu in reprisal for assassination of several Italian officers on Greek soil. Corfu Incident was ended when Italy, at behest of the other Great Powers, evacuated Corfu, and Greece apologized. In World War II, Corfu was again occupied by Italy. The island's cap., Corfu (pop. 30,739), is a commercial port. The near-by Achilleion palace was built for Elizabeth of Austria.

Cori, Carl Ferdinand (kō'rē), 1896–, and his wife, **Gerty Theresa (Radnitz) Cori,** 1896–, American biochemists, who shared (with Houssay) the 1947 Nobel

Prize in Physiology and Medicine for research on carbohydrate metabolism and enzymes. Both were associated with Washington Univ. from 1931.

coriander, aromatic herb (*Coriandrum sativum*). Yields oil used as flavoring, in medicine, and in liqueurs.

Corinth, Lovis (lô′vēs kô′rĭnt), 1858–1925, German postimpressionist painter.

Corinth (kŏ′rĭnth), Gr. *Korinthos*, city (pop. 12,715), Greece, in NE Peloponnesus; a port on Gulf of Corinth. Trades in silk, olive oil, fruits. Founded 1858 after destruction of Old Corinth by earthquake; rebuilt after another quake (1928). Old Corinth, 3 mi. SW of Corinth, is now a village (pop. 1,473). Strategically situated and protected by the ACROCORINTHUS, it was a wealthy, powerful, and cultured city of ancient Greece. A Dorian town existing from Homeric times, it became under PERIANDER and his successors a flourishing seapower and colonized Syracuse, Corfu, Potidaea. Rivalry with Athens and alliance with Sparta brought on the PELOPONNESIAN WAR (431–404 B.C.). After the Macedonian occupation Corinth led the ACHAEAN LEAGUE until its conquest and destruction by Rome (146 B.C.). Caesar restored it and reestablished the ISTHMIAN GAMES. Held by VILLEHARDOUIN family in the 13th cent., later by various Italian princes, Corinth fell to Turkey (1458), and to Venice (1687). Turkey recovered it 1714; lost it to Greek insurgents 1822. The **Gulf of Corinth,** an inlet of the Ionian Sea, 80 mi. long, 3–20 mi. wide, lies between central Greece (N) and the Peloponnesus (S), which are connected by the **Isthmus of Corinth,** 20 mi. long, 4–8 mi. wide. The isthmus is crossed by the ancient Isthmian Wall, repeatedly restored by Byzantine emperors to defend the Peloponnesus. Parallel to wall runs the Corinth Canal (built 1881–93; damaged in World War II), which connects Gulf of Corinth with Saronic Gulf.

Corinth, city (pop. 9,785), NE Miss., near Tenn. line. Farm trade and processing center. Strategic rail center in Civil War, captured by H. W. Halleck's Union troops after battle of SHILOH (May, 1862), and defended by Gen. Rosecrans against Confederates under Gens. Van Dorn and Price (Oct. 3–4, 1862).

Corinth, Gulf of: see CORINTH, Greece.

Corinth, Isthmus of: see CORINTH, GREECE.

Corinthian order, latest and most ornate of the orders of architecture, reaching full development in the middle of the 4th cent. B.C. Little used by the Greeks, although the temple of Zeus at Athens (begun 2d cent. B.C. and completed by Hadrian 2d cent. A.D.) was the first great Corinthian temple. The Greek Corinthian column is more slender than the Ionic. Its capital, supposedly originated by Callimachus, is decorated with acanthus leaves. The Romans used the order in many works of imperial architecture. See *ill.,* p. 47.

Corinthians (kŭrĭn′thĕŭnz), epistles of New Testament written to Christians at Corinth by St. Paul. First Corinthians, written probably early in A.D. 55, is one of longest and most important of epistles. It covers various aspects of Christian conduct, counsels against factionalism, incest, litigation, sensuality, and answers questions on marriage and celibacy. Contains many famous passages, e.g., institution of Eucharist (11.17-34); an eloquent panegyric on Christian love (13). Second Corinthians is shorter, written perhaps within a year of the other. Contains Paul's defense of his mission, citing his authority, and accounting for his actions.

Coriolanus (kô′rēŭlā′nŭs), legendary Roman patrician. The story goes that Coriolanus offered to give state grain to the starving people in return for abolition of the tribunate of the people. He was expelled from Rome. Joining the Volscians in an attack on Rome (possibly 491? B.C.), he was moved by the tears of his wife and his mother to spare the city. The frustrated Volscians killed him. The story is used for Shakspere's drama.

Cork, Richard Boyle, 1st earl of: see BOYLE, RICHARD.

Cork [Irish,= swamp], maritime county (2,881 sq. mi.;

pop. 343,668), S Ireland, Munster Prov.; largest Irish county. Has rocky coastline with several bays and harbors. Interior has both mountains and fertile valleys. Farming, fishing, and dairying main occupations. Mfg. (textiles, whisky, flour, and leather goods) mostly around county town, **Cork,** county borough (pop. 75,-595), on Lee R. near Cork Harbour. Occupied by the Danes (9th cent.), Cromwell (1649), and Marlborough (1690). In 1920 disturbances lord mayor was murdered. Harbor entrance is fortified; Cobh and Passage are important ports, and Haulbowline and Spike Isls. are military and naval depots. Exports mainly farm produce, cloth, and fish. Site of Univ. Col. and two cathedrals.

cork oak, evergreen oak (*Quercus suber*), native to Mediterranean region. Its thick but light bark or cork is used to make many things (e.g., bottle stoppers, life preservers, insulating material).

Corliss, George Henry, 1817–88, American inventor and international authority on steam-engine.

corm, short, thickened underground stem, resembling a bulb. The gladiolus and the crocus form corms. See *ill.,* p. 783.

cormorant (kôr′mŭrŭnt), large aquatic bird, an expert swimmer, related to the gannet and pelican, found in temperate or tropical areas, usually on the sea, but also on inland waters. Plumage is thick, usually dark; the body is 2–3 ft. long; the feet are webbed; the long bill is hooked. Used in Orient to catch fish.

corn, in agr., name given to leading grain crop of a region. In England, it means WHEAT, in Scotland and Ireland, OATS. Grain called corn in America is Indian corn or maize (*Zea mays*), a grass, domesticated and cultivated long before white man's arrival. Indians grew several kinds. In U.S. it is used as foodstuff, for making starch, sugar, etc., as grain feed and fodder.

Cornaro, Caterina (kätärē′nä kôrnä′rō), 1454–1510, queen of Cyprus, a celebrated Venetian beauty. Ruled from death of husband, James II of Cyprus (1473), until 1489, when Venice recalled her and annexed the island. Portrait by Titian (Uffizi, Florence).

Corn Belt, W part of U.S. Midwest with soil and climate best suited to grow corn and corn-fed livestock (esp. hogs). Iowa and Ill. are heart of area.

corn borer or **European corn borer,** small moth, in its larval stage a serious pest to corn. Probably reached U.S. from S Europe c.1910; found near Boston 1917. Has one or two broods a season. Mature larva pinkish, with brown head, and c.1 in. long. Often attacks other plants, such as dahlia.

Corneille, Pierre (pyĕr′ kôrnā′yù), 1606–84, French dramatist, master of classical tragedy. *Le Cid* (1637), his masterpiece, is based on Spanish sources (see CID). Among his other plays, the most successful are the tragedies, *Horace* (1640), *Cinna* (1640), and *Polyeucte* (1643), and the comedy *Le Menteur* (1643). In grandiose, dignified style, Corneille exalts the will, subordinating passion to duty. He lived to see Racine replace him in popular favor.

cornel: see BUNCHBERRY; DOGWOOD.

Cornelia, fl. 2d cent. B.C., Roman matron, daughter of Scipio Africanus Major, wife of Ti. Sempronius Gracchus, mother of the Gracchi. Devoted herself to her children after her husband's death, raising them well. When asked by a wealthy lady about her jewels, Cornelia pointed at her sons, saying, "These are my jewels!"

Cornelius, one of first Gentile converts; traditionally first bishop of Caesarea. Acts 10.

Cornelius, Peter von, 1783–1867, German painter who helped revive art of fresco painting. Did fresco decorations in the Glyptothek. Favorite themes were religious or philosophical.

Cornell, Ezra, 1807–74, American capitalist, founder of Cornell Univ. A founder and director of the Western Union Telegraph Co. (formed 1855). His son, **Alonzo B. Cornell,** 1832–1904, was governor of N.Y. (1880–83), associate of Roscoe Conkling.

Cornell, Katharine, 1898–, American actress. Since 1916 has appeared in plays such as *The Green Hat, The Barretts of Wimpole Street,* and *Candida.*

Cornell College: see MOUNT VERNON, Iowa.

Cornell University, mainly at Ithaca, N.Y.; nonsectarian, with land-grant, state, private support; coed.; chartered 1865, opened 1868. Named for Ezra CORNELL. First president was A. D. WHITE. Has colleges of architecture, arts and sciences, engineering, medicine (in New York city); schools of law, nutrition, business administration; N.Y. state colleges of agr. and schools of industrial and labor relations, home economics, veterinary medicine.

corner, the securing of all or nearly all the supply of any commodity so that buyers must pay exorbitant prices. In stock exchanges, corners are made possible by short selling on MARGIN. Corners may be unintentional or deliberately planned. Joseph's corner of Egyptian grain is described in the Bible. U.S. Supreme Court in 1913 held that a corner in a commodity entering into general use or into interstate commerce is illegal.

Corner Brook, town (pop. 10,276, with Corner Brook West), of W N.F., Canada, on Bay of Islands. Paper mills, iron foundries, and furniture works.

cornet: see WIND INSTRUMENTS.

cornflower, annual plant (*Centaurea cyanus*) with blue, purple, pink, or white flower heads. Also called bachelor's button, ragged sailor, bluebottle.

Corning. 1 City (pop. 2,104), SW Iowa, WSW of Creston. Icarian communistic settlement was near here, 1858–98 (see CABET, ÉTIENNE). **2** City (pop. 17,684), S N.Y., NW of Elmira and on Chemung R.; settled 1788. Famous for glass industry (begun 1868); 200-in. telescope mirror for Mt. Palomar, Calif., Observatory was made here.

Cornish, Vaughan, 1862–1948, English geographer. Dealt with relation of geography to military strategy, action of waves and tides, scenery preservation.

Cornish, town (pop. 989), SW N.H., near Connecticut R. N of Claremont. Resort and art colony. Birthplace of S. P. Chase. "Aspet," summer estate of Augustus Saint-Gaudens, is now a memorial.

Cornish, Brythonic language of Celtic subfamily of Indo-European languages. See LANGUAGE (table).

Corn Islands, two islands off E Nicaragua, opposite Bluefields. Leased to U.S. in 1916 in Nicaragua Canal project.

corn laws, regulations dating from 1361 restricting export or import of grain, especially in England. Laws of 1791 and 1815 forbade import unless prices were high. Food costs rose. Resentment led to Anti-Corn-Law League's campaign and repeal of laws by Robert Peel, 1846.

Corno, Monte, Italy: see GRAN SASSO D'ITALIA.

Cornplanter, c.1740–1836, half-breed chief of the Seneca Indians. Fought for British in New York in American Revolution.

cornucopia (kôr″nŭkō′pēŭ) [Latin,= horn of plenty], in Greek religion, broken-off horn of goat Amalthaea, which became full of whatever owner desired. It is symbol of plenty.

Cornwall, Barry, 1787–1874, English writer of sentimental songs; real name Bryan Waller Procter.

Cornwall (kôrn′wôl), maritime county (1,365 sq. mi.; pop. 345,612), SW England; co. town Bodmin. Peninsula ending in promontory Lands End, region is low-lying plateau with market and dairy farms in fertile valleys. County includes Scilly Isles, famous for flower exports. Cornish tin mines known early to Greek traders. History distinct from rest of England. Cornish tongue did not die out until 18th cent. Great fishing center. Climate and picturesque coast towns make it popular with tourists.

Cornwall, town (pop. 16,899), SE Ont., Canada, on St. Lawrence R. and SE of Ottawa. At NE end of Cornwall Canal (11 mi. long, 6 locks), it is a port with dry dock. Mfg. of textiles, clothing, chemicals, furniture;

processing of dairy products from surrounding area.

Cornwallis, Charles Cornwallis, 1st Marquess, 1738–1805, British general. Led fateful CAROLINA CAMPAIGN in American Revolution. Defeat in YORKTOWN CAMPAIGN ended fighting. Later was governor general of India and viceroy to Ireland.

corolla (–rŏl′–), part of FLOWER, usually brightly colored and just within CALYX. May be united as in morning glory or separate petals as in rose. See *ill.*, p. 783.

Coromandel Coast (kŏrōmăn′dŭl), E coast of Madras, India, between Point Calimere and Kistna R. Name probably derives from Cholomandalam, i.e., country of the Cholas, an ancient dynasty.

Corona, city (pop. 10,223), S Calif., ESE of Los Angeles. Ships citrus fruit (esp. lemons). Mfg. of pottery, glass, orchard equipment, chemicals.

corona (kŭrō′nŭ), envelope surrounding sun (outside the chromosphere), believed to consist of fine particles luminous from their own light and reflected sunlight. Pale yellow inner corona is ringed by pearly white halo of outer corona, visible during total eclipse and also by means of coronagraph.

Coronado, Francisco Vásquez de, c.1510–1554, Spanish explorer in America. Unsuccessfully sought fabled wealth of Seven Cities of Cibola and QUIVIRA, but expedition acquainted Spanish with Pueblo Indians and opened Southwest.

Coronado (kŏ″rŭnä′dō), residential and resort city (pop. 17,171), S Calif., on peninsula on W side of San Diego Bay.

coronary thrombosis: see THROMBOSIS.

coronation, ceremony of crowning sovereign on accession to throne. Has origins of great antiquity and ritual; usually has some religious as well as political significance (e.g., anointing with oil). In England medieval pageantry retained. English rulers crowned at Westminster Abbey since 1066. **Coronation Stone,** on which Scottish kings were crowned at Scone, was brought to Abbey in 1296 by Edward I and is now part of the coronation chair. Traditionally Jacob's "pillow," it was long Stone of Destiny of Irish kings before removal to Scotland. Stolen 1950 by Scottish nationalists but soon returned.

Coronea (kŏr′ŭnē′ŭ), town of anc. Greece, in Boeotia, ENE of Thebes. Here in 447 B.C. Athenians were defeated by Thebans, and in 394 B.C. Spartans won a hollow victory over Thebans.

Corot, Jean Baptiste Camille (zhä′ bätēst′ kämē′yŭ kôrō′), 1796–1875, French landscape painter of the Barbizon school. Spent most of his life in Fontainebleau or Ville d'Avray. Depicted the misty hours before dawn, using mainly silvery grays and greens and creating a poetic effect.

corporal punishment, physical chastisement of an offender, as in capital punishment, flogging, mutilating, or branding. Known from the dawn of history, it was opposed by humanitarians in 18th cent., and generally punishments have become less severe in Western countries.

corporation, organization enjoying legal personality for purpose of carrying out certain activities. Though there are many kinds (e.g., ecclesiastic, municipal, cooperative), business corporations organized for profit are commonly meant. Crude forms known in ancient Rome, but modern corporations developed with spread of commerce in Renaissance and growth of industry in 18th and 19th cent. In U.S. most operate under state charters (first general incorporation law in N.Y. 1811). As legal person corporation may hold property, carry on business, and even commit crimes (punishable by fine). Increasing power and narrowing of control to a few owners by holding companies (organized by controlling shares in other corporations) has caused opposition and some restriction by law.

corporative state, governmental economic system, organized with guilds (or corporations) of employers and employees; thus combines capitalism and syndicalism. As exemplified by Fascist Italy, corporative state gives government unlimited control over economic life. Spain and Portugal have modified corporative system.

Corpus Christi (kôr′pùs krĭs′tē) [Latin,= body of Christ], feast of the Roman Catholic Church, celebrated on the Thursday after Trinity Sunday (or on the following Sunday) to commemorate institution of the Eucharist. In many countries the day is marked with great processions and with much show of flowers.

Corpus Christi (krĭs′tē), city (pop. 108,287), S Texas, on Corpus Christi Bay at entrance of Nueces Bay (inlet at mouth of Nueces R.). Bay discovered Corpus Christi Day, 1519. Trading post founded here 1840; land claimed by Texas and Mexico. Boomed in Mexican War; briefly captured (1862) by Federal troops in Civil War. Livestock trade grew in late 18th cent. Recovering from 1919 hurricane, city developed as oil center. A deepwater port, it refines and ships oil, zinc, and other chemicals and processes cotton, milk, sea food, and truck. Seat of great naval air training base. Has resort beaches.

Corpus Christi College: see CAMBRIDGE UNIVERSITY and OXFORD UNIVERSITY.

corpuscles, cells carried in body fluids, especially blood plasma. Red blood corpuscles, yellowish biconcave disks containing hemoglobin (protein combined with iron and carrying oxygen), en masse give blood its red color; 4,500,000 to 5,000,000 are normally found per cu. mm. of human blood. Several types of white cells exist (see WHITE CORPUSCLE), totaling 6,000 to 10,000 per cu. mm. See *ill.,* p. 633.

Corpus Juris Civilis (kôr′pùs jōo′rĭs sĭvĭ′lĭs), most comprehensive code of Roman law, compiled (529–35) under Justinian I, by commission of jurists headed by TRIBONIAN. Four parts are the Codex or Code (collection of imperial constitutions), the Digest of Pandects (selections from classical jurists), the Institutes (textbook of elementary rules), and the Novels or Novellae (constitutions later than the Codex). *Corpus* was main source of modern CIVIL LAW.

Correggio (kùrĕ′jō), 1494–1534, Italian baroque painter, b. Correggio. His real name was Antonio Allegri. Greatly influenced Italian art of the 16th and 17th cent. by bold use of foreshortening and soft, moving contrasts of color, light, and shade. His most famous work is the grand fresco, *Assumption of the Virgin,* on the cupola of Parma cathedral.

Corregidor (kùrĕ′gĭdôr″), fortress island, area c.2 sq. mi., off BATAAN peninsula of Luzon, Philippines. First fortified by the Spanish, its defenses were further strengthened by the U.S. after 1898. In World War II U.S. troops under Lt. Gen. Wainwright fought on hopelessly for a month here after fall of Bataan; they surrendered May, 1942.

Corrèze (kôrĕz′), department (2,273 sq. mi.; pop. 254,-601), S central France, in Limousin; cap. Tulle.

Corrientes (kôrēĕn′tĕs), city (pop. 56,544), cap. of Corrientes prov., NE Argentina, port on Paraná R. in cattle and agr. district.

corrosion: see RUSTING.

Corry, city (pop. 7,911), NW Pa., SE of Erie. Mfg. of furniture and metal products.

Corsica (kôr′sĭkù), Fr. *Corse,* island (3,367 sq. mi.; pop. 267,873), a department of Metropolitan France, in Mediterranean, SE of France and N of Sardinia. Its cap., Ajaccio, and Bastia are the chief towns and ports. Largely mountainous (Monte Cinto reaches 8,982 ft.). Olive oil, wine, timber are main exports. Poor communications. Large areas are wild, covered by undergrowth (*maquis*), offering ideal hideout to bandits. Blood feuds and banditry were traditional until suppression in 20th cent. Outside chief towns an Italian dialect is spoken. Corsica was seized in turn by the Romans (3d cent. B.C.), Vandals (5th cent. A.D.), Arabs (9th cent.), Pisans (1077), and Genoese (1312). In 1755 Pasquale PAOLI successfully rebelled against Genoa, but French intervention led in 1768 to cession of Corsica to France. The Bonapartes, including Napoleon I, originated here. In 1794 Paoli returned, expelled French, united Corsica with British crown; but in 1796 France recovered it. In World War II German-Italian occupation (1942–43) was ended by local rebellion aided by Free French task force.

Corsicana (kôrsĭkă′nù), city (pop. 19,211), E central Texas, SSE of Dallas, in oil, agr., and cattle region. Processes and ships cotton, food and dairy products, and oil. First important commercial oil well (1895) and first refinery of Texas were here.

Corte Real, Gaspar (gùshpär′ kôr′tù rēäl′), c.1450–1501?, Portuguese explorer. Made two voyages seeking Northwest Passage. May have discovered Greenland (1500) and touched North America. Lost on second voyage. His brother, Miguel Corte Real, was lost searching for him.

Cortés, Hernán, or **Hernando Cortez** (ĕrnän′ kôrtäs′, hĕrnän′dō kôrtĕz′), 1485–1547, Spanish conquistador, conqueror of Mexico. After service in Hispaniola and Cuba, he went (1519) under a commission of the Cuban governor Diego de Velázquez to conquer Mexico. There he was aided by a Spanish survivor of an earlier expedition and by an Indian girl, Malinche (renamed Marina on becoming Christian). He won over some peoples subordinate to the Aztec empire and got the help of Tlaxcalans after defeating them. His march on the Aztec cap., Tenochtitlán, ended triumphantly when Emperor Montezuma received him as a descendant of the god Quetzalcoatl. Cortés made Montezuma hostage and governed through him. He had, however, renounced allegiance to Velázquez and in 1520 had to return to the coast to defeat a force sent by Velázquez under Pánfilo de Narváez. While he was gone the Spanish under Pedro de Alvarado were driven from Tenochtitlán. Cortés rallied his forces and in 1521 besieged and took the city, destroying the Aztec empire. In 1524–26 he led an expedition to Honduras, putting the last puppet Aztec emperor, Cuauhtémoc, to death en route. He returned to find the governing power taken from him and though he was made marqués del Valle de Oaxaca he was not able to reestablish power in long wrangles with other administrators. He died in Spain, neglected by the court.

Cortes (kôr′täs), representative assembly in Spain. Local cortes originated in 12th–13th cent. in Leon, Castile, Aragon, Catalonia, Navarre, Valencia; continued to 19th cent., though much curtailed after Spanish unification (15th cent.). Local cortes were composed of three estates: clergy, nobles, commons. First all-Spanish Cortes met at Cádiz 1812. Since then, its status as parliament has been affected by frequent constitutional changes.

Cortez, Hernando: see CORTÉS, HERNÁN.

Cortez (kôrtĕz′), town (pop. 2,680), SW Colo., near Mesa Verde Natl. Park, Yucca House Natl. Monument, in an agr. and livestock area.

cortin: see ADRENAL GLAND.

Cortina d'Ampezzo (kôrtē′nä dämpĕd′zō), Alpine resort, NE Italy, in heart of Dolomites.

Cortland, city (pop. 18,152), central N.Y., S of Syracuse; settled 1791. Rail center in farm area. Wood, metal (esp. wire), food products.

Cortona, Pietro da (pyä′trō dä kôrtō′nù), 1596–1669, Italian painter and architect; real name Pietro Berrettini. Frescoes in Barberini Palace, Rome.

Cortot, Alfred (kôrtō′), 1877–, French pianist and conductor, authoritative interpreter of Chopin. For many years he played trios with Jacques Thibaud, violinist, and Pablo Casals, cellist.

Coruña, La (kùrū′nù, Span. lä kôrōo′nyä), city (pop. 92,-189), cap. of La Coruña prov., NW Spain, in Galicia; Atlantic port. Of pre-Roman origin; flourished as port and textile center in Middle Ages; sacked by Drake 1598. Scene of Peninsular War battle in which Sir John Moore was mortally wounded (1809). Also spelled Corunna in English.

corundum (kùrŭn′dùm), a mineral, aluminum oxide.

The finer varieties are used as gems, the coarser as abrasives. Emery is impure corundum. The chief corundum gems are ruby, sapphire, and topaz.

Corunna, Spain: see CORUÑA, LA.

Corvallis (kôrvăl′ĭs), city (pop. 16,207), NW Oregon, on Willamette R. and SSW of Salem, in dairy, fruit, and timber area; settled 1846. Seat of Oregon State Col. (land-grant, state supported; coed.; chartered 1858).

Corvinus, Matthias: see MATTHIAS CORVINUS.

Coryate, Thomas (kŏr′ēāt), 1577?–1617, English traveler. His *Crudities* (1611) reports his journey that covered much of the Continent.

Corybantes (kôr″ĭbăn′tēz), in Greek religion, dancers who accompanied goddess CYBELE on her journeys.

Corydon (kŏr′ĭdŭn), town (pop. 1,944), S Ind., W of Louisville, Ky.; laid out 1808. Territorial cap. 1813–16, state cap. 1816–25. Scene of only Indian battle of Civil War (July 8, 1863).

Cos, island in the Dodecanese: see KOS.

Cosenza (kôzĕn′tsä), city (pop. 30,038), Calabria, S Italy. Chief city of anc. Brutii. Alaric I is said to be buried here under Busento R., which was temporarily diverted from its course. Medieval castle built by Emperor Frederick II. Cathedral.

Cosgrave, William Thomas (kŏz′grāv), 1880–, Irish statesman. After Sinn Fein split (1922) he stood by Free State. Was president of executive council of Ireland, 1922–32. After defeat by De Valera, was opposition leader until his resignation in 1944.

Coshocton (kŭshŏk′tŭn), city (pop. 11,675), E central Ohio, N of Zanesville, at junction of Walhonding and Tuscarawas rivers; laid out 1802. Mfg. of iron and steel products and plastics.

cosmetics to enhance personal appearance have been used since prehistoric times. The ancient Egyptians, Greeks, Romans used them; in Middle Ages, known beauty aids were supplemented by those brought home by Crusaders. Renaissance saw beginning of lavish use, which continued until virtual disappearance of make-up in 19th cent. Revival came at turn of century; manufacture of cosmetics is now huge industry.

cosmic rays, radiation of unknown origin coming to earth from outer space, carrying large amounts of energy and able to penetrate nearly all substances. Primary rays believed to be chiefly protons; many of these collide with air particles. The nuclei of atoms destroyed in collisions break into particles which probably become secondary cosmic rays. Tertiary and quaternary rays said to be formed similarly.

cosmogony (kŏzmŏ′gùnē), any theory of the origin of the world, of man, and of the universe in a philosophic, scientific setting. See NEBULAR HYPOTHESIS; PLANETESIMAL HYPOTHESIS.

cosmos (kŏz′mùs), garden annual of genus *Cosmos* with crimson, pink, white, or orange flowers.

Cossa, Baldassarre (bäldäs-sär′rä kôs′sä), c.1370–1419, Neapolitan churchman, antipope as John XXIII in the Great SCHISM. When he was a cardinal he deserted the cause of Gregory XII and supported the Council of PISA, intended to end the schism between Rome and Avignon popes. When Antipope Alexander V died, Cossa was elected (1410). He courted the favor of Emperor SIGISMUND and aided Louis II of Anjou against Lancelot (an ally of Gregory) in Naples. He convened the Council of CONSTANCE under pressure from Sigismund and reluctantly promised to abdicate if his rivals would. They did, but he fled and tried to maintain his position. He was forced to return and was held prisoner until 1418.

Cossa, Francesco, or **Francesco del Cossa** (fränchä′skō dĕl kôs′sä), c.1435–1477?, Italian painter, identified with the schools of Ferrara and Bologna.

Cossacks (kŏ′săks), peasant-soldiers of several regions in Russia who until 1918 held certain privileges of self-government in return for military service. They were descended from fugitive serfs who settled frontier steppes in 16th and 17th cent. and defended them against Turks and Tatars (see DON COSSACKS; ZAPO-

ROZHE COSSACKS). Their prominence in social revolts of 17th–18th cent. cost them many privileges. Cossacks took important part in conquest and colonization of new territories (e.g., SIBERIA, KUBAN). Before 1917 their 11 communities numbered c.4,000,000. Most of them fought against the Bolsheviks in civil war of 1918–20.

Costa, Isaäc da (ē′sä-äk dä kôs′tä), 1798–1860, Dutch poet. Of an aristocratic Jewish family, he entered (1822) the Reformed Church, and much of his poetry is fervently Christian.

Costa Mesa (kŏ′stù mā′sù), village (pop. 11,844), S Calif., S of Santa Ana, in citrus fruit area.

Costa Rica (kŏ′stù rē′kù) [Span.,= rich coast], republic (19,650 sq. mi.; pop. 800,875), Central America, between the Caribbean (NE) and the Pacific (S and W). The NE area is a broad jungle plain, the NW is jungles and low mountains. The heart of the country is the central plateau in the mountain belt; here are the cap., CARTAGO (founded 1563), HEREDIA, and Alajuela. The small Indian population made Spanish conquest easy, and colonists had relatively small landholdings. Part of the captaincy general of Guatemala before gaining independence from Spain, Costa Rica was later part of Iturbide's empire (1821–23) and a member of the Central American Federation (1823–38). Coffee, introduced in the 19th cent., became the dominant crop. In 1874 M. C. Keith founded Limón and developed banana plantations on the Caribbean coast (many now abandoned because of leaf blight). The plateau cities are connected by rail and highways and are connected with the Pacific port, PUNTARENAS. Costa Rica is traditionally democratic and has been active in Pan-American organizations. Took part in World War II on the Allied side and joined the United Nations (1943).

Coster, Charles de: see DE COSTER, CHARLES.

Côte-d'Or (kōt-dôr′), department (3,392 sq. mi.; pop. 335,602), E France, in Burgundy; cap. Dijon. World-famed vineyards.

Cotentin (kôtätē′), peninsular region of Normandy, N France, projecting into English Channel; roughly identical with Manche dept. Historic cap. Coutances; chief towns are Cherbourg, Saint-Lô. Agr., apple orchards. Heavy fighting in World War II (1944).

Côtes-du-Nord (kōt′dü-nôr′), department (2,787 sq. mi.; pop. 526,955), NW France, in Brittany; cap. Saint-Brieuc.

Cöthen, Germany: see KÖTHEN.

Cotman, John Sell, 1782–1842, English landscape painter, best known for water colors and drawings.

Cotopaxi (kōtōpăk′sē), active volcano, 19,344 ft. high, N central Ecuador.

Cotswold Hills, broken limestone plateau in Gloucestershire, England, extending c.50 mi. NE from Bath. Crest is Thames-Severn watershed. Region famous for Cotswold sheep and picturesque houses.

Cottage Grove, city (pop. 3,536), W central Oregon, on Coast Fork (near dam) of WILLAMETTE R.

cottage holding, in England, agr. tract of three acres or less, producing food for family whose cash income is from some other source. See also SMALL HOLDING.

cotter, cottar, or **crofter,** in Highland Scotland, an agr. tenant who rents a croft (small farm).

Cotton, (Thomas) Henry, 1907–, British golfer. Won British Open (1934, 1937), Professional Golfers' Association of America (1932, 1939, 1946) championships, many others.

Cotton, John, 1584–1652, Puritan clergyman in England and Mass. Bay Colony. Getting into difficulty as Puritan vicar of St. Botolph's, Boston, Lincolnshire, he migrated (1633) to America. The city of Boston renamed to honor him. Responsible for exile of Anne Hutchinson and expulsion of Roger Williams. Helped mold Congregational Church.

Cotton, Sir Robert Bruce, 1571–1631, English antiquarian. His collection of books, manuscripts, coins, and antiquities now is in British Museum.

GREEK

ROMAN

MEDIEVAL
FRENCH c.1250

EARLY RENAISSANCE
FRENCH c.1430

EARLY TUDOR
ENGLISH c.1540

ELIZABETHAN
ENGLISH c.1600

LOUIS XIV
FRENCH c.1690

LOUIS XVI
FRENCH c.1780

EMPIRE
FRENCH c.1805

TIME OF GEORGE IV
ENGLISH c.1820

EARLY VICTORIAN
AMERICAN c.1850

MID-VICTORIAN
AMERICAN c.1870

cotton, most important of vegetable fibers, used from prehistoric times in many lands. The plant, a perennial of genus *Gossypium,* bears capsules (bolls) containing seeds (forming c.⅔ of bulk of boll), each surrounded by downy white or creamy fibers (c.¾ in.–1½ in. long), easily spun into thread. Usually grown as annual; thrives in temperate climate with well-distributed rainfall, as in U.S. COTTON BELT, where upland varieties are mainly grown; sea-island and American-Egyptian cotton are produced in W U.S. U.S., India, China, USSR, Egypt, Brazil are chief producers. Bolls were long hand picked; machine picking, now increasing, is aided by use of chemical to rid plants of leaves before stripping bolls. BOLL WEEVIL is most harmful of many insect pests and diseases. Cotton mfg., a huge industry, esp. in Great Britain and U.S., involves cleaning, ginning, carding, and spinning in order to get thread strong enough for weaving. Innumerable commodities, in addition to textiles, are made from cotton. Linters yield CELLULOSE; seeds, containing c.20% oil, yield **cottonseed oil,** used in refined state in cookery, as ingredient of margarine and cosmetics, and in crude state as industrial raw material.

Cotton Belt, term applied to part of U.S. formerly devoted mainly to cotton. Area included N.C., S.C., Ga., Ala., Miss., La., Ark., Okla., Texas, and sections of Va., Ky., Tenn., Fla., and Mo. Mainly diversified crops now, though cotton still important. Texas now main cotton grower, and it is also grown in Calif., Ariz., and N.Mex.

cotton gin (jĭn), machine for separating cotton fiber from seeds. Roller gin known from ancient times. Saw gin invented 1793 by Eli Whitney consisted of revolving toothed cylinder which pulled lint through grate. Modern mechanized adaptation has series of circular saws which draw fiber through grid.

cottonmouth: see WATER MOCCASIN.

cottonseed oil: see COTTON.

cottonwood: see POPLAR.

Cottrell, Frederick Gardner (kŏ′trŭl), 1877–1948, American chemist. He was an authority on nitrogen fixation and mineral fertilizers and developed Cottrell method of dust precipitation, using an electric current at high potential.

Cotulla (kŭtū′lŭ), city (pop. 4,418), SW Texas, NNE of Laredo. Tourist stop on Pan-American Highway.

Coucy, Robert de (rōbĕr′ dü kōōsē′), d. 1311, French architect who helped build Rheims cathedral.

Coué, Émile (kōōā′), 1857–1926, French psychotherapist known for formula, "Day by day, in every way, I am getting better and better."

Coughlin, Charles Edward (kŏ′glĭn), 1891–, Roman Catholic priest in U.S., b. Canada. Bitterly opposed New Deal policies through press and radio.

Coulanges, Numa Denis Fustel de: see FUSTEL DE COULANGES, NUMA DENIS.

coulomb (kōō′lŏm), quantity of electricity that current of one AMPERE transfers in one second. **Coulomb's law:** force of attraction or repulsion between two charges is inversely proportional to square of distance between them and directly proportional to product. Established by **Charles Augustin de Coulomb,** 1736–1806, French physicist, for whom coulomb named.

Coulter, John Merle, 1851–1928, American botanist, b. China. A pupil of Asa Gray, he edited sixth ed. of Gray's *Manual.* Influential in founding Boyce Thompson Inst. for Plant Research. Founded and edited (for 50 years) the *Botanical Gazette.*

council, ecumenical (ĕ″kūmĕ′nĭkŭl, ē″-) [Gr.,= universal], council of church authorities accepted by the Church as official. Their decrees are called canons if ratified by the pope. Roman Catholics recognize the following ecumenical or general councils: (1) 1 Nicaea, 325; (2) 1 Constantinople, 381; (3) Ephesus, 431; (4) Chalcedon, 451; (5) 2 Constantinople, 553; (6) 3 Constantinople, 680; (7) 2 Nicaea, 787; (8) 4 Constantinople, 869; (9) 1 Lateran, 1123; (10) 2 Lateran, 1139; (11) 3 Lateran, 1179; (12) 4 Lateran, 1215; (13)

1 Lyons, 1245; (14) 2 Lyons, 1274; (15) Vienne, 1311; (16) Constance, 1414; (17) Basel and Ferrara-Florence, 1431, 1438; (18) 5 Lateran, 1512; (19) Trent, 1545; (20) Vatican, 1869. The Orthodox recognize the first seven and also the continuation of 3 Constantinople (the Trullan Synod). At the time of the Great Schism the theory was advanced that the general council, rather than the pope, was supreme in the Church. The chief proponent was John Gerson, and this conciliar theory flourished at the Councils of Pisa and Constance, later failing.

Council Bluffs, city (pop. 45,429), SW Iowa, on the Mississippi opposite Omaha, Nebr.; settled 1846 by Mormons on sites of trading post (1820s) and Indian mission (estab. 1838–40 by Father De Smet). Supply point during 1849–50 gold rush. Grew after being made E terminus of Union Pacific RR 1863. Has railroad shops, grain elevators, and stockyards. Mfg. of metal, wood, and food products. Monument commemorates 1804 meeting of Lewis and Clark with the Indians.

Council Grove, city (pop. 2,722), E central Kansas, SW of Topeka and on Neosho R. Treaty made here with Osage Indians, 1825. Site later became a campground on Santa Fe Trail. Methodist Indian mission (1849) still stands.

Council of Europe, Council of Foreign Ministers, Council of Ten, etc.: see EUROPE, COUNCIL OF; FOREIGN MINISTERS, COUNCIL OF; TEN, COUNCIL OF.

counterpoint, in music, the art of combining melodies, each of which is independent of the others, although together they form a homogeneous whole. Five types of counterpoint have been defined: note against note; two notes against one; four notes against one; syncopation; and florid counterpoint, which combines the other four. See also POLYPHONY.

Counts, George S(ylvester), 1889–, American educator, professor of education at Teachers College, Columbia Univ., after 1927. Advocated teachers' unions and was president (1939–42) of American Federation of Teachers. Has taken part in liberal politics. Wrote many books on history and democracy.

Couperin, François (frãswä′ kōōpŭrĕ′), 1668–1733, French organist, harpsichordist, and composer, called "le Grand" to distinguish him from other members of his musically prominent family. His four books of harpsichord suites influenced Bach.

Couperus, Louis Marie Anne (kōōpā′rōōs), 1863–1923, Dutch novelist. His works, popular at home and abroad, include a collection of four realistic novels, *The Book of the Small Souls* (1901–3).

Courbet, Gustave (güstäv′ kōōrbä′), 1819–77, French painter, b. Ornans. An opponent of vested authority, whether aesthetic or political. Showed his avowed realism in his painting such works as *Funeral at Ornans* and *Painter's Studio;* won prestige but aroused much official criticism. In 1873, after participating in the Commune, he fled to Switzerland where he died in exile and poverty.

coureurs de bois (kōōrûr′ dübwä′) [Fr.,= wood runners], in French regime in Canada unlicensed traders who played active part in fur trade and exploration.

Courier, Paul Louis (pŏl′ lwĕ′ kōōryä′), 1772–1825, French author and classical scholar. After the Restoration he wrote political pamphlets which place him among his nation's most brilliant stylists.

Courland or **Kurland** (kûr′lŭnd, kōōr′länt), region and former duchy, W Latvia; historic cap. JELGAVA. Conquered by LIVONIAN KNIGHTS in 13th cent. When the order disbanded (1561), its grand master became first duke of Courland, under Polish overlordship. Under Russian influence from early 18th cent., Courland was annexed by Russia in third Polish partition (1795). Became part of Latvia 1918.

court, in general, official body charged with adjudicating legal cases. In ancient Egypt and Babylonia courts were semi-ecclesiastic; in Greece assemblies had court functions; in Rome emerged secular complex system of courts, staffed with professional jurists. Britain since Judicature Act of 1873 has high court of justice (with divisions of chancery; probate, divorce, and admiralty; Queen's—or King's—Bench) and court of appeal. In U.S. two systems are Federal courts (district courts, circuit courts of appeals, and at head, Supreme Court) and state courts (including many types, e.g., police courts, court of probate).

Courtois, Bernard (bĕrnär′ kŏ̄ortwä′), 1777–1838, French chemist. He discovered and isolated iodine.

Courtrai (kŏ̄orträ′), Flemish *Kortrijk*, town (pop. 40,-085), West Flanders, W Belgium, on Lys R. Textile center since medieval times. Scene of first BATTLE OF THE SPURS (1302). Church of Notre Dame (13th cent.) contains Van Dyck's *Elevation of the Cross.*

court tennis, believed to have been originated about 14th cent. in France, forerunner of most modern racquet games. Played on indoor cement court 110 ft. by 38 ft., surrounded by four walls 30 ft. high.

Cousin, Jean (zhã kŏ̄ozĕ′), c.1490–c.1560, French painter. His treatise on portraiture and some of his glass paintings are attributed by some to his son and pupil, **Jean Cousin,** c.1522–c.1590.

Cousin, Victor, 1792–1867, French philosopher, minister of education under Louis Philippe. In that period he was practically dictator of education and philosophy. His own philosophy was eclectic in the extreme because Cousin believed that all conflicting doctrines held part of the truth ready for the intuitive eye to discern.

Cousin-Montauban, Charles Guillaume: see PALIKAO.

Cousins, Samuel, 1801–87, English mezzotint engraver.

Coustou (kŏ̄ostŏ̄o′), family of French sculptors. **Nicolas Coustou,** 1658–1733, and brother, **Guillaume Coustou,** 1677–1746, worked at Marly and Versailles. Guillaume's son, **Guillaume Coustou,** 1716–77, was also a sculptor.

Couthon, Georges (zhôrzh′ kŏ̄otŏ̄′), 1755?–1794, French revolutionist. Fanatic Jacobin. Shared with Robespierre, Saint-Just in triumvirate of Terror. Fell on 9 Thermidor; guillotined.

Couza, Alexander John: see CUZA.

Covadonga (kō′vädōn′gä), hamlet, N Spain, in Asturias. Scene (716?) of first Christian victory over Moors.

Covarrubias, Miguel (mĕgāl′ kōvär-rŏ̄o′bēäs), 1902–, American artist, b. Mexico. Best known for his caricatures and drawings for *Vanity Fair.*

covenant (kŭ′vŭnŭnt) [O. Fr.,= agreement], in Bible and theology, explicit promise of God to man. In law, contract under seal or agreement by deed. In Scottish history (kŭvŭnănt′), pact by opponents of episcopacy, known as COVENANTERS. Covenants in Bible are not contractual, but free promises of God: e.g., His covenants with Israel culminating in Law of Moses, and known as Old Covenant. In law, covenants follow same rules as other contracts; variously classified, all are characterized by explicit promise of covenantor to covenantee.

Covenanters, in Scottish history, groups of people bound by oath to defend Presbyterianism. Covenant of 1581 sought to combat Catholicism. Covenant of 1638 opposed innovations of Archbishop LAUD, especially use of English Book of Common Prayer. They resisted king's armies in BISHOPS' WARS (1639–40) and supported Parliament in PURITAN REVOLUTION only after acceptance (1643) of Solemn League and Covenant pledging Presbyterian state church in England and Ireland. Their power broken by Cromwell's conquest of Scotland in 1650. After Restoration, Covenanters were alternately coerced and persuaded to accept episcopacy but stubbornly resisted. Troubles ended with Glorious Revolution (1688).

Covent Garden (kŭ′vŭnt), London opera house. Located in produce market district, it is on site of famous theater (opened 1732) associated with Garrick, the Kembles, and others. Present theater built 1858. Patti and Caruso sang here.

Coventry (kŏv′ŭntrē), city (pop. 258,211), Warwickshire, England. Founded 14th cent., has old buildings.

Has been important center for airplane and munitions mfg. since 1914. Legend of Lady Godiva and Peeping Tom, celebrated by Tennyson, perpetuated until recently by pageants. City suffered intensely destructive air raid Nov. 14–15, 1940. Hundreds of buildings destroyed, including the 14th-cent. cathedral, and thousands made homeless. Phrase "to send to Coventry" means to ostracize socially.

Coventry, town (pop. 9,869), W R.I., SW of Providence. Mfg. of textiles.

cover crop, temporary crop sown to protect soil (e.g., from erosion), increase nutrients (e.g., nitrogen from legumes), or to improve texture by being plowed under. Valuable in rehabilitating land.

Coverdale, Miles, 1488–1569, English translator of Bible, bishop of Exeter (1551–53). Published translation 1535. Later collaborated in Great Bible (1539), edited "Cranmer's Bible" (1540), and helped on first Book of Common Prayer.

covered wagon: see CONESTOGA WAGON; PRAIRIE SCHOONER.

Coverley, Sir Roger de: see ROGER DE COVERLEY.

Covington (kŭv′–). **1** City (pop. 5,192), N central Ga., SE of Atlanta. Textile and lumber mills. **2** City (pop. 64,452), N Ky., on Ohio R. where Licking R. enters; settled 1812, laid out 1815. Bridges connect with Cincinnati and Newport. Rail focus with breweries, distilleries, meat and tobacco packing plants, and mfg. of X-ray equipment, tools, and wire goods. **3** Town (pop. 5,113), SE La., near L. Pontchartrain, in agr. (strawberries, tung oil) area; settled 1769. Has lumbering and mfg. of wood preservatives. Resort. **4** Town (pop. 5,860), western Va., SW of Staunton, in Jackson R. valley. Paper, pulp, and rayon plants. Iron and coal fields near.

Coward, Noel, 1899–, English playwright, actor, director, composer. His versatile, sophisticated works include dramas (e.g., *Private Lives,* 1930), musicals (e.g., *Bittersweet,* 1929), and films (e.g., *In Which We Serve*).

cowbird, New World bird of oriole and blackbird family. Male eastern, or common, cowbird (cow blackbird) is glossy black and c.8 in. long with brown head and breast. Most species lay eggs in other birds' nests; birds usually incubate the cowbird eggs and feed the young at expense of their own.

Cowdry, Edmund Vincent (kou′drē), 1888–, American biologist, authority on cells and tissues.

Cowell, Henry Dixon (kou′ŭl), 1897–, American composer and pianist. He experimented with new musical resources (e.g., in piano compositions he introduced the tone cluster, played with the arm or fist). In 1927 he founded *New Music,* a quarterly for the publication of music by contemporary composers.

Cowes (kouz), urban district (pop. 17,154), Isle of Wight, England, near Southampton. Seaport, resort, and shipbuilding center, it is headquarters of the Royal Yacht Club and holds annual regattas.

Cowles, Henry Chandler (kōlz), 1869–1939, American botanist, a pioneer in plant ecology.

Cowley, Abraham (kŏ̄o′–, kou′–), 1618–67, English poet and essayist. One of the cleverest of the metaphysical poets, he was notable for precociousness and wit. Among volumes of his works are *Poetical Blossoms* (1633), *The Mistress* (1647), *Poems* (1656). Prose essays, simple in style, much praised.

Cowley, Hannah: see DELLA-CRUSCANS.

cowpea or **black-eyed bean,** leguminous plant (*Vigna sinensis*), a forage and cover crop in S U.S.

Cowpens (kou′pĭnz), town (pop. 1,879), NW S.C., ENE of Spartanburg. National battlefield site marks battle (Jan. 17, 1781) of CAROLINA CAMPAIGN near by.

Cowper, William Cowper, 1st **Earl** (kŏ̄o′pŭr), c.1664–1723, English jurist. Took leading part in union of England with Scotland 1706. As first lord chancellor of Great Britain (1707–10) presided at trial of Henry Sacheverell.

Cowper, William (kŏ̄o′pŭr, kou′–), 1731–1800, English

poet. Subject to melancholia, he was placed with the Unwin family at Huntington and later at Olney. His writings include intensely religious *Olney Hymns* (1779); *The Task* (1785). Pictures of rural life foreshadow romanticism. Also known for shorter poems, "John Gilpin," "To Mrs. Unwin," "To Mary," and longer *The Castaway*. Letters much admired.

cowpox, infectious viral disease of cows, related to SMALLPOX. Similar disease affects horses and sheep.

cowrie or **cowry** (kou'rē), marine gastropod mollusk found in warm waters. Shells of various species used among primitives as money and adornment.

cowslip: see MARSH MARIGOLD; PRIMROSE; SHOOTING STAR; VIRGINIA COWSLIP.

Cox, Jacob Dolson, 1828–1900, Union general in Civil War and American statesman. Served ably in Antietam and Atlanta campaigns. Secretary of Interior (1869–70) under Pres. Grant; advocated civil service reform, opposed spoilsmen in Republican party. Father of **Kenyon Cox,** 1856–1919, painter and art critic.

Cox, Palmer, 1840–1924, American writer-illustrator of the Brownie stories for children.

Coxey, Jacob Sechler, 1854–1951, American social reformer. Interested in unemployment and monetary problems. Farmer-Labor presidential candidate 1932, 1936. Led **Coxey's Army,** band of unemployed men who marched to Washington, D.C., following Panic of 1893, to petition Congress for measures which they hoped would relieve unemployment and distress. Reached Washington with c.500 men instead of the proclaimed 100,000; its leaders were arrested for walking on Capitol lawn.

coyote (kī'ō'tē, kī'ōt) or **prairie wolf,** small wolf (*Canis*) native to W North America, with thick, long, tawny fur and a bushy black-tipped tail. It hunts small animals and in packs attacks larger mammals. It is a scavenger and a destroyer of rodents. Cry is yelping, doglike.

Coypel (kwäpĕl'), family of French painters. **Noël Coypel,** 1628–1707, worked on decorations of royal palaces. His son, **Antoine Coypel,** 1661–1722, painted Aeneid series for Palais-Royal. Antoine's half-brother, **Noël Nicolas Coypel,** 1692–1734, and son, **Charles Antoine Coypel,** 1694–1752, were also well-known painters.

Coysevox, Antoine (kwäzvôks'), 1640–1720, French sculptor who did much of the sculpture at Versailles.

Cr, chemical symbol of the element CHROMIUM.

Crab, the, in astronomy: see ZODIAC.

crab, crustacean with broad, flat outer skeleton, short abdomen bent under body, stalked eyes, five pairs of legs (the first with claws). Crabs are chiefly marine, but some are fresh-water, some land forms. Omnivorous feeders, some are scavengers, others predatory. See also KING CRAB; HERMIT CRAB.

crab apple, type of apple tree and its small, sour fruit used in preserves and jellies. Siberian crab (*Malus baccata*) is widely grown. Other species and varieties, e.g., Bechtel's crab with double flowers, are grown for ornament.

Crabbe, George, 1754–1832, English poet, a physician and clergyman. His strong, drab poetry (as in long poems, *The Village,* 1781; *The Parish Register,* 1807; and *The Borough,* 1810) on the life of the poor illustrates realistic aspect of romanticism.

Crabtree, Lotta, 1847–1924, American actress. A pupil of Lola Montez, she was a popular child actress in Calif. mining camps before a successful career in generally shoddy plays. Retired 1891.

Cracow (krä'kō, krä'cou), Pol. *Kraków,* city (pop. c.347,500), S Poland, on the Vistula; cap. of Poland from 14th cent. to 1595. Commercial and mfg. center; seat of Jagiellonian Univ. (founded 1364); episcopal see from c.1000. Kings of Poland continued to be crowned and buried at Cracow after fire of 1595 caused transfer of cap. to Warsaw. Cracow passed to Austria in third Polish partition (1795); was made a republic (with surrounding dist.) under

protection of Austria, Russia, and Prussia by Congress of Vienna (1815); was annexed by Austria after insurrection of 1846; reverted to Poland 1919. Noted landmarks include royal castle (Wawel), rebuilt 16th cent.; 14th-cent. Gothic cathedral; 13th-cent. Church of Our Lady, with altarpiece by Veit Stoss; 14th-cent. cloth hall.

Craddock, Charles Egbert, pseud. of **Mary Noailles Murfree,** 1850–1922, American novelist, author of novels and stories of Tennessee people.

Crafton, borough (pop. 8,066), SW Pa., W residential suburb of Pittsburgh. Mfg. of stoves.

Craig, (Edward) Gordon, 1872–, English stage designer, producer, and actor; son of Ellen Terry. His poetic, mysterious stage designs and productions for Ibsen's *Vikings* and Shakspere's *Much Ado about Nothing* (1903) and *Hamlet* (Moscow Art Theatre, 1912) greatly contributed to modern theater development.

Craig, James: see CRAIGAVON, JAMES CRAIG, 1st VISCOUNT.

Craig, Sir James Henry, 1748–1812, British soldier, governor in chief of Canada (1807–11), b. Gibraltar. Led English army into Italy (1805–6) and occupied Sicily. As governor in chief of Canada, opposed to representative government and to French Canadians, he dissolved assembly of Lower Canada (1809).

Craigavon, James Craig, 1st **Viscount** (krägä'vùn), 1871–1940, Ulster statesman. Organized resistance against Home Rule. First prime minister of N. Ireland from 1921 until his death.

Craigenputtock, moorland home of the Carlyles (1828–34) near Dumfries, S Scotland.

Craigie, Sir William A., 1867–, British lexicographer. Generally considered the foremost lexicographer of his time, he was joint editor of *New English Dictionary* (commonly called *Oxford Dictionary*) 1901–33 and was chief editor of *A Dictionary of American English on Historical Principles* (issued in parts after 1936; pub. as 4 vols., 1938–43).

Craik, Dinah Maria Mulock: see MULOCK.

Craiova (kräyô'vä), city (pop. 84,574), SW Rumania; historic cap. of Oltenia.

Cram, Ralph Adams, 1863–1942, American architect, an exponent of Gothic architecture. Wrote chiefly on medieval architecture and thought.

Cranach or **Kranach, Lucas** (both: lōō'käs krä'näkh), the elder, 1472–1553, German artist, whose real name was Müller or Sunder. Court painter to three electors of Saxony. A master of piquant line and silhouette in nudes, portraits, and religious paintings. Was a friend and supporter of Luther. His son and pupil **Lucas Cranach,** the younger, 1515–86, continued in his tradition.

cranberry, low creeping evergreen bog plant (*Vaccinium oxycoccus*), with red, tart berries used for sauces and jellies. Cultivated on commercial scale in parts of Mass., N.J., and Wis.

Cranbrook Foundation, school, art academy, and science institute, at Bloomfield Hills, Mich., near Pontiac. Buildings designed by Saarinen.

Crane, Hart, 1899–1932, American poet, author of *The Bridge* (1930) and other poems. Suicide by drowning.

Crane, Stephen, 1871–1900, American novelist, journalist, poet. After *Maggie: a Girl of the Streets* (1893), *The Red Badge of Courage* (1895; a Civil War novel) brought fame and career as war correspondent. Wrote epigrammatic free verse and short stories. Died in Germany of tuberculosis.

Crane, Walter, 1845–1915, English illustrator, painter, and decorator. Founded Arts and Crafts Exhibition Society of London in 1888.

crane, large wading bird of Old World chiefly. Some are in North America, e.g., the whooping crane (nearly extinct), sandhill crane, little brown crane, and Florida crane. Cranes perform rhythmical dance in mating season.

crane, machine using free end of a fixed beam to hoist and transfer heavy loads. Actuated anciently by manual or animal power, modern cranes run by steam, electric, Diesel, and hydraulic, as well as manual power. Cranes used inside include bridge or overhead traveling crane (along steel girder spanning fixed rails). Outside cranes include the gantry (mounted on structure over operating area), the rotary, derrick, and hammerhead (steel tower supports cantilever-type truss with power generator at short end, load-carrying device at other). Locomotor crane revolves on turntable mounted on rail car, caterpillar tread, truck, or pontoons. See *ill.*, page 619.

crane fly: see DADDY LONGLEGS.

Cranford, residential township (pop. 18,602), NE N.J., W of Elizabeth. Printing, mfg. of metal goods.

cranium: see SKULL.

Cranmer, Thomas (krăn′mŭr), 1489–1556, English churchman. Came to attention of HENRY VIII in 1529 by proposing method by which king could divorce Katharine of Aragon without recourse to Rome. Made Archbishop of Canterbury 1533; was subservient to king. As a regent for Edward VI, he largely determined course of English Church. Placed English Bible in churches; revised BOOK OF COMMON PRAYER 1552. Supported claim of Lady Jane Grey to throne. Under Catholic Mary I, was tried for treason, convicted of heresy, and burned at the stake.

Cranston, industrial city (pop. 55,060), central R.I., SW of Providence. Mfg. of textiles, metal and wood products, rubber goods, chemicals, plastics.

crape myrtle (krāp), shrub (*Lagerstroemia indica*), with crinkled flowers, grown in S U.S.

craps: see DICE.

Crapsey, Adelaide, 1878–1914, American poet; originator of the cinquain—a delicate, compressed five-line verse, modeled on Japanese *hokku.*

Crashaw, Richard (krä′shô), 1612–49, English poet, generally considered one of the metaphysical poets, and chief "baroque" poet in English. Son of Puritan clergyman, he turned to the High Church. On the Continent after the Puritans took over Cambridge (1643), he became a Roman Catholic (1646). His intense religious poetry includes richly ornamental poetry on St. Theresa. Chief volumes are *Steps to the Temple* and *Delights of the Muses* (1646; enlarged 1648) and *Carmen Deo Nostro* (1652).

Crassus (krä′sùs), family of anc. Rome. One well-known member was **Lucius Licinius Crassus** (lĭsĭ′nēùs), d. 91 B.C., orator and political leader. As consul in 95 B.C. he promoted the Licinian Law, intended to banish from Rome all who had gained citizenship by illegal means. This restrictive measure helped to bring on the Social War. Most noted was **Marcus Licinius Crassus,** d. 53 B.C., who managed by personal charm and ambition to become the richest man in Rome. His devices were not always admirable; it is said that as a supporter of Sulla he got property of proscribed persons and also that he had an efficient fire-fighting organization that would not act until the owner of a burning building sold it to Crassus. He earned prestige by helping to defeat the revolt of Spartacus. Politically ambitious, he was consul with POMPEY in 70 B.C., but they disagreed. Julius CAESAR persuaded him to join in the First Triumvirate (Caesar, Pompey, Crassus) and held the organization together. Crassus, assigned the province of Syria, had military ambitions and undertook a campaign against the Parthians. He was routed at Carrhae (53 B.C.) and was murdered by treachery.

crater (krā′tŭr), cuplike mouth of the vent of a volcano or geyser. Water sometimes fills the crater of an extinct volcano, as in Crater Lake, Oregon.

Crater Lake National Park: see NATIONAL PARKS AND MONUMENTS (table).

Craters of the Moon National Monument: see NATIONAL PARKS AND MONUMENTS (table).

crawfish: see CRAYFISH.

Crawford, F(rancis) Marion, 1854–1909, American romantic novelist, b. Italy (where he spent much of his life). His popular novels (e.g., *Saracinesca,* 1887; *The White Sister,* 1909) had a remote, exotic air and frequently historical or Oriental backgrounds.

Crawford, Isabella Valancy, 1850–87, Canadian poet, b. Ireland. Her verse was not recognized until after her death.

Crawford, Thomas, 1813–57, American sculptor, best known for his figure *Armed Freedom* on the dome of the Capitol at Washington.

Crawford, William Harris, 1772–1834, American statesman. U.S. Senator from Ga. (1807–13). U.S. Secretary of the Treasury (1816–25). Unsuccessful presidential candidate in 1824.

Crawford Notch, scenic pass, c.5 mi. long, in White Mts., N central N.H., through which Saco R. flows.

Crawfordsville, city (pop. 12,851), W Ind., S of Lafayette; laid out c.1822. Farming and stock-raising center; metal products. Seat of Wabash Col.

crayfish or **crawfish,** fresh-water crustacean smaller than related, similar lobster, and found in most areas except Africa. Usually they live in ponds, streams, or swamps; a few are partially terrestrial. They eat small aquatic animals and carrion. Developing eggs are carried on female's swimming legs.

Crazy Horse, d. 1877, Indian leader, chief of Oglala Sioux. Aided Sitting Bull in defeat of Custer (1876). Surrendered in 1877 but he was accused of planning a revolt and was shot.

cream of tartar, substance obtained from crystalline crust (argol), formed in wine-fermenting tanks. Argol is dissolved, decolorized, and purified and the crystalline product when dried and powdered is cream of tartar. Used in baking and to make ROCHELLE SALT and TARTAR EMETIC.

Creasy, Sir Edward Shepherd (krē′sē), 1812–78, English historian. Best known for *Fifteen Decisive Battles of the World* (1821; see BATTLE).

Crébillon, Prosper (prôspĕr′ krābēyō′), 1674–1762, French classical dramatist, author of *Rhadamiste et Zénobie* (1711) and *Catilina* (1748). His son, **Claude Crébillon** (klōd) (Crébillon fils), 1707–77, brought the licentious tale to perfection with *Le Sopha* (1745).

Crécy (krē′sē, Fr. kräsē′), in English also spelled **Cressy,** small town, N France, N of Abbeville. Here in 1346 Edward III of England defeated Philip VI of France in a major battle of Hundred Years War. French nobles were decimated by English longbows, which appeared for first time on Continent. Among combatants were EDWARD THE BLACK PRINCE and the blind king of Bohemia, JOHN OF LUXEMBURG.

Credi, Lorenzo di: see LORENZO DI CREDI.

credit, financial system to facilitate transfer of capital from those who own it to those who can use it in expectation of profit. Credit depends on trust of the person giving money or goods to another in the ability and honesty of the borrower. Modern business relies heavily on use of credit, from simple delivery of goods with later payment of purchase price to gigantic loans for building or expanding a business. Little known in the ancient world, credit developed with commerce. Excess credit in a community brings inflation; too little brings deflation. See DEBT.

Crédit Mobilier of America (krē′dĭt mōbĭlyä′), ephemeral construction company, connected with building of Union Pacific RR and with one of the major financial scandals in U.S. history. Led by Oakes AMES and Thomas C. DURANT, inner stockholders of Union Pacific set up Crédit Mobilier and made contracts with themselves, at profits of $7,000,000–$23,000,000. To forestall investigations or interference by Congress, Ames sold or assigned shares of stock to members of Congress at par, though shares were worth twice as much. Scandal broke during 1872 presidential campaign. Congressional investigation resulted in censures, no prosecutions.

creed [Latin *credo* = I believe], summary of basic doctrines of faith. Several have been of fundamental importance in Christianity. **1** The Nicene Creed, usually said to be a revision at the First Council of Constantinople (381) of the creed adopted by the First Council of Nicaea (325) to settle problems raised by Arianism. Actually the original creed was a simple statement including a declaration on the nature of Christ. The Nicene Creed may have been composed by St. Cyril of Jerusalem. In the Roman Catholic Church since the 9th cent. it has said, "the Holy Ghost . . . Who proceedeth from the Father *and the Son (Filioque).*" The Orthodox Church quarrels with the italicized words. **2** See ATHANASIAN CREED. **3** The Apostles' Creed, familiar in most of the more conservative Western churches, probably arose in the 2d or 3d cent. but did not reach its present form before 650. Essentially similar to the Nicene Creed (though simpler), it has two significant differences; it has the statement that Christ descended into Hell, not in the Nicene; it says "resurrection of the body," where the Nicene has "resurrection of the dead." **4** The Augsburg Confession (1530) is the official Lutheran statement, written by Melanchthon, endorsed by Luther. **5** The Thirty-nine Articles is the basic statement of faith for Anglican and Episcopal churches; its present form dates from the reign of Elizabeth I. **6** The Westminster Confession (1645–47) is a pronouncement of Calvinist doctrine in English, basic in the development of Presbyterianism and in Congregationalism.

Cree Indians, tribe, formerly located in Manitoba, of Algonquian linguistic stock. One branch, the Plains Cree, moved SW into buffalo territory. Culture of the Woodland Cree (in N) like that of Ojibwa.

Creek Indians, confederacy of more than 50 Indian towns (or tribes) mostly in Ala. and Ga. and mostly of Natchez-Muskogean linguistic stock. Had advanced agr. In Creek War of 1813–14, they massacred many at Fort Mims but were defeated by Andrew Jackson. Moved to the Indian Territory, they became one of FIVE CIVILIZED TRIBES.

creeper, name for various small birds with long decurved bills and usually inconspicuous plumage. True creepers (Certhiidae) are Old World family related to wrens and nuthatches; represented by one New World species, the brown creeper and its subspecies. Related are the Mexican or Sierra Madre, Rocky Mt., Sierra, and California creepers.

Crefeld, Germany: see KREFELD.

Creighton University: see OMAHA, Nebr.

Crémazie, (Joseph) Octave (krämäzē'), 1827?–1879, French Canadian poet. Poems were strongly influenced by nationalism and romanticism; of great importance in French Canadian poetry.

crème de menthe, mint-flavored LIQUEUR.

Crémieux, Isaac (or Adolphe) (ēzäk' krāmyû'), 1796–1880, a French minister of justice. Abolished slavery in colonies and secured full citizen's rights for Jews in Algeria.

Cremona (krāmō'nä), city (pop. 54,564), Lombardy, N Italy, on Po R., in rich agr. dist. Was Roman colony; independent commune in Middle Ages; conquered by Milan 1344. Famous for violins made by Amati, Guarneri, Stradivari. Impressive main square has cathedral (12th–16th cent.), 13th-cent. town hall.

creole [perhaps from Span.,= servant or child], in Latin America, native descendants of French and Spanish conquerors. In S U.S., descendants of French settlers as distinct from "Cajuns," descendants of Acadian exiles. The idea that Creole means part-Negro persons is incorrect though mixed bloods and Negroes may be called Creole.

Creon (krē'ŏn), in Greek legend, uncle of OEDIPUS. Regent of Thebes after banishment of Oedipus, he helped Eteocles, son of Oedipus, wrest kingdom from his brother POLYNICES. Forbade funeral rites for Polynices, and killed Antigone for defying him.

creosote (krē'ŭsōt), volatile, heavy oily liquid, a strong antiseptic, obtained by distillation of wood tar. Active principle is guaiacol. Creosote oil is used as preservative of timber and meat.

crepe (krāp), thin silk fabric with crinkled texture. Hard-finished crepe (crape) is used for mourning; soft crepes include crepe de Chine. Wool, rayon, cotton threads can be given crepe weave.

Crépy, Treaty of (krāpē'), 1544, concluded between Emperor Charles V and FRANCIS I of France at Crépy-en-Laonnois (formerly Crespy), N France. Charles renounced claim to Burgundy; Francis renounced claims to Naples, Flanders, Artois.

Crerar, Henry Duncan Graham (krēr'är), 1888–, Canadian general in World War II. After serving as chief of Canadian general staff, and in several commands, he was given command in 1944 of Canadian Army Overseas.

Crerar, John (krēr'är), 1827–89, American capitalist and philanthropist. Provided for the **John Crerar Library,** Chicago, noted for scientific and technical reference library and many special collections.

Cres, Yugoslavia: see CHERSO.

Cresap, Michael (krē'săp), 1742–75, American frontiersman and soldier. Accused by some of starting Lord Dunmore's War (1774). In American Revolution he marched his company so fast to support patriots at Boston—550 mi. in 22 days—that he died of exhaustion.

Cresilas (krē'sĭlŭs), fl. c.450 B.C., Greek sculptor. His statue of Pericles is the earliest Greek portrait statue that has been identified.

Crespy, Treaty of: see CRÉPY, TREATY OF.

cress: see NASTURTIUM; PEPPERGRASS; WATER CRESS.

Cressent, Charles (krēsä'), 1685–1768, French cabinetmaker, one of originators of Regence style. Studied under Boulle.

Cressida: see TROILUS AND CRESSIDA.

Cressy, France: see CRÉCY.

Creston, city (pop. 8,317), SW Iowa, SW of Des Moines, in livestock-raising area. Has food-processing plants and railroad shops.

Crestview, town (pop. 5,003), NW Fla., near Choctawhatchee Natl. Forest.

Cretaceous period (krētā'shŭs), third period of the MESOZOIC ERA of geologic time. It was marked by extensive submergence and vast changes in the earth's surface and life. By middle Cretaceous a seaway extended from the Gulf of Mexico to the Arctic. Late Cretaceous saw uplift and withdrawal of the water; conditions resembling the Carboniferous prevailed, and coal deposits accumulated. Near the close of the period came the Laramide revolution, and the first generation of the Rockies was born. Cretaceous marine life included reptiles, some resembling fish and some of huge size. Dinosaurs were still dominant on land, but primitive mammals were beginning to appear. Before the end of the period such modern plant forms as willow, elm, birch, oak, and maple were abundant. See also GEOLOGY, table.

Crete (krēt), Gr. *Krete,* largest island (3,235 sq. mi.; pop. 438,239), of Greece, in the E Mediterranean, c.60 mi. SE of mainland; cap. Canea. Extending c.160 mi. E-W, it is S limit of Aegean Sea. Candia is the largest city. Largely mountainous, it rises to 8,058 ft. in Mt. Ida. Agr. (olive oil, fruit, vegetables); wine growing; stock raising, dairying. There are iron and lignite deposits. Crete's ancient MINOAN CIVILIZATION, named after mythical King MINOS, was one of the world's oldest; it reached its height c.1600 B.C., then ended suddenly and mysteriously. Impressive remains have been found at CNOSSUS. Later Dorian settlers founded many flourishing city states, including Cnossus and Cydonia (modern Canea). Crete became an important trade center but played no vital political part in the Greek world. Conquered by Rome (68–67 B.C.) it later was held by Byzantium (except during Arab occupation, 826–961), then fell to Venice (1204) and to Turkey (1669; last two Venetian forts were ceded 1715). The Cretan insurrection of 1896–97 led to war between Greece and Turkey. Greece was utterly defeated, but the Great

Powers forced Turkey to evacuate Crete (1898) and occupied the island until 1909. Union with Greece, proclaimed 1908, became official in 1913. Antimonarchist uprising by followers of VENIZELOS was suppressed after some fighting (1935). In World War II Anglo-Greek forces were evacuated to Crete (April, 1941); in May they were overwhelmed in a German airborne invasion. Late in 1944 the Germans were isolated by British ships and surrendered to guerrilla forces.

cretinism (krē′tĭnĭzŭm), condition, usually congenital, resulting from lack of thyroid secretion. Cretins are often feeble-minded and dwarfed.

Creusa (krēoō′sù), in Greek and Roman legend, princess of Corinth. When Jason wished to marry Creusa, his wife, MEDEA, killed her.

Creuse (krûz), department (2,164 sq. mi.; pop. 188,-669), central France, in Marche; cap. Guéret.

Creusot, Le (lù krûzō′), city (pop. 17,133), Saône-et-Loire dept., E central France, in coal-mining region. Seat of large Schneider plants (steel and munitions). Heavily damaged in World War II.

crevasse (krùvăs′), crack in surface of a glacier caused by stresses developed as ice moves. The word is also applied to a crack in a river levee.

Crèvecœur, J. Hector St. John (krĕvkûr′), 1735–1813, American author and agriculturist, b. France. He introduced culture of European crops in America and wrote *Letters from an American Farmer* (1782).

Creve Coeur (krĕv′ koŏr′), village (pop. 5,499), N central Ill., near Peoria, in agr. and coal area.

Crewe (krōō), municipal borough (pop. 52,415), Cheshire, England; an important railway junction.

Crichton, James (krī′tùn), 1560?–1582, Scottish adventurer and scholar, called the Admirable Crichton. Attracted much attention in Italy (1579) by personal charms and scholarship; reputedly spoke 12 languages. Was killed in a street brawl.

cricket, insect of order Orthoptera related to grasshopper and katydid. Typical species have long antennae and powerful hind legs. Some are winged. Most are nocturnal. They often destroy vegetation; some also eat insects. Males "chirp" by rubbing one front wing against other, causing vibration; pitch and rate vary with temperature.

cricket, national sport of England. Played with bats and ball by two opposing teams of 11 men on level, closely cut green turf preferably measuring about 525 ft. by about 550 ft., with two wickets 66 ft. apart. Cricket was played in medieval England. London Cricket Club drew up (1774) first authoritative set of rules. Marylebone Cricket Club, governing body of game, founded 1787.

Crile, George Washington (krīl), 1864–1943, American surgeon. He was an authority on thyroid operations and surgical shock and author of technical and popular scientific works.

crime, legally, act in violation of the law consciously committed by a sane adult. Punishment is meted out by the government. Causes of crime are complex. Former beliefs in hereditary criminality and link of crime with physical characteristics are now generally discarded, and emphasis of study has shifted to environmental and psychological factors—poverty, family background, emotional disorders. With increasing complexity of industrial society came more laws and more crime. Offenses against property (e.g., theft) more common in cities, but crimes of violence (e.g., murder, rape) equally common in urban and rural areas. General attitude toward crime has changed since humanitarian movement began late in 18th cent. Emphasis now is placed on crime prevention and rehabilitation of criminal.

Crimea (krīmē′ù), Rus. *Krim,* anc. *Chersonesus Taurica,* peninsula (c.10,000 sq. mi.; pop. c.1,050,000), S European RSFSR, on N shore of Black Sea, connected with mainland by PEREKOP Isthmus. Cities: Simferopol, Sevastopol, Kerch, Feodosiya, Eupatoria.

Consists of wheat and cotton-growing steppe in N; Crimean or Yaila Mts. (highest point 5,062 ft.) in S; and subtropical littoral ("Russian Riviera"), growing fruit, wine, tobacco, with famous resorts such as Yalta. KERCH peninsula (E) has mineral wealth and heavy industries. Early inhabitants, Cimmerians, were followed in 8th cent. B.C. by Scythians. Coast was colonized by Ionian Greeks 7th cent. B.C. Ruled by a Thracian dynasty after 438 B.C., the "kingdom of the Cimmerian Bosporus" was annexed c.110 B.C. by Mithridates VI of Pontus and soon afterward by Rome. Between 3d and 13th cent. A.D. the Crimea was overrun by Goths, Huns, Khazars, Cumans, Mongols. Coast was controlled by Byzantium 6th–12th cent., then by Genoa, which set up prosperous colonies, notably at FEODOSIYA. In 1475 Crimea fell to the TATARS, whose khans were vassals to Ottoman sultans from 1478. From their cap. at BAKHCHISARAI the khans conquered ports of S Russia, pushed their raids as far as Moscow and Poland. In 1774 Catherine II forced Turkey to declare the khanate independent; in 1783 she annexed it to Russia. Many Russian, Greek, and other settlers came. The Crimea was a battleground in the Crimean War (1854–56), in both world wars, and in the Russian civil war, when in 1920 it became the last refuge of the Whites. Its status as autonomous soviet republic, created 1921, was abolished during World War II; the Tatar pop., charged with aiding the Germans, was deported.

Crimean War (krīmē′ùn), 1853–56, between Russia and allied powers of Turkey, England, France, Sardinia. General causes: see EASTERN QUESTION. Pretext: quarrel between Russia and France over guardianship of Palestinian holy places. Turkey having turned down Russian demands, Russia occupied Moldavia and Walachia, and Turkey declared war (1853). France and England joined Turkey in 1854; Sardinia in 1855. Main campaign, centered on siege of SEVASTOPOL in Crimea, was marked by futile gallantry (e.g., battle of BALAKLAVA) and scandalous condition of hospitals (which prompted the work of Florence NIGHTINGALE). Peace treaty (see PARIS, CONGRESS OF) checked Russian influence in SE Europe.

criminal law, distinct body of legal rules governing the definition and trial of crimes (acts deemed detrimental to the state), a part of public law. The state rather than a private individual seeks out and punishes the offender. In England criminal law developed out of common law; principles brought by settlers to British American colonies. In U.S. some important fundamental rules are: no act is a crime unless defined as such in law; accused is considered innocent until proved guilty; bills of attainder (legislative decrees declaring guilt without trial) and *ex post facto* laws (which define as crimes acts committed before the law was adopted) are forbidden.

crinoid (krī′noid, krī′–), marine animal, an echinoderm of class Crinoidea, related to starfish and sea urchin, and found in deep sea and tropical waters. Crinoids include sea lily and feather star. The body is usually a central disk with plumelike arms; many forms have stalks.

Cripple Creek, city (pop. 853; alt. 9,375 ft.), central Colo., SW of Colorado Springs. Started as mining camp after 1891 gold discovery. Had c.50,000 pop. in 1901. Production declined, but mining continued. New veins found and worked after 1934; old mines reactivated after drainage tunnel built, 1941.

Cripps, Sir Stafford, 1889–1952, British statesman; nephew of Beatrice Webb. Brilliant lawyer, was solicitor general in Labour government 1930–31. Expelled from Labour party 1939 for urging united front with communists; readmitted 1945. Under Churchill was ambassador to USSR (1940), lord privy seal and leader in Commons (1942), and envoy to India (1942) with self-government plan. In Labour government initiated (1945) Britain's austerity program. As minister of economic affairs and chancellor of exchequer (1947–50) virtually controlled British economy until ill health forced his resignation.

Crispi, Francesco (fränchä'skō krē'spē), b. 1818 or 1819, d. 1901, Italian premier (1887–91, 1893–96). Fostered colonial expansion.

Crispin and Crispinian, Saints, 3d cent., missionaries in Gaul martyred under Diocletian. They were brothers, both shoemakers. Feast: Oct. 25. The "Crispin Crispinian" speech in Shakspere's *Henry V*, Act IV, refers to the feast.

Crispus, Christian convert. Acts 18.8; I Cor. 1.14.

Cristobal (krĭstō'bûl), Span. *Cristóbal* (krĕstō'bäl), town (pop. 417), Panama Canal Zone, near the Atlantic end of Canal; American residential quarter for Colón.

Cristus, Petrus: see CHRISTUS, PETRUS.

criticism, judging or evaluating works of art or literature. Canons have changed with tastes of different periods. In early 20th cent., neo-humanism was rivaled by economic and sociological theories of interpretation. Psychology and semantics have strongly affected recent criticism. Notable in history of criticism have been Aristotle, Horace, Alexander Pope, Lessing, Sainte-Beuve, Matthew Arnold, Saintsbury, Vernon L. Parrington, I. A. Richards, and T. S. Eliot.

Critius (krĭ'shûs) and **Nesiotes** (nēshēō'tēz), 5th cent. B.C., Greek sculptors during the Persian Wars.

Crittenden, John Jordan, 1787–1863, American statesman. U.S. Attorney General (1841, 1850–53). As U.S. Senator (1855–61) from Ky., he attempted to conciliate North and South by **Crittenden Compromise,** proposal to settle slavery issue through constitutional amendments, including restoration of Missouri Compromise line; plan was defeated.

Crivelli, Carlo (krēvĕl'lē), b. c.1430, d. after 1493, Venetian religious painter, active in the Marches. His *Pietà* in Metropolitan Mus.

Crna Gora, Yugoslavia: see MONTENEGRO.

Croaghpatrick (krō'äpä'trĭk), mountain, Co. Mayo, Ireland. Connected by legend with St. Patrick, its summit has long been a place of pilgrimage.

Croatan (krō"ûtän'), unexplained word derived incorrectly from letters CROATOAN, which were found carved on tree of ROANOKE ISLAND in 17th cent., claimed by some to indicate that the "lost colony" had joined Indians.

Croatia (krōä'shù), Croatian *Hrvatska,* autonomous republic (21,611 sq. mi.; pop. 3,749,039), NW Yugoslavia; cap. Zagreb. W section is crossed by DINARIC ALPS; E part is agr. plain, drained by Sava and Drava rivers. Republic consists of Croatia proper, SLAVONIA, DALMATIA, and most of ISTRIA. Chief cities: ZAGREB, FIUME, OSIJEK, SPLIT, ZARA. Part of Pannonia prov. under Rome, region was settled in 7th cent. by Slavic Croats, who accepted Roman Catholicism (9th cent.) and set up a kingdom (10th cent.). From 1091 to 1918 (except during Turkish occupation, 1526–1699; French occupation, 1809–13; and Austrian annexation, 1849–68), Croatia was in personal union with Hungary—i.e., the kings of Hungary were also kings of Croatia, which, however, was governed by native bans and had its own diet. United with Serbia in 1918 (see YUGOSLAVIA), Croatia despite intense nationalist agitation secured autonomy only in 1939. After Germany invaded Yugoslavia (1941), a nationalist and terrorist group—the Ustachi—declared Croatia an independent kingdom under the nominal rule of Aimone, duke of Spoleto (an Italian prince) and under the dictatorship of their leader, Ante Pavelich. In 1943 Croatia passed under German control, but a large part of the people joined the anti-German partisan forces. In 1946 Croatia became one of Yugoslavia's six constituent republics.

Croce, Benedetto (bänädĕt'tō krō'chä), 1866–1952, Italian philosopher and critic. His broad idealistic thought is reflected in his *Philosophy of the Spirit* (1902–17), divided into four parts: *Aesthetic as Science of Expression and General Linguistic; Logic as the Science of Pure Concept; Philosophy of the Practical;* and

History: Its Theory and Practice. Minister of education 1920–21, he lived in retirement under Fascism.

crochet work (krōshā'), form of knitting in which a hook is used to draw thread into patterns of interconnected loops. Used in making lace, bedspreads, tablecloths, apparel (e.g., hats and bags).

Crocker, William, 1876–1950, American botanist, director of Boyce Thompson Inst. for Plant Research from 1921. Known for research on plant growth.

Crockett, David (Davy), 1786–1836, American frontiersman. U.S. Representative from Tenn. (1827–31, 1833–35), known for backwoods humor. Died at the ALAMO. Supposed author of autobiographical exploits.

Crockett, town (pop. 5,932), E Texas, SSE of Palestine, in lumber and farm area. Replica of first Spanish mission (1690) in E Texas near by.

crocodile (krŏ'kŭdĭl), large carnivorous reptile of order Crocodilia. It has tough scales on top, bony plates underneath, powerful jaws, short legs, and a vertically flattened tail. American species, inhabiting fresh (sometimes salt) water near S Fla., in West Indies, and Central and N South America, is not hostile to humans.

crocus, low plant of genus *Crocus,* with grasslike foliage and purple, yellow, or white flowers (usually goblet shaped) in spring or autumn. See also MEADOW SAFFRON; SAFFRON.

Croesus (krē'sûs), d. 546? B.C., king of Lydia after 560 B.C. He was to the Greeks a symbol of wealth. Allied himself with Egypt and Babylonia against Cyrus the Great of Persia and was defeated and captured.

crofter: see COTTER.

Croghan, George (krō'gûn), d. 1782, American Indian agent, b. Ireland. Became deputy superintendent of Indian Affairs in 1756 under Sir William Johnson. Responsible for much of Johnson's success.

Croker, Richard, 1841–1922, American politician, boss of Tammany Hall (1886–1902), b. Ireland. Abdicated after Tammany defeat in 1901 election.

Cro-Magnon man: see MAN, PRIMITIVE.

Cromarty, county: see ROSS AND CROMARTY.

Cromarty Firth, deep narrow inlet of Firth of Moray in Ross and Cromarty co., Scotland. An excellent anchorage, it was a naval base in World War I.

Crome, John, 1768–1821, English landscape painter, founder of Norwich School; often called Old Crome. Influenced by Gainsborough and Dutch masters. His son, **John Bernay Crome,** 1794–1842, painted landscapes in father's style.

Cromer, Evelyn Baring, 1st earl of, 1841–1917, British administrator and diplomat in Egypt. Was virtual ruler 1883–1907, reforming Egyptian finances, administration, and education.

Crommelynck, Fernand (fĕrnä' krômŭlĕk'), 1888–, Belgian poet and dramatist, author of tragic farce *Le Cocu magnifique* (1921).

Cromwell, Oliver, 1599–1658, lord protector of England. Was strong Puritan in Parliament. Prominent in PURITAN REVOLUTION because of military ability (esp. at Edgehill 1642 and Marston Moor 1644). In struggle between largely Presbyterian Parliament and Puritan army, he proposed army reorganization (1644). Given command with Baron Fairfax; defeated Charles I at Naseby. After flight of Charles in 1645, he lost hope of dealing with king and was leader in demand for his execution. Led cruelly punitive expedition to Ireland (1649) where he continued policy of settling English. Invaded Scotland 1650; defeated Charles II and royalist Scots. Dissolved Rump Parliament 1653; tried to replace it with feeble Barebone's Parliament appointed by himself. PROTECTORATE estab. 1653 with Cromwell as lord protector. Declined the crown 1656. New constitution (1657) strengthened his powers. Tried to build up Protestant league abroad but policy was governed by need for foreign trade. Navigation Act (1651) led to first DUTCH WAR (1652–54). War with Spain (1655–58) was over trade rights. Opinions of him vary widely. Favored religious toleration and democracy, but tolerated only Jews and non-Anglican Protestants and could not work with Parliament. His military genius and force of character are recognized but necessities of governing forced him into cruelty and intolerance. Dependence of Protectorate on him was shown when his son, **Richard Cromwell**, 1626–1712, succeeded him as lord protector, 1658. Army and Parliament struggled for power until Commonwealth was reestab. 1659. He lived abroad, 1660–80, and later in England under assumed name. A man of virtue and dignity, he was forced into a situation beyond his talents.

Cromwell, Thomas, earl of Essex, 1485?–1540, English statesman. Legal secretary to Cardinal Wolsey; avoided implication in his fall and attracted attention of Henry VIII. Carried out suppression of monasteries (some of whose wealth he received). Made lord great chamberlain 1539; negotiated Henry's marriage to Anne of Cleves to secure German alliance. This failed and he was convicted of treason and heresy and beheaded.

Cronstadt, RSFSR: see KRONSTADT.

Cronstedt, Axel Fredrik, Baron (äk'sùl frä'drĭk krōōn'stĕt), 1722–65, Swedish mineralogist. Discovered nickel in niccolite; one of first to recognize importance of chemical constituents of minerals.

Cronus (krō'nùs), Gr. *Kronos* [time], in Greek legend, the youngest TITAN, son of URANUS [heaven] and GAEA [earth]. He led Titans in revolt against Uranus and ruled the world. Father by RHEA of the great gods—ZEUS, Poseidon, Demeter, Hera, and Hestia. Fated to be overthrown by one of his children, he tried unsuccessfully to destroy them. Zeus later led the Olympian gods against his father in successful revolt called TITANOMACHY. He is equated with Roman Saturn.

Crook, George, 1828–90, U.S. general. An able Indian fighter, especially against Paiute and Snake Indians in Idaho, in Sioux War of 1876, and against Apaches under Geronimo. Noted for patience and integrity in dealing peaceably with Indians.

Crookes, Sir William (krŏoks), 1832–1919, English chemist, physicist. He discovered thallium; studied radioactivity, selenium, rare earths, diamonds. He invented a high-vacuum tube, the **Crookes tube**: a glass bulb with air exhausted and anode and cathode set in walls. When high-voltage current is used, electrons come from cathode and cause yellow-green fluorescence of the glass.

Crooks, Ramsay, 1787–1859, American fur trader, b. Scotland. Second in command to John Jacob Astor in American Fur Co.

Crookston, city (pop. 7,352), NW Minn., on Red Lake R. and SE of Grand Forks, N.Dak. Trade center in agr. (grain, sugar beets, potatoes) area.

croquet (krōkā'), lawn game in which players hit wooden balls with wooden mallets through series of wire arches (9 or 10). A favorite game in Ireland in 18th cent., also popular in France, England, U.S.

Crosby, Bing, 1904–, American singer and moving-picture actor, whose real name is Harry Lillis Crosby. A popular singer with dance bands, he gained enormous success on the radio. Popularized many songs (e.g., *White Christmas*). He also won fame as an actor in films (e.g., *Going My Way*).

Cross, Wilbur L(ucius), 1862–1948, American educator and public official. Professor of English at Yale (1902–30); dean of graduate school (1916–30); authority on the English novel. As Democratic governor of Conn. (1931–39), he brought about much reform legislation.

crossbow, medieval military weapon consisting of a bow set on a stock to give it greater strength than an ordinary bow. It was used to fire stones and metal as well as arrows (sometimes flaming, used to ignite buildings under siege). A late form was the arbalest,

which worked with a kind of ratchet. The advantage of the crossbow was power. This was in the end outweighed by clumsiness—as evidenced by the victory of English longbowmen over Genoese crossbowmen (fighting for the French) at Crécy (1346).

cross vine: see BIGNONIA.

Crothers, Rachel (krŭ'dhùrz), 1878–, American dramatist. Her comedies, notable for craftsmanship and clever dialogue, include *A Man's World* (1909), *Let Us Be Gay* (1929), and *Susan and God* (1937).

Croton, short river, SE N.Y., flowing S and SW to Hudson R. near Ossining. Paralleled by **Croton Aqueduct** (38 mi. long; built 1837–42), which carries water from Croton basin reservoirs to New York city. Aqueduct begins at Croton L. in Croton R.; crosses Harlem R. into New York over High Bridge. Supplemented by a second aqueduct (built 1885–91).

Crotona (krōtō'nù), anc. city, S Italy, on E coast of Calabria, a city founded (8th cent.) by Greeks. Reached its height in 6th cent. B.C., when Pythagoras had his school here and the army, led by the athlete Milo, defeated Sybaris (510 B.C.). Declined later. Called Cotrone from Middle Ages to 1928.

Croton Aqueduct: see CROTON, river.

crow, partially migratory black bird of same family as the raven, magpie, jay, rook, and European jackdaw. American or eastern crow is c.19 in. long with wingspread of c.3 ft. It destroys injurious insects and rodents, but also eats some eggs, nestlings, and grain. It is easily tamed.

crowberry, low, alpine evergreen plant (*Empetrum*), with berrylike fruits. It is suited to rockeries.

crowfoot: see BUTTERCUP.

Crow Indians or **Absaroka**, tribe ranging chiefly about Yellowstone R., of Siouan linguistic stock. Had typical Plains culture.

Crowley (krou'lē), city (pop. 12,784), SW La., SW of Baton Rouge; founded 1886. Processes and ships rice, and has rice experiment station.

Crowninshield, Frederic, 1845–1918, American decorative artist. Work includes murals and landscapes.

Crown Point. 1 Residential city (pop. 5,839), NW Ind., S of Gary. Mfg. of monuments and signs. **2** Town (1940 pop. 1,661), NE N.Y., on L. Champlain and N of Ticonderoga; a summer resort. French fort, built 1731, was demolished 1759 in French and Indian Wars. British fort, built 1759, was captured by Green Mountain Boys (1775) but abandoned in Saratoga campaign (1777). Crown Point Reservation is here.

Croydon, county borough (pop. 249,592), Surrey, England; a suburb of London. Airport, formerly important, used by military during World War II.

Cruden, Alexander, 1701?–1770, British scholar, a London bookseller and proofreader. His *Complete Concordance to the Holy Scriptures* (1737) is basis of later biblical concordances.

Cruikshank, George (krŏŏk'–), 1792–1878, English caricaturist and illustrator. Etchings include notable illustrations for *Oliver Twist*.

cruiser, large, fast, moderately armed warship, intermediate between battleship and destroyer. Modern cruisers fall in two classes: battle cruisers (in effect small battleships, representing an effort to combine maximum gun caliber, armor protection, and speed); and light cruisers (of moderate tonnage, lightly armed, and very fast).

Crusades, wars undertaken by European Christians between 11th and 14th cent. to recover the Holy Land, particularly JERUSALEM, from Islam. The movement began in France, when Pope URBAN II at the Council of Clermont (1095) exhorted Christendom to war, promising that the journey would count as full penance and that a general truce would protect the homes of the absent ones. From the crosses distributed at this meeting the Crusaders took their name. Religious motives dominated at first, but worldly considerations were never absent, and the conflict between spiritual and material aims grew increasingly serious: the nobles hoped for loot and territorial aggrandizement; the Italian cities expanded trade with the Near East; all were lured by travel and adventure. The **First Crusade**, 1095–99, began with the march of several undisciplined hordes of French and German peasants, led by WALTER THE PENNILESS, PETER THE HERMIT, and others. They started out by massacring the Jews in the Rhineland; incensed the Bulgarians and Hungarians, who attacked and dispersed them; reached Constantinople in shreds; crossed over to Asia Minor; and were promptly defeated by the Turks. The organized host, led by Count RAYMOND IV of Toulouse, GODFREY OF BOUILLON, BOHEMOND, and TANCRED, followed in 1097. All save Raymond and Tancred swore fealty to the Byzantine Emperor, ALEXIUS I, binding themselves to accept him as overlord of their conquests. Their victorious campaign was crowned by the conquest of Jerusalem (1099). The establishment of the Latin Kingdom of JERUSALEM and of the orders of KNIGHTS HOSPITALERS and KNIGHTS TEMPLARS followed. The **Second Crusade**, 1147–99, preached by St. BERNARD OF CLAIRVAUX after the fall of EDESSA (1144) was led by Emperor Conrad III and by Louis VII of France. It ended in dismal failure. In 1187 SALADIN captured Jerusalem. The **Third Crusade**, 1189–92, led by Emperor FREDERICK I, PHILIP II of France, and RICHARD I of England, failed to recapture the city, but Richard I negotiated a truce by which Christians were granted free access to the Holy Sepulchre. The **Fourth Crusade**, 1202–4, began in France but was completely diverted from its purpose by its leader, Enrico Dandolo, for the benefit of Venice. To pay for their passage, the Crusaders assisted the Venetians to recover Zara from Hungary (1202). Despite violent papal condemnation after the sack of that Christian city, the host next turned toward Constantinople, ostensibly to restore ISAAC II on his throne. In 1204 they stormed and sacked the city, divided the spoils with Venice, and set up the Latin Empire of CONSTANTINOPLE. The pathetic **Children's Crusade** of 1212 was preached by a visionary French peasant boy, Stephen of Cloyes. Thousands of children set out for Holy Land but instead were sold into slavery by unscrupulous skippers. Another group, of German children, made their way by land; they perished of hunger and disease. The **Fifth Crusade**, 1217–21, preached by Innocent III, was aimed at Egypt and failed. The **Sixth Crusade**, 1228–29, undertaken by Emperor FREDERICK II, was actually a peaceful visit. Frederick made a truce with the Moslems, securing the surrender of the Holy Places. Sporadic warfare soon broke out again. The Christian rout by the Egyptian MAMELUKES at Gaza (1244) led to the **Seventh Crusade**, 1248–54, led by LOUIS IX of France. Despite Louis's gallantry, the enterprise failed; his death cut short the **Eighth Crusade** (1270). The **Ninth Crusade**, 1271–72, led by Prince Edward (later Edward I of England) was abortive. In 1291 Acre, the last Christian stronghold, fell. The term *crusade* was also applied to other expeditions, sanctioned by the pope, against heretics and heathens (e.g., the WENDS, the ALBIGENSES) and, more loosely, to campaigns of the 15th–16th cent. against the Turks.

crustacean (krŭsta′shŭn), animal of class Crustacea of phylum Arthropoda. Examples are CRAB, LOBSTER, SHRIMP, CRAYFISH, BARNACLE, water flea or daphnia, cyclops, pill bug, sow bug. They have jointed appendages and a horny outer skeleton. Breathing organs are gills. Colorless blood usually circulated by a heart. Some are omnivorous, some eat flesh only, some plants only. Many are parasites.

Cruveilhier, Jean (zhā′ krüvěyā′), 1791–1874, French physician, pioneer in descriptive pathology.

Cruz, Juana Inés de la: see JUANA INÉS DE LA CRUZ.

Cruz, Ramón de la (rämōn′ dä lä krooth′), 1731–94, Spanish dramatist, best known for *sainetes*, short realistic comedies of Madrid lower-class life. Also

wrote tragedies and a Spanish version of *Hamlet*.

cryolite or **kryolite** (krī′ulĭt), a mineral, fluoride of sodium and aluminum, used in making lampshades, hard glass, porcelain. Found in Greenland.

cryptography (krĭptŏ′grŭfē) [Gr.,= hidden writing], art of secret writing, employed from anc. times. A cryptogram is a secret message and also the form in which it is couched. Forms include codes, ciphers, invisible writing, and other devices which make true meaning discernible only to the one holding the proper key. Codes used in business are usually systems of pronounceable words with meanings listed in code books held by firms involved. Ciphers often consist of unpronounceable words made up by transposition of letters within the message or substitution of one letter for another or of a number for a letter. A famous cipher was that devised by Francis Bacon (1605). In modern times official government cryptography, the solution of cryptograms, and even the general methods employed are jealously controlled by governments, since codes and ciphers are used for secret messages in peacetime as well as in war.

crystal, solid having definite internal structure owing to atomic arrangement and definite external form (polyhedron bounded by natural plane surfaces) which is the manifestation of its internal structure. Crystallization is the assumption of crystal form when a substance passes from liquid or gaseous state to solid state or when it goes out of solution. Crystalline species are grouped, according to their type of symmetry, into 32 classes, which in turn are grouped into six systems: cubic or isometric, hexagonal, tetragonal, orthorhombic, monoclinic, triclinic.

Crystal City, city (pop. 7,198), SW Texas, SW of San Antonio, in irrigated winter-garden area. Spinach is main product.

Crystal Palace, building erected in Hyde Park, London, for the Great Exhibition in 1851. Served for a time as a museum. Torn down in 1941 because it served as a guide to enemy air raiders.

Cs, chemical symbol of the element CESIUM.

Csaba, Hungary: see BEKESCSABA.

Csepel (chě′pěl), city (pop. 46,171), central Hungary, on Csepel isl. (30 mi. long) in the Danube, near Budapest. Aluminum and iron mills; mfg. of machinery and munitions.

Ctesibius (tĭsĭ′bēŭs), 2d cent. B.C., Alexandrian Greek reputed first to perceive and apply expansive power of air as motive force.

Ctesiphon (tě′sĭfŏn), ruined anc. city, near Baghdad, Iraq, on the Tigris at mouth of the Diyala. Was cap. of Parthian kings and later of Sassanidae.

Cu, chemical symbol of the element COPPER.

Cuauhtémoc (koō-outä′mōk), d. 1525, Aztec emperor. After the Spanish were driven from the Aztec cap., he fought valiantly until the city was taken and he was made captive. Taken along on the march to Honduras, he was hanged by order of Cortés. Also Cuauhtemoctzín, Guatémoc, Quauhtémoc.

Cuba (kū′bù, Span. koō′vä), republic (44,218 sq. mi.; pop. 4,778,583, incl. Isle of Pines), occupying all the island of Cuba, westernmost and largest of the West Indies; cap. HAVANA (largest city of the West Indies). The island (c.700 mi. long, averaging 50 mi. in breadth) lies at the entrance to the Gulf of Mexico, with the Atlantic on the N, the Caribbean on the S; its W tip is 90 mi. from Key West, Fla. The chief ports besides Havana are SANTIAGO DE CUBA, MATANZAS, CIENFUEGOS, and GUANTÁNAMO. The mountains (in several groups) have deposits of iron, manganese, copper, nickel, chromium, and barite, and the forests of the interior yield timber and naval stores, but Cuba has been mainly dependent for exports on sugar, fine tobacco, and coffee. Other products are tropical fruits, henequen, sponges, hides, and winter vegetables. After discovery by Columbus (1492), Cuba was explored by the Spanish, and by 1511 a colony was firmly planted. Expeditions went out to conquer other territories (notably Mexico), and the island, "the Pearl of the Antilles," was a gathering point for Spanish treasure fleets from the New World. It was much harassed by French and English buccaneers. The native Arawak Indians soon died out, and the sugar plantations were worked with the labor of imported Negroes. The Negro element has contributed much to Cuban life. In the early 19th cent., when most of Latin America won independence from Spain, Cuba remained in the empire. There were intermittent revolts and filibustering expeditions, rising to a climax in the TEN YEARS WAR (1868–78). Spain retained control until a new revolt precipitated the SPANISH-AMERICAN WAR (1898), in which Cuba gained independence with U.S. help. Its history thereafter was dominated by the question of relationship with the U.S. and with the problem of a one-crop economy. U.S. military occupation of the island lasted until 1902, and the Platt Amendment (see PLATT, ORVILLE H.) giving the U.S. the right to intervene led to new occupations (1906–9, 1912). U.S. citizens owned many plantations and industries, and "Yankee imperialism" in Cuba was much decried in Latin America until a new basis for relationship was estab. in the administration of F. D. Roosevelt. A sugar boom in World War I led to later false prosperity ("the dance of the millions") and then almost total collapse. Diversification of agr. has been forwarded to avoid the ills of one-crop economy. Political life in Cuba has been stormy and intermittently marked by dictatorships (e.g., that of Gerardo Machado). After 1940 the dominant figure was Fulgencio BATISTA, who became president for the second time by a coup d'état in 1952.

Cubberley, Ellwood Patterson, 1868–1941, American educator. At Stanford Univ. after 1898, he was professor of education after 1906, dean of the school of education from 1917 to 1933. Wrote *A History of Education* (1920).

cube, in geometry, a regular solid bounded by six equal squares perpendicular to one another.

cubeb (kū′bĕb), dried, unripe berry of a climbing pepper plant, *Piper cubeba,* native to East and West Indies. Used medicinally and as a condiment.

cube root, see ROOT, in mathematics.

cubism, a movement primarily in painting, originating c.1910 in France. One of the earliest forms of modern abstract art, it tended to reduce painting to design in space based on three-dimensional geometry. While it no longer flourishes, many are indebted to its discipline. Picasso, Braque, and Gris were among the early cubists.

Cuchulain (kōŏkū′lĭn, kōō′khōŏlĭn) [Irish,= the hound of Culan], Irish legendary hero of Ulster. He is central figure of Ulster legends, of which greatest is *Táin Bó Cúalnge* [the cattle raid of Cooley], wherein he defends his province singlehanded against armies of the rest of Ireland.

cuckoo (kōō′kōō), name for certain birds abundant in tropics, widespread in both hemispheres except in colder regions. They are usually insectivorous, arboreal, and have slightly decurved bills, long tails, and usually dull plumage. Many cuckoos make no nests but lay eggs in nests of other birds. Family includes ROAD RUNNER, ani, trogon, and KINGFISHER. Black-billed and yellow-billed cuckoos of U.S. are slender, long-billed, olive-brown birds which eat destructive insects. Maynard's cuckoo and California cuckoo are other related birds. The cuckoo has featured largely in English literature as early herald of spring from Middle English "Sumer Is Icumen In," through Wordsworth, to present day.

cucumber, fruit of *Cucumis sativus,* an annual vine. It is eaten either raw or pickled.

cucumber tree: see MAGNOLIA.

Cúcuta (kōō′kōōtä), city (pop. 37,323), NE Colombia, c.10 mi. from Venezuelan border on E cordillera of Andes, in rich coffee-raising region. Congress of 1821 met here to draft constitution for Greater Colombia.

Cudahy (kŭ′dùhē), city (pop. 12,182), SE Wis., on L. Michigan between Milwaukee and South Milwaukee; city and its meat-packing industry founded 1892.

Cuenca (kwĕng′kä), city (pop. 46,428; alt., c.8,000 ft.), S central Ecuador; founded 1557. In rich agr. basin of Ecuadorian Andes, it produces grains, subsistence crops, and cattle. Panama hats are woven here.

Cuenca, city (pop. 23,038), cap. of Cuenca prov., E central Spain, in New Castile. Medieval castle; 13th-cent. cathedral.

Cuernavaca (kwĕrnävä′kä), city (pop. 14,336), cap. of Morelos, central Mexico; popular tourist and health resort. Palace built here by Cortés now is decorated with murals by Diego Rivera. Maximilian and Carlotta frequently stayed in Cuernavaca.

Cuero (kwâ′rō), city (pop. 7,498), S Texas, on Guadalupe R. and NW of Victoria. Processes poultry, cotton, milk, and farm products. Annual Turkey Trot.

Cueva, Beatriz de la (bäätrēs′ dä lä kwä′vä), d. 1541, governor of Guatemala, only woman to govern major American political division in Spanish times. Succeeded her husband, Pedro de Alvarado, to position but was killed a few weeks later in flood.

Cueva, Juan de la (hwän′ dä lä kwä′vä), 1550?–1610?, Spanish dramatist, precursor of Lope de Vega. Wrote *Los siete infantes de Lara* (presented 1579).

Cui, César (Antonovich) (tsäzär′ küē′), 1835–1918, Russian composer and critic. He proclaimed the ideals of the nationalist composers, especially the Russian Five, of which he was a member. His own works include operas, songs, orchestral and salon music.

Cuiabá (kōōyùbä′), city (pop. 24,119), cap. of Mato Grosso state, W Brazil, at head of navigable Cuiabá R.; founded in gold rush of 18th cent.

Culbertson, Ely (ē′lē kŭl′bùrtsùn), 1893–, American expert on contract bridge, b. Rumania of American-Russian parentage. Became a leading figure in the playing of bridge. After World War II he wrote and lectured widely on world peace. His writings include *The Contract Bridge Blue Book* (1930) and *Must We Fight Russia?* (1946).

Culiacán (kōōlēäkän′), city (pop. 22,025), cap. of Sinaloa, NW Mexico; founded 1531. It figured prominently in Spanish colonial period as point of departure for expeditions to N, notably that of Coronado (1540). Surrounding area produces tropical fruits, sugar, cotton, some minerals.

Culion (kōōlyôn′), island (150 sq. mi.; pop. 7,328), one of Calamian Isls., Philippines. Has leper colony.

Cullen, Countee, 1903–46, American Negro poet.

Cullman, city (pop. 7,523), N Ala., N of Birmingham. Ships strawberries, cotton, timber.

Culloden Moor (kŭlō′dùn), moorland, Inverness-shire, Scotland. Scene of decisive defeat (1746) of Prince Charles Edward by English troops.

Culpeper or **Colepeper, Thomas Culpeper, 2d Baron** (both: kŭl′pĕ″pùr), 1636–89, British colonial governor of Va. (1675–83).

cultivation, working soil to improve its condition, by means of tools (e.g., hoe, plow) or machinery. Includes mixing, loosening, adding humus, destroying weeds; aided by IRRIGATION and ROTATION OF CROPS.

culture, in anthropology, the way of life of a society, without implication of refinement or advanced knowledge. Culture is historically transmitted, primarily through language, and is the attribute that most distinguishes man from the animals.

Culver City, residential city (pop. 19,720), S Calif., between Los Angeles and the Pacific coast; laid out 1913. Has moving-picture studios. Los Angeles International Airport is here.

Culver-Stockton College, at Canton, Mo.; coed. (probably first W of the Mississippi); chartered 1853, opened 1855 by Disciples of Christ as Christian Univ., renamed 1917.

Cumae (kū′mē), anc. city of Campania, Italy; a Greek colony. A powerful city, it was conquered by Samnites (5th cent. B.C.), later rose and declined under Roman control, disappeared only in 13th cent. A.D.

Cumans (kū'munz), nomadic people of Turkic language; also called Kipchaks and, in Russian, Polovtsi. Conquered S Russia and Walachia (11th cent.); warred with Byzantium, Hungary, Kiev. After defeat by Mongols (c.1245), part of Cumans fled to Hungary, where they merged with Magyars.

Cumberland, Richard, 1732–1811, English dramatist, author of sentimental plays such as *The Brothers* (1769), *The West Indian* (1771), *The Wheel of Fortune* (1795).

Cumberland, county (1,520 sq. mi.; pop. 285,347), N England, next to Scotland; co. town Carlisle. Low in N, county is mountainous in SW and E. Scafell Pike (3,210 ft.) highest point in England. Pastoral area, with some mining, quarrying, textile mfg., and smelting. Scene of centuries of border strife between England and Scotland. The region, with Westmoreland and Lancashire known as LAKE DISTRICT, popular with 19th-cent. literary figures.

Cumberland. 1 City (pop. 37,679), NW Md., on North Branch of Potomac R. and W of Hagerstown; laid out 1785 on site of trading post and around Fort Cumberland (hq. of Gen. Braddock 1755). Railroad shipping point with mfg. of rayon, clothing, and tires. Gateway through Appalachians to Ohio valley, city became E end of Cumberland or NATIONAL ROAD, division point for Baltimore & Ohio RR, and W terminus of Chesapeake and Ohio Canal. **2** Town (pop. 12,842), NE R.I., between Blackstone R. and Mass. line. Mfg. of textiles and metal goods. Has Ballou Meetinghouse (c.1740).

Cumberland, river formed on Cumberland Plateau in E Ky. by juncture of Poor and Clover forks, and flowing 693 mi. SW then NW through Ky. and Tenn. to Ohio R. above Paducah, Ky. Locks, dams, levees, and canals improve navigation and irrigation; power projects planned. TVA authorized to market power from three dams.

Cumberland Gap, natural mountain pass, near point where Va., Ky., and Tenn. meet. Discovered 1750; WILDERNESS ROAD ran through it. Gap was held by both sides during Civil War. National historical park authorized.

Cumberland House, Hudson's Bay Co. fur-trading post, W Man., Canada, on Cumberland L., near The Pass. Built 1774 by Samuel Hearne; first permanent settlement on Saskatchewan R. and the company's first interior post. Commanded fur trade and exploration routes to upper Saskatchewan and Churchill rivers.

Cumberland Island: see SEA ISLANDS.

Cumberland Plateau or **Cumberland Mountains,** SW division of Appalachian Mts. Extends NE-SW through S W.Va., SW Va., E Ky., E Tenn., and N Ala. Rises E from Great Valley of E Tenn., and slopes roughly W. Source of Cumberland and other rivers. Has coal and timber resources.

Cumberland Presbyterian Church, branch of Presbyterian Church in U.S. It arose as revival movement in "Cumberland country" of Tenn. and Ky. Its presbytery was dissolved by synod but reorganized (1810) as independent body. Negro organization set apart (1869) as Colored Cumberland Presbyterian Church.

Cumberland Road: see NATIONAL ROAD.

Cumberland Valley, part of great Appalachian valley, N of Shenandoah Valley, extending from Potomac R. in Md. to the Susquehanna in Pa. Had much Civil War action.

cumin (kŭm'ĭn), low annual herb (*Cuminum cyminum*) with threadlike foliage; native to Mediterranean region. Seedlike aromatic fruits used in bread, soup, and cheese; oil used in liqueurs.

Cummings, E(dward) E(stlin), 1894–, American poet. His lyrics are marked by imaginative virtuosity, flashing originality, and crisp romanticism. They also have startling typographical effects (e.g., omission of capital letters). Notable also is his prose work, *The Enor-*

mous Room (1922; on his war internment in France).

Cummings, Homer S(tillé), 1870–, U.S. Attorney General (1933–39). Strong supporter of New Deal.

Cummington, town (pop. 620), W Mass., E of Pittsfield. Birthplace of Bryant; his home is memorial.

Cunard, Sir Samuel (kūnärd'), 1787–1865, Canadian pioneer of regular transatlantic steam navigation. With others he formed company which in 1840 initiated first regular mail service between North America and Britain. This was beginning of Cunard Line, which was united with White Star Line in 1934.

Cunaxa (kūnăk'sù), town, Babylonia, near the Euphrates; scene of victory (401 B.C.) of Artaxerxes II over Cyrus the Younger—victory only because Cyrus had been killed. The retreat of the Ten Thousand after the battle is told in the ANABASIS.

cuneiform (kūnē'ĭfôrm) [Latin,= wedge shaped], writing developed in lower Tigris and Euphrates valley, probably by Sumerians. Characters consist of arrangements of four kinds of wedge strokes impressed into brick or stone. History of the script is parallel to that of Egyptian HIEROGLYPHIC (see also ALPHABET; INSCRIPTION). Babylonians and Assyrians used cuneiform writing extensively, but it existed outside Mesopotamia, notably among the Hittites. A very late use was in Old Persian, written in the era of the Achaemenidae, whose greatest monument is that of Darius I at BEHISTUN. Key finds have been made at Nineveh, Lagash, Erech, Tel-el-Amarna, Susa, and Boghazkeui. The Assyrian king Assur-bani-pal had a huge cuneiform library at Nineveh. Sir Henry C. Rawlinson and G. F. Grotefend were great interpreters of cuneiforms.

Cunha, Euclides da (ā"ōōklē'dĭsh dä kōo'nyù), 1866–1909, Brazilian writer. Best-known work is account which he wrote as "on the spot" reporter of revolt in W Bahia: *Os sertões* (1902; Eng. tr., *Rebellion in the Backlands,* 1944), a study of conditions, prospects, and national soul of Brazil.

Cunha, Tristão da (trĕshtä'ō), c.1460–c.1540, Portuguese navigator. Led 15 ships to India (1506); took Socotra in hope of controlling Red Sea.

Cunningham, Allan, 1784–1842, Scottish poet, collector of *The Songs of Scotland, Ancient and Modern* (1825), which includes his own "A Wet Sheet and a Flowing Sea." His son, **Sir Alexander Cunningham,** 1814–93, English archaeologist, army engineer, headed archaeological survey of India (1861–65, 1870–85).

Cunninghame-Graham, Robert: see GRAHAM, ROBERT.

Cunninghame Graham, R(obert) B(ontine), 1852–1936, Scottish author, whose sketches and tales reflect his life and travels in Latin America, Morocco, and Spain.

Cunobelinus: see CYMBELINE.

Cupid [Latin,= desire], Roman equivalent of EROS, Greek god of love; also called Amor. Son of Venus and Mars. For his own love story, see PSYCHE.

Curaçao (kōōrä'sou'), Dutch colony (366 sq. mi.; pop. 95,000), West Indies; cap. WILLEMSTED. Includes widely separated islands, some off Venezuela (Curaçao, Bonaire or Buen Ayre, Aruba), some in NW Leeward Isls. (St. Martin—S part, St. Eustatius, Saba). Though discovered by Spanish (1499) and occupied briefly by English (1798, 1807–14) the islands have been under Dutch control since 1634. Discovery and exploitation of petroleum in Venezuela greatly increased importance of Curaçao and Aruba.

curaçao (kyōōrùsō'), LIQUEUR distilled from dried orange peel and spirits, flavored with rum. Grand Marnier and Cointreau kinds have a brandy base.

curare (kyōōrä're), aqueous poisonous extract of certain South American plants, used by South American Indians as arrow poison. Causes muscle paralysis. It is used in medicine to relax muscles.

curb market, originally, unorganized customary street meetings of brokers; now well organized and state regulated. Primary function is to introduce new securities, but a curb market lists both estab. securities

---

and those which later "graduate" to stock exchange.

curculio (kûrkū′lēō), any typical snout beetle with a beak which is long and decurved in some, short and wide in others. Over 1,800 U.S. species, including serious pests: apple and plum curculios, imbricated snout beetle, many species of WEEVIL.

Curia Regis: see PARLIAMENT.

Curia Romana: see CARDINAL.

Curicó (kūrēkō′), city (pop. 19,165), cap. of Curicó prov., central Chile; founded c.1743; market for cattle and agr. produce. Flour mills and distilleries are main industries.

Curie, Pierre (pyĕr kyōōrē′), 1859–1906, and his wife, **Marie Sklodowska Curie** (märē′ sklôdôf′skä), 1867–1934, b. Poland, French chemists and physicists. Pierre's early work was on crystallography, effects of temperature on magnetism, and piezoelectricity (form of electric polarity) discovered in crystals. Marie studied uranium, radioactive element in pitchblende. In 1898 she reported a probable new element in pitchblende; Pierre joined this research. They discovered polonium and radium (1898), isolated one gm. of radium salts (1902), and determined atomic weights and properties of both elements. They shared with Becquerel the 1903 Nobel Prize in Physics for radioactivity work. Marie Curie won 1911 Nobel Prize for isolation of metallic radium. Their daughter **Ève (Denise) Curie**, 1904–, author, lecturer, and pianist, is known especially for her biography of Mme Curie. See also JOLIOT-CURIE, IRÈNE.

Curitiba (kōōrētē′bù), city (pop. 141,349), cap. of Paraná state, SE Brazil. Founded in 17th-cent. gold rush. Immigration into Paraná hinterland in 20th cent. has made it center of agr. and ranch area with some mfg. Univ. of Paraná is here.

curium (kyōō′rēùm), radioactive element identified in 1944 (symbol = Cm; see also ELEMENT, table). Emits alpha particles, highly active (half life about five months).

curlew (kûr′lū), name for a number of large shore birds of both hemispheres. Among them are the long-billed curlew (rare) of E U.S.; Hudsonian and Eskimo (rare) curlews, which migrate from arctic breeding grounds to South America; bristle-thighed curlew; and some godwits and ibises. See ill., page 105.

curling, winter sport played on ice court by teams of four. Each player hurls squat, circular stone, weighing 44 lbs., at tees or fixed goals, placed 38 yds. apart. Stones nearest tee count for score.

Curran, John Philpot, 1750–1817, Irish statesman, trial lawyer, and orator. Opposed repressive policy of British in Ireland. Defended Wolfe Tone, Lord Edward Fitzgerald, and other anti-British rebels. His daughter was in love with Robert EMMET.

currant, shrub of genus *Ribes,* native to colder climates. Its tart black, red, or white berries are used for jellies and sauces. The shrub is a host of white-pine blister rust but an immune variety has been developed.

current, electric: see ELECTRICITY.

Currie, Sir Arthur William (kŭ′rē), 1875–1933, Canadian commander in World War I.

Currier & Ives, American lithographers and print publishers of scenes and events of 19th-cent. American life. Nathaniel Currier (1813–88), who founded the firm in 1835, was joined in 1850 by J. Merritt Ives, an artist.

Curry, John Steuart, 1897–1946, American painter. Known primarily for scenes of his native Kansas.

curry, pungent Eastern dish based on meat, fish, eggs, or vegetables, usually served with rice, and spiced with curry powder, a compound of turmeric, fenugreek, ginger, black and cayenne pepper, coriander, caraway, and sometimes other ingredients.

cursive: see PALEOGRAPHY.

Curtea-de-Arges (kōōr′tää-dā-är′zhĕsh), town (pop. 9,180), S central Rumania; a former cap. of Walachia. Has 16th-cent. Byzantine cathedral (burial place of Rumanian kings).

Curtin, Andrew Gregg, 1817–94, Civil War governor of Pa. Rallied state to cause of Union. Later served as Democrat in U.S. Congress (1881–87).

Curtis, Benjamin Robbins, 1809–74, Associate Justice of U.S. Supreme Court (1851–57). Dissented in DRED SCOTT CASE. Chief counsel to Andrew Johnson at impeachment trial. His brother, **George Ticknor Curtis,** 1812–94, lawyer and writer, was one of the defense counsel in Dred Scott Case. Wrote classic Federalist interpretation of Constitution.

Curtis, Cyrus H(ermann Kotzschmar), 1850–1933, American publisher. In Philadelphia after 1876, he bought a publication which became (1883) the *Ladies' Home Journal.* Founded (1890) Curtis Publishing Co. Bought the *Saturday Evening Post* (1897), the *Country Gentleman* (1911), and several newspapers.

Curtis, George Ticknor: see CURTIS, BENJAMIN ROBBINS.

Curtis, George William, 1824–92, American author, editor, and orator. His most popular book was a series of essays, *Prue and I* (1856). He was long one of the editors of the magazines *Harper's Monthly* and *Harper's Weekly.* Campaigned against slavery and for civil service reform and woman suffrage. Chancellor of New York Univ. after 1890.

Curtis Institute of Music, in Philadelphia; founded 1924. Operates entirely on scholarship basis with faculty made up chiefly of concert artists.

curvature of the spine, abnormal curves of spinal column. Causes include faulty posture, pathological bony changes, and congenital factors. Lateral curvature (scoliosis) is more common than backward (kyphosis) or forward (lordosis).

curve, in mathematics, a line no part of which is straight; sometimes considered to be any one-dimensional group of points (straight line is then included as a special curve). In analytic geometry plane curve is used mainly as graph of equation or function; properties of algebraic curves (i.e., those with algebraic equations) depend largely on degree of the equation; transcendental curves (nonalgebraic) are dependent on the particular function. Plane curves include CIRCLE; ELLIPSE; HYPERBOLA; PARABOLA. Twisted (skew) curve does not lie all in one plane.

Curzola, Yugoslavia: see KORCULA.

Curzon, George Nathaniel, 1st Marquess Curzon of Kedleston, 1859–1925, British statesman. As viceroy of India (1899–1905) promoted reforms, pacified NW border. As foreign secretary presided at Lausanne Conference 1922–23. Paved way for Dawes Plan.

Cusa, Alexander John: see CUZA.

Cusa, Nicholas of: see NICHOLAS OF CUSA.

Cush (kŭsh), in Bible, eldest son of Ham. Descendants lived in "land of Cush"—usually referring to Ethiopia (roughly modern Anglo-Egyptian Sudan). The Bible also mentions an Asiatic nation called Cush (perhaps same as historical group with similar name which flourished c.1500 B.C. in E Mesopotamia). Gen. 10.6–8; 1 Chron. 1.8–10.

Cushing, Caleb (kōō′shĭng), 1800–1879, American statesman. First U.S. commissioner to China, negotiated opening of Chinese ports to U.S. trade. U.S. Attorney General (1853–57).

Cushing, Harvey Williams, 1869–1939, American neurosurgeon, noted for brain surgery and as teacher and author. He won the 1925 Pulitzer Prize in biography for his life of Sir William Osler.

Cushing, city (pop. 8,414), central Okla., near Cimarron R. and SW of Tulsa. Trade and industrial center of agr., oil, and stock area.

Cushitic (kŭshĭ′tĭk), group of Hamitic languages, spoken S of Egypt. See LANGUAGE (table).

Cushman, Pauline, 1835–93, Union spy in Civil War, known for her services in Tenn. in 1863.

Cushny, Arthur Robertson (kŭsh′nē), 1866–1926, Scottish physician and pharmacologist, noted for study of action of digitalis on heart and for text on pharmacology.

Custer, George Armstrong, 1839–76, American army officer. Youthful general in Civil War; made spectacular record. Custer's last stand, during campaign against the Sioux in 1876, is still much debated: on the Little Bighorn on June 25, he and over 200 men were killed by the Indians. Battlefield is now a national monument in Mont. His wife, **Elizabeth Bacon Custer,** 1842–1933, devoted much of her life to upholding his memory.

Custer, resort city (pop. 2,017), SW S.Dak., SSW of Rapid City. Oldest town in the Black Hills, it was laid out 1875. Wind Cave Natl. Park, Jewel Cave and Fossil Cycad national monuments, and Mt. Rushmore Natl. Memorial are near.

Custer Battlefield National Monument: see NATIONAL PARKS AND MONUMENTS (table).

Custine, Adam Philippe, comte de (ädä' fēlēp' kõt' dù küsten'), 1740–93, French general in French Revolutionary Wars. Guillotined on charge of treason after failure of 1793 campaign.

customs, government taxes, imposed since early times, on imports or exports. Two common types are specific duty (on quantity of goods) and ad valorem duty (on price). See PROTECTION.

Custozza (kōōstôd'zä), village, N Italy, near Verona. Scene of Austrian victories over Sardinia (1848), and over Italy (1866).

Cutch: see KUTCH.

Cutler, Manasseh (mùnä'sù), 1742–1823, American clergyman, scientist, and colonizer. Wrote first systematic description and classification of New England flora. Aided in forming OHIO COMPANY OF ASSOCIATES. Helped estab. Marietta, Ohio, 1788.

Cutler, Charles A(mmi), 1837–1903, American librarian, a minister. A pioneer in subject cataloguing, he used letters instead of numbers. His classification is basis of Library of Congress system.

cutter, small, one-masted sailing vessel, with rig similar to the SLOOP. Notable for speed, cutters used in service between England and France 1800–1830. Also used as revenue cutters to pursue smugglers; the name was retained for later steam-type revenue vessels. Similarly, vessels of the coast guard are called cutters. See *ill.,* p. 865.

cutting, method of plant propagation in which part of stem, leaf, or root is cut off and produces a new plant by forming buds and roots. Cuttings are made of chrysanthemums, grapes, African violets, and shrubs.

cuttlefish, marine mollusk of warm and temperate coastal waters with shield-shaped body, distinct head, well-developed eyes, and 10 arms. Its internal limy plate, the cuttlebone, is used in abrasives, fertilizers, and as source of lime for cage birds. Artist's sepia is made from a dried glandular secretion.

Cuttyhunk, Mass.: see ELIZABETH ISLANDS.

cutworm, larva of various noctuid or owlet moths. Eggs are laid in midsummer. After hatching, larva eats young shoots and roots, and in autumn goes underground, emerging in spring. Cutworms work by night, destroying more than they eat.

Cuvier, Georges Léopold Chrétien Frédéric Dagobert, Baron (zhôrzh lāôpôld' krätyē' frädärēk' dägôbēr' bärō' küvyä'), 1769–1832, French zoologist and geologist, a founder of comparative anatomy and paleontology. He rejected theories of continuous evolution and supported catastrophism.

Cuxhaven (kōōks'häfùn), city (pop. 47,174), Lower Saxony, N Germany; transatlantic port at mouth of Elbe R., c.60 mi. NW of Hamburg. Chartered 1907; transferred from Hamburg to Hanover prov. 1937. Naval yard was often bombed in World War II.

Cuyahoga (kī'ùhō'gù), river of NE Ohio, rises near Chardon, flows SW then N to L. Erie at Cleveland.

Cuyahoga Falls, city (pop. 29,195), NE Ohio, near Akron on Cuyahoga R.; laid out 1837. Mfg. of machinery, rubber products, tools, and paper products.

Cuyp or **Kuyp** (koip), family of Dutch painters of Dordrecht. **Jacob Gerritszoon Cuyp** (yä'kōp gĕ'rĭt-zōn), 1594–c.1651, was a portrait and landscape painter. His nephew **Benjamin Cuyp,** 1616–52, did peasant scenes. Jacob's son and pupil **Aelbert Cuyp** (äl'bürt), 1620–91, was a leading Dutch landscapist.

Cuyuna, iron range in Minn.: see MESABI.

Cuza, Alexander John (kōō'zä), 1820–73, first prince of Rumania; also known as Couza, Cusa, or Alexander John I. Elected prince of both Moldavia and Walachia 1859; recognized by Turkey as prince of united Rumania 1861. Was forced to abdicate 1866 because of his corrupt regime.

Cuzco (kōō'skō), city (pop. 45,158; alt., 11,207 ft.), cap. of Cuzco dept., S Peru. Site was probably actually occupied by pre-Incan tribes, but legend has city founded by first Incan ruler, Manco Capac. Pizarro entered it in 1533. Today's population is predominantly Indian. Cuzco is center for agr. produce and has woolen textile mills.

cyanide (sī'ùnīd), salt or ester of hydrocyanic (prussic) acid. Both sodium and potassium cyanide are corrosive and systemic water-soluble poisons, giving off prussic acid in presence of moisture. Used in insecticides, casehardening, electroplating. **Cyanide process** for extracting gold and silver from ore: gold or silver dissolved in cyanide solution, then precipitated from solution by another metal.

cyanogen (sīā'nùjĭn), colorless, inflammable, poisonous gas composed of carbon and nitrogen. Chemically active. **Cyanogen chloride:** poisonous liquid with low boiling point, used as poison gas.

Cybele (sī'bùlē), in Phrygian religion, the Great Mother of the Gods. She rode in a chariot drawn by lions and attended by Corybantes and Dactyls. Her worship, involving fertility rites, was imported to Greece, where she was identified with Demeter and Rhea.

Cyclades (sī'klùdēz), Gr. *Kyklades,* Aegean island group (1,023 sq. mi.; pop. 129,015), Greece, stretching SE from Attica and including DELOS, NAXOS, Andros, Tenos, Melos, Paros, Keos, and Syros; chief town Hermopolis (on Syros). Mountainous, with mild, dry climate, islands produce wine, fruit, olive oil, wheat, tobacco. Became Athenian dependency 479 B.C.; later belonged to Rome and Byzantium. After 1204, they formed major part of the duchy of the Archipelago, ruled by Italian nobles and by Venice until its fall to the Turks (1566).

cyclamen (sĭk'–), tuberous-rooted pot plant (*Cyclamen indicum*), native to Mediterranean region. It has nodding flowers with reflexed white, purple, or rose petals.

cycle (sī'kùl), in astronomy, time required to bring about recurrence of same relative positions or aspects of heavenly bodies. Important cycles include revolution of earth about sun (365 days 5 hr. 48 min. 46 sec.); revolution of moon about earth (c.29½ days); solar cycle (c.28 years), marking same relative position of earth and sun; solar ECLIPSE cycle (18 or 19 years); PRECESSION OF THE EQUINOXES; SUNSPOT cycle.

cyclone (sī'klōn), low-pressure storm area, almost circular, with wind blowing spirally inward (clockwise in N Hemisphere, counterclockwise in S Hemisphere). Extratropical cyclone a term for large storms of temperate latitudes. See also HURRICANE; TORNADO.

Cyclops (sī'klŏps), plural **Cyclopes** (sīklō'pēz), in Greek religion, one of a group of one-eyed giants, descended from Uranus and Gaea. Some were shepherds, others worked in smithy of Hephaestus. In battle called the TITANOMACHY they forged a thunderbolt which enabled Zeus to vanquish the Titans.

cyclotron (sī'klùtrŏn), magnetic resonance accelerator invented by E. O. Lawrence. Rapidly oscillating electric current in constant magnetic field makes particles accelerate in curved paths. They move with increasing speeds in widening circles until they reach chamber's edge, where they escape into receptacle and bombard atoms therein. Cyclotron has made it possible to make ordinary elements radioactive, leading to element transmutation, discovery of new elements, production of radioactive isotopes. See *ill.*, page 773.

Cydonia: see CANEA, Crete.

cymbals: see PERCUSSION INSTRUMENTS.

Cymbeline (sĭm′būlēn) or **Cunobelinus** (kū″nōbĭlī′nŭs), fl. A.D. 40, British king; wealthy and powerful ruler. Gave his name, but little else, to Shakspere's play.

Cymru and **Cymry:** see WALES.

Cynewulf (kĭn′ŭwŏolf), fl. early 9th cent.?, Old English religious poet of Northumbria or Mercia. *Elene* best of his four extant poems.

Cynics (sĭ′nĭks), members of a Greek school of philosophy, founded by Antisthenes. On the principle that "Virtue is the only good," the Cynics viewed all else—riches, honor, freedom, even other beings—as worthy only of contempt. Their criticisms were harsh, their manners uncouth. Among cynics were Diogenes of Sinop, Crates, and Menippus.

Cynoscephalae (sĭnŭsĕ′fŭlē), two hills in Thessaly; scene of the victory of Pelopidas in 364 B.C. and of Flamininus over Philip V of Macedon in 197 B.C.

Cynthiana, city (pop. 4,847), N Ky., NE of Lexington. Scene of two raids by Gen. J. H. Morgan in Civil War. Has log house where Henry Clay appeared as lawyer, covered bridge (c.1837), and burying ground (1793).

cypress, coniferous evergreen tree. True cypress (*Cupressus*) is native to S Europe, China, and W U.S. Monterey cypress (*Cupressus macrocarpa*) native to limited region in Calif. Italian cypress of classical literature is *C. sempervirens.* Bald cypress (*Taxodium distichum*), common in swamps of SE U.S., produces upright root projections called knees. Other evergreens called cypress are of genus *Chamaecyparis.*

Cyprian, Saint (sĭ′prēun), d. 258, Father of the Church, bishop of Carthage. Though stern in his demands on Christians, he sturdily opposed the teachings of NOVATIAN that Christians who had lapsed under persecution should not be readmitted to the Church. In pleading for unity of the Church he estab. orthodox doctrines. Feast: Sept. 16.

Cyprus (sī′prŭs), Gr. *Kypros,* British colony (3,572 sq. mi.; pop. 450,114), island in E Mediterranean; cap. Nicosia. Pop. mostly Greek, but also Turkish. A wide plain lies between two mountain ranges which rise to Mt. Olympus (6,406 ft.). Island rich in agr. products, mainly wine, wheat, olives, and tobacco. Minerals include copper, name derived from Cyprus. Excavations show neolithic culture existed 4000–3000 B.C. Ancient Cyprus ruled by many countries, including Phoenicia, Egypt, Greece, and Rome. Christianity introduced by apostles Paul and Barnabas. During Third Crusade, given (1192) to French LUSIGNAN dynasty. Later ruled by Venetians and Turks. Placed under British administration (1878), Cyprus received colonial status 1925. Used by British as detention center for "illegal" Jewish immigrants to Palestine 1945–48.

Cyrano de Bergerac, Savinien (sävēnyē′ sĕränō′ dù bĕrzhùräk′), 1619–55, French author. His *Voyages to the Moon and Sun* (1657–62; Eng. tr., 1923) are two satirical, utopian romances. A swaggering personality, he was romanticized by Edmond Rostand in the drama *Cyrano de Bergerac* (1897).

Cyrenaica (sĭrūnā′ĭkù, sī–), region about anc. CYRENE, N Africa. Became Roman province. Name revived for Italian province.

Cyrenaics (sĭrĭnā′ĭks, sĭrĭ–), members of Greek school of philosophy of 5th and 4th cent. B.C., founded by Aristippus. All were hedonistic, i.e., they held pleasure to be the highest good, but they varied in defining pleasure. Some stressed spiritual satisfactions, others advocated mere painlessness.

Cyrene (sīrē′nē), anc. port, center of anc. Cyrenaica. A Greek colony (7th cent. B.C.), it was a kingdom with much commerce (wheat, wool, silphium) and some development of art. Cyrene became powerful over other cities and held nominal independence until the marriage of Berenice (d. 221? B.C.) to Ptolemy III.

There were severe Jewish outbreaks in Cyrene against Roman Emperor Trajan, and the city declined after severe punishment.

Cyril (of Jerusalem), Saint (sĭ′rùl), 315?–386?, bishop of Jerusalem, Doctor of the Church. He opposed Arianism and may have been the actual author of the Nicene Creed. Feast: March 18.

Cyril (of Alexandria), Saint, d. 444, patriarch of Alexandria, Doctor of the Church. He was stern in attack on heretics and nonbelievers. His fight against NESTORIANISM came to a triumphant conclusion in the Council of EPHESUS (431). He for a time alienated the churchmen of Antioch but reached a compromise with them. His writings on the Trinity, though orthodox, contained seeds of later heresies of EUTYCHES and MONOPHYSITISM. Feast: Feb. 9.

Cyril and Methodius, Saints (–thō′–), d. 869 and 885 respectively, Greek Christian missionaries, brothers. Sent to convert the Moravians (863), they met opposition of the German rulers and were haled back to Rome on charges of heresy. They were cleared, but Cyril died before he could return to the field. Methodius returned, was "deposed" by the Germans from the archbishopric of Moravia, and was restored by the pope. Methodius completed the Slavic translation of religious works begun by Cyril (after whom the Cyrillic alphabet is named, though he did not invent it). Feast: July 7.

Cyrus the Great, d. 529 B.C., king of Persia, who estab. rule of Achaemenidae. Herodotus says he overthrew his grandfather Astyages. He created a firm Persian Empire, including not only Media but all the Near East. Croesus of Lydia, Nabonidus of Babylonia, Amasis II of Egypt—all fell before him. He did not actually conquer Egypt but prepared for later Persian conquest there. He affected the Greek cities of Asia Minor and recreated the power of the Jews in Palestine. His successor was Cambyses.

Cyrus the Younger, d. 401 B.C., Persian prince, son of Darius II, who favored him and gave him large commands. After the death of Darius he was accused of a plot against his brother, ARTAXERXES II. Pardoned, he soon began a rebellion and hired a Greek force (the Ten Thousand) to help him. He won much local help, but in battle with Artaxerxes at CUNAXA (401 B.C.) he was killed and his army defeated. See also ANABASIS; XENOPHON.

Cythera (sĭthēr′ù), Gr. *Kythera,* island (109 sq. mi.; pop. 7,932), Greece, southernmost of IONIAN ISLANDS; chief town Kythera (pop. 1,235), on S shore. Cult of Aphrodite was centered here.

cytoplasm: see PROTOPLASM.

Cyzicus (sĭ′zĭkùs), ancient city of Asia Minor, on Cyzicus Peninsula (modern Kapidagi Peninsula), NW Turkey; a port on Sea of Marmara. Colonized by Greeks from Miletus 756 B.C., it was a member of the Delian League and rivaled Byzantium. Alcibiades defeated Spartan fleet off Cyzicus 410 B.C.

Czajkowski, Michael (chĭkôf′skē), 1804–86, Polish novelist. Took part in Polish insurrection of 1831, later went to Turkey and fought in Crimean War against Russia. Wrote novels on the life of Cossacks and South Slavs and on Polish history.

Czartoryski, Adam Jerzy, Prince (yĕ′zhĭ chärtôrĭ′skē), 1770–1861, Polish-Russian statesman, a close adviser of Alexander I. Russian foreign minister 1803–6. Created Polish school system; persuaded Alexander to grant Polish constitution of 1815. Opposing later Russian policies, he headed the Polish provisional government of 1830–31; after failure of the insurrection he lived in exile at Paris.

Czech language (chĕk), a Western Slavic language of Indo-European family. See LANGUAGE (table).

Czechoslovakia (chĕk″ōslōvăk′ēù), Czech *Československo,* republic (49,354 sq. mi.; pop. 12,196,730), central Europe, bordering on Poland (N), USSR (E), Hungary and Austria (S), and Germany (W and N); cap. PRAGUE. Other large cities: BRNO, BRATISLAVA,

MORAVSKA OSTRAVA. (For geography, economy, and history before 1918, see articles on constituent provinces: BOHEMIA; MORAVIA; SILESIA; SLOVAKIA.) Population is largely Slavic (c.8,100,000 Czechs, 3,100,000 Slovaks, 115,000 Ukrainians); of the once large German and Magyar minorities (c.3,200,000 and 700,000, respectively, before World War II) less than a million remain. Roman Catholicism is the majority religion, but there are large Protestant (notably Hussite) and Eastern Orthodox groups. During World War I Czech units fought on the Allied side, and in 1918 Czechoslovakia emerged as independent republic from the ruins of the Austro-Hungarian Monarchy. Its creation was largely the work of its first and second presidents, T. G. MASARYK and Eduard BENES. The most favored of the Austro-Hungarian "successor states," Czechoslovakia was rich in agr. land, forests, minerals; had well-developed industries; and benefited from a liberal, democratic constitution. Its weakness lay in the disaffection of its German and Magyar minorities and the separatism of Slovakia, which were fostered by Germany and Hungary in the hope of obtaining a revision of their frontiers. Against this threat, the government relied on its alliance with France and on the LITTLE ENTENTE. The rise of Hitler and Western appeasement resulted in 1938 in the MUNICH PACT, through which Germany obtained the Bohemian borderlands; Poland and Hungary shared in the spoils. The truncated state, renamed Czecho-Slovakia, was altogether dissolved in March, 1939, when Germany created and occupied the "Protectorate of Bohemia and Moravia," while Slovakia became nominally independent. The destruction of LIDICE was symbolic of the brutality of German occupation during World War II. In 1945 Czechoslovakia was liberated by U.S. and Russian forces. Pre-Munich Czechoslovakia was restored (except for RUTHENIA, ceded to USSR). The expulsion of the German population was authorized by the Potsdam Conference (1945). A coalition government was in power until Feb., 1948, when the Communists (who formed the largest single party, but not an absolute majority) seized the power. Their leader, Klement Gottwald, succeeded Benes as president. Under Russian influence, Czechoslovakia was transformed into a "people's republic." All opposition was suppressed. The constitution of 1949 abolished the provinces and divided the country into two constituent states—the Czech Lands (Bohemia, Moravia, Silesia) and Slovakia. After Gottwald's death (1953), Antonin Zapotocky was chosen president.

Czernowitz, Bukovina: see CHERNOVTSY.

Czerny, Karl (chĕr'nē), 1791–1857, Austrian pianist. Best known for his technical studies for the piano, which are much used in instruction.

Czestochowa (chĕn"stŭkô'vǔ), city (pop. 101,255), S Poland, on Warta R. Has iron, textile, chemical, and food industries. Chiefly famed for its monastery on Jasna Gora [mountain of light], with image of Our Lady, a major shrine of pilgrimage. In 1655 the monastery, defended by a handful of soldiers, withstood Swedish siege for 40 days. The Swedes withdrew, and the alleged miracle fired Poland to successful resistance to the invaders. Since then Our Lady of Czestochowa, venerated as the "Queen of Poland," has been a symbol of national survival.

Czolgosz, Leon F. (chŏl'gŏsh), c.1873–1901, American anarchist, assassin of Pres. McKinley.

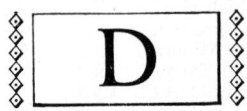

Dabo, Leon (dä'bō), 1868–, American landscape and mural painter.

Dabrowski, Jan Henryk (yän' hĕn'rĭk dämbrôf'skē), 1755–1818, Polish general. Organized and led Polish legions in Napoleon's campaigns.

Dacca (dă'kù), city (pop. 213,218), cap. of East Bengal, Pakistan. Its glory as 17th-cent. Mogul cap. is reflected in Bara Katra palace. Formerly famous for muslins. Mfg. and trade center of E Pakistan. Seat of Univ. of Dacca.

Dachau (dä'khou), town (pop. 23,567), Upper Bavaria, near Munich. Site of a notorious concentration camp under Hitler regime.

D'Ache, Caran: see CARAN D'ACHE.

dachshund: see HOUND.

Dacia (dä'shù), region of Roman Empire, roughly modern Transylvania and Rumania. Its people were called Getae by the Greeks, Daci by the Romans. With advanced material culture they resisted Domitian, who in A.D. 90 paid them tribute to keep them quiet. Trajan planted colonies in Dacia (A.D. 105), and it became a Roman province until Aurelian had to withdraw the colonists. Their legacy to the area was the Romance language, Rumanian.

Da Costa, Isaäc: see COSTA, ISAÄC DA.

Da Costa, Jacob Mendez (dù kŏ'stù), 1833–1900, American physician, outstanding teacher, and author of works on diagnosis and functional heart disease.

Dada (dä'dä) or **Dadaism** (dä'däĭzm), international and nihilistic movement (1916–21) among European artists and writers. A doctrine of utter formlessness, it attacked all conventional standards of aesthetics and behavior, thus encouraging surrealism and other later radical movements.

daddy longlegs, name for harvestman (a relative of the spider) and for crane fly (an insect related to mosquito). Harvestman has small body, eight slender legs. It sucks fluids from fruits, other vegetable matter, and insects (some say it eats whole insects). Crane fly has a slender body and two pairs of wings.

Dadeville, town (pop. 2,354), E central Ala., near Martin L. At near-by Horseshoe Bend of Tallapoosa R. a state monument marks Andrew Jackson's defeat of Creek Indians in March, 1814.

Daedalus (dĕ'dùlùs), in Greek myth, builder of labyrinth for the Minotaur; father of ICARUS.

daffodil: see NARCISSUS.

Dafydd ap Gwilym (dä'vĭdh ăp gwī'lĭm), 1340?–1400?, Welsh poet. Introduced new meters and new themes. Most notable are his nature poems.

Dagenham (dä'gùnùm), urban district (pop. 114,588), Essex, England. Huge Ford plant estab. 1929.

Dagestan or **Daghestan** (dägùstän'), autonomous soviet socialist republic (14,750 sq. mi.; pop. c.900,000),

SE European RSFSR, between Terek R., Greater Caucasus, and Caspian Sea; cap. Makhachkala. Mostly bare inaccessible mountains. Wine, cotton, corn in irrigated lowlands. Population, mostly Moslems, includes c.30 nationalities. Ceded to Russia by Persia 1813; native revolts until 1877.

Dagobert I (dăg'ōbûrt), d. c.639, Frankish king (629?–639). Last of MEROVINGIANS to exercise personal rule.

Dagon, Philistine god, perhaps a fish god. Probably his was a fertility cult.

Daguerre, Louis Jacques Mandé (lwē' zhăk' mädä' dägâr'), 1789–1851, French scene painter and physicist, inventor of the daguerreotype. With C. M. Bouton he also invented the diorama.

dahlia (dăl'–), tuberous-rooted perennial of genus *Dahlia,* native to Mexico. Widely grown for late-blooming colorful, composite flowers of many types (e.g., large double, single, pompon). See *ill.,* p. 783.

Dahlstjerna, Gunno Eurelius (gŭ'nō ā-ōōrā'lēŭs däl'shĕr"nä), 1661–1709, Swedish poet, first to use native themes.

Dahomey (dähō'mē), French overseas territory (c.45,560 sq. mi.; pop. 1,458,000), SE French West Africa, on Slave Coast of Gulf of Guinea; cap. Porto Novo. Cotton, palm oil, and coffee are exported. Under French rule since 1894.

Dáil Éireann (dôl' ā'rôn, dīl' â'rûn [Irish,= diet of Ireland], popular representative body of National Parliament of republic of IRELAND. Second chamber, the Senate, has little power; prime minister responsible to Dáil. Members of first Dáil, elected to British Parliament, proclaimed republic 1919.

Daimler, Gottlieb (dăm'lùr), 1834–1900, German engineer, inventor, automobile manufacturer. Contributed to development of automobile industry by improving the internal-combustion engine.

daimyo or **daimio** (both: dīm'yō), great feudal barons of Japan. Owned vast tax-free estates (built up after 8th cent.); in 12th cent. held more power than imperial government until Yoritomo established system of centralized feudalism.

Daingerfield, Elliot (dān'jùrfĕld), 1859–1932, American religious and landscape painter.

Daingerfield, town (pop. 1,668), E Texas. Metallurgical plant built in World War II near by.

Dairen (dī'rĕn'), Chinese *Talien,* Rus. *Dalny,* industrial city (pop. 543,690), S Manchuria, on LIAOTUNG peninsula; port on Korea Bay, S terminus of South Manchurian RR. Included in Kwantung leased territory 1898–1945. Opened 1906 to foreign trade by Japan. After World War II included in Port Arthur naval base under joint Sino-Soviet control.

dairying, industry producing milk and milk products, the largest single source of income of U.S. farmer. Supplies c.20% of average food intake. Butter and market milk account for about two thirds of production; rest goes into cheese, by-products, farm uses. Creameries process and market dairy products; many are farmers' cooperatives, esp. in Denmark.

daisy, name for many plants of composite family with petallike rays. True daisy of literature is English daisy (*Bellis perennis*), a low biennial with white, pink, or red flowers. Common white field or oxeye daisy (*Chrysanthemum leucanthemum*) is naturalized in U.S. from Europe. The Shasta daisy is a species of *Chrysanthemum.* See also MARGUERITE; PYRETHRUM.

Dakar (dùkär'), city (pop. c.185,400), Senegal, cap. of French West Africa, a major Atlantic port at tip of Cape Verde peninsula. A naval base and stopover point for transoceanic air lines. In World War II held by Vichy forces from 1940 until Dec., 1942, when it peaceably joined the Allies.

Dakin's solution, dilute (0.5%) solution of sodium hypochlorite. It is unstable, liberating chlorine, thus valuable as surgical antiseptic and for wound dressing. It was named for **Henry Drysdale Dakin,** 1880–1952, British-born American chemist.

Dakota Indians: see SIOUX INDIANS.

Daladier, Édouard (ādōōär' dälädya'), 1884–, French politician. Three times premier (1933, 1933–34, 1938–40); minister of war 1936–40. Signed MUNICH PACT (1938). One of defendants in RIOM trial (1942); interned by Germans until 1945.

Dalai Lama: see LAMAISM.

Dalarna (dä'lärnä") or **Dalecarlia** (dälükär'lēū), historic province of central Sweden, nearly identical with KOPPARBERG co. In 1521 peasants of Dalarna, under GUSTAVUS I, freed Sweden from Danish rule. Old rural customs and home industries have survived.

D'Albert, Eugen Francis Charles: see ALBERT, EUGEN FRANCIS CHARLES D'.

Dalcroze, Émile Jaques: see JAQUES-DALCROZE.

Dale, Sir Henry Hallett, 1875–, English scientist. Shared 1936 Nobel Prize in Physiology and Medicine for study of acetylcholine agent in transmission of nerve impulses.

Dalecarlia, Sweden: see DALARNA.

D'Alembert's principle. Jean le Rond d'Alembert introduced (1742) and estab. (1743) a principle of mechanics which shows that Newton's third law of motion applies to bodies free to move as well as to stationary bodies.

Dalen, Nils Gustaf (nīls' gŭs'täv dälän'), 1869–1937, Swedish scientist. Won 1912 Nobel Prize chiefly for invention of automatic regulator for acetylene-gas lights used for railway signals, beacons, buoys.

Dalhart (dăl'härt), city (pop. 5,918), N Texas, NW of Amarillo in Panhandle. Has railroad shops, stockyards, and grain elevators. Near by is Rita Blanca Creek, dammed for irrigation.

Dalhousie, James Andrew Broun Ramsay, 1st marquess of (dălhōō'zē), 1812–60, British statesman. As governor general of India (1847–56) annexed Sikh territory of the Punjab 1849, promoted economic and social reforms, and annexed princely states with no natural heirs.

Dalhousie (dălhou'zē) town (pop. 4,939), N N.B., Canada, at mouth of Restigouche R. Fishing port and seaside resort with lumber and paper mills.

Dalhousie University: see HALIFAX, N.S.

Dali, Salvador (sälvädhôr' dä'lē), 1904–, Spanish surrealist painter. Tried futurism and cubism before he turned to surrealism. With fine draughtsmanship he expresses an irrational dream world.

Dalin, Olof von (ōō'lôv fŭn dälän'), 1708–63, Swedish historian, lyric poet, and journalist, foremost literary figure of his day. Founded periodical, the *Swedish Argus.* Also wrote poetical satires, drama, and popular history.

Dalkeith (dŭlkēth'), burgh (pop. 8,786), Midlothian, Scotland. Important grain center, it also has metal works. Near one of few oil fields in England. Dalkeith House seat of duke of Buccleuch.

Dallas, Alexander James, 1759–1817, U.S. Secretary of the Treasury (1814–16), b. West Indies. Restored confidence in U.S. currency during critical period. His son, **George Mifflin Dallas,** 1792–1864, was Vice President of the United States (1845–49). As minister to Great Britain (1856–61), he signed Dallas-Clarendon Convention (1856), which set basis for settlement of difficulties in Central America.

Dallas, city (pop. 434,462), N Texas, E of Fort Worth at head of Trinity R. Settled 1841; growth augmented 1858 by French from disbanded Fourierist Colony. A cotton center, it makes gin machinery, processes, weaves, and ships cotton; regional style center. Has oil processing and related industries and mfg. of auto and aircraft parts. Expanded in World War II. Financial, industrial, and cultural center of much of Southwest, it is second largest Texas city. Here are SOUTHERN METHODIST UNIVERSITY, symphony orchestra, Little Theatre, and U.S. airfield. Old reservoir, White Rock L., is now in park; new one, L. Dallas (see TRINITY, river), near Denton. Annual state fair held.

Dalles, The, Oregon: see THE DALLES.

Dalmatia (dălmā'shù), coastal region of Yugoslavia, extending along Adriatic from Fiume to Kotor. Interior forms part of Dinaric Alps. Coastline, famed for beauty, has many islands, bays, and harbors. ZARA, SPLIT, DUBROVNIK are main ports and cities. From the 10th cent. Dalmatia was divided among Croatia, Serbia, and Venice, which controlled the islands and main ports. Venetian possessions passed to Austria in 1797. In 1919 Yugoslavia received all Dalmatia except Zara and several islands, which were given to Italy but which passed to Yugoslavia in 1947.

Dalmatian dog: see HUNTING DOGS.

Dalrymple, earls of Stair; Viscount Stair: see STAIR, JAMES DALRYMPLE, VISCOUNT.

Dalrymple, Alexander (dăl'rĭmpùl, dălrĭm'pùl), 1737–1808, British hydrographer. Traveled in the S Pacific for the East India Co. For the British admiralty he collected charts, memoirs, and records and wrote accounts of the South Seas.

Dalton, John (dôl'tùn), 1766–1844, English scientist. He revived the ATOMIC THEORY and applied the concept to a table of atomic weights and in formulating **Dalton's law:** total pressure of a mixture of gases equals sum of pressures of gases in the mixture, each gas acting independently.

Dalton, city (pop. 15,968), NW Ga., in Appalachian Valley. Major producer of candlewick bedspreads; mfg. also of yarn, hosiery, and lumber. Confederate hq. in Civil War after CHATTANOOGA CAMPAIGN, it fell to Sherman in ATLANTA CAMPAIGN (1864).

Dalton plan: see PROGRESSIVE EDUCATION.

Dalton's law: see DALTON, JOHN.

Daly, Augustin, 1838–99, American theatrical manager. A playwright and drama critic, made debut as manager with his melodrama *Under the Gaslight.* Opened his first theater 1869. Later started Daly's Theatre where he presented magnificent productions of Shakspere and of French and German adaptations.

Daly, Marcus, 1841–1900, American copper magnate, b. Ireland. Estab. Anaconda Copper Mining Co. in Mont. and became fabulously rich. His fierce and long-lasting rivalry with William A. CLARK dominated Mont. politics and economy.

Daly, Thomas Augustine, 1871–1948, American humorous poet, known for Italian-dialect verse.

Daly City, residential city (pop. 15,191), W Calif., adjoining San Francisco, in truck and dairy area.

Dam, Henrik (hăn'rĕk däm'), 1895–, Danish biochemist. For identification and studies of vitamin K he shared 1943 Nobel Prize in Physiology and Medicine. Also worked on role of vitamin E in nutrition.

dam, barrier of rock, earth, masonry, concrete, timber (seldom used), or some combination, which restrains water. Rock or earth dams usually have upstream surface made watertight. Masonry and concrete dams are either gravity type (resist water only with own weight) or single- or multiple-arched type. Single-arched dams are usually constructed in narrow canyon having rock walls to withstand tremendous thrust of horizontal, upstream arch. Multiple-arched dams employ buttresses. Many modern dams serve multiple purposes—provide irrigation, aid flood control, provide power for hydroelectric plants.

Damão (dämä'ō) or **Daman** (dùmän'), district (176 sq. mi.; pop. 63,521) of Portuguese India; cap. Damão. Consists of three separate enclaves within Bombay state. Acquired 1558 by Portugal.

Damariscotta (dăm"ùrĭskŏt'ù), town (pop. 1,113), S Maine on Damariscotta R. and SE of Augusta. Has St. Patrick's Church (1803), said to be oldest Roman Catholic church in New England. Near the river are seemingly ancient mounds.

Damascene, John: see JOHN OF DAMASCUS, SAINT.

Damascus (dùmä'skùs), Arabic *Esh-Sham*, city (pop. 303,952), S Syria, cap. of Syria, on Barada R. Dates from unknown antiquity. Successively held by Assyrians and Persians. Conquered 332 B.C. by Alexander the Great, after whose death it fell prey to other conquerors, notably Armenians. In 64 B.C. it passed to Romans under Pompey, becoming one of cities of Decapolis. On road to Damascus Paul was converted to Christianity. With Arab occupation (begun 635) city became Moslem; great Christian church, built A.D. c.375 under Emperor Theodosius I, became Great Mosque. Seat of Omayyad caliphate 661–750. City prospered and became known for fine metalwork (esp. swords). Fell to Mongols under Hulagu Khan in 1260, sacked by Tamerlane in 14th cent. Was under Ottoman Turks 1516–1918. Captured 1918 by the British, it was under French mandate 1920–1941. Became cap. of independent Syria 1943.

damask (dă'mùsk), fabric whose ground and pattern are of different weaves: e.g., ground may be in twill with the design in satin. True damasks, unlike brocade, are flat and reversible.

Damian, Peter: see PETER DAMIAN, SAINT.

Damien, Father (dä'mēùn, dämyē'), 1840–89, Belgian missionary priest named Damien de Veuster. After working as a missionary among the natives of Hawaii, he was transferred at his own request to the leper colony on Molokai, where he labored among the afflicted until he himself died of leprosy.

Damietta (dămēē'tù), city (pop. 53,620), NE Egypt; textile center. As Tamiathis it was twice captured by Crusaders in 13th cent. Destroyed 1250, later rebuilt by Egyptians.

Damocles (dă'mùklēz), in classic legend, Syracusan at court of Dionysius. To demonstrate dangers of high estate, the ruler gave a banquet in his honor; Damocles was happy until, looking up, he saw a sword suspended above his head by a single hair.

Damodar (dä'mōdär), river, c.340 mi. long, India, in Bihar and West Bengal. Major multi-purpose project (8 dams) is in its valley.

Damon and Pythias (dä'mùn, pĭ'thēùs), two faithful Syracusan friends. When Pythias, condemned to death, was freed to arrange his affairs, Damon stayed as pledge. On Pythias' return, tyrant Dionysius, impressed, freed both and asked to be their friend.

Damophon (dä'mùfōn), fl. 2d cent. B.C., Greek sculptor. Did colossal heads of Demeter and Artemis.

damp, in mining, any of several gases. Firedamp, found in coal mines, is mostly methane and, mixed with air, is highly combustible. Afterdamp is gaseous mixture remaining after firedamp explosion. Chokedamp, mostly carbon dioxide, is imperceptible and when in quantity is dangerous to life.

Dampier, William (dăm'pēr), 1651?–1715, English explorer and buccaneer. Fought in Dutch War (1673), managed plantation in Jamaica, took part as buccaneer against Spanish America (1679–81). Wrote masterly hydrographic treatise. As commander of expedition in S Pacific, discovered Dampier Archipelago and Dampier Strait, named New Britain as island.

Damrosch (dăm'rŏsh), German-American family of conductors, composers, and educators. **Leopold Damrosch,** 1832–85, came to New York in 1871. He founded the New York Symphony Society in 1878. Many works of Brahms and Wagner received their first American performances under his baton. His compositions include violin concertos, cantatas, and a symphony. His son, **Frank Damrosch,** 1859–1937, supervised music in New York public schools. In 1905, he helped organize the Institute of Musical Art (later a unit of the Juilliard School). Another son of Leopold Damrosch, **Walter Damrosch,** 1862–1950, first conducted at the Metropolitan Opera. Later he conducted both the New York Philharmonic and the New York Symphony. He directed a series of music education programs on the radio for children. His compositions include operas and choral works.

damsel fly: see DRAGONFLY.

Dan [Heb.,= judge]. **1** Son of Jacob, ancestor of one of 12 tribes of Israel. Tribe finally settled in N Palestine. Samson was famous Danite. Many references in Genesis, Exodus, Numbers. **2** City at N extremity of Palestine, hence expression "from Dan to BEER-SHEBA." Jeroboam erected golden calf here.

Dan, river rising in SW Va. in piedmont and flowing c.180 mi. E to the Roanoke in S Va., twice crossing N.C. line.

Dana, Charles A(nderson) (dā'nù), 1819–97, American newspaper editor. Was at Brook Farm. Later was associated (1847–62) with Horace Greeley on the New York *Tribune*. Became (1864) Assistant Secretary of War. As editor and part owner of the New York *Sun* (1868–97) he estab. high standards of readability and hired many famous writers.

Dana, Edward Salisbury: see DANA, JAMES DWIGHT.

Dana, Francis, 1743–1811, American diplomat. Accompanied (1779) John Adams to Paris and was sent (1780) to the court of Catherine the Great of Russia. Stayed there 1781–83, although he was never recognized. His son, **Richard Henry Dana,** 1787–1879, was a poet and essayist. His son, **Richard Henry Dana,** 1815–82, was an author and lawyer. Shipped as a common seaman around Cape Horn to Calif. Narrative of this voyage, *Two Years before the Mast* (1840), became a classic.

Dana, James Dwight, 1813–95, American geologist, author of standard works on geology and mineralogy and studies of volcanoes, coral, and crustaceans. He taught at Yale 1850–90. His son, **Edward Salisbury Dana,** 1849–1935, taught physics at Yale (1890–1917) and also wrote on mineralogy.

Dana, John Cotton, 1856–1929, American librarian, long director of Newark Museum. Inaugurated many progressive library projects.

Dana, Richard Henry: see DANA, FRANCIS.

Danaë (dă'nāē), in Greek legend, daughter of Acrisius. Zeus visited her in a shower of gold, and she bore him PERSEUS.

Danaüs (dă'nāŭs), in Greek myth, brother of Aegyptus; he had 50 daughters, the Danaïds or Danaïdes, Aegyptus had 50 sons. When the sons demanded Danaïds as brides, Danaüs told each one to slay her husband. Only Hypermnestra failed to kill her husband, Lynceus, and their descendants were the Danaï, another name for the Greeks.

Danbury, city (pop. 22,067) in Danbury town (pop. 30,337), SW Conn., NW of Bridgeport; settled 1684. Hat mfg. center since 1780. Noted annual fairs (since early 1800s). Military depot in Revolution.

Danbury Hatters' Case, decided in 1908 by U.S. Supreme Court. The holding that hatters' union, which had boycotted products of a nonunion hat manufacturer in Danbury, Conn., was subject to injunction and treble damages set precedent for Federal Court interference in labor activities.

Danby, Thomas Osborne, earl of, 1631–1712, English statesman. One of chief ministers of Charles II. Impeached and imprisoned 1678–84, later joined Whigs in inviting William of Orange to England. Was virtual premier 1690–95.

dance. Among primitive people, dancing developed as natural expression of united feeling and action, usually of ritualistic, ceremonial nature. In dances of religious ecstasy (esp. in the Orient, Africa) trancelike states are induced. In many Pacific isls. and in the Orient there are dances performed entirely in a sitting posture. Primitive dances survive today in FOLK DANCE. Dance played an important role in developing drama in Greece, India, and Japan (see JAPANESE DRAMA). Dancing as social activity and BALLET are of relatively recent origin. Dancing reached a height in France during Louis XIV's reign—era of the saraband, pavan, MINUET, and gavotte. Later forms include the Spanish bolero, German WALTZ, American fox trot, and S American tango. Early in the 20th cent. dance as an art form was profoundly affected by Isadora DUNCAN, who paved the way for, and Mary WIGMAN, who actually founded, "modern dance"—the somewhat inappropriate name for nonballetic 20th-cent. theater dance. As developed by Martha GRAHAM,

Hanya Holm, Doris HUMPHREY, Charles Weidman, and others, modern dance became a medium for expressing complex emotions and abstract ideas. Such media as films and television also are developing and transmuting dance forms.

dandelion, common, milky-juiced perennial plant (*Taraxacum officinale*), with a rosette of toothed leaves and bright yellow flower heads borne on hollow stalks. Young leaves are edible both cooked and in salad; wine made from flowers. See *ill.*, p. 783.

Dandolo, Enrico (ĕnrē'kō dän'dōlō), c.1108–1205, doge of Venice (1192–1205). Led Fourth Crusade to capture Zara and Constantinople (see CRUSADES). Of the same family was **Andrea Dandolo** (ändrā'ä), c.1307–1354, doge of Venice (1343–54). Reformed laws; wrote chronicle of Venetian history.

Danegeld (dān'gĕld"), medieval land tax, originally raised to buy off raiding Danes. First levied in England by Æthelred in 991; collected irregularly until 1163. In France monks of Saint-Denis paid a Danegeld in 845 and several times later.

Danelaw (dän'lô"), originally body of law which prevailed in part of England occupied by Danes after treaty of King ALFRED with Guthrum (886). Soon applied to area in which Danish law prevailed. Had four main regions: Northumbria; shires dependent on boroughs of Lincoln, Nottingham, Derby, Leicester, and Stamford; East Anglia; SE Midlands.

Danforth, Thomas, 1703–86, American pewterer, founder of a family of celebrated pewterers. First shop was in Norwich, Conn.

Dania (dā'nēù), city (pop. 4,540), SE Fla., on the Atlantic just S of Fort Lauderdale; settled 1896 by Danes. Seminole Indian Reservation is near.

Daniel [Heb.,= God is my judge], prophet, central figure of book of DANIEL.

Daniel, Samuel, 1562–1619, English poet known chiefly for *Delia* (1592), a collection of sonnets.

Daniel, book of Old Testament. Some parts occur only in Greek and are placed in Apocrypha in AV, but are included in Western canon (see SUSANNA; BEL AND THE DRAGON; THREE HOLY CHILDREN). Book tells story of Daniel, a Jew living in 6th cent. B.C., who was taken in captivity into court of Nebuchadnezzar, where he rose to power and was called Belteshazzar. Proverbial for wisdom, he was hero of many stories, e.g., his interpretation of Nebuchadnezzar's dreams; his reading of handwriting on wall; his escape from lion's den; his apocalyptic visions. Book also tells of his three friends who faced ordeal of fiery furnace. Critics question date of book, its authorship and historical accuracy, but agree on its inspirational value as story of uncompromising faith.

Daniels, Josephus, 1862–1948, American statesman, newspaper editor, and author. Was editor in Raleigh, N.C., after 1884. U.S. Secretary of the Navy (1913–21); ambassador to Mexico (1933–42). Wrote *The Wilson Era* (1944–46). His son **Jonathan Worth Daniels,** 1902–, succeeded to editorship of Raleigh *News and Observer* in 1948.

Danielson, Conn.: see KILLINGLY.

Danilo (dänē'lô), princes of MONTENEGRO. **Danilo I** (Danilo Petrovich of Niegosh), 1677–1735, reigned 1696–1735. Instigated massacre of Moslems (1703; "Montenegrin Vespers"); began traditional alliance with Russia against Turkey. **Danilo II,** 1826–60, reigned 1851–60. Secularized the prince-bishopric by transferring his ecclesiastic functions to an archbishop. Defeated Turks at Ostrog (1853) and Grahovo (1858). Assassinated.

Danish language, North Germanic language of Indo-European family. See LANGUAGE (table).

Danish West Indies: see VIRGIN ISLANDS OF THE U.S.

Dannemora (dă"nùmô'rù), village (pop. 4,122), NE N.Y. Clinton State Prison is here.

D'Annunzio, Gabriele (gäbrēā'lä dän-nōōn'tsyō), 1863–1938, Italian author and adventurer, a leader of the decadents. A strong nationalist, he led an expedition to free Fiume (1919) and was an early idol of fascism. Poems, novels, and plays include *Canto novo* [new song] (1882) and the play *Il sogno d'un tramonto d'autunno* (1898). His love affair with Eleanora Duse is described in the novel *Il fuoco* (1900).

Dansville, village (pop. 5,253), W central N.Y., S of Geneseo, in agr. area. Here Clara Barton founded (1881) first local chapter of American Red Cross.

Dante (Alighieri) (dän'tā älēgyä'rē), 1265–1321, Italian poet, author of the DIVINE COMEDY, b. Florence. *La vita nuova* [the new life] (1292), a prose narrative with inserted lyrics, told of his love for a beautiful girl, identified by many as Beatrice Portinari. He went into exile with the White Guelphs (1302). He died in exile in Ravenna. Dante also wrote in Italian many fine lyrics and an unfinished encyclopedic work, the *Convivio.* His Latin works include an unfinished treatise (*De vulgari eloquentia*), on Italian language and poetics, and a masterful apology for world government (*Monarchia*).

Danton, Georges Jacques (zhōrzh' zhäk' dätō'), 1759–94, French revolutionist. A lawyer, he won immense popularity through his powerful oratory. As a leader of the CORDELIERS he championed the extreme left in the National Assembly and was instrumental in overthrowing the monarchy (1792). As head of the provisional republican government and minister of justice he set up the Revolutionary Tribunal and dominated the first Committee of Public Safety (1793). The rise of the extremists led by ROBESPIERRE led Danton to seek a relatively moderate course. His struggle with Robespierre was, however, personal rather than ideological. Danton gradually lost his influence. Early in 1794 he was arrested on a charge of conspiracy and, after a mock trial, guillotined.

Danube (dă'nūb), Ger. *Donau,* Hung. *Duna,* Serbo-Croatian *Dunav,* Rumanian *Dunarea,* river, c.1,750 mi. long, Central and SE Europe; largest in Europe after Volga. Draining c.320,000 sq. mi., it rises in the Black Forest (SW Germany) and flows generally SE through S Germany, E Austria, Hungary, NE Yugoslavia, and SE Rumania into the Black Sea. It forms sections of the Czechoslovak-Hungarian border and of the borders of Rumania with Yugoslavia, Bulgaria, and the USSR. After passing the IRON GATE it broadens steadily and at Galati it divides into a swampy delta. Its course passes Ulm (where it becomes navigable), Regensburg, Passau, Linz, Vienna, Bratislava, Esztergom, Budapest, Belgrade, Galati, and Izmail. Among some 300 affluents are the Inn, Drava, Theiss, Sava, and Pruth. A vital traffic artery, the Danube also is a link of many cultures. It was the N border of the Roman Empire; its fertile plains have attracted many invaders. In 1919 it was placed under an international commission, which was dissolved in 1940. The Belgrade convention of 1948, which the U.S., Great Britain, and France refused to sign, created a navigation commission composed of the riparian nations only (excluding Germany and Austria).

Danvers, town (pop. 15,720), NE Mass., NW of Salem; settled 1636. Mfg. of shoes and metal products.

Danville. 1 City (pop. 37,864), E Ill., on Vermilion R. at Ind. line; plotted 1827. Center of agr. and coal area with railroad shops. Mfg. of brick, food, and zinc products. Abraham Lincoln had law office here for five years. **2** City (pop. 8,686), central Ky., SSW of Lexington; settled 1775. Rail hub with stockyards, flour and lumber mills, and mfg. of clothing and furniture. One of state's oldest settlements, seat of govt. 1784–92. Kentucky constitutional conventions held here (setting preserved). Seat of Centre Col. of Kentucky (Presbyterian; coed.; 1819). **3** Borough (pop. 6,994), NE central Pa., on Susquehanna R. and NE of Harrisburg. Has iron and steel works. **4** City (pop. 35,066), S Va., SE of Roanoke and on Dan R.; founded 1793. One of world's largest bright-leaf tobacco markets, it has cotton mills and mfg. of tex-

tiles and furniture. Operates Pinnacles of Dan hydroelectric project. Was last cap. of the Confederacy in April, 1865.

Danzig (dăn'sĭg), Pol. *Gdańsk,* city (pop. 117,894; 1941 pop. 267,251), a Baltic seaport on a branch of the Vistula; transferred to Polish administration 1945. The ancient cap. of Pomerelia, it was settled by German merchants; joined the Hanseatic League 13th cent.; passed to the Teutonic Knights 1308; became an autonomous state under Polish overlordship 1466; passed to Prussia 1793; was a free city 1807–14; was restored to Prussia 1814. It was the cap. of West Prussia prov. until 1919, when the Treaty of Versailles again made it a free city, united with Poland by a customs union and supervised by a League of Nations high commissioner. After 1935 the local National Socialist party gained control over the legislature and agitated for reunion with Germany. Hitler's demand for Danzig was the chief direct cause of World War II. Danzig was annexed to Germany Sept. 1, 1939; it fell to the Russian army early in 1945. The construction of the Polish port of GDYNIA after World War I reduced its importance as a port. Virtually destroyed in World War II, Danzig lost all its fine medieval architecture; only the port escaped destruction. Most of the German population was expelled after 1945 and replaced by Poles.

Daphne (dăf'nē), in Greek myth, nymph who attracted love of Apollo. Pursued by him, she prayed for escape and was changed into a laurel tree.

Daphnis (dăf'nĭs), in Greek literary legend, shepherd in love with a Naiad. Made blind for unfaithfulness, he played sad songs upon his shepherd's pipes and thus began pastoral melody.

Daphnis and Chloë (dăf'nĭs, klō'ē), Greek pastoral romance attributed to one Longus of 3d cent. A.D.

Da Ponte, Lorenzo (lôrĕnd'zō dä pōn'tä), 1749–1838, Italian poet and librettist, a pioneer in spreading Italian culture in the U.S. Wrote librettos for Mozart's *Così fan tutte* (1790), *The Marriage of Figaro* (1786), and *Don Giovanni* (1787). Came to U.S. in 1805, was made professor at Columbia Univ. 1830.

D'Arblay, Madame: see BURNEY, FRANCES.

Darby, John Nelson, 1800–1882, a founder of PLYMOUTH BRETHREN. He formed congregations on the Continent and in U.S. and Canada.

Darby, borough (pop. 13,154), SE Pa., SW suburb of Philadelphia; settled 1682. Has colonial landmarks. Mfg. of boats, textiles, and clothing.

Dardanelles (därdŭnĕlz'), strait, c.40 mi. long, 1–4 mi. wide, connecting the Aegean with the Sea of Marmara and dividing the Gallipoli peninsula of European Turkey from Asiatic Turkey. Called the Hellespont in antiquity; scene of legend of HERO and Leander. Controlling navigation between the Black Sea and the Mediterranean, the Dardanelles and BOSPORUS straits have been important from the dawn of history. Ancient Troy prospered near W entrance of Hellespont. Xerxes and Alexander the Great crossed it by a bridge of boats (c.481 B.C.; 334 B.C.). Under the Byzantine and Ottoman empires the Straits were essential to defense of Constantinople; with the decay of Turkey (see EASTERN QUESTION), their status became an international problem. In 1841 the Great Powers agreed to close the Straits to all but Turkish warships in peacetime. This was reaffirmed by the Congress of Paris (1856). In World War I the Allied GALLIPOLI CAMPAIGN failed to force the Straits. The Treaty of SÈVRES (1920) internationalized the Straits zone, but the Conference of LAUSANNE (1923) restored it to Turkey on condition of demilitarization. In 1936, by the MONTREUX CONVENTION, Turkey was permitted to refortify it.

Dardanus (där'dŭnŭs), in Greek mythology, founder of Troy; son of Zeus and the Pleiad Electra.

Dare, Virginia, b. 1587, on Roanoke Isl., first white child of English parents born in America.

Dares Phrygius (dâ'rēz frĭ'jĕŭs), supposed author of a

history of Trojan War. Latin MS of 5th cent. A.D. was popular source for medieval stories.

Dar-es-Salaam (där′-ēs-sŭläm′), city (pop. 69,227), cap. of Tanganyika; a port on the Indian Ocean.

Dariel, Georgian SSR: see DARYAL.

Darien (dâ″rēēn′, dâ′rēēn′, Span. däryän′), E part of Panama. Properly today Isthmus of Darien is that part of Isthmus of Panama between Gulf of Darien and Gulf of San Miguel, but formerly name was applied to entire isthmus. Visited by Bastidas (1501) and Columbus (1502). Arias de Ávila (Pedrarias) succeeded ENCISO as governor in 1514 and established harsh rule over entire isthmus.

Darien. 1 (dâ″rēēn′) Residential town (pop. 11,767), SW Conn., on Long Isl. Sound E of Stamford. 2 (dā′rēĭn) City (pop. 1,380), SE Ga., N of Brunswick. Founded 1736 by Scotch Highlanders recruited by Oglethorpe to supersede Spanish influence. Site of Fort King George (1721–27), first English settlement in Ga., is near.

Darien Scheme, Scottish colonial project. Scottish Parliament chartered trading company 1695. Efforts made to estab. colony on Isthmus of Panama failed (1698–99) with loss of many lives and great losses to Scottish investors. Showed Scotland's commercial disadvantage outside British "realm."

Darío, Rubén (rōōbĕn′ därē′ō), 1867–1916, Spanish American poet, b. Nicaragua. Spent many years in diplomatic service. Was leader of MODERNISMO. His poems have elegance and grace strengthened by vigor and power, technical mastery, and achieve poetic universality. First important volume was *Azul* [blue] (1888).

Darius (dûrī′ŭs), kings of anc. Persia. **Darius I** (the Great), c.549–485? B.C., reigned 521–485? B.C. Succeeding his cousin Cambyses after the fall of a false claimant, he put down rebellions, then set up the administrative system under satraps (governors responsible only to him, with checks by the army and police). This system lasted even beyond the fall of the empire to Alexander the Great. Darius campaigned against the Scythians but is best remembered as the king against whom the Ionian Greek cities revolted (c.500 B.C.), thus beginning the PERSIAN WARS. His first expedition against Greece was turned back by storms, his second defeated at MARATHON (490 B.C.). Succeeded by XERXES I. **Darius II**, d. 404 B.C., son of Artaxerxes I, succeeded his half brother Xerxes II and reigned 423?–404 B.C. Succeeded by Artaxerxes II, but CYRUS THE YOUNGER claimed the throne. **Darius III**, d. 330 B.C., was raised to the throne (336 B.C.) by the eunuch Bagoas, who had murdered Artaxerxes III and his heir. Darius had Bagoas killed but could not estab. his rule firmly. His empire fell to ALEXANDER THE GREAT, who defeated his armies at Issus (333 B.C.) and Gaugamela (331 B.C.) and pursued Darius into Bactria, where he was murdered by his cousin, the satrap Bessus. Called Darius Codomannus.

Darius the Mede, in Bible, called son of Ahasuerus and king of Chaldeans after defeat of Belshazzar; exact identity unknown. Dan. 5.31; 9.1; 11.1.

Darjeeling (därjē′lĭng), resort town (pop. 25,873), N West Bengal, India, in Himalaya foothills, alt. c.7,000 ft. Tea-growing center.

Dark Ages: see MIDDLE AGES.

dark horse, in U.S. politics, a comparatively unknown man chosen by a major party as candidate for public office, especially the presidency. Usually chosen to break a deadlocked national convention. W. H. Harrison was first important dark horse.

Darlan, Jean François (zhä′ fräswä′ därlä′), 1881–1942, French admiral. Important member of VICHY GOVERNMENT from 1940; received command of armed forces 1942; advocated collaboration with Germany. After Allied landing in N Africa (Nov., 1942) went over to Allies, who made him high commissioner in N Africa. Assassinated by an antifascist.

Darling, river of SE Australia, 1,702 mi. long, mainly in New South Wales; longest tributary of Murray R. Explored by Charles Sturt in 1844.

Darlington, county borough (pop. 84,861), Durham, England; railroad center. Has locomotive works, iron, steel, and woolen mills. Locomotive which drew first passenger train (1825) preserved here.

Darlington, town (pop. 6,619), NE S.C., NW of Florence. Center of cotton, tobacco, and lumber area.

Darmstadt (därm′stät, därm′shtät), city (pop. 94,132), former cap. of Hesse-Darmstadt (see HESSE), W Germany. Commercial center; chemical industry. Severely damaged in World War II.

Darnley, Henry Stuart or **Stewart, Lord,** 1545–67, claimant to English throne and second husband of MARY QUEEN OF SCOTS. Son of powerful earl of Lennox, he claimed succession to Elizabeth through his grandmother, Margaret Tudor. Catholic sympathies, claim on throne, and perhaps his handsome appearance induced Mary to marry him (1555). He proved vicious and dissipated, and she did not make him royal consort. Joined in murder of David Rizzio (1566); was soon without friends. Plot formed to murder him, probably under earl of Bothwell. Killed under mysterious circumstances. Father of James I.

Darrow, Clarence (Seward), 1857–1938, American lawyer. After defending (1894) Eugene V. Debs during the Pullman strike, he gave up his lucrative practice to champion the "underdog." Defended many labor leaders (e.g., William J. Haywood) and over 100 persons charged with murder (e.g., Leopold and Loeb). Opposed W. J. Bryan in the SCOPES TRIAL.

Dartford, urban district (pop. 40,544), Kent, England. Wat Tyler's rebellion broke out here. England's first paper mill built here in Elizabeth's time.

Dartmoor, picturesque upland c.25 mi. long, Devonshire, England. Includes ancient Royal Forest of Dartmoor. Has copper, tin, and iron mining, granite quarrying, and grazing. In the middle of Dartmoor, near Princetown, is **Dartmoor Prison**, built 1806–9. Housed French captives in Napoleonic Wars, American captives in War of 1812. Made a convicts' prison 1850. In World War I conscientious objectors were imprisoned here.

Dartmouth (därt′mŭth), industrial town (pop. 15,037), S N.S., Canada, on Halifax Harbour opposite Halifax; settled 1751. Has sugar refineries, shipbuilding, and iron founding.

Dartmouth (därt′mŭth), municipal borough (pop. 5,842), Devonshire, England. Site of Royal Naval Col. Richard I embarked here for the Crusades.

Dartmouth, town (pop. 11,115), SE Mass., on Buzzards Bay SW of New Bedford; settled c.1650. Quaker center with 18th-cent. Friends' meetinghouse.

Dartmouth College, at Hanover, N.H.; nonsectarian, for men; chartered 1769, opened 1770 by Eleazar WHEELOCK. A state college connected (1868–93) with Dartmouth became Univ. of New Hampshire (see DURHAM). Dartmouth stresses liberal arts. Its famous outing club holds a winter carnival.

Dartmouth College Case, decided by the U.S. Supreme Court in 1819. New Hampshire legislature amended (1816) the college charter to make it a public institution. Trustees, represented by Daniel Webster, argued that the state had violated a contract and won the case. The opinion rendered by John Marshall was that a charter is in effect inviolable.

Darwin, Erasmus, 1731–1802, English poet. A physician who cultivated a botanic garden, he wrote *The Botanic Garden* (1789–91) and *Zoonomia* (1794–96), more important as science than literature. His grandson **Charles (Robert) Darwin**, 1809–82, was a naturalist. He studied medicine and ministry before becoming official naturalist on the *Beagle*. His explorations, observations, and investigations led to his formulating a concept of EVOLUTION, known as DARWINISM, set forth in his *Origin of Species* (1859). A. R. WALLACE worked out a similar theory independently. His son **Francis Darwin,** 1848–1925, a botanist, assisted his father and edited his biography and letters. **Sir George Howard Darwin,** 1845–1912, brother of Francis, was an astronomer and mathematician and an authority on cosmogony. His son, **Sir Charles Galton Darwin,** 1887–, a physicist, served as director of the National Physical Laboratory (1938–49).

Darwin, port (pop. 2,538), cap. of Northern Territory, Australia, on inlet of Timor Sea. Originally called Palmerston, renamed for Charles Darwin. Important for its airport on Singapore-Sydney route. A key Allied base in World War II.

Darwinism, concept of EVOLUTION set forth by Charles Darwin. Observing the tendency of organisms to increase geometrically while numbers of given species remained about stable, he deduced a struggle for survival. He emphasized individual variation within a species and survival of those with most favorable variations, some being transmitted to offspring. This principle of natural selection is, with modifications, almost universally accepted by scientists.

Daryal (däryăl') or **Dariel** (däréěl'), gorge, c.5,900 ft. deep, Georgian SSR, in central Greater Caucasus, below Mt. Kazbek. Formed by Terek R.; traversed by road linking Dzaudzhikau (Vladikavkaz) with Tiflis. Famed for wild grandeur. Known in antiquity as Caucasian or Iberian Gates.

dasheen: see TARO.

Dass, Petter, 1647–1707, Norwegian poet, author of still-popular *Norway's Trumpet.*

date, long-lived, tall palm (*Phoenix dactylifera*) and its edible, brown fruit (1–3 in. long) borne in heavy, pendent clusters. A principal food in many desert and tropical regions from early times. Trees are now cultivated in SW U.S. and Mexico.

Dathan (dā'–), rebel with KORAH against Moses. Brother of Abiram.

Datia (dŭ'tēä), town (pop. 22,086), Vindhya Pradesh, India. Has superb 17th-cent. Hindu palace. Was cap. of Rajput state of Datia, founded c.1626.

dative: see CASE.

Daubigny, Charles François (shärl' fräswä' dōbēnyē'), 1817–78, French landscape painter, best known for his scenes of the banks of the Seine and the Oise. Usually classed with the Barbizon school, although he never lived in Barbizon.

Daudet, Alphonse (älfōs' dōdä'), 1840–97, French author. He wrote with charm and gentle satire of his native Provence in *Lettres de mon moulin* (1866) and *Tartarin de Tarascon* (1872), his most enduring works. *Froment jeune et Risler aîné* (1874), *Le Nabab* (1877), *Numa Roumestan* (1881), *Sapho* (1884), and *L'Immortel* (1888) are novels of social criticism and satire. *Le Petit Chose* is autobiographical. His son, **Léon Daudet** (läō'), 1867–1942, author, edited the royalist, extreme rightist daily *Action française* and wrote valuable memoirs (6 vols., 1914–21; partial Eng. tr., 1925).

Daugherty, Harry M(icajah) (dô'ûrtē), 1860–1941, U.S. Attorney General (1921–24). Accused of taking part in Teapot Dome scandal, but case was dismissed.

Daughters of the American Revolution, patriotic society in U.S., open to women whose ancestors aided patriot cause in Revolution. Organized 1890.

Daulatabad (doulŭtŭbäd'), village, S Hyderabad, India. The Chand Minar (1294) is a noted moslem minaret.

Daumier, Honoré (ônôrä' dōmyä'), 1808–79, French lithographer, cartoonist, and painter. Satirized the bourgeois society of his day, producing c.4,000 lithographs, now considered masterpieces of the art. Imprisoned for 6 months in 1832 for his political cartoon *Gargantua*. Painted c.200 small canvases, including *The Good Samaritan* (Metropolitan Mus.).

Daun, Leopold, Graf von (lä'ōpôlt gräf' fŭn doun'), 1705–66, Austrian field marshal. Drove French from Bohemia (1742) in War of Austrian Succession; defeated Frederick II of Prussia at Kolin (1757), but lost at Torgau (1760), in Seven Years War.

Dauphin (dô'fĭn), town (pop. 6,007), W Man., Canada, on Vermilion R. and NW of Winnipeg. Agr. and milling center. Riding Mountain Natl. Park is S.

dauphin (dô'fĭn, Fr. dōfě'), title of eldest son (sometimes grandson) of a king of France. See DAUPHINÉ; LOST DAUPHIN.

Dauphiné (dōfēnä'), region and former province, SE France, in Hautes-Alpes, Isère, and Drôme depts.; historic cap. Grenoble. In E, Alps culminate in the BARRE DES ÉCRINS. Vineyards and silkworm raising in lower districts. Cities: Grenoble, Vienne, Valence. As part of kingdom of ARLES, region was ruled by counts of Vienne, who took title "dauphin" (etymology uncertain). Dauphin Humbert II sold it to Philip VI of France (1349). Dauphiné was governed by eldest sons of French kings until accession of Louis XI, who incorporated it with France, although technically it was part of Holy Roman Empire. Title "dauphin" thenceforth was merely honorific.

Dauthendey, Max (doutĕn'dä), 1867–1918, German poet and novelist. Wrote many volumes of exotic, impressionistic verse and a number of novels and plays (e.g., *Caprices of an Empress,* 1910).

Davao (dävou'), city (pop. 111,263), SE Mindanao, Philippines, on Davao Gulf; hemp-producing center.

D'Avenant or **Davenant, Sir William** (dăv'ŭnŭnt), 1606–68, English poet, dramatist, theater manager. A royalist, he was imprisoned in 1651, released through efforts of Milton and others.

Davenport, George, 1783–1845, American Indian trader, b. England. Managed fur-trading post at Rock Island, Ill. Davenport, Iowa, named for him.

Davenport, John, 1597–1670, Puritan clergyman, b. England. Founded New Haven, Conn. (1637–38), with Theophilus EATON. Important figure in colony.

Davenport, city (pop. 74,549), E Iowa, on the Mississippi. Forms, with ROCK ISLAND, MOLINE, and EAST MOLINE (all in Ill.), economic unit called Quad Cities. Founded 1836 by George Davenport on site of early trading post, it prospered with coming (1856) of first railroad to bridge the Mississippi and with heavy river traffic of late 19th cent. Rail, commercial, and industrial center, it has mfg. of machinery and other metal products, clothing, beer, and foodstuffs. Credit Isl., a park, is site of War of 1812 battle.

David, Saint, d. 588?, patron saint of Wales, first abbot of Menevia (SAINT DAVID'S). His shrine was an important place of pilgrimage in the Middle Ages. On his feast, March 1, the national Welsh festival is celebrated.

David [Heb.,= beloved], d. c.972 B.C., shepherd boy who became king of Hebrews (c.1012–c.972 B.C.). One of greatest of Hebrew national heroes, celebrated not only for his valor as a warrior but for his ability as a ruler and for his gifts as a poet and musician as well. Among popular stories about him: his victory over Goliath, his friendship with Jonathan, his love for Bath-sheba, the revolt of his son Absalom. Many Psalms ascribed to him. Under David, Hebrews changed from loose confederation of tribes to strong national state. According to Gospels, Jesus was of House of David. 1 Sam. 17.12–1 Kings 2.12; 1 Chron. 11–29.

David, kings of Scotland. **David I,** 1084–1153, was king 1124–53. In struggle for English crown between Matilda (his niece) and Stephen, he fought for Matilda without success; made peace 1141. His rule was wise and momentous. **David II** (David Bruce), 1324–71, was king 1329–71. Edward III and Edward de BALIOL invaded Scotland 1332. David invaded England 1346, was captured, and held until 1357.

David or **Davit, Gerard** (gä'rärt dä'vĕt), c.1450–1523, painter of the early Flemish school.

David, Jacques Louis (zhäk' lwē' dävēd'), 1748–1825, French painter. His *Andromache* and *Oath of the Horatii* established him as the leading exponent of the classical reaction. His *Mme. Recamier* and *Assassination of Marat* are renowned. He was an ardent republican despite his honored position as painter to Louis XVI. Later served Napoleon.

David, Pierre Jean: see DAVID D'ANGERS.

David, Sir Tannatt William Edgeworth (dā'vĭd), 1858–1934, British geologist. As geologist for the Shackleton antarctic expedition, he led the party which first reached the south magnetic pole.

David d'Angers (dävēd' däzhā'), or **Pierre Jean David** (pyĕr' zhä'), 1788–1856, French sculptor. A typical work is the group on pediment of the Panthéon.

David Harum: see WESTCOTT, EDWARD NOYES.

Davids, (Thomas William) Rhys (rēs), 1843–1922, English Orientalist, a leading authority on Buddhism and on Pali texts.

Davidson, George, 1825–1911, American geographer and astronomer, b. England. Staff member of U.S. Coast and Geodetic Survey (1845–95). Directed charting of Pacific coast for navigation (1850–60). Surveyed Delaware R.; mapped Philadelphia area for fortification (1860–66). Directed Survey's Pacific coast work (1867–87). Built first Pacific coast observatory in San Francisco 1879. Made valuable meteorological and astronomical studies.

Davidson, Jo, 1883–1952, American sculptor, best known for busts of famous contemporaries.

Davies, Arthur Bowen (dā'vēz), 1862–1928, American painter. His romantic work includes symbolic pictures of the female nude in idyllic landscapes. Largely responsible for famous Armory Show of 1913.

Davies, Sir John (dā'vĭs), 1569–1626, English poet, author of *Nosce Teipsum* (1599; a philosophical poem) and *Hymns to Astraea* (1599).

Davies, Joseph E(dward) (dā'vēz), 1876–, American diplomat. Ambassador to USSR (1937–38), ambassador to Belgium (1938–40). His book, *Mission to Moscow* (1945), pictures conditions in USSR.

Dávila, Gil Gonzáles: see GONZÁLES DE ÁVILA, GIL.

Dávila, Pedrarias: see ARIAS DE ÁVILA, PEDRO.

Da Vinci, Leonardo: see LEONARDO DA VINCI.

Davis, Alexander Jackson, 1803–92, American architect, exponent of the Greek-revival style.

Davis, Arthur Powell, 1861–1933, American civil engineer and hydrographic authority on many important irrigation and water-supply projects.

Davis, Benjamin Oliver, 1877–, American general. First Negro general in U.S. army (1940).

Davis, Charles Henry, 1807–77, American naval officer. In Civil War he repulsed Confederate fleet near Fort Pillow (May, 1862); annihilated fleet before Memphis, captured June (June, 1862).

Davis, David, 1815–86, Associate Justice of U.S. Supreme Court (1862–77). His decision in *Ex parte Milligan* (1866), denouncing arbitrary military power, became a bulwark of civil liberty in U.S.

Davis, Elmer (Holmes), 1890–, American author and radio commentator, director (1942–45) of the Office of War Information.

Davis, Henry Winter, 1817–65, American political leader. U.S. Representative from Md. (1855–61, 1863–65). Opposed Reconstruction program of Pres. Lincoln with more radical plan of his own.

Davis, Jefferson, 1808–89, American statesman, President of CONFEDERACY (1861–65). U.S. Senator from Miss. (1847–51). Secretary of War (1853–57). Again Senator (1857–61), he resigned at secession of Miss. Provisional president of Confederacy, then regular president; inaugurated Feb., 1862. Administration stormy as he assumed strong centralized power, thus weakening states' rights policy for which South had seceded. Lee surrendered without his approval. Captured and confined at Fort Monroe for two years; released 1867, never prosecuted.

Davis or **Davys, John,** c.1550–1605, British navigator. In seeking Northwest Passage, clarified much arctic geography N of Labrador. Discovered Falkland Isls. (1592). Lost his life in East Indies fighting Japanese pirates. Invented useful quadrant.

Davis, John William, 1873–, American lawyer, public

official. U.S. Congressman (1911–13). Nominated as compromise Democratic presidential candidate in 1924 after two-week convention deadlock; won only 136 electoral votes.

Davis, Richard Harding, 1864–1916, American correspondent for all major wars of his era, author of romantic stories and plays. His mother, **Rebecca Harding Davis,** 1831–1910, was the author of several novels dealing with the effect of social problems on individuals.

Davis, Stuart, 1894–, American painter of abstractions. Studied with Robert Henri.

Davis, William Morris, 1850–1934, American geographer. Global traveler, authority on land forms, prolific contributor to geographical journals, he helped advance science of physiography.

Davis, Mount, peak (3,213 ft.), SW Pa., in the Alleghenies near Md. line. Highest point in state.

Davis Mountains, W Texas, SE of El Paso, rising to 8,382 ft. in Mt. Livermore (or Baldy Peak or Old Baldy). Parks and scenery attract visitors.

Davisson, Clinton Joseph, 1881–, American physicist. He shared the 1937 Nobel Prize for demonstrations confirming Louis de Broglie's theory of wave nature of moving electrons.

Davis Strait, between Greenland and Baffin Isl., connecting Atlantic Ocean and Baffin Sea, 180–400 mi. wide. John Davis sailed through it 1787.

Davit, Gerard: see DAVID, GERARD.

Davos (dävōs'), town (resident pop. 10,332), Grisons canton, E Switzerland. Winter sports; health resort for tuberculosis.

Davout, Louis Nicolas (lwē' nēkôlä' dävoo'), 1770–1823, marshal of France, duke of AUERSTEDT, prince of Eckmühl; one of Napoleon's ablest lieutenants.

Davy, Sir Humphry (dā'vē), 1778–1829, English chemist and physicist. He investigated laughing gas; isolated sodium, potassium, calcium, barium, boron, magnesium, and strontium; did electrochemical research; established elementary nature of chlorine; and advanced theory that hydrogen is characteristic of acids.

Davys, John: see DAVIS, JOHN.

Dawes, Charles G(ates) (dôz), 1865–1951, American statesman and banker. Vice President of United States (1925–29). Forwarded **Dawes Plan** in 1924 to Reparations Commission of the Allied nations. Plan provided for reduction in payment of REPARATIONS and the stabilization of German finances.

Dawes, Henry Laurens, 1816–1903, U.S. Senator from Mass. (1875–93). Sponsored **Dawes Act,** 1887, passed by U.S. Congress to provide for granting of individual landholdings to civilized Indians who would renounce their tribal holdings. Began the absorbing of Indians into body politic. **Dawes Commission,** commission to Five Civilized Tribes, was created by Congress in 1893. It reorganized Indian Territory by getting consent of chiefs to substitute individual for tribal land holding.

Dawes Plan: see DAWES, CHARLES GATES.

Dawson or **Dawson City,** town (pop. 783), territorial cap., W Yukon, Canada, at junction of Yukon and Klondike rivers. Trade center of a mining region, it is usually reached via Skagway, Alaska, the White Pass RR, or by boat from White Horse. In 1898 gold rush Dawson was a boom town.

Dawson Creek, village (pop. 3,589), E B.C., Canada, near Alta. border, NE of Prince George. S terminus of Alaska Highway, connected by railroad and highway to Edmonton.

Day, Benjamin Henry, 1810–89, American journalist. Founded the New York *Sun* (1833) and made it a cheap popular paper before selling it (1838) to Moses Y. Beach. His son, **Benjamin Day,** 1838–1916, invented the Benday process for reproducing maps and illustrations.

Day, Clarence (Shepard), 1874–1935, American humorist, author of *This Simian World* (1920), *God* *and My Father* (1932), *Life with Father* (1935), *Life with Mother* (1937).

Day, Edmund Ezra, 1883–1951, American educator. Professor of economics, Univ. of Michigan (1923–27) and dean of school of business administration. President of Cornell Univ. (1937–49).

Day, John, 1522–84, English printer. Designed and made type, including musical notes and the first Anglo-Saxon type. Printed (under another title) first English edition of John Foxe's *Book of Martyrs* (1562).

Day, Thomas, 1748–89, English social reformer. His *History of Sandford and Merton* (3 vols., 1783–89), contrasts "natural" and conventional education.

Daye, Stephen, c.1594–1668, British settler in Mass., a locksmith, usually called first printer in English American colonies. Supervised Cambridge Press, first colonial printing plant. Published *Bay Psalm Book* (1640), first book printed in colonies. Actual printing was probably done by his son, **Matthew Daye,** c.1620–1649, a trained printer.

Day Lewis, C(ecil), 1904–, English writer, b. Ireland, author of several volumes of highly praised poetry and (under pseud. Nicholas Blake) of detective stories.

daylight-saving time, time reckoned later (usually one hour) than standard time. Adopted by federal law in U.S. as wartime measure (1918–19) and during World War II, its use was continued as summer time at option of state and local governments by turning clocks ahead in spring and back in autumn.

day lily, Old World perennial of genus *Hemerocallis*, with yellow, orange, or reddish flowers. Species often cultivated include fragrant lemon day lily and widely naturalized tawny day lily.

Dayton. 1 City (pop. 8,977), N Ky., on Ohio R. and near Covington, opposite Cincinnati. **2** City (pop. 243,872), SW Ohio, NW of Cincinnati and on Great Miami R. at influx of Mad and Stillwater rivers; settled 1796. Shipping and industrial center for agr. area, it has mfg. of cash registers, refrigerators and air conditioning equipment, precision tools, lighting equipment, motors, and aircraft and auto parts. Chief U.S. aviation center with many installations, both governmental and private. Wright brothers started experimental air plant here 1911. Here are Univ. of Dayton (R.C.; coed.; 1850), Dayton Art Inst., P. L. Dunbar Mus., Newcom Tavern (1796), and old courthouse (1850). **3** City (pop. 1,870), E Tenn., near Tennessee R. and NNE of Chattanooga. Scene of SCOPES TRIAL.

Daytona Beach (dātō′nū), resort city (pop. 30,187), NE Fla., on Atlantic coast S of St. Augustine and on Halifax R. (lagoon), in citrus-fruit area. Founded 1870 in area where Spanish monks estab. missions in 16th and 17th cent. Present city formed 1926 by consolidation of Seabreeze, Daytona, and Daytona Beach. Beach (c.25 mi. long) is often used for auto races (since 1903). Seat of Bethune-Cookman Col. (Negro; coed.; 1904).

DDT: see INSECTICIDE.

Dead, Book of the: see BOOK OF THE DEAD.

deadly nightshade: see NIGHTSHADE.

Dead Sea, salt lake, on border of Jordan and Israel; 49 mi. long, 3–10 mi. wide, 1,292 ft. below sea level, c.1,300 ft. deep. Lies in the Ghor, a great depression. Far saltier than the ocean, it yields minerals (esp. potash and bromides). It is the biblical Salt Sea, Sea of the Plain, and East Sea.

Deadwood, city (pop. 3,288), W S.Dak., in Deadwood Gulch in the Black Hills, and near Lead; settled 1876 after discovery (1875) of gold here. City's boom-and-bust cycles followed fortunes of near-by gold and silver mines. Tourist center, it has Adams Memorial Mus. and graves of Wild Bill Hickok and Calamity Jane. Grave of Deadwood Dick is near.

Deadwood Dick, American frontiersman, celebrated in many dime novels. Original is supposedly Richard W. Clarke (1845–1930), an Englishman who came to the

gold diggings of the Black Hills and became a scout.

deafness, partial or complete loss of hearing. Causes include infections, especially in the head; diseases, e.g., scarlet fever, syphilis; obstructions of auditory canal; and bone formation in ear labyrinth capsule. Electrical aids are commonly employed. School for education of deaf estab. 1755 in Paris by C. M. de l'EPÉE. Other pioneers in teaching deaf include A. M. and A. G. BELL, and T. H. Gallaudet and his sons. Most of the deaf can be taught to speak; others use manual alphabet.

Deak, Francis (dĕ′äk), Hung. *Deák Ferenc*, 1803–76, Hungarian statesman. Opposed extremism of Louis KOSSUTH during revolution of 1848–49; became leader of his nation after defeat of revolutionists. Insisted on recognition of Hungary as separate kingdom, but in union with Austria; negotiated, in cooperation with Julius · ANDRASSY, creation of AUSTRO-HUNGARIAN MONARCHY (1867).

Deakin, Alfred, 1856–1919, Australian statesman. Helped federation of Australian states. Was three times prime minister.

Deal, municipal borough (pop. 24,276), Kent, England. Reputed landing place of Caesar 55 B.C. One of CINQUE PORTS, it has official residence (Walmer Castle) of Lord Warden. Naval station and shipbuilding center.

Deal Island, off Eastern Shore, Md., in Tangier Sound N of Crisfield. Has seafood industry.

De Amicis, Edmondo (ädmōn′dō dä ämē′chēs), 1846–1908, Italian author of travel books and novel *Cuore: an Italian Schoolboy's Journal* (1886; Eng. tr., 1887).

Dean, Jerome Herman (Dizzy Dean), 1911–, American baseball pitcher, outstanding right-hander. With St. Louis Cardinals (1932–38). Original name possibly Jay Hanna Dean.

Dean, Forest of, ancient royal forest, Gloucestershire, England.

Deane, Silas, 1737–89, American Revolutionary patriot and diplomat. As diplomatic agent in France, secured commercial and military aid for colonies and recruited foreign officers.

Dearborn, Henry, 1751–1829, American general. U.S. Secretary 'of War (1801–9). Relieved of command of N frontier in War of 1812 because of his inaction. Fort Dearborn named for him.

Dearborn, city (pop. 94,994), SE Mich., on the River Rouge and W of Detroit; settled 1795. Home of Ford Motor Co., it also has mfg. of aircraft parts and metal products. Here are Edison Inst. of Technology, GREENFIELD VILLAGE, and birthplace of Henry Ford.

Dearborn, Fort, U.S. army post on Chicago R., estab. 1803; named for Henry Dearborn. Site of Indian attack in 1812. Chicago grew around rebuilt fort.

death. In man, death is definite if no heartbeat is detectable by stethoscope for some time, if circulation is not backed up by cord around arm or leg, or if rigor mortis has set in. Heart may beat after breathing ceases; nervous system stimulation is possible for short time after heart stops beating, thus resuscitation sometimes possible.

Death Valley, SE Calif., deep and arid basin E of Panamint Range and W of Amargosa Range. Annual average rainfall is 1.4 in. Summer temperatures are among world's highest, but climate is mild from Nov. to May. Has alkali and salt flats, briny pools, and grotesque rocks. Badwater, 280 ft. below sea level, is lowest point in Western Hemisphere. Valley named in 1849 by party of gold seekers. Borax deposits discovered in 1880s. Small animals enliven the solitude; peculiar plants attract scientists. Panamint Indians (valley's only inhabitants for centuries) live in model village here. Here are Scotty's Castle, ostentatious home of Walter Scott (Death Valley Scotty) and resorts. Includes **Death Valley National Monument:** see NATIONAL PARKS AND MONUMENTS (table).

Deauville (dōvēl′), seaside resort (pop. 5,438), Calvados dept., N France, on English Channel.

De Bary, Heinrich Anton (hīn'rĭkh än'tōn dù bärē'), 1831–88, German botanist, authority on fungi.

Debierne, André Louis (ädrā' lwē dùbyĕrn'), 1874–, French chemist. He discovered actinium and worked with the Curies on radioactivity.

Deborah, Israel's only woman judge. Helped Barak defeat Sisera and free Israel from King Jabin. Song of Deborah one of great poems in Bible. Judges 4; 5.

De Bow, J(ames) D(unwoody) B(rownson), 1820–67, American editor. Began publishing monthly *De Bow's Review* 1846. Also a statistician.

Debrecen (dĕ'brĕtsĕn), city (pop. 125,936), E Hungary. Commercial center. Historic stronghold of Hungarian Protestantism. Univ. (chartered 1912) grew out of Calvinist college (founded 1588). Hungarian independence was proclaimed at Debrecen by revolutionary government April 14, 1849. Formerly spelled Debreczen.

Debs, Eugene V(ictor), 1855–1926, American Socialist leader. Advocate of industrial unionism and a pacifist; imprisoned 1895 for violating injunction in strike at Pullman, Ill., and in 1918 under Espionage Act. Presidential candidate five times. Widely revered as martyr for his principles.

debt, obligation in services, money, or goods owed by one party (debtor) to another (creditor). If debtor fails to pay, a court may assign payment out of his property. In ancient times debtors unable to pay were sold into slavery, and imprisonment for debt persisted into 19th cent. Today in the West relief is afforded by BANKRUPTCY.

debt, public, indebtedness of a government expressed in money terms. Such debts typically result from revenue deficiencies, wars, and expenses for public works or emergency projects. Modern form of debt is public loan through government bonds, treasury notes, and other instruments. Ultimate security of public debt is willingness of public to pay taxes and ability of government to collect.

Debussy, Claude (klōd' dùbüsē'), 1862–1918, outstanding composer of the French impressionist movement. His piano music includes the *Suite bergamasque* (containing *Clair de Lune*); *The Children's Corner;* 24 preludes, including *La Cathédrale engloutie;* and 12 etudes. Among his orchestral works are *L'Après-midi d'un Faun, Nocturnes,* and *La Mer.* He also wrote many songs and an opera, *Pelléas et Mélisande.*

Debye, Peter Joseph Wilhelm (dĕbī'), 1884–, American physicist, b. Netherlands. He won the 1936 Nobel Prize for work on structure of molecules.

decadents (dĭkā'dùntz, dĕ'kùdùntz), name loosely applied to late 19th-cent. artists and writers who strove to express morbid and macabre elements in human emotions; often confused with French SYMBOLISTS, who influenced the movement. They were most evident in England (e.g., Oscar Wilde, Ernest Dowson, Aubrey Beardsley).

Decalogue: see TEN COMMANDMENTS.

Decameron, The (dĭkă'mùrùn), or **Il Decamerone** (ēl däkämärō'nä) [Gr.,= 10 parts], collection of 100 charming and often licentious tales by Giovanni Boccaccio, written 1348–53.

decathlon (dĭkăth'lŏn), composite contest consisting of broad jump, high jump, discus throw, shot put, javelin throw, pole vault, 100-meter, 400-meter, and 1500-meter flat races, 110-meter hurdle race.

Decatur, Stephen (dĕkā'tùr), 1779–1820, American naval officer. Became famous in TRIPOLITAN WAR. In Algerine War (1815) he forced dey of Algeria to sign treaty ending American tribute to Algeria. Responsible for toast, ending, "may she always be in the right; but our country, right or wrong."

Decatur. 1 City (pop. 19,974), N Ala., on Tennessee R. and N of Birmingham; founded 1820. Processes and ships iron, steel, textiles, timber, fertilizer, foodstuffs. Has shipyards. Uses TVA power. Almost destroyed in Civil War. **2** City (pop. 21,635), NW Ga., an Atlanta suburb at foot of Stone Mt. Seat of Agnes Scott Col. (for women; founded 1889). **3** City (pop. 66,269), central Ill., E of Springfield and on Sangamon R. (here dammed to form L. Decatur); founded 1829. Distributing point for agr., oil, and coal area, it has railroad shops, mfg. of chemicals, plastics, and metal products, and corn and soybean processing. Has log cabin courthouse where Lincoln practiced and, near by, site of first Lincoln home in Ill. Grand Army of the Republic organized here 1866. Seat of James Millikin Univ. (coed.; 1901). **4** City (pop. 7,271), NE Ind., SSE of Fort Wayne. Food and cement products and motors.

Decazes, Élie (ālē' dùkäz'), 1780–1860, French premier (1819–20) under LOUIS XVIII; a moderate.

Deccan (dĕ'kän"), region, S India. Historically defined as all India S of Narbada R., thus including the CARNATIC.

December: see MONTH.

Decembrist Conspiracy, military revolt at St. Petersburg, Russia, at the accession of NICHOLAS I (Dec., 1825). The plotters, belonging to liberal revolutionary societies, hoped to place Nicholas's brother Constantine on the throne and to obtain a constitution. The revolt was crushed by artillery fire; five of the leaders were hanged.

decimal system (dĕ'sĭmùl), notation system for number writing based upon powers of 10. Number is written as row of digits, each standing for a certain power of 10. Each place left of decimal point raises to higher power of 10; each place to right divides by 10 or raises to a negative power of 10. Decimal is name for any number in system; sometimes only for proper fraction in system, not a mixed number. Decimal system of Melvil Dewey is system for classification of library books.

Decius (dē'shùs), 201–51, Roman emperor (249–51). Sent to put down a mutiny against Philip the Arabian, he headed it instead, defeated and killed Philip, and became emperor. Persecuted the Christians vigorously. He was killed trying to repel the Goths in Moesia.

Decker, Thomas: see DEKKER, THOMAS.

Declaration of Independence, adopted July 4, 1776, by delegates of Thirteen Colonies, announcing their separation from Great Britain and making them into the United States. Written almost wholly by Thomas Jefferson. Opening paragraphs state idea of government based on theory of NATURAL RIGHTS.

Declaration of Rights: see BILL OF RIGHTS.

Declaration of the Rights of Man, historic French document, drafted by Sieyès (1789), embodied as preamble of French constitution of 1791. Based on J. J. Rousseau's theories and on American Declaration of Independence, it asserted the equality of all men, the sovereignty of the people, the inalienable rights of the individual to "liberty, property, security."

Decorah (dĭkô'rù), city (pop. 6,060), NE Iowa, NNE of Waterloo. Seat of Luther Col. (Evangelical Lutheran, coed.; opened 1861, chartered 1865), a center of Norwegian-American culture.

Decoration Day: see MEMORIAL DAY.

decorations, civil and military. Practice of rewarding achievements grew from medieval custom of conferring knighthood. In Great Britain this still exists in such orders as Garter, Thistle, and Bath. In Europe such orders have tended to lose feudal connotations. Among best known are Order of Golden Fleece (1429 or 1430, Austria and Spain); Dannebrog and Elephant (1219 and 1462, Denmark); Annunciata and SS. Maurice and Lazarus (1362 and 1434, Italy); papal order of Golden Spur (1559); Black Eagle, Red Eagle, and Pour le Mérite (Prussia); White Eagle and Polonia Restituta (Poland); and Legion of Honor (France). Military decorations for heroism include Croix de Guerre (France); Iron Cross (Germany); Distinguished Service Order, Royal Victoria Order, and Order of the British Empire (England); Congressional Medal of Honor (1862), Distinguished Service Cross,

Distinguished Service Medal, Distinguished Flying Medal, Purple Heart (1782), and silver and bronze stars (U.S.); and Red Star, Victory, Lenin, Suvarov, and Alexander Nevsky awards (USSR).

De Coster, Charles Théodore Henri (dù kŏ'stùr, Fr. shärl' tãōdôr' ārē' dù kôstĕr'), 1827–79, Belgian author. His chief work, *La légende et les aventures héroïques, joyeuses et glorieuses d'Ulenspiegel et de Lamme Goedzak* (1867; Eng. trs., 1918, 1921), is written in archaic style and based on the Germanic folk hero Till Eulenspiegel.

decree, in British and U.S. law, final decision of a court of equity or in equitable actions, differing from a judgment (of a court of law) in being less rigid and not limited to the award of money damages. Can be more easily enforced by proceedings for CONTEMPT OF COURT. Familiar are the INJUNCTION and the decree of DIVORCE.

Dedham (dĕ'dùm), town (pop. 18,487), E Mass., SW of Boston; settled 1635. Oldest frame house in U.S., Fairbanks house (1636), is here. Scene of Sacco-Vanzetti trial. Mfg. of paper products.

Dee, John, 1527–1608, British scientist and astrologer. Drew up geographical materials on newly found lands for Queen Elizabeth and urged adoption of Gregorian calendar. His interest in the occult led to accusations of sorcery and fame as a magician.

Dee, rivers in Scotland; **1** Aberdeenshire and Kincardine; famous for its beauty, flows 90 mi. past Balmoral Castle to North Sea; **2** Kirkcudbrightshire.

Dee, river of Wales and England, flowing 70 mi. to Irish Sea. Expanse of sand of shallow estuary at low tide is Kingsley's "Sands of Dee."

Deepwater, village (1940 pop. 798), SW N.J., on Delaware R. below Penns Grove. E terminus of Del. Memorial Bridge; S terminus of N.J. Turnpike.

deer, ruminant mammal of family Cervidae found over most of world except Australia. Males usually have antlers, which are shed annually. If they lack antlers (e.g., the MUSK DEER and Chinese river deer) their upper canines are long and serve as weapons. Deer are polygamous. They eat herbaceous plants, lichens, and mosses. The white-tailed deer, a source of many necessities for American Indians and settlers, was nearly exterminated through years of slaughter, but is restored in parts of the U.S. See also CARIBOU; ELK; MOOSE; REINDEER; WAPITI.

Deere, John, 1804–86, American manufacturer of agr. implements, pioneer maker of steel plows. His factory at Moline, Ill. became world-known.

Deerfield, town (pop. 3,086), NW Mass., on Deerfield R. and N of Northampton. Seat of Deerfield Acad. for boys (chartered 1797, opened 1799).

Deerfield, river, c.70 mi. long, rising in S Vt. and flowing S into NW Mass., then SE to Connecticut R. near Greenfield, Mass. Furnishes power.

Deering, William, 1826–1913, American farm machinery manufacturer. He developed the first successful grain binder.

Deer Park, village (pop. 7,241), SW Ohio, a NE suburb of Cincinnati.

Defense, United States Department of, created 1947; reorganized 1949. James V. Forrestal, who pioneered in its organization, became first Secretary of Defense. Department guards U.S. security and coordinates activities of army, navy, and air force. Its organization has eliminated much overlapping and duplication.

defense mechanism, psychoanalytic expression indicating unconscious mode of behavior designed to ward off anticipated or imagined criticism or condemnation. These "dynamisms" include rationalization—substitution (for ego's sake) of socially acceptable for unsocial motives; repression—barring of distressing ideas from consciousness; regression—to infantile behavior, gratifications; projection—assignment to others of own ego-repudiated urges; identification—reaction to others' desires as if one's own; sublimation—redirection of libido to constructive ends; conversion—transfor-

mation of psychological conflict into actual physical symptoms.

Defense Mobilization, Office of, created 1950 by executive order of U.S. Pres. Harry S. Truman to direct and control mobilization activities of executive branch of government, including control over production, procurement, man power, stabilization, and transport activities. Charles Edward Wilson was first director (1950–52).

Deffand, marquise du: see DU DEFFAND.

Defiance, city (pop. 11,265), NW Ohio, at junction of Auglaize and Maumee rivers SW of Toledo; settled 1790. Mfg. of machinery and machine tools. Here was Fort Defiance (1794); near by was Fort Winchester (1812). Seat of Defiance Col.

Defoe or **De Foe, Daniel,** 1660–1731, English writer, author of ROBINSON CRUSOE. A pamphleteer and journalist, he won the favor of William III with his poem, *The True-born Englishman* (1701), but strong anti-Tory sentiment in *The Shortest Way with Dissenters* (1702) brought imprisonment under Anne. His *Review* (1704–13) was an early and influential journal. Besides his *Life and Strange, Surprizing Adventures of Robinson Crusoe* (1719), he wrote *Moll Flanders* (1722); *Journal of the Plague Year* (1722; fictitious), *The Fortunate Mistress; . . . or Roxana* (1724) and various other pieces of vigorous, journalistic prose.

De Forest, Lee, 1873–, American inventor. Pioneered in development of wireless telegraphy, sound pictures, television; granted over 300 patents.

De Funiak Springs (dē fū'nēăk), town (pop. 3,077), NW Fla., NW of Panama City. Fresh-water spring here is c.1 mi. in circumference.

Degas, (Hilaire Germain) Edgar (ĕdgär' dùgä'), 1834–1917, French impressionist painter. Fanatic in his self-criticism and despairing of attaining perfection in oils, he turned in his middle life to pastels. Ballet dancers, modistes, and women at their toilet were among his favorite subjects. His later works, daring in composition, free in execution, and immensely effective in color, greatly influenced such men as Gauguin and Picasso.

De Gasperi, Alcide (älchē'dä dä gä'spärē), 1881–, Italian premier (1945–), leader of Christian Democrats.

De Gaulle, Charles: see GAULLE, CHARLES DE.

degree, academic, bestowed on student fulfilling stated requirements or on eminent person as honor. Usual degrees in U.S.: Bachelor of Arts (B.A. or A.B.), of Science (B.S.), of Laws (LL.B.); Master of Arts (M.A. or A.M.), of Science (M.S.); Doctor of Philosophy (Ph.D.), of Medicine (M.D.), of Laws (LL.D.), of Divinity (D.D.), of Letters (Litt.D.).

De Haven, Edwin Jesse, 1816–65, American arctic explorer. Led fruitless search for Sir John Franklin and party (1850); discovered Grinnell Land.

De Heem, Jan Davidszoon: see HEEM, JAN DAVIDSZOON DE.

Dehmel, Richard (rīkh'ärt dā'mùl), 1863–1920, German poet. His works, some of which lean toward social themes but away from naturalism, include the collection *Erlösungen* [redemptions] (1891), *Schöne wilde Welt* [fair wide world] (1913), and the novel in verse *Zwei Menschen* [two souls] (1903).

Dehn, Adolf (Arthur) (dān), 1895–, American lithographer and painter. Became known through his satiric figures in black and white.

De Hooch or **De Hoogh, Pieter:** see HOOCH, PIETER DE.

Dehra (dâ'rù) or **Dehra Dun** (dōōn), city (pop. 78,228), NW Uttar Pradesh, India. Site of temple (1699) of Ram Rai, founder of Hindu Udasi sect.

Deira (dē'îrù), Anglian kingdom between the Humber and the Tyne, united (late 6th cent.) with Bernicia to form Northumbria.

Deirdre (dēr'drē, –drä, dâr'–), heroine of Irish story. Reared to be wife of King Conchobar of Ulster; she fell in love with Naoise and fled to England with him and his brothers. On their return home Conchobar slew the brothers, and Deirdre died on their grave.

deists (dē'ĭsts), group of rationalists of 17th and 18th cent. who rejected formal religion and supernatural revelation but argued that the course of nature demonstrates the existence of God. There were deistic elements in the thinking of Voltaire, Rousseau, Franklin, and Jefferson. The religious orthodox called them freethinkers.

De Kalb, Johann: see KALB, JOHANN.

De Kalb (dē kălb'), city (pop. 11,708), N Ill., W of Chicago. Center of agr. area. Mfg. of canned food, machinery, and musical instruments.

Deken, Agatha: see WOLFF, ELISABETH.

Dekker or **Decker, Thomas,** 1572?–1632, English dramatist, author of *The Shoemaker's Holiday* (1600), *Old Fortunatus* (1600). Collaborated with Middleton on *The Honest Whore* (1604; Part II, 1630) and *The Roaring Girl* (1611), with Massinger on *The Virgin Martyr* (1622). Also wrote pamphlets and satirical *The Gull's Hornbook* (1609).

de Koven, Reginald, 1859–1920, American composer. He is best known for his operettas, especially *Robin Hood* (1890), which has the song *Oh, Promise Me*.

de Kruif, Paul (dù krīf'), 1890–, American writer on scientific subjects. Works include *Microbe Hunters* (1926) and *Hunger Fighters* (1939).

Delaborde, Henri, Comte (ärē' kōt' dùläbôrd'), 1811–99, French historical painter and art critic, best known for writings on Flandrin and Ingres.

Delacroix, Ferdinand Victor Eugène (fĕrdänā' vēktôr' ûzhĕn dùläkrwä'), 1798–1863, leading French romantic painter. Studied with Guérin but early revolted against academicism. Aroused controversy by using bright color and dynamic treatment, as in *Dante and Vergil* (c.1822), *Massacre of Scio,* and scenes of Morocco (visited 1832). As a colorist he ranks among the great French painters.

de la Mare, Walter (dĕl'ùmâr"), 1873–, English poet and novelist. His work is marked by rich imagination in poetry and prose. Some of his poetry is primarily for children (e.g., *Peacock Pie,* 1912). Best-known novel *Memoirs of a Midget* (1921).

Delambre, Jean Baptiste Joseph (zhä' bätēst' zhôzĕf' dùlä'brù), 1749–1822, French astronomer and mathematician, noted for astronomical computations and work in spherical geometry.

De Lancey (dù lăn'sē), family of political leaders, soldiers, and merchants prominent in colonial N.Y. **Étienne De Lancey** or **Stephen De Lancey,** 1663–1741, b. France, became one of New York city's wealthiest merchants. His son, **James De Lancey,** 1703–60, was chief justice of provincial supreme court (1733–60) and served as lieutenant governor (1753–55, 1757–60). Later members of family supported the British in American Revolution.

De Land (dē lănd'), resort city (pop. 8,652), NE Fla., N of Orlando and SE of L. George, in citrus-fruit area; founded 1876. Seat of John B. Stetson Univ. (Baptist; coed.; 1883). Near-by Ponce de Leon Springs empty c.94,000 gal. a minute.

Delano (dē'lūnō), city (pop. 8,717), S central Calif., NNW of Bakersfield in San Joaquin Valley. Ships truck, fruits, grain, wine. Cotton gin.

Delany, Martin Robinson (dùlä'nē), 1812–85, American Negro leader. Furthered return of American Negroes to Africa in 1850s.

Delaroche, Hippolyte (ēpôlēt' dùlärôsh'), 1797–1856, French historical and portrait painter, commonly called Paul Delaroche.

de la Roche, Mazo, 1885–, Canadian novelist, known for her books about Whiteoak family of "Jalna."

De la Rue, Warren (dĕ'lùrōō), 1815–89, British scientist and inventor, a pioneer in celestial photography and inventor of a photoheliograph.

Delaware, state (1,978 sq. mi.; pop. 318,085), E U.S.; one of Thirteen Colonies; cap. DOVER. WILMINGTON only large city. On NE part of peninsula between Chesapeake Bay and Delaware Bay (joined at Delaware City by canal). Bordered E by the Atlantic,

Delaware Bay, Delaware R. Major part of state lies in Atlantic coastal plain, rising to rolling uplands in N. Industrial life dominated by Du Pont Co. Easy laws on business incorporation bring many large corporations to state. Farming (esp. poultry) also important. Region was contested by Dutch and English. First Dutch settlement (1631) was short-lived. NEW SWEDEN founded 1638, captured by Dutch 1655. Seized by British 1644, transferred to William Penn 1682. Became sovereign state 1776. First to ratify Constitution. Remained loyal to Union in Civil War, but pro-Southern feeling grew during war. Industrial growth accelerated by World War II.

Delaware, city (pop. 11,804), central Ohio, on Olentangy R. and N of Columbus; laid out 1808. Trade center in farm area with mfg. of motor vehicles and rubber goods. Birthplace of R. B. Hayes. Seat of Ohio Wesleyan Univ. (coed.; opened 1844 by Methodists; absorbed Ohio Wesleyan Female Col. in 1877).

Delaware, river, 315 mi. long, rising in the Catskills, SE N.Y., and flowing SE between N.Y. and Pa. to Port Jervis, then generally S between N.J. and Pa. to Delaware Bay. Trenton and Camden (N.J.), Philadelphia and DELAWARE WATER GAP (Pa.), and Wilmington and New Castle (Del.) are on its course. Major bridges are at Trenton, Philadelphia, Wilmington, and near Newcastle. Chesapeake and Delaware Canal links river with Chesapeake Bay. Delaware Aqueduct on headstream is part of New York city water supply. Interstate bodies have been formed to plan use of river's water. Washington Crossing villages (N.J. and Pa.) are at point where Washington crossed river (1776) before capture of Trenton.

Delaware, University of: see NEWARK, Del.

Delaware and Raritan Canal, N.J., abandoned canal connecting Delaware and Raritan rivers between Bordentown and New Brunswick; completed 1834.

Delaware Bay, inlet of the Atlantic between N.J. and Del., receiving Delaware R.

Delaware City, town (pop. 1,363), N Del., on Delaware R. and S of Wilmington, near E end of Chesapeake and Delaware Canal. Fort Du Pont is here.

Delaware Indians, members of related Indian tribes, once living in region of Delaware R., later in Susquehanna valley, of Algonquian linguistic stock. Called themselves Lenni-Lenape or Lenape. Friendly with Dutch; made famous treaty (1682) with William Penn. Iroquois drove them W into Ohio (1720). Defeated (1794) by Anthony Wayne. Later they moved to Kansas and Texas and were finally removed to the Indian Territory.

Delaware Water Gap, borough (pop. 734), E Pa. where Delaware R. cuts through Kittatinny Mt., near Stroudsburg. Scenic summer resort.

De la Warr, Thomas West, Baron (dĕ'lùwùr), 1577–1618, first governor of Virginia colony, b. England. Delaware was later named for him.

Delcassé, Théophile (tāôfēl' dĕlkäsā'), 1852–1923, French foreign minister (1898–1905, 1914–15), one of chief architects of Entente Cordiale and Triple Entente (see TRIPLE ALLIANCE AND TRIPLE ENTENTE).

Deledda, Grazia (grä'tsēä dälēd'dä), 1875–1936, Italian novelist, b. Sardinia. Among novels are *Elias Portoliu* (1903), *Cenere* (1904; Eng. tr., *Ashes,* 1908), *La Madre* (1920). Won Nobel Prize for 1926.

De Lee, Joseph Bolivar, 1869–1942, American obstetrician and gynecologist. Improved obstetrical methods through his practice, teaching, and writing.

Delémont (dùlämō'), Ger. *Delsberg,* town (pop. 6,625), Bern canton, W Switzerland, in Jura. Château was residence of prince-bishops of Basel 1528–1792. Prince-bishopric, which did not include Basel itself, passed to France 1792, to Bern 1815.

De Leon, Daniel (dē lē'ŏn), 1852–1914, American socialist leader, b. Curaçao; came to U.S. 1872. A doctrinaire Marxist, he split with Socialist Labor party. Favored industrial rather than trade unions. Helped found the Industrial Workers of the World.

Delescluze, Charles (shärl' dùlāklüz'), 1809–71, French journalist and radical leader. Often exiled and imprisoned. Led resistance of COMMUNE OF PARIS of 1871. When defeat became inevitable, he threw himself into line of fire and was killed.

Delft, municipality (pop. 62,018) and town, South Holland prov., W Netherlands, near The Hague. Famous for ceramics known as delftware. Its aspect has changed little since Jan Vermeer, who was born here, painted his famous *View of Delft.* The Gothic Nieuwe Kerk contains the tomb of William the Silent, who was assassinated at Delft.

delftware. Earliest delftware was a faïence of late 16th cent., brown with opaque white glaze and polychrome decoration in Oriental style. Modern delftware (usually blue and white) is of average quality.

Delhi dĕ'lē), state (574 sq. mi.; pop. 1,743,992), N India. Within state are sites of several dynastic seats. Earliest center was 12th-cent. citadel of Chauhan Rajput, containing Lal Kot or Red Fort (built 1052) and famous Kulb Minar and Iron Pillar. Located just SW of Delhi city, it became nucleus of first cap. of DELHI SULTANATE in 1206. Just E of New Delhi, on legendary site of cap. of ancient Pandava dynasty, is Mogul fort Purana Kila. State cap. is **Delhi** (pop. 542,984), on Jumna R. In 1638 it became Mogul cap. of Shah Jehan, who built beautiful palace within Red Fort. It contained fabulous Peacock Throne, carried off by Nadir Shah in 1739. Occupied 1803 by the British. Became cap. of India in 1912, succeeded 1931 by adjacent city of **New Delhi** (pop. 116,784), notable for its new government buildings based on Palladian-classic style. Residence of India's president is here. Scene of Gandhi's assassination (Jan. 30, 1948).

Delhi Sultanate, Moslem state, ruling most of India 1206–1526. Founded by Kutb-ud-din, Afghan general, who took Delhi in 1192. His dynasty (called Slave dynasty because of his slave origin) was succeeded by the Kulji (1290–1320) and Tughlak (1321–98). Sultanate was crushed 1398 by Tamerlane.

Delian League, confederation of Greek states under leadership of Athens, with original hq. at temple of Apollo in Delos. The first Delian League, 478–404 B.C., was formed with Ionian cities to oppose the Persian kings. After the successful outcome of the PERSIAN WARS, it was made into an Athenian maritime empire that lasted until Sparta won the long-drawn PELOPONNESIAN WAR (404 B.C.). After Conon reestablished Athenian naval power at Cnidus (394 B.C.), a new league was formed (378 B.C.). This lasted, with Athenian-Theban quarrels, until dissolved by the victory of Philip II of Macedon at Chaeronea (338 B.C.).

Délibes, (Clément) Léo (dālēb'), 1836–91, French composer. He wrote several operas, of which *Lakmé* is best known, and ballets (e.g., *Coppélia*).

Delilah (dĭlī'lù), courtesan hired by Philistines to betray SAMSON. Judges 16.4–20.

delirium tremens (trē'mĕnz), disordered mental state, occasional result of continued alcoholic excess. Tremors and hallucinations common.

Delisle, Guillaume (gēyôm' dùlēl'), 1675–1726, French geographer, founder of modern cartography. Noted for highly accurate world map (1700), first without errors of Ptolemy.

Delius, Frederick (dēl'yùs), 1862–1934, English composer. His works, which combine elements of romanticism and impressionism, include an opera, *A Village Romeo and Juliet;* a choral work, *Sea Drift;* and orchestral pieces, *Brigg Fair* and *On Hearing the First Cuckoo in Spring.* He also composed chamber music, concertos, and songs.

Dell, Floyd, 1887–, American author of reformist articles, novels (e.g., *Moon-Calf,* 1920), and plays (e.g., *The Angel Intrudes,* 1918).

Della Casa, Giovanni: see CASA.

Della-Cruscans (dĕl'ù-krùs'kùnz) [from Accademia della Crusca, founded for linguistic purity, Florence,

16th cent.], group of English poets in Italy who published *The Florence Miscellany* (1785). Chief follower in England was Hannah Cowley (1743–1809).

Della Porta: see PORTA.

Della Quercia, Jacopo: see QUERCIA.

Della Robbia (dĕ"lù rŏ'bĕù, Ital. dĕl'lä rôb'byä), Florentine family of sculptors famous for enameled terra cotta or faïence. The atelier founded by **Luca della Robbia** (lōo'kä), 1400?–1482, was continued by his nephew **Andrea della Robbia** (ändrā'ä), 1435–1525?, and by Andrea's sons, **Luca II della Robbia,** c.1480–c.1550, **Giovanni della Robbia** (jōvän'-nē), 1469–c.1529, and **Girolamo della Robbia** (jērō'lämō), 1488–1566. Andrea did the famous medallions on the Foundling Hospital in Florence.

Dells of the Wisconsin or **The Dells,** scenic gorge (c.8 mi. long) of Wisconsin R., central Wis., near city of Wisconsin Dells. Of sandstone carved by river into curious forms, often beautifully colored.

De Long, George Washington, 1844–81, American arctic explorer. Lost with most of his men in attempted dash to North Pole, under auspices of U.S. navy and private backing. Expedition proved essential facts about polar drift and that Wrangel Isl. was not southern tip of a northern continent.

Delorme, Marion (märyō' dùlôrm'), 1613?–1650, French courtesan, mistress of CINQ MARS, whom she sought to avenge during Fronde.

Delorme or **de l'Orme, Philibert** (dùlôrm' fēlēbĕr'), c.1515–1570, great French architect of the Renaissance who designed the Tuileries.

Delos (dē'lŏs), island (c.1 sq. mi.), in the Aegean off Greece, one of the Cyclades; in Greek legend the birthplace of Apollo and Artemis. Of great commercial importance in ancient times, it had the treasury of the Delian League until it was removed (454 B.C.) to Athens. Sacked by Mithridates VI of Pontus in 88 B.C., Delos never recovered.

Delphi (dĕl'fī), locality in Phocis, Greece, near foot of Mt. Parnassus, seat of Delphic oracle. Oracle, which answered all questions, public or private, arose from worship of an earth-goddess, possibly Gaea. It passed to Apollo and was his preeminent shrine, with oracle housed in temple built in 6th cent. B.C. Oracles, spoken by priestess Pythia, were interpreted in verse by a priest; answers were revered and had great influence in Greece. Delphi was unifying influence in otherwise fragmented life of Greece, meeting place of Delphic Amphictyony, and seat of Pythian games. Shrine was later despoiled by Romans under Sulla and Nero.

delphinium: see LARKSPUR.

Delphos (dĕl'fùs), city (pop. 6,220), NW Ohio, NW of Lima. Mfg. of motors and food products.

Delray Beach (dĕlrā'), resort city (pop. 6,312), SE Fla., on Atlantic coast S of Palm Beach. Polo center. Holds annual gladiola festival.

Del Rio, city (pop. 14,211), SW Texas, port of entry on Rio Grande opposite Villa Acuña, Mexico; founded 1868. Makes wine and leather goods and ships wool, mohair, and farm produce.

Deluge, in Bible, overwhelming flood which covered earth and destroyed every living thing except family of NOAH and creatures in ARK. Gen. 6–8; Isa. 54.9; Mat. 24.38; Luke 17.27; Heb. 11.7; 1 Peter 3.20; 2 Peter 2.5. Flood stories resembling biblical one found in folklore of many cultures, e.g., Babylonian, Greek, Indian, aboriginal Australian, American Indian.

delusion, false belief based on misinterpretation of reality. Passing delusions are not abnormal, but fixed delusions (e.g., of persecution, external influence, grandeur) characterize paranoia, schizophrenia. Social psychologists study delusions for their crucial role in development of mass hysteria.

De Mabuse, Jan: see MABUSE, JAN DE.

dementia praecox: see SCHIZOPHRENIA.

Demerara, river, British Guiana: see GUIANA.

Demeter (dĭmē'tùr), in Greek legend, earth-goddess of corn, harvest, and fruitfulness; daughter of Cronus

SMALL CAPITALS = cross references. Pronunciation key on inside end pages. Abbreviations: p. 2.

and Rhea and mother of PERSEPHONE by Zeus. She and her daughter were chief figures in ELEUSINIAN MYSTERIES. Her festival, Thesmophoria, was held in autumn. Identified with Roman Ceres.

Demetrius (dĭmē′trēŭs), kings of Macedon. **Demetrius I** (Poliorcetes), c.337–283 B.C., aided his father ANTIGONUS I in the wars of the DIADOCHI until they were defeated at Ipsus (301 B.C.). Managed to get the throne of Macedon (294 B.C.), but his enemies drove him to take refuge with Seleucus I. He was father of ANTIGONUS II. **Demetrius II**, d. 229 B.C., reigned 239–229 B.C. His heir was young Philip V.

Demetrius, kings of Syria. **Demetrius I** (Soter), c.187–150 B.C., reigned 162–150 B.C.; son of Seleucus IV. A hostage in Rome, Demetrius escaped, killed his cousin Antiochus V, took the throne, but was beset by rebellion, notably that of Alexander Balas and the Maccabees. Demetrius was defeated. **Demetrius II** (Nicator), d. c.125 B.C., got the aid of Ptolemy VI against Alexander Balas, married Cleopatra (already the wife of Alexander), and took the throne in 146 B.C. Captured by Parthians (141 B.C.), he returned, regained the throne (128 B.C.), but again lost it and died fighting the Egyptians.

Demetrius, in Russian history: see DMITRI.

De Mille, Cecil B(lount), 1881–, American film director, noted for "spectacle" films. His niece, **Agnes De Mille**, 1905?–, is a dancer and choreographer. Her ballets include *Three Virgins and a Devil, Rodeo,* and *Fall River Legend.* Her choreography for musical comedies (e.g., *Oklahoma!*) made ballet popular on the Broadway stage.

Deming (dĕm′ĭng), village (pop. 5,672), SW N.Mex., in valley of Mimbres R. (here underground). Trade center for agr., grazing, mining area. Resort.

democracy [Gr.,= power of the people], government under control of the people as a whole rather than that of a class, group, or individual; by extension, in such phrases as social democracy and economic democracy, control of human institutions by and in the interest of the people. Democracy was born in the Greek city-states. The Roman Republic had principle of representation of people, basic to modern democratic republics. General democracy all but disappeared under the Roman Empire and in the Middle Ages, emerged again in modern times, greatly advanced by the Puritan, American, and French revolutions. Among names influential in growth of democratic theory are J. J. Rousseau, John Locke, Thomas Jefferson, and Abraham Lincoln. U.S. founded on democracy. Democratic forms adopted in most Western countries by 20th cent. Challenged recently by fascism and communism (which have rule by proletarian class, though theoretic aim is complete economic democracy).

Democratic party, in U.S. history. Arose, under Thomas JEFFERSON, in opposition to Alexander Hamilton and Federalist party; emphasized personal liberty and limitation of powers of Federal government. Early party name of Democratic Republican yielded to Democratic by 1828. Election of Jefferson in 1800 had virtual force of a revolution; victory of radical group under Andrew JACKSON in 1828 represented second revolution. Arguments over slavery created or deepened splits within party; Civil War all but destroyed it. Party revived in disputed election of 1876. End of Reconstruction brought emergence of "solid South," a bulwark of Democratic strength thereafter, except for rare instances. With nomination of W. J. BRYAN in 1896 on a "free silver" platform, radicals again gained ascendant. His defeat posed problem of keeping together party's diverse factions—Southern and Western farmers, big-city industrial classes, a few of the wealthy. Leader appeared in idealistic liberal, Woodrow WILSON. Economic depression helped to sweep F. D. ROOSEVELT and Democrats into power in 1932, and party was again identified as reform party with New Deal. Roosevelt died in office in 1945, in fourth

term, and Harry S. TRUMAN became President. In 1948, despite disaffection of the South, due to Negro civil-rights issue, and of dissidents under Henry WALLACE, Truman brought Democrats to surprising victory. Republican victory under Dwight D. Eisenhower in 1952 ended 20-year rule of Democratic party and seemed to forecast two-party system in once "solid South."

Democritus (dĭmŏk′rĭtŭs), c.460–c.370 B.C., Greek philosopher. A materialist, he held that the world was made up of tiny particles, imperceptible to the senses but indivisible and indestructible. These are atoms and by constant motion they combine to make the universe. The true nature of things can be discovered only by thought, for sense perceptions are confusing.

Demopolis, city (pop. 5,004), W Ala., SSW of Tuscaloosa at confluence of Black Warrior and Tombigbee rivers; founded 1818 by Bonapartist exiles.

De Morgan, William (Frend), 1839–1917, English novelist. A designer of glass and tiles, he began on retirement to write long leisurely novels such as *Joseph Vance* (1906), *Alice-for-Short* (1907), *Somehow Good* (1908), *An Affair of Dishonour* (1910).

Demosthenes (dĭmŏs′thŭnēz), 384?–322 B.C., Greek orator, one of the greatest orators of all time. His fame rests chiefly on his orations against the conquering Philip II of Macedon—three *Philippics* and three *Olynthiacs* (asking aid for the city of Olynthus). Other orations are *On the Peace, On the False Legation* (against his rival, Aeschines), and *On the Crown* (a defense of himself against Aeschines). Even after Philip triumphed, Demosthenes was honored until he was exiled on obscure charges of financial corruption. Returning after the death of Alexander the Great, he failed to rebuild Greek strength and took poison when fleeing before Antipater.

demotic: see HIEROGLYPHIC.

Dempsey, William Harrison (Jack Dempsey), 1895–, American boxer. Won heavyweight championship from Jess Willard (1919), lost title to James J. (Gene) Tunney (1926). Dempsey was again defeated by Tunney (1927) in fight involving controversial "long count" in seventh round.

Demuth, Charles (dā′mooth), 1883–1935, American water-color painter. Shows influence of cubism.

Denain (dŭnē′), town (pop. 22,299), Nord dept., N France. Coal fields, ironworks. Scene of French victory (1712) in War of Spanish Succession.

Denbighshire (dĕn′bĕshĭr) or **Denbigh**, maritime county (669 sq. mi.; pop. 170,699), N Wales; co. town Denbigh. Largely high pastoral moorland with agr. in valleys. Mineral resources (coal, iron, lead, and slate) around Wrexham.

Denikin, Anton Ivanovich (ŭntôn′ ēvä′nŭvĭch dyĭnyē′kĭn), 1872–1947, Russian general. Commanded anti-Bolshevik forces in S Russia 1918–20.

Denis, Saint (dĕn′ĭs, dŭnē′), 3d cent.?, patron saint of France. Said to have been first bishop of Paris and to have been martyred on Montmartre. The name is a form of Dionysius. Feast: Oct. 9.

Denis, Maurice (môrēs′ dŭnē′), 1870–1943, French muralist and writer on art.

Denison, city (pop. 17,504), N Texas, near Red R. NNE of Dallas. Grew around ante-bellum stagecoach station. Rail division point and shipping center, it processes cheese, milk, cotton, wheat, peanuts. Mfg. of machinery, metal goods. Birthplace of Pres. Eisenhower. **Denison Dam** is NW, in Red R. between Denison and Durant, Okla.; completed 1943–44, for flood control, power. Main dam is 165 ft. high, 15,200 ft. long. Its reservoir, L. Texoma, is one of largest artificial lakes in U.S. and much used for recreation.

Denison University: see GRANVILLE, Ohio.

Denmark, Dan. *Danmark,* kingdom (16,576 sq. mi.; pop. 4,279,151), NW Europe, southernmost of Scandinavian countries; cap. Copenhagen. Except for JUTLAND peninsula, bordering on Germany, Denmark consists of several Baltic isls., notably ZEALAND, FYN,

FALSTER, LAALAND, LANGELAND, BORNHOLM. Overseas possessions are GREENLAND and the FAEROE ISLANDS. A low-lying, highly cultivated country, Denmark specializes in dairying and stock raising and has important commercial and fishing fleets. Form of government is parliamentary democracy (see RIGSDAG). Ruling house: Schleswig-Holstein-Sonderburg-Glucksburg. Reigning king: Frederick IX. Established Church is Lutheran. In the Viking Age (see VIKINGS) Danes took important part in Norse raids of W Europe. Harold Bluetooth (d. c.985) was their first Christian king. His son SWEYN conquered England, and CANUTE united Denmark, England, and Norway from 1018 to 1035. S Sweden was part of Denmark to 1658. Danish hegemony over the N was first estab. under Waldemar I and Waldemar II (12th–13th cent.); WALDEMAR IV restored Danish power but was successfully challenged by the HANSEATIC LEAGUE (14th cent.). His daughter MARGARET created (1397) the KALMAR UNION of Denmark, Sweden, and NORWAY; the union with Norway lasted to 1814, but that with Sweden never was effective and ended in 1523. The house of Oldenburg, from which the present dynasty is descended, acceded in 1448 with CHRISTIAN I, who also united SCHLESWIG and HOLSTEIN with the Danish crown. The Reformation was introduced by Christian III. Danish participation in the Thirty Years War (see CHRISTIAN IV) and the wars of FREDERICK III caused 17th-cent. Denmark to lose its leading position to Sweden. An absolute monarchy was estab. under Christian V, and colonial imperialism resulted in the creation of trade monopolies in ICELAND and the VIRGIN ISLANDS. Important social reforms (e.g., abolition of serfdom, 1788) marked the late 18th cent., especially under the ministries of STRUENSEE and A. P. BERNSTORFF. Denmark sought to maintain neutrality in the French Revolutionary and Napoleonic wars but was attacked by England and joined the French camp. As a result, the Congress of Vienna deprived it of Norway. The complex question of SCHLESWIG-HOLSTEIN led to the German-Danish war of 1848–49 and to war with Prussia and Austria in 1864, in which Denmark lost both duchies. (N Schleswig was restored to Denmark after a plebiscite, 1920.) Of more lasting importance was the internal reform of 19th-cent. Denmark, which transformed its poor peasantry into the most prosperous small farmers in Europe. This achievement was largely due to the educational efforts of Bishop GRUNDTVIG and to the cooperative movement. Neutral in World War I, Denmark was occupied (1940–45) by German forces in World War II. It joined the UN (1945), the European Recovery Program (1948), and the North Atlantic Treaty (1949).

Dennie, Joseph, 1768–1812, American Federalist journalist, editor of anti-Jefferson weekly.

Dennis, resort town (pop. 2,499), SE Mass., on Cape Cod NE of Yarmouth. Has summer theater.

density, measurement of a quantity of matter in a unit volume of a substance. It is usually expressed in grams per cubic centimeter; grams per liter, or pounds per cubic foot and is calculated by dividing the MASS by the volume occupied at standard temperature and pressure. SPECIFIC GRAVITY of solid or liquid is density compared with that of water; that of gas is compared with hydrogen or air.

Dent du Midi or **Dents du Midi** (both: dä′ dü mēdē′), Alpine mountain group, Vaud canton, SW Switzerland, rising to 10,696 ft. in Haute Cime.

dentistry, science of treatment and care of teeth and associated oral structures. Important contributions to evolution of modern dentistry made by Ambroise Paré, John Hunter, Pierre FAUCHARD, G. V. BLACK, C. A. HARRIS, and many others. Progress aided by development of X ray, local anesthetics, artificial dentures, drilling machine, and methods of preparing fillings and inlays. As dentistry became field separate from medicine, training schools multiplied and educa-

tional requirements became stringent. Preventive and corrective treatment and education in care of teeth stressed today.

Denton, city (pop. 21,372), N Texas, NW of Dallas, NE of Fort Worth; founded 1855. Seat of North Texas State Col. and Texas State Col. for Women (1901). Processing and mfg. center in varied farm area. L. Dallas is near.

D'Entrecasteaux Islands (dătrŭkăstō′), volcanic group, area c.1,200 sq. mi., off SE New Guinea, part of Territory of Papua. Named for the French navigator Entrecasteaux.

Dents du Midi, Switzerland: see DENT DU MIDI.

Denver, city (pop. 415,786; alt. 5,280 ft.), state cap., N central Colo., on South Platte R.; settled 1858, made territorial cap. 1867. Rich gold, silver strikes of '70s and '80s boomed Denver. At this time, H. A. W. TABOR built opera house, and Silver Dollar saloon flourished. As transportation, processing, distributing center for huge agr. and livestock area, growth was steady by 1900. It is now metropolis of the Rockies, largest city in Colo., financial center. Has stockyards, oil refineries, rail shops, fruit and vegetable canneries, flour mills; mfg. of mine and farm machinery, furniture, rubber and cotton goods; motorcar assembly. Large tourist trade. Has fine climate. Here are hq. for many Federal agencies, a U.S. mint, mountain parks, Colorado Mus. of Natural History, zoological gardens, Denver Art Mus., Lowry Air Force Base. Seat of Loretto Heights Col. (R.C.; for women; 1891); Univ. of Colorado medical school; **University of Denver** (Methodist; coed.; chartered and opened 1864 mainly by John Evans).

deodar or **deodar cedar:** see CEDAR.

De Patinir, De Patenier, or **De Patiner, Joachim:** see PATINIR, JOACHIM DE.

De Paul University: see CHICAGO, Ill.

DePauw University: see GREENCASTLE, Ind.

De Pere (dĭ pēr′), city (pop. 8,146), NE Wis., on Fox R. and S of Green Bay. Father Allouez founded mission here 1671. Mfg. of paper, boats, and brick.

Depew, Chauncey (Mitchell) (dĭpū′), 1834–1928, American railroad president and orator. President (1885–99) and chairman of board (1899–1928) of New York Central lines. Noted as after-dinner speaker.

Depew, village (pop. 7,217), W N.Y., near Buffalo. Mfg. of textiles, metal products, cereals.

De profundis (dā prōfoon′dēs), one of penitential psalms, Ps. 130 (or 129). See PSALMS.

Deptford (dĕt′fŭrd), metropolitan borough (pop. 75,-694), SE London, England; industrial district. Noted in Elizabethan times for cattle market and royal dockyard. Christopher Marlowe was killed here.

De Quincey, Thomas (dĭ kwĭn′sē), 1785–1859, English essayist. Settled (1816) at Grasmere, near Wordsworth and Coleridge. The opium habit overcame him for a time and inspired "Confessions of an English Opium-Eater" (in London Magazine, 1821). Became prolific contributor of essays and critical articles to journals.

Derain, André (ändrä′ dŭrē′), 1880–, French painter. Associated with the fauvists, but his art shows an assimilation of various other influences.

Derbent (dyĭrbyĕnt′), city (pop. 23,097), SE Dagestan, SE European RSFSR; Caspian fishing port. Founded 5th or 6th cent. A.D. by Persians at Iron Gates (called Caspian or Albanian Gates by ancients), a defile between Caucasus and Caspian, on a major commercial route. Ceded by Persia to Russia 1813. Remains of 6th-cent. Caucasian Wall (or Alexander's Wall), built by Persians to stem N invaders.

Derby, Edward George Geoffrey Smith Stanley, 14th **earl of** (där′bē), 1799–1869, British statesman. As Whig colonial secretary he pushed through abolition of slavery 1833. Influenced by Robert PEEL he became a Conservative. Was colonial secretary 1841–45. As head of two ministries (1852, 1858–59), he was a great force in liberalizing the Tory party.

Derby, England: see DERBYSHIRE.

Derby (dûr'bē), city (pop. 10,259), SW Conn., at junction of Naugatuck and Housatonic rivers; founded 1642. Metal and rubber products. Yale holds annual spring regatta on the Housatonic here.

Derby (där'bē, dûr'bē), famous horse race held annually since 1780 at Epsom Downs, near London, England. The name derby is also applied to other well-known horse races, notably Kentucky Derby (dûr'bē), held annually since 1875 at Churchill Downs, Louisville, Ky.

Derbyshire (där'bĕshïr) or **Derby**, county (1,002 sq. mi.; pop. 826,336, central England. Area flat in S, rising to Peak district in N. Has rich coal deposits in E section. Heavily cultivated; dairy farming and sheep raising are important. County town, **Derby**, borough (pop. 141,264) on Derwent R., is a rail center. Has mfg. of cars (Rolls-Royce), pottery (Derby ware), textiles, and paper. Birthplace of Herbert Spencer. George Eliot lived here.

Derby ware, delicate, richly decorated English china produced at Derby since c.1750. Became Royal Crown Derby in 1890 by permission of Queen Victoria. Most Derby marks show a crown over a D.

Derg, Lough (lŏkh' dĕrg'), lakes, Ireland. **1** Expansion of Shannon R. (length, 23 mi.; width, 1–5 mi.) on borders of Counties Galway, Tipperary, and Clare. **2** SE Donegal. Station Isl. here, traditional place of St. Patrick's Purgatory, has extensive religious establishments and is noted place of pilgrimage.

De Ridder, city (pop. 5,799), SW La., E of Sabine R. Center of sheep raising, lumbering, and agr. area.

Dermot McMurrough or **Diarmuid mac Murchada** (both: dûr'mùt mùkmŭ'rù), d. 1171, Irish king who brought the English into Ireland. Banished 1166. Promised aid by Richard Strongbow and other adventurers, he returned to Ireland in 1168. With the invaders, he had conquered SE Ireland, including Dublin, by 1170.

Derna (dĕ'rnä), town (pop. 20,782), E Cyrenaica, Libya, a Mediterranean port. Occupied 1805 by U.S. in Tripolitan War. In World War II it changed hands several times 1941–42.

Derry, Northern Ireland: see LONDONDERRY.

Derry, town (pop. 5,826), SE N.H., SE of Manchester, in agr. and resort area. Has horse races on ice (since 1928). Robert Frost farmed and taught here.

Derwent (dûr'wùnt), rivers in England. **1** Cumberland, in the Lake District. **2** Derbyshire, tributary of the Trent. **3** Yorkshire, tributary of the Ouse.

Derwentwater, oval lake, 3 mi. long and 1 mi. wide, Cumberland, England. Formed by widening of Derwent R., it is surrounded by wooded hills. Lodore waterfalls are at upper end.

Derzhavin, Gavril Romanovich (gùvrēl' rùmä'nùvĭch dyïrzhä'vĭn), 1743–1816, Russian classical poet; poet laureate to Catherine II. His fame rests chiefly on his *Ode to God* (Eng. tr., 1861).

De Sanctis, Francesco (fränchäs'kō dä sängk'tēs), 1818–83, Italian literary critic, notable for *Saggi Critici* [critical essays] (1866) and *History of Italian Literature* (1871).

Desargues, Gérard (zhärär' dùzärg'), 1593–1662, French mathematician, engineer, founder of modern geometry. He discovered the involution and transversal theorems named for him and worked on conic sections.

Descartes, René (rùnä' dākärt'), 1596–1650, French philosopher, mathematician, and scientist. His teachings are called Cartesian from his name in Latin (Renatus Cartesius). Studied at the Jesuit school at La Flèche and the Univ. of Poitiers; served in the army of Maurice of Nassau; retired to Holland for research and reflection (1628); accepted the invitation of Queen Christina (1649), but died soon after reaching Sweden. A mathematical genius, he worked out the treatment of negative roots and a system of notation in algebra; originated Cartesian coordinates and Cartesian curves and is said to have founded analytic geometry. He attempted to apply mathematical methods to philosophy (notably in *Discourse on Method*), and discarding authoritarian scholasticism, he founded his system on universal doubt. One thing, he says, cannot be doubted: doubt itself. The action of the mind proves reality; his motto was *Cogito, ergo sum* [I think, therefore I am]. He refined scholastic arguments for the existence of God and held God to be the link between the mechanical world of the senses and the rational world of the mind. In physical science he rejected tradition but relied on rationalization, mathematics, and logic rather than experiment. He made numerous advances in optics (notably in reflection and refraction of light), in psychology, and in physiology. His influence on modern thought is incalculable.

Deschanel, Paul (pôl' dāshänĕl'), 1855–1922, president of France (1920).

Deschutes (dāshōōts'), river rising in W central Oregon in Cascade Range, flowing NNE to Columbia R. near The Dalles. Used for power, irrigation.

desert (dĕ'zùrt), arid region, at least partly covered by sand, with scanty vegetation, limited and specially adapted animal life. High-altitude deserts, often perpetually covered with ice or snow, are not usually considered with deserts of warm regions. One fifth of world's land is desert. Largest desert regions lie between 20° and 30° N and S of equator, where mountains block trade winds or atmospheric high-pressure areas cause descending air currents and lack of precipitation. Other factors: amount of sunshine, water evaporation rate, temperature range, annual rainfall. Europe, only continent without deserts, has semideserts around Black and Caspian Seas, in Ukraine, and in the N Caucasus. The GOBI, in Asia, is desert because of remoteness from water. The SAHARA, in Africa, is largest desert; second largest is central and W Australian desert region. North American deserts include MOJAVE DESERT, IMPERIAL VALLEY, and DEATH VALLEY. Desert plants, widely spaced, have stems and leaves adapted to lessen water loss; roots form spreading network penetrating down to 50 ft. North American desert animals include birds, mice, foxes, deer, snakes, lizards, and spiders.

desertion, in military law, the abandonment of a place of duty without leave and with the intention not to return. It is punishable in war time by death. In maritime law, the abandonment of a ship by a seaman without leave. In family law, willful abandonment of the spouse or children of a marriage without consent of the other party or parties. In most states, desertion is ground for DIVORCE.

Desiderio da Settignano (dāzēdā'rēō dä sĕt"tēn-yä'nō), 1428–64, Florentine sculptor, known for church decorations and marble busts of women and children.

Desiderius, d. after 774, last Lombard king in Italy. Attacked Pope ADRIAN I, who appealed to Charlemagne. Charlemagne (who had married and later repudiated Desiderius' daughter) invaded Italy (773) and captured and deposed Desiderius (774).

De Sitter, Willem: see SITTER, WILLEM DE.

De Smet, Pierre Jean (dē smĕt'), 1801–73, missionary in U.S. Pacific Northwest, a Jesuit, b. Belgium. Often mediated between Indians and whites.

Des Moines (dù moin'), city (pop. 177,965), state cap., S central Iowa, largest city of state, at junction of Des Moines and Raccoon rivers, in heart of Corn Belt. Estab. 1843 as Fort Des Moines, it was settled by homesteaders 1845. Transportation, industrial, insurance, and commercial center, it has mfg. of food, metal, rubber, and clay products, and printing and publishing. Adopted Des Moines (commission) plan of city government 1907. Here are state historical collections, Fort Des Moines, and DRAKE UNIVERSITY. Camp Dodge is near by.

Des Moines, river rising in SW Minn. and flowing c.535 mi. SSE across Iowa to Mississippi R. at Keokuk.

Desmond, ancient division of Munster prov., Ireland,

including present Co. Cork and Co. Kerry. The Fitz-geralds became powerful earls of Desmond.

Desmoulins, Camille (kämē′yù dämōōlē′), 1760–94, French revolutionist and journalist, early leader of CORDELIERS. His oratory led to storming of Bastille, July 14, 1789. Executed with Danton.

De Soto, Hernando (Span. dā sō′tō), c.1500–1542, Spanish explorer. Led unsuccessful treasure hunt, on which he died, from Fla. to Okla. (1539–42).

De Soto (dĭ sō′tō), city (pop. 5,357), E Mo., SSW of St. Louis. Railroad shops and apparel factories.

Despenser, Hugh le (hū′ lù dĭspĕn′sùr), d. 1265, chief justiciar of England. Supported barons against Henry III, fought in Baron's War, and was killed at Eve-sham 1265. Two best-known members of this family were **Hugh le Despenser**, the elder, 1262–1326, and **Hugh le Despenser**, the younger, d. 1326. The elder Despenser became chief adviser to EDWARD II. The younger Despenser later joined his father and the king. Were banished by barons 1321; returned to Eng-land 1322 and became real rulers of the kingdom. Hat-ed by barons; were executed when Isabella returned from France and seized control 1326.

Despiau, Charles (shärl′ dāpēō′), 1874–1946, French sculptor. Studied under Rodin. Best known for his bronze busts and nudes of young women.

Des Plaines (dĕs plānz′), city (pop. 14,994), NE Ill., on Des Plaines R. and near Chicago; founded in 1830s. Mfg. of electrical equipment. Annual Methodist en-campment.

Des Plaines, river rising in SE Wis. and flowing c.110 mi. S and SW to join Kankakee R. near Joliet, Ill. This combined stream is Illinois R.

Des Prés, Josquin: see JOSQUIN DES PRÉS.

Dessalines, Jean Jacques (zhä′ zhäk′ dĕsälĕn′), c.1758–1806, Negro emperor of Haiti (1804–6), born a slave. Served under Toussaint L'Ouverture in wars of libera-tion. Was named governor (1801), later crowned em-peror, Jacques I. Because of his despotic rule, he was murdered.

Dessau (dĕ′sou), city (pop. 88,139), former cap. of AN-HALT, central Germany, at junction of Elbe and Mulde rivers. Produces machinery. Seat of BAUHAUS school 1925–32.

Destaing, Charles Hector: see ESTAING.

destroyer, warship of 1,500 to 2,000 tons, very fast, with powerful torpedo armament, a few medium-caliber guns, and anti-aircraft artillery. Introduced in 1892, much improved in World War I. Equipped with new electronic devices, destroyers proved highly effective against submarines during World War II and were used for convoying larger naval vessels and merchant ships. In battle, they rely on speed and maneuverability.

detective story, popular type of fiction in which solution of a crime is traced step by step. Poe's *Murders in the Rue Morgue* is considered first modern detective story. Mystery story, an allied type in which there is no de-tective and often no crime, only unexplained situa-tion, is exemplified by Wilkie Collins' *Woman in White.* Famous detective-story writers include Conan Doyle, E. C. Bentley, Agatha Christie, Georges Si-menon, Dashiell Hammett, Raymond Chandler, Erle Stanley Gardner, and S. S. Van Dine.

detergent (dĕtûr′jùnt), substance that aids in dirt re-moval by reducing surface tension of water. Soap is a good detergent but has the disadvantages of forming insoluble compounds with salts of hard water and of decomposing in acid solutions. Synthetic detergents produced in quantities after 1930.

Detmold (dĕt′mōlt), city (pop. 30,192), former cap. of LIPPE, NW Germany. Near by is monument to vic-tory of ARMINIUS over Romans.

detonator (dĕ′tùnä″tùr), type of explosive that reacts rapidly and is used to set off more inert explosives. Commonly used are fulminate of mercury mixed with potassium chlorate. Term is also applied to equipment to set off chemical detonator.

Detroit (dĭtroit′) city (pop. 1,849,568), SE Mich., on Detroit R. and between lakes St. Clair and Erie. State's largest city and fifth largest in U.S., it is a great transportation center with mfg. of motor vehicles, air-craft, railroad cars, and rubber and metal products. Its carriage industry helped Henry Ford and others make Detroit the center of world's auto industry. Set-tled 1701 by French; British took over in 1760 and withstood long siege in PONTIAC'S REBELLION (1763). Has been American since 1796, except for short Brit-ish occupation in War of 1812. Territorial and state cap. 1805–47. Grew rapidly (esp. in 1830s) with de-velopment of land and water transportation. Became important in last half of 19th cent. through shipping, shipbuilding, and manufacturing. Notable sights are Ambassador Bridge, spanning river for 2 mi. to Wind-sor, Ont., and Belle Isle, a park in the river with sym-phony shell and yacht basins. Detroit includes inde-pendent cities of HAMTRAMCK and HIGHLAND PARK. Seat of Univ. of DETROIT and Wayne Univ. (city, county support; coed.; formed 1933 from five city colleges opened 1868–1927).

Detroit, river, c.28 mi. long, flowing from L. St. Clair, between SE Mich. and S Ont., S into L. Erie. Forms part of international boundary.

Detroit, University of, at Detroit; R.C. (Jesuit), coed.; opened 1877, chartered as college 1881, became uni-versity 1911.

Detroit Lakes, city (pop. 5,787), NW Minn., E of Moor-head. Lake resort and farm trade center.

Dettifoss (dĕ′tĭfôs), fall, c.200 ft. high, in Jokulsa R., NE Iceland, the most powerful in the country.

Dettingen (dĕ′tĭngùn), village, NW Bavaria, on Main R. Here in 1743 allies under George II of England defeated French in War of Austrian Succession.

Deucalion (dūkā′lēùn), in Greek mythology, son of Prometheus and father of Hellen. He and his wife, Pyrrha, only survivors of a great flood, were told to cast behind them bones of their mother, the stones of the earth. These became human beings.

deuterium: see HYDROGEN.

deuterocanonical books: see OLD TESTAMENT.

deuteron: see HYDROGEN.

Deuteronomy (dūtùrŏn′ùmē) [Gr.,= second law], book of Old Testament, last of 5 books of Law (Pentateuch or Torah) ascribed by tradition to Moses. It gives the final words of Moses—his last instructions to his peo-ple and his blessing of them. Book ends with death of Moses.

deutzia (dū′tsèù), ornamental shrub of genus *Deutzia,* with abundant white, pink, or purple blooms.

Deux-Sèvres (dû-sĕv′rù), department (2,337 sq. mi.; pop. 312,756), W France, in Poitou; cap. Niort.

De Valera, Eamon (ā′mùn dĕ″ vùlä′rù), 1882–, Irish statesman, b. New York. Imprisoned (1916) for part in Easter Rebellion. Made president of Sinn Fein 1917. As head of DÁIL ÉIREANN raised funds in U.S. 1919–20. After period of virtual war against British rule, Irish Free State was estab. 1921. Opposing Free State, he left the Dáil in 1922. Nominal leader of re-publicans, he deplored subsequent civil war. Re-enter-ing Dáil in 1927 with his party, the FIANNA FÁIL, he became prime minister in 1938. Kept Ireland neutral in World War II. Defeated 1948, he was returned to office 1951.

developer, in PHOTOGRAPHY, solution used to prepare NEGATIVE after exposure of film. It acts on silver salts that were affected by light.

Deventer (dĕ′vĕntùr), municipality (pop. 44,089) and town, Overijssel prov., E central Netherlands, on the Ijssel. Produces machinery, textiles, carpets. It was a medieval center of piety and learning (Thomas à Kempis and Erasmus studied here) and member of the Hanseatic League. There are many medieval and Ren-aissance buildings.

Devereux, Robert: see ESSEX, ROBERT DEVEREUX, EARL OF.

devil: see SATAN.

Devil Postpile National Monument: see NATIONAL PARKS AND MONUMENTS (table).

Devils Island, Fr. *Île du Diable,* tiny island off French Guiana. Until 1946 used as penal colony, largely for political prisoners.

Devils Lake, city (pop. 6,427), NE N.Dak., WNW of Grand Forks, near salty Devils L. (c.30 mi. long; steadily receding). Rail junction, resort, and trade center in livestock and grain area.

Devils Tower National Monument: see NATIONAL PARKS AND MONUMENTS (table).

De Vinne, Theodore L(ow) (dù vĭ′nē), 1828–1914, American printer, most famous of his day. By example and through his writings he advanced the cause of good printing.

Devolution, War of, 1667–68, between France and Spain, caused by complicated legal claim of Louis XIV to Spanish Netherlands. The French overran the Spanish Netherlands and Franche-Comté, but made peace when the United Provs. formed anti-French TRIPLE ALLIANCE with England and Sweden (see AIX-LA-CHAPELLE, TREATY OF).

Devon, county, England: see DEVONSHIRE.

Devonian period (dĭvō′nēŭn), fourth period of the PALEOZOIC ERA of geologic time. It began with the continents mainly dry; later large areas were flooded and thick sediments deposited. The OLD RED SANDSTONE was laid down. Fish in great numbers dominated marine life, among them sharks, lungfish, armored fish, and ganoids. Amphibians emerged in this period. Invertebrates included trilobites, corals, starfish, and sponges. On land, forests of giant ferns and fernlike trees appeared. See also GEOLOGY, table.

Devonport, Devonshire, England: see PLYMOUTH.

Devonshire, Spencer Compton Cavendish, 8th duke of, 1833–1908, English statesman. Led Liberal Unionists who broke (1886) with Gladstone over HOME RULE for Ireland.

Devonshire or **Devon,** maritime county (2,612 sq. mi.; pop. 798,283), SW England; co. town Exeter. Surface largely hilly, rises to 2,000 ft. in Dartmoor. Has many rivers and streams. Mainly agr. and pastoral (Devonshire cream famous); there is also fishing, mining, and quarrying. Of great maritime importance in Elizabethan times, county is associated with Ralegh, Drake, Hawkins, and Grenville. Pilgrim Fathers sailed from Plymouth.

De Vos, Cornelis: see VOS, CORNELIS DE.

De Voto, Bernard (Augustine) (dù vō′tō), 1897–, American writer. He was editor (1936–38) of the *Saturday Review of Literature* and attracted attention when writing a column in *Harper's Magazine.* His writings include novels as well as literary criticism and historical works; notable are *Mark Twain's America* (1932) and *Across the Wide Missouri* (1947). Has edited Mark Twain manuscripts.

Devoy, John, 1842–1928, Irish-American journalist and leader of FENIAN MOVEMENT. In U.S. founded *Irish Nation* and (1903) *Gaelic–American.* Secured American support for Irish Land League movement and 1916 rebellion. Backed Irish Free State.

dew, water formed by condensation of atmospheric water vapor as air cools (above freezing point). Dew point is temperature at which condensation begins.

Dewar, Sir James (dū′ûr), 1842–1923, British chemist and physicist. He worked on properties of matter at low temperatures, liquefaction of gases; he liquefied and solidified hydrogen and was co-inventor of cordite. Invented **Dewar flask:** two flasks, one inside other, with vacuum between, silvered to cause heat reflection; keeps liquid hot or cold.

dewberry, trailing bramble of genus *Rubus,* similar to blackberry, but with earlier and larger fruit.

De Wet, Christian Rudolf (dù vĕt′), 1854–1922, Boer general, prominent in the South African War. Opposed entry of South Africa into World War I and led an unsuccessful revolt.

Dewey, George, 1837–1917, American admiral, hero of battle of Manila in SPANISH-AMERICAN WAR. Briefly boomed for President in resulting enthusiasm.

Dewey, John, 1859–1952, American philosopher and educator, long associated with Columbia Univ. His philosophy, called instrumentalism, is related to pragmatism. He held truth to be evolutionary, not fixed or eternal, and that the modes and forms of human activity are instruments for solving psychological and social problems—instruments that change with the problems. He recognized democracy as a primary source of ethical value. In education he abandoned belief in authoritarian methods and the use of rote practices, arguing for learning by experience, motivated by a sense of the student's need. This was the basic principle that underlay the 20th-cent. progressive education theory and movement. Among his many works are *Psychology* (1887), *The School and Society* (1899), *Democracy and Education* (1916), *Experience and Nature* (1925), *Art as Experience* (1934), and *Logic: the Theory of Inquiry* (1938).

Dewey, Melvil, 1851–1931, American library pioneer, originator of Dewey decimal system, a scheme of book classification using numbers 000 to 999 to cover the general fields of knowledge and narrowing the system to fit special subjects by the use of decimal points. Librarian of Columbia Col., Dewey estab. first school for training librarians. A founder of American Library Association. Advocated spelling reform. Organized Lake Placid Club.

Dewey, Thomas E(dmund), 1902–, governor of N.Y. (1942–). Unsuccessful Republican presidential candidate (1944, 1948).

De Witt, Jan, and **Cornelius de Witt:** see WITT.

Dexter, Timothy, 1747–1806, American merchant and eccentric. Made a fortune by buying up depreciated Continental Congress currency, which was later reclaimed at full value. Author of *A Pickle for the Knowing Ones* (1802), remarkable for its individual spelling and absence of punctuation.

dextrin, a carbohydrate with same general formula as starch, but with a smaller, less complex molecule. It is an intermediate product in starch hydrolysis. Commercial type is powder that forms adhesive paste when mixed with water; used in adhesives and for sizing cotton cloth.

dextrose: see GLUCOSE.

Dezhnev, Cape, RSFSR: see EAST CAPE.

Dhar (där), town (pop. 22,015), Madhya Bharat, India. Rajput cap. and cultural center 9th–18th cent. Taken by Mahrattas in 1730.

diabase (dī′ŭbās), an igneous rock common in intrusive masses. The Hudson Palisades and Connecticut valley trap rock hills are largely diabase.

Diabelli, Antonio (dēäbĕl′ē), 1781–1858, Austrian music publisher. Published works of Beethoven, Schubert.

diabetes (dīŭbē′tēz, –bē′tĭs), continued excessive secretion of urine. *Diabetes mellitus,* a serious form caused by INSULIN deficiency, results in excess sugar in blood and usually also in urine. Often marked by loss of weight; acidosis and coma may follow. Treated by diet and insulin injections.

Diadochi (dīā′dŭkī) [Gr.,= successors], generals and administrators of ALEXANDER THE GREAT who attempted to take over his empire on his death (323 B.C.). Chief among them were Antipater (and his son Cassander), Perdiccas, Antigonus I, Ptolemy I, Seleucus I, and Lysimachus. Rivalry led to a dreary succession of wars. The main events were the victory of Antipater over Perdiccas for the regency (321 B.C.); the coalition against Antigonus after Antipater's death (319 B.C.), which brought the defeat of Antigonus and his son, Demetrius I, at Ipsus (301 B.C.); and the victory of Seleucus I over Lysimachus (281 B.C.). The result was the irrevocable splitting of the empire into smaller empires, notably under the descendants of Ptolemy, Seleucus, and Antigonus.

Diaghilev, Sergei Pavlovich (sĭrgā′ päv′lŭvĭch dyä′gĭlyĭf), 1872–1929, Russian ballet impresario. In Paris founded (1909) Diaghilev's Russian Ballet with painter Bakst, choreographer Fokine. Dancers included Pavlova and Nijinsky. Productions include *The Afternoon of a Faun, The Rite of Spring.*

dialect, variety of a language. In 20th-cent. scientific usage, a dialect is language of a person or group considered as it varies from that of other members of same speech community (which includes all speakers whose native language is intelligible to other—but not necessarily all other—members of the group). With increasing isolation differences may accumulate to the point of mutual unintelligibility. An example is Dutch-German speech community, extending from Flanders to Schleswig and to Styria, yet speakers of Flemish and Styrian dialects cannot understand each other. In the area there are standard languages (i.e., official Dutch and German) which are mutually unintelligible because developed from mutually unintelligible dialects.

dialectic, in philosophy, method of logical procedure, originating in the question-answer-resolution method of Socrates, developed by Plato into a method of reducing the many and the contradictory into systematic organized concepts. Kant used the term for his method of demonstrating metaphysics (as opposed to knowledge derived from phenomena). Hegel based his philosophy on the logic of dialectic, moving from thesis (statement) through antithesis (counterstatement) to synthesis (joining of the two in higher truth); he also held that this process underlay movement in history.

dialectical materialism, method of historical analysis developed by Karl Marx and Friedrich Engels, fundamental in the method of Socialists and Communists. Basically derived from Hegel's dialectic, the theory is notable for thorough-going materialism and insistence that history proceeds only from economic drives. Thus, opposing classes are born of economic stress and must inevitably struggle until the working class gains power and a classless and stateless society ultimately emerges. See MARXISM.

dialysis (dīă'lĭsĭs), in chemistry, a method of separating a colloid from a substance in true solution by using a membrane permeable only to one. Molecular particles of solution pass through membrane; particles of colloid are too large.

diamond, crystallized pure carbon, valued as a gem. It is the hardest substance known, and inferior stones are used as abrasives. Earliest sources were stream gravels (see MINING). Most of the world's gem supply comes from the pipes of old volcanoes in South Africa; Brazil is a source of carbonados (black diamonds).

Diamond Head, extinct crater, 761 ft. high, SE Oahu, T.H. Once burial grounds of ancient Hawaiians. U.S. Fort Ruger on plateau.

Diamond Necklace, Affair of the, scandal which took place in 1784–86 at the French court. An adventuress, calling herself the comtesse de Lamotte, persuaded Cardinal de ROHAN that he could gain Queen Marie Antoinette's favor by buying her a diamond necklace worth nearly $1,000,000. The necklace, assembled by two jewelers, was bought on installment by the cardinal in the queen's name. When he could not meet the payments, the jewelers brought a complaint. It was discovered that Mme de Lamotte's husband had absconded with the necklace to London (where it was broken up and sold). At the trial (1785) the cardinal was acquitted but disgraced; Mme de Lamotte was branded and imprisoned, but escaped. CAGLIOSTRO, at first suspected of complicity, was acquitted. Although the queen had no part in it, the affair revealed a moral laxity at her court which increased her unpopularity.

Diana, in Roman legend, goddess of the moon, of forests, of animals, and of women in childbirth; identified with Greek Artemis. Her temple at Aricia was a shrine of women.

Diane de Poitiers (dyän' dü pwätyä'), 1499–1566, mistress of Henry II of France.

dianthus: see PINK.

Diarmuid mac Murchada: see DERMOT MCMURROUGH.

diarrhea (dīūrē'ŭ), frequent discharge of watery feces, resulting from irritation or nervous stimulation of intestines. Tissues and blood lose fluids and minerals which need to be replaced.

diastase (dī'ŭstās) or **amylase** (ă'mĭlās), an enzyme that converts starch to sugar and thus is important in digestion and fermentation. It is present in some plants and in saliva (as ptyalin) and pancreatic fluid (as amylopsin).

diathermy: see ELECTROTHERAPY.

diatom (dī'ŭtŏm"), microscopic plant form of algae group. Diatoms exist as single cells or joined as colonies in fresh or salt water, in moist soil, and on moist surfaces of other plants. They are most abundant in arctic and other cold regions. Diatomaceous earth and the more compact rock, diatomite, are formed from shells of dead diatoms. Diatomite, found in parts of U.S., is used industrially, especially for insulating against both heat and sound. See *ill.,* p. 633.

Diaz, Armando (ärmän'dō dē'äts), 1861–1928, Italian field marshal. Routed Austrians at Vittorio Veneto and accepted their surrender (Nov., 1918).

Díaz, Bartholomew (dē'ăz), d. 1500, Portuguese navigator. First European to round Cape of Good Hope (1488), thus opening sea route to India.

Díaz, Porfirio (pôrfē'rēō dē'äs), 1830–1915, Mexican statesman, a mestizo who became president (1876) and remained in power until 1911. His regime saw material prosperity in Mexico grow largely through investment of foreign capital, but oppressed masses were neglected and education stagnated. A revolution led by Madero was successful. Díaz died in exile.

Diaz de la Peña, Narciso Virgilio (dyäz' dü lä pänyä'), 1807?–1876, French landscape and figure painter of the Barbizon school, b. Bordeaux.

Díaz del Castillo, Bernal (bĕrnäl' dē'äth dĕl kästē'lyō), c.1492–1581, Spanish conquistador, author of *The True History of the Conquest of New Spain* (1632; Eng. tr., 5 vols., 1908–16).

Dibon (dī'–) or **Dibon-gad,** anc. city, E of Dead Sea, now a ruin called Dhiban. MOABITE STONE found here.

Dice, one of the HORAE.

dice [plural of *die*], small cubes usually made of ivory, bone, wood, similar materials. The six sides are numbered by dots from 1 to 6, so placed that sum of dots on opposite sides equals 7. Most popular dice game in U.S. is craps. Dice also used in poker dice, backgammon, parcheesi, many other games. Dice known to the ancient Egyptians and the Babylonians and were very popular among the Greeks and Romans.

Dick, George Frederick: see DICK TEST.

Dickens, Charles, 1812–70, English novelist, one of the outstanding writers of fiction in English. His childhood was poverty-stricken, and at 12 he worked in a blacking warehouse. Was a court and parliamentary reporter before he began writing sketches (first collected as *Sketches by Boz,* 1836). He was commissioned to write *Posthumous Papers of the Pickwick Club* (1836–37; connected humorous sketches) and began the long series of major novels: *Oliver Twist* (as book 1838), *Nicholas Nickleby* (1839), *The Old Curiosity Shop* (1841), *Barnaby Rudge* (1841), *Martin Chuzzlewit* (1843), *Dombey and Son* (1848), *David Copperfield* (1850), *Bleak House* (1853), *Hard Times* (1854), *Little Dorrit* (1857), *A Tale of Two Cities* (1859), *Great Expectations* (1860–61), *Our Mutual Friend* (1865), *The Mystery of Edwin Drood* (1870; unfinished). Also wrote Christmas books and stories (e.g., *A Christmas Carol,* 1843) and many short stories. Visit to United States in 1842 brought highly critical *American Notes* (1842) and section of *Martin Chuzzlewit.* Married Catherine Hogarth (1836) and had 10 children; separated from her in 1858, possibly because of interest in an actress, Ellen Ternan. His novels are remarkable for depicting quirks of character, for rich panoramas of social scenes, for sentimentality, for crusades against social evils (e.g., imprisonment for debt, legal delays, bad education). Edited magazines, was interested in drama and amateur theatricals.

Dickinson, Emily, 1830–86, American poet. She spent almost all of her life in Amherst, Mass., mostly in seclusion, seeing only a limited number of persons. Whether or not she had a brief and abortive love affair is hotly argued. Certainly she began c.1862 writing the short, frequently cryptic lyrics that have made her one of America's major poets. Her fame began when Mabel L. Todd and T. W. Higginson edited and published her poems (1890–91). Other volumes were issued later, the publications accompanied by vigorous quarreling among her editors.

Dickinson, G(oldsworthy) Lowes, 1862–1932, British author, internationalist and pacifist. Of his varied work perhaps best known is *The Greek View of Life* (1896).

Dickinson, John, 1732–1808, American patriot and statesman. A conservative, his *Letters from a Farmer in Pennsylvania* (1767–68) criticized Townshend Acts and recommended conciliation.

Dickinson, Jonathan, 1688–1747, American Presbyterian clergyman, founder and first president of Col. of New Jersey (now Princeton Univ.).

Dickinson, city (pop. 7,469), SW N.Dak., on Heart R. Ships livestock and wheat. Lignite mines.

Dickinson College: see CARLISLE, Pa.

Dickson City, borough (pop. 8,948), NE Pa., on Lackawanna R. and NE of Scranton. Has anthracite mining and produces metal products.

Dick test, skin test for determining susceptibility to scarlet fever. American physician, **George Frederick Dick,** 1881–, and wife Gladys Dick developed test and immunity serum and isolated streptococcus causing disease.

dictator, originally, a Roman magistrate appointed to rule the state in time of crisis; now, any absolutist or autocrat. Modern dictators may, as head of party or personal following, seize power or may come to office constitutionally and later create dictatorship. Typically they rely on an official party, secret police, and heavy propaganda. Hitler and Mussolini outstanding examples, and Russia under Communist rule developed a party dictatorship with large elements of personal dictatorship. See also CAUDILLO.

dictionary, published list of forms of a language, with content governed by some specific purpose. Descriptive dictionaries (e.g., foreign-language dictionaries) attempt, ideally, to give objectively exact meaning of all forms of their languages. The modern dictionary of its own standard language is often prescriptive, for it attempts to establish certain forms as preferable (as in dictionary of the French Acad.). In 20th cent. American dictionary makers began to replace notions of purity (esp. based on ETYMOLOGY) by criteria of use. The sound line of English dictionaries may be said to begin with *Universal Etymological English Dictionary* (1721) and *Dictionarium Britannicum* (1730), by Nathan Bailey. Samuel Johnson used Bailey's second work to prepare *A Dictionary of the English Language* (1755). His definitions are basic in later lexicography. The next great lexicographer was an American, Noah Webster, whose *Spelling Book* appeared in 1783. His more advanced *Compendious Dictionary of the English Language* (1806) and his larger work, *An American Dictionary of the English Language* (1828), followed. Authorized publishers have made a series of skillful revisions, which have caused Webster's dictionaries to retain popularity. *The Century Dictionary,* an American work in six volumes, with encyclopedic features, was completed in 1891. In England dictionary work after Johnson progressed with John Walker's dictionary (1791), which gave special care to pronunciation, and later with that of the Philological Society, published 1884–1928 as *New English Dictionary, Oxford English Dictionary,* or *Murray's Dictionary* (for Sir J. A. H. Murray, one of the editors), in which examples of

usage were collected and organized, with dates given.

Dictys Cretensis (dĭk'tĭs krētēn'sĭs), supposed hero of Trojan War. Latin MS of his "diary" (A.D. 4th cent.) was popular source for medieval stories.

Didache (dĭ'dŭkē) [Gr.,= teaching], collection of Christian moral precepts, directions for baptism and the Eucharist, and instructions to ministers. It is in Greek, is also called in English *The Teaching of the Twelve Apostles,* and probably dates from before A.D. 100.

Diderot, Denis (dŭnē' dēdŭrō'), 1713–84, French philosopher, a leading figure of the ENLIGHTENMENT and a universal genius of the modern era. His life work was the editorship of the ENCYCLOPÉDIE (1747–72). His philosophy, scattered in numerous writings, combines extreme skepticism with bold materialism. As a playwright, he created the "bourgeois drama" with *Le Père de famille* (1758). *La Religieuse* and *Jacques le fataliste,* novels, and *Le Neveu de Rameau,* a satire in dialogue (all pub. posthumously) are, like all his works, highly individualistic and personal in style. In his *Salons* (1759–71) he pioneered in modern art criticism. Late in life he enjoyed the patronage of Catherine II, whom he visited at St. Petersburg (1773–74).

Dido (dī'dō), in Roman legend, founder and queen of Carthage. Of several versions of her story the most famous is in Vergil's *Aeneid,* which tells how she loved Aeneas and how, when he had to leave her, she destroyed herself on her own funeral pyre.

Didot, François (frässwä' dēdō'), 1689–1757, Parisian printer. His son, **François Ambroise Didot** (äbrwäz'), 1730–1804, was called by Benjamin Franklin Bache "the best printer of this age and even the best that has ever been seen." Scholarly and typographic excellence of Didot's books is unquestioned. He designed some "modern" type and improved and secured adoption of Pierre Simon Fournier's "point" system of type measurement. His sons, **Pierre Didot,** 1761–1853, and **Firmin Didot** (fĕrmē'), 1764–1836, continued family tradition of printing excellence, choosing and editing texts conscientiously and also producing good inexpensive books for students.

Didrikson, (Mildred) Babe (dĭ'drĭksŭn), 1913–, American athlete. Broke four records at Olympic games of 1932. Has won many golf titles. Married George Zaharias 1938.

Didymus: see THOMAS, SAINT.

Diels, Otto Paul Hermann, 1876–, German chemist. He shared 1950 Nobel Prize for discovering and developing method of producing synthetically certain complex compounds.

Diemen, Anton van (än'tŏn vän dē'mŭn), 1593–1645, Dutch colonial official. Became governor general of Dutch East India Co. in 1636. Sent out Abel TASMAN on exploring voyages. Van Diemen's Land was original name of Tasmania.

Dieppe (dēĕp'), town (pop. 20,877), Seine-Inférieure dept., N France; fishing port and resort on English Channel. Scene (1942) of Allied commando raid in World War II.

Diesel engine (dē'zŭl), internal-combustion type of engine invented by Rudolf Diesel (1858–1913, German engineer). Since patented in 1892, it has developed into competitor of steam engine, steam turbine, and electric motor, particularly for marine work and for driving locomotives, trucks, electric generators, and pumps. Instead of igniting fuel by spark as in gasoline engines, it uses compression of air to raise air temperature to igniting point. Although heavier than gasoline engines, the Diesel uses cheaper fuel (crude oil). See *ill.,* p. 303.

Dies irae (dē'ās ē'rā) [Latin,= day of wrath], hymn of the Roman Catholic Church, part of the Requiem Mass, a description of the Last Judgment. Its plainsong tune has been used in instrumental music, as in Berlioz's *Symphonie fantastique.* Verdi and Mozart composed original music for it.

diet, daily intake of food. For maintenance of physical and mental health it should include adequate daily amounts of proteins (e.g., from meat, fish, eggs, legumes, milk, cheese); carbohydrates, i.e., starches (grain products, potatoes, rice) and sugar (fruits, honey, moderate amount of other sweets); fats; and a sufficient intake of minerals (calcium, phosphorus, iron, copper, iodine) and VITAMINS, as well as water. Obesity is caused by a diet with more calorie (i.e., energy) value than the body requires. Special diets are needed in certain diseases and to correct obesity or underweight.

diet, a deliberative or legislative assembly. The diet (Ger. *Reichstag*) of the HOLY ROMAN EMPIRE was summoned irregularly. Emperor Charles IV organized it into three bodies—ELECTORS, princes, and representatives of imperial cities (1356). In 1648 it became a federal body, above the emperor; from 1663 it met at Regensburg. For the federal diet (Ger., *Bundesrat*), of 1815–66, see GERMAN CONFEDERATION. Parliamentary bodies of some other countries have also been called diets. See also WORMS, DIET OF.

Dieulafoy, Marcel Auguste (dyûläfwä'), 1844–1920, French archaeologist. Discovered palaces of Darius and Artaxerxes at Susa while exploring in Persia (1885). Aided by his wife, **Jeanne** (or **Jane) Rachel Magre Dieulafoy,** 1851–1916.

differential, in automobile a set of gears used on driving axle (usually the rear) to divide torque of common power source (drive shaft) equally between two rear wheels, at the same time allowing each wheel to revolve at its own speed.

diffraction. Light travels in straight lines through a uniform, transparent medium. When an opaque object partly blocks its path, the rays that just pass the edges are bent slightly. This is diffraction; it occurs when light waves pass through narrow slits. A **diffraction grating** is used for producing spectra and for direct measurement of wave lengths of lines in certain spectra. Sound waves are also diffracted.

diffusion, uniform distribution of molecules of one substance through those of another in apparent contradiction to laws of gravity. Rate is inversely proportional to square root of density of diffusing gas (Graham's law). It is seen also in liquids and in some solids in contact with others.

Digby, earls of Bristol: see BRISTOL, JOHN DIGBY, 1ST EARL OF.

Digby, Sir Kenelm, 1603–65, English writer, man of affairs. Varied career included brief piracy, loyal support of king in civil war. A Roman Catholic, he tried to convert Cromwell. Promotion of a panacea, the "powder of sympathy," overshadowed real scientific achievements.

Digby, fishing and resort town (pop. 2,047), W N.S., Canada, on Bay of Fundy opposite St. John, N.B.

Digest: see CORPUS JURIS CIVILIS.

digestion, conversion of food in alimentary canal into simple, soluble form which can pass into the circulation and be used by tissues. In man, it occurs chiefly by the action of SALIVA, BILE, and juices of STOMACH, PANCREAS, and INTESTINE.

Diggers, members of small English religio-economic movement (fl. 1649–50), so called because of efforts to cultivate wastelands. Offshoot of LEVELERS; favored egalitarian communism. Leader was Gerrard Winstanley (1609?–1660?). Colonies, estab. in Surrey, were destroyed by mob violence 1650.

Dighton (dī'tŭn), town (pop. 2,950), SE Mass., on Taunton R. and S of Taunton. Origin of inscriptions, probably Indian, on Dighton Rock is uncertain.

digitalis: see FOXGLOVE.

Dijon (dēzhô'), city (pop. 92,686), cap. of Côte-d'Or dept., E France; historic cap. of Burgundy. Chief trading center for Burgundy wine. Reached its flower under Duke Philip the Good (15th cent.). Among art treasures are funeral statues of dukes by Claus SLUTER and his disciples in former ducal palace (12th cent.; rebuilt 17th and 18th cent.); several 13th-cent. churches, including cathedral; 16th-cent. palace of justice

(once housing parlement). University founded 1722.

dill, Old World annual (*Anethum graveolens*), with aromatic seeds used for pickling and flavoring.

Dillard University: see NEW ORLEANS, La.

Dillinger, John, 1902–34, American bank robber. In 1933 he terrorized the Midwest with an organization of criminals, killing 16 persons before he was shot by FBI agents.

Dillon, town (pop. 5,171), NE S.C., near N.C. line NE of Florence, in farm (cotton, tobacco) area.

Dilthey, Wilhelm (vĭl'hĕlm dĭl'tī), 1833–1911, German philosopher. Argued for analytic psychology as base for philosophy, a central spiritual science distinct from natural sciences. He stressed history and development of ideas, to the exclusion of metaphysics.

DiMaggio, Joseph Paul (dĭmä'jēō), 1914–, American baseball outfielder. Joe DiMaggio estab. (1941) major league record by hitting safely in 56 consecutive games.

dime novels, swift-moving, thrilling novels, mainly about American Revolution, frontier period, or Civil War. First sold in 1860 for 10 cents. Among most famous were those about DEADWOOD DICK and Nick CARTER. Quality of stories was lowered by imitators after 1880, and dime novels acquired bad name.

Dinah (dī'nŭ), daughter of Jacob. Gen. 30.21; 34.1–31.

Dinan (dēnä'), town (pop. 11,111), Côtes-du-Nord dept., NW France. Medieval ramparts and 14th-cent. castle of dukes of Brittany still stand.

Dinant (dēnä'), town (pop. 6,925), Namur prov., S Belgium, on Meuse R. Railroad junction; market center. Fortified since Merovingian times, it was noted in Middle Ages for metalware.

Dinard (dēnär'), town (pop. 7,353), Ille-et-Vilaine dept., NW France, facing Saint-Malo across inlet of English Channel. Bathing resort.

Dinaric Alps (dīnā'rĭk), mountain range, occupying one third of Yugoslavia and part of Albania. Prolongs Alps along E coast of Adriatic; includes KARST in N. Highest peak (8,714 ft.) is in Albania.

D'Indy, Vincent: see INDY, VINCENT D'.

Dinesen, Isak (ē'säk dē'nŭsŭn), pseud. of Karen, Baroness Blixen, 1885–, Danish author. Notable among her works in English are *Seven Gothic Tales* (1934), *Winter's Tales* (1943), autobiographical *Out of Africa* (1937).

dingo (dĭng'gō), wild dog of Australia, similar to the fox but larger, with short legs and a brown coat marked on the back with black. Hunts its prey (rabbits, sheep, poultry) chiefly at night. Genus *Canis*.

Diniz, Port. **Dinis** (dĭnēzh'), 1261–1325, king of Portugal (1279–1325). His reign was generally peaceful. A patron of literature, founder of Coimbra Univ. (originally at Lisbon), he also increased the royal domain (particularly at the expense of the Templars) and greatly encouraged farming. Nicknamed "the farmer." His queen was St. Elizabeth of Portugal.

dinosaur (dī'nŭsôr), extinct land reptile of the MESOZOIC ERA, ranging in length from 2½ to c.90 ft. Some were herbivorous, others carnivorous. They died out by the end of the Cretaceous period.

Dinosaur National Monument: see NATIONAL PARKS AND MONUMENTS (table).

Dinwiddie, Robert, 1693–1770, colonial governor of Va. (1751–58), b. Scotland. Sent George Washington on unsuccessful mission to forestall French in Ohio valley in 1754. Aided Braddock's campaign.

Dio: see DION.

Diocletian (dīŭklē'shŭn), 245–313, Roman emperor (284–305), b. Salona, Dalmatia, of humble parents. An army commander, he was chosen to succeed after Numerian was murdered, and he killed the suspected murderer, Arrius Aper. Ruled jointly with Carinus, who had been joint emperor with Numerian, until Carinus was killed. Later to defend the empire with responsible officials he made MAXIMIAN joint emperor (286) and CONSTANTIUS I and GALERIUS Caesars (subemperors). This policy succeeded brilliantly:

Britain was restored, the Persians were subdued, and some barbarians driven out. The empire throve. There was, however, severe persecution of the Christians; economic measures turned out badly; and the division of the empire formally instituted by Diocletian led to much warfare after he and Maximian abdicated (305). Diocletian retired to a splendid castle at Salona.

Diodorus Siculus (dīŭdô′rŭs sĭ′kūlŭs), d. after 21 B.C., Sicilian historian. Author of world history ending with Gallic Wars; in Greek, in 40 books, of which I–IV and XI–XX are fully preserved.

Diogenes (dīŏj′ŭnēz), c.412–323 B.C., Greek Cynic philosopher. Lived in Athens, where he stressed belief in the simple life by living in a tub. When Alexander the Great asked what he might do for Diogenes, the philosopher answered, "Only step out of my sunlight." Diogenes is also said to have gone about in daylight carrying a lantern and looking for a "man" (i.e., someone showing proper human virtues).

Diomed (dī′ŏmĕd), **Diomede** (–mēd), or **Diomedes** (dī″ōmē′dēz), in Greek legend. **1** One of the EPIGONI, prominent in the Trojan War. **2** Son of Ares who fed his horses on human flesh. HERCULES killed him.

Diomede Islands (dī′ŭmēd), group of three islands in Bering Strait between Alaska and Siberia. USSR–U.S. boundary and International Date Line pass between two larger islands.

Dion Cassius (Cassius Dio Cocceianus) (dī′ŭn kă′shŭs), c.155–235?, Roman historian, b. Bithynia. He held high imperial office but is known for his history of Rome, written in Greek and now only partly extant. Also Dio Cassius.

Dion Chrysostom (krĭ′sŭstŭm, krĭsō′stŭm) [Gr.,= golden-mouthed], d. after A.D. 112, Greek sophist and rhetorician. Author of 80 extant orations.

Dionne quintuplets (dēŏn′), five daughters (Annette, Emélie, Yvonne, Cécile, and Marie) born to Oliva Dionne and his wife at Callender, Ont., on May 28, 1934. In 1935 the Ontario legislature made them wards of the province. Allan Roy Dafoe was their physician.

Dion of Syracuse (dī′ŭn), 409?–354? B.C., Greek political leader in Sicily. Brother-in-law of Dionysius the Elder, he knew Plato and philosophically favored moderate government. Led a force from Athens to overthrow Dionysius the Younger (357 B.C.) and commanded Sicily until murdered by an Athenian companion.

Dionysia (dīŭnĭ′shĕŭ), in Greek religion, festivals to honor god Dionysus. Resembling the Bacchanalia, they stressed fertility. From them developed the dithyramb, the choral procession, and Greek drama (see COMEDY and TRAGEDY).

Dionysius (dīŭnĭ′shĕŭs), tyrants of Syracuse. **Dionysius the Elder**, c.430–367 B.C., rose as representative of the poor to become tyrant (406 B.C.). He kept the people in obedience through fear of the Carthaginians. Led expeditions against Italian cities and the Carthaginians. Patronized literature and the arts. His son, **Dionysius the Younger**, fl. 368–344 B.C., succeeded him, tried to maintain popularity, but lost it to DION OF SYRACUSE (357 B.C.). After Dion's murder he regained power, but was expelled by Timoleon (344 B.C.).

Dionysius of Halicarnassus (hă″lĭkärnă′sŭs), fl. 1st cent. B.C., Greek rhetorician and historian. Author of *Antiquities of Rome*.

Dionysius the Areopagite, Saint (dīŭnĭ′shĕŭs, ârēŏp′ŭjĭt), 1st cent. Athenian Christian, converted by St. Paul; traditionally first bishop of Athens and a martyr. He is sometimes confused with St. Denis (their names are different forms of the same one). In the Middle Ages some letters and treatises important in scholasticism were attributed to him. Actually they were written (in Greek) in 5th- or 6th-cent. Palestine. Their author is now called Pseudo-Dionysius.

Dionysius the Elder: see DIONYSIUS.

Dionysius the Younger: see DIONYSIUS, tyrants.

Dionysus (dīŭnī′sŭs), in Greek legend, god of fertility and wine, patron of choral song and drama; son of Zeus and Semele. His worship (said to have been imported from Thrace) was full of enthusiasm and emotionalism, as in the DIONYSIA. Pan and Silenus were his companions, and he was surrounded by the BACCHAE. His grave was supposedly at Delphi, which was sacred to him in winter; thus he achieved a sort of parity with Apollo. He was chief deity in ORPHIC MYSTERIES and shared in ELEUSINIAN MYSTERIES. As nature god he was confused with Bacchus.

Diophantus (dīŭfăn′tŭs), 3d cent., Greek algebraist, pioneer in solving a type of indeterminate algebraic equations. This work is now known as Diophantine analysis.

Dioscorides, Pedanius (pĭdā′nĕŭs dīŭskô′rĭdēz), 1st cent. A.D. Greek physician, author of standard work on materia medica.

Dioscuri: see CASTOR AND POLLUX.

dip, in stock raising, antiseptic solution to kill skin parasites. Applied by dipping animals in tank.

diphtheria (dĭfthēr′ĕŭ), communicable disease caused by toxin produced by bacterium and characterized by membranous film in air passages. Incubation period is two to five days. Toxoid used for immunization. Antitoxin given after exposure and to treat disease. SCHICK TEST determines susceptibility. See *ill.,* p. 633.

diplomatic service, body of agents maintained by a government to conduct its relations with foreign nations. First ambassadors acted only on specific missions. In early Middle Ages Venice set up first permanent system of resident ambassadors in foreign caps., and permanent legations became general by end of 18th cent. Congress of Vienna (1815) adopted classification of officers now widely accepted: ambassador, minister plenipotentiary, envoy extraordinary, minister, chargé d'affaires. Diplomats enjoy "diplomatic immunity," their residences rights of EXTERRITORIALITY. One function of diplomats is to observe political, economic, and military trends subject to international restrictions barring espionage. A diplomat is responsible usually to his own foreign minister. His business is carried on with foreign minister of country to which he is accredited in form of memorandums, oral and written notes, and formal notes. Diplomatic language has patterns and gradations which may seem meaningless but which often smooth difficult situations. Diplomatic service is distinguished from CONSULAR SERVICE, though often they are combined, as in U.S. under Rogers Act of 1924. Foreign Service Act of 1946 set up merit system for protection of staff.

Dipoenus (dīpē′nŭs) and **Scyllis** (sĭ′lĭs), c.580 B.C., Greek sculptors, mentioned by Pliny the Elder.

Dirac, Paul Adrien Maurice (dĭräk′), 1902–, English physicist. Shared 1933 Nobel Prize for work in developing Heisenberg's theory of quantum mechanics.

direct current: see ELECTRICITY; GENERATOR.

direction finder, name for various radio, radar, and other electronic devices used to navigate ship, plane, or other craft.

Directoire style (dērĕktwär′), in French interior decoration and costume, the style of the Directory (1795–99); transition between Louis XVI and Empire styles. Departed from ornateness of aristocratic regime and emphasized classic design (esp. Pompeian forms). Furniture was more massive, with painted or waxed wood surfaces. See *ill.,* p. 356. Wallpaper and plain walls replaced tapestries and wainscoting. Women wore tight skirts, low necklines, and high waistlines.

Directory, Fr. *Directoire,* French government from 1795 to 1799. Its executive branch consisted of five directors, chosen by the two legislative chambers. Its history was marked by corruption, coups d'état, inflation, and, in 1799, military disaster. Sieyès and Barras, who were directors in 1799, helped Bonaparte in overthrowing the Directory and establishing the Consulate by the coup d'état of 18 Brumaire.

SMALL CAPITALS = cross references. Pronunciation key on inside end pages. Abbreviations: p. 2.

dirigible balloon: see AIRSHIP.

Dis, Roman name for PLUTO.

Disarmament Conference, 1932–37. In 1926 preparatory commission for general disarmament met under League of Nations auspices at Geneva. First general conference met in Feb., 1932 (including members of League, USSR, and U.S.), and drafted plans for budgetary restrictions of armaments, limitation of armed forces, and permanent committee to advise on execution of treaty. France opposed draft and offered substitute. In resulting deadlock Germany demanded either world disarmament to her level or right to rearm. Germany withdrew from conference and League in Oct., 1933. Sporadic meetings were held until indefinite postponement in April, 1937. UN commission dealing with problem has had little success thus far.

disciple: see APOSTLE.

Disciples of Christ, Protestant religious body in U.S., estab. in early 19th cent. by Thomas and Alexander Campbell in W Pa. With other groups they finally formed the "Disciples" and "Christians." Progressive group is called Disciples of Christ. Stress is on the simple gospel and on Bible alone as basis of faith. See CHRISTIANS; CHURCHES OF CHRIST.

Discobolus (dĭskŏ'bŭlŭs) [Gr.,= discus thrower], statue by Myron. Only copies of it remain.

disease, departure from health resulting from changes in structure or function of tissues. See also COMMUNICABLE DISEASES.

disease carrier, person or animal harboring and capable of distributing to others the causative agent of a disease. Carrier may be immune to, or recovered from the disease. Famous example was cook known as Typhoid Mary. Typhoid fever and diphtheria are spread by human carriers; malaria, by mosquitoes.

disinfectant, agent which destroys organisms causing disease. Contaminated materials are disinfected by burning, boiling, sterilizing by steam under pressure, or by the use of a GERMICIDE.

Disko (dĭ'skŏ), island, area 3,312 sq. mi., off W Greenland. Telluric iron has been found; lignite is mined. Godhavn is on S shore.

Dismal Swamp, SE Va. and NE N.C. Now c.20 mi. long, it was once much larger and almost impenetrable; trees and plants have fallen into it, creating much organic material. Visited by William Byrd (1728) and George Washington (1763; as member of draining commission). Canal (1828) connects Chesapeake Bay and Albemarle Sound. Much subsequent drainage and lumbering has been undertaken. L. Drummond, at center, is c.5 mi. long. Scene of Harriet B. Stowe's novel *Dred*.

Disney, Walt (dĭz'nē), 1901–, producer of animated cartoons. Studied at Acad. of Fine Arts in Chicago. Began making comic films in Hollywood in 1923 and became known through his "Mickey Mouse" series. His *Snow White and the Seven Dwarfs* (1938) was the first full-length animated cartoon.

dispensary: see CLINIC.

dispersion. 1 In chemistry, the dispersal of fine particles of one substance through another. According to size and nature of particles a dispersion is classed as a SOLUTION, COLLOID, SUSPENSION, or emulsion. **2** In physics, the separation of beam of white light by prism into various colors of SPECTRUM because of unequal refraction.

Disraeli, Benjamin, 1st **earl of Beaconsfield** (dĭzrā'lē), 1804–81, British statesman and author of Jewish descent. His novels (e.g., *Coningsby,* 1844, and *Sybil,* 1845) gave him a place in English literature. Elected to Parliament 1837; became leader of Tory protectionists. Succeeded DERBY as prime minister 1867. His REFORM BILL of 1867 enfranchised c.2,000,000 men; greatly benefited CONSERVATIVE PARTY. His second ministry (1874–80) had an aggressive foreign policy—annexation of Fiji Isls. (1874) and of the Transvaal (1877); war against Afghans and Zulus (1878–79). Purchase of controlling share of Suez Canal stock

strengthened Britain in the Mediterranean. After Russo-Turkish War he induced Turkey to cede Cyprus to Great Britain. Through Congress of Berlin he reduced Russia's power in the Balkans. Favorite of Queen Victoria, he had her crowned Empress of India (1876). His twofold policy of democracy and imperialism revitalized the Tory party. His father, **Isaac D'Israeli,** 1761–1848, was an author. His best-known work is *Curiosities of Literature* (2 ser., 1791; 1823).

dissenters: see NONCONFORMISTS.

dissociation, in chemistry, separation of molecules into simpler parts. It occurs at high temperatures (thermal dissociation) and when a substance dissolves (electrolytic dissociation, see ION).

distemper, in veterinary medicine, any of several infectious diseases of animals, especially canine distemper, a serious contagious catarrhal disease of young dogs.

distillation, process for purifying a substance, for separating substances from one another, and for breaking down a substance into fractional parts. In purifying water, for example, the impure water is heated to its boiling point and steam, the vapor thus formed, is led into condenser tubes where it is cooled and condensed to form liquid called the distillate. Impurities with higher boiling point than the water are left in the original container. "Double distilled" and "triple distilled" products have undergone further distillations. Many alcoholic beverages are distilled. In **fractional distillation** a liquid mixture of substances with different boiling points is repeatedly distilled at different temperatures and the parts or fractions obtained from each distillation are drawn off and condensed separately. This process is used in refining petroleum, yielding such fractions as gasoline, benzine, kerosene, fuel and lubricating oils, paraffin. **Destructive distillation** involves heating, out of free contact with air, materials such as wood, coal, or oil shale, and collecting separately the portions driven off. Wood thus yields acetic acid, methyl or wood alcohol, charcoal, and hydrocarbons. Coal yields coal gas, coal tar, coke, and ammonia. In **steam distillation,** steam is introduced at high temperatures to carry off volatile matter.

Distinguished Service Cross, Distinguished Service Medal, and **Distinguished Service Order:** see DECORATIONS, CIVIL AND MILITARY.

District of Columbia (pop. 802,178), E U.S., Federal district (c.70 sq. mi.) on E bank of Potomac R., coextensive with city of WASHINGTON, cap. of U.S. Estab. by congressional acts of 1790, 1791. Md. and Va. granted land on each side of river, including towns of Alexandria and Georgetown. Alexandria was returned to Va. 1846. Territorial government estab. 1871, present system 1878. Governed by Congress through executive board of presidential appointees. Inhabitants have no voice in local government, no representation in Congress, no vote for President.

dithyramb (dĭ'thĭrăm), in anc. Greece, choral lyric, a hymn to the god Dionysus. The TRAGEDY seems to have been developed from it.

Ditmars, Raymond L(ee) (dĭt'märz), 1876–1942, American naturalist and author, authority on snakes.

Diu (dē'ōō), district (14 sq. mi.; pop. 19,731), of Portuguese India; consists mainly of Diu isl. off S tip of Kathiawar peninsula, W India. Diu town was acquired 1535 by Portugal.

Dives (dī'vēz), rich man of parable. Luke 16.19–31.

dividend, that part of a corporation's net earnings which is distributed to its stockholders, usually at regular intervals. In U.S. dividends may be paid in bonds, stocks, cash, or scrip. Businesses being terminated may issue liquidation dividends.

Divine, Father, c.1882–, American Negro leader of Peace Mission movement, begun in Harlem section of N. Y. city. Born in Ga. as George Baker, he moved (c.1915) to North as Major M. J. Divine, later Father Divine. Many accept him as personification of God. Movement is nonsectarian and interracial.

Divine Comedy, Italian epic poem in *terza rima* by DANTE. Dante called it *Commedia* because it ended happily; *Divina* was added in the 16th cent. The narrator is led by Vergil through Hell and Purgatory, by Beatrice through Paradise.

divine right, doctrine that sovereigns derive their right to rule by birth alone, inheriting it from their ancestors, according to the law of God and of nature. A ruler claiming divine right rejects responsibility to his subjects. The theory, much argued in 17th-cent. England, ended there with the Revolution of 1688.

diving. Since the early days of his history and in all parts of the world man has developed the skill of plunging into water for pleasure and for profit (e.g., diving for pearls, coral, sponges). Yet deep-water diving was not possible until the early 19th cent. when Augustus Siebe devised diving dress for prolonged stays under water. The "open-type" dress was essentially a helmet with a pipe to supply air and a waterproof jacket. This type required that the diver stay upright, and Siebe therefore designed a less dangerous "closed-type" suit, which covered the diver entirely except for his hands. Later deep-water suits have merely been improvements on this. Waterproofed canvas, rubber, metal, and plastics are usual materials for making them. They have made possible much exploration of the ocean depths as well as recovery of valuable articles in sunken ships. Types of diving bells have also been used for investigating the underwater world—two notable examples being the bathysphere, a windowed steel globe invented by Otis Barton and used by him and William Beebe (who went to a depth of 3,028 ft. off Bermuda in 1934), and the somewhat similar benthoscope, which Barton invented and took to a depth of 4,500 ft. (off Calif., 1949). Shallow-water diving was developed as a sport late in the 19th cent. and fancy diving contests are a usual part of all swimming meets, the divers being rated for precision, grace, and skill. The use of diving helmets (usually with breastplates) became popular for sport, including spear fishing, after the 1930s. Invention of the aqualung allows diving to 100 ft. or more without diving suit.

division, a basic arithmetical operation; the symbol is ÷ or /. The inverse of multiplication, it is the process of finding a number by which to multiply the divisor to get a product equal (with remainder added) to the dividend. Quotient results from dividing one number by another; dividend is number divided; divisor is number by which dividend is divided; remainder is units left over. For division other than of whole numbers, see FRACTION.

divorce, dissolution of a marriage by court judgment. Partial dissolution (divorce "from bed and board") is effected by judicial SEPARATION. Divorce is distinct from nullity of marriage, which is a decree that the marriage was originally illegal. In U.S., divorce powers belong to the individual states, and policies are varied; all attempts to reach some agreement about different laws has failed. Generally in all courts chief grounds are adultery, DESERTION, and cruelty. After decree is final both parties may remarry, and the wife is entitled to ALIMONY at the discretion of the court.

Dix, Dorothea Lynde, 1802–87, American reformer, pioneer in movement for more humane treatment of the insane.

Dix, Fort, U.S. army training center, SE of Trenton, N.J. Built in World War I, it was the largest army training center in U.S. in World War II.

Dixie, song composed by Daniel Emmett in 1859, the patriotic song of the Confederacy during Civil War. Dixie now regarded as those states lying below Mason-Dixon line; originally "Dixie's Land" referred to a Manhattan farm owned by Johaan Dixie.

Dixon, Thomas, 1864–1946, American novelist, a Baptist clergyman. His militantly Southern novel *The Clansman* (1905) was the basis for the film *The Birth of a Nation* (1915).

Dixon, city (pop. 11,523), N Ill., on Rock R. and SW of Rockford, in agr. area; founded 1830. Wire and dairy products. Statue of Lincoln as captain in Black Hawk War is on Dixon Blockhouse site.

Dixville Notch, 2-mi. pass in White Mts., N N.H.

Diyarbakir (dēyärbĕkĕr'), city (pop. 45,495), E central Turkey, on the Tigris. Commercial center. Occupies site of ancient Amida. Also spelled Diarbekr.

Djibouti or **Jibuti** (jĭboō'tē), town (pop. c.22,000), cap. of French Somaliland, on inlet of Gulf of Aden. Major port on shipping lanes to Suez Canal and chief outlet for Ethiopian exports.

Djokjakarta, Indonesia: see JOGJAKARTA.

Dmitri (dùmē'trē) or **Demetrius,** d. 1591, son of Ivan IV of Russia. He was murdered, probably by order of Boris GODUNOV. In 1604 an impostor, pretending that he was Dmitri, invaded Russia with Polish aid and claimed the throne from Boris. Crowned tsar in 1605, he married Marina, a Polish noblewoman. In 1606 he was killed in an insurrection. Another false Dmitri appeared in 1607, was recognized by Marina as her husband, received Polish aid, and successfully invaded Russia. He was killed (1610), as were two later impostors who claimed to be Dmitri's son. Michael Romanov's election (1613) ended the confusion, known as the Time of Troubles.

Dneprodzerdzhinsk (dùnyĕ"prùdzĭrzhĕnsk'), city (pop. 147,829), S central Ukraine, on the Dnieper, near Dnepropetrovsk. Steel mills, chemical plants.

Dneproges (dùnyĕprügĕs'), suburb of Zaporozhe, Ukraine, on the Dnieper, site of largest dam and hydroelectric power station in Europe (capacity over 500,000 kw per hour). Its construction (1927–32) raised level of Dnieper 123 ft., made river navigable. H. L. Cooper was chief among American consultant engineers. Destroyed in World War II; rebuilt 1947. Originally named Dneprostroi.

Dnepropetrovsk (dùnyĕ"prüpĕtrôfsk'), city (pop. 500,-662), central Ukraine, on the Dnieper bend. River port, rail center, heavy industries. Growth began late 19th cent. with exploitation of Donets Basin coal, Krivoi Rog iron, and Nikopol manganese. Receives power from Dneproges. Suffered in World War II, when fighting raged in area. Named Ekaterinoslav or Yekaterinoslav until 1926.

Dneprostroi, Ukraine: see DNEPROGES.

Dnieper (nē'pùr), Rus. *Dnepr,* river, 1,420 mi. long, Belorussia and Ukraine. Anc. name is Borysthenes. Rises in Valdai Hills, flows S past Smolensk, Kiev, Dnepropetrovsk, Zaporozhe (site of DNEPROGES dam), Kherson into Black Sea, describing vast bend between Kremenchung and Nikopol. Navigable in nearly entire length since construction of Dneproges; linked by canals with Bug, Niemen, Western Dvina.

Dniester (nē'stùr), Rus. *Dnestr,* river, 850 mi. long, SW European USSR. Rises in Carpathians; flows generally SE, partly along border between Ukraine and Moldavian SSR; joins Black Sea SW of Odessa. Navigable below Mogilev-Podolski. Formed Rumanian-USSR border 1918–40.

Doab (dō'äb), in India, a tract of land between two rivers. The Doab, unqualified by any names, designates tract between Ganges and Jumna rivers.

Doane, George Washington, 1799–1859, Episcopal bishop of N.J. (1832–59). Author of a number of hymns, including *Softly Now the Light of Day.*

Doane College, at Crete, Nebr.; coed.; 1872.

Dobbs Ferry, residential village (pop. 6,268), SE N.Y., on the Hudson above Yonkers. Masters School for girls is here.

Döbereiner, Johann Wolfgang (yō'hän vŏlf'gäng dü'-bùrīnùr), 1780–1849, German chemist. He discovered similar triads of elements, a step in development of PERIODIC LAW.

Doberman pinscher, sleek, short-haired dog developed originally in Germany. The coat is predominantly black, brown, or blue marked with rust; males stand 24–27 in. at the shoulder, females 23–25 in. The body is well knit and muscular and the dog has a proud bearing. It needs considerable exercise.

Döblin, Alfred (dûblēn'), 1878–, German novelist, best known for *Berlin Alexanderplatz* (1929; Eng. tr., 1931), which shows the influence of James Joyce.

Dobrich, Bulgaria: see TOLBUKHIN.

Dobruja (dō'brōōjù), region, SE Rumania and NE Bulgaria. Constanta is the chief city of the Rumanian section (5,998 sq. mi.; pop. 503,217); Tolbukhin, of the Bulgarian section (2,971 sq. mi.; pop. 318,772). Largely agr.; forests inland. Region was part of Roman Moesia, later of Byzantine Empire and of medieval Bulgaria. Under Ottoman rule from 15th cent. to 1878, when Congress of Berlin awarded most of it to Rumania. Bulgaria forced to cede S Dobruja to Rumania in 1913, recovered it in 1940.

Dobson, (Henry) Austin, 1840–1921, English author of light verse in French forms (rondeau, villanelle, ballads) and of essays on 18th-cent. literature.

Docetism (dōsē'tĭzùm), early Christian heretical movement, holding that Christ was not a man, but a mere phantasm who only seemed to live and to suffer. Gnostics held a similar belief.

dock, weedy plant of genus *Rumex*, widely distributed. It has small flowers and winged fruits. Common species are large curled dock, spinach dock, and canaigre (a food of Indians of SW U.S.). Species with arrowhead-shaped foliage are called sorrel, e.g., sheep sorrel of pastures.

documentary film: see MOVING PICTURES.

Dodd, William E(dward), 1869–1940, American historian and diplomat, long at the Univ. of Chicago. He was ambassador to Germany (1933–37), and his diary (pub. 1941) records early days of Nazism there. He was an authority on the history of the South.

dodder, leafless parasitic plant of genus *Cuscuta*, with small flowers. Often a pest in fields of alfalfa, clover, and flax.

Dodds, Harold Willis, 1889–, American educator. Authority on economics and politics in Latin America, he has had international posts. A professor of politics at Princeton after 1927, he became president in 1933.

Dodecanese (dōdĕ"kùnēs', –nēz, dō"dĕ–), island group (1,044 sq. mi.; pop. 120,000), Greece, in the SE Aegean, between Asia Minor and Crete; chief city Rhodes. Despite its name [12 islands], it consists of c.20 islands and islets, notably RHODES, Karpathos, Kalymnos, Patmos, Astypalaia, Kasos, Telos, Syme, Leros, Nisyros, Chalke, Kastellorizo. Mostly mountainous. Agr., livestock raising, sponge fishing. With fall of Rhodes to Suleiman I (1522), Dodecanese came under Turkish rule. Islands were occupied by Italy 1912; formally ceded to Italy 1922; awarded to Greece 1947.

Dodge, Grenville Mellen, 1831–1916, Union general in Civil War and railroad builder. Greatest achievement was as chief engineer (from 1866) in building of Union Pacific RR.

Dodge, Henry, 1782–1867, American frontiersman, governor of Territory of Wisconsin (1836–41, 1845–48), U.S. Senator (1848–57).

Dodge, Mary Mapes, 1831–1905, American editor of *St. Nicholas* magazine, author of juvenile classic, *Hans Brinker; or, The Silver Skates* (1865).

Dodge City, city (pop. 11,262), SW Kansas, on Arkansas R. and on old Santa Fe Trail; laid out 1872 near Fort Dodge (1864). Called the "cowboy capital" it flourished as cattle town and, after 1872, as railhead. Now a distributing center for wheat and livestock area. City hall is on site of Boot Hill, burial ground of early cowboys.

Dodgson, Charles Lutwidge: see CARROLL, LEWIS.

dodo, flightless forest-dwelling bird of Mauritius, extinct since late 17th cent. Although related to pigeon, it was larger than the turkey.

Dodona (dōdō'nù), in Greek religion, oldest oracle, in inland Epirus, sacred to Zeus and Dione.

Dodsley, Robert, 1703–64, English publisher, compiler of a well-known collection of plays (12 vols., 1744)

and projector (with Burke) of *Annual Register* (1758).

Doeg (dō'ĕg), Edomite who massacred priests at Nob at Saul's command. 1 Sam. 21.1–9; 22.6–23.

Doenitz, Karl (dû'nĭts), 1891–, German admiral. Commanded submarine operations in World War II; chief naval commander from 1943. Named by Hitler as his successor, he ordered unconditional surrender of Germany to Allies (May 7, 1945). Sentenced to imprisonment for 10 years at Nuremberg war crimes trial (1946).

dog, domesticated mammal. Evidence that dogs were domesticated in the late Paleolithic period shows them to be the first domestic animals. A theory that only certain kinds of dogs were descended from wolves and that others were descended from jackals, coyotes, and foxes has been largely disproved by comparative studies of the teeth of dogs and those of the other animals. The generally accepted conclusion is that dogs of both hemispheres developed originally in Asia from the wolf. By selective breeding of dogs, man has perpetuated and intensified certain characteristics and eliminated others. For some of the better-known types see CHOW; HOUND; HUNTING DOGS; POODLE; SHEEP DOGS; SPANIELS; TERRIERS; TOY DOGS. See also SEEING-EYE DOGS.

dogfish, name for small sharks of several families of both hemispheres, found chiefly in temperate but also in tropical waters. Commonest is the spiny dogfish (*Squalus acanthias*), of the family Squalidae. It is 3–4 ft. long. In front of each dorsal fin is a stout spine, supplied with poison. It destroys food fish and nets.

Dogger Bank (dô'gùr, dō'–), extensive sand bank, central North Sea, between England and Denmark, covered by shallow water. It has fisheries.

dogtooth violet, adder's tongue, or **trout lily,** wild flower of genus *Erythronium*, with pendent, lilylike spring blossoms and mottled foliage.

dogwood or **cornel,** shrub or tree of genus *Cornus,* chiefly of N Hemisphere. Best known, flowering dogwood (*Cornus florida*), has white or pink flowers (botanically they are bracts), in spring. Its hard wood is used for shuttles, door handles. See also BUNCHBERRY.

dogy or **dogie** (both: dō'gē), cowboys' name for orphan or scrubby calf, sometimes for all cattle.

Dohnanyi, Ernst von (dō'nänyē), 1877–, Hungarian composer, pianist, and conductor. His compositions include four operas, chamber music, concertos, piano pieces, orchestral suites, and the witty *Variations on a Nursery Tune* for piano and orchestra.

Doisy, Edward Adelbert, 1893–, American biochemist. Shared 1943 Nobel Prize in Physiology and Medicine for discovery of the chemical nature of vitamin K.

Dolci, Carlo or **Carlino** (kär'lō, kärlē'nō dōl'chē), 1616–86, Florentine painter. Excelled in sorrowful heads of Christ and the Mater Dolorosa.

doldrums (dōl'drùmz) or **equatorial belt of calms,** area just N of equator, circling earth between two trade-wind belts. Characterized by low pressure, light variable winds, squalls, thunderstorms.

Dole, Sanford Ballard, 1844–1926, American statesman of Hawaiian Isls., b. Honolulu. Became first president of republic of Hawaii 1894. Was first governor of Territory of Hawaii 1900–1903.

Dôle (dōl), town (pop. 16,340), Jura dept., E France, on Doubs R. Stronghold and cap. of Franche-Comté until conquest (1674) by Louis XIV, who transferred the parlement and university (founded c.1422) to Besançon. Birthplace of Pasteur.

Dolet, Étienne (ātyěn' dôlā'), 1509–46, French scholar and printer. Wrote treatises on grammar and history and a famous commentary on the Latin language. Printed these and a translation of the Bible. He was finally accused of heresy, imprisoned, and executed.

doll. Small figures were early used as cult objects. In Christian era the Nativity was represented by crèche dolls. From 15th cent. styles were spread by exchange of fashion dolls. Play dolls probably used by children in ancient Egypt, Greece, and Rome; commonly used in Europe by 17th cent. Made of many materials.

Dollfuss, Engelbert (ĕng'ŭlbĕrt dôl'fŏŏs), 1892–1934, chancellor of Austria (1932–34). A Christian Socialist, he opposed both National Socialists and Social Democrats, was driven into alliance with native fascists of E. R. von STARHEMBERG. After ruthlessly suppressing a Socialist rising, he made Austria a one-party, corporative state, under constitution drafted by SCHUSCHNIGG (1934). He was assassinated by Austrian Nazis.

Döllinger, Johann Joseph Ignaz von (yō'hän yō'zĕf ĭg'näts fŭn dû'lĭng-ùr), 1799–1890, German theologian, church historian, leader of OLD CATHOLICS. Ordained (1822) as a Roman Catholic priest, he was long associated with the Univ. of Munich and a leading member (1845–52) of Catholic party in Frankfurt Parliament. Spurned dogma of papal infallibility pronounced by Vatican Council (1870) and was excommunicated in 1871. Although in sympathy with Old Catholics, he never intended a separate church to emerge from the movement and he never was formally a member of the Old Catholic Church.

dolmen (dŏl'mĕn, dōl–), rough stone structure, consisting usually of two uprights and a capstone. Characteristic megalithic monument, probably erected as substitute for cave burial.

dolomite (dŏ'lŭmĭt). **1** A mineral, calcium magnesium carbonate. **2** A carbonate rock composed chiefly of dolomite, similar to limestone but harder.

Dolomites (dŏ'lŭmīts), Alpine group, N Italy, famed for striking outline and vivid colors of its DOLOMITE rocks. Marmolada (10,964 ft.) is highest peak. Many resorts, e.g., Cortina d'Ampezzo.

dolphin. 1 Gregarious mammal, a toothed whale found in most oceans, sometimes in rivers. Its length is 4–30 ft., usually 5–14 ft. Pointed muzzle distinguishes dolphin from true porpoise. Common Atlantic and Mediterranean dolphin has bearlike jaws; bottle-nosed dolphin inhabits all but polar seas; killer whale or grampus (*Orcinus* or *Orca*) has a large, black and white mottled body, and it attacks seals, porpoises, fish, sea birds, and, in packs, large whales. River dolphins are found in Asia and South America. **2** Name for the coryphene, a small swift, iridescent, spiny-finned fish of warm seas.

Dolton, residential village (pop. 5,558), NE Ill., S suburb of Chicago, in truck-farm area.

Dom (dōm), peak, 14,923 ft. high, Valais canton, S Switzerland; highest in Mischabelhörner group.

Domagk, Gerhard (gär'härt dō'mäk), 1895–, German chemist and pathologist. Because of Nazi decree he declined 1939 Nobel Prize in Physiology and Medicine awarded for discovery of use of prontosil, forerunner of SULFA DRUGS.

Domenichino (dōmānēkē'nō) or **Domenico Zampieri** (dōmä'nēkō tsämpyä'rē), 1581–1641, Italian painter of the Carracci school.

Domenico Veneziano (dōmä'nēkō vānätsēä'nō), c.1400–1461, Florentine painter who introduced the technique of finishing tempera works with an oil glaze.

Domesday Book (dōmz'dä, dōomz'dä), record of general survey of England made at order of William I, 1086. It ascertained economic resources of most of the country for purposes of more accurate taxation. Unsurpassed in medieval history for speed and thoroughness, it is invaluable historical source.

domestication, of plants and animals. All major plant crops and domestic animals (except the dog, tamed earlier) were brought into man's service during Neolithic period. Archaeological evidence has fixed points of origin of many crops. No new animals are known to have been domesticated during recorded history, although BREEDING has produced improved types.

domicile, one's legal residence, the permanent home to which one has the intention of returning after a temporary absence. Question of domicile is especially important in tax laws and in legal matters concerning domestic relations.

Dominic, Saint (dŏ'mŭnĭk), 1170?–1221, Castilian churchman, named Dominic Guzmán, founder of the Dominicans. He and his bishop (of Osuna) were sent to preach to the Albigenses in S France, and did so with some success. In 1216 he was given a house at Toulouse for his growing band of preachers, and Pope Honorius III allowed him to form them into an order devoted to study and preaching. Tradition says that the first rosary was given to him by Our Lady in a vision. Feast: Aug. 4.

Dominica (dōmĭnē'kù), island (304 sq. mi.; pop. 47,-624), British West Indies. Discovered by Columbus (1493), it changed hands frequently. Detached from Leeward Isls., it became separate colony in 1940. People, largely Negro, speak a French patois.

Dominican Republic (dùmĭ'nĭkùn), republic (19,129 sq. mi.; pop. 2,121,083), West Indies, occupying the E two thirds of Hispaniola; cap. TRUJILLO. The whole island was first settled as the Spanish colony of SANTO DOMINGO, but later the W part became a French colony (present HAITI). After revolution had broken out in Haiti, Spain ceded all to France (1795), but triumphant Haitians conquered the W section (1801). The Spanish-speaking Dominicans opposed this union and there were numerous changes of domination—French, independent, Spanish, Haitian—before the Dominican Republic was estab. 1844. Even later one president planned reunion with Spain and another negotiated a treaty of annexation to the U.S., but both schemes fell through. The country had political and economic difficulties. Bankruptcy in 1905 brought a U.S. customs receivership (lasting to 1941), and U.S. marines occupied the country (1916–34). Rafael TRUJILLO MOLINA came to power in 1930 and thereafter tried to bring about material advancement, though his rule was widely criticized elsewhere as dictatorial. Sugar is the chief export. Others are cacao and coffee.

Dominicans (dùmĭ'nĭkùnz), Roman Catholic religious order, founded by St. Dominic 1216. More officially the order of Preachers (O.P.). Beginning as a band of preachers in S France, the order spread very rapidly and it is today one of the most important in the Church. Members (friars) are admitted not to specific houses but to the order as a whole. The heads of houses and of provinces are elected for set terms. Dominicans, who wear a white habit with a black mantle (worn while preaching), were formerly called Black Friars. Devoted to study, preaching and teaching, the order has supplied many eminent theologians, notably St. Thomas Aquinas. The Dominicans were prominent in the Inquisition. In the 19th cent. in France and England they forwarded social reform. The order came to the U.S. soon after 1800 (first U.S. province 1805). There is an order of contemplative Dominican nuns and a large third order (including many nuns devoted to teaching and good works).

dominion, territory controlled by a particular government. Commonly refers today to one of autonomous divisions of BRITISH EMPIRE.

Dominion Day, celebrated in Canada, July 1, anniversary of confederation of the provinces (1867).

dominoes, game played with pieces (most often 28) called dominoes—oblong pieces of wood, bone, or ivory, with one face blank, other marked with dots. Game introduced in Europe via Italy in 18th cent.

Domitian (dōmĭ'shùn), A.D. 51–A.D. 96, Roman emperor (A.D. 81–A.D. 96); son of Vespasian and successor of his brother Titus. Obsessed with the idea of law and order, he became a despot. Plots against him ended when his wife had him murdered. Nerva succeeded.

Domrémy-la-Pucelle (dōrämē-lä–püsĕl'), village, Vosges dept., E France, in Lorraine. Birthplace of Joan of Arc. Her house still stands, as do church and font where she was baptized.

Don, river of Yorkshire, England, 70 mi. long.

Don, river, 1,222 mi. long, S European RSFSR, rising SE of Tula, flowing SE, then SW, into Sea of Azov. Its eastward bend comes to within 40 mi. of the Volga at Stalingrad (Volga-Don canal here completed 1952). Navigable from Voronezh, accessible to seagoing vessels as far as Rostov, the Don is an important artery for grain, coal, lumber shipments. Chief tributary, the Donets, links it with industrial Donets Basin. The ancient Tanais, the Don has been a trading channel since Scythian times. In 16th cent. COSSACKS founded virtually independent republic of the **Don Cossacks** along its lower course. Stenka RAZIN was their most famous ataman. Gave nominal allegiance to tsar in 1614 but retained self-government until collapse of PUGACHEV rebellion (1775). Famed for their songs and choirs.

Don, river of Aberdeenshire, Scotland; 82 mi. long. Empties into North Sea near Aberdeen.

Donaghadee (dŏn″ŭkhŭdē′), urban district (pop. 3,398), Co. Down, N Ireland. Irish port nearest to Great Britain; connected by cable with Scotland.

Donatello (Donato di Niccolò di Betto Bardi) (dŏnŭtĕ′lō), c.1386–1466, Florentine painter of the early Renaissance. In *St. George* he abandoned earlier Gothic style for realism, climaxed in later works such as *David* and *St. John Baptist* (all: Bargello). The equestrian *Gattamalata*, made 1453 for Padua, was first of its kind since antiquity.

Donati, Giovanni Battista (jōvän′nē bät-tē′stä dōnä′tē), 1826–73, Italian astronomer. He pioneered in spectral analysis of comets and discovered six comets including Donati's comet (June 2, 1858).

Donatism (dō′nŭtĭzŭm), heretical movement of the 4th cent. in N Africa, led by Donatus of Casa Nigra and the later Donatus the Great. In the Roman persecutions they took the position that those who lapsed from the faith could not be readmitted fully to the Church. Bishops and priests who had given up sacred books to the government were, they held, traitors and had lost their sacramental powers. Opposed, they seceded from the Church and had a formidable church of their own, but they were condemned by the Synod of Arles (314). Extreme Donatists in Numidia terrorized the orthodox, but the teaching of St. Augustine destroyed the Donatist theology, and by 450 it had lost power in N Africa.

Donatus, fl. 333, Roman grammarian; teacher of St. Jerome. His *Ars grammatica* [elements of grammar] was the standard elementary Latin grammar throughout the Middle Ages.

Donauwörth (dō′nouvûrt″), town (pop. 7,298), Swabia, W Bavaria, on the Danube. Noted for medieval architecture. In Thirty Years War city fell to Swedes 1632, to imperials 1634.

Donbas, USSR: see DONETS BASIN.

Doncaster (dŏng′kŭstŭr), county borough (pop. 81,896), West Riding of Yorkshire, England, on the Don. Has coal mines, railroad shops, and steel mills. Near-by racecourse long estab.

Don Cossacks: see DON, river.

Donders, Franciscus Cornelius (fränsĭ′skŭs kôrnā′lĭŭs dôn′dŭrs), 1818–89, Dutch ophthalmologist, pioneer in study of the eye and its disorders. Wrote treatise on accommodation and refraction (1864).

Donegal (dŏ′nĭgôl), maritime county (1,865 sq. mi.; pop. 136,317), Ulster prov., Ireland; co. town Lifford. Coastline irregular and indented; interior rugged and hilly (Mt. Errigal 2,466 ft.). Mainly agr. and pastoral (no large towns), but boggy soil makes farming hard. Deep-sea fishing important. Was ancient kingdom of Tyrconnell.

Donegan, Horace William Baden, 1902–, American Episcopal bishop, b. England; made Bishop of N.Y. in 1950.

Donelson, Andrew Jackson (dŏ′nŭlsŭn), 1799–1871, American diplomat, nephew of and private secretary to Andrew Jackson. Successfully negotiated annexation of Texas.

Donelson, Fort, Confederate fortification on Cumber-

land R. at Dover, Tenn., commanding river approach to Nashville. Captured Feb. 16, 1862, by U. S. Grant, opening way for Union advance on Nashville.

Donets (dŭnyĕts′), river, 655 mi. long, S European RSFSR and S Ukraine, flowing generally SE into lower Don R. Navigable 140 mi. The **Donets Basin**, abbreviated as **Donbas**, SW of the river, is one of main coal-producing and industrial areas of Russia and Ukraine. Stalino is largest of many industrial cities producing steel, heavy machinery, chemicals. Scene of heavy fighting in World War II.

Doniphan, Alexander William (dŏ′nĭfŭn), 1808–87, American soldier. Led 3,600-mi. march into Mexico during Mexican War, taking Chihuahua and Saltillo.

Donizetti, Gaetano (gäätä′nō dōnēdzĕt′tē), 1797–1848, Italian composer. His melodic operas range from serious to pure *opera buffa*. Best known are: *Lucia di Lammermoor* (1835); *La Fille du regiment* (1840); *L'elisir d'amore* (1832) and *Don Pasquale* (1843).

Don Juan (dŏn jōō′ŭn, Span. dōn hwän′), legendary hero of many literary works, supposedly based on life of Don Juan Tenorio of Seville. Don Juan seduces girl, then kills her father. He invites statue of the father to a feast; it comes, seizes the libertine, and drags him to hell. Subject of Mozart's opera *Don Giovanni*; also used by Molière, Byron, Balzac, Robert Browning, and Shaw.

donkey: see ASS.

Donna, city (pop. 7,171), S Texas, WNW of Brownsville, in irrigated lower Rio Grande valley. Has canneries and dehydrating plants.

Donne, John (dŭn), 1572–1631, English poet, a clergyman; generally considered the greatest of the metaphysical poets. Reared a Roman Catholic, he later became an Anglican divine. Secretary to Sir Thomas Egerton, lord keeper of the great seal, he earned a reputation for his clever, often sensual, lyrics and for essays and verse satires, but his court career was ruined by discovery of his secret marriage to Anne More, Egerton's niece by marriage. Later he earned a reputation as a writer of exalted religious poetry as in *An Anatomy of the World* (1611) and *Of the Progresse of the Soul* (1612)—both written as elegies for the daughter of a patron and called the First and the Second Anniversary—took orders (1615), and became a preacher well-known for eloquence. His poetry is remarkable not only for its deep religious feeling (notably solemn in the *Holy Sonnets*) but for virtuosity, with long-drawn, complicated figures called "conceits," exquisite melody and rhyme, and sharp wit to underline his philosophical utterances. His prose works also have distinction as in *Biathanatos* (1644; a qualified apology for suicide), the *Pseudo-Martyr* (1610), and his sermons.

Donnelly, Ignatius, 1831–1901, American author and political reformer. His *Atlantis: the Antediluvian World* (1882; rev. ed., 1949) argued that ATLANTIS was seat of world's original civilization. He championed underdog; helped found Populist party.

Donner Party (dŏ′nŭr), group of emigrants to Calif. who in winter of 1846-47 met with tragedy. Prominent in group were two families named Donner. In Oct. party was trapped by snow in passes at what is now Donner L. in the Sierra Nevada; survivors were driven to cannibalism before rescue. Only about half of party reached Calif. **Donner Lake** is today a popular mountain resort, near Truckee. Near-by **Donner Pass** has U.S. weather observatory.

Donnybrook, suburb of Dublin, Ireland; site of famous fair suppressed 1855 because of disorderliness.

Donora, borough (pop. 12,186), SW Pa., on Monongahela R. and S of Pittsburgh. Mfg. of wire, steel, and zinc products.

Don Quixote (de la Mancha) (dŏn′ kēhō′tä dä lä män′chä, Eng. dŏn kwĭk′sŭt), romance satirizing chivalry, masterpiece of Miguel de CERVANTES SAAVEDRA and one of the great works of world literature (first part pub. 1605, and, after a spurious continuation by Alonso Fernández de Avellaneda, second part pub. 1615). Don Quixote, a country gentleman whose mind is addled by chivalric romances, undertakes absurd adventures, riding his nag Rosinante and aided by a squire, the shrewd and realistic peasant Sancho Panza. His lady is a country girl whom he calls Dulcinea del Toboso. The tone is not sharp but compassionate; humor, pathos, and philosophy are blended.

Dooley, Mr.: see DUNNE, FINLEY PETER.

Doolittle, Hilda, pseud. **H. D.,** 1886–, American poet, abroad after 1911, one of the IMAGISTS.

Doomsday Book: see DOMESDAY BOOK.

Doon (dōōn), river of Ayrshire, Scotland. Robert Burns sang of its beauties.

Door Peninsula, NE Wis., between Green Bay and L. Michigan. Crossed by waterway at Sturgeon Bay. Visited 17th cent. by French. Has cherry growing.

Doppler, Christian Johann (krĭs'tyän yō'hän dô'plùr), 1803–53, Austrian physicist and mathematician. **Doppler's principle:** as distance between source of sound or light and observer becomes less or greater, frequency of waves received increases or decreases respectively. Effect called **Doppler effect.** Examples: rise in pitch of sound with decreased distance between source and observer; in light, this causes shift of color toward violet end of spectrum.

Dorcas or **Tabitha,** Christian woman raised from dead by St. Peter. She sewed for the poor. Acts 9.36–43.

Dorchester, Guy Carleton, 1st **Baron:** see CARLETON, GUY.

Dorchester, municipal borough (pop. 11,623), county town of Dorsetshire, England, on Frome R. Birthplace of Thomas Hardy, it is Casterbridge of his novels. Has Roman remains.

Dorchester, district (since 1870) of Boston, Mass. Estab. 1630, it was important in colonial history.

Dordogne (dôrdô'nyù), department (3,561 sq. mi.; pop. 387,643), SW France, in Périgord; cap. Périgeux. It is crossed by the **Dordogne** river, 305 mi. long, rising in Auvergne mts. and joining the Garonne N of Bordeaux to form the Gironde.

Dordrecht (dôr'drĕkht) or **Dort** (dôrt), municipality (pop. 68,217) and town, South Holland prov., SW Netherlands, on Lower Merwede R. Rail junction, river port; mfg. of machinery and chemicals. Chartered 1220, it was the scene of William the Silent's proclamation as stadholder (1572) and of the Synod of Dort 1618–19; see REMONSTRANTS). Has 14th-cent. Gothic church (Groote Kerk).

Doré, (Paul) Gustave (pōl' güstäv' dôrā'), 1833?–1883, French illustrator and engraver. His illustrations for *Don Quixote, Paradise Lost, Divine Comedy,* and other classics are famous.

Dore, Mont, France: see MONT-DORE.

Doria, Andrea (ändrā'ä dō'rēä), 1468–1560, Genoese admiral and statesman. Fought in French service in ITALIAN WARS until 1528, when he suddenly went over to Emperor Charles V. Helped Charles capture Tunis (1535) but failed at Algiers (1541). Virtual dictator of Genoa, yet preserved republican institutions.

Dorians, members of one of the traditional branches of the Greek peoples, supposedly the last comers (just before 1,000 B.C.). Sparta and Crete were Dorian centers. The Dorian dialect was considered harsh by Athenians but gave rise to the choral lyric. Doric style is one of great simplicity.

Doric order, the earliest of Greek architectural orders. Appeared in definite form in 7th cent. B.C., and perfected in 5th cent. B.C., especially in the PARTHENON. The Greek Doric column has no base, a massive, fluted shaft, and a simple capital. The Tuscan order, estab. in 16th-cent. Italy, is a simplified form of Doric. See *ill.,* p. 47.

Dormont, borough (pop. 13,405), SW Pa., SW residential suburb of Pittsburgh; settled c.1790.

dormouse, small, squirrellike nocturnal rodent of the Old World. Lives in bushes and trees, feeding on nuts and acorns and hibernating in winter. The family includes a number of genera, e.g., *Glis, Muscardinus, Dryomys, Eliomys,* and *Glirulus.*

Dorpat, Estonia: see TARTU.

Dorr, Thomas Wilson, 1805–54, leader of Dorr's Rebellion (1842) in R.I. Urging universal manhood suffrage, Dorr's party estab. its own government, resorted to arms. New state constitution of 1843, liberalizing voting requirements, was result.

Dorset, Charles Sackville, 6th **earl of:** see SACKVILLE, CHARLES.

Dorset, Thomas Sackville, 1st **earl of:** see SACKVILLE, THOMAS.

Dorset, town (pop. 1,150), SW Vt., N of Manchester. Artists' and writers' resort. First commercial marble quarry in U.S. opened here 1785. Conventions that led to Vt. independence held here 1775 and 1776.

Dorsetshire or **Dorset,** maritime county (973 sq. mi.; pop. 291,157), S England; co. town Dorchester. Rolling country crossed by chalk ranges, it has fine harbor at Poole and agr. in fertile valleys. Sheep raising and dairy farming chief occupations. Marble quarried. Pre-Roman remains include large earthwork, Maiden Castle. Thomas Hardy wrote of region in "Wessex" novels.

Dort, Netherlands: see DORDRECHT.

Dortmund (dôrt'mòont), city (pop. 500,150), North Rhine-Westphalia, NW Germany. A major industrial center of the RUHR, on Dortmund-Ems Canal. Heavily damaged in World War II.

Dorval, town (pop. 5,293), S Que., Canada, on S shore of Montreal Isl. Resort and site of Montreal international airport. Offshore is Dorval isl.

Dorylaeum (dôrĭlē'ùm), city of N Phrygia, now in NW Turkey. An important trade center in Roman times, it later declined. Here (1097) Crusaders defeated the Seljuk Turks.

Dos Passos, John (Roderigo), 1896–, American author of novels with broad social themes. *Manhattan Transfer* (1925) was followed by two trilogies, *U.S.A.* (separate vols., 1930–36; about industrial society) and *District of Columbia* (separate vols., 1939–49; about American politics).

Dosso Dossi (dôs'sō dôs'sē), 1479?–1542, Italian painter of the Ferrarese school. His real name was Giovanni de Luteri.

Dost Mohammed (dōst'), 1793–1863, emir of Afghanistan. Fought against the British in first Afghan War (1839–42). Later tried to play Russian interests against the British.

Dostoyevsky, Feodor Mikhailovich (fyô'dùr mēkhī'lùvĭch důstùyěf'skē), 1821–81, Russian novelist, one of the giants of modern literature. He won his first success with *Poor Folk* (1845). Arrested 1849 for membership in a Fourierist circle, he was sentenced to death; while he was waiting for death, his sentence was commuted to hard labor in Siberia. The shock of the experience and the hardship of Siberian life (described in *The House of the Dead,* 1862) aggravated his epilepsy and caused him to turn to religion. He returned to St. Petersburg 1859. His chronic financial difficulties were increased by his passion for gambling. His novels are characterized by deep psychological insight; compassion for all men, even the vilest of whom he thought capable of redemption; and morbid preoccupation with guilt and crime. His greatest novels are *Crime and Punishment* (1866), *The Idiot* (1869), *The Possessed* (1872), *The Brothers Karamazov* (1879–80). *Notes from the Underground* (1864) and other short novels are equally powerful. All his major works are translated by Constance Garnett and others.

Dothan (dō'thăn), ancient city, central Palestine. Near here Joseph was sold into slavery, Syrians were blinded at Elisha's prayer. Gen. 37.17; 2 Kings 6.13. Dothaim: Judith 4.6; 7.3,18; 8.3.

Dothan (dō'thùn), city (pop. 21,584), extreme SE Ala., near Chattahoochee R. and Fla. line. Farm trade center; processes livestock, cotton, peanuts.

Douai (dōōā'), town (pop. 35,509), Nord dept., N

France, in Flanders. Coal mining; machinery. Here Philip II of Spain estab. college (R.C.) where Douay Bible was prepared. Taken by Louis XIV 1667; rebuilt 18th cent. Despite heavy damage in both World Wars, most old buildings still stand.

Douaumont (dōō-ōmō′), fort on VERDUN battlefield, NE France. Lost and retaken by French 1916. Graves of 10,000 unidentified soldiers are near by.

double bass: see VIOLIN.

Doubleday, Abner, 1819–93, alleged originator of BASE-BALL, a Union general in Civil War. Said to have created game 1839 at Cooperstown, N.Y.

doublet, in W Europe until late 17th cent., a close-fitting, usually sleeveless upper garment for men. Doublet of defense was body armor.

Doubs (dōō), department (2,031 sq. mi.; pop. 298,255), E France, in Franche-Comté; cap. Besançon. The **Doubs** river, 267 mi. long, rises in the French Jura, flows NE, makes loop into Switzerland, then continues SW to join Saône near Chalon, c.60 mi. W of its source.

Doughty, Charles Montagu (dō′tē, dou′tē), 1843–1926, English traveler, author of *Travels in Arabia Deserta* (1888).

Doughty, Thomas (dou′tē), 1793–1856, American painter of the Hudson River school.

Douglas, Scottish noble family, divided into two branches. **William de Douglas, lord of Douglas,** d. 1298, was first to take title. Joined William Wallace revolt 1297, was captured, and died in Tower of London. His son, **Sir James de Douglas, lord of Douglas,** 1286?–1330, was called Black Douglas or Douglas the Good. Deprived of his estates by Edward I, became terror of border. Joined Robert I, fought at Bannockburn, and was a regent of Scotland. After death of Robert I, started for Palestine to bury king's heart but was killed in Spain. His nephew, **William Douglas, 1st earl of Douglas and Mar,** 1327?–1384, added lands to family holdings. His son, **James Douglas, 2d earl of Douglas and Mar,** 1358?–1388, married daughter of Robert II. Killed at battle of Otterburn. His uncle, **Archibald Douglas, 3d earl of Douglas,** 1328?–1400?, was illegitimate son of Sir James de Douglas. Acquired large estates. At his death, family most powerful in Scotland. His son, **Archibald Douglas, 4th earl of Douglas,** 1369?–1424, married daughter of Robert III 1390. Fought against Henry IV and Henry V. Tried and acquitted for murder of heir to Scottish throne. Joined the French and was killed at Verneuil. His son, **Archibald Douglas, 5th earl of Douglas,** 1391?–1439, was twice imprisoned by James I who feared his power. After James's death (1437) he was most powerful man in Scotland. His son, **William Douglas, 6th earl of Douglas,** 1423?–1440, was beheaded (together with his brother) by advisers of James II and family power was temporarily broken. Succeeded by his great-uncle, **James Douglas, 7th earl of Douglas,** 1371?–1443. His son, **William Douglas, 8th earl of Douglas,** 1425?–1452, reunited family estates by marrying his cousin. His brother, **James Douglas, 9th earl of Douglas,** 1426–88, rebelled twice (1452, 1455) against James II, was defeated, and fled to England. Captured 1483, spent rest of his life in prison. With him, power of older or "Black" Douglas branch ended. Younger or "Red" Douglas branch descended from illegitimate son of William Douglas, 1st earl of Douglas and Mar, and Margaret Stuart, countess of Angus. **Archibald Douglas, 5th earl of Angus,** 1449?–1514, was chancellor of Scotland 1493–98. In revolt against James III 1487–88, earned nickname of Bell-the-Cat by capture of king's favorite. Father of Gawin DOUGLAS. His grandson, **Archibald Douglas, 6th earl of Angus,** 1489?–1557, married Margaret Tudor, sister of Henry VIII and widow of James IV, and attempted to gain control of her son, James V. She divorced him 1528 and he fled to England. Returned 1542 and was restored to power. His grandnephew, **Archibald Douglas, 8th earl of Angus,** 1555–

88, supported his uncle, the earl of MORTON, and opposed James Stuart, earl of Arran.

Douglas, Clifford Hugh, 1879–, English social economist, author of theory of SOCIAL CREDIT.

Douglas, David, 1798–1834, Scottish botanist, one of the first travelers in Oregon country and Calif. The Douglas fir (or spruce) is named for him.

Douglas, Gawin (gä′wĭn) or **Gavin** (găv′ĭn), 1474?–1522, Scottish poet and churchman. Member of the powerful DOUGLAS family, he was involved in political disputes after 1515. A major poet of the Chaucerian tradition, his works include *The Palace of Honour, King Hart,* and a translation of the *Aeneid* (one of first classical translations into English).

Douglas, George, pseud. of George Douglas Brown, 1869–1902, Scottish novelist, author of *The House with the Green Shutters* (1901).

Douglas, James, 2d duke of Queensberry: see QUEENS-BERRY, JAMES DOUGLAS, 2D DUKE OF.

Douglas, James, 2d earl of Douglas and Mar: see DOUGLAS, family.

Douglas, James, earls of Douglas: see DOUGLAS, family.

Douglas, James (d. 1581): see MORTON, JAMES DOUGLAS, 4TH EARL OF.

Douglas, Sir James, 1803–77, Canadian fur trader and colonial governor, b. Scotland. In 1846 he succeeded to command of Hudson's Bay Co. territory W of the Rockies. Appointed governor of Vancouver Isl. (1851) and also became governor of new colony of British Columbia in 1858. Retired 1864.

Douglas, Sir James de Douglas, lord of: see DOUGLAS, family.

Douglas, (George) Norman, 1868–1952, English writer, best known for novel *South Wind* (1917) and sketches in *Old Calabria* (1915).

Douglas, Paul H(oward), 1892–, American economist and U.S. Senator (1948–) from Ill., b. Salem, Mass.; an authority on wages and social security.

Douglas, Stephen A(rnold), 1813–61, American statesman. U.S. Representative from Ill. (1843–47); U.S. Senator (1847–61). Responsible for SQUATTER SOVEREIGNTY aspects of COMPROMISE OF 1850 and KANSAS-NEBRASKA BILL; championed popular sovereignty as way of settling North-South controversy peacefully. Lincoln-Douglas debates featured his 1858 campaign for reelection; at Freeport, on Aug. 27, 1858, he asserted that people of a territory could exclude slavery. Freeport doctrine made him anathema to Southern Democrats. Democratic national convention of 1860 nominated him for President, but Southern delegates broke away. In election he won only 12 electoral votes, but stood second in popular votes. Douglas, it is now held, was one of few men in his era with truly broad national vision.

Douglas, William: see DOUGLAS, family.

Douglas, William O(rville), 1898–, Associate Justice of U.S. Supreme Court (1939–).

Douglas. 1 City (pop. 9,442), extreme SE Ariz., at Mexican line. Copper-smelting and ranching center, resort. **2** City (pop. 7,428), S central Ga., NW of Waycross. Tobacco market and processing center.

Douglas and Mar, earls of: see DOUGLAS, family.

Douglas fir or **Douglas spruce,** huge coniferous evergreen (*Pseudotsuga taxifolia*) of W North America. Named for David Douglas, it is not a true fir or spruce. Wood valued for construction.

Douglass, Frederick, c.1817–1895, American abolitionist, son of slave mother. Escaping in 1838, he took surname from Scott's *The Lady of the Lake.* At Rochester, N.Y., estab. and edited *North Star* for 17 years in abolitionist cause.

Douglas spruce: see DOUGLAS FIR.

Douhet, Giulio (jōō′lyō dōōā′), 1869–1930, Italian military theorist, a general. Held that command of air could win a war despite land and sea power.

Doukhobors: see DUKHOBORS.

Doulton ware, English pottery produced at Lambeth after 1815, first by John Doulton, then by his descendants. Includes brown stoneware and faïence. Now known as Royal Doulton.

Doumer, Paul (pôl' dōōmâr'), 1857–1932, president of France (1931–32).

Doumergue, Gaston (gästō' dōōmĕrg'), 1863–1937, president of France (1924–31). Headed a rightist coalition cabinet in Feb.–Nov. 1934.

Doura: see DURA.

Douro (dō'rōō) or **Duero** (dōōā'rō), river, c.475 mi. long, Spain and Portugal; Douro is Port., Duero Span. name. Rises in N central Spain, flows generally W into Atlantic beyond Oporto. Hydroelectric plants.

Dove (dŭv), river rising in Derbyshire, England, and forming much of Derbyshire-Staffordshire border. Its water-course was a haunt of Izaak Walton. Glen of Dovedale celebrated by artists and poets.

dove, name for certain smaller birds of pigeon family; name often used synonymously with pigeon. European rock dove is probably ancestor of domesticated pigeons. Mourning dove, native to North America, is common.

Dover, municipal borough (pop. 35,217), on a bay beneath chalk cliffs, Kent, England. Chief of CINQUE PORTS, called "key to England." Easternmost English port (21 mi. from France), it was important naval base World War I and constant target of German long-range guns World War II. Subterranean caves and tunnels in the cliffs, once used by smugglers, were shelters 1940–44. Important travel and shipping port to the Continent. Noteworthy are Shakespeare Cliff and Dover Castle.

Dover. 1 City (pop. 6,223), state cap., central Del. on St. Jones R. near Silver L. and S of Smyrna; settled 1683. Shipping and canning center of farm and fruit region. Statehouse (partly built 1722) has been capitol since 1777. 2 City (pop. 15,874), SE N.H., near Piscataqua R. NW of Portsmouth; settled 1623, held 1633–41 by Lord Saye and Sele. Mfg. of leather goods, machinery, and wood products. Woodman Inst. has historical and natural science collections. 3 Town (pop. 11,174), N N.J., NW of Morristown; settled 1722. Former iron center and port on old Morris Canal. Mfg. of metal products, machinery, and rock wool. Picatinny Arsenal and U.S. naval rocket experiment station are near. 4 City (pop. 9,852), E Ohio, on Tuscarawas R. and SSW of Canton. Mfg. of steel, electric light bulbs, clay products, and chemicals.

Dover, Strait of, separates England from France and connects English Channel with North Sea. Width 21 mi. between Dover and Cape Gris-Nez near Calais. Called Pas de Calais by French.

Dovrefjell (dô'vrüfyĕl), rough plateau of central Norway, culminating in Snohetta (Nor. Snøhetta; 7,498 ft. high) and dividing country in two.

Dow, Lorenzo, 1777–1834, American evangelist, who introduced camp meetings into Ireland and England.

Dowagiac (dōwô'jăk), city (pop. 6,542), SW Mich., SW of Kalamazoo, in farm and lake region. Mfg. of stoves, furnaces, and heaters.

Dowie, John Alexander (dou'ē), 1847–1907, founder of Christian Catholic Apostolic Church in Zion, b. Scotland. In Australia became interested in faith healing. Came to U.S. (1888); founded church in Chicago (1896) and community in Zion, Ill. (1901). Deposed as leader in 1905.

Down, maritime county (952 sq. mi.; pop. 241,105, excluding Belfast, which is partly within county), Ulster prov., N. Ireland; co. town Downpatrick. Coastline indented by Strangford Lough and Dundrum Bay; beautiful Mourne Mts. rise in south. Area extensively cultivated (oats, potatoes, wheat, and flax). There are many linen mfg. towns.

Downers Grove, village (pop. 11,886), NE Ill., just W of Chicago; settled 1832. Metal products.

Downing, Andrew Jackson, 1815–52, American horticulturist, rural architect, and landscape gardener, author of many books on gardening and landscaping. He planned the grounds of the Capitol, the White House,

and the Smithsonian Institution in Washington, D.C.

Downing, Major Jack: see SMITH, SEBA.

Downing College: see CAMBRIDGE UNIVERSITY.

Downing Street, London. British colonial and foreign offices located here. No. 10 residence of first lord of Treasury, usually prime minister. Figurative use of term means government in power.

Downpatrick (dounpă'trĭk), urban district (pop. 3,878), co. seat of Co. Down, N. Ireland. Has long been a religious center and place of pilgrimage as tomb of Ireland's saints—Patrick, Colomba, and Bridget of Kildare. Holy wells of Struell near by.

Downs, the, low chalk hills, SE England. N. Downs range in Surrey and Kent separated by the WEALD from S. Downs in Sussex. Excellent sheep pasturage.

dowry, property a woman brings to her husband at marriage. Institution apparently originated in marriage gift made by family of the bride to the groom, estab. as custom in many peoples from earliest days. Known to Greece, Rome, India, medieval Europe, and modern civil-law countries. Generally on divorce the husband must return dowry.

Dowson, Ernest (Christopher) (dou'–), 1867–1900, English lyric poet, one of the best-known poets of the decadents. Perhaps most familiar of his delicate, highly musical poems is that with the refrain "I have been faithful to thee, Cynara! in my fashion." A Roman Catholic, he also wrote religious poetry. His brief, wretched life was ended by tuberculosis.

doxology, sacred hymn of praise. Best-known doxologies of Christian church are "Gloria in Excelsis," "Gloria Patri," and Thomas Ken's "Praise God from Whom All Blessings Flow," sung to the tune Old Hundred from the Genevan Psalter.

Doyle, Sir A(rthur) Conan, 1859–1930, English author, creator of Sherlock Holmes, most celebrated of all fictional detectives. Among detective stories are A Study in Scarlet (1887), The Sign of the Four (1890), The Memoirs of Sherlock Holmes (1894), The Hound of the Baskervilles (1902), The Return of Sherlock Holmes (1905). Doyle in later life was a spiritualist.

Doylestown, borough (pop. 5,262), SE Pa., N of Philadelphia. Trade center in agr. area. Seat of Natl. Farm School.

Drachenfels (drä'khùnfĕls), cliff, 1053 ft. high, on the Rhine, S of Bonn, W Germany. Legendary scene of Siegfried's triumph over the dragon. Ruins of Drachenburg castle, on top of cliff, date from 12th cent. Popular excursion point.

Draco or **Dracon,** fl. 621 B.C., Athenian lawgiver, at least semilegendary. Said to have assigned death penalty for many offences; hence Draconian means harsh.

Dracut (drā'kŭt), textile town (pop. 8,666), NE Mass., on Merrimack R. and N of Lowell.

draft riots, in Civil War. Nation-wide opposition to Union conscription act of March 3, 1863, broke into bloody riots in New York city (July 13–16, 1863). Huge mob overpowered police and militia, seized Second Ave. armory, set fires, and assaulted abolitionists and Negroes. Damage over $1,500,000, with est. 1,000 casualties.

Draga, queen of Serbia: see ALEXANDER, king of Serbia.

Drago, Luis María (lōōēs' märē'ä drä'gō), 1859–1921, Argentine statesman, jurist, and writer on international law. His protest against coercion of Venezuela by Great Britain, Germany, and Italy (1902) became known as the **Drago Doctrine** (a corollary to Monroe Doctrine). It set forth principle that no public debt should be collected from sovereign American state by armed force or through occupation of American territory by foreign power. Modified form was approved at Hague Conference (1907).

dragon, in mythology, composite winged reptilic beast, generally said to have lion's claws, eagle's wings, and serpent's tail. The conception, dating from Babylonian times, is widespread, and is sometimes used as national symbol. Story of slaying of a dragon by a hero appears frequently in literature.

SMALL CAPITALS = cross references. Pronunciation key on inside end pages. Abbreviations: p. 2.

dragonfly, large insect of order Odonata, which includes also the damsel fly. Found in most parts of world, they are numerous in South America and Japan. Eggs are laid in or near water, and nymphs (the young) are aquatic. Metamorphosis is incomplete. Adults have four membranous wings; some surpass swallow in flying speed and agility. They eat larvae and adult insects. See *ill.*, p. 469.

dragon's blood, red resin obtained from certain plants, including *Dracaena draco*. Used in photoengraving.

drainage, in mining, accomplished by causing surface or subterranean water to flow by gravity into reservoirs or sumps dug at lowest level, whence it is usually pumped out.

drainage basin: see CATCHMENT AREA.

Drake, Daniel, 1785–1852, American physician, author of a study on relation of disease to geography in valley of Mississippi R.

Drake, Edwin Laurentine, 1819–80, American oilwell driller. He sank the first U.S. well to strike oil, Aug. 27, 1859.

Drake, Sir Francis, 1540?–1596, English navigator, admiral, first Englishman to circumnavigate world (1577–80). From 1572 commanded marauding expeditions against Spanish, taking rich booty from treasure ships and Spanish possessions in the Americas for treasury of Queen Elizabeth, who finally knighted him and openly recognized his exploits. Commanded sea forces against rebellious Ireland; destroyed a Spanish fleet at Cádiz (1587) and participated in destruction of the Armada (1588). Died of dysentery during last and unsuccessful expedition against Spanish West Indies.

Drake, Joseph Rodman, 1795–1820, American poet, satirist, a physician, author of "The Culprit Fay" and light satirical verse (with Fitz-Greene HALLECK).

Drakensberg (drä'künzbûrg), mountain range, South Africa. Extends c.700 mi., rises to 11,425 ft. at Thabantshonyana.

Drake University, at Des Moines, Iowa; coed.; chartered, opened 1881 by Disciples of Christ; named for F. M. Drake. Includes College of the Bible.

Drammen (drä'mùn), city (pop. 26,994), SE Norway, on Drammen R. and at head of Drammen Fjord. Wood products. **Drammen** river, c.25 mi. long, SE Norway, empties into Drammen Fjord, a branch of Oslo Fjord. Lumber mills; hydroelectric plants.

Draper, John William, 1811–82, American scientist, philosopher, and historian, b. England. He helped organize medical school of New York Univ., taught chemistry and physiology there, and became its president 1850. Conducted important research on radiant energy. His works include *Human Physiology* (1856), containing the first published microphotographs; *History of the Intellectual Development of Europe* (1863). His son **Henry Draper,** 1837–82, taught physiology at New York Univ. (1870–82) and was a pioneer in astronomical photography and spectroscopy.

draughts: see CHECKERS.

Drava or **Drave** (both: drä'vù), Ger. *Drau*, river, c.450 mi. long, central Europe; tributary of the Danube. Rises in Italian Alps; flows E through Carinthia (Austria), then SE, forming part of Hungarian-Yugoslav border, past Villach, Maribor, and Osijek.

Dravidian (drùvĭ'dēùn), name of largest group of inhabitants of India before coming of Aryans. Also name of group in S India today presumably descended from prehistoric Dravidians.

Dravidian languages, family of languages of S India; see LANGUAGE (table). Attempts have been made to connect them with other groups.

drawbridge, movable bridge, usually over stream or river in situation requiring maintenance of waterborne traffic, but prohibiting erection of fixed bridge high enough to allow passage under it. In fortresses surrounded by ditch or moat, it was part of defense system. Common types include the lifting, bascule, and swing bridges. See *ill.*, p. 131.

Drayton, Michael, 1563–1631, English poet. Sonnet beginning "Since there's no help, come let us kiss and part" most famous in *Ideas Mirrour* (1594, 1619) and other volumes. Notable longer poems, panoramic *Poly-Olbion* (1612–22) and charming *Nymphidia* (1627).

dream, mental activity of disputed duration, associated with sleep and commonly made up of visual images. Like hallucinations, dreams are not usually aroused by sense impressions; somatic disturbances (e.g., toothache, indigestion) and external stimuli occasionally affect form but not content. Dream interpretation vigorous among ancient, primitive, and superstitious peoples. Freud, an early exponent of scientific dream study, distinguished manifest content (the experienced dream-image) from latent content (meaning). Dream-images are symbols—universal, cultural, or personal (translatable through free association). Symbolism protects dreamer from recognition of attempted fulfillment of impulses that consciousness forbids. Freud believed dreams insure sleep by draining force of emotional disturbances that would waken sleeper. Jung considered them testing ground for possible future steps. Adler emphasized compensatory function.

Drebbel, Cornelis Jacobszoon (kôrnā'lĭs yä'kôp-sōn drĕ'bùl), 1572–1634, Dutch inventor, physicist, and mechanician who settled in England. His many inventions include "perpetual motion" machine and a diving boat (first navigable submarine).

dredging, process of underwater excavation to clear or deepen channels and entrances of harbors, docks, rivers, and canals. Modern dredging equipment divisible into four main classes. The **grab dredge,** for small operations, consists of grab buckets operated by cranes. Bucket is similar to clamshell bucket used ashore, as is the **dipper dredge** (known as boom and dipper assembly) used extensively in canal construction. **Ladder-bucket dredge,** operated usually from self-propelling vessel built with well in center open to water, consists of endless succession of buckets operating through the well and discharging, as they rise, into a chute projecting to hopper barge, or to hopper in dredge itself. **Suction dredge** used principally to remove sand and mud through flexible pipe extended to bottom, by means of centrifugal pump.

Dred Scott Case, argued before U.S. Supreme Court in 1856–57. Brought as a test case; concerned status of Dred Scott, a Negro who had lived with his master for several years in free territory. Chief Justice R. B. Taney delivered court's opinion that a Negro "whose ancestors . . . were sold as slaves" was not entitled to rights of a Federal citizen and had no standing in court, and that Missouri Compromise was unconstitutional. John McLean and B. R. Curtis dissented. Verdict further enflamed North-South controversy. Decision later nullified by FOURTEENTH AMENDMENT.

Dreiser, Theodore (drī'sùr), 1871–1945, American author. His first novel (*Sister Carrie*, 1900) was suppressed by the publisher, but his later novels (including *Jennie Gerhardt*, 1911; *The Titan*, 1914; *An American Tragedy*, 2 vols., 1925) won acclaim for their power despite their ponderous style.

Drenthe (drĕn'tù), province (1,011 sq. mi.; pop. 271,-909), NE Netherlands, bordering on Germany; cap. Assen. Stock raising, dairy farming.

Dresden (drĕz'dùn), city (pop. 467,966; 1939 pop. 630,-216), cap. of Saxony, E Germany, on the Elbe. Mfg. center (machine tools, optical instruments, glass, chemicals) and large inland port. Originally a Slavic settlement; settled by Germans 13th cent.; residence of electors (later kings) of Saxony 1547–1918. In late 17th and 18th cent. it became a center of the arts, outstanding for baroque and rococo architecture. City was about three quarters destroyed in World War II. Former landmarks include Zwinger palace and museum; Hofkirche [court chapel]; cathedral. Many art treasures, including Raphael's *Sistine Madonna*, were removed to Russia. "Dresden china," despite name, was made in Meissen. Napoleon defeated allies near Dresden in 1813. For Treaty of Dresden (1745), see AUSTRIAN SUCCESSION, WAR OF THE.

Drew, Daniel, 1797–1879, American capitalist. Bold and scheming, he helped manipulate Erie RR stock (1866–68) to defeat attempt of Cornelius Vanderbilt to gain control. Drew was bankrupt by 1876.

Drew, Louisa Lane, 1820–97, American actress, b. London. From girlhood appeared in support of era's leading actors until she married (1850) John Drew (1827–62). They co-starred at his Arch St. Theater, Philadelphia. On his death she assumed its management. Her children were Sidney, Georgiana (see BARRYMORE), and **John Drew,** 1853–1927, who joined the Daly company in 1875. Acted in Daly's Shaksperian productions. Under Charles Frohman did modern comedies with Maude Adams.

Drewrys Bluff (drōō'rēz), height on S bank of James R., E central Va., S of Richmond, scene of two battles in Civil War. Union gunboats repulsed here (May 15, 1862). B. F. Butler defeated by inferior Confederate force under Beauregard (May 16, 1864). Also called Drewry Bluff, Drury's Bluff.

Drew University: see MADISON, N.J.

Drexel Institute of Technology: see PHILADELPHIA, Pa.

Dreyer, John Louis Emil (drī'ûr), 1852–1926, Danish astronomer in Great Britain, compiler of standard catalogue of nebulae and clusters (1888; supplements, 1895, 1908).

Dreyfus Affair (drā'fūs, drī'–), began 1894 with the discovery of a schedule (the famous *bordereau*) addressed to Maj. Schwartzkoppen, German military attaché in Paris, which listed secret French documents that the writer promised to furnish. A court martial convicted Capt. Alfred Dreyfus (1859–1935) of treason on the slim evidence that the handwriting on the *bordereau* was similar to his. Dreyfus never ceased to protest his innocence, but his being both a Jew and an Alsatian weighed heavily with his bigoted judges. He was sentenced to degradation and to life imprisonment on Devils Isl. (1894). The case flared up again in 1896, when Col. Georges PICQUART discovered evidence pointing to Maj. Ferdinand Walsin ESTERHAZY as the real author of the *bordereau*. Picquart was silenced by the authorities, but in 1897 Dreyfus's brother Mathieu independently made the same discovery and energetically pressed for a new trial. The case now became a major political issue, dividing all France into two violent partisan groups for 10 years. Royalists, militarists, and (with a few notable exceptions) Catholics made up the anti-Dreyfusard camp; republicans, socialists, and anti-clericalists professed faith in Dreyfus's innocence. The anti-Dreyfusards, by dint of patriotic forgeries and pious perjuries, prevailed at first; Esterhazy was acquitted by a court martial and Émile Zola was sentenced for his article "J'accuse" (1898), which had accused the authorities of framing Dreyfus. However, when Maj. Henry, who had forged evidence against Dreyfus at the Esterhazy trial, committed suicide in 1898, revision of the Dreyfus case became imperative. The court of appeals ordered a new court martial, but surprisingly the military court at Rennes found Dreyfus guilty again (1899). Though Pres. Loubet pardoned him, agitation for complete exoneration continued until 1906, when the supreme court of appeals (a civil court) cleared Dreyfus, who was reinstated as a major. Publication of the Schwartzkoppen papers (1930) conclusively proved his innocence. The Dreyfus Affair discredited the monarchists and clericalists and hastened separation of Church and state in France.

drift, mixture of clay, sand, and boulders left by an ice sheet. Unstratified drift is also called boulder clay. Stratified drift was deposited by glacial streams.

Driftless Area, over 10,000 sq. mi. largely in SW Wis., but also in SE Minn., NE Iowa, NW Ill. Area, un-

touched by continental glacier which once covered surroundings, has no glacial drifts.

Drin (drēn), largest river of Albania, c.170 mi. long, formed by White and Black Drin, which rise in Yugoslavia and join in NE Albania. Flows W and S through deep gorges into Adriatic.

Drinkwater, John, 1882–1937, English writer, author of many plays (e.g., *Abraham Lincoln,* 1918; *Bird in Hand,* 1927), biographies, poetry.

Drogheda (drô'ŭdù, droi'dù) urban district (pop. 15,-715), Co. Louth, Ireland, on the Boyne. POYNINGS's Law enacted here in 1494. Town taken and inhabitants massacred by Cromwell 1649. Battle of the Boyne fought near here 1690.

Drogobych (drûgô'bĭch), Pol. *Drohobycz,* city (1931 pop. 32,622), W Ukraine, SW of Lvov; center of important petroleum and natural gas fields. Under Austria 1772–1918; ceded by Poland to USSR 1945.

Droitwich (droit'wĭch), municipal borough (pop. 6,453), Worcestershire, England, on Salwarpe R. Has canal to the Severn. Noted for its brine baths and salt trade.

Drôme (drōm), department (2,533 sq. mi.; pop. 268,-233), SE France, in Dauphiné; cap. Valence.

Drontheim, Norway: see TRONDHEIM.

Droysen, Johann Gustav (yōhän' gōōs'täf droi'zùn), 1808–84, German historian. Known for *Geschichte der preussischen Politik* (14 vols., 1855–86) and biography of Yorck von Wartenburg (3 vols., 1851–52).

drug addiction, craving for drug resulting in need for increasing quantity to produce effect and in nervous disturbances when not under its influence. Chief habit-forming drugs are opium, cocaine, hashish, marijuana, alcohol, and nicotine.

drugs, substances used internally or externally for cure, alleviation, or prevention of disease. They include inorganic substances, alkaloids and other plant derivatives, and hormones, vaccines, serums, and other substances derived from animals. SULFA DRUGS and ANTIBIOTIC SUBSTANCES are valued in treating infections. Many countries list standards and tests in official PHARMACOPOEIA. U.S. legislation to safeguard users began 1906, was superseded by Federal Food, Drug, and Cosmetic Act of 1938; laws enforced by Food and Drug Administration.

druids, priests and medicine men of Celtic peoples, especially in Gaul and Great Britain. Practiced herbal medicine and ruled in ritualistic religion based on sun worship and belief in immortality of soul. They had a confederation which was politically powerful and fostered revolt against Rome. Druidic system finally yielded to Christianity. Many prehistoric ruins such as Stonehenge, once attributed to druids, appear to have other sources.

drum: see PERCUSSION INSTRUMENTS.

drumlin, smooth oval hill of glacial DRIFT, elongated in the direction of ice movement.

Drummond, Thomas, 1797–1840, Scottish engineer, inventor. He took part in trigonometrical survey of United Kingdom 1820; devised Drummond light (using incandescent properties of lime) to aid observations in murky weather.

Drummond (of Hawthornden), William, 1585–1649, Scottish poet. A friend of Ben Jonson, he wrote graceful sonnets, elegies, hymns (as in *Flowres of Sion,* 1623). His prose *Cypresse Grove* (1623) is on death.

Drummond, William Henry, 1854–1907, Canadian poet, b. Ireland. His verse portrays French Canadians, using habitants' own dialect of English.

Drummond, Lake: see DISMAL SWAMP.

Drummond Island: see MANITOULIN ISLANDS.

Drummond light: see DRUMMOND, THOMAS.

Drummondville, city (pop. 14,341), S Que., Canada, on St. Francis R. and ENE of Montreal. Rayon-milling center, with textile mfg. and printing.

Drumright, city (pop. 5,028), central Okla., WSW of Tulsa, in oil region. Oil refineries.

Drury College: see SPRINGFIELD, Mo.

Drury Lane, London street and district; site of Drury

Lane Theatre. Original 17th-cent. theater was a cockpit. Present theater designed by Benjamin Wyatt 1812.

Druses (drōō'zĭz), people of S Syria and Lebanon who inhabit hills of the Hauran, much of the Lebanon and the Anti-Lebanon. They believe in divinity of 11th-cent. Fatimite caliph, Hakim. Massacred Christians in 19th cent., fought against French control of Syria and Lebanon 1925–26.

Drusus (drōō'sùs), Roman family. **Marcus Livius Drusus,** d. 109? B.C., was tribune of the people with C. GRACCHUS (122 B.C.) and led the senatorial attack on Gracchus, succeeding by dubious means. He was consul in 112 B.C. His son **Marcus Livius Drusus,** d. 91 B.C., also led the senatorial party and by generous sums of money and wholesale grant of citizenship he won the allegiance of the Italians. The senate turned against him and by withdrawing the citizenship laws provoked the SOCIAL WAR. A member of family by adoption was LIVIA DRUSILLA, mother of **Nero Claudius Drusus Germanicus** (Drusus Senior), 38 B.C.–9 B.C., who as stepson of Augustus got an army command early and fought against Rhaetians, Gauls, and Germans. His sons were Germanicus Caesar and Claudius I. The son of his brother Tiberius was **Drusus Caesar** (Drusus Junior), d. A.D. 23, who served against the Germans, awoke the jealousy of Sejanus, and died, supposedly of poison, at the instance of Sejanus.

Dryburgh Abbey (drī'bùrù), Berwickshire, Scotland. Built 1150, now a beautiful ruin. Contains Sir Walter Scott's tomb.

dry cell: see CELL, in electricity.

Dryden, John, 1631–1700, English poet, dramatist, and critic. First came to notice with *Heroick Stanzas* (1659) commemorating Oliver Cromwell, but welcomed Charles II with *Astraea Redux* and rose to prominence in the Restoration. He was made poet laureate in 1668. He was converted to Catholicism and on the accession of William III lost the laureateship and court patronage but continued prominent. Among his long poems are *Annus Mirabilis* (1667), *Absalom and Achitophel* (first part 1681; second part, with Nahun Tate, 1682; on the plot in favor of Monmouth), *MacFlecknoe* (1682; a satirical attack on Thomas Shadwell), *Religio Laici* (1682; a defense of Protestantism), and *The Hind and the Panther* (1687; on his conversion to Catholicism). Two of his best-known shorter pieces are his "Ode to the Memory of Mrs. Anne Killigrew" and "Alexander's Feast." He was also a prolific writer of plays—comedies such as *Marriage-à-la-Mode* as well as tragedies, including *The Conquest of Granada, Aureng-Zebe,* and *All for Love* (his version of the Antony and Cleopatra story). His essays are much admired for their style, and he also wrote brilliant critical prefaces, prologues, and discourses; his *Essay of Dramatick Poesy* (1668) is notable. He also translated and adapted much Latin literature.

dry farming produces crops in low-rainfall areas, without irrigation. Aided by drought-resistant strains, deep soil, crop rotation, and fallowing.

dry ice, solid CARBON DIOXIDE, formed when liquefying pressure is removed and liquid is allowed to evaporate in a confined space. Some liquid becomes gas at once, drawing heat from remaining liquid, which "freezes" to solid.

drying oil, an oil (from either plants or animals), which oxidizes easily and forms resistant film when exposed to air. Used in paints, varnishes, etc.

dry rot, fungus disease that attacks seasoned timber, often causing it to collapse. Certain fungus diseases of fruits and vegetables are also called dry rot.

Dry Tortugas (tôrtōō'gùz), island group off S Fla., W of Key West. On Garden Key (sometimes called Shark Isl.) is Fort Jefferson Natl. Monument (see NATIONAL PARKS AND MONUMENTS, table), a Civil War prison.

Dual Alliance, 1879–82: see TRIPLE ALLIANCE AND TRIPLE ENTENTE.

dualism, any philosophical system that explains the universe in terms of two distinct and exclusive principles—e.g., form and matter, mind and matter, being and nonbeing. In religion, dualism usually means belief in an ultimate evil principle as well as an ultimate good principle. This appeared in striking form in Zoroastrianism, in Gnosticism, and in Manichaeism.

Dual Monarchy: see AUSTRO-HUNGARIAN MONARCHY.

Duane, James (dūan'), 1733–97, American Revolutionary statesman. Member of Continental Congress (1774–83). Helped draft Articles of Confederation.

Duane, William, 1760–1835, American journalist. Editor (1798–1822) of Philadelphia *Aurora,* leading Jeffersonian organ. Arrested under both Alien Act and Sedition Act; vindicated. His son, **William John Duane,** 1780–1865, was U.S. Secretary of Treasury (June–Oct., 1833). Replaced after refusing Pres. Jackson's request to transfer government deposits from Bank of the United States to state banks.

Duarte (dwär'tù), 1391–1438, king of Portugal (1431–1438). Called the "philosopher-king," he was better known for his learning than for his indecisive statesmanship. Brother of Henry the Navigator.

Duban, Jacques Félix (zhäk' fālĕks' dübä'), 1797–1870, French architect, a leader of the Neo-Greek movement in France, 1830–50. Helped restore the color adornment of Sainte-Chapelle, Paris.

Du Barry, Jeanne Bécu, comtesse (zhän' bäkü' kŏtĕs' dü bärē'), 1743–93, last mistress of Louis XV. Of extremely vulgar background, she was notorious for her extravagance but did not seek political influence. Guillotined in Revolution.

Du Bartas, Guillaume de Salluste (gēyōm' dù sälüst' dü bärtäs'), 1544–90, French poet and Huguenot soldier. Wrote epic poem on creation (1578).

Dubawnt, river, SE Mackenzie dist. and W Keewatin dist., Northwest Territories, Canada. Rises NE of L. Athabaska and flows 580 mi. NE through Dubawnt L to Thelon R. W of Aberdeen L.

Du Bellay, Joachim (zhōäshē' dü bĕlä'), 1522?–1560, French poet of the PLÉIADE. Wrote its manifesto, *La Deffence et illustration de la langue francoyse* (1549), and sonnet collections such as *Les Regrets* (1558), nostalgic poems of Rome.

Dubinsky, David (dōobĭn'skē), 1892–, American labor leader, b. Poland. President after 1932 of International Ladies Garment Workers Union, he led it into the C.I.O. in 1936, but broke with C.I.O. in 1938 and later rejoined A.F. of L. He advocated political action; helped to found American Labor Party, Liberal Party, and Americans for Democratic Action.

Dublin, county (327 sq. mi.; pop. 636,193), Leinster prov., Ireland. City area, including Wicklow Mts. and Liffey R., dominated by Dublin. Rural area has farming, cattle, and fishing. Has several large suburban towns.

Dublin, Irish *Baile Átha Cliath* (bä'lē ä klē'), county borough (pop. 506,051), cap. of Ireland and co. seat of Dublin Co., on Dublin Bay at mouth of Liffey R. Harbor with shipyards and docks connected with interior by two canals. Chief industries brewing (Guinness), distilling, linen milling, and mfg. of chemicals, soap, textiles, carpets, lace, and machinery. Site of Univ. of Dublin (or Trinity Col. founded 1591) which has famous Book of KELLS, Univ. Col. (R.C.), and Natl. Gallery of Art. Dublin Castle (c.1200) houses government offices. Leinster House seat of Irish Parliament. City became seat of English government and center of Pale 12th cent. Black Monday massacre of English residents occurred 1209. Cromwell landed here 1649 after city's surrender to parliamentarians. Dublin saw much bloodshed 19th and 20th cent.—Robert EMMET's insurrection 1803, FENIAN MOVEMENT uprising 1867, murder of Lord Cavendish 1882, and Easter Rebellion 1916. ABBEY THEATRE world famous, as are many Dublin literary figures (e.g., Swift, Yeats, and Joyce).

Dublin, city (10,232), central Ga., on Oconee R. and

SE of Macon. Farm and timber market. Mfg. of cotton products, woolen textiles, and lumber.

Dubois, Guillaume (gēyōm' dübwä'), 1656–1723, French cardinal, chief adviser (1715–23) to the regent, Philippe d'Orléans. Astute diplomat.

du Bois, Guy Pène (dü bwä') 1884–, American painter and art critic, b. Brooklyn, N.Y.

Du Bois, W(illiam) E(dward) B(urghardt) (dübois'), 1868–, American Negro author, editor of *Crisis*.

Du Bois (dōō'bois), city (pop. 11,497), central Pa., NE of Pittsburgh; settled 1812. Has railroad shops, coal mining, and metal and textile plants.

Du Bois-Reymond, Emil (ā'mēl dü bwä'-rāmō'), 1818–96, German physiologist, authority on muscle and nerve action and accompanying electrical changes.

Dubos, René Jules (rünä' zhül dübō'), 1901–, American bacteriologist, b. France. He isolated gramicidin from soil bacteria.

Dubrovnik (dōō'brôvnĭk), Ital. *Ragusa*, city (pop. 16,-060), Croatia, NW Yugoslavia; Adriatic port and resort. Founded by Greek refugees c.7th cent. A.D., it became a powerful, virtually independent merchant republic (under Venetian rule 13th–14th cent.; later tributary to Turkey). Seized by French (1806), it was awarded to Austria at Congress of Vienna (1815). A medieval center of Serbo-Croatian culture, city retains much medieval architecture, including city walls.

Dubuque, Julien (dübūk'), 1762–1810, pioneer settler of Iowa, b. Quebec.

Dubuque (dübūk'), city (pop. 49,671), NE Iowa, on bluffs above the Mississippi; organized 1837 and named for Julien Dubuque. Rail, trade, and industrial center and river port for agr. area, it has railroad shops and shipyards and mfg. of food, metal, and wood products. Seat of Univ. of Dubuque, Clarke Col., and Loras Col. (R.C.; mainly for men; opened as pioneer theological seminary 1839, chartered as college 1894). Grave of Dubuque near by.

Du Cange, Charles du Fresne, sieur (shärl' dü frĕn' syûr dü käzh'), 1610–88, French medieval scholar, compiler of *Glossarium mediae et infimae Latinitatis*, greatest collection ever made of forms of early medieval Latin and of oldest Romance.

Ducas (dü'kùs), Greek family of Constantinople. Four members were Byzantine emperors—Michael VII, ALEXIUS V, John III, and Constantine I.

Duccio (di Buoninsegna) (dōōt'chēō dē bwōnēnsä'nyä), fl. 1278–1319, Italian painter, founder of Sienese school. Only authenticated work is double altar in Siena cathedral. Rucellai Madonna (in Santa Maria Novella, Florence) is attributed to him.

Du Cerceau: see ANDROUET.

Du Chaillu, Paul (Belloni) (dü shäyü'), 1831?–1903, French-American explorer in Africa, b. probably in Paris. Backed by Philadelphia Acad. of Natural Sciences, explored Gabun country in Africa (1855–59). Published account upsetting previous ideas of region's geography. Second expedition (1863–65) visited unknown tribes, verified reports of a Pygmy race.

Duchamp, Marcel (märsĕl' düshä'), 1887–, French painter. Famous work is *Nude Descending a Staircase*, painting depicting continuous action with series of overlapping figures. Was a leader of the Dadaists.

Duchesne, Père: see HÉBERT, JACQUES RENÉ.

duck, waterfowl smaller than related goose and swan. Accurately, duck refers to female and drake to male. Usually divided into three groups: river or fresh-water ducks (mallard, wood duck, black duck, teal), sea ducks (canvasback, scoter, eider, redhead), and mergansers or fish-eating ducks. Domestic meat producers are Pekin or Peking, Aylesbury, and Rouen ducks, all descendants of mallard duck. See *ill.*, p. 105.

Duck Lake, central Sask., Canada, SW of Prince Albert. Saw first encounter of Riel's Rebellion, 1885.

Ducommun, Élie (ālē' dükômü'), 1833–1906, Swiss journalist and pacifist. Organized Internatl. Peace Bureau at Berne (1891). Shared 1902 Nobel Peace Prize with C. A. Gobat.

ductless gland: see GLAND.

Duddell, William Du Bois (dŭdĕl'), 1872–1917, English consulting electrical engineer. His research on resistance of electric arc led to Poulsen arc.

Du Deffand, Marie de Vichy-Chamrond, marquise (märē' dü vēshē'-shärō' märkēz' dü dēfä'), 1697–1780, French woman of letters. Her salon was frequented by the leaders of the Enlightenment. Mme du Deffand's later years were made tragic by blindness and by her attachment to Horace Walpole, one of the chief recipients of her brilliant correspondence.

Dudley, John: see NORTHUMBERLAND, JOHN DUDLEY, DUKE OF.

Dudley, Joseph, 1647–1720, colonial governor of Mass. (1702–15). Unpopular because of earlier connection with rule of Sir Edmund Andros.

Dudley, Plimmon Henry, 1843–1924, American civil and metallurgical engineer, inventor of instruments for testing and ways of improving railroad beds.

Dudley, Robert: see LEICESTER, ROBERT DUDLEY, EARL OF.

Dudley, town (pop. 5,261), S central Mass., near Conn. line SW of Worcester. Mfg. of textiles.

duel, prearranged armed fight between two persons to settle a point of honor. Presumably arose from wager of battle (form of trial in which formal fight between accuser and accused settled the case). Duels popular in 16th-cent. France, later in England. Student duels prominent in 19th-cent. German universities, revived by Nazis. In U.S. most famous duel was that in which Aaron Burr killed Alexander Hamilton. Alexander Jackson was also known as a duelist. Dueling now illegal in all Western countries.

due process of law: see FOURTEENTH AMENDMENT.

Duer, William (dü'ûr), 1747–99, American Revolutionary patriot and capitalist, b. England. One of largest contractors supplying army during Revolution. Became Assistant Secretary of Treasury in 1789; sued by government for irregularities in his work. Imprisoned for debt. His son, **William Alexander Duer,** 1780–1858, American jurist and educator, was president of Columbia Col. (1829–42). There he estab. scientific courses not requiring Latin and increased instruction in modern languages.

Duero, river: see DOURO.

Dufay, Guillaume (gēyōm' düfä'), c.1400–1474, leading composer of the Burgundian (sometimes called Netherlands) school. His style united Gothic, Italian, and English elements. He wrote three-part vocal chansons, Masses, songs with instrumental accompaniment, and motets.

Dufour, Guillaume Henri (gēyōm' ārē' düfōōr'), 1787–1875, Swiss general. Led federal forces to victory over SONDERBUND (1847). Wrote military treatises. Helped estab. International Red Cross (1864).

Dufourspitze: see ROSA, MONTE.

Dufy, Raoul (räōōl' düfē'), 1877–1953, French painter and illustrator, with decorative, calligraphic style and subtle use of brilliant color.

Du Gard, Roger Martin: see MARTIN DU GARD.

Dugdale, Richard Louis (dŭg'dāl), 1841–83, American social investigator, author of a study on criminality in the "Jukes" family.

dugong (dōō'gŏng), herbivorous aquatic mammal. (*Dugong* or *Halicore*) of Red Sea, Indian Ocean, and Australian waters. Like the manatee of same order (Sirenia) it is called sea cow. Brownish or grayish, 7–9½ ft. long, it has flexible front flippers and a two-lobed, flat tail. Hunted for hide, tusks, oil, and palatable flesh, it is now scarce.

Duguay-Trouin, René (rünä' dügā'-trōōē'), 1673–1736, French admiral. Enlisted as privateer 1689. By 1709 he had captured 300 merchantmen, 20 warships. Took Rio de Janeiro 1711.

Du Guesclin, Bertrand (dügĕs'klĭn, bĕrträ' dü gĕklē'), c.1320–1380, constable of France (1370–80), one of most popular heroes of France, particularly in his native Brittany. Most notable achievement was his

Duhamel reconquest of English-held France (1370–74; see HUNDRED YEARS WAR).

Duhamel, Georges (zhôrzh' düämĕl'), 1884–, French author. Best known for novel, *Cycle de Salavin* (1920–32; Eng. tr., 1936), whose "hero," Salavin, is unable to adjust himself to society.

Duisburg (düs'bŏŏrk), city (pop. 408,877), North Rhine-Westphalia, NW Germany, at junction of Ruhr and Rhine rivers. Industrial center of RUHR dist. (steel, machinery, textiles) and large inland port. Armaments industry drew World War II air raids which destroyed three quarters of the city.

Dukas, Paul (dükä'), 1865–1935, French composer of symphonic poem *The Sorcerer's Apprentice* (1897) and opera *Ariane et Barbe-Bleue* (1907).

Duke, James Buchanan, 1856–1925, American processor of tobacco products and benefactor of Duke Univ.

Duke University, at Durham, N.C.; for men and women; opened 1838, chartered 1841 by Friends and Methodists as Union Col. Reorganized as Normal Col. (1852) and again as Trinity Col. (1859; Methodist); moved to Durham 1892. Renamed 1924 for benefactor J. B. Duke. Has two undergraduate colleges, Trinity and Woman's. Tobacco culture and medical research are noted.

Dukhobors or **Doukhobors** (both: dŏŏ'kŭbôrz) [Rus.,= spirit wrestlers], religious sect that arose among Russian peasants in 17th cent.; now more properly Christians of the Universal Brotherhood. They believe in absolute equality of men and resist all authority, civil or ecclesiastic. This attitude brought persecution in Russia. Alexander I allowed them to settle on the Sea of Azov, but later resistance to military conscription caused their removal to a barren section now in Georgian SSR. This they brought to blossom, but in 1887 military conscription again reached them. In the 1890s with the help of Leo Tolstoy and of the Quakers most of them moved to Saskatchewan, Canada. Again they created a thriving community—under the leadership of Peter Veregin after he was allowed to leave Siberia and, after his death, under his son, another Peter Veregin. Trouble with their neighbors and the government led to spectacular demonstrations, notably the "nudist strikes." A small group of more ascetic Dukhobors split from the main body as the Sons of Freedom. Some Dukhobors presumably remain in Russia; a few are in the Paraguayan Chaco.

dulcimer (dŭl'sŭmŭr), stringed musical instrument. Consists of wooden box strung with strings which are struck with mallets instead of being plucked. Oriental in origin; appeared in Europe in Middle Ages.

Du Lhut, Daniel Greysolon, sieur: see DULUTH.

Dulles, John Foster (dŭ'lŭs), 1888–, U.S. delegate to the United Nations (1945–48, 1950); grandson of John Watson Foster. Chosen (1952) by Eisenhower to be Secretary of State.

Dulong, Pierre Louis (pyĕr' lwē dülō'), 1785–1838, French physicist and chemist. Dulong and Petit's law: specific heats of elements are inversely proportional to their atomic weights; specific heat is constant for all solid elements.

Duluth or **Du Lhut, Daniel Greysolon, sieur** (Fr. dülüt'), 1636–1710, French explorer in Canada. He won the L. Superior and upper Mississippi region for France.

Duluth (dŭlŏŏth'), city (pop. 104,511), NE Minn., at W end (and head of navigation) of L. Superior; harbor shared with Superior, Wis. Site visited in 17th cent. by explorers, including sieur Duluth; permanently settled after 1850. Grew as trade and shipping center for lumber area, became one of world's chief ore shipping points after discovery in 1890s of Mesabi and Vermilion iron ranges. Now commercial and industrial center of N Minn. and entrance to resort area, it has foundries, shipyards, flour and lumber mills, canneries, creameries, and mfg. of farm and telephone equipment, metal and wood products, and clothing. Dock facilities for handling ore, grain, and

other products are extensive. Here are Aerial Lift Bridge and a branch of state university.

Dulwich (dŭl'ĭj), residential suburb, S London, England. Has a well-known public school, Dulwich Col. (founded 1613).

duma (dŏŏ'mä), Russian representative body, particularly the Imperial Duma (lower house) estab. 1906 as a result of 1905 Revolution.

Dumas, Alexandre (älĕksä'drù dümä'), known as **Dumas père** (pĕr'), 1802–70, French author, partly of African descent. He wrote many historical adventure novels, notably *The Three Musketeers* (1844), *Twenty Years After* (1845), *The Count of Monte Cristo* (1844–45). Among his dramas *La Tour de Nesle* (1832) is best known. He employed many collaborators. His son, **Alexandre Dumas,** known as **Dumas fils** (fēs'), 1824–95, French dramatist and novelist, wrote *La Dame aux camélias* (1852; known in English as *Camille;* basis of Verdi's *La Traviata*), *Le Demi-Monde* (1855), *Le Fils naturel* [the natural son] (1858), mainly plays of moral or social theme. He is also considered a creator of the modern comedy of manners.

Dumas (dōō'mùs), city (pop. 6,127), N Texas, N of Amarillo in Panhandle. Oil, gas, and wheat center with chemical plants.

Dumas fils: see DUMAS, ALEXANDRE (1824–95).

Dumas père: see DUMAS, ALEXANDRE (1802–70).

Du Maurier, George (Louis Palmella Busson) (dü môr'ēä), 1834–96, English artist and novelist, b. Paris. His best-known novels are *Peter Ibbetson* (1892) and *Trilby* (1894). Was an illustrator on *Punch* staff. His granddaughter, **Daphne Du Maurier,** 1907–, has written popular novels, notably *Rebecca* (1938).

Dumbarton (dŭmbär'tùn), burgh (pop. 23,703), co. town of Dumbartonshire, Scotland. Shipbuilding center, it also has mfg. of aircraft, pharmaceuticals, whisky, soap, and hosiery. Chief town of ancient kingdom of Strathclyde.

Dumbarton Oaks, estate, now in Washington, D.C.; scene of a conference (1944) at which the U.S., Great Britain, the USSR, and China reached an agreement to create the United Nations.

Dumbartonshire or **Dunbartonshire** (dŭn–), county (241 sq. mi.; pop. 164,263), central Scotland; co. town Dumbarton. Bordered on E by Loch Lomond, on S by Clyde estuary, and on W by Loch Long. It is mountainous region (up to 3,000 ft.) with little agr. Cattle and sheep raised. Industries include fishing, shipbuilding, and cotton mfg.

Dumdum (dŭm'dŭm), town (pop. 39,434), S West Bengal, India. The deadly soft-nosed (dumdum) bullets, banned in 1899 by Hague Conference, were first made here. Its large airport serves Calcutta.

Dumfriesshire (dŭmfrēs'shĭr) or **Dumfries,** border county (1,073 sq. mi.; pop. 85,656), SW Scotland. Surface largely hilly with agr. in valleys. Salmon fishing and cattle grazing important; limestone and sandstone quarried. There are many beautiful lochs. Scene of much border warfare until 18th cent. County town, **Dumfries,** burgh (pop. 26,320), includes Maxwelltown across Nith R. Has Burns's mausoleum.

Dummer, Jeremiah, 1645–1718, American silversmith. His mark is ID over a fleur-de-lis in a heart.

Dumont (dŏŏ'mŏnt), suburban borough (pop. 13,013), NE N.J., NE of Hackensack; settled 1730.

Dumouriez, Charles François (shärl' fränswä' dümŏŏrēä'), 1739–1823, French general in French Revolutionary Wars. Victor at Valmy and Jemappes (1792); conquered Belgium, invaded Netherlands, but deserted to Austrians after his defeat at Neerwinden (1793).

Dunant, Jean Henry (zhä' ērē' dùnä'), 1828–1910, Swiss philanthropist. Brought about founding of Red Cross. Shared 1910 Nobel Peace Prize with Passy.

Dunbar, Paul Laurence, 1872–1906, American Negro poet, b. Dayton, Ohio. Wrote *Lyrics of Lowly Life* (1896).

Dunbar, William, c.1460–c.1520, Scottish poet strongly influenced by Chaucer. Noted for inventiveness and metrical skill. "Dance of the Sevin Deidly Synnis" most characteristic poem.

Dunbar (dŭnbär'), burgh (pop. 4,115), East Lothian, Scotland, at mouth of Firth of Forth; resort and fishing port. Has remains of castle to which Mary Queen of Scots was abducted by Bothwell 1567. Cromwell defeated Covenanters here 1650.

Dunbar, city (pop. 8,032), W W.Va., on Kanawha R. WNW of Charleston. Mfg. of glass and farm tools.

Duncan I, d. 1040?, king of Scotland (1034–1040?). He was murdered by his general Macbeth.

Duncan, Isadora, 1878–1927, American dancer. Early failures preceded triumphs (1903–8) in Budapest, Berlin, London, and finally in U.S. A daring, dynamic innovator, she danced barefoot in flowing robes. Greatly influenced modern dance through her concert tours and schools. She died at Nice, accidentally strangled by her scarf.

Duncan, city (pop. 15,325), S Okla., S of Chickasha; founded 1892. Supply and trade center for oil, cattle, and agr. area, it processes oil and cotton and has mfg. of oil-field equipment.

Duncansbay Head or **Duncansby Head,** 210 ft. high, northeastern extremity of Scotland, in Caithness.

Dundalk (dŭndôk'), urban district (pop. 18,562) co. seat of Co. Louth, Ireland, on Dundalk Bay of Irish Sea; seaport. Industries include export of farm produce, brewing, shipbuilding, and fishing. Railroad center with large car works.

Dundas, town (pop. 6,846), S Ont., Canada, at head of Burlington Bay and NW of Hamilton. Head of Desjardins Canal. Mfg. of machinery and clothing.

Dundee, John Graham of Claverhouse, 1st Viscount (klă'vŭrŭs), c.1649–1689, Scottish Jacobite chieftain and soldier, known as Bonnie Dundee. Hated by Covenanters whom he tried to suppress 1678–88. Fought for James II in Glorious Revolution; raised force to restore him but was killed in battle of Killiecrankie. Subject of ballads and novels.

Dundee (dŭndē'), independent burgh (pop. 177,333), Angus, Scotland, on Firth of Tay. Has docks and various industries. Dundee marmalade famous. Site of Univ. Col., part of Univ. of St. Andrews. City early adopted doctrines of Reformation.

Dundonald, Thomas Cochrane, 10th earl of, 1775–1860, British naval commander in Napoleonic wars. Commanded Chilean navy in liberation of Chile and Peru and Greek navy in war against Turkey 1827.

Dunedin (dŭnē'dĭn), city (pop. 65,771; metropolitan pop. 83,351), SE South Isl., New Zealand; port at base of Otago Peninsula; founded 1848. Seat of Univ. of Otago (1869). Woolen mills.

Dunellen (dŭnē'lŭn), borough (pop. 6,291), N central N.J., SW of Newark; laid out 1868. Mfg. of concrete mixers, adhesives; pumps, printing presses.

Dunes, Battle of the, 1658, victory of French and English under Turenne over Spanish under John of Austria and Louis II de Condé; fought near Dunkirk, France.

Dunfermline (dŭmfûr'lĭn), burgh (pop. 44,710), Fifeshire, Scotland. Residence of Scottish kings from 11th cent. Abbey is burial place of Robert I and others. Birthplace of Andrew Carnegie, town is hq. of Carnegie Trusts. Has textile mills and metal foundries.

Dunkards, Dunkers, or **Tunkers,** a popular name for a sect of German Baptist brethren, divided into five denominations. Name derived from German "to dip," baptism being by immersion. Having evolved in Germany from Pietism, the sect was brought (1719) to Pa. It bans war, oaths, alcohol, tobacco, worldly amusements. Members wear simple, plain garb.

Dunkirk (dŭn'kûrk), Fr. *Dunkerque,* town (1946 pop. 9,869; 1936 pop. 28,450), Nord dept., N France; fishing port on North Sea. A key city in centuries-long struggle between France and its neighbors, Dunkirk often changed masters, passed permanently to France

1662. In 1940 (May 26–June 4) it was scene of one of most memorable naval actions in history when some 300,000 Allied troops, cut off by German advance on Channel ports, were evacuated to England. Dunkirk was left in ruins. Germans held out here against Allies until May, 1945.

Dunkirk, city (pop. 18,007), W N.Y., on L. Erie. Mfg. (heaters, silk, tool steel, glass) and fisheries.

Dunlap, William, 1766–1839, American playwright, prolific writer of Gothic romances and tragedies. Adapted many French and German works. Was theater manager (1796–1805), a founder of Natl. Academy of Design, and author of books on theater and design.

Dunmore, John Murray, 4th earl of, 1732–1809, British colonial governor of Va. Led Indian campaign in 1774, known as Lord Dunmore's War. Opposed colonists until forced to return to England in 1776.

Dunmore, borough (pop. 20,305), NE Pa., near Scranton; settled 1783. Produces coal and textiles.

Dunmore's War: see DUNMORE, JOHN MURRAY, 4TH EARL OF.

Dunn, Gano, 1870–1953, American electrical engineer of large-scale projects and designer of electrical equipment for production.

Dunn, town (pop. 6,316), central N.C., S of Raleigh. Farm trade center with lumber and flour mills.

Dunne, Finley Peter, 1867–1936, American humorist, journalist. His Irish-American "Mr. Dooley" excelled in deflating politicians' pretensions.

Dunnet Head, promontory, Caithness, Scotland, forming N extremity of Great Britain proper.

Dunois, Jean, comte de (zhä' kõt' dŭ dünwä'), c.1403–1468, French general, called the Bastard of Orléans; natural son of Louis d'Orléans. In charge of defense of Orléans when Joan of Arc relieved it (1429); joined Joan in subsequent campaign; took part in capture of Paris (1436).

Dunoyer de Segonzac, André: see SEGONZAC.

Dunsany, Edward John Moreton Drax Plunkett, 18th Baron (dŭnsăn'ē, –sā'–), 1878–, Anglo-Irish author. Plays (e.g., *A Night at an Inn,* 1916), prose tales (e.g., *The Gods of Pegana,* 1905) of Lord Dunsany are halfsatire, half-fantasy.

Dunsinane (dŭn"sĭnān'), one of Sidlaw Hills, Perthshire, Scotland. Has ruins of fort, called Macbeth's Castle, supposedly scene of Macbeth's defeat by earl of Northumbria, as told by Shakspere.

Dunsmuir (dŭnz'mūr), city (pop. 2,256), N Calif., S of Mt. Shasta. Hunting and fishing resort. Lava Beds Natl. Monument is near.

Duns Scotus, John (dŭnz' skō'tŭs), d. 1308, British or Irish scholastic philosopher, a Franciscan, called the Subtle Doctor. There is no authentic list of his works, but some are definitely known. He was the founder of Scotism, opposed to Thomism (i.e., the school of St. Thomas Aquinas) in Roman Catholicism. He denied that individuality comes from matter; said that knowledge of finite truths rests on the ultimate Truth, which is God; argued that God's possible existence, demonstrable from sense experience, involves his necessary existence; and held that the state got its sanction from consent of the people and that private property is not sanctioned by natural law.

Dunstable (dŭn'stŭbŭl), municipal borough (pop. 17,-108), Bedfordshire, England. Traces of Stone and Bronze Age exist. Excavations in 1926 produced relics of woman of c.2000 B.C.

Dunstan, Sir Wyndham Rowland, 1861–1949, English chemist, expert on alkaloids, authority on tropical agriculture and mineralogy.

Dunster, Henry, c.1612–1659, first president of Harvard (1640–54), b. England.

duodecimal system, notation system corresponding to decimal system but based on 12 instead of 10. Since 12 has more factors than 10 more fractions can be expressed evenly. System common in British and American measure (e.g., inches, feet) in contrast to metric system, which has a thorough-going decimal base.

Dupleix, Joseph François, marquis (zhōzĕf' frănswä' märkē' düplĕks'), 1697–1763, French governor of Pondichéry, India (1741–54). Captured Madras (1746); held Pondichéry against British (1748); formed plan of establishing French supremacy in India. By armed force and by diplomacy he made himself master of the Carnatic and most of Deccan (1749–51,) but British intervention under Robert Clive and fear of war with England induced the French government to recall him. Died in poverty.

Duplessis, Maurice Lenoblet (mōrēs' lùnôblä' dü-plĕsē'), 1890–, premier and attorney general of Quebec, Canada (1936–39, 1944–).

Du Pont (dü pŏnt'), French-American family. **Pierre Samuel Du Pont de Nemours** (dù nùmōōr'), 1739–1817, was a French economist, one of the PHYSIO-CRATS. Also active in politics. He migrated to U.S. in 1799. His son, **Eleuthère Irénée Du Pont** (älûtēr' ēränä'), 1771–1834, b. Paris, set up a powder mill near Wilmington, Del., in 1802. He developed an extensive business, which he named E. I. du Pont de Nemours & Company (firm's present name). **Samuel Francis Du Pont**, 1803–65, American naval officer, was grandson of Pierre Samuel du Pont de Nemours. In Civil War he led successful attack on Port Royal, S.C. (1861). Against his own will, he led unsuccessful attack on Charleston (1863). **Pierre Samuel Du Pont**, 1870–, served as president of family business for many years. Under him the company developed scores of chemical manufactures, acquired many other industries.

Dupré, Jules (zhül' düprä'), 1811?–1889, French landscape painter of the Barbizon school.

Dupuy de Lôme, Stanislas (stänēsläs' düpüē' dù lōm'), 1816–85, French naval engineer. Built first French armored ship. Demonstrated (1872) practicability of dirigible balloon.

Dupuytren, Guillaume, Baron (gēyōm' bärō' düpüētrē'), 1777–1835, French surgeon, influential as a clinical teacher and through his writings.

Duquesne (dùkän'), city (pop. 17,620), SW Pa., on Monongahela R. and near Pittsburgh; settled 1789. Mfg. of iron, steel, and chemicals.

Duquesne, Fort, on site of PITTSBURGH, Pa. Strategic position at junction of Monongahela and Allegheny rivers made it major objective in last of French and Indian Wars. Abandoned by French to British in 1758 and renamed Fort Pitt.

Duquesne University: see PITTSBURGH, Pa.

Duquesnoy, François (fräswä' dükĕnwä'), 1594–1643?, Flemish sculptor, also called François Flamand. Worked mostly in Italy. Did reliefs of children.

Du Quoin (dōō koin'), city (pop. 7,147), S Ill., N of Cairo. Center of agr. and coal region.

Dura (dōō'rù), anc. city on the Euphrates, E of Palmyra; also called Europos, Doura, and Doura-Europus. A prominent post from the 3d cent. B.C. to the 3d cent. A.D., it fell to ruins. Excavations after 1922 gave much information on Hellenistic and Roman Mesopotamia.

duralumin (dōōrăl'yùmĭn), alloy of aluminum, copper, magnesium, manganese. Because of lightness and tensile strength, is used in dirigible frameworks.

Duran, Carolus: see CAROLUS-DURAN.

Durance (düräs'), rapid river, c.180 mi. long, SE France, rising in Dauphiné Alps and joining Rhone near Avignon. Fertile valley.

Durand, Asher Brown (düränd'), 1796–1886, American painter, a founder of Hudson River school.

Durango (dōōräng'gō), state (47,691 sq. mi.; pop. 629,-502), N Mexico; cap. Durango (pop. 33,412). Mountains in W are rich mining area; semiarid plains to E are ranch country; farther E is fertile LAGUNA DISTRICT. Gómez Palacio is chief city. Francisco de Ibarra undertook its exploration and colonization in 1562.

Durango (dōōräng'gō), city (pop. 7,459; alt. c.6,500 ft.), SW Colo., on Animas R., in farm, ranch, mine

area. Mining of carnotite for uranium. Processes uranium, vanadium. Mesa Verde Natl. Park is W, Fort Lewis School of Agriculture near by.

Durant, Thomas Clark, 1820–85, American railroad builder, chief figure in construction of Union Pacific RR. Organized CRÉDIT MOBILIER.

Durant, city (pop. 10,541), SE Okla., near Red R. and Denison Dam, settled c.1870. Commercial and processing center for agr. region (esp. cotton).

Durazzo (dōōrät'sō), Albanian *Durrës*, town (pop. 14,031), Albania; Adriatic port. Founded c.625 B.C. as Epidamnus, a joint colony of Corinth and Corcyra, whose quarrel over it precipitated the PELOPON-NESIAN WAR (431 B.C.). Renamed Dyrrhacchium c.300 B.C., it passed under Epirus; fell to Rome 229 B.C.; became a major Roman naval and military base. Passing to Byzantine Empire, Durazzo was often seized by foreigners, notably by the Angevin kings of Naples, who made it a duchy in 1267, and by Venice, which held it from 1392 until its fall to the Turks in 1501. Majority of pop. accepted Islam. City has many mosques; three early Byzantine towers; Venetian fortifications.

Durban (dûr'bùn), city (pop. 339,247), Natal, South Africa, a port on Natal Bay and Natal's largest city. Exports coal, manganese, chrome.

Düren (dü'rùn), city (pop. 35,121), North Rhine-Westphalia, NW Germany, on Roer R. between Aachen and Cologne. Most of city was pulverized in World War II bombings and shellings.

Dürer, Albrecht (äl'brĕkht dü'rùr), 1471–1528, German artist, famous for prints and drawings of keen observation and rich detail; b. Nuremberg, where he studied with Michael Wolgemut. In 1494 he estab. own studio in Nuremberg and did woodcuts for the *Apocalypse* and *Great Passion*. Visited Venice 1505–7. During his most fertile period (1507–20) he painted several great altarpieces and created his most celebrated engravings, including *Melancholia*, *The Knight*, and *St. Jerome in His Study*. Visited the Netherlands 1520. Was a friend of Luther. Wrote on human proportions, perspective, geometry, and fortifications.

duress, actual or threatened violence or imprisonment to force a person, directly or indirectly, to enter into an agreement or perform some other act against his will. To void such a contract, duress must be shown to have been such as to overcome the party's mind and will. See also COERCION.

Durfee, William Franklin (dûr'fē), 1833–99, American engineer and producer of first steel by Bessemer process in America.

Durham, John George Lambton, 1st earl of, 1792–1840, British liberal statesman. Promoted Reform Bill of 1832. As Governor General of Canada he prepared masterly *Report on the Affairs of British North America* (1839), supporting self-government and reforms but opposing French nationalism in Canada.

Durham (dŭ'rùm), maritime county (1,015 sq. mi.; pop. 1,463,416), N England, one of most densely populated English counties. Has dairy farming and cattle raising, but mainly industrial (rich coal deposits) and iron, steel, chemical, and glass industries. Shipbuilding along Tyne R. Sunderland and Hartlepool are important seaports. County ruled by bishops of Durham until 1836. The county town, **Durham,** municipal borough (pop. 19,283), has 11th-cent. castle occupied by Univ. of Durham. Cathedral, begun 1093 and one of England's finest examples of Norman architecture, contains relics of St. Cuthbert.

Durham. 1 Town (pop. 4,770), SE N.H., SW of Dover. Seat of Univ. of New Hampshire (land-grant, state supported; coed.), which was chartered 1866, opened 1868 as state college of agr. and mechanic arts at DARTMOUTH COLLEGE, moved 1893, and became a university 1923. **2** City (pop. 71,311), central N.C., in piedmont NW of Raleigh; settled c.1852. Great center for marketing and processing tobacco, it also has textile and hosiery mills. Tobacco industry grew after Civil War, with J. B. Duke as leader. Hq. of largest Negro life insurance company in U.S. Seat of DUKE UNIVERSITY.

Durkheim, Émile (ämēl' dürkĕm'), 1858–1917, French sociologist. Influenced by Comte, he held that religion and morality originated in the collective mind of society.

Durkin, Martin P(atrick), 1894–, U.S. Secretary of Labor (1953–). President of plumbers' and steamfitters' union (1943–52).

Durres, Albania: see DURAZZO.

Duryea, Charles Edgar (door'yā), 1862–1938, American inventor and automobile manufacturer. With his brother, J. Frank Duryea (1870–), he built one of first practical internal-combustion automobiles.

Duryea, borough (pop. 6,655), NE Pa., on Lackawanna R. SW of Scranton. Has coal mines and silk mills.

Duse, Eleonora (dōō'zŭ, Ital. ālāōnō'rä dōō'zä), 1859–1924, Italian actress. Made debut at 14 as Juliet. Later vehicles included Sardou's *Fédora,* Goldoni's *La Locandiera,* and Ibsen's *Lady from the Sea.* Her acting combined simplicity with emotional power. For some years a romantic attachment existed between Duse and Italian poet D'Annunzio.

Dushan, Stephen: see STEPHEN DUSHAN.

Düsseldorf (dü'sŭldôrf), city (pop. 498,347), cap. of North Rhine-Westphalia, NW Germany, at junction of Rhine and Düssel rivers. Industrial and commercial center; steel, machinery, textiles. Cap. of duchy of Berg from 1288; passed to Prussia 1814. Largely ruined by World War II air raids. Birthplace of Heinrich Heine. Has famous art academy (founded 1819).

dust, atmospheric, minute particles of matter (chiefly inorganic) settling from or suspended in air. Sources: city activities, blown dry earth, volcanic eruptions, ocean salt spray, organic matter (e.g., pollen), and meteorite combustion.

Dust Bowl, areas of U.S. prairie states where dust storms carry off topsoil which has lost its natural cover of grass by overgrazing, burning over, or plowing. Remedies include planting of cover crops, trees, and much grass to anchor soil.

Dutch East India Company: see EAST INDIA COMPANY, DUTCH.

Dutch East Indies: see INDONESIA.

Dutch Guiana: see GUIANA.

Dutch Harbor, village on Amaknak isl. in Unalaska Bay, which indents Unalaska, off W Alaska. One of few good harbors in ALEUTIAN ISLANDS, known early to Russian fur traders. Became transshipping point for Nome after 1899 gold strike. U.S. naval base, estab. 1940, was important in World War II. Attacked by Japanese planes 1942.

Dutch language, West Germanic language of Indo-European family. See LANGUAGE (table).

Dutchman's-breeches, North American wild flower (*Dicentra cucullaria*) related to bleeding heart. It has drooping racemes of yellow-tipped white flowers and ferny foliage.

Dutchman's-pipe, twining vine (*Aristolochia durior*) of E U.S. It has pipelike flowers and heart-shaped leaves. Flowers can trap and later release insects.

Dutch New Guinea: see NEW GUINEA.

Dutch Reformed Church: see REFORMED CHURCH IN AMERICA.

Dutch Wars. 1 1652–54, war between English and Dutch. Marked crisis between two nations' rivalry as carriers of world trade; precipitated by English search and seizure of Dutch merchant ships and by English Navigation Act of 1651, directed against Dutch trade with British possessions. Sea fight between Robert Blake and Maarten TROMP, May, 1652, opened hostilities. Tromp's victory over Blake off Dungeness, Nov., 1652, gave Dutch control of Channel; control was broken by British victory at Portland (1653). After victory off Gabbard's Shoal, British blockaded

Dutch coast. Tromp attacked blockading fleet, July 31, 1653, and was defeated. Peace signed April, 1654. Dutch agreed to salute British flag in British seas, to pay compensation for English losses, and to submit territorial claims to arbitration. **2** 1664–67, another war between Dutch and English. Dutch had continued to threaten English commercial supremacy. In 1664 British raided Dutch colonies on African coast and took New Netherland in North America. England declared war, March, 1665. Duke of York (later James II) won battle of Lowestoft in June, 1665; in Sept., bishop of Munster, an English ally, overran E province of Netherlands, but was soon expelled. Louis XIV of France declared war on England, Jan., 1666, but took little part in war. British fleet under Monck and Prince Rupert was defeated in Four Days battle or battle of the Downs (June 1–4, 1666) by Michiel de RUYTER and Cornelis Tromp; in Aug. they defeated Dutch and destroyed shipping along Dutch coast. Charles II having let the navy fall into unprepared state, De Ruyter exacted heavy losses in raid in the Thames, 1667. In Treaty of Breda (July, 1667), trade laws were modified to favor Dutch, conquests of war were retained (English received N.Y., N.J., and Del.; Dutch kept Surinam), and English and French made mutual restoration of conquests. **3** 1672–78, first of great wars of Louis XIV of France. Aimed at destruction of Dutch rivalry to French trade and expansion of French empire. Having gained allies in CHARLES II of England, in Sweden, and several German states, Louis overran S provinces of Netherlands, May, 1672. His advance on Amsterdam was stopped when Dutch opened the dikes. De Ruyter defeated English and French fleets at Southwold Bay. Dutch peace offers having been spurned, a revolution took place, and William of Orange (later WILLIAM III of England) took over from Jan de WITT, July, 1672. In 1673 Dutch received support of Spain, the emperor, Brandenburg, Denmark, and other powers, and England made peace 1674, but French victories on land (Maastricht, Seneff, Sinzheim, Cassel, Freiburg) under Louis II de CONDÉ and TURENNE and the 1676 naval campaign of Abraham Duquesne gained peace at Nijmegen (1678–79). Maastricht was ceded to Dutch, and French restrictive tariffs were modified in their favor. In subsequent treaty with Spain, France got Franche-Comté and chain of border fortresses in return for evacuating Spanish Netherlands. In treaty with the emperor (1679), France was confirmed in possession of Freiburg and part of Lorraine.

Dutch West India Company, trading and colonizing company, chartered by Dutch republic 1621, organized 1623. Founded NEW NETHERLAND (New York). Given trading rights on African coast between Tropic of Cancer and Cape of Good Hope, on American coast between Newfoundland and Straits of Magellan. Company had almost complete power in its territory.

Dutch West Indies: see WEST INDIES.

Dutton, Clarence Edward, 1841–1912, American geologist. He served in 1875 with John W. Powell on U.S. Geological Survey in the Rocky Mt. region. He introduced the term *isostasy,* and was a pioneer advocate of the isostatic theory (see CONTINENT).

Duun, Olav (ō'läv dōōn'), 1876–1939, Norwegian novelist, author of a monumental series, *The People of Juvik* (6 novels; 1918–23).

Duveen, Joseph, 1st Baron Duveen of Millbank, 1869–1939, English art dealer. Benefactor of many museums and galleries, notably the Natl. Gall. in London. Helped form several American art collections.

Duveneck, Frank (dū'vŭnĕk), 1848–1919, American portrait and genre painter, an inspired teacher.

Duvergier de Hauranne, Jean (zhä' düvĕrzhyä' dü ōrän'), 1581–1643, French theologian, one of the molders of JANSENISM. A friend of Cornelis Jansen and of the ARNAULD family, he helped make Port-Royal a Jansenist stronghold. He had trouble with the Jesuits and with Cardinal Richelieu, who had him imprisoned (1638–42).

du Vigneaud, Vincent (dū věn′yō), 1901–, American biochemist, known for research including chemistry of insulin, protein, sulphur compounds, and biotin.

Duxbury, resort town (pop. 3,167), SE Mass., on Duxbury Bay and SE of Boston. Plymouth colonists including John Alden, Miles Standish, and William Brewster settled here. Alden's house still stands.

dvi-manganese: see RHENIUM.

Dvina (dvēnä′) or **Northern Dvina,** Rus. *Severnaya Dvina,* river, 455 mi. long, N European RSFSR, formed near Veliki Ustyug by two affluents. Flows NW, empties into White Sea below Archangel. Navigable May–Nov., it carries much commerce. Connected with MARIINSK SYSTEM.

Dvina or **Western Dvina,** Lettish *Daugava,* Rus. *Zapadnaya Dvina,* river, 620 mi. long, E Europe, rising in Valdai Hills, RSFSR, and flowing W through Belorussia and Latvia into the Gulf of Riga of the Baltic Sea. Navigable from Vitebsk. Connected by canal with Berezina.

Dvorak, Anton (än′tôn dvôr′shäk), Czech *Antonín Dvořák,* 1841–1904, Czech composer. Much of his music is nationalistic in spirit and influenced by Brahms and Wagner. He is best known for his symphony in E Minor, *From the New World,* written while he was in the U.S., and for his Slavonic Dances. He wrote nine symphonies, chamber works, a violin concerto, a cello concerto, and overtures.

dwarf, a plant, animal, or person whose size is less than normal; proportions sometimes abnormal. Human dwarfs usually have normal size parents.

dwarf cornel: see BUNCHBERRY.

Dwiggins, W(illiam) A(ddison), 1880–, American type designer, calligrapher, and book designer. Brought to type and book designing fresh boldness of advertising work. Designed clean, spare type faces (notably Electra and Caledonia) for linotype composition.

Dwight, Timothy, 1752–1817, American author and educator; grandson of Jonathan Edwards. An army chaplain in Revolutionary Army, he was later a Congregational pastor at Greenfield Hill, Conn. A famous preacher and writer of verse (one of CONNECTICUT WITS), he is perhaps better known as able president of Yale (1795–1817). His brother, **Theodore Dwight,** 1764–1846, also belonged to Connecticut Wits and was a conservative political leader. Theodore's son, **Theodore Dwight,** 1796–1866, wrote travel books and forwarded antislavery movement. A grandson of Timothy Dwight (1752–1817), **Theodore William Dwight,** 1822–92, headed Hamilton College law school, then was sole member of Columbia School of Law, later headed it. Another grandson of Timothy Dwight (1752–1817) was **Timothy Dwight,** 1828–1916, who helped to reorganize the Yale Divinity School and, as

president of Yale (1886–98), helped change it from college to university.

Dy, chemical symbol of the element DYSPROSIUM.

Dyck, Sir Anthony van: see VAN DYCK, SIR ANTHONY.

dye, substance used to color materials. Natural dyes obtained from plants (e.g., alizarin), animals (e.g., COCHINEAL), minerals (e.g., OCHER) have been largely replaced by synthetic dyes. Most of these are prepared from coal tar, from aromatic hydrocarbons such as benzene (see also ANILINE) or anthracene. Some materials can be dyed directly, others require use of MORDANT. Dyes may be acid or basic. Vat dye is so named for the method of application. Method of attachment of dye to material it colors may be chemical reaction between dye and fibers or may be absorption of dye by fiber. Dyeing was practiced centuries ago by Chinese, Persians, and Indians.

Dyer, Mary, d. 1660, Quaker martyr in Mass., b. England. Banished, she returned to Boston twice to minister to imprisoned Quakers. Arrested both times, reprieved in 1659, but hanged in 1660.

Dyersburg, city (pop. 10,885), W Tenn., near Mississippi R. NNE of Memphis; laid out 1825. Mfg. of textiles, cotton, grain, timber, and dairy products.

Dying Gaul, statue in Capitoline Mus., Rome. Example of Pergamene school of Greek sculpture (c.200 B.C.). Depicts fallen Galatian warrior.

Dykh-Tau (dĭkh″-tou′), peak, 17,054 ft. high, USSR, in central Greater Caucasus.

Dykstra, Clarence Addison (dĭk′strü), 1883–1950, American educator, civic administrator. City manager of Cincinnati 1930–37. President of Univ. of Wisconsin 1937–45. Provost of Univ. of California at Los Angeles 1945–50.

dynamics: see MECHANICS.

dynamite, explosive made from nitroglycerin and a porous substance; charge is set off by DETONATOR. It was discovered 1866 by A. B. NOBEL.

dynamo: see GENERATOR.

dyne (dīn), unit of force in centimeter-gram-second system producing an acceleration in a one-gram mass of one centimeter per second for each second the force acts.

dysentery, intestinal inflammation resulting from swallowing certain microorganisms, parasitic worms, or irritating substances. Amoebic dysentery is caused by a protozoan; bacterial, by bacillus.

dysprosium (dĭsprō′shēŭm), metallic element (symbol = Dy; see also ELEMENT, table) found in certain minerals with other metals of the RARE EARTHS. It is the most highly magnetic substance.

Dzaudzhikau (dzoujĭkou′), city (pop. 127,172), cap. of North Ossetian ASSR, SE European RSFSR, on Terek R., at foot of Caucasus. Metallurgy (zinc, lead, silver). Founded 1874 as Vladikavkaz; was military, political center of Russian Caucasus.

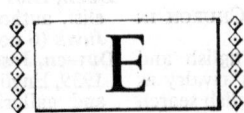

Ea (ā′ä), Sumerian water-god, widely known in Mesopotamia. Eridu was one center of his worship.

Ead-. For some Anglo-Saxon names beginning thus, see ED-; e.g., for Eadward, see EDWARD.

Eads, James Buchanan (ēdz), 1820–87, American engi-

neer. He invented a diving bell (c.1841) to salvage wrecks in Mississippi; built fleet of Civil War ironclads, St. Louis steel-arch bridge, and system of jetties which made New Orleans an ocean port.

Eagels, Jeanne, 1894–1929, American actress, noted

especially for her portrayal of Sadie Thompson in *Rain*.

eagle, large predatory bird related to kite, hawk, and falcon, and of world-wide distribution. American or bald or white-headed eagle is U.S. national emblem; other forms are southern and northern bald eagles, and golden or mountain eagle. Eagles eat fish, sometimes carrion.

Eagle Pass, city (pop. 7,276), W Texas, port opposite Piedras Negras, Mex. Ships spinach, has creameries, cotton gins, and food processing plants. Connected by rail and highway to Mexico City.

Eakins, Thomas (ā'kǐnz), 1844–1916, American painter and sculptor. Painted humble types and scenes of everyday world with uncompromising realism.

Eames, Emma (āmz), 1865–1952, American soprano, b. China, of American parentage. Sang at the Metropolitan Opera, New York, 1891–1909. Among her famous roles were Aïda, Juliet, and Micaela.

Eames, Wilberforce (ēmz), 1855–1937, American bibliographer, long at New York Public Library, an expert of Americana and literature on Indians. Edited Vols. XV–XX of Sabin's *Dictionary of Books Relating to America*.

ear, organ of HEARING in mammals. External ear and auditory canal are separated by eardrum from middle ear which contains three bones (malleus, incus, stapes) and opens into EUSTACHIAN TUBE. Internal ear, labyrinth of temporal bone, contains three semicircular canals important for equilibrium.

Earhart, Amelia (âr'härt), 1898–1937, American aviator. First woman to fly Atlantic: as passenger in 1928, solo in 1932. Flew Honolulu to California, 1935. Lost in Pacific during 1937 round-the-world flight attempt. She married George Palmer Putnam in 1931.

Earle or **Earl, Ralph,** 1751–1801, American portrait and landscape painter, pupil of Benjamin West.

Early, Jubal Anderson, 1816–94, Confederate general. Prominent in battle of Chancellorsville and in Gettysburg campaign. In Wilderness campaign (1864), defeated David Hunter and Lew Wallace. Burned Chambersburg, Pa., for refusal of ransom. After defeats by P. H. Sheridan in 1864, and at Waynesboro in 1865, he was removed from command.

early man: see MAN, PRIMITIVE.

Earn, Loch (lŏkh' ûrn'), lake in Perthshire, Scotland. Ardvorlich House, on its shore, is Darlinvarach of Scott's *Legend of Montrose*. Earn R. flows 46 mi. from the lake to estuary of the Tay.

earth, fifth largest PLANET of the SOLAR SYSTEM and third from sun (average distance c.93,000,000 mi.). The earth rotates on its axis (which is perpendicular to plane of the equator) causing day and night. It revolves in an elliptical orbit about the sun in 365¼ days; this, with the fact that the axis is tipped 23½° to the plane of the orbit, causes change of seasons. The earth is slightly flattened at the poles, its equatorial diameter being c.7,926 mi. and polar diameter c.26 mi. less. Land is said to occupy 57,469,928 sq. mi. of the surface and water to cover 139,480,841 sq. mi. Theory of isostasy postulates that the various segments of the crust are in balance (see CONTINENT). Earth's age is estimated at from two to three billion years. See *ill.*, p. 927.

earthquake, trembling or shaking of earth's surface, commonly caused when rock masses slip along a FAULT. Other causes are violent volcanic activity and the collapse of roofs of caves. Tremors involve longitudinal, transverse, and surface waves (which produce the most severe shocks). Seismic sea waves (erroneously called tidal waves) are caused by submarine earthquakes. See also SEISMOLOGY.

earthworm, segmented worm (phylum Annelida or Annulata) found over most of world except in deserts and cold regions; valuable to agriculture because it improves condition of soil. *Lumbricus terrestris* (common in Europe and the Americas) has no head but is sensitive to light and vibrations; it goes underground in winter, drought, and on bright days. Moves by

circular and longitudinal muscles, aided by rows of bristles along sides; muscular gizzard grinds leaves and other food. Each individual produces both eggs and sperms; two worms exchange sperm cells and each worm secretes a cocoon (placed in ground) in which fertilization occurs and young develop.

earwig, popular name of rather small, mostly nocturnal insect of order Dermaptera, usually black or brown but in tropics some are brightly colored. Pincerlike organs are attached to end of abdomen. Metamorphosis is gradual. In temperate zones, they are often garden or household pests.

easement, in law, right to limited use of another's land. It is either a personal privilege, which cannot be transferred without consent of the landowner (easement in gross) or a right attached to the land (servitude or easement appurtenant), which is transferred with sale or lease. Servitude (derived from Roman law) comes from use of land for prescribed time without protest of owner or from necessity of using another's land (as in drainage).

Easley, cotton-milling city (pop. 6,316), NW S.C., W of Greenville.

East Alton, village (pop. 7,290), SW Ill., on the Mississippi adjoining Alton. Mfg. of ammunition.

East Anglia (ăng'glĕu), kingdom of Anglo-Saxon England, comprising the modern counties of Norfolk and Suffolk. Settled in 5th cent. by Angles, it was one of most powerful kingdoms of late 6th cent. Became an underkingdom of MERCIA against which it later rebelled (825) to submit to Wessex. Danish invading army was quartered (865–66) in East Anglia and later conquered (869) the state entirely. Treaty of 886 made region a part of DANELAW. After 917 East Anglia was an earldom of England.

East Aurora, village (pop. 5,962), W N.Y., SE of Buffalo. Mfg. of metal and leather goods. Site of Roycroft Shops (1895–1939) of Elbert HUBBARD.

East Avon: see AVON 2, river, England.

Eastbourne, county borough (pop. 57,801), Sussex East, England. Popular resort on the coast, the city is backed by the South Downs.

East Cape, northeastern extremity of Asia, RSFSR, on Chukchi Peninsula and on Bering Strait. Official name (since 1898) is Cape Dezhnev, for Russian navigator who first reached it (1648).

Eastchester, village (pop. 3,096), S Alaska, just SE of Anchorage.

Eastchester, town (pop. 27,174), SE N.Y., E of Yonkers; settled 1664. Became a township 1788. Middle section became independent city of Mt. Vernon 1892, S part annexed by New York city 1895. Now includes residential villages of Bronxville (pop. 6,778) and Tuckahoe (pop. 5,991; marble quarrying). Bronxville is seat of Sarah Lawrence Col. (for women; chartered 1926, opened 1928; experimental college without fixed requirements; curriculum based on individual needs and interests of students, who are largely responsible for self-direction.

East Chicago, city (pop. 54,263), NW Ind., on L. Michigan SSE of Chicago; settled 1888. Largest port in state. Produces coke, chemicals, gypsum, petroleum, and metal products. Indiana Harbor, its lake front, is connected with Grand Calumet R.

East China Sea, arm of Pacific Ocean, between China and Japan, connected with South China Sea by Formosa Strait.

East Cleveland, city (pop. 40,047), NE Ohio, suburb of Cleveland. Here are Nela Park, hq. of General Electric laboratories, and Forest Hill Park, former Rockefeller estate.

East Detroit, residential city (pop. 21,461), SE Mich., suburb of Detroit; settled 1827.

Easter, chief Christian feast, anniversary of resurrection of Jesus Christ. Falls between March 22 and April 25 inclusive (see CALENDAR), following LENT and HOLY WEEK. Roman Catholics must perform "Easter duty" (i.e., they must receive communion at some

---

SMALL CAPITALS = cross references. Pronunciation key on inside end pages. Abbreviations: p. 2.

time between Ash Wednesday and Trinity Sunday).

Easter Island, island (c.46 sq. mi.; pop. 563), in Pacific c.2,350 mi. W of Chile, to which it belongs. Has long been known for indecipherable petroglyphs and monolithic stone heads (30 to 40 ft. tall, average weight, 5 to 8 tons), whose origin is unknown.

Eastern Empire: see ROME; BYZANTINE EMPIRE.

Eastern Question, the European problem presented by the decline and disintegration of the OTTOMAN EMPIRE after c.1700. Western powers, notably England and Prussia, took alarm at Russian expansion in RUSSO-TURKISH WARS of 18th cent. Austro-Russian plan to partition Turkey (with Constantinople and DARDANELLES going to Russia) was thwarted, but Turkish disintegration continued in 19th cent. with rise of independent Balkan states. Russian setbacks in CRIMEAN WAR (1853–56) and at Congress of BERLIN (1878) did not stop Russian influence in Balkans. Russian interference and encouragement of pan-Slavism clashed with Austro-German imperialism in East (*Drang nach Osten*), nearly caused war in crisis over BOSNIA AND HERCEGOVINA, and was a major factor leading to World War I. See also KUCHUK-KAINARJI, TREATY OF; ADRIANOPLE, TREATY OF; SAN STEFANO, TREATY OF; and articles on Balkan countries.

Eastern Rumelia: see RUMELIA.

East Flanders, province (1,147 sq. mi.; pop. 1,223,073), NW Belgium; cap. GHENT. Fertile soil; textile mfg. Population is mostly Flemish-speaking. For history, see FLANDERS.

East Friesland (frēz'lùnd), region, extreme NW Germany, separated from Netherlands by the Dollart (estuary of Ems R.); chief city Emden. Region includes E FRISIAN ISLANDS, in North Sea. Became county of Holy Roman Empire 1454; duchy 1654; passed to Prussia 1744; to Hanover 1815.

East Galloway, county, Scotland: see KIRKCUDBRIGHTSHIRE.

East Gary, town (pop. 5,635), NW Ind., near L. Michigan. Surgical instruments.

East Grand Forks, city (pop. 5,049), NW Minn., on Red R. opposite Grand Forks, N.Dak., in farm area.

East Greenwich, town (pop. 4,923), central R.I., SW of Providence. Textiles (since c.1790). Northeastern Naval Air Station is at near-by Quonset Point.

East Ham, county borough (pop. 120,873), Essex, England; suburb of London. Has extensive shipyards, docks, chemical factories, and ironworks.

East Hampton, resort and residential village (pop. 1,737), on E Long Isl., SE N.Y., near Southampton. Home of J. H. Payne is here.

Easthampton, town (pop. 10,694), W Mass., S of Northampton; settled 1664. Textiles, metal products.

East Hartford, town (pop. 29,933), central Conn., across Connecticut R. from Hartford; settled c.1640. Aircraft mfg.

East Haven, town (pop. 12,212), S Conn., E of New Haven. Metal goods.

East India Company, British, 1600–1858, chartered by Parliament for monopoly of trade with Eastern Hemisphere. Soon limited itself to Indian trade, chiefly textile export. Abolished 1698, restored 1708, it grew virtually supreme in India after Clive's victories over French rivals (1745–61). It acquired territory for military establishments and was placed by Parliament under cabinet control (1773). Warren Hastings was first governor general of the Indian possessions. Monopoly was abolished 1813; activities became purely administrative 1833. Sepoy Rebellion (1857) hastened crown's direct assumption of Indian rule.

East India Company, Dutch, 1602–1798, chartered by States-General to aid war of liberation against Spain and to expand trade. Drove British and Portuguese from Indonesia, Malaya, Ceylon; monopolized trade of Spice Islands; founded colony at Cape of Good Hope (S Africa). Its possessions became part of Dutch colonial empire.

East India Company, French, 1664–1769, chartered by

Louis XIV to compete with British trade in India. Briefly merged into Compagnie des Indes, 1719–20 (see MISSISSIPPI SCHEME). Dissolved after British victories over DUPLEIX and LALLY (1745–61).

East Indies, name used primarily for Indonesia (formerly Netherlands East Indies), but also more widely to include SE Asia. It once referred mainly to India.

Eastlake, city (pop. 7,485), NE Ohio, NE of Cleveland. Post office is Willoughby.

East Lansing, residential city (pop. 20,325), S Mich., on Cedar R. adjoining Lansing; settled c.1850. Seat of MICHIGAN STATE COLLEGE OF AGRICULTURE AND APPLIED SCIENCE.

East Liverpool, city (pop. 24,217), NE Ohio, on Ohio R. and N of Steubenville; settled 1798. Mfg. of clay products, machinery, and steel.

East Lothian (lō'dhēùn), formerly **Haddingtonshire,** county (267 sq. mi.; pop. 52,240), SE Scotland; co. town Haddington. Chief river is the Tyne. Rich lowlands extensively cultivated; sheep raised in highlands. Other occupations are fishing, coal mining, brick making, and distilling.

East Lyme (līm), town (pop. 3,870), SE Conn., W of Niantic Bay. Has Thomas Lee House (1664) and Little Red Schoolhouse (1734?).

Eastmain, river rising in central Que., Canada, and flowing W 375 mi. to James Bay. Near mouth is 1685 Hudson's Bay Co. post.

Eastman, George, 1854–1932, American inventor, industrialist, philanthropist, founder of Eastman Kodak Co. He invented a dry-plate photographic process, devised roll film, Kodak camera, and a process for color photography.

Eastman, Joseph Bartlett, 1882–1944, U.S. government administrator. Appointed (1919) by Pres. Wilson to Interstate Commerce Commission. Director of Office of Defense Transportation (1941–44).

Eastman, Max, 1883–, American author. Edited (1913–17) the *Masses* until it was suppressed in World War I. His works include *Enjoyment of Poetry* (1913), *Enjoyment of Laughter* (1936), and his autobiography, *Enjoyment of Living* (1948).

Eastman School of Music: see ROCHESTER, N.Y.

East Moline (mōlēn'), city (pop. 13,913), NW Ill., on the Mississippi. Industrial suburb of MOLINE.

Easton. 1 Town (pop. 6,244), SE Mass., SW of Brockton. Mfg. of metal products. **2** City (pop. 35,632), E Pa., on Delaware R. near mouth of Lehigh R. and N of Philadelphia; laid out 1752. In canal days was coal-receiving port. Has mfg. of machinery and metal products. Seat of Lafayette Col. (Presbyterian; for men; 1826).

East Orange, city (pop. 79,340), NE N.J., mainly a residential suburb of New York and Newark; settled 1678. Seat of Upsala Col. (Lutheran; coed.; 1893) and Panzer Col. of Physical Education and Hygiene.

East Palestine, city (pop. 5,195), NE Ohio, at Pa. line S of Youngstown, in coal and clay area. Mfg. of clay and steel products.

East Paterson, borough (pop. 15,386), NE N.J., near Paterson. Mfg. of paper, leather, metal products.

East Peoria, city (pop. 8,698), N central Ill., on Illinois R. opposite Peoria.

East Pittsburgh, borough (pop. 5,259), SW Pa., on Monongahela R. and near Pittsburgh. Braddock's army defeated here 1755 by French and Indians. Has mfg. of electrical equipment.

East Point, city (pop. 21,080), NW Ga., an Atlanta suburb. Mfg. of cotton and metal products, fertilizer, and batteries. Has creosoting plants.

Eastport, resort city (pop. 3,123), SE Maine, on Moose Isl. in SE PASSAMAQUODDY BAY. Fishing and sardine canning (since c.1875). Tidal variation averages 18 ft.

East Providence, town (pop. 35,871), E R.I., on Seekonk R. opposite Providence; originally in Mass., inc. as a R.I. town 1862. Mfg. of food, petroleum, and steel products and building materials and chemicals. Narragansett race track near by.

SMALL CAPITALS = cross references. Pronunciation key on inside end pages. Abbreviations: p. 2.

East Prussia, former province (14,283 sq. mi.; 1939 pop. 2,333,301) of Prussia; historic cap. KÖNIGSBERG. On 1938 map it was separated from the rest of Germany by the Polish Corridor and the Free City of Danzig, and bordered on Poland, Lithuania, Memel, and the Baltic Sea. It is a heavily wooded and largely agr. region, dotted by many lakes (as in MASURIA). At the POTSDAM CONFERENCE (1945), East Prussia was partitioned between the USSR (which received c.6,100 sq. mi., incl. Königsberg) and Poland (received the rest, incl. Allenstein, Elbing, Marienburg). Transfers, subject to ratification in final peace treaty with Germany, are not considered final by U.S. For earlier history, see PRUSSIA.

East Ridge, town (pop. 9,645), E Tenn., Chattanooga suburb.

East Riding: see YORKSHIRE, England.

East River, New York city, navigable tidal strait (c.16 mi. long and 600–4,000 ft. wide) connecting Upper New York Bay with Long Isl. Sound and separating Manhattan and the Bronx from Brooklyn and Queens. Hell Gate channel (long dangerous to ships because of strong tidal currents and rocks) connects it with HARLEM RIVER (link to the Hudson). Lined with piers and shipyards. Welfare, Wards, Randalls, and Rikers islands are in it. Crossed by many bridges (e.g., Brooklyn, Queensboro, Triborough, Hell Gate, Bronx-Whitestone) and tunnels (subway, rail, vehicular).

East Rochester, village (pop. 7,022), W N.Y., SE of Rochester. Pianos, farm machinery, chemicals.

East Rockaway, resort and residential village (pop. 7,970), SE N.Y., on SW Long Isl. near Lynbrook.

East Rutherford, borough (pop. 7,438), NE N.J., NE of Newark. Mfg. of clothing, chemicals, and asbestos and metal products.

East Saint Louis (loo'is), city (pop. 82,295), SW Ill., on the Mississippi (here checked by large levees) opposite St. Louis (connecting bridges); platted 1816. Large railroad yards and shops, stockyards, meat-packing plants and oil refineries. Mfg. of chemicals, metal products, glass, fertilizer, flour, and feed. Coal mines and rock quarries near by. City had violent race riots 1917. Has Parks Col. of Aeronautical Technology of St. Louis Univ. Cahokia Mounds are NE.

East Stroudsburg, borough (pop. 7,274), E Pa., N of Stroudsburg. Has railroad shops, printing, and mfg. of textiles.

Eastview, NE suburb of Ottawa (pop. 13,799), SE Ont., Canada, on Rideau Canal. Has lumbering, woodworking, and flour milling.

Eaton, John Henry, 1790–1856, U.S. Senator from Tenn. (1818–29), Secretary of War (1829–31). Social snubbing of his second wife (see Margaret O'NEILL) helped disrupt Pres. Jackson's cabinet.

Eaton, Theophilus, 1591–1657, Puritan leader in Conn., b. England. Founded New Haven (1637–38) with John DAVENPORT. Governed colony there.

Eaton, William, 1764–1811, U.S. Army officer, celebrated for exploit in Tripolitan War. Devised plan to win war against Tripoli by supporting claimant to rule of Tripoli. Set off on long overland march with small band to take Tripoli from rear. War ended with truce (1805) before he arrived.

Eau Claire (ō' klâr'). **1** Town (pop. 9,238), central S.C., suburb of Columbia. **2** City (pop. 36,058), W Wis., on Chippewa R. at mouth of Eau Claire R., in dairy area. Built on site of 18th-cent. trading post, it developed as lumbering center. Farm trade center with mfg. of metal and rubber products.

eau de Cologne (ō" dù kùlōn'), dilute perfume introduced c.1709 in Cologne, Germany, by Jean Marie Farina. Probably was a modification of formula made before 1700 by Paul Feminis, an Italian in Cologne; it was based on bergamot and other citrus oils.

Ebal, Mount (ē'–), central Palestine. Hebrews were cursed here for violating God's commands. Joshua built altar and monument inscribed with Mosaic law. Deut. 11.29; 27.4,13; Joshua 8.30–33.

Eber (ē'bùr), variant of HEBER.

Ebert, Friedrich (frē'drĭkh ā'bùrt), 1871–1925, first president of the German republic (1919–25); a Social Democrat.

Eberth, Karl (kärl ā'bùrt), 1835–1926, German bacteriologist and anatomist, authority on pathological anatomy. Bacterial genus *Eberthella* named for him.

Ebner-Eschenbach, Marie, Baronin von (mär'ē bärō'nĭn fün āb'nur-ĕsh'ùnbäkh), 1830–1916, Austrian author. Her *Novellen,* famed for "poetic realism," include *The Two Countesses* (1855; Eng. tr., 1893), *The Child of the Parish* (1887; Eng. tr., 1893), and the dog story *Krambambuli* (1894; Eng. tr., 1913–15).

Éboli, Ana de Mendoza de la Cerda, princesa de (ä'nä dä mändō'thä dä lä thâr'dä, ā'bōlē), 1540–92, Spanish noblewoman. A famous beauty (though she had lost an eye when a girl), she probably was loved by Philip II but lost his favor through her liaison with Antonio PÉREZ. Shared Pérez's disgrace when he was accused of Escobedo's murder. Spent years after 1579 in prison and exile.

ebony, handsome, dark heartwood of several tropical trees, especially of persimmon genus. Used for ornaments, tableware, inlay, piano keys.

Eboracum: see YORK, England.

Ebro (ē'brō, ā'brō), river, c.575 mi. long, NE Spain, flowing from Cantabrian Mts. SE, along foot of Pyrenees, past Saragossa, to Mediterranean. Irrigation canals; hydroelectric plants.

Eça de Queiroz, José Maria (zhōōzā' mùrē'ù ā'sù dù kārôsh'), 1846?–1900, realistic Portuguese novelist, author of *A ilustre casa de Ramires* (1900), and *A cidade e as serras* (1901).

Ecbatana (ĕkbā'tùnù, –būtä'nù), cap. of anc. Media, at the foot of Mt. Elvend. Later the summer residence of Persian and Parthian kings. Modern Hamadan is on the site.

eccentric, in mechanics, device by which rotary motion in one part of machine becomes longitudinal motion in another part. Cam is similarly used.

Ecclesiastes (ĕklē"zēäs'tēz), book of Old Testament. In ancient times ascribed to Solomon. A philosophical essay, somewhat cynical in tone, it opens with theme that "all is vanity" and continues with passages in praise of wisdom and mercy. Book is example of wisdom literature (see WISDOM).

Ecclesiasticus, in Western canon, book of Old Testament; placed in Apocrypha in AV. Called also Wisdom of Jesus the Son of Sirach. Theme of book is the excellence of wisdom. Among well-known passages: praise of wisdom and protest against determinism (14.20–15.20); praise of God for works of nature (43); praise of famous men who added to Israel's glory (44–50). Example of wisdom literature (see WISDOM).

Echegaray, José (hōsā' āchägärī'), 1832–1916, Spanish dramatist, a mathematician and economist. A common theme in his romantic realistic dramas is the clash of honor and duty. Well known are *O locura o santidad* (1876), *El hijo de don Juan* (1892), *El gran Galeoto* (1881). Shared with Mistral 1904 Nobel Prize in Literature.

Echeverría, Esteban (ästā'vän ā"chävĕrē'ä), 1805–51, Argentine romantic poet, prose writer, and revolutionary propagandist against dictator Rosas.

echinoderm (īkī'nùdûrm, ĕ'kĭnù–), invertebrate marine animal of phylum Echinodermata, having a calcareous, often spiny, outer skeleton and tube feet controlled by a water-vascular system. Many forms have five or more arms. Examples of the group are STARFISH, SEA URCHIN, CRINOID.

Echmiadzin (ĕchmēädzēn'), town (1926 pop. 8,436), central Armenian SSR, W of Erivan. Dates from 6th cent. B.C.; cap. of Armenia 2d–4th cent. A.D. Called Vagarshapat until 1945. The near-by monastery, seat of the catholicus (head) of the Armenian Church, is famous for its gardens and its cathedral (traditionally dated from 4th cent.).

Echo, in Greek mythology, mountain nymph who

helped Zeus in a love affair by distracting Hera with her chatter. As penalty, she could only repeat last words of someone else. In unrequited love for Narcissus, she pined away into nothing but her voice.

echo, phenomenon caused by reflection of sound waves. When wave strikes a reflecting surface, it is partly absorbed and partly reflected. When echo is reflected again and again from different surfaces the effect is called reverberation.

Eck, Johann Maier von (yō′hän mī′ùr fŭněk′), 1486–1543, German Catholic apologist. Disputed with Martin Luther at Leipzig (1519).

Eckermann, Johann Peter (yōhän′ pā′tùr ĕ′kùrmän), 1792–1854, German scholar and author, long a secretary to Goethe. He wrote *Conversations with Goethe* 1836–48; Eng. tr., 1850), an invaluable key to Goethe's thought.

Eckhart, Meister (mīs′tùr ĕk′härt), c.1260–c.1328, German mystical theologian. A Dominican, he awoke 14th-cent. mystical movement in Germany. He was accused of connection with the Beghards, and Pope John XXII condemned 17 of his propositions as heretical (1329).

Eclectic school, in painting: see CARRACCI.

eclipse (ēklĭps′, ĭ–), in astronomy, partial or complete obscuring of one heavenly body by another. Spherical opaque bodies cast cone-shaped shadows away from sun; when one opaque body shining by reflected light lies in shadow of another, it is eclipsed. Lunar eclipse (entire period lasting c.4 hr. and period of totality c.1 hr. 42 min.) occurs if moon's orbit crosses ecliptic when earth lies between sun and moon (full moon); it is visible from all parts of earth's surface where moon is above horizon. Solar eclipse occurs when sun and moon are on same side of earth (at new moon) if sun is not more than 18°5′ from point where moon's orbit crosses ecliptic and if moon and earth are close enough for moon's relatively short shadow to reach earth. Solar eclipse is visible at different moments from different points as moon's shadow moves eastward. Total eclipse visible about once in 400 years from any one place; maximum possible duration 7 min. 30 sec. at equator when sun is directly overhead; duration decreases as latitude increases. In true shadow (umbra), all direct sun rays are cut off; in surrounding partial shadow (penumbra) there is illumination from part of sun's face. If apex of moon's cone-shaped umbra does not reach earth, annular (ring) eclipse is observable from region on earth directly beyond apex of umbra. During total solar eclipse moon appears as dark object moving across face of sun, daylight fades, temperature drops. At totality sun's corona and prominences glow around black disk of moon. Nearly similar solar eclipses occur in cycles of c.18 years. Also important in astronomy are eclipses of Jupiter's satellites. See *ill.,* p. 927.

ecliptic (ēklĭp′tĭk, ĭ–), great circle in heavens which marks sun's apparent yearly course, actually the path of earth's revolution about sun. Obliquity of the ecliptic, the cause of changing seasons, is inclination at c.23.5° angle of plane of ecliptic (earth's orbit) to plane of celestial equator (imaginary extension of equator into sky).

Ecnomus, Cape: see LICATA, Sicily.

École des Beaux-Arts (ākôl′ dā bōzär′), French national school of fine arts in Paris, founded 1648 as École académique. Has three departments: painting and graphic arts, sculpture, and architecture. Free to those who pass entrance examination. Prepares students to compete for PRIX DE ROME.

ecology, scientific study of plants and animals in relation to environmental conditions, e.g., temperature, soil, light, wind, and moisture. It is also concerned with interrelations in plant and animal communities, and stages (succession) leading to final development (known as climax community or area) for a particular region. Ecology as a social science (relation of man to natural environment) developed in 20th cent.

Economic and Social Council, constituent organ of the UN. Undertakes investigation of economic and social conditions throughout the world and reports its suggestions for action to the General Assembly and other organs of the UN.

Economic Cooperation Administration: see EUROPEAN RECOVERY PROGRAM.

economic planning, from the budgeting of a family's needs to the control of a nation's business and industry, has a long history. In one form or another it was practiced by governments in Egypt, Greece, and Rome, and, through craft and mercantile guilds, in the Middle Ages. In modern times doctrines such as SOCIALISM, COMMUNISM, and FASCISM propose dominant control, but all governments have some degree of economic planning: public works, taxation, tariff agreements, fair trade laws, immigration laws—all have their origin in economic considerations. Most industrial countries have over-all economic planning.

economics (ē″kùnŏ′mĭks, ĕ″–), study of the supplying of man's physical needs. Not well developed in ancient and medieval times, economics took form with that growth of commerce which began in the 16th cent. and gave rise to the policy of MERCANTILISM. The 18th-cent. PHYSIOCRATS advocated LAISSEZ FAIRE—allowing business to follow freely the "natural laws" of economics. The effect on economic theory of the INDUSTRIAL REVOLUTION was reflected in Adam SMITH, advocate (1776) of free trade and the division of labor; MALTHUS, who believed population outruns subsistence; and RICARDO, with his theory of diminishing returns. The early exponents of socialism, such as Saint-Simon, Proudhon, and Fourier, attacked the belief in the necessity of private property and competition, and *Das Kapital,* by Karl MARX, appeared as the major work in socialist economics.

Economy, Pa.: see AMBRIDGE, Pa.; HARMONY SOCIETY.

Ecorse (ēkôrs′), city (pop. 17,948), SE Mich., on Detroit R. and S of Detroit; settled c. 1815. Mfg. of metal products, chemicals, and auto parts.

Écrins, Barre des, France: see BARRE DES ÉCRINS.

Ecuador (ĕ′kwùdôr) [Span.,= Equator, which traverses the country], republic (108,478 sq. mi.; pop. 3,076,-933), W South America, on the Pacific; cap. QUITO. Two ranges of the Andes cross the country. There are many active volcanoes (including Chimborazo and Cotopaxi), and frequent earthquakes cause much damage. The highlands, with fertile intermontane valleys, support the main bulk of the population (in which the percentage of sedentary agr. Indians is high). E of the Andes is a largely unexplored wilderness of plains and rain forest, sparsely populated by "wild" Indians. W of the Andes is the hot, humid Pacific coast. From the port of GUAYAQUIL are exported cacao, petroleum, gold and cyanide precipitates, tagua nuts, and Panama hats. Francisco Pizarro sent Benalcázar into the region in 1533 to forestall Pedro de Alvarado. Unimportant in the colonial region (when it was the presidency of Quito), it was liberated from Spain by Sucre in the victory at Pichincha (1822) and was incorporated into Bolívar's republic of Greater Colombia. On dissolution of that union Ecuador became a separate republic (1830). In 1832 Ecuador gained the Galápagos Isls., but recurrent border disputes with neighboring countries did not bring Ecuador much gain. In 1948 the Quito Charter recommended a customs union and political and cultural cooperation among Colombia, Venezuela, Ecuador, and Panama.

ecumenical council: see COUNCIL, ECUMENICAL.

ecumenical movement (ĕ″kūmĕ′nĭkùl, ĕ″–), term for a movement aimed at the unification or reunion of the Protestant churches of the world and ultimately of all Christians. The Evangelical Alliance (1846) was an early attempt in this direction, and the Federal Council of Churches of Christ (U.S.) was estab. 1908. Several world-unity conferences have been held (e.g., first meeting of the WORLD COUNCIL OF CHURCHES, 1948).

Some Protestant denominations have been consolidated (e.g., formation in U.S. of the Methodist Church by three Methodist groups, 1939).

Edam (ē'dŭm, Dutch ādäm'), town (pop. 3,741), North Holland prov., NW Netherlands, on the Ijsselmer. Important market for famous Edam cheese.

Edda (ĕ'dù), title of two works in old Icelandic. Edda of Snorri Sturluson or *Prose Edda* was intended as a guide to scaldic poetry, has rules of that poetry as well as much mythology. *Poetic Edda,* also called Elder Edda (though compiled later) is a collection of 33 or 34 heroic lays (incomplete).

Eddington, Sir Arthur Stanley, 1882–1944, British astronomer, physicist. Contributed to study of evolution, motion, and internal constitution of stars. He was a leading exponent of the theory of relativity and a prolific author of scientific works.

Eddy, Mary Baker, 1821–1910, discoverer of principles of CHRISTIAN SCIENCE, and founder of the church based on them. In frail health from childhood, she was interested in the problem of health and faith and formulated doctrine and system which became Christian Science, dating from 1866. Her *Science and Health* appeared 1875. In 1877 she married Asa Gilbert Eddy. She planned *Manual* for conduct of church and all details of its upbuilding, and was pastor of Mother Church, Boston.

Eddystone (ĕ'dĭstŭn), lighthouse, on dangerous rocks off coast of Cornwall, England. First light here built 1696. Present structure (built 1878–82) fourth lighthouse at site.

Eddyville, city (pop. 1,840), SW Ky., near Kentucky Dam on Cumberland R. and E of Paducah. Ruins of iron furnace where William KELLY invented steelmaking method are near by.

edelweiss (ā'dŭlvīs), low-growing perennial (*Leontopodium alpinum*) of high Alps. Its small yellow flower heads are surrounded by woolly-white bracts.

Eden, (Robert) Anthony, 1897–, British foreign minister. Became noted for support of League of Nations 1934–35. Foreign minister 1935–38, he resigned in opposition to Neville Chamberlain's "appeasement" of Axis. Was foreign minister in Churchill's war cabinet (1940–45) during alliance of Great Britain, USSR, and U.S. and building of UN. On fall of Labour Government (1951) he again became foreign secretary.

Eden, in Bible: see EDEN, GARDEN OF.

Eden, name of several rivers in England and Scotland. Principal one flows 65 mi. NW from Westmorland, England, into Solway Firth.

Eden, Garden of, in Bible, first home of man. God created the garden, with its trees of knowledge and of life, as home for Adam and Eve, until, eating of forbidden fruit, they were banished. Gen. 2; 3. In Babylonia there was legend of a holy place with tree of life inhabited by a god and goddess.

Edenhall, village, Cumberland, England, on Eden R. Family seat of Musgraves, whose luck (according to legend) depended on keeping unbroken an enameled goblet taken from the fairies near St. Cuthbert's Well; basis of Longfellow's "Luck of Edenhall."

Edenton, town (pop. 4,468), NE N.C., SW of Elizabeth City. Townswomen had "Edenton Tea Party," boycotting English goods 1774. Historic buildings include courthouse (1767) and St. Paul's Church (1736).

Edessa (ĭdĕ'sù), anc. city of Mesopotamia, modern URFA, Turkey. Center of a kingdom, later a Roman city, it was under Byzantine Empire a religious center. Fell to Arabs 639; captured by Crusaders 1097. BALDWIN I was count of Edessa before becoming king. City fell to Moslems in 1144.

Edgar or **Eadgar** (ĕd'gŭr), 943?–975, king of England (959–75). With a reign of orderly prosperity he won title of the Peaceful. He initiated widespread monastic reforms and granted practical autonomy to the Danes in England (see DANELAW) in return for their loyalty. Political unity ended with his death.

Edgar Atheling (ă'thŭlĭng), 1060?–1125?, English

prince. Chosen to succeed to throne on Harold's death, but submitted (1067) to WILLIAM I. Fled to Scotland, and, after unsuccessful uprising (1069), he later settled in France. He led (1097) English expedition which dethroned Donald III and seated Atheling's nephew Edgar on Scottish throne.

Edgartown, resort town (pop. 1,508), SE Mass., on E Martha's Vineyard; main center for the island.

Edge Hill, ridge on border of Warwickshire and Oxfordshire, England. Scene of first great battle of the civil war 1642.

Edgeworth, Maria, 1767–1849, Irish novelist. Wrote realistic novels of Ireland (notably *Castle Rackrent* (1800), *Belinda* (1801), *The Absentee* (1812), *Ormond* (1817). Also wrote children's stories.

Edina (ēdī'nù), village (pop. 9,744), E Minn., SW suburb of Minneapolis.

Edinburg (ĕ'dĭnbûrg), city (pop. 12,383), S Texas, WNW of Brownsville. Processes citrus fruits, truck, and cotton. Oil and gas wells in area.

Edinburgh, Philip Mountbatten, duke of (ĕ'dĭnbùrù), 1921–, husband of ELIZABETH II of Great Britain. Descended from kings of Greece, Denmark, and England, he became a British citizen before his marriage in 1947. Served in British navy in World War II.

Edinburgh (ĕ'dĭnbùrù), independent burgh (pop. 466,770), cap. of Scotland and co. town of Midlothian, near Firth of Forth. Often referred to in literature as Dunedin, it has nickname of "Auld Reekie." City is built on a series of ridges. Became burgh 1329 and capital 1437. Town sacked by English 1544. After Act of Union 1707 Parliament House, now seat of Supreme Law Courts, ceased to be meeting place of national assemblies. Noteworthy are HOLYROOD palace, Norman Chapel of St. Margaret, the cathedral, Royal Botanic Gardens, and Princes St. There are several art museums, and Natl. Library have valuable manuscripts. Univ. of Edinburgh (1583) has noted medical school. City developed as center of learning and literature in 18th and early 19th cent. (*Edinburgh Review* founded 1802) and is associated with many famous men of learning. Industries—engineering, tanning, making of machine tools, chemicals and biscuits—are mostly in suburbs. LEITH is city's port.

Edinburghshire, county, Scotland: see MIDLOTHIAN.

Edirne, Turkey: see ADRIANOPLE.

Edison, Thomas A(lva), 1847–1931, American inventor. His early inventions include a transmitter and receiver for automatic telegraph, a system of transmitting four simultaneous messages, and an improved stock-ticker system. He invented a carbon telephone transmitter and the first successful phonograph. In 1879 he produced the first commercially practical incandescent lamp; developed complete system of electricity distribution for use with it. Later (1881–82) he developed first central electric-light power plant in world. Edison demonstrated synchronization of moving pictures and sound; produced superior storage battery; developed kinetoscope; built and ran experimental electric railroad. He held over 1,300 patents.

Edisto (ĕ'dĭstō), river rising in W central S.C. and flowing 90 mi. SE and S to the Atlantic, separating near ocean to form Edisto Isl.

Edman, Irwin, 1896–, American philosopher; teacher at Columbia after 1918. Achieved wide popularity, particularly in the field of aesthetics. His works include *Philosopher's Holiday* (1938), *Arts and the Man* (1939), and *Philosopher's Quest* (1947).

Edmond, city (pop. 6,086), central Okla., N of Oklahoma City. Farm trade center with oil fields. Wiley Post memorial near by.

Edmonds, Walter L(umaux), 1903–, American author of historical novels, mostly about N.Y. state, such as *Rome Haul* (1929), *Drums Along the Mohawk* (1936), *Chad Hanna* (1940).

Edmonton, city (pop. 159,631), provincial cap. (since 1905), central Alta., Canada, on North Saskatchewan R. Transportation and distribution center for Peace and Athabaska river area and for N Mackenzie region, it is S terminus of Alaska Highway. Has important fur trade, grain elevators, lumber and flour mills, oil refineries, woodworking and meat-packing plants, and major airport. Seat of Univ. of ALBERTA. Fort Edmonton was built 1794, rebuilt 1819 after 1807 destruction by Indians.

Edmonton, urban district (pop. 104,244), Middlesex, England, near London. Associated with Charles Lamb, Keats, and Cowper.

Edmund, Saint (Edmund Rich), 1170?–1240, English churchman: archbishop of Canterbury under HENRY III, with whom he vainly struggled.

Edmund Crouchback: see LANCASTER, HOUSE OF.

Edmund Ironside, d. 1016, king of England (1016). Son of ÆTHELRED, he was prominent in fighting against CANUTE. On Æthelred's death, Edmund was proclaimed king although Canute received support of over half of England. Courage and bravery earned him name of Ironside. After battle of Assandun, he and Canute came to terms and partitioned England.

Edmundston, town (pop. 10,753), NW N.B., Canada, at Maine border, on St. John R. at mouth of Madawaska R. Pulp-milling center, fishing and hunting base. Settled c.1785 by Acadians as Petit Sault.

Edom (ē'dŏm), **Idumaea,** or **Idumea** (both: īdūmē'ù), mountainous country, called also Mt. Seir, given to Esau and his descendants. Extended from Dead Sea to Gulf of Aqaba. Edomites were often in conflict with their neighbors, especially the Hebrews; later they moved to S Judah and were finally subdued by the Maccabees.

Edrisi: see IDRISI.

Education, United States Office of, estab. 1867 as independent governmental agency, transferred 1869 to Dept. of the Interior, transferred 1939 to Federal Security Agency. Created to collect and disseminate information on education and to promote better U.S. educational standards. Expanded functions now include administering funds appropriated as aids to education, conducting special studies.

Edward, kings of England. **Edward I,** 1239–1307, was king 1272–1307. Son of Henry III, he fought for him in BARONS' WAR (1263–67) and was responsible for triumph. Conquest of Wales was followed by long campaign against Scotland. Made notable efforts to extend English rule to all of Britain. His legal reforms (notably Statutes of WESTMINSTER) earned him name of the English Justinian. Restricted private and church courts and prohibited land grants to church without his permission. His Model Parliament (1295) marked greater representation of barons, merchants, and clergy whose resistance to war taxation forced king to confirm previous charters (e.g., Magna Carta). His promise to collect taxes only with consent of parliament became basis of "no taxation without representation." His son, **Edward II,** 1284–1327, was king 1307–27. The dominant strains of his reign were internal dissension and the loss of Scotland. His insistence on having Piers GAVESTON at court caused rebellion of barons, who later killed Gaveston. Edward's later favorites, the Hugh Despensers, virtually ruled 1322–26. They made a truce with Robert the Bruce and recognized him as king of Scots. Queen Isabella refused to return from France while the Despensers ruled, entered an adulterous alliance with Roger de Mortimer, and invaded England (1326). The Despensers were executed and Edward forced to abdicate. Brutally mistreated, he was finally killed by henchmen of Isabella and Mortimer. His son, **Edward III,** 1312–77, was king 1327–77. Real power was held by Isabella and Mortimer until Edward seized it in 1330. He supported Edward de Baliol against Scottish king David II, but, despite his victory at Halidon Hill in 1333, Scottish question remained unsettled. HUNDRED YEARS WAR, which was to dominate his reign, began in 1337. He and his son, EDWARD THE BLACK PRINCE, took an active part in the war, the first phase of which

ended with Treaty of London in 1359. War was renewed after various treaties and truces, but, like the Scottish wars, was inconclusive in Edward's reign. Parliament, which withheld money grants and forced concessions from king, now began to take on form it was to retain. Black Death (see PLAGUE) decimated the population and brought about social changes in demands of lower classes for higher wages and social advancement. Edward quarreled with the Church, and religious unrest found a spokesman in John WYCLIF. There was rivalry between court party headed by JOHN OF GAUNT (supported by Edward's mistress Alice Perrers) and parliamentary party led by Black Prince and Edmund Mortimer. **Edward IV,** 1442–83, son of Richard, duke of York, became king (1461–70) as leader of York party (see ROSES, WARS OF) after his defeat of Lancastrians and capture of HENRY VI. Edward's disaffected cousin, earl of Warwick, fled to France and formed alliance with MARGARET OF ANJOU, queen of deposed Henry VI. They returned to England with troops and replaced Henry on throne. Their final defeat by Edward led to Henry's death in the Tower (1471) and quiet end to Edward's reign. His son, **Edward V,** 1470–83, boy king (1483), was pawn of conflicting ambitions of his uncles, Richard, duke of Gloucester, and Earl Rivers. Gloucester confined the king and his younger brother to the Tower, had them declared illegitimate, and took the throne as RICHARD III. More than 20 years later Sir Thomas More declared the princes had been smothered in their sleep on Gloucester's orders. Shakspere's *Richard III* deals with their fate. **Edward VI,** 1537–53, succeeded his father Henry VIII as king (1547–53) under council of regency controlled by his uncle and protector, Edward SEYMOUR, duke of Somerset. Tudor absolutism was relaxed by liberalizing treason and heresy laws. Government moved slowly towards Protestantism. Somerset's sympathy with yeomen's problems led to overthrow by his rival, John Dudley, duke of NORTHUMBERLAND. He secured ascendancy over the king and persuaded him to settle crown on Lady Jane GREY. Resulting struggle for throne ended in victory of Mary I. **Edward VII,** 1841–1910, was king 1901–10. Eldest son of Queen Victoria, he was prince of Wales for 60 years. Cooperated reluctantly in Herbert Asquith's attempt to limit veto power of House of Lords. Improved international understanding by traveling on continent, by promoting alliance with France, and by arbitration treaties with other powers. Father of George V, whose eldest son, **Edward VIII** (1894–), was king 1936. As prince of Wales he attracted attention by interest in social reform problems. The issue of his marriage to Wallis Warfield Simpson (see duchess of WINDSOR) precipitated a crisis with the cabinet headed by Stanley Baldwin. Their fear of a threat to constitutional procedure forced his abdication in 1936. As duke of Windsor he married Wallis Warfield 1937. Was governor of the Bahamas 1940–45.

Edward Nyanza (nīän'zù), lake, area 830 sq. mi., in Great Rift Valley, central Africa, on border of Belgian Congo and Uganda; alt. 3,240 ft. Discovered 1899 by Stanley. Also called L. Edward.

Edwards, Jonathan, 1703–58, American theologian and metaphysician. His strict Calvinist preaching brought GREAT AWAKENING to New England. His masterpiece, *The Freedom of the Will* (1754), sets forth metaphysical and ethical arguments for determinism.

Edwardsville. 1 City (pop. 8,776), SW Ill., NE of St. Louis, in coal area. Metal products. **2** Borough (pop. 6,686), NE Pa., on Susquehanna R. near Wilkes-Barre. Coal mining.

Edward the Black Prince, 1330–76, son of Edward III of England. Was first duke (of Cornwall) ever created in England (1337). He fought in battle of Crécy and siege of Calais. In 1356 he won battle of Poitiers and captured John II of France. Edward III created a principality of his French holdings, and the Black Prince maintained a brilliant court at Bordeaux after

1363. He aided Peter I (of Castile and Leon) in keeping his throne against rebellious Castilians, but the taxes he was forced to levy in Aquitaine resulted in war with Charles V of France. Bad health forced him to resign his principalities in 1372. Opposed his brother, JOHN OF GAUNT, who had become virtual ruler of England with the aging of Edward III. He died before his father but his son succeeded to the throne as Richard II.

Edward the Confessor, d. 1066, king of England (1042–66). Son of Æthelred, he grew up in France and returned to succeed Harthacanute. Governed well and freed his people from heavy taxes. Strife with powerful noble, Earl GODWIN, was heightened by Edward's favor of the Normans in England. Godwin and his family were exiled (1051) but soon returned. During their absence Edward received William, duke of Normandy, and probably promised him the succession. Since both William and Harold III of Norway had claims to the English throne, Edward recognized Godwin's warlike son, HAROLD, as his heir. Crisis was resolved by the NORMAN CONQUEST. Edward's piety won him name of Confessor.

Edward the Elder, d. 924, king of Wessex (899–924). Son of Alfred and joint king with him, he played an active part in wars with the Danes. Gradually became ruler of all England S of the Humber.

Edward the Martyr, d. 978, king of England (975–78), son of Edgar. Murdered at Corfe, his body was removed to Shaftesbury. Miracles occurred there and he was regarded as a saint and martyr.

Edwin or **Eadwin** (both: ĕ'dwĭn), 585?–632, king of Northumbria (616–32). Kept from the throne by Æthelfrith, he was restored by Rædwald and became overlord of all the Anglo-Saxon kingdoms except Kent.

Eeckhout, Gerbrand van den (gĕr'bränt vän dĕn āk'hout), 1621–74, Dutch painter, a close follower of Rembrandt.

eel, edible fish of family Anguillidae of order Apodes. Common fresh-water eel (*Anguilla*) found in Atlantic waters of North America, Europe, and in Mediterranean. Minute scales embedded in skin cover snakelike body; dorsal and anal fins are continuous around tail. Females grow to c.4 ft. long; males to c.2 ft. American and European species breed in Atlantic Ocean S and SE of Bermuda. They hatch as tiny, flattened, transparent larvae which travel back to ancestral shores, developing as elvers. Females swim up rivers, while males remain near mouth. Sexually mature adults migrate to breeding grounds, reproduce, and die.

Efate: see NEW HEBRIDES.

efficiency: see INDUSTRIAL MANAGEMENT; MACHINE; WORK.

Effingham, city (pop. 6,892), SE central Ill., SE of Decatur, in agr., dairy area. Rail and mfg. (food products) center. L. Kanaga (resort) borders city.

efflorescence: see HYDRATE.

Égalité, Philippe: see ORLÉANS, family.

Egan, Pierce, 1772–1849, English sports writer of the Regency.

Egbert, d. 839, king of Wessex (802–39), son of an underking of Kent. He eventually secured submission of Kent, East Anglia, Mercia, and Northumbria, thus gaining overlordship of all the Anglo-Saxon kingdoms.

Eger (ā'gùr), Czech *Cheb,* city (pop. 14,533; 1939 pop. 35,507), NW Bohemia, Czechoslovakia. Commercial center. Town hall and castle were scene of assassination of Wallenstein and his officers (1634). German-speaking pop. expelled after World War II.

Eger (ĕ'gĕr), Ger. *Erlau,* city (pop. 32,482), NE Hungary, on Eger R., in wine-growing region. Created bishopric by St. Stephen (now an archiepiscopal see), it is called the "Rome of Hungary" for its many churches. Its fortress withstood Turkish siege in 1552, fell through treachery in 1596, was razed after Francis II Rakoczy used it in his fight against Austria.

Egeria (ējēr'ēù), in Roman religion, water goddess. She was invoked as a goddess of childbirth. Because she was adviser to King Numa, her name has been applied to all women of culture who advise writers and artists.

Egerton, Thomas: see ELLESMERE, THOMAS EGERTON, BARON.

egg: see OVUM.

Egge, Peter (pā'tùr ĕ'gù) 1869–, Norwegian novelist, author of *Hansine Solstad* (1925).

Eggleston, Edward, 1837–1902, American author, a Methodist clergyman, circuit rider in Indiana, best known for *The Hoosier Schoolmaster* (1871).

eggnog, beverage of eggs beaten with milk or cream, sweetened and flavored. It often contains spirits or wine. It is a traditional Christmas drink.

eggplant, tropical vegetable (*Solanum melongena*) widely grown for purple or white fruit.

Egham (ĕg'ùm), urban district (pop. 24,515), Surrey, England, on the Thames. Near by are Virginia Water, an artificial lake, and RUNNYMEDE.

Eginhard, Frankish historian: see EINHARD.

eglantine: see SWEETBRIER.

Eglon (ĕg'–), king of Moab: see EHUD.

Egmont, Lamoral, count of (lä'mōräl), 1522–68, Flemish statesman, governor of Brabant and Artois. Though a devout Catholic and a loyal servant of Philip II of Spain, he intervened in behalf of the persecuted Protestants. Duke of ALBA had him and count of HOORN arbitrarily arrested (1567) and beheaded after an irregular trial. Their death stirred the Netherlanders to open rebellion. Egmont is central figure in tragedy by Goethe, with overture and incidental music by Beethoven.

ego: see PSYCHOANALYSIS.

egret (ēgrĕt'), name for several heron species in both hemispheres. Slaughtered in nesting colonies for white, silky plumage (called aigrettes) used in millinery, they were nearly exterminated before they were protected by law.

Egypt, kingdom (386,198 sq. mi.; pop. 19,087,304), occupying NE corner of Africa and Sinai peninsula of SW Asia; cap. CAIRO, chief port ALEXANDRIA. Bounded on W by Libya and on S by ANGLO-EGYPTIAN SUDAN. Mainly a plateau, split by the Nile into Western Desert and Eastern Desert. Some 95% of population lives in fertile valley and delta of the Nile. Chief export crop is cotton, and oil, salt, and potash are exploited. Chief industry is cotton spinning and weaving. Some 91% of population is Moslem; 8% is Christian (Coptic); and there is small minority of Jews. Earliest known date in world history is that of adoption of Egyptian calendar in 4241 B.C. A widely accepted dating system divides Egyptian history into 30 dynasties (3400–332 B.C.). In c.3400 B.C. Menes united two earlier kingdoms to create centralized Egyptian state, with cap. at Memphis. Fall of Old Kingdom in 25th cent. B.C. was followed by dark age. Unity restored in 2160 B.C. by IX dynasty, with cap. at Thebes; Middle Kingdom reached its height in 2000 B.C. After its fall (1788 B.C.) Egypt passed under the Hyksos (apparently Semites from east), who were expelled 1580 B.C. by native founder of New Kingdom. Weakened by decline of royal power, Egypt came under rule of the Nubians in 712 B.C. and later, briefly, under the Assyrians. Returned to orderly native rule in c.663 B.C., but again came under foreign rule in 525 B.C. with conquest by Cambyses of Persia. Regained freedom in 405 B.C. by successful revolt. Alexander the Great took Egypt unopposed in 332 B.C. His brief empire faded, and Egypt fell to his general Ptolemy who became king as Ptolemy I, with cap. at Alexandria. Rising power of Rome early overshadowed Egypt, and even the wily efforts of CLEOPATRA failed to regain power for Egypt. Octavian annexed Egypt to Rome and killed Ptolemy XIV (last of the Ptolemies). Christianity was welcomed in Egypt, and several of most famous Doctors of the Church were Egyptians; Coptic Church arose out of MONOPHYSITISM. Arabic conquest (639–42) made Egypt an integral part of

Moslem world. In 10th cent. Egypt fell to FATIMITE family, who founded Cairo as their capital. During period of Ayyubite dynasty (founded by Saladin) Egypt came under control of the MAMELUKES (1250–1517). Ottoman Turks conquered Egypt in 1517, but by 18th cent. their rule had become almost nominal. Napoleon's occupation of Egypt (1798–1801) was undertaken ostensibly to restore Turkish rule in region but actually to sever British trade lines with India; his withdrawal was forced by Anglo-Turkish forces. MOHAMMED ALI, who rose to power in 1805 as Egyptian pasha (governor), became founder of present royal line. With growing independence from Ottoman rule the title khedive (viceroy) was granted to ISMAIL PASHA. In World War I the British (who had brought Egypt under their control 1883–1907) made it a British protectorate. Agitation by WAFD party led to granting of independence in 1923, with FUAD I as Egypt's first constitutional monarch. Anglo-Egyptian treaty of 1936 promised eventual withdrawal of all British troops. In World War II Egypt was defended by the British (see NORTH AFRICA, CAMPAIGNS IN); it did not declare war against the Axis until Feb., 1945. Under FAROUK I, Egypt (as member of ARAB LEAGUE) attacked Israel in 1948. In Aug., 1952, an army coup forced Farouk's abdication and estab. reform government under Gen. NAGUIB.

Egyptian architecture reached formulation prior to 3000 B.C. Lack of wood and availability of clay and stone led to development of an architecture of massive and static quality. Immensely thick walls, containing only a few small openings, were covered with colorful pictorial and hieroglyphic carvings. Columns were confined to halls and inner courts, and supported flat stone roofs. Belief in existence after death resulted in sepulchral architecture of impressiveness and permanence. Remains of Old Kingdom (3400–2475 B.C.) are chiefly tombs of monarchs (see PYRAMID). Tombs of Middle Kingdom (2475–1788 B.C.) were tunneled out of rock cliffs. New Empire (1580–1090 B.C.) was great period of temple construction, exemplified by temple at KARNAK.

Egyptian art. Characteristic stylistic conventions appear with beginning of Old Kingdom period (3400–2475 B.C.). Relief sculpture and painting show human figure with eyes and shoulders in front view, head, pelvis, legs, and feet in profile view. Little attempt at plastic or spatial illusionism; color applied in flat tones. Sculpture in the round emphasized symmetry and minimized suggested movement. Painting served primarily as accessory to sculpture. In Middle Kingdom Period (2475–1788 B.C.) painting and sculpture became increasingly formalized. In Empire period (1580–1090 B.C.) they tended toward greater elasticity of line and boldness of design; a masterpiece of period is painted limestone bust of Queen Nefretete. Art of Saite period (8th cent. B.C.) returned to simplicity of Old Kingdom style. Egyptian art began to decline during Ptolemaic dynasty and was eventually stifled by infiltration of Greek and Roman forms.

Egyptian language, chief of the anc. Hamitic languages. See HIEROGLYPHIC and LANGUAGE (table).

Egyptian religion. Although documentary evidence on religion of ancient Egypt is rich and varied, interpretations are difficult because of its complexity and contradictions. Gods are identical and yet coexist, and contradictory myths explaining creation of world and natural phenomena were simultaneously accepted. Gods had relationship to various animals and were represented as part animal and part human—e.g., Ptah and Serapis, the great gods, with the Apis bull; Nut and Hathor, mother goddesses, with the cow; Bast, mother goddess, with the cat; and Horus, sun-god, with the hawk. Sun worship was very important in Egypt. The one attempt to establish monotheism there—the reforms of IKHNATON—was aimed at making sungod the sole deity. Horus, Ra, and Amon were sungods. Great emphasis was placed on cult of the dead;

hence building of PYRAMID as tomb of king and preservation of body by embalming and mummification. There was belief in immortality of body and of vital spirit or ka. King as successor to god and himself a god was chief priest. Many Egyptian gods, notably ISIS, Horus, and Serapis, became popular in Greece and Rome.

Egyptians, Gospel of the: see PSEUDEPIGRAPHA.

Ehrenburg, Ilya (Grigoryevich) (ĕlyä′ grĭgôr′yùvĭch ā′rŭnbōŏrk), 1891–, Russian novelist and journalist. Among translated works are *The Love of Jeanne Ney* (1924); *The Tempering of Russia* (1944; reports on World War I and II). Received Stalin Prize twice (1942, 1948).

Ehrlich, Paul (poul′ âr′lĭkh), 1854–1915, German bacteriologist. He shared 1908 Nobel Prize in Physiology and Medicine for work in immunology. Discovered drugs effective against syphilis.

Ehud (ē′hŭd), man who assassinated King Eglon of Moab and freed Israel from Moabite oppression. He later became a judge of Israel. Judges 3.12–30.

Eichendorff, Joseph, Freiherr von (yō′zĕf frī′hĕr fūn ī′khùndôrf), 1788–1857, German poet. His lyric nature poems are spontaneously musical and have attracted many composers, notably Schumann. Some have passed into folklore. *Memoirs of a Good-for-Nothing* (1826; Eng. tr., 1866), a delightful short novel, shows German romanticism at its best.

Eichholtz, Jacob (īk′hōlts), 1776–1842, American portrait painter, pupil of Gilbert Stuart.

Eider (ī′dùr), river, 125 mi. long, N Germany, separating Holstein from Schleswig. Flows W into North Sea.

Eifel (ī′fùl), plateau, NW Germany, N of Moselle R. and E of the Ardennes. Barren area with deep valleys, extinct volcanoes, crater lakes. Highest point 2,447 ft.

Eiffel, Alexandre Gustave (ī′fùl, Fr. älĕksä′drù güstäv′ äfĕl′), 1832–1923, French engineer, bridge and viaduct builder, authority on aerodynamics. He designed the **Eiffel Tower** (984 ft. high) erected for the Paris exposition of 1889.

Eight, The, group of American artists in New York, formed in 1908 to exhibit paintings. Comprised Arthur B. Davies, Maurice Prendergast, Ernest Lawson, William Glackens, Everett Shinn, Robert Henri, John Sloan, and George Luks. These men of widely different tendencies were bound by common opposition to academism and were stigmatized as "the ashcan school." They organized Armory Show of 1913 which introduced modern European art to a reluctant but curious America.

Eijkman, Christian (krĭs′tyän īk′män), 1858–1930, Dutch physician. Shared 1929 Nobel Prize in Physiology and Medicine for work on cause of beriberi.

Eikon Basilike (īkŏn bùsĭ′lĭkē) [Gr.,= royal image], work generally believed an autobiography by Charles I of England. Later John GAUDEN claimed authorship and started long controversy. Also Icon, Ikon.

Eildon Hills (ēl′dùn), three conical hills, Roxburghshire, Scotland. Associated with legends of Thomas of Erceldoune.

Eilshemius, Louis Michel (īlshē′mēùs), 1864–1941, American painter of numerous landscapes. His work first won notice at Armory Show of 1913.

Eindhoven (īnt′hō′vùn), municipality (pop. 134,527), North Brabant prov., S Netherlands. Mfg. of electrical appliances, radios, plastics, textiles. In World War II Allied airborne troops landed successfully here (Sept., 1944).

Einhard (īn′härd) or **Eginhard** (ā′gĭnhärd), c.770–840, Frankish historian. Known for biography of Charlemagne, a prime contemporary source book.

Einsiedeln (īn′zē″dùln), town (pop. 8,392), Schwyz canton, central Switzerland. Benedictine abbey (founded 9th cent.) has fountain with statue of Blessed Virgin; noted place of pilgrimage.

Einstein, Albert (īn′stīn), 1879–, American theoretical physicist, b. Germany. He won the 1921 Nobel Prize for contributions to theoretical physics, especially for work on the photoelectric effect. He postulated (1905) light quanta or photons, comparable to energy quanta, and on these based his explanation of the photoelectric effect; he developed the quantum theory of specific heat. In 1905 he set forth his special theory of relativity on electrodynamics of moving bodies and equivalence of mass and mechanical energy. In 1911 he asserted the equivalence of gravitation and inertia and c.1916 completed the mathematical formulation of his general theory of relativity which included gravitation as a determiner of curvature of space-time continuum and represented gravitation as a field rather than a force. His mathematical expression of the theory appeared in 1950. In 1939 he stressed the urgency of investigating the use of atomic energy in bombs.

Einthoven, Willem (vī′lùm īnt′hōvùn), 1860–1927, Dutch physiologist. Won 1924 Nobel Prize in Physiology and Medicine for development of electrocardiograph which makes graphic records of heart action.

Eire: see IRELAND.

Eisenach (ī′zùnäkh), city (pop. 51,834), Thuringia, central Germany. Mfg. of electrical supplies, chemicals. Birthplace of J. S. Bach; residence of Luther, 1498–1501. German Social Democratic party formed here by Bebel and Liebknecht at Socialist congress of 1869. WARTBURG is near by.

Eisenhower, Dwight D(avid) (ī′zùnhou″ùr), 1890–, American general, 33d President of the United States (1953–), b. Denison, Texas. Commanded Allied forces in North Africa in World War II. Appointed supreme commander of Allied Expeditionary Force in 1943; integrated forces in battle for Europe. Made general of the army ("five-star general") in 1944. U.S. army chief of staff 1945–48. President of Columbia Univ. 1948–53. Appointed supreme commander of Allied forces in Europe (NATO) in 1950; resigned post 1952. Successful Republican presidential candidate in 1952. His nickname is Ike.

Eisenstadt (ī′zùnshtät), town (pop. 7,626), cap. of Burgenland, E Austria. Haydn resided here under patronage of Esterhazy family.

Eisenstein, Sergei Mikhailovich (sĭrgā′ mĕkhī′lùvĭch āzùnshtyān′), 1898–1948, Russian film director. Won world wide fame (1925) with *Potemkin*. Other films include *Alexander Nevsky* (1938) and *Ivan the Terrible* (1944; Part II withheld by Soviet Film Trust).

Eisleben (īs′lābùn), city (pop. 29,652), Saxony-Anhalt, central Germany, at foot of Harz mts. Copper-mining center for 750 years. Houses where Martin Luther was born and died still stand.

Eisner, Kurt (kŏŏrt īs′nùr), 1867–1919, German Socialist. Organized revolution which overthrew Bavarian monarchy (1918); was first republican premier of Bavaria. A separatist, he opposed the reestablishment of a federal Germany. Assassinated by an anti-Semitic nationalist.

eisteddfod (āstĕdh′vōd) [Welsh,= session], Welsh festival. Contests are held in all arts and crafts, with special emphasis on music and poetry. National Eisteddfod held annually in August; local eisteddfods held throughout year. Important in preserving Welsh language and culture.

ejido (āhē′dō) [Span.,= common land], in Mexico, agricultural land expropriated from large private holdings and redistributed to small farmers. Common holding practiced by Aztecs, reinstituted under Cárdenas. First large-scale ejido estab. in LAGUNA DISTRICT (1936).

Ekaterinburg, RSFSR: see SVERDLOVSK.

Ekaterinodar, RSFSR: see KRASNODAR.

Ekkehard (ĕ′kùhärt), name of several monks of St. Gall, Swiss monastery. **Ekkehard I** wrote the *Waltharilied* (c.930), a Latin epic. **Ekkehard II**, fl. 10th cent., appears in Scheffel's novel *Ekkehard*. **Ekkehard IV**, fl. 11th cent., revised *Waltharilied* and contributed to chronicle of St. Gall.

Ekron (ĕ′krŏn), Philistine city, ESE of Jaffa, last for-

eign city to keep Ark of the Covenant before its return to Israel. Now called Akir.

El. For Arabic and Spanish names beginning thus and not listed here, see second element; e.g., for El Alamein, see ALAMEIN; for El Salvador, see SALVADOR.

Elagabalus: see HELIOGABALUS.

Elah (ē′lù), **1** Died c.885 B.C., king of Israel (c.886–c.885 B.C.), successor of Baasha. He was murdered by Zimri, who succeeded him. 1 Kings 16.8–14. **2** Valley in which David slew Goliath.

El Alamein, Egypt: see ALAMEIN.

Elam (ē′lùm), anc. Asiatic country, N of Persian Gulf, now in W Iran. A civilization began in 5th millennium B.C. Cap. was SUSA, and country is often called Susiana. In 18th cent. B.C. it overthrew Babylonia. Golden age came after 1200 B.C. Fell to ASSUR-BANI-PAL (c.645 B.C.).

eland (ē′lùnd), the largest living African antelope. Bull may be 6 ft. high at shoulder and weigh over 1,200 lb. Spiral horns extend straight upward.

elasticity, ability of matter to return to original shape or volume after distortion. Elasticity is measured in the amount of force a substance can resist without permanent deformity; smallest force that brings this about is elastic limit.

Elath (ē′–), ancient port, on Gulf of Aqaba. Built by King Uzziah of Judah, lost by King Ahaz. Also appears as Eloth. Was on or near site of modern Aqaba.

Elba (ĕl′bù), island (86 sq. mi.; pop. 29,462), off Tuscany, central Italy, in Tyrrhenian Sea; chief town Portoferraio. Iron mines. Principality 1814–15 under exiled Napoleon.

Elbasan (ĕlbäsän′), town (pop. 14,968), central Albania; center of fertile agr. region.

Elbe (ĕl′bù), Czech *Labe*, river, c.700 mi. long, Czechoslovakia and Germany, rising in N Bohemia and flowing NW through Bohemia, Saxony, and N Germany (past Dresden, Magdeburg, and Hamburg) into North Sea. Connected by canal system with Oder and navigable for 525 mi., it is a major European waterway. Germany repudiated (1938) its internationalization by Versailles Treaty.

Elberfeld, Germany: see WUPPERTAL.

Elbert, Mount: see SAWATCH MOUNTAINS.

Elberton, city (pop. 6,772), NE Ga., ENE of Athens near Savannah R. State's granite center.

El-beth-el, name given by Jacob to place at BETHEL where God appeared to him. Gen. 35.7.

Elbing (ĕl′bĭng), Pol. *Elblag*, city (pop. 20,924; 1939 pop. 85,952), former East Prussia, E of Danzig (under Polish administration since 1945); port on Elbing R. near its mouth on Baltic Sea. Was member of Hanseatic League. The city passed to Poland 15th cent., to Prussia 1772.

Elbrus, Mount (ĕl′brŏōs), highest mountain of Caucasus and Europe, NW Georgian SSR, formed by two extinct volcanic cones, respectively 18,481 and 18,356 ft. high.

Elburz (ĕlbŏōrz′), mountains, N Iran, S of Caspian Sea. Highest is Mt. Demavend (c.18,600 ft. high).

El Cajon (ĕl kähōn′), city (pop. 8,653), S Calif., E of San Diego, in avocado, citrus fruit, and grape region.

El Campo (ĕl kăm′pō), city (pop. 6,237), S Texas, SW of Houston. Market center for oil, cattle, dairy, and agr. area. Mfg. of food and metal products; meat packing plants.

El Centro (ĕl sĕn′trō), city (pop. 12,590), SE Calif., S of Salton Sea; laid out 1905. Shipping center for IMPERIAL VALLEY truck and livestock.

El Cerrito (ĕl sùrē′tō), residential city (pop. 18,011), W Calif., on San Francisco Bay.

elder or **elderberry,** deciduous tree or shrub of genus *Sambucus,* widely distributed. Common elderberry (*Sambucus canadensis*) has purple berries in late summer used to make wine and jelly. Other species, e.g., European elder (*S. nigra*), are sometimes grown for ornament.

Eldon, John Scott, 1st earl of, 1751–1838, English

statesman and jurist. As attorney general he drew up repressive laws of 1793–98. Lord chancellor almost continuously 1801–27 and virtual prime minister 1807–12, he was a reactionary Tory. Opposed Catholic Emancipation and liberal reform.

El Dorado (ĕl′ dŭrä′dō) [Span.,= the gilded man], mythical country sought by adventurers in North and South America. Used figuratively to mean any country of wealth or land of desire.

El Dorado (ĕl dŭrä′dú). **1** City (pop. 23,076), S Ark., near La. line; settled 1843. Oil center of the state (after 1921) and a farm trade center, with lumber and cotton mills. **2** City (pop. 11,037), SE Kansas, on Walnut R. and ENE of Wichita; laid out 1868. Refines and ships oil.

Eldorado Mines, Canada: see PORT RADIUM.

Eleanor Crosses: see ELEANOR OF CASTILE.

Eleanor of Aquitaine (ăkwĭtān′), 1122?–1204, queen of HENRY II of England; daughter of William X, duke of Aquitaine. Her marriage to LOUIS VII of France was annulled in 1152. Shortly thereafter she married Henry, then duke of Normandy. Two of her sons became kings of England—RICHARD I and JOHN. Henry's infidelities (see ROSAMOND) caused her to estab. (1170) her own court at Poitiers. Aided her sons in an unsuccessful revolt (1173) against Henry (who confined her for many years) and helped Richard secure the throne. Her court was the scene of much artistic activity.

Eleanor of Castile (kăstēl′), d. 1290, queen consort of EDWARD I of England. After her death Edward supposedly had Eleanor Crosses erected to mark stages of her funeral journey at Lincoln, Grantham, Stamford, Geddington, Northampton, Stony Stratford, Woburn, Dunstable, St. Albans, Waltham, Westcheap, and Charing. Three are extant, though restored.

Eleatic school (ēlēă′tĭk), Greek pre-Socratic school of philosophy at Elea, Italy, including Xenophanes, PARMENIDES, Melissus, and ZENO. Taught that being is ultimate reality and that sense perceptions and change are illusory.

elecampane (ĕ″lŭkămpān′), hardy Old World herb (*Inula helenium*) naturalized in U.S. It has yellow-rayed flowers. Its thick root was formerly used as cough remedy and in horse medicine.

election, organized voting to choose candidates for office. Greek officials, though occasionally elected, were more often selected by lot than elected by balloting, and in Rome the popular assemblies elected the tribunes. Popular suffrage and elections, practically abandoned in Middle Ages, have grown principally along with democracy. In England, elections, associated with parliamentary procedures from the 13th cent., were regularized after 1688 and led to the secret ballot in 1872. In the U.S., the Seventeenth Amendment provided for the popular election of Senators, the Fourteenth (1868) and Fifteenth (1870) for the enfranchisement of the Negro, and the Nineteenth (1920) for the enfranchisement of women.

electoral college, in U.S. government, the body of electors in the states which chooses the President and Vice President. The Constitution provides that each state may appoint a number of electors equal to the whole number of the state's U.S. Senators and Representatives. Congress is authorized to count their votes. To win, a presidential candidate must have a majority in the electoral college (not necessarily a majority of popular votes). Twelfth Amendment (1804) enjoins electors to vote for President and Vice President separately and provides that, in case no candidate has a majority of the electoral vote, the House of Representatives (voting by state, with one vote for each state) shall choose the President from among the three candidates highest on electoral list. Present popular election of electors superseded earlier choice by state legislatures; prevailing general-ticket system enables a party to carry whole state if it achieves a plurality vote.

electors. In theory, the head of the HOLY ROMAN EMPIRE was elected by a number of princes called elec-

tors; until 1562 his title was king of the Romans unless he was crowned emperor by the pope. In practice, in all elections but one after 1438, a member of the house of HAPSBURG was chosen. The Golden Bull (so called because of its golden seal), issued by Charles IV in 1356, designated as upper house of the DIET the seven prince-electors; archbishops of Mainz, Trier, and Cologne; king of Bohemia; count palatine of the Rhine; duke of Saxony; margrave of Brandenburg. The palatine vote was transferred (1623) to duke of Bavaria, but in 1648 an eighth vote was created for the count palatine. A ninth vote was given to the dukes of Hanover (after 1714 also kings of England). Elections took place amid great pomp at Frankfurt.

Electra (ĭlĕk′trù), in Greek mythology. **1** Daughter of Agamemnon and Clytemnestra. She helped her brother ORESTES avenge murder of their father by their mother. Portrayed by Aeschylus, Sophocles, and Euripides. **2** One of the Pleiades; daughter of Atlas and mother by Zeus of Dardanus. **3** Daughter of Oceanus and mother of Iris and the Harpies.

electric circuit, unbroken path along which current of electricity flows. A simple circuit can be set up with electric cell, two conducting wires (one attached to negative and one to positive pole of cell), small lamp and socket to which free ends of wires from cell are attached. When wires are made fast, circuit is "closed," lamp will light. External circuit is part in which current flows from cell along wire to lamp, through lamp, and back along other wire to cell; internal circuit is where current flows from one electrode to another through electrolyte of cell. When wires are disconnected, circuit is "open" or broken. In practice this is done by switches and fuses. Series circuit is one in which current flows through its parts one after another; negative electrode of one cell is connected with positive electrode of another. Resistance to flow of current in series circuit is sum of the separate resistances; voltage is sum of voltages for different parts; current strength is same throughout circuit. In parallel circuit current flows through all parts at same time; like electrodes are connected, i.e., negative with negative, positive with positive. Resistance is less than that of part having least resistance; voltage same for all parts; current strength is sum of current strengths in different parts. Parallel circuit is most commonly used. Devices connected in series must all operate at same time. Series circuit generally used for street lighting, in windings of generators and motors, and transformers when high voltages are needed. See *ill.,* p. 293.

electric eye: see PHOTOELECTRIC CELL.

electric fish, name for various fish with organs (usually from modified muscle tissue) producing electricity to kill or paralyze prey or enemies. Electric eel (*Electrophorus*), a fresh-water fish related to carp, has organs producing 450–600 volts. Others are electric ray or torpedo (species in warm waters of Europe and U.S.); fresh-water electric catfish (*Malapterurus*); and U.S. Atlantic coast marine stargazer (*Astroscopus*).

electricity [from Gr.,= amber; named by Wm. Gilbert]. Modern electron theory views matter as basically electrical and the ATOM, basic unit of matter, as composed of negative charges (electrons), positive charges (protons), and neutral charges (neutrons). Electrons move within atom in orbits around nucleus and sometimes move to another atom. Loss of an electron leaves atom positively charged; gain of an electron charges it negatively. Static electricity is concerned with nature, strength, and effect of charge on bodies; ways of charging a body include bringing it close to a charged body (see INDUCTION), rubbing a glass rod with silk, and rubbing a hard rubber rod with flannel. Capacity to receive and hold charge varies; some metals, called good conductors, pass charge on rapidly; some other materials are poor conductors (see INSULATION). Current is generally said to flow from positive to negative but actually both positive and negative charges move either way in electrolytic and gaseous conductors. Electric

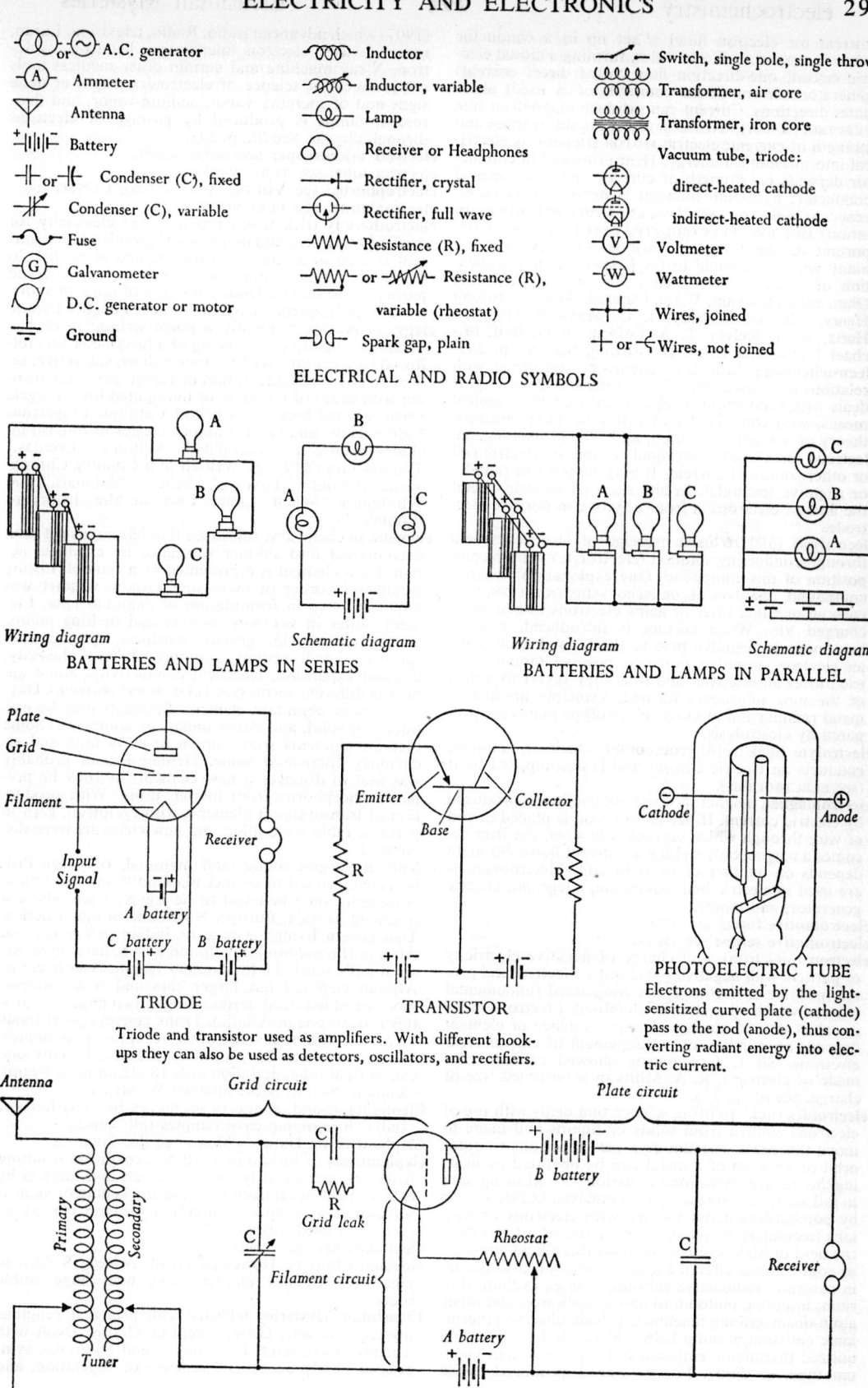

ELECTRICAL AND RADIO SYMBOLS

A.C. generator — Inductor — **Switch, single pole, single throw**
Ammeter — Inductor, variable — **Transformer, air core**
Antenna — Lamp — **Transformer, iron core**
Battery — Receiver or Headphones — Vacuum tube, triode:
Condenser (C), fixed — Rectifier, crystal — direct-heated cathode
Condenser (C), variable — Rectifier, full wave — indirect-heated cathode
Fuse — Resistance (R), fixed — **Voltmeter**
Galvanometer — or — Resistance (R), — **Wattmeter**
D.C. generator or motor — variable (rheostat) — **Wires, joined**
Ground — Spark gap, plain — or — Wires, not joined

Wiring diagram   *Schematic diagram*   *Wiring diagram*   *Schematic diagram*
BATTERIES AND LAMPS IN SERIES   **BATTERIES AND LAMPS IN PARALLEL**

Plate
Grid
Filament
Receiver
Input Signal
A battery
C battery   B battery
TRIODE

Emitter   Collector
Base
R   R
TRANSISTOR

Triode and transistor used as amplifiers. With different hook-ups they can also be used as detectors, oscillators, and rectifiers.

Cathode   Anode
PHOTOELECTRIC TUBE
Electrons emitted by the light-sensitized curved plate (cathode) pass to the rod (anode), thus converting radiant energy into electric current.

Antenna   Grid circuit   Plate circuit
Primary   Secondary
C
R
Grid leak
C
Filament circuit
B battery
Rheostat
C
Receiver
A battery
Tuner
Ground   **DIAGRAM OF A SIMPLE RADIO CIRCUIT**

current (or electron flow) is set up in a conductor when it connects cell electrodes, forming a closed electric circuit; one-direction flow called direct current; generator current (if no commutator is used) alternates directions. Current can produce magnetism (see ELECTROMAGNET); GALVANOMETER measures force and strength of current; electric MOTOR transforms electrical into mechanical energy. Heat produced in conductor depends on strength of current and resistance of conductor; light-bulb filament is heated to incandescence, as is electric ARC. Passage of current through solutions (see ION; ELECTROLYTE; ELECTROLYSIS) is important to metallurgy in various ways. Among the many who contributed to the knowledge and utilization of electricity are Henry Cavendish, Coulomb, Ohm, Joule, Galvani, Volta, Oersted, Ampère, Joseph Henry, Michael Faraday, J. C. Maxwell, Heinrich Hertz, W. T. Kelvin, T. A. Edison, A. G. Bell, Michael Pupin, and E. H. Armstrong. See ill., p. 293.

electrochemistry, branch of chemistry concerned with relations between chemical reactions and electricity. It deals with production of electric current by chemical means, with conductivity of solutions, ELECTROLYSIS, theory of ION and ionization, and related phenomena.

electrode (ŭlĕk′trōd), a terminal or pole of electric cell or other source of current. It may be positive (anode) or negative (cathode). In any external electric circuit the flow of electrons is from negative to positive electrode.

electrolysis (ŭlĕktrŏ′lŭsĭs), passage of electric current through conducting solution (electrolyte) with decomposition of this compound. One explanation: when a compound dissolves it undergoes DISSOCIATION, i.e., each atom either loses or gains electrons to become a charged ION. When current is introduced, positive ions move to negative pole (cathode) and each gains an electron, negative move to positive (anode) and each loses an electron, and thus they revert to atoms of the new substances formed. Principle applied in metal refining and PLATING; electrotype plates are prepared by electrolysis.

electrolyte (ŭlĕk′trŭlīt), compound which, in solution, conducts an electric current and is decomposed by it (see ELECTROLYSIS).

electromagnet, magnet in which magnetism is produced by electric current. If bar of soft iron is placed in coil of wire through which current is flowing, the iron becomes a magnet only so long as current flows. Strength depends on number of turns in coil. Electromagnets are used in electric bell, telephone, telegraph, electric generator, and motor.

electromotive force: see VOLT.

electromotive series: see METAL.

electron (ŭlĕk′trŏn), unit charge of negative electricity or particle with negative (−) charge. Electron and proton (positive or + charge) are considered fundamental units of which all matter is composed. Electrons move in orbits around nucleus of atom; valence of element depends on number and arrangement of extranuclear electrons. Sir J. J. Thomson showed cathode rays made of electrons; R. A. Millikan determined size of charge. See ill., p. 773.

electronics (ĭlĕk′trŏ′nĭks), science that deals with use of electrons emitted from solids or liquids and made to move through a vacuum or a gas. Electrons in outer orbit of an atom of a metal can be liberated by heating the surface (thermionic emission); by allowing light to fall on certain surfaces (as in PHOTOELECTRIC CELL); by bombarding metal surface with electrons or with ions (secondary emission); and by use of intense electric field of high positive potential (high-field emission or cold-cathode effect). Electron emission also occurs in naturally radioactive substances (e.g., radium, thorium, uranium, plutonium) and in cyclotron and other atom-disintegrating machines. Edison observed thermionic emission in lamp bulb (1883). Sir J. A. Fleming utilized thermionic emission in his two-element vacuum tube, or diode; Lee de Forest produced triode

(1907) which advanced radio. Radio, television, Loran, radar devices, electron microscope, betatron, cyclotron, X-ray machine and certain other medical tools are products of science of electronics. Light of neon signs and of mercury-vapor, sodium-vapor, and fluorescent lamps is produced by passage of electrons through the gas. See ill., p. 293.

electron microscope: see MICROSCOPE.

electron tube: see TUBE, VACUUM.

electrophorus: see VOLTA, ALESSANDRO, CONTE.

electroplating: see PLATING.

electrotherapy (ĭlĕk″trōthĕ′rŭpē), use of electricity for medical treatment and diagnosis. Galvanic (direct) current is used to destroy skin tumors and blemishes, to stimulate surface circulation, to introduce charged particles into tissues. Diathermy (use of long- or short-wave high-frequency currents) reaches deeper tissues.

elegy, in poetry, originally a poem written in elegiac verse, i.e., a couplet consisting of a hexameter line followed by a pentameter line, now a short, subjective, reflective poem of lamentation or regret, generally dealing with death or unhappy or unrequited love. Elegiac verse reached height in work of Catullus, Propertius, Callimachus, and Ovid. Famous elegies in English include Spenser's "Astrophel," Milton's "Lycidas," Thomas Gray's "Elegy Written in a Country Churchyard," Arnold's "Thyrsis," Shelley's "Adonais," and Whitman's "When Lilacs Last in the Dooryard Bloom'd."

element, in chemistry, substance that has not as yet been decomposed into simpler substance by chemical action. Each element is represented by a symbol. Listing elements in order of increasing ATOMIC WEIGHT was important step in formulation of PERIODIC LAW. Elements differ in VALENCE, boiling and melting points, density and specific gravity, hardness, specific heat, spectrum, radioactivity, compressibility, elasticity, thermal expansion, electrical conductivity. Some appear in different forms (see ALLOTROPY; ISOTOPE). Oxygen is most abundant element. Elements may be gas, liquid, or solid, and either metals or nonmetals. Some metallic elements were known to early man and alchemists discovered some. Hennig Brandt probably was first to discover a new element; in 1669 he prepared phosphorus from human urine. With production of transuranium elements with cyclotron, gaps in periodic table were filled and new elements were discovered.

elephant, largest living land mammal, of order Proboscidea, related to extinct mammoth and mastodon. Ancestral home believed to be Egypt, from where it migrated to Asia, Europe, North and South America. Two genera living: Asiatic or Indian (*Elaphas*), and African (*Loxodonta*) now found S of Sahara only. African bulls reach 11 ft. shoulder height, Asiatic c.9 ft. African elephant has larger ears and tusks; longer, more wrinkled trunk terminating in two fingerlike protuberances (one in Asiatic). Trunk conveys plant foods to mouth and sucks up water to spray into mouth. Adults mature at 25 yrs.; at 50 are old. Usually one calf born at time; gestation lasts 18–22 months. Pygmy elephant (5–7 ft. high) inhabits W Africa.

Elephanta, island, area c.14 sq. mi., in Bombay harbor, India. Brahmanic cave temples (8th cent.).

Elephant Butte Dam, N.Mex.: see RIO GRANDE.

elephantiasis (ĕ″lŭfăntī′ŭsĭs, –fŭn–), condition resulting from obstruction of lymphatic vessels and marked by enlargement of affected part and thickening of skin. It sometimes accompanies filariasis (disease caused by parasitic roundworms).

elephant's ear: see TARO.

elephant's-foot or **Hottentot bread,** twining S African vine (*Testudinaria elephantipes*), with huge edible roots.

Eleusinian Mysteries (ĕl″ūsĭ′nĕ̈un), principal religious mysteries of anc. Greece, held at Eleusis. Dealt with legends of Demeter, Persephone, and Dionysus, symbolized yearly decay and renewal of vegetation, and

Element	Symbol	Atomic Number	Atomic Weight	Melting Point	Boiling Point	Valence
actinium	Ac	89				
aluminum	Al	13	26.97	659.7°C.	1800°C.	3
americium	Am	95				
antimony (stibium)	Sb	51	121.76	630.5°C.	1380°C.	3, 5
argon	A	18	39.944	−189.2°C.	−185.7°C.	0
arsenic	As	33	74.91	sublimes at 615°C.		3, 5
astatine	At	85				
barium	Ba	56	137.36	850°C.	1140°C.	2
berkelium	Bk	97				
beryllium	Be	4	9.02	1350°C.	1500°C.	2
bismuth	Bi	83	209	271.3°C.	1450°C.	3, 5
boron	B	5	10.82	2300°C.	2550°C.	3
bromine	Br	35	79.916	−7°C.	58.8°C.	1, 3, 5, 7
cadmium	Cd	48	112.41	320.9°C.	767°C.	2
calcium	Ca	20	40.08	810°C.	1170°C.	2
californium	Cf	98				
carbon	C	6	12.010	3500°C.	4200°C.	2, 4
cerium	Ce	58	140.13	640°C.	1400°C.	3, 4
cesium	Cs	55	132.91	28.5°C.	670°C.	1
chlorine	Cl	17	35.457	−101.6°C.	−34.7°C.	1, 3, 5, 7
chromium	Cr	24	52.01	1615°C.	2200°C.	2, 3, 6
cobalt	Co	27	58.94	1480°C.	3000°C.	2, 3
copper	Cu	29	63.57	1083°C.	2300°C.	1, 2
curium	Cm	96	242			
dysprosium	Dy	66	162.46			3
erbium	Er	68	167.2			3
europium	Eu	63	152.0			2, 3
fluorine	F	9	19	−223°C.	−187°C.	1
francium	Fr	87				
gadolinium	Gd	64	156.9			3
gallium	Ga	31	69.72	29.7°C.	1600°C.(†)	2, 3
germanium	Ge	32	72.6	958.5°C.	2700°C.	4
gold	Au	79	197.2	1063°C.	2600°C.	1, 3
hafnium	Hf	72	178.6	(1700°C.)	3200°C.(†)	4
helium	He	2	4.003	−272°C.(‡)	−268.94°C.	0
holmium	Ho	67	164.94			3
hydrogen	H	1	1.0080	−259.14°C.	−252.7°C.	1
indium	In	49	114.8	155°C.	1450°C.(*)	3
iodine	I	53	126.922	113.5°C.	184.3°C.	1, 3, 5, 7
iridium	Ir	77	193.1	2350°C.(*)	4800°C.(†)	3, 4
iron	Fe	26	55.84	1535°C.	3000°C.	2, 3
krypton	Kr	36	83.7	−169°C.	−151.8°C.	0
lanthanum	La	57	138.92	826°C.	1800°C.	3
lead	Pb	82	207.21	327.4°C.	1620°C.	2, 4
lithium	Li	3	6.940	186°C.	1220°C.(†)	1
lutetium	Lu	71	175			3
magnesium	Mg	12	24.32	651°C.	1107°C.(*)	2
manganese	Mn	25	54.93	1260°C.	1900°C.(*)	2, 3, 7 (4, 6)
mercury	Hg	80	200.61	−38.87°C.	356°C	1, 2
molybdenum	Mo	42	96	2620°C.	3700°C.(*)	3, 4, 6
neodymium	Nd	60	144.27	840°C.		3
neon	Ne	10	20.183	−248.67°C.	−245.9°C.	0
neptunium	Np	93				
nickel	Ni	28	58.69	1455°C.	2900°C.	2, 3
niobium	Nb	41	92.91	1950°C.	3300°C.(†)	3, 4, 5
nitrogen	N	7	14.008	−209.86°C.	−195.81°C.	3, 5
osmium	Os	76	190.2	2700°C.(*)	5300°C.(†)	2, 3, 4, 6, 8
oxygen	O	8	16	−218.4°C.	−183°C.	2
palladium	Pd	46	106.7	1553°C.	2200°C.(*)	2, 4
phosphorus	P	15	30.98	See PHOSPHORUS		3, 5
platinum	Pt	78	195.23	1773.5°C.	4300°C.	2, 4
plutonium	Pu	94				
polonium	Po	84	210			
potassium	K	19	39.096	62.3°C.	760°C.	1
praseodymium	Pr	59	140.92	940°C.		3
promethium	Pm	61				
protactinium	Pa	91	231			
radium	Ra	88	226.05	960°C.(*)	1140°C.(*)	2

(*) Approximately. (†) Over. (‡) Under.

ELEMENTS (continued)

Element	Symbol	Atomic Number	Atomic Weight	Melting Point	Boiling Point	Valence
radon (niton)	Rn	86	222			0
rhenium	Re	75	186.31	3000°C.(*)		
rhodium	Rh	45	102.91	1985°C.	2500°C.(†)	3
rubidium	Rb	37	85.48	38.5°C.	700°C.	1
ruthenium	Ru	44	101.7	2450°C.(*)	2700°C.(†)	3, 4, 6, 8
samarium	Sm	62	150.43	1300°C.(†)		3
scandium	Sc	21	45.10	1200°C.	2400°C.	3
selenium	Se	34	78.96	220°C.	688°C.	2, 4, 6
silicon	Si	14	28.06	1420°C.(*)	2600°C.(*)	4
silver	Ag	47	107.88	960.5°C.	1950°C.(·)	1
sodium	Na	11	22.997	97.5°C.	880°C.	1
strontium	Sr	38	87.63	800°C.(*)	1150°C.(*)	2
sulphur	S	16	32.06	113°–119°C.	444.6°C.	2, 4, 6
tantalum	Ta	73	180.88	2850°C.(*)	4100°C.(†)	5
technetium	Tc	43				
tellurium	Te	52	127.61	452°C.	1390°C.(*)	2, 4, 6
terbium	Tb	65	159.2			3
thallium	Tl	81	204.39	303.5°C.	1650°C.(*)	1, 3
thorium	Th	90	232.12	1845°C.(*)	3000°C.(†)	4
thulium	Tm	69	169.4			3
tin	Sn	50	118.7	231.89°C.	2260°C(*)	2, 4
titanium	Ti	22	47.9	1800°C.(*)	3000°C.(†)	3, 4
uranium	U	92	238.07	1850°C.(‡)		4, 6
vanadium	V	23	50.95	1710°C.(*)	3000°C.	3, 5
wolfram	W	74	183.92	3370°C.	5900°C.(*)	6
xenon	Xe	54	131.3	−140°C.	−109.1°C.	0
ytterbium	Yb	70	173.04	1800°C.		3
yttrium	Y	39	88.92	1490°C.	2500°C.	3
zinc	Zn	30	65.38	419.47°C.	907°C.	2
zirconium	Zr	40	91.22	1900°C.(*)	2900°C.(†)	4

(*) Approximately.   (†) Over.   (‡) Under.

elevator, device for vertical transportation. Term is applied to both enclosed structures and open ones used in buildings, ships, and mines and also to continuous-belt device with buckets for handling bulk material. Power elevators, often run by steam, were used from middle of 19th cent. Elisha Graves Otis in 1853 introduced elevator with safety device in case cable should break. Sir William Armstrong's introduction of hydraulic crane (1846) led to hydraulic elevators, which began to replace steam elevators in early 1870s. Toward close of 19th cent. electric elevators came into use.

Elfsborg, Sweden: see ALVSBORG.

Elgar, Sir Edward, 1857–1934, English composer. Music composed for Queen Victoria's Diamond Jubilee (1897) brought him recognition; he was knighted in 1904. Perhaps his best-known works are the *Variations on an Original Theme* (called the *Enigma Variations*) and the five marches, *Pomp and Circumstance.*

Elgin, Thomas Bruce, 7th **earl of** (ĕl'gĭn), 1766–1841, British soldier and diplomat. Brought to England the so-called ELGIN MARBLES from Athens. His son, **James Bruce,** 8th **earl of Elgin** (1811–63), governor general of Canada (1847–54), implemented plan for responsible government outlined by his father-in-law, the earl of DURHAM. Negotiated with U.S. the reciprocity treaty of 1854. His son, **Victor Alexander Bruce,** 9th **earl of Elgin,** 1849–1917, was viceroy of India 1894–99 and colonial secretary 1905–8.

Elgin (ĕl'jĭn), city (pop. 44,223), NE Ill., on Fox R. and WNW of Chicago; founded 1835. Rail and trade center with mfg. of dairy products, watches, wood products, and clothing; and publishing.

Elgin Marbles (ĕl'gĭn), ancient sculptures taken from Athens to London in 1806 by Thomas Bruce, 7th earl of Elgin. Consist of PARTHENON frieze and part of the ERECHTHEUM. They are now in British Museum.

Elginshire, county, Scotland: see MORAYSHIRE.

El Greco: see GRECO, EL.

Eli (ē'lī), high priest and judge of Israel, teacher of Samuel. 1 Sam. 1–4.

Elia: see LAMB, CHARLES.

Eliakim (ēlī'ŭkĭm), king of Judah: see JEHOIAKIM.

Elias (ēlī'ŭs), Greek form of ELIJAH.

Eli, Eli, lama sabachthani? (ē'lī, lä'mü säbăk'thŭnī; ä'lē, lä'mäsäbäkh'thänē) or **Eloi, Eloi, lama sabachthani?** (ē'loi; ä'loi) [*Eli, Eloi:* Heb. or Aramaic,= Lord; *lama sabachthani?:* Aramaic,= why hast thou forsaken me?], cry of Jesus on the cross. Mat. 27.46; Mark 15.34. Seemingly a quotation of Ps. 22.1.

Elihu (ēlī'hū) [Heb.,= he is my God], one of Job's comforters. Job 32.2–37.24.

Elijah (ēlī'jŭ) or **Elias** (ēlī'ŭs) [Heb.,= God's God], fl. c.875 B.C., Hebrew prophet. His mission was to destroy cults of Baal brought into Israel by Jezebel, wife of King Ahab. He is the hero of many stories (e.g., his raising of widow's son from the dead; his contest of faith with priests of Baal; his being fed by ravens; his experience of the still, small voice on Mt. Horeb). He departed from earth in a chariot of fire, leaving his sacred mantle and the continuation of his work to his disciple Elisha. Elijah appeared in the Transfiguration. He is prominent in the Koran. 1 Kings 17–19; 21.17–29; 2 Kings 1–2; Mal. 4.5; Mat. 11.14; 16.14; 17.3; Luke 4.25; John 1.21; James 5.17.

Elijah ben Solomon, 1720–97, Hebrew scholar, called the Gaon [genius] of Vilna. Fought spread of Hasidic mysticism among Jews of Poland and Lithuania.

Eliot, Charles W(illiam), 1834–1926, American educator, president of Harvard Univ. (1869–1909). Under his guidance many changes were made—e.g., introduction of elective system—the university grew, and standards were raised. Eliot also fostered development of Radcliffe Col. He was later a member of the General Education Board, a trustee of the Carnegie Foundation for the Advancement of Teaching, and an emissary abroad of the Carnegie Endowment for Internatl. Peace. He edited *The Harvard Classics* ("President Eliot's Five-Foot Shelf") to further adult education.

Eliot, George, 1819–80, English novelist, real name Mary Ann or Marian Evans. She defied convention to live a happy life with George Henry LEWES, mentor of her literary career. Her novels picture middle-class life in realistic terms with stern moral interest: in *Adam Bede* (1859), *The Mill on the Floss* (1860), *Silas Marner* (1861), *Middlemarch* (1871–72), *Daniel Deronda* (1876). *Romola* (1862–63) is a historical romance of Savonarola's Italy, and *Felix Holt* (1866) is a political novel. Also wrote poems. After Lewes's death she married John W. Cross (1880).

Eliot, Sir John, 1592?–1632, English statesman. Promoter of PETITION OF RIGHT (1628), he refused to submit to Charles I and died in prison.

Eliot, John, 1604–90, English missionary in colonial Mass., called the Apostle to the Indians. Estab. villages for Christian natives.

Eliot, T(homas) S(tearns), 1888–, English poet and critic, b. St. Louis, Mo., studied at Harvard, Sorbonne, Oxford. His poetry, highly influential and much imitated, is complex with allusions and references in intellectual, often difficult, language and subtle music. Early poems—in *Prufrock and Other Observations* (1917), *The Waste Land* (1922), "The Hollow Men" —express disillusion and despair over modern life in nervous rhythms. Later he became an Anglo-Catholic, and his poems broadened with religious meaning as in *Ash Wednesday* (1930), *Four Quartets* (1943). His early poetic dramas (e.g., *Sweeney Agonistes,* 1932) were strictly literary, but later (e.g., *Murder in the Cathedral,* 1935; *Family Reunion,* 1939; *The Cocktail Party,* 1950) were successfully produced. His critical essays, stressing classical standards, did much to revive interest in Elizabethan and Jacobean authors. Awarded the 1948 Nobel Prize in Literature.

Elis (ē'lĭs), region of anc. Greece, W Peloponnesus, noted for horses and for games at OLYMPIA.

Elisabethville, city (pop. 67,980), SE Belgian Congo; founded 1910. Chief city of Katanga, a rich mining area. Copper, tin, gold, uranium refineries.

Elisha (ēlī'shù) or **Eliseus** (ĕlĭsē'ùs) [both: Heb.,= God is salvation], fl. 875 B.C., Hebrew prophet. He continued the work of ELIJAH under successors of Ahab. His miracles include raising of the dead boy, curing of Naaman's leprosy, and timely aid to widow in debt. 1 Kings 19.16–21; 2 Kings 2.9; 13.14–21; Luke 4.27.

Elizabeth, Saint, mother of St. John the Baptist and cousin of the Virgin MARY. Luke 1. Feast: Nov. 5.

Elizabeth, Saint, 1207–31, daughter of Andrew II of Hungary, wife of Louis II of Thuringia; noted for devotion to the needy.

Elizabeth, 1837–98, empress of Austria and queen of Hungary, consort of Francis Joseph; a Bavarian princess. Her life was marked by tragedy, notably the death of her son, Archduke RUDOLF, and her own assassination by an Italian anarchist at Geneva.

Elizabeth, 1709–62, empress of Russia (1741–62); daughter of Peter I and Catherine I. Gained throne by deposing IVAN VI. Rid Russia of German influence; successfully warred against Prussia in SEVEN YEARS WAR. Founded Moscow Univ. Her nephew, Peter III, succeeded her.

Elizabeth, 1876–, queen of Belgium, consort of ALBERT I; a Bavarian princess. Revered for her hospital work in World War I, interest in improvement of social conditions, and patronage of arts.

Elizabeth, 1596–1662, queen of Bohemia and countess palatine, consort of FREDERICK THE WINTER KING; daughter of James I of England. Nicknamed "Queen of Hearts" for her beauty. After her husband's defeat (1620) she lived in poverty in Holland; returned to England 1661. Among her 13 children were Prince RUPERT and SOPHIA, electress of Hanover.

Elizabeth I, 1533–1603, queen of England (1558–1603). Daughter of HENRY VIII and Anne BOLEYN, she was declared illegitimate after her mother's execution. Parliament reestab. her in succession in 1544. Imprisoned as rallying point for discontented Protestants, she regained freedom by outward conformity to Catholicism. On her succession England's low fortunes included religious strife, a huge government debt, and failure in wars with France. Her reign took England through one of its greatest periods. It produced such men as Shakspere, Spenser, Francis Bacon, and Walter Ralegh. It saw the country united to become a first-rate European power with a great navy. It saw commerce and industry prosper and colonization begin. Her Tudor concept of strong rule and need for popular support helped her select excellent counselors. She reestab. Anglicanism and measures against Catholics grew harsher. Important measures enacted included stabilization of labor conditions, currency reforms, poor laws, and acts to encourage agr., commerce, and mfg. Elizabeth began a policy of peace and her series of diplomatic maneuvers eventually defeated Spain and stalemated France. Treaty of Edinburgh (1560) started policy of supporting Protestant lords against Catholics. After abdication of MARY QUEEN OF SCOTS from Scottish throne, Elizabeth gave her refuge, kept her prisoner, and executed her only after plots to seat Mary on English throne. By marriage negotiations with Francis, duke of Alençon and Anjou, she secured (1572) defence alliance against Spain and, later, French aid for the Dutch against Spain, who now emerged as England's main enemy. Philip II of Spain, whose offer of marriage Elizabeth had refused in 1559, planned Spanish Armada expedition as reprisal against English raids on Spanish shipping. Defeat of Armada broke power of Spain. Vain, fickle in bestowing favors (see 2d earl of ESSEX and earl of LEICESTER), prejudiced, vacillating, and parsimonious, she was also highly aware of responsibility of rule and immensely courageous.

Elizabeth II, 1926–, queen of Great Britain (1952–), eldest daughter of GEORGE VI. She married (1947) Philip Mountbatten, duke of Edinburgh. They have two children: Prince Charles (1948–) and Princess Anne (1950–). Her mother, **Elizabeth,** 1900–, queen consort of George VI, is the daughter of the 14th earl of Strathmore.

Elizabeth, 1843–1916, queen of Rumania, consort of Carol I; a German princess. Wrote extensively, under pseud. Carmen Sylva, in German, French, English, Rumanian. Her works include *Pensées d'une reine* (1882); *The Bard of Dimbowitza* (1891; Rumanian folk tales).

Elizabeth, city (pop. 112,817), NE N.J., S of Newark, on Newark Bay and Arthur Kill (Goethals Bridge to Staten Isl.). English bought site from Indians 1664; called Elizabethtown until 1740. Became first provincial cap. of N.J.; assembly met here 1668–82. School that became Princeton Univ. opened here 1747. Village raided and partly burned by British in Revolution. Industrialization began in late 1800s; Singer sewing-machine factory opened 1873. Mfg. of machinery, printing presses and type, paper containers, chemicals, and radio, auto, and aircraft parts. Also oil refining, bookbinding, and railroad shops. Has Nathaniel Bonnell House (before 1682), Belcher Mansion (before 1750), and Elias Boudinot's home (c.1750).

Elizabeth City, town (pop. 12,685), NE N.C., port on Pasquotank R. N of Albemarle Sound; founded 1793. Commercial and fishing center with lumber, hosiery, and cotton mills. Resort with U.S. coast guard base.

Elizabeth Farnese (färnā'sā), 1692–1766, queen of Spain, second wife of PHILIP V; niece of duke of Parma. She dominated her weak husband; secured Naples and Parma for her sons Charles and Philip.

SMALL CAPITALS = cross references. Pronunciation key on inside end pages. Abbreviations: p. 2.

Elizabeth Islands, chain forming SE boundary of Buzzards Bay, off SE Mass. Cuttyhunk (discovered 1602, settled 1641) is farthest W; Naushon (nô'shùn), 7 mi. long, is largest. Penikese Isl. had summer school of marine biology estab. by Louis Agassiz.

Elizabeth of Valois (välwä'), 1545–68, queen of Spain, third wife of Philip II; daughter of Henry II of France. She had been originally promised to Philip's son CARLOS, but the story of a tragic love between her and Carlos is unfounded.

Elizabethton, town (pop. 10,754), NE Tenn., at junction of Watauga and Doe rivers; one of state's earliest settlements. Sycamore Shoals Monument commemorates organization of WATAUGA ASSOCIATION 1772, Richard Henderson's Cherokee treaty 1775, and formation of Revolutionary force. Rayon mills. Unaka Natl. Forest near by.

Elizabethtown. 1 City (pop. 5,807), central Ky., S of Louisville; settled 1780. Trade center for agr. and limestone area. Thomas Lincoln lived here for time. Garrison captured by Gen. J. H. Morgan in Civil War, Dec., 1862. Indian mounds have yielded artifacts. Fort Knox near by. **2** Borough (pop. 5,083), SE Pa., SE of Harrisburg. Trade center for agr. area.

elk, member of deer family, genus *Alces* (or *Alce*), found in reduced numbers in parts of N Europe and Asia. Smaller but similar to American MOOSE.

Elk City, city (pop. 7,962), W Okla., in dairy region. Has cooperative medical center (1929).

Elkhart, city (pop. 35,646), N Ind., at junction of Elkhart and St. Joseph rivers and E of South Bend; settled 1832. Shipping and trading center for agr. area. Rail junction with mfg. of metal, rubber, and clay products.

Elkhorn City or **Praise,** town (pop. 1,349), E Ky., in Cumberlands, SE of Pikeville and near scenic Breaks of Big Sandy R.

Elkhorn Tavern: see PEA RIDGE.

Elkins, Stephen Benton, 1841–1911, American statesman. U.S. Secretary of War (1891–93). As U.S. Senator from W.Va. (1895–1911), he authored Elkins Act of 1903 against REBATE system.

Elkins, city (pop. 9,121), N W.Va., on Tygart R. and SE of Clarksburg. Center for timber and mining area with foundry and lumber products. Seat of Davis and Elkins Col.

Elk Island National Park, central Alta., Canada, E of Edmonton; estab. 1913. Canada's chief fenced preserve of buffalo and other prairie animals.

Elk Mountains, range of Rocky Mts., W central Colo. Its highest point, Mt. Carbon (also called Castle Peak), rises to 14,259 ft.

Elko, city (pop. 5,393), NE Nev., on Humboldt R. and N of Diamond Mts. Shipping point for ranches and mines.

Elkton. 1 City (pop. 1,312), S Ky., E of Hopkinsville near Tenn. line. Birthplace of Jefferson Davis (with memorial park, monument) near by. **2** Town (pop. 5,245), NE Md., NE of Baltimore. Until state changed marriage laws (1938), town was Gretna Green of the East. Mfg. of toys, paper, clothing, and fireworks.

Ellensburg, city (pop. 8,430), central Wash., on Yakima R., in lumber, dairy, agr., mining area. Center of Yakima reclamation project.

Ellesmere, Thomas Egerton, Baron, c.1540–1617, lord chancellor of England. He took part in trial of Mary Queen of Scots (1586) and was a favorite and adviser of Queen Elizabeth. Originally a friend of the 2d earl of Essex, he was a witness against him at the trial which resulted in his execution. Retained by James I, he upheld James's harsh policy toward Puritans and was severe to Catholics. He was a man of learning and an incorruptible judge.

Ellesmere Island, area 77,392 sq. mi., most northerly and second largest of Arctic Archipelago, Franklin dist., Northwest Territories, Canada, in Arctic Ocean. Largely covered by ice cap in SE. Central area called Grinnell Land.

Ellice Islands (ĕl'ĭs), group of atolls (9.5 sq. mi.; pop. 4,487), S Pacific; with Gilbert Isls. constitutes a British colony. Most important of nine islands are Funafuti and Nanumea. Main export is copra. Occupied 1943 by U.S. forces.

Ellicott, Andrew, 1754–1820, American surveyor. As surveyor of capital at Washington (1792), he issued an altered city plan. Surveyed U.S.–Fla. boundary (1796–1800) and Ga.–S.C. boundary (1811–12).

Ellicott City, village (1940 pop. 2,682), N Md., on Patapsco R., W of Baltimore. Near by is Doughoregan Manor (c.1720), home of Charles Carroll.

ellipse (ĭlĭps'), closed plane curve of which sum of distances between point on curve and two fixed points (foci) is same for all points on curve. Center is point halfway between foci; major axis is chord passing through foci; vertices are two points at which major axis intersects curve. Ellipse is also conic section (other than circle) formed by plane cutting all elements of cone in same nappe.

Ellis, Havelock, 1859–1939, English psychologist. A qualified physician, his major work, *Studies in the Psychology of Sex* (1897–1928), greatly influenced the public attitude toward sex problems.

Ellis, William, 1794–1872, English nonconformist missionary. He developed a form of writing for the Hawaiian language and set up at Tahiti first printing press in the South Seas. Also wrote a history of Madagascar.

Ellis Island, SE N.Y., in Upper New York Bay, SW of Manhattan isl.; c.27 acres. Government property since 1808. Nation's chief immigration station 1892–1943. Now a detention center for deportees and immigrants whose entry is questioned.

Ellora (ĕlō'rù), village, NW Hyderabad, India. Buddhist, Brahman, and Jain rock-cut temples (3d–13th cent.) extend over a mile. The Kailasa, Dravidian temple carved from a single mass of rock, has some of India's greatest sculptural treasures.

Ellsworth, Henry Leavitt, 1791–1858, American agriculturist who helped bring about establishment of Dept. of Agriculture.

Ellsworth, Lincoln, 1880–1951, American explorer. Financial supporter and associate of Roald Amundsen in arctic aviation ventures. Flew over North Pole in 1926. Accomplished first flight over Antarctica in 1935. Published several accounts of his experiences.

Ellsworth, Oliver, 1745–1807, American statesman. Advanced "Connecticut compromise" at FEDERAL CONSTITUTIONAL CONVENTION. Chief Justice of U.S. Supreme Court (1796–99).

Ellwood City, borough (pop. 12,945), W Pa., NW of Pittsburgh; settled 1890. Mfg. of metal products.

elm, deciduous tree of genus *Ulmus* of wide distribution. Among North American species are American or white elm (*Ulmus americana*), a favorite shade tree, and slippery elm (*U. fulva*). Elm wood is hard and durable. The Dutch elm disease, caused by a fungus carried by beetles, has exterminated many plantings in U.S. of both American and European species.

Elman, Mischa (ĕl'mùn), 1891–, Russian-American violinist. Since his debut in New York (1908), he has toured widely in Europe and the U.S.

Elmhurst, residential city (pop. 21,273), NE Ill., W of Chicago, in truck-farm area; settled 1843.

Elmira, city (pop. 49,716), S N.Y., on Chemung R. and W of Binghamton; settled 1788. Distributing and mfg. (milk bottles, fire-fighting equipment and chemicals, office equipment, business machines) center. Here are Arnot Art Gall., Elmira State Reformatory (see Z. R. BROCKWAY), Mark Twain's grave, **Elmira College** (nonsectarian; for women; opened 1855), first women's college to grant degrees (1859) for work equivalent to that offered in men's colleges.

Elmo, Saint: see PETER GONZALEZ, SAINT.

El Monte, city (pop. 8,101), S Calif., E of Los Angeles, in truck and dairy area. A lion farm is near by.

El Morro National Monument: see NATIONAL PARKS AND MONUMENTS (table).

Elmwood, city (pop. 1,613), N central Ill., WNW of Peoria. Birthplace of Lorado Taft, whose statue to his parents, *Pioneers of the Prairies,* is here.

Elmwood Park, village (pop. 18,801), NE Ill., residential suburb W of Chicago.

Elohim (ĕlōhĕm', ēlō'hǐm), common Hebrew name of God.

Eloi, Eloi, lama sabachthani?: see ELI, ELI, LAMA SABACHTHANI?

Eloth (ē'lŏth), the same as ELATH.

El Paso (ĕl pă'sō), city (pop. 130,485), W Texas, port of entry on Rio Grande opposite JUÁREZ, Mexico. Largest U.S.–Mex. border city, its past is bound with that of Juárez. Both in El Paso del Norte region to which missionaries, soldiers, and traders came in 17th cent. Missions founded at YSLETA and elsewhere, but main settlement was in Juárez. First El Paso house built 1827. Settlement grew after U.S.–Mex. border was estab. and after railroad came (1881). Has refineries, mfg. of food and wine products, cement, and textiles. International trade most important. Seat of Texas Western Col. Here are Fort Bliss (with guided missiles experiment station), army hospital, and U.S. airfield. Elephant Butte Dam (N.Mex.) irrigates area.

Elphinstone, George Keith, 1746–1823, British admiral. In wars of American and French revolutions, he was noted for the reduction of Charleston (1780) and the capture of Capetown (1795).

El Reno, city (pop. 10,991), central Okla., near North Canadian R. and W of Oklahoma City; settled 1889. Market center with flour mills and railroad shops. U.S. reformatory and Fort Reno are near by.

El Segundo (ĕl sǐgŭn'dō), city (pop. 8,011), S Calif., WSW of Los Angeles; founded 1911. Oil refineries. Mfg. of aircraft and chemicals.

Elsheimer, Adam (ä'däm ĕls'hīmŭr), 1578–1610?, German painter. Biblical and mythological pictures notable for landscape backgrounds and light effects.

Elsinore (ĕl'sĭnôr'), Dan. *Helsingør,* city (pop. 21,010), NE Zealand, Denmark; a port on the Oresund opposite Halsingborg. Flourished until 1857 as toll-collection station for ships passing through Oresund. Kronborg castle (built 1577–85; restored 1635–40) is sometimes used for performances of Shakspere's *Hamlet,* which is laid in Elsinore.

Elssler, Fanny (ĕl'slŭr), 1810–84, Austrian ballet dancer. Made her debut in 1833 and was very popular in London, Paris, and U.S. until her retirement in 1851. Her forte was folk dancing.

Eluard, Paul (pôl' ālwär'), 1895–1952, French poet. Was long associated with surrealism, later with Communism. Among his volumes of poetry are *Mourir de ne pas mourir* (1924), *Poésie et vérité* (1942), *Au rendez-vous allemand* (1945). Was active in anti-German resistance during World War II.

Elvehjem, Conrad Arnold (ĕlvā'ùm), 1901–, American biochemist. His research led to use of niacin (part of vitamin B complex) in treating pellagra. He discovered that copper is essential to hemoglobin formation and made many other valuable contributions.

Elvend or **Elwend** (both: ĕlvĕnd'), mountain, c.11,600 ft. high, W Iran, SW of Hamadan. Has rock inscriptions of Darius and Xerxes.

Elwood, city (pop. 11,362), E central Ind., NNE of Indianapolis. Canning center for tomato-growing area, it ships grain and livestock. Mfg. of metal products. W. L. Willkie born here.

Ely. 1 City (pop. 5,474), NE Minn., on Vermilion iron range, in wooded lake region. Resort center with hq. of Superior National Forest. **2** City (pop. 3,558), E Nev., in rich copper area. Lehman Caves Natl. Monument is near.

Ely, City of, urban district (pop. 9,989), Isle of Ely, England, NNE of Cambridge. Ely cathedral (begun 1083), one of largest in England, has architecture of varied periods. Within its grounds are Tudor palace of the bishop, a theological college, and King's Grammar School, founded by Henry VIII.

Ely, Isle of, administrative county (372 sq. mi.; pop. 89,038), E England; administrative center March. Region of extensive fens, now drained for agr. Historically a part of CAMBRIDGESHIRE.

Elymas (ē'lĭmăs), the same as BAR-JESUS.

Elyria (ĭlēr'ēù), city (pop. 30,307), N Ohio, on Black R., SW of Cleveland; settled 1817. Trade center of agr. area, it has mfg. of aircraft, electrical products, and motor vehicles.

Elysian fields (ĭlĭ'zhùn) or **Elysium** (ĭlĭ'zhēùm), in Greek religion, happy otherworld for heroes favored by the gods. Identified with Isles of the Blest or Fortunate Isls., and, in Vergil, part of underworld.

Elzevir, Louis (ĕl'zùvùr, –vēr), 1540–1617, Dutch publisher, whose name also appears as Elsevier and Elzevier. The business he founded in 1583 at Leiden was continued by his descendants until 1712, and the name is still used. They owned presses and type and hired good editors and printers to turn out legible inexpensive books. Because of types designed for the house by Christopher van Dyck, the type known in English-speaking countries as "old-style" is called "Elzevir" on the Continent.

Emancipation, Edict of, March 3, 1861 (N.S.), edict by which Alexander II freed all Russian serfs (c.22,000,000—one third of total pop.). Provisions for peasants' purchase of land were complex and cumbersome, made private ownership of land nearly impossible until belated reform of STOLYPIN (1906).

Emancipation Proclamation. Despite insistence of abolitionists, Pres. Lincoln, in early Civil War, did not issue edict freeing slaves lest it alienate loyal border states. But on July 22, 1862, he read a draft to his cabinet. After successful Antietam campaign he issued preliminary edict, and on Jan. 1, 1863, the formal Emancipation Proclamation. It did not free all slaves in U.S., but only those in states in rebellion "as a fit and necessary war measure for suppressing said rebellion." Designed to deplete Southern manpower reserve in slaves and to enhance Union cause abroad.

embalming (ĕmbä'mǐng), treatment for preserving a corpse. Practiced by ancient peoples, notably Egyptians. Bodies can now be preserved indefinitely.

Embargo Act of 1807, passed Dec. 22, 1807, by U.S. Congress in answer to British ORDERS IN COUNCIL restricting neutral shipping and to Napoleon's opposing CONTINENTAL SYSTEM. Forbade all international trade to and from American ports in attempt to persuade England and France of the value and rights of a neutral commerce. In Jan., 1809, prohibition was extended to inland waters and land commerce to halt trade with Canada. England and France stood firm, and enforcement of act was difficult, especially in New England. Acts replacing it effectually dissolved whole purpose of embargo.

embezzlement, misappropriation of another's property by a wrongdoer who is in lawful possession. Since common law considered only "felonious taking" as larceny, the misuse of funds by the legal administrator for selfish ends is covered in England and U.S. by statutes making embezzlement a distinct crime or enlarging definition of larceny to include it.

embroidery, ornamental needlework in thread, fiber, or leather thongs, applied to a fabric or to leather. As an art it is probably older than weaving; primitive peoples used embroidered skins. From ancient times, the East has produced rich embroideries; the art came to Europe through Byzantine influence. From 12th to 14th cent., church embroidery (e.g., altar-cloths, vestments) flourished; later, secular embroidery, such as that on the rich costumes of Elizabethan England, reached its height. Advent of machinery caused decline of embroidery, but eyelet, cutwork, and other light forms are still done.

SMALL CAPITALS = cross references. Pronunciation key on inside end pages. Abbreviations: p. 2.

embryo (ĕm′brēō), name for developing young of animal and plant. Embryology is the scientific study of development up to hatching or birth. Exact duration of embryo stage is not well defined; in mammals the young in later prenatal stages is called fetus. In all animal reproduction involving union of sperm and egg cells, a series of cell divisions begins soon after fertilization; succeeding stages vary. In many forms, a blastula, a hollow ball consisting of one layer of cells, develops and later becomes two-layered cuplike gastrula; in higher forms, a third cell layer develops. Various body parts develop from each layer.

Emden (ĕm′dŭn), city (pop. 36,762), Lower Saxony, NW Germany, chief city of East Friesland; a North Sea port at mouth of Ems R. and on Dortmund-Ems Canal. Shipyards, herring fisheries. Dates from 10th cent. Heavily damaged in World War II.

emerald, green gem variety of BERYL. The finest come from South America. Oriental emerald is a variety of corundum.

Emerson, Ralph Waldo, 1803–82, American essayist, poet, and philosopher, b. Boston. Educated at Harvard for the Unitarian ministry, he became pastor of the Old North Church, Boston, in 1829 but retired in 1832 because of doctrinal difficulties. A trip to Europe broadened his acquaintance with the literary world of his day and wide reading in English, Continental, classic, and Oriental literature stimulated his thought. He settled in Concord, Mass., which became a center of American culture. He gained notice as a lecturer, his Phi Beta Kappa address at Harvard, *The American Scholar* (1837), being especially remarkable in its call for American intellectual freedom. He became a spokesman for a group that included his friends Thoreau and Margaret Fuller, and the principles of TRANSCENDENTALISM shone forth in his lectures and writings. His lectures (which were yearly more famous) were based on the *Journal* he had kept since Harvard days, and his essays were closely linked to the lectures. These *Essays* (1st series, 1841; 2d series, 1844), still much read today, generally set forth his sturdy belief that the individual can find redemption only in his own soul; among them are "The Over-Soul," "Compensation," and "Self-Reliance." Though technically he left much to be desired as a poet, some of his short lyrics are familiar to all American readers, such as "Brahma," "The Rhodora," and "The Concord Hymn." Among his many volumes are also *Nature* (1836; new ed., 1849), *English Traits* (1856; lectures after a trip to England in 1847), *Addresses and Lectures* (1849), and *Representative Men* (1850).

emery: see CORUNDUM.

Emesa: see HOMS, Syria.

Emigrant Aid Company, formed 1854 to promote organized antislavery immigration to Kansas from the Northeast. Name associated exclusively with New England Emigrant Aid Co., though other Kansas aid societies were subsequently formed. Founder Eli Thayer received 10% of all money he collected. Amos A. Lawrence was treasurer. Company sent out 1,240 settlers. Natl. Kansas Committee, formed at Buffalo, N.Y., 1856, as joint endeavor of aid societies, divided over problem of how to handle proslavery excesses. Whole movement was virtually ended by 1857. The movement, although it did little toward making Kansas a free state, captured public attention and engendered much bitterness and hate.

emigration: see IMMIGRATION; MIGRATION.

Emilia-Romagna (āmē′lyä-rōmä′nyä), region (8,542 sq. mi.; pop. 3,338,721), N central Italy, extending S from Po R.; cap. BOLOGNA. Other cities: FERRARA, FORLÌ, MODENA, PARMA, PIACENZA, RAVENNA, REGGIO EMILIA, RIMINI. Fertile agr. plain; few industries. Annexed to Sardinia 1860. For earlier history, see articles on individual cities; ROMAGNA.

Eminescu, Mihail (yĕmĕnĕ′skoͦo), 1850–89, foremost Rumanian poet, whose last name was originally Iminovici. His poetry has been widely translated.

Emmanuel, in Bible: see IMMANUEL.

Emmanuel. For Byzantine and Portuguese rulers thus named, see MANUEL.

Emmanuel College: see CAMBRIDGE UNIVERSITY.

Emmanuel Philibert, 1528–80, duke of Savoy (1553–80), called Ironhead. In Spanish service, he fought the French, who had occupied Savoy; won a brilliant victory at Saint-Quentin (1557); recovered Savoy at Treaty of Cateau-Cambrésis (1559). An energetic reformer, he restored his duchy to prosperity, shifted his cap. to Turin, made Savoy an Italian rather than French state.

Emmaus (ĕm′äus), place near Jerusalem where Cleopas and another disciple met the risen Christ. Luke 24.13.

Emmaus (ĕm′äus), borough (pop. 7,780), E Pa., S of Allentown; settled c.1740 by Moravians. Mfg. of commercial gases and rubber products.

Emma Willard School: see TROY, N.Y.

Emmental (ĕ′mùntäl), valley of Emme R., Bern canton, Switzerland. Produces fine cheese.

Emmet, Robert, 1778–1803, Irish patriot. After an unsuccessful attempt at a French-aided uprising in Ireland (1803), he was captured and hanged. He made a stirring speech from the gallows and became a great hero of Irish patriots.

Emmett, city (pop. 3,067), SW Idaho, on Payette R. and SE of Payette, in BOISE PROJECT.

Emmitsburg, town (pop. 1,261), N Md., near Pa. line NE of Hagerstown. Seat of Mt. St. Mary's Col. and St. Joseph's Col.

Emory University, near Atlanta, Ga.; mainly for men; chartered 1836, opened 1838 by Methodists, became a university 1915. Cooperates with Agnes Scott Col. (for women; 1889) at near-by Decatur.

emotion, term loosely used synonymously with feeling. In psychology: a response to stimuli involving physiological changes, tending to stimulate further activity. Fear, love, anger (primary responses) are roused directly by external stimuli, indirectly through memory, and expressed variously according to individual and to culture. Psychosomatic medicine has shown that tension from unrelieved emotions may cause physical disorders.

Empedocles (ĕmpĕ′dùklēz), c.495–c.435 B.C., Greek philosopher. Taught that two opposing forces—harmony and discord—combine indestructible material particles into varying forms.

Empire State Building, in central Manhattan, New York city, on Fifth Ave. between 33d and 34th streets, built 1930–31. Tallest building in the world; 1,250 ft. high, 102 stories.

Empire style, manner of interior decoration evolved in France from Directoire style and identified with reign of Napoleon I. Roman forms were used to emphasize grandeur of Napoleonic era, and symbols of imperial pomp added to traditional classic motifs. Staple wood was mahogany, but rosewood and ebony also used. Brass and ormolu mounts were chief ornaments. Style fell into disuse c.1840. Simplified form was adopted in England and U.S.; a German bourgeois adaptation is Biedermeier. See *ills.*, pp. 229, 356.

empiricism, philosophical doctrine that all knowledge is derived from experience. Opposed to RATIONALISM, it denies innate ideas and a priori truth and stresses generalizations based only on observation (experience). Basic to scientific method, it dominated British philosophy from Francis Bacon to John Stuart Mill.

employment bureau, establishment for bringing together the employer offering work and the employee seeking it. In England the first employment bureau was opened 1855; a national system was established 1909. France has had public employment agencies since 1916. In the U.S. the first state regulation of private agencies was in Mass. in 1848. Regulations requiring licensing have been enacted in 41 states. The U.S. government has operated employment offices since 1907. In 1918 the Employment Service of Dept. of Labor was estab. The state agencies, brought directly under

Federal operation in 1942, were turned back to the states in 1946. In 1948 the U.S. Employment Service was transferred to the Federal Security Agency.

Emporia. 1 City (pop. 15,669), E central Kansas, near Neosho R. and SW of Topeka; founded 1857. Trade and rail center in dairy and grain area. William Allen WHITE made the Emporia *Gazette* famous. **2** Town (pop. 5,664), S Va., on Meherrin R. and S of Petersburg. Shipping and processing center for agr. (cotton) and timber area.

Ems or Bad Ems (bät′ ĕms′), town (pop. 8,454), Rhineland-Palatinate, W Germany, on Lahn R. It is one of Europe's oldest watering places.

Ems, river, 208 mi. long, NW Germany, rising near Paderborn and flowing NW into North Sea near Emden. Wide mouth is called the Dollart. Much of its course is paralleled by the Dortmund-Ems Canal. Oil and natural gas were discovered after 1940 in the Emsland (region about lower course).

Ems dispatch, July 12, 1870, incident leading to Franco-Prussian War. The Spanish throne had been offered to a Hohenzollern prince. France having protested, the prince refused the offer, but the French ambassador Benedetti, meeting William I of Prussia at Ems, demanded assurance that no Hohenzollern should ever seek the Spanish throne. William turned him down flatly but politely. Seeking to goad France into declaring war, Bismarck published the interview in skillfully altered and insulting language, with complete success.

emu (ē′mū), large flightless bird of Australia, related to cassowary and ostrich. A swift runner, it is 5–6 ft. tall. It is almost extinct.

emulsion: see SUSPENSION.

encephalitis lethargica: see SLEEPING SICKNESS.

Encina or Enzina, Juan del (both: hwän′ dĕl änthē′nä), 1469?–1530, Spanish dramatist, musician, poet, a priest.

Enciso, Martín Fernández de (märtēn′ fĕrnän′däth dä ĕnthē′sō), fl. 1509–19, Spanish conquistador and geographer. Refounded colony in Darien (1509), but was replaced by Pedrarias (1514). Wrote commentary on flora and fauna in New World.

enclosure of land: see INCLOSURE.

encomienda (änkōmyän′dä), system of tributary labor adapted in Spanish America, modeled on that imposed in Spain on conquered Moors. It permitted conquistadors receiving land grants from crown to exact tribute from Indians living thereon. In return Indians received the protection of owner and subsistence rights on the land. See also REPARTIMIENTO.

encyclical: see BULL.

encyclopedia, either a general compendium of knowledge in all fields or a work which aims to be comprehensive in some one field. *Natural History* of Pliny the Elder is often considered the most ancient encyclopedia because it aimed at encompassing all knowledge. Various medieval scholars attempted to make all knowledge available to less informed. Example of modern encyclopedia—including alphabetical arrangement of material and bibliographies—was set by John Harris (c.1667–1719) in his *Lexicon technicum* (1704). *The Encyclopaedia Britannica* was first published in 1771. Famous French ENCYCLOPÉDIE was completed in 1772. The German *Brockhaus' Konversations-Lexikon* was first issued in 1796–1808. On this was based *The Encyclopaedia Americana*, edited by Francis Lieber (13 vols., 1829–33). Among the encyclopedias limited to a single branch of knowledge are the *Encyclopaedia of the Social Sciences* and *The Catholic Encyclopedia*.

Encyclopédie (äsĕklōpädē′), French encyclopedia, in 28 vols., edited by DIDEROT, published 1751–72. D'ALEMBERT, coeditor until 1758, wrote "Preliminary Discourse"; other collaborators included MONTESQUIEU, QUESNAY, J. J. ROUSSEAU, VOLTAIRE. Banned by the government in 1759, it was clandestinely printed with the secret tolerance of the police chief. The emphasis of the *Encyclopédie* is on science, crafts, mechanics; it contains no biographic articles. Its outlook is deliberately rationalist and materialistic. It had great influence on European learning.

Endecott or Endicott, John, c.1588–1665, first governor of Mass. Bay colony (1628–30).

endemic disease: see COMMUNICABLE DISEASES.

Enderbury Island, area 4 sq. mi., Phoenix Isls., central Pacific, near CANTON ISLAND; under Anglo-American control since 1939.

Enderby Land, area in Indian Ocean sector of Antarctica. Claimed by British because of John Biscoe's discovery (1831); not visited again until 1929.

Endicott, John: see ENDECOTT, JOHN.

Endicott, village (pop. 20,050), S N.Y., on Susquehanna R and W of Binghamton and Johnson City, with which it forms the Triple Cities; settled c.1795. Shoes, business machines, and foundry products.

endive (ĕn′dīv; Fr. ēdēv′), salad plant (*Cichorium endivia*) with crisp curly or broad leaves; related to chicory. Commonly blanched.

endocrine gland: see GLAND.

endogamy: see MARRIAGE.

En-dor, village, Palestine, S of Mt. Tabor. Here Saul consulted famous witch. 1 Sam. 28.7; Ps. 83.10.

Endymion (ĕndĭ′mēŭn), in Greek legend, shepherd of Mt. Latmos, loved by Selene (the moon). He was given immortality and eternal sleep.

energy, in physics, defined usually as ability to do work. It includes heat, light, sound, electricity, and chemical energy. **Potential energy** of a body is work capacity because of its position. **Kinetic energy** of a body is work capacity because of its motion. **Law of conservation of energy** states that although its form may change, energy can neither be created nor destroyed. **Chemical energy** is a form involved in chemical reaction. Solar energy, considered ultimate energy source, is utilized in PHOTOSYNTHESIS.

Enesco, Georges (zhôrzh ĕnĕs′kō), 1881–, Rumanian violinist, composer, and conductor. Most popular are his two Rumanian Rhapsodies for orchestra.

Enfield, urban district (pop. 110,458), Middlesex, England, N of London. Site of Royal Small Arms factory which makes Enfield rifles.

Enfield, town (pop. 15,464), N Conn., on Connecticut R. at Mass. line; settled c.1680. Had Shaker settlement c.1780–1915. Town includes mfg. village of Thompsonville (pop. 9,633; textiles, wood products).

Engadine (ĕng′gŭdēn), upper part of Inn R. valley, Grisons canton, E Switzerland. BERNINA group rises at S end. Many tourist and health resorts, e.g., St. Moritz, Pontresina. Pop. largely Romansh-speaking and Protestant.

Engelberg (ĕng′ŭlbĕrk), village, Obwalden half-canton, central Switzerland. Winter and summer resort. Has 12th-cent. Benedictine abbey.

Engels, Friedrich (frē′drĭkh ĕng′ŭls), 1820–95, German socialist, one of the two founders, with Karl MARX, of modern COMMUNISM. After organizing (1845–50) revolutionary movements in Europe, he lived in England, collaborating with Karl Marx on the *Communist Manifesto* (1848); after Marx's death, edited 2d and 3d volumes of *Das Kapital*. He elaborated theories of MARXISM and DIALECTICAL MATERIALISM, fundamental to communism. Basic to communist literature are his *Landmarks of Scientific Socialism* (1878) and *The Origin of the Family, Private Property, and the State* (1884).

Enghien, Louis Antoine Henri de Bourbon-Condé, duc d' (lwē ätwän′ ärē′ dù bŏŏrbō′-kŏdä′ dük dägē′), 1772–1804, French prince. Emigrated with his father, Louis Henri Joseph de Condé. Unjustly suspected by Napoleon of participation in conspiracy of CADOUDAL, he was kidnaped from Baden, court-martialed, and shot within few hours.

engine: see DIESEL ENGINE; INTERNAL-COMBUSTION ENGINE; STEAM ENGINE; *ill.*, p. 303.

engineering, science dealing with design, construction,

SMALL CAPITALS = cross references. Pronunciation key on inside end pages. Abbreviations: p. 2.

and operation of structures, machines, engines, and other devices used in industry and everyday life. Until Industrial Revolution engineering embodied only civil engineering (construction of tools, roads, bridges, etc.) and military engineering (construction of fortifications, engines of war, etc.); afterward mechanical engineering developed separately for design and construction of machinery. Vast field of modern engineering includes aeronautical, agricultural, chemical, civil, electrical, geological, industrial or management, marine, mechanical, and metallurgical engineering.

England, John (ing'glùnd), 1786–1842, Irish-American churchman, b. Ireland. Catholic bishop of Charleston, S.C. after 1820, he was a devoted American, interested especially in the needs of the Negroes.

England, largest political division (all figures without Monmouthshire: 50,327 sq. mi.; pop. 41,147,938) of island of Great Britain in British Isles; core of British Empire. To the W is WALES; to the N is SCOTLAND (above Solway Firth). Cut off from continent of Europe by English Channel, Straits of Dover, and North Sea, England's growth was determined by defensibility from attack, mild climate, and geographic accessibility by S ports and E and W river estuaries. The 38 (or 39) political divisions, the counties or shires, are Bedfordshire, Berkshire, Buckinghamshire, Cambridgeshire, Cheshire, Cornwall, Cumberland, Derbyshire, Devonshire, Dorsetshire, Durham, Essex, Gloucestershire, Hampshire, Herefordshire, Hertfordshire, Huntingdonshire, Kent, Lancashire, Lincolnshire, Middlesex, Monmouthshire (often included in Wales), Norfolk, Northamptonshire, Northumberland, Nottinghamshire, Oxfordshire, Rutland, Shropshire, Somerset, Staffordshire, Suffolk, Surrey, Sussex, Warwickshire, Westmoreland, Wiltshire, Worcestershire, and Yorkshire. S and SE are low and fertile; marshy NE has been mostly reclaimed. W is rough country, ending in peninsula of Cornwall. N of the Humber the Pennine Chain leads to scenery of Lake District and to Scotland. For the last 200 years England's chief wealth has derived from great industries of the Black country (based on coal and iron fields N of large Midlands plain), from the industrial centers of Lancashire and Yorkshire, and from shipping and mfg. of leading cities—London (capital), Manchester, Liverpool, Leeds, Sheffield, Birmingham, Bristol, Bradford, and Hull. In 19th cent. England led the world in exports of manufactures. A limited monarchy, England is joined with Scotland and N. Ireland in the United Kingdom of Great Britain and N. Ireland. Legislative and actual sovereignty reside in PARLIAMENT. Executive authority, nominally vested in the crown, lies with a cabinet responsible to parliament. The estab. church is the Church of England. Education Act of 1944 attempted coordination of all secondary and public schools, including Eton, Harrow, Rugby, and Winchester. Oxford and Cambridge are oldest and most noted of the 11 universities, the others being Birmingham, Bristol, Durham, Leeds, Liverpool, London, Manchester, Reading, and Sheffield.

Celt and Roman, Saxon and Dane. For history of these early invaders and settlers, see BRITAIN. By 865 the Danes (term for all Norse invaders) had conquered England until resistance by ALFRED and his successors finally ended the DANELAW. New invasions led to CANUTE becoming Danish ruler of all England in 1017. The ANGLO-SAXONS had important effects on English culture—they developed Christianity, stimulated trade and the growth of towns, and brought central government from tribal chieftainships to a monarchy controlling executive and judicial powers. Period was ended by the NORMAN CONQUEST in 1066.

Feudal England. Norman king William I marked a new point in English history. His strong rule and efforts at centralization were typified in DOMESDAY survey. Political and military FEUDALISM were introduced. Under his successors baronial wars produced noted English constitutional document, the MAGNA CARTA

(1215). Increased royal holdings in France led to the first Anglo-French struggles and to the HUNDRED YEARS WAR (1337). Subsequent dynastic Wars of the ROSES were ended by accession of Henry VII (1485) of family of Tudor, with whom modern English history begins.

Tudor and Stuart. Tudor period was a glorious one. REFORMATION, introduced by Henry VIII, ran parallel with the flowering of the Renaissance. Trade expanded. Succession to throne was a vital issue in reigns of Edward VI, Mary I, ELIZABETH I. STUART period, introduced by James I, was dominated by PURITAN REVOLUTION, culminating in civil war (1642). Parliamentarian victory led to execution of CHARLES I (1649) and to the Protectorate under Oliver CROMWELL. Reaction against puritanism was shown by the Restoration of CHARLES II. Supremacy of parliament final after overthrow of James II by the Glorious Revolution of 1688 and the accession of WILLIAM III and Mary. WHIG and TORY party government developed under Sir Robert Walpole. Colonial expansion and rivalries led to wars of European alliances, mainly with France. Tudors, Stuarts, and Cromwell continued conquest of Ireland. Under Queen ANNE Scotland was joined to England by Act of Union in 1707. For later history see GREAT BRITAIN and BRITISH EMPIRE.

In a World of Industry. England's leadership in INDUSTRIAL REVOLUTION in 19th cent. was derived from industrial Midlands. Attendant depressions produced CHARTISM. Expanding trade caused enormous growth of cities. World War II brought huge damage from air raids. War was followed by nationalization of industry, loss of England's financial supremacy to U.S., and shrinkage of empire. England reemerged as the center of the British Commonwealth of Nations.

The royal rulers of England since William the Conqueror have been: *Norman*—William I, 1066–87; William II, 1087–1100; Henry I, 1100–1135. *Stephen*—Stephen, 1135–54. *Plantagenet*—Henry II, 1154–89; Richard I, 1189–99; John, 1199–1216; Henry III, 1216–72; Edward I, 1272–1307; Edward II, 1307–27; Edward III, 1327–77; Richard II, 1377–99. *Lancaster* —Henry IV, 1399–1413; Henry V, 1413–22; Henry VI, 1422–61 and 1470–71. *York*—Edward IV, 1461–70 and 1471–83; Edward V, 1483; Richard III, 1483–85. *Tudor*—Henry VII, 1485–1509; Henry VIII, 1509–47; Edward VI, 1547–53; Mary I, 1553–58; Elizabeth I, 1558–1603. *Stuart*—James I, 1603–25; Charles I, 1625–49 (executed 1649; Commonwealth and Protectorate, 1649–60; Charles II in exile); Charles II, 1660–85; James II, 1685–88. *Orange*—William III, 1688–1702, and Mary II, 1688–94. *Stuart*—Anne, 1702–14. *Hanover*—George I, 1714–27; George II, 1727–60; George III, 1760–1820; George IV, 1820–30; William IV, 1830–37; Victoria, 1837–1901. *Saxe-Coburg-Gotha*—Edward VII, 1901–10. *Windsor*—George V, 1910–36; Edward VIII, 1936; George VI, 1936–52; Elizabeth II, 1952–.

England, Church of, official church of England. Its break with Roman Church came when Henry VIII withdrew from allegiance to pope and announced that the king would be head of English church; this move was confirmed by Act of Supremacy of 1534. Henry suppressed monasteries and authorized Great Bible (1539). First Book of Common Prayer was adopted 1549. Under Mary, England came again under Catholic communion, but Elizabeth restored Protestantism. Act of Supremacy of 1559 defined constitutional position of Church and relation to the crown. Under James I rising tide of Puritanism necessitated Hampton Court Conference (1604), where king upheld estab. doctrine. Under Charles I measures of Archbishop Laud against Calvinists contributed to civil war (1642). The Long Parliament estab. Presbyterianism (1646). With Restoration (1660) episcopacy was restored and the Prayer Book was made the only legal service book by Act of Uniformity (1662), which also required episcopal ordination of all ministers. Thereafter, de-

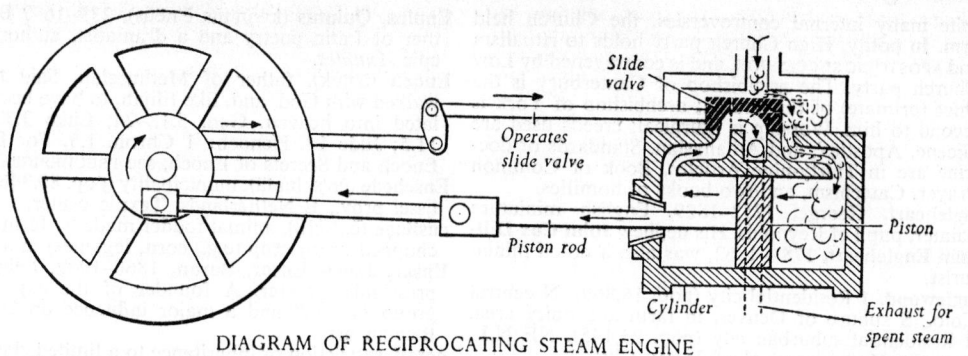

DIAGRAM OF RECIPROCATING STEAM ENGINE

The slide valve admits steam alternately on either side of the piston. Arrows indicate the direction of force.

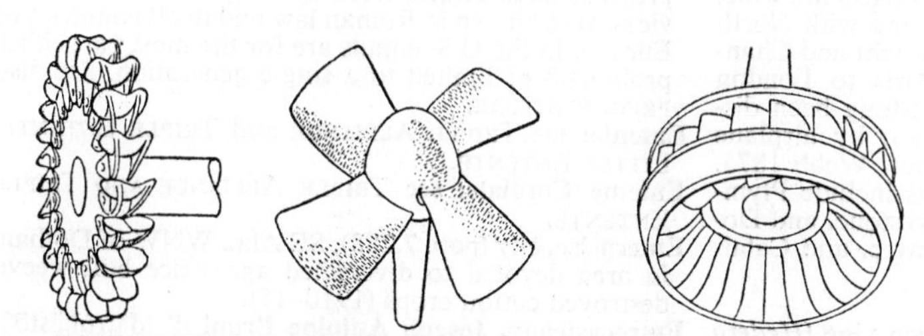

PELTON TYPE   PROPELLER TYPE   FRANCIS TYPE

WATER TURBINES

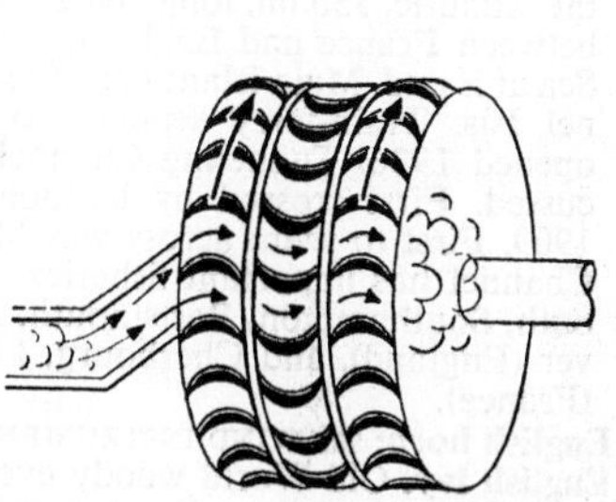

DIAGRAM OF A STEAM TURBINE

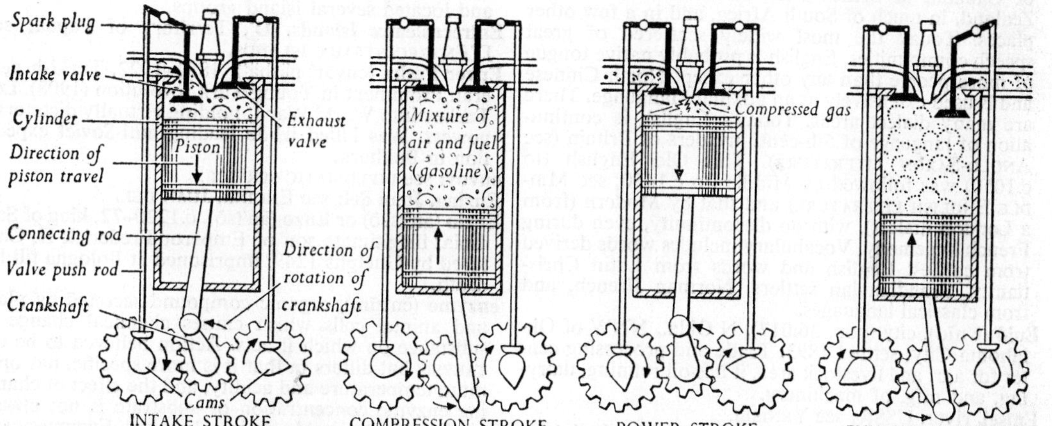

INTAKE STROKE   COMPRESSION STROKE   POWER STROKE   EXHAUST STROKE

DIAGRAM OF A FOUR-CYCLE (FOUR-STROKE-CYCLE) INTERNAL-COMBUSTION ENGINE

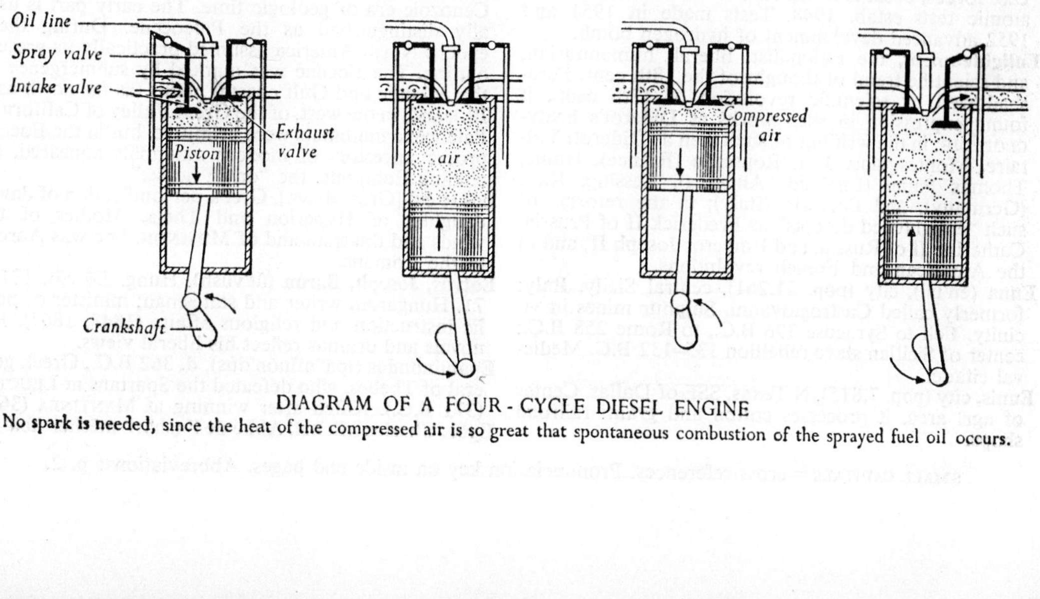

DIAGRAM OF A FOUR-CYCLE DIESEL ENGINE

No spark is needed, since the heat of the compressed air is so great that spontaneous combustion of the sprayed fuel oil occurs.

spite many internal controversies, the Church held firm. In polity, High Church party holds to ritualism and APOSTOLIC SUCCESSION, and is contravened by Low Church party. The archbishop of Canterbury is the chief (primate) of the church; archbishop of York is second to him. Worship is liturgical; creeds used are Nicene, Apostles', and Athanasian. Standards of doctrine are in Thirty-nine Articles, Book of Common Prayer, Catechism, and two books of homilies.

Engleheart, George, 1752–1829, English miniature painter, pupil of Reynolds. His nephew **John Cox Dillman Engleheart,** 1784–1862, was also a noted miniaturist.

Englewood. 1 Residential city (pop. 16,869), N central Colo., S suburb of Denver, in farm and dairy area. **2** Residential suburban city (pop. 23,145), NE N.J., near the Hudson and N of Jersey City.

English Channel, Fr. *La Manche* = the sleeve; arm of the Atlantic, 350 mi. long and 21 mi. to c.150 mi. wide, between France and England, connecting with North Sea at E end. Main islands are Isle of Wight and Channel Isls. Train-ferry service from Paris to London opened 1936. Tunneling Channel has long been discussed. First crossed by balloon 1785; by airplane 1909. First to swim across was Matthew Webb 1875. Channel has important fisheries. Ports include Plymouth, Southampton, Portsmouth, Folkestone, and Dover (England), and Cherbourg, Le Havre, and Calais (France).

English horn: see WIND INSTRUMENTS.

English ivy, Old World woody evergreen vine (*Hedera helix*), a ground or wall cover and house plant.

English language, language prevalent in U.S. and much of Canada, in British Isles, in Australia and New Zealand, in much of South Africa, and in a few other places. Today the most widely scattered of great speech communities, English is probably native tongue of more people than any other except North Chinese and is used extensively as an auxiliary language. There are many dialect areas. Today's English is continuation of language of 5th-cent. invaders of Britain (see ANGLO-SAXON LITERATURE). This Old English (to c.1050) was followed by Middle (to c.1450; see MIDDLE ENGLISH LITERATURE) and that by Modern (from a London dialect), with no discontinuity, even during French hegemony. Vocabulary includes words derived from earliest English and words from Latin Christianity, Scandinavian settlers, Norman French, and from classical languages.

Enid (ē'nĭd), city (pop. 36,017), N Okla., NNW of Oklahoma City; settled 1893. Trade and processing center for agr. and livestock area, it has oil refining, dairying, and mfg. of machinery.

Enisei, river, USSR: see YENISEI.

Eniwetok (ĕnĭwē'tŏk), circular atoll of Marshall Isls., central Pacific; comprises 40 islets. Captured 1944 by U.S. forces, became naval base 1945. Installations for atomic tests estab. 1948. Tests made in 1951 and 1952 advanced development of hydrogen bomb.

Enlightenment, the rationalist, liberal, humanitarian, and scientific trend of thought of the 18th cent. Foreshadowed by scientific revolution of 17th cent., it found expression in such works as Diderot's ENCYCLOPÉDIE; in the writings of such men as Diderot, Voltaire, Montesquieu, J. J. Rousseau (France), Hume, Thomas Paine (England, America), Lessing, Kant (Germany), and Beccaria (Italy); in the reforms of such "enlightened despots" as Frederick II of Prussia, Catherine II of Russia, and Emperor Joseph II; and in the American and French revolutions.

Enna (ĕn'nä), city (pop. 21,261), central Sicily, Italy; formerly called Castrogiovanni. Sulphur mines in vicinity. Fell to Syracuse 396 B.C., to Rome 258 B.C.; center of Sicilian slave rebellion 135–132 B.C. Medieval citadel.

Ennis, city (pop. 7,815), N Texas, SSE of Dallas. Center of agr. area, it processes cotton and grain; railroad shops.

Ennius, Quintus (kwĭn'tŭs ĕ'nēŭs), 239–169? B.C., father of Latin poetry and a dramatist, author of the epic *Annales.*

Enoch (ē'nŭk), father of Methuselah. Said to have walked with God, and, like Elijah, to have been translated into heaven. Gen. 5.18–24; Luke 3.37; Heb. 11.5; Jude 14. Henoch: 1 Chron. 1.3. For Book of Enoch and Secrets of Enoch, see PSEUDEPIGRAPHA.

Enschede (ĕn'skhŭdā), municipality (pop. 80,346), Overijssel prov., E Netherlands. Textile center.

ensilage (ĕn'sŭlĭj), animal fodder made by fermenting a chopped green crop (e.g., corn, legumes) in a SILO.

Ensor, James Ensor, Baron, 1860–1949, Belgian impressionist painter. A founder of the experimental group *Les XX* and a major influence on 20th-cent. Belgian art.

entail, restriction of inheritance to a limited class of descendants for at least several generations in order to preserve large estates from disintegration. Similar devices were known in Roman law and in all countries of Europe. In the U.S. entails are for the most part either prohibited or limited to a single generation. See also PRIMOGENITURE.

Entente: see TRIPLE ALLIANCE and TRIPLE ENTENTE; LITTLE ENTENTE.

Entente Cordiale: see TRIPLE ALLIANCE AND TRIPLE ENTENTE.

Enterprise, city (pop. 7,288), SE Ala., WNW of Dothan, in area devoted to diversified agr. since boll weevil destroyed cotton crops (1910–15).

Entrecasteaux, Joseph Antoine Bruni d' (dātrŭkästō'), 1739–93, French navigator. In command of expedition to search for La Pérouse (1791–92), he explored coast of New Caledonia, Tasmania, and New Holland, and located several island groups.

Entrecasteaux Islands, D', Territory of Papua: see D'ENTRECASTEAUX ISLANDS.

Enver Pasha (envâr' päshä'), 1881–1922, Turkish general. Prominent in Young Turk revolution (1908). Led Turkey into World War I, holding virtually dictatorial powers. Was killed while leading anti-Soviet expedition in Bukhara.

envoy: see DIPLOMATIC SERVICE.

Enzina, Juan del: see ENCINA, JUAN DEL.

Enzio (ān'tsēō) or **Enzo** (ān'tsō), c.1220–72, king of Sardinia; illegitimate son of Emperor Frederick II. Captured by Guelphs 1249; imprisoned at Bologna till his death.

enzyme (ĕn'zīm), organic compound secreted by plant and animal cells which causes chemical change in substance on which it acts. Action believed to be CATALYSIS but differs in that it is more specific, has optimum temperature and acidity, and the effect of changing enzyme concentration or substrate is not always predictable by simple chemical theory. Enzymes catalyze digestion, oxidation, other metabolic processes.

Eocene epoch, first epoch of the TERTIARY PERIOD and Cenozoic era of geologic time. The early part is usually distinguished as the Paleocene. During these epochs North America assumed practically its present outline. The Eocene was marked by submergence of the Atlantic and Gulf coastal plains (as far north as S Ill.), and, in the west, of the Great Valley of California. Paleocene mammals were primitive, but in the Eocene proper ancestors of modern mammals appeared, including Eohippus, the "dawn horse."

Eos (ē'ŏs) [Gr.,= dawn], Greek personification of dawn, daughter of Hyperion and Theia. Mother of the winds and the stars and of MEMNON. She was Aurora to the Romans.

Eotvos, Joseph, Baron (ût'vûsh), Hung. *Eötvös,* 1813–71, Hungarian writer and statesman; minister of public instruction and religious affairs (1848, 1867). His novels and dramas reflect his liberal views.

Epaminondas (ĭpă″mĭnŏn'dŭs), d. 362 B.C., Greek general of Thebes, who defeated the Spartans at LEUCTRA (371 B.C.). Killed after winning at MANTINEA (362).

Epée, Charles Michel, Abbé de l' (shärl' mēshĕl' äbä' dŭ lāpā'), 1712–89, French Jansenist. Developed manual system of communications for deaf-mutes.

Épernay (āpĕrnä'), town (pop. 18,716), Marne dept., NE France, in Champagne, on Marne R. A center of champagne industry.

Ephesians (–fē'–), epistle of New Testament, traditionally written by St. Paul to Christians of Ephesus from his captivity at Rome (A.D. c.60). Book contains: doctrine of mystical body of Christ; example of ideal harmony of husbands and wives; famous metaphor of the Christian as a soldier.

Ephesus (ĕ'fŭsŭs), anc. Ionian Greek city of Asia Minor, in modern Turkey; a wealthy seaport. Under Rome became leading city of Asia. Temple of Diana (Artemis) was one of the Seven Wonders of the World. Ephesus was later a center of Christianity.

Ephesus, Council of, 431, third ecumenical council called to deal with NESTORIANISM. St. CYRIL of Alexandria was the leader of the faction that after a struggle succeeded in exiling Nestorius and condemning his doctrines. The council declared Mary might be called the Mother of God, since God and Christ were one person, a doctrine further defined later by the Council of CHALCEDON. For the Robber Synod (Latrocinium) of Ephesus, see EUTYCHES.

ephod (ē'fŏd, ĕ'fŏd), sacred linen garment worn by high priests of Israel; apparently somehow used in divination. Ex. 28; Judges 8.27; 17.5; 18.14; 1 Sam. 2.28; 14.3; 22.18; 23.6,9; 30.7; Hosea 3.4.

Ephraim (ē'frŭm), son of Joseph, ancestor of one of 12 tribes of Israel. Tribe occupied region around Shiloh. Gen. 41.52; 46.20; 48.14–20; Joshua 16; 1 Chron. 7.20. Samuel was of house of Ephraim.

Ephraim, city (pop. 1,987; alt. 5,543 ft.), central Utah, S of Provo. Irrigated by Sanpete project.

Ephrata (ĕ'frŭtŭ), borough (pop. 7,027), SE Pa., NE of Lancaster; settled 1728–33 by Seventh-Day Baptists as communal religious community. Was famous for music; estab. early printing press. Buildings preserved as shrine by state. Center of agr. area with mfg. of clothing, textiles, and furniture.

Ephratah (ĕ'frŭtŭ) or **Ephrath:** see BETHLEHEM.

epic, long narrative poem, elaborate and dignified, in which theme is treated in heroic proportions and in grand style. Story of hero is usually unifying subject. Epics are generally classed as those conceived and composed by one mind (Vergil's *Aeneid,* Milton's *Paradise Lost*) and those by various unknown poets working at different times on popular legends concerning heroes (BEOWULF and ROLAND); Greek epics, the *Iliad* and the *Odyssey,* embrace both groups. Some epics embody ideals of a nation, e.g., Finnish KALEVALA and *The Lusiads* of Camões. Other epics include the *Jerusalem Delivered* of Tasso, *The Faerie Queene* of Spenser, and the Spanish CID.

Epictetus (ĕpĭktē'tŭs), b. c.60 A.D., Roman Stoic philosopher.

Epicurus (ĕpĭkū'rŭs), 341–270 B.C., Greek philosopher. Defined philosophy as the art of making life happy, with intellectual pleasure or serenity the only good. His teaching (Epicureanism) later debased to "eat, drink, and be merry" formula—opposite of his belief. See also LUCRETIUS.

Epidaurus (ĕpĭdô'rŭs), anc. city, NE Peloponnesus, Greece. To the temple of Asclepius here came many health seekers.

epidemic disease: see COMMUNICABLE DISEASES.

Epigoni (ĕpĭg'ŭnī) [Gr.,= the offspring], in Greek legend, sons of the SEVEN AGAINST THEBES. Led by Adrastus, they conquered Thebes and gave the kingdom to THERSANDER.

epigraphy: see INSCRIPTION.

epilepsy, condition marked by attacks usually accompanied by loss of consciousness and convulsions. Most cases begin in youth; seizures vary in frequency and duration. Treatment includes rest.

Epimetheus (ĕpĭmē'thĕŭs, –thŭs) [Gr.,= afterthought], in Greek religion, Titan. Brother of Prometheus, who

warned him against marrying PANDORA—but in vain.

Épinal (āpēnäl'), town (pop. 21,939), cap. of Vosges dept., E France, in Lorraine. Famous for *images d'Épinal*—popular colored portrayals of melodramatic events long printed here.

Épinay, Louise de la Live d' (lwĕz' dü lä lēv' dāpēnā'), 1726–83, French patroness of letters, friend of Diderot and Grimm. She was a benefactress of J. J. Rousseau, who broke with her in 1757 and calumnied her in his *Confessions.*

epinephrine: see ADRENALINE.

Epiphania: see HAMA, Syria.

Epiphany (ĭpĭ'fŭnē) [Gr.,= showing], a prime Christian feast, celebrated Jan. 6; called also Twelfth Day, Little Christmas, and Manifestation of Christ to the Gentiles. Its eve is TWELFTH NIGHT. It commemorates three events—baptism of Jesus (Mark 1), visit of Wise Men to Bethlehem (Mat. 2), and miracle at Cana (John 2). Feast is more ancient than Christmas and technically more important, ranking after Easter and Whitsunday. The term *epiphany* (without capital letter) means a manifestation (usually of divine power) or a moment of intuitive perception.

epiphyte: see AIR PLANT.

Epirus (ĕpī'rŭs), anc. country of W Greece, on Ionian Sea. Reached its height in 3d cent. B.C. under PYRRHUS. Sided with Macedon against Rome, was sacked (167 B.C.), and passed under Roman rule. In A.D. 1204, as result of Fourth Crusade, an independent state, the **despotat of Epirus,** was set up here by a branch of Angelus family. It became nominally dependent on the empire of NICAEA (c.1246), passed to Serbs and Albanians (14th cent.) and to Turks (15th cent.).

Episcopal Church, Protestant, in the United States of America, in communion with the Anglican church. Services in America were first held (1607) in Jamestown, Va. In 1689 King's Chapel was opened in Boston, and Trinity Church in N.Y. city. Col. of William and Mary was founded 1693, King's Col. (now Columbia Univ.) 1754. After Revolution American Anglicans organized, with Samuel Seabury first bishop (1784). First General Conference (1789) approved name of church, and adopted constitution and revised Book of Common Prayer. Church spread rapidly in U.S. Standards of doctrine are Apostles' and Nicene creeds and Thirty-nine Articles.

Episcopal Church, Reformed: see REFORMED EPISCOPAL CHURCH.

Episcopius, Simon (ĕpĭskō'pĕŭs), 1583–1643, Dutch theologian; originally named Bisschop or Bischop. As leader of Arminians or REMONSTRANTS, he formulated in his *Institutiones theologicae* (1650) the doctrines of Jacob Arminius.

epistemology (ĭpī"stŭmŏ'lŭjē), branch of philosophy devoted to theories of knowledge, its origin and nature. Empirical epistemology teaches that all knowledge comes from experience; rationalistic epistemology holds that the mind contributes innate ideas.

epistle, a formal letter. Of books of New Testament, 21 are epistles. Those traditionally ascribed to St. Paul are Romans, 1 and 2 Corinthians, Galatians, Ephesians, Philippians, Colossians, 1 and 2 Thessalonians, 1 and 2 Timothy, Titus, Philemon, Hebrews. Catholic, or General Epistles are James, 1 and 2 Peter, 1, 2, and 3 John, Jude. Use of letters as literary form popular in 18th cent. when the novel was epistolary. Celebrated epistles are those of Petrarch, Pascal, Swift, and (in verse) Pope and Dryden.

Epping Forest, NNE of London, England, the anc. Royal Waltham Forest. Originally included all Essex. Has been a 5,600-acre public park since 1882.

Epsom and Ewell (yoo'ŭl), urban district (pop. 68,049), Surrey, England. DERBY and Oaks horse races are run on Epsom Downs.

Epstein, Jacob (ĕp'stīn), 1880–, sculptor, b. New York city. Studied under Rodin; worked chiefly in England. His massive creations done in startlingly unconventional style have caused much controversy. Some of best work is bronze portraiture.

equal temperament, in music, a system of tuning based on the arbitrary division of the octave into 12 equal semitones. The octave is the only acoustically correct interval; other tones of scale are adjusted or tempered so that, in keyboard instruments, a single key can represent two tones—for example, both F sharp and G flat. Scale thus derived is called a tempered scale. Bach supported this system with his *Well-Tempered Clavier,* containing preludes and fugues in all major and minor keys. See also TEMPERAMENT.

equation. 1 in mathematics, a statement of the equality of two quantities or algebraic expressions. If equation contains only numbers, it is called numerical; if it has letters as well as numbers, literal; if literal equation is true for all values of the variable, it is called an identical equation; if not, it is called a conditional equation. To solve equation, obtain value or values of variables which satisfy it. **2** in chemistry, an equation represents a reaction, the first member of the equation consisting of the formulas for the reacting substances and the second member the formulas for the resulting products. An arrow (——►) is used instead of an equals sign and its direction shows the direction in which the reaction is proceeding. In physics, equations are means of expressing fundamental relationships.

equatorial belt of calms: see DOLDRUMS.

equinox (ē′kwĭnŏks), in astronomy, either of two points of intersection of ECLIPTIC and celestial equator. Night and day are of equal length over entire earth on dates when sun's center crosses celestial equator southward (vernal equinox, about March 21) or northward (autumnal equinox, about Sept. 23). See also PRECESSION OF THE EQUINOXES. See *ill.,* p. 927.

equites (ē′kwĭtēz) [Latin,= horsemen, knights], original cavalry of the Roman army, later selected (to number 3,600) on basis of wealth. By the 1st cent. B.C. had become the influential capitalist class.

equity, principles of justice developed by chancellor and court of chancery in England to make up for inadequacies of common law. Equity originally drew many of its principles from Roman and canon law. Contest with common law was important in 16th and 17th cent. In 1875 common law and equity amalgamated by Judicature Acts in England. In U.S. most states have also done away with distinction between equity and common law.

Er, chemical symbol of the element ERBIUM.

era of good feeling, phrase applied to period 1817–23 in U.S. history, when, the Federalist party having declined, there was little open party feeling. Under the surface, however, vast sectional issues and personal rivalries were shaping themselves to break loose in campaign of 1824.

Erasistratus (ĕrŭsĭ′strŭtŭs) 3d cent. B.C., Greek physician, a founder of medical school at Alexandria.

Erasmus (ĭrăz′mŭs) or **Desiderius Erasmus** (dĕsĭdēr′-ēŭs), 1469?–1536, Dutch humanist. A Catholic priest and teacher, he had great influence after 1500. Acquainted with most scholars of the day, he was the broadest of humanists. Edited Greek and Latin works, including those of Church Fathers. Wrote satires (*The Praise of Folly,* 1509; *The Education of a Christian Prince,* 1515). His position with regard to the Reformation caused enmity of Luther.

Erastus, Thomas (ĭră′stŭs), 1524–83, Swiss physician and theologian, b. Lieber or Liebler. Opposed Calvinist doctrine and punitive power of church. Term **Erastianism** represents approval of dominance of civil authority in punitive matters, and, by extension, dominance of state over church.

Erato, Muse of the poetry of love: see MUSES.

Eratosthenes (ĕrŭtŏs′thŭnēz), c.275–c.195 B.C., versatile Greek scholar, head of Alexandria library. Especially noted for measuring circumference and tilt of earth and for map of known world.

Erbil (ĕr′bĭl), town (pop. 26,086), NE Iraq. On site of ARBELA, it has an old Turkish fort.

erbium (ûr′bēŭm), rare metallic element (symbol = Er; see also ELEMENT, table; metals of the RARE EARTHS).

Ercilla y Zúñiga, Alonso de (älōn′sō dä ĕrthī′lyä ē thōō′nyēgä), 1533–94, Spanish author of epic poem, *La Araucana,* about Araucanians, whom he had fought.

Erckmann-Chatrian (ĕrkmän′-shätrēä′), joint authorship of Émile Erckmann (āmēl′), 1822–99, and Alexandre Chatrian (älĕksä′drŭ), 1826–90. They wrote historical romances and plays set in native Lorraine, e.g., *Madame Thérèse* (1863) and *L'Ami Fritz* (1864; adapted into a play 1876).

Erdelyi, John (ĕr′dālyĭ), Hung. *Erdélyi,* 1814–68, Hungarian writer and critic, prominent in the Hungarian language reform movement. Edited (1846–48) the first collection of Hungarian folk poetry.

Erebus (ĕ′rĭbŭs) [Gr.,= darkness], in Greek mythology, gloomy part of underworld on way to Hades.

Erebus, Mount, volcanic peak, more than 13,300 ft. high, on Ross Isl., in the Ross Sea off Antarctica. Discovered 1841 by Sir James C. Ross.

Erech (ē′rĕk) or **Uruk** (ōō′rōōk), anc. Sumerian city of Mesopotamia, on Euphrates, near Ur; long the cap. of Lower Babylonia.

Erechtheum (ĭrĕk′thēŭm), temple in Pentelic marble on the Acropolis, Athens; built c.420–409 B.C., probably designed by Mnesicles. Contains finest examples of Greek IONIC ORDER. On S portico is Porch of the Caryatids, with its six draped female figures which support its entablature. Used as a church in Justinian's reign and as a harem during Turkish rule. Much damaged in Greek revolution of 1827. Part of it is included in ELGIN MARBLES.

Erechtheus (ĕrĕk′thūs), ancient mythological king of Athens; son of Hephaestus and Gaea. He invented four-wheeled chariot and founded Panathenaea.

Eretria (ĕrē′trĕu), anc. city of Greece, on Euboea. Mother-city of colonies in N Aegean, it supported the Ionian revolt against Persia (499 B.C.). Darius I destroyed it (490 B.C.).

Erfurt (âr′fōort), city (pop. 174,633), cap. of Thuringia, central Germany. Mfg.; center of gardening and truck-farming region. Bishopric of Erfurt, founded 741 by St. Boniface, passed to electors of Mainz 1664, to Prussia 1802. Occupied by French 1806–13, it was scene of Congress of Erfurt (1808), where Napoleon I and Alexander I renewed their alliance of 1807. City was incorporated into Thuringia in 1946, replaced Weimar as cap. 1948. Univ. of Erfurt (1392–1816) had Luther as student. Erfurt Program, adopted by German Social Democrats at party congress of 1891, marked triumph of Marxist doctrines over those of Lassalle. Erfurt's cathedral and Church of St. Severus (both 13th cent.) are notable.

erg, unit of work and energy in centimeter-gram-second system. It is the work done by one DYNE acting through distance of one centimeter. Joule is 10,000,000 ergs.

Eric, kings of Sweden. **Eric IX** (The Saint), d. 1160. Forcibly converted Finland to Christianity. Murdered by a Danish pagan, he became patron saint of Sweden. **Eric XIV,** 1533–77, reigned 1560–68. In conflict with nobility, he had Nils Sture and other powerful nobles assassinated. His unpopularity and soon evident insanity led to his deposition and imprisonment.

Ericsson, John (ē′rĭksŭn), 1803–89, Swedish-American inventor and marine engineer, b. Sweden. Chiefly remembered as designer and builder of the *Monitor* (see MONITOR).

Ericsson, Leif: see LEIF ERICSSON.

Eric the Red, fl. 10th cent., Norse chieftain, discoverer and colonizer of Greenland. Vainly resisted the introduction of Christianity there by his son, Leif Ericsson.

Eridu (ā′rĭdōō), anc. Sumerian city of Mesopotamia, near the Euphrates, not far from Ur. It perhaps was in existence in 8th millennium B.C. and was a center of the worship of Ea.

Erie, city (pop. 130,803), NW Pa., on L. Erie SW of Buffalo; laid out 1795. Only Pa. port on Great Lakes, it has mfg. of electrical and metal products. Site fortified by French, then British. In 1843 first all-iron battleship was assembled here. Was station on Underground Railroad.

Erie, Lake, 241 mi. long, 30–57 mi. wide, fourth in size and shallowest of the Great Lakes. Lies c.572 ft. above sea level, maximum depth 210 ft., area 9,950 sq. mi. Bordered N by Ontario, S by N.Y., Pa., and Ohio, W by small portion of Mich. Connected with L. Huron by natural channel, with L. Ontario by Niagara R. and by Welland Canal. N.Y. State Barge Canal and Hudson R. connect it with the Atlantic. Partially icebound and largely closed to navigation from mid-December to April. Principal U.S. ports include Buffalo, N.Y.; Erie, Pa.; Cleveland and Toledo, Ohio; and Detroit, Mich. First white man to see lake was probably Louis Jolliet (1669). Forts and trading posts were built on shores. Great Britain controlled area after French and Indian Wars until War of 1812 when international boundary was set. In War of 1812 at **battle of Lake Erie** (Sept. 10, 1813) British were defeated by U.S. fleet under O. H. PERRY.

Erie Canal, artificial waterway, extending from Albany to Buffalo and connecting the Hudson with L. Erie. Authorized by N.Y. in April, 1817; completed 1825. Later converted into NEW YORK STATE BARGE CANAL. The Erie furthered New York city's financial development, opened Eastern markets to farm products of the Great Lakes region, fostered immigration to Old Northwest, helped create numerous large cities.

Erie Indians, sedimentary tribe of Iroquoian linguistic stock, in region E and S of L. Erie in 17th cent. Enemies of the Iroquois Confederacy, they were almost exterminated after 1656.

Erie Railroad. Incorporated 1832 as New York and Erie Railroad Co. Struggle for control among railroad barons after Civil War, with victory for Jay Gould, was main phase of company's unstable financial history in 19th cent. Beginning as a short N.Y. railroad, it had by 1880 branch lines to Chicago, and E terminus at Jersey City. Reorganized 1895 as Erie Railroad Co. After reorganization of 1941, company yielded a dividend for first time in 69 years.

Erigena, John Scotus (skō′tŭs ĕrī′jĭnŭ), c.810–880, scholastic philosopher. Identified philosophy and theology and made a four-fold division of nature, a creative cycle that begins and ends with God.

Erin (ĕr′ĭn, ēr′ĭn), poetic name of IRELAND.

Erinyes (ērĭn′ē-ēz), in Greek religion, Furies or goddesses of vengeance, represented as three maidens, winged, with snakes in their hair. Born from blood of Uranus which fell on land. They pursued criminals and tormented them in Hades. Euphemistically, also called Eumenides [favorable ones], their title in the chorus in the *Eumenides* of Aeschylus.

Eris (ē′rĭs) [Gr.,= discord], in Greek legend, female personification of strife. In revenge for not being invited to a wedding, she threw the APPLE OF DISCORD.

Eritrea (ĕrĭtrē′ŭ), former Italian colony (45,754 sq. mi.; pop. c.1,087,000), NE Africa, on Red Sea; cap. Asmara; now part of Ethiopia. Bounded on W by Anglo-Egyptian Sudan and on S by Ethiopia. Desert coastal strip adjoins rugged plateau of interior. Fertile valleys in central part. Inhabited by pastoral nomads of Ethiopian stock. Products include citrus fruits, cereal, cotton, and hides. Eritrea was virtual possession of Ethiopia until 16th cent., when it fell to Ottoman Turks. Divided among local chieftains from 17th to mid-19th cent. Became Italian colony in 1890. British troops expelled the Italians in April, 1941. In 1949 the UN awarded most of Eritrea to Ethiopia; all unified under Ethiopia 1952.

Erivan (ĕrīvän′), Armenian *Yerevan,* city (pop. c.300,-000), cap. of Armenian SSR, on Zanga R., beautifully set among orchards and mountains. Founded 7th cent. A.D.; cap. of Armenia under Persian rule; after 15th

cent. passed back and forth between Persia and Turkey; ceded by Persia to Russia 1828. New machinery, textile, chemical industries quadrupled pop. after 1926.

Erlach, Johann Bernhard Fischer von: see FISCHER VON ERLACH, JOHANN BERNHARD.

Erlangen (ĕr′läng-ùn), city (pop. 49,886), Middle Franconia, N Bavaria, on Regnitz R. Has important mfg. of medical equipment (X-ray machines, hearing aids). Under margraves of Bayreuth-Kulmbach (house of Hohenzollern) from 1402; to Prussia 1792; to Bavaria 1810. University was founded at Bayreuth 1742, transferred to Erlangen 1743; Schelling and Schleiermacher taught here. City was rebuilt after a fire (1706), has baroque architecture.

Erlanger, Joseph (ûr′läng-ùr), 1874–, American scientist. Shared 1944 Nobel Prize in Physiology and Medicine for work in physiology, especially nerve action.

Ermak, Cossack leader: see YERMAK.

ermine (ûr′mĭn), name for various species of weasel and their fur. Fur trappers use name weasel for North American skins and stoat for chief species (*Mustela erminea*) of N Europe and Asia. The pelts (the most valuable white with black markings) make wraps, coats, and trimmings; black tails are used in Europe with ermine robes of royalty.

Ermine Street, early Roman road in Britain said to have extended from London to Lincoln.

Erne, river of Ireland and N. Ireland, flowing 72 mi. from Lough Gowna to Donegal Bay in the Atlantic.

Ernest I, 1784–1844, duke of Saxe-Coburg-Gotha; brother of Leopold I of Belgium, uncle of Victoria of England, father of Victoria's consort, Albert. Succeeded to Coburg 1806; acquired Gotha 1826.

Ernst, Max (mäks′ ĕrnst′), 1891–, German surrealist painter. Was a Dadaist in his early period.

Eros (ī′rŏs, ē′rŏs) [Gr.,= love], in Greek mythology, god of love. He is the force of love in all its manifestations. Pictured by some as one of oldest gods, born from Chaos. Associated with Dionysus in Orphic Mysteries, he was worshiped as Protogonos, first-born. More usually, he was called son of Ares and Aphrodite and pictured as winged youth or child armed with bows and arrows. Identified with Roman Cupid or Amor. For his own love story, see PSYCHE.

erosion, wearing away of the earth's surface by running water, waves, glaciers, wind. Streams transport rock fragments formed by weathering, and these particles serve as cutting tools. Sea coasts are worn back by waves and the rock waste they carry. A glacier erodes by grinding boulders against its bed. In arid regions wind is an important erosive agent, transporting sand as dunes.

Errigal, Mount (ĕrēgôl′), 2,466 ft. high, Co. Donegal, Ireland; highest point in the county.

Erskine, John, 1879–1951, American author and musician, teacher of English at Amherst (1903–9) and Columbia (1909–37). He is best remembered for his tongue-in-cheek satiric novels, notably *The Private Life of Helen of Troy* (1925). He appeared as a concert pianist and was president of the Juilliard School of Music (1928–37).

Erskine, Thomas, 1st Baron Erskine, 1750–1823, British jurist. A great trial lawyer, he defended Thomas Paine's *The Rights of Man* against charge of sedition. Caused liberal revision of libel laws.

Ervine, St. John (Greer) (sĭn′ jùn, ûrvĭn), 1883–, British dramatist, b. Ireland. Among his plays are *John Ferguson, Jane Clegg,* and *The First Mrs. Fraser.* Also wrote novels.

Eryri, Wales: see SNOWDON.

erysipelas (ĕrùsĭ′pùlùs, –lĭs, īrù–), acute febrile disease attended by inflammation of skin and underlying tissues. Results from invasion of break in skin by hemolytic streptococcus.

Eryx (ē′rĭks), ancient city, W Sicily, Italy. Long a bone of contention between Carthage and Syracuse; destroyed by Carthaginians c.260 B.C. Cyclopic walls and Phoenician inscriptions remain.

Erzberger, Matthias (mätē′äs ĕrts′bĕrgùr), 1875–1921, German statesman, leader of Catholic Center party. Headed delegation which signed armistice of Nov., 1918. Assassinated by a nationalist.

Erzerum or **Erzurum** (both: âr′zùrōom), city (pop. 54,-360), NE Turkey, in Armenia. Agr. trading center. Long of strategic and commercial importance.

Erzgebirge (ĕrts′gùbǐr″gù) or **Ore Mountains,** Czech *Krušné Hory,* mountain range of Bohemia (Czechoslovakia) and Saxony (Germany), extending c.100 mi. SE from the Elbe. Highest point, Mt. Klinovec (Ger. *Keilberg*), in Czechoslovakia, is at 4,080 ft. Important silver and iron mines exploited 14th–19th cent., notably at JACHYMOV. Now uranium, wolframite, lead, tin, copper, and sulphur are mined. Among the many spas, CARLSBAD and MARIENBAD are best-known. Intensive mfg. (textiles, machinery). Czech part of Erzgebirge was annexed by Germany in 1938, but was restored in 1945.

Erzsebetfalva, Hungary: see PESTSZENTERZSEBET.

Erzurum, Turkey: see ERZERUM.

Esaias (ēzā′yùs), variant of ISAIAH.

Esar-Haddon (ē″sär-hä′dùn), king of Assyria (681–668 B.C.), son of SENNACHERIB. Put down revolts, defeated the Chaldaeans; conquered Egypt (673–670); curbed Elam. Succeeded by Assur-bani-pal.

Esau (ē′sô), [Heb.,= hairy], son of Isaac, tricked out of his inheritance by his twin, Jacob. He settled on Mt. Seir. As ancestor of Israel's enemies, the Edomites, he is called EDOM. Gen. 25–28; 32; 33; 36; Deut. 2.4,5; Joshua 24.4; Jer. 49.7–22; Heb. 12.14–17.

Esbjerg, Dan. *Esbjaerg* (ĕs′byĕr), city (pop. 48,205), SW Jutland, Denmark; a North Sea port.

Escambia (ĕskăm′bēù), river rising in SE Ala. (called Conecuh [kùnĕ′kù] there). Flows 231 mi. SW, then S through NW Fla. to Escambia Bay, which is an arm of Pensacola Bay.

Escanaba, city (pop. 15,170), W Upper Peninsula, N Mich., on inlet of Green Bay and NE of Menominee; settled 1852. Ships much iron ore, has fishing and mfg. of wood products. Resorts in area.

escarpment or **scarp,** a long cliff, bluff, or steep slope. It is usually the result of erosion or of geologic faulting; often both causes are involved.

Escaut (ĕskō′), French name of SCHELDT river.

Esch, town (pop. 26,851), grand duchy of Luxembourg, on Alzette R. Steel center.

Eschenbach, Wolfram von: see WOLFRAM VON ESCHENBACH.

Eschweiler (ĕsh′vīlùr), city (pop. 35,446), North Rhine-Westphalia, NW Germany, near Aachen. Center of a soft-coal basin; iron and steel mills.

Escondido (ĕskùndē′dō), city (pop. 6,544), S Calif., N of San Diego, in valley yielding citrus, grapes, poultry, and dairy products; laid out 1885. Mexican War battle at near-by San Pasqual (1846).

Escorial (ĕskô′rēùl, Span. äskōrēäl′) or **Escurial,** former royal residence near Madrid, Spain. Built 1563–84, it comprises massive palace, monastery, church; contains royal tombs. Decorated by noted artists; has fine collection of Spanish painting.

Esdraelon (ĕs′drùē′lùn), fertile plain, central Palestine, drained by Kishon R., extending from SE foot of Mt. Carmel to Jordan valley. In ancient times a battleground, especially around MEGIDDO (see also GILBOA). Called also plain of JEZREEL or of Megiddo.

Esdras (ĕz′–) [Gr. from Heb. Ezra], name given in Western canon to four books of Old Testament and PSEUDEPIGRAPHA. Esdras 1 and 2 are same as AV EZRA and Nehemiah; Esdras 3 and 4 are pseudepigrapha, called, in Apocrypha of AV, Esdras 1 and 2. In Greek Bibles, Ezra and Nehemiah together are called 1 Esdras and pseudepigrapha are called 2 and 3 Esdras. Pseudepigrapha are (1) Greek translations of portions of 2 Chron., Ezra, and Nehemiah, and (2) an account of visions of Ezra.

Esenin, Sergei Aleksandrovich: see YESENIN.

Esher (ē′shùr), urban district (pop. 51,217), Surrey, England. Wolsey's Tower, remains of "Esher Place" occupied by Cardinal Wolsey, is here.

Esk, name of several rivers in Scotland. N and S Esk in Midlothian join and enter Firth of Forth; Black and White Esk of Dumfriesshire join and enter Solway Firth; and N and S Esk of Kincardine and Angus flow into the North Sea.

esker (ĕs′kùr), long, narrow, winding ridge of stratified DRIFT. Eskers resemble abandoned railway embankments; probably were deposited by streams flowing beneath a retreating ice sheet.

Eskilstuna (ĕ′skǐlstü″nä), city (pop. 53,577), SE Sweden. Center of Swedish cutlery industry.

Eskimo (ĕ′skùmō), native inhabitant of the arctic and subarctic regions of North America. Estimated Eskimo pop. c.30,000. Despite their wide dispersal they are highly uniform in language, physical type, and culture; Mongoloid features point to an Asiatic origin. The ingenuity of their material culture is essential to survival in the Arctic.

Eskimo dog: see CHOW.

Eskisehir (ĕskĕ′shĕhĕr), city (pop. 88,459), W central Turkey; probably identical with ancient Dorylaeum. Export center for meerschaum, chromium, magnesite; agr. market; railroad junction; cotton and tile mfg. Mineral springs.

espalier (ĕspăl′yùr), tree (usually a fruit such as apple or pear) or vine trained to grow flat against wall or trellis. Plants so trained take up little space and are ornamental (often fan or fork shaped).

Española: see HISPANIOLA.

Espartero, Baldomero (bäldōmä′rō ĕspärtä′rō), 1793–1879, Spanish general. After his victory over the CARLISTS in civil war of 1836–39 he was created duque de la Victoria. As regent he ruled dictatorially (1841–43), was forced to flee by an uprising. Served as premier 1854–56.

Esperanto: see UNIVERSAL LANGUAGE.

Espinel, Vicente Martínez (vēthän′tä märtē′nĕth äspēnĕl′), 1550–1624, Spanish poet, novelist, musician. Added fifth string to guitar. Created 10-line stanza. Wrote picaresque novel, *Vida del escudero Marcos de Obregón* (1618).

Espiritu Santo: see NEW HEBRIDES.

Espronceda, José de (hōsä′ dä äsprōnthä′dhä), 1808–42, Spanish romantic poet, author of *El estudiante de Salamanca* and *El diablo mundo* (1841).

Espy, James Pollard (ĕ′spē), 1785–1860, American meteorologist. Developed a convection theory of storms. His work in War and Navy departments laid basis for scientific weather forecasting.

Esquimalt (ĕskwī′môlt), W suburb of Victoria, on Vancouver Isl., B.C., Canada. Here is chief naval station and naval dockyard in W Canada.

Essad Pasha (ĕ′sät pä′shä), 1863–1920, Albanian dictator (1914–16). Expelled the king (William, prince of Wied), who had appointed him premier. Defeated by the Austrians (1916); was assassinated.

Esseg, Yugoslavia: see OSIJEK.

Essen (ĕ′sùn), city (pop. 605,125), North Rhine-Westphalia, NW Germany. Center of RUHR dist.; seat of KRUPP steel works. Three quarters destroyed in World War II air raids.

Essenes (ĕ′sēnz), members of a Jewish religious order (2d cent. A.D.). They believed in immortality, but not in resurrection. Ceremonial purity was rigidly practiced. Property was held communally; trading and slavery were prohibited.

essential oils: see OILS.

Essex, Robert Devereux, 2d earl of (dĕ′vùrōo), 1567–1601, English nobleman, favorite of Queen Elizabeth. His position involved him in rivalry with Sir Walter RALEGH. He angered (1590) the queen by his secret marriage to Sir Philip Sidney's widow. Advised by Francis Bacon he entered politics, hoping to seize power from the aging Lord Burghley. Elizabeth, wary of his demands, conferred power on Robert Cecil. Made lord lieutenant of Ireland (1599), Essex was sent there to quell rebellion of earl of Tyrone. He failed, was confined on his return to England, and later banned from court. He unsuccessfully tried to oust opposing party and estab. his own party about queen in 1601. He was arrested, Elizabeth signed the death warrant, and he was executed. His son, **Robert Devereux, 3d earl of Essex,** 1591–1646, was restored (1604) to his estates by James I. He fought with royal army in first Bishops' War and later commanded parliamentary forces. After failure and disgrace in 1644, he relinquished his command.

Essex, kingdom of Anglo-Saxon England. Probably settled in early 6th cent., it eventually included modern counties of Essex, London, Middlesex, and most of Hertfordshire. Having early accepted Christianity the kingdom lapsed into heathenism until reconverted by Cedd in 7th cent. Long dominated by MERCIA, Essex joined other kingdoms in 9th cent. in submitting to Wessex and became an earldom. Became part of DANELAW in 886; was later retaken (917) by Edward the Elder of Wessex. Its most famous later earl was Byrhtnoth, defeated (991) at Maldon.

Essex, maritime county (1,528 sq. mi.; pop. 2,043,574), E England, on N bank of Thames estuary; co. town Chelmsford. Chief products are fish, oysters, fruits, and vegetables. SW portion, in Greater London area, has mfg. of chemicals, machinery, textiles, and cement. There are popular coastal resorts. Area near London and coast much bombed in World War II.

Essex Junction, village (pop. 2,741), in Essex town (pop. 3,931), NW Vt., E of Burlington and on Winooski R. Has annual Champlain Valley Exposition.

Essex Junto, group of New England merchants, so called because many of them came from Essex co., Mass. Opposed radicals in Mass. in American Revolution and supported the Federalists. Later encouraged disaffection of Hartford Convention.

Esslingen (ĕs'lĭng-ùn), city (pop. 70,610), Württemberg-Baden, SW Germany, on Neckar R. Produces machinery, textiles. Free imperial city from 1219; passed to Württemberg 1803. Swabian League was founded here (1488). Has 13th-cent. castle.

Established Church: see ENGLAND, CHURCH OF; SCOTLAND, CHURCH OF; IRELAND, CHURCH OF.

Estaing, Charles Hector, comte d' (shärl' ĕktôr' kõt' dĕstĕ'), 1729–94, French admiral. Commanded French fleet sent to aid American revolutionists, 1778–80. His planned attack on Newport, R.I., was undone by a storm (1778). Cooperated with Benjamin LINCOLN in unsuccessful attack on Savannah (1779). Was guillotined as a royalist.

estate. 1 In law of property, manner of owning realty and realty itself; more broadly any property held or bequeathed. **2** In constitutional law, one of the classes given a separate voice in government in Middle Ages and later. Three estates were nobility, clergy, commons (townspeople of substance, bourgeoisie, "third estate"). By extension "fourth estate" means newspapers.

Estates-General: see STATES-GENERAL.

Este (ĕ'stä), Italian noble family; branch of the GUELPHS. Derives name from town of Este, near Padua. Ruled FERRARA (1240–1597; from 1471 as dukes) and MODENA (1288–1796; from 1452 as dukes). Court of the Este family at Ferrara in 15th–16th cent. was a major center of literature and art. **Isabella d'Este,** 1474–1539, wife of Francesco GONZAGA, and her sister **Beatrice d'Este,** 1475–97, wife of Ludovico SFORZA, were brilliant ladies of the Renaissance and patronesses of Leonardo and Ariosto. Their brother, **Alfonso d'Este I,** 1476–1534, duke of Ferrara and Modena (1505–34), also was a lavish patron. In the Italian Wars he sided first with France against Pope Julius II (who in 1510 declared him forfeit of his fiefs), later with Emperor Charles V against Pope Clement VII (who had to reinstate him in 1530). He was the second husband of Lucrezia BORGIA. His brother, **Ippolito I, Cardinal d'Este** (ĕp-pô'lētō), 1479–1520, was long the

patron of Ariosto, who dedicated *Orlando furioso* to him. Alfonso's son, **Ippolito II, Cardinal d'Este,** 1509–72, built the famous Villa d'Este at Tivoli, near Rome. The direct male line of dukes died out 1597; in 1598 Pope Clement VIII incorporated Ferrara into Papal States, despite claims of cadet line, which retained Modena. Deposed by Bonaparte 1796, last duke died 1803. His daughter married Archduke Ferdinand of Austria, a son of Emperor Francis II, who founded line of Austria-Este. Their descendants were dukes of Modena, Massa, and Carrara 1815–59.

ester, compound formed by a reaction, esterification, between alcohol and acid. Esters react with water under some conditions to form alcohol and acid; some saponify, i.e., yield soap and glycerin when heated with hydroxide. Common fats and oils are ester mixtures. Esters are used for flavoring; and in making perfumes, paints, explosives.

Esterhazy (ĕ'stùrhä"zē), Hung. *Esterházy,* Hungarian noble family; princes of Holy Roman Empire since 1712. Best-known are **Paul Anton, Fürst Esterhazy von Galantha** (gä'läntä), d. 1762, and his brother and successor to the title, **Nikolaus Joseph, Fürst Esterhazy von Galantha,** 1714–90, because of their patronage of Haydn, who was in their service 1761–90. Nikolaus Joseph was extremely lavish with his immense wealth, built the famous château of Esterhaz on the Neusiedler Lake, endowed Haydn with handsome pension in his will.

Esterhazy, Ferdinand Walsin (Fr. fĕrdēnä' välsĕ' ĕstĕräzĕ'), 1847–1923, French army officer, claiming membership in old Hungarian Esterhazy family. His guilt in selling military secrets to Germany was pinned on Captain Dreyfus (see DREYFUS AFFAIR). He was later dismissed from the army.

Estes Park (ĕs'tēz), resort town (pop. 1,617; alt. c.7,500 ft.), N central Colo., in the Rockies NNW of Denver. Hq. for Rocky Mt. Natl. Park. Two power dams of COLORADO–BIG THOMPSON PROJECT are near.

Esther, book of Old Testament. It tells of a Jewish girl, named originally Hadassah, who became queen of Persian king Ahasuerus (Xerxes). A wicked courtier, Haman, tried to incite a massacre of the Jews, but Esther, with aid of her uncle Mordecai, saved her people. The feast of Purim commemorates this. Chapters 10.4–16 are in Apocrypha in AV but are in Western canon.

Estherville, city (pop. 6,719), NW Iowa, on West Fork of Des Moines R. near Minn. line. Center for livestock, farm, and lumber area. Site of Fort Defiance (1862) is preserved near by.

esthetics: see AESTHETICS.

Estienne, Étienne (ätyĕn'), Latin **Stephanus,** family of printers and scholars in Paris and Geneva. **Henri Estienne,** d. 1520, was a printer in Paris by 1502. His son, **Robert Estienne,** b. 1498 or 1503, d. 1559, printed scholarly works, many edited by himself. Specialized in editions of classical authors, dictionaries—his own Latin thesaurus (1541) is a masterpiece—and critical editions of the Bible. Geofroy Tory designed his printer's mark (the Olive Tree) and Claude Garamond designed some of his type faces. A Protestant, he found himself in trouble and moved to Geneva (1550). His brother **Charles Estienne,** c.1504–1564, took over the Paris shop in 1551. Educated in medicine and in the classics, he wrote on many subjects. Got out an early French encyclopedia, a treatise on dissection, and *Praedium rusticum* [country property]. Robert's son, **Henri Estienne,** 1531?–1598, was the greatest scholar of the family. He took over the Geneva business, and though his books were not so good typographically as his father's, he brought out editions of Greek and Latin works notable for accuracy and textual criticism. He compiled a notable *Thesaurus Graecae linguae* (1572). Championed the use of French as a literary language. Trouble with Geneva authorities, begun by his satirical *Apologie pour Herodote* (1566), forced him to leave Geneva and later caused imprisonment. Became wandering scholar.

Estonia, Estonian *Eesti,* republic (17,400 sq. mi.; 1934 pop. 1,126,413), NE Europe, bounded by RSFSR (E), Latvia (S), and Baltic Sea (N and W); cap. Tallinn. Its inclusion (1940) into USSR is not recognized by U.S. A generally flat, dairy-farming country, it also has shale oil, timber, fisheries. Estonians speak a Finnic language, are mostly Lutherans. Country, part of historic LIVONIA, was ruled by Livonian Knights from 13th cent.; passed to Sweden 1561; was conquered by Russia 1710 (formally ceded by Sweden 1721). Descendants of German knights formed ruling class till 1917. Independence from Russia was proclaimed 1918; peace treaty with Russia was signed 1920. Democratic rule ended 1934, when Pres. Konstantin Päts began authoritarian regime. USSR secured military bases 1939 and in 1940 occupied Estonia and made it constituent Soviet republic. Occupied by Germany 1941–44.

Estournelles de Constant, Paul Henri Benjamin, baron d' (pôl′ ãrě′ bězhämě′ bärô′ dãtŏŏrněl′ dù kôstä′), 1852–1924, French diplomat and pacifist. Shared 1909 Nobel Peace Prize with Auguste Beernaert.

Estrées, Gabrielle d' (gäbrěěl′ děsträ′), 1573–99, famous beauty, mistress of Henry IV of France.

Estremadura (ěshtrůmůdŏŏ′rů), historic province, SW Portugal, now divided among provs. of Estremadura (2,064 sq. mi.; pop. 1,379,533; cap. Lisbon), Ribatejo, and Beira Litoral. Contains fertile valley of Tagus R. Agr., orchards, vineyards, forests.

Estremadura (ěstrůmůdŏŏ′rů), Span. *Extremadura,* region (16,059 sq. mi.; pop. 1,253,924), W central Spain, bordering on Portugal. Cities: Badajoz, Cáceres. Arid tableland except for fertile Tagus and Guadiana valleys. Sheep grazing, hog raising.

Estremoz, Port. *Estremós* (ěshtrůmôsh′), city (pop. 6,765), Alentejo, Portugal. Famous for white marble and pottery. Castle was built by King Diniz.

Eszek, Yugoslavia: see OSIJEK.

Esztergom (ě′stěrgôm), Ger. *Gran,* city (pop. 22,171), N Hungary, on the Danube. Birthplace of St. Stephen; seat of archprimates of Hungary since 1198. Has beautiful domed cathedral (built 19th cent.). Primate's palace contains museum and rich library. Also a warm-spring spa.

Eteocles (ētē′ŏklēz), in Greek legend, son of Oedipus. He defended kingdom of Thebes, usurped from his brother, POLYNICES, in war of SEVEN AGAINST THEBES.

Ethan [Heb.,= strong], a wise man. 1 Kings 4.31; title of Ps. 89. May be same as Ethan of 1 Chron. 2.6.

ethanol: see ETHYL ALCOHOL.

Ethel–. For some Anglo-Saxon names beginning thus, see ÆTHEL–; e.g., for Ethelbald, see ÆTHELBALD.

ether, in chemistry, term used for ethyl ether, compound of ethyl radical (C_2H_5) and oxygen. Colorless liquid, volatile, inflammable; used as organic solvent and anesthetic. In physics and astronomy, it is hypothetical medium that transmits light and heat and fills all unoccupied space. Invisible, odorless, it does not interfere with motions of bodies through space. Many deny its material existence.

Etherege, Sir George (ěth′ůrĭj), 1635?–1691, English Restoration dramatist, author of witty, licentious comedies of manners.

Ethical Culture movement, originating in Society for Ethical Culture founded in New York city (1876) by Felix Adler. It stresses ethical factor in life, apart from theological or metaphysical considerations. The society holds religious services; it lays emphasis on education and pioneered in kindergarten and adult education. In England, Stanley Coit founded society (1887). Internatl. Union of Ethical Culture Societies estab. 1896.

ethics, study and evaluation of human conduct in light of moral principles. Historically, various theories have developed as to man's conscience and responsibility for his actions. The intuitionists (e.g., ROUSSEAU) hold that conscience is innate and instigates moral action.

Empiricists (e.g., COMTE, LOCKE, John Stuart MILL) instead explain it as a by-product of experience. Some philosophers seek an absolute ethical criterion in religion. Idealists (e.g., PLATO, KANT) see basis of ethics in metaphysics. Some (e.g., HEGEL, MARX) teach that the state is the arbiter of morals, others (e.g., DEWEY, Felix ADLER) that the individual controls.

Ethiopia (ēthēŏ′pēů) or **Abyssinia** (ăbĭsĭ′nēů), empire (c.400,000 sq. mi.; pop. c.15,500,000), E central Africa; cap. Addis Ababa. Comprises low-lying deserts and mountainous plateau rising to 15,158 ft. at Ras Dashan. In NE is Tana L., source of Blue Nile. Exports include coffee, grains, hides, and gold. Ethiopia's main link with outside world is its single railroad, from Addis Ababa to Jibuti. According to tradition, founded in c.1000 B.C. by Solomon's first son, borne by queen of Sheba (identified with Ethiopia), but records go back only to 1st cent. A.D. In 4th cent. ruler was converted to Coptic Christianity. Judaism probably introduced from Yemen. Rise of Islam (7th cent.) deprived Ethiopia of its coast. Period of chaos followed, but order was restored in 13th cent., when new dynasty was founded. Portuguese embassies and missionaries arrived in 16th cent. Emperor was converted to Roman Catholicism, but Coptic Church was fully restored mid-17th cent. and all foreigners expelled. Civil strife of next two centuries ended 1889, when MENELIK II became dominant with help of Italy. Claiming that Menelik had agreed to establishment of protectorate, Italy invaded Ethiopia 1895. Decisive battle of Aduwa compelled Italy to recognize Ethiopia's independence. HAILE SELASSIE, who ascended throne in 1930, faced renewed Italian threat, culminating in full-scale invasion (1935). Economic sanctions imposed against Italy by League of Nations were soon abandoned. Ethiopia was incorporated into Italian East Africa until 1941, when it was liberated by British troops. Unification with ERITREA was finally achieved in 1952.

Ethiopic (ēthēŏp′ĭk), subgroup of Semitic languages. See LANGUAGE (table).

ethnology: see ANTHROPOLOGY.

ethyl (ě′thĭl), in chemistry, organic radical of carbon and hydrogen (C_2H_5). Compounds in which it occurs are called ethane derivatives.

ethyl alcohol, ethanol, or **grain alcohol,** colorless liquid alcohol with strong affinity for water. Absolute alcohol, a poison, is ethyl alcohol free of water. It burns in air, reacts with acids and active metals, is prepared by fermentation of sugar or starch. Used as industrial solvent; biological preservative; to make essences, tinctures, medicines; as fuel. It is denatured by addition of poison.

ethylene (ě′thĭlēn), colorless gas with faint odor, sweet taste. Forms explosive mixture with oxygen. Used in illuminating gas, as anesthetic, to bring out color of citrus fruit. It is an unsaturated HYDROCARBON with two atoms of carbon joined by double bond, each holding two hydrogen atoms. It is first member of **ethylene series;** each member has twice number of hydrogens as carbons. Lower members, gases; middle, liquids; higher, solids.

Étienne, family of printers: see ESTIENNE.

Etna, borough (pop. 6,750), SW Pa., on Allegheny R. near Pittsburgh. Mfg. of iron and steel products.

Etna or **Aetna** (ět′nů), active volcano, 10,700 ft. high, on E coast of Sicily, Italy. Shape and height of central cone often changed by eruptions. There are c.260 lesser craters. Its densely populated, fertile base is subtropical; the top has snow most of the year. Observatory at 9,650 ft. First known eruption 475 B.C. Those of 1069 and 1669 were particularly destructive.

Eton (ē′tůn), urban district (pop. 3,250), Buckinghamshire, England. Chiefly known for **Eton College,** largest of famous English public schools, founded by Henry VI 1440. Unlike other similar schools, Eton is controlled by elected student representatives. Closely allied with King's Col., Cambridge. Many outstanding

Englishmen educated here. Since World War II more scholarships granted to poorer students. Has annual cricket match with Harrow.

Etowah, river rising in N Ga. in the Blue Ridge and flowing 141 mi. SW to Rome, where it joins the Oostanaula to form the Coosa. Allatoona Dam (completed 1950; for flood control, power, navigation), near Cartersville, is first project in plan to develop Alabama-Coosa river system.

Etruria (ĭtrōō'rēŭ), anc. land, W Italy, now Tuscany and W Umbria. See ETRUSCAN CIVILIZATION.

Etruscan civilization (ĭtrŭ'skŭn), highest civilization in Italy before rise of Rome. Modern research upholds Herodotus that the Etruscans came (c.800 B.C.) from Asia Minor, possibly Lydia. In language and culture they differed from other Italians. Their wealth was based partly on knowledge of metalworking. They made fine pottery and improved agr. The oligarchical Etruscan cities (e.g., Tarquinii, Caere, Veii, Clusium) formed a loose confederacy. By 500 B.C. their civilization was at its height and included the Umbrian cities and part of Latium. In 5th and early 4th cent. B.C. Rome beat them back, capturing Veii after long struggles (396 B.C.). Invading Gauls in N aided disintegration.

Ettrick Forest, former woodland and royal hunting ground famous in legend, Selkirkshire, Scotland.

Ettrick Water, river of Selkirkshire, Scotland, flowing c.32 mi. from Capel Fell NE to the Tweed.

etymology, historical derivation of linguistic forms, especially words. Study had prestige for centuries because of an accepted theory that knowledge of the history of a word made its meaning clearer. This study revealed the regular relations of sounds in Indo-European languages (as in Grimm's law). In 20th cent. linguists continued to use etymology to learn how meanings change, but they came to consider that the meaning of a form at a given time must be understood without reference to its history if it is to be understood at all.

Eu, chemical symbol of the element EUROPIUM.

Euboea (ūbē'ŭ), Gr. *Evvoia,* Aegean island (1,457 sq. mi.; pop. c.162,800), Greece, off Boeotia and Attica; chief city CHALCIS (connected with mainland by drawbridge across EURIPOS). Island is mostly mountainous. Agr., cattle raising. Euboea belonged to Athenian empire from 506 B.C.; passed to Macedon 338 B.C.; to Rome 191 B.C. After the Fourth Crusade it passed to Venice (1209), which lost it to the Turks in 1470. Its Venetian name was Negropont.

eucalyptus (ūkŭlĭp'tŭs) or **gum tree,** large tree or shrub of genus *Eucalyptus,* native to Australia and Asia. Some, e.g., blue gum and red gum, are widely planted on W coast of U.S. Various species yield timber and medicinal oils.

Eucharist (ū'kŭrĭst) [Gr.,= thanksgiving], Christian SACRAMENT which repeats Jesus' giving bread and wine at the Last Supper. Catholics believe that in the sacrament bread and wine actually become the body and blood of Christ by transubstantiation. Partaking of the bread and wine is called communion. Performance of the sacrificial ritual is called the liturgy, and the Roman liturgy is the Mass. For Protestant communion, see LORD'S SUPPER.

Eucken, Rudolph Christoph (oi'kŭn), 1846–1926, German philosopher. His "activism" stressed experience as the source of value. Awarded 1908 Nobel Prize in Literature.

Euclid (ū'klĭd), fl. c.300 B.C., Greek mathematician famous for his *Elements,* a collection of theorems and problems forming basis of geometry.

Euclid, city (pop. 41,396), N Ohio, on L. Erie, NE of Cleveland; settled 1798. Mfg. of electrical goods and office machinery. Here is Natl. American Shrine of Our Lady of Lourdes.

Eudes (ūdz, ûd) or **Odo,** c.860–898, French king (888–98); great-uncle of Hugh Capet. As count of Paris he defended his city against the Normans (885–87).

Eudoxus of Cnidus (ūdŏk'sŭs, nīdŭs), 408?–355? B.C., Greek astronomer and mathematician, credited with calculating length of solar year and discovering certain parts of Euclidean geometry.

Eufaula (ūfô'lŭ), city (pop. 6,906), SE Ala., on Chattahoochee R. and SE of Montgomery. Ships cotton; produces textiles, lumber products.

Eugene III, d. 1153, pope (1145–53), a CISTERCIAN, friend of BERNARD OF CLAIRVAUX. His rule was disturbed by Arnold of Brescia. Eugene promoted the disastrous Second Crusade.

Eugene IV, 1383–1447, pope (1431–47). Opposed antipapal acts of Council of BASEL, but was driven by Roman rebellion to exile at Florence (1434). In 1437 he ordered the council to Ferrara, but leaders at Basel refused to obey and declared Eugene deposed. Meanwhile the Council of FERRARA-FLORENCE met.

Eugene, city (pop. 35,879), W Oregon, at head of navigation on Willamette R. and S of Salem; settled 1846. Has creameries, fruit canneries, wool and lumber mills. Main seat of Univ. of Oregon (state supported; coed.; chartered 1872, opened 1876; medical and dental schools at Portland).

Eugene of Savoy, Prince, 1663–1736, French general in imperial service; son of a prince of Savoy-Carignano and of Olympe MANCINI. Louis XIV having refused him a commission, he entered service of Emperor Leopold I (1683). Defeated Turks at Zenta (1697) and Belgrade (1717), making possible victorious Treaty of PASSAROWITZ (1719). In War of the SPANISH SUCCESSION he shared in victory of Blenheim with Marlborough (1704); defeated French at Oudenarde (1708) and Malplaquet (1709); negotiated Peace of Rastatt (1714). His only major defeat was inflicted on him by his cousin Vendôme (Cassano, 1705).

eugenics (ūjĕ'nĭks), study of methods to improve human race physically and mentally. It is directed chiefly toward discouraging propagation by unfit and encouraging it in the fit. Some states have laws relating to sterilization of mental defectives, but many problems are involved in carrying out such laws. Probably the greatest hope lies in education and in euthenics (bettering the environment).

Eugénie (Fr. ûzhānē') (Eugenia María de Montijo de Guzmán), 1826–1920, empress of the French, consort of Napoleon III; a Spanish noblewoman famed for her beauty. Fled to England when Second Empire was overthrown (1870).

Euhemerus (ūhē'mŭrŭs), fl. c.300 B.C., Cyrenaic philosopher who developed a theory of mythology holding that gods were deified heroes (euhemerism).

Eulenspiegel, Till (oi'lŭn-shpē'gŭl), N German peasant clown of the 14th or 15th cent., immortalized all over Europe by chapbooks describing his tricks, particularly on upper class persons. Subject of tone poem by Richard Strauss and of literary treatment by De Coster. Also spelled Tyl Ulenspiegel.

Euler, Leonhard (lā'ônhärt oi'lŭr), 1707–83, Swiss mathematician. A founder of higher mathematics, known especially for work on calculus of variations, trigonometry, and analytic mathematics and mechanics. His work in astronomy, hydrodynamics, and optics was also notable. Eulerian equation and Euler's formula named after him.

Euler-Chelpin, Hans von (häns fūn oi'lŭr kĕl'pĭn), 1873–, Swedish chemist, b. Germany. He shared 1929 Nobel Prize for work on sugar fermentation and chemistry of enzymes.

Eumenides: see ERINYES.

Eunice (ūnī'sē, ū'nĭs) [Gr.,= good victory], mother of Timothy; a Christian. 2 Tim. 1.5; Acts 16.1.

Eunice (ū'nĭs), town (pop. 8,184), SW La., W of Baton Rouge. Trade center for oil, cotton, and rice area.

Eunomia, one of the HORAE.

euonymus (ūŏn'ĭmŭs) or **spindle tree,** shrub or vine of genus *Euonymus.* Some are evergreen and some have winged stems and brilliant autumn foliage and fruits. See also BURNING BUSH.

Eupatoria (ūpùtô'rĕu), Rus. *Yevpatoriya* or *Evpatoriya*, city (pop. 23,512), RSFSR, in W Crimea; Black Sea port. Founded 1st cent. A.D.; named for Eupator, king of Pontus. Occupied by allies in Crimean War, by Germans in World War II. Old section contains ruins of Tatar fortress, 16th-cent. mosque.

Eupen (oi'pùn), town (pop. 14,462), Liége prov., SE Belgium. Wool mfg. Districts of Eupen and MALMÉDY (c.380 sq. mi.; pop. 60,000) were transferred from Germany to Belgium by Treaty of Versailles (1919). Population is predominantly German-speaking.

Euphranor (ūfrā'nùr), fl. 364 B.C., Greek painter and sculptor. His statues were praised by Pliny.

Euphrates (ūfrā'tēz), river of SW Asia, rising in E Turkey. Flows c.1,675 mi. to Iraq, there joining TIGRIS R. to form the SHATT EL ARAB. Lower course irrigates Iraq's great date plantations. With the Tigris it watered Mesopotamia, birthplace of early civilization.

Euphrosyne, one of the GRACES.

euphuism (ū'fūīzùm), in English literature, a highly artificial style derived from the *Euphues* (1579) of John Lyly. Has come to mean any artificial and high-flown style.

Eupompus (ūpŏm'pùs), fl. 4th cent. B.C., Greek painter, founder of Sicyonic school.

Eurasia (yōorā'zhù, –shù), land mass comprising continents of Europe and Asia.

Eure (ûr), department (2,331 sq. mi.; pop. 315,902), N France, in Normandy; cap. Évreux.

Eure-et-Loir (ûr-ā-lwär'), department (2,293 sq. mi.; pop. 285,110), N France, in Beauce; cap. Chartres.

Eureka, city (pop. 23,058), N Calif., on Humboldt Bay, in heart of redwood country; founded 1850. Lumber milling and commercial fishing.

Euric (yōo'rĭk), d. c.484, Visigothic king of Spain (466–c.484). Conquered nearly all Iberian peninsula and part of Gaul; made Toulouse his cap.; issued first code of Visigothic law.

Euripides (yōorĭ'pĭdēz), b. 480 or 485 B.C., d. 406 B.C., Greek tragic poet. Author of perhaps 92 plays, 19 extant. Most important: *Alcestis, Medea, Hippolytus, Andromache, Trojan Women, Electra, Iphigenia in Tauris, Iphigenia in Aulis,* and *Bacchae.* A realist, with an interest in contemporary people and problems and with an iconoclastic attitude toward the gods. Used the *deus ex machina* [god from a machine] to resolve a play's problem.

Euripos (yōorĭ'pùs), strait, 130 ft. to 1 mi. wide, between Euboea and Greek mainland.

Europa (yōorō'pù), in Greek religion, Phoenician princess; daughter of Agenor. Zeus (taking the form of a bull) took her to Crete, where she bore him Minos. She later married king of Crete.

Europe, continent (with adjacent islands c.4,000,000 sq. mi.; pop. c.550,000,000), a vast peninsula of the Eurasian land mass. Separated from Asia by Ural mts., Ural R., Caspian Sea, Caucasus, Black Sea, Bosporus, and Dardanelles; from Africa by Mediterranean Sea and Strait of Gibraltar. It is washed in the N by the Arctic Ocean (incl. Barents Sea, White Sea), in the W by the Atlantic, with which the Irish, North, Baltic, Mediterranean, and Black Seas are connected. A huge mountain chain (Pyrenees, Alps, Carpathians, Balkans, Caucasus) crosses continent from W to E. Highest points: Mt. Elbrus (18,481 ft.), Mont Blanc (15,772 ft.). Between the mountainous Scandinavian peninsula and this chain extends the great European plain—largely fertile soil, with steppe, forest, lake, and tundra dists. in E and N. S of the mountain chain are the fertile Po and Danubian plains and the mountainous Balkan, Italian, and Iberian peninsulas. Among chief rivers are (from E to W) the Volga, Don, Dnieper, Danube, Oder, Elbe, Rhine, Loire, Garonne, and Tagus. Climate, though greatly varied, is subject to moderating prevailing westerly winds. The states of Europe, grouped here by geographic regions, are: E Europe—USSR (incl. Lithuania, Latvia, Estonia) and Poland; SE Europe—

Rumania, Hungary, Yugoslavia, Albania, Bulgaria, Greece, Turkey; Scandinavia—Sweden, Norway, Denmark, Finland; Central Europe—Austria, Czechoslovakia, Germany (now split into E and W Germany), Switzerland, Liechtenstein; W Europe—Belgium, Netherlands, Luxembourg, France, Monaco; S Europe—Italy, Free Territory of Trieste, San Marino, Vatican City, Spain, Portugal, Andorra; British Isles—United Kingdom of Great Britain and Northern Ireland, republic of Ireland; and Iceland. Turkey and USSR lie only partly in Europe. Great Britain, France, Portugal, Spain, Netherlands, Belgium, Denmark, and Norway have overseas possessions.

Europe, Council of, international body created 1949 as first step toward a federation of European states; hq. at Strasbourg, France. Consists of a committee of ministers and a consultative assembly. Members as of 1952: Belgium, Denmark, France, [West] German Federal Republic, Great Britain, Greece, Iceland, Ireland, Italy, Luxembourg, Netherlands, Norway, Saar Territory, Sweden, Turkey.

European Coal and Steel Community: see SCHUMAN PLAN (under SCHUMAN, ROBERT).

European corn borer: see CORN BORER.

European Defense Community, term for nations to be covered by a proposed European army. Includes France, West Germany, Belgium, the Netherlands, Luxembourg, and Italy. If ratified, army will be associated with NORTH ATLANTIC TREATY Organization.

European Recovery Program, name popularly given project instituted at Paris Economic Conference (July, 1947) to foster post-war economic recovery in certain European countries. Took form when U.S. Secretary of State George C. Marshall—for whom program was also called Marshall Plan—urged (June, 1947) integration of U.S. economic aid to European countries. The Economic Cooperation Administration (ECA) administered program 1948–51; activities then transferred to Mutual Security Agency.

europium (yōorō'pēùm), rare metallic element of rare earths (symbol = Eu; see also ELEMENT, table).

Europos or **Europus:** see DURA.

Eurydice, nymph, wife of ORPHEUS.

Eurymedon (yōorĭ'mùdŏn), small river of anc. Pamphylia, S Asia Minor. Here in the Persian Wars Cimon defeated the Persians (c.467 B.C.).

eurythmics (yōorĭdh'mĭks) [as if Gr.,= good rhythm], system of musical training through harmonious bodily movements; first advanced by Émile Jaques-Dalcroze. Method begins with a set of gymnastics in response to music. Finally, student is able to improvise an interpretation, through gesture language, of an entire composition. System has influenced ballet and acting.

Eusebius of Caesarea (ūsē'bēùs sēzùrē'ù) or **Eusebius Pamphili** (păm'fĭlī), c.263–339?, Greek historian. Wrote *Ecclesiastical History,* in 10 books.

Eustace II (ū'stĭs), d. 1093, count of Boulogne, kinsman by marriage of Edward the Confessor. Over his visit to England (1051) Earl Godwin of Wessex broke with Edward. His great-grandson, **Eustace IV,** d. 1153, count of Boulogne, was the son of Stephen of England. Died before his father.

Eustachi, Bartolomeo (bär"tōlōmā'ō ā"ōostä'kē), d. 1574, Italian anatomist, discoverer of many structures recorded in remarkable drawings (1552, published 1714). Discoveries include **Eustachian tube** (ūstā'kĕun, –shùn), the auditory canal equalizing air pressure between throat and middle ear.

Euterpe, Muse of music or of lyric poetry: see MUSES.

Eutyches (ū'tĭkēs), c.378–c.452, archimandrite in Constantinople, sponsor of Eutychianism, the first phase of MONOPHYSITISM, and leader of opponents of NESTORIANISM. His chief doctrine was that Christ's humanity was absorbed in his one divine nature. His teachings were denounced and he was deposed (448), but the so-called Robber Synod at Ephesus (449) reinstated him. At the synod St. Flavian, who opposed Eutyches, was manhandled and died. Theodoret was

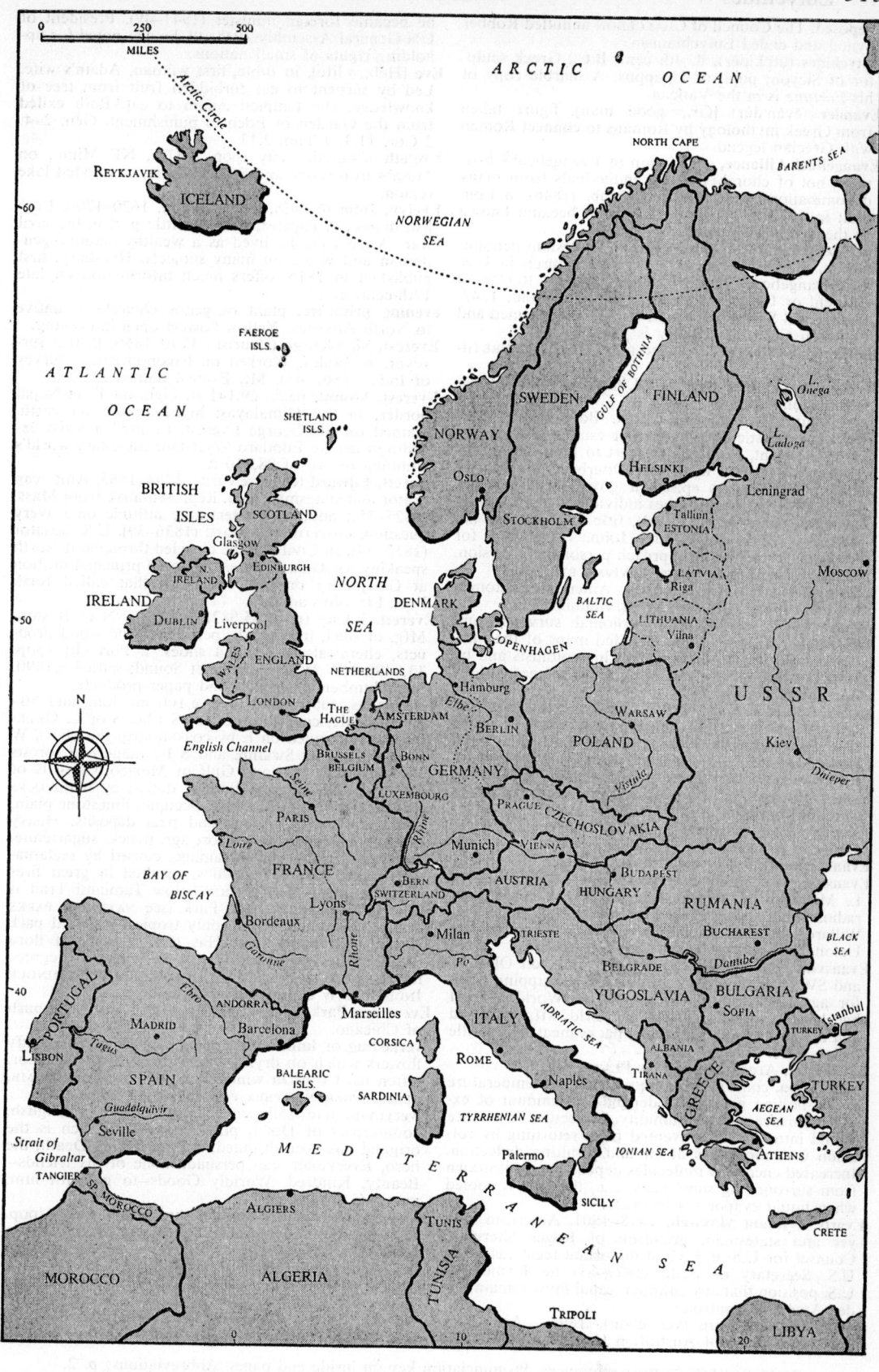

deposed. The Council of CHALCEDON annulled Robber Synod and ended Eutychianism.

Eutychides (ūtĭ'kĭdēz), fl. 4th cent. B.C., Greek sculptor of Sicyon; pupil of Lysippus. A marble copy of his *Fortune* is in the Vatican.

Evander (ēvăn'dûr) [Gr.,= good man], figure taken from Greek mythology by Romans to connect Roman with Grecian legend.

Evangelical Alliance, association of Evangelical Christians, not of churches but of individuals from many denominations and countries. Estab. (1846) in London; in 1923 the largest association became known as the World's Evangelical Alliance.

Evangelical and Reformed Church, Protestant denomination, merger (1934) of Reformed Church in U.S. and Evangelical Synod of North America. Reformed Church, or German Reformed Church, estab. 1747. Evangelical Synod was union (1840) of Reformed and Lutheran Christians. Polity is presbyterian.

Evangelical Church: see EVANGELICAL UNITED BRETHREN CHURCH.

Evangelical United Brethren Church, Protestant denomination, merger (1946) of Evangelical Church and United Brethren in Christ. Both bodies grew from evangelistic efforts. Former estab. (1807) under Jacob Albright, Lutheran convert to Methodism; latter founded (1800) by P. W. Otterbein and Martin Boehm. Church has episcopal government and Arminian doctrine, and stresses individual responsibility.

evangelist (from Gr.,= Gospel], title first given to SS. Matthew, Mark, Luke, and John. Now used for Protestant preachers who preach personal conversion. See also CAMP MEETING and REVIVAL, RELIGIOUS.

Evans, Herbert McLean, 1882–, American anatomist and embryologist, discoverer of vitamin E.

Evans, Lewis, c.1700–1756, colonial surveyor and geographer, b. Wales. His detailed maps of the middle colonies were used by migrating colonists and by Braddock. He drew attention to Ohio, suggested how to wrest it from French.

Evans, Luther H(arris), 1902–, American librarian and political scientist. Appointed librarian of Congress 1945. Member UNESCO executive board since 1949.

Evans, Maurice, 1901–, Anglo-American actor-manager. Noted for Shakspere productions (esp. *Hamlet*).

Evans, Oliver, 1755–1819, American inventor of grain-handling machinery and pioneer builder of high-pressure steam engines. He built the first steam river dredge in America.

Evans, Mount: see FRONT RANGE.

Evanston, residential city (pop. 73,641), NE Ill., on L. Michigan N of Chicago; settled 1826. Mfg. of radios and metal products. Once home of Frances E. Willard; hq. of Woman's Christian Temperance Union. Seat of NORTHWESTERN UNIVERSITY.

Evansville, city (pop. 128,636), SW Ind., on Ohio R. and SW of Indianapolis; settled 1817. Shipping point for agr. and coal-mining region. In World War II had largest inland shipyards in world. Mfg. of wood and metal products, and flour; packs meat. Evansville Col. is here.

Eva Perón, Argentina: see LA PLATA.

evaporation, conversion of liquid to gas at temperature below boiling point; rate depends on amount of exposed surface and on humidity. Molecules at surface bound into air, are prevented from returning by collision with molecules of air and resulting deflection. Increased energy of molecules depends on heat drawn from surrounding substances, e.g., the skin is cooled when liquid evaporates from it.

Evarts, William Maxwell, 1818–1901, American lawyer and statesman; grandson of Roger Sherman. Counsel for U.S. in several important legal cases. As U.S. Secretary of State (1877–81) he formulated U.S. position that any isthmian canal must remain under American control.

Evatt, Herbert Vere (vēr ě'vŭt), 1894–, Australian statesman. Judge of Australian High Court 1930–40,

he became foreign minister (1941–49). President of UN General Assembly 1948–49, he was noted for upholding rights of small nations.

Eve [Heb.,= life], in Bible, first woman, Adam's wife. Led by serpent to eat forbidden fruit from tree of knowledge, she tempted Adam to eat. Both exiled from the Garden of Eden in punishment. Gen. 2–4; 2 Cor. 11.3; 1 Tim. 2.13.

Eveleth (ēv'ŭlĕth), city (pop. 5,872), NE Minn., on Mesabi iron range and S of Virginia, in wooded lake region.

Evelyn, John (ēv'ūlĭn, ēv'lĭn, ēv'lĭn), 1620–1706, English diarist. A royalist, he took little part in the civil war. After 1652 he lived as a wealthy country gentleman and wrote on many subjects. His diary, first published in 1818, offers much information on late 17th-cent. life.

evening primrose, plant of genus *Oenothera,* native to North America. Yellow flowers open in evening.

Everest, Sir George (ē'vûrĭst), 1790–1866, British surveyor, b. Wales. Worked on trigonometrical survey of India (1806–43). Mt. Everest named for him.

Everest, Mount, peak, 29,141 ft. high, on Tibet-Nepal border, in the Himalayas; highest point on earth. Named for Sir George Everest. In 1952 a Swiss expedition led by Edouard Wyss-Dunant estab. world's climbing record of 28,210 ft.

Everett, Edward (ēv'rĭt, ē'vûrĭt), 1794–1865, American orator and statesman. U.S. Representative from Mass. (1825–35); adopted conservative attitude on slavery question. Governor of Mass. (1836–39). U.S. Senator (1853–54). In Civil War he traveled throughout North speaking for Union cause. Delivered principal oration at Gettysburg on same occasion that called forth Pres. Lincoln's address.

Everett. 1 City (pop. 45,982), E Mass., N of Boston. Mfg. of steel, iron goods, petroleum and wood products, chemicals, coke, and shoes. **2** Port city (pop. 33,849), NW Wash., on Puget Sound; settled c.1890. Ships lumber, fish, dairy and paper products.

Everglades, subtropical area, c.100 mi. long and 50–75 mi. wide, covering most of S Fla., S of L. OKEECHOBEE. Bounded on E by coastal strip (beaches), W by Big Cypress Swamp, and S by mangrove forests along Florida Bay and Gulf of Mexico. Consists of saw grass savannas and water dotted by hammocks (island-like clumps of trees). Occupies limestone plain, partly covered by muck and peat deposits. Heavy rainfall. Fringe areas support agr. (truck, sugar cane) and stock raising. Overdrainage, caused by reclamation projects of early 1900s, resulted in great fires in 1939. Most of S portion below Tamiami Trail is now in Everglades Natl. Park (see NATIONAL PARKS AND MONUMENTS, table), only tropical national park within U.S. boundaries. Has great variety of flora (some of it virgin) and fauna (esp. herons, egrets, ibises, pelicans, spoonbills). Reservation of SEMINOLE INDIANS is W of lower Everglades.

Evergreen Park, village (pop. 10,531), NE Ill., S suburb of Chicago.

everlasting or **immortelle,** plant with papery or chaffy flowers which on drying retain their form and color. Often used thus in winter bouquets are COCKSCOMB, GLOBE AMARANTH, SEA PINK, STRAWFLOWER.

Everyman, late 15th-cent. morality play in English, counterpart of Dutch play *Elckerlijc.* Which is the original has been disputed. Summoned by Death, the hero, Everyman, can persuade none of his friends—Beauty, Kindred, Worldly Goods—to go with him, except Good Deeds.

Evesham (ēv'shŭm, ē'shŭm), municipal borough (pop. 12,066), Worcestershire, England, on Avon R. in productive fruit and vegetable region. Scene of royalists' victory over Simon de Montfort 1265.

Évian (āvyä') or **Évian-les-Bains** (-lä-bě'), resort, Haute-Savoie dept., E France, on L. Geneva. Mineral spa.

evidence, in law, sum of all facts stated in a trial, including documents and testimonial evidence of witnesses under oath. Particular evidence may be excluded by the judge on grounds that it is irrelevant (having no bearing on the case), immaterial (having no direct connection with substance of the case), or incompetent (outside the knowledge of the witness; e.g., hearsay evidence). In civil suits each party must prove its affirmative contentions; in criminal suits, the burden of proof rests on the plaintiff (prosecutor).

evolution, concept that animals and plants developed by gradual, continuous change from earlier forms. This concept, known as organic evolution (in contrast to inorganic evolution or origin of the physical universe) conceives of life as having arisen from simple primordial protoplasmic mass, probably in sea. Evolutionary concepts appeared in early Greece; during 15 centuries of Christian era under Church restraint, none developed until glimpses of later evolutionary theory began to appear after mid-16th cent. Invention of microscope and classification studies contributed to development. Charles Darwin, after 20 years of gathering evidence, formulated evolutionary theory later known as DARWINISM (and similar independent work of Alfred Russel Wallace). Darwin presented his theory in 1859, when first edition of his *Origin of the Species* appeared. Influence of theory upon scientific thought and philosophy incalculable. The concept was later enlarged by the growth of science of genetics, based on Mendel's laws of inheritance and extended through the work of T. H. Morgan, H. J. Muller, and others.

Évora (e'vôrŭ), city (pop. 21,851), S Portugal, chief city of Alentejo. The Ebora of Roman times, it has impressive ruins ("temple of Diana"). Commercial center under Moors; captured by Portuguese 1166. Cathedral dates from 12th cent. Former Jesuit univ. (1559–1758) now a high school.

Evpatoriya, RSFSR: see EUPATORIA.

Évreux (āvrû'), town (pop. 16,645), cap. of Eure dept., N France, in Normandy. Counts of Évreux were also kings of NAVARRE 1349–1425. Cathedral (14th–17th cent,) damaged in World War II.

Ewald, Georg Heinrich August von (gā'ôrk hīn'rīkh ou'gōost fün ā'vält), 1803–75, German Orientalist and philologist, an authority on Hebrew and the Bible. He was one of the seven professors of the Univ. of Göttingen who protested the revocation of the Hanoverian constitution (1837).

Ewald, Johannes (ā'väl), 1743–81, Danish romantic poet. Author of dramas *Rolf Krage* (1770; first original Danish tragedy), and *The Fishers* (1779; containing the Danish national anthem). Name also spelled Evald.

Ewbank, Thomas (ū'băngk), 1792–1870, American inventor of methods of manufacturing metal tubing, author of works on water-lifting machines and travel. As U.S. patent commissioner he improved patenting methods.

Ewell, Richard Stoddert (ū'ŭl), 1817–72, Confederate general. Supported Stonewall Jackson in Shenandoah Valley (1862). Succeeded Jackson in command (1863) and ably led Lee's advance in Gettysburg campaign. Fought in Wilderness campaign (1864), and defended Richmond (1865).

Ewing, Sir James Alfred, 1855–1935, Scottish engineer and physicist. His research in magnetism disclosed phenomenon of hysteresis, and he advanced the knowledge of crystalline structure of metals. His studies of earthquakes in Japan were significant.

Excalibur: see ARTHURIAN LEGEND.

Excelsior, resort village (pop. 1,763), E Minn., on L. Minnetonka and E of Minneapolis.

Excelsior Springs, city (pop. 5,888), W Mo., NE of Kansas City. Health resort (mineral springs). Frank and Jesse James lived near by.

exchange, mutual transfer of goods, money, or services. Barter, a pure form of exchange, is replaced in modern society by money and price system. The value of exchanged items is set mainly by the market de-

mand. In commerce, an exchange is a place where trading goes on, such as a STOCK EXCHANGE.

Exchequer, Court of (ĕkschĕ'kŭr), British governmental agency. Originated after Norman Conquest as a financial committee of the Curia Regis. By end of 13th cent. the court of appeal was separated from the exchequer or treasury. After 1830 a single Court of Exchequer emerged as court of appeal intermediate between common-law courts and House of Lords. The Judicature Act of 1873 made it the exchequer division of the high court of justice.

excise: see INTERNAL REVENUE.

excommunication, formal expulsion of a person from a religious community, particularly notable in Judaism (e.g., expulsion of Spinoza) and Roman Catholicism. Elaborate Catholic form involves pronouncement of anathema and public exclusion from Church and was important in Middle Ages. In wider sense any "fallen away" Catholic is excommunicate.

excretion, elimination of useless matter by living organism. In man, organs that form excretions include skin, lungs, kidneys, and large intestine.

Exe (ĕks), stream of Somerset and Devonshire, England, flowing from Exmoor to the English Channel.

executors and administrators. An executor is the person designated in a will to carry out its provisions. An administrator is appointed for same purpose by the court, if there is no capable executor named or living or also if a person dies without a will.

Exeter (ĕk'sŭtŭr), county borough (pop. 75,479), co. town of Devonshire, England, above Exe R. Strategically located, town was besieged by Danes, William the Conqueror, Yorkists, and religious factions. Great cathedral contains remarkable oak throne of the bishops; chapter house has EXETER BOOK. Severely bombed in World War II.

Exeter. 1 Town (pop. 5,664), SE N.H., SW of Portsmouth; settled 1638. Cap. of N.H. in Revolution. Birthplace of Lewis Cass and D. C. French. Seat of Phillips Exeter Acad. (nonsectarian; for boys; chartered 1781, opened 1783 by John Phillips). **2** Borough (pop. 5,130), NE Pa., on Susquehanna R. and NE of Wilkes-Barre. Coal mining.

Exeter College: see OXFORD UNIVERSITY.

Exile: see CAPTIVITY.

existentialism (ĕgzīstĕn'shŭlīzŭm, ĕksĭ–). Although there are three main developments of this philosophic school, the basic beliefs are commonly held–the problem of human existence is the major one; reason, by itself, is an inadequate method of explanation; anguish is an emotion common to men confronting life's problems; and morality demands participation. Soren Kierkegaard developed a Christian existentialism in which anguish is relieved by transcendent faith in God. Martin Heidegger and Jean Paul Sartre deny existence of God and stress man's absolute freedom to choose, with resulting anguish and despair. Jacques Maritain has approached a Christian existentialism, based upon St. Thomas Aquinas, in which desire to be and fear of nothingness are rendered powerless by faith in God.

Exmoor, high moorland, Somerset and Devonshire, England. Largely a wasteland, with hills, valleys, and wooded glens, underlain by slate and sandstone. Grazing ground for sheep and small Exmoor ponies.

Exmouth (ĕks'mouth), urban district (pop. 17,232), Devonshire, England; port and summer resort.

Exodus (ĕk'sŭdŭs), book of Old Testament, second of books of Law (Pentateuch or Torah), ascribed by tradition to Moses. Some of the most important events of biblical history occur in Exodus, e.g., the deliverance of Hebrews in Egypt from bondage, the institution of Passover, the parting of the Red Sea, and the giving of the Ten Commandments. A most solemn moment is the appearance of God to Moses in the burning bush revealing His name as I Am.

exogamy: see MARRIAGE.

expanding universe: see UNIVERSE.

SMALL CAPITALS = cross references. Pronunciation key on inside end pages. Abbreviations: p. 2.

expansion, in physics, increase in volume resulting from temperature increase; contraction is reverse. When heat is applied, rate of vibration and distance between molecules increases; increased volume results. Degree of expansion is specific property of each liquid and solid; amount per unit volume per one-degree temperature rise is coefficient of cubical expansion. Coefficient of linear expansion is increase per unit of length per degree rise in temperature. Expansion coefficient about same for all common gases at ordinary temperatures; Kelvin scale of temperature is based on this number.

Exploits, largest river of N.F., Canada, rising in Long Range and flowing NE to Exploits Bay. Grand Falls and Bishop's Falls have hydroelectric plants.

exploration was undertaken by primitive peoples in search of supplies, and most regions of the world were discovered by them. Recorded exploration contributing to Western civilization began c.3000 B.C. An Egyptian-sponsored expedition is said to have sailed around Africa c.600 B.C. Ancient Greeks probably sailed beyond Britain c.330 B.C., having previously explored the Mediterranean and Black Sea regions. Romans penetrated well into Europe and traded directly with China. Crusades turned European attention to Eastern riches. Important achievements after 1400 that revealed extent of globe include reaching of India by Vasco da Gama, discovery of America by Columbus, and first circumnavigation of globe under Magellan. The 16th cent. brought Spanish exploration of the Americas. Much of North American interior explored by French in 17th cent. Spanish and Portuguese monopoly of trade routes challenged by English and Dutch voyages in the Pacific. Australian interior was explored by mid-19th cent., and most of Africa by end of century. Arctic, antarctic, and deep-sea exploration begun in 19th cent. was expanded in 20th cent. Scientific interest and desire for natural resources and strategic bases motivate most modern exploration; explorer is aided by vast technological advances.

explosive, substance undergoing decomposition or combustion rapidly with evolution of heat and production of large volume of gas, which exerts enormous sudden pressure causing blasting of rocks, etc. Some explosives are not truly explosive but are mixtures of substances which undergo very rapid combustion; others are compounds which liberate much energy during rapid decomposition. Most high explosives are prepared from nitric acid. Some high explosives are set off by a DETONATOR.

exponent (ĕk'spōnŭnt), in mathematics, a number, letter, or algebraic expression written above and to the right of another number, letter, or expression called the base. Exponent indicates power to which base is to be raised.

export: see BALANCE OF TRADE.

exposition. Word has wider meaning but is applied typically to international exhibitions or fairs, designed to register the state of civilization. Fine and industrial arts lend themselves well to such expositions. Later expositions emphasize scientific and technological progress. They help to raise standards of popular taste, to lessen provincialism, and to promote international understanding. London, Paris, Vienna, Zurich, New York, Chicago, and San Francisco have housed famous expositions (popularly called worlds' fairs).

expressionism, term for movement in art following impressionism, used generally to describe any art work in which representation of nature is subordinated to expression of emotion. Used more specifically to classify modern art characterized by intuitive, spontaneous distortion for emotional effect. In literature the effort to project spiritual actualities rather than naturalistic records of events was of most importance in the drama and the novel. Outstanding among expressionist playwrights of post–World War I period was the German Ernst Toller. Movement gained much from

work of the experimental stage designers of the period.

exterritoriality or **extraterritoriality,** privilege of alien of exemption from local jurisdiction in foreign country. Applies to officials of UN while performing duties; and to a nation's official personnel and residences, public vessels in port, and sometimes armed forces. Nonofficial residents have enjoyed exterritoriality in many foreign countries, custom persisting longest in Egypt and China. It was resented, however, and legal reforms led to abolition. China in World War I abolished rights of Central Powers, in World War II of Italy and Japan. In 1924 USSR abandoned rights, followed by Britain and U.S. in 1943, and France in 1946.

extortion, unlawful obtaining of money or property through wrongful use of fear, force, or authority of office.

extradition (ĕkstrŭdĭ'shŭn), delivery of a person suspected or convicted of a crime by the state where he has taken refuge to the state asserting jurisdiction over him. International extradition is normally governed by special treaties, and it is usual for neighboring countries to grant extradition more readily than countries remote from each other. The first U.S. treaty with an international extradition clause was Jay's Treaty (1794). In the 19th cent. many extradition treaties were concluded by Western nations. Usually extradition for political crimes is excluded, though a nation may refuse asylum to a political fugitive. In the U.S., Congress has established a uniform law for state-to-state extradition; it provides that any person properly charged shall be extradited.

extra-sensory perception: see PSYCHICAL RESEARCH.

extraterritoriality: see EXTERRITORIALITY.

Extremadura, Spain: see ESTREMADURA.

extreme unction: see SACRAMENT.

extroversion and **introversion,** terms introduced by C. G. Jung for opposed psychological types. The extrovert's general activity or drive (libido) is directed toward external world, the introvert's upon himself. Everyone has both tendencies, with one generally dominant as a result of both temperament and environment. Extreme extrovert behavior becomes an irrational flight from self, the acting out of feelings in society, as in hysteria. Extreme introvert retreats into inner world, with fantasies displacing reality. Jung saw schizophrenia as introvert's psychosis.

Eyck, Huybrecht van (hoi' brĕkht vän īk') or **Hubert van Eyck,** c.1370–1426, and **Jan van Eyck** (yän) c.1390–1441, founders of Flemish school of painting; brothers. Inaccurately credited with discovery of oil painting, but they were first to use a resin or oil medium in naturalistic painting to achieve greater spacial depth and richness of color. Controversy as to part taken by each in their masterpiece *The Adoration of the Lamb* (Ghent). Attributed to Jan is portrait of Arnolfini and his wife (Natl. Gall., London).

Eyde, Samuel (sä'mōŏĕl ā'dù), 1866–1940, Norwegian engineer, co-developer of Birkeland-Eyde process for nitrogen fixation.

eye, organ of vision consisting of eyeball enclosing refracting media. Outermost fibrous layer of eyeball comprises white, opaque sclera at back and sides and transparent cornea in front. Vascular, pigmented middle layer consists of chorioid (or choroid) under the sclera; iris, behind cornea and perforated by pupil; and ciliary body connecting chorioid and iris rim. Over inner layer, the retina, lie optic nerve fibers. Refracting media consist of transparent lens behind iris; jellylike vitreous humor between retina and lens; and aqueous humor between lens and cornea. See *ill.,* p. 595.

Eyja Fjord (ā'ù fyôrd"), longest fjord in Iceland (37 mi.), on N coast. At its head is Akureyri.

Eylau (ī'lou), town (pop. 7,485), former East Prussia, near Königsberg; inc. into USSR 1945 and renamed Bagrationovsk. Here in Feb., 1807, Napoleon I fought a bloody but indecisive battle against Russian and Prussian forces (in which Prince Bagration distinguished himself). Also known as Preussisch Eylau.

Eyre, Lake (âr), shallow salt lake, area 3,430 sq. mi., NE South Australia; frequently dry.

Ezechiel: see EZEKIEL.

Ezekias (ĕzŭkī'ŭs): see HEZEKIAH.

Ezekiel or **Ezechiel** (both: ēzē'kēēl) [Heb.,= God strengthens], book of Old Testament, an account of the prophetic career of the priest Ezekiel (fl. 592 B.C.). Central point is the fall of Jerusalem, what goes on before being prophetic of doom, the rest inspired by hope of restoration. Among famous passages are chapters 18, 21, 26–28, 31–32, 37.

Ezra [Heb.,= help] and **Nehemiah** (nēŭmī'ŭ) [Heb.,= consoled by God], in AV, books of Old Testament; called 1 and 2 ESDRAS in Western canon; a single work in Hebrew canon. Ezra (fl. after 460 B.C.) was a priest and scribe; Nehemiah (fl. 444 B.C.) was cupbearer to Artaxerxes I and later governor of Jerusalem. Books tell of return of Jews to Palestine from captivity. Important events are the reading of the Law to the assembled people, the signing of a covenant, and the completion of the wall.

Ezzelino da Romano (ĕt"sālē'nō dä rōmä'nō), 1194–1259, Italian Ghibelline leader, lord of Verona, Vicenza, Padua. A supporter of Emperor Frederick II, he dominated N Italy after 1237; was excommunicated by Pope Innocent IV 1254; suffered defeat shortly before his death. Reputedly a cruel tyrant; mentioned in Dante's *Inferno*.

F, chemical symbol of element FLUORINE.

Faber, Frederick William (fā'bŭr), 1814–63, English theologian, adherent of the Oxford movement; friend of J. H. Newman. Founded community at Birmingham which became the Oratory of St. Philip Neri (1848) and an oratory at London (1849).

Fabian Society, influential English socialist society, developed 1884 out of the Fellowship of the True Life (1883). Among its outstanding exponents were G. B. Shaw and Sidney and Beatrice Webb. Fabians repudiated the Marxist class struggle, believing in natural development of socialism. They helped found the British Labour Party in 1900.

Fabius (fā'bēŭs), family name of several Romans. **Quintus Fabius Maximus Rullianus** (kwĭn'tŭs, măk'sĭmŭs rŭlēā'nŭs) or **Rullus** (rŭ'lŭs), d. c.291 B.C., renowned as a general for his victory over Etruscans, Samnites, and allies at Sentinum (295 B.C.). His descendant, **Quintus Fabius Maximus Verrucosus** (vĕrōōkō'sŭs), d. 203 B.C., opponent of HANNIBAL in the Second PUNIC WAR, was called Cunctator (kŭngk'tŭtôr) [Latin,= delayer] because of his tactics, which have given the term Fabian to any waiting policy. Tired of his masterly inaction, the Romans replaced him as consul and were defeated at Cannae.

fable, short moral story, often one in which characters are beasts or inanimate objects. One of oldest collections is Indian PANCHATANTRA. Fables of AESOP were earliest to be written down. In medieval times began satirical series about REYNARD THE FOX. Great French fabulist was LA FONTAINE. John Gay and Dryden continued tradition of beast fable in England. Use of fable to mean general narrative with a lesson is demonstrated in J. R. Lowell's *Fable for Critics* (1848).

Fabre, Jean Henri (zhä ärē' fä'brŭ), 1823–1915, French entomologist and author, known for observations and studies of insect behavior. Chief work is *Souvenirs entomologiques* (10 vols., 1879–1907); English translations of parts of this work include *The Life of the Spider* (1912); *The Wonders of Instinct* (1918); *The Marvels of the Insect World* (1938).

Fabriano, Gentile da: see GENTILE DA FABRIANO.

Fabricius, Hieronymus (hīŭrō'nŭmŭs), 1537–1619, Italian anatomist, teacher of William Harvey at Padua. His discoveries include valves in veins.

Fackenthal, Frank Diehl (fă'kŭnthôl), 1883–, American educator and administrator. He served Columbia Univ. 1906–48 as, successively, chief clerk, secretary, provost, and acting president.

facsimile (făksĭ'mŭlē), in communication, a radio or wire transmission system for pictures and other graphic matter. By light-beam and photoelectric-cell arrangement light and dark areas of material are translated into transmittable tones; receiver reproduces them on chemically treated paper.

factor, in arithmetic, any number dividing a given number evenly without any remainder.

Facundo Quiroga, Juan: see QUIROGA, JUAN FACUNDO.

fading, in radio, irregular variation in strength and quality of received signal. Chief cause considered changing altitude and density of Kennelly-Heaviside layer; transmitted wave reflects unevenly, arrives out of phase. Automatic volume control corrects.

Faenza (fään'tsä), city (pop. 23,823), Emilia-Romagna, N central Italy, in Romagna. Renaissance cathedral and palace. Richly colored ceramics, called faïence, made here since 12th cent.

Faerie Queene, The: see SPENSER, EDMUND.

Faeroe Islands or **Faroe Islands** (both: fâ'rō), Dan. *Faerørne,* Faeroese *Føroyar,* group of 21 volcanic islands (c.540 sq. mi.; pop. 29,178), in N Atlantic Ocean, between Iceland and the Shetlands; Danish crown possession. Stromo (with cap., Thorshavn) and Ostero isls. are largest. Transferred from Norway to Denmark 1814; under British protection in World War II; obtained home rule 1948. Faeroese language is akin to Icelandic. Fish and wool are main exports.

Fages, Pedro (pā'dhrō fä'häs), fl. 1767–96, Spanish governor of Alta Calif. (1782–91). Notable for encouraging colonization, agr., and missionary work.

Fahrenheit, Gabriel Daniel (fä'rŭnhīt, Ger. gä'brēĕl dä'nyĕl fä'rŭnhīt), 1686–1736, German physicist. He devised Fahrenheit TEMPERATURE scale and substituted mercury for alcohol in thermometer.

fair. Before transportation and marketing developments made distribution of goods to all markets easy, marketing opportunities arose from religious observances which brought widely separated people together. Markets or fairs of this kind developed in Greece and Rome. Their advantages multiplied during the Middle Ages in Europe, the greatest period being the 13th–14th cent. Always a business institution for buying, selling, and bartering, they declined under competition with continuous marketing; a few (e.g., at Leipzig) survived. The typical American fair (e.g., at Danbury, Conn.) is dissimilar, being an exhibition of farm and home products ranked by judges for excellence of quality.

Fairbairn, Sir William (fâr'bârn), 1789–1874, Scottish engineer, builder of iron ships and railroad bridges.

Fairbanks, Douglas, 1883–1939, American film actor, whose real name was Douglas Elton Ulman. After 1915 he made such swashbuckling films as *The Mark of Zorro, Robin Hood,* and *The Thief of Bagdad.* He was married (1920–35) to Mary Pickford.

Fairbanks, Thaddeus, 1796–1866, American inventor of the platform scale, patented 1831.

Fairbanks, town (pop. 5,771), central Alaska, on Chena Slough, where Chena R. enters the Tanana. Transportation, distribution, and financial center for Tanana R. area and all of inland Alaska. Grew as mining camp after 1902 gold discovery; hydraulic mining succeeded placer mining. Building of Alaska RR increased town's importance. Richardson Highway from Valdez on coast reaches Fairbanks, which became terminus of ALASKA HIGHWAY in World War II. Has one of chief airports of territory; army air base near. Near by is Univ. of ALASKA.

Fairborn, city (pop. 7,847), NW Ohio, ENE of Dayton; formed 1950 by consolidation of Fairfield and Osborn. Wright-Patterson Air Force Base near by.

Fairbury, city (pop. 6,395), SE Nebr., near Kansas line. Flour, meat and dairy products.

Fairchild, David Grandison, 1869–, American botanist. He organized and was later in charge of division of plant exploration and introduction in U.S. Dept. of Agriculture. His works include *The World Was My Garden* (1938); *The World Grows Round My Door* (1947).

Fair Employment Practices Committee (FEPC), established (1941) during World War II to eliminate discriminatory employment practices. Suspended (1946) for lack of funds. A few states have established similar bodies. After 1946 efforts were made to establish a permanent U.S. FEPC.

Fairfax, Thomas, 3d Baron, 1612–71, English soldier-statesman. Commanded the New Model Army that crushed Charles I in 1645. Fearing military dictatorship, he opposed Cromwell. Was instrumental in return of Charles II to the throne (1660).

Fairfax, Thomas Fairfax, 6th Baron, 1693–1781, British proprietor of Northern Neck of Va. Claim to land between Rappahannock and Potomac rivers, disputed by Va., confirmed in 1745.

Fairfax, town (pop. 1,946), N Va., W of Washington, D.C. In old courthouse are wills of George and Martha Washington. Mount Vernon, Gunston Hall (1755–58), and Pohick Church (1774) are in county.

Fairfield. 1 City (pop. 13,177), N central Ala., near Birmingham; founded c.1910. Steel goods. **2** Industrial town (pop. 30,489), SW Conn., on Long Isl. Sound SW of Bridgeport; settled 1639. Metal goods, chemicals. Burned by British, 1779. **3** City (pop. 5,576), SE Ill., E of Mount Vernon, in agr. area. Mfg. of auto parts. **4** City (pop. 7,299), SE Iowa, E of Ottumwa. Has mfg. of washing machines and farm equipment. Here are Parsons Col. and Old Settlers Park (with log cabin built 1836). **5** Town (pop. 5,811), S Maine, on Kennebec R. above Waterville. Pulp and woolen mills. **6** See FAIRBORN, Ohio. **7** Town (pop. 1,428), NW Vt., E of St. Albans. C. A. Arthur's birthplace is near.

Fairhaven, resort town (pop. 12,764), SE Mass., Acushnet R. mouth opposite New Bedford; settled 1670. Boatbuilding.

Fairhope, resort town (pop. 3,354), SW Ala., on Mobile Bay. Founded (1894–95) by followers of Henry George, it remained a single-tax town until 1937.

Fair Isle, rocky island (pop. 108), off N Scotland. Known for knitted hosiery of bright, many-colored designs. Also a famous bird migration station.

Fair Lawn, borough (pop. 23,885), NE N.J., near Paterson; includes planned community of Radburn.

Fairmont. 1 City (pop. 8,193), S Minn., near Iowa line. Resort and shipping center of agr. area. **2** City (pop. 29,346), N W.Va., on Monongahela R.; founded 1843. Center of coal area, it has mfg. of glass and sheet aluminum.

Fair Oaks: see PENINSULAR CAMPAIGN.

Fairport, village (pop. 5,267), W N.Y., SE of Rochester and on Erie Canal. Tin cans and chemicals.

fairy, in legend of British Isles, supernatural being similar to humans and usually beautiful but having magical powers and generally ill-disposed toward men. Shakspere led in conventionalizing fairies, which became popular in 16th-cent. English literature and were connected with various classical names and ideas. On the Continent, supernatural beings were linked with pagan gods. **Fairy tales** are characterized by appearance of supernatural beings and magic. Great adapters of popular fairy tales were Charles Perrault, the brothers Grimm, and Hans Christian Andersen.

Faisal: see FEISAL.

Faiyum, Egypt: see FAYUM.

Faizabad, Uttar Pradesh, India: see FYZABAD.

Falange (fä'länj), Spanish political party, founded 1933 as Falange Española Tradicionalista by José Antonio Primo de Rivera. Based on FASCISM; emphasized Spanish national tradition. Sided with Insurgents in civil war of 1936–39; emerged as strongest party but was absorbed by Franco into one-party government (1942).

Falashas (–lä'–) [Ethiopic,= emigrant], group of Abyssinians of Jewish affinity.

falcon (fôl'kŭn, fô'kŭn), name for numerous species of long-winged, swift birds of prey, found throughout the world. They have strong hooked, notched bills and eat birds, small mammals, and insects. Duck hawk (American variety of Old World peregrine), pigeon hawk, sparrow hawk, and prairie falcon are American falcons. The female of some species is trained for **falconry,** hunting birds and small animals for masters. Known to ancient Chinese, Persians, Egyptians.

Falfurrias (fălfūr'ēŭs), city (pop. 6,712), S Texas, SW of Corpus Christi. Center of agr. and oil area with recycling and gypsum plants and cotton gins.

Falguière, Jean Alexandre Joseph (zhä' ălĕksä'drü zhôzĕf' fälgyĕr'), 1831–1900, French sculptor, noted for monuments and portrait statues.

Faliero or **Falier, Marino** (märē'nō fälyä'rō, fälēĕr'), 1274–1355, doge of Venice (1354–55). Joined in plot against patricians to overthrow oligarchic government and make him dictator. Plot was discovered, Faliero and accomplices executed.

Falkberget, Johan (yōhän' fälk'bĕrgù), 1879–, Norwegian novelist. Wrote of miners in *Lisbeth of Jarnfjeld* (1915), trilogy *Christianus Sextus* (1927–35), and *Night Bread* (1940).

Falkirk (fôl'kûrk), burgh (pop. 37,528), Stirlingshire, Scotland. In mining and mfg. region, it produces chemicals and leather goods. Has annual stock fairs. English defeated Scots here 1298; Gen. Hawley defeated by Prince Charles Edward's Jacobites 1746.

Falkland, Lucius Cary, 2d Viscount (fôk'lŭnd), 1610?–1643, English statesman and literary figure. Represented Charles I in attempts to make peace with Parliament. He supposedly let himself be killed in battle rather than fight either king or Parliament.

Falkland Islands (fô'klŭnd), islands, S Atlantic, c.300 mi. E of Strait of Magellan. Ownership disputed by Argentina and Great Britain. Group administered as British crown colony (4,618 sq. mi.; pop. 2,268); cap. Stanley. Spanish name *Islas Malvinas*.

Falkner, William: see FAULKNER, WILLIAM.

Fall, Albert Bacon, 1861–1944, U.S. Secretary of the Interior (1921–23). Convicted in 1929 for his part in TEAPOT DOME conspiracy.

Falla, Manuel de (mänwĕl' dā fäl'yä), 1876–1946, Spanish composer. Notable among his compositions are *La vida breve,* an opera; *Nights in the Gardens of Spain,* for piano and orchestra; the ballets *El Amor Brujo* and *The Three-cornered Hat.*

Fallada, Hans (häns' fä'lädä), pseud. of Rudolf Ditzen, 1893–1947, German novelist. Best remembered for *Little Man, What Now?* (1932; Eng. tr., 1933).

fallen arches: see FLAT FOOT.

Fallen Timbers, state park, NW Ohio, on Maumee R., near Maumee. Site of battle where Anthony Wayne's forces decisively defeated hostile Indians 1794.

Fallières, Armand (ärmä' fälyĕr'), 1841–1931, president of France (1906–13). Under him law of separation of Church and state was carried out; Dreyfus Affair was concluded (1906).

falling star: see METEOR.

fall line, boundary between upland region and coastal or tidewater plain. Marks place where rivers drop to plain in falls or rapids. Since falls supply water power for industries, fall-line cities rival ports in economic importance.

Fallon (fäl'ŭn), city (pop. 2,400), W Nev., ENE of Carson City. Trade center for ranches and for Newlands project.

Fallopius (fŭlō'pēŭs), 1523–62, Italian anatomist, noted teacher at Padua. His discoveries include **Fallopian tubes** leading from ovaries to uterus.

fallow land, in agr., land plowed but not seeded, to conserve moisture and check weeds. ROTATION OF CROPS is now often preferred.

Fall River, industrial city (pop. 111,963), SE Mass., at Taunton R. mouth on Mt. Hope Bay; settled 1656. Mfg. of textiles (first cotton mill built 1811), metal, rubber, and paper products.

Falls Church, city (pop. 7,535), N Va., W of Washington, D.C. The Falls Church was built 1767–69 on site of earlier church (1734).

Falls City, city (pop. 6,203), extreme SE Nebr., on Nemaha R., near Kansas line. Railway division point in livestock, grain, and dairy area.

Falmouth (fäl'mŭth), municipal borough (pop. 17,036), Cornwall, England; port and fishing town. Has excellent harbor guarded by two castles. Unusually warm climate; subtropical plants thrive.

Falmouth. 1 Town (pop. 4,342), SW Maine, on Casco Bay. One of earliest settlements in Maine (c.1632), it included Portland until 1786. Nearly destroyed by British in 1775. **2** Town (pop. 8,662), SE Mass., on extreme SW Cape Cod; settled 1660. Includes Woods Hole resort (1940 pop. 549). Has U.S. fish and wildlife station, marine biological institute, and Oceanographic Inst. (1930; endowed by Rockefeller Foundation), which maintains research ship *Atlantis.*

False Decretals (dĭkrē'tŭlz), collection of partly spurious documents treating of canon law, published c.847–852 probably in France. Compiler called himself Isidore Mercator (hence term Pseudo-Isidorian Decretals). By incorporation in GRATIAN the False Decretals received authority in medieval canon-law texts. One of the great forgeries of history, they were first exposed by Nicholas of Cusa and Juan de Torquemada (15th cent.).

false imprisonment, complete restraint upon a person's liberty of movement against his will and without legal justification, either by a private person or by an official improperly issuing a warrant for arrest. If the restrainer is an official, release may be had through HABEAS CORPUS.

Falstaff (fôl'stäf), famous jovial companion of Prince Hal (later Henry V) in Shakspere's play *Henry IV.* Also leading character in Shakspere's *Merry Wives of Windsor.* The character was originally called Sir John Oldcastle (as in Shakspere's source on Henry V) but has no resemblance to the real Sir John Oldcastle—nor to the historical Sir John Fastolf, whose name may have suggested the name Falstaff.

Falster (fäl'stŭr), island (198 sq. mi.; pop. 45,665), S Denmark, in the Baltic Sea; cap. Nykobing.

Falun (fä'lŭn"), town (pop. 16,858), central Sweden, co. seat and industrial center of KOPPARBERG CO. Oldest

Swedish industrial company was organized in 12th cent. to operate its copper mine, now exhausted.

Famagusta (fämägōo'stä), city (pop. 16,194), on E Cyprus; chief port of island. Seat of Venetian governors (15th–16th cent.); thought to be main scene of Shakspere's *Othello.* Ruins include so-called Tower of Othello, 13th-cent. Gothic cathedral, and Venetian governors' palace. A British naval base, it was bombed in World War II.

family, social group consisting of parents and their children. Other close relatives and even servants and slaves may be added, forming the "large" or "joint" family, an important economic and biological unit. Commonest unit in Western civilization is one male, one female, and their children. Hebrew and Roman law gave the father almost complete control over the family. In modern times the family unit has been affected by the legal equalization of women (beginning in 19th cent.), removal from the family of economic tasks, and state interest in children's education. The changed relationships of the members of the family to each other and to the community are thought to contain the germ of many psychological and sociological maladjustments.

Family Compact. 1 Name of three agreements (1733, 1743, 1761) between French and Spanish branches of Bourbon family. The last provided for Spanish entry into Seven Years War on French side. **2** Term popularly applied to small, powerful group of men who dominated government of Upper Canada from late 18th cent. to the beginnings of responsible government under the Baldwin-LaFontaine ministry (1848–51). Opposition movement developed into the Reform party. Religious differences embittered the struggle, since the Family Compact (term first appeared c.1828) was composed almost entirely of members of the Church of England. Chateau Clique was name given to similar powerful group in French Lower Canada.

Fanariots: see PHANARIOTS.

Faneuil Hall (fǎn'l, fǎn'yūl), public market and hall given to Boston by merchant Peter Faneuil, 1742. Burned 1761, then rebuilt; enlarged by Bulfinch, 1806. Called "the cradle of liberty" because of Revolutionary meetings held here.

Fannin, James Walker (fǎ'nĭn), 1804?–1836, hero in Texas Revolution, b. Ga. Distinguished himself in first victories of 1835. Captured after evacuating Goliad, shot at Santa Anna's orders.

Fanning, Edmund, 1769–1841, American trader and explorer. Discovered Fanning Isl., Washington Isl., and other islands (1783). Became agent for group of New York city merchants to promote and organize South Sea trading expeditions.

Fanning Island, atoll, 15 sq. mi., central Pacific, NW of Christmas Isl. Added 1916 to British colony of Gilbert and Ellice Isls. Cable relay station here connects Canada and Suva, Fiji.

Fantin-Latour, Ignace Henri Jean Théodore (fätēlätoor'), 1836–1904, French painter and lithographer. Best known for portrait groups of famous contemporaries.

Faraday, Michael (fǎ'rŭdā"), 1791–1867, English scientist. He developed the first dynamo, the precursor of modern dynamos and generators. From his discovery of electromagnetic induction stemmed the development of electrical machinery for industry. He formulated laws of electrolysis.

Farallon Islands (fǎ'rŭlŏn), Calif., two groups of small rocky islands in the Pacific W of the Golden Gate; part of San Francisco. Here are bird sanctuary and U.S. radar station.

farce [Latin,= stuffing], light, comic theatrical piece. Form of comedy in which characters and events are greatly exaggerated to produce broad, simple humor. Examples are Latin comedies of Plautus and Terence, but term is derived from *farces* of medieval France. Early English farce is *Ralph Roister Doister* (pub. 1566). Molière and Henry Fielding also wrote farces.

In more recent times farce is used in slapstick comedies of American moving pictures.

farcy: see GLANDERS.

Far Eastern Territory, former administrative division, RSFSR, in E and NE Siberia. Its vast area is now divided into KHABAROVSK TERRITORY and MARITIME TERRITORY. Khabarovsk was cap., Vladivostok chief port. Russian colonization began 17th cent.; SE sections ceded by China 1858 and 1860. During civil war and Allied intervention following 1917 Revolution, much of area was occupied by Japanese. In 1920 local Bolsheviks organized Far Eastern Republic, with cap. at Chita, but Japanese held Vladivostok until 1922. Territory was organized 1926, redivided 1938.

Farel, Guillaume (gēyōm' färĕl'), 1489–1565, French reformer, associate of Calvin in Swiss Reformation.

Farewell, Cape, southernmost point of Greenland, on Egger Isl.

Fargo, William George, 1818–81, American pioneer expressman. Helped found American Express Co. (1850). By 1852 he and Henry Wells organized Wells, Fargo & Co. to handle express service between New York and San Francisco.

Fargo, city (pop. 38,256), E N.Dak., largest city in state, on Red R.; settled 1871. Rail center and river port. Chief distributing point in region, it handles agr. machinery and foodstuffs, processes food, has mfg. of fur coats, luggage, and electrical apparatus. Seat of North Dakota Agricultural Col. (state and land-grant supported; coed.; 1890).

Faribault (fä'rĭbō), city (pop. 16,028), SE Minn., S of Minneapolis at confluence of Cannon and Straight rivers, in farm area; platted 1854. Alexander Faribault, French fur trader, built port here 1826. Became Episcopal center with work of J. L. Breck and Bishop H. B. Whipple. Seat of pioneer school for feebleminded and of schools for the deaf and the blind. Mfg. of food products and household equipment.

Faridun: see FERID ED-DIN ATTAR.

Farinelli, Carlo Broschi (brŏ'skē färēnĕl'lē), 1705–82, Italian male soprano, greatest of the *castrati*, official singer to Philip V of Spain.

Farley, James A(loysius), 1888–, American political leader, U.S. Postmaster General (1933–36, 1937–40). As Democratic Natl. Committee chairman, he managed successful 1932 and 1936 F. D. Roosevelt presidential campaigns.

Farm Credit Administration (FCA), agency of U.S. Dept. of Agriculture supervising loans to farmers and agricultural cooperatives. The Federal Farm Loan Act of 1916 established land banks as a centralized source of farm-mortgage credit. In 1933 the FCA took over the land banks, and additional farm-credit measures were taken. By 1940 the FCA held 40 per cent of all outstanding farm mortgages. The original plan that the farm-credit system would be cooperatively owned was not achieved.

Farmer, Fannie Merritt, 1857–1915, American expert on cookery, editor of *The Boston Cooking School Cook Book* (1896; many times reissued and translated).

Farmer-Labor party, in U.S. history, political organization formed 1920 by former members of the older Progressive party together with farm and labor representatives, chiefly from Middle West. Advocated socialistic program. Party particularly strong in Minn. Dissolved 1924, reorganized later, but lost strength as New Deal incorporated some of its reforms.

farming: see AGRICULTURE.

farming, in taxation, the collection of taxes through private contractors. Tax farmers pay a lump sum; difference between that sum and sum actually collected is their profit or loss. Practiced since ancient times (e.g., by publicans in Rome), the system was most fully applied in 18th-cent. France, where indirect taxes were collected by the farm general (a body consisting of 40 financiers). Notorious for extortion, some 30 farmers general were executed in French Revolution.

Farmingdale, village (pop. 4,492), SE N.Y., on W Long Isl. near Mineola. Large aircraft factories. Long Isl. Agricultural and Technical Inst. is here.

Farmington. 1 Town (pop. 7,026), central Conn., SW of Hartford. Has Miss Porter's School for girls. Includes Unionville village (pop. 2,197; metal goods). **2** Town (pop. 4,677), W central Maine, NW of Augusta. Gateway to Rangeley Lakes and Dead R. resort regions. **3** Town (pop. 3,637), NW N.Mex., on San Juan R. Distributing point for Navajo reservation. Aztec Ruins, Chaco Canyon natl. monuments are near.

Farmville, town (pop. 4,375), S Va., on Appomattox R. and E of Lynchburg. Near by is Hampden-Sydney Col. (at Hampden-Sydney, Va.; for men: opened by Presbyterians as academy 1776, chartered as college 1783).

Farnborough, urban district (pop. 27,702), Hampshire, England. Site of important RAF stations, it includes part of Aldershot military camp. Empress Eugenie lived here (1881–1920) and is buried (with Napoleon III) in crypt of church she built.

Farne Islands, group of islets off Northumberland coast, England. Sheltered St. Cuthbert in 7th cent. Scene of Grace Darling's heroism at wreck of *Forfarshire* in 1838.

Farnese (färnā'zā), Italian noble family, long prominent in Rome, which ruled duchy of PARMA and PIACENZA 1545–1731. Duchy was created out of papal lands by Pope PAUL III (Alessandro Farnese) in favor of his natural son Pierluigi. Pierluigi's son and heir Ottavio married MARGARET OF PARMA. Their son, **Alessandro Farnese,** 1545–92, duke of Parma and Piacenza (1586–92), fought under his uncle, John of Austria, at Lepanto (1571) and in the Netherlands. Succeeding John as Spanish governor of the Netherlands (1578), he took Tournai, Maastricht, Breda, Bruges, Ghent, and Antwerp from the rebels, thus securing continued possession of S Low Countries for Spain. In 1509 he led an army to support the League against Henry IV of France. He relieved Paris (1590) and Rouen (1592), but died from a wound. After male line of family died out, ELIZABETH FARNESE secured Parma and Piacenza for her son Philip.

Farnese Bull, sculptured group attributed to Apollonius of Tralles and his brother Tauriscus of 1st or 2d cent. B.C. Shows Dirce being tied to an infuriated bull. A copy in Naples national museum was formerly in Farnese Palace.

Farnese Hercules, marble statue by Glycon, Athenian sculptor of 1st cent. B.C. Once in the Farnese Palace, now in Naples national museum.

Farnese Palace, in Rome, designed by Antonio da Sangallo for Cardinal Alessandro Farnese (Pope Paul III). Begun before 1514 and completed by Giacomo della Porta; Michelangelo also worked on it. Built of huge blocks taken from Colosseum and theater of Marcellus. Halls decorated by Annibale Carracci.

Farnesina (färnāzē'nä), Renaissance villa, Rome, Italy. Built 1508–11 by Peruzzi. Frescoes by Raphael and pupils.

Farnsworth, Philo Taylor, 1906–, American inventor. Demonstrated television system (1927); developed Orthicon or "dissector tube."

Faro (fä'rō), town (pop. 19,695), cap. of Algarve prov., S Portugal; seaport. Exports fish, cork.

faro (fâ'rō) [for *Pharaoh*, from old French card design], gambling game played with pack of 52 cards. First played in France and England, especially popular in American gambling houses in 19th cent.

Faroe Islands: see FAEROE ISLANDS.

Farouk I (färook'), 1920–, king of Egypt (1937–52), son and successor of Fuad I. Revolt led by Gen. Naguib forced his abdication and his infant son, Fuad II, was proclaimed king.

Farquhar, George (fär'kŭr, –kwŭr), 1678–1707, British Restoration dramatist, b. Ireland. Best known of his licentious, naturalistic comedies is *Beaux' Stratagem* (1707).

Farragut, David Glasgow, 1801–70, American admiral,

hero of New Orleans and Mobile Bay in Civil War. Commanding West Gulf Blockading Squadron (1862), he boldly sailed up the Mississippi past Forts St. Philip and Jackson to defeat Confederate flotilla, enabling B. F. Butler to take New Orleans. In 1864 he moved on Mobile. Forcing defenses in Mobile Bay, he defeated Franklin Buchanan, thus closing last Gulf port of Confederate blockade-running. The outstanding naval commander in war, honored by rank of admiral, created for him in 1866.

Farrar, Geraldine (fürär'), 1882–, American operatic soprano; pupil of Lilli Lehmann. Sang at the Metropolitan Opera, New York, 1906–22. Her most famous roles were in *La Bohème, Madame Butterfly,* and *Carmen.*

Farrell, James T(homas) (fă'rŭl), 1904–, American novelist. Wrote realistically of Chicago's Irish population in the *Studs Lonigan* trilogy (1923–35).

Farrell, city (pop. 13,644), W Pa., on Shenango R. at Ohio border and adjoining Sharon. A rail center, it has steel and iron works.

Fars (färs) or **Farsistan** (färsĭstän'), region (75,476 sq. mi.; pop. 1,403,583), SW Iran, corresponding to Seventh Prov. Almost identical with ancient Persis, nucleus of Persian Empire. Chief city is Shiraz, chief port Bushire.

farsightedness, vision defect resulting when light rays focus behind retina. It is caused by shortness of the eyeball from front to back.

Farsistan, Iran: see FARS.

fascism (fă'shĭzŭm). In narrower sense, Fascism was political and economic system in Italy under MUSSOLINI; it developed after 1922 and lasted until Italy's defeat in World War II. In wider sense, the term *fascism* has been applied rather loosely to similar ideologies elsewhere; e.g., to NATIONAL SOCIALISM in Germany, and to Franco's regime in Spain. Fascism in general has been negative reaction against socialism and democratic equalitarianism, its roots reaching back to reaction of ruling classes against French Revolution. It plays upon national pride and prejudice and often exploits ANTI-SEMITISM, and sets itself up as champion of law and order against threat of mob rule. In Italy particularly social unrest was mixed with nationalist dissatisfaction over poor fruits of victory after World War I. Governmental paralysis enabled Mussolini to become premier by a show of force. He posed as strong-armed savior of Italy from anarchy and Communism. With strong organization and party militia, Black Shirts, he set up dictatorship. Use of Roman fasces as emblem gave regime name Fascist. Fascism differed from Communism in two respects: it followed Darwinian theory of survival of fittest, making youth and struggle paramount; and its organization was based on representation by classes, making CORPORATIVE STATE. Masses were won by paternalistic methods of works and relief, but real power was in hands of élite.

Fashoda Incident (fŭshō'dŭ), 1898, diplomatic dispute between France and Great Britain caused by rivalry for control of upper Nile region. While British troops under Kitchener were quelling Mahdist revolt in N Sudan, a French–Ethiopian party led by J. B. Marchand entered S Sudan and took town of Fashoda (now Kodok). Upon British insistence the French withdrew from area and in March, 1899, yielded their claims to upper Nile region. Peaceful settlement mainly due to efforts of Delcassé.

fat: see FATS AND OILS.

fata morgana, optical illusion: see MIRAGE.

Fatehpur Sikri (fŭtŭpŏŏr' sĭk'rē), town, W Uttar Pradesh, India. On site of Mogul cap. founded 1569 by Akbar and abandoned 1584. Remains present a nearly intact Mogul city.

Fates, in Greek mythology, three goddesses who controlled lives of men; daughters of Zeus and Themis. Known as Moerae or Moirai; they were Clotho, who spun web of life, Lachesis, who measured its length,

and Atropos, who cut it off. Roman Fates were called Parcae (see PARCA) and Germanic, NORNS.

Fathers of the Church, orthodox Christian writers of early times (See PATRISTIC LITERATURE). One of many groupings distinguishes eight Doctors of the Church: (Greek Church) St. Basil the Great, St. Gregory Nazianzen, St. John Chrysostom, St. Athanasius; (Latin Church) St. Ambrose, St. Jerome, St. Augustine, St. Gregory the Great.

fatigue, in physiology, decreased ability or inability of tissue or organ to respond to stimulus because of continual stimulation without adequate rest. Believed to result from accumulation of waste products and using up of nutritive material in cells.

Fatima (fă'tĭmŭ), 606?–632, daughter of Mohammed by his first wife. Wife of Ali, mother of Husein; reputedly the ancestress of Fatimites.

Fátima (fä'tēmŭ), hamlet, W Portugal, near Leiria. Near-by shrine of Our Lady of the Rosary became a great Roman Catholic center of pilgrimage after apparitions of Virgin Mary to shepherd children in 1917.

Fatimite (fă'tĭmīt) or **Fatimide** (fă'tĭmĭd), family claiming to hold the CALIPHATE on basis of alleged descent from FATIMA, a daughter of Mohammed the Prophet. In c.904 Obaidallah, leader of Syrian Shiite group, went to NW Africa, where he was hailed as the long-awaited Mahdi. In 909 he claimed the caliphate in opposition to the Abbasids. Conquered Cyrenaica and Libya. His successors consolidated his empire and conquered Sicily, W Arabia, Palestine, and Syria. Cairo became Fatimite cap. with conquest of Egypt in 969. The sixth Fatimite caliph, Hakim, proclaimed 1020 that he was a reincarnation of God; his claim is still espoused by DRUSES. Fatimite rule officially came to an end when SALADIN entered Cairo in 1171.

fats and oils, simple or mixed glyceryl esters of organic acids of fatty-acid series, important in diet and industry. Fats usually are solid; oils, liquid. They are derived from both plants and animals. Vegetable oils are obtained by cold pressing of cleaned fruits or seeds; this is followed by warm pressing which yields industrial grades. Vegetable fats are usually made by hydrogenation of oils: hydrogen is brought into contact with heated oil in presence of catalyst. Fats and oils in the diet are an energy source; cod-liver oil contains vitamins A and D. See also OILS; PETROLEUM.

Fauchard, Pierre (pyĕr' fōshär'), 1678–1761, French dentist, a founder of modern dentistry.

Faulhaber, Michael von (mĭkh'äĕl fŭn foul'häbŭr), 1869–1952, German cardinal, archbishop of Munich, an unflinching opponent of the Nazis.

Faulkner, William (fôk'nŭr), 1897–, American novelist, b. Miss. His major novels are studies of family disintegration and of degeneration in an imaginary Miss. county. Though they are explicitly about the Deep South, they deal with universal problems of man and evil. Among them are *The Sound and the Fury* (1929), *As I Lay Dying* (1930), *Sanctuary* (1931), *Light in August* (1932), *Absalom, Absalom!* (1936), and *Intruder in the Dust* (1948). His literary style is often long-drawn and confused to represent the thoughts of his characters, and incidents in the novels are sometimes macabre. Has also written notable short stories. Was awarded the Nobel Prize in Literature for 1949. Earlier used the spelling Falkner.

fault, in geology, a fracture in the earth's surface, with displacement on one side of the fault plane relative to the other. This displacement may be horizontal, vertical, or oblique, or both horizontal and vertical. The immediate cause of faults is stretching and compression of the earth's crust; the remote causes are probably the same as those of folding, since faulting and folding alike are involved in mountain making. Faults are responsible for most earthquakes.

faun (fôn), in Roman religion, creature similar to Greek SATYR, half man and half goat.

Faunus (fô'nŭs), in Roman religion, popular god of nature, protector of farmers and herdsmen, identified with Greek PAN. He was attended by many little fauns.

Faure, Élie (ālē' fōr'), 1873–1937, French art historian. Related history of art to progress of human culture.

Faure, Félix (fäleks' fōr'), 1841–99, president of France (1895–99). His term was marked by the Dreyfus Affair.

Fauré, Gabriel (gäbrēēl' fōrā'), 1845–1924, French composer. His works, largely of a refined, intimate quality, include nocturnes and barcarolles for piano, chamber music, operas, a Requiem, and many songs.

Faust (foust) or **Faustus** (fô'stùs), in German legend, a learned doctor who sold his soul to the devil (Mephistopheles) in exchange for youth, knowledge, and magical power. Supposedly based on the life of one Dr. Johann Faust (d. 1541), the subject has been used in literature since 1570. The *Volksbuch* of Johannes Spies (1587), an early version, was the basis of Marlowe's *Dr. Faustus* (1593). GOETHE wrote a masterpiece on Faust (treated also by other authors, including Thomas Mann). Musical treatments of the legend include those by Berlioz, Gounod, Liszt, and Wagner.

Fausta (fô'stù), d. c.326, wife of Constantine I, daughter of Maximian, mother of Constantine II, Constantius II, and Constans I. Constantine I is supposed to have had her murdered after discovering that she had brought about the murder of his son Crispus through false accusations.

Faustina (fôstī'nù), name of two Roman empresses. **Faustina,** the elder, c.104–141, was wife of Antoninus Pius. **Faustina,** the younger, c.125–176, was wife and companion of Marcus Aurelius. Called *Mater Castrorum* [mother of camps].

fauvism (fō'vĭzùm) [Fr. *fauve* = wild beast], name adopted by group of French painters including Matisse, Derain, and Braque for short-lived art movement which preceded cubism. Essentially an expressionistic movement, marked by bold distortion and vivid color used for emotive effect.

Favre, Jules (zhül' fä'vrù), 1809–80, French statesman. A republican, he was a leading opponent of the July Monarchy and of Napoleon III. Served in provisional governments of 1848 and 1871.

Fawkes, Guy: see GUNPOWDER PLOT.

Fay, Charles Ernest (fā), 1846–1931, American mountain climber, known as "dean of American mountain climbing." First president (1902–8) American Alpine Club. Mt. Fay in Canadian Rockies named for him.

Fay, Sidney B(radshaw), 1876–, American historian, authority on European diplomatic history, known for *The Origins of the World War* (1928; 2d ed., 1939).

Fayetteville. 1 City (pop. 17,071), NW Ark., in the Ozarks; founded 1828. Farm trade center; has canning and woodworking. Captured by both sides in Civil War. Several battles fought near here (e.g., Pea Ridge). Main seat of Univ. of Arkansas (land-grant, state supported; coed.; chartered 1871, opened 1872, called Arkansas Industrial Univ. until 1899). **2** City (pop. 34,715), S central N.C., at head of navigation on Cape Fear R. and SSW of Raleigh; founded 1739 by Scots. Has textile and lumber mills. State cap. 1789–93; state convention ratified U.S. Constitution 1789. Occupied 1865 by Sherman, who destroyed arsenal. Fort Bragg, U.S. military reservation, near by. **3** Town (pop. 5,447), S Tenn., SSE of Nashville, in farm area. Has old inn (1813). Near by is site of Camp Blount, scene of troop-mustering for Andrew Jackson's campaign against the Creek Indians.

Fayum or **Faiyum** (both: fīyōōm'), fertile region, N Egypt, W of the Nile. Produces cereals, fruits, sugar cane, and cotton. Rich in archaeological remains, it has yielded many 8th-cent. papyri in ancient Egyptian and Arabic. Chief city, Fayum (pop. 72,465), is trade and rail center; cotton spinning.

Fe, chemical symbol of the element IRON.

Fear, Cape, promontory on Smith Isl., off SE N.C., at mouth of Cape Fear R. Lighthouse. Lightship off Frying-Pan Shoals (extend c.20 mi. to sea).

Feather, river rising in N Calif. in the Sierra Nevada and flowing S to Sacramento R. above Sacramento.

Rich gold strikes made here. Supports power projects.

feathers, skin outgrowths characteristic only of birds. Considered modified scales, they grow in definite areas called feather tracts or pterylae; each feather develops from papilla of cells of both layers of the skin embedded in a pit; blood supply nourishes it until feather is grown, then discontinues. Contour or body feathers consist of shaft bearing barbs with small barbules that have microscopic interlocking projections. Down feathers lack projections. Bristles are modified feathers.

February: see MONTH.

February Revolution, 1848, French revolution which overthrew LOUIS PHILIPPE (abdicated Feb. 24) and set up Second Republic. Caused by increasingly reactionary policy of king and his chief minister, GUIZOT, and by dissatisfaction of workers, whose condition had deteriorated in Industrial Revolution. Provisional government, which included Lamartine and LEDRU-ROLLIN, was predominantly bourgeois and moderate. At first, concessions were made to the radicals: right to work was guaranteed, national workshops (planned by Louis BLANC) were created. Deliberate sabotage and eventual dissolution of workshops led to JUNE DAYS rebellion, which was bloodily suppressed. After completion of republican constitution Louis Napoleon was elected president (Dec., 1838; see NAPOLEON III). February Revolution set off similar outbreaks in most of Europe; all were eventually suppressed.

Fécamp (fākā'), town (pop. 16,072), Seine-Inférieure dept., N France; fishing port on English Channel. Famous for benedictine liqueur invented here by monks. Abbey church is a splendid example of 12th-cent. Norman architecture.

Fechner, Gustav Theodor (fĕkh'nùr), 1801–87, German philosopher, founder of psychophysics.

Federal Art Project: see WORK PROJECTS ADMINISTRATION.

Federal Bureau of Investigation, division of U.S. Dept. of Justice, created 1908, given present name 1935. J. Edgar HOOVER is director. FBI investigates Federal law violations, including crimes pertaining to internal security.

Federal Capital Territory: see AUSTRALIAN CAPITAL TERRITORY.

Federal Communications Commission, independent executive agency of U.S. government estab. by Federal Communications Act of 1934. Replaced Federal Radio Commission (estab. 1927). FCC has jurisdiction over all radio and television activities.

Federal Constitutional Convention, in U.S. history, held at Philadelphia, May to Sept., 1787. Under Articles of Confederation the central government was too weak to be effective, incapable of enforcing obligations entered into with foreign nations, impotent to quell internal disorder or maintain economic stability among the states. The wealthy and conservative class and the investors in Western territories favored a stronger central government. All states except R.I. sent delegates to convention. George Washington presided. Convention's only real division lay between smaller states, wishing to retain their power, and larger states, wishing to have power fall where population and wealth lay. Disagreement centered on composition of new Congress. A compromise measure proposed by Oliver Ellsworth finally won approval; this provided for Congress as it is now constituted. James Madison was chief drafter of Constitution; Gouverneur Morris also worked on it. Document went to states for ratification. Despite opposition, a sufficient majority to make Constitution binding had ratified it by the end of June, 1788.

federal government, a union of states which delegate some powers to the central government. It is always stronger than a confederation, having power over individuals as well as over the local governments. Federal powers usually include war, coinage, foreign relations, and commerce. Federal government has developed out of confederations, of which there are many examples, from the Greek city-states to such groups as the Hanseatic League (13th cent.), the Swiss Confederation (1291), and the U.S. (1781; superseded by a more centralized federation in 1789).

Federalist Papers, series of 85 essays written by Alexander Hamilton, James Madison, and John Jay in 1788 explaining and urging adoption of the Federal Constitution, then before the states for decision. Widely published in newspapers, they helped greatly to secure the Constitution's adoption.

Federalist party, in U.S. history. When political division appeared in Pres. Washington's cabinet the party that emerged to champion views of Alexander HAMILTON was Federalist party. It was conservative, favoring a strong centralized government, encouragement of industries, attention to needs of great merchants and landowners, and establishment of a well-ordered society. Pro-British in foreign affairs. Geographically, they were concentrated in New England, with strong element in Middle Atlantic states. After Democratic victory of 1800, Federalist party remained powerful locally, but leadership passed to reactionaries, rather than moderates. Federalist opposition to EMBARGO ACT OF 1807 and to War of 1812 resulted in HARTFORD CONVENTION. Successful issue of war ruined party; by election of 1824 it was virtually dead.

Federal Power Commission, independent executive agency of U.S. government estab. by Federal Water Power Act of 1920. Commission controls activities of privately-operated hydroelectric and natural-gas projects on navigable rivers and public lands. Also supervises various parts of Federal hydroelectric projects.

Federal Reserve System, central banking system of the U.S., established 1913. Each of 12 reserve banks (at Boston, N.Y., Philadelphia, Cleveland, Richmond, Atlanta, Chicago, St. Louis, Minneapolis, Kansas City, Dallas, San Francisco) serves a national region. All national banks belong to this system and must maintain reserves on deposit with their regional reserve banks. The operation of the reserve system is on a nonprofit basis. System seeks to maintain sound national monetary and credit conditions; it has markedly improved American banking.

Federal Theatre Project: see WORK PROJECTS ADMINISTRATION.

Federal Trade Commission (FTC), U.S. government commission (set up 1914) serving to check monopolies, prevent fraudulent advertising, investigate doubtful business practices, and preserve competition. Its attempts at legal enforcement of its cease-and-desist orders, in cases where violations are observed, have frequently been frustrated by differing court interpretations of the intent and phrasing of antitrust laws. It now seeks to obtain voluntary adoption of its recommendations wherever possible.

Federal Writers' Project: see WORK PROJECTS ADMINISTRATION.

federation: see FEDERAL GOVERNMENT.

Fedor. For Russian rulers thus named, see FEODOR.

feeble-mindedness, state of arrested mental development. In U.S. three degrees are recognized: idiots (I.Q., 0–25) who have mental age up to three years, need constant supervision; imbeciles (I.Q., 26–50), mental age 3–7 years, can learn simple tasks, rarely reading; morons (I.Q., 51–70), mental age 8–12 years, can do manual labor as complex as operation of lathe or sewing machine under supervision. Less than 10 percent show physical defects: cretinism, stunted growth owing to underactive thyroid gland; Mongolism, mongoloid appearance caused by unknown influence on embryo; microcephalia, small skull, receding forehead, resulting from fetal injury; hydrocephalia, large head, protruding forehead, cause unknown, high infant mortality rate. Disease, glandular disturbance, birth injury, as well as heredity cause mental deficiency. In U.S. only 10 percent of feeble-minded are in institutions.

Fehling's solution (fā'lǐngs) is used to test for glucose,

fructose, and other reducing agents. Discovered by Hermann von Fehling (1812–85) German chemist. Two solutions, cupric sulphate and alkaline Rochelle salt, are combined just before use; when heated with reducing agent red precipitate forms.

Fehmgericht: see VEHMGERICHT.

Feininger, Lyonel (fī'nǐng-ûr), 1871–, American painter. Until 1907 worked as illustrator and cartoonist. Taught at the Bauhaus in Germany (1919–32) and at colleges in U.S.

Feisal or **Faisal** (both: fī'sùl), kings of Iraq. **Feisal I,** 1885–1933, reigned 1921–33. In 1916 joined T. E. Lawrence in Arab revolt against Turkey. Became king of Syria in 1920 but deposed in same year by the French. Won Iraqi throne with British support. **Feisal II,** 1935–, succeeded his father, Ghazi I, in 1939. State affairs are conducted by a regent. Visited U.S. 1952.

Feke, Robert (fēk), c.1705–c.1750, early American portrait painter, b. Oyster Bay, N.Y. Worked in Newport, New York, Philadelphia, and Boston.

feldspar or **felspar,** mineral of many widely distributed varieties. It has clean cleavage planes in two directions. It is colorless when pure but occurs in pinkish, red, white, gray, and other colors. As constituents of granite and other crystalline rocks the feldspars form part of the earth's crust.

Felix V, antipope: see AMADEUS VIII.

Felixstowe (fē'lĭkstō), urban district (pop. 15,080), Suffolk East, England. It is a fishing port, seaplane base, and summer resort (yachting).

Feller, Robert William Andrew (Bob Feller), 1918–, American baseball pitcher. Right-handed ace of Cleveland Indians (1936–). Holds two major-league records —most strikeouts in one game (18, against Detroit Tigers, 1938), most strikeouts in one season (348, 1946). Pitched 3 no-hitters.

Fellows, Sir Charles, 1799–1860, English archaeologist, who discovered 15 anc. cities in Asia Minor. Brought back group of marbles, now in British Mus.

felony, grave crime, in contrast to a misdemeanor, or petty crime. Felonies in Great Britain and U.S. are usually tried by jury and carry with them as possible consequences imprisonment, loss of citizenship, or (for an alien) deportation.

felspar: see FELDSPAR.

felt, fabric made by matting (felting) together the fibers of wool, hair, or fur. Woven felt is a coarse fabric with nap first raised by teaseling, then ironed flat; true felt, however, is a fiber mass compressed to desired thickness. As an art, feltmaking antedates weaving.

Felton, William Harrell, 1823–1909, American political leader. After Civil War he was leading independent Democrat of Ga., opposing reactionary machine politics. U.S. Representative (1875–81). His second wife, **Rebecca Latimer Felton,** 1835–1930, was first woman to enter U.S. Senate, serving briefly in 1922 by appointment.

Femgericht: see VEHMGERICHT.

feminism, movement for political, social, and educational equality for women and men. Prior to Industrial Revolution women had no personal or property rights. Early leaders in England such as Mary Astell and Mary WOLLSTONECRAFT pleaded in vain. In U.S. active feminist movement dates from 1848 convention at Seneca Falls, N.Y., where Elizabeth Cady STANTON, Lucretia MOTT, and others issued a declaration of independence for women. Sparked by leaders such as Mrs. Stanton and Susan B. ANTHONY, movement spread rapidly. See also WOMAN SUFFRAGE.

fencing, sport of attack and defense with foil, épée, saber, and similar weapons, by two opponents. Held on strip 40 ft. long, about 6 ft. wide. In 1920 the sport was first included in the Olympics.

Fénelon, François de Salignac de la Mothe (frăswä' dù sălēnyäk' dù lä môt' fănülō'), 1651–1715, French theologian and author, archbishop of Cambrai. Wrote *Télémaque* (1699) for young duke of Burgundy, his pupil. Defended QUIETISM.

Feng Yu-hsiang (fŭng' yü'–shyäng), 1880–1948, Chinese general, called the Christian General. Fought with Chang Tso-lin and Wu P'ei-fu, 1920–26, for control of N China and Manchuria. Later, though an opponent of Chiang Kai-shek, he held high posts in Nationalist government.

Fenian movement (fē'nĕun), Irish secret revolutionary society (organized c.1858) for independence from England by force. Under James Stephens (1825–1901), the main appeal in Ireland was to the nonagrarian population and was opposed by the Catholic Church. Risings and terrorism led first to suppression by the British but finally to their attention to Irish problems. In U.S. John O'Mahony was the leader of embittered Irish emigrants whose attempts to invade Canada increased Anglo-American tension at end of Civil War—although Fenian raids fostered Canadian confederation. By 1914 Fenian influence was drawn into the new SINN FEIN organization founded by a former Fenian.

Fenn College: see CLEVELAND, Ohio.

fennel, Old World herb (*Foeniculum vulgare*) with fine, licorice-scented foliage and seeds used to flavor sauces, bread, liqueurs. Finochio or sweet fennel has bulbous-based stalk eaten like celery.

Fens, the, district W and S of the Wash, England. Includes parts of Bedford, Norfolk, Cambridge, Huntingdon, and Lincoln counties. Extending c.70 mi. from N to S and c.35 mi. from E to W, it is traversed by several streams. Originally a swampland; Romans attempted drainage and built roads. First effective drainage developed by Cornelius Vermuyden (Dutch) after 1621. District now has fertile soil and is largely cultivated.

Fenton, Reuben Eaton, 1819–85, U.S. Senator from N.Y. (1869–75). Fought with Sen. Roscoe Conkling over distribution of patronage; Conkling won.

Feodor (fyô'dùr), tsars of Russia. **Feodor I,** 1557–98, son of Ivan the Terrible, reigned 1584–98. Dominated by his brother-in-law and successor, Boris GODUNOV. **Feodor II,** 1589–1605, succeeded his father Boris Godunov; was killed the same year at accession of first false DMITRI. **Feodor III,** 1656–82, succeeded his father Alexis 1676. Crippled; energetic reformer. His brother Ivan V and half-brother Peter I jointly succeeded him. Name sometimes appears as Theodore.

Feodosiya (fä"ŭdô'sĕu), city (pop. 28,656), RSFSR, E Crimea, on Black Sea. Grain export center; health resort. Founded 6th cent. B.C. by Greek colonists as Theodosia; known as Caffa or Kaffa in Middle Ages, when Genoese had flourishing colony here, from which they virtually monopolized Black Sea trade. Fell to khan of Crimea 1475, to Russia 1783. Twice occupied by Germans in World War II. Ruins of Genoese fortifications.

Ferber, Edna, 1887–, American novelist, playwright, author of novels (e.g., *So Big,* 1924; *Show Boat,* 1926, later a musical), stories, plays.

fer-de-lance (fâr"dù-läs'), poisonous snake, c.5–6 ft. long, related to bushmaster and rattlesnake and found in tropical America and some of West Indies. It hunts at night.

Ferdinand, emperors, kings of Hungary and Bohemia. **Ferdinand I,** 1503–64, younger brother of Emperor CHARLES V, was brought up in Spain at court of his grandfather Ferdinand the Catholic. Charles gave him Austria (1521), had him crowned German king (1531), put him in charge of German affairs, and abdicated in his favor (1558). Meanwhile, Ferdinand had inherited Hungary and Bohemia from his brother-in-law, LOUIS II of Hungary (1526). In Hungary, he fought against rival claimants JOHN I and JOHN II, whom Sultan SULEIMAN I was supporting. Eventually, Ferdinand kept NW Hungary and the royal title but had to pay tribute to sultan. In Bohemia, Ferdinand vigorously pushed the Catholic Reform and established Hapsburg absolutism by abolishing most of local liberties (1547). In Germany he dealt with the PEASANTS' WAR

and other rebellions and negotiated the PEACE OF AUGSBURG (1555). His grandson **Ferdinand II,** 1578–1637, succeeded his cousin MATTHIAS as king of Bohemia (1617) and Hungary (1618) and as emperor (1619). In 1619 the Bohemian nobles rebelled against him (because of his strong anti-Protestant stand) and elected FREDERICK THE WINTER KING. Thus the THIRTY YEARS WAR began. Ferdinand defeated Frederick (1620). His generals won major victories, but Ferdinand's Edict of Restitution (1629) provoked renewed opposition. He almost certainly instigated the murder of WALLENSTEIN (1634). The war reached its conclusion under his son, **Ferdinand III,** 1608–57, who succeeded him as king of Hungary (1626) and Bohemia (1627) and as emperor (1637). Under him the war took a disastrous turn, and he reluctantly accepted the Peace of WESTPHALIA (1648).

Ferdinand, 1793–1875, emperor of Austria (1835–48). Was subject to fits of insanity. A council of state, dominated by METTERNICH, governed in his name. Fled Vienna after outbreak of 1848 revolution; abdicated in favor of nephew Francis Joseph.

Ferdinand, 1861–1948, tsar of Bulgaria (1908–18); a prince of Saxe-Coburg-Gotha. Was chosen to succeed Alexander of Battenberg as prince of Bulgaria (1887); took advantage of Young Turk revolution (1908) to declare full independence of Bulgaria and proclaim himself tsar. First triumphed, then lost, in BALKAN WARS (1912–13). In World War I he joined Central Powers (1915). Was forced to abdicate in favor of his son, Boris III. Died in Germany.

Ferdinand II, king of Aragon: see FERDINAND V, Spanish king of Castile.

Ferdinand, kings of Portugal. **Ferdinand I,** 1345–83, nicknamed "the Handsome" and "the Inconstant"; reigned 1367–83. Leonor Teles, whom he married after securing dubious annulment of earlier marriage, had a baleful influence on his reign. He fought three unsuccessful wars against Henry II and John I of Castile. In 1382 he abandoned his ally, JOHN OF GAUNT, and made peace with John I, to whom he gave his daughter and heiress Beatrice in marriage. Portugal would thus have gone to Castile after his death if a revolution had not given the throne to John of Aviz (see JOHN I of Portugal). **Ferdinand II,** 1816–85, oldest son of Ferdinand, duke of Saxe-Coburg-Gotha, was titular king of Portugal (1837–55) through his marriage with MARIA II.

Ferdinand, 1865–1927, king of Rumania (1914–27). Entered World War I on Allied side (1916); annexed Bessarabia (1918); intervened in Hungary to break up Communist government of Bela Kun (1919); acquired Transylvania and SE Hungary in peace treaties. Agr. reforms and universal suffrage were introduced during his reign. His consort was MARIE of Rumania. Succeeded by grandson MICHAEL.

Ferdinand, Spanish kings. **Ferdinand I** (the Great), d. 1065, king of Castile (1035–65) and Leon (1037–65); son of Sancho III of Navarre. Reduced Moorish emirs of Saragossa, Badajoz, Seville, and Toledo to vassalage. Divided his kingdom among three sons. **Ferdinand III,** 1199–1252, king of Castile (1217–52) and Leon (1230–52). Crusaded successfully against Moors. Canonized a saint of Roman Church (1671). **Ferdinand IV,** 1285–1312, king of Castile and Leon (1295–1312). Conquered Gibraltar. **Ferdinand V** or **Ferdinand the Catholic,** 1452–1516, king of Castile and Leon (1474–1504); king of Aragon (as Ferdinand II, 1479–1516), king of Sicily (1468–1516), king of Naples (1504–16); son of John II of Aragon. Married ISABELLA I of Castile (1469), shared kingship of Castile with her until her death (1504), when he became regent for his daughter JOANNA. The Catholic Kings, as Ferdinand and Isabella are called, completed the reconquest of Spain from the Moors by taking GRANADA (1492); expelled JEWS and Moors from Spain (1492; 1502); instituted Spanish INQUISITION; financed expedition of Christopher COLUMBUS (1492); divided world with Portugal by Treaty of TORDESILLAS (1494). Their reign thus was crucial in the history of the world as well as of Spain. Ferdinand also took a leading part in the ITALIAN WARS and annexed most of NAVARRE (1512). His grandson, Emperor CHARLES V, inherited the Spanish empire from him. **Ferdinand VI,** b. 1712 or 1713, d. 1759, king of Spain (1746–59); son of Philip V and Marie Louise of Savoy. Sent his stepmother Elizabeth Farnese into retirement. Kept Spain neutral in Seven Years War. **Ferdinand VII,** 1784–1833, king of Spain (1808–33). Deposed his father CHARLES IV, but was lured to Bayonne by Napoleon I, who forced him to renounce throne in favor of Charles IV, who in turn was forced to resign his rights to Napoleon (1808). Imprisoned in France until 1814, when he was restored to Spanish throne. He disappointed his liberal supporters by abolishing constitution of 1812. A revolution in 1820 forced him to reinstate it, but in 1823 French military intervention (sanctioned by Holy Alliance) restored him to full authority, and he revoked the constitution once more. He set aside the Salic law to give the succession to his daughter ISABELLA II; the Carlist Wars resulted (see CARLISTS). During his reign Spain lost its colonies on N and S American mainland.

Ferdinand, kings of the Two Sicilies. **Ferdinand I,** 1751–1825. In 1759 he became king of Naples as Ferdinand IV, of Sicily as Ferdinand III. Succeeding his father, who had become king of Spain as Charles III. Promoted absolutism under influence of Queen MARIE CAROLINE and Sir John ACTON. Suppressed PARTHENOPEAN REPUBLIC (1799), but after joining Third Coalition against Napoleon I (1805) he lost Naples to French (1806–15). After his restoration he styled himself king of the Two Sicilies as Ferdinand I (1816), ruled despotically. **Ferdinand II,** 1810–59, reigned 1830–59. During revolutionary outbreaks of 1848–49, he ordered bombardments of Messina and Palermo, thus earning nickname "King Bomba."

Ferdinand the Catholic: see FERDINAND V.

Fergana Valley or **Ferghana Valley** (fĕrgä'nù), region, central Asiatic USSR, in Uzbek SSR, Tadzhik SSR, and Kirghiz SSR. Fergana Range (part of Tien Shan system) rises in NE, Pamir in S. Drained by SYR DARYA R., valley consists partly of desert, partly of densely populated irrigated steppe (cotton, grapes, fruit). Kokand is chief city. One of world's oldest cultivated regions, valley has long been a major silk-producing area, with such ancient trade centers as MARGELAN and OSH. Arabs introduced Islam 8th cent. Valley passed under rule of shahs of KHOREZM (12th-14th cent.), of Jenghiz Khan, of Tamerlane, and of Uzbek khans of KOKAND (16th–19th cent.). Russian conquest completed 1876.

Fergus Falls, city (pop. 12,917), W Minn., SE of Fargo, N.Dak.; settled 1857. Dairy and wood products.

Ferguson, James Edward, 1871–1950, governor of Texas (1915–17). Impeached and removed from office. His wife, **Miriam A. Wallace Ferguson,** 1875–, known as Ma Ferguson, became governor in 1925; served again 1933–35. Ferguson was actual, though not nominal, governor.

Ferguson, suburban city (pop. 11,573), E Mo., NW of St. Louis; settled c.1874.

Fergusson, Robert, 1750–74, Scottish poet, author of "Auld Reekie."

Ferid ed-Din Attar (fĕrēd' ĕdēn' ùtär'), d. c.1229, Persian poet, a Sufi; one of greatest mystic poets of Islam. Also called Faridun.

Fermanagh (fùrmă'nù), inland county (653 sq. mi.; pop. 53,040), N. Ireland, in Ulster; co. town Enniskillen. Erne R. divides county almost in half. Hilly land, largely devoted to grazing. Exports include butter, eggs, and oats. Pottery and linen are made, and some limestone and sandstone quarried.

Fermat, Pierre de (pyěr' dù fěrmä'), 1601–65, French mathematician, known as founder of modern theory of numbers and calculus of probabilities.

fermentation, chemical change caused by enzyme action. Formation of lactic acid in milk and production of vinegar are fermentation. Alcoholic fermentation is most important commercially. Pasteur proved it is caused by yeast; later it was found that yeast enzyme system of which zymase is chief component is responsible. Reaction involves production of alcohol and carbon dioxide from simple sugars; it is a source of both industrial alcohol and alcoholic beverages.

Fermi, Enrico (ĕnrē'kō fěr'mē), 1901–, American physicist, b. Italy. Won 1938 Nobel Prize for work on radioactive substances. He greatly aided atomic bomb project by research (1934–38) and active participation after 1939 when he came to U.S.

fern, flowerless perennial plant of which there are more than 6,000 species, widely distributed, especially in tropics. They range in form from the climbing fern to the TREE FERN. Those of North America usually have green fronds (leaves) rising from a rootstalk. Reproduction is by asexual spores usually found on backs of fronds or on special frond stalks. Valued as ornamental plants for growing in shade and as house plants (e.g., Boston fern).

Fernández or **Hernández, Gregorio** (grāgō'rēō fěrnändäth, ěrnän'däth), c.1576–1636, Spanish baroque sculptor of religious figures.

Fernández de Córdoba, Francisco (fränthē'skō fěrnän'däth dä kōr'dhōbä), d. 1518?, Spanish explorer. Died of wounds suffered in battle with Mayas in Yucatan.

Fernández de Córdoba, Francisco, d. 1526?, Spanish conquistador. Sent by Pedrarias (1524) to take Nicaragua from González de Ávila, he tried to seize territory for himself; he was captured and executed.

Fernández de Córdoba, Gonzalo (gōnthä'lō), 1453–1515, Spanish general, called the Great Captain. Took part in conquest of Granada; expelled French from Naples twice (1495, 1503). First Spanish viceroy of Naples.

Fernández de Lizardi, José Joaquin (hōsā' hwäkēn' fěrnän'däs dä lēsär'dē), 1776–1827, Mexican journalist, novelist, and dramatist, author of novel *El Periquillo Sarniento* (1816–30).

Fernández de Moratín, Leandro (lään'drō fěrnän'däth dä mōrätēn'), 1760–1828, Spanish dramatist, author of comedies after the manner of Molière.

Fernández Navarrete, Juan: see NAVARRETE, JUAN FERNÁNDEZ.

Fernandina (fûrnändē'nù), city (pop. 4,420), NE Fla., on Amelia Isl. at mouth of St. Marys R. Site of Spanish fort in 1680s. Changed hands many times in 18th cent. Declared free port in 1808, it developed rapidly as base of pirates, slave traders, smugglers. Permanently captured by U.S. 1817. Fort Clinch (built 1847–61) captured by Union troops, 1862.

Fernando da Noronha (fěrnän'dō dù nùrō'nyä), islands in Atlantic, off NE Brazil. Discovered by Portuguese (1503). Long used as a penal colony by Brazil, it is now military base.

Fernán González (fěrnän' gônthä'läth), d. 970, count of Castile. Won virtual independence from Leon. Hero of 13th-cent. popular epic poem.

Ferndale, city (pop. 29,675), SE Mich., N residential suburb of Detroit. Mfg. of metal products and synthetic resins.

Fernel, Jean François (zhä fräswä' fěrněl'), 1497–1558, French physician and author of influential works on medicine, mathematics, and astronomy.

Ferney-Voltaire (fěrnā'-vôltěr'), village, Ain dept., E France, near Geneva. Voltaire bought seigniory 1758; lived here till 1778; founded still flourishing pottery industry.

Ferrar, Nicholas (fē'rùr), 1592–1637, English theologian, founder of religious community at Little Gidding, Huntingdonshire.

Ferrara (fär-rä'rä), city (pop. 58,187), Emilia-Romagna, N central Italy. Agr. center. Its past splendor as princely cap. of the ESTE family is recalled by its palaces and works of art. It declined after passing to Papal States (1598). Notable buildings include Palazzo dei Diamanti, Schifanoia palace, 14th-cent. moated castle, Romanesque cathedral. It was the birthplace of Savonarola.

Ferrara-Florence, Council of, 1438–45, second part of 17th ecumenical council of Roman Church (see BASEL, COUNCIL OF). Chief goal at Ferrara was to end Schism of East and West. Promoted by Byzantine Emperor John VII, who hoped Christian union might save his empire from the Turks. Leading figure was Bessarion, archbishop of Nicaea. In Jan., 1439, the council moved to Florence, and in July the pope issued the bull *Laetentur coeli,* announcing the religious union of E and W churches. After the Eastern delegates went home, the party opposing union gained power. The council moved to the Lateran (1443) and devoted itself to reuniting smaller, non-Orthodox E churches and the Holy See.

Ferrari, Gaudenzio (goudän′tsēō fĕr-rä′rē), c.1480–1546, Italian religious painter, a leading member of Lombard school.

Ferraris, Galileo (gälēlä′ō fär-rä′rēs), 1847–97, Italian physicist and electrical engineer. He discovered the rotary magnetic field and thereby promoted the development of alternating-current motors.

Ferrel, William (fĕ′rŭl), 1817–91, American meteorologist. Worked on government coast and geodetic survey (1867–82); did research on tides, currents, winds, storms. Formulated **Ferrel's law:** because of earth's rotation moving bodies on earth's surface are deflected to right in N Hemisphere, to left in S Hemisphere; amount varies with velocity of motion and latitude (zero at equator, greatest near poles).

Ferrer, José (Vicente), 1912–, American actor, director, and producer, b. Puerto Rico. After his debut in 1935 he won acclaim in such varied plays as *Charley's Aunt, Othello* (as Iago), and *Cyrano de Bergerac* and such films as *Joan of Arc, Cyrano de Bergerac,* and *Moulin Rouge.*

Ferrer, Vincent: see VINCENT FERRER, SAINT.

Ferrero, Guglielmo (gōōlyĕl′mō fā-rä′rō), 1871–1942, Italian man of letters and historian. Noted for works on Roman history, notably *The Greatness and Decline of Rome* (Eng. tr., 5 vols., 1907–9).

ferret. American (black-footed) ferret is largest and very rare North American weasel. It inhabits Great Plains; chief prey is prairie dog. It is c.2 ft. long, yellow-buff marked with brown, with black band across eyes, black-tipped tail, and black feet. Old World ferret is domesticated polecat (c.14 in. long) used in hunting.

Ferri, Ciro (chē′rō fĕr′rē), 1634–89, Italian painter, pupil and follower of Pietro da Cortona.

Ferris wheel, huge, revolving wheel for carrying passengers in cars suspended on the wheel, built by George W. Ferris, American engineer, for World's Columbian Exposition (1893).

Ferrol, El (ĕl fĕröl′), officially **El Ferrol del Caudillo** (dĕl koudhĕ′lyō), city (pop. 40,664), NW Spain, in Galicia, on the Atlantic. Important naval base. Birthplace of Francisco Franco.

Ferry, Jules (zhül′ fĕrē′), 1832–93, French statesman. Minister of education (1879–80, 1882); premier (1880–81, 1883–85). Established modern French educational system on secular, anticlerical basis. Built up French colonial empire in Africa, Indo-China.

ferry, a passage across water by boat, provided for the public upon payment of toll. Ferries include rowboats for transport of persons, flat-bottomed barges (carrying vehicles, persons, or animals) propelled by hand or by utilizing water currents, and power-driven ferryboats. Trains can be carried across the English Channel by ferry.

Fersen, Hans Axel, Count (häns′ äk′sŭl fĕr′sŭn), 1755–1810, Swedish soldier. Served in French army from 1779; became a favorite of Marie Antoinette; helped to plan flight of royal family (1791) and himself drove their coach out of Paris. Made marshal of Sweden 1801. Killed by a mob after Swedish revolution.

fertility rites, magico-religious rites to insure ample food and birth of children. In primitive cultures natural phenomena, such as cycle of vegetation, were personified and symbolized in mythical marriages of earth-goddess and sun-god and birth and death of their progeny. Myths of death and resurrection of the hero-god (e.g., Adonis) were the basis of elaborate fertility rites, frequently phallic in nature. Later MYSTERIES apparently grew out of fertility rites. The sacred drama was developed from them. Survivals in disguised form abound (e.g., Maypole dance and carnivals).

fertilization, in biology, a process in plant and animal reproduction, involving union of two unlike sexual cells, or gametes (SPERM and OVUM). Process occurs in seed-producing plants after POLLINATION. **Cross-fertilization,** in botany, refers to fusion of sperm of one flower with ovum of another, in contrast to self-fertilization (fusion of sperm and ovum in one flower).

fertilizer, material containing nitrogen, phosphorus, potash, and other elements essential to plant growth, applied to soil or other growing medium. Fertilizers may be organic (e.g., animal manures, bone meal), or inorganic or commercial (e.g., nitrate of soda, superphosphate).

fescue (fĕs′kū), annual or perennial grass (*Festuca*), used for pasture, forage, or lawns.

Fessenden, William Pitt (fĕ′sŭndŭn), 1806–69, American statesman. U.S. Representative from Maine (1841–43). U.S. Senator (1855–64, 1865–69). U.S. Secretary of the Treasury (1864–65). Made excellent record in public finance.

Festival of Lights, Jewish festival: see HANUKKAH.

Festus, Sextus Pompeius, fl. at some time between A.D. 100 and 400, Roman lexicographer. His surviving work, *On the Meaning of Words,* an abridgment of the lost glossary of M. Verrius Flaccus, is an important source for Roman antiquities.

Festus, city (pop. 5,199), E Mo., on the Mississippi below St. Louis. Shoes, textiles, grain products.

Fetterman, William Judd, 1833?–1866, American army officer. **Fetterman massacre** occurred when, despite his unfamiliarity with frontier conditions and methods of Indian fighting, he volunteered to lead supply party of 80 men, ignored orders not to leave trail, and was ambushed by Indians under Red Cloud. Entire party was killed.

fetus or **foetus** (both: fē′tŭs), unborn offspring of a viviparous animal, especially in later stages of development. In earlier prenatal life the offspring is called an embryo. Circulatory system is separate from maternal system; nourishment and oxygen are received through placenta.

Feuchtwanger, Lion (lē′ōn foikht′väng-ŭr), 1884–, German author; in U.S. after 1940. Historical novels include *The Ugly Duchess* (1923), *Jud Süss* (1925; U.S. ed., *Power*), and the *Josephus* trilogy (1923–42). All these have been translated into English.

feudalism, social order in W Europe from end of Charlemagne's empire to rise of absolute monarchies. Basic character was local, agricultural political economy. Usual unit was manor—peasants, VILLEIN and SERF, held land from lord of manor, the seigneur, who gave protection and use of land in return for personal services and dues. This was MANORIAL SYSTEM. In ideal feudal society, ownership of all land was vested in king. Under him was hierarchy of nobles, highest holding from him directly, lesser ones from them, and so on to seigneur, holding single manor. Holding was by fief, acquired by formal ceremony of INVESTITURE. Basically system rested upon unsettled conditions of time and a lord's need for armed warriors. The KNIGHT was the typical warrior. Gradations of nobility were based on both land-holding and military service. The Church had great influence in shaping feudalism; it owned much land, and its hierarchy somewhat paralleled feudal system. The system probably had its roots in disruption of decaying Roman institutions by inroads and settlements of Germans. It spread from

France to Spain, to Italy, and later to Germany and E Europe. Frankish form was imposed on England by William the Conqueror (1066). System disappeared gradually with rise of monarchies that broke down local systems, but it persisted in France until French Revolution (1789), in Germany and Japan until 19th cent., and in Russia until 1917.

Feuerbach, Ludwig, 1804–72, German philosopher. Abandoned Hegelianism for materialism, asserting religion is but a symbolic "dream."

Feuermann, Emanuel (foi′ürmän), 1902–42, virtuoso cellist, b. Kolomea, Galicia. Taught in Europe and America. Gave concerts in U.S. after 1935.

Feuillants (fûyä′), political club of French Revolution. Formed 1791 by right-wing JACOBINS led by Barnave. Advocated constitutional monarchy, peace policy. Suppressed by Jacobins in 1792.

feverfew, strong-scented perennial herb (*Chrysanthemum parthenium*), with small daisylike flowers.

fever therapy, treatment of disease by artificially produced fever. High temperature can destroy organisms causing disease without injuring patient. Original method of injecting microbes to produce fever, introduced 1917 by Wagner-Jauregg, is largely replaced by use of electric cabinets or blankets, hot baths, radiation, injection of foreign proteins.

Fez, city (pop. 200,946), French Morocco, at central point on routes to Tangier, Rabat, and Marrakesh. Fez was cap. of several dynasties (8th–19th cent.). Consists of old city (founded 808), new city (founded 1276), and European suburb. Has c.100 mosques and ancient Moslem university. Noted for native industries, it gave its name to the brimless felt cap.

Fianna Fail (fē′ŭnŭ fäl′) [Irish,= Fenians of Ireland], Irish political party (organized 1926). Led by Eamon DE VALERA, it opposed Irish Free State. In control of the government after 1932, it advocated complete separation from Great Britain. Defeated (1948) by a coalition, it returned to power in 1951.

fiber, threadlike strand, usually pliable and capable of being spun into yarn. Of about 40 commercially important kinds, those of animal origin (mainly composed of protein) include silk and wool and the hair of the goat (mohair), llama (alpaca), vicuña, camel, horse, rabbit, beaver, hog, badger, sable; vegetable fibers (containing mostly cellulose) include cotton, kapok, flax, hemp, Manila hemp, istle, ramie, sisal hemp, Spanish moss. Rayon and nylon are best-known synthetic fibers. Chief inorganic fiber is asbestos.

Fibiger, Johannes (yôhä′nŭs fē′bēgŭr), 1867–1928, Danish pathologist. Won 1926 Nobel Prize in Physiology and Medicine for his research on cancer.

Fibonacci, Leonardo (lāonär′dō fēbōnät′chē), late 12th, early 13th cent., Italian mathematician, also called Leonardo da Pisa. Wrote early work on algebra and arithmetic, standard for centuries; organized, extended known geometry and trigonometry.

Fichte, Johann Gottlieb (yō′hän gôt′lēp fīkh′tù), 1762–1814, German philosopher and political leader. His ethical idealism was a development of Kantianism. His *Addresses to the German People* (1808) awoke liberal nationalism.

Fichtelgebirge (fikh′tùlgùbēr′gù), mountain range, Upper Franconia, NE Bavaria, near Czech border. Highest point 3,447 ft. (Schneeberg). Many resorts.

Ficino, Marsilio (märsē′lyō fēchē′nō), 1433–99, Florentine humanist. He translated Plato into Italian, wrote works of Platonic philosophy, and forwarded humanism as head of Cosimo de′ Medici′s academy.

Field, Cyrus West, 1819–92, American promoter of first Atlantic cable. Unsuccessful attempts of 1857–58 preceded success of *Great Eastern* in laying a cable in 1866. His brother, **David Dudley Field,** 1805–94, a lawyer, worked in behalf of law reform. His codes of procedure for N.Y. were adopted by several other states; strongly influenced English Judicature Acts of 1873 and 1875. Also worked to establish a code of international law. Another brother, **Stephen Johnson**

Field, 1816–99, was U.S. Supreme Court Justice (1863–97). As member of Calif. legislature in 1850s, he estab. legal recognition of mining camp usages and regulations.

Field, Eugene, 1850–95, American poet, journalist. In Chicago *Daily News* (later the *Record*) his column, "Sharps and Flats," helped establish the newspaper columnist. His poems of childhood include "Little Boy Blue" and "Wynken, Blynken, and Nod."

Field, John, 1782–1837, composer and pianist, b. Dublin, settled in Russia. Chopin′s nocturnes were modeled after those of Field.

Field, Marshall, 1834–1906, American merchant. As head of Marshall Field and Co. from 1881, he pioneered in modern retailing practices. Benefactor of Art Institute of Chicago, Univ. of Chicago, Chicago Museum of Natural History (formerly Field Museum of Natural History). His grandson, **Marshall Field III,** 1893–, has devoted himself to various social projects. Backed New York city liberal newspaper *PM* (1940–48). Started Chicago *Sun* in 1941; merged it with Chicago *Times* in 1948.

Field, Stephen Johnson: see FIELD, CYRUS WEST.

Fielding, Henry, 1707–54, English novelist. Began career by writing comedies, farces, and parodies, with many attacks on Walpole′s government. These helped bring about the censorship of the Licensing Act (1737), and Fielding had to give up drama. His first novel *Joseph Andrews* (1742) was undertaken to burlesque Richardson′s *Pamela*. Strong satire laces the vigorous prose of his other fine realistic novels. *Tom Jones* (1749) is generally considered a masterpiece of world literature. Other novels are *Jonathan Wild* (1743), *Amelia* (1752).

Field Museum of Natural History: see CHICAGO NATURAL HISTORY MUSEUM.

Field of the Cloth of Gold, meeting ground of Henry VIII of England and Francis I of France, near Calais, France (1520); so called because of splendor of pageantry. Projected Franco-English alliance did not come off.

Fields, Lewis Maurice: see WEBER, JOSEPH.

Fiene, Ernest (fē′nù), 1894–, American painter, b. Germany. Best known for landscapes of New England and New York. A popular teacher.

Fiesole (fyä′zōlā), town (pop. 2,647), Tuscany, central Italy, on hill above Florence. Once an important Etruscan and Roman town (Faesulae). Has Roman theater, baths; Romanesque cathedral. Near-by Church of San Domenico has Fra Angelico paintings.

Fife or **Fifeshire,** maritime county (505 sq. mi.; pop. 306,855), Scotland, between Firths of Forth and Tay; co. town Cupar. Part of central Scottish Lowlands, well cultivated terrain rises to Lomond Hills. One of most prosperous Scottish counties, it has coal mining, linen mfg., brewing, and shipbuilding. Once home of the Picts, county has long been called kingdom of Fife. Saint Andrews, famous golfing resort, is seat of oldest Scottish University.

Fifth Avenue, famous street of Manhattan, New York city, from Washington Square to Harlem R. Business and shopping center between 34th and 59th Street; passes Empire State Building, New York Public Library, Rockefeller Center, and St. Patrick′s Cathedral. From 59th to 110th streets it borders Central Park. Runs through Harlem N of the park.

Fifth Monarchy Men, religious group during Puritan Revolution in England, millennarians expecting second coming of Christ, who would set up fifth monarchy (earlier four being Assyrian, Persian, Greek, and Roman empires). Opposed church and civil government.

Fifty-four forty or fight, phrase commonly used by extremists in controversy with Great Britain over Oregon country. They held that U.S. rights extended to lat. 54° 40′ N, the recognized S boundary of Russian America. Phrase was used by Democrats as 1844 campaign slogan. Boundary set in 1846 at 49°.

fig   328   Finland

fig, a tree (*Ficus carica*), native to Mediterranean region and long grown for its commercially valuable fruit, now cultivated in California and Gulf states. Some varieties require pollination by fig wasp before setting fruit.

figured bass, in music, a system of notation in which the notes of the bass part have figures written below them to indicate which chords are to be played. Also called thorough bass and *basso continuo.* Used much in harpsichord and organ music of baroque era. Now chiefly used as device for teaching harmony.

Fiji (fē'jē), island group (7,056 sq. mi.; pop. 259,638), S Pacific; most important British colony in the Pacific. Comprises 250 islands, of which 80 are inhabited. Main islands are Viti Levu, with Suva, cap. of colony, and Vanua Levu; gold mines on both islands. Crops include sugar cane, tropical fruits, rice, and cotton. Discovered 1643 by Tasman, annexed 1874 by Great Britain. Missionaries arriving in 1835 helped abolish cannibalism. Fijians, of Melanesian origin, make up only c.40% of population. Indian laborers, imported 1879–1916 under indenture system, are chiefly engaged in sugar industry. Governor of Fiji is also British high commissioner of Western Pacific.

filament, in incandescent lamp, threadlike wire (usually tungsten) wound in center of bulb, which becomes hot when current runs through it. In vacuum tube an uncoiled filament is used.

filament battery: see BATTERY, ELECTRIC.

Filaret, Vasily Drosdov: see PHILARET, VASILY DROSDOV.

filbert: see HAZEL.

Filene, E(dward) A(lbert) (filēn', fi–), 1860–1937, American merchant. As president of Boston firm of William Filene's Sons he pioneered in scientific methods of retail distribution.

filibuster, in 17th cent., buccaneer who plundered Spanish colonies in New World. In 19th cent., adventurer who led privately organized armed forays into friendly countries; e.g., from U.S. into Cuba and Mexico. Term now denotes obstructionist tactics in legislative bodies.

Filipino: see PHILIPPINE ISLANDS.

Fillmore, Millard, 1800–1874, 13th President of the United States (July, 1850–March, 1853). U.S. Representative from N.Y. (1833–35, 1837–43); promoted high tariff of 1842. Vice President of the U.S. (1849–50); succeeded to presidency on death of Zachary Taylor. Signed Compromise of 1850; tried to enforce Fugitive Slave Act. Upheld nonintervention in foreign disputes and approved treaty opening Japan to Western commerce. Unsuccessfully strove to make Whigs a national party to conciliate sectional struggle. Hoping to unite North and South, he joined KNOW-NOTHING MOVEMENT; its presidential candidate in 1856.

Fillmore, city (pop. 1,890), W central Utah. Territorial cap. 1851–56.

film, photographic: see PHOTOGRAPHY.

Filson, John, c.1747–1788, Kentucky pioneer, b. Pa. Author of *Discovery, Settlement, and Present State of Kentucke* (1784), containing alleged autobiography of Daniel Boone. Boone's subsequent high reputation mainly stems from this work.

filtration: see WATER.

fin, locomotive organ of fish consisting of cartilaginous or bony rays covered by thin tissue. In some (e.g., eel) single fin extends from back around tail along ventral surface. Majority have one, two, or three dorsal fins, a tail fin, an anal fin (called median or unpaired fins). Paired fins are pectoral (behind gills) and pelvic (position varies; sometimes lacking). Some (e.g., salmon, catfish) have adipose fin (fatty tissue without support) behind dorsal fin.

finch, member of largest bird family (Fringillidae). Finches have cone-shaped bills and eat chiefly seeds. Among the finches are SPARROW, GROSBEAK, CANARY, GOLDFINCH, BULLFINCH, chaffinch, INDIGO BUNTING, JUNCO, purple finch, hawfinch. See *ill.*, p. 105.

finder. The discoverer of lost property is treated differently in the various countries. In some he has the right to retain it against anyone except the owner. In most countries, however, he is obligated to deliver the property to the police, though he is entitled to a legally fixed reward against the owner. In some states (e.g., New York) the finder becomes the owner, if the article after delivery to the police is not claimed within a certain period.

Findlay, city (pop. 23,845), NW Ohio, on Blanchard R. and S of Toledo; laid out 1821. Mfg. of auto tires and tubes and agr. machinery; oil refineries. Findlay Col. is here.

Fingal: see FINN MAC CUMHAIL.

Fingal's Cave, unusually beautiful cavern, on Staffa Isl., Inner Hebrides, Scotland. Associated with many legends. Mendelssohn composed an overture called *The Hebrides* or *Fingal's Cave.*

Finger Lakes, W central N.Y., group of long, narrow glacial lakes in N-S valleys, in scenic resort and agr. (fruits, esp. grapes, vegetables, wheat) region between Geneseo and Syracuse. From W to E lakes are Conesus; Hemlock; Canadice; Honeoye; Canandaigua (kănŭndā'gwŭ) (c.15 mi. long); Keuka (kū'kŭ) (c.18 mi. long); Seneca (largest; extends c.35 mi. N from Watkins Glen to Geneva; on E shore is Sampson, where U.S. naval training station, estab. 1942, functioned for a time after 1946 as an emergency college for veterans); Cayuga (kàyōō'gŭ) (longest; c.38 mi. long; joined by canal to the Barge Canal, by Seneca R. to Seneca L.; on cliffs near S end are Cornell Univ. and Taughannock Falls, 215 ft. high); Owasco (c.11 mi. long); Skaneateles (skĭnēăt'lŭs) (15 mi. long; Syracuse water supply; at N end is Skaneateles resort village, pop. 2,331); Otisco.

fingerprint, an impression of the inside of the end of a finger or thumb, used for identification because the arrangement of lines is thought to be unique with each person. First practical classifications of fingerprints were those of Sir Francis Galton and Juan Vucetitch in 1891.

Fini, Tommaso di Cristoforo: see MASOLINO DA PANICALE.

Finiguerra, Maso or **Tommaso** (mä'zō, tôm-mä'zō fēnē-gwĕr'rä), 1426–64, Florentine goldsmith and engraver, who probably introduced copperplate engraving process into Italy.

Finistère (fēnēstâr'), department (2,714 sq. mi.; pop. 724,735), NW France, at the tip of Brittany; cap. Quimper.

Finisterre, Cape, rocky promontory, extreme NW Spain, on Atlantic. Here English navy twice defeated French (1747, 1805).

Fink, Albert, 1827–97, American engineer, b. Germany. Designed a truss bridge known by his name. After Civil War he helped regulate Southern railway freight rates.

Fink, Mike, 1770?–1822, American frontier hero, river boatman. A notable shot and fighter, he is said to have ended by shooting one companion and being shot by another.

Finland, Finnish *Suomi,* republic (117,970 sq. mi., with water surface 130,160 sq. mi.; pop. 4,076,624), N Europe; cap. Helsinki. Bounded in W and S by the Gulf of Bothnia and Gulf of Finland (branches of Baltic Sea); in NW by Sweden and Norway; in N and E by USSR. Central and S Finland is covered by thousands of interconnected lakes. N section (a part of LAPLAND) rises to 2,000–3,000 ft. Half of population is agr., although only 7% of land is arable. Forests cover c.70% of area; timber and timber products form chief exports. Major part of economic life is carried on by cooperatives. Most Finns are Lutherans. There is a small Swedish-speaking minority. Conquered and Christianized by Sweden (12th cent.), Finland was made a grand duchy (16th cent.), and was ceded by Sweden to Russia in 1809. With its own parliamentary constitution, Finland enjoyed semi-independence as Russian grand duchy, though Russian rule was tightened after 1890.

Full independence was proclaimed in 1917. Communists were defeated in civil war by Marshal MANNERHEIM; republic was established 1919. Land reforms made 90% of farmers independent. After outbreak of World War II, Russia demanded demilitarization of Finnish fortifications facing Leningrad (the Mannerheim Line) and cession of military bases. Finland refused, and Russian troops invaded Finland (Nov., 1939). Despite heroic and, at first, successful resistance, Russia won the war and by the peace treaty of March, 1940, obtained part of Karelian Isthmus, Vyborg, and other border sections. To recover its territories, Finland joined in the German attack on Russia (1941). Forced to capitulate in Sept., 1944, it kept its promise to expel German troops. N Finland suffered much in resulting German-Finnish warfare. Peace treaty between Finland and principal Allies (except U.S., which had not been at war with Finland) was signed at Paris in 1947. In addition to territories ceded in 1940, Finland ceded Petsamo and leased Porkkala area to USSR. Democratic government continued under Pres. Juho K. Paasikivi (elected 1946), despite recurrent tension with Communist party and USSR. Finland was the only country to honor its debts to U.S. after World War I.

Finlay, Carlos Juan, or **Charles John Finlay,** 1833–1915, Cuban physician of Scotch and French blood. In 1881 he suggested that yellow fever is carried by the mosquito (he specified genus *Stegomyia* as carrier in 1882). Reed Commission of 1900 undertook experiments which proved his theories.

Finlay, river of N B.C., Canada, rising in Stikine Mts. and flowing 210 mi. SE to join Parsnip R. at Finlay Forks and form chief tributary of the Peace.

Finnish language, one of the Finno-Ugric languages. See LANGUAGE (table).

Finn mac Cumhail, Fionn mac Cumhail, or **Finn Mac-Cool** (all: fĭn′ mŭkōōl′), a central hero in the Irish legend of OSSIAN and the original of Macpherson's Fingal. Leader of corps of professional fighters, the Fenians, in 3d cent.

Finnmark (fĭn′märk), county (18,799 sq. mi.; pop. 58,-790), N Norway, forming northernmost part of Scandinavian peninsula; cap. Vadso. NORTH CAPE is on one of numerous islands off coast. A plateau rising to barren glaciated mountains, Finnmark is largest and least populated county of Norway. Fishing, reindeer raising (mainly by Lapps) are main sources of livelihood.

Finno-Ugric languages: see LANGUAGE (table).

finochio: see FENNEL.

Finsbury, metropolitan borough (pop. 35,347), N London, England. Site of Bunhill Fields (Bunyan, Blake, Defoe, and Isaac Watts buried here), John Wesley's chapel and house, Sadler's Wells Theatre (home of English ballet), and mint of Bank of England.

Finsen, Niels Ryberg (nēls rü′bĕr fĭn′sùn), 1860–1904, Danish physician. Won 1903 Nobel Prize in Physiology and Medicine for method of treating certain diseases by light-ray therapy.

Finsteraarhorn (fĭn″stürär′hôrn″), peak 14,032 ft. high, Switzerland; highest of the Bernese Alps.

Fiorenzo di Lorenzo (fyōrän′tsō dē lōrän′tsō), b. c.1440, d. after 1521, Italian painter, b. Perugia. May have been master of Perugino.

fir, tall, coniferous evergreen tree (*Abies*), widely distributed. North American kinds include BALSAM FIR, silver fir, and red and white firs.

Firbank, (Arthur Annesley) Ronald, 1886–1926, English writer. His mannered short novels highly esteemed by some critics.

Firdausi (fürdou′sē) (Abul Kasim Mansur), c.940–1020, Persian poet, author of *Shah Namah* (great Persian epic, which set standard for Persian poetry).

fire. For nature of fire, see COMBUSTION and FLAME. There is no record of any human community without use of fire, an exclusively human property. Ideas of indispensability and mysterious force have made fire a sacred object (in Zoroastrianism and other sun-wor-

shiping religions it is a god). In Greece, fire in colony was kindled from that of mother city as tie between them. In Rome, cult of Vesta, goddess of hearth, was strong. Story of Prometheus, the fire bringer, is a great Greek myth. Greek philosophers regarded fire as one of the four elements.

fire apparatus, devices to combat fire or escape from it. Fire-fighting apparatus is designed to remove one or more of the conditions essential to burning: fuel, oxygen, and heat. For ordinary combustible materials (wood, paper, cloth), water is commonly used, serving to cool burning substance and help exclude oxygen. Since water spreads fires of liquid (e.g., gasoline, alcohol, oil, paint) and electrical types, they require chemicals. Soda and acid mixture is commonly used in metal extinguishers indoors. Addition of chemical detergents to water gives it greater penetrating power and this mixture is used for both forest fires and indoor fires (liquid, electrical, or ordinary). Foam-type extinguishers emit carbon dioxide foam from a cylindrical container. Vapor-type extinguishers include those of liquid carbon tetrachloride, which forms heavy vapor shutting off oxygen; and liquid carbon dioxide under pressure, which flakes upon release, vaporizes, and forms layer of gas over fire. Numerous chemicals are used in dry form. Sprinkler systems, from which excessive heat automatically releases water, are employed in many buildings. Motorized equipment includes pumping engines, hook-and-ladder trucks, searchlight apparatus, rescue wagons, smoke ejectors, water towers, chemical apparatus, and salvage weapons. Fireboats are used at sea and on water fronts.

firebrick, heat-resistant brick used in construction of kilns, furnaces, ovens, and fireplaces, especially in metalworking industries. Firebrick should not fuse below 1600° C. and should resist chemical decomposition. Its composition varies according to intended use.

fire clay, a clay high in percentage of silica and alumina, and offering great resistance to heat. Used in making firebrick and metalworking utensils such as crucibles and retorts.

firedamp: see DAMP.

fire-eaters, in U.S. history, term applied by Northerners to Southern proslavery extremists before Civil War. Led by R. B. Rhett and W. L. Yancey, they urged secession as early as 1850.

fire extinguisher: see FIRE APPARATUS.

firefly, luminescent carnivorous beetle (often called lightning bug) of family Lampyridae, more numerous in tropical than in temperate regions. Light organs on abdomen are several layers of small cells acting as reflectors and a lower layer of luminescent or photogenic cells, all permeated by nerves and by air tubes permitting oxidizing of luciferin in presence of enzyme called luciferase. Color of light (yellow, greenish, bluish, or reddish) varies with species, as do intensity and intervals between flashes. Light believed to be related to attraction between sexes. Males, females, larvae, and eggs of some forms emit light.

Fire Island, SE N.Y., c.30 mi. long, off S shore of Long Isl., between Great South Bay and the Atlantic. Has several resorts and a lighthouse (1858). Ferries from Bay Shore and Babylon.

fire lands: see WESTERN RESERVE.

Firenze, Italy: see FLORENCE.

fireproofing, method of making combustible materials resistant to fire. Usually it is a treatment with solution or coating which merely retards ignition. Wood can be impregnated with ammonium phosphate solution; paints can be made fire-retardant by using certain pigments (antimony oxide and calcium carbonate) or chlorinated resins, chlorinated oils, chlorinated paraffins. Asbestos and cement are mixed to make fireproof board. Fireproof doors are made of steel or of wood pressed between metal covering sheets; sometimes they are closed by automatic devices to check spread of fire. Hollow clay tile, brickwork, gypsum, plaster, and concrete are fire-resistant building construction materials. Steel fails rapidly above 1000° F. and must be protected when used in construction; very heavy slow-burning timber is sometimes used. Textiles are made flameproof by being dipped in or brushed with certain chemical solutions. Asbestos, which is noncombustible and a nonconductor of heat, is used for insulation, roofing, and many other purposes and the fibers can be woven into flexible cloth used in many products.

Firestone, Harvey Samuel, 1868–1938, American manufacturer of rubber products.

fireworks: see PYROTECHNICS.

Firkins, Oscar W., 1864–1932, American critic, a professor at the Univ. of Minnesota.

first aid. The immediate treatment of a patient in case of emergency while awaiting the arrival of a physician is often a means of saving life and also may result in a better and more rapid recovery. Prevention of further injury is important. Essential knowledge includes that of the proper bandage for a wound; that of the treatment of bleeding, fracture, sprain, dislocation, fainting, bites and stings, burns and scalds, poisoning (in all such cases call doctor), sunstroke, and heat exhaustion; and that of the method of artificial respiration for drowning and asphyxia. See also Red Cross literature.

Asphyxia. Symptoms: blue color; gasping; unconsciousness. Treatment: remove cause, e.g., a foreign body or gas; use artificial respiration.

Bites. Symptoms: wound. Treatment: bandage part on side towards heart. Use antivenin for snake bite. Cauterize with nitric acid for bite of rabid dog and follow with vaccination.

Bleeding. Symptoms: external wound; pallor; weakness if internal. Treatment: local pressure; temporary tourniquet for severe arterial bleeding.

Burns. Symptoms: redness; blistering; charring. Treatment: coat with oily material. If from acid, first use baking soda. If from alkali, first use vinegar. Caution: treat for shock.

Dislocation. Symptoms: pain; swelling; deformity of the joint. Treatment: rest; cold or hot wet applications. Caution: do not move.

Drowning. Treatment: artificial respiration. Caution: patient should be on stomach, with head low and mouth and nose unobstructed.

Fainting. Symptoms: pallor; cold; rapid pulse. Treatment: elevate legs. When conscious, give stimulants.

Foreign body in eye. Symptoms: pain; redness; tears. Treatment: wash out with clean water; remove with clean cloth. Caution: do not touch cornea, the eyeball covering over pupil and iris.

Fracture. Symptoms: pain; deformity of bone. Treatment: splint the whole limb. Caution: do not move until splint is in place. Treat for shock.

Heat exhaustion. Symptoms: pale, clammy skin; weakness; subnormal temperature. Treatment: rest; stimulants. Caution: no cold application to skin.

Poisoning. Symptoms: corrosive stain around mouth from irritants; depression from narcotics. Treatment: emetic; soothing liquids such as eggs, milk, oils.

Shock. Symptoms: pallor; cold; weak breathing; weak pulse. Treatment: head low; warmth; stimulants; treat cause of shock. Caution: do not move; avoid contact if electric shock.

Sprain. Symptoms: pain; swelling. Treatment: rest, cold wet applications.

Sunstroke. Symptoms: headache; unconsciousness; fever; red, dry, hot skin. Treatment: rest; cold applications to skin; cool drinks. Caution: no stimulants.

Wound. Treatment: remove foreign body; apply clean dressing and bandage. Caution: treat for bleeding and shock.

firth or frith, name applied to an estuary in Scotland. For Firth of Clyde, see CLYDE.

Firuzabad (fīrŏŏ′zübäd″), ruined city, S Iran, S of Shiraz. Palace built by Artaxerxes.

Fischart, Johann (yōhän′ fī′shärt), c.1545–c.1590, German satirist. Wrote an imitation of Rabelais, *Geschichtklitterung* (1575), and religious satires.

Fischer, Emil (ä′mēl fi′shùr), 1852–1919, German organic chemist. Won 1902 Nobel Prize for work on structure and synthesis of sugars, purines, and purine base derivatives, e.g., caffeine.

Fischer, Hans (häns), 1881–1945, German organic chemist. Won 1930 Nobel Prize for studies of chlorophyll and synthesis of hemin (salt of a constituent of hemoglobin).

Fischer von Erlach, Johann Bernhard (yō′hän bĕrn′härt fī′shùr fün ĕr′läkh), c.1656–1723, Austrian architect. His baroque buildings, notably the Karlskirche and Schönbrunn palace, give a definite stamp to Vienna.

Fish, Hamilton, 1808–93, American statesman. U.S. Representative from N.Y. (1843–45); U.S. Senator (1851–57). U.S. Secretary of State (1869–77); one of ablest to hold that office. Greatest achievement was bringing about treaty of Washington (see WASHINGTON, TREATY OF), accomplished amid great difficulties. Settled VIRGINIUS affair. Long chairman of board of trustees of Columbia Col. His son, **Hamilton Fish,** 1849–1936, was long a Republican leader in N.Y. His son, **Hamilton Fish,** 1888–, was a U.S. Representative from N.Y. and isolationist leader.

fish, aquatic gill-breathing vertebrate animal with fins, skin with mucous glands and usually scales or plates, and no distinct neck. Lamprey and hagfish (cyclostomes) are primitive, elongated creatures without paired fins, attaching themselves by suctorial mouths to larger fish on whose tissues they feed. Cartilaginous fish (including shark and ray) are more highly developed. Highest in scale are bony fish (those with true bone in skeleton), which includes most fresh-water and marine species. Whale shark (said to reach 50 ft. length) is largest living fish; smallest is goby (c.⅜ in. long) of Philippines. Fish move by contracting body muscles, moving fins, and expelling water through gill slits (giving thrust). They eat plankton, aquatic animals, plants, and refuse. See also CLIMBING PERCH; ELECTRIC FISH; FIN; FLYING FISH; GILL.

Fisher, Dorothy Canfield, 1879–, American novelist, chiefly of Vermont. Among her works are *The Bent Twig* (1915), *The Brimming Cup* (1916, *The Deepening Stream* (1930), *Seasoned Timber* (1939), and children's books.

Fisher, Geoffrey Francis, 1887–, archbishop of Canterbury after 1945, an educator for 21 years, bishop of Chester (1932–39), of London (1939–45).

Fisher, John (Saint John Fisher), 1459–1535, English cardinal, a very learned man. Opposed divorce of Henry VIII and Katharine of Aragon, and was imprisoned (1534). Pope Paul III in defiance made Fisher a cardinal (1534). Bishop Fisher was beheaded. Canonized by Roman Church 1935. Feast: June 22.

fisher, large species of marten (genus *Martes*) of N U.S. and Canada. It is over 3 ft. long and the beautiful fur is brown shading to black. It hunts other mammals and robs traps by night. Also called pekan, black cat, and Pennant's marten.

Fisher, Fort, Confederate outpost on peninsula between the Atlantic and Cape Fear R., defending port of Wilmington, N.C., in Civil War. Taken by Adm. D. D. Porter and Gen. A. T. Terry on Jan. 15, 1865.

fisheries. From earliest times and almost universally fisheries have had industrial and commercial importance. Largest grounds are in N Atlantic off Labrador and Newfoundland, yielding cod, herring, mackerel, haddock, and bluefish. Pacific fisheries of Japan, sardine fisheries of Baltic and North Sea, and inland fisheries of Russia are among largest. Fishing on high seas is subject to international agreements. Treaties covering rights of Americans to fish on entire Atlantic coast date from Treaty of Paris (1783); final agreement was made 1910 by North Atlantic Coast Fisheries Arbitration at The Hague. In 1882 Great Britain, Germany, France, Denmark, and Belgium signed North Sea Fisheries Convention, and other pacts in 1901 and

1904, ending lawlessness in that area. Pacific has been subject of many controversies, e.g., Japanese right to fish in Siberian waters, and celebrated BERING SEA FUR-SEAL CONTROVERSY.

Fishers Island, SE N.Y., c.8 mi. long, off NE tip of Long Isl. and SE of New London, Conn. Summer-resort and residential area, with Long Isl. coast guard hq. Discussions regarding island's annexation to Conn. held in the 1940s.

fish hawk: see OSPREY.

Fishkill Landing: see BEACON, N.Y.

Fisk, James, 1834–72, American financial buccaneer. Manipulation of Erie RR stock by him and Jay Gould wrecked the road. Fisk had a part in BLACK FRIDAY scandal.

Fiske, Bradley Allen (fĭsk), 1854–1942, American naval officer and inventor. Aide for naval operations (1913–17). Invented electric range-finder and other instruments for shipboard use.

Fiske, John, 1842–1901, American philosopher and historian; b. Edmund Fisk Green. In early lectures and books he thought to reconcile orthodox belief with science. Later he lectured and wrote many popular books on American history of years 1000–1865.

Fiske, Minnie Maddern, 1865–1932, American actress, long a leading figure in the theater. On stage at three, she starred at 15. A great interpreter of intellectual drama, she introduced Ibsen to U.S. Also won fame as Becky Sharp, Tess of the D'Urbervilles. Did famous revival of Sheridan's *Rivals*.

Fisk University, at Nashville, Tenn.; Negro; nonsectarian; coed.; opened 1866, chartered 1867 by Congregationalists (American Missionary Assn.), Western Freedmen's Aid Commission of Cincinnati, aided by C. B. Fisk. Fisk Jubilee Singers have toured U.S. and Europe.

Fitch, (William) Clyde, 1865–1909, American playwright. His plays are psychological studies (e.g., *The Girl with The Green Eyes,* 1902; *The Truth,* 1907; and *The City,* 1909), and historical romances (e.g., *Beau Brummel,* 1890).

Fitch, John, 1743–98, American inventor, believed to be first to invent American steamboat. Unable to commercialize his invention and robbed of recognition, he committed suicide.

Fitchburg, city (pop. 42,691), N Mass., N of Worcester; settled c.1730. Mfg. of paper, metal products, electrical machinery, tools, and textiles.

Fitzgerald, Irish noble family. **Maurice Fitzgerald,** d. 1176, Anglo-Norman invader of Ireland, aided Dermot McMurrough and acquired vast Irish landholdings. From his sons descend the two branches of the Fitzgeralds, the earls of Kildare and the earls of Desmond. **Thomas Fitzgerald, 10th earl of Kildare,** 1513–37, rebelled against the pro-English Ormondes in 1534 and was hanged with five of his uncles. To avenge his death **Gerald Fitzgerald, 15th earl of Desmond,** d. 1583, made allies of his relatives in Kildare. Was defeated in life-long fight against pro-English Butlers of Ormonde. **James Fitzgerald, 20th earl of Kildare** and **1st duke of Leinster,** 1722–73, defeated attempts to divert surplus Irish revenues to the Crown. His son, **Lord Edward Fitzgerald,** 1763–98, Irish patriot, fought (1779–81) in American Revolution in British army from which he was later expelled for republicanism. Joined United Irishmen in French-aided rebellion and was captured (1798) by the English.

FitzGerald, Edward, 1809–83, English poet, adapter of the Persian Rubaiyat of Omar Khayyam in three well-known English versions (1859, 1868, 1872).

Fitzgerald, F(rancis) Scott (Key), 1896–1940, American novelist. Pictured the jazz age in *This Side of Paradise* (1920), *All the Sad Young Men* (short stories, 1926), *The Great Gatsby* (1925), and *Tender Is the Night* (1934).

Fitzgerald, Gerald, earl of Desmond; James and Thomas, earls of Kildare; and **Maurice:** see FITZGERALD, family.

Fitzgerald, city (pop. 8,130), S central Ga., SSE of Macon; founded 1895 by Union veterans. Processing and shipping center for farm area. Jefferson Davis was taken prisoner by Union troops near here in 1865.

Fitzgibbon, John: see CLARE, JOHN FITZGIBBON, 1ST EARL OF.

Fitzherbert, Maria Anne, 1756–1837, wife (1785–95) of George IV. The marriage, illegal under English law, was ignored when the then prince of Wales married Caroline of Brunswick.

Fitzmaurice, Henry Charles Petty: see LANSDOWNE, HENRY CHARLES PETTY, 5TH MARQUESS OF.

Fitzmaurice, William Petty: see SHELBURNE, WILLIAM PETTY FITZMAURICE, 2D EARL OF.

Fitzpatrick, Thomas, c.1799–1854, American trapper, fur trader, and guide, one of greatest of MOUNTAIN MEN, b. Ireland.

Fitzsimmons, Robert, 1862–1917, British boxer. Won heavyweight championship 1897 by defeating James J. Corbett, lost title 1899 to James J. Jeffries.

Fiume (fyōō′mä), Serbo-Croatian *Rijekav,* city (pop. 72,120), Croatia, NW Yugoslavia; Adriatic seaport. Chief port of Hungary until World War I. Contested by Italy and Yugoslavia after 1918, it was seized by Italian free corps under D'ANNUNZIO 1919; made a free state by Treaty of Rapallo of 1920; occupied by Italy 1922. Treaty of Rome (1924) gave Yugoslavia the suburb of Susak, which became its leading port. Fiume was occupied by Yugoslavs 1945, formally ceded by Italy 1947.

Five Civilized Tribes, inclusive term for portions of Cherokee, Chickasaw, Choctaw, Creek, and Seminole tribes settled in E Okla. Were officially recognized as domestic dependent nations, with constitutional governments modeled on those of American states. This status was lost after Civil War because of support rendered to Confederacy.

Five Forks, crossroads near Dinwiddie Courthouse, SW of Petersburg, Va., scene of last important battle of Civil War, April 1, 1865; a Union victory.

Five Nations: see IROQUOIS CONFEDERACY.

Five-Year Plan, Rus. *Pyatiletka,* program adopted 1928 with primary objective of industrializing USSR. Subsequent five-year plans became standard feature of Soviet economic planning (see UNION OF SOVIET SOCIALIST REPUBLICS).

flag. Flags and standards—either a piece of cloth or figure on spear—have been used at least since early Egyptian times. Biblical references to them are many. Early Greeks and Romans used standards. Later Romans used vexillum, square flag on crosspiece suspended from end of a spear. Constantine adopted labarum bearing Christian symbol. Early flags usually had religious significance. In medieval times many flags were used. The Dannebrog of Denmark, red ensign, swallow-tailed, bearing a white cross, is no doubt oldest existing flag. An early French flag was oriflamme of abbey of St. Denis. It was replaced by Bourbon white flag sprinkled with fleurs-de-lis, succeeded in turn by the tricolor at time of the Revolution. British flag (Union Jack) is formed by crosses of St. George, St. Andrew, and St. Patrick, national saints, respectively, of England, Scotland, and Ireland. On Jan. 2, 1776, first flag of U.S. was raised by George Washington at Cambridge, Mass. On June 14, 1777, Congress delineated general form of present U.S. flag. This was revised in 1818 to provide that 13 alternate red and white stripes, denoting original 13 colonies, remain fixed and a white star be added to the blue union for each state at its admission to the Union. In armies and navies of the world, flags are used for signaling. Special codes govern display of flags—e.g., flag at half-mast denotes mourning.

Flag Day, anniversary of adoption of American flag in 1777. In 1895, June 14 was set in U.S. as Flag Day. It is not a legal holiday.

flagellants (flǎ′jŭlŭnts, flŭjĕ′lŭnts), groups of Christians who practiced public flagellation as a penance. Appeared as a movement in 12th cent. in N Italy. It was put down by the church, but there were later occasional flare-ups (e.g., at time of Black Death, 1348–49). In 1349 Pope Clement VI prohibited the practice. Most important heretical sects were the Bianchi of Italy and France (1399) and a group led by Karl Schmid or Schmidt in Thuringia (1414). There was a short-lived rebirth of practice within the Church after the Reformation. In Spanish America flagellant orders persisted; in New Mexico the Penitentes still practice secret rites.

flageolet: see WIND INSTRUMENTS.

Flagg, Ernest, 1857–1947, American architect. In 1908 built Singer Building in New York which marked a revolutionary height (612 ft.).

Flagg, James Montgomery, 1877–, American painter and magazine illustrator. Made posters as official artist for New York state during World War I.

Flagler, Henry Morrison, 1830–1913, American capitalist. Early associate of John D. Rockefeller. His backing of Fla. developments was chiefly responsible for state's growth as winter playground.

Flagstad, Kirsten (fläg'stät), 1895–, Norwegian soprano. First appeared at the Metropolitan Opera, New York, in 1935 in Wagner's *Die Walküre*. She is considered the greatest Wagnerian soprano of her time.

Flagstaff, city (pop. 7,663), N Ariz., near San Francisco Peaks, NE of Prescott, in lumbering, ranching area; founded 1881. Tourist center near pueblo ruins, Mormon L., Sunset Crater, Walnut Canyon. Has Lowell Observatory (1894). Indian powwow in July.

Flaherty, Robert J(oseph) (flä'ûrtē), 1884–1951, American moving-picture producer. His *Nanook of the North* (1922) was the first full-length documentary film. His other films include *Tabu* (1931), *Man of Aran* (1934), and *Louisiana Story* (1949).

Flamand, François: see DUQUESNOY, FRANÇOIS.

flame, result of chemical reaction of a gas heated above kindling temperature with another gas, usually oxygen (see COMBUSTION); heat and light are produced. Luminosity is usually caused by foreign matter; shape of flame is commonly a hollow cone. BUNSEN BURNER increases heat by mixing gas with air before igniting. **Flame test** is used to identify metals. Salt of metal introduced into Bunsen burner flame produces a characteristic color: barium, yellow-green; calcium, reddish-orange; copper, bluish-green; potassium, violet; lithium, crimson; sodium, yellow; strontium, red.

flamingo (flŭmĭng'gō), large, gregarious wading bird. Found in marshes and lagoons of both hemispheres; it has vermilion plumage with black-edged wings. Rare American flamingo nests in Bahamas and other islands. See *ill.,* p. 105.

Flaminian Way, principal Roman road to Cisalpine Gaul, 215 mi. long, built by C. Flaminius (220 B.C.).

Flamininus, Titus Quinctius (tī'tùs kwĭngk'shùs flămĭnī'nùs), c.230–175 B.C., Roman general, known as Liberator of Greece. Defeated Philip V of Macedon at Cynoscephalae (197 B.C.). Crushed Sparta (195) and forced king of Bithynia to give up Hannibal.

Flaminius, Caius (kā'ùs flūmĭ'nēùs), d. 217 B.C., Roman statesman, general, constructor of Circus Flaminius and Flaminian Way.

Flamsteed, John (flăm'stēd), 1646–1719, English astronomer, compiler of noted star catalogue. First astronomer royal.

Flanders, former county in the Low Countries, extending W of Scheldt R. along North Sea; now divided between Belgium (see EAST FLANDERS; WEST FLANDERS) and France. In Belgian Flanders, Flemish is spoken by most inhabitants (Flemings). A county from 862, Flanders soon came under overlordship of France (though later acquisitions in the E were held in fief from the Holy Roman Empire). Direct line of counts died out 1191 and was succeeded by counts of HAINAUT. The cities, notably GHENT, BRUGES, YPRES, and COURTRAI, enjoyed virtual independence.

Their cloth industry (which is still important) was the largest in Europe (13th cent.), but intense industrialization brought such modern problems as economic crises and class war. In the chronic struggle between the French kings and the counts of Flanders the lower classes generally sided with the *Clauwaerts* (supporters of the counts), the upper classes with the *Leliaerts* (supporters of the kings). Routed at Bouvines (1214), the *Clauwaerts* triumphed in the BATTLE OF THE SPURS (1302). However, despite the efforts of Jacob and Philip van ARTEVELDE, the French party won out eventually at Roosebeke (1382). In 1384 PHILIP THE BOLD became count of Flanders. Under his successors (see BURGUNDY) Flemish commerce and art reached their flower, but industry declined and local liberties were curtailed. The death of MARY OF BURGUNDY (1482) brought Flanders under Hapsburg rule (for subsequent history until 1797, see NETHERLANDS, AUSTRIAN AND SPANISH). Annexed by France in 1797 and awarded to the Netherlands in 1815, Flanders became part of Belgium in 1830 and was divided into two provinces. It has long been a traditional battleground. In World War II, Battle of Flanders began with German invasion of Low Countries (May 10, 1940) and ended with Allied evacuation at Dunkirk (June 4, 1940).

Flanders, French, region and former province, N France, on North Sea, bordering on Belgium; historic cap. Lille. Rich coal fields; industries. Part of county of Flanders until annexed by France (1662–78). Flemish is still widely spoken.

Flandrau, Charles Macomb (flăn'drō), 1871–1938, American author. Wrote pictures of college life in *Harvard Episodes* (1897), *The Diary of a Freshman* (1901), and *Sophomores Abroad* (1935). His best-known work is a travel book, *Viva Mexico!* (1908).

Flandrin, Jean Hippolyte (zhä' ēpôlēt' flädrē'), 1809–64, French painter, a follower of Ingres. Best known for religious paintings.

Flatbush: see BROOKLYN, New York city borough.

flatfish, fish of order Heterosomata with compressed body and, in adult form, both eyes on same side of head. Larvae are bilaterally symmetrical at first; asymmetry of adult involves skeletal and digestive changes, migration of one eye. Includes flounder, halibut, sole, plaice, turbot.

flat foot, condition of human foot in which entire sole rests on ground. This depression of the arches is caused by distorted alignment of bones forming longitudinal arch, which extends from heel to toes on inner side of foot, and transverse arch extending across foot in metatarsal region. Distortion usually results from muscle weakness and consequent straining and stretching of ligaments.

Flathead, river formed by three forks in NW Mont. Flows S through Flathead L. to Clark Fork. In South Fork is Hungry Horse Dam for power, irrigation, and flood control.

Flathead Indians, tribe of Salishan linguistic stock in Bitterroot river valley, W Mont. in 19th cent. After introduction of the horse, adopted Plains area culture. Suffered heavily in wars with Blackfoot.

Flat River, city (pop. 5,308), E Mo., ESE of Potosi. Lead-mining center.

Flattery, Cape: see JUAN DE FUCA STRAIT.

Flaubert, Gustave (güstäv' flōbĕr'), 1821–80, French novelist. An untiring stylist striving for complete objectivity and exactitude of expression, he produced *Madame Bovary* (1857), *Salammbô* (1862), *Éducation sentimentale* (1869), *The Temptation of St. Anthony* (1874), *Three Tales* (1877; including "A Simple Heart" and "St. Julian the Hospitaler"), and *Bouvard et Pécuchet* (1881), his unfinished satire on the French bourgeois and all his works and thoughts.

Flavian (flā'vēùn), epithet given to three Roman emperors, Vespasian, Titus, and Domitian.

flax, annual plant (*Linum usitatissimum*), grown for its fiber and seed. A plant domesticated in man's early history, it was chief source of textile fiber, but is now largely replaced by other fibers. Still grown in USSR, in Belgium for fine LINEN, and in U.S. and Argentina for flaxseed, the source of linseed oil. Other flax species are grown in gardens.

Flaxman, John, 1755–1826, English artist, known for memorial sculptures, notably those in Westminster Abbey.

flea, wingless, leaping insect. Mouth parts of the adult can pierce skin and suck blood of mammals and birds. Dog flea and cat flea also attack man. Human flea is abundant in warmer parts of Europe and Asia. Flea parasitic on rodents transmits bubonic PLAGUE. CHIGOE is a flea. See *ill.,* p. 469.

Flecker, James Elroy, 1884–1915, English writer of poetry (e.g., *The Golden Journey to Samarkand,* 1913) and plays (e.g., *Hassan*).

Fleet Prison, former London jail. Rebuilt several times, finally demolished 1845–46. Mainly notable for incarceration of debtors. "Fleet marriages," clandestine and irregular, performed here by debtor clergymen. System abolished under George II.

Fleet Street, center of journalism in London. Named for Fleet R., now a sewer under Farringdon St. Many buildings destroyed in bombings 1940–41.

Flémalle, Master of: see CAMPIN, ROBERT.

Fleming, Sir Alexander, 1881–, Scottish bacteriologist. He shared 1945 Nobel Prize in Physiology and Medicine for work on penicillin, which he discovered. He also discovered lysozyme.

Fleming, Sir John Ambrose, 1849–1945, English electrical engineer, a leader in developing the use in England of electric lighting, telephone, and telegraph. He invented a thermionic valve.

Fleming, Sir Sandford, 1827–1915, Canadian civil engineer, b. Scotland. Appointed chief engineer of Canadian Pacific Railway (1871); surveyed route W from Fort William. Introduced idea of 24-hour-a-day standard time and urged its adoption. Was the chief influence in laying of Pacific cable from Canada to Australia.

Flemington, borough (pop. 3,058), W N.J., NNW of Trenton. Scene of Hauptmann's trial for the kidnaping and murder of Charles A. Lindbergh, Jr., 1935.

Flemish [adjective for Flanders], Germanic language (see LANGUAGE, table), very closely allied to Dutch. The distinction is made on a more or less political basis, the Flemings being the Germanic-speaking people of Belgium (in earlier days, those of Flanders). Dutch and Flemish literature have maintained affinity to the present day, with Flemish authors contributing notably. The great period of Flemish painting (1400–1600) began with the brothers Van Eyck. After the 18th cent. Flemish painting, sculpture, and architecture generally showed decided French influence.

Flensburg (flĕns'bŏŏrk), city (pop. 102,045), Schleswig-Holstein, N Germany; a port on Baltic Sea. Shipbuilding; mfg. of machinery, chemicals, foodstuffs.

Fletcher, Giles, the elder, c.1548–1611, English writer and diplomat. An envoy to Russia in 1588, he published *Of the Russe Common Wealth* (1591), which was suppressed. Also wrote a number of Latin poems. His son, **Phineas Fletcher,** 1582–1650, was a poet whose best-known work is *Purple Island* (1633; an involved, somewhat scientific poem on the human body). His brother, **Giles Fletcher,** the younger, b. 1585 or 1586, d. 1623, was also a poet. His best poem is *Christ's Victory and Triumph* (1610), a baroque devotional work.

Fletcher, John, 1579–1625, prolific English dramatist, frequent collaborator with others. Often composed larger part of plays written with Francis BEAUMONT. With Shakspere wrote *The Two Noble Kinsmen* and *Henry VIII* (1613). Extravagant in plot, facile in poetic style, his own best work includes the comedies *The Woman's Prize* and *Rule a Wife and Have A Wife* (1624) and the tragicomedy *The Island Princess.* In later years collaborated with various other drama-

tists but most frequently with Philip MASSINGER.

Fletcher, John Gould, 1886–1950, American poet. *Preludes and Symphonies* (1922) typifies imagist verse. Later work (e.g., *XXIV Elegies,* 1935) shows more exacting forms.

Fletcher, Phineas: see FLETCHER, GILES.

Flettner, Peter: see FLÖTNER, PETER.

Fleurus (flûrüs'), town (pop. 6,949), Hainaut prov., Belgium. Scene of Protestant victory in Thirty Years War (1622); of French victory in War of the Grand Alliance (1690); and of a decisive French victory in French Revolutionary Wars (1794).

Fleury, André Hercule de (ädrä' ĕrkül' dù flûrē'), 1653–1743, French cardinal, chief minister to Louis XV. Virtually ruled France, 1726–43. Restored finances, strove for peace, but was unwillingly drawn into wars of Polish and Austrian successions.

Flexner, Abraham, 1866–, American educator. His report (1910) to Carnegie Foundation for the Advancement of Teaching hastened reforms in American medical schools. He was first director of Inst. for Advanced Study at Princeton (1930–39). His brother, **Simon Flexner,** 1863–1946, noted pathologist, was director (1920–35) of Rockefeller Institute.

flicker, large North American woodpecker, the only brown woodpecker. Northern or yellow-shafted flicker has many local names (e.g., yellowhammer, high hole). Southern form is similar. In flight the white rump patch is prominent. Red-shafted flicker found in W U.S.

Fliegende Holländer: see FLYING DUTCHMAN.

flight, sustained progress through air by aircraft or animal. Science of flight included in study of aerodynamics, the physics of air (and other gases) in motion. Balloons and airships inflated with lighter-than-air gas stay aloft by ARCHIMEDES' PRINCIPLE. Airplanes, autogiros, helicopters, and gliders sustained by forward motion, their airfoils developing lifting air pressure on under surfaces and reduced air resistance on upper surfaces. Engine-driven craft are pulled or pushed by propellers (air screws) or jets. Mechanical flight was first suggested by natural flight of birds. The leading edge of the slightly concave wings of birds is rather sharp and feathers are small and close-fitting, so streamlined surface meets the air. On trailing edge of each wing the interlocking of larger feathers forms surface that simulates action of ailerons of plane. In all of three general types of bird flight—flapping, soaring, gliding—principal flight feathers overlap so that air pressure on underside of wing causes feathers to form airtight surface; on upstroke feathers part enough to allow some air to pass through, thus reducing pressure against which wings must work. Form and size of wings and speed of flight vary; most bird flight ranges from 10 to 60 mi. an hour. See *ill.,* p. 19.

Flinders, Matthew, 1774–1814, English naval captain and hydrographer, noted for his charting and coast surveys of Australia and Tasmania (1795–99, 1801–3). W. M. Flinders Petrie was his grandson.

Flinders Island: see FURNEAUX ISLANDS.

Flinders Petrie, Sir William Matthew: see PETRIE.

Flin Flon (flĭn' flŏn), town (pop. 9,899), W Man., Canada, at Sask. border, NNW of The Pas. Important mining and smelting center (copper, zinc, gold, silver, cadmium).

Flint, Timothy, 1780–1840, American author of several works on the West.

Flint, county, Wales: see FLINTSHIRE.

Flint, city (pop. 163,143), S Mich., on Flint R. and NW of Detroit; settled 1819 as fur-trading post. One of state's chief automobile centers with mfg. of metal products, cement blocks, and furniture. Has General Motors Inst. of Technology.

Flint, municipal borough (pop. 14,257), Flintshire, Wales. Castle was scene of Richard II's submission to Bolingbroke in 1399.

Flint, river rising S of Atlanta, Ga., and winding 330

mi. generally S, past Albany (head of navigation), to join Chattahoochee R. and form Apalachicola R. in SW corner of Ga. at Fla. line. Power dams.

flint, variety of QUARTZ often found in chalk and limestone. Since it was easy to chip, primitive man made tools and weapons of flint. It was long used with steel for fire making and to discharge flintlock guns.

Flintshire or **Flint,** county (256 sq. mi.; pop. 145,108), NE Wales; co. town Mold. Uplands devoted to pasturage; farming in fertile valleys. Has rich coal, metal, clay, and limestone deposits, and mfg. of pottery, chemicals, and artificial silk.

Flodden, hill, Northumberland, England; scene of battle of Flodden Field (1513) where English defeated Scots under James IV, who was killed. Battle is described in Scott's *Marmion*.

Flood, in the Bible: see DELUGE.

flood plain, level land along lower course of large river formed by deposition of sediment during floods. Often extensive, extremely fertile.

Flor, Roger de, d. c.1306, German soldier of fortune, b. Italy. Led band of Spanish adventurers (Catalan company) in service of Byzantium; defeated Turks but oppressed native population and was assassinated. His followers set up duchy of Athens (1311).

Flora [from Latin, = flower], Roman goddess of flowers. Her temple was near the Circus Maximus.

Flora, city (pop. 5,255), SE Ill., ENE of Centralia. Center of oil and agr. area with mfg. of shoes.

Floral Park, residential village (pop. 14,582), SE N.Y., on W Long Isl. near Mineola.

Florence, Ital. *Firenze,* city (pop. 271,975; with suburbs 321,176), cap. of Tuscany, central Italy, on Arno R. Of Roman origin, it rose to prominence after 1200, when it gained autonomy and grew into a commercial and cultural center of world importance. Despite civil strife between GUELPHS AND GHIBELLINES —later between Black and White Guelphs—Florence waged successful warfare against rival cities, notably PISA, which it absorbed within its growing territories. The silk, wool, and jewelry industries brought enormous wealth. In the 15th cent. the MEDICI family of merchants and bankers took the power, but the republican constitution was ostensibly retained. Twice exiled (1494–1512, 1527–30), the Medici were both times restored through foreign intervention; in the first of these revolutions SAVONAROLA and MACHIAVELLI played leading parts. In 1569 Cosimo I de' Medici was made grand duke of Tuscany (for later history, see TUSCANY). Florence was the cap. of Italy 1865–70. The cradle and chief jewel of the Italian RENAISSANCE, Florence saw an enormous outburst of creativeness in the 14th–16th cent.: Dante, Boccaccio, Fra Angelico, Brunelleschi, Donatello, Da Vinci, Raphael, Michelangelo, and Cellini are among the best-known of the many geniuses who were born or worked in Florence. Probably the world's greatest repository of art, Florence abounds in famous churches, palaces, museums, and monuments. Among these are the Gothic Cathedral of Santa Maria del Fiore; the near-by baptistery, with doors by Ghiberti; the churches of Santa Croce, Santa Maria Novella, and San Lorenzo; the Palazzo della Signoria (city hall) and the near-by Loggia; the UFFIZI, Strozzi, and Pitti palaces; and the BARGELLO. Each of these contains works by the most famous Renaissance artists. Many historic buildings suffered bomb hits in World War II; all bridges except the famous Ponte Vecchio were blown up.

Florence. 1 City (pop. 23,879), NW Ala., on Tennessee R. near MUSCLE SHOALS and Wilson Dam (provides power); laid out 1818. Region yields minerals, cotton. Mfg. of textiles, heaters; lumber milling; meat packing. Large aluminum plant near by (1941). **2** Resort town (pop. 1,776), S Ariz., on Gila R. and SE of Phoenix near Coolidge Dam (irrigation). **3** City (pop. 22,513), E central S.C., ENE of Columbia; founded in 1850s. Rail focus and mfg. (metal prod-

ucts, fertilizer) and trade center for farm, tobacco, and livestock area. Important point during Civil War. Has national cemetery.

Florence, Council of: see FERRARA-FLORENCE, COUNCIL OF.

Flores, Indonesia: see SUNDA ISLANDS.

Florey, Sir Howard Walter, 1898–, Australian pathologist. He shared 1945 Nobel Prize in Physiology and Medicine for work on penicillin.

Florianópolis (flō"rēŭnä'pŭlĭs), city (pop. 49,290); cap. and chief port of Santa Catarina state, SE Brazil, on Santa Catarina Isl.; founded 1700.

Florida, state (58,560 sq. mi.; pop. 2,771,305), extreme SE U.S., admitted 1845 as 27th state (slaveholding); cap. TALLAHASSEE. Other cities are TAMPA, JACKSONVILLE, MIAMI, SAINT PETERSBURG. Low peninsula, mostly in coastal plain, washed on E by the Atlantic and W by Gulf of Mexico. Rolling hills in NW, EVERGLADES in S; interior has numerous lakes (e.g., OKEECHOBEE) and extensive swamps. Climate mainly subtropical. State's largest industry is tourism, but agr. (esp. citrus, truck, sugar cane), cattle raising, lumbering (pine, cypress), fishing (esp. shrimp, sponges), mining (e.g., phosphates), food processing, naval stores are important. Region explored by PONCE DE LEÓN 1513; French settlements under René de LAUDONNIÈRE failed (1562–66); settlement begun by Spanish at SAINT AUGUSTINE (1565), oldest city in U.S. Spain ceded colony to England in 1763; returned to Spain 1783 (see WEST FLORIDA CONTROVERSY). Sold to U.S. in 1819. Became a territory (with present boundaries) in 1822. Wars with SEMINOLE INDIANS impeded development. Fla. joined Confederacy 1861, but suffered little in Civil War and Reconstruction. Drainage of the Everglades, growth of railroads and hotels, and land booms have aided development in 20th cent. Fla. prospered in World War II from army, navy, air force installations.

Florida, village, NE central Mo., SW of Hannibal. Birthplace of Mark Twain.

Florida, ship: see CONFEDERATE CRUISERS.

Florida, Straits of, SE and S of Fla., between Florida Keys and Cuba. Here the Gulf Stream passes from Gulf of Mexico to the Atlantic.

Florida, University of, at Gainesville; land-grant and state supported, mainly for men; opened 1853 as seminary at Ocala, moved 1906 after union of state schools. The General Col. (jr.; 1935) pioneered in modern curriculum and guidance plans. Has Inter-American Inst.

Florida Agricultural and Mechanical College, at Tallahassee; Negro, land-grant and state supported; coed.; 1887.

Floridablanca, José Moñino, conde de (hōsä' mōnyē'nō kōn'dä dä flōrē'dhäbläng'kä), 1728–1808, Spanish statesman. As ambassador to Rome he secured suppression of Society of Jesus (1773). As premier (1777–92) he consolidated absolutism, pushed program of economic reform, promoted peace, but was drawn into war with England in American Revolution.

Florida Keys, chain (c.150 mi. long) of small coral and limestone islands or reefs, forming S tip of Fla. Separated from mainland by Florida Bay and from Cuba by Straits of Florida. Joined to mainland by Key Largo (the largest, c.30 mi. long) by a highway (opened 1944), which also links the islands from here to KEY WEST. Many are habitable and have commercial fisheries and resorts. Devastated by hurricane in Sept., 1935.

Florida Southern College: see LAKELAND.

Florida State University, at Tallahassee; coed.; chartered and opened 1905 as Florida State Col. for Women, renamed 1947.

Florio, John (flō'rēō), 1553?–1625, English author, best remembered for his translation (1603) of the essays of Montaigne.

Florissant, city (pop. 3,737), E Mo., on the Missouri and near St. Louis. Settled 1785 by French, it was later called St. Ferdinand by Spanish. Has Church of St. Ferdinand (1821) and Jesuit St. Stanislaus Seminary (1823, rebuilt 1840–49). Father De Smet was ordained here, 1827.

Flötner or Flettner, Peter (pā'tŭr flût'nùr, flĕt'nùr), c.1485–1546, German medalist and craftsman, a pioneer of German Renaissance.

Flotow, Friedrich von (flō'tō), 1812–83, German composer of operas, of which *Martha* is best known.

flotsam, jetsam, and ligan (flŏt'sùm, jĕt'sùm, lī'gùn), in maritime law, goods lost at sea, distinguished from wreck, goods which come to shore. Flotsam refers to goods floating on surface, jetsam to those thrown overboard and generally partly submerged. Ligan (or lagan) designates goods which go down with a ship, or sunken goods marked with a buoy. The return of such is obligatory; flotsam and jetsam are returned only upon claim by owner. Rules of salvage apply.

flounder, name used for any FLATFISH (except true sole of Europe) or sometimes only for certain members of family Pleuronectidae. Many are also called flukes. Flesh is delicate. Flattened body has whitish underside and brown or olive, often mottled, upperside. In many species color and pattern are changeable to blend with background. Found chiefly in salt water, but some swim up rivers. Abundant in North America and parts of Europe.

flour, the finely ground meal of grain or of such plants as the potato, cassava, peas, or beans; it is the chief ingredient of bread. Wheat flour predominates in U.S., Canada, W Europe; millet and durra are used in India and China, while rye, buckwheat, rice, corn, and other grains lead in other areas. Wheat flour is separated into grades by milling. Composition depends upon type of wheat and processing; Gluten is chief protein, starch the principal carbohydrate.

Flower, George, 1788–1862, pioneer settler of Ill., b. England. With Morris Birkbeck, undertook settlement scheme which led to founding of Albion, Ill.

flower, specialized part of a seed plant containing organs of reproduction. Outermost parts are usually green sepals of CALYX, within which are the often showy, colored petals of the COROLLA. Innermost are the organs of reproduction: the male organs (or stamens) bear powdery pollen, and the female organ (the pistil or pistils) is enlarged at the base to form the ovary containing eggs. Some flowers have both stamens and pistil, others are unisexual. Fruit and seed develop after POLLINATION, which results in fertilization of the egg. See *ill.*, p. 783.

flowering maple: see ABUTILON.

flowering quince, spiny, Asiatic shrub (*Chaenomeles*), with early spring flowers ranging from white to red. Yellowish fruits, similar to related quince, are sometimes used in preserves. *Chaenomeles japonica* is called Japanese quince or japonica.

Floyd, John Buchanan, 1807–63, U.S. Secretary of War (1857–60) and Confederate general. In quarrel over Fort Sumter, and because of irregularities in War Dept., he resigned by request and became secessionist. Equally incompetent in war, he was removed from command after his defeat at Fort Donelson.

fluke, parasitic flatworm of class Trematoda, phylum Platyhelminthes. In parts of Orient, humans may become infested with liver fluke by eating raw fish, by lung fluke from raw crab. Blood flukes are prevalent in Egypt, parts of tropical America; enter body through drinking water or skin of bather. Intestinal flukes attack man and pigs. Liver fluke *Fasciola hepatica* is cause of liver rot, fatal to sheep and other herbivorous animals. See also FLOUNDER.

fluorescence, emission of light of visible color from substance stimulated by light waves or other means. Light is given off only during stimulation. Rock fluorescence known for many years. Sir George G. Stokes named fluorescence and discovered it can be induced by ultraviolet light. Stokes's law states: wave length of fluorescent light is (with few exceptions)

greater than that of the exciting radiation. Visible light, infrared, X rays, radio waves, cathode rays, friction, heat, or pressure can all cause fluorescence. Fluorescent lights are long, sealed, glass tubes with electrode at each end; argon and small amount of mercury are inside tube. Inner surface of tube is coated with fluorescent powders; when electric discharge is maintained through mercury vapor, ultraviolet light so produced causes excitation of coating, producing fluorescent light.

fluorine (floo'ùrēn), most active nonmetallic element (symbol = F; see also ELEMENT, table); yellowish, poisonous, corrosive gas. It is a member of HALOGEN series. Its compounds are used in metallurgy, in etching, and also in making insecticides. It does not occur free in nature.

fluorite (floo'ùrīt) or **fluorspar** (floo'ùrspär), a mineral, calcium fluoride, varied in color. Used as a flux in metallurgy; also in preparation of hydrofluoric acid, opal glass, and enamel.

fluoroscope (floo'rùskōp), device used in medical diagnosis. Bismuth salts are given to patient, who is placed between screen and X-ray source; since X rays cannot penetrate salts, course of bismuth through alimentary canal is seen.

fluorspar: see FLUORITE.

Flushing (flŭ'shĭng), Dutch *Vlissingen,* municipality (pop. 20,217), Zeeland prov., SW Netherlands; a port on S coast of Walcheren isl. Terminus for boats crossing English Channel; oil refineries, shipyards, machinery and metallurgical plants. One of first Dutch towns to rebel against Spain (1572), Flushing has strategic position at mouth of Scheldt R. British took it from French 1809, from Germans 1944.

Flushing: see QUEENS, New York city borough.

flute: see WIND INSTRUMENTS.

Fly, largest river of New Guinea, 650 mi. long; rises in NE, flows to Gulf of Papua. Forms part of boundary between Netherlands New Guinea and Territory of Papua.

fly, name for many winged insects; accurately only for certain members of order Diptera, including housefly, gnat, midge, and mosquito. One pair of wings is functional; vestiges of second pair, knobbed threadlike structures called halteres, aid in balancing. Many flies are disease carriers and crop destroyers; some parasitize harmful insects. See *ill.*, p. 469.

flycatcher, name for various members of Old World songbird family, Muscicapidae. For some members of New World tyrant flycatcher family (Tyrannidae), see KINGBIRD; PEWEE; PHOEBE; SCISSOR-TAILED FLYCATCHER.

flying animals. Only large animal group moving chiefly by FLIGHT are birds and insects. Among mammals only BAT is capable of true flight. See also FLYING FISH; FLYING SQUIRREL; LIZARD.

Flying Dutchman, according to sailors, ominous apparition of a ship seen near Cape of Good Hope. The legend of its blasphemous captain, doomed to sail forever, is used in Wagner's *Der fliegende Holländer.*

flying fish, name for various gliding fish of warm seas, usually traveling in schools. In some only the pectoral or anterior paired fins are enlarged and winglike as in members of genus *Exocoetus,* usually c.1 ft. long, seen in N Atlantic. Others (Catalina flying fish, *Cypselurus,* c.18 in. long) have enlarged pelvic or hind paired fins. After swimming rapidly in water, then "taxiing" along surface propelled by tail movements, they rise into air, sometimes to 25 ft.

flying squirrel, name chiefly for certain nocturnal tree squirrels of Asia, North America, and Europe. Using furry skin fold around body which spreads parachutelike, they glide, rather than fly, from heights. Tail is used as rudder. North American tree squirrel (*Glaucomys*) is 9–14 in. long.

flywheel, heavy, metal wheel attached to drive shaft of an engine or other machine; its weight is concentrated at the circumference. It is used to equalize energy exerted and work done, thereby regulating velocity.

Foch, Ferdinand (fĕrdēnä' fôsh'), 1851–1929, marshal of France. In World War I he stopped Germans at the Marne (1914); became chief of French general staff (1917); headed Allied supreme command 1918.

focus, in optics, point of convergence of rays after reflection by mirror or refraction by LENS is real focus. Virtual focus is imaginary point from which rays seem to have diverged after reflection by convex mirror or refraction by diverging lens.

foetus: see FETUS.

fog, cloudlike aggregation of water droplets immediately above land or water. If light, usually called mist. Forms when moisture content of air increases above saturation point (e.g., when cold air is in contact with warm body of water or warm rain) or when air cools below dew point, causing radiation fog (earth at night after losing heat by radiation cools adjacent air), advection fog (warm air flows on cold surface), and upslope fog (ascending air expands, cools).

Fogazzaro, Antonio (äntō'nyō fōgät-tsä'rō), 1842–1911, Italian novelist, author of *Piccolo mondo antico* (1896; Eng. tr., *The Patriot*, 1906).

Foggia (fôd'jä), city (pop. 57,234), Apulia, S Italy. Important communications center and wheat market. Damaged in World War II, when it was a German air base. Has cathedral (12th cent., much restored).

foie gras (fwä grä'), livers of specially fattened geese, a delicacy usually prepared as *pâté de foie gras* (containing wine, truffles, other seasonings) in vicinity of Strasbourg and Toulouse, France.

Foix (fwä), town (pop. 6,026), cap. of Ariège dept., S France, on Ariège R. Counts of Foix rose to great power in 11th cent., acquired BÉARN 13th cent., inherited NAVARRE 1479. Their titles and lands passed by marriage to house of ALBRET 1494. Foix was incorporated into French royal domain 1607.

Fokine, Michel (mēshĕl' fōkēn', Rus. fô'kyĭn), 1880–1942, Russian ballet dancer and choreographer; a founder of modern ballet. Helped form Diaghilev's Russian Ballet (Paris, 1909). Among his works are *The Dying Swan* (for Pavlova), *Les Sylphides*, *Petrouchka, Scheherazade,* and *L'Oiseau de feu.*

fold, in geology, a bend in stratified rocks, which normally are horizontal (see STRATIFICATION). Arches are called anticlines; troughs, synclines. Folds are often formed far below the surface and are exposed by erosion. The top of an anticline may be eroded till only the worn-down stumps remain. The cause of folding is related to compression of the earth's crust involved in mountain building.

Folengo, Teofilo (tāō'fēlō fōlĕng'gō), 1491–1544, Italian burlesque poet, author of *Baldus,* a burlesque on chivalric romance.

Foley, John Henry, 1818–74, Irish sculptor; studied in London. Designed seal of the Confederacy.

Folger, Henry Clay, 1857–1930, American capitalist and collector of Shaksperiana. With help of his wife, Emily Jordan Folger, acquired one of the largest collections. Endowed **Folger Shakespeare Library,** Washington, D.C., dedicated 1932.

folk dance, primitive, tribal, or racial form of the DANCE. Term also includes characteristic national dances, country dances, and figure dances in costume to folk tunes. Good examples are the Spanish fandango, Bohemian polka, Hungarian czardas, Irish jig, Highland fling, English morris and maypole dances, and the American Virginia reel.

Folkestone (fōk'stùn), municipal borough (pop. 45,200), Kent, England, on the Channel; summer resort and seaport. Bombed World War II.

folklore, in its widest extent, body of oral traditions, art, and superstitions of any society. It includes folk dances, folk songs, folk tales, and folk medicine. Its study was originally domain of the antiquarian, but rise of European romanticism and of nationalism made this a serious pursuit. Folk tales have been collected, and folk heroes (e.g., Robin Hood in England, the Cid in Spain, and Paul Bunyan in U.S.) have received much attention. Today anthropologists regard folk tales as imaginative expression by a social group of its desires, attitudes, and cultural values. Almost every country now has a folklore society.

folk school, form of adult education originated in Denmark by Bishop Nikolai GRUNDTVIG in mid-19th cent. Idea was to stimulate intellectual life of young adults of rural Denmark, foster patriotism and religion, and provide agricultural and vocational training. First school estab. 1844. Folk-school idea spread through Europe and even to U.S.

folkways, term coined by William Graham Sumner (c.1907) to define more clearly the patterning of behavior usually denoted as custom. Included traditions, laws, manners, usages, mores, and the like, which make up the culture of a group.

Follen, Charles (Karl Theodor Christian Follen) (fŏ'lùn), 1796–1840, American educator, b. Germany. Appointed to Harvard faculty in 1825, he taught first course in German offered in America. Later became identified with reform movements. His wife, **Eliza Lee (Cabot) Follen,** 1787–1860, influential as a writer in Unitarian movement, led in antislavery and feminist causes.

Folsom culture, early North American culture known through artifacts first found near Folsom, N. Mex. The findings suggest the presence of man in North America c.10,000 or more years ago.

Fond du Lac (fŏn' dù lăk"), city (pop. 29,936), E Wis., at S end of L. Winnebago and SSE of Oshkosh; settled c.1835. Has railroad shops, limestone quarries, and metal products plants (tools, machinery). Resort.

Fonseca, Gulf of (fônsä'kä), inlet of Pacific, c.50 mi. long and 30 mi. wide, Central America. Harbor shared by Nicaragua, Honduras, and Salvador. Rights for Nicaragua Canal given to U.S. by Nicaragua disputed by other nations.

Fontaine, Pierre François Léonard (fōtĕn'), 1762–1853, French architect, associate of Charles PERCIER, with whom he fostered Empire style in France.

Fontainebleau (fōtĕnblō'), town (pop. 13,498), Seine-et-Marne dept., N France, SE of Paris. The vast Forest of Fontainebleau was a favorite hunting ground of French kings. In the magnificent Renaissance palace, built by Francis I, Pope Pius VII was imprisoned (1812–14) and Napoleon I abdicated (1814).

Fontana, Domenico (dōmä'nēkō fōntä'nä), 1543–1607, Italian architect, who played leading part in rebuilding of Rome. Designed Lateran palace and parts of the Vatican; helped finish dome of St. Peter's.

Fontana, Prospero (prō'spärō), 1512–97, Italian painter. Worked mainly in Bologna. His daughter **Lavinia Fontana,** 1552–1614?, was a portrait painter in Bologna and Rome.

Fontane, Theodor (tä'ōdōr fôntä'nù), 1819–98, German author. He is best known for his ballads and for the novels *L'Adultera* (1882), *Irrungen, Wirrungen* (1888; Eng. tr., *Trials and Tribulations*), and *Effi Briest* (1895; Eng. tr., 1913–15).

Fontanne, Lynn (fōntän'), 1887?–, American actress. Acts with her husband Alfred LUNT (e.g., in *The Guardsman, Reunion in Vienna, O Mistress Mine*).

Fonte, Jacopo della: see QUERCIA.

Fontenelle, Bernard le Bovier de (bĕrnär' lù bôvyä' dù fōtùnĕl'), 1657–1757, French author. His *Entretiens sur le pluralité des mondes* (1686) is a model of scientific popularization.

Fontenoy (fōn'tùnoi, Fr. fōtùnwä'), village, Hainaut prov., Belgium, SE of Tournai. Here in 1745 French under Maurice de Saxe won celebrated victory over British and allies under duke of Cumberland in War of Austrian Succession.

Fontenoy, village, N central France, near Auxerre. Reputed site of a battle in which Charles II of France and Louis the German checked their brother, Emperor LOTHAIR I (841). Battle led to Oath of STRASBOURG and

Treaty of VERDUN. Also known as Fontenay, Fontanet, or Fontenailles.

Foochow (fōō'chou'), commercial city (pop. 331,273), cap. Fukien prov., China, on Min R. One of treaty ports opened 1842 at end of Opium War. In mid-19th cent. was China's leading tea-exporting center.

food adulteration, the intentional debasement of quality of foods offered for sale, has been dealt with from consumer's standpoint only since mid-19th cent., when new knowledge made close analysis possible. First British food law passed in purchaser's interest came in 1860; in U.S., Pure Food and Drugs Act of 1906, often amended and later superseded, came only after stormy campaign. Federal and local regulations now govern content, handling, labeling, and advertising of food, drugs, and cosmetics, and certain aspects of importation and interstate traffic.

Food and Agriculture Organization (FAO), agency of UN. Estab. in Oct., 1945; under UN in Dec., 1946. FAO contributes to expanding world economy by bettering rural conditions, improving production and distribution, and raising level of nutrition.

food poisoning, any of a number of illnesses marked by gastrointestinal disturbances and caused by eating food contaminated by poisonous substances. The term "ptomaine poisoning" is now generally replaced because ptomaines (produced by action of decay bacteria on proteins) are not known to cause illness. Substances causing food poisoning include inorganic chemicals; organic substances derived from animals and plants (e.g., certain mushrooms); and bacterial toxins, especially toxins produced by species of *Staphylococcus, Salmonella,* and *Clostridium* (see BOTULISM).

food preservation has been practiced since remotest times; early products of experiment were cheese, butter, wine, bacon, parched grain. Advances came with scientific investigation (notably by Pasteur) of causes of putrefaction. Basic preserving processes include drying, heating (as in CANNING and PASTEURIZATION), refrigeration (both freezing and chilling), exclusion of air, and use of such substances as salt, sugar, vinegar, smoke, alcohol, and saltpeter. Use of certain chemicals is generally limited by legislation.

fool, absurdly irresponsible person, often subject to spells of mirth or melancholy. Some fools are benevolent, others cunningly malevolent. In all countries from ancient times to 18th cent., dwarfs, cripples, and idiots provided amusement at court. Court fools were not necessarily deformed or mentally deficient. Keen, witty men often obtained powerful patronage as fools. Clowns and jesters were common in Elizabethan drama.

foot, organ in most higher vertebrates, used chiefly for support and locomotion. In man seven bones form heel; five parallel metatarsals form long arch and their lower ends form transverse arch. Each toe has three phalanges except great toe, which has two. See also FLAT FOOT. See *ill.,* p. 595.

foot and mouth disease or **hoof and mouth disease,** communicable virus disease of cattle and other clovenfooted animals. It causes great losses to cattle industry and is more prevalent in Europe and South America than in U.S. It is characterized by eruption of blisters on mucous membranes, especially of mouth, feet, and udder. Control is by slaughter and deep burial of infected animals, disinfection of area occupied, and strict quarantine.

football, in U.S., game played by two opposing teams of 11 men on level field 100 by 53⅓ yd. Game originally developed from Greek *harpaston.* American football similar to rugby, dating from 1823 in England. Rutgers and Princeton played (1869) first intercollegiate football game in America at New Brunswick, N.J. Organized professional football in U.S. dates from 1920.

Foote, Andrew Hull, 1806–63, American naval officer. In Civil War he gave brilliant support to Union army in victories at Fort Henry, Fort Donelson, and Island No. 10, and was made rear admiral but had to retire.

Foote, Arthur William, 1853–1937, American organist, composer, and teacher. His compositions include sacred choruses, chamber music, and choral settings of Longfellow's poems.

Foote, Henry Stuart, 1804–80, U.S. Senator (1847–52), governor of Miss. (1852–54). Fought states' rights doctrines in the Senate and later opposed Jefferson Davis in Confederate congress; supported Republicans after the war.

Foote, Lucius Harwood, 1826–1913, American minister to Korea (1883–84), first regular diplomat from a Western power to that country.

foot-pound: see WORK.

Foot Resolution, offered 1829 by Samuel A. Foot in U.S. Senate. Instructed committee on public lands to inquire into limiting of public-land sale. Jacksonian Democrats, encouraging migration W, opposed resolution; New England manufacturing interests, demanding a ready labor supply, backed it. Advocates of states' rights identified themselves with interests of West. Touched off dramatic debates of 1830 between Robert HAYNE and Daniel WEBSTER.

Foppa, Vincenzo (vēnchän'tsō fôp'pä), c.1427–c.1515, Italian painter, founder of Lombard school. Worked in Pavia and Milan.

Forain, Jean Louis (zhā' lwē' fôrē'), 1852–1931, French painter, etcher, and lithographer. Best known for political cartoons in manner of Daumier.

Foraker, Joseph Benson (fôr'ŭkŭr), 1846–1917, American political leader. U.S. Senator from Ohio (1897–1909). Old Guard Republican; accused of accepting retainers from Standard Oil Co.

foraminifera (fŭrä″mŭnī'fŭrŭ), members of an order of protozoa most of which have a shell. They inhabit all oceans, and there are a few species in fresh and brackish water. Discarded skeletons of genus *Globigerina* form on ocean bottom a deposit which solidifies into chalk.

Forbes, John, 1710–59, British general in French and Indian Wars. Captured Fort Duquesne 1758.

Forbes, John Murray, 1813–98, American capitalist. Under his direction the Michigan Central and Chicago, Burlington & Quincy railroads were marked by financial stability.

Forbes-Robertson, Sir Johnston, 1853–1937, English actor. On stage from 1874, he had his first great success in 1889. Appeared as Hamlet (1898) and in such plays as *The Passing of the Third Floor Back.*

Forbidden City, China: see CHINESE ARCHITECTURE.

Forbush, Edward Howe (fôr'boosh), 1858–1929, American ornithologist, state ornithologist of Mass. from 1908 and director of division of ornithology of state board of agr. (1893–1908; 1921–).

force, in physics, is commonly defined as any "push" or "pull" acting on a body or as that effort acting to change its state of motion (i.e., its acceleration or direction of movement) or state of rest. Forces are measured in pounds, grams, or kilograms, depending upon system of weights used. For every force there is an equal and opposite force. Both direction and magnitude enter into effect of a force upon a given body. Forces can produce rotation of certain bodies, e.g., of a lever bar free to revolve about its center. A rotating part is acted upon by centrifugal force, i.e., a force acting to make it fly off at a tangent from its path around the center. This force must be balanced, if equilibrium is to be maintained, by a centripetal force, i.e., a force acting in the opposite direction and toward the center, holding the body in its regular path. Forces acting on the various parts of structures and machines are factors determining stress and strain and STRENGTH OF MATERIALS. Certain force measurements are based on velocity imparted to a given mass in a certain unit of time. The DYNE is unit of force in cgs (centimeter-gram-second) system; in English system it is the poundal. See also GRAVITATION; MAGNETISM; PRESSURE; VOLT. See *ill.,* p. 619.

force bill, popular name for several laws in U.S. history, notably act of March 2, 1833, and Reconstruction acts of 1870 and 1871. First force bill, passed in response to ordinance of NULLIFICATION of S.C., empowered Pres. Jackson to use army and navy, if necessary, to enforce laws of Congress, specifically the tariff measures at issue. In second set of force bills, radical Republicans strengthened their Reconstruction program by imposing severe penalties on those Southerners who tried to obstruct it. Act of May 31, 1870, penalized anyone preventing qualified citizens (in this case Negroes) from voting, and placed congressional elections under exclusive Federal control. Act of April 20, 1871, inspired by activities of Ku Klux Klan, declared acts of armed combinations tantamount to rebellion and empowered President to suspend privilege of habeas corpus in lawless areas.

Ford, Edsel Bryant: see FORD, HENRY.

Ford, Ford Madox, 1873–1939, English author. As editor of literary reviews he greatly influenced modern writing. Taught Joseph Conrad English and collaborated with him. Originally Ford Madox Hueffer.

Ford, Henry, 1863–1947, American industrialist, pioneer automobile manufacturer. An inexpensive, standardized car, resulting from mass production, helped make Ford world's largest automobile producer. Had employee profit-sharing plan; opposed union organization until 1941. Estab. FORD FOUNDATION. His son, **Edsel Bryant Ford,** 1893–1943, was president of Ford Motor Co. 1919–43. **Henry Ford II,** 1917–, succeeded his grandfather as president in 1945.

Ford, John, b. 1586, English dramatist, author of verse plays, including '*Tis Pity She's a Whore* (1633). Collaborated with Dekker and Rowley in *The Witch of Edmonton,* 1621.

Ford, Worthington Chauncey, 1858–1941, American historian and editor. He was chief of the manuscripts division of the Library of Congress (1902–9) and editor of the Mass. Historical Society (1909–29). Works he edited include the writings of George Washington (14 vols., 1889–93) and of John Quincy Adams (7 vols., 1913–17). Joint editor of *Winnowings in American History* (15 vols., 1890–91), together with his brother, **Paul Leicester Ford,** 1865–1902. He edited many early U.S. writings, including those of Thomas Jefferson (10 vols., 1892–99), and wrote biographies (notably *The True George Washington,* 1896) and novels (e.g., *Janice Meredith,* 1899; *The Honorable Peter Stirling,* 1894).

Ford City, borough (pop. 5,352), W Pa., on Allegheny R. NE of Pittsburgh. Mfg. of glass products.

Ford Foundation, incorporated 1936 with funds from Henry Ford and Edsel B. Ford for general purpose of advancing human welfare. Greatly expanded program was inaugurated in 1950 with five main aims: to support activities directed toward world peace; to secure greater allegiance to basic principles of freedom and democracy; to advance economic well-being of people everywhere; to promote educational and cultural activities; and to support scientific study.

Fordham University (fôr′dŭm), in the Bronx, New York city; R.C. (Jesuit), partly coed.; opened 1841 as St. John's Col., chartered 1846 as university, renamed 1905. Noted for seismography work.

Fords Island, T.H.: see PEARL HARBOR.

Forefathers' Day, celebrated by New Englanders Dec. 21, to commemorate landing of Pilgrims in 1620 on Plymouth Rock. It was first observed in 1769.

Foreign Legion, French volunteer infantry regiment, created 1831 for pacification of Algeria, where it is normally stationed. Enlisted men are mostly foreigners. Important in French colonial expansion, Legion also fought gallantly in World War I. It was renovated and reorganized 1946.

Foreign Ministers, Council of, informal body set up at Yalta Conference Feb., 1945 by U.S., British, and Russian ministers. France was admitted 1946. After POTSDAM CONFERENCE, group met in London, then in Moscow in late 1945. It decided on certain peace treaties, an 11-power Far Eastern Commission and Council for Japan, and an atomic energy commission within UN. It steered Paris peace conference of 1946 and subsequent decisions; but failed in 1947 to draft peace treaties with Germany and Austria. Revived in June, 1949, it achieved ending of Soviet blockade of Berlin.

foreign missions: see MISSIONS.

foreign service: see DIPLOMATIC SERVICE; CONSULAR SERVICE.

Forel, Auguste or **August** (ōgüst′ fôrĕl′), 1848–1931, Swiss psychiatrist and entomologist. As a boy he began his studies of ants on which he wrote a number of books and which later influenced his approach to psychiatry. He promoted humane treatment of the insane and contributed to study of hypnotism and of sexual problems.

Forel, François Alphonse (fräswä′ älfôs′), 1841–1912, Swiss physician and naturalist. He taught anatomy and physiology at Univ. of Lausanne and studied Swiss glaciers and lakes.

Foreland, North, and **South Foreland;** headlands of Kent, England. Both are chalk cliff formations. Defeat of Dutch in 1666 associated with Forelands.

forest, plant community in which trees are dominant. Three main types of forests: equatorial or tropical rain-belt forests, found especially in basins of Amazon and Congo rivers and marked by luxuriant growth of a variety of trees; and deciduous and coniferous forests, both occurring mainly in temperate latitudes. Some conifers are found in the tropics at high altitudes, and at low altitudes of subarctic regions. Mixed stands of deciduous trees and conifers occur in temperate zones. Generally conifers are the climax growth of regions above about 40° N lat.; below this, deciduous trees usually dominate. Forests are of vital importance in conservation of water and wildlife, prevention of erosion and floods, for timber supply, and for recreation. Great areas of U.S. forest land are now preserved as NATIONAL FORESTS, national parks, and state, county, and municipal parks. **Forestry** or silviculture is the scientific development and management of forests.

Forester, C(ecil) S(cott), 1899–, British author of superior adventure stories (notably those about naval hero Horatio Hornblower).

Forest Hill, village (pop. 15,305), S Ont., Canada, residential suburb of Toronto.

Forest Hills. 1 See QUEENS, New York city borough. **2** Borough (pop. 6,301), SW Pa., E suburb of Pittsburgh.

Forest Park, village (pop. 14,969), NE Ill., W residential suburb of Chicago. Has greenhouses.

Forfarshire: see ANGUS, county.

forgery, willful fabrication or alteration of a written document (private or public—e.g., birth or marriage certificate) with the intent fraudulently to injure the interests of another. In the U.S. forgery ordinarily is a state crime, but to send forged documents through the mail may constitute Federal crime.

forget-me-not, plant (*Myosotis*) with small flowers, usually blue, used in borders and rock gardens.

forging, working metals by heating, then hammering and rolling. Metal is heated to red or white heat in forge; charcoal and coke are usual fuels. Heated metal is removed with tongs to anvil, hammered to desired shape, and thrust into water for tempering. Like founding, forging was practiced prehistorically, probably first in Asia. Early importance of metals is indicated by names Bronze Age and Iron Age.

Forlì, Melozzo da: see MELOZZO DA FORLÌ.

Forlì (fôrlē′), city (pop. 33,505), Emilia-Romagna, N central Italy, in Romagna. Free commune from 11th cent.; later a principality; passed to Papal States 1504. Citadel (14th cent.); art gallery.

formaldehyde (fôrmăl′dŭhīd), simple gaseous ALDEHYDE with suffocating odor. Used to make dyes, plastics, resins; subject to POLYMERIZATION. **Formalin,** 40% water solution of formaldehyde, used as antiseptic, disinfectant, biological preservative.

formic acid, colorless, corrosive organic acid, lowest member of fatty-acid series. It is a compound of hydrogen, carbon, and oxygen. Found in red ants, sting of bees, and other insects.

Formosa (fôrmō′sù) [Port.,= beautiful], Chinese *Taiwan,* island (13,808 sq. mi.), off SE coast of Chinese mainland; with PESCADORES isls. forms Formosa province (13,886 sq. mi.; pop. 7,617,753) of China; cap. Taipei. Mountainous, rises to c.13,600 ft. at Mt. Morrison. Produces rice, sugar cane, and oolong tea. Lumbering (oak, cypress, camphor), mining (mainly coal, gold, copper). Portuguese came 1590, followed 1624 by the Dutch, who were dominant until 1662, when they were ousted by Koxinga, Chinese general of Southern Ming dynasty. Brought under Ch'ing dynasty in 1683, ceded 1895 to Japan, restored to China after World War II. In 1949 became last refuge of Nationalists under Chiang Kai-shek. In Feb., 1953, the U.S. lifted the 7th Fleet's blockade of Formosa, thus presumably freeing Chiang to attack the Communist-held mainland of China.

formula, in chemistry, a written expression which indicates elements, in proportion by weight, making up one molecule of a chemical COMPOUND. Formula of water is H_2O: symbol H = hydrogen, O = oxygen; subscript 2 shows that there are 2 atoms of hydrogen. Formula also shows that 2 parts of hydrogen by weight (2 × its ATOMIC WEIGHT of 1) and 16 parts of oxygen (1 × 16) are combined to form 18 parts by weight of water. Structural formula shows arrangement of atoms.

formula, in mathematics and physics, a statement in symbols of relationship between certain quantities. Quantities are expressed usually by letters, relationships by algebraic symbols.

Forres (fŏ′rĭs), burgh (pop. 4,462), Morayshire, Scotland; ancient town with many legends. One of possible places where Macbeth murdered Duncan.

Forrest, Edwin, 1806–72, American actor, one of the era's great tragedians. His roles included Othello, Lear, Macbeth, and Hamlet. Married (1837) Catherine Sinclair, an English actress, who brought (1852) sensational divorce suit against him. Violent rivalry with MACREADY and demonstrations instigated by Macready and Forrest adherents culminated in the Astor Place riot (1849), but failed to dim Forrest's reputation as an actor.

Forrest, John Forrest, 1st Baron, 1847–1918, Australian explorer and statesman. Led coastal expedition from Perth to Adelaide (1870). Surveyor general of Western Australia (1883); first premier (1890–1901).

Forrest, Nathan Bedford, 1821–77, Confederate general. Commanded cavalry units in Tenn. (1862–63); in N Miss., where his victories menaced Sherman's communications; and again in Tenn. (1864) under J. B. Hood. Probably greatest Confederate cavalryman, he is the hero of many legends in South. To him is attributed the formula for victory: "Git there fustest with the mostest men."

Forrestal, James V(incent) (fŏ′rĭstäl), 1892–1949, U.S. Secretary of the Navy (1944–47) and first Secretary of Defense (1947–49). A suicide.

Forrest City, city (pop. 7,607), E Ark., at Foot of Crowley's Ridge. Trade center for agr. area.

Forster, E(dward) M(organ), 1879–, English novelist. Lived in Italy, India, Egypt. His novels are noted for crisp style and subtle irony: *Where Angels Fear to Tread* (1905), *The Longest Journey* (1907), *A Room with a View* (1908), *Howard's End* (1910), *A Passage to India* (1924). Also wrote short stories, essays, and literary criticism.

Forsyth, John, 1780–1841, American statesman. U.S. Senator from Ga. (1818–19, 1829–34); supported Pres. Jackson in nullification controversy in Ga. U.S. Secretary of State (1834–41).

forsythia (–sĭth′ēù), Old World shrub (*Forsythia*) with abundant yellow flowers appearing in spring before the leaves.

Fort, Paul (pōl′ fôr′), 1872–, French symbolist poet, noted for use of "rhythmical prose," as in *Ballades françaises* (1897).

Fortaleza (fôrtùlä′zù), city (pop. 213,605), cap. of Ceará state, NE Brazil; Atlantic port, founded 1609. Long a center of great sugar plantations; today important also for cotton.

Fort Atkinson, city (pop. 6,280), S Wis., SE of Madison. Trade center of dairy region.

Fort Beauséjour National Park: see BEAUSÉJOUR, FORT.

Fort Benton, city (pop. 1,522), N central Mont., at head of navigation on Missouri R. and NE of Great Falls. Grew around fur-trading post (1846). Reached by steamboat in 1859, it became supply point for gold seekers and cattlemen.

Fort Bridger State Park, SW Wyo., E of Evanston and on Blacks Fork of Green R. The supply post, founded 1843 by James BRIDGER, was held by Mormons 1853–57, then leased by U.S. as fort until 1890.

Fort Collins, city (pop. 14,937), N Colo., N of Denver and on Cache la Poudre R.; settled around fort (1864–71). Trade, processing center in irrigated area (grain, sugar beets, livestock). Dams of COLORADO-BIG THOMPSON PROJECT are near. Seat of Colorado Agricultural and Mechanical Col. (land-grant; coed.; 1879); includes Fort Lewis School near Durango.

Fort Davis, village, W Texas, SE of El Paso in Davis Mts. Much visited for mountain scenery. Near by is McDonald Observatory (1932; Univ. of Texas and Univ. of Chicago).

Fort-de-France (fôr-dù-fräs′), city (pop. 48,576), cap. of Martinique dept., French West Indies; chief port of island. It exports sugar and rum.

Fort Dodge, city (pop. 25,115), central Iowa, on Des Moines R. and NNW of Des Moines; settled c.1846. Fort Clarke estab. here 1850, renamed Fort Dodge (for Henry Dodge) 1851, abandoned 1853. Rail and industrial center of agr. and mining area with mfg. of gypsum, clay, and food products.

Fort Donelson National Military Park: see NATIONAL PARKS AND MONUMENTS (table).

Fort Erie, town (pop. 7,572), S Ont., Canada, on Niagara R. (bridged) opposite Buffalo, N.Y. Has steel mills, gold refineries, mfg. of aircraft and auto parts. Some U.S. firms have branch units here. Fort built 1764 by British. Taken by Americans in War of 1812 and successfully defended in 1814. Merged 1934 with Bridgeburg.

Fort Fairfield, town (pop. 5,791), NE Maine, on Aroostook R. at N.B. line. Potato-growing center.

Fort Frances, town (pop. 8,038), W Ont., Canada, on Rainy R. opposite International Falls, Minn. Hunting and camping center with paper, pulp, and lumber mills. Built as Hudson's Bay Co. post.

Fort Frederica National Monument: see NATIONAL PARKS AND MONUMENTS (table).

Fort George, river, central and W Que., Canada, longest river (520 mi.) flowing into Hudson Bay from the East. Formerly called Big R.

Fort Gibson, town (pop. 1,496), E Okla., E of Muskogee. Founded 1824 as army post for coming of Five Civilized Tribes; served until 1857. Natl. cemetery and Fort Gibson Dam near by.

Forth, river of Scotland. Flows c.50 mi. from Stirlingshire to Alloa. **Firth of Forth** extends c.50 mi. from Alloa to North Sea and is 1–18 mi. wide. Crossed at Queensferry by cantilever railroad bridge (5,330 ft. long). Rosyth, on bay, is a naval base. Several other rivers flow into the firth.

fortification. Defense structures appeared with the beginning of organized warfare. By the Middle Ages, the walled city and the castle were the standard fortifications. Masonry walls, however, failed to withstand artillery, which came into use about the 15th cent. Subsequent fortifications featured posts for the defenders' artillery and a far-flung defense perimeter around the main fortress. Extensive systems of intricate fortifications were used in Europe during the recent two great wars. As emphasis fell again on mobile warfare, the accent has returned to temporary, even improvised, fortifications designed primarily to delay an invader until reinforcements arrive.

Fort Jefferson National Monument: see NATIONAL PARKS AND MONUMENTS (table).

Fort Kent, town (pop. 5,343), N Maine, on St. John R. and NNW of Presque Isle. Potato processing.

Fort Laramie National Monument: see NATIONAL PARKS AND MONUMENTS (table).

Fort Lauderdale (lô'dŭrdāl), city (pop. 36,328), SE Fla., N of Miami, on Atlantic coast and on navigation canal to L. Okeechobee; settled around fort built (1837) in Seminole War. Ships fruits and vegetables. Fishing and yachting resort. Port Everglades and a Seminole Indian reservation are near.

Fort Lee, borough (pop. 11,648), NE N.J., on the Hudson, connected with upper Manhattan by George Washington Bridge. Fort here abandoned Nov. 20, 1776, by Gen. Greene after Fort Washington, across the river, was taken by British. Early center of moving-picture industry.

Fort McHenry National Monument and Historical Shrine: see NATIONAL PARKS AND MONUMENTS (table).

Fort McMurray, village, N Alta., Canada, on Athabaska R. Chief base for air travel to central Northwest Territories. Built 1790 as fur-trading post.

Fort Madison, city (pop. 14,954), SE Iowa, on the Mississippi below Burlington; settled 1833. Fort Madison, U.S. trading post, here 1808–13. Rail hub with mfg. of food products and writing equipment.

Fort Marion National Monument, renamed (1942) Castillo de San Marcos National Monument: see NATIONAL PARKS AND MONUMENTS (table).

Fort Matanzas National Monument: see NATIONAL PARKS AND MONUMENTS (table).

Fort Morgan, city (pop. 5,315), NE Colo., NE of Denver and on South Platte R. Trade, processing center for rich farm, dairy, livestock region.

Fort Myers, city (pop. 13,195), SW Fla., near Gulf of Mexico. Grew around fort built (1841) in Seminole War, held by Federals in Civil War. Ships citrus fruit, winter vegetables, and fish. T. A. Edison wintered and experimented here.

Fort Necessity National Battlefield Site: see NECESSITY, FORT.

Fort Nelson, village, N B.C., Canada, on Alaska Highway and Fort Nelson R. and N of Dawson Creek. Hudson's Bay Co. post here estab. c.1800.

Fort Payne, city (pop. 6,226), NE Ala., NE of Gadsden, in farm area, with mineral deposits.

Fort Peck Dam, NE Mont., in Missouri R. above mouth of Milk R. Built 1933–40 to control floods and improve navigation, it is used also for irrigation and power. One of world's largest earth-filled dams, it is 21,026 ft. long and 250 ft. high.

Fort Pierce, city (pop. 13,502), SE Fla., port on Indian R. (here connected to the Atlantic by an inlet). Grew around fort built 1838. Ships citrus fruit, vegetables, and lumber.

Fort Pulaski National Monument: see NATIONAL PARKS AND MONUMENTS (table).

Fortress Monroe: see MONROE, FORT.

Fort Scott, city (pop. 10,335), SE Kansas, N of Pittsburg near Mo. line. Grew up around military post (estab. 1842, abandoned 1855, rebuilt in Civil War). Rail and trade center in dairy and farm area.

Fort Smith, city (pop. 47,942), NW Ark., at Okla. line where Arkansas and Poteau rivers join. Founded 1817 as military post; was supply point in gold rush of 1848. State's chief industrial center, it has mfg. of furniture, glass, textiles, and metal and wood products and processing of zinc, oil, and gas. Mule market. Rail and trade center for farm area. Has Civil War

cemetery and the Old Fort and other old buildings.

Fort Stockton, city (pop. 4,444), W Texas, on plateau W of Pecos R. Grew around army post (1859). Near Comanche Springs (once camp site for Indians and California overlanders). Tourist center.

Fort Sumner, village (pop. 1,982), E N.Mex., NNE of Roswell. Near by are Alamogordo Dam and cemetery with grave of Billy the Kid.

Fort Sumter National Monument: see SUMTER, FORT.

Fort Thomas, residential city (pop. 10,870), N Ky., on Ohio R. in Cincinnati metropolitan area. Fort Thomas, U.S. army post, estab. here 1887.

Fortuna fôrtū'nù) [Latin,= fortune], in Roman religion, popular oracular goddess of chance.

Fortunate Isles or **Isles of the Blest,** in classical and Celtic legend, islands in Western Ocean, eternal home of souls of favored mortals. Long thought to be Canary or Madeira Isls.

Fortunatus (Venantius Honorius Clementianus Fortunatus), d. c.600, last Gallic Latin poet, author of the hymn *Vexilla Regis prodeunt*.

Fortune, Robert, 1813–80, British botanist. He introduced in England the kumquat and many other plants which he collected in the Orient. His experiments led to the growing of tea in India.

Fort Valley, city (pop. 6,820), S central Ga., E of Columbus. Center for peach-growing area.

Fort Wayne, city (pop. 133,607), NE Ind., where St. Joseph's and St. Mary's rivers form Maumee R. Miami Indians, who early resisted taking of site by French (who built Fort Miami here 1704), then by British, were subdued by Anthony Wayne, who built (1794) fort that bore his name. After further Indian fighting in War of 1812 town grew with fur trade. Now state's second largest city, key rail and shipping point of agr. and dairying region. Mfg. of electrical and metal products; food processing.

Fort William, city (pop. 34,947), W Ont., Canada, on NW shore of L. Superior at mouth of Kaministikwia R. With twin city, Port Arthur, is W Canadian lake port and shipping center. Terminus of Canadian National and Canadian Pacific railways. Has grain elevators and paper, pulp, lumber, and flour mills, foundries, machine shops, and shipyards. Fort Kaministiquia built here 1717, and Fort William estab. 1801 as post of North West Co.

Fort William, burgh (pop. 2,661), Inverness-shire, Scotland, on Loch Linnhe, near Ben Nevis; tourist center for Highlands. Fort (built by General Monck 1655) was twice besieged by Jacobites, whose relics are in a museum. Has important aluminum industry.

Fort Worth, city (pop. 278,778), N Texas, at junction of Clear and West forks of Trinity R. and W of Dallas; settled 1843. Army Fort Worth estab. 1847. Was cowtown after Civil War. Railroad (1876) aided growth. Industrial and transportation center of cattle and agr. area with stockyards, grain elevators and mills, and meat packing plants; also refineries and aircraft plants. Grew through two World Wars. Here are TEXAS CHRISTIAN UNIVERSITY and U.S. military air base. Served by three reservoirs on West Fork.

Forty Fort, residential borough (pop. 6,173), NE Pa., on Susquehanna R. near Wilkes-Barre. Militia marched from fort here in WYOMING VALLEY massacre 1778.

forum, market and meeting place in anc. Roman towns in Italy; consisted of open square surrounded by public buildings. Old Roman Forum extended SE from Capitoline Hill, later reaching almost to Colosseum. Arch of Augustus was entrance to Forum proper. In NE were Basilica Aemilia and the curia, where the senate met. Temple of Saturn housed the treasury. In imperial times new fora, with marble pavements and grandiose colonnades, were built to NE, from Basilica of Constantine to valley between Capitoline and Quirinal. Decay of Old Forum began in 4th cent.; in Middle Ages the fora were stripped to provide materials for new monuments.

Foscolo, Ugo (ōō'gō fō'skōlō), 1778–1827, Italian poet

and patriot. His novel *The Last Letters of Jacopo Ortis* (1796–1802; Eng. tr., 1818), modeled on Goethe's *Werther*, stirred Italian hearts for generations. His "graveyard" poem *Sepolcri* (1807) is notable.

Fosdick, Harry Emerson, 1878–, American clergyman. Pastor Park Ave. Baptist Church (1926) and its successor, Riverside Church, New York (1930–46). Noted for Modernist stand in controversies of 1920s.

Fosse Way (fŏs), Roman road in England, supposed to have linked present Exeter, Bath, Cirencester, Leicester, and Lincoln.

fossil, organic remains or impressions preserved in sedimentary rocks from the geologic past. Favorable conditions included burial in asphalt, mud, or other materials which prevent decay. Fossilization is usually confined to skeletons or hard parts, but entire mammals of the late Pleistocene have been found frozen in ice. Footprints of land animals and tracks of marine invertebrates are regarded as fossils. Petrified wood and other petrified plant and animal remains form when the original structure is slowly replaced by mineral matter.

Fossil Cycad National Monument: see NATIONAL PARKS AND MONUMENTS (table).

Foster, John Watson, 1836–1917, American diplomat. Minister to Mexico (1873–80), Russia (1880–81). Secretary of State (1892–93). Represented U.S. in arbitration of Bering Sea Fur-Seal Controversy.

Foster, Stephen Collins, 1826–64, American composer. His knowledge of the Negro was gained from minstrel shows, for which he wrote many of his songs. He had little business acumen, and despite the popularity of his songs, died in extreme poverty. Among his best-loved songs are *Oh! Susannah* (1848), *Camptown Races* (1850), *Old Folks at Home* (1851), *My Old Kentucky Home* (1853), *Jeanie with the Light Brown Hair* (1854), and *Old Black Joe* (1860).

Foster, William Z(ebulon), 1881–, American Communist leader. Three-time presidential candidate.

Fostoria, city (pop. 14,351), NW Ohio, S of Toledo; estab. 1854. Trade center for farm area with stockyards and mfg. of wood products and auto parts.

Fothergill, John (fŏ'dhŭrgĭl), 1712–80, English physician, a Quaker, noted for his London practice, for botanic garden at Upton, Essex, and for work to improve jails and sanitation.

Fotheringhay (fŏdh'ŭrĭng-gā), village, Northamptonshire, England. Castle was birthplace of Richard III and scene of Mary Queen of Scots' execution.

Foucault, Jean Bernard Léon (zhä' bĕrnär' lāŏ' fōōkō'), 1819–68, French physicist. He determined velocity of light in air; found that speed of light in other media is reduced in proportion to index of refraction. He devised the Foucault PENDULUM.

Fouché, Joseph (zhôzĕf' fōōshä'), 1759–1820, French police minister (1799–1802, 1804–10); created duke of Otranto 1809. A lifelong opportunist, he sided with every party in power from the French Revolution through the Bourbon restoration. Through his private spy system he discovered the CADOUDAL plot (1804), thus earning a return to favor. Sometimes considered the father of the modern police state, he created a ruthlessly efficient system of criminal and political police. After his second dismissal (because of secret dealings with England) he held several high posts but never regained his power.

Foucquet: see FOUQUET.

Fouillée, Alfred (fōōyā'), 1838–1912, French philosopher. Developed motor theory of consciousness, making ideas agents of change and progress.

founding or **casting,** shaping of metals by melting and pouring into molds. Foundry is place where this is done. Sand or loam mold (held to desired form by wooden pattern) used to cast iron or steel. Pattern is made slightly large to allow shrinkage when metal solidifies. Rapid cooling increases hardness of casting. Metal molds are used in type founding and also in die-casting.

Fountains Abbey, ruined 12th-cent. abbey, West Riding of Yorkshire, England, SW of Ripon.

Fouqué, Friedrich, Freiherr de la Motte- (frē'drĭkh frī'hĕr dù lä môt'-fōōkā'), 1777–1843, German Romantic poet, best known for the fairy tale *Undine* (1811; many trs.).

Fouquet or **Foucquet, Jean** or **Jehan** (all: zhä' fōō-kā'), c.1415–c.1480, founder of 15th-cent. school of French painting which shows influence of Van Eycks and early Florentines. Famous for kneeling portrait of Etienne Chevalier (Louvre) and for illuminations in duc de Berry's Book of Hours (Chantilly).

Fouquet or **Foucquet, Nicolas** (nēkōlä'), 1615–80, French statesman, superintendent of finance (1653–61). Mismanaged treasury, accumulated huge private wealth. Denounced by Colbert and resented by Louis XIV for his ostentatious entertainments, he was brought to trial (1661) and sentenced (1664) to banishment. The king "commuted" the sentence to life imprisonment. Fouquet was a patron of La Fontaine and Molière.

Fouquier-Tinville, Antoine Quentin (ätwän' kätē' fōōkyä-tēvēl'), 1746–95, French revolutionist, chief prosecutor in Revolutionary tribunal during REIGN OF TERROR. Guillotined after fall of Robespierre.

Fourcroy, Antoine François, comte de (ätwän' fräswä' kŏt dù fōōrkrwä'), 1755–1809, French chemist. Pioneer in animal and plant chemistry; collaborated in reforming chemical nomenclature.

Four Forest Cantons, Ger. *Vier Waldstätten,* cantons of UNTERWALDEN, SCHWYZ, URI, and LUCERNE; first Swiss communities to win freedom. Lake of the Four Forest Cantons is called in English Lake of LUCERNE.

Four Freedoms. In message to Congress (Jan. 6, 1941, Pres. F. D. Roosevelt stated that Four Freedoms should prevail throughout world—freedom of speech and expression, freedom of worship, freedom from want, and freedom from fear. These were substantially incorporated in ATLANTIC CHARTER.

Four-H or **4-H clubs,** organizations under Dept. of Agr. for boys and girls in rural areas. They aim to improve methods of agr. and home economics and to promote good citizenship. Name is derived from fourfold purpose of improving head, heart, hands, health. Groups are very active.

Four Horsemen of the Apocalypse (ŭpŏk'ŭlĭps), allegorical figures in Bible. Rev. 6.1–8. Rider on white horse has many interpretations—one is that he represents Christ; rider on red horse is war; rider on black horse is famine, and rider on pale horse, death.

Fourier, Charles (shärl' fōōryä'), 1772–1837, French social philosopher. Projected social utopia organized in small economic units (phalanxes) of 1,620 persons. Doctrine of **Fourierism** spread to America under auspices of Prosper Considérant, Albert Brisbane, Horace Greeley. BROOK FARM was for a time Fourierist; most successful community was at Red Bank, N.J.

Fourier, Jean Baptiste Joseph, Baron (fōō'rēä", Fr. zhä' bätēst' zhôzĕf' bärō' fōōryä'), 1768–1830, French mathematician and physicist. Noted for research on heat and numerical equations; he originated Fourier's theorem on vibratory motion and Fourier series which provided method for representing discontinuous functions by trigonometric series.

Four Lakes, S Wis., chain of lakes (Mendota, largest; Monona, Waubesa, Kegonsa). Madison is between first two. Univ. of Wisconsin is on Mendota.

Fournier, Pierre Simon (fōōrnyä'), 1712–68, Parisian type founder. Devised first point system for measuring type. Wrote *Manuel typographique* (1764–66).

Fourteen Points, formulation of a peace program, presented by U.S. Pres. Woodrow Wilson in address before Congress on Jan. 8, 1918. Message was intended to reach people and liberal leaders of Central Powers as a seductive appeal for peace, in which purpose it was successful, and to provide a framework for peace discussions. Message made Wilson moral leader of the Allies, but after the Armistice opposition to the points quickly crystallized, and actual treaty (see VERSAILLES, TREATY OF) represented a compromise or defeat of many of them.

Fourteenth Amendment, to the U.S. Constitution (1868). Section 1 established the basis of U.S. citizenship and forbade states to abridge privileges and immunities of U.S. citizens, to deprive any person of life, liberty, or property without due process of law, or to deny any person equal protection of law. The U.S. Supreme Court used Section 1 extensively to limit restrictive state legislation (e.g., the states were forbidden to favor or suppress any religious establishment). The equal-protection clause became the main weapon of Negroes in their fight for equality. It was also a claim for corporations seeking immunities of citizens.

fourth dimension: see SPACE TIME.

Fourth of July, Independence Day, or **July Fourth,** U.S. patriotic holiday par excellence, commemorating adoption of Declaration of Independence. Observance began during American Revolution.

Fowke, Gerard (fouk), 1855–1933, American archaeologist. Noted for study of the Ohio valley. Investigated aboriginal remains in E U.S. (1885–88, 1891–93). Explored Vancouver Isl. (1898). Made ethnological studies in Hawaiian Isls. (1920).

Fowler, H(enry) W(atson), 1858–1933, English lexicographer. He and his brother, F. G. Fowler, collaborated on *The King's English* (1906) and on an abridgment of *Oxford English Dictionary* (1911). After F. G. Fowler died in 1918 H. W. Fowler completed alone *A Dictionary of Modern English Usage* (1926).

Fowliang (foo'leäng'), town (pop. 86,744), Kiangsi prov., China, on Chang R. Founded 6th cent. Long celebrated as porcelain-making center.

Fox, Charles James, 1749–1806, English Whig statesman and orator. Disliked by George III, he was a friend of the prince of Wales (George IV). Opponent of Lord North, he attacked British policy in the American war. Was foreign secretary for brief periods (1782, 1783, 1806). Supported repeal of Poynings's Law in 1782. Opposed William Pitt by demanding British nonintervention in French Revolution. Urged abolition of slave trade (passed in 1807 after his death) and political freedom for dissenters.

Fox, George, 1624–91, English founder of Society of FRIENDS. He turned from organized religion to direct, personal relationship with God through "inward light" of Christ and began to preach in 1647. Despite persecutions and imprisonments he won many followers. Plan of organization was set up in 1668, with first London Yearly Meeting in 1671. His writings include his noted journal (1694; preface by William Penn).

Fox, John, Jr., 1862–1919, American novelist, b. Ky., author of *The Little Shepherd of Kingdom Come* (1903), *The Trail of the Lonesome Pine* (1908).

Fox or **Foxe, Luke,** 1586–1635, English explorer. Sought Northwest Passage; explored W shore of Hudson Bay, satisfied himself there was no passage through it (1631).

Fox, Margaret, 1836–93, American spiritualist. She claimed connection with spirit world and toured U.S. and Europe with her sisters. In 1888 she admitted that effects were fraudulent.

Fox, river, c.176 mi. long, rising in central Wis. and flowing SW to within c.1½ mi. of Portage, on Wisconsin R., with which it is connected by ship canal. Thence flows NE to Green Bay, at Green Bay city. Drains L. Winnebago. Above lake it is known as Upper Fox R., below lake as Lower Fox. Route of early explorers, missionaries, traders into Wis. and Northwest; forts, missions, and trading posts were estab. along course. Jolliet and Marquette were first white men to reach the Mississippi by way of Fox-Wisconsin portage 1673.

fox, predatory intelligent animal of dog family. Fur is usually long and thick; tail bushy, and longer than the wolf's. It eats small animals, berries, and fruits. Red fox (*Vulpes*) inhabits parts of Europe, Asia, N Africa, most of U.S., and Canada. Usually the coat is reddish, the tail white-tipped, the ears black-tipped. Silver, black, and cross fox (yellowish to pale orange) are color phases which may appear in any red fox litter. Breeders have developed platinum fox. Arctic fox has circumpolar range. Gray fox found over most U.S. and through Mexico to N South America.

Foxboro or **Foxborough,** town (pop. 7,030), SE Mass., W of Brockton. Mfg. of precision instruments.

Foxe, John, 1516–87, English clergyman, author of *Book of Martyrs.* In Strasbourg appeared (1554; in Latin) story of Protestant martyrs to c.1500. At Basel appeared (1559) first complete edition. John Day issued (1563) first complete English edition.

Foxe, Luke: see Fox, LUKE.

foxglove, Old World biennial or perennial plant of genus *Digitalis.* It has handsome, spirelike spikes of purple, pink, or white bell-shaped flowers in early summer. Its leaves yield the drug digitalis.

Fox Indians: see SAC AND FOX INDIANS.

Fox Islands: see ALEUTIAN ISLANDS.

fox terrier: see TERRIER.

Foyle, river of Co. Tyrone, N. Ireland. Its navigable estuary is called Lough Foyle.

F. P. A.: see ADAMS, FRANKLIN PIERCE.

Fra Angelico: see ANGELICO, FRA.

Fracastoro, Girolamo (jērō'lämō fräkästō'rō), 1483–1553, Italian physician, authority on epidemic diseases. He wrote a poem on syphilis from which the disease takes its name.

Frackville, borough (pop. 6,541), E Pa., NNW of Pottsville. Anthracite mining.

fraction, in arithmetic, expression representing a part, or several equal parts, of a unit. In writing ⅖, number 5 is denominator (total number of parts into which unit is divided); number 2 is numerator (number of equal parts taken of unit). When the numerator is less than the denominator, the fraction is called proper; when the reverse is true it is improper. To add two fractions, denominators must be like, or be make like, after which numerators are added together; or, for subtraction, subtracted. To multiply fractions, multiply numerators together and denominators together. To divide, invert divisor; then multiply. In algebraic fractions procedure is the same.

fracture, a breaking, especially of a bone. Types include simple, in which overlying skin is unbroken; compound, in which broken bone communicates with external wound; and greenstick, in which one side of bone is broken, other side bent.

Fra Diavolo (frä" dēä'vōlō) [Ital.,= brother devil], 1771–1806, Neapolitan bandit and soldier whose real name was Michele Pezza. Taking up the cause of the Bourbon rulers of Naples, he fought the French, who captured and hanged him. Auber's opera, *Fra Diavolo,* is in no way historical.

Fragonard, Jean Honoré (zhä ōnôrä' frägônär'), 1732–1806, French painter. Studied with Chardin and Boucher. Painted scenes of love and gallantry for the French court.

Framingham, town (pop. 28,086), E Mass., WSW of Boston; settled 1650. Mfg. of autos, paper products, shoes, and carpets. Seat of Massachusetts State Teachers Col. (for women; chartered 1838, opened 1839 in Lexington); oldest existing U.S. school for teachers; estab. by Horace MANN.

France, Anatole (änätôl' fräs'), pseud. of **Jacques Anatole Thibault** (zhäk', tēbō'), 1844–1924, French author. The style of his early works is charming and ironic, as in *Le Crime de Sylvestre Bonnard* (1881), *Le Livre de mon ami* (1885), *Thaïs* (1890), *La Rôtisserie de la Reine Pédauque* (1893), *Le Lys rouge* (1894). Following the Dreyfus Affair, in which he supported Zola, he turned to political satire with *Penguin Island* (1908) and *La Révolte des anges* (1914). Awarded 1921 Nobel Prize in Literature.

France, republic (212,700 sq. mi.; pop. 40,502,513), W

Europe, bordering on English Channel (N), Atlantic Ocean (W), Spain (SW), Mediterranean (S), Italy, Switzerland, Germany (E), Luxembourg, and Belgium (NE); cap. Paris. Called Metropolitan France, it is the chief member of the FRENCH UNION and consists of the 89 departments of continental France and the island-department of CORSICA. Its central natural feature is the MASSIF CENTRAL. N of that rugged mountain mass and of the LOIRE R. extend the fertile Paris basin, drained by the SEINE and MARNE, and the hilly landscapes of NORMANDY and BRITTANY. W and SW of the Massif Central the Aquitanian plain, drained by the GARONNE and DORDOGNE, stretches to the Atlantic and the PYRENEES; S of the Massif is the coastal plain of LANGUEDOC. A chain of mountains parallels the E border—the ARDENNES, VOSGES, and JURA, and the ALPS of SAVOY, DAUPHINÉ, and PROVENCE (highest point MONT BLANC). Despite extreme administrative centralization, the old provinces (abolished 1789) retain striking diversity and are basic cultural, economic, and geographic units—e.g., ALSACE, AUVERGNE, Brittany, CHAMPAGNE, GASCONY, TOURAINE). Nearly self-sufficient in agr., France is a country of small, independent farmers and of many small towns. Only PARIS, MARSEILLES, LYONS, and BORDEAUX have more than 250,000 inhabitants. Wine and luxury articles are among chief exports. Natural resources include coal (NORD dept.), iron (LORRAINE), hydroelectric power (RHONE valley). Lille, Saint-Étienne, Roubaix, Clermont-Ferrand, Le Creusot are important industrial centers. Le Havre, Rouen, Cherbourg, Saint-Nazaire, Nantes, Bordeaux, Marseilles are the chief ports. Though some German, Flemish, and Basque are spoken in border regions, as well as Breton in lower Brittany, Latin culture predominates, as does Roman Catholicism. Separation of Church and state dates from the struggle of 1905–6.

Medieval France. Roman conquest of GAUL was completed by Caesar 51 B.C. A Christian, Latin, highly civilized, prosperous country by the 5th cent. A.D., Gaul was suddenly reduced by Germanic invaders to chaos and barbarism. The FRANKS, emerging as sole masters under CLOVIS I, ruled Gaul as part of their empire under the dynasties of the MEROVINGIANS (481 –751) and CAROLINGIANS (751–987). CHARLES MARTEL saved Gaul from Arabic conquest; CHARLEMAGNE gave it an era of order and cultural rebirth; the treaties of VERDUN (843) and MERSEN (870) made France a separate kingdom; the decline of Carolingian rule hastened the establishment of FEUDALISM and the MANORIAL SYSTEM. Powerful feudal lords easily usurped the authority of the weak kings. In 987 began the dynasty of the direct Capetians (Hugh Capet, Robert II, Henry I, Philip I, Louis VI, Louis VII, Philip II, Louis VIII, Louis IX, Philip III, Philip IV, Louis X, John I, Philip V, Charles IV). Their rule was a patient uphill struggle for control over the nobles and robber barons, extension of the royal domain, and revival of commerce; in this they were aided by the rising urban bourgeoisie. The reform of the CLUNIAC ORDER, the prestige of the SORBONNE, and its leading role in the CRUSADES gave France cultural supremacy in medieval Christendom. These gains were lost in the HUNDRED YEARS WAR with England, which devastated France and nearly ended its national existence (1337–1453). The VALOIS kings, aided by such heroes as DU GUESCLIN and JOAN OF ARC, emerged victorious; LOUIS XI (reigned 1461–83) created a new, unified France under a strong royal authority.

From Renaissance to Revolution. The later Valois kings—CHARLES VIII, LOUIS XII, FRANCIS I—wasted much effort on their imperialist struggle with Spain (see ITALIAN WARS); under the last Valois—Henry II, Francis II, Charles IX, Henry III—France bled in bitter civil strife (see RELIGION, WARS OF). Nevertheless, French culture in the 16th cent., stimulated by the Renaissance, went through a golden age which continued through the 17th cent. HENRY IV, first Bour-

bon king, ended the civil war and restored prosperity. The reigns of LOUIS XIII (1610–43) and LOUIS XIV (1643–1715), parts of which were dominated by cardinals RICHELIEU and MAZARIN, made France a nearly absolute monarchy and in a series of costly wars raised it to the chief power of Europe. But the quest for glory strained the treasury and drained the people. LOUIS XV's wars were no less ruinous but brought no glory; LOUIS XVI's intervention in the American Revolution made France bankrupt. At the same time the bourgeoisie had risen to prosperity and increasingly resented an antiquated system which restricted its economic activities (see MERCANTILISM), drained it through an iniquitous and inefficient fiscal system, misspent the revenues, and to some extent barred it from the government. This, rather than royal absolutism—which in fact was limited by custom and law— was the chief factor leading to the revolution of 1789. *Modern France.* The upheaval that shook Europe from 1789 to 1815 is covered in the articles FRENCH REVOLUTION; FRENCH REVOLUTIONARY WARS; NAPOLEON I. France emerged from it a uniform, bureaucratic state, dominated by its bourgeoisie, whom the Industrial Revolution brought into its own. The Bourbon Restoration was shortlived (see LOUIS XVIII; CHARLES X). The July Revolution of 1830 set up the monarchy of LOUIS PHILIPPE, overthrown in turn by the FEBRUARY REVOLUTION of 1848. The Second Republic was changed into the Second Empire by NAPOLEON III (1852), whose rule ended disastrously in the FRANCO-PRUSSIAN WAR (1870). French prosperity and colonial expansion continued under the Third Republic (1871–1940), but political disunity was a constant cause of instability. At tremendous sacrifice, France won in WORLD WAR I, but it was unable to deal with the crises of the post-war period. In WORLD WAR II France had to conclude an ignominious armistice (1940). While Gen. Charles de GAULLE continued to lead the Free French movement from London, France itself was partly under direct German occupation, partly under the subservient VICHY GOVERNMENT of Marshal Pétain; after the Allied invasion of N Africa (1942) all France came under German occupation. Liberated in 1944, France was slow in recovering from the sufferings of occupation, the destruction of war, and the shock to its economy. The Fourth Republic began with the new bicameral constitution of 1946. A member of the UN, France also joined in the European Recovery Program (1948) and the North Atlantic Treaty (1949).

Francesca, Piero della: see Piero DELLA FRANCESCA.

Francesca da Rimini (fränsĕ′skù, Ital. fränchä′skä dä rē′mēnē), 13th-cent. heroine of tragic verse. Her love for Paolo, brother of her crippled husband, was immortalized in Dante's *Divine Comedy.*

Franceschi, Piero de': see PIERO DELLA FRANCESCA.

Franche-Comté (fräsh-kôtā′), region and former province, E France, in Haute-Saône, Doubs, and Jura depts.; historic cap. Dôle (until 1676), later BESANÇON. A mountainous region (JURA in E. VOSGES in N), it has forests, pastures, agr. Mfg. of clocks, machinery, plastics. Free County of Burgundy or Franche-Comté was created 9th cent.; passed with kingdom of Arles to Holy Roman Empire 1034. Philip the Bold of Burgundy acquired it by marriage (15th cent.); through his daughter, Mary of Burgundy, it passed to the Spanish Hapsburgs, but it retained considerable autonomy. A battleground in the Wars of Religion and the Thirty Years War, it was twice laid waste. Louis XIV conquered it twice (1668, 1674) and obtained its cession from Spain in 1678.

franchise, a right specifically conferred by the government, especially that business franchise conferred by a municipality for the use of its streets to furnish public utilities. In politics, franchise is the right to vote.

Francia (frän′chä), c.1450–1517, Italian painter of early Bolognese school.

Francia, José Gaspar Rodríguez (hōsä′ gäspär′ rōdrē′-

gās frän′syä), 1760–1840, dictator of Paraguay (1814–40) and creator of national independence, known as El Supremo. By keeping Paraguay from foreign intercourse he stimulated internal growth and strong nationalistic spirit.

Franciabigio (frän″chäbē′jō), 1482–1525, Florentine painter. Collaborated on several works with his master, Andrea del Sarto.

Francis, Saint (Francis of Assisi), 1182?–1226, founder of the Franciscans, one of the greatest of Christian saints, b. Assisi, Italy. His original name was Giovanni di Bernardone, but he was called Francesco [Frenchman] from his father's travels in France. Was briefly a soldier, but at 22 he turned from worldly things and became devout. In 1209 he set out to preach, and from the first he won others by his humility, his joyful poverty, his singular devotion to other men, and his religious fervor. A little group of men gathered about him, and they went to Rome, where they were permitted to form a band of friars. These new Franciscans went about Italy, and soon they were preaching in foreign lands. Francis went abroad too and was in the Holy Land when dissension in the order led to his return. He held an assembly (1221), at which, with typical self-abnegation, he laid down command. He went on preaching and leading an ascetic life, and he wrote the rule for his order. In 1224 in a vision he received the stigmata (painful wounds corresponding to the wounds of the crucified Christ). He was well loved in his time and mourned throughout Italy when he died. Stories clustered about his holy, simple life, some of them later collected in *The Little Flowers of St. Francis;* very familiar are the stories of his preaching to the birds and of his taming a wolf at Gubbio by gentleness. He may have written the joyous appreciation of nature called *Hymn of the Sun.* Feast: Oct. 4.

Francis, emperors of the Holy Roman Empire. **Francis I,** 1708–65. Married MARIA THERESA 1736; elected emperor 1745 (see AUSTRIAN SUCCESSION, WAR OF THE). Earlier, he had been duke of LORRAINE (1729–37) and grand duke of TUSCANY (1737–65). Ruled ably in Tuscany, but left imperial government largely in hands of Maria Theresa. Father of Joseph II, Leopold II, Marie Antoinette. **Francis II,** 1768–1835, succeeded his father Leopold II as emperor and king of Hungary and Bohemia (1792). Was defeated four times in FRENCH REVOLUTIONARY WARS (1797, 1801) and in wars against NAPOLEON I (1805, 1809). Took title emperor of Austria as **Francis I** in 1804; dissolved Holy Roman Empire in 1806. Gave his daughter Marie Louise in marriage to Napoleon (1810). Joined new coalition against Napoleon 1813; presided over Congress of VIENNA (1814–15). With his minister METTERNICH he dominated HOLY ALLIANCE and German Confederation. His son Ferdinand succeeded him.

Francis, kings of France. **Francis I,** 1494–1547, son-in-law of Louis XII, reigned 1515–47. Resuming ITALIAN WARS, he won at MARIGNANO (1515). He lost in imperial election of 1519 to CHARLES V, his life-long rival. Despite failure to win English alliance at FIELD OF CLOTH OF GOLD he attacked Charles (1521), was routed and captured at Pavia (1525). Having, in his words, "lost all save life and honor," he obtained freedom by signing Treaty of Madrid (1526), in which he renounced territorial claims. His creation of the League of Cognac (with Pope Clement VII, Henry VIII of England, Venice, and Florence) precipitated a second war (1527–29), which ended, unfavorably, with the Treaty of CAMBRAI. A third war (1536–38) was inconclusive. In 1542, in alliance with SULEIMAN I of Turkey, he again attacked Charles (allied with Henry VIII). Peace with Charles (1544; see CRÉPY, TREATY OF) and with Henry (1546) confirmed his previous failures. A typical Renaissance monarch, unscrupulous, spendthrift, and dissolute, Francis also was a patron of arts and letters. Da Vinci, Cellini, and Rabelais were among his protégés. His grandson **Francis II,**

1544–60, son of Henry II, reigned 1559–60. Married Mary Queen of Scots (1558). Government was in hands of Charles and François de GUISE. Reprisals against Conspiracy of AMBOISE antagonized Protestants.

Francis, kings of the Two Sicilies. **Francis I,** 1777–1830, reigned 1825–30. His rule was reactionary and corrupt. **Francis II,** 1836–94, reigned 1859–61. Fought against RISORGIMENTO. His capitulation at Gaeta to Victor Emmanuel II (1861) led to proclamation of united Italy.

Francis, c.1554–1584, French prince, duke of Alençon and Anjou; youngest son of Henry II of France. One of suitors for hand of Elizabeth of England. In 1580 William the Silent offered him the rule of Netherlands (then in rebellion against Spain). He accepted, set sail from England in 1582, but was expelled by his subjects and lost Elizabeth's support when he tried to obtain absolute power (1583). His death opened French succession to Henry of Navarre (Henry IV).

Francis II, 1453–88, duke of Brittany (1458–88). Sought to preserve Breton independence from France. Joined League of Public Weal against LOUIS XI, who forced him to sign Peace of Ancenis (1468). Died shortly after his rout by Charles VIII (1488), who eventually married his daughter ANNE OF BRITTANY.

Francis Borgia, Saint (bôr′jù), 1510–72, Spanish Jesuit, third general of his order (1565–72). A member of the Borgia family, he was great-grandson of Pope Alexander VI and was duke of Gandia and a wealthy courtier of Emperor Charles V. After his wife's death (1546) he went to join St. Ignatius Loyola in Rome to become a Jesuit. Gave money to build the Roman College. After ordination in 1551, he built up the order and took charge of foreign missions (including those to America). As general of the Society of Jesus, he sent missionaries to N and E Europe and did much to promote the Catholic Reform. Edited the Jesuit rule and the *Spiritual Exercises.* Feast: Oct. 10.

Franciscans (frănsĭ′skŭnz), members of the religious orders following the rule of St. FRANCIS (approved by the pope 1223). They include three organizations of friars: the Friars Minor (formerly called Observants; they use the abbreviation O.F.M.), the Friars Minor Capuchin (see CAPUCHINS), and the Friars Minor Conventual. The Franciscans began as friars living in absolute poverty without property, but later generations relaxed this custom, and there were recurrent moves within the order to return to "pure" poverty. These caused some dissension, particularly that led by zealots called Spirituals; briefly they were very powerful in Italy, and one of their heroes was pope as CELESTINE V, but had to abdicate. In 1322 the pope settled the matter by putting Franciscans on the same basis as other orders as to property holding. Later another move toward primitive practice produced the Observants, who were made independent in 1517. Friars wishing still more strict observance of the rule became the Capuchins in 1525. The Franciscans were prominent at the medieval universities and contributed to scholasticism. They also were vigorous missionaries and did much work in many parts of the New World. St. CLARE, a follower of St. Francis, founded an order of Franciscan nuns (also called Poor Clares). There are also many members of the third order, both men and women, some living as laymen in the world, others in religious communities. Formerly the Franciscans were called the Gray Friars, but their habit now is typically brown.

Francis Ferdinand, 1863–1914, Austrian archduke, heir apparent of his great-uncle, Emperor Francis Joseph. Was assassinated, with his wife, by a Serbian nationalist at Sarajevo (June 28). Serbia's partial rejection of stiff Austrian ultimatum (July 23) led to WORLD WAR I.

Francis Joseph, 1830–1916, emperor of Austria (1848–1916), king of Hungary (1867–1916); nephew of FERDINAND, who abdicated in his favor. Subdued Hungary and defeated Sardinia (1849), but lost Lombardy in Italian War of 1859, Venetia in AUSTRO-PRUSSIAN WAR of 1866. Reorganized in 1867, his empire became the AUSTRO-HUNGARIAN MONARCHY. His private life was beset by the tragedies of his wife, ELIZABETH; his brother, MAXIMILIAN of Mexico; his son, Archduke RUDOLF. Charles I succeeded him.

Francis of Sales, Saint, 1567–1622, Savoyard Roman Catholic preacher, Doctor of the Church. Of an aristocratic family, he joined the priesthood contrary to his father's wishes and rose to become bishop coadjutor (1599) and bishop (1602) of Geneva. With St. Jane Frances de Chantal he founded the Order of the Visitation for women. His eloquent sermons moved to religion and converted many Protestants. Their burden was love of God and love of man. Two treatises *L'Introduction à la vie dévote* and *Treatise on the Love of God* are masterpieces of religious writing. Feast: Jan. 29.

Francis Xavier, Saint (zā'vyür), 1506–52, Basque Jesuit missionary, called the Apostle to the Indies. Friend of St. IGNATIUS OF LOYOLA, with whom he and five others formed the Society of JESUS; he was ordained with Ignatius (1537). After 1540 he spent the last 11 years of his life as a missionary in India and the Far East.

Franck, César (sāzär' frăk'), 1822–90, Belgian-French composer and organist. Much of his finest music was for organ. Among his most significant works are the Symphony in D Minor; *Variations symphoniques* for piano and orchestra; *Les Béatitudes,* oratorio; a violin sonata; *Trois Chorals* for organ; *Prélude, choral et fugue,* for piano.

Franck, Hans: see LÜTZELBURGER, HANS.

Franck, James, 1882–, German physicist. He shared 1925 Nobel Prize for discovery of laws governing effect of impact of electron on atom.

Franco, Francisco (fränthē'skō frän'kō), 1892–, Spanish generalissimo and dictator. Joined Insurgents in civil war of 1936–39 (see SPAIN); became chief of government in 1936, *Caudillo* [leader] in 1937, premier in 1939, regent (pending installment of a king) in 1947. Dissolved all parties except FALANGE (1937); dissolved Falange 1942. Kept Spain out of World War II despite commitments to Mussolini and Hitler.

Franco-German War: see FRANCO-PRUSSIAN WAR.

Franconia (frăngkō'nēŭ), Ger. *Franken,* duchy of medieval Germany. Created 9th cent., it extended from W bank of the Rhine eastward along Main R. Emperor Otto I broke it up into two nominal duchies—W or Rhenish Franconia (incl. archbishoprics of Mainz and Speyer, free cities of Frankfurt and Worms, Rhenish Palatinate, landgraviate of Hesse) and E Franconia (incl. bishoprics of Würzburg and Bamberg, margraviates of Ansbach and Bayreuth, free city of Nuremberg). Titular dukes of W Franconia furnished Franconian or Salian dynasty of emperors (1024–1125; see HOLY ROMAN EMPIRE). In E Franconia the ducal title, long in disuse, was revived by bishops of Würzburg (15th cent.). E Franconia passed to Bavaria in 1806–15 and was later divided into the provinces of **Lower Franconia** (cap. Würzburg), in the Main valley, NW Bavaria; **Middle Franconia** (cap. Ansbach), in hilly region of N Bavaria, with Nuremberg, Fürth, and Erlangen; and **Upper Franconia** (cap. Bayreuth), which includes the wooded Frankenwald plateau and the Fichtelgebirge, in NE Bavaria.

Franconia Mountains, range in White Mts., NW N.H., rising to 5,249 ft. in Mt. Lafayette. To W is **Franconia Notch,** c.6-mi. pass, with Old Man of the Mountain or the Profile ("Great Stone Face" of Hawthorne's story) and the Flume. Tramway (1938) mounts Profile Mt. near Echo L. **Franconia** town (pop. 549), NW of notch, is ski resort.

Franco-Prussian War or **Franco-German War,** July 19, 1870–Jan. 28, 1871. By his publication of EMS DISPATCH, Bismarck deliberately goaded the aggressive French government into declaring war on Prussia, which was joined by the other German states. A brilliant campaign, led by H. K. B. von Moltke, resulted

in French rout at Sedan, where NAPOLEON III was captured (Sept. 1). French resistance continued under a provisional government but became useless after surrender of BAZAINE at Metz (Oct. 27). Paris, however, resisted Prussian siege until Jan., 1871, despite growing famine, and refused to accept preliminary peace signed at Versailles (see VERSAILLES, TREATY OF, 1871) until May, when COMMUNE OF PARIS was suppressed by regular French forces. Chief results of war were creation of German Empire under William I of Prussia (proclaimed at Versailles on Jan. 18, 1871); cession of Alsace-Lorraine to Germany; establishment of Third Republic in France.

Frankenstein: see SHELLEY, MARY WOLLSTONECRAFT.

Frankfort. 1 City (pop. 15,028), W central Ind., NW of Indianapolis; laid out 1830. Trade center for apple region. Food and metal products. **2** City (pop. 11,916), state cap. (since 1792), N Ky., on Kentucky R. and E of Louisville; settled 1779, organized by Gen. James Wilkinson 1786. Trade and shipping center for farm and limestone area with mfg. of whisky, shoes, and twine. Here are present capitol (1909), old capitol (1827–30), Liberty Hall (1796, perhaps designed by Thomas Jefferson), cemetery with graves of Daniel and Rebecca Boone, and Kentucky State Col. for Negroes (land grant; coed.; 1886).

Frankfurt (frăngk'fŭrt, Ger. frängk'fŏŏrt) or **Frankfurt-am-Main** (äm-mīn'), city (pop. 523,923), Hesse, W Germany, on Main R. Historic, cultural, industrial, commercial, financial, and publishing center; river port. Produces chemicals, pharmaceutic articles, machinery, electrical equipment, clothing. Seat of university (opened 1914). Founded on site of Roman settlement; a royal residence under Carolingians; free imperial city from 1372; site of imperial elections from 1356 (see ELECTORS). Emperors-elect were crowned at Church of St. Bartholomew, then proceeded amid medieval pageantry to banquet at city hall, the Römer. Semiannual fairs, first mentioned 1240, brought city prosperity. Jews played important part until Nazi regime; Rothschild family originated here. Frankfurt accepted Reformation (1530), belonged to Schmalkaldic League (1536–47), was seat of diet of GERMAN CONFEDERATION (1815–66). In 1848–49 the Frankfurt Parliament met here at Church of St. Paul to plan unification of Germany; it adopted a federal constitution (excluding Austria) and offered imperial crown to FREDERICK WILLIAM IV of Prussia, whose refusal caused the failure of the whole scheme. Having sided with Austria in Austro-Prussian War, Frankfurt was annexed by Prussia (1866) and incorporated into Hesse-Nassau prov. After World War II, when it was in great part destroyed, Frankfurt became hq. of U.S. occupation forces. Its historic landmarks, including the Römer, the Catholic Church of St. Bartholomew, the Protestant Church of St. Paul, and the house where Goethe was born, have been largely rebuilt.

Frankfurt, Treaty of, 1871: see VERSAILLES, TREATY OF, 1871.

Frankfurt-an-der-Oder (–än-dĕr-ō'dŭr), city (pop. 51,-577), Brandenburg, E Germany, on Oder R. Mfg. of machinery, textiles, frankfurter sausages.

Frankfurter, Felix, 1882–, Associate Justice of U.S. Supreme Court (1939–), b. Austria. Has long public record in support of liberal tradition.

frankincense, resin of E African and Arabian tree of genus *Boswellia.* It is gathered in lumps for use in incense for religious ceremonies—a use it has had since Old Testament times (Ex. 30.34).

Frankland, Sir Edward, 1825–99, English chemist. He evolved the theory of valence; made studies of flame, luminosity, and gases; discovered helium.

Franklin, Ann Smith, 1696–1763, American printer. Succeeded her husband, James Franklin, Benjamin Franklin's brother, in commercial printing business. Published Newport, R.I., *Mercury,* and printed legal documents, paper money of R.I., and almanac series.

Franklin, Benjamin, 1706–90, American statesman,

printer, scientist, and writer, b. Boston. Went to Philadelphia as printer (1723). His common-sense philosophy and wit won attention, especially in his *Poor Richard's Almanack*, published 1732–57. Helped estab. (1751) present Univ. of Pennsylvania. Experiment with kite in a thunderstorm proved identity of lightning and electricity. Deputy postmaster general of colonies (1753–74). Proposed plan of union for colonies at ALBANY CONGRESS (1754). Agent for several colonies in England before American Revolution. Helped draft Declaration of Independence, which he signed. Successful diplomatic agent to France for new republic. Chosen commissioner (1781) to negotiate peace with Great Britain. Popular figure in France and England. Took part in Federal Constitutional Convention (1787). His autobiography is well known. His natural son, **William Franklin,** c.1730–1813, last royal governor of N.J., sided with Loyalists in American Revolution.

Franklin, Sir John, 1786–1847, British explorer in N Canada. Led two expeditions into arctic regions (1819–22, 1825–27). Set out in 1845 to seek Northwest Passage. Entire expedition of 129 men lost. More than 40 rescue parties subsequently sought traces of expedition, gaining immense geographical knowledge. Evidence of expedition's tragic fate finally discovered in 1850s.

Franklin, William: see FRANKLIN, BENJAMIN.

Franklin, provisional district: see NORTHWEST TERRITORIES, Canada.

Franklin. 1 Village, SE Idaho, at Utah line; founded 1860 by Mormons. Idaho's first permanent settlement. **2** City (pop. 7,316), S central Ind., S of Indianapolis. Trade center of agr. area. Mfg. of automobile parts and rayon. **3** Town (pop. 6,144), S La., on Bayou Teche. Processing center of sugar area. **4** Town (pop. 8,037), including Franklin village (pop. 5,348), SE Mass., near R.I. line, SW of Boston. Mfg. of woolens and foundry products. Birthplace of Horace Mann. **5** City (pop. 6,552), S central N.H., N of Concord. Merrimack R. is formed here. Mfg. of paper, textiles, and metal products. Birthplace of Daniel Webster. **6** City (pop. 5,388), SW Ohio, S of Dayton. Mfg. of paper products and clothing. **7** City (pop. 10,006), NW Pa., on Allegheny R.; laid out 1795. Has oil wells and refineries and mfg. of machinery and metal products. **8** Town (pop. 5,475), central Tenn., on Harpeth R. and S of Nashville, in farm area. Has phosphate mines and lumber mills. Scene of Civil War fighting 1864.

Franklin, State of, government (1784–88) formed by inhabitants of Washington, Sullivan, and Greene counties in present E Tenn. after N.C. ceded (June, 1784) its western lands to U.S. Government under John Sevier passed out of existence when terms of its officers expired.

Franklin and Marshall College: see LANCASTER, Pa.

Franklin Institute, in Philadelphia; for the promotion of mechanic arts; chartered and opened 1824, first of its kind in U.S. Named for Benjamin Franklin. An important research center, it includes Fels Planetarium, applied-science museum, technical library, Bartol Research Foundation (physics, now housed at Swarthmore Col.), and Biochemical Research Foundation. Has published journal since 1825; makes awards for work in physical sciences.

Franklin Park, village (pop. 8,899), NE Ill., W suburb of Chicago.

Franks, group of Germanic tribes which by the 3d cent. A.D. had settled along the Rhine (Salian Franks in N, Ripuarian Franks in S). Salian Franks moved into Gaul in 4th cent. A.D. as Roman allies. Their leader CLOVIS I united all Franks under his kingship (481), accepted Christianity, founded dynasty of MEROVINGIANS. He and his successors conquered most of W and central Europe, but the Frankish empire was usually divided into several kingdoms, notably NEUSTRIA, AUSTRASIA, and BURGUNDY. In 8th cent. began rule of CAROLINGIANS, which culminated under CHARLE-

MAGNE. After Treaty of MERSEN (870), kingdom of W Franks became France; that of E Franks, Germany.

Franz, Robert (fränts'), 1815–92, German composer of about 350 lieder, intimate songs, which have some of the feeling of folk song.

Franzen, Frans Michael (fränsän'), 1772–1847, early Swedish romantic poet, a bishop, b. Finland.

Franz Josef Land (fräns' jō'zŭf, fränts' yō'zĕf), archipelago, c.8,000 sq. mi., in the Arctic Ocean, N of Novaya Zemlya. Claimed by USSR 1926. Its 85 islands include settlements and government observation stations, but are 90% covered by ice interspersed with poor lichen vegetation. Discovered by Karl Weyprecht and Julius van Payer (1873); explored by Fridtjof Nansen (1895–96) and others.

Franz Joseph: see FRANCIS JOSEPH.

Frascati (fräskä'tē), town (pop. 10,660), Latium, central Italy, in Alban Hills near site of anc. Tusculum. Noted for its wine and its fine Renaissance villas (e.g., Villa Aldobrandini, Villa Torlonia). Damaged in World War II.

Frasch process extracts sulphur from deposits. Three concentric pipes are sunk in bed; water heated above melting point of sulphur is sent down outer pipe, air under pressure down inner and sulphur is forced to surface through middle pipe. Process was named for Herman Frasch, 1851–1914, German-born American chemist.

Fraser, James Earle, 1876–, American sculptor. Best known for monuments and statues of the American Indian, notably *The End of the Trail.* Designed Indian head and buffalo for five-cent piece. His wife, **Laura Gardin Fraser,** 1889–, is also a sculptor.

Fraser, Simon, 1776?–1862, Canadian explorer and fur trader. Explored Fraser R. to its mouth while establishing trading posts for North West Co.

Fraser, chief river of B.C., Canada. Rises on W slope of the Rockies and flows c.350 mi. NW to Prince George, then c.500 mi. S and W to the Strait of Georgia S of Vancouver. Chief tributaries are Nechako, Quesnal, Thompson, Chilcotin, Blackwater and Lillooet rivers. Navigable to Yale, c.80 mi. from the mouth. Above this is scenic Fraser R. canyon. Discovered 1793 by Alexander Mackenzie and named for fur trader Simon Fraser. Gold discovered on upper reaches 1859, after which Cariboo Road opened area to settlement.

Fraserburgh (frā'zŭrbŭrŭ), burgh (pop. 10,444), Aberdeenshire, Scotland. Has a fine harbor and is one of chief herring fishing centers in Scotland.

fraternal orders, social organizations offering members a fellowship reminiscent of code and spirit of medieval guild. Local "lodges," in such orders as FREEMASONRY (oldest in the U.S.) and the Odd Fellows, use symbolic rituals. Orders may be restricted to one sex only, or may be mixed.

fraud, willful misrepresentation intended to deprive another person of some right. It may also constitute the crime of false pretenses. Fraud may be interposed as defense in a suit based on a contract to which the defendant was fraudulently induced.

Frauenfeld (frou'ŭnfĕlt), town (pop. 11,026), cap. of Thurgau canton, N Switzerland. Aluminum and food industries. Has 11th-cent. castle.

Fray Bentos (frī bān'tōs), city (pop. 9,500), SW Uruguay, port on Uruguay R.; founded 1859 as Independencia. Has large meat-packing plants.

Frayser's Farm: see SEVEN DAYS BATTLES.

Frazee, John, 1790–1852, American pioneer sculptor. Did busts of Daniel Webster and John Marshall.

Frazer, Sir James George, 1854–1941, Scottish classicist and anthropologist, known especially for *The Golden Bough,* a study of magic and religion.

Fréchette, Louis Honoré (frāshĕt'), 1839–1908, French Canadian poet. First Canadian poet whose works were crowned by French Academy. His verse shows genuine feeling for nature and for heroic history of French Canada.

Fredegunde (frē″dŭgŭn′dù), c.545–597, Frankish queen. Married CHILPERIC I of Neustria after inducing him to murder his wife Galswintha (567). Resulting feud with BRUNHILDA of Austrasia continued until 613 under her son CLOTAIRE II.

Frederic, Harold, 1856–98, American novelist. A newspaperman, he was after 1884 a foreign correspondent for the New York *Times*. Of his novels, his masterpiece was *The Damnation of Theron Ware* (1896; a study of moral degeneration).

Frederica, town, S central Del., S of Dover. At near-by Barratt's Chapel annual services commemorate formation of Methodist Episcopal Church.

Frederick, emperors and German kings. **Frederick I** or **Frederick Barbarossa** [Ital.,= red beard], c.1122–1190, of the house of HOHENSTAUFEN, succeeded his uncle Conrad III as German king (1152), pacified Germany by proclaiming a general land peace (1152), and was crowned emperor by Pope ADRIAN IV (1155). In four subsequent campaigns in Italy he struggled against the papacy (notably ALEXANDER III) and the cities of Lombardy (see LOMBARD LEAGUE). Though victorious at first, he was excommunicated by Alexander, defeated at Legnano (1176), and forced to accept the Lombard League's demands in the Peace of Constance (1183). He succeeded, however, in breaking the power of his Guelphic rival, HENRY THE LION, in 1180–81. In 1189 he set out on the Third Crusade. He drowned in Cilicia. Legend has him still alive, awaiting German unification in the KYFFHÄUSER. His grandson, **Frederick II**, 1194–1250, was the son of Emperor HENRY VI and of Empress CONSTANCE. Pope Innocent III invested him with Sicily (1197) and promoted his election as antiking to OTTO IV (1212). He was crowned king at Aachen after Otto's formal deposition (1215) and emperor at Rome (1220). His long-delayed crusade (1228–29), actually a state visit, resulted in the peaceful cession of Jerusalem, Nazareth, and Bethlehem to the Christians and his own coronation as king of Jerusalem. This treaty was denounced by Pope GREGORY IX and soon broken by the Moslems. Sporadic warfare between emperor and pope flared into a life-and-death struggle in 1239 and reached its culmination under INNOCENT IV, who declared Frederick deposed and excommunicated (1245). Frederick died of dysentery while the war was turning in his favor. It was left for his son CONRAD IV and his grandson CONRADIN to see the final downfall of their house and the triumph of the papacy. An Italian by birth and temperament, Frederick left German affairs largely to his sons Henry (whom he had imprisoned in 1235 after a rebellion) and Conrad IV. Henry made sweeping concessions to the German princes, and under Conrad Germany fell into anarchy. In Sicily, Frederick promoted far-seeing legal and fiscal reform and expanded commerce and industry. His universal gifts made him a patron and student of medicine, mathematics, astronomy, and poetry. His court at Palermo was of oriental splendor. **Frederick III**, 1415–93, duke of Styria (1435–93) and of Austria (1457–93), became head of the house of HAPSBURG at the death of his cousin Albert II. Elected German king (1440) and crowned emperor (1452), he overcame his many rivals and enemies by dint of sheer indolence and longevity. Through his marriage policy he came near to realizing his motto, AEIOU (*Austriae est imperare orbi universo:* "it is Austria's destiny to rule the whole world"). The marriage of his son MAXIMILIAN I with MARY OF BURGUNDY was indeed the cornerstone of Hapsburg world power. **Frederick III**, 1831–88, emperor of Germany, king of Prussia (March–June, 1888); son of William I, father of William II. He was a liberal and a patron of art and learning. His consort, Victoria, daughter of Queen Victoria of England, was known after his death as Empress Frederick.

Frederick, Danish kings. **Frederick III**, 1609–70, king of Denmark and Norway (1648–70). Lost Skane, Halland, and Blekinge to Sweden in Treaties of Roskilde (1658) and Copenhagen (1660). His minister GRIFFENFELD drew up "King's Law" (*Kongelov*), which made Denmark an absolute hereditary monarchy (1665). **Frederick IV**, 1671–1730, king of Denmark and Norway (1699–1730). Joined alliance with Poland and Russia against Charles XII of Sweden in NORTHERN WAR. In peace treaties of 1720–21 he renounced claims to S Sweden but obtained ducal Schleswig. Consolidated absolutism; abolished serfdom. **Frederick V**, 1723–66, king of Denmark and Norway (1746–66). His reign was period of commercial prosperity. **Frederick VI**, 1769–1839, king of Denmark (1808–39) and of Norway (1808–14). After English attack on Copenhagen (1807) he allied himself with Napoleon I and was punished at Congress of Vienna by transfer of Norway to Sweden. **Frederick VII**, 1808–63, king of Denmark (1848–63). The vexed SCHLESWIG-HOLSTEIN question caused trouble throughout his reign. **Frederick VIII**, 1843–1912, king of Denmark (1906–12) was the father of Christian X of Denmark and Haakon VII of Norway. **Frederick IX**, 1899–, king of Denmark (1947–), succeeded his father Christian X.

Frederick, kings of Prussia. **Frederick I**, 1657–1713, elector of Brandenburg (1688–1713), was crowned first king of PRUSSIA in 1701. **Frederick II** or **Frederick the Great**, 1712–86, succeeded his father FREDERICK WILLIAM I in 1740. Despised by his father as effeminate esthete (he cultivated music, philosophy, and poetry), he spent a miserable youth. In 1730 he planned to flee abroad and barely escaped execution as a deserter. As soon as he became king, Frederick showed unexpected qualities of leadership and decision. With a spurious claim on parts of SILESIA, he opened the War of the AUSTRIAN SUCCESSION with a surprise attack on Maria Theresa (1740); having secured Silesia, he abandoned his allies and made peace (1745). This war and the SEVEN YEARS WAR (1756–63) made Prussia the foremost military power of Europe and established Frederick as one of the great military geniuses of all time. Frederick also was the prime mover for the first partition of POLAND (1772), which vastly increased his kingdom. The War of the BAVARIAN SUCCESSION (1778–79) and his creation of the Fürstenbund [league of princes] (1785), thwarted the schemes of Emperor JOSEPH II. A "benevolent despot," he promoted important legal and social reforms. His stormy friendship with VOLTAIRE is well known, as are his philosophical midnight suppers at SANS SOUCI. His writings, mostly in French, are collected in *Œuvres de Frédéric le Grand* (33 vols., 1846–57). His poetry is mediocre, his prose excellent. Though idolized by German nationalists, he despised German cultural aspirations. His philosophy was skeptical and materialistic. A champion of religious tolerance, he disliked all religions. He composed passable flute concertos and other music. Childless, he was succeeded by his nephew, Frederick William II. **Frederick III:** see FREDERICK III, emperor of Germany.

Frederick I, c.1372–1440, elector of Brandenburg (1415–40); as Frederick VI, burgrave of Nuremberg. Emperor Sigismund rewarded his good services by investing him with Brandenburg, of which he was the first Hohenzollern ruler.

Frederick, electors palatine. **Frederick III** (the Pious), 1515–76, reigned 1559–76. Inclining toward Calvinism, he caused HEIDELBERG CATECHISM to be drawn up (1563). **Frederick IV**, 1574–1610, reigned 1592–1610. Promoted and headed PROTESTANT UNION. **Frederick V:** see FREDERICK THE WINTER KING.

Frederick III (the Wise), 1463–1525, elector of Saxony (1486–1525). Founded Univ. of Wittenberg (1502). A protector of Luther, he gave him asylum at the Wartburg but himself remained a Catholic.

Frederick. 1 City (pop. 18,142), NW Md., near Monocacy R.; settled 1746. Trade and mfg. (clothing, brushes, electrical apparatus) center in farm area. Seat of Hood Col. (Evangelical and Reformed; for women; 1893). Here are homes of R. B. Taney and Barbara Frietchie, and Francis Scott Key Monument. Confederate victory near by in Civil War. **2** City (pop. 5,467), SW Okla., near Red R., in farm area. Processes cotton.

Frederick Augustus, rulers of Saxony. **Frederick Augustus I** and **Frederick Augustus II,** electors: see AUGUSTUS II and AUGUSTUS III, kings of Poland. **Frederick Augustus III,** 1750–1827, elector (1763–1806), became king of Saxony as **Frederick Augustus I** in 1806 after concluding a separate peace with Napoleon I. Napoleon also made him titular duke of Warsaw (1807–14). He abandoned his alliance with Napoleon a little later than everybody else and as a result lost half his kingdom to Prussia at the Congress of Vienna (1815).

Frederick Barbarossa: see FREDERICK I, emperor.

Frederick Henry, 1584–1647, prince of Orange; son of William the Silent. As stadholder of the Netherlands (1625–47) he secured (1635) French and Swedish alliance in Thirty Years War; captured 's Hertogenbosch (1629), Maastricht (1632), and Breda (1637) from Spaniards. In 1631 stadholderate of United Provs. was made hereditary in his family. His rule is known as "The Golden Age of Frederick Henry" because of its great artists (Rembrandt, Frans Hals) and scientists, and the commerce, prosperity, and prestige of the Netherlands.

Frederick Louis, 1707–51, prince of Wales, eldest son of George II of England. His opposition to the king was furthered by Bolingbroke and William Pitt. Father of George III.

Fredericksburg. 1 Town (pop. 3,854), S central Texas, W of Austin; founded 1846 by Germans whose customs, architecture, and speech persist. **2** City (pop. 12,158), N Va., on Rappahannock R. and N of Richmond; settled 1671. Trade center in agr. area with mfg. of apparel and food products. Tourist center. Points of interest include Mary Washington's home (1774–89); "Kenmore," home of Washington's sister; Rising Sun Tavern (c.1760); James Monroe's law office; and home of J. P. Jones. Near by are George Washington Birthplace Natl. Monument and Fredericksburg and Spotsylvania County Battlefields Memorial, commemorating battles of Fredericksburg, CHANCELLORSVILLE, Wilderness, and Spotsylvania Courthouse (see WILDERNESS CAMPAIGN). Seat of Mary Washington Col. (now affiliated with Univ. of Virginia).

Fredericksburg, battle of, in Civil War, fought Dec. 13, 1862, at Fredericksburg, Va. A. E. Burnside, aiming for Richmond, sent his Union troops across Rappahannock R. in frontal assault on James Longstreet's impregnable position. A severe Union defeat, with losses of over 12,000.

Frederick the Fair, c.1286–1330, German antiking (1314–26), duke of Austria. Elected by Hapsburg party as rival king to Emperor LOUIS IV. Renounced his rights in 1326.

Frederick the Great: see FREDERICK II, king of Prussia.

Frederick the Winter King, 1596–1632, king of Bohemia (1619–20), as Frederick V elector palatine (1610–20). The Protestant diet of Bohemia chose him king after deposing FERDINAND II. The expected help from his father-in-law, James I of England, did not materialize, and he was disastrously defeated at the White Mountain (1620). Nicknamed the Winter King for his short tenure, he was stripped of all his territories. Through his daughter Sophia he was grandfather of George I of England.

Frederick William, kings of Prussia. **Frederick William I,** 1688–1740, reigned 1713–40; known as the soldier-king. Laid foundation for Prussian greatness by creating efficient army and administration. Notoriously avaricious, he left surplus in treasury, avoided warfare. His tastes were coarse, and he despised his gifted heir, FREDERICK II. **Frederick William II,** 1744–97, nephew of Frederick II, reigned 1786–97. Defeat-

ed in French Revolutionary Wars, he made separate peace in 1795. Shared in Polish partitions of 1793, 1795. An amateur cellist, he was a patron of Mozart. His son, **Frederick William III,** 1770–1840, reigned 1797–1840. He accepted the harsh Treaty of TILSIT (1807) after his defeat at Jena by Napoleon I. Though weak and vacillating, he had the aid of such men as Karl vom und zum STEIN, K. A. von HARDENBERG, and SCHARNHORST, who reformed the Prussian state and prepared the way for the Prussian "War of Liberation" against Napoleon (1813–14). Joining the Holy Alliance in 1815, he became increasingly reactionary. His elder son, **Frederick William IV,** 1795–1861, reigned 1840–61. A romanticist, mystic, and half-hearted liberal, he crushed the revolution of March, 1848, and turned down the imperial crown offered him by the FRANKFURT Parliament (1849), arguing that a monarch by divine right could not receive authority from an elected assembly. His scheme for a German union was prevented by Austria in the Treaty of OLMÜTZ (1850). In 1857 his mental unbalance necessitated the regency of his brother and successor William I.

Frederick William, known as **the Great Elector,** 1620–88, elector of Brandenburg (1640–88). Secured E Pomerania and other territories at Peace of Westphalia (1648); rebuilt his devastated state after Thirty Years War; obtained full sovereignty over Prussia at Peace of OLIVA (1660). His victory over Charles XI of Sweden at Fehrbellin (1675) in third Dutch War increased his prestige. His son became king of Prussia as Frederick I (1701).

Frederick William, 1771–1815, duke of Brunswick; son and successor of CHARLES WILLIAM FERDINAND. Dispossessed of his duchy by Napoleon (1806), he seized it in a dashing raid by his free corps, the "Black Brunswickers" (1809), but soon had to flee to England. Was killed in the Waterloo campaign.

Fredericton, city (pop. 16,018), provincial cap. (since 1788), S central N.B., on St. John R. and NW of St. John; founded 1785 by United Empire Loyalists. Seat of Univ. of New Brunswick (provincially supported; coed.; opened 1800). Hunting and fishing center with lumbering and mfg. of wood and leather products.

Frederikshaab (frĭdh′rĭks-hôp′), district (pop. 1,432) and settlement (pop. 634), SW Greenland. District has important cryolite mines at Ivigtut.

Fredonia, village (pop. 7,095), W N.Y., near L. Erie and S of Dunkirk. Makes wine and grape juice.

free association: see ASSOCIATION; PSYCHOANALYSIS.

Free Church of Scotland: see SCOTLAND, FREE CHURCH OF.

Freedmen's Bureau, U.S. government agency, estab. by act of March 3, 1865, under name "bureau of refugees, freedmen, and abandoned lands," to aid and protect newly freed Negroes in South after Civil War. Organized under War Dept., bureau provided relief work for both blacks and whites in war-stricken areas, regulated Negro labor, managed abandoned and confiscated property, and supported education for Negroes. In its relief and educational activities bureau compiled an excellent record, often marred, however, by excesses of its local agents. Ultimately, bureau became little more than a political machine, organizing the black vote for Republican party. Work of bureau was discontinued in 1869, but its educational activities were carried on for another three years.

freedom: see LIBERTY.

freedom of speech, of the press, of the seas: see SPEECH, FREEDOM OF, etc.

Freehold, borough (pop. 7,550), E central N.J., E of Trenton; settled before 1700, called Monmouth Courthouse 1715–1801. Farm trade center with rug works and liquor distilleries. Monument (1884) commemorates Revolutionary battle (see MONMOUTH, BATTLE OF). Has race track and 18th-cent. buildings.

Freeland, borough (pop. 5,909), NE Pa., NE of Hazleton. Coal-mining center with mfg. of clothing.

Freeman, Douglas Southall, 1886–, American editor

and historian, biographer of R. E. Lee and George Washington.

Freeman, Edward Augustus, 1823–92, English historian. Major work was *History of the Norman Conquest* (6 vols., 1867–79). Others included history of Sicily and Byzantine history in Middle Ages.

Freeman, Mary (Eleanor) Wilkins, 1852–1930, American author. Wrote on New England life as in *A New England Nun and Other Stories* (1891).

Freeman's Farm, battle of: see SARATOGA CAMPAIGN.

Freemasonry, teachings and practices of the secret fraternal order of Free and Accepted Masons. Not restricted to stoneworkers, it retains much of the spirit and code of the medieval masons' guild. Charity is enjoined on Masons and practiced by them. Custom is the supreme authority in the order, and its teachings include obedience to the law of the land. There has been strong opposition to such secret societies (see ANTI-MASONIC PARTY). The order—always an independent national group—has had adherents in many parts of the world, George Washington and Goethe among them.

Freeport. 1 City (pop. 22,467), N Ill., W of Rockford; settled 1835. Center of agr. and dairy area producing cheese, toys, and batteries. Douglas expounded famous "Freeport doctrine" in Lincoln-Douglas debate here 1858. Near by occurred battle with Black Hawk's Indian forces. **2** Town (pop. 3,280), SW Maine, on Casco Bay. Papers preliminary to admission of Maine into Union as a state signed here, 1820. Desert of Maine, sandy region, is near by. **3** Residential and resort village (pop. 24,680), SE N.Y., on S shore of Long Isl.; settled c.1650. Deep sea fishing. Clothing and machinery. **4** City (pop. 6,012), S Texas, at mouth of Brazos R. SSW of Houston. Port with chemical (esp. sulphur) plants. Center of Brazosport area. Intracoastal Waterway crosses Brazos R. here.

Freer, Charles Lang (frēr), 1856–1919, American art collector and industrial capitalist. Gave his collection and the building which houses it to Smithsonian Institution of Washington, D.C. Freer Gallery of Art is best known for its collection of works of Whistler and of Oriental masters.

freesia, fragrant flower (*Freesia*) native to S Africa. Grown from corms, largely in greenhouses, for winter and spring cutting. Five to seven white or yellow tubular blossoms are borne near tip of stem.

free silver. Free coinage of silver became a popular proposal in U.S. soon after panic of 1873 and a major political issue in the next quarter century. Hard times of 1873–78 stimulated advocacy of cheap money; GREENBACK PARTY flourished in local elections. Inflationists, not getting paper-money expansion, turned to silver. Silver-mining interests also wanted silver coinage. BLAND-ALLISON ACT of 1878 and SHERMAN SILVER PURCHASE ACT of 1890 represented compromises. POPULIST PARTY demanded free silver. Nomination of W. J. BRYAN in 1896 made free silver major issue of presidential campaign. McKinley's victories of 1896 and 1900, coupled with increasing gold supplies and returning prosperity, minimized free silver as a political issue.

Free-Soil party, in U.S. history, a political party born 1847–48 out of rising opposition to extension of slavery into territories newly acquired from Mexico. In 1848, vote for its ticket gave N.Y. to the Whigs, made Zachary Taylor President. Following Compromise of 1850 party's Barnburner element returned to Democratic party, but radical antislavery men kept organization alive until 1854, when new Republican party absorbed it.

freethinkers, those who reach religious conclusions by reasoning, rejecting supernatural authority and ecclesiastical tradition. Name used in England c.1713 to denote esp. deists. In France it was associated with time of Revolution. In U.S. chief groups founded were American Rationalist Association, American Secular Union, Freethinkers of America.

Freetown, city (pop. 64,576), cap. of Sierra Leone; port on the Atlantic. Founded 1788 by the British as settlement for freed slaves.

free trade, commerce without restrictive duties. Domestic free trade is customary, but international commerce is frequently subjected to taxation. Theoretical basis for free trade is territorial division of labor: each region producing what it can most cheaply and best. France has generally followed an anti-free-trade policy, as have other European nations. The U.S. has generally followed a high-tariff policy. In England, Adam Smith endorsed free trade, the repeal of the corn laws in 1846 furthered it, and Gladstone reestablished it in 1869. (After the First World War England reintroduced an empire protection system.) Trade barriers have been increasingly viewed as promoting international discord, and in Europe attempts are being made to further free trade. See CUSTOMS; PROTECTION.

free verse or **vers libre** (vĕr' lē'brü), term loosely used for rhymed or unrhymed verse made free of conventional and traditional limitations and restrictions in regard to metrical structure. Cadence, especially cadence of common speech, is often substituted for rhythmical meter. Term applied to irregular poetry of Whitman and to some of the poetry of such writers as Ezra Pound, Amy Lowell, H. D., John Gould Fletcher, and T. S. Eliot.

freezing: see MELTING POINT; REFRIGERATION.

Freiberg (frī'bĕrk), city (pop. 42,303), Saxony, E Germany. Mfg. of precision instruments. Was long a lead and silver-mining center; has mining academy (founded 1765).

Freiburg, Switzerland: see FRIBOURG.

Freiburg im Breisgau (Ger. frī'boŏrk ĭm brīs'gou), city (pop. 109,822), S Baden, W Germany, at the edge of Black Forest. Archiepiscopal see; seat of famous university (founded 1457); since 1945 cap. of French-occupied Baden. Founded 1120; passed to Hapsburgs, with rest of BREISGAU, 1368. Scene of French victory over imperials in Thirty Years War (1644). Held by France 1677–97 and 1744–48; passed to Baden 1805. Has splendid 13th-cent. cathedral and other historic buildings.

Freising (frī'zĭng), city (pop. 25,326), Upper Bavaria, on Isar R. Mfg. of agr. machinery, brewery implements, textiles. Founded 724. Prince-bishopric until 1803; diocese was united with that of Munich 1817. Cathedral was started in 8th cent.

Frelinghuysen, Frederick Theodore (frē'lĭnghī"zŭn), 1817–85, U.S. Secretary of State (1881–85). Urged reciprocity agreements with Latin America; generally carried on a patient, pacifistic policy.

Fremantle, principal port (pop. 18,791) of Western Australia, SW of Perth, at mouth of Swan R. and at terminus of Trans-Australian RR; founded 1829. Exports are wheat, wool, and fruit.

Frémiet, Emmanuel (ĕmänüĕl' främyä'), 1824–1910, French sculptor, noted for studies of animals and portrait statues.

Frémont, John Charles (frē'mŏnt), 1813–90, American explorer, soldier, and political leader. His enthusiastic reports of explorations in West did much to publicize that region. Prominent in liberating Calif. from Mexico; governor there in 1847 until his quarrel with S. W. Kearny. U.S. Senator (1850–51). Republican candidate for President in 1856. Removed from command of Western Dept. in Civil War. Lost fortune in railroad venture (1870). Governor of Arizona Territory (1878–82). The Pathfinder, as he was called, is one of most controversial figures of Western history. His wife, **Jessie Benton Frémont,** 1824–1902, daughter of Thomas H. Benton, encouraged and aided her husband. Wrote accounts of her experiences to support household when their fortune was lost.

Fremont (frē'mŏnt). **1** City (pop. 14,762), E Nebr., on Platte R. and WNW of Omaha; founded 1856. Trade center in prairie region, it produces grain, livestock, and dairy products. Seat of Midland Col. **2** City (pop.

16,537), N Ohio, on Sandusky R. and SE of Toledo. Trade center of agr. area with mfg. of auto parts and clothing. Two post-War of 1812 towns united 1829, named Fremont 1849. Has home and tomb of Pres. R. B. Hayes.

Fremstad, Olive (Nayan) (frĕm'stăd), 1870?–1951, Swedish-American soprano; pupil of Lilli Lehmann. Sang at the Metropolitan Opera, New York, 1903–14. Best known for Wagnerian roles.

French, Daniel Chester, 1850–1931, American sculptor. Executed first commission *The Minuteman* (Concord, Mass.) at age of 23. Among other works is the heroic Lincoln in Lincoln Memorial, Washington, D.C.

French Academy, first and chief constituent of the IN-STITUT DE FRANCE. Founded 1635 by Cardinal Richelieu; suppressed 1793; reinstated 1803. Its chief aim was the governance of French literary effort, grammar, orthography, and rhetoric. Its dictionary (1694; 8th ed., 1932–35) and grammar (1932) are noted for conservatism. Another function is the awarding of prizes. Its 40 members (often called "the forty immortals") are self-perpetuating; elections may be vetoed by head of state. Members include mostly literary men but also other eminent Frenchmen, such as ecclesiastics and military men. Among prominent authors who failed to be admitted were Molière, Rousseau, Balzac, Stendhal, Flaubert.

French and Indian Wars, 1689–1763, name given to North American colonial wars between England and France in late 17th and 18th cent., roughly linked to wars of European coalitions. Ultimate aim was domination of eastern part of continent; wars were marked by capture of seaboard strongholds and Western forts and attacks on frontier settlements, including Indian border warfare. First war was King William's War, corresponding to European War of the GRAND AL-LIANCE (1688–97), marked principally by frontier attacks on British colonies. Queen Anne's War (1701–13) corresponded to the War of the SPANISH SUCCES-SION. King George's War (1745–48) was connected with War of the AUSTRIAN SUCCESSION. Last and most important conflict, called simply French and Indian War (1754–60), was linked to SEVEN YEARS WAR. British captured French forts in the West, Lord AMHERST captured Louisburg (1758), and Quebec fell to the British (see ABRAHAM, PLAINS OF). Treaty of Paris (1763) ended French control in Canada and the West.

French Broad River, rising in W N.C. in the Blue Ridge and flowing 204 mi. NE, NNW past Asheville into Tenn., joining Holston R. near Knoxville to form Tennessee R.

French Cameroons: see CAMEROONS.

French Congo: see FRENCH EQUATORIAL AFRICA.

French East India Company: see EAST INDIA COMPANY, FRENCH.

French Equatorial Africa, group of four French overseas territories (c.970,000 sq. mi.; pop. c.4,131,000), W Africa; cap. Brazzaville. Called French Congo until 1910. Border with Belgian Congo on E is partly marked by Congo R. Constituent territories are Gabon, Middle Congo, Ubangi-Shari, and Chad. Products include hardwood, cotton, coffee, and peanuts. As members of French Union the territories are represented in French parliament.

French Establishments in Oceania, colony (1,554 sq. mi.; pop. 55,734) formed 1903 to embrace 105 islands constituting French possessions in S Pacific; cap. Papeete on Tahiti, Society Isls. Popularly called French Oceania. Includes SOCIETY ISLANDS, MARQUESAS Is-LANDS, TUBUAI ISLANDS, TUAMOTU ISLANDS, GAMBIER ISLANDS.

French Guiana: see GUIANA.

French Guinea (gĭ'nē), overseas territory (c.95,000 sq. mi.; pop. c.2,125,000), French West Africa, on the Atlantic; cap. Conakry. Has swampy coastal zone and mountainous interior. Produces rubber, lumber, coffee, palm oil, and hides. Represented in French parliament.

French horn: see WIND INSTRUMENTS; also *ill.,* p. 667.

French India, overseas territory (193 sq. mi.; pop. 317,-259) of France, in India; cap. Pondichéry. Comprises four settlements, Karikal, Mahé, Pondichéry, and Yanaon. Formerly included Chandernagor.

French Indo-China: see INDO-CHINA.

French language, Romance language. See LANGUAGE (table).

French Lick, resort town (pop. 1,946), S Ind., NW of Louisville, Ky. Mineral water is obtained from sulphur springs here. Was a French trading post in colonial times.

Frenchman Bay, inlet of the Atlantic, S Maine, extending c.20 mi. inland between Mt. Desert Isl. and the mainland.

French Oceania: see FRENCH ESTABLISHMENTS IN OCE-ANIA.

French Revolution, political upheaval which began in France in 1789 and which affected the whole world. Historians differ widely as to its "causes"—some see it as an intellectual movement, born from the liberal ENLIGHTENMENT of the 18th cent.; some, as a rebellion of the underprivileged classes against feudal oppression; some, as the assertion of the new capitalist bourgeoisie against an outdated and restrictive social and economic system. It is now generally held that the oppressive features of the *ancien régime* have been much exaggerated. The immediate cause of the revolution was without doubt the bankrupt state of the public treasury. The wars of the 17th and 18th cent., an iniquitous and inefficient system of taxation, waste, and intervention in the American Revolution had resulted in a gigantic public debt, which neither NECKER, nor CALONNE, nor LOMÉNIE DE BRIENNE was able to reduce. As last resort, LOUIS XVI called the STATES-GENERAL, which, it was hoped, would pass the necessary fiscal reforms. It convened at Versailles on May 5, 1789. From the start, the deputies of the third estate, joined by many members of the lower clergy and by a few nobles, pressed for sweeping political and social reforms that far exceeded the assembly's powers. Defying the king, they proclaimed themselves the National Assembly (June 17) and took an oath not to separate until a constitution had been made. The king yielded, but his dismissal of Necker led to the storming of the BASTILLE by an excited mob (July 14). Louis XVI, ever anxious to avoid bloodshed, gave in once more: Necker was recalled; the commune was estab. as city government of Paris; the National Guard was organized. On Aug. 4 the Assembly abolished all feudal privileges. Rumors of counterrevolutionary court intrigues were exploited by extremist demagogues, and on Oct. 5 a mob marched on Versailles and forcibly moved the royal family and the Assembly to Paris. Honoré de MIRABEAU, foreseeing the uncontrolled revolution that the king's weakness was about to unleash, tried to restore strength to the executive branch, but the Constituent Assembly (as the National Assembly was now called) drafted a constitution which reduced the executive to impotence (1791; its preamble was the famous DECLARATION OF THE RIGHTS OF MAN). Anticlerical legislation was capped when the clergy was required to take oaths to civil authority (1790), a measure which alienated many pious rural districts from the Revolution. The king decided to join those nobles who had already fled abroad (émigrés), but his flight (June 20–21, 1791) was arrested at Varennes. Brought back to Paris, Louis accepted the new constitution. In the Legislative Assembly the republican GIRONDISTS and the extreme JACOBINS and CORDE-LIERS gained the upper hand. "Liberty, Equality, Fraternity" became the watchword. Meanwhile, the émigrés were inciting other European courts to intervene. The Declaration of PILLNITZ played into the hands of the Girondists, who hoped that a foreign war would rally the nation to the republican cause. With the declaration of war on Austria (April 20, 1792) the

FRENCH REVOLUTIONARY WARS began. Early reverses led to rumors of treason by the king and, particularly, Queen MARIE ANTOINETTE. A mob stormed the Tuileries palaces and massacred the SWISS GUARDS (Aug. 10, 1792); all police power was seized by the Paris commune (dominated by DANTON and MARAT); the Assembly suspended the king and ordered elections for a new body, the National Convention; and hundreds of royalist prisoners were killed by "spontaneous" mobs in the September Massacres. The Convention on Sept. 21 abolished the monarchy, set up the First Republic, and proceeded to try the king for treason. Louis's execution (Jan., 1793) led to royalist uprisings, notably in the VENDÉE, and was followed by the REIGN OF TERROR, in which ROBESPIERRE and his associates triumphed in turn over the more moderate Girondists and over his rivals Danton and HÉBERT. The republican constitution never became active; the Committee of Public Safety and the Revolutionary Tribunal reigned supreme. Robespierre's final excesses frightened the Convention into the coup d'état of 9 THERMIDOR (July 27, 1794), which resulted in his execution and in a period of relative reaction. Under the new constitution of 1795 the DIRECTORY came into existence. Its rule, which was marked by corruption, intrigues, run-away inflation, and bankruptcy, was ended by Bonaparte's coup d'état of 18 BRUMAIRE (Nov. 19, 1799). With the establishment of the CONSULATE (followed 1804 by Napoleon's empire), the victory of the moneyed bourgeoisie became final. Together with the French Revolutionary and Napoleonic wars, the French Revolution tore down the ancient structure of Europe, opened the path for 19th-cent. liberalism, and hastened the advent of nationalism and the era of modern, total warfare.

French Revolutionary calendar, official calendar of France, 1793–1805. It was computed as from Sept. 22, 1792. Year was divided into 12 months of 30 days— Vendémiaire, Brumaire, Frimaire, Nivôse, Pluviôse, Ventôse, Germinal, Floréal, Prairial, Messidor, Thermidor, Fructidor; the 5 remaining days, called sansculottides, were feast days; in leap years the extra day (last of year) was Revolution Day. Months were divided into three decades; every 10th day (*décadi*) was day of rest. Example: 18 Brumaire of year VIII = Nov. 9, 1799.

French Revolutionary Wars, 1792–1802, general European war precipitated by the FRENCH REVOLUTION. The Declaration of PILLNITZ was used by the revolutionists as pretext for declaring war on Austria (April, 1792). Meeting little resistance at first, allied Austrian and Prussian armies invaded France, but the cannonade of VALMY proved a turning point. Late in 1792 the French overran the Austrian Netherlands, crossed the Rhine into Germany, and seized Savoy and Nice from Sardinia, while the National Convention proclaimed its determination to carry the revolution to all Europe. This and the execution of Louis XVI led to the formation of the First Coalition (Austria, Prussia, England, Holland, Spain). In the emergency, the Committee of Public Safety was created in France (see REIGN OF TERROR) and a *levée en masse* (universal conscription) was ordered. Guided by Lazare CARNOT, the committee raised new armies which, by the end of 1793, had driven the allies from France. The French again took the offensive in the Low Countries (1794). Holland, transformed into the BATAVIAN REPUBLIC, made peace in 1795, as did Prussia and Spain (Treaties of Basel, 1795). Against Austria and Sardinia, Carnot now evolved a plan of three-pronged attack: Jourdan was to advance SE from the Low Countries; Moreau was to strike at S Germany; Bonaparte was to strike at Piedmont and Lombardy, cross the Alps, and join Jourdan and Moreau. Only the Italian campaign, where one victory followed another (see NAPOLEON I) was completely successful and ended with the Treaty of CAMPO FORMIO (1797). England alone stayed in the war. Bonaparte's hope to strike at England by way of Egypt and India failed utterly and resulted in the destruction of the French fleet at Aboukir (1798). French interference in Italy, Switzerland, and Egypt led to the Second Coalition (England, Russia, Austria, Turkey, Portugal, Naples). Hastening back to France from Egypt, Bonaparte estab. himself as First Consul and set about to repair French losses in Italy and Switzerland. Faulty cooperation between the Austrians and Russians facilitated the victory of Masséna over the Russians at Zurich (Sept., 1799), followed by Suvarov's epic retreat across the Alps and the defection of Russia from the coalition. In 1800 Bonaparte crossed the St. Bernard and routed the Austrians at Marengo. Moreau's victory at Hohenlinden (Dec., 1800) demolished Austrian resistance. Austria consented to the Peace of LUNÉVILLE (1801) and the Second Coalition collapsed. England continued the war alone, expelling the French from Egypt and destroying the neutral Danish fleet (see COPENHAGEN, BATTLE OF), but after Pitt's retirement it also made peace with France and its allies (Spain and Batavian Republic) in the Treaty of AMIENS (1802). Peace was shortlived, for in 1803 began the Wars of NAPOLEON I.

French Sudan (sōōdăn'), French overseas territory (c.448,200 sq. mi.; pop. c.3,080,000), French West Africa; cap. Bamako. Drained by Senegal and Niger rivers in fertile S part. Much of country is arid. Under French control since 1896, it is represented in French parliament.

French Union, according to French constitution of 1946, the French republic and associated states. French republic consists of: Metropolitan France (France proper and Corsica); Algeria; the overseas departments and territories of Martinique, Guadeloupe, Réunion, French Guiana, French West Africa, French Equatorial Africa, Madagascar, Comoro Isls., French Somaliland, French India, New Caledonia, French Establishments in Oceania, Saint-Pierre, and Miquelon; the UN trusteeships of Togoland and the Cameroons; the Anglo-French condominium of New Hebrides. The associated states are Morocco, Tunisia, and Indo-China. President of France is also president of French Union. Parliamentary body of French Union consists of a high council and an assembly; these are distinct from the council and national assembly of the French republic.

French West Africa, group of eight French overseas territories (c.1,800,000 sq. mi.; pop. c.15,996,000); cap. Dakar. Comprises DAHOMEY, FRENCH GUINEA, FRENCH SUDAN, IVORY COAST, MAURITANIA, NIGER, SENEGAL, and UPPER VOLTA.

French West Indies: see WEST INDIES.

Freneau, Philip (frēnō'), 1752–1832, American poet. A Revolutionary prisoner on brig *Aurora*, he wrote "The Prison Ship." Was a Jeffersonian journalist, but his fame rests on lyrics ("The Wild Honeysuckle," "The Indian Burying Ground," "Eutaw Springs.")

frequency: see RADIO FREQUENCY; SOUND; VIBRATION; WAVE.

frequency modulation, radio transmitting and receiving system, called FM in contrast to older AM system (amplitude modulation). FM reduces static; improves fidelity. Amplitude of carrier wave is constant; its frequency varies.

Frescobaldi, Girolamo (jērō'lämō fräskōbäl'dē), 1583–1644, Italian organist and composer, organist at St. Peter's in Rome between 1608 and 1643. He wrote toccatas, fugues, and other works for organ.

Fresno (frĕz'nō), city (pop. 91,669), central Calif., SE of San Francisco; founded 1872. Railroad, processing, and shipping center in San Joaquin Valley (raisins, figs, sweet wine). Lumbering and mfg. of machinery, clothing, cottonseed and olive oil.

Freud, Sigmund (froid, Ger. zēk'mŏont froit'), 1856–1939, Austrian psychiatrist, founder of PSYCHOANALY-

SIS. His collaboration with Josef Breuer on use of hypnosis to treat hysteria marked beginning of psychoanalysis, revealed that symptoms of hysteria, traceable to early psychic trauma, represent undischarged emotional energy (conversion). He and Breuer separated over Freud's growing conviction that undefined energy causing conversion was sexual. Freud replaced hypnosis with free ASSOCIATION. His theories roused bitter antagonism. He was joined in 1906 by Eugen Bleuler, Jung, and Adler, but later Jung and Adler formed their own schools (1911–13) in protest against Freud's emphasis on infantile sexuality and the Oedipus complex. Basic structure of analysis is still Freudian and disagreement is in emphasis on concepts largely originated by Freud. After 1923 he used psychoanalytic theory in cultural studies. He greatly influenced anthropology, education, art, and literature.

Frey and Freyja (frī, frī′yù), Scandinavian god and goddess, brother and sister, deities of fertility, love, and matrimony and of light and peace. Frey's chief shrine was at Uppsala, Sweden.

Freycinet, Louis Claude Desaulses de (dùsōls′ dù frāsēnā′), 1779–1842, French marine officer. Commanded, and edited findings of, scientific expedition to South Pacific on the *Uranie* (1817–20).

Freyre, Gilberto (jĕlbĕr′tō frā′rù), 1900–, Brazilian sociologist and anthropologist, known for social history of plantation system in NE Brazil.

Freytag, Gustav (gō̄′stäf frī′täk), 1816–95, German author. His most lasting works include the comedy *The Journalists* (1852; Eng. tr., 1888) and the novels *Debit and Credit* (1855; Eng. tr., 1856) and *The Lost Manuscript* (1861; Eng. tr., 1865).

Friant Dam, central Calif., in San Joaquin R., E of Fresno; completed 1944. It is one of world's largest dams (320 ft. high, 3,430 ft. long) and a key unit of CENTRAL VALLEY project. Forms Millerton L.

friar's balsam, alcoholic solution of benzoin, storax, aloes, tolu balsam. Used for wounds, ulcers.

Fribourg (Fr. frēboōr′), Ger. *Freiburg*, canton (645 sq. mi.; pop. 157,919), W Switzerland, on N slopes of Bernese Alps. Agr., cattle raising, cheese production (Gruyère). City of **Fribourg** (pop. 28, 767), its cap., on Sarine R., was founded 1157, joined Swiss Confederation 1481. Largely Catholic, it is an episcopal see and has a Catholic university and a cathedral (14th–15th cent.).

Frick, Henry Clay, 1849–1919, American capitalist. Key figure in coke industry. Engineered expansion of Carnegie Steel Co. Largely responsible for antiunion policy of steel industry. His New York city mansion, together with art collection and large endowment, was willed to public as a museum.

friction, resistance between surfaces moving against one another. Factors on which it depends include nature of surfaces in contact, magnitude of force holding them together (including gravity), their weight, their chemical natures, and the attractive force between different materials. So-called **coefficient of friction:** quotient obtained by dividing the value of force necessary to move one body over another at constant speed by the weight of the body. Coefficient varies with type of surface even though weight of body is constant, but it is constant for any two given kinds of materials. **Fluid friction** is observed in flow of liquids and gases. It is affected by increased velocities and streamlining is attempt to minimize it.

Friday: see WEEK.

Friedel, Charles (shärl frēdĕl′), 1832–99, French chemist, mineralogist, co-developer of Friedel-Crafts reaction for production of hydrocarbons and ketones.

Friedland (frēt′länt), Czech *Frýdtlant*, town (pop. 4,308), N Bohemia, Czechoslovakia. Castle was seat of duchy awarded to Wallenstein in 1625.

Friedland, small town, former E Prussia, near Königsberg; renamed Pravdinsk after transfer to USSR (1945). Napoleon's victory at Friedland over Russians led to Treaty of Tilsit (1807).

Friedlander, Leo (frēd′ländùr), 1890–, American sculptor. His many decorative works include groups for R.C.A. Building in New York.

Friedrichshafen (frē′drĭkshä″fùn), town (pop. 20,477), S Württemberg, SW Germany, on L. of Constance. Mfg. of machine parts. Zeppelin works here were destroyed by World War II air raids.

Friends, Society of, religious body originating in England in 17th cent. under George Fox. He believed that a person needed no spiritual intermediary but could find understanding and guidance through "inward light" supplied by Holy Spirit. Fox's followers were known as Religious Society of Friends, popularly called Quakers because they trembled with emotion in meetings. They refused to worship in estab. churches, to take oaths, and to bear arms in war. They rejected social and official titles and used "plain" forms of address (notably "thee" and "thou"). Mission effort took them to Asia, Africa, and America. Persecuted in New England, they found refuge in R.I. and in colony estab. (1682) for them by William Penn. in Pa. In 1827 they split into "Hicksites" under Elias Hicks, who stressed inner guidance, and "Orthodox" group, with guidance by church elders. Meetings of Friends are periods of silent meditation, only those urged by "Inner Light" offering prayer or exhortation. Friends are noted for activity in education and social welfare. The American Friends Service Committee and the Service Council of the British Society of Friends were jointly awarded the 1947 Nobel Peace Prize.

Fries, John, c.1750–1818, American rebel. Stirred Pennsylvania Germans into uprising (called Fries's Rebellion) against assessors and collectors of Federal property taxes (1799). Arrested, sentenced to death, but pardoned by Pres. John Adams.

Frieseke, Frederick Carl (frē′zĭkù), 1874–1939, American painter. Developed a highly popular style influenced by French impressionism.

Friesland (frēz′lùnd) or **Frisia** (frī′zhù), province (1,249 sq. mi.; pop. 459,361), N Netherlands; cap. Leeuwarden. Comprises several of W FRISIAN ISLANDS. Intensive dairying and cattle raising. Frisians, a Germanic people, were conquered by Franks in 8th cent.; they have preserved their language. Medieval Frisia, under counts of HOLLAND, extended from Scheldt R. in W to Weser R. in E. After 1433 Frisians defied authority of their successive new masters—the dukes of Burgundy, Duke Albert of Saxony, and the Hapsburgs—until they were subdued by Emperor Charles V (1523). Friesland joined the United Provs. 1579. It appointed its own stadholders until 1748, when its stadholder, Prince William IV of Orange, became sole and hereditary stadholder of the Netherlands. EAST FRIESLAND, in Germany, had a separate history after 1454.

Friesz, Othon (ōtō′ frēĕs′), 1879–, French painter. Calligraphic style was influenced by impressionism.

frigate (frĭ′gĭt), originally a long, narrow type of vessel propelled by oars or sails in the Mediterranean. Now denotes a warship, with raised quarterdeck and forecastle, of about the same tonnage as the destroyer.

Frigg or Frigga, in Germanic mythology, wife of Woden. Originally an earth-goddess, she became confused with Scandinavian Freyja and thus was worshiped as goddess of fertility and love. From her likeness to Venus, the Latin day of Venus became in Germanic-speaking countries *Frigg's day* or *Friday*.

frijole (frēhō′lē), used mostly in plural **frijoles**, in Mexico and Spanish American countries, any cultivated bean of genus *Phaseolus;* in particular, small black bean second only to maize as article of diet.

Frioul (frēool′), Romance language. See LANGUAGE (table).

Frisia: see FRIESLAND.

Frisian Islands (frī′zhùn), chain of islands off North Sea coast of Netherlands, Germany, and Denmark. W Frisian Isls., belonging to Netherlands, include Texel, Vlieland, Tershelling, Ameland. E Frisian Isls., in Germany, include Norderney, Borkum. N Frisian Isls., off Schleswig-Holstein, Germany, and S Jutland, Denmark, include Sylt, Föhr, Romo. Fishing, cattle raising are important on all the islands. Many bathing resorts.

Frisian language, Germanic language of Frisian Isls. and near-by coasts, the language most like English. See LANGUAGE (table).

Frithjof (frēt'yôf), hero of Icelandic saga (late 13th or early 14th cent.). Swedish poet Esaias Tegner used legends of him in *Frithjof's Saga* (1825).

Friuli (frēōō'lē), historic region, NE Italy and NW Yugoslavia, between E Alps and Adriatic. Includes a fertile plain and part of KARST region. Chief cities: Udine, Gorizia (both in Italy). Once a Lombard duchy 6th–8th cent.), Friuli was later divided into county of Gorizia (E) and county of Friuli (W). W Friuli (with Udine) passed to patriarchs of Aquileia (11th cent.), to Venice (1420), and to Austria (1797). Gorizia passed to Austria in 1500. Italy received W Friuli in 1866 and the rest in 1919, but by the Italian peace treaty of 1947 E Friuli (except Gorizia) was ceded to Yugoslavia, where it forms part of Slovenia. The remaining Italian part of Friuli was merged with what is left of VENEZIA GIULIA to form the autonomous province of **Friuli-Venezia Giulia** (vänä'tsyä jōō'lyä) (2,948 sq. mi.; pop. 837,000); cap. Udine.

Frobenius, Leo (lā'ō frōbā'nēŏos), 1873–1938, German archaeologist and anthropologist, authority on prehistoric art and culture (esp. African).

Frobisher, Sir Martin (frō'bĭshŭr), 1535?–1594, English mariner. Licensed by Queen Elizabeth, backed by merchants, he made three fruitless voyages (1576, 1577, 1578) to arctic regions seeking Northwest Passage. Commanded a ship in Sir Francis Drake's West Indies expedition (1585). Knighted for role in defeat of Spanish Armada (1588). Discovered (1576) **Frobisher Bay,** arm of the Atlantic, 150 mi. long, 20–40 mi. wide, cutting into SE Baffin Isl., Northwest Territories, Canada. There is a trading post and an air base at its head.

Froding, Gustaf, Swed. **Fröding** (frû'ding), 1860–1911, Swedish lyric poet.

Froebel, Friedrich Wilhelm August (frä'bŭl, frō–, Ger. frē'drĭkh vĭl'hĕlm ou'gŏost frû'bŭl), 1782–1852, German educator and founder of KINDERGARTEN system. In 1837 he founded first kindergarten and in 1849 first kindergarten training school. His educational system, based on unity of nature, or God, reflects influence of Fichte and Schelling. He stressed importance of pleasant surroundings, self-activity, and physical training in child development. Most important work is *Menschenerziehung* (1826; Eng. tr., *The Education of Man,* 1877).

frog, amphibian living usually in quiet fresh water or woods. Skin is smooth, usually green or brown, often spotted; in some species produces irritating or poisonous secretions. Most frogs hibernate underwater in mud over winter and lay eggs (which are fertilized as they are laid) in early spring. Gelatinous covering secreted by female causes eggs to adhere in mass, giving buoyancy, protection. In 3–10 days, small tadpole hatches; by summer's end metamorphosis from fishlike form to lung-breathing, tailless, carnivorous adult is completed (except in BULLFROG). Growth to adult size takes several years. Edible U.S. frogs include leopard, pickerel, and green frogs, common and southern bullfrogs, and Oregon red-legged frog. See also TREE FROG.

Frohman, Charles, 1860–1915, American theatrical manager and producer. Bronson Howard's *Shenandoah* (1889) made him a successful producer. Known for ability to develop talent, he launched stars (e.g., Julia Marlowe, Maude Adams, Ethel Barrymore) and playwrights (e.g., Clyde Fitch, Barrie, Rostand). His brother, **Daniel Frohman,** 1851–1940, managed small theatrical companies c.1871; settled in N.Y. 1879. Augustin Daly's business manager for a time, he later

was manager and part owner of Lyceum theater.

Froissart, Jean (zhä' früwäsär'), c.1337–1410?, French chronicler, poet, and courtier. His chronicle covers history of W Europe from early 14th cent. to 1400, i.e., first half of Hundred Years War. Historically it suffers from inaccuracy and unobjectiveness, but in literary merit ranks high and brings whole era to life. Standard English translation is by John Bourchier, Lord Berners.

Fronde (frŏd), 1648–53, series of outbreaks in France during minority of Louis XIV. Caused by rivalry between Parlement of Paris and royal authority (as championed by MAZARIN); by the discontent of the great nobles; by the excessive fiscal burden of the people. The **Fronde of the Parlement,** 1648–49, began with the Parlement's refusal to register a fiscal edict. The court retired to Rueil; government forces under Louis II de CONDÉ blockaded Paris until a compromise peace was arranged. The arrest of the overbearing Condé, by Mazarin's orders, precipitated the much more serious **Fronde of the Princes,** 1650–53. Although Condé was released and Mazarin left for voluntary exile (1651), Condé with the support of several powerful nobles and the provincial parlements of S France waged open warfare on the government and even concluded an alliance with Spain, then at war with France. Defeated at the Faubourg Saint-Antoine (1652), he was given shelter in Paris through the intervention of Mlle de MONTPENSIER. His arrogance soon alienated the Parisians, and the Fronde disintegrated. In 1653 Mazarin returned to Paris, but Condé continued to wage war at the head of a Spanish army until the Peace of the PYRENEES (1659).

Frontenac, Louis de Buade, comte de (frŏn'tĭnäk), 1620–98, French governor of New France (1672–82, 1689–98). Dealt successfully with Indians, encouraged explorations, and aided in establishment of forts. Sought to restrain British in French and Indian Wars. Reestab. **Fort Frontenac,** on site of Kingston, Ont., Canada, in 1696. La Salle was made commandant of original fort (1673). Its capture by British in 1758 gave them control of L. Ontario.

frontier, borderland, in various senses. May be used to mean actual border between two countries or region about an international boundary. In U.S. history, however, it means border area of white settlement, vital in conquest of land between Atlantic and Pacific. Theory that frontier was a governing factor (if not the governing factor) in developing U.S. civilization as distinct from that of other nations was announced by F. J. Turner in 1893. Thesis is that American democracy was shaped by the frontier, by the contest of settler with wilderness. In the contest man learned self-reliance; he became assured of equality with other men and resentful of class distinctions and any attempt at civic and social coercion. Belief that the frontier shaped American thought and character is now almost universally accepted. It has been pointed out, however, that other factors (e.g., industrialization) were of telling weight, that individualism on the frontier has been perhaps overemphasized, and that the frontier farming community was possibly not as classless as has been pictured.

Front Range, part of Rocky Mts., extending c.300 mi. SE and S from E central Wyo. to S central Colo. and rising to 14,274 ft. in Grays Peak. Forms part of Continental Divide in Colo. Includes Laramie and Medicine Bow mts. and most of Rocky Mt. Natl. Park, where highest peak is Longs Peak (14,255 ft.). Range also includes PIKES PEAK; Mt. Evans (14,260 ft.), with Inter-Univ. High Altitude Laboratory at summit; Arapahoe Peak (13,506 ft.), with glacier on E face; and James Peak (13,260 ft.), cut by Moffat Tunnel, railroad tube (6.4 mi. long; built 1923–27).

Front Royal, town (pop. 8,115), N Va., on S Fork of Shenandoah R. and S of Winchester, at N end of Skyline Drive near Shenandoah Natl. Park and George Washington Natl. Forest. Mfg. of chemicals and rayon. In Shenandoah Valley campaign Stonewall Jackson routed Union troops here (1862).

Frost, Arthur Burdett, 1851–1928, American illustrator and cartoonist, best known for illustrations for "Uncle Remus" stories.

Frost, Edwin Brant, 1866–1935, American astronomer, authority on astrophysics. Director of Yerkes Observatory (1905–32).

Frost, Robert, 1875–, American poet, b. San Francisco; in New England after 1885. Won recognition while in England, where *A Boy's Will* (1913) and *North of Boston* (1914) appeared; was famous after return to U.S. Later volumes of lyrical, dramatic, and reflective poetry include *West-running Brook* (1928) and *A Further Range* (1936). Four times awarded Pulitzer Prize.

frost or **hoarfrost,** feathery ice deposit caused by direct condensation of water vapor in crystalline form on surfaces at below-freezing temperatures. Frost-occurrence factors: topography, altitude, latitude, relation to land and water. Killing (to vegetation) frosts occur variously (Sept. 1–June 1 in Rocky Mt. region; Dec. 1–Mar. 1 along Gulf coast, parts of Calif., Ariz.).

Frostburg, resort and trading town (pop. 6,876), NW Maryland, W of Cumberland in coal area.

Froude, James Anthony (frōōd), 1818–94, English historian. Wrote voluminously on many historical and biographical topics. Major work is *The History of England from the Fall of Wolsey to the Defeat of the Spanish Armada* (12 vols., 1856–70).

fructose (frōōk'tōs), **levulose** (lĕ'vūlōs), or **fruit sugar,** found in honey and fruits; sweeter than cane sugar. It is a carbohydrate with same chemical formula as GLUCOSE.

fruit, fully developed seed-producing organ of a FLOWER. Botanically it is the ripened ovary. Seedlike fruit (see GRAIN) of grasses is commonly called seed, and many food fruits are popularly called vegetables (e.g., beans, tomatoes). Fleshy fruits include the pome (e.g., apple, pear), berry (raspberry), and drupe (cherry, peach). See also NUT. See *ill.*, p. 783.

Fruita (frōō'tù), town (pop. 1,463), W Colo., NW of Grand Junction. Colorado Natl. Monument is near.

fruit fly, name for certain insects of family Trypetidae whose larvae bore through fruits and other plant parts. Damagers of North American fruit include apple or blueberry maggot, currant and gooseberry fruit fly, cherry fruit fly. Mexican, West Indian, and papaya fruit flies are serious pests farther south. Mediterranean fruit fly is a pest in many areas. Fruit (or vinegar) flies of genus *Drosophila* are much used in genetic research.

fruit sugar: see FRUCTOSE.

Frunze, city (pop. c.140,000), cap. of Kirghiz SSR, on branch of Turksib RR; center of rich agr. area. Founded 1873 as Pishpek; renamed 1927.

Fry, Christopher, 1907–, English dramatist. His verse plays, often compared in style to those of the Elizabethans, include *The Lady's Not for Burning* (1948), *Venus Observed* (1950), and *A Sleep of Prisoners* (1951).

Fry, Roger (Elliott), 1866–1934, English art critic and painter. Helped to introduce postimpressionists to England.

Fuad I (fōōäd'), 1868–1936, first king of modern Egypt (1917–36), son of deposed khedive, Ismail Pasha. Became sultan in 1917, acquired title of king in 1922. Autocratic rule opposed by Wafd party. Succeeded by his son Farouk I.

fuchsia (fū'shù), tropical American shrub (*Fuchsia*), with graceful, pendulous flowers in various shades of red and purple. Grown outdoors in mild climates and as pot or summer bedding plant elsewhere.

fuchsine (fōōk'sĭn) or **magenta,** bright red biological dye composed of aniline derivatives.

fuel, material combustible in presence of air to produce usable heat. Chemical principle of COMBUSTION is essentially same for all fuel forms: rapid oxidation involving union of carbon and hydrogen (important fuel constituents) with oxygen, and liberation of heat energy (exothermic reaction). Fuels are valued in terms of heat (in calories or in B.T.U.) that a unit weight can produce.

Fuertes, Louis Agassiz (fūĕr'tēs), 1874–1927, American artist and naturalist. He is known for his paintings of birds which appeared in leading American ornithological works and for murals and habitat groups in the American Mus. of Natural History.

Fuessli, Johann Heinrich: see FUSELI, HENRY.

Fugger (fōō'gùr), German family of merchant princes at Augsburg. Its fortune reached its zenith with Jacob Fugger II (1459–1525), who held a virtual monopoly in the mining and trading of silver, copper, and mercury. He lent immense sums to Emperor Maximilian I and financed the election of Charles V, who ennobled the family and granted them sovereign rights over their vast land holdings. Owning merchant fleets and palatial establishments throughout Europe, the Fuggers were also noted patrons of art and learning. Their fortunes declined with the Hapsburgs, whose wars they financed.

fugitive slave laws, in U.S. history, Federal acts of 1793 and 1850 providing for return between states of escaped Negro slaves. As Northern states abolished slavery they relaxed enforcement of 1793 law; abolitionism brought the UNDERGROUND RAILROAD. Many Northern states passed personal liberty laws allowing fugitives jury trial; others forbade state officials to help capture alleged fugitive slaves or to lodge them in state jails. As a concession to the South, COMPROMISE OF 1850 incorporated a more rigorous fugitive slave law. Required "all good citizens" to help execute it; heavily penalized anyone aiding fugitive slaves; denied fugitive jury trial and right to give testimony. New personal-liberty laws of Northern states contradicted 1850 legislation; abolitionists fearlessly defied it. Trials of fugitive slave cases increased sectional hostility. Both acts were repealed by Congress on June 28, 1864.

fugue (fūg) [Fr., from Ital.,= flight], in music, a polyphonic composition of several parts or voices, wherein a melody, phrase, or motive is used in more than one voice. The melody (called the subject) makes its entry in each voice successively. The various devices of COUNTERPOINT may, or may not, be used. Fugue writing reached its peak in the music of Bach; declined after Beethoven; has attracted much interest in 20th cent.

Fujiyama (fōō"jēyä'mä) or **Mount Fuji,** sacred mountain, 12,389 ft. high, central Honshu, Japan; highest point in Honshu. Symmetrical cone with dormant volcanic crater at summit.

Fukien (fōō'kyĕn'), province (46,376 sq. mi.; pop. 11,-053,860), SE China, on Formosa Strait; cap. Foochow. Largely mountainous. Chief rivers are Min and Lung. Leading ports (Foochow, Amoy) export sugar cane and tobacco. Rice crop is large but inadequate for population's needs. Declined as great tea center but still known for fine tea. Lumbering and fishing are important. Mining (coal, manganese) is minor industry.

Fukuoka (fōōkōō'ōkä), city (pop. 328,548), N Kyushu, Japan; port on Hakata Bay. Textile mfg. Seat of Kyushu Imperial Univ.

Fulda, Ludwig (lōōt'vĭkh fōōl'dä), 1862–1939, German playwright. His works include *Der Talisman* (1893) and *The Pirate* (1911; adapted by S. N. Behrman 1942). Also translated Ibsen, Molière, Shakspere, and Spanish dramatists.

Fulda (fōōl'dä), city (pop. 42,238), Hesse, W Germany, on Fulda R. Grew around Benedictine abbey founded 744 by St. Boniface. From this abbey Christianity spread through central Germany. Abbots held temporal power under Holy Roman Empire; became prince-bishops 1752. Secularized 1802, Fulda passed to Electoral Hesse in 1815. Still an episcopal see, Fulda is meeting place of annual conference of Catholic bishops of Germany. Buildings, restored after World War II, include baroque cathedral, where St. Boniface is buried; Church of St. Michael (9th cent.); baroque château.

Fulham (fool'ùm), metropolitan borough (pop. 122,047), London. Has a palace of the bishops of London.

Fulk (fùlk), 1092–1143, king of Jerusalem (1131–43), count of Anjou (1109–29). Journeyed to Holy Land 1120 and again 1129, when he made over Anjou to his son Geoffrey IV (Geoffrey Plantagenet). Married daughter of Baldwin II of Jerusalem, whom he succeeded as king.

Fuller, George, 1822–84, American portrait, figure, and landscape painter.

Fuller, Henry Blake, 1857–1929, American author. His novels are divided into romantic novels laid in Europe (e.g., *The Chevalier of Pensieri-Vani,* 1890) and realistic works about the Chicago scene (e.g., *The Cliff-Dwellers,* 1893). Also wrote short stories and newspaper editorials and book reviews.

Fuller, (Sarah) Margaret, 1810–50, American writer, lecturer, b. Mass. Translated Eckermann's *Conversations with Goethe* (1839), was a feminist (*Woman in the Nineteenth Century,* 1845), a transcendentalist, and a literary critic. In Rome, she married Marchese Ossoli; in 1850, en route to U.S., they drowned in a shipwreck.

Fuller, Melville Weston, 1833–1910, Chief Justice of U.S. Supreme Court (1888–1910). Leaned toward strict construction of Constitution.

Fuller, Thomas, 1608–61, English writer, a moderate Anglican clergyman, compiler of antiquary *Worthies of England* (1662), author of *History of the Holy Warre* (1639) and *The Holy State and the Profane State* (1642).

fuller's earth, a sedimentary clay which has the property of absorbing basic colors. Chiefly used in clarifying petroleum and refining edible oils.

Fullerton, city (pop. 19,050), S Calif., SE of Los Angeles. Processes citrus fruits, vegetables, and walnuts. Oil-field center.

fulminate (fùl'mĭnāt), commonly a name for explosive, crystalline mercury salt of fulminic acid, used as detonator when mixed with potassium chlorate.

Fulton, Robert, 1765–1815, American inventor, engineer, painter. His *Clermont,* launched in 1807, though not first steamboat in America, was first to be commercially successful in American waters.

Fulton. 1 City (pop. 10,052), central Mo., NE of Jefferson City, in farm area. Mfg. of firebrick and shoes. Seat of Westminster Col. (Presbyterian; for men; 1851). **2** City (pop. 13,922), N N.Y., on Oswego R. and the Barge Canal and NW of Syracuse. Mfg. of candy, textiles, paper, and aluminum products.

Fulvia (fùl'vēù), d. 40 B.C., Roman woman. Her third husband was Marc ANTONY. She led an unsuccessful revolt against Augustus (40 B.C.).

fumitory, Old World herb (*Fumaria officinalis*) with red-tipped purplish flowers. It is naturalized in North America. Climbing fumitory or Allegheny vine (*Adlumia fungosa*) is a North American vine.

Funafuti: see ELLICE ISLANDS.

Funchal (foonshäl'), city (pop. 58,856), chief city of Madeira isl., Portugal. Port and resort. Cathedral built 15th cent.

function, in mathematics, quantity having numerical value (a variable) which varies with value of one or more other such quantities (independent variables). For example, the distance a body falls is a function of the time it is allowed to fall.

fundamentalism, conservative religious movement in Protestant denominations early in 20th cent. Aim was to maintain traditional interpretations of Bible and fundamental doctrines of faith against what they considered threat of scientific discoveries. There were bitter controversies. In 1925, William Jennings Bryan, a fundamentalist leader, won state's case in famous SCOPES TRIAL.

Fundamental Orders, in U.S. history, basic law of Conn. colony, 1639–62. Contained preamble and 11 orders, including voting restrictions. Placed welfare of community over that of individual.

Fundy, Bay of, inlet of the Atlantic (100 mi. long, 60 mi. wide at entrance), between N.B. and SW N.S., Canada. In its upper arms, Chignecto Bay and Minas Basin, its tides or bore rise to 70 ft. Some flatlands have been diked off and reclaimed. Annapolis Royal, on N.S. shore, is oldest settlement in Canada. St. John, N.B., is chief port.

Fundy National Park, 79.5 sq. mi., S N.B., Canada, on Bay of Fundy and ENE of St. John; estab. 1949.

Fünfkirchen, Hungary: see PECS.

fungicide, chemical used for spraying or dusting on plants, or applied to seeds, soils, woods, or fabrics to destroy fungi. Sulphur, copper (BORDEAUX MIXTURE), and organic mercury compounds are used to destroy or prevent fungus diseases of plants.

fungus (fùn'gùs), plural **fungi** (fùn'jī), simple plant lacking true roots, stems, and leaves and belonging like algae to lowest division of plant kingdom. Unlike algae the fungi have no chlorophyll and must get food from living or dead organic matter. Examples are BACTERIA, MUSHROOM, YEAST. See *ill.,* p. 633.

Funk, Casimir (kă'zĭmēr foongk'), 1884–, American biochemist, credited with discovery of vitamins.

Funston, Frederick, 1865–1917, U.S. general. Captured Emilio AGUINALDO in 1901. Commanded occupying troops at Veracruz in 1914.

fur, hairy covering of an animal, especially the skins of such animals as have thick, soft, close-growing hair next to the skin itself and coarser protective hair above it. Term *fur* extends to dressed sheep and lamb skins prepared for wearing with hair kept on and (usually) curled (persian lamb, karakul, astrakhan, and mouton). Since prehistoric days man has used furs for clothing. Some of the more prized furs are sable, marten, mink, ermine, and chinchilla. Staple for great fur-trading days in North America was beaver. Fur trade reached its peak in wilderness of North America and Asia from 17th to early 19th cent. Effect in opening wilderness was even more striking in Canada. Important fur-trading companies were HUDSON'S BAY COMPANY, NORTH WEST COMPANY, and AMERICAN FUR COMPANY. Advance of settlement, depletion of beaver and other fur-bearing animals, and decline in importance of beaver hat ended day of fur trader in 1840s in U.S. and S Canada. Later threat of extinction of fur seal led to BERING SEA FUR-SEAL CONTROVERSY. Preparation and sale of furs remains, however, a very considerable business; fur farming has become in U.S. and Canada a major industry in 20th cent.

furfural (fûr'fùrăl") or **furfuraldehyde,** ALDEHYDE of pyromucic acid. It is a colorless, oily liquid with aromatic odor. Used as solvent and in making deodorants, disinfectants, preservatives, etc.

Furies, goddesses of vengeance: see ERINYES.

Furka (foor'kä), road, central Switzerland, linking Uri and Valais cantons. Built 1864–66, it crosses Furka Pass, 7,971 ft. high. A rail line goes through Furka Tunnel.

Furman University: see GREENVILLE, S.C.

Furneaux Islands (fûr'nō), group in Bass Strait between Tasmania, to which it belongs, and Australia; discovered 1773. Largest is Flinders Isl. Sheep, dairy products, tin.

Furness, hilly district of Lancashire, England. In SW are rich iron mines and great engineering works which center at Barrow-in-Furness.

Furniss, Harry, 1854–1925, British caricaturist and illustrator of many books, including works of Dickens, Thackeray, and Lewis Carroll.

Fürth (fürt), city (pop. 99,503), Middle Franconia, Bavaria, on Regnitz R., near Nuremberg. Produces machinery, precision instruments, textiles.

furze, spiny Old World shrub (*Ulex europaeus*), also called gorse. It has scalelike leaves and fragrant yellow

EGYPTIAN
Seat of plaited string
15th Century B.C.

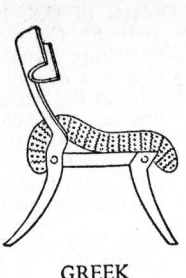

GREEK

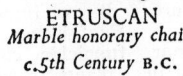

ETRUSCAN
Marble honorary chair
c.5th Century B.C.

ROMAN
Marble

**CENTRAL
EUROPEAN**
c.10th Century

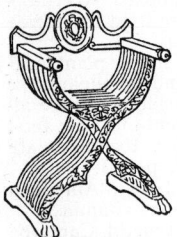

ITALIAN
Savonarola chair
15th Century

FLORENTINE
Strozzi chair
15th Century

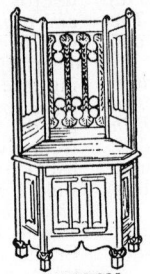

SPANISH
15th-century Gothic

SPANISH
16th Century

CHINESE
18th Century

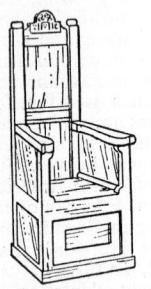

ENGLISH – *Tudor*
Late 16th Century

ENGLISH
Queen Anne
Early 18th Century

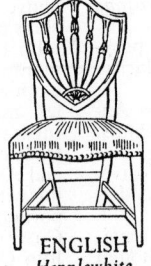

ENGLISH
Hepplewhite
Late 18th Century

ENGLISH
Adam
Late 18th Century

ENGLISH
Chippendale
Late 18th Century

ENGLISH
Sheraton
Late 18th Century

FRENCH
Louis XV
18th Century

FRENCH
Louis XVI
Late 18th Century

FRENCH
Directoire
Late 18th Century

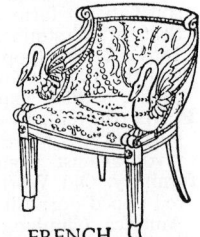

FRENCH
Empire
Early 19th Century

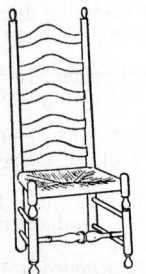

AMERICAN
Pennsylvania
Early 18th Century

AMERICAN
New England Windsor
Late 18th Century

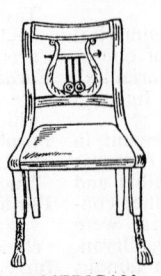

AMERICAN
Duncan Phyfe
Early 19th Century

AMERICAN
Hitchcock
19th Century

AMERICAN
c.1950

pealike flowers. Often used as sand binder in the U.S.

fuse, electric, safety device in electric circuit; when current exceeds safe amount, fuse breaks circuit, stopping flow of electricity.

Fuseli, Henry (fū'zĭlē), 1741–1825, Anglo-Swiss artist, b. Zurich; also called Johann Heinrich Fuessli or Füssli. Famous for dramatic drawings. Was a friend of William Blake.

fusel oil (fū'zŭl), oily colorless liquid with disagreeable odor and taste. It is a mixture of alcohols and fatty acids used as a solvent.

Fushun (foo'shoon), city (pop. 279,604) in, but independent of, Liaotung prov., Manchuria, in important coal-mining area.

fusion, in physics: see MELTING POINT; HEAT.

Füssli, Johann Heinrich: see FUSELI, HENRY.

Fust, Johann, d. 1466, printer at Mainz. Johann Gutenberg, unable to repay Fust's loans, had to give Fust his press and types. Fust and his partner, Peter Schöffer, were first to print in colors and among the first to use Greek type (1465). Issued first dated book (1457).

Fustel de Coulanges, Numa Denis (nümä' dünē' füstĕl' dù kōōlãzh'), 1830–89, French historian. His *Histoire des institutions politiques de l'ancienne France* (6 vols., 1882–92) opened way for new thought on early medieval history.

futurism, Italian school of painting, sculpture, and literature which flourished 1909–c.1915. Futurists strove to portray dynamic character of 20th-cent. life. They glorified danger, war, and machine age, and in theory favored growth of fascism.

Fyn (fün), island (1,149 sq. mi.; pop. 338,013), Denmark, in Baltic Sea, between Little Belt (W) and Great Belt (E); chief city Odense. Second largest Danish island. Fertile lowland; it has dairy farming and cattle breeding.

Fyne, Loch (lōkh fīn'), arm of Firth of Clyde, Argyllshire, Scotland. Famous for its herring fisheries. Leading city on Loch is Inverary.

Fyt, Jan (yän' fĭt'), 1611–61, Flemish animal painter and etcher. Collaborated with Rubens and Jordaens.

Fyzabad or **Faizabad** (fī'zŭbăd), city (pop. 57,632), E central Uttar Pradesh, India. Cap of kingdom of Oudh (1724–75). Its suburb, Ajodhya or Ayodhya, is sacred to Hindus; mentioned in Ramayana.

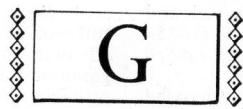

Ga, chemical symbol of the element GALLIUM.

Gabirol: see IBN GABIROL, SOLOMON BEN JUDAH.

Gablonz, Czechoslovakia: see JABLONEC NAD NISOU.

Gabriel (gā'–) [Heb.,= man of God], archangel, the divine herald. In Bible he appears to Daniel, to Zacharias, and to the Virgin Mary in the Annunciation. Dan. 8.16; 9.21; Luke 1.19,26,27. Christian tradition makes Gabriel the archangel trumpeter of the Last Judgment. 1 Thes. 4.16. In Islam, Gabriel revealed the Koran to Mohammed. Feast: March 24.

Gabriel, Jacques Ange (zhäk' äzh' gäbrēĕl'), c.1698–1782, French architect, who designed Place de la Concorde (Paris) and finished Petit Trianon (Versailles).

Gabrieli, Giovanni (gäbrēä'lē), 1557–1612, Italian organist and composer. His music shows the beginnings of baroque techniques; thus, his *Sonata pian' e forte* employs the baroque use of contrasts in dynamics and contains elements of modern orchestration.

Gabrilowitsch, Ossip (ô'sĭp gäbrĭlô'vĭch), 1878–1936, Russian-American pianist and conductor. Conductor of the Detroit Symphony Orchestra, 1918–36.

Gad, son of Jacob, ancestor of one of 12 tribes of Israel. Tribe settled in GILEAD. Gen. 30.11; 35.26; 49.19; Num. 2.14; 13.15; 32.1,2,34; Deut. 3.12; 33.20; Joshua 13.24; 1 Chron. 5.18,26; 12.8,14.

Gadara (gä'–), anc. city, SE of Sea of Galilee, in the Decapolis. The "country of the Gadarenes"—or Gergesenes or Gerasenes—given in Bible as scene of miracle of the possessed swine probably refers not to this city but to obscure town on E shore of Sea of Galilee. Mat. 8.28; Mark 5.1; Luke 8.26.

Gaddi (gäd' de), family of Florentine artists. **Gaddo Gaddi** (gäd'dō), c.1260–c.1333, painter and mosaicist, was probably an associate of Cimabue and Giotto. His son, **Taddeo Gaddi,** c.1300–c.1366, was godson and pupil of Giotto, whom he assisted for 24 years. Also painters were Taddeo's sons, **Agnolo Gaddi,** c.1350–96, and **Giovanni Gaddi,** d. 1383.

gadolinium (gădŭlĭ'nēŭm), rare metallic element of RARE EARTHS (symbol = Gd; see also ELEMENT, table).

Gadsden, James, 1788–1858, American railroad promoter and diplomat. Urged construction of railroad from South to the Pacific. Minister to Mexico (1853–56); negotiated GADSDEN PURCHASE. Recalled for exceeding instructions.

Gadsden, industrial city (pop. 55,725), NE Ala., on Coosa R. and NE of Birmingham, in mining area; founded c.1845. Alabama City annexed 1932. Metalworking (iron, steel). Rubber tires, textiles.

Gadsden Purchase, strip of land purchased (1853) by U.S. from Mexico. Pres. Franklin Pierce wanted to insure U.S. possession of Mesilla Valley near the Rio Grande—most practicable route for southern railroad to the Pacific. James GADSDEN negotiated purchase. Area of 45,535 sq. mi., purchased for $10,000,000, now forms extreme S N.Mex. and Ariz. S of the Gila.

Gadshill (gădz'hĭl), low hill, Kent, England. Scene of Falstaff's robberies in Shakspere's *Henry IV*.

Gaea (jē'ù) [Gr.,= earth], Greek earth-goddess; daughter of Chaos, mother of Uranus and Pontus. Mother by Uranus of Cyclopes and Titans, by Pontus of five sea-deities. Worshiped as mother of all things, a counselor of gods and men. Oracles of Delphi and Olympia traced their origin to her.

Gaelic (gā'lĭk), Celtic languages spoken in Ireland (Irish) and Highland Scotland (Scottish or Scottish Gaelic). It may include Manx. Erse is sometimes a synonym for Gaelic. See LANGUAGE (table).

Gaelic literature, literature of Gaelic-speaking Ireland and Scotland. Irish literature is divided into Old Irish (before 900), Middle Irish (until 1350), Late Middle or Early Modern Irish (until 1650), and Modern Irish (from 1650). Old Irish works survive in Middle Irish copies (e.g., Book of Leinster). Middle Irish literature consists of two groups of romances or sagas—the Red Branch or Ulster cycle and the Fenian cycle. Red

Branch deals with pagan heroes (e.g., *Cuchulain*). Fenian cycle, later in origin, is gentler, and Christianity is introduced during time of *Ossian*. Form of sagas is prose with interspersed verse dialogue. Poetic revival and rise of modern Irish prose (16th–17th cent.) culminated in work of Geoffrey Keating. Poetry after time of Cromwell (1649) was in hands of wandering poets. Depopulation of Ireland after potato famine of 1847 brought great decrease in number of those who spoke Gaelic. Late 19th cent. brought Gaelic revival, led by the Gaelic League and Douglas Hyde. Scottish Gaelic literature has been separate since 16th cent. Rebellion (1745) of Charles Edward Stuart led to great outburst of poetry by such men as Alexander Macdonald. Controversy over *Ossian* of James MACPHERSON renewed interest in Gaelic. Some Highland writers have used Gaelic in 19th–20th cent.

Gaeta (gää′tä), city (pop. 4,967), S Latium, central Italy; Mediterranean port on Gulf of Gaeta. Long a stronghold of kingdom of Naples. On its fall to Victor Emmanuel II of Sardinia after long siege (1860–61), the kingdom of Italy was proclaimed.

Gaffney, city (pop. 8,123), NW S.C., NE of Spartanburg near N.C. line. Has textile mills. Seat of Limestone Col. (for women; 1845).

Gafsa (gäf′sù), anc. *Capsa*, town (pop. 11,320), S central Tunisia, in an oasis. Exports phosphates, dates, and olives. Surrounding region has yielded artifacts of an upper Paleolithic culture (Capsian) of N Africa and S Europe.

Gág, Wanda (gäg), 1893–1946, American artist and writer for children; noted for her lithographs.

Gage, Thomas, d. 1656, English traveler. Lived and traveled among Indians of Central America (1625–37). Wrote *The English-American: His Travail by Sea and Land* (1648).

Gage, Thomas, 1721–87, British general. Commanded British forces in North America (1763–73). As governor of Mass. (1774–75) he enforced coercive measures on eve of American Revolution.

gag rules, procedural rules in force in U.S. House of Representatives from 1836 to 1844. Southerners, aided by Northern Democrats, secured their passage to prevent discussion of antislavery proposals in the House. Repealed following John Quincy Adams's successful fight to secure right of petition. Their effect was to strengthen cause of abolitionists.

Gaillard, David DuBose (gā′lùrd), 1859–1913, American army engineer. Directed construction of central division of Panama Canal, including excavation of Culebra (now Gaillard) Cut, most difficult portion of undertaking.

gaillardia (gälär′–), annual or perennial plant (*Gaillardia*) of W U.S. It has showy red or yellow daisy-like flower heads, used for cutting.

Gaines's Mill: see SEVEN DAYS BATTLES.

Gainesville. 1 City (pop. 26,861), N central Fla., SW of Jacksonville; founded c.1854 on site of trading post (1830). Resort. Industrial and shipping center for tung oil, naval stores, lumber, citrus fruit, and vegetables. Seat of Univ. of FLORIDA. Paynes Prairie, a marsh, is near. **2** City (11,936), N Ga., near Chattahoochee R. NE of Atlanta, in Blue Ridge foothills. Textile mfg. and poultry processing. Brenau Col. (for women; 1878) is here. **3** City (pop. 11,246), N Texas, on Elm Fork of Trinity R. NNW of Dallas; founded 1850 on Calif. trail. Center of oil and agr. area processing cotton, grains, and oil. Railroad shops. Has annual community circus.

Gainsborough, Thomas (gānz′bùrù), 1727–88, English portrait and landscape painter. Began as apprentice to a London silversmith. At peak of career his popularity rivaled that of Reynolds. Famous for elegance of his portraits (esp. of women), which have a light and airy quality. Greens and blues predominate in his work. Among famous paintings is *The Blue Boy* (Huntington Art Gall., San Marino, Calif.).

Gainsborough, urban district (pop. 17,509), Lincoln-shire, England, on Trent R. It is St. Ogg's of George Eliot's *Mill on the Floss*. Town estab. very early; Old Hall supposedly built by John of Gaunt.

Gaiseric (gī′sùrĭk) or **Genseric** (gĕn′sùrĭk, jĕn′–), c.390–477, king of the VANDALS (428–77). Invaded Roman Africa from Spain (429); took Carthage 439; won control of Mediterranean through his pirate fleets; sacked Rome 455. When he made peace with Zeno (476), he held N Africa, Sicily, Sardinia, Corsica, Balearic Isls.

Gaithersburg, town (pop. 1,755), W central Md., NW of Washington, D.C. U.S. Coast and Geodetic Survey runs international latitude observatory here.

Gaius (gā′ùs, gī′–), 2d cent. A.D., Roman jurist, known for his *Institutes*, a legal textbook used in the compilation of the Corpus Juris Civilis.

galactose: see LACTOSE.

Galahad, Sir: see ARTHURIAN LEGEND.

Galápagos Islands (gùlä′pùgōs) [Span.,= tortoise], Pacific archipelago (2,966 sq. mi.; pop. 1,346), c.650 mi. W of Ecuador, to which they belong. Discovered in 1535, the islands have biological interest. Visited by Charles Darwin (1835).

Galatea (gälùtē′ù), in Greek mythology, beautiful statue made by the sculptor PYGMALION. Aphrodite granted his prayer that it might come to life.

Galati or **Galatz** (gäläts′), city (pop. 80,411), E Rumania, in Moldavia; a major port on the lower Danube. It was the seat of Danube Navigation Commission from 1856 to 1939.

Galatia (gùlä′shù), anc. territory of central Asia Minor, in the present Turkey (around Ankara). So called from its inhabitants, the Gauls, who conquered it in 3d cent. B.C. and increased territory to extend from Bithynia and Pontus on N to Pamphylia on S. Their advance was checked c.230 B.C. by Attalus I of Pergamum. Fell to Romans 189 B.C., became Roman province 25 B.C. Chief city was Ancyra (present Ankara.)

Galatians (gùlä′shùnz), epistle of New Testament, written by St. Paul to Christians of central Asia Minor. The Galatians had acquired the belief that rigid obedience to the Law of Moses was the means of salvation. This, Paul thought, would vitiate the whole of Christian freedom won for men on the Cross. He states that man is justified in the sight of God by faith, rather than by adherence to the Law. This doctrine is of great importance in Christian theology.

Galatz, Rumania: see GALATI.

Galax (gā′lăks), town (pop. 5,248), SW Va., SW of Roanoke. Mfg. of furniture, caskets, and glass products. Galax plant gathered and shipped.

galax (gā′lăks″), low-growing evergreen plant (*Galax aphylla*), native to mountain woods from Va. to Ga. Its spikes of white flowers and heart-shaped leaves are used by florists.

Galaxy: see MILKY WAY SYSTEM.

Galba (Servius Sulpicius Galba) (găl′bù), 3 B.C.–A.D. 69, Roman emperor. An able soldier, he was proclaimed emperor on Nero's death (68) but soon was killed in a rebellion. Otho became emperor.

Galdhoppigen: see JOTUNHEIM.

Galdós, Benito Pérez: see PÉREZ GALDÓS, BENITO.

Gale, Zona, 1874–1938, American novelist, b. Portage, Wis. Won notice for her idealized stories of small-town life (e.g., *Friendship Village*, 1908). Her later novels were realistic and her best-known work, *Miss Lulu Bett* (1920), was satiric.

Galeed (gā′lēĕd) or **Mizpah** (mĭz′pù), cairn, raised by Jacob and Laban to mark their covenant. So-called "Mizpah benediction" given here was mutual warning, not a blessing. Gen. 31.44–55. Also called Jegar-sahudutha.

Galen (gā′lùn), c.130–c.200, physician of Greek parentage, systematizer of contemporary medical learning. His authority was almost undisputed until the 16th cent. He wrote many treatises; about 83 of his medical works are extant.

Galena, city (pop. 4,648), extreme NW Ill., on Galena

R. near the Mississippi. Lead mined here since early 18th cent. From 1807, when U.S. took mines under its protection, to 1860's, busy steamboat port and center of NW Ill. and SW Wis. lead area. Home of U. S. Grant is state museum.

galena (gŭlē'nù) or **lead glance,** lustrous, blue-gray crystalline mineral, an important ore of lead and in some areas of silver. It is chiefly lead sulphide, but often contains silver and sometimes copper, zinc, or other elements.

Galena Park, city (pop. 7,186), S Texas, E suburb of Houston, absorbed 1948 by Houston.

Galerius (gŭlēr'ĕùs), d. 310, Roman emperor (305–10). Appointed Caesar by Diocletian in 293, he succeeded (305) to empire in the East when Constantius I succeeded in the West. After Constantius' death, Galerius recognized Severus as coemperor, but after they were defeated by the troops of Maxentius, he supported Licinius. A confused fight for power was still going on when Galerius died.

Galesburg, city (pop. 31,425), W Ill., WNW of Peoria; founded 1836. Rail center (with shops) and livestock market. Mfg. of bricks and metal products. Seat of KNOX COLLEGE. Town and college founded by N.Y. Presbyterians under G. W. Gale. Birthplace of Carl Sandburg.

Galiani, Ferdinando (färdēnän'dō gälyä'nē), 1728–87, Italian economist. His *Della moneta* [on money] (1750), and *Dialogues sur le commerce des blés* (1770), set forth modern theory of value and historical approach to economics.

Galich (gä'lĭch), Pol. *Halicz,* city (pop. 4,386), NW Ukraine, on the Dniester. The seat of the dukes of Przemysl from c.1134, it later became the cap. of the duchy of Galich, which in 1188 was united with Vladimir (see VLADIMIR-VOLYNSKI). In 13th cent. Galich-Vladimir (which then included GALICIA and VOLHYNIA), extended E to Kiev. Under Tatar overlordship from 1245, duchy was partitioned in 1366 between Poland and Lithuania. City, now insignificant, has medieval remains.

Galicia (gŭlĭ'shù), former Austrian crownland, now in NW Ukraine; chief city Lvov (Lemberg). The W section of old duchy of GALICH and Vladimir, it passed to Poland 1366, to Austria 1772. Polish population enjoyed limited autonomy 1861–1918. A battleground during World War I, Galicia was contested by Poland and Ukrainian republic in 1918–20. Poland secured all Galicia and was confirmed in possession by Treaty of Riga with USSR (1921). By Polish-Soviet Treaty most of Galicia (incl. Lvov and Drogobych oil fields) passed to USSR.

Galicia, region (10,984 sq. mi.; pop. 2,495,860), NW Spain, bordering on Atlantic Ocean and on Portugal. Largely mountainous. Fishing, cattle raising, agr. Chief cities: Santiago de Compostela, La Coruña, Vigo, El Ferrol, Pontevedra. Galician dialect, akin to Portuguese, has a great literary past. Region was conquered from Moors by kings of Asturias 8th–9th cent.

Galigaï, Leonora: see CONCINI, CONCINO.

Galilee (gä'lĭlē), agr. region, N Palestine, chief scene of ministry of Jesus. The lake, countryside, and towns —Cana, Capernaum, Tiberias, Nazareth—are repeatedly referred to in the Gospels. Jesus was called the Galilean. Joshua 20.7; 21.32; 1 Kings 9.11; 2 Kings 15.29; Isa. 9.1; Mat. 26.69–75; John 7.52.

Galilee, Sea of, fresh-water lake, 13 mi. long, 3–7 mi. wide, NE Palestine. It has fisheries. In Old Testament called Chinnereth or Chinneroth; in New Testament called Galilee, Gennesaret, or Tiberias. Modern Arabic name is Bahr Tabariyeh. In Jesus' time there were nine flourishing towns on its shores.

Galilei, Vincenzo (vēnchän'tsō gälēlā'ē), d. 1591, Italian lutanist, singer, writer, and composer; father of Galileo. A pioneer of the baroque era, he was one of the first to compose recitatives.

✓ **Galileo** (gä"lĭlē'ō), It. *Galileo Galilei,* 1564–1642, Italian astronomer, mathematician, and physicist whose investigation of natural laws laid the foundations of modern experimental science. He formulated mathematically many physical laws and is credited with conclusions foreshadowing Newton's laws of motion. Constructed the first complete astronomical telescope (1609). His astronomical discoveries confirmed Copernican theory of solar system which he supported in his dialogue on the two chief systems of the world (published 1632). He was forced by the Inquisition, however, to abjure belief that earth moved about sun.

Galion, city (pop. 9,952), N central Ohio, SW of Mansfield. Mfg. of road machinery and vehicles.

Galitzin or **Galitsin:** see GALLITZIN.

Gall, c.1840–1894, war chief of Sioux Indians. Refused to accept treaty of 1868 confining him to reservation. Joined Sitting Bull in defeat of Custer (1876). Surrendered at Poplar, Mont., and became farmer on reservation.

gall (gôl), abnormal growth of plant tissue produced by stimulus of external agent. Commonest agents are gall insects (certain aphids, wasps, midges, beetles, thrips, moths) and mites. Usually gall maker produces same type of gall even on different hosts. Galls are source of tannin and of good quality permanent ink.

Gallait, Louis (lwē' gälä'), 1810–87, Belgian historical painter. Headed a school of historical painting in Brussels.

Galla Placidia (gä'lù plùsĭ'dēù), d. 450, West Roman empress; daughter of Theodosius I. Long a hostage among the Visigoths, she married ATAULF (414) but was returned to her brother HONORIUS after Ataulf's death. Her second husband through her influence was made coemperor as CONSTANTIUS III. After 425 she was regent for her son VALENTINIAN III.

Gallas, Matthias, Graf von (mätē'äs gräf' fŭn gä'läs), 1584–1647, Austrian field marshal in Thirty Years War. Sided with emperor against his superior, WALLENSTEIN; succeeded to Wallenstein's command and to most of his duchy of Friedland. Won major victory at NÖRDLINGEN (1634).

Gallatin, Albert (gä'lùtĭn), 1761–1849, American statesman and financier, b. Switzerland. Member, U.S. Congress (1795–1801). As U.S. Secretary of the Treasury 1802–14), he reshaped country's financial policy from Federalist to Jeffersonian principles. Key figure in negotiating Treaty of Ghent. Authority on banking and finance.

Gallatin, town (pop. 5,107), N Tenn., NE of Nashville near Cumberland R. Tobacco, farm, and livestock center with mfg. of shoes. Town, with Union garrison, captured Aug., 1862 by Gen. J. H. Morgan.

Gallatin, river, 120 mi. long, SW Mont., Rising in NW Yellowstone Natl. Park and flowing N between Madison and Gallatin ranges, then NW to join Madison and Jefferson Rivers to form the Missouri.

gall bladder: see BILE.

Galle, Johann Gottfried (yō'hän gôt'frēt gä'lù), 1812–1910, German astronomer. He discovered the planet Neptune from calculations of Leverrier.

Galle (gäl), city (pop. 49,038), SW Ceylon, port on Indian Ocean. Flourished under Portuguese rule (1507–1640).

Gallegos, Rómulo (rō'mōōlō gäyä'gōs), 1884–, Venezuelan novelist, president of Venezuela (Feb.–Nov., 1948). Best-known novel is *Doña Bárbara* (1929; Eng. tr., 1931).

galleon (gä'lēùn), type of ocean-going sailing vessels used by Spanish in 15th and 16th cent. They were cumbersome three-masted, square-rigged ships with high bow and stern, the latter ornamented with carvings. Though they were much used to bring goods from the Americas, their service in Spanish Armada brought defeat by smaller, swifter English ships (1588).

galley, type of long, narrow vessels of anc. and medieval times, propelled usually by oars, sometimes by sails. Earliest type was sometimes 150 ft. long with 50 oars, decked at bow and stern but otherwise open. Benches along sides were for chained rowers (slaves, prisoners), while center was for cargo. Usual number of banks of oars was three (triremes); smaller biremes had two banks. Galleys allegedly grew to as many as 40 banks; these were abandoned for smaller vessels by 1st cent. B.C. When used for war, sides were raised to protect rowers. Romans used hooks for grappling and carried bridges for boarding other vessels. French and Venetians used galleys in the Mediterranean until 17th cent.

gallic acid, colorless, crystalline solid organic acid usually obtained from tannins. Used as astringent and disinfectant.

Gallicanism (găˈlĭkŭnĭzŭm), theory that the French monarch had special rights in the Roman Catholic Church in France. It was put forward with the doctrine that the pope was subordinate to the ecumenical council (the conciliar theory), which emerged from the Univ. of Paris during the Great SCHISM and was confirmed by Charles VII in the Pragmatic Sanction of Bourges (1438). Francis I repealed the act after the Concordat of 1516 in which the papacy surrendered rights of appointment. The concordat was revoked in 1561, and the struggle resumed. LOUIS XIV in his trouble with INNOCENT XI had an assembly of bishops pass the "Four Gallican Articles of 1682," putting both councils and kings above the pope. Innocent XII managed to quiet the trouble in 1693, and Louis abandoned Gallican theory. Its effect was felt later in Jansenism, in the Revolutionary Civil Constitution of the Clergy, and in clauses added by Napoleon to the Concordat of 1801. Gallicanism has been impossible since the enunciation of papal infallibility of the Vatican Council (1869).

Galli-Curci, Amelita (gälˈlē-kō͞orˈchē), 1889–, Italian-American coloratura soprano. She made her American debut (Chicago, 1916) as Gilda in *Rigoletto;* she sang with the Chicago Opera Co. until 1926 and with the Metropolitan, New York, 1921–30.

Gallic Wars (găˈlĭk), campaigns of Caesar as proconsul of GAUL (58–51 B.C.). His first task was to prevent the Helvetii from entering SW Gaul. Next the Aedui asked his help against the German ARIOVISTUS. In 57 he pacified Belgica. In 56 he attacked the Veneti. In 55 he went to the Low Countries and crossed the Rhine. In 54 he invaded Britain. Next, some Belgian tribes led by AMBIORIX raised a revolt which Caesar dispersed. In 53 all central, E, and N Gaul revolted under VERCINGETORIX. With incredible speed and brilliant tactics Caesar crossed the Alps and stifled the uprising. The prime source is his own commentary, *The Gallic Wars.*

Galli da Bibiena: see BIBIENA, GALLI DA.

Gallieni, Joseph Simon (zhôzĕfˈ sēmōˈ gälyānēˈ), 1849–1916, French general. As military governor of Paris early in World War I, he vitally contributed to the victory of the Marne (Sept., 1914), sped troops from Paris to front in commandeered taxicabs. Made marshal posthumously (1921).

Gallienus (găˈlēˈnŭs), d. 268, Roman emperor, colleague of his father, VALERIAN (253–60), and alone (260–68). Dissolution of the empire started in his reign.

Gallipoli (gŭlĭˈpŭlē), Turkish *Gelibolu,* city (pop. 16,-496), European Turkey; a port near the neck of the Gallipoli Peninsula, which extends c.60 mi. to the SW between the Aegean Sea and the Dardanelles. Peninsula was scene of **Gallipoli campaign,** April, 1915–Jan., 1916, an Allied expedition in World War I to gain the Dardanelles, capture Constantinople, and make contact with Russia through the Black Sea. Idea of forcing Straits was originally Winston Churchill's. A naval expedition having failed (March), British troops landed on peninsula, French on Asiatic shore. Allies, whose cooperation was poor, were prevented from joining by stubborn Turkish resistance (directed by Liman von Sanders) and had to withdraw. Sir Ian Hamilton and, after Oct., Sir Charles Munro were the Allied commanders.

Gallipolis (găˈlĭpŭlēsˈ), city (pop. 7,871), SE Ohio, on Ohio R. Mfg. of furniture and food products.

Gallitzin (gŭlĭtˈsĭn), Rus. *Golytsin,* Russian princely family; also spelled Galitzin, Galytzin. **Vasily Vasilyevich Gallitzin** (vēsēˈlyē vŭsēˈlyŭvĭch), d. 1619, helped to enthrone first false Dmitri. **Vasily Vasilyevich Gallitzin,** 1643–1714, lover and adviser of SOPHIA ALEKSEYEVNA, was banished to Siberia by Peter I (1689). **Boris Alekseyevich Gallitzin** (bŭrēsˈ ŭlyĭksyāˈĭvĭch), 1654–1714, tutor of Peter I, helped him to depose Sophia. **Dmitri Mikhailovich Gallitzin** (dŭmēˈtrē mēkhīˈlŭvĭch), 1665–1737, diplomat and general, was exiled by Empress Anna for seeking to limit her power (1730). **Dmitri Alekseyevich Gallitzin,** 1735–1803, Russian ambassador to Paris (1765–73), was a friend of Diderot and Voltaire. His son, **Demetrius Augustine Gallitzin,** 1770–1840, became a Roman Catholic, went to America. Ordained 1795; worked in SW Pennsylvania as frontier missionary; was known as Father Smith. Founded Catholic colony of Loretto near Gallitzin, Pa. **Aleksandr Nikolayevich Gallitzin** (ŭlyĭksänˈdŭr nyĭkŭlīˈŭvĭch), 1773?–1844, was minister of education under Alexander I; a liberal.

gallium (găˈlēŭm), silver-gray metallic element (symbol = Ga; see also ELEMENT, table), widely distributed in small quantities. Since it is liquid over a wide temperature range it is sometimes used in high-temperature thermometers.

Galloway, Joseph, c.1731–1803, American colonial leader. Urged conciliation and written constitution as means of avoiding conflict prior to American Revolution and later remained loyal to the king.

Galloway, district of SW Scotland, comprising Wigtownshire and Kirkcudbrightshire. Black, hornless Galloway cattle bred here.

gallstone: see CALCULUS, in medicine.

Gallup, George Horace, 1901–, American public opinion statistician, originator of the Gallup poll. Founded (1935) American Institute of Public Opinion.

Gallup, town (pop. 9,133; alt. 6,503 ft.), NW N.Mex., on Puerco R. and near Ariz. line; founded c.1879. Rail and trade center in coal, wool, and livestock area, and in heart of Indian country. Scene of annual intertribal rites.

Galois, Évariste (āvärēstˈ gälwäˈ), 1811–32, French mathematician. He contributed to theories of equations, numbers, and functions and was a pioneer in establishing theory of groups in algebraic solutions.

Galswintha (gälswĭnˈthŭ), d. 567, Frankish queen, sister of BRUNHILDA and wife of CHILPERIC I, by whom she was murdered.

Galsworthy, John, 1867–1933, English novelist and dramatist. Many plays concern social problems (e.g., *Strife,* 1909). Novels portray the limited social consciousness and viewpoint of upper-middle-class families of Victorian era. Many are grouped in three trilogies, *The Forsyte Saga* (1922), *A Modern Comedy* (1928), *The End of the Chapter* (1935). He also wrote short stories, *Caravan* (1925), and poems (in a collected edition, 1934). Received 1932 Nobel Prize in Literature.

Galt, John, 1779–1839, Scottish novelist, founder of CANADA COMPANY (1826). Novels and stories portray Scottish country life. His son, **Sir Alexander Tilloch Galt,** 1817–93, was a Canadian statesman, b. England. A leader for confederation of Canadian provinces. As minister of finance (1858–62, 1864–66) he defended protective tariff. Dominant member of Halifax Fisheries Commission. First Canadian high commissioner in London (1880–83).

Galt, city (pop. 19,207), S Ont., Canada, on Grand R. and WNW of Hamilton. Has textile and lumber mills and mfg. of clothing, shoes, and machinery.

Galton, Sir Francis (gôlˈtŭn), 1822–1911, English scientist, founder of eugenics (term coined by him); cousin of Charles Darwin.

Galuppi, Baldassare (bäldäs-säˈrä gälōō͞pˈpē), 1706–85, Italian composer of oratorios, chamber music, and operas. Immortalized in Browning's poem "A Toccata of Galuppi's."

Galvani, Luigi (lwā'jē gälvä'nē), 1737–98, Italian physician. After observing contraction of frog's leg when touched with metal, he made an arc of two different metals and used it to cause muscle contractions. He held that tissue was the electricity source; Volta said the arc was. This controversy stimulated research.

galvanizing, term commonly used for process of coating a metal (usually iron or steel) with zinc, which resists oxidation and moisture. Methods include dipping, electroplating, and baking.

galvanometer, instrument for determining presence of a current in a conductor, the direction of flow, and strength of current. It is based on Hans C. Oersted's discovery that magnetic needle is deflected by passage of electric current along a conductor; magnetic needle tends to turn at right angles, the extent of turn being, in general, dependent upon strength of current. Modern galvanometers have fixed magnet and movable coil. Ammeter is a form of galvanometer with scale to indicate number of amperes. Voltmeter is moving-coil galvanometer which has high-resistance coil and which indicates number of volts of current—the greater the electromotive force of the current, the greater the deflection of the needle.

Galveston (găl'vùstùn), port city (pop. 66,568), on Galveston Isl., S Texas. Island lies across Galveston Bay (inlet of Gulf of Mexico) entrance. Spanish knew it early; probable scene of Cabeza de Vaca's shipwreck (1528). Explored late 18th cent., later outlaw country (esp. for pirates of Jean Lafitte). Settled in 1830s, city progressed despite yellow fever, hurricanes, and Union blockade and brief occupation 1862. Sea wall built after 1900 hurricane. Two causeways connect with mainland. Stores, processes, and ships cotton, sulphur and other chemicals, foodstuffs, and metals. Has fishing and shrimping. Beach resort. Fort Travis (1898) and Fort Crockett (1897–99) were active in World War II. Seat of Univ. of Texas medical school.

Gálvez, José de (hōsā' dā gäl'vĕth), 1720–87, Spanish colonial administrator, visitor general to New Spain (1765–72). Upon return to Spain was responsible for two important changes in Spanish colonial policy: more liberal trade policy to replace earlier narrow mercantilism; system of intendancies. His brother, **Matías de Gálvez** (mätē'äs), 1717–84, was Spanish colonial administrator; viceroy of New Spain (1783–84). Matías's son, **Bernardo de Gálvez**, c.1746–1786, became Spanish governor of Louisiana in 1777. Aided patriot cause in American Revolution. After Spain declared war on England (1779), he captured Baton Rouge and Natchez (1779), Mobile (1780), and Pensacola (1781). Succeeded his father as viceroy.

Galway (gôl'wä), maritime county (2,293 sq. mi.; pop. 165,201), W Ireland, in Connaught. Lough Corrib divides the county; W is Connemara, with picturesque mountains, and E a rolling plain. The Shannon is chief river, and Aran Isls. chief islands. Industries mainly agr. and fishing. The county town is **Galway,** urban district (pop. 20,370), on Galway Bay. A fort for men of Connaught (1124), it saw later fighting. Has good harbor and exports agr. produce, salmon, herring, marble, woolen goods. Site of University Col.

Galway Bay, inlet of the Atlantic, 30 mi. long and 23 mi. wide at entrance on W Ireland coast, in counties Galway and Clare. Aran Isls. at entrance.

Gama, Vasco da (vă'skō dù gä'mù), c.1460–1524, Portuguese navigator, first European to reach India by sea (1497–99). Voyage around Africa made wealth of Indies accessible to Europe and made possible growth of Portuguese wealth and empire. On second voyage (1502) he estab. Portuguese power in Indian waters and on African coast by harsh methods.

Gamaliel of Jabneh, fl. A.D 100, Hebrew leader. He added the 18 benedictions to the daily prayers in an attempt to retain the spirit of Judaism after the destruction of Jerusalem.

Gambetta, Léon (lāō' gäbĕtä'), 1838–82, French statesman. In FRANCO-PRUSSIAN WAR (1870–71) organized French resistance in provinces. Played important part in creation of Third Republic, was premier 1881–82. Republican and anticlerical, he steered mid-course between radicals and royalists, advocated revenge against Germany.

Gambia (găm'bēù), British colony and protectorate (4,033 sq. mi.; pop. c.250,000), W Africa, on the Atlantic; cap. Bathurst. A narrow enclave in Senegal, it borders both banks of Gambia R., the chief trade artery of region. The colony (69 sq. mi.) comprises St. Mary's Isl. (site of Bathurst) and several inland areas. Largely inhabited by Moslem Negro tribes. Exports peanuts. The Portuguese, who estab. settlements here in mid-15th cent., were succeeded by the British in early 17th cent. Present boundaries estab. 1888.

Gambier (găm'bēr), village (pop. 1,037), central Ohio, E of Mt. Vernon. Here is Kenyon Col. (for men; chartered 1824 as Episcopal theological seminary); publishes literary quarterly *Kenyon Review.*

Gambier Islands (găm'bēr) or **Mangareva** (män"gärä'vä), coral group, S Pacific; part of FRENCH ESTABLISHMENTS IN OCEANIA. Mangareva (pop. 553) is largest island. Discovered 1797 by the British, annexed 1881 by France. Produces copra and coffee.

gamboge (gămbōj'), reddish yellow gum RESIN (from tree sap) used as paint pigment and as a purgative.

Gambrinus (gămbrī'nùs), mythical Flemish king, to whom is attributed invention of beer.

gamma ray: SEE RADIOACTIVITY.

Gammer Gurton's Needle, second extant English comedy, acted 1566 at Christ's College, Cambridge. Once attributed to John Still (later bishop of Bath and Wells), but more probably by William Stevenson, fellow of the college.

Gander, town (pop. including airport personnel, c.3,000), E N.F., Canada. Main North American terminal for air service to Europe. Was a major Allied base in World War II.

Gandhi, Mohandas Karamchand (mō"hùndàs' kŭ"rùmchŭnd gän'dē), 1869–1948, great Indian leader. Educated in India and London; admitted to the bar in 1889. While in South Africa he fought for rights of Indians in that country. Returned 1915 to India and began working for India's independence. Gave up Western ways to lead life of abstinence in accordance with Hindu ethics; advocated revival of home industries (esp. cloth weaving). Asserting man's unity under one God, he preached Christian and Moslem scriptures along with the Hindu; vigorously espoused abolition of untouchability. Several times leader of INDIAN NATIONAL CONGRESS he opposed British policy with *Satyagraha* [Sanskrit = truth force] or, in English, nonviolent resistance. Imprisoned 1930 for violating state salt monopoly by publicly extracting salt from sea water, but released 1931 to attend London conference on India. Called the Mahatma [great souled], he was so widely revered that he could exact political concessions by threatening "fasts unto death." Called for *Satyagraha* in 1942, when the British rejected offer to cooperate in war if India were freed at once; interned until 1944. A major figure in conferences leading to India's freedom (1947), he was deeply disappointed by partition of India. Shot fatally on Jan. 30, 1948, by a Hindu who blamed him for the partition.

Gandzha, Azerbaijan SSR: see KIROVABAD.

Ganges (găn'jēz), river, c.1,560 mi. long, in N India and E Pakistan, rising in Himalayas in N Uttar Pradesh and flowing to Bay of Bengal; most sacred Hindu river. Especially holy bathing sites at Allahabad and at Benares.

gannet (găn'ĭt) or **solan goose** (sō'lùn), large white sea bird related to pelican. Common gannet of N Atlantic dives for fish from high in air to deep in water. Boobies are related tropical sea birds.

Gannett, Henry, 1846–1914, American geographer. Chief geographer of U.S. Geological Survey after

1882; improved system of census taking. His efforts led to establishment of U.S. Board of Geographical Names (1890); its chairman until 1910.

Gannett Peak, Wyo.: see WIND RIVER RANGE.

Ganso, Emil, 1895–1941, American painter and etcher, b. Germany.

Ganymede (găʹnĭmēd), in Greek mythology, beautiful boy seized by Zeus to be his cupbearer.

Garamond, Claude (găʹrùmŏnd; Fr., klōdʹ gärämōʹ), d. 1561, Parisian designer and maker of printing types. His designs were used by the Estiennes and Bodoni and were used as a base for designs used by the Elzevir family. His roman and italic types were the first to be primarily designed for metal type, not imitated after handwriting. His roman also helped make roman standard rather than black letter. Modern Garamond types do not closely resemble his.

Garand, John C(antius) (găʹrùnd), 1888–, American inventor of the Garand semiautomatic rifle (on principle of expanding gas), b. Canada.

Garay, Juan de (hwänʹ dù gärīʹ), c.1528–83, Spanish conquistador in South America. Refounded Buenos Aires (1580) from Asunción.

Garbo, Greta, 1905–, American film actress, whose real name is Gustafsson, b. Sweden. Her beauty and restrained acting won fame in such films as *Anna Christie, Queen Christina, Camille,* and *Ninotchka.*

Garborg, Arne Evensen, 1851–1924, Norwegian poet and novelist. Championed use of Landsmaal, the language of the peasants.

García (y Iñigues), Calixto (kälēkʹstō gärsēʹä ē ēnyēʹgĕs), 1836–98, Cuban revolutionist, leader in Ten Years War and Spanish-American War. Elbert Hubbard's essay *A Message to Garcia* has made his name famous.

García, Manuel del Popolo (mänwĕlʹ dĕl pōpōʹlō gärthēʹä), 1775–1832, Spanish tenor, teacher, impresario, and composer. His opera company included his wife, his son, and his daughter, Maria MALIBRAN. He was first to produce opera in Italian in New York. His son, **Manuel Patricio García** (pätrēʹthyō), 1805–1906, inventor of the laryngoscope, taught in Paris and London. Jenny Lind was his pupil.

García Calderón, Francisco (fränsēʹskō gärsēʹä käldärōnʹ), Peruvian writer. Lived in France many years. Wrote (in French) *Latin America: Its Rise and Progress* (Eng. tr., 1913).

García Lorca, Federico (fädhārēʹkō gärthēʹä lôrʹkä), 1899–1936, Spanish poet and dramatist, steeped in the folklore of his native Andalusia. With *Romancero gitano* [gypsy balladeer] became his generation's most popular poet. Also wrote farces and tragedies. Shot by the Franco forces in the civil war.

Garcilaso de la Vega (gärthēläʹsō dä lä väʹgä), 1503?–1536, Spanish lyric poet of the Renaissance, a courtier and soldier. Wrote sonnets, odes, eclogues; adapted 11-syllable Italian verse to Spanish.

Garcilaso de la Vega (gärsēläʹsō dä lä väʹgä), 1539?–1616, Peruvian historian; son of Spanish conquistador and Incan princess; called the Inca. Writings (notably *Royal Commentaries of Peru*) tell of conquest of Peru and legends of the Inca.

Gard (gär), department (2,271 sq. mi.; pop. 393,279), S France, in Languedoc; cap. Nîmes. The Gard R., a tributary of the Rhone, is crossed at Remoulins by PONT DU GARD aqueduct.

Garda, Lake (gärʹdä), Ital. *Lago di Garda* or *Benaco,* lake (143 sq. mi.; 32 mi. long), N Italy, between Lombardy and Venetia. Fed by Sarca R., drained by the Mincio. N tip, with Riva di Trento, is Alpine resort. Shores are dotted with vineyards, resorts.

Garden, Mary, 1877–, American operatic soprano, b. Scotland. She made her U.S. debut (New York, 1907) with the Manhattan Opera Co. as Thaïs. Other famous roles were Louise, Mélisande, Salomé.

Gardena (gärdēʹnù), city (pop. 14,405), S Calif., S of Los Angeles. Fruit, truck, and poultry farms.

Garden City. 1 City (pop. 10,905), SW Kansas, on Arkansas R.; founded 1878. Center of an irrigated farm and dairy area, it refines beet sugar. **2** Residential city (pop. 9,012), SE Mich., near Dearborn, in farm area. **3** Village (pop. 14,486), SE N.Y., on W Long Isl. near Hempstead; founded c.1869. Has large publishing business; mfg. of greases and aerial and marine instruments. Seat of Adelphi Col. (coed.; 1896). Mitchell Air Force Base is near.

garden city, community surrounded by a rural belt, owned by inhabitants, with predetermined maximum population and area. Scheme originated as preventative of urban crowding following Industrial Revolution. Original proponents were Robert Owen, James Silk Buckingham, and Charles Fourier. A number of such cities have been built since 1851 in England and America, but outside of England most such cities have become simply satellite suburbs of a larger industrial city, rather than communities whose industries have a self-sufficient labor force.

gardenia, subtropical shrub (*Gardenia jasminoides*), also known as Cape jasmine. It has fragrant white flowers and glossy evergreen leaves. Grown outdoors in mild regions, as house plant in cold areas.

Garden of the Gods: see COLORADO SPRINGS.

Gardiner, Sir Christopher, fl. 1630–32, personage in early history of Mass. Bay colony. When Puritans arrived at Mass. Bay to found colony (1630), they found him and a young woman. Later discovered to be agent of Sir Ferdinando Gorges, whose claims to Mass. he aided.

Gardiner, Samuel Rawson, 1829–1902, English historian. Wrote a thorough, careful history of Puritan Revolution in England, covering years 1603–60. Also edited constitutional documents of Revolution. Editor (1891–1901) *English Historical Review.*

Gardiner (gärdʹnùr), city (pop. 6,649), SW Maine, on Kennebec R. below Augusta. First technical school in U.S. estab. here (1823) by Benjamin Hale. E. A. Robinson grew up here. Mfg. of shoes and textiles.

Gardiners Island, 3,000 acres, SE N.Y., between flukes of E Long Isl.; settled 1639 by Lion Gardiner. Site of first permanent English settlement in present N.Y.

Gardner, Erle Stanley, 1889–, American writer of detective stories featuring fictional lawyer, Perry Mason.

Gardner, Ernest Arthur: see GARDNER, PERCY.

Gardner, Isabella Stewart, 1840–1924, American art collector. Her collection and Fenway Court, which houses it, were willed to Boston as a museum.

Gardner, Percy, 1846–1937, English classical archaeologist and author of works on Greek art, history, and coins. While professor of archaeology at Oxford (1887–1925) he built up the archaeology department and its library and collections. His brother **Ernest Arthur Gardner,** 1862–1939, was director of British School of Archaeology at Athens (1887–95), professor of archaeology (1896–1929) and vice chancellor at Univ. of London, and author of works on Greek art and history.

Gardner, city (pop. 19,581), N central Mass., NNW of Worcester; settled 1764. Mfg. of furniture (from c.1805), metal products, stoves, and machinery.

Garfield, James A(bram), 1831–81, 20th President of the United States. U.S. Representative from Ohio (1863–80). Elected President in 1880 after being chosen by Republicans as compromise candidate. By appointing J. G. Blaine, political foe of Roscoe CONKLING, as Secretary of State, Garfield declared war with most important faction of his party. He won first battle by getting his appointee for New York port collectorship approved. Began prosecution of STAR ROUTE frauds. Constantly harassed by office seekers, he was shot by one of them, Charles J. Guiteau, on July 2, 1881; on Sept. 19 he died. Chester A. Arthur succeeded to presidency.

Garfield, city (pop. 27,550), NE N.J., on Passaic R. and ENE of Passaic. Mfg. of machinery, mechanical equipment, pharmaceuticals, rubber goods, textiles.

Garfield Heights, city (pop. 21,662), NE Ohio, SE suburb of Cleveland; founded 1904.

SMALL CAPITALS = cross references. Pronunciation key on inside end pages. Abbreviations: p. 2.

garfish, marine fish with long, slender body and long, pointed, toothed beak. It is found in most temperate and warm waters. Sometimes it enters rivers. Some of the 50 known species reach length of 5–6 ft. Swift and predatory, they swim near surface.

Garibaldi, Giuseppe (jōōzĕp'pä gärēbäl'dē), 1807–82, Italian patriot and soldier, hero of the RISORGIMENTO; b. Nice. Fled abroad after taking part in an unsuccessful republican plot (1835); fought in civil wars of Brazil and Uruguay (1835–46); returned to Italy and fought with Sardinian forces against Austria (1848–49) and with Mazzini's Roman republic against French interventionists (1849). Renouncing his republican ideal, he gave support to the policy of CAVOUR and VICTOR EMMANUEL II. In 1860, with Victor Emmanuel's connivance, he led 1,000 volunteer "Red Shirts" in spectacular conquest of Sicily and Naples. After handing his conquests over to Victor Emmanuel, who thus became king of Italy, Garibaldi retired to his home on Caprera isl. He twice attempted to conquer the Papal states, but was stopped by Italian troops at Aspromonte (1862) and by French and papal troops at Mentana (1867).

Garigliano (gärēlyä'nō), name of LIRI R., S central Italy, below junction with Rapido R.; empties into Tyrrhenian Sea. Scene of bitter fighting (1943–44) during battle for CASSINO.

Garland, Augustus Hill, 1832–99, American lawyer, U.S. Attorney General (1885–89). In *Ex parte Garland* (1867), Garland, a former Confederate, won plea to resume practice before U.S. Supreme Court.

Garland, Hamlin, 1860–1940, American writer of stories of the Middle Western prairie country. Wrote *Main-travelled Roads* (1891; stories), novels, and autobiographical classic, *A Son of the Middle Border* (1917).

Garland, town (pop. 10,571), N Texas, NE of Dallas. Industrial suburb producing aircraft and seismic instruments.

garlic, perennial herb (*Allium sativum*), native to Europe and closely related to onion. The bulb is used as food flavoring.

Garmisch-Partenkirchen (gär'mĭsh-pär"tŭnkĭr'kŭn), town (pop. 25,022), Upper Bavaria. Winter resort at foot of ZUGSPITZE.

Garmo Peak, USSR: see STALIN PEAK.

Garneau, François Xavier (gärnō'), 1809–66, French Canadian historian. His *Histoire du Canada* (3 vols., 1845–48; 2d ed., with added material, 1852) covers Canadian history to union of two Canadas. Later editions by author's grandson brought work up to date. History has influenced and stimulated French Canadian literature, especially poetry.

Garner, John Nance, 1869–, Vice President of the United States (1933–41).

garnet, name given to a group of widely distributed crystalline minerals some of which are gems. They are commonly red and are double silicates. Garnets are rather soft, hence not highly valued.

Garnett, Richard (gär'nĭt), 1835–1906, English librarian and author. Served at the British Mus. with distinction. Wrote biographies (of Carlyle, Emerson, Milton, Coleridge, and others), essays, and critical works. His son, **Edward Garnett,** 1868–1937, was a critic who encouraged many great writers. His wife, **Constance (Beach) Garnett,** 1862–1946, made widely read translations from the Russian. Their son, **David Garnett,** 1892–, was a partner in the Nonesuch Press and wrote the fantastic short novel, *Lady into Fox* (1923), and other works.

Garnett (gär'nĕt), city (pop. 2,693), E Kansas, S of Lawrence. Birthplace of Edgar Lee Masters.

Garnier, Jean Louis Charles (gärnyä'), 1825–98, French architect, who built the Paris OPÉRA.

Garnier, Marie Joseph François, 1839–73, French explorer and naval officer usually known as Francis Garnier. Accompanied Doudart de Lagrée's expedition through Indo-Chinese area unfamiliar to Europeans

(1866–68). Captured Hanoi on Tonkin expedition (1873). Wrote accounts of experiences.

Garofalo, Il (ēl gärō'fälō), 1481–1559, Italian painter of Ferrarese school. Real name was Benvenuto Tisi or Tisio.

Garonne (gärôn'), river, 402 mi. long, SW France, rising in Pyrenees. It flows NE to Toulouse, then swings NW, and below Bordeaux joins the Dordogne to form the GIRONDE.

Garonne, Haute, France: see HAUTE-GARONNE.

gar pike, fresh-water fish of E and S U.S., Central America, Mexico, West Indies. It has a cylindrical body, platelike scales, snoutlike jaws, sharp teeth. Flesh is unpalatable. Gars eat more useful fish. Garfish is name for salt-water gar.

Garrett, João Batista de Almeida: see ALMEIDA.

Garrick, David, 1717–79, English actor and manager. Accompanied Dr. Johnson to London and set up a wine shop. Launched theatrical career by acting in his own *Lethe* (1740) and by association with Peg Woffington. Was London's idol after playing Richard III in 1741. Other roles included Hamlet, Lear, and Abel Drugger (in Jonson's *Alchemist*). His simple diction and manner swept declamatory actors from the stage. As manager of the Drury Lane after 1747, he made important stage reforms. Appeared last in 1776. He was a member of Dr. Johnson's circle.

Garrison, William Lloyd, 1805–79, American abolitionist. Founded the *Liberator* (1831), in which paper he waged uncompromising antislavery campaign for 35 years. Although a nonresistant and a believer in moral persuasion, his militant style antagonized many. His opposition to political action divided abolitionists. A founder of American Anti-Slavery Society (1833), its president 1843–65. Opposed Civil War until Emancipation Proclamation.

Garry, Fort, early trading post on site of present city of Winnipeg, Man. Founded 1821. Until city was founded (1860s), it was seat of authority in Manitoba region. Louis Riel captured it in rebellion of 1869. Sold in 1882, it was torn down except for the gate. Lower Fort Garry, on Red R., 19 mi. below Fort Garry, was built 1831 and still stands.

Garter, Order of the, oldest and most important order of knighthood in England. Instituted c.1346 by Edward III, it was originally limited to 25 members. Motto is *Honi soit qui mal y pense* [evil be to him who evil thinks]. Title is abbreviated K.G.

garter snake, common harmless North American snake, usually c.2 ft. long. Common form of NE U.S. varies, but usually is blackish or brownish with three yellow stripes. Young born alive in litters of 30 to 65. Ribbon snake is a garter snake found in wet places.

Garvey, Marcus, 1887–1940, American Negro leader, b. Jamaica. Plans for an African settlement ended when he was charged with fraud.

Gary, Elbert H(enry), 1846–1927, American industrialist, a lawyer. Chairman of board of directors of U.S. Steel Corp. (1903–27). Helped found GARY, Ind. Promoted employee benefits, but refused labor union recognition and insisted on the open shop.

Gary, city (pop. 133,911), NW Ind., at end of L. Michigan SE of Chicago. On U.S. Steel Corp. land, city was chartered and named for E. H. Gary, 1906. Great world steel center, midway between iron-ore beds of NW U.S. and coal of E and SE, it also has oil refining and mfg. of chemicals and cement. Calumet rivers have been made into lake harbors. The **Gary plan** was developed 1908–15 in the school system here by W. A. Wirt. It increases utilization of school plant by alternating classes between regular and special teachers, by running two schools simultaneously, and by coordinating various levels of schooling. Also called platoon system.

gas. 1 In general usage, any substance appearing in gaseous state at ordinary temperature and pressure; may be compound, element, or mixture. POISON GAS is used in chemical warfare, in insecticides, fumigation;

LAUGHING GAS in anesthesia. Illuminating gases include air gas, natural gas. **2** In physics, one of the three states of matter, i.e., that state in which a substance is without definite shape or volume. Gases are classed with liquids as fluid. Molecules of gas move faster and are farther apart than those of liquids or solids. Cohesion between molecules is small; when not confined gas is capable of unlimited DIFFUSION. Volume can be reduced by compression; gases undergo liquefaction after being cooled below critical temperature. At constant temperature volume of gas decreases in direct proportion to increase in pressure (Boyle's law). At fixed volume, increase in pressure and in temperature are directly proportional. Dalton's law deals with mixtures of gases. At constant pressure, volume of gas is directly proportional to temperature. Kelvin temperature scale is used in calculating changes in volume and pressure on gases when temperature change is involved. Avogadro discovered that there are same number of molecules in equal volumes of gases under standard conditions. Each molecule of an elemental gas has two atoms; molecular weight is twice the atomic weight. If molecular weight of any gas is measured at standard conditions, the volume (gram-molecular volume) is 22.4 liters. When gas diffuses into a liquid and is held there it is said to have undergone absorption.

Gasca, Pedro de la (pā'drō dā lä gä'skä), c.1485–1567?, Spanish colonial administrator. A priest and lawyer, he was sent to Peru (1547), where he restored order. Repealed New Laws of Las Casas.

Gascoigne, George (găskoin'), c.1539–1577, English poet. He was the first to write an essay on prosody (in *The Posies of George Gascoigne,* 1575). Also wrote first prose comedy in English (*Supposes,* 1566), introduced nondramatic blank verse (in *The Steele Glass,* 1576).

Gasconade (găskùnād'), river rising in S Mo. in the Ozarks and flowing c.265 mi. NE to the Missouri near Gasconade, E of Jefferson City.

Gascony (gă'skùnē), Fr. *Gascogne,* region and former province, SW France, in Landes, Gers, Hautes-Pyrénées, Basses-Pyrénées, Lot-et-Garonne, Tarn-et-Garonne, and Haute-Garonne depts.; historic cap. Auch. Agr., fishing (along Atlantic coast), cattle raising, winegrowing, brandy mfg. (in Armagnac dist.) are main occupations. Basque is still spoken in old Basque provs., notably in and around Bayonne. Part of Roman Aquitania, region was inhabited by BASQUES, who created duchy of Vasconia or Gascony in 7th cent. A.D. Duchy fell into anarchy in 9th cent.; was united in 11th cent. with AQUITAINE, whose later history it shared. Recovered by France at end of Hundred Years War, Gascony consisted of several fiefs, held mainly by the counts of ARMAGNAC and of FOIX and the lords of ALBRET; all these passed, through marriage and inheritance, to Henry of Navarre, who after becoming king of France as Henry IV incorporated them with the royal domain (1607).

gas engine: see INTERNAL-COMBUSTION ENGINE.

Gaskell, Elizabeth (Cleghorn Stevenson), 1810–65, English novelist. Known especially for *Mary Barton* (1848) and *Cranford* (1853; a charming tale of British village life). She also wrote a controversial biography of Charlotte Brontë (1857).

gasoline, volatile fuel oil obtained by fractional distillation of petroleum and also from natural gas. Chief uses are as gas-engine fuel and organic solvent.

Gaspar: see WISE MEN OF THE EAST.

Gasparri, Pietro (pyā'trō gäspär'rē), 1852–1934, Italian cardinal. Directed great codification of canon law and received cardinal's hat from Pius X (1907); as papal secretary of state in World War I, worked for peace; under Pius XI concluded the LATERAN TREATY (1929).

Gaspee (gă'spē", gäspē'), British revenue cutter, burned (June 10, 1772) at Gaspee Point in Narragansett Bay, R.I. Ship sent to enforce revenue laws; burning was act of defiance by colonists.

Gaspé Peninsula (găspā'), tongue of land (150 mi. long, 60–90 mi. wide), E Que., Canada, extending E into the Gulf of St. Lawrence between St. Lawrence R. (N) and Chaleur Bay (S). **Gaspé Bay** is a deep inlet at E end of the peninsula. The resort and market village of **Gaspé** (pop. 1,692) is near the head of the bay. **Cape Gaspé** is at the E end of the peninsula. Population (chiefly French Canadian) is scattered in villages along coast. Fishing, the major industry, is supplemented by lumbering, pulp milling, and some agr. Excellent hunting and fishing is found in the heavily forested and mountainous interior. Since a highway has been completed (1928) encircling the peninsula, tourists have been attracted by the charm of picturesque villages and fine scenery.

Gasperi, Alcide de: see DE GASPERI, ALCIDE.

Gassendi, Pierre (gäsädē), 1592–1655, French materialist philosopher and scientist. Opposed Aristotelian authority; as vigorous rival of Cartesian school, revived atomic theory; sought to reconcile mechanism and theology.

Gasser, Herbert Spencer (gä'sùr), 1888–, American physiologist. Shared 1944 Nobel Prize in Physiology and Medicine for work on electrophysiology of nerves. Became director of Rockefeller Institute in 1935.

Gasset, José Ortega: see ORTEGA Y GASSET, JOSÉ.

Gastein (gä'stīn), valley and resort area in Salzburg, W central Austria. Bad Gastein, a fashionable bathing place, has radium thermal springs; its water is also piped to Bad Hofgastein. By Gastein Convention (1865) Austria assumed administration of Holstein, Prussia that of Schleswig.

Gastonia (găstō'nēù), city (pop. 23,069), W central N.C., in piedmont. Mfg. of textiles and tire fabric. Near by is Kings Mountain battlefield.

gastric juice: see STOMACH.

Gatchina (gä'chēnù), city (pop. 18,589), RSFSR, SSW of Leningrad. Developed around imperial summer residence (built 1766–70). Palace (now museum) looted by Germans in World War II.

Gate City, town (pop. 2,126), SW Va., near Tenn. line. Near by is Natural Tunnel (75–100 ft. high, c.900 ft. long).

Gates, Horatio, 1727–1806, American Revolutionary general, b. England. National hero after success of SARATOGA CAMPAIGN. Commanded Carolina campaign until disgraceful defeat at Camden, S.C. (1780).

Gates, Sir Thomas, fl. 1585–1621, British colonial governor of Va. (1611–14). One of grantees in original charter to found colony.

Gateshead (gäts'hĕd), county borough (pop. 115,017), Durham, England, on Tyne R. opposite Newcastle. Has locomotive works, railroad shops, shipbuilding, and mfg. of glass, iron goods, cables and chemicals. Near by are coal mines and grindstone quarries.

Gath, Philistine city, on borders of Judah; birthplace of Goliath; refuge of David during years when he was outlawed.

Gatineau (gä'tĭnō"), village (pop. 5,771), SW Que., Canada, on N shore of Ottawa R. and E of Hull.

Gatineau, river of SW Que., Canada, flowing from the Laurentians 230 mi. S to Ottawa R. at Hull.

Gatlinburg, resort city (pop. 1,301), E Tenn., SE of Knoxville near foot of Mt. Le Conte. Near hq. of Great Smoky Mts. Natl. Park.

Gatling, Richard Jordan, 1818–1903, American inventor of Gatling multiple-firing gun, precursor of machine gun. His name gave rise to slang word *gat.*

Gatti-Casazza, Giulio (jōō'lyō gät'tē-käzät'sä), 1869–1940, Italian operatic manager. Director of La Scala Opera Co., Milan, 1898–1908; director of Metropolitan Opera, New York, 1908–35.

Gatun Lake, artificial lake (alt. 85 ft.; area 163.38 sq. mi.), Panama Canal Zone, formed by impounding of Chagres R. Used as part of canal route. Gatun Dam, 1½ mi. long, 115 ft. high, controls level of lake.

gaucho (gou'chō), cowboy of Argentine pampa, typically a mestizo, a skillful horseman, lover of adventure. Played important part in national life of Argentine (also Uruguay and Paraguay) 18th–19th cent. Glorified in José Hernández' *Martín Fierro.*

Gaudeamus igitur (gou″däā′mōōs ĭ′gĭtōōr″) [Latin,= let us rejoice therefore], student song; based on songs dating back to at least 13th cent. Present variant forms did not appear in print until 18th cent. Probably originated in parodies of, and borrowings from, religious songs. Brahms used its tune in his *Academic Festival Overture.*

Gauden, John (gô′dùn), 1605–62, English bishop, who claimed authorship of the EIKON BASILIKE (1649).

Gaudier-Brzeska, Henri (ăr€′ gōdyä′-bùrzĕskä′), 1891–1915, French sculptor, the chief exponent of vorticism in sculpture.

Gauguin, Paul (pôl′ gōgĕ′), 1848–1903, French painter, b. Paris. At 35 he gave up a successful banking career to devote himself to art. Allied himself with impressionists and contributed to their last exhibition (1886). During next five years spent some time in Martinique, Brittany, and Arles (with Van Gogh). In 1891 went to Tahiti where he painted some of his finest pictures; except for one brief trip to France spent rest of his life in South Seas. Died in Marquesas Isls. His paintings, neglected in his time, are now highly prized. His figure compositions, gorgeous in color, place him among the great postimpressionists.

Gaul (gôl), Latin *Gallia,* anc. name for the land S and W of the Rhine, W of the Alps, and N of the Pyrenees. The name was extended by the Romans to include N Italy. The name is derived from its settlers of the 4th–3d cent. B.C.—invading Celts, called Gauls by the Romans. Julius CAESAR conquered Gaul in the GALLIC WARS (58–51 B.C.). He is the best ancient source and has immortalized its three ethnic divisions, Aquitania, Gaul proper (central France), and Belgica. It was rapidly Romanized.

Gauley Bridge, unincorporated village (pop. 1,134), S central W.Va. The death from silicosis of a number of workers building a tunnel near here (1930–32) led to a congressional investigation.

Gaulle, Charles de (shärl dù gōl′), 1890–, French general and politician. In World War II he opposed armistice of 1940; fled to England; organized "Free French" forces, which fought successfully in Syria, Madagascar, N Africa; was sentenced to death *in absentia* by a French military court. In 1943 he became co-president with Gen. GIRAUD of the French Committee of Natl. Liberation at Algiers. Despite coolness of U.S. government, he succeeded in ousting his rival Giraud from the committee, which in June, 1944, proclaimed itself the provisional government of France. Elected president of France in 1945, he resigned 1946 when he lost leftist support. In 1947 he became head of the Reunion of the French People, a generally rightist movement which became a major factor in French politics. In his book *The Army of the Future* (1934; Eng. tr., 1941), De Gaulle correctly predicted the strategy and tactics of motorized warfare.

Gaunt, John of: see JOHN OF GAUNT.

Gaur (gour), anc. city of West Bengal, India. Center of Moslem culture (1198–1575). Has fine Golden Mosque. A stone in Kadam Rasul Mosque supposedly bears imprint of Mohammed's foot.

Gauss, Christian (gous), 1878–1951, American educator, dean of Princeton Univ. from 1925 to 1945.

Gauss, Karl Friedrich (kärl frē′drĭkh gous′), 1777–1855, German mathematician and astronomer. He made important contributions to theory of numbers, solving of binomial equations, geometry of curved surfaces, and method of least squares, and also in geodesy. He pioneered in applying mathematical theory to electricity and magnetism. Unit of intensity of magnetic field was called gauss until 1932 when gauss was applied to unit of magnetic induction.

Gautama: see BUDDHA.

Gautier, Théophile (tāôfēl′ gōtyä′), 1811–72, French poet, novelist, and critic. His aesthetic creed, illus-

trated in the carefully tooled poems of *Émaux et camées* [enamels and cameos] (1852), influenced the Parnassians. His best-known novels are *Mademoiselle de Maupin* (1835) and *Le Capitaine Fracasse* (1863), all translated into English.

Gavarni (gävärnē′), 1804–66, French caricaturist and lithographer, whose real name was Guillaume Sulpice Chevalier. His work appeared in the periodicals *Charivari* and *Illustration.*

Gavarnie, Cirque de (sĕrk′ dù gävärnē′), gigantic natural amphitheater in central Pyrenees, SW France. From its bottom, at c.5,740 ft., it rises in concentric circles and is enclosed by crests over 9,000 ft. high. The famous Brèche de Roland is a cleft in one of crests. Near by is a waterfall 1,385 ft. high.

Gaveston, Piers (pērz′ gä′vùstùn), d. 1312, favorite of EDWARD II of England. Had great influence with Edward and in his absence acted as regent. His greed and arrogance aroused the barons' hostility; they twice banished him and then put him to death.

Gavle, Swed. *Gävle* (yĕv′lù), city (pop. 46,834), co. seat of Gavleborg co., E Sweden; a Baltic Sea port. Produces wood pulp, textiles, tobacco, chemicals. Chartered 1446; oldest and largest city of Norrland.

gavotte, originally a peasant dance of the Gavots, inhabitants of the Gap region, France; introduced at court of Louis XIV; used by Lully in ballets and operas, by Bach and Couperin in keyboard suites.

Gawain, Sir: see ARTHURIAN LEGEND; PARSIFAL.

Gay, John, 1685–1732, English playwright and poet. Friend of wits and courtiers of his day, he is famous for realistic, satiric *Beggar's Opera* (1728), a ballad opera still revived. Also wrote verse, *The Shepherd's Week* (1714), and essays, *Trivia* (1716).

Gay, Walter, 1856–1937, American painter. Studied and lived mostly in Paris. Noted for paintings of elegant 18th-cent. interiors.

Gaya (gī′ù), commercial city (pop. 105,223), central Bihar, India. Has noted Vishnuite temple.

gay-feather: see BLAZING STAR.

Gay Head, W tip of Martha's Vineyard, in Gay Head town (pop. 88), SE Mass. Has lighthouse (1799) on high clay cliffs.

Gay-Lussac, Joseph Louis (zhôzĕf lwē gä′-lüsäk), 1778–1850, French chemist and physicist. Discovered cyanogen; made advances in industrial chemistry; collaborated in isolating boron; invented alcoholometer, hydrometer; discovered Charles's law independently. **Gay-Lussac's law** of combining volumes: volumes of gases that interact to give gaseous product are in ratio of small whole numbers to each other and each has similar relation to volume of product.

Gayoso de Lemos, Manuel (mänwĕl′ gĭō′sō dä lā′mōs), c.1752–1799, Spanish governor of Louisiana (1797–99). Intrigued to separate American West from U.S.

Gaza, Theodore (gä′zù, gä′zù), c.1398–c.1478, Greek scholar and humanist of the Renaissance. When Turks attacked Constantinople, he went to Italy. His Greek grammar was printed (1495) by Aldus Manutius.

Gaza (gä′-), or **Ghuzzeh** (gü′-), town (pop. c.18,000), SW Palestine, near the Mediterranean; in anc. times a chief city of the Philistines. Here Samson brought down temple on his captors and himself. Town has long been meeting place of caravans between Egypt and Syria.

gazelle (gùzĕl′), graceful antelope of genus *Gazella.* Number of species are found chiefly in Africa, also in central and SW Asia and India. They are small (2–3 ft. high) and fleet, usually fawn color, but some are marked with black and white.

gazetteer, originally one who wrote gazettes; now a dictionary of geographical names (of a region, of certain classes, or of the world). First used in its modern sense after publication of Lawrence Echard's geographical index, *Gazetteer's or Newsman's Interpreter* (1703). Such lists have been made since the 6th cent., but general gazetteers date only from the 19th cent. Well-known gazetteers include Johnston's (Scotland,

1850), Blackie's (Scotland, 1850), Bouillet's (France, 1857), Ritter's (Germany, 1874), Longman's (England, 1895), Garollo's (Italy, 1898), Lippincott's (U.S., 1865; latest revised issue *The Columbia Lippincott Gazetteer of the World,* 1952).

Gaziantep (gä″zēäntĕp′), formerly **Aintab** (īntäb′), city (pop. 72,743), S Turkey. Textile mfg. Taken by Saladin 1183. Fell after six-month siege (1920–21) to the French in occupation of Syria, but it was returned to Turkey 1921.

Gd, chemical symbol of the element GADOLINIUM.

Gdansk: see DANZIG.

Gdynia (gŭdĭn′yu̇), city (pop. c.117,700), NW Poland; a Baltic seaport on gulf of Danzig. Constructed after 1921 to end Poland's dependence on Danzig. Damaged in World War II.

Ge, chemical symbol of the element GERMANIUM.

gearing, in a machine, device for transmitting motion by means of teeth or friction wheels. **Spur gearing** utilizes wheels with teeth at right angles to their shafts. **Bevel gearing,** accomplished by inclined tooth edges, transmits motion to shafts intersecting drive shaft. **Screw** or **worm gearing** transmits by screwlike action. **Friction gearing** transmits motion, without use of teeth, by friction of two surfaces in contact.

Geary, John White (gĕr′ē), 1819–73, American politician, Union general in Civil War. As governor of "bleeding" Kansas (1856–57), he helped bring peace to territory. Governor of Pa. 1866–73.

Gebal (gē′–), biblical name of BYBLOS.

Gedaliah (gĕdŭlī′u̇), governor of Jews not carried off in Captivity. He was treacherously murdered. Day of death still observed as Jewish fast. Jer. 40–41.

Geddes, Norman Bel, 1893–, American scenic designer. Originated modernistic style in shop-window displays. *The Miracle* is perhaps his most popular work.

Geddes, Sir Patrick, 1854–1932, Scottish biologist and sociologist. Interested in the evolution of sex, he sought to relate biological knowledge with civic welfare and to city planning.

Gedeon (gĕ′dēun), same as GIDEON.

Gegenbaur, Karl (kärl gā′gu̇nbou″u̇r), 1826–1903, German comparative anatomist, influential as a teacher and through his writings.

Gehenna: see HELL.

Gehrig, (Henry) Lou(is) (lōō gâ′rĭg), 1903–41, American baseball infielder. As first baseman (1925–39) of N.Y. Yankees, estab. major-league record of playing 2,130 consecutive league games. Had lifetime batting average of .341, batted .361 in seven world series. Four times won American League most-valuable-player award.

Geiger, Abraham (ä′brähäm gī′gu̇r), 1810–74, German rabbi, Semitic scholar, foremost exponent of the reform movement, a chief rabbi of Berlin.

Geiger counter (gī′gu̇r), instrument for detection and quantitative determination of ionizing particles, such as beta rays and cosmic rays. Variously designed, it usually consists of a thin metal cylinder (forming one electrode) and a needle (or a thin wire as the other electrode) enclosed by glass tube in which a gas is also sealed. Current passes from electrode to electrode when the counter is near radioactive substances. Emanations, however faint, ionize the gas, allowing current to jump gap and close circuit, activating audible indicator. Instrument named for Hans Geiger (1882–1945), German physicist.

Geijerstam, Gustaf af (äv yā′yu̇rstäm), 1858–1909, Swedish novelist, author of realistic studies of peasant life and of "problem novels."

geisha (gā′shu̇), trained Japanese professional entertainer, skilled in dancing and in repartee. Her status varies; she may or may not be a courtesan. Many live luxuriously and influence state policies. She may marry, but always bears a certain stigma.

Geissler tube (gīs′lu̇r), a gas discharge tube in which light is produced when electricity is passed through gas in the tube. It is used in spectroscopy. It was named for **Heinrich Geissler,** 1814–79, German mechanic and inventor.

Gela (jē′lu̇), city (pop. 31,918), SW Sicily, Italy, on Mediterranean; founded c.690 B.C. by Greek colonists. Reached its height under tyrants Gelon and Hippocrates (5th cent. B.C.). Modern Gela (known as Terranova di Sicilia until 1927) was founded by Emperor Frederick II in 1230.

Gelasius II (jĭlā′shĕu̇s), d. 1119, pope (1118–19), elected in protest against weakness of PASCHAL II in struggle with Emperor Henry V over INVESTITURE. Thrown in prison by emperor's party, he was delivered by the people, but advance of Henry with an army forced Gelasius to flee to Gaeta, then to France. Henry set up Gregory VIII as antipope.

gelatin, glutinous material, an animal jelly, obtained from supporting structures of vertebrates. Pure product is brittle, transparent, colorless, odorless, tasteless; it dissolves in hot water, congeals when cold. It swells to an elastic mass in cold water. Some of its many uses are: in making confectionery, jellied soups, and molded meats and salads, in preserving meat and fruit, in electrotyping, photography, waterproofing, dyeing, as bacteriologic culture medium, coating for pills and capsules, and emulsifying agent. Glue and size are impure forms. AGAR is vegetable gelatin.

Gelderland, Guelderland, or **Guelders** (gĕl′dürlü̇nd, gĕl′du̇rz), province (1,922 sq. mi., pop. 1,028,127), E and central Netherlands; cap. Arnheim. Drained by Ijssel, Lower Rhine, and Waal rivers, which enclose fertile agr. lowland in SW. Duchy of Gelderland was conquered by Charles the Bold of Burgundy 1473; passed to Hapsburgs after his death; joined United Provs. of Netherlands 1579. Part of province, including ducal cap., Geldern, was ceded to Prussia 1715.

Gelibolu, Turkey: see GALLIPOLI.

Gellius, Aulus (jĕl′yu̇s), fl. 2d cent., Latin writer, a lawyer; author of *Noctes Atticae,* a collection valuable for its quotations from lost works.

Gelon (jē′lŏn), d. 478 B.C., Greek Sicilian ruler. Tyrant of Gela, he ruled Syracuse (485–478 B.C.), dominating Greek Sicily. In 480 he crushed the Carthaginians under Hamilcar. He was succeeded by HIERO I.

Gelsenkirchen (gĕl′zu̇nkĭr′khu̇n), city (pop. 310,108), North Rhine–Westphalia, NW Germany, adjoining Essen; a major industrial and coal-mining center of RUHR dist. Heavily damaged in World War II.

gem, substance of mineral or organic origin used for adornment. Beauty, rarity, and durability determine value. Beauty depends mainly on optical properties, which impart luster, color, and fire; durability on HARDNESS. Other properties include form of crystal, index of refraction, cleavage, type of fracture. Gems most prized are DIAMOND, RUBY, SAPPHIRE, EMERALD, PEARL (organic); some semiprecious stones are AQUAMARINE, AMETHYST, GARNET, TOURMALINE, TOPAZ, TURQUOISE, MOONSTONE, JADE, CHRYSOBERYL.

Gemara: see TALMUD.

Gemini [Latin,= twins] (jĕ′mĭnē), third sign of ZODIAC. The twins were Castor and Pollux.

Geminiani, Francesco (fränchä′skō jämēnyä′nē), d. 1762, Italian violinist and composer of music for strings. He wrote on methods of playing stringed instruments (e.g., *The Art of Playing the Violin*).

Gemniczer, Wenzel: see JAMNITZER.

gender, in grammar, subclassification of a form class (or part of speech) in which members of the subclass have characteristic features of agreement with other words. The term *gender* is usually restricted to such a classification of nouns or nounlike words and is not usually considered to include NUMBER. In French *la viande* [the meat] and *le vin* [the wine] are distinguished by *la* and *le* as different genders, *la* being feminine, *le* masculine (because most French nouns referring to females are feminine, most referring to males are masculine). German, Russian, and Latin have three genders—masculine, feminine, and neuter. A two-gender distinction between animate and inanimate is widespread (as in Algonquian languages). English nouns may be divided into gender classes according to personal pronoun used to refer to them; these do not match sex classes (e.g., *she* for *ship*). The grammatical device of concord or agreement is bound up with gender distinctions; thus in Romance languages adjectives "agree" with the corresponding nouns in being masculine or feminine.

gene (jēn), ultimate unit in transmission of hereditary characters in plants and animals. Genes are believed to be contained within chromosomes and to control development of specific morphological characters by control of biochemical reactions. See also GENETICS.

General Land Office, estab. 1812 in U.S. Treasury Dept. and transferred in 1849 to U.S. Dept. of the Interior. Managed and disposed of public domain. Emphasized conservation of remaining public land after 1900. Consolidated in 1946 with Grazing Service into Bureau of Land Management.

general strike, cessation of work by all or a majority of workers in a region. The motive is economic if the strike is directed against employers, political if it seeks to eventuate in governmental concessions or governmental overthrow. It has been advocated by syndicalists and anarchists, and has been a powerful weapon of European labor.

generator, machine for changing mechanical into electrical energy, using principle of electromagnetic INDUCTION. Simple generator consists of coil of wire rotating between two magnetic poles; as turning coil cuts magnetic lines of force, electric current is generated in coil, from which metal strips (brushes) lead current into closed circuit. Turning coil cuts lines of force first in one direction then another, so current flows first in one then another direction (AC or alternating current). One-direction current (DC or direct current) obtained by using device called commutator, but current remains pulsating. Commercial generators avoid pulsation by use of more complicated structure involving so-called ARMATURE. In dynamo, the ELECTROMAGNET is commonly used.

Genesee, river, c.158 mi. long, rising in N Pa. in the Alleghenies and flowing N through N.Y. to L. Ontario at Rochester. In beautiful, fertile valley.

Genesis (jĕ′nŭsĭs) [Gr.,= origin], first book of Old Testament, first of the five books of Law (the Pentateuch or Torah), ascribed by tradition to Moses. It is a religious account of the creation of the world and of man, of man's first fall from grace, of the great Deluge. It tells the stories of the great religious patriarchs: Noah, Abraham, Isaac, and Jacob—who later became Israel. Book ends with story of Joseph and the migration of Jacob's family to Egypt. For religious conceptions derived from opening chapters, see SIN and GRACE. Importance of Genesis in Jewish and Christian thought is inestimable.

Genesis, Little: see PSEUDEPIGRAPHA.

Genêt, Edmond Charles Édouard (zhŭnā′), 1763–1834, French minister to U.S. (1793–94), known as Citizen Genêt. Welcomed by pro-French Jeffersonians, his efforts to raise troops against Spanish Florida and to commission privateers against British commerce were not approved by Pres. Washington. His recall was demanded.

genetics (jŭnĕ′tĭks), scientific study of heredity. The basis of the science was the work of Gregor MENDEL rediscovered in 1900 independently by Hugo De Vries, K. E. Correns, and Erich Tschermak-Seysenegg. Mendel's principles were modified and extended by discovery of CHROMOSOME and GENE as physical basis of transmission of hereditary characters; by discoveries such as those related to tendency of certain characters to be inherited together, of some characters to be sex-linked, and of interaction of different genes to determine presence of characters. Work of T. H. Morgan and his followers on *Drosophila melanogaster* (fruit fly) was important to progress of genetics in U.S. See also HEREDITY; MUTATION.

Geneva (jŭnē′vŭ), Fr. *Genève,* canton (109 sq. mi.; pop. 201,505), SW Switzerland, at SW tip of L. of Geneva, almost entirely surrounded by French territory. Rural section produces fruits, vegetables, wine. Its cap., **Geneva** (pop. 144,422), lies on both sides of the Rhone, which emerges here from the lake. It is a cultural and financial center, mfg. machinery and watches. Included in Roman Gaul, Geneva early became an episcopal see, shared history of first and second kingdoms of BURGUNDY and passed to Holy Roman Empire 1033. Though citizens won extensive rights of self-rule (1387), these rights were increasingly encroached on by the dukes of Savoy, whose representatives shared the authority with the bishops. In alliance with Swiss cantons of Fribourg and Bern, the citizens expelled the bishops in 1533 and accepted the Reformation, preached by Guillaume Farel, in 1536. Under CALVIN Geneva became the focal point of the Reformation. An attempt by Charles Emmanuel I of Savoy to recapture the city was repulsed (1602). Huguenot refugees contributed to growing prosperity of Geneva, which was a cosmopolitan intellectual center by the 18th cent. Under French occupation 1798–1814, Geneva joined Switzerland as a canton 1815. It is the seat of the Internatl. Red Cross, the Internatl. Labor Organization, and several UN bodies. The huge Palais des Nations housed the League of Nations until it was taken over by the UN. Univ. of Geneva originated with academy founded by Calvin. Historic monuments include cathedral, city hall. Its fine parks and splendid situation make Geneva a cosmopolitan resort. It is the birthplace of J. J. Rousseau. The **Lake of Geneva** or **Lake Leman,** between Switzerland and France, is 45 mi. long, 2–9 mi. wide. The Rhone is its main feeder and only outlet. N (Swiss) shore is bounded by vineyards and orchards and dotted with resorts. From S (French) shore rise the French Alps. Scenery has been celebrated by many writers.

Geneva (jŭnē′vŭ). **1** City (pop. 5,139), NE Ill., W of Chicago and on Fox R. **2** City (pop. 17,144), W central N.Y., at N end of Seneca L. and SE of Rochester; settled 1788. Farm trade center with mfg. of canned goods, machinery, heaters, and optical goods. Seat of The Colleges of the Seneca, corporate title since 1943 of Hobart Col. (affiliated Episcopalian; for men; chartered 1822) and William Smith Col. (nonsectarian; for women; opened 1908). **3** See PROVO, Utah.

Geneva, Lake, c.8 mi. long, SE Wis., near Ill. line. Shores have summer homes. Yerkes Observatory is at Williams Bay near W end.

Geneva, Lake of: see GENEVA, Switzerland.

Geneva Arbitration: see ALABAMA CLAIMS.

Geneva Convention: see RED CROSS.

Geneva Protocol: see PROTOCOL.

Genevieve, Saint, d. 512, patron saint of Paris, a nun said to have averted an attack of Attila on Paris. Feast: Jan. 3.

Genghis Khan: see JENGHIZ KHAN.

genie, an older name for JINNI.

Génissiat Dam, France: see RHONE.

genista: see BROOM.

genitive: see CASE.

Gennesaret (gĕnĕ′sŭrĕt): see GALILEE, SEA OF.

Genoa (jĕ′nŭwŭ), Ital. *Genova,* city (pop. 512,313; with suburbs 634,646), cap. of Liguria, NW Italy, on the Mediterranean. Chief Italian port; industrial center (shipyards, automobiles, airplanes). City flourished under Romans; became free commune, governed by consuls, c.10th cent. Its growth as a commercial and Mediterranean power brought wars with Pisa and Venice (13th–14th cent.). Genoa acquired colonies and trading privileges in wars from Spain to the CRIMEA; its expansion was largely financed by a group of merchants who in 1408 founded a powerful bank, the Banco San Giorgio. After 1339 the republic (which came to include most of Liguria) was governed by doges elected for life. The foreign possessions were gradually lost, and internal strife made possible intervention by France and Milan. Genoese power was briefly revived by Andrea DORIA (16th cent.), but his rule was followed by periods of Spanish, French, and Austrian control. Austrians were expelled 1746, but in 1768 Genoa lost Corsica to France. Annexed to France in 1805, Genoa and Liguria were united in 1815 with the kingdom of Sardinia. City was heavily damaged in World War II. Notable buildings include Cathedral of San Lorenzo (rebuilt 1100) and the doges' palace. The harbor section is very picturesque. Univ. of Genoa was founded 1812. Birthplace of Christopher Columbus, Mazzini, Paganini.

Genoa. 1 Village (pop. 1,026), E central Nebr., W of Columbus and on Loup R. Pawnee village has been excavated near by. **2** Town, W Nev., SW of Carson City; founded c.1849. First permanent settlement in the state.

Genoa, Conference of, 1922, international conference held at Genoa, Italy, to discuss economic reconstruction of Europe after World War I. Main item was Russian debt, which the Soviets had repudiated. Some progress was made, but announcement of German-Soviet Treaty of RAPALLO cut negotiations short.

genocide, attempt to destroy a national, ethnic, racial, religious, or political group. Genocide was made an international crime by a UN convention, unanimously adopted in 1948. The convention took effect in 1950 after ratification by 20 nations. It had not been ratified in April, 1953, by either the U.S. or USSR. See also WAR CRIMES.

gens (jĕnz), ancient Roman family group, counterpart of clan or sib in other societies. Descent was traced in male line only, from common ancestor worshiped by all. Marriage within gens was discouraged.

Genseric: see GAISERIC.

gentian (jĕn'shŭn), perennial or annual plant of widely distributed genus *Gentiana,* bearing predominantly blue flowers, usually in autumn. Two species native to E North America are fringed gentian (*Gentiana crinita*), a biennial and difficult to grow, and bottle, or closed, gentian (*G. saponaria*). Others are prized for rock gardens.

Gentile da Fabriano (dä fäbrēä'nō), c.1370–1427?, Italian painter, first great representative of Umbrian school. Retained gilt ornament and glowing color of early Umbrian painters. Influenced Venetians. Masterpiece is *The Adoration of the Magi.*

Gentileschi, Orazio (ōrä'tsēō jäntēlä'skē), c.1562–1647, Florentine mural and portrait painter. In 1626 settled in England at invitation of Charles I. His daughter **Artemisia Gentileschi** (ärtämē'zyä), 1590–c.1642, was a renowned portraitist.

gentlemen's agreement, in business, an informal, private, usually verbal agreement among rivals as to prices charged, goods handled, or areas served. They are outlawed in the U.S. by antitrust legislation. In U.S. and Japanese history the gentlemen's agreement was the understanding arrived at (1907) in the administration of Theodore Roosevelt, with Ishii the Japanese negotiator. It provided that Japan should stop emigration of Japanese workers to the U.S. and the U.S. should halt discrimination against Japanese. The U.S. immigration laws of 1924 automatically ended this agreement.

Gentz, Friedrich von (frē'drĭkh fŭn gĕnts'), 1764–1832, German publicist. Conducted polemics against Napoleon; became Metternich's secretary 1812. The brain of the Holy Alliance, he was secretary at congresses of Vienna, Aachen, Troppau, Laibach, Verona.

geodesy (jēō'dŭsē) or **geodetic surveying,** theory and practice of determining points on the earth's surface and dimensions of areas so large that the curvature of the earth must be taken into account.

Geoffrey IV, known as **Geoffrey Plantagenet** (plăntăj'-ŭnĕt) [O.Fr.,= sprig of broom; he usually wore a sprig in his helmet], 1113–51, count of Anjou (1129–51); son of FULK. Married MATILDA, daughter of Henry I of England (1128?); claimed Normandy in her name

and completed its conquest 1144. Went on crusade with Louis VII (1147). His son became Henry II of England.

Geoffrey of Monmouth, c.1100–1154, English author, bishop of St. Asaph after 1152. His largely fictional *Historiae regum Britanniae* is a source for Arthurian legend.

Geoffroy Saint-Hilaire, Étienne (ātyĕn' zhôfrōoä' sētēl-ĕr'), 1772–1844, French zoologist, member of Napoleon's scientific staff in Egypt. His theory that all animals conform to single structural plan was opposed by Cuvier. His son, **Isidore Geoffroy Saint-Hilaire** (ēzēdôr'), 1805–61, also a zoologist, was an authority on deviations from normal structure.

geography, science that observes, catalogues, analyzes, correlates facts of area differentiation on earth's surface. First systematic study was Greek: Aristotle demonstrated world's sphericity, delimited its habitable parts; Strabo's interest in human adaptation to physical setting enlarged scope of study beyond mathematical relationships; study culminated in Ptolemy. Arabs carried learning through Middle Ages. Marco Polo's travels, growing Eastern trade, and exploration voyages revived geographic interest beyond Moslem world. The 16th and 17th cent. textbooks (Varenius) and maps (Mercator) formulated sound theoretical geography. Modern era began late 18th cent. with Alexander von Humboldt and Karl Ritter. Two basic methods of approach are systematic and regional. Systematic approach was spurred by growth of physical and social sciences; regional approach integrates results of systematic method, focuses them on specific place or area—meeting demand for inventory of resources of newly discovered regions. These approaches are actually interdependent. Two branches of geography are physical and human (or cultural). First, based on physical sciences, studies features of world's surface in relation to cosmic influences; climate, land form, soil are examined as to origin, classified as to distribution; flora and fauna are brought into areal pattern. Human (economic, social, political) geography studies man's relation to environment, also his conscious adaptation of himself to it and it to his needs. Geography integrates data of other sciences in terms of areal differentiation. Cartographers, gazetteer compilers, scientific expeditions, university studies, Federal agencies, and geographic institutes promote modern geographic knowledge.

Geological Survey, United States, bureau organized under Dept. of the Interior (1879) to explore surface and geological structure of country, investigate natural resources, classify public lands, and issue papers, bulletins, and maps based on surveys.

geology (jēŏ'lŭjē), the science of the earth with respect to its structure, rocks, surface features. Its branches include petrology, structural geology, geomorphology, physiography, cosmology, and economic and historical geology. Geologic history includes five grand divisions or eras: ARCHEOZOIC, PROTEROZOIC, PALEOZOIC, MESOZOIC, CENOZOIC. Each is supposed to have marked a new stage in life development, and to have ended with profound structural changes. The geologic cycle, repeated again and again, consists of a period of mountain building, followed by one of erosion and, in turn, by renewed uplift. Time elapsed since deposition of oldest known rocks is probably at least a billion and a half years. See table, pp. 370–71.

geometry, branch of mathematics dealing with space properties and relations of figures in space. Elementary, Euclidean, axiomatic geometry includes plane (study of figures lying entirely in one plane), solid (three-dimensional figures), and spherical (figures drawn on spherical surface). More advanced geometries have a less formally stressed axiomatic basis. Analytical geometry includes geometric relations between curves, using algebraic relations between equations corresponding (by coordinate system) to curves; descriptive includes study of reproducing solid figures on a plane; differential includes theory of properties of figures describable in terms of calculus. Modern geometry includes study of non-Euclidean spaces, Riemannian geometry, spaces of abstract elements, and topology.

geomorphology, study of origin and evolution of earth's topographic features. Developed after 1890 as a result of William M. Davis's concept of the geomorphic cycle, theory that land forms pass through a series of well-organized stages in an inorganic evolution.

geopolitics, geographical principles applied to world politics. Chief exponent was Karl Haushofer, adviser to Hitler. He held growing nations must gain *Lebensraum* [living space], specifically Germany at expense of Great Britain (one of the "oceanic nations") and Russia (which is the "heart land" of Eurasia, the "world island").

George, Saint, 4th cent.?, patron of England, perhaps a soldier in the imperial army who died for the faith in Asia Minor. Ancient patron of soldiers, he was adopted in medieval England. In old plays and art St. George is the slayer of the dragon (the tale was popularized in *The Golden Legend*). His red cross appears on the Union Jack.

George, kings of Great Britain and Ireland. **George I** (George Louis), 1660–1727, was king 1714–27. Great-grandson of James I, he was the first British sovereign of house of HANOVER under Act of SETTLEMENT. His indifference to government led to first real cabinet and rise of the Whigs to power. Quadruple Alliance guaranteed Hanoverian succession in 1718. His son, **George II** (George Augustus), 1683-1760, was king 1727–60. More active in government, in War of AUSTRIAN SUCCESSION he was last British king to lead troops in person. His wife, CAROLINE OF ANSPACH, furthered long dominancy (1721–42) of Robert WALPOLE. Whigs united behind policy of William PITT (the elder) in SEVEN YEARS WAR (1756–63). King's grandson, **George III** (George William Frederick), 1738–1820, was king 1760–1820. Ended long Whig control by securing Pitt's resignation in 1761. Wanting to rule personally, he found amenable minister (1770–82) in Lord North whose policy of coercion led to AMERICAN REVOLUTION. Notable Tory ministry of the younger William Pitt (1783–1801) saw the end of royal attempts to control the ministry. His reign saw changes effected by Industrial Revolution; a flowering of arts and letters. King's insanity led to regency (1811) of his son, **George IV** (George Augustus Frederick), 1762–1830, who was king 1820–30. Ruling through Tory ministers, he was the leader of a profligate society and was personally hated. Succeeded by William IV. **George V** (George Frederick Ernest Albert), 1865–1936, king 1910–36, was the second son of Edward VII. Interested in empire affairs, he visited India in 1911. In 1916 he gave up all German titles and changed the name of the royal house from Saxe-Coburg-Gotha to Windsor. His second son, **George VI,** 1895–1952, became king of Great Britain (Ireland being then independent) in 1936 when his brother, Edward VIII, abdicated. With his consort, Elizabeth, he made royal visits to France (1938), Canada and U.S. (1939), and South Africa (1947). In World War II he visited bombed areas and toured theatres of war. His eldest daughter, Elizabeth II, succeeded him.

George V, 1819–78, last king of Hanover (1851–66). Sided against Prussia in Austro-Prussian War; lost Hanover to Prussia. He was blind.

George, kings of the Hellenes. **George I,** 1845–1913, second son of Christian IX of Denmark, was elected 1862 to succeed Otto I on Greek throne. Introduced democratic constitution (1863); acquired Thessaly and part of Epirus (1881) and Crete (1908). Was assassinated. His grandson was **George II,** 1890–1947. Reigned 1922–23; exiled 1923–35; restored 1935. Countenanced dictatorship of METAXAS. In exile during Axis occupation of Greece in World War II, he returned 1946 after plebiscite had decided in favor of monarchy. Civil war with Communists continued under his brother Paul, who succeeded him.

George, David Lloyd: see LLOYD GEORGE, DAVID.

George, Henry, 1839–97, American economist, founder of the single-tax movement. He believed a single tax on land would meet all costs of government and even leave a surplus. In 1879 he wrote *Progress and Poverty,* the Bible of the movement.

George, Stefan (shtä′fän gāôr′gŭ), 1868–1933, German poet. Influenced by the French symbolists, he perfected a style of classic, polished beauty and hardness which raised him to the position of major poet and had tremendous influence on the younger generation. His lyric cycles include *Hymnen* (1890), *Algabal* (1892), *Die Bücher der Hirten* [book of the shepherds] (1895), *Das Jahr der Seele* [the soul's year] (1897), *Der Teppich des Lebens* [tapestry of life] (1899), *Das neue Reich* [the new kingdom] (1928).

George, river of N Que., Canada, flows N 365 mi. into Ungava Bay on Hudson Strait.

George, Fort, B.C., Canada: see PRINCE GEORGE.

George, Lake, 33 mi. long and 1–3 mi. wide, NE N.Y., in foothills of the Adirondacks and S of L. Champlain, into which it drains. Center of resort area. Discovered and named Lac du Saint Sacrement by Isaac Jogues, 1646; renamed by Sir William Johnson, 1755. At S end is Lake George village (pop. 1,005), year-round sports center. Has ruins of Fort William Henry (1755) and Fort George (1759; in near-by L. George Battleground Park), battle scenes in French and Indian and Revolutionary wars.

George Junior Republic, community at Freeville, N.Y., founded 1895 by W. R. George, and similar communities elsewhere, for neglected and maladjusted adolescents. Community is self-governing, but all must work. Schooling is provided.

George of Podebrad (pô′dyĕbrät), 1420–71, administrator (1448–58) and king (1458–71) of Bohemia. Came to power as leader of UTRAQUISTS. Was excommunicated by Pope Paul II (1466); expelled MATTHIAS CORVINUS, whom Catholic nobles had proclaimed king in 1469. Restored peace and prosperity to Bohemia.

George Pepperdine College: see LOS ANGELES, Calif.

Georgetown, city (pop. 73,509), cap. and largest city of British Guiana; port on Demerara R.

Georgetown. 1 Part (since 1895) of Washington, D.C., on Potomac R. near confluence of Rock Creek; settled c.1665. It was part of land granted by Md. in 1790 to U.S. government for national cap. Has fine old houses, e.g., DUMBARTON OAKS. Here is Georgetown Univ. (Jesuit; for men; opened 1791, chartered 1815; oldest R.C. college in U.S.). **2** City (pop. 5,516), N Ky., N of Lexington. Processing center in bluegrass agr. area. Seat of Georgetown Col. **3** Village (pop. 2,200), SW Ohio, SE of Cincinnati. Has boyhood home of U. S. Grant, whose birthplace is at near-by Point Pleasant. **4** City (pop. 6,004), E S.C., at head of Wynah Bay, c.15 mi. from ocean, where Pee Dee, Waccamaw, Black, and Sampit rivers enter bay. Port, resort, and shipping center with lumber and paper mills. Has Church of Prince George (1740s). **5** City (pop. 4,951), central Texas, N of Austin at head of San Gabriel R. Seat of Southwestern Univ. (Methodist; coed.; 1873).

Georgetown University: see GEORGETOWN, D.C.

George Washington Birthplace National Monument: see NATIONAL PARKS AND MONUMENTS (table).

George Washington Bridge, vehicular suspension bridge over Hudson R. between Manhattan borough of New York city and Fort Lee, N.J.; main span is 3,500 ft. long; constructed 1927–31.

George Washington University, at Washington, D.C.; nonsectarian, coed.; chartered 1821 as Columbian Col., became a university 1873, renamed 1904.

Georgia, USSR: see GEORGIAN SOVIET SOCIALIST REPUBLIC.

Georgia, state (58,876 sq. mi.; pop. 3,444,578), SE U.S.; one of Thirteen Colonies; cap. ATLANTA. Other cities are SAVANNAH, AUGUSTA, MACON, ROME, ATHENS.

Time	Geologic Development	Life Forms
AZOIC TIME		
3000–5000 million years ago.*	Formation of the earth; lands and seas developed.	No life forms.

PRE-CAMBRIAN TIME. Lasted c.1000–1500 million years. Includes two eras.

Time	Geologic Development	Life Forms
1. ARCHEOZOIC ERA	Much volcanic activity. Mountain ranges formed, then eroded to hills. Minerals deposited.	Rudimentary life forms probably existed.
2. PROTEROZOIC ERA	Iron, copper, and other metallic ores deposited. Glacial periods at least twice. At end of period, volcanic disturbances in North America, followed by erosion of mountains.	Simple marine life: probably soft-bodied wormlike animals; algae.

PALEOZOIC ERA. Age of invertebrates and marine forms; lasted c.300 million years.*

Time	Geologic Development	Life Forms
Cambrian period Began c.505 million years ago, lasted c.80 million years.*	Seas covered much of world; conditions unstable, with many periods of uplifts. Highlands mostly leveled. Climate generally mild.	Marine invertebrates: trilobites dominant; primitive snails; first shells. Calcareous marine algae. Lichens in some regions.
Ordovician period Began c.425 million years ago, lasted c.65 million years.	Fully half of North America covered by seas periodically. Greatest deposition of limestones, marbles, and slates. Great disturbances at end of period; Taconics (N.Y.) thrust up. No sharp geological gradations in climate.	Great numbers of marine animals; some corals, gastropods, clams. Continued dominance of marine invertebrates. First primitive, fishlike vertebrates.
Silurian period Began c.360 million years ago, lasted c.35 million years.	Seas flooded inland basin of North America; great salt beds deposited in E U.S. Mountains eroded, but Appalachians continued high and volcanic. In late period, lands emerged almost completely; arid deserts formed in E U.S.	Sea scorpions most distinctive; also mollusks, corals (reefs), primitive vertebrate fish. Animals similar to scorpions, possibly the first air-breathing forms. Beginnings of land plants.
Devonian period Began c.325 million years ago, lasted c.45 million years.	About 40% of U.S. under water at times, but emerged gradually and completely. North America connected with Europe by land bridge. Volcanic activity. Second upthrusting of Appalachian chain. At close of period E coast rose while W sank. Climate mild.	Age of fishes: marine and armored; also lungfish. Primitive land vertebrates (amphibians); wingless insects and spiders. Ferns, mosses, horsetails; forests of tree ferns. Primitive evergreens.
Carboniferous period (in North America, Mississippian and Pennsylvanian) Began c.280 million years ago, lasted c.50 million years.	Lands flooded several times. Almost 80% of world's coal beds formed from marshy vegetation—in U.S., especially in Pa. Mountains formed in North America, Europe, and Asia. At end of era E North America largely dry. Air warm and moist.	Fish abundant. First land vertebrates (reptiles). Insects larger than at any other period: giant dragonflies, c.800 species cockroaches. Tree ferns, scale trees, primitive conifers; first seed plants.
Permian period Began c.230 million years ago, lasted c.25 million years.	Lands rose, swamps dried up, and some deserts formed. Widespread aridity. Salt beds formed in Kansas, Germany, and USSR. At end of period, world-wide mountain making. Ice over parts of world.	Reptiles (four-legged, not large, and mostly sprawling) developed in number and variety. Some insects (beetle, dragonfly) survived ice age. Spore-bearing ferns and conifers survived aridity.

MESOZOIC ERA. Age of reptiles; lasted c.130 million years.

Time	Geologic Development	Life Forms
Triassic period Began c.205 million years ago, lasted c.40 million years.	Marked erosion of mountains in E North America; at close of period, complex faulting and tilting known as Palisade disturbance. Parts of W U.S. invaded by sea; waters retreated late in period. Climate mild; aridity and semiaridity widespread but some areas were moist.	Vertebrate animals included fresh-water fishes, aquatic reptiles (e.g., ichthyosaur), and dinosaurs (many bipedal) which became dominant life by mid-period. Forests chiefly conifers and cycads; also ferns, tree ferns, scouring rushes.

* All figures vary widely among authoritative sources.

Time	Geologic Development	Life Forms

MESOZOIC ERA (continued)

Jurassic period
Began c.165 million years ago, lasted c.30 million years.*

Pacific coastal region of North America submerged during most of period; deposition of sediments (esp. red beds) and volcanic matter. At close of period vast disturbances formed Sierra Nevada, Cascade, and coastal ranges. Gold-quartz veins formed in Sierras. In E North America land continuously elevated and eroded. Period best defined in Europe; rich fossil beds.

Reptiles dominated land, sea, air (winged reptile, pterosaur). Chief land animals dinosaurs. First bird (archaeopteryx). Modern insects: bees, moths, flies. Cycads dominant plant life; also conifers, ginkgos, tree ferns.

Cretaceous period or Chalk age
Began c.135 million years ago, lasted c.60 million years.

Greatest submergence of continents: 50% of North America submerged. Most of world chalk supply formed, chiefly from limy skeletons of foraminifera. Coal and oil in W U.S. At close of era vast disturbances, Appalachians rose again, Andes formed, seas retreated. Climate generally mild but a cold age late in period.

Dinosaurs included Tyrannosaurus and armored, horned, and duck-billed forms. At close of period dinosaurs became extinct. Marsupials and primitive placental mammals evolved. Flowering plants appeared; deciduous trees became dominant. Sequoias widely distributed.

CENOZOIC ERA. Age of mammals and modern seed plants. Period variously estimated from c.60–75 million years; 75 million used here.

Paleocene and Eocene epochs **
Began c.75 million years ago, lasted c.36 million years.

Mountain building continued in early period, followed by erosion. Atlantic and Gulf coasts partly submerged. Climate mild in most of world.

Modern birds. Primitive mammals: Eohippus (early horse, c.1 ft. high), ancestors of cat, dog, elephant, camel; small primates. Vegetation fairly modern: seed-bearing plants.

Oligocene epoch
Began c.39 million years ago, lasted c.11 million years.

Erosion continued; volcanoes on Pacific coast and in parts of Europe. North America increasingly emergent; N Atlantic coast and most of Pacific coast dry land.

Mammals dominant: cat and dog families supreme; three-toed horse; mastodon; true carnivores. Primates walked erect; primitive anthropoid ape.

Miocene epoch
Began c.28 million years ago, lasted c.16 million years.

In mid-era, great mountain making: Sierras and Rockies rose again, as well as Himalayas, Andes, and Alps. Volcanic activity in W U.S. Climate cooler and drier.

Modern birds. Horse further developed; camels abundant and varied. Great ape in Europe. Cooler climate reduced forests and resulted in more plains. More modern trees.

Pliocene epoch
Began c.12 million years ago, lasted c.11 million years.

Land still rose; volcanoes on Pacific coast and inland. At end of era, Sierras, Cascades, Rockies, Appalachians lifted. Climate increasingly cooler and drier.

Horse evolved almost to modern form; mastodons migrated from Old World to W North America. Manlike apes: gibbon, gorilla. Beginning of Old Stone Age: earliest implements of man, antedating any skeleton of man himself thus far discovered.

Pleistocene epoch or Ice age
Began c.1 million years ago.

Glaciers covered parts of Americas, Europe, and Asia four or five times; disappeared from N.Y. c.38,000 years ago and from Sweden c.12,000 years ago. Great Lakes formed when ice last disappeared. Erosion in nonglacial regions; volcanoes on Pacific coast.

Four species elephants in North America, including mastodon and mammoth; also camels, sabretooth tiger. Camels and horse survived glacial eras but died out in U.S. before advent of man. Beginning extinction of mammals and rise of man: Piltdown, Java, Peking, Heidelberg, Neanderthal, Cro-Magnon (known for cave paintings).

Recent
Began c.25,000 years ago.

Most glaciers melted and lands became warm. Deserts formed in parts of world.

Neolithic man developed after last glacial age, at least 20,000 B.C. Beginnings of civilization: pottery, community life, agriculture, domestication of animals. Copper and Bronze Ages began 5000–2000 B.C. and Iron Age 3000–800 B.C.

* All figures vary widely among authoritative sources.

** The epochs Paleocene through Pliocene are sometimes classed as Tertiary period, and the subsequent time as Quaternary period.

Chief rivers are the SAVANNAH, forming boundary with S.C., the OCMULGEE, the CHATTAHOOCHEE, and the SAINT MARYS. Coastal plains rise to piedmont plateau and to mountains in N. Agr. (cotton, tobacco, peanuts, corn, peaches, pecans, truck); mfg. of cotton textiles, wood products; food processing. Leading producer of kaolin, fuller's earth, naval stores. Hernando De Soto crossed Ga. 1540; Spanish later estab. SEA ISLANDS missions. English-Spanish struggle for possession resulted in English ownership. James E. OGLETHORPE founded Savannah 1733. Tory and patriot sentiment divided in Revolution; British held most of state. First Southern state to ratify Constitution, but early took strong states' rights stand. Seceded from Union 1861; suffered in Civil War from ATLANTA CAMPAIGN of W. T. SHERMAN, especially in his march to the sea. Industry rose after war. Recent progressive force was liberal governorship of Ellis G. Arnall (1943–47).

Georgia, Strait of, channel, c.150 mi. long, between mainland of B.C. and Vancouver Isl., Canada, connecting Puget Sound and Queen Charlotte Sound. Forms part of inland waterway to Alaska.

Georgia, University of, at Athens; land-grant and state supported, for men and women. Had the first state university charter (1785). Its first college (Franklin) opened 1801. Abraham Baldwin and Lyman Hall were instrumental in its founding.

Georgia Institute of Technology, at Atlanta; state supported, for men; chartered 1885, opened 1888.

Georgian Bay, NE arm of L. Huron, S Ont., Canada (120 mi. long, 65 mi. wide), separated from main part of lake by Saugeen Peninsula and Manitoulin Isl. Connects with L. Ontario via Severn R., L. Simcoe, and Trent Canal. The **Georgian Bay Islands National Park** (3,458 acres; estab. 1929) includes 30 islands in the bay.

Georgian Soviet Socialist Republic or **Georgia,** constituent republic (c.29,400 sq. mi.; pop. c.3,600,000), USSR, in W Transcaucasia; cap. TIFLIS. Extending S from crest of Greater Caucasus, it borders on Black Sea in W, on Turkey in S. KURA and RION are chief rivers. Climate and vegetation vary from subtropical coastal region of MINGRELIA in W to high mountain crest and dry Kura steppe in E. Fruit, tea, tobacco, silk, wine are grown in warmer districts. Manganese at Chiatura. Batum, Poti, Sukhum are chief ports. Main political subdivisions are ABKHAZ ASSR, ADZHAR ASSR, S OSSETIA. About two thirds of pop. are Georgians, speaking a S Caucasian language. Minorities include Russians, Armenians, Greeks, various Moslem peoples. Georgian church is one of oldest Orthodox Eastern foundations. Known in antiquity as COLCHIS (in W) and Iberia (in E), Georgia became a kingdom c.4th cent. B.C., with cap. at MTSKHET. Persian Sassanidae ruled it 3d–4th cent. A.D.; branch of Armenian Bagratid dynasty 6–19th cent., with interruptions caused by numerous invasions. Greatest flowering under Queen Thamar (12th–13th cent.). Pressed by its Moslem neighbors, Georgia accepted Russian overlordship in 18th cent. Last king abdicated 1801. Additional territories ceded by Turkey between 1803 and 1829. Briefly independent after 1917, Georgia became soviet republic 1921.

Georgian style, in English architecture of the reigns (1714–1820) of George I, George II, and George III. Based on principles of Andrea Palladio introduced into England by Inigo Jones and Sir Christopher Wren. Emphasized classic correctness, which made symmetry the essential feature. Typical Georgian house was brick structure with courses and cornices of white stone and trimmings of white painted woodwork. Corridors in interiors were an innovation. Notable examples of public architecture of the period include St. James's Club, by Robert Adam; Somerset House, by Sir William Chambers; Bank of England, by Sir John Soane; and St. Martin's-in-the-Fields, by James Gibbs. American buildings of the period, closely resembling

their English prototypes, are usually called Colonial.

Georgia State College for Women: see MILLEDGEVILLE.

Georgia State Womans College: see VALDOSTA.

Gera (gā′rä), city (pop. 89,212), Thuringia, E central Germany; until 1918 cap. of principality of REUSS (younger line). Textile center.

geranium, name for widely grown house and bedding plant of genus *Pelargonium,* native to S Africa. Many varieties have showy flowers; others are grown for their scented leaves. Native American wild geranium or crane's-bill belongs to the genus *Geranium.*

Gérard, François Pascal Simon, Baron, 1770–1837, French portrait and historical painter, a favorite pupil of David.

Gerard, James Watson (jürärd′), 1867–1951, U.S. ambassador to Germany (1913–17).

Gerbert: see SYLVESTER II, pope.

Géricault, Jean Louis André Théodore (zhā′ lwē′ ädrā′ tāödôr′ zhārēkō′), 1791–1824, French painter, who helped to introduce romanticism into France. In 1819 he exhibited his famous *Raft of the Medusa* (Louvre), which brought violent protests from those of classical school. Acclaimed in London, where he produced many fine paintings of horses. Exerted great influence on French painting.

Gérin-Lajoie, Antoine (zhārē′-läzhwä′), 1824–82, French Canadian author. Most popular works are two novels which idealize simple life of French Canadian habitants.

Gerizim (gĕ′rùzĭm), mountain, central Palestine. Samaritans considered it the only proper place of worship; 300-year-old Samaritan temple was destroyed by Maccabean leader, John Hyrcanus, c.130 B.C.

Gerlachovka, Czechoslovakia: see TATRA.

germ, term applied to any minute disease-causing organism, including certain bacteria, viruses, protozoa, molds, and rickettsia. Theory that disease is caused by introduction of germs into another living organism was accepted following Pasteur's experiments and Lister's use of antiseptics to reduce infection. Germ plasm is living material inherited through sex cells. A seed or portion of seed is often called germ.

German, Sir Edward, 1862–1936, English composer. Known for incidental music to plays, e.g., *Henry VIII, Nell Gwynn,* and for light operas. Knighted 1928.

German Baptist Brethren: see DUNKARDS.

German Confederation, 1815–66, estab. by Congress of Vienna. Membership consisted of the sovereign states and free cities of Germany; the emperor of Austria; the king of Denmark (as duke of Holstein and Lauenburg); the king of Hanover; and the king of the Netherlands (as duke of Luxembourg). The federal diet, which met at Frankfurt under presidency of Austria, was reduced to impotence through unanimity rule; suspended 1848–50, when the FRANKFURT Parliament was meeting, it resumed under Austrian leadership after Treaty of OLMÜTZ. AUSTRO-PRUSSIAN WAR led to dissolution of the confederation and establishment of NORTH GERMAN CONFEDERATION.

German East Africa, former German colony, area c.370,000 sq. mi., E Africa. Divided into three parts after World War I. Kionga was annexed to Mozambique, and TANGANYIKA and RUANDA-URUNDI became mandated territories held by Great Britain and Belgium, respectively.

Germanic languages, subfamily of Indo-European, of which English and German, standard language of Germany, are members. See LANGUAGE (table).

Germanic laws, codes adopted (5th–9th cent.) after the Germanic invaders of the Roman Empire had created governments. Since law then applied to the person rather than the territory or governmental unit, there were codes for the Germans themselves (called *leges barbarorum*) and, in S Europe, other codes for Romans under German rule (*leges Romanorum*). Although all except the Anglo-Saxon were in Latin and all imitated the form of the Roman law code, the *leges barbarorum* are now accepted as incorporating much of the older Germanic customary law. They are largely concerned with penal law and particularly with COMPOSITION for personal injuries. Some of the more important codes, however, show strong Roman influence. The Visigoths in Spain had a series of notable codes: that of King Euric (5th cent.), the *Breviary of Alaric* (or *Lex Romana Visigothorum*) in 506, and the *Lex Visigothorum* or *Liber iudiciorum* (later translated as the *Fuero juzgo* and applying to Goths and Romans alike) of c.654. Notable also was the *Edictum Rotharis* (643), which with a collection of Italian legislation of the Holy Roman Empire became the basis for the later renaissance of Roman law in Italy.

Germanic religion. Tacitus' *Germania* and *Beowulf* are our best sources on it. It was polytheistic, with "Olympian" and underworld gods. Its principal gods were Woden, Tiw, Frey and Freyja, and an earth-goddess. Sacrifices, oracles, and fertility rites were practiced. Mythology was not highly developed, but there was much story-telling, and from later works (such as NIBELUNGENLIED) mythical ideas can be gained. Ideas of death and afterworld were similar to those of the Greeks. In Iceland, sources of its mythology are the Eddas, the oldest direct material on Germanic myth. Norse mythology differs from that of other Germanic peoples because of Christian influence, isolation of Old Norse, and longer development of the system.

Germanicus Caesar (jŭrmăʹnĭkŭs), 15 B.C.–A.D. 19, Roman general; son of Drusus Senior, nephew of TIBERIUS. Fought well against the Germans, but was replaced by his brother Drusus. He was later poisoned at Tiberius' request. CLAUDIUS I was his brother. AGRIPPINA II and CALIGULA were his children.

germanium (jŭrmăʹnēŭm), rare, gray, brittle metallic element (symbol = Ge; see also ELEMENT, table). It resembles tin and lead and occurs in a few minerals.

German language, a Germanic language. See LANGUAGE (table).

German measles: see MEASLES.

German New Guinea: see NEW GUINEA, TERRITORY OF.

German Order: see TEUTONIC KNIGHTS.

German Reformed Church: see EVANGELICAL AND REFORMED CHURCH.

Germans, great ethnic complex of Europe, a basic stock in the composition of the peoples of Scandinavia, Germany, Austria, Switzerland, N Italy, the Low Countries, France, and England. They lived in N Germany and along the Baltic Sea before their great expansion S, SE, and W in the early Christian era. Prime sources for their culture and distribution are works of Caesar and Tacitus. The Teutons and Cimbri whom Marius defeated in 102–101 B.C. may have been Germans. Germans became increasingly troublesome to the Roman Empire; attacks were made by the VANDALS in the W and by the OSTROGOTHS in the E. The Germans probably retained a certain ethnic solidarity until the 2d or 3d cent., but later broke up into many peoples. Chief among these were the ALEMANNI, the FRANKS, the ANGLO-SAXONS, the Burgundii (see BURGUNDY), the LOMBARDS, the SAXONS, and the VISIGOTHS. The Scandinavians, a large group, included the Icelanders, who produced the first Germanic literature (see OLD NORSE LITERATURE).

German silver or **nickel silver,** silver-white alloy of copper, zinc, nickel in varying proportions. Hard, tough, and resistant to corrosion, it is used in tableware and in heating coils.

German Southwest Africa: see SOUTH-WEST AFRICA.

Germantown, residential section of Philadelphia, Pa.; settled by Germans c.1683. Early American center of printing and publishing. Annexed to Philadelphia 1854. In Revolution British were quartered here; Washington defeated here 1777. Howe House and other colonial buildings stand.

Germany, Ger. *Deutschland* or *Deutsches Reich,* largest country of Central Europe, stretching from the Baltic Sea and the North Sea on the N to the Alps

on the S. Lacking a peace treaty with its enemies of World War II, it remains in 1953 without settled boundaries, unified government, or well-defined status. In 1949 two separate republics came into existence: (1) Federal Republic of [West] Germany (c.94,900 sq. mi.; 1950 pop. 47,585,872; temporary cap. Bonn), under U.S., British, and French occupation, consisting of the states of BAVARIA, WÜRTTEMBERG-BADEN, HESSE, and BREMEN (U.S. zone); NORTH RHINE-WESTPHALIA, LOWER SAXONY, SCHLESWIG-HOLSTEIN, and HAMBURG (British zone); RHINELAND-PALATINATE, WÜRTTEMBERG-HOHENZOLLERN, and BADEN (French zone); and W BERLIN. (2) [East] German Democratic Republic (c.41,400 sq. mi.; 1946 pop. 18,489,713; cap. E Berlin), under Russian occupation, consisting of the states of BRANDENBURG, MECKLENBURG, THURINGIA, SAXONY, and SAXONY-ANHALT. N Germany is generally level and low lying. Central Germany, with the HARZ mts. and Thuringian Forest, and S Germany, with the mountains of SWABIA and FRANCONIA and the Bavarian Alps (highest peak, ZUGSPITZE) are generally mountainous and forest-covered. The RHINE, WESER, ELBE, ODER, and DANUBE are the principal rivers. The heaviest industrial concentrations are in the NW (N Rhineland and RUHR dist., with Cologne, Düsseldorf, and Essen); at Berlin; and in Saxony (with Leipzig, Dresden, and Chemnitz). Other major commercial and industrial centers: Munich, Stuttgart, Nuremberg (S); Frankfurt, Mannheim (W); Dortmund, Duisburg (NW); Hanover, Magdeburg (N); and the port cities of Hamburg, Bremen, Kiel, and Lübeck. For its huge metallurgical industry Germany depends largely on Ruhr coal and on imported ores. Other major industrial products are textiles, chemicals, electrical machinery. In 1945 the SAAR TERRITORY and the E provinces of SILESIA, POMERANIA, and EAST PRUSSIA were detached from Germany, which thus lost some of its chief industrial, mining, and agr. districts. About 25% of the population is engaged in agr. In the Federal Republic of [West] Germany, Protestants have a slight majority over Catholics, with Catholicism prevailing in the S and W. E Germany is predominantly Lutheran.

Germany before 1871. In antiquity, Germany was inhabited by a number of Germanic tribes (see GERMANS). Rome conquered (1st cent. B.C.–1st cent. A.D.) the regions along the Rhine and parts of S Germany, but further conquest was stopped at the battle of TEUTOBURG FOREST (A.D. 9). In the 4th–5th cent. German tribes invaded the Roman Empire, while the Slavs occupied the lands E of the Elbe. The FRANKS soon subjugated other German tribes and created a vast empire in Germany and Gaul (see also MEROVINGIANS; CAROLINGIANS; CHARLEMAGNE). Christianization of Germany, begun by St. BONIFACE, was completed in the 12th–13th cent. with the German colonization of the lands E of the Elbe (see WENDS; TEUTONIC KNIGHTS). From divisions of the Frankish empire (9th cent.) came a separate kingdom under LOUIS THE GERMAN. Weakened by foreign invaders (Norsemen, Slavs, Magyars) and by the rise of powerful feudal princes (the dukes of FRANCONIA, SWABIA, BAVARIA, SAXONY, and LOTHARINGIA), the kingship recovered authority under HENRY I and OTTO I (crowned as emperor, 962). German history then overlapped with that of the HOLY ROMAN EMPIRE. The feudal structure of Germany proved persistent. The great "stem duchies" were broken up by the emperors in the 10th–12th cent., but still lesser principalities and free cities made Germany a loose federation over which the emperors presided with varying degrees of effectiveness. After the Thirty Years War (1618–48) imperial control was nominal, and within the federal structure arose two powerful rival states—AUSTRIA (i.e., the far-flung, multinational Hapsburg empire) and the modern, centralized kingdom of PRUSSIA. Austro-Prussian rivalry was temporarily in-

terrupted by Napoleon I, who swept aside the Holy
Roman Empire (1806) and created the CONFEDERA-
TION OF THE RHINE. The Congress of Vienna (1814–
15) reduced the number of sovereign German states
but retained the federal structure by creating the
GERMAN CONFEDERATION. The liberal-nationalist revolution of 1848 was easily suppressed and the FRANK-
FURT Parliament vainly sought to create a unified
Germany. However, under the leadership of BIS-
MARCK, Prussia eliminated Austria from German
affairs (see AUSTRO-PRUSSIAN WAR, 1866), and at the
end of the FRANCO-PRUSSIAN WAR William I of Prussia was proclaimed emperor of Germany (1871). The
new empire, increased by ALSACE and LORRAINE, was
united by a common ruler, a federal diet (Reichstag),
and a customs union (see ZOLLVEREIN), but it remained a confederation of kingdoms (Prussia, Bavaria, Württemberg, Saxony), grand duchies (Baden,
Hesse, Saxe-Weimar, Mecklenburg), lesser principalities, and Hanseatic cities (Hamburg, Bremen, Lübeck).

From Bismarck to Hitler. In half a century, Germany
had evolved from a feudal, disunited, socially and
industrially retarded area into the chief military and
economic power of the Continent. The phenomenal
speed of industrial and commercial expansion continued after 1871 and, combined with the program of
colonial and naval expansion under WILLIAM II, became a serious threat to England. As long as Bismarck
held power (i.e., until 1890) the government sought
peaceful relations with its neighbors, but William II's
aggressive diplomacy helped to bring about WORLD
WAR I (1914–18). Germany in 1914 was at the peak
of its prosperity. By 1918, it was exhausted by the
war. A Social Democratic revolution forced the abdication of William II and the conclusion of an armistice. In 1919 Germany accepted the harsh Treaty of
VERSAILLES and adopted the republican constitution
drafted at Weimar. The "Weimar Republic" retained
the federal structure of the empire, with some minor
territorial adjustments. It was beset from the beginning by extremist agitation (both nationalist and
Communist), mass unemployment, and a currency
inflation that wiped out the nation's savings. Pres.
Ebert, who steered a middle course, was succeeded by
HINDENBURG. After 1925 came economic recovery,
while the foreign policy of STRESEMANN restored
Germany as a great power. However, the world economic crisis that began in 1929 again plunged Germany into near-bankruptcy. Both Communism and
NATIONAL SOCIALISM made great electoral gains. By
1932 Hitler's party was the largest single party in the
Reichstag; in Jan., 1933, disunion among his opponents made possible the appointment of HITLER as
chancellor.

Third Reich and Collapse. Within a year, Hitler
estab. absolute dictatorship, virtually abolished the
powers of the state governments, and reduced all
German life to Nazi control. Repudiating the Treaty
of Versailles, he began a program of intensive rearmament, remilitarized the Rhineland (1936), and annexed Austria (March, 1938). Allied with Fascist
Italy from 1936 (see AXIS), Germany interfered in the
Spanish civil war of 1936–39, and was allowed by
the Western Powers to seize part of Czechoslovakia
in Sept., 1938 (see MUNICH PACT). Bohemia and
Moravia were annexed altogether in April, 1939, along
with the Memel dist., and Germany began to demand
DANZIG and part of the POLISH CORRIDOR. After concluding a nonaggression pact with the USSR (Aug.,
1939), Germany invaded Poland and began WORLD
WAR II. Despite spectacular victories up to 1942, the
war ended with Germany's unconditional surrender
in May, 1945, and left the German cities in ruin.
According to decisions made at the YALTA and POTS-
DAM conferences, Germany was divided into four
occupation zones; Berlin, under four-power occupation, received special status. Dissension between the

USSR and the West paralyzed the Allied control
council, from which the USSR withdrew in 1948. The
REPARATIONS question was a major factor in the failure to arrive at a general peace treaty. The Soviet
blockade of W BERLIN (1948–49) widened the rift
between E and W Germany, which in 1949 became
two separate republics. While E Germany underwent
increasing sovietization, W Germany, under supervision of a three-power Allied High Commission, became a federal, parliamentary democracy. Its chancellor, Conrad Adenauer, headed (as of 1953) a
coalition cabinet of Christian Democrats and other
conservatives. Economic recovery was remarkably
speedy, but many problems remained: aside from the
influx of millions of Germans who had been expelled
(or had fled) from Poland, Czechoslovakia, and other
countries, and aside from the danger of a Nazi revival, there was the constant threat of aggression from
the E and the unwillingness of all Germans to accept
a permanent division of their country. In 1951 W
Germany and the Western Powers signed a peace
contract by which W Germany was to obtain nearly
complete jurisdiction over internal affairs and foreign
trade, but which gave the Allies the right to maintain
security forces in Germany. The contract was made
contingent on W Germany's joining the SCHUMAN
PLAN (which it did) and furnishing troops for a projected European army; it was ratified (1952) by the
U.S. and Great Britain but not (as of March, 1953)
by Germany and France. Chief factors in the delay
of ratification were French-German differences over
the Saar Territory and the opposition of German
Social Democrats (and many others) to the army plan.

germicide (jûr′mŭsĭd), chemical capable of killing
germs. It may be ineffective against resistant spores
formed by some germs. Many are injurious to living
tissue. Some body secretions act as germicides toward
certain disease-causing organisms.

germination, in a seed, the growth of the embryo (after
period of dormancy) and emergence of young plant
from seed. Suitable conditions of temperature, moisture, and oxygen are necessary. Seed viability ranges
from a few days to (rarely) 50 years or more. Use of
germination tested seed prevents planting of old or
inferior seed. For parts of a seedling, see *ill.,* p. 783.

Gérôme, Jean Léon (zhă′ lăō′ zhărōm′), 1824–1904,
French historical and genre painter.

Gerona (hārō′nä), city (pop. 28,752), cap. of Gerona
prov., NE Spain, in Catalonia. Textile mfg. Heroically
resisted French in Peninsular War 1808–9. Notable
Gothic cathedral.

Geronimo (jŭrŏ′nŭmō), c.1829–1909, chief of a Chiricahua band of the Apache Indians. Terrorized Ariz.
by brutal raids in 1880s.

Gerry, Elbridge (gĕ′rē), 1744–1814, American statesman. Supported patriot activities before and during
American Revolution. Opponent of strong central government. Had a part in XYZ AFFAIR. Governor of
Mass. (1810, 1811); Vice President of U.S. (1813–14).
Name used by opponents in political practice called
gerrymander (jĕ′rēmăn″dŭr), rearrangement of voting
districts so as to favor party in power. Origin of term,
though not origin of practice, was in such an arrangement made in Mass. when Elbridge Gerry was governor.

Gers (zhĕr), department (2,429 sq. mi.; pop. 190,431),
SW France, at foot of Pyrenees, in Armagnac region
of Gascony; cap. Auch.

Gershon, Levi ben: see GERSONIDES.

Gershwin, George, 1898–1937, American composer.
Songs from his musical comedy scores (e.g., *Embrace-
able You* and *The Man I Love*) are masterpieces of
their kind. His principal larger compositions are *Rhapsody in Blue* (1923), the classic example of symphonic
jazz; Piano Concerto in F (1925); *An American in
Paris* (1928); and *Porgy and Bess* (1935), a folk opera
from which comes the well-known *Summertime.*

Gerson, John (Jean Charlier de Gerson) (gûr′sün),

1363–1429, French ecclesiastical statesman. With Pierre d'AILLY (his teacher at Paris), he sought to end the Great SCHISM by advancing the conciliar theory (basically, doctrine that councils are superior to the pope; later declared heretical) for Council of Pisa. Attended Council of CONSTANCE, and helped to end the schism and condemn John Huss. Wrote much and, as chancellor of the Univ. of Paris, opposed teaching of Occam and began change to realism.

Gersonides (gürsö'nĭdēz) or **Levi ben Gershon** (lē'vī bĕn gûr'shùn), 1288–1344, Jewish philosopher, author of *Milchamoth Adonai* [the wars of the Lord], a criticism of the philosophy of Maimonides.

Gersoppa Falls (gürsö'pù) cataract of Sharavati R., on Mysore-Bombay border, India. Highest of four cascades is c.830 ft.

Gesenius, Wilhelm (vĭl'hĕlm gāzā'nyṓs), 1786–1842, German Orientalist, known for his *Hebrew Grammar;* one of first to open Semitic to scientific study.

Gessner, Salomon (zä'lōmôn gĕs'nùr), 1730–88, Swiss poet, landscape painter, and etcher. His poems and "idyllic prose pastorals" (e.g., *The Death of Abel,* 1758) were very popular and had great influence on European literature.

Gestalt (gùshtält'), school of psychology interpreting phenomena as organized wholes greater than the sums of their parts. The term was coined in Germany by Charles von Ehrenfels (1890). Early experimentation led to the laws of membership character (i.e., each element of a pattern through its dynamic participation in that pattern alters its individuality), and of *Prägnanz,* the dynamic attribute of self-fulfillment in all structured wholes. Structural correspondence between sensory and extrasensory mental processes was postulated.

Gestapo: see SECRET POLICE.

Gesta Romanorum (jĕ'stù rō"mùnô'rùm) [Latin,= deeds of the Romans], medieval collection of Latin stories, each tale characterized by a moral.

gestation: see PREGNANCY.

Gethsemane (gĕthsē'mùnè), olive grove or garden, near foot of Mt. of Olives, E of Jerusalem, scene of the agony and betrayal of Jesus. Mark 14.32; Mat. 26.36.

Gettysburg, borough (pop. 7,046), S Pa., near Md. border; named for James Gettys, grantee of land from William Penn. Seat of Gettysburg Col. (Lutheran; coed.; 1832) and Lutheran Theological Seminary. Gettysburg Natl. Military Park is shrine of Civil War battle (see GETTYSBURG CAMPAIGN). At dedication of national cemetery here Abraham Lincoln delivered the **Gettysburg Address** Nov. 19, 1863.

Gettysburg campaign, June–July, 1863, of Civil War. After victory at Chancellorsville, R. E. Lee undertook second invasion of North via Shenandoah Valley into S Pa. At Chambersburg he learned Army of Potomac under G. G. Meade was concentrating N of Potomac. Two armies met just W of Gettysburg. On July 1 Federals were driven to Cemetery Hill, S of town. Meade, in strong position, consolidated forces. On July 2 Confederates failed in assaults both on Union left at Round Top and Little Round Top and on its right at Cemetery Hill. On July 3 Lee sent Longstreet with G. E. Pickett's division in famous charge against Union center; briefly successful, it was beaten back. On July 4 Lee withdrew. Confederate defeat, turning point of war.

geyser (gī'zùr), a hot spring that intermittently erupts steam and hot water. Geysers occur only in New Zealand, Iceland, Yellowstone Park. Some build up cones of mineral matter about their vents.

Geysir (gā'sĭr), hot spring, SW Iceland, W of Reykjavik. Eruptions (at intervals of several weeks) last c.20 minutes. Max. height of jet is 200 ft.; max. temperature 180°F. Neighborhood has many hot springs. English name *geyser* derives from Geysir.

Gezelle, Guido (gē'dō khùzè'lù), 1830–99, Flemish lyric poet, a Roman Catholic priest, b. Bruges; forerunner of the Flemish literary revival.

Gezer (gē'–), natural fortress, Palestine, on ridge overlooking the road between Jerusalem and Jaffa. In Bible, important in the wars of Joshua, David, and the Maccabees; several times a scene of battle in the Crusades.

Ghats (gôts, gäts), two mountain ranges of S India. Eastern Ghats extend c.875 mi. along E coast and merge in S with Western Ghats, which parallel W coast for c.1,000 mi., with Palghat Gap as only major break. Anai Mudi Peak (8,841 ft.) in SW is highest point.

Ghazali, Al-: see AL-GAZEL.

Ghazipur (gä'zēpṓr"), town (pop. 31,326), SE Uttar Pradesh, India, on Ganges R.; opium mfg. Tomb of Lord Cornwallis.

Ghazni (gŭz'nē), town (pop. 25,000), E Afghanistan. Flourished under Turkish Ghaznivid dynasty (962–c.1152), founded by Mahmud of Ghazni, whose domain reached from Persia to the Punjab. Held by British in Afghan wars (1839–42).

ghee: see BUTTER.

Ghent (gĕnt), Flemish *Gent,* Fr. *Gand,* city (pop. 166,797; with suburbs 228,798), cap. of East Flanders prov. and historic cap. of Flanders, N Belgium, at confluence of Scheldt and Lys rivers and at focus of a canal network. Second largest port and chief textile center of Belgium; episcopal see; seat of university (founded 1816); art center. City grew around fortress built by first count of Flanders on a small island (9th cent.). A major cloth-mfg. center by the 13th cent., it witnessed bitter social strife between the "lesser folk" and the rich bourgeoisie. Under Jacob and Philip van ARTEVELDE Ghent led Flanders in struggle against the French. Ghent's liberties were curtailed by Philip the Good after an insurrection (1453); Mary of Burgundy restored them through the Great Privilege, signed at Ghent (1477). Emperor Charles V, who was born and reared at Ghent, abrogated its liberties after another rebellion (1540). By the Pacification of Ghent, signed here 1576, the provinces of the Netherlands allied themselves with William the Silent to drive out the Spanish. Capture of Ghent by Alessandro Farnese (1584) completed Spanish reconquest of Flanders. Among landmarks of Ghent are ruins of Abbey of St. Bavon (10th cent.) and of castle of counts (12th cent.); Cathedral of St. Bavon (13th–16th cent.); cloth hall (16th cent.); and 14th-cent. belfry, with famous carillon. Flemish painting flourished here in 15th cent. with Hugo van der Goes and the brothers Van Eyck. The **Treaty of Ghent,** signed here Dec. 24, 1814, ended War of 1812 between U.S. and Great Britain. Provision for restoring territories and places taken by either party represented diplomatic victory for U.S.

Gherardesca, Ugolino della: see UGOLINO DELLA GHERARDESCA.

ghetto (gĕ'tō), section of a city (usually walled) in which Jews were obliged to live after 14th cent. In 1870 the last ghetto (in Rome) was abolished.

Ghibellines: see GUELPHS and GHIBELLINES.

Ghiberti, Lorenzo (lōrän'tsō gēbĕr'tē), c.1378–1455, Florentine sculptor. In 1401 he won competition for bronze doors of Florence baptistery. His superb panels on N and S doors show scenes from life of Christ and Old Testament.

Ghilan, Iran: see GILAN.

Ghirlandaio or **Ghirlandajo, Domenico** (both dōmā'nēkō gērländä'yō), 1449–94, Florentine painter. Studied with Baldovinetti and later taught Michelangelo. Magnificent frescoes in Santa Trinità and Santa Maria Novella (both in Florence) are famous for contemporary portraits and settings. His son **Ridolfo Ghirlandaio** (rēdôl'fō), 1483–1561, was also a painter.

Ghor (gôr) or **Ghur** (gṓr), mountainous region, W central Afghanistan. Powerful Moslem dynasty was estab. here in 12th cent.

ghost dance, central ritual of messianic religion instituted by Paiute Indian, Wovoka. It included dancing, shaking, and hypnotic trances. After 1887 spread among Western tribes.

Ghur, Afghanistan: see GHOR.

Ghuzzeh: see GAZA.

Giacosa, Giuseppe (jōōzĕp'pä jäkō'zä), 1847–1906, Italian dramatic poet. His plays include *I triste amori* (1888) and *La Dame de Challant* (1891; written for Bernhardt). With Luigi Illica, he wrote librettos for Puccini's *La Bohème, Tosca,* and *Madame Butterfly.*

giant, manlike being of great size and strength. Giants appear in mythology of various peoples (Greeks, Germans, Celts). No evidence of such beings is known. Gigantism in humans results from over-secretion in childhood of growth hormone of anterior lobe of pituitary gland.

Giant Mountains: see RIESENGEBIRGE.

Giant's Causeway, headland on N coast of Co. Antrim, N. Ireland, extending 3 mi. along coast. Thousands of basaltic columns form three natural platforms. Built, according to legend, for giants to cross to Scotland.

Giauque, William Francis (jēōk'), 1895–, American chemist. Won 1949 Nobel Prize in Chemistry for studies of properties of substances at extremely low temperatures. He is codiscoverer of the second and third isotopes of oxygen.

Gibbon, Edward, 1737–94, English historian, author of monumental *Decline and Fall of the Roman Empire.* It was conceived on a visit to Rome. Appearing in six volumes (1776–83), it met wide acclaim. Standard edition is J. B. Bury's (7 vols., 1896–1900). Gibbon also wrote an autobiography.

gibbon (gĭ'bùn), smallest of anthropoid apes (genera *Hylobates* and *Symphalanga*) found in SE Asia and East Indies. Gibbons have slender bodies and very long arms; they travel through trees with speed and agility and on ground often walk erect. They live in family groups and are monogamous.

Gibbons, Grinling, 1648–1721, English wood carver and sculptor. Employed by Sir Christopher Wren to do architectural decorations for his buildings, notably St. Paul's.

Gibbons, James, 1834–1921, American cardinal. Became bishop of Baltimore (1877), cardinal (1886). Notable for praising the blessings of American democracy for the Church. He persuaded the pope to lift the ban on the Knights of Labor.

Gibbons, Orlando, 1583–1625, English composer and organist, the last of the great Elizabethans. His works include madrigals, English anthems and services, and music for strings and for virginal.

Gibbs, James, 1682–1754, English architect, distinguished exponent of Georgian style. His finest works are St. Martin's-in-the-Fields (1722–26) and St. Mary-le-Strand (1714–17).

Gibbs, Josiah Willard, 1839–1903, American mathematical physicist, known especially for contributions in field of thermodynamics.

Gibraltar (jĭbrôl'tùr), town (pop. 28,460, including garrison), constituting a British crown colony. Located at NW end of Rock of Gibraltar (one of PILLARS OF HERCULES), a peninsula of S Spain at E end of Strait of Gibraltar. Strait connects the Atlantic and the Mediterranean. Gibraltar Bay, an inlet of the Strait, has safe enclosed harbor of c.450 acres. Rock, 2¾ mi. long and ¾ mi. wide, rises to height of 1,408 ft. Of Jurassic limestone, its caves have produced valuable archaeological finds. Has been an English possession since 1704. Town, a free port, serves as coaling station and port of call. Naval station and fortress, its population is kept small. Underground tunnels built in World War II. Since the war, Spain has renewed its claims on Gibraltar.

Gibson, Charles Dana, 1867–1944, American illustrator, a leading exponent of black-and-white art in America. Creator of Gibson Girl.

Gibson, W(ilfrid) W(ilson), 1878–, English poet of Georgian group, writing on the obscure and lowly.

Giddings, Franklin Henry, 1855–1931, American sociologist. Based explanation of social phenomena on principle of "consciousness of kind."

Gide, André (ädrä' zhēd'), 1869–1951, French author and intellectual leader. Of Calvinist background, he projected the conflict between the wish for self-fulfillment and the barriers of convention into semi-autobiographical fiction, such as *L'Immoraliste* (1902; Eng. tr., 1930), *Strait Is the Gate* (1909; Eng. tr., 1924), and *The Counterfeiters* (1925; Eng. tr., 1927). His lucid, gemlike style also illuminates his journals (1939; Eng. tr., 4 vols., 1947–51) and translations. Awarded Nobel Prize in Literature in 1947.

Gide, Charles (shärl), 1847–1932, French economist, expert on monetary problems. Played important role in cooperative movement.

Gideon (gĭ'dēùn) or **Gedeon** (gĕ'–), judge of Israel. Called by an angel of the Lord to free Israel from Midianite oppressors, he won a spectacular victory with only 300 men. An interesting event is his oracle of the fleece. Judges 6–8; Heb. 11.32. Jerubbaal: Judges 6.30–32; 7.1. Jerubbesheth: 2 Sam. 11.21.

Gideons, givers of Bibles: see BIBLE SOCIETIES.

Gideonse, Harry D(avid) (gĭ'dēùnz), 1901–, American educator, president of Brooklyn Col. after 1939.

Gielgud, John (gĭl'gŏod), 1904–, English actor. Made his stage debut in 1921. Has played Hamlet (his greatest role) many times in U.S. and England.

Giers, Nikolai Karlovich (nyĭkŭlī' kär'lùvĭch gēyĕrs'), 1820–95, Russian foreign minister (1882–95). Promoted peace policy.

Giessen (gē'sùn), city (pop. 46,701), Hesse, W Germany, in Upper Hesse, on Lahn R. Seat of well-known Protestant university 1607–1945. Heavily damaged in World War II.

Giffard (zhē'fär), town (pop. 8,097), S Que., Canada, on the St. Lawrence and NE of Quebec city.

Gijón (hēhōn'), city (pop. 72,053), N Spain, in Asturias; Atlantic port on Bay of Biscay. Exports minerals. Fishing; mfg. Dates from pre-Roman times.

Gila (hē'lù), river, rising in mountains of W N.Mex. and flowing W across all of Ariz., to Colorado R. at Yuma, Ariz. Early peoples in "Valley of the Sun" farmed by irrigation. Near head is U.S. "unimproved" Gila Wilderness Area (entered via Silver City, N.Mex., but not by auto). Has irrigation dams in N.Mex., COOLIDGE DAM in Ariz. Other projects are on lower Gila and its tributaries, notably in SALT RIVER VALLEY.

Gila Cliff Dwellings National Monument: see NATIONAL PARKS AND MONUMENTS (table).

gila monster (hē'lù), a species of *Heloderma,* only genus of poisonous lizards. Found in deserts of SW U.S. It averages c.18 in. long. Tuberclelike scales cover the skin and the stout, clumsy body is black with a marbled pattern of orange or pink, yellow, or dull white. The tail is a food reservoir. Poison glands are in lower jaw; grooved teeth (carrying venom) are far back in mouth. Mexican gila monster is black and yellow.

Gilan or **Ghilan** (both: gēlän'), region, NW Iran, between Elburz Mts. and Caspian Sea; formerly a province. Held by Russia 1723–32. Was Soviet republic (1920–21). Produces rice, fruit, and silk.

Gilberd, William: see GILBERT, WILLIAM.

Gilbert, Cass, 1859–1934, American architect. Built the 60-story Woolworth Building, New York, and Supreme Court Building, Washington, D.C.

Gilbert, Charles Kendall, 1878–, American Episcopal bishop. Editor of the *Churchman* (1912–18); suffragan bishop of N.Y. (1930–46); bishop (1947–50).

Gilbert, Grove Karl, 1843–1918, American geologist. He was appointed senior geologist when the U.S. Survey was created in 1879 and published many reports, including a notable one on extinct Lake Bonneville.

Gilbert, Sir Humphrey, 1539?–1583, English soldier, navigator, and explorer; half brother of Sir Walter Ralegh. Knighted (1570) for Irish campaign services. His *Discourse* (1576), arguing existence of Northwest Passage, long motivated English exploration. Claimed Newfoundland for Queen Elizabeth and assumed authority over fishermen's colony already there (1583). Lost on return voyage.

Gilbert or **Gilberd, William,** c.1540–1603, English scientist and physician, noted for pioneer studies of magnetism described in his *De magnete* (1600; Eng. tr., 1893, 1900).

Gilbert, Sir W(illiam) S(chwenck), 1836–1911, English playwright and poet. Wrote amusing, cynical *Bab Ballads* (1869). In 1871 he began his long collaboration with composer Arthur Sullivan, resulting in popular satiric operettas: *Trial by Jury* (1875), *H.M.S. Pinafore* (1878), *The Pirates of Penzance* (1879), *Patience* (1881), *Iolanthe* (1882), *Princess Ida* (1884), *The Mikado* (1885), *Ruddigore* (1887), *The Yeomen of the Guard* (1888), *The Gondoliers* (1889).

Gilbert and Ellice Islands (ĕl'ĭs), British colony (375 sq. mi.; pop. 36,000), central and S Pacific, estab. 1915 and placed under Western Pacific High Commission at Suva, Fiji; cap. Tarawa. Includes GILBERT ISLANDS, ELLICE ISLANDS, OCEAN ISLAND, FANNING ISLAND, WASHINGTON ISLAND, CHRISTMAS ISLAND, and part of PHOENIX ISLANDS. Chief exports of colony are copra and phosphate.

Gilbert Islands, group of atolls (144 sq. mi.; pop. 27,-824), central Pacific, belonging to Great Britain. Discovered 1764 by Capt. Byron, group became a British protectorate 1892; included in Gilbert and Ellice Isls. colony 1915. Occupied 1941 by the Japanese. After fierce fighting Tarawa and Makin isls. were regained 1943 by U.S. forces.

Gilboa (-bō'-), ridge, Palestine, on E edge of plain of Esdraelon. Here Saul and Jonathan were defeated and killed. 1 Sam. 28.4; 31; 2 Sam. 1.21.

Gilder, Richard Watson (gĭl'-), 1844–1909, American editor, poet, editor of *Century* magazine.

Gildersleeve, Virginia (Crocheron), 1877–, American educator. She was dean of Barnard Col. (1911–47) and only woman member of U.S. delegation to the San Francisco Conference (1945).

gilds: see GUILDS.

Gilead (gĭl'ēăd), mountainous region, NE of Dead Sea; allotted to Reuben, Gad, and Manasseh. Noted for spices, myrrh, and balm. Also called Mt. Gilead and Land of Gilead.

Giles, William Branch (jīlz), 1762–1830, American statesman. Anti-Federalist U.S. Representative from Va. (1790–98, 1801–03); U.S. Senator (1804–15). Opposed Albert Gallatin and James Monroe.

Gilgamesh (gĭl'gŭmĕsh), hero of a Babylonian epic of c.3,000 lines written on 12 tablets. Tells of adventures of Gilgamesh, how he spurned Ishtar, how he wandered with his friend Enkidu (half bull and half man), and how he sought key to immortality possessed by Ut-napishtim, his ancestor.

Gill, Sir David (gĭl), 1843–1914, Scottish astronomer, astronomer royal of Cape of Good Hope (1879–1907); a leader in use of photography in star cataloguing.

Gill, Eric (Rowland), 1882–1940, English sculptor and wood engraver. Some of best work is religious sculpture. His books give his views on art and life.

gill (gĭl), respiratory organ of many aquatic animals. In fish, gill is chief respiratory organ throughout life. Blood in tiny vessels permeating gill filaments absorbs oxygen, releases carbon dioxide; filaments are attached to the outer edge of cartilaginous or bony branchial (or gill) arch. Projections from inner edge of arch are gill rakers; these are present except in fish eating whole fish or other large food and serve to strain food from water which enters mouth and leaves through gill clefts. Gills differing in structure are found in developing amphibians (also in adult of some forms), in mollusks, echinoderms, crustaceans, and aquatic insect larvae.

Gillette, William, 1853–1937, American actor and playwright. Permanently associated with *Sherlock Holmes* —play and stage character he created after Conan Doyle. Appeared also in Barrie plays.

Gillmore, Quincy Adams, 1825–88, Union general in Civil War. Known especially for service as commander of Dept. of the South (1863–64, 1865).

gillyflower: see STOCK; WALLFLOWER.

Gilman, Charlotte Perkins, 1860–1935, American feminist, reformer, and writer; great-granddaughter of Lyman Beecher. Edited *Forerunner.*

Gilman, Daniel Coit, 1831–1908, American educator. He helped to found Sheffield Scientific School at Yale. After serving 1872–75 as president of Univ. of California, he became first president (1875–1901) of Johns Hopkins Univ. He was president of Carnegie Inst. of Washington, 1902–4.

Gilmer, Thomas Walker, 1802–44, U.S. Secretary of the Navy (Feb., 1844). His death from gun explosion while on the *Princeton* with other government officials raised question of succession to presidency in event of wholesale death of public officials.

Gil Vicente: see VICENTE, GIL.

Gimbel, Adam, 1817–96, American merchant, founder of a family of merchants and philanthropists, b. Bavaria. His sons furthered the Gimbel department store business in Philadelphia, New York city, and many other cities.

gin, spirituous liquor distilled chiefly from fermented cereals and flavored with juniper berries. Types include London, sloe (flavored with sloes instead of juniper), dry (distilled several times).

ginger, tropical perennial plant (*Zingiber officinale*) and its rootstalk, a commercially important spice. It is marketed as preserved or green ginger, mostly in China, or as dried or cured ginger. It is used in cookery and medicine; the oil flavors ginger ale.

ginger ale, sweetened carbonated beverage flavored with ginger. Ginger beer is unrelated fermented drink brewed from ginger and bitter vegetables.

Ginkel, Godart van, 1st earl of Athlone (văn gĭng'kŭl, äthlōn'), 1630–1703, Dutch general in service of WILLIAM III of England. In War of Grand Alliance he was commander in chief in Ireland (1690–91); captured Ballymore and Athlone, defeated forces of James II at Aughrim, and took Limerick.

ginkgo (gĭngk'gō) or **maidenhair tree,** deciduous tree (*Ginkgo biloba*), with fan-shaped leaves. It is native to China but widely planted elsewhere for shade and ornament. It is a survivor of group of trees that existed in geologic times.

ginseng (jĭn'sĕng"), perennial herb (*Panax*) of North America and Asia. Asiatic ginseng (*Panax schinseng*) has long been prized by Chinese as a panacea. Demand for ginseng led to cultivation of a substitute for export, the American *P. quinquefolium*.

Gioberti, Vincenzo (vĕnchän'tsō jōbĕr'tē), 1801–52, Italian statesman; a priest and philosopher. Premier of Sardinia 1848–49. Advocated at first a federation of Italian states under papal arbitration; later a unified, constitutional monarchy.

Gioia or **Gioja, Melchiorre** (both: mälkyôr'rä jō'yä), 1767–1829, Italian economist, an early advocate of unification of Italy. An opponent of Adam Smith, he insisted on economic duty of the state.

Giolitti, Giovanni (jōvän'nē jōlēt'tē), 1842–1928, Italian premier (1892–93, 1903–5, 1906–9, 1911–14, 1920–21). A leftist but no Socialist, he favored labor unions, promoted social reform, opposed participation in World War I and Fascism.

Giono, Jean (zhä' jônō'), 1895–, French novelist. His novels, mostly laid in his native Provence, exalt the soil. They include *Colline* (1920; Eng. tr., *Hill of Destiny,* 1929) and *Regain* (1930; Eng. tr., *Harvest,* 1939). A short story, *The Baker's Wife,* was successfully filmed in 1938.

Giordano, Luca (lōō'kä jōrdä'nō), 1632–1705, Neapolitan painter, pupil of Ribera and Cortona. Executed frescoes in Naples, in Florence, and in Madrid and in Toledo.

Giordano, Umberto, 1867–1948, Italian composer of operas (e.g., *Andrea Chénier, Madame Sans-Gêne*).

Giorgio, Francesco di (fränchä'skō dē jōr'jō), 1439–1502, Italian artist, b. Siena. Paintings show influence of Filippo Lippi. Did sculpture for choir of Siena cathedral. Was also an engineer.

Giorgione (jôrjō′nā), c.1478–1510, Venetian painter, fellow student of Titian under Giovanni Bellini. A great innovator, he initiated fusion of forms and subordination of local color to the pervading tone. His works have luminous color and poetic sensibility. Extant works include *Concert champêtre* (Louvre) and *Venus and Cupid in a Landscape* (Natl. Gall., Washington, D.C.).

Giotto (jôt′tō), c.1266–c.1337, Florentine artist. Tremendously influenced course of European painting. Turned from Italo-Byzantine conventionalism to study of nature, achieving lifelike, expressive faces and illusion of movement. Tradition says he was a pupil of Cimabue. Undoubtedly influenced by naturalistic trend in sculpture begun by the Pisani and by Franciscan movement in religion. Earliest extant works are probably frescoes in Church of St. Francis, Assisi. Most famous works are the 38 biblical frescoes in Scrovegni (Arena) Chapel, Padua. Among many works attributed to him are frescoes in Church of Santa Croce, Florence. Succeeded Arnolfo di Cambio as chief architect of Santa Maria del Fiore, Florence; designed its richly decorated campanile.

Giovanni da Bologna: see BOLOGNA, GIOVANNI DA.

Giovanni delle Bande Nere: see MEDICI, GIOVANNI DE' (under MEDICI, *Younger line*).

giraffe (jǐrăf′), ruminant mammal (genus *Giraffa*) of Africa living in open country S of Sahara. The tallest animal, it may be 18 ft. from hoof to crown and can outrun most enemies. Its short horns are covered with skin and hair. It is protectively colored with large sandy to chestnut angular spots, closely spaced. It eats chiefly acacia and mimosa leaves, using extensible tongue and mobile lips; can live without water for long intervals.

Giralda (jǐräl′dù, Span. hēräl′dä), tower adjoining cathedral of Seville, Spain. Built 1163–84 as minaret for mosque which originally stood on cathedral's site. Converted 1568 into bell tower by addition of Renaissance superstructure (123 ft. high). Original Moorish section is 197 ft. high.

Girard, Stephen (jǐrärd′), 1750–1831, American merchant, banker, and philanthropist, b. France. A merchant in Philadelphia, he set up a bank, and helped finance U.S. in War of 1812. Bequeathed money to found Girard College, free educational institution for poor white orphan boys.

Girard, city (pop. 10,113), NE Ohio, on Mahoning R. and NW of Youngstown; settled c.1800. Mfg. of steel, leather goods, and metal products.

Girard College: see GIRARD, STEPHEN.

Giraud, Henri Honoré (ārē′ ônôrā′ zhērō′), 1879–1949, French general. Captured by Germans in both world wars, he escaped both times. After his second and more dramatic escape (1942), he landed with the Allies in N Africa, succeeded Darlan as high commissioner of French N and W Africa, and briefly was co-president, with his rival De GAULLE, of the French Committee of Natl. Liberation (1943). He was commander in chief of the Free French armed forces until April, 1944.

Giraudoux, Jean (zhä′ zhērōdoō′), 1882–1944, French novelist and dramatist. Among his novels are *Suzanne et le Pacifique* (1921) and *Siegfried et le Limousin* (1922; adapted into a play 1928). His plays include *Amphitryon 38* (1929) and *The Madwoman of Chaillot* (1945).

Girgenti, Italy: see AGRIGENTO.

Girl Scouts, organization founded 1912 at Savannah, Ga., by Mrs. Juliette Gordon Low (who had been a leader of Girl Guide troops in England), to promote good citizenship, sociability, and outdoor life among girls from 7 to 16.

Gironde (zhērōd′), department (4,141 sq. mi.; pop. 858,381), SW France, in Guienne; cap. Bordeaux. Includes Bordeaux wine region. Crossed by the **Gironde,** an estuary 40 mi. long and 3–7 mi. wide, formed by junction of Garonne and Dordogne rivers 12 mi. N of Bordeaux; great artery of wine trade.

Girondists (jǐrŏn′dǐsts), Fr. *Girondins,* group of moderate republicans in French Revolution; so called because early members were mostly deputies from Gironde dept. (1791). Among leaders were Brissot de Warville, Vergniaud, Condorcet, Dumouriez. In June, 1793, the Jacobin and Cordelier extremists expelled the Girondists from the Convention and had their leaders executed. The assassination of Marat by Charlotte Corday brought further persecution. Joined by the royalists, the Girondists rose in revolt in the provinces, but their efforts were drowned in blood.

Girtin, Thomas, 1775–1802, English water-colorist. He was among first to abandon the tinted drawing and to paint directly in water color.

Girton College (gûr′tùn), English college for women, founded (1869) at Hitchin, Hertfordshire, by Emily Davies. Moved (1873) to Cambridge. Recognized as a college of CAMBRIDGE UNIVERSITY in 1948.

Girty, Simon (gûr′tē), 1741–1818, American frontiersman, known as the white renegade. Joined British in 1778. Led or participated in many savage Indian raids; known for his cruelty.

Gissing, George, 1857–1903, English author. His novels (best known is *New Grub Street,* 1891) were influenced by Dickens and the French naturalists. Wrote semiautobiographical *Private Papers of Henry Ryecroft* (1903).

Gist, Christopher (gǐst), c.1706–1759, American frontiersman. Explored Ohio valley region for Ohio Co. (1750). Served as guide on Braddock's expedition (1755).

Giulio Romano (joō′lyō rōmä′nō), c.1492–1546, Italian artist, whose real name was Giulio Pippi. Favorite pupil of Raphael, some of whose Vatican frescoes he completed. Architect to duke of Mantua (1524) and briefly of St. Peter's. Sometimes called the first academic painter.

Giusti, Giuseppe (joōzĕp′pä joō′stē), 1809–50, Italian poet and patriot. His satires (notably the lyrical "Saint Ambrose") were generally nationalistic.

Gizeh or **Giza** (both: gē′zù), market town (pop. 68,520), Egypt, on the Nile opposite Cairo. Pyramid of Khufu (Cheops) and Great Sphinx are near by.

Gjellerup, Karl Adolf (yĕ′lùroŏp), 1857–1919, Danish poet and novelist. Early novels are largely autobiographical; later writings show influence of Buddhism. Shared with Henrik Pontoppidan the 1917 Nobel Prize in Literature.

Glace Bay (glās), coal-mining town (pop. 25,586), Cape Breton Isl., N.S., Canada, on NE coast. Good harbor and large fishing fleet.

glacial periods (glā′shùl), times in past geologic history when owing to excessively cold climate great ice sheets extended over the land. Most recent ice invasion occurred in PLEISTOCENE. See table, pp. 370–71.

glacier, slowly moving ice mass formed from accumulated snow. Chief types are valley, piedmont, and continental. Valley glaciers are ice tongues which start in mountain snow fields and follow stream valleys. A piedmont glacier forms when valley glaciers unite. Greenland and Antarctica now have the only continental ice sheets (see PLEISTOCENE EPOCH). Ice is an important agent of erosion and transportation, having shaped the present topography of Canada and much of N U.S.

Glacier Bay National Monument: see NATIONAL PARKS AND MONUMENTS (table).

Glacier National Park: see NATIONAL PARKS AND MONUMENTS (table).

Glackens, William (James), 1870–1938, American landscape and genre painter and illustrator. First exhibited with The EIGHT. His work shows influence of French impressionists.

Gladewater, city (pop. 5,305), E Texas, W of Shreveport, La. and near Sabine R. Boomed after 1930 discovery of East Texas oil field.

gladiolus (glădēō′lùs), tender cormous-rooted plant

(*Gladiolus*), native to Africa. It has sword-shaped leaves and long stalks of flowers of many pastel as well as vivid colors.

Gladkov, Feodor Vasilyevich (fyô'dùr vŭsē'lyùvĭch glŭtkôf'), 1883–, Russian author. Won fame with novel *Cement* (1926; Eng. tr., 1929), describing post-revolution reconstruction.

Gladstone, William Ewart, 1809–98, British statesman, dominant personality of the Liberal Party 1868–94. As chancellor of exchequer (1852–55, 1859–66), he promoted free trade and fairer tax distribution. Was prime minister four times—1868–74, 1880–85, 1886, 1892–94. A man of no fixed political principles, he achieved notable reforms—Irish land act, changes in civil service, vote by ballot, abolition of the sale of army commissions, parliamentary reform, and educational expansion. Constant advocacy of Irish HOME RULE ended his last ministry. He was a great orator and a master of finance.

Glamis (glämz; in Shakspere glä'mĭs), parish and village, Angus, Scotland. Macbeth was thane of Glamis; castle here wrongly claimed as scene of Duncan's murder. Birthplace of Elizabeth, queen consort of George VI.

Glamorganshire (glùmôr'gùnshĭr) or **Glamorgan,** maritime county (813 sq. mi.; pop. 1,201,989), S Wales, on Bristol Channel; co. seat Cardiff. Has rich coal deposits in N, dairy farming and cattle grazing on coastal plain. Great mineral wealth (iron and copper) make it one of chief industrial areas of British Isles. Severe industrial depression struck area in 1920s; conditions now improved. Cardiff and Swansea important ports.

gland, organ which forms a SECRETION from material extracted by its cells from body fluids. Varies from single cell to many cells, or system of tubes uniting into a duct (e.g., salivary glands, breast, liver). Hormones, secretions of endocrine or ductless glands (e.g., thyroid, adrenals), are taken up directly by blood. Some glands (e.g., liver, testis) produce both a hormone and a secretion which flows from a duct.

glanders, chronic bacterial disease (*Pfeifferella mallei*) of horses and other animals, which also attacks man. There are various forms but all cause lesions in the lungs. When the disease infects skin tissue, it is known as farcy.

Glarus (glä'rùs), canton (264 sq. mi.; pop. 37,674), central Switzerland, S of the Wallensee; cap. Glarus (pop. 5,695). Mountainous and pastoral; hydroelectrical and textile industries. Glarus joined Swiss Confederation 1352. Inhabitants are mainly German-speaking Protestants.

Glasgow, Ellen (gläs'gō), 1874–1945, American novelist, b. Va. Among her realistic novels are *Barren Ground* (1925), *The Romantic Comedians* (1926), and *Vein of Iron* (1935). *A Certain Measure* (1943) contains her critical prefaces.

Glasgow (gläs'gō, –kō), independent burgh (pop. 1,089,-555), Scotland, on the Clyde. Largest city in Scotland, it is mostly in Lanarkshire but partly in Renfrewshire and Dumbartonshire. Most important seaport of Scotland, it has huge shipyards. Other industries include tanning, weaving, brass casting, and many manufactures. Has art museums and Univ. of Glasgow, founded 1451, whose undergraduates wear short red gowns.

Glasgow. 1 City (pop. 7,025), S Ky., E of Bowling Green. Trade center for agr., timber, and oil area with mfg. of clothing and food products. **2** City (pop. 3,821), NE Mont., on Milk R. and near Fort Peck Dam, in Milk R. project.

Glaspell, Susan (gläs'pěl), 1882–1948, American writer. A novelist, she became interested in the Provincetown Players (after her marriage to George Cram Cook) and wrote plays (e.g., *Alison's House*, 1930).

Glass, Carter, 1858–1946, U.S. Secretary of the Treasury (1918–20), U.S. Senator from Va. (1920–46). Active in framing of Federal Reserve System.

Glass, Hugh, fl. 1822–33, trapper in American West. Experience while on expedition in Missouri river country of being mauled by a grizzly bear, left for dead, and dragging himself 100 mi. to Fort Kiowa is told in John G. Neihardt's *Song of Hugh Glass.*

glass, hard substance, usually brittle and transparent. Its composition varies but it is commonly made chiefly of silicates, an alkali (usually soda or potash), and lime (as stabilizer), fused at high temperatures. Materials are boiled down, skimmed, and cooled; then molten glass (called metal) is ladled or poured into molds and pressed, or is blown (sometimes into molds), or is drawn. Shaped glass is annealed—usually by carrying it on rollers through annealing ovens (lehrs). Most common hollow vessels (e.g., light bulbs) are machine blown but much fine ware is still made by glass blowers using blowpipes. Methods of decoration include cutting, copper-wheel engraving, etching with hydrofluoric acid, enameling, gilding, and painting. Sheet glass is drawn into sheets by a continuous process; plate glass is rolled, ground, and polished; safety glass is made of plate glass so tempered that it crumbles when broken or it is laminated (two or more sheets are cemented by a plastic that prevents it from scattering if broken). Glass can be drawn into continuous filaments (fiber glass) or produced in short staple fibers (glass wool). Other forms include foam glass, glass blocks, and polaroid glass. Glass is used in architecture, illumination, electrical transmission, and for making instruments, spectacles, utensils, and containers. Many art treasures are fashioned in glass. First glass objects made by man were of natural glass such as obsidian and rock crystal. Manufactured glass dates from prehistoric times in Far East, India, and Egypt, but its place and date of origin are unknown. The art spread to Europe and the Romans were especially skilled in it. After the time of the Crusades Venice, Bohemia, France, and England, in turn, became noted for special kinds of glass. In America Sandwich glass (made 1825–88) became widely known. The glass-pressing machine (invented c.1827) brought about great changes in the industry. See also STAINED GLASS.

Glassboro, borough (pop. 5,867), SW N.J., S of Camden. Farm trade center with glassworks.

Glassport, borough (pop. 8,707), SW Pa., on Monongahela R. and SSE of Pittsburgh. Produces glass, steel, and refined oil.

glass snake, legless burrowing lizard of genus *Ophisaurus* of S and central U.S. It averages c.2 ft. long; shiny body is gray or greenish brown, sometimes striped, above; the sides are darker with light lines; ventral surface is whitish. Its long tail breaks easily from body; new, usually shorter, tail without real backbone grows to replace it. The glass snake has eyelids, ear openings, broad tongue; eats insects, worms, and small snakes.

Glastonbury, municipal borough (pop. 5,081), Somersetshire, England. Place of many legends. One tells that Joseph of Arimathea founded England's first Christian church here. He rested his staff, which rooted and grew into Glastonbury thorn. Another says Glastonbury is Isle of Avalon of Arthurian legend. Abbey dates from 8th cent.

Glastonbury, town (pop. 8,818), central Conn., on Connecticut R. below Hartford. Textiles, metals.

Glatz (gläts), Pol. *Kłodzko,* city (pop. 22,814), Lower Silesia, on Glatzer Neisse R., transferred to Polish administration 1945. Was cap. of a county created 1462. The **Glatzer Gebirge** (glä'tsùr gùbĭrgù), a range of the Sudetes, rises to 4,672 ft. at Czech border. For **Glatzer Neisse R.,** see NEISSE.

Glauber's salt, hydrated sodium sulphate, a compound of sodium, sulphur, and oxygen, with 10 molecules of water. On exposure to air it effloresces (gives up water of crystallization). It is used as a mild laxative. It was named for Johann Rudolf Glauber (1604–68), German alchemist.

glaucoma (glôkō′mù), eye disease marked by increased pressure within eyeball and often resulting in impaired vision or blindness.

Glaucus (glô′kùs), in Greek legend, sea-god who loved SCYLLA.

Glazunov, Aleksandr (Konstantinovich) (ŭlyĭksändr′ gläzoo′nôf), 1865–1936, Russian composer. He wrote eight symphonies, a piano and a violin concerto, ballets (e.g., *Raymonda, The Seasons*), and chamber music.

Gleiwitz (glī′vĭts) Pol. *Gliwice*, city (pop. c.128,200), Upper Silesia, transferred to Polish administration 1945. It is a center of the KATOWICE mining region.

Gleizes, Albert Léon (älbĕr′ lāō′ glēz′), 1881–, French cubist painter and illustrator.

Glencoe (glĕn′kō), residential village (pop. 6,980), NE Ill., N suburb of Chicago.

Glencoe (glĕnkō′), valley of Coe R., Argyllshire, Scotland, overhung by lofty mountains. Macdonald clan massacred here by the Campbells in 1692.

Glen Cove, city (pop. 15,130), SE N.Y., on N shore of Long Isl., in summer resort area; settled 1668. Mfg. of office supplies, clothing, and radios.

Glendale. 1 City (pop. 8,179), S central Ariz., NW of Phoenix. Agr. trade point in SALT RIVER VALLEY. **2** Suburban city (pop. 95,702), S Calif., N of Los Angeles; laid out 1886 on site of first Spanish land grant in Calif. Mfg. of petroleum products, aircraft, and glass. Has Forest Lawn Memorial Park, cemetery containing reproductions of great works of art.

Glendale, battle of: see SEVEN DAYS BATTLES.

Glendive (glĕn′dīv), city (pop. 5,254), E Mont., on Yellowstone R. and NE of Miles City. Center of farm, stock, and poultry area. Has railroad shops.

Glendower: see OWEN GLENDOWER.

Glen Echo, resort town (pop. 356), W central Md., near Potomac R. Clara Barton had house near by.

Glen Ellyn, residential village (pop. 9,524), NE Ill., W suburb of Chicago.

Glenolden, borough (pop. 6,450), SE Pa., SW suburb of Philadelphia. Mfg. of pharmaceuticals.

Glen Ridge, suburban residential borough (pop. 7,620), NE N.J., NW of Newark.

Glen Rock, borough (pop. 7,145), NE N.J., SW of Ridgewood.

Glens Falls, city (pop. 19,610), E N.Y., on Hudson R. (water power) and N of Saratoga Springs; settled 1763. Has paper and lumber mills, makes clothing and food and metal products. Birthplace of C. E. Hughes.

Glenview, residential village (pop. 6,142), NE Ill., N suburb of Chicago.

Glenwood Springs, city (pop. 2,412), NW Colo., on Colorado R. Mineral springs resort.

glider, engineless aircraft similar to airplane, using gravity and natural air currents to obtain forward motion. Otto Lilienthal demonstrated (1890–96) superiority of curved over flat surfaces. Other pioneers: Percy Pilcher, England; Henri Farman, France; Octave Chanute and John J. Montgomery, U.S. Chanute first used movable plane parts to obtain stable flight. Wright brothers added landing skids. Troop-transport gliders towed by airplane were used for World War II invasions.

Glière, Reinhold (Moritzovich) (rīn′hŏlt glēēr′), 1875–, Russian composer. His music is nationalistic. Most popular of his many works are the ballet *The Red Poppy* and the Third Symphony, *Ilya Mourometz.*

Glinka, Mikhail (Ivanovich) (mēkhŭyĕl glǐn′kä), 1804–57, first of the Russian nationalist composers. Known for his operas, *A Life for the Tsar* and *Russlan and Ludmilla.*

Glittertind, mountain of Norway: see JOTUNHEIM.

Gliwice, Upper Silesia: see GLEIWITZ.

Globe, city (pop. 6,419), E Ariz., near Pinal Mts., in mining, ranching area; settled 1876. Built by silver boom, it then became big copper center, later (c.1918) superseded by Miami, Ariz.

globe, spherical body used to illustrate the earth (terrestrial globe) or sky (celestial globe). Terrestrial globe represents sizes and shapes of continents without distortion of shape, mistakes in relative area, or inaccuracy of angles and direction, except that while globes are spheres, earth's equatorial diameter exceeds the polar one by 27 mi. Probably oldest globe was made by Crates, Greek geographer, 2d cent. B.C. First modern globes made by Martin Behaim (1492), by Leonardo da Vinci soon after. On celestial globes star positions correspond to actual ones on sky; if globe is in correct position a line drawn from its center to any star on surface, if extended, focuses actual star.

globe amaranth, annual plant (*Gomphrena globosa*) with chaffy dome-shaped flowers in various colors. Used as an EVERLASTING.

globeflower, perennial (*Trollius*) of N temperate regions with white, yellow, orange, or purple blooms, similar to buttercups but larger.

Globe Theatre, London playhouse, built 1598. Most of Shakspere's plays were first presented there. Puritans destroyed it in 1644.

glockenspiel: see PERCUSSION INSTRUMENTS.

Glogau (glō′gou), Pol. *Głogów*, town (1939 pop. 33,-500; 1946 pop. 1,681), Lower Silesia, on the Oder; transferred to Polish administration 1945. Cap. of principality of Glogau under Piast dynasty (1249–1506); under Bohemian suzerainty from 1331; passed to Prussia 1745. Destroyed in World War II.

Glomma (glō′mä), chief river of Norway, rising in highlands S of Trondheim Fjord and flowing c.375 mi. S into the Skagerrak. Large falls at Sarpsborg furnish power for industrial concentration.

Gloria in excelsis (ĕksĕl′sĭs) [Latin,= glory in the highest], the *Angelic Hymn* or greater doxology, anc. Christian hymn; an amplification of Luke 2.14. In the Roman Mass it follows the *Kyrie;* in Anglican communion it is just before the benediction. Omitted from both services at certain seasons.

Glorious Revolution, in English history, the events of the years 1688–89 resulting in deposition of JAMES II. His overt Catholicism and the birth of a Catholic heir united Tories and Whigs in opposition. Seven nobles invited William of Orange and his consort Mary, Protestant daughter of James, to come to England's aid. After Bloodless Revolution they ruled jointly as WILLIAM III and Mary II. Their acceptance of the BILL OF RIGHTS showed final ascendancy of parliament over "divine right of kings."

glory lily, tropical tuberous-rooted climbing plant (*Gloriosa*), with lilylike yellow and red flowers.

Gloucester, Gilbert de Clare, earl of: see GLOUCESTER, RICHARD DE CLARE, 7TH EARL OF.

Gloucester, Humphrey, duke of (glô′stùr), 1391–1447, English nobleman; son of Henry IV. Fought for his brother (Henry V) in France and served (1420–21) as regent of England during Henry's absence. After the accession of the infant Henry VI, he was powerful in the regency and (after 1435) heir to the throne. His influence waned and in 1447 he was arrested on charges of plotting Henry's death. He died in custody. A patron of Oxford Univ., his gift of books formed nucleus of the Bodleian Library.

Gloucester, Richard de Clare, 7th earl of, 1222–62, English nobleman. He vacillated between support of Henry III and baronial party. Gloucester and his rival, Simon de MONTFORT, were most powerful political figures of the time. His son, **Gilbert de Clare, 8th earl of Gloucester,** 1243–95, was first a leader of the barons under Simon de Montfort. Henry III surrendered to him (1264) after the battle of Lewes. He later aided the accession of Edward I (1272) and married (1290) Edward's daughter. His son, **Gilbert de Clare, 9th earl of Gloucester,** 1291–1314, was several times regent of England and was killed at Bannockburn.

Gloucester, Robert, earl of, d. 1147, English nobleman; illegitimate son of Henry I. Earldom created c.1121 for him. Refused to claim throne at his father's death (1135) and supported STEPHEN. Later quarreled with him, declared for MATILDA (Robert's half-sister), and was leader of the Angevin party.

Gloucester, Thomas of Woodstock, duke of, 1355–97, English nobleman; seventh son of Edward III. Was a leader (1388) of baronial opposition to his nephew, RICHARD II. Made peace with the king (1389), but later intrigues caused his arrest and conviction for treason. Richard probably had him killed.

Gloucester, England: see GLOUCESTERSHIRE.

Gloucester (glŏ'stŭr), city (pop. 25,167), NE Mass., on Cape Ann, at head of Gloucester Harbor; settled 1623. Fishing (for over three cent.) and fish-processing center. Summer resort and artists' colony since late 19th cent. Hammond Mus. has art collections. Bronze *Fisherman* is memorial to Gloucestermen lost at sea.

Gloucester City, city (pop. 14,357), SW N.J., on Delaware R.; settled 1682 by Friends. Mfg. of asbestos, cork and paper products, and chemicals.

Gloucestershire or **Gloucester** (glŏ'stŭrshĭr), county (1,255 sq. mi.; pop. 938,618), W England. Includes Cotswold Hills (sheep grazing) in E; fertile Severn valley (dairy farming) in center; and Forest of Dean in W. Mfg. centered around Bristol. Rich in ecclesiastical remains. County seat is **Gloucester,** county borough (pop. 67,268), on Severn R., an industrial city and site of a cathedral.

Gloversville, city (pop. 23,634), E central N.Y., N of Johnstown. Glove-mfg. center since early 19th century; other leather goods, and textiles.

glowworm, name for luminescent larva and wingless female of certain beetles or fireflies chiefly of families Lampyridae and Phengodidae. Common European glowworm is wingless female of beetle *Lampyris noctiluca;* cells of abdominal segments emit greenish light.

gloxinia, tuberous-rooted Brazilian plant (*Sinningia speciosa*), with richly colored bell-shaped flowers and velvety foliage. It is grown as a summer pot plant.

glucinum: see BERYLLIUM.

Gluck, Alma (glook), 1884–1938, American soprano, b. Rumania. Sang at Metropolitan Opera, New York, 1909–1912, and afterwards in concerts. One of the first singers to make phonograph records.

Gluck, Christoph Willibald von (krĭs'tôf vĭ'lēbält), 1714–87, operatic composer, b. Bavaria, studied in Prague and Italy. His early operas were in Italian tradition. With *Orfeo ed Euridice* (1762) he began his reform of opera, giving greater unity to text and music and eliminating meaningless coloratura in arias. To Ranieri Calzabigi, librettist of *Orfeo* and of *Alceste* (1767) he credited much of his new operatic style. *Iphigénie en Tauride* (1779) is considered his masterpiece.

glucose, dextrose, or **grape sugar.** Commonly *glucose* is term for sweet sirupy liquid (called corn sirup), really a mixture. Chemically *glucose* indicates d-glucose, dextroglucose, or dextrose, a white, crystalline solid carbohydrate found in fruit juices. There are a number of forms with the same formula (6 carbon atoms; 12, hydrogen; 6, oxygen), differing in arrangement or optical properties. Presence of glucose is shown by FEHLING'S SOLUTION.

glue: see ADHESIVE.

gluten (glōo'tŭn), albuminous substance, tough, elastic, almost tasteless, found in northern wheat.

glycerin, glycerine, or **glycerol,** colorless, odorless liquid ALCOHOL, used in perfume, cosmetics, some inks, explosives, antifreeze mixtures, and in medicine. It is a by-product of soapmaking.

glycogen (glī'kŭjĕn), form of carbohydrate stored in animal cells; also called animal starch. It is made of d-glucose molecules. Some animal cells convert glucose into glycogen for storage. It resembles plant starch in physical properties.

Glycon: see FARNESE HERCULES.

Glyndebourne Festivals (glīn'bôrn), operatic festivals, begun 1934 in Sussex, England. First few devoted to Mozart; later other composers included. Became a second Salzburg during World War II.

Glyptothek (glüp"tōtāk'), museum in Munich, founded by Louis I of Bavaria. Designed by Leo von Klenze, built 1816–30. Destroyed in World War II, but collection (ancient and modern sculptures) was saved.

Gnadenhutten (jĭnä'dŭnhŭ"tŭn), village (pop. 895), E central Ohio, on Tuscarawas R. and W of Steubenville. State park marks site of Gnadenhutten massacre (1782) of 96 Christian Indians by white men.

gnat (năt), name for various small flies of order Diptera. BLACK FLY is pest to humans and most other warm-blooded animals. Several fungus gnat species injure mushrooms and various greenhouse plants. Potato scab gnat bores through tubers; gall gnats and midges damage plants.

Gneisenau, August, Graf Neithardt von (ou'goost gräf' nīt'härt fŭn gŭnī'zŭnou), 1760–1831, Prussian field marshal. Won fame in Napoleonic Wars for his defense of Kolberg (1807); was Blücher's chief of staff 1813–15.

gneiss (nīs), rock which shows alternating light and dark bands. Usually it is metamorphosed granite.

Gneist, Rudolf von (rōo'dôlf fŭn gŭnīst'), 1816–95, German jurist. Tried to reform the Prussian constitution and to make administration a cooperative function of citizens, local officials, and central administration.

Gnesen, Poland: see GNIEZNO.

Gniezno (gŭnyĕz'nô), Ger. *Gnesen,* town (pop. 30,-292), Poland, NE of Poznan. Legendary cradle and first cap. of Polish nation; metropolitan see of Poland from 1000 (transferred to Poznan 1821). Under Prussian rule 1793–1919.

Gnosticism (nŏs'tĭsĭzŭm) [from Greek *gnosis* = knowledge], religious and philosophical movement, arising in the Hellenistic era. Its fundamental doctrine was that salvation is to be obtained through knowledge rather than through faith or good works. Gnostics generally accepted a strong dualism of good and evil and adopted many magical practices. Some Jewish sects (the Essenes and Therapeutae), affected by Gnosticism, rejected the Old Testament idea of God as Righteousness and substituted that of Divine Wisdom. Early Christian Gnostics rejected the Jewish foundations of Christianity and the Old Testament. Redemption through Wisdom (Sophia) was the basis of the complex doctrines of Valentinus and other 2d cent. Gnostics. They divided men into three classes: the Gnostics, sure of salvation; non-Gnostic Christians who might be saved through faith in Christ; and all others, who are incapable of salvation. Gnosticism merged with MANICHAEISM. The MANDAEANS are the only surviving Gnostic sect. The movement had a great effect on early Christianity by forcing the new religion to define doctrines in declaring Gnosticism heretical. Present knowledge of the movement is based on Coptic texts and wisdom literature of the PSEUDEPIGRAPHA.

gnu (nōo), S African antelope resembling the ox. White-tailed gnu (genus *Connochaetes*) or black wildebeest is believed extinct in wild state. It is dark brown or blackish; long hair tufts stand erect on muzzle, and hang from throat and between forelegs; the broad head has horns and an upright mane. Males stand c.4 ft. high at the shoulder. Brindled gnu (genus *Gorgon* or *Connochaetes*) or blue wildebeest exists in small herds; it is bluish gray with brown on the sides, larger than the white-tailed gnu and with a narrower head.

Goa (gō'ù), district (1,348 sq. mi.; pop. 540,925) of Portuguese India, on coast of Bombay. Founded by Afonso de Albuquerque. Its original cap., Old Goa, is site of St. Francis Xavier's tomb. Present cap., Pangim or New Goa (pop. 14,213), is also cap. of

Portuguese India (which includes Damão and Diu).

goat, ruminant animal with hollow horns, related to sheep. Probably it was domesticated in Persia from wild bezoar goat or pasan. True goats belong to genus *Capra,* family Bovidae; they are raised for milk, wool, flesh. Milk goats are common in Old World and are increasing in U.S.

Goat Island, N.Y.: see NIAGARA FALLS.

goatsbeard, tall perennial plant (*Aruncus sylvester*), with handsome spikes of small white flowers. The unrelated purple goatsbeard, better known as salsify or oyster plant (*Tragopogon porrifolius*), is grown as a vegetable for its edible roots.

Gobelins, Manufacture nationale des (gōbùlĕ′), state-controlled tapestry manufactory in Paris. Founded as dye works in mid-15th cent. by brothers, Gilles and Jehan Gobelin. Purchased 1662 by Louis XIV. Famous Gobelin tapestries include the set based on Raphael's frescoes in Vatican.

Gobi (gō′bē), Mandarin *Sha-mo,* sandy desert, area 500,000 sq. mi., in China and Mongolia; average alt. c.3,000 ft. Winds have stripped off most of its soil. Small number of pastoral Mongols inhabit scanty grasslands. Many paleontological finds have been made here.

Gobineau, Joseph Arthur, comte de (zhōzĕf′ ärtür′ kōt′ dù gōbēnō′), 1816–82, French author and diplomat. *The Inequality of Human Races* (1853–55; Eng. tr., 1915) was an early and influential attempt at proving the supremacy of the "Nordic race."

God, the divinity of the great monotheistic religions, Judaism, Christianity, and Islam. In the Old Testament the most celebrated form of his name was the ineffable (not to be spoken) name represented by the four letters transcribed as YHWH (the tetragrammaton). The origin of this is unknown; the reconstruction *Jehovah* is mistaken, and the form *Yahweh* is not now widely accepted. Because the name was ineffable the Hebrews used substitutes such as *Adonai* [my Lord] and *Elohim* (a plural form). *El* is not related to *Elohim* but is connected with *Allah,* used by Arabs (Moslem and Christian) as the name for God. The general conception of God in all three religions is that of a Being infinite, all powerful, all good, all creating, all knowing, loving but judging mankind, transcendent over and immanent in the world. He is often treated as a personality, though not necessarily in an anthropomorphic sense. The 19th-cent. rationalists argued that the Hebrew God was originally simply the chief of many gods and that He absorbed the attributes of His fellow divinities. Gradually He was considered as more and more powerful until He became the one God (though still preferring the Hebrews). In recent times in the Western world the term God has come to be applied to any overriding universal concept (such as the world soul or the Absolute). Scholasticism produced several demonstrations of the existence of God that are still current. One is the argument from First Cause: every effect in the world has its cause but this chain must lead back to the primary cause of the whole existing universe, which must have been itself both cause and effect (i.e., God). The cosmological argument is that the relations extant in the world must have their base in some independent, absolute existence (God), since all that is in the world is relative. The teleological argument is that the world operates on a great plan and toward set ends; therefore a master planner (God) must exist. The ontological argument is that since the human mind can reach the highest conception, which is God, that conception must have existence, for if not there could be a higher conception—one including existence. In the Western world the word god written without a capital letter is used for all the gods of polytheism (see MYTH).

Goddard, Henry Herbert, 1866–, American psychologist, director of research (1906–18), Training School for Feeble-Minded Children, Vineland, N.J. He is noted for systematic hereditary studies, especially for *The Kallikak Family* (1912).

Goderich (gŏd′rĭch), town (pop. 4,934), S Ont., Canada, on L. Huron, NW of London. Farming and fishing center and lake port with grain elevators, saltworks, flour and lumber mills.

Godesberg, Germany: see BAD GODESBERG.

Godey, Louis Antoine (gō′dē), 1804–78, American publisher of *Godey's Lady's Book.*

Godfrey of Bouillon (boōyō′), c.1058–1100, duke of Lower Lorraine, leader of First Crusade. Elected king of Jerusalem, which he helped capture, but took title "protector of the Holy Sepulchre." His brother Baldwin succeeded him.

Godhavn (gôdh′houn), settlement (pop. 319), W Greenland, on S shore of Disko isl. Administrative center of N Greenland. Fishing base.

Godiva, Lady (gōdī′vù), fl. c.1040–1080, wife of Leofric, earl of Mercia and lord of Coventry. Legends claim she rode naked through the town to get her husband to lower heavy taxes of the people. The only man who looked became known as Peeping Tom.

Godkin, E(dwin) L(awrence), 1831–1902, American editor, b. Ireland. His fearless and perceptive criticism made the *Nation* and the New York *Evening Post,* which he edited, influential in reform.

Godolphin, Sidney Godolphin, 1st earl of, 1645–1712, English statesman. By financial ability as lord treasurer aided victories of Marlborough (with whom he was politically associated after marriage of their children). Queen Anne dismissed him in 1710.

Godoy, Manuel de (mänwäl′ dā gōdoi′), 1767–1851, Spanish statesman. Favorite of Queen MARÍA LUISA; chief minister to CHARLES IV after 1793. Favored war on revolutionary France, but made peace 1795. *Príncipe de la Paz* [prince of the peace] was one of many titles showered on him. The corruption of his regime and his increasing subservience to France led to his overthrow by Ferdinand VII (1808).

God Save the King (or Queen), English national anthem. Both words and music of uncertain origin. Tune probably evolved from folk and plain song elements; present tune (often ascribed to Henry Carey) and words appeared in 1745. See also AMERICA.

Godthaab (gôt′hôp), town (pop. 970), cap. of S Greenland and of Godthaab dist. (pop. 1,962); a port on Godthaab Fjord of SW Greenland. Founded 1721 by Hans Egede, it was first Danish colony in Greenland. Has U.S. and Canadian consulates.

Godunov, Boris (būrĕs′ gŭdoōnôf′), c.1551–1605, tsar of Russia (1598–1605). A favorite of Ivan IV, he ruled Russia as regent during reign of Feodor I (1584–98). He probably had Feodor's brother DMITRI murdered (1591). Chosen successor to Feodor, Boris ruled capably but lost popular support. He died during the false Dmitri's invasion of Russia. His son, Feodor II, lost his throne to the impostor. Boris's life is the subject of a drama by Pushkin, basis of Moussorgsky's opera.

Godwin or **Godwine** (both: gŏd′wĭn), d. 1053, English statesman. Earl of Wessex, he was chief adviser to Canute and most powerful earl in England. After king's death he supported claims to throne of Harthacanute. Opposed the French favorites of Harthacanute's successor, Edward the Confessor, and was exiled (1051). Invaded England (1052) and regained his former importance.

Godwin, Mary: see WOLLSTONECRAFT, MARY.

Godwin, William, 1756–1836, English author and political philosopher. His materialism pervaded his anarchistic tract, *An Enquiry concerning the Principles of Political Justice and Its Influence on General Virtue and Happiness* (1793) and also his novel *The Adventures of Caleb Williams* (1794). In 1797 he married Mary Wollstonecraft. Their daughter, Mary, became wife of SHELLEY.

Godwin-Austen, Mount, or **K2,** peak, 28,250 ft. high, Kashmir, in Karakorum range; second highest in world.

Godwine: see GODWIN (d. 1053).

Goebbels, (Paul) Joseph (poul' yō'zĕf gû'bŭls), 1897–1945, German National Socialist (Nazi) propaganda minister (1933–45), an able orator and writer. Worked on principles of self-justification of power and inculcating "the big lie" by varied repetition. Died by suicide when Berlin was being conquered.

Goering or **Göring, Hermann Wilhelm** (hĕr'män vĭl'hĕlm gû'rĭng), 1893–1946, German National Socialist (Nazi) leader. An air force hero of World War I, he joined the party early. President of the Reichstag from 1932, he became in 1933 air minister for Germany and Prussian premier. He founded the Gestapo (secret police), which he headed until 1936; directed German economy with dictatorial powers, 1937–43 (invented slogan "guns instead of butter"); was designated by Hitler as successor (1939). Also boasted such unique titles as "imperial marshal" and "imperial master of the hunt." In World War II he was responsible for initiating total air war. Excessively fond of pomp and pageantry, he amassed fabulous wealth and art collection. Surrendered to U.S. troops 1945. Chief defendant at Nuremberg war crimes trial (1945–46); sentenced to death but took poison before scheduled hanging.

Goes, Hugo van der (hōō'gō vän dĕr gōōs'), d. 1482, Flemish painter. Realism and rich detail mark portraits and Portinari altarpiece (Uffizi).

Goethals, George Washington (gō'thŭlz), 1858–1928, U.S. army engineer. Chief engineer of Panama Canal (1907–14). Governor of Canal Zone (1914–16).

Goethe, Johann Wolfgang von (yō'hän vôlf'gäng fŭn gû'tŭ), 1749–1832, German poet, dramatist, novelist. His universal genius also embraced other fields, notably science. After a happy childhood in Frankfurt, he studied law at Leipzig and later at Strasbourg, where he came under the spell of the STURM UND DRANG movement. In 1773 he won recognition with his drama *Götz von Berlichingen* (see BERLICHINGEN, GÖTZ VON). While a lawyer at Wetzlar (1772), he fell unhappily in love with Charlotte Buff; he overcame his despair by writing *The Sorrows of Young Werther* (1774), an epistolary novel of morbid sensitiveness. It made him famous overnight. In 1775 he accepted an invitation to the court of Charles Augustus, duke of Saxe-Weimar, where he remained for the rest of his life. For 10 years he served the duke as chief minister. Goethe's first trip to Italy (1786–88) fired his enthusiasm for the classical ideal. His drama *Egmont* (1788) still shows traces of *Sturm und Drang*, but the drama *Iphigenie auf Tauris* (1779, rewritten 1787), *Römische Elegien* (1788), and the domestic epic *Hermann und Dorothea* (1797) are pure products of classicism. His two great novels, *Wilhelm Meisters Lehrjahre* (1796) and *Die Wahlverwandtschaften* [elective affinities] (1809), aside from their intrinsic merit, showed the way for the German novel of character development and the German psychological novel. His friendship with Schiller, begun in 1794, had a stimulating effect on both men. In 1808 he published the first part of his life work, FAUST, completed shortly before his death. Increasingly aloof in his old age, Goethe became more and more the Olympian divinity, to whose shrine at Weimar all Europe flocked. Literary products of his later years include *Dichtung und Wahrheit* (1811–33), his charming autobiography, and *Westöstlicher Diwan* (1819), a collection of exquisite lyrics inspired by readings of Persian poets. Goethe attached equal importance to his scientific and his poetic work. His discovery of the intermaxillary bone in man (1784) was important to the theory of evolution; his work in botany showed great intuitive insight; his *Zur Farbenlehre* (1810) was a stubborn attack on Newton's theory of light. His philosophy, greatly influenced by Spinoza, was a mystic pantheism. Most of his best-known works have been translated into English, as have been many of his lyrics and ballads.

Gog, leader who, according to prophecy, will come from land of Magog, attack Israel, and be defeated. Ezek. 38–39. Rev. 20.8 warns of Gog and Magog.

Gogarty, Oliver St. John (gō'gŭrtē), 1878–, Irish wit, a surgeon. In youth a friend of James Joyce, he has since written much criticism of him.

Gogebic (gōgē'bĭk), range, c.80 mi. long, extending W from W Upper Peninsula, N Mich., into N Wis. Known for its iron content.

Gogh, Vincent van (văn gō', Dutch, vĭnsĕnt' vän khôkh'), 1853–90, postimpressionist painter, b. Netherlands. Decided to become a painter only 10 years before his death. His early pictures were dark, but after moving in 1886 to Paris, where he met Pissarro, Degas, and Gauguin, he began to paint the brilliantly colored and dynamic pictures that later made him famous. Despite periodic fits of insanity he succeeded in producing numerous, now-popular works.

Gogmagog (gŏg'măgŏg), low chalk hills, Cambridgeshire, England.

Gogol, Nikolai Vasilyevich (nyĭkŭlī' vŭsē'lyŭvĭch gô'gŭl), 1809–52, Russian author. Won his first success with romantic tales of Cossack life, as in *Evenings on a Farm near Dikanka* (1831) and "Taras Bulba" (1835). With his later short stories, notably "The Overcoat," and with his satiric novel and masterpiece, *Dead Souls* (1842), he founded the great school of Russian realism. In a religious and moral crisis, Gogol destroyed the second part of *Dead Souls*. His fame as a dramatist rests on *Revizor* (*The Inspector-General*, 1836), a satire of provincial officialdom. All his major works are available in English.

Goiás (goiäsh'), state (240,333 sq. mi.; pop. 1,234,740), central Brazil; cap. Goiânia (pop. 41,584). On landlocked plateau, it has some rivers in Amazon system, some in Paraná system.

goiter: see THYROID GLAND.

Golan (gō–), one of the cities of refuge, E of the Jordan. Deut. 4.43; Joshua 20.8; 21.7; 1 Chron. 6.71.

Golconda (gŏlkŏn'dŭ), deserted city, Hyderabad, India. Was cap. of Moslem kingdom of Golconda (1512–89). Declined after conquest by Aurangzeb in 1687. Famed diamond trade made Golconda a byword for wealth.

gold, metallic element (symbol = Au [Latin *aurum*]; see also ELEMENT, table). Very ductile and malleable, it can be beaten into gold leaf. It is a good conductor of electricity and is chemically inactive. Usually it is hardened by being alloyed with other metals. The gold content of an alloy is stated in carats (a carat being 1/24 by weight of the total mass; because of this "pure" gold is 24 carats fine). Gold is a favored metal for the backing of currency. The quest for gold has had an important and colorful place in history. Chief producers are Union of South Africa, USSR, Canada, and U.S.

Goldberg, Rube, 1883–, American cartoonist. Known for his panels showing fabulously involved machinery for simple operations.

Goldberger, Joseph, 1874–1929, American medical research worker, discoverer of cause of pellagra.

Gold Coast, British colony and protectorates (91,690 sq. mi.; pop. 4,095,276), W Africa, on Gulf of Guinea; cap. Accra. Bordered on N by French West Africa. Comprises crown colony of Gold Coast (23,490 sq. mi.; pop. 2,194,466) with cap. at Cape Coast, British TOGOLAND, and inland protectorates of NORTHERN TERRITORIES and ASHANTI. Has swampy coast and forested interior. Gold is produced in NW area. Other products are manganese, bauxite, diamonds, hardwoods, and cacao. In 1482 the Portuguese estab. first European settlement in area. British crown colony was created 1874. Since 1951 the natives have enjoyed considerable self-rule.

Golden, resort city (pop. 5,238), N central Colo., just W of Denver, in area yielding coal, gold, clay, farm produce; founded 1859. Territorial cap. 1862–67. Seat of COLORADO SCHOOL OF MINES. Grave of Buffalo Bill is on near-by Lookout Mt.

SMALL CAPITALS = cross references. Pronunciation key on inside end pages. Abbreviations: p. 2.

Golden Ass, The, Latin novel: see APULEIUS, LUCIUS.
Golden Bough, The: see FRAZER, SIR JAMES GEORGE.
golden bull. 1 In history of Holy Roman Empire: see ELECTORS. **2** In Hungarian history: see ANDREW II.
Golden Fleece, in Greek mythology, magic fleece of a ram. Fleece was hung in a wood guarded by a dragon in Colchis. JASON and Argonauts sought this fleece, which they took after fulfilling tasks assigned by Aeëtes, king of Colchis.
Golden Gate, strait, 5 mi. long and 1–2 mi. wide, W Calif., between San Francisco Bay and the Pacific.
Golden Gate Bridge (built 1933–37) crosses strait from San Francisco to Marin co. Longest single-span suspension bridge in world (4,200 ft. between towers; over-all length 9,266 ft.). See *ill.,* p. 131.
golden glow, double-flowered yellow variety of a North American coneflower (*Rudbeckia laciniata*).
Golden Horde, Mongol host, so called because of magnificence of the camp of its leader BATU KHAN. Their empire (see TATARS) was founded in mid-13th cent. and comprised most of Russia, with cap. at Sarai (near modern Stalingrad). At first tributary to Great Khan at Karakorum, Golden Horde took part in Kublai Khan's conquest of S China. Islam became official religion after 1314. Ascendancy of grand duke of Moscow after 1380 brought decline; after 1405 empire broke up into independent khanates of Astrakhan, Kazan, Crimea, Sibir.
Golden Horn: see ISTANBUL.
Golden Legend, The, popular collection of saints' lives written in the 13th cent. by JACOBUS DE VORAGINE; originally entitled *Legenda sanctorum.*
goldenrod, perennial plants of large North American genus *Solidago.* Their spikes or panicles of fluffy yellow (rarely white) flowers brighten fields and roadsides in late summer. Goldenrod pollen now rarely considered a cause of hay fever.
Golden Rule, a saying of Jesus, "As ye would that men should do to you, do ye also to them likewise." Luke 6.31; Mat. 7.12.
Golden Valley, village (pop. 5,551), E Minn., W suburb of Minneapolis.
Goldfield, town (pop. of district 336), SW Nev., S of Tonopah. Gold discovery here of 1902 brought a rush in 1903. Peak production was reached 1910, then fell off rapidly.
goldfinch, name for several finches of Europe and America. North American eastern goldfinch (thistle bird or wild canary) is olive yellow, but in spring the male becomes vivid yellow and black. There are several forms in W U.S. See *ill.,* p. 105.
goldfish, fresh-water fish of carp and minnow family, used in aquariums and ponds. It was domesticated from wild form in China centuries ago; reverts to type upon escape. Bizarre varieties are bred.
Goldman, Edwin Franko, 1878–, American bandmaster. Organized the Goldman Band (1918), for which he wrote many marches. Author of books on band techniques.
Goldman, Emma, 1869–1940, American anarchist, b. Russia. Her speeches attracted wide attention, she was imprisoned for advocating birth control (1916) and for obstructing the draft (1917). She was deported (1917) to Russia, which she left in 1921.
Goldoni, Carlo (kär'lō gōldō'nē), 1707–93, Italian dramatist. He wrote real and witty comedy to replace *commedia dell' arte* on Italian stage. His plays include *La bottega del caffè* (1751) and *La locandiera* (1753). His memoirs (1787) are in French.
Goldsboro, city (pop. 21,454), E central N.C., near Neuse R. and SE of Raleigh; settled c.1840. Trades and ships tobacco, cotton, and truck.
Goldsborough, Louis Malesherbes, 1805–77, American naval officer. In Civil War, commanded North Atlantic Blockading Squadron in support of successful expedition against N.C. coast (1862).
Goldsmith, Oliver, 1730?–1774, English poet, dramatist, and novelist, b. Ireland. Unsuccessful as physi-

cian, he turned to writing. Fame, won with "Chinese letters" of *The Citizen of the World* (1762), grew with poems *The Traveller* (1764) and *The Deserted Village* (1770). He wrote one novel, *The Vicar of Wakefield* (1766; a masterpiece of domestic literature), and popular comedies (notably *She Stoops to Conquer,* 1773). The anonymous children's classic *Little Goody Two-Shoes* (1765) is sometimes attributed to him. Eccentric but lovable, he was a close friend of Reynolds, Burke, Garrick, and Samuel Johnson.
gold standard: see BIMETALLISM and MONEY.
golem (gō'lùm) [Heb.,= embryo], in medieval Jewish legend, an automaton given life through the invocation of religious symbols.
golf, game played with specially made clubs and balls on outdoor course called links. Game identified with Scotland, where it has been popular since 15th cent. Royal and Ancient Golf Club of St. Andrews, Scotland, founded 1774, became international shrine of golf; its basic rules accepted throughout the world. U.S. Golf Association, founded 1894, governing body of game in U.S. Standard golf course, usually more than 6,000 yd. around, is divided into 18 holes of varying length.
Golgi, Camillo (kämēl'lō gōl'jē), 1844–1926, Italian physician, noted as neurologist and histologist. Shared 1906 Nobel Prize in Physiology and Medicine for work on structure of nervous system.
Golgotha (gōl'gùthù), the same as CALVARY.
Goliad (gō'lēăd), city (pop. 1,584), S Texas, on San Antonio R. SE of San Antonio. Spanish mission moved here 1749 from Lavaca Bay (Goliad then La Bahia). Captured twice (1812, 1821) by filibusters from U.S. Texans regained it in Texas Revolution. Mexicans defeated and massacred Col. J. W. FANNIN and troops, March 19–27, 1836. Restored mission and presidio ruins now in state park.
Goliardic songs (gōlēär'dĭk), Late Latin poetry written by "wandering scholars." The origin of the name is uncertain. Songs, resembling medieval hymns in form but not in content, were usually licentious and attacked the church. Number of vagabond scholars grew so great as to become a plague in the 13th cent., but it is no longer thought that they actually organized a burlesque religious order. Church began (c.1230) to take strong measures against them, and they gradually declined.
Goliath (gōlī'ûth), Philistine giant, killed by young David. 1 Sam. 17; 21.9; 22.10; 2 Sam. 21.19.
Gombos, Julius, Hung. *Gömbös Gyula* (gûm'bûsh dyōō'lō), 1886–1936, Hungarian premier (1932–36); a nationalist and revisionist leader.
Gomel (gô'mĭl), city (pop. 144,169), SE Belorussia. Varied light industries. Dates from 12th cent.; to Russia in first Polish partition (1772). Pre-World War II Jewish pop. (c.40%) was largely exterminated by the Germans.
Gómez, Juan Vicente (hwän' vēsän'tä gō'mĕs), 1857–1935, ruler of Venezuela (1908–35), a *caudillo.* Of Indian and white parentage, he grew up as nearly illiterate cattle herdsman. Supported Cipriano CASTRO (1899), then replaced Castro as president (1908). Ruled Venezuela—not always as president—until his death. Though tyrannical, he was honest and industrious and improved his country economically, largely through encouraging foreign investments.
Gomorrah or **Gomorrha,** city, destroyed with SODOM.
Gompers, Samuel (gŏm'pùrz), 1850–1924, American labor leader, b. London. Helped found (1881) the Federation of Organized Trades and Labor Unions, which became (1886) the American Federation of Labor, of which he was president, except for 1895, until his death. He rejected cooperative business plans and socialist or radical programs, maintaining that the just aims of labor were simply shorter hours, more wages, and greater freedom.
Gonaïves (gônäēv'), city (pop. 13,534), NW Haiti, a port on Gulf of Gonaïves. In 1804 Haitian independ-

ence was proclaimed here, and DESSALINES, first of the Negro emperors, was crowned.

Gonçalves Dias, Antonio (äntô′nyŏ gônsäl′vĭsh dē′ûsh), 1823–64, Brazilian romantic poet.

Goncharov, Ivan Aleksandrovich (ēvän′ ŭlyĭksän′drŭvĭch gŭnchŭrôf′), 1812–91, Russian novelist; author of *Oblomov* (1858; Eng. tr., 1915), a minute portrayal of the indolent Russian gentleman.

Goncourt, Edmond (Huot) de (ĕdmô′ üŏ′ dù gŏkōōr′), 1822–96, and **Jules (Huot) de Goncourt** (zhül), 1830–70, French authors, brothers. Together, in their own nervous, telegraphic style, they wrote art criticism (much promoting Japanese art), naturalistic novels, as *Renée Mauperin* (1864) and *Germinie Lacerteux* (1865), and the famous *Journal des Goncourt* (9 vols., 1887–96), an intimate picture of Parisian society. Edmond founded the Goncourt Academy to award annual prizes for fiction.

Gondola, Giovanni: see GUNDULIC, IVAN.

gondola (gŏn′dùlù), boat used on canals of Venice since 11th cent. Long, narrow, and flat-bottomed, with high tapering prows and sterns, gondolas average 30 by 4 ft. The gondolier propels the boat with one oar from stern. Curtained cabin in center holds four to eight persons. Once gaily colored, law now requires that gondolas be black.

gong: see PERCUSSION INSTRUMENTS.

Góngora y Argote, Luis de (lwēs′ dä gŏn′gōrä ē ärgō′tä), 1571–1627, last great Spanish poet of the Golden Age, a priest. Stylistic refinement and somewhat exaggerated elegance gave rise to Gongorism, equivalent to euphuism in England.

gonorrhea (gŏnùrē′ù), an infectious venereal disease caused by gonococcus. It is commonly transmitted to genital organs by direct contact; may spread to adjacent structures or be carried to other parts of body by lymphatic system. Gonococcus, transmitted to infant at birth from genital tract of mother, sometimes causes conjunctivitis and blindness (preventable by silver-nitrate treatment).

Gonville and Caius College: see CAMBRIDGE UNIVERSITY.

Gonzaga (gŏntsä′gä), Italian princely family. Senior line ruled MANTUA 1328–1627 (first as captains general, from 1433 as marquesses, from 1530 as dukes) and acquired MONTFERRAT in 1536. After its extinction (1627) it was succeeded by a younger line, which by marriage had acquired the French duchies of NEVERS and RETHEL; this in turn became extinct 1708. Another branch ruled GUASTALLA (1539–1746). Many rulers of Mantua were lavish patrons of art and letters, notably **Francesco Gonzaga,** d. 1519, who married Isabella d′ESTE. In the Italian Wars he preserved Mantuan independence with difficulty, siding first with Venice, then with France, then with Pope Julius II.

Gonzaga University: see SPOKANE, Wash.

Gonzales (gùnzä′lĭs), city (pop. 5,659), S central Texas, near Guadalupe R. and ENE of San Antonio. First battle of Texas Revolution fought near by, Oct. 2, 1835. Park marks battlefield. Region yields cotton and poultry.

González de Ávila, Gil (hēl′ gŏnthä′lĕth dä ä′vēlä), d. 1543, Spanish conquistador. Conquered Nicaragua (1522); his claims usurped by Francisco Fernández de Córdoba (1524).

González de Ávila, Gil, 1578?–1658, Spanish historian. Royal chronicler of Castile and Indies, he wrote history of the Church in Spanish colonies.

Gooch, George Peabody, 1873–, English historian. An editor of *Cambridge History of British Foreign Policy, 1783–1919* (3 vols., 1922–23). His *History and Historians in the Nineteenth Century* (1913; 2d ed., 1946) is among best in modern historiography.

Good Hope, Cape of: see CAPE PROVINCE.

Goodhue, Bertram Grosvenor, 1869–1924, American architect. Evolved a distinctive style for his ecclesiastical work, which was Gothic in form yet permeated with a modern spirit.

Gooding, city (pop. 3,099), S Idaho, W of Shoshone, in MINIDOKA PROJECT.

Goodman, Benny (Benjamin David Goodman), 1909–, American clarinetist and dance band leader. In 1934 he organized his own orchestra, which became nationally famous. His contributions to the development of swing music earned him the title "king of swing." He also appeared as solo clarinetist with many symphony orchestras and in chamber ensembles.

Goodnews Bay, inlet of Kuskokwim Bay, SW Alaska. Platinum and osmiridium are found here.

Goodnight, Charles, 1836–1929, Texas cattleman, a pioneer in improving cattle breeds. He laid out Goodnight cattle trail to Wyoming in 1866.

Goodrich, Samuel Griswold, pseud. **Peter Parley,** 1793–1860, American editor and writer of juvenile stories. His *Peter Parley Tales* were sugar-coated moralistic stories of instruction. Edited periodicals, including *The Token* and juvenile *Robert Merry's Museum.*

Goodspeed, Edgar Johnson, 1871–, American Greek scholar. He is principally known for his new translation of the Bible: *The New Testament—an American Translation* (1923) and *The Complete Bible—an American Translation* (with J. M. P. Smith, 1939).

Good Thief or **Penitent Thief,** the thief crucified with Jesus who did not mock Him but accepted Him; Jesus promised him Paradise that day. Luke 23.39–43. His feast is March 25. Tradition names him Dismas or Desmas, the other thief Gesmas.

Goodwin Sands, 10 mi. stretch of shoals and shifting sands, off E coast of Kent, England. Formerly scene of many shipwrecks. Sands were supposedly once a fertile isle, property of Earl Godwin.

Goodyear, Charles, 1800–1860, American inventor, originator of rubber vulcanization (1839; patent 1844). His son **Charles Goodyear,** 1833–96, was pioneer in use of sewing machine for shoe manufacturing.

Goole, urban district (pop. 19,227), W Riding of Yorkshire, England; a port. Has shipbuilding and passenger lines to several continental ports.

goose, wild and domesticated bird related to duck and swan. Accurately, goose is the female, gander the male. Common Canada or wild goose of North America migrates in V-shaped flocks in spring and autumn. Other wild geese are BRANT, the blue, the snow, and the white-fronted or laughing geese. Domestic are Toulouse or gray goose, African and Embden geese, and oriental breeds (from wild Chinese goose).

Goose Bay, village of SE Labrador on Goose Bay. Has large air base and radio station built in World War II for transatlantic transport.

gooseberry, shrub (*Ribes*) of temperate regions and its fruit, a berry used in preserves. It is related to the currant and is a host to white pine blister rust.

Goose Creek, Texas: see BAYTOWN.

Goosport, village (pop. 8,318), SW La., near Lake Charles.

gopher (gō′fùr) or **pocket gopher,** burrowing rodent of North America and Central America. In U.S. chief genera are western (*Thomomys*) and eastern (*Geomys*) gophers. Gophers are gray, buff, or dark brown and 7–14 in. long. They have fur-lined pouches opening on outside of cheeks for carrying food and nesting material. They live and forage mostly underground, feeding on roots and tubers.

Gorboduc (gôr′bùdùk), legendary early British king who created murderous strife by dividing his realm between two sons. The story is treated in early English tragedy (1562) by Thomas Norton and Thomas SACKVILLE.

Gorchakov, Aleksandr Mikhailovich, Prince (ŭlyĭksän′dùr mĕkhī′lùvĭch, gŭrchŭkôf′), 1798–1883, Russian foreign minister (1856–82). Sought to nullify Treaty of Paris which closed Crimean War. Though friendly to Prussia and hostile to Austria, kept Russia neutral in Austro-Prussian and Franco-Prussian wars and helped form THREE EMPERORS' LEAGUE. Opposed

Russo-Turkish War of 1877–78; represented Russia at Congress of BERLIN.

Gordian I (Marcus Antonius Gordianus Africanus) (gôr'dēŭn), d. 238, Roman emperor. Ruled (238) with his son, **Gordian II**, 192–238, who was killed in Carthage. The father committed suicide. Gordian II's son, **Gordian III**, c.223–244, was emperor (238–44).

Gordian knot: see GORDIUS.

Gordin, Jacob Mikhailovich, 1853–1919, American writer of Yiddish plays, b. Russia.

Gordius (gôr'dēŭs), legendary king of Phrygia and founder of Gordium. Pole of his wagon was tied to yoke with intricate knot. Oracle said that he who untied it would rule all Asia. Alexander the Great severed it with his sword. Hence the figure "to cut the Gordian knot," meaning to solve a perplexing problem with one bold stroke.

Gordon, Charles George (Chinese Gordon), 1833–85, British soldier and administrator. Commander of Chinese army that suppressed the Taiping Rebellion. Was governor of Egyptian Sudan 1877–80. Trying to crush power of the Mahdi, he was killed in the siege of Khartoum. Popular indignation at his death was partial cause of fall of Gladstone government in 1885.

Gordon, Lord George, 1751–93, English agitator, responsible for the tragic Gordon riots in London (June 2–7, 1780). Protestant demonstration against removal of civil restrictions from Catholics; became an orgy of destruction and plunder.

Gordon, John Brown, 1832–1904, Confederate general and Ga. statesman. Served brilliantly in Wilderness campaign and Shenandoah Valley (1864). A leader in Ga. politics after war; governor 1886–90.

Gordon, Sir John Watson-, 1788–1864, Scottish portrait painter. Succeeded Raeburn as leading portraitist in Scotland.

Gordon, Leon, 1830–92, Russian-Hebrew novelist and poet, leader in renaissance of Hebrew culture.

Gordon riots: see GORDON, LORD GEORGE.

Gore Range: see PARK RANGE.

Gorgan, Iran: see GURGAN.

Gorgas, William Crawford (gôr'gŭs), 1854–1920, American disease and sanitation expert, surgeon general of U.S. (1914–19). Cleansed Havana and the Canal Zone of yellow fever.

Gorges, Sir Ferdinando (gôr'jĭz), c.1566–1647, British colonizer, proprietor of Maine. A leading figure in Plymouth Co. Conducted long struggle with Mass. Bay and Salem colonies over patent rights.

Gorgons (gôr'gŭnz), in Greek myth, female monsters. Winged and snake-haired, the three hideous creatures turned to stone all men who looked on them. Chief Gorgon was MEDUSA (killed by Hercules).

Gorham, town (pop. 2,639), NE N.H., on Androscoggin R. below Berlin, within sight of Presidential Range. Resort and lumber center, it has paper mills and holds winter carnival.

gorilla, anthropoid ape (genus *Gorilla*) native to W equatorial Africa. Largest of the great apes, males reach 5–6 ft. in height, and weigh 300–600 lb. Usually terrestrial, they walk on all fours, hands doubled under. They are chiefly vegetarian. Females and young sleep in tree platform nests; males sleep at base. Threatened by extinction, they are now protected.

Göring, Hermann Wilhelm: see GOERING.

Gorizia (gôrē'tsēä), Ger. *Görz,* city (pop. 30,265), Friuli-Venezia Giulia, NE Italy, in FRIULI, on Isonzo R. Under Austria 1500–1918. Bitterly contested in World War I.

Gorki, Maxim (mŭksyēm gôr'kē), pseud. of Aleksey Maximovich Pyeshkov, 1868–1936, Russian author. After years of vagabondage, he began writing in 1892. Among his early short stories, "Twenty-six Men and a Girl," "Chelkash," and "Malva" are well known in English, as are his novels *Foma Gordeyev* (1899) and *Mother* (1907) and his drama *The Lower Depths* (1902). A Marxist from his youth, he sought social

realism in his descriptions of the outcasts of society, in whom he saw the hope of the future. Living abroad after 1905, he returned to Russia in 1928, where he was given the highest honors. Late novels include *The Artamanov Affair* (1925; Eng. tr., *Decadence,* 1927) and *The Life of Klim Samgin* (1927–36; Eng. tr., in four separate vols., 1930–38), covering the whole revolutionary period from 1880 to 1934. He also wrote *My Childhood* (1913; Eng. tr., 1915) and *Reminiscences* (Eng. tr., 1946).

Gorki or **Gorky,** formerly **Nizhni Novgorod** (nyēzh'nyē nôv'gŭrŭt), city (pop. c.900,000), central European RSFSR, on right bank of the Volga and at mouth of the Oka. Major transportation and industrial center (rolling stock, heavy machinery, electric equipment, chemicals). Univ., technical schools. Founded 1221 as outpost by prince of Vladimir; became seat of a principality 1350; fell to Moscow 1393. Site of famous annual fairs 1817–1930. Renamed 1932 for Maxim Gorki, who was born here. Old section contains 13th-cent. kremlin, with palace and two cathedrals.

Görlitz (gûr'lĭts), city (pop. 85,686), Saxony, E Germany, on Görlitzer Neisse R.; chief city of Lusatia. Mfg. of textiles, machinery, glass, beer. A flourishing medieval duchy under Bohemian overlordship, it passed to Saxony 1635, to Prussia 1815, again to Saxony 1945. Jakob Boehme lived here. For **Görlitzer Neisse** river, see NEISSE.

Gorman, Arthur Pue, 1839–1906, U.S. Senator from Md. (1881–99, 1903–6). Led in making Wilson-Gorman Tariff Act of 1894 a high-tariff act.

Gorno-Badakhshan, Tadzhik SSR: see MOUNTAIN-BADAKHSHAN.

gorse: see FURZE.

Gorton, Samuel, c.1592–1677, one of founders of R.I., b. England. He settled Warwick (1642), where he preached unorthodox religious views.

Görz: see GORIZIA, Italy.

Gosforth (gŏz'fûrth). **1** Village, Cumberland, England; site of famous Viking cross. **2** Urban district (pop. 24,424), Northumberland, England; coal-mining center. George Stephenson built his first locomotive here in 1814.

goshawk (gŏs'hôk), fearless, relentless hawk of Old World and North America. Eastern goshawk male is c.22 in. long, female c.24 in. As adults both have black crown, white stripe over red eye, blue-gray upper parts, and white, gray-barred lower parts. Western goshawk has darker plumage. Goshawks destroy poultry and game birds. See *ill.,* p. 105.

Goshen (gō'–), fertile part of Egypt occupied by Israelites during bondage. Gen. 47.6; Ex. 8.22; 9.26.

Goshen. 1 City (pop. 13,003), N Ind., on Elkhart R. and SE of South Bend; settled c.1830. Agr. distribution center. Metal and wood products. Large Mennonite population. **2** Village (pop. 3,311), SE N.Y., SE of Middletown. Good Time (scene of the Hambletonian) and Historic or Harriman harness-racing tracks are here.

Goslar (gôs'lär), city (pop. 40,735), Lower Saxony, central Germany, at N foot of Harz mts. Mining center since its foundation in 10th cent. (formerly silver; now copper, lead, zinc, iron, sulphur). A favorite residence of early German emperors. A free imperial city until 1802, it was awarded to Hanover 1815, transferred to Brunswick 1941. City has preserved its medieval character. Much Romanesque and Gothic architecture (notably the 11th-cent. Kaiserhaus, built for Henry III).

Gosnold, Bartholomew (gŏz'nōld), fl. 1572–1602, English explorer and colonizer. Explored coast from Maine to Narragansett Bay (1602). Commanded *God Speed* in first settlement of Va. (1606).

Gospel [M.E.,= good news; cf. *evangel* from Gr.,= good news], one of the four biographies of Jesus in New Testament. The gospels are named MATTHEW, MARK, LUKE, and JOHN. First three called SYNOPTIC GOSPELS because of apparent relationship. Solemn

SMALL CAPITALS = cross references. Pronunciation key on inside end pages. Abbreviations: p. 2.

reading of the Gospel of the day is special feature of liturgy of many churches. Formerly a book of the Gospels was used instead of Bible for the oath in courts in Christian countries. Illumination of the Gospels became an art (e.g., the Lindisfarne Gospels, the Book of Kells). For apocryphal Gospels, see PSEUDEPIGRAPHA.

Gosport (gŏs'–), municipal borough (pop. 58,246), Hampshire, England; port on Portsmouth Harbour.

Gosse, Sir Edmund W(illiam), 1849–1928, English poet, critic, and literary biographer.

Gossen, Herman Heinrich (hĕr'män hīn'rĭkh gô'sùn), 1810–58, German economist, anticipated (1854) theory of marginal utility of Jevons and others.

Gota, Swed. *Göta älv,* river, 56 mi. long, SW Sweden, draining Vanern lake into the Kattegat. Forms part of **Gota Canal,** 240-mile system of rivers, lakes, and canals, from Goteborg to Stockholm.

Gotaland or **Gotarike:** see SWEDEN.

Goteborg (Swed. yûtùbôr'yù) or **Gothenburg** (gö'thùnbûrg), Swed. *Göteborg,* city (pop. 353,991), SW Sweden, co. seat of Goteborg and Bohus co.; a seaport at mouth of Gota R. on Kattegat. Second largest city of Sweden; shipyards, machinery mfg. Seat of Lutheran bishop. Founded 1619, city was planned by Dutch architects and retains many stately old buildings. University was founded 1887.

Goteborg licensing system: see LIQUOR LAWS.

Gotha (gō'thù, Ger. gō'tä), city (pop. 57,639), Thuringia, central Germany. Mfg. center (railroad cars, machinery); printing (mainly cartography). *Almanach de Gotha,* reference work on European royalty and nobility, was published here from 1764 to World War II. Passed to Ernestine line of Wettin dynasty 1485; cap. of Saxe-Gotha 1640–1826; cap. of Saxe-Coburg-Gotha 1826–1918. Historic buildings include ducal palaces (17th and 18th cent.). City was damaged in World War II.

Gotham (gō'tùm), village, Nottinghamshire, England. Inhabitants reputed to do ridiculous things (e.g., trying to drown an eel). Stories may stem from efforts to prevent King John from living there. Hence, Gotham (gō'thùm), name for New York city, first used by Washington Irving and others in *Salmagundi Papers.*

Gothenburg: see GOTEBORG.

Gothic architecture, style of building practiced in Europe, 13th–15th cent.; sometimes called pointed style because of use of pointed arch and vault. Style is found in its most consistent form in France. Evolving from ROMANESQUE ARCHITECTURE, the Gothic structure consisted basically of open skeleton of stone supporting stone vaulting. Diagonal ribs were introduced to support and strengthen groined vaults, and advent of pointed arch in early 12th cent. made possible a structure of greater height. Flying buttresses (arches of masonry leaning on parts of outer walls to counteract pressure of the vaults) gave greater stability to the structure. Earliest complete expression of skeleton method of construction was Notre Dame, Paris (1163–c.1230); loftiest and most fully evolved French church is Amiens cathedral (1220–88). In England the transition from Norman style to Gothic was made in latter half of 12th cent. Building of Westminster Abbey was directly influenced by the French, but distinctive national styles were evolved. German architecture (e.g., Cologne cathedral) borrowed from France in 13th cent. In Spain and Italy decorative elements tended to overshadow purely structural aspects of Gothic architecture. Medieval artists everywhere produced magnificent sculptures and stained glass as architectural decorations. See *ill.,* p. 47.

Gothic language, East Germanic language. Earliest literary remains in any Germanic tongue are in Gothic Bible of Ulfilas. See LANGUAGE (table).

Gothic revival, a 19th-cent. style of architecture and decoration imitating arts of Middle Ages. Reached its peak in c.1850. In England it gained support of the Church and many medieval structures were restored. Came into conflict with classic revival, with respective exponents taking sides in "battle of the styles." A triumph for Gothicists was building of Houses of Parliament in Perpendicular Gothic in 1840. Revival of interest in arts and crafts, with medieval work as inspiration, was led by William Morris. Movement spread to France, where Viollet-le-Duc became its chief exponent, and to U.S., where it was influenced by Victorian taste and, despite some masterpieces, tended to become trivial and ugly.

Gothic romance, a type of novel which flourished in late 18th and early 19th cent. in England. Mystery of each tale is heavily tinged with horror derived from gloomy background of medieval architecture and with terror of the supernatural. *Castle of Otranto* by Horace Walpole was forerunner of type which flourished in works of Mrs. Ann Radcliffe, M. G. Lewis, and C. R. Maturin.

gothic type: see TYPE.

Goths: see OSTROGOTHS; VISIGOTHS.

Gotland (gôt'lùnd), Baltic island, SE Sweden, off coast of Kalmar co. With several smaller islands it forms a county (1,224 sq. mi.; pop. 59,505). Agr., fishing. For its colorful history, see article on its cap., WISBY.

Gottfried von Strassburg (gôt'frēt fŭn shträs'bŏŏrk), fl. 13th cent., German poet. Ranks among greatest medieval writers for his epic *Tristan* (c.1210), which brings the story to the point where Tristan meets Isolt (see TRISTRAM AND ISOLDE). The poem was concluded by Ulrich von Türheim and Heinrich von Freiberg.

Gottheil, Gustav (gôt'hīl), 1827–1903, American reform rabbi, b. Prussia, a leader of reform Judaism.

Gotthelf, Jeremias (yärämē'äs gôt'hĕlf), 1797–1854, Swiss author whose real name was Albert Bitzius; a Protestant clergyman. A forerunner of German naturalism, he crusaded against the materialism of his time in the novels *Uli der Knecht* [Ulric the farmhand] (1840) and *Uli der Pächter* [Ulric the tenant] (1849), written partly in Swiss-German idiom.

Göttingen (gù'tĭng-ùn), city (pop. 78,438), Lower Saxony, W central Germany, in Hanover, on Leine R. Mfg. of optical and precision instruments. Its famous university was founded 1737 by Elector George Augustus (later George II of England). When King Ernest Augustus revoked Hanoverian constitution (1837), seven professors (incl. Jakob and Wilhelm Grimm) protested and were summarily dismissed. In late 19th cent. university became a world center for study of mathematics and physics.

Gottsched, Johann Christoph (yō'hän krĭs'tôf gôt'shät), 1700–1766, German poet and critic. He married the famous actress Karoline Neuber. As professor at Leipzig Univ., he dominated the literary scene of the German Enlightenment, advocated classical drama on French model. His influence waned after the attacks of Bodmer and Lessing.

Götz von Berlichingen: see BERLICHINGEN, GÖTZ VON.

Goucher College: see TOWSON, Md.

Gouda (gou'dù, Dutch khou'dä), municipality (pop. 37,283), South Holland prov., W Netherlands. Pottery mfg.; cheese trade. Has Gothic city hall.

Goudy, Frederic William, 1865–1947, American type designer. The most prolific type designer in history (Kennerley, Deepdene, and Garamont are among more than 100 faces), he also wrote about his craft.

Goujon, Jean (gōōzhŏ'), c.1510–c.1566, French Renaissance sculptor, known for decorations in low relief for buildings. Associated with Pierre Lescot, architect of the Louvre.

Gould, Jay, 1836–92, American capitalist. Helped defeat Cornelius Vanderbilt for control of ERIE RAILROAD. He and James FISK caused BLACK FRIDAY panic. Later, Gould controlled four Western railroads. His son, George Jay Gould, 1864–1923, inherited all his father's holdings and, through daring policies, seemed to have a transcontinental system in his grasp. By 1918, however, he lost all his roads.

Gould, Thomas Ridgeway, 1818–81, American sculptor of portrait busts and statues.

Gounod, Charles (shärl′ gōonō′), 1818–93, French composer. He wrote church music, e.g., *La Rédemption* and *Messe à Sainte Cécile,* but his fame rests chiefly on his operas *Faust* and *Romeo and Juliet.*

gourd (gōrd), fruit of vinelike tender annual plants of several genera related to cucumber, melon, and pumpkin. The dried cleaned fruit shells have been used from ancient times as drinking cups, dippers, bowls, etc., in tropical and Asiatic countries. In U.S. they are mostly grown for decoration.

Gourgues, Dominique de (gōorg′), c.1530–1593, French soldier and adventurer. Avenged massacre of Huguenot colony of Jean RIBAUT by slaughtering Spanish garrison on Fla. coast (1568).

Gourlay, Robert Fleming (gōor′lē), 1778–1863, Scottish writer and agitator. Came to Upper Canada in 1817. Led agitation against control of land grants by Family Compact. Banished from province (1819). Sentence was nullified in 1842. Wrote account of Upper Canada (1822) and autobiographical work (1843).

Gourmont, Rémy de (rāmē′ dü gōormō′), 1858–1915, French critic. Chief apologist for SYMBOLISTS.

gout, disease characterized by joint inflammation, much uric acid in blood, and deposits of sodium urate crystals about joints. It tends to recur.

Gouthière, Pierre (pyĕr′ gōotyär′), 1740–1806, French metalworker, foremost artist of ornamental bronzes of period of Louis XVI.

Gouverneur (gŭ″vürnōor′), resort village (pop. 4,916), N N.Y., S of Ogdensburg. Named for Gouverneur Morris, whose mansion still stands.

Govan (gŭ′vün), parish (pop. 364,801) of SW Glasgow, Scotland. Has extensive shipbuilding yards and mfg. of chemicals, asbestos, and machine tools.

government ownership: see PUBLIC OWNERSHIP.

Government Printing Office, United States, authorized by joint Congressional resolution (1860), purchased for $135,000 (1861). Its activities, defined by the Printing Act of 1895, include executing orders of Congress and the various Federal offices for printing and binding, distributing government publications, and reprinting documents for public purchase.

Governors Island, 173 acres, SE N.Y., in Upper New York Bay, S of Manhattan isl. (ferry connections). Bought from Indians in 1637 by Dutch governor of New Netherland. Present name adopted in 1784 because colonial governors lived here. Historic landmarks include Fort Jay (early 19th cent.) and Castle Williams (military prison; built 1807–11). Became hq. of 2d Corps Area in 1878.

Gower, John (gou′ür, gôr), d. 1408, English poet, contemporary and friend of Chaucer. Author of *Confessio Amantis* (c.1393; collection of tales in English verse illustrating Seven Deadly Sins) and of other poems in English, French, and Latin.

Gower (gou′ür), peninsula, c.15 mi. long and 5 mi. wide, Glamorganshire, Wales, SW of Swansea.

Gowrie, earls of: see RUTHVEN, family.

Goya (y Lucientes), Francisco José de (fränthē′skō hōsa′ dä gō′yä ē lōothēän′tĕs), 1746–1828, Spanish artist, b. near Saragossa. Gained royal notice with his witty scenes of popular life for tapestry designs. As court painter to Charles III and Charles IV, he did candidly realistic portraits. Most Madrid notables, including the duchess of Alba, posed for him. Mordant social satire fills the three series of etchings: *Caprichos, Proverbios,* and *Tauromaquía* [bullfight]. The great *Desastres de la guerra* [disasters of war] is a terrifying series of etchings, suggested by Peninsular War. At 70 he retired to his villa, which he decorated with macabre paintings, such as *Saturn Devouring his Children* (Prado). Spent last years in Bordeaux. Generally conceded to be greatest painter of his time.

Goyen, Jan Josephszoon van (yän′ yō′zŭfsōn vän gō′yün), 1596–1656, Dutch landscape painter, one of first to subordinate detail to atmospheric effect.

Gozzi, Carlo, Conte (kär′lō kōn′tä gôt′tsē), 1720–1806, Italian dramatist. He defended the *commedia dell' arte* against Goldoni. His *Fiaba dell' amore delle tre melarance* (1761) inspired Prokofiev's *The Love for the Three Oranges,* and his *Re Turandot* (1762) was made into an opera by Puccini. His brother **Gasparro Gozzi** (gä′spärō), 1713–86, stimulated critical interest in Dante.

Gozzoli, Benozzo (bänôt′tsō gôt′tsōlē), 1420–97, Florentine painter, whose real name was Benozzo di Lese. Assisted Fra Angelico, whose influence is seen in his decorative style. Famous for frescoes in San Gimignano and in Campo Santo, Pisa.

GPU: see SECRET POLICE.

Graaf, Reinier de (rīnēr′ dü gräf′), 1641–73, Dutch physician, noted for studies on pancreatic juice and generative organs. He discovered the follicles of the ovary known as Graafian follicles.

Grabbe, Christian Dietrich (krĭs′tyän dē′trĭkh grä′bŭ), 1801–36, German dramatist. His powerful dramas are marked by genius and bizarreness—e.g., *Don Juan und Faust* (1829), *Napoleon* (1831).

Graça Aranha, José Pereira da (zhōoza′ pĕrä′rŭ dü grä′sü ärä′nyŭ), 1868–1931, Brazilian novelist.

Gracchi (grä′kī), two Roman statesmen and reformers; brothers, sons of CORNELIA. **Tiberius Sempronius Gracchus,** d. 133 B.C., the elder, alarmed by the growth of wealth of the few, stood for tribunate in 133 B.C. as an avowed reformer. He passed the Sempronian Law (see AGRARIAN LAWS), to redistribute public lands. At the next election he renominated himself, and the senate postponed the election. In a great riot the following day he was murdered. **Caius Sempronius Gracchus** (kā′ŭs), d. 121 B.C., publicly committed himself to avenging his brother and completing his work. Elected tribune (123 B.C.), he initiated a series of remarkable social reforms. He was reelected (122) and proceeded with further schemes, checking the power of consuls and senate. In 121 he was defeated. When repeal of his measures was proposed, riots ensued and he was killed.

grace, in Christian theology, free favor of God towards men necessary for their salvation. Natural graces (e.g., gift of life) are distinguished from supernatural graces, by which God makes man (depraved through original sin) capable of enjoying eternal life. Supernatural grace, keystone of the whole Christian theological system, is usually defined as actual grace, which turns the soul to God, or sanctifying grace, which perpetuates this conversion. Most theologies, except CALVINISM, distinguish prevenient grace, which makes man's will free, from cooperating grace, by which God assists to salvation the free man who seeks it. Grace may be so powerful that a man cannot escape conversion (efficacious grace), or it may be of lesser strength so that a man can reject it though always sufficient for conversion if he accepts it (sufficient grace). As to the means of grace, there is serious cleavage regarding the SACRAMENT. Catholics hold the sacrament actually confers grace; Protestants that it is the sign, not the means, of grace. Certain Christian systems have developed other ideas of grace (e.g., the Society of FRIENDS, who deny original sin). A blessing or benediction is sometimes called grace (notably in grace before and after meals, universally advocated by Christians).

Graces, three Greek goddesses, daughters of Zeus and Eurynome—Aglaia (ăglä′ŭ), Thalia (thălī′ŭ), and Euphrosyne (ūfrŏs′īnē). They were personifications of beauty and charm. Called Charites by Greeks and Gratiae by Romans.

Gracián, Baltasar (bältäsär′ gräthyän′), 1601–58, Spanish philosopher, scholar, satirist, a Jesuit, notable for epigrams. Among his works is *El criticón,* 1651–57.

grackle, name for some members of family of New World orioles and blackbirds. Purple or common grackle of Atlantic coast is black with metallic hues, iridescent in sun. It eats grain and insects and is a cannibalistic nest robber. Bronze grackle found inland, W to Rocky Mts., Florida and boat-tailed grackles in S U.S.; great-tailed or jackdaws in Texas and Mexico.

Graecia Magna: see MAGNA GRAECIA.

Graefe or **Gräfe, Albrecht von** (both: äl'brěkht fŭn grä'fù), 1828–70, German ophthalmologist, noted for eye surgery and as a teacher. His father, **Karl Ferdinand von Graefe** (kärl fěr'dēnänt), 1787–1840, was a pioneer in plastic surgery.

Graetz, Heinrich: see GRÄTZ, HEINRICH.

grafting, method of propagation in which two parts of closely related plants are united so that they grow as one. The scion (a bud or shoot) united with the stock retains its own characteristics. Either seedlings or mature trees may be grafted. The method is particularly important in growing fruit, notably in orange and grapefruit groves.

Grafton. 1 Town (pop. 8,281), S central Mass., SE of Worcester. Mfg. of textiles, leather, and abrasives. **2** City (pop. 7,365), N W.Va., near Fairmont. Rail junction with mfg. of glass products.

Graham, James: see MONTROSE, JAMES GRAHAM, 5TH EARL and 1ST MARQUESS OF.

Graham, Martha, American dancer and teacher of the dance; a leading figure in modern dance. With Denishawn company 1919–23; she made independent debut 1926. Her compositions include *Frontier, Every Soul Is a Circus, Letter to the World* and *Judith.*

Graham, Robert, later **Robert Cunninghame-Graham,** d. 1797?, Scottish poet, author of lyric, "If Doughty Deeds My Lady Please."

Graham, Robert Bontine Cunninghame: see CUNNINGHAME GRAHAM, ROBERT BONTINE.

Graham, Thomas, 1805–69, Scottish chemist. He distinguished between colloids and crystalloids, and discovered DIALYSIS. His research on diffusion led to **Graham's law:** rate of diffusion of gas is inversely proportional to square root of density.

Graham. 1 Textile-mill town (pop. 5,026), central N.C., E of Greensboro. **2** City (pop. 6,742), N Texas, S of Wichita Falls. Has cottonseed and flour mills, meat packing and carbon-black plants, and oil refineries. Possum Kingdom L. is near.

Graham Coast: see PALMER PENINSULA.

Grahame, Kenneth, 1859–1931, English writer of children's books, author of *The Wind in the Willows* (1908), a classic.

Graham Island, largest of the Queen Charlotte Isls., W B.C., Canada, in the Pacific Ocean.

Graham Land: see PALMER PENINSULA.

Graham of Claverhouse: see DUNDEE, JOHN GRAHAM OF CLAVERHOUSE, 1ST VISCOUNT.

Grail, Holy, a feature of medieval legend and literature. Appears variously as a chalice, cup, or dish and sometimes as a stone or caldron into which a bleeding lance drips blood. Identified by Christians as chalice of the Last Supper. It would be revealed only to a pure knight; Grail Quest appears in different stories. In Arthurian legend purest knight is variously Parsifal or Galahad. Legend has features of Christian story, Celtic myth, and ancient fertility cults.

grain, name for cereal grasses, certain other plants (e.g., buckwheat), and their edible fruits, which whole or ground supply the main food of man and some domestic animals. Principal grain crops are wheat, Indian corn, oats, barley, rye, and rice; all staple grain crops were domesticated in Neolithic period. In preparing the seedlike fruits of these plants for many uses the husk, outer coat, or bran is removed. To make whole-wheat flour whole part of the bran is removed; for graham flour whole grain is used.

grain alcohol: see ETHYL ALCOHOL.

Grainger, Percy (Aldridge), 1882–, Australian-American pianist and composer; friend and disciple of Grieg, whose music he often played. Known for his adaptations of folk music, e.g., *Molly on the Shore, Shepherd's Hey, Mock Morris,* and *Country Gardens.*

Gram, Hans Christian Joachim (gräm, Dan. häns krĭs'-

tyän yō'äkĭm gräm'), 1853–1938, Danish physician. He developed a differential staining method useful in identification and classification of bacteria. Bacteria that retain the dye after immersion in decolorizer are Gram positive; others, Gram negative.

Gramont or **Grammont, Philibert, comte de** (fēlēbĕr' kŏt' dù grämō'), 1621–1707, French courtier. Exiled by Louis XIV, he was prominent at court of Charles II of England (1663–64). His brother-in-law, Anthony HAMILTON, wrote the celebrated *Mémoires du comte de Grammont,* a racy and thoroughly amoral account of his time.

Grampians, mountain system, cutting NE–SW across central Scotland, separating Highlands from Lowlands. Highest peak is Ben Nevis (4,406 ft.). Wild, magnificent scenery on N side; deer forests on more gently sloping S side.

Gran, Hungary: see ESZTERGOM.

Granada (gränä'dhä), city (pop. 21,743), W Nicaragua, on L. Nicaragua; founded 1524. Was long stronghold of landed aristocracy. Controls extensive commerce on lake.

Granada, city (pop. 140,941), cap. of Granada prov., S Spain, in Andalusia, picturesquely situated in view of the Sierra Nevada. It became in 1238 the cap. of the kingdom of Granada, the last Moorish foothold in Spain, and flourished as a center of Moslem art and culture. Long torn by feuds among the noble families, notably the Zegris and Abencerrages, the kingdom fell to Ferdinand and Isabella of Castile during the reign of Boabdil. The city itself fell in 1492 after a long siege. Its Moorish fortress, the ALHAMBRA, is its most famous monument. Near by is the imposing palace of Emperor Charles V. The late Gothic and plateresque cathedral (16th cent.) is adjoined by a chapel containing the tombs of Ferdinand and Isabella.

Granados (y Campiña), Enrique (ĕnrē'kä gränä'dōs ē kämpē'nyä), 1867–1916, Spanish composer. *Goyescas,* a set of piano pieces which later formed the basis for an opera of the same name, is his best-known work.

Granby, city (pop. 21,989), S Que., Canada, on North Yamaska R. and E of Montreal. Has textile mills and mfg. of furniture and rubber products.

Grand Alliance, War of the, 1688–97, war between France and the powers of the League of AUGSBURG, known as Grand Alliance after 1689. Louis XIV had been promised the support of James II of England, who however was overthrown by William III. French support of counterrevolution in Ireland was frustrated by William's victory at the Boyne (1690). On the sea, also, England was victorious at La Hogue (1692), but on land the French defeated the allies at Fleurus (1690), Namur (1692), Neerwinden (1693), and Marsaglia (1693). The Treaty of RYSWICK ended the war, which in America was known as King William's War (see FRENCH AND INDIAN WARS).

Grand Army of the Republic, organization estab. by Union veterans of Civil War. First post formed at Decatur, Ill., April 6, 1866; first national encampment at Indianapolis, Nov. 20, 1866. Aims were to preserve friendships, honor fallen comrades, aid widows and handicapped, and increase pensions. Members were mostly Republicans; added to that party's strength until 1900. Parallel Southern group, United Confederate Veterans, was founded in 1889. The 83d and last G.A.R. encampment met Aug. 28–31, 1949, at Indianapolis, with 6 of 16 surviving members present.

Grand Bank, town (pop. 2,148), S N.F., Canada, on SE shore of Fortune Bay. Important base for Grand Banks fisheries.

Grand Banks, submarine plateau off SE N.F., Canada, extends 420 mi. E–W and 350 mi. N–S, with depths of 22–100 fathoms. Mostly in the Labrador Current, with E edge in Gulf Stream. Meeting of warm and cold air results in persistent fogs. Probably most important cod-fishing region in world. Fishing endangered by icebergs.

Grand Canal. 1 Chinese *Yun-ho* [transit river], largest canal of China, c.1,000 mi. long, extending from Hangchow to Tientsin. Oldest portion (connecting Yellow and Yangtze rivers) was completed in 7th cent.; remainder built 13th–14th cent. Silting has reduced canal's former economic importance. **2** See VENICE.

Grand Canyon, gorge, c.1 mi. deep, 4–18 mi. wide, and 217 mi. long, of Colorado R., NW Ariz. Visible strata show still-continuing record of geologic change beginning with Archeozoic era. Varicolored layers, steep and embayed rims, and eroded rock forms in chasm catch the light of sun and shadow and glow with changing hues of intense beauty. Discovered by G. L. de Cardenas (1540); boat party taken through by J. W. Powell (1869). Much of canyon now included in Grand Canyon Natl. Park and Grand Canyon Natl. Monument (see NATIONAL PARKS AND MONUMENTS, table).

Grand Coulee, city (pop. 2,741), NE central Wash., on Columbia R. and WNW of Spokane. Work base for **Grand Coulee Dam,** built 1933–41 for power, irrigation, flood control. One of world's largest dams (4,300 ft. long; 550 ft. high). Impounds Roosevelt L. (151 mi. long), a recreational area.

Grand Detour, unincorporated village, N Ill., SW of Rockford and on Rock R. Leonard ANDRUS and John DEERE associated in building first Grand Detour steel plow here 1837.

Grand Falls. 1 Town (pop. 2,365), W N.B., Canada, on St. John R. Falls here attract many visitors. Has large hydroelectric development. **2** Town (pop. c.4,508), central N.F., Canada, on Exploits R. and NW of St. John's. Has large paper mills and hydroelectric plant.

Grand Falls, spectacular waterfalls of upper Hamilton R., S Labrador. River drops 245 ft., then flows 12 mi. through canyon over series of rapids in a total fall of 1,038 ft. Discovered 1839 by John McLean of Hudson's Bay Co., but forgotten and rediscovered 1891.

Grand Forks, city (pop. 26,836), E N.Dak., at junction of Red and Red Lake rivers, N of Fargo; settled 1871. Second largest city in state. Distributing center for spring-wheat region, it has grain elevators, flour mills, creameries, and meat-packing plants. Seat of Univ. of North Dakota (state supported; coed.; chartered 1883, opened 1884).

Grandgent, Charles Hall (grǎn'jŭnt), 1862–1939, American philologist and distinguished student of Italian language and Italian literature.

Grand Haven, city (pop. 9,536), S Mich., on L. Michigan at mouth of Grand R. and NW of Grand Rapids. Port, fishing and mfg. center. Ships grapes and celery. Resort.

Grand Island. 1 City (pop. 22,682), S Nebr., near Platte R., W of Lincoln; settled 1857 by Germans. Rail and processing center for livestock (horses, mules, cattle), dairy, and agr. (grain, fruit, beet sugar) area. U.S. Central Monitoring Station, radio-broadcasting checking point, is near. **2** See NIAGARA, river.

Grand Island, N Mich., in L. Superior N of Munising; one of largest Mich. islands (c.13,000 acres). Wooded area, it is a resort with game refuge.

Grand Junction, city (pop. 14,504), W Colo., at junction of Gunnison and Colorado rivers near Utah line; founded 1881. Resort. Ships and processes livestock, farm produce. Colorado Natl. Monument is near.

Grand Lake. 1 Lake, c.2 mi. long, N central Colo., at W edge of Rocky Mt. Natl. Park and in Colorado-Big Thompson project. Resort; has annual yacht race. **2** See GRAND RIVER DAM.

Grand Manan, island (pop. c.2,457), c.16 mi. long and c.7 mi. wide, S N.B., Canada, in Bay of Fundy near entrance to Passamaquoddy Bay. Summer resort and fishing center. Settled after Revolution by Loyalists; claims disputed by U.S. until 1817.

Grand'Mère (grä'měr"), city (pop. 11,089), S Que., Canada, on St. Maurice R. and NNW of Trois Rivières. Here are hydroelectric station, paper and woolen mills, and lumbering.

Grand Portage (pôr'tĭj), nine-mile carrying place, famous in American fur trade, in extreme NE corner of present Minn. Led from L. Superior N to widening of Pigeon R.

Grand Prairie, city (pop. 14,594), N Texas, WSW of Dallas. Industrial suburb with aircraft mfg.

Grand Pré (grän' prā, Fr. grä prā'), agr. village, N N.S., Canada, on Minas Basin. Old village, founded near by c.1675, was early home of Acadians and of Evangeline, heroine of Longfellow's poem.

Grand Rapids. 1 City (pop. 176,515), S Mich., on Grand R. and NW of Lansing. State's second largest city and most famous furniture mfg. and market center in U.S.; it also has mfg. of railroad equipment, metal products, chemicals, paint, and food products. Here are furniture museum and Calvin Col. **2** Village (pop. 6,019), N central Minn., on the Mississippi and NW of Duluth. Mfg. of paper and dairy products.

Grand River. 1 River, 165 mi. long, S Ont., Canada, flows into L. Erie at Port Maitland. Navigable for 70 mi. from mouth. **2** Former name of the OTTAWA river, E Ont. and W Que., Canada.

Grand River. 1 See COLORADO, river. **2** River rising in S Michigan and flowing c.260 mi. N, NW and W past Lansing and Grand Rapids (head of navigation) to L. Michigan at Grand Haven. **3** River rising in SW N.Dak. and flowing c.209 mi. ESE through S.Dak. to Missouri R. near Mobridge. **4** River in Okla.: see NEOSHO, river, and GRAND RIVER DAM.

Grand River Dam, NE Okla., in Grand R. (local name of NEOSHO R.) and SE of Vinita. Built for flood control and power (completed 1940). It is 6,565 ft. long, also called Pensacola Dam. Created Grand L.

Grandson (gräsō'), town (pop. 1,726), Vaud canton, Switzerland, on L. of Neuchâtel. Here Swiss defeated Charles the Bold 1476. Also spelled Granson.

Grand Teton National Park: see NATIONAL PARKS AND MONUMENTS (table).

Grandview Heights, city (pop. 7,659), central Ohio, W suburb of Columbus.

Grangemouth, burgh (pop. 15,305), Stirlingshire, Scotland, on the Forth estuary. Has extensive docks and shipyards.

Granger, Francis (grän'jŭr), 1792–1868, American political leader. Defeated as Anti-Masonic party nominee in 1830 and 1832. Later became a leader of conservative Whigs.

Granger movement, American agrarian movement taking its name from the Natl. Grange of the Patrons of Husbandry, organization founded in 1867 by Oliver H. Kelley and others. Local units were called granges and the members grangers. Expanded rapidly after Panic of 1873. Though originally estab. for social and educational purposes, local granges became political forums, channels of protest against economic abuses; sought correction partly through cooperative enterprises. Their political activity secured passage in Ill., Wis., Minn., and Iowa of so-called Granger laws, dealing with railroad and storage rates. So-called Granger Cases challenged constitutionality of these laws (see MUNN VS. ILLINOIS). Inadequacy of state regulation led to demands for national legislation. After 1876 other groups led agrarian protest and granges returned to being social organizations.

Grangesberg, Sweden: see KOPPARBERG.

Grangeville, city (pop. 2,544), N central Idaho, in wheat section of the Camas Prairie and old Nez Percé country. Outfitting point in 1898 gold rush.

Granicus (grŭnī'kŭs), anc. name of small river of Mysia, Asia Minor; now the Turkish Kocabas. Here Alexander the Great defeated Persians in 334 B.C., and Lucullus defeated Mithridates VI in 73 B.C.

granite, hard igneous rock of coarse structure, commonly containing quartz, feldspar, mica. It takes a high polish, and is used for buildings, monuments.

Granite City, industrial city (pop. 29,465), SW Ill., on the Mississippi above St. Louis. Rail center producing metal products and chemicals.

SMALL CAPITALS = cross references. Pronunciation key on inside end pages. Abbreviations: p. 2.

Graniteville, village (pop. 3,362), W S.C., near Aiken. Founded 1846 as state's first mill town by William GREGG.

Granjon, Robert (grän'jùn, Fr. rōbĕr' gräzhõ'), fl. 1545–88, French designer of type. Worked in Paris, Lyons, Antwerp, and Rome. Created *caractères de civilité,* intended as a French equivalent of italic; though beautiful, they lost out in competition with more legible italic. He is honored by having a later type face named for him.

Gran Paradiso (grän" pärädĕ'zō), mountain, 13,323 ft. high, NW Italy, in Alps S of Aosta. It is the highest peak entirely in Italian territory.

Gran Quivira National Monument: see NATIONAL PARKS AND MONUMENTS (table).

Gran Sasso d'Italia (grän säs'sō dētä'lyä), mountain group, Abruzzi, S central Italy, highest of the Apennines. Culminates at 9,557 ft. in Monte Corno or Corno Grande.

Granson, Switzerland: see GRANDSON.

Grant, Ulysses S(impson), 1822–85, commander in chief of Union army in Civil War, 18th President of the United States (1869–77); originally named Hiram Ulysses Grant. Captured Fort Henry and Fort Donelson in 1862, then fought controversial battle of Shiloh. VICKSBURG CAMPAIGN (1862–63) was great success. Became supreme commander in the West, Oct., 1863. After CHATTANOOGA CAMPAIGN, became commander in chief, March, 1864. Directed WILDERNESS CAMPAIGN (1864) against Lee. Accepted Lee's surrender at APPOMATTOX COURTHOUSE (1865). His campaigns were successful largely because he practiced elementary military doctrine that destruction of enemy's main armies was principal objective in warfare. Made a full general in 1866, first U.S. citizen after Washington to hold that rank. Successful Republican candidate for presidency in 1868; possibly most ill-fitted man for that office nation ever had. Punitive radical reconstruction program was pushed with new vigor; monetary legislation favorable to commercial and industrial interests was passed (see GREENBACK). Grant, though honest himself, associated with disreputable politicians and financiers. In foreign affairs, however, much was accomplished by Secretary of State Hamilton Fish. Grant's *Personal Memoirs* (2 vols., 1885–86) are among the great military narratives of history.

Granta, river, England: see CAM.

Grantham (grăn'tùm, grăn'thùm), municipal borough (pop. 23,405), Lincolnshire, England. Here Richard III condemned duke of Buckingham to death (1483) and Cromwell won first victory over royalists (1643). Site of George Hotel described in Dickens's *Nicholas Nickleby.*

Grants Pass, city (pop. 8,116), SW Oregon, W of Medford and on Rogue R. Trade center of farm and lumber area. Oregon Caves Natl. Monument is S.

Granvelle, Antoine Perrenot de (ätwän' pĕrùnõ' dù grävĕl'), 1517–86, cardinal, statesman in service of Emperor Charles V and King Philip II of Spain; b. Besançon, France. As chief adviser to MARGARET OF PARMA (1556–64), he brought Spanish troops and Inquisition into Netherlands. His unpopularity stirred up rebellion and necessitated his recall.

Granville, John Carteret, 1st Earl, 1690–1763, British statesman. Ambassador to Sweden (1719–21), he mediated treaties ending the Northern War. Secretary of state 1721–24, he clashed with Robert Walpole and became (1730–42) leader of the opposition which brought about Walpole's downfall. Became unpopular for favoring George II's Hanoverian policies. Was president of the privy council 1751–63.

Granville, village (pop. 2,653), central Ohio, NE of Columbus. Seat of Denison Univ. (Baptist; coed.; 1831).

Granville-Barker, Harley Granville, 1877–1946, dramatist, actor, producer of G. B. Shaw's plays. Wrote plays (e.g., *Madras House*), translated others.

grape, woody vine of genus *Vitis,* widely cultivated in N Hemisphere, and its fruit. Varieties of *Vitis vinifera* are native to Mediterranean region and have been cultivated there from ancient times (now also grown in Calif.). They are used for making most WINE and are source of the RAISIN. In U.S. grapes grown E of the Rockies are hybrids or are derived from native species.

grapefruit or **pomelo,** citrus fruit (*Citrus paradisi*), related to orange and lemon, and originally native to SE Asia. The large globular fruit grows in bunches and weighs up to 4–5 lb. Fla., Texas, and Calif. lead in U.S. production.

grape hyacinth, bulbous plant of genus *Muscari,* bearing clusters of dainty blue or white flowers in spring.

grape sugar: see GLUCOSE.

graphite (gră'fīt), allotropic form of CARBON, also called plumbago and black lead, soft and greasy with metallic luster. It is used in "lead" of pencils, stove polish, some paints, as a lubricant, etc.

Grasmere, village, Westmoreland, England. Dove Cottage, Wordsworth's home 1799–1808, now a museum. De Quincey and Coleridge also lived here. Grave of Wordsworth, his family, and Hartley Coleridge.

grass, any plant of important and widely distributed family Gramineae. Grasses, which have hollow, jointed stems and bladelike leaves, include hay and pasture grasses, the cereals (see GRAIN), sugar cane, and bamboo. See also LAWN.

Grasse, François Joseph Paul, comte de (kõt' dù gräs'), 1723–88, French admiral. Played crucial part in YORKTOWN CAMPAIGN of American Revolution by blockading York and James rivers, thus bottling up Cornwallis at Yorktown.

Grasse (gräs), town (pop. 13,731), Alpes-Maritimes dept., SE France, in hills above Cannes, in a flower-growing dist. Center of French perfumery industry.

grasshopper, name for leaping insect of order Orthoptera. Common grasshoppers and locusts belong to short-horned grasshopper family. Long-horned family includes katydid, meadow grasshopper, Mormon, sand, and cave or camel crickets. Most grasshoppers have firm but flexible forewings, membranous underwings, powerful jumping legs, and strong jaws. Many are herbivorous, some carnivorous. See *ill.,* p. 469.

grass-of-Parnassus, perennial plant (*Parnassia*) with green-veined white flowers. Grows in damp places.

Grass Valley, city (pop. 5,283), N central Calif., NE of Sacramento, in gold-mining area. Homes of Lola Montez and Lotta Crabtree preserved here.

Gratian (grā'shùn), 359–83, West Roman emperor (375–83). Ruled with his brother, VALENTINIAN II. In 378 he made Theodosius I emperor of the East. He took St. Ambrose as adviser and attacked paganism. In 383 he was assassinated by MAXIMUS.

Gratian, fl. 1140, Italian founder of the science of CANON LAW, a monk who taught at Bologna. His great work, the *Decretum,* or *Concordia discordantium canonum,* appeared c.1140. A private synthesis, it was used by later popes and became the kernel of the *Corpus juris canonici.*

Grattan, Henry, 1746–1820, Irish patriot statesman. Through his fight to repeal Poynings's Law (1782) the Irish Parliament became free from the English government. Gained Catholics the right to vote in Ireland (1792) and consent for them to sit in Parliament. This latter right was overruled by George III, thus encouraging the Rising of '98.

Gratz, Barnard (grăts), 1738–1801, American merchant, b. Upper Silesia. With his brother Michael Gratz (1740–1811) he estab. firm that acquired land in Ohio, Ky., Ind., and Ill. for pioneer settlement and ran boats on Ohio R. Michael's daughter, **Rebecca Gratz,** 1781–1869, known for her philanthropies in Philadelphia, is remembered chiefly as probable prototype of Rebecca in Scott's *Ivanhoe.*

Grätz or **Graetz, Heinrich** (both: hīn'rĭkh grĕts'), 1817–91, German-Jewish historian, champion of orthodox Judaism, author of *History of the Jews* (1853–75).

Gratz, Rebecca: see GRATZ, BARNARD.

Graubünden, Switzerland: see GRISONS.

Grau San Martín, Ramón (rämōn' grou' sän märtēn'), 1887–, president of Cuba (Sept., 1933–Jan., 1934, 1944–48), a physician, professor of Univ. of Havana.

gravel, rock fragments rounded by water, coarser than sand and classed according to size as pebble, cobble, or boulder gravel. Quartz is commonest constituent. Used in road building and in concrete.

Gravelines (grävlēn'), small Channel port, Nord dept., N France. Scene of Spanish victory over French (1558).

Gravenhage, 's, Netherlands: see HAGUE, THE.

Graves, Frank Pierrepont, 1869–, American educator, commissioner of education and president of Univ. of the State of New York from 1921 to 1940.

Graves, Robert (Ranke), 1895–, English poet, critic, and novelist, best known for historical novels, such as *I, Claudius* (1934). Interested in myth (both in fiction and socio-religious history).

Gravesend (grāv'zēnd'), municipal borough (pop. 45,043), Kent, England, on S bank of the Thames. Has long been official reception place of London's distinguished visitors and starting place of expeditions. Station of pilots and customhouse officers. Has shipbuilding and mfg. Hq. of Royal Thames Yacht Club. Grave of Pocahontas.

Graves's disease: see THYROID GLAND.

gravitation. Law of gravitation states that all bodies in universe have a mutual attraction for one another. This attractive force is in direct proportion to product of masses of bodies concerned and varies inversely as square of distance between them. Gravitation constant is force exerted by a body with mass of 1 gm. upon another body with same mass at a distance of 1 cm. Law of gravitation was first stated by Isaac Newton but work of Johannes Kepler contributed to it, and experiments of Cavendish helped to establish its universality. **Gravity,** although commonly used synonymously with gravitation, is more accurately defined as that force operating between other bodies and the earth. This force is the cause of a body's having weight; the force is considered to act upon the whole body at a definite point (the center of gravity) within the body. The force of gravity varies slightly in different places, therefore the weight also varies accordingly. Gravity gives to a falling body a uniform acceleration; the value for this acceleration generally used as a standard is 32 ft. per second per second at sea level.

Gray, Asa, 1810–88, American botanist and taxonomist. As Harvard professor and through his writing, he helped popularize study of botany. He was author of *Manual of the Botany of Northern United States* (1848) known in numerous revisions.

Gray, Robert, 1755–1806, American sea captain, discoverer of Columbia R. (1792). First American to circumnavigate globe (1787–90).

Gray, Thomas, 1716–71, English poet; friend of Horace Walpole. His early poems were classical (e.g., odes "To Spring," "On a Distant Prospect of Eton College," both 1742). Most familiar of his works is "An Elegy Written in a Country Churchyard" (1750). "The Progress of Poesy" (1754) is a critical poem. Later verse was near-romantic (e.g., "The Descent of Odin," 1761). He refused the laureateship in 1757 and was made professor of ancient history at Cambridge in 1768.

Gray Eminence: see JOSEPH, FATHER.

grayling, game fish related to salmon, found chiefly in clear, cold, fresh waters of N Hemisphere. It has a high dorsal fin, is usually vivid with mixed purples and blues, sometimes marked with other colors. Its flesh is delicious. Generic name *Thymallus* refers to wild thyme odor. Common grayling (*Thymallus thymallus*) found in European rivers.

Grays Harbor, a Pacific inlet, W Wash., at mouth of Chehalis R. Aberdeen and Hoquiam are on N shore.

Gray's Inn: see INNS OF COURT.

Grayson, David: see BAKER, RAY STANNARD.

Grays Peak: see FRONT RANGE.

Graz (gräts), city (pop. 226,271), cap. of Styria, SE Austria, on Mur R. Second largest city of Austria. Metallurgy; mfg. of machinery. Has Gothic cathedral, several medieval churches (13th–15th cent.), 16th-cent. Landhaus [provincial parliament], museum. Kepler taught at Graz univ. (founded 1585).

Graziani, Rodolfo (rōdōl'fō grätsëä'nē), 1882–, Italian marshal. Viceroy of Ethiopia (1936–37); governor of Libya (1940–41). Resigned after rout by British. Trial for high treason suspended 1949.

greasewood, spiny shrub (*Sarcobatus vermiculatus*) native to alkali soils of W U.S. Leaves are eaten by cattle and hard yellow wood is used as fuel.

Great Australian Bight, wide bay of Indian Ocean, indenting S coast of Australia.

Great Awakening, wave of religious revivals in American colonies in later half of 18th cent. It began in N.J. under the evangelical preaching of Gilbert Tennent. In New England, where the Congregationalists played a leading role, it was stirred by Jonathan Edwards. It was spread by the tour (1739–41) of George Whitefield and by the preaching of Samuel Davies among the Presbyterians of Va. It led to missionary work among Indians by Samuel Kirkland and others. It also caused bitter disputes that resulted in doctrinal changes; swayed social and political thought; and served to build up intercolonial relations and to create a democratic spirit in religion.

Great Barrier Reef, 1,250 mi. long, largest coral reef in world, in Coral Sea, forming natural breakwater for coast of Queensland, Australia. Contains islets with coral gardens and unusual marine life.

Great Barrington, town (pop. 6,712), SW Mass., on Housatonic R., in the Berkshires near N.Y. line. Summer resort and ski center.

Great Basin, interior region of W U.S., E of Sierra Nevada, W of Rocky Mts., NW of Colorado Plateau, NE of Sonoran Desert. Its more than 200,000 sq. mi. comprise most of Nev., W half of Utah, parts of Idaho, Oregon, and SE Calif. Its rugged N–S ranges are divided by deep, flat valleys. Altitude varies from c.10,-000 ft. above sea level to 280 ft. below in Death Valley. Little rain falls, streams do not reach ocean (e.g., Humboldt R., Carson R.), most lakes are saline. In ancient era, N part was covered by Bonneville (Great Salt L. is a remnant) and Lahontan Lakes. Basin is scene of silver, gold, other mining, and some irrigated farming.

Great Bear Lake, 200 mi. long and 25–110 mi. wide, N central Mackenzie dist., Northwest Territories, Canada. Drained W by Great Bear R. (flows c.100 mi. to Mackenzie R.). PORT RADIUM on E shore. Discovered by North West Co. traders c.1800. Fort Franklin built on SW shore by Sir John Franklin 1825.

Great Belt: see BELT, GREAT.

Great Bend, city (pop. 12,665), central Kansas, on Arkansas R. and on old Santa Fe and Chisholm trails; settled 1871. Trade center for wheat and oil region.

Great Berkhampstead, Berkhampstead, or **Berkhampstead** (all: bûrk'ŭmstĕd, bärk'–), urban district (pop. 10,777), Hertfordshire, England. Site of 11th-cent. royal castle associated with many historical figures. Birthplace of William Cowper.

Great Britain, largest of the British Isles. Politically the name is given to England, Scotland, and Wales since Act of Union of 1707. With NORTHERN IRELAND they form the United Kingdom (which earlier included all of IRELAND). Island was originally called BRITAIN. For history, see ENGLAND, SCOTLAND (until 1707), and WALES (until 1284).
The Growth of Empire. After 1707 Union the government remained as described under England. Founding of BANK OF ENGLAND (1694) showed growing English dominance of world trade and finance. After victories over Holland and France, the empire was expanded in late 18th cent. under the Georges and party leaders

Sir Robert WALPOLE, William PITT, Charles James Fox, and Edmund BURKE. After victories of War of the AUSTRIAN SUCCESSION and SEVEN YEARS WAR Britain's predominance was confirmed in India by Robert Clive and Warren Hastings; in North America by the conquests of James Wolfe. Loss to empire through the AMERICAN REVOLUTION was soon made up by settlements in Australia and New Zealand and by victories in FRENCH REVOLUTIONARY WARS and over NAPOLEON I. Rapid internal changes were caused by the INDUSTRIAL REVOLUTION. Irish grievances were only intensified by union with England (1800).

Commercial Leadership of the World. In the reign of VICTORIA (1837–1901) prosperity reached a peak. REFORM BILLS brought political reforms, and economic legislation removed the worst social abuses. Pressure from the new LIBERAL PARTY ended slavery (1832). The CORN LAWS were repealed in 1846. Robert Peel's advocacy of free trade split the CONSERVATIVE PARTY. A policy of colonial representative self-government contrasted with further conquests in INDIA. Britain's commercial interests led to OPIUM WAR with China (1840); its European diplomacy to participation in CRIMEAN WAR. Dominating statesmen of late 19th cent. were Liberal William GLADSTONE and Conservative Benjamin DISRAELI. Problems of empire expansion (see BRITISH EMPIRE) led to SOUTH AFRICAN WAR. Creation of the civil service improved government administration. The growth of trade unions increased the power of labor.

Before the Second World War. The reigns of Edward VII and George V saw tariff and social reforms, reduction of the power of the House of Lords by LLOYD GEORGE, the TRIPLE ALLIANCE and TRIPLE ENTENTE, WORLD WAR I, and the Treaty of VERSAILLES (1918). Problems mounted—reparations, WAR DEBTS, and new relation with Irish Free State. The LABOUR PARTY won its first victory (1924). 1931 saw a government crisis and a world-wide depression from which Britain recovered only slowly. Premiership of Neville CHAMBERLAIN (1937–40) saw policy of preferential tariffs maintained, decline of LEAGUE OF NATIONS, appeasement of Axis by MUNICH PACT (1938), delayed rearmament, pact with Poland, Soviet-German accord, and outbreak of World War II.

The Second World War and Social Change. After British defeat in Norway, Winston CHURCHILL became war-time coalition prime minister. DUNKIRK was followed by widely destructive air bombings of Britain. Outstanding military leaders were Bernard Montgomery, Archibald Wavell, and Lord Louis Mountbatten. After increasing aid from U.S. the ATLANTIC CHARTER was proclaimed in 1941. Britain took part in international conferences of CASABLANCA, CAIRO, MOSCOW, TEHERAN, and YALTA. Living standards were lowered drastically. German surrender (1945) was followed by a Labour government headed by Clement Attlee. Britain withdrew from India (1948), turned over problem of PALESTINE to UN, and signed a 50-year pact with France, Belgium, Luxembourg, and the Netherlands. Programs of nationalization of industry, socialized medicine, and housing and educational reforms were started. After termination of LEND-LEASE large U.S. loans (see EUROPEAN RECOVERY PROGRAM) failed to stop depletion of Britain's dollar reserve and devaluation of the pound. Conservatives returned to office (1951) under Churchill. For list of British kings see ENGLAND.

Great Chebeague Island (shǐbēg'), SW Maine, in Casco Bay. Resort and residential island.

great Dane: see HOUND.

Great Divide: see CONTINENTAL DIVIDE.

Great Dividing Range, general name for mountains and plateaus roughly paralleling E and SE coasts of Australia. Includes Australian Alps.

Great Falls, city (pop. 39,214), N central Mont., on Missouri R. opposite mouth of Sun R. (irrigation) and near falls for which city is named; founded 1883.

Largest city in state. Industrial and commercial center for a power development and for an agr. and mining area. Processes zinc, copper, oil, flour, and livestock. A U.S. Air Force base is near.

Great Fish, river: see BACK, SIR GEORGE.

Great Glen, depression extending NE–SW across Scotland. Traversed by CALEDONIAN CANAL.

Great Lakes, five fresh-water lakes, central North America, between Canada and U.S. Stretching 1,610 mi., they are L. SUPERIOR, L. MICHIGAN (entirely in U.S.), L. HURON, L. ERIE, and L. ONTARIO, out of which flows SAINT LAWRENCE R. French traders first saw lakes in c.1612. War of 1812 ended long English-French struggle for region, and settlement was fast. Erie Canal opening in 1825 accelerated commerce. Huge quantities of iron ore, grain, coal, oil, steel, and manufactured products are shipped out from April until Dec. when winter closes most ports. Shipbuilding and fishing are major industries. The lakes are linked to Mississippi R. and Gulf of Mexico by Illinois R. waterway, to Hudson R. and the Atlantic by N.Y. State Barge Canal.

Great Lakes-Saint Lawrence Seaway and Power Project, proposal by U.S. and Canada to deepen the waterway from W end of L. Superior to the Atlantic via Saint Lawrence R., for passage of ocean-going vessels and creation of water-power sites. Most attention would be given to river between Montreal and L. Ontario, where canals by-passing rapids are too shallow. Bills for joint development failed to pass U.S. Congress in 1932, 1941, 1952.

Great Meadows: see NECESSITY, FORT.

Great Miami (mīǎ'mū) or **Miami,** river rising in W Ohio and flowing generally SW c.160 mi., past Dayton, to Ohio R. at Ind. line. Little Miami R., to E, enters Ohio R. at Cincinnati.

Great Mother of the Gods, in ancient religions, Mother Earth, goddess of motherhood and of wild things, the symbol of fertility. She was worshiped under many names—Gaea, Rhea, Demeter, Artemis, and Aphrodite in Greece; Magna Mater and Bona Dea in Rome; Cybele in Phrygia; Isis in Egypt; Astarte in Phoenicia; and Ishtar in Babylonia and Assyria. See FERTILITY RITES.

Great Neck, village (pop. 7,759), SE N.Y., on N shore of Long Isl., in summer-estate area.

Great Northern Peninsula or **Petit Nord Peninsula,** NW part of N.F., Canada, extending 170 mi. NNE from Bonne Bay (SW) and White Bay (E) to Cape Bauld (N). Long Range lies along W coast.

Great Ouse, river, England: see OUSE 1.

Great Plains, high, extensive grasslands of W U.S. and Canada; generally level, treeless, semiarid. Bounded W by Rocky Mts., S by Llano Estacado and South Plains of Texas Panhandle, E by level prairies of Mississippi valley. In U.S. they include W parts of N.Dak., S.Dak., Nebr., Kansas, Okla.; E parts of Mont., Wyo., Colo., N.Mex.; and NW Texas. Plateau's elevation slopes gently from 6,000 ft. on W to the 2,000 ft. of prairies on E. Flowing E are the rivers Platte, Republican, Kansas, Arkansas, Cimmaron, and Canadian rivers. Wheat raising on this natural grazing land has caused some drought.

Great Rift Valley, geological FAULT system of E Africa and SW Asia, marked by chain of lakes. Ranges in elevation from 1,300 ft. below sea level (Dead Sea) to 6,000 ft. above in S Kenya.

Great Salt Lake, N Utah, W of Wasatch Range. Largest lake W of Mississippi R. (75 mi. long, 50 mi. wide, averages 13 ft. deep, but dimensions fluctuate greatly). Crossed by railroad. A remnant of anc. L. Bonneville fed by Weber, Jordan, Bear rivers; has no outlet. Only brine shrimp survive in extreme salinity. Some islands become peninsulas in low water. Long promontory extends from N shore. Salt wastelands to W now used for auto racing. Lake yields commercial salt. Explored 1825 by James Bridger.

Great Salt Plains Dam, NW Okla., in Salt Fork (Arkansas R. tributary); 5,700 ft. long, 68½ ft. high, completed 1948. Built for flood control and wildlife refuge.

Great Sand Dunes National Monument: see NATIONAL PARKS AND MONUMENTS (table).

Great Schism: see SCHISM, GREAT.

Great Slave Lake, 11,170 sq. mi., S Mackenzie dist., Northwest Territories, Canada, 300 mi. long and 30–140 mi. wide. Drained at W end by Mackenzie R. Discovered 1771 by Samuel Hearne. Gold found in 1930s on N shore and town of Yellowknife estab. as mining center. Receives the Hay (SW) and the Mackenzie (S), which is called **Great Slave** or **Slave River** between L. Athabaska and Great Slave L.

Great Smoky Mountains, part of Appalachian system, W N.C. and E Tenn., between Asheville and Knoxville, and between French Broad and Little Tennessee rivers. Part set aside for national park (estab. 1930). Rise to 6,642 ft. in Clingman's Dome. Folk and Indian museums and trails for hikers are to be found.

Great South Bay, SE N.Y., Atlantic arm between S shore of Long Isl. and barrier beach. Extends c.45 mi. from inlet near Rockaway Beach (W) to Moriches Bay. Both shores are rimmed with resorts and residential communities.

Great Stone Face: see FRANCONIA MOUNTAINS.

Great Wall of China: see CHINA, GREAT WALL OF.

Great Whale, river, rising in N central Que., Canada, and flowing 365 mi. W to Hudson Bay.

Great Yarmouth, Norfolk, England: see YARMOUTH.

grebe (grēb), diving bird related to loon and found on lakes and oceans over most of world. It has short wings, a vestigial tail, smooth plumage, and long, individually webbed toes. Grebes swim and fly well, but walk clumsily. Nests are on floating vegetation or fastened to water plants. Pied-billed grebe is well known in W Hemisphere. See *ill.,* p. 105.

Greco, El (ĕl grĕ′kō), c.1541–1614, Greek painter in Spain, b. Candia, Crete; real name was Domenicos Theotocopoulos. Studied in Venice. Settled 1577 in Toledo, where he painted the famous *View of Toledo* (Metropolitan Mus.). In his own day he enjoyed little popularity, but modern criticism ranks him among the great baroque artists. His typical paintings have elongated, distorted figures and vibrant color contrasted with subtle grays; pervading tone is one of religious ecstasy. Works are best seen in Toledo, Madrid, and the Escorial.

Greece, Gr. *Hellas* or *Ellas,* kingdom (50,147 sq. mi.; pop. 7,460,203), SE Europe, in S Balkan Peninsula and on islands in surrounding Ionian and Aegean Seas (largest EUBOEA and CRETE; islands variously grouped; see CYCLADES, DODECANESE, IONIAN ISLANDS, SPORADES). Continental Greece is cut sharply into two sections at the Isthmus of Corinth. S portion is the Peloponnesus, with Patras as its largest center. More populous and prosperous N has most of the cities, notably the cap., ATHENS, and the ports, PIRAEUS (part of Greater Athens), SALONICA, and KAVALLA. The country is hilly to mountainous, cut by short rivers, some with very fertile valleys. Though predominantly agr., Greece does not grow enough food for its population, and the land has been much eroded because of centuries of goat and sheep raising. The chief exports are tobacco, olive oil, raisins, currants, dried figs, and wine. Some minerals (iron ore, magnesite, chromite, and emery) and sponges are also shipped out. The prevailing religion is the Greek Orthodox.

Ancient Greece. The region had seen the rise and fall of splendid civilizations (see MINOAN CIVILIZATION, MYCENAEAN CIVILIZATION) before Greek-speaking peoples migrated in waves and thoroughly entrenched themselves. Traditional branches of the Greeks are Aeolians, Ionians, and Dorians, who supposedly arrived at different times, the last coming before 1000 B.C. In the mountain-divided lands they developed many independent CITY-STATES, which engaged in a constant succession of wars and alliances. Most important of these were to be Athens, SPARTA, THEBES,

and CORINTH. Even before the era celebrated in the poems of Homer the Greeks had looked to the sea and had begun to spread colonies across the Mediterranean that were ultimately to create a net of city-states from the Ionian shores of Asia Minor to Sicily, S Italy, and even to S France and Spain (see MAGNA GRAECIA). All the cities were united by a feeling of being Hellenes; they had common shrines (as at DELPHI) and common celebrations (as the OLYMPIC GAMES). Nevertheless, political disunity was so strong that even when the Persians threatened the Ionian cities there was only a half-hearted union to oppose them in the PERSIAN WARS (500–449 B.C.). When the war was successful the greatest period of Greek history was begun. The city-states, and Athens in particular, felt a surge of cultural development scarcely equaled in world history. Prosperity came to Athens with the aid of the DELIAN LEAGUE, and the age of Pericles was one of glory. Drama and poetry, art, architecture, and philosophy flourished, and Greece became the fountainhead of later Western civilization. The list of great men whose words still echo is astonishing, and the list continued to grow after political misfortune set in; Aeschylus, Sophocles, Euripides, Aristophanes, Phidias, Socrates, Plato, and Aristotle are all well known to all the West. Though Athens lost to Sparta in the PELOPONNESIAN WAR (431–404 B.C.), Athenian thought prevailed. Even in politics, though the city-states varied from monarchy to aristocracy, oligarchy, and tyranny, the idea of democracy was born in Greece. Sparta's short-lived triumph was followed by the hegemony of Corinth and of Thebes, but all soon yielded to the conquest of PHILIP II of Macedon at Chaeronea (338 B.C.). Ironically, this defeat made it possible for Philip's son, ALEXANDER THE GREAT, to carry Greek civilization across the known world. While Greece itself fell prey to wars and conquest (despite the efforts of the Achaean League and the Aetolian League), HELLENISTIC CIVILIZATION spread, and though the Romans by 146 B.C. had reduced Greece to a political cipher, they looked up to the Greeks as bearers of civilization. When the Roman Empire was split (A.D. 395), the E portion, the BYZANTINE EMPIRE, was thoroughly Greek in tradition.

Medieval and Modern Greece. Greece was not an important factor in Byzantine history, and was frequently overrun by barbarians. In the 11th cent. began the Turkish inroads and Norman attacks. The Fourth Crusade led (1204) to disintegration of the empire and creation of the Latin Empire of Constantinople. When the Byzantine Empire was restored (1261–1453), only parts of Greece were recovered, European rulers holding the rest until all fell to the Turks (by 1456). Greece was unimportant in the Ottoman Empire. With the awakening of nationalism in the early 19th cent. the Greeks dreamed of independence and in 1821 commenced a rebellion that, with the leadership of the Ypsilantis and the aid of European liberals, succeeded. In 1827 CAPO D'ISTRIA became president of a Greece whose independence was assured by the battle of Navarino (1827), the Russo-Turkish Treaty of Adrianople (1829), and wide recognition (1832). Civil struggles continued, and the Bavarian king imposed on the Greeks, OTTO I, was finally deposed (1862) and succeeded by GEORGE I. A war with Turkey (1896–97) to obtain Crete was unsuccessful, but later international pressure forced incorporation of Crete into Greek territory (1913). In the Balkan Wars Greece got SE Macedonia and W Thrace. When in World War I King CONSTANTINE insisted on neutrality and resisted joining the Allies even after the Salonica campaigns, the political leader Venizelos led a movement that forced Constantine's abdication (1917) in favor of his son, ALEXANDER. After the war the Greeks were given most of European Turkey and the Bulgarian coast. An attempt to invade Asia Minor led to defeat by the Turks (1922).

Under a League of Nations commission Greece and Turkey then exchanged nationals to make their boundary an ethnic as well as a political one. Constantine, who had returned as ruler after the death of Alexander (1920), was deposed again (1922) and succeeded by GEORGE II, who was in turn deposed in 1923 but was restored in 1935 after Greece suffered many warring years as a republic. Shortly Greece was under the dictatorship of METAXAS. In World War II Greece was neutral until invaded by the Italians from Albania (1940). The Greeks gave a good account of themselves, but in 1941 the Germans attacked and were shortly triumphant over resistance of the Greeks and British allies. There resulted organized guerrilla warfare that was successful though there was strife between leftist (ELAS) and rightest (EDES) guerrillas. After the Germans were expelled with some British help (1944), attempts were made to restore the war-ridden country, but bad conditions were made worse by internal strife. Though George II was recalled by plebiscite (1946), Communist-led leftists opposed him and set up a rival government. In 1947 Truman announced U.S. support to anti-Communists, and U.S. aid was poured into Greece. The Communist forces were defeated and some headway made in clearing up the appalling economic conditions left by the war. In 1947 George II died and was succeeded by his brother PAUL. Admission of Greece into the North Atlantic Treaty Organization was made final early in 1952. A new constitution was adopted in 1951.

Greek Anthology, collection of Greek epigrams or short poems, including poetry down to the decay of Byzantium. Edited and added to successively by ancient and medieval scholars; versions of 10th and 14th cent. most used.

Greek architecture began with advent of the Dorians in Greece (before 1000 B.C.) and was evolved between 10th and 6th cent. B.C. The Heræum at Olympia, most ancient temple yet discovered, illustrates beginning of Doric style. Chief Greek works were produced between 700 B.C. and Roman occupation (146 B.C.). Great age was reign of Pericles, in which the architects Callicrates, Mnesicles, and Ictinus flourished and in which the perfected DORIC ORDER appeared in PARTHENON and PROPYLAEA. The Greeks laid masonry without mortar but with joints cut to great exactness. Colors and gilding were used to emphasize decorative sculpture. The IONIC ORDER, evolved in Greek colonies of Asia Minor, was used extensively at Miletus. It appeared after 500 B.C. in Greece proper, where its only great example is the ERECHTHEUM. Latest and most ornate Greek style, CORINTHIAN ORDER, was little used. After shift of power from Greece proper to Asia Minor, Hellenistic architecture arose (4th–3d cent. B.C.) with florid elements, more complicated design, and a new emphasis on city planning. See *ill.,* p. 47.

Greek art may be said to have begun with pottery making (c.900–700 B.C.), marked by abstract, mathematical systems of design. New interest in representation arose between 700 and 600 B.C. Sculpture emerged as dominant artistic form in archaic period (c.625–480 B.C.) with statues of nude walking youths, *kouroi,* which suggest Egyptian prototypes, and draped female figures, which suggest Near Eastern influence. Painters of archaic period depicted many mythological and contemporary scenes as decoration for vases; outstanding masters were Euthymides and Euphronius. Early classical or transitional period (c.480–450 B.C.) tried to find balance between naturalism and abstraction. Classical period or Golden Age (c. 450–400 B.C.) aimed to represent the ideal human being, both in form and in character. Significant sculptures of the period are from Athenian Acropolis. In late classical period (400–300 B.C.) emphasis on emotion was increased (esp. in sculptures of Scopas). Among great sculptors who flourished 500–300 B.C. were Praxiteles, Lysippus, Myron, Cresilas, Timotheus, and Bryaxis; the painters included Apollodorus, Zeuxis, Parrha-

sius, and Apelles. Hellenistic period was last phase of Greek art; its best-known masterpiece is *Victory of Samothrace.*

Greek Church: see ORTHODOX EASTERN CHURCH.

Greek fire, inflammable substance, a "liquid" fire, said to have been invented by Callinicus of Heliopolis who, at Constantinople in reign of Constantine Pogonatus, used it to set fire to enemy ships. Byzantine Greeks used it in early Middle Ages. Chemical nature not known, but probably contained sulphur, various easily inflammable materials, and a substance (e.g., lime) which reacts with water to produce heat.

Greek language, Indo-European language. Modern Greek is derived from the standard Greek (or Koine) of Hellenistic world. The New Testament is written in a form of this. See LANGUAGE (table).

Greek music. Music in ancient Greece was evidently a highly developed art. Few examples are extant, but something about it can be learned from secondary sources, e.g., the third book of Plato's *Republic* and writings on musical theory by Aristoxenus of Tarentum (fl. 4th cent. B.C.). Early Greek music was inseparable from poetry and dancing. Its melodic system was based on the MODE. Music was believed to have an emotional and moral influence. Chief instruments were the oboe-like aulos (used in festivals of Dionysus) and a kind of lyre called the kithara (sacred to Apollo). Notation was indicated by letters. There were two such systems, one vocal and one instrumental. Early in Greek music's history, its relation to physics was recognized. See *ill.,* p. 667.

Greek religion. Sources and history of Greek myth are subject of much argument and conjecture. Religious beliefs in ancient Greece were complex and often contradictory. There was a basic animism, but it was complicated by confusion with local deities. Even in Homer's time, when gods were pictured anthropomorphically, no code of ethics or morals was connected with them. Cults of mortal heroes were common from earliest times. Later, heroes and gods became inextricably mixed in legends. Characteristics and stories of the great gods were drawn from many sources: some stemmed from early worship of the Greeks outside the peninsula, some came from Minoan and Mycenaean civilizations, and some were brought in from Asia and Egypt. ZEUS was ruler of OLYMPIAN gods, whose home was Mt. Olympus but who wandered freely about the world. There were also underworld gods. These dwelt in Hades, ruled by Pluto and PERSEPHONE. The underworld and the cycle of vegetation were the base for ELEUSINIAN MYSTERIES. Other MYSTERIES, such as ORPHIC MYSTERIES were connected with worship of DIONYSUS. Mysteries were important for their strong ethical and moral teachings, and their priests were exalted, as were those of the great oracles (see ORACLE; DELPHI). By 5th cent. B.C. literal belief in gods was fading in minds of the educated, and dematerialization of gods into great forces enabled poets and philosophers to picture a cosmos in which moral struggle was paramount.

Greek revival: see CLASSIC REVIVAL.

Greeley, Horace, 1811–72, American newspaper editor, founder of New York *Tribune* (1841). Sought to provide for laboring classes a cheap paper that would be both clean and intelligent. Staff included distinguished talent; his editorials made paper widely known. Supported protective tariff; other causes he advocated included many social reforms. The *Tribune* was popular in the West; many had acted upon Greeley's advice, "Go West, young man, go West." One of first editors to join Republican party. His humanitarian hatred of war often embarrassed Lincoln's administration; at end of Civil War he advocated amnesty for all Southerners. Though an early supporter of U. S. Grant, Greeley encouraged growth of LIBERAL REPUBLICAN PARTY. Party's unsuccessful candidate for President in 1872.

Greeley, city (pop. 20,354), N Colo., NNE of Denver

near South Platte R. Rail, trade, processing center for irrigated farms (grain, sugar beets). Cooperative Union Colony was founded here in 1870 by an agent of Horace Greeley.

Greely, Adolphus Washington, 1844–1935, American army officer and arctic explorer. Commanded U.S. expedition to establish one of chain of international circumpolar meteorological stations (1881). Rescued with few survivors (1884). Noted builder of army telegraphic communications. Directed relief operations after San Francisco earthquake. Awarded Congressional Medal of Honor (1935).

Green, Anna Katharine, 1846–1935, American detective-story writer. Her thrillers (e.g., *The Leavenworth Case,* 1878) popularized the master detective.

Green, Duff, 1791–1875, American journalist and politician. His paper, the *United States Telegraph,* supported Pres. Jackson until Green turned to support of J. C. Calhoun and to defense of South on slavery and tariff issues. Later was diplomatic agent to Texas and Mexico.

Green, George, 1793–1841, English mathematician. He worked on equilibrium of fluids and was first to introduce potential as applied to theories of magnetic and electric fields.

Green, Henry, pseud. of Henry Vincent Yorke, 1905–, English novelist, an industrialist. His novels, somewhat experimental in style, combine the comic spirit with a sympathetic detachment. They include *Living* (1929), *Loving* (1945), *Back* (1946), *Nothing* (1950), *Doting* (1952).

Green, Hetty (Howland Robinson), 1835–1916, American financier. Managed inherited fortune so shrewdly that she was considered greatest woman financier in the world.

Green, John Richard, 1837–83, English historian. His *A Short History of the English People* (1874) stressed social rather than political change.

Green, Julian, 1900–, French writer, of American origin. Studied in U.S. Author of somber psychological tales (*The Closed Garden,* 1927; Eng. tr., 1928), journals (1938–39; Eng. tr., *Personal Record*), and reminiscences (*Memories of Happy Days,* 1942).

Green, Paul, 1894–, American author, b. N.C. His works include plays (e.g., *In Abraham's Bosom,* 1926), short stories, and a novel (*Laughing Pioneer,* 1932). Has also written symphonic dramas (*The Lost Colony,* 1937; *The Common Glory,* 1948) dealing with American history.

Green, Samuel Swett, 1837–1918, American librarian. One of the founders and president (1891) of American Library Association; author of *The Public Library Movement in the United States, 1853–1893* (1913).

Green, Seth, 1817–88, pioneer American pisciculturist, credited with making large-scale fish breeding practical. He transplanted Atlantic shad to Pacific.

Green, Thomas Hill, 1836–82, English neo-Hegelian philosopher. Asserted that consciousness made knowledge possible, thus setting idealism against prevailing empiricism and sensationalism. His *Prolegomena to Ethics* (1883) was an influential book.

Green, William, 1873–1952, American labor leader, president of American Federation of Labor (1924–52). Built up A.F. of L.; led fight with C.I.O.

Greenaway, Kate, 1846–1901, English illustrator of children's books and water-color painter.

greenback. In 1862 U.S. government first issued, on a temporary basis, legal tender notes (popularly called greenbacks) which were placed on a par with notes backed by specie. By end of Civil War such notes were outstanding to amount over $400,000,000. In accordance with Funding Act of 1866 Secretary of State Hugh McCulloch began retiring them. Hard times in 1867 led to demand that currency should be inflated rather than contracted; Congress suspended retirement. In 1868 a compromise left greenbacks to amount of $356,000,000 in circulation. Law creating them was declared constitutional in later LEGAL TEN-

DER CASES. Following Panic of 1873 agrarians wanted currency inflated with more greenbacks. Conservatives triumphed with Resumption Act of 1875, which fixed Jan. 1, 1879, as date for redeeming greenbacks in specie. Congress provided in 1878 that greenbacks then outstanding ($346,681,000) remain permanent part of currency.

Greenback party, in U.S. history, political organization formed in years 1874–76 to promote currency expansion. Members were principally Western and Southern farmers; stricken by Panic of 1873, they wanted inflated currency because it would wipe out farm debts contracted in times of high prices. Failing to capture the Democratic party in 1874, Greenback party nominated Peter Cooper for President in 1876; got only 81,737 votes. In 1878, however, the Greenback-Labor party, representing a union of labor and greenback supporters, polled over 1,000,000 votes and elected 14 Representatives to Congress. Party dissolved after 1884 election. Many members later became Populists.

Green Bay, city (pop. 52,735), NE Wis., at mouth of Fox R. and on Green Bay. Here Jean Nicolet estab. trading post 1634, and Father Allouez a mission 1669. Oldest permanent settlement in Wis., estab. 1701. Augustin LANGLODE chief early fur trader. French had fort here from 1717, which British held from 1761 until PONTIAC'S REBELLION. U.S. Fort Howard built 1816. Furs lost importance after opening of Erie Canal and expansion of lumbering and farming. Shipping, wholesale, and jobbing trade center; processing paper and cheese. Has professional football team, Green Bay Packers.

Green Bay, W arm of L. Michigan, c.100 mi. long, indenting NE Wis. and along Mich. Upper Peninsula.

Greenbelt, town (pop. 7,074), W central Md., near Washington, D.C.; chartered 1937. Garden city constructed by the Federal Resettlement Administration as model community (others are Greenhills, Ohio, and Greendale, Wis.). Businesses are cooperatively owned.

greenbrier: see SMILAX.

Greencastle, city (pop. 6,888), W central Ind., WSW of Indianapolis. Rail and trade center for agr. and livestock area. Produces zinc and lumber. Seat of DePauw Univ. (Methodist; coed.; 1837).

Greendale, village (pop. 2,752), SE Wis., near Milwaukee. A Federal Resettlement Association garden city (see GREENBELT, Md.).

Greene, Graham, 1904–, English writer. Earlier novels gave literary merit to "shockers" (e.g., *Brighton Rock,* 1938); later deal with Catholic themes (e.g., *The Heart of the Matter,* 1948; *The End of the Affair,* 1951). Also powerful short stories.

Greene, Nathanael, 1742–86, American Revolutionary general. Commander in CAROLINA CAMPAIGN.

Greene, Robert, 1558?–92, English dramatist, poet, miscellaneous writer. His short romantic "novels" (e.g. *Pandosto,* 1588) were popular. His plays, pseudo-historical in tone, include *Friar Bacon and Friar Bungay* (1594) and *James IV* (1598). Among his many didactic tracts, those on cony-catching show sordid London underworld.

Greeneville, town (pop. 8,721), NE Tenn., SW of Johnson City, in tobacco and farm area. Cap. of State of FRANKLIN 1785–88. Has Andrew Johnson Natl. Monument (his home, tailor shop, grave), monument to Gen. J. H. Morgan (killed here in Civil War). Tobacco experiment station and Tusculum Col. (coed.; 1794) are near by.

Greenfield. 1 City (pop. 6,159), central Ind., E of Indianapolis. Birthplace of J. W. Riley. **2** Town (pop. 17,349), including Greenfield village (pop. 15,075), NW Mass., near junction of Deerfield R. with Connecticut R.; settled 1686. Mfg. of metal products. E terminus of Mohawk Trail.

Greenfield Village, reproduction of early American village, estab. 1933 by Henry Ford at Dearborn, Mich., as part of Edison Inst. About a typical New England village green are grouped public buildings and other structures, including Edison's Menlo Park workshop, Noah Webster's birthplace, Stephen Foster's home. Mills and craft shops illustrate early methods.

Greenhills, village (pop. 3,005), SW Ohio, near Cincinnati; estab. 1938 by Federal Resettlement Administration. See GREENBELT, Md.

greenhouse, enclosed glass house used for growing plants in regulated temperatures and humidity. In size range from lean-to type attached to home to large commercial buildings or hothouses for growing flowers and vegetables out of season.

Greenland, Dan. *Grønland,* Danish colony (c.840,000 sq. mi.; pop. 21,412), island, largely within Arctic Circle, between Canada (W) and Iceland (E); max. length 1,660 mi., max. width 750 mi. Geologically part of Canadian shield, Greenland is covered by an ice sheet (over 8,000 ft. thick in some places) ringed with mountains, except for c.132,000 sq. mi. of coastland. Numerous glaciers (Humboldt is largest), which "calve" icebergs, debouch into coastal fjords. Over 90% of pop. lives on warmer W coast. Natives are mostly of mixed Danish and ESKIMO ancestry. Greenland is administered by board of governors at Copenhagen. Important settlements are Godthaab and Godhavn. Chief resources are minerals (esp. cryolite at Ivigtut; also lignite and graphite). Agr. and sheep grazing are limited to SW, but Peary Land supports musk oxen. There are cod and halibut fisheries, and seals and walruses are hunted. Entire trade of Greenland is a state monopoly. Island was discovered and colonized (c.982) by ERIC THE RED, but it fell into neglect in 14th and 15th cent. and was not rediscovered until 16th cent. Then coast was charted by seekers of Northwest Passage. Modern colonization was begun (1721) by a Norwegian missionary, Hans Egede. Greenland was explored and mapped by many arctic explorers in 19th and 20th cent. In World War II, U.S. estab. (1940) a consulate at Godthaab and received permission to set up military bases. In late 1952 a huge strategic air base was under construction at THULE. A plan for raising Greenlanders' economic, educational, and hygienic standards was drafted in 1946.

Greenland Sea, arm of Arctic Ocean, off NE coast of Greenland. Main outlet of Arctic Ocean to Atlantic. Due to ice it is rarely open to navigation.

Green Mountain Boys, popular name of partisan armed bands in present Vt. Defended region against New York control in NEW HAMPSHIRE GRANTS controversy. Chief leader was Ethan ALLEN. In American Revolution they captured Ticonderoga in 1775 and won victory at Bennington in 1777.

Green Mountains, range of the Appalachians extending from Que. (N) to Mass. (S); generally low (2–3,000 ft.), but rising to 4,393 ft. in Mt. Mansfield, NW of Montpelier. This peak, highest in Vt., has pre-1860 hotel at summit and deep gorge, Smugglers Notch, at foot. There are many streams (water power) and fertile valleys. Noted for scenic beauty; many resorts. Yield marble and granite.

Greenock (grē′nŭk, grī′–), burgh (pop. 76,299), Renfrewshire, Scotland, on S shore of Firth of Clyde. A port, it has shipbuilding and varied mfg. Has unusually heavy rainfall. Birthplace of James Watt.

Greenough, Horatio (grē′nō), 1805–52, American sculptor, b. Boston. Worked in Florence 1829–51. His colossal statue of Washington is in Smithsonian Institution building, Washington, D.C.

Green River. 1 River rising in central Ky. and flowing 370 mi. WNW to Ohio R. near Evansville, Ind. **2** River, 730 mi. long, rising in W Wyo. in Wind River Range and flowing through W Wyo. and E Utah, with loop in NW Colo., to Colorado R. in SE Utah. Largest tributary of the Colorado, it receives Yampa, White, Black Fork, Duchesne, Price, and San Rafael rivers. Large U.S. reclamation project planned.

Greensboro, city (pop. 74,389), central N.C., E of Winston-Salem in piedmont; settled 1749. Rail junc-

tion and textile center. Seat of Bennett Col. (Negro; Methodist; for women; 1873); Woman's Col. of Univ. of NORTH CAROLINA; Agricultural and Technical Col. of North Carolina (Negro; land-grant, state supported; coed; chartered 1891, opened 1893); and Guilford Col. (Friends; coed; 1834). Birthplace of O. Henry. Battle of Guilford Courthouse was near.

Greensburg. 1 City (pop. 6,619), SE Ind., SE of Indianapolis. Trade center for agr., oil, and gas area. Ships tobacco. **2** City (pop. 16,923), SW Pa., SE of Pittsburgh; settled 1782. Mfg. of plumbing supplies and metal products. Seat of Seton Hill Col. (R.C.; for women; 1883).

Greenville. 1 City (pop. 6,781), S Ala., SSW of Montgomery, in cotton, truck, pecan area. **2** City (pop. 6,668), S Mich., NE of Grand Rapids. Potato market; mfg. of refrigerators. **3** City (pop. 29,936), W Miss., on Mississippi R. and NW of Jackson. Trade, processing, and shipping center of Mississippi-Yazoo delta (cotton). Flood of 1927 caused building of higher levees and creation of L. Ferguson. **4** Town (pop. 16,724), E N.C., on Tar R. and ESE of Raleigh; founded 1786. Tobacco market. **5** City (pop. 8,859), W Ohio, NW of Dayton. Trade center of agr. area. Gen. Anthony Wayne built Fort Greenville 1793, and negotiated Treaty of Greenville 1795 with Indians, who ceded large part of Old Northwest to U.S. **6** Borough (pop. 9,210), W Pa., near Ohio border NNE of Sharon. Trade center in agr. area. **7** City (pop. 58,161), NW S.C., in piedmont near Blue Ridge on Reedy R., laid out 1797. A main SE U.S. industrial and commerical center, it processes textiles and farm produce, and has packing plants and other industries. Center of milltown region. Has biennial Southern Textile Exposition. Seat of Furman Univ. (Baptist; 1825; coordinated with Greenville Woman's Col. 1933). **8** City (pop. 14,-727), E Texas, NE of Dallas; settled 1846. Cotton growing, processing, and shipping center with oil refineries.

green vitriol: see COPPERAS.

Greenwich (grĭ′nĭj), metropolitan borough (pop. 91,-492) of SE London, England, on the Thames. Located here are the Royal Naval Col., Greenwich Hospital (on the site of a former palace where Henry VIII, Mary I, and Elizabeth were born), and the Natl. Maritime Mus. The Royal Observatory was located until 1946 on a hill in Greenwich Park selected by Sir Christopher Wren. Geographic longitude is still figured from the prime meridian here.

Greenwich. 1 (grĕ′nĭch) Residential and resort town (pop. 40,835), extreme SW Conn., on Long Isl. Sound at N.Y. state line. Purchased from Indians 1640; raided by British 1779. Includes villages, e.g., Riverside, Old Greenwich, Cos Cob. Printing and publishing. Has Edgewood and Rosemary Hall schools. Audubon Nature Center (1943) is near. **2** (grēn′wĭch) Village, SW N.J., SW of Bridgeton. Scene of a tea-burning "party" 1774.

Greenwich Village (grĕ′nĭch), district of lower Manhattan borough of New York city, lying roughly between 14th St. (N) and Houston St. (S), Washington Square (E) and Hudson R. (W). Separate village in colonial times, it became, successively, exclusive residential area, tenement area, and (c.1910) home and workshop of nonconformist artists, writers, and theater people. Many artists still live here. Visitors are attracted by lingering aura of bohemianism which surrounds picturesque streets and buildings. Holds semiannual outdoor art exhibits.

Greenwood. 1 City (pop. 18,061), W central Miss., on Yazoo R. and N of Jackson; settled 1834. Processing, marketing, and shipping center of cotton area. **2** City (pop. 13,806), W S.C., WNW of Columbia; settled 1824. Has textile and lumber mills, foundries, and machine shops. Buzzard Roost hydroelectric development near by.

Greenwood Lake, c.7 mi. long, SE N.Y. and N N.J., in mountain resort area.

Greer, town (pop. 5,050), NW S.C., NE of Greenville. Has textile mills.

Greet, (Sir Philip) Ben, 1857–1936, English actor and theatrical manager. Noted for productions of Shakspere and of morality play, *Everyman.*

Gregg, Josiah, 1806–50, American trader, historian of Sante Fe Trail. Wrote *Commerce of the Prairies* (1844), classic of American frontier history.

Gregg, William, 1800–1867, "father of Southern cotton manufacture." Estab. Graniteville, S.C. (1846), first Southern mill town.

Gregorian chant: see PLAIN SONG.

Gregory I, Saint (the Great), c.540–604, pope (590–604), Doctor of the Church. A Roman prefect, he gave his property to the Church and bécame a monk. Though he resisted each promotion, his abilities carried him finally to the papacy. His rule was notable for the firmness with which he defended his office and Rome, attacking Donatism in Africa, refusing to recognize the patriarch of Constantinople as ecumenical (an act that helped split East and West), treating with attacking Lombards (592) after the imperial exarch failed to act. Gregory did much to shape the history of the Church for centuries; he encouraged the spread of monasticism, made laws for the lives of the clergy, and sent missionaries to England. He wrote much and well (commentaries on Job; saints' lives; *Pastoral Care*) and contributed to development of Gregorian chant or PLAIN SONG.

Gregory VII, Saint, d. 1085, pope (1073–85) (Hildebrand; Ital., *Ildebrando*). A Benedictine, he became a notable figure under Pope Gregory VI, and under Leo IX launched the Hildebrandine reform, aimed at correcting chief Church abuses of simony, lay INVESTITURE, and violation of clerical celibacy. As chief figure in the curia under Leo's successors, he transferred papal election from the Romans to the college of cardinals and formed an alliance with the Normans of S Italy. A powerful antireform party grew among laymen who feared church domination; with this ambitious German King HENRY IV sided. Hildebrand, made pope (1073) as Gregory VII, pressed his reform and sent papal legates throughout Europe enforcing his decrees. The quarrel between Henry and Gregory came to an open break in 1076. The pope excommunicated Henry, who, losing his support, humbled himself before Gregory at Canossa. In 1080 the two again fell out. Henry, again excommunicated, set up GUIBERT OF RAVENNA (Clement III) as antipope. Gregory's appeal to the Christian world failed, and when the German civil war ended Henry marched into Italy. He took Rome (1083) and Gregory retired into the Castel Sant' Angelo. The Normans under ROBERT GUISCARD rescued him but were quickly expelled from Rome. Gregory went with them; he died in Salerno after a year of exile. His last words were said to be, "I have loved justice and hated iniquity, therefore I die in exile." His extreme assertion of papal prerogative and devotion to reform made him one of the most powerful and greatest of the popes. He was canonized in 1728. Feast: May 25.

Gregory IX, 1145–1241, pope (1227–41); nephew of Innocent III. He excommunicated Emperor FREDERICK II for delaying to fulfill his vow to go on crusade (1227). Imperialists in Rome then revolted, and the pope fled to Viterbo and Perugia. Later, in a struggle over Italian liberties Gregory again excommunicated Frederick and ordered his dethronement. Frederick prevented German publication of the bulls and blocked a general council. Gregory died as Frederick was about to attack Rome.

Gregory XI, 1330–78, pope (1370–78), a Frenchman (Pierre Roger de Beaufort). He received prophetic warnings from St. Bridget of Sweden and St. CATHERINE OF SIENA to remove papacy from Avignon to Rome, but Avignon court was opposed and Italy inhospitable. He defeated Bernabò Visconti of Milan with hired aid of Sir John de Hawkwood (1374). A struggle with Milan and Florence ensued, ending with the interdict on Florence. Gregory finally consented to Catherine's pleas and moved to Rome (1376–77). Gregory first condemned Wyclif. Elections after his death began the Great SCHISM.

Gregory XII, c.1327–1417, pope (1406–15). He agreed before his election during course of Great SCHISM to resign if Avignon antipope Benedict XIII (Pedro de LUNA) would also resign. The agreement failed, and Gregory created four new cardinals despite agreement against new creations. But the cardinals united in convoking the Council of Pisa (1409), which declared pope and antipope deposed, and elected a new antipope, Alexander V. After years of confusion the Council of CONSTANCE recognized Gregory as canonical pope, after which he resigned.

Gregory XIII, 1502–85, pope (1572–85), best known for his reformed Gregorian CALENDAR. He was prominent in the Catholic Reform at Council of TRENT (1545, 1559–63). As pope, he proposed deposition of Queen Elizabeth, refused to compromise with German Protestants, and held public thanksgiving at Rome for the massacre of St. Bartholomew's Day (having been told it was suppression of a rebellion). Issued new edition of the canon law. His government of Papal States was execrable.

Gregory XVI, 1765–1846, pope (1831–46); a conservative, much denounced by European liberals. His most famous act was condemnation of LAMENNAIS (1832).

Gregory, Augusta (Persse) Gregory, Lady, 1859–1932, Irish author and playwright. A founder of the ABBEY THEATRE, she devoted many years to managing and directing it and writing for it. Her journals are a vivid source of Irish literary history.

Gregory, Horace, 1898–, American poet and critic.

Gregory, James, 1638–75, Scottish mathematician. He invented a reflecting telescope and a photometric mode of measuring the distance of stars.

Gregory Nazianzen, Saint (năzēăn'zĭn), c.330–390, Cappadocian theologian, Doctor of the Church. An intimate of St. Basil the Great, he was chosen bishop of Constantinople (379), but on the failure of the First Council of Constantinople, he retired. Feast: May 9.

Gregory of Nyssa, Saint (nĭs'ŭ), d. 394, bishop of Nyssa, Cappadocia (after 371); brother of St. BASIL THE GREAT; one of great orthodox Catholic writers on Trinity, redemption, grace. Feast: March 9.

Gregory of Tours, Saint, 538–94, French historian, bishop of Tours (from 573), author of *History of the Franks.* Feast: Nov. 17.

Greiz (grīts), city (pop. 45,410), Thuringia, central Germany; until 1918 cap. of principality of REUSS (older line). Textile, paper, chemical mfg.

Grenada (grĭnā'dŭ), island (c.119 sq. mi.), British West Indies. Part of Grenada colony (133 sq. mi., pop. 72,-387), in Windward Isls; cap. Saint George's.

Grenada (grĭnā'dŭ), city (pop. 7,388), N central Miss., on Yalobusha R. and NW of Greenwood, in cotton and timber area.

grenadine: see POMEGRANATE.

Grenfell, Sir Wilfred (Thomason), 1865–1940, English Protestant medical missionary. Served 40 years in Labrador and Newfoundland among fishermen and Eskimo.

Grenoble (grünô'blǔ), city (pop. 97,287), cap. of Isère dept., SE France, on Isère R.; historic cap. of Dauphiné. Mfg. (paper, cement); electrical industries. Famous university estab. 1339. Among notable buildings are cathedral (12th–13th cent.), Church of St. André (13th–14th cent., with tomb of Bayard), and Renaissance palace of dauphins. Birthplace of Stendhal. Grande CHARTREUSE is near by.

Grenville, George, 1712–70, British prime minister (1763–65). Initiated unpopular prosecution of John Wilkes and caused unrest in America by ill-advised STAMP ACT (1765). His son, **George Nugent Temple Grenville, 1st marquess of Buckingham,** 1753–1813, Whig member of Parliament (1774–79), opposed Lord

North's policy of coercion of the American colonies. His brother, **William Wyndham Grenville, Baron Grenville,** 1759–1834, was William Pitt's foreign secretary 1791–1801. In 1806 he formed the "ministry of all the talents" which abolished the slave trade.

Grenville, Sir Richard, 1542–91, English naval hero. Commanded fleet carrying first colonists to ROANOKE ISLAND in 1585. On an expedition to capture Spanish treasure ships in 1591, his ship *Revenge* became separated from the rest of the fleet. He tried to break through the Spanish line, fought 15 ships, and was mortally wounded.

Grenville, William Wyndham Grenville, Baron: see GRENVILLE, GEORGE.

Gresham's law (grĕ′shŭmz), economic principle that "bad money drives out good," i.e., when debased money is in concurrent circulation with money of high value in terms of precious metals, the good money disappears. Named for Sir Thomas Gresham (1519?–1579), English merchant and financier, though it has now been shown that he did not originate it.

Gretchaninov, Aleksandr (Tichonovich) (ŭlyĭksän′dùr grĕchänĕ′nŏf), 1864–, Russian composer. Although he wrote symphonies and operas, he is best known for his many songs and sacred choral works. Settled in the U.S. 1939.

Gretna, city (pop. 13,813), SE La., S of New Orleans. Industrial and residential suburb.

Gretna Green or **Gretna,** parish (pop. 2,857), Dumfriesshire, Scotland. Famous as a place of runaway marriages 1754–1856.

Grétry, André Ernest (ädrä′ ĕrnĕst′ grātrē′), 1741?–1813, French composer, master of the *opéra comique.* His masterpiece is *Richard Cœur-de-Lion.*

Greuze, Jean Baptiste (zhä′ bäptĕst′ grûz′), 1725–1805, French genre and portrait painter. Tried to paint according to Diderot's aesthetic theories.

Greville, Fulke: see BROOKE, FULKE GREVILLE, 1ST BARON.

Grévy, Jules (zhül grāvē′), 1807–91, president of France (1879–87); a moderate republican.

Grew, Joseph C(lark), 1880–, American diplomat. U.S. ambassador to Japan from 1932 until Pearl Harbor, he was earlier ambassador to Turkey (1927–32) and twice served as Undersecretary of State (1924–27, 1944–45).

Grew, Nehemiah, 1641–1712, English botanist, physician. He practiced medicine in London and made important microscopic studies of plants. His observations of sex in plants were probably the first.

Grey, Charles Grey, 2d Earl, 1764–1845, British prime minister (1830–34). Put through Wilberforce's act to abolish African slave trade (1807). Secured passage of Reform Bill of 1832 by forcing William IV to threaten to create enough Whig peers to carry it in the House of Lords. His grandson, **Albert Henry George Grey, 4th Earl Grey,** 1851–1917, English statesman, was liberal member, House of Commons (1880–86); opposed Home Rule Bill of 1886. Governor general of Canada (1904–11).

Grey, Lady Jane, 1537–54, candidate for the throne of England; greatniece of Henry VIII. Married to the son of duke of Northumberland who persuaded Edward VI to name her as his successor. Unwillingly proclaimed queen (1553), she was imprisoned after nine days and Mary I became queen. Her father joined Wyatt's rebellion and she was beheaded.

Grey, Zane, 1875–1939, American writer of many Wild West tales (e.g., *Riders of the Purple Sage,* 1912).

greyhound: see HOUND.

Greylock, peak, Mass.: see BERKSHIRE HILLS.

Grey of Fallodon, Edward Grey, 1st Viscount (fă′lōdùn), 1862–1933, British statesman. Foreign secretary (1905–16), he worked long but fruitlessly to avert war in Europe.

Griboyedov, Aleksandr Sergeyevich (ŭlyĭksän′dùr sĭrgä′ŭvĭch grĕbùyĕ′dùf), 1795–1829, Russian playwright, author of *The Misfortune of Being Clever*

(1825; Eng. tr., 1914), a satire on Moscow society.

Gridley, Charles Vernon, 1844–98, U.S. naval officer. To him Adm. Dewey said, "You may fire when you are ready, Gridley," at Manila in 1898.

Grieg, Edvard (ĕd′vär grēg′), 1843–1907, Norwegian composer. He often used Norwegian folk themes in his music. Apart from the Piano Concerto in A Minor, his most successful work was in the small forms—songs and piano and chamber music. His suites for Ibsen's *Peer Gynt* are very popular.

Grien, Hans Baldung: see BALDUNG, HANS.

Grierson, Sir George Abraham, 1851–1941, Irish philologist. He directed compilation of the great *Linguistic Survey of India* (19 vols., 1894–1927).

Griffenfeld, Peder Schumacher, Count (pä′dhùr shōō′mäkhùr, grī′fùnfĕlt), 1635–99, Danish statesman; created count 1673. Secretary to Frederick III, 1665–70; chief minister to Christian V, 1671–76. Introduced absolute monarchy; centralized administration; promoted trade, industry, peace. Opposition of nobles and army led to his fall and trial on trumped-up treason charges. Death sentence was commuted to life imprisonment.

Griffes, Charles Tomlinson (grĭ′fĭs), 1884–1920, American composer. His best-known works combine elements of romanticism and impressionism (e.g., *The Pleasure Dome of Kubla Khan* and *The White Peacock*).

Griffin, city (pop. 13,982), W central Ga., S of Atlanta, in cotton, truck, and fruit area; laid out 1840. Textile mfg. and food processing.

griffin, in anc. and medieval mythology, animal represented as a cross between lion and eagle. Conspicuous in Assyrian and Persian sculpture. In heraldry it symbolizes vigilance. Origin traced to Hittites.

Griffith, Arthur, 1872–1922, Irish statesman, founder of SINN FEIN. Served cause by propaganda in his newspapers. Commanded revolution in De Valera's absence. First president (1922) of Free State.

Griffith, David Wark, 1875–1948, American film director and producer. Began (1908) association with Biograph Company as scenarist and actor, then as director. Evolved many film techniques (e.g., cross-cutting, flashback, fade-in, fade-out). His experiments were summed up in first notable long American film, *Birth of a Nation* (1915). Among his other films are *Intolerance* (1915), *Broken Blossoms* (1919), and *Orphans of the Storm* (1921).

Grignard, Victor (vēktôr′ grēnyär′), 1871–1935, French chemist. He shared 1912 Nobel Prize for work in organic synthesis based on discovery of **Grignard reagent:** halogen compound used with other substances to synthesize organic compounds.

Grijalva, Juan de (hwän′ dä grēhäl′vä), d. 1527, Spanish explorer. Led expedition to Yucatan (1518).

Grillparzer, Franz (fränts′ grīl′pärtsùr), 1791–1872, Austrian dramatist. His plays, notable for power and poetic beauty, include *Der Traum: ein Leben* (1817–34); *Des Meeres und der Liebe Wellen* (1819); the posthumous *Die Jüdin von Toledo.*

Grimaldi, Giovanni Francesco (jōvän′nē fränchä′skō grēmäl′dē), 1606–80, Italian painter and architect, called Il Bolognese.

Grimaldi, Joseph (grĭmäl′dē), 1779–1837, English pantomime actor and clown. A master of grimace and of stagecraft, he was so popular that his songs were demanded long after his death.

Grimké, Angelina Emily (grĭm′kē), 1805–79, American abolitionist and feminist, b. Charleston, S.C. She and her sister, **Sarah Moore Grimké,** 1792–1873, settled in North and worked for freedom of slaves and woman's rights. Their nephew, **Archibald Henry Grimké,** 1849–1930, son of slave mother, was a lawyer, author, and crusader for Negro advancement.

Grimm, Friedrich Melchior, Baron (frē′drĭkh mĕl′khĕôr grĭm′), 1723–1807, French author, b. Germany. His *Correspondance littéraire* (1st complete ed., 1829–30) was a private newsletter service which throws a unique light on intellectual life of 18th-cent. Paris. He was a friend of Diderot.

Grimm, Jakob (yä′kôp), 1785–1863, German philologist; a founder of comparative philology. His chief contributions were formulation of GRIMM'S LAW; German grammar (1819–37); *German Mythology* (1835; Eng. tr., 1880–88). With his brother **Wilhelm Grimm** (vĭl′hĕlm), 1786–1859, he collected and published German folktales, world-famous as *Grimm's Fairy Tales* (1812–15).

Grimmelshausen, Hans Jakob Christoffel von (häns′ yä′kôp krĭs′tôfŭl fŭn grĭ′mŭlshou″zŭn), 1625?–1676, German author. His satirical *The Adventuresome Simplicius Simplicissimus* (1669) is a picaresque, partly autobiographical novel of the Thirty Years War.

Grimm's law, principle of relationships in Indo-European languages, first observed by Jakob Grimm in 1822. It shows that primitive tenues (k, t, p) become aspirates in Low German (e.g., English) and mediae in High German (German); that primitive aspirates (gh, dh, bh) become mediae in Low German, tenues in High German; and that primitive mediae (g, d, b) become tenues in Low German, aspirates in High German. In English, aspirates are h, th, f; mediae, g, d, b; tenues, k, t, p. In German, mediae are h, d, f; tenues, k, t, p; aspirates, ch, z, f.

Grimsby, county borough (pop. 94,527), Lincolnshire, England, at mouth of Humber R.; largest fishing port in Great Britain. Has over 100 acres of docks.

Grindelwald (grĭn′dŭlvält), resort in Bernese Alps, Switzerland, at foot of the Eiger. Celebrated for grandeur of scenery.

grindstone, abrasive stone mounted so that it rotates and can sharpen edges of tools and other instruments.

Grinnell, Josiah Bushnell, 1821–91, American pioneer, clergyman, and abolitionist. Lost pastorate in Washington, D.C., after antislavery sermon. Went West following Horace Greeley's advice to him, "Go West, young man, go West!" Founded Grinnell, Iowa.

Grinnell, city (pop. 6,828), central Iowa, between Des Moines and Iowa City; founded 1854 by J. B. Grinnell. **Grinnell College** (nonsectarian; coed.) chartered 1847 as Iowa Col., opened 1848 at Davenport by pioneer Congregational missionaries. Moved 1859 when Grinnell donated land and building; college named for him 1909.

Gris, Juan (hwän′ grēs′), 1887–1927, Spanish cubist painter. Settled in Paris 1906. Produced mostly still lifes in oil and collage.

Griselda (grĭzĕl′dŭ), in medieval story, heroine who patiently endures many trials imposed by her husband to test her devotion.

Gris-Nez, Cape (grē-nā′), cliff near Calais, N France, projecting into Strait of Dover, 21 mi. from English coast. Lighthouse.

Grisons (grēsônz′, Fr. grēsō′), Ger. *Graubünden,* canton (2,746 sq. mi.; pop. 136,050), E Switzerland; cap. Chur. Largest but least populated of Swiss cantons. Pastures, forests, hydroelectric stations; some agr. in valleys. ENGADINE valley and other resorts attract many tourists. German, Romansh (a Rhaetic dialect), and Italian are official languages. Part of ancient Rhaetia, region passed to Ostrogoths 493, to Franks 537. Bishops of Chur exercised considerable temporal power after 9th cent., but their control was broken after 1367 by three local leagues of towns; the Gray League gave the canton its name. Joining Swiss Confederation as allies, the leagues conquered Valtellina from Milan in 1512 (lost 1797). In the Thirty Years War the country was torn by civil war between Protestants and Catholics and by French and Spanish intervention. Forced by Napoleon to enter the Helvetic Republic (1799), Grisons became a Swiss canton (1803) after Napoleon's mediation.

Griswold, town (pop. 5,728), SE Conn., NE of Norwich. Includes Jewett City borough (pop. 3,702; textiles).

Grocyn, William (grō′sĭn), 1446?–1519, English humanist. An associate of John Colet and Linacre, he reputedly introduced teaching of Greek at Oxford.

Grodno (grôd′nô), city (pop. 49,818), Belorussia, on the Niemen. Mfg. of agr. machinery, textiles, tobacco. Seat of Polish diets 1673–1793. Passed to Russia 1795; to Poland 1921; to Russia 1945.

grog, name given to unsweetened mixture of spirits and water, hot or cold; formerly, rum and water.

Grolier de Servières, Jean, vicomte d'Aguisy (grōl′yŭr, Fr. grôlyā′), 1479–1565, French collector of fine books.

Gromyko, Andrei Andreyevich (ŭndrā′ ŭndrā′ŭvĭch grŭmī′kŭ), 1909–, Russian diplomat. Soviet ambassador at Washington 1943–46, chief permanent delegate to UN 1946–48, chief deputy foreign minister 1949–52, and ambassador to England 1952–.

Grongar Hill, Caermarthenshire, Wales. It is celebrated in a poem by John Dyer.

Groningen (khrō′nĭng-ŭn), province (867 sq. mi.; pop. 449,862), N Netherlands, on North Sea coast. Cattle raising, dairying, agr. History is that of its cap., the municipality of **Groningen** (pop. 132,021), an agr. trading center. Nominally under bishops of Utrecht from 11th cent., city joined Hanseatic League 1284; gained control over central Friesland (i.e., modern Groningen prov.); joined United Provs. 1579. University was founded 1614.

Gronlund, Laurence (grōn′lŭnd), 1846–99, American socialist, b. Denmark. Wrote the *Cooperative Commonwealth* (1884), the first adequate exposition of German socialism in English.

Groote, Gerard or **Geert** (khā′rärt, khärt′, khrō′tŭ), 1340–84, Dutch Roman Catholic reformer. A Carthusian deacon, he preached in Netherlands, founded Brothers of the Common Life (later joined with Augustinian canons), urged monastic reform. *The Following of Christ* is attributed to him by some.

Groote Eylandt (grōōt ī′lŭnd), area 950 sq. mi., off N Australia, largest island in Gulf of Carpentaria. Aboriginal reservation.

Gropius, Walter (väl′tŭr grō′pēōōs), 1883–, German architect, one of leaders of modern "functional" architecture. Headed the famous BAUHAUS, 1919–28. Set of buildings he designed for it at Dessau in 1926 is one of his finest achievements. Worked in London 1934–37, came to U.S. 1937.

Gropper, William, 1897–, American painter. Contributed radical cartoons to periodicals, notably the *New Masses.* Won recognition as a painter when he first exhibited his oils in 1936.

grosbeak (grōs′bēk), name used (generally in combination) for various birds, especially of finch family. They have large, conical bills and bright summer plumage, and are 8–9 in. long. Rose-breasted grosbeak, pine grosbeak, western or black-headed grosbeak, and common European grosbeak (hawfinch) are well known.

Groseilliers, Médard Chouart, sieur des (mādär′ shwär′ syûr dü grôsāyā′), 1618?–c.1690, French trader and explorer in North America. Brother-in-law of Pierre E. RADISSON; his companion on journeys.

Gros Morne (grō′ môrn′), mountain, 2,666 ft. high, W N.F., Canada, in Long Range. Highest point in Newfoundland.

Gross, Samuel David, 1805–84, American surgeon, influential as teacher and writer. He invented surgical instruments and techniques.

Grosse Pointe (grōs point′), residential city (pop. 6,283), SE Mich., suburb of Detroit, on L. St. Clair. Also near Detroit are residential villages, **Grosse Pointe Farms** (pop. 9,410), **Grosse Pointe Park** (pop. 13,075), and **Grosse Pointe Woods** (pop. 10,381).

Grosseteste, Robert (grōs′tĕst), c.1170–1253, English prelate; chief founder of Oxford Franciscan school. As bishop of Lincoln after 1235, he fought efforts of HENRY III to control appointments and supported reforms of Simon de Montfort; upheld the papal prerogative but censured INNOCENT IV for exactions. His studies of Aristotle were the basis for scholastic thought of THOMAS AQUINAS. Very learned, he wrote hundreds of works.

Grossglockner (grōs'glôknùr), highest peak of Austria, 12,460 ft. high, in the Hohe Tauern. First ascended 1800. The Grossglocknerstrasse, a highway rising to 8,215 ft., now crosses near peak.

Grossgörschen, Germany: see LÜTZEN.

Grosswardein, Rumania: see ORADEA.

Grosvenor Square (grōv'nùr), fashionable residential square, W London. Site of American Embassy; hq. American troops in London World War II. Statue of F. D. Roosevelt erected here 1949.

Gros Ventre Indians (grō vä'trù) [Fr.,= big belly], name for two quite distinct North American Indian tribes. One was the Atsina, a detached band of the Arapaho, of Algonquian linguistic stock. The other was the Hidatsa Indians, of Siouan stock.

Grosz, George (grōs), 1893–, German painter and caricaturist in America. Famous in post-war Germany for his vitriolic, satirical drawings of bourgeois society. Came to U.S. 1933.

Grote, George, 1794–1871, English historian of ancient Greece. His *History of Greece* (12 vols., 1846–56) is a classic of historical writing.

Grotefend, Georg Friedrich (gä'ôrk frē'drïkh grō'tùfênt), 1775–1853, German archaeologist and philologist. Deciphered cuneiform inscriptions of Persia.

Grotius, Hugo (grō'shùs), 1583–1645, Dutch jurist, author of *De jure belli ac pacis* (1625) [concerning the law of war and peace]. The book is on natural law and is generally considered the first definitive text on international law.

Groton (grō'tùn). **1** Town (pop. 21,896), including Groton borough (pop. 7,036), SE Conn., on Thames R. (bridged to New London, 1943); settled c.1650. Has U.S. submarine base. **2** Town (pop. 2,889), N Mass., NW of Boston. Seat of Groton School for boys (1884). Among famous graduates was F. D. Roosevelt.

Grouchy, Emmanuel, marquis de (ēmänüël' märke' dù grōōshē'), 1766–1847, marshal of France. Was largely responsible for Napoleon's disaster in WATERLOO CAMPAIGN by letting Prussians join English.

ground bass (bās), short musical phrase constantly reiterated in the bass of a composition, with variations in the upper parts. Popular during baroque era; used by Purcell, Bach, and Buxtehude.

ground hog: see WOODCHUCK.

ground ivy, creeping perennial plant (*Glecoma*, or *Nepeta, hederacea*) also called gill-over-the-ground, naturalized in North America. It has small purple flowers and rounded leaves.

ground pine: see CLUB MOSS.

groundsel, common name for large, varied, widely distributed plant genus *Senecio* of daisy family. Includes such plants as golden groundsel, purple ragwort, CINERARIA, dusty miller, and german ivy. Groundsel bush (*Baccharis halimifolia*) native to U.S. coastal regions, has downy white seed heads.

ground squirrel, rodent of squirrel family. The name is used chiefly for those of genus *Citellus* (or *Spermophilus*) of North America, Europe, and Asia, and also for the African ground squirrel *Xerus,* and for the chipmunk.

group insurance: see INSURANCE.

grouse (grous), game bird of colder parts of N Hemisphere (c.25 species). It is henlike and terrestrial, and has red, brown, and gray plumage. American grouse include eastern ruffed grouse (called also partridge or pheasant), SAGE GROUSE, PTARMIGAN, and PRAIRIE CHICKEN.

Grove, Sir George, 1820–1900, English musicographer, whose *Dictionary of Music and Musicians* (1879–89) is a standard reference work. First director of the Royal Col. of Music, 1883–94.

Grove, Robert Moses (Lefty Grove), 1900–, American baseball pitcher. In 1931 he won 31, lost 4, equaled American League record of 16 consecutive victories.

In 17 years in major leagues, he won 300, lost 141, struck out more than 2,000 batters.

Grove City, borough (pop. 7,411), W Pa., NNW of Pittsburgh. Mfg. of engines.

growth, in biology, development of plant or animal from early stages. Involves increase in size, cell division (see *ill.,* p. 633), differentiation of tissues; often called growth by intussusception (from within), in contrast to growth by accretion (addition of materials externally, as in crystal growth).

Grozny (grôz'nē), city (pop. 172,468), RSFSR, at N foot of Greater Caucasus. Center of rich oil dist., linked by pipe lines with Caspian, Black Sea, Donets Basin. Major German objective in World War II, but Germans were stopped c.50 mi. to W (1942).

Grub Street, in London, since 1830 named Milton St. Once famous as home of poor authors, it was used as symbol of hack work by Dr. Johnson and others.

Grün, Hans Baldung: see BALDUNG, HANS.

Grundtvig, Nikolai Frederik Severin, 1783–1872, Danish writer and educator, founder of the Danish folk school.

Grünewald, Mathias (mätē'äs grü'nùvält), c.1480–c.1530, German religious painter. Famous for *Isenheim Altarpiece* (Colmar) which portrays passion of Christ with dramatic realism.

Grünwald, battle of, 1410: see TANNENBERG.

Grütli, Switzerland: see RÜTLI.

Gruyère (grüyèr'), Ger. *Greierz,* area in Fribourg canton, Switzerland. Known for its cattle and for Gruyère cheese. Town of Gruyères has well-preserved medieval architecture.

Guadalajara (gwä"dhälähä'rä), city (pop. 229,235), cap. of Jalisco, W Mexico, second largest city of Mexico; modern commercial city with picturesque survivals of colonial period. Permanently settled (1542), it was later seat of *audiencia* of Nueva Galicia and center of reformists in war against Spain (1810–21) and War of Reform (1858–61). Famous for handmade glassware and pottery.

Guadalajara, city (pop. 21,466), cap. of Guadalajara prov., central Spain, in New Castile, on Henares R. Near by is battlefield where Loyalists defeated Insurgents, mostly Italian "volunteers," March, 1937.

Guadalcanal (gwädùlkùnäl'), volcanic island (2,500 sq. mi.; pop. c.14,000), S Pacific, one of SOLOMON ISLANDS. Largely jungle, rises to c.8,000 ft. Occupied 1942 by the Japanese, regained 1943 by U.S. forces. Battles of Cape Esperance and Lunga Point were important U.S. victories.

Guadalquivir (gwä"dhälkēvēr'), river, c.350 mi. long, S Spain, in Andalusia, flowing from Sierra de Cazorla SW through fertile region, past Córdoba and Seville (head of navigation), into Atlantic.

Guadalupe (Span. gwädhälōō'pä), village, W central Spain, in Estremadura. Noted for shrine of Our Lady of Guadalupe, whose cult was transferred (16th cent.) to Guadalupe Hidalgo, Mexico.

Guadalupe Hidalgo (gwähdälōō'pä ēdäl'go), shrine, central Mexico, suburb of Mexico city; one of principal shrines in Christendom. In 1531, an Indian, Juan Diego, had vision of Virgin at place renamed Guadalupe in honor of shrine in Spain; Hidalgo was added in 1810 to honor revolutionary priest, Hidalgo y Costilla. **Treaty of Guadalupe Hidalgo,** signed and ratified in 1848, ended Mexican War. In it Mexico recognized Texas as U.S. possession and ceded most of present SW U.S.; U.S. agreed to pay Mexico $15,000,000 and assumed American claims against Mexico.

Guadalupe Mountains (gwä'dùlōōp), SE N.Mex. and W Texas. In Texas are El Capitan (8,078 ft.) and Guadalupe Peak (8,751 ft.), state's highest point, W of which are salt lakes and flats.

Guadalupe Victoria (gwädhälōō'pä vēktōr'yä), 1786?–1843, Mexican general, president of Mexico (1824–29). Active in revolution against Spain from 1811, he adopted the name of the revolutionary standard (his real name, Manuel Félix Fernández).

Guadarrama, Sierra de (sēē'rä dä gwädhärä'mä), mountain range, central Spain, N of Madrid, culminating in Peñalara peak (7,972 ft.).

Guadeloupe (gôdŭlōōp', gwä–), overseas department of the French Republic (687 sq. mi.; pop. 278,864), in Leeward Isls., West Indies; cap. BASSE-TERRE. Discovered by Columbus, 1493, it was abandoned by Spain 1604. French settled it 1635, but English contended for its ownership until 1815.

Guadiana (gwädhyä'nä), river, c.500 mi. long, central Spain and S Portugal. Flows W past Ciudad Real and Badajoz, then S, forming Spanish-Portuguese border till it empties in Gulf of Cádiz.

Guaira, La (lä gwī'rä), town (pop. 10,103), N Venezuela, port on Caribbean.

Guam (gwäm), island (203 sq. mi.; pop. 58,754), W Pacific, belonging to U.S.; largest, most populous, and southernmost of MARIANAS ISLANDS. AGANA is seat of government. Inhabited mainly by Chamorros. Discovered 1521 by Magellan, it came under Spanish rule in late 17th cent. Taken 1898 by U.S., under Dept. of Navy since 1917. Fell Dec. 9, 1941, to the Japanese invaders. Regained July, 1944, by U.S. and became major air and naval base.

guanaco (gwänä'kō) or **huanaco** (hwänä'kō), wild South American mammal (genus *Lama*) of camel family of Andes. Llama and alpaca were probably domesticated from it. Its shoulder height is c.3½ ft. and it has a dark face, brown back and sides, and light under parts. Indians use its flesh, hide, bones.

Guanajuato (gwänähwä'tō), state (11,805 sq. mi.; pop. 1,317,629; average alt. c.6,000 ft.), central Mexico, on central plateau. Leading mining state of Mexico, it produces silver, gold, mercury, lead, tin, copper, opals. Principal cities are Celaya (pop. 22,766), LEÓN, Irapuato (pop. 32,377), Guanajuato (cap.; pop. 23,521).

guano (gwä'nō), fertilizer of dried excrement of sea birds collected from equatorial coasts.

Guantánamo (gwäntä'nämō), city (pop. 42,423), SE Cuba. Large sugar center on Guantánamo Bay (with U.S. naval station).

Guaraní Indians (gwäränē'), people of Tupi-Guaraní linguistic stock in S Brazil and Paraguay. Lived in patrilineal communities, practiced seminomadic agr. Called Tupí in Brazil.

Guardi, Francesco (fränchä'skō gwär'dē), 1712–93, Venetian landscape painter. Developed more brilliant style than that of his master Canaletto.

guardian and ward, relationship, in which a ward—an infant, insane person, or spendthrift—and (in most cases) his property are placed under the management and control of a guardian. Generally the guardian is appointed by the court; in some countries appointed by one of the parents (in others by the father only).

Guarini, Giovanni Battista (jōvän'nē bät-tē'stä gwärē'nē), 1537–1612, Italian poet, author of the pastoral drama *Pastor Fido* (1590), rival of Tasso.

Guarneri (gwärnä'rē) or **Guarnerius,** family of violinmakers of Cremona, Italy, beginning with **Andrea Guarneri** (ändrā'ä), c.1626–1698, a pupil of Niccolò Amati. His grandnephew, **Giuseppi Guarneri** (jōōzĕp'pä), 1687?–1745, called "del Gesù" because he signed his labels with a cross and the letters IHS, was the greatest craftsman of the family.

Guastalla (gwästäl'lä), town (pop. 3,934) and former duchy, Emilia-Romagna, N Italy. Bought by Gonzaga family 1539; duchy from 1621; passed to Parma 1748. Napoleon I gave it to his sister Pauline (1806); it reverted to Parma on his downfall, was transferred to Modena 1847.

Guatemala (gwätämä'lä), republic (42,042 sq. mi.; pop. 2,786,403), Central America, just S of Mexico, most populous of Central American countries; cap. GUATEMALA. Tropic areas on Pacific and Caribbean coasts and jungles of Petén yield produce, but cool highlands from border of Mexico to borders of Salvador and Honduras have most of the population. Except in urban areas—notably Guatemala and QUETZALTENAN-

GO—Indian patterns of life persist. The chief ports are San José and Puerto Barrios; chief exports are bananas and coffee. Near W coast is a chain of volcanoes. The Maya-Quiché had a notable civilization before the Spanish conquest under Pedro de Alvarado. The first capital was Ciudad Vieja, the second Antigua, the third Guatemala. Though a captaincy general, it was of little importance in the Spanish Empire. Gained independence in 1821 and was briefly part of Iturbide's Mexican Empire. Guatemala was the nucleus of the Central American Federation (1825–38) and since that time, under such leaders as Rafael Carrero, Manuel Estrada Cabrera, and Justo Rufino Barrios, has tried to gain hegemony in Central America. Border disputes have been numerous. In World War II Guatemala declared war against the Axis countries (1941), and in 1945 became a member of the United Nations.

Guatemala, city (pop. 283,100), S central Guatemala, cap. and largest city of republic, in highland valley. Founded 1776 as cap. after Antigua was abandoned; rebuilt after destruction by earthquake (1917–18).

Guatémoc: see CUAUHTÉMOC.

guava (gwä'vŭ), small tree (*Psidium*) native to tropical America, and its fruit, a fleshy berry with many hard seeds. Guava jelly is made from the fruit. Both strawberry guava (*Psidium littorale*) with round red fruit, and common guava (*P. guajava*) are grown in Fla. and Calif.

Guayaquil (gwīūkēl'), city (pop. 262,624), W Ecuador, on Guayas R.; Pacific port and largest city of Ecuador; founded by Benalcázar 1535. Historic meeting between Bolívar and San Martín occurred here 1822.

Guaymas (gwī'mäs), city (pop. 8,796), Sonora, NW Mexico, a port on Gulf of California; a popular resort for gulf fishing. Exports agr. and fish products of area.

Gubbio (gōōb'byō), town (pop. 7,432), Umbria, central Italy. Was anc. town of Umbrians (IGUVINE TABLES found here). Flourished in Middle Ages, first as free commune, later under dukes of Urbino. Fine ceramics made here in 16th cent. City retains much medieval architecture.

Gudbrandsdal (gōōd'bränsdäl"), valley, central Norway, extending from Mjosa L. NW to Dovrefjell. Rich agr. and timber district; horse breeding. Many valley farmers trace ancestry to saga times; population preserves own dialect, customs.

Guden (gōō'dŭn), Dan. *Gudenaa*, river, 98 mi. long, Jutland, Denmark. Only important Danish river; partly navigable. Flows N and NE to the Kattegat.

Gudmundsson, Kristmann, 1902–, Icelandic writer of Norwegian novels.

Gudrun or **Kudrun,** name of principal female character of the Icelandic *Laxdaelasaga*, a stalwart heroine; also of a character in the *Volsungasaga* (corresponding to Kriemhild in the *Nibelungenlied*).

Guelderland or **Guelders,** Netherlands: see GELDERLAND.

Guelph (gwĕlf), city (pop. 27,386), S Ont., Canada, on Speed R. and NW of Hamilton; founded 1827 by John Galt. Has knitting and paper mills, meat packing, woodworking, and varied mfg. Site of Ontario Agricultural Col.

Guelphs (gwĕlfs), European dynasty, tracing descent from Guelph I or Welf I (9th cent.), father-in-law of Emperor Louis I. Guelph d'Este IV (d. 1101), duke of Carinthia from 1055 and duke of Bavaria from 1070, was common ancestor of Italian house of ESTE and of the German Guelphs, who ruled Bavaria and Saxony to 1180 (see HENRY THE PROUD; HENRY THE LION). In feud with house of HOHENSTAUFEN, German Guelphs lost all but the duchy of BRUNSWICK. The line of Brunswick-Lüneburg or HANOVER ascended the British throne in the person of George I (1714). Because of Salic law of succession, Hanover was separated from British crown when Victoria became queen of England (1837). After the deposition of GEORGE V of Hanover (1866), the so-called Guelphic party sought to restore the kingdom, but with no success.

Guelphs and Ghibellines (gĭ'bŭlēnz, –lĭnz), opposing political factions in later Middle Ages. They originated 12th cent. in the rivalry between the German Guelphs or Welfs and the Hohenstaufen emperors. (See HENRY THE PROUD; HENRY THE LION.) The name Ghibelline probably derives from the Hohenstaufen castle of Waiblingen. The struggle continued in Italy, where the Guelphs at first were the papal party in the struggle between emperors and popes. The Guelphs included many important cities (e.g., LOMBARD LEAGUE, Bologna, Florence, Genoa) and the Angevin kings of Naples. The Ghibellines included several noble families and petty tyrants, such as Ezzelino da Romano, the Della Scala of Verona, the Visconti of Milan, and several cities (e.g., Pisa, Arezzo). The cities themselves were often divided, and bloody strife resulted. The party names soon lost their original connotations, and local feuds disturbed party alignments—as in Florence, where the Guelphs split into Blacks and Whites. The names fell into disuse by the 15th cent.

Guercino (gwĕrchē'nō), 1591?–1666, Italian eclectic painter; real name was Giovanni Francesco Barbieri. Work shows influence of Caravaggio and Guido.

Guericke, Otto von (ô'tō fŭn gā'rĭkŭ), 1602–86, German physicist. Made first air pump; devised Magdeburg hemispheres for demonstrating air pressure.

Guérin, Pierre Narcisse, Baron, 1774–1833, French painter, exponent of the classicism of David.

Guernica (gĕrnē'kä), historic town, Vizcaya prov., N Spain. Oak of Guernica, former meeting place of Vizcayan diet, symbolizes lost liberties of Basques. In 1937 German planes, in aid of Insurgent forces, bombed the defenseless town. The action, which provoked widespread indignation, inspired Picasso's famous painting.

Guernsey, one of the CHANNEL ISLANDS.

Guernsey cattle: see CATTLE.

Guerra Junqueiro, Abílio (äbē'lyō gĕ'rŭ zhōōnkā'rō), 1850–1923, Portuguese poet, author of violent satiric poems and also of touching lyrics.

Guerrero (gĕrā'rō) [for Vicente Guerrero, revolutionary leader], state, SW Mexico, on Pacific; cap. Chilpancingo (pop. 8,834). Extremely mountainous except for narrow coastal strip around ACAPULCO. Silver works at TAXCO are famous. Prominent in war against Spain (1810–21), it was not a state until 1849.

Guerrière: see CONSTITUTION, ship.

Guesclin, Bertrand du: see DU GUESCLIN, BERTRAND.

Guess, George: see SEQUOYAH.

Guest, Lady Charlotte (Bertie), 1812–95, English author, translator of MABINOGION.

Gueux (gŭ) [Fr.,= beggars], nickname given to the Dutch and Flemish noblemen and burghers (both Protestant and Catholic) who in 1566 signed a petition protesting against Spanish encroachments on their traditional liberties. The petition was a toned-down version of the Compromise of Breda (1566), which pledged the signers to resist Spanish oppression. The nickname was taken up by the patriots in the ensuing struggle. Patriotic privateers chartered in 1569 by William the Silent were called Beggars of the Sea; their chief success was the raising of the siege of LEIDEN (1574).

Guevara, Antonio de (äntō'nyō dā gāvä'rä), 1480?–1545, Spanish novelist, author of didactic *Libro llamado Relox de príncipes* (1529).

Guevara, Luis Vélez de: see VÉLEZ DE GUEVARA.

Guggenheim (gōō'gŭnhīm), family of American industrialists and philanthropists. **Meyer Guggenheim,** 1828–1905, b. Switzerland, made fortune from metal smelting and refining. His son, **Daniel Guggenheim,** 1856–1930, was largely responsible for combining Guggenheim interests with the American Smelting and Refining Co. in 1901. The Daniel and Florence Guggenheim Foundation is his principal philanthropy. His brother, **Simon Guggenheim,** 1867–1941, estab. (1925), with his wife, the John Simon Guggenheim Memorial Foundation, which grants fellowships to scholars, writers, and artists. Another brother, **Solomon Robert Guggenheim,** 1861–1949, estab. foundation to increase appreciation of non-objective art.

Guiana (gēä'nä), region, NE South America, roughly bounded by the Orinoco basin, the Casiquiare channel (connecting the Orinoco with the Río Negro), the Amazon basin, and the Atlantic. The narrow coastal region is rainy and hot. The vast, unexploited interior includes the Guiana Highlands as well as broad savannas and vast rain forests. The region includes SE Venezuela and part of N Brazil as well as the three colonies called Guiana. The westernmost of these is **British Guiana** (83,000 sq. mi.; pop. 375,701), a crown colony; cap. GEORGETOWN on the Demerara R. (colony still sometimes called Demerara). The population is polyglot—a few whites and Indians, many East Indians, and many Negroes. Sugar, rum, rice, hardwoods, gold, diamonds (the Mazaruni fields are rich), and bauxite are exported. British settlement in Guiana began in present Dutch Guiana by 1630, and the Dutch settled Essequibo, Berbice, and Pomeroon in present British Guiana. In the course of continental and colonial wars involving the Dutch, the British, and the French, the areas changed hands often, and it was not until the Congress of Vienna that the present division of the three colonies was more or less fixed. Discovery of gold in British Guiana led to British expansion and to the VENEZUELA BOUNDARY DISPUTE. **Dutch Guiana** (55,143 sq. mi.; pop. 211,804) is between British and French Guiana; cap. PARAMARIBO. Colony called also Netherlands Guiana, Surinam, and Suriname. The population includes Javanese, East Indians, and Jewish refugees, as well as Dutch and Negroes (many of them bush Negroes or maroons, descended from escaped slaves). Rum, timber, coffee, and bauxite are exported. The Dutch first estab. colonies (beginning 1616) in present British Guiana, and the Dutch West India Co. encouraged settlement. Ultimate settlement in 1815 gave Dutch their present territory. The easternmost of the three, **French Guiana** (c.34,740 sq. mi.; pop. 28,537), a department of Metropolitan France, comprises the colony proper and the interior Territory of Inini; cap. CAYENNE. The name—and even more the name of Devil's Isl. in the colony—was made notorious as a penal colony until 1946.

Guiana Highlands, mountainous tableland, mostly in Venezuela, bounded by Orinoco and Amazon basins and coastal lowlands of British Guiana. Tablelands rise in escarpments and create magnificent waterfalls in rivers which pour over edges. Gold and some diamonds have been mined.

Guibert of Ravenna (gwī'bŭrt, gēbĕr'), d. 1100, antipope as Clement III (1080–1100). Led antireform party which repudiated Pope Alexander II. HENRY IV made him archbishop of Ravenna (1072). Henry, excommunicated in 1080 by GREGORY VII, declared Gregory deposed and enthroned (1084) Guibert, who then crowned Henry emperor.

Guicciardini, Francesco (fränchä'skō gwēt-chärdē'nē), 1483–1540, Italian historian and statesman. Served Florentine government and Pope Leo X. His history of Italy during 1492–1534 (period of the Italian Wars) is masterwork of Italian historical literature of Renaissance.

Guido d'Arezzo (gwē'dō därĕt'tsō) or **Guido Aretinus** (ârŭtī'nŭs), c.990–1050, Italian Benedictine monk, important in the history of musical notation. He added two lines to the two already serving as a staff, using the spaces as well as the lines. His chief contribution was the solmization syllables (a system to denote tones by syllables), called the Aretinian syllables or Guido's scale. He had observed that each line of a certain hymn began a note higher than the previous line, so, as an aid to memorizing, he named each of the tones of the hexachord (a group of six consecutive notes) after the first syllable of each line of the hymn: *Ut quEant laxis; REsonare fibris; MIra gestorum; FAmuli* tuorum; *Solve* polluti; and so on. As the octave superseded the hexachord, an additional *si* or *ti* was added; *ut* was replaced by the more singable *do*. These syllables became the basis of various systems of MUSICAL NOTATION (see also SOLFEGE) used today.

Guido Reni (rā'nē), 1575–1642, Italian painter, b. near Bologna. Studied briefly with the Carracci. In 1600 made first of many trips to Rome, where he became rival of Caravaggio. Later he estab. own academy in Bologna. Eclecticism and voluptuous sentimentality of such baroque paintings as *Aurora* (Rospigliosi Palace, Rome) made him one of favorite artists of 17th and 18th cent.

Guienne (gēēn', gwēēn'), Fr. *Guyenne*, region and former province, SW France; historic cap. Bordeaux. Synonymous with AQUITAINE until Hundred Years War. Largely under English rule 1152–1453. Guyenne prov. in 17th–18th cent. consisted of present Gironde, Dordogne, Lot, Lot-et-Garonne, and Aveyron depts.—i.e., the regions of BORDEAUX, AGEN, PÉRIGORD, QUERCY, and ROUERGUE.

Guildford, municipal borough (pop. 47,484), co. town of Surrey, England. Identified with Astolat of Arthurian Legend. Grave of Lewis Carroll.

guilds or **gilds**, economic and social groups of people in same business or craft, typical of W Europe in Middle Ages. Membership was never by class but by profession or trade. Primary functions were to control profession or trade in a locality, to set standards of workmanship and price, to protect business from capricious exactions, to prevent encroachment from other localities, and to establish status for guild members in society. Similar groups both of merchants and of craftsmen were known from early Greek times, some of them extremely powerful. Merchant guilds had vast effect on what is known as Commercial Revolution. No less important were craft guilds, which grew rapidly in 12th cent. Generally members were masters, apprentices, and journeymen. Masters owned shops and trained apprentices, bound to them. Journeymen were men who had finished training but could not attain status of masters, limited in number. Guilds reflected medieval desire for orderly society, and often dominated municipal government, e.g., LIVERY COMPANIES of London. Increasing power of nations in 15th and 16th cent. reduced power of guilds, which, by 17th cent., had withered in England, but persisted on Continent until French Revolution.

guild socialism, type of socialism developed in England, advocating industrial self-government through worker-controlled guilds; originated by A. J. Plenty in 1906. Aspects of Marxism and SYNDICALISM were adopted. Control of industry was emphasized, rather than political reform. Movement eventually waned, although it influenced British trade unions.

Guilford, town (pop. 5,092), S Conn., on Long Isl. Sound E of New Haven. Has some of state's oldest houses, e.g., Whitfield House (1639–40, restored 1936). Dairy products, truck, metal goods, sea food.

Guilford College: see GREENSBORO, N.C.

Guillaume, Charles Édouard (shärl' ädwär' gēyōm'), 1861–1938, French physicist. Won 1920 Nobel Prize for discovery of several alloys, among them invar and platinite.

Guillaume de Lorris (dù lōrēs'), c.1215–c.1278, French poet, author of first part of ROMAN DE LA ROSE.

Guillén, Jorge (hôr'hä gēlyän'), 1893–, Spanish intellectual lyric poet.

Guimarãis or **Guimarães** (both: gē"mùrã'ēsh), city (pop. 12,568), NW Portugal, SE of Braga. Seat of Henry of Burgundy and his son, Alfonso I of Portugal. Favorite royal residence; noted old castle.

Guimerà, Angel (än'zhĕl gēmärä'), 1845–1924, Catalan romantic poet and dramatist.

Guinea, Gulf of, inlet of the Atlantic, W Africa. Extends from W Gold Coast to mouth of Congo R.

guinea fowl, breed of domestic poultry related to the pheasant and developed from wild species of Africa.

It is in demand for its delicate, but gamelike flesh.

guinea pig, domesticated form of the cavy (genus *Cavia*), descended from wild South American species. In North America it is chiefly a laboratory animal used for testing serums, antitoxins, and for experiments in genetics and nutrition.

Guinegate (gēngät'), village, Pas-de-Calais dept., N France, near Saint-Omer. Scene of two French defeats: 1479, by Archduke Maximilian, in war over Burgundian succession; 1513, by English and imperialists, in second BATTLE OF THE SPURS.

Guinevere: see ARTHURIAN LEGEND; also spelled Guenever or Guenevere.

Guiney, Louise Imogen (gī'nē), 1861–1920, American Catholic poet and essayist; in England after 1901.

Guipúzcoa, Spain: see BASQUE PROVINCES.

Guiscard, Norman rulers of Sicily: see ROBERT GUISCARD and ROGER I.

Guise (gēz, gwēz), French ducal family, founded as cadet branch of house of LORRAINE by **Claude de Lorraine, 1st duc de Guise** (klōd' dù lōrĕn'), 1496–1550, whom Francis I made duke and peer. His daughter MARY OF GUISE married James V of Scotland and was the mother of Mary Queen of Scots. His sons **François de Lorraine, 2d duc de Guise** (fräswä'), 1519–63, and **Charles de Guise, Cardinal de Lorraine**, c.1525–1574, controlled French politics in the reign of Francis II, first husband of Mary Queen of Scots. Championing the Catholic cause against the Huguenots, they cruelly suppressed the conspiracy of AMBOISE (1560). After Francis's death they opposed the tolerant policy of CATHERINE DE' MEDICI and provoked the outbreak of the Wars of RELIGION (1562). François defeated the Huguenots at Dreux, but was assassinated shortly afterward. Charles negotiated for Spanish help and held power at court in 1567–70. **Henri de Lorraine, 3d duc de Guise** (ärē'), 1550–88, son of François, helped to plan the massacre of SAINT BARTHOLOMEW'S DAY and after 1576 formed the Catholic LEAGUE. Immensely ambitious and popular, he instigated the revolt of Paris against King HENRY III (1588) and took control of the city. After an ostensible reconciliation the king had him murdered. His brother, **Louis de Lorraine, Cardinal de Guise**, 1555–88, was killed at the same time. Leadership of the League devolved upon their brother, Charles, duc de MAYENNE. **Henri de Lorraine, 5th duc de Guise**, 1614–64, conspired against Richelieu (1641); fought in Naples against Spain (1647–48, 1654); later was grand chamberlain at court of Louis XIV.

guitar: see STRINGED INSTRUMENTS.

Guitry, Lucien Germain (gētrē'), 1860–1925, French actor. Was among first exponents of realistic drama in plays by Zola, France, and Bernstein. His actor son, **Sacha Guitry** (säshä'), 1885–, is also a prolific, witty dramatist and film director.

Guizot, François (fräswä' gēzō'), 1787–1874, French statesman and historian; leading intellectual exponent of the bourgeois monarchy of LOUIS PHILIPPE. He dominated the cabinet from 1840, was premier 1847–48. His complacency led to FEBRUARY REVOLUTION of 1848. Ranking high as historian, he wrote *Histoire de la révolution d'Angleterre* (2 vols., 1826–27); *General History of Civilization in Modern Europe* (1829–32; Eng. tr., 3 vols., 1846).

Gulf. For names beginning thus, see second part; e.g., for Gulf of Mexico, see MEXICO, GULF OF.

Gulfport, city (pop. 22,659), SE Miss., on Mississippi Sound W of Biloxi; settled 1891. Resort and sea port (fine artificial harbor) processing sea-food, naval stores, lumber, tung oil, and cotton. Has large VA hospital.

Gulf Stream, ocean current found (1513) by Ponce de León. It originates in Gulf of Mexico, passes through Straits of Florida, flows NE parallel to U.S. coast, separated from it by narrow "cold wall" of water. Temperature is 80°F. at beginning, drops as stream moves N. Stream slows up and spreads out, finally merges

SMALL CAPITALS = cross references. Pronunciation key on inside end pages. Abbreviations: p. 2.

with North Atlantic Drift (lat. 40°N, long. 60°W). Stream results from general vertical circulation of ocean; cold water from N sinks down, warm water of equatorial region rises and flows N above cold current.

gulfweed, a SEAWEED of genus *Sargassum,* a brown alga of tropical waters, which commonly floats in large patches in Sargasso Sea and Gulf Stream.

Gulick, Luther Halsey (gū'lĭk), 1865–1918, American pioneer in physical education. He helped to originate game of basketball and in 1910 helped found Camp Fire Girls.

Gulistan, Treaty of, 1813, between Russia and Iran, ended Russo-Persian War begun in 1804. Persia ceded khanates forming present Azerbaijan SSR, renounced claims to Georgia, Dagestan.

gull, aquatic bird of tern family found near all oceans and many inland waters. Sea gull is a common name for herring gull (a subspecies of common European gull) found on Atlantic and Pacific coasts of Canada and U.S., as well as inland. Larger and heavier than terns, gulls have webbed·feet and hooked bills. They are useful as scavengers.

Gullah, dialect spoken by Negroes of the Sea Isls., SE U.S. Originally a mixture of W African words with English, it is now a very corrupt form of English.

Gulliver's Travels (1726), political, social satire by Jonathan SWIFT. Despite the satire, its fairy-tale quality has made it a children's classic.

Gullstrand, Allvar (äl'vär gŭl'stränd), 1862–1930, Swedish ophthalmologist. Won 1911 Nobel Prize in Physiology and Medicine for study of optical images and of light refraction in eye.

gum, term for a variety of plant substances, many not true gums. True gums are complex organic materials; some are soluble in water, others are insoluble but absorb large amounts of water. Gum arabic is typical; it is used in making inks, adhesives, confections; as fabric filler; as emollient.

gumbo, a name for OKRA. In W U.S. it is name for rich, black alluvial soil, sticky or soapy when wet.

Gumplowicz, Ludwig (lŏŏt'vĭkh gŏŏm'plŏvĭch), 1838–1909, Austrian sociologist. Held that social development rose out of conflict, first among races, then among states, then among other social groups.

gum tree: see EUCALYPTUS; BLACK GUM; SWEET GUM.

guncotton, explosive formed by action of cold nitric and sulphuric acids on cotton. Burns when ignited; explodes with detonator. Used in torpedoes, in blasting (mixed with nitroglycerin), in underwater blasting and mines; in making smokeless powder.

Gundulic, Ivan (ē'vän gŏŏndŏŏ'lĭch), Ital. *Giovanni Gondola,* 1588–1638, Croatian poet. Held high office in his native Dubrovnik (Ragusa). His chief work, *Osman* (1626), is an epic of the Polish-Turkish wars.

gun metal, a BRONZE, an alloy of copper, tin, and zinc in varying proportions. Originally used for making guns; now used for casting machine parts.

Gunnarsson, Gunnar, 1889–, Icelandic novelist. Early works in Danish, later in Icelandic.

Gunnison, town (pop. 2,770; alt. c.7,680 ft.), W central Colo., on Gunnison R., in resort, mining, irrigated-farm area.

Gunnison, river formed in W central Colo. and flowing c.180 mi. W and NW to Colorado R. at Grand Junction. Courses through Black Canyon of the Gunnison (a national monument). Some water diverted for irrigation by Gunnison Tunnel (1905–9), 30,582 ft. in length.

gunpowder, explosive mixture of potassium nitrate (75%), sulphur (10%), and carbon (15%). Formerly much used in blasting and in weapons. In guns, because of the large residue of solid matter, it has been superseded by smokeless powder. Though some have called Roger Bacon or Berthold Schwarz the inventor, it is now agreed that gunpowder was invented in Asia (probably 9th-cent. China). Introduction to Europe in 14th cent. revolutionized warfare.

Gunpowder Plot, frustrated plan to blow up the British houses of Parliament and King James I on Nov. 5, 1605, the opening day of Parliament. A rising of English Catholics was to follow. Plot was exposed by a warning to a relation of one of the plotters not to attend Parliament on that day. Guy Fawkes, a conspirator, was arrested as he entered the cellar of the House of Lords. Nov. 5 is still celebrated as Guy Fawkes Day and effigies of him are burned.

Gunsaulus, Frank Wakeley (gŭnsô'lùs), 1856–1921, American Congregational clergyman and lecturer, president of Armour Inst. of Technology (now Illinois Inst. of Technology) after 1893.

Gunter, Edmund, 1581–1626, English mathematician and astronomer. He invented a portable quadrant, Gunter's surveyors chain, Gunter's sector or scale; discovered variation of magnetic compass. Probably was first to use terms *cosine* and *cotangent.*

Guntersville, city (pop. 5,253), NE Ala., port on Tennessee R. near Guntersville Dam (TVA), and in farm and resort area. Textile mills.

guppy or **rainbow fish,** small fish (*Lebistes reticulatus*) abundant in parts of South America. It is a popular aquarium fish. It can survive temperatures of 65°–100° F. Rainbow-colored, inch-long male has black bars and spots. Female is greenish gray, c.1½ in. long. Adults are cannibalistic. They produce 12–25 living young every few weeks.

Gupta (gŏŏp'tù), dynasty, 320?–544?, of N India, founded by Chandragupta I. It saw a golden age of Hindu culture.

Gurgan (gŏŏrgän') or **Gorgan** (gōr–), town (pop. 21,-376), NE Iran, c.25 mi. E of the Caspian in area known as Hyrcania in anc. times. Flourished c.1800 during rise of Kajar dynasty, which originated here. Formerly ealled Asterabad.

Gurkha (gŏŏr'kù), ethnic group of Nepal, of mixed Mongol-Rajput extraction and predominantly Hindu in religion. The British formerly recruited large military contingents from this group.

Gustavus (gùstä'vùs), kings of Sweden. **Gustavus I** (Gustavus Vasa), 1496–1560. His father, Erik Johansson, was a Swedish senator murdered in the Stockholm massacre (1520). Gustavus led the peasants of Dalarna in the rebellion against CHRISTIAN II of Denmark, defeated the Danes, and was elected king by the Riksdag in 1523. Thus the KALMAR UNION of Denmark, Norway, and Sweden was dissolved. Gustavus's reign was marked by the establishment of a national Protestant Church (1527) and by the Swedish-Danish victory over Lübeck (1537), which freed Sweden from economic subjection to the Hanseatic League. He reigned firmly, made the crown hereditary in the Vasa family, transformed Sweden into a modern, national state. **Gustavus II** (Gustavus Adolphus), 1594–1632, reigned 1611–32. Helped by his chancellor, Axel OXENSTIERNA, he insured internal stability by granting concessions to the nobles and ended the KALMAR WAR by buying off the Danes (1613). His resumption in 1621 of intermittent warfare with Poland gained him a large part of Livonia when a truce was made at Altmark (1629). Meanwhile, however, he had been drawn into an alliance with Christian IV of Denmark (1628) and with France (1629); to both powers he promised to intervene on the Protestant side in the THIRTY YEARS WAR. Gustavus landed in Pomerania (1630) and in a spectacular sweep through Germany defeated the imperials at Breitenfeld (1631), at the Lech (April, 1632), and at Lützen (Nov., 1632). In that last battle, he was killed. His daughter Christina succeeded him. **Gustavus III,** 1746–92, reigned 1771–92. By a coup d'état (1772) he restored the royal prerogatives lost by his predecessors. He waged successful war on Russia (1788–90). His reform policies and his autocratic tendencies earned him the hatred of the nobles, one of whom murdered him. His son and successor, **Gustavus IV** (Gustavus Adolphus), 1778–1837, joined the third coalition against Napoleon I (1805). He lost Swedish Pomerania to French occupation and Finland to Russia (1808). His despotism and mental unbalance led to his enforced abdication (1809). He died in Switzerland. **Gustavus V**, 1858–1950, reigned 1907–50. Sweden evolved toward advanced democracy and economic prosperity; kept neutral in both world wars. His son **Gustavus VI** (Gustavus Adolphus), 1882–, succeeded him in 1950.

Gustavus Adolphus: see GUSTAVUS II, GUSTAVUS IV, and GUSTAVUS VI, kings of Sweden.

Gustavus Adolphus College: see SAINT PETER, Minn.

Gutenberg, Johann (gōō'tŭnbûrg; Ger. gōō'tŭnbĕrk), c.1397–1468, German printer, generally considered the first European to print from movable type, though some claim that honor for Laurens Janszoon Koster, for Pamfilo Castaldi, or for some unknown. Little is known of his life. His father's name was Gensfleisch, and the name Gutenberg was derived from his mother. He is believed to have lived in Strasbourg, where he may have made his great invention in 1436 or 1437. He founded a print shop in Mainz (apparently his birthplace), where he issued the MAZARIN BIBLE. Mainz became the center of the new printing trade, but Gutenberg had to give up his press and types to Johann FUST for debt. See PRINTING and TYPE.

Guthrie, city (pop. 10,113), central Okla., near Cimarron R. N of Oklahoma City, in farm and dairy area; founded 1889. Territorial, state cap. until 1910. Langston Univ. (Negro; land-grant, state supported; coed.; 1897) is near.

Gutiérrez Nájera, Manuel (mänwĕl' gōōtyĕ'rĕs nä'härä), 1859–95, Mexican poet, showing transition from romanticism to modernism.

gutta-percha, solidified milky juice or latex of various Malayan evergreen trees (esp. *Palaquium gutta*). It is nonelastic and insoluble in water; pliable when heated in water. Of great value as insulation for submarine cables; also used in golf balls, telephone receivers, adhesives, waterproofing materials, etc.

Guttenberg (gŭ'tŭnbûrg), town (pop. 5,566), NE N.J. near the Hudson and NE of Jersey City. Textiles.

Gutzkow, Karl (kärl gŏōts'kō), 1811–78, German author; a leader of the Young Germany group. His drama *Uriel Acosta* (1847; Eng. tr., 1913–15) is considered his best work, but he is known chiefly as a radical polemicist.

Guyenne: see GUIENNE.

Guy of Chauliac: see CHAULIAC, GUY DE.

Guy of Lusignan: see LUSIGNAN.

Guyon, Jeanne Marie Bouvier de la Motte (zhän' märē' bōōvyä' dù lä môt' güēyō'), 1648–1717, French mystic, author of works on QUIETISM. Confined by government to convent because of heretical opinions and correspondence with Miguel de MOLINOS, she was released through aid of Mme de Maintenon but was later imprisoned in Bastille (1695–1702).

Guys, Constantin (gois), 1805?–1892, French draughtsman, b. Holland. Did superb drawings in line and wash, first reproduced in *Illustrated London News*.

Guzmán, Nuño de (nōō'nyō dä gōōthmän') d. 1544, Spanish conquistador. As head of first *audiencia* of New Spain (1529), he ruled so notoriously that he was forced to leave Mexico city. Conquered Nueva Galicia; founded Culiacán and Guadalajara.

Guzmán Blanco, Antonio (äntō'nyō gōōsmän' blän'kō), 1829–99, president of Venezuela. A *caudillo*, he dom-

inated the nation 1870–88 as a benevolent despot. After overthrow of his regime, he lived in Paris until his death.

Guzmán de Alfarache: see ALEMÁN, MATEO.

Gwalior (gwä'lēôr), former princely state, Madhya Bharat, India. Founded in 18th cent. by Ranoji Sindhia, a Mahratta chief. Town of **Gwalior** (pop. 34,488) is near Lashkar and lies at foot of a hill fort containing ornate palaces and shrines.

Gwilt, Joseph (gwĭlt), 1784–1863, British architect, known chiefly for his encyclopedia of architecture (8 vols., 1842).

Gwin, William McKendree, 1805–85, American politician. U.S. Senator from Calif. (1850–55, 1857–61). Spokesman for Calif. slavery interests. Involved in political battles with antislavery rival, David C. BRODERICK.

Gwinnet, Button, c.1735–1777, American Revolutionary patriot, signer of Declaration of Independence, b. England. His signature, one of the rarest of American holographs, is very valuable.

Gwyn or **Gwynn, Nell** (Eleanor), 1650–87, English actress, notable in comic roles. Charles II's mistress after 1669, she bore him two sons.

gymnastics, exercises for balanced development of body. In Greece the gymnasium was originally the place of training for the Olympic games. Modern gymnastics date from early 19th cent., when Ludwig Jahn estab. *Turnplätze* in Berlin. In U.S., principal gymnastics events are side and long horse, parallel and horizontal bars, Indian club swinging, rope climbing, flying rings, tumbling.

Gyor (dyûr), Hung. *Györ*, Ger. *Raab*, city (pop. 57,192), NW Hungary, on Raab R. Chief textile center of Hungary; mfg. of machinery. Episcopal see since 1001; cathedral was built 12th cent., rebuilt 17th cent. Scene of decisive Austrian victory over Hungarian revolutionists (1849).

gypsum (jĭp'sŭm), name for hydrated calcium sulphate. Alabaster and satin spar are varieties. Plaster of Paris is obtained from gypsum.

gypsy or **gipsy,** nomadic people numbering roughly 1,000,000, found on every continent. They are probably partly of East Indian origin and speak an Indo-Iranian language called Romany. Disinclined to assimilate, they hold to own customs. Usually depend on trading for living.

gypsy moth, European insect with larva destructive to forest and fruit trees. It appeared in U.S. c.1869 and is confined to NE portion. Adult male is yellowish brown; female whitish; dark lines mark forewings of each. Larva is c.2 in. long, dark brown or black with yellow markings and rows of blue and red tubercles bearing hairs. Air sacs on hairs make the larva buoyant; it can be carried by wind.

gyroscope (jī'rŭskōp), rotating wheel movable about a second axis. This secondary motion, called "precession," is the azimuthal motion of the spin axis of the top. Gyroscope was invented in 1852 by Foucault and was used to demonstrate earth's rotation. With later invention of electric rotor its uses grew to include giant gyroscopic ship stabilizers, directional instruments such as gyrocompass (unaffected by magnetic variations), automatic pilot for guiding aircraft, and other devices.

H, chemical symbol of element hydrogen.

Haag, Den, Netherlands: see HAGUE, THE.

Haakon (hä'kun, Nor. hô'kōōn), kings of Norway. **Haakon I** (the Good), c.915–961, son of Harold I, was brought up as Christian at court of King Athelstan in England. Displaced his brother Eric as king c.935. Strengthened national army and fleet; sought unsuccessfully to introduce Christianity. **Haakon IV** (Haakon Haakonsson), 1204–63, a grandson of Sverre, was formally recognized as king in 1223 after overcoming rival claimants. Under him medieval Norway reached its zenith. He acquired Greenland and Iceland, carried out legal reforms, held a splendid court. He died during an expedition in the Orkney Isls. **Haakon VII,** 1872–, second son of Frederick VIII of Denmark, was elected to Norwegian throne 1905. Married Maud, daughter of Edward VII of England. Headed government in exile in England during World War II.

Haarlem (här'lùm), municipality (pop. 156,856), cap. of North Holland prov., W Netherlands, near North Sea. World center of tulip breeding and bulb exporting since 17th cent. Mfg. of machinery, textiles. Chartered 1245; sacked 1573 by Spanish. Center of 17th-cent. Dutch painting; Frans Hals, Ruisdael worked here. Landmarks include Church of St. Bavo (Groote Kerk, 15th cent.) and city hall (begun 1250; former palace of counts of Holland). Formerly also spelled Harlem.

Habakkuk or **Habacuc** (both: hùbă'kŭk, hă'–), book of Old Testament, a set of poems on the triumph of justice and divine mercy over evil. Identity and time of prophet unknown. A prophet of this name appears in story of Bel and the Dragon. Also Habbacuc.

Habana, Cuba: see HAVANA.

habeas corpus (hā'bēùs kôr'pùs) [Latin,= you may have the body], writ directed by a judge to some person who is detaining another; it commands that the person in custody shall be brought at a specified time to a specified place for a specified purpose. It was known in England as early as the 14th cent. and came to be in England and later in the U.S. the prime remedy for false imprisonment and illegal detention without a judicial hearing. The U.S. Constitution provides that the privilege of the writ shall not be suspended unless, when in cases of rebellion or invasion, public safety may require suspension.

Haber, Fritz (hä'bùr), 1868–1934, German chemist. He won the 1918 Nobel Prize. The **Haber process** for commerical synthesis of ammonia by direct combination of hydrogen and nitrogen was his invention.

Habsburg, family: see HAPSBURG.

hackberry, deciduous tree of genus *Celtis,* widely distributed, and often grown for ornament. It has warty bark, elmlike leaves, small edible fruit.

Hackensack, city (29,219), NE N.J., on Hackensack R. and NW of New York city; settled 1639 by Dutch. Has mfg. of pumps, metal products, glass, and furniture. Several Revolutionary engagements fought here. Has Dutch Reformed church (1696).

Hackensack, river rising in SE N.Y., W of Haverstraw, and flowing c.50 mi. S into N.J., past Hackensack and through Hackensack Meadows to Newark Bay.

Hackney, metropolitan borough (pop. 171,337), NE London, England; once exclusive residential area.

Hadassah (hùdă'sù), Hebrew name of ESTHER.

Hadassah (hùdă'sù), the women's Zionist organization of America; founded 1912 by Henrietta Szold. Maintains medical and child welfare services in Israel, educational services in U.S.

Haddington, burgh (pop. 4,497), co. seat of East Lo-

thian, Scotland, on the Tyne. Cruciform parish church is called "Lamp of the Lothians."

Haddingtonshire: see EAST LOTHIAN, Scotland.

haddock, food fish of N Atlantic similar to cod. Black lateral line runs from gill to tail. Its averages 2–4 lb., with maximum of c.17 lb. Flesh is tender, white, flaky. Smoked haddock is finnan haddie.

Haddonfield, borough (pop. 10,495), SW N.J., suburb of Camden; settled 1682. Has Indian King Tavern (1750), where first state legislature met, 1777.

Haden, Sir Francis Seymour (hā'dùn), 1818–1910, English etcher. His writings did much to familiarize the public with Rembrandt's etchings.

Hades, Greek underworld: see HELL and PLUTO.

Hadhramaut, Arabia: see HADRAMAUT.

Hadley, Henry Kimball, 1871–1937, American composer and conductor. Typical of his well-constructed and facile music are the opera *Cleopatra's Night* and the orchestral works *Salome* and *The Culprit Fay.*

Hadramaut or **Hadhramaut** (both: hädrùmout'), region, Arabia, on Gulf of Aden and Arabian Sea, occupying roughly the central portion of Aden protectorate. Called Hazarmaveth in Bible.

Hadrian: see also ADRIAN.

Hadrian (hā'drēùn), A.D. 76–138, Roman emperor (117–38), b. Spain. A ward of TRAJAN, he distinguished himself as commander and administrator and was named to succeed to the throne. His rule was vigorous, and he traveled about the empire, stabilizing government and beautifying cities with new architecture. He abandoned Trajan's aggressive policy in Asia, fixing the Euphrates as a boundary; had great walls built in Germany and Hadrian's Wall in Britain. In Palestine he put down the uprising under Bar Kochba and built a temple of Jupiter Capitolinus on the ruined Temple, renaming Jerusalem as Aelia Capitolina. Patronized the arts, and his regard for his favorite Antinoüs is recorded in many statues. Chose ANTONINUS PIUS as his successor. Name also appears as Adrian.

Hadrian's Mole: see CASTEL SANT' ANGELO.

Hadrian's Wall, anc. Roman wall, 73½ mi. long, across narrow part of Great Britain from Wallsend on Tyne R. to Bowness at head of Solway Firth. Built A.D. c.121–127 by Emperor Hadrian. Fragments remain of wall (6 ft. high and 8 ft. thick) and stone forts along it. British government preserves wall, one of largest Roman remains.

Haeckel, Ernst Heinrich (ĕrnst' hīn'rĭkh hĕ'kùl), 1834–1919, German biologist and philosopher. He evolved a mechanistic form of monism based on Darwin's theories. His studies of invertebrate marine organisms are well known. Although often erroneous, his theories stimulated research.

haemo-, for words beginning thus: see HEMO-.

Hafiz (häfēz'), d. 1389?, Persian poet, known for lyrics and drinking songs. Was a teacher of the Koran. Moslem critics interpret his poems allegorically.

hafnium (häf'nēùm), widely distributed metallic element (symbol = Hf; see also ELEMENT, table).

Hafrs Fjord or **Hafs Fjord** (both: häfs'fyôrd), inlet of North Sea, SW Norway, near Stavanger. HAROLD I won decisive victory here, 872.

Hagar (hā'gùr) [Heb.,= flight], handmaid of Sarah and mother of Ishmael by Abraham. Sent into desert because of Sarah's jealousy, she was comforted by an angel. Gen. 16: 21.9–21. St. Paul used Hagar as symbol for bondage of the Old Law. Gal. 4.2. Also Agar.

Hagen, Walter (hā'gùn), 1892–, American golfer. Won

SMALL CAPITALS = cross references. Pronunciation key on inside end pages. Abbreviations: p. 2.

U.S. Natl. Open (1914, 1919), British Open (1922, 1924, 1928, 1929), U.S. Professional Golfers Association championships (1921, 1924–27), many other titles.

Hagen (hä′gùn), city (pop. 146,099), North Rhine-Westphalia, NW Germany. Industrial center of Ruhr dist. Heavily damaged in World War II.

Hagerstown, city (pop. 36,260), NW Md., NW of Frederick; settled c.1740. Trade center of agr. area with mfg. of organs and aircraft. Has Confederate cemetery.

haggada: see HALAKAH.

Haggai (hă′gāī), book of Old Testament, written in Jerusalem after the return from captivity. It urges renewal of work on restoring the Temple and contains a Messianic prophecy (2.7). In Vulgate: Aggeus.

Haggard, Sir H(enry) Rider, 1856–1925, English novelist, author of romantic adventure stories (e.g., *King Solomon's Mines,* 1885; *She,* 1887).

Hagia Sophia (hä′jù sōfē′ù, hä′jù, hä′gyù) [Gr.,= Holy Wisdom] or **Santa Sophia,** originally a Christian church at Constantinople, now a museum of Byzantine art; supreme masterpiece of Byzantine architecture. On site of earlier churches (destroyed by fire) built in 360 by Constantine II and in 415 by Theodosius II. Present fireproof structure was built 532–37 by Justinian on designs of Anthemius of Tralles and Isidorus of Miletus. With Turkish conquest of city in 1453, it became a mosque. Nave is covered by lofty central dome (102 ft. in diameter, 184 ft. high) in which opens a luminous corona of 40 arched windows. All interior surfaces are sheathed with polychrome marbles and gold mosaic. Four slender minarets rise at outer corners of building. A cross surmounts the dome.

Hague, Frank, 1876–, Democratic political boss, mayor of Jersey City, N.J. (1917–47).

Hague, The (hāg), Dutch *'s Gravenhage* or *Den Haag,* municipality (pop. 532,998), cap. of South Holland prov. and *de facto* cap. of Netherlands, near the North Sea. Seat of royal court, legislature, supreme court of justice, and foreign embassies. City is almost entirely residential. It grew around palace begun 1250 by William, count of Holland, the Binnenhof, which now houses the legislature. As residence of stadholders of United Provs. in 17th–18th cent. it grew into a major diplomatic and intellectual center. Since First Hague Conference (1899) it also has been the center for promotion of internatl. justice and arbitration; Peace Palace (completed 1913) has housed Permanent Court of Arbitration, Permanent Court of Internatl. Justice, and, since 1945, Internatl. Court of Justice. Other landmarks include royal palace; Gevangenenpoort (14th-cent. prison, where brothers De Witt were murdered 1672); Mauritshuis (residence of John Maurice of Nassau, now a museum containing outstanding paintings by Rembrandt); 16th-cent. city hall; and Nieuwe Kerk [new church], with Spinoza's tomb.

Hague Conferences (hāg), term for the Internatl. Peace Conference of 1899 and the Second Internatl. Peace Conference of 1907, both proposed by Russia and held at The Hague. Failed to effect an arms reduction, but modified some of the rules of war. First conference estab. (1899) the Permanent Court of Arbitration, known popularly as the **Hague Tribunal.** Each member nation may appoint up to four members of a panel of judges from which arbitrators are picked when two or more nations submit a dispute for arbitration. More than 20 international disputes have been arbitrated. After World War I the Tribunal lost most of its importance to the World Court.

Hahn, Otto (ô′tō hän), 1879–, German chemist and physicist. Won 1944 Nobel Prize for splitting uranium atom and discovering possibility of chain reactions. Atom bomb was based on this work.

Hahnemann, Samuel (hä′nùmùn), 1755–1843, German physician, founder of homeopathy.

Hahnemann Medical College and Hospital, in Philadelphia; chartered 1848 as Homeopathic Medical Col. of Pennsylvania. United 1869 with Hahnemann Medical Col. of Philadelphia (1866–67); assumed present name 1885.

Haida Indians (hī′dù), North American Indian tribe, on Queen Charlotte Isls. and Prince of Wales Isl. Language is only one of Haida family. They belong to Pacific Northwest culture area.

Haidar Ali: see HYDER ALI.

Haifa (hī′fä), seaport (pop. c.130,000), NW Israel, on the Mediterranean, at foot of Mt. Carmel; chief port of Israel. Terminus of pipe line from Iraq.

Haig, Douglas Haig, 1st Earl, 1861–1928, British soldier. In World War I he was British commander in chief after 1915. Maintained confidence of the public despite antagonism of Lloyd George.

hail, pellets or lumps of ice, snow, or rime, falling usually over small areas in hot weather at onset of thunderstorm. The freezing nuclei of hailstones are carried by turbulent winds and grow between wetting and freezing until heavy enough to fall.

Haile Selassie (hī′lē sùlä′sē), 1891–, emperor of Ethiopia, originally named Tafari Makonnen; grandson of Menelik II. Was governor of several provinces during reign of Lij Yasu. When emperor became a Mohammedan, Haile Selassie (a Coptic Christian and then known as Ras Tafari) forced his deposition and put Menelik's daughter Judith on the throne, with himself as regent. Crowned emperor in 1930. During Italian invasion (1935–36) he personally led troops against the enemy. Fled to England 1936, returned in early 1941 to regain his throne.

Hailey, resort city (pop. 1,464), S central Idaho, E of Boise. Has hot springs.

Haileybury, town (pop. 2,346), E Ont., Canada, N of North Bay, on L. Timiskaming. Center of mining region. Popular ski resort.

Hainan (hī′nän′), island (13,000 sq. mi.; pop. 2,500,000), off Kwantung prov., China, in South China Sea. Separated from mainland by Hainan Strait (10–15 mi. wide). Agr., lumbering, and iron mining. Occupied 1939–45 by the Japanese, fell 1950 to Communists.

Hainaut (ěnō′), province (1,437 sq. mi.; pop. 1,247,-299), SW Belgium, bordering on France; cap. Mons. Formerly spelled Hainault. Drained by Scheldt, Sambre, and Dender rivers. Agr.; cattle raising and dairying in S. Important coal mines (Borinage dist.); metallurgy (at Charleroi); textile mfg. (at Tournai). Population is mainly French-speaking. Hainaut became a county in 9th cent., was part of Lotharingia. In 1191 Flanders passed to counts of Hainaut by marriage. Baldwin VI (as Baldwin IX, count of Flanders) became emperor of Constantinople as BALDWIN I (1204). In 1278 the two counties were separated: Flanders passed to Guy of Dampierre, a great-grandson of Baldwin; Hainaut passed to John of Avesnes, another great-grandson, who also became count of Holland. With HOLLAND, Hainaut passed to the houses of Burgundy (1433) and Hapsburg (1482). (For later history, see NETHERLANDS, AUSTRIAN AND SPANISH). Parts of Hainaut were annexed to France 1659, 1678.

Haines, village (pop. 338), SE Alaska, on Chilkoot Inlet of Lynn Canal, SSW of Skagway. Fur-trading post estab. 1867, U.S. army post later. Has good harbor, fishing, and fur farming. Haines Cutoff built in World War II to connect with Alaska Highway at Haines Junction, Yukon territory, provides short route from Panhandle to interior.

Haines City, city (pop. 5,630), central Fla., ENE of Tampa and NNW of L. Kissimmee. Ships citrus.

Haiphong (hī′fông′), city (pop. 142,956), Indo-China, on arm of Thaibinh R. delta near Gulf of Tonkin; main port and naval base of Tonkin.

hair, modified skin structure, consisting of a shaft and a root which is expanded into hair bulb embedded in dermis of skin. Life cycle of scalp hair is about four years.

hairworm or **horsehair worm,** long, slender, unsegmented roundworm usually included in phylum Nemathelminthes. Larvae are parasitic, usually in body of an aquatic insect larva, later in another insect. Once mature they escape from second host into water, where they live as adults.

Haiti (hā′tē), Fr. *Haïti* (äētē′), republic (c.10,700 sq. mi.; pop. 3,111,373), West Indies, on W third of Hispaniola (rest occupied by DOMINICAN REPUBLIC); cap. PORT-AU-PRINCE. The island (called also Haiti and SANTO DOMINGO) belonged to the Spanish, but English and French buccaneers used Haiti region as a base, and French colonists developed sugar plantations with Negro slaves in 17th cent. Spain ceded Haiti (then Saint-Domingue) to France in 1697. French Revolution caused uprising of slaves, which was successful under TOUSSAINT L'OUVERTURE. Spain ceded all the island to France in 1795, but Toussaint conquered it all, and the Haitians resisted Napoleon's punitive force under Gen. Leclerc and even kept up resistance after Toussaint was captured by trickery. Independence, proclaimed in 1804, was achieved. Jacques DESSALINES and Henri CHRISTOPHE became emperors, then Alexandre Pétion, J. P. Boyer, and Faustin SOULOUQUE ruled. Political trouble continued, and financial trouble followed. The U.S. exercised customs receivership (1905–41), and U.S. naval control was strong until 1934. Haiti produces coffee, cotton, sugar, sisal, bananas, and cacao, diversification being enforced by law since the collapse of the sugar market in 1926. Mulattoes dominate the political scene, and most of the population (95% Negro) lives on bare subsistence from farms. Practice of *vodun* (voodoo) rites has been much studied. Border clashes with the Dominican Republic continue and are sometimes violent.

Hakluyt, Richard (hă′klo͞ot), 1552?–1616, English geographer. Noted for *The Principal Navigations, Voyages, Traffics, and Discoveries of the English Nation* (3 vols., 1598–1600), called by J. A. Froude "the prose epic of the English nation."

Hakodate (häko′dätä), city (pop. 211,441), extreme SW Hokkaido, Japan; port on Tsugaru Strait. Shipbuilding center and chief port of island.

Hakone (hä″kō′nä), resort region of mountains, lakes, and hot springs, central Honshu, Japan.

halakah or **halacha** (both: hälä′khä, häläkhä′), the part of the MIDRASH and the TALMUD which embraces the legal statutes of the unwritten commentaries based upon the teachings of the Old Testament. Contrasting is the haggada, the literary element of the Oral Law, which illustrates application of the law by parables.

Halbe, Max (mäks′ häl′bŭ), 1865–1945, German naturalist dramatist. Best known for *Jugend* (1893; Eng. tr., *When Love Is Young,* 1904).

Halberstadt (häl′bŭrshtät), city (pop. 47,652), Saxony-Anhalt, central Germany. Has many fine medieval buildings, notably Liebfrauenkirche (12th cent.) and cathedral (13th–17th cent.; heavily damaged in World War II).

Halcyone (hälsī′ŭnē) [Gr.,= kingfisher], in Greek mythology, daughter of Aeolus. At death of her husband she leaped into the sea. The gods, from compassion, changed the pair into kingfishers, and Zeus forbade the winds to blow for 14 days at the winter solstice, the time when halcyons breed. Hence the expression "halcyon days," a time of tranquillity.

Haldane, John Scott (hôl′dān), 1860–1936, English scientist, known for studies in respiration and gasometry of blood, industrial hygiene, safety and health in mines. His son, **J(ohn) B(urdon) S(anderson) Haldane,** 1892–, is known for application of mathematics to biology and for expositions of science for layman.

Haldimand, Sir Frederick (hôl′dĭmŭnd), 1718–91, British general and colonial governor of Quebec (1778–84), b. Switzerland.

Hale, Edward Everett, 1822–1909, American author of *The Man without a Country* (1863). A Unitarian clergyman, he was famous as a preacher. His sister, **Lucretia Peabody Hale,** 1820–1900, is best remem-

bered for her amusing stories for children, *The Peterkin Papers* (1880).

Hale, George Ellery, 1868–1938, American astronomer, authority on solar vortices and magnetic fields, inventor of spectroheliograph. He organized the Mt. Palomar, Yerkes, and Mt. Wilson observatories.

Hale, Lucretia Peabody: see HALE, EDWARD EVERETT.

Hale, Sir Matthew, 1609–76, English jurist, author of scholarly works on criminal law (*Pleas of the Crown,* 1678; *History of the Pleas of the Crown,* 1685).

Hale, Nathan, 1755–76, American patriot in American Revolution. Hanged by British as spy. Remembered for reputed last words, "I only regret that I have but one life to lose for my country."

Hale, Sarah Josepha (Buell), 1788–1879, American author, long editor of *Godey's Lady's Book.* "Mary Had a Little Lamb" is attributed to her.

Haleakala (hä″lää″kälä′), mountain, 10,032 ft. high, on E Maui, T.H. World's largest extinct crater, 20 mi. in circumference, 2,000 ft. deep.

Haledon (hāl′dŭn), borough (pop. 6,204), NE N.J., NW of Paterson. Textiles, labels, pharmaceuticals.

Hales, Alexander of: see ALEXANDER OF HALES.

Hales, John, 1584–1656, English clergyman and scholar, often called the Ever-Memorable. His lectures on Greek at Oxford, his preaching, and his writings won him renown.

Hales, Stephen, 1677–1761, English physiologist, a clergyman (curate of Teddington), noted for experimental studies in plant and animal physiology.

Halévy, Jacques Fromental (zhäk′ frômätäl′ älāvē′), 1799–1862, French operatic composer. His one successful opera was *La Juive* (1835). Father-in-law and teacher of Bizet, he was father of **Ludovic Halévy** (lüdôvēk′), 1834–1908, author of the librettos of Offenbach's most successful operettas and, with Henri Meilhac, of the libretto of Bizet's *Carmen* (1875).

Halévy, Joseph (zhôzěf′ älāvē′), 1827–1908, Jewish-French Orientalist. Deciphered Sabean and Himyaritic inscriptions and argued that Sumerian literature was merely Babylonian literature in secret writing.

Halevy, Judah: see JUDAH HA-LEVI.

Halévy, Ludovic: see HALÉVY, JACQUES FROMENTAL.

Half-Way Covenant, doctrinal decision of Congregational churches in New England regarding membership in 1662. Original rule had permitted children of "converted" adults to share in covenant. New rule included also grandchildren even though their parents had not been converted. Decision, nicknamed Half-Way Covenant, caused dissension and secession.

Haliburton, Thomas Chandler, pseud. **Sam Slick,** 1796–1865, Canadian author, a jurist. His popular series of the sayings and doings of Sam Slick, Yankee peddler, were collected in *The Clockmaker* (1836) and in later volumes.

halibut, important food fish, largest of flatfish, of genus *Hippoglossus.* Two species are known, one in N Atlantic and one in N Pacific. Females sometimes weigh 500 lb., males rarely over 50 lb.

Halicarnassus (hä″lĭkärnă′sŭs), anc. city of Caria, SW Asia Minor. Widow of ruler MAUSOLUS (4th cent. B.C.) built him a great tomb (see MAUSOLEUM).

Halicz, Ukrainian SSR: see GALICH.

Halifax, Charles Montagu, earl of (hă′lĭfäks, hă′lŭ–), 1661–1715, British statesman. Wrote (with Matthew Prior) *The City Mouse and the Country Mouse* (1687). Persuaded Commons to estab. (1692) national debt. Adopted plan to found Bank of England and was made (1694) chancellor of the exchequer. Prime minister 1697–99.

Halifax, Edward Frederick Lindley Wood, 1st earl of, 1881–, British statesman. Governor general of India 1926–31. As foreign secretary (1938–40) he played a large part in negotiating the MUNICH PACT. Ambassador to U.S. 1941–46.

Halifax, city (pop. 85,589), provincial cap., S N.S., Canada, on Halifax Harbour on the Atlantic. Largest city and chief port of N.S. All-year port is main Canadian winter terminal for transatlantic shipping. Industries include oil and sugar refining, shipbuilding, and meat packing. Has large fishing fleet. Founded 1749, it became a naval base in 1758 expedition against Louisburg, in American Revolution, and in War of 1812. Important naval and air base in both World Wars. The Citadel, fortress built 1794–97, overlooks town and harbor. Seat of Dalhousie Univ. (nonsectarian; coed.; 1838) and associated or affiliated Univ. of King's Col. (opened 1790, became first Canadian university by royal charter in 1802, moved from Windsor, N.S., 1923), Nova Scotia Technical Col., and St. Mary's Col. The Halifax *Gazette* (1752), first Canadian newspaper, continues as the *Nova Scotia Royal Gazette*.

Halifax, county borough (pop. 98,376), West Riding of Yorkshire, England. Noteworthy are Akroyd museum and art gallery. Defoe supposedly wrote part of *Robinson Crusoe* here. Industries include mfg. of carpets, cotton, wool, and worsteds.

Halifax, town (pop. 346), N N.C., on Roanoke R. and NE of Raleigh. Had state's first constitutional convention 1776. Some 18th-cent. buildings.

Hall, Basil, 1788–1844, British naval officer and traveler. Commanded vessels on voyages of exploration. His *Travels in North America* (3 vols., 1829) form valuable description of America.

Hall, Charles Francis, 1821–71, American arctic explorer. Made two expeditions (1860–62, 1864–69) seeking Sir John Franklin's party. Added much to geographical knowledge of area. Led government North Pole expedition (1871).

Hall, Charles Martin, 1863–1914, American chemist, a founder of Aluminum Company of America. He discovered electrolytic process that made large-scale aluminum production possible.

Hall, Granville Stanley, 1846–1924, American psychologist, educator. He was the first president of Clark Univ. (1889–1920). His work *The Contents of Children's Minds on Entering School* (1894) initiated the child-study movement in U.S.

Hall, James, 1793–1868, American author of works on the West, a magazine editor.

Hall, James, 1811–98, American geologist and paleontologist. His work served as a basis for later geological histories of North America.

Hall, Marshall, 1790–1857, English physician and physiologist, pioneer in study of reflex action.

Hall, Fort, trading post, SE Idaho, on Snake R. and near present Pocatello. Built 1834. Important stopping point on Oregon Trail.

Hallam, Arthur Henry (hăl′ŭm), 1811–33, English poet. Tennyson's *In Memoriam* is an elegy for him.

Halland (hä′länd), Swed. *Hallands län,* county (1,901 sq. mi.; pop. 163,363), SW Sweden, on the Kattegat; co. seat Halmstad. This area was conquered from Denmark by Charles X of Sweden, 1658.

Halle (hä′lŭ), city (pop. 222,505), cap. of Saxony-Anhalt, E central Germany, on Saale R. Center of an important salt-mining dist.; chemical and machine-building industries. Ruled in Middle Ages by archbishops of Magdeburg; accepted Reformation 1544; was awarded to Brandenburg (i.e., the later Prussia) 1648. Famous university was founded 1694; it absorbed Wittenberg Univ. 1817. First Bible Society was founded here 1710. Among many fine buildings are Gothic Red Tower and Marienkirche, on medieval market place. Birthplace of Handel.

Halleck, Fitz-Greene, 1790–1867, American poet. With Joseph Rodman Drake wrote satirical verse in "Croaker" papers. Also known for "Marco Bozzaris" and elegy on Drake.

Halleck, Henry Wager, 1815–72, Union general in Civil War. Commanded Dept. of the Missouri (1861–62). Gained unwarranted prestige from victories under his command. General in chief at Washington (1862–64); exerted little influence as military adviser to President and Secretary of War.

Hallelujah (hă″lŭlōō′yù) or **Alleluia** (ă″lŭlū′yù) [Heb., = praise the Lord], expression of joy in Hebrew worship; cf. Pss. 104–6, 111–13; 115–17; 135; 146–50. Used in Christian liturgy, especially at Easter.

Haller, Albrecht von (äl′brĕkht fŭn hä′lŭr), 1708–77, Swiss scientist and author. Especially noted for researches in experimental physiology, he was distinguished also as botanist, writer on bibliography and medical history, poet, and novelist.

Hallet, Étienne Sulpice (ātyĕn′ sülpēs′ älā′), 1755–1825, French architect, known in U.S. as Stephen Hallet. Became supervisor of execution of William Thornton's design for the Capitol, Washington, D.C., but was dismissed for attempted alterations.

Halley, Edmund (hă′lē), 1656–1742, English astronomer, astronomer royal from 1720. First to predict (1682) return of a comet (Halley's comet).

hallmark, plate mark or impress on silver or gold work officially approving purity of metal. Introduced by statute in England in 1300 and enforced by Goldsmiths' Hall, London. Other marks include date mark (usually a letter) and maker's initials.

Hall of Fame, national shrine estab. 1900 at New York Univ. with aid of $250,000 donation by Mrs. Finley J. Shepard. Names of 50 outstanding Americans were inscribed on bronze tablets in 1900. Other names were added later.

Halloween, Oct. 31, evening before feast of All Saints. Tales and customs concerned with witches and ghosts on Halloween are Celtic in origin.

hallucination, false sensory perception lacking external stimulus. Most psychiatrists consider hallucinations symbolic of repressed wishes; they help reveal emotional conflicts, especially in schizophrenic patients. Some hallucinations are caused by emotional stress or great fatigue, e.g., the fata morgana or imagined oasis of desert travelers.

Halmahera (hälmähä′rä) or **Jailolo** (jīlô′lô), island (c.6,870 sq. mi.; pop. including near-by Morotai 83,-743), E Indonesia; largest of the Moluccas. Mountainous, volcanic. Products include nutmeg, resin, sago, and rice. In World War II it was major Japanese air base, neutralized by Sept., 1944.

Halmstad (hälm′städ″), industrial town (pop. 35,276), co. seat of Halland co., SW Sweden, seaport on the Kattegat. Mineral baths are near.

halo, in physics, circle of light around sun or moon, produced when light from either is refracted and reflected by atmospheric ice crystals. Most complex and brilliant near poles. Corona is similar.

halogen (hă′lŭjŭn), member of a family of very active elements. FLUORINE is lightest, most active; CHLORINE, BROMINE, and IODINE are least active. All are monovalent, nonmetallic, and form negative ions.

Hals, Frans (fräns′ häls′), c.1580–1666, Dutch painter, b. Antwerp. Spent most of his life in Haarlem. Painted both single and group portraits as well as studies of low-life types. His bold brushwork gives his work an air of vivacity and informality. Used heavy browns in early period; later alternated blacks and grays with brilliant color. His *Laughing Cavalier* is among widely known works. Also painters were his son Frans Hals, c.1620–c.1669, and his brother **Dirk Hals,** c.1591–1656, noted for festivals and drinking scenes.

Halsey, William F(rederick) (hôl′sē), 1882–, American admiral. Commanded naval action in South Pacific area and in Philippines in World War II. Admiral of the fleet 1945–47.

Halsingborg (hĕlsĭng′bôryù), Swed. *Hälsingborg,* city (pop. 71,718), Malmohus co., S Sweden, seaport on the Oresund opposite Elsinore, Denmark. Trade center and stronghold from 9th cent., it was ceded 1658 by Denmark to Sweden, seized and plundered 1676 by Danes, and regained 1710 by Sweden. Its products include copper, sugar, beer, and superphosphates. To NE is only coal field in Sweden. Formerly also spelled Helsingborg.

Halsted, William Stewart (hôl′stĕd), 1852–1922, American surgeon, professor at Johns Hopkins. His many surgical innovations include use of rubber gloves.

Halys, river of Asia Minor: see KIZIL IRMAK.

Ham [Heb.,= swarthy], son of Noah and father of Cush, Mizraim, Phut, and Canaan. Gen. 9; 10. Hamitic languages named after him; see LANGUAGE, table.

Hama (hä′mä), city (pop. c.70,000), N Syria, on Orontes R. Was Hittite center in ancient times. Called Hamath in Bible, it was renamed Epiphania by Antiochus IV. Once famed for fine textiles, now a trade center for grain-producing area.

Hamadan (hä′mŭdăn), city (pop. 103,874; alt. 6,280 ft.), W Iran, at foot of Mt. Elvend; market center. On site of Ecbatana, cap. of Media. Traditional tomb of Esther is here.

Haman (hä′−), courtier of Ahasuerus. He ordered the massacre of the Jews but was thwarted by Esther and Mordecai and was hanged. Esther 3–7. Also Aman.

Hamar (hä′mär), city (pop. 10,183), SE Norway, on Mjosa L. It is center of rich agr. area, with mfg. of machinery and leather goods. Founded 1152 as an episcopal see by Nicholas Breakspear (later Pope Adrian IV), it is now a Lutheran see. Remains of 12th-cent. cathedral survive, but modern city dates only from 19th cent.

Hamasa (hämä′sä), anthology of beautiful early Arabic poems, gathered by Abu Tammam (c.805–c.845).

Hamath, Syria: see HAMA.

Hambidge, Jay (hăm′bĭj), 1867–1924, American writer and artist. His measurements of classical works of art led to his discovery of mathematical principles which he believed had been consciously used by ancient Egyptian and Greek designers. These principles, called dynamic symmetry, were developed into an extensive system of application.

Hambletonian (hămbŭltō′nĕŭn), 1849–76, American trotting horse, foundation sire of trotting horses bearing his name. Hambletonian Stake Race for three-year-old trotters held annually at Goshen, N.Y.

Hamburg (hăm′bûrg, Ger. häm′boork), state (288 sq. mi.; pop. 1,604,600), N Germany. It consists mainly of the free Hansa city of **Hamburg,** on the Elbe near its mouth on the North Sea. Largest German seaport; shipyards; mfg. (machinery, chemicals); fishing fleet. A cultural center, it has a university (founded 1919) and several technical and medical institutes. Founded by Charlemagne, Hamburg soon grew to commercial importance and became a free imperial city. Its alliance with Lübeck (1241) was the basis of the HANSEATIC LEAGUE. Hamburg joined the German Confederation (1815), the German Empire (1871), the Weimar Republic (1919), and the Federal Republic of [Western] Germany (1949). In 1938 its outlying port, CUXHAVEN, was ceded to Prussia in exchange for ALTONA. Half the city and many lives were destroyed by air raids in World War II. Postwar reconstruction was rapid. The state has been under British occupation since 1945.

Hamburg. 1 Borough (pop. 1,305), NW N.J., N of Dover. "Gingerbread Castle" here has fairy-tale scenes. **2** Village (pop. 6,938), W N.Y., S of Buffalo.

Hamden, town (pop. 29,715), S Conn., N of New Haven; settled c.1664. Site of Eli Whitney's arms factory is marked, his model barn (1816) preserved. Metals.

Hameln (hä′mŭln) or **Hamelin** (hä′mŭlĭn), city (pop. 48,086), Lower Saxony, NW Germany, in Hanover, on Weser R. Scene of legend of PIED PIPER OF HAMELIN.

Hamhung (häm′hoong′), Jap. *Kanko,* city (1944 pop. 112,184), N Korea; industrial center.

Hamilcar Barca (hä′mĭlkär, hùmĭl′kär), d. 228 B.C., Carthaginian commander. Gave a good account of himself in Sicily in the First Punic War. When the peace settlement surrendered Sicily, he withdrew without submission. He ruthlessly put down an insurrection of the mercenaries (238 B.C.) and became practically dictator of Carthage. Set out (237 B.C.) to conquer Spain and was successful until he fell in battle. Father of HANNIBAL.

Hamilton, Scottish noble family. **James Hamilton, 2d Baron Hamilton** and **1st earl of Arran,** 1477?–1529, grandson of King James II, was regent (1522–24) for boy king, James V, whom he helped to keep prisoner. His son, **James Hamilton, 2d earl of Arran,** d. 1575, joined English party as a Protestant, then French party as a Catholic. Again Protestant, he fled Scotland when Mary Queen of Scots married Darnley. Tried unsuccessfully to marry Mary to his son, **James Hamilton, 3d earl of Arran,** 1530–1609, who later became insane. Succeeded as head of the family by his brother, **John Hamilton, 1st marquess of Hamilton,** 1532–1604, nearest heir to Scottish throne after James VI. Banished after his part in murder of earl of Murray, he later enjoyed the king's favor. His grandson, **James Hamilton, 3d marquess** and **1st duke of Hamilton,** 1606–49, was Charles I's chief adviser for Scottish affairs. Tried to pacify the Covenanters. Fought for the king at Preston in 1642 and was found guilty of treason by same court which condemned Charles. His brother, **William Hamilton, 2d duke of Hamilton,** 1616–51, was also favored by Charles I. Signed for the Scots the treaty known as the engagement with Charles in 1647.

Hamilton, Alexander, 1757–1804, American statesman, b. West Indies. Supported patriot cause and fought in American Revolution. Through FEDERALIST PAPERS he did much to get Constitution ratified. Strong exponent of centralized government. A leader of FEDERALIST PARTY. As first Secretary of the Treasury, he estab. Bank of the United States. Favored strengthening Federal government at expense of the states, tying administration more or less tightly to moneyed interests, and following a pro-British foreign policy. Though Jeffersonianism was more popular, Hamilton's vision of the future America as a wealthy, industrial land proved more accurate than Jefferson's agrarian dream. Hamilton was killed in a duel by Aaron Burr, whom he had kept from the presidency in 1800 and from the governorship of N.Y. in 1804.

Hamilton, Andrew Jackson, 1815–75, provisional governor of Texas (1865–66). Pursued wise and courageous course, but much of his work was undone by radical Republican plan of Reconstruction.

Hamilton, Anthony, c.1645–1719, Scottish author of the French *Mémoires du comte de Grammont* (1713?), based on the reminiscences of his brother-in-law, Philibert de GRAMONT. It is a thoroughly amoral but vastly entertaining account of the times.

Hamilton, Emma, Lady, c.1765–1815, English beauty. Mistress (and later wife) of Sir William Hamilton, ambassador to Naples, she had great influence with the queen of Naples. After 1798 she was the mistress of Horatio NELSON whose daughter she bore in 1801. There are many portraits of her by Romney.

Hamilton, Henry, d. 1796, British army officer. In American Revolution, accused of being a "hair buyer" —i.e., one who paid bounties to Indians for scalps taken in frontier raids. Captured by George Rogers Clark at Vincennes (1779).

Hamilton, James, earls of Arran, and **James, 3d marquess and 1st duke of Hamilton:** see HAMILTON, family.

Hamilton, James, 1786–1857, U.S. Representative (1822–29), governor of S.C. (1830–32). Presided over convention which passed nullification ordinance. Diplomatic agent in Europe for Texas (1839).

Hamilton, John, 1st marquess, and **William, 2d duke, of Hamilton:** see HAMILTON, family.

Hamilton, Sir William, 1788–1856, Scottish philosopher. Revived Scottish "common sense" school of metaphysics.

Hamilton, city (pop. c.3,000) and cap. of Bermuda; chief port and center of governmental, commercial, and social life.

Hamilton, city (pop. 208,321), S Ont., Canada, on Hamilton Harbour at head of L. Ontario, SW of Toronto; laid out 1813. Lake port, rail and air center.

Has steel, cotton, and knitting mills, automobile plants, and railroad shops. In fruitgrowing region. Seat of McMaster Univ. (Baptist; coed.; 1887).

Hamilton, burgh (pop. 40,173), Lanarkshire, Scotland. Rudolf Hess landed on near-by Hamilton estate after his flight from Germany in May, 1941.

Hamilton. 1 Village (pop. 3,507), central N.Y., SW of Utica. Seat of Colgate Univ. (nonsectarian; for men; opened as Baptist seminary 1820. Named for William Colgate, a benefactor, 1890). **2** City (pop. 57,951), SW Ohio, on Great Miami R. and N of Cincinnati; settled on site of Fort Hamilton (1791). Trade center for agr. area with mfg. of paper products, machinery, and steel and iron products. Boyhood home of W. D. Howells.

Hamilton, river, 600 mi. long, S Labrador. Rises as Ashuanipi R. from Ashuanipi L. and flows in arc N then SE through series of lakes to the GRAND FALLS where it becomes the Hamilton. Below it flows SE to Lake Melville.

Hamilton, Mount, 4,372 ft. high, W Calif., in Diablo Range near San Jose. Lick Observatory (built 1876–88) of Univ. of California is here.

Hamilton College: see CLINTON, N.Y.

Hamilton Inlet, large bay on SE Labrador coast. Rigolet, Hudson's Bay Co. post, is at its narrows.

Hamitic languages: see LANGUAGE (table).

Hamlet, town (pop. 5,061), S N.C., near S.C. line. Trade and shipping center for fruit area.

Hamlin, Alfred Dwight Foster, 1855–1926, American architect and teacher. Taught architecture at Columbia Univ. His son, **Talbot Faulkner Hamlin,** 1889–, is author of several books on architecture.

Hamlin, Hannibal, 1809–91, Vice President of the United States (1861–65). U.S. Senator from Maine (1848–57, 1869–81). Minister to Spain (1881–82).

Hamline University: see SAINT PAUL, Minn.

Hamm (häm), city (pop. 59,372), North Rhine-Westphalia, NW Germany, on Lippe R. Railroad and industrial center in Ruhr dist.

Hamm, village, grand duchy of Luxembourg. Has large American military cemetery.

Hammarskjold, Dag (däg' häm'ärshüld'), 1905–, Swedish statesman, secretary general of the United Nations (1953–). Was Swedish deputy minister of finance 1936–45, assistant foreign minister 1949–51, and deputy foreign minister 1951–53.

hammer, tool known since Neolithic period. It evolved from club weighted at striking end by hammerstone. Stone hammer is emblem of Thor. Power hammer came into use c.1840. See also PNEUMATIC APPLIANCES AND TOOLS.

Hammerfest (hä'mùrfĕst), city (pop. 3,538), Finnmark co., N Norway, port on Kval isl.; inc. 1789. Though it is northernmost city of Europe, harbor is always ice free. It is fishing, whaling, and sealing center. Germans, who used it as naval base in World War II, demolished it upon retreating.

Hammersmith, metropolitan borough (pop. 119,317), W London, England. Has St. Paul's School for boys (founded 1509), attended by Milton and Pepys. Site of Kelmscott Press and Doves Press.

Hammerstein, Oscar (hä'mùrstīn), 1847–1919, German-American operatic impresario. He brought many famous singers to the U.S. and introduced such operas as *Louise, Pelleas et Melisande,* and *Elektra.* His grandson, **Oscar Hammerstein 2d,** 1895–, is a lyricist and librettist. His musicals (e.g., *Oklahoma!, South Pacific*) with the composer Richard Rodgers have made theatrical history by running for great lengths of time and by using serious plots.

Hammett, Dashiell, 1894–, American writer of "tough" detective stories (e.g., *The Maltese Falcon,* 1930).

Hammond, James Henry, 1807–64, governor of S.C. (1842–44). Early advocate of secession. Elected to U.S. Senate in 1857, he made famous "Cotton is King" speech there.

Hammond, John Hays, 1855–1936, American mining engineer. Employed by Cecil Rhodes in South Africa. Involved in Jameson raid (1895–96), captured and sentenced to death, released on payment of fine. Promoted many mining and hydroelectric projects. His son, **John Hays Hammond, Jr.,** 1888–, gained note as inventor and electrical engineer. His inventions include torpedoes for coastal defense, incendiary projectiles, telegraphic apparatus.

Hammond. 1 City (pop. 87,594), NW Ind., near L. Michigan between Gary and Chicago, on Grand Calumet R.; settled 1851. Mfg. of railroad cars, metal, petroleum and wood products, and surgical supplies. **2** City (pop. 8,010), SE La., E of Baton Rouge. Rail and trade center of strawberry-growing area.

Hammonton, town (pop. 8,411), S central N.J., SE of Camden. Farm trade center with canneries.

Hammurabi (hämōōrä'bē), fl. 2100 B.C., king of BABYLONIA and founder of its greatness. His code of laws is one of the most famous of ancient documents.

Hampden, John, 1594–1643, English statesman; cousin of Oliver Cromwell. Popular hero of the parliamentarians after his attempted arrest (1642) by Charles I helped to precipitate the civil war.

Hampden, Walter (hăm'dùn), 1879–, American actor. Has acted in classical repertory (London, 1901), Ibsen, and Shakspere. With his own company after 1923 did such plays as Rostand's *Cyrano de Bergerac.*

Hampden-Sydney College: see FARMVILLE, Va.

Hampshire (hămp'shĭr) or **Hants** (hănts), maritime county (1,649 sq. mi.; pop. 1,292,211), S England; co. town WINCHESTER. Officially Southampton since 1888, county no longer includes Isle of WIGHT. Undulating region devoted to sheep raising and dairy farming, it also has shipbuilding and large maritime trade. SOUTHAMPTON and Portsmouth major ports. Has many literary and historical associations.

Hampshire sheep: see SHEEP.

Hampstead (hămp'stĭd), metropolitan borough (pop. 95,073), NW London, England. Associated with artists and writers. On a hill above is **Hampstead Heath,** a public park of 869 acres.

Hampton, Wade, 1818–1902, Confederate general. Succeeded J. E. B. Stuart as cavalry corps commander (1864). Restored home rule as governor of S.C. (1876–79). Until 1890 he was dominant in S.C. politics.

Hampton, former urban district, now part of Twickenham, Middlesex, England. Site of David Garrick's house. **Hampton Court Palace** was built by Cardinal Wolsey in 1515 as his private residence. After his downfall, it was a royal residence until time of George II. Has an art gallery and public gardens. **Hampton Court Conference** was held (1604) to find agreement between Puritans and Established Church, with results most unsatisfactory to Puritans.

Hampton. 1 Town (pop. 2,847), SE N.H., S of Portsmouth. Hampton Beach is a resort. **2** City (pop. 5,966), SE Va., port on HAMPTON ROADS opposite Norfolk; settled 1610. One of oldest continuous English settlements in U.S. Sacked by British 1813; burned by Confederates 1861. Processes and ships seafood. Near by is Langley Field, U.S. Army air base. Seat of **Hampton Institute** (Negro; nonsectarian; coed.; opened 1868, founded by American Missionary Assn. through efforts of S. C. Armstrong). B. T. Washington studied here. Indians attended 1878–1923. Best-endowed school for Negroes in country.

Hampton Court Conference and **Hampton Court Palace:** see HAMPTON, England.

Hampton Institute: see HAMPTON, Va.

Hampton Roads, roadstead, SE Va., outlet of James, Nansemond, and Elizabeth rivers into Chesapeake Bay. One of finest natural harbors and one of busiest U.S. seaports; port of Newport News, Hampton, Portsmouth, and Norfolk. In Civil War, scene of fight between ironclads MONITOR AND MERRIMAC. The **Hampton Roads Peace Conference** was a meeting to end Civil War, held Feb. 3, 1865, on board Union transport *River Queen* here. Lincoln presented Union terms. They were unacceptable to South, and meeting failed.

hamster, small rodent of temperate parts of Europe and W Asia. It has a thickset body c.6 in. long and a hairy tail ½ in. long. Usually it is brown or gray (sometimes black or marked with black) above with white under parts. It has a rather broad head, round ears, and large internal cheek pouches. In the wild state it eats small animals in summer and grain stored underground in winter.

Hamsun, Knut (kŭnōōt häm'sōōn), 1859–1952, Norwegian novelist. His wandering life brought him twice to U.S., where he had many jobs. His best-known novels—*Hunger* (1890), *Pan* (1894), and *The Growth of the Soil* (1917)—are uncompromisingly realistic. Awarded 1920 Nobel Prize in Literature. In World War II sympathized with Germans in Norway.

Hamtramck (hămträ'mĭk), city (pop. 43,355), SE Mich., within confines of Detroit. Mfg. of automobiles, metal products and machinery. Public schools here undertook notable plan for education for democracy 1923.

Hamun-i-Helmand (hämōōn'-ē-hĕl'mŭnd), lake, area 5,000 sq. mi., on border of Iran and Afghanistan.

Han (hän), dynasty of China, which ruled 202 B.C.– A.D. 220. Ruled 400 years with only one break, caused by Hsin dynasty (A.D. c.9–c.25) which divided Early or Western Han period from Later or Eastern Han. Era of expansion and cultural growth. First Chinese dictionary and encyclopedic history compiled; Buddhism introduced. Collapse of Han was followed by c.350 years of petty states.

Han, river, c.750 mi. long, in Shensi and Hupeh provs., China. At junction with Yangtze R. are Hankow, Wuchang, and Hanyang.

Hananiah (hănŭnī'ù), one of the THREE HOLY CHILDREN.

Hancock, John, 1737–93, American Revolutionary patriot, signer of Declaration of Independence. Advocated resistance to British. President of Continental Congress (1775–77).

Hancock, Winfield Scott, 1824–86, Union general in Civil War. Conspicuous as leader of 2d Corps at Gettysburg; foremost in repulsing Confederate attacks, notably Pickett's charge on July 3, 1863.

Hancock, city (pop. 5,223), extreme N Mich., on Portage L. On Keweenaw Waterway ship canal, in copper region. Mfg. of metal products.

Hand, Learned, 1872–, American jurist; judge of Federal District Court 1909–24, of U.S. Court of Appeals 1924–51. *The Spirit of Liberty,* a collection of his papers and addresses, was published in 1952.

hand, terminal portion of arm. Human hand has eight bones in wrist, five parallel metacarpals, and three phalanges in each finger and two in thumb. Actions of small hand muscles and arm tendons permit intricate motions. See *ill.,* p. 595.

handball, indoor and outdoor game played on one-wall or four-wall court. In one-wall game, court is 20 ft. by 34 ft. In four-wall game, court is 23 ft. by 46 ft., surrounded by three walls 23 ft. high and back wall 12 ft. high. Four-wall handball, played in England and Ireland for many centuries, was introduced in U.S. in 1870s.

Handel, George Frideric, 1685–1759, German-English composer, b. Halle. After traveling through Germany and Italy, presenting his early operas, he finally settled in England in 1712. Much of his finest music is to be found in his operas, e.g., *Atalanta, Berenice,* and *Serse* (containing the tenor aria now known as *Largo*). His great oratorio, *The Messiah,* was presented in Dublin in 1742. Among other oratorios are *Samson, Judas Maccabeus,* and *Esther.* His orchestral suites, *Fireworks Music* and *Water Music,* are popular today. He also wrote many songs, sonatas, and concertos for various solo instruments and instrumental combinations, and an anthem for the coronation of George II, still used at coronations today. He was buried in Westminster Abbey.

Handy, W(illiam) C(hristopher), 1873–, American Negro composer. First to set down the blues. His songs, such as *Memphis Blues, St. Louis Blues,* and *Beale Street Blues,* are classic examples of their type.

Hanford, city (pop. 10,028), S central Calif., S of Fresno. Trade and processing center in San Joaquin Valley.

Hangchow or **Hang-chou** (both: hăng'chou'), city (pop. 517,559), cap. Chekiang prov., China; port on Tsientang R. at head of Hangchow Bay. Commercial and cultural center on scenic West Lake; S terminus of Grand Canal. Exports silk, tea, and paper fans. Founded A.D. 606. Cap. of Southern Sung dynasty in 12th cent. Occupied 1937–45 by the Japanese.

Hanko (häng'kō), Swed. *Hangö,* city (pop. 6,836), SW Finland, icefree port on small peninsula in Baltic Sea; summer resort. Following Finnish-Russian War (1939–40) Hanko peninsula was leased to USSR as naval base. Returned to Finland 1944 in exchange for lease on Porkkala dist.

Hankow (häng'kou''), commercial city (pop. 749,952) in, but independent of, Hupeh prov., China, at junction of Han and Yangtze rivers. Port (accessible to ocean-going ships) opened to foreign trade 1858.

Hanna, Marcus Alonzo (Mark Hanna), 1837–1904, American capitalist and politician. Handled 1896 campaign of William McKinley for presidency. U.S. Senator from Ohio (1897–1904). A great party boss who exemplified union between business and politics for purposes of economic policy.

Hannah [Heb.,= grace], mother of Samuel. 1 Sam. 1; 2.1–26. Anna and Ann are variants of Hannah.

Hannibal [Punic,= grace of Baal], 247–182? B.C., Carthaginian general, one of the great military geniuses of all time; son of Hamilcar Barca, of the great Barca family. In the Punic Wars he succeeded his brother-in-law, Hasdrubal, as commander in Spain (221 B.C.). With a small force of picked troops he set out to invade Italy, crossed the Alps with full baggage train and elephants, and with his cavalry overran the Po valley. He wiped out a Roman force and in 217 set out toward Rome. After defeating the Romans again at L. Trasimeno, he went to S Italy and gained many allies. At Cannae (216 B.C.) he won one of the most brilliant victories of history, but he failed to get proper support from Carthage and could not take Rome. In 207 B.C. his brother Hasdrubal was defeated on the Metaurus, and Hannibal had to draw back. Recalled (203) to defend Carthage against Scipio, he was decisively beaten in the battle of Zama (202). After peace was concluded (201 B.C.), he was chief ruler in Carthage, governing well, but Rome demanded him as a prisoner, and he went into exile, finally poisoning himself to avoid being given to the Romans.

Hannibal, city (pop. 20,444), NE Mo., on the Mississippi and S of Quincy, Ill.; founded 1819. A river port and rail center, it has mfg. of shoes and wood and metal products. Birthplace of MARK TWAIN, who is commemorated by various structures here.

Hanno, fl. c.470? B.C., Carthaginian navigator. Supposedly explored NE coast of Africa.

Hannover, Germany: see HANOVER.

Hanoi (hä'noi), city (pop. 237,146), Indo-China; cap. of Tonkin, port on Red River. Shipping center for agr. and industrial products, mainly rice and leather. Consists of old Annamese town and modern European-style quarter. Seat of Chinese rulers of Annam, 7th–15th cent. Continued as chief government center after French occupation in late 19th cent. Was cap. of Viet Nam government 1945–46.

Hanover (hä'nōvùr), Ger. *Hannover,* former province (14,960 sq. mi.; 1939 pop. 3,457,477) of Prussia, NW Germany, stretching from Dutch border and N Sea (NW) to Harz mts. (SE); since 1946 part of LOWER SAXONY. Cities include Hanover, Osnabrück, Hildesheim, Emden, Lüneburg, Celle, Göttingen. Mostly agr. lowland (grain, potatoes, sugar beets). Part of old duchy of BRUNSWICK, the region constituted the duchy of Brunswick-Lüneburg until 1692, when Duke Ernest Augustus was raised to rank of elector and his duchy became the electorate of Hanover. Personal union of England and Hanover under Hanoverian dynasty began 1714 with George I (see HANOVER, HOUSE OF). Hanover formed part of Jérôme Bonaparte's kingdom of Westphalia (1807–13). After restoration of its dynasty, it was raised to a kingdom (1815) and became member of GERMAN CONFEDERATION. Because of Salic law of succession it was separated from British crown when Victoria became queen of England (1837). Ernest Augustus, son of George III, who became king of Hanover, began his reactionary reign by rescinding the constitution but was forced to restore it in 1848. His son, George V, succeeded in 1851. As a result of his pro-Austrian stand in the Austro-Prussian War (1866) he lost his kingdom, which became a Prussian province. Hanover city (pop. 441,615), on Leine R., is a commercial center and has varied and important industries. The cap. of the former kingdom and province of Hanover, it became the cap. of Lower Saxony in 1946. It was more than half destroyed in World War II.

Hanover. 1 Town (pop. 6,259), W N.H., NW of Lebanon near Connecticut R. Seat of DARTMOUTH COLLEGE. **2** Borough (pop. 14,048), SE Pa., SW of York. Harness-racing horses bred in area. First Civil War battle N of Mason-Dixon line fought here 1863. **3** Village, E Va., N of Richmond. Patrick Henry lived here for many years.

Hanover, house of, royal family, of Guelphic origin (see HANOVER, province). Succeeded to English throne by Act of Settlement (1701) through a claim based on descent from James I. The first of five Hanoverian kings of Great Britain was (1714) George I, elector of Hanover. With Victoria (1837) the crowns of Hanover and Great Britain were separated.

Hanseatic League (hăn″sēă′tĭk, hăn″zē–), mercantile league of medieval German towns. It came into existence gradually. Originally a *hansa* seems to have been a company of individual traders to foreign lands. The principal establishments of Hansa companies were at WISBY, NOVGOROD, BERGEN, BRUGES, and London (see STEELYARD, MERCHANTS OF THE). To protect themselves against piracy and to overcome foreign competition and trade restrictions, the mercantile cities drew closer. In 1241 LÜBECK and HAMBURG signed a treaty of mutual protection. Some 70 other cities joined. The League was formally organized in 1358. In 1370 it forced on WALDEMAR IV of Denmark the Treaty of Stralsund, which gave it trade monopoly in Scandinavia for more than a century. After a steady decline, the league dissolved in the 17th cent., but the name "Hansa city" has lived on in Bremen, Hamburg, and Lübeck.

Hanson, Howard, 1896–, American composer; director, after 1924, of the Eastman School of Music, Rochester, N.Y., where he estab. American Composers Concerts. His Second, or Romantic, Symphony and an opera, *Merry Mount,* are among his most popular works.

Hanson, John, 1715–83, first "President of the United States in Congress Assembled." First President (1781–82) to serve one-year term under Articles of Confederation, but his duties were merely those of a presiding officer.

Hants: see HAMPSHIRE.

Hanukkah (hä′nŏŏkä), Jewish holiday, the Festival of Lights or the Feast of the Maccabees (also transliterated Chanukah). It celebrates the rededication of the Temple of Jerusalem in 165 B.C. The festival usually occurs in December and lasts eight days.

Hanyang (hän′yäng′), city (pop. 69,483), E Hupeh prov., China, at junction of Han and Yangtze rivers, near Hankow and Wuchang. Steel mills.

Hapeville, residential city (pop. 8,560), NW Ga., S suburb of Atlanta.

Hapsburg or **Habsburg** (both: hăps′bûrg, Ger. häps′bŏŏrk), ruling house of AUSTRIA from 1282 to 1918. Original holdings of family, which can be traced to 10th cent., were in NW Switzerland and Alsace. Name is taken from Habsburg castle, now in ruins, in Aargau, Switzerland. By 13th cent. family held most of Upper Alsace, Switzerland, and Baden. Count Rudolf IV of Hapsburg was elected (1273) German king as RUDOLF I. He confiscated Austria, Styria, Carinthia, Carniola from Ottocar II of Bohemia (1276) and in 1282 made these duchies hereditary family possessions. SWITZERLAND was soon lost, but Tyrol was added in 1363. All Hapsburg possessions as a whole were held together by a family law and could not be alienated from family nor inherited by females. With the election of Albert II as German king (1438), the imperial office, though theoretically still elective, became vested in the house of Hapsburg (for list of Hapsburg emperors, see HOLY ROMAN EMPIRE). Three marriages made the Hapsburgs a world power: (1) that of Maximilian I with MARY OF BURGUNDY, which brought the Low Countries; (2) that of their son, Philip I, to Joanna of Castile, which gave their elder son, Emperor CHARLES V, Spain and the Spanish empire; (3) that of Philip and Joanna's younger son, Ferdinand, with Anna, sister of Louis II of Hungary and Bohemia, which in 1526 brought these two crowns to the Hapsburgs. Thus the Hapsburg empire, "where the sun never set," stretched from the Carpathians to the Philippines. In the division made by Charles V, his son Philip II received the Spanish empire, including Sicily, Naples, Milan, and the Netherlands (see NETHERLANDS, AUSTRIAN AND SPANISH); Ferdinand, as FERDINAND I, became emperor and retained Austria, Bohemia, Hungary, and various German territories. Imperial wars of the 17th cent. weakened authority and cost them Alsace, Franche-Comté, Artois, and parts of Flanders and Hainaut, but at the same time they recovered Hungary from Turkey. The Spanish branch ended in 1700 with Charles II; the resulting War of the SPANISH SUCCESSION (1701–14) forced Austria to give up its claim to Spain but gave it the Austrian Netherlands and Milan. The PRAGMATIC SANCTION made it possible for a woman, MARIA THERESA, to inherit the Hapsburg lands; in the War of the AUSTRIAN SUCCESSION (1740–48) she defended her inheritance against a coalition, losing only SILESIA. Her husband, the grand duke of Tuscany, became emperor as FRANCIS I (1745). With their son, JOSEPH II, one of the greatest Hapsburg monarchs, began the line of **Hapsburg-Lorraine.** TUSCANY was ruled by a separate branch 1790–1860; Modena, acquired by marriage, was ruled by branch of Austria-Este (see ESTE) until 1859. The main branch was continued by Leopold II and by Francis II, who in 1804 took title "Emperor of Austria" as Francis I. From this point, the history of the Hapsburgs became that of Austria and, after 1867, the AUSTRO-HUNGARIAN MONARCHY. After the death of Emperor Charles I (abdicated 1918), the claims of the dynasty passed to his son, Archduke OTTO.

hara-kiri (hä′rŭ-kēr′ē, hä′rŭ-) Japanese form of honorable suicide. Before 1868 was obligatory for disobedience or disloyalty to emperor. Still occasionally performed voluntarily after misfortune.

Harald: see HAROLD.

Haran (hä′răn) or **Harran** (hä′răn), anc. city of Mesopotamia, now in SE Asiatic Turkey, SE of Urfa. A trade center, seat of the temple of the Assyrian moon-god, it was also the home of Abraham's family after the migration from Ur. As Carrhae in Roman times it was the scene of a disastrous defeat of Romans by Parthians (53 B.C.).

Harbin (här′bĭn), city (pop. 760,000), cap. Sungkiang prov., Manchuria; port on Sungari R. Transportation hub of N Manchuria. Founded 1897 by Russia as construction settlement on Chinese Eastern RR. Soybean products are main export.

Hardanger Fjord (härdäng′ŭr fyôrd′), second largest

fjord of Norway, penetrating 114 mi. from the Atlantic into SW Norway. At head of a S branch is Skjeggedalsfoss (waterfall, 525 ft. high); Voringfoss (535 ft. high) is near head of an E branch. The Hardangerfjell, mountain mass extending inland from fjord, rises to 6,153 ft. in the Hardangerjokel. Picturesque villages and scenery make region a favorite of tourists.

Hardee, William Joseph, 1815–73, Confederate general. An able leader in Army of Tennessee. Surrendered to W. T. Sherman in N.C. in April, 1865.

Harden, Sir Arthur (här'dŭn), 1865–1940, English biochemist. Shared 1929 Nobel Prize for research in alcoholic fermentation; he established the character of zymase and discovered that other yeast enzymes are also concerned with fermentation.

Harden, Maximilian (mäk″sēmē'lyän här'dŭn), 1861–1927, German journalist whose real name was Witkowski. An admirer of Bismarck, he attacked the regime of William II in his weekly, *Die Zukunft*.

Hardenberg, Friedrich von: see NOVALIS.

Hardenberg, Karl August, Fürst von (kärl' ou'gŏost fürst' fün här'dŭnbĕrk), 1750–1822, Prussian minister of foreign affairs (1804–6) and chancellor (1810–22). Continued reform program begun by Karl vom und zum STEIN; abolished trade monopolies; turned feudal land into freeholds; emancipated Jews. Persuaded Frederick William III to join coalition against Napoleon (1813). After 1815 he came increasingly under the conservative sway of Metternich.

hardening of the arteries: see ARTERIOSCLEROSIS.

hardhack or **steeplebush,** a North American spirea (*Spiraea tomentosa*) with clusters of rose or white flowers.

Harding, Chester, 1792–1866, American portrait painter. Worked in London and Boston.

Harding, Stephen: see STEPHEN HARDING, SAINT.

Harding, Warren G(amaliel) (gŭmā'lēŭl), 1865–1923, 28th President of the United States (1921–23). U.S. Senator (Republican) from Ohio (1915–21). His noncommittal utterances in presidential campaign of 1920 (he coined the word *normalcy* to express social and economic conditions he promised the nation) helped win him election. One achievement of his administration was calling of the Washington Conference (see NAVAL CONFERENCES). He died suddenly in San Francisco, Aug., 1923. Exposure of TEAPOT DOME scandal and lesser scandals came later; as a result, his administration has been stigmatized as one of most corrupt in U.S. history.

hardness, the resistance a substance offers to being scratched. Mohs's scale (named for Friedrich Mohs) ranges from softest to hardest: talc, 1; gypsum, 2; calcite, 3; fluorite, 4; apatite, 5; feldspar, 6; quartz, 7; topaz, 8; corundum, 9; diamond, 10. The hardness of many minerals falls between those listed; e.g., barite is 3.3.

hardpan, condition of soil or subsoil in which particles become bound together in an impervious mass. It is a serious handicap to farming.

Hardy, Thomas, 1840–1928, English novelist and poet, b. Dorsetshire. Fame came in 1874 with novel *Far from the Madding Crowd*. Novels laid in his native region (which he called Wessex) include *The Return of the Native* (1878), *The Mayor of Casterbridge* (1886), *The Woodlanders* (1887), *Tess of the D'Urbervilles* (1891), *Jude the Obscure* (1896). They are generally gloomy and naturalistic studies of character and environment. Adverse criticism led him to turn to poetry. His pessimism was expressed in such books as *Wessex Poems* (1898); a poetic drama, *The Dynasts* (1904–8); and *Moments of Vision* (1917; lyrics). He also wrote distinguished short stories, such as *Wessex Tales* (1888).

hare, mammal of North America, Europe, Asia, and Africa, formerly considered a rodent, now usually placed in order Lagomorpha. True hares (genus *Lepus*) have longer ears and hind legs than rabbits. At birth they are covered with hair and the eyes are open. Varying hare or snowshoe rabbit and jack

rabbit (with ears sometimes c.⅓ body length) are native to North America; arctic hare has circumpolar distribution; European hare native to central and W Europe is introduced in North America.

harebell, bluebell, or **bluebells-of-Scotland,** slender wiry-stemmed perennial bellflower (*Campanula rotundifolia*), with dainty blue bell-shaped blossoms.

Harfleur (ärflûr'), town (pop. 5,052), Seine-Inférieure dept., N France; a Channel port at mouth of the Seine. Captured 1415 by Henry V of England.

Hargreaves, James, d. 1778, Englishman credited with invention of spinning jenny (see SPINNING).

Hari, Mata: see MATA HARI.

Hariri (härē'rē), 1054–1122, Arabian writer of Basra. Chief work is the popular *Makamat*, a kind of picaresque novel, consisting of 50 episodes.

Hari Rud (hä'rē rōōd'), anc. *Arius*, river, 650 mi. long, rising in central Afghanistan. Forms part of Iran-Afghanistan and Iran–USSR boundaries. Called Tedzhen in USSR.

Harkness, E(dward) S(tephen), 1874–1940, American philanthropist. Extended philanthropies especially to colleges, hospitals, and museums.

Harlan, John Marshall, 1833–1911, Associate Justice of U.S. Supreme Court (1877–1911). On the whole, a strict constructionist; known as a "dissenter."

Harlan, city (pop. 4,786), E Ky., in the Cumberlands near Va. line. Shipping center for coal mines of Harlan co., where only after 20 years of bitter strife between coal operators and miners were the mines unionized (1941).

Harlech (här'lĕkh), village, Merionethshire, Wales. Its heroic defense against Yorkists (1468) is theme of Welsh battle song, *The March of the Men of Harlech*. Has best golf course in Wales.

Harleian Library (här'lēŭn), collection of manuscripts and legal documents, formed by Robert Harley, 1st earl of Oxford, and his son Edward Harley, 2d earl of Oxford. Purchased by British government in 1753; now in British Museum library.

Harlem, congested residential and business section of upper Manhattan borough of New York city, bounded roughly by Central Park and 110th St. (S), East R. (E), Harlem R. (NE), 168th St. (N), Amsterdam Ave. and Morningside Park (W). Estab. 1658 as Dutch settlement of Nieuw Haarlem. In Revolutionary battle of Harlem Heights, the Continentals stopped British advance up Manhattan isl. (Sept. 16, 1776). Largely rural until modern transportation linked it to lower Manhattan in 19th cent. Largest Negro community (pop. over 400,000) in U.S. grew up here after 1910.

Harlem River, navigable tidal channel 7 mi. long, in New York city, separating Manhattan from the Bronx. With Spuyten Duyvil Creek (spī'tŭn dī'vŭl) (1-mi. ship canal) on W, it connects Hudson R. with Hell Gate channel of EAST RIVER. Bridges.

Harlequin (här'lŭkwĭn), stock PANTOMIME character. A nimble, witty, grotesque rogue, he plays opposite Columbine, sometimes as her father.

Harley, Robert, 1st earl of Oxford and **Earl Mortimer,** 1661–1724, English statesman. Had great influence on Queen Anne through his cousin, Lady Masham, and was virtual prime minister 1711–14. Began SOUTH SEA BUBBLE scheme. Secretly negotiated end of War of Spanish Succession in 1713. Struggled for power with Henry ST. JOHN and was forced out of office. His library was basis of HARLEIAN LIBRARY.

Harlingen (här'lĭnjŭn), city (pop. 23,229), S Texas, NW of Brownsville; founded c.1904. Processes and ships cotton, truck, and citrus fruit.

Harmhab (härm'häb), fl. 1350 B.C., king of anc. Egypt. Powerful under Ikhnaton and Tut-ankh-amen, he himself became king and founder of the XIX dynasty. He suppressed corruption in government and restored prosperity. RAMSES I succeeded him. Also appears as Horemheb.

Harmodius and Aristogiton (härmō'dēŭs, ä″rĭstōjī'tŭn), d. c.514 B.C., Athenian patriots. Hipparchus the tyrant tried to win the affection of Aristogiton away from Harmodius and, spurned, insulted Harmodius' sister. The two friends planned to kill Hipparchus and his brother Hippias. They did kill Hipparchus but not Hippias. Harmodius was killed on the spot, Aristogiton executed. The two were regarded as heroes by liberty-loving Athenians.

harmonica. 1 In music, the simplest of the free-reed instruments; also called the mouth organ. The reeds, set in a narrow wooden or metal case, are supplied with holes through which air is drawn or blown. Most harmonicas have only a diatonic scale. **2** Musical glasses, introduced 1743, improved by Benjamin Franklin. Franklin's instrument consisted of a graduated series of glass bowls fitting inside one another and supported by a spindle which revolved the edges of the bowls through a water trough. Fingertips touching the moistened edges produced the sound. Both Mozart and Beethoven composed for it.

Harmony, borough (pop. 912), W Pa., WSW of Butler. First settlement (1805) of HARMONY SOCIETY.

harmony, in music, the simultaneous sounding of two or more tones, which produces chords. The study of harmony examines chords and their relation to each other. The idea of chords was definitely estab. about the 16th cent. Before then, music was polyphonic, and although sounds resembling chords did occur, horizontal and melodic considerations took precedence over vertical or harmonic ones. In 1722, Rameau presented theories that form the basis for the highly complicated rules of harmony. During the 18th cent., the concept of TONALITY became general. Freer uses of tonality developed in the 19th cent., and the 20th cent. saw the evolution of ATONALITY and some breakdown of the old laws of harmony.

Harmony Society, religious society founded by German Separatists led by George Rapp. Harmonists held property in common and subscribed to celibacy. Several communities (Harmony, Pa., in 1805; New Harmony, Ind., in 1814; and Economy, Pa., in 1825) were created in the U.S.

Harmsworth, Alfred Charles William: see NORTHCLIFFE.

Harnack, Adolph von (ädôlf fŭn här'näk), 1851–1930, German theologian and church historian, noted for *Lehrbuch der Dogmengeschichte* (4 vols., 1886–1900).

Harney, William Selby, 1800–1889, American general. Ranking cavalry officer in Mexican War, he fought brilliantly at Cerro Gordo (1847). In early Civil War he commanded Dept. of the West; his conciliatory policy lost him his command in 1861.

Harney Peak: see BLACK HILLS.

Harnosand (härnûsänd'), Swed. *Härnösand,* city (pop. 15,263), co. seat of Vasternorrland co., NE Sweden, seaport (ice-bound in winter) at mouth of Angerman R. Exports timber, tar, cellulose, and wood pulp. It is a Lutheran episcopal see. Settled in 14th cent. and inc. 1585. It was sacked 1721 by Russians.

Harold, 1022?–1066, king of England (1066), rival of WILLIAM I. Son of GODWIN, he belonged to most powerful noble family in reign of Edward the Confessor. Exiled in 1051, family returned and recovered power in 1053. Driven by wind to French coast, he was seized and forced to take oath to support William's claim to English throne. Returning home he renounced oath. In a revolt of the Northumbrians, Harold sided against his brother Tostig. Family was thus divided at death of Edward, who named Harold his heir. William at once invaded in S and Tostig, with Harold III of Norway, invaded from N. Harold defeated and killed Tostig and Harold III. Opposed William at Hastings and was killed.

Harold, kings of Norway. **Harold I** (Harold Fairhair), Norse *Harald Haarfagre,* c.850–c.933, became first king of Norway after victory at Hafrs Fjord over several petty kings (872). Many Viking rulers fled to Iceland as a result; others (e.g., ROLLO) conquered and settled Normandy. **Harold III,** Norse *Harald*

Hardhrádhi [stern council], d. 1066, half-brother of OLAF II, entered Byzantine service after Olaf's defeat (1030). He returned in 1042, joined revolt against MAGNUS I, became joint ruler with Magnus 1046, sole ruler 1047. In 1066 he took part with TOSTIG in invasion of England; fell at STAMFORD BRIDGE.

Harold Bluetooth, d. c.985, first Christian king of Denmark (935–85).

Harold Harefoot, d. 1040, king of England (1037–40). Illegitimate son of Canute, he struggled with his half-brother Harthacanute for control of England.

Haroun-al-Rashid: see HARUN-AL-RASHID.

harp, stringed musical instrument of anc. origin, whose strings are plucked with the fingers. Modern harp consists of three parts—sound box, neck, and pillar. Strings are stretched from sound box to neck, where tuning pegs are fastened. The harp was originally diatonic. More strings were added to make it chromatic, but its capabilities were still limited. Introduction of double-action pedals (c.1810) made it possible to raise the pitch of a string either a tone or a semitone, thus increasing the possibilities of the instrument and making it popular in the orchestra.

Harper, William Rainey, 1856–1906, American educator and Hebrew scholar. He became professor of Semitic languages at Yale in 1886. In 1891 he was appointed first president of Univ. of Chicago.

Harpers Ferry, town (pop. 822), E W.Va., on bluffs at confluence of Potomac and Shenandoah rivers, c.55 mi. NW of Washington, D.C. Scene of John Brown's raid on U.S. arsenal, Oct. 16, 1859. Key to Shenandoah Valley in Civil War, it changed hands several times, being finally taken by Union forces in 1863.

harpsichord: see PIANO.

Harpy, in Greek religion, predatory monster with head of a woman and body, wings, and claws of a bird.

harpy, large bird of prey found from S Mexico to Brazil. It is 38–40 in. long.

Harran, anc. city of Mesopotamia: see HARAN.

Harriman, E(dward) H(enry), 1848–1909, American railroad executive. Gained control of several Western railroads. Attempt to control Chicago, Burlington & Quincy RR was blocked by James J. HILL. His son, **W(illiam) Averell Harriman,** 1891–, was ambassador to the USSR (1943–46), U.S. Secretary of Commerce (1946–48), and director of the Mutual Security Agency (1951–53).

Harriman, city (pop. 6,389), E Tenn., W of Knoxville and near Tennessee R. Rail and trade center in farm area. Mfg. of wood products and blankets.

Harrington, James, 1611–77, English political writer. His utopian *Commonwealth of Oceana* (1656) influenced democratic thought in America and elsewhere.

Harris, Chapin Aaron, 1806–60, American dentist, pioneer in modern dentistry, noted for writings and as founder of *American Journal of Dental Science* and of first school of dentistry.

Harris, Frank, 1856–1931, British-American author, b. Ireland; educ. in U.S.; a magazine editor in London and New York. Created scandal with partly fictional memoirs, *My Life and Loves* (3 vols., 1923–27).

Harris, Joel Chandler, 1848–1908, American Southern author, a newspaper editor, famous for "Uncle Remus" stories in Negro dialect.

Harris, Roy, 1898–, American composer; pupil of Nadia Boulanger. Among his works are *When Johnny Comes Marching Home,* an "American Overture"; *Symphony for Voices,* to poems by Whitman; *Folksong Symphony;* and a piano quintet. While he is not a strict modernist, he occasionally uses such devices as polytonality and irregular metrical patterns.

Harris, Thomas Lake, 1823–1906, American Christian mystic, founder of Brotherhood of the New Life, b. England. Estab. at Wassaic, N.Y. (1861), the community was moved to Amenia, N.Y. (1863), and to Brocton, near Buffalo (1867), where it was known as Salem-on-Erie. In 1875 Harris and part of the group settled in Calif.

Harris, Townsend, 1804–78, American diplomat. Appointed first U.S. consul general to Japan in 1855, raised to minister in 1859. Negotiated commercial treaty (1858).

Harris, Hebrides, Scotland: see LEWIS WITH HARRIS.

Harrisburg. 1 City (pop. 10,999), S Ill., N of Paducah, Ky., in coal, grain, and timber area; platted in 1850s. Produces wood products, flour, and brick. **2** City (pop. 89,544), state cap. (since 1812), SE Pa., on Susquehanna R.; laid out 1785. Settled by German religious sects and Scotch-Irish, it grew as canal and rail center. Has mfg. of steel, clothing, and lumber products.

Harrison, William Henry, 1773–1841, 9th President of the United States (1841). Governor of Indiana Territory (1800–1812); primarily responsible for opening Ohio and Indiana to white settlement. Won battle of Tippecanoe against Indians, Nov. 6–7, 1811. In War of 1812, as commander in Northwest, he won battle of the Thames (see THAMES, BATTLE OF THE). U.S. Representative (1816–19) and Senator from Ohio (1825–28). The Whigs, presenting Harrison as a rugged Westerner and using "Tippecanoe and Tyler too" as a slogan, waged first "rip-roaring" campaign in U.S. history to elect him President. He died a month after taking office. His grandson, **Benjamin Harrison,** 1833–1901, was 23rd President of the United States (1889–93). Served in Civil War. U.S. Senator (Republican) from Ind. (1881–87). As President he approved all regular Republican measures, including highly protective McKinley Tariff Act. His moderate stand on civil service reform displeased both reformers and spoilsmen. First Pan-American Conference was held in his administration (1889).

Harrison. 1 City (pop. 5,542), NW Ark., in the Ozarks. Commercial center for agr. area. Wood products, cheese, and flour. Diamond Cave is near. **2** Town (pop. 13,490), NE N.J., industrial suburb of Newark. Mfg. of steel, elevators, pumps, machine parts, gases, and ink. **3** Town (pop. 13,577), including residential Harrison village (1940 pop. 6,307), SE N.Y., between Mamaroneck and Rye.

Harrisonburg, city (pop. 10,810), N Va., in Shenandoah Valley, NNE of Staunton; settled 1739. Trade center in agr. area. Mfg. of textiles, shoes, and furniture. Hq. of George Washington Natl. Forest.

Harrod, James, 1742–93, American frontiersman. In 1774 he founded first settlement in Ky., later named Harrodsburg in his honor.

Harrodsburg, city (pop. 5,262), central Ky., S of Frankfort; founded 1774 by James Harrod. Oldest settlement in state; G. R. Clark was early leader. Trades in livestock, grain, and cattle. Resort. Near by are replica of Fort Harrod and cabin where Nancy Hanks and Thomas Lincoln were married.

Harrow or **Harrow-on-the-Hill,** urban district (pop. 219,463), Middlesex, England. Seat of Harrow (founded 1571), one of England's great public schools.

Harsha (hûr′shù), d. 647, Indian emperor. Conquered all N India 606–12. His cap. at Kanauj was artistic and literary center. Turned from Hinduism to Buddhism.

Hart, Albert Bushnell, 1854–1943, American historian. Harvard professor (1883–1926) and prodigious worker, responsible for over 100 volumes written or edited by him. Editor of and contributor to "American Nation" series (28 vols., 1904–18) and *Epochs of American History* (4 vols., 1891–1926). Editor or coeditor of many series, notably *Guide to the Study and Reading of American History* (1896; revised ed., 1912), an important bibliography.

Hart, Charles Henry, 1847–1918, American writer and art expert. Director of Pennsylvania Academy of Fine Arts (1882–1902).

Hart, George Overbury, 1868–1933, American watercolor painter. Traveled widely to paint scenes depicting everyday life of people everywhere.

Hart, William S., 1870–1946, American stage and film actor. After a long stage career (1895–1914), he entered films and became the model of the strong, silent man of the West.

Harte, (Francis) Bret, 1836–1902, American writer. A gold seeker, teacher, and journalist, he wrote stories (e.g., "The Luck of Roaring Camp," "The Outcasts of Poker Flat"), novels, and humorous poems of the West. Last years spent in England.

hartebeest (här′tĭbēst″), name for certain African antelopes. Usually it refers to genus *Alcelaphus* (or *Bubalis*); sometimes to *Damaliscus*, the bontebok and blesbok. The bubal hartebeest (*Alcelaphus buselaphus*) is believed by some to be extinct. It is reddish or fawn, stands c.3½ ft. at the shoulder, and has ringed, pointed, curved horns. The larger red hartebeest (*A. caama*) is native to S Africa.

Hartford. 1 City (pop. 177,397), state cap., central Conn., on Connecticut R.; settled 1635–36 on site of Dutch trading post (1633). State's largest city and financial, industrial, and commercial center. It is internationally famous for insurance business (since 1794). Mfg. of firearms, typewriters, airplane parts, tools, and brushes. Hartford *Courant*, founded 1764, is one of oldest U.S. newspapers. Was home of Connecticut Wits. Birthplace of Noah Webster, John Fiske, and elder J. P. Morgan. Harriet Beecher Stowe and Mark Twain lived here. Has old statehouse (1796; designed by Bulfinch), capitol (1872), state library and supreme court building (1910; with Stuart's full-length *Washington*), Trinity Col. (for men; 1823), and parts of Univ. of Connecticut. Charter Oak stood here until 1856. Tradition says that Conn. charter was hidden in this tree when Sir Edmond Andros demanded it (1687). **2** Town (pop. 5,827), E Vt., on Connecticut R. Includes White River Junction, industrial and rail center (pop. 2,365).

Hartford City, city (pop. 7,253), E Ind., N of Muncie. In agr., gas and oil area. Jute board, hardware mfg.

Hartford Convention, Dec. 15, 1814–Jan. 4, 1815, meeting of 26 delegates to consider the problems of New England in the War of 1812, held at Hartford, Conn. Grew out of opposition to embargo acts and to war. It recommended that New England secession, which extremists had urged, if it came at all, should be gradual and should be executed in peaceful times. Importance of meeting is twofold: it continued the view of states' rights that was the refuge of minority groups; it virtually destroyed the Federalist party politically, since the Federalists, who had sponsored the convention, were unable to regain lost prestige.

Hartford Wits: see CONNECTICUT WITS.

Harthacanute (här′thăkùnūt), d. 1042, king of Denmark (1035–42) and of England (1040–42), son of Canute. Ruled in Denmark until the death of Harold Harefoot, then in England. Left throne to Edward the Confessor.

Hartlepool (härt′lē–, härt′ùl–), municipal borough (pop. 17,217), Durham, England; a seaport. Has extensive docks and trade in coal and timber.

Hartley, Marsden, 1878–1943, American landscape and still-life painter. Early paintings were abstract; later work largely representational. Also wrote poetry.

Hartmann, Eduard von (härt′män), 1842–1906, German philosopher. His philosophy of the "unconscious" (meaning forces of nature) stressed struggle in man between impulse and reason.

Hartmann von Aue (härt′män fün ou′ù), c.1170–c.1220, German poet. He wrote lyrics, chivalric romances (*Erec, Iwain*), a religious legend (*Gregorius*, which inspired Thomas Mann's *The Holy Sinner*), and the idyl *Der arme Heinrich* (used by Longfellow for his *Golden Legend*).

Hartsville, town (pop. 5,658), NE S.C., ENE of Columbia. Mfg. of textiles, bricks, furniture, and paper.

Harun-al-Rashid (härōōn-äl-räshēd′, hăʹrōōn-äl-räʹ-shĭd), c.764–809, 5th ABBASID caliph (786–809). Imprisoned the Barmecides, a powerful Persian family who had helped him become caliph. Under him

Baghdad was at its height as a cultural center. Figures prominently in *Thousand and One Nights*.

Harunobu (Harunobu Suzuki) (hä'rōō'nō'bōō), c.1725–1770, Japanese artist. Introduced multiple color printing with wood blocks.

Harvard, John, 1607–38, chief founder of Harvard Col. He bequeathed half his estate and his library toward the college, which was named for him.

Harvard, town (pop. 3,983), E eentral Mass., NW of Boston. In town is "Fruitlands," once scene of co-operative community of Bronson ALCOTT.

Harvard, Mount: see SAWATCH MOUNTAINS.

Harvard University, first New England college, mainly at Cambridge, Mass.; nonsectarian, mainly for men; founded 1636 by Mass. Bay colony, opened 1638, chartered 1650. Named after John HARVARD, 1639. Closely allied with Congregational Church, later with the Unitarian until 1851. In Pres. Charles W. Eliot's administration (1869–1909), Harvard Col. became great university. He introduced elective system. Under A. Lawrence Lowell tutorial system and general examinations were begun. J. B. Conant was president 1933–53. Includes Harvard Col. and, among others, graduate schools of divinity (1816), law (1817), arts and sciences (1872; with journalism), and some professional schools at Boston. Radcliffe Col. (nonsectarian; for women) is associated but not corporately connected with Harvard. Classes began 1879; Society for the Collegiate Instruction of Women (known as Harvard Annex) chartered 1882; rechartered and renamed 1894. Elizabeth C. Agassiz was president, 1879–1903. Instruction is given by Harvard faculty. Harvard has one of largest libraries in America. Maintains several astronomical observatories in U.S. and one near Bloemfontein, Union of South Africa. Has Fogg Mus. of Art (1894), Univ. Mus. containing Peabody Mus. of Archaeology and Ethnology (1866) and Mus. of Comparative Zoology (1859), several botanical collections. Harvard-Yenching Inst. (for aid in China) founded 1928. Has traditional sports rivalry with Yale Univ. Harvard Univ. Press founded 1913.

harvestman: see DADDY LONGLEGS.

Harvey, Gabriel, 1545?–1630, English poet and miscellaneous writer; friend of Spenser, bitter opponent (in pamphlets) of Thomas Nashe.

Harvey, William, 1578–1657, English physiologist, discoverer of circulation of blood and function of heart as pump. His theory was stated in 1616, published 1628. Known also for research in embryology.

Harvey, city (pop. 20,683), NE Ill., just S of Chicago. Mfg. of engines and machinery.

Harwich (här'ij), municipal borough (pop. 13,488), Essex, England; port and chief naval station on E coast. Frequently bombed 1940–41.

Harz (härts), densely forested mountain range, central Germany, extending c.60 mi. between Elbe and Weser rivers and occupying parts of Lower Saxony and Saxony-Anhalt. Upper Harz, in NW, is rich in silver, iron, lead, copper; culminates in the BROCKEN. There are many resorts.

Hasa, El (el hä'sù), region, NE Saudi Arabia, on Persian Gulf. Extensive oil drilling.

Hasan (hä'sùn), c.625–c.669, 5th caliph; son of Ali and Fatima (Mohammed's daughter). Succeeded Ali as caliph, 661; abdicated under Omayyad pressure. His brother, HUSEIN, took up the family cause. He is a saint of the Shiites.

Hasbrouck Heights (häz'brŏŏk), residential borough (pop. 9,181), NE N.J., S of Hackensack; settled c.1685. Teterboro airport is near.

Hasdrubal (häz'drōŏbùl), name of two Carthaginian generals. **Hasdrubal,** d. 221 B.C., succeeded his father-in-law, Hamilcar Barca, as commander in Spain, increased the Carthaginian empire, founded Cartagena. He was succeeded by his brother-in-law HANNIBAL. Another brother-in-law, **Hasdrubal,** d. 207 B.C., took command in Spain when Hannibal left for Italy. He fought against the Scipios and, to avoid a disaster,

crossed the Alps to Italy. There on the Metaurus he was killed in battle (207 B.C.), and his head was thrown into Hannibal's camp. The defeat marked the beginning of Carthaginian decline.

hashish (hä'shĭsh), name used chiefly in Asia for narcotic and intoxicating substance prepared from hemp plant and sometimes limited to extract of leaves. It is chewed, smoked, or taken as liquid.

Hasidim (häsē'dĭm) or **Assideans** (äsĭdē'ŭnz) [Heb.,= pious], originally the most rigid adherents of Judaism. The sect developed between 300 B.C. and 175 B.C. When Antiochus IV decreed that the Jews must offer sacrifices to the Greek gods, the Hasidim led the resistance. The modern sect of Hasidim was founded in Europe in the 18th cent. by BAAL-SCHEM-Tov. It opposed the inflexible rationalism of the Talmud and is characterized by a belief in the immediate coming of the Messiah and emotional exaltation in prayer. The Talmudists in 1781 pronounced the Hasidim heretics. The sect still has adherents. The name is also transliterated as Chassidim.

Hasmoneans: see MACCABEES.

Hassam, Childe (chĭld' hä'sùm), 1859–1935, American painter and etcher. His landscapes and interiors show strong influence of impressionism.

Hasse, Johann Adolph (hä'sù), 1699–1783, German composer. Although he wrote in all forms, he was chiefly known for operas written in the Italian tradition, e.g., *Alessandro nell' Indie* and *Arminio*.

Hasselt (hä'sùlt), city (pop. 29,369), cap. of Limburg prov., E Belgium.

Hassler, Ferdinand Rudolph, 1770–1843, American geodesist, b. Switzerland. Helped organize U.S. Coast and Geodetic Survey. His original survey of Atlantic seacoast has not had to be repeated.

Hastings, Warren, 1732–1818, first governor general of British India (1774–84). Began as clerk for East India Company (1750). His aggressive policy of judicial and financial reform rebuilt British prestige in India but met with opposition. When he returned to England after resigning he was charged with high crimes by Edmund BURKE and was impeached (1787). Was finally acquitted in 1795.

Hastings, county borough (pop. 65,506), Sussex East, England, on S coast. One of the CINQUE PORTS. Famous as scene of battle of Hastings (Oct. 14, 1066) between Normans under William the Conqueror and Saxons under HAROLD. One of history's most celebrated battles, it was won by William's smaller but better trained and equipped force after a whole day's fighting. It was first and most decisive victory of NORMAN CONQUEST.

Hastings. 1 City (pop. 6,096), S Mich., WSW of Lansing and on tributary of Grand R. Mfg. of metal products. Indian mounds near by. **2** City (pop. 6,560), E Minn., SE of St. Paul and on the Mississippi at mouth of St. Croix R.; farm trade center. **3** City (pop. 20,211), S Nebr., S of Grand Island; founded 1872. Rail and trade center for wheat region. Mfg. of farm equipment, wheat and corn products. Seat of Hastings Col. (Presbyterian; coed.; 1882).

Hastings-on-Hudson, residential village (pop. 7,565), SE N.Y., on E bank of the Hudson N of Yonkers. Mfg. of chemicals, copper wire, and cables.

Hatay, Turkey: see ALEXANDRETTA, SANJAK OF.

Hathaway, Anne: see SHAKSPERE, WILLIAM.

Hatshepsut, Egyptian queen: see THUTMOSE I.

Hatteras, Cape (hä'tùrùs), promontory on low sandy island, off E N.C., E of Pimlico Sound. Dangerous because of frequent storms; marked by lighthouses since 1798. Has recreational area.

Hattiesburg, city (pop. 29,474), SE Miss., on Leaf R. and SE of Jackson; settled early 1880s. Rail, trade, and industrial center of farm and timber area, it has mfg. of explosives, chemicals, naval stores, and silk. U.S. Camp Shelby near by.

Hauff, Wilhelm (vĭl'hĕlm houf'), 1802–27, German author. *Lichtenstein* (1826) was a popular historical novel. English translations of his tales are *Fairy Tales* (1910) and *Caravan Tales* (1912).

Haugesund (hou'gŭsōōn), city (pop. 18,407), Rogaland co., SW Norway, fishing port and fish-processing center on North Sea. Near-by Viking monuments include grave of Harold I.

Hauptmann, Bruno Richard, 1899–1936, convicted kidnaper and murderer of infant son of Charles A. Lindbergh, b. Germany. Electrocuted after sensational trial at Flemington, N.J.

Hauptmann, Gerhart (gĕr'härt houpt'män), 1862–1946, German poet, dramatist, novelist. After his naturalistic plays *Before Dawn* (1889) and *The Weavers* (1892), he turned to a romantic medium in the dream play *Hannele* (1893) and in *The Sunken Bell* (1897). The tragedies *Drayman Henschel* (1899) and *Rose Bernd* (1903) mark a return to realism. His novels, notably *The Fool in Christ, Emanuel Quint* (1910) and *The Heretic of Soana* (1918), show his mastery of prose. Awarded the 1912 Nobel Prize in Literature; ranks among foremost modern German writers.

Hauran (hourän'), district, SW Syria, E of Jordan R. Many caverns (once inhabited) are in mountainous NE. Region has volcanic peaks and rich lava soil. Inhabited mainly by Druses. At least part of Hauran belonged to biblical kingdom of BASHAN; it marked NE boundary of the Promised Land. Some 300 ancient towns, with buildings and furniture made of lava, have been located.

Hausa or **Haussa** (both: hou'sù, –sä), Negro people, largely Moslem, numbering over 5,000,000 of N Nigeria and Niger territory. They practice agr. and trading. Their language is a lingua franca in much of W Africa.

Hauser, Kaspar (käs'pär hou'zùr), 1812?–1833, German foundling; possibly an impostor. Appeared in Nuremberg as a "wild boy" (1828), claiming to have spent years in a dark prison hole. Rehabilitated, he wrote his autobiography (1829); was adopted by earl of Stanhope (1832); died of a knife wound, possibly self-inflicted. The theory that he was a son of the grand duke of Baden has not been substantiated. Subject of a novel by Jakob Wassermann.

Haushofer, Karl (kärl' hous'hōfùr), 1869–1946, German geographer, chief exponent of GEOPOLITICS. A professor at Munich, he became one of Hitler's advisers on foreign affairs. Died by suicide.

Haussmann, Georges Eugène, Baron (ōsmän'), 1809–91, French city planner, largely responsible for layout of present-day Paris. Boulevard Haussmann named in his honor.

Haute-Garonne (ōt"-gärôn'), department (2,458 sq. mi.; pop. 512,260), S France; cap. Toulouse. S part lies in Pyrenees.

Haute-Loire (–lwär'), department (1,931 sq. mi.; pop. 228,076), S central France, in Auvergne; cap. Le Puy.

Haute-Marne (–märn'), department (2,416 sq. mi.; pop. 181,840), NE France, in Champagne; cap. Chaumont.

Hautes-Alpes (ōt"zälp'), department (2,178 sq. mi.; pop. 84,932), SE France, in Dauphiné; cap. Gap.

Haute-Saône (ōt"-sōn'), department (2,075 sq. mi.; pop. 202,573), E France, in Franche-Comté; cap. Vesoul.

Haute-Savoie (–sävwä'), department (1,775 sq. mi.; pop. 270,468), E France, in Savoy; cap. Annecy.

Hautes-Pyrénées (–pērănä'), department (1,751 sq. mi.; pop. 201,954), SW France, bordering on Spain; cap. Tarbes.

Haute-Vienne (–vyĕn'), department (2,145 sq. mi.; pop. 336,313), W central France; cap. Limoges.

Haut-Rhin (ō"-rĕ'), department (1,354 sq. mi.; pop. 471,705), E France, in Alsace; cap. Colmar.

Havana (hùvă'nù), Span. *La Habana*, city (pop. 659,883), W Cuba, cap. of Havana prov. and Cuba; largest city and chief port of the West Indies; founded c.1515. Its position has been strategic historically and commercially. After Cuban independence (1898), U.S. forces improved sanitary conditions in Havana, now popular winter resort. Principal exports: sugar,

fruits, tobacco. MORRO CASTLE is at harbor entrance.

Havelok the Dane, English 14th-cent. metrical romance, telling the story of a prince brought up as a peasant who comes into his own.

Haverford, village (pop. 2,529), SE Pa., W of Philadelphia. Seat of Haverford Col. (Friends; for men; opened 1833), with notable Quakeriana collection.

Haverhill (hā'vùrĭl), city (pop. 47,280), NE Mass., on Merrimack R. and NE of Lawrence; settled 1640. A leading U.S. shoe producer. Whittier's birthplace preserved.

Haverstraw, industrial village (pop. 5,818), SE N.Y., on W bank of the Hudson opposite Ossining.

Havre (hā'vùr), city (pop. 8,086), N Mont., NE of Great Falls and on Milk R. (irrigation); founded 1887. Ships livestock. Has railroad shops.

Havre, Le (lù ä'vrù), city (pop. 105,491), Seine-Inférieure dept., N France, at mouth of the Seine. Chief French transatlantic port. Founded 1517. Heavily damaged in World War II.

Havre de Grace (hăv'ùr dù grăs'), city (pop. 7,809), NE Md., on Chesapeake Bay at mouth of Susquehanna R. (bridged 1940), NE of Baltimore. Trade and resort center in agr. area with canneries and commercial fisheries. Has famous race track.

Hawaii (hùwī'ē, hävä'ē), island (4,021 sq. mi.; pop. 68,350), largest and southernmost of Hawaiian Isls. Dominated by mountain masses of MAUNA LOA, MAUNA KEA, and Hualalai. Climate ranges from tropical heat of S coastal areas to icy chill of mountain summits. Major Hawaiian producer of sugar cane; coffee and sisal also grown. Large cattle ranch at foot of Mauna Kea. Hilo on NE coast is chief port.

Hawaii, University of, at Honolulu; land grant and territorial, coeducational. Chartered 1907, opened 1908 as Col. of Agr. and Mechanic Arts; known as Col. of Hawaii 1911–20. Colleges of arts and sciences, agr., applied science, and education.

Hawaiian Islands, group of 20 islands (6,420 sq. mi.; pop. 499,794), central Pacific, c.2,400 mi. from San Francisco. A territory of U.S. since 1900, officially known as Territory of Hawaii; governor is appointed by U.S. President and Congress. Cap. HONOLULU. Islands, formerly called Sandwich Isls., are of volcanic origin and are fringed with coral reefs. Climate is notably fine. OAHU, HAWAII, MAUI, KAUAI, and MOLOKAI are main islands. Sugar cane and pineapples are chief products and basis of principal industries; coffee, rice, sisal, and cotton also grown. Many ethnic and cultural groups are represented in population. Islands discovered by Capt. James Cook 1778. KAMEHAMEHA I became sole sovereign 1810. Missionaries arrived 1820. Queen LILIUOKALANI was deposed 1893; S. B. DOLE was president of republic before annexation to U.S. in 1898. Tourist trade grew in 1930s. Plebiscite of 1940 showed Hawaiians in favor of statehood. U.S. entrance into World War II came with Japanese attack on Pearl Harbor, and the islands became an armed base for Pacific fighting.

Hawaii National Park: see NATIONAL PARKS AND MONUMENTS (table).

Hawick (hô'ĭk), burgh (pop. 16,718), Roxburghshire, Scotland. Castle at near-by Branksome is Branksome Hall of Scott's *Lay of the Last Minstrel.* Woolen and hosiery mfg. center.

hawk, bird of prey of same family as eagle, kite, osprey. It is short winged and swift flying and has sharp claws and a hooked bill. Completely harmful North American hawks are sharp-shinned hawk, Cooper's or chicken hawk, GOSHAWK. Largely beneficial are American, rough-legged, broad-winged, red-tailed, and red-shouldered hawks which eat insects and rodents. Marsh hawk sometimes kills game. Name hawk is applied to some birds of FALCON family. See *ill.,* p. 105.

Hawkesbury, town (pop. 7,194), SE Ont., Canada, on Ottawa R. and W of Montreal. Has paper and lumber mills.

Hawkins or **Hawkyns, Sir John,** 1532–95, English mariner. In profitable slave trading expeditions he sold African Negroes in Spanish ports. As treasurer and comptroller of the navy he improved ship construction. Fought against the Spanish Armada (1588) as did his son, **Sir Richard Hawkins**, 1562?–1622. Served under his father and Drake. Captured by Spanish while raiding South America, he was imprisoned 1597–1602. Later served in Parliament.

Hawksmoor, Nicholas, 1661–1736, English architect. Known chiefly for work done under Sir Christopher Wren and Sir John Vanbrugh. His own designs show influence of Italian baroque.

hawkweed, perennial plant of genus *Hieracium*, widely distributed, generally considered a weed but sometimes cultivated in rocky soil. It has small dandelion-like flower heads of yellow, orange, or red.

Hawley-Smoot Tariff Act, enacted 1930 by U.S. Congress. Highest protective tariff act in U.S. history. Retaliatory foreign tariffs caused sharp decline in U.S. foreign trade.

Haworth, Sir Walter Norman (härth), 1883–1950, English biochemist. Shared 1937 Nobel Prize in Chemistry for work on carbohydrates and vitamin C.

Haworth (hô'ŭth, hou'–), part of Keighley, West Riding of Yorkshire, England. Has home of Brontë family, now a museum and library. All the Brontës but Anne are buried here.

hawthorn, thorny shrubs or small trees of genus *Crataegus*, particularly prevalent in E North America. Clusters of white or red flowers in spring are followed by showy, variously colored fruits sometimes used in jelly. Much used in landscaping in U.S. and England.

Hawthorne, Charles Webster, 1872–1930, American portrait and genre painter, a noted teacher.

Hawthorne, Nathaniel, 1804–64, American novelist and short-story writer, b. Salem, Mass. After graduation from Bowdoin Col. (1825) he spent years in seclusion in his home doing literary hack work and winning notice with his short stories (collected in *Twice-told Tales*, 1837; 2d series 1842). He secured a job as measurer at the Boston customhouse, then tried (1841) life at Brook Farm. He married Sophia Peabody in 1842 and through her grew to know well Emerson, Thoreau, Margaret Fuller, and other transcendentalists. His *Mosses from an Old Manse* (1846) was written in Concord. He was a surveyor of the port at Salem (1846–49) and was made consul to Liverpool by his friend Franklin Pierce. His novels, like many of his short stories, deal with the gloomy, brooding spirit of Puritanism: *The Scarlet Letter* (1850), *The House of the Seven Gables* (1851), *The Blithedale Romance* (1852; based on the Brook Farm experience), and *The Marble Faun* (1860; laid in Italy). His *Wonder-Book* (1852) and *Tanglewood Tales* (1853; named for an estate near Lenox, Mass., where he lived) are children's classics. His notebooks have been subjected to much scholarly study. Hawthorne, with his superb creation of dark-hued atmosphere, his symbolism, and his blend of realistic detail and romantic—even melodramatic—theme, stands as a major American novelist.

Hawthorne. 1 City (pop. 16,316), S Calif., SW of Los Angeles, in oil and truck area. Mfg. of aircraft. **2** Borough (pop. 14,816), NE N.J., NNE of Paterson; settled 1850. Mfg. of chemicals, clothing, and metal goods.

Hay, John, 1838–1905, American author and diplomat. Assistant private secretary to Pres. Lincoln. Wrote *Pike County Ballads* (1871) and, with J. G. Nicolay, *Abraham Lincoln: a History* (10 vols., 1890). As U.S. Secretary of State (1898–1905), Hay was responsible for Open Door policy in China (1899) and for the HAY-PAUNCEFOTE TREATY.

Hay, river, rising in NE B.C., Canada, and flowing c.350 mi. across NW Alta. into Great Slave L.

hay, wild or cultivated plants (e.g., timothy, alfalfa, clover), dried and cured for livestock feed.

Haya de la Torre, Víctor Raúl (vĕk'tôr räōōl' ä'yä dä

lä tô'rĕ), 1895–, Peruvian leader, founder of APRA (Alianza Popular Revolucionario Americana) party, which advocates overthrow of Peruvian oligarchy.

Haydn, Franz Joseph (hī'dùn), 1732–1809, Austrian composer. Most of his music was written in the 29 years he was musical director for the Princes Esterhazy. The number of his symphonies is usually set at 104. Many bear nicknames, e.g., Toy, London, Surprise, and Clock. Outstanding also are symphonies No. 88 in G and No. 99 in E Flat. His early string quartets influenced Mozart. Haydn also wrote sonatas, songs, Masses, chamber music, and *The Seven Last Words*, originally written for orchestra, but later arranged as a choral work. His last great works were the oratorios, *The Creation* and *The Seasons*.

Haydon, Benjamin Robert, 1786–1846, English painter, whose admirers included the great literary figures of his day. His *Lazarus* in Natl. Gall., London.

Hayes, Carlton J(oseph) H(untley), 1882–, American historian and diplomat. Noted especially for studies in nationalism, *Essays on Nationalism* (1926) and *The Historical Evolution of Modern Nationalism* (1931). Ambassador to Spain (1942–45), he was influential in keeping Spain neutral in World War II.

Hayes, Helen, 1900–, American stage and film actress. One of her well-known roles was the queen in Laurence Housman's *Victoria Regina* (1935–39).

Hayes, Isaac Israel, 1832–81, American arctic explorer. Led expedition in search of open seaway to North Pole (1860–61). Wrote several books on his experiences.

Hayes, Patrick Joseph, 1867–1938, American cardinal (created 1924), archbishop of New York (1919–38). Organized the Catholic Charities of New York; sponsored social reform.

Hayes, Roland, 1887–, American Negro tenor. He is recognized in Europe and the U.S. as a great singer of both Negro spirituals and of art songs.

Hayes, Rutherford B(irchard), 1822–93, 19th President of the United States (1877–81). Served in Civil War. U.S. Representative (1865–67). Governor of Ohio (1868–72, 1876–77). In 1876 an electoral commission appointed by Congress decided disputed presidential elections in S.C., Fla., La., and Oregon in his favor and against Samuel J. TILDEN. His administration was generally conservative and efficient. Reconstruction era was ended. His conciliatory policy toward the South and his interest in civil service reform alienated important Republican party groups. An advocate of hard money, he provided for resumption of specie payments in gold.

Hayes, river of NE Man., Canada, rising NE of L. Winnipeg and flowing generally NE c.300 mi. to Hudson Bay. Chief route of Hudson's Bay Co. traders from Hudson Bay to L. Winnipeg.

hay fever, inflammation of mucous membrane of nose and eyes resulting from specific sensitivity to foreign substance, usually pollen of plants.

Hay-Herrán Treaty (hā"-ĕrän'), concerning Panama Canal, signed by U.S. Secretary of State John Hay and Foreign Minister Tomás Herrán of Colombia on Jan. 22, 1903. Provided that New Panama Canal Co. might sell its properties to U.S.; Colombia was to lease a strip of land across the Isthmus of Panama to U.S. for canal construction; U.S. was to pay Colombia $10,000,000 and, after nine years, an annuity of $250,000. U.S. Senate ratified treaty, but Colombian congress declined ratification.

Haymarket Square riot, outbreak of violence in Chicago on May 4, 1886. Demonstration for an eight-hour working day, largely staged by anarchists, caused a crowd of some 1,500 to gather at Haymarket Square. Policemen attempted to disperse the meeting; a bomb exploded and rioting ensued. Eleven persons were killed, over 100 were wounded. A trial convicted eight anarchist leaders of inciting violence; four of them were hanged. Incident was frequently used by adversaries of organized labor to discredit the waning

Knights of Labor movement and oppose organization.

Hayne, Paul Hamilton, 1830–86, Southern lyric poet of the Charleston group, called "the last literary cavalier." Wrote of the South and the Civil War. Friend of Henry Timrod.

Hayne, Robert Young, 1791–1839, American statesman. U.S. Senator from S.C. (1823–32); in famous debate of Jan., 1830, with Daniel WEBSTER, he upheld doctrines of states' rights and nullification. Governor of S.C. (1832–34).

Haynes, Elwood, 1857–1925, American automobile manufacturer and inventor, designer of one of earliest gasoline automobiles (tested 1894).

Hay-Pauncefote Treaty (hā"-pôns'foot), negotiated in 1901 by U.S. Secretary of State John Hay and Julian Pauncefote, 1st Baron Pauncefote of Preston, British ambassador to U.S. Replaced CLAYTON-BULWER TREATY. Estab. supremacy of U.S. in the Caribbean. Original treaty, signed Feb. 5, 1900, was ratified, with amendments, by U.S. Senate; Great Britain refused ratification. Revised treaty represented a compromise. It provided that U.S. might construct a transisthmian canal and have full control of it, retained nominally the principle of neutrality under sole guarantee of U.S., and provided that the canal be open to ships of all nations on equal terms. Panama Canal Act (1912), exempting from tolls U.S. ships engaged in coastwise trade, was protested by Great Britain as a treaty violation; Pres. Wilson secured repeal of act in 1914.

Hays, Arthur Garfield, 1881–, American lawyer, long director of the American Civil Liberties Union.

Hays, Will(iam) H(arrison), 1879–, president of the Motion Picture Producers and Distributors of America (1922–45). Headed voluntary censorship of moving-picture moral code (the "Hays Code").

Hays, city (pop. 8,625), W central Kansas, W of Salina; founded 1867 near Fort Hays (estab. 1865, abandoned 1889). Center of a wheat and oil area.

Hayward, city (pop. 24,292), W Calif., SE of Oakland; founded 1854. Poultry center. Fruit canning.

Haywood, William Dudley (Big Bill Heywood), 1869–1928, American labor leader. Helped found INDUSTRIAL WORKERS OF THE WORLD. Joined Socialist party, but was ejected for advocating violence. Imprisoned for sedition in World War I, he escaped (while awaiting a new trial) in 1921 to Russia.

Hazael (hă'zāĕl, hŭzā'ŭl), fl. 840 B.C., king of Damascus; murderer and successor of Benhadad **2.** In Bible, he is designated by Elijah and Elisha as God's scourge to punish Baal-worshipers. He ravaged Judah and Israel. 1 Kings 19.15; 2 Kings 8–10.

Hazard, Paul (pôl' äzär'), 1878–1944, French scholar, one of the outstanding authorities on comparative literature. He taught at the Sorbonne, Collège de France, and Columbia Univ. In 1939 he was elected to French Acad. Though made president of Univ. of Paris in 1941, he was rejected by Germans.

Hazard, city (pop. 6,985), E Ky., on North Fork of Kentucky R., in Cumberland foothills. Trading and shipping center of coal area (also oil, gas, timber). Frontier Nursing Service near by.

haze, diminished transparency of air owing to suspension in it of dust or salt particles, or water droplets. Optical haze or "shimmer" caused when unequally heated air, varying in density, refracts light unequally.

hazel, hazelnut, or **filbert,** shrub or small tree of genus *Corylus.* It is often grown for ornament but European species (*Corylus maxima*) is grown commercially for its nut crop.

Hazel Park, city (pop. 17,770), SE Mich., N residential suburb of Detroit.

Hazleton, city (pop. 35,491), E Pa., S of Wilkes-Barre; settled 1780. Coal-mining center with mfg. of textiles, clothing, and paper goods.

Hazlitt, William, 1778–1830, English essayist, literary and dramatic critic. Works include *Characters of Shakespear's Plays* (1817), *Lectures on the English*

Poets (1818), *Lectures on the English Comic Writers* (1819), *Table Talk* (1821–22), and *The Spirit of the Age* (1825). With Coleridge he led in reinterpreting Shakspere and Elizabethan drama. His perceptive essays, such as "On Going a Journey" and "My First Acquaintance with Poets," are noted for their lucid style.

H.D.: see DOOLITTLE, HILDA.

He, chemical symbol of the element HELIUM.

Head, Sir Francis Bond, 1793–1875, British administrator in Canada. Lieutenant governor (1835–37). His reactionary policy and alliance with Family Compact estranged moderate reformers and drove W. L. Mackenzie and other radical reformers to open rebellion in 1837.

head-hunting, taking the head of a slain enemy. It occurs in many parts of the world and often is associated with attempt of the taker to gain status.

health: see HYGIENE; PUBLIC HEALTH.

health insurance, plan for prepayment of medical care, effected by compulsory national insurance. Initiated (1883) by Bismarck, it was adopted in other countries after World War I. Fear of government "regimentation" of medicine has restricted its spread, particularly in the U.S., where voluntary plans were begun as early as 1850. In 1947 there were in the U.S. 24,000,000 subscribers to voluntary health plans, which, although helpful, fail to cover many people and must limit benefits to avoid prohibitive rates.

Healy, George Peter Alexander, 1813–94, American painter. Did portraits of eminent Americans and Europeans, including Guizot and Lincoln.

hearing, sense by which sound is appreciated. Vibrations are collected by outer EAR, transmitted by eardrum to bones of middle ear, and pass to spiral tube (cochlea) of inner ear where fluid-filled sacs convey them to specialized cells in organ of Corti which generate nerve impulses reaching brain.

Hearn, Lafcadio (lăfkä'dēō hûrn'), 1850–1904, multinational author of works in English, b. Ionian Isls. of Irish-Maltese parents; in U.S. 1869–90. In Japan after 1890, he became a Japanese citizen. Representative works are *Chita* (1889), a Louisiana romance; *Japan: An Attempt at an Interpretation* (1904).

Hearne, Samuel (hûrn), 1745–92, British fur trader, explorer in N Canada. His expedition to mouth of Coppermine R. opened unknown territory.

Hearst, George (hûrst), 1820–91, American mining magnate, U.S. Senator from Calif. (1886–91). His wife, Phoebe Apperson Hearst (1842–1919), became a prominent philanthropist and donated freely to Univ. of California. Their son, **William Randolph Hearst,** 1863–1951, was a journalist and publisher. After managing the San Francisco *Examiner* for his father, he bought (1895) the N.Y. *Morning Journal* and demanded (1897) war with Spain. Outdoing other "yellow" journalists, he founded a news empire including 30 big dailies (also magazines, moving-picture interests). Influential in N.Y. politics, he opposed U.S. entry in World War I, all internationalism.

Heart, river rising in SW N.Dak. and flowing E to Missouri R. at Mandan. Part of MISSOURI RIVER BASIN PROJECT.

heart, cone-shaped, muscular organ which maintains CIRCULATION OF THE BLOOD. In man and other mammals it lies in the chest and is enclosed in a sac (pericardium). The mammalian heart consists of four chambers, two auricles lying above two ventricles; right and left sides are separated by septum which in prenatal life has opening between auricles. Diseases of the heart have attracted much medical attention in the 20th cent. (see ANGINA; THROMBOSIS). See also BLOOD; PULSE. See *ill.*, p. 595.

heat, form of ENERGY into which others are convertible. It is also described as the energy of motion that the molecule possesses. Sun is the most important source of heat. Heat results from friction, chemical reactions, compression of substances, impact, passage of electric current over a high resistance. It is measured qualitatively by THERMOMETER; CALORIE and BRITISH THERMAL UNIT indicate amount of heat. Specific heat of substance is amount of heat needed to raise temperature of 1 gm. of the substance 1°C. Heat needed to change unit mass of substance from solid to liquid at melting point is latent heat of fusion; amount needed to change substance from liquid to gas at boiling point is heat of vaporization. Heat is transmitted by CONDUCTION, CONVECTION, and RADIATION. Relationship between mechanical energy and heat was first determined by Sir James P. Joule.

heath, level or rolling wasteland covered with dry-land shrubs, such as heather in Great Britain. Heath land is sometimes cultivated, as in Denmark.

heather, low evergreen shrub (*Calluna vulgaris*) of Old World, with scalelike foliage and red, rose, purple, or white nodding flowers in late summer. Also known as heather, but more properly called heath, are shrubs of closely related genus *Erica*. They have needlelike leaves and bell-shaped white, rose, or yellow flowers in winter and early spring.

heating. Methods began with open fire, progressed to fireplace with chimney, stove, and to modern hot-air, hot-water, steam-heating, and radiant-heat systems. VENTILATION must be considered when designing heating equipment. Open grate system is inefficient. Stove is more efficient but does not create natural ventilation. Heating by hot-air or hot-water system has many advantages over older methods. Use of solar energy for heating buildings is being studied.

heatstroke: see SUNSTROKE.

heaven, in Christian theology, the state of bliss in which God is seen face to face; abode of souls of the good, reunited to their glorified bodies after the RESURRECTION. Roman Church teaches that many must prepare for heaven by suffering in purgatory. Popular notion of heaven is of place full of material delights. Islamic heaven often thought to contain fleshly pleasures, but passages of Koran describing it may be allegorical. See ELYSIAN FIELDS; FORTUNATE ISLES; VALHALLA.

heaves, respiratory disease of horses causing chronic cough, wheezing, difficulty in exhaling, and indigestion. It is relieved by low-roughage diet, feeding only clean hay, and rest after feeding.

Heaviside, Oliver (hĕ'vēsīd), 1850–1925, English physicist. He contributed to development of telephony and predicted existence of conducting layer in upper atmosphere known as Kennelly-Heaviside layer and also as Heaviside layer.

heavy hydrogen: see HYDROGEN.

heavy spar: see BARITE.

heavy water: see WATER.

Hebbel, Friedrich (frē'drĭkh hĕ'bŭl), 1813–63, German dramatist. Ranking him as a leading tragic poet, his plays include *Maria Magdalena* (1844), *Herod and Mariamne* (1850), *Agnes Bernauer* (1852), and the trilogy *The Nibelungs* (1855–60).

Hebe (hē'bē), in Greek mythology, goddess of youth; daughter of Zeus and Hera. She had power to make old people young again, and is said to have rejuvenated HERCULES after his ascent to Olympus.

Heber (hē'bŭr), man's name from which Hebrews supposedly taken. Luke 3.35. Eber: Gen. 10.21.

Heber (hē'bŭr), city (pop. 2,936; alt. 5,595 ft.), N central Utah, NE of Provo. Hot-water pools of extinct geysers near by.

Hébert, Jacques René (zhäk' rünä' äbĕr'), 1757–94, French revolutionist. Edited a virulent paper, *Père Duchesne;* led CORDELIERS after Marat's death; promoted worship of Reason. Largely responsible, during Reign of Terror, for tightening maximum price laws and Law of Suspects. His power over Paris commune threatened position of Robespierre, who had him and his followers guillotined on a concocted charge of conspiracy. Hébert's fall marked triumph of propertied middle classes.

Hébert, Louis (äbĕr'), d. 1627, French pioneer, known as first Canadian farmer. Settled in Quebec in 1617.

Hébert, Louis Philippe, 1850–1917, most noted Canadian sculptor and monument designer of his time. His son, Henri Hébert, was also a sculptor.

Hebrew language, Semitic language of the Canaanite group. See LANGUAGE (table).

Hebrew literature. The earliest great work is the OLD TESTAMENT. From the 2d cent. until the 6th, the TALMUD, the great anonymous encyclopedic work, and the MIDRASH were compiled. In the 4th cent. the TARGUM to the Pentateuch and to the Prophets was finished. The 6th and 7th cent. saw the development of the MASORA in Palestine, while in Babylonia commentaries on the Talmud were written until the suppression of the academies (11th cent.). Jewish literary activity then shifted to Spain, where fine poetry and philosophy were written. In the 14th cent. the great work of CABALA, the *Zohar,* appeared. Famous scholars and authors of Hebrew literature in the Middle Ages were Solomon ben Judah IBN GABIROL, RASHI, MAIMONIDES, and Joseph ben Ephraim CARO. After the 14th cent., the Jews, driven from country to country, clung to their existing literature, especially the Old Testament. Modern Hebrew literature began with Moses MENDELSSOHN. Important names of the more recent period are the novelist Solomon Yakob Abramovich, whose pen name was MENDELE MOCHER SFORIM, and the poet Hayyim Nahman BIALIK. The rise of Zionism made Palestine the Hebrew publication center. Outside of Israel, Jews usually write in the vernacular or in YIDDISH, the literary use of which developed rapidly in the 19th cent.

Hebrew music: see JEWISH MUSIC.

Hebrews. For history, see JEWS; for religion, see JUDAISM.

Hebrews, epistle of New Testament. Tradition ascribes it to St. Paul, but few critics agree. It is treatise on the superiority of the new religion over the old and proclaims the ascendancy of Christ over the angels and Moses. It describes the new priesthood under Christ replacing that of Aaron and speaks of the sacrifice by Christ of himself as taking away sin. Hebrews is a call to faith, urging dynamic action in following Christ—even unto martyrdom. Its teachings are very important in history of theology.

Hebrews, Gospel according to the: see PSEUDEPIGRAPHA.

Hebrew University, at Jerusalem. First proposed 1882, formally opened 1925. Originally comprised institutes of chemistry, microbiology, and Jewish studies (all opened 1924). Includes school of agr. (1940), Hebrew Univ.-Hadassah Medical School (1949), and Weizmann Inst. of Science (merged 1950 with the university).

Hebrides (hĕ'brĭdēz) or **Western Islands,** group of more than 500 islands, off W and NW Scotland. Less than a fifth inhabited. Outer Hebrides, extending 130 mi., separated from mainland and from Inner Hebrides by straits of Minch and Little Minch and Sea of the Hebrides. Mild, humid climate and beautiful scenery draw tourists. Chief occupations fishing, farming, sheep grazing, quarrying, and mfg. of tweeds. Tales of Scott and William Black helped familiarize islands. There has been much emigration, particularly to Canada in 20th cent.

Hebrides, New: see NEW HEBRIDES.

Hebron (hē'–), city (1946 est. pop. 26,390), Israel, SW of Jerusalem. Modern Arabic name: El-Khalil. Bible first mentions it as site where Abraham estab. family tomb. Was David's capital before Jerusalem. Hebron figured in every Palestinian war—Maccabean, Roman, and Crusaders'. Also appears in Bible as Kirjath-arba and Mamre. Hebron is a shrine of Moslems and Jews.

Hecate (hĕ'kŭtē, hĕ'kĭt), in Greek mythology, mysterious moon-goddess. Attendant of Persephone in underworld where she had power to conjure up spirits of dead and hence was goddess of ghosts. In upper world she haunted graveyards and crossroads.

Hecht, Selig (hěkt), 1892–1947, American biophysicist, pioneer in applying physiochemical principles to sensory physiology. He determined minimal quantal requirements at threshold of vision. Wrote scientific works for laymen (e.g., *Explaining the Atom*, 1947).

Hecker, Isaac Thomas, 1819–88, American Roman Catholic priest, founder (1858) of Paulist Fathers. Associated with New England transcendentalists, was converted to Catholicism (1844) and ordained priest (1849). Worked among immigrants. Founded Paulist organ, *Catholic World.*

Hector, in the *Iliad,* leader of Trojan forces in Trojan War, greatest Trojan hero; son of Priam and Hecuba, brother of Paris, husband of Andromache, and father of Astyanax. Slain by Achilles in revenge for death of PATROCLUS.

Hecuba (hě'kyoōbù), in Greek legend, queen of Troy, wife of PRIAM. After Trojan War she was taken as slave by Odysseus. She is a prominent character in two plays by Euripides.

hedge, ornamental or protective barrier of shrubs, e.g., box, privet, barberry, or yew. Formal hedges were once pruned to resemble statuary.

hedgehog, insectivorous, nocturnal, hibernating Old World mammal with spines among its hairs. American porcupine is incorrectly called hedgehog. European hedgehog is of genus *Erinaceus;* related forms are in Africa and Asia.

Hedin, Sven (Anders) (hēdēn'), 1865–1952, Swedish explorer in central Asia. Wrote scientific and popular accounts of travels in Kunlun and Trans-Himalaya ranges, Tibet, and Sinkiang prov., China.

Hedjaz, Saudi Arabia: see HEJAZ.

hedonism, philosophy that holds pleasure to be the chief goal of man. Pleasure may be variously defined —from the mere satisfaction of sensual desires (as with the Cyrenaics) to a lofty belief in rationally ascetic control of desires (as in the school of Epicurus). All materialistic philosophies contain elements of hedonism (thus utilitarianism stresses the chief ethical and social aim of life as the greatest good for the greatest number).

Hedrick, Ulysses Prentiss, 1870–1951, American horticulturist, authority on fruit cultivation, and author of many works including *History of Horticulture in America to 1860* (1950).

Heem, Jan Davidszoon de (yän' dä'vētsōn dù häm'), 1606–c.1683, celebrated Dutch still-life painter, known for fruit and flower pieces.

Hegel, Georg Wilhelm Friedrich (gā'ôrk vĭl'hĕlm frē'drĭkh hā'gùl), 1770–1831, German philosopher, formulator of an idealistic philosophy that has had enormous influence since his day. He taught at various universities, being a professor at Jena, Heidelberg, and Berlin. His idealism, set forth in a series of books (*Phenomenology of Mind,* 1807; *Science of Logic,* 1812–16; *Encyclopedia of the Philosophical Sciences,* 1817; *Philosophy of Right,* 1821), is all-embracing and highly unified, welding together a world view with theories of ethics, aesthetics, history, politics, and religion. The system is complicated, and no brief statement does justice to it. Fundamentally he believed in an enveloping Absolute. The world soul is seen through contemplation of dialectical knowledge. In this dialectic, one concept (thesis) inevitably evokes its opposite (antithesis), and the two interact to form a new concept (synthesis), which in turn becomes a new thesis. Thus the idea of being evokes the idea of not being, and the two necessarily produce the synthesis, becoming. The universe is thus in a state of perpetual self-creation. The absolute is the active principle in this process. History also shows the progress from lower to higher manifestations of the principle. Thus cultures conflict, and the higher is triumphant. In art also different periods succeed each other. In religion Christianity was considered as succeeding to nature religions, and Christ is the union of God and man, of spirit and matter. Various later philoso-

phers developed differing aspects of this system. Hegelian dialectic appealed strongly to the Socialists and was developed into Marxian dialectical materialism.

hegira or **hejira** (hējī'rù, hě'jīrù), flight of the prophet MOHAMMED from Mecca, June, 622, to Yathrib (Medina). Since the foundation of Islam was laid in Medina, Mohammedan era dates from the hegira. Abbreviation A.H. is used in West with year number to mean After the Hegira.

Heiberg, Johan Ludvig (hī'bâr), 1791–1860, Danish poet, dramatist, critic, and director of the Natl. Theater. His play, *The Hill of the Elves* (1828), very popular.

Heidegger, Martin (hī'dĕgùr), 1889–, German philosopher. Professor at Marburg (1923–28) and Berlin (1928–33), he became rector at Berlin in 1933. He considered and adapted ideas put forward by Kierkegaard and Husserl and created a system of thought which has been labeled atheistic existentialism. Viewing man as oppressed by anguish and forlornness in his brief existence in the finite world, Heidegger rejected the conventional religious answers to man's problem and argued that by questioning man may learn the nature of existence and, accepting it, may assert his essence and destiny by "resolute decision." One of his best-known works is *Sein und Zeit* (1927). Jean Paul Sartre became his disciple.

Heidelberg (hī'dùlbĕrk), city (pop. 115,750), Württemberg-Baden, W Germany, on Neckar R., beautifully situated in a region of orchards and vineyards. It is best known for its university, founded 1386. The cap. of the Rhenish PALATINATE until 1720, it was devastated by the imperials in 1622, by the French in 1689 and 1693. There was only minor damage in World War II. The famous castle dates from the 15th–17th cent. The **Heidelberg Catechism,** a profession of faith of German Reformed (Calvinistic) Church was drawn up at the request of Elector Frederick III and was published 1563.

Heidelberg College: see TIFFIN, Ohio.

Heidenstam, Verner von (hā'dùnstäm), 1859–1940, Swedish lyric poet, novelist, and essayist. Opposed naturalism and in his novels evoked a patriotic sense of the continuing unity of Sweden's history. Awarded 1916 Nobel Prize in Literature.

Heifetz, Jascha (yä'shù hī'fĭts), 1901–, Russian-American violinist, known for his virtuosity. Studied at St. Petersburg Conservatory with Leopold Auer. Came to the U.S. 1917.

Heilbronn (hīlbrôn'), city (pop. 64,544), Württemberg-Baden, W Germany, in Württemberg, on Neckar R. Mfg. of machinery, tools. Free imperial city 1281–1803. In World War II old city was largely destroyed. Götz von Berlichingen was imprisoned (1522) in the Götzenturm, a tower built in 1392.

Heilungkiang: see MANCHURIA.

Heine, Heinrich (hīn'rĭkh hī'nù), 1797–1856, German author, of Jewish parentage. His *Buch der Lieder* [book of songs] (1827) placed him among the greatest German poets. Lyrics have musical, folklike quality (as in "Lorelei"), often spiced with subtle irony or dissonant endings, have attracted many composers, notably Schubert, Schumann, Mendelssohn, Brahms. His prose travel sketches, beginning with *Die Harzreise* (1826), show the same mixture of lyric emotion and corrosive wit. In 1831, drawn by his revolutionary sympathies, he left Germany for Paris, where he died after eight years of tragic sickness, confined to his "mattress grave." There he wrote the verse satires *Atta Troll* and *Deutschland; Neue Gedichte* (1847) and *Letzte Gedichte* (1853), in which his verse takes on an increasingly bitter and tragic tone; prose essays on German literature and philosophy (in French); and political reports for a German newspaper. Nearly all his work has been translated into English, although his verse often defies translation.

Heisenberg, Werner (vĕr'nùr hī'zùnbĕrk), 1901–, German physicist. Won 1932 Nobel Prize for theory of quantum mechanics and discovery of allotropic forms of hydrogen.

Heiser, Victor George (hī'zŭr), 1873–, American physician, authority on public health, associated with Rockefeller Foundation (1915–34). His works include *An American Doctor's Odyssey* (1936); *Toughen Up, America* (1941).

Hejaz or **Hedjaz** (both: hĕjäz') region, NW Saudi Arabia, on Gulf of Aqaba and Red Sea. Mainly a mountain range and plateau, lying between coastal strip and interior desert. Holy cities of Mecca and Medina are here. Husein ibn Ali overthrew Turkish rule in 1916, but was ousted 1924 by Ibn Saud.

hejira: see HEGIRA.

Hekla (hĕk'lä), volcano, 4,746 ft. high, SW Iceland. Since 1004 many eruptions have been recorded.

Held, Anna, 1873?–1918, American musical comedy actress, b. Paris. Famed for her beauty and for her tempestuous private life.

Helen, in Greek legend, daughter of Leda and Zeus. From many suitors she chose MENELAUS. When PARIS awarded APPLE OF DISCORD to Aphrodite, she, in return, gave him the fairest of women, Helen, whom he carried off to Troy, thus causing TROJAN WAR. After the war Helen returned with Menelaus to Sparta. She bore him only one child, Hermione.

Helena, Saint (hĕ'lŭnŭ), c.248–328?, mother of Constantine the Great. Converted to Christianity in 313, she is said to have gone to Jerusalem, where she found the True Cross and the Holy Sepulcher.

Helena (hĕ'lŭnŭ). **1** City (pop. 11,236), E Ark., on Mississippi R. and SW of Memphis, Tenn. A rail center and river port, it ships cotton, lumber, and farm products. Canning, woodworking, and mfg. of cottonseed oil and hosiery. **2** City (pop. 17,581), state cap., W central Mont., NNE of Butte near Missouri R.; founded in Last Chance Gulch after 1864 gold discovery. Became territorial cap. 1874, replacing Virginia City. Also had silver strikes. Center of mining, ranching, and agr. (Prickly Pear valley) area. Seat of Carroll Col. (R.C.; for men; 1910) and Fort Harrison army post (now a VA hospital).

Helgoland (hĕl'gōlänt) or **Heligoland,** island, area less than 150 acres, Germany, in North Sea off the Elbe estuary. Consisting of red sandstone, it rises c.160 ft. above sea and is covered by grazing land. Once a Danish possession, it was ceded to England 1814; traded to Germany for Zanzibar 1890. It served as German naval base in World War II; fortifications were blown up by British 1947.

Helicon (hĕ'lĭkŏn), Gr. *Elikon,* mountain group, Boeotia, Greece. In Greek legend, abode of the MUSES.

helicopter (hĕ'lĭkŏptŭr), rotor aircraft obtaining lift and propulsion from engine-driven rotors. It differs from the autogiro, the rotor of which is moved by aerodynamic forces resulting from propulsion in the conventional manner by engine-driven propeller. Helicopter is valuable for air-sea rescue and aeromagnetic surveying; it can maneuver and hover at nearly zero ground speed. See *ill.,* p. 19.

Heligoland, German island: see HELGOLAND.

Heliodorus (hē″lēŏdō'rŭs), fl. 175 B.C., Syrian political leader. Murdered Seleucus IV in vain hope of getting the throne. In 2 Mac. 3 he is said to have been prevented by three angels from taking the treasure from the Temple at Jerusalem.

Heliogabalus (hē″lēŏgă'bŭlŭs), c.205–222, Roman emperor (218–22). He was Varius Avitus Bassianus, a priest of the sun-god of Emesa, cousin and, according to his mother, son of CARACALLA. The troops in Syria chose him as emperor on the defeat of Macrinus, the legitimate heir. He had a reign notorious for the indecency of the rites of his sun-god and of his own life. He and his mother were killed in an uprising of Praetorian guards. His cousin, Alexander Severus, succeeded. Also Elagabalus.

heliograph (hē'lēŭgrăf), signaling device consisting of a mirror reflecting sunlight and shuttered to permit interruption of light beam for long and short signal flashes. Heliostat similarly reflects light beam on distant spot. Spectroheliograph, combining heliostat and spectroscope, is used by scientists to photograph sun.

Hélion, Jean (ālyō'), 1904–, French abstractionist painter. Settled in U.S. in 1932.

Heliopolis (hēlēŏ'pŭlĭs) [Gr.,= city of the sun], anc. city, N Egypt, near Cairo, center of the worship of Ra (or Re), who was long the state deity. It was under the New Empire (c.1580–c.1090 B.C.) seat of the viceroy of N Egypt. Obelisks called Cleopatra's Needles were erected here. Its school of philosophy was said to have been visited by Plato. Egyptian name was On.

Heliopolis, anc. Syrian city: see BAALBEK.

Helios (hē'lēŏs) [Gr.,= sun], in Greek religion, sungod; son of Hyperion and Theia, husband of nymph Clymene, and father of PHAËTHON. Each day he drove a golden chariot from his palace in the E to his palace in the W. In Rhodes he was national god, and Colossus represented him. He symbolized material aspects of the sun, Apollo its spiritual aspects. In the *Odyssey* Helios shipwrecked Odysseus for eating his sacred cattle. He was called Sol by Romans.

heliotrope (hē'–), tender perennial plant (*Heliotropium arborescens*) with fragrant purple flower clusters. Commonly called garden heliotrope is a valerian (*Valeriana officinalis*).

helium (hē'lēŭm), colorless, odorless, tasteless, inert gaseous element (symbol = He; see also ELEMENT, table). Because of its lightness (only hydrogen is lighter) and noninflammability it is used in balloons and airships. Used in pressure chambers for divers and caisson workers because of low solubility in human blood. U.S. controls production. Alpha rays from radium are helium nuclei. See *ill.,* p. 773.

hell, in Christian theology, eternal abode of those damned by God's judgment and forever denied sight of Him. It is ruled by Satan (Lucifer, the devil). Tradition and legend have made of it a place of fire and brimstone, with the damned souls undergoing physical torment. The vivid description of hell (Inferno) by Dante is known over the Western world. The Islamic idea of hell is similar to the Christian. The Sheol or Tophet of the ancient Jews was a gloomy place where the souls of the dead wander about unhappy; the name Gehenna (from Hinnom) is used in the New Testament. The Greeks believed that the souls of the dead (good and evil) went to an underworld, Hades, ruled by the god Hades (also called Pluto) and his wife Persephone. Its entrance was guarded by Cerberus, and Hades was surrounded by the river Styx, across which Charon ferried the dead. Tartarus below Hades was a place of torment for the very wicked. The Romans also called the underworld Hades and Orcus, Dis (also a name for Pluto) and Avernus. The Hel of the Icelandic *Edda* is probably a borrowing from Christianity.

Hellas, name for GREECE.

hellebore (hĕl'ŭ–), name for winter- or spring-blooming Eurasian perennial plants of genus *Helleborus*. The Christmas rose (*Helleborus niger*) has evergreen leaves and its flowers (usually white) resemble wild roses and often bloom in winter. Roots of North American false hellebores (*Veratrum*) yield veratrine used in insecticides.

Hellen, in Greek mythology, ancestor of Hellenes or Greeks.

Hellenism, culture, ideals, and pattern of life of Greece, as represented in Athens at the time of Pericles; frequently contrasted with Hebraic seriousness in the Old Testament. Hellenism gave way to Hellenistic civilization in 4th cent. B.C., but any modern attempt to revive Greek ideals is called Hellenism.

Hellenistic civilization, widespread, Greek-tinctured culture that grew out of the efforts of ALEXANDER THE GREAT to spread Hellenism with his conquests across the known world. After his death (323 B.C.) the

DIADOCHI estab. dynasties that helped to give that world political disunity but at the same time Greek unity of trade and learning. A new culture in art, letters, and science developed. Alexandria and Pergamum were notable centers. Physical comfort increased for the well-to-do, education was general among the wealthy. Literature grew to vast proportions and learning (as distinct from knowledge and philosophy) came into being. Though accused of being derivative and ponderous, literature had great richness. Libraries were built, anthologies compiled. Sculpture developed, and some of the most familiar statues of the present day (e.g., the Venus of Milo, the Dying Gaul) are Hellenistic. Philosophy became the field of all the educated. The triumph of Rome meant the Roman absorption of Hellenistic culture, not its extinction.

Hellertown, borough (pop. 5,435), SE Pa., near Delaware R. and S of Bethlehem. Mfg. of electrical products and commercial gases.

Hellespont: see DARDANELLES.

Hell Gate, N.Y.: see EAST RIVER.

Helmand (hĕl′mŭnd), river, c.700 mi. long, rising in central Afghanistan. Flows to Hamun-i-Helmand on Iranian border. Vital irrigation works.

Helmholtz, Hermann Ludwig Ferdinand von (hĕr′män lōōt′vĭkh fĕr′dĕnänt fŭn hĕlm′hôlts), 1821–94, German scientist. He extended the application of law of conservation of energy and formulated it mathematically; contributed to thermo- and electrodynamics. He extended Young's theory of color vision; explained lens accommodation in eye; invented ophthalmoscope. He was an authority on acoustics.

Helmont, Jan Baptista van (yän bäptī′stä vän hĕl′mônt), 1577–1644, Flemish scientist. He discovered carbon dioxide, distinguished gases from solids and liquids, and is credited with introducing the term *gas* in present scientific sense.

Heloise: see ABELARD, PETER.

Helper, Hinton Rowan, 1829–1909, American author. A Southerner, he wrote *The Impending Crisis of the South* (1857), an attack on slavery as an economic evil that delighted Republicans. Later wrote anti-Negro books.

Helsingborg: see HALSINGBORG.

Helsingfors, Finland: see HELSINKI.

Helsingor, Denmark: see ELSINORE.

Helsinki (hĕl′sĭngkē), Swed. *Helsingfors,* city (pop. 375,981), cap. of Finland; a Baltic seaport on Gulf of Finland. Intellectual, commercial, administrative center of Finland. Mfg. of paper, tobacco, sugar, liquor, textiles, machinery. Called White City of the North for its cleanliness and buildings of native granite. Founded 1550, it grew rapidly after cap. was moved here from Turku (1812). Outstanding sites include university (moved here from Turku 1828), railway station (designed by Saarinen), national archives, opera house, Church of St. Nicholas. Slightly damaged in World War II. Olympic games were held here 1952.

Helst, Bartholomeus van der (hĕlst′), c.1613–1670, Dutch portrait painter. *Banquet of the Civic Guard* (Rijks Mus.) is considered his masterpiece.

Helvellyn (hĕlvĕl′ĭn), mountain, 3,118 ft. high, Cumberland and Westmorland, England.

Helvetia (hĕlvē′shù). **1** Latin name of Switzerland; short for *Confoederatio Helvetica.* **2** Roman administrative district of Upper Germany, 1st cent. B.C.–5th cent. A.D. It occupied W part of modern Switzerland. The Helvetii, a predominantly Celtic people, tried to conquer S Gaul in 58 B.C., were defeated by Julius Caesar at Bibracte.

Helvetic Republic, 1798–1803: see SWITZERLAND.

Helvétius, Claude Adrien (hĕlvē′shùs; Fr. ĕlväsyüs′), 1715–71, French philosopher, one of the Encyclopedists. After serving as farmer-general and as chamberlain to the queen he retired in 1751. His philosophy as set forth in *Essays on the Mind* (1758) held that all men are born with equal ability and that educa-

tional influences create distinctions. He argued that all intellectual activity arises from sensation, even the soul being at first a capacity for sensation. He regarded self-interest as the sole motive for action and influenced the utilitarians. In France he was condemned by the Sorbonne.

Hemans, Felicia (Dorothea Browne), 1793–1835, English poet, noted for sentimental poems, such as "Casabianca" and "The Landing of the Pilgrims."

hematite (hĕ′mŭtīt), a mineral, an oxide of iron, important as an ore. It occurs in red earthy masses and gray to black crystals.

Hemingway, Ernest, 1898–, American writer, notable for terse, direct style and realistic tone. Among his novels are *The Sun Also Rises* (1926), *A Farewell to Arms* (1929), *For Whom the Bell Tolls* (1940). Favorite theme, also expressed in vigorous short stories (as in *Men without Women,* 1927) is struggle of man mutilated by environment. Nonfictional *Death in the Afternoon* (1932) concerns bullfighting.

Hemling, Hans: see MEMLING, HANS.

hemlock, name for several plants, especially coniferous evergreen trees of genus *Tsuga,* native to North America and Asia. They are popular ornamentals with small cones and flattened leaves on horizontal branches. The poison hemlock (*Conium maculatum*) by which Socrates died, a perennial meadow plant with flattened clusters of white flowers, is naturalized in North America. Similar to it is the North American water hemlock (*Cicuta maculata*), sometimes grown in bog gardens.

hemoglobin: see CORPUSCLES.

Hémon, Louis (lwē′ āmō′), 1880–1913, French Canadian novelist, b. France. Wrote *Maria Chapdelaine* (1913), story of pioneer life in Quebec.

hemophilia (hē″mŭfĭ′lĕù, hĕ″–), rare disease marked by delayed CLOTTING OF BLOOD. Death sometimes results from bleeding after even minor injuries. Inherited by males only, it is transmitted as a sex-linked character only through females.

hemorrhage (hĕ′mŭrĭj), escape of blood from heart or blood vessels. Bleeding from arteries is red and of rhythmic flow; from veins, it is dark and of constant flow. See also HEMOPHILIA.

hemorrhoids (hĕ′mŭroidz) or **piles,** dilated veins at anus. They often result from constipation, poor circulation, and pressure on rectum.

hemp, tall annual plant (*Cannabis sativa*), native to Asia but cultivated elsewhere for its bast fiber, also called hemp, and as a source of the narcotic drug marijuana. It has large, digitately divided narrow leaves and inconspicuous male and female flower spikes on separate plants. Cordage, paper, canvas, etc., are made from the bast fiber. Dried plant parts, especially female flowers, are the source of marijuana and hashish; the U.S. government restricts its cultivation.

Hempstead. 1 Residential village (pop. 29,135), SE N.Y., on W Long Isl. and E of Jamaica; settled 1644. Hofstra Col. (coed.; 1935) is here. **2** Town (pop. 1,395), S Texas, NW of Houston. Near-by "Liendo" was plantation home of Elizabeth Ney.

Hems, Syria: see HOMS.

henbane, weedy annual Old World plant of nightshade family. Black henbane (*Hyoscyamus niger*) is naturalized in E North America. It has yellow flowers and is poisonous, especially to poultry.

Hench, Philip Showalter, 1896–, American physician. An authority on rheumatic diseases, he has long been associated with Mayo Clinic and Mayo Foundation (of Univ. of Minnesota). He shared 1950 Nobel Prize in Physiology and Medicine for work on hormones of the cortex of adrenal glands.

Henderson, Alexander, 1583–1646, Scottish churchman. Opposed English domination of Church of Scotland. As moderator of general assembly he conferred with Charles I on Presbyterian aims of Covenanters.

Henderson, Leon, 1895–, American economist, head of Office of Price Administration (1941–42).

Henderson, Richard, 1735–85, American colonizer in Ky. Chief promoter of TRANSYLVANIA COMPANY. Important figure in early frontier expansion.

Henderson. 1 City (pop. 16,837), W Ky., on Ohio R. and S of Evansville, Ind.; founded 1797. Mfg. and shipping of tobacco, wood, food, and cotton products. J. J. Audubon lived here (1810–19); Audubon Memorial Park near by. **2** City (pop. 10,996), N N.C., NNE of Raleigh; settled 1814. Tobacco market with cotton and flour mills. **3** City (pop. 6,833), E Texas, WSW of Shreveport, La. First gusher of rich East Texas oil field struck near by, 1930. Shawnee Indian village site near.

Hendersonville, city (pop. 6,103), W N.C., in Blue Ridge SSE of Asheville. Resort with farm trade and textile mills.

Hendon, urban district (pop. 155,835), Middlesex, England. Has RAF airfield, scene of June Display.

Hendrix College: see CONWAY, Ark.

Hengist and Horsa (hĕng′gĭst, hôr′sù), traditional names of two leaders of 5th-cent. Germanic invasion of Britain. Supposedly invited to help Britons against Picts and Scots, they settled in Kent.

Henie, Sonja (sō′nyù hĕ′nē), 1913–, Norwegian-American skater. Won Olympic figure-skating championship (1928, 1932, 1936).

Henle, Jacob (yä′kôp hĕn′lù), 1809–85, German anatomist and pathologist, noted for work on microscopic structure of tissues.

Henley, William Ernest, 1849–1903, English lyric poet, critic, and editor. Best known of his poems "England, My England" and "Invictus." He wrote plays with Stevenson and edited literary reviews.

Henley-on-Thames (-tĕmz), municipal borough (pop. 7,970), Oxfordshire, England, at base of the Chilterns, on the Thames. Scene of annual Henley rowing regatta (begun 1839) in which several English and some American crews take part.

Henlopen, Cape (hĕnlō′pùn), SE Del., at mouth of Delaware Bay opposite Cape May, N.J. Lightship.

henna, Old World tropical shrub (*Lawsonia inermis*) with small fragrant flowers. From its dried leaves henna dye is made.

Hennepin, Louis, 1640–1701?, Franciscan Recollect friar, explorer in North America. With Michel Aco he explored the upper Mississippi valley.

Henri, Robert (hĕn′rī), 1865–1929, American painter and teacher, b. Cincinnati. His teachings helped to destroy tradition of academicism and to inspire development of living art for America. One of The EIGHT, he sponsored first exhibit in America without a jury. Excelled in dramatic portraits.

Henrietta Maria, 1609–66, queen consort of Charles I of England, daughter of Henry IV of France. Her dealings with the pope, foreign powers, and army officers increased suspicion of Charles and fear of a Catholic uprising which partly led to civil war.

Henrietta of England (Henrietta Anne), 1644–70, duchess of Orléans, called Madame; sister of Charles II of England and wife of Philippe I d'ORLÉANS. Negotiated Treaty of Dover with Charles II in behalf of Louis XIV. An unfounded rumor ascribed her sudden death to poison.

Henry, emperors and German kings. **Henry I** or **Henry the Fowler,** 876?–936, duke of Saxony, was elected king 919 to succeed Conrad I. He won Lotharingia from allegiance to France (925), defeated the Magyars (933), built many walled towns in E border regions. His queen, St. Matilda (d. 968) founded many monasteries. His son Otto I succeeded him. **Henry II,** 973–1024, duke of Bavaria, was elected German king 1002; crowned king of the Lombards 1004; crowned emperor at Rome 1014. He and his empress, Kunigunde, were canonized saints of the Roman Church. **Henry III,** 1017–56, was crowned joint king with his father Conrad II in 1028; became sole king 1039; was crowned emperor 1046. Under him the medieval empire reached its greatest power. He supported the re-

forms of the CLUNIAC ORDER. In 1046 he deposed three rival claimants to the papacy at the Synod of Sutri and caused the election of a reform-minded German (Clement II). Popes Leo IX and Victor II were also his candidates (1048, 1055). His son, **Henry IV,** 1050–1106, succeeded him as king (1056). During his minority archbishops Anno of Cologne and ADALBERT of Bremen held the power. Beginning his personal rule in 1065, Henry restored his authority in the duchies, notably Saxony. His appointments of bishops in 1075 met the condemnation of Pope GREGORY VII (see INVESTITURE), whom Henry declared deposed (1076). Gregory in turn declared Henry excommunicated and deposed, and Henry, threatened with revolt, made his humiliating journey to CANOSSA, where the pope gave him absolution (Jan., 1077). Nevertheless, the German nobles elected Rudolf of Swabia antiking. Civil war resulted, and in 1080 Gregory renewed his excommunication of Henry. But Henry was now supported by a large party. Invading Italy (1081), he drove Gregory from Rome in 1084 and was crowned emperor by GUIBERT OF RAVENNA. He was forced to abdicate in 1105 by his rebellious son, **Henry V,** 1081–1125, who had the support of Pope Paschal II. The new king soon fell out with the pope over the question of lay investiture. In 1111, at Rome, he took the pope and cardinals prisoners. To obtain his release, Paschal conceded to Henry the right to invest at will and crowned him emperor. The struggle was continued with popes Gelasius II and Calixtus II until a final compromise was reached in 1122 (see WORMS, CONCORDAT OF). Henry's widow, Matilda, married Geoffrey Plantagenet. **Henry VI,** 1165–97, succeeded his father Frederick I as German king (1190) and was crowned emperor in 1191. As husband of CONSTANCE, heiress of Sicily, he took possession of that kingdom in 1194, after the death of TANCRED of Lecce. In the same year good fortune delivered RICHARD I of England into his power, whom he forced to swear fealty as vassal. He died on his way to lead a crusade to Holy Land. His son, who later became Emperor Frederick II, succeeded him in Sicily; his brother Philip of Swabia, succeeded him as German king. **Henry VII,** c.1275–1313, count of Luxemburg, was elected German king to succeed Albert I (1308). He vainly sought to restore imperial authority in Italy by ending the strife between Guelphs and Ghibellines. Crowned king of the Lombards (1311) and emperor (1312), he died in the middle of a campaign in S Italy. He was the father of John of Luxemburg.

Henry, kings of England. **Henry I,** 1068–1135, king 1100–1135, was the youngest son of William I. On death of his brother William II, he obtained crown by a coup d'état which excluded his brother Robert II, duke of Normandy, who was on crusade. Robert invaded England (1101) but was bought off by Henry. Henry invaded Normandy (1105) and imprisoned his brother for life. Was involved in a struggle with ANSELM over investiture. His attempts to secure succession for his daughter MATILDA later led to long civil war between STEPHEN and Matilda. **Henry II,** 1133–89, king 1154–89, was son of Matilda and Geoffrey IV. Duke of Normandy, he married ELEANOR OF AQUITAINE, thus gaining vast territories in France. Invaded England and forced Stephen to acknowledge him as heir. He restored order to war-ravaged England, subdued barons, centralized power of government in royal authority, and strengthened royal courts. His long controversy with THOMAS À BECKET concerned sole jurisdiction of ecclesiastical courts over clergymen accused of crimes. Henry adopted Constitutions of Clarendon (1164) which brought such men into lay courts; Becket protested and fled to France. Soon after his return and continued insistence on ecclesiastical prerogative, Thomas was murdered by four knights in Canterbury Cathedral. Henry was forced by public indignation to do penance. During his reign he gained N counties of England from Scotland and subdued N Wales. He was also involved in family struggles—revolt of his son Henry, and intrigues of sons Geoffrey, RICHARD I, and JOHN. Richard, with Philip II of France, defeated the aged king, who died. He was the founder of ANGEVIN or Plantagenet line. **Henry III,** 1207–72, king 1216–72, was the son of John. Became king under a regency; was granted full powers in 1227. Against advice of HUBERT DE BURGH, chief justiciar and greatest power in government, he led unsuccessful expedition to Gascony and Brittany. Dismissed De Burgh in 1232 and began a reign of extravagance, absolutism, and general incapacity. Spent vast sums on futile wars in Gascony. Henry's absolutism, and his attempt to put his son Edmund, earl of Lancaster, on Sicilian throne eventually led to outbreak of BARONS' WAR (1263). Simon de MONTFORT, leader of barons, won at Lewes and summoned (1265) his famous representative Parliament. Edward (later Edward I) led royal troops to victory at Evesham where Montfort was killed. From 1267 Edward was actually ruler and Henry king in name only. **Henry IV,** 1367–1413, king 1399–1413, was son of JOHN OF GAUNT. Opposed RICHARD II in 1387 and was one of lords appellant who ruled England for a year. After accusing duke of Norfolk of treason against Richard he was banished for six years. In the absence of Richard (whose rule was unpopular) he landed in England in 1399 and claimed throne, thus founding Lancastrian dynasty. Put down rebellions by Richard's followers, by the Scots and the Welsh, and by the Percies. Maintained prerogatives of the crown against Parliament, but he left crown enormously in debt. His son, **Henry V,** 1387–1422, king 1413–22, presided over privy council during his father's illness. As prince (Shakspere's Prince Hal) he had led armies against Welsh Owen Glendower and been active in royal victory over the Percies. Rebellion by the Lollards continued after his accession until 1417. Determined to regain lands which he sincerely but mistakenly believed to be his, he invaded France in 1415, thus reopening HUNDRED YEARS WAR. Announced his claim to French throne and defeated the French at Agincourt. Henry conquered Normandy (1417–19) and in 1420 married CATHERINE OF VALOIS. Fell ill and died in 1422. Despite early recklessness he ruled with justice and industry and restored civil order and nationalism. His charm, military genius, and care for less fortunate subjects made him a popular hero even though his wars left the crown heavily in debt. His son, **Henry VI,** 1421–71, king 1422–61 and 1470–71, became king when less than a year old. During his early years England was under protectorate of his uncles, John of Lancaster and Humphrey, duke of Gloucester. The English, after their defeat by Joan of Arc, attempted to protect their French interests by crowning Henry king of France at Paris (1431) but their cause became hopeless. Rebellion of Jack Cade was one of many riots showing dissatisfaction with government. Struggle between factions headed by Queen, MARGARET OF ANJOU, and Edmund Beaufort, duke of SOMERSET, and by Richard, duke of YORK, developed into dynastic battle between Lancasters and Yorkists called Wars of the ROSES. In battle of St. Albans (1455) Somerset was killed and Henry captured. York, who had been made protector and named successor to Henry (whose mind had given way), was killed in 1460 but his son Edward defeated Lancastrians and was proclaimed king as EDWARD IV in 1461. He later fled to Holland and Henry was restored briefly. Edward retook crown and Henry died in the Tower in 1471. **Henry VII,** 1457–1509, king 1485–1509, became head of house of Lancaster at Henry VI's death. Invaded England from Brittany (1485) and at battle of Bosworth Field defeated forces of RICHARD III. Married Elizabeth, daughter of Edward IV, uniting houses of York and Lancaster and founding Tudor dynasty. Sent Edward POYNINGS to Ireland in 1494 to consolidate British rule there. Peace treaty (1499) between Scotland and

England was followed by marriage of Henry's daughter, Margaret, to James IV of Scotland. Henry estab. Tudor tradition of autocratic rule tempered by justice and brought order out of chaos. Estab. (1487) court of Star Chamber. His reign saw end of Wars of the Roses and is generally considered beginning of modern English history. His son, **Henry VIII,** 1491–1547, king 1509–47, married his brother's widow, KATHARINE OF ARAGON, who bore him a daughter, Mary. His chief minister, Thomas WOLSEY, concluded an alliance with France but Henry (despite FIELD OF THE CLOTH OF GOLD) joined (1522) Emperor Charles V in war against France. England prospered internally under Wolsey (who had almost complete control). Court was a center of learning and the pope gave Henry title of "Defender of the Faith" for treatise against Luther. Henry now wished to marry Anne BOLEYN but Pope Clement VII resisted his demands for a divorce from Katharine. Wolsey's failure in the affair caused his downfall and Thomas Cromwell became chief minister. An antiecclesiastical policy was begun and subservient Thomas Cranmer became archbishop of Canterbury. Henry married Anne (1533) and was excommunicated. Papal powers were now transferred to king who became supreme head of English church. Break with Rome was complete and Church of ENGLAND was estab. Anne had one daughter, Elizabeth. The marriage ended when Anne was convicted of adultery and beheaded. Ten days later Henry married Jane Seymour who died in 1537 giving birth to Edward VI. Dealt harshly with such rebellions as the Pilgrimage of Grace. Licensed (1537) publication of Bible in English. His marriage (1540) to ANNE OF CLEVES (whom he disliked and divorced) led to execution of Cromwell. He then married Catherine HOWARD who suffered (1542) Anne Boleyn's fate. In 1543 Catherine Parr became his sixth queen. War with Scotland began again (1542) and Henry made unsuccessful attempts to unite the two kingdoms. Wales was officially incorporated into England (1536) but conquest of Ireland proved too expensive. End of his reign saw gradual move toward Protestantism. He remained immensely popular despite his advancement of personal desires under guise of public policy or moral right. His political insight, however, steadily grew better; he gave England a comparatively peaceful reign.

Henry, kings of France. **Henry I,** c.1008–1060, reigned 1031–60. He was a powerless tool of the great feudal lords. **Henry II,** 1519–59, son of Francis I, reigned 1547–59. Was dominated by Anne de Montmorency, by his mistress Diane de Poitiers, and by François and Charles de Guise. He continued his father's struggle against Emperor Charles V; recovered Calais from England (1558). Treaty of CATEAU-CAMBRÉSIS ended French pretensions to Italy (1559). He was accidentally killed in a tournament. His queen was Catherine de' Medici. His third son, **Henry III,** 1551–89, was elected king of Poland in 1573 but returned to France in 1574 to succeed his brother Charles IX. His reign was almost continually disturbed by the Wars of RELIGION. The death in 1584 of his brother Francis made him the last male member of the house of Valois. His recognition of Henry of Navarre (later Henry IV) as heir presumptive was opposed by Henri, 3d duc de GUISE, head of the Catholic LEAGUE (the "War of the Three Henrys" resulted). Having procured the murder of Guise (1588), the king was faced with a revolt of the League and was expelled from Paris. Henry of Navarre came to his aid, but Henry III was assassinated in the siege by Jacques Clément, a fanatic monk. Henry III was notorious for his vices. **Henry IV** (Henry of Navarre), 1553–1610, first BOURBON king of France, was the son of Antoine de Bourbon and JEANNE D'ALBRET. On her death he succeeded to the kingdom of Navarre (1572). He took leadership of the Huguenot (Protestant) party in 1569. His marriage in 1572 with MARGARET OF VALOIS was the occasion for the massacre of SAINT BARTHOLOMEW'S DAY. Henry saved his life by abjuring Protestantism, but in 1576 he escaped from his virtual imprisonment at court and returned to Protestantism. When in 1584 HENRY III named him heir presumptive, the Catholic LEAGUE, headed by Henri, 3d duc de GUISE, refused to recognize him as heir and persuaded Henry III to send an army to force his conversion. In the resulting "War of the Three Henrys," Henry of Navarre defeated Henry III at Coutras (1587) but came to the king's support in the troubles of 1588, and after Henry III's death (1589) defeated the League forces at Arques (1589) and Ivry (1590); he was unable to enter Paris until 1594, after he had abjured Protestantism—allegedly with the remark, "Paris is worth a Mass." His war with Spain, the ally of the League, ended in 1598 with the Treaty of VERVINS. In 1598 also he established religious toleration through the Edict of NANTES. With his minister SULLY he spent the rest of his reign restoring order, industry, and trade. His slogan, "A chicken in every peasant's pot every Sunday," has remained famous. In 1600 he married Marie de' Medici, having had his earlier marriage annulled. He was stabbed to death by RAVAILLAC. His gallantry and wit, his concern for the common people, and his exploits with the ladies have become legendary. **Henry V:** see CHAMBORD, HENRI, COMTE DE.

Henry II or **Henry of Trastamara** (trăstümä′rù), 1333? –1379, Spanish king of Castile and Leon (1369–79); natural son of Alfonso XI. In his struggle against his half-brother PETER THE CRUEL he was aided by Du Guesclin, Peter by Henry the Black Prince. Though defeated at Najéra (1367), he routed and killed Peter in 1369. His son JOHN I succeeded him.

Henry, Joseph, 1797–1878, American physicist, first secretary and director of Smithsonian Institution (estab. 1846). He improved the electromagnet, discovered self-inductance, and independently of Michael Faraday he discovered principle of the induced current (basic to dynamo, transformer, and many other devices).

Henry, O., pseud. of **William Sydney Porter,** 1862– 1910, American short-story writer, notable for unexpected twist at end of stories. Charged with fraud in an Austin, Texas, bank, he fled to Central America, later returned to imprisonment, then lived as a writer in New York. Many stories (as in *The Four Million,* 1906) picture great-city life.

Henry, Patrick, 1736–99, American patriot and orator. Spurred colonial revolt in the South by oratory; he was responsible for the phrase, "Give me liberty or give me death." Later fought to add Bill of Rights to the Constitution.

Henry, William: see HENRY'S LAW.

Henry, Cape, SE Va., at entrance to Chesapeake Bay E of Norfolk. Jamestown settlers landed here April 26, 1607. Site included in Colonial Natl. Historical Park 1939.

Henry, Fort, fortification, SE Ont., Canada, on St. Lawrence R. overlooking Kingston harbor. Built 1812, demolished 1832, rebuilt 1832–36. Prisoners' camp in both World Wars.

Henry Clay, suburb (pop. 6,104) of Lexington, Ky.

Henry E. Huntington Library and Art Gallery: see HUNTINGTON, COLLIS POTTER.

Henryetta, city (pop. 7,987), E central Okla., S of Tulsa. Has coal mines and processes zinc, oil, and glass.

Henry of Burgundy, d. 1112 or 1114, count of Portugal. A brother of Eudes, duke of Burgundy, he was called by Alfonso VI of Leon to help in the fight against the Moors and was assigned a portion of land which under his son, Alfonso I, became the independent kingdom of Portugal.

Henry of Flanders, c.1174–1216, Latin emperor of Constantinople (1206–16); brother of Baldwin I. Fought successfully against Bulgarians.

Henry of Navarre: see HENRY IV, king of France.

Henry of Trastamara: see HENRY II, Spanish king.

Henry's law states that amount of gas that dissolves in liquid is proportional to pressure of gas above liquid. Named for William Henry (1774–1836), English chemist and physician.

Henryson, Robert, c.1425–c.1506, Scottish poet, imitator of Chaucer. His *Testament of Cresseid* is a sequel to *Troilus and Criseyde.* Also wrote the lively *Moral Fables of Aesop* and *Robene and Makyne.*

Henry Street Settlement: see WALD, LILLIAN D.

Henry the Fowler, German king: see HENRY I.

Henry the Lion, 1129–95, Guelphic duke of Saxony (1142–80) and Bavaria (1156–80); son of HENRY THE PROUD. Emperor Frederick I restored the two duchies to him in the hope of restoring peace between the Guelphs and the Hohenstaufen. Henry took part in Frederick's early Italian campaigns; was a leader in the Wendish Crusade of 1147; and extended his power over the Wendish lands of NE Germany, where he introduced Christianity. The growth of his power resulted in friction with Frederick, who in 1180 seized upon a pretext for confiscating Henry's fiefs. Bavaria and Saxony, last of the great German duchies, thus were subdivided into a patchwork of small principalities. Henry went into exile to England but returned 1189, recovered parts of Saxony (Brunswick and Lüneburg), and was left in possession of them by the Peace of Fulda (1190). His younger son became emperor as Otto IV.

Henry the Navigator, 1394–1460, Portuguese prince, patron of exploration; son of John I of Portugal. Founded naval arsenal, observatory, school for study of geography and navigation. His navigators explored W coast of Africa, penetrated into Sudan and Senegal, estab. slave and gold trade (but Henry in 1455 forbade kidnaping of Negroes). He also fought in Moroccan campaigns and exerted considerable political influence, but his chief importance was his contribution to art of navigation and progress of exploration.

Henry the Proud, c.1108–1139, Guelphic duke of Bavaria (1126–39) and Saxony (1137–39). He helped his father-in-law, Emperor LOTHAIR II, against the HOHENSTAUFEN. CONRAD III of Hohenstaufen defeated him in the imperial elections of 1138 and deprived him of his duchies. Henry was in the process of reconquering them when he died, leaving HENRY THE LION as his heir.

Henson, Josiah, 1789–1883, reputed original of Uncle Tom in *Uncle Tom's Cabin.* Escaped from slavery and became leader of community of escaped Negroes in Canada. Autobiography published 1849.

Henty, G(eorge) A(lfred), 1832–1902, English journalist and writer of boys' books. Wrote 80 tales of adventure as popular in America as in England.

hepatica or **liverwort,** low woodland wild flower (genus *Hepatica*) of the temperate zone. It has three-lobed leaves and white or lilac blooms in spring.

Hephaestus (hēfĕ′stŭs), in Greek religion, Olympian god of fire and metalwork; son of Zeus and Hera and father of Erechtheus. He was usually represented as a bearded man, with mighty shoulders and arms, but lame. A comic figure on Olympus, he was butt of many jokes. Once he split Zeus' aching head, and the goddess Athena sprang forth. His favorite abodes on earth were volcanic islands where he had workshops manned by the Cyclopes. As the craftsman's god he was worshiped at industrial centers such as Athens. In Trojan War he supported the Greeks. Romans called him Vulcan.

Hepplewhite, George (hĕ′pŭlhwīt), d. 1786, English cabinetmaker and furniture designer. His style is marked by such details as slight tapering legs with spade feet, chair backs in shield, oval, hoop, and interlaced heart forms. Used mahogany, satinwood, and beechwood, with painted or inlaid decoration (esp. of classical motifs). See *ill.,* p. 356.

Heptameron: see MARGARET OF NAVARRE.

Hera (hēr′ù), in Greek religion, queen of Olympian gods, protectress of women; daughter of Cronus and Rhea, sister and wife of Zeus, and mother of Hephaestus and Ares. A jealous wife, she persecuted Zeus, his earthly mistresses, and their progeny. The Trojan Prince Paris did not award to her APPLE OF DISCORD, and she in revenge supported Greeks in Trojan War. She had especially fine temples at Argos and Samos. Romans called her JUNO.

Heraclea (hĕrŭklē'ù), anc. Greek city, S Italy, not far from the Gulf of Taranto. Here Pyrrhus defeated the Romans 280 B.C.

Heraclea Pontica (pŏn'tĭkù), anc. Greek city, on S shore of the Black Sea, site of modern Eregli, Turkey; large commercial center (5th–6th cent. B.C.).

Heracles, another name for HERCULES.

Heraclitus (hĕrŭklī'tùs), c.535–c.475 B.C., Greek philosopher of Ephesus. He held that the only reality is change and that permanence is an illusion. All things carry with them their opposites, and therefore being and not being are in everything and the only real state is one of transition. Heraclitus believed that fire was the underlying substance of the universe.

Heraclius I (hĕrŭklī'ùs, hĭrā'klēus), c.575–641, Byzantine emperor (610–41). Recovered Syria, Palestine, and Egypt from Persia (622–28), only to see them fall to the Moslem Arabs (629–41). Favored MONOTHELETISM.

Herakleion, Crete: see CANDIA.

Heralds' College, body first chartered in 1484 by Richard III of England. Purpose is to assign coats of arms and trace lineages. Officials are called Garter king-of-arms, other kings-of-arms, heralds, and pursuivants. Officials also proclaim accession of king and attend at state occasions.

Herat (hĕrät'), anc. *Aria,* city (pop. c.80,000), cap. of Herat prov., NW Afghanistan, on Hari Rud R. On trade route from Persia to India, it was taken by various conquerors, notably Alexander the Great and Tamerlane. Disputed by Persians and Afghans until mid-19th cent.

Hérault (ārō'), department (2,403 sq. mi.; pop. 461,100), S France, in Languedoc; cap. Montpellier.

herb (ûrb, hûrb), botanically any plant lacking woody tissue as distinguished from shrubs or trees. More specifically, it is a plant used either medicinally or for its flavor or scent.

herbarium, collection of dried plant specimens used in study of botany. They are mounted on heavy paper and arranged according to genera. Notable herbariums in U.S. include Gray Herbarium at Harvard Univ. and those at the National Museum and the New York and Missouri botanical gardens.

Herbart, Johann Friedrich (yō'hän frē'drĭkh hĕr'bärt), 1776–1841, German philosopher, professor at Königsberg and Göttingen. He made important contributions to psychology and education. To Herbart the universe was made up of simple independent "reals" and change came from shifting relationships of these "reals" in their efforts at self-preservation. In education he emphasized the conscious effort to relate learning to the learner's former experience and stressed moral education.

Herbert, A(lan) P(atrick), 1890–, English humorist. One of his many books is novel *The Water Gipsies* (1930).

Herbert, George, 1593–1633, English religious poet. His poems (posthumously pub. as *The Temple: Sacred Poems and Private Ejaculations,* 1633) are some of the finest of metaphysical poetry, marked by deep feeling, precise language, and metrical versatility. His brother, **Edward Herbert,** 1st **Baron Herbert of Cherbury,** 1583–1648, was a philosopher and poet. Precursor of deism, he wrote *De religione laici* (1645). In *Poems* (1665) he published secular metaphysical verse.

Herbert, Mary: see PEMBROKE, MARY HERBERT, COUNTESS OF.

Herbert, Victor, 1859–1924, Irish-American composer and conductor. He began his career playing cello; was conductor of the Pittsburgh Symphony Orchestra, 1898–1904. His operettas (e.g., *Babes in Toyland*

1903; *Mlle Modiste,* 1905; *The Red Mill,* 1906; *Naughty Marietta,* 1910; and *Sweethearts,* 1913) have been much revived.

Herbert, William: see PEMBROKE, WILLIAM HERBERT, 3D EARL OF.

Herbert of Cherbury: see HERBERT, GEORGE.

Hercegovina: see BOSNIA AND HERCEGOVINA.

Herculaneum (hûrkyōōlā'nèùm), anc. city, S Italy, on the Gulf of Naples, at the foot of Mt. Vesuvius, notable chiefly because it was buried (along with Pompeii) by the eruption of Vesuvius in A.D. 79. Excavations have uncovered walls, statues, books, and the like in fine preservation.

Hercules (hûr'kyōōlēz) or **Heracles** (hĕ'rùklēz), most popular hero in Greek and Roman legends, famous for his extraordinary strength and courage. Son of Zeus and Alcmene, he was hated by Hera, who sought to kill him by sending two serpents to his cradle, but these he strangled; later she sent madness upon him, so that he slew his wife and children. As advised by Delphic oracle, he sought (and achieved) purification at court of King Eurystheus, who demanded of him 12 labors: killing Nemean lion, nine-headed Hydra, and man-eating Stymphalian birds; cleaning stables of Augeas; procuring golden apples of Hesperides and girdle of Hippolyte; and capturing fleet-footed Cerynean hind, mad Cretan bull, flesh-eating mares of Diomed, Erymanthian boar, cattle of Geryon, and three-headed watchdog of Hades, Cerberus. Later he joined Calydonian hunt and expedition of Argonauts. At his death he ascended to Olympus, where he married Hebe. He was widely worshiped. Hero of plays by Sophocles, Euripides, and Seneca. Most famous statue of him is *Farnese Hercules* in Naples.

Hercules, Pillars of: see PILLARS OF HERCULES.

Hercules'-club, small North American tree (*Aralia spinosa*) with a stout thorny trunk, huge compound leaves, and a large flower cluster at the top of the tree.

Herczeg, Francis (hĕr'tsĕg), Hung. *Herczeg Ferenc,* 1863–, Hungarian dramatist, novelist, short story writer.

Herder, Johann Gottfried von (yō'hän gôt'frēt fŭn hĕr'dùr), 1744–1803, German philosopher, poet, and critic. Studied theology and after winning attention by literary criticism he became (1776) court preacher at Weimar at the instance of Goethe, whom he influenced. He was a leader in the *Sturm und Drang* movement in German literature, a passionate opponent of the cool rationalism of 18th-cent. Enlightenment and a precursor of the romantics. Herder sought to develop a philosophy of history showing the march of man's progress. His most ambitious work was *Outlines of the Philosophy of Man* (1784–91). He did much to introduce foreign literature (notably Shakspere, Ossian, and English and Romance folk songs) to German intellectuals and stirred interest in the science of language.

Heredia, José María (hōsā' märē'ä ärā'dhēä), 1803–39, Cuban journalist and poet. Though his poetry is classic in form, he was in temperament a romantic.

Heredia, José María de, 1842–1905, French poet, b. Cuba. *Les Trophées* (1893), a collection of sonnets of classic inspiration, brings to perfection the ideals of the PARNASSIANS.

heredity (hùrē'dĭtē), transmission, through reproductive process, of factors in plants and animals which cause offspring to resemble parents. First scientifically founded concepts, those of Gregor J. MENDEL, indicated that characters are inherited as units independently of each other. Studies of chromosomes, genes, MITOSIS, meiosis, and sex-linked characters shed light on mechanism of heredity. Constancy of transmission of hereditary characters from generation to generation does not preclude changes required by evolutionary concept since MUTATION can occur. See also GENETICS.

Hereford, England: see HEREFORDSHIRE.

Hereford (hûr'fùrd), city (pop. 5,207), N Texas, SW of

Amarillo in Panhandle. Center of cattle and agr. area. Noted for low rate of dental decay attributed to fluorine in soil.

Hereford cattle: see CATTLE.

Herefordshire or **Hereford,** county (842 sq. mi.; pop. 127,092), W England, on Welsh border. Has undulating terrain, rising to Black Mts. and Malvern Hills. Mainly agr. and pastoral region famous for orchards and cattle. Scene of border warfare with Welsh. The county town is Hereford, municipal borough (pop. 32,490), on the Wye. Has cathedral dating from 11th cent., scene every third year of Festival of the Three Choirs, held other years at Gloucester and Worcester. White Cross near town marks end of great plague, 1347. Birthplace of Nell Gwyn and David Garrick.

Hereward the Wake (hĕ'rĭwûrd), fl. 1070, thane of Lincolnshire. A leader of resistance against William I, he was folk hero of conquered Anglo-Saxons.

Herford, Oliver (hûr'fûrd), 1863–1935, American humorist, b. England; author and illustrator of many popular volumes of light verse (e.g., *Rubáiyát of a Persian Kitten,* 1904).

Herford (hĕr'fôrt), city (pop. 50,431), North Rhine-Westphalia, NW Germany. Varied mfg. (furniture, chocolate, textiles). An old Westphalian city, it was founded 823.

Herisau (hā'rĭzou), town (pop. 13,464), cap. of Ausser-Rhoden half canton, Appenzell, Switzerland. Embroideries, cotton textiles, machinery.

Héristal, Belgium: see HERSTAL.

Herkimer (hûr'kĭmŭr), village (pop. 9,400), central N.Y., on Mohawk R. and SE of Utica; settled c.1725 by Palatines. Farm trade center with mfg. of clothing and furniture.

hermandad (ĕrmändädh') [Span.,= brotherhood], league of towns in medieval Spain. *Hermandades* were formed as protection against lawless nobles. Ferdinand and Isabella founded the Holy Hermandad for all Spain to act as permanent police force. Local *hermandades,* greatly modified, continued to 1835. Mexican Acordada was similar organization.

Hermann, d. A.D. 21: see ARMINIUS.

Hermannstadt, Rumania: see SIBIU.

Hermaphroditus (hûrmă"frŭdī'tŭs), beautiful son of Hermes and Aphrodite. He and his consort became one body, with characteristics of both the male and the female.

Hermes (hûr'mēz), in Greek religion, Olympian god; son of Zeus and Maia. He had great variety of functions: god of commerce, of cheats and thieves, of luck (and hence gamblers), of athletic contests, and of eloquence; messenger of the gods; and conductor of souls to Hades. Lyre and flute were his inventions. He was thought of as a merry youth with much cunning, and he inspired riotous festivals. In art he is usually shown wearing a winged hat and winged sandals and carrying the CADUCEUS. His Roman equivalent is Mercury.

Hermes Trismegistus (trĭsmŭjĭ'stŭs), name given to reputed author of books of occult wisdom. Hermes here means Thoth, Egyptian god of learning. *Hermetic Books* encompassed wisdom of ancient Egypt. Hermetical philosophy was popular in 17th cent. and is still used by believers in the occult.

Hermione (hûrmī'ŭnē), in Greek legend, only child of Helen and Menelaus and wife of Orestes.

Hermitage, museum in Leningrad. Rebuilt in 19th cent. as a museum in Neo-Greek style from Catherine II's pavilion palace. Fine collection includes Spanish and French paintings and rare Greek jewelry.

Hermitage, home of Andrew Jackson, central Tenn., near Nashville. House built 1819–31, rebuilt 1835. Jackson and wife buried here. Has church (1823) built by him.

hermit crab, crustacean with soft, asymmetrical, usually coiled abdomen. It is chiefly a marine animal but in the tropics some are largely land forms. Most hermit crabs occupy shells of snails or other gastropod mollusks, thus protecting the abdomen with a portable shelter.

Hermite, Charles (shärl ĕrmēt'), 1822–1901, French mathematician. He made valuable contributions to theory of numbers, theory of elliptic functions, and theory of equations.

Hermite, Tristan l': see TRISTAN L'HERMITE.

Hermon, Mount, on Syria-Lebanon boundary, near Palestine. Highest of its three peaks rises to c.9,000 ft. Snow-capped in winter and spring, it was sacred landmark in ancient Palestine. Mentioned in Bible as Hermon, Sion, Senir, and Shenir.

Hermopolis (hûrmŏ'pŭlĭs), city (pop. 18,925), Syros Isl., Greece, chief city and port of the CYCLADES.

Hermosa Beach (hûrmō'sù), resort and residential city (pop. 11,826), S Calif., on Santa Monica Bay.

Hermosillo (ĕrmōsē'yō), city (pop. 18,601), cap. of Sonora, NW Mexico, on Sonora R.; trading and manufacturing center in tropical-fruit district.

Hernandarias: see ARIAS DE SAAVEDRA, HERNANDO.

Hernández. For some Spaniards thus named, see FERNÁNDEZ.

Hernández, José (hōsā' ĕrnän'dĕs), 1834–86, Argentine poet, author of classic of gaucho literature, *Martín Fierro* (1872).

Herndon, Angelo, 1913–, American Negro labor organizer. A Communist, he led a demonstration against the Ga. relief administration and was the subject of a celebrated civil liberties case.

Herndon, William Henry, 1818–91, law partner and biographer of Abraham Lincoln. Much of *Herndon's Lincoln: the True Story of a Great Life* (3 vols., 1889) ran counter to established legend.

Herne (hĕr'nù), city (pop. 111,249), North Rhine-Westphalia, NW Germany; a center of Ruhr dist.

hernia or **rupture,** protrusion of any internal organ from cavity in which it is normally located. Common form is protrusion of a loop of intestine through weak point in wall of abdomen or groin.

Hero, in late Greek legend, priestess of Aphrodite in Sestos. Her lover, Leander, swam the Hellespont nightly to see her. He drowned one night, and she threw herself into sea.

Hero, mathematician: see HERON OF ALEXANDRIA.

hero, in Greek religion, dead person of note who was given reverence and worship as quasi-divine. Heroes were regarded as ghosts to be appeased, and rites were like those for underworld gods. Heroes might be actual dead men, real or imaginary ancestors, or "faded gods," those demoted to human status.

Herod, dynasty reigning in Palestine at time of Christ. Founder of family fortune was Antipater (ăntĭp'ŭtùr), d. 43 B.C., who was in favor with Caesar after defeat of Pompey and who had gained power in Palestine by aiding Hyrcanus II (see MACCABEES). His son, Herod the Great, d. 4 B.C., gave family its name. Through Marc Antony, Herod secured title of King of Judaea (37 B.C.–4 B.C.); after battle of Actium he made peace with Octavian (Augustus). Herod married 10 times, and the various families intrigued against each other. In his last years Herod was subject to insanity and executed his sons Aristobulus (ăr"ĭstōbū'lŭs), Alexander, and Antipater. It was this Herod who was ruling at time of Jesus' birth and who ordered massacre of the Innocents. Mat. 2; Luke 5. He divided his kingdom among his sons Archelaus, Herod Antipas, and Philip. Archelaus (är"kēlā'ùs), d. after A.D. 6, ruled Judaea and Idumaea (4 B.C.–A.D. 6). Mat. 2.22. Herod Antipas (ăn'tĭpăs), d. after A.D. 39, tetrarch of Galilee and Peraea, was the Herod who executed John the Baptist and who was ruling at Jesus' death. He repudiated his wife to marry Herodias (hērō'dĕus), daughter of his half brother Aristobulus, divorced wife of his half brother Herod Philip, and mother of Salome. Her vaulting ambition caused his ruin, and Caligula banished him (A.D. 39). Mat. 14; Mark 6; Luke 3; 23; Acts 13. Herod the Great's son Philip, d. A.D. 34, was made tetrarch of region E of Galilee.

The eldest son of Aristobulus became Herod Agrippa I, d. A.D. 44. Caligula made him king (A.D. 39) of Philip's tetrarchy and of region W of Damascus. On Claudius' accession he was made ruler of S Syria and of Palestine E and W of Jordan R. His son, Herod Agrippa II, d. c.100, was a poor ruler who alienated his subjects. St. Paul spoke before him. Acts 25; 26. After fall of Jerusalem he went to Rome. As a dynasty the Herods were neither good nor capable rulers; they depended largely on power of Rome and are usually blamed for state of virtual anarchy in Palestine as Christian era began.

Herodotus (hĕrŏ'dŭtŭs), 484?–425? B.C., Greek historian, called father of history. His work, the first comprehensive attempt at secular narrative history, marks start of Western history writing. It deals primarily with Persian Wars, but its rich diversity of contemporary information makes it an important source book on ancient Greece.

heroic couplet, a verse form: see PENTAMETER.

heroin: see OPIUM.

heron (hĕ'rŭn), large wading bird of most temperate parts of world, abundant in the tropics and subtropics. It has a long, sharp bill, long neck and legs, and large wings. Many nest in large colonies. Among American species are great and little blue herons, little green heron, black-crowned and yellow-crowned night herons, and Louisiana heron.

Heron of Alexandria (hĕr'ŏn) or **Hero,** mathematician, inventor; birth and death dates probably between 2d cent. B.C. and 3d cent. A.D. He wrote on measurement of geometric figures, studied mechanics and pneumatics, and invented many devices operated by water, steam, and compressed air.

Herophilus (hĭrŏ'fŭlŭs), fl. 300 B.C. Greek anatomist, a leader of Alexandria school of medicine.

Herrera, Fernando de (fĕrnän'dō dā' ĕrā'rä), 1534–97, Spanish poet, notable for graceful sonnets and love lyrics, heroic odes.

Herrera, Francisco de (fränthē'skō), the elder, 1576–1656, Spanish religious painter, a founder of naturalistic school of Seville. A teacher of Velazquez. His son, **Francisco de Herrera** the younger, 1622–85, studied in Rome, where he painted still lifes. Designed baroque Saragossa cathedral.

Herreshoff, John Brown (hĕ'rŭs-hŏf), 1841–1915, American yacht and speedboat builder. He and his brother, **Nathaniel Greene Herreshoff,** 1848–1938, introduced radical features of design in sailing yachts after 1891. The *Gloriana* won them a reputation, and they subsequently produced five successful defenders of the *America*'s Cup.

Herrick, Robert, 1591–1674, English poet, usually called greatest of CAVALIER POETS. Took orders c.1627 and lived at Dean Prior in Devon. The volume *Hesperides* (1648) contains his *Noble Numbers* (sacred songs) and bucolic love lyrics (e.g., "Night-Piece: To Julia," song opening "Gather ye rosebuds," and "Cherry-ripe") and epigrams. Among sacred poems is the touching "Litany to the Holy Spirit." Herrick's poetry is notable for its simple naïveté, melody, and perfectly chosen words.

Herrick, Robert, 1868–1938, American novelist. His realistic novels include *The Web of Life* (1900), *Clark's Field* (1914), and *The End of Desire* (1932).

Herrin, city (pop. 9,331), S Ill., N of Cairo. Trade center of coal area. Site of "Herrin Massacre" (1922), local clash in country-wide coal strike, which resulted in death of about 25 persons.

herring, common food fish in N Atlantic waters of North America and Europe. There are many species; common herring is *Clupea harengus,* which travels in huge schools. It is c.1 ft. long, blue above and silver on the sides. In spring or autumn it lays c.30,000 eggs, which sink to bottom and develop; young mature in three years.

Herrings, battle of the, 1429, episode in siege of Orléans. An English wagon train, led by Sir John Fastolf,

repulsed a French attack at Rouvray by using wagons with herring barrels as barricade.

Herriot, Édouard (ādwär' ĕryō'), 1872–, French politician. As leader of Radical Socialists, who dominated French politics 1899–1940, he played a prominent part in the chamber of deputies, in several cabinets, and as premier (notably 1924–25, 1932). Favored conciliatory foreign policy, payment of war debts to U.S. Imprisoned by Germans 1942–45. Has been mayor of Lyons since 1904 (except 1941–45). Has strongly advocated a United States of Europe. Also known as scholar and author (notably of a biography of Beethoven, Eng. tr., 1935).

Herrnhut (hĕrn'hoŏt'), town (pop. 2,024), Saxony, E Germany. Founded 1722 by ZINZENDORF as colony of MORAVIAN CHURCH.

Herron, George Davis, 1862–1925, American clergyman. Became Christian Socialist, helped organize RAND SCHOOL OF SOCIAL SCIENCE. Aided President Wilson in peace negotiations after World War I.

Herschel, Sir William, 1738–1822, English astronomer, b. Germany, originally named Friedrich Wilhelm Herschel; pioneer systematizer of sky exploration and cataloguing of heavenly bodies. His many discoveries with reflecting telescopes which he constructed include the planet Uranus (1781). He concluded that solar system as a whole moves through space. His sister Caroline (1750–1848) worked with him. His son **Sir John Frederick William Herschel,** 1792–1871, confirmed and extended his observations and cataloguing of nebulae and double stars.

Hersey, John (hûr'sē), 1914–, American author and journalist. A former war correspondent, he wrote works on events of World War II. They include *Hiroshima* (1946) and the novels *A Bell for Adano* (1944) and *The Wall* (1950).

Hershey, uninc. village, S central Pa., E of Harrisburg. Owned by the Hershey company, it makes chocolate confectionery.

Herstal (hĕr'stäl), town (pop. 27,092), Liége prov., E Belgium; suburb of Liége. Also known as Héristal. Mfg. of arms. Residence of early Carolingian mayors of the palace and of Charlemagne.

Hertford, England: see HERTFORDSHIRE.

Hertford College: see OXFORD UNIVERSITY.

Hertfordshire (här'fŭrdshĭr, härt–), **Hertford,** or **Herts** (härts, hûrts), inland county (632 sq. mi.; pop. 609,–735), S England. Agr. county with level terrain, it produces wheat, hay, vegetables, and flowers. St. Albans an important urban center. County prominent in military history, particularly during Wars of the Roses. The county town, **Hertford,** municipal borough (pop. 13,890), was important in Saxon times. First national church council held here 673. Haileybury Col., important English public school, near here.

Hertogenbosch, 's: see 's HERTOGENBOSCH.

Herts: see HERTFORDSHIRE.

Hertwig, Oscar (ôs'kär hĕrt'vĭkh), 1849–1922, German embryologist. He discovered that fertilization consists of union of male and female germ cells.

Hertz, Gustav (goŏs'täf hĕrts'), 1887–, German physicist. Shared 1925 Nobel Prize for work on effect of impact of electrons on atoms.

Hertz, Heinrich Rudolf (hûrts, Ger. hīn'rĭkh roŏ'dôlf hĕrts'), 1857–94, German physicist. In the course of his experiments confirming J. C. Maxwell's electromagnetic theory, he produced and studied electromagnetic waves (known also as hertzian waves or radio waves).

Hertzog, James Barry Munnik, 1866–1942, South African military and political leader. Commanded a division of Boer forces in South African War 1899–1902. Organized (1913) nationalist party for independence from British Empire. Prime minister (1924–39) in coalition government with Labour party.

Hervey Islands: see COOK ISLANDS.

Hervey of Ickworth, John, Baron (här'vē, hûr'vē), 1693–1743, English statesman and memoir writer. Vice chancellor and privy councilor, Lord Hervey influenced Queen Caroline. Bitterly attacked by Pope. Author of *Memoirs of the Reign of George II.*

Herzen, Aleksandr Ivanovich (ŭlyĭksän'dŭr ēvä'nŭvĭch hâr'tsĭn), 1812–70, Russian revolutionary leader and writer. Lived abroad after 1847, attacking tsarist autocracy in various writings and in the influential periodical, *Kolokol* (1857–62).

Herzl, Theodor (tā'ōdôr hĕr'tsŭl), 1860–1904, Hungarian journalist, founder of modern Zionism. Aroused by the Dreyfus Affair, he devoted his life to the creation of a Jewish state, which he advocated in his booklet *Der Judenstaat.*

Hesiod (hē'sēŭd, hē'–), fl. 8th cent.? B.C., Greek poet. Little-known, self-styled Boeotian farmer; author of the didactic *Works and Days* (advice to farmers) and of the *Theogony.*

Hesperides (hĕspĕ'rĭdēz) [Gr.,= in the west], in Greek religion, nymphs; daughters of Atlas. On an enchanted island in the western sea they guarded tree bearing golden apples, which HERCULES took.

Hess, Germain Henri (hĕs, Fr. zhĕrmē' ärē ĕs'), 1802–50, Swiss-Russian chemist, a founder of thermochemistry. Hess's law: amount of heat liberated or absorbed in chemical reaction is constant regardless of number of stages occurring, if same original substances and end products are involved.

Hess, Dame Myra, 1890–, English pianist. Made her London debut, 1907; first appeared in the U.S., 1922.

Hess, Rudolf (rōō'dôlf hĕs'), 1894–, German National Socialist leader. Hitler made him deputy Führer and minister without portfolio (1933). Hess created worldwide sensation by his secret airplane flight to Scotland (1941), where he was imprisoned. Of doubtful sanity, he was sentenced to life imprisonment at Nuremberg war-crimes trial (1946).

Hess, Victor Francis, 1883–, American physicist. Shared 1936 Nobel Prize for discovering cosmic rays.

Hess, Walter Rudolf, 1881–, Swiss physiologist. Shared 1949 Nobel Prize in Physiology and Medicine for work on control of organs by certain areas of the brain.

Hesse, Hermann (hĕr'män hĕ'sŭ), 1877–, German novelist and poet, son of missionaries in India. Concerned with man's spiritual loneliness, his novels include *Peter Camenzind* (1904), *Demian* (1919; Eng. tr., 1923), *Der Steppenwolf* (1927; Eng. tr., 1929), *Narziss und Goldmund* (1930; Eng. tr., *Death and the Lover,* 1932), and *Das Glasperlenspiel* (1943; complete ed., 1945; Eng. tr., *Magister Ludi,* 1949). Awarded 1946 Nobel Prize in Literature.

Hesse, Philip of: see PHILIP OF HESSE.

Hesse (hĕ'sē, hĕs), Ger. *Hessen,* state (8,153 sq mi.; pop. 4,303,920), Federal Republic of [W] Germany, between Thuringia and the Rhine; cap. Wiesbaden. It is a generally hilly, agr., and forested region, with famous vineyards along the Rhine. Industries are concentrated at Frankfurt (chemicals), Kassel (machinery), and Darmstadt. The Taunus area is famed for its resorts. Hesse has no historical unity. Its name is derived from the landgraviate of Hesse, which in 1247 became an immediate fief of the Holy Roman Empire. After the death (1567) of PHILIP OF HESSE, who introduced the Reformation, Hesse underwent several subdivisions among branches of the ruling family: Hesse-Kassel and Hesse-Darmstadt were the chief divisions. The rulers of the 18th-cent. Hesse improved their finances by letting mercenaries for hire (notably to the English in the American Revolution). In 1803 the landgrave of Hesse-Kassel was raised to the rank of elector; Hesse-Kassel henceforth was known as Electoral Hesse (Ger. *Kurhessen*). Napoleon I in 1806 raised the landgraviate of Hesse-Darmstadt to a grand duchy and in 1807 annexed Electoral Hesse to the kingdom of Westphalia under his brother Jérôme. The Congress of Vienna (1814–15) restored Electoral Hesse and awarded it and Hesse-Darmstadt substantial territorial gains. In 1866 Electoral Hesse, NASSAU, and the free city of Frankfurt, having all three

sided with Austria in the Austro-Prussian War, were annexed by Prussia and merged in Hesse-Nassau prov., with its cap. at Kassel. Hesse-Darmstadt continued under its grand dukes until 1918 (after 1871 as a member of the German Empire) and joined the Weimar Republic in 1919. After World War II all of former Prussian Hesse-Nassau and all of Hesse-Darmstadt E of the Rhine were consolidated into the single state of Hesse under U.S. occupation. The section W of the Rhine (called Rhenish Hesse and containing MAINZ and WORMS) was incorporated into French-occupied Rhineland-Palatinate.

Hesse-Nassau, Germany: see HESSE; NASSAU.

Hessian fly, widely distributed wheat pest, a gall gnat, said to have been carried across the Atlantic from its native Europe by Hessian troops. The larvae injure plants by removing sap from stem; control methods include late planting of seed and plowing under infected wheat.

Hestia (hĕ'stēŭ), in Greek mythology, old and honored virgin goddess of the hearth and domestic life and guardian of state's welfare; daughter of Cronus and Rhea. Identified with Roman Vesta.

Heston and Isleworth (īz'ŭlwûrth), urban district (pop. 106,636), Middlesex, England; residential suburb of London. Site of a large airport.

Hetch Hetchy Valley, in Yosemite Natl. Park, central Calif., on Tuolumne R. O'Shaunessy Dam (built 1923, enlarged 1938) turned valley into lake 7 mi. long, supplying San Francisco with water and power.

Hevelius, Johannes (hīvē'lēŭs, Ger. yōhä'nŭs hāvā'lēōōs), 1611–87, astronomer, b. Danzig. He was a pioneer in the study of the moon's surface.

Hevesy, Georg von (gā'ôrk fŭn hĕ'vĕshē), 1885–, Hungarian physicist and chemist. Won 1943 Nobel Prize for work on use of isotopes as indicators in studying chemical processes.

Hewitt, Abram Stevens (hū'ĭt), 1822–1903, American industrialist and political leader; son-in-law of Peter Cooper. Promoted advanced methods of ironmaking and steelmaking. U.S. Representative from N.Y. (1875–79, 1881–86).

hexameter (hĕksă'mŭtŭr) [Gr.,= measure of six], in prosody, a line to be scanned in six feet. In dactylic hexameter, most celebrated hexameter measure, each foot may have a long syllable followed by two shorts, except last, which has only two syllables, the first being long; any of first four feet may have two long syllables. Dactylic hexameter appears in first, and purest, form in Homer. Stress accent in modern languages substitutes for quantitative differences of classical meters; hence English dactylic hexameter has singsong effect when read aloud. The alexandrine is most common modern hexameter.

Hexapla (hĕk'sŭplŭ) [Gr.,= sixfold], polyglot version of Old Testament made by Origen. Mainly in six columns —Hebrew text. Greek transliteration of it, and four Greek versions. Fragments survive.

Heymans, Corneille (kôrnä'yŭ hī'mäns), 1892–, Belgian physiologist. Won 1938 Nobel Prize in Physiology and Medicine for study of regulation of respiratory center.

Heyse, Paul (poul' hī'zŭ), 1830–1914, German realistic author. His voluminous work includes novels (*Children of the World,* 1872; Eng. tr., 1882), dramas, and *Novellen* (notably *L'Arrabbiata,* 1855; Eng. tr., *The Fury*). Was awarded 1910 Nobel Prize in Literature.

Heyward, DuBose (dùbōz'), 1885–1940, American author, b. Charleston, S.C., author of *Porgy* (1925)—a story of Negro life, later made into a play and an opera (*Porgy and Bess;* score by George Gershwin).

Heywood, John, c.1497–c.1578, English dramatist, most famous writer of the interlude, short comic dialogue (e.g., *The Play of the Weather,* 1533; *The Four P's*).

Heywood, Thomas, 1574?–1641, English playwright and actor. Of his numerous plays *A Woman Killed with Kindness* (pub. 1607) is notable.

Hezekiah (hĕzŭkī'ŭ), d. c.698 B.C., king of Judah (c.727–c.698 B.C.), successor of Ahaz. Resisted two invasions of Sennacherib of Assyria; the second was ended by plague in Assyrian army. Hezekiah, one of best of Judah's kings, abolished idolatry and listened to Isaiah and Micah. 2 Kings 18–20; 2 Chron. 29–32; Isa. 36–39; Prov. 25.1. Ezekias: Mat. 1.10.

Hf, chemical symbol of the element HAFNIUM.

Hg, chemical symbol of the element MERCURY.

Hialeah (hīŭlē′ŭ), residential city (pop. 19,676), SE Fla., part of Greater Miami; settled 1921. Hialeah Park race track is here.

Hibbing, village (pop. 16,276), NE Minn., on Mesabi iron range and NW of Duluth; laid out 1893. Moved to present site after 1917 to make way for world's largest open-pit iron mine.

hibernation (hī″bŭrnā′shŭn), practice among certain animals of passing part of cold season in more or less dormant state. It is believed that the habit arose as protection against cold when food was scarce, or as an alternative to migration (like migration, probably is connected with reproductive life). Hibernation is possible only for those animals able to store enough food in their bodies to carry them over until food is again available. In hibernation bodily activity is at a low ebb. Deepness of sleep varies; on warmer winter days, some emerge. Aestivation (dormant period of escape from heat when water is scarce) occurs chiefly among amphibians, reptiles, fishes.

Hibernia: see IRELAND.

hibiscus (hībĭs′kŭs), annual or perennial shrub or small tree of widely distributed genus *Hibiscus,* many of which are known as rose mallow. Variously colored flowers are large and showy (esp. in tropical forms). See also ROSE OF SHARON.

hiccup or **hiccough,** sharp sound associated with spasm of larynx and diaphragm and produced when inhaled air strikes closed glottis.

Hickam Field (hĭ′kŭm), U.S. Air Force base, on Oahu, T.H., near Pearl Harbor. Bombed Dec. 7, 1941, by the Japanese.

Hickok, Wild Bill, 1837–76, American frontier marshal in Kansas. Real name was James Butler Hickok. Known as a marksman in encounters with outlaws. Murdered in Deadwood, S.Dak.

Hickory, city (pop. 14,755), W central N.C., NW of Charlotte in piedmont; founded 1874. Annexed Highland and West Hickory 1931. Mfg. of textiles, cordage, wagons, and metal products. Seat of Lenoir Rhyne Col. (Lutheran; coed.; 1891).

hickory, deciduous nut-bearing tree of genus *Carya,* chiefly native to North America. One species, the PECAN, is an important nut tree of U.S. Others include shagbark hickory (*Carya ovata*), shellbark hickory (*C. laciniosa*), and mockernut (*C. tomentosa*), all found in E and SE U.S. The pignut (*C. glabra*) has small bitter nuts. Hickory wood, hard and strong, is valued commercially for tool handles, furniture, etc.

Hicks, Edward, 1780–1849, American painter, best known for *The Peaceable Kingdom,* of which c.25 versions are extant.

Hicks, Elias, 1748–1830, American preacher of Society of FRIENDS. In schism of 1827 he led liberal separatist party called Hicksites.

Hicksville, residential village (1940 pop. 6,835), SE N.Y., on W Long Isl.

Hidalgo (ēdhäl′gō), state (8,058 sq. mi.; pop. 840,760), central Mexico. Largely mountainous, Hidalgo has plains in S and W and fertile valleys within central plateau. Mining, the main industry, has centered at PACHUCA (cap.). Conquered 1530 by Spanish, territory was not made separate state until 1869.

Hidalgo y Costilla, Miguel (mēgĕl′ ēdhäl′gō ē kōstē′yä), 1753–1811, Mexican revolutionist and a national hero, a priest. Hidalgo was among the creoles who met at Querétaro to plan revolution against Spain. On Sept. 16, 1810, he issued the *grito de Dolores* which precipitated the revolt. The banner of Our Lady of Guadalupe was his standard. Initially successful in encounters with Spanish forces, he was finally defeated at

Calderón Bridge, betrayed, degraded by Inquisition, and shot.

Hidari Jingoro (hēdä′rē jēn′gōrō), c.1594–1633, Japanese sculptor, famous for delicate wooden friezes of birds and flowers.

Hidatsa Indians (hēdät′sä), North American tribe, also known as the Minitari and the Gros Ventre of the River, of Siouan linguistic stock. In 18th cent. they lived on upper Missouri, in N.Dak. Were typical of "village Indians" of Plains area, cultivating corn and organizing annual buffalo hunt.

Hideyoshi (Hideyoshi Toyotomi) (hēdä′yōshē), 1536?– 1598, Japanese dictator. Succeeded NOBUNAGA and completed unification of Japan by defeating powerful feudal barons. In 1592 began fruitless campaign to conquer China by way of Korea. As civil ruler he encouraged foreign trade and froze class structure by banning change of occupation. First tolerated but later persecuted Christian missionaries.

hieratic: see HIEROGLYPHIC.

Hiero (hī′ūrō), Greek tyrants of Syracuse. Also Hieron. **Hiero I** was tyrant 478–467 B.C., succeeding his brother Gelon. He was a patron of literature and was victor over the Etruscans in a naval battle at Cumae (474 B.C.). **Hiero II,** d. c.215 B.C., was, because of his ability, chosen tyrant (c.270 B.C.). At first an ally of the Carthaginians, he saw the rising power of Rome and as an ally aided the Romans in the Punic Wars. He encouraged his relative, Archimedes, who made him great engines for warfare.

hieroglyphic (hī″rŭglĭ′fĭk, hī″ŭrŭ–) [Gr.,= priestly carving], pictographic writings of anc. Egypt (by extension also those of Crete, Asia Minor, and Central America and Mexico). Interpretation of Egyptian hieroglyphics, begun by CHAMPOLLION, is quite complete. Hieroglyphics are conventionalized pictures used chiefly to represent meanings that seem arbitrary and are seldom obvious. Egyptian hieroglyphics were already perfected in the I dynasty. They began to go out of use in Middle Kingdom; in New Empire they were no longer well understood, and from 500 B.C. their use was a *tour de force.* A given hieroglyphic might be put to three uses (though very few were used for all three), i.e., as an ideogram, as a phonogram, or as a determinative. Phonograms, controlling factor in progress of hieroglyphic writing, became basis of an alphabet. A developed cursive (the hieratic) was used in the Middle Kingdom. This was later supplanted by the demotic, so conventionalized that its hieroglyphic origin was not discernible.

Hieron, tyrants of Syracuse: see HIERO.

Higginson, Thomas Wentworth, 1823–1911, American author, a Unitarian minister. An abolitionist, he headed the first regiment of Negroes in the Civil War. After being wounded, he devoted himself to writing essays on reforms, popular history, biography. Edited poems of Emily Dickinson.

high-bush cranberry or **cranberry bush,** name for two tall viburnum shrubs, *Viburnum opulus,* native to Europe, and the North American *V. trilobum.* Both have flat-topped white flower clusters and red berries.

High Church: see ENGLAND, CHURCH OF.

Highgate, residential suburb of London, England. Dick Whittington supposedly was resting at foot of Highgate Hill when he heard Bow Bells recalling him to London.

Highland, residential town (pop. 5,878), NW Ind., SW of Gary. Truck farming.

Highland Park. 1 City (pop. 16,808), NE Ill., Chicago suburb on L. Michigan; settled 1834. Ravinia Park here is Chicago summer music center. U.S. Fort Sheridan is near. **2** City (pop. 46,393), SE Mich., within confines of Detroit; laid out 1818. Mfg. of automobiles, trucks, and steel tubing. **3** Residential borough (pop. 9,721), E N.J., on Raritan R. opposite New Brunswick. **4** Town (pop. 11,405), N Texas, N suburb of Dallas.

Highlands, mountainous country in Scotland, N of line

running from Moray Firth to Dumbarton. Late Middle Ages produced clan system and dress (kilt, tartan, sporran, tam, dirk) outlawed by British in drastic suppression of Highland support of Jacobites in 18th cent. With decline of Scottish Gaelic language in 19th cent., revival of dress and use of bagpipes were allowed. Rugged beauty and persisting old customs are depicted in romantic literature.

High Point, city (pop. 39,973), central N.C., SW of Greensboro in piedmont; laid out 1853. Mfg. of furniture, hosiery, and textiles.

High Point: see KITTATINNY MOUNTAIN.

Hightstown, borough (pop. 3,712), central N.J., ENE of Trenton. Seat of Peddie School for boys.

Hildebrand: see GREGORY VII, SAINT.

Hildesheim (hĭl'dŭs-hīm), city (pop. 71,821), Lower Saxony, SE of Hanover. Was seat of a prince-bishopric until 1803; passed to Hanover 1815. Its wealth of medieval architecture was largely destroyed in World War II – e.g., the 11th-cent. Romanesque cathedral and the Knochenhaueramtshaus [butchers' guildhouse], built in 1529.

Hildreth, Richard, 1807–65, American historian. Chief work *The History of the United States* (6 vols., 1849–52), written from Federalist viewpoint.

Hill, Ambrose Powell, 1825–65, Confederate general. His 3d Corps initiated fighting at Gettysburg, and he directed battle on July 1, 1863. Led corps in Wilderness campaign (1864). Killed in action at Petersburg (1865).

Hill, Archibald Vivian, 1886–, English physiologist. Shared 1922 Nobel Prize in Physiology and Medicine for work on thermodynamics of muscular activity.

Hill, Daniel Harvey, 1821–89, Confederate general. Served with distinction in Peninsular campaign and Antietam campaign (1862). Protesting Braxton Bragg's command in Chattanooga campaign, he was himself removed by Jefferson Davis.

Hill, James J(erome), 1838–1916, American railroad builder, b. Canada. His extension of St. Paul and Pacific RR to Seattle, completed 1893, was probably greatest feat of railroad building in U.S. Formed Great Northern Railway Co. in 1890. With J. P. Morgan, in 1901, he defeated E. H. Harriman in struggle for the Chicago, Burlington & Quincy.

Hillah or **Hilla** (both: hĭl'lŭ), town (pop. 51,361), Iraq, on branch of Euphrates R. Largely built of materials taken from ruins of near-by Babylon.

Hillel (hĭl'ĕl), fl. 30 B.C.–A.D. 10, Jewish scholar, b. Babylon. Laid the foundation of a systematic interpretation of the Midrash. Many of his teachings approximate those of Christ.

Hilliard, Henry Washington (hĭl'yŭrd), 1808–92, U.S. Representative from Ala. (1845–51). A Whig, chief opponent of secession in Ala.

Hilliard, Nicholas, 1537–1619, first true miniaturist in England; court painter to Elizabeth and James I.

Hillman, Sidney, 1887–1946, American labor leader, b. Lithuania. Became (1915) president Amalgamated Clothing Workers, helped found C.I.O., American Labor Party, and World Federation of Trade Unions. A moderate, he promoted labor-management cooperation and sought labor support for political platforms favored by labor, especially the New Deal. Headed (1943–46) C.I.O. Political Action Committee.

Hillquit, Morris, 1869–1933, American lawyer and Socialist leader, b. Latvia, entered U.S. 1886. Led right-wing Socialists against radical leadership of Daniel De Leon in 1897 and founded the Social Democratic party, which evolved into the present Socialist party. Was a prominent pacifist.

Hillsboro. 1 Town (pop. 2,179), S N.H., WSW of Concord. Here is Franklin Pierce home (1804; restored 1925). **2** Town (pop. 1,329), central N.C., NW of Durham. Early cap. of N.C. province; scene of disturbances in REGULATOR MOVEMENT. Birthplace of T. H. Benton. **3** City (pop. 5,126), SW Ohio, E of Cincinnati. Trade center in agr. area. Woman's Temperance Crusade

founded here 1873. **4** City (pop. 5,142), NW Oregon, W of Portland. Quick freezes fruits and vegetables. **5** City (pop. 8,363), N central Texas, SSW of Dallas. Processes cotton, textiles, and dairy products.

Hillsdale, city (pop. 7,297), S Mich., on St. Joseph R. and SW of Jackson. Mfg. of machinery. Has an arboretum.

Hillside, township (pop. 21,007), NE N.J., SW suburb of Newark. Mfg. of metal, rubber, asbestos, cork, paper goods, hydrogen, pharmaceuticals, plastics.

Hilo (hē'lō), city (pop. 27,198), co. seat of Hawaii co., on NE Hawaii, T.H.; port on Hilo Bay. Commercial center of island. Main export is sugar.

Hilprecht, Hermann Volrath (hĕr'män fôl'rät hĭl'-prĕkht), 1859–1925, American Assyriologist, noted authority on cuneiform writing. He was scientific director of four expeditions (1895–1914) to Nippur.

Himachal Pradesh (hĭmä'chŭl prä'dĕsh), state (10,600 sq. mi.; pop. 989,437), NW India, in Himalayas; cap. Simla. Produces timber, wheat, rice, and corn. Formed 1948 by merger of 21 former Punjab states.

Himalayas (hĭmä'lŭyŭz, hĭmŭlä'ŭz) [Sanskrit,= abode of snow], Asiatic mountain system, c.1,500 mi. long, in Pakistan, Kashmir, India, Tibet, China, Nepal, Sikkim, and Bhutan. Comprises three nearly parallel ranges: Greater Himalayas, which include Mt. EVEREST (world's highest peak) and Kanchenjunga; Lesser Himalayas, enclosing noted Vale of Kashmir; and Outer Himalayas. A range N of Brahmaputra R. is sometimes called Trans-Himalayas. The ranges form almost insuperable barrier between Tibet and India and give rise to many great rivers, notably the Indus, Ganges, and Brahmaputra.

Himeji (hēmā'jē), city (pop. 197,299), S Honshu, Japan; railroad and mfg. center.

Himera (hĭ'mŭrŭ), anc. Greek city, N Sicily. Here according to tradition Gelon of Syracuse defeated the Carthaginians (480 B.C.), but in 408 B.C. Carthaginians destroyed the city.

Himmler, Heinrich (hīn'rĭkh hĭm'lŭr), 1900–1945, German National Socialist leader. Headed SS (see NATIONAL SOCIALISM) from 1929; became head of entire German police system in 1936 (see SECRET POLICE) and minister of the interior in 1943. After putting down a conspiracy against Hitler in July, 1944, he acted as virtual dictator of Germany. The most ruthless of Nazi leaders, he was responsible for the death of millions in forced-labor and extermination camps and ended up by terrorizing his own party hierarchy. He died by taking poison shortly after his arrest by the British.

Himyaritic, Semitic language. See LANGUAGE (table).

Hincks, Sir Francis, 1807–85, Canadian journalist and statesman, b. Ireland. Became editor in 1838 of Toronto *Examiner,* a Reform party newspaper. As premier in joint Hincks-Morin administration (1851–54) he sought a reciprocal trade treaty with U.S. and promoted railroad construction. Minister of finance (1869–73).

Hindemith, Paul (hĭn'dŭmĭth), 1895–, German-American composer and violist; became U.S. citizen 1946. Early compositions were often atonal; later works display a return to tonality. Among his works are the symphony (1934) drawn from his own opera *Mathis der Maler;* a song cycle, *Das Marienleben* (1924; revised 1949); the viola concerto *Der Schwanendreher* (1935); the ballet *Nobilissima Visione* (1938); and *Ludus Tonalis* (1943) for piano.

Hindenburg, Paul von (Paul von Hindenburg und Beneckendorff) (hĭn'dŭnbûrg, Ger. –bōŏrk), 1847–1934, German field marshal and president, b. Poznan (then in Prussia). In World War I he and his chief of staff, LUDENDORFF, routed the Russians at TANNENBERG (1914) and occupied Poland. In 1916 Hindenburg became chief commander of the Central Powers. After the armistice of 1918, he led his troops back in sufficiently good order to prevent a radical revolution. Though a monarchist, he was elected president of the Reich in 1925. He was a tool in the hands of the reactionary Junker class. With Socialist help, he defeated Hitler in the presidential elections of 1932, but in Jan., 1933, largely through the intrigues of PAPEN, he was persuaded to appoint Hitler as chancellor. He continued as a figurehead till his death.

Hindenburg, Pol. *Zabrze,* city (pop. 104,184), Upper Silesia; transferred to Polish administration 1945. A center of Katowice mining and industrial region.

Hindi (hĭn'dē), Indo-European languages of N India. See LANGUAGE (table).

Hinduism, Western term for religious beliefs and practices of most of the people of India. Corresponding Indian term is *dharma* [law]. It has no fixed scriptural canon, but VEDA, *Brahmanas,* and *Bhagavad-Gita* have elaborate theological commentary. Brahmanism substituted (c.550 B.C.) for Vedic religion a complex system of ritual and theosophy expounded in *Brahmanas* and *Upanishads. Brahmanas* regulate sacrifices to gods and personify moral qualities. *Upanishads,* foundation of modern Hindu philosophy, develop doctrine of a universal soul or being to which individual souls will be reunited after maya (illusion of time and space) is conquered. Buddhism and Jainism, which flourished from c.300 B.C. to A.D. c.400 in India, attacked this complex ritual and theology. However, Brahmanism adopted features of those religions and codified its own ritual in *Laws of Manu.* Several schools of interpretation of *Upanishads* appeared (see VEDANTA) and YOGA was developed. A later stage of Hinduism is represented by *Tantras* and *Puranas. Tantras* are mainly prescriptions for securing divine favor; *Puranas* comprise poems addressed mainly to Siva (or Shiva) the Destroyer and Vishnu the Preserver. These and Brahma, a remote deity who created the universe and is equated with it, form triad at center of modern Hinduism. Many cults, with widely variant practices, exist side by side. Modern Hinduism, always more than a religion, is a complete way of life. Conditions have forced much modification (e.g., child marriage, rite of suttee, and untouchability are now illegal). Still widely observed is sacredness of animals (esp. cow and snake). Pilgrimages to sacred shrines are a marked feature of Hinduism.

Hindu Kush (hĭn'dŏŏ kŏŏsh'), mountain system, central Asia, lying mainly in NE Afghanistan and extending E to Pakistan. Culminates in Tirich Mir (25,263 ft.). Crossed by passes (10,000–17,000 ft.), which were used by conquerors of India.

Hindu music. In the music of India, only one voice part carries the melody. The tonal system divides the octave into 22 segments, each roughly equivalent to one quarter of the whole tone of Western music. The most important scale, called *sa-grama,* closely resembles our C major scale. Melody is based on the system of *ragas* or melody types which are used as the basis of an improvisation. There are 60-odd *ragas,* each having its own rules for improvising in that *raga.* Each has its own ethical and emotional properties; each is associated with a certain season or time of day. Traditionally, a night *raga,* sung by a skilled performer at noon, could produce darkness. *Gamakas,* the ornaments or graces of *ragas,* are very important. The accompanying rhythm is based on certain constantly repeated rhythm patterns called *talas.* Among instruments used are various types of drums, the vina (in modern times, a kind of zither), and kinds of bagpipes, lutes, fiddles, oboes, trumpets, flutes, cymbals, and gongs.

Hindustan (hĭn"dŏŏstăn') [Persian,= Hindu land], a term applied to various areas of India and Pakistan. Sometimes refers to region between Narbada R. and the Himalayas, but sometimes limited to mean N central India. Since partition of Indian subcontinent (1947) it has sometimes been applied to the largely Hindu state of India as opposed to Moslem Pakistan.

Hindustani (hĭndŏŏstän'ē), standard Indo-European language of Hindus. See LANGUAGE (table).

Hingham (hĭng'ŭm), town (pop. 10,665), E Mass., on Boston Bay arm. Shipbuilding during World War II.

Hinkle, Beatrice Moses (Van Geisen), 1874–1953, American psychiatrist. Opened first U.S. psychotherapeutic clinic (1908) at Cornell Medical Col. She wrote *The Re-Creating of the Individual* (1923).

Hinnom, valley, near Jerusalem. Despised as place of Moloch worship and dump for Jerusalem's refuse. Tophet was in the valley. In New Testament, Gehenna, a form of Hinnom, meant HELL, perhaps because of fires of Moloch or dump fires always burning there.

Hinsdale, residential village (pop. 8,676), NE Ill., just W of Chicago.

Hinsley, Arthur, 1865–1943, English cardinal, Roman Catholic archbishop of Westminster (after 1935).

Hinton, city (pop. 5,780), S W.Va., SE of Beckley. Agr. shipping point with railroad shops.

Hipparchus, tyrant of Athens: see HIPPIAS.

Hipparchus (hĭpär'kŭs), 2d cent. B.C., Greek astronomer. Ptolemy based his geocentric theory of the universe largely on conclusions of Hipparchus whose researches are recorded in Ptolemy's *Almagest.*

Hippias (hĭp'ēŭs), 6th–5th cent. B.C., tyrant of Athens. He and his brother Hipparchus governed jointly after the death of their father PISISTRATUS until Hipparchus was killed by Harmodius and Aristogiton (c.514 B.C.). Hippias then reigned alone until overthrown by the Alcmaeonidae and the Spartans. He advised the Persians in the campaign ending at Marathon.

Hippocrates (hĭpŏ'krŭtēz), c.460–c.370 B.C., Greek physician, recognized as father of medicine. Placed medicine on scientific basis through practice of bedside observation of disease. Hippocratic writings (including those of disputed authorship) appeared in many translations; some are in Loeb Library. Hippocratic oath, administered to many graduates in medicine, is said to represent his ideals of ethical professional conduct.

Hippodamus (hĭpŏ'dŭmŭs), fl. 5th cent. B.C., Greek architect, earliest known planner of cities. Designed Piraeus (port of Athens) and Rhodes.

Hippolyte (hĭpŏ'lītē), in Greek mythology, queen of the Amazons; daughter of Ares. HERCULES captured her girdle.

Hippolytus, Saint (hĭpŏ'lītŭs), c.160–235, antipope (217 –35), a theologian. Urging a Neoplatonic theology rejected by the popes, he left the Church to become the first antipope. Later officially reconciled, he died a martyr in Maximin's persecution. Feast: Aug. 13.

Hippolytus, in Greek myth, son of Theseus and Antiope or Hippolyte. His stepmother, Phaedra, loved him, but, rebuffed by him, she accused him of dishonoring her. Poseidon then caused his death.

Hippomenes, in Greek legend, winner of ATALANTA.

hippopotamus (hĭpŭpŏ'tŭmŭs), herbivorous mammal (genus *Hippopotamus*) of Africa, related to pig. It has short legs, a broad body, tough gray or brown hide, and a wide mouth. Its incisors and lower canines are large tusks, a source of "ivory." Frequents water and eats aquatic plants. Pygmy hippopotamus (genus *Choeropsis*) is in W Africa.

Hippo Regius: see BÔNE, Algeria.

Hiram (hī'–). **1** Fl. 1000 B.C., king of Tyre, friend of David and Solomon. Sent magnificent gifts for Temple. 2 Sam. 5.11; 1 Kings 5; 9; 10. Huram: 2 Chron. 2; 8; 9. **2** Artisan in metals, sent to Solomon by King Hiram to work on ornamentation of Temple. 1 Kings 7.13–45. Huram: 2 Chron. 4.11–22.

Hiram College, at Hiram, Ohio, SE of Cleveland; coed.; opened 1850. Has well-known plan for intensive study of one subject for nine weeks.

Hirohito (hērō'hētō), 1901–, emperor of Japan. Became regent 1921. Under reign name of Showa succeeded his father Yoshihito in 1926. Publicly rejected concept of imperial divinity in 1946. Constitution of 1947 deprived him of all real power.

Hiroshige (Hiroshige Ando), 1797–1858, Japanese landscape painter and color-print artist. *Mishima in Morning Fog* and *Rain at Shono* are typical.

Hiroshima, city (pop. 224,100), SW Honshu, Japan; port on Inland Sea. Mfg. of textiles and rubber goods. Founded 16th cent. as castle city on delta of Ota R. In World War II was target (Aug. 6, 1945) of first atomic bomb.

Hishigawa, Moronobu: see MORONOBU.

Hispaniola (hĭs″pănyō′lù), island (c.30,000 sq. mi.), West Indies, between Cuba and Puerto Rico. Haiti occupies W third and Dominican Republic the remainder. Discovered by Columbus 1492. In Spanish the name is Española.

Hiss, Alger, 1904–, American public official. In Aug., 1948, Whittaker Chambers charged that Hiss, while in the Dept. of State, helped to transmit confidential government documents to the Russians. After denying the charges, Hiss stood trial twice and was finally convicted of perjury (Jan., 1950) and sentenced to a five-year prison term.

Hitchcock, Alfred (Joseph), 1899–, English film director. Brilliant creator of suspense in such films as *The Lady Vanishes*, *Rebecca*, and *Spellbound*.

Hitchcock, Frank Harris, 1869–1935, U.S. Postmaster General (1909–13). Estab. parcel post and postal savings banks; promoted founding of air mail.

Hitchcock, Lambert, 1795–1852, American chairmaker. Village erected by his factory in Conn. was called Hitchcockville (now Riverton). The **Hitchcock chair,** now sought by collectors, is a factory product of good wood, painted black over red and often having designs stenciled in colors or bronze. Seats are of wood, cane, or rush. See *ill.,* p. 356.

Hitchcock, Thomas, Jr., 1900–1944, American polo player. Probably greatest polo player of all time, he received highest polo rating from U.S. Polo Association, a 10-goal handicap, 1922–40 (except in 1935, when he had 9-goal rating).

Hitchcock chair: see HITCHCOCK, LAMBERT.

Hitler, Adolf, 1889–1945?, German dictator, founder and leader (Ger. *Führer*) of NATIONAL SOCIALISM; b. Braunau, Upper Austria, the son of an Austrian customs official. Studied at Munich; moved to Vienna 1907, where he was refused admission to art academy and spent years of utmost poverty. His violent anti-Semitism began in that period. In 1913 he moved to Munich. He enlisted in the Bavarian army in World War I; became a corporal, received Iron Cross for bravery, and was gassed. After the war he and a few malcontents founded at Munich the National Socialist German Workers' party (NSDAP). Still small but well-disciplined and backed by such men as LUDENDORFF, the NSDAP sought to gain control over Bavaria by a coup d'état, the so-called "beer-hall putsch" of Nov. 8–9, 1923. The plot was put down by the army, on whose support Hitler had counted; 14 Nazis were killed. Hitler was sentenced to five years at Landsberg fortress, where he wrote *Mein Kampf* [my battle], the bible of Nazism, but he was released after 13 months. The depression after 1929 helped in the spectacular growth of the NSDAP. Hitler and his propaganda chief GOEBBELS blamed all ills on Jewish capitalism, Communism, the Treaty of Versailles, and the Social Democrats and promised a millennium for pure-blooded Germans. Secretly backed by a few great industrialists (who hoped to use him as a tool for their own ends), he controlled a powerful press and a private militia. Though he lost the 1932 presidential election to Hindenburg, his party became the largest in the Reichstag. In Jan., 1933, Hindenburg appointed him chancellor. Even with his allies, the monarchist German National party, Hitler had no absolute majority in the Reichstag. To estab. his dictatorship, he outlawed the Communists, whom he accused of setting the REICHSTAG fire, and in March, 1933, an obedient Reichstag voted him dictatorial powers. Hitler placed Germany under the absolute rule of the NSDAP, which took control not only of the state but

of all German life, including youth activities (through the Hitler Jugend). Within his party, he crushed opposition in the "blood purge" of 1934. Anti-Semitism was enacted into law. Concentration camps were set up to take care of all suspected enemies of the regime. Only in the churches was some opposition left alive. In 1934, 88% of the voters favored the union of the presidency and the chancellorship in the person of the Führer. Hitler's aggressive foreign policy, though long abetted by English and French appeasement (see (MUNICH PACT) led GERMANY on the road to WORLD WAR II (1939–45). Late in 1941 Hitler personally took over the conduct of the war in Russia, with disastrous results. To save Germany from total defeat, a group of high military and civil officials resolved upon assassinating Hitler. The bomb placed under his chair failed to kill him, and the conspiracy was put down ruthlessly by the police chief, HIMMLER. On April 30, 1945, with the Allies closing in from all sides, Hitler committed suicide at Berlin, together with Eva Braun, his mistress, whom he had just married. No trace of their burned bodies was found, and there are persistent though dubious rumors that Hitler actually escaped into hiding. His appointed successor, Adm. DOENITZ, arranged for the unconditional surrender of Germany a few days later. The ruin and misery that Hitler's folly and cruelty brought upon the world and his own people is beyond computation.

Hittites (hĭt′tīts), anc. people of Asia Minor and Syria, who had a culture that is still imperfectly known despite many inscriptions that have been uncovered (notably at Boghazkeui). Most inscriptions in cuneiform are in Hittite or Kanesian and in Babylonian, with some in Luish, Khattish, and Khurrish (the last two not related to Hittite). One reconstruction has it that the Hittites created a powerful federation of cities in Cappadocia by c.1800 B.C., then moved S, and finally came into conflict with Ramses II of Egypt. Supposedly their state was destroyed in late 12th cent. B.C. by Thracians, Phrygians, and Assyrians. Lydia was one of the successor states.

Hittorff, Jacques Ignace (hĭ′tôrf, Fr. zhäk′ ēnyäs′ ētôrf′), 1792–1867, French architect, a leader of classic revival in France. Chief work is church of St. Vincent de Paul, Paris. Designed fountains for Place de la Concorde and the column in Place Vendôme (both in Paris).

hives (urticaria), skin eruption, marked by raised areas (wheals) which burn and itch, thought to be an allergic reaction. Causative agents include foods, drugs, infections, insect bites, tapeworm.

Hjalmaren (yĕl′märùn), Swed. *Hjälmaren*, lake, area 190 sq. mi., central Sweden. It is connected with Malaren L. and Abroga R.

Hjort, Johan (yōhän′ yòort′), 1869–1948, Norwegian oceanographer and biologist, authority on fisheries.

Ho, chemical symbol of the element HOLMIUM.

Hoadly, Benjamin, 1676–1761, bishop of Bangor, Wales, center of BANGORIAN CONTROVERSY.

Hoar, Ebenezer Rockwood, 1816–95, American lawyer, U.S. Attorney General (1869–70). One of Grant's few excellent appointments. U.S. Senate rejected his nomination to U.S. Supreme Court in 1870.

hoarfrost: see FROST.

Hoban, James (hō′bùn), c.1762–1831, American architect, b. Ireland. Designed and built the White House (1792–99); rebuilt it after its burning in 1814 by the British.

Hobart (hō′bùrt), city (pop. 56,640; metropolitan pop. 76,534), cap. and principal port of Tasmania, Australia, on Derwent estuary; founded 1804. Seat of Univ. of Tasmania. Woolen mills.

Hobart. 1 City (pop. 10,244), NW Ind., SE of Gary; settled c.1849. Mfg. of clay products. **2** City (pop. 5,380), SW Okla., N of Wichita Mts., in a farming and oil producing area.

Hobart College: see GENEVA, N.Y.

Hobbema, Meindert (mīn′dùrt hô′bùmä), 1638–1709,

great Dutch landscapist; probably studied with Jacob van Ruisdael. His woodland and village scenes are luminous and full of life. Much of work is in England, where it influenced later English landscapists.

Hobbes, Thomas, 1588–1679, English philosopher. In his works, both in Latin and in English, he set forth a rationalist materialism, which offended the religious. His view was strongly mechanistic. His best-known work, the *Leviathan* (1651), made him the first of the great English political theorists. This argues that men in their natural existence are self-seeking, brutish, and constantly at war with one another. To escape the dangers of this anarchy groups of men agree to set up an artificial body for maintaining peace. They submit absolutely to the sovereign, who is, however, obliged to protect the people and to promote truth. Hobbes implies that if the sovereign failed in this duty the citizens would have a right to revolt. In his psychology he was a strict sensationalist.

hobblebush or **wayfaring tree,** a viburnum (*Viburnum alnifolium*) of E North America. It has long straggling branches which often root at the tips.

Hobbs, city (pop. 13,875), SE N.Mex., on Llano Estacado, near Texas line. Trade center for livestock and farm region. Hq. for rich oil fields found in 1927.

Hobby, Oveta Culp, 1905–, American public official and journalist. Organized and directed WAC in World War II. Executive vice president of Houston *Post.* Became Secretary of Health, Education, and Welfare in 1953.

Hoboken (hō′bōkŭn), town (pop. 31,941), Antwerp prov., N Belgium, on Scheldt R.; part of greater Antwerp. Shipyards; copper, tin, and silver refineries; wool-processing plants.

Hoboken (hō′bōkŭn), city (pop. 50,676), NE N.J., on the Hudson opposite lower Manhattan (ferry, Lincoln Tunnel, subway connections). Commercial and industrial center (since mid-19th cent.) and ocean port (marine and rail terminals) with shipbuilding and mfg. of food products, electrical equipment, machinery, furniture, chemicals, and scientific instruments. Seat of STEVENS INSTITUTE OF TECHNOLOGY. Dutch trading and farming began c.1630. Indians deeded land to Stuyvesant 1658. John STEVENS bought site 1784, and laid out town 1804. He operated (1811) first steam ferry between New York and Hoboken, built (c.1825) and ran first locomotive to pull a train on tracks in U.S. Noted early 19th-cent. authors gathered at John Jacob Astor home (1828).

Hobson, John Atkinson (hŏb′sŭn), 1858–1940, English economist. Criticized classical economics, holding that economic theory should be a guide to resolution of problems of social welfare.

Hobson, Richmond Pearson, 1870–1937, American naval officer. Gained notice by his effort to sink collier *Merrimac* to block harbor of Santiago in Spanish-American War.

Hoche, Lazare (läzär′ ōsh′), 1768–97, French general. Pacified VENDÉE (1794–96); failed in invasion of Ireland (1796); defeated Austrians at Neuwied (1797).

Hochelaga (hō″shŭlä′gŭ, –lä′gŭ), former Indian village, Canada, discovered by Jacques Cartier in 1535. At foot of Mt. Royal in what is now central part of Montreal. Capital of Hochelagan people, chief inhabitants of St. Lawrence valley. Recent excavations have unearthed early cultural remains.

Ho Chi-minh (hō′ chē-mĭn′), 1890?–, Indo-Chinese revolutionary leader. Visited Moscow 1925–27. Leader of Viet Minh (League for Independence of Viet Nam), he headed VIET NAM provisional government in 1945. Warfare begun 1946 between the French and Ho's regime was still raging in 1953.

Höchstädt (hûkh′shtĕt), village, W Bavaria, on Danube R., near battlefield of BLENHEIM. Scene of French victory over Austrians (1800).

hockey, game played on field or ice. Field hockey, played in England for several centuries, has been popu-

lar in U.S. since 1901, especially among college girls. Played on level field measuring 50 to 60 yd. by 90 to 100 yd. by two teams of 11 players. Ice hockey, played exclusively by men, originated in Canada and was probably standardized by McGill Univ. students in 1870s. Game is played on regulation ice rink 200 ft. by 85 ft. by teams of six players.

Hodgenville (hŏj′ĭnvĭl), town (pop. 1,695), central Ky., S of Louisville. Abraham Lincoln Natl. Historical Park, with cabin said to be his birthplace, is near by.

Hodmezovasarhely (hôd′mĕzŭvä″shärhä), Hung. *Hódmezövásárhely,* city (pop. 61,776), S Hungary. A typical "peasant city," it occupies 294 sq. mi.

Hoe, Richard March, 1812–86, American inventor, manufacturer of first U.S. flat bed and cylinder press, and designer (1846–47), of the first Hoe rotary press.

hoe, usually a flat blade set in long handle and used for loosening soil and weeding; probably the first exclusively agricultural implement. Forerunner was forked stick or antler; from it adz and plow were evolved.

Hoek van Holland: see HOOK OF HOLLAND.

Hofer, Andreas (ändrä′äs hō′fŭr), 1767–1810, Austrian patriot; a Tyrolean innkeeper. Led peasants of TYROL in revolt against Bavaria (1809) and was made governor of Tyrol by the Austrians. Betrayed to the French, he was shot at Mantua.

Hoffman, Charles Fenno, 1806–84, American author. Associated with many periodicals. His works, which were widely popular, include a travel book (*A Winter in the West,* 1935), a novel (*Greyslaer: a Romance of the Mohawk,* 1840), and lyrics.

Hoffman, Malvina, 1887–, American sculptor. Studied under Rodin. Best known for portrait busts; did 100 bronzes of racial types for Field Mus., Chicago.

Hoffmann, E(rnst) T(heodor) A(madeus) (ĕrnst′ tā′ōdōr ämädä′ōōs hôf′män), 1776–1882, German author, composer, and artist. Was active as conductor and as jurist. Himself an eccentric personality, he was a master of fantastic fiction, which his poetry and flashes of psychological insight raised to the highest level. His works include *The Serapion Brethren* (1819–22), *The Devil's Elixir* (1815–16), *Kater Murr, the Educated Cat* (1820–21). These and many selected tales have been translated into English. *The Nutcracker and the Mouse-King* served as basis for Tchaikovsky's ballet; three other tales were used for Offenbach's opera *Tales of Hoffmann.*

Hoffmann-Donner, Heinrich (hīn′rĭkh hôf′män-dô′nŭr), 1809–94, German author of *Struwwelpeter* [slovenly Peter] (1845), widely known children's book.

Hofmann, August Wilhelm von (ou′gōōst vĭl′hĕlm fŭn hôf′män), 1818–92, German organic chemist. He was first to prepare rosaniline and its derivatives, thereby laying basis for aniline dye industry.

Hofmann, Joseph (hôf′mŭn), 1876–, Polish-American pianist. Made his American debut (1887) at the Metropolitan Opera House. Director (1924–38) of the Curtis Inst. of Music, Philadelphia.

Hofmannsthal, Hugo von (hōō′gō fŭn hôf′mänstäl), 1874–1929, Austrian dramatist and poet. His *Electra* (1903), *Der Rosenkavalier* (1911), *Ariadne auf Naxos* (1912), *Die Frau ohne Schatten* [the woman without a shadow] (1919), and *Die ägyptische Helena* (1928) were set to music by Richard Strauss. Also famous is his adaptation of *Everyman* (*Jedermann,* 1911).

Hofstra College: see HEMPSTEAD, N.Y.

hog: see SWINE.

Hogan, Ben (hō′gŭn), 1912–, American golfer. Won many tournaments, including P.G.A. championship (1946, 1948) and U.S. Open (1948).

Hogarth, William (hō′gärth), 1697–1764, English painter and engraver. Won fame and financial security with his engravings, notably the three series *The Harlot's Progress, The Rake's Progress,* and *Marriage à la Mode,* which reveal his power as a satirist. Also made didactic prints (e.g., *Gin Lane*) to spur social reform. In his own time he won little recognition as a serious painter, although he produced some magnificent canvases, including the famous *Shrimp Girl* (Natl. Gall., London).

Hogben, Lancelot (Thomas) (hŏg′bĕn), 1895–, English scientist and author. Known for work in genetics and endocrinology and for popular science books.

hog cholera, infectious, very contagious, often fatal virus disease of hogs. It can be prevented by vaccination.

Hogg, James, 1770–1835, Scottish poet, the "Ettrick Shepherd." Known for his rustic verse, such as *The Mountain Bard* (1807) and *The Queen's Wake* (1813).

Hog Island, in Delaware R., SE Pa. Government shipyard in World War I. Acquired by Philadelphia 1930 as airport and shipping and mfg. area.

Hogue, La (lä ôg′) or **La Hougue** (lä ōōg′), harbor on English Channel, NW France, on NE coast of Cotentin peninsula. Scene of English-Dutch naval victory over French (1692).

Hohenfriedberg (hōŭnfrēt′bĕrk), village, Silesia, near Breslau. Scene of decisive victory of Frederick II of Prussia over Austro-Saxon forces (1745).

Hohenlinden (hōŭnlĭn′dŭn), village, Upper Bavaria. Scene of French victory over Austrians (1800).

Hohenlohe-Schillingsfürst, Chlodwig, Fürst zu (klŏt′vĭkh fürst′ tsōō hō′ŭnlōŭ-shĭ′lĭngsfürst), 1819–1901, chancellor of Germany (1894–1900).

Hohenstaufen (hō″ŭnshtou′fŭn), German dynasty; dukes of Swabia from 1079; emperors and German kings 1138–1254; kings of Sicily 1194–1266 (see CONRAD III; FREDERICK I; HENRY VI; PHILIP OF SWABIA; FREDERICK II; CONRAD IV; MANFRED; CONRADIN). Their chief rivals were the Guelphs (see GUELPHS AND GHIBELLINES), who sided with the popes in their struggle with the Hohenstaufen emperors.

Hohenwald (hō′ŭnwôld), town (pop. 1,703), central Tenn., SW of Nashville. Near by is Meriwether Lewis Natl. Monument.

Hohenzollern (hō″ŭntsō′lŭrn), German dynasty, named for its ancestral castle in Swabia. Frederick of Hohenzollern (d. c.1200) became burgrave of Nuremberg 1192. His sons founded the two main lines of the house—the Swabian line (see HOHENZOLLERN, former province) and the Franconian line, which received the margraviates of ANSBACH and BAYREUTH (which later passed to separate branches) and, in 1415, the electorate of BRANDENBURG. In 1525 ALBERT OF BRANDENBURG created the duchy of Prussia, which passed to the main line of Brandenburg in 1618. Elector FREDERICK WILLIAM (reigned 1640–88) vastly increased his territories, which his son Frederick I transformed in 1701 into the kingdom of PRUSSIA. From 1871 to 1918 the Hohenzollern kings of Prussia were also emperors of Germany (William I, Frederick III, William II).

Hohenzollern, former province (441 sq. mi.; pop. 85,-863), of Prussia, SW Germany, in Swabia, between Württemberg and Baden; cap. Sigmaringen. After World War II it became part of WÜRTTEMBERG-HOHENZOLLERN. Mountainous; agr., forestry. Zollern or Hohenzollern castle, in N, gave name to Prussia's ruling house. About 1600 territory split into two counties, later principalities, ruled by two branches of the Swabian Hohenzollern line—**Hohenzollern-Hechingen** and **Hohenzollern-Sigmaringen.** Both houses yielded their rights to Prussia 1849. Charles of Hohenzollern-Sigmaringen became king of Rumania as Carol I.

Hohe Tauern (hō′ŭ tou′ŭrn), range of E Alps, S Austria, in Salzburg, Carinthia, and E Tyrol. Rises to 12,-460 ft. in GROSSGLOCKNER.

Hokan, hypothetical linguistic family of North America deriving from unproven unification of a number of Western and Eastern stocks.

Hokkaido (hōkī′dō), island (c.30,000 sq. mi.; pop. 3,852,821), N Japan; cap. Sapporo. Northernmost, second largest, and most sparsely populated of the four major islands of Japan. Rugged interior with many volcanic peaks; c.60% of area is forested. Ishikari R. in W is second largest in Japan. Has severe winters. Chief products: coal, lumber, paper, iron. One of

world's major fishing centers. Until 1800 Ainus outnumbered the Japanese. Formerly called Yezo.

Hokusai (hō′kōōsī), 1760–1849, Japanese artist, the foremost figure of ukiyoye school. Accurately depicted Japanese scenes and contemporary life. A famous color-print series is *Hundred Views of Fuji.* His landscapes had much influence on Western art.

Holbach, Paul Henri Thiry, baron d' (ôlbäk′; also German hôl′bäkh), 1723–89, French philosopher, b. the Palatinate. A friend of Diderot, Condorcet, and Rousseau, he was an Encyclopedist. He is remembered chiefly as a stalwart opponent of all positive religion. Man, he held, was innately moral but perverted by education.

Holbein, Hans (hôl′bīn), the elder, c.1460–1524, German painter, designer of stained glass, and silverpoint portraitist. His son **Ambrosius Holbein,** c.1494–1519, is best known for book illustrations and portraits. The other son, **Hans Holbein,** the younger, 1497–1543, was an outstanding artist of German Renaissance. Spent early half of life in Basel, where he enjoyed friendship of Erasmus, whose *Praise of Folly* he illustrated and of whom he painted many portraits. In 1526 he visited England, where he painted Sir Thomas More and other eminent persons. Settled in England after brief return to Basel. Became painter to Henry VIII in 1536 and made many portraits of the king and his wives. As impressive as his paintings are numerous preliminary portrait drawings, remarkable for sensitivity of line and characterization. Among other famous works are his woodcuts, which include *Dance of Death* series and illustrations for Luther's Bible.

Holberg, Ludvig, Baron (lōōdh′vĕ, hōl′bĕr), 1684–1754, Danish dramatist and historian, b. Norway. One of the great figures of Danish literature, he was first to use Danish as a literary medium. *The Danish Stage* (1731) is a collection of 15 comedies.

Holborn (hō′bŭrn), metropolitan borough (pop. 24,-806), central London, England. Has British Mus., Univ. of London, Gray's Inn and Lincoln's Inn, Royal Col. of Surgeons, and Hatton Garden, all damaged by bombing in World War II. Known for its diamond trade.

Holbrook, Josiah (hōl′brŏŏk), 1788–1854, American educator. He founded the LYCEUM movement at Millbury, Mass., in 1826.

Holbrook (hōl′brŏŏk), town (pop. 2,336), E central Ariz., on Little Colorado R. and SE of Winslow. To E is Petrified Forest Natl. Monument.

Holden, city (pop. 1,765), W Mo., SE of Kansas City. Carry Nation lived here.

Holdenville, city (pop. 6,192), SE central Okla., SE of Shawnee. Trade center for farm and oil region. Site of Fort Holmes near by.

Hölderlin, Friedrich (frē′drĭkh hûl′dŭrlĭn), 1770–1843, German poet. Before he became insane at 36 he wrote lyric poetry of deep and intensely personal content, in classic meter and in free rhythms, which place him among the foremost German poets. Equally notable for its blending of classical and romantic elements is the epistolary novel *Hyperion* (1797–99).

holding company: see CORPORATION.

Holinshed, Raphael, d. c.1580, English chronicler. His *Chronicles of England, Scotland, and Ireland* (1577) was source for many English history plays.

Holland, former county of the Holy Roman Empire and, from 1579 to 1795, chief member of the United Provs. of the Netherlands; historic cap. The Hague. The name is popularly applied to the entire Netherlands. Created a county in 10th cent., Holland originally also controlled ZEELAND and FRIESLAND. It was seized in 1299 by John of Avesnes, count of HAINAUT, and was ruled by his successors till 1433, when Duke Philip the Good of Burgundy wrested it from Jacqueline, countess of Hainaut, Holland, Zeeland, and Friesland. After the death of Mary of Burgundy (1482) Holland was taken over by Maximilian of Austria (later Emperor Maximilian I), who suppressed a Dutch

---

SMALL CAPITALS = cross references. Pronunciation key on inside end pages. Abbreviations: p. 2.

rebellion in 1490. The ports and cities of Holland—e.g., Amsterdam, Rotterdam, The Hague, Leiden, Delft—rose to prosperity in the 15th and 16th cent., and Holland led in the struggle for Dutch independence from Spain (16th–17th cent.). Its history became virtually identical with that of the NETHERLANDS. In 1840 Holland was divided into NORTH HOLLAND and SOUTH HOLLAND provs.

Holland, resort city (pop. 15,858), S Mich., SW of Grand Rapids and on Black R. and Black L.; founded 1847 by Dutch. Mfg. of metal and rubber products. Has tulip growing and annual tulip festival. Here are Hope Col. and Netherlands Mus.

Holland, Parts of: see LINCOLNSHIRE, England.

Holland House, residence of the Holland family in Kensington, London, made famous in first half of 19th cent. by hospitality of Henry Richard Vassall Fox, 3d Baron Holland. Did much for English liberalism by providing an intellectual center for scientists, writers, and statesmen.

Hollandia (hŏlăn'dēŭ), trading post (district pop. 6,228), cap. of Netherlands New Guinea, on Humboldt Bay, N New Guinea. In World War II it was Japanese air base, taken 1944 by U.S. troops.

Holland Land Company, a Dutch venture active in the settlement of much of W N.Y. and some of NW Pa. Organized 1796. Company developed its holdings, planned town sites, and sold lands directly to settlers on liberal terms.

Hollar, Wenzel or **Wenceslaus** (hŏ'lŭr, –lär), 1607–77, Bohemian etcher. Works included portraits, architectural studies, still lifes, and religious scenes. Worked mainly in England.

Hollidaysburg, borough (pop. 6,483), S Pa., S of Altoona and on Juniata R. Has railroad shops and plants for metal products and explosives.

Hollidays Cove, W.Va.: see WEIRTON.

Hollingworth, Leta Stetter, 1886–1939, American educator and psychologist. From 1916 until her death she taught at Teachers Col., Columbia Univ. She was noted for her studies in child psychology.

Hollins College: see ROANOKE, Va.

Hollister, city (pop. 4,903), W Calif., E of Monterey Bay. Pinnacles Natl. Monument is near.

holly, handsome evergreen or deciduous tree or shrub of widely distributed genus *Ilex* with berrylike fruits of various colors. Male and female flowers are often on different plants. English holly (*Ilex aquifolium*), with glossy spiny evergreen leaves and bright red berries, is closely associated with Christmas tradition. The similar American holly (*I. opaca*) may reach 50 ft. in the South. Other hollies include inkberry, winterberry, and commercially important MATE.

hollyhock, a tall biennial or perennial plant (*Althaea rosea*), with large leaves and showy single or double flowers of various colors.

Hollywood. 1 Part (pop. c.185,000) of Los Angeles (since 1910), S Calif.; founded in late 1880s. Center of moving-picture industry, though many of the studios are now outside. Hollywood's first picture was made in 1911. The word Hollywood now means American film industry in general—its morals, manners, and characteristics. Community is also a Western broadcasting center for radio and television. Hollywood Bowl, Griffith Park, and estates of many cinema stars are here. **2** City (pop. 14,351), SE Fla., on Atlantic coast N of Miami; founded 1921 as planned resort.

Holmes, John Haynes, 1879–, American clergyman (undenominational), minister (1907–49) of the Community Church, New York city; founder of Natl. Association for the Advancement of Colored People and of American Civil Liberties Union.

Holmes, Oliver Wendell, 1809–94, American author and physician, b. Cambridge, Mass.; grad. Harvard. He brought out a volume of *Poems* in 1836, and verse written throughout his life was to provide familiar poems for Americans (e.g., "Old Ironsides," "The Chambered Nautilus," "The Deacon's Masterpiece;

or, The Wonderful One-Hoss Shay," and "Lord of all being, Throned afar"). He also wrote medical pamphlets of considerable importance. Sketches, contributed to the *Atlantic Monthly,* gave rise to several collections (e.g., *The Autocrat of the Breakfast-Table,* 1858; *The Professor at the Breakfast-Table,* 1860). These and his poems made him a sort of apostle of good humor, but his unsuccessful novels (*Elsie Venner,* 1861; *The Guardian Angel,* 1867; *A Mortal Antipathy,* 1885) were anti-Calvinist and "medical" and have been recently called the first American psychological novels. His son, **Oliver Wendell Holmes,** 1841–1935, was Associate Justice of U.S. Supreme Court (1902–32). Known as the "great dissenter," he by his clear, forceful opinions gained the notice of the nation's liberals. He believed in respecting human rights more than property rights. His writings (e.g., *The Common Law,* 1881) are much admired.

Holmes, William Henry, 1846–1933, American geologist and anthropologist. He served with U.S. Geological Survey, contributing pioneer reports on Yellowstone, Grand Canyon, and other areas. His interest in cliff dwellings of the Southwest turned him to archaeology. From 1910 to 1920 he was curator of anthropology at U.S. National Museum.

holmium (hōl'mēŭm), metallic element of rare earths (symbol = Ho; see also ELEMENT, table).

Holofernes (hŏlŭfûr'nēz, hōlō'–), invading general killed by JUDITH to save her city. Judith 2–13.

Holst, Gustav (hōlst), 1874–1934, English composer. Among his compositions are *The Mystic Trumpeter* (1904), for voice and orchestra; *The Planets* (1914–16), a suite for orchestra; and *The Perfect Fool* (1920–22), an opera.

Holst, Hermann Eduard von (fŭn hôlst'), 1841–1904, American historian. Main work, *The Constitutional and Political History of the United States* (7 vols., 1876–92), studies struggle to preserve Union.

Holstein (hōl'stīn, Ger. hôl'shtīn), former duchy, N Germany; the part of Schleswig-Holstein S of the Eider R.; cap. Kiel. Created a county of the Holy Roman Empire in 1111, Holstein was ruled until 1459 by the house of Schauenburg, which in 1386 also received SCHLESWIG. In 1459 it passed by inheritance to Christian I of Denmark, of the house of OLDENBURG, who in 1460 estab. the relationship of Denmark, Schleswig, and Holstein as a personal union. Holstein was raised to a duchy in 1474. For subsequent history, see SCHLESWIG-HOLSTEIN.

Holstein, Friedrich von (frē'drĭkh fŭn hôl'shtīn), 1837–1909, German civil servant, the "Gray Eminence" of the German foreign office. Holding a relatively obscure post, he was a powerful influence in shaping German foreign policy after the fall of his enemy, Bismarck. Resigned 1906.

Holstein-Friesian cattle: see CATTLE.

Holt, Henry, 1840–1926, American publisher and author. Joined (1866) the publishing firm which became (1873) Henry Holt & Co. Founded (1913) the *Unpopular Review.* Wrote novels and an autobiography.

Holt, Joseph, 1807–94, judge advocate general of U.S. army (1862–75). Followed Pres. Lincoln's desires in extending military jurisdiction over civil affairs.

Holt, Luther Emmett, 1855–1924, American physician, specialist in children's diseases, author of *Care and Feeding of Children* (1894).

Holtby, Winifred, 1898–1935, English novelist and journalist. Edited *Time and Tide* after 1926. Her novel *South Riding* (1936) widely known.

Holtville, city (pop. 2,472), SE Calif., SE of Salton Sea in IMPERIAL VALLEY. Ships truck.

Holy Alliance, formed 1815, agreement among Alexander I of Russia (its sponsor) and the rulers of Austria and Prussia. Its wording, which reflects Alexander's confused mysticism, bound the sovereigns to conduct themselves according to Christian principles and was later interpreted to mean that the political status of Europe as of 1815 was divinely inspired and should remain unchanged forever. All sovereigns of Europe adhered to the alliance save three—George IV of England (who could not for constitutional reasons) and the pope and the sultan (who could not for religious reasons). The QUADRUPLE ALLIANCE of 1814, though distinct from the Holy Alliance, became soon confused with it and under the leadership of Metternich acted as its instrument. The defection of England from the Quadruple Alliance (1822) did not prevent the survival of the Holy Alliance as a spiritual climate until the Revolution of 1848.

Holy City: see ALLAHABAD; BENARES; JERUSALEM; MECCA; ROME.

Holy Cross, College of the: see WORCESTER, Mass.

Holy Cross National Monument: see NATIONAL PARKS AND MONUMENTS (table).

Holy Ghost or **Holy Spirit,** in Christian doctrine, third Person of the Trinity, often defined as the aspect of God immanent in the world; the giver of faith, the Paraclete (Comforter or Strengthener). Descended upon the apostles at first Pentecost, giving them the gift of tongues (Acts 2). The dove is symbol of the Holy Ghost.

Holy Grail: see GRAIL, HOLY.

Holyhead (hŏl′lēhĕd), urban district (pop. 10,569), on Holyhead Isl., Wales, small island off W coast of Anglesey. Chief port for mail and passenger service to Dublin. Also a fishing port and resort.

Holy Island, England: see LINDISFARNE.

Holy Land: see PALESTINE.

Holy League. 1 In French history: see LEAGUE. **2** In Italian history, alliance formed 1510 by Pope Julius II with Venice, Swiss Confederation, Spain, England, Emperor Maximilian I, and others to expel LOUIS XII of France from Italy. Swiss routed French at Novara (1513), but league broke up when Julius died.

Holyoke, city (pop. 54,661), SW Mass., on Connecticut R. (water power) above Springfield; settled 1745. Mfg. of paper and metal products and textiles.

holy orders: see ORDERS, HOLY.

Holy Roman Empire, political body embracing most of central Europe from 962 to 1806; "Roman" because it claimed succession to imperial Rome; "holy" because it originally claimed supremacy over Christendom. Its universality was never recognized in the E by the Byzantine emperors and only briefly in the W, where England, France, and Spain developed into separate states. A constantly evolving organism, the Holy Roman Empire was a mixture of conflicting theories and realities. CHARLEMAGNE in 800 recreated a Western Empire and sought to restore the order and unity Europe had known under Rome; this empire broke up under his successors (LOUIS I, LOTHAIR I, LOUIS II, CHARLES II, CHARLES III, ARNULF). The union of GERMANY and ITALY under OTTO I and his imperial coronation (962) created a new empire, based on FEUDALISM. Its rulers were chosen by the princes of Germany (after 1356, by a fixed number of ELECTORS) unless crowned emperor by the pope, they bore the title German king or king of the Romans. Customarily, after being crowned king at Aachen, the emperor-elect proceeded to Rome to be crowned emperor there. To keep the succession in his family, he normally had his heir elected king of the Romans in his lifetime. After 1562 the emperors-elect dispensed with coronations by the pope and were crowned at Frankfurt. The emperors exercised direct rule only over their hereditary family domains (e.g., the Saxon dynasty, over Saxony; the Hapsburg dynasty, over Austria); they also held immediate jurisdiction over the free imperial cities (e.g., Frankfurt, Regensburg, Augsburg), which they chartered in the 12th–13th cent. The rest of the empire they controlled only to the extent to which they controlled the DIET, which might even depose them. They succeeded, in the 10th–12th cent., in breaking up the powerful "stem duchies" (see GERMANY) and raised a multitude of lesser temporal and ecclesiastic princes to the rank of

immediate vassals. This process was completed by FREDERICK I, who also brought to a head the long-standing rivalry between emperors and popes. One factor in that bitter struggle was that both popes and emperors claimed supremacy over Christendom—the popes in spiritual matters, the emperors in temporal matters, but with no agreement as to ultimate rights in administration and authority. From this arose the quarrel over INVESTITURE (settled 1122 by the Concordat of WORMS). Another factor was the dual role of the emperors as kings of both Germany and Italy and the dual role of the popes as both spiritual and temporal rulers. If the emperors stayed N of the Alps, they lost effective control over Italy; if they invaded Italy (as they did at irregular intervals) to reassert their authority, the popes as a rule managed to stir up trouble in Germany, thus forcing the invader to hasten back. Frederick I lost out in his struggle against the LOMBARD LEAGUE, which had papal backing; FREDERICK II, who was also king of Sicily, shifted his center of interest to Italy, which he temporarily subdued, but after his death (1250) the papacy emerged triumphant and imperial rule over Italy was lost. After an interregnum which put Germany at the mercy of robber barons, feuding nobles, and rival kings, a new phase began with the election of RUDOLF I of Hapsburg (1273). The HAPSBURG dynasty, which became permanently entrenched after 1438, directed its primary attention to its own aggrandizement and to its hereditary domains, which under CHARLES V stretched around the entire globe, far beyond the boundaries of the Holy Roman Empire. The victory of the princes and the towns in the PEASANTS' WAR (1524–26) prolonged serfdom and feudalism for another three centuries; the REFORMATION destroyed even the religious unity of the empire and offered the German princes a pretext for rebelling against Hapsburg supremacy in the THIRTY YEARS WAR (1618–48). The Peace of WESTPHALIA dissolved the empire in all but its name. Some 300 princes obtained virtual sovereignty, limited only by vague provisions forbidding alliances directed against the emperor. Hapsburg power was further weakened by France in the wars of Louis XIV (17th cent.) and by PRUSSIA in the War of the AUSTRIAN SUCCESSION and the SEVEN YEARS WAR (18th cent.). The FRENCH REVOLUTIONARY WARS and Napoleon I swept away the empire. In 1803 the diet deposed and indemnified the majority of princes, creating a smaller number of larger states; in 1804 Francis II took the title Francis I, emperor of Austria; in 1806 the empire was dissolved. The following is a list of German kings and emperors from 919.

Saxon dynasty (919–1024): Henry I, Otto I, Otto II, Otto III, Henry II.

Salian or Franconian dynasty (1024–1125): Conrad II, Henry III, Henry IV, Henry V.

Lothair II (reigned 1125–37; duke of Saxony).

Hohenstaufen dynasty (1138–1254): Conrad III, Frederick I, Henry VI, Philip of Swabia (antiking: Otto IV), Frederick II, Conrad IV (antiking: William, count of Holland).

Interregnum (1254–73): Richard, earl of Cornwall and Alfonso X of Castile, rivals.

Hapsburg, Luxemburg, and other dynasties: Rudolf I (1273–91; Hapsburg); Adolf of Nassau (1292–98); Albert I (1298–1308; Hapsburg); Henry VII (1308–13; Luxemburg); Louis IV (1314–46; Wittelsbach); Charles IV (1346–78; Luxemburg); Wenceslaus (1378–1400; Luxemburg); Rupert (1400–1410; Wittelsbach); Sigismund (1410–37; Luxemburg).

Hapsburg dynasty (1438–1740): Albert II, Frederick III, Maximilian I, Charles V, Ferdinand I, Maximilian II, Rudolf II, Matthias, Ferdinand II, Ferdinand III, Leopold I, Joseph I, Charles VI.

Interregnum (1740–42).

Charles VII (emperor, 1742–45; elector of Bavaria).

Francis I (emperor, 1745–65; ex-duke of Lorraine; husband of Maria Theresa).

Hapsburg-Lorraine dynasty (1765–1806): Joseph II, Leopold II, Francis II.

Holyrood (hŏ'lērōōd) [i.e., holy cross], former residence of Scottish kings, in Edinburgh. David I founded abbey here in 1128. Its Chapel Royal contains remains of several kings. Present building begun 1501; rebuilt after fire of 1650. Scene of murder of David Rizzio (1566).

Holy Sepulcher, church in Jerusalem on the supposed site of Jesus' tomb, officially the Church of the Resurrection. St. HELENA is said to have pointed out the site. Most of the church is controlled by the Orthodox, though other Christian groups have sections.

Holy Spirit: see HOLY GHOST.

Holy Week, week before Easter marked by commemoration of Jesus' passion and death. Chief days are Palm Sunday, Maundy Thursday, Good Friday, and Holy Saturday (Lent ends Saturday at noon).

Holywell (hŏ'lēwĕl), urban district (pop. 8,196), Flintshire, Wales. Gothic chapel (place of pilgrimage for Roman Catholics) covers St. Winifred's Well, which, legend says, sprang up on the spot where St. Winifred was beheaded.

Holywood, urban district (pop. 6,316), Co. Down, N. Ireland. Has ruins of 13th-cent. monastery on the site of one founded in the 7th cent.

Holz, Arno (är'nō hôlts'), 1863–1929, German poet; an influential critic and a founder of the naturalistic school.

Homburg (hôm'bŏŏrk), town (pop. 27,670), Hesse, W Germany; officially called Bad Homburg. Famous spa and fashionable resort. Until 1866 cap. of landgraviate of Hesse-Homburg.

Home, Daniel Dunglas, 1833–86, American spiritualist medium. He claimed to have discovered his gifts at 13 and from 1850 on had triumphant career in U.S. and Europe. His séances produced highly physical manifestations of spirits. Many efforts were made to expose him but none was successful.

Home, John, 1722–1808, Scottish dramatist, author of successful tragedy *Douglas* (1756), which has speech beginning, "My name is Norval."

Homedale, village (pop. 1,411), SW Idaho, on Snake R. near Oregon line, in OWYHEE project.

home economics deals with homemaking and the relation of the home to the community. Formerly (called domestic science) it was limited to problems of food (nutrition and cookery), clothing, sewing, textiles, home equipment and maintenance, and hygiene; today it includes also aspects of family relations, parental education, consumer education, institutional management. Scientific aspects preceded the social, economic, and aesthetic phases. In U.S., home economics on college level dates from the '70s; teaching of cooking and sewing in public schools began in the '80s.

home missions: see MISSIONS.

homeopathy (hōmēŏ'puthē), system of medicine based on principle that disorders are cured by small doses of drugs producing effects similar to the disorder. It was originated by Samuel Hahnemann and gained great popularity (now somewhat dwindled).

Home Owners' Loan Corporation, established (1933) to refinance urban mortgage debt and stabilize depreciated real estate. HOLC lent $3,000,000,000, of which 90 per cent had been liquidated by 1949.

Homer, first Greek poet. His actual existence much debated in 19th cent., but most recent scholars say that such a poet lived before 700 B.C. Legend says that he was blind and that seven cities claimed him. Narrative poems, the ILIAD and the ODYSSEY, are masterpieces of world literature and models for all later epics. The HOMERIC HYMNS, a comic poem (MARGITES), and a mock epic (*The Battle of the Frogs and the Mice*) anciently attributed to him.

Homer, Louise, 1871?–1947, American operatic contralto. Sang at the Metropolitan Opera, New York, 1900–19; at the Chicago Opera until 1924. She sang the principal contralto roles in *Aïda, Il Trovatore,* and

Hansel and Gretel, but considered Orpheus, in Gluck's opera, her greatest role.

Homer, Winslow, 1836–1910, American landscape, marine, and genre painter. Many of his studies of everyday life date from Civil War period when he was a popular magazine illustrator. Best known for his dramatic interpretations of the sea in water color.

Homeric Hymns (hōmĕ'rĭk), hexameter poems, complimentary to the gods, composed c.800–400 B.C., anciently attributed to Homer.

Home Rule. Economic conditions in Ireland gave rise to demand for autonomy. Home Rule movement began in 1870 and was strengthened by rise of Charles Stewart PARNELL who unified Irish party in British Parliament. Accompanied by a campaign of violence in Ireland. First Home Rule Bill introduced by Gladstone (1886) failed to pass. Second Home Rule Bill (1893) was passed by House of Commons but defeated by House of Lords. Third Home Rule Bill passed by Commons (1912) led to threats of civil war and House of Lords excluded Ulster. Bill never took effect because 1916 rebellion led to recognition of the Irish Free State with dominion status in 1921. Since 1949 Republic of Ireland has had no legal ties to Britain. N. Ireland is governed under the Fourth Home Rule Bill of 1920.

home rule, municipal, system permitting cities to draft and amend their own charters without state interference. Adopted first (1875) in Missouri and now also used in other states, it has not—because of great variation from state to state and court strictures—accomplished all that was expected of it.

Homestead, borough (pop. 10,046), SW Pa., on Monongahela R. adjoining Pittsburgh. Iron and steel works (now largely in Munhall borough) were scene of bitter **Homestead strike** (1892). Pinkerton men, hired by Carnegie company, and strikers met in armed battle in which a number of men were killed or wounded. Strike broken when governor called out Natl. Guard.

Homestead Act, 1862, passed by U.S. Congress. It gave a quarter section of unoccupied public land to homesteader for nominal fee after five years' residence. It replaced earlier government practice of selling land for purposes of revenue.

Homestead National Monument of America: see NATIONAL PARKS AND MONUMENTS (table).

Homestead strike: see HOMESTEAD, Pa.

homicide (hŏ'mŭsīd), taking of human life. A homicide is considered excusable if it results from an accident not amounting to culpable negligence. Justifiable homicide is defined variously but generally includes legal execution of criminals, killing committed to prevent a felony or arrest a felon, and killing in self-defense (i.e., committed by someone reasonably fearing death or serious injury at the hands of the person slain). Other homicides are criminal; if committed with malice aforethought the homicide is murder, otherwise manslaughter—though statutes in various states use different terminology.

hominy, hulled corn, coarsely broken or ground. As a pioneer food it was prepared by soaking grains in weak wood lye. Now marketed as hominy grits.

Homma, Masaharu (mäsä'härōō hōmä'), 1888?–1946, Japanese general. Led invasion of Philippines 1941; ordered Bataan "death march." Hanged 1946 as war criminal.

Homs (hôms), anc. *Emesa,* city (pop. c.100,000), W Syria, on Orontes R. and S of Hama. The Roman emperor Heliogabalus was originally a priest of Homs temple to Baal. Here Aurelian defeated Zenobia's forces in 272. Name also written as Hems.

Honan (hō'nän', hŭnän'), province (55,000 sq. mi.; pop. 25,000,000), N central China; cap. Kaifeng. Mountainous with fertile valleys in SW and N. Main products: rice, silk, cotton, peanuts. Some coal and iron mined. Earliest region of Chinese settlement.

Honduras (hŏndōō'rŭs), republic (59,160 sq. mi.; pop. 1,533,625), Central America, bordering on Nicaragua, Salvador, and Guatemala, with Caribbean and Pacific coasts; cap. TEGUCIGALPA. The N (Caribbean coast) has on its W half vast banana plantations owned by U.S. companies; principal ports are Trujillo, La Ceiba, Tela, and Puerto Cortés. S (Pacific) coast largely semiarid and unproductive; has small port of Amapala. Between the coasts are mountain ranges, ending in the E in jungles and swamps of MOSQUITO COAST. Silver mining developed Comayagua and Tegucigalpa, and silver is still exported. First visited by Columbus (1502), it was reached by Cortés (1524) and conquered and settled by Pedro de Alvarado. Gained independence from Spain (1821) then was part of Iturbide's Mexican Empire and a member of the CENTRAL AMERICAN FEDERATION (1825–38). Great Britain long controlled all the Mosquito Coast and the BAY ISLANDS, and Honduras has been involved in long border struggles with neighbors. The country is generally self-sufficient in foodstuffs, but foreign capital is the basic factor in the economy.

Hone, Philip, 1780–1851, American diarist. A successful businessman, he was (1825) mayor of New York. His diary (1828–51) is an invaluable historical record.

Honegger, Arthur (hŭ′nēgŭr), 1892–, Swiss-French composer. His music, often polytonal, ranges from satire to the intensely religious. Besides *Pacific 231,* his best-known works are largely theatrical, such as ballets, the operas *Judith* and *Antigone,* and the oratorio *King David.*

Honesdale, borough (pop. 5,662), NE Pa., on Lackawaxen R. and NE of Scranton. Mfg. of shoes and textiles. First regular trial run of a locomotive in U.S. made here 1829. Was W terminus of Delaware and Hudson Canal.

honey, sweet, viscid fluid produced by the bee from nectar of flowers. Taken into worker bee's honey sack, nectar is converted by enzymes there into glucose and fructose sugars. The bees put the fluid in open wax cells of the honeycomb; after evaporation to proper consistency, it is sealed in. Average bee colony requires for its own use 400–500 lb. of honey a year; at least 20,000 trips to field are needed to make 1 lb. Production on commercial scale is in apiaries. Color and flavor of honey depend upon the kind of flower nectar used.

honey locust, thorny leguminous deciduous tree (*Gleditsia triacanthos*) native to E U.S. and widely planted as a shade tree. It has fragrant flowers and the fruits are long pods often used as cattle feed.

honeysuckle, ornamental shrub or vine of genus *Lonicera,* widely distributed in N Hemisphere. White, red, or purple flowers, usually fragrant, are followed by variously colored berries.

Hong Kong (hŏng′ kŏng′), Chinese *Hsiang-chiang,* British crown colony (391 sq. mi.; pop. 1,850,000), S China, adjoining Kwantung prov.; cap. Hong Kong (Victoria). Comprises Hong Kong isl. (32 sq. mi.) ceded by China in 1842; Kowloon peninsula (c.3 sq. mi.), ceded 1860; and the New Territories (359 sq. mi.), on adjoining mainland area with Mirs Bay, leased in 1898 for 99 years. Hong Kong city is chief port and distributing center for S China; also an international air hub. Surrendered Dec. 25, 1941, to Japan; restored to the British after World War II. Refugees from Communist-held area of China swelled colony's population 1948–49.

Honolulu (hŏnůlōo′lōo), city (pop. 248,034), cap. Territory of Hawaii, on SE shore of Oahu. With Palmyra it constitutes Honolulu co. (pop. 353,020). Chief port of Hawaiian Isls. and vital stopover point for air service between U.S. mainland and Orient. Lies on narrow plain between the sea and Koolau Range. Famous bathing beach at Waikiki. Notable institutions are Univ. of HAWAII, Bishop Mus. (1889), and Acad. of Arts (1926). Iolani Palace (former home of Hawaiian kings) is territorial capitol. Succeeded Lahaina, Maui, as Hawaiian cap. in 1845. Has sugar refineries, pineapple canneries. Pearl Harbor naval base near by.

Honorius I (hŏnô′rēŭs), pope (625–38). Wrote a letter apparently supporting the heresy of MONOTHELETISM. He and the letter were condemned by the Third Council of Constantinople, but this condemnation is held not to affect the doctrine of papal infallibility because Honorius was not speaking *ex cathedra.*

Honorius II, d. 1130, pope (1124–30). As adviser to Paschal II, he concluded the Concordat of Worms (1122) with German King Henry V. Supported Lothair II, who yielded to church demands on episcopal election. Quarreled with Henry I of England.

Honorius III, d. 1227, pope (1216–27), an Italian, successor of Innocent III. He had been tutor to Frederick II, crowned him, and tried in vain to get the emperor to go on crusade.

Honorius, 384–423, West Roman emperor (395–423); son of Theodosius I. His brother Arcadius inherited the East. Honorius had his guardian STILICHO murdered in 408. He held out at Ravenna against ALARIC I (409–10) but made peace with the Visigoths in 412. In 421 he had to make his brother-in-law joint emperor as CONSTANTIUS III. His reign marked important stage in decline of Western Empire.

Honshu (hŏn′shōo), island (c.88,000 sq. mi.; pop. 58,-769,968), central Japan, between Sea of Japan and the Pacific; largest and most important island of Japan. Largely mountainous, rises to 12,389 ft. at Fujiyama; Mt. Asama highest of active volcanoes. Chief lowland area is Kanto Plain in central part. Climate ranges from extreme cold of N to subtropical warmth of S. Frequent earthquakes. Agr. and raw-silk production are widespread. Heavy industry at Yokohama, Tokyo, Nagoya, Osaka, Kobe.

Honthorst, Gerard van (gĕr′ärt vän hŏnt′hŏrst), 1590–1656, Dutch painter, called Gerardo dalle Notti for his preference for nocturnal scenes.

Hooch or **Hoogh, Pieter de** (both: pē′tûr dù hōkh), b. c.1629, d. after 1677, noted Dutch genre painter. Typical themes are quiet domestic interiors, often with housewives and children.

Hood, John Bell, 1831–79, Confederate general. Commanded in ATLANTA CAMPAIGN. Advanced to Nashville, Tenn., where forces were virtually annihilated by G. H. Thomas. Resigned command Jan., 1865.

Hood, Raymond M(athewson), 1881–1934, American architect. Designed Daily News Building (New York).

Hood, Thomas, 1799–1845, English poet, known today especially for poems of sentiment and social protest ("The Bridge of Sighs" and "The Song of the Shirt"). Also wrote humorous verse and prose.

Hood, Mount: see CASCADE RANGE.

Hood College: see FREDERICK, Md.

Hood River, city (pop. 3,701), N Oregon, on Columbia R., E of Portland, and near Mt. Hood. Area noted for fruits (esp. apples). Annual music fete.

hoof, horny epidermal casing at end of digits of an ungulate mammal. In some animals (pig, sheep, cattle) hoof is cloven, in others (horse, zebra) solid.

hoof and mouth disease: see FOOT AND MOUTH DISEASE.

Hooft, Pieter Corneliszoon (hōft), 1581–1647, Dutch historian and poet, author of a classic history (1642, incomplete) of the Netherlands from 1555 to 1584. A fine lyric poet, he introduced into Dutch the tones of French and Italian Renaissance love poetry.

Hoogh, Pieter de: see HOOCH, PIETER DE.

Hooghly (hōo′glē), river, c.200 mi. long, West Bengal, India; arm of Ganges R. Shipping artery to major industrial area around Calcutta. On it is town of Hooghly, founded 1537 by the Portuguese.

Hooke, Robert, 1635–1703, English scientist. He was first to formulate the theory of planetary movements as a mechanical problem. He improved astronomical instruments; devised practical system of telegraphy; invented spiral watch spring; constructed first arithmetical machine and Gregorian telescope. He described cells in plant tissues. **Hooke's law:** within the limit of elasticity, the stress on a body is in direct proportion to strain.

Hooker, Joseph, 1814–79, Union general in Civil War. Known as "Fighting Joe." Commanded Army of the Potomac; defeated at Chancellorsville (1863). Commanded ably in Chattanooga campaign.

Hooker, Richard, 1554?–1600, noted English theologian. His *Of the Laws of Ecclesiastical Polity* formulated concepts of Anglicanism and influenced civil as well as ecclesiastical government.

Hooker, Thomas, 1586–1647, Puritan clergyman in American colonies, chief founder of Hartford, Conn. (1635–36), b. England.

Hooke's law: see HOOKE, ROBERT.

Hook of Holland, Dutch *Hoek van Holland,* port (pop. 2,536), South Holland prov., SW Netherlands, on North Sea; an outer port of Rotterdam. Terminus for Channel crossings from Harwich, England.

hookworm (ancylostomiasis), disease in man caused by certain parasitic nematode worms lodged in intestine. Anemia results from blood sucking and bleeding. Worm eggs passed from intestine of victim develop into larva stage in warm, moist soil, then burrow into skin of persons in contact with infected soil and travel by way of body fluids to lungs and thence to pharynx where they are swallowed.

Hoopeston (hoop'stŭn), city (pop. 5,992), E Ill., N of Danville. Canning (corn, beans) center.

Hoorn or **Horn, Philip de Montmorency, count of** (both: hôrn), 1518?–1568, Netherlands nobleman. Joined EGMONT in protesting Spanish abuses in the Netherlands. Was beheaded after an irregular trial. He is a national hero.

Hoosac Range (hoo'sŭk), S continuation of Green Mts. in SW Vt. and NW Mass., E of the Berkshires. Pierced by 5-mi. railroad tunnel (built 1852–73).

Hooton, Earnest Albert (hoo'tŭn), 1887–, American anthropologist, specialist on early man and primates.

Hoover, Herbert (Clark), 1874–, 30th President of the United States (1929–33), b. Iowa. Before 1915 he engaged in world-wide mining and engineering activities. Headed food administration and war relief bureaus during and after World War I. As U.S. Secretary of Commerce (1921–29), he reorganized and expanded department. Stock market crash of 1929 ushered in an economic depression which continued throughout his administration as president. Hoover recommended extensive public works, appointed commissions to study urgent problems. Destitute farmers were aided by Federal Farm Board. RECONSTRUCTION FINANCE CORPORATION was created. Congress, which had a Democratic majority after 1930 election, passed Emergency Relief Act and created Federal home loan banks. Veterans seeking a bonus marched on Washington; Hoover ordered Federal troops to oust them from Federal property. Disarmament conferences were ineffective (see NAVAL CONFERENCES); debt moratorium which Hoover proposed in 1931 to alleviate Germany's financial situation had no practical results. Hoover left office in 1933 during serious banking crisis. Handled world food problems in 1946. Headed "Hoover Commission" (1947–49), which studied and advised on organization of the executive branch of government.

Hoover, J(ohn) Edgar, 1895–, American administrator, director of the FEDERAL BUREAU OF INVESTIGATION (1924–).

Hoover Dam, in Black Canyon, at Nev.-Ariz. line, in Colorado R.; built 1931–36. One of world's largest, 727 ft. high, 1,282 ft. long. Key unit of projects on Colorado R., it provides water power (mainly to Calif.), flood control, and irrigation. Formerly called Boulder Dam (1933–47). L. Mead, reservoir, 115 mi. long, is resort center.

Hoover Library on War, Revolution, and Peace, at Stanford Univ., Palo Alto, Calif.; estab. 1919 by Herbert Hoover. Contains mostly materials on period of World War I and afterward. Housed in Hoover Tower since 1941.

hop, perennial twining vine (*Humulus lupulus*) grown from early times for brewing purposes. The conelike female flowers, "hops," contain lupulin, a bitter-tasting yellow powder added to beer.

Hopatcong, Lake (hōpăt'kŏn), c.7 mi. long and 3 mi. wide, N N.J., NW of Dover. Summer resort.

Hope, Anthony, pseud. of Sir Anthony Hope Hawkins, 1863–1933, English novelist, known for his romantic *Prisoner of Zenda* (1894).

Hope, city (pop. 8,605), SW Ark., ENE of Texarkana. Shipping center for farm products (esp. watermelons), it has cotton processing, woodworking.

Hopeh or **Ho-pei** (both: hŏ'pä, hŭ'bä'), province (50,-000 sq. mi.; pop. 27,000,000), N China, on Gulf of Chihli of Yellow Sea; cap. Paoting. Bounded in N along Great Wall by Manchuria. Lies entirely on alluvial plain. Crops include wheat, millet, kaoliang, and soybeans. Major coal mines here. Chief centers are Peking and Tientsin. Held 1937–45 by the Japanese; under Chinese Communists since 1949. Formerly called Chihli.

Hope Island: see SPITSBERGEN.

Hopewell. 1 Borough (pop. 1,869), W N.J., N of Trenton. John Hart lived here. Has historical museum. Home for juvenile delinquents near here is former Lindbergh estate (deeded to state 1941). **2** City (pop. 10,219), E Va., at junction of James and Appomattox rivers; founded 1913 as munitions center. Mfg. of rayon, chemicals, and cans. City Point (annexed 1926) was Grant's base of operations in 1864–65.

Hopewell Village, national historic site, SE Pa., SE of Birdsboro. Restored iron-making village of 18th and 19th cent.

Hophni (hŏf'nī), wicked son of Eli. See PHINEHAS.

Hopi Indians (hō'pē), tribe of Pueblo Indians, formerly called Moki, or Moqui. Almost all speak Hopi language (Uto-Aztecan family). They live in pueblos, practice sedentary farming (corn, beans, squash), with irrigation. The highly developed Hopi culture is typical of Southwest Indians.

Hopkins, Sir Frederick Gowland, 1861–1947, English biochemist. Shared 1929 Nobel Prize in Physiology and Medicine for pioneer work on vitamins. Authority on carbohydrate metabolism and muscular activity.

Hopkins, Gerard Manley, 1844–89, English poet. Followed Newman into Roman Catholicism, and became a Jesuit. Wrote best poetry after shipwreck called forth "Wreck of the Deutschland." His *Poems,* edited by Robert Bridges, appeared in 1918, and have had much influence on 20th-cent. poets.

Hopkins, Harry (Lloyd), 1890–1946, American public official. Intimate friend of Pres. F. D. Roosevelt, held high posts as his special assistant.

Hopkins, Johns, 1795–1873, American financier and philanthropist. In 1867 he founded a free hospital and Johns Hopkins Univ. at Baltimore.

Hopkins, Mark, 1802–87, American educator. He was professor of philosophy at Williams until his death and president of the college from 1836 to 1872. He was also president of American Board of Commissioners for Foreign Missions, 1857–87.

Hopkins, Samuel, 1721–1803, New England clergyman and theologian. He adopted doctrine of Jonathan Edwards as basis of his own, called Hopkinsianism.

Hopkins, Stephen, 1707–85, colonial governor of R.I., American Revolutionary patriot, signer of Declaration of Independence. Governor for nine years between 1755 and 1768.

Hopkins, village (pop. 7,595), E Minn., SW suburb of Minneapolis, in truck-farm area. Mfg. of farm machinery.

Hopkinson, Francis, 1737–91, American writer and musician, signer of Declaration of Independence. Considered first native American composer. Wrote political satires.

Hopkinsville, city (pop. 12,526), S Ky., WSW of Bowling Green. Tobacco and livestock market with mfg. of clothing. Jefferson Davis Memorial Park near by.

Hopkinton, town (pop. 1,831), S N.H., W of Concord.

Long Memorial Library holds New Hampshire Antiquarian Society collection. Congregational Church (1789) has a Paul Revere bell.

Hoppe, William Frederick (Willie Hoppe) (hŏ′pē), 1887–, American billiards champion. Generally acknowledged world's billiard champion since 1906.

Hopper, DeWolf, 1858–1935, American singer and comedian. Associated (1895–1904) with Weber and Fields, he later sang in Gilbert and Sullivan operettas (e.g., Bunthorne in *Patience*). Made recitation "Casey at the Bat" famous.

Hopper, Edward, 1882–, American painter. Excels in realistic pictures of sunlit streets and houses.

Hoppner, John, 1758–1810, English portrait painter, known for idealized portraits of women and children. Was a protégé of George III.

hops: see HOP.

Hoquiam (hō′kweŭm), city (pop. 11,123), W Wash., on Grays Harbor adjoining ABERDEEN; settled 1859.

Hor, mountain (4,383 ft.), SW Jordan, overlooking ruins of Petra. Peak was scene of Aaron's death. Num. 20. Called Jebel Nebi Harun in Arabic. The Hor of Num. 34.7 is probably Mt. Hermon.

Horace (Quintus Horatius Flaccus), 65 B.C.–8 B.C., Latin lyric poet. Vergil introduced him to MAECENAS, who became his patron. His *Satires* and *Epodes* (35–29 B.C.) established him as leading lyric poet in Rome. The *Odes, Epistles,* and *Ars Poetica,* products of his mature years at Sabine farm, display his mastery of phrase and poetic form. His verse, though it owes something to the Greek Archilochus, reflects an emancipated Roman cultivation of the arts and the true spirit of the Augustan Age. He was an urbane Epicurean, and the pungency, beauty, and descriptive power of his verse influenced greatly English poetry.

Horae (hō′rē), three Greek symbolic personages, controlling order of nature and recurrence of seasons; daughters of Zeus and Themis. They were Irene, (īrē′nē), i.e., Peace, Dice (dī′sē), i.e., Justice, and Eunomia (ūnō′mēū), i.e., Order.

Horatius (hōrā′shŭs), legendary Roman hero. He and two companions held Lars Porsena's Etruscan army at bay while the Romans cut down the Sublician Bridge to protect the city. He then swam the Tiber safely and was given as much land as he could plow around in a day.

Horeb, mountain where God appeared to Moses in burning bush. Ex. 3–4.17. May be same as Mt. SINAI.

horehound, aromatic Old World perennial herb (*Marrubium vulgare*) with woolly-white foliage. Used to make horehound candy and cough and cold remedies.

Horemheb: see HARMHAB.

hormone: see GLAND and SECRETION.

Hormuz (hôr′mŭz″) or **Ormuz,** island, off S Iran, in Strait of Hormuz between Persian Gulf and Gulf of Oman. Town of Hormuz was chief trade center for Persian Gulf area, 16th–17th cent. Portuguese under Afonso de Albuquerque took the island (1507–14), but lost it (1622) to Persian-English forces.

Horn, Philip de Montmorency, count of: see HOORN.

horn, in biology, organ projecting from head of animal and used chiefly in offense and defense. Three main types among mammals: hollow, permanent, unbranched horns, each horn overlying a bony core growing on skull (as in cattle, sheep, buffalo, musk oxen, Old World antelopes, related animals); branched horns or antlers of DEER family composed of true bone, usually shed annually; and that of the PRONGHORN, with characteristics of both bovine and deer types. Rhinoceros horns derive entirely from epidermis of skin of snout; probably are modified hairs.

horn, in music: see WIND INSTRUMENTS.

Horn, Cape, headland, 1,391 ft. high, S Chile, most southerly point of South America, in archipelago of Tierra del Fuego. Discovered and first rounded by Willem Schouten in 1616.

Hornaday, William Temple (hôr′nŭdā), 1854–1937, American naturalist, leader in wildlife conservation.

hornbeam, deciduous tree of genus *Carpinus* native to N Hemisphere. American hornbeam, blue beech, or ironwood (*Carpinus caroliniana*) has strong wood used for tool handles, etc. The hop hornbeam (*Ostrya virginiana*), also called ironwood, and of same family, has wood of similar strength and value.

horned toad, lizard, several species of which live in deserts of SW U.S. and Mexico. Body (3–5 in. long) is broad and flattened, the tail short and thin, and the legs short. Spines are on the head; some scales on sides and back are sharp. It is protectively colored, usually dull grays and browns.

Hornell, city (pop. 15,049), S N.Y., S of Rochester. Mfg. of textiles, clothing, and furniture.

hornet: see WASP.

Horney, Karen, 1885–1952, American psychiatrist, b. Germany. She was founder (1941) and dean of American Inst. of Psychoanalysis. She modified orthodox Freudian analysis by emphasis on social factors, holding that environmental disturbances cause "basic anxiety" that forces one to meet problems in new ways (neurotic because rigid and compulsive).

Hornsby, Rogers, 1896–, American baseball player and manager. Had lifetime batting average of .358 in 19 major-league seasons, hit (1924) .424, a 20th-cent. major-league record, was Natl. League batting champion seven times.

horoscope: see ASTROLOGY.

Horowitz, Vladimir (hô′rōwĭts), 1904–, Russian-American pianist, known for his technical virtuosity; son-in-law of Toscanini. Made his American debut in 1928 with the New York Philharmonic.

Horsa: see HENGIST AND HORSA.

horse. The horse family (Equidae) is now represented by only one genus (*Equus*) which includes the horse, the ASS, the ZEBRA, and the QUAGGA (extinct from 1872). Evolution of the horse from its tiny primitive ancestor (*Eohippus*) occurred in North America, whence it reached the Old World over a now vanished land bridge. Horses became extinct in America about the time the Indians arrived. One of the last animals to be domesticated, the horse was probably first tamed by central Asian nomads. First used in hunting and war, it did not supersede the ox for farm work until the 19th cent. Modern draft horses owe much of their quality to the breeding of heavy chargers in the Middle Ages. The Percheron, of French origin, is the chief draft breed in America. The Arabian breed has the longest history; it and the thoroughbred are primarily saddle horses. All wild horses now living, except the TARPAN, are descended from tame horses. See also MUSTANG.

Horse Cave, town (pop. 1,545), S Ky., E of Mammoth Cave Natl. Park. Resort of cave area; Hidden River Cave underlies part of town.

horse chestnut, deciduous tree (*Aesculus hippocastanum*) of Mediterranean region, widely planted for ornament and shade. It has pyramidal clusters of white or salmon flowers and nonedible chestnutlike fruits.

horsefly, large, swift, hairy fly of family Tabanidae, a common pest of stock and sometimes of humans. Male sucks flower nectar; female sucks blood as well. Some transmit disease. In North America are nearly 200 species of genus *Tabanus.* Genus *Chrysops* includes smaller horseflies; some attack man. Eggs are laid on plants or stones close to water.

horsehair worm: see HAIRWORM.

horse latitudes, two belts of calms (with generally fair weather) between trade winds and prevailing westerlies; about 30° or 35° N and S.

horsepower, unit of power (rate of doing work) originated by James Watt. He determined experimentally that a horse can do work equal to 33,000 foot-pounds per minute; this unit is now standard in computing power generated by an engine.

horse-radish, perennial herb (*Armoracia lapathifolia*) native to S and central Europe and naturalized in North America. The grated roots are mixed with vinegar to make a sharp sauce for meats and sea food.

SMALL CAPITALS = cross references. Pronunciation key on inside end pages. Abbreviations: p. 2.

horsetail, perennial rushlike plants of genus *Equisetum*, related to ferns and club mosses. They have jointed hollow stems and small scaly leaves.

Horsley, Samuel, 1733–1806, English bishop and scientist, particularly remembered for controversy (c.1783–1790) with Joseph Priestley concerning doctrine of Christ's incarnation.

Horsley, Sir Victor, 1857–1916, English surgeon, a specialist in surgery of the ductless glands and the nervous system.

Horta (hôr′tû), city (pop. 8,184), cap. of Horta dist., Portugal, on Fayal isl., one of Azores.

Horthy (de Nagybanya), Nicholas (hôr′tē dù nŏ′dyûbä′nyŏ), Hung. *Nagybányai Horthy Miklós,* 1868–, Hungarian admiral and statesman. Headed counterrevolutionary government during Communist dictatorship of Bela Kun (1919); was regent of HUNGARY 1920–44. Forced to resign by German pressure after his attempt to make an armistice with Russia, he fled to Bavaria, where he later was briefly held a prisoner by the U.S. army (1945).

horticulture, a branch of agr.; includes cultivation of ornamental plants, market gardening, fruit growing, landscape gardening. Known to prehistoric peoples and in civilizations of both East and West. Formal gardening developed first in irrigated regions of Orient. Crusaders disseminated in Europe many ideas gathered from Eastern gardens. Horticulture has become a complex science; the Dept. of Agr., state experiment stations, agr. colleges, and horticultural societies in the U.S. provide information.

Horus (hō′rùs), sun-god, one of great gods of EGYPTIAN RELIGION, often identified with Amon. A popular myth tells how he avenged death of father, Osiris, aided by his mother, ISIS, and the god Thoth.

Hosanna [perhaps Heb.,= save now; cf. Ps. 118.25,26], word shouted in greeting to Jesus as He entered Jerusalem. Mat. 21.9,15; Mark 11.9,10; John 12.13. Mistaken by early Christians as a joyous salutation; in this sense widely used in Christian worship today.

Hosea (hōzē′ù) or **Osee** (ōsē′), book of Old Testament, written by prophet of 8th cent. B.C. Book contains allegory comparing the idolatrous Israel to a faithless woman; sermons against moral decadence; promise that after punishment will come redemption.

Hoshea (hōshē′ù). **1** See JOSHUA. **2** Died after 722 B.C., last king of Israel (c.730–722 B.C.). A vassal of king of Assyria, he rebelled. Israel was invaded, Hoshea taken prisoner. 2 Kings 15.30; 17.

Hospitalers: see KNIGHTS HOSPITALERS.

Host, in Roman Catholic communion: see EUCHARIST.

hostage (hŏ′stïj), person delivered by a constituted authority to another as guarantee that some stated promise will be executed or some stated loyalty upheld. In the Middle Ages the practice of giving hostages for fulfillment of treaty obligations was common and was governed by a strict code of feudal honor; this practice was generally abandoned in the 18th cent. The fundamental idea was that the hostage might be killed if the obligation was not fulfilled. By extension the seizure of civilians in an occupied country is called taking of hostages. The practice has been known since early times. In World War II the Germans used it ruthlessly in an attempt to put down resistance movements. Germans responsible for the massacre of such hostages were tried as war criminals.

Hostos, Eugenio María de (āŏŏhā′nyŏ märē′ä dā ō′stōs), 1839–1903, Latin American philosopher, sociologist, writer, and political and educational reformer, b. Puerto Rico.

hothouse: see GREENHOUSE.

Hotin, Ukraine: see KHOTIN.

Hot Springs. 1 Resort city (pop. 29,307), SW central Ark., in Ouachita Mts. SW of Little Rock; settled 1807. It is in Hot Springs Natl. Park. **2** See TRUTH OR CONSEQUENCES, N.Mex. **3** City (pop. 5,030), SW S.Dak., SSW of Rapid City, near Cheyenne R. and the Black Hills. Health resort with hot sulphur springs. Fossil Cycad and Jewel Cave national monuments and Wind Cave Natl. Park are near. **4** Famous resort, western Va., WSW of Staunton, in a valley of the Allegheny Mts.

Hot Springs National Park: see NATIONAL PARKS AND MONUMENTS, table.

Hotspur: see PERCY, SIR HENRY.

Hottentots (hŏ′tûntŏts″), people ⍺f S and SW Africa numbering c.20,000 and resembling the Bushmen in language and physical type. They were forced into the interior by Dutch. Economy based on herding with some farming and metallurgy.

Hötzendorf, Franz Conrad von: see CONRAD VON HÖTZENDORF, FRANZ.

Houdin, Jean Eugène Robert (zhä′ ûzhĕn′ rōbĕr′ ōōdĕ′), 1805–71, French conjurer and magician. He was noted for his optical illusions and for fact that he made no claim that his devices were supernatural.

Houdini, Harry (hōōdē′nē), 1874–1926, American magician and writer. Born Erich Weiss, he took his stage name after the French magician Houdin. He was world famed for escapes from bonds and noted for his exposure of fraudulent mediums and their phenomena.

Houdon, Jean Antoine (zhä′ ätwän′ ōōdō′), 1741–1828, French sculptor. His portrait sculpture has hardly been surpassed (esp. his *Voltaire* in Comédie Française). Bronze copy of his *Washington* and his *Bathers* are in Metropolitan Mus.

Houghton, Richard Monckton Milnes, 1st Baron (hō′tûn, hou′–), 1809–85, English author, philanthropist, and patron of letters.

Houghton (hō′tûn), village (pop. 3,829), extreme N Mich., opposite Hancock on Keweenaw Waterway. Here are Michigan Col. of Mining and Technology and mainland hq. of Isle Royale Natl. Park.

Hougue, La, France: see HOGUE, LA.

Houlton (hōl′tûn), town (pop. 8,377), including Houlton village (pop. 6,029), E Maine, NNE of Bangor, near N.B. line. Potato-growing and resort center.

Houma (hō′mù), city (pop. 11,505), SE La., on Bayou Terrebonne and SW of New Orleans; founded 1834. On Intercoastal Waterway, it processes and ships seafood, fur, oil, and sugar cane.

hound. Certain hunting dogs of various breeds are known as hounds. Usually hounds are classified as to whether they follow the prey chiefly by scent (e.g., dachshund, beagle, foxhound, bloodhound, and great Dane) or by sight (e.g., greyhound, Afghan hound, Irish wolfhound, and borzoi or Russian wolfhound). The dachshund is distinguished by its long body and short legs—a body three times as long as the dog is high at the shoulder being considered a good proportion. It has an elongated, tapered head, forefeet that turn outward, and ears of medium length. Its coat may be smooth, wiry, or long-haired. The beagle is a small (not over 15 in. high), smooth-haired dog with ears of medium length. The larger foxhound is bred for speed and used in packs. Like the beagle, it has the typical hound markings—black saddle, tan on legs, hips, and shoulder, with a varying amount of white. The bloodhound has very long soft ears and thin, loose skin falling in folds around head and neck. It combines the hound colors of black or red with tan or tawny, stands 25–27 in. high, and weighs c.90 lb. Its remarkable sense of smell makes it valuable in following a trail in police work. It has a gentle disposition. The great Dane (c.30 in. at shoulder), is a sleek, short-haired dog of obscure origin. In color it varies from brindle, fawn, or black, to white with black spots. It is powerful and fast and makes an excellent watch dog. The greyhound is a tall (28–31 in. at shoulder), slender dog with narrow pointed nose and short hair; it is usually gray in color. Graceful and very swift, it is trained for racing and sometimes achieves speeds of 35 mi. per hour or more. Related to the greyhound is the Afghan hound. Its coat is thick and silky; its head has a topknot; and its legs and ears are feathered. The term *wolfhound* is applied to several breeds of dogs but especially to the Irish wolfhound and the borzoi or Russian wolfhound. The Irish wolfhound is more robust than the greyhound but less massive than the great Dane. Tallest of dogs, it may reach 36 in. at the shoulder, weighs at least 120 lb., and is cream, brindle, or gray to black in color. The borzoi is 30 in. high, weighs 75–105 lb., and has a long narrow head. It is usually white marked with lemon, tan, black, or gray.

Hounslow, suburb in Heston and Isleworth urban district, Middlesex, England, W of London; once an important coach stop. Hounslow Heath, near here, was noted as a resort for highwaymen.

hours of labor: see LABOR, HOURS OF.

Housatonic (hŏŏsŭtŏn′ĭk), river rising in the Berkshires, W Mass., and flowing c.130 mi. S through Conn. to Long Isl. Sound at Milford.

House, E(dward) M(andell), 1858–1938, American statesman. Col. House (a Texas state title) was a confidant of Pres. Woodrow Wilson. Helped to draft Treaty of Versailles, particularly concerned with drawing up of Covenant of the League of Nations.

housefly, common name of *Musca domestica,* found over most of world. It visits excrement and other filth and transports bacteria, protozoa of many diseases (typhoid fever, cholera, dysentery) in its digestive system, on hairy body, and sticky foot pads. Breeds in manure and other decaying organic matter; larvae are white maggots. It ejects a liquefying material on food before eating it. See *ill.,* p. 469.

House of Commons: see PARLIAMENT; WESTMINSTER PALACE.

House of David: see BENTON HARBOR, Mich.

House of Lords: see PARLIAMENT; WESTMINSTER PALACE.

House of Representatives: see CONGRESS OF THE UNITED STATES.

housing, the living accommodations provided for people in a community. Housing for workers during Industrial Revolution was constructed by employers on a profit basis. First housing legislation in U.S. was N.Y. tenement house law of 1867. Government housing began in World War I. Housing shortages in Europe in the '20s resulted in government construction of workers' apartments. In England the GARDEN CITY was developed. In 1934, U.S. set up the Federal Housing Administration to insure private loans and mortgages; in 1937 the U.S. Housing Authority was established; and in 1942 the Federal Public Housing Authority was formed. Mass production methods, such as prefabrication, are now widely used.

Housman, A(lfred) E(dward), 1859–1936, English poet. A classical scholar, he edited Manlius, Juvenal, and Lucian. He is best known for his lyrics, such as "Bredon Hill" and "Loveliest of Trees." Volumes include *A Shropshire Lad* (1896), *Last Poems* (1922), and *Collected Poems* (1940). His brother **Laurence Housman,** 1865–, author and artist, is best known for *Victoria Regina* (1934), a dramatic biography compiled from his play cycle *Palace Plays* (1930–33).

Houssay, Bernardo Alberto (bĕrnär′dhō älbĕr′tō o͞o′sī), 1887–, Argentine physiologist. Shared 1947 Nobel Prize in Physiology and Medicine for demonstrating role of pituitary secretion in inhibiting body's use of insulin.

Houston, Sam(uel) (hū′stùn), 1793–1863, American frontier hero and statesman of Texas. Commanding Texas revolutionary troops, he captured Santa Anna at battle of SAN JACINTO (April 21, 1836). First president of Texas republic 1836–38; again president 1841–44. U.S. Senator 1846–59. Governor of Texas 1859–61; his refusal to join the Confederacy brought about his removal.

Houston (hū′stùn) [for Gen. Samuel Houston], city, (pop. 596,163), S Texas, on Gulf Coast plain NW of Galveston Bay. Harrisburg (now part of Houston) settled 1823; Houston settled 1836. Cap. of Texas republic 1837–39. Grew in 19th cent. as railroad and shipping center. Great expansion came with ship canal (1912–14; making it deepwater port), and development of Gulf Coast oil fields. One of main U.S. ports and Texas' largest city, it has mfg. of metals, chemicals, food products, and paper; also oil refineries. World War II brought many industries, including shipbuilding. Seat of RICE INSTITUTE and Texas Medical Center. Battlefield of SAN JACINTO is near by.

Hovenden, Thomas, 1840–95, American genre painter, b. Ireland; studied in New York and Paris.

Hovenweep National Monument: see NATIONAL PARKS AND MONUMENTS (table).

Hovey, Richard (hŭ′vē), 1864–1900, American poet, author of *Songs from Vagabondia* (1894; with Bliss Carman).

Howard, British noble family. First called Hereward, their career in England goes back to 10th cent. A Hereward fought against William I. His descendants were created earls of Arundel (1139), Barons Maltravers (1330), earls of Surrey and dukes of Norfolk (1483), Barons Fitzalan (1627), earls of Norfolk (1644), and Barons Herries (1884). **John Howard,** 1st **duke of Norfolk,** 1430–85, adherent of the house of York in the Wars of the Roses, was killed at Bosworth fighting for Richard III. His son, **Thomas Howard,** 2d **duke of Norfolk,** 1443–1524, was imprisoned after Bosworth but released by Henry VII. Arranged the marriage of Margaret Tudor and James IV of Scotland. Became leading general of England and defeated (1513) the Scots at Flodden. He is the ancestor of all the living Howards in the main line. His son, **Thomas Howard,** 3d **duke of Norfolk,** 1473–1554, bitterly opposed Cardinal Wolsey. Supported the marriage of his niece, Anne Boleyn, to Henry VIII but later presided at her trial and execution. Remained Catholic although he conducted campaign against Pilgrimage of Grace in 1536. Accused of treason (1546), he was saved by death of Henry. Mary I released him (1553) and he led campaign against Wyatt's rebellion. His power had waned since the execution of his niece, **Catherine Howard,** 1521?–1547, queen of England, fifth wife of Henry VIII. Married in 1540, she was accused (1541) of immoral conduct and confessed. Beheaded largely to rid Henry of Howard family influence. **Henry Howard, earl of Surrey,** c.1517–1547, was the son of the 3d duke of Norfolk. A poet, he introduced new forms (chiefly blank verse) into English poetry. Arrested with his father on questionable treason charges, he was beheaded. His son, **Thomas Howard,** 4th **duke of Norfolk,** 1536–72, was favored by Elizabeth but jealous of the earl of Leicester. Became a candidate for the hand of Mary Queen of Scots and aroused Elizabeth's suspicions. Imprisoned (1569–70), he became involved in a Spanish plot on his release and was beheaded. His brother, **Henry Howard, earl of Northampton,** 1540–1614, was a courtier known for his great learning and lack of principle in public life. His cousin, **Charles Howard,** 1st **earl of Nottingham,** 1536–1624, was lord high admiral of England and commanded (1588) the forces against the Spanish Armada. **Thomas Howard,** 1st **earl of Suffolk,** 1561–1626, was son of the 4th duke of Norfolk. Commanded squadron that attacked Spanish treasure fleet in 1591. Became lord high treasurer in 1614. His daughter, Frances, and her husband, the earl of Somerset, were tried (1615) and convicted of the murder of Sir Thomas Overbury. Convicted (1619) of fraud and embezzlement as treasurer, Suffolk never regained power. **William Howard,** 1st **Viscount Stafford,** 1614–80, was the son of Thomas Howard, 2d earl of ARUNDEL. Falsely accused at the time of Popish Plot, he was convicted on false testimony of Titus Oates and others and beheaded. Other prominent Howards have included **Charles Howard,** 1st **earl of Carlisle,** 1629–85; **Frederick Howard,** 5th **earl of Carlisle,** 1748–1825, viceroy of Ireland and guardian of Lord Byron; and **Esme William Howard,** 1st **Baron Howard of**

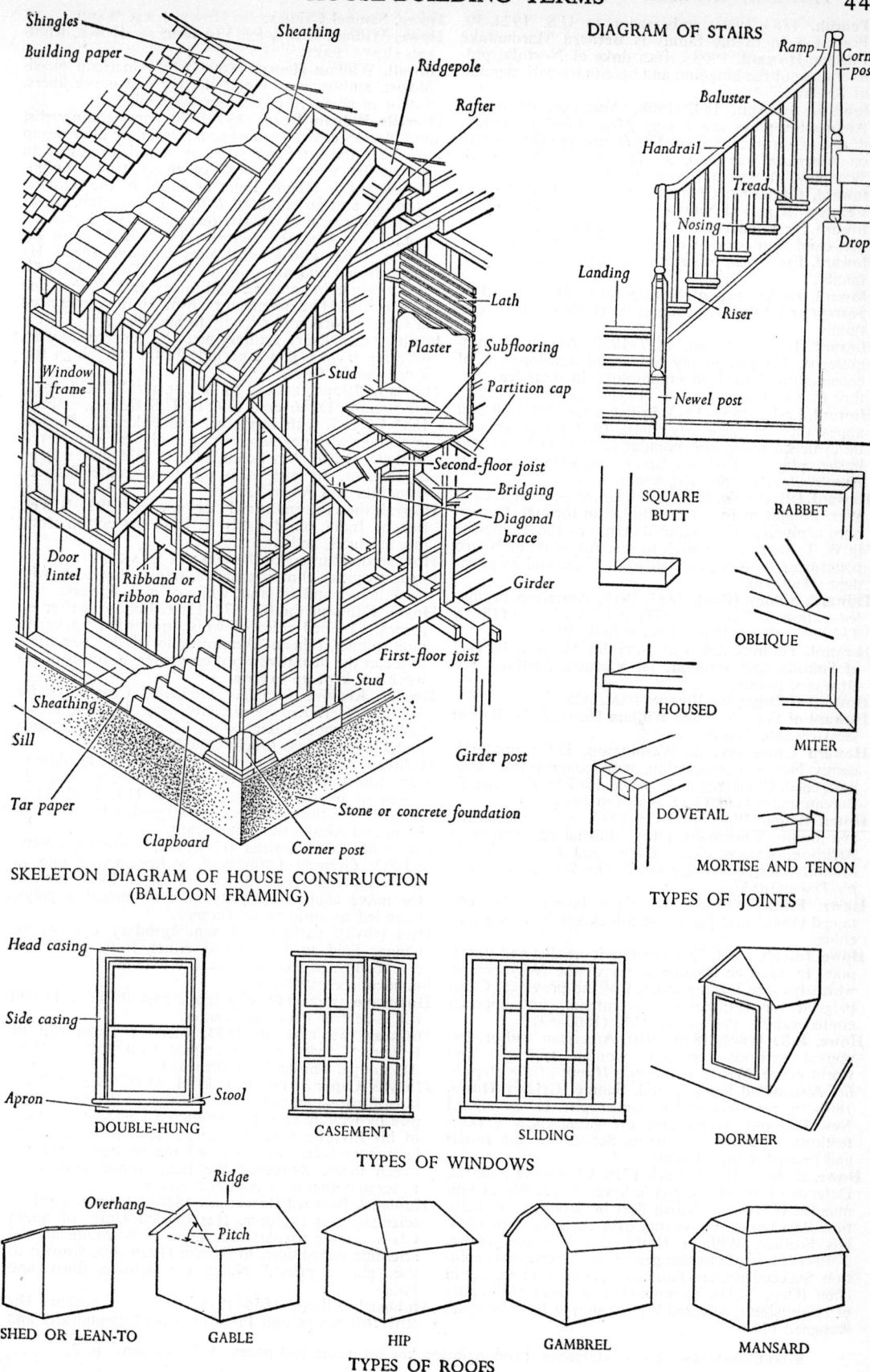

DIAGRAM OF STAIRS

Ramp · Corner post · Baluster · Handrail · Tread · Nosing · Drop · Landing · Riser · Newel post

Shingles · Building paper · Sheathing · Ridgepole · Rafter · Lath · Plaster · Subflooring · Partition cap · Stud · Window frame · Second-floor joist · Bridging · Diagonal brace · Door lintel · Ribband or ribbon board · Girder · First-floor joist · Sheathing · Stud · Sill · Girder post · Tar paper · Clapboard · Corner post · Stone or concrete foundation

SKELETON DIAGRAM OF HOUSE CONSTRUCTION (BALLOON FRAMING)

TYPES OF JOINTS

SQUARE BUTT · RABBET · OBLIQUE · HOUSED · MITER · DOVETAIL · MORTISE AND TENON

Head casing · Side casing · Apron · Stool

DOUBLE-HUNG · CASEMENT · SLIDING · DORMER

TYPES OF WINDOWS

Ridge · Overhang · Pitch

SHED OR LEAN-TO · GABLE · HIP · GAMBREL · MANSARD

TYPES OF ROOFS

Penrith, 1863–1939, ambassador to U.S. 1924–30. Present head of the family is **Bernard Marmaduke Fitzalan-Howard,** 1908–, 16th **duke of Norfolk,** premier duke of the kingdom and hereditary earl marshal of England.

Howard, Bronson, 1842–1908, American dramatist. Among his plays are *Young Mrs. Winthrop* (1882; drama of social criticism), *The Henrietta* (1887; satire on American business), *Shenandoah* (1888; a Civil War play), and *Aristocracy* (1892).

Howard, Catherine; Charles, 1st **earl of Carlisle; and Charles,** 1st **earl of Nottingham:** see HOWARD, family.

Howard, Sir Ebenezer, 1850–1928, English town planner, chief founder of English garden-city movement.

Howard, Frederick, 5th **earl of Carlisle:** see HOWARD, family.

Howard, Henry, earl of Northampton; Henry, earl of Surrey; and John, 1st **duke of Norfolk:** see HOWARD, family.

Howard, Leland Ossian, 1857–1950, American entomologist. He profoundly influenced development of economic and medical entomology in America. Author of *The Insect Menace* (1931) and other works.

Howard, Leslie, 1893–1943, British actor. After his first appearance (in *Peg o' My Heart,* 1917) his air of gentle cynicism made him popular in U.S. and England in such plays as *Berkeley Square* and such films as *Of Human Bondage* and *Pygmalion.*

Howard, Oliver Otis, 1830–1909, Union general in Civil War. Fought in East from Bull Run through Gettysburg campaign. Commanded Army of the Tennessee in W. T. Sherman's march to sea. Advocate of Negro betterment, a founder of Howard Univ. and its president (1869–73).

Howard, Sidney (Coe), 1891–1939, American dramatist, author of *They Knew What They Wanted* (1924), *The Silver Cord* (1926), *Yellow Jack* (1934).

Howard, Thomas, dukes of Norfolk; Thomas, 1st **earl of Suffolk; and William,** 1st **Viscount Stafford:** see HOWARD, family.

Howard College: see BIRMINGHAM, Ala.

Howard of Penrith, Esme William Howard, 1st **Baron:** see HOWARD, family.

Howard University, at Washington, D.C.; predominantly Negro, nonsectarian, with congressional support, coed. Chartered and opened 1867 by Freedmen's Bureau under Gen. O. O. HOWARD and others.

Howe, Ed(gar Watson), 1853–1937, American editor and author. Known for pithy editorial paragraphs in Atchison, Kansas, *Daily Globe* and *E. W. Howe's Monthly.* Wrote realistic novel, *The Story of a Country Town* (1883).

Howe, Elias, 1819–67, American inventor. He obtained (1846) first patent on a lock-stitch sewing machine.

Howe, Joseph, 1804–73, Canadian journalist and statesman. In 1828 he became editor of the *Novascotian,* which became leading journal of the province. Campaigned for responsible government, but opposed confederation. Premier of N.S. (1860–63).

Howe, Julia Ward, 1819–1910, American author. Espoused reforms—abolition, woman suffrage, and world peace. Wrote *The Battle Hymn of the Republic.* Also aided her husband, **Samuel Gridley Howe,** 1801–76, reformer and philanthropist. He organized New England Asylum for the Blind (now Perkins Institution and Massachusetts School for the Blind) and headed it for 44 years.

Howe, Richard Howe, Earl, 1726–99, British admiral. Defended English channel in Seven Years War. Commanded (1776–78) British fleet in American Revolution. Best known for victory over the French in 1794. His brother, **William Howe,** 5th **Viscount Howe,** 1729–1814, was a British general in American Revolution. Succeeded Gen. Thomas Gage as commander in chief (Oct., 1775). Commanded in successful battle of Long Island; defeated Washington at BRANDYWINE. Resigned 1778.

Howe, Samuel Gridley: see HOWE, JULIA WARD.

Howe, William Howe, 5th **Viscount:** see HOWE, RICHARD HOWE, EARL.

Howell, William Henry, 1860–1945, American physiologist, authority on blood clotting and nerve fibers, author of standard physiology textbook.

Howells, William Dean, 1837–1920, American novelist and literary critic. Trained as a printer, he later began to write, and after five years as American consul in Venice he wrote the first of many travel books, *Venetian Life* (1866). Later as editor of the *Atlantic Monthly* and an editor of *Harper's Magazine,* he set forth his critical ideas. His own novels were realistic (e.g., *Their Wedding Journey,* 1872; *A Modern Instance,* 1882; *The Rise of Silas Lapham,* 1885). He was a friend and an editor of Mark Twain. Howells also wrote light comedies and farces. In *Criticism and Fiction* (1891) he defended realism. He was interested in social reform and friendly to Socialism.

howitzer (hou′ĭtsŭr), artillery piece longer than mortar, differing from a gun especially in the very high trajectory of its fire.

Howland Island, area 1 sq. mi., central Pacific near the equator. Discovered 1842 by U.S. traders, claimed 1857 by U.S. with Jarvis Isl. and Baker Isl. Became important with development of Pacific air commerce. Settled 1935 by Americans, placed 1936 under Dept. of Interior. Its airfield is on direct route between Honolulu and Australia.

Howrah (hou′rä), industrial city (pop. 379,292), S West Bengal, India, on Hooghly R. Produces cotton cloth, jute products, and steel.

Hoy, second largest of the ORKNEY ISLANDS.

hoya, tropical climbing shrub (*Hoya carnosa*) with thick leaves and fragrant white or pink flowers.

Hoyle, Edmond (hoil), 1672–1769, English writer on games. Codified rules of whist, quadrille, backgammon, piquet, others. "According to Hoyle" has come to mean the definitive word on games. Editions of his work are kept up to date.

Hradec Kralove (hrä′dĕts krä′lôvĕ), Czech *Hradec Králové,* Ger. *Königgrätz,* city (pop. 19,242), E Bohemia, Czechoslovakia, on the Elbe. Battle of SADOWA or Königgrätz was fought near by (1866).

Hrdlicka, Ales (ä′lĕsh hŭrd′lĭchkä), 1869–1943, American anthropologist, b. Bohemia. He organized division of physical anthropology at U.S. Natl. Mus. His investigations of supposed migration tracks in Siberia and Alaska were significant.

Hroswitha or **Roswitha** (rōswĭ′thŭ, rôsvē′tä), c.940–c.1002, German Latin poet, a Benedictine nun at Gandersheim. Wrote lyrics; six saints' lives, notable for naïve charm and piety; and six morality plays, intended as antidote to Terence.

Hsia (shyä), earliest and semilegendary dynasty of China. Said to have ruled either from c.2205 to c.1766 B.C. or from c.1994 to c.1523 B.C.

huanaco: see GUANACO.

Huancayo (wän-kī′ō), city (pop. 28,680; alt. c.11,000 ft.), S central Peru; agr. center.

Huáscar (wäs′kär), d. 1533, Inca of Peru; son of Huayna Capac. Shared empire with half brother, Atahualpa, who had him drowned.

Huayna Capac (wī′nä kä′päk), d. 1525, Inca of Peru, last of great emperors. His decision to divide his empire by leaving recently conquered kingdom of Quito to his favorite son, Atahualpa, and the rest to his legitimate heir, Huascar, and the resultant war between them, weakened the Inca empire and made Francisco Pizarro's conquest easier.

Hubbard, Bernard Rosecrans, 1888–, American priest, scientist, and explorer. Has headed Univ. of Santa Clara geology department since 1926. Made annual scientific expeditions to Alaska (1926–43). Known as the "glacier priest." Noted for lectures, films, and books.

Hubbard, Elbert, 1856–1915, American author. His Roycroft Shops and Press promoted handicrafts and bookmaking. Wrote *Little Journeys* to homes of the great and the inspirational *Message to Garcia* (1899).

Hubbardton, town (pop. 332), W Vt., NW of Rutland, near L. Bomoseen. Near here, troops under Seth WARNER, covering St. Clair's retreat from Ticonderoga, were routed by British, July 7, 1777.

Hubbell, Carl (Owen), 1903–, American baseball pitcher. Left-handed N.Y. Giant ace won 24 consecutive games in 1936–37 seasons, won 253 major-league games.

Hubble, Edwin Powell, 1889–, American astronomer, noted for systematic investigation of nebulae outside of Milky Way system.

Hubert de Burgh (dù bûrg'), d. 1243, chief justiciar of England (1215–32) under John and Henry III. After Henry assumed power in 1227 trouble increased between Hubert and king whose foreign favorites opposed him. Tried to prevent (1230) expedition to France and resisted drain of money to papacy. In 1232 he was accused of disloyalty to crown and imprisoned. Was later reconciled with the king.

Hubertusburg, Peace of (hōōbĕr'tōōsbōŏrk), 1763, treaty between Austria and Prussia, at end of Seven Years War, signed at Hubertusburg castle in Saxony. Prussia retained Silesia; Saxony was restored to prewar boundaries.

Huch, Ricarda (rēkär'dä hōōkh'), 1864–1947, German novelist. Her historical novel of the Thirty Years War, *Der grosse Krieg in Deutschland* (1912–14), ranks among the best of its kind.

huckleberry, North American shrub of genus *Gaylussacia* of heath family. Common huckleberry (*Gaylussacia baccata*) is valued for its black edible fruit, usually picked from wild plants. Evergreen box huckleberry (*G. brachycera*) is often cultivated.

Huddersfield, county borough (pop. 129,021), West Riding of Yorkshire, England. An important textile-milling center, it also has other mfg.

Hudibras: see BUTLER, SAMUEL (1612–80).

Hudson, Henry, fl. 1607–11, English navigator and explorer. Ascended Hudson R., establishing Dutch claims to region, later explored Hudson Bay for English, both while seeking Northwest Passage.

Hudson, Manley O(ttmer), 1886–, American jurist. Specialist in international law, he was a justice on the Permanent Court of Arbitration (1933–45) and also served on the Permanent Court of Internatl. Justice (1936–46).

Hudson, W(illiam) H(enry), 1841–1922, English author and naturalist, b. Buenos Aires of American parents. Wrote romances laid in South America—*The Purple Land* (1855) and classic *Green Mansions* (1904). *Far Away and Long Ago* (1918) is autobiographic.

Hudson. 1 Town (pop. 8,211), E Mass., NE of Worcester; settled 1699. Mfg. of shoes and textiles. 2 City (pop. 11,629), E N.Y., on E bank of Hudson R. (bridged to Catskill); settled 1662. Mfg. of matches, cement, and food and leather products.

Hudson, river, c.315 mi. long, rising in NE N.Y. in L. Tear of the Clouds near Mt. Marcy in the Adirondacks and flowing generally S, forming N.Y.-N.J. line for c.17 mi. near its mouth in Upper New York Bay. Port region is called North R. Chief tributary is Mohawk R. One of the world's important highways, the Hudson is linked to the Great Lakes, L. Champlain, and St. Lawrence R. by N.Y. State Barge Canal. Tidal to Albany, head of channel for ocean-going vessels; Troy is at head of 12-ft. channel. At New York city (max. width here 4,400 ft.) Holland and Lincoln tunnels, railroad tunnel, subways, ferries, and George Washington Bridge link N.Y. and N.J. Above New York city river widens at Tappan Zee. First explored by Henry Hudson 1609. Major highway for Indians and early settlers. Has many historic, literary, and artistic associations.

Hudson Bay, great inland sea, 850 mi. long and 650 mi. wide, area c.475,000 sq. mi., E central Canada. Lies generally SE of Northwest Territories, to which

bay and islands belong. Has important cod and salmon fisheries. CHURCHILL is chief port on bay, connected to interior by Hudson Bay RR. Among rivers draining into bay are the CHURCHILL, NELSON, ALBANY, Abitibi, and SEVERN. Hudson's Bay Co. posts estab. at the rivers' mouths. Bay open to navigation from mid-July to Oct. Discovered 1610 by Henry Hudson and named for him.

Hudson Bay Railway, part of Canadian Natl. Railways system, 510 mi. long, extending from The Pas, Man., to Churchill, Man., on W coast of Hudson Bay. Built 1910–29; designed to reduce rail and sea rates from grain-producing provinces to Liverpool.

Hudson Falls, village (pop. 7,236), E N.Y., on Hudson R.; settled 1761. Mfg. of paper.

Hudson River school, 1825–75, in American landscape painting. Influenced by European romanticism. So called because the artists classified with the school were attracted by scenic beauty of Hudson R. valley. Group included Thomas Doughty and Thomas Cole.

Hudson's Bay Company. Organized 1668 by English merchants and courtiers to open fur trade with Indians in Hudson's Bay region of North America and to discover Northwest Passage to Orient. Permanent charter issued 1670. French contested claim to region; warfare ended with British in control. Company was harshly criticized in middle of 18th cent. for failure to discover Northwest Passage. NORTH WEST COMPANY became chief rival. RED RIVER SETTLEMENT scheme under earl of SELKIRK brought disaster to company. Amalgamation with North West Co. in 1821 marked beginning of period of true monopoly. Governorship (1821–60) of Sir George Simpson marked peak of company's fortune. Company territory transferred to Canada (1869) by governmental order for £300,000. In 20th cent. company expanded into retail trade and mfg. of all sorts. In 1930 Canadian stores were segregated in separate organization and London portion again turned to fur trade.

Hué (hwä), city (pop. c.40,000), Indo-China; cap. of Annam, on Hué R. near South China Sea. Probably founded by Chinese in 3d cent.

Huelva (wĕl'vä), city (pop. 50,837), cap. of Huelva prov., SW Spain, in Andalusia, on Odiel R. near Atlantic. Exports copper and sulphur from near-by Río Tinto mines.

Huerta, Victoriano (vēktōryä'nō hwĕr'tä), 1854–1916, Mexican general and president (1913–14). Served under Porfirio Díaz. After successful revolution of Madero (1911), Huerta supported him until 1913, then opposed him and was made president. His reactionary rule brought trouble with U.S. and revolutions led by Carranza, Villa, and Zapata, and he was forced to resign. Died in U.S.

Huesca (wā'skä), city (pop. 16,943), cap. of Huesca prov., NE Spain, in Aragon. Dates from Roman times. Residence of kings of Aragon 1096–1118. Has Gothic cathedral.

Hügel, Friedrich, Baron von (frē'drĭkh bärōn' fŭn hü'gǔl), 1852–1925, British Catholic philosopher, b. Florence. The independent thought in his writings, stressing inner security and moral responsibility, profoundly influenced modern Catholicism.

Huggins, Sir William, 1824–1910, English astronomer, pioneer in spectroscopic analysis of stars and in spectroscopic celestial photography.

Hugh Capet (kā'pĭt, kǎ'pĭt), c.938–996, king of France (987–96); son of HUGH THE GREAT and first of the CAPETIANS.

Hughes, Charles Evans, 1862–1948, U.S. Secretary of State (1921–25), Chief Justice of Supreme Court (1930–41). Lost presidential election to Woodrow Wilson in 1916 in very close contest.

Hughes, David Edward, 1831–1900, American inventor of an improved type-printing telegraph and of a microphone.

Hughes, Howard Robard, 1869–1924, American inventor of the widely used cone-shaped oil drill.

Hughes, John Joseph, 1797–1864, American Roman Catholic clergyman; bishop coadjutor (after 1838), bishop (after 1842), and first archbishop (after 1850) of New York.

Hughes, (James) Langston, 1902–, American Negro poet. His lyrics and songs (e.g., *The Weary Blues,* 1926), dramas, and fiction deal with Negro problems.

Hughes, Thomas, 1822–96, English author of the classic of school life, *Tom Brown's School Days* (1857), which idealizes Dr. Thomas Arnold of Rugby.

Hugh le Despenser: see DESPENSER, HUGH LE.

Hugh of Lincoln, Saint, d. 1200, bishop of Lincoln (1186–1200), b. Burgundy. Spokesman of the barons (1198) in their refusal of money to Richard I, he was also in conflict with John. Noted for charity, love of the poor, and holiness. Partially rebuilt Lincoln Cathedral. Feast: Nov. 17.

Hugh of Lincoln, Christian boy supposed to have been murdered by Jews in the 13th cent.

Hugh of Saint Victor, d. 1141, French or German scholastic philosopher. Headed the school of the monastery of St. Victor, Paris, after 1133 and made it a center of learning and of opposition to the teachings of Abelard. Hugh himself wrote learned theological works (notably one on the sacraments) and also works on mysticism. Also Hugo.

Hugh the Great, d. 956, French duke; son of King Robert I, father of HUGH CAPET. Waived succession in favor of RAOUL; placed LOUIS IV on French throne (936), later quarreled with him; virtually ruled France after 954.

Hugo, Victor (Fr. vēktôr′ ügō′), 1802–85, French poet, dramatist, and novelist. The preface to his drama *Cromwell* (1827) and the production of the tragedy *Hernani* (1830), which caused a riot, placed him at the head of the romanticists. Other plays include *Le Roi s'amuse* (1832; basis of Verdi's *Rigoletto*) and *Ruy Blas* (1838). After the tragic death of his daughter (1843), his poetry turned from the lush romanticism of earlier collections such as *Les Orientales* (1829) to the philosophic content of *Les Contemplations* (1856). Though created peer and viscount under Louis Philippe, Hugo soon turned to republicanism and ardently advocated reform. He opposed Napoleon III, fled abroad in 1851, and took residence in Jersey (till 1855), then in Guernsey till Napoleon's fall in 1870, when he returned to Paris in triumph. In the poems of *Les Châtiments* (1853) he vituperated Napoleon III. *La Légende des siècles* (1859) is an epic evocation of history. Hugo's great novels are *Notre Dame de Paris* (1831), *Les Misérables* (1862), and *Toilers of the Sea* (1866), on which his popularity in the English-speaking world is founded.

Hugo, city (pop. 5,984), SE Okla., near Red R. Rail and farm center processing peanuts and creosote.

Huguenots (hū′gŭnŏts), the Calvinist Protestants of France. Presbyterian church was founded in France at synod of 1559 and gained many followers among all classes. After the Wars of RELIGION (1562–98), Henry IV promulgated the Edict of NANTES, which gave the Huguenots complete toleration and estab. Protestantism in 200 towns. Cardinal RICHELIEU used an uprising (1621–22) against the introduction of Catholicism into Béarn as a pretext for depriving the Huguenots of all their strongholds save La Rochelle and Montauban. Another Protestant uprising (1625) led to the capture of La Rochelle by Richelieu (1628) and to the peace of Alais (1629), which stripped the Huguenots of all political power. Mounting persecution of Protestants under Louis XIV culminated in 1685 with the revocation of the Edict of Nantes. Countless Huguenots fled to England, Holland, Germany, Switzerland, and America, where they contributed substantially to civic and industrial life. In the Cévennes, the Protestant CAMISARDS long fought Louis XIV's troops (1702–10).

Huitzilopochtli (wē″tsēlōpōcht′lē), Aztec god of war. Human beings, especially prisoners of war, were sacri-ficed to him at the splendid temple of Tenochtitlán.

Hulagu Khan (hōōlä′gōō khän′), 1217–65, Mongol conqueror; grandson of Jenghiz Khan. Sacked Baghdad 1258, but westward move was checked 1260 by Mamelukes of Egypt. His Persian khanate lasted until 1335.

Hull, Cordell, 1871–, U.S. Secretary of State (1933–44). Consistently pursued a course making for sound international economic relations and constructive good will toward nonaggressor nations.

Hull, William, 1753–1825, American general. In command of Detroit in War of 1812, he lost it to British on Aug. 16, 1812. Court-martialed, he was saved only by his Revolutionary War record.

Hull, city (pop. 43,483), SW Que., Canada, on Ottawa R. at mouth of Gatineau R., opposite Ottawa. Paper and lumbering center with iron and steel foundries and hydroelectric station.

Hull, officially **Kingston-upon-Hull,** county borough (pop. 299,068), East Riding of Yorkshire, England, on the Humber. One of chief ports for Yorkshire and Lancashire, it also has extensive mfg. There are steamship lines to the Continent. It is an ocean fishing base. Town has several museums, grammar school (founded 1486), University Col., and Trinity House (estab. 1369, for sailors). Heavily bombed 1941.

Hull House: see ADDAMS, JANE.

humanism, movement in thought in the Renaissance, characterized chiefly by a revolt against medieval religious authority and attitudes and a great spread of classical learning. The rediscovery of Greek and Latin works was a main preoccupation of scholars, and the classic secular (humanistic) attitudes were generally adopted. The new learning more or less coincided with the religious upheaval of the Reformation, and many humanists became Protestants, though others clung to the old religion. The humanists formed a sort of intellectual community, which continued from the 14th cent. until shattered by the religious struggle in the late 16th cent.; numbered among them were such men as Boccaccio, Petrarch, Pico della Mirandola, Budé, the Scaligers, Reuchlin, Ulrich von Hutten, Erasmus, John Colet, and Sir Thomas More. The term *humanism* has been used for other later movements, most particularly in the 20th cent. by F. C. S. Schiller, Irving Babbitt, and C. F. Potter.

Human Rights, Commission on, division of the Economic and Social Council of the United Nations. Drew up Universal Declaration of Human Rights, adopted by UN on Dec. 10, 1948. A proposed Covenant on Human Rights received a setback when U.S. announced (1953) that it would not sign such a covenant.

Humber, navigable estuary of Trent R. and Ouse R., on E coast of England. It is 40 mi. long and 1–8 mi. wide. Encroachment of sea has destroyed former ports. Hull and Grimsby are chief cities.

Humberstone, village (pop. 3,895), S Ont., Canada, on L. Erie at S end of Welland Ship Canal. Humberstone Lock is one of world's largest lift locks.

Humbert, kings of Italy. **Humbert I,** 1844–1900, reigned 1878–1900. Was assassinated. **Humbert II,** 1904–, was made lieutenant general of the realm 1944, succeeded his father Victor Emmanuel III on his abdication (1946). Referendum of 1946 estab. republic, and Humbert went into exile.

Humboldt, Alexander, Freiherr von (älĕksän′dừr frī′hĕr fŭn hōōm′bōlt), 1769–1859, German explorer, scientist, and natural philosopher. His expedition to Cuba, Central and South America (1779–1804), noted for systematic observations, initiated era of scientific exploration. Estab. use of isotherms. In his great work on natural science, *Cosmos* (5 vols., 1845–62), he sought to formulate known facts about universe into uniform conception of nature. His brother **Wilhelm, Freiherr von Humboldt** (vǐl′hĕlm), 1767–1835, was Prussian minister of education (1809–10), reformed school system, founded Univ. of Berlin. In 1819 he left government service in protest against reactionary regime. A friend of Goethe and Schiller, he also wrote a work on Kavi, the ancient language of Java, important in history of philology.

Humboldt, city (pop. 7,426), W Tenn., NNW of Jackson. Rail, mfg., and trade center for farm area.

Humboldt, river rising in NE Nev. and flowing W and S c.300 mi. into Humboldt Sink near Humboldt Range. Named by J. C. Frémont, it was followed by Utah emigrants bound for Calif. Rye Patch Dam, built 1935–36, serves Humboldt project around Lovelock.

Humboldt Glacier, NW Greenland, largest known glacier. It debouches into Kane Basin. E. K. Kane discovered it on his expedition of 1853–55.

Hume, David (hūm), 1711–76, Scottish philosopher and historian. He pressed the analyses of Locke and Berkeley into a determined, thorough-going skepticism. He found in the mind nothing but a series of sensations and the cause-effect relation in the natural world as apparent only because two sensations were customarily joined. Rejecting the possibility of knowledge that is certain, he fell back on common sense and faith. His essays (e.g., *Treatise of Human Nature,* 1739–40; *Essays Moral and Political,* 1741–42; *Philosophical Essays,* 1748; *An Enquiry Concerning the Principles of Morals,* 1750; *Political Discourses,* 1752) are marked by the purity of literary style that made his *History of England* (1754–62) long standard despite errors in fact. He was patron of Rousseau in his English exile, but later the two quarreled bitterly.

humidity, primary climatic element, atmospheric state regarding moisture content. Measured as absolute humidity (moisture per unit volume of natural air); relative humidity (ratio of moisture content to moisture-holding capacity of air at given temperature); specific humidity (moisture per unit mass of natural air); and mixing ratio (moisture per dry-air unit mass). Hygrometer used to measure humidity.

hummingbird, small perching bird of New World. Most of c.750 species and subspecies are native to Central and South America. They have brilliant plumage with a metallic sheen and long, slender, sometimes curved bills. In seeking insects and nectar of flowers they carry on cross pollination. Giant hummer of Andes (c.8½ in. long) is largest; smallest, Helena's hummingbird or fairy hummer of Cuba (c.2¼ in. long). Ruby-throated hummingbird is only species in N U.S.

Humperdinck, Engelbert (hŭm′pûrdǐngk), 1854–1921, German composer and teacher. Apart from the opera *Die Königskinder,* he is known chiefly for his first opera, *Hansel and Gretel* (1893).

Humphrey, Doris, American dancer and choreographer. Long associated with Charles Weidman. Her outstanding works include *New Dance; With My Red Fires.*

Humphrey, George M(agoffin), 1890–, U.S. Secretary of the Treasury (1953–). President of M. A. Hanna Co., steel mfg. firm, Cleveland (1929–52).

Humphreys, Andrew Atkinson, 1810–83, American army engineer, Union general in Civil War. Known for topographic and hydrographic survey of Mississippi delta (1850–61).

Humphreys, David, 1752–1818, American diplomat and poet. Active in U.S. service abroad. One of the CONNECTICUT WITS. His poetry is largely patriotic and didactic.

Humphreys, Joshua, 1751–1838, American ship designer, responsible in 1790s for successful frigates (*United States, Constitution,* and others).

Humphrey's Peak: see SAN FRANCISCO PEAKS.

humus, decayed vegetable and animal matter, essential to productive soil. It aids plant growth by conserving moisture, loosening soil particles to admit air and water, and by releasing mineral nutrients. Sandy and clay soils lack humus to varying degrees.

Hunan (hōō′nän′), province (80,000 sq. mi.; pop. 28,-000,000), S central China; cap. Changsha. Largely hilly. Watered by Siang, Yuan, and Tsz rivers which drain through Tungting L. into the Yangtze. Major producer of tea, rice, and minerals (lead, zinc, coal, antimony, tin, tungsten).

Hundred Days, March 20–June 28, 1815, period of attempt by NAPOLEON I to rebuild empire after return from Elba. See also WATERLOO CAMPAIGN.

Hundred Years War, 1337–1453, between England and France. Basic cause: the kings of England, who as dukes of GUIENNE were vassals of the French kings, opposed the centralizing policies of the French crown and showed increasing reluctance to do homage to France for their continental possessions. Contributing causes: claim of EDWARD III to the French crown as a grandson of Philip IV; territorial disputes between Edward and PHILIP VI of France; English-French rivalry in Flanders; Philip's support of Scotland against England. First phase of war (1337–60) began when Edward proclaimed himself king of France. Allied with the Flemings under Jacob van ARTEVELDE, he defeated the French navy at Sluis (1340); routed the French at CRÉCY (1346); took CALAIS (1347); and routed and captured JOHN II of France at Poitiers (1356). The Treaty of BRÉTIGNY (1360) gave England Calais and W and SW France. Second phase of war (1369–73) was brought on by the oppressive taxation of EDWARD THE BLACK PRINCE and resulted in the reconquest by DU GUESCLIN of most of the lost French territories. After a period of quiescence, HENRY V of England renewed the war in 1415. Victorious at AGINCOURT, he later won the alliance of PHILIP THE GOOD of Burgundy (1419) and in 1420, by the Treaty of TROYES, was recognized by Charles VI as regent and heir of France. The dauphin (later CHARLES VII) refused to accept his disinheritance, and desultory warfare recommenced after Charles VI's death (1422). By 1429 the English and Burgundians were masters of nearly all France N of the Loire, but in that year JOAN OF ARC appeared, relieved besieged ORLÉANS, defeated the English at Patay, and saw Charles VII crowned at Rheims. The tide turned, and in 1435, when by the Treaty of ARRAS Burgundy passed over to the French camp, the final phase of the war began. The French reconquered Paris (1436), Normandy (1449–50), and all Guienne but Bordeaux (1449–51). The capture of Bordeaux (1453) left only Calais in English hands. England, torn by the Wars of the Roses, made no attempt at reconquest and henceforth turned its interest to sea power rather than to expansion on the Continent. France, laid waste and reduced to anarchy by the war, recovered under Charles VII and Louis XI, who took advantage of the virtual destruction of the feudal class to rebuild a centralized monarchy. The Hundred Years War saw the transition from medieval to modern warfare (artillery) and from feudalism to the first awakening of national consciousness.

Huneker, James Gibbons (hŭ′nĭkŭr), 1860–1921, American essayist, critic of music, art, and drama.

Hungarian language, Finno-Ugric language. See LANGUAGE (table).

Hungary, Hung. *Magyarország,* republic (33,935 sq. mi.; pop. c.9,205,000), SE Europe, in the Danubian plain; cap. Budapest. E of the Danube the Great Hungarian Plain (Hung. *Alföld*) extends beyond the border to the Carpathians; W of the Danube are the Little Alfold, with L. BALATON, and the Bakony, Vertes, and Mecsek mts. Present frontiers, except for minor changes in 1947, were estab. by Treaty of TRIANON (1920), which stripped Hungary of two thirds of former area (incl. its Adriatic coast). Though it has mineral resources (coal, manganese, bauxite, petroleum) and industrial concentrations (esp. at Budapest, Gyor, Miskolc), Hungary is predominantly agr. (wheat, maize, livestock, poultry, wine). Irrigation has reduced the former PUSZTA to a small area around Debrecen. Chief industrial products: textiles, machinery, processed foods, chemicals. Population is c.66% Catholic, 25% Protestant (mainly Calvinist).

Part of the Roman provinces of Pannonia and Dacia, Hungary was later conquered by the Huns, Ostrogoths, Avars, and (9th cent.) MAGYARS. Magyar expansion in W was halted by Emperor Otto I at the Lechfeld (955). St. STEPHEN, first king of Hungary, completed the Magyars' Christianization. A feudal society came into being. The power of the magnates (great nobles), who were to play a major role until 1918, was only temporarily curbed by the Golden Bull of ANDREW II (1222). Hungary was occupied by the Mongols in 1241–42. In 1301 the ARPAD dynasty died out. The kingship was elective, but dynastic ties influenced the royal elections. Hungary was ruled after 1308 by the ANGEVIN dynasty and after 1386 by other foreign houses (mostly in personal union with Bohemia and Poland; see esp. JAGIELLO dynasty). The double marriage treaty of 1515 (see ULADISLAUS II) prepared the advent of HAPSBURG rule in 1526. Medieval Hungary reached its zenith under LOUIS I (14th cent.) and under MATTHIAS CORVINUS (15th cent.), whose reign interrupted that of the Jagiellos. John HUNYADI successfully led the resistance against Turkish conquest, but the defeat and death of Louis II at MOHACS (1526) plunged Hungary into chaos. Ferdinand of Austria (see FERDINAND I, emperor) contested the succession with the Zapolya family (see JOHN, kings of Hungary), and in 1541 Turkey annexed most of the country. The resulting threefold partition of Hungary (confirmed by treaty, 1606) lasted until the reconquest of Turkish Hungary by the Hapsburgs after 1683: W Hungary remained under the Hapsburgs, who kept the royal title; central Hungary was a Turkish province; TRANSYLVANIA, ruled by its own princes, shifted its allegiance back and forth between the sultans and the emperors. By 1711, the rebellion of Francis II RAKOCZY having failed, all Hungary and Transylvania was firmly under Hapsburg control. Religious freedom had been guaranteed by the treaty of 1606 between BOCSKAY and the emperor. The peasantry, subjected to serfdom after its rebellion of 1514, was freed in 1781 by Emperor Joseph II. Magyar opposition to Hapsburg rule remained strong and flared up in the Revolution of 1848. The short-lived Hungarian republic (April–Aug., 1849) under KOSSUTH was put down by Austrian and Russian troops. Hungarian self-rule was abolished until 1867, when Hungary became a constitutional kingdom in personal union with Austria (see AUSTRO-HUNGARIAN MONARCHY). Except in CROATIA, which enjoyed some autonomy, the Slavic and Rumanian minorities (in SLOVAKIA, RUTHENIA, DALMATIA, and the BANAT OF TEMESVAR) were held in virtual subjection by Magyar nationalism. After the collapse of the Dual Monarchy in World War I, Hungary was proclaimed an independent republic (1918) and reduced by the Treaty of Trianon to its predominantly Magyar core. (Large Magyar minorities passed to Czechoslovakia, Rumania, and Yugoslavia.) The Communist dictatorship of BELA KUN (1919) was put down by Rumanian intervention, and in 1920 Hungary became a kingdom without a king, with Adm. HORTHY DE NAGYBANYA as regent. The authoritarian and reactionary regimes of premiers Bethlen and Gombos were tempered by the parliament but blocked a much-needed agrarian reform. Hungarian agitation for treaty revision met the hostility of the LITTLE ENTENTE and eventually caused Hungary to join the AXIS powers in World War II (1941). Invaded by Russian troops in 1944, Hungary made an armistice in Jan., 1945; heavy fighting between Germans and Russians continued. Peace was signed in Paris in 1947. It confirmed the restoration of territories ceded to Hungary by Slovakia in 1938 and by Rumania in 1940, and it provided for $300,000,000 in reparations to the USSR. Hungary became a republic in 1946. Land reforms were introduced by a coalition government of moderates and leftists. In 1948 a coup d'état imposed Communist totalitarianism on the country, which in 1949 became a People's Republic under virtual economic and political control of the USSR.

Hunkers, conservative faction of the Democratic party in N.Y. in the 1840s, so named because they were supposed to "hanker" or "hunker" after office. Opposed the BARNBURNERS. Generally controlling party machinery and patronage, they favored internal improvements and liberal chartering of state banks; opposed antislavery agitation.

Huns, nomadic people from N central Asia. Organized into hordes, they were indomitable horsemen living off the countries they ravaged. They first appeared 3d cent. B.C., when the Great Wall of China was built to contain them. They occupied China from 3d cent. A.D. to 581. About 372 A.D. they invaded the Volga valley and advanced W, pushing the OSTROGOTHS and VISIGOTHS before them, thus starting the waves of migrations that destroyed the Roman Empire. In 432 they forced Emperor Theodosius II to pay tribute. ATTILA, from his hq. in Hungary, levied tribute in nearly all central and E Europe but was defeated in Gaul (451). The Huns withdrew after his death, and little is known of their later movements.

Hunt, Holman, 1827–1910, English painter, a founder of the Pre-Raphaelite brotherhood.

Hunt, (James Henry) Leigh, 1784–1859, English poet, critic, and essayist. Edited weeklies *Examiner* and *Liberal;* contributed to many others. A friend of contemporary writers, he strongly influenced Keats. Some lyrics (e.g., "Abou Ben Adhem," "Jenny Kissed Me"), essays, and autobiography still much read.

Hunt, Richard Morris, 1828–95, American architect, brother of William Morris Hunt; an exponent of 19th-cent. eclecticism. His Tribune Building, New York, was one of first elevator buildings. His son, **Richard Howland Hunt,** 1862–1931, also an architect, led movement against unrestricted skyscraper building.

Hunt, William Morris, 1824–79, American painter, a follower of Barbizon School. As teacher and painter in Boston he exerted wide influence on American art.

Hunt, Wilson Price, 1782?–1842, American explorer, leader of the overland expedition (1810–12) to Astoria, Oregon.

Hunter, John, 1728–93, Scottish pioneer in comparative anatomy and in surgery. His noted anatomical collection was acquired by the Royal College of Surgeons. His brother, **William Hunter,** 1718–83, was famed as obstetrician and as head of influential school of anatomy.

Hunter, Robert Mercer Taliaferro (tŏ'lŭvŭr), 1809–87, American statesman. U.S. Representative from Va. (1837–43, 1845–47); a leading states' rights Democrat. U.S. Senator (1847–61). Participated in Confederate government.

Hunter, William: see HUNTER, JOHN.

Hunter College: see NEW YORK, COLLEGE OF THE CITY OF.

hunting dogs. Many breeds of dogs used in hunting are not expected to kill the game which they track down, but rather to flush game or to fetch game after it has been shot. Among these are the pointer and the several kinds of retrievers and setters. The pointer is a large, lean, smooth-coated dog weighing c.60 lb. When it comes upon game birds, it points them with its nose, remaining motionless until the bird attempts to fly. It is usually white marked with liver, orange, or yellow. The retriever has a thick coat and generally stands 22–25 in. at shoulder and weighs 65–80 lb. It is bred for fetching game already shot by the hunter, especially game that has fallen in water. In addition to a keen sense of smell, it must have a soft mouth for carrying game without damage. Breeds of retrievers include the Labrador retriever, a hardy dog whose short straight coat is usually black; the Chesapeake Bay retriever, varying from dark brown to faded tan; the golden retriever; and the curly-coated retriever, usually black or liver in color. Generally setters have silky coats with feathered legs and tail. The English setter is white marked with tan, black, lemon, or liver; the Gordon setter has a very glossy coat of black or tan; the Irish setter is a golden chestnut or mahogany red. The Dalmatian or coach dog was sometimes used in hunting, but was specially trained and long used to trot along beside a carriage. It is short-haired, stands 19–23 in. at shoulder, and is white spangled with round, clearly defined, black or dark brown spots.

Huntingdon, England: see HUNTINGDONSHIRE.

Huntingdon, borough (pop. 7,330), S Pa., E of Altoona. Mfg. of paper, boilers, and radiators. Seat of Juniata Col. (Church of the Brethren; coed.; 1876).

Huntingdonshire or **Huntingdon,** inland county (365 sq. mi.; pop. 69,273), E central England. Mainly agr., it has some paper mfg. and brewing. County town is **Huntingdon,** municipal borough (pop. 5,282), birthplace and home of Oliver Cromwell.

hunting leopard: see CHEETAH.

Huntington, Anna Hyatt: see HYATT, ANNA VAUGHN.

Huntington, Collis P(otter), 1821–1900, American railroad builder. Helped organize Central Pacific RR. Gained for himself and partners practical control of transportation in West. President of Southern Pacific after 1890. Left most of fortune to his nephew, **Henry E(dwards) Huntington,** 1850–1927. Endowed his estate at San Marino, near Pasadena, Calif., for public use. Has fine gardens and the **Henry E. Huntington Library and Art Gallery** with largest collection of incunabula in America; many rare documents, manuscripts and books, with accent on American and British past. Special art treasures are Gainsborough's *Blue Boy,* Reynolds's *Mrs. Siddons as the Tragic Muse,* and Thomas Lawrence's *Pinkie.* The library gives research fellowships and scholarships.

Huntington, Ellsworth, 1876–1947, American geographer. Accompanied expeditions to central Asia (1903, 1905–6). Taught at Yale (1907–15); as research associate (1917–47) he made notable climatic and anthropogeographic studies.

Huntington, Henry Edwards: see HUNTINGTON, COLLIS POTTER.

Huntington, William Reed, 1838–1909, American Episcopal clergyman. Noted pastor (from 1883) of Grace Church, New York city.

Huntington. 1 City (pop. 15,079), NE Ind., on Little R. and SW of Fort Wayne. Farm trade center producing rubber goods, furniture, and metal products. **2** Residential and resort town (pop. 47,506), including Huntington village (pop. 9,324), SE N.Y., on NW Long Isl. near Oyster Bay. Site of Nathan Hale's capture marked in Huntington Bay village. Birthplace of Walt Whitman is in West Hills. **3** City (pop. 86,353), W W. Va. on Ohio R. and WNW of Charleston; founded 1871 as W terminus of Chesapeake & Ohio RR. Largest city in state and commercial center for wide area. Mfg. of monel metal, railroad equipment, steel rails, and glass. Here is Marshall Col. (coed.; 1837).

Huntington Beach, coastal city (pop. 5,237), S Calif., SE of Long Beach. Oil wells and refineries.

Huntington Library and Art Gallery: see HUNTINGTON, COLLIS POTTER.

Huntington Park, city (pop. 29,450), S Calif., residential and industrial suburb of Los Angeles. Mfg. of iron and steel products and oil-field equipment.

Huntsville. 1 City (pop. 16,437), N Ala., between Tennessee R. and Tenn. line; settled 1807. Textiles, shoes, farm implements. Site of constitutional convention (1819); briefly, state cap. **2** City (pop. 9,820), E central Texas, N of Houston. Home of Sam Houston, it has memorials to him (grave, restored home). Processes cotton, lumber, and dairy produce.

Hunyadi, John (hŏon′yŏdĭ), c.1385–1456, Hungarian national hero, leader of resistance against the Turks. Was voivode of Transylvania 1441–46; regent of Hungary 1446–53 (for Ladislaus V). His chief victory (together with St. John Capistran) was that of Belgrade (1456), which staved off Turkish conquest of Hungary for 70 years. Matthias Corvinus was his son.

Hupeh or **Hupei** (both: hōo′pā′, hōo′bā′), province (70,-000 sq. mi.; pop. 25,000,000), central China; cap. Wuchang. Largely an alluvial plain; drained by Yangtze and Han rivers. Major iron mines in SE. Produces rice, cotton, and wheat. Trade centered at urban hub comprising Hankow, Wuchang, Hanyang.

Hur, man who upheld hand of weary Moses during battle, thus insuring Hebrew victory. Ex. 17.12; 24.14.

Hurd, Peter, 1904–, American painter of Western scenes and types. Uses realistic style.

hurling, game popular in Ireland, played on field 80 yd. by 140 yd. by two teams of 15 players each with a cork-centered ball and a wooden stick (the hurley).

Huron, city (pop. 12,788), E central S.Dak., on James R. and E of Pierre; laid out 1879. Shipping and trade center for agr. area. Has meat-packing plants and creameries. Seat of Huron Col. (Presbyterian; coed.; 1883).

Huron, river rising in S Mich. and flowing c.97 mi. SE to L. Erie S of Detroit.

Huron, Lake, 206 mi. long, 183 mi. wide, second largest of Great Lakes. Lying 579.79 ft. above sea level, it has maximum depth of 750 ft., area of 23,010 sq. mi. Bounded N and E by Ontario, W by Mich. Drains L. Superior and L. Michigan and empties into L. Erie. Its large Georgian Bay indents Ont.; Saginaw Bay is in Mich. Islands include Mackinac and the Manitoulins. Iron ore, grain, coal, limestone, other articles are shipped. Ports include Bay City, Alpena, and Cheboygan in Mich., and Goderich, Collingwood, and Midland in Canada. L. Huron has violent storms, and is icebound from about mid-Dec. until early April. Probably first of Great Lakes visited by white men, possibly by Étienne Brulé c.1612.

Huronian: see PROTEROZOIC ERA.

Huron Indians, confederation of four North American Indian tribes, who spoke Wyandot language (Iroquoian family). Their culture was of the Eastern Woodlands area. In early 17th cent. occupied region around L. Simcoe and near Georgian Bay, Ontario. The Hurons were friendly to the French, and the confederacy was destroyed by the Dutch-supported Iroquois (1649).

hurricane, tropical cyclone originating in doldrums, on W side of oceans, probably from convective heating. Most frequent in late summer or autumn in N Hemisphere, late winter or spring in S Hemisphere. Called typhoon in India and China.

Hurtado de Mendoza, Diego (dyä′gō ōortä′dhō dā mändō′thä), 1503–75, Spanish writer, a diplomat under Charles V. Banished by Philip II to Granada, he wrote an unbiased account of the Moorish rebellion. Also wrote poetry. Picaresque novel *Lazarillo de Tormes* sometimes attributed to him.

Husein (hōosīn′), c.626–680, Moslem saint of the Shiites; second son of ALI and FATIMA. On death of his brother Hasan he unsuccessfully claimed caliphate. Tomb at KERBELA is holy place for Shiites. Name also spelled Hussein.

Husein ibn Ali (ĭ′bŭn ä′lē), 1856–1931, Arabian leader; father of Abdullah of Jordan and Feisal I of Iraq. Led revolt against Turkish rule and made himself king of the HEJAZ in 1916. Overthrown 1924 by Ibn Saud.

Hu Shih (hōo′ shŭ′), 1891–, Chinese writer and diplomat. Educated in China and U.S. (Cornell and Columbia univs.). Leader in Chinese literary renaissance; advocated simplification of written language. Ambassador to U.S. (1938–1942).

husky: see CHOW.

Huss, John, Czech *Jan Hus* (yän′ hōos′), 1369?–1415, religious reformer. He attacked abuses of clergy, earning their hostility, but was supported by Queen Sophia and Emperor Wenceslaus, who made him rector of Univ. of Prague. He was involved in controversy of rival popes Gregory XII and Benedict XIII, and he won enmity of John XXIII, who excommunicated him. At castle near Tabor, Huss wrote chief works, including *De ecclesia.* Emperor Sigismund invited him to defend views at Council of Constance (1414); but by unfair means he was condemned as heretic and burned. See HUSSITES.

Hussein: see also HUSEIN.

Hussein I (hōōsīn'), 1935–, king of Jordan (1952–), son and successor of Talal; grandson of Abdullah.

Husseini (Amin el Husseini) (hōōsā'nē; ämēn' ĕl), 1896?–, Arab political leader. Appointed mufti of Jerusalem in 1921. Arrested 1937 for instigation of anti-Semitic riots but escaped to Lebanon and later to Iraq. Broadcast Nazi propaganda from Berlin in World War II. Listed as war criminal, he found asylum in Egypt in 1946.

Husserl, Edmund (hōōs'ûrl), 1859–1938, German philosopher. His theories on the relationship of the conscious mind and objects—the basis of the system of *phenomenology*—have had great influence.

Hussites, followers of John Huss in Bohemia and Moravia. In 1420 they drew up Four Articles of Prague, demanding freedom of preaching, communion in both kinds for laymen and priests, limited property holding by Church, and civil punishment of mortal sin. In Hussite Wars movement divided into moderate UTRAQUISTS (some of whom in 16th cent. fused with Lutherans and were called Evangelicals) and radical TABORITES (from whom stemmed Moravian Church).

Hussite Wars, 1419–36, conflict caused by the rise of the HUSSITES in Bohemia and Moravia. Its nature was religious and national (Hussite Czechs vs. Catholic Germans) as well as social (radical TABORITES, largely recruited among peasantry, vs. moderate UTRAQUISTS, backed by Czech nobility). The Hussites took up arms in 1419 to prevent the succession of Emperor SIGISMUND to the Bohemian crown. Under the leadership of ZIZKA and, after 1425, of PROCOPIUS THE GREAT, the Hussites defeated Sigismund (1420, 1422), invaded Silesia (1425–26) and Franconia (1429–30), and repulsed several anti-Hussite crusades. Hussite delegates at the Council of BASEL accepted the so-called Compactata, by which the Utraquists were taken back into the Catholic Church (1433), but the Taborites refused to compromise. In the resulting civil war, the Taborites were routed at Lipany (1434); the Compactata were ratified and Sigismund was recognized as king of Bohemia in 1436. The later wars against GEORGE OF PODEBRAD were of primarily political nature, though Hussitism was the ostensible issue.

Hutchins, Robert Maynard, 1899–, American educator. He was dean of Yale Law School, 1927–29, and helped organize Inst. of Human Relations at Yale. In 1929 he became president of Univ. of CHICAGO, where his title was chancellor after 1945. He instituted "Chicago plan" there. In 1946 he was on leave to promote "great books" program. He resigned in 1950 to become associate director of Ford Foundation.

Hutchinson, Anne, c.1591–1643, religious leader in New England, b. England. Banished from Mass. Bay colony as antinomian heretic, she and followers founded Portsmouth, R.I. (1638).

Hutchinson, Thomas, 1711–80, colonial governor of Mass. (1771–74) and historian. Unpopular with colonists because he upheld British measures. Wrote history of Mass. Bay colony.

Hutchinson, city (pop. 33,575), S central Kansas, on Arkansas R. and NW of Wichita; laid out 1871. Rail, trade, and mfg. center of area yielding salt, oil, wheat, and livestock.

Hutten, Ulrich von (ōōl'rĭkh fŭn hōō'tŭn), 1488–1523, German humanist, poet, and political reformer. Wrote in Latin, later in German. Was poet laureate of Maximilian I (1517). Supported Johann REUCHLIN; joined with Franz von SICKINGEN (1519); supported Luther. Sickingen's defeat forced him into exile in Switzerland (1522).

Hutterische Community (hōō'tĕ'rĭshŭ) or **Hutterian Brethren** (hŭtĕr'ĕŭn), religious communistic group founded (1874) at Tabor, S.Dak. by immigrant descendants of followers of Jacob Hutter. Closely allied with Mennonites in matters of doctrine and principles.

Hutton, James, 1726–97, Scottish geologist. He formulated the theory of UNIFORMISM as opposed to long accepted belief known as CATASTROPHISM.

Huxley, T(homas) H(enry), 1825–95, English biologist. While assistant surgeon on H.M.S. *Rattlesnake* he collected marine life in Pacific areas (1846–50). A supporter of Darwin, he wrote on evolution, and also on anatomy, physiology, and other fields of science. His son **Leonard Huxley,** 1860–1933, was a poet, general writer, and editor of *Cornhill Magazine.* Leonard's son **Julian S(orell) Huxley,** 1887–, biologist and author, was director general of UNESCO (1946–48). His works include *The Living Thoughts of Darwin* (1939) and *Heredity East and West* (1949). Another son of Leonard, **Aldous (Leonard) Huxley,** 1894–, gained early fame by satirical novels and short stories (*Crome Yellow,* 1921; *Antic Hay,* 1923; *Point Counter Point,* 1928; *Brave New World,* 1932, depicting a repulsive Utopia). Later novels reflect his interest in Eastern mysticism, though mordant criticism of the modern world continued in such works as *Eyeless in Gaza* (1936). Has also written popular history as in *Grey Eminence* (1941) and *The Devils of Loudun* (1952).

Huygens, Constantijn (kōnstäntīn' hoi'gŭns), 1596–1687, Dutch poet. Noted for descriptive and satirical poems, he wrote in French, Italian, Latin, Dutch. His son, **Christiaan Huygens** (krīs'tyän), 1629–95, was a mathematician and physicist. He improved telescopic lenses and discovered a satellite and the rings of Saturn. He was first to use pendulum in clocks. **Huygens's principle:** every point on wave front of light is source of new waves.

Huysmans, Cornelis (hois'mäns), 1648–1727, Flemish painter of landscapes and religious subjects. His brother and pupil, **Jan Baptist Huysmans,** 1654–1716, also painted landscapes.

Huysmans, Joris Karl (zhōrēs' kärl' üēsmäs'), 1848–1907, French novelist. First a naturalist, he became a Catholic convert. His novel, *À rebours* (1884; Eng. tr., *Against the Grain,* 1922), is a self-portrait. *La Cathédrale* (1898; Eng. tr., 1898) shows his magnificent prose and mystic symbolism.

Hvar (khvär), Gr. *Pharos,* Ital. *Lesina,* Adriatic island, 120 sq. mi., Yugoslavia, off Dalmatia. Chief town, Hvar, has 12th-cent. Byzantine cathedral.

Hwaining, China: see ANKING.

Hwang Ho: see YELLOW RIVER.

Hwangpoo, China: see WHANGPOO.

Hyacinth, in Greek myth, beautiful youth loved by Apollo, who accidentally killed him with a discus. Flower named for him sprang up from his blood.

hyacinth, bulbous plant of genus *Hyacinthus* native to Mediterranean region and S Africa. Common or Dutch hyacinth became so popular in 18th cent. that 2,000 kinds were said to be grown in Holland. It has a single dense spike of fragrant flowers in the spring but can be made to bloom earlier indoors.

Hyannis, Mass.: see BARNSTABLE.

Hyatt, Anna Vaughn, 1876–, American sculptor, noted for studies of animals. A well-known statue is *St. Joan of Arc.* Married Archer M. Huntington.

Hyatt, John Wesley, 1837–1920, American inventor of CELLULOID and of Hyatt filter for chemical purification of water while it is in motion.

Hyattsville, town (pop. 12,308), W central Md., NE residential suburb of Washington, D.C.

hybrid (hī'brĭd), term of plant and animal breeders for offspring of two different species or genera. In genetics it is usually a term for offspring of two parents differing in any genetic character.

Hyde, Edward: see CLARENDON, EDWARD HYDE, 1ST EARL OF.

Hyde Park, 363 acres, in W London. Was once a deer park where races were held. Duke of Hamilton and Lord Mohun fought their fatal duel here. The Serpentine, artificial lake, was constructed 1733. Distinctive features of the park are Marble Arch, meeting place of soapbox orators; Rotten Row, famous bridle path; and the Albert Memorial.

Hyde Park, town (pop. 6,136), E N.Y., on E bank of Hudson R. N of Poughkeepsie; settled c.1740. Here are Franklin D. Roosevelt and Vanderbilt Mansion national historic sites.

Hyderabad (hī′dùrùbăd″), state (82,313 sq. mi.; pop. 18,652,964), S central India, almost entirely within Deccan plateau. Produces cotton, wheat, rice, and tobacco. Chief industry is cotton spinning and weaving. Conquered in late 17th cent. by Mogul empire. In 1724 the Mogul viceroy, Asaf Jah, won Hyderabad's independence and founded present dynasty, whose ruling head is called the Nizam. Predominantly Hindu state was formally joined to Indian republic in 1950. **Hyderabad,** city (pop. 739,159), the cap., was founded 1589 as cap. of Golconda kingdom; major commercial center.

Hyderabad, city (pop. 134,693), central Sind prov., W Pakistan; trade center. In 1950 succeeded Karachi as cap. of province.

Hyder Ali or **Haidar Ali** (both: hī′dùr ä′lē), d. 1792, Indian maharaja. Though illiterate and a Moslem, he rose to become highest military leader in Hindu state of Mysore. Seized power in 1761, made himself maharaja in 1766. Defeated the British in 1767, but he and his son Tippoo Sahib were defeated 1781 by Warren Hastings.

Hydra (hī′drù) [Gr.,= watery (snake)], in Greek mythology, water serpent with nine heads. When one head was cut off, two new ones grew. HERCULES conquered monster by burning neck after severing each head.

hydrangea (hīdrăn′jù), ornamental deciduous shrub of genus *Hydrangea,* native to Asia and the Americas. It has flat-topped or rounded clusters of blue, white, or pink flowers. Used in landscaping and as potted plant.

hydrate (hī′drāt), substance formed by chemical combination of a compound and one or more molecules of water (number of molecules is specific for substance). This water is called water of crystallization; it is given off on heating or in some hydrates at ordinary temperatures (efflorescence).

hydraulic brake: see BRAKE.

hydraulic machine, machine actuated by motion or pressure of fluid (liquid or gas). Water under pressure is used as power agent for presses, riveters, winches, and other machines. Power derived from falling water drives TURBINE and the water wheel. Hydraulic elevator, jack, and press are based on PASCAL'S LAW. Certain machines are driven by accumulator (consisting chiefly of cylinder enclosing weighted ram) which keeps liquid at fixed pressure.

hydraulic press, hydraulic machine (also called hydrostatic press), invented by Joseph Bramah. Consists essentially of two liquid-filled cylinders of very unequal diameter, connected by pipe and each fitted with piston. Pressure exerted on smaller piston is transmitted through liquid and forces up larger piston.

hydraulics: see HYDRAULIC MACHINE; MECHANICS.

hydrocarbon (hī″drōkär′bùn), organic compound of carbon and hydrogen in varying proportions. Hydrocarbons are divided into series in which each member has definite relation to one preceding and following (a difference of one carbon and two hydrogen atoms); examples are methane series, ethylene series, acetylene series, benzene series, anthracene series. Many common natural substances are complex mixtures of these compounds, e.g., petroleum, asphalt, methane. They vary in chemical activity, resist ordinary reagents, burn in air. Many important compounds are derivatives of hydrocarbons.

hydrochloric acid, aqueous solution of hydrogen chloride, a strong acid of great commercial importance. It reacts with most metals, and with their oxides and hydroxides, forming chlorides. It is used for cleaning metal; in producing chlorides, glue, dyes, glucose; and in medicine. Muriatic acid is a solution of 30–35% by weight.

hydrocyanic (–sīā′nĭk) or **prussic** (prŭ′sĭk) **acid,** colorless, volatile, very poisonous liquid with almond odor. Water solution is a weak acid; salts are cyanides. It is used in the laboratory, as poison gas in war, and as a fumigant.

hydrodynamics: see MECHANICS.

hydroelectric power: see POWER.

hydrogen (hī′drùjùn), colorless, odorless, tasteless gaseous element (symbol = H; see also ELEMENT, table). It is the lightest known gas, explosive when mixed with air or oxygen, and burns with a hot blue flame. It is slightly soluble in water; can be liquefied under pressure; is active at high temperatures; is a powerful reducing agent; forms many important compounds. Discovered in 1766 by Henry Cavendish, it was named in 1783 by Lavoisier. Heavy hydrogen, deuterium, is isotope with atomic weight 2; it and its atomic nuclei (deuterons) are important in research. Tritium is radioactive isotope, atomic weight 3. See *ill.,* p. 773.

hydrogenation of oils (hī″drùjùnā′shùn), treatment of vegetable oils with hydrogen, in presence of catalyst, at high temperature under pressure. It forms a product resembling solid animal fats.

hydrogen bomb derives energy from union of nuclei of low atomic weight. Atomic bomb probably would have to be used as detonator to get needed amount of heat for this fusion. Most likely ingredients are hydrogen isotopes. The thermonuclear reactions involved are believed to be same as those producing heat of sun. Energy yield of bomb has no foreseeable peacetime applications; potentially more harmful than atomic bomb. Tests which advanced its development made at Eniwetok (1951, 1952). See *ill.,* p. 773.

hydrogen-ion concentration: see ION.

hydrogen peroxide (pùrŏk′sīd), colorless, unstable liquid with metallic taste; has two atoms of both hydrogen and oxygen. Used as bleaching agent and in cleansing wounds (germicidal value disputed).

hydrolysis (hīdrŏ′lùsĭs), type of chemical reaction in which water (dissociated into hydrogen and hydroxyl ions) is involved. It is common in many life processes, e.g., in digestion, food substances (carbohydrates, fats and oils, and proteins) are decomposed by action of water in presence of enzymes. Final product of hydrolysis of starch is glucose; of fats and oils, products are glycerin and fatty acids; and of proteins, amino acids. Some salts undergo hydrolysis in water solution, others do not. Some reactions involving water are not hydrolysis, e.g., when a metal or water reacts to form a base and liberate hydrogen.

hydrometer (hīdrŏ′mùtùr), device to determine directly the SPECIFIC GRAVITY of a liquid. Usually it is a thin glass tube closed at both ends, with a bulb at one end filled with mercury or fine shot so that it will float upright in liquid being tested. Scale is so calibrated that reading at level of surface of liquid gives specific gravity. Density can be calculated from specific-gravity readings. Commercial hydrometers usually are calibrated for 20°C.

hydrophobia [from Greek,= hatred of water] (hī″drùfō′bêù) or **rabies** (rā′bēz), acute infectious disease caused by virus which affects nervous system. It is transmitted by bite of rabid animal. Spasm of pharynx on swallowing results in fear of drinking water. Pasteur developed method of preventing disease by inoculation 1884 and first used it on human patient 1885.

hydroponics: see SOILLESS GARDENING.

hydrostatics: see MECHANICS.

hydroxide (hīdrŏk′sīd), term commonly used for a BASE, although some compounds with hydroxyl (OH) radical show acid properties. Others have both acidic and basic characteristics (i.e., are amphoteric); still others are neutral.

hydroxyl radical: see HYDROXIDE; RADICAL.

hyena (hīē′nù), nocturnal Old World mammal. Its front legs are longer than hind ones. It eats mostly carrion. Striped hyena of Asia Minor, Persia, India, and N Africa and brown hyena or strand wolf of S Africa both belong to genus *Hyaena*. Spotted hyena (*Crocuta*) in Africa S of Sahara is largest form (2½ ft. high at shoulder). It has a maniacal cry and is said to rob graves and steal children.

hygiene (hī'jĕn), science of health and its preservation. Community aspects are handled by PUBLIC HEALTH and SOCIAL HYGIENE programs. Field of MENTAL HYGIENE developed after recognition of health role of mental and emotional factors.

hygrometer (hīgrŏ'mŭtŭr), instrument for measuring moisture content of air. In the condensing, or dew-point hygrometer, fluid in a tube is evaporated, thereby drawing heat from surrounding air; since air holds less moisture as temperature decreases, excess moisture condenses on tube. From temperatures recorded, when condensation begins, by thermometers within tube and outside it, moisture content is calculated. Other hygrometers are based on use of substance that expands or contracts as moisture varies or of substance that absorbs moisture from air with consequent weight increase. In the psychrometer moisture content is determined by difference in temperatures recorded by two thermometers, the bulb of one kept moist, the other dry.

Hyksos (hĭk'sōs), invaders of anc. Egypt, probably Semitic people. They took the kingship (c.1675 B.C., according to one date) from decadent rulers and kept it a century or more (XV–XVII dynasties) until driven out by Amasis I. By false etymology they are called the Shepherd Kings. Little is known of them.

Hymen or **Hymenaeus** (hīmŭnē'ŭs), Greek personification of marriage, represented as beautiful youth carrying bridal torch and wearing veil.

Hymettus (hīmĕ'tŭs), Gr. *Hymettos,* mountain group, Attica, Greece. Mt. Hymettus (3,367 ft.) famed since antiquity for its honey. Marble quarries.

hymn, song of praise, devotion, or thanksgiving, especially of a religious nature. Early Christian hymnody consisted mainly of the Psalms and other biblical texts chanted in unison. Metrical Latin hymns developed in 4th cent. Great medieval hymns include *Dies irae, Stabat Mater Dolorosa,* and *Pange lingua.* In the Reformation, the Lutheran chorale developed; Luther wrote several (e.g., *A Mighty Fortress,* which has a famous setting by J. S. Bach). Calvinism contributed the Genevan Psalter, containing the tune *Old Hundred.* The English hymn developed largely in the 18th cent. with the sacred texts of Cowper, Watts, and Wesley. An early collection of hymns in America was the *Bay Psalm Book* (pub. 1640).

hyoscine: see SCOPOLAMINE.

Hypatia (hīpā'shŭ), d. 415, Alexandrian Neoplatonic philosopher, a woman renowned for beauty, learning, and eloquence; said to have been murdered by monks at the instigation of St. Cyril of Alexandria, an enemy of the prefect who was Hypatia's lover.

hyperbola (hīpûr'bŭlŭ), a plane curve such that difference between distances from any point on it to two fixed points (*foci*) is same for all points on curve. It is also a conic section formed by a plane cutting both nappes of the cone. Center is halfway between foci; principal axis is straight line through foci; vertices are intersections of axis with curve. *Latus rectum* is chord through either focus perpendicular to principal axis. Asymptotes are lines in same plane which curve approaches as it approaches infinity. Equilateral hyperbola is one whose asymptotes are perpendicular.

Hyperboreans (hī"pŭrbô'rēŭnz, –bôrē'ŭnz), in Greek legend, people dwelling in bliss in the Far North.

Hyperion (hīpēr'ēŭn), in Greek religion, Titan; son of Uranus and Gaea and father of Helios, Selene, and Eos by Theia.

hypertension: see BLOOD PRESSURE.

hypnotism, Braid's term (1842) for animal magnetism or mesmerism (see MESMER). It is induced in a relaxed subject by monotonous repetition of words and gestures—some people are not affected. In slight hypnosis consciousness remains, actions are remembered; in deep hypnosis, sensory system and muscles are affected, supernormal feats cause no fatigue, are forgotten. Hypnosis heightens suggestibility, was used to treat and study hysteria. Briefly used by Freud in psychoanalysis, it is still used in some therapy and in study of mental activities.

hypochondria (hī"pŭkŏn'drēŭ), the neurotic reaction marked by habitual preoccupation with health and with imagined or negligible physical defect.

Hyrcania: see GURGAN.

Hyrcanus, John (hûrkā'nŭs), name of two of the MACCABEES.

hyssop (hĭs'ŭp), aromatic perennial herb (*Hyssopus officinalis*) native to Old World. It has small violet-blue, white, or pink flowers. Once used as flavoring, it is now grown chiefly for ornament.

hysteria, in general usage, highly emotional and irrational conduct, reflected in bodily disturbance. Psychologists define it as a conversion NEUROSIS. Occasionally hysteria creates organic sickness (see PSYCHOSOMATIC MEDICINE). In late 19th cent., the psychological origin of hysteria was recognized, and hypnosis was used for its cure.

Hythe (hīdh), municipal borough (pop. 9,218), Kent, England; summer resort and one of CINQUE PORTS. School of Small Arms is here.

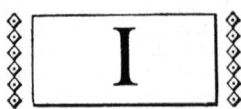

I, chemical symbol of element IODINE.

iambic pentameter: see PENTAMETER.

Iamblichus (ĭăm'blĭkŭs), d. c.330, Syrian Neoplatonic philosopher; pupil of Porphyry.

Iapetus (īă'pĭtŭs), in Greek mythology, Titan; son of Uranus and Gaea and husband of CLYMENE.

Iasi, Rumania: see JASSY.

Ibadan (ēbä'dän), city (pop. 387,133), SW Nigeria, inhabited by the Yoruba. Consists mainly of mud huts. Cacao, cotton, and palm oil are exported.

Ibagué (ēbägä'), city (pop. 27,448), W central Colombia; founded 1550; a commercial center.

Ibáñez, Vicente Blasco: see BLASCO IBÁÑEZ.

Iberia (ībēr'ēŭ), anc. name of a country in Transcaucasia, roughly E part of Georgian SSR.

Iberian Gates, Georgian SSR: see DARYAL.

Iberian Peninsula, SW Europe, comprising SPAIN and PORTUGAL, between Atlantic and Mediterranean. Separated from main continent by Pyrenees, from N Africa by Strait of Gibraltar. Named for the **Iberians,**

anc. people believed to have migrated from Africa in Neolithic period. They merged with the Celts (who came later) into "Celtiberian" nation.

Iberville, Pierre le Moyne, sieur d' (pyĕr' lü mwän' syûr' dēbĕrvēl'), 1661–1706, French Canadian naval officer and colonizer. Led attacks on British settlements in North America. Estab. colony in lower Mississippi valley with brother, sieur de BIENVILLE.

Iberville (ē'bûrvĭl), town (pop. 5,185), S Que., Canada, on Richelieu R. and SE of Montreal. Trade center in dairy region.

ibex (ī'bĕks), gregarious, sturdy, agile wild goat (*Capra*) living at snow line of mountains of Asia, Europe. It is brown or gray, 2½–3½ ft. high at the shoulder, and has long ridged horns curving backward.

ibis (ī'bĭs), wading bird of warm parts of both hemispheres. Usually it nests in colonies. Its body is c.2 ft. long; the bill is long, slender, decurved, and grooved from nostril to tip. In North America are white ibis, white-faced and eastern glossy ibises, and wood ibis (really a stork).

Ibiza, island, Spain: see IVIZA.

Ibn Batuta (ĭ'bŭn bätōō'tä), 1304?–1378?, Moslem traveler, b. Tangier. More widely traveled than any known medieval man, he wrote valuable accounts of the Near and Far East.

Ibn Ezra, Abraham ben Meir (mâr' ĭ'bŭn), 1092?–1167, Jewish poet, biblical critic, astronomer; inspiration of Robert Browning's "Rabbi Ben Ezra."

Ibn Gabirol, Solomon ben Judah (ĭ'bŭn gäbē'rôl), c.1021–1058, Jewish poet and philosopher, known also as Avicebron. Wrote *The Well of Life,* an attempt to explain man's purpose in life.

Ibn Khaldun (ĭ'bŭn khäldōōn'), 1332–1406, Arab historian. In *Kitab al-Ibar* [universal history] he treats history as science and outlines philosophy of history. Deemed greatest of Arab historians.

Ibn Saud (Abdu-l-Aziz ibn Saud) (ĭ'bŭn säōōd'), c.1880–, founder of SAUDI ARABIA. Triumphed over his rival, HUSEIN IBN ALI, in 1924 and declared himself king of the HEJAZ and NEJD. Remained neutral during World War II. A leader in anti-Zionist movement among Arab states.

Ibn Tufail (ĭ'bŭn tōōfil'), 12th-cent. Spanish-Arabian philosopher and physician. Wrote *Hayy ibn Yaqzan,* a philosophical romance.

Ibn Zohr: see AVENZOAR.

Ibrahim Pasha (ĭbrähēm' pä'shä), 1789–1848, Egyptian general; son of MOHAMMED ALI. Led Turkish forces against Wahabis in Arabia (1816–19) and rebel Greeks (1825–28). Conquered Turkish-held Syria (1832–33), but European troops forced his withdrawal 1838.

Ibsen, Henrik, 1828–1906, Norwegian dramatist, one of the outstanding figures in modern world theater. A satirical verse play, *Love's Comedy* (1862) was followed by dramatic poems *Brand* (1866) and *Peer Gynt* 1867) and a series of powerful, realistic social plays in prose (*The Pillars of Society,* 1877; *A Doll's House,* 1879; *Ghosts,* 1881; *An Enemy of the People,* 1882; *The Wild Duck,* 1884; *Rosmersholm,* 1886; *The Lady from the Sea,* 1888; *Hedda Gabler,* 1890; *The Master Builder,* 1892; *Little Eyolf,* 1894; *John Gabriel Borkman,* 1896; *When We Dead Awaken,* 1899). His uncompromising insistence in presenting natural characters in conflict with social custom and environment brought a fresh breath into the theater. G. B. Shaw was one of his disciples.

Ica (ē'kä), city (pop. 21,437), SW Peru; commercial center for irrigated valley of Ica R.

Icaria: see CABET, ÉTIENNE.

Icarus, in Greek myth. He flew too near the sun with wings made by his father, Daedalus. Wax joints of the wings melted, and he fell into the sea.

ice action, an agent of erosion. Freezing (and expansion) of water in cracks breaks up rocks; glaciers and shore ice wear away land by friction.

Ice Age: see PLEISTOCENE EPOCH.

iceberg, ice mass detached from glacier or ice sheet and floating on ocean. About one ninth of mass projects above water.

ice cream, frozen confection made from milk fat and solids, sugar, and flavoring, and often containing a stabilizer (e.g., starch, gelatine), eggs, fruits, or nuts. Agitation during freezing produces light, smooth texture. Similar desserts include parfaits, mousses, frozen custards, ices, sherbets. Probably originated as a frozen ice in 17th-cent. Italy.

Iceland, Icelandic *Island,* republic (c.40,000 sq. mi.; pop. 141,042), westernmost state of Europe, occupying Iceland isl. and several smaller islands in the Atlantic just S of Arctic Circle, c.600 mi. W of Norway; cap. REYKJAVIK. Iceland is a plateau, averaging 2,000 ft. high and culminating in vast icefields, of which VATNAJÖKULL is largest. Deep fjords indent the coast. Many of the more than 100 volcanoes are still active (highest is Mt. HEKLA). Hot springs such as the GEYSIR abound. Climate is mild and humid because of North Atlantic Drift. Iceland is only c.25% habitable, and most cities are on the coast. Island lacks timber, but has extensive grazing (sheep, horses, cattle). Agr. (hay, potatoes, turnips) is limited. Fishing is most important industry, codfish and herring constituting chief export. Iceland is governed by parliamentary democracy. Here social-security legislation is very advanced. Most citizens are Lutherans. High educational level is due to ancient tradition and ingrained civilization rather than to formal schooling. Irish monks visited Iceland before 9th cent., but abandoned it on arrival of Norse settlers (c.850–870). In 930 a general assembly, the ALTHING, was estab., and c.1000 Christianity was introduced. However, memory of paganism was preserved in literature of 13th-cent. Iceland, where OLD NORSE LITERATURE reached its greatest flowering (modern Icelandic is virtually same language as that of the sagas). Attempt of SNORRI STURLUSON to establish full control of King Haakon IV of Norway over Iceland failed, but in 1261–64 king obtained acknowledgment of his sovereignty by the Icelanders. With Norway, Iceland passed under the Danish crown (1380). In 17th and 18th cent. pirates ruined trade: epidemics and a general volcanic eruption (1783) killed many; and creation (1602) of a private trading company at Copenhagen, with exclusive rights to Iceland trade, caused economic ruin. Foreign traders were not admitted until 1854. Home rule was finally granted in 1874, and in 1918 Iceland was declared a sovereign state in personal union with Denmark. During World War II, when British and U.S. forces were based in Iceland, the Althing assumed king's prerogatives, and on June 17, 1944, after popular referendum, kingdom of Iceland became an independent republic. Iceland was admitted to the UN in 1946, and joined in European Recovery Program and North Atlantic Treaty.

Icelandic language, North Germanic language. See LANGUAGE (table).

Icelandic literature. The Eddas and sagas of early Icelandic literature (see OLD NORSE LITERATURE) had a lasting effect on later writing. Literature declined after the loss of Iceland's independence (1261–64), but in the 14th cent. arose the *rimur,* a type of narrative poem. After the Protestant Reformation, religion dominated literature until the period of enlightenment (1750–1835). The romantic revival, begun in the 1830s, stressed nationalism as well as romantic elements. The classic Iceland style was developed in 19th and 20th cent. by such men as the short-story writer Jonas Hallgrimsson; the novelist Jon Thoroddsen; the poets Grimur Thomsen, Benedikt Grondal, and Steingrimur Thorsteinsson; and the dramatist Matthias Jochumsson. The historian Jon Sigurdsson helped to promote Icelandic language and literature. Realism appeared to challenge romanticism with attacks on the Church and social institutions; important in the movement were short-story writer Gestur Palsson; the Icelandic Canadian poet Stephen G. Stephansson. A more introspective type of literature also developed. Various strains enriched Icelandic literature, as in the neoromantic movement and "proletarian" writing. Among 20th-cent. figures have been Jon Trausti (pseud. of Gudmundur Magnusson), Sigurdur Nordal, Kristmann Gudmundson, and Halldor K. LAXNESS.

Iceland moss, a grayish paper-thin lichen (*Cetraria islandica*) of northern countries and found as far south as N U.S. It has long been used in Scandinavian countries for human food and for fodder.

Iceland spar, transparent calcite characterized by double refraction. Used for prisms of polarizing microscopes and other optical instruments.

ice plant, low fleshy plant (*Mesembryanthemum,* or *Cryophytum, crystallinum*) of warm, dry, barren regions. It is a useful ground cover or pot plant.

Ichabod (ĭ'kŭbŏd) [Heb.,= inglorious], grandson of Eli. 1 Sam. 4.21; 14.3. Name given disparagingly to Daniel Webster in poem by John Greenleaf Whittier.

Ichang or **I-ch'ang** (both: ē'chäng), city (pop. 80,979), SW Hupeh prov., China, on Yangtze R.; terminus for ocean-going vessels from Shanghai.

Ickes, Harold L(eClaire) (ĭ'kŭs), 1874–1952, U.S. Secretary of the Interior (1933–46). Long a progressive known for his bluntness in action, he called himself a "curmudgeon."

Icknield Street (ĭk'nēld), Saxon name for an early road in Britain from Berkshire Downs to the Chilterns.

Icolmkill, Inner Hebrides, Scotland: see IONA.

Icon Basilike: see EIKON BASILIKE.

Iconium (īkō'nēŭm), anc. city of Asia Minor, included in various regions as boundaries shifted. In Galatia when Paul visited it as a missionary. Modern Konya, Turkey is here.

iconoclasm (īkō'nŏklăzŭm) [Gr.,= image-breaking], opposition to religious use of images. Use of religious pictures and statues was an early feature of Christian worship (see ICONOGRAPHY and CATACOMBS). After the 5th cent., however, images came to be associated with superstitions, and iconoclasm flourished in Monophysite center of Asia Minor and was perhaps influenced by iconoclasm of Islam, Judaism, Manichaeism, and the Paulicians. Emperors Leo III, Constantine V, Leo IV, and Leo V favored iconoclasm, but Empress IRENE restored the images. Iconoclasm was rejected at the Second Council of NICAEA. The controversy gave Byzantine art a spiritual bent, away from naturalism.

iconography (ī"kŏnŏg'–), broadly, act of representation by pictures and images, which may or may not have a symbolic as well as a literal meaning; also the study of such figural representations. Systematic investigation of the history of art has shown that each major phase or epoch has developed an iconography of its own, and the term is necessarily qualified (e.g., iconography of Egyptian deities, iconography of Napoleon, Byzantine iconography). The aim of iconographic research is to recover and express the thought behind a certain type, particularly if the type became a symbol. Christian iconography is extremely rich and varied. It began with the catacombs and developed a complex language of symbols. Every medieval artist had to learn the characters of this sacred "writing" and also the sacred "mathematics" that dictated position, group, symmetry, and number of figures in representation. The symbolic code (as in representing the Holy Ghost as a dove) has invited men to look at one thing and see the figure of another. The essence of Christian iconography lies in the expression and reading of the spiritual meaning intended in the art.

Ictinus (ĭktī'nŭs), 2d half of 5th cent. B.C., one of greatest architects of Greece. Designed PARTHENON with Callicrates as associate.

id: see PSYCHOANALYSIS.

Ida, Mount, 8,058 ft. high, central Crete; island's highest mountain. Also known as Psiloriti.

Ida, Mount, range in Phrygia, Asia Minor. Here in legend Paris was reared and fell in love with Oenone.

Idaho, state (82,808 sq. mi.; pop. 588,637), NW U.S.;

admitted 1890 as 43d state; cap. BOISE. Other cities are POCATELLO and IDAHO FALLS. SNAKE R. forms part of W boundary. Along Mont. boundary is BITTERROOT RANGE of Rockies. Farming (wheat, oats, alfalfa, potatoes, sugar beets, fruits, livestock, dairy products); mining (lead, silver, zinc, copper, gold, phosphate); lumbering. New atomic energy processing plant was begun at Arco in 1949. Lewis and Clark expedition of 1805 preceded activities of Canadian and American fur traders in region. Franklin was first permanent settlement (1860). Discovery of gold that year led to rapid settlement. Idaho Territory set up in 1863. Indian troubles occurred until late 1870s. Boomed in late 19th cent. through silver and lead mines and growth of railroads. Now has irrigation and power projects (see BOISE PROJECT, MINIDOKA PROJECT). State has increasing tourism (e.g., at the popular resort of Sun Valley).

Idaho, University of: see MOSCOW.

Idaho Falls, city (pop. 19,218), SE Idaho, on Snake R. and NNE of Pocatello. Settled in 1860s; named Idaho Falls in 1890–91. Chief city of upper Snake valley; trade and processing center for irrigated farms (esp. potatoes), stock ranches, dairies.

Idaho Springs, resort city (pop. 1,769; alt. c.7,500 ft.), N central Colo., just W of Denver. Had first major gold strike in Colo., 1859. Hot mineral springs.

Ida Mountains (ī'dŭ), range, NW Turkey, SE of site of anc. Troy. Its modern name is Kazdagi. Rises to c.5,800 ft. at Mt. Gargarus.

idealism, in metaphysics, belief that the underlying reality of the universe resides in ideas, ideal forms, or an absolute. It is opposed by all types of materialism and relativistic beliefs. The classic statement of idealism was that of Plato. In modern times Hegel was the most thorough-going philosopher in his doctrines of the Absolute and the unchanging laws by which change takes place. Among later idealists Bernard Bosanquet and A. N. Whitehead may be named. Subjective idealism, represented by Bishop Berkeley, is the belief that all reality exists only in personal consciousness. Outside metaphysics the term is used in several wide senses (e.g., in art, tendency to represent things as artist thinks they should be rather than as they are).

idiocy: see FEEBLE-MINDEDNESS.

Idlewild: see QUEENS, New York city borough.

idol [Gr.], image believed to possess supernatural power because it is dwelling place of supernatural being. Represents fixation of a spiritual force in a material object. Whereas fetish or charm has inherent power, idol must be consecrated before it can be worshiped. It is animal or human in form, and is treated as though alive. Idolatry has inspired many great works of art. Ritual use of idols dates from late Paleolithic times and still prevails in large sections of today's world.

Idomeneus (īdŏ'mĭnūs, –mĭnēŭs), in Greek legend, aged Cretan king who led Cretan troops in the Trojan War. Caught in a storm at sea when returning home, he vowed that if the ship was saved he would sacrifice to Poseidon the first living thing he met after landing. This was his son, whom he sacrificed.

Idrisi or **Edrisi** (īdrē'sē, ĕ–), b. 1099?, d. after 1154, Arabian geographer. He compiled a description of the earth (1154), most important geographic work of the period.

Idumaea or **Idumea:** see EDOM.

idyl (ī'dŭl), short poem. Ancient idyls, especially those of Bion and Moschus, were intended as little selections in style of longer poems, such as elegies or epics. Since some of the ten famous idyls by Theocritus dealt with pastoral or rural scenes term *idyl* came to be restricted to gently flowing, artistic pieces on rural subjects. Tennyson in his *Idylls of the King* used term in looser original sense.

Ie-jima: see OKINAWA.

Ieyasu (Ieyasu Tokugawa) (ēā'äsōō), 1542–1616, Japanese dictator, founder of TOKUGAWA shogunate. Victory over rival barons in battle of Sekigahara (1601) made him successor to Hideyoshi as supreme leader of Japan. Secured title of shogun 1603, set up cap. at Yedo (Tokyo). First tolerated, then persecuted Christian missions, but encouraged foreign trade. Name also spelled Iyeyasu.

If, Château d', France: see CHÂTEAU D'IF.

Ifni (ĭf'nē), Spanish possession (676 sq. mi.; pop. 45,-852), NW Africa, enclave on Atlantic coast of SW Morocco. Ceded by Morocco in 1860.

Iggdrasill, another spelling for YGGDRASILL.

igloo (ĭ'gloo), dome-shaped dwelling of the Eastern Eskimo constructed from snow blocks. It is usually a temporary shelter only.

Ignatius of Antioch, Saint (ĭgnā'shŭs, ăn'tēŏk), d. c.110, bishop of Antioch, Christian martyr. Wrote epistles to Christian communities to combat heresy. First to use word *Catholic;* he enjoined obedience to bishop, deacons, and presbyters. Feast: Feb. 1.

Ignatius of Constantinople, Saint, c.800–877, Greek patriarch of Constantinople. A son of Emperor MICHAEL I, he was castrated and imprisoned by LEO V (813) to prevent his accession. In 846 or 847 he was made patriarch by Empress Theodora, who approved his zeal against iconoclasm. After her banishment St. Ignatius was asked to resign, and MICHAEL III made PHOTIUS patriarch. Under BASIL I, St. Ignatius was restored and was declared legal patriarch by Fourth Council of Constantinople.

Ignatius of Loyola, Saint (loiyō'lŭ), 1491–1556, Spanish founder of the Jesuits (see JESUS, SOCIETY OF). A courtier and then a soldier, he was converted to the religion in 1521 when recovering from wounds. At Monserrat, at Manresa, and at various other places he studied and prepared himself. In 1534 he and six companions took together vows of chastity and poverty and agreed to go to the Holy Land. War prevented their journey, but they were ordained (1537), received by the pope (1538) and kept at Rome. In 1539 Pope Paul III accepted Ignatius' *Formula,* which (called in revised form the *Constitutions*) is still the charter of the Jesuits. Ignatius was general of the order until his death. He was a leader in the Catholic REFORM, but his chief interests were foreign missions and education of boys rather than reconversion of Protestants. He was a mystic as well as a practical leader, and his *Spiritual Exercises* (begun just after his conversion) is a contemplative devotional work. His idea of the Jesuit as a "soldier of Christ" is based on St. Paul (Eph. 6.10–17). Feast: July 31.

igneous rock: see ROCK.

ignis fatuus: see WILL-O'-THE-WISP.

ignition, device for igniting an explosive mixture. Ignition system in automobiles uses electric spark which ignites compressed mixture of air and gasoline vapor in the cylinders. Necessary high-voltage current is obtained from magneto or by battery-ignition system (with engine-driven generator) and is used directly, or indirectly through storage battery. System consists of storage battery, circuit breaker, induction coil (condenser), distributor, and wiring. Low voltage from battery is increased to high voltage by flowing into primary winding of coil and setting up magnetic flux. When circuit breaker is opened low-voltage current ceases and magnetic field collapses; this induces in secondary winding of coil a high voltage which then goes to distributor for relay to spark plugs; these are "fired" in definite order to insure even movement of pistons in cylinder and smooth running of engine.

Igor (ē'gŭr), 1150–1202, Russian prince. Led unsuccessful expedition against Cumans 1185. Hero of Russian epic, *The Lay of the Host of Igor,* discovered in 1795 and attributed to 12th cent.; used by Borodin for opera, *Prince Igor.*

Igorot (ĭgŭrōt'), proto-Malayan people of N central Luzon isl. They live under village-state form of organization and practice rice-terrace agr. Were formerly head-hunters.

Iguala (ēgwä'lä), city (pop. 12,756), Guerrero, SW Mexico. Famous as place where Iturbide proclaimed **Plan de Iguala,** Feb. 24, 1821, providing that Roman Catholicism should be only religion; Mexico should be independent of Spain; all races in Mexico should be equal.

iguana (ĭgwä'nŭ), large lizard of tropical America, West Indies, some Pacific isls. Common tropical American species is greenish (blending with the tree branches which it frequents), 3–6 ft. long, and has a crest of spiny scales from neck to tail. It eats leaves, fruit, sometimes small animals.

Iguassú Falls (ēgwŭsoo'), in Iguassú R., South America. Higher and wider than Niagara, they belong partly to Argentina, partly to Brazil. Also Iguazú.

Iguvine Tables (ĭ'gyoovĭn), several inscribed bronze tablets discovered in 1444 at Gubbio, where most of them are still preserved. They proved helpful in understanding ancient Umbrian language and supplied information on ancient Italian religious rites.

Ij or **Y,** Dutch *IJ* (all: ī), inlet of the Ijsselmeer, NW Netherlands, on which Amsterdam is located. Receives Amstel R. and is connected by canals with North Sea and with Lek and Waal rivers.

Ijssel, Dutch *IJssel* (both: ī'sŭl), river, 72 mi. long, E and central Netherlands. Branches from the Lower Rhine near Arnhem and flows N into the Ijsselmeer near Kampen. The Hollandsche Ijssel, in W Netherlands, branches from Lek R. and flows WSW to the Meuse just E of Rotterdam. Also Yssel.

Ijsselmeer, Dutch *IJsselmeer* (both: ī'sŭlmār"), shallow fresh-water lake, N and central Netherlands. It was formed from old ZUIDER ZEE by construction of a dam (completed 1932) extending 19 mi. between North Holland and Friesland provinces. Ijssel R. is chief feeder. Large areas (293 sq. mi. in all) have been reclaimed from the former Zuider Zee since 1932. Largest is Northeast Polder (185 sq. mi.). Parts of the polders flooded in World War II have since been salvaged. Former Zuider Zee was an important fishing ground.

Ikhnaton (ĭknä'tŭn) or **Akhenaton** (ä"kŭnä'tŭn) [Egyptian,= Aton is satisfied], d. c.1358 B.C., king of Egypt (c.1375–c.1358 B.C.) of the XVIII dynasty, son of Amenhotep III. Beginning reign as Amenhotep IV, he changed his name on undertaking a complete reform in an attempt to unify political, social, and artistic life under a monotheism, centered about the sun-god Aton. The priests opposed him and domestic and foreign affairs brought ruin, but his period was one of the greatest of Egyptian art. A statue bust of his queen Nefretete (also Nofretete, Nepretiti, Nephretiti) is a familiar treasure of world art.

Ikon Basilike: see EIKON BASILIKE.

Île-aux-Noix, Fort (ēl-ō-nwä'), French fort in Canada, on Île aux Noix, an island in Richelieu R., c.30 mi. SE of Montreal. Built 1759. Fort surrendered to British in 1760. Named Fort Lennox, it fell to Americans in 1775 and became base of operations against Quebec until it was evacuated in 1776. Present fortifications (now included in Fort Lennox Natl. Historic Park; 210 acres) were started in 1782 and maintained as a military post until 1870.

Île-de-France (ēl-dü-fräs'), region and former province, N France, in Seine, Seine-et-Oise, Oise, and Aisne depts.; historic cap. Paris. Other cities: Beauvais, Compiègne, Fontainebleau, Soissons, Versailles. The center of the Paris basin, a fertile depression watered by the Seine, Marne, and Oise rivers, it is a vast agr. area, supplying Paris and its suburbs with fruit, vegetables, dairy products. There are many large and beautiful forests (e.g., at Fontainebleau, Compiègne, Rambouillet). The cradle of the French monarchy, the region grew out of the county of Paris, whose count, Hugh Capet, became king in 987. The crown enlarged its domains, acquiring parts of Beauce, Brie, the Vexin, and other neighboring areas, and in the 15th cent. the region was made a province.

Île Jésus (ēl zhāzü') or **Jesus Island,** island (93 sq. mi.;

pop. 37,843), S Que., Canada, between Mille Îles R. and Rivière des Prairies. Market gardening and dairy center.

Îles du Salut (ēl dü sälü'), small archipelago, off French Guiana, including Devil's Island. Also Safety Islands.

Ilf, Ilya (Arnoldovich) (ēlyä' ûrnôl'dŭvĭch ēlf'), pseud. of I. A. Fainzilber, 1897–1937, Russian humorist. With Y. P. Petrov (pseud. of Y. P. Katayev, 1903–42), he wrote *Little Golden Calf* (1933), a satire of capitalist survivals in Soviet society, and *Little Golden America* (1937), after a tour in the U.S.

Iliad (ĭ'lēŭd) [from Gr. *Ilion* = Troy], Greek epic in 24 books by HOMER, telling of the wrath of ACHILLES and its consequences in the Trojan War.

Ilion: see TROY, anc. city of Asia Minor.

Ilion (ĭ'lēŭn), village (pop. 9,363), E central N.Y., on Mohawk R. and the Barge Canal and SE of Utica. Mfg. of firearms (see REMINGTON, ELIPHALET) and typewriters.

Ilium: see TROY, anc. city of Asia Minor.

Illampú (ēyämpōō'), peak, 21,275 ft. high, E Bolivia, in Andes near L. Titicaca.

Ille-et-Vilaine (ēl"-ä-vēlĕn'), department (2,697 sq. mi.; pop. 578,246), NW France, in Brittany; cap. Rennes.

Illimani (ēyēmä'nē), mountain (21,184 ft. high), E Bolivia, in Andes.

illinium: see PROMETHIUM.

Illinois, state (55,947 sq. mi.; pop. 8,712,176), N central U.S.; admitted 1818 as 21st state (free); cap. SPRINGFIELD. CHICAGO largest city; other cities are PEORIA, ROCKFORD, EAST ST. LOUIS, DECATUR, JOLIET, ELGIN. Bounded W by Mississippi R., S by Ohio R., NE by L. Michigan. Region of well-watered plains. Farming (livestock, corn, oats, hay, soybeans, truck, fruit); mining (coal, oil, fluorspar, silica sand). Processes meat, food, oil; mfg. of steel, farm machinery; printing, publishing. Transportation center of Midwest. Explored by Marquette and Jolliet (1673), La Salle (1679). Region went to British after last French and Indian War (1763). Won by U.S. in American Revolution after capture by G. R. CLARK of CAHOKIA and KASKASKIA (1778). Became separate territory 1809. Land speculation, factory of Cyrus H. McCORMICK (1847) and rail development of 1850s marked state's rise. Abraham LINCOLN and Stephen DOUGLAS won national attention by their debates on slavery issue in senatorial race (1858). Industry expanded greatly after Civil War. Farmers joined GRANGER MOVEMENT and resisted dominance of railroads. Labor-management tension reflected in HAYMARKET SQUARE RIOT (1886) and strike at PULLMAN (1894). Industrial position in nation was strengthened in World War II.

Illinois, river formed in NE Ill. by junction of Des Plaines and Kankakee rivers. Flows 273 mi. SW past Peoria to the Mississippi at Grafton. Link in shipping route between Great Lakes and Gulf of Mexico; part of Illinois Waterway system.

Illinois, University of, at Urbana, Champaign, and Chicago; land-grant, state-supported, coed.; chartered 1867, opened 1868 as Illinois Industrial Univ., renamed 1885. Has institute of labor and industrial relations. Rush Medical College in Chicago (chartered 1837, affiliated with Univ. of Chicago 1898–1941) is affiliated. Pioneered in vocational education. Has betatron. Also has an Alma Mater group by alumnus Lorado Taft.

Illinois College: see JACKSONVILLE.

Illinois Indians, group of North American Indian tribes of Algonquian linguistic stock. In 17th cent. were scattered over S Wis., N Ill., and parts of Iowa and Mo. They were of Eastern Woodlands area culture, but also hunted buffalo. Wars with Iroquois and with Lake tribes (provoked by assassination of Pontiac) reduced Illinois Indians almost to nothing.

Illinois Institute of Technology: see CHICAGO.

Illuminati (ĭlōō"mĭnä'tī, –nä'tē) [Latin,= the enlightened], members of a rationalist society founded by Adam Weishaupt (after 1776) and flourishing briefly.

It was connected with Freemasonry, was condemned by the Roman Catholic Church, and dissolved (1785) in Bavaria by the government. Later groups have also used the name, and the Rosicrucians call themselves Illuminati.

illuminating gas: see GAS; METHANE; NATURAL GAS.

illumination, in art, the decoration of manuscripts and books with colored and metal pictures, especially initial-letter and marginal decorations. Used in many medieval writings copied in monasteries and cathedral schools. A beautiful example is the Irish Book of Kells (8th cent.), at Trinity Col., Dublin.

illumination of streets and buildings: see LIGHTING; PHOTOMETRY.

Illyria (ĭlĭ'rēŭ) and **Illyricum** (ĭlī'rĭkŭm). In prehistoric times Indo-European tribes (Dalmatians and Pannonians) migrated to the N and E shores of the Adriatic in region later known as Illyria. Warlike and given to piracy, they withstood Greek influence and defeated Macedon. The Romans conquered the Illyrian kingdom and created the province of Illyricum (167 B.C.) from part of it. Later the region was Dalmatia and Pannonia. Today Illyria means the Adriatic coast N of central Albania.

Ilmen (ĭl'mŭn), lake (c.400 sq. mi.), NW European RSFSR. Empties through Volkhov R. into L. Ladoga. Novgorod and Staraya Russa are near its shores.

Iloilo (ē"lōē'lō), commercial city (pop. 110,122), on SE Panay, Philippines; port on Iloilo Strait. Seat of Central Philippine Col. of Jaro.

image, in optics, likeness of object produced when light rays from object are reflected from mirror or refracted by lens. A real image, one formed by light rays coming from an object and converging before producing an image, can be thrown on a screen. A virtual image formed by prolongations of rays (not by rays themselves) cannot be thrown on screen, e.g., image from plane mirror. Size of image and whether it is erect or inverted, real or virtual, depend on distance from lens and type of lens or mirror used.

imagists, Anglo-American school of poetry, stressing concentration, hard clear images, new rhythms, and use of common speech. Founded by Ezra Pound, taken over by Amy Lowell. Richard Aldington, Hilda Doolittle, and John Gould Fletcher were imagists.

imam (ĭmäm'), in Islam, leader, especially in Friday prayer at mosque. As synonym for caliph, applied by Shiites to caliphs descended from ALI. After OMAYYAD family had held caliphate for centuries, the believers in Ali's supremacy (esp. Fatimites) adopted theory that Alid caliphs were really carrying on their rule secretly and that one Alid caliph (the MAHDI) would be restored to public rule before the end of the world. The fervor of Alid followers has led to rebellions in some Moslem countries.

imbecility: see FEEBLE-MINDEDNESS.

Immanuel or **Emmanuel** [Heb.,= God with us], Isaiah's name for child who was to be a sign of Judah's deliverance. A name of Jesus. Isa. 7.14; 8.8; Mat. 1.23.

Immermann, Karl (kärl' ĭ'mŭrmän), 1796–1840, German author. Successful as playwright in his lifetime, he survives chiefly through his novel *Die Epigonen* (1836), a satire on his contemporaries, and through short novels, e.g., *Der Oberhof*.

immigration, entrance of a person into a new country where he intends to establish permanent residence. There was a great influx of Europeans into the U.S. in the 19th cent., c.38,000,000 immigrants entering the U.S. between 1820 and 1920; Chinese and Japanese also began to immigrate. But restrictions were imposed (against Chinese) in 1882–the first against any group–and in 1917, 1921, and 1924 there were further restrictions, the last establishing the quota system whereby entrants were limited to 3% annually of the number of natives residing in the U.S. in 1910. In 1924, Asiatics were almost wholly excluded; a "national origins" plan made for more restrictions. The Chinese Exclusion Act was repealed in 1943, and a small quota set up. In 1952 Congress passed, over President Truman's veto, a new immigration law (the so-called McCarran Act) that, though it removed racial barriers to allow a small number of Asians to enter annually, reaffirmed the "national origin" feature of the 1921 and 1924 laws.

immunity, resistance to disease. Natural immunity arises from body's inherent ability to destroy invading organisms by action of certain white blood corpuscles and antibodies in blood. Immunity is acquired by surviving the disease or by inoculation or vaccination. Active immunity arises from antibodies produced in tissues; passive immunity results from introducing defense factors (e.g., antitoxin) into body and lasts for shorter time than active.

impala or **pallah,** antelope (*Aepyceros*) of E and S African bush country. It is reddish brown shading to whitish on under parts; shoulder height c.3 ft. Only male has horns (long, curved, lyre-shaped).

impatiens, touch-me-not, or **balsam,** annual or perennial plant of genus *Impatiens* with seed pods that burst at a touch when ripe. Annual garden balsams (*Impatiens balsamina*) have camellialike flowers. Wild jewelweed (*I. biflora*), native to moist soil in North America, has orange spurred flowers.

impeachment, formal accusation made by a legislature against a public official charging crime or serious misconduct. Also loosely used to describe the ensuing trial. In England, House of Commons presented articles of impeachment of House of Lords, who rendered judgment. Impeachment of Warren Hastings (1788–95) was one of last English cases. U.S. Constitution gives House of Representatives right to impeach U.S. officials (but not members of Congress). Senate tries cases; vote of two thirds of those present necessary to convict. Famous case was that of Pres. Andrew Johnson (impeached, but not convicted).

Impellitteri, Vincent R. (ĭmpĕl″ītĕ′rē), 1900–, American public official, mayor of New York city (1950–), b. Italy. Refused the Democratic nomination, he was elected as an independent, a political upset.

Imperial, city (pop. 1,759), SE Calif., oldest community in IMPERIAL VALLEY; founded 1902.

Imperial Conference, assembly of representatives of self-governing members of British Empire, held about every four years. First called Colonial Conferences (1887–1906) and dealt with defense problems. Since 1907 economic problems have been discussed. Dominion premiers now attempt to unify Empire policy. Decisions have no legal power, but are influential.

imperialism, broadly, extension of rule or influence by one people over another. Empires have existed since dawn of history, as in Egypt, Mesopotamia, Assyria, and Persian Empire. Ancient imperialism reached climax in Roman Empire and in Byzantine Empire and later Ottoman Empire. In West imperialism emerged with rise of modern national states and age of exploration and discovery; and term is normally restricted to this modern type of empire building. Through colonies European hegemony was introduced by force, with an assumed superiority over native people. Spanish and Portuguese built "trading" empires, British and French true "settlement" empires, all motivated by MERCANTILISM. U.S. spread westward with idea of manifest destiny, but was not an empire until Spanish-American War. Anti-imperialism has grown steadily since American Revolution, and has led U.S. to grant independence to Philippines, and anti-imperialist sentiment following World War II. British and French empires have gradually loosed their hold upon dependent nations as agitation for nationalism has spread.

Imperial Valley, below-sea-level area of old Colorado Desert in SE Calif. and N Lower California, Mexico. Occupies Salton Sink S of SALTON SEA. Rainfall is scanty, and there are sudden, extreme changes in temperature (32°F.–115°F.). Colorado R. irrigation of its rich soils (begun c.1900, hindered by floods) succeeded by 1907. Irrigation now supplied to c.1,000,000 acres

(mainly via ALL-AMERICAN CANAL), which produce truck, fruit, dates, grain, alfalfa, cotton, and dairy products. Centers include Brawley, Calexico, El Centro, Holtville, and Imperial in Calif., and Mexicali, Mexico.

import: see BALANCE OF TRADE.

impressionism, in painting, a late 19th-cent. French school. Its adherents attempted to depict quick visual impressions, often painted directly from nature. By using broken color they produced a luminous effect and were particularly successful with sunlight. Movement originated in 1870s and became popular in 90s, when most of its exponents had already left it. Most consistent impressionists were Monet, Sisley, and Pissarro. Others associated with school were Renoir and Degas. The term is used also in music for a late 19th-cent. French movement, typified in works of DEBUSSY. Characterized by breakdown of tonality and attempt to convey vague impression of mood.

impressment, enforcement of conscription. May be applied either to property or to persons in peace or war by virtue of a state's sovereign authority, except that constitutional limitations and legal regulations must be respected. In most modern democracies impressment in the historic sense of a "press gang" actually seizing and carrying an individual into service has been abandoned. Impressment of American sailors by the British was a cause of the War of 1812.

In, chemical symbol of the element INDIUM.

inbreeding, mating of closely related living things. Chief use is to insure preserving of desirable characters among purebred animal offspring. Inbreeding through too many generations reduces chances of diversity of characters in offspring and sometimes lessens vigor and reproductive ability.

Inca (ĭng′kù), pre-Colombian Indian empire (c.650,000 sq. mi.; pop. c.6,000,000), centered at Cuzco, Peru. The name Inca specifically refers to emperor and is used loosely to mean his people. Founded c.1200, empire reached its greatest extent under Huayna Capac (1493–1527), who was succeeded by his sons Huascar and Atahualpa. Atahualpa won in ensuing civil war, but Spanish, under Francisco Pizarro, conquered empire in 1553. Through a genius for organization, the Inca had welded together many peoples speaking different languages and exercised close control. The state was responsible for welfare of subjects, and owned everything except houses and movable household goods. Taxes were collected in labor. Populations were shifted at government's discretion for economic and control purposes. The Inca were skilled in engineering and agriculture, their activities in those fields running to road, bridge, drainage, and irrigation construction, and use of fertilizer. Highly developed arts and crafts included textiles, metallurgy, and ceramics.

incest (ĭn′sĕst), sexual relations between persons to whom marriage is prohibited because of blood relationship. Degree of proscribed relationship varies from group to group; in some societies marriage between clan members is taboo; in others even brother-sister marriage is accepted (e.g., among Egyptian and Inca royalty).

Inchcolm (ĭnch′kŭm), small island in Firth of Forth, Fifeshire, Scotland. Has ruins of Abbey of St. Columba (founded 1123).

Inchon, Korea: see CHEMULPO.

incinerator (ĭnsĭ′nùrātùr), furnace for burning combustible refuse. Usually it consists of a brick-lined combustion chamber fitted with stationary or mechanically-operated grates, charging holes, stoking and removal openings, ducts, and valves; often there are forced-draft blowers supplying air for combustion and a flue conducted through tall chimney.

inclined plane, a simple machine, of ancient origin, using a slanted plane up which the load or resistance is moved. Work put into the machine equals the effort multiplied by length of the plane; work output is product of the load and the height of the plane. Applications include the screw, wedge, chisel, carpenter's plane, and ax. See *ill.,* p. 619.

inclosure or **enclosure,** in agr., the practice of setting apart land formerly subject to common rights. Followed shift from the manorial system to free cultivation. In England it began in 12th cent., grew after development of Flemish wool trade in 14th cent., and reached its peak in late 17th cent. Caused shift of the poor to urban centers. Also helped efficient tillage and reclamation of wasteland.

income tax. Experiments on taxation of income were tried in medieval Italy and 19th-cent. England. A permanent income tax was adopted in England 1874, and a temporary one in U.S. 1862–72. The U.S. income-tax law of 1894 was declared unconstitutional, but the 16th Amendment legalized the income tax in 1913. The various states have levied income taxes since 1789; since 1919 most states have adopted them.

incorporation: see CORPORATION.

incubator, artificially heated apparatus for hatching eggs. Crude incubators were devised in ancient times; the Chinese have long used baskets heated by layers of wheat. Modern incubators are usually operated by electricity with automatic controls for heat, air, and moisture, and devices for turning eggs. Small models are used for premature babies.

incunabula (ĭn″kyŏŏnă′byŏŏlù), books of the "cradle" days of printing (15th cent.) by such printers as Gutenberg, Jenson, Caxton, and Aldus Manutius. There are many well-known European collections. Notable American collections are in Washington (Library of Congress), New York (Pierpont Morgan Library and others), Providence (John Carter Brown Library and Annmary Brown Memorial), and San Marino, Calif. (Henry E. Huntington Library).

Independence. 1 City (pop. 11,335), SE Kansas, on Verdigris R. near Okla. line; founded 1869. Oil refining and grain processing. Site of Rebel Creek battle (1863) is near. **2** City (pop. 36,963), W Mo., near Kansas City; settled 1825. Produces farm machinery and stoves. Was starting point in mid-19th cent. for SANTA FE TRAIL, OREGON TRAIL, and California Trail travelers. Hq. of Reorganized Church of Jesus Christ of Latter-Day Saints. Home of Harry S. Truman.

Independence, Declaration of: see DECLARATION OF INDEPENDENCE.

Independence Day: see FOURTH OF JULY.

Independence Hall, building in Philadelphia on Independence Square. Houses Liberty Bell and historical museum. Scene of proclamation of Declaration of Independence, Continental Congress, and Constitutional Convention.

Independents, in religion, name given to Christian congregations claiming freedom from ecclesiastical and civil authority. In England called Brownists (see BROWNE, ROBERT) or SEPARATISTS until in 17th cent. name Independents became popular.

Independent Treasury System. Pres. Andrew Jackson secured transfer of government funds from BANK OF THE UNITED STATES to state banks, but Panic of 1837, at least partially brought on by transfer of government surplus to states, showed evils of that arrangement. Pres. Van Buren proposed an independent treasury isolated from all banks. A law to this end was passed in 1840, but the Whigs, victorious in national election, repealed it. Objections of Pres. John Tyler on constitutional grounds prevented establishment of another Bank of the United States. Following Democratic return to power, an act of Aug., 1846, ordered public revenues retained in the Treasury building and in subtreasuries (see SUBTREASURY) in various cities. Treasury was to pay out its own funds and be completely independent of banking and financial system of the nation. In practice, however, specie tended to accumulate in the Treasury to detriment of business. Civil War put strain on Treasury and proved interdependence of Treasury and banks; NATIONAL BANK was created. Old theory of absolute independence was in practice abandoned by 1898. Federal Reserve Act of 1913 marked true end of Independent Treasury.

Index, in full *Index librorum prohibitorum,* list of books forbidden to its members by the Roman Catholic Church. It includes only works that have been brought before the Holy See for judgment and have been officially declared inimical to faith or morals. Catholics are obliged also to avoid any other works that are injurious but are not on the Index, and for critical and scholarly purposes are allowed to read those that are.

index, of a book or periodical, a list, nearly always alphabetical, of the topics treated. Seeks to direct reader to every subject and proper name about which any information is given in book. Index to periodical is less specific. In 16th cent. term *index* began to be commonly applied to such a list. In 1848 in U.S., William F. Poole issued index to most widely circulated periodicals of the time. *Poole's Index* was superseded in 1907 by *Readers' Guide to Periodical Literature.* Various fields of knowledge have special indexes. Newspaper indexes include that to the New York *Times* (from 1913).

index number, figure showing change in price or quantity in ratio to a number taken as norm, or base, often expressed in percentage. Index of wages divided by index of cost of living is index of purchasing power, or real wages.

India, subcontinent, S Asia, cut off from most of the continent by lofty Himalayas. In it are PAKISTAN and republic of **India,** officially also called *Bharat* (1,138,-814 sq. mi.; pop. 356,891,624); member of British Commonwealth of Nations; cap. New Delhi. Comprises 27 states, including Bombay, Delhi, Hyderabad, Madras, Mysore, and Punjab. SIKKIM and BHUTAN are protectorates. Republic is bounded NE by Burma and China, N by Tibet and Nepal, and NW by W Pakistan, with E Pakistan forming an enclave in NE India. Small enclaves on E and W coasts constitute FRENCH INDIA and PORTUGUESE INDIA. S half is huge peninsula jutting between Arabian Sea and Bay of Bengal. Great Indian rivers are Ganges, Brahmaputra, and Indus. Agr. output is inadequate for feeding vast population. Crops include rice, cotton, jute, and tea. Among natural resources are valuable forests (esp. teak and ebony) and deposits of mica, manganese, coal, copper, and iron. Heavy industry is centered at Jamshedpur (iron and steel), Bombay (textiles), and Calcutta (jute products). Largest cities and main ports are Bombay, Calcutta, and Madras. Much of Indian life is still largely based on CASTE system, despite official disapproval. Relief from life of poverty is found in religious rites (mainly Hindu and Moslem) and in pilgrimages to holy cities, notably Benares. Earliest known civilization on subcontinent is that of MOHENJO-DARO (fl. 4000–2000 B.C.). Aryans first entered India from NW in c.1500 B.C. and developed a Brahmanic civilization, in which basic tenets of HINDUISM were formulated. BUDDHISM and JAINISM emerged in 6th cent. B.C. Hinduism was at first the religion of MAURYA empire (325–184 B.C.), founded after Alexander the Great's invasion of N India (c.326 B.C.); but in 3d cent. B.C. ASOKA estab. Buddhism as state religion. During Gupta dynasty (A.D. 320?–c.544?) and reign of Harsha (606–47), Hindu culture enjoyed a golden age. After 8th cent., Rajputs dominated NW. Moslem power began with raids of Mahmud of Ghazni in 11th cent. and establishment (1206) of DELHI SULTANATE. MOGUL empire, founded 1526 by BABER, flourished under AKBAR, SHAH JEHAN, and AURANGZEB. Meanwhile the Portuguese had taken Goa in 1510; in 18th cent., while MAHRATTAS and SIKHS were weakening the empire, the British and French carved out colonial domains. Victories of Robert CLIVE over DUPLEIX ended all European threats to power of British East India Co. Warren HASTINGS as governor general did much to solidify Clive's gains. SEPOY REBELLION (1857) led to abolition of East India Co. and transfer of Indian rule to the crown. Movement for independence became important when Gandhi assumed leadership of INDIAN NATIONAL CONGRESS. Desire of Congress to form united front against Britain was balked by MOSLEM LEAGUE (led by Mahomed Ali Jinnah), which agitated for a separate Moslem state. When India became free in 1947, Congress agreed reluctantly to the partition. Dominion of India became a sovereign republic on Jan. 26, 1950. In 1951 she launched a five-year plan (aided in 1952 by Point Four grants from U.S.) to develop her resources. Rival claims to control over KASHMIR strained her relations with Pakistan.

Indiana, state (36,291 sq. mi.; pop. 3,934,224), N central U.S.; admitted 1816 as 19th state (free); cap. INDIANAPOLIS. Other cities are FORT WAYNE, GARY, SOUTH BEND, EVANSVILLE, TERRE HAUTE. Bounded S by Ohio R., SW by Wabash R., NW by L. Michigan. Farming (corn, wheat, livestock, grains, fruit, truck, poultry, dairying); mining (coal, limestone, oil). Mfg. of steel, motor vehicles, machinery, chemicals; food processing; rail and machine shops. French estab. first permanent settlement at VINCENNES c.1735. British took over region in 1763. G. R. CLARK took Vincennes in American Revolution. Process of subduing Indians continued through indecisive battle of TIPPECANOE (1811). Indiana Territory created 1800. State hurt by Panic of 1837. Supported Union in Civil War despite activities of KNIGHTS OF THE GOLDEN CIRCLE. Farmers and laborers fought for rights against rising industry in late 19th cent. Present economy is aided by mfg., but farmers' problems remain.

Indiana, borough (pop. 11,743), W Pa., NE of Pittsburgh; settled c.1772. Coal mining center with mfg. of tires, food products, and clay products.

Indian Affairs, Bureau of, created (1824) in U.S. War Dept. and transferred (1849) by act of Congress to U.S. Dept. of the Interior. Had jurisdiction over Indian trade and removal of Indians to reservations in the West. Developed primarily into land-administering agency. Now also provides educational facilities and other services.

Indiana Harbor, Ind: see EAST CHICAGO.

Indianapolis, city (pop. 427,173), state cap. (since 1825), central Ind., on White R. and SE of Chicago; settled 1819. State's largest city, it is a banking, transportation, and farm trade center with large stockyards. Mfg. of building materials, metal products, pharmaceuticals, and packed meat. Has home and burial place of J. W. Riley, American Legion national hq., and annual motor races on near-by speedway. Seat of Butler Univ. (Disciples of Christ; coed.; chartered 1850, opened 1855; John Herron Art Institute affiliated), and Indiana Univ. units.

Indian art and architecture is essentially decorative and often highly symbolic. Historical period began c.250 B.C. with Buddhist shrines, temples, and stupas (memorial mounds), which show Persian and Greek influence. Paintings were mainly frescoes. Jain work (100 B.C.–A.D. 1300) flourished as Buddhism waned (from 3d cent.), resulting in impressive temples with pointed domes. Hindu style, which borrowed much from the Jains, is marked by pyramidal roof and great richness of detail. Finest example of late Indian Moslem style, characterized by graceful dome, arch, and minarets, is the TAJ MAHAL. As architectural decoration sculpture was more important than painting. Decorative arts (e.g., damascening and jewelry making) have been carried to perfection.

Indiana University, mainly at Bloomington; state supported, coed.; chartered as seminary 1820, opened 1824; became college 1828; university 1838. Has institute of criminal law and criminology.

Indian breadroot: see BREADROOT.

Indian literature. An extensive written literature in vernacular languages of the subcontinent of India did not appear until 16th cent. Its development was spurred by emergence of Hindu pietistic movements which encouraged popularizing of SANSKRIT LITERATURE. Great

classics, e.g., *Ramayana,* were put into popular verse form. Classical Persian poetry was basis for Urdu verse written for Mogul court. In early 19th cent. popular prose began to flourish with introduction of printing presses and establishment of vernacular schools. Literature today includes works in English and major languages of India and Pakistan. Best-known writers of modern India include Tagore, Iqbal, R. K. Narayan, Sudhin N. Ghose, and Sarojini Naidu. See PALI LITERATURE and PRAKRIT LITERATURE.

Indian mallow: see VELVETWEED.

Indian millet: see PEARL MILLET.

Indian music of North America is primarily a vocal art. It is entirely melodic, having no harmony or polyphony. Intonation is uncertain, resulting from the use of forced muscular tension in the vocal chords. Drums and rattles are the chief percussion instruments; wind instruments are mainly flutes and whistles. A song is considered a means of communication with supernatural powers; definite results, (e.g., victory, rain, or health) are expected. There is no system of notation; songs are handed down from generation to generation. Certain ceremonial and medicinal songs are believed to be owned by the singer and to have been received by him in a dream. Only the owner of such a song may sing it, unless he chooses to sell it and share the mystical properties that accompany it. Most love songs associated with Indians actually show strong European influence.

Indian Mutiny: see SEPOY REBELLION.

Indian National Congress, political organization of India, founded 1885. Original purpose was to make India a British dominion by constitutional means. In 1917 the militants, led by GANDHI, forced resignation of moderates and began call for *Swaraj* [complete independence]. Their chief weapon, nonviolent disobedience campaign, was first used on large scale in 1919. Party's refusal to cooperate with the British in World War II led to arrest of its leaders. Outlawed 1942–45. In conferences leading to India's independence (1947), party was forced to bow to demand of MOSLEM LEAGUE for separate state of Pakistan. With NEHRU as leader the Congress kept its dominant position in Republic of India (estab. 1950).

Indian nut: see PINE.

Indian Ocean, third largest ocean of world, extending from India to Antarctica and from E Africa to Tasmania; stretches c.4,000 mi. along equator and c.6,000 mi. N to S. Greatest known depth, c.24,000 ft., is near Java. Its great seasonal winds (monsoon) bring rain to SE Asia. Only northern part is important for shipping.

Indianola (ĭn″dēŭnō′lŭ), city (pop. 5,145), S Iowa, S of Des Moines. Seat of Simpson Col. (Methodist; coed.; 1860).

Indian paintbrush or **painted cup,** parasitic annual or perennial plant (*Castilleja*), with many species native to W U.S. They bear flowerlike red bracts.

Indian pipe, low funguslike saprophytic woodland plant, waxy white or salmon, of genus *Monotropa,* found in North America and Asia. It has scalelike leaves and pipe-shaped flowers which form seeds.

Indian River, lagoon, c.120 mi. long, E Fla., paralleling coast and extending S from N of Titusville to Stuart. Resorts border its shores. Its fertile valley produces citrus fruit.

Indians, American, peoples who occupied North America, Middle America, and South America before the coming of the Europeans. Most authorities today believe that the Indians came into the W Hemisphere from Asia via the Bering Strait in a series of migrations (the waves accounting for many linguistic families). Common origin is taken to explain the common physical features—coarse, straight black hair, dark eyes, sparse body hair, and brownish skin color. They supposedly brought with them their Neolithic culture; most Indians made fire with a drill, had domesticated dogs, made baskets, and used stone tools. In Middle America and South America high material cultures were built up before the coming of the white man: MAYA, TOLTEC, AZTEC, INCA, and CHIBCHA. The development of powerful city-states and, in the case of the Inca, a true empire, was accompanied by a rich architectural and artistic development. Some tribes, however (e.g., those of Tierra del Fuego) had very sparse material culture. Other groups had intermediate culture, some agricultural, and some dependent on gathering, hunting, and fishing. Among the agricultural societies, maize was generally the basic crop. Anthropologists distinguish so-called culture areas (as Eastern Woodlands, Plains). In 1492 Indians N of Mexico numbered 900,000, but by 1870 they had dwindled to 300,000. In 1945, there were 400,000. In most Central and South American countries, the Indian strain predominates, and in the 20th cent. a movement for reviving and preserving Indian culture (*indianismo*) has been strong.

Indian Territory, in U.S. history, name generally applied to country set aside for Indians by Indian Intercourse Act (1834) and more particularly applied to territory to which Cherokee, Creek, Seminole, Choctaw, and Chickasaw tribes were removed between 1820 and 1845. E part of present Okla., N of Red R., became known as Indian Territory as Indians were gradually forced into settlement there. Tribes other than original five also moved there. Extinction of Territory came in 1907 with entrance of Okla. into the Union.

Indian turnip: see JACK-IN-THE PULPIT.

India-rubber tree: see RUBBER PLANT.

Indic languages, group of Indo-Iranian subfamily of Indo-European languages. See LANGUAGE (table).

indiction (ĭndĭk'shŭn), a period of 15 years or a year in such a period. Probably suggested by an Egyptian fiscal period, dating by indiction was adopted by the Roman Empire in 4th cent., was practiced by the Byzantine Empire and throughout Europe, and is still occasionally used by the Roman Church.

indictment (ĭndīt'mŭnt) formal written charge of a crime made by a public prosecutor before a grand jury. The grand jury in turn may offer the charge against the accused. A person suspected of crime may also be brought to trial by presentment (accusation issued by the grand jury though the prosecutor has not offered a formal bill of indictment) or by information (accusation made directly by prosecutor without consideration by grand jury; not permissible in capital or otherwise infamous crime). When an indictment or a presentment is approved, the foreman of the grand jury marks it "true bill."

indigo, the most important blue dye. Known in ancient India and Egypt, it was introduced into Europe in 16th cent. It is obtained from leguminous plants of genus *Indigofera* by fermentation of macerated plants; these liberate colorless indican which oxidizes to blue indigo when stirred. Adolf von Baeyer first synthesized it.

indigo bunting or **indigo bird,** small bird of FINCH family. Male summer plumage in suitable light is metallic blue; female and young have brown sparrowlike plumage. Breeds from N.B. to Ga., W to N.Dak. and central Texas; winters from S Mexico to Panama.

Indio, city (pop. 6,450), SE Calif., ESE of Redlands. Trade center in COACHELLA VALLEY. Joshua Tree Natl. Monument is near.

indium, silver-white, metallic element (symbol = In; see also ELEMENT, table) resembling aluminum. It is relatively soft, malleable, and ductile.

Indo-Aryan, group of the Indo-Iranian subfamily of Indo-European languages. Broader uses on a racial basis are now obsolete. See LANGUAGE (table).

Indo-China (ĭn'dōchī"nù), group (272,200 sq. mi.; pop. 27,000,000) of three states (VIET NAM, comprising Cochin China, Annam, and Tonkin; LAOS; and CAMBODIA) in SE Asia, on E Indo-Chinese peninsula. Borders on Burma, Thailand, and Malaya. Associated with France within French Union, which the three states joined in 1950.

Indo-European, family of languages to which English belongs. It includes more speakers than any other family. See LANGUAGE (table).

Indo-Iranian, subfamily of Indo-European languages. See LANGUAGE (table).

Indonesia, republic (575,893 sq. mi.; pop. c.80,000,000), Malay archipelago, SE Asia; cap. Jakarta. Comprises Sunda Isls. (including JAVA and SUMATRA), Lesser Sundas (including BALI), CELEBES, the MOLUCCAS, part of BORNEO and TIMOR, and thousands of smaller islands. A major producer of tin and oil, with rich deposits of manganese, gold, silver, copper, and zinc. Agr. and forest products include rice, rubber, quinine, tobacco, sugar, coffee, tea, and pepper. Early in Christian era, area came under influence of Indian civilization through influx of Buddhist and Hindu monks; great native empires that emerged after 7th cent. were strongly linked to Hinduism and Buddhism. Islam, introduced by Arab traders in 13th cent., eventually became dominant religion. By 16th cent., when Portuguese traders appeared, Indonesia had disintegrated into many small weak states. The Portuguese were soon ousted by Dutch East India Co., which succeeded also in removing rivalry of British East India Co. (1610–23). After liquidation of company (1798), area came under direct rule of Dutch government; known thereafter as Netherlands East Indies. Dutch rule was broken 1811–15 when islands were occupied by the British under Raffles. In World War II, nationalists were active throughout Japanese occupation (begun early 1942); in Aug., 1945, they estab. Republic of Indonesia, which claimed rule over Java, Madura, and Sumatra. Dutch opposition led to warfare, which did not subside even after Dutch recognition of republic by Cheribon agreement (1947). Finally, after Hague conference (mediated by UN), Indonesia became a sovereign country on Dec. 28, 1949. Called the United States of Indonesia, it comprised the nationalist-sponsored republic of Indonesia and 15 Dutch-supported states. Federation gave way in Aug., 1950, to unified republic (headed by SUKARNO), linked to Netherlands only through loose union under Dutch crown. In 1952 Indonesians were still disputing Dutch claim to W New Guinea.

Indore (ĭndôr'), former princely state, W central India; since 1948 part of Madhya Bharat. Indore, city (pop. 203,695), was its cap., founded early 18th cent. It is now summer cap. of Madhya Bharat. Major cotton-milling center.

Indra (ĭn'drù), in Vedic religion and in Hinduism, god of sky and storms, a beneficent deity of Aryan invaders of India. With rise of Brahmanism, he was displaced by trinity of Brahma, Vishnu, and Siva. See also VEDA.

Indre (ē'drù), department (2,666 sq. mi.; pop. 252,075), central France, in Berry, crossed by Indre R.; cap. Châteauroux.

Indre-et-Loire (ēdrãlwär'), department (2,378 sq. mi.; 349,685), N central France, in Touraine; cap. Tours.

induction. Electrostatic induction is the production of an electric charge on a body by bringing it near a charged body. This "charging by induction" can be done, for example, by bringing a negatively charged body near an uncharged body; negative charges in the uncharged body are repelled and some will leave the uncharged body if there is a conductor through which they can run off into the ground. If ground connection is removed before charged body is withdrawn, the originally uncharged body will be positively charged since negative charges have become less than number of positive charges. Electromagnetic induction is accomplished by movement of conductor across field of a magnet or movement of magnetic field over the conductor. Self-induction (or inductance), also called electromagnetic inertia, is the setting up of an electromotive force in a conductor which opposes the change of a current, i.e., it retards both an increase and a decrease, so current cannot be instantaneously started or stopped.

indulgence (ĭndŭl′jŭns). The Roman Catholic Church teaches that a sinner, forgiven through the sacrament of penance, must yet make satisfaction for his sins here or in purgatory. But Christ and his saints have by their good works earned a superfluity of satisfaction to God for human sins, and this accumulated grace is called doctrinally the Infinite Treasury of Merits. From this satisfaction the Church as God's ministry remits punishment the sinner would otherwise have to undergo. Official statement of this remission is an indulgence, which may be gained by Catholics in many ways (e.g., prayers, visiting churches). Until the Council of TRENT, there were many abuses in granting indulgences (esp. their purchase for money), and it was these abuses that LUTHER first denounced.

Indus (ĭn′dŭs), river, c.1,900 mi. long, rising in Himalayas in W Tibet. Flows through Kashmir and W Pakistan (where it is joined by Panjinad R.) to Arabian Sea. An ancient civilization (see MOHENJO-DARO) flourished on its banks.

Indus Civilization: see MOHENJO-DARO.

industrial diseases: see OCCUPATIONAL DISEASES.

industrial management, the highly organized modern method of carrying on industrial operations. Growth of manufacturing required special supervision of machinery and elimination of inefficiency. The first sustained effort in this direction was made in the 1880s by F. W. Taylor of the Midvale Steel Co. The motions of workers were studied to speed up production by cutting out excess movements. Such time and motion studies of the flow of materials through the plant became a major item of inquiry, as did product design. Relations with workers became the subject of industrial psychology. Soon after 1910 U.S. firms estab. the first personnel departments, and much attention was given to improving worker morale by providing better facilities and new incentives, such as chance for advancement and, occasionally, a voice in management. Other items that have come to be the concern of management include safety devices, better sanitation, rest, eating, and recreation facilities, health insurance, and pensions.

Industrial Revolution. The term refers primarily to the period in English history, roughly 1750–1850, in which striking changes in economic structure were produced by transition from stable agr. and commercial society to modern industrialism. Voyages of 15th and 16th cent. opened the way for world-wide commerce. Capitalism appeared in 17th cent. Machines were made of wood and driven by water and wind power. In 18th cent. the change to steam power was made by James Watt. England became world textile center and there were such inventions as Arkwright's spinning frame (1769) and Edmund Cartwright's power loom (1785). Coke was used in iron production; coal mines and the use of steel became of paramount importance. Factories and industrial towns sprang up. In 19th cent. railroads and steamboats wrought new changes. Electricity and the gasoline engine have produced further changes. Spread has been world wide. Germany (after 1850), U.S. (after Civil War), and Japan (in 20th cent.) have been transformed by industrialism. Accompanying economic philosophy was laissez faire doctrine of Adam Smith. Later interpretations have been attempted by Karl Marx, Socialism, and the Manchester school. Industrialism has divided society into opposing classes of capital and labor, brought about world economic interdependence, and introduced many economic problems as well as causing a world-wide rise in the level of material goods.

industrial union, one composed of all the workers in a given industry, regardless of skill, craft, or occupation. All American unions were craft unions until the 1870s. Knights of Labor, Industrial Workers of the World, and the C.I.O. have advocated organizations cutting across craft lines. An industrial union is called a vertical union (including workers of all levels of skills), as opposed to horizontal or craft unions.

Industrial Workers of the World (I.W.W.), revolutionary industrial union, organized in Chicago in 1905. Among its leaders were Eugene V. Debs, William D. Haywood, and Daniel De Leon. Members were nicknamed the Wobblies. Aimed to unite all skilled and unskilled workers for purpose of overthrowing capitalism and achieving socialist society. Its methods were direct action, propaganda, the boycott, and the strike; it opposed sabotage, arbitration, collective bargaining, and political affiliation. About 150 strikes were carried out, but from a probable strength of 100,000 in 1912 it had dropped to less than 10,000 by 1930. Its contributions include the temporary organization of migrant and Negro workers, union of skilled and unskilled labor, and influence on later unions.

Indy, Vincent d' (vĕsā′ dēdē′), 1851–1931, French composer; pupil of Franck. His compositions include *Symphony on a French Mountain Air* for piano and orchestra; symphonic variations, *Istar;* songs, chamber music, piano works, and three symphonies.

inertia (ĭnûr′shǔ), in physics, resistance of body at rest to being set in motion and that of body in motion to being accelerated, retarded, or changed in direction. Force must be applied to overcome it.

Inez de Castro: see CASTRO, INÉS DE.

infallibility (ĭnfăl″ǔbĭ′lūtē), in Christian thought, inability of Church to err as a teaching authority. The idea is widely rejected by Protestants. There is disagreement as to which organ of Church is protected by God from teaching error. Orthodox hold ecumenical councils infallible; Roman Catholics agree but do not accept conciliar acts unratified by the pope. The dogma that the pope's pronouncements made ex cathedra on faith and morals are infallible was enounced by the Vatican Council (1870).

infant, human baby from birth to about two years. Development and characteristics vary greatly. Average birth weight 6½–7½ lb.; height, 20–21 in. Weight usually is doubled at 5–6 months, trebled at one year. Height increases c.5 in. in first 6 months, 8 to 10 in. by end of year. Skull bones, sutures, and posterior of two fontanels (called "soft spots") close in several weeks; larger, front fontanel at about one year. Teeth usually begin to erupt at 5–8 months; first dentition (20 teeth) complete at 24–30 months. At first human milk or substitute formula provides essential nutrients except vitamins C and D. Cereals and strained foods are added gradually. Injections immunizing against diphtheria, smallpox, and other diseases are advisable during first year. Affectionate care is needed for healthy development.

infantile paralysis: see POLIOMYELITIS.

infectious diseases: see COMMUNICABLE DISEASES.

inferiority complex, Adler's term for a COMPLEX of emotionally toned ideas centered on real or imaginary handicaps. The attempt to compensate for feelings of inferiority leads to behavior aimed at proving them unjustified. Failure to compensate successfully ends in NEUROSIS. Successful compensation is directed to valuable social or personal ends.

infinity, in mathematics, term for quantity larger than any number; indicated by symbol ∞. In geometry, a position an infinite distance from the portion of space considered.

inflection, in grammar. In most languages words can be arranged in formally similar sets, such that members of each set have a common feature (stem, root, or base), and members of different sets have features in common not included in the stem; these features are often called inflections. Examples of languages with extensive inflections are Latin, Eskimo, and Arabic; of those with few inflections, Chinese. Typical Latin noun or adjective is inflected for CASE and NUMBER; adjectives are inflected for gender. Latin verbs have overlapping categories of inflection, MOOD, VOICE, TENSE, person, and number. Some linguists distinguish between inflection and agglutination, which is inflection with relative looseness of fusion between stem and inflectional feature. In 19th cent. theory was widely held that agglutination was more primitive than inflection. This theory is now abandoned.

influenza (ĭn″flŏoĕn′zủ), contagious, infectious disease characteristically occurring in epidemic and pandemic outbreaks. Cause is thought to be a virus. It is attended by rapid progressive inflammation of mucous membranes of respiratory tract.

infrared rays (ĭn″frŭrĕd′), invisible rays of wave length longer than visible light and having a heating effect.

infusorial earth (ĭn″fyŏosô′rêul), name sometimes used for diatomaceous deposits built up from remains of microscopic plant life. It is not generally approved as a term.

Inge, William Ralph (ĭng), 1860–, Anglican prelate and author, dean of St. Paul's Cathedral (1911–34). His pessimism earned him name of "gloomy dean."

Ingelow, Jean (ĭn′jủlō), 1820–97, English author of verse (e.g., "High Tide on the Coast of Lincolnshire, 1571"), novels (e.g., *Off the Skelligs*, 1872), children's books (e.g., *Mopsa the Fairy*, 1869).

Ingemann, Bernhard Severin (ĭng′ŭmän), 1789–1862, Danish poet. Poems in *Holger Danske* (1837) became popular national songs. Also wrote religious lyrics in *Morning and Evening Songs* (1839) and historical novels.

Ingermanland (ĭng′gŭrmŭnlănd), historic region, RSFSR, S of Gulf of Finland, between L. Peipus and L. Onega; also called Ingria. Subject to Great Novgorod, later to Moscow, in Middle Ages; conquered by Sweden 1617; restored to Russia 1721. Peter I built St. Petersburg (Leningrad) in Ingermanland.

Ingersoll, Charles Jared (ĭng′gùrsôl), 1782–1862, American political leader and author. U.S. Representative from Pa. (1813–15, 1841–49). Some of his publications urge more intellectual independence and national self-sufficiency.

Ingersoll, Robert Green, 1833–99, American orator, a lawyer. Nominated James G. Blaine for President in famous "plumed knight" speech (1876). Known as "the great agnostic"; his lectures on religion won wide attention. Called Bob Ingersoll.

Ingersoll, town (pop. 6,524), S Ont., Canada, on Thames R. and ENE of London. Mfg. of furniture, hardware, and tools.

Ingham, Charles Cromwell (ĭng′ŭm), 1796–1863, American painter, b. Ireland. Achieved fame in New York as painter of beautiful and fashionable women.

Inglewood, city (pop. 46,185), S Calif., industrial and residential suburb of Los Angeles; laid out 1887. Oil refining and mfg. of aircraft. Has race track.

Ingoldsby, Thomas: see BARHAM, RICHARD HARRIS.

Ingolstadt (ĭng′gôlshtät), city (pop. 40,270), Upper Bavaria, on the Danube. Produces textiles, automobiles. Dates from 8th cent. Unsuccessfully besieged by Gustavus II of Sweden 1632. The university, founded 1772, was transferred to Landshut in 1800, to Munich in 1826. The Gothic minster (15th cent.) and other medieval buildings survived damage in World War II.

Ingres, Jean Auguste Dominique (zhä′ ŏgüst′ dômēnĕk′ ē′grủ), 1780–1867, French painter, a master draughtsman and portraitist; b. Montauban. Studied with J. L. David and became bulwark of classicism in a romantic era. Lived mainly in Rome, where he spent his later years as director of French Acad.

Ingush, people of Caucasus: see CHECHEN.

Inisfail (ĭ″nĭsfāl′) [Irish,= island of destiny], literary name for Ireland.

initiative and referendum, the initiating of a law by popular petition (initiative) and the referring to popular vote a law passed by the legislature (referendum). In the U.S., individual states require signatures of from 5 to 8 percent of the electorate for an initiative. The referendum is required in most states for constitutional amendments.

injection, introduction of liquid into body. Types include intradermal, into skin tissue; intramuscular, into muscle; intravenous, into vein; spinal, beneath outer membrane of spinal cord. Usually administered by means of a needle and syringe or a container which introduces fine spray into tissues.

injunction, formal written order of a court (decree) commanding or prohibiting a certain act, usually granted by a judge without a jury. Originally only prohibitive (negative) injunctions were granted, but later courts broadened the practice to include positive commands. Interlocutory injunctions are those issued while an action is pending and tend to protect a plaintiff's interests so that the final judgment may be of use to him. A final injunction is the judgment of the court after all the evidence has been heard. In case of disobedience of an injunction, the defendant is tried for contempt of court. In labor disputes injunctions were formerly very widely used (see CONSPIRACY).

ink. India or China ink, a permanent black ink, made of lampblack or ivory black mixed with glue or gum, probably known in China from c.1200 B.C. Standard black ink containing tannic acid, probably known from 2d cent., is much used because it flows freely. Aniline dyes generally used in colored inks.

Inkerman (ĭng′kùrmùn, Rus. ēn-kĭrmän′), E suburb of Sevastopol, RSFSR, scene of costly allied victory (1854) in Crimean War.

Inkster, village (pop. 16,728), SE Mich., residential suburb of Detroit; settled 1825.

Inland Sea, scenic body of water in Japan, between Honshu on N and Kyushu and Shikoku on S. Many pine-covered islets.

Inman, Henry, 1801–46, American portrait, genre, and landscape painter.

Inn, river, 320 mi. long, rising in Engadine valley, Switzerland, and flowing NE through Austria and Bavaria, joining the Danube at Passau.

inn, in Great Britain, means a hotel, public house, tavern, or coffeehouse where lodging is provided. A tavern, in usual sense, provides only food and drink. In U.S., inns usually are small rural houses for transients, or, occasionally, resort establishments. The hotel has emerged since late 17th cent.

Inner Hebrides, Scotland: see HEBRIDES.

Inner Mongolia: see MONGOLIA.

Inner Temple: see INNS OF COURT; TEMPLE, THE.

Inness, George (ĭ′nĭs), 1825–94, American landscape painter. Early work was in Hudson River school tradition. Later influenced by Barbizon school, but achieved free and colorful personal style. A Swedenborgian, he sought the mystical in nature. His son, **George Inness, Jr.**, 1854–1926, was a landscape and animal painter.

Innisfree, small island, Co. Sligo, Ireland, in Lough Gill. Celebrated by W. B. Yeats in his poem "Lake Isle of Innisfree."

Innocent I, Saint, d. 417, pope (401–17). Upheld supremacy of the papacy; supported St. John Chrysostom and condemned Pelagius; tried vainly to prevent Alaric's sack of Rome (410). Feast: July 28.

Innocent II, d. 1143, pope (1130–43), a Roman. Opposed by Antipope Anacletus II, Innocent won the support of Bernard of Clairvaux and Emperor Lothair II and prevailed over Anacletus' successor, Victor IV. Convened Second Lateran Council and condemned some teachings of Abelard and Arnold of Brescia.

Innocent III, b. 1160 or 1161, d. 1216, pope (1198–1216), an Italian named Lotario di Segni; one of the most prominent figures of medieval history. A learned theologian and jurist, he held the theory that supremacy of the spirit over the flesh meant that the Church ruler (the pope) should have superiority over lay rulers of states—a theory later carried to an extreme by Boniface VIII but not held in present Roman Catholic doctrine. To establish papal supremacy Innocent was active in political affairs. In the Holy Roman Empire he arbitrated the dispute of PHILIP OF SWABIA and OTTO IV in Otto's favor (1201); later favored Philip (1207–8); crowned Otto (1209) after Philip's murder, only to excommunicate him (1210) and bring about the election of FREDERICK II, who was his ward. In England, Innocent by setting aside two claimants for the archbishopric of Canterbury and naming Stephen Langton infuriated King John; in the quarrel Innocent put England under the interdict and formally deposed the king (1212). John submitted and received England and Ireland as a fief from the pope. Later he declared that the Magna Carta was not binding on John because extorted by force and without the knowledge of his overlord (Innocent). In France, the pope could not establish political power over Philip II but did force him to bow to canon law in the matter of a divorce. In Italy he reclaimed and reorganized papal territories and was recognized as overlord of Tuscany, but he failed to subdue N Italian cities. Thus in all Europe he went far to put his theory of papal supremacy into effect, though history was to make his victories hollow. He promoted the Fourth Crusade and protested when the Crusaders instead of going to the Holy Land attacked the Byzantine Empire; nevertheless he recognized the Latin Kingdom of Constantinople which they set up, and by efforts to spread the Latin rite in that kingdom embittered relations between the Eastern and Western churches. Similarly he protested when the crusade he had started against the Albigenses was turned to political and economic ends by Simon de Montfort, but his protests were vain; he later urged St. Dominic's mission. Innocent was vigorous in internal Church affairs and dominated the Fourth LATERAN COUNCIL (1215). He wrote extensively and his *De contemptu mundi* [on contempt of this world] was popular in the Middle Ages.

Innocent IV, d. 1254, pope (1243–54), a Genoese. His reign was occupied chiefly in a contest with the Hohenstaufen rulers. He opposed Emperor FREDERICK II and had to flee to Lyons, where he convened a council (1245) that declared Frederick deposed. Innocent supported counterclaimants to the throne against Frederick, CONRAD IV, and MANFRED. Just before his death he supported young CONRADIN as claimant to the Sicilian throne. Heavy taxes to support these contests brought criticism on Innocent (from Robert Grosseteste among others).

Innocent VIII, 1432–92, pope (1484–92), a Genoese. Papal affairs were largely directed by his friend Giuliano della Rovere (later Julius II). He originally planned a crusade against the Turks, but later he obtained Djem, the brother of the sultan, from Pierre d'Aubusson (who became a cardinal) and the French king, Charles VIII. Innocent threatened BAJAZET II with recognizing the captive Djem as sultan.

Innocent XI, 1611–89, pope (1676–89), an Italian, noted for his saintliness and desire for reform. Engaged in a quarrel with LOUIS XIV, who actively promoted GALLICANISM. He denounced not only Louis's Gallican statement (1682) but also revocation of the Edict of Nantes (1685).

Innsbruck (ĭnz'brŏŏk, Ger. ĭns'–), city (pop. 94,599), cap. of Tyrol, W Austria, on the Inn. Its beautiful situation, in the Alps, and its architectural treasures make it a favorite tourist resort. Landmarks include 16th-cent. Hofkirche, a Franciscan church, with a monument to Emperor Maximilian I by Peter Vischer; 15th-cent. Fürstenburg palace. The university was founded 1677.

Inns of Court, collective name of the four legal societies in London which have exclusive right of admission to the bar. They are Lincoln's Inn, Gray's Inn, the Inner Temple, and the Middle Temple (see also TEMPLE, THE); all date from before the 14th cent. Names come from the buildings in which masters taught law to "apprentice" lawyers.

inoculation, in strict sense, insertion of virus into a wound to immunize by producing mild form of a disease or to produce disease for experimental purposes. Value in preventing smallpox proved by Edward JENNER.

Inonu, Ismet (ĭsmĕt' ĕnŭnü'), 1884–, Turkish general. Premier under Ataturk 1923–24, 1925–37; president of Turkey 1938–50.

inquest, inquiry by a coroner's jury into the cause of a death. Procedure is generally like that of a grand jury. Among verdicts returnable are natural death, accidental death, suicide, and murder.

Inquisition. 1 The medieval Inquisition began c.1233 when the pope commissioned certain Dominicans to investigate the ALBIGENSES in S France. As it evolved in France, N Italy, Germany, and the Papal States (where it continued to the 19th cent.), the Inquisition soon resorted to judicial torture, but it rarely condemned accused heretics to burning; imprisonment was the usual punishment. The medieval clerical inquisitors were eager to receive abjurations of heresy and to avoid trials; sentences could be enforced only by the local authorities ("secular arm"). **2** The Spanish Inquisition, estab. 1478 by Ferdinand and Isabella, and first headed by Tomás de TORQUEMADA, was independent of the medieval Inquisition and was controlled by the Spanish kings. Originally supposed to spy out converted Jews and Moors who were insincere, it soon evolved into a form of thought police from which no Spaniard was safe. It was far better organized, harsher, and freer with the death sentence than the medieval Inquisition. Its attempted introduction into the Netherlands led to rebellion. It was driven from Naples in 1510 and was abolished in Spain in 1820. **3** In 1512 Paul III assigned the medieval Inquisition to the Congregation of the Inquisition or Holy Office. The modern Congregation of the Holy Office has the decision as to questions of faith, morals, heresy, and some matrimonial cases, and also has the duties of censorship (the Index).

insanity or **lunacy,** in law, mental aberration or defect which may relieve a person from certain legal consequences of his acts. Criminal and civil insanity differ from concepts of psychopathology (see NEUROSIS; PSYCHOSIS). There is much medical criticism of legal categories. Strictest U.S. jurisdictions limit insanity to ignorance of the nature of one's acts, inability to distinguish right from wrong, i.e., crimes committed in frenzy or by idiots, but paranoiacs may be judged sane. Less strict jurisdictions include PARANOIA and sudden irresistible impulse (temporary insanity). Less mental aberration is required for civil insanity; extreme deficiency of intelligence or marked defect in reason may suffice. Harmless lunatics may be placed under guardianship on application to court. Dangerous lunatics may be committed to institutions on application of close relatives or public authorities; court approval, and sometimes a jury verdict of insanity, must be given. Asylum detention may be reviewed by habeas corpus proceedings.

inscription, writing on durable material. The art is called epigraphy. Modern inscriptions are made for permanent, monumental record, as on gravestones, cornerstones, and building fronts. First writing was probably everywhere done on hard materials, mainly stones, clay, metal, bone, and ivory. When light materials were developed, it was possible to distinguish between temporary writing and permanent recording. Outside Western history epigraphy was important in New World (MAYA, TOLTEC, AZTEC) and in China. Earliest Chinese inscriptions are on bronze (c.1800 B.C.). First Sanskrit inscriptions date from some centuries later than Prakrit inscriptions of ASOKA (3d cent. B.C.). Western epigraphy began in Mesopotamia (CUNEIFORM inscriptions, probably Sumerian, c.4000 B.C.; a similar Eastern instance is epigraphy at Mo-HENJO-DARO, c.3000 B.C.) and in Egypt (HIEROGLYPHIC inscriptions from 4th millennium B.C.). Influences of Egyptian epigraphy are found everywhere in Arabian peninsula in inscriptions of 1st millennium B.C. In the Mediterranean earliest epigraphy of Greek culture appears in AEGEAN CIVILIZATION and MINOAN CIVILIZATON. From expansion of Greece through career of Rome epigraphy flourished everywhere, and inscriptions are literally innumerable. Greek influence was decisive in Italy, first in inscriptions of ETRUSCAN CIVILIZATION. There are also many inscriptions in Italic languages, notably the IGUVINE TABLES. Latin epigraphy began with religious documents, but by end of the republic it was touching every phase of life. Germanic RUNES and Celtic OGHAM writings are European alphabets used in inscriptions of the early Christian era. Modern monumental inscription is in the same tradition as Latin epigraphy.

insect, air-breathing arthropod of class Insecta, with distinct head, thorax, and abdomen, three pairs of legs, one pair of antennae. The adult usually has one or two pairs of wings. Many (e.g., BUTTERFLY, MOTH, MOSQUITO, BEE, HOUSEFLY) undergo complete metamorphosis, passing through egg, larva, pupa, and adult stages. Grasshopper and some others undergo gradual metamorphosis (the young resembles the adult). Some primitive wingless ones hatch in adult form and grow in size only. Fossil records indicate that insects are earth's oldest inhabitants; c.$\frac{9}{10}$ of all animals are insects; a few hundred of 500,000 known species are harmful. Many are useful for cross-pollination (see POLLINATION); some are enemies of harmful insects and some form chief food of some fish, reptiles, birds, mammals. Men eat white ants in Brazil; grasshoppers in China. Silk, honey, cochineal, and lac are insect products. See *ill.,* p. 469.

insecticide (ĭnsĕk'tŭsīd), substance used to destroy insect pests. Some insecticides are effective only against specific insects, some are toxic, some can be used only under certain conditions. They are applied by dusting, spraying, fumigating (release of a gas), or by aerosol method (insecticide and liquefied gas are packed in container and released as fine mist under gas pressure). Stomach poisons are used against chewing insects; arsenical poisons (e.g., PARIS GREEN) are the oldest widely applied stomach poisons. Others are fluorine compounds, copper salts, organic poisons, synthetics. Contact poisons (those that penetrate body covering or enter breathing pores) include compounds of sulphur and nicotine, petroleum oils, coal-tar derivatives, pyrethrum (from flowers), rotenone (from derris and other plants), and DDT (dichloro-diphenyl-trichloroethane), which has a long-lasting residual effect.

insectivorous plants: see BLADDERWORT; PITCHER PLANT; VENUS'S-FLYTRAP.

Inside Passage, natural, protected waterway, c.950 mi. long, off coast of British Columbia and SE Alaska. Threads through ALEXANDER ARCHIPELAGO. From Seattle, Wash., to Skagway, Alaska, route uses channels and straits between islands and mainland giving protection from storms and open waters of ocean. Known to early explorers. Of great scenic beauty, it is route generally used by steamers between U.S. and Alaska.

installment buying and selling, payment at specified intervals in set amounts for goods taken on credit. Goods belong legally to seller until fulfillment of payment. Practice originated in Paris in 19th cent. and now is applied to purchase of goods of all kinds. It is usually state regulated, and was severely curbed by the Federal government during World War II to reduce inflation.

instinct, controversial term generally indicating an innate tendency, disposition, or drive to action rising from vital needs of an organism, expressed in activity not based on past experience. It is seen in adult insects which emerge from pupa stage after complete bodily changes but with immediate command over food-getting and reproductive structures. In mammals gregariousness is ascribed to herd instinct and maternal activities of suckling and caring for young, to parental instinct. In man instinctive action, with specific goals but no specific means of reaching them, is distinguished from reflex action with its specific response to a stimulus. However, some psychologists claim that adult human behavior is too complex, too much modified by civilization and individual intelligence to be explained adequately on the basis of instinct.

Institut de France (ēstētü' dù fräs'), cultural institution of the French state, founded 1795 to replace five royal academies suppressed in 1793. Subsequent reorganizations restored, within the framework of the Institut, the earlier academies, though the names of several were changed. They are: FRENCH ACADEMY; Académie des Inscriptions et Belles-Lettres (history and archaeology; originally founded 1663); Académie des Sciences (1666); Académie des Beaux-Arts (1648); Académie des Sciences morales et politiques (1795).

Institute for Advanced Study, at Princeton, N.J.; chartered 1930, opened 1933; founded by Louis Bamberger and Mrs. Felix Fuld as research and experimental center beyond the graduate level. Abraham Flexner was first director; succeeded by Frank Aydelotte (1939–47); Einstein is faculty member. Owns Gest Oriental Library; shares many resources with Princeton Univ.

Institutes: see CORPUS JURIS CIVILIS.

instrumental: see CASE.

instrumentalism: see DEWEY, JOHN.

insulation (ĭn"sŭlā'shŭn), use of materials to prevent passage of heat or electricity. Common heat insulators are asbestos, glass, stone, wood, wool; all are poor conductors. They prevent flow of heat in either direction. Air spaces and vacuums are effective insulators. In conduction of electricity, the conductor acts as a guide for the current and must be insulated at every point of contact to prevent leakage. Ordinary wires are usually insulated by thin rubber coating wrapped with cotton.

insulin (ĭn'sŭlĭn), active principle of hormone secreted by groups of cells (islands of Langerhans) in pancreas. It regulates sugar metabolism in body and glycogen storage in liver. Banting and Best first prepared it in a form effective in treatment of diabetes.

Insull, Samuel, 1859–1938, American public-utilities financier, b. England. Vindicated of charges of embezzlement and using mails to defraud following collapse (1932) of his public-utilities empire.

insurance or **assurance,** device for indemnifying or guaranteeing an individual against loss out of a fund to which many individuals exposed to the same risk have contributed certain specified amounts, called premiums. The amount of the premium is determined by the law of averages as calculated by actuaries. Anticipations of modern insurance were to be found in ancient times, among the Babylonians. By the middle of the 14th cent., as evidenced by the earliest known insurance contract (Genoa, 1347), marine insurance was practically universal in Europe. Life insurance began in England in 1583. Fire, burglary, and other forms of insurance were gradually added, so that insurance may now be obtained against any conceivable risk. Since the late 19th cent., the state has entered the field of social insurance (see SOCIAL SECURITY and HEALTH INSURANCE).

Insurgents, in U.S. history, Republican Senators and Representatives who in 1909–10 revolted against conservative party policies of N. W. Aldrich and J. G. Cannon. Many joined PROGRESSIVE PARTY.

intelligence is usually defined as the general ability of the organism to utilize understanding gained in past experience to deal with similar or new situations. Potential intelligence is somewhat related to heredity, while environment largely determines the extent of its realization. **Intelligence tests** help determine individual ability to learn. Alfred Binet's first scale of tests (1905) inaugurated testing movement. Some psychologists doubt that such tests actually measure intelligence, but they have been valuable in education (to assign class groups and judge aptitude for high school or college) and in industry (to determine suitability for particular positions). Tests are a heterogeneous series of questions, problems, tasks, of varying difficulty to

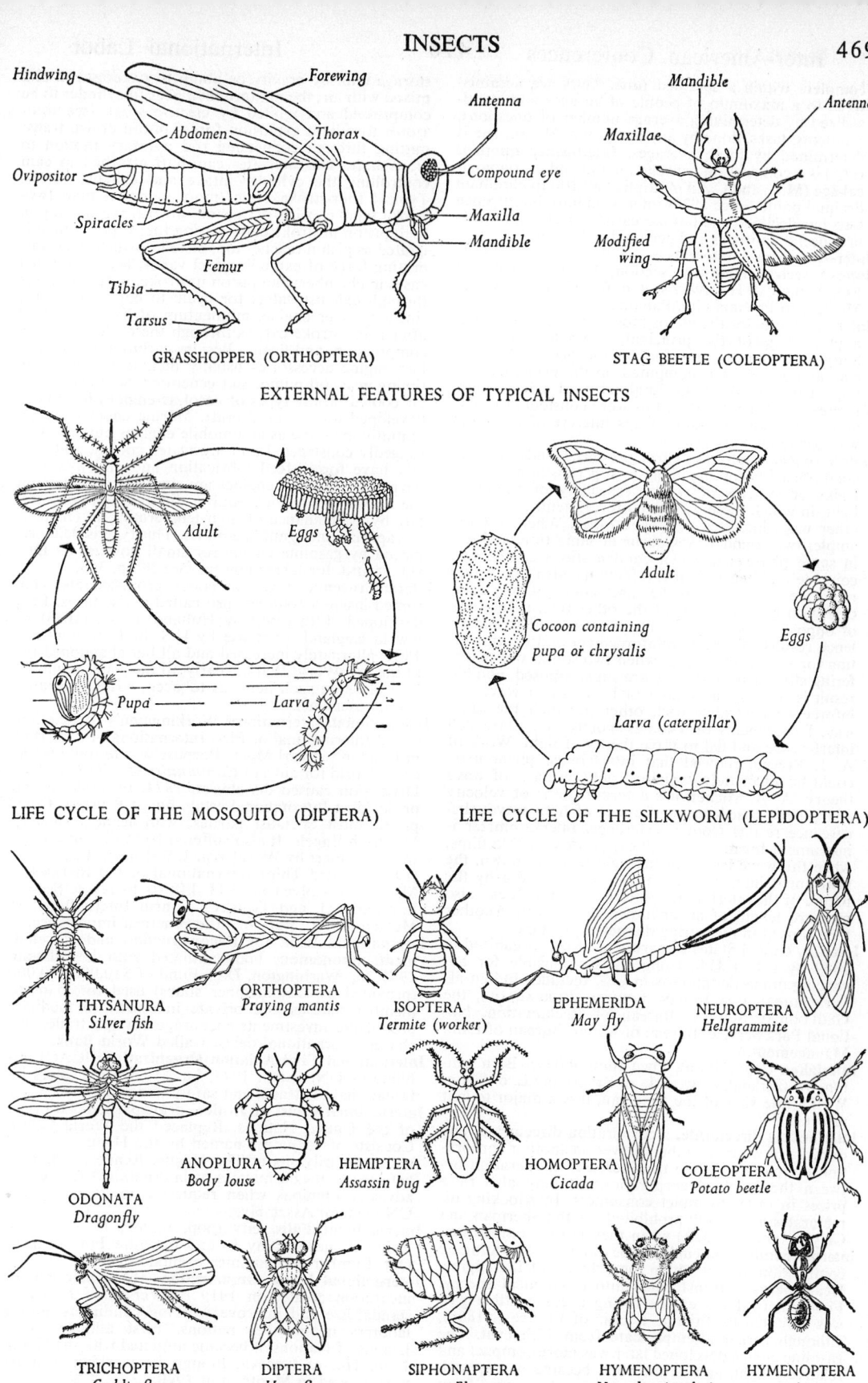

GRASSHOPPER (ORTHOPTERA)

Hindwing, Forewing, Antenna, Abdomen, Thorax, Ovipositor, Compound eye, Spiracles, Maxilla, Mandible, Femur, Tibia, Tarsus

STAG BEETLE (COLEOPTERA)

Mandible, Antenna, Maxillae, Modified wing

EXTERNAL FEATURES OF TYPICAL INSECTS

LIFE CYCLE OF THE MOSQUITO (DIPTERA)

Adult, Eggs, Pupa, Larva

LIFE CYCLE OF THE SILKWORM (LEPIDOPTERA)

Adult, Eggs, Cocoon containing pupa or chrysalis, Larva (caterpillar)

THYSANURA
Silver fish

ORTHOPTERA
Praying mantis

ISOPTERA
Termite (worker)

EPHEMERIDA
May fly

NEUROPTERA
Hellgrammite

ODONATA
Dragonfly

ANOPLURA
Body louse

HEMIPTERA
Assassin bug

HOMOPTERA
Cicada

COLEOPTERA
Potato beetle

TRICHOPTERA
Caddis fly

DIPTERA
Housefly

SIPHONAPTERA
Flea

HYMENOPTERA
Honeybee (worker)

HYMENOPTERA
Ant

REPRESENTATIVE INSECT ORDERS (NOT DRAWN TO THE SAME SCALE)

complete within a specified time. Tests are administered to a maximum of people of all ages and standardized by determining average number of questions, problems, tasks, done by any age group. Mental age is determined by those averages. **Intelligence quotient** (I.Q.) is a comparison between mental and chronological age (M.A. and C.A.) multiplied by 100 to eliminate decimal point. Since 1920s interest in pure intelligence tests has declined and has increased in tests that measure special aptitudes and personality factors.

Inter-American Conferences: see PAN-AMERICANISM.

Inter-American Highway, section, 3,349 mi. long, of PAN AMERICAN HIGHWAY system from Nuevo Laredo, Mexico, to Panama city, Panama.

interest, charge for the use of money, usually figured as a percentage of the principal, computed annually. Simple interest is computed on the principal alone; compound interest is computed on the principal plus unpaid interest. In 1545, England fixed a legal max. interest; higher rates than this were considered usury, although among certain groups interest of any kind was condemned as usurious.

interference, in physics, effect produced under certain conditions by combination or superposition of two trains or systems of waves, especially of sound or light, in which these waves reinforce, neutralize, or in other ways interfere with each other. When, for example, two sound waves occur at same time and are in same phase, i.e., when condensations of the two coincide and hence their rarefactions, also, the waves reinforce each other; if the rarefactions of one coincide with condensations of the other (i.e., if they are of opposite phase) they neutralize each other and silence results. Alternate reinforcement and neutralization (or weakening) occur when two sound waves differing slightly in frequency are superimposed; audible result is series of pulsations or beats. Light waves reinforce or neutralize each other in much the same way. Experiments of Thomas Young first illustrated interference and led to wave theory of light. Work of A. J. Fresnel showed that interference phenomena could be adequately explained only on basis of wave theory. A. A. Michelson's determinations of velocity of light are based on interference of light waves. Iridescence results from interference. **Interferometer** is instrument for measuring thickness of very thin films; when the wave length of the light used is known, the instrument indicates the thickness of the film by the nature of the interference patterns it forms. It can also measure length of an unknown light wave. Another type is used in measuring diameters of stars.

Interior, United States Department of the, organized in 1849 by act of U.S. Congress. Responsible for advancing domestic interests in U.S. Includes Indian affairs bureau (see INDIAN AFFAIRS, BUREAU OF), the GEOLOGICAL SURVEY, Bureau of Reclamation, National Park Service, Bureau of Mines, Bureau of Land Management.

Interlaken (ĭn'tùrläkùn), town (pop. 4,059), Bern canton, Switzerland, between L. of Brienz and L. of Thun. With a fine view of the Jungfrau, it is a major tourist resort.

interlocking directorate, a corporation directorate, one or more of whose members serves on another corporation directorate. While this increases cooperation between the involved corporations, it may also raise prices in order to mulct consumers. Interlocking directorates are legally prohibited (by the Sherman and Clayton antitrust acts) when they lessen competition.

internal-combustion engine, type of engine operating by combustion of fuel within the cylinder of the engine. Heat energy is transformed into mechanical energy. First practical gas engine (using a combustible gas) was invented by Étienne Lenoir of France (c.1860), although earlier attempts date from 17th cent. The gasoline engine developed later was more compact and relatively light, and its use soon became widespread. In typical automobile gasoline engine, fuel is fed from

storage tank by gravity or pump to CARBURETOR and mixed with air; the mixture then goes to cylinder to be compressed and ignited by electric spark (see IGNITION). Resultant explosion forces piston down, transmitting through connecting rod a rotary motion to crankshaft. This activates camshaft attached to cam controlling the cylinder intake and exhaust valves. Typical four-stroke cycle (more common than two-stroke type) consists of: piston downstroke sucking in fuel; piston upstroke compressing fuel vapor, which is ignited as piston reaches top; piston downstroke transmitting force of exploding fuel vapor, leaving burned gases in chamber; and piston upstroke, expelling gases through exhaust valve, for cycle to begin again. (In single-cylinder engine, momentum of heavy flywheel after firing stroke carries through the cycle of intake, compression, and firing.) Besides carburetor, automobile engine accessories usually include water pump, timing gear, oil pump, and generator. Some types are air cooled. Many types of gasoline engines have been developed for use in aircraft. Marine engines are essentially the same as automobile engines but are more ruggedly constructed and are water cooled, and usually have forced-feed lubrication and an oil-cooling device. Oil-burning engines are similarly designed but the heavier grade fuel requires different ignition, usually by maintenance of high temperature in chamber to vaporize and ignite the oil jet. This type is being replaced by gasoline engine for small powers; by DIESEL ENGINE for larger powers. See *ill.,* p. 303.

internal revenue, taxes on goods produced and consumed inside a country, also called excise taxes. First developed (17th cent.) by Holland; estab. (1643) by law in England. First use by U.S. in 1791; repealed 1802; alternately increased and all but abandoned until the two World Wars. Nearly all the states regularly levy taxes on such items as tobacco, gasoline, liquor, and amusements.

International. International Workingmen's Association, called International or First International, estab. 1864 in London by Karl Marx. Purpose was to unite workers of world for aims of *Communist Manifesto* (1848). Dissension caused dissolution 1874. In 1889 Second or Socialist International estab. hq. at Brussels. Comprised most Socialist parties, with leaders such as Friedrich Engels. It also suffered from dissension and was torn apart by World War I. Bolshevik Revolution (1917) created Third International or COMINTERN at Moscow, dissolved in 1943. Efforts to revive Second International, and Trotsky's Fourth International in Mexico (1937), were of little practical importance.

International Bank for Reconstruction and Development, autonomous body affiliated with UN. Estab. 1945, hq. Washington, D.C. Fund of $10,000,000,000 (provided by UN member states) used for loans to member nations and private investors, to facilitate productive investment, encourage foreign trade, discharge international debts. Called World Bank.

International Civil Aviation Organization (ICAO), affiliate of UN. Estab. 1947, hq. Montreal. Fosters international air trade, and safety and economy.

International Court of Justice, principal judicial organ of the United Nations. Replaced the World Court. Consists of 15 judges named by the Hague Tribunal and ordinarily sits at The Hague. Renders judgment between states on matters of international law. Gives advisory opinions when requested to do so by the UN General Assembly.

International Falls, city (pop. 6,269), N Minn., on Rainy R. near Rainy L. and opposite Fort Francis, Ont. Lumber and summer excursion center.

International Labor Organization (ILO), autonomous institution created in 1919 by Versailles Treaty to standardize and improve working conditions among laborers in member nations. First affiliated with League of Nations, it became affiliated with the UN in 1946. Hq. at Geneva, though its working quarters were moved to Montreal in 1940.

International Monetary Fund, autonomous body affiliated 1947 with UN; hq. Washington, D.C. Fund of $8,000,000,000 used, on application of member nations, to buy foreign currencies to discharge international indebtedness.

International Red Cross: see RED CROSS.

International Refugee Organization: see UNITED NATIONS RELIEF AND REHABILITATION ADMINISTRATION.

International Telecommunication Union (ITU), UN agency, estab. 1934 by merging two existing organizations, hq. Geneva. Operates under Internatl. Telecommunication Convention (adopted 1947, effective 1949). Allots radio frequencies, furthers low rates, and perfects communications in rescue work.

International Trade Organization (ITO), proposed specialized agency of UN to administer and implement a code of principles or rules of fair dealing in international trade. Code is contained in Havana Charter, drawn up at Havana Conference, Nov. 21, 1947–March 24, 1948. Interim Commission was estab. to prepare ground for ITO. Tariff concessions reached in a series of three tariff conferences between 1947 and 1950 were incorporated in the schedules of the General Agreement on Tariffs and Trade (GATT).

Interstate Commerce Commission, estab. 1887 by U.S. Congress as a result of mounting indignation over railroad malpractices. Board was to regulate common carriers in interstate commerce and in foreign commerce within U.S. ICC was designed chiefly to prevent railroads from charging exorbitant rates and from engaging in discriminatory practices (e.g., the REBATE), but its activities were limited by numerous Supreme Court decisions won by railroads. Hepburn Act of 1906, however, extended commission's jurisdiction to include intraterritorial commerce and express, sleeping-car, and pipe-line (exclusive of those carrying water or gas) companies; empowered ICC upon complaint and after a full hearing to reduce rates adjudged unreasonable. Later extensions of board's jurisdiction included power to regulate communications, motor carriers engaged in interstate commerce, and water-borne carriers operating coastwise, intercoastally, and upon inland U.S. waters; power to fix rates without previous complaint; power to evaluate property of common carrier companies; power to deal with labor disputes in interstate commerce.

intertype, trade name of machine that makes slugs, each doing work of a line of hand-set type. Similar to LINOTYPE, they have interchangeable matrices. Developed and produced by Internatl. Typesetting Machine Co. (organized 1912). See MONOTYPE.

intestine or **bowel,** tubular portion of alimentary canal extending from stomach to anus. Food mass is carried along within the intestine by contractions of muscular walls. In small intestine (tube c.23 ft. long), bile, pancreatic juice, and secretion from glands in its lining complete digestion of proteins, fats, carbohydrates; digested nutrients pass through lining into blood and lymph. Large intestine (c.5 ft. long) continues from cecum (blind portion forming right angle with small intestine) as the ascending, transverse, and descending colon, the rectum, anal canal, anus. See *ill.,* p. 595.

Intolerable Acts, name given by American patriots to five laws (including QUEBEC ACT) adopted by Parliament in 1774, limiting political and geographical freedom of colonists. Four of laws punished Mass. for Boston Tea Party.

Intracoastal Waterway, route, c.3,100 mi. long, part natural, part artificial, providing protected water passage from Boston, Mass., to Brownsville, Texas, along Atlantic and Gulf of Mexico coasts. Authorized by Congress, maintained toll free by U.S. Corps of Engineers. Minimum depth 7 ft. Important works are Cape Cod Canal, Chesapeake and Delaware Canal, Okeechobee Waterway, cut from Pensacola Bay to Mobile Bay, New Orleans–Rigolets Cut, and channel from Port Arthur to Corpus Christi, Texas. Final section (Corpus Christi-Brownsville) completed 1949.

introversion: see EXTROVERSION AND INTROVERSION.

intuitionism, philosophic theory that man may have or obtain knowledge (and truth) directly and immediately, quite apart from his experience or his reasoning. A distinction is made between intellect and intuition, between rational argument and suprarational comprehension (e.g., a mystic's knowledge of God). Intuitionists in ethics argue that a human being has an inborn moral sense.

Inverness-shire (ĭn″vŭrnĕs′shĭr) or **Inverness,** maritime county (4,211 sq. mi.; pop. 84,924), NW Scotland. Largest Scottish county, it includes many of the HEBRIDES. Caledonian Canal follows Great Glen diagonally across county through several lochs. Mountainous region, it has highest peak in Great Britain (Ben Nevis, 4,406 ft.). Chief occupation is sheep grazing; quarrying and fishing are also important. The county town is **Inverness,** burgh (pop. 28,115), called "Capital of Highlands." Scene of Great Highland Gathering in September, it has museums of Highland lore. Castle is on site of Macbeth's Castle, said to be scene of Duncan's murder.

invertebrate (ĭnvûr′tŭbrāt), any animal without a backbone. Invertebrates are divided into phyla including protozoa, sponges, coelenterates (jellyfish, sea anemone, coral), echinoderms (starfish and related forms), flatworms, roundworms, segmented worms, mollusks, arthropods. In size they range from microscopic protozoans to giant SQUID.

investiture, in FEUDALISM, ceremony by which an overlord transferred a fief to his vassal. After oath of fealty, lord "invested" him with fief, usually by giving a clod or stick or stone, or other token of land or office given. Ceremony imposed on lord duties of suzerain, chiefly protection of vassal's interests. Clerical investiture was of great importance as dispute about it was phase of struggle between Church and state in Middle Ages. Fundamental trouble lay in dual role of bishops and abbots as both spiritual and temporal lords. Always both king and pope were interested in election and installation of bishops. Quarrel was touched off by divergence between Emperor Henry IV and Pope Gregory VII. After long conflict agreement was reached by Henry V and Pope Calixtus II in Concordat of WORMS (1122), a victory for Church. In England William the Conqueror had trouble with the Church. Agreement (1107) by Henry I and Anselm gave investiture to Church, with homage to king.

Io (ī′ō), in Greek religion, princess of Argos, who was transformed into heifer by either Zeus or Hera. Hera persecuted her, but Argus guarded her. A gadfly drove her to Egypt, where she became a woman again. Sometimes identified with Egyptian Isis.

Ioannina (yôä′nēnä), city (pop. 32,268), NW Greece, in Epirus; also spelled Janina, Yannina. Agr. center; silk and textile mfg. Was under Turkish rule 1438–1913. Scene of severe fighting in World War II. Famous as residence of ALI PASHA.

iodine (ī′ŭdīn), the least active HALOGEN, it is a dark gray to purple-black, lustrous, crystalline solid element (symbol = I; see also ELEMENT, table). Undergoes SUBLIMATION when heated; its vapor is violet. It forms many compounds; is found in salt deposits and in some seaweed. Used in treating goiter, as antiseptic (in alcoholic solution and as iodoform), and in making certain drugs and dyes.

Iola (ī′ōlŭ), city (pop. 7,094), SE Kansas, W of Fort Scott. Center of dairy, grain, and livestock area.

Iolo Marganwg (yō′lō môrgä′nōōg), bardic name of Edward Williams, 1746–1825, Welsh poet, who led in Welsh revival.

Ion (ī′ŭn, ī′ŏn), in Greek mythology, son of Apollo and Creusa, who became ancestor of the Ionians.

ion (ī′ŏn). To explain the fact that some substances conduct current only in aqueous solution, S. A. Arrhenius advanced the theory (1887) that molecules dissociate and parts conduct. According to theory of ion, some of the molecules break up into two parts—one with positive (+) charge, one with negative (−). Particles are called ions. Each particle with + charge is an atom that has lost an electron; each with − charge has gained an electron. When electric current is introduced (see ELECTROLYSIS), particles with + charge are attracted to cathode (− pole); those with − charge to anode (+ pole). At the poles, the particles gain or lose electrons to become neutral, combine with other atoms to form molecules. Substances that conduct electricity are called electrolytes (e.g., sodium chloride); those that do not, nonelectrolytes (e.g., sugar). Acids, bases, and salts are, in general, electrolytes. Some substances ionize when melted; important industrial processes are based on this. Acidity or alkalinity of substance in solution depends on concentration of hydrogen ions (H^+) or hydroxyl ions (OH^-). Indicators show which ions are present in greater concentration. Litmus is an indicator that turns red in acid solution (excess of H^+); blue in basic solution (excess of OH^- ions). Hydrogen-ion concentration is indicated by pH.

Iona (ī̄ō′nủ) or **Icolmkill** (ĭ′kŏmkĭl′), island of Inner Hebrides, in Argyllshire, off W Scotland. It is c.3½ mi. long and 1½ mi. wide. At this early center of Celtic Christianity St. Columba landed in 563. It has many ancient remains. Cathedral dates from 12th or 13th cent. Cemetery reputed to be burial place of kings from several countries.

Ionia (ī̄ō′nēủ), anc. Greek region of Asia Minor occupying a narrow coastal strip of what is today W Turkey and the neighboring Aegean Isls. Here Ionian Greek settlers founded colonies, presumably before 1000 B.C. Athens claimed to be mother city of them all. There came to be 12 important cities, among them Miletus, Ephesus, and Samos. After conquest by several empires came under Persian power. In 500 B.C. they revolted against Darius. Athens supported them, and the PERSIAN WARS ensued. Continued rich and important under Roman and Byzantine Empires. After the Turkish conquest their culture was destroyed.

Ionia, city (pop. 6,412), S Mich., on Grand R. and E of Grand Rapids, in agr. area. Mfg. of furniture and auto parts.

Ionian Sea (ī̄ō′nẽủn), part of Mediterranean Sea, between SE Italy and Greece. Connected with Adriatic Sea by Strait of Otranto. In it are the **Ionian Islands,** chain (752 sq. mi.; pop. 219,562), off W Greece. They include CORFU, CEPHALONIA, ZANTE, CYTHERA, Ithaca, Paxo, Leucas. Largely mountainous. Agr., fruit growing, cattle raising, fishing, soapmaking. Islands passed from Byzantine Empire to Venice in 14th–15th cent. Though ceded by Venice to France in 1797, they were under Russo-Turkish occupation 1799–1807 and under English occupation from 1809. Treaty of Paris made them a British protectorate (1815). England ceded them to Greece 1864.

Ionic order, in architecture. Distinctive feature is spreading, scroll-shaped capital. Originated in Asia Minor in 6th cent. B.C. In 5th cent. appeared in Greece, where its only complete example is ERECHTHEUM. Greek Ionic columns are fluted and slender; Roman versions are heavier. A variant, called Scamozzi Ionic order, is named after Vincenzo Scamozzi, Italian Renaissance architect who standardized it. See *ill.*, p. 47.

ionization: see ION.

ionosphere (ī̄ō′nủsfẽr), a series of concentric ionized layers in upper atmosphere. It makes possible long-distance wireless communication by reflecting radio waves back to earth. Independently discovered by Oliver Heaviside and A. E. Kennelly; both entire ionosphere and highly ionized layer are known also as Kennelly-Heaviside layer. See *ill.*, p. 19.

Iowa, state (56,280 sq. mi.; pop. 2,621,073); N central U.S., in Middle West; admitted 1846 as 29th state (free); cap. DES MOINES. Other cities are SIOUX CITY, DUBUQUE, CEDAR RAPIDS. Bounded E by Mississippi R., W by Missouri and Big Sioux rivers. State is largely a gently rolling plain. Farming includes grains (esp.

corn), livestock, dairying. Has bituminous coal and gypsum deposits. Mfg. of food, meat, dairy products, machinery (agr. and industrial), railroad equipment, buttons. Region explored by French and fur traders. Indians leased land to Julien DUBUQUE in late 18th cent. Part of Louisiana Purchase; most Indian claims abandoned after BLACK HAWK WAR (1832). Iowa Territory organized by 1838. Supported Union in Civil War. Farmers joined GRANGER MOVEMENT, GREENBACK PARTY, and POPULIST PARTY in hard times of late 19th cent. An agr. commonwealth, Iowa tends toward stable, conservative norm.

Iowa, river, 329 mi. long, rising in N central Iowa and flowing SE across state. Joined by Cedar R. at Columbus Junction, it enters the Mississippi between Muscatine and Burlington.

Iowa, State University of, at Iowa City; state supported, coed.; chartered 1847, opened 1855. Has child-welfare research station and state historical society. Campus, on both sides of Iowa R., includes old capitol, begun 1840.

Iowa City, city (pop. 27,212), E Iowa, on both sides of Iowa R. and S of Cedar Rapids; founded 1839 as cap. of Iowa Territory. Was cap. 1841–57. Became supply center for western trails with opening of railroad 1855. Mfg. of dairy, food, wood, and paper products. Seat of State Univ. of IOWA. Near by are villages of AMANA SOCIETY and birthplace of Herbert Hoover.

Iowa Indians, tribe of Siouan linguistic stock, formerly on the Platte R. Were presumably once part of the Winnebago people and shared culture of Eastern Woodlands and Plains areas.

Iowa State College of Agriculture and Mechanic Arts, at Ames; land-grant and state supported, coed.; chartered 1858, opened 1868. Has atomic, industrial science, and veterinary research institutes, and Guatemala Tropical Research Center.

ipecac (ĭ′pĭkăk″), drug obtained from dried roots and rhizomes of a tropical creeping shrub. Contains toxic, emetic alkaloids capable of destroying amoebae and occasionally used in treatment of certain parasitic diseases.

Iphigenia (ĭ″fủjủnī̄′ủ), in Greek legend, daughter of Clytemnestra and Agamemnon. His ships becalmed at Aulis en route to Trojan War, Agamemnon sacrificed her to Artemis, but goddess rescued her and took her to Tauris as a priestess for her temple. Here she saved Orestes from sacrifice and fled with him to Greece.

Ipiranga or **Ypiranga** (both: ē″pēr
äng′gú), stream, São Paulo, SE Brazil, where Pedro issued Grito de Ypiranga, declaring independence of Brazil from Portugal, Sept. 7, 1822.

Ippolitov-Ivanov, Mikhail (Mikhailovich) (mēkhŭyēl′ ēpủlyē′tủf-ēvä′nủf), 1859–1935, Russian composer; pupil of Rimsky-Korsakov. His music is nationalistic. His best-known work is his orchestral *Caucasian Sketches.* He also composed operas, choral works, and chamber music.

Ipsus (ĭp′sủs), town, anc. Phrygia, Asia Minor, the modern Ipsili Hissar. Here ANTIGONUS I was defeated and slain by other Diadochi (301 B.C.).

Ipswich, county borough (pop. 104,788), Suffolk East, England. Town is very old and has many historical houses and buildings. Industries include shipping and mfg. of agr. machinery.

Ipswich, town (pop. 6,895), NE Mass., NNE of Salem and on Ipswich R. (crossed by bridge built 1764); area, called Agawam, settled 1633. Hosiery.

Iquitos (ēkē′tōs), city (pop. 34,231), NE Peru, on Amazon, c.2,300 mi. up the river; founded 1863. Was important port in wild-rubber boom of early 20th cent.

Ir, chemical symbol of the element IRIDIUM.

Ira (ī̄′rủ), chief officer of David. 2 Sam. 20.26.

Irak: see IRAQ.

Irala, Domingo Martínez de (dōmēng′gō märtē′näs dä ērä′lä), d. 1556 or 1557, first governor of Paraguay elected by free vote of colonists. Moved inhabitants of Buenos Aires to Asunción (1539).

Iran (ērän', īrän'), kingdom (630,000 sq. mi.; pop. c.18,-387,000), SW Asia, widely known in English as Persia; cap. TEHERAN. Bounded on N by USSR and Caspian Sea, on S by Gulf of Oman and Persian Gulf, on W by Iraq, and on E by Afghanistan and Pakistan. On great plateau surrounded by Elburz and Zagros ranges. Great salt deserts are in interior. Trans-Iranian RR links Caspian Sea with Persian Gulf. People are predominantly SHIITES in religion. Wheat and rice are grown; opium and tobacco are state monopolies. Main industrial products are carpets and rugs, but supreme source of wealth is oil. In ancient times the area was the heart of a great empire (see PERSIA). Safavid dynasty (1499–1736) reached its peak under Shah Abbas I. After brief period of Afghan rule, NADIR SHAH estab. Afshar dynasty in 1736. It was succeeded by Zand dynasty (1750–94) and by Kajar or Qajar dynasty (1794–1925), founded by Aga Mohammed Khan. In 19th cent. Iran fell under increasing pressure of European nations. Lost Caucasian lands to Russia by treaties of 1813 and 1828. Divided into British and Russian spheres of influence 1907–19. Agreement with Great Britain in 1919 ambiguously affirmed Iran's independence, while Russians withdrew in 1921. New dynasty was founded 1925 by REZA SHAH PAHLEVI, whose abdication in favor of his son MOHAMMED REZA SHAH PAHLEVI was forced by the British and Russians who in World War II had again occupied Iran. Teheran Conference in 1943 guaranteed independence of Iran. Foreign troops were withdrawn 1946 after a short-lived, Soviet-supported autonomous movement in Azerbaijan had been suppressed under UN direction. Intense nationalism, spurred by Communist Tudeh party, resulted in nationalization of British-owned oil industry in 1951 by Premier MOSSADEGH. Ousting of Anglo-Iranian Oil Co. and subsequent British blockade against Iran led to virtual collapse of the vital industry, which severely strained the national economy. Iran broke off diplomatic ties with Britain in 1952, and despite U.S. mediation the oil dispute remained unsettled in early 1953. Iran is a constitutional monarchy with a legislature consisting of an upper house (senate) and a lower house (Majlis).

Iranian languages, group of Indo-Iranian subfamily of Indo-European languages. See LANGUAGE (table).

Iraq or **Irak** (both: ēräk'), kingdom (c.168,000 sq. mi.; pop. 4,799,500), SW Asia; cap. Baghdad. Bordered on E by Iran, on S by Saudi Arabia, and on N by Turkey. Roughly co-extensive with ancient MESOPOTAMIA. Population concentrated on banks of TIGRIS and EUPHRATES rivers. In dry SE area, dates and cotton are grown with aid of irrigation. In mountainous north oil is exploited by British companies. Chief port is Basra. Most Iraqi are Arabic-speaking Moslems. Fiercely resisted subjugation by Ottoman Turks in 16th cent. Supported Allies in World War I and welcomed British occupation (begun 1915). Treaty of Sèvres (1920) made it a League of Nations mandate under the British. Country became a kingdom under FEISAL I in 1921, but British mandate continued until 1932. Pro-British elements controlled Iraq at outset of World War II but nationalist opposition strengthened as British lost Middle East territory in early phase of war. In 1941 the British defeated pro-Axis usurper Rashid Ali al Gailani and recalled Emir Abdul Illah, regent for FEISAL II. Declared war on Axis powers in 1943. Anti-British sentiment, fed mainly by British control of oil industry, reappeared after the war. In 1948 Iraq joined other ARAB LEAGUE nations in unsuccessful war against Israel.

Ireland, John, 1838–1918, American Catholic prelate, first archbishop of St. Paul (1888–1918), b. Ireland, came to St. Paul as a child. A well-known public figure, he stirred controversy by advocating state support and inspection of Catholic schools and by opposing foreign-language church schools.

Ireland, William Henry, 1777–1835, English forger of Shaksperian documents and manuscripts. Exposed, he admitted hoax in *Authentic Account* (1796).

Ireland [Irish *Eire* (â'rù); to it are related the poetic *Erin* and, perhaps, the Latin *Hibernia*], island (31,-839 sq. mi.; pop. 4,329,587), second largest of British Isles. Lies W of Great Britain, from which it is separated by the North Channel, the Irish Sea, and St. George's Channel. At present divided into political regions—NORTHERN IRELAND (cap. Belfast) and the republic of Ireland (26,601 sq. mi.; pop. 2,958,878; cap. Dublin). Island has 32 counties and, historically, four provinces. ULSTER is divided between N. Ireland (counties Antrim, Down, Armagh, Fermanagh, Tyrone, and Londonderry) and republic (counties Monaghan, Cavan, and Donegal). Other three provinces are in republic—LEINSTER has counties Louth, Meath, Dublin, Kildare, Wicklow, Carlow, Wexford, Kilkenny, Laoighis, Offaly, Westmeath, and Longford; MUNSTER has Tipperary, Waterford, Cork, Kerry, Limerick, and Clare; CONNAUGHT has Leitrim, Roscommon, Galway, Mayo, and Sligo. Island has a large central plain, extremely fertile, roughly enclosed by a highland rim. In N are Mourne Mts., Sperrin Mts., and those of Antrim; in W are mountains of Connemara and Mayo; and in S are mountains of Galty, Knockmealdown, and Kerry. Heavy rains (over 80 in. annually in S) account for brilliant green grass of "emerald isle." Off W coast are many islands (including Aran and Blasket Isls.) and in interior are many lakes and wide stretches of rivers called loughs. SHANNON R., 250 mi. long, provides electric power for much of the republic. Lagan, Foyle, Liffey, and Lee are among other rivers. Economy is mainly agr., chief products being dairy goods and flax. Fine linen and laces are world famous. Industrial activity is concentrated in Belfast area and adjoining area in the republic. Population of republic is overwhelmingly Catholic. Protestants outnumber Catholics in N. Ireland, but number of Catholics has increased in recent years, and the traditional religious difference between sections seems about to upset.

Ireland to 1169. Ireland was invaded before the Christian era by several Celtic tribes who left their culture. Anglo-Saxons and Romans did not affect the island. Ireland enjoyed golden age of its culture until 8th cent. when Norsemen began their raids. People were organized into clans owing allegiance to one of five provincial kings (of Ulster, Munster, Leinster, Connaught, and Meath) who in turn served high king of all Ireland at Tara. Despite constant clan fighting, literary and artistic culture flourished (see GAELIC LITERATURE). In 5th cent. St. PATRICK completed the island's conversion to Christianity. Later Irish religious leaders included St. Columba, St. Columban, and St. Bridget. In 1014 Brian Boru broke the hold of Norse invaders. There followed 150 years of freedom from foreign interference. Overlordship of Ireland was granted in 12th cent. to Henry II of England by Pope Adrian IV. English in 1169 began conquest. Anglo-Irish struggle was to continue intermittently for nearly 800 years.

Ireland to Union of 1800. Anglo-Norman rapacity in Ireland led to landlord-tenant problem. Irish were denied benefit of English law and their own law was split apart. English control lessened, however, until Henry VIII became first monarch to bring all Ireland under English control. POYNINGS'S LAW (1495) gave legislative initiative to English Parliament. By 16th cent. Irish people were sunk in desperate poverty which was to last for centuries. The Protestant English imposed the PENAL LAWS upon the Catholic Irish. In Elizabeth's reign three serious rebellions were crushed. Scotch settlers were planted in Ulster. A rebellion began in 1641 which lasted ten years, cost 600,-000 lives, and was brutally crushed by Cromwell (who massacred Irish at Drogheda). Irish support of James II led to new Penal Laws and economic exploitation after battle of the Boyne (1690). In 1782 Henry GRAT-

TAN obtained an independent Parliament which proved ineffective. After rebellion under Wolfe TONE, England and Ireland were united (1800), and Irish were unwillingly represented in English Parliament.

Ireland under the Union, 1800–1921. Agitation led by Daniel O'Connell caused Catholic Emancipation Act to be passed in 1829. Other causes for Irish discontent persisted. Church of Ireland was not disestab. until 1869. Evils of absentee landlordism grew more serious (see IRISH LAND QUESTION). Potato blight struck Ireland in 1840s. In five years ending 1851 c.1,000,000 Irish died of starvation and disease and some 1,600,-000 emigrated, mostly to U.S. FENIAN MOVEMENT was organized. By 1870 PARNELL had arisen as a leader. HOME RULE movement was gradually superseded by SINN FEIN. Easter Rebellion of 1916 led to guerrilla warfare in 1918. English tried to suppress it with auxiliaries known as Black and Tans, who terrorized country (1920) and met increasing resistance. Irish cause was strengthened by literary and cultural revival of late 19th cent.; by such writers as G. B. Shaw, W. B. Yeats, and James Joyce; and by Abbey Theatre. *Irish Free State and the Republic.* Irish Free State was estab. (1921) as result of negotiations between British and Eamon DE VALERA. Six N Protestant counties accepted dominion status as N. Ireland. Split of Sinn Fein into right- and left-wing groups led to a period of civil war. William Cosgrave was president 1922–32. Succeeded by De Valera who estab. (1937) sovereign country of Ireland (officially Eire) associated in foreign policy with British Commonwealth of Nations. Trade war between England and Ireland ended. During World War II Ireland remained neutral and protested Allied military activity in N. Ireland. Outlawed Irish Republican Army continued to agitate for end of separation of N. Ireland from Eire. In 1948 De Valera was voted out of power and a coalition chose John Costello new premier. Republic of Ireland Bill of 1949 estab. independent nation. Executive power is vested in prime minister and legislative power in the DÁIL ÉIREANN. De Valera was again returned to office in 1951.

Ireland, Church of, principal Anglican church in Ireland. Unlike Church of England, it has been disestablished since 1889. Represents minority of population.

Irenaeus, Saint (īrĭnē′ŭs), c.125–c.202, bishop of Lyons, Gaul, b. Asia Minor, author of *Against the Heresies* (against GNOSTICISM).

Irene (īrēn′, īrē′nē), 752–803, Byzantine empress (797–802). As regent for her son Constantine VI after 780, she bent all her efforts on suppression of ICONOCLASM. Constantine's misconduct led to his deposition (797); Irene had him blinded and ascended the throne. She was deposed and exiled by Nicephorus I (802).

Irene, one of the HORAE.

Ireton, Henry (ī′ŭrtŭn), 1611–51, English parliamentarian general in Puritan Revolution; husband of Oliver Cromwell's daughter. As lord deputy of Ireland (1650) he carried on Cromwell's policy of dispossessing the Irish in favor of Englishmen.

Iriarte, Ignacio (ēgnä′thyō ēryär′tä), 1620–85, Spanish landscape painter, who often collaborated with Murillo.

Iriarte, Tómas de (tōmäs′ dā ēryär′tä), 1750–91, Spanish poet and critic. Wrote *Fabulas literárias* (1782).

iridescence (ĭ′rĭdĕ′sŭns), exhibition of changing, shifting color bands by certain surfaces (e.g., in mother-of-pearl). It results from breaking up of white light and INTERFERENCE of light rays caused by irregularities in the surface.

iridium (ĭrĭ′dĕŭm), rare, silver-white metallic element (symbol = Ir; see also ELEMENT, table). It resembles platinum, is very hard, and one of the heaviest elements known. Alloys are used for making standard weights and other apparatus resistant to action of atmosphere, contact points of electrical apparatus, and fountain pen points.

Irigoyen, Hipólito (ēpō′lētō ērēgō′yän), 1850?–1933, Argentine political leader, president of the republic (1916–22, 1928–30).

Iris, in Greek religion, goddess of the rainbow; daughter of Electra and attendant of Zeus and Hera.

iris, stately perennial plant of genus *Iris* from which the fleur-de-lis is thought to have been derived. Native American irises are called blue flags. Violet-scented rootstalks of some Old World irises, especially *Iris florentina*, are sold commercially as orrisroot, which is powdered and used in perfume, sachet, etc. The bearded irises of June gardens include several thousand varieties; beardless kinds include Japanese and Siberian irises. These all have creeping rootstalks. Spanish, Dutch, and English irises are grown from bulbs. See *ill.,* p. 783.

Irish Free State: see IRELAND.

Irish Land Question. The problem of Irish land ownership, which came to a crisis in 19th cent., goes back many centuries. Feudal landholding system was imposed on Ireland in 12th cent. The Tudors, Cromwell, and William III continued land confiscations. 18th cent. Penal Laws increased difficulty of landowning by Catholics. CATHOLIC EMANCIPATION did not materially help. Hatred for England grew through great famine of 1840s and influx of speculators after Encumbered Estates Act of 1849. The violent Fenian movement, the Reform Act of 1867, and support by Gladstone led to first land act (1870). Agitation of Michael Davitt and Charles Stewart Parnell led to Land Act (1881) giving the farmer the "three F's"—fair rent, fixity of tenure, and freedom from sale. Main issue then became land purchase by the tenant. Agitation of William O'BRIEN led to Wyndham Act (1903) and Amended Land Purchase Act (1909). By 1921 Irish tenants owned two thirds of the land; the rest was confiscated by law and given to the tenants. Issue of land annuity payments to England led to trade war with settlement in favor of Ireland in 1938.

Irish language, one of the Goidelic group of the Celtic subfamily of Indo-Iranian languages. It is also called Gaelic and Erse. See LANGUAGE (table).

Irish literature: see GAELIC LITERATURE.

Irish moss, reddish or purplish seaweed (*Chondrus crispus*), found off coasts of Ireland and E U.S. When cooked it yields gelatine used as pudding or as textile sizing.

Irish Sea, part of the Atlantic, 130 mi. long, up to c.130 mi. wide, between Ireland and Great Britain. Connected with the Atlantic by North Channel and (on S) St. George's Channel.

Irish terrier: see TERRIER.

Irish wolfhound: see HOUND.

Irkutsk (īrkōōtsk′), city (pop. 243,380), RSFSR, in S central Siberia, W of L. Baikal, on Angara and Irkut rivers and on Trans-Siberian RR. River port; mfgr. of aircraft, cars, mining equipment; educational center. Chartered 1683.

Irnerius (ûrnēr′ēŭs), c.1055–c.1130, Italian teacher and commentator on Roman law, founder of the school at Bologna.

iron, silver-white metallic element (symbol = Fe; see also ELEMENT, table), lustrous, ductile, malleable, attracted by magnet. It rusts easily. Chemically active, it forms ferrous (divalent), and ferric (trivalent) compounds. The fourth most abundant element, it comprises about 5% of earth's crust. Its compounds occur in soil, sand, plants, animals. Deficiency causes anemia in humans and some animals. Three forms of commercial iron: cast iron, wrought iron, STEEL. **Cast iron** is made when pig iron, prepared in BLAST FURNACE, is remelted and poured into molds to make castings. Usually has 92–94% iron, 2–6% carbon, small amounts of silicon, sulphur, manganese, phosphorus. Used in making machine parts, ranges, stoves, pipes, radiators. **Wrought iron** is made by purifying melted pig iron in puddling furnace; relatively pure, with 0.1–0.2% carbon. Used for rivets, bolts, water pipes, chains, anchors, fire bars, ornamental ironwork.

Iron Age, period of industrial development that begins with the general use of iron and continues in the present. Beads of meteoric iron shaped by rubbing were worn in Egypt c.4000 B.C., but the oldest known hammered object is a dagger made there before 1350 B.C. Casting of iron was known in ancient Greece, where the Iron Age began c.1000 B.C. From previous times the Iron Age inherited staple farm crops, animals, wheeled vehicles, and a variety of tools and implements. Glass and pottery making, spinning, weaving, and writing developed.

Iron Cross: see DECORATIONS, CIVIL AND MILITARY.

Irondequoit (ŭrŏn'dĭkwoit"), town (pop. 34,417), W N.Y., N of Rochester and on L. Ontario; settled 1791.

Iron Gate, narrow, mountainous gorge of the Danube, between Orsova and Turnu-Severin, on the Rumanian-Yugoslav border.

Iron Guard, Rumanian nationalistic, anti-Semitic, terrorist organization, founded 1924 by Corneliu Zelea Codreanu. Banned 1933, it carried on under different name. It helped Ion Antonescu into power (1940), but he suppressed it after a rebellion (1941).

Iron Mask, Man with the, mysterious French prisoner of state, brought to Bastille in 1698, buried 1703 under name Marchioly. Wore black velvet (not iron) mask to prevent identification. Wild speculation as to his identity was started by Voltaire's *Age of Louis XIV,* reached fantastic proportions in Dumas Père's *Le Vicomte de Bragelonne.* Actually, most modern students agree that the Iron Mask was one Count Mattioli, secretary to the duke of Mantua, whom Louis XIV had kidnaped for political reasons; but other theories still flourish.

Iron Mountain, city (pop. 9,679), W Upper Peninsula, N Mich., near Wis. line. Distributing point for iron ore of Menominee range. Winter sports center.

Iron Mountain, elevation, 325 ft. high, central Fla., near L. Wales. Singing Tower, with carillon of 71 bells, and bird sanctuary estab. here by Edward Bok and opened 1929.

Ironton. 1 Resort city (pop. 1,148), SE Mo., SW of St. Louis, in the Ozarks. Union troops under Thomas Ewing defeated Sterling Price's Confederates at nearby battle of Pilot Knob (Sept. 27, 1864). **2** City (pop. 16,333), S Ohio, on Ohio R. opposite Ashland, Ky.; laid out 1848. Mfg. of iron and steel goods and cement; limestone quarries.

Ironwood, city (pop. 11,466), extreme W Upper Peninsula, N Mich., on Montreal R. at Wis. line; founded 1885. Trade center for Gogebic iron range; has some of world's deepest mines.

ironwood: see HORNBEAM.

Iroquoian (ĭrŭkwoi'yŭn), North American Indian linguistic stock, in N.Y., Pa., E Canada, and in S U.S. (Tuscarora, Cherokee). See LANGUAGE, table.

Iroquois Confederacy or **Iroquois League** (ĭ'rŭkwoi), Indian confederation consisting of Mohawk, Oneida, Onondaga, Cayuga, and Seneca tribes; founded c.1570 by prophet Deganawidah and disciple Hiawatha; also called Five Nations. Gave name to Iroquoian linguistic family. Despite some intertribal warfare, the confederacy was tight knit, the main Onondaga village serving as meeting place of the council. Material culture, based on hunting and agr., was most advanced of Eastern Woodlands area, exhibiting also traits of SE area. Iroquois were second to no other Indians N of Mexico in political organization, statecraft, and military prowess. In second half of 17th cent. they conquered neighboring tribes and dominated area bounded by Kennebec, Ottawa, Illinois, and Tennessee rivers. Were allies of British against the French in French and Indian Wars and (excepting the Oneida) American Revolution. Sir William Johnson held their loyalty. In the Revolution Cornplanter, Red Jacket, and Joseph Brant were Iroquois leaders against the patriots. The Cherry Valley and Wyoming Valley massacres incensed Americans, and John Sullivan led a punitive expedition (1779) against them and Walter

Butler, the Tory leader, defeating them near Elmira.

Irrawaddy (ĭrŭwŏ'dē), chief river of Burma, c.1,300 mi. long, rising in NW and flowing to Bay of Bengal. Chief tributary is Chindwin R.

irredentism (ĭrĭdĕn'tĭzŭm), Italian nationalist movement for annexation of *Italia irredenta* [unredeemed Italy]— the ethnically Italian territories left to Austria after 1866 (e.g., Trentino, Trieste, part of Dalmatia). Chief motive for Italian entry into World War I.

irrigation, artificial watering of arable lands. It is used chiefly in regions with an annual rainfall under 20 in., but also in areas of greater rainfall to supply the high water requirements of certain crops, e.g., rice. Irrigation has been practiced from ancient times. Methods include free-flooding of entire areas from canals and ditches; check-flooding, in which water is guided over strips of land between levees; furrow method in which water is run between crop rows; and surface-pipe and sprinkler systems. Large-scale irrigation is commonly a part of multiple-purpose water projects combining irrigation, water supply, hydroelectric power production, and flood control.

Irtysh (ĭrtĭsh'), river, 1,844 mi. long, China and USSR, chief tributary of Ob. Rises in Sinkiang, flows generally NW through W Siberia past Semipalatinsk, Pavlodar, Omsk, Tobolsk. Navigable April–Nov. Reached by Russians 1594.

Irving, Edward, 1792–1834, Scottish preacher, a founder of CATHOLIC APOSTOLIC CHURCH, whose members are often called Irvingites. His emphasis on the supernatural and on the second coming of Christ and his other teachings caused expulsion (1833) from Church of Scotland.

Irving, Sir Henry, 1838–1905, English actor and manager, originally named Brodribb. Had acting successes in such dramas as *Eugene Aram* and *Hamlet.* Became (1878) manager of London's Lyceum Theatre where he reigned (with leading lady Ellen Terry) until 1903, presenting spectacular Shakspere productions. He was the first English actor knighted.

Irving, Washington, 1783–1859, American author, b. New York city. Began early contributing essays to periodicals, styled *Letters of Jonathan Oldstyle, Gent.* (1802–3) and after a tour in Europe joined William Irving and James K. Paulding in a series called *Salmagundi* (1807–8), and under the pseudonym Diedrich Knickerbocker he produced the comic *History of New York* (1809). Sent (1815) to England to manage the Liverpool branch of the family hardware business, he saw that fail and turned definitely to literature. Essays and stories, appearing serially and collected as *The Sketch Book of Geoffrey Crayon, Gent.* (1820) made his reputation. This was followed by others in *Bracebridge Hall* (1822) and *Tales of a Traveller* (1824). He was attached to the embassy at Madrid after 1826 and turned to writing of things Spanish: a biography of Columbus (1828), *The Conquest of Granada* (1829), and *The Alhambra* (1832). After returning to the U.S., he wrote several works on the American West: *A Tour of the Prairies* (1835); *Astoria* (1836; written with his nephew, Pierre Irving, for John Jacob Astor); and *The Adventures of Captain Bonneville, U.S.A.* (1837). Except for service as minister to Madrid (1842–46), he lived most of his later years at "Sunnyside," near Tarrytown, N.Y. (and in Irvington), now a sort of shrine to him. Completed biography of Washington (5 vols., 1855–59). One of the first American writers to receive wide recognition abroad, Irving has been held in affectionate regard by Americans ever since his own time. Some essays and tales (e.g., "Rip Van Winkle" and "The Legend of Sleepy Hollow") are known to most Americans. He was notable for effortlessly smooth style, good humor, and playful satire.

Irvington. 1 Town (pop. 59,201), NE N.J., W suburb of Newark; settled 1692 as Camptown, renamed 1852. Mfg. of metal and rubber goods and leather. **2** Residential village (pop. 3,657), SE N.Y., on E bank of

Hudson R. S of Tarrytown; settled c.1655. Renamed 1854 for Washington Irving, who bought "Sunnyside" estate in 1835. Columbia Univ. maintains "Nevis," once estate of Alexander Hamilton's son.

Irwell, river of Lancashire, England.

Isaac, Byzantine emperors. **Isaac I,** 1005–1061, first of Comnenus dynasty, was proclaimed emperor by the army in 1057 but abdicated, ostensibly because of bad health, in 1059. Uncle of Alexius I. **Isaac II** (Isaac Angelus), d. 1204, proclaimed emperor by the people in 1185, was deposed and blinded in 1195 by his brother ALEXIUS III. His son, ALEXIUS IV, appealed to the host of the Fourth Crusade (see CRUSADES), which restored father and son as joint emperors in 1203. Their overthrow by ALEXIUS V (1204) led to the sack of Constantinople by the Crusaders.

Isaac [Heb.,= laughter], only son of Abraham and Sarah, father of Jacob and Esau. Offered as sacrifice to God by Abraham in act of supreme faith; saved by divine intervention. Tricked into blessing Jacob instead of Esau. Lived longest and most peaceful life of all the patriarchs. Gen. 21–27; 35.29; 49.31; Amos 7.9,16; Mat. 8.11; Heb. 11.17; James 2.21.

Isaacs, Jorge (hôr′hä ē′säks), 1837–95, Colombian novelist, author of idyllic romance, *María* (1867).

Isabeau of Bavaria (ēzäbō′), 1371–1435, consort of CHARLES VI of France. In league with Burgundy, she helped bring about the Treaty of TROYES (1420), which disinherited her own son, Charles VII.

Isabel, 1846–1921, princess imperial of Brazil; daughter of Pedro II, wife of comte d'Eu. As regent, during father's absence, she signed law abolishing slavery (1889). After downfall of empire, lived in Paris.

Isabella, 1292?–1358, queen consort of EDWARD II of England; daughter of Philip IV of France. Mistreated by her husband, she hated royal favorites, the Despensers. Visited France (1325), formed a liaison with Roger MORTIMER, and invaded England. King abdicated and was murdered. Isabella and Mortimer ruled until Edward III seized power in 1330.

Isabella, Spanish queens. **Isabella I** or **Isabella the Catholic,** 1451–1504, queen of Castile and Leon (1474–1504), consort of Ferdinand II of Aragon, who became Ferdinand V of Castile. Her claim to Castile was contested in civil war by JUANA LA BELTRANEJA until 1479. For the crucial reign of Ferdinand and Isabella, called the Catholic monarchs, see FERDINAND V. **Isabella II,** 1830–1904, queen of Spain (1833–68), succeeded her father Ferdinand VII under the regency of her mother MARIA CHRISTINA. Her accession was challenged by her uncle Don Carlos; the Carlist Wars resulted (see CARLISTS). She married her cousin, Francisco de Asís (1846). Her rule was troubled by continuous party conflicts and frequent rebellions. Deposed in 1868, she went into exile in France. In 1870 she abdicated her rights in favor of her son Alfonso XII.

Isabey, Jean Baptiste (zhä bäptēst′ ēzäbā′), 1767–1855, French portrait painter and miniaturist. Portrayed, among others, Marie Antoinette and Napoleon III. His son, **Eugène Louis Gabriel Isabey,** 1804–86, was a marine and genre painter.

Isaiah (īzā′yù) [Heb.,= salvation of God] or **Isaias** (īsā′yùs), book of Old Testament. A collection of prophecies attributed to Isaiah (fl. 710 B.C.), one of major prophets. Message partly political, urging recognition of Assyrian power and opposing Egyptian alliance. Book falls into two major sections of prophecies (1–35 and 40–66) concerning the fate of Israel and Judah, with a prose section (36–39) that mainly parallels 2 Kings 18.13–20.19. Has Messianic allusions (8–12; 40–42; 53). Later biblical mention includes Mat. 1.23; 4.15; 13.14. Esaias: Mat. 3.13.

Isaiah, Ascension of: see PSEUDEPIGRAPHA.

Isaias: see ISAIAH.

Isauria (īsô′rēù), anc. district of Asia Minor, N of the Taurus range, in present S central Turkey. A wild region, it was inhabited by bands who lived by

depredations on land and sea traffic. They were only partially checked by the Romans and not subdued until the arrival of the Seljuk Turks.

Iscariot: see JUDAS ISCARIOT.

Ischia (ēs′kyä), rocky island (18 sq. mi.; pop. 30,418), S Italy, at entrance of Bay of Naples. Health resort, celebrated for warm mineral springs. Wine.

Ischl or **Bad Ischl** (bät′ ī′shùl), town (pop. 14,004), Upper Austria, in the SALZKAMMERGUT. Famous spa; after 1822 summer residence of imperial family.

Isère (ēzer′), department (3,180 sq. mi.; pop. 574,019), SE France, in Dauphiné; cap. Grenoble. Named for Isère R., tributary of the Rhone.

Iseult: see TRISTRAM AND ISOLDE.

Isfahan (īsfùhän′), anc. *Aspadana,* city (pop. 204,598), central Iran, midway between Teheran and Shiraz. Cap. of Persia 1051–63, 1072–92, 1590–1722. Here are Abbas I's palace and the superb imperial mosque (built 1585–1612). The Julfa quarter, originally Armenian, was founded 1605 by Shah Abbas. City endured massacres by Tamerlane (1387) and by Ghalzai Afghans (1723). Occupied by Russian troops 1916. Traditionally known for metalwork, it is now a textile center.

Ish-bosheth (īsh-bō′shēth, īsh′bōshēth), son of Saul. Contested throne with David for 7 years. 2 Sam. 2; 3; 4. Esh-baal: 1 Chron. 8.33; 9.39.

Isherwood, Christopher (ī′–), 1904–, English writer. Collaborated with Auden on plays (e.g., *The Dog beneath the Skin,* 1935; *The Ascent of the F6,* 1936). Among his novels are two on Berlin (1935, 1939; reissued as *The Berlin Stories,* 1946) and *Prater Violet* (1945). Other works on travels and interest in Eastern mysticism.

Ishii, Kikujiro, Viscount (kē″kōō″jērō′, īshē′), 1867?–1945, Japanese diplomat. In 1907–8 aided in negotiating GENTLEMEN'S AGREEMENT with U.S. Negotiated Lansing-Ishii agreement (1917) with U.S., reaffirming Open Door policy in China.

Ishmael [Heb.,= God hears], son of Abraham and Hagar, half brother of Isaac. Sent, with Hagar, into desert because of family quarrel. Settled in wilderness; became noted archer. Gen. 16.4–16; 17.18–26; 21.8–21; 25.9,12–17; 28.9; 1 Chron. 1.29–30. Honored as forefather of the Arabs by Moslems who esteem him as the Hebrews do Isaac; thus, use of name Ishmael for a social outcast is unknown in Islam though common in Judaism and Christianity.

Ishpeming (īsh′pùmǐng), city (pop. 8,962), W Upper Peninsula, N Mich., W of Marquette. Center of Marquette iron range. Mining, quarrying and dynamite mfg. Ski tournaments held since 1888.

Ishtar (īsh′tär), in Babylonian and Assyrian religion, goddess of fertility. She corresponds to Phoenician Astarte, Greek Aphrodite, and Roman Venus. As her cult grew, it absorbed others, and Ishtar became common name for goddess. She was a form of the ancient GREAT MOTHER OF THE GODS.

Isidore of Seville, Saint, c.560–636, Spanish encyclopedist, bishop of Seville, best known for his voluminous *Etymologiae* or *Origines,* a compendium of knowledge.

Isidorus of Miletus (īzǐdô′rùs, mīlē′tùs), name of two architects who helped rebuild Hagia Sophia, one in A.D. 532–37, the other in A.D. 553.

Isis (ī′sĭs), in Egyptian religion, nature goddess, whose worship, originating c.1700–1100 B.C., expanded throughout Egypt and Mediterranean world. She became prototype of all goddesses, and her cult was one of most antagonistic forces met by early Christians. In mythology of Egypt she was faithful wife and sister of OSIRIS and mother of Horus. After Osiris was slain by their brother, Set, and his body scattered in pieces, Isis gathered these together; Osiris was then restored and became ruler of dead. The legend symbolizes the sun (Osiris) overwhelmed by night (Set), followed by birth of the sun of a new day (Horus) from the eastern sky (Isis). Isis was universal mother and mistress of all magic. Centers of her worship were at Memphis, Abydos, and Philae, where her cult prevailed until A.D. 560.

Isis: see THAMES, river, England.

Iskander Beg, Albanian hero: see SCANDERBEG.

Iskenderun (ĭskĕn'dŭroŏn), formerly **Alexandretta** (ă"lĭgzăndrĕ'tŭ), city (pop. 22,946), SW Turkey, on inlet of the Mediterranean. Was port for Alep until 1937. See ALEXANDRETTA, SANJAK OF.

Isla, José Francisco de (hōsä' fränthē'skō dā ē'slä), 1703–81, "el Padre Isla," Spanish Jesuit preacher, author of the satirical novel *Historia del famoso predicador Fray Gerundio de Campazas* (1758).

Islam (ĭs'lŭm, ĭsläm') [Arabic,= submission to God], religion of which MOHAMMED was the prophet; adherents are called Moslems or Muslims (popularly also Mohammedans). The latest of the three great monotheisms, it drew upon the other two (Judaism and Christianity); Abraham and Jesus are in the list of prophets preceding Mohammed. It is generally held that Jesus will return as the MAHDI at the end of the world. Islam is based on the sacred book, the Koran, revealed by God (called Allah in Arabic) to Mohammed. The concepts of God and of heaven and hell are akin to those in Judaism and Christianity. Five duties are prescribed for every Moslem: (1) At least once in his life the believer must say with full acceptance, "There is no god but God and Mohammed is his prophet." (2) He must pray five times daily, facing toward Mecca, and he must say Friday noonday prayers in the mosque. (3) He must give alms generously—above the amount absolutely prescribed by law. (4) He must keep the fast of Ramadan. (5) He must, if he can, once in his life make the pilgrimage (Hajj) to Mecca. This last provision has made the pilgrimage the greatest in the world and a great unifying force in Islam. In addition to the Koran, Islam accepts the Sunna, collections of Traditions (moral sayings and anecdotes) of Mohammed. These were collected as early as the 9th cent. by BUKHARI and others. There are contradictions in the Sunna, but they are resolved by the doctrine of Ijma, which expresses the agreement of Islam; every Moslem holds that a belief held by the greater part of Islam is infallibly true; the principle has made the religion flexible. There was early a great split in Islam between SUNNITES and SHIITES, and this has persisted. The WAHABI defection was the only important later sectarian movement among Sunnites, but many groups developed among the Shiites (e.g., Assassins, Fatimites, Karmathians). The original split was over the CALIPHATE, which was the crowning institution of the theocratic structure of Islam. Though secularism has modified the unity somewhat, in theory the civil law in Mohammedan countries is not separate from religious law; religion governs all aspects of life. There have developed some four different systems of interpretation of the law in Sunnite Islam, all regarded as orthodox. Islamic philosophy is in effect part of theology; the greatest philosopher was Al-Gazel. Rationalism and mysticism (see SUFISM) both grew up in Islam, but were equally absorbed. The spread of the religion after its founding by Mohammed was phenomenally rapid in the 7th and 8th cent., and it soon was dominant from Spain (see MOORS) to India. It is today spread across Asia to the S Pacific, prevails in N Africa (with its intellectual center at Cairo), and is still gaining converts in the rest of Africa. There are also Mohammedan groups in Europe (Albania, Bosnia, and sections of Russia), but only scattered communities in the New World.

island, relatively small body of land surrounded entirely by water. As oceans form continuous water mass, continents are, strictly speaking, islands. Largest island is Greenland, followed by New Guinea, Borneo, Madagascar, Baffin Isl., Sumatra, Honshu, Great Britain. Islands are continental if created by submergence of coastal highlands with only summits left above water, or by sea's breaking through an isthmus or peninsula. Great Britain, Japanese archipelago, Sicily are continental; submarine banks show former coherence of each with mainland. Islands are oceanic if created by ascent of ocean floor, as through volcanic action, or by coral growth (atoll). In rare cases coastal island reunites with mainland.

Island No. 10, formerly a Tenn. island (not now extant) in Mississippi R. near New Madrid, Mo. Scene of Civil War campaign (March 3–April 7, 1862). A Union victory.

Islay (ī'lä, ī'lŭ), island (pop. 4,970) of the Inner Hebrides, off W Scotland, in Argyllshire. It is 25 mi. long and 19 mi. wide. A tower commemorates American soldiers and sailors drowned in torpedoing of the *Tuscania* in 1918. Industries include farming, dairying, distilling, and fishing.

Isle La Motte (īl" lŭ mŏt'), island, 6 mi. long and 2 mi. wide, NW Vt., in L. Champlain and W of St. Albans. Comprises Isle La Motte town (pop. 295), settled permanently c.1788 on site of French Fort Ste Anne (1665), first European settlement in Vt. Black marble quarries.

Isle of. For names beginning thus, see second element; e.g., for Isle of Ely, see ELY, ISLE OF.

Isle Royale National Park: see NATIONAL PARKS AND MONUMENTS (table).

Isles of Shoals, group of seven islands off SW Maine and SE N.H., SE of Portsmouth, N.H. Appledore (Maine) and Star (N.H.) islands have resort hotels; White Isl. (N.H.) has lighthouse.

Isles of the Blest: see FORTUNATE ISLES.

Isleta (ĭslĕ'tŭ), Indian pueblo village (1948 pop. 1,462), W central N.Mex., on Rio Grande and S of Albuquerque; discovered 1540. Seat of a Franciscan mission from c.1621 until Pueblo revolt of 1680. Captured by Spanish 1681. Mission revitalized as San Augustín de Isleta in early 1700s. Holds annual feast of St. Augustine. PUEBLO INDIANS here are mainly prosperous farmers. Language Tanoan.

Islington (ĭz'–), metropolitan borough (pop. 235,645), N London, England; industrial district. Site of Pentonville Prison and Holloway Gaol for Women.

Islip (ī'slĭp), residential and resort town (pop. 71,465), including Islip village (pop. 5,254), SE N.Y., on S shore (Great South Bay) of Long Isl.

Ismail (ĭsmäēl'), 1499–1524, shah of Persia (1502–24), founder of Safavid dynasty. Made Shiism the official religion of Persia.

Ismail, Ukraine: see IZMAIL.

Ismailia (ēs"mäīlē'ä), city (pop. 68,338), Egypt, at midpoint of Suez Canal. Founded 1863 by Lesseps as operational base for construction of canal.

Ismail Pasha (ĭsmäēl' pä'shä), 1830–95, ruler of Egypt (1863–79), son of Ibrahim Pasha; first to bear the title khedive (viceroy). His schemes, such as building of Suez Canal, put Egypt seriously in debt, forcing him to sell his stock (c.44%) in Suez Canal to Great Britain, and to submit in 1876 to joint Anglo-French management of Egyptian government. Deposed 1879 in favor of his son Tewfik Pasha.

isobars (ī'sŭbärz") or **isobaric lines** (ī"sŭbă'rĭk), weathermap lines connecting points of equal barometric pressure to define cyclones, anticyclones.

Isocrates (īsŏ'krŭtēz), 436–338 B.C., Greek orator, a pupil of Socrates and perhaps the greatest teacher in Greek history. *Panegyricus* was considered his most celebrated oration.

Isolde: see TRISTRAM AND ISOLDE.

isomerism (īsŏ'mŭrĭzŭm), in chemistry, condition in which two or more compounds have same molecular formula but different atomic arrangement. Structural isomers have different structural formulas and properties. Sterioisomerism depends on arrangement of atoms in space. Optical isomerism depends on difference in effect of compounds on polarized light; optical isomers have same structural formulas and same general properties.

isomorphism (ī″sōmôr′fĭzùm), similarity of crystal form and chemical composition between two substances.

Isonzo (ēzōn′tsō), river, 86 mi. long, Yugoslavia and Italy. Fiercely contested in World War I.

isotope (ī′sùtōp), in chemistry, one of two or more elements identical in chemical activity but differing in ATOMIC WEIGHT. Weight difference probably caused by difference in number of neutrons in nucleus; identical properties result from atoms having same number and arrangement of electrons outside nucleus. Radioactive isotopes are used as tracers in research.

Israel (ĭz′rēul) [as understood by Hebrews,= prevailing with God], in Bible, name given to Jacob as ancestor of the Hebrews, God's chosen people. The 12 tribes of Israel—Reuben, Simeon, Judah, Zebulun, Issachar, Dan, Gad, Asher, Naphtali, Benjamin, Ephraim, Manasseh—were named for 10 sons and 2 grandsons (sons of Joseph) of Jacob. For 13th tribe, see LEVI. When Hebrew kingdom was divided under REHOBOAM, N part called Israel, S part Judah.

Israel (ĭz′rēul), republic (8,050 sq. mi.; pop. c.1,414,- 500), W Asia, on the Mediterranean; cap. JERUSALEM. Boundaries are not permanently fixed; at present Lebanon is N, Syria and Jordan E, and Egypt SW. Grains are grown mainly in Galilee in N, citrus fruits in coastal area. Irrigation and dry-farming methods used in the NEGEV. Agr. cooperatives are widespread. Industrialization is being advanced, mainly at HAIFA and TEL-AVIV. Haifa and Jaffa are chief ports. For early history see PALESTINE. The nearly all-Jewish state of Israel grew out of ZIONISM. After World War II many backed an independent state for Palestinian Jews (1945 pop. c.500,000) which would also be a homeland for surviving European Jews and Jews in Arab countries. Palestinian Arabs (1945 pop. c.1,000,000) and Arab states opposed a Jewish state and demanded independence for all Palestine, with Jews a protected minority. British decision to admit only 2,000 displaced European Jews a month, until 100,000 had been admitted, led to attacks on British military installations by Jewish terrorist groups. In 1947 the UN divided Palestine into a Jewish state, an Arab state, and a small international zone, including Jerusalem. Despite Arab opposition the state of Israel was proclaimed at Tel-Aviv on May 14, 1948. Ensuing war between ARAB LEAGUE countries and Israel was ended Jan., 1949, by UN mediation supervised first by Count Folke BERNADOTTE and later by Ralph Bunche. The war had increased Israel's holdings about one half. In Jan., 1949, Chaim Weizmann was elected president; Ben Gurion became prime minister as leader of dominant party in *Knesset* (parliament). Itzhak Ben-Zvi succeeded Weizmann in 1952.

Israëls, Jozef (yō′zùf ēs′räĕls), 1824–1911, outstanding Dutch genre painter of 19th cent. Realistically depicted pathetic scenes from life of peasants and fishermen.

Issachar (ĭ′sùkùr), son of Jacob, ancestor of one of 12 tribes of Israel. Tribe allotted land W of Jordan R. Gen. 30.18; 49.14; 46.13; Num. 1.29; 2.5; Deut. 27.12; 33.18; Joshua 19.17; 1 Chron. 7.1–5.

Issus (ĭ′sùs), anc. town, SE Asia Minor. Here in 333 B.C. Alexander the Great defeated DARIUS III.

Istanbul (ī″stänbōōl′, Turkish ĭstäm′bōol), city (pop. 1,000,022), Turkey, on both sides of the BOSPORUS; name was officially changed from Constantinople 1930. (For history, see CONSTANTINOPLE.) The cap. of Turkey until 1922 and still its chief commercial center and seaport, Istanbul also is the seat of a university (founded 1453; reorganized 1933) and is the see of three patriarchs (Greek Orthodox, Latin-rite Roman Catholic, Armenian). Only the European side of Istanbul corresponds to historic Constantinople. Rising on both sides of the Golden Horn, an inlet of the Bosporus, it is built on seven hills. Several miles of medieval city walls and forts still stand. The commercial quarter of Galata and the quarters of Pera (formerly reserved for foreigners) and Haskoy (Jew-

ish quarter) are outside the walls. A famous bridge crosses the Golden Horn into Stambul, the core of the city, abutting on the Bosporus and the Sea of Marmara. In the NW are the former Greek quarter of Phanar and the Byzantine imperial palace of Blachernae. The Asiatic part of Istanbul includes Kadikoy (anc. Chalcedon) and Uskudar (also known as Scutari). The chief monument from Byzantine times is the HAGIA SOPHIA. Masterpieces of Turkish architecture include the 16th-cent. mosques of Bajazet II, Suleiman I, and Ahmed I; the Seraglio (former palace of sultans); and the Dolma Bagtche and Yildiz Kiosk (sultans' residences in 19th and 20th cent.). Istanbul is also famed for its polyglot population and its beautiful environs.

Isthmian games (ĭs′mēun), athletic events organized c.581 B.C. Held at Corinth in spring of first and third years of Olympiad. Contests generally like OLYMPIC GAMES, but conducted on smaller scale.

Istria (ĭs′trēu), Serbo-Croatian *Istra*, mountainous peninsula, c.2,000 sq. mi., projecting into N Adriatic and bounded in N by Karst plateau; chief city Pola. Population is Yugoslav and Italian. Nominal Byzantine rule ceased in 8th cent. A.D., and area was partitioned by Venice, Carinthia, the patriarchs of Aquileia, and the counts of Gorizia. By the 15th cent. Venice held the SW, Austria the NE, and in 1797 all passed to Austria. Awarded to Italy in 1919, Istria was again partitioned in 1947, the major part going to Yugoslavia, the remainder to the Free Territory of Trieste.

Italian East Africa, former Italian colony, comprising ERITREA, Italian SOMALILAND, and ETHIOPIA.

Italian language, one of the Romance or Romanic group of the Italic subfamily of Indo-European languages. See LANGUAGE (table).

Italian Somaliland: see SOMALILAND, ITALIAN.

Italian Wars, 1494–1529. Rivalry among the states of Renaissance ITALY invited imperialist intervention of the rising national states, especially France and Spain. Alignments of Italian and foreign powers shifted constantly. In the first phase (1494–95) CHARLES VIII of France conquered Naples but was forced to abandon it by a coalition of Spain, the emperor, the pope, Venice, and Milan. In the second phase (1499–1504) LOUIS XII of France occupied Milan, Genoa, and (jointly with Spain) Naples. French-Spanish disagreement flared into warfare (1502); Louis lost at Cerignola and at the Garigliano; the Treaties of Blois (1504–5) gave Milan and Genoa to France but pledged Naples to Spain. The third phase (1508–16) consisted of three subphases: the victorious campaign of the League of CAMBRAI against Venice (1509); the formation of the HOLY LEAGUE and the expulsion of the French from Lombardy by the Swiss (1510–13); the victory of Francis I at Marignano (1515), followed by the Peace of Noyon, which restored Milan to France. The wars between FRANCIS I and Emperor Charles V opened 1521. Defeated and captured at Pavia (1525), Francis bought his freedom by the Treaty of Madrid (1526), in which he renounced all claims in Italy. He promptly repudiated the treaty and formed the League of Cognac with Pope Clement VII, Henry VIII of England, Venice, and Florence, thus beginning a fifth war. Charles's troops sacked Rome (1527), while the French seized Genoa and with the help of Andrea DORIA laid siege to Naples. Doria's defection (1528) forced Francis to accept the Treaty of CAMBRAI (1529). After three more wars, fought largely outside Italy, Spain retained supremacy in Italy by the Treaty of CATEAU-CAMBRÉSIS.

Italic languages, subfamily of Indo-European languages. Latin superseded the other two important groups (Oscan and Umbrian) and was the only one to survive antiquity; from it the Romanic languages are derived. See LANGUAGE (table).

Italy, Latin and Ital. *Italia,* republic (116,235 sq. mi.; pop. 47,021,000), S Europe; cap. Rome. N Italy is separated by the ALPS from France, Switzerland, Austria, Yugoslavia. Central and S Italy, traversed by the APENNINES, form a boot-shaped peninsula between the Tyrrhenian and Adriatic seas and contain VATICAN CITY and SAN MARINO. Of the 19 regions making up Italy, five enjoy autonomous rights—the islands of SICILY and SARDINIA and the border regions of Val d'AOSTA, TRENTINO-ALTO ADIGE, and FRIULI-VENEZIA GIULIA. The other regions are: LIGURIA, PIEDMONT, LOMBARDY, VENETIA, EMILIA-ROMAGNA, MARCHES, TUSCANY, UMBRIA, LATIUM, CAMPANIA, BASILICATA, ABRUZZI E MOLISE, CALABRIA, APULIA. N Italy, with the fertile Po plain and the commercial and industrial centers of MILAN, GENOA, and TURIN, is the richest part of the country. Central Italy contains such historic and cultural centers as FLORENCE, PISA, BOLOGNA, RAVENNA, ROME. S Italy, with NAPLES as chief city, is scarred by poverty. The varied beauty of the Italian landscape conceals the harshness of its rocky, eroded soil, intensely and patiently worked by a frugal population. Fruit, wine, olive oil, cheese are among the exports; food staples and basic raw materials are largely imported. Industries (silk, textiles, automobiles, machinery, chemicals, luxury goods) depend largely on export markets and imported raw materials; hydroelectric power, sulphur, mercury, and marble are the only important natural resources. Roman Catholicism is the official religion of this overwhelmingly Catholic country, but freedom of worship is guaranteed.

Ancient and Medieval Italy. About the 8th cent. B.C. the Etruscans settled in N Italy, the Greeks along the S coasts (see ETRUSCAN CIVILIZATION; MAGNA GRAECIA). A Celtic invasion (5th cent. B.C.) drove the Etruscans S, until they were stopped by the SAMNITES. Italian history from the 5th cent. B.C. to the 5th cent. A.D. is largely that of rising ROME and of the Roman Empire. The barbarian invasions (5th cent.; see VISIGOTHS, HUNS, ODOACER, OSTROGOTHS) destroyed the Western Empire and Italian unity. THEODORIC THE GREAT preserved Roman institutions, but after his death the papacy alone remained a stable element. JUSTINIAN I reconquered Italy (535–54), but his successors were defeated by the LOMBARDS. Byzantine rule persisted for some time in Ravenna, the PENTAPOLIS, and along the S coast. In Rome, Pope GREGORY I resisted Lombard conquest and laid the foundation for the PAPAL STATES. The persisting Lombard threat to Rome brought the intervention of PEPIN THE SHORT (751) and CHARLEMAGNE (800), who enlarged the papal domain and estab. Frankish hegemony over Italy. After the divisions of the Carolingian empire (9th cent.), Italy gradually slipped from imperial control and fell into anarchy. The coronation of OTTO I as king of Italy (961) and Roman emperor (962) created the HOLY ROMAN EMPIRE, but despite their frequent incursions the German emperors could never establish control over Italy. S Italy, conquered by the Normans (11th cent.), passed, after a period of HOHENSTAUFEN rule, to the Angevins of Naples and the Aragonese kings of Sicily. The cities in the N (where the LOMBARD LEAGUE had defied imperial authority) and in central Italy became separate and warring states, some under princes (the VISCONTI, the SFORZA, the GONZAGA, the ESTE, the MALATESTA), some as republics. VENICE and GENOA built huge commercial empires, while merchants of FLORENCE, SIENA, and LUCCA gained power and wealth. Despite constant struggles between and within cities (see GUELPHS AND GHIBELLINES), the city-states had great prosperity, dominated European finances through their great bankers (e.g., the MEDICI), and produced the miraculous cultural flowering known as the RENAISSANCE.

Disintegration and Rebirth. With the ITALIAN WARS, beginning 1494, Italy became the battleground of French and Hapsburg imperialism. The Treaty of CATEAU-CAMBRÉSIS (1559) gave Sicily, Naples, and Milan to Spain. The Wars of the 17th and 18th cent. completed Italian subjection to foreign rule. By 1748

Naples, Sicily, Parma, and Piacenza were ruled by branches of the Spanish Bourbons; Milan, Mantua, Tuscany, and Modena were under Austrian rule. Venice, Genoa, Lucca, still independent, were declining. The Papal States and the kingdom of SARDINIA, under the rising house of SAVOY, made up the rest. All this was swept away by the FRENCH REVOLUTIONARY WARS and the rise of NAPOLEON I, who remade the Italian map several times. The Congress of Vienna (1814–15) more or less restored the pre-Napoleonic status quo. Austria, receiving Lombardy and Venetia, held a paramount position, but could not for long suppress the nationalist movement for unification (see RISORGIMENTO). The Italy of which VICTOR EMMANUEL II became king in 1861 still lacked Venetia (acquired in AUSTRO-PRUSSIAN WAR of 1866) and Rome. Florence was the cap. In 1870 Italian troops annexed Rome; the resulting conflict with the papacy was resolved only in 1929 (see LATERAN TREATY).

Modern Italy. From 1861 to 1922 Italy was ruled under the relatively liberal Sardinian constitution of 1848 by Victor Emmanuel II, Humbert I, and Victor Emmanuel III. Italy acquired colonies (Somaliland, Eritrea, Libya), expanded industrially, and found an outlet for overpopulation in mass emigration to the Americas. Though a member of Triple Alliance with Germany and Austria, it entered World War I on Allied side (1915). At the Paris Peace Conference of 1919 it obtained S Tyrol, Trieste, Istria, part of Carniola, several Dalmatian isls., and the Dodecanese, but not all the territory it had been secretly promised. Italian seizure of FIUME (1921) was symptomatic of nationalist discontent. Political and social unrest furthered the growth of FASCISM, and in 1922 MUSSOLINI seized the power. He gradually created a totalitarian corporative state and sought to solve the problem of overpopulation through "dynamic expansion." His conquest of ETHIOPIA (1935–36), his intervention in Spain (1936–39), and his seizure of ALBANIA (1939) were followed by formal alliance with Germany (1939; see AXIS). In 1940 Italy entered World War II; by 1943 it had lost Africa and Sicily to the Allies. The king dismissed Mussolini, appointed BADOGLIO as premier, and surrendered Italy to the Allies, who eventually recognized Italy as "cobelligerent" against Germany. The Italian campaign was slow, arduous, and destructive. Rome fell in 1944; in May, 1945, the German troops surrendered. The Italian peace treaty of 1947 deprived Italy of most of VENEZIA GIULIA (including TRIESTE), of its colonies, and some lesser territories. Its economic sufferings were only partially relieved by UNRRA aid and, later, by the European Recovery Program. King Humbert II was deposed by a popular referendum (1946) which made Italy a republic. Premier De Gasperi, a Christian Democrat, headed a series of anti-Communist coalition cabinets after 1945. Though barred by Russian opposition from the UN, Italy became an important partner in the North Atlantic Treaty (1949).

Itasca, Lake (ītă′skŭ), small shallow lake in NW central Minn., SSW of Bemidji. Identified by H. R. Schoolcraft as source of the Mississippi, but later geographers consider source to be above lake.

itch: see SCABIES.

Ithaca (ĭ′thĭkŭ, ĭ′thŭkŭ), Gr. *Ithake,* mountainous island (37 sq. mi.; pop. 7,083), W Greece, one of the IONIAN ISLANDS; chief town Ithaca (pop. 3,120). Famed as home of ODYSSEUS.

Ithaca, city (pop. 29,257), W central N.Y., at S end of Cayuga L. and SW of Syracuse in FINGER LAKES region; settled c.1790. Seat of CORNELL UNIVERSITY and Ithaca Col. Mfg. of guns, machines, salt, fertilizers, and cement.

Ito, Hirobumi, Prince (hērō′bōōmē, ē′tō), 1841–1909, Japanese statesman, the outstanding figure in modernization of Japan. Sent abroad 1882 to study foreign governments. Drafted constitution of 1889, largely on Prussian model. Was twice premier 1892–96, 1899–

1901; first president of Seiyukai party. Responsible for agreement (1905) which made Korea a virtual protectorate.

Itsuku-shima (ĕtsŏŏkŏō'shĭmä), sacred islet in Inland Sea, Japan. Has a 9th-cent. Buddhist temple and ancient Shinto shrine with huge torii. Known also as Miya-jima.

Iturbide, Agustín de (ägŏŏstēn' dā ētŏōrbē'dā), 1783–1824, Mexican revolutionist, emperor of Mexico (1822–23). Commander of royalist troops, he united with the insurgents and proclaimed the Plan of IGUALA. Instead of liberal state that separatists had planned, Iturbide had himself made emperor (1822). Forced to abdicate (1823), he fled to Europe. Returning to Mexico (1824), he was tried and shot.

Ituzaingó, battle of (ē''tōōsĭn-gō'), fought in S Uruguay, Feb. 20, 1827. Argentine-Uruguayan forces defeated Brazil. Argentina and Brazil both claimed Uruguay but in peace treaty (1828), an independent Uruguay emerged as buffer state.

Itzá (ētsä'), Maya Indians of Yucatán and Petén (Guatemala), probable founders of Chichén Itzá (c.514). Moved c.1450 to L. Petén, remained there until driven from their capital, Tayasal (1697).

Iuka (īū'kù), town (pop. 1,527), NE Miss., near Tennessee R. Has ante-bellum houses and mineral springs. In Civil War battle (Sept. 19, 1862), Federal troops defeated Confederates here.

Ivan II (Ivan Asen), d. 1241, tsar of Bulgaria (1218–41). Bulgaria reached its zenith under his rule. He made it the strongest Balkan power but was essentially a man of peace.

Ivan (ī'vän, ī'vùn, Rus. ēvän'), rulers of Russia. **Ivan III** (the Great), 1440–1505, grand duke of Moscow (1462–1505), expanded Muscovite state, freed Muscovy from allegiance to Golden Horde (1480). Married niece of last Byzantine emperor, claimed successorship of Moscow to East Roman Empire. His grandson, **Ivan IV** (the Terrible), 1530–84, acceded as grand duke of Moscow 1533, had himself crowned tsar 1547. Conquered Kazan (1552) and Astrakhan (1557) from Tatars, thus beginning Russia's eastward expansion, which was carried into Siberia by the Cossack YERMAK. Warfare with Poland and Sweden over Baltic Coast ended to his disadvantage (1558–82). He began and encouraged trade relations with England. At home, Ivan crushed power of boyars (high nobles), favored common people, strengthened tsarist autocracy, and estab. special corps (*Oprichnina*) to fight rebellion. The death of his first wife (1560; six others followed her) apparently affected his mental balance. He was given to alternate fits of cruel rage (in one of which he killed his eldest son) and of prayerful repentance. Two sons survived him—FEODOR I and DMITRI—but his favorite, Boris GODUNOV, inherited the actual power. **Ivan V**, 1666–96, tsar (1682–96), succeeded his brother Feodor III jointly with PETER I under regency of SOPHIA ALEKSEYEVNA. Feeble-minded, he was excluded from affairs of state. He was the father of Empress Anna, who was succeeded in 1740 by her infant grand-nephew, **Ivan VI**, 1740–64, a German by birth. In 1741 he was deposed by Empress Elizabeth, and in 1764 he was murdered in Schlüsselburg fortress on orders of Catherine II.

Ivanovo (ēvä'nùvŭ), city (pop. 285,069), RSFSR, 155 mi. NE of Moscow. Major textile center. Chartered 1328. First textile mill 1751. Called Ivanovo-Voznesensk until c.1930.

Ives, Charles, 1874–, American composer. In the insurance business for 32 years, he was at the same time composing music in a modern idiom. Most of his works were unknown until 1939. Among his works are symphonies, suites (including *Three Places in New England*), sonatas, chamber music, and songs. His Third Symphony won the Pulitzer Prize in 1947.

Ivigtut (ē'vĭgtŏŏt), town (pop. 141), SW Greenland,

port SE of Frederikshaab. Here is world's largest cryolite mine. Site of a U.S. base in World War II.

Iviza, Span. *Ibiza* (ēvē'thä), island (221 sq. mi.; pop. 33,961), one of the Balearic Isls., Spain; chief town Iviza (pop. 9,644).

ivory, type of dentine present only in the tusks (prolongations of the upper pair of second incisors) of the elephant. Africa, the principal source of supply, furnishes the best and largest tusks. The chief commercial uses are for piano keys, billiard balls, handles, and decorative objects. In art, ivory is an excellent material for miniature painting and has been used through the ages for inlay work and intricate carvings. The civilizations of Egypt, Mesopotamia, Assyria, Babylon, Greece, Rome, India, China, and Japan are represented by works in ivory. Imitations and substitutes for ivory include celluloid and vegetable ivory (tagua).

Ivory Coast, French overseas territory (c.127,800 sq. mi.; pop. c.2,031,000), French West Africa, on Atlantic coast, between Liberia and Gold Coast; chief port and cap. Abidjan. Has coastal lowland, forested plateau, and high savannas. Exports include cotton, cacao, palm oil, and hardwoods. Portuguese traders settled here in 16th cent. Became French protectorate 1891, incorporated 1904 into French West Africa. Represented in French parliament.

ivory nut: see TAGUA.

Ivrea (ēvrā'ä), town (pop. 8,737), Piedmont, NW Italy, on Dora Baltea R. Medieval marquisate of Ivrea passed to Savoy in 14th cent.

Ivry-la-Bataille (ēvrē'-lä-bätä'yù), village near Évreux, N France, where Henry IV of France won a major victory over the League (1590).

ivy, name referring usually to English ivy but also to other climbing plants, e.g., poison ivy, Boston ivy, ground ivy. Kenilworth ivy (*Cymbalaria muralis*) is a house or garden plant often seen on old ruins in Europe; grape ivy (*Cissus rhombifolia*) is a house plant. See *ill.*, p. 783.

Iwasa Matabei (ēwä'sä mätäbä'), c.1578–1650, Japanese landscape and genre artist, a founder of ukiyoye school of painting, characterized by popular color prints of topical interest.

Iwo Jima (ē'wō jē'mù), volcanic island (c.8 sq. mi.; pop. 1,051), most important and largest of Volcano Isls., W Pacific. In S is Mt. Suribachi (extinct volcano). Sulphur mining. In World War II the site of Japanese air base, taken in early 1945 by U.S. forces.

I.W.W.: see INDUSTRIAL WORKERS OF THE WORLD.

Ixion (ĭk'sèùn), in Greek mythology. He was chained to revolving, fiery wheel in Hades as punishment for fathering centaur monsters by Hera.

Ixtacihuatl (ēs''täsē'wätùl) [Aztec,= white woman], dormant volcano, 17,342 ft. high, central Mexico, near POPOCATEPETL. Known also as Sleeping Woman.

Iyeyasu: see IEYASU.

Izhevsk (ē'zhĭfsk), city (pop. 175,740), cap. of Udmurt ASSR, E European RSFSR. Metal industry includes machinery and arms mfg.

Izmail (ēzmŭēl'), Rumanian *Ismail*, city (pop. 17,569), SW Ukraine, on the Danube delta and on Rumanian border. Commercial center; naval base. A Turkish fortress from 16th cent., it was captured by the Russians in 1770 and 1790. Ceded to Russia 1812, it shared later history of BESSARABIA.

Izmir, Turkey: see SMYRNA.

Izu-shichito (ē'zŏōshĭchĭtō), volcanic island group, extending c.300 mi. S of Tokyo Bay, Japan. O-shima is largest island.

Izvolsky, Aleksandr Petrovich (ŭlyĭksän'dùr pĕtrô'vĭch ēzvôl'skē), 1856–1919, Russian foreign minister (1906–10). Ended Russo-English rivalry in Middle East by establishing zones of influence (1907). After Austria annexed Bosnia and Hercegovina (1908), he prepared for war by strengthening Triple Entente.

Jabbok, river of Jordan, the modern Wadi Zerka, which enters Jordan R. N of Jericho. On its S bank Jacob wrestled with angel. Gen. 32.22.

Jabesh-gilead (jă′bĕsh-gĭl′lēăd), city of Gilead. Saul saved its people from atrocities at the hands of the Ammonites. At his death the grateful city buried him.

Jablonec nad Nisou (yä′blŏnĕts näd nē′sō), Ger. *Gablonz,* city (pop. 23,112), NE Bohemia, Czechoslovakia. Mfg. center for Bohemian glass.

jaborandi (jăb″ŭrăn′dē), tropical American shrub (*Pilocarpus),* yielding poisonous drug jaborandi which contains pilocarpine used in medicine.

Jachymov, Czech *Jáchymov* (yä′khĭmôf), Ger. *Joachimsthal,* town (pop. 6,806), NW Bohemia, Czechoslovakia. A major mining center for radium, uranium, and lead, it also has radioactive springs. Its former rich silver mines are now little exploited. From the Joachimsthaler, a coin struck here in the 16th cent., came the words *Thaler* and *dollar.*

jackal (jă′kôl), nocturnal wild mammal (genus *Canis*) of dog family, found in SE Europe, Asia, Africa. It eats carrion, plant food, and animals. It resembles the wolf but is smaller.

jack-in-the-pulpit or **Indian turnip,** American woodland perennial (*Arisaema triphyllum*). Small flowers are borne on club-shaped spadix enveloped by purplish-striped hooded spathe and are followed by cluster of red berries. Cooked roots were eaten by Indians.

jackscrew: see SCREW.

Jackson, Andrew, 1767–1845, 7th President of the United States (1829–37). Decisive victory as U.S. commander in battle of New Orleans made him the military hero of War of 1812. His popularity almost elected him President in 1824. Idol of the democratic West, an expansionist, man of action, he led what later came to be called Jacksonian democracy—government for the good of the small man, of the frontier farmer and the backwoodsman, the laborer and the mechanic of Eastern cities. His sweeping victory of 1828 led to conflict between reformers and settled proponents of order. KITCHEN CABINET was powerful; party was paramount and SPOILS SYSTEM was born. Social slights offered Margaret O'NEILL helped break up the cabinet; John C. CALHOUN provoked further estrangement through his NULLIFICATION doctrine and his resignation from the vice presidency. Jackson's fight against the BANK OF THE UNITED STATES was an important factor in election of 1832, in which he defeated Henry CLAY. Second administration was dominated by bank issue. Jackson sponsored Specie Circular in 1836, stipulating that all public lands must be paid for in specie; it helped hasten Panic of 1837. After presidency he retired to his estate, the Hermitage, in Tenn.

Jackson, Claiborne Fox, 1806–62, governor of Mo. (1860–61). Opponent of Union cause, called by him "unholy crusade." After conflict with Union troops Jackson was deposed.

Jackson, Helen (Fiske) Hunt, 1830–85, American writer, pseud. H. H. Notable for historical account of the Indian problem, *A Century of Dishonor* (1881), and novel on the theme, *Ramona* (1884).

Jackson, Robert H(oughwout) (hou′ŭt), 1892–, Associate Justice of U.S. Supreme Court (1941–). On leave (1945–46) as U.S. chief counsel at Nuremberg war-crimes trial.

Jackson, Thomas Jonathan known as **Stonewall Jackson,** 1824–63, Confederate general. At first battle of Bull Run, he and his brigade won sobriquet by standing "like a stone wall." He won renown by his Shenandoah Valley campaign (1862). Supported Lee in Seven Days battles, and was largely responsible for victory in second battle of Bull Run. Ably led Confederate right at Fredericksburg (Dec., 1862). Mortally wounded at battle of CHANCELLORSVILLE. Next to Lee he was Confederacy's greatest general.

Jackson. 1 Town (pop. 6,772), SE La., N of Baton Rouge. **2** City (pop. 51,088), S Mich., on Grand R. and W of Detroit; settled 1829. Industrial and commercial center of agr. area, it has mfg. of auto and aircraft parts. Founding of Republican party here (July 6, 1854) marked by tablet. **3** City (pop. 98,271), state cap., W central Miss., on Pearl R. State's largest city and railroad and shipping center. Processes cotton, lumber, textiles, and natural gas. Laid out as state cap. 1821; named for Andrew Jackson. Center of military activity in VICKSBURG CAMPAIGN; largely destroyed by Sherman 1863. Points of interest include old capitol (1839) and Confederate monument. **4** Resort town (pop. 344), E N.H., NNW of Conway; winter sports center. **5** City (pop. 6,504), S Ohio, SE of Chillicothe. Has steel mills, foundries, and coal mines. **6** City (pop. 30,207), W Tenn., NE of Memphis; settled 1819. Rail and trade center of agr. area, it has mfg. of wood, steel, and meat products. Seat of Lane Col. (Negro; Methodist Episcopal; coed.; 1882). Has Indian mounds and "Casey" Jones monument. **7** Resort town (pop. 1,244; alt. c.6,200 ft.), NW Wyo. Gateway to Grand Teton and Yellowstone national parks. Trade center for hunting, dude-ranch, and livestock area in **Jackson Hole,** fertile valley, 48 mi. long and 6–8 mi. wide, partly in Grand Teton Natl. Park. Abundant game (esp. elk). Snake R. waters valley and flows through Jackson L. (18 mi. long, 4 mi. wide).

Jackson, Port, or **Sydney Harbour,** inlet of the Pacific, E New South Wales, Australia, forming Australia's finest harbor. Sydney on S shore connected with N suburbs by Sydney Harbour Bridge (1932) with arch span of 1,650 ft. Shipyards on Cockatoo Isl. Port was Allied naval base in World War II.

Jacksonville. 1 City (pop. 204,517), NE Fla., second largest city in state and deepwater port on St. Johns R. near its mouth on the Atlantic. One of chief coastal commercial centers of the South, it is a rail, air, and highway focus. City has many wood- and metal-processing industries; also food processing, boatbuilding, and fishing. Lewis Hogan settled here in 1816. City laid out 1822 and named for Andrew Jackson. Growth interrupted by Seminole and Civil wars. Commerce developed in late 1800s with building of good harbor and railroads. Points of interest are municipal docks and yards, war-memorial fountain, and Confederate monument. Has naval air training station (1940). **2** City (pop. 20,387), W central Ill., W of Springfield; laid out 1825. Rail and trade center in grain area with mfg. of apparel and metal products. S. A. Douglas and W. J. Bryan lived here. Was Underground Railroad station. Seat of Illinois Col. (coed.; 1830) and MacMurray Col. for Women (Methodist; 1847). **3** City (pop. 8,607), E Texas, NE of Palestine. Shipping, packing, and processing truck (esp. tomatoes).

Jacksonville Beach, resort city (pop. 6,430), NE Fla., on Atlantic coast ESE of Jacksonville.

Jacob [Heb.,= supplanter]. **1** Son of Isaac, brother of Esau. As ISRAEL, ancestor of the Hebrews. By bargaining and trickery he gained the inheritance and

SMALL CAPITALS = cross references. Pronunciation key on inside end pages. Abbreviations: p. 2.

481

blessing that Isaac intended for Esau. Jacob's life was filled with cruel disappointments (his discovery that after his years of labor to obtain Rachel, Leah was his first bride; the conduct of his wayward older sons), with spiritual revelations (his vision of the ladder to heaven; his wrestling with the angel), and with great joy (his reunion with Joseph in Egypt). Gen. 25–50; Hosea 12.2–4, 12; Mal. 1.2; Acts 7.12–16; Heb. 11. 20, 21. **2** Father of St. Joseph. Mat. 1.15, 16.

Jacob, Max (mäks′ zhäkôb′), 1876–1944, French writer and painter. His poems, plays, novels, and short stories, and paintings in their extreme symbolism to some extent anticipated surrealism. He was a Catholic convert and a mystic. Died in a concentration camp.

Jacobi, Abraham (jùkō′bē), 1830–1919, American physician, a pioneer in pediatrics. His wife **Mary Putnam Jacobi**, 1842–1906, also a physician, taught at medical schools in New York city and was the first woman member of several medical societies.

Jacobi, Friedrich Heinrich (yäkō′bē), 1743–1819, German philosopher. Argued that philosophy cannot maintain distinct realms of experience and that unity is based on faith, knowledge on intuition and reason.

Jacobi, Karl Gustav Jakob (kärl gōōs′täf yä′kôp yäkō′bē), 1804–51, German mathematician, noted for his work on elliptical functions, differential determinants, and theory of numbers.

Jacobi, Mary Putnam: see JACOBI, ABRAHAM.

Jacobins (jăk′ùbĭnz), political club of French Revolution; so called for original meeting place, a monastery of the Jacobins (Parisian name of Dominicans). Founded 1789, it first was led by such moderates as Mirabeau, Sieyès, Lafayette. Jacobins and FEUILLANTS dominated Legislative Assembly (1791–92). Split of Jacobins and GIRONDISTS occurred when Girondist majority advocated war as a means to discredit monarchy; Jacobins (mainly Parisian deputies) opposed war, advocated direct reform, became increasingly radical and republican. In the Convention the Jacobins and CORDELIERS were called the MOUNTAIN. Among their new leaders were DANTON, ROBESPIERRE. After the fall of the Girondists (June, 1793), Jacobins began REIGN OF TERROR, liquidated the extremist Cordeliers and the moderate Danton (1794), and governed dictatorially till Robespierre's fall on 9 THERMIDOR.

Jacobite Church (jă′kŭbĭt), Christian church of Syria, Iraq, and India, founded (6th cent.) as part of the Monophysite heresy by Jacob Baradaeus, aided by Empress Theodora. Church is out of communion with both Roman Catholics and Orthodox. Its head is the patriarch of Antioch (at Homs), its rite is the Antiochene, its liturgical language Syriac. One group (the "Syrian Catholics") since 17th cent. has resumed relations with the pope, but keeps its practices and rite (head is another patriarch of Antioch, at Beirut). On the other hand in the 17th cent. most Malabar Christians left communion with the pope and became "Malabar Jacobites" with Antiochene rite; later a group became "Reformed Jacobites," and in 20th cent. another portion returned to communion with Rome (the "Malankarese Catholics"). The Malabar Christians who did not become Jacobites at all are "Syro-Malabar Catholics" (Chaldean rite).

Jacobites (jă′kŭbĭts), adherents of exiled branch of the house of STUART after Revolution of 1688. Sought restoration of JAMES II; later advanced claims of his descendants until 1807 when direct Stuart line ended. Included many Catholics, high churchmen, extreme Tories, and the NONJURORS. Two major risings in 18th cent. are known as "the '15" and "the '45." After the death of Queen Anne (1714) Henry St. John and the 6th earl of MAR attempted intrigue and revolt to crown James Edward Stuart; he was defeated at Preston (1715). The abortive invasion of Charles Edward Stuart (Bonnie Prince Charlie), which was crushed at Culloden Moor in 1745, was the last serious action of Jacobitism as an important political force.

Jacobs, Helen (Hull), 1908–, American tennis player. Won U.S. women's singles title 1932–35, British women's singles crown 1936.

Jacobs, W(illiam) W(ymark), 1863–1943, English author, known for humorous short stories of London docks (as in *Many Cargoes,* 1896; *Snug Harbour,* 1931) and for horror tale, "The Monkey's Paw."

Jacobsen, Jens Peter, 1847–85, Danish novelist, creator of a prose style. His *Marie Grubbe* (1876) is a historical novel. Also wrote poetry.

Jacobus de Voragine (vùrä′jīnē), c.1230–1298, Italian hagiographer. Chiefly remembered as compiler of the GOLDEN LEGEND, he was archbishop of Genoa (1292–98) and was beatified in 1816.

Jacopone da Todi (yäkōpō′nä dä tō′dē), 1230?–1306, Italian religious poet, a Franciscan tertiary, probable author of the hymn *Stabat Mater Dolorosa.*

Jacquard loom: see LOOM.

Jacque, Charles Émile (shärl āmēl′ zhäk′), 1813–94, French painter of Barbizon school.

Jacquerie (zhäk″ùrē′), 1358, revolt of French peasants (nicknamed *Jacques*) against nobles and pillaging soldiers. Put down by Charles II of Navarre. Thousands were massacred in retaliation.

jade, name for two silicate minerals, jadeite and nephrite, used as gems, ranging in color from white to green. Jade is especially prized by Chinese and Japanese, who attribute to it magical properties.

Jadwiga (yädvē′gä), 1371–99, Polish queen (1383–99); daughter of Louis I of Hungary and Poland. Married Ladislaus Jagiello, grand duke of Lithuania (see LADISLAUS II of Poland), who accepted Christianity. She is nationally venerated as a saint.

Jael (jāl), heroine in time of Deborah. She murdered the Canaanite general, Sisera. Judges 4; 5.

Jaén (hään′), city (pop. 48,003), cap. of Jaén prov., S Spain, in Andalusia. The seat of a small Moorish kingdom, it was conquered by Castile 1246. Has imposing cathedral (16th–18th cent.), palaces, ruins of Moorish castle.

Jaffa (jä′fù), city (est. pop. 101,580), W Israel, on the Mediterranean; chief port for Jerusalem. Mentioned in Old Testament in connection with Jonah. City often changed hands in fighting between Maccabees and Syrians. Destroyed by Vespasian A.D. 68. Held by Crusaders in 12th cent. Fell to Napoleon in 1799 and to the British in 1917. Largely inhabited by Arabs until 1948, when Israel captured it. Jaffa is the Japho of Joshua 19.46; elsewhere in Bible it appears as Joppa.

Jaffna (jäf′nù), peninsula, N Ceylon, separated from India by Palk Strait. Chief city is Jaffna (pop. 62,922). Occupied in 17th cent. by the Portuguese and Dutch.

Jaffrey, resort town (pop. 2,911), SW N.H., near Mt. Monadnock.

Jagannath, India: see PURI.

Jagiello (yägyĕ′lō) or **Jagello** (yägĕ′lō), Pol. *Jagiełło,* ruling dynasty of Poland and Lithuania (1386–1572), Hungary (1440–44, 1490–1526), and Bohemia (1471–1526). Founded by Ladislaus Jagiello, grand duke of Lithuania, who became king of Poland as LADISLAUS II. His successors were Ladislaus III, Casimir IV, John I, Alexander I, Sigismund I, and Sigismund II. See also ULADISLAUS II and LOUIS II, kings of Hungary and Bohemia.

jaguar (jă′gwär), largest New World predatory cat (*Panthera*) ranging from SW U.S. to S central Argentina. Black spots and rosettes mark its yellow fur; occasionally an all black jaguar occurs. Males reach 6–7 ft. body length.

Jahn, Friedrich Ludwig (frē′drĭkh lōōt′vĭkh yän′), 1778–1852, German patriot; a high school teacher in Berlin. Hoped to promote national revival by organizing gymnastic associations (Ger. *Turnvereine*); became known as *Turnvater.* Imprisoned as political agitator 1819–25.

Jahve, Jahveh, Jahweh (jä′vĕ, –wĕ), modern reconstructions of anc. Hebrew name of God (which could be neither spoken nor written). Other forms are Jehovah and Yahweh.

jai alai: see PELOTA.

jail: see PRISON.

Jailolo: see HALMAHERA.

Jainism (jī′nĭzŭm), Indian religion held by c.1,500,000 people. Rose with Buddhism in 6th cent. B.C. as protest against Hinduism. Tradition teaches a succession of 24 Tirthankanas (saints) originated the religion; last was prophet Vardhamana, called Mahavira [the great hero] and Jina ["the victor"]. Basis of Jain doctrine is belief that everything in universe, even matter, is eternal. Spirits retain consciousness of identity through successive incarnations which are determined by cumulative effect of conduct. Nirvana—release from body and matter—may be attained after nine incarnations. For the yati [ascetic] 12 years of self-denial earn Nirvana. For salvation all must be guided by three gems: right faith, cognition, conduct. For Jainist writings, see PRAKRIT LITERATURE.

Jaipur (jī′poŏr), former princely state in Rajputana, India; since 1949 part of Rajasthan. Estab. in 12th cent. **Jaipur,** city (pop. 175,810), cap. of Rajasthan, was cap. of Jaijur state; financial center. Famed for jewelry, enamels, and muslins. Maharaja's palace and a university. Rajput palace is at near-by deserted city of Amber.

Jairus (jāī′–), man whose daughter Jesus raised from the dead. Mat. 9.18–26; Mark 5.22–43; Luke 8.41–56.

Jakarta, formerly **Batavia,** city (pop. 533,015), cap. of Indonesia, on NW Java. Its port, Tanjungpriok (5 mi. NE), is country's largest. Seat of a university. Produces textiles, rubber goods, machinery, and chemicals. Exports minerals, rubber, tea, and spices. The Dutch founded a fort here in 1619. Seat of British rule in Java, 1811–15. In World War II it was briefly hq. of Allied Far East Command.

Jalalabad (jŭlä″läbäd′), town (pop. c.20,000), E Afghanistan, on Kabul R. near Khyber Pass. Held by British in First Afghan War (1839–42). Trade center.

Jalapa (hälä′pä), city (pop. 6,605), cap. of Veracruz, E Mexico; agr. center and health resort.

Jalisco (hälē′skō), state (31,152 sq. mi.; pop. 1,744,700), W Mexico, on Pacific; cap. Guadalajara. Has coastal plains in W, volcanic mountains in center (L. Chapala is here), and productive plateau in E. Products are maize, wheat, fruits, minerals, timber. Explored 1522, settled 1529, Jalisco led in the liberal reform movement of 1858.

jam: see JELLY AND JAM.

Jamaica (jŭmā′kŭ), island (4,411 sq. mi.; pop. 1,297,900), British West Indies, S of Cuba and W of Haiti. Comprising crown colony of Jamaica is the island itself, Turks and Caicos Isls., and Cayman Isls.; cap. Kingston. Discovered by Christopher Columbus 1494; settled by Diego Columbus 1509. Attacked by English (1596, 1643), Jamaica was formally ceded to Great Britain 1670. Population, largely Negro, is overcrowded and unemployment is high. Agr. products include fruits, spices, coffee, tobacco, cacao.

Jamaica: see QUEENS, New York city borough.

Jamaica Bay, SE N.Y., shallow inlet, c.18½ sq. mi., indenting SW Long Isl. in Brooklyn and Queens boroughs and opening SW into the Atlantic via Rockaway Inlet (bridged). Part of Port of New York.

Jambres: see JANNES AND JAMBRES.

James, Saint [ultimately from Jacob]. **1** One of the Twelve Apostles, called St. James the Greater, son of Zebedee, brother of St. John. Killed by Herod Agrippa. Mark 3.17; 5.37; 9.2; 10.35–45; 14.33; Mat. 20.20–29; Acts 12.1–2. Patron saint of Spain, where he is called Santiago. Feast: July 25. **2** One of the Twelve Apostles, called St. James the Less, son of Alphaeus. Mat. 10.3; Mark 15.50; Acts 1.13. Bible tells of a James who was kinsman of Jesus and head of church at Jerusalem (Acts 15; 21.18; Gal. 1.19; 2.8). One tradition says he is same as James the Less; another

claims he is a different person. Epistle of James is commonly ascribed to him. Feast: May 1.

James I (the Conqueror), 1208–76, king of Aragon and count of Barcelona (1213–76). Conquered Balearic Isls. and Valencia from Moors; brought Murcia under Castilian control. In Treaty of Corbeil (1258) he and Louis IX of France renounced their respective claims to territories in S France and Spain. Wrote chronicle of his reign.

James, kings of England. **James I,** 1566–1625, king 1603–25, was the son of Lord Darnley and MARY QUEEN OF SCOTS. Became James VI of Scotland on his mother's abdication (1567). During his minority Scotland was ruled by regents and saw complicated struggle between pro-French Catholic party and pro-English Protestant faction. Began personal rule in 1583. Allied himself (1586) with Elizabeth and accepted calmly his mother's execution in 1587. Succeeded Elizabeth in 1603. From Hampton Court conference (1604) grew movement which produced Authorized (King James) version of the BIBLE. Inconsistent policy toward English Catholics angered them and Protestants alike. Despite GUNPOWDER PLOT of 1605, James was suspected of favoring Catholics. His reliance on incompetent favorites (Robert Carr, earl of SOMERSET, and George Villiers, 1st duke of BUCKINGHAM) and his extravagance furthered discontent. House of Commons became rallying point of opposition to crown. In 1611 James dissolved Parliament and (except for Addled Parliament) ruled without it until 1621. James acceded (1624) to wish of Commons for war with Spain. His reign saw beginnings of English colonization in North America. **James II,** 1633–1701, king 1685–88, was son of Charles I and brother and successor of Charles II. Escaped to France (1648) in Puritan Revolution. Returned to England as lord high admiral in 1660, but resigned after Test Act (1673). His marriage (1673) to MARY OF MODENA brought close ties to Catholic and imperial policies of Louis XIV and increased Whig hatred of him. His daughter Mary married Protestant prince of Orange (later WILLIAM III). Exiled after accusations of Titus Oates about the Popish plot, he was recalled in 1680. After failure of Parliament to exclude him from succession and the abortive RYE HOUSE PLOT, Charles's death brought him to throne in 1685. His unpopularity was increased by Bloody Assizes of Baron Jeffreys of Wem; by the trial of seven bishops (1688) who opposed his declaration of indulgences giving religious toleration; and by his autocratic methods with a hostile parliament. Birth of James Edward Stuart as possible Catholic heir led to Glorious Revolution of 1688. James fled to France. In 1689 he attempted to restore himself in Ireland but was defeated at battle of the Boyne (1690). Died in exile.

James, kings of Scotland. **James I,** 1394–1437, king 1424–37, was the son of Robert III. Fearful for his safety because of king's brother, Robert STUART, duke of Albany, Robert sent James to France in 1406. Captured by the English and held prisoner until 1424, he was treated as a royal guest and well educated. Before his return to Scotland he married Joan Beaufort. He brought peace to Scotland by ruthless methods, but his popularity was lessened by his vindictiveness, cupidity, and quick temper. He was assassinated by a group of nobles. Thought to be the author of a number of fine poems. His son, **James II,** 1430–60, king 1437–60, had successive earls of Douglas as regents during his minority. Allied himself with the 8th earl of Douglas (whom he later slew) and from 1449 ruled in his own right. Invaded England in Wars of the Roses and was accidentally killed. His son, **James III,** 1451–88, king 1460–88, was seized at his mother's death by Boyd family who ruled until 1469. He reigned in a turbulent period, and was murdered by nobles at Sauchieburn. His son, **James IV,** 1473–1513, king 1488–1513, was popular, and his reign was a profitable one for Scotland. Married (1502) Margaret Tudor, daughter of Henry VII of England. Relations with England deteriorated with accession of Henry VIII. James invaded England and was killed at battle of Flodden in 1513. His son, **James V**, 1512–42, king 1513–42, was the object of a struggle between his regents. Held captive, he escaped (1528) and allied himself with France against Henry VIII. Married MARY OF GUISE in 1538. War broke out with England (1542). He died shortly thereafter. **James VI**, king of Scotland: see JAMES I, king of England.

James, kinsman of St. Jude. Luke 6.16.

James, Henry, 1811–82, American student of religious and social problems, b. Albany, N.Y. He rejected the Calvinism taught at Princeton Theological Seminary and was much influenced by Swedenborgian teachings. He became a member of Fourierist circles and a friend of literary men. He spent much time in Europe and, following his own theories of education, had his sons spend much time there. One son, **William James**, 1842–1910, became one of the most eminent of American philosophers and psychologists. He was a teacher at Harvard (1872–1907), at first of physiology and anatomy, later of psychology and philosophy. He considered consciousness as active and purposeful. Will and interest are primary, and knowledge is an instrument. The true is "only the expedient in our way of thinking." Ideas only lead the way to the objective world. For this basic theory of knowledge he borrowed from C. S. Peirce the word PRAGMATISM. In his "radical empiricism" James rejected all transcendent principles and argued that all experience is organized by "conjunctive relations," which are themselves direct experience. His works, notable for lucid and trenchant literary style, include *Principles of Psychology* (1890), *The Will to Believe* (1897), *The Varieties of Religious Experience* (1902), and *Pragmatism* (1907). His brother, **Henry James**, 1843–1916, was one of the most celebrated of American novelists. When studying law at Harvard he determined to devote himself to literature. He decided to settle in Europe and made his home in England after 1876, becoming a British citizen in 1915 as a gesture of his sympathies in World War I. A recurrent theme in his fiction is the contrast between ingenuous, though often charming, Americans and cultured, sophisticated Europeans and between the raw American scene and the centuries-laden, rich civilization of Europe, all on a level of wealth and social position. Among his novels and novellas are *A Passionate Pilgrim, and Other Tales* (1875), *Daisy Miller* (1879), *Washington Square* (1881), *The Portrait of a Lady* (1881), *The Bostonians* (1886), *The Awkward Age* (1899), *The Wings of the Dove* (1902), *The Ambassadors* (1903), and *The Golden Bowl* (1904). Among his short stories, all of high quality, "The Turn of the Screw" is perhaps most familiar. All his fiction is remarkable for conscious refinement of art. He frequently uses the device of the "detached observer" to study the minute reactions in speech and action that limn the psychological variations in character. He also wrote dramas, largely unsuccessful on the stage; travel books that are urbane and deep; literary criticism (including prefaces to later editions of his own work) that has had great influence; and autobiographical works including *A Small Boy and Others* (1913).

James, Jesse (Woodson), 1847–82, American outlaw. In 1866 he and his brother Frank (Alexander Franklin James, 1843–1915) became leaders of gang which robbed and murdered through most of central states.

James, Thomas, 1593?–1635?, English navigator and explorer. In 1631 he explored James Bay (named for him) while seeking Northwest Passage.

James, William: see JAMES, HENRY.

James. 1 River rising in central N.Dak. and flowing 710 mi. SSE across the Dakotas to Missouri R. near Yankton, S.Dak. Often called the Dakota. **2** River formed in western Va. and flowing 340 mi. E to Chesapeake Bay through Hampton Roads. Bridged just N of Newport News. River's lower course rich in historical association. Jamestown founded here 1607. In Civil War river was avenue of Union attempts to take Richmond.

James, epistle of New Testament, ascribed by one tradition to St. James the Less. Book gives various admonitions applying mostly to everyday aspects of Christian behavior; urges Christians to "be doers of the word, not hearers only" (1.22). Scriptural source cited for extreme unction is here (5.14–15). One of later books to be accepted as canonical.

James, Protevangelium of: see PSEUDEPIGRAPHA.

James Bay, S arm of Hudson Bay, 275 mi. long, 135 mi. wide, E central Canada, between Ont. and Que. Posts on bay include Rupert's House, Fort Albany, Moose Factory, Fort George, and Eastmain. Discovered 1610 by Hudson and named for Capt. Thomas James, who explored it 1631.

James Island: see CHARLESTON, S.C.

Jameson, Sir Leander Starr, 1853–1917, British colonial administrator and statesman in South Africa. Made famous unauthorized Jameson Raid from Rhodesia into Boer colony of Transvaal (1895).

James Peak: see FRONT RANGE.

Jamestown. 1 City (pop. 43,354), W N.Y., on Chautauqua L. and SW of Buffalo; founded c.1806. Mfg. of furniture, textiles, toys, tools, and machines. Known for cooperative community services. **2** City (pop. 10,-697), SE N.Dak., on James R. and E of Bismarck; settled 1872, when army post was estab. to protect railroad workers. Rail and trade center of wheat and livestock area. **3** Resort town (pop. 2,068), S R.I., coextensive with Conanicut Isl. (kŭnăn'ĭkŭt), c.9 mi. long and 1–2 mi. wide, in Narragansett Bay (bridged 1940 to North Kingston). Beavertail Light, on S tip of island, was estab. before 1750. **4** First permanent English settlement in America founded here (May 13, 1607) on peninsula (now island) in James R., SE Va., NW of Norfolk. Early hardships diminished as new settlers and supplies arrived and tobacco culture was introduced. As seat of Virginia government, saw first representative assembly in New World here 1619. Village restored after being largely destroyed in Bacon's Rebellion, but declined when cap. was moved to Williamsburg 1699. Few relics remaining include church tower (c.1639), old cemetery, utensils, and building foundations. Included in Colonial Natl. Park except for 22 acres owned by a state society.

Jamestown weed: see JIMSON WEED.

Jami (jä'mē), 1414–92, Persian poet, whose works include the collections *Haft Aurang* (poems) and *Baharistan* (short stories).

Jamitzer, Wenzel: see JAMNITZER, WENZEL.

Jammes, Francis (fräsēs' zhäm'), 1868–1938, French poet. Influenced by symbolists, but distinctive in his optimism and rustic simplicity, as in *De l'angélus de l'aube a l'angélus du soir* (1898). Later wrote religious verse in classical style.

Jammu and Kashmir: see KASHMIR.

Jamnia (jăm'nēŭ), biblical *Jabneel* and *Jabneh*, anc. town, W Israel. A Philistine center, it was sacked by Judas Maccabeus and later rebuilt. After fall of Jerusalem, Vespasian allowed the rabbi Johanan ben Zaccai to settle here as leader of the Jews. Except for short period, city remained center of Judaism until revolt of Bar Kokba in 130. Fortified by Crusaders in Middle Ages. Near site of ancient city is modern settlement, Yavne (pop. 350).

Jamnitzer, Jamitzer or **Gemniczer, Wenzel** (věn'tsŭl yäm'nĭtsŭr, –mĭtsŭr, gěm'nĭtsŭr), 1508–85, leading member of a German family of goldsmiths and engravers.

Jamshedpur (jŭm"shĕdpoŏr'), city (pop. 148,711), SE Bihar, India; major steel center.

Jamtland (yĕmt'länd), Swed. *Jämtlands län*, county (19,966 sq. mi.; pop. 144,137), NW Sweden, bordering on Norway; co. seat Ostersund. It consists, roughly, of historical provinces of Jamtland in N and

Harjedalen in S, both conquered 1645 by Sweden from Norway. There are health and winter resorts, dairy farms, and lumber camps. Formerly spelled Jemtland.

Jamuna: see BRAHMAPUTRA.

Janacek, Leos (lä'ōsh yä'nächĕk), Czech *Janáček,* 1854–1928, Czech composer and collector of Slav folk music. Among his works are an orchestral rhapsody, *Taras Bulba;* and an opera, *Jenufa.*

Janesville, city (pop. 24,899), S Wis., SE of Madison and on Rock R.; settled 1835. Industrial and commercial center in dairy and tobacco area with mfg. of autos and fountain pens.

Janet: see CLOUET, JEAN.

Janet, Pierre (pyěr' zhänä'), 1859–1947, French physician and psychologist. He contributed greatly to knowledge of mental pathology and origins of hysteria, chiefly by use of hypnosis. He founded automatic psychology and first described psychasthenia.

Janina, Greece: see IOANNINA.

Janizaries (jä'nĭzě"rēz) or **Janissaries** (–sě"rēz), élite corps of old Ottoman army, recruited from forced levies of Christian youths and trained in strict discipline. Janizaries later gained enormous power and often made and unmade sultans. In 17th cent. membership became largely hereditary; conscription of Christians gradually ceased. Mahmud II liquidated them in a massacre (1826).

Jan Mayen (yän' mī'ùn), island (144 sq. mi.; pop. 8), Norwegian possession (since 1929) in Arctic Ocean, c.300 mi. E of Greenland. It is narrow strip of tundra, rising to 8,347 ft. in Mt. Beerenberg, an extinct volcano. Has meteorological and wireless station. Discovered 1607 by Henry Hudson.

Jannes and Jambres (jä'nēz, jăm'brēz), opponents of Moses. 2 Tim. 3.8. By tradition, names of Pharaoh's magicians. Ex. 7.11. See PSEUDEPIGRAPHA.

Jansen, Cornelis (kôrnä'lĭs yän'sùn), 1585–1638, Dutch Roman Catholic theologian, professor at Louvain and bishop of Ypres. He and DUVERGIER DE HAURANNE sought to reform Christian life by returning to teachings of St. Augustine. From his posthumously published *Augustinus* (1642) grew up the movement called **Jansenism** (jänsùnĭ'zùm), which stressed greater personal holiness and austerity and made much of the necessity of divine grace for conversion and of predestination. The Jansenists were called "Calvinists" by their opponents, but actually they were bitter opponents of Calvinism and held that the Catholic Church was necessary to salvation. Members of the ARNAULD family became leaders in the movement, and PORT-ROYAL was its center. The Jansenists' teachings of predestination, discouragement of frequent communion for the faithful, and attacks on the Jesuits raised a storm in the Church. In 1653 some Jansenist doctrines were condemned, and in 1656 Antoine Arnauld was expelled from the Sorbonne. The able Blaise PASCAL came to Arnauld's defense. Trouble continued, complicated by the relationship of Jansenism with GALLICANISM, the use Louis XIV made of it to combat the pope. Clement XI condemned a vernacular New Testament with Jansenist notes by Pasquier Quesnel. A Jansenist declaration in 1702 that the pope's infallibility is limited to declaring propositions (and not particular statements) heretical brought matters to a head. The bulls *Vineam Domini* (1705) and *Unigenitus* (1713) practically put the Jansenists out of the Church. Port-Royal was closed, and most Jansenists fled from France. Some submitted; others founded an independent church in the Netherlands. There are Jansenist bishops of Utrecht, Haarlem, and Deventer. The first bishop of the OLD CATHOLICS was consecrated by Jansenists.

Janson, Nicolas: see JENSON, NICOLAS.

Janssen or **Jansen, Zacharias** (zäkhärē'äs yän'sùn), late 16th-early 17th cent., Dutch spectaclemaker credited with making first compound microscope.

January: see MONTH.

Janus (jā'nùs), in Roman religion, god of "beginnings" both temporal and spatial. As spatial god he presided over gates and doors; as temporal god, over first hour of day, first day of month, and first month of year (named for him). He was represented with two bearded heads set back to back.

Japan, Japanese *Nippon,* empire (140,681 sq. mi.; 1950 pop. 83,199,637), occupying an archipelago off E coast of Asia; cap. Tokyo. Its four main islands are HONSHU, KYUSHU, SHIKOKU, HOKKAIDO. Before World War II it included KOREA, S half of SAKHALIN, KURILE ISLANDS, FORMOSA, PESCADORES isls., BONIN ISLANDS, Kwantung leased territory (see LIAOTUNG), Caroline Islands, Marshall Islands, Marianas Islands. According to tradition empire was founded 660 B.C. by Emperor Jimmu, descendant of sun goddess. Foundation for Japanese state was laid in 5th cent. by Yamato clan whose priest-chief later assumed role of emperor. Japan borrowed heavily from Chinese culture, 6th–8th cent.; Buddhism was introduced and influenced in native religion, SHINTO. By 9th cent. authority of imperial government was reduced by rising power of Fujiwara family and Buddhist priesthood. In 12th cent. YORITOMO Minamoto became master of Japan and the first to bear title of SHOGUN. First European contact made by Portuguese 1542; Christianity introduced by St. Francis Xavier 1549. The 16th-cent. dictators NOBUNAGA and HIDEYOSHI were succeeded by IEYASU, founder of TOKUGAWA shogunate (1603–1867). Opening of Japan to the West by Commodore PERRY in 1854 was a factor in overthrow of shogunate and subsequent MEIJI restoration (1868). With policy of Westernization Japan rapidly became a modern industrial state and military power. New constitution of 1889 created a diet consisting of house of peers and elected house of representatives. Victory in FIRST CHINO-JAPANESE WAR (1894–95) and RUSSO-JAPANESE WAR (1904–5) established Japan as world power. Annexed Korea 1910; after World War I won mandate over former German islands in the Pacific. Manchuria occupied in 1931 and puppet state of MANCHUKUO estab. After 1937 SECOND CHINO-JAPANESE WAR was intensified. In 1940 pact signed with Germany and Italy. Rise of Gen. Tojo to premiership in Oct., 1941 marked height of militarist power over Japan; on Dec. 7 Japan struck at Pearl Harbor, Singapore, and other possessions of U.S. and Great Britain. Rapidly made sweeping gains in Pacific and Asia (see WORLD WAR II), but by end of 1942 tide had begun to turn. With explosion of atomic bombs in Hiroshima and Nagasaki, Japan capitulated and surrendered unconditionally Sept. 2, 1945. Allied occupation (following terms laid down by POTSDAM CONFERENCE) began under command of Gen. MacArthur (replaced 1951 by Gen. Ridgway). New democratic constitution, making lower house dominant and enfranchising women, was adopted 1946. Peace treaty was signed Sept., 1951 at San Francisco by all major Allied powers except USSR. It ended Allied occupation, but some U.S. troops remained in areas specified by defense pact (Sept., 1951).

Japan, Sea of, part of Pacific Ocean between Japan and Korea.

Japan Current or **Kuroshio** (koōrōshē'ō) warm ocean current of the Pacific. A northward flowing branch of North Equatorial Current, it runs E of Formosa and Japanese archipelago. Near lat. 35° N it divides: E branch nears Hawaiian Isls.; N branch skirts Asia coast, merges with cold Oyashio current.

Japanese architecture. Building art of China came to Japan with introduction of Buddhism in 6th cent. The temple Horyu-ji (near Nara) was completed c.650; it is oldest known example of wood architecture extant and is basis of all later Japanese design. Wood has always been favored material. Chief features of traditional Japanese design are interior columns, thin exterior walls of woodwork, plaster, and rice paper, and curved overhanging roofs. Pavilion called Phoenix Hall in temple at Uji represents peak of native design. Emphasis on ornamentation began in 14th cent. and became increasingly important during Tokugawa shogunate (1603–1867). Striking example of late style is group of lavishly decorated temples at Nikko. All Buddhist temples have courtyards approached by terraces and wide flights of stairs. Accessory structures include square PAGODA (often omitted) and drum tower. Shinto temple (still in pre-Buddhist form) is severely simple and roofed with bark thatch. At approach to it is gateway called *torii.* Typical native dwelling, as developed in Tokugawa era, is elegantly simple. Interior is subdivided by sliding screens; main spaces have *tokonoma* (alcoves for display of flower arrangement or a painting). For public and commercial buildings Western methods are now used.

Japanese art is based on Chinese art, which was introduced in 6th cent. with Buddhism by way of Korea. Kose no Kanaoka (9th cent.), first notable native master, adopted T'ang traditions of Chinese painting. In 11th cent. Motomitsu estab. the Yamato, or native, school, which still leaned heavily on Chinese style. Painters of Tosa school (13th–14th cent.) were aristocrats, who confined their work to the court. Toba Sojo (late 12th cent.) satirically represented various personages as animals in amusing poses; he and later caricaturists expressed the people's incisive humor. Next era produced painters who worked in classic Chinese tradition, with SESSHU and JOSETSU among leading exponents. Emerging in same period was KANO school. Linked with original movements in Japanese art are KORIN and IWASA MATABEI, founder of ukiyoye school of color prints, whose exponents included HOKUSAI, HIROSHIGE, and HARUNOBU. The 18th cent. produced the Shijo naturalistic school and the Ganku school of Chinese traditions. Mid-19th cent. contact with European culture had negative effect on native art. Traditional method of painting requires Chinese ink and water colors, applied on paper or silk placed flat on the floor. Mounted on silk brocade or paper, pictures are of two types: *kakemono* (hanging picture) and *makimono* (scroll portraying series of scenes). Early sculptors (Chinese and Koreans) made spirited wooden images and small bronzes of Buddhist deities, which show Greco-Indian influences (7th–8th cent.). Stone sculptures are few; but exquisite ivory carvings are numerous. Among highly-developed minor arts are porcelain and lacquer work, arms and armor, enamels, cloisonné, and damascening.

Japanese beetle, name for destructive insect related to June bug. Discovered (1916) in New Jersey, it spread so widely that extermination was impossible. Adult is c.½ in. long, has a metallic green head and thorax, and brown wing covers. It skeletonizes leaves and destroys fruits and flowers. Eggs are laid in summer on ground; larvae feed on roots, winter underground, and emerge in June or July.

Japanese drama. The lyric drama, *no* or *noh,* originated in pantomimic dance performed at ancient Shinto and Buddhist festivals. Most of c.250 extant *no* plays were written in 15th cent. Restraint and symbolism characterize both acting and staging of *no;* vocal recitative is indispensable, and wooden masks are used. Farcical interlude, *kyogen* (dialogue or monologue, without music), developed along with *no* to provide comic relief. *No* appealed mainly to intellectual tastes; by 17th cent. need for popular fare had been filled by *kabuki,* a form utilizing bizarre make-up and exaggerated stylized acting. Dramatic ballad, *joruri,* used in *kabuki,* was adapted also to the puppet show (introduced early 16th cent.). In late 19th cent. translations of European plays were successfully introduced.

Japanese ivy: see BOSTON IVY.

Japanese literature. Japan had no written language until late 3d cent. A.D., when Chinese was intro-

duced by Korean scholars. Early in 8th cent. a method of writing Japanese was evolved by adapting Chinese ideographs to spoken Japanese. This system was used in writing of *Kojiki* (712), sacred book of Shinto, which gives basis for myth of emperor's divine origin, but other principal works of the period were written in pure Chinese. In 9th cent. simplification of written language by use of two syllabaries opened golden age of letters. By early 11th cent. such writers as Lady MURASAKI were adding luster to literature in native language (as opposed to classical Chinese). Basic forms of JAPANESE DRAMA were evolved, 12th–17th cent. Under Tokugawa shogunate (17th–19th cent.) written language was standardized and freer verse forms (e.g., *haikai* or *hokku*) began to replace the *tanka,* the classical form. After 1868 Japanese writing was deeply influenced by Western literature.

Japanese music. Much of Japanese music was borrowed from other countries, especially China. Forms of sacred music include: the *gagaku,* ancient ceremonial music, brought from China, 5th cent. A.D.; Buddhist hymns dating from the 6th cent.; the *bugaku,* ceremonial dance music, imported from China in the 7th cent.; and the *kagura,* native to Japan, principally vocal, and used for the most solemn religious rites. Historically midway between sacred and secular music is the music for *no* drama (see JAPANESE DRAMA). Secular music dates from the 16th cent. with the importation of the *samisen* (a type of lute). Other instruments include the *koto* (a zither) and many kinds of flutes, oboes, drums, and gongs. Japanese scales are all five-toned. Those borrowed from China are without semitones; native scales have semitones. There is no harmony as we understand the term. Rhythm background provided by drums forms no pattern recognizable to Western ears. Western music was introduced into Japan in the late 19th cent. and is now an integral part of Japanese culture.

Japanese quince: see FLOWERING QUINCE.

Japheth (jā′fĕth), son of Noah, ancestor of those who were to occupy the isles of the Gentiles. This was taken to mean the Mediterranean lands of Europe and Asia Minor. Gen. 5.32; 6.10; 9.27; 10.1–5.

Japho: see JAFFA.

japonica: see FLOWERING QUINCE.

Japurá (zhǔ″pōōrä′), river, over 1,000 mi. long, rising in Colombia as Caquetá and flowing SE across Brazil into Amazon.

Jaques-Dalcroze, Émile (zhäk″-dälkrōz′), 1865–1950, Swiss educator and composer. Developed the Dalcroze system of EURYTHMICS.

Jarnac (zhärnäk′), town (pop. 3,624), Charente dept., W France. Scene of Catholic victory over Huguenots, where Louis I de Condé was killed (1569).

Jarrow, municipal borough (pop. 28,541), Durham, England, on the Tyne estuary. Industries include iron foundries and shipbuilding. Scene of labors of the Venerable Bede, who died here.

Jarves, James Jackson (jär′vĭs), 1818–88, American art critic and collector of Italian works of art.

Jarvis, John Wesley, 1781?–1839, American portrait painter, b. England.

Jarvis Island, area 1 sq mi., central Pacific near equator, 1,100 mi. E of Howland Isl. Claimed 1857 by U.S., placed 1936 under Dept. of Interior. On Hawaii–New Zealand air route.

jasmine or **jessamine,** shrub or climbing plant of genus *Jasminum* of tropical or semitropical regions. The scented flowers, mostly white or yellow, are often used in tea; the oil is used in perfumery. For Cape jasmine, see GARDENIA.

Jason, in Greek mythology, hero who claimed kingdom of Ioclus, which his uncle, Pelias, had stolen from his father, Aeson. Pelias would return it only in exchange for GOLDEN FLEECE, owned by Aeëtes, king of Colchis, where Jason led the Argonauts in ship *Argo.* He secured the fleece with aid of MEDEA, who loved him and who returned with him to Ioclus. He was also a hero of Calydonian hunt. In one legend Jason committed suicide; in another he was crushed by beam of the *Argo*.

Jasper. 1 City (pop. 8,589), NW central Ala., NW of Birmingham, in coal area. Processes cotton, timber. **2** City (pop. 5,215), SW Ind., NE of Evansville. Mfg. of desks; coal mining.

Jasper National Park, 4,200 sq. mi., W Alta., in Canadian Rocky Mts.; estab. 1907. Game reserve and recreation center, noted for spectacular mountain scenery. Jasper is park hq. and station on Canadian National RR.

Jaspers, Karl (kärl yäs'pŭrs), 1883–, German philosopher, associated with existential school developed by KIERKEGAARD, and Heidegger. His philosophy is subjective and nonrational.

Jassy (yä'sē) or **Iasi** (yäsh), city (pop. 94,075), E Rumania; historic cap. of Moldavia. Textile mfg.; food industries. See of Orthodox archbishop. Former large Jewish population was massacred in World War II at German instigation (1941). Has a university (founded 1860) and several fine churches in Byzantine style (15th-17th cent.). For Treaty of Jassy (1792), see RUSSO-TURKISH WARS.

Játiva (hä'tēvä), city (pop. 17,496), Valencia prov., E Spain. Noted for its Spanish-Moorish castle and several fine churches and palaces. Was residence of Borgia or Borja family.

jaundice (jôn'dĭs), condition attended by yellowish discoloration of tissues and excretions resulting from bile pigments in blood. Causes include obstruction of bile duct and virus infections.

Jauregg, Julius Wagner: see WAGNER-JAUREGG.

Jaurès, Jean (zhä' jōrĕs'), 1859–1914, French Socialist leader and historian. An idealist and pacifist, he advocated a peaceful revolution to obtain economic equality. Was killed by a fanatic nationalist on eve of World War I, which he desperately sought to avert. His *Histoire socialiste de la Révolution française* is an economic interpretation.

Java (jä'vù), island (48,842 sq. mi.; pop. 39,755,902, including offshore islands), INDONESIA, S of Borneo, from which it is separated by Java Sea, and SE of Sumatra. Cultural, political, and economic center of Indonesia. Chain of volcanic mountains rises to 12,-060 ft. Climate is warm and humid, soil highly fertile. Exports quinine, rubber, sugar, and teak. Oil fields are in NE. Native arts include silver craft and batik work. A home of early man (see MAN, PRIMITIVE); remains of Java man or *Pithecanthropus erectus* found here 1891. Religion is predominantly Moslem, but Hinduism and Buddhism have strongly affected native culture. Highly developed arts include the *wayang* or shadow play employing puppets and musical accompaniment. Largest city is JAKARTA (cap. of Indonesia). Other centers include JOGJAKARTA and SURAKARTA. Hindus colonized central and E Java in 7th cent. Rise of Hindu-Javanese state of Majapahit (founded 1293) marked peak of Javanese history; it ruled over much of Indonesia and Malay Peninsula. Islam, introduced in 13th cent., produced Moslem state of Mataram. Following the Portuguese, the Dutch arrived 1596; after 1619 Dutch East India Co. gradually absorbed remnants of Javanese empire. Early in World War II Java was exposed to Japanese invasion by Allied defeat in battle of Java Sea (Feb., 1942).

Javanese music, of uncertain origin, is remarkable in its orchestral development. It is based on two pentatonic systems—*pelog*, which has semitones, and *slendro* (or *salendro*), which is composed of whole tones. *Slendro* is considered masculine, *pelog* feminine. The *gamelan*, an orchestra of tuned percussion instruments, originated in Java, but is only rarely heard there today. See BALINESE MUSIC.

Jaxartes: see SYR DARYA.

Jay, John, 1745–1829, American statesman. Urged moderate policy as delegate to Continental Congress. As the Secretary of Foreign Affairs (1784–89) he recognized need of a more powerful central government; wrote five of the FEDERALIST PAPERS. First Chief Justice of U.S. Supreme Court (1789–95). American signer of JAY'S TREATY. His son, **William Jay,** 1789–1858, a jurist, was an active abolitionist. His son, **John Jay,** 1817–94, a lawyer, served as minister to Austria (1869–74).

jay, common name for certain birds of the crow family, found in Europe, Asia, and the Americas. Well known in America are BLUE JAY and Canada jay (often called camp robber) which is gray, with a white throat and black cap.

Jay's Treaty, concluded in 1794 between U.S. and Great Britain to settle difficulties arising mainly out of violations of Treaty of Paris of 1783 and to regulate commerce and navigation. Treaty, signed in England by John Jay and Baron Grenville, provided for British evacuation of Northwestern posts, unrestricted navigation of the Mississippi, and equal privileges to vessels in Great Britain and the East Indies, but placed severe restrictions on American trade in the West Indies. It did not allow indemnity for those Americans whose Negro slaves were carried off by Britain's evacuating armies, guarantee protection to American seamen against impressment, or secure recognition of principles of international maritime law. Therefore, it aroused indignation in America, and appropriations to carry it into effect were delayed until May, 1796.

jazz, style of music regarded as one of the most distinctive of American contributions to the art of music, characterized by its highly emotional melodic line and its strongly marked, syncopated rhythms. Originated in the late 19th cent. among Negro musicians of New Orleans but not fully developed until c.1910. The word itself is of uncertain origin. The original jazz ensemble was small and composed principally of the trumpet, cornet, trombone, clarinet, various percussion instruments, and sometimes saxophone and piano. Emphasis was on the ability of the individual player to improvise. As the size of the ensemble grew, more formal arrangements became necessary. Jazz was not seriously or critically studied until the 1930s. Outstanding names in its history have been Jellyroll Morton, Louis Armstrong, and Bix Beiderbecke.

Jean Baptiste de la Salle, Saint: see JOHN BAPTIST DE LA SALLE, SAINT.

Jean de Meun (zhä' dù mœ'), d. 1305, French poet, author of second part of the ROMAN DE LA ROSE.

Jeanne d'Albret (zhän' dälbrä'), 1528–72, queen of Navarre (1555–72); daughter of Henri d'Albret and Margaret of Navarre; mother of Henry IV of France. Unlike her turncoat husband, Antoine de Bourbon, she was a staunch Protestant.

Jeanne d'Arc: see JOAN OF ARC.

Jeannette (jŭnĕt'), city (pop. 16,172), SW Pa., ESE of Pittsburgh; laid out 1888. Mfg. of glass, rubber, and metal products.

Jean Paul: see RICHTER, JOHANN PAUL FRIEDRICH.

Jeans, Sir James (Hopwood), 1877–1946, English astronomer, mathematician, physicist. With H. A. Jeffreys he developed the tidal theory of origin of solar system. His works include *The Universe Around Us* (1931), *Through Space and Time* (1934), *Science and Music* (1937), *Physics and Philosophy* (1942).

Jebail: see BYBLOS.

Jebb, Sir Richard (Claverhouse), 1841–1905, British classical scholar. He was noted for his standard editions and translations of Greek writers and for his *Growth and Influence of Greek Poetry* (1893).

Jebus (jē'–), **Jebusi,** or **Jebusite,** name of tribe occupying Jerusalem before the Hebrews.

Jedburgh (jĕd'bùrù), burgh (pop. 4,083), co. town of Roxburghshire, Scotland. Border town, it suffered from Scottish-English strife; "Jedburgh Justice" (hanging first, trying after) became an unpleasant byword.

Jedda, Saudi Arabia: see JIDDA.

Jedidiah (jĕdĭdī'ù) [Heb.,= beloved of God], name given by Nathan to baby Solomon. 2 Sam. 12.24, 25.

Jeffers, Robinson (jĕ'fûrs), 1887–, American poet. His works, stressing civilized man's divorce from nature, include *Tamar and Other Poems* (1924), *Roan Stallion* (1925), and *The Double Axe & Other Poems* (1948). Several of his plays (esp. his free translation of *Medea,* 1947) have been produced.

Jefferson, Joseph, 1829–1905, American actor. After 20 years as strolling player, he joined (1857) Laura Keene's company. Was famous as Asa Trenchard in *Our American Cousin* and as Bob Acres in Sheridan's *Rivals.* Seeking an original play, he and Dion Boucicault adapted (1865) Washington Irving's *Rip Van Winkle,* a long-time stage favorite.

Jefferson, Thomas, 1743–1826, 3d President of the United States (1801–9), author of DECLARATION OF INDEPENDENCE, and apostle of agrarian democracy. In Va. legislature (1776–79) he laid groundwork for abolition of entail and primogeniture, for establishment of religious freedom, and for a public school system. Served as minister to France (1785–89), U.S. Secretary of State (1790–93). Growing opposition to Alexander Hamilton and his policies associated Jefferson with group called Republicans, forerunners of present DEMOCRATIC PARTY. While serving as Vice President (1797–1801), he drafted Kentucky Resolutions (see KENTUCKY AND VIRGINIA RESOLUTIONS). He was elected President following a long deadlock with Aaron Burr in the House of Representatives, largely because Hamilton considered Burr the more dangerous man and gave support to Jefferson. First President inaugurated in Washington, which he had helped to plan, he instituted a republican simplicity there. Notable achievements of his first administration were LOUISIANA PURCHASE and LEWIS AND CLARK EXPEDITION. In his second administration attempts to enforce measures such as EMBARGO ACT OF 1807 brought strong opposition. In retirement at his beloved MONTICELLO, Jefferson secured the founding of Univ. of Virginia and continued his activities as scientist, architect, and philosopher-statesman. He had complete faith that a people enlightened by free education could under democratic-republican institutions govern themselves better than under any other system.

Jefferson, river, 207 mi. long, rising in SW Mont., W of Yellowstone Natl. Park, and flowing W and NW (as Red Rock R.), then NE (as Beaverhead R.). Becomes Jefferson R. at entrance of Ruby and Big Hole rivers, then flows E to join Madison and Gallatin rivers at Three Forks. Main headstream of Missouri R.

Jefferson, Fort: see DRY TORTUGAS.

Jefferson, Mount: see PRESIDENTIAL RANGE.

Jefferson City. 1 City (pop. 25,099), state cap., central Mo., on the Missouri; laid out 1822. Trade and mfg. center of agr. area, it has railroad shops, printing plants, and mfg. of shoes, clothing, wood and grain products. Here are Lincoln Univ. (Negro; land grant; coed.; 1866) and a national cemetery. **2** Town (pop. 3,633), E Tenn., ENE of Knoxville. Seat of Carson-Newman Col. (Baptist; coed.; 1851). Cherokee Dam near by.

Jefferson Medical College (for men; 1825), in Philadelphia.

Jefferson Memorial: see THOMAS JEFFERSON MEMORIAL.

Jeffersonville, city (pop. 14,685), S Ind., on Ohio R. (bridged to Louisville, Ky.); settled 1802. Port with many shipyards. Mfg. of wood and foundry products.

Jeffreys of Wem, George Jeffreys, 1st Baron, 1648–89, English lord chancellor. In the Bloody Assizes after the duke of Monmouth's rebellion (1685) he caused c.300 to be hanged, c.800 transported, and many imprisoned or whipped.

Jeffries, James J., 1875–1953, American boxer. Won (1899) heavyweight championship from Bob Fitzsim-

mons, retired undefeated 1905. Return to ring, lost title to Jack Johnson (1910).

Jegar-sahadutha: see GALEED.

Jehannet: see CLOUET, JEAN.

Jehoahaz (jĕhō'ùhăz) or **Joahaz** (jō'–). **1** Died c.804 B.C., king of Israel (c.820–c.804 B.C.), son of Jehu. 2 Kings 13.1–9; 14.1. **2** Fl. 609 B.C., king of Judah (c.609 B.C.), son of Josiah. Deposed and taken to Egypt by Pharaoh Necho, who made Jehoiakim king instead. 2 Kings 38.30–35; 2 Chron. 36. Shallum: 1 Chron. 3.15; Jer. 22.11. **3** See AHAZIAH **2.**

Jehoash (jĕhō'ăsh) or **Joash** (jō'–). **1** Died c.789 B.C., king of Israel (c. 804–c.798 B.C.). Successful in wars against Damascus and Judah. 2 Kings 13; 14. **2** Died c.802 B.C., king of Judah (c.841–c.802 B.C.), son of Ahaziah **2.** When his father was murdered and Athaliah seized the throne and massacred the royal family, Jehoash, a baby, was saved by his uncle and aunt, Jehoida and Jehosheba. He was placed on throne 6 years later in coup d'état. 2 Kings 11.

Jehoiachin (jĕhoi'ùkĭn), fl. c.598 B.C., king of Judah (c.598 B.C.). Captured by Nebuchadnezzar; imprisoned in Babylon. Later freed and honorably treated. 2 Kings 24.6–16; 25.27–30. Also variously called Jeconiah, Jechonias, and Coniah.

Jehoiada (jĕhoi'ùdù), high priest. With his wife, Jehosheba, he saved the baby Jehoash and led conspiracy against Athaliah that put Jehoash **2** on the throne. 2 Kings 11; 12; 2 Chron. 22–24.

Jehoiakim (jĕhoi'ùkĭm), d. c.598 B.C., king of Judah (c.609–c.598 B.C.), successor of JEHOAHAZ **2.** Restored idol worship; burned book of Jeremiah's prophecies. Died just before Nebuchadnezzar took Jerusalem. Originally called Eliakim, took name of Jehoiakim on becoming king. 2 Kings 23.24–24.6. Jer. 36.

Jehol (juhōl'), Chinese *Jeho,* province (40,000 sq. mi.; pop. 5,000,000), SW Manchuria; cap. Chengteh. Bounded in S by Hopeh along Great Wall. Largely rugged and rocky. Agr. (wheat, barley, kaoliang, corn, soybeans) limited by meager rainfall. Large coal mines. Originally inhabited by Mongolian leagues; Chinese control dates from Ming dynasty.

Jehoram (jĕhō'rùm) or **Joram** (jō'–). **1** Died c.846 B.C., king of Israel (c.852–c.846 B.C.), successor of Ahaziah **1.** Killed in Jehu's coup d'état; last of house of Ahab in Israel. 2 Kings 1.17, 18; 3; 4. **2** Died c.846 B.C., king of Judah (c.851–c.846 B.C.), son of Jehoshaphat. His wife was ATHALIAH. Succeeded by Ahaziah **2.** 2 Kings 8.16–24; 2 Chron. 21.

Jehoshaphat (jĕhō'shùfăt) or **Josaphat** (jŏs'–). **1** Died c.851 B.C., king of Judah (c.870–c.851 B.C.), son of Asa. A "good" king, he made many religious reforms. Often allied with kings of Israel. 1 Kings 22; 2 Kings 3; 2 Chron. 12–20. **2** Recorder under David and Solomon. 2 Sam. 8.16; 1 Kings 4.3. **3** Father of Jehu. 2 Kings 9.2,14. Also Joshaphat.

Jehosheba (jĕhō'shĕbù), princess of Judah; daughter of Jehoram **2,** aunt of Jehoash **2.** See JEHOIADA.

Jehovah (jùhō'vù, jĕ–), modern reconstruction of the anc. Hebrew ineffable (to be neither spoken nor written) name of God.

Jehovah's Witnesses, sect founded in U.S. in 1872 by Charles Taze Russell, also called Russellites. Doctrine centers on second coming of Christ. Sect has no churches or ministers, but circulates views by *The Watch Tower Announcing Jehovah's Kingdom.*

Jehu (jē'hū), d. c.820 B.C., king of Israel (c.846–c.820 B.C.). Anointed king by Elisha. Jehu murdered Jehoram **1** and Ahaziah **2** and massacred the royal family. His skill as a charioteer is proverbial. 2 Kings 9.

Jekyll, Gertrude (jē'kĭl), 1843–1932, English horticulturist and author of many works on gardening.

Jekyll Island: see SEA ISLANDS.

Jelgava (yĕl'gävä), Ger. *Mitau,* city (pop. 34,099), Latvia, SW of Riga. Agr. center; varied mfg. Founded by Livonian Knights 1266; cap. of Courland 1561–1795. Notable buildings include Trinity Church (16th cent.) and ducal palace (18th cent.).

Jellicoe, John Rushworth Jellicoe, 1st Earl, 1859–1935, British admiral. In World War I he was commander in chief of the Grand Fleet (1914–16) and first sea lord (1916–17). Commanded at battle of JUTLAND. Governor general of New Zealand 1920–24.

jelly and jam, both preparations of fruit and sugar. Jelly is produced by cooking the juice of fresh fruit with sugar to the concentration at which jelly is formed. Good jelly depends upon proper balance of sugar, acid, and PECTIN. Jam is made from crushed or sliced fruit cooked with sugar until thick or until somewhat jelled. In preserves, unlike jam, the fruit retains its form.

jellyfish, popular name for the medusa, the gelatinous, umbrella-shaped, free-swimming form of marine invertebrate related to coral polyp and sea anemone. Most species pass through both medusa and polyp or hydroid stage. Jellyfish capture small animals by means of tentacles with stinging cells.

Jemappes (zhùmäp′), town (pop. 12,812), Hainaut prov., SW Belgium, near Mons; coal-mining center. Here in 1792 French defeated Austrians in one of first important battles of French Revolutionary Wars.

Jemez (hā′mäs), Indian pueblo village (1948 pop. 892), NW central N.Mex., W of Santa Fe. Diminished from several pueblos in 1500s to one by 1680, when PUEBLO INDIANS revolted against Spanish. Captured by Spanish in 1694. Jemez Indians rose again in 1696, killed the missionary, and fled to Navajo lands. Some finally returned and built present village c.1700. Language Tanoan. Annual feast to San Diego.

Jemima (jēmī′–) [Heb.,= dove], first daughter of Job after his misfortune. Job 42.14.

Jemtland, Sweden: see JAMTLAND.

Jena (yā′nä), city (pop. 82,722), Thuringia, central Germany, on Saale R. Industrial and cultural center. Great Zeiss plant (optical and precision instruments) was partially removed by Russians after World War II. Chartered 13th cent., Jena later passed to Saxe-Weimar-Eisenach; was incorporated with Thuringia 1920. Napoleon I decisively defeated Prussians here 1806. Univ. of Jena (founded 1558) reached height in late 18th–early 19th cent., when Schiller, Hegel, Fichte, and A. W. von Schlegel taught here.

Jenghiz Khan or **Genghis Khan** (both: jĕng′gĭs kän′), 1167?–1227, Mongol conqueror. Succeeded his father, Yekusai, as chieftain of Mongolian confederacy. In 1206 completed conquest of Mongolia and made Karakorum his capital. Began conquest of N China in 1213; by 1215 held most of Ch′in empire. Conquered Turkistan, Transoxania, and Afghanistan (1218–24). Kublai Khan was his grandson.

Jenkins, town (pop. 6,921), E Ky., in Cumberlands on Va. line near Pound Gap. Has coal mining.

Jenkins′s Ear, War of, 1739–41, struggle between England and Spain. Based on commercial rivalry, it led into the larger War of the Austrian Succession. Propaganda effect of claim by shipmaster Robert Jenkins that Spanish coast guards cut off his ear forced Sir Robert Walpole to declare war.

Jenkintown, residential borough (pop. 5,130), SE Pa., N of Philadelphia. Seat of Beaver Col. (Presbyterian; for women; 1853).

Jenner, Edward, 1749–1823, English physician, originator of inoculation with cowpox virus to immunize against smallpox. He first demonstrated his method in 1796 on James Phipps.

Jenner, Sir William, 1815–98, English physician, known especially for distinguishing between typhus and typhoid fever.

Jennewein, Carl Paul (jĕ′nùwīn), 1890–, American architectural sculptor, b. Germany.

Jenney, William Le Baron, 1832–1907, American architect and engineer. In 1883 built the 10-story Home Insurance Building (Chicago), generally known as first skyscraper.

Jennings, Sarah, duchess of Marlborough: see MARLBOROUGH, JOHN CHURCHILL, 1ST DUKE OF.

Jennings. 1 City (pop. 9,663), SW La., E of Lake Charles. Agr. center with rice mills and cotton gins. **2** Town (pop. 15,282), E Mo., just N of St. Louis near the Mississippi.

Jensen, Johannes V(ilhelm), 1873–1950, Danish author. Interest in biological science shown in the epic *The Long Journey* (1909–20). Created a distinctive literary form in short essays (called "myths"). Awarded the 1944 Nobel Prize in Literature.

Jenson or **Janson, Nicolas,** d. c.1480, Venetian printer, b. France. Excellence of designs of roman type inspired many of his successors. He produced many beautiful works after 1470. The Aldine Press used his types from 1480.

jeopardy (jĕ′pùrdē), danger of punishment involved in trial for crime. In U.S. interesting chiefly for double jeopardy, prohibited by U.S. constitution, which would make a man liable for trial for the same offense more than once. If the trial was abortive (e.g., if it ended with the jury unable to reach a verdict) or if a new trial is ordered after review by a court of appeal, a new trial does not constitute double jeopardy.

Jephthah (jĕf′thù), judge of Israel. Because of rash vow, he had to sacrifice his daughter, an only child. Judges 11.1–12.7. Jephthae: Heb. 11.32.

Jeremiah (jĕrĭmī′ù) or **Jeremias,** book of Old Testament. Tells story of Jeremiah (fl. 600 B.C.), one of the major prophets, who preached in Jerusalem under Josiah and his successors. He foresaw nothing but doom in Judah′s foreign policy and urged the people to turn from futile resistance to Babylon and concern themselves with domestic reform and their own religious welfare. For such unpopular advice, he was imprisoned. Released after fall of Jerusalem (586 B.C.). Among Messianic passages in book: 14.8–9; 23.5–6; 30.9–24; 32.37–44. Other references to Jeremiah in Bible: 2 Chron. 35.25; Dan. 9.2; Mat. 2.18; Heb. 8.8. See also LAMENTATIONS; BARUCH.

Jeremy, Epistle of [Eng. form of Jeremiah] (jĕ′rĭmē), name given to sixth chapter of BARUCH.

Jerez de la Frontera (hārāth′ dā lä frŏntä′rä), city (pop. 65,166), SW Spain, in Andalusia, near Cádiz. Export center for sherry (named after town).

Jericho (jĕ′rĭkō), anc. city, Palestine, N of Dead Sea. Its spectacular capture by Joshua marked Hebrew entry into Canaan, the Promised Land; its fall to Babylonia centuries later marked end of kingdom of Judah. Sacked and rebuilt by many conquerors—among them Herod the Great, who made it his winter residence. Recent excavations reveal walls said to be those of original Jericho.

Jeroboam I (jĕrùbō′ùm), d. c.910 B.C., first king of N kingdom of Israel after it broke away from Rehoboam. Notorious for fostering idolatry and restoring worship of golden calf. 1 Kings 11.26–14.20; 2 Chron. 10; 13. **Jeroboam II,** d. c.749 B.C., king of Israel (c.789–c.749 B.C.), son of Jehoash 1. Amos and Hosea prophesied under him. 2 Kings 14.16,23–29.

Jerome, Saint (jâr′ùm, jùrōm′), c.347–419?, Christian scholar, Doctor of the Church, one of the Latin Fathers; full name in Latin Sophronius Eusebius Hieronymus. Studies (partly at Rome) made him proficient in pagan learning, but after a vision at Antioch (375) he renounced this scholarship and fled to the desert, where he devoted himself to scriptural studies. These, after he was ordained in 378, he continued under St. Gregory Nazianzen in Constantinople. Went (382) to Rome, where he became secretary to Damasus I and at the pope′s request began work on a new version of the Bible. He was spiritual adviser to a number of Roman ladies, including St. Paula, who founded a monastery for him in Bethlehem. There Jerome lived from 386 to his death. His scholarly editing of Latin translations of the Bible together with some of his own translations of some portions from the Hebrew were the basis of the VULGATE. Also wrote exegetical works, tracts (often attacking the opinions of others with some violence), lives of Christian writers, and brilliant letters. Feast: Sept. 30.

Jerome, Jerome K(lapka), 1859–1927, English humorist and playwright, best known for play *The Passing of the Third Floor Back* (1907; still revived).

Jerome, William Travers, 1859–1934, American lawyer. Prominent in cause of reform in New York city. Led campaign against crime and political corruption.

Jerome of Prague, d. 1416, Bohemian religious reformer. With Huss (1407) he urged Bohemian control of Univ. of Prague. Defended Huss (1415) before Council of Constance, but was himself imprisoned and burned (1416) as a heretic.

Jersey, largest of the CHANNEL ISLANDS.

Jersey cattle: see CATTLE.

Jersey City, commercial and industrial city (pop. 299,-017), NE N.J., opposite lower Manhattan (ferry, Holland Tunnel, subway connections) on peninsula bounded on W by Hackensack R. and Newark Bay, E by Hudson R. and New York Bay. Part of Port of New York, second largest N.J. city, important rail and steamship terminal. Produces packed meat, ink, chemicals, cans, and metal, petroleum, and graphite products. Area acquired by Michiel Pauw as Pavonia patroonship 1630. Paulus Hook (connected with Manhattan by ferry c.1764), Communipaw, and Harsimus (first permanent N.J. settlement) set up as trading posts. Near-by Dutch village of Bergen (settled before 1620) had first municipal government in N.J. (1661), first church (1660; Dutch reformed), first school (1662). Jersey town, Bergen, Hudson City, and Greenville formed Jersey City 1836. Has medical center. Home and hq. of Frank HAGUE, long-time Democratic boss of N.J. U.S. Supreme Court voided city's laws curbing civil liberties 1939.

Jersey Shore, borough (pop. 5,595), N central Pa., on Susquehanna R. and W of Williamsport, in farm area. Mfg. of metal products.

Jerseyville, city (pop. 5,792), W Ill., NNW of Alton. Trade and shipping center of agr. area.

Jerusalem, Arabic *El Kuds,* city (est. 1946 pop. 164,-440), central Palestine, on rocky ridge of Judaean Hills, SE of Tel Aviv. The New City was in 1949 made cap. of Israel; the Old City is in Jordan. Jerusalem is the Holy City of Jews and Christians and one of the chief shrines of Islam. Often called Zion in Jewish and Christian literature, it is the symbol of the City of God (Rev. 21.2). Almost all holy sites of the three faiths are in the Old City. Moslems visit the Haram esh-Sherif, a sacred enclosure, with the Dome of the Rock or Mosque of Omar (built on the old Mt. Moriah) and the Mosque of Aksa. Part of the wall of the Haram is believed to be made from stones from Solomon's Temple; this, the Wailing Wall, is sacred to Jews. Christians revere especially the Church of the Holy Sepulcher which stands on the traditional site of Calvary. The Old City is surrounded by a wall built by Suleiman I (1542). E of the Old City is the valley of Kidron, across which lie the Garden of Gethsemane and the Mt. of Olives; N is Mt. Scopus, with Hadassah Medical Center, the Natl. Library, and Hebrew Univ. New City (W) is political and economic center, with government buildings, schools, Palestine Archaeological Museum, monasteries, and synagogues. Jerusalem is rich in bold Old and New Testament associations. Churches and shrines marking sites connected with biblical and other holy persons are innumerable. City dates back to at least 15th cent. B.C. It may be the Salem mentioned in Gen. 14.18. David made it his capital after taking it from the Jebusites; Solomon glorified it with his Temple; here Judah's kings clung to their waning power; many of the great Hebrew prophets spoke in its streets. It fell in 586 B.C. to Babylonia; was rebuilt by Ezra and Nehemiah after return from exile. It was city of the Maccabees and of the Herods. Early Roman emperors were enemies of the Holy City; Titus razed its buildings and destroyed its

Temple (A.D. 70). After the revolt of Bar Kokba the Romans made Jerusalem a pagan shrine called Aelia Capitolina (134). With the conversion of Constantine to Christianity, Jerusalem underwent a revival. His mother, St. Helena, is said to have discovered and restored many of its holy places. Moslems believe city was visited by Mohammed, treated it well when it fell into their hands in 637, made it their chief shrine after Mecca; but the molesting of Christian pilgrims and destruction of the Church of the Holy Sepulcher by fanatics led to the Crusades. Jerusalem fell to Crusaders in 1099 (see JERUSALEM, LATIN KINGDOM OF). In 1187, Moslems, led by Saladin, again took the city, and it was to remain almost constantly under Moslem control until it was taken by the British in World War I; it was later the center of British mandate of Palestine. When the mandate ended, both Arabs and Jews were determined to control Jerusalem. After considerable fighting, the Jews surrendered the Old City but held the New.

Jerusalem, Latin Kingdom of, state created in Syria and Palestine by leaders of First Crusade after conquest of Jerusalem (1099; see CRUSADES). Organized along lines of feudal theory, it consisted of the royal domain of Jerusalem (incl. subfiefs, e.g., counties of Jaffa and Ashkelon, lordships of Krak and Montreal), and of the fiefs of Antioch, Edessa, and Tripoli, over which the kings held only nominal overlordship. Kingship was elective (in theory); Assises of Jerusalem (the law of the country) reflected ideal feudal law. In practice, royal authority was weakened by independence of feudal lords and by rise of great military orders—KNIGHTS TEMPLARS and KNIGHTS HOSPITALERS. Internal dissensions facilitated advance of neighboring Moslems. Edessa fell 1144; Jerusalem 1187; Acre, last stronghold, 1291. Reigning kings of Jerusalem were Baldwin I, Baldwin II (house of Bouillon); Fulk, Baldwin III, Amalric I, Baldwin IV, Baldwin V (Angevin dynasty). Titular kingship passed to various princes, notably Emperor Frederick II, and later was borne by kings of Cyprus.

Jerusalem artichoke: see ARTICHOKE.

Jerusalem cherry: see NIGHTSHADE.

Jervis, John, earl of St. Vincent (jär'vĭs, jûr–), 1735–1823, British admiral. His victory over a much larger Spanish fleet off Cape St. Vincent (1797) was largely due to an unauthorized attack by Horatio Nelson. First lord of the admiralty 1801–6.

Jervis Bay (jär'vĭs), inlet of the Pacific, E New South Wales, Australia. Harbor and 28 sq. mi. of peninsula sheltering it were transferred 1915 to commonwealth for a port to be linked by rail with Canberra, 85 mi. inland.

jessamine: see JASMINE.

Jesse, father of David. Name came to symbolize the royal line and Messianic hopes involving it. Ruth 4.17–22; 1 Sam. 16.1–18; 17.12,58; 1 Chron. 2.12, 13; Isa. 11.1,10; Mat. 1.5,6; Luke 3.32. Jesus has been called Jesse's Rod and the Virgin Mary Jesse's Root. Jesus' family tree, depicted with Jesse as source, was popular subject of medieval art.

jester: see FOOL.

Jesuit: see JESUS, SOCIETY OF.

Jesuit Estates Act, adopted 1888 by Quebec legislature, partly to indemnify the Society of Jesus for Jesuit property confiscated after Pope Clement XIV had suppressed the society. It caused a violent controversy and was vetoed by the Canadian House of Commons.

Jesuit Martyrs of North America, designation for six Jesuit missionaries and two assistants who were beatified in 1925 and canonized in 1930 for having suffered martyrdom in 1648–49 at the hands of the Iroquois.

Jesuit Relations, reports by French Jesuit missionaries in New France. Important historical sources of French exploration and Indian conditions.

Jesus or **Jesus Christ.** The name *Jesus* is Greek for the

Hebrew *Joshua* [savior]; Christ is Greek translation of the Hebrew *Messiah* [anointed]. Primary sources for life of Jesus are the four Gospels of MATTHEW, MARK, LUKE, and JOHN, and the epistles of the New Testament. The apocryphal gospels (see PSEUDEPIGRAPHA) and traditional sayings ascribed to Jesus (see AGRAPHA OF JESUS) are unreliable. Scholarly analysis of life of Jesus was not extensively begun until end of 19th cent. The facts of his career are subject to question (a small group even denying his historicity). In Christian teaching, Jesus was born of Mary, wife of Joseph, a carpenter of Nazareth, who had brought his wife to Bethlehem for the Roman tax-census. The Christian era is computed (according to a 6th-cent. reckoning) to begin with Jesus' birth, A.D. 1. Date is placed several years too late; Jesus was probably born between 8 B.C. and 4 B.C. According to the Gospels, wonderful events surrounded the birth of Jesus (e.g., the Annunciation to Mary, the appearance of the heavenly host, the adoration of the shepherds and the Wise Men). Jesus lived at a critical time in Jewish history. The Jews were restive under Roman rule as administered by the corrupt house of HEROD; Judaism was under control of the Pharisees and scribes who upheld the letter of Mosaic law. The simple people of Galilee and Judaea were eager for the promised Messiah and deliverance from Roman domination. Shortly before A.D. 30, an ascetic preacher, John the Baptist, made a stir in the Jordan valley, urging people to repent and prepare for the Messiah. Among those he baptized was his cousin Jesus. Jesus went from his baptism to solitude and meditation, thence to emerge on his three-year mission. He went about as a wandering teacher, accompanied by a small band of disciples (see APOSTLE). His extraordinary powers (see MIRACLE) and his PARABLES, spoken in the language of the people instead of the pedantries of the priestly scholars, attracted great crowds. His living of the principles he taught, his denunciation of the hypocrisy of Pharisees and scribes, his preference for the company of the miserable and the oppressed, reached the hearts of the people. At the end of three years, he went with his disciples to Jerusalem for the Passover. Jerusalem was seething with unrest at this feast of Jewish independence. Jesus' arrival was marked by an outburst of Messianic enthusiasm, alarming to those in power. After Jesus had created a scene in the Temple by beating the usuring money-changers, the ruling clique decided to destroy this man whom they could see only as a revolutionary leader and violent reformer. They bribed one of his companions, JUDAS ISCARIOT, to betray him. Jesus ate a farewell supper with his disciples and went out of the city to pray in the Garden of Gethsemane. There he was arrested. He was rushed to trial before the ecclesiastical court of the Sanhedrin. His claims to be the Messiah and the Son of God convicted him of blasphemy, a crime carrying the death penalty in Jewish law. Since only the Roman governor (at this time Pontius Pilate) could order a man's death, the court, in turning Jesus over to Pilate, emphasized Jesus' claims of kingship, thus charging him with treason against Rome. Pilate tried to evade action, but he dared not brave popular opinion, which was now aroused against Jesus. He yielded and delivered Jesus to be crucified. Jesus died and was buried, deserted by all but his mother and a few friends. About three days later, some of the women visiting the tomb found it open and the body of Jesus gone. An angel told them that he had risen from the dead. Later they saw him and spoke with him; his disciples met with him, and many others as well. Here the Gospels end, but the book of Acts tells how, 40 days after the Resurrection, Jesus ascended into heaven in sight of his disciples. In orthodox theology, Jesus is God made man, the second person of the Trinity, born of Mary, a virgin; he was crucified to make atonement to God for man; he rose from the dead and ascended into heaven, and he shall come again with glory to judge the living and the dead; he founded, through his disciples, the Church to continue his work on earth. The Christian calendar revolves around Christmas (Dec. 25), the day set aside to celebrate the birth of Jesus; and Easter, with its movable feasts and fasts, commemorating the Resurrection. In Christianity, split as it is into many parts, two vital facts may be observed: the inspiring nature of the Gospels, and the consciousness of the reality of Jesus. Incidents of his life have long been the inspiration of artists in every medium of art.

Jesus. 1 Son of Sirach, author of ECCLESIASTICUS. **2** or **Jesus Justus,** Jewish convert in Rome. Col. 4.11. **3** Greek form of JOSHUA.

Jesus, Society of, religious order of the Roman Catholic Church. Its members are called Jesuits (jĕz′wĭts, jĕzh′ūĭts) and sign the initials S.J. after the names. Originally called *Compañia de Jésus* [Span.,= (military) company of Jesus], when founded (1534–39) by St. IGNATIUS OF LOYOLA (for founding, see article on him) and six companions. Ignatius drafted the rules which still govern the society. Training of those who enter the order is long and rigorous, involving much study. Jesuits have been particularly active as missionaries, as educators, and as scientists. Though not (as frequently asserted) founded to combat the Reformation, Jesuits were active leaders in the Catholic REFORM, laboring with some success to convert Protestants in S and W Germany, France, Hungary, and Poland in 16th and 17th cent. They also made daring attempts to reconvert England. From their beginning Jesuits have always been active in foreign missions. One of the original band, St. FRANCIS XAVIER, went as far afield as the Far East. In India, China, and Japan, Jesuit missions flourished long, and though many were washed away in blood, the Jesuits did estab. Catholicism in the Orient. They were also active in the New World, not only creating the much-discussed reductions (Indian settlements) in Paraguay but also working in all parts of Latin America and in New France (Canada). From Quebec the "black robes" went out into the wilderness of present Canada and N U.S. to convert the Indians, even penetrating as far as Oregon. Six Jesuits and two of their lay helpers, murdered by the Indians in the 1640s, became the Jesuit Martyrs of North America (most celebrated are Isaac Jogues and Jean Brébeuf). Their zeal and solidarity and their peculiar devotion to the Holy See aroused the jealousy of some other orders and the hatred and fear of some ecclesiastical vested interests and especially of the absolute monarchs of Catholic Europe, who wanted to be free of all papal influence. The pope's power was weakened, and by 1700 the Jesuits were his chief support. They were the object of violent and concerted abuse. Some color was lent to charges of commercialism by a notable scandal. The accusations that they were given to intrigue and were lax in receiving penitents back into the Church have been hotly debated. Some of the claims against them were scurrilously false and were perhaps the basis for ridiculous statements repeated even today (e.g., that they have a secret constitution; that there are secret male and female affiliates; that they have special privileges; that they accept the doctrine that "the end justifies the means"; that they have revolutionary intentions). The princes had their way. The order was suppressed in Portugal 1759, in France 1764, in Spanish dominions 1767, and Clement XIV was compelled to dissolve the order in 1773. Frederick the Great and Catherine the Great refused to publish the papal brief, so the order continued in Russia and Prussia. It was reestablished as a world order on general demand in 1814 and has since resumed and expanded its missionary and educational work. There are notable Jesuit schools and colleges in the U.S. (e.g., Georgetown, Fordham, St. Louis universities).

Jesus College: see CAMBRIDGE UNIVERSITY; OXFORD UNIVERSITY.

Jesus Island: see ÎLE JÉSUS, Que.

jet, black variety of lignite coal. Compact, takes good polish, and is easily worked into beads and other ornaments. Yorkshire, England, is chief source.

Jethou: see CHANNEL ISLANDS.

Jethro (jĕth'rō), Midianite priest of Sinai; father-in-law of Moses. Ex. 2.21; 3.1; 4.18; 18. Reuel: Ex. 2.18; Raguel: Num. 10.29. Hobab: Judges 4.11.

jet propulsion, forward "thrust" resulting from rearward expulsion of mass of gas under high pressure generated by combustion in jet engine. Any apparatus using jet propulsion is essentially a reaction motor based on Newton's law that every action has an equal and contrary reaction. Two general types of reaction machines are rocket or chemical-fuel motor and airstream or turbojet engine, based on gas turbine engine. First flight entirely by rocket power was made in Germany (1929). R. H. Goddard, an American, developed liquid fuels for rockets. A jet engine for powering full-size airplane was developed (1939) by Frank Whittle, an Englishman. Various types of engines and augmentation devices later used and supersonic speeds were reached. See *ill.,* p. 19.

jetsam: see FLOTSAM, JETSAM, AND LIGAN.

Jevons, William Stanley (jĕ'vŭnz), 1835–82, English economist and logician. He developed the theory, mathematically demonstrated, that value is determined by utility. Wrote *The Theory of Political Economy* (1871), *The Principles of Science* (1874).

Jewel Cave National Monument: see NATIONAL PARKS AND MONUMENTS (table).

jewelweed: see IMPATIENS.

Jewett, Charles Coffin, 1816–68, American librarian. Worked out catalogue rules internationally used.

Jewett, Sarah Orne, 1849–1909, American novelist, b. Maine. Her stories and sketches of the Maine coast (as in *The Country of the Pointed Firs,* 1896) are delicate local-color pieces.

Jewett City, Conn.: see GRISWOLD.

Jewish Autonomous Oblast, RSFSR: see BIROBIDZHAN.

Jewish literature: see HEBREW LITERATURE; YIDDISH.

Jewish music. According to the Bible, music making was common among the ancient Jews on all important occasions. Instruments mentioned include the *kinnor* (a lyre), the *ugab* (a flute?), and the *shofar* (a ram's horn; still used today). With the formation of the kingdom of Israel, music was systematized with a professional group of musicians in the Temple. New instruments, apparently including varieties of harp, oboe, and organ appeared. Biblical passages were chanted on set modal patterns. After the destruction of the Temple (A.D. 70), instrumental music disappeared, but some of the chants survive today. Jewish music influenced early Christian plain song. With the growing importance of the synagogue came the rise of the cantor, a singer who performed the solo chants in the service. Among North European Jews in the Middle Ages, traditional melodies were corrupted under the influence of German folk song. During the Renaissance, there was a reintroduction of ancient elements by Oriental Jews. Cantors returned to improvisation in the Oriental modes and developed a very distinct type of coloratura. In the 17th cent., this art was found all over Europe. Instruments, especially the organ, were reintroduced into the synagogue. In the early 19th cent., an extreme reform movement eliminated the cantor and set traditional Jewish hymns to the tunes of Protestant chorales. A more moderate reform restored the cantor, returned to traditional chants, but at the same time made use of new music written by Jewish composers for the synagogue. Ernest BLOCH is the leading figure in the attempt to create a Jewish national music.

Jews [from Judah], descendants of the tribes of ISRAEL, adherents of the religion of JUDAISM. Before the Second World War they numbered c.16,000,000; between 5,000,000 and 6,000,000 were massacred during the war. More than half the Jews speak YIDDISH. According to the OLD TESTAMENT, their ancestor was Terah of Ur of the Chaldees, from whom descended the patriarchs Abraham, Isaac, and Jacob. Ancient Jewish history begins with their settlement in Egypt, as farmers, many centuries before Christ. Moses led the persecuted group out of Egypt; at Mt. Sinai he gave them the Decalogue. The Jews then conquered Canaan and united under Saul, their first king, who was defeated by the Philistines. The next king, David, conquered the enemies of the Jews. His son, King Solomon, built the first temple (see TEMPLE). Disruption followed, and the two kingdoms then formed, Israel and Judah, warred during much of the following two centuries (935 B.C.–725 B.C.). In 722 the Israelites (the LOST TRIBES) were exiled. The Temple, destroyed in 586 B.C. by the Babylonians, was rebuilt in 516 B.C. The Jews regained their independence under the MACCABEES, but in 70 A.D. Jerusalem was destroyed by the Romans. With the fall of the Roman Empire, Jews appeared in Western Europe, where from the 9th to the 12th cent. they enjoyed a golden age of literary activity (notably in Spain). From the time of the Crusades until the 19th cent. the Jews were persecuted and driven from many countries. The rise of capitalism improved the conditions of the Jews throughout Europe, as did the revolutionary movements of the 19th cent. The emancipation of the Jews brought forth two opposed movements: cultural assimilation, begun by Moses MENDELSSOHN, and ZIONISM, founded by Theodor HERZL in 1896. A wave of persecution starting in Russia (1881) and moving westward to France slowly abated until 1933, when with the rise to power in Germany of the Nazis, persecution of the Jews became violent. After the massacres of the Second World War, many sought refuge in Palestine, where a Jewish state (see ISRAEL) was established in 1948.

Jex-Blake, Sophia, 1840–1912, English physician, active in opening medical profession to women.

Jezebel (jĕ'–), d. c.846 B.C., wife of AHAB, mother of Ahaziah **1,** Jehoram **1,** and Athaliah. Willful and cruel, she led Israel into idolatry and persecuted the prophets. Killed in Jehu's coup d'état; her body thrown to the dogs. 1 Kings 16.31; 18; 21; 2 Kings 9.1–10, 30–37. Reference in Rev. 2.20 obscure.

Jezreel (jĕz'rēĕl), anc. city, Palestine, in plain of Esdraelon, between Megiddo and Jordan R.; residence of King Ahab, whose family is often called the house of Jezreel.

Jhansi (jän'sē), city (pop. 103,254), S Uttar Pradesh, India. Founded 1613 by Bundela Rajputs. Trade center. Mfg. of brassware and silk cloth.

Jhelum (jā'lŭm) anc. *Hydaspes,* river, c.500 mi. long, in Kashmir and W Pakistan; westernmost of five rivers of Punjab.

Jibuti, French Somaliland: see DJIBOUTI.

Jidda (jĭ'dù) or **Jedda** (jĕ'dù), city (pop. 60,000), Hejaz, Saudi Arabia, on Red Sea; port of Mecca. Handles huge influx of pilgrims. Just outside is reputed tomb of Eve.

jigger: see CHIGOE.

Jiménez, Juan Ramón (hwän' rämōn' hēmä'näth), 1881–, Spanish lyric poet. Simplicity of style and obscure depths of meaning make his poems (as in *Diario de un poeta recien casado,* 1917) among the most admired in Spanish literature.

Jiménez de Cisneros, Francisco (fränthē'skō hēmä'näth dä thēsnä'rōs), 1436–1517, Spanish cardinal and statesman. Archbishop of Toledo from 1495; inquisitor general from 1507. Led expedition which captured Oran (1509); founded Univ. of Alcalá; had Polyglot Bible compiled. Became regent on death of Ferdinand V (1516) but was summarily dismissed by Charles I (Emperor Charles V). Formerly spelled Ximenes.

Jiménez de Quesada, Gonzalo (gŏnthä'lō hēmä'nāth dä käsä'dhä), c.1499–1579, Spanish conquistador in Colombia. Setting out 1536 to explore Magdalena R. in search of El Dorado, he defeated Chibchas; founded Bogotá 1538. His claims, disputed by Federmann and Benalcázar, were verified by Spain 1550. A later expedition (to Orinoco R., 1569) was disastrous.

Jimson weed or **Jamestown weed,** coarse tropical annual plant (*Datura stramonium*) naturalized in North America. It has rank smelling foliage, trumpet-shaped white or purple flowers, and spiny fruits. Contains a narcotic poison similar to belladonna.

Jinnah, Mahomed Ali (mùhŏ'mĭd ä'lē jĭ'nù), 1876–1948, founder of Pakistan. Admitted to the bar in England 1896, returned to India to practice law. First supported INDIAN NATIONAL CONGRESS and advocated Hindu-Moslem unity, but after 1934 (when he won control of MOSLEM LEAGUE) he agitated for separate state of Pakistan. Gained power during World War II by supporting the British; forced Congress to accept partition of India (1947). Became first governor general of dominion.

jinni (jĭnē'), plural **jinn** (jĭn), in Arabic folklore and in Moslem literature, creature like man but having certain supernatural powers, especially those of changing size and shape. Jinn may be good or evil. They appear constantly in the *Thousand and One Nights.* Also spelled genie.

jiujitsu or **jiujutsu:** see JUJUTSU.

Joab (jō'ăb), David's nephew, commander of his armies. An able administrator but often cruel, as in his killing of Abner, Absalom, and Amasa. Executed by Solomon for supporting Adonijah. 2 Sam. 2.12–32; 3.22–31; 8.16; 10.7–14; 11; 12.26; 14; 18; 19.1, 5–7; 20.7–23; 24.1–9; 1 Kings 1; 2.5, 6, 28–34.

Joachim, Saint (jō'ûkĭm), in tradition, father of the Virgin, husband of St. ANNE.

Joachim, Joseph (yō'äkēm), 1831–1907, Hungarian violinist; friend of Mendelssohn, Brahms, and Schumann. Considered a master interpreter of great violin works, he composed cadenzas for violin concertos of Beethoven and Brahms.

Joachimsthal, Czechoslovakia: see JACHYMOV.

Joad, C(yril) E(dwin) M(itchinson) (jōd), 1891–1953, English rationalist philosopher.

Joahaz: see JEHOAHAZ.

Joanes, Vicente: see MACIP, VICENTE JUAN.

Joanna (jōä'nù), queens of Naples. **Joanna I,** 1326–82 (reigned 1343–81), was also countess of Provence. The murder of her husband, Andrew of Hungary (probably with her complicity) in 1345 brought recurrent warfare with Andrew's brother, Louis I of Hungary. She successively adopted Charles of Durazzo (see CHARLES III of Naples) and Louis of Anjou (see LOUIS I of Naples) as heirs. Charles imprisoned her and probably had her murdered. **Joanna II,** 1371–1435, succeeded her brother Lancelot in 1414. Her reign was beset by court intrigues and by rival claims of LOUIS III of Naples. Her successive adoptions as heirs of ALFONSO V of Aragon, Louis, and RENÉ of Anjou plunged Naples into warfare from which Alfonso emerged victorious after her death.

Joanna (the Mad), 1479–1555, Spanish queen of Castile and Leon (1504–5); daughter of Ferdinand V and Isabella I. Married PHILIP I, after whose death her insanity became apparent. She never ruled, her father being regent 1504–6; Philip I, 1506–7; her father again, 1507–16. Her son, Emperor Charles V, governed as joint ruler 1516–55.

Joanna, in Bible, wife of Herod's steward, follower of Jesus. One of those who visited Jesus' tomb and found it empty. Luke 8.3; 24.10.

Joan of Arc, 1412?–1431, French saint and national heroine, called the Maid of Orléans; daughter of a farmer of Domrémy, in Lorraine. She early began to hear "voices"—of St. Michael, St. Catherine, and St. Margaret—exhorting her to bear aid to the dauphin,

CHARLES VII, then kept from his throne by the English. After many rebuffs, she was authorized by Robert de Baudricourt, military governor of Vaucouleurs, to journey to the dauphin (1429). She adopted male attire, which she was to keep till her last days. Meeting the dauphin at Chinon, she convinced him of her mission. After some more delays she was given troops, succeeded in lifting the siege of ORLÉANS, took other places along the Loire, routed the English at PATAY, and persuaded Charles to march on Rheims, where he was crowned, with Joan standing beside him (1429). She was eager to push her victories, which had turned the tide of the Hundred Years War, but the king's advisers and his indolence inclined him to negotiations with Burgundy, England's ally. After besieging Paris without success (1429), Joan in 1430 went to relieve Compiègne but was captured by the Burgundians who later sold her to the English. An irregular trial before an ecclesiastic court at Rouen, headed by Pierre CAUCHON, ended with her condemnation for heresy and sorcery (1431). She was burned at the stake. Rehabilitated in a new trial (1456), she was canonized in 1920. Feast: May 30.

João de Deus: see RAMOS, JOÃO DE DEUS.

João Pessoa (zhwä'õ pùsõ'ù), city (pop. 90,853), cap. of Paraíba state, NE Brazil; Atlantic port founded 1589. Exports cotton, sugar, minerals.

Joash: see JEHOASH.

Job (jōb), book of Old Testament. A dramatic dialogue concerned with problem of good and evil in the world. In prologue in heaven, plan is laid to test Job, a truly good man. Property, family, and health are taken from him. Some friends who come to "comfort" him accuse Job of some great sin; Job protests his innocence. He learns that God's judgment is beyond man's understanding. In epilogue, all that Job lost is restored to him. Ethical problem not explicitly resolved. Parts of original text may be lost, new parts added at later date.

Job's-tears, tall tropical grass (*Coix lacryma-jobi*) with bony, white or gray beadlike fruits.

Jocasta, mother of OEDIPUS.

Jocelin de Brakelond (jŏs'lĭn dù brăk'lŏnd), fl. 1200, English monk whose chronicle of Bury St. Edmunds (1173–1202) is simple, vigorous, vivid.

Jodhpur (jŏd'pōŏr) or **Marwar** (mär'wär), former princely state, part of Rajasthan, India, since 1949. Estab. in early 13th cent. by Rathor Rajputs. Placed under British protection 1818. **Jodhpur,** city (pop. 126,842), cap. of former state, was founded 1459. Site of several palaces. Trade center with light mfg.

Joel, book of Old Testament. Joel, an otherwise unknown prophet, vividly describes plague of locusts, urges people to repent. Has Messianic prophecy (2.28–32; 3). Peter used Joel as text. Acts 2.

joe-pye weed, tall North American perennial (*Eupatorium purpureum*) bearing pinkish or purple flower clusters in the autumn.

Joffre, Joseph Jacques Césaire (zhôzĕf' zhäk' säzĕr' zhô'frù), 1852–1931, marshal of France. French commander in chief in World War I until 1916; chairman of Allied War Council 1916–18. Won first battle of the Marne (1914); nearly lost Verdun (1916).

Jogjakarta (jŏg"yäkär'tä) or **Djokjakarta** (jŏk"–), town (pop. 136,646), S Java, Indonesia, at foot of Mt. Merapi. Cultural center, known for artistic life and handicrafts. After World War II it was cap. of original republic of INDONESIA (1945–50).

Jogues, Isaac (ēzäk' zhôg'), 1607–46, Jesuit missionary and martyr in New World, b. France. Discovered L. George (1646). Murdered by hostile Mohawks. Canonized in 1930.

Johanan ben Zaccai (jōhä'nùn bĕn zä'kāī), Palestinian rabbi, contemporary of the apostles. Preserved Jewish law and the ritual of temple worship.

Johannesburg (jōhä'nĭsbûrg), city (pop. 603,470), S Transvaal, South Africa; founded 1886. Largest city of South Africa, industrial center of the WITWATERS-

RAND. Textile milling, metalworking. Seat of a university.

John, Saint, one of the Twelve Apostles; brother of James, son of Zebedee. Accepted since ancient times as author of the fourth Gospel, three epistles, and Revelation. Was apparently the disciple "whom Jesus loved" (John 13.24; 19.26). As Jesus was dying, He committed His mother to John's care. According to 2d-cent. authorities John was exiled for a time on Patmos (Rev. 1.9), died at Ephesus c.100. Variously called St. John the Evangelist, St. John the Divine (i.e., theologian), and the Beloved Disciple. Feast: Dec. 27.

John VIII, d. 882, pope (872–82). Opposed St. Ignatius of Constantinople and recognized Photius as patriarch, thus temporarily reconciling E and W churches. Crowned Charles II (the Bald) and helped Charles III (the Fat) to the imperial throne.

John XII, c.937–964, pope (955–64), a Roman. Called in Otto I to help him against Berengarius, king of Italy, and was confirmed in the Patrimony of St. Peter, but shortly turned against Otto. Otto conquered Rome and called a synod to depose John and elect an antipope, Leo VIII. John retook Rome (964) but was soon murdered. His life was immoral, his pontificate a disgrace.

John XXI, d. 1277, pope (1276–77), a Portuguese, called Petrus Hispanus and reputed to be the author of a textbook on logic. Actually 19th canonical pope named John but called himself John XXI.

John XXII, 1244–1334, pope (1316–34), a Frenchman, chosen after a delay as successor to Clement V. He quarreled with Emperor Louis IV (who was assisted by Marsilius of Padua and William of Occam). Louis invaded Italy and set up as antipope Pietro Rainalducci, who shortly had to submit to John, but the pope's claims to authority over the empire came to nothing. Because of confused numbering also called John XXI.

John XXIII, antipope: see COSSA, BALDASSARRE.

John, Byzantine emperors. **John I** (Tzimisces), c.925–976, gained the throne by murdering Nicephorus II (969), whose anticlerical legislation he revoked. Extended Byzantine power against Russians and Arabs. **John II** (Comnenus), 1088–1143, succeeded his father Alexius I in 1118, despite the intrigues of his sister Anna Comnena to put her husband on the throne. He unsuccessfully tried to cancel Venetian commercial privileges. **John III** (John Ducas Vatatzes), d. 1254, emperor of Nicaea (1222–54), took Salonica from Latin Empire of Constantinople (1246), thus nearly completing reunion of dismembered Byzantine Empire. **John V** (Palaeologus), 1332–91, reigned 1341–76 and 1379–91. His throne was usurped during his minority by John VI and from 1376 to 1379 by his son Andronicus IV. **John VI** (Cantacuzene), c.1292–1383, usurped throne of John V (1341–55). Called Ottoman Turks to his aid and allowed Stephen Dushan to build up Serbian empire. Retired to a monastery. **John VIII** (Palaeologus), 1390–1448, reigned 1425–48. Sought to secure Western aid against Turks by agreeing to union of Eastern and Western churches at Council of Florence (1439).

John, kings of Aragon and counts of Barcelona. **John I,** 1350–95, reigned 1387–95. Patron of learning; held brilliant court. **John II,** 1397–1479, reigned 1458–79. Also inherited Sicily (1458). Married Blanche, heiress of Navarre (1425). After her death (1442) conflict broke out between John and his son, CHARLES OF VIANA, whose death in 1461 was followed by further troubles in Catalonia until 1472. John's son Ferdinand II (Ferdinand V of Castile) inherited Aragon, Catalonia, Sicily; his son-in-law, the count of Foix, inherited Navarre.

John, 1167?–1216, king of England (1199–1216), youngest son of Henry II. Supported his brother, Richard I, against his father in 1189. While Richard was on the Third Crusade, he had himself declared heir and conspired to keep Richard in captivity. Succeeded Richard to exclusion of his nephew, Arthur I of Brittany. Arthur's supporters, aided by PHILIP II of France, revolted and John was finally forced to surrender most of his French possessions. Excommunicated and deposed by INNOCENT III, he surrendered England to the pope and received it back as fief (1213). Barons, intensely opposed to John, united and forced him to sign (1215) the MAGNA CARTA. Tyrannical, treacherous, and cruel, he is the subject of one of Shakspere's chronicle plays.

John, kings of France. **John I** (the Posthumous), 1316, son of Louis X, lived only a few days. **John II** (the Good), 1319–64. His reign (1350–64) was troubled by HUNDRED YEARS WAR and internal disturbances, notably his quarrels with CHARLES II of Navarre and the JACQUERIE. Captured by English at Poitiers (1356), he was released by Treaty of BRÉTIGNY (1360). In 1364 one of hostages who had taken his place in England escaped; John, to save his honor, returned to England, where he died. During his absences, his son (later CHARLES V) was regent.

John, kings of Hungary. **John I** (John Zapolya), 1487–1540; son of Stephen ZAPOLYA. Voivode of Transylvania (1511–26), he was chosen king by the Hungarian nobles after Louis II's death at MOHACS (1526). Louis's brother-in-law, Ferdinand of Austria (later Emperor FERDINAND I) challenged the succession in a series of campaigns, but in 1529 Sultan Suleiman I intervened and set up John as puppet king. John was succeeded by son **John II** (John Sigismund Zapolya), 1540–71. Suleiman, on pretext of protecting the infant's interests, invaded Hungary in 1541 (thus beginning 150 years of Turkish rule) and made John prince of Transylvania. Deposed by the pro-Austrian party in Transylvania (1551), John was recalled in 1556 on Turkish pressure. Austro-Turkish peace of 1562 left him in possession of Transylvania, with the rest of Hungary divided between Austria and Turkey. In 1664 the Transylvanian diet estab. Calvinism as state religion.

John, kings of Poland. **John II** (John Casimir), 1609–72. His reign (1648–68) is known in Polish history as the Deluge. Cossack rebellion under CHMIELNICKI led to war with Russia (1654–67) and cession of E Ukraine. Invasion by CHARLES X of Sweden (1655) was checked by miracle of CZESTOCHOWA, but in Peace of OLIVA John had to cede N Livonia to Sweden and to grant Elector Frederick William of Brandenburg full sovereignty over Prussia, in exchange for aid against Sweden. Abdicated in 1668; retired to a French monastery. **John III** (John Sobieski), 1624–96, reigned 1674–96. He briefly restored Polish prestige when, in 1683, he led his forces to relieve Vienna from Turkish siege. Pursuing the Turks into Hungary, he formed a Holy League with the pope, Emperor Leopold I, and Venice (1684), but he failed to wrest Moldavia and Walachia from Turkey. His death marked virtual end of Polish independence.

John, kings of Portugal. **John I** (the Great), 1357?–1433, illegitimate son of Pedro I, grand master of the Knights of Aviz. When his half-brother Fredinand I died (1383), Portugal was ruled by a regency for Ferdinand's daughter Beatrice, wife of John I of Castile. John of Aviz cooperated with Nun' Álvares Pereira in the national revolt against Spanish hegemony and in 1385 was elected king. The great victory of Aljubarrota (1385) assured Portuguese independence. John's reign, one of the most glorious in Portuguese history, was marked by an alliance with England, the beginnings of Portuguese colonial and maritime expansion, the capture of Ceuta from the Moors (1415), and the flowering of Portuguese literature. **John II** (the Perfect), 1455–95, reigned 1481–95. Asserted royal supremacy over nobles; fostered exploration (but refused to aid Columbus); signed Treaty of TORDESILLAS with Spain. Patron of Renaissance art and learning. **John III** (the Fortunate), 1502–57. His reign (1521–57) marked the height of the Portuguese empire but saw the beginning of decadence in Portugal itself. He introduced the Inquisition; imported African slaves. **John IV,** d. 1656, duke of Braganza, descended from Manuel I and in illegitimate line from John I, became king in 1640 when Portugal cast off Spanish rule. Founder of Braganza dynasty. **John V** (the Magnanimous), 1689–1750, reigned 1706–50. **John VI,** 1769–1826, became regent for his insane mother, Maria I, in 1799. Joined second coalition against France; defeated, he accepted humiliating Treaty of Badajoz (1801). Fled to Brazil when French attacked Portugal (1807); succeeded to throne 1816; returned to Portugal 1820. In 1824, after a turbulent reign, he retired to Brazil, which had become an independent empire under his son PEDRO I, leaving Portugal under regency of his daughter Isabella.

John, Spanish kings of Castile and Leon. **John I,** 1358–90, reigned 1379–90; son of HENRY II. Sought to unite Portugal and Castile; defeated by Portuguese at Aljubarrota (1385). JOHN OF GAUNT challenged his succession, but made peace 1388 and married his daughter to John's heir. **John II,** 1405–54, reigned 1406–54. Left government to Alvaro de LUNA. Notable as a patron of literature.

John, in Bible. **1** See JOHN, SAINT. **2** See JOHN THE BAPTIST. **3** See MARK, SAINT. **4** See MACCABEES.

John, Augustus (Edwin), 1879–, British painter and etcher, b. Wales. A leading portrait painter.

John, epistles of New Testament, called First, Second, and Third John; ascribed to St. John the Apostle. 1 John is homily on blending of mystical and practical religion. Discusses God as light (1.5–2.28), God as righteousness (2.29–4.6), God as love (4.7–5.12). 2 John, shortest book of Bible, warns against false teachers who deny historical reality of Jesus. 3 John is protest against a certain church leader's failure to receive teaching missionaries.

John, Gospel according to Saint, book of New Testament, traditionally ascribed to John the Apostle. A biography of Jesus in essay form, its aim is to show that Jesus is a vital force in the world now and forever and that He lived on earth in order to reveal Himself to men in the flesh. The acts of Jesus as a human being introduce discourses on His mystical nature. Thus, the feeding of the multitude is told, and following is sermon on the Bread of Life. Book begins with the famous philosophical passage identifying Jesus as the Word (see LOGOS). There follow two main sections, the ministry of Jesus (1.19–12.50) and the Passion and Resurrection (13–21). Unique position of Jesus Christ in Christian theology as God and man, which involves dogmas of the Trinity, the Incarnation, and the Atonement, is first enunciated in this Gospel.

John Baptist de la Salle, Saint (säl), 1651–1719, French educator. At Rheims he formed the first order devoted solely to Christian education, Brothers of the Christian Schools (Christian Brothers; 1684). In 1685 he founded first normal school at Rheims to train his teachers. Name in French: Jean Baptiste de la Salle. Feast: May 15.

John Bosco, Saint, 1815–88, Italian priest at Turin, founder (1841) of the Salesian order for work with boys and in foreign missions, and of Daughters of Mary Auxiliatrix, for work with girls.

John B. Stetson University: see DE LAND, Fla.

John Capistran, Saint (kŭpĭ'strŭn), 1385?–1456, Italian preacher, a Franciscan. Preached against the Hussites (1451) and led a wing of Hunyadi's army in great victory of Belgrade (1456).

John Carter Brown Library: see BROWN, JOHN CARTER.

John Chrysostom, Saint (krĭ'sŭstŭm, krĭsŏ'stŭm) [Gr.,= golden-mouth], c.347–407, Doctor of the Church, greatest Greek Father. Made patriarch of Constantinople (398), he undertook reforms and defied the imperial powers. Illegally deposed by Empress Eudoxia and Theophilus, bishop of Alexandria (403), he was recalled when people rioted. Later he was exiled by Arcadius. St. John's many authoritative homilies and commentaries, in excellent Greek style, had great influence.

John Crerar Library: see CRERAR, JOHN.

John Damascene, Saint: see JOHN OF DAMASCUS, SAINT.

John Day, river, NE Oregon, rising in Blue Mts. and flowing 281 mi. W and N to Columbia R. near The Dalles. Used for power and irrigation.

John Fisher, Saint: see FISHER, JOHN.

John Frederick I (the Magnanimous), 1503–54, elector of Saxony (1532–47). Divided his lands with his brother Ernest (1542). A member of Schmalkaldic League, he was captured by Emperor Charles V at Mühlberg (1547) and had to renounce electorate in favor of his cousin MAURICE of Saxony.

John Henry, legendary Negro strong man, celebrated in Southern American Negro ballads and "tall tales."

John Mark: see MARK, SAINT.

John Maurice of Nassau, 1604–79, Dutch general; grandnephew of William the Silent. As governor of Brazil (1636–43), for the Dutch West India Company, he conquered NE Brazil from Portuguese, built up state of Pernambuco, made broad plans for development. Subsequently held commands in Thirty Years War and Dutch Wars. His residence at the Hague is the celebrated Mauritshuis.

Johnny Appleseed: see CHAPMAN, JOHN.

John of Austria, 1547?–1578, Spanish admiral and general; natural son of Emperor Charles V. Won decisive naval victory against Turks at LEPANTO. As governor general of Netherlands (1576–78) Don John fought rebels with inconclusive success.

John of Austria, 1629–79, natural son of Philip IV of Spain. While governor of the Netherlands, he was defeated by French in battle of the Dunes (1658). Took over regency for Charles II in 1677.

John of Brienne (brēĕn'), c.1148–1237, French crusader. Became, through marriage, titular king of Jerusalem (1210); captured Damietta in Fifth Crusade (1219); became regent for the Latin emperor, Baldwin II (1228); defended Constantinople against Greeks and Bulgars (1236). Father-in-law of Frederick II.

John of Damascus, Saint, or **Saint John Damascene** (dä'mŭsĕn), c.675–749, Syrian theologian, Doctor of the Church. Reared at court of the caliph in Damascus, he entered a Palestinian monastery (c.726) and spent most of his life in writing against iconoclasm and defending orthodoxy. *The Fountain of Wisdom* is his theological masterpiece.

John of Gaunt, 1340–99, duke of Lancaster; fourth son of Edward III of England. By his first marriage (see LANCASTER, HOUSE of) he became one of most influential nobles in England. Served under his brother, Edward the Black Prince, in Hundred Years War. Aided Peter the Cruel of Castile and married his daughter. As viceroy for senile Edward III he espoused cause of court party and, for a time, ruled England. Fought (1386–88) for his claim to throne of Castile against John I. Helped keep peace between Richard II and hostile barons. His eldest son became Henry IV. By his third marriage, he was ancestor of the house of Tudor. Patron of Chaucer.

John of Lancaster, 1389–1435, duke of Bedford; son of Henry IV of England and brother of Henry V. Made protector of Henry VI (1422), he devoted himself to English affairs in France.

John of Leiden, c.1509–1536, Dutch Anabaptist leader. In revolt in Münster (1534) he set up theocracy and was leader of a communistic, chaotic state until in 1535 Anabaptists were ousted and their leaders tortured and executed.

John of Luxemburg, 1296–1346, king of Bohemia (1310–46); son of Emperor Henry VII. Was elected king after marriage with Elizabeth, daughter of Wenceslaus II of Bohemia. The blind king is best remembered for his gallant death at Crécy, where he fought as ally of Philip VI of France; he commanded that his charger be led into the thick of the fight. His son was Emperor Charles IV.

John of Procida (prō′chĕdä), c.1210–c.1298, Italian Ghibelline conspirator. Prepared uprising of SICILIAN VESPERS (1282).

John of Salisbury (sôlz–), c.1115–1180, English scholastic philosopher. Studied at Paris and traveled much. Was secretary to St. Thomas à Becket, and later bishop of Chartres (1176–80). His *Metalogicus* sums up the scholastic knowledge of his time; his *Polycraticus* urged independence of church and state.

John of the Cross, Saint, Span. *Juan de la Cruz,* 1542–91, Spanish mystic, founder of the Discalced Carmelites, friend of St. Theresa of Ávila. His mystical poetry and treatises have had great influence on modern Catholicism. Feast: Nov. 24.

John o' Groats House, locality in Caithness, Scotland; often erroneously named as N point of Scotland. House, now gone, was supposedly built by a Dutchman in the 16th cent.

John Scotus: see DUNS SCOTUS; ERIGENA.

Johns Hopkins University, at Baltimore, Md.; nonsectarian, partly coed.; chartered 1867, opened 1876 with bequest from Johns Hopkins. Its medical school, connected with the noted hospital, is one of world's largest. Has continually excelled in laboratory and research work; institute for cooperative research estab. 1946. Had first university press in U.S.

Johnson, Andrew, 1808–75, 17th President of the United States (1865–69). Completely self-educated. A tailor in Greeneville, Tenn. U.S. Representative (1843–53); governor of Tenn. (1853–57); U.S. Senator (1857–62). Interested in securing legislation providing Western land for laboring class; as a war Democrat he vigorously supported Lincoln. U.S. Vice President (1865). As President he was denounced by radical Republicans for his RECONSTRUCTION program. After passage over his veto of bill extending life of FREEDMEN'S BUREAU, his administration was the record of one humiliation after another. His efforts to remove from office E. M. STANTON, whom he rightly suspected of conspiring with congressional leaders, led to impeachment proceedings. On Feb. 24, 1868, the House passed a resolution of impeachment against him even before it adopted 11 articles detailing the reasons for it. Most important of the charges, which were purely political, was that he had violated the TENURE OF OFFICE ACT in the Stanton affair. By a narrow margin the Senate failed to convict. Important achievement of his administration in foreign affairs was purchase of Alaska (1867), negotiated by W. H. Seward. Again U.S. Senator in 1875.

Johnson, Eastman, 1824–1906, American portrait and genre painter. Influenced by Dutch masters.

Johnson, Edward, 1884–, Canadian operatic tenor. He sang at the Metropolitan Opera, New York, after 1922, and was its general manager 1935–50.

Johnson, E(mily) Pauline, 1862–1913, Canadian poet. Her poems of Indian life were highly popular.

Johnson, Guy: see JOHNSON, SIR WILLIAM.

Johnson, Herschel Vespasian, 1812–80, American statesman. U.S. Senator from Ga. (1848–49). Nominated by National Democrats as Vice President (1860). Opposed secession of Ga. in 1861, but in Confederate senate he upheld states' rights policies.

Johnson, Hiram (Warren), 1866–1945, American political leader, U.S. Senator from Calif. (1917–45). A founder of Progressive party; its candidate for Vice President in 1912. A Republican supporter of F. D. Roosevelt in 1932. He was a consistent isolationist and opponent of the League of Nations.

Johnson, Hugh (Samuel), 1882–1942, American army officer, government administrator. Supervised World War I draft. Head of National Recovery Administration (1933–34).

Johnson, Jack (John Arthur Johnson), 1876–1946, American boxer. Defeated Tommy Burns (1908), claimed world's heavyweight championship. Johnson definitely won title by knocking out James J. Jeffries (1910), lost championship to Jess Willard (1915).

Johnson, James Weldon, 1871–1938, American author, founder of the National Association for the Advancement of Colored People. Among his works are *Autobiography of an Ex-Colored Man* (fictional, 1912) and *God's Trombones* (Negro sermons in verse, 1927); *Along This Way* (autobiography, 1933). His brother, **(John) Rosamond Johnson,** 1873–, is the composer of several hundred songs, including *Lift Every Voice and Sing* (for which J. W. Johnson wrote the words). His *Rolling Along in Song* (1937) is an anthology of American Negro songs.

Johnson, Sir John: see JOHNSON, SIR WILLIAM.

Johnson, Martin Elmer, 1884–1937, American explorer and author. Photographed wildlife and native tribes on expeditions to South Sea Isls., Borneo, and particularly Africa. His wife, **Osa Helen (Leighty) Johnson,** 1894–1953, was his companion on all expeditions and co-author of accounts of their adventures.

Johnson, Reverdy, 1796–1876, American lawyer and statesman. One of ablest constitutional lawyers of his day. U.S. Senator from Md. (1845–49, 1863–68). U.S. Attorney General (1849–50). Opposed secession. Minister to Great Britain (1868–69).

Johnson, Richard Mentor, 1781–1850, Vice President of the United States (1837–41). U.S. Representative from Ky. (1807–19, 1829–37); U.S. Senator (1819–29). Elected Vice President by U.S. Senate.

Johnson, Rosamond: see JOHNSON, JAMES WELDON.

Johnson, Samuel, 1696–1772, American clergyman, educator, and philosopher. He was first president (1756–63) of King's Col. (now Columbia Univ.). His son, **William Samuel Johnson,** 1727–1819, was a statesman and also president of Columbia Col. (1787–1800). Active in political affairs in Conn.; representative at Continental Congress (1784–87). U.S. Senator (1789–91).

Johnson, Samuel, 1709–84, English author. His first major work was in satiric verse, *London* (1738) and *The Vanity of Human Wishes* (1749). His *Rambler* essays appeared 1750–52. Despite extreme difficulties he published in 1755 *A Dictionary of the English Language,* which won immediate fame. His "Idler" essays appeared 1758–60, and his moralizing fable *Rasselas* in 1759. In 1763 he met James BOSWELL, his future biographer, and in 1764, with Reynolds, Goldsmith, Burke, and others he formed his famous "Club." In 1765 began his long friendship with Mr. and Mrs. Henry Thrale. He published in 1765 an edition of Shakspere (with preface and notes still highly valued). After a tour of Hebrides appeared *A Journey to the Western Islands of Scotland* (1775). Last major work was *Lives of the Poets* (1779–81), full of personal but illuminating criticism. His prose is ponderous, but often incisive and always distinguished; his critical judgments were often prejudiced, but always shrewd and interesting. Johnson was dictator of literary taste in London and, because of his literary judgment and his integrity, the dominating literary figure of his age.

Johnson, Walter (Perry), 1887–1946, American baseball pitcher. Right-handed Washington Senator ace, acknowledged fastest hurler in baseball history, he won 414, lost 276 in 21 major-league seasons. His major-league records include most shutouts (113), most strikeouts (3,497), most consecutive scoreless innings pitched (56).

Johnson, Sir William, 1715–74, British colonial leader in America, b. Ireland. Influence over Indians made him a key figure in French and Indian Wars and in control of land afterwards. Founded Johnstown, N.Y. (1762). His son, **Sir John Johnson,** 1742–1830, was a Loyalist leader in American Revolution. Failed in plan to organize settlers and Indians of Mohawk region against patriots. Served in Saratoga campaign. **Guy Johnson,** c.1740–1788, Loyalist leader in colonial N.Y., b. Ireland, was son-in-law of Sir William Johnson. Superintendent of Indian affairs (1774–82). Directed raids against patriot frontier settlements in American Revolution.

Johnson, William Samuel: see JOHNSON, SAMUEL (1696–1772).

Johnson City. 1 Village (pop. 19,249), S N.Y., near Binghamton. With Binghamton and Endicott, forms the Triple Cities, noted for shoes. **2** City (pop. 27,864), NE Tenn., ENE of Knoxville; settled before 1800. Tobacco market and rail center (with shops), has mfg. of wood products, textiles, bricks, foundry and limestone products. VA hospital here.

Johnson C. Smith University: see CHARLOTTE, N.C.

Johnston, Albert Sidney, 1803–62, Confederate general. Commanded operations in West. Death at Shiloh (April 6, 1862) was severe loss to South.

Johnston, Joseph Eggleston, 1807–1901, Confederate general. For vital part played in first victory at Bull Run, made commander of Army of Northern Virginia. Opposed McClellan in PENINSULAR CAMPAIGN. Lost Vicksburg campaign (1863). Commanded Army of Tennessee in ATLANTA CAMPAIGN. Probably peer of R. E. Lee as defensive general.

Johnston, Mary, 1870–1936, American novelist. Among her 30-odd works, combining romance with historical accuracy, are *To Have and to Hold* (1900) and *Audrey* (1902).

Johnston, town (pop. 12,725), NE R.I., just W of Providence. Mfg. of textiles.

Johnston Island (pop. 69), central Pacific, c.715 mi. SW of Honolulu. Discovered 1807 by British, claimed 1858 by U.S. Became naval air station 1941.

Johnstown. 1 City (pop. 10,923), E central N.Y., near Mohawk R., NW of Albany. Founded 1762 by Sir William JOHNSON, whose home, Johnson Hall, remains. Glove center with mfg. of other leather goods and knitted goods. Last Revolutionary battle in N.Y. fought near by, Oct. 25, 1781. **2** City (pop. 63,232), SW Pa., on Conemaugh R. and ESE of Pittsburgh; settled 1794. Industrial area with coal mining and mfg. of iron and steel and machinery. Johnstown flood (May 31, 1889) resulted in great loss of life and property damage.

John the Baptist, Saint, fl. A.D. c.29, prophet, cousin of JESUS, son of Zacharias and Elizabeth. An ascetic, he urged people to repent and prepare for the Messiah. Venerated by Christians as forerunner of Jesus, whose coming he heralded. Jesus was baptized by him before beginning His mission. At instigation of Herodias (see HEROD) and SALOME, John was beheaded. Mat. 11.1–19; 17.11–13; Mark 6.16–19; Luke 1; 3; John 1. Birthday observed June 24; feast of his beheading, Aug. 29.

John the Fearless, 1371–1419, duke of Burgundy (1404–19); son of PHILIP THE BOLD. Captured by Turks at Nikopol (1396), but ransomed. Inherited his father's feud with Louis d'ORLÉANS, whom he had murdered (1407). During the resulting struggle between ARMAGNACS AND BURGUNDIANS he controlled Paris 1411–13 and again from 1418. Connived with English in Hundred Years War but continued to negotiate with Armagnacs. Assassinated during interview with the dauphin (later Charles VII).

Johore (jōhôr′), state (7,321 sq. mi.; pop. 738,251), S MALAYA, at S tip of Malay Peninsula opposite Singapore; cap. Johore Bahru. Largely jungle, with great rubber plantations. Iron is mined. Accepted British protectorate 1914. Ruled by a sultan, it was one of Unfederated Malay States until 1948, when it joined Federation of Malaya.

joint, in anatomy, articulation between bones. Types of joints allowing free movement are ball-and-socket (hip), hinge (knee), gliding (wrist). Joints may be immovable as in skull or permit limited movement as in spinal column.

Joinville, Jean, sire de (zhã′ sēr′ dù zhwēvēl′), 1224?–1317?, French chronicler, biographer of Louis IX (St. Louis). Went on Seventh Crusade 1248–54. His memoirs of St. Louis are invaluable record of the king, of feudal France, and of the Crusade.

Jokai, Maurice (yō′koi), 1825–1904, Hungarian novelist, a prolific, popular writer. Many novels have been translated into English (e.g., *An Hungarian Nabob; Black Diamonds*).

Jokulsa (yû′külsou), Icelandic *Jökulsá,* river, c.125 mi. long, rising in central Iceland and flowing N into Axar Fjord. DETTIFOSS waterfall is on it.

Joliet, Louis: see JOLLIET, LOUIS.

Joliet (jō′lĕĕt″), city (pop. 51,601), NE Ill., SW of Chicago and on Des Plaines R.; settled 1831. Rail center near limestone quarries and coal mines. Mfg. of wallpaper, chemicals, steel, food, and oil products.

Joliette (zhôlyĕt′), city (pop. 16,064), S Que., Canada, on L'Assumption R. and NNE of Montreal. Has steel and paper mills, mica mining, and quarrying. Seat of Seminaire de Joliette.

Joliot-Curie, Frederic (frådārēk′ zhôlyō′-kürē′), 1900–, and **Irène Joliot-Curie** (ērēn′), 1897–, French scientists. They shared 1935 Nobel Prize in Chemistry for artificial production of radioactive substances by bombarding certain elements with alpha particles.

Jolliet or **Joliet, Louis** (both: jō′lĕĕt″, jō″lĕĕt′, Fr. lwē′ zhôlyã′), 1645–1700, French explorer, b. Canada; joint discoverer with Jacques MARQUETTE of upper Mississippi R.

Jonah (jō′–), **Jonas,** or **Jona,** book of Old Testament. Tells of Jonah, a prophet, who tried to avoid his mission by sailing away. His presence on ship was a curse; a violent storm arose. Jonah agreed to be thrown overboard. He was swallowed by a fish and after three days left on shore, alive and now ready to preach. Jonah's escape from fish regarded as foreshadowing resurrection of Jesus. Story alluded to later in Bible: Mat. 12.39–41; 16.4; Luke 11.29–30.

Jonas, Greek form of Hebrew JONAH.

Jonathan (jŏn′–). **1** Oldest son of Saul, brave and gallant hero. Killed at battle of Mt. Gilboa. His close friendship with David is proverbial. 1 Sam. 13; 14.18–20; 20.16–18; 31.1,2. **2** One of the MACCABEES.

Jones, Anson, 1798–1858, last president of the Texas republic (1844–46).

Jones, Casey, 1864–1900, American locomotive engineer famous in ballad and song. Real name was John Luther Jones. His application of brakes saved passengers in crash of *Cannon Ball* express on April 30, 1900, at Vaughan, Miss.; Jones was killed.

Jones, Sir Edward Burne-: see BURNE-JONES.

Jones, Henry Arthur, 1851–1929, English playwright. His plays (e.g., *Wealth,* 1889; *The Liars,* 1897) dealt with social problems.

Jones, Inigo, 1573–1652, earliest of England's great architects. Traveled in Italy, where he closely studied Renaissance buildings of Palladio. In 1619 began his finest work, the royal banquet hall in Whitehall, London, which marked starting point for classic architecture of late Renaissance and Georgian periods in England. Designed settings for masques performed at court of James I and Charles I.

Jones, Jesse (Holman), 1874–, U.S. Secretary of Commerce (1940–45). A director of RFC 1932–39; chairman of board 1933–39.

Jones, John Paul, 1747–92, American naval hero, b. near Kirkcudbright, Scotland. Raided shores of British Isles in command of *Ranger* (1778). Captured frigate *Serapis* (1779) but his own ship, *Bon Homme Richard,* sank; this memorable victory was little noticed at the time. Later served in Russian navy.

Jones, Mary (Harris), 1830–1930, American labor agitator, called Mother Jones.

Jones, Owen, 1809–74, English architect, best known for writings on decorative arts.

Jones, Robert Edmond, 1887–, American stage designer. Studied with G. P. Baker and Max Reinhardt. His designs include those for *Desire under the Elms, The Green Pastures,* and *The Iceman Cometh.*

Jones, Robert Tyre, Jr. (Bobby Jones), 1902–, American golfer. Won Natl. Open (1923, 1926, 1929), Natl. Amateur (1924–25, 1927–28), British Open (1926–27). First golfer to win (1926) Natl. and British Open tournaments same year. Only golfer ever to score "grand slam"—winning (1930) Natl. Open, Natl. Amateur, British Open, and British Amateur.

Jones, Rufus M(atthew), 1863–1948, American writer on mysticism of Society of Friends. A teacher at Haverford Col. (1893–1934) and a founder of American Friends Service Committee (1917).

Jones, Sir William, 1746–94, English philologist and jurist, one of greatest scholars of England. He was famous in jurisprudence and for translations from Greek (a speech of Isaeus) and Oriental languages (e.g., Laws of Manu, the *Sakuntala* and *Hitopadesa*, all Sanskrit). Wrote a Persian grammar.

Jones Beach, state park, 2,413 acres, on sandy island off S shore of Long Isl., SE N.Y.; estab. 1929. Noted outing resort with 2½ mi. of beaches and boardwalk and a marine stadium.

Jonesboro. 1 City (pop. 16,310), NE Ark., NW of Memphis, Tenn.; founded 1859. Distributing center for area producing cattle, poultry, corn, fruit, truck, cotton, and rice. Seat of Arkansas State Col. (coed.; chartered 1909, opened 1910). **2** Town (pop. 1,126), NE Tenn., near Johnson City; laid out 1779. State's oldest town, first cap. of State of FRANKLIN. Andrew Jackson entered law practice, fought duel here (1788).

Jongkind, Johann Barthold (yōhän′ bär′tôlt yông′kĭnt), 1819–91, Dutch landscape painter and etcher. Worked mainly in France. Paintings have elements of both naturalism and impressionism.

Jonkoping, Swed. *Jönköping* (yûn′chû″pĭng), city (pop. 44,685), co. seat of Jonkoping co., S central Sweden, on Vattern L.; chartered 1284. Has some of world's largest match factories (founded 1844). In 1620 Gustavus Adolphus gave it special privileges after citizens had burned it to avoid sack by Danes.

Jonquière (zhŏkyěr′), town (pop. 21,618), S Que., Canada, on Sable R. and WSW of Chicoutimi. Has railroad workshops and pulp mills.

jonquil: see NARCISSUS.

Jonson, Ben, 1572–1637, English dramatist and lyric poet, an actor. His life and works bridge the Elizabethan and Jacobean periods. His comedies, such as *Every Man in His Humour* (1598), *Every Man Out of His Humour* (1599), were capped by *Volpone* (1606), *Epicoene* (1609), *The Alchemist* (1610), and *Bartholomew Fair* (1614). His tragedies *Sejanus* and *Catiline* were much praised in his time. His nondramatic poems showed the same neoclassic influence as his plays. Of his graceful lyrics the most familiar today is "Song to Celia" ("Drink to me only with thine eyes"). He had much influence on a group of younger poets called "the tribe of Ben." Shakspere said of him, "He was not of an age, but for all time," and his tomb in Westminster Abbey has the inscription, "O rare Ben Jonson."

Jonsson, Einar (ā′när yōn′sôn), 1874–, Icelandic sculptor and painter. His work is housed in a special museum in Reykjavik, Iceland.

Joplin, city (pop. 38,711), SW Mo., at edge of the Ozarks and W of Springfield; settled c.1840. Rail center in important lead and zinc area, it ships and processes food, metal, and leather products.

Joppa, Palestine: see JAFFA.

Joram (jō′–), kings of Israel and Judah: see JEHORAM.

Jordaens, Jacob (yä′kôp yôr′däns), 1593–1678, Flemish painter. Like his master Rubens he excelled in large allegorical paintings and portraits. Ranks among great masters of Flemish school.

Jordan, David Starr, 1851–1931, American scientist and educator. From 1891 to 1913 he was first president of Stanford Univ. and afterwards chancellor, 1913–16. He was director (1910–14) of World Peace Foundation and president (1915) of World Peace Congress. A leading ichthyologist, he served on U.S. and international commissions for fisheries.

Jordan, Dorothea or **Dorothy**, 1762–1816, British actress, whose real name was Bland. Exuberant and charming, she excelled in such roles as Lady Teazle

and Rosalind. Mistress of the duke of Clarence (later William IV), she bore him many children.

Jordan, kingdom (c.37,000 sq. mi.; 1948 pop. c.450,-000), SW Asia; cap. Amman. Formerly called Transjordan or Transjordania. Bordered by Saudi Arabia on E and S and by Israel on W. Only outlet to the sea is Aqaba, port on Gulf of Aqaba. Mainly arid and mountainous. Wheat, barley, and grapes are grown. Roughly corresponds to biblical lands of Edom, Gilead, and Moab, and to lordships of Montreal and Krak in Latin Kingdom of Jerusalem. Under Turkish rule from 16th cent. to 1918. In 1920 it was part of short-lived kingdom of Syria. Originally part of British mandate of PALESTINE, it was estab. as semi-independent emirate under ABDULLAH in 1923. Agreement of 1928 made Britain suzerain, with right to maintain garrisons. In 1946 mandate was ended and kingdom proclaimed. Treaty in 1948 provided for annual British subsidy for its famed Arab Legion. After partition of Palestine (1948) it joined other members of ARAB LEAGUE in armed attack against Israel. When truce was made in 1949 its forces held most of the Palestinian area that had been designated Arab territory by UN. Annexation in 1950 of occupied area (c.2,500 sq. mi.) was strongly resented by other Arab countries.

Jordan, the great river of Palestine, rising in Anti-Lebanon mts. and flowing c.200 mi. S to Dead Sea. Jordan contains S half of river; N half marks part of Israel-Jordan and Israel-Syria borders. Jordan valley is called the Ghor and is northernmost part of Great Rift Valley. Often mentioned in the Bible; it was scene of baptism of Christ.

Jordan, river, N central Utah, flowing c.60 mi. N, from Utah L., past Salt Lake City, to Great Salt L.

Josaphat (jŏ′sùfăt), in Bible: see JEHOSHAPHAT.

Joseph, Saint, husband of Mary, a carpenter of Nazareth, descended from royal line of David. Mat. 1; Luke 2; John 1; Mat. 13.55. Highly honored by Orthodox and Roman Catholics as foster father of Jesus and chaste spouse of Mary the Virgin. Feast: March 19.

Joseph, emperors (also kings of Hungary and Bohemia). **Joseph I**, 1678–1711. His reign (1705–11) was taken up with the War of the SPANISH SUCCESSION and the rebellion of Hungary under Francis II RAKOCZY. **Joseph II**, 1741–90, son of Francis I and MARIA THERESA. Ruled Hungary, Bohemia, and hereditary Hapsburg lands jointly with his mother from 1765 till her death (1780). Succeeded Francis I as emperor 1765. A revolutionary reformer and "benevolent despot," he sought to raise the miserable condition of his people and to centralize his administration by a series of radical decrees, but his impatience undid much of his work in his own lifetime. Falling far short of his aim of abolishing hereditary and ecclesiastic privileges, he nevertheless abolished serfdom and feudal dues (1781); enabled peasants to buy land cheaply; granted wide religious tolerance (1781); abolished judicial torture; humanized the penal code; created two degrees of appeal. He took anticlerical measures, forbidding religious orders to obey foreign generals and suppressing all contemplative orders, and was unmoved by a personal visit of Pope PIUS VI. His schemes for a single land tax and for providing free food and medical care for the indigent were failures. His bullying attempts to centralize all administration provoked revolts in the Austrian Netherlands and in Hungary. His plan to annex Bavaria was frustrated by the War of the BAVARIAN SUCCESSION; his project to exchange his part of the Netherlands for Bavaria was thwarted by Frederick II of Prussia, who formed the *Fürstenbund* [princes' league] for the purpose (1785). His anti-Turkish alliance with Catherine II of Russia brought Austria no advantage.

Joseph, 1715–77, king of Portugal (1750–77). His reign was dominated by his minister POMBAL.

Joseph, in Bible. **1** Favored son of Jacob. Sold into slavery by his jealous brothers, he was taken to Egypt. Imprisoned because of false accusation by the wife of his master (Potiphar), but released after he interpreted Pharaoh's dream. He became governor of Egypt and was reunited with his father and brothers when he helped them during a famine. Gen. 30; 37; 39–50. Story has been expanded in Joseph and Asenath (see PSEUDEPIGRAPHA) and in works of Thomas Mann. **2** See JOSEPH, SAINT.

Joseph (Chief Joseph), c.1840–1904, American Indian leader, chief of the Nez Percé Indians. Since his tribe refused to recognize land cessions made to U.S. in 1863, he undertook to lead them to Canada (1877). Forced to surrender to U.S. troops.

Joseph, Father, 1577–1638, French Capuchin monk, confidant and agent of Cardinal Richelieu; called "Gray Eminence"; lay name François Leclerc du Tremblay. He dreamed of restoring Catholicism throughout Europe but advanced a policy of supporting Protestant states and the Turks against the house of Hapsburg. Rumor made him the cardinal's evil genius, but actually he was probably simply a tool.

Joseph Barsabas, competitor of Matthias for place among the disciples left vacant by Judas Iscariot. Matthias was chosen. Acts 1.23.

Josephine (Marie Josèphe Rose Tascher de la Pagerie), 1763–1814, empress of the French, b. Martinique. Her first husband, Alexandre de BEAUHARNAIS, was guillotined 1794, but she escaped persecution through friendship with Barras. Married Napoleon Bonaparte 1796. He ignored her many indiscretions but had marriage annulled (1809) because of her alleged sterility. Died in retirement at Malmaison.

Joseph of Arimathea, Saint (ă″rǐmùthē′ù), man who gave body of Jesus decent burial. Mat. 27.57–61; Mark 15.42–47; Luke 23.50–56; John 19.38–42. Grateful Christendom has always honored him.

Josephus, Flavius (flă′vēùs jōsē′fùs), A.D. 37–A.D. 95?, Jewish historian and soldier. Thoroughly Romanized, he won the favor of Vespasian. Wrote *The Jewish War; Antiquities of the Jews; Against Apion* (a defense of the Jews); and an autobiography.

Joses (jō′–) [Gr.,= Heb. Joseph]. **1** Kinsman of Jesus. Mark 6.3; Mat. 13.55. **2** Brother of James the Less; may be same as **1.** Mat. 27.56; Mark 15.40,47.

Josetsu (jō″sā′tsoō), fl. 1425, Japanese landscape painter, a priest. His work has characteristics of Ming painting.

Joshua (jō′–) or **Josue** (jō′sūē), book of Old Testament. Its hero is Joshua, successor of Moses as leader of the Hebrews. Moses had brought the people to edge of Canaan, the Promised Land; it was Joshua's task to lead them into the country, conquer it, and divide the land among the tribes. Well-known events of book: fall of Jericho; battle in Ajalon valley where the sun stood still. Other forms of Joshua are Jehoshua, Jehoshuah, Jeshua, and Jesus.

Joshua tree: see YUCCA.

Joshua Tree National Monument: see NATIONAL PARKS AND MONUMENTS (table).

Josiah (jōsī′ù) or **Josias** (jōsī′ùs), d. c.610 B.C., king of Judah (c.641–c.610 B.C.). Chief event of his reign was discovery of old book of the law, apparently Deuteronomy, in the Temple. Josiah had it read publicly and led a reform movement to concentrate worship at Jerusalem. He later fell in battle against Egypt. 2 Kings 22–23; 2 Chron. 34–35.

Josika, Baron Nicholas (yō′shĭkŏ), 1794?–1865, Hungarian novelist, first to write Hungarian historical novel.

Josquin des Prés (zhōs′kĕn dĕprā′), c.1450–1521, Flemish composer, considered by his contemporaries as the greatest of his age. Wrote masses and motets.

Jostedalsbreen (yô′stŭdälsbrā′ŭn), glacier, area 340 sq. mi., Sogn og Fjordane co., W Norway, W of Jotunheim mts. Largest icefield on European mainland, it rises to 6,700 ft.

Josue, variant of JOSHUA.

Jotham (jō′–). **1** Only son of Gideon not killed by Abimelech. Told parable of the trees electing bramble as king. Judges 9.5–21. **2** Died c.731 B.C., king of Judah (c.535 B.C.–c.731 BC); contemporary of Isaiah, Hosea, Micah. 2 Kings 15.5,32–38.

Jotunheim (yō′toōnhäm), mountain group, central Norway, highest of Scandinavia, rising to 8,098 ft. in Galdhoppigen and to 8,048 ft. in Glittertind. JOSTEDALSBREEN glacier is W. Supports summer grazing. In Norse mythology, it was home of the giants.

Jouett, Matthew Harris, 1783–1827, American portrait painter, b. Ky. Studied with Gilbert Stuart.

Jouhaux, Léon (lāō′ zhoō-ō′), 1879–, French Socialist labor leader. Headed Confédération Générale du Travail from 1909 but left it in 1947 to found anti-Communist Internatl. Confederation of Free Trade Unions. Played prominent role at Internatl. Labor Organization. Was awarded 1951 Nobel Peace Prize.

Joule, James Prescott (joōl), 1818–89, English physicist. Made studies in electricity, thermodynamics, and was first to determine mechanical equivalent of heat. Electrical unit the **joule** (joul) is named for him. It is work done in one second in maintaining current of one ampere in resistance of one ohm.

Jourdan, Jean Baptiste (zhä′ bäptēst′ zhoōrdä′), 1762–1833, marshal of France. Fought in American Revolution and in FRENCH REVOLUTIONARY WARS.

journalism, collection and periodical publication of news. Includes writing for, editing, and managing such media as the NEWSPAPER and the PERIODICAL. Journalism had real beginnings at end of 18th cent. Until freedom of speech was instituted, journalism served as handmaiden of politics or a means of business. Growth of individualistic leadership in newspaper field in U.S. in 19th cent. (see GREELEY, HORACE; BOWLES, SAMUEL; DANA, CHARLES) in turn influenced other journalistic media. In 20th cent. power of individualistic journalist declined in face of technological advances, growth of news agency, vast strides in reporting techniques, broadening of education and reform, and growth of advertising. Earliest school of journalism in U.S. was estab. at Univ. of Missouri in 1908.

Jouvenet, Jean (zhä′ zhoōvùnä′), 1644–1717, French painter, known for religious pictures. Worked in Paris studio of Charles Le Brun.

Jove, another name for JUPITER.

Jovellanos, Gaspar Melchor de (gäspär′ mĕlchôr′ dä hōvĕlyä′nōs), 1744–1811, Spanish philosophical poet (as in *Epístola de Fabio a Anfriso*), a statesman and economist.

Jovian (jō′vēun), c.331–364, Roman Emperor (363–64). Returned Christianity to privileged position it had enjoyed before Julian the Apostate.

Jowett, Benjamin (jou′ĕt), 1817–93, English Greek scholar, an Anglican clergyman, master of Balliol College, Oxford, and vice chancellor of Oxford, one of greatest educators England has had. His translations of dialogues of Plato are famous.

Joyce, James, 1882–1941, Irish novelist, b. Dublin; spent almost all adult life in "exile" on Continent. First published works were poems in *Chamber Music* (1907; later included with *Pomes Penyeach* and *Ecce Puer* in *Poems,* 1937). His *Dubliners* (1914) was a linked collection of stories, his *Portrait of the Artist As a Young Man* (1916) a novel that foreshadowed the two great novels that made Joyce a major figure of world literature—*Ulysses* (1922; banned in U.S. for indecency until 1933) and *Finnegans Wake* (1939). His labyrinthine prose explores many levels of meaning, both conscious and unconscious, and employs many linguistic devices, including many-faceted puns. His influence on writing has been great, though he has few direct imitators.

Juana Inés de la Cruz (hwä′nä ēnäs′ dä lä kroōs′), 1651–95, Mexican poet, generally considered greatest lyric poet of colonial Spanish America. Became a nun in Mexico at 16 or 17, devoting her life to pursuit of knowledge. Her poems are marked by spontaneity and sincerity. Family name Asbaje.

Juana la Beltraneja (hwä'nä lä bĕltränä'hä), 1462–1530, Castilian princess. Her legal father was Henry IV of Castile; her presumed actual father, Beltrán de la Cueva, a courtier. Henry designated first his sister (later ISABELLA I), then Juana as successor. His death brought war between the two (1474–79). Juana, though aided by her husband Alfonso V of Portugal, lost and retired to a convent.

Juan de Fuca Strait (jōō'ùn dē fū'kù), inlet, c.100 mi. long, 15–20 mi. wide, connects Pacific Ocean with Puget Sound and Strait of Ga., between Vancouver Isl. (N) and Wash. state (S). Cape Flattery (Wash.), discovered 1778 by Capt. Cook, is at its entrance.

Juanes, Juan de: see MACIP, VICENTE JUAN.

Juan Fernández (hwän' fērnän'däs), group of small islands (pop. 434), c.400 mi. W of Valparaiso, Chile, belonging to Chile. Thought to be locale of Daniel Defoe's *Robinson Crusoe*.

Juan-les-Pins (zhüä'-lä-pē'), town (pop. 2,764), Alpes-Maritimes dept., S France, on the Cap d'Antibes; a resort of French Riviera.

Juárez, Benito (bänē'tō hwä'räs), 1806–72, Mexican liberal statesman and national hero, an Indian. Led liberal opposition to conservative government of Santa Anna and was acting president during War of the Reform (1858–61). During French attempt at establishment of Mexican empire under Maximilian (1864–67), Juárez moved his capital to El Paso del Norte (now Juárez). His sturdy resistance defeated the French and destroyed the empire. Reelected president 1871, he died while suppressing a revolution led by Porfirio Díaz.

Juárez (hwä'räs), city (pop. 48,881), Chihuahua, N Mexico, on Rio Grande opposite El Paso, Texas. Originally El Paso del Norte, it included settlements on both sides of river until close of Mexican War (1848). Name of Mexican town changed (1888) to honor Benito Juárez.

Juba (jōō'bù), c.85 B.C.–46 B.C., king of Numidia. Fought for Pompey and ended his life after Caesar won at Thapsus. His young son, **Juba II**, d. A.D. c.20, was educated in Rome and was given rule, probably in Numidia, then in Mauretania, by Augustus. Was very learned.

Jubal, originator of musical instruments. Gen. 4.21.

Jubbulpore (jùbùlpôr'), city (pop. 178,339), N Madhya Pradesh, India. Ordnance-mfg. center.

jubilee, in Bible, a year when slaves were freed and debts forgiven. It occurred once in 50 years. Lev. 25.8–55. Name now used to mean celebration of a 50-year or longer period (e.g., Diamond Jubilee of Queen Victoria, 1897). In Roman Catholic Church name is applied to a holy year when special privileges are given by the Church for pilgrimages to Rome. Recent such jubilee years were 1929 and 1950.

Jubilees, Book of: see PSEUDEPIGRAPHA.

Juda. 1 See JUDAH. **2** See JUDE, SAINT.

Judaea or **Judea** (both: jōōdē'ù), Greco-Roman name (from Judah) for S Palestine, southernmost of Roman divisions of Palestine. At time of Christ it was part of province of Syria and a kingdom ruled by the Herods.

Judah I, 135?–220?, Jewish leader, called *ha-Nassi* [prince], editor of the Mishna (see TALMUD), president of Sanhedrin.

Judah, son of Jacob and ancestor of one of 12 tribes of Israel; a leader in family counsels, spokesman for his brothers before Joseph in Egypt. Tribe of Judah settled in S Palestine; gave its name to kingdom. Royal and Messianic line of David was of this tribe. Gen. 29.35; 35.23; 37.26; 38; 43.3; 44.14; 46.12,28; 49.8; Num. 2.3; 10.14; 13.6; 26.22; 34; Joshua 15.1; 1 Chron. 2–5. Juda: Luke 3.33; Heb. 7.14; Rev. 5.5; 7.5. Judas: Mat. 1.2.

Judah, Theodore Dehone, 1826–63, American railroad builder. Promoted idea of railroad across mountains E from Central Valley of Calif. Central Pacific RR Co. was formed, with Judah as chief engineer.

Judah, southern of the two kingdoms after division of Hebrew nation under REHOBOAM (N kingdom was Israel); cap. Jerusalem; dynasty, the house of David.

Judah ha-Levi or **Judah Halevy** (both: hä''lē'vī), 1085?–1140?, Spanish rabbi, Hebrew poet, philosopher, author of *Sefer ha-Kuzari*, which argues for superiority of religious truths arrived at through intuition over those formulated through logic.

Judaism (jōō'dùïzùm, –dē–) [from Judah; cf. Jews], religion of the Jews, oldest of the great monotheistic religions. It is the complex of law, tradition and doctrine consisting of the OLD TESTAMENT and the TALMUD. Its outstanding feature is its belief in an omnipotent God, and in his law, the TORAH, given by him to Moses, the leader of Israel, whom God had chosen as his people in the time of Abraham, the father of Israel. The great text of Judaism, the Shema, begins "Hear, O Israel: the Lord our God is one Lord" (Deut. 6.4.–9). Circumcision of males is practised as a sign of God's covenant with his people. The synagogue is primarily a place of meeting; the most elaborate feast of Judaism, the PASSOVER, is celebrated in the home. The rabbi is primarily a teacher. The principal Jewish sects of ancient times were the ESSENES, SADDUCEES, and the PHARISEES. In more modern times, the cabalists (see CABALA) and the HASIDIM are notable. In the 18th cent. appeared a new movement, Reformed Judaism. Unlike orthodox Jews, the reformed reject many of the restrictions of the Law, use the vernacular in religious ceremonies, and reduce much of the ritual. One group, the "conservatives," retains some orthodox customs. Judaism demands the recognition of God and the observance of the Law. The importance of the Law is seen in the development and preservation of the exalted ethical standards of Judaism.

Judas [Gr.,= Judah], in Bible. **1** See JUDE, SAINT. **2** See MACCABEES. **3** See JUDAS ISCARIOT.

Judas Iscariot (ĭskă'rēùt), disciple who for 30 pieces of silver betrayed Jesus, identifying him for capture by kissing him. Judas hanged himself. Blood money went to buy potter's field, thenceforth called Aceldama. Mat. 26.20–25,47–49; 27.3–10; Acts 1.16–20.

Judas Maccabeus: see MACCABEES.

Judas of Galilee (gă'lĭlē), fl. A.D. 7, a leader of the ZEALOTS, a revolutionary Jewish sect.

Judas tree: see REDBUD.

Jude, Saint, or **Saint Judas** [Jude an Eng. form to distinguish him from Judas Iscariot], one of the Twelve Apostles. Also called Thaddaeus and Lebaeus. Epistle of Jude ascribed to him. Mat. 10.3; 13.55; Mark 3.18; Luke 6.16. Juda: Mark 6.3. Feast: Oct. 28.

Jude, epistle of New Testament. Traditionally ascribed to St. Jude the Apostle, but many critics disagree. Book shows the danger of heresy in the church by citing examples from Old Testament.

Judea: see JUDAEA.

Judges, book of Old Testament; sequel to Joshua in biblical history, telling of the Hebrews in Canaan from death of Joshua up to time of Samuel. There are many well-known stories about these violent times when men took the law into their own hands. Leaders, mostly heroes of war, were called judges; among them were Samson, Gideon, Jephthah, Ehud, and Deborah.

judgment, final decision of a court of law. It can be altered by a court of appeal, which rectifies error, but cannot be reconsidered from the beginning like a decree. In criminal cases the judge gives a sentence in accord with the verdict of a jury. In civil cases, a judge normally awards damages (including legal costs). When a debtor fails to pay, the sheriff may seize his property.

Judith [Heb.,= the Jewess], book of Old Testament, placed in Apocrypha in AV, before Esther in Western canon. Tells of time when Palestine was occupied by foreign army led by Holofernes. Judith, a Jewish widow of great beauty, entered the enemy camp, gained the favor of Holofernes, and murdered him. The invaders, without a leader, were easily routed by the Jews. Story repeated in an Anglo-Saxon epic.

judo: see JUJUTSU.

Judson, Adoniram (ădŭnī'rŭm), 1788–1850, American Baptist missionary. After two years in India as Congregational worker, he became a Baptist and transferred to Burma, where he spent most of his life as pioneer in Protestant mission work. Judson's first wife, Ann (Hasseltine) Judson (1789–1826), founded a girls' school at Rangoon. His second wife, Sarah (Hall) Boardman Judson (1803–45), translated *Pilgrim's Progress* into Burmese. His third wife, Emily (Chubbuck) Judson (1817–54), was an author, whose pseudonym was Fanny Forester.

Judson, Edward Zane Carroll: see BUNTLINE, NED.

Juggernaut, India: see PURI.

Jugoslavia: see YUGOSLAVIA.

Jugurtha (jŏŏgûr'thŭ), c.156–104 B.C., king of Numidia, grandson of Masinissa. He was finally defeated after long warfare with the Romans through treachery of his father-in-law, Bocchus of Mauretania.

Juilliard School of Music (jŏŏl'yärd), in Manhattan borough of New York city; coed.; chartered 1926. In 1946, its two units, Juilliard Graduate School (1924) and Inst. of Musical Art (1905; founded by Frank Damrosch and James Loeb), were amalgamated.

Juiz de Fora (zhwēzh' dù fô'rù), city (pop. 86,819), S Minas Gerais state, E Brazil; industrial city.

jujube (jŏŏ'jŏŏb), deciduous or evergreen spiny shrub or tree of genus *Zizyphus* of tropics and subtropics of both hemispheres. Long grown by Chinese for fruit used fresh, dried, or preserved.

jujutsu (jŏŏjŏŏt'sŏŏ, –jĭt'–) or **jiujitsu** (jŏŏjĭt'sŏŏ), Japanese method of defense and offense without weapons in personal encounter. Requires extensive training and detailed knowledge of anatomy. Probably imported from China, jujutsu was long exclusive property of Japanese nobility. By 20th cent. jujutsu had attracted attention in Europe, America. Judo, outgrowth of jujutsu, was taught in U.S. Army in World War II.

Jujuy (hŏŏhwē'), city (pop. 41,955), cap. of Jujuy prov., NW Argentina, on Jujuy R.; founded 1593; center of cattle and agr. area. Minerals and timber exploited near by.

juke box: see PHONOGRAPH.

Jukes: see DUGDALE, RICHARD LOUIS.

julep or **mint julep,** alcoholic beverage, traditional in the S U.S. containing bourbon whisky, crushed mint leaves, crushed ice, sugar.

Julia, feminine name in the family of the Caesars. **1** Died 54 B.C., daughter of Julius Caesar and wife of Pompey. It was only after her death that warfare broke out between the two. **2** 39 B.C.–A.D. 14, daughter of Augustus, wife of M. Claudius Marcellus, M. Vipsanius Agrippa, and Tiberius. Banished for gross immorality to the island of Pandataria, she died of starvation. **3** 18 B.C.–A.D. 28, daughter of Julia **2** and Agrippa, also banished for immorality.

Julian, George Washington, 1817–99, American abolitionist, U.S. Representative from Ind. (1849–51, 1861–71). In later life a Liberal Republican and then a Democrat.

Juliana, 1909–, queen of Netherlands (1948–); daughter of Wilhelmina. Married (1937) Prince Bernard of Lippe-Biesterfeld.

Julianehaab (yŏŏlyä'nŭhôp"), town (pop. 936), SW Greenland; cap. of Julianehaab colony (pop. 4,186), most populous part of Greenland. It is chief trade center in S Greenland and port in cattle-raising area.

Julian the Apostate, 331?–363, Roman emperor (361–63); nephew of Constantine I. Both a scholar and an able general, he unsuccessfully tried to restore paganism, which to him meant the glory of antiquity. He did not institute systematic persecution of Christians and ruled justly and humanely.

Jülich (yü'lĭkh), former duchy, NW Germany, between Cologne and Aachen; historic cap. Jülich (pop. c.8,-000). At first a county, Jülich was united with county of BERG (1348) and made a duchy (1356). After extinction of Jülich line, both Jülich and Berg passed to

dukes of CLEVES (1524); to Palatinate-Neuburg branch of Wittelsbach dynasty (1666); to France (1806); to Prussia (1815).

Julier (yŏŏl'yŭr), pass, 7,507 ft. high, Grisons canton, Switzerland; a link between Engadine and Italy. Modern road was built 1820–40.

Julius I, Saint, pope (337–52). When called upon for his opinion in the Arian controversy, he summoned a council at Rome (340). The Arians did not come, and Julius wrote them a letter, chiding them for lack of sincerity and asserting the papal claim to jurisdiction over the whole church. Feast: April 12.

Julius II, 1443–1513, pope (1503–13). As Giuliano della Rovere, created cardinal by his uncle Sixtus IV. As pope he completed work of Cesare Borgia (his enemy) of restoring Papal States to the Church. A warrior, he took a vigorous part in the Italian Wars. In 1512 Julius assembled the Fifth LATERAN COUNCIL, which condemned Gallicanism in France, abolished simony in the college of cardinals. A patron of art, he favored Raphael (for whom he sat), Michelangelo, and Bramante. He laid the cornerstone of St. Peter's.

Julius Caesar: see CAESAR, JULIUS.

Jullundur (jŭ'lŭndŭr), city (pop. 135,283), central Punjab, India. Taken by Ranjit Singh 1811. Trade center with mfg. of silk fabrics.

July: see MONTH.

July Revolution, 1830, French revolution which deposed CHARLES X and created the bourgeois July Monarchy under LOUIS PHILIPPE. It resulted from the opposition of the propertied middle class, led by such men as THIERS, and of the radical workers in Paris to Charles's reactionary policies. The repressive, ultraroyalist July Ordinances under ministry of J. A. de POLIGNAC brought matters to a head. Revolution was over in two days.

Jumna (jŭm'nù), river, c.850 mi. long, rising in N Uttar Pradesh, India. Its junction with the Ganges at Allahabad forms one of bathing sites most sacred to Hindus.

Junagarh (jŏŏ'nùgär") or **Junagadh** (jŏŏ'nùgäd"), former princely state, India, on Kathiawar peninsula; since 1949 part of Saurashtra. **Junagarh,** town (pop. 58,111), formerly cap. of state, was Rajput stronghold until 15th cent.

junco or **snowbird,** bird of FINCH family. Slate-colored junco is a winter resident in E North America. About the size of a sparrow, it is dark gray with white abdomen. Other juncoes are in W and S U.S.

Junction City, city (pop. 13,462), NE Kansas, at head of Kansas R. and W of Topeka; founded 1858. Rail and trade center in agr. and dairy area. Fort RILEY is near by.

June: see MONTH.

Juneau, Solomon Laurent (jŏŏnō', jŏŏ'nō), 1793–1856, French Canadian fur trader and founder of Milwaukee, Wis. Moved to fur post at Milwaukee in 1818; surveyed town site, built first store, became first mayor (1846).

Juneau (jŏŏ'nō), city (pop. 5,956), territorial cap., (since 1900), SE Alaska, at foot of Mt. Juneau and Mt. Roberts, on Gastineau Channel; settled 1881 following 1880 gold discovery. Bridge connects with Douglas town on Douglas Isl., across channel. Has gold mining, salmon fishing, fur farming, and lumbering. Port with ice-free harbor, seaplane base, and airport. Has U.S. and territorial offices and Alaska Historical Library and Mus.

June beetle, June bug, or **May beetle,** nocturnal blackish or mahogany-colored beetle of scarab family. Larvae (white grubs) eat underground roots.

Juneberry: see SHADBUSH.

June bug: see JUNE BEETLE.

June Days, 1848, in French history, insurrection of Parisian workers, brought on by government sabotage of national workshops established by Louis BLANC. Workers had played major part in FEBRUARY REVOLUTION, felt cheated of its fruits. Rebellion was ruthlessly put down by military in four days' fighting.

Jung, Carl Gustav (kärl gōōs'täf yŏong'), 1875–, Swiss psychiatrist, founder of school of analytical psychology. As first president of International Psychoanalytic Association he was second only to Freud in the movement; they worked together until differences of approach caused a formal break (1913). Jung conceived of libido as primal, nonsexual energy and postulated two systems in the unconscious: the personal (repressed events of personal life) and the collective unconscious (archetypes of inherited tendencies). He introduced terms EXTROVERSION AND INTROVERSION.

Jünger, Ernst (yüng'ùr), 1895–, German writer. Wrote novels of World War I—e.g., *Storm of Steel* (1919; Eng. tr., 1929); diaries of World War II.

Jungfrau (yŏong'frou) [Ger.,= Virgin], peak, 13,653 ft. high, Switzerland, in Bernese Alps. First ascended 1811. The Jungfraujoch (–yôkh") is a mountain saddle 11,342 ft. high, highest point in Europe reached by rail. Has scientific institute and weather station.

Juniata (jōōnēä'tù), river of Pa., rising in Alleghenies and flowing 150 mi. E to Susquehanna R. above Harrisburg.

Junín (hōōnēn'), small town, W central Peru. Near here Bolívar aided by Sucre won first important battle (1824) in liberation of Peru from Spain.

juniper, evergreen tree or shrub of genus *Juniperus,* with berrylike fruits and needle- or scale-shaped leaves. Dwarf or pyramidal forms of the common juniper (*Juniperus communis*) of N Hemisphere are used in landscaping. Their fruits flavor gin. Wood of red cedar, a juniper (*J. virginiana*) native to E U.S., is much used for chests and closets; its oil is used in medicine and perfumery.

Junius, English political controversialist, anonymous writer of letters to London *Public Advertiser* (notably Jan., 1769–Jan., 1772) attacking the king's party and George III himself. Mystery of identity added interest to letters. Authorship ascribed to Sir Philip Francis, to Lord Shelburne, or to Laughlin Macleane, secretary to Shelburne.

Juno (jōō'nō), in Roman religion, queen of gods; sister and wife of Jupiter. Like Greek goddess HERA, she was protector of women.

Junot, Andoche (ädōsh' zhünō'), 1771–1813, French general. Commanded French invasion of Portugal (1807); was driven out by Wellington (1808). Created duke of Abrantès by Napoleon. His wife, Laure Junot, duchesse d'Abrantès (1784–1838) was socially prominent during Restoration and left lively memoirs.

Jupiter [Latin,= God the father], in Roman religion, supreme god, also called Jove; son of Saturn and Ops and brother and husband of Juno. Identified with Olympian god Zeus.

Jupiter, in astronomy, largest PLANET (mean diameter c.86,728 mi.) of solar system. It revolves around the sun in 11 years 314.8 days at mean distance of 483,310,000 mi. in an orbit between Mars and Saturn. Mean rotation period is 9 hr. 55 min. It is enveloped by atmosphere and has 12 satellites. See *ill.,* p. 927.

Jura (zhürä'), department (1,952 sq. mi.; pop. 216,386), E France, in Franche-Comté; cap. Lons-le-Saunier.

Jura (jōō'rù), mountain range, E France (Jura and Doubs depts.) and W Switzerland (Vaud, Neuchâtel, and Bern cantons). Extends in parallel ridges from the Rhine R. at Basel to Rhone R. at Geneva; rises above 5,500 ft. Pine forests, pastures, agr. Watch industry in many towns (e.g., Le Locle, La Chaux-de-Fonds). Many resorts. Formed of sandstone and limestone rich in fossils, Jura gives name to Jurassic period. Mountains of S Württemberg are called the Swabian Jura.

Jurassic period (jōōrä'sĭk), second period of the MESOZOIC ERA of geologic time. As in Triassic period E North America was continuously elevated and subject to erosion which reduced the Appalachians to a peneplain. Deserts at first prevailed in SW U.S., but this region was later flooded from the N, and sediments were deposited. The period's close was marked

by mountain making and lava intrusions in the W; to the E, by upwarping of the Appalachian peneplain. Reptiles dominated sea, land, air. Plant life included cycads, conifers, tree ferns. See also GEOLOGY, table.

Jurieu, Pierre (pyĕr' zhüryû'), 1637–1713, French Protestant theologian and Calvinist controversialist. Took refuge in Rotterdam after publication (1681) of *La Politique du clergé de France,* an attempt to preserve Huguenot liberties. Attacked Arnauld, Bossuet, and others in controversial works.

jurisprudence, study of the nature, origin, and development of law. Prevailing concept from 13th to 19th cent. was that of natural law—that laws took their sanction from a law of nature estab. by divine ordinance. In 19th cent. there grew up theories that law depends only on sovereign decree or custom of the culture, divorced from theology or morality. Other schools of thought are the historical (that law is the product of development) and the sociological (that law expresses the dominant social pattern in a nation or the community.)

Juruá (zhōōrwä'), river, c.1,200 mi. long, rising in E Peru, flowing generally NE through Brazil to Amazon. Important during wild-rubber boom.

jury, in Anglo-Norman times, body of men brought together to decide from personal knowledge in an inquest what the facts were. Institution gradually developed until it became before the 18th cent. the symbolic and actual protection against tyranny for all Englishmen. It was incorporated into the U.S. constitution. Judgment of a man's "peers" as to facts of a case are considered to be binding, above the decision of a judge. A group of prospective jurors (panel) is called the venire. In choosing a petit jury (for trial), counsel may challenge the whole group or any individuals as unfit according to counsel's opinion. A grand jury usually has 12 to 23 members, a petit jury 12 (or less, according to state law). A petit jury takes an oath to reach a fair decision on evidence (the VERDICT). On the Continent jury trials are restricted to criminal cases of great importance.

Jusserand, Jean Jules (zhä' zhül' zhüsùrä'), 1855–1932, French diplomat and scholar. As ambassador to Washington (1902–15) he was extremely popular. Among his works are *English Wayfaring Life in the Middle Ages* (1889) and an incomplete autobiography (1933).

Jussieu (zhüsyû'), name of a French family of botanists. **Antoine de Jussieu** (ätwän' dù), 1686–1758, was director of the Jardin des Plantes, Paris, and editor of botanical works. His brother **Bernard de Jussieu** (bĕrnär'), 1699–1777?, was director of gardens at Trianon, Versailles, and developer of a classification system. Another brother, **Joseph de Jussieu** (zhôsĕf'), 1704–79, traveled in South America and introduced into Europe many plants (e.g., heliotrope) from there. A nephew, **Antoine Laurent de Jussieu** (lōrä'), 1748–1836, elaborated Bernard's system of classification in his *Genera plantarum* (1789). He was professor at the Museum of Natural History, Paris, and organized its botanical collection. His son, **Adrien de Jussieu** (ädrēē'), 1797–1853, was also professor of botany at the museum.

Justice, United States Department of, created by act of Congress in 1870. Office of U.S. Attorney General became nucleus of department. Act of 1870 also set up office of Solicitor General to represent government in Supreme Court cases and empowered creation of assistants to aid Attorney General in administering department. Department furnishes legal counsel in Federal cases, provides means for enforcing Federal laws, and officially construes laws—subject to court decisions —under which government officials act. Department consists of seven specialized divisions (e.g., Antitrust Division), three bureaus (e.g., FEDERAL BUREAU OF INVESTIGATION), and two boards.

Justin I, c.450–527, Byzantine emperor (518–27). Chief of imperial guard, he seized power on death of Anastasius I. He was illiterate and entrusted the government to his nephew, Justinian I.

Justinian I, 483–565, Byzantine emperor (527–65); nephew of JUSTIN I. His reign was a rebirth of imperial greatness. His generals BELISARIUS and NARSES recovered Africa from the Vandals and Italy from the Ostrogoths. The *Nika* riot, caused by discontent with heavy taxation and his hostility to Monophysitism, was crushed by the firm stand of Empress THEODORA (532). Justinian advocated caesaro-papism—the supremacy of the emperor over the Church—and in 553 called the Second Council of Constantinople in an attempt to reconcile the Monophysites. His chief accomplishment was the codification of Roman law (see CORPUS JURIS CIVILIS). He also had the Church of HAGIA SOPHIA built.

Justin Martyr, Saint, A.D. c.100–c.165, Christian apologist, b. Palestine. Converted to Christianity at 30, he was finally martyred with disciples at Rome. Two undisputed works (in Greek) remain, both philosophic defenses of Christian doctrine—the *Apology* and the *Dialogue*.

Justin Morgan, 1792–1821, American horse, foundation sire of Justin Morgan breed, which preceded Hambletonian strain as favored type of trotting horse in U.S.

jute (joōt), annual tropical plant (*Corchorus capsularis*) grown for fiber which lies between outer bark and central wood. The fiber, widely used, is cheap, easily spun and dyed. Burlap, webbing, twines, backing yarns for carpets and linoleum, oakum, paper, etc., are made from jute. Calcutta is leading manufacturer and exporter, but the plant can be grown in any hot humid country.

Jutes: see ANGLO-SAXONS; KENT, KINGDOM OF.

Jutland, Dan. *Jylland,* Ger. *Jütland,* peninsula, N Europe, comprising continental Denmark and German SCHLESWIG N of Eider R.; bounded on N by the Skagerrak and W by North Sea. Danish Jutland, including adjacent islands, has area of 11,411 sq. mi. and pop. of 1,826,056. Dairying and cattle raising are chief occupations on fertile and densely populated E coast. Aarhus, Aalborg, and Frederikshavn are main ports here. Jutland has many lakes and is crossed by Guden R. South Jutland is name applied in Denmark to N part of former duchy of Schleswig. The **battle of Jutland,** May 31, 1916, chief naval engagement of World War I, was fought c.60 mi. W of Jutland coast; also known as battle of the Skagerrak. Although the German fleet, brilliantly commanded by admirals Hipper and Scheer, suffered lighter losses than the British (under Beatty and Jellicoe), it was forced to return to its bases, where it remained bottled up.

Juvenal (Decimus Junius Juvenalis) (joō'vŭnŭl), 1st–2d cent. A.D., Roman satirical poet. His 16 savage satires, in denouncing the criminal excesses, immorality, and tyranny of the Romans, give a vivid picture of the society.

juvenile delinquency, behavior of children and adolescents which in adults would be judged criminal (see CRIME). Maximum age of juveniles is variously defined, from 14 to 21 years. Delinquency frequently arises from bad family situations, and it persists in slum neighborhoods. Though juvenile corrective institutions have been separated from regular prisons since early 19th cent., the separate judgment of youth was developed only after 1899 in the juvenile court, and the rehabilitation of delinquents, though benefiting from improved psychiatric and sociological programs, is still recognizably inadequate.

juvenile literature. First books for children were Latin texts of 7th cent., school texts of Venerable Bede, and colloquy of Ælfric in 10th cent. William Caxton printed for children Aesop's fables in 1484. Invention of hornbook in 15th cent. made books readily available. Chapbooks were sold in 17th and 18th cent. John Newbery (1713–67), publisher and author, made small attractive volumes expressly for children. The 18th cent. produced school of writers of didactic literature. The 19th cent. produced such works as fairy tales of brothers Grimm in Germany, tales of Hans Christian Andersen, Edward Lear's *Book of Nonsense* (1846), Lewis Carroll's *Alice in Wonderland* (1865), Stevenson's *Treasure Island* (1883), and Kipling's *Jungle Book* (1894). Series were popular in America; the didactic *Rollo* series of Jacob Abbott and the *Elsie Dinsmore* series were followed by the Horatio Alger books and the Oliver Optic books. From the 19th cent. came works by James Fenimore Cooper, Mark Twain, Howard Pyle, Louisa May Alcott, and Joel Chandler Harris. Recent children's books of note have been written by Kenneth Grahame, Selma Lagerlof, Hugh Lofting, P. L. Travers, and A. A. Milne.

Jylland: see JUTLAND.

K

K, chemical symbol of the element POTASSIUM.

K2: see GODWIN-AUSTEN, MOUNT.

Kaaba or **Caaba** (both: kä'bù, kä'ùbù), most sacred building, housing the sacred Black Stone; goal of the pilgrimage to Mecca, center of Islam. Its sanctity is earlier than Islam.

Kabardian Autonomous Soviet Socialist Republic (kùbär'dĕùn), autonomous republic (4,550 sq. mi.; pop. c.300,000), S European RSFSR, on N slopes of Greater Caucasus; cap. Nalchik. Includes peaks of Mt. Elbrus, Koshtan-Tau, Dykh-Tau. Kabardians (c. 60% of pop.), a Moslem Circassian group, support themselves by agr., stock raising.

kabuki: see JAPANESE DRAMA.

Kabul (kä'bool, city (pop. 300,000), cap. of Afghanistan, on Kabul R., in fruit-growing region. Early cap. of Baber (1504–19). Succeeded Kandahar as cap. of Afghanistan in 1773. Figured prominently in First Afghan War (1839–42).

Kachin State (kùchĭn'), constituent unit (33,871 sq. mi.; pop. 427,625) of Union of Burma, N Upper Burma; cap. Myitkyina; largely autonomous. Many of inhabitants are Kachins or Jinghpaws.

Kaffa, RSFSR: see FEODOSIYA.

kaffir or **kaffir corn:** see SORGHUM.

Kaffraria, South Africa: see KAFIRS.

Kafirs or **Kaffirs** (both: kä'fŭrz), Bantu-speaking Negro people (c.500,000) of South Africa. Chiefly in Kaffraria, region in E Cape Prov., Union of South Africa.

Kafka, Franz (fränts' käf′kä), 1883–1924, German novelist and essayist, b. Prague, Czechoslovakia, of a Jewish family. Among his works are *The Trial* (1925), *The Castle* (1926), and *Amerika* (1927), all translated into English. In prose remarkable for clarity and precision, Kafka presents a world at once real and dreamlike in which modern man, burdened with guilt, isolation, and anxiety, makes a futile search for personal salvation.

Kagawa, Toyohiko (tōyō′hēkō kä″gä′wä), 1888–, Japanese Christian social worker. Influential in organizing cooperatives and in labor problems. Arrested in World War II for pacifism. Author of poetry, novels, essays, and religious studies.

Kagera, river: see NILE.

Kagoshima (kä″gō′shĭmä), city (pop. 170,416), S Kyushu, Japan; port on inlet of East China Sea. Mfg. of porcelain ware, clothing, and tinware. St. Francis Xavier landed here in 1549. Was seat of powerful lords of Satsuma.

Kahlenberg (kä′lŭnbĕrk), mountain, 1,585 ft. high, Lower Austria, near Vienna, of which it commands a beautiful view. A favorite excursion point.

Kahn, Albert, 1869–1942, American architect, b. Germany. His firm in Detroit applied technique of mass production to architecture; designed many factories and war plants.

Kahn, Otto (Hermann), 1867–1934, American banker and patron of the arts, b. Germany. In U.S. after 1893, he joined Kuhn, Loeb, & Co. Took part in many international finance organizations. Helped finance many theatrical and musical groups. A director of the Metropolitan Opera Co. 1903–31.

Kahoolawe (kähō′ōlävä), uninhabited island (45 sq. mi.), Hawaiian Isls. Leased to a private citizen.

Kailas (kīläs′), peak, 22,028 ft. high, SW Tibet, in Himalayas. Home of Hindu god Siva, it is goal of pilgrimages.

Kairouan (kīrwän′), city (pop. 32,299), Tunisia; sacred city of Islam. Founded 670, it was seat of Arab governors in W Africa until 800. First cap. of Fatimites was estab. here in 909. Has famous 9th-cent. mosque. Noted for carpet industry.

Kaisaria, Turkey: see KAYSERI.

Kaiser, Georg (gä′ôrk kī′zùr), 1878–1945, German playwright. His plays, which he called thought dramas, have social themes. *From Morn to Midnight* (1916; produced in New York 1922), *The Corals* (1917; a trilogy), and *Gas* (1918) are translated into English.

Kaiserslautern (kī″zùrslou′tùrn), city (pop. 62,395), Rhineland-Palatinate, W Germany. Machine and textile mfg.

Kaiser Wilhelm Canal: see KIEL CANAL.

Kalamata (kälŭmä′tù), Gr. *Kalamai,* city (pop. 38,363) S Greece, in SW Peloponnesus; a port on the Gulf of Messenia. Fisheries, silk and cigarette mfg., distilleries.

Kalamazoo (kăl″ŭmùzōō′), city (pop. 57,704), SW Mich., on Kalamazoo R. at junction with Portage Creek; settled 1829. Industrial and commercial center in agr. area, it has mfg. of paper, metal products, and pharmaceuticals. Seat of Kalamazoo Col.

Kalamazoo, river rising in S Mich. and flowing c.138 mi. NW past Battle Creek and Kalamazoo to L. Michigan.

Kalaupapa, T.H.: see MOLOKAI.

Kalb, Johann (Ger. yō′hän kälp′), 1721–80, general in American Revolution, known as "Baron de Kalb" (dē kälb), b. Germany. Mortally wounded in battle of Camden, S.C. (1780).

Kalckreuth, Leopold Karl Walter, Graf von (kälk′-roit), 1855–1928, German genre painter, one of the Secessionists, who emphasized realism in subject matter. Pictured peasant life.

kale, nonheading cabbage variety (*Brassica oleracea acephala*) with curly leaves, grown for greens and, in Europe, for fodder. Sea kale (*Crambe maritima*) is N

European coastal plant sometimes used as a potherb.

kaleidoscope (kŭlī′dŭskōp), cylindrical tube, one end containing two mirrors set at angle of 60° and many particles of varicolored glass which can move between two glass disks. Other end has eyepiece. When tube is rotated, glass forms many patterns, always symmetrical because of reflection in mirrors.

Kalevala (kä′lĕvä″lä), Finnish national epic, a compilation of folk verses dealing with the deeds of three semidivine brothers of gigantic stature. Known to scholars as early as 1733, verses were collected in 19th cent. by Zakarias Topelius and Elias LÖNNROT. Effect on Finnish art has been great.

Kalgan, China: see CHANGKIAKOW.

Kali (kü′lē), in Hinduism, primarily the black goddess of death and evil, though she has other and more attractive aspects. As consort of Siva, she represents the female principle. The name was also given earlier to one of the tongues of the fire-god Agni.

Kalidasa (kä″lĭdä′sù), fl. 5th cent.?, Indian poet and dramatist, often regarded as greatest figure in classical Sanskrit literature. Three surviving verse dramas (including *Sakuntala*) relate fanciful or mythological tales of lovers separated by adversity but reunited by happy chance. Two epics mingle delicate descriptions of nature with battle scenes. Also wrote shorter lyrical poems.

Kalinin, Mikhail Ivanovich (mēkhŭyēl′ ēvä′nùvĭch kŭlyē′nyĭn), 1875–1946, Russian revolutionist, first president of USSR (officially: chairman of presidium of supreme council of USSR) 1922–46.

Kalinin, formerly **Tver,** city (pop. 216,131), RSFSR, NW of Moscow and on the Volga. It is an industrial center (railway cars, machinery, textiles). The seat of a powerful principality in 14th–15th cent., it was annexed to Moscow c.1486. Renamed 1933 for M. I. Kalinin. It was briefly held by the Germans in 1941 and was heavily damaged.

Kaliningrad, Russian name of KÖNIGSBERG.

Kalisch, Poland: see KALISZ.

Kalispel Indians: see PEND D'OREILLE INDIANS.

Kalispell (kä′lĭspĕl″), city (pop. 9,737), NW Mont., on Flathead R. and near Glacier Natl. Park. Trade center of agr., mining, and lumbering region.

Kalisz (kä′lēsh), Ger. *Kalisch,* city (pop. 48,092), W Poland. Mfg. of clothing, food, machinery. By Convention of Kalisz (1813) Prussia promised Russia to declare war on Napoleon I.

Kalm, Peter (pä′tùr kälm′), 1716–79, Swedish scientist. His *Travels in North America,* recording his observations of natural history, plantations, and agriculture, was the first account of its kind by a trained scientist. It was published between 1753 and 1761; was republished in 1937. Genus *Kalmia* (mountain laurel) is named for Kalm.

Kalmar (käl′mär), city (pop. 27,049), co. seat of Kalmar co., SE Sweden, Baltic port opposite Oland isl. across Kalmar Sound. Its medieval castle, the Kalmarnahus, has withstood 24 sieges. Here in 1397 was effected the **Kalmar Union** of Denmark, Sweden, and Norway under Queen MARGARET. Since kingship was elective in all three countries, a lasting union under the Danish crown proved impossible. Sweden definitively left the union in 1523 (see GUSTAVUS I). The **Kalmar War,** 1611–13, between Denmark and Sweden, took its name from the fall of Kalmar to the Danes early in the conflict. Gustavus II bought off the Danish claims at the Peace of Knared.

Kalmucks (käl′mŭks) or **Kalmycks** (käl′mĭks), Asiatic people, a branch of Oirat Mongols. They migrated from Altai region to lower Volga basin c.1636 and became vassals of Russia. To avoid Russian colonization, a large part of Kalmucks E of the Volga migrated to China in 1771, but were decimated along their arduous route. The others stayed on, clinging to their Lamaist Buddhist faith and to their traditional ways. During the Russian civil war of 1917–20 many migrated to Central and W Europe. The Kalmuck Autonomous Soviet Socialist Republic (28,650 sq. mi.; pop. 220,723; cap. Elista) was estab. 1935 and dissolved 1943, the Kalmucks having allegedly collaborated with the German invaders. Many fled to Germany and became "displaced persons"; those who remained were "resettled" elsewhere in USSR.

Kaluga (kŭlōō′gŭ), city (pop. 89,484), W European RSFSR, on Oka R. Machinery mfg. It was scene of murder of second false Dmitri (1610). Center of action in World War II, 1941.

Kalymnos (kä′lēmnôs), Greek island (41 sq. mi.; pop. 11,864); part of DODECANESE. Sponge-fishing center.

Kama (kä′mŭ), river, 1,262 mi. long, E European RSFSR; chief tributary of the Volga, which it joins below Kazan. Navigable about half the year, it is an important transportation route.

Kamakura (kämä′kōōrä), city (pop. 55,168), central Honshu, Japan. Known for *daibutsu*, 42-ft.-high bronze figure of Buddha, cast in 1252. Was eastern cap. of Ashikaga shogunate (1333–1573).

Kamchatka (kämchăt′kŭ), peninsula (104,200 sq. mi.), Khabarovsk Territory, RSFSR, in NE Siberia. It separates Sea of Okhotsk (W) from Bering Sea and Pacific Ocean. Beyond Cape Lopatka (S tip) lie the Kurile Isls. Petropavlovsk is main center. Two volcanic ranges, which rise to 15,666 ft. in Klyuchevskaya Sopka, enclose central valley (N–S), drained by Kamchatka R. (335 mi. long). There are hot springs, peat marshes, forests, petroleum, and coal deposits. Fishing, fur trapping, lumbering, and reindeer raising are chief occupations. The sparse population is mainly Russian, but in N part dwell native Kamchatkans and Koryaks. It was discovered 1697, and its conquest by Russia was completed 1732.

Kamehameha I (Kamehameha the Great) (kämä′hämä′hä), 1758–1819, Hawaiian monarch. United the islands in 1810, estab. law and order.

Kamehameha, Fort, at Pearl Harbor, Oahu, T.H.; hq. of coast defenses of Oahu; estab. 1909.

Kamenev, Lev Borisovich (lyĕf′ bŭrē′sŭvĭch kä′mĭnyĭf), 1883–1936, Russian Communist leader whose real name was Rosenfeld; brother-in-law of Trotsky. One of triumvirate (with Stalin and Zinoviev) which succeeded Lenin in 1924. Joined Trotsky's opposition 1925; twice expelled from party (1927, 1932); executed after 1936 treason trials.

Kamerlingh Onnes, Heike (hī′kŭ kä′mŭrlĭng ô′nŭs), 1853–1926, Dutch physicist. Won 1913 Nobel Prize chiefly for study of properties of helium.

Kamet (kä′mĕt), peak, 25,447 ft. high, on Tibet-India border, in Himalayas. Ascended 1931 by British expedition under F. S. Smythe.

kamikaze (kä′mēkä′zä) [Jap.,= divine wind], typhoon that destroyed Kublai Khan's fleet, foiling his invasion of Japan in 1281. In World War II, term used for Japanese suicide pilots (esp. active at Okinawa) who crashed their planes into enemy ships.

Kaministikwia or **Kaministiquia** (both: kŭmĭ″nĭstĭ′kwēŭ), river, c.60 mi. long, rising in W Ont., Canada, and flowing S, then E to L. Superior at Fort William. Was alternate route to the GRAND PORTAGE.

Kamloops (kăm′lōōps), town (pop. 8,099), S B.C., Canada, on Thompson R. Trading post estab. here 1812. Growth spurred by Cariboo gold rush. Canadian Pacific RR reached here 1885. Center of agr., mining, and lumbering area.

Kamperduin, Netherlands: see CAMPERDOWN.

Kanab (kŭnăb′), resort city (pop. 1,287), S Utah, near Ariz. line. Vivid countryside provides location for much film making (esp. "westerns"). Zion and Grand Canyon national parks are near.

Kanaoka (känä′ōkä), c.850–c.931, Japanese landscape and figure painter, founder of Kose school.

Kanawha (kŭnô′wŭ), river formed in SW W.Va. and flowing 97 mi. NW past Charleston to Ohio R. at Point Pleasant. Valley has chemical mfg. and mining.

Kanazawa (kä″nä′zäwä), city (pop. 231,441), central Honshu, Japan, on Sea of Japan. Mfg. of silk textiles,

porcelain, and lacquer ware. Park has noted gardens.

Kanchenjunga (kän″chŭnjōōng′gŭ), mountain, 28,146 ft. high, on Sikkim-Nepal border, in Himalayas; third highest in world. German expedition in 1931 climbed 26,220 ft. Also spelled Kinchinjunga.

Kanchipuram, India: see CONJEEVERAM.

Kandahar (kän″dŭhär′), city (pop. c.60,000) S Afghanistan. Cap. of Afghanistan, 1747–73. Held by the British in 19th-cent. Afghan Wars. Trade center in fruit-growing area.

Kandinsky, Vasily (vŭsē′lyē kŭndyēn′skē), 1866–1944, Russian abstract painter in Germany. With Klee he initiated German expressionism.

Kandy or **Candy** (kăn′dē), city (pop. 50,767), central Ceylon. Was cap. of independent kingdom of Ceylon, 1592–1815. Site of temple supposedly containing one of Buddha's teeth. Surrounding area has tea and rubber plantations.

Kane, Elisha Kent, 1820–57, American arctic explorer. Accompained first Grinnell expedition (1850) seeking lost Franklin party. Interest in his published account made possible second expedition (1853–55), which discovered Kane Basin.

Kane, borough (pop. 5,706), NW Pa., NW of Ridgeway. Oil wells and refineries; health resort.

Kaneohe Bay (kä′nāōhä), E Oahu, Hawaiian Isls. U.S. naval air station here.

kangaroo, vegetarian MARSUPIAL of Australia and Tasmania. The front limbs are small and the long, powerful hind limbs enable the animal to leap swiftly over the ground; the long muscular tail aids balance while leaping and is a prop when standing or moving slowly. In the large kangaroos and wallaroos (genus *Macropus*) the hind foot of adults is more than 10 in. long; in the smaller kangaroos or wallabies (members of several genera) the hind foot is 6–10 in. long. Tree kangaroos (genus *Dendrolagus*) are partially arboreal; rat kangaroos are smallest forms.

Kaniapiskau (känyŭpĭ′skô″), river, NE Que., Canada, issues from **Kaniapiskau Lake,** on St. Lawrence-Hudson Bay watershed. Flows 450 mi. generally NNW to form Koksoak R. with Larch R.

Kankakee (kăngkŭkē′), city (pop. 25,856), E Ill., on Kankakee R. and SW of Chicago. Industrial and shipping center in agr. area. Mfg. of brick, tile, clothing, furniture, and paint; limestone quarries.

Kankakee, river, c.135 mi. long, rising near South Bend, N. Ind., and flowing SW to Kankakee, Ill., then NW to Des Plaines R. below Joliet to form the Illinois.

Kannapolis (kŭnăp′ŭlĭs), cotton-mill "company town" (pop. 28,448), W central N.C., NNE of Charlotte; founded 1906.

Kano (kä′nō), family or school of Japanese painters. Its forerunner, **Kano Masanobu** (mäsä′nōbōō), c.1453–c.1550, painted landscapes, birds, and figure pieces, chiefly in ink, with touches of palest tints. His son, **Kano Motonobu** (mōtō′nōbōō), c.1476–1559, actual founder of school, gave it its character—the subordination of color to design. The painting of **Kano Eitoku** (ä′tōkōō), 1543–90, grandson of Motonobu, is characterized by energy, ease, and inventiveness. His grandson, **Kano Tanyu** (tänyōō′), 1602–74, was so original and versatile that he really created a school of his own.

Kano (kä′nō), city (pop. 89,162), N Nigeria. Built in 16th cent. on site of 9th-cent. settlement. Flourished as caravan center in 19th cent. Now an important transport center, with international airport. Chief town of Nigeria's peanut industry.

Kanpur: see CAWNPORE.

Kansa Indians, North American tribe of Siouan linguistic stock, known also as Kansas and Kaw Indians. They were at the mouth of the Kansas R. in the 18th cent., later moved farther W, were settled on a reservation at Council Grove until 1873, then were moved to present Okla., near the related Osage Indians. Had a typical Plains culture.

Kansas, state (82,276 sq. mi.; pop. 1,905,299), central

U.S. (has geographical center of U.S.); admitted 1861 as 34th state (free); cap. TOPEKA. Other cities are KANSAS CITY, WICHITA. Bounded NE by Missouri R. Major rivers are the KANSAS, ARKANSAS. Rises from Mississippi valley plains of E to GREAT PLAINS in W. Agr. of grain (esp. wheat, corn); cattle, hogs, dairy products, poultry. Mfg. of cement, agr. implements, airplanes, food and dairy products, metal goods, lumber products; meat packing, oil refining. Mining (oil, natural gas, coal, lead, zinc). Part of Louisiana Purchase except for SE corner (ceded by Texas in 1850). Part of INDIAN TERRITORY until made separate territory under KANSAS-NEBRASKA BILL (1854). Violence between proslavery and antislavery factions filled years before Civil War (see BROWN, JOHN). Agr. developed after war. Grasshopper plague (1874), droughts, depression of 1880s caused hardship. Farmers supported POPULIST PARTY until conditions improved, then returned to allegiance to Republican party. State marked by conservative, moral tone. Government subsidies, storage elevators for grain, and conservation measures have been introduced to stabilize the basically agr. economy of the state.

Kansas, sometimes called the **Kaw,** river formed by junction of Smoky Hill and Republican rivers in NE Kansas. Flows c.170 mi. E to the Missouri at Kansas City. Drains Kansas and parts of Nebr. and Colo.

Kansas, University of, mainly at Lawrence; state supported, coed.; chartered 1864, opened 1866 with aid from A. A. Lawrence.

Kansas City, two adjacent cities of same name, one (pop. 129,553) in Kansas, the other (pop. 456,622) in Mo., at junction of Missouri and Kansas (or Kaw) rivers, almost in geographical center of U.S. Each is second largest city of its state. They are a great commercial, industrial, transportation, and cultural center, with stockyards, grain elevators, oil refineries, and railroad shops, and food-processing, soap, and metal products plants. Surrounding area was starting point of many westward expeditions; Santa Fe and Oregon trails passed through here. Several early 19th-cent. settlements were foundations for these present-day cities. One was Westport (in Mo.) where Confederate forces were decisively defeated on Oct. 21–23, 1864, thus ending last Confederate invasion of Far West. Kansas City, Kansas, has Univ. of Kansas Hospitals. Kansas City, Mo., has Nelson Gall. of Art and Univ. of Kansas City (coed.; 1929). Kansas City *Star* was founded by W. R. Nelson, 1880. Political reform move in 1937 led to deposing of T. J. PENDERGAST.

Kansas-Nebraska Bill, legislation by which U.S. Congress estab. territories of Kansas and Nebraska, more properly Kansas-Nebraska Act, since it became law on May 30, 1854. Sectional conflict over slavery and over location of transcontinental railroad made territorial organization a serious problem. Southerners, wanting no free territory W of Mo., had already defeated four attempts to organize a single territory for the area. Bill, presented by Stephen A. Douglas, provided for "popular sovereignty" (see SQUATTER SOVEREIGNTY) and creation of two territories instead of one. An amendment specifically repealed Missouri Compromise. Bill caused sectional division to grow beyond reconciliation. Proslavery and antislavery forces exerted pressure to determine "popular" decision in Kansas in their own favor (see EMIGRANT AID COMPANY); result was "bleeding" Kansas. Opponents of bill founded new Republican party.

Kansas State College of Agriculture and Applied Science, at Manhattan; land-grant, state supported, coed.; chartered and opened 1863.

Kansu (gän'soo'), province (150,000 sq. mi.; pop. 7,000,-000), NW China; cap. Lanchow. Climate conditioned by nearness of Gobi Desert. Agri. (opium, cotton, tobacco), stock raising. Leading Chinese producer of petroleum; coal also mined.

Kant, Immanuel (känt), 1724–1804, German philosopher, one of the greatest figures in the history of philosophy. He lived a quiet life at Königsberg, becoming professor of logic and metaphysics at the university and quietly evolving a system of thought that influenced all succeeding philosophers in one way or another. His great works are *Critique of Pure Reason* (1781), *Foundations of the Metaphysics of Ethics* (1785), *Critique of Practical Reason* (1788), *Critique of Judgment* (1790), and *Religion within the Boundaries of Pure Reason* (1793–94). In them he set forth intricate and well-knit arguments that defy brief summary. He distinguished sharply between the things of our experience (phenomena), which can be fitted into categories of our understanding (including causality and substantiality) and things-in-themselves (noumena), which the intellect cannot actually fathom. To illustrate the failure of the intellect to deal with things-in-themselves, he set up the antinomies, logical contradictions of principles which cannot be resolved; thus, he demonstrated that space and time are infinite and that they are finite, that God exists and that he does not exist. Yet though we cannot *know* the noumenal realm, we can know that it exists. Ethics and aesthetics are grounded in it. Moral conduct rests upon the categorical imperative, which may be expressed as, "Act as if the maxim from which you act were to become through your will a universal law of nature" and also as "So act as to treat humanity, whether in your own person or that of another, in every case as an end in itself, never as a means." Faith, not knowledge, justifies belief in freedom of the will, immortality, and God.

kaolin: see CHINA CLAY.

kaolinite (kā'ulĭnīt), crystallized clay mineral forming main constituent of kaolin and china clay. It is a hydrous aluminum silicate resulting chiefly from weathering of feldspar.

Kapilavastu (kä"pĭluvä'stoo), town, S Nepal. A pillar marks birthplace of Buddha.

kapok (kā'pŏk, kä'–), tropical tree of Bombacaceae family and the fiber (floss) obtained from its ripe pods. Light, resilient, and resistant to water and decay, the fiber has been of commercial value since 1890s for filling and insulation. Oil from seed kernels is used for soap and as edible oil.

Kappel or **Cappel** (kä'pùl), village, Switzerland, S of Zurich. Here ZWINGLI fell in battle (1531).

Kapteyn, Jacobus Cornelius (yäkö'bùs kôrnā'lĭùs käptīn'), 1851–1922, Dutch astronomer, authority on Milky Way system. Computed positions of many stars of S Hemisphere.

Kapuas (kä'pooäs), longest river of Borneo, rising on Sarawak border, flowing 710 mi. to South China Sea.

Karabakh, USSR; see MOUNTAIN-KARABAKH.

Karachi (kùrä'chē), city (pop. 1,005,000), W Pakistan, on Arabian Sea. After it passed to the British in 1843 it became main port for NW India. Became cap. of Pakistan in 1947 and grew phenomenally (1941 pop. 386,655). Country's chief port, it ships grains, salt, hides, and wool.

Karafuto, former Japanese possession: see SAKHALIN.

Karaganda (kä"rùgùndä'), city (pop. c.220,000), Kazakh SSR, in Kazakh Hills. Center of one of largest coal basins in USSR, developed after 1928.

Karageorge (kä"rùjôrj', kä"räjôr'jä) [Turkish,= Black George], Serbo-Croatian *Czerny George*, 1752?–1817, Serbian patriot. An illiterate peasant, he led Serbian insurrection against Turks (1804), took Belgrade (1806), was proclaimed hereditary chief of Serbia (1808). Abandoned by his Russian allies in 1812, he fled to Austria. On his return to Serbia he was murdered at instigation of MILOSH Obrenovich. From him is descended the **Karageorgevich** (kä"rùjôr'jùvĭch) dynasty of Serbia and Yugoslavia—Prince ALEXANDER and Kings PETER I, ALEXANDER, and PETER II. The family was long in feud with the OBRENOVICH dynasty.

Karaites (kâ'rŭīts), Jewish anti-Talmudic sect, founded c.765 in Persia, which proclaimed freedom of individual to interpret Bible according to his own conception. At present has some adherents in Crimea.

Karajich, Vuk Stefanovich (vŏŏk′ stĕfä′nôvĭch kä′-räyĭch), 1787–1864, Serbian philologist and folklorist. He adopted Serbian vernacular as his literary language, introduced phonetic spelling, and invented new letters to complete the Cyrillic alphabet. In 1847 he translated the New Testament into Serbian.

Karakalpak Autonomous Soviet Socialist Republic (kä″rükülpäk′), autonomous republic (61,600 sq. mi.; pop. c.600,000), NW Uzbek SSR, comprising part of Ust-Urt plateau, Kizil Kum desert, and Amu Darya delta on Aral Sea; cap. Nukus. Produces cotton and alfalfa. Population consists mostly of Turkic Karakalpaks, Uzbeks, Kazakhs—all Moslems.

Karakoram (kä″rükō′rŭm), mountain system, N Kashmir, extending c.300 mi. Main range (sometimes called Mustagh) has large glaciers and includes Mt. GODWIN-AUSTEN, second highest peak in world.

Karakorum (kä″rükō′rŭm), ruined city, Mongolian People's Republic. Was cap. of Jenghiz Khan.

Kara Kul (kä′rŭ kŏŏl′), mountain lake, area 140 sq. mi., Tadzhik SSR, in the Pamir, near Chinese border; alt. 12,980 ft. and depth 775 ft.

karakul sheep: see SHEEP.

Kara Kum (kä″rŭ kŏŏm′), large desert, Turkmen SSR, S of Amu Darya R. Crossed by Trans-Caspian RR. Here is MERV oasis. Seminomadic population raises goats, camels, karakul sheep. Sulphur mines.

Karaman (kärämän′) or **Caraman,** town (pop. 13,605), S Turkey, N of Taurus mts. Taken by a Turkic tribe c.1250, it became the cap. of the emirate of Karamania, a successor state of the Seljuk empire. Karamania, which once comprised most of Asia Minor, fell to the Ottoman Turks in the mid-15th cent. There are ruins of a castle and two fine college-mosques.

Karamzin, Nikolai Mikhailovich (nyĭkŭlī′ mēkhī′lŭvĭch kŭrŭmzēn′), 1766–1826, Russian historian and novelist. Wrote *Letters of a Russian Traveler* (1792) and an 11-volume history of Russia (1818–24).

Kara Sea, section of Arctic Ocean, between W Siberia and Novaya Zemlya. Receives Ob, Yenisei, Pyasina, and Taimyra rivers. Navigable Aug.–Sept.

Karbala, Iraq: see KERBELA.

Karelo-Finnish Soviet Socialist Republic or **Karelia** (kürēl′yů), constituent republic (68,900 sq. mi.; pop. c.600,000), USSR, in NE Europe, between Finland and the White Sea; cap. Petrozavodsk. A glaciated plateau stretching from Kola Peninsula in N to L. Ladoga and L. Onega in S, it is covered by thousands of lakes and by dense coniferous forests. Karelia has important lumber industries (paper, furniture, prefabricated houses); marble, quartzite, and porphyry quarries; iron, magnetite, and lead-zinc ores. Majority of population is Russian; the rest are Karelians and Finns, whose written languages are identical. W Karelia, conquered by Swedes in 12th cent., shared history of Finland till 1940. E Karelia, conquered by Novgorod in 13th cent., became an autonomous republic of RSFSR in 1923; in 1940 it was made a constituent republic, enlarged by most of the territory ceded by Finland after the Finnish-Russian War. The **Karelian Isthmus** is a land bridge 90 mi. long and 25–70 mi. wide, connecting Russia and Finland, between the Gulf of Finland and L. Ladoga. It contains the cities of Leningrad and Vyborg. Until 1940 all except its S end belonged to Finland, which built the MANNERHEIM LINE across it. The Russo-Finnish peace treaty of 1940 and the Finnish peace treaty of 1947 gave the whole isthmus to the USSR; N part went to Karelo-Finnish SSR; S part to RSFSR.

Karenni State (kürě′nē), constituent unit (4,506 sq. mi.; pop. 70,493) of Union of Burma, in Upper Burma; cap. Loikaw. Largely autonomous. Produces tungsten and teak. People are mainly Karens.

Karens (kürĕnz′), members of Thai-Chinese cultural group, one of most important minorities in Burma (esp. in Karenni State). Some are pagan, but many are Christian and Buddhist.

Karfiol, Bernard (kär′fēōl), 1886–1952, American painter, known for nudes, landscapes, portraits.

Karikal: see FRENCH INDIA.

Karkonosze, Polish name of RIESENGEBIRGE.

Karlfeldt, Erik Axel, 1864–1931, Swedish lyric poet. He was posthumously awarded the 1931 Nobel Prize in Literature, which he had refused in his lifetime.

Karlovy Vary, Czechoslovakia: see CARLSBAD.

Karlowitz, Treaty of (kär′lōvĭts), 1699, between Turkey and the Holy League (the emperor, Venice, Poland). Turkey ceded Hungary, Crotia, Slavonia to Emperor Leopold I; Podolia to Poland; Peloponnesus to Venice.

Karlsbad, Czechoslovakia: see CARLSBAD.

Karlsburg, Rumania: see ALBA-IULIA.

Karlsefni, Thorfinn: see THORFINN KARLSEFNI.

Karlskrona (kärlskrōō′nä), city (pop. 30,997), co. seat of Blekinge co., S Sweden. A Baltic port built on islands and on mainland, it is hq. of Swedish navy (since 1680). Fortifications and docks are cut out of granite. Sometimes spelled Carlskrona.

Karlsruhe (kärls′rŏŏù), city (pop. 198,014), Württemberg-Baden, W Germany, near the Rhine, with which it is linked by canal. Industrial center (metallurgy, food mfg.). Has several institutes of higher learning; well-known theaters and art galleries. Founded 1715, it was laid out in a semicircle, with streets converging radially upon ducal palace (heavily damaged in World War II). Was cap. of Baden-Durlach 1715–71; of Baden 1771–1945. Formerly spelled Carlsruhe.

Karlstad (kärl′städ), city (pop. 35,651), co. seat of Varmland co., W central Sweden, port on Vanern L. and on Thingvalla isl. It is a Lutheran episcopal see. It has lumber, pulp, and textile mills and shipyards. Union of Norway and Sweden was severed by treaty signed here, 1905.

Karlstadt, Reformation leader: see CARLSTADT.

Karmathians or **Carmathians,** crypto-Moslem sect, similar to ASSASSIN sect. An independent political force, they conquered Arabia early in the 10th cent., defied Abbasid caliph, and rocked Islam (c.930) by taking the black stone from the Kaaba, keeping it 10 years. They declined after 1000.

Karnak (kär′näk), town (pop. 10,865), central Egypt, on the Nile. Near LUXOR, it occupies part of the site of THEBES. Most notable of ancient ruins here is temple of Amon (XVIII dynasty), with its impressive Great Hall of Columns.

Karo, Joseph ben Ephraim: see CARO.

Karolyi, Count Julius, Hung. *Károlyi Gyula* (kä′rôlyĭ dyōō′lō), 1871–, Hungarian premier (1931–32). Though a nationalist, he abandoned Hungarian agitation for a revision of Treaty of Trianon in an effort to obtain foreign loans. His brother, **Count Michael Karolyi,** Hung. *Károlyi Mihály* (mĭ′hĭ), 1875–, a socialistic liberal, became premier of Hungary after abdication of Charles IV (1918). Elected president of the provisional republic (1919), he reluctantly surrendered the government to the Communists. He was Hungarian ambassador in Paris 1947–49.

Karpathos (kär′päthôs), Ital. *Scarpanto,* Greek island (111 sq. mi.; pop. 7,396); part of DODECANESE.

Karrer, Paul (kä′rür), 1889–, Swiss chemist. Shared 1937 Nobel Prize for work on vitamins, flavins, and carotinoids.

Kars (kärs), city (pop. 20,524), NE Turkey, in Armenia. Long an important fortress, it was taken by the Russians in 1828, 1855, and 1878. Kars dist. was formally ceded to Russia at Congress of Berlin (1878) but was returned to Turkey in 1921.

Karst, Ital. *Carso,* Serbo-Croatian *Kras,* barren limestone plateau, NW Yugoslavia. Characterized by deep fissures, caves (see POSTOJNA), underground channels. The name karst applies also to similar geological formations elsewhere.

Karun (kärōōn′), biblical *Ulai,* anc. *Euloeus,* river, 500 mi. long, rising in SW Iran and flowing into Shatt el Arab on Iraq border.

Kaschau, Czechoslovakia: see KOSICE.

Kashmir (kăshmēr'), officially **Jammu and Kashmir** (jŭ'-mōō), state (82,258 sq. mi.; pop. 4,370,000), N Indian subcontinent; summer cap. Srinagar, winter cap. Jammu. Mainly mountainous. Vale of Kashmir (valley of Jhelum R.) is most populous area; produces wheat and rice. Formerly renowned for cashmere shawls. Was under Hindu rulers until 14th cent., when it fell to Moslems who converted most of the people to Islam. Moslem rule was overthrown 1819 by Ranjit Singh, aided by the Rajput Gulab Singh (a Hindu), who became raja and his heirs the maharajas of Kashmir. After partition of India (1947) Moslem tribesmen, aided in 1948 by Pakistan forces, sought control of state; opposed by Hindu maharaja (who acceded to India) and by Indian troops which occupied most of area. Dispute was brought 1948 before UN, which effected a ceasefire early in 1949. Both sides agreed to plebiscite, but no agreement had been reached in late 1952 on how it should be held.

Kashmiri language (kăshmē'rē), language of Indic or Indo-Aryan group of Indo-Iranian subfamily of Indo-European languages. See LANGUAGE (table).

Kasimir: see CASIMIR.

Kaskaskia (kăskă'skēŭ), village (pop. 112), Ill., on Kaskaskia Isl. in the Mississippi at junction with Kaskaskia R. Settled by Jesuits 1703. French had fort here 1733–55; destroyed by British 1763. George Rogers Clark took possession for U.S. in 1778. Cap. of Illinois Territory 1809–18. Fort Kaskaskia State Park is near by.

Kaskaskia, river rising in E central Ill., near Urbana, and flowing c.320 mi. SW to the Mississippi NW of Kaskaskia.

Kasner, Edward (kă'snŭr), 1878–, American mathematician, known especially for studies of relativity, horn angles, invariants, polygonic functions.

Kassa, Czechoslovakia: see KOSICE.

Kassaba or **Cassaba** (kăsă'bä), city (pop. 25,139), W Turkey, NE of Smyrna; modern Turgutlu. Famed for type of melon named after it.

Kassel (kä'sŭl), city (1939 pop. 216,141; 1950 pop. 161,-322), Hesse, W Germany, on Fulda R.; also spelled Cassel. Center of locomotive and machinery industries; during World War II a center of armaments production. Virtually obliterated by Allied bombings. Paintings of celebrated gallery (itself destroyed) were saved. Kassel was after 1567 the cap. of the landgraviate of Hesse-Kassel (raised to electorate 1803); cap. of kingdom of Westphalia 1807–13; cap. of Hesse-Nassau prov. 1866–1945.

Kasserine Pass, gap, 2 mi. wide, W Tunisia, in an extension of Atlas Mts. Here in World War II German attack was contained by Allies in decisive battle (Feb., 1943) of Tunisian campaign.

Kasson, John Adam (kă'sŭn), 1822–1910, American political leader and diplomat. U.S. Representative from Iowa (1863–67, 1873–77, 1881–84). U.S. minister to Austria-Hungary (1877–81), to Germany (1884–85).

Katahdin (kŭtä'dĭn), mountain, 5,268 ft. high, between branches of Penobscot R. in N central Maine. Highest point in Maine.

Katayama, Tetsu (tĕtsōō kätäyä'mä), 1887–, Japanese statesman. Leader of Social Democratic party, prime minister of coalition cabinet (1947–48).

Katayev, Valentin Petrovich (vŭlyĭntyēn' pētrô'vĭch kŭtī'ŭf), 1897–, Russian author. His novels *The Embezzlers* (1926), *Time, Forward!* (1932), and *The Wife* (1944), all translated into English, portray Soviet life. Also wrote popular comedies.

Katharine or **Katherine.** For some persons thus named, see CATHERINE.

Katharine of Aragon, 1485–1536, queen of England, daughter of Ferdinand and Isabella of Spain and first wife of HENRY VIII. She did not produce a male heir and her political importance waned after the collapse (1525) of the Spanish alliance. Henry, infatuated with Anne Boleyn, tried to have the marriage annulled. Pope denied the divorce, and Henry married Anne

secretly. Led to English Reformation. Katharine never accepted the decision that her marriage was invalid. She was confined and died after a prolonged illness.

Katkov, Mikhail Nikiforovich (mēkhŭyēl' nyĭkē'fŭrŭvĭch kŭtkôf'), 1818–87, Russian journalist. Became a reactionary and Slavophile adviser of Alexander III.

Katmai National Monument: see NATIONAL PARKS AND MONUMENTS (table).

Kato, Takaakira, Viscount (tä"kä-ä'kērä kä'tō), 1859–1926, Japanese statesman. Largely responsible for Twenty-one Demands presented to China. As prime minister (1924–25) he cut budget and army strength, sponsored manhood-suffrage law.

Katowice (kätôvē'tsĕ), Ger. *Kattowitz,* city (pop. 128,-290), cap. of Silesia prov., SW Poland. It is the center of an important mining district (coal, iron, zinc, lead) which also contains the industrial centers of Beuthen, Chorzow, Gleiwitz, Hindenburg. Katowice has metallurgical, chemical, electrical, and other industries. Inc. 1867, it passed from Prussia to Poland in 1921.

Katrine, Loch (lŏkh kăt'rĭn), lake, c.8 mi. long and 1 mi. wide, Perthshire and Stirlingshire, Scotland. Outlet flows to Teith R. In 1859 Loch became source of water supply for Glasgow.

Kattegat (kă'tĭgăt"), strait, 137 mi. long and 37–c.100 mi. wide, between Sweden and Jutland, Denmark. It connects with North Sea through the Skagerrak, with Baltic Sea through the Oresund, Great Belt, and Little Belt. Goteborg (Sweden) and Aarhus (Denmark) are chief ports. Also spelled Cattegat.

Kattowitz, Poland: see KATOWICE.

katydid, insect of long-horned grasshopper family. Most of c.7,000 species are green and eat plants. Produce sound by rubbing forewings together.

Katyn (kūtĭn'), village, RSFSR, W of Smolensk. Mass grave of some 10,000 Polish officers, imprisoned after Poland's defeat in 1939, was found in a near-by forest by German occupation forces in 1943. Russians, though they denied having committed the massacre, refused international investigation. They later accused Germans of the crime.

Kauai (kou"wī'), island (551 sq. mi.; pop. 29,683), one of the Hawaiian Isls. In central mountain mass are Kawaikini (5,170 ft.), the highest peak, and scenic WAIALEALE. Produces sugar, rice, and pineapples. Lihue is principal town.

Kauffman, Angelica, 1741–1807, Swiss historical and portrait painter. As protégée of Sir Joshua Reynolds she enjoyed great success in England and Italy.

Kaufman, George S. (kôf'mŭn, kouf'–), 1889–, American playwright. Sole author of only one play (*The Butter and Egg Man,* 1925), he has collaborated on many, including *Of Thee I Sing* (with Morrie Ryskind, 1931, score by George Gershwin), *You Can't Take It with You* (with Moss Hart, 1936), and *Stage Door* (with Edna Ferber, 1936).

Kaukauna (kôkô'nŭ), city (pop. 8,337), E Wis., on Fox R. and E of Appleton. Railroad shops, creameries, stone quarries, and paper mills.

Kaulbach, Wilhelm von (vĭl'hĕlm fŭn koul'bäkh), 1805–74, German historical painter.

Kaunas (kou'näs), Rus. *Kovno,* city (pop. 154,109), central Lithuania. It is an active port on the Niemen, with food and textile mfg. A Lithuanian stronghold against the Teutonic Knights in medieval times, Kaunas passed to Russia in third Polish partition (1795). It was the provisional cap. of Lithuania 1918–40, VILNA being held by Poland. The Germans, who occupied Kaunas 1941–44, massacred nearly all the Jews (c.30% of prewar population) and destroyed most of city before withdrawing. The university was founded 1922.

Kaunitz, Wenzel Anton, Fürst von (vĕn'tsŭl än'tōn fürst' fŭn kou'nĭts), 1711–94, Austrian chancellor and foreign minister under Maria Theresa, Joseph II, and Leopold II. His astute diplomacy created the anti-Prussian coalition that led to the SEVEN YEARS WAR and secured a share for Austria in the Polish partition of 1772.

Kautsky, Karl Johann (kärl yō'hän kout'skē), 1854–1938, German-Austrian socialist, co-founder of the Independent Social Democratic party in Germany, and a dominant figure in Second International. He opposed Lenin and Bolshevism as well as those who advocated revision of Marxist doctrines.

Kavalla or **Kavala** (both: kävä'lä), city (pop. 49,667), E Macedonia, Greece; an Aegean port on the Gulf of Kavalla. Chief Greek tobacco center. Taken by Bulgaria from Turkey in first Balkan War; ceded to Greece after second Balkan War (1913).

Kaveri: see CAUVERY.

Kaw, river: see KANSAS, river.

Kawartha Lakes (kùwôr'thù), group of 14 lakes in Lindsay-Peterborough area, S Ont., Canada. Popular resort region.

Kawasaki (käwä'sä'kē) city (pop. 252,923), central Honshu, Japan, on Tokyo Bay. Steel mills, shipyards.

Kaw Indians: see KANSA INDIANS.

Kay, John, 1704–64, English inventor of fly shuttle, patented 1733, important in mechanical weaving.

kayak: see CANOE.

Kayseri (kī'sērē), anc. *Caesarea Mazaca,* city (pop. 65,489), central Turkey. Agr. center; cotton and tile mfg. Was important in Byzantine and Seljuk empires. Also known as Kaisaria.

Kazakh Soviet Socialist Republic (käzäk') or **Kazakhstan** (kä"zäkstän'), second largest constituent republic (1,063,200 sq. mi.; pop. c.6,000,000) of USSR, in central Asia, bordering on Caspian Sea (W) and China (E); cap. Alma-Ata. It consists of the dry Caspian and Turan lowlands, the arid Ust Urt plateau, and the Kazakh hills, and it contains the Aral Sea and L. Balkhash. In the E and S rise the Altai and Ala-Tau ranges. The Irtysh, Ural, Ili, and Syr Darya are the chief rivers. Wheat is grown in black-earth steppes of N; camels and sheep are raised in arid central section; irrigated S plains grow rubber-bearing plants, cotton, rice, fruit, and other crops. Industry is based on rich mineral resources (copper, coal, lead, zinc, iron). The Kazakhs (57% of pop.) are a Turkic-speaking Moslem group of warlike ancestry. Area came under Russian rule in 19th cent.

Kazan (kùzän'), city (pop. c.500,000), cap. Tatar ASSR, E European RSFSR, near the Volga, where its port and shipyards are. A major industrial and commercial center, it has mfg. of locomotives, aircraft, agr. machinery, synthetic rubber, gunpowder, and textiles. There are various cultural institutions including a university (founded 1804). Founded 1401, Kazan was cap. of a powerful khanate, which was conquered 1552 by Ivan IV. In 18th cent. it became an E outpost of Russian colonization. Of the Moslem period of Kazan little remains except the Suyumbeka tower in the 16th-cent. kremlin.

Kazanlik (kä"zänlīk'), town (pop. 19,386), central Bulgaria, in a valley famous for its rose fields. Long a mfg. center for attar of roses.

Kazbek, Mount (kŏzbĕk'), peak, 16,541 ft. high, N Georgian SSR, in central greater Caucasus, above DARYAL gorge. Its glaciers give rise to Terek R. First scaled 1868.

Kazvin or **Qazvin** (both: käzvēn'), city (pop. 60,013), NW Iran. Was cap. of Persia, 1514–90. A mosque of Harun-al-Rashid is here. Trades in silk, fruit, and rice. Carpet making.

Kea or **Keos,** Greek island of the CYCLADES.

Kealakekua Bay (kä'ùläkākōō'ù), W Hawaii, T.H., in Kona district. On shore is British monument to Capt. James Cook, killed here by natives in 1779.

Kean, Edmund, 1787?–1833, English actor. His triumph (1814) as Shylock is a landmark in theatrical history. Other great roles of his brief career include Iago, Lear, and Richard III. Kean's intensity and insight made him one of England's greatest actors. His son, **Charles John Kean,** 1811?–1868, was an actor whose forte was melodrama. Played opposite his wife, **Ellen Tree Kean,** 1808–80. Her first appearance (1829) estab. her as a comedienne. Retired after her husband's death.

Keansburg, resort borough (pop. 5,559), E N.J., on Raritan Bay and ESE of Perth Amboy.

Kearney, Dennis (kär'nē), 1847–1907, American political agitator, b. Ireland. In 1870s he inflamed Californians against Chinese labor. Formed a working-men's party which achieved reform measures.

Kearney (kär'nē), city (pop. 12,115), S Nebr., on Platte R. and SW of Grand Island; founded 1871. Trade, processing, and rail center in Great Plains grain and livestock area. Site of Fort Kearney (1848–71), estab. to protect Oregon Trail, is near.

Kearny, Stephen Watts (kär'nē), 1794–1848, American general in Mexican War. Commanded Army of the West. Took Santa Fe and Los Angeles; served as military governor of California territory until May, 1847. His cousin, **Lawrence Kearny,** 1789–1868, was an American naval officer. Commanding East India squadron (1840–43), he opened negotiations which led to a U.S.–China commercial treaty, signed 1844. **Philip Kearny,** 1814–62, nephew of S. W. Kearny, was a Union general in Civil War. Led 1st N.J. Brigade in Peninsular campaign and second battle of Bull Run. Killed at Chantilly. Noted for courage and dash, idolized by his men.

Kearny (kär'nē), town (pop. 39,952), NE N.J., E of Newark on tidal wastelands (under reclamation) between Passaic and Hackensack rivers. Shipyards, drydocks; mfg. of lineoleum, aluminum ware, chemicals, electrical products, and paint.

Kearsarge (kēr'särj"), Union ship in the Civil War. See CONFEDERATE CRUISERS.

Keats, John, 1795–1821, English lyric poet. Educated for surgery, he turned to poetry under influence of Charles Cowden Clarke. *Poems* (1817) included "Sleep and Poetry" and "I stood tip-toe upon a little hill." His long poem *Endymion* (1818) was cruelly attacked by critics. In that year he developed tuberculosis, and began his passionate, hopeless love for Fanny Brawne. His *Lamia, Isabella, The Eve of St. Agnes, and Other Poems* appeared in 1820. He sailed soon after to Italy in search of health with his friend Joseph Severn, but died in Rome. Despite a tragically brief life, Keats is one of greatest English poets. Among the poems that are masterpieces of romanticism are "Ode to a Nightingale," "Ode on a Grecian Urn," "To Autumn," "Ode to Melancholy," and the unfinished narrative "Hyperion." "The Eve of St. Agnes" and "La Belle Dame sans Merci" show romantic medievalism at its best. His most familiar sonnets are "On First Looking into Chapman's Homer," "When I have fears that I may cease to be," and "Bright star! would I were steadfast as thou art."

Keble, John (kē'bùl), 1792–1866, English clergyman and poet. His devotional poems in *The Christian Year* (1827), based on Book of Common Prayer, won him a professorship of poetry at Oxford. His sermon "National Apostasy," given in 1833, Newman called the beginning of OXFORD MOVEMENT. Wrote many hymns.

Keble College: see OXFORD UNIVERSITY.

Kebnekaise (kĕb'nùkī"sù), glaciated peak, 6,965 ft. high, Norrbotten co., N Sweden; highest in Sweden.

Kecskemet, Hung. *Kecskemét* (kĕch'kēmāt), city (pop. 87,269), central Hungary; center of fruit export.

Kedah (kē'dù), state (3,660 sq. mi.; pop. 554,581), NW MALAYA, on Strait of Malacca; cap. Alor Star. Ruled by a sultan. Siam transferred sovereignty over Kedah to Great Britain in 1909.

Kedesh (kē'-), one of the cities of refuge, N Palestine. It is frequently mentioned in the Bible. Also Kedesh-naphtali.

Keeler, James Edward, 1857–1900, American astronomer. Discovered many nebulae and confirmed theory that Saturn's rings are composed of meteoric particles.

Keelung (kē'lōong') or **Kilung,** Jap. *Kirun,* city (pop. 145,240), Formosa, China; also Chilung (jē'lōong'). Naval base on East China Sea. Shipbuilding, food processing. In 17th cent. occupied first by the Spaniards, later by the Dutch. Came under Chinese control in 1683; held by Japan 1895–1945.

Keene, Laura, c.1826–1873, Anglo-American actress and manager. Her most famous production was Taylor's *Our American Cousin,* given (Ford's Theater, Washington, 1865) when Lincoln was shot.

Keene, city (pop. 15,638), SW N.H., W of Manchester, in resort area; settled 1736. Mfg. of wood products, textiles, machinery, and shoes. Has railroad shops. A summer theater is here.

Keewatin (kēwä'tĭn), provisional district: see NORTHWEST TERRITORIES, Canada.

Keewatin: see ARCHEOZOIC ERA.

Kefauver, (Carey) Estes (kē'fävŭr), 1903–, U.S. Senator from Tenn. (1949–). Headed Senate crime investigating committee.

Keighley (kēth'lē), municipal borough (pop. 56,938), West Riding of Yorkshire, England. Products include textiles, leather, and paper.

Keitel, Wilhelm (vĭl'hĕlm kī'tŭl), 1882–1946, German field marshal. Chief of combined German general staff in World War II. Was hanged after Nuremberg war-crimes trial.

Keith, Sir Arthur (kēth), 1866–, British anthropologist and anatomist, authority on human evolution.

Keith, George, 1638–1716, Scottish preacher. At first a Friend, he estab. (1684) in America Christian Quakers, separatists denounced by William Penn 1692. Ordained priest (1700) in Church of England.

Keith, George, 1693?–1778, 10th earl marischal of Scotland. A leader in the Jacobite rebellion of 1715 and the Spanish expedition to Scotland (1719), he fled to the Continent. Held various high offices under Frederick the Great. His brother, **James Francis Edward Keith,** 1696–1758, also took part in the Jacobite rebellion and fled abroad. After service in Spain and Russia he was made (1747) a Prussian field marshal and rendered great service in the Seven Years War. Killed in the battle of Hochkirch.

Keith, George Keith Elphinstone, Viscount: see ELPHINSTONE, GEORGE KEITH.

Keith, James Francis Edward: see KEITH, GEORGE (1693?–1778).

Keith, Minor Cooper, 1848–1929, American magnate, founder of United Fruit Co. Dominated banana trade, greatly altered economic life of Central America.

Kekulé von Stradonitz, Friedrich August (frē'drĭkh ou'gōŏst kā'kōōlä fŭn shträ'dōnĭts), 1829–96, German chemist. Worked in organic chemistry, especially on benzene, for molecular structure of which he developed ring theory.

Kelantan: see MALAYA.

Keller, Gottfried (gôt'frēt), 1819–90, Swiss novelist, one of the major German prose writers. Among his chief works are the autobiographical novel *Der grüne Heinrich* (1854–55) and a collection of short novels, *People of Seldwyla* (1856–74; Eng. tr., 1929).

Keller, Helen (Adams), 1880–, American author and lecturer, blind and deaf from the age of two, grad. Radcliffe 1904. Her teacher and companion was Anne Sullivan Macy. Helen Keller gained world fame for her aid to the handicapped.

Kellermann, François Christophe (fräswä' krĕstôf' kĕlĕrmän'), 1735–1820, marshal of France; created duke of Valmy 1808. He and Dumouriez stopped Prussians at Valmy (1792).

Kelley, Hall Jackson, 1790–1874, American propagandist who urged settlement of Oregon.

Kelley, Oliver Hudson, 1826–1913, American agriculturist, a founder of the Natl. Grange of the Patrons of Husbandry, the central influence in the GRANGER MOVEMENT of the 1870s.

Kelley, William Darrah (dă'rŭ), 1814–90, U.S. Representative from Pa. (1861–90). Called "Pig Iron" Kelley for his protectionism and his allusions to iron industry of Pa. Humanitarian in his views.

Kellogg, Edward, 1790–1858, American economist. His scheme of government loans at low interest rates was backed by many radical political parties in U.S.

Kellogg, Frank B(illings), 1856–1937, American statesman. As U.S. Secretary of State (1925–29) he promoted KELLOGG-BRIAND PACT. Judge of Permanent Court of Internatl. Justice (1930–35).

Kellogg, city (pop. 4,913), N Idaho, between Coeur d'Alene and Wallace. Grew around Bunker Hill and Sullivan mines (discovered 1885), now combined as one of world's largest lead producers. Sunshine Mine is a leading U.S. silver producer.

Kellogg-Briand Pact (–brēä'), agreement, signed Aug. 27, 1928, condemning war and agreeing to peaceful settlement of international differences. More properly known as the Pact of Paris. Primary moving forces were Aristide BRIAND of France and F. B. KELLOGG of U.S. Effectiveness of pact vitiated by its failure to provide for enforcement.

Kells, town, Co. Meath, Ireland. Has relic of an ancient monastery founded by St. Columba. Here was found the **Book of Kells,** beautifully illuminated manuscript of the Latin Gospels, written probably 8th cent. Now in Trinity Col. library in Dublin.

Kelly, George, 1887–, American dramatist. Wrote satirical comedies (e.g., *The Torchbearers,* 1922; *The Show-off,* 1924) and drama *Craig's Wife* (1925).

Kelly, Howard Atwood, 1858–1943, American surgeon, influential professor of gynecology and obstetrics at Johns Hopkins (1889–1919). He was also an authority on American medical history.

Kelly, James Edward, 1855–1933, American sculptor of war memorials and historical subjects.

Kelly, William, 1811–88, American inventor. He independently discovered basic principle of Bessemer process and estab. his priority right. Conflict between Bessemer and Kelly interests was settled by consolidation of the rival companies.

Kelowna (kĭlō'nŭ), city (pop. 8,517), S B.C., Canada, ENE of Vancouver. Center of agr. area.

kelp, name for various species of brown algae, or seaweeds, found in waters along Atlantic and Pacific coasts. Some, e.g., *Macrocystis,* have fronds up to 200 ft. long; others are small. They are a source of potassium and iodine.

Kelso, lumber city (pop. 7,345), SW Wash., near Columbia R. and adjoining Longview. Timber, fish, fruit, and dairy industries.

Kelt: see CELT.

Kelvin, William Thomson, 1st Baron, 1824–1907, British mathematician and physicist. Inventor of many improvements in transmission of messages by submarine cables, of the reflecting galvanometer, and a siphon recorder for telegraphic messages; he also contributed to thermodynamics. He coordinated the various theories of heat, established on a firm basis Joule's law of conservation of energy, and introduced the Kelvin or absolute scale of TEMPERATURE.

Kemal Pasha, Mustafa: see ATATURK, KEMAL.

Kemble, Roger, 1721–1802, English actor and manager. Father of 12 children, he founded one of England's most distinguished acting families. His eldest son, **John Philip Kemble,** 1757–1823, was educated for the priesthood, but turned to the stage. Managed Drury Lane 1783–1802 (gaining fame in Shaksperian roles opposite his sister, Sarah Kemble SIDDONS) and Covent Garden, 1803–8. His brother, **George Stephen Kemble,** 1758–1822, played at Covent Garden and Haymarket. Managed Edinburgh Theater, 1792–1800. His youngest brother, **Charles Kemble,** 1757–1854, excelled in comic roles. Toured U.S. (1832–34) with his elder daughter, **Fanny Kemble** (Frances Ann Kemble), 1809–93. Her debut (1829) at Covent Garden as Juliet brought her fame, which she increased in such roles as Lady Macbeth, Portia, and Beatrice. In England she wrote against slavery during U.S. Civil War. Her sister, **Adelaide Kemble,** 1814–79, was a singer, notable in Italian operatic roles.

Kemerovo (kĕ'mŭrō"vō), city (pop. 132,978), RSFSR,

in S central Siberia, on Tom R. and on a branch of Trans-Siberian RR. Coal-mining center of Kuznetsk Basin, with chemical industries.

Kemi (kĕ'mē), city (pop. 23,959), NW Finland, on Gulf of Bothnia and at mouth of Kemi R. Lumber and cellulose industry.

Kemp, Will(iam), fl. 1579–1600, English comic actor and dancer, known as a player in Shakspere's company and for his morris dance from London to Norwich (1599).

Kempe, Margery (kĕmp), d. 1438 or after, English religious enthusiast. Her autobiography, perhaps the earliest in English, was known only in part until 1934.

Kempener, Pieter de (kĕm'pùnùr), c.1503–1580, Flemish religious painter. Worked in Italy and Spain.

Kempis, Thomas à: see THOMAS À KEMPIS.

Ken, Thomas, 1637–1711, English prelate and hymn writer. Bishop of Bath and Wells, he was deprived of his see in 1691 for refusing oath of allegiance to William III. His best-known hymn is the doxology, *Praise God from Whom All Blessings Flow*.

Kenai Peninsula (kē'nī), S Alaska, jutting into Gulf of Alaska, between Prince William Sound and Cook Inlet. Kenai Mts. cross it from NE to SW. Coastal climate mild, with abundant rainfall; growing season adequate for many crops. Forest, mineral, fishing resources; good farmland in W section. Alaska RR crosses peninsula from Seward. Kenai Natl. Moose Range (1941) is in N.

Kendal, Dame Madge, 1849–1935, English actress, whose maiden name was Margaret Robertson. Made her debut as Ophelia in 1865. Co-starred often with her husband, William Kendal (1843–1917), e.g., in Shakspere's *As You Like It* and in Sheridan's *Rivals*.

Kendall, Amos (kĕn'dùl), 1789–1869, American journalist and statesman. Leading member of Pres. Jackson's KITCHEN CABINET; defended Jackson's policies in Washington *Globe*. U.S. Postmaster General (1835–40); thoroughly reorganized department.

Kendall, Edward Calvin, 1886–, American biochemist. Shared 1950 Nobel Prize in Physiology and Medicine for work on hormones of the cortex of adrenal glands. Other contributions include isolation of thyroxin, preparation (with others) of cortisone by partial synthesis, and investigations (with co-workers) of effects of cortisone and ACTH (adrenocorticotropic hormone from the pituitary gland) on rheumatoid arthritis and rheumatic fever. Associated with Mayo Clinic from 1914 and with Mayo Foundation (of Univ. of Minnesota) from 1921.

Kendall, George Wilkins, 1809–67, American journalist. Cofounder of New Orleans *Picayune* (1837). His articles during Mexican War made him first modern war correspondent.

Kendall, William Sergeant, 1869–1938, American painter, best known for portraits of children.

Kendallville, city (pop. 6,119), NE Ind., NNW of Fort Wayne. Ships onions. Mfg. of metal products. Mulholland Mus. has Indian and pioneer relics.

Kenilworth (kĕn'ùl–), urban district (pop. 10,738), Warwickshire, England. Has ruins of noted castle celebrated in Scott's *Kenilworth*. Built c.1120, it was later the property of Simon de Montfort and of John of Gaunt. Earl of Leicester entertained Queen Elizabeth here lavishly in 1575.

Kenilworth ivy: see IVY.

Kenites, wilderness tribe, friendly to the Hebrews, with whom they came into Palestine.

Kenmore, residential village (pop. 20,066), W N.Y., near Buffalo; settled 1889. Mfg. of chemicals, machinery, and wood, metal, and rubber products.

Kennan, George, 1845–1924, American authority on Siberia. Explored Siberia and other parts of Russia. His articles were for many years only reliable source of information on the area. His grandnephew, **George F(rost) Kennan**, 1904–, became a diplomat. Originated (1947) U.S. policy of "containment" of Russia. He was made ambassador to USSR (1952), but his recall was demanded by Russian government. Retired 1953.

Kennebec (kĕn'ùbĕk), river, c.150 mi. long, flowing S from Moosehead L., NW Maine, to the Atlantic, receiving Dead and Androscoggin rivers. Furnishes power at Skowhegan, Waterville, and Augusta. Champlain explored it, 1604 and 1605.

Kennebunk (kĕn'ĭbŭngk), town (pop. 4,273), SW Maine, SW of Portland, in resort area; settled c.1650. Has Revolutionary church, with Paul Revere bell (1803).

Kennebunkport or **Kennebunk Port** (both: kĕn"ĭbŭngkpôrt'), town (pop. 1,522), SW Maine, on coast SE of Kennebunk; renamed from Arundel, 1821. Summer resort, especially for authors, artists, and actors.

Kennedy, John Pendleton, 1795–1870, American novelist, author of *Horse-Shoe Robinson* (1835). Was a member of Congress (1838–44) and Secretary of the Navy (1852–53).

Kennelly, Arthur Edwin (kĕ'nùlē), 1861–1939, American electrical engineer, b. India. His theory (advanced 1902, independently of Oliver Heaviside) that layer of ionized air in upper atmosphere deflects electromagnetic waves toward earth was later verified; the deflecting layer is called Heaviside layer, Kennelly-Heaviside layer, and ionosphere.

Kenner, farm trade and industrial town (pop. 5,535), SE La., near New Orleans.

Kennesaw Mountain (kĕn'ùsô): see NATIONAL PARKS AND MONUMENTS (table).

Kenneth I (Kenneth mac Alpin), d. 858, traditional founder of the kingdom of Scotland.

Kennett (kĕn'ĭt), city (pop. 8,685), SE Mo., near St. Francis R. and Ark. line, in cotton area. Has cotton gins and compresses.

Kennewick, city (pop. 10,106), SE Wash., on Columbia R. opposite Pasco, near influx of Snake R. Fruit and dairy products and wheat. Boomed in World War II by atomic-energy plant near Richland (NW).

Kenny, Elizabeth, 1886–1952, Australian nurse, originator of a system of treating infantile paralysis patients. Her method was based on use of hot, moist applications and passive exercise.

Kénogami (kānō'gùmē), town (pop. 9,895), S Que., Canada, on Sable R. and W of Chicoutimi. Here are hydroelectric station, paper and pulp mills.

Kenora (kùnô'rù), town (pop. 8,695), W Ont., Canada, at N end of L. of the Woods. Fishing, hunting, and canoeing base. Here are paper, pulp, lumber, and flour mills, boatbuilding, and fur trading.

Kenosha (kĭnō'shù), industrial city (pop. 54,368), SE Wis., on L. Michigan and S of Milwaukee; settled 1835. Mfg. of autos, mattresses, and metal products. Liberal German refugees came in 1850s.

Kensett, John Frederick, 1818–72, American landscape painter of Hudson River school.

Kensico Reservoir, N.Y.: see CATSKILL AQUEDUCT.

Kensington, metropolitan borough (pop. 168,054), W London, England; largely a residential district. Kensington Gardens, adjoining Hyde Park, includes Long Water (the Serpentine of Hyde Park), Round Pond, and Flower and Broad Walks. Kensington Palace, former royal residence, is W of gardens. South Kensington is site of part of British Mus., Victoria and Albert Mus., Imperial Inst., Science Mus., Royal Col. of Art, Royal Col. of Science, and Albert Hall.

Kensington Rune Stone, found near Kensington, Minn., in 1898. Contains account of Norse exploration party. Authenticity of stone much disputed.

Kent, James, 1763–1847, American jurist, first professor of law at Columbia College. Chancellor Kent had great influence on law in New York and U.S., principally through his *Commentaries on the American Law* (1826–30).

Kent, Rockwell, 1882–, American painter, wood engraver, and lithographer.

Kent, maritime county (1,525 sq. mi.; pop. 1,563,286), SE England; co. town Maidstone. North Downs cross county E to W. Largely agr. and pastoral, the region has growing industry as London urban area encroaches in W. Strategic location on path to the Continent has always made Kent important. Many religious houses were estab. in Middle Ages; Canterbury was goal of many pilgrimages (Chaucer's *Canterbury Tales*). Coast was heavily fortified in World Wars 1 and II against possible invasion.

Kent. 1 Resort town (pop. 1,392), W Conn., on Housatonic R. in hills at N.Y. line. Has Kent School for boys (prep.; Episcopal; 1906). **2** City (pop. 12,418), NE Ohio, NE of Akron. Mfg. of motor vehicles and electrical apparatus. Seat of Kent State Univ.

Kent, kingdom of, one of the states of the Anglo-Saxon heptarchy in England. Settled in mid-5th cent. by the Jutes, perhaps under Hengist and Horsa. St. Augustine of Canterbury led first Catholic mission to England here in 597. Became a province of Mercia, then of Wessex. Was one of the most advanced areas in pre-Conquest England.

Kent, Maid of: see BARTON, ELIZABETH.

Kenton, Simon, 1755–1836, American frontiersman. Joined Daniel Boone in settlement at Boonesboro. Took part in expeditions of G. R. Clark. Participated in many Indian raids.

Kenton, city (pop. 8,475), W central Ohio, on Scioto R. and NW of Marion. Mfg. of candy, machinery, and tools. Has limestone quarries.

Kentucky, state (40,395 sq. mi.; pop. 2,944,806); admitted 1792 as 15th state (slaveholding); cap. FRANKFORT. Other cities are LOUISVILLE, COVINGTON, LEXINGTON. Hilly in E and W (coal areas); gently rolling in center, with bluegrass region in N and Pennyroyal plateau in S. Bordered N by Ohio R., SW by the Mississippi, E by Big Sandy R. and the Tug Fork. Chief rivers are the TENNESSEE, CUMBERLAND, LICKING, KENTUCKY. Processes whisky (esp. bourbon), tobacco, meat, food; farms tobacco, corn, hay, rye, soybeans, potatoes. Mines coal, oil, natural gas, feldspar. Horse breeding and training are important. First permanent settlement, HARRODSBURG, founded 1774. Daniel BOONE founded BOONESBORO 1775. Early settlers menaced by Indian raids. Resolutions (see KENTUCKY AND VIRGINIA RESOLUTIONS) passed in objection to Alien and Sedition Acts (1798). Remained in Union during Civil War but supplied men to both sides. Industrial development came after war, but farmers met hard times. Marked by turbulent political and economic life (feud between tobacco growers and buyers; industrial strife in mines in 1930s). Agr. has progressed from one-crop (tobacco) system. Internal improvements and extension of education effected in 20th cent.

Kentucky, river formed in central Ky., and flowing 259 mi. NW to the Ohio at Carrollton.

Kentucky, University of, mainly at Lexington; land-grant, state supported, coed.; opened 1865 as part of Kentucky Univ. (now Transylvania College), became state college 1878, and university 1908. College of pharmacy is at Louisville.

Kentucky and Virginia Resolutions, passed in 1798 and 1799 in opposition to ALIEN AND SEDITION ACTS. Kentucky Resolutions, written by Thomas Jefferson, with advice of John Breckinridge, stated that Federal government had no right to exercise powers not specifically delegated to it by the Constitution. If it did assume such powers, states had right to judge constitutionality of acts. Virginia Resolutions, written by James Madison, were somewhat milder. Resolutions were later considered first notable statement of STATES' RIGHTS theory.

Kentucky State College for Negroes: see FRANKFORT.

Kentucky University: see KENTUCKY, UNIVERSITY OF; LEXINGTON, Ky.

Kenya (kēn'yù), British colony and protectorate (224,-960 sq. mi.; pop. 5,377,393), E Africa, on Indian Ocean; cap. Nairobi. Lies across equator. Protectorate (within colony) is coastal strip, leased from sultan of Zanzibar. Arid in N, but more fertile in S, where wheat, peanuts, coffee, tea, sisal, and cotton are grown. Coastal area was settled in 7th cent. by Arab and Per-

sian traders in slaves and ivory. Under Portuguese control, 16th–17th cent. The British expanded their influence in mid-19th cent. through British East Africa Co. and made Kenya a protectorate in 1895. In 1920 the leased coastal strip was named Kenya Protectorate, while rest of region became crown colony. Ruled by an appointed governor with advice and consent of legislative council, composed mainly of white representatives. In late 1952 the British began taking measures to suppress the terroristic Mau Mau secret society, which aimed to oust the whites from Kenya.

Kenyon College: see GAMBIER, Ohio.

Keokuk (kē'ùkŭk), c.1780–1848, American Indian, chief of Sac and Fox tribes. Refused to aid British in War of 1812. Keokuk, Iowa, named for him.

Keokuk, city (pop. 16,144), SE Iowa, on the Mississippi at foot of Des Moines R. rapids; platted 1837 on 1829 trading post site. U.S. ship canal (1877) around rapids superseded 1913 by Keokuk Dam (power; impounds L. Keokuk). U.S. dry docks and locks here are among largest ever built. Center of farm area with mfg. of food, metal, and wood products. Has Natl. Cemetery. Mark Twain worked here.

Keos or **Kea,** Greek island of the CYCLADES.

Kepler, Johannes (yōhä'nùs kĕplùr), 1571–1630, German astronomer, evolver of laws of planetary motion.

Kepler's laws, summarized, are: (1) Orbit of each planet is an ellipse, of which sun's center is one of the foci; (2) Radius vector of each planet (line joining its center with that of sun) moves over equal areas in equal times; (3) Square of period of each planet's revolution around sun is proportional to cube of its mean distance from sun.

Keppler, Joseph, 1838–94, American cartoonist and founder of *Puck,* b. Vienna.

Kerak, El, Jordan: see KRAK.

Kerbela (kûr'bùlù) or **Karbala** (kär–), city (pop. 122,-719), central Iraq, at edge of Syrian Desert. Here is tomb of HUSEIN, a great shrine of pilgrims of Moslem Shiite sect.

Kerch (kyĕrch), city (pop. 104,471), S European RSFSR, in E Crimea; a fortified Black Sea port on Kerch Peninsula. Has iron and steel mills, coking plant, shipyards, fisheries, and canneries. Founded by Greek colonists in 6th cent. B.C., it became a Genoese colony in 13th cent. Conquered by Crimean Tatars in 1475, by Russians in 1771. German-held in World War II. A museum contains Greco-Scythian antiquities. Church of St. John the Baptist dates from 8th cent. Kerch is on **Kerch Strait,** shallow channel, 25 mi. long, connecting Sea of Azov (N) and Black Sea and separating the Crimea (N) from Taman peninsula. Known to ancients as Cimmerian Bosporus.

Kerensky, Aleksandr Feodorovich (kùrĕn'skē, Rus. ùlyìksän'dùr fyô'dùrùvĭch kâ'rĭnskē), 1881–, Russian revolutionist. A moderate Socialist, he succeeded Prince Lvov as provisional premier in July, 1917. His vacillation enabled Lenin to overthrow his government in November (see RUSSIAN REVOLUTION). Settled in U.S. (1940).

Kerguelen (kûr'gùlĕn), subantarctic island of volcanic origin, in S Indian Ocean, belonging to the French since 1893.

Kerman (kĕrmän'), anc. *Carmana,* city (pop. 50,048), SE Iran. A walled city with citadel and 11th-cent. mosque. Ravaged in 1794 by Aga Mohamad Khan. Noted for fine rugs.

Kermanshah (kĕrmän"shä'), city (pop. 88,622), W Iran. Dating from 4th cent. it was royal summer residence of Medes and Sassanians. Trade center in grain-producing area. Oil refinery.

kermes (kûr'mēz), natural red dye from bodies of females of scale insects parasitic on oak trees.

Kermit, town (pop. 6,912), W Texas, S of N.Mex. line and N of Pecos R. Oil and cattle center near carbon-black plants.

Kern, Jerome, 1885–1945, American composer of musical comedies. He wrote *Sally* (1920), containing the song *Look for the Silver Lining; Sunny* (1925); *Roberta* (1933), containing *Smoke Gets in Your Eyes;* and, perhaps his greatest work, *Show Boat* (1929), containing *Ol' Man River*.

Kern, river rising in the S Sierra Nevada, E Calif., and flowing 155 mi. S and SW past Bakersfield to a reservoir in what was Buena Vista L. Irrigates S San Joaquin Valley with the aid of Friant-Kern Canal (see CENTRAL VALLEY). Upper gorge (in Sequoia Natl. Park) is spectacular canyon.

kerosene, colorless, oily mixture of hydrocarbons, obtained from fractional distillation of PETROLEUM. It is also prepared from coal, oil shale, wood. It is used as fuel, illuminant, insecticide.

Kerrville, city (pop. 7,691), S central Texas, on Guadalupe R. and NW of San Antonio. Resort town shipping wool, mohair, dairy products, and poultry.

Kerry, maritime county (1,815 sq. mi.; pop. 133,893), W Ireland, in Munster; co. town Tralee. Consists of mountainous peninsulas extending into the Atlantic. Carrantuohill (3,414 ft.) is highest point in Ireland. Lakes of Killarney attract tourists. Farming, dairying, and fishing chief occupations.

Kesselring, Albert (äl'bĕrt kĕ'sŭlrĭng), 1887–, German field marshal in World War II. Commanded in Italy 1943–45. Was sentenced to life imprisonment after war-crimes trial (1946–47).

Kesteven, Parts of: see LINCOLNSHIRE, England.

Keswick (kĕs'ĭk), urban district (pop. 4,868), Cumberland, England, in Lake District. Southey and Coleridge lived here, and Southey's tomb is here. Has ancient Druids' Circle near by. **Keswick Convention** is interdenominational religious gathering held annually since 1875.

Ketchikan (kĕ'chĭkăn″), town (pop. 5,305), on Revillagigedo Isl., in Alexander Archipelago, SE Alaska. Supply point for miners in 1890s gold rush; now salmon industry center. With good port on Inside Passage, it is distribution center for lumbering, fur-farming, and mining area. Has U.S. coast guard and lighthouse service stations.

kettledrum: see PERCUSSION INSTRUMENTS.

Keuka College: see PENN YAN, N.Y.

Keuka Lake: see FINGER LAKES.

Kewanee (kĭwä'nē), city (pop. 16,821), NW Ill., SE of Rock Island, in coal and farm area. Mfg. of metal products; oil refining.

Keweenaw (kē'wĭnô), peninsula, extreme N Mich., jutting NE from W Upper Peninsula into L. Superior. Portage L. and ship canal cut across it, making upper portion an island and creating important waterway. Known for copper and as resort. Towns include Houghton, Hancock, and Calumet.

Kew Gardens (kū), Surrey, England, on the Thames, W of London. Royal Botanic Gardens is official name. They cover 288 acres and contain thousands of species of plants, four museums, and laboratories and hothouses. Rare plants destroyed in 1940 bombing. Near by is Kew Palace, once home of George III.

Key, Ellen, (kā), 1849–1926, Swedish author and feminist; advocate of education for motherhood.

Key, Francis Scott (kē), 1779–1843, American poet, author of STAR-SPANGLED BANNER. Was U.S. attorney for the District of Columbia (1833–41).

Keyes, Sir Roger John Brownlow (kēz), 1872–1945, British admiral. In World War I he commanded the Dover patrol that raided Zeebrugge and Ostend. In World War II he was director of combined operations (1940–41) and organizer of the commando forces.

Key Largo: see FLORIDA KEYS.

Keynes, John Maynard, 1st **baron of Tilton** (kānz), 1883–1946, English economist and monetary expert, studied at Cambridge. Until 1929 a classical economist believing in free economy, Keynes came to support both government large-scale economic planning and spending to promote employment. He profoundly influenced economic policy in democratic nations. Wrote *Economic Consequences of the Peace* (1919),

The General Theory of Employment, Interest, and Money (1936).

Keyport, borough (pop. 5,888), E N.J.; resort and fishing center on Raritan Bay SE of South Amboy.

Keyser, Cassius Jackson (kī'zür), 1862–1947, American mathematician, author of works in mathematics, logic, and mathematical philosophy.

Keyser, Thomas de (kī'zür), c.1596–1667, Dutch portrait and figure painter.

Keyser (kī'zür), city (pop. 6,347), in E Panhandle of W.Va., on North Branch of Potomac R. and SW of Cumberland, Md. Lumber mills and railroad shops. Important supply base in Civil War.

Keyserling, Hermann, Count (kī'sürlĭng), 1880–1946, German philosopher and man of letters, b. Estonia. Traveled widely and was influenced by Oriental mysticism. His most popular work was *The Travel Diary of a Philosopher* (1925).

Key West, city (pop. 26,433), occupying Key West island, westernmost of FLORIDA KEYS, S Fla. Southernmost city of U.S. Granted to Juan Pablo Salas in 1815, it was sold to an American, 1822. Formerly a ship-salvage point and next a cigar-mfg. center. Now a resort and sponge-fishing center. Here are U.S. naval station, naval air station, and coast guard base (Fort Taylor, built 1844–46). Terminus of highway spanning the keys from the mainland. Has lighthouse (1846) and two Civil War forts.

Khabarovsk (khŭbûrôfsk'), city (pop. c.300,000), RSFSR, in E Siberia, on Amur R. and on Trans-Siberian RR. Has oil refinery and auto, aircraft, and agr. machinery plants. It is cap. of **Khabarovsk Territory,** administrative division (965,400 sq. mi.; pop. c.1,250,-000), a part of former FAR EASTERN TERRITORY. Extends from Okhotsk and Bering seas to Arctic Ocean; separated (SW) from Manchuria by Amur R. It includes KAMCHATKA peninsula and CHUKCHI PENINSULA. Stanovoi, Kolyma, and Anadyr ranges traverse it SW–NE. Rich in gold, iron, coal, petroleum, and nonferrous metals. In N there is reindeer raising, seal hunting, and fur trapping.

Khachaturian, Aram (Ilich) (ŭräm' khä″chŭtōoryän'), 1904?–, Russian composer, of Armenian parentage. His music contains many themes from Russian folk music. Among his works are a piano concerto, a violin concerto, and the ballets *Gayne* and *Masquerade.*

Khafre (khä'frā) or **Chephren** (kĕf'rĕn), fl. 2869? B.C., king of IV dynasty of Egypt, builder of the second pyramid at Gizeh.

Khania, Crete: see CANEA.

Kharga (khär'gü), large oasis (pop. 11,155), S central Egypt; accessible by railroad. Produces dates, cotton, grain. Ruins of ancient temples.

Kharkov (kär'kôf), city (pop. 833,432), SE Ukraine. Major industrial and engineering center at junction of six railroad lines, with mfg. of machinery, electrical goods, locomotives, precision instruments, and machine tools. Seat of a university (founded 1804). Founded by Cossacks in early 17th cent., it grew rapidly after industrialization of S Ukraine in late 19th cent. Thoroughly modernized and a showpiece of Soviet accomplishment, it was more than half destroyed in World War II.

Khartoum (kärtōōm'), city (pop. 71,400), cap. of Anglo-Egyptian Sudan, on the Blue Nile. Founded in 1820s by Mohammed Ali. Razed 1885 by Mahdists, who besieged and killed Gen. Charles GORDON. Recovered 1898 by Lord Kitchener. Mainly a commercial and educational center.

Khayyam, Omar: see OMAR KHAYYAM.

Khazars (käzärz'), anc. Turkic people, partly nomadic, who appeared in Transcaucasia in 2d cent. A.D. and subsequently settled in S Russia between the Volga and the Don (cap. at Itil). In 7th cent. they conquered the Crimea and levied tribute from E Slavs. They embraced Judaism c.740, but kept complete religious tolerance. Khazar empire fell when Sviatoslav, duke of Kiev, defeated its army, 969. Some say Khazars were ancestors of many Russian Jews. Also spelled Chazars.

Kherson (khĕrsôn'), city (pop. 97,186), SW Ukraine, on the Dnieper, 15 mi. above its mouth on Black Sea. Founded 1778 by Potemkin as port and shipbuilding center. Population was 25% Jewish until World War II, when city was German-held, 1941–43.

Khingan, Great (khǐng-gän'), mountain range, W Manchuria; rises to 5,670 ft. Its offshoot, the **Lesser Khingan,** forms watershed between Amur and Sungari rivers; rises to 4,665 ft.

Khios, Greek island: see CHIOS.

Khiva (kē'vù), city (1932 pop. c.23,700), Uzbek SSR, near Kara-Kum desert. Carpet mfg. Its medieval Moslem splendor is preserved. In late 16th cent. it became cap. of **khanate of Khiva,** the successor of KHOREZM Empire, S of Aral Sea and of Amu Darya R. Independent until 1873 when it became Russian protectorate. In 1920 it was fully annexed to USSR.

Khmelnitsky, Bohdan: see CHMIELNICKI, BOHDAN.

Khmer Empire (kùmâr'), Indo-Chinese kingdom (6th–15th cent.) roughly corresponding to modern Laos and Cambodia. Declined after series of wars with the Annamese, Chams, and Siamese. Khmer civilization was largely formed by Hindu influences. Its great achievement in architecture and sculpture is revealed by ruins at ANGKOR THOM.

Khokand, Uzbek SSR: see KOKAND.

Khorezm (khǔrĕ'zùm), medieval empire, the predecessor of khanate of KHIVA, central Asia, contained by Caspian and Aral seas, Amu Darya R., and Persia; cap. URGENCH. Converted to Islam by Arab conquerors in 18th cent. Under Seljuk Turks it subdued Bukhara, Samarkand, and most of Persia, 12th–13th cent. Conquered by Jenghiz Khan, 1218–24.

Khorramshahr, Iran: see KHURRAMSHAHR.

Khorsabad (khôrsäbäd'), village, NE Iraq, near Tigris R. Built on site of Assyrian city, founded 8th cent. B.C. by Sargon. Its mounds were excavated by P. E. Botta in 1842 and 1851. Cuneiform tablets in Elamite language were discovered in 1932.

Khosru (khŏsrōō'), Sassanid kings of Persia. **Khosru I** (Noshirwan), d. 579, reigned 531–79. Extended rule over Bactria, Arabia, and parts of Armenia and Caucasia. Fought the Byzantine emperors. His grandson, **Khosru II** (Parvis), d. 628, was aided by Emperor Maurice in ousting usurper Bahram. Avenged murder of Maurice by taking Byzantine territory until defeated by Heraclius. Name also appears as Chosroes.

Khotin (khŭtyĕn'), city (pop. 7,579), W Ukraine, on Dniester R. Agr. market center. It was a leading town of Moldavia in 17th–18th cent. From 1812 it shared history of BESSARABIA. Also spelled Hotin.

Khufu (khōō'fōō) or **Cheops** (kē'ŏps), fl. 2900? B.C., king of anc. Egypt, founder of the IV dynasty; builder of greatest pyramid at Gizeh.

Khurramshahr or **Khorramshahr** (khōram"shä'hùr), town (pop. 20,000), SW Iran, on Shatt el Arab, 10 mi. NW of Abadan; chief overseas trade port of Iran. Handled lend lease to USSR in World War II.

Khyber Pass (kī'bùr), on border of W Pakistan and Afghanistan; c.28 mi. long and rising to c.3,500 ft. Trade route between Kabul and Peshawar, it has road and railway. One of main routes in ancient times for invasion of India. Was vitally important to the British in 19th-cent. Afghan Wars.

Kiangsi (kyäng'sē'), province (65,000 sq. mi.; pop. 14,-000,000), SE China; cap. Nanchang. Wide Kan R. valley, bordered by hills, extends N to Poyang L. Major producer of rice, tungsten. Coal mining, lumbering, porcelain mfg. Communists estab. control here after 1927 split with Kuomintang.

Kiangsu (kyäng'sōō'), province (35,000 sq. mi.; pop. 40,000,000), E China, on Yellow Sea. Since 1949 divided into North Kiangsu (cap. Yangchow) and South Kiangsu (cap. Wusih). Consists of alluvial plain and much of delta of Yangtze R. Many large lakes linked by Grand Canal. Major crops are cotton, grain, soybeans, and rice. Industry limited largely to textile mfg.

in urban centers (esp. Shanghai, Soochow, and Wusih). Held 1937–45 by the Japanese; fell to Chinese Communists 1949.

Kiangtu, China: see YANGCHOW.

Kiaochow (kyou'chou'), former German territory, area c.400 sq. mi., S Shantung prov., China; cap. Tsingtao. Leased by Germany 1898, held 1914–22 by Japan.

Kickapoo Indians, Indian tribe of Algonquian linguistic stock, in SW Wis. in late 17th cent. Were of Eastern Woodlands culture, but also hunted buffalo. Joined in war against Illinois Indians (c.1769); fought against the Americans in the Revolution and War of 1812, and supported the Sac and Fox in the Black Hawk War. Some went to Mexico (c.1852) but were later induced to return to present Okla.

Kicking Horse, river of SE B.C., Canada, rising on W slopes of the Rockies and flowing SW and NW to the Columbia. **Kicking Horse Pass,** 5,339 ft. high, NW of L. Louise, is highest point of Canadian Pacific route. Connects Bow and Kicking Horse rivers.

Kid, Thomas: see KYD, THOMAS.

Kidd, William, c.1645–1701, British privateer. Commissioned as a privateer (1696), he was arrested (1699) on charges of piracy. Hanged after a probably unfair trial. Has become semilegendary as cruel Captain Kidd with huge hidden treasure.

Kidderminster, municipal borough (pop. 37,423), Worcestershire, England. Kidderminster carpets have been made here since 1735.

Kiddush (kǐ'dùsh) [Heb.,= sanctification], a prayer of benediction said at the beginning (and sometimes the end) of the Sabbath and other Hebrew festivals.

kidnaping, the unlawful and wilful taking away of a person by force, threat or deceit with intent to cause him to be detained against his will. The object is usually ransom, and the victim is usually a child—though neither condition need be true. Kidnaping differs from abduction (which requires intent of sexual intercourse) and from false imprisonment which does not involve "taking away." Strong public sentiment over such cases as the kidnaping of the Lindbergh child (1932) led to very severe Federal and state legislation.

kidneys, in the human body two reddish, bean-shaped organs c.4 in. long, lying below ribs near spine. Urine is secreted in outer zone, collects in tubules of inner part, and passes through ureter to bladder.

Kidron (kǐd'–) or **Cedron** (sē'–), deep valley between Jerusalem and Mount of Olives.

Kiel (kēl), city (pop. 253,857), cap. of Schleswig-Holstein, N Germany. A major Baltic seaport, it was the chief German naval station until 1945, when its installations were dismantled. Kiel was chartered 1242, was the seat of the dukes of Holstein, and with Holstein passed to Prussia in 1866. Its university was founded 1665. A sailors' mutiny at Kiel touched off the German revolution of 1918. Kiel is connected with the North Sea by the **Kiel Canal** (also known as Kaiser Wilhelm Canal), an artificial waterway 61 mi. long, opened 1895. Its E terminus is on the Elbe estuary opposite Cuxhaven.

Kielce (kyĕl'tsĕ), city (pop. 49,960), S Poland. Trade center; metal- and woodworking industries.

Kielland, Alexander Lange (khĕ'län), 1849–1906, Norwegian author of novels dealing with social reform (e.g., *Skipper Worse,* 1882).

Kierkegaard, Soren, Dan. *Søren* (sû'rùn kyĕr' kùgôr), 1813–55, Danish philosopher, writer on religion, a minister whose unorthodox teaching plunged him in trouble with the national church. He believed that man must find truth within himself and that the religious person suffers greatly because of the opposition of temporal existence and eternal truth. Religion for him is intensely personal and mystical. His ideas influenced later existentialism, and his books (among them *Either/Or,* 1843; *Stages on Life's Way,* 1845) have been read all over the world. His aesthetic teachings have influenced several literatures.

Kiev (kēēf'), city (pop. 846,293), cap. of Ukrainian SSR, on Dnieper R. One of largest cities of USSR, it is a leading industrial (machinery, rolling stock, radio equipment, textiles), cultural, and commercial center; see of a metropolitan of Russian Orthodox Church. Its university was estab. here 1833. A Slavic settlement on trade route between Scandinavia and Constantinople, it passed from Khazars to Varangians under Oleg in 882. It was cap. of medieval RUSSIA, but declined and became tributary to Mongols in 1240. Passed in 14th cent. to Lithuania, which was united with Poland in 1569. In 1654 Cossacks voted union of UKRAINE with Russia. Kiev changed hands several times in Russian civil war (1917–20), and was devastated in World War II by Germans, who also decimated the inhabitants. Cathedral of St. Sophia and Lavra monastery (formerly a pilgrim's shrine), both dating from 11th cent., indicate Kiev's close link with Byzantium and its role as cradle of Christianity in Russia.

Kilauea (kē'läwä'ù), crater, 4,000 ft. high, on Hawaii, T.H., on SE slope of MAUNA LOA; one of world's largest active craters. Has circumference of c.8 mi.; surrounded by rocky wall 200–500 ft. high. In its floor is fiery pit called Halemaumau.

Kildare (kĭldâr'), inland county (654 sq. mi.; pop. 64,-849), S Ireland, in Leinster; co. town Kildare. Flat agr. region, it has the Bog of Allen and the fertile plain of Curragh. History associated with St. Bridget and legendary Finn mac Cumhail.

Kilgore, city (pop. 9,638), E Texas, E of Tyler. Enriched by 1930 discovery of East Texas oil field, it has many wells even amongst houses.

Kilimanjaro (kĭ"lĭmùnjä'rō), mountain, NE Tanganyika; highest in Africa. Extinct volcanic cone. Its two main peaks are Mt. Kibo (19,565 ft.) and Mt. Mawenzi (17,300 ft.)

Kilkenny (kĭlkĕ'nē), inland county (796 sq. mi.; pop. 66,712), SE Ireland, in Leinster. Flat agr. region, it has a coal field around Castlecomer. Area is roughly same as ancient kingdom of Ossory. The county town is **Kilkenny,** urban district (pop. 10,291), on Nore R. Strife between two sections (Englishtown and Irishtown) may account for stories of Kilkenny cats, who ate each other up. Swift, Berkeley, and Congreve went to school here. Has 12th-cent. castle and two cathedrals.

Killarney, urban district (pop. 5,947), Co. Kerry, Ireland. Tourist center for three Lakes of Killarney. Lough Leane has Ross Isl. and "sweet Innisfallen" of Thomas Moore's poem.

killdeer, a North American upland PLOVER.

Kill Devil Hill National Memorial: see KITTY HAWK, N.C.

Killeen (kĭlēn'), city (pop. 7,045), central Texas, SW of Waco. Farm market near Camp Hood.

Killiecrankie, Pass of (kĭlĭkräng'kē), Perthshire, Scotland, through which flows Garry R. Battle of Killiecrankie (1689) was fought at N end of pass.

Killigrew, Thomas, 1612–83, English dramatist, a theater manager in the time of Charles II.

Killingly, town (pop. 10,015), NE Conn., NE of Willimantic at R.I. line; settled c.1700. Includes Danielson borough (pop. 4,554; textiles, metal goods).

Kill Van Kull: see NEW YORK BAY.

Kilmainham (kĭlmā'ùm), suburb of Dublin, Co. Dublin, Ireland. Parnell was imprisoned here when he signed (1882) "Treaty of Kilmainham" with Gladstone.

Kilmer, Joyce, 1886–1918, American poet, a journalist. Wrote popular verse, the most familiar example being "Trees." Killed in World War I.

kilowatt: see WATT.

Kilpatrick, William Heard, 1871–, American philosopher. He was professor of the philosophy of education at Teachers Col., Columbia Univ., 1918–38.

Kilpatrick, Old or West, parish (pop. 55,641), Dumbartonshire, Scotland; one of the places claiming to be St. Patrick's birthplace.

Kilung, Formosa: see KEELUNG.

Kilwinning (kĭlwĭ'nĭng), burgh (pop. 6,553), Ayrshire, Scotland. Traditional birthplace of Freemasonry in Scotland. Has celebrated archery meets.

Kimball, (Sidney) Fiske, 1888–, American architect and writer. Specialized in restoration of old houses, notably Monticello, Va.

Kimberley, mining town and district (pop. 5,933), SE B.C., Canada, NW of Cranbrook. Has large silver, lead, and zinc mines. Here is Sullivan Mine.

Kimberley, city (pop. 52,576), Cape Prov., South Africa; founded 1871; diamond-cutting center. Its great diamond mines are controlled by a trust organized 1888 by Cecil Rhodes. In South African War it was besieged by Boer forces, Oct., 1899–Feb., 1900.

Kimhi (kĭm'hē) or **Kimchi** (kĭm'khē), family of Hebrew scholars and grammarians. **Joseph ben Isaac Kimhi,** 1105?–1170, introduced the long and short divisions of vowels. **Moses Kimhi,** d. 1190, son of Joseph, wrote *The Paths of Knowledge,* a grammatical textbook. **David Kimhi,** 1160?–1235, another son, wrote *Book of Completeness,* a Hebrew grammar.

Kimpton, Lawrence A(lpheus), 1910–, American educator, chancellor of Univ. of Chicago (1951–).

kin, group of people who have, or believe they have, a common ancestry, which is traced through either the male or female line or through both (see CLAN; GENS).

Kinabalu or **Kinibalu, Mount** (both: kĭ"nùbùlōō'), peak, 13,455 ft. high, British North Borneo; highest peak of Borneo.

Kincardineshire (kĭngkär'dĭnshĭr) or **Kincardine,** maritime county (379 sq. mi.; pop. 47,341), E Scotland; co. town Stonehaven. Has rocky coast and mountainous interior. Sheep grazing, fishing, and quarrying are main occupations; oats and barley chief crops. County sometimes called the Mearns (mârns). Dunnottar Castle located near Stonehaven.

Kinchinjunga: see KANCHENJUNGA.

kindergarten [Ger.,= garden of children], system of preschool education. FROEBEL designed (1837) system less formal than that of elementary schools. Children's creative play instincts are used to develop cooperation and application and to prepare them for school. In U.S. many public school systems include kindergartens.

Kinderhook (kĭn'–), village (pop. 853), SE N.Y., NE of Hudson; has House of History of Columbia Co. Historical Society. Martin Van Buren born and buried here; to S is Van Buren home, "Lindenwald."

Kindi or **Al-Kindi** (Abu Yusuf Yakub ibn Ishak Al-Kindi) (älkĭn'dē), 9th cent. Arabian philosopher. Sought to show harmony of views of Plato and Aristotle. Not accepted by orthodox Moslems, his ideas influenced medieval Christian scholars.

Kineo, Mount (kĭn'ēō), 1,806 ft. high, central Maine, on peninsula in Moosehead L. Summer resort.

King, Charles: see KING, RUFUS.

King, Clarence, 1842–1901, American geologist. He persuaded Congress to authorize 40th Parallel Survey (1867–72), of which he was chief geologist. He organized and served as first director of the U.S. Geological Survey (1879). His publications in geology were significant.

King, Ernest Joseph, 1878–, American admiral, commander in chief of U.S. fleet (1941–45). Made admiral of fleet ("five-star admiral") in 1944.

King, Grace Elizabeth, 1852–1932, American author. Her sketches of New Orleans life include *Monsieur Motte* (1888) and *Balcony Stories* (new ed., 1925).

King, Rufus, 1755–1827, American statesman. Delegate to Federal Constitutional Convention (1787). U.S. Senator from N.Y. (1789–96, 1813–25); minister to Great Britain (1796–1803, 1825–26). Supported Federalists. His son, **Charles King,** 1789–1867, was an editor and educator. During his presidency of Columbia Col., 1849–64, the school moved from Park Place to Madison Ave. and 49th St.

King, Thomas Starr, 1824–64, American Unitarian clergyman, lecturer, and author. Influential in keeping Calif. loyal to Union in Civil War. Wrote *The White Hills* (1860).

King, William Lyon Mackenzie, 1874–1950, Canadian statesman, prime minister for over 21 years; grandson of W. L. Mackenzie. Chosen leader of Liberal party in 1919. Served as prime minister 1921–30, except for brief interval in 1926, and again 1935–48. Concluded with Pres. Roosevelt the Ogdensburg Agreement (1940) and Hyde Park Declaration (1941) by which Canada and U.S. agreed to create a permanent joint board of defense and to cooperate in production of defense materials.

kingbird, North American flycatcher. Eastern species, also called tyrant flycatcher and bee martin, eats some bees but chiefly noxious insects. It is dark gray above, light gray and white below with a white-banded black tail and an orange crest.

King Charles Land: see SPITSBERGEN.

king crab or **horseshoe crab,** marine arthropod (*Limulus*) having a cephalothorax (fused head and thorax) covered by domed, horseshoe-shaped carapace, a triangular abdomen with carapace, and spinelike tail or telson. It has one pair of simple eyes, one of compound eyes, and six pairs of legs.

King Edward VII Land, peninsula, Antarctica, extending NW from Marie Byrd Land into Ross Sea. Discovered and named by Robert F. Scott 1902. Now generally called Edward VII Peninsula.

kingfisher, member of family of birds most abundant in Malayan region and on Pacific isls. but found on all continents. American kingfishers, chiefly fisheaters, live near lakes, ponds, or coast; usually they have large, crested heads, long, heavy bills, and short bodies and tails.

King George's War: see FRENCH AND INDIAN WARS.

Kinglake, Alexander William, 1809–91, English traveler and historian. *Eöthen* (1844), an account of his journey to the Far East, is a classic travel book.

Kingman, town (pop. 3,342), NW Ariz., SE of Hoover Dam and SW of Grand Canyon. Stock raising, mining.

King Philip's War: see PHILIP (King Philip).

King Ranch, S Texas, S and W of Corpus Christi, hq. at Kingsville. Covers c.1,000,000 acres in several divisions (Santa Gertrudis is home ranch). Has Santa Gertrudis cattle, a new breed; race horses; oil wells; and farming. Founded c.1853 by Richard King, ex-Rio Grande steamboat captain. Now managed by grandson Robert Kleburg. Divisions made 1935, but ranch still one of world's largest.

Kings, county, N.Y.: see BROOKLYN, borough.

Kings, river rising in the Sierra Nevada, E Calif., and flowing W and SW until it almost disappears in sands of San Joaquin Valley. Some of its waters reach Tulare L. Traverses Kings Canyon Natl. Park.

Kings, books of Old Testament, called 1 and 2 Kings in AV, 3 and 4 Kings in Western canon (1 and 2 SAMUEL called 1 and 2 Kings in Western canon). They narrate the history of the Hebrews from the death of David to the fall of Judah. Among notable events are the golden reign of Solomon and the building of the Temple; the division of the kingdom under Rehoboam into Israel (N) and Judah (S); the end of the notorious house of Ahab; and the inspiring careers of the prophets Elijah and Elisha.

Kings Bay, inlet, 16 mi. long, in NW coast of West Spitsbergen. It was base (1926) of successful polar flights by R. E. BYRD and AMUNDSEN.

Kings Canyon National Park: see NATIONAL PARKS AND MONUMENTS (table).

King's College: see CAMBRIDGE UNIVERSITY; COLUMBIA UNIVERSITY.

King's College, University of: see HALIFAX, N.S.

King's County, Ireland: see OFFALY.

Kingsford, city (pop. 5,038), W Upper Peninsula, N Mich., on Menominee R. and near Iron Mountain. Large Ford Motor Co. holdings here.

Kingsley, Charles, 1819–75, English clergyman and novelist. His views on Christian socialism were embodied in *Alton Locke* (1850). A controversy with J. H. NEWMAN led to Newman's *Apologia*. Kingsley is best known for *Westward Ho!* (1855), *Hereward the Wake* (1866), and *The Water-Babies* (1873).

King's Lynn, Lynn Regis (rē′jĭs), or **Lynn,** municipal borough (pop. 26,173), Norfolk, England. Once a major port, it dates from Saxon times.

Kings Mountain, town (pop. 7,206), SW N.C., near S.C. line; textile center. On ridge, just S of state line, British force was defeated (1780) in CAROLINA CAMPAIGN of American Revolution. Site marked by national military park (estab. 1931).

king snake, nonvenomous, egg-laying constrictor snake of North America. Common form of E U.S. is 3–5 ft. long, black or brown with yellow or white rings or bands forming chainlike pattern. It and related milk snake are useful destroyers of rodents.

Kings Park, village (pop. 10,960), SE N.Y., near N shore of Long Isl., E of Huntington, in agr. area.

Kings Peak: see UINTA MOUNTAINS.

Kings Point, residential village (pop. 2,445), SE N.Y., on NW Long Isl. near Great Neck. A U.S. merchant marine academy was estab. here in 1942.

Kingsport, city (pop. 19,571), NE Tenn., on Holston R. and NNW of Johnson City near Va. line. On site of old Wilderness Road fort (1761). Book printing; mfg. of book cloth, paper, chemicals, cement, and cellulose acetate yarn.

Kingston, city (pop. 33,459), S Ont., Canada, on N shore of L. Ontario, near head of St. Lawrence R. and at S end of Rideau Canal. Mfg. of locomotives, machinery, chemicals, and aluminum; grain elevators. Seat of Queen's Univ. (coed.; 1841) and Royal Military Col. Fort Frontenac (1673) important in French and Indian Wars. City founded 1784 by United Empire Loyalists. Used as naval base in War of 1812. Cap. of United Canada 1841–44.

Kingston, port (pop. 109,056), cap. and largest city of Jamaica, British West Indies; founded 1693; made cap., 1872.

Kingston. 1 City (pop. 28,817), SE N.Y., on W bank of the Hudson S of Albany; settled 1652 by Dutch. Grew as E terminus of Delaware and Hudson Canal. Clothing, textiles, refrigerators, and brick. Has senate house (1676; meeting place of first N.Y. state legislature) and museum. Ashokan Reservoir near. **2** Borough (pop. 21,096), NE Pa., on Susquehanna R. opposite Wilkes-Barre; settled 1769. Coal mining and mfg. of cigars, rayon, and nylon. Victory of British and Indians here 1788 prefaced the Wyoming Valley massacre. **3** See SOUTH KINGSTOWN, R.I.

Kingston-on-Thames (-tĕms), municipal borough (pop. 40,168), Surrey, England; residential suburb of London. Site of Saxon coronations and of last battle of civil war (1648). Has metalworking and mfg.

Kingston-upon-Hull, Yorkshire, England: see HULL.

Kingstown, port (pop. 14,766), cap. of SAINT VINCENT, British West Indies.

Kingsville, city (pop. 16,898), S Texas, S of Corpus Christi; settled 1902. Hq. of KING RANCH. Processes oil, farm produce, and chemicals. Seat of Texas Col. of Arts and Industries.

King William Island, S Franklin dist., Northwest Territories, Canada, in Arctic Ocean, an island of the ARCTIC ARCHIPELAGO. Discovered 1831 by Sir John Ross. Sir John Franklin and party were lost here 1847–48. Roald Amundsen's winter hq. 1903–4.

King William's War: see FRENCH AND INDIAN WARS.

Kinibalu, Mount: see KINABALU, MOUNT.

Kinnarodden: see NORTH CAPE, Norway.

Kino, Eusebio Francisco (ā͞o͞osā′vyō fränsē′skō kē′nō), c.1644–1711, Jesuit missionary explorer in American Southwest, b. Segno, in the Tyrol.

Kinross-shire (kĭnrŏs′-shĭr), inland county (81 sq. mi.; pop. 7,418), Scotland; co. town Kinross. Level plain surrounded by hills. Agr. is chief occupation; there is some mfg. of woolens and linen.

Kinston, city (pop. 18,336), E N.C., on Neuse R. and NW of New Bern; founded 1762. Processes, trades, and markets tobacco, lumber, and cotton.

Kintyre (kĭntīr′) or **Cantire** (kăntīr′), peninsula, 42 mi. long and 10 mi. wide, Argyllshire, Scotland. S extremity is 13 mi. from N. Ireland.

Kioto, Japan: see KYOTO.

Kiowa (kī′ũwù), city (pop. 1,561), S Kansas, SW of Wichita near Okla. line. Here in 1900 Carry Nation gained notoriety by wrecking a saloon.

Kiowa Indians (kĭ′ũwù), North American tribe, occupying W Mont. in 17th cent., later ranging through the West. Language only one of Kiowan stock. Shared Plains area culture, but had several distinctive traits, including a pictographic calendar and the worship of a stone image. Allied with the Comanche, they waged many bloody wars against whites and Cheyenne, Sioux, Navaho, and Osage.

Kipchaks, Turkic people: see CUMANS.

Kipling, Rudyard, 1865–1936, English poet, novelist, and story writer, b. India. His many popular works include poems in *Departmental Ditties* (1886) and *Barrack-Room Ballads* (1892); stories in *Plain Tales from the Hills* and *Soldiers Three* (both 1888); novel *The Light That Failed* (1890); children's stories such as *The Jungle Book* (1894), *Captains Courageous* (1897), *Kim* (1901), and *Just So Stories* (1902). Familiar poems are "Mandalay," "Gunga Din," and *Recessional* (1897). He interpreted India, the army, and British imperialism, and was England's first Nobel Prize winner in literature (1907).

Kirby, William, 1817–1906, Canadian author, b. England. His *Le Chien d'Or,* also published as *The Golden Dog* (1877), helped popularize historical novel in Canadian fiction.

Kirby-Smith, Edmund: see SMITH, EDMUND KIRBY.

Kircher, Athanasius (ätänä′zyōōs, kĭr′khùr), 1601?–1680, German Jesuit archaeologist, mathematician, biologist, and physicist. He was possibly first to hold that disease and putrefaction were caused by presence of invisible living bodies. He also perfected the aeolian harp.

Kirchhoff, Gustav Robert (gōōs′täf rō′bĕrt kĭrkh′hôf), 1824–87, German physicist. With Bunsen he worked on spectroscope, discovered cesium and rubidium. He explained Fraunhofer lines in solar SPECTRUM.

Kirghiz Soviet Socialist Republic (kĭrgēz′) or **Kirghizia** (kĭrgē′zhù) or **Kirghizstan** (kĭrgēstän′), constituent republic (c.76,000 sq. mi.; pop. c.1,500,000) of USSR, in central Asia, bordering on China (SE); cap. Frunze. Mountainous country in Tien Shan and Pamir systems, rising to 24,406 ft. in Pobeda Peak, with grazing in highland valleys. Crop production concentrated mainly in FERGANA VALLEY and Issyk Kul basin. Industry is based on mineral resources (e.g., mercury, antimony, uranium). The Kirghiz, a Moslem, Turko-Mongolian pastoral people, migrated here in 16th cent. They were formerly known as Kara Kirghiz to distinguish them from the Kazakhs (formerly called Kirghiz). With khanate of Kokand they passed to Russia in 1876.

Kirin: see MANCHURIA.

Kirjath-arba: see HEBRON.

Kirk, Grayson L(ouis), 1903–, American educator, president of Columbia Univ. (1953–). Was professor of government and of international relations.

Kirkaldy of Grange, Sir William (kûrkôl′dē), c.1520–1573, Scottish soldier and politician. Associated with brutal murder of Cardinal Beaton, he later became prominent Protestant leader to whom Mary Queen of Scots surrendered at Carberry in 1557.

Kirkcudbrightshire (kûrkōō′brēshĭr), maritime county (899 sq. mi.; pop. 30,742), SW Scotland; co. town Kirkcudbright. NW part is wild and hilly. Agr. is chief occupation; cattle grazing is important. Region is sometimes called East Galloway.

Kirke, Sir David, 1596–1654, French-born English merchant adventurer. Attacked the French in Canada

and Nova Scotia; forced surrender of Quebec (1629). Became governor and colonizer (1638) of Newfoundland which the Commonwealth later took away from him because he was royalist.

Kirkland, Samuel, 1741–1808, American missionary to the Oneida Indians. Founded an academy which developed into Hamilton Col.

Kirkland Lake, town (pop. c.19,734), E Ont., Canada, N of Sudbury. Center of gold-mining region.

Kirksville, city (pop. 11,110), N Mo., N of Moberly; founded c.1841. In a dairy, livestock, poultry, and coal area, it also has mfg. of shoes.

Kirkuk (kĭrkōōk′), town (pop. 69,035), NE Iraq. Its great oil fields are linked by pipe line to Mediterranean ports of Tripoli and Haifa.

Kirkwall (kûrk′wôl, –wùl), burgh (pop. 4,376), cap. of Orkney Isls., Scotland. Has a good harbor and carries on trading, fishing, and boatbuilding.

Kirkwood, city (pop. 18,640), E Mo., W suburb of St. Louis; laid out 1852.

Kirov, Sergei Mironovich (sĭrgä′ myĭrô′nùvĭch kē′rùf), 1888–1934, Russian Communist leader, one of Stalin's closest aides. His assassination was officially laid to a Trotskyist conspiracy and led to treason trials and party purge of 1930s.

Kirov, formerly **Vyatka** (vyät′kǔ), city (pop. 143,181), E European RSFSR, on Vyatka R. Rail junction. Mfg. of machine tools; sawmilling, food processing. Used as place of political exile in 19th cent.

Kirovabad (kē′rùvùbät′), city (pop. 98,743), W central Azerbaijan SSR. Formerly named Gandzha or Ganja, it was cap. of a khanate under Persian suzerainty until Russian conquest in 1804. Renamed 1935. Produces copper sulphate, cotton textiles, wine.

Kirsehir (kĕrshĕ′hēr), town (pop. 14,168), central Turkey. Noted for carpet mfg.

Kiruna (kē′rünä), village (pop. 19,023), Norrbotten co., N Sweden. It is center of Lapland iron-mining dist. Ore, c.70% pure, is shipped to Baltic port of Lulea and Atlantic port of Narvik (Norway). Founded as model town after opening of mines. (c.1900).

Kisfaludy, Charles (kĭsh′fŏlŏodē), 1788–1830, Hungarian dramatist, founder of the Hungarian national drama. *Tatars in Hungary* (1819), first of his many successes, was first genuinely dramatic Hungarian play. His brother, **Alexander Kisfaludy,** 1772–1844, founded the Hungarian school of lyric poetry.

Kish. 1 Father of Saul. 1 Sam. 9.1; 10.21. Cis: Acts 13.21. **2** Uncle of Saul. 1 Chron. 8.30; 9.36.

Kish, anc. city in the Euphrates valley, E of Babylon. Occupied from early times, it was in the 4th millennium B.C. a powerful Sumerian city.

Kishinev (kĭshĕnyôf), Rumanian *Chisinau,* city (pop. c.102,000), cap. of Moldavian SSR. First mentioned c.1420, it was the cultural, spiritual, commercial and (after annexation by Russia, 1812) political center of BESSARABIA. Population was 40% Jewish until World War II.

Kishon, river of central Palestine, flowing NW through Esdraelon to the Mediterranean. On its banks Barak defeated Sisera, Elijah slew the prophets of Baal.

Kiska, island, c.20 mi. long, off W Alaska, in Rat Isls. group of ALEUTIAN ISLANDS, between Adak and Attu. Mountainous, rising to nearly 4,000 ft. in Kiska Volcano. Occupied and garrisoned 1942 by Japanese, it was cut off 1943 by recapture of Attu, and abandoned by Japanese, Aug., 1943. U.S. forces made it an air and naval base.

Kislovodsk (kēslùvôtsk′), city (pop. 51,289), S Stavropol Territory, RSFSR, in central Greater Caucasus; health resort.

Kissimmee, Lake, fresh-water lake, c.15 mi. long and 5 mi. wide, central Fla., N of L. Okeechobee.

Kitasato, Shibasaburo (shĭbä′säbōorō kē′täsä′tō), 1852–1931, Japanese physician, authority on infectious diseases. Discovered, simultaneously with Yersin in 1894, bacterium causing PLAGUE.

Kit-Cat Club, London social and political club, active

c.1700–1720. Organized by Whig supporters of the Hanoverian dynasty.

Kitchen Cabinet, popular name for group of intimate, unofficial advisers of Pres. Andrew Jackson. Administration policies were formed in its meetings. Members, all able journalists, included the elder Francis P. BLAIR, Duff GREEN, and Amos KENDALL. John H. Eaton of regular cabinet met with group; Martin Van Buren enjoyed its confidence.

Kitchener, Horatio Herbert Kitchener, 1st Earl, 1850–1916, British field marshal and statesman. As commander in chief of Egyptian army, he reconquered (1896–98) the Sudan and became its governor general. In SOUTH AFRICAN WAR he used fortified blockhouses and systematic denudation of farm lands to conquer the Boers (1900–1902). As secretary for war in World War I he expanded army from 20 to 70 divisions (1914–16). On voyage to confer with the tsar, he was drowned when his ship was sunk under mysterious circumstances.

Kitchener, city (pop. 44,867), S. Ont., Canada, in Grand R. valley W of Toronto. Important mfg. center with tanning and meat packing. Settled 1806 by Germans from Pa. Called Berlin to 1916.

kitchen midden, refuse heap left by a prehistoric community. Valuable in archaeological study.

kite, bird of prey allied to hawk and eagle and noted for flying grace. It eats mainly small reptiles and insects. In U.S. are found the swallow-tailed, white-tailed, Everglade, and Mississippi kites.

Kittanning (kǐtă'nǐng), borough (pop. 7,731), W Pa., on Allegheny R. and N of Pittsburgh. Coal mining and mfg. of clay and metal products.

Kittatinny Mountain (kǐtŭtǐn'ē), ridge of Appalachian system, chiefly in extreme NW N.J. Extends SW from Shawangunk Mt., SE N.Y., to Blue Mt., E Pa. Rises to 1,801 ft. in High Point, highest summit in N.J., affording view of three states and surrounded by state park (c.10,900 acres), year-round forest recreational area. Delaware R. cuts ridge forming DELAWARE WATER GAP.

Kittery, town (pop. 8,380), including Kittery village (pop. 6,692), extreme SW Maine, at mouth of Piscataqua R. (bridged here) opposite PORTSMOUTH, N.H.; settled 1622; inc. 1647 as first town in Maine. John Paul Jones's *Ranger* (1777) and the Civil war vessel *Kearsarge* built here. U.S. Naval Base is on islands in river.

Kittredge, George Lyman, 1860–1941, American scholar; professor of English at Harvard 1896–1936. He was an authority on Chaucer, Shakspere, the English language, balladry, and witchcraft.

Kitty Hawk, peninsula, NE N.C., E of Albemarle Sound. Scene of Wright brothers' glider and aircraft experiments (1900–1903). Kill Devil Hill Natl. Memorial commemorates first successful flight.

Kitzbühel (kǐts'bü"hùl), town (pop. 7,282), Tyrol, W Austria. Winter resort and skiing center.

Kiushu, Japan: see KYUSHU.

kiva (kē'vù), underground ceremonial chamber of Pueblo Indians. Used, by men only, for secret ceremonies, lounging, and as a workshop for weaving.

Kiwanis International (kīwä'nĭs), organization of business and professional men, founded 1915. Local clubs are active in business and civic affairs.

kiwi (kē'wē), flightless bird (*Apteryx*) of New Zealand. Its wings are vestigial and it walks with back hunched. Nocturnal in habit, it hunts worms, insects, and grubs largely by scent.

Kiyonaga (kyō'nägä), 1752?–1815, Japanese designer of woodcuts of Torii school, best known for cuts of beautiful women and of warriors.

Kizil Irmak (kǐ'zǐl ǐrmäk'), anc. *Halys*, river, 715 mi. long, rising in N central Turkey and flowing in a wide arc to the Black Sea.

Kizil Kum or **Kyzyl-Kum** (both: kēzēl' kōom'), desert, USSR, in central Asia, E of Aral Sea between Amu Darya and Syr Darya rivers.

Kladno (kläd'nô), city (pop. 19,166), central Bohemia, Czechoslovakia, in coal-mining dist. Iron and steel plants.

Klagenfurt (klä'gùnfŏort), city (pop. 62,792), cap. of Carinthia, S Austria, on Glan R., in mountain lake area. Episcopal see. Winter sports center.

Klaipeda: see MEMEL.

Klamath, river, c.270 mi. long, rising in Upper Klamath L., SW Oregon, and flowing SW into NW Calif. and across to the Pacific.

Klamath Falls (klä'mùth), city (pop. 15,875), SW Oregon, on Upper Klamath L. near Calif. line; settled c.1866. Irrigation project (1900) and railroad (1909) aided growth. Lumbering, farming (potatoes, grain, alfalfa), and livestock center.

Klamath Indians, North American tribe, of Lutuamian linguistic stock, living in 19th cent. in SW Oregon. Got food by hunting, fishing, and root digging. They were friendly to the whites but hostile towards Indians of N Calif.

Klausenburg, Rumania: see CLUJ.

Klaypeda: see MEMEL.

Kléber, Jean Baptiste (zhä' bäptēst' kläbĕr'), 1753–1800, French general. Left in command in Egypt after Bonaparte's return to France, he defeated the Turks at Heliopolis (1800). Was assassinated by Moslem fanatic.

Klebs, Edwin (kläps), 1834–1913, German-American pathologist, pioneer in study of infectious diseases.

Klee, Paul (poul' klä'), 1879–1940, German expressionist painter, b. Switzerland. Taught at the Bauhaus. Works are notable for piquancy of design.

Klein, Felix (fä'lĭks klīn), 1849–1925, German mathematician, noted for work in geometry, theory of functions, and program for unifying geometry by study of equivalence in transformation groups.

Kleist, Heinrich von (hīn'rĭkh fùn klīst'), 1777–1811, German poet. His unhappy life ended in suicide. His plays *Der zerbrochene Krug* [the broken jug] (1806), *Das Käthchen von Heilbronn* (1807), *Penthesilea* (1808), and *Der Prinz von Homburg* (1821) rank among the finest of the German theater, for their dramatic skill, emotional power, and bold poetry. He also wrote a remarkable short novel, *Michael Kohlhaas* (1808; Eng. tr., 1949).

Klenze, Leo von (lä'ō fùn klĕn'tsù), 1784–1864, German architect. Built Glyptothek (Munich) and part of Hermitage (Leningrad).

Kleve, Germany: see CLEVES.

Klinger, Friedrich Maximilian von (frē'drĭkh mäk"sēmē'lyän fùn klĭng'ùr), 1752–1831, German dramatist. His play *Wirrwarr; oder, Sturm und Drang* [confusion; or, storm and stress] (1776) gave the *Sturm und Drang* period its name.

Klinger, Max (mäks'), 1857–1920, German sculptor, painter, and etcher.

Klondike (klŏn'dīk), region of Yukon territory, NW Canada, just E of Alaska border. Gold strike on Klondike Creek led to Klondike stampede of 1897–98. Thousands of prospectors rushed into area, numbering c.18,000 in 1898. Since that time gold production has declined.

Klopstock, Friedrich Gottlieb (frē'drĭkh gôt'lēp klôp'shtôk), 1724–1803, German poet. His greatest work is the epic *Messias* (1748–83).

Klosterneuburg (klōs"türnoi'bŏork), city (pop. 13,710), Lower Austria, on the Danube near Vienna. Its Augustinian monastery (consecrated 1163) has a noted library with many incunabula.

Kloster-Zeven, Convention of (klō'stùr-tsä'fùn), 1757. Early in Seven Years War duke of Cumberland, defeated by French at Hastenbeck, capitulated at the former Benedictine abbey near Zeven (a small town NE of Bremen, Germany) and allowed the French to occupy Hanover. English government disavowed convention and dismissed Cumberland.

Knaus, Ludwig (lŏod'vĭkh knous'), 1829–1910, German genre painter, who used coloring in manner of

Dutch masters. His paintings were often anecdotal.

Kneller, Sir Godfrey (nĕl'ûr), 1646–1723, English portrait painter, b. Germany. Succeeded Lely as court painter to Charles II. Many portraits are in Hampton Court.

Knickerbocker (nĭ'kûrbŏ"kûr), family name, which came to be used as a term for all early N.Y. Dutch and was immortalized by Washington Irving's pseudonym Diedrich Knickerbocker.

knight. 1 In ancient history, a noble of second class who in military service furnished own mount and equipment. In Rome knights (*equites*) ranked between senatorial class and citizens. **2** In medieval history, armed and mounted warrior belonging to nobility. With growth of FEUDALISM term applied to landholders as well as to nobility. Knighthood, in true meaning, was never hereditary but had to be earned. In late Middle Ages son of a noble served as page and as squire before being knighted. Knighthood was conferred by overlord with accolade (blow, usually with flat of sword, on neck or shoulder). Military tenure was subject to law of PRIMOGENITURE, leading to a class of landless knights. In Crusades these formed great military orders such as KNIGHTS TEMPLARS, KNIGHTS HOSPITALERS, and TEUTONIC KNIGHTS. Secular orders also grew up, e.g., orders of Garter and of Thistle in England, Order of the Golden Fleece in Burgundy. Title knight (Ger. *Ritter*, Fr. *chevalier*) was later used as noble title. In modern England knighthood is not title of nobility, but is conferred by king on commoners or nobles for civil or military achievements. Knight is addressed as Sir; a woman knighted, as Dame.

knighthood and chivalry. Ethical ideals of FEUDALISM found highest expression in 12th and 13th cent. They originated in France and Spain and spread over Continent and England. They were fusion of Christian and military ideals, with piety, bravery, loyalty, and honor as virtues. Chivalrous love glorified womanhood (finding supreme expression in cult of the Virgin) and rendered homage in noblest sense. Virtues were proved in battle and tournament. Medieval secular literature dealt primarily with knighthood and chivalry, with ARTHURIAN LEGEND and CHANSONS DE GESTE as patterns. ROMAN DE LA ROSE and work of CHRESTIEN DE TROYES also were influential. For lyric poetry of age of chivalry, see TROUBADOUR; TROUVÈRE; MINNESINGER.

Knights Hospitalers (hŏ'spĭtůlûrz), members of the military religious Order of the Hospital of St. John of Jerusalem, called also Knights of St. John and Knights of Jerusalem. The order grew out of a hospital estab. 11th cent. to care for pilgrims in Holy Land. Reconstituted as a military order, it soon grew in wealth and power, with subsidiary establishments (preceptories) all over Europe. Its knights, with their colleagues and rivals, the Templars, took part in all the military ventures of the Latin Kingdom and of the Crusaders. After the Saracens took Jerusalem (1187) the order moved to Acre, then (1291) to Cyprus. Their conquest of Rhodes (1310) and the material benefits derived from the dissolution of the Knights Templars marked the beginning of a period of increasing power. Dominating the Mediterranean, the Knights of Rhodes, as they were called, checked Moslem piracy but often turned to piracy themselves. Under Pierre d'Aubusson they heroically defended Rhodes against Mohammed II (1480), but they had to capitulate to Suleiman I in 1522. In 1530 Emperor Charles V gave them the island of MALTA, which became their fixed home. Under Jean de la Valette they defended Malta against the Turks, whose menace remained acute until the battle of Lepanto (1571). Thereafter the Knights of Malta carried on their charitable hospital work in relative peace until Napoleon seized Malta in 1798. Remnants of the order survived in Europe, and in 1879 the pope restored the office of grand master; but, as reconstituted, the order bears little relation to the old Knights of Malta. The Hospitalers were called also Knights of the White Cross for the white cross worn on their black robes.

Knights of Columbus (K.C. or K. of C.), American Roman Catholic society for men, founded 1882, at New Haven, Conn.

Knights of Jerusalem: see KNIGHTS HOSPITALERS.

Knights of Labor, American labor organization, started 1869. Organized on an industrial basis, with women, colored workers, and employers welcomed. With the motto "an injury to one is the concern of all," it championed the 8-hour day and abolition of child labor. Reached its apex in 1886, under Terence V. Powderly, with a membership of 702,000. It collapsed from financial and factional difficulties.

Knights of Malta and **Knights of Rhodes:** see KNIGHTS HOSPITALERS.

Knights of Saint Crispin, union of shoemakers organized in 1867. At one time it was the largest trade union in the U.S. By 1878 it was defunct, many of its members having joined the Knights of Labor.

Knights of Saint John of Jerusalem: see KNIGHTS HOSPITALERS.

Knights of the Golden Circle, secret order of Southern sympathizers in North in Civil War. First "castle" estab. 1854 in Cincinnati. Active in Ky., Ind., Ohio, Ill., and Mo. Membership mostly Peace Democrats, opposed to war and increasing Federal power. In 1863 named Order of American Knights, in 1864 organized as Order of the Sons of Liberty; C. L. Vallandigham, leading Copperhead, was commander. Numbered over 200,000 in 1864; with mounting Union victories soon dissolved.

Knights of the White Camellia: see KU KLUX KLAN.

Knights Templars, in medieval history, members of military religious order of Poor Knights of Christ, called also Knights of the Temple of Solomon. Like their rivals, KNIGHTS HOSPITALERS and TEUTONIC KNIGHTS, Templars formed in period of CRUSADES. Nucleus was band of nine knights headed by Hugh de Payens who united c.1118 for protection of pilgrims. Group increased, adopted Benedictine rule, and had quarters beside Solomon's Temple. They rapidly became one of most powerful bodies in Europe, and their dashing military exploits won great fame throughout Crusades. They held Acre till citadel fell in 1291, then retired to Cyprus. Through receipts of many gifts and lands they became wealthy, and were bankers of Europe. Their financial control aroused jealousy of Philip IV of France, who accused order of many crimes and abuses and persecuted it 1308–14. Last grand master, Jacques de Molay, was burned 1314, and order came to an end.

knitting, construction of fabric by using needles to interlock loops of yarn. In hand knitting, two needles are used to produce flat work; tubular shapes (e.g., hose) are made with several double-pointed needles or a single circular needle. Knitting machines produce fabric either in horizontal courses, as in hand knitting, or in vertical chains interlocked so as to produce run-resistant qualities.

Knobelsdorff, Georg Wenzeslaus von (knō'bŭlsdôrf), 1699–1753, German architect, who designed Sans Souci (Potsdam) and State Opera House (Berlin).

Knossos: see CNOSSUS.

Know-Nothing movement, in U.S. history. During 1840s in Eastern cities where Roman Catholic immigrants especially had concentrated and been welcomed by Democrats, local nativistic societies formed to combat "foreign" influences and uphold "American" view. Native American party, stemming from American Republican party (formed in N.Y. in 1843), became a national party in 1845. In 1850s many secret orders grew up. All inquiries of supposed members were met with a statement to the effect that they knew nothing; hence members were called Know-Nothings. They sought to elect only native Americans to office and to estab. a 25-year residence qualification for citizenship. Allied with a Whig faction, Know-Nothings in 1854 swept Mass. and Del. polls. In 1855 they adopted name American party, yielded much of their secrecy. Slavery issue split them apart; Millard Fillmore, party candidate for President in 1856, polled small vote. Movement continued until 1860, mainly in Eastern cities and in border states among Southern Unionists.

Knox, Frank, 1874–1944, U.S. Secretary of the Navy (1940–44). Opposed to New Deal, he was appointed by Pres. F. D. Roosevelt to help create national unity in defense preparations.

Knox, Henry, 1750–1806, patriot general in American Revolution. Directed artillery in many battles. U.S. Secretary of War (1785–94).

Knox, John, 1505?–1572, Scottish religious reformer, founder of Scottish Presbyterianism. Originally a Catholic priest, he attached himself to George Wishart and became a Protestant. Preached (1549–54) in England, was a royal chaplain briefly, and helped revise second Book of Common Prayer. After accession of Mary I he went into exile on the Continent, chiefly at Geneva where he consulted with Calvin. Scottish Protestant nobles made their first covenant in 1557 (see SCOTLAND, CHURCH OF) and invited Knox's help against Mary of Guise. After a civil war (1559–60) the reformers forced withdrawal of the French and won their freedom and dominance of the new religion. Knox, as minister of Edinburgh, tried to abolish pope's authority and condemn creeds and practices of old church. He attacked the religion of Mary Queen of Scots. Her abdication led to estab. of Church of Scotland. His single-minded zeal made him the outstanding leader of the Scottish Reformation but closed his mind to tolerance.

Knox, Philander Chase, 1853–1921, U.S. cabinet officer. Attorney General (1901–4). Secretary of State (1909–13); protected financial interests abroad, policy attacked as "dollar diplomacy."

Knox, Fort [for Henry Knox], U.S. military reservation, 33,000 acres, N Ky., c.30 mi. SW of Louisville; estab. 1917 as training camp; used since 1936 to store bulk of nation's gold bullion.

Knox College, at Galesburg, Ill.; nonsectarian, coed.; chartered 1837, opened 1841 by Congregationalists and Presbyterians under G. W. Gale. Manual-labor college until 1857. In 1930 absorbed Lombard Col. (chartered 1851, opened 1852). Old Main Hall, where Lincoln debated with Douglas, was made national historic shrine 1936.

Knoxville. 1 City (pop. 7,625), S Iowa, SE of Des Moines, in farm and mine area. **2** City (pop. 124,769), E Tenn., on Tennessee R.; settled c.1786. Cap. of Territory South of the River Ohio (1792–96), twice state cap. (1796–1812, 1817–19). Loyal to Union in Civil War, held by Confederates until abandoned by Gen. A. E. Burnside's Federals, Sept., 1863. Subsequent siege by Longstreet (Nov.–Dec., 1863) failed. Livestock and tobacco market and industrial and commercial center for farm, marble, and mine area, it has mfg. of textiles, clothing, marble and wood products. Seat of Univ. of TENNESSEE. Near Norris Dam and Great Smoky Mts. Natl. Park. Has graves of John Sevier and William Blount, Blount Mansion (1792), and Chisholm Tavern (1791).

Knut: see CANUTE.

Knutson, Paul: see PAUL KNUTSON.

koala (kōä′lü), arboreal marsupial animal (genus *Phascolarctos*) of Australia. It is grayish, thickly furred, tailless, usually 2–2½ ft. high, and has a protuberant, curved, black nose, and large furry ears. Each foot has five toes with claws fitted for climbing and grasping. It often sleeps by day, and at night it eats leaves and shoots of certain eucalyptus trees. Mother carries single cub (c.¾ in. long at birth) in pouch for first six months; cub emerges, uses pouch two months more, and is carried in arms or on back until it is a year old. The koala is harmless and defenseless.

Kobe (kō′bä), city (pop. 607,079), S Honshu, Japan; major port on Osaka Bay. Industrial center (shipbuilding, sugar refining, mfg. of chemicals). Includes ancient port of Hyogo, opened 1868 to foreign trade. Seat of two universities, a nautical college, and several ancient Buddhist temples.

Koblenz, Germany: see COBLENZ.

Koch, Robert (rō′bĕrt kôkh′), 1843–1910, German bacteriologist. He developed techniques of bacteriological culture and discovered causative organisms of many infectious diseases including anthrax (1876), tuberculosis (1882), cholera (1884). Won 1905 Nobel Prize in Physiology and Medicine for developing tuberculin test for tuberculosis.

Kochanowski, Jan (yän kôkhänôf′skē), 1530–84, greatest Polish Renaissance poet. Of especial note is his Polish version of Psalms of David.

Kocher, Emil Theodor (ā′mēl tā′ōdōr kô′khur), 1841–1917, Swiss surgeon. Won 1909 Nobel Prize in Physiology and Medicine for work on thyroid gland.

Kodaly, Zoltan (zôl′tän kō′dälē), 1882–, Hungarian composer. Worked with Bartok in collecting folk tunes and, like Bartok, has used them in his own compositions. Among his works are an opera, *Hary Janos*; the *Psalmus Hungaricus* for chorus and orchestra; and the *Dances of Galanta* for orchestra.

Kodiak Island (kō′dēăk), 100 mi. long, 10–60 mi. wide, off S Alaska, on Shelikof Strait. Mountainous, heavily wooded in N and E; good pasturage in S for cattle, sheep. Kodiak bear is native here. Discovered 1764 by Stepan Glotov, it had first permanent Russian settlement in Alaska, planted by Grigori Shelekhov on Three Saints Bay 1784, moved to Kodiak village 1792. Center of fur trade until Aleksandr Baranov moved hq. to Sitka. Salmon fishing now chief occupation; Karluk R. famous for salmon run. U.S. navy estab. base at Womens Bay 1940.

Koestler, Arthur (kĕst′lur), 1905–, Hungarian-born author. Led adventurous life as newspaper correspondent; in England since 1941. An ex-radical, he found his chief theme in anti-Communism. Among his works are *Spanish Testament* (1937), *The Yogi and the Commissar* (1945), and novels *Darkness at Noon* (1941), *Thieves in the Night* (1946), and *The Age of Longing* (1951).

Koffka, Kurt, 1886–1941, American psychologist, b. Germany. A founder of GESTALT psychology, he taught at Cornell, Univ. of Wisconsin, Smith College (after 1928).

Koh-i-noor, name of a diamond associated through centuries of India's history with deeds of violence. In 1849 came into possession of the British and after being recut was placed among crown jewels.

kohlrabi (kōl′rä′bē), vegetable (*Brassica oleracea gongylodes* or *B. caulorapa*) with turniplike edible swollen stems, closely allied to cabbage.

Kokand or **Khokand** (both: kōkănd′), city (pop. 84,665), Uzbek SSR, in Fergana Valley. Important city since 10th cent., it was cap. of Kokand khanate from 16th cent. until Russian conquest, 1876. Textile mfg. (silk and cotton).

Kokomo (kō′kūmō), city (pop. 38,672), N central Ind., N of Indianapolis; founded c.1843. Farm trade center. Elwood Haynes, inventor, tested first practical automobile here, 1894. Metal, glass, and food products.

Koko Nor (kōkō nōr′), Chinese *Tsing Hai*, salt lake (2,300 sq. mi.), NE Tsinghai prov., China.

Kokoschka, Oskar (ôs′kär kōkôsh′kä), 1886–, Austrian expressionistic painter and playwright, now living in England.

Koksoak, river, NE Que., Canada, formed by Kanaipiskau and Larch rivers SW of Fort Chimo. Flows 90 mi. NE and N to Ungava Bay.

Kokura (kōkōō′rä), city (pop. 168,119), N Kyushu, Japan; port on Inland Sea. Industrial center (steel, cotton textiles, porcelain, chemicals).

kola, tropical tree (*Cola acuminata*) native to Africa and grown in warm regions for seeds known as kola (or cola) nuts. They contain caffeine, oil, and a gluco-side (kolanin). Native peoples chew the fresh nuts. Some nuts are exported for use in beverages and medicine.

Kola Peninsula (kō′lu̇), area c.50,000 sq. mi., N European RSFSR, an E extension of Scandinavian peninsula between Barents (N) and White seas. Rich mineral deposits. Russians live along coasts, Lapps inland. MURMANSK is chief city.

Kolar Gold Fields (kōlär′), city (pop. 133,859), E Mysore, India; India's chief gold-mining center.

Kolbe, Georg (gä′ôrk kōl′bu̇), 1877–1947, German sculptor. Worked in Paris under Rodin.

Kolchak, Aleksandr Vasilyevich (u̇lyĭksän′du̇r vūsē′lyu̇vĭch ku̇lchäk′), 1874–1920, Russian admiral and counterrevolutionist. Commanded Black Sea fleet in World War I. After October Revolution of 1917 he organized anti-Bolshevik government in Siberia, was recognized by Allies, and assumed dictatorship 1918. Successful at first; defeated 1919; retreated to Irkutsk and was captured and shot.

Kolding (kôl′dĭng), city (pop. 31,017), E Jutland, Denmark; a port on Kolding Fjord (inlet of Little Belt). Shipbuilding; machinery and dairy mfg.

Kolhapur (kōlu̇po͞or′), city (pop. 95,918), S Bombay, India. Was cap. of former princely state of Kolhapur, which merged 1949 with Bombay. Textile mfg.

Kolin, Czech *Kolín* (kô′lēn), city (pop. 19,820), central Bohemia, Czechoslovakia, on the Elbe. Varied mfg. Scene of victory of Austrians under Daun over Frederick II of Prussia (1757).

Kollar, Jan, Czech *Kollár* (yän′ kô′lär), 1793–1852, Slovak poet who wrote in Czech. His ardent pan-Slavism is reflected in his best-known poem, *The Daughter of Slava* (1821–24).

Kölliker, Albert von (äl′bĕrt fu̇n kû′lĭku̇r), 1817–1905, Swiss anatomist and physiologist. His microscopic studies of animal tissues advanced development of embryology and histology.

Kollwitz, Käthe (Schmidt) (kā′tu̇ shmĭt′ kôl′vĭts), 1867–1945, German lithographer, best known for her superb studies of poor people. Was ardent socialist and pacifist.

Kolmar, France: see COLMAR.

Köln, Germany: see COLOGNE.

Kolomna (ku̇lôm′nu̇), city (pop. 75,139), central European RSFSR, on Moskva R., SE of Moscow. Mfg. of locomotives and rolling stock. Founded 1177, it passed 1301 to Moscow. It was important in defense of Moscow against Tatars until 16th cent.

Kolomyya (ku̇lu̇mĭ′yu̇), Ger. *Kolomea,* Pol. *Kołomyja,* city (1931 pop. 33,385), W Ukraine, in Galicia, on Pruth R. Petroleum refining. Was important as Polish frontier city 15th–16th cent.; ruled by Austria 1772–1918; ceded by Poland to USSR 1945.

Kolozsvar, Rumania: see CLUJ.

Kolyma (kōlē′mu̇), river, c.1,500 mi. long, RSFSR, in NE Siberia. Flows N into Arctic Ocean. It is partially navigable June–Oct. There are rich gold mines along upper course. **Kolyma Range** (c.6,000 ft. high) parallels E shore.

Komandorski Islands (kŏmu̇ndôr′skē), group (including Bering Island) off Kamchatka Peninsula, RSFSR, in SW Bering Sea. Foggy, composed of volcanic rock, and subject to frequent earthquakes, they are whaling and sealing base, populated mostly by Aleuts.

Komarno, Slovak *Komárno* (kô′märnô) or **Komarom,** Hung. *Komárom* (kô′märôm), city of Czechoslovakia and Hungary. Komarno (pop. 15,461), on left bank of the Danube, belongs to Slovakia; has machinery and textile mfg., flour mills. Komarom (pop. 8,876), on right (Hungarian) bank, has lumber and textile industries. There are port installations on both banks. Entire city belonged to Hungary until partition after World War I.

Komi Autonomous Soviet Socialist Republic (kō′mē), autonomous republic (156,200 sq. mi.; pop. c.450,000), NE European RSFSR, extending W from the N Urals;

cap. Syktyvkar. Nearly half the area is permanently frozen. The sparse population is concentrated in S, where there is farming, lumbering, and stock raising. Coal mines in Pechora Basin. Inhabitants are mostly Komi, a Finnic people, closely related to Permyaks and formerly known as Zyrians.

Komsomolsk (ku̇msu̇mōlsk′) or **Komsomolsk-on-Amur,** city (pop. c.150,000), S Khabarovsk Territory, RSFSR, in E Siberia. Industrial center of Soviet Far East; steel and lumber mills, shipyards, aircraft plants, petroleum refineries. Founded 1932.

Kona (kō′nu̇), district, W Hawaii, T.H.; coffee belt of Hawaiian Isls. Among relics of ancient Hawaii is City of Refuge at Honaunau. First American missionaries landed at Kailua Bay in 1820.

Konev, Ivan Stepanovich (ēvän′ styĭpä′nu̇vĭch kô′nyĭf), 1897–, Russian field marshal in World War II. Took part in capture of Berlin.

Konia, Turkey: see KONYA.

Königgrätz: see HRADEC KRALOVE; SADOWA.

Königsberg (kû′nĭkhsbĕrk), since 1945 **Kaliningrad** (ku̇lyē″nyĭngrät′), city (1939 pop. 372,164), historic cap. of East Prussia; transferred to USSR in 1945 and inc. into RSFSR. It is an ice-free Baltic seaport and produces freight cars, machinery, processed foods. Founded 1255 as fortress of Teutonic Knights, it joined Hanseatic League 1340. Residence of dukes of Prussia 1525–1618; coronation city of kings of Prussia from 1701. Its university, founded 1544, reached greatest fame when Kant taught there; the building, like most of the city, was destroyed in World War II during a two-month siege by the Russians (1945). Kaliningrad, built up after war in NW section of Königsberg, has a Russian population.

Königshütte, Poland: see CHORZOW.

Königsmark, Countess Maria Aurora (märē′ä ourō′rä kû′nĭksmärk), 1666?–1728, Swedish noblewoman, mistress of Augustus II of Poland and Saxony. Their son Maurice became known as Marshal de SAXE.

Konoye, Fumimaro, Prince (fo͞o″mēmärō′ kōnoi′), 1891–1945, Japanese statesman. Of ancient Fujiwara family. Premier 1937–39, 1940–41. Forsook liberalism to advance Japanese aggression in China. Resigned 1941 when talks with U.S. failed; succeeded by Gen. Tojo. Suicide prevented trial as war criminal.

Konstanz, Germany: see CONSTANCE.

Konya or **Konia** (kôn′yä), city (pop. 64,509), S central Turkey. Center of rich agr. area; mfg. of carpets, textiles, leather goods. The ancient ICONIUM, it reached its peak after becoming the seat of the powerful Seljuk sultanate of Iconium or Rum, in Asia Minor (11th cent.). After the Seljuks' defeat by allied Mongols and Armenians (late 13th cent.), the territory passed to the emirs of Karaman, then to the Ottoman Turks (15th cent.). Konya remained important as religious center of the whirling dervishes, whose order was founded here in 13th cent. It has kept several medieval mosques and its old city walls. In 1832 Egyptians under Ibrahim Pasha routed Turks at Konya.

Koo, (Vi Kuiyuin) Wellington (ko͞o′), 1887–, Chinese diplomat; educated at Columbia Univ. At various times minister of foreign affairs and prime minister. Ambassador to France (1932–41) and to Great Britain (1941–46). Chief Chinese delegate to San Francisco conference (1945) which founded UN. Ambassador to U.S. since 1946.

Koolau Range (kō′u̇lou′), mountain chain, Oahu, T.H., rising to 3,105 ft. Cut by two scenic passes, Nuuanu Pali (c.1,200 ft. high) and Waimanalo Pali.

Kootenai (ko͞o′tĭnā) (in Canada, Kootenay), river, rising in SE B.C., Canada, and flowing into NW Mont., W into N Idaho, then N to Kootenay L. in B.C. Part of Columbia R. system.

Kootenai Indians, North American tribes, of distinct linguistic stock (the Kootenai), living in 18th cent. in N Mont., N Idaho, and SE British Columbia. Culture was essentially that of Plateau area till coming of horse changed their culture to that of the Plains.

SMALL CAPITALS = cross references. Pronunciation key on inside end pages. Abbreviations: p. 2.

Kootenay Lake, SE B.C., Canada, E of the Selkirk range, an expansion of Kootenay (in U.S., Kootenai) R. To E, on Alta. line, is **Kootenay National Park,** estab. 1920.

Kooweskoowe: see ROSS, JOHN.

Kopparberg, Swed. *Kopparbergs län* (kô″pärběryùs lĕn′), county (11,648 sq. mi.; pop. 267,019), central Sweden, virtually identical with historical DALARNA prov.; cap. FALUN. Copper mines, from which name derives, are now exhausted, but rich iron mines are worked in Grangesberg dist. in S. There are iron, steel, and lumber mills. It includes Domnarvet metalworks.

Köprülü, family of grand viziers: see KUPRILI.

Korah (kō′rù), Levite leader (with Abiram and his brother Dathan) of revolt against Moses. Rebels ended by being consumed by fire and earthquake. Num. 16; 26.9–11; Deut. 11.6. Core: Jude 11.

Koran or **Quran** (kŏrän′, –rän′) [Arabic,= reading], sacred book of Islam; after the Bible, the world's most influential book. Moslems consider it a series of revelations by God to Mohammed. Canonical text (in classical Arabic) estab. A.H. 30 (A.D. 651–52) under the Caliph Othman according to the 114 suras [chapters] of Zaid ibn Thabit, the Prophet's secretary. All variant texts were destroyed. Moslems memorize the Koran, consider all science a commentary on it.

Korbel, Mario (kôr′bùl), 1882–, American sculptor, b. Bohemia. Did fountains and dancing figures.

Korça or **Korçë,** Albania: see KORITSA.

Korcula (kôr′chŏŏlä), Ital. *Curzola,* Serbo-Croatian *Korčula,* Adriatic island, area 107 sq. mi., off Dalmatia, Yugoslavia. Chief town, Korcula (pop. 2,012), has fine medieval cathedral and fortifications.

Korea (kôrē′ù, kù–), Korean *Choson,* Jap. *Chosen,* country (85,228 sq. mi.; 1944 pop. 25,900,142), E Asia. Occupies a mountainous peninsula bounded on N by Yalu and Tumen rivers (forming borders of Manchuria and USSR), on W by Korea Bay, on S by Korea Strait and Yellow Sea, and on E by Sea of Japan. Has c.3,400 offshore islands. Principal mountain range extends along E coast, rising to 8,337 ft. at Mt. Kwanmo. Gold, iron, tungsten, and coal are chief mineral resources. There is valuable timberland. N Korea is largely industrial, while S Korea is predominantly agr. (crops include rice, barley, soybeans, and tobacco). Long coast line provides extensive fishing grounds. Religion of most Koreans is a mixture of Buddhism, Confucianism, and native shamanism; Christians are a small minority. Recorded history begins in 12th cent. B.C., when a Chinese scholar Ki-tze founded a colony at Pyongyang. In 7th cent. A.D. the native Silla kingdom, aided by China, estab. rule over all Korea. Country was occupied 1592–96 by the Japanese dictator HIDEYOSHI in his campaign to conquer China. It became a vassal state of China in early 17th cent. Long known as the Hermit Kingdom, Korea was forced to abandon isolationism by accepting a commercial treaty with Japan in 1876. Japan's victories in First CHINO-JAPANESE WAR (1894–95) and RUSSO-JAPANESE WAR (1904–5) led to annexation of Korea in 1910. In World War II, Korea was promised independence by U.S., Britain, and China at Cairo Conference (1943). At war's end, the country was divided into occupation zones—the Russians N and Americans S of 38th parallel. When cooperation between the two proved impossible, the division was formalized by establishment of two regimes, Republic of Korea in S (cap. Seoul) and People's Republic of Korea in N (cap. Pyongyang). After the election held in S Korea under UN supervision (1948), Syngman RHEE was elected first president by the parliament. By mid-1949 all occupation troops had been withdrawn. On June 25, 1950, N Korea invaded S Korea and was promptly declared an aggressor by UN Security Council (from which USSR was voluntarily absent). The swift advance of the invaders was stopped in Aug. by UN forces (under supreme command of Gen. MACARTHUR) who held a perimeter defense 50 mi.

from Pusan on SE coast. A counterattack, featuring invasion of Inchon on Sept. 15, carried UN forces to Manchurian border, but entrance of Chinese Communists into the war in Nov. again turned the tide; UN troops were forced to retreat far below 38th parallel until early 1951 when UN forces began a counterattack, driving the enemy back of the 38th parallel. Truce talks, begun July, 1951, at Kaesong and continued in the fall at Panmunjom, were deadlocked by July, 1952, on the issue of prisoner exchange (the Communists rejecting UN proposal for voluntary repatriation). After Oct., 1952, when truce talks were indefinitely postponed, fighting became heavier, with each side vying for control of strategic hills in central Korea. In 1953 the Communists abruptly agreed to Allied proposal for exchange of sick and wounded prisoners, which was begun on April 20, with the Allies returning 5,800 and the Communists 600; at the same time truce talks were resumed.

Korin (Korin Ogata) (kō′rēn), c.1655–1716, Japanese artist, renowned for his lacquer work.

Koritsa (kôrĭt′sù), Albanian *Korçë* or *Korça,* city (pop. 24,035), SE Albania. Commercial and agr. center of a fertile plain. Long claimed by Greeks, who occupied it in Balkan Wars and both world wars.

Kornilov, Lavr Georgyevich (lä′vùr gēyôr′gyĭvĭch kùr-nyē′lùf), 1870–1918, Russian general. Kerensky made him commander in chief after February Revolution of 1917 but dismissed him in Sept. He refused to accept his dismissal, was arrested, escaped after the Bolshevik Revolution, and led an army of counterrevolutionary volunteers in S Russia. Forced to fall back on the Kuban, he was killed in action and was succeeded by Denikin.

Korolenko, Vladimir Galaktionovich (vlŭdyē′mĭr gù-lùktyô′nùvĭch kùrùlyĕn′kù), 1853–1921, Russian author and liberal publicist. Best known for his short stories (many tr. into Eng.).

Koros, Hung. *Körös* (kù′rùsh), river of E Hungary, formed by three headstreams rising in Transylvania (Rumania) and flowing c.50 mi. W into the Theiss.

Kortrijk, Belgium: see COURTRAI.

Korzybski, Alfred (Habdank) (kôrzĭb′skē), 1879–1950, Polish-American scientist, b. Warsaw. Founded system of General Semantics. Wrote (1933) *Science and Sanity,* on distinction between words and objects.

Kos (kŏs, kôs), Latin *Cos,* Aegean island (111 sq. mi.; pop. 18,545), Greece, second largest of the DODECANESE, 2½ mi. off Asia Minor; chief city Kos (pop. 7,955). Important cultural center in Roman times; home of Hippocrates.

Kosciusko, Thaddeus (kŏ″sēù′skō), 1746–1817, Polish general. Fought for patriot cause in American Revolution. Champion of Polish independence, he led an unsuccessful rebellion against Russian and Prussian control (1794) and became one of the great heroes of Poland.

Kosciusko (kŏ″sēù′skō), city (pop. 6,753), central Miss., NE of Jackson, in dairy area.

Kosciusko, Mount (kŏzēŭ′skō), 7,305 ft. high, SE New South Wales, in Australian Alps; highest peak of Australia.

kosher [Heb.,= proper, i.e., fit for use], term applied to food which complies with the Jewish dietary laws. Kosher meat is the flesh of animals which chew the cud and have cloven hoofs; both meat and fowl must be slaughtered by a specially trained pious Jew and must be salted and soaked to remove all traces of blood. Kosher fish are those which have scales (mollusks and eels are forbidden). The laws forbid cooking and eating of milk with meat and also the use of the same kitchen or table utensil for handling both meat and milk. It is widely held that many of these laws stem from the health preservation measures of ancient Palestine.

Koshtan-Tau (kŭshtän″-tou′), peak, 16,880 ft. high, USSR, in central Greater Caucasus.

Kosice (kô′shĭtsä), Ger. *Kaschau,* Hung. *Kassa,* Slovak

Košice, city (pop. 51,689), SE Slovakia, Czechoslovakia. Textile, machinery, food, and tobacco mfg. Episcopal see. Belonged to Hungary until 1918 and reverted to it 1938–45. Has fine residences of former Magyar nobility and 14th-cent. Gothic Cathedral of St. Elizabeth.

Kosovo, Yugoslavia: see Kossovo.

Kossak, Sophia (kô'säk), Pol. *Zofja Kossak-Szczucka,* 1890–, Polish author. Among her works in English translation are the historical novels *The Blaze* (1922), *The Leper King* (1937), and *Blessed Are the Meek* (1938).

Kossel, Albrecht (äl'brĕkht kô'sùl), 1853–1927, German physiological chemist. Won 1910 Nobel Prize in Physiology and Medicine for work on proteins, cells, and cell nuclei.

Kossovo, Serbo-Croatian *Kosovo* (kô'sôvô), plain in SW Serbia, Yugoslavia. Scene of decisive Turkish victory over Serbs, Bulgarians, and allies (1389) and of another Turkish victory over Hungarians under Hunyadi (1448). Just before first battle of Kossovo, Sultan Murad I was stabbed to death by a Serb posing as deserter.

Kossuth, Louis (kŏsōoth', Hung. kôsh'ōot), Hung. *Kossuth Lajos,* 1802–94, Hungarian revolutionary hero. One of the principal figures in the Hungarian revolution of March, 1848, he was a liberal and an extreme nationalist. When Austria prepared to move against Hungary, Kossuth became head of the government of national defense; in April, 1849, he became president of the newly proclaimed Hungarian republic. He resigned in August, when Russian troops came to aid the Austrians, and spent the rest of his life in exile.

Koster, Laurens Janszoon (lou'rùns yän'sōn kô'stùr), c.1370–c.1440, Dutch sexton [*koster*], to whom some have attributed the use of movable type in printing prior to Gutenberg.

Kostroma (kùstrùmä'), city (pop. 121,205), central European RSFSR, on the Volga. Linen-milling center. Annexed to Moscow 1364. Michael Romanov was elected tsar here in 1613. Has Uspenski Cathedral (c.1250).

Kotelny Island or **Kotelnyy Island** (both: kōtĕl'nē), 100 mi. long, 60 mi. wide, largest of Anjou group of New Siberian Islands. Arctic observation post on NW coast.

Köthen (kû'tùn), city (pop. 42,588), Saxony-Anhalt, E central Germany. Lignite mines; sugar mills; textile mfg. Until 1847 residence of dukes of Anhalt-Köthen. Formerly spelled Cöthen.

Kotka (kôt'kä), city (pop. 24,528), S Finland; a seaport on Gulf of Finland and at southern end of *Päijänne* waterway. Main Finnish paper, pulp, and timber export center.

Kotor (kô'tôr), Ital. *Cattaro,* town (pop. 5,402), Montenegro, SW Yugoslavia, on the bay of Kotor (Serbo-Croatian *Boka Kotorska,* Ital. *Bocche di Cattaro*), an inlet of the Adriatic. Was held by Venice from 15th cent. till 1797, when it passed to Austria. An important Austrian naval base, it passed to Yugoslavia in 1918. Has medieval fortifications; cathedral (built 9th cent., rebuilt 17th cent.).

Kotzebue, August von (ou'gōost fün kôt'sùbōo), 1761–1819, German playwright, author of many popular melodramas. After a stay in Russia he returned to Germany as paid agent of Alexander I. His assassination by a student led to suppression of German student organizations by Carlsbad Decrees. His son, **Otto von Kotzebue,** 1787–1846, Russian naval officer and explorer, commanded two voyages around world (1815–17, 1823–26). Discovered and explored Kotzebue Sound (1816).

Koussevitzky, Serge (sĕrzh' kōosùvĭt'skē), 1874–1951, Russian-American conductor. Began his career playing the double bass. Made his conducting debut in Berlin, 1908. Was conductor of the Boston Symphony Orchestra (1924–49); director of the Berkshire Symphonic Festivals after 1936.

Kovel (kô'vùl), Pol. *Kowel,* city (1931 pop. 27,650), W Ukraine, in Volhynia. Agr. processing center. Passed to Russia from Poland 1795; reverted to Poland 1921; was ceded to USSR 1945.

Kovno, Lithuania: see Kaunas.

Kowel, Ukraine: see Kovel.

Kowloon: see Hong Kong.

Koyukuk (kùyōo'kōok), river rising on S slope of Brooks Range, N Alaska, and flowing c.450 mi. SW to the Yukon near Koyukuk village. Partially explored by H. T. Allen 1855. Gold is mined at headwaters.

Kr, chemical symbol of the element krypton.

Krafft-Ebing, Richard von (rīkh'ärt fün kräft-ā'bĭng), 1840–1902, German physician and neurologist, authority on psychological aspect of mental disorders and their medico-legal relations.

Kraft or **Krafft, Adam** (both: ä'däm kräft'), c.1455–1509, German sculptor of Nuremberg. Most famous work was Tabernacle for Church of St. Lawrence, Nuremberg.

Krak (kräk) or **El Kerak** (ĕl kĕ'räk), town (pop. c.10,000), S central Jordan; trade center. As the ancient Kir Moab it was walled citadel of Moabites. Lordship of Krak and Montreal was one of chief baronies of Latin Kingdom of Jerusalem. In 1131 Knights Hospitalers built castle (called Krak des Chevaliers), which still stands. Taken 1188 by Saladin. Krak was seat of an archbishop from early Christian era until 1910, when Christians were expelled by Turks.

Krakatoa (kräkùtō'ù), volcanic island, Indonesia, in Sunda Strait between Java and Sumatra. Its explosion in 1883 caused great destruction in surrounding area and scattered debris across Indian Ocean as far as Madagascar.

Krakow, Poland: see Cracow.

Kramer, Jack (John Albert Kramer), 1921–, American tennis player. Won (1946–47) national singles, British singles. As professional he won U.S. singles (1948), world singles (1949).

Kranach, Lucas: see Cranach, Lucas.

Krasicki, Ignacy (ēgnä'tsē kräsēts'kē), 1735–1801, Polish writer and archbishop. Noted for prose and verse satires (including *Monachomania,* on monastic life), fables, and novels.

Krasinski, Sigismund (kräsē'nyùskē), Pol. *Zygmunt Krasiński,* 1812–59, Polish poet, an ardent Slavophile. His works include the dramatic poems *The Undivine Comedy* (1835; Eng. tr., 1875) and *Irodon* (1836; Eng. tr., 1927).

Krasnodar (krùs"nùdär'), city (pop. 203,946), SE European RSFSR, port on lower Kuban R. Rail hub and industrial center (oil refineries, machinery plants, steel foundries). Founded 1794 as Ekaterinodar (after Catherine II), it became hq. of Kuban Cossacks. Renamed 1920. German-held in World War II. It is cap. of **Krasnodar Territory,** administrative division (32,800 sq. mi.; pop. c.3,000,000), RSFSR, extending E from Sea of Azov and Black Sea into Kuban Steppe, its main agr. region. Subtropical Black Sea littoral, with health resorts, produces citrus fruits, essential oils, tea, and wine. Rich oil fields at Maikop. N section was annexed to Russia 1783; Black Sea littoral ceded by Turkey 1829; the rest, Circassia, was annexed 1864.

Krasnoyarsk (krùsnùyärsk'), city (pop. c.300,000), RSFSR, in S central Siberia, on Yenisei R. and on Trans-Siberian RR. Transportation center, with machinery, lumber, and textile mills. Founded 1628. It is cap. of **Krasnoyarsk Territory,** administrative division (928,000 sq. mi.; pop. c.2,100,000), RSFSR, extending across Siberian steppe, forest, and tundra to Arctic Ocean. Includes Taimyr Peninsula. In arable S section dwells 94% of population (Russian, Turkic, Mongol peoples). Farther N are gold, coal, and graphite deposits. Organized 1934.

Krasnoye Selo (kräs'nùyù syīlô'), city (pop. over 10,000), RSFSR, SW of Leningrad. Peter III was murdered in a near-by palace in 1762. City was a summer resort for St. Petersburg society before 1917.

Kraszewski, Joseph Ignatius (kräshĕf'skē), Pol. *Józef*

Ignacy Kraszewski, 1812–87, Polish writer. Translated works include the historical romances *Memories of the Countess Cosel* and *Count Bruehl,* the romance *Iermola,* and the comedy *The Jew.*

Kravchinski, Sergei Mikhailovich: see STEPNIAK, S.

Krefeld (krā'felt), city (pop. 170,482), North Rhine-Westphalia, NW Germany, on the Rhine and NW of Düsseldorf. Silk and rayon mfg. (estab. 18th cent. by Frederick II); mfg. of quality steel, machinery, dyes. About 70% destroyed in World War II. Formerly spelled Crefeld.

Kreisler, Fritz (krī'slùr), 1875–, Austrian-American violinist. Made his debut as a child prodigy. After studying medicine, then art, he returned to the violin and became world famous. His compositions include numerous short works for violin (e.g., *Liebesleid* and *Caprice Viennois*), and a few works that he originally played as being by old masters and later revealed to be his own.

Kremenchug (krĕmĭnchōok'), city (pop. 89,553), central Ukraine, on the Dnieper. River-rail center, with machinery mfg. German-held in World War II.

Kremer, Gerhard: see MERCATOR, GERARDUS.

kremlin, Rus. *kreml,* citadel of several Russian cities, which served as administrative and religious center and offered protection against military attacks in Middle Ages. Among most famous kremlins are those of Astrakhan, Kazan, Moscow, Nizhni Novgorod, Novgorod, and Pskov. That of Moscow, known simply as **the Kremlin,** occupies historic core of the city. Triangular in shape, it contains such structures as Uspenski Cathedral (late 15th cent.), where tsars were crowned; Arkhangelski Cathedral (14th–17th cent.), with tsars' tombs; and 300-ft. bell tower of Ivan the Great, with golden cupola. The Grand Palace, built in 19th cent., was rebuilt under Soviet regime to house supreme council (parliament) of USSR. Other buildings are used as government offices and residences for some high officials.

Kremsier (krĕm'zēr), Czech *Kroměříž,* town (pop. 17,-626), Moravia, Czechoslovakia, on Morava R. Here the Austrian constituent assembly or Reichstag, transferred from Vienna, wrote a federal constitution for the Hapsburg empire in 1848–49. Felix zu Schwarzenberg rejected the constitution and dissolved the assembly.

Krenek, Ernst (krĕ'nĕk), Czech *Křenek,* 1900–, Austrian-American composer. Well schooled in the traditions of the past, he is at the same time an innovator (e.g., he wrote a jazz opera, *Jonny spielt auf,* 1926. He adopted (1928) the 12-tone technique (see ATONALITY) originated by Arnold Schönberg and wrote an opera *Karl V* (1933) in it. He has also composed chamber, orchestral and choral music, and a piano concerto.

Kreuger, Ivar (ē'vär krōō'gùr), 1880–1932, Swedish financier. In 1913 he formed a match trust, which became an international financial agency. Speculation and fraud brought Kreuger some $500,000,000 (about half from U.S. creditors) but wrecked the trust. He died by suicide.

Kreutzer, Rodolphe (kroi'tsùr), 1766–1831, French composer and violinist. A prolific composer, he is best remembered for his 40 etudes for violin. Beethoven's Kreutzer Sonata is dedicated to him.

Kreymborg, Alfred (krām'bôrg), 1883–, American poet and anthologist, originally one of the imagists.

Krishna (krĭsh'nù), eighth avatar of the god Vishnu, very popular in Hinduism; one of the more joyful expressions of deity.

Krishnamurti, Jiddu (jĭ'dōō krĭsh"nùmōōr'tē), 1895–, Hindu religious leader. Mrs. Annie Besant met him in 1907, proclaimed him the incarnation of Maitreya, the world teacher. Toured England and America with her (1926–27), later repudiated her claims.

Kristiania, Norway: see OSLO.

Krivoi Rog (krēvoi' rôk'), city (pop. 197,621), S central Ukraine, on Ingulets R. Industrial center of iron-mining region with ore reserves of over 1,000,000,000

tons. In World War II Germans held city and destroyed most industrial installations.

Krk (kŭrk), Ital. *Veglia,* Adriatic island, area 165 sq. mi., Croatia, NW Yugoslavia, off Dalmatian coast. Chief town, Krk, has medieval walls, castle, and cathedral.

Krkonose: see RIESENGEBIRGE.

Krochmal, Nachman Kohen (näkh'män kō'hĕn krôkh'-mäl), 1785–1840, Jewish historian, b. Galicia; a founder of modern Jewish scholarship and a leader of the Jewish enlightenment.

Kroeber, Alfred Louis, 1876–, American anthropologist. He taught at Univ. of Calif. (1901–1946) and is author of many works on cultural anthropology.

Krogh, August (ou'gōost krôkh), 1874–1949, Danish physiologist. Won 1920 Nobel Prize in Physiology and Medicine for work on regulation of capillary blood supply in muscle.

Kroll, Leon (krōl), 1884–, American painter, perhaps best known for his studies of women.

Kromeriz, Czechoslovakia: see KREMSIER.

Kronecker, Leopold (lā'ōpôlt krō'nĕ"kùr), 1823–91, German mathematician. He was a pioneer in the field of algebraic numbers and in formulating relationship between theory of numbers, theory of equations, and elliptic functions.

Kronstadt, Rumania: see BRASOV.

Kronstadt (krōn'stät), city (pop. c.50,000), RSFSR, on island of Gulf of Finland, near Leningrad; also spelled Cronstadt. Founded 1703 by Peter I as port and fortress; now base of Soviet Baltic fleet. Port lost commercial value after dredging of deep-sea canal to St. Petersburg (1875–93). Mutinies of naval garrison played a part in revolutions of 1905 and 1917. City defended Leningrad in World War II.

Kropotkin, Peter (krōpŏt'kĭn), 1842–1921, Russian anarchist, a prince who became interested in the peasants and renounced his title. Escaped prison in Russia and, after a three-year imprisonment in France, lived thereafter in England. Returned to Russia after Revolution, despite his opposition to Bolshevism.

Krout, John Allen, 1896–, American historian, long a professor and dean at Columbia Univ. He has written texts and scholarly works. Became vice president and provost of Columbia in 1953.

Krüdener, Julie de (dù krü'dùnùr), 1764–1824, Russian pietist. Before her conversion she wrote a sentimental novel, *Valérie* (1804), which caused some scandal. Later she preached her mystic faith throughout Europe. Under her spell, Alexander I of Russia created the Holy Alliance (1815).

Kruger, Stephanus Johannes Paulus (krōō'gùr), 1825–1904, South African statesman, known as Paul Kruger or Oom Paul. Played important role in history of TRANSVAAL as pioneer, soldier, farmer, and politician. With Joubert and Pretorius he negotiated Pretoria agreement with the British (1881) restoring independence to the Boer state. As president (1883–1900) he implacably opposed the policies of Cecil Rhodes. After outbreak of SOUTH AFRICAN WAR he went to Europe on futile mission to win support for the Boers. Died in Switzerland.

Krugersdorp (krōō'gùrzdôrp), town (pop. 71,885), S Transvaal prov., South Africa. Named for Paul Kruger. Gold-mining center.

Krupp (krōop), family of German armament manufacturers, settled in Essen since 16th cent. **Friedrich Krupp,** 1787–1826, began the modern concern with a steel plant; his son, **Alfred Krupp,** 1812–87, the "cannon king," specialized in armaments. Great financial expansion took place under his son, **Friedrich Albert (Fritz) Krupp,** 1854–1902; under the latter's son-in-law, **Gustav Krupp von Bohlen und Halbach,** 1870–1950, the Krupp works became the center for German rearmament after 1933. His son, **Alfred Krupp von Bohlen und Halbach,** 1907–, was sentenced to imprisonment for 12 years as a war criminal (1948).

Krusevac, Serbo-Croatian *Kruševac* (krōō'shĕväts),

town (pop. 14,104), Serbia, Yugoslavia, SE of Belgrade. Was a cap. of medieval Serbia.

Krusne Hory: see ERZGEBIRGE.

Krutch, Joseph Wood (krōōch), 1893–, American author, long a professor at Columbia Univ. Among his works are *The Modern Temper* (philosophical, 1929) and many books on drama and literature (e.g., *The American Drama since 1918*, 1939; *Samuel Johnson*, 1944).

Krylov, Ivan Andreyevich (ēvän' ŭndrä'ŭvĭch krĭlôf'), 1768–1844, Russian poet, celebrated for his fables.

kryolite: see CRYOLITE.

krypton (krĭp'tŏn), inert, colorless, odorless, tasteless, gaseous element (symbol = Kr; see also ELEMENT, table). It forms no known compounds.

Kuala Lumpur (kwä'lu lōōm'pŏōr), town (pop. 175,-961), SW Malaya; cap. of Selangor and of Federation of Malaya. Trade center.

Kuban (kōōbän'), river, 584 mi. long, Georgian SSR and RSFSR, rising in the Greater Caucasus and flowing N, then W into Sea of Azov and Black Sea via two arms. Kuban Steppe, a major grain region, is on lower course. After Russian annexation of the khanate of Crimea (1783), of which the area was a part, Cossacks were settled here to protect it from Circassian mountaineers. Cossacks fought against Bolsheviks in 1917. Scene of heavy fighting in World War II.

Kubelik, Jan (kōō'bulĭk), 1880–1940, Czech violin virtuoso. Made his debut in Vienna in 1898; first appeared in the U.S. in 1901.

Kublai Khan (kōō'blĭ kän'), 1215?–1294, Mongol emperor, founder of Yüan dynasty of China. In 1260 became khan of empire founded by his grandfather Jenghiz Khan. Defeated Sung dynasty of China in 1279. Failed in campaign to conquer Japan, SE Asia, and Indonesia. Fostered Chinese scholarship and arts; favored Buddhism but tolerated other religions. His cap. at Cambuluc was visited by Marco Polo.

Kuching (kōō'chĭng), city (pop. 37,949), on W Borneo; cap. of Sarawak. Ships sago flour and pepper.

Kuchuk Kainarji, Treaty of (kōōchōōk' kĭnär'jē), 1774, peace treaty between Russia and Turkey. Khanate of Crimea was declared independent, except for Kerch, which passed to Russia. Russia also gained right to intervene on behalf of the Moldavian and Walachian principalities (which, however, were restored to Turkish overlordship) and certain rights of representation on behalf of the sultan's Greek Orthodox subjects. The treaty prepared Russia's annexation of the Crimea (1783) and marked Russian ascendancy over Turkey (see EASTERN QUESTION). It was signed at village of Kainardzha, now in Bulgaria; other spellings include Kutchuk and Kainardji.

Kudrun, Germanic heroine: see GUDRUN.

kudzu (kōōd'zōō), perennial leguminous vine (*Pueraria thunbergiana*), native to Japan, with broad leaves and purple flowers. Of rapid growth, it is used in S U.S. as a ground cover and forage or cover crop.

Kuhn, Richard (rĭkh'ärt kōōn'), 1900–, Austrian chemist. Won 1938 Nobel Prize for work on carotinoids, vitamins, isolation of riboflavin; Nazi decree prevented his acceptance of the award.

Kuhn, Walt (kūn), 1880–1949, American painter. Known for portrait studies of circus and back-stage types. Helped assemble the famed Armory Show.

Kuibyshev (kwē'bĭshĕf), formerly **Samara** (sümä'rä), city (pop. c.600,000), E European RSFSR, river port and rail center on the Volga. Mfg. of aircraft, locomotives, machinery, ball bearings, synthetic rubber, textiles; oil refining. Founded 1586 as Muscovite stronghold, it was attacked by Nogai Tatars in 1615 and Kalmucks in 1644; gates opened to Cossack rebels in 1670. Became chief grain center of the Volga. Seat of anti-Bolshevik government in 1918. Renamed 1935. In World War II central government was here.

Ku Klux Klan (kū' klŭks" klăn', kōō'), name of two distinct secret societies in U.S. history. **1** Original Ku Klux Klan was organized by ex-Confederates at Pulas-

ki, Tenn., in Dec., 1865, to oppose radical Republican RECONSTRUCTION, maintain "white supremacy." Absorbed many smaller groups as it spread. Its practices played upon fears and superstitions of the blacks. General organization of local Klans was effected in April, 1867; Gen. N. B. Forrest was made leader. Disbandment ordered in Jan., 1869; local organizations continued. Success in keeping Negroes from polls enabled ex-Confederates to gain political control in many states. Congressional legislation attempted to combat Klan (see FORCE BILL). In Lower South dominant group was more conservative Knights of the White Camellia. **2** Second Ku Klux Klan was founded in 1915; first meeting was held on Stone Mt., Ga. Added to "white supremacy" an intense nativism, anti-Catholicism, anti-Semitism. After 1920 it spread throughout North and South. Controlled politics in many communities. Texas, Okla., Ind., Oregon, Maine were particularly under its influence. Klan frequently took extra-legal measures, some of them extreme. Large membership of mid-1920s declined to estimated 30,-000 by 1930. After World War II attempt at revival failed when state after state specifically barred the order. It still exists in incipient form in several Southern states, notably Ga.

Kulikovo, battle of (kōōlyĭkô'vu), 1380, fought near Don R., SE of Tula, with victory for Grand Duke Dmitri Donskoi of Moscow over the Golden Horde. It made Moscow the center of strengthened resistance to Mongol domination.

Kulm, Poland: see CHELMNO.

Kulmbach, Hans von (kōōlm'bäkh), c.1476–1522, German painter and engraver; follower of Dürer.

Kulpmont, borough (pop. 5,199), E Pa., SE of Sunbury. Anthracite mining and mfg. of clothing.

Kulturkampf (kōōltōōr'kämpf") [Ger.,= conflict of cultures], 1873–87, the conflict between the German government under Bismarck and the Roman Catholic Church. Bismarck saw in political Catholicism, as represented by the Center party (founded 1870), a threat to the unified German state. With a series of drastic laws he sought to intimidate the clergy and to break down the Catholic school system. His measures merely strengthened the Catholic party. In 1887, fearing the rise of socialism, Bismarck rescinded his anti-Catholic measures and reached a *modus vivendi* with Pope LEO XIII.

Kum, Qum, or **Qom** (all: kōōm), city (pop. 52,637), N central Iran, on Trans-Iranian RR; Shiite pilgrimage center.

Kumamoto (kōōmä'mōtō), city (pop. 245,841), W Kyushu, Japan; mfg. center. Seat of Kumamoto Medical Univ. Was important castle town in 16th cent.

Kumasi (kōōmä'sē), city (pop. 70,705), cap. of Ashanti, W Africa; second city of Gold Coast. Center of cacao trade.

Kumbakonam (kōōmbŭkô'num), city (pop. 67,008), S Madras, India, on Cauvery R.; Brahmanic cultural center. Silk and cotton weaving, jewelry making. Name formerly spelled Combaconum.

kumquat (kŭm'kwŏt), ornamental evergreen shrub of genus *Fortunella*, native to China and closely related to the orange. It has sweet-scented white flowers and small, orange fruits which can be eaten fresh or in preserves.

Kun, Bela (bä'lô kōōn'), 1886–?, Hungarian communist. As head of coalition government of Communists and Social Democrats (1919) he set up dictatorship of the proletariat, raised Red Army, overran Slovakia. Forced out of Slovakia by Allies and defeated by Rumanian army of intervention, Kun fled abroad. According to unconfirmed rumor he died in a Russian prison after Communist party purges of 1930s.

Kunersdorf (kōō'nŭrsdôrf"), village in E Brandenburg, where Frederick II of Prussia suffered a critical defeat by Austrians and Russians (1759).

Kungalv (kŭng'ĕlv"), Swed. *Kungälv*, city (pop. 3,632), SW Sweden, N of Goteborg and on the Kattegat. One of chief cities of medieval Norway, it was plundered 1135 by Wends, seized 1368 by Hansa merchants, and ceded 1612 to Sweden.

Kung Hsiang-hsi (kōong shyäng'shē'), better known as **H. H. Kung**, 1881–, Chinese banker and political leader. Educated at Oberlin Col. and Yale Univ. Important in Kuomintang government since 1927. Married SOONG Ai-ling.

Kuniyoshi, Yasuo (yäsōō-ō' kōon"ēyō'shē), 1892–, American painter, b. Japan. His decorative work is Oriental in spirit, Western in technique.

Kunlun (kōon'lōon'), mountain system of central Asia, between Himalayas and Tien Shan. Forms N boundary of Tibet, rises to 25,340 ft. on Tibet-Sinkiang border.

Kunming (kōon'ming'), commercial city (pop. 300,-297), cap. Yunnan prov., S China. In World War II it was vital supply point at E end of Burma Road.

Kuomintang (kwō'mintäng') [Chinese,= national people's party]. Organized 1912 by SUN YAT-SEN with program calling for independent republic and moderate socialism. Suppressed 1913 by Yüan Shih-kai; set up unrecognized governments at Canton in 1918 and 1921. Reorganized 1922 with Russia's help. At party congress (1924) coalition including Communists adopted Sun's political principles. Its army under CHIANG KAI-SHEK advanced N from Canton to gain military control of country. Government established at Nanking received diplomatic recognition 1928; by 1930 all China under its control except for N regions held by Communists (purged in 1927). Until 1947 Kuomintang barred participation of minority parties in official Chinese government. Civil war (begun after World War II) forced Nationalists to take refuge on Formosa in 1950.

Kuopio (kōō'ôpēō), city (pop. 33,305), central Finland, on L. Kallavesi, in principal forest region of Finland and at head of Saima lake system. Timber industries.

Kuprili (kùprē'lē), Turkish-Albanian family, many members of which served as grand viziers; also spelled Köprülü. It rose into prominence with **Mohammed Kuprili**, 1583–1661, grand vizier of Mohammed IV from 1656. Though an upstart and illiterate, he restored some of its former prestige to the Ottoman Empire, notably by reorganizing the fleet and by his conquest of Transylvania (1658). The power of the family ended with Abdullah Kuprili (d. 1735), acting vizier from 1723.

Kuprin, Aleksandr Ivanovich (ùlyĭksän'dùr ēvä'nŭvĭch kōō'prĭn), 1870–1938, Russian author. His novels *The Duel* (1905) and *Yama: the Pit* (1909) are well known. The volumes *The River of Life* (1916) and *Sasha* (1920) include some of his best short stories.

Kura (kōōrä'), anc. *Cyrus,* river, 940 mi. long, chief river of Georgian and Azerbaijan republics, in Transcaucasia. From Turkish Armenia it flows NE, then SE to Caspian Sea. Lower course irrigates cotton-growing plain.

Kurdistan (kûr'dĭstän", kōōrdĭstän'), extensive plateau and mountainous region, c.74,000 sq. mi., inhabited by Kurds or Carduchis, and occupying parts of E Turkey, Soviet Armenia, NE Iraq, and NW Iran. Ethnically related to the Persians, the Kurds are a nomadic pastoral people of c.2,500,000; their leading industry is carpet mfg. Majority are fanatic Sunnite Moslems. A warlike people, the Kurds have struggled for centuries for autonomy from Ottoman rule, and at the Paris Peace Conference (1919) reaffirmed claims to independence. The Treaty of Sèvres (1921) provided for a free Kurdish state, but the amending Treaty of Lausanne (1923) failed to mention Kurdistan. Kurdish revolts in Turkey (1925, 1930) and in Iran (1946) were suppressed.

Kurds: see KURDISTAN.

Kure (kōō'rä), city (pop. 185,740), SW Honshu, Japan, on Hiroshima Bay. Major naval base and port.

Kure Island (kōō'rä), formerly **Ocean Island**, atoll in NW part of Hawaiian group. Annexed 1886 by Hawaii; under U.S. navy since 1936.

Kurhessen, Germany: see HESSE.

Kurile Islands (kōō'rĭl), island chain (5,700 sq. mi.; pop. 17,549), RSFSR, in N Pacific, between Kamchatka and Hokkaido. Comprises 50 islands, mainly volcanic. Sulphur mining, hunting, and fishing. Became Japanese possession 1875; annexed 1945 by USSR in accordance with Yalta agreement.

Kurisches Haff (kōō'rĭshùs häf'), coastal lagoon, 56 mi. long, Lithuania and former East Prussia. Separated from Baltic Sea by Kurische Nehrung, a thin sandspit which leaves only a narrow opening at the Memel channel in the N. The Niemen empties into the Kurisches Haff.

Kurland: see COURLAND.

Kuropatkin, Aleksey Nikolayevich (ùlyĭksyä' nyĭkùlī'-ùvĭch kōōrŭpät'kĭn), 1848–1925, Russian general. Took part in Skobelev's 500-mile march from Tashkent to Geok-Tepe (1881). As minister of war from 1898 he opposed the policy leading to Russo-Japanese War of 1904–5, but after its outbreak he took command in Manchuria. Though blameless in the Russian defeat at Mukden, he resigned.

Kuroshio: see JAPAN CURRENT.

Kursk (kōōrsk), city (pop. 119,972), S central European RSFSR. Rail junction and mfg. center (esp. machinery). Seat of a principality in 11th cent., it was destroyed 1238 by Mongols and not rebuilt until 1586. Scene of heavy fighting in World War II.

Kurusu, Saburo (sä"bōōrō' kōōrōō'sù), 1888–, Japanese diplomat. Signed Berlin Pact Sept., 1940. Special envoy to U.S. in 1941 for negotiations cut short by Japanese attack on Pearl Harbor.

Kuskokwim (kŭs'kōkwĭm), river rising on NW slopes of Alaska Range, W Alaska, and flowing SW to Kuskokwim Bay of Bering Sea. Mining in upper reaches.

Küssnacht (kùs'näkht), village, Schwyz canton, Switzerland, on L. of Lucerne. A chapel commemorates legendary shooting of Gessler by William Tell.

Kutais (kōōtūēs') or **Kutaisi**, city (pop. 81,479), W Georgian SSR, on Rion R. Mfg. of machinery, chemicals, textiles. Founded in 6th cent. B.C., it was cap. of ancient Imeritia. Taken by Russia in 1804.

Kutch or **Cutch** (kŭch), state (exclusive of the Rann 8,461 sq. mi.; pop. 567,825), W India; cap. Bhuj. Mostly barren. Rann of Kutch is salt waste (9,000 sq. mi.), mainly in N, bounded W by Arabian Sea.

Kutchuk Kainardji or **Kutchuk Kainarji, Treaty of:** see KUCHUK KAINARJI, TREATY OF.

Kut-el-Amara (kōōt'-ĕl"-ùmä'rù), town, Iraq, on the Tigris and c.100 mi. S of Baghdad; scene of bitter fighting in World War I. It was taken 1915 by the British under Gen. Charles Townshend, who after his failure to take Baghdad retreated to his base and withstood a five-month siege by superior Turkish forces before surrendering (1915–16). British recovered town in 1917. Construction of a dam across Tigris was completed 1939.

Kutna Hora, Czech *Kutná Hora* (kōōt'nä hô'rä), city (pop. 12,119), central Bohemia, Czechoslovakia. Its silver mines largely created power of medieval kings of Bohemia. After its capture by Zizka in Hussite Wars, city was for two centuries the center of Bohemian Protestantism. Its rich medieval architecture includes two Gothic churches (14th cent.) and "Italian Court," a castle once used both as a mint and as a royal residence (begun 12th cent.).

Kutuzov, Mikhail Ilarionovich (mēkhŭyēl' ēlŭryôn'ùvĭch kōōtōō'zùf), 1745–1813, Russian field marshal. Fought brilliantly in Russo-Turkish Wars, replaced Barclay de Tolly as commander in chief against Napoleon (1812), and fought bloody battle of BORODINO but then resumed Barclay's Fabian tactics. Pursued *Grande Armée* into Germany and was created prince of Smolensk shortly before his death.

Kuwait (kōōwīt', –wät'), independent state (c.6,000 sq. mi.; pop. c.170,000), Arabia, near head of Persian Gulf; British protectorate. Mainly desert. Major producer of oil.

Kuyp, family of Dutch painters: see CUYP.

Kuznetsk Basin (kōōznyĕtsk′), abbreviation **Kuzbas,** richest coal basin of USSR, area c.10,000 sq. mi., RSFSR, in S central Siberia, between Kuznetsk Ala-Tau (E) and Salair Ridge. Vast reserves are of high quality and great variety. Mining centers are Anzhero-Sudzhensk, Kemerovo, and Leninsk-Kuznetski. New metallurgical industry is centered at Stalinsk.

Kwajalein (kwä′jūlān), atoll (pop. 832), central Pacific, largest of Marshall Isls. District headquarters of U.S. Trust Territory of the Pacific Isls. Captured 1944 by U.S. forces.

Kwakiutl Indians (kwä′kēōō″tùl), Indian tribes of Wakashan linguistic stock, on N Vancouver Isl. and adjacent mainland of Canada. Their culture was typical of Pacific Northwest Coast.

Kwangchowan, China: see CHANKIANG.

Kwang Hsü (gwäng′ shü′), 1872–1908, emperor of China (1875–98). Enthroned by his aunt, dowager empress and regent Tz'u Hsi; began personal rule 1889. Forced by her to abdicate because he favored reforms.

Kwangsi (gwäng′shē′), province (85,000 sq. mi.; pop. 15,000,000), S China; cap. Kweilin. Bounded SW by Viet Nam. Mainly a tableland, dissected by headstreams of West R. Exports cassia and camphor.

Kwangtung (gwäng′dŏong′), province (85,000 sq. mi.; pop. 32,000,000), S China, on South China Sea; cap. Canton. Includes HAINAN isl. On its coast are foreign enclaves of MACAO and HONG KONG. Mainland Kwangtung touches in extreme W on Viet Nam. Has tropical monsoon climate with high humidity. Largely mountainous; agr. restricted to river valleys and delta lowlands, notably Canton R. delta. Silk is leading export. Mineral resources include tungsten, manganese, coal, and iron. Bulk of population formed by Cantonese. Kwangtung was scene of early activity of Kuomintang party.

Kwantung Territory, China: see LIAOTUNG.

Kweichow (gwä′jō′), province (65,000 sq. mi.; pop. 11,-000,000), SW China; cap. Kweiyang. Mainly a high plateau with many deep river valleys, notably that of

the Wu. Produces grains, beans, lacquer, and timber.

Kweilin (gwä′lĭn′), commercial city (pop. 130,790), cap. Kwangsi prov., S China, on Kwei R. Cotton mills. Seat of a university.

Kyd or **Kid, Thomas,** 1558–94, English dramatist, exponent of "tragedy of blood." His best-known work is *Spanish Tragedy* (1592).

Kyffhäuser (kĭf′hoizùr), forested mountain, c.1,550 ft. high, N Thuringia, central Germany. It is crowned by the ruined castles of Rothenburg and Kyffhausen and by a huge, atrocious monument to Emperor William I. A legend, originally applied to Emperor Frederick II, has been later transferred to Emperor Frederick I (Barbarossa), who is said to be waiting in a cave of the mountain for the right time to return and restore German greatness.

Kyosai, Shofu (shô′fōō kyō′sĭ), 1831–89, Japanese painter, illustrator, and cartoonist.

Kyoto or **Kioto** (kyō′tō), city (pop. 999,660), S Honshu, Japan; chief cultural center of Japan. Seat of Kyoto Imperial Univ., Doshisha Univ., and many ancient Buddhist temples. Long known for hand-crafted products (cloisonné, bronzes, damascene work, porcelain, lacquer ware, fabrics). Founded 8th cent. Was cap. of Japan from 794 to 1868, when it was succeeded by Tokyo. In World War II it was the only major Japanese city to escape bombing.

Kyrie eleison (kĕ′rēā ālā′ēsōn) [Gr.,= Lord, have mercy], in Roman Catholic Church, prayer of the Mass, following introit, the only part of the ordinary (section that does not change with the day) said in Greek. There are many notable musical settings.

Kyushu or **Kiushiu** (kyōō′shōō), island (c.13,770 sq. mi.; pop. 11,398,976), S Japan; third largest, southernmost, and most densely populated of four major islands of Japan. Connected with Honshu (just N) by tunnel under Shimonoseki Strait. Mountainous with many hot springs. In N is Japan's chief coal field. Mild climate favors agr. (rice, tobacco, oranges). Chief ports are Nagasaki, Moji, Kagoshima, and Sasebo.

Kyzyl-Kum, Uzbek SSR: see KIZIL KUM.

La. For names beginning thus and not listed here, see second element; e.g., for La Guaira, see GUAIRA, LA.

La, chemical symbol of the element LANTHANUM.

Laaland or **Lolland** (both: lô′län), low island (479 sq. mi.; pop. 87,150), Denmark, in Baltic Sea, S of Zealand. Sugar beets are main crop. Nakskov and Maribo are chief cities.

Labadie, Jean de, or **Jean de la Badie** (zhä′ dù lä bädē′), 1610–74, French mystic. A Catholic priest, he became a Protestant minister (c.1650). In Holland he estab. the Labadists, a religious community dedicated to simple living, holding goods and children in common. Movement was ended by 1732.

Laban (lā′–), father of Leah and Rachel, uncle of Jacob. Gen. 24.29–60; 29–31.

Labé, Louise (lwēz′ läbā′), c.1520–1566, French poet. Her sonnets and elegies are outstanding love poems.

Labiche, Eugène (ûzhĕn′ läbēsh′), 1815–88, French playwright. His best-known comedy is the farcical *Le*

Voyage de M. Perrichon (with Édouard Martin, 1860).

La Boétie, Étienne de (ātyĕn′ dù lä bôāsē′), 1530–63, French judge, remembered for his friendship with Montaigne and as author of a fiery and original attack on despotism, *Discours sur la servitude volontaire; ou, Contr'un* (Eng. tr., *Anti-Dictator,* 1942).

labor, term used both for the effort of performing a task and for the social group doing the work. In the ancient world the status of labor was low, since most physical work was done by slaves. During the feudal period, skilled artisans were influential citizens. With the introduction of machinery, status of labor was again depressed. Since 19th cent., labor has become organized (see UNION, LABOR) so as to bargain collectively with employers and to place pressure on governments. See STRIKE, CHILD LABOR, MIGRATORY LABOR, SLAVERY.

labor, in medicine: see BIRTH.

labor, hours of. Until the Industrial Revolution, the

work day varied from 11 to 14 hr. With the growth of capitalism and the introduction of machinery, longer hours began to prevail. The great competition for work forced workers to accept whatever conditions employers imposed. A day of 16 hr. was not uncommon, with 14 to 15 hr. the accepted working day. First law on the length of a working day was passed (1833) in England, limiting miners to 12 hr. and children under 13 to 8 hr. The 10-hr. day was legally established in 1848, and shorter hours at the same pay were achieved gradually thereafter. In the U.S., the 8-hr. day was generally accepted by 1912. The WAGES AND HOURS ACT of 1938 recognizes 40 hrs. as the maximum ordinary work week.

Labor, United States Department of, organized in 1913 under Secretary of Labor by act of U.S. Congress. Began in 1884 as Bureau of Labor in U.S. Dept. of Interior. Department includes following major units: Bureau of Labor Statistics; Women's Bureau; U.S. Employment Service; Bureau of Labor Standards; Bureau of Apprenticeship; Wage and Hour and Public Contracts Divisions; Bureau of Veterans' Reemployment Rights.

Labor Day, holiday celebrated in U.S. and Canada on first Monday in Sept. to honor the workingman.

labor law, legislation dealing with workers. The earliest English factory law dealt (1802) with the health, safety, and morals of child textile workers. Labor unions were legalized in 1825, but agreements among their members to seek better hours and wages were punishable as conspiracy until 1871. In the U.S., the Norris-LaGuardia act (1932) outlawed the use of injunctions in labor disputes, the Wagner Act (establishing the NATIONAL LABOR RELATIONS BOARD; 1935) required employers to accept collective bargaining, and the WAGES AND HOURS ACT (1938) set up minimum standards of hours and wages in basic industries; the TAFT-HARTLEY LABOR ACT (1947) sharply modified the acts of 1932 and 1935 and introduced an 80-day injunction procedure in labor disputes affecting the national welfare.

Labor Relations Act: see NATIONAL LABOR RELATIONS BOARD; TAFT-HARTLEY LABOR ACT.

labor union: see UNION, LABOR.

La Bourdonnais, Bertrand François Mahé de (bĕrträ′ fräswä′ mää′ dù lä boördônä′), 1699–1753, French naval officer in service of French India Co. Captured Madras (1746). After a quarrel with Dupleix he was recalled, tried for treason, and acquitted.

Labour party, British political party. Founded in 1900 as result of long history of trade-union activity that became effective after Reform Act (1867) enfranchised the urban workers. Aided by Fabian Society (founded 1883). Until 1918 it was a federation of trade unions and socialist groups, with no individual members. Split in World War I over British participation in the war. Ramsay MACDONALD became first Labour prime minister in 1924. After domestic reforms, recognition of USSR, and peace efforts in the Ruhr, he was overthrown over a forged letter supposedly written by Grigori Zinoviev. Labour was returned to power in 1929. Hampered by deepening economic crisis, MacDonald formed (1931) a coalition ministry and was read from the party. Moving to the left, party advocated nationalization of industries and opposition to any foreign war. By 1937 new leaders were Herbert Morrison, Ernest BEVIN and Clement ATTLEE. Intellectual leaders were Hugh Dalton and Harold Laski. Labour entered coalition government in World War II. Won 1945 elections; Attlee became prime minister. Passed national health bill, nationalized important industries, and estab. the dominions of India and Pakistan (1947). The 1951 election restored Conservatives to power. Left wing of party, headed by Aneurin Bevan, has been challenging moderate leadership of Attlee.

Labrador (lă′brùdôr″), dependency of NEWFOUNDLAND, E Canada (c.110,000 sq. mi.; pop. 7,890), at mouth of Gulf of St. Lawrence; cap. Battle Harbour. Population (largely Algonquin Indians and Eskimo) scattered along Atlantic coast with a few white settlers in fishing villages and missions (e.g. Carteret, Battle Harbour, Rigolet, Hopedale, Nain). Icy Labrador Current and lack of transportation facilities discourage settlement and development of mineral and hydroelectric resources. Probably explored by Vikings c.1000, and later by Cabot (1498), Corte Real (1500), and Cartier (1534). Became British after Treaty of Paris (1763), with jurisdiction given to N.F. 1763–64 and again in 1809. Moravian missions, estab. in 1760s, shared fur trade with Hudson's Bay Co., which virtually controlled peninsula until 1870. Claims to NE peninsula (called Ungava) settled 1927 by British Privy Council.

Labrador Current: see OCEAN CURRENTS.

labradorite (lă′brùdôrīt″), variety of FELDSPAR, usually gray, brown, or green. Some varieties showing color play of red, yellow, blue, green (labradorescence) are used for decorative purposes.

La Brea (lù brā′ù), area in Los Angeles, S Calif. Tar pits here yielded prehistoric remains.

La Bruyère, Jean de (zhä′ dù lä brüyĕr′), 1645–96, French writer; tutor at the house of the prince de Condé. His great work is *Les Caractères* (1688), in small part translations of THEOPHRASTUS, but mainly a series of brilliant character sketches, maxims, and short essays. Though he applied his strong moral views to the contemporary scene, he was a detached observer, rather than a reformer.

Labuan (lùboō′ùn), island (35 sq. mi.; pop. 8,500), off NW Borneo, attached to British colony of North Borneo since 1946.

laburnum (lùbûr′nùm), small ornamental tree (*Laburnum anagyroides*), native to Europe, widely grown in U.S. It has sprays of yellow flowers in spring.

lac (lăk), resinous exudate from bodies of female scale insects from which SHELLAC is prepared. Insects feed on sap of trees, which form resinous secretion around bodies of female and young. Crude material is stick-lac. When purified and red coloring is removed, it is seed-lac from which shellac is made. Red coloring is sometimes used as dye and pigment.

Lacaille, Nicolas Louis de (nēkôlä′ lwē dù läkä′yù), 1713–62, French astronomer, noted for calculations. Recorded positions of many stars of S Hemisphere.

Laccadive Islands (lă′kùdīv), group of coral atolls (10 sq. mi.; pop. 18,355), in Arabian Sea, off Malabar Coast of India; part of Madras state.

lace, patterned openwork fabric made by hand or by machine. General types of handmade laces include needlepoint, bobbin lace, tatting, and crochet work. Needlepoint, the most costly, is worked with a needle in variations of the buttonhole stitch; Venetian point or *punto in aria* developed in Italy from reticella cutwork. From the early laces patterned in France after Venetian point, developed *point de France;* among later French laces are Alençon, Argentan, and Valenciennes. Brussels is a name used for either needlepoint or bobbin lace of a certain style. Pillow, bone, or bobbin lace, woven with bobbins, includes *point d'Angleterre* (similar to Flemish point), Valenciennes (fine, diamond-meshed), Mechlin (very filmy), torchon (simple and loose), Honiton (English lace with net foundation and appliqués of delicate braid), duchesse (exquisite patterns, with much raised work), Maltese (coarse), and Chantilly (delicate mesh, ornate patterns). Crocheted lace reached its finest development in Ireland. There are also knitted laces and those made by knotting (e.g., tatting, macramé). Machine-made lace dates from late 18th cent.

Lacedaemon (lăsùdē′mùn), in Greek mythology, ruler of LACONIA or Lacedaemon; son of Zeus. He gave his capital the name of his wife, Sparta.

La Chaise, François d'Aix de (fräswä′ dăks′ dù lä shĕz′), 1624–1709, French Jesuit, confessor of Louis XIV. Held considerable influence. Père-Lachaise cemetery in Paris is named for him.

Lachaise, Gaston (läshāz'), 1882–1935, American sculptor, b. Paris. Famous for his female nudes.

Lachesis, one of the FATES.

Lachine (lùshēn'), city (pop. 27,773), S Que., Canada, on Montreal Isl., at E end of L. St. Louis; settled 1675. Iron and steel founding and mfg. of tires, wires, and tiles. Is SW terminus of **Lachine Canal** connecting L. St. Louis and St. Lawrence R. at Montreal (opened 1825).

Lachish (lā'kĭsh), anc. Amorite city, S Palestine. Captured by Joshua; later besieged by Sennacherib.

Lachute (lùshoot'), town (pop. 6,179), SW Que., Canada, on North R. and W of Montreal. Woolen and paper mills, lumbering, and dairying.

Lackawanna (lăkùwä'nù), city (pop. 27,658), W N.Y., on L. Erie S of Buffalo. Iron and steel. Has Our Lady of Victory basilica, charitable institutions.

Lackawanna, river rising in NE Pa. and flowing 50 mi. SSW through anthracite region to Susquehanna R. near Pittston.

Laclede, Pierre (pyĕr' läklĕd'), c.1724–1778, French pioneer in U.S. As fur trader with René Auguste CHOUTEAU, helped found St. Louis (1763–64).

Laclos, (Pierre) Choderlos de (pyĕr' shôdĕrlō' dù läklō'), 1741–1803, French author and general. His savage novel of manners, *Les Liaisons dangereuses* (1782; Eng. tr., *Dangerous Acquaintances,* 1924), had great influence.

Lac Mégantic, Que.: see MÉGANTIC.

Lacombe (lùkōm'), town (pop. 2,277), S central Alta., Canada, S of Edmonton. A dominion government experimental farm is here.

Laconia (lùkō'nĕù) or **Lacedaemon** (lăsùdē'mùn), anc. region, S Peloponnesus, Greece. On the Eurotas, the main river, stood SPARTA, the cap.

Laconia, city (pop. 14,745), central N.H., N of Concord. Resort center. Hosiery, textile machinery, and wood products. Holds annual international dog-sled derby. To N are Lakeport, hq. of U.S. mail boat on L. Winnipesaukee, and The Weirs, resort.

Lacordaire, Jean Baptiste Henri (zhä' bätēst' ärē' läcôrdĕr'), 1802–61, French Roman Catholic preacher. A liberal, he was a collaborator of LAMENNAIS, but after the pope condemned the liberal program, he submitted. Later he was a famed preacher at Notre Dame in Paris; joined the Dominicans (1840). Favored the Revolution of 1848 and went into exile after coup d'état of Napoleon III.

Lacoste, René (rùnä' läkôst'), 1905–, French tennis player. Member French team that won Davis Cup, 1927.

La Crosse (lù krôs), city (pop. 47,535), W Wis., on the Mississippi (bridged) at confluence of Black and La Crosse rivers, in dairy area. Site of late 18th cent. fur-trading post. Mfg. of farm equipment, air-conditioning systems, and rubber footwear. Park has U.S. fish hatchery.

lacrosse (lùkrôs'), national sport of Canada since 1867. Played by two teams of 10 players on grass-covered playing field 60 to 70 yd. wide by 110 yd. long. Lacrosse gained following in U.S. after 1880s, particularly in North Atlantic states. Women's lacrosse team has 12 players.

La Cruz, Ramón de: see CRUZ, RAMÓN DE LA.

Lactantius (lăktăn'shùs), c.260–340, Christian apologist, b. Africa. Converted to Christianity, he became a member of Constantine's household. His writings on Christian doctrine and Christian history show his wide knowledge of pagan rhetoric and literature.

lactic acid, colorless organic acid, present in sour milk and formed in animals as result of muscle contraction. Usually prepared commercially by bacterial fermentation of glucose. Used in tanning and dyeing and in medicine.

lactose (lăk'tōs) or **milk sugar,** white crystalline carbohydrate with 12 carbon, 22 hydrogen, 11 oxygen atoms. It has the same formula as sucrose and maltose but differs in structure. Found in mammalian milk and cells of mammary gland, it is important in diet of young mammals. When hydrolyzed (by acid or enzyme) it yields glucose and galactose.

La Cueva, Juan de: see CUEVA, JUAN DE LA.

Ladd, William, 1778–1841, American peace advocate. He proposed (1840) plan for a world congress and court of nations.

Ladies' Peace: see CAMBRAI, TREATY OF.

Ladislas. For rulers thus named, see LADISLAUS; LANCELOT; ULADISLAUS.

Ladislaus, Hung. *László,* kings of Hungary. **Ladislaus I** (Saint Ladislaus), 1040–95, reigned 1077–95. Conquered Croatia 1091; compelled CUMANS to accept Christianity and allowed them to settle in certain parts of Hungary; reformed law code. Was noted for his valor and chivalry. **Ladislaus V** (Ladislaus Posthumus), 1440–57; posthumous son of the German king, Albert II. Duke of Austria by birth, he was claimed as king by the Bohemian diet and in 1444 was also elected king of Hungary, but his guardian, Emperor Frederick III, refused to let him leave his court until 1452. In 1453 he was crowned king of Bohemia and entered Hungary, but actual rule was exercised by GEORGE OF PODEBRAD in Bohemia and by John HUNYADI in Hungary.

Ladislaus, king of Naples: see LANCELOT.

Ladislaus, Pol. *Władysław,* kings of Poland. **Ladislaus I** (the Short), 1260–1333, crowned king 1320, restored unified Polish kingdom after 82 years of division. **Ladislaus II** or **Ladislaus Jagiello** (yägyĕ'lō), 1350?–1434, grand duke of Lithuania (1377–86), acceded to the Polish throne in 1386 by marrying Queen JADWIGA. He was baptized and converted Lithuania to Christianity. Though Lithuania was ruled by other members of the JAGIELLO dynasty (see WITOWT), Ladislaus' marriage was the basis of the eventual union of the Polish and Lithuanian nations. The victory over the Teutonic Knights at Tannenberg (1410) and the First Peace of TORUN (1411) were the main events of his reign. His son **Ladislaus III,** 1424–44, succeeded him in Poland and as Uladislaus I was elected king of Hungary (1440). He led two crusades against the Turks and was defeated and slain at Varna. The name also appears as Wladislaw, Wladyslav, and Wladislas.

Ladoga, Lake (lä'dōgù), largest lake in Europe, area c.7,000 sq. mi., S Karelo-Finnish SSR and NW European RSFSR, NE of Leningrad. Max. depth 732 ft. The Svir (from L. Onega), Vuoksi (from Saima lake system of Finland), and Volkhov (from L. Ilmen) are the main feeders; Neva R. is main outlet. Because of difficult navigation the S shore of L. Ladoga is paralleled by the Ladoga Canals, 100 mi. long, connecting Svir and Neva rivers. N shore belonged to Finland until its cession to USSR in 1940 (confirmed 1947). Valaam isl., in N part of lake, has famous Russian monastery dating from 12th cent.

ladybird or **ladybug,** beetle of the family Coccinellidae. It is oval, reddish, or yellow spotted with black or black spotted with red or yellow; most species eat aphids and other harmful insects. Australian ladybird was imported by U.S. to eat cottony-cushion scale which is destructive to citrus fruit. Injurious herbivorous species are the Mexican bean beetle and the squash beetle.

Lady Margaret Hall: see OXFORD UNIVERSITY.

Lady of the Lake: see ARTHURIAN LEGEND.

Ladysmith, town (pop. 14,221), W Natal, South Africa. Named for wife of Sir Harry Smith, governor of Cape Colony. British forces were besieged here, 1899–1900, during Boer War. Cotton milling.

lady's-slipper or **moccasin flower,** wild flower of genus *Cypripedium* of orchid family, native to north temperate zone. There are white-, yellow-, and pink-flowered species in North America.

Lae (lä'ĕ), town, on E New Guinea, Territory of New Guinea, on Huon Gulf. Serves air transport lines into near-by gold fields. Occupied 1942 by Japanese, regained 1943 by Allied forces.

Laënnec, René Théophile Hyacinthe (rùnā′ tãôfēl′ yäsět läänēk′), 1781–1826, French physician. He invented the stethoscope and used it in diagnosis.

Laertes (lāûr′tēz), in Greek mythology, king of Ithaca; father of Odysseus. He joined the Calydonian hunt and was one of the Argonaut heroes.

La Farge, John (lù färzh′), 1835–1910, American artist, writer, and worker in stained glass. A man of wide culture, he did much to create a tradition of the fine arts in America. His grandson, **Oliver La Farge**, 1901–, writer and anthropologist, is best known for his novel, *Laughing Boy* (1929).

Lafayette or **La Fayette, Marie Joseph Paul Yves Roch Gilbert du Motier, marquis de** (märē′ zhôzěf′ pôl′ ēv′ rôk zhēlběr′ dü môtyā′ märkē′ dù läfäyět′), 1757–1834, French general and statesman. Despite opposition by his government, he sailed for America in 1777 to join Washington's army. Was made major general by Congress; was wounded at Brandywine (1777) and was at Valley Forge. After a trip to France (1779–80), where he negotiated for French aid, he played a vital part in the YORKTOWN CAMPAIGN. Active in the French Revolution, he became commander of the National Guard (July 15, 1789) and in 1792 commanded an army. A moderate, he sought to save the monarchy but in his irresolution missed his opportunity, deserted his army, and was imprisoned in Austria (1792–97). His triumphal tour of the U.S. in 1824–25 has passed into legend. He also took part in the July Revolution.

La Fayette, Marie Madeleine Pioche de la Vergne, comtesse de (märē′ mädülēn′ pyôsh′ dù lä věr′nyù, kōtěs′), 1634–92, French novelist. Mme de La Fayette's classic masterpiece, *La Princesse de Clèves* (1678), was the first French psychological novel.

Lafayette (lā′fēět′). **1** City (pop. 35,568), W Ind., on Wabash R. and NW of Indianapolis; settled 1825. Grain and livestock market; coal. Mfg. of rubber, paper, and metal products. Battle of TIPPECANOE fought near by, Nov., 1811. Seat of PURDUE UNIVERSITY. **2** City (pop. 33,541), S La., on Vermilion R. N of Vermilion Bay; laid out c.1824 by Acadians. Shipping and commercial center for agr. and mineral area, it has sugar refineries, cotton and cottonseed-oil processing plants, machine and railroad shops, and creameries. Seat of Southwestern Louisiana Inst. (coed.; 1898).

Lafayette, Mount: see FRANCONIA MOUNTAINS.

Lafayette College: see EASTON, Pa.

Lafayette Escadrille (ēskùdrīl′), group of American volunteer aviators in World War I in French air service. In Jan., 1918, outfit was reorganized in U.S. army as 103d Pursuit squadron.

Laffite or **Lafitte, Jean** (both: zhā′ läfēt′), c.1780–c.1825, leader of a band of privateersmen and smugglers. Preyed on Spanish commerce off La. and Texas. Aided U.S. in battle of New Orleans.

La Follette, Robert M(arion) (lùfō′lĭt), 1855–1925, American statesman. Under his governorship of Wis. reform legislation known as Wisconsin Idea was instituted. As U.S. Senator (1906–25) he took courageous, independent stands; supported reform, opposed both war measures and international peace bodies. As PROGRESSIVE PARTY presidential candidate in 1924 he polled 5,000,000 votes. Known as "Fighting Bob" La Follette. His wife, **Belle Case La Follette**, 1859–1931, was an ardent feminist and able adviser to her husband. Their older son, **Robert M(arion) La Follette, Jr.**, 1895–1953, U.S. Senator (1925–47), generally backed New Deal legislation. Another son, **Philip (Fox) La Follette**, 1897–, was governor of Wis. (1931–33, 1935–39).

La Follette (lù fŏl′ĭt), city (pop. 5,797), E Tenn., on Norris L. and NNW of Knoxville at E base of Cumberland Plateau. Coal-mining center.

La Fontaine, Henri (ärē′ läfŏtěn′), 1854–1943, Belgian jurist. Headed Internatl. Peace Bureau from 1907; was awarded 1913 Nobel Peace Prize.

La Fontaine, Jean de (zhā′ dù), 1621–95, French poet,

author of the famous *Fables choisies* (1668–94), 12 books of c.230 fables. Their material is largely based on Aesop, Phaedrus, and other classics (see FABLE), but La Fontaine's subtle originality, exquisite charm, and perfection of verse place him beside Molière and Racine. As a poet of nature, he stands unique in 17th-cent. French literature. Though popular with children, his fables are essentially satires, sometimes bitter and cynical, always sophisticated; their appeal is universal. Other works include *Contes et nouvelles en vers* (1664), imitations in verse of Boccaccio and Ariosto.

LaFontaine, Sir Louis Hippolyte, 1807–64, Canadian statesman. Formed the Baldwin-LaFontaine ministry (1842–43) with Robert Baldwin. Second Baldwin-La-Fontaine ministry (1848–51) was notable for its reforms and achievement of responsible government.

Laforgue, Jules (zhül′ läfôrg′), 1860–87, French poet, one of the SYMBOLISTS.

Lafourche, Bayou (bī′ō läfōosh′, bī′ōō), SE La., flowing to Gulf of Mexico. Former Mississippi R. outlet, now dammed at Donaldsonville.

Lagan (lā′gùn), river of N. Ireland, rising in Co. Down and flowing 45 mi. to Belfast Lough at Belfast.

Lagash (lā′gäsh) or **Shirpurla** (shĭrpōor′lù), anc. city of SUMER, S Babylonia. Flourished c.3000 B.C., rivaled Kish and Umma until it was destroyed, and rose to new supremacy under Gudea (c.2450 B.C.).

Lagerkvist, Par (Fabian), (pâr′ fä′bēän lä′gùrkvĭst), 1891–, Swedish poet, dramatist, and novelist. His writings reflect his interest in political and social problems; his verse has had a marked influence on Swedish poetry. Among his novels are *The Dwarf* (1944) and *Barabbas* (1950). Awarded the 1951 Nobel Prize in Literature.

Lagerlof, Selma, Swed. *Lagerlöf* (lä′gùrlûv), 1858–1940, Swedish novelist. Winner of 1909 Nobel Prize in Literature, she was also the first woman to be elected (1914) to the Swedish academy. Popular stories (many laid in Varmland prov.) are *The Story of Gosta Berling* (1894), *The Ring of the Lowenskolds* (1931), and *The Wonderful Adventures of Nils* (1906).

Lagos (lä′gōs), city (pop. 90,193), cap. of Nigeria, port on lagoon just off Gulf of Guinea. Comprises Lagos and Iddo isls. and a mainland section. Notorious slave market from 18th to mid-19th cent. Ceded 1861 to British. In 1886 Lagos and surrounding area became self-governing colony and protectorate, which in 1906 was combined with protectorate of Southern Nigeria. Exports include palm oil and cacao.

Lagos (lä′gōosh), city (pop. 6,938), SW Portugal, in Algarve, on the Atlantic. It was the starting point of Portuguese explorers at the time of Henry the Navigator and now harbors important sardine and tuna fishing fleets.

La Grande (lä gränd′), city (pop. 8,635), NE Oregon, E of Blue Mts. and SE of Pendleton. Processes and ships fruit, livestock, lumber; rail shops.

Lagrange, Joseph Louis, Comte (zhôzěf′ lwē′ kôt lä-gräzh′), 1736–1813, French mathematician and astronomer, b. Turin. Calculus of variations is in part based on his method of solving isoperimetrical problems; he also made notable contributions in application of differential calculus to theory of probabilities and in solution of equations. He made studies on the libration of the moon and on satellites of Jupiter and made calculations of the motions of the planets.

La Grange (lù gränj′). **1** City (pop. 25,025), W Ga., SW of Atlanta near Chattahoochee R. Textile center, with sawmills. La Grange Col. is here. City was a center of state-wide textile strike, 1934. **2** Residential village (pop. 12,002), NE Ill., W suburb of Chicago; settled in 1830s. Aluminum products.

LaGuardia, Fiorello H(enry) (fēùrě′lō lùgwär′dēù), 1882–1947, U.S. Congressman (1917–19, 1923–33) and Fusion mayor of New York city (1934–45). Fought for labor reforms in Congress. Executed vast program of municipal improvement. Because of his first name jocularly called "the Little Flower."

LaGuardia Field: see QUEENS, New York city borough.

Laguna (lŭgōō′nù), Indian pueblo village (1948 pop. 2,932), W central N.Mex., W of Albuquerque. Most recent of N.Mex. pueblos; founded 1699. Western Keresan language. Annual feast to San José.

Laguna Beach (lùgōō′nù), residential and resort city (pop. 6,661), S Calif., SE of Los Angeles. Artists' colony.

Laguna District [Span.,= lake, so called from shallow lakes on plain], irrigated area (c.900,000 acres), E Durango and W Coahuila, Mexico. Land was redistributed (1936) on *ejido* system by Lázaro Cárdenas.

La Halle, Adam de: see ADAM DE LA HALLE.

La Hire (lä ēr′), c.1390–c.1443, French commander in Hundred Years War; real name Étienne de Vignolles. Helped Joan of Arc in victory of Patay (1429).

La Hire or **La Hyre, Laurent de** (both: lä ēr′), 1606–56, French portrait and historical painter.

Lahontan, Louis Armand, baron de (läōtã′), 1666–c.1713, French explorer in America. His admiration of Indian life influenced European thought.

Lahontan, Lake (lùhŏn′tùn, läōtã′), extinct lake of enormous size in W Nev. and NE Calif. Brought into existence by glacial age, it vanished soon after Pleistocene epoch; several lakes in Nev. are remnants. Area rich in fossils.

Lahore (lùhôr′), city (pop. 849,000), cap. of Punjab prov., W Pakistan. Flourished under Mogul rule, 16th–17th cent. Was Sikh cap. in 19th cent. Notable remains of Moslem art are palace of Jahangir and Shalimar gardens (1667). Punjab Univ. and famed museum of Indian antiquities are here. Mfg. and financial center.

Lahti (lä′tē, läkh′tē), city (pop. 45,190), central Finland. Center of Finnish furniture industry.

La Hyre, Laurent de: see LA HIRE, LAURENT DE.

Laibach (lī′bäkh), German name of LJUBLJANA, Yugoslavia. At the **Congress of Laibach,** 1821, widening of the breach between Great Britain and the powers of the Holy Alliance became apparent. The congress countenanced the suppression by Austrian forces of the insurrection in Naples.

laissez faire (lĕ″sä fâr′), doctrine that an economic system functions best without governmental interference. Historically, it was a reaction against MERCANTILISM, wherein governments imposed controls on industry and trade in order to strengthen the state. The French PHYSIOCRATS first formulated the doctrine, and it was developed by Adam SMITH, who maintained that competition, motivated by self-interest, would regulate economic life more effectively than would the state. This originally radical individualistic doctrine came to be a principle of classical economics and political conservatism. Theoretically, the theory of laissez faire is still insisted on by private enterprise as an antidote to socialism, but the tendency of business combinations to evolve into monopolies has led to a shift in emphasis from individualism to the importance of private profit as an incentive to progress.

Laius, father of OEDIPUS.

La Jolla (lù hoi′yù), resort and residential part of San Diego, S Calif. Sea beaches, caves, and cliffs attract visitors. Scripps Inst. of Oceanography of Univ. of California is here.

La Junta (lù hōōn′tù, hŭn′tù), city (pop. 7,712), SE Colo., on Arkansas R. below Pueblo. Trade and rail center in sugar-beet, grain region. Has museum commemorating BENT'S FORT.

Lake, Simon, 1866–1945, American designer of submarines. His type was at first disregarded by the U.S. navy, but it was used by Germans in World War I and was later adopted by the Allies.

lake, body of standing water surrounded by land. Most lakes originate in glacial action by excavation and filling in of depressions or by damming of rivers by ice or moraine. Lakes are also caused by interference in river courses, by filling in of extinct volcanic craters, by volcanic separation of parts of ocean. Lakes disappear because of detrital deposits and lowering of affluent streams in humid climate, or (in arid regions) because of greater evaporation than precipitation. World's largest lakes are Caspian Sea, L. Superior, Victoria Nyanza, Aral Sea, L. Michigan, L. Huron. World's highest lake is L. Titicaca, 12,500 ft. above sea level; lowest, the Dead Sea, 1,292 ft. below sea level.

lake, in dyeing, insoluble compound formed in the material by action between organic dye and MORDANT.

Lake Bluff, village (pop. 2,000), NE Ill., on L. Michigan N of Chicago. Great Lakes Naval Training Station is just N.

Lake Charles, city (pop. 41,272), SW La., on L. Charles, port on deepwater channel from Gulf of Mexico; settled 1852. Shipping center for rice, oil, lumber, and cotton area with mfg. of turpentine, fertilizer, and chemicals. Has rice and lumber mills, refineries, cotton gins.

Lake City. 1 City (pop. 7,571), N Fla., W of Jacksonville near Suwannee R.; founded in 1830s. Tobacco and lumber products. Has U.S. veterans' hospital. **2** Town (pop. 5,112), E central S.C., S of Florence, in truck and tobacco area. **3** Town (pop. 1,827), E Tenn., NNW of Knoxville, near Norris Dam.

Lake District, region (c.30 mi. in diameter) of mountains and lakes in Cumberland, Westmoreland, and Lancashire, England. Has 15 lakes and some of England's highest peaks. Area a favorite resort of artists and writers. Wordsworth, Coleridge, and Southey called Lake poets; Keats, Shelley, and other poets have also lived here.

lake dwelling, habitation built over shallow waters of lake or marsh, supported by piles or artificial mounds. Prehistoric lake dwellers lived in Africa, Asia, and New World; most famous were the Neolithic inhabitants of European Alpine region.

Lake Forest, residential city (pop. 7,819), NE Ill., on L. Michigan N of Chicago. Seat of Lake Forest Col.

Lake Geneva, resort city (pop. 4,300), SE Wis., on L. Geneva and SW of Milwaukee.

Lake George, N.Y.: see GEORGE, LAKE.

Lakehurst, borough (pop. 1,518), E N.J., SW of Lakewood. Site of U.S. naval air station with facilities for dirigibles. First used by the *Shenandoah* 1923. U.S. terminal for transatlantic airships from 1924 until the *Hindenburg* burned here, 1937.

Lakeland, city (pop. 30,851), central Fla., E of Tampa in lake region. Settled in 1870s, it developed after railroad came in 1884. Processing and shipping center for citrus fruits. Mfg. of machinery and boats. Seat of Florida Southern Col. (Methodist; coed.; 1886). Has Hindu temple.

Lake of the Woods, c.70 mi. long, N Minn., SE Man., and W Ont. Fed by Rainy R. and drained by Winnipeg R. Separates Northwest Angle, northernmost land of continental U.S., from rest of Minn. Resort center with fish and game.

Lake Placid, resort village (pop. 2,999), NE N.Y., in the Adirondacks, surrounding Mirror L. and at S end of L. Placid (4 mi. long, 1–2 mi. wide). Noted eastern sports center. Scene of 1932 Olympic winter games. Near are famous bobsled run (opened 1930), farm and grave of John Brown.

Lake Success, village (pop. 1,264), SE N.Y., on NW Long Isl. Temporary hq. of the UN 1946–51.

Lakeville, Conn.: see SALISBURY.

Lake Wales, resort city (pop. 6,821), central Fla., W of L. Kissimmee and E of Tampa. Processes and ships fruit. Shrine of Ste Anne des Lacs (scene of annual R.C. pilgrimage) is near.

Lakewood. 1 See SKOWHEGAN, Maine. **2** Inland resort township (pop. 9,970), E N.J., SSE of Freehold. Former Rockefeller estate, now a state reserve, is near. **3** City (pop. 68,071), NE Ohio, on L. Erie, W suburb of Cleveland. Mfg. of metal products.

Lake Worth, resort city (pop. 11,777), SE Fla., on Atlantic coast just S of Palm Beach.

Lalande, Joseph Jérôme de (zhôzĕf′ zhärōm′ dù läläd′),

1732–1807, French astronomer, influential teacher and author, and establisher of annual Lalande Prize (1802) in astronomy.

Lalique, René (rùnà′ lälĕk′), 1860–1945, French designer of jewelry and glass.

Lally, Thomas Arthur, baron de Tollendal, comte de (tômä′ ärtür′ bärö′ dù tôlädäl′ kôt′ dù lälē′), 1702–66, French general of Irish parentage; governor of French India (1758–61). His surrender to the English at Pondichéry ended the French empire in India. After a highly irregular trial in France he was executed for treason. His son, with Voltaire's aid, secured his posthumous rehabilitation (1778).

Lalo, Édouard (ādwär′ lälö′), 1823–92, French composer. His works include an opera, *Le Roi d'Ys* (1888), and *Symphonie espagnole* for violin and orchestra.

Lamaism, BUDDHISM of Tibet and Mongolia; in doctrine differing but slightly from Mahayana (Indian) Buddhism from which it was derived. Tradition says the religion was imported by Indian and Chinese wives of a 7th-cent. king. A later king invited an Indian monk to found monastery near Lhasa (749), beginning Red Hat sect which still exists. Another Indian monk, Atisa, in 11th cent. reformed Lamaism and tried to eliminate elements of Bon (native religion). Translation of Sanskrit writings into *Kanjur* and *Tanjur*, Lamaist scriptures, was begun. The Saskya monastery was after the conversion of Kublai Khan given temporal rule of W Tibet. Under lama [priest] Tsong-kha-pa, Atisa's sect was reformed (15th cent.) as celibate Yellow Hat order, and in 1640 its 5th Ta-lai or Dalai Lama was given temporal rule of all Tibet by Mongol prince. Hierarchical priesthood developed; palace monastery was built near Lhasa. Dalai Lama is considered divine and is believed to be reincarnated immediately on death, perpetuating succession (14th installed 1940). Second to him is the abbot Panchen Lama (or Tashi). Saints, gods, spirits, and genii are worshiped.

Lamar (lùmär′), **Lucius Quintus Cincinnatus,** 1825–93, American statesman. U.S. Representative from Miss. (1857–60, 1873–77); U.S. Senator (1877–85). U.S. Secretary of the Interior (1885–88); Associate Justice of U.S. Supreme Court (1888–93).

Lamar, Mirabeau Buonaparte, 1798–1859, Texas statesman, b. Ga. As president of Texas (1838–41) he secured recognition of Texas independence by European countries; carried out vigorous Indian policy; laid foundations of present Texas public education system; founded capital at Austin.

Lamar (lùmär′), city (pop. 6,829), SE Colo., on Arkansas R. and E of Pueblo. Farm processing center.

Lamarck, Jean Baptiste Pierre Antoine de Monet, chevalier de (zhä bäptēst′ pyĕr′ ätwän′ dù mônà′ shùvälyä′ dù lämärk′), 1744–1829, French naturalist. Noted as introducer of evolutionary theories, of term *Invertebrata,* and for classification of invertebrates. Regarded founder of invertebrate paleontology. His skill as a botanist was first shown in his *Flore français* (1778). **Lamarck's theory of evolution** is based on belief that organism passes to offspring characteristics developed because of need created by its environment. This is known as the theory of inheritance of acquired characteristics, which is no longer accepted by Western scientists.

Lamarque (lùmärk′), village (pop. 7,359), S Texas, NW of Galveston. In agr. (strawberries, truck), oil area.

Lamartine, Alphonse de (älfôs′ dù lämärtēn′), 1790–1869, French poet, novelist, and statesman. Author of *Les Méditations poétiques* (1820; including well-known "Le Lac") and of *Harmonies* (1829), in which he expressed his personal lyricism in musical verse. His religious orthodoxy turned to pantheism in *Jocelyn* (1836) and *La Chute d'un ange* (1838). He wrote *Histoire des Girondins* (1847) in praise of the Girondists. After the FEBRUARY REVOLUTION of 1848, he headed the provisional government. Politically idealistic, democratic, and pacific, his moderation eventu-

ally caused his supporters to desert him. Later works include the novel *Graziella* (1849).

Lamb, Lady Caroline: see MELBOURNE, WILLIAM LAMB, 2D VISCOUNT.

Lamb, Charles, 1775–1834, English essayist. A friend from boyhood of Coleridge, he worked as a clerk at India House (1792–1825). Collaborated with his sister Mary in *Tales from Shakespear* (1807). His *Specimens of English Dramatic Poets* (1808) estab. his reputation as a critic, and his famous *Essays of Elia* (collected 1823, 1833) marked him as the great master of the familiar literary style. Despite personal and family handicaps, he was able to give to his essays the warm, humorous quality of his personality.

Lamb, William: see MELBOURNE, WILLIAM LAMB, 2D VISCOUNT.

lamb: see MUTTON; SHEEP.

Lambeth, metropolitan borough (pop. 230,105), S London, England, S of the Thames. Site of Lambeth Palace (chief residence of Archbishop of Canterbury and scene of Lambeth conferences), St. Thomas's Hospital (9th cent.), and Doulton ware potteries.

lamb's quarters, European annual weed (*Chenopodium album*) of goosefoot family, naturalized in North America. It has small green flowers and whitish leaves used for greens when young.

Lambton, John George: see DURHAM, JOHN GEORGE LAMBTON, 1ST EARL OF.

Lamennais or **La Mennais, Felicité Robert de** (fälēsētä′ röbĕr′ dù lämùnä′), 1782–1854, French Roman Catholic apologist. Leader of a liberal group, he was aided by MONTALEMBERT and LACORDAIRE in founding (1830) the journal *Avenir,* which forwarded ultramontanism, opposed Gallicanism, and maintained that the Church could not be free under royal government. In clash with the royalist clergy, he appealed to Pope Gregory XVI, who condemned liberal doctrines in encyclical *Mirari vos.* Lamennais retired for two years, emerged as a non-Christian, and died outside the Church. Ironically he probably did more than any other man to end Gallicanism and forward papal power. His *Paroles d'un croyant* (1834) expresses liberal humanitarianism.

Lamentations, book of Old Testament, ascribed to Jeremiah, a series of poems mourning the fallen Jerusalem. Chapters 1–4 are each divided into equal groups of lines; initial letters of the groups form an alphabetical acrostic in Hebrew.

La Mesa (lù mä′sù), city (pop. 10,946), S Calif., near San Diego, in citrus, truck, and poultry area.

Lamesa (lùmē′sù), city (pop. 10,704), NW Texas, S of Lubbock on S Llano Estacado; settled 1903. Center of agr. and cattle area with cotton gins and cottonseed oil mills.

La Mettrie, Julien Offray de (lä mĕtrē′), 1709–51, French physician and materialist philosopher. Explained man's mind and all his actions on a mechanical basis. Wrote *Man, the Machine* (1748).

Lamia (lā′mēù), in Greek mythology, grief-crazed woman whose name was used to frighten children. Her own children were killed by Hera, jealous of Zeus' love for her, and thereafter Lamia, envious of happy mothers, stole and killed their children.

Lamia (Gr. lämē′ä), city (pop. 25,843), E central Greece. Founded c.5th cent. B.C. as chief city of Malis; became an ally of Athens. Gave its name to Lamian War (323–322 B.C.) waged by the united Greeks against Antipater, who was besieged here.

Lammermuir Hills (lămûrmūr′, lä′mùrmūr) or **Lammermoor Hills** (–mōōr′), broad range of hills, East Lothian and Berwickshire, Scotland.

Lamont, Thomas W(illiam), 1870–1948, American banker. A partner of J. P. Morgan & Co. after 1910. Served abroad as U.S. financial adviser in 1920s and 1930s. Benefactor of Harvard.

La Motte-Fouqué: see FOUQUÉ.

lamp, lighting device, originally a vessel for holding oil burned through a wick. Used since Paleolithic

SMALL CAPITALS = cross references. Pronunciation key on inside end pages. Abbreviations: p. 2.

period. Forms include float-wick lamp (wick was supported above oil), primitive open-cruse type, and spouted saucer type, e.g., Betty lamp of American colonists. Circular wick with open center eliminated smokiness; it was invented 18th cent. by Aimé Argand who also introduced glass lamp chimney. In mid-19th cent. kerosene superseded other oils for lamps. For the electric lamp, see LIGHTING.

lampblack: see SOOT.

Lampedusa (lämpädōō′zä), Mediterranean island (77 sq. mi.; pop. 3,821), between Malta and Tunis, belonging to Italy. Sponge and sardine fishing.

Lampman, Archibald, 1861–99, Canadian nature poet, author of *Among the Millet* (1888).

Lamy, Jean Baptiste (zhä′ bätēst′ lämē′), 1814–88, Roman Catholic archbishop in U.S. Southwest, b. France. Willa Cather's *Death Comes for the Archbishop* (1927) is based on his career.

Lanai (lŭnī′), island (141 sq. mi.; pop. 3,136), one of Hawaiian Isls., W of Maui. Formerly used only for cattle grazing; after 1922 developed as pineapple-growing center.

Lanarkshire (lă′nŭrkshĭr, lă′närk–) or **Lanark,** county (892 sq. mi.; pop. 1,614,125), S central Scotland. In Clyde R. valley, it has level plain in N and mountains in S. Extensive mfg. and rich mineral deposits in and near Glasgow. Central agr. region has cattle, sheep, and dairying. County town is **Lanark,** burgh (pop. 6,219), on Clyde R. New Lanark, just S, scene of social experiments by Robert Owen.

Lancashire (lăng′kŭshĭr, –shŭr), **Lancaster** (lăng′kŭstŭr), or **Lancs** (lăngks), county (1,878 sq. mi.; pop. 5,116,-013), NW England, on Irish Sea. E and N parts in Lake District; W and S are lowlands with rich coal and iron deposits. FURNESS separated from rest of county by Morecombe Bay. Most populous county of England with one of world's great industrial regions centered around MANCHESTER and LIVERPOOL. Has textiles (notably cotton), much mfg., and large shipyards. County also a duchy, vested in the sovereign. County town is **Lancaster,** municipal borough (pop. 51,650), on Lune R. Has textile and other mfg. and flour mills.

Lancaster, earls and dukes of: see LANCASTER, HOUSE OF; JOHN OF GAUNT.

Lancaster, John of: see JOHN OF LANCASTER.

Lancaster, Joseph, 1778–1838, English Quaker educator. In 1801 he founded a free elementary school using a type of MONITORIAL SYSTEM. Later, he came to America to lecture and promote his ideas.

Lancaster, England: see LANCASHIRE.

Lancaster. 1 City (pop. 2,402), central Ky., S of Lexington. Site of Kennedy House, said to have been used in *Uncle Tom's Cabin,* is near by. 2 Town (pop. 3,601), central Mass., NE of Wachusett Reservoir. Has one of Bulfinch's finest churches (1817). Birthplace of Burbank. 3 Village (pop. 8,665), W N.Y., E of Buffalo; settled 1810. Steel, wood, and glass products. 4 City (pop. 24,180), S central Ohio, SE of Columbus and on Hocking R.; founded 1800. Mfg. of flint glass and farm machinery. Birthplace of W. T. Sherman. 5 City (pop. 63,774), SE Pa., on Conestoga R. and W of Philadelphia; settled c.1721. Center of Pa. Dutch region and one of richest agr. areas in nation, it has large stockyard and mfg. of tobacco, linoleum, and watches. Seat of Franklin and Marshall Col. (Evangelical-Reformed; for men; formed 1853 by merger of Franklin Col. and Marshall Col.). Munitions center in Revolution. Continental Congress met here briefly in 1777. State cap. 1799–1812. Was W terminus of Lancaster Turnpike. Birthplace of Robert Fulton. Pres. Buchanan is buried here and his near-by home is historic memorial. 6 Town (pop. 7,159), N S.C., NNE of Columbia near N.C. line. Textile mills and farms.

Lancaster, house of (lăng′kŭstŭr), royal family of England. Title began in 1267 when Henry III gave it to his second son, **Edmund, earl of Lancaster,** 1245–96,

called Edmund Crouchback from a cross he wore on crusade. He had been made titular king of Sicily in 1254 but the title lapsed. His son, **Thomas, earl of Lancaster,** 1277?–1322, opposed Piers Gaveston and the Despensers under Edward II, led the baronial party, and was executed for treason. His brother, **Henry, earl of Lancaster,** 1281?–1355, was chief adviser to Edward III in his seizure of power from his mother. His son, **Henry, duke of Lancaster,** 1299?–1361, was made duke for victories in the Hundred Years War. He died without male issue and the title passed to JOHN OF GAUNT, fourth son of Edward III, who married Henry's daughter, Blanche. His son became the first Lancastrian king as HENRY IV. Others were HENRY V and HENRY VI. Struggle with the rival house of YORK led to Wars of the ROSES.

Lancelot or **Ladislaus,** c.1376–1414, king of Naples (1386–1414); son of Charles III. His reign was consumed by his struggle with the rival claimant, Louis II of Naples, and with the antipope John XXIII. He had Rome sacked in 1413.

Lancelot, Sir: see ARTHURIAN LEGEND.

Lancret, Nicolas (nēkôlä′ läkrä′), 1690–1743, French painter, whose style is suggestive of Watteau. Painted balls, fairs, and other festivities.

Lancs, county, England: see LANCASHIRE.

Lander, city (pop. 3,349), W central Wyo., on Popo Agie R. Tourist center in dude-ranch area near Fort Washakie, Wind River Indian Reservation hq.

Landes (länd′), region of Gascony, SW France; a sandy, marshy area stretching for c.100 mi. along Atlantic coast. Sheep grazing. Part has been reclaimed through drainage and forestation. It occupies part of Gironde dept. and most of **Landes** dept. (3,614 sq. mi.; pop. 248,395; cap. Mont-de-Marsan).

land-grant colleges and universities, institutions benefiting from Morrill Act of 1862. These now number 69. Hatch Act (1887) provided for research and experiment stations, Smith-Lever Act (1914) for extension work in agriculture and home economics.

Landis, Kenesaw Mountain, 1866–1944, American jurist, commissioner of baseball (1921–44). He did much to restore public faith in baseball after 1920 "Black Sox" scandal.

Landon, Alf(red) M(ossman), 1887–, governor of Kansas (1933–37) and unsuccessful Republican candidate for President (1936).

Landon, Letitia Elizabeth, pseud. L.E.L., 1802–38, English poet and novelist, whose contributions in verse to the *Literary Gazette* had wide appeal.

Landor, Walter Savage, 1775–1864, English author, best known for *Pericles and Aspasia* (1836) and especially for prose dialogues, *Imaginary Conversations* (1824–53). His verse is of wide range.

Landowska, Wanda (ländôf′skä), 1877–, Polish-French harpsichordist, pianist, and teacher. Made her American debut in 1923. She has done much to revive interest in the harpsichord and its music.

Landsberg an der Warthe (länts′běrk än děr vär′tù), Po. *Gorzów Wielkopolski,* town (1939 pop. 48,053; 1946 pop. 19,796), E Brandenburg, on Warthe R.; transferred to Polish administration 1945. Trade and transportation center.

Landseer, Sir Edwin Henry (lăn′sēr), 1802–73, English animal painter, extremely popular in his day.

Lands End, promontory, Cornwall; SW extremity of England. Has granite cliffs 100 ft. high.

Landskrona (länskrōō′nä), seaport city (pop. 25,089), Malmohus co., S Sweden, on the Oresund; founded 1413. It has shipyards, flour mills, sugar refineries, and metalworks. Town was burned 1428 by Hansa merchants and devastated in 16th- and 17th-cent. wars. Its citadel was built 1540. Swedes defeated Danes in naval battle here, 1677.

landslide, slipping of a mass of rock and earth down a slope. Main cause is saturation with water, which increases weight, lessens friction. Caused also by earthquakes. Landslides dam streams and destroy forests, farm land, habitations, life, and cause floods.

Landsmaal: see NORWEGIAN LANGUAGE.

Landsteiner, Karl (kärl länt'shtīnŭr), 1868–1943, American medical research worker, b. Vienna. For discovery of human blood groups, he won 1930 Nobel Prize in Physiology and Medicine. With A. S. Wiener, he identified Rh blood factor (1940).

Lane, James Henry, 1814–66, American politician, called "Liberator of Kansas." Encouraged antislavery men to emigrate to Kansas; secured Free State control of legislature. U.S. Senator (1861–66).

Lane, Joseph, 1801–81, American general in Mexican War, territorial governor of Oregon (1848–50). Also superintendent of Indian affairs there.

Lane, Sir Ralph, c.1530–1603, leader of first attempted English settlement in America, on ROANOKE ISLAND, N.C. (1585).

Lane, Ralph Norman Angell: see ANGELL, SIR NORMAN.

Lanett (lŭnĕt'), cotton-milling city (pop. 7,434), E Ala., on Chattahoochee R. and ENE of Montgomery.

Lanfranc (lăn'frăngk), d. 1089, Italian churchman, archbishop of Canterbury. A theologian and scholar trained in France under BERENGAR OF TOURS, he founded the famous school at Bec and wrote (against Berengar) a widely popular treatise on transubstantiation. He was a friend of William the Conqueror, and after the Norman Conquest reluctantly became archbishop of Canterbury. A strong reformer, he did much to root out abuses in the English church and came into conflict with King William II.

Lang, Andrew, 1844–1912, Scottish scholar and man of letters. He wrote graceful poetry in French forms, as in *Ballades in Blue China* (1880, 1881). His anthropological theory of myth appears in *Myths, Literature, and Religion* (2 vols., 1887). Lang is best known, however, for prose translations of the *Odyssey* (1879, with S. H. Butcher), the *Iliad* (1883, with Walter Leaf and Ernest Myers), and *Aucassin and Nicolete* (1887).

Lang, Cosmo Gordon, 1864–1945, English churchman, archbishop of York (1908–28), archbishop of Canterbury (1928–42). He exercised some influence in the abdication of Edward VIII.

Langdell, Christopher Columbus (lăng'dŭl), 1826–1906, American teacher of law. As dean of Harvard Law School after 1875, he introduced (with J. B. Ames) the "case method" of law study, which was then at Columbia and later almost universally accepted.

Langdon, John, 1741–1819, American statesman. Largely responsible for N.H. ratifying Constitution as ninth state, thus making instrument effective. U.S. Senator (1789–1801).

Lange, Christian Louis (krĭs'tyän lōō'ē läng'ŭ), 1869–1938, Norwegian pacifist and Nobel Prize winner (1921).

Langeland (läng'ŭlän), island (110 sq. mi.; pop. 20,-354), Denmark, in Baltic Sea, between Fyn and Laaland. Produces grain. Langeland Belt, strait, joins Great Belt and Baltic Sea.

Langensalza (läng"ŭnzäl'tsä), town (pop. 16,013), Thuringia, central Germany. Has kept part of medieval walls and castle. Scene of victory of Emperor Henry IV over rebellious Saxons and Thuringians (1075); of Prussians over Hanoverians (1866). Bad Langensalza, near by, has sulphur springs.

Langerhans, islands of, in medicine: see PANCREAS.

Langlade, Augustin (ōgüstē' lägläd'), c.1695–c.1771, French Canadian fur trader. Estab. fur trade at Green Bay, Wis. His son, **Charles Michel de Langlade,** 1729–1800, aided in fur trading and was a leader in French and Indian Wars.

Langland, William, c.1332–c.1400, supposed author of PIERS PLOWMAN, b. probably Ledbury, near Welsh Marches; lived in London. Took minor orders, but because of marriage never became priest.

Langley, Samuel Pierpont, 1834–1906, American scientist. A pioneer in mechanics-of-flight studies and heavier-than-air flight experiments. Flew models successfully (1896), but full-scale aircraft, financed by War Dept., in 1903 could not be launched. Reconstructed in 1914, it flew. Invented bolometer (instrument for recording variations in heat radiation); pioneered in studies of infrared radiation. Helped to popularize astronomy. Secretary of Smithsonian Institute from 1887.

Langmuir, Irving (lăng'mŭr), 1881–, American chemist. He contributed to development of radio vacuum tube, introduced atomic-hydrogen welding. Won 1932 Nobel Prize for work in surface chemistry—development of new technique for molecule study, which has applications in research on immunology.

Langres (lä'grü), town (pop. 5,624), Haute-Marne dept., NE France, surrounded by wooded Langres Plateau. Medieval fortifications. Cutlery industry. Birthplace of Diderot.

Langston University: see GUTHRIE, Okla.

Langtry, Lillie, 1852–1929, English actress, called the Jersey Lily. A noted beauty, she was painted by Millais and Burne-Jones. *Lady Windermere's Fan* was written by Wilde as a vehicle for her.

Langtry [for Lillie Langtry], village, W Texas, on Rio Grande near mouth of the Pecos. Near old town of Langtry where "law west of Pecos," Judge Roy Bean, meted out whisky and justice at his saloon.

language, systematic human vocal communication. It is a distinctive, exclusive, and universal mark of the human species, but its origin is unknown. When languages resemble each other in a systematic way they are held to be genetically related. Though scientifically estab., such relationships have always been on the basis of sounds of the languages and the way the sounds are grouped in systematic patterns; no certainty has been attained in comparing the fundamental grammatical structures of languages. Maximal groups of related languages are called families and stocks. For a survey of the important languages by families, see tables on pp. 535–37. In the tables asterisks indicate extinct languages and locations are general.

Languedoc (lägdôk'), region and former province, S France; historic cap. Toulouse. It consists of Lower Languedoc, along Mediterranean coast, with cities of Nîmes, Montpellier, and Narbonne; of the fertile Garonne plains, with Toulouse as center (agr., wine growing); and of part of the Massif Central (incl. the Cévennes, Vivarais, and Velay). Languedoc corresponds roughly to Narbonensis prov. of Roman Gaul, the later Septimania. Its history before its incorporation into the French royal domain (1271) is largely that of the county of TOULOUSE.

langue d'oc and langue d'oïl (läg dôk', dôël', dô'yü), names of the two principal groups of medieval French dialects, *oc* and *oïl* being their respective words for *yes. Langue d'oc* was spoken S of a line running roughly from Bordeaux to Grenoble. The *langue d'oïl* dialect of the Paris region gradually developed into modern French. Both *langue d'oïl* and *langue d'oc* (e.g., Provençal) dialects (*patois*) persisted, however, in some rural regions.

Lanier, Sidney (lŭnēr'), 1842–81, American poet, b. Ga. A Confederate soldier, he was imprisoned and lost his health. Lanier was a musician (flutist with Peabody Orchestra, Baltimore) and devoted much attention to the relationship of music and poetry—the subject of his *Science of English Verse* (1880). His own poems show the use of musical principles as in "The Symphony" and "The Marshes of Glynn." Some of his shorter poems, notably "The Song of the Chattahoochee" and "A Ballad of Trees and the Master" have lasting popularity.

Lanka: see CEYLON.

Lannes, Jean (zhä' län'), 1769–1809, marshal of France; one of Napoleon's chief lieutenants. Fell at Essling.

The Indo-European Languages

SUBFAMILY	GROUP		PRINCIPAL LANGUAGES
Germanic	W	High	Bavarian, Swiss Alemannic, Pennsylvania Dutch, Alsatian—Swabian Franconian—Old* and Middle* High German, German—Yiddish
		Low	Old Saxon*, Plattdeutsch (Modern Low German) Lower Franconian*, Dutch, Flemish, Afrikaans
			Anglo-Frisian 1. Frisian 2. Old English*, Middle English*—Middle Scots* English: British, American, Colonial, etc., each with standard and dialect variations—Scottish
	N		Old Norse*, Icelandic—Norwegian, incl. Landsmaal Old Swedish*, Swedish—Danish, Dano-Norwegian— Faroese
	E		Gothic*
Celtic	Continental		Gaulish*
	Brythonic		Middle Welsh*, Welsh—Cornish*—Breton
	Goidelic		Old*, Middle*, and Modern Irish, Scottish Gaelic, Manx
Italic	Latin and Romanic (Romance)		Umbrian*
			Old: Old Latin*, Classic Latin*, Medieval Latin*
			Middle: Vulgar Latin*—Old Italian*, Old French*
			Italian, standard (Tuscan) and dialects Sardinian—Dalmatian*—Rumanian Rhaeto-Romanic: Romansh, Ladin or Frioul French, Canadian F., Louisiana F.—dialects of N France Provençal, dialects of S France—Catalan Spanish, American S., Philippine S.—Judeo-Spanish Portuguese, Brazilian Portuguese—Galician
			Oscan*
Albanian			Albanian
Hellenic or Greek			Ionian*, Homeric G.*—Classical Attic*, Hellenistic G.*, Koine*, Biblical G.* (OT, NT), Byzantine G.*— Modern G.
			Doric*, Choral Doric*, Corinthian*—Aeolic*—Cyprian*
Slavic or Slavonic	E		Russian—Ukrainian, Ruthenian—White Russian
	S		Slovene, Serbo-Croat, Bulgarian—Old Church Slavonic*
	W		Polish—Sorbian or Wendish—Czech, Slovak
Baltic			Old Prussian*, Lithuanian, Lettish
Indo-Iranian	Iranian		Western: Avestan*, Old Persian*—Pahlavi*, Sogdian* Persian—Caspian dialects—Kurdish
			Eastern: Baluchi, Afghan or Pushtu, Pamir dialects
			Northern: Ossetian
	Indic or Indo-Aryan		Old: Vedic*, Sanskrit*
			Middle: Prakrit* (several languages), Pali*
			Northwestern languages, Kashmiri, et al.—Romany Lahnda, Sindhi, Gujarati, Marathi—Bhili, Rajasthani Panjabi, Pahari, W. Hindi—standard Hindustani and Urdu—E. Hindi, Bihari Bengali, Oriya, Assamese Singhalese or Sinhalese
Tokharian*			Tokharian A* (of Turfan), Tokharian B* (Kuchean)
Armenian			Classical Armenian*, Armenian
Anatolian*			Hittite* (Kanesian), Hieroglyphic Hittite* Luwian*, Lycian*, Lydian*

The Mongolic or Mongolian Languages

Eastern	Literary Mongolian, Mongolian proper or Halha, incl. new standard language of Urga South Mongolian, incl. Harachin, Chahar, Ordos Buryat, incl. new standard, Selenga, et al.
Western	Oirat, incl. Kalmuck, Kobdo Oirat Afghanistan Mongol

The Finno-Ugric Family

Finno-Permian Group

1. Finnish
   incl. Estonian
   Lappish
   Mordvinian
   Cheremiss

2. Permian
   Zyrian (or Komi)
   Udmurt (Votyak)

Ugric Group

Obi Ugric
Vogul, Ostyak
Hungarian or Magyar

The Malayo-Polynesian Languages

Indonesian Group

Malagassy

W	N	Formosan Philippine Tagalog Bisayan Ilocano Igorot Magindanao
		Eastern Chamorro Palau NE Celebes
	W	Malay Sumatran Nias, et al. Maduran, Bugi Balinese, Macassar
	S — E	Javanese Sundanese Borneo Dyak Sumba, et al.

E: Aru, Savu, et al.

Micronesian Group

Caroline
Yap
Ponape
Gilbertese
Marshallese
Nauru
Marianas

Melanesian Group

S Melanesian
Central Melanesian
Fijian
S Solomons
N Melanesian
Santa Cruz

Polynesian Group

W	Vaitupu (Ellices) Samoan, Tongan, et al.
E	Maori Rarotonga Tahitian Society Tuamotu Marquesan Hawaiian Rapanui (Easter Isl.)

An asterisk (*) indicates a dead language.

LINGUISTIC FAMILIES (continued)

The Semitic and Related Groups

GROUP	LANGUAGE	GROUP	LANGUAGE
Akkadian	Babylonian*, Assyrian* Nuzi Akkadian*	Ethiopic	Geez* Tigrigna Tigré Amharic Gafat Harari Gauragé
Canaanite	Old Canaanite* Moabite* Phoenician*, Punic* Hebrew*, New Hebrew Ugaritic*	Hamito-Semitic	Egyptian* Coptic*
Aramaic	W Aramaic: Biblical*, Palestinian*, Modern Syriac* Mandean* Neo Syriac	Hamitic	Old Libyan* Modern Berber: 1. Tuareg, Kabyle, et al. 2. Riff, Algerian, et al. Guanche* (Canaries)
Arabic	Classical Arabic Arabian Arabic Iraqi Arabic Syrian Arabic Egyptian Arabic Western Arabic, incl. Maltese, Andalusian Arabic*	Cushitic	Beja Afar and Saho Somali Galla Agaw—Bilin Sidama—Gonga
	Himyaritic*—Soqotri		

The Turkic Languages

East Turkic	Oirat Altai, North Altai, Abakan, Kizil, Baraba, Uigur, et al.
West Turkic	Kirghiz, Irtysh, Bashkir, Volga Kirghiz, et al.
Tatar or Central Turkic	Kashgar, Yarkand, Sart, Taranchi, Uzbek, et al.
South Turkic	Turkmen, Azerbaijanian and Caucasian Turkic Standard Turkish and related (Anatolian or Ottoman) dialects Crimean Turkish
Yakut	
Chuvash	

The Sino-Tibetan or Indo-Chinese Languages

Tibeto-Burman	Standard Tibetan, Tibeto-Himalayan, North Assamese Bodo, Kachin, Naga (all in S Assam)
Burman	Standard Burmese, Burmese dialects Karen language and others
Chinese	Standard Written Chinese, Ancient* and Modern North Chinese Central Coastal Chinese Kiangsi dialects Cantonese and Hakka
Tai or Thai	Standard Siamese, Southeastern Tai, incl. Laos Eastern Tai, incl. Lakya of Hainan Northern Tai, incl. Shan

The Dravidian Family

Tamil (Coromandel Coast)
Malayalam (S Malabar)
Kanarese (Malabar Coast)
Kulu
Kota
Toda
Telugu (N Coromandel Coast)
Central Dravidian
Gondhi
Kurukh, Malto
Bhil
Kolami
Naiki
Brahui (Baluchistan)

The Siouan Stock

GROUP	LANGUAGE
Eastern	Catawba
Ohio	Ofo*, Biloxi*, Tutelo*
Missouri	Hidatsa, Crow
Mississippi or Chiwere	Iowa, Oto, Missouri* Winnebago
Dhegiha	Omaha, Ponca, Quapaw, Osage, Kansa*
Mandan	
Dakota	Sioux Assiniboin

Native Linguistic Families of the U.S. and Canada

FAMILY	SUGGESTED KINSHIP	FORMER LOCATION
Eskimo-Aleut		Arctic America Aleutians, Alaska
Eyak		Copper R. delta
Athapascan		separate table
Tlingit	Athapascan	SE Alaska, NW B.C.
Haida	Athapascan	Queen Charlotte Isl.
Tsimshian	Penutian	Prince Rupert region
Wakashan	Algonquian	Coastal B.C., Wash.
Salishan	Algonquian	separate table
Kootenai	Algonquian	SE B.C. and vicinity
Chimakuan	Algonquian	Cape Flattery, Wash.
Chinook	Penutian	Lowest Columbia R.
Shahaptin incl. Yakima, Nez Percé	Waiilatpuan Lutuamian Penutian	S Washington N and central Oregon E central Idaho
Waiilatpuan incl. Cayuse	Shahaptin Penutian	N Oregon
Kalapuya	Penutian	Upper Willamette R.
Siuslaw—Yakonan, incl. Lower Umpqua	Penutian	Middle coast of Oregon
Coos	Penutian	Coos R., SW Oregon
Lutuamian incl. Klamath and Modoc	Shahaptin Waiilatpuan Penutian	S Oregon
Takelma	Penutian	Rogue R., SW Oregon
Karok	Hokan	Extreme NW Calif.
Yurok—Wiyot	Algonquian	Klamath R., NW Calif.
Chimariko	Hokan	NW California
Shasta—Achomawi	Hokan	N and NE California
Penutian	Tsimshian et al.	Central California
Yana*	Hokan	NE California
Washo	Hokan	Lake Tahoe region
Yuki	Hokan	Round Valley, Calif.
Pomo	Hokan	Calif. coast N of S.F.
Esselen*	Hokan	Coast S of San Francisco
Salinan*	Hokan	San Luis Obispo coast
Chumashan*	Hokan	Santa Barbara coast
Uto-Aztecan		separate table
Yuman	Hokan	separate table
Zuñi		Zuñi, N.Mex.
Keresan	Hokan	N.Mex.; see PUEBLO INDIANS
Tanoan	Uto-Aztecan	separate table
Kiowa	Tanoan Uto-Aztecan	NW Okla. and neighboring Kan., Texas
Algonquian		separate table
Siouan	Hokan	separate table
Tonkawa*	Hokan	Austin region, Texas
Karankawa*	Hokan	Middle Texas coast
Caddoan	Hokan	separate table
Atacapa*	Tunica	SW La., SE Texas
Natchez-Muskogean	Hokan	separate table
Yuchi	Siouan	E Tenn., E Ga.
Iroquoian	Caddoan Hokan	1. N.Y. state and vic. 2. Va. and Carolinas

An asterisk (*) indicates a dead language.

LINGUISTIC FAMILIES OF THE AMERICAS (concluded)

The Athapascan Stock

GROUP	LANGUAGE
Northern	Kutchin
(in Alaska,	Sarsi, Beaver, Sekani
NW Canada)	Chipewyan, Yellowknife, Slave
Northwestern	Hoopa, (Upper) Umpqua*, et al.
Apachean	Navaho, Apache, Lipan, Kiowa Apache

The Salishan Stock

Inland	Okanogan
	Flathead
	Coeur D'Alene
	Shuswap
Coastal	Bella Coola
	Clallam
	Nisqualli
	Puyallup
	Tillamook

The Algonquian Stock

Central and Eastern	1. Cree, Montagnais, Naskapi
	Menominee
	Fox, Sauk, Kickapoo
	Shawnee
	Miami*, Illinois*
	Potawatami
	Ojibwa, Ottawa, Algonquin
	Delaware
	Powhatan*
	2. Natick*, Narragansett*
	Mohegan*, Pequot*
	Penobscot, Abnaki
	Passamaquoddy, Malecite
	Micmac
Blackfoot	Blackfoot, Piegan, Blood
Cheyenne	
Arapaho	Arapaho, Atsina, Nawathinehena

The Natchez-Muskogean Stock

Natchez	
Muskogean	W: Choctaw, incl. Chickasaw
	E: Alibamu, Creek, incl. Seminole

The Tanoan Stock

Tiwa	Taos, Picuris
	Sandia, Isleta, Isleta del Sur
Towa	Jemez, Pecos*
Tewa	San Juan, S. Clara, San Ildefonso, Nambé, Pojoaque*, Tesuque, Hano

The Caddoan Stock

Pawnee	Pawnee proper, Skiri Pawnee, Arikara
	Kitsai or Kichai
	Wichita (two languages)
Caddo	Caddo proper
	Haina

The Yuman Stock

NW—Arizona	Yavapaí, Walapai, Havasupai
Colorado—Gila	Mohave, Halchidhoma, Kavelchadom, Maricopa, Yuma
Colorado Delta	Cocopa, Halyikwamai, Kahwan
S Calif.—Lower Calif.	Diegueño, Kamia, Akwa'ala, Kiliwa

The Uto-Aztecan Stock

GROUP	LANGUAGE	LOCATION
Southern-Californian	Cahuilla, Luiseño, et al.	S Calif.
Hopian	Hopi, Bannock, et al.	NE Ariz., S Idaho, to E Calif.
Utan	Ute, Paiute, et al.	W Colo. to SE Calif.
Shoshonean	Shoshone, Comanche	SW Wyo. to Calif., Central Texas
Taracahitian	Tarahumara, Yaqui, et al.	Chihuahua, Sonora, Sinaloa
Aztecoidan	Cora, Huichol	Jalisco, Nayarit
	Nahuatlan, et al.	Middle America
Piman	Pima—Papago, Tepehuan, et al.	Gila R. to Nayarit

The Mayan Stock

Huastec		Tampico area
Yucatec	Maya	Yucatán
Quichoid	Cakchiquel, Quiché, et al.	Chiapas and Central America
Mamoid	Mam, Aguacatec, Jacaltec	
Chiapan	Tzeltal, Tzotzil Tabasco Chontal	Chiapas, Tabasco, Guatemala

Native Stocks of Latin America

STOCK	LOCATION
Seri (Hokan kinship?)	Sonora coast
Tarascan	Michoacán
Otomí	Hidalgo, Mexico state
Matlatzinca	Mexico state
Totonac	Vera Cruz, Puebla
Subtiaba-Tlapanec (Hokan kinship?)	1. Nicaragua 2. Guerrero
Puebla Popoloca—Mazatec	Puebla, Oaxaca
Zapotec	Oaxaca
Mixtec	Oaxaca, Guerrero
Huave (Penutian kin?)	Oaxaca
Mixe-Zoque (Penutian?)	Vera Cruz, Oaxaca
Chinantec	Oaxaca
Oaxaca Chontal	Oaxaca
Xinca	SE Guatemala
Miskito—Suma—Matagalpa or Misumalpa	Honduras, Salvador Mosquito Coast
Chorotega	Nicaragua, Costa Rica
Cariban	West Indies, Caribbean coasts
Arawakan	Amazonia
Chibchan	Costa Rica to Colombia
Kechua	Bolivia, Perú plateau
Aymar	Titicaca region
Tupí-Guaraní	Coastal, central Brazil, Paraguay
Gê	Maranhão and vicinity
Araucanian	Chile

An asterisk (*) indicates a dead language.

lanolin (lă′nŭlĭn), greasy yellow substance from wool. It is used as ointment base, in finishing and preserving leather, in some varnishes and paints.

Lansbury, George, 1859–1940, British Labour party leader. Founded (1912) and edited the *Daily Herald*, the voice of British labor. Pacifist and reformer, he headed Labour party in Parliament 1931–35.

Lansdale, borough (pop. 9,762), SE Pa., N of Philadelphia. Mfg. of clothing and metal products.

Lansdowne, Henry Charles Keith Petty Fitzmaurice, 5th marquess of (lănz′doun), 1845–1927, British statesman. As foreign secretary tried to end England's diplomatic aloofness by alliances.

Lansdowne, borough (pop. 12,169), SE Pa., SW residential suburb of Philadelphia. Metal products.

Lansford, borough (pop. 7,487), E Pa., S of Hazleton. Anthracite mining and mfg. of clothing.

Lansing, Robert, 1864–1928, U.S. Secretary of State (1915–20). Authority on international law. Advocated U.S. joining in World War I with Allies. Disapproved Covenant of League of Nations as part of peace treaty.

Lansing. 1 Village (pop. 8,682), NE Ill., S suburb of Chicago near Ind. line. **2** City (pop. 92,129), state cap. (since 1847), S Mich., at junction of Grand and Cedar rivers; settled 1837. Development came with railroads (1870s) and automobile industry (1901). Mfg. of automobiles, buses, trucks, automotive equipment, metal products, chemicals, and paints.

Lanston, Tolbert, 1844–1913, American inventor of a typesetting machine, MONOTYPE (patented 1887).

lantana (lăntă′nŭ), tropical shrubs of genus *Lantana*. *Lantana camara*, grown as bedding or greenhouse plant, has clusters of red or yellow flowers.

lanthanum (lăn′thŭnŭm), relatively common metallic element of rare earths (symbol = La; see also ELEMENT, table). It is gray-white, ductile, malleable.

Laoag (läwäg′), municipality (pop. 44,406), on NW Luzon, Philippines. Trade center for rice area.

Laocoön (lāŏk′ōŏn), in Greek legend, priest of Apollo who warned the Trojans not to touch wooden horse made by the Greeks in Trojan War. Two sea serpents, sent (according to different versions) by Athena, Poseidon, or Zeus, killed Laocoön and his two sons. Struggle is represented by Greek statue now in the Vatican. Pliny names Agesander, Athenodorus, and Polydorus, Greek sculptors of 1st cent. B.C., as creators of the work.

Laodicea (lāŏ″dĭsē′ŭ), anc. city of Asia Minor; under Rome a Christian center and seat of one of the Seven Churches.

Laoighis (lā′ĭsh) or **Leix** (lā′ĭsh, lāks), inland county (664 sq. mi.; pop. 49,697), S central Ireland, in Leinster; co. town Port Laoghise. Formerly Queen's Co. Mostly level, it has Slieve Bloom Mts. in N. Agr. and dairying are main occupations.

Laon (läő′), city (pop. 14,868), Aisne dept., N France. Its famous Church of Notre Dame (12th–13th cent.; a cathedral until French Revolution) dominates the plain from a rocky height.

Laos (lä′ōs), kingdom (91,400 sq. mi.; pop. 1,169,000), NW INDO-CHINA; cap. Vientiane. Bounded on N by China, E by Viet Nam, S by Cambodia, and W by Burma and Thailand. Drained by Mekong R. Mainly a rugged plateau cut by deep valleys. Chief exports include coffee, benzoin, and opium. Under Siamese control from early 19th cent. to 1893, when sovereignty was shifted to France. Monarchy estab. 1947. Joined French Union as associated state in 1950. In April, 1953, the French suffered a setback in the Indo-Chinese war when Viet Minh troops invaded Laos from Viet Nam.

Lao-tze or **Lao-tzu** (both lou′dzŭ), b. c.604 B.C., Chinese philosopher, legendary founder of TAOISM.

La Paz (lä päs′), city (pop. 319,600), W Bolivia, *de facto* cap. and largest city of Bolivia (Sucre is *de jure* cap.); founded 1548. In a narrow valley (alt. c.12,-000 ft.), it lacks fuel and power and has little mfg.

Chief tourist attractions are near-by Illimani and L. Titicaca.

La Paz, city (pop. 10,401), cap. of S territory, Lower California, Mexico; pearl fishing center.

Lapeer (lŭpēr′), city (pop. 6,143), S Mich., E of Flint and on South Bend of Flint R., in grain and dairy area. Mfg. of metal products.

La Pérouse, Jean François de Galaup, comte de (dù gälő′ kőt′ dù lä pārōōz′), 1741–c.1788, French navigator. Led French government expedition in 1785 to explore Pacific, seeking Northwest Passage. He discovered (1787) **La Pérouse Strait,** a channel, 25 mi. wide, separating Hokkaido, Japan, from Sakhalin, USSR. Sometimes called Soya Strait.

lapis lazuli (lă′pĭs lăz′yōōlī, –lē), a gem, deep blue, violet, or greenish blue, usually flecked with yellow iron pyrites. Found in Afghanistan, Chile, Siberia, Burma, U.S. Formerly made into vases, bowls; used also for beads, small ornaments.

Laplace, Pierre Simon, marquis de (pyĕr′ sēmő′ märkē′ dù läpläs′), 1749–1827, French astronomer and mathematician, evolver of scientific form of NEBULAR HYPOTHESIS. His research on motions of heavenly bodies was published in his *Mécanique céleste* (1799–1825). His notable work in mathematics includes development of theory of probabilities.

Lapland, Finnish *Lappi*, Nor. *Lapland*, Swed. *Lappland*, vast region of N Europe, largely within Arctic Circle. It includes Finnmark, Troms, and part of Nordland counties (Norway); historic Lappland prov., now comprising Norrbotten and Vasterbotten counties (Sweden); N Finland; and Kola peninsula (RSFSR). Region is mountainous in N, rising to 6,965 ft. in the KEBNEKAISE (Sweden), and consists largely of tundra in NE. It has extensive forests and many lakes and rivers. Its rich mineral resources include highgrade iron ore (esp. at KIRUNA, Sweden), copper (Sulitelma, Norway), nickel (Pechenga, RSFSR), and apatite (Kirovsk, RSFSR). Narvik and Murmansk are important ports. **Lapps** or **Laplanders,** the indigenous population (c.30,000) are concentrated mainly in Norway, where they are called Finns. Largely nomadic, they follow their reindeer herds, fish, and hunt. They are believed to have come from central Asia and to have been pushed N by other migrations. Though nominally conquered by Sweden and Norway in Middle Ages, their Christianization was not completed until 18th cent. Finno-Ugric language.

La Plata (lä plä′tä), city (pop. 302,073), cap. of Buenos Aires prov., E Argentina, SE of Buenos Aires. Founded 1882 as cap. of prov. after Buenos Aires had been federalized. Has large meat-packing plants. Renamed Eva Perón (1952).

La Plata, Río de: see PLATA, RÍO DE LA.

La Pointe (lù point′), town, on Madeline Isl. (largest of APOSTLE ISLANDS), N Wis. French fortified trading post here 1693–98, 1718–59. American Fur Co. had post here early 19th cent.

Laporte, Roland (rōlä′ läpôrt′), 1675–1704, French leader of the CAMISARDS, known as Roland. Betrayed, he fell defending himself.

La Porte (lù pôrt′), city (1951 special census pop. 20,-414), NW Ind., E of Gary; settled 1830. Produces road-building material, machinery, and furniture. Resort with many lakes.

Lapps: see LAPLAND.

Laptev Sea (lăp′tyĭf), section of Arctic Ocean, bounded by E Siberia (S), Severnaya Zemlya and Taimyr Peninsula (W), and New Siberian Isls. (E). Navigable in Aug. and Sept.

lapwing, crested plover of Old World, also called green plover or pewit. It has a deep, iridescent green back, greenish-black crown and crest, black throat and upper breast, white under parts, and fawn tail coverts.

Larache (läräsh′), Arabic *El Araish*, city (pop. 41,286), W Spanish Morocco; port on the Atlantic. Near site of Phoenician settlement, which was later a Roman colony. Held by Spain 1610–89. Exports include grain, skins, and fruit.

Laramie (lă'rùmē), city (pop. 15,581; alt. 7,145 ft.), SE Wyo., on Laramie R. and WNW of Cheyenne; settled 1868. Transportation, trade, and industrial center for cattle and sheep region; mfg. of building materials. Seat of Univ. of Wyoming (land-grant, state supported; coed.; chartered 1886, opened 1887). Near by is site of Fort Sanders, estab. 1866 to protect Overland Trail and railroad workers.

Laramie, river rising in N Colo. in S Medicine Bow Mts. Flows 216 mi. NE to North Platte R. in Wyo.

Laramie, Fort, Wyo.: see NATIONAL PARKS AND MONUMENTS (table).

Laramie Mountains: see FRONT RANGE.

larceny, unlawful taking and carrying away of the property of another with intent to deprive the owner of its use or to appropriate it to the use of the perpetrator or of someone else. Usually distinguished from EMBEZZLEMENT and from false pretenses, larceny is in some U.S. states defined to include them. Grand larceny, usually a felony, differs from petty larceny, usually a misdemeanor, as to the value of the property stolen.

larch or **tamarack** (tă'mùrăk), tree of genus *Larix.* Larches are conifers of the pine family but are not evergreen. Widely distributed in N Hemisphere, they are grown for ornament and lumber. American larch or hackmatack is *Larix laricina.* Timber of *L. occidentalis* of W U.S. used in construction.

Larchmont, suburban village (pop. 6,330), SE N.Y., on Long Isl. Sound between New Rochelle and Mamaroneck. Yachting center.

Larcom, Lucy (lär'kùm), 1824–93, American poet. A worker in the Lowell, Mass., cotton mills, she attracted the interest of Whittier by her sweet and idealistic poems.

Lardner, Ring(gold Wilmer), 1885–1933, American short-story writer. A sports reporter, he turned to fiction and gained fame with vigorous stories in *You Know Me Al* (1916), *How to Write Short Stories* (1924), and other volumes. Pungent idiom of the sports world and the street made him a much-imitated master of tough and sardonic humor.

Laredo (lùrā'dō), city (pop. 51,910), SW Texas, on Rio Grande (bridged) opposite Nuevo Laredo, Mexico. Founded by Spanish in 1750s, it grew as post on road to other Texas cities. Mexican after Texas Revolution, city went to U.S. after Mexican War. Border city and port of entry, it developed through ranching and farming and discovery of oil and gas. Has antimony smelter, foundries, refineries, hat factory, and meatpacking plants.

La Reine, Fort (lä rěn'), S Man., on Assiniboine R., near the present Portage la Prairie. Built 1738 by Vérendrye.

lares and penates (lâ'rēz, pùnā'tēz), in Roman religion, household gods. Each household had one lar and two penates. The lar was a youth bearing cup and drinking horn; penates were dancing youths, also with drinking horns. The three images stood together in a niche, and offerings were made to them before meals and on festive occasions.

Largillière, Nicolas de (lärzhēlyär'), 1656–1746, French portrait painter. Influenced by Rubens.

Largo Caballero, Francisco (fränthē'skō lär'gō käbälyä'rō), 1869–1946, Spanish Socialist leader. Led in overthrow of monarchy (1931). Premier of Loyalist government 1936–37. Died in Paris.

Larissa (lùrĭ'sù, Gr. lä'rēsä), city (pop. 41,163), N Greece, on the Peneus; cap. of Thessaly. Was annexed by Macedon 4th cent. B.C.; became a Roman ally 196 B.C. Partly destroyed in World War II.

lark, member of large family of perching birds, chiefly of Old World and best known through SKYLARK. Horned larks belong to the only American species. MEADOW LARK belongs to blackbird family.

Larkspur, residential town (pop. 2,905), W Calif., N of San Francisco and near Mt. Tamalpais. Larkspur Canyon near by has redwood grove.

larkspur or **delphinium,** annual or perennial plant of genus *Delphinium* with handsome spires of flowers. Annual kinds are commonly called larkspur and are white, pink, red, or purple; perennials, known as delphinium, are usually white or blue.

Larksville, borough (pop. 6,360), NE Pa., near Wilkes-Barre. Anthracite mining.

La Rochefoucauld, François, duc de (fräswä' dük dù lä rôshfōōkō'), 1613–80, French author. He described his part in the FRONDE (he was wounded at the Faubourg Saint-Antoine) in his remarkable memoirs, but his great work is *Réflexions ou sentences et maximes morales* (1665), in which he viewed selfishness (*amour-propre*) as mainspring of human behavior. His style, peerless in its hard brilliance and incisive clarity, made the maxim a major genre in French literature.

La Rochejaquelein, Henri du Vergier, comte de (ārē' dù vĕrzhyä' kōt dù lä rôshzhäkùlē'), 1772–94, French commander of counterrevolutionary army in the VENDÉE. Fell in battle.

Lars Porsena or **Lars Porsenna** (lärz' pôr'sùnù, pôrsĕ'nù), semilegendary king of Clusium, Etruria. Conquered Rome and reinstated TARQUIN family (c.500? B.C.), though legend says that heroism of the Romans caused him to abandon the conquest.

larva (lär'vù), term for stage between egg and pupa in life of insects with complete metamorphosis, and for nymph stage of insects with incomplete metamorphosis. It is sometimes used also for immature stages of other animals (e.g., mollusks, crustaceans, fish, amphibia). Grubs are larvae of beetle, bee, and some related insects; maggots are larvae of certain flies; mosquito larvae are wrigglers or wigglers. Larvae usually eat ravenously; many do great damage to crops, foods, etc.

larvae (lär'vē), in Roman religion, ghosts of the dead. To keep them from returning to frighten the living, rites, the Lemuria, were celebrated silently at night in May. See MANES.

larynx (lă'rĭngks), voice organ lying above windpipe. Composed of cartilages, membranes, and two elastic vocal cords extending from front to back wall.

Las. For names beginning thus and not listed here, see second element; e.g., for Las Palmas, see PALMAS, LAS.

La Salle, Jean Baptiste de: see JOHN BAPTIST DE LA SALLE, SAINT.

La Salle, Robert Cavelier, sieur de (rōbĕr' kävùlyä' syûr' dù lä säl'), 1643–87, French explorer in North America. Commanded Fort Frontenac, developed trade, built forts. Descended the Mississippi to mouth (1682), claiming entire valley for France. Murdered by own men in futile attempt to reach mouth of the Mississippi by sea.

Lasalle (lùsäl') or **Ville Lasalle,** residential town (pop. 11,633), S Que., Canada, SW of Montreal and on St. Lawrence R.

La Salle (lù säl'), city (pop. 12,083), N Ill., on Illinois R. adjoining Peru, in agr. and mining area; laid out 1837. Mfg. of meat, glass, metal, and zinc products and cement. Near by is Starved Rock.

Las Animas (läs ä'nēmäs), city (pop. 3,223), SE Colo., E of Pueblo. Kit Carson Mus. and site of Bent's Fort are near.

Lascaris, Constantine (kŏn'stùntēn lä'skùrĭs), d. 1501?, Greek grammarian. After fall of Constantinople he came to Italy. His Greek grammar (1476) was first book printed in Greek characters.

Las Casas, Bartolomé de (bärtōlōmä' dā läs kä'säs), 1474–1566, Spanish missionary and historian, called Apostle to the Indies. Ordained a priest in Hispaniola 1510, he worked most of his life (in Hispaniola, Peru, Guatemala) for abolition of Indian slavery and for bettering the lot of all Indians. Largely through his efforts the New Laws (1542) were adopted to protect Indians in colonies. Wrote monumental *Historia de las Indias.*

Las Cruces (läs krōō'sĭs), town (pop. 12,325), SW N.Mex., on Rio Grande and NNW of El Paso, Texas, in irrigated farm (cotton, grain, sugar beets, fruit, vegetables) and dairy area; founded 1848. Near by are Tortugas, Indian village, and New Mexico Col. of Agr. and Mechanic Arts (land-grant; coed.; 1889).

Lashio (läsh'yō), town (pop. 4,638), cap. of Shan State, E Upper Burma; head of Burma Road.

Lashkar (lŭsh'kŭr), city (pop. 113,718), winter cap. of Madhya Bharat, India; commercial and rail center. Palace of maharaja of Gwalior is here.

Lasker, Emanuel (ämä'nōōĕl), 1868–1941, German chess player. Won (1894) world's championship by defeating Steinitz, lost (1921) title to Capablanca.

Laski, Harold J(oseph) (lă'skē), 1893–1950, English political scientist, economist, and writer, chairman (1945–46) of the British Labour party, grad. Oxford. He was a member of the executive committee of the Fabian Society and a professor at London School of Economics and Univ. of London. His numerous books include *Reflections on the Revolution of Our Time* (1943) and *The American Democracy* (1948). He taught and lectured much in the U.S.

Lassalle, Ferdinand (fĕr'dĕnänt läsäl'), 1825–64, German socialist. In contrast to Marx, he emphasized the role of the state and favored a state system of workers' cooperatives. He greatly influenced the German politics of his day and helped establish the first German workers' political party.

Lassen Peak (lă'sŭn, lä'–), 10,453 ft. high, in Cascade Range, N Calif., is only active volcano in U.S. Included in **Lassen Volcanic National Park:** see NA-TIONAL PARKS AND MONUMENTS (table).

Last Supper, of Jesus and His disciples at the time of the Pasch just before His crucifixion (Mat. 26.17–30; Mark 14.12–26; Luke 22.7–39; John 13–17; 1 Cor. 11.23–29). For the sacrament, see EUCHARIST and LORD'S SUPPER. It has been a favorite subject of painting; best known is that of Leonardo da Vinci.

Las Vegas (läs vā'gŭs). **1** City (pop. 24,624), S Nev., near Colorado R.; settled 1855 by Mormons and abandoned 1857. U.S. army built Fort Baker here, 1864. In ranching and mining area, city grew after railroad arrived in 1905. Now a resort, famed for gambling and divorces. Atomic Energy Commission installations are near. **2** City (pop. 7,494; alt. 6,398 ft.), sometimes called East Las Vegas, N N.Mex., ESE of Santa Fe. Forms one community with Las Vegas town (pop. 6,269; settled c.1835), sometimes called West Las Vegas. Mountain and health resort with dude ranches near by. Shipping center in agr., sheep, and cattle area. Seat of New Mexico Highlands Univ.

Latakia (lătŭkē'ŭ), city (pop. c.35,000), W Syria, port on Mediterranean opposite Cyprus. Was ancient Phoenician city and the Roman Laodicea ad Mare. Incorporated into Syria 1942. Now known for special type of tobacco.

La Tène (lä tĕn'), anc. Celtic settlement, L. Neuchâtel, Switzerland. Tenian culture of second Iron Age, spanning period from 6th cent. B.C. to end of 1st cent. B.C., was so named for antiquities found here.

Lateran (lă'tŭrŭn), name of group of buildings of SE Rome facing the Piazza San Giovanni. Occupies land once belonging to the Laterani and given to the Church by Constantine. The basilica, known as St. John Lateran, is cathedral of Rome, the pope's church, and first-ranking church in Roman Catholic world. Original basilica, built perhaps before 311, was restored 5th–10th cent.; rebuilt and altered 14th–18th cent. Original Lateran palace was replaced in 16th cent. by present palace.

Lateran Councils, 9th–12th and 18th ecumenical councils of the Roman Catholic Church. **1** 1123, summoned by CALIXTUS II. Confirmed Concordat of Worms (1122) ending the INVESTITURE controversy. Forbade clerical marriage or concubinage. **2** 1139, convened by Innocent II to heal the wounds left by schism of antipope Anacletus II (d. 1138). **3** 1179,

convened by ALEXANDER III after the Peace of Venice (1178) had reconciled Emperor Frederick I. Most important canon gave papal election exclusively to the cardinals. **4** 1215, convened by INNOCENT III as pinnacle of his pontificate. Its decrees included a statement of faith, definition of transubstantiation, laws for trials of clergy, arrangements for a new crusade. Made annual confession and communion at Easter time minimal requirements for church membership. **5** 1512–17, convened by JULIUS II, continued by LEO X, called to counter an attempt (1510) by Louis XII of France to revive the conciliar theory (see SCHISM, GREAT). The council ratified a papal agreement with France, the Concordat of 1516. It also republished the bull of Julius (1503) declaring that simony invalidated a papal election.

Lateran Treaty, concordat between the Holy See and Italy, signed in 1929 in the Lateran Palace by Cardinal GASPARRI for PIUS XI and by MUSSOLINI for Victor Emmanuel III. Unification of Italy (completed 1871) brought confiscation by the state of all papal possessions except a few buildings. The pope was then granted an annual indemnity, but subsequent popes refused indemnity and looked upon themselves as prisoners. These problems, called the Roman Question, were solved by the treaty, which provided for a sovereign and independent new state called Vatican City and a guarantee of the pope's inviolability by the Italian government.

Lateur, Frank: see STREUVELS, STIJN.

latex: see RUBBER.

lathe (lādh), machine tool to hold and turn wood or metal while it is cut into form desired. The term is also used for loom frame carrying the reed which parts the warp and beats up the weft and for a type of potter's wheel.

Lathrop, Rose Hawthorne, 1850–1926, American Roman Catholic nun; daughter of Nathaniel Hawthorne. She and her husband (the author George Parsons Lathrop) were converted to Catholicism in 1891. She worked much in and near New York city for the care of the poor afflicted with incurable cancer. After her husband's death (1898), she became a nun, and as Mother (Mary) Alphonsa founded a community of Dominican nuns.

Latimer, Hugh (lă'tĭmŭr), c.1485–1555, English bishop and martyr. Refused to recant Protestantism at his trial after accession of Catholic Mary I; was burned at the stake with Nicholas RIDLEY.

Latin America, Spanish-speaking, Portuguese-speaking, and French-speaking countries of North America (S of the U.S.), South America, Central America, and West Indies. The 20 republics are Argentina, Bolivia, Brazil, Chile, Colombia, Costa Rica, Cuba, Dominican Republic, Ecuador, El Salvador, Guatemala, Haiti, Honduras, Mexico, Nicaragua, Panama, Paraguay, Peru, Uruguay, and Venezuela. Term also used to include Puerto Rico, French West Indies, and other islands of West Indies where Romance languages are spoken.

Latin Empire of Constantinople: see CONSTANTINOPLE, LATIN EMPIRE OF.

Latini, Brunetto (brōōnĕt'tō lätē'nē), d. 1294?, Italian scholar. Teacher of Dante, he is immortalized in *The Divine Comedy*.

Latin Kingdom of Jerusalem: see JERUSALEM, LATIN KINGDOM OF.

Latin language, Italic language of anc. Rome, standard tongue of most of the Roman Empire. It continued in Romance languages. Schoolbook Latin is that of Cicero and Caesar. The Latin of the Christian Fathers is still official language of Roman liturgy in Roman Catholic Church.

Latins, in anc. times, inhabitants of Latium. Their many small settlements united against Etruscans and Samnites, came under dominance of Rome (338 B.C.). All Latins were granted Roman citizenship after the SOCIAL WAR of 90 B.C.

Latin Way: see ROMAN ROADS.

Latium (lā'shēŭm), Ital. *Lazio*, region (6,634 sq. mi.; pop. 2,654,924), central Italy, between the Apennines and the Tyrrhenian Sea; cap. Rome. It includes the CAMPAGNA DI ROMA and the former PONTINE MARSHES. The Tiber is the chief river. Region produces wine, olive oil, cereals, vegetables. Inhabited by the LATINS in ancient times, Latium later shared the history of the PAPAL STATES until its annexation by Italy (1870).

La Tour, Georges de (zhôrzh' dù lä tōōr'), 1593–1652, French painter. Used bold nocturnal light effects and simplified, solid forms, as in *Education of the Virgin* (Frick Coll., N.Y.).

La Tour, Maurice Quentin de (mōrēs' kắtē' dù lä tōōr'), 1704–88, French portraitist in pastel.

La Tour d'Auvergne, Théophile Corret de (tăôfēl' kôrā' dù lä tōōr' dōvĕr'nyù), 1743–1800, French officer, celebrated for his bravery. Though a nobleman, he fought for the French Revolution and fell in battle. He refused promotion above grade of captain, was officially called "first grenadier of France."

La Trappe: see TRAPPISTS.

La Trémoille or **La Trimouille, Georges de** (zhôrzh' dù lä trămoi'yù or trēmōō'yù), c.1385–1446, French nobleman, favorite of Charles VII from 1427 to 1433. Probably in Burgundian pay, he favored negotiated peace, opposed Joan of Arc.

Latrobe, Benjamin Henry (lùtrōb'), 1766–1820, American architect, b. England. Came to U.S. in 1796, became surveyor of public buildings in 1803. Introduced Greek forms, important in classic revival; his Bank of the U.S. (now the old Philadelphia Custom House) was based on the Parthenon. Built first American cathedral, the Roman Catholic cathedral in Baltimore (1805–18). Designed Sedgely (1800), a residence near Philadelphia, an early example of Gothic revival in America. A son, **Benjamin Henry Latrobe,** 1806–78, was an eminent engineer. Another son, **John Hazlehurst Boneval Latrobe,** 1803–91, was a lawyer and philanthropist, who supported African colonization of Liberia.

Latrobe, borough (pop. 11,811), SW Pa., ESE of Pittsburgh. Coal mining and mfg. of metal products. Seat of St. Vincent Col.

Latter-Day Saints, Church of Jesus Christ of, religious sect founded (1830) in N.Y. by Joseph SMITH. Its members are called MORMONS, and hq. are in Salt Lake City. Beliefs are based on Bible, Book of Mormon, revelations to Smith (in *Doctrines and Covenants*), and *The Pearl of Great Price* (sayings ascribed to Moses and Abraham). Church is organized with Twelve Apostles. It is marked by importance of revelation and by stress on the interdependence of spiritual and temporal life.

Latter Day Saints, Reorganized Church of Jesus Christ of, separatist group from Mormon Church. Estab. 1852. Hq. since 1904 at Independence, Mo.

Lattimore, Owen, 1900–, American author and educator. Author of books on Far East, and editor of *Pacific Affairs* (1934–41). Director (from 1938) of School of Internatl. Affairs at Johns Hopkins. Adviser (1941–42) to Chiang Kai-shek, and economic adviser (1945–46) Japanese Reparations Commission. Cleared 1950 of espionage charges. Indicted (Dec., 1952) on charges of perjury growing out of hearings before congressional committee.

La Tuque (lä tük'), town (pop. 9,538), S Que., Canada, on St. Maurice R. and NW of Quebec. Pulp-milling center with hydroelectric station.

Latvia (lăt'vēŭ), Lettish *Latvija*, republic (24,900 sq. mi.; 1935 pop. 1,950,502), NE Europe, bordering on Baltic Sea (W), Estonia (N), RSFSR (E), and Lithuania (S); cap. RIGA. Its incorporation in 1940 into the USSR as a constituent republic has not been recognized by U.S. (as of 1953). Latvia is a generally hilly, agr. plain (dairying, stock raising, timber). Industries produce fine and heavy machinery. Population is largely Lutheran, except in Roman Catholic Latgale region, in the NE. The regions of Kurzeme and Zemgale, S of Western Dvina R., share the history of COURLAND, of which they were part; Latgale and Vidzeme, N of the Dvina, were part of LIVONIA. With the third Polish partition (1795), all Latvia was in Russian hands, but the German "Baltic barons," settled since the times of the Livonian Knights, remained the dominating class. Devastated in World War I, Latvia was proclaimed independent in 1918 but was invaded in 1919 by Soviet troops. Peace was restored in 1920. In 1934 the parliamentary regime was replaced by a rightist dictatorship under Karlis Ulmanis. USSR secured military bases in 1939, and in 1940 occupied Latvia and made it a constituent Soviet republic. Occupied by Germans 1941–44.

Laud, William, 1573–1645, English churchman, archbishop of Canterbury. Worked with Charles I to oust all Puritans from church positions. Parliamentarians opposed his persecution of nonconformists by tyrannical courts. By decreeing Anglican prayer book compulsory in Scotland he precipitated Bishops' Wars. Condemned by House of Commons through bill of attainder, he was executed.

laudanum: see OPIUM.

Lauderdale, James Maitland, 8th earl of (măt'lŭnd, lō'dŭrdāl), 1759–1839, Scottish statesman and author. Long an ardent Whig, he finally became a Tory. Wrote many tracts (e.g., *Inquiry into the Nature and Origin of Public Wealth,* 1804).

Lauderdale, John Maitland, duke of (lô'dŭrdāl), 1616–82, Scottish politician. Imprisoned (1651–60) for support of Charles II. An unpopular member of the CABAL, he was powerful in Scotland.

Laudon or **Loudon, Gideon Ernst, Freiherr von** (both: gē'dâôn ĕrnst' frī'hĕr fŭn lou'dôn), 1717–90, Austrian field marshal. Defeated Frederick II at Kunersdorf (1759); captured Belgrade from Turks (1789).

Laudonnière, René Goulaine de (rùnā' gōōlĕn' dù lōdônyĕr'), fl. 1562–82, French colonizer in Fla. Estab. Fort Caroline near mouth of St. Johns R. (1564). Escaped massacre of settlement by Pedro MENÉNDEZ DE AVILÉS.

Laue, Max von (mäks fŭn lou'ù), 1879–, German physicist. Won 1914 Nobel Prize for method of measuring wave lengths of X rays by using a crystal.

Lauenburg (lou'ŭnbōōrk), former duchy, N Germany, on the lower Elbe; chief city Lauenburg an der Elbe (pop. 11,137). Duchy of Saxe-Lauenburg was held from 1181 by a branch of the Ascanian house of Saxony, upon whose extinction in 1689 it passed to Hanover. Transferred to Danish crown in 1815 (but as member of German Confederation), it was seized by Prussia in Danish War of 1864 and incorporated into Schleswig-Holstein in 1865. Bismarck was created duke of Lauenburg (1890) but never used the title.

laughing gas, colorless gas with sweet taste and odor. It is a compound of nitrogen and oxygen, nitrous oxide. Widely used as dental anesthetic; laughing hysteria is common aftereffect.

Launcelot of the Lake, Sir: see ARTHURIAN LEGEND.

Launceston (lôn'sĕstŭn, lŏn'–), city (pop. 37,717), on N Tasmania, Australia; port at junction of the North Esk and South Esk; founded 1805. Second largest city of state. Exports dairy products, flour, lumber.

Laura, beloved lady of Petrarch, thought to have been Laura de Noves (1308?–1348), wife of Hugo de Sade.

Laurel. 1 Town (pop. 4,482), W central Md., NE of Washington, D.C. Has large race track. **2** City (pop. 25,038), SE Miss., SE of Jackson on Tallahala Creek; founded 1881. Processes lumber and farm products. Near U.S. Indian school and reservation.

laurel of history and classical literature is an evergreen tree, *Laurus nobilis,* native to Mediterranean region, and called also bay and sweet bay. To the ancients it symbolized victory and merit. Its leaves, sold as bay leaves, are used as flavoring for meats and soups. See also CALIFORNIA LAUREL; MOUNTAIN LAUREL.

Laurencin, Marie (märē′ lōräsē′), 1885–, French painter. Her work usually has a young girl as the subject, done in pastel colors with a flat surface.

Laurens, Henry (lô′rŭnz), 1724–92, American Revolutionary statesman. Promoted colonial opposition to Britain. President of Second Continental Congress (1777–78). His son, **John Laurens**, 1754–82, patriot officer in American Revolution, drew up terms for surrender of Cornwallis.

Laurens, city (pop. 8,658), NW S.C., NW of Columbia. Mfg. of textiles and glass.

Laurent, Robert (lô′rŭnt), 1890–, American sculptor. Known for sensitive interpretations of the figure.

Laurentian Mountains, range in S Que., Canada, N of St. Lawrence and Ottawa rivers. Resort area.

Laurentian Plateau (lôrĕn′shŭn, lŭ–), roughly shield-shaped region of rock (also called Canadian shield), the first part of the North American continent permanently elevated above sea level. It is the earth's greatest area of exposed Archaean rocks—largely of granite, gneiss, and schist. During the Pleistocene epoch ice sheets gouged out numerous lake basins, taking away much of the soil. The region is rich in natural resources, including minerals, forests, fur.

Lauria, Roger of: see ROGER OF LORIA.

Laurier, Sir Wilfrid (lô′rēä), 1841–1919, Canadian statesman, prime minister (1896–1911). Sought to develop dominion within framework of empire.

Laurinburg, town (pop. 7,134), S N.C., near S.C. line, SW of Fayetteville. Mfg. of cotton products and textiles.

Lausanne (lōzän′), city (pop. 107,225, incl. Ouchy, its port on L. of Geneva), cap. of Vaud canton, SW Switzerland. Watchmaking; printing; tourism. Seat of Swiss federal tribunal. Was ruled by its bishops till 1536, when it was conquered by Bern and accepted the Reformation. School of theology, a famous center of Calvinism, was founded 1537, was made a university 1890. Bernese rule ended 1798, when Lausanne became cap. of liberated Vaud.

Lausanne, Conference of, 1922–23, peace conference held to write a new peace treaty with Turkey, whose new government under Kemal Pasha (see ATATURK) did not recognize the earlier Treaty of SÈVRES. The treaty, signed 1923, restored E Thrace, the Straits Zone, the Smyrna dist., and other territories to full Turkish sovereignty; abolished foreign zones of influence and capitulations; demanded no reparations. The Straits were to remain demilitarized and subject to an international convention (see DARDANELLES). A separate agreement between Turkey and Greece provided for compulsory exchange of minorities.

Lausitz and Lausitzer Neisse: see LUSATIA; NEISSE.

Lautrec, Henri de Toulouse: see TOULOUSE-LAUTREC.

Lauzon (lōzō′), town (pop. 9,643), S Que., Canada, on St. Lawrence R. and NE of Lévis. Has large dry dock. Shipbuilding and lumbering.

Lauzun, Antonin Nompar de Caumont, duc de (ātōnē′ nōpär′ dù kōmō′ dük dù lōzŭ′), 1633–1723, marshal of France. Despite Louis XIV's opposition, he seems to have secretly married Mlle de Montpensier (c.1681), with whom he quarreled and separated 1684. He brought James II's family to safety from England to France (1688) and in 1689–90 commanded the Irish expedition which ended in defeat at the Boyne.

lava (lä′vù), igneous rock erupted by a volcano on the earth's surface or the ocean floor or from a fissure. The term is applied both to liquid and hardened rock. Lavas are composed chiefly of silica and metallic oxides, varying in color and texture. Before it is exposed to the air lava is called magma. Conflicting theories have been proposed to explain the heat and liquidity of magma, its source, and the cause of its rise in the earth.

Lava Beds National Monument: see NATIONAL PARKS AND MONUMENTS (table).

Lavaca Bay: see MATAGORDA BAY.

Laval, François Xavier de (läväl′), 1623?–1708, French prelate in Canada, first bishop of Quebec (1674–88). Under his strong leadership Quebec church became vital force of colonial life. Founded a seminary, later nucleus of Laval Univ. Fought bitterly with governors. Appears as a character in Willa Cather's novel *Shadows on the Rock.*

Laval, Pierre (pyěr′), 1883–1945, French politician. At first a socialist, later a conservative, he was twice premier (1931–32, 1935–36). Publication of the Hoare-Laval plan, which proposed to appease Italy by giving it a large part of Ethiopia, caused his fall in 1936. An advocate of Franco-German cooperation, he reached new prominence after the fall of France (1940). In 1940 Marshal Pétain made him foreign minister but soon dismissed him as an intriguer. Reinstated, with full dictatorial powers, in 1942, Laval to all appearances acted as a tool of Germany (see VICHY GOVERNMENT). In 1945, after a much-criticized trial for treason, he was executed.

Laval, town (pop. 28,171), cap. of Mayenne dept., NW France, on Mayenne R. Linen mfg.

Lavalleja, Juan Antonio (hwän′ äntō′nyō lävayä′hä), c.1786–1853, Uruguayan revolutionist. Led the Thirty-three Immortals in declaration of independence from Brazil in 1825. After Uruguay became independent (1827), Lavalleja and Fructuoso Rivera both sought presidency. Rivera won, but Lavalleja led revolts. One of a triumvirate chosen (1852) to govern Uruguay, he died before serving.

La Vallière, Louise de (lwēz′ dù lä välyěr′), 1644–1710, French noblewoman. Became Louis XIV's mistress in 1661; bore him four children. He made her a duchess (1667) but left her for Mme de Montespan.

Laval University: see QUEBEC, Que.

Lavater, Johann Kaspar (yō′hän käs′pär lä′vätùr), 1741–1801, Swiss preacher and theological writer. Remembered for his work on physiognomy.

lavender, aromatic shrubby herb (*Lavendula officinalis*) native to Mediterranean region. It has gray foliage and spikes of small purple flowers. Its flowers are valued for scenting linens, and oil of lavender is used in toiletries and perfumery.

Laveran, (Charles Louis) Alphonse (älfōs′ lävùrä′), 1845–1922, French physician. Won 1907 Nobel Prize in Physiology and Medicine for work on protozoa in disease causation. Found cause of malaria (1880).

La Vérendrye, Pierre Gaultier de Varennes, sieur de: see VÉRENDRYE.

Lavery, Sir John (lä′vùrē), 1856–1941, British painter, leader of Glasgow school of painting.

Lavisse, Ernest (ĕrnĕst′ lävēs′), 1842–1922, French historian, professor at Sorbonne. Noted for brilliant editorship of several collectively written histories of France, in which he wrote some of best volumes.

Lavoisier, Antoine Laurent (ätwän′ lōrä′ lävwäzyä′), 1743–94, French chemist, physicist, a founder of modern chemistry. He was one of the first to introduce quantitative chemical methods. He determined the nature of combustion and the role of oxygen in respiration. His classification was the basis of distinction between elements and compounds and of the system of chemical nomenclature. As one of the farmers general he was guillotined during the Reign of Terror.

La Voisin, French poisoner: see POISON AFFAIR.

Lavongai (lävông′ī), volcanic island (c.460 sq. mi.; pop. c.5,000), SW Pacific, in BISMARCK ARCHIPELAGO and part of Territory of New Guinea.

Law, Andrew Bonar (bŏ′nùr), 1858–1923, British Conservative statesman. In 1916 he became chancellor of exchequer under Lloyd George. Led revolt from wartime coalition government (1922) and became prime minister. Soon resigned because of ill-health.

Law, John, 1671–1729, Scottish financier in France. Set up (1716) Banque générale, with paper currency issue guaranteed by the state. Acquired commercial monopoly in Louisiana (1717) and set up huge stock company. This was merged (1720) with the bank. Frenzied speculation led to wholesale ruin (see MISSISSIPPI SCHEME).

Law, William, 1686–1761, English clergyman, nonjuror, noted for controversial, devotional, and mystical writings, which wielded great influence. He was a chief figure in the Bangorian Controversy.

Law, the, in Judaism: see TORAH.

Lawes, Sir John Bennet, 1814–1900, English agriculturist. He founded experimental farm at Rothamsted and developed superphosphate which marked beginning of chemical fertilizer industry.

Lawes, Lewis E(dward), 1883–1947, American penologist, warden (1920–41) at Sing Sing Prison, N.Y.

law merchant: see COMMERCIAL LAW.

lawn, grass turf or greensward in private grounds or public park. Requires good soil, frequent watering and mowing, occasional rolling and fertilizing. Grasses often used in N U.S. are redtop and other bent types, bluegrass (esp. Kentucky bluegrass), fescue grass, and white clover. In S U.S. lawns are often of Bermuda grass, St. Augustine grass, carpet grass, Korean lawn grass. Lawn may be started with seed, runners or stolons (if creeping bents, Bermuda, or carpet grass is used), or blocks of sod.

Lawnside, borough (1,566), SW N.J., SE of Camden. Site bought by abolitionists for Negroes, 1840. Almost all inhabitants are Negroes.

Lawrence, Saint, d. 258, Roman martyr, supposed to have been roasted to death on a gridiron. Feast: Aug. 10.

Lawrence, Abbott, 1792–1855, American textile manufacturer and statesman. A founder of Lawrence, Mass. While U.S. minister to Great Britain (1849–52) he helped relieve tension over proposed isthmian canal and status of Mosquito Coast. His nephew, **Amos Adams Lawrence,** 1814–86, was a colonizer and philanthropist. He backed EMIGRANT AID COMPANY in settlement of Kansas. Aided founding of Univ. of Kansas and Lawrence Col. at Appleton, Wis.

Lawrence, Charles, 1709–60, governor of Nova Scotia, b. England. Mainly by his orders the Acadians were deported (see ACADIA).

Lawrence, D(avid) H(erbert), 1885–1930, English author. He wrote of primitive and natural passions, trying to show instinctive forces in man that might bring happiness. Novels include *Sons and Lovers* (1913), *The Rainbow* (1915), *Women in Love* (1920), *The Plumed Serpent* (1926), and *Lady Chatterley's Lover* (1928). He also wrote stories, essays, and other works (e.g., *Mornings in Mexico,* 1927). Traveled in search of health, spending some time in N.Mex.

Lawrence, Ernest Orlando, 1901–, American physicist. Won 1939 Nobel Prize for invention of CYCLOTRON and research in atomic structure.

Lawrence, James, 1781–1813, American naval hero. Commanded *Chesapeake* in battle with British frigate *Shannon* (1813). His dying command, "Don't give up the ship!" became popular naval battle cry.

Lawrence, Sir Thomas, 1769–1830, English portrait painter. Succeeded Reynolds as painter in ordinary to the king (1792) and was knighted in 1815. The fashionable portrait painter of his day, he was perhaps most successful in studies of children, notably *The Calmady Children* (Metropolitan Mus.) and *Pinkie* (Huntington Gall.). Another well-known portrait is that of Mrs. Siddons (Natl. Gall., London).

Lawrence, T(homas) E(dward), 1888–1935, British adventurer, soldier, and scholar. Joined revolt of Feisal I in World War I and helped defeat the Turks. Feeling that the Arabs had been betrayed in British actions after the war, he joined RAF under an assumed name. "Lawrence of Arabia" attracted much popular attention by his exotic career. Wrote *The Seven Pillars of Wisdom* (1935; abridged version, *Revolt in the Desert,* 1927) and translated the *Odyssey.*

Lawrence, William, 1850–1941, American Episcopal

bishop of Mass. (1893). Founder Church pension system. His son, **William Appleton Lawrence,** 1889–, became bishop of Western Mass. in 1937.

Lawrence. 1 City (pop. 23,351), NE Kansas, on Kansas R. and WSW of Kansas City. Founded 1854 for New England Emigrant Aid Co. by Charles ROBINSON, it was named for A. A. Lawrence. Had first church (1854) of Kansas settlers. Political center of the Free Staters, it was actual, though not legal, cap. for a time after 1857. Proslavery raid (1856) led to Pottawatamie killings by John BROWN. Town sacked 1863 by W. C. QUANTRILL. Processing and shipping center for grain-growing and truck-farming area. Seat of Univ. of KANSAS and Haskell Inst. (1884), largest Indian school in U.S. **2** Industrial city (pop. 80,536), NE Mass., on Merrimack R. (water power) and NE of Lowell. Settled 1655; laid out 1845 as industrial town by Boston capitalists, who built dam, mills, workers' dwellings. Became a world center for woolens. Mfg. also of cotton goods, shoes; paper, rubber, plastic products; radio equipment, machinery. Scene of labor strife (I.W.W.) in 1912.

Lawrenceburg. 1 City (pop. 4,806), SE Ind., on the Ohio and W of Cincinnati, in agr. area. **2** City (pop. 5,442), S Tenn., SSW of Nashville, in dairy, livestock, and cotton area.

Lawrence College of Wisconsin: see APPLETON.

Lawrenceville. 1 City (pop. 6,328), SE Ill., WNW of Vincennes, Ind., in agr. area. Refines oil; mfg. of oilwell and telephone equipment. **2** Village (pop. 1,056), W N.J., near Trenton. Has transoceanic radiotelephone transmitting station and Lawrenceville School for boys (prep.; nonsectarian; estab. 1810).

Lawrie, Lee (lô'rē), 1877–, American sculptor. His *Prometheus* at Rockefeller Center, New York.

Lawson, Ernest, 1873–1939, American landscape painter, one of The EIGHT. Painted in impressionistic style.

lawsuit: see PROCEDURE.

Lawton, city (pop. 34,757), SW Okla., near Wichita Mts.; founded 1901. Commercial and industrial center of agr. area (esp. cotton). Oil, asphalt, and granite deposits near. U.S. Fort Sill, Fort Sill Indian school, and Medicine Park close by.

laxative, substance used to stimulate elimination of wastes from intestines. Various kinds act by irritating intestines to increased muscular action, by increasing bulk in tract, or by lubricating tract. Their use may inhibit normal intestinal action, prevent absorption of essential food elements, or cause rupturing of appendix.

Laxness, Halldor (Kiljan) (häl'dōr kĭl'yän läkhs'nĕs), 1902–, Icelandic novelist. Early works had religious, later had Communist, tinge. In novel cycles *Salka Valka* (1931–32) and *Independent People* (1934–35) he created a new modern style in Icelandic literature.

Layamon (lä'ümŭn, –mŏn, lī'–, lä'mŭn), fl. c.1200, first prominent Middle English poet, author of *Brut,* chronicle of early history of Britain.

Layard, Sir Austen Henry (lā'ürd), 1817–94, English archaeologist and diplomat. Excavated in Mesopotamia and Babylon (1842–51). Minister to Spain (1869–77). Ambassador to Constantinople (1877–80).

Lazarillo de Tormes (läthärē'lyō dä tôr'mäs), Spanish picaresque novel published before 1554. Formerly ascribed to Hurtado de Mendoza.

Lazarus (lä'–). **1** Brother of Mary and Martha, raised from the dead by Jesus. John 11.1–44; 12.1–5. **2** Beggar-hero of parable told by Jesus. Luke 16.19–25.

Lazarus, Emma, 1849–87, American poet, b. N.Y. city, best known for *Songs of a Semite* (1882); *Poems* (1889). Her Statue of Liberty poem (1886) is carved inside the pedestal of the statue.

Le. For names beginning thus and not listed here, see second element; e.g., for Le Havre, see HAVRE, LE.

Leacock, Stephen (Butler), 1869–1944, Canadian economist and humorist, b. England. Head of department of political science and economics at McGill Univ. (1908–36). Best known for his many volumes of humorous essays and stories, including many parodies.

Lead, city (pop. 6,422), W S.Dak., in the Black Hills near Wyo. line; laid out 1876 after discovery of gold here. Site of Homestake Mine, largest gold mine in the U.S.

lead, heavy metallic element (symbol = Pb; see also ELEMENT, table), one of the oldest metals used by man. Light silver when freshly cut, it darkens on exposure to air. It is soft, malleable, of low tensile strength, and a poor conductor. It is a component of many alloys. Used for covering cables, as lining for laboratory sinks, in electrolytic cells, in chambers for making sulphuric acid, in storage battery plates. Compounds (all poisons) are used in paints, glass, gasoline, in thickening oils, in construction.

lead poisoning, industrial disease (also called plumbism and painter's colic) caused by absorption of lead through respiratory or digestive tracts. It may result from drinking from receptacles containing lead. Supervision of working conditions in industries using lead has reduced incidence of disease.

Leadville, mining city (pop. 4,081; alt. c.10,200 ft.), central Colo., near headwaters of Arkansas R. SW of Denver. Area had brief gold boom, c.1860. Lead with high silver content caused new boom, 1877. One of world's great silver camps by 1880 (c.40,000 pop.), it declined with repeal of Sherman Silver Act in 1893, but soon revived with new gold boom. Fortunes made fast, often lost fast. History of H. A. W. TABOR symbolizes Leadville's story. Some mining and smelting still carried on (near-by Climax has large molybdenum output). Tourism.

Leaf, river of N Que., Canada, issuing from L. Minto, and flowing c.300 mi. NE to Ungava Bay.

leaf, one of the chief vegetative organs of a plant. Green color is caused by pigment CHLOROPHYLL, necessary for PHOTOSYNTHESIS, the process by which carbohydrates (sugar and starch) are formed. Thus leaves are ultimate basis of most animal life. Autumn coloration of leaves is caused by low temperatures and other factors which destroy chlorophyll and make visible other pigments. Combinations of these pigments are present in variegated leaves; white leaves, often produced by blanching, result from lack of pigments. See *ill.,* p. 783.

leafhopper, any of numerous species of small leaping insects of family Cicadellidae, order Homoptera. Found over most of world; nearly all plants are damaged by some species.

leaf insect, leaf-eating, usually arboreal insect, order Phasmatida (formerly included in Orthoptera). Walking leaf is winged tropical species resembling leaf; WALKING STICK resembles a twig.

League or **Holy League,** 1576–98, organization of French Catholics, aimed at suppression of Protestantism during Wars of RELIGION; founded by Henri, 3d duc de GUISE. King HENRY III, fearing Guise's ambition, proclaimed himself its head and dissolved it in 1577, but in 1585 the League was revived to prevent the succession of Henry of Navarre (see HENRY IV), who ultimately defeated it in spite of the support it received from Spain.

League of Nations, former international organization, predecessor of UNITED NATIONS, which had as aims maintenance of peace, arbitration of international disputes, and promotion of international cooperation. It was product of World War I and ideas of General SMUTS, Léon BOURGEOIS, and Lord Robert Cecil. Pres. Woodrow WILSON incorporated proposal into FOURTEEN POINTS and was chief figure in founding of League at Paris Peace Conference in 1919. Basis of League was Covenant, included in Treaty of VERSAILLES. Geneva was hq. League consisted of assembly composed of all members; council composed of Great Powers (England, France, Italy, and Japan, later also Germany and USSR); and several allied bodies, e.g., WORLD COURT and INTERNATIONAL LABOR ORGANIZATION. Covenant had 26 articles concerning organiza-

tion, need for disarmament, guarantees of territorial status quo against aggression, provision for arbitration and conciliation with SANCTION against aggressors. It provided for treaties, MANDATE system of colonial administration, international cooperation in labor and humanitarian enterprises. League suffered severe handicap in refusal of U.S. to join and in insistence of all members upon their national sovereignty. A general DISARMAMENT CONFERENCE was called, but was unsuccessful. League failed, moreover, because powerful nations could not be coerced into mutual compromise or acceptance of its decisions. However, among problems settled by League were Swedish-Finnish dispute over ALAND ISLANDS (1920); status of N SCHLESWIG and Upper SILESIA, settled by plebiscites (1920, 1921); population exchanges of Greece, Turkey, and Bulgaria after Treaty of Lausanne of 1923; and Yugoslav-Hungarian dispute after assassination (1934) of King ALEXANDER of Yugoslavia. League extended much aid to refugees, especially Armenians; helped suppress white slave and opium traffic; pioneered in health surveys; extended aid to needy states, e.g., Austria; and furthered international cooperation in many fields. Early failures were Polish refusal to accept League decision in VILNA dispute; shelving of Geneva Protocol because of British opposition; and split of France and LITTLE ENTENTE with Great Britain. League's decay began with Second CHINO-JAPANESE WAR in 1931 and withdrawal of Japan from League. League was unable to stop war of Bolivia and Uruguay over Chaco (1932–35). Adolf Hitler began to rearm, withdrew Germany from League 1933, remilitarized Rhineland 1934, denounced Treaty of Versailles 1936, and seized Austria 1938. Italy under Mussolini attacked ETHIOPIA 1935, disregarding economic sanction by League. Japan resumed war with China 1937, and appeasement policy of dominant League members—Great Britain and France—reached apex in MUNICH PACT 1938, which virtually discarded League as international instrument. League dissolved itself, April, 1946, and transferred its services and real estate to UN.

League of Women Voters, organized in Chicago in Feb., 1920. Purposes are to educate women in use of vote and through educational and research campaigns to improve the general political, economic, and social structure.

Leah, Jacob's unloved first wife; mother of Reuben, Simeon, Levi, Judah, Issachar, Zebulun. Gen. 29–30.

Leahy, Frank (William) (lā′hē), 1908–, American football coach. Head coach Boston College 1939–41; athletic director and head coach Notre Dame 1941–43, 1946–. In four complete seasons through 1949, Notre Dame played 38 straight games without defeat (though with two ties).

Leamington, town (pop. 6,950), S Ont., Canada, on L. Erie and SE of Windsor. Port, resort, and agr. center with canneries.

Leamington (lĕ′mĭngtŭn), officially Royal Leamington Spa, municipal borough (pop. 36,345), Warwickshire, England; health resort with mineral springs.

Leander, lover of HERO.

Lear (lēr), legendary English king, turned out by two elder daughters, then welcomed by third, whom he had disinherited. Subject of Shakspere's great tragedy.

Lear, Edward, 1812–88, English artist and humorist, known for illustrated limericks and poems (as in *A Book of Nonsense,* 1846).

Leaside, NE suburb of Toronto (pop. 16,233), S Ont., Canada. Mfg. of trucks.

leather, skin or hide of mammals, reptiles, or birds tanned to prevent decay and to impart flexibility and toughness. Pelts usually are dehaired, submitted to TANNING process, made pliable with fats, and desired finish is produced by process such as glazing, coloring, lacquering, suèding, or embossing. The pelt or leather is split by machine into flesh and grain (hair-side) layers to achieve required thickness. Artificial leather has fabric base usually coated with synthetic substance.

Leavenworth (lĕ'vŭnwûrth), city (pop. 20,579), NE Kansas, on the Missouri and NW of Kansas City. Oldest city in Kansas, it was settled 1854 by proslavery Missourians. Had state's first newspaper (1854). Was supply point for westbound travelers. Trade center for agr. and coal area, it has flour milling, meat packing, metalworking, and mfg. of furniture.

Leavenworth, Fort, U.S. military post, on Missouri R. and near Leavenworth, Kansas. Built 1827 to protect traffic of old Santa Fe Trail. At present it includes a command and general staff school and a Federal penitentiary.

Lebanon (lĕ'bŭnŭn), republic (3,927 sq. mi.; pop. 1,165,- 208), SW Asia; cap. Beirut. Bordered on W by the Mediterranean, on N and E by Syria, and on S by Israel. Valley of El Bika (which produces grain and fruit) lies between coastal Lebanon Mts. and Anti-Lebanon range (on E border). In ancient times the region was dominated by Hittites and Aramaeans; it later became center of PHOENICIAN CIVILIZATION. With Syria the area came under Roman dominion and was included in Byzantine Empire until part of it fell to Arabs in 7th cent. Despite enmity of the DRUSES, the MARONITES remained strong enough to keep the region predominantly Christian. After the Crusades, area was under Ottoman control until World War I, after which Levant States (Syria and Lebanon) were put under French mandate. Lebanon became a republic under the mandate in 1926; treaty of 1936 (not ratified by France) provided for freedom after three-year transition period. In World War II, Vichy control overthrown by British and Free French forces, June–July, 1941. Lebanon became free on Jan. 1, 1944. Joined Arab League in 1945.

Lebanon. 1 City (pop. 7,631), central Ind., NW of Indianapolis, in dairying region. Metal products. **2** City (pop. 4,640), central Ky., SE of Louisville. A national cemetery is near. **3** City (pop. 6,808), S central Mo., NE of Springfield, in an Ozark timber and farm area. Has garment factory and food-processing plants. **4** Town (pop. 8,495), W N.H., S of Hanover and near Connecticut R. Wood products and woolens. **5** City (pop. 5,873), NW Oregon, SSE of Salem, in fruit (esp. strawberries) and grain region. Paper and lumber mills. **6** City (pop. 28,156), E Pa., ENE of Harrisburg; settled c.1720. Center of rich agr. area with mfg. of iron and steel products and textiles. **7** Town (pop. 7,913), central Tenn., E of Nashville in timber and farm area. The HERMITAGE is near. Mfg. of wood and cloth products.

Lebanon, anc. *Libanus,* mountain range, Lebanon, paralleling Mediterranean coast. Rises to 10,131 ft. Famed in ancient times for its huge cedars.

Leblanc, Nicholas, 1742–1806, French chemist. He developed the **Leblanc process** for commercial preparation of soda from common salt. Salt is treated with sulphuric acid to yield sodium sulphate; this is reduced by carbon to give sodium sulphide. Sodium carbonate (soda) is formed by reaction between this and limestone. This process was largely displaced by the Solvay process.

Lebrun, Albert (älbĕr' lŭbrü'), 1871–1950, last president of Third Republic of France. Elected 1932 and reelected 1939, he was deprived of all authority by Marshal Pétain in 1940. In 1944 he recognized Charles de Gaulle as provisional president of France.

Le Brun, Charles (shärl' lŭ brü'), 1619–90, French artist. In 1648 he founded Royal Academy to replace guilds. As painter to Louis XIV he directed decorative works at Versailles and Chateau de Vaux.

Lebrun, Élisabeth Vigée-: see VIGÉE-LEBRUN.

Lecce (lĕt'chä), city (pop. 42,622), S Apulia, S Italy. Was a semi-independent county, 1053–1463. Has many baroque churches and palaces.

Lech (lĕkh), river, c.175 mi. long, rising in Vorarlberg, Austria, and flowing NE through Bavaria, past Augsburg, into the Danube. In 1632 Gustavus II of Sweden defeated Tilly, who was mortally wounded, on the Lech near its confluence with the Danube. On the **Lechfeld,** a plain near Augsburg, Otto I decisively defeated the Magyars in 955.

Lecky, William Edward Hartpole, 1838–1903, British historian. His major work, *History of England in the Eighteenth Century* (8 vols., 1878–90), ranks him as literary historian very near to Gibbon.

Leclerc, Charles Victor Emmanuel (shärl' vĕktôr' ĕmänüĕl' lŭklĕr'), 1772–1802, French general; first husband of Pauline Bonaparte. In 1801 he led the expedition against TOUSSAINT L'OUVERTURE in Haiti. His treacherous arrest of Toussaint led to a native revolt under DESSALINES, who expelled the French. Leclerc died of yellow fever on Tortuga.

Leclerc, Jacques Philippe (zhäk' fēlēp'), 1902–47, French general. His real name was Philippe, comte de Hauteclocque. In World War II he led Free French forces in epic march from Lake Chad to Tripoli (Dec., 1942–Jan., 1943); took part in Tunisian campaign (1943) and in liberation of Paris (1944).

Lecompton (lùkŏmp'tùn), city (pop. 263), NE Kansas, on Kansas R. and E of Topeka. Territorial cap. 1855–58. Here was formulated proslavery **Lecompton Constitution.** Slavery clause was approved in Dec., 1857, as Free State men declined to vote. Pres. Buchanan urged Congress to admit Kansas under this constitution, but bill could not pass the House. Submitted to popular vote, constitution was decisively rejected in Aug., 1858.

Leconte de Lisle, Charles (shärl' lŭkôt' dü lēl'), 1818–94, French poet, the leading Parnassian. A pessimist, he saw death as only reality and drew inspiration from antiquity, as in *Poèmes antiques* (1852), *Poésies barbares* (1862), and *Poèmes tragiques* (1884).

Le Corbusier (lù kôrbüzyä'), pseud. of Charles Édouard Jeanneret, 1887–, Swiss architect. His first experimental studies (1915) showed a new and radical attitude toward technical and aesthetic problems of building. His famous "Citrohan" model for dwellings (1921) expressed new construction methods. Exerted wide influence on modern architecture by his writings. A prize winner in competition (1927) for Geneva palace of League of Nations, he was chosen in 1946 as one of group of architects to design UN headquarters in New York.

Lecouvreur, Adrienne (ädrēĕn' lŭkōŏvrûr'), 1692–1730, French actress. After her debut in 1717, she was the idol of the public until her mysterious death. Her romance with Maurice de Saxe was tragic.

Leda (lē'dù), in Greek mythology, wife of Tyndareus, king of Sparta, and by him mother of Clytemnestra. In one legend, Zeus visited Leda as swan, and she bore two eggs; from one issued Helen and from the other came Castor and Pollux.

Ledo Road: see BURMA ROAD.

Ledru-Rollin, Alexandre Auguste (älĕksä'drü ōgüst' lùdrü'-rôlē'), 1807–74, French politician. An active promoter of the FEBRUARY REVOLUTION of 1848, he was minister of the interior in Lamartine's government and introduced universal suffrage. Passing to the opposition after the JUNE DAYS, he formed the Social Democratic party but was soon after forced to flee to England (1849).

Ledyard, John (lĕd'yùrd), 1751–89, American adventurer. Failed to secure funds in U.S. or France for expedition to find Northwest Passage. Attempted to walk across Europe and through Siberia; arrested at Yakutsk and sent back.

Lee, Virginia family, of which Robert E. LEE was most distinguished member. **Richard Lee,** d. 1664, American colonist, b. England, was the founder of the Lee family of Va. **Arthur Lee,** 1740–92, was an American Revolutionary diplomat, agent of Continental Congress to secure French aid. Recalled after quarrel with Silas Deane. His brother, **Francis Lightfoot Lee,** 1734–97, served in Continental Congress (1775–80) and signed Declaration of Independence. Another brother, **Richard Henry Lee**, 1732–94, also served in Continental Congress (1774–80, 1784–87) and signed Declaration of Independence. U.S. Senator (1789–92). A fourth brother, **William Lee**, 1739–95, diplomatic agent of Continental Congress, was unable to obtain support from Austria or Prussia. Unofficial U.S.-Dutch treaty he helped draft became cause of war between Great Britain and the Netherlands. **Henry Lee**, 1756–1818, American Revolutionary cavalry general, usually known as Light-Horse Harry Lee, was a cousin of these four brothers and father of Robert E. Lee.

Lee, Ann, 1736–84, religious visionary, founder of SHAKERS in America, b. England. She formed (1776) first Shaker settlement at present Watervliet, N.Y.

Lee, Arthur: see LEE, family.

Lee, Charles, 1731–82, American Revolutionary general, b. England. Settled in Va. (1773). Traitorously aided British when captured in 1776. Later exchanged, but court-martialed for disobedience at battle of Monmouth (1778). Criticism of Washington led to dismissal (1780).

Lee, Fitzhugh: see LEE, ROBERT E.

Lee, Francis Lightfoot: see LEE, family.

Lee, George Washington Custis: see LEE, ROBERT E.

Lee, Henry: see LEE, family.

Lee, Jason, 1803–45, American pioneer in Oregon, a Methodist missionary. Missions founded by him and his associates were centers of settlement.

Lee, John Doyle, 1812–77, American Mormon leader. Executed for leading massacre (1857) at MOUNTAIN MEADOWS.

Lee, Light-Horse Harry: see LEE, family.

Lee, Nathaniel, 1653?–1692, English dramatist. He wrote poetic tragedies with classical backgrounds, notably *The Rival Queens* (1677).

Lee, Richard, and **Richard Henry Lee:** see LEE, family.

Lee, Robert E(dward), 1807–70, general in chief of Confederate armies in Civil War; son of Henry Lee. Superintendent of West Point (1852–55). Though he loved the Union and the army, he was loyal to Va. when it seceded. Became military adviser to Jefferson Davis and, from June 1, 1862, commander of Army of Northern Virginia. He checked G. B. McClellan's threat to Richmond in SEVEN DAYS BATTLES (June 26 –July 2), and defeated John Pope in second battle of Bull Run (Aug. 29–30). McClellan, however, checked his first Northern invasion, ANTIETAM CAMPAIGN (Sept.). He defeated A. E. Burnside at Fredericksburg (Dec. 13, 1862), and Joseph Hooker at CHANCELLORS-VILLE (May 2–4, 1863). Assumed full blame for failure of GETTYSBURG CAMPAIGN. In 1864 he repulsed U. S. Grant's attacks in WILDERNESS CAMPAIGN, but could not prevent long siege of Petersburg. Appointed general in chief, Feb., 1865. Surrendered to Grant at Appomattox Courthouse, April 9, 1865. After war he was president of Washington Col. (now Washington and Lee Univ.). A great commander, a man of exalted character, Lee was idolized by South and has become an American hero. His son, **George Washington Custis Lee**, 1832–1913, was a Confederate general. Succeeded his father as president of Washington and Lee Univ. (1871–97). Another son, **William Henry Fitzhugh Lee**, known as Rooney Lee, 1837–91, was a Confederate cavalry general. Served creditably under J. E. B. Stuart. **Fitzhugh Lee**, 1835–1905, Confederate cavalry general, was a nephew of R. E. Lee. Brilliantly covered retreat from Antietam campaign.

Lee, Sir Sidney, 1859–1926, English editor of *Dictionary of National Biography*.

Lee, William: see LEE, family.

Lee, William Henry Fitzhugh: see LEE, ROBERT E.

Leech, John, 1817–64, English caricaturist and illustrator, associated mainly with *Punch* magazine.

leech, annelid worm, round or slightly flattened, with segments externally divided by secondary rings, and a suction disk at each end of the body. Leeches live chiefly in fresh water (a few on land and in sea) in temperate and tropical regions. Most are bloodsuck-

ers. Leech of genus *Hirudo* was formerly much used by physicians to bleed patients.

leechee: see LITCHI.

Leech Lake, large lake, N central Minn., SE of Bemidji and lying mainly within Leech Lake Indian Reservation. Used as reservoir.

Leeds, county borough (pop. 504,954) and city, W. Riding of Yorkshire, England; center of industrial district (to W and S) and important transportation junction. Has mfg. of woolen and metal goods, chemicals, and glass. Yorkshire Col. (1874) became Univ. of Leeds in 1904. Triennial music festivals are held. Near-by Kirkstall Abbey founded 1152.

leek, hardy garden vegetable (*Allium porrum*), closely related to onion. Leafstalk and basal leaves, which have a mild onion flavor, are blanched and served like asparagus, or used in soups and stews. Its leaves are worn by the Welsh on St. David's day.

Lee Mansion National Memorial, N Va., across Potomac R. from Washington, D.C., in Arlington Natl. Cemetery. As Arlington House was home of R. E. Lee, inherited by his wife. Abandoned by Lees in Civil War; was used as field hospital after first battle of Bull Run. Made memorial 1925.

Leesburg, city (pop. 7,395), N central Fla., between Harris and Griffin lakes. Head of navigation on Oklawaha R. system. Processes and ships fruit and truck.

Leeuwarden (lā'vär"dün), Frisian *Lieuwert*, municipality (pop. 72,008), cap. of Friesland prov., N Netherlands; chartered 1435. An agr. and dairying center, it is important cattle market. Has mfg. of clothing and artificial silk. It was gold- and silver-working center, 16th–18th cent.

Leeuwenhoek, Antony van (än'tōnē vän lā'vünhook"), 1632–1723, Dutch student of natural history. He made powerful lenses and simple microscopes and, using them, was first to see protozoa and bacteria; he gave first complete description of red blood cells.

Leeward Islands (loo'ürd, lū'ürd, lē'ürd), N group of Lesser Antilles in West Indies, extending SE from Puerto Rico to Windward Isls. Principal islands are VIRGIN ISLANDS of the U.S., GUADELOUPE (French), St. Eustatius and Saba (Dutch), SAINT MARTIN (jointly owned by Dutch and French) and British Leeward Isls. colony (ANTIGUA, SAINT KITTS, Nevis, Montserrat, and British Virgin Isls.). Discovered by Columbus (1493). A long contest between England, France, and Spain for possession was finally resolved at end of Napoleonic Wars (1815).

Le Fanu, (Joseph) Sheridan (lĕ'fŭnū), 1814–73, Irish novelist and journalist, known for tales of mystery and terror, notably *Uncle Silas* (1864).

Lefebvre, Jules Joseph (zhül' lüfĕ'vrü), 1836–1912, French figure painter, a popular teacher.

Lefkosha, Turkish name of NICOSIA, Cyprus.

Le Gallienne, Richard (lùgǎl'yŭn), 1866–1947, English literary critic, man of letters; a contributor to *Yellow Book*. Lived long in U.S. His daughter, **Eva Le Gallienne**, 1899–, American actress, producer, played in dramas by Molnar, Ibsen and others. Founded (1926) Civic Repertory Theatre and (1946, with Margaret Webster) American Repertory Theatre.

Legal Tender cases, lawsuits before U.S. Supreme Court testing Legal Tender Act of 1862. Passed to meet wartime currency needs, act authorized issue of greenbacks without any reserve or specie basis. Declared unconstitutional in 1870, act was held valid in 1871 and 1884.

Legaré, Hugh Swinton (lùgrē'), 1797–1843, American statesman. U.S. Attorney General (1841–43). A founder of *Southern Review;* its editor 1828–32.

Legaspi (lùgà'spē), town (pop. 15,780), on SE Luzon, Philippines; port on Albay Gulf.

Legendre, Adrien Marie (ädrēē' märē' lùzhà'drù), 1752–1833, French mathematician. He is noted for work on theory of numbers and elliptical integrals, and for the invention (independently of Gauss) of method of least squares. Collaborated in drawing up centesimal trigonometric tables. Wrote influential mathematical works.

Léger, Alexis Saint-Léger (ălĕksēs' sē-lāzhā' lāzhā'), pseud. **Saint-Jean Perse,** 1887–, French poet, statesman. He was Briand's aide and in 1933 became general secretary of ministry of foreign affairs. He is considered by many as greatest French poet of his age. His poetry includes *Éloges* (1910), *Anabase* (1924; Eng. tr. by T. S. Eliot, 1930), *Exil* (1942).

Léger, Fernand (fĕrnā' lāzhā'), 1881–, French painter. A modified cubist, he depicts the machine in dynamic style. Created two abstract designs for auditorium of UN General Assembly building, New York.

Leghorn (lĕg'hôrn), Ital. *Livorno,* city (pop. 109,067), Tuscany, central Italy; third largest port on Italian W coast. Seat of naval academy. Was developed in 16th cent. by the Medici; in 1590 Ferdinand I made it a free port and opened it to religious and political refugees. Damage in World War II includes cathedral and 16th-cent. synagogue.

legion, large unit of the Roman army. Varied in number (from 3,000 to 6,000 men in Caesar's time); divided into cohorts (in turn, divided into centuries). Primarily heavy infantry, the soldiers carried armor, weapons, provisions, and camping equipment. They accomplished the Roman conquests, but were finally vulnerable to highly mobile cavalry and guerrilla warfare of their enemies.

Legion of Honor: see DECORATIONS, CIVIL AND MILITARY.

legitimation, the act of giving a child born out of wedlock the status of legitimacy. Subsequent marriage of the parents is the general form in the U.S., though some states require special proceedings and in others one or both parents may adopt the child.

Legnano (lānyä'nō), city (pop. 31,959), N Italy, NW of Milan. Scene of defeat of Emperor Frederick I by Lombard League (1176).

Legros, Alphonse (älfôs' lügrō'), 1837–1911, French painter of religious subjects, portraits, and peasant scenes. Taught in London.

Leguiá, Augusto Bernardino (ougōōs'tō bĕrnārdē'nō lāgē'ä), 1863–1932, president of Peru (1908–12, 1919–30). His acceptance of Tacna-Arica compromise coupled with economic depression, his financial dealings, and his dictatorial rule caused his overthrow.

legume (lĕ'gūm), common name for pulse or pea family (Leguminosae) which contains plants of ornamental and economic value, e.g., peas, beans, clover, acacia, wisteria, lupine. Some legumes are used as green manure to increase nitrogen of the soil.

Lehar, Franz (lā'här), 1870–1948, composer of operettas, b. Komarno (then in Hungary); after 1889 he lived in Vienna. *The Merry Widow* (1905) was his outstanding success.

Lehi (lē'hī), place, SW Palestine, where Samson slew Philistines with jawbone of an ass. Judges 15.9–20.

Lehigh, river rising in NE Pa. and flowing 103 mi. S and W through coal and mfg. region to Delaware R. at Easton.

Lehighton, borough (pop. 6,565), E Pa., on Lehigh R. and NNW of Allentown. Textile mills.

Lehigh University, at Bethlehem, Pa.; nonsectarian, mainly for men; chartered and opened 1866.

Lehman, Herbert H(enry) (lē'mǔn), 1878–, American statesman. Notable Democratic governor of N.Y. (1932–42). U.S. Senator (1949–).

Lehman Caves National Monument: see NATIONAL PARKS AND MONUMENTS (table).

Lehmann, Lilli (lā'män), 1848–1929, German operatic soprano. Sang in the first Bayreuth Festival, 1876. Appeared at the Metropolitan Opera, New York, 1885–90. She was also a great lieder singer and a noted teacher.

Lehmann, Lotte, 1888–, German-American soprano. Made her American debut in Chicago as Sieglinde in *Die Walküre* in 1930. Appeared at the Metropolitan Opera, New York, 1934–46. As a concert artist, she was known for her singing of lieder.

Lehmbruck, Wilhelm (vĭl'hĕlm lām'brŏŏk), 1881–1919, German sculptor. His female nudes have a Gothic elongation.

Leibl, Wilhelm (vĭl'hĕlm lī'bŭl), 1844–1900, German genre and portrait painter. Lived most of his life as a Bavarian peasant. Intensely realistic style.

Leibniz or **Leibnitz, Gottfried Wilhelm, Baron von** (līp'nĭts), 1646–1716, German philosopher and mathematician, who was also learned in science, history, and law. Served as a diplomat in service of archbishop of Mainz and was long in Paris. He developed the infinitesimal calculus (1675–76) without knowing of Newton's work in the field. Later he served the duke of Brunswick and became first president of the Prussian academy of science (he had suggested its founding). His philosophy—expressed in such works as *Monadology* (1714) and *Principles of Nature and Grace* (1714) and many letters and essays—rests fundamentally on the conception of the universe as made up of an infinite number of units of spiritual force or matter, which he called monads. These, being substance, cannot interact, but each reflects the universe in itself (thus making perception possible). There is a hierarchy of monads rising up to God, the supreme monad, who allows freedom of the will but still shapes the world as the best of all possible worlds.

Leicester, Robert Dudley, earl of (lĕ'stŭr), 1532?–1588, English courtier and favorite of Queen ELIZABETH. Involved in plot to place Lady Jane Grey upon throne, he was later pardoned. Elizabeth for a time thought of marrying him. Leader at court (from c.1564) of Puritan party which desired war with Spain, he commanded (1585–87) an unsuccessful expedition to the Low Countries.

Leicester, England: see LEICESTERSHIRE.

Leicester of Holkham, Thomas William Coke, earl of (kŏŏk, hōl'kùm), 1752–1842, English politician and agriculturist. For over 50 years he represented Norfolk in Parliament. His improvement of breeds of livestock and development of his estate led to more scientific farming.

Leicestershire (lĕ'stŭrshĭr) or **Leicester** (lĕs'tŭr), inland county (832 sq. mi.; pop. 630,893), central England. Primarily agr. and pastoral county, it makes well-known Stilton cheese. Has famous fox-hunting centers. Defeat of Richard III by Henry VII at Bosworth (1485) ended Wars of the Roses. County town is **Leicester,** county borough (pop. 285,061), an ancient town with Roman and Norman remains. Richard III was buried here. Has ruins of abbey where Wolsey died. Long an industrial city; manufactures include shoes and hosiery.

Leiden or **Leyden** (both: lī'dùn), municipality (pop. 86,-914), South Holland prov., W Netherlands, on Old Rhine R., NE of The Hague. Though mfg. of textiles (since Middle Ages) and machinery are important, it is famed chiefly for its university (founded 1575), oldest in the Netherlands. Univ. of Leiden was center of Protestant theological learning and of science and medicine in 17th and 18th cent. LEYDEN JAR was invented here. ELZEVIR family made Leiden a printing center after 1580. Leiden dates from Roman times. In 1574 it was saved from surrender to the Spanish when William the Silent ordered dikes cut to flood surrounding land, thus enabling GUEUX fleet to sail to its relief. Home of many of the Pilgrims before 1620. Birthplace of Rembrandt and Jan Steen. Landmarks include the Hoglandsche Kerk (15th cent.) and the Pieterskerk (14th cent.).

Leif Ericsson (lēf'), fl. 1000, Norse discoverer of America, b. probably in Iceland; son of ERIC THE RED. One old Norse saga (the more widely accepted) says discovery was accidental, but another says he voyaged W from Greenland intentionally, then wintered at VINLAND.

Leighton, Clare (lā'tùn), 1899–, English print maker and illustrator. Known for woodcuts and engravings.

Leighton, Frederick Leighton, Baron, 1830–96, English painter. His popular pictures generally depicted subjects taken from antiquity.

Leighton, Robert, 1611–84, Scottish prelate. A noted Presbyterian preacher, he signed Covenant (1643). He accepted (1661) bishopric of Dunblane and sought a basis for union of Presbyterianism and episcopacy.

Leinster (lĕn'stŭr, lĭn'–), province (7,580 sq. mi.; pop. 1,281,117), Ireland, comprising counties of Carlow, Dublin, Kildare, Kilkenny, Laoighis, Longford, Louth, Meath, Offaly, Westmeath, Wexford, and Wicklow. Most populous and fertile of provinces, it constitutes most of central Irish plain.

Leipzig (līp'sĭg, Ger. līp'tsīkh), city (pop. 607,655), largest city of Saxony, E Germany, on Pleisse R., in Russian zone of occupation. A major commercial, industrial, and cultural center, it was until World War II the center of German book and music publishing and of the European fur trade. It has mfg. of textiles, steel, machinery, and chemicals and two great yearly industrial fairs. Its famous university was founded 1409. Chartered 1174, Leipzig soon rose to commercial importance. Leibniz and Richard Wagner were born at Leipzig; J. S. Bach was cantor of the Church of St. Thomas, 1723–50; Mendelssohn made the Gewandhaus concerts (begun 1743 in a former guildhouse) internationally famous; the Leipzig conservatory of music achieved world fame. City was heavily damaged in World War II. Among damaged buildings are the Church of St. Thomas and the former supreme court of Germany. Other landmarks include 13th-cent. Pauline church; Auerbach's Keller, an inn made famous by Goethe's *Faust;* the stock exchange (1682); the 17th-cent. Church of St. John (with Bach's tomb); and Wagner's house of birth. The **battle of Leipzig,** Oct. 16–19, 1813, also called Battle of the Nations, was a decisive allied victory over Napoleon I. During the battle most of Napoleon's German auxiliary forces went over to the allies. A large monument commemorates the battle, which cost c.120,000 casualties.

Leiria (lārē'ù), city (pop. 7,208), SW Portugal, in Estremadura. It played a prominent part in history of medieval Portugal. Its castle, built 12th cent., dominates city from a cliff.

Leisler, Jacob (lī'slŭr), 1640–91, leader of insurrection in colonial N.Y. (1689–91), b. Germany. A Protestant champion, he seized control of colony until captured by English forces and hanged.

Leith (lēth), former burgh (part of Edinburgh since 1920), Midlothian, Scotland, on S shore of Firth of Forth; Scotland's second largest seaport. Has fishing, fish curing, and varied mfg.

Leitha (lī'tä), Hung. *Lajta,* river, 112 mi. long, formed in E Austria by two headstreams and flowing NE and E to an arm of the Danube in NW Hungary. Historic boundary between Austria (Cisleithania) and Hungary (Transleithania).

Leitrim (lē'trĭm), county (589 sq. mi.; pop. 44,591), NW Ireland, in Connaught; Co. town Carrick-on-Shannon. Area is mountainous in N and level S of Lough Allen. Grazing and agr. are chief occupations, but soil and climate are poor.

Leix, county, Ireland: see LAOIGHIS.

Leixões (lāthō'ēsh), seaport of OPORTO, Portugal.

Lek (lĕk), navigable river, 40 mi. long, central Netherlands. It flows W from the Lower RHINE to the New Maas (see MEUSE). Crossed by Merwede Canal.

Lekain (lùkē'), 1728–78, French actor, whose real name was Henri Louis Cain. Protégé of Voltaire, he was one of the great tragic actors of his time. Used natural diction and costuming.

L. E. L.: see LANDON, LETITIA ELIZABETH.

Leland, Charles Godfrey: see BREITMANN, HANS.

Lely, Sir Peter (lē'lē), 1618–80, Dutch portrait painter. Real name was Pieter van der Faes. Succeeded Van Dyck as painter to the English court.

Leman, Lake: see GENEVA, Switzerland.

Le Mars (lù märz'), city (pop. 5,844), NW Iowa, on Floyd R. and NE of Sioux City. Agr. trade and mfg.

Lemberg, Ukraine: see LVOV.

Lemercier, Jacques (lùmĕrsyā'), c.1585–1654, French architect of the Renaissance. Designed many churches for the Jesuits. Built Richelieu's Paris residence (later transformed into Palais-Royal) and entire town of Richelieu in W central France.

lemming, rodent related to mouse. Common or brown lemming (genus *Lemmus*) of arctic and antarctic regions has long, brownish, grayish, or black fur. In periods of overpopulation and food scarcity lemmings, especially in Scandinavia, swarm overland, through water, despite obstacles, eating vegetation on way; if they reach sea before urge subsides they swim until drowned. Collared lemming (*Dicrostonyx*) of circumpolar range turns white in winter. Lemming mouse (*Synaptomys*) of North America is related form; species called bog lemming found S to NE U.S.

Lemnos (lĕm'nŏs), Aegean island (186 sq. mi.; pop. 23,842), Greece. Fishing, livestock, agr. Kastron is chief town and port. Sacred to Hephaestus in antiquity. After the fall of Constantinople (1204) during the Fourth Crusade, Lemnos became a Latin principate; belonged to Venice (1464–79), to Turkey (1479–1912).

lemon, citrus tree and its fruit (*Citrus limonia*) probably native to India. Unknown to Greeks and Romans, it was introduced in 12th or 13th cent. by Arabs into Spain; from there it reached Mediterranean basin and then spread into most tropical and subtropical regions. Lemons are an important crop in Calif. They are high in vitamins and are main source of commercial citric acid. Lemon oil is extracted from the skin.

lemon balm, perennial Eurasian herb (*Melissa officinalis*), naturalized in North America. Its lemon-flavored leaves are used as seasoning. It is sometimes called bee balm.

Lemonnier, Pierre Charles (pyĕr' shärl' lùmônyā'), 1715–99, French astronomer. He is especially noted for studies of moon, terrestrial magnetism, and atmospheric electricity.

Lemoyne, residential borough (pop. 4,605), SE Pa., on Susquehanna R. opposite Harrisburg. Northernmost point of Confederate advance, 1863.

lemur (lē'mùr), primitive Old World arboreal primate with a foxlike muzzle and huge eyes. Tails, if present, are frequently long and bushy. Usually lemurs are gregarious and many are chiefly nocturnal. They eat insects, fruits, small birds, eggs, lizards. True lemur is confined to Madagascar and neighboring islands. Related animals are galagos ("bush baby") of S Africa, African potto, Oriental slow loris and slender loris, indri or endrina, sifaka, mouse lemur, and aye-aye of Madagascar. The tarsier is usually considered intermediate between lemur and New World monkey.

Lena (lē'nù), river in RSFSR, the easternmost and longest (2,648 mi.) of Siberia. Rising near L. Baikal, it flows NE, then NW to empty through 150-mile-wide delta into Laptev Sea. Navigable for 2,135 mi. Coal, oil, and gold are found along its course.

Le Nain (lù nē'), family of French painters consisting of three brothers: **Antoine Le Nain** (ätwän'), 1588?–1648, **Louis Le Nain** (lwē), 1593?–1648, and **Mathieu Le Nain** (mätyû'), 1607–77. They came to Paris from Laon c.1629. Collaborated in much of their work, which portrayed humble people in everyday settings, as in *Mendicants* (Metropolitan Mus.).

Lenape: see DELAWARE INDIANS.

Lenard, Philipp Eduard Anton (fē'lĭp ā'dŏŏärt än'tōn lā'närt), 1862–1947, German physicist. Won 1905 Nobel Prize for research on cathode rays.

Lenau, Nikolaus (nē'kōlous lā'nou), pseud. of Nikolaus Niembsch von Strehlenau, 1802–50, German romantic poet, b. near Timisoara (then in Hungary). His lyrics, imbued with melancholy and pessimism, and his epic *Faust* (1836) are his best-known works. He became insane in 1844.

Lenbach, Franz von (fränts' fŭn län'bäkh), 1836–1904, German portrait painter, eminent in his day.

Lenclos, Ninon de (nēnō' dù läklō'), b. 1620?, d. 1705

or 1706, French beauty and wit. Her salon at Paris gathered many famous figures of her time. The Great Condé, La Rochefoucauld, and Saint-Évremont were among her many lovers.

lend-lease. Lend-Lease Act, passed by U.S. Congress (1941), gave President power to sell, transfer, lend, or lease necessary war supplies to nations whose defense was vital to U.S. in World War II. By end of war most of United Nations had been declared eligible for lend-lease aid, though not all demanded or received it. Certain countries (e.g., Great Britain, Belgium) provided "reverse lend-lease" to American forces overseas. End of lend-lease aid was announced Aug. 31, 1945. Total aid given exceeded $50,600,000,000.

L'Enfant, Pierre Charles (pyĕr' shärl' läfä'), 1754–1825, American architect, b. France. Volunteered as a private in American Revolution. His plans for capital at Washington were rejected in 1792, but in 1901 were used as basis for city's development.

Lenglen, Suzanne (süzän' läglĕn'), 1899–1938, French tennis player. French women's singles champion (1920–23; 1925–26); British women's singles champion (1919–23; 1925).

Lenin, Vladimir Ilyich (lĕ'nĭn, Rus. vlŭdyē'mĭr ĭl'yĕch lyĕ'nĭn), 1870–1924, Russian revolutionist, founder of Soviet Russia; b. Simbirsk (now Ulyanovsk) as V. I. Ulyanov, the son of a school official. Studied law at Kazan and St. Petersburg but gave up legal practice to turn to the study of Marx and to revolutionary activities; was twice exiled to Siberia. He left Russia in 1900; in 1903, at London, he brought about split of Russian Social Democratic party into BOLSHEVISM AND MENSHEVISM. Back in Russia in 1905–7, he was responsible for the participation of the Bolsheviks in the imperial Duma. In Switzerland during World War I, Lenin, denouncing imperialism as the last stage of capitalism, called on the proletariat to oppose the imperialist war by a world-wide struggle against all capitalism. After the outbreak of the RUSSIAN REVOLUTION (Feb., 1917) the German government helped Lenin to return to Russia, in the correct assumption that he would disrupt the Russian war effort. In Nov., 1917, Lenin overthrew the Kerensky government, became chairman of the Council of People's Commissars, and estab. the "dictatorship of the proletariat." He saw the revolution through to victory in the civil war of 1918–20; the UNION OF SOVIET SOCIALIST REPUBLICS was founded. In 1921 he introduced the NEW ECONOMIC POLICY as an expedient to raise Russia from economic ruin. The COMINTERN (founded 1919) was largely his creation. As chairman of the Communist party and of the Council of People's Commissars, he ruled as virtual dictator. His death opened a contest for his succession from which Stalin emerged victorious. His mausoleum in the Red Square at Moscow is a Communist shrine. His elaboration of Marxism, called Leninism, has as its main features his analysis of imperialism; his insistence on the necessity of a strongly organized and disciplined Communist party to prepare and guide the proletarian revolution; his uncompromising atheism; and his willingness to resort to opportunism (though he remained dogmatically opposed to gradualist compromise or to any revision of Marxist doctrine). Regarded by Stalinists and Trotskyites alike as the liberator of the proletariat, he is considered by other Socialists as a despot who betrayed and enslaved the working class. His writings and speeches have been translated into English.

Leningrad (lĕ'nĭngrăd), second largest city (pop. 3,191,-304) of USSR, in RSFSR, at S end of Karelian Isthmus; former cap. of Russia. Named St. Petersburg until 1914, Petrograd 1914–24. Its founder, Peter the Great, ordered (1703) his new capital, "a window looking on Europe," built on newly conquered delta through which the NEVA enters Gulf of Finland. Italian and French architects planned a spacious city of classical beauty, which became a brilliant international, cultural, and social center. It also had become the chief industrial center of Russia, with large armament plants, when St. Petersburg workers precipitated the 1905 revolution and carried out Russian Revolution of 1917. Moscow replaced it as cap. in 1918. In the course of World War II Leningrad, protected by KRONSTADT, withstood a two-year German siege (1941–43). Principal thoroughfare of the city is Nevsky Prospekt, where points of interest include Winter Palace, HERMITAGE mus., and Falconet's equestrian statue of Peter the Great. Among other notable sites are the university (founded 1819) and fortress of SS. Peter and Paul (city's oldest building). Leningrad is the principal port and foremost machine- and electrical-goods mfg. center of USSR. Suburbs include PUSHKIN, with the Summer Palace, and former imperial residences of PETERHOF and GATCHINA.

Lenin Peak, 23,382 ft. high, Tadzhik SSR, in Trans-Alai range in central Asia; second-highest point in USSR. Formerly called Kaufmann Peak.

Lenni-Lenape: see DELAWARE INDIANS.

Lennox, Matthew Stuart or **Stewart,** 4th **earl of,** 1516–71, Scottish nobleman. Leader of the Catholic nobles, he married his son, Lord DARNLEY, to Mary Queen of Scots. Became regent (1570), but queen's party declared war against him and he was killed.

Lennox, Fort: see ÎLE-AUX-NOIX, FORT.

Lennoxville, town (pop. 2,895), SE Que., Canada, on St. Francis and Massawippi rivers and E of Sherbrooke. Seat of Univ. of Bishop's Col. (Anglican; coed.; 1843).

Lenoir (lùnôr'), town (pop. 7,888), W N.C., in Blue Ridge foothills. Resort with furniture mfg.

Lenoir City, industrial city (pop. 5,159), E Tenn., SW of Knoxville and on Tennessee R., in timber and farm area. Fort Loudon Dam near.

Lenoir Rhyne College: see HICKORY, N.C.

Lenôtre or **Le Nôtre, André** (ädrä' lùnō'trù), 1613–1700, French landscape architect. His designs for formal gardens at Versailles and Fontainebleau exerted wide influence.

Lenox, James, 1800–1880, American bibliophile and philanthropist. His fine collection of paintings and books in Lenox Library (now part of New York Public Library).

Lenox, resort town (pop. 3,627), W Mass., in the Berkshires S of Pittsfield. Scene of annual BERKSHIRE SYMPHONIC FESTIVAL at "Tanglewood," former estate, mainly in adjoining Stockbridge town; estate has Hawthorne's cottage (burned 1890; rebuilt, dedicated as shrine 1948).

Lens (läs), town (pop. 34,134), Pas-de-Calais dept., N France. Industrial center in coal dist. French victory over imperials at Lens (1648) was last important battle of Thirty Years War.

lens, circular piece of glass with two curved surfaces or with one curved and the other plane. All light rays passing through lens are bent (by REFRACTION) except those that pass through optical center. Converging lenses bend emerging light rays inward and toward each other; such lenses (e.g. double convex and plano-convex) are thicker at the center than at edges. Diverging lens causes rays to be bent outward and away from each other; such lenses (e.g., double concave and plano-concave) are thicker at the edges than at the center. Each curved surface of lens is considered part of the surface of a sphere; the center of that sphere is called center of curvature. Line through optical center connecting centers of curvature is principal axis. The distance from the principal focus to optical center is called focal length. Aberration is the phenomenon of an inexact focus. IMAGE formed by lens varies according to curvature of the surfaces. Devices in which lenses are used include CAMERA, MICROSCOPE, SEARCHLIGHT, SPECTACLES, STEREOSCOPE, TELESCOPE.

Lent [Old Eng.,= spring], Latin *Quadragesima,* Christian period of fasting and penitence preparatory to Easter. In the West, penitential season begins with Septuagesima, ninth Sunday before Easter. Lent begins on Ash Wednesday, 40th weekday prior to Easter, and ends at noon on Holy Saturday, the day before Easter. The last week of Lent is Holy Week.

lentil, leguminous Old World annual plant (*Lens esculenta*) grown for its beanlike seeds, also called lentils. It has long been a staple food.

Lenz, Jakob (yä′kôp lĕnts′), 1751–92, German author of the STURM UND DRANG period. He befriended Goethe at Strasbourg but later lampooned him; died in poverty and insanity. Wrote plays of social criticism (*Der Hofmeister,* 1774; *Die Soldaten,* 1776) and poetry which suggests his inner conflict.

Leo I, Saint (the Great), c.400–461, pope (440–61), Doctor of the Church; one of greatest early pontiffs. With aid of Valentinian III fought Manichaeism in Italy. Subduing St. Hilary of Arles, he confirmed the authority of pope over bishops. In Nestorian-Monophysite controversy he wrote the celebrated *Tome of Leo* on natures of Christ, later adopted at Council of CHALCEDON. Persuaded ATTILA (452) and his Huns not to sack Rome. Feast: April 11.

Leo III, Saint, d. 816, pope (795–816). He was attacked by family of his predecessor, ADRIAN I, who hoped to render him unfit for the papacy. He recovered and fled to Charlemagne, who came to Rome, where he was crowned. Leo worked to unite East and West and did much to beautify Rome.

Leo IX, Saint, 1002–54, pope (1049-54). A relative of Emperor Conrad II, educated and made bishop (1027) at Toul. Initiated reform of clergy in which chief figure was Hildebrand (later GREGORY VII). The heresy of BERENGAR OF TOURS also occupied the pope. Leo was defeated at Civitella (1053) by the Normans of S Italy. Michael Cerularius, patriarch of Constantinople, attacked the pope (1042), and Leo excommunicated him (1054)—an act that began the formal schism of East and West.

Leo X, 1475–1521, pope (1513–21) (Giovanni de′ Medici). Son of Lorenzo de′ MEDICI, he was made a cardinal in boyhood and was head of the family before he was 30. His chief fame rests on his patronage of RAPHAEL, continuation of St. Peter's by Bramante, and on his literary circle. Fifth LATERAN COUNCIL failed to effect desired reforms and the Protestant REFORMATION began when Martin LUTHER posted his theses (1517). Leo excommunicated the reformers (1520) but did not give the crisis much attention.

Leo XIII, 1810–1903, pope (1878–1903), an Italian named Gioacchino Pecci. He devoted himself to forming Catholic attitudes appropriate to the modern world and issued several encyclicals to that end. *Immortale Dei* (1885) charted the course for Catholics as responsible citizens in modern democratic states. *Rerum novarum* (1891), one of the most important of all encyclicals, outlined Catholic social ideals, pointing to the abuses of capitalism and the deficiencies of Marxism. To meet intellectual attacks on the Church he declared the philosophy of St. Thomas Aquinas official and founded the Inst. of Thomistic Philosophy at Louvain. In his reign the KULTURKAMPF was ended in Germany with a victory for the Church (1887).

Leo, Byzantine emperors. **Leo I** (the Great or the Thracian), d. 474, reigned 457–74. Broke the power of the Germans in the Roman army but failed in a naval expedition against Vandals (468). **Leo III** (the Isaurian), c.680–740, reigned 717–40. He checked the Arabs (717–18) and reorganized the empire. His civil code, the *Ecloga,* is characterized by Christian feeling. Popes Gregory II and Gregory III opposed his ICONOCLASM and defied his expeditions against Rome. **Leo V** (the Armenian), d. 820, reigned 813–20. Reviving iconoclasm, he deposed the patriarch Nicephorus (815) and persecuted Theodore of Studium. He was murdered. **Leo VI** (the Wise or the Philosopher), 862?–912, reigned 886–912. His accession forced the resignation of PHOTIUS. His *Basilica,* a modernization of the law of Justinian I, was published 887–93 and

was intended to supersede the *Ecloga* of Leo III.

Leo (lē′ō) [Latin,= lion], fifth sign of ZODIAC.

Leo Africanus, early 16th cent., Moorish traveler in Africa and near East. Wrote description of African journeys, long only known source on Sudan.

Leoben (lāō′bŭn), city (pop. 35,785), Styria, S central Austria, on Mur R. Industrial center of coal-mining area. Armistice preliminary to Treaty of CAMPO FORMIO was signed here 1797.

Leochares (lēō′kŭrēz), 4th cent. B.C., Greek sculptor. Possibly the creator of *Apollo Belvedere* (Vatican).

Leominster (lĕ′mĭnstŭr), city (pop. 24,075), N Mass., N of Worcester. Plastics and machinery.

León, Juan Ponce de: see PONCE DE LEÓN, JUAN.

León, Luis Ponce de (lwēs′ pōn′thä dā lāōn′), 1527?–1591, Spanish lyric poet, monk and mystic. He translated the Song of Songs, wrote notable odes and some prose works.

León (lāōn′), city (pop. 74,155), Guanajuato, central Mexico; founded 1576. Once the second largest city in Mexico, it is still an agr. and mining center, with some mfg. (leather goods, fabrics).

León (lāōn′), city (pop. 31,008), NW Nicaragua, second largest city of republic; founded 1524 on L. Managua; moved (1610) after earthquake. Stronghold of liberal forces after independence from Spain (1821), it was the rival of Granada. Now trade center of agr. area.

Leon (lē′ŏn), Span. *León,* region and former kingdom (20,594 sq. mi.; pop. 1,732,082), NW Spain, bordering on Portugal. Chief cities: Leon, Palencia, Salamanca, Valladolid, Zamora. Mostly a dry plateau crossed by the Duero. Cantabrian Mts. in N have coal mines, forests, minerals. Conquered from the Moors by the kings of Asturias (8th–9th cent.), the region became the kingdom of Leon and Asturias. It was twice united with the neighboring kingdom of Castile (1037–65, under Ferdinand I of Castile; 1072–1157, under Alfonso VI, Urraca, and Alfonso VII) before a permanent union was effected by Ferdinand III (1230). Its historic cap., Leon (pop. 43,260), is an agr. and commercial center dating from Roman times. Conquered from Moors 882, it replaced Oviedo as cap. in 10th cent.; declined when Valladolid became favorite royal residence. Among its many ancient buildings is the Gothic cathedral (13th–14th cent.).

Leonardo da Pisa: see FIBONACCI, LEONARDO.

Leonardo da Vinci (lēōnär′dō dä vēn′chē), 1452–1519, Italian artist and scientist, the supreme example of Renaissance genius, b. Vinci. The natural son of a Florentine notary and a peasant girl, he was apprenticed in 1466 to Verrocchio in Florence. The unfinished *Adoration of the Magi* (Uffizi), painted in 1481, shows his early mastery of dramatic chiaroscuro. Went to Milan c.1482, became court artist to Lodovico Sforza. While in Milan he wrote his *Trattato della pittura,* began his notebooks (dealing with problems of hydraulics, mechanics, anatomy, geology, and botany), and with the help of his pupil Ambrogio de Predis painted the *Madonna of the Rocks* (2 versions: Louvre and Natl. Gall., London). Also of this period is the *Last Supper* fresco (Milan). Returned to Florence 1500 and served Cesare Borgia as military engineer, and painted the *Mona Lisa* (Louvre). Back in Milan (1506–13) he served the French king Louis XII as architect and engineer, while continuing his activities as painter, sculptor, and teacher; here he did *St. Anne, Mary and the Child* (Louvre). From 1513 to c.1515 he worked for Pope Leo X in Rome, where he did the young *St. John the Baptist* (Louvre). Invited by Francis I, he went to France, where for the rest of his life he was left free to conduct research.

Leoncavallo, Ruggiero (rōōd-jä′rō lä″ōn-kävä′lō), 1858–1919, Italian composer. He wrote several operas and songs (e.g., *Mattinata*), but his opera *Pagliacci* (1892) was his one outstanding success.

Leonia (lēō′nyù), borough (pop. 7,378), NE N.J., near W approach to George Washington Bridge.

Leonidas (lēō′nĭdùs), d. 480 B.C., king of Sparta. When

the Persians invaded Greece under Xerxes (480), he and his men held the pass at THERMOPYLAE and were all killed.

Leonov, Leonid (lyäûnyēt' lyâô'nŭf), 1899–, Russian novelist of psychological and social realism. Among his novels in praise of Soviet policies are *The Thief* (1927), *Sot* (1930), *The Road to the Ocean* (1935), and *Chariot of Wrath* (1944).

leopard, mammal of cat family (genus *Panthera,* or, in some classifications, *Felis*) found in Africa and Asia. It is also called panther or pard. It has thick fur, the ground color yellow-buff, rusty, or gray, patterned with black rosettes. Black leopard often occurs in litter of normal color. Snow leopard, irbis, or ounce lives at high altitudes in Tibet and Himalayas. Leopards prey on monkeys, dogs, other mammals, and birds and reptiles.

Leopardi, Giacomo, Conte (jä'kōmō kōn'tä läōpär'dē), 1798–1837, Italian poet. He wrote lyric poetry that ranks with Petrarch's and prose unequaled in Italian for simplicity and purity. His lyrics express agnosticism and pessimism. His prose works show tender wit and irony.

Leopold, emperors (also kings of Bohemia and Hungary). **Leopold I,** 1640–1705. The salient events of his reign (1658–75) were his wars with Louis XIV of France; the rebellion of THOKOLY (1678); the Turkish siege of VIENNA (1683); and the victorious Treaty of KARLOWITZ with Turkey (1699). He was fortunate in having such able generals as Montecuccoli, Charles V of Lorraine, and Eugene of Savoy. **Leopold II,** 1747–92, as Leopold I grand duke of Tuscany (1765–90), succeeded his brother JOSEPH II as emperor in 1790. Though he had proved himself an able reformer in Tuscany, he was obliged to revoke most of his brother's reforms to pacify his Hungarian, Bohemian, and Belgian subjects. He was the last crowned king of Bohemia. In 1791, to aid his brother-in-law, Louis XVI of France, he instigated the Declaration of Pillnitz, which helped precipitate the FRENCH REVOLUTIONARY WARS a few weeks after his death.

Leopold, kings of the Belgians. **Leopold I,** 1790–1865, third son of Francis Frederick, duke of Saxe-Coburg-Saalfeld, was elected king of newly formed Belgium in 1831. Called "Uncle of Europe," he was the husband of Princess Charlotte (daughter of George IV of England); brought about marriage of his niece, Queen Victoria, with his nephew, Prince Albert. **Leopold II,** 1835–1909. His reign (1865–1909) was one of industrial and colonial expansion (see BELGIAN CONGO). Notorious for his ruthless greed and his dissolute private life. **Leopold III,** 1901–, succeeded his father Albert I in 1934. Lost his wife, Queen Astrid (a Swedish princess) in an automobile accident (1935). In 1936 he announced that Belgium would remain neutral in any armed conflict. In World War II, after Germany invaded Belgium (May, 1940), he led Belgian resistance but on May 28 he surrendered his armies to Germany, despite the opposition of his ministers. He was held a prisoner of war by the Germans, first at his castle at Laken, after 1944 in Germany. Accusations of treason and collaboration with Germany prevented his return to Belgium until 1950 and embittered Belgian postwar politics. In 1951 he abdicated in favor of his son Baudouin. In 1941 he had married a commoner, whom he later created princess of Réthy.

Leopold I, 1676–1747, prince of Anhalt-Dessau (1693–1747). As field marshal in the Prussian army he organized infantry under Frederick William I and distinguished himself under Frederick II.

Leopoldville, city (pop. c.137,000), cap. of Belgian Congo, on Congo R. Founded 1887 by Henry Stanley, named for Belgian king, Leopold II. Main base of navigation on the Congo.

Leovigild (lēō'vĭgĭld"), d. 586, Visigothic king of Spain (568–86). Made notable additions to Visigothic laws.

Lepage, Jules Bastien-: see BASTIEN-LEPAGE, JULES.

Lepanto, battle of (lĭpăn'tō), Oct. 7, 1571, naval battle fought off Lepanto (see NAUPAKTOS), Greece, between fleet of the Holy League, commanded by JOHN OF AUSTRIA, and Turkish fleet, commanded by Ochiali Pasha. Allies (mostly Spanish, Venetian, and papal ships) virtually destroyed Turkish fleet, captured or killed c.15,000 Turks, liberated c.10,000 Christian galley slaves. Among allied wounded was Cervantes. Allied victory ended threat of Turkish naval supremacy in Mediterranean.

lepidodendron (lĕ"pĭdōdĕn'drŭn), extinct tree, genus *Lepidodendron,* many species of which flourished in the Carboniferous period. They grew to heights of 50–100 ft., with diameter of 4–6 ft.

Lepidus (lĕ'pĭdŭs), family of anc. Rom. **Marcus Aemilius Lepidus** (ēmĭ'lēŭs), d. 77 B.C., raised an army to challenge the senatorial leader, CATULUS, but was defeated. His son, **Marcus Aemilius Lepidus,** d. 13 B.C., was consul with Caesar (46 B.C.). With ANTONY and Octavian (AUGUSTUS) formed the Second Triumvirate. After victory at Philippi he governed Africa and conquered Sicily, but Augustus later deprived him of his offices.

leprosy, infectious disease caused by a bacterium. Lepromatous or cutaneous form is marked by hard, nodular swellings in skin and mucous membranes of throat, nose, eyes. In the neural type, less acute, germs accumulate in nerves and cause partial loss of sensation. It is transmitted chiefly by close contact with patient for months or years. Incubation period commonly is 5–20 years. Most prevalent in tropics and subtropics; endemic in parts of Fla., Texas, La. In U.S. patients are treated at National Leprosarium, Carville, La. Disease is ancient; segregation laws date from c.7th cent.

Lerdo de Tejada, Miguel (mēgēl' lĕr'dhō dä tähä'dhä), d. 1861, Mexican liberal statesman, a leader of the Revolution of Ayutla. Initiated Ley Lerdo (1856), which provided for forced sale of all real property of Catholic Church. His younger brother, **Sebastián Lerdo de Tejada** (sävästyän'), 1820?–1889, was also an important liberal in Revolution of Ayutla. After the death of Júarez, he served as provisional president (1872–76) and was driven from office by Porfirio Díaz.

Lérida (lā'rēdhä), city (pop. 35,061), cap. of Lérida prov., NE Spain, in Catalonia, on Segre R. Center of fertile agr. region. Ancient Ilerda, it was scene of Caesar's victory over Pompey's generals (49 B.C.). Held by Moors A.D. 714–1149. Seat of a university c.1300–1717. A key defense point for Barcelona in civil war of 1936–39, it fell to Insurgents 1938. Has medieval castle, Romanesque cathedral.

Lerma, Francisco Gómez de Sandoval y Rojas, duque de (fränthēs'kō gō'mĕth dä sändōväl' ē rō'häs dōō'kä dä lĕr'mä), 1552?–1625, chief minister of Philip III of Spain from 1598 to 1618. His corruption led to his downfall. Was later compelled to give up part of wealth he had appropriated in connection with expulsion of Moriscos (1609).

Lermontov, Mikhail Yurevich (mēkhüyēl' yōōr'yĭvĭch lyĕr'mŭntŭf), 1814–41, Russian author. His masterpiece is the *The Demon* (1829–41; Eng. tr., 1930), an autobiographical poem laid in the Caucasus, where he spent much of his life. His novel *A Hero of Our Time* (1840; Eng. tr., 1928) foreshadows Gogol in its realism and its characteristic theme of frustration. Second only to Pushkin as a lyricist, he died, like Pushkin, in a duel.

Lerwick (lûr'wĭk, lĕ'rĭk), burgh (pop. 5,538), Mainland Isl., co. town of Shetland Isls., Scotland; most northerly town of British Isles.

Le Sage, Alain René (älĕ' rùnä' lù säzh'), 1668–1747, French author. *Turcaret* (1709), a comedy of character, satirizes the new plutocracy. His masterpiece is the classic *Gil Blas de Santillane* (1715–35; Eng. tr. by Tobias Smollett, 1749), a picaresque novel distinguished for its wit and realism.

Lesbos (lĕz'bŏs), Aegean island (632 sq. mi.; pop. 134,-054), Greece, off W Turkey, also called Mytilene; chief city Mytilene. Center of civilization in 7th cent.

SMALL CAPITALS = cross references. Pronunciation key on inside end pages. Abbreviations: p. 2.

B.C.; home of poets Sappho and Alcaeus. Joined Delian League and revolted unsuccessfully against Athens (428 B.C.). Aristotle and Epicurus lived here.

Lescarbot, Marc (lĕskärbō′), fl. 1599–1619, lawyer, poet, and historian of New France, b. France.

Lescaze, William (lĕskäz′), 1896–, American architect, born and trained in Switzerland.

Les Cheneaux Islands (lā shĕn′ō), group of 35 small islands, S of E Upper Peninsula, N.Mich., in L. Huron NE of Straits of Mackinac. Annual regatta.

Leschetizky, Theodor (lĕshŭtĭts′kē), 1830–1915, Polish pianist and teacher; pupil of Czerny. Among his pupils were Paderewski and Gabrilowitsch.

Lescot, Pierre (lĕskō′), c.1510–1578, French architect of early Renaissance. Beginning in 1546 he built earliest parts of the palace that later became the Louvre. All his known works have sculptural decoration by Jean Goujon.

lese majesty or **leze majesty** (both: lēz′ mă′jĭstē) [Latin *laesae maiestatis* (*crimen*) = (crime of) violating majesty], offense against the dignity of the sovereign or of a state. First appeared in Rome as offense against the state and, later, against the person of the emperor. Since the disappearance of absolute monarchy, the crime has tended to decline, although acts of TREASON are still criminal. In the U.S., attacks on public officials are protected by the right of free speech if not attended by threats of violence.

Lesina, Yugoslavia: see HVAR.

Leslie, Frank, 1821–80, American engraver and publisher of family periodicals, b. England. Real name was Henry Carter. Illustrations made by his artists on the battlefield in Civil War now have historical value. His second wife, **Miriam Florence (Folline) Leslie,** c.1836–1914, ably managed the business after his death. An ardent feminist, she wrote several books.

lespedeza, plant of genus *Lespedeza,* also called bush clover. Common lespedeza or Japanese clover (*Lespedeza striata*), an annual, is forage crop in S U.S. and a means of enriching soil and checking erosion. It grows to c.18 in., has branched stems, three-parted leaves, small pink or purplish flowers.

Lespinasse, Julie de (zhülē′ dü lĕspēnäs′), 1732–76, French woman of letters; niece of Mme DU DEFFAND. In 1764 she treacherously left her aunt's house to found her own literary salon, taking her friend D'Alembert and other lights along with her. Her letters to the comte de Guibert remain a classic chronicle of unhappy love (written 1773–76; Eng. trs., 1901, 1929).

Lesseps, Ferdinand Marie, vicomte de (fĕrdēnä′ märē′ vēkōt′ dü lĕsĕps′), 1805–94, French diplomat and engineer who planned and supervised Suez Canal and attempted Panama Canal.

Lesser Slave Lake, 60 mi. long and 3–10 mi. wide, central Alta., Canada, NNW of Edmonton. Drains E into Athabaska R. by Lesser Slave R.

Lessing, Gotthold Ephraim (gôt′hôlt ā′frä̆im), 1729–81, German author, chief figure of the ENLIGHTENMENT in Germany. His dramatic criticism (*Hamburgische Dramaturgie,* 1767–69) attacked the imitators of French classicism and held Shakspere up as a model for German playwrights; his *Laokoon* (1766) is a classic of modern aesthetics. His own dramatic works include the tragedies *Miss Sara Sampson* (1755) and *Emilia Galotti* (1779); the comedy *Minna von Barnhelm* (1767), a very successful piece; and the noble drama of ideas, *Nathan der Weise* (1779), a plea for peaceful coexistence of religious faiths. His friend Moses MENDELSSOHN is said to have been the model for Nathan. Lessing was drawn into interminable polemics on theological, aesthetic, and antiquarian subjects. All these are characterized by his sharp wit and erudition. In his *Die Erziehung des Menschengeschlechts* (1780) [the education of mankind] he sketched the evolution of mankind, through progressive stages of revealed religion, toward a divinely ordained society.

Le Sueur, Eustache (ûstäsh′ lù süûr′), 1617–55, French religious painter. Best works in Louvre.

Le Tellier, Michel (mēshĕl′ lù tĕlyä′), 1603–85, French statesman, chancellor of France under Louis XIV. Father of Louvois.

Lethbridge, city (pop. 22,947), S Alta., Canada, on Oldman R. and SE of Calgary. Center of coal-mining, ranching, and agr. area. Has grain elevators, food processing plants, and clothing mills. Hq. of Royal Canadian Mounted Police in Alta.

Lethe (lē′thē) [Gr.,= oblivion], in Greek mythology, river of forgetfulness in Hades. Its waters were partaken of both by arriving dead and by departing souls being reincarnated into world of the living.

Lethington, William Maitland of: see MAITLAND, WILLIAM.

Leticia (lātē′sēä), town, SE Colombia, on upper Amazon. Border dispute in region between Colombia and Peru was decided by League of Nations (1934)—first instance of action by an international body in an area covered by Monroe Doctrine.

Leto (lē′tō), in Greek religion, mother by Zeus of Apollo and Artemis. Hera, in jealousy, caused her to wander, but Zeus chained floating island of Delos to bottom of the sea; here she bore the twins. They took tragic revenge on NIOBE for insulting Leto.

Lettish, Baltic language of Latvia. It belongs to the Indo-European family. See LANGUAGE (table).

lettre de cachet (lĕ′trù dù käshā′), in French law under the *ancien régime,* a private, sealed document sent as an official communication from the king to an individual or a group. It was much used in the 16th and 17th cent. to give notice of imprisonment or exile, and the victim had no recourse. It was used by the revolutionists as a symbol of tyranny.

lettuce, annual garden plant (*Lactuca sativa*), cultivated from antiquity. Varieties include head or cabbage lettuce, the leaf or loose type, and Cos lettuce or romaine which forms long, upright leaves. It is grown on large scale in U.S.; much of winter crop comes from Fla. and Calif.

Leucas or **Leukas,** one of IONIAN ISLANDS.

Leucippus (lūsĭ′pùs), 5th cent. B.C., Greek philosopher, reputed founder of atomic theory and teacher of DEMOCRITUS.

leucocyte: see WHITE CORPUSCLE.

Leuctra (lōok′trù), village of anc. Greece, in Boeotia, 7 mi. SW of Thebes. Here the Thebans under Epaminondas defeated Sparta (371 B.C.).

Leukas or **Leucas,** one of IONIAN ISLANDS.

leukemia (lōokē′mèù), serious malady marked by abnormal increase of white blood cells (leucocytes) or their precursors. It is thought to be a malignant disease of bone marrow which spreads by way of blood. Usually it is attended by anemia.

Leuna (loi′nä), town (pop. 9,918), Saxony-Anhalt. Center of German synthetic chemical industry.

Leuthen (loi′tùn), village near Breslau, Lower Silesia. Scene of brilliant victory of Frederick II of Prussia over Austrians (1757).

Leutze, Emanuel (loit′sù), 1816–68, American historical painter, b. Germany. Works include mural on staircase of Capitol, Washington, D.C., and *Washington Crossing the Delaware* (Metropolitan Mus.).

Levant (lùvănt′) [Ital.,= east], region of the E shore of the Mediterranean from Egypt to, and including, Turkey. Syria and Lebanon are sometimes called the Levant States.

Le Vau, Louis (lù vō′), 1612–70, French architect, who designed the nucleus of palace of Versailles.

levee (lĕ′vē), embankment along a river to keep high waters from flooding adjacent plain. Levees are built by piling earth on cleared, leveled surface. Broad at the base, they narrow to a level crown on which temporary embankments or sacks of soil can be placed as protection from unusually high waters. Since intensity of flood discharge increases in channel leveed on both banks and since silt deposits raise level of river beds, levee-system planning and use of auxiliary measures are vital. In U.S., levee systems are along Mississippi and Sacramento rivers; in Europe, dikes of Holland are form of levee, and embankments are used along Danube, Vistula, and Po.

Levelers, extremist English Puritan sect active (1647–49) during Puritan Revolution. Leader was John LIL-BURNE. Aims were religious and social equality. Movement was crushed by Cromwell.

leveling: see SURVEYING.

Levelland (lĕ'vŭlănd"), town (pop. 8,264), NW Texas, W of Lubbock on Llano Estacado. Center of agr. (cotton, grains) and oil area.

Leven, Loch (lŏkh lē'vŭn). **1** Lake, between Inverness-shire and Argyllshire, Scotland. **2** Lake, Kinross-shire, Scotland. Leven R. flows from lake E through Fife-shire to Firth of Forth.

Lever, Charles James (lē'vŭr), 1806–72, Irish novelist, author of *Charles O'Malley* (1841), *Arthur O'Leary* (1844) and *Tom Burke of "Ours"* (1844).

lever, simple machine consisting of bar or rod either attached or supported at some point (fulcrum) along its length. A force applied anywhere along bar or rod tends to rotate it about the fulcrum. A small force properly distant from fulcrum will overcome larger force closer to fulcrum. This principle is basic to its many practical applications, e.g., in forceps, scissors, pliers, spades, wheelbarrow, beam balance, and other devices. See *ill.,* p. 619.

Leverrier, Urbain Jean Joseph (ürbĕ' zhä' zhôzĕf' lüvĕryä'), 1811–77, French astronomer. He discovered, independently of J. C. Adams, planet Neptune. He completed revision of planetary theories 1875.

Levi (lē'vī), son of Jacob, ancestor of the LEVITES. Tribe did not have its own allotment in Canaan. Gen. 29.34; 34; 46.11; 49.5–7.

Levi, Carlo (kär'lō lā'vē), 1902–, Italian writer, painter, and anti-Fascist leader, a physician. His powerful novel, *Christ Stopped at Eboli* (1945), is based on his experiences as an exile in Lucania.

leviathan (lĕvī'–), in Bible, huge beast, possibly the crocodile. Job 41; Pss. 74.14; 104.26; Isa. 27.1.

Levi ben Gershon: see GERSONIDES.

Levi-Civita, Tullio (tōōl'lyō lā'vē-chē'vētä), 1873–1942, Italian mathematician, known for researches in pure geometry, hydrodynamics, and absolute differential calculus (on which Einstein in part depended).

levirate marriage: see MARRIAGE.

Lévis (lē'vĭs, Fr. lāvē'), city (pop. 13,162), S Que., Canada, on St. Lawrence R. opposite Quebec; settled 1647. Base for Wolfe's siege of Quebec 1759. Port with shipbuilding, woodworking, and mfg. of trucks and chemicals.

Levites (lē'–), among anc. Hebrews, a religious caste, descendants of Levi, son of Jacob. Not counted as one of the 12 tribes of Israel; held no portion of land in Canaan. Instead certain cities were given a quota of Levites to support. Levites were Temple servants at Jerusalem; later were teachers of the Law. Ex. 6.16; 32.26–28; 38.21; Num. 1; 3–5; 8; Deut. 18; Joshua 21; 1 Chron. 6; 9; 15; 23; 2 Chron. 17.8,9; 19.8–11; 20.19–21; 23; Ezra 7.24; 8.20.

Leviticus (lĕvī'tĭkŭs), book of Old Testament, third of books of Law (the Pentateuch or Torah), named for the Levites. Book contains: general liturgical laws governing worship, sacrifice, and purification; specific rules regarding individual conduct.

Levkosia, Greek name of NICOSIA, Cyprus.

levulose: see FRUCTOSE.

Lévy-Bruhl, Lucien (lüsyĕ' lāvü-brül'), 1857–1939, French philosopher, sociologist, and ethnologist, known for research and writings on primitive mentality.

Lewes, George Henry (lōō'ĭs), 1817–78, English author. As editor of *Fortnightly Review* (1865–66) he won fame as a critic. Most noted work is *Life of Goethe* (1855). He guided, lived with, and finally married George ELIOT.

Lewes (lōō'ĭs, –ĭz, lū'–), municipal borough (pop. 13,-104), co. town of Sussex East, England; farm center. Scene of victory by Simon de Montfort over Henry III (1264). Has archaeological museum.

Lewes (lōō'ĭs), resort town (pop. 2,904), SE Del., at mouth of Delaware Bay NW of Rehoboth Beach. Harbor protected by Delaware Breakwater. Deep-sea fishing. Site of first European settlement on the Delaware; settled 1631 by Dutch.

Lewes (lōō'ĭs), river, upper course of Yukon R., rising in N B.C. and Yukon territory, Canada, and flowing c.300 mi. NW to Pelly R. at Fort Selkirk.

Lewis. For rulers thus named, see LOUIS.

Lewis, Cecil Day: see DAY LEWIS, CECIL.

Lewis, C(live) S(taples), 1898–, British writer, noted for advocacy of Christianity in such books as *The Screwtape Letters* (1942).

Lewis, John L(lewellyn), 1880–, American labor leader. Head of UNITED MINE WORKERS OF AMERICA (1920–); built up union, won power for himself. Taking his union from the American Federation of Labor, he helped form and headed (1935–40) the CONGRESS OF INDUSTRIAL ORGANIZATIONS, which he left in 1940. His aggressive strike tactics have led to conflicts with courts and government but greatly benefited the union.

Lewis, Matthew Gregory, 1775–1818, English author of "Gothic" horror tales; known as "Monk" Lewis from his extravagant thriller *The Monk* (1796).

Lewis, Meriwether, 1774–1809, American explorer, leader of LEWIS AND CLARK EXPEDITION.

Lewis, Morgan, 1754–1844, American general, governor of N.Y. (1804–7). In War of 1812 he captured Fort George, commanded at battle of Sackets Harbor.

Lewis, Sinclair, 1885–1951, American novelist. Important among many realistic and satirical novels are *Main Street* (1920), *Babbitt* (1922), *Arrowsmith* (1925), *Elmer Gantry* (1927), *It Can't Happen Here* (1935). Awarded Nobel Prize for 1930.

Lewis, (Percy) Wyndham, 1886–, English writer and painter. A leader in artistic movement called vorticism, he won more fame with more conventional paintings. His novels and essays are satirical.

Lewis, Hebrides, Scotland: see LEWIS WITH HARRIS.

Lewis. 1 Early name of SNAKE R. **2** River rising in Cascade Range, SW Wash., and flowing c.95 mi. SW to the Columbia NW of Vancouver. Furnishes power.

Lewis and Clark Cavern National Monument: see MORRISON CAVE STATE PARK.

Lewis and Clark expedition, 1803–6, military exploring expedition across the North American continent. Headed by Pres. Jefferson's private secretary, Meriwether Lewis, aided by William Clark. Purpose was to search out route to the Pacific and to gather information about Indians and Far West. Following a winter of training, the members set out in 1804 from St. Louis up the Missouri. Their Indian woman guide, SACAJAWEA, aided them in crossing the Rockies. After wintering on the coast, they began their return journey, splitting temporarily to follow separate routes along the Marias and the Yellowstone, and arrived in St. Louis, Sept. 23, 1806. Their expedition, of which many records were kept, opened vast new territories to knowledge.

Lewisburg. 1 Borough (pop. 5,268), central Pa., on W branch of Susquehanna R. and NW of Sunbury. Mfg. of textiles and lumber products. Seat of Bucknell Univ. (Baptist; coed.; 1846). **2** Town (pop. 5,164), central Tenn., S of Nashville. Livestock, dairy, and timber center. Mfg. of shoes and stoves.

lewisite: see POISON GAS.

Lewisohn, Ludwig (lōō'ĭzōn), 1882–, American writer of criticism, novels (e.g., *The Island Within*, 1928), autobiography (*Up Stream*, 1922; *Mid-Channel*, 1929; *Haven*, 1940), and works on Jews and Zionism. Also translated German literature.

Lewiston. 1 City (pop. 12,985), NW Idaho, at junction of Snake and Clearwater rivers and at Wash. line. Site visited by Lewis and Clark, 1805. Founded 1861 after gold was found on Clearwater R. First cap. of Idaho Territory (1863–64). Had Idaho's first newspaper (1862). Lumber, fruit, livestock center. **2** Industrial city (pop. 40,974), SW Maine, at falls (power) of Androscoggin R. (bridged here) opposite Auburn; settled 1770. Second largest city in Maine. Mfg. of textiles (since early 19th cent.), shoes, wood and metal products, and brick. Seat of Bates Col. (coed.; 1863).

Lewistown. 1 City (pop. 2,630), central Ill., SW of Peoria. Source of *Spoon River Anthology* by E. L. Masters, whose home it was. Indian mounds are near. **2** City (pop. 6,573), central Mont., SE of Great Falls; laid out 1882. Scene of gold rush in 1880s. Trade center of agr. (grain), stock-raising, and mining region. Mfg. of building materials and oil refining. **3** Borough (pop. 13,894), central Pa., on Juniata R. and NW of Harrisburg; settled as trading post 1754. Mfg. of metal products and rayon.

Lewis with Harris, island (825 sq. mi.; pop. 28,042), off NW Scotland, most northerly of Outer Hebrides. Lewis, N part, in Ross and Cromarty co.; Harris, in Inverness-shire. Little cultivated, it has fishing and stock raising. Harris tweeds made here.

Lexington. 1 City (pop. 55,534), N central Ky., SE of Frankfort in bluegrass region; founded 1779. Thoroughbred horse-raising center and tobacco market, it processes tobacco and liquor and has railroad shops. Seat of Univ. of KENTUCKY and Transylvania Col. (Disciples of Christ; coed.; chartered 1780 and 1783, opened at Danville 1785, moved 1789). Called Kentucky Univ. for some years after affiliation with that school; pioneer medical and law schools closed 1915. Alumni include Jefferson Davis and J. C. Breckenridge. Here are homes of J. H. Morgan, Henry Clay, and Mary T. Lincoln, U.S. hospital for drug addicts, veterans' hospital, and national cemetery. **2** Residential town (pop. 17,335), E Mass., NW of Boston; settled c.1640. Monument on the green marks site of first battle of the Revolution (April 19, 1775) (see LEXINGTON AND CONCORD, BATTLES OF). **3** City (pop. 5,074), W Mo., on the Missouri and E of Kansas City, in a coal and farm area. Besieged and captured (Sept., 1861) by Missouri militia under Gen. Sterling Price in Civil War. **4** City (pop. 5,068), S Nebr., on Platte R. and SE of North Platte, in grain region. Center of irrigation and power project. **5** City (pop. 13,571), central N.C., S of Winston-Salem in Yadkin valley; settled 1775. Has flour, lumber, and cotton mills. **6** Town (pop. 5,976), western Va., in Shenandoah Valley NNW of Lynchburg; laid out 1777. Partially burned in Civil War. R. E. Lee and Stonewall Jackson buried here. Seat of WASHINGTON AND LEE UNIVERSITY, and Virginia Military Inst. (state supported; for men; opened 1839; called West Point of the South).

Lexington and Concord, battles of, opening engagements of American Revolution, April 19, 1775. A British infantry column, sent to capture colonial military stores at Concord, encountered armed resistance at Lexington, fought another engagement at Concord, and withdrew to Boston.

Leyden, Lucas van: see LUCAS VAN LEYDEN.

Leyden, Netherlands: see LEIDEN.

Leyden jar, early form of electrical CONDENSER. Modern form is a glass jar partially coated, inside and out, with tin foil and closed by a nonconducting stopper with brass rod knobbed at one end, connected to foil at other.

Leysin (lāzē'), village, Vaud canton, Switzerland, with sanatoriums for tubercular diseases.

Leyte (lā'tā), island (2,785 sq. mi.; pop. 835,532), one of Visayan Isls., Philippines, just SW of Samar. Produces sugar cane, rice, hemp, and corn. U.S. forces defeated the Japanese in decisive battle of Leyte Gulf (Oct., 1944).

leze majesty: see LESE MAJESTY.

Lhasa (lä'sŭ), city (pop. c.20,000; alt. 12,087 ft.), cap. of Tibet. Center of Lamaism. Near by are Potala (main palace of Dalai Lama) and three great monasteries.

Holiest temple in city is Jokang, which contains jeweled image of Buddha. Traditional hostility of Tibetan clergy to foreigners has led Lhasa to be called Forbidden City.

L'Hôpital or **L'Hospital, Michel de** (both: mēshěl' dŭ lōpētäl'), c.1505–1573, chancellor of France under Catherine de' Medici. Favored religious toleration. Was forced out of office by the Guises (1567).

Li, chemical symbol of the element LITHIUM.

Liaosi, province: see MANCHURIA.

Liaotung (lyou'dŏong'), province (40,000 sq. mi.; pop. 11,000,000), S Manchuria; cap. Antung. Bounded SE by Korea along Yalu R.; occupies peninsula jutting into Yellow Sea. Tip of Liaotung peninsula leased 1898 by the Russians from China as Kwantung Territory (including Dairen and PORT ARTHUR); after Russo-Japanese War lease taken over by Japan 1905. After World War II most of Kwantung Territory included 1945 in Port Arthur naval-base district under joint Sino-Soviet control. Liaotung is Manchuria's chief industrial area; produces iron and coal.

Liaquat Ali Khan (lēä'kŭt ä'lē kän'), 1895–1951, political leader of Pakistan, educated in India and at Oxford. Headed Moslem League, 1946–47. With creation of Pakistan (1947) he became its prime minister. Shot fatally on Oct. 16, 1951, by fanatic Afghan who wanted autonomy for Pathan tribes.

Liard (lē'ärd"), river of W Canada, 570 mi. long, rising in SE Yukon and flowing ESE into B.C., then N to Mackenzie R. in Mackenzie dist. Navigable to Fort Liard, 165 mi. from its mouth.

Libanus: see LEBANON, mountain range.

Libau, Latvia: see LIEPAJA.

Libby Prison, Richmond, Va., used for captured Union officers in Civil War, formerly tobacco warehouse. Living conditions were notoriously bad, causing death of thousands.

libel and **slander,** two forms of defamation (exposure to hatred, contempt, ridicule, or pecuniary loss). Libel requires some permanent form (e.g., a writing or picture), whereas slander is committed orally, by gesture, or the like. In both cases the defamation must affect a living person (thus attacking a large group such as doctors or lawyers is unactionable). Truth is generally a defense; however, sometimes even a false statement is excusable, if based on a normally reliable source such as a reputable credit-rating agency. Some abusive terms are libelous or slanderous per se, regardless of the character of the person attacked. Broader protection under the law is granted by rights of privacy, which may not be invaded.

Liber (lī'bŭr) [Latin,= free], in Roman religion, god of fertility and wine. Identified with Bacchus. His consort **Libera** (lī'bŭrŭ) was identified with Persephone or Ariadne. Liberalia was their festival.

Liberal, city (pop. 7,134), SW Kansas, near Okla. line. Grazing, agr., gas fields.

liberal arts, term originally used to mean studies suited to freemen. In the Middle Ages included the trivium (grammar, logic, rhetoric) and the quadrivium (arithmetic, geometry, astronomy, music). In modern times the liberal arts have been considered to be studies based primarily on the humanities as opposed to specialized, vocational, or purely scientific training.

Liberal party, in British history, organization that grew out of Whig party. Lord John RUSSELL is credited with the party's name. Its policies were free trade, religious liberty, abolition of slavery, and extension of franchise. W. E. GLADSTONE sponsored great reforms (e.g., REFORM BILLS). First Irish Home Rule Bill (1886) split the two-party system on greater class basis. Great Whig landowners joined Conservatives. In the 1890s an imperialist group dominated the party. An external threat was the new Labour party. Sir Henry Campbell-Bannerman's reorganization led to Liberal victory in 1906. David LLOYD GEORGE headed World War I coalition (1916–22). Party has declined and is now negligible.

Liberal party, in U.S. history, organized 1944 in New York city by AMERICAN LABOR PARTY dissenters favoring New Deal policies and opposing spread of totalitarianism. Its platform called for a strong UN, greater national development program, extension of civil liberties.

Liberal Republican party, in U.S. history, organization formed in 1872 by Republicans discontented at political corruption and policies of Grant's first administration. Leaders included Carl Schurz, Horace GREELEY. Party urged civil service reform and an end to Reconstruction program of radical Republicans. U. S. Grant, however, was reelected.

Liberec (lĕ'bĕrĕts), Ger. *Reichenberg,* city (pop. 29,690), N Bohemia, Czechoslovakia, on the Lausitzer Neisse. Textile mfg. (wool, cotton, linen, silk).

Liberia (lībē'rēu), republic (c.43,000 sq. mi.; est. pop. 1,600,000), W Africa, on the Atlantic, between British Sierra Leone and French Ivory Coast; cap. Monrovia. Founded 1822 by American Colonization Society as colony of freed slaves from U.S. Became a free republic in 1847, with its government modeled on that of U.S. To further economic progress a 99-year lease to c.1,000,000 acres was granted to Firestone Co. for development of rubber plantations. In World War II the U.S. developed defense bases in Liberia, building a large air field and modernizing Monrovia harbor. By agreement with the government a group of American businessmen began far-reaching program in 1949 to further country's economic and social development. Railroad was built to link Monrovia with iron mines in interior; cacao growing and use of lumber resources were encouraged.

Liberius (lībēr'ēus), pope (352–66). Urged Emperor Constantius to call the Council of Arles (353), where, however, papal legates, subdued by imperial favor toward ARIANISM, voted against St. ATHANASIUS. Liberius, refusing to be coerced, was banished; an antipope, Felix, was set up. In 358 Liberius was allowed to return as pope, and after the death of Constantius he openly avowed his orthodoxy and reasserted the primacy of Rome.

Liberty, vacation and health resort village (pop. 4,658), SE N.Y., in the Catskills.

liberty, general term for the sum of specific liberties or freedoms, such as religious liberty, political liberty, and freedom of speech. Fundamental is personal liberty, the physical freedom to come and go as one pleases. Freedom of worship and of private religious judgment were greatly restricted before the Protestant Reformation, and political liberties, such as the right to vote, were little known before the 19th cent. Anarchism, individualism, socialism, and nationalism all represent different ways of seeking human liberty. Stages in the process of acquiring liberties are exemplified by the struggle for the MAGNA CARTA in 1215, the Habeas Corpus Act (1679), the feminist movement in the 19th and 20th cent., and the demands of ethnic minorities and colonies for political rights. Such philosophers as Locke, Rousseau, and Jefferson popularized the notion that the individual possesses certain natural rights or liberties. Since the French Revolution, liberty has become closely connected with equality of opportunity: the freedom to develop one's potentialities.

Liberty, Statue of, colossal statue, on Bedloe's Isl. in New York harbor, commanding entrance to New York city. Designed by F. A. Bartholdi, it commemorates French and American revolutions. Statue (152 ft. high and made of copper sheets) is in form of woman with uplifted arm holding a torch; its base is 11-pointed star, and the c.150-ft.-high pedestal is of concrete faced with granite. Presented in 1884 to U.S. by Franco-American Union, became national monument in 1924.

Liberty Bell, historic relic now exhibited in Independence Hall, Philadelphia. Hung in steeple of Hall 1753; rung July, 1776, to proclaim Declaration of Independence; hidden in Allentown (1777–78) during British occupation of Philadelphia; moved to tower 1781. Bell was cracked in 1835.

Liberty party, in U.S. history, antislavery political organization founded in 1840 by those abolitionists, under James G. BIRNEY, who repudiated W. L. Garrison's nonpolitical stand. Vote given Birney in 1844 threw presidency to J. K. Polk. In 1848 party united with antislavery Whigs and Democrats to form FREE-SOIL PARTY.

Libertyville, village (pop. 5,425), NE Ill., NNW of Chicago; center of farm area.

Libon (lī'bŏn), 5th cent. B.C., Greek architect. Built the Doric temple to Zeus at Olympia.

Libra (lī'bru) [Latin,= the balance], seventh sign of ZODIAC.

library. Earliest known library was a collection of clay tablets in Babylonia in 21st cent. B.C. There were ancient Egyptian temple libraries, and the library of Assur-bani-pal (d. 626? B.C.) in Nineveh was the most noted before Greek times. The temple at Jerusalem contained a sacred library. In Greece private book collections date from 6th cent. B.C., first public library from 330 B.C. Most famous libraries of antiquity were those of ALEXANDRIA and PERGAMUM. First Roman libraries were brought from Greece, Asia Minor, and Syria. Continental and English libraries are successors of the monastic libraries that preserved learning for centuries. The Arabs collected (9th to 15th cent.) many libraries. In 15th cent. the Vatican Library, oldest public library in Europe, was formed. Sorbonne library at Paris was founded in 1257. Many other great university libraries were opened in the 14th cent. Among the chief modern libraries are the BIBLIOTHÈQUE NATIONALE, Paris; the BRITISH MUSEUM, London; the BODLEIAN LIBRARY, Oxford; the VATICAN LIBRARY, Rome; the AMBROSIAN LIBRARY, Milan; the Laurentian, Florence; the Lenin Library, Moscow; the LIBRARY OF CONGRESS, Washington, D.C.; the NEW YORK PUBLIC LIBRARY; the libraries at Harvard. A public library had been opened in Boston in 1653. First circulating library in U.S. chartered in Philadelphia in 1732. Late 19th cent. brought free access to books, and Andrew Carnegie funds helped create many new libraries. Three widely used book-classification systems are those of Melvil DEWEY, Charles Ammi CUTTER, and Library of Congress.

Library of Congress, U.S. national library, at Washington, D.C., estab. 1800. An act of 1870 provided that copies of all books copyrighted in U.S. must go to Library of Congress. Now open to the public as a reference library. Mainly supported by congressional appropriations.

library school. Since Melvil Dewey estab. (1887) at Columbia Univ. a school for training library workers, over 30 have come into operation in U.S. and Canada (e.g., at Univ. of Illinois, Pratt Institute, Los Angeles Public Library). Univ. of Chicago was first graduate school to confer doctoral degree in library science. There are now library schools in Europe and South America.

libretto [Ital.,= little book], the text of an opera or an oratorio. Outstanding librettists have been Pietro Metastasio, Philippe Quinault, Lorenzo Da Ponte, W. S. Gilbert, and Hugo von Hofmannsthal. Wagner tried to achieve a perfect union of text and music by writing his own librettos.

Libreville (lēbrüvēl'), town (pop. 9,900), SW French Equatorial Africa, port on Gulf of Guinea. Hardwoods are exported.

Libya (lī'bēu), kingdom (c.680,000 sq. mi.; est. pop. 1,168,000), N Africa, fronting on the Mediterranean; winter cap. Tripoli, summer cap. Bangasi. Comprises Tripolitania, Cyrenaica, and Fezzan. Much of Libya is desert. Dates, olives, and oranges are grown in coastal oases. Area was successively ruled by Carthage, Rome, and the Vandals. Vying for control over it in Middle Ages were Arabia, Morocco, and Egypt. Spain and

Knights of Malta briefly held dominion in 16th cent. Was under Ottoman rule from 1551 to 1911, when seized by Italy. Its development as Italian colony began only in 1930s, when c.20,000 colonists were brought from home country. Libya was important battleground in World War II (see NORTH AFRICA, CAMPAIGNS IN). In accordance with UN decision of 1949, Libya became independent on Dec. 24, 1951, with Idris I (former titular king of Cyrenaica) as ruler.

Licata (lēkä′tä), anc. *Phintias*, city (pop. 30,641), S Sicily, Italy. It is a seaport shipping sulphur, asphalt, cheese. Founded 3d cent. B.C., it was refuge of people of Gela after Gela's destruction. Off near-by Cape Ecnomus Romans won in 256 B.C. a decisive battle in the Punic Wars. Licata was an Allied landing point in invasion of Sicily (1943).

lichen (lī′kŭn), slow-growing simple plant form, usually gray, but often red, rust, or brown, found on rocks or tree stumps from arctic to tropics. A lichen is composed of algae and fungi living together. When growing on rocks, lichens by their acids start the long process of weathering by which rocks are changed into soil.

Lichfield, municipal borough (pop. 10,624), Staffordshire, England. Market town, famous for its three-spired cathedral (13th–14th cent.) and associations with Dr. Johnson, who was born and lived here.

Lichnowsky, Karl Max, Fürst (līkhnôf′skē), 1860–1928, German diplomat; ambassador to London 1912–14. In a privately printed pamphlet (1916) he accused his government of failing to support him in his efforts to avert World War I; its publication in the U.S. (1917) caused his expulsion from the Prussian house of lords.

Licinius (līsĭn′ēŭs), d. 325, Roman emperor. Coemperor with Galerius, he later allied himself with CONSTANTINE I and defeated Maximin in 313, becoming sole ruler in the East. Later defeated twice and put to death by Constantine.

Licinius Calvus Stolo, Caius (kā′yŭs, kăl′vŭs stō′lō), fl. 375 B.C., tribune to whom are attributed the Licinian Rogations. These laws limited the amount of public land held by one person, regulated debts, and ordained that one consul must be plebeian.

Licking, river rising in E Ky., SE of Salyersville, and flowing 320 mi. NW to Ohio R. opposite Cincinnati. G. R. Clark's group met here 1780 for march up the Little Miami. Battle of Blue Licks (1782) occurred in Licking valley. Partly navigable, it is a busy trade route.

licorice (lĭk′ŭrĭs), Old World perennial plant (*Glycyrrhiza glabra*) and the sweet substance obtained from its roots, used medicinally and in confectionery.

Lidice (lĭ′dĭsē, Czech lĭ′dyĭtsē), village (former pop. 446), central Bohemia, Czechoslovakia, near Kladno. In reprisal for assassination of Reinhard Heydrich, Nazi "protector" (i.e., governor) of Bohemia and Moravia, the Germans razed Lidice, killed all men, deported women and children (1942).

Lido di Venezia (lē′dō dē vānä′tsyä), beach resort near Venice, Italy.

Lie, Jonas (lē), 1880–1940, American landscape and marine painter, b. Norway.

Lie, Jonas Lauritz Idemil (yō′näs lou′rĭts ē′dŭmēl lē′), 1833–1908, Norwegian novelist. His stories of ordinary family life (e.g., *The Pilot and His Wife,* 1874) were the first modern Norwegian novels.

Lie, Marius Sophus (mä′rēŏŏs sō′fŏŏs lē′), 1842–99, Norwegian mathematician, noted for studies of differential equations and for continuous transformation groups.

Lie, Trygve (Halvdan) (trüg′vŭ hälv′dän lē′), 1896–, Norwegian statesman. Foreign minister of Norway from 1941, he was chosen in 1946 first secretary general of the United Nations. Pursued conciliatory policy. His resignation took effect 1953. Dag Hammarskjold was chosen to succeed him.

Lieber, Thomas: see ERASTUS, THOMAS.

Lieberman, Max, 1847–1935, German genre painter, who depicted life of workers and peasants.

Liebig, Justus, Baron von (yŏŏs′tŏŏs bärōn′ fŭn lē′bĭkh), 1803–73, German chemist. In almost 50 years of teaching he profoundly influenced the training of leading chemists. He improved organic analysis and made valuable contributions to agricultural chemistry including the development of artificial fertilizers.

Liebknecht, Wilhelm (vĭl′hĕlm lēp′kŭnĕkht), 1826–1900, German Socialist leader. Influenced by Karl Marx, he founded with his disciple Bebel the German Social Democratic party (1869). Was imprisoned for two years under Bismarck's anti-Socialist laws. Served in Reichstag 1874–1900. His son, **Karl Liebknecht,** 1871–1919, served in Reichstag as member of radical wing of Social Democrats from 1912. Refused to support government in World War I; founded SPARTACUS PARTY. After failure of Spartacist revolt of 1919 he and Rosa LUXEMBURG were arrested and killed while being carried to prison.

Liebler, Thomas: see ERASTUS, THOMAS.

Liechtenstein (lĭkh′tŭnshtīn″), sovereign principality (62 sq. mi.; pop. 11,218), in the Alps between Austria and Switzerland; cap. Vaduz. The Rhine forms its W boundary. Pastures, agr. Much revenue is derived from moderate taxes on internatl. holding companies with hq. at Vaduz. Ruling prince is Francis Joseph II (acceded 1938). Elected diet has 15 members. There is no army. Population is Roman Catholic and German-speaking. Principality was created 1718 as immediate fief of Holy Roman Empire by uniting county of Vaduz and barony of Schellenberg, acquired by the old Austrian family of Lichtenstein. A member of German Confederation from 1815, it sided with Austria in Austro-Prussian War of 1866 but was overlooked in peace treaty, thus remaining technically at war with Prussia. Liechtenstein family was prominent under the Hapsburg empire, but after World War I the principality became oriented toward Switzerland, whose currency it accepted in 1921. It entered a custom union with Switzerland in 1924 and is represented abroad by the Swiss government.

lied and lieder: see SONG.

lie detector, any scientific instrument recording bodily changes (e.g., in respiration, pulse rate, blood pressure) caused by telling of lies. W. M. Marston (1914–15), John A. Larson (1921), Leonarde Keeler (1926), were noted for such devices. W. G. Summers's psychogalvanometer (1936) measures electrical changes on skin. Usually lie detector evidence is legally inacceptable because of similarity of physical changes caused by emotional factors (such as feelings of guilt) to those caused by lies.

Liége (lyäzh), Flemish *Luik,* province (1,526 sq. mi.; pop. 973,911), E Belgium, in industrial Meuse valley and agr. Ardennes plateau. Chief cities: Liége, Verviers, Spa, Seraing. Coal mining, metallurgy, wool mfg. Population is largely French-speaking (see WALLOONS); EUPEN and MALMÉDY dists. are German-speaking. Province shared history of prince-bishopric of Liége, of which it was a part. The cap., **Liége** (pop. 432,471, incl. suburbs), on the Meuse and at the head of the Albert Canal, is a commercial, industrial, and transportation center as well as the cultural cap. of French-speaking Belgium. Mfg. of arms (at Herstal), machinery, beer, flour. Episcopal see. Seat of university (founded 1817). A trading center from the 10th cent., Liége became the cap. of a prince-bishopric which comprised most of modern Liége prov. and parts of Limburg and Namur provs. The rising guilds took part in city government, and in 1373 the bishop's officials were placed under supervision of a tribunal of 22 persons; this Peace of the Twenty-Two remained in force (with interruptions) till 1792. In 1467 Charles the Bold of Burgundy, who had imposed his protectorate on Liége, punished the rebellious citizens by abolishing communal liberties. The citizens, encouraged by Louis XI of France, rose against Charles, but

Charles forced Louis to assist him in repressing the revolution and sacked Liége (1468). Though still a sovereign member of the Holy Roman Empire, the bishopric was in practice dependent on Spain and Austria from 16th cent. to 1792 (see NETHERLANDS, AUSTRIAN AND SPANISH). Despite its strong fortifications it fell to the Germans in 1914 and 1940. Liberated by U.S. troops (1944), it was bombarded by rocket weapons during Battle of the Bulge (1944–45), but the principal buildings and thoroughfares of the handsome city suffered little damage.

Liegnitz (lēg′nĭts), Pol. *Legnica*, city (pop. 24,357), Lower Silesia; transferred to Polish administration 1945. Textile mfg. It was the seat of a principality ruled by a branch of the PIAST dynasty from 1248 till 1675, when it passed to Austria; ceded to Prussia 1742. At near-by Wahlstatt the Mongols defeated the Germans and Poles (1241), and the Prussians under Blücher defeated the French (1813).

Liepaja (lēĕ′päyä), Ger. *Libau*, city (pop. 57,098), SW Latvia; an ice-free port on Baltic Sea. Steel mills, paper mills, shipyards. First mentioned 1263, it passed with Courland to Russia in 1795 and was an important commercial center in late 19th and early 20th cent.

Liestal (lēs′täl), town (pop. 7,211), cap. of half-canton of Basel-Land, NW Switzerland. Textiles.

Lieven, Dorothea, Princess (lē′vùn), 1785–1857, Russian noblewoman; wife of the Russian ambassador to London (1812–34). A brilliant personality, she was a friend of Metternich, Wellington, and Guizot; her Paris salon (after 1834) was noted, as was her witty correspondence (*The Private Letters of Princess Lieven*, 1938).

life insurance: see INSURANCE.

Liffey (lĭf′fē), river of Ireland, flowing 50 mi. from Co. Wicklow through Dublin to Dublin Bay.

lift: see ELEVATOR; LOCK, CANAL.

ligan: see FLOTSAM, JETSAM, AND LIGAN.

light, form of energy not yet adequately explained by any one theory. Corpuscular (or emission) theory of Newton said light consists of minute particles (corpuscles) emitted from luminous bodies and traveling through space. This was superseded by wave theory of Christiaan Huygens. This states that light consists of waves traveling in luminiferous ether at high velocity with transverse vibration at right angles to direction of wave and proceeding in straight lines. Electromagnetic theory of J. C. Maxwell classes visible light as form of electromagnetic radiation occurring in waves shorter than infrared but longer than ultraviolet. QUANTUM THEORY says light is form of radiant energy given off from luminous bodies in tiny quantities called photons. Light is often described in terms of effect on eye (see VISION). As such, it is limited to radiations of wave length between infrared and ultraviolet; neither infrared nor ultraviolet rays can be "seen" by man. Light is said to be energy that makes visible the bodies producing it and those reflecting it. PHOTOMETRY deals with measurement of relative intensity of light source and illumination. Transparent objects let light pass through them; translucent objects let light through but scatter rays; opaque objects do not permit light passage. Light travels in straight lines through uniform transparent substance; its velocity in air is c.186,000 mi. per second. Explanation of REFRACTION is based on differences in velocity in different media. When light rays strike bodies through which they cannot pass, some are absorbed, some undergo reflection. Color of light depends on wave length. White light is all colors combined; its composition is determined by its dispersion. Light is involved in PHOTOSYNTHESIS. Studies of light can be traced from the early Greeks, through the discoveries of optical instruments (e.g., microscope, telescope) and the work of many investigators including Snell, Descartes, Thomas Young, Fresnel, Malus, Fizeau, Foucault, Helmholtz, Michelson, and Morley.

lighthouse, structure equipped to give optical or radio-electrical guidance to ships and airplanes. In 1789 U.S. Congress took over lighthouses formerly privately operated. Lighthouse Board appointed in 1852 was superseded in 1910 by Lighthouse Service, which was transferred to U.S. coast guard (1939) from Dept. of Commerce. From 1934, so-called remote-control stations began to replace lighthouses; these have radio apparatus to operate lamps, fog signals, radio beacon.

lighting. Earliest methods of lighting, by open fire, firebrands, and torches, were followed by development of LAMP, CANDLE, and lantern. All still survive in various civilizations and for various uses. The lantern, enclosed in glass or equipped with a chimney, is to some extent superseded by the flashlight. Use of gas for lighting was stimulated by invention of Bunsen burner and Welsbach mantle. Illuminating gases include coal gas, air gas, acetylene, water gas, and producer gas. First development in electric lighting was arc lamp evolved from carbon arc. Carbon-arc street lamps appeared in Cleveland in 1879 and came into wide use. Mercury-arc lamp was developed in 1903. Arc lights are used in floodlights, some searchlights, spotlights, and projectors. In 1879 Edison patented the first commercially practical incandescent lamp (one in which current passes through filament offering high resistance and enclosed in a vacuum). Neon lamp was invented in 1911 by Georges Claude. Fluorescent lamp consists of tube containing argon and trace of mercury and with inner walls coated with fluorescent powder; electric current causes mercury vapor to emit ultraviolet radiation which causes power to fluoresce. Sodium vapor lamps are among those used experimentally for highway lighting.

lightning: see THUNDERSTORM.

light-year, unit of distance (c.5.87 million million mi.) based on speed of light (186,000 mi. per sec.), used for measurements in space. An object is one light-year distant when its light takes one year to reach observer.

Ligne, Charles Joseph, prince de (shärl′ zhôzĕf′ prēs′ dù lē′nyù), 1735–1814, Austrian courtier and field marshal, of an ancient family of Hainaut. His remark on the Congress of Vienna (*Le congrès danse, mais ne marche pas*—the congress dances but takes no steps) has remained famous. His memoirs and correspondence (Eng. tr. of selections, 1927) mirror his charm, gaiety, and metropolitanism.

lignite (lĭg′nīt) or **brown coal,** a carbonaceous fuel intermediate between PEAT and COAL, brown or yellowish in color and woody in texture. Its flame is smoky and heating power low.

lignum vitae (lĭg′nùm vī′tē), tropical American evergreen tree (*Guaiacum,* or *Guajacum, officinale*). Valued for its hard resinous wood and gum resin used in certain drugs.

Ligny (lēnyē′), village, Namur prov., central Belgium, NE of Charleroi and near Fleurus. Here Napoleon defeated Prussians early in WATERLOO CAMPAIGN (1815).

Liguori, Alfonso Maria de': see ALPHONSUS LIGUORI.

Liguria (lĭgyŏo′rēù), region (2,098 sq. mi.; pop. 1,466,810), NW Italy, extending along Mediterranean (called here the Ligurian Sea) from the French border to La Spezia; cap. GENOA. Coastal strip forms Italian RIVIERA; inland rise the Ligurian Alps (W) and Ligurian Apennines (E). Fishing, gardening, wine growing, agr. are main occupations. Ancient Ligurii occupied Mediterranean coast from Rhone to Arno, but Celtic migrations and Phoenician, Greek, and Carthaginian colonists displaced them in 4th cent. B.C. Region was subdued by Romans in 2d cent. B.C. During later Middle Ages Genoa gradually gained control of most of Liguria, which shared the history of its cap. from the 16th cent. until its annexation to Sardinia (1815).

lilac, flowering shrub of genus *Syringa,* native to Europe and Asia, and widely grown in America since colonial times. The fragrant purple, white, or rosy-pink flowers are usually borne in cone-shaped clusters in late spring. The term French lilac refers to modern double-flowered hybrids.

SMALL CAPITALS = cross references. Pronunciation key on inside end pages. Abbreviations: p. 2.

Lilburne, John, 1614?–1657, English political leader and pamphleteer for the LEVELERS. Spent much of his life in prison or exile for agitation.

Liliencron, Detlev, Freiherr von (dĕt′lĕf frī′hĕr fŭn lē′lyŭnkrōn), 1844–1909, German lyric poet.

Lilienthal, David E(li) (lī′lyŭnthôl), 1899–, American public official. Appointed a director of TVA in 1933; its chairman 1941–46. As chairman of U.S. Atomic Energy Commission (1947–49) he pioneered in civilian control of U.S. atomic-energy program.

Lilienthal, Otto (ô′tō lē′lyŭntäl), 1848–96, German aeronautical engineer and pioneer experimenter with heavier-than-air flight. Improved gliders. His brother, **Gustav Lilienthal** (gōōs′täf), 1849–1933, was associate in experiments.

Lilith (lī′lĭth), in Talmudic tradition, a female demon; in legend, Adam's first wife.

Liliuokalani (lēlēōō″ōkälä′nē), 1838–1917, last reigning queen of Hawaiian Isls. (1891–93). Dethroned in 1893, formally renounced royal claims in 1895. Lived much in U.S. thereafter. Wrote many songs (e.g., *Aloha Oe* or *Farewell to Thee*).

Lille (lēl), city (pop. 179,778), cap. of Nord dept., N France. Textile mfg. center (gave its name to lisle). Seat of a university (founded 1887) and of an important art museum. Was chief city of county of Flanders; after 1668 cap. of French Flanders prov. Its huge citadel was built by Vauban. Other landmarks include old stock exchange (17th cent.) and unfinished cathedral (begun 1854).

Lillehammer (lī′lühämür), town (pop. 6,565), co. seat of Opland co., SE Norway, N of Oslo and on N end of L. Mjosa; founded 1827. It is commercial and tourist center for the fertile Gudbransdal. Its folk museum exhibits old buildings of the region.

Lillie, Beatrice, 1898–, English comedienne, b. Canada. Made her debut in 1914. Won an international reputation for sophisticated wit in such shows as *Charlot's Revue* (1922, 1924), *Seven Lively Arts* (1945), *An Evening with Beatrice Lillie* (1952).

Lillo, George, 1693–1739, English playwright. In *The London Merchant; or, The History of George Barnwell* (1731) he created first modern melodrama.

Lilly, John: see LYLY, JOHN.

Lilly, William (c.1468–1522): see LILY, WILLIAM.

Lilly, William, 1602–81, English astrologer. Somewhat popular as a prophet and caster of horoscopes, he issued an annual almanac and foretold events. His best-known work is *Christian Astrology* (1647).

Lily, William, c.1468–1522, English scholar, first headmaster of St. Paul's School, and co-author of the Eton Latin grammar. Also Lilly, Lyly.

lily, ornamental perennial plant of genus *Lilium,* with scaly bulb. The flowers, often fragrant, are of great diversity in form and color. Widely cultivated are the Madonna lily of Europe, the Easter lily, the goldenrayed lily of Japan, and the regal and tiger lilies of China. Others, including the meadow lily and Turk's cap lily, are native to North America. In religion and art the lily symbolizes purity.

Lilybaeum (lĭlĭbē′ŭm), anc. city of Sicily (modern Marsala); founded by Carthage 396 B.C. Withstood long Roman siege (250–242 B.C.).

lily of the valley, perennial spring-blooming plant (*Convallaria majalis*), native to Europe, Asia, and mountains of SE U.S. Its dainty, white, bell-shaped, fragrant flowers are borne on a stalk which rises between two shiny leaves. It thrives in shade.

Lima (lē′mä), city (pop. 533,645), W Peru, cap. and largest city of Peru; founded 1535 by Francisco Pizarro. Its port is Callao. Its cultural supremacy on continent was contested in colonial times only by Bogotá and in magnificence and political prestige its only peer in Spanish America was Mexico city. Univ. of San Marcos, founded here in 1551, is one of finest in South America.

Lima (lī′mù), city (pop. 50,246), NW Ohio, N of Dayton; laid out 1831. Mfg. of railroad equipment, machinery, and electrical goods. Has limestone quarries.

Liman von Sanders, Otto (ô′tō lē′män fŭn zän′dúrs), 1855–1929, German general. Reorganized Turkish army (1913); commanded Turks in GALLIPOLI CAMPAIGN (1915–16).

Limassol (lēmäsôl′), city (pop. 22,799), S Cyprus, a Mediterranean port. Has a large wine trade.

Limburg, Fr. *Limbourg,* province (930 sq. mi.; pop. 475,716), NE Belgium, bordering on the Netherlands; cap. Hasselt. Crossed by Meuse R. and Albert Canal. Agr.; coal mining. Population is largely Flemish. Most of province was included in prince-bishopric of Liége until 1792 and formed part of Dutch province of Limburg, 1815–39.

Limburg, province (840 sq. mi.; pop. 684,105), SE Netherlands, bordering on Belgium and Germany; cap. MAASTRICHT. Contains chief coal deposits of Netherlands. Population is mostly Roman Catholic. Former duchy of Limburg comprised S part of the modern Dutch province and E portion of modern Liége prov., Belgium. Limbourg, a small town E of Liége, was the cap. The duchy was divided between United Netherlands and Spanish Netherlands 1648; united (with altered boundaries) in 1815 under kingdom of the Netherlands. Dutch-Belgian treaty of 1839 divided it into Dutch and Belgian provinces of Limburg.

lime, small citrus tree (*Citrus aurantifolia*) and its green fruit, similar to the lemon. Native to SE Asia, it is susceptible to frost injury and is cultivated in U.S. only in S Fla. Limes are high in vitamins and yield citric acid.

lime or **quicklime,** calcium oxide, a common, white amorphous solid. It is made by heating LIMESTONE in kiln. Used to make porcelain, glass, alkalies; in sugar purification; in treating soils; as insecticide. A basic anhydride, it reacts with water to form calcium hydroxide. This process is slaking, product is **slaked lime,** a white bulky powder. It is used in mortar, plaster, whitewash; to counteract soil acidity; in refining beet sugar. In solution it forms limewater. **Lime-sulphur,** a mixture of calcium sulphides, is an insecticide.

Limehouse, district of docks, warehouses, and factories of London, England, on the Thames. Noted as the Chinese district of London.

Limerick (lĭ′mùrĭk), county (1,037 sq. mi.; pop. 142,559), S Ireland, in Munster. An agr. plain, dairy farming and salmon fishing are chief occupations. Has hydroelectric plant on Shannon R. County town is **Limerick,** county borough (pop. 42,970), a seaport at head of Shannon estuary and only town of any size in county. Cap. of Munster under Brian Boru. Last stronghold of James II, it has stone on which treaty was signed (1691) giving Irish and Catholics certain rights. Has Protestant (12th cent.) and Catholic cathedrals and Norman castle.

limestone, sedimentary rock composed wholly or in part of calcium carbonate (calcite). Ordinarily it is white, but impurities (carbon, iron oxide) give it variety of colors. Formed by consolidation of marine invertebrate skeletons or from chemical precipitation. Important uses: flux in smelting iron ore, source of lime, ingredient of Portland cement, building stone. Varieties include chalk, dolomite, and marble.

lime-sulphur: see LIME.

limewater, solution of calcium hydroxide (or slaked lime). Used to test for carbon dioxide, in treating acid burns, and as an antacid.

Lim Fjord (lēm′ fyôrd″), strait, c.110 mi. long, cutting across N Jutland, Denmark, and connecting North Sea with the Kattegat. It broke through to the North Sea in 1825. Aalborg is chief port on it.

liming (lī′mĭng), application to soil of calcium in various forms, e.g., marl, chalk, limestone, shells, or hydrated lime. It neutralizes soil, improves texture, increases activity of soil bacteria. Oversupply may be injurious to plants.

Limoges (lēmôzh′), city (pop. 99,535), cap. of Haute-Vienne dept., S central France, on Vienne R.; historic cap. of LIMOUSIN. It was burned and its people were massacred by Edward the Black Prince (1371) and it was devastated again in the Wars of Religion (16th cent.). The famous Limoges enamel industry, fully developed by the 13th cent., reached its peak with Léonard LIMOUSIN. Turgot, as intendant of Limoges (1761–74), introduced its celebrated china manufactures. Limoges has a cathedral (13th–16th cent.), a notable ceramics museum, and an art gallery. Birthplace of Renoir.

limonite (lǐ′mŭnīt), **brown hematite**, or **bog iron**, yellow to dark brown hydrated iron oxide, used as pigment and iron ore.

Limousin or **Limosin, Léonard** (lāônär′ lĕmōōzĕ′, lĕmōzĕ′), c.1505–c.1577, French painter, member of family of Limoges enamel artists.

Limousin (lĕmōōzĕ′), region and former province, S central France, in Corrèze and Haute-Vienne depts.; historic cap. LIMOGES. Hilly region with fertile agr. lowlands. The viscounty of Limoges (part of Aquitaine) passed under English rule in 1152; was annexed to France by Philip II in 1204; ceded back to England by Louis IX in 1259; ravaged by Edward the Black Prince in Hundred Years War; and recovered for France by Du Guesclin. A fief of the Bourbon-Vendôme family, it became part of the royal domain after the accession of Henry IV (1589).

Limpopo (lǐmpō′pō), river, c.1,000 mi. long, rising in Transvaal prov., South Africa. Flows through Mozambique to empty into Indian Ocean. Also called Crocodile R.

Linacre or **Lynaker, Thomas** (both: lǐ′nŭkùr), 1460?–1524, English humanist and physician. He wrote a Latin grammar (c.1523), translated many of Aristotle's and Galen's works into Latin, and founded Royal Col. of Physicians and readerships in medicine at Oxford and Cambridge. Erasmus and Sir Thomas More were among his pupils.

Linares (lēnä′rĕs), city (pop. 31,720), S Spain, in Andalusia. Silver and lead mines near by.

Lincoln, Abraham, 1809–65, 16th President of the United States. Born in log cabin in Hardin co., Ky. (now in Larue co.), the son of Thomas Lincoln and of Nancy Hanks, he grew up on the frontier as family moved forward. Mostly self-schooled. Story of early love affair with Ann RUTLEDGE is now discredited. Moving to Springfield, Ill., in 1837, he practiced law there. U.S. Representative (1847–49). As Republican candidate for U.S. Senate in 1858, Lincoln made his mark in debates with Stephen A. DOUGLAS. He was not an abolitionist, but he regarded slavery as an "injustice" and an evil; opposed its extension. Elected President in 1860. His wise control after CIVIL WAR began practically amounted to dictatorship. Cabinet was rent by internal jealousies and hatred; radical abolitionists condemned him as too mild; conservatives were gloomy over war's progress. He was in constant trouble with the generals. EMANCIPATION PROCLAMATION and Gettysburg Address express high moral tone he sought to give Northern cause. His second inaugural address included memorable phrase, "With malice toward none; with charity for all"; presaged a peace without conquest, RECONSTRUCTION without destruction. Assassinated by John Wilkes BOOTH in 1865. Became object of adulation and symbol of American democracy. His wife, **Mary Todd Lincoln,** 1818–82, met and married Lincoln in 1842. Many unkind comments have been made about her, especially by W. H. Herndon. Of the four sons she bore, only **Robert Todd Lincoln,** 1843–1926, lived to manhood. He was a lawyer and a public official. Papers of his father which he owned he left to Library of Congress; in 1947 these papers were opened to the public.

Lincoln, Benjamin, 1733–1810, American Revolutionary general. Served in Saratoga campaign (1777). Failed to take Savannah (1779); surrendered at Charleston (1780). Helped suppress Shays's Rebellion in Mass. (1787).

Lincoln, Mary Todd and **Robert Todd:** see LINCOLN, ABRAHAM.

Lincoln, England: see LINCOLNSHIRE.

Lincoln. 1 City (pop. 14,362), central Ill., NNE of Springfield, in farm and coal area; settled in 1830s. Platted and promoted (1853) with aid of Abraham Lincoln, who practiced law here 1847–59. Mfg. of china and cigars. 2 City (pop. 98,884), state cap. (since 1867), SE Nebr., W of the Missouri, in prairie region; founded 1864. Second largest city and educational center of state, it is rail, trade, and industrial center for extensive grain and livestock area. Food processing, oil refining, and mfg. of bricks and farm, printing, and office equipment. Modern capitol completed 1934. Seat of Univ. of NEBRASKA, Union Col. (Seventh-Day Adventist; coed.; 1891), and Nebraska Wesleyan Univ. (coed.; 1887). W. J. Bryan lived here, 1887–1916. 3 Town (pop. 11,270), NE R.I., on Blackstone R. and N of Providence. Limestone quarrying since colonial times. Textiles.

Lincoln, Mount: see PARK RANGE.

Lincoln City, settlement, SW Ind., NE of Evansville; laid out 1872 on site of Thomas Lincoln's farm. Park near by has Nancy Hanks Lincoln Memorial (with her grave) and site of Lincoln cabin, built 1816.

Lincoln College: see OXFORD UNIVERSITY.

Lincoln Heights, suburban city (pop. 5,531), SW Ohio, N of Cincinnati.

Lincoln Memorial, monument in Potomac Park, Washington, D.C., designed by Henry Bacon; dedicated 1922. Has heroic statue of Lincoln by Daniel Chester French and murals by Jules Guérin.

Lincoln Park, city (pop. 29,310), SE Mich., residential suburb SW of Detroit.

Lincolnshire or **Lincoln,** maritime county (2,665 sq. mi.; pop. 706,574), E England. Has three administrative districts—Parts of Holland in SE, Parts of Kesteven in SW, and Parts of Lindsey. Low, flat, and marshy region, it has many dykes and canals. Agr. and fishing are main occupations; there is some shipbuilding and mfg. Has many medieval churches and remains. County town is **Lincoln,** county borough (pop. 69,-412), in Parts of Lindsey; a transportation center. An ancient British fort, it was important under Romans and Danes. Cathedral (built 1075–1501) has famous bell "Great Tom of Lincoln" in 271 ft. tower. Lincoln Castle, many times besieged, was begun in 1068 by William I.

Lincoln's Inn: see INNS OF COURT.

Lincolnton, textile-mill town (pop. 5,423), W central N.C., NW of Charlotte.

Lincoln University: see JEFFERSON CITY, Mo.

Lind, Jenny, 1820–87, Swedish soprano. Made her debut in 1838 as Agathe in Weber's *Der Freischütz.* In 1841 studied with Manuel García. Under the management of P. T. Barnum she toured (1850–52) the U.S. Called "the Swedish nightingale," she was the greatest coloratura soprano of her time.

Lindau (lǐn′dou), town (pop. 19,768), Württemberg-Hohenzollern, SW Germany, on an island in L. of Constance. With its district (120 sq. mi.; pop. 57,-970) it belonged to Bavaria until in 1945 it was incorporated into French occupation zone.

Lindbergh, Charles A(ugustus), 1902–, American aviator. Nonstop, solo New York–to–Paris transatlantic flight in 1927 brought sudden fame. Kidnaping and death of his son in 1932 caused them to move to England in 1935. With Alexis Carrel invented (1936) a "mechanical heart." Resigned army reserve commission following criticism of his antiwar speeches. Served U.S. in Europe and Pacific as civilian consultant in World War II. His wife, **Anne (Spencer) Morrow Lindbergh,** 1907–, daughter of Dwight W. Morrow, accompanied and aided her husband on long flights and wrote several books.

Linden, city (pop. 30,644), NE N.J., SSW of Elizabeth; site bought from Indians 1664. Oil refinery; mfg. of pharmaceuticals, motors, and chemicals.

linden or **basswood,** ornamental deciduous tree of genus *Tilia* of N Hemisphere. Fragrant flowers are attractive to bees. Wood is valued for Venetian blinds, inexpensive furniture, and other articles.

Lindenhurst, village (pop. 8,644), SE N.Y., on S shore of Long Isl. near Babylon. Mfg. of machinery, aircraft and marine instruments, and cabinets.

Lindesnes (lĭn'dùsnĕs) or **the Naze** (näz), cape, extreme S Norway, on North Sea at entrance of the Skagerrak. Its beacon was first (1650) in Norway.

Lindisfarne (lĭn'dĭsfärn) or **Holy Island,** small island off Northumberland coast, England. Celtic Christianity first estab. in England here in 635. St. Cuthbert was famous bishop. Lindisfarne Gospels or Book of Durham, illuminated Latin manuscript now in British Mus., was written here before 700.

Lindsay or **Lyndsay, Sir David,** c.1490–c.1555, Scottish Protestant poet. Wrote several satires against Catholic Church (e.g., *The Testament and Complaynt of Our Soverane Lordis Papyngo,* 1530) and long morality play of religious and political criticism, *Ane Pleasant Satyre of the Three Estaitis* (1540).

Lindsay, (Nicholas) Vachel (vā'chùl), 1879–1931, American poet, b. Ill. He lived as a prairie troubadour, selling his rhymes for bread. Among his works are *The Congo* (1914), *The Chinese Nightingale* (1917), *Johnny Appleseed* (1928).

Lindsay, town (pop. 9,603), S Ont., Canada, NE of Toronto, in lake district. Woolen, flour, lumber mills.

Lindsay, town (pop. 5,060), S central Calif., SE of Fresno. Processes and ships oranges and olives.

Lindsey, Ben(jamin Barr), 1869–1943, American judge and reformer. He pioneered in establishing juvenile courts. Advocated trial marriages.

Lindsey, Parts of: see LINCOLNSHIRE, England.

Línea, La (lä lē'nää), fortified city (pop. 35,101), S Spain, on Strait of Gibraltar. Its position at border of neutral zone which separates it from the British colony gives it strategic importance.

Line Islands, group of 10 islands (including Palmyra and Christmas Isl.) in central and S Pacific, S of Hawaiian Isls. and extending N-S. Roughly separated into two groups by the equator.

linen, fabric or yarn made from the fiber of flax. Probably the earliest vegetable fiber in use, linen has been found in Egyptian tombs more than 3,500 years old. It was the principal European textile of the Middle Ages; Flanders has been famed for it since the 11th cent. Today, Ireland is chief producer of fabric; the greatest quantity of flax fiber is grown in Russia, the finest in Belgium. The amount of handwork involved until recently in processing linen restricted the development of the industry in the U.S.

Linfield College: see McMINNVILLE, Oregon.

lingua franca (lĭng'gwù frăng'kù) [language of the Franks], spoken language, usually hybrid, used for limited communication among peoples of mutually unintelligible languages. The original lingua franca was used for commerce in the Mediterranean after the Crusades. Similar polyglot tongues include pidgin English, Chinook jargon, and Swahili. Occasionally term is applied to a formal language (e.g., French as language of diplomacy).

linguistics, scientific study of language. Its central aspect is descriptive study of a given language. Comparative or historical linguistics, study of relation of languages to each other, was developed especially in 19th-cent. Germany. The descriptive field developed notably in U.S. Linguistics, an anthropological science, has contacts with other sciences, e.g., with physics through PHONETICS. Some parts of language study are not apparently amenable to attack by scientific methods and are not, therefore, fields of linguistics at all. See PHILOLOGY.

Liniers, Jacques de (Span. lēnēärz'; Fr. lēnyä'), 1753–1810, French officer in Spanish service, viceroy of Río de la Plata. Was twice successful in recapturing Buenos Aires from British invaders (1806, 1807).

Linkoping, Swed. *Linköping* (lĭn'chů"pĭng), industrial city (pop. 54,552), co. seat of Ostergotland co., SE Sweden, on Gota Canal. It has rail shops, ironworks, sugar refineries, and textile mills. It has been an episcopal see since 1120. Its cathedral was begun 1230.

Linlithgow (lĭnlĭth'gō), burgh (pop. 3,929), co. town of West Lothian, Scotland. Linlithgow Palace, former residence of Scottish kings, was birthplace of James V and Mary Queen of Scots.

Linlithgowshire, Scotland: see WEST LOTHIAN.

Linnaeus (lĭnē'ùs), 1707–78, Swedish botanist. His name was originally Karl von Linné. A founder of modern systematic botany, he established the binomial method of designating plants and animals. The 1758 edition of his *Systema naturae* (1735) is used as basis of Linnaean nomenclature.

Linnhe, Loch (lŏkh lĭ'nē), inlet, Argyllshire, Scotland, extending 20 mi. NE from Firth of Lorne.

linoleum (lĭnō'lēùm), resilient floor or wall covering of jute or burlap surfaced with mixture of powdered cork, oxidized linseed oil, gums or other ingredients, and coloring matter. Patented 1863 by English rubber manufacturer, Frederick Walton.

linotype, trade name of machine that makes slugs, each doing the work of a line of hand-set type. Patented by Ottmar Mergenthaler (1885), it was first used at the N.Y. *Tribune* (1886). Operated by a keyboard, it assembles brass matrices into a line, casts the slug, distributes the matrices.

linseed, seed of flax plant from which **linseed oil,** an amber fatty oil, is made. Used as DRYING OIL in paint and varnish, in making linoleum, oilcloth, and ink, and in medicine. **Linseed cake,** made by pressing flaxseed (after removing most of the oil) into cakes, is a concentrated livestock feed.

Linton, William James, 1812–97, Anglo-American wood engraver and political reformer. Edited and wrote for several radical periodicals in England. In 1867 he moved to U.S., where he helped to revive art of wood engraving.

Linton, city (pop. 5,973), SW Ind., SSE of Terre Haute. Coal mining.

Linyü, China: see SHANHAIKWAN.

Lin Yutang (lĭn' yü'täng'), 1895–, Chinese-American writer; in U.S. since c.1928. His books have been written largely in English. They include *My Country and My People* (1935), *The Importance of Living* (1937), and *Chinatown Family* (1948, a novel).

Linz (lĭnts), city (pop. 185,177), cap. of Upper Austria, on the Danube. River port; mfg. center (iron and steel works, machinery, textiles, chemicals). Dates from Roman times. Episcopal see.

lion, mammal (*Felis leo* or genus *Panthera*) of cat family, found in Africa, SW Asia, W India. It is extinct in Europe, much of Asia, Asia Minor. Lions are yellow to brown, short-haired, and the tail is tipped by a dark tuft. Usually the male has black or tawny mane. Male (with tail) is 9–10 ft. long, up to 500 lb. Lions hunt antelope, zebra, other animals, and also eat carrion. Usually only old or weak lions attack man.

Lion, Gulf of, Fr. *Golfe du Lion,* bay of the Mediterranean, S France, from Spanish border to Toulon.

Lions International, organization of business and professional men, founded 1914 by Melvin Jones. Furthers community projects.

Lipari Islands (lĭ'pùrē) or **Aeolian Islands** (ēō'lēùn), volcanic group (44 sq. mi.; pop. 17,697), Italy, N of Sicily, in Tyrrhenian Sea. In ancient mythology, the residence of the wind god Aeolus. The chief islands are Lipari; Vulcano (mythical site of fire god's workshop), with a volcano emitting sulphur vapors; and Stromboli, with an active volcano 3,040 ft. high. The islands have long been a place of political exile. Pumice stone, wine, and currants are the chief exports.

Lipchitz, Jacques (zhäk' lēpshēts'), 1891–, French sculptor, b. Lithuania. Was allied with cubists. Known for skeletal constructions and transparents (made by melted-wax technique).

Li Po (lē′ pō′, bō) or **Li Tai Po** (tī′), c.700–762, Chinese poet of T'ang dynasty. Largely traditional in theme, his poems describe grief of separated lovers, beauty of nature, and the solace found in wine. He conveys exquisitely his sense of mystery in the universe. The 2,000 extant poems are said to comprise only a tenth of his output.

Lippe (lĭ′pŭ), former state (469 sq. mi.; 1939 pop. 187,-220), NW Germany, between Teutoburg Forest and Weser R.; cap. Detmold. Was incorporated in 1946 with North Rhine-Westphalia. Region is mainly agr. It is crossed by Lippe R., a tributary of the Rhine. A lordship from 12th cent. and a county from 16th cent., it was subdivided several times after 1613. Two counties (after 1720, principalities) emerged—Lippe or Lippe-Detmold and SCHAUMBURG-LIPPE. Lippe joined German Confederation 1815; German Empire 1871; Weimar Republic 1919. In 1897 the contested succession to Lippe was awarded to Count Ernest of Lippe-Biesterfeld. His son, Prince Leopold, abdicated 1918; his nephew, Bernhard zu Lippe-Biesterfeld (b. 1911), married (1937) Juliana who became queen of the Netherlands.

Lippi (lĭp′pē), name of two Florentine painters of 15th cent. **Fra Filippo Lippi** (frä′ fēlēp′pō), c.1406–1469, also called Lippo Lippi, was a Carmelite. Master of color and graceful line (as shown by *Coronation of the Virgin*), he taught Botticelli, Benozzo Gozzoli, and Il Pesellino. Enjoyed patronage of the Medici. His son, **Filippino Lippi** (fēlēp-pē′nō), c.1457–1504, studied under Botticelli. Finished Masaccio's frescoes in Brancacci Chapel, Florence.

Lippmann, Gabriel (gäbrēěl′ lēpmän′), 1845–1921, French physicist. Won 1908 Nobel Prize for discovery of method for photographic reproduction of colors through use of interference process.

Lippmann, Walter (lĭp′mùn), 1889–, American essayist, an editor on *New Republic* and N.Y. *World*. After 1931 wrote syndicated column on world affairs for N.Y. *Herald Tribune.*

Lipsius, Justus (lĭp′sēŭs), 1547–1606, Flemish scholar, authority on Roman literature, history, and antiquities. His edition of Tacitus is famous.

Lipton, Sir Thomas (Johnstone), 1850–1931, British merchant and yachting enthusiast. Opened (1876) a grocery store which he expanded into a large chain of stores. Made five unsuccessful attempts to win the *America*'s Cup yachting trophy.

liquefaction, in physics, change of substance from solid or gaseous state to liquid. It is held to be a change in kinetic energy of molecules. Change from solid to liquid or liquid to gas requires heat; change from gas to liquid or liquid to solid requires taking away heat. Liquefaction of gas can be effected by subjecting gas to high pressure and cooling it below its critical temperature.

liqueur (lĭkŭr′), strong alcoholic beverage made by distilling spirits flavored with herbs, fruits, or other substances and usually sweetened. Liqueurs contain from c.27% to 80% alcohol.

liquid, one of three states of matter in which substance has definite volume but no definite shape. Since liquids flow into shape of containing vessel they are classed with gases as fluids. Liquid changes to gas at its boiling point, to solid at its freezing or melting point. By fractional distillation liquids in a mixture can be separated from each other because they vaporize at their own distinct boiling points. Cohesion between molecules of liquid is not sufficient to prevent water at free surface from bounding off at ordinary temperatures (see EVAPORATION). Liquids exhibit SURFACE TENSION and CAPILLARITY. DIFFUSION can occur between two liquids. In general, liquids expand when heated, contract when cooled; they exert pressure on sides of a container and on any body immersed in them; pressure is transmitted undiminished in all directions. Liquids exert a buoyant force on immersed body (see ARCHIMEDES' PRINCIPLE; SPECIFIC GRAVITY).

liquid air, air that has been liquefied by compression and cooling to very low temperatures. It must be kept in Dewar flask since at ordinary temperatures it absorbs heat rapidly and reverts to gaseous state. Used for freezing other substances and as source of nitrogen, oxygen, argon (and other inert gases).

liquor laws, legislation restricting or controlling the manufacture and sale of alcoholic beverages. Intent is often to prevent immoderate use of intoxicants as well as to raise revenue. Licensing and direct taxation are the favorite methods of control. In Sweden was inaugurated (1865) the Goteborg licensing system, which eliminated private profit from sale of spirits. National PROHIBITION was attempted in the U.S. 1919–33. Local option to prohibit sale of liquor is retained by some states and cities.

Liri (lē′rē), river of S central Italy, rising in Apennines and flowing into Tyrrhenian Sea near Gaeta. Below its junction with the Rapido it is called Garigliano (combined length of Liri and Garigliano, 98 mi.). Hydroelectric stations. In World War II, Allies gained access to Rome through Liri valley after long and bitter fighting, notably at Cassino (1943–44).

Lisa, Manuel (lē′sů), 1772–1820, American fur trader. Led expeditions in upper Missouri R. region. Helped form Missouri Fur Co.

Lisbon (lĭz′bùn), Port. *Lisboa,* city (pop. 783,919), cap. of Portugal and of Estremadura prov., on mouth of Tagus R. A thriving Atlantic port, it is also an important center of transoceanic air transport. See of an archbishop (titular patriarch). University was founded 1910. Built on seven hills, Lisbon is dominated by the old Castel São Jorge. Lisbon's importance dates from its conquest from the Moors by Alfonso I (1147). Though largely rebuilt after the great earthquake of 1755, it has preserved several medieval buildings, especially the old Alfama quarter around the cathedral. The Renaissance Monastery of São Vicente contains the tombs of the Braganza kings. At Belém, on N shore of the Tagus near the sea, is the magnificent monastery built by Manuel I to commemorate Vasco da Gama's discovery of the route to India. Camões was born in Lisbon.

Lisburn (lĭz′bûrn, lĭs′–), urban district (pop. 14,778), Co. Antrim, N. Ireland. Main industry, linen mfg., introduced by Huguenots in 1594. Episcopal seat of a Catholic and a Protestant diocese.

Lisieux (lēzyû′), town (pop. 11,569), Calvados dept., N France, one of oldest towns of Normandy. The shrine of St. Theresa of the Child Jesus is a major place of pilgrimage.

Lismore (lĭsmôr′, lĭz–), market town (pop. 1,174), Co. Waterford, Ireland. In 7th cent., town had an abbey and a great school. Lismore Castle has medieval Irish manuscript, the Book of Lismore.

Lismore (lĭz′môr, lĭzmôr′), island, c.10 mi. long and 1½ mi. wide, Argyllshire, Scotland, in Loch Linnhe. Has several old castles. Book of the Dean of Lismore (16th cent.) is one of the oldest and most valuable of Gaelic collections.

Lissoy, Co. Westmeath, Ireland: see AUBURN.

List, Friedrich (lĭst), 1789–1846, German economist. Forced to emigrate (1825) to U.S. for advocating reforms. Returned (1832) as U.S. consul at Leipzig. Favored commercial association of German states. Many of his ideas were adopted.

Lister, Joseph Lister, 1st **Baron** (lĭ′stûr), 1827–1912, English surgeon, founder of antiseptic surgery. He proved the value of use of carbolic acid as ANTISEPTIC and of heat sterilization of instruments in decreasing postoperative infections (1865). Introduced absorbable ligature, drainage tube, and other operative techniques.

Liszt, Franz (lĭst), 1811–86, Hungarian pianist and composer. He was regarded as the greatest pianist of his age, and all the principal artistic figures of the time were among his friends. He lived with Mme d'Agoult, 1833–44, and their daughter Cosima was the wife of Hans von Bülow and later of Wagner. His colorful life was as romantic as his music. He developed the tone poem (e.g., *Les Préludes*) which influenced Wagner and Richard Strauss. His *Années de pélérinage,* his Hungarian Rhapsodies, his etudes and concertos for piano, and his Dante and Faust symphonies are his chief works.

Li Tai Po: see Li Po.

Litchfield. 1 Town (pop. 4,964), W Conn., SW of Torrington. Includes part of Bantam L. Here, Judge Tapping Reeve started first school in U.S. for law only (1784–1833). Birthplace of Ethan Allen, Henry Ward Beecher, and Harriet Beecher Stowe. **2** City (pop. 7,208), S central Ill., S of Springfield, in coal and farm area. Mfg. of radiators and shoes.

litchi or **leechee,** small Chinese tree (*Litchi chinensis*), with nutlike fruit in a thin rough shell. The Chinese use fruit fresh, dried, or preserved; for commerce it is dried. Now grown in S Fla. and Calif.

litharge (lǐ′thärj), yellow monoxide of lead made by heating lead in air. It is used in making paints, glass, etc., and in treating rubber.

lithium (lǐ′thēŭm), silvery-white metallic element (symbol = Li; see also ELEMENT, table). It is an alkali metal, very soft, and the lightest of metals. Its compounds color a flame bright red and are used in pyrotechnics. It is alloyed with aluminum, lead, beryllium; certain lithium salts are used to increase capacity of storage cells, others are used in medicine.

lithography (lǐthŏ′grŭfē), type of surface printing, used both as an art process and as a commercial printing process. A lithograph is printed from a stone except in commercial lithography, which uses grained metal plates. The drawing is usually made in reverse directly on a slab of stone with a lithographic crayon or ink that contains soap or grease. The fatty acid of this material forms an insoluble soap on the surface, which will accept the greasy printing ink and reject water. Next, the design is fixed against spreading by treatment with a gum arabic and nitric acid solution. The drawing is washed off with turpentine and water and is then ready to be inked with a roller and printed. The process was invented c.1796 by Aloys Senefelder in Germany. He used limestone, which is still considered the best material for lithography as an art process.

lithopone (lǐ′thŭpōn), white pigment, a mixture of barium sulphate and zinc sulphide. It is used in interior paints and cheaper enamels.

Lithuania (lǐthōŏā′nĕŭ), Lithuanian *Lietuva,* republic (c.25,000 sq. mi.; pop. c.3,000,000), NE Europe, on the Baltic Sea; cap. Vilna. Its incorporation in 1940 into the USSR as a constituent republic has not been recognized by the U.S. (as of 1953). A flatland drained by the Niemen, Lithuania is largely agr. (dairying, stock raising). The population is largely Roman Catholic. In the 13th cent. the Liths or Lithuanians, who were then still pagans, formed a unified state to defend themselves against the LIVONIAN KNIGHTS and TEUTONIC KNIGHTS. Under the grand dukes Gedimin and Olgerd (14th cent.) Lithuania acquired all Belorussia, much of the Ukraine, and sections of Great Russia, becoming one of the largest states of medieval Europe. In 1386 Grand Duke Jagiello became king of Poland as LADISLAUS II and was baptized. The union of Poland and Lithuania under the JAGIELLO dynasty was at first a close alliance of two independent nations. Under WITOWT (reigned 1392–1430) Lithuania reached its greatest power, but it declined under the pressure of the expanding grand duchy of Moscow. In 1569 Lithuania and Poland united as a single state. The upper classes became thoroughly polonized. Russia annexed all Lithuania in the Polish partitions of 1772–95. In 1918 Lithuania proclaimed its independence. It successfully resisted attacks by Bolshevik troops but became involved in lengthy international disputes after the Polish seizure of VILNA (1920) and the Lithuanian seizure of the

MEMEL TERRITORY (1923). Kaunas was the cap. until the recovery of Vilna in 1940. The virtual dictatorship of Augustine Voldemaras (1926–29) was succeeded by that of Antanas Smetona (1929–39); a constitution along corporative (fascist) lines became law in 1938. Lithuania was forced in 1939 to grant military bases to the USSR. In 1940 it was occupied by Soviet troops and inc. into the USSR. During German occupation (1941–44) in World War II, its Jewish minority (c.7%) was largely exterminated.

Lithuanian, Baltic language of Lithuania. It belongs to Indo-European family. See LANGUAGE (table).

Lititz (lǐ′tǐts), borough (pop. 5,568), SE Pa., N of Lancaster. Mfg. of chocolate, pretzels, shoes, and textiles.

litmus, organic dye that turns blue in alkalies and red in acids, therefore classed as indicator. It is used in form of treated paper and is prepared chiefly in Netherlands from certain lichens.

Little, Lou, 1893–, American football coach. Head coach at Columbia since 1930.

Little America, Antarctic exploration base, on Ross Shelf Ice, S of Bay of Whales. Estab. 1929 by Richard E. Byrd and used subsequently by him and other explorers.

Little Belt: see BELT, GREAT.

Little Bighorn, river rising in N Wyo., in Bighorn Mts. and flowing N to enter S Mont. and join Bighorn R. at Hardin. Scene, June 25, 1876, of defeat and death, at hands of the Sioux, of G. A. CUSTER. Battlefield is now national monument.

Little Colorado, river, rising in W N.Mex. near Ariz. line and flowing NW 315 mi. across Ariz. to Colorado R. in the Grand Canyon.

Little Compton, town (pop. 1,556), SE R.I., between Sakonnet R. and Mass. line. R.I. Red fowl originated here. John and Priscilla Alden's daughter Elizabeth buried here. Includes Sakonnet resort.

Little Entente (äntänt′, ätät′), defensive alliance formed after World War I by Czechoslovakia, Rumania, and Yugoslavia and supported by France. Purpose was to preserve territorial status quo estab. by treaties of Versailles, Saint-Germain, Trianon, and Neuilly and to prevent union between Germany and Austria. It was effectively ended when Czechoslovakia was dismembered by Munich Pact (1938).

Little Falls. 1 City (pop. 6,717), central Minn., on the Mississippi and NNW of St. Cloud. Farm trade center with mfg. of food and wood products. **2** Township (pop. 6,405), NE N.J., SW of Paterson. Laundry plant. **3** City (pop. 9,541), E central N.Y., SE of Utica, on Mohawk R. (water power) and the Barge Canal. Mfg. of clothing and footwear.

Littlefield, city (pop. 6,540), NW Texas, NW of Lubbock on Llano Estacado. Processes cotton, grains, poultry, and dairy products.

Little Flower of Jesus: see THERESA, SAINT (Theresa of the Child Jesus).

Little Masters, term applied to a group of 16th-cent. German engravers, mostly followers of Dürer. Group includes Albrecht Altdorfer, Heinrich Aldegrever, the Beham brothers, and Georg Pencz.

Little Minch, Scotland: see MINCH.

Little Missouri, river rising in NE Wyo. and flowing 560 mi. NE and E to the Missouri in W N.Dak.

Little Rock, city (pop. 102,213), state cap., central Ark., on Arkansas R. and in Ouachita foothills; laid out 1820. Rail focus and state's largest city and commercial center, it is in diversified-farming, mining (bauxite, coal, clay), timber, oil, and natural-gas region. Has large cotton trade. Mfg. of cottonseed and wood products and chemicals. Seat of Univ. of Arkansas medical school. Old capitol (1836) is now war memorial. Birthplace of Gen. Douglas MacArthur. NORTH LITTLE ROCK is across the river.

Little Russia: see UKRAINE.

Little Sioux (sōō), river rising in SW Minn. near Iowa line and flowing SW 221 mi. across NW Iowa to the Missouri S of Sioux City. Tributaries include Maple

R., West Fork, and Elliott Creek. Included in flood-control and soil-conservation program (1947) affecting large areas in NW Iowa.

Little Tennessee, river rising in Blue Ridge, NE Ga., and flowing N into N.C., then WNW around the Smokies into Tenn. to Tennessee R. Has Fontana and Cheoah dams in N.C., and Calderwood Dam in Tenn.

Littleton, Sir Thomas, 1422–81, English jurist, author of a short work on the types of estates in land in England (*Tenures*).

Litvinov, Maxim Maximovich (mŭksyēm′ mŭksyē′mŭvĭch lyĭtvē′nŭf), 1876–1952, Russian foreign commissar (1930–39) whose real name was Wallach. Advocated cooperation with Western powers, firm stand against Axis. Replaced by Molotov shortly before German-Soviet pact. Ambassador to U.S. 1941–43.

Liutprand (lēoōt′pränd), d. 744, Lombard king of Italy (712–44). Favored Roman law; created a centralized state by curbing powers of local dukes and bishops; expanded his domain N into Bavaria; died at Ravenna in campaign against Byzantine exarchs.

Livadiya (lyĭvä′dyĕŭ), Black Sea resort near Yalta, RSFSR, in S Crimea. Its former imperial palace (built 1910–11), now a sanatorium, was F. D. Roosevelt's residence during Yalta Conference (1945).

Live Oak, city (pop. 4,064), N Fla., E of Tallahassee. Chief bright-leaf-tobacco market of Fla.

liver, large, reddish-brown gland. In man, it lies below diaphragm chiefly on right side; it is divided into four unequal lobes. Functions include secretion of bile; conversion of glucose into a starch (glycogen), which is reconverted when need arises; storage of antianemic principle; conversion of protein wastes; destruction of worn-out red corpuscles. See *ill.*, p. 595.

liver fluke: see FLUKE.

Liverpool, seaport (pop. 789,532), Lancashire, England, on Mersey R. Greatest port in W Britain and one of world's leading trade centers, it has docks over 7 mi. long. Europe's leading cotton market, its importance has declined since World War II. Connected by tunnel with Birkenhead. Cathedral, when finished, will be England's largest. Univ. of Liverpool chartered 1903. Heavily bombed 1940–41.

liverwort, small flowerless plant usually growing in moist places and considered intermediate between aquatic algae and terrestrial mosses and ferns. Among the genera are *Marchantia* and *Riccia*.

livery companies, name for English GUILDS in city of London. Chartered largely by Edward III in 14th cent. For ceremonies, they assumed distinctive livery or costume and distinctive badge, and thus attired have formed colorful part of municipal pageants and royal coronations down to present time. Attained political power under Edward III, having right to elect common council of city of London. They were incorporated, held lands and other wealth, and administered schools, e.g., St. Paul's and Merchant Taylors'. Their character has changed with rise of capitalism and competitive system, but there are still some 75 livery companies today, 12 of them known as the great companies.

Livia Drusilla (lĭv′ĕŭ droōsĭl′ŭ), c.55 B.C.–A.D. 29, mother of Roman emperor TIBERIUS and of Drusus Germanicus. In 38 B.C. Augustus forced her to be divorced and marry him. After Tiberius' accession she tried to control government.

Livingston, family of American statesmen, diplomats, and jurists. **Robert Livingston,** 1654–1728, b. Scotland, acquired wealth and lands in N.Y. and exerted control in the provincial assembly. His grandson, **Robert R. Livingston,** 1718–75, was a Whig political leader in N.Y. His son, the younger **Robert R. Livingston,** 1746–1813, a famous lawyer, negotiated the Louisiana Purchase as minister to France. His brother, **Edward Livingston,** 1764–1836, jurist and statesman, was Secretary of State (1831–33) under Andrew Jackson and also minister to France (1833–35). Another grandson of Robert Livingston (1654–1728) was **Peter**

Van Brugh Livingston, 1710–92. A Whig supporter preceding American Revolution, he was president of first provincial congress (1775). His brother, **Philip Livingston,** 1716–78, signed the Declaration of Independence and was an original promoter of King's Col. (now Columbia Univ.). Another brother, **William Livingston,** 1723–90, was first governor of N.J. under state constitution of 1777. William's son, **Henry Brockholst Livingston,** 1757–1823, was a justice of U.S. Supreme Court (1806–23).

Livingston. 1 City (pop. 7,683), S Mont., on Yellowstone R. and N of Yellowstone Natl. Park. Rail, tourist, and trade center in agr. and mining area. **2** Township (pop. 9,932), NE N.J., near Passaic R. and NW of Newark.

Livingstone, David (lĭ′vĭngstŭn), 1813–73, Scottish missionary and explorer in Africa. Missionary in Bechuanaland (1841–52). Discovered Victoria Falls (1855). When he had been long unheard from, H. M. STANLEY was sent in search of him and found him (1871).

Livingstone, town (pop. 7,899), S Northern Rhodesia, near Victoria Falls; tourist center. Named for the explorer David Livingstone. Was cap. of Northern Rhodesia, 1911–35.

Livius Andronicus (lĭ′vēŭs ăndrŭnī′kŭs), fl. 3d cent. B.C., Roman poet who introduced Greek literature into Rome. Founded Latin comedy.

Livonia (lĭvō′nēŭ) or **Livland,** region of NE Europe, on the Baltic Sea, comprising present ESTONIA and N LATVIA. It is named for the Livs, a Finnic people, who were conquered by the LIVONIAN KNIGHTS (13th cent.). Reducing the Livs to serfdom, the knights formed a powerful state which also comprised S Latvia. Its chief cities—Riga, Tartu, Tallinn—were German in culture and were members of the Hanseatic League. The dissolution of the Livonian Order (1561) was followed by a contest for its domains among Poland, Russia, and Sweden. COURLAND (i.e., S Latvia) became a duchy under Polish overlordship. Latgale (NE Latvia) passed to Poland and, in 1772, to Russia. Estonia passed to Sweden; Vidzeme (NW Latvia) passed first to Poland, then (1629) to Sweden; both Vidzeme and Estonia were conquered by Peter I in 1710 and formally ceded to Russia in 1721. Livonia was a Russian province (government) 1783–1918.

Livonian Knights, German military religious order, founded c.1202 by the bishop of Riga to Christianize the Baltic countries; also called the Brothers of the Sword and Knights Swordbearers. Habit: white robe with red cross and sword. They conquered COURLAND and LIVONIA but were routed by the Lithuanians at Siauliai (1236) and as a result formed a union with the TEUTONIC KNIGHTS until 1525. Weakened by the Reformation and by Russian attacks, they disbanded in 1561 but kept their vast estates. The "Baltic barons," who dominated the Baltic provs. until World War I, were largely descended from the knights.

Livorno, Italy: see LEGHORN.

Livy (Titus Livius) (lĭ′vē), 59 B.C.–A.D. 17, Roman historian. His life work was the *History of Rome,* 35 of the original 142 books surviving; there are fragments of others, and all but two are known through epitomes. Noted for his freedom of expression and masterly style.

Lizard, the, promontory, Cornwall, England. S extremity is southernmost point of Great Britain.

lizard, reptile of tropical and temperate regions. The body is scaly, most species have four limbs, and usually eyelids and ear openings are present. Tail in many forms is easily broken off and regenerated. The tongue may be short and wide or long and forked. Many lizards can undergo color changes. Most are insectivorous; few are herbivorous or omnivorous. Some lay eggs; some bear live young. Size ranges from few inches to 8–12 ft. in komodo or dragon lizard. Flying lizards, which glide from tree to tree, live in Malay Archipelago; frilled lizards in N Australia. See also CHAMELEON; GILA MONSTER; GLASS SNAKE; HORNED TOAD; IGUANA.

Ljubljana (lyōō'blyänä), Ger. *Laibach,* city (pop. 120,-994), cap. of Slovenia, NW Yugoslavia, on Sava R. It is a trade center with varied mfg. and a Roman Catholic archiepiscopal see. University was founded 1919. Until 1918 it was cap. CARNIOLA, part of Austria. Scene of Congress of LAIBACH (1821).

llama (lä'mù), South American domesticated hoofed mammal (*Lama*) of camel family, believed to be descended from guanaco. Smaller than camel, it has no hump and somewhat resembles a sheep. Llamas are brown, white, black, or piebald. They live in herds up to snow line in Andes.

Llandudno (lăndŭd'nō, –dĭd'nō), urban district (pop. 16,712), Caernarvonshire, Wales, on a point of land jutting into the Irish Sea; a popular resort.

Llanelly (lănĕ'lē, –ĕ'thlē), municipal borough (pop. 34,-329), Caermarthenshire, Wales. Has important coal exports and metal works.

Llano Estacado (lä'nō ĕstŭkä'dō) [Span.= staked plain], S grasslands of Great Plains plateau, E N.Mex. and W Texas. On S is Cap Rock escarpment, which runs across Texas Panhandle SW almost to SE N.Mex. High N plains around Amarillo are distinguished from the somewhat lower South Plains, centered around Lubbock. All are wind-swept grasslands, formerly cattle country, now dotted by farms (irrigated and dry) and by oil and gas fields.

llanos (yä'nōs), Spanish American term for prairies, specifically those of Orinoco basin in Venezuela and part of E Colombia. Despite the bad climate, in colonial and early republican times *llaneros* (comparable to gauchos of Argentine pampa) herded several million head of cattle here.

Llewelyn ap Gruffydd (lōōĕ'lĭn äp grōō'fĭdh, thlōōĕ'lĭn, grĭ'fĭdh), d. 1282, first prince of Wales (1267). Had great power in N Wales but English invasions brought total disaster. He was one of the last fighters for Welsh liberties.

Lloyd George, David, 1st **Earl Lloyd-George of Dwyfor** (dōōĕ'vôr), 1863–1945, British statesman. Liberal anti-imperialist member of Parliament for 54 years from 1890. Opposed South African War. Chancellor of exchequer under Herbert Asquith, he ended veto power of House of Lords by taking social insurance issue to the people in 1910 election. Prime minister in coalition cabinet (1916–22). One of the "Big Four" at Paris Peace Conference in 1919. Opposed appeasement policy before World War II.

Lloyd's, London insurance underwriting corporation of some 300 individual syndicates. Founded late 17th cent., it is now international in scope. Deals mainly with marine insurance, but insures against many kinds of risk.

loam, soil composed of clay, sand, and silt, with particles of many sizes rather evenly mixed. Loams are gritty, plastic when moist, and retain more water and contain more nutriment than sandy soil.

Loanda, Angola: see LUANDA.

Lobachevsky, Nikolai Ivanovich (nyĭkûlī' ēvä'nùvĭch lūbŭchĕf'skē), 1793–1856, Russian mathematician. He pioneered in non-Euclidean geometry and originated a system of geometry which challenged Euclid's fifth postulate.

lobbying, practice of influencing legislation or government officials by agents who serve special interests. The pressure may be exerted through data, publicity, threat of political reprisals, or pledges of support. Lobbyists are required by law to register, but lobbying is nevertheless frequently condemned as an abuse of representational government.

lobelia (lōbē'lyù), annual or perennial plant (genus *Lobelia*) with tubular flowers. Annuals for window boxes or gardens are compact or trailing forms of blue or white S African *Lobelia erinus.* The scarlet cardinal flower (*L. cardinalis*) is a choice North American wild flower.

Lobito (lōbē'tō), town (pop. 13,592), Angola; port on the Atlantic. Terminus of railroad to rich copper-mining area of Katanga, Belgian Congo.

Lob Nor or **Lop Nor** (both: lôp' nôr'), marshy salt-lake depression, E Sinkiang prov., China.

Lobos Islands (lō'bōs) or **Seal Islands,** off coast of NW Peru; valuable for deposits of guano.

lobster, marine crustacean, with five pairs of jointed legs, the first pair having pincerlike claws. An outer skeleton, usually greenish brown, covers the body and appendages. Lobsters move slowly on land and rapidly in water, on ocean bottom. Female with eggs is called "berried lobster." Common American lobster is *Homarus americanus.* Chief U.S. fisheries are in Maine and Mass.

Locarno (lōkär'nō), town (pop. 7,747), Ticino canton, S Switzerland. Tourist resort. Here in 1925 was signed the **Locarno Pact,** a series of treaties of mutual guarantee and arbitration entered into by England, France, Germany, Italy, Belgium, Czechoslovakia, and Poland. The major treaty guaranteed the W boundaries of Germany as fixed by the Treaty of Versailles of 1919. Germany also agreed to demilitarize a strip of the Rhineland and was guaranteed entry into the League of Nations. A serious flaw of the treaties, which were intended as the foundation of European security, was the absence of a guarantee of Germany's E frontier. Briand, Stresemann, and Austin Chamberlain were the chief framers of the pact.

locative (lŏk'–), in grammar of certain languages (e.g., Sanskrit), CASE referring to location.

Loch (lŏkh, lŏk). For names of Scottish lakes and inlets beginning thus, see second part of name: e.g., for Loch Long, see LONG, LOCH. See also LAKE.

Lochner, Stephan (shtē'fän lŏkh'nùr), d. 1451, German painter, main representative of Cologne school.

lock, canal, enclosed water area for raising or lowering a vessel from one water level to another, used in rivers and canals where course is not level and at dock entrances. To pass to higher level, water in lock is lowered to level of floating vessel, gate is opened, ship moves in, and gate is closed. Water enters lock from higher level until water level in two is the same. Procedure is reversed when vessel goes from higher to lower level.

lock and key. Lock usually consists of sliding, pivoted, or rotary bolt guarded by an obstacle either fixed (warded) as in most padlocks or movable (tumbler) and controlled by a key with a flat, pipe, or pin shank. In the time lock, used since c.1875, a clock mechanism prevents opening until set time.

Locke, David Ross: see NASBY, PETROLEUM V.

Locke, John, 1632–1704, English philosopher, founder of British empiricism. In political exile in Holland (1683–89) he completed his famous *Essay concerning Human Understanding.* A practical psychology, it held that the mind at birth is a blank upon which human experience inscribes all knowledge. After the Glorious Revolution (1688) he returned to England. In *Two Treatises on Government* (1689) he justified constitutional monarchy. He contradicted Hobbes by asserting the original state of nature was good, and men equal and independent. The state, he held, was formed by social contract and should be guided by belief in natural rights. This was in essence a plea for democracy, which bore fruit in the U.S. Constitution. His empiricism was expanded by Berkeley and Hume, and the men of the Enlightenment regarded him as the prophet of reason.

Lockhart, John Gibson, 1794–1854, Scottish lawyer and literary critic; son-in-law of Sir Walter Scott. His biography of Scott (7 vols., 1837–38) is a classic. He was editor of *Quarterly Review* 1825–53.

Lockhart, city (pop. 5,573), S central Texas, SSE of Austin. Center of agr., dairying, and oil area. Texans defeated Comanches (1840) at battle of Plum Creek to NE.

Lock Haven, city (pop. 11,381), N Pa. on W branch of

Susquehanna R. and SW of Williamsport; settled 1769. Mfg. of aircraft and building materials.

lockjaw: see TETANUS.

Lockland, city (pop. 5,736), SW Ohio, near Cincinnati. Mfg. of aircraft, building materials.

lockout, dismissal and prevention of reemployment, adopted by employers to resist labor demands or to break a strike by importing new workers. Lockouts have generally been considered legal when not in violation of the terms of a joint agreement.

Lockport. **1** City (pop. 4,955), NE Ill., N of Joliet, at locks connecting Chicago Sanitary and Ship Canal with Des Plaines R. Also has locks of old Illinois and Michigan Canal. **2** City (pop. 25,133), W N.Y., on the Barge Canal and NE of Buffalo; settled 1816 around locks of old Erie canal. Steel, paper, food products.

Lockyer, Sir (Joseph) Norman (lŏk′yûr), 1836–1920, English astronomer, pioneer in spectroscopic examination of stars. Authority on solar physics and chemistry.

Locofocos (lō″kōfō′kōz), name given in derision to members of faction that split off from Democratic party in N.Y. Name arose when members worked by light of candles and "locofoco" matches at Tammany Hall meeting on Oct. 29, 1835. As Friends of Equal Rights or Equal Rights party, the group, anti-bank and reformist, urged a vague but fervid leveling program. United with Workingman's party, group for several years disturbed and revitalized regular parties. After adoption of ideas by Van Buren Democrats in 1837, Equal Rights men returned to Democratic party.

locomotive, a railroad engine. Pioneer locomotive builders include Richard TREVITHICK; George STEPHENSON, who demonstrated practicability of steam engine in 1829 with famous *Rocket;* John Stevens, who built c.1825 the first U.S. locomotive; Peter Cooper, whose *Tom Thumb* (1830) was first practical American locomotive; Mathias Baldwin, constructor in 1832 of *Old Ironsides;* and J. B. Jervis, who introduced in 1832 swivel truck at forward end which increased safe passage around corners. Modern reciprocating engine consists essentially of steam engine and boiler; superheated steam admitted to cylinders causes pressure on pistons which is transmitted to driving wheels connected by side rods. Electric locomotives, introduced c.1895, are used chiefly on steep grades and on runs of high traffic density. Diesel-electric locomotives, introduced in U.S. c.1924, are used as switching engines and on many runs.

locomotor ataxia (lōkùmō′tùr ùtăk′sēù) or **tabes dorsalis** (tā′bēz dôrsā′lĭs), chronic progressive disease of nervous system. Impairment of the senses determining position and vibrations results in muscular incoordination accompanied by uncertainty in walking. Occurs in syphilitic individuals.

locoweed, leguminous plant of W U.S. which when eaten by cattle causes in them a nervous disorder. Common kinds are species of *Astragalus* and *Oxytropus.*

Locris (lō′krĭs), region of anc. Greece, in three regions (separated chiefly by Phocis), N of Boeotia. Locrians, long settled, rivaled Phocians. They founded a colony in S Italy.

locust, name used both for any grasshopper with antennae shorter than body and for those short-horned forms that migrate in swarms. The 17-year locust is a CICADA.

locust, leguminous deciduous tree or shrub (genus *Robinia*) native to U.S. and Mexico. The common locust is black, or yellow locust (*Robinia pseudoacacia*) sometimes called acacia or false acacia. It has clusters of fragrant flowers similar to sweet peas. The wood is durable. It is attacked by locust borer.

Lodge, Henry Cabot, 1850–1924, U.S. Senator from Mass. (1893–1924). A conservative, party-line Republican, he bitterly opposed Pres. Wilson's peace policy and led the attack on Treaty of Versailles and League of Nations. His grandson, **Henry Cabot Lodge, Jr.,** 1902–, U.S. Senator from Mass. (1937–44, 1947–53),

became head of the U.S. mission to the UN in 1953.

Lodge, Sir Oliver (Joseph), 1851–1940, English physicist. He contributed to wireless telegraphy; studied electrons, the ether, lightning. He was interested in reconciling science and religion and in psychical research.

Lodge, Thomas, 1558?–1625, English writer. Prose tales interspersed with poems most important (e.g., *Rosalynde*, 1590). Also wrote poem *Scillaes Metamorphosis* (1589) and tuneful sonnet-cycle *Phillis* (1593).

Lodi (lō′dē), city (pop. 23,305), Lombardy, N Italy, on Adda R. Here Bonaparte defeated the Austrians on May 10, 1796.

Lodi (lō′dī). **1** City (pop. 13,798), central Calif., N of Stockton. Produces wine and olive oil. **2** Borough (pop. 15,392), NE N.J., NE of Passaic. Dye works; mfg. of machinery.

Lodomeria: see VLADIMIR-VOLYNSKI, USSR.

Lodore (lōdôr′), waterfalls, Cumberland, England; celebrated in Southey's "The Cataract of Lodore."

Lodz (lōdz, loōj, Pol. woōj), Pol. *Łódź*, industrial city (pop. c.622,500), Poland, SW of Warsaw. Incorporated in 15th cent., it passed to Prussia 1793, to Russia 1815; reverted to Poland 1919. From 1820 to 1900 it developed into cap. of Polish industry, producing chiefly textiles and clothing.

Loeb, Jacques (lōb), 1859–1924, American physiologist, b. Germany. Known for tropism theory and for experiments in inducing parthenogenesis and regeneration by chemical stimulus.

Loeb, Solomon, 1828–1903, American banker, b. Germany. A founder of banking house of Kuhn, Loeb and Co. in New York city. His son, **James Loeb,** 1867–1933, was a banker and philanthropist. Founded and endowed Loeb Classical Library; helped found part of present JUILLIARD SCHOOL OF MUSIC.

Loeffler, Charles Martin (lĕf′lùr), 1861–1935, American composer, b. Alsace. His works include the *Pagan Poem* (1909) for orchestra, *Canticle of the Sun* (1925) for solo voice and orchestra, *Evocations* (1931) for women's chorus and orchestra, and chamber works.

loess (lō′ĭs), unstratified yellowish clay soil, believed to have been carried by wind. Extensive deposits occur along the Mississippi and in NW U.S., where it is largely of glacial origin, and in China, where it is of desert origin. Loess is rich in organic matter and very fertile, but easily eroded.

Loewi, Otto (lō′ē), 1873–, German pharmacologist and physiologist. Shared 1936 Nobel Prize in Physiology and Medicine for study of chemical transmission of nerve impulses. He came to U.S. in 1940.

Loewy, Raymond Fernand (lō′ē), 1895–, American industrial designer, b. France.

Löffler, Friedrich (frē′drĭkh lûf′lùr), 1852–1915, German bacteriologist. He related diphtheria to causative organism now known as Klebs-Löffler bacillus.

Lofoten (lō′fōtùn) and **Vesteralen** (vĕ′stùrôlùn; Nor. *Vesterålen*), two contiguous island groups (c.2,000 sq. mi.; pop. c.80,000), off NW Norway, in Norwegian Sea, 1–50 mi. off mainland. Entirely within Arctic Circle, they extend c.150 mi. NE–SW. Climate is tempered by North Atlantic Drift. The MAELSTROM is S of Moskenes isl. Vesteralen group, S of Lofoten group, includes Hinnoy, largest island of Norway. Herring and cod fisheries of Lofoten and Vesteralen isls. are among world's largest. Vesteralen is also spelled Vesteraalen.

Lofting, Hugh, 1886–1947, American writer of juvenile stories, b. England. Author and illustrator of "Dr. Doolittle" stories.

Logan, James, 1674–1751, American colonial statesman and scholar, b. Ireland, of Scottish parents. Adviser to William Penn, he supported proprietary rights in Pa. Acting governor of province (1736–38). Engaged in botanical research.

Logan, John Alexander, 1826–86, American politician, Union general in Civil War. Fought in Vicksburg and Atlanta campaigns. U.S. Congressman (1867–71); U.S.

Senator (1871–77, 1879–86). Inaugurated MEMORIAL DAY (1868).

Logan, Sir William Edmond, 1798–1875, Canadian geologist. Head of Geological Survey of Canada (1843–69); constructed maps and sections. Work summarized in *The Geology of Canada* (1863).

Logan. 1 City (pop. 5,972), S central Ohio, on Hocking R. and SE of Columbus. Mfg. of shoes, foundry products, pottery, and tools. **2** City (pop. 16,832), N Utah, N of Ogden and on Logan R.; founded 1859 by Mormons. Processing center for irrigated farm, dairy area. Here are Mormon temple and tabernacle and UTAH STATE AGRICULTURAL COLLEGE. Near by are Logan Canyon and Logan Peak. **3** City (pop. 5,079), S W.Va., on Guyandot R. and SSW of Charleston, in mine and farm area.

Logan, Mount, 19,850 ft. high, extreme SW Yukon, just E of Alaska; highest peak in Canada and second highest in North America.

loganberry, blackberrylike plant of genus *Rubus,* grown on Pacific coast for its large red-purple fruit.

Logansport, city (pop. 21,031), N Ind., at junction of Wabash and Eel rivers NE of Lafayette; settled c.1826. Farm produce shipping center with mfg. of fire apparatus, radiators, farm equipment.

logarithm (lŏ′gŭrĭdhm). Each positive number has logarithm, which is power to which third number (called base) must be raised to obtain that positive number. Logarithms of numbers using 10 as the base are called common logarithms; if base is *e* (approximately 2.718) they are natural logarithms. Since logarithms are exponents, they satisfy rules of exponents and hence simplify calculations.

Log College: see TENNENT, WILLIAM.

Logos (lŏ′gŏs) [Gr.,= Word], concept of Greek and Hebrew metaphysics. The central idea is that Logos links God and man. HERACLITUS held the Logos was fire, ordering and animating the world. The Stoics called God as the active law guiding the world the Logos. The Old Testament idea of Wisdom of God active in the world was merged with ancient Hebrew concept of active Word of God. NEOPLATONISM adapted the idea of the Logos into the system of emanations. PHILO taught that God, remote from the world, acts in it through mediation of the Logos (Divine Reason). Gospel of St. John states that the Logos, eternal God, took flesh and became man in time; the Logos is Jesus.

logwood, leguminous tree (*Haematoxylon campechianum*), native to Central America and grown in parts of N South America and West Indies. Its brown-red heartwood yields haematoxylin dye.

Lohengrin (lō′ŭn-grĭn), in medieval German story, a knight of the Grail, son of Parzifal. Led by a swan to rescue Princess Elsa of Brabant, he then marries her. When she asks his name, in violation of a pledge, he must return to the castle of the Grail, and the swan, now revealed as Elsa's brother, reappears. Its fullest form is in German epic (c.1285–90) ascribed to Wolfram von Eschenbach. Story was used by Wagner.

Loir (lwär), river, 193 mi. long, N central France, rising S of Chartres and flowing generally SW to the Sarthe N of Angers.

Loire (lwär), department (1,853 sq. mi.; pop. 631,591), E central France, in Lyonnais; cap. Saint-Étienne. The **Loire river,** 625 mi. long, is the longest of France. Rising in Cévennes mts., it flows NW to Orléans, then swings SW to the Atlantic at Saint-Nazaire. Nevers, Blois, Tours, Angers, and Nantes are also on or near its course. The Allier, Cher, Vienne, and Maine are its chief tributaries. The Loire valley, a region of rich fields, gardens, and vineyards, has fostered traditions of civilized living which have become the heritage of all France. The châteaux of the Loire—notably Blois, Amboise, Chambord, Chenonceaux, and Chinon—are synonymous with French history and civilization.

Loire-Inférieure (lwär″-ēfâryûr′), department (2,693 sq. mi.; pop. 665,064), NW France, in S Brittany; cap. Nantes.

Loiret (lwärā′), department (2,630 sq. mi.; pop. 346,-918), N central France; cap. Orléans.

Loir-et-Cher (lwär-ā-shĕr′), department (2,479 sq. mi.; pop. 242,419), N central France; cap. Blois.

Lois (lō′ĭs), grandmother of Timothy. 2 Tim. 1.5.

Loisy, Alfred (Firmin) (älfrĕd′ lwäzē′), 1857–1940, French biblical critic. Ordained a Roman Catholic priest (1879), he later became the leader of Catholic MODERNISM. His teachings were condemned by the Holy See, and he was excommunicated (1908).

Loki (lō′kē), in Norse myth, personification of the evil principle. He caused trouble for the other gods.

Lolland, Denmark: see LAALAND.

Lollardry (lŏ′lŭrdrē) or **Lollardy,** 14th-cent. English movement for religious reform led by John WYCLIF and his "poor priests." Abuses in the Church, the great wealth of high churchmen, the appalling poverty of the poor—these contributed to making Lollardry popular. The chief teachings of the Lollards (mostly expressed in a memorial to Parliament in 1395) were that the clergy should be rigidly poor; that the doctrines of the sacraments (especially transubstantiation) were false; that the ordinary believer could arrive at true doctrine solely by reading the Bible for himself; and that celibacy of priests and nuns was unnatural and wrong. The movement gained much momentum by 1400, and the high clergy and the government feared the Lollards. In 1401 a parliamentary statute was passed against them. The Lollards grew fanatic and even entered on a small rebellion under Sir John Oldcastle. This was easily put down (1414), and the movement went underground. Just how much influence it had on the later Reformation is a matter of dispute. Many Lollard doctrines were reflected by the Hussites.

Lombard, Peter: see PETER LOMBARD.

Lombard, residential village (pop. 9,817), NE Ill., W suburb of Chicago.

Lombard League. When in 1158 Emperor Frederick I at the Diet of Roncaglia asserted the imperial authority over all Lombard communes, the rival towns of Lombardy united against him and in 1167 formed a single league, backed by Pope Alexander III. The League defeated Frederick at Legnano (1176) and in the Peace of Constance (1183) received confirmation of the freedom of the communes. Revived in 1226 against Frederick II, the League was defeated at Cortenuova (1237) and split into Guelph and Ghibelline cities.

Lombardo (lōmbär′dō), Italian family of sculptors and architects. Emigrants from Lombardy c.1450, they were leaders in architectural Renaissance in Venice. The most distinguished of them were **Pietro Lombardo,** c.1435–1515, who worked on court façade of the doge's palace, and his sons, **Antonio Lombardo,** c.1458–1516?, and **Tullio Lombardo,** c.1455–1532.

Lombards (lŏm′bŭrdz, -bärdz), Latin *Langobardi,* anc. Germanic people. In 568 they invaded N Italy under ALBOIN and estab. a kingdom with Pavia as cap. Their conquests spread to most of Italy save Byzantine and papal holdings of Ravenna, Pentapolis, Rome, and along coast. Kingdom soon split into duchies (notably Spoleto and Benevento), but in 584 Authari restored Lombard kingdom, which reached its flower under LIUTPRAND (d. 744). Arians at first, Lombards later accepted Catholicism and assimilated Latin culture. Their attacks on Rome brought forth Frankish intervention under PEPIN THE SHORT (751) and CHARLEMAGNE (772), who after his victory over DESIDERIUS was crowned with iron crown of Lombard kings. This crown, also used for coronations of later emperors, is now kept at MONZA. Duchy of Benevento survived until Norman conquest (11th cent.). Lombards gave their name to Lombardy.

Lombard Street, London. Street of banks and financial houses named for Lombard moneylenders who settled here in 12th cent.

Lombardy (lŏm′bŭrdē), Ital. *Lombardia,* region (9,189

sq. mi.; pop. 5,836,479), N Italy, bordering on Switzerland, in the S Alps and the Po valley; cap. MILAN. Other cities include BERGAMO, BRESCIA, COMO, CREMONA, MANTUA, PAVIA. The Po valley, irrigated since Roman times, is a rich grain region. The mulberry is extensively cultivated for silk production. Lombardy is the chief industrial region of Italy. Conquered from its Gallic inhabitants by the Romans (3d cent. B.C.), the region became the Roman province of Cisalpine Gaul. In A.D. 569 it became the center of the kingdom of the LOMBARDS, and in 774 it was added by Charlemagne to his empire. In 11th cent. power gradually passed from feudal lords to autonomous communes. These united against imperial pretensions as the LOMBARD LEAGUE (1167) but fell apart in 13th cent. Lombard merchants and bankers had a major share in revival of European economy. Rivalry among cities favored the rise of two families who shared Lombardy between themselves—the VISCONTI dukes of Milan (succeeded by the SFORZA) and the GONZAGA of Mantua. Parts of Lombardy passed to Venice (e.g., Bergamo) and to the Swiss (e.g., the Ticino). After the ITALIAN WARS of the 16th cent., Lombardy was ruled by Spain (1535–1713), Austria (1713–96), France (1796–1814), and Austria (as Lombardo-Venetian kingdom, in union with Venetia, 1815–59). Annexed to Sardinia 1859.

Lombok, island (1,825 sq. mi.; pop. 701,290), Indonesia, one of Lesser Sundas. Products include coffee, sugar, cotton, and indigo. Noted by the naturalist A. R. Wallace as being part of dividing line between fauna of Asia and that of Australia.

Lombroso, Cesare (chā'zärä lōmbrō'zō), 1835–1909, Italian criminologist. Maintained (1876) theory (now outmoded) that the criminal is an atavistic type marked by distinct physical and psychological traits.

Loménie de Brienne, Étienne Charles (ātyĕn' shärl' lōmānĕ' dù brēĕn'), 1727–94, French statesman; archbishop of Toulouse (1763–88) and of Sens (1788–91). Succeeded Calonne in control of finances (1787); exiled the Parlement of Paris to Troyes because of its opposition to his proposed fiscal reforms; left office in popular disfavor (1788). He was made a cardinal in 1788. Died in prison during Terror.

Lomond, Loch (lŏkh lō'mùnd, –mùn), lake, between Dumbartonshire and Stirlingshire, Scotland. Largest (23 mi. long and 5 to less than 1 mi. wide) and one of most beautiful of Scottish lakes, it has Ben Lomond (3,192 ft. high) overlooking N end.

Lomonosov, Mikhail Vasilyevich (mēkhũyĕl' vũsē'lyùvĭch lũmùnô'sùf), 1711–65, Russian scientist and writer. His experiments anticipated mechanical nature of heat and kinetic theory of gases. A founder of modern Russian literature, he reformed Russian literary language and altered character of Russian prosody by adopting principle of tonic rather than syllabic versification.

Lomonosov, formerly **Oranienbaum** (ōrä'nyùnboum), city (pop. over 10,000), RSFSR, on Gulf of Finland near Leningrad. Site of a palace built 1714 by Peter I and of Catherine II's "Chinese Palace" (built 1768). Was renamed 1948.

Lompoc (lŏm'pōk), city (pop. 5,520), S Calif., NW of Santa Barbara. Produces flowers and seeds. Near by are kieselguhr quarries and oil fields.

London, Jack (John Griffith London), 1876–1916, American novelist and short-story writer. A sailor, a gold seeker in the Klondike, and a newspaperman, he wrote adventure tales romantic in effect though rawly realistic in setting and character (e.g., *The Call of the Wild,* 1903; *The Sea-Wolf,* 1904; *White Fang,* 1905). Championed the socialistic I.W.W. and wrote socialist novels (e.g., *Martin Eden,* 1909) and tracts.

London, city (pop. 95,343), S Ont., Canada, on Thames R. and SW of Toronto. Trade and mfg. center of agr. region. Seat of Univ. of Western Ontario (coed.; 1878) and affiliated Huron and Ursuline colleges. Site selected as future capital of Upper Canada 1752,

but the city not actually founded until 1826.

London, cap. of United Kingdom and chief city of the British Empire, on both sides of the Thames. Greater London (c.693 sq. mi.; pop. 8,346,137), includes parts of the counties of Essex, Kent, Hertfordshire, Middlesex, and Surrey. Administrative county of London (117 sq. mi.; pop. 3,348,336) includes 28 metropolitan boroughs, each with own mayor and council, responsible to London Co. Council. Present form of municipal government began in 12th cent. Core of London is the City (1 sq. mi.; pop. 5,268). London lost its importance when Romans left in 5th cent.; emerged again (886) under Alfred. Nucleus of TOWER OF LONDON was built by William I. The LIVERY COMPANIES became important in 13th–14th cent. Medieval London saw beginnings of INNS OF COURT, SAINT PAUL'S CATHEDRAL, and WESTMINSTER ABBEY. In 1665 the great plague took c.75,000 lives, and in 1666 great fire destroyed most of city. Rebuilt by Christopher Wren. Galleries and museums include British Mus., Victoria and Albert Mus., Tate Gallery, Natl. Gallery, and Wallace Coll. Univ. of LONDON is in Bloomsbury. Among famous streets are Fleet St., the STRAND, PICCADILLY, WHITEHALL, PALL MALL, Downing St., Lombard St., Bond St., and Regent St. In World War II many historic buildings and many ancient churches were destroyed or damaged.

London, village (pop. 5,222), central Ohio, WSW of Columbus. Mfg. of metal products.

London, Declaration of, international code of maritime law, especially as related to war, proposed in 1909 by leading European naval powers, U.S., and Japan, after meeting in conference at London, England, in 1908. Dealing with many controverted points (e.g., blockade, contraband, prize), it largely restated existing law but showed greater regard for rights of neutrals. Declaration was ratified by U.S. senate but not by many other powers; thus it never went into effect officially.

London, University of, founded in London, England, in 1836 to give examinations and degrees. Teaching functions were added in 1898. Now has many affiliated colleges, institutions, and schools (e.g., London School of Economics and Political Science).

London Bridge, granite, five-arched bridge over the Thames, in central London. 928 ft. long, present structure was built 1824–31. First bridge built in 963. Only bridge over the Thames until 18th cent.

London Company, corporation granted charter (1606) by James I to locate colonies in America. Given tract of land fronting 100 mi. on the sea and extending 100 mi. inland somewhere between lat. 34° and 41° N. Company expedition founded Jamestown (1607). Charter of 1609 replaced local council with absolute governor. Third charter (1612) made company self-governing, but disagreement over policies created dissension. Company dissolved in 1624 following unfavorable investigation.

London Conference, name of several international meetings held at London, England, the most important of which are listed below. At the **London Conference of 1830–31** the chief powers of Europe agreed to estab. Greece as independent principality, with boundaries fixed by London Protocol of 1829. The conference also considered the revolt of the Belgians against William I of the Netherlands. Mediation was unsuccessful, but late in 1831 joint French and British intervention compelled William to evacuate Belgium. The **London Conference of 1838–39,** which prepared the final Dutch-Belgian separation treaty, divided disputed Luxembourg and Limburg between Dutch and Belgian crowns. For the **London Conference of 1852,** see SCHLESWIG-HOLSTEIN; for the **London Conference of 1908,** see LONDON, DECLARATION OF.

Londonderry or **Derry,** maritime county (804 sq. mi.; pop. 155,520), N. Ireland, in Ulster. Largely mountainous area whose damp, cold climate allows little agr. Chief occupations are linen making, distilling, and fishing. *Londonderry Air* probably from region

SMALL CAPITALS = cross references. Pronunciation key on inside end pages. Abbreviations: p. 2.

originally. County town is **Londonderry** or **Derry**, county borough (pop. 50,099), on Foyle R., a major Irish seaport. Chief export is cattle. Varied industries include linen weaving and distilling. Given to City of London corporation in 1608 and name changed to Londonderry. City withstood siege of James II's forces for 105 days in 1689. U.S. naval base in World War II.

Long, Crawford Williamson, 1815–78, American physician, pioneer in use of ether anesthesia (1842).

Long, Huey P(ierce), 1893–1935, American political leader in La. As governor (1928–31) and U.S. Senator (1931–35) he promoted a "Share-the-Wealth" program by ruthless and demagogic means. Assassinated at Baton Rouge.

Long, Perrin Hamilton, 1899–, American physician, known for research on sulfa drugs.

Long, Stephen Harriman, 1784–1864, American explorer. In 1817 he explored the upper Mississippi region; in 1819–20, the Rocky Mts.

Long, Loch (lŏkh), inlet, c.20 mi. long, between Argyllshire and Dumbartonshire, Scotland.

Long Beach. 1 City (pop. 250,767), S Calif., on harbor on San Pedro Bay and S of Los Angeles; laid out 1882. Year-round resort. Mfg. of aircraft, soap, and tires. Has shipyards and canneries. Refines and ships oil from wells of Signal Hill, independent city (pop. 4,040) within Long Beach. **2** Resort city (pop. 15,586), SE N.Y., on S shore of Long Isl., S of Rockville Centre; inc. as a city 1922.

Long Branch, SW residential suburb of Toronto (pop. 8,727), S Ont., Canada, on L. Ontario.

Long Branch, city (pop. 23,090), E N.J., N of Asbury Park; settled 1740. Presidents Grant and Garfield had homes here. Noted resort since early 19th cent.

Longchamp, William of (lŏng'shămp), d. 1197, chancellor of England (1190–91), bishop of Ely. Joined (1189) Richard I against Henry II. Upon Richard's accession, William rose rapidly to become acting head of both church and state. Rebellion of John and the barons drove him from England in 1191.

Longchamp (lôshä'), famous racecourse of Paris, France, in the Bois de Boulogne.

Longfellow, Henry Wadsworth, 1807–82, American poet, b. Portland, Maine; long a professor of modern languages and belles lettres. His poetry was highly popular in his time, and his kindly figure loomed large on the literary horizon. Many of his short sentimental and "inspirational" verses are still familiar to every American schoolchild (e.g., "A Psalm of Life," "Excelsior," "The Village Blacksmith"), as are some of his longer tales in verse (e.g., *Evangeline,* 1847, based on the expulsion of the Acadians; *The Song of Hiawatha,* 1855, a sentimental treatment of Indian legends; *The Courtship of Miles Standish,* 1858; "Paul Revere's Ride" in *Tales of a Wayside Inn,* 1863). He helped introduce much foreign literature to the U.S., using the meter of the Finnish *Kalevala* for *Hiawatha,* translating Dante, and modeling some verse on Spanish forms. He also wrote an early travel book, *Outre-Mer* (1833–34), and the prose romance *Hyperion* (1839).

Longford (lông'fûrd), inland county (403 sq. mi.; pop. 36,218), Ireland, in Leinster; co. town Longford. Level area with many lakes, bogs, and marshes. Dairy farming is chief occupation.

Longhi, Pietro (pyä'trō lông'gē), 1702–85, Venetian genre painter. His son, **Alessandro Longhi,** 1733–1813, was a portrait painter and engraver.

Longinus (Dionysius Cassius Longinus) (lŏnjī'nùs), c.213–273, Greek rhetorician, philosopher. Only slight fragments of his work survive, and his fame rests on a classic treatise of literary criticism incorrectly attributed to him, *On the Sublime,* or *Longinus on the Sublime,* which treats what would be called now "loftiness of style."

Long Island, 118 mi. long and 12–20 mi. wide (pop. 5,237,909), SE N.Y., extending ENE from Hudson R. mouth and separated from Staten Isl. by the Narrows

of New York Bay, from Manhattan and the Bronx by East R., from Conn. by Long Isl. Sound. Along c.75 mi. of its S shore is a barrier beach sheltering large bays from the Atlantic. E end terminates in 2 flukes, the longer in Montauk Point (mŏn'tôk"), easternmost point in N.Y. state. Counties (E–W) are Kings (Brooklyn borough) and Queens (parts of New York city), Nassau, Suffolk. Has many resorts and parks (e.g., Jones Beach), fine estates, commuters' suburbs (W portion), farms (potatoes, truck) and fishing villages. Settled 1636; both Dutch and English estab. colonies here before English gained control in 1664. Extensive settlement occurred after development of New York city and building of railroads and highway system.

Long Island, battle of, in American Revolution, Aug. 27–30, 1776. To protect New York city and lower Hudson valley from British, George Washington sent force to defend Brooklyn Heights on Long Isl. British, under Sir William Howe, laid siege. Washington evacuated army and retreated N, fighting delaying actions.

Long Island City: see QUEENS, New York city borough.

Long Island Sound, Atlantic arm, c.90 mi. long and 3–20 mi. wide, separating Long Isl. from N.Y. and Conn. mainland. Extends from Block Isl. Sound to East R. (connection to New York Bay). Coastal shipping route; pleasure boating, fisheries.

Long Island University: see BROOKLYN, N.Y.

Longmeadow, suburban town (pop. 6,508), SW Mass., on Connecticut R. just S of Springfield.

Longmont, city (pop. 8,099), N Colo., N of Denver, in rich farm area, with coal mines.

Long Parliament: see PARLIAMENT.

Longs Peak: see FRONT RANGE.

Longstreet, Augustus Baldwin, 1790–1870, American humorist; author of *Georgia Scenes* (1835), realistic sketches filled with frontier humor.

Longstreet, James, 1821–1904, Confederate general. Fought at Bull Run, in Peninsular campaign, at Fredericksburg. At Gettysburg his delay in offensive may have cost Lee the battle. Distinguished himself in Wilderness campaign. Considered poor strategist but excellent tactician. Career still disputed.

Longueuil (lōgû'yù), residential city (pop. 11,103), SW Que., Canada, on St. Lawrence R. opposite Montreal.

Longueville, Anne Geneviève, duchesse de (än' zhùnù-vyĕv' düshĕs' dù lôgvēl'), 1619–79, French beauty and politician, a leader of the FRONDE; sister of Louis II de Condé. Made her peace with court 1653.

Longview. 1 City (pop. 24,502), E Texas, W of Shreveport, La. and near Sabine R. Boomed after 1930 discovery of East Texas oil fields. **2** Inland port city (pop. 20,339), SW Wash., at junction of Cowlitz and Columbia rivers (latter bridged to Oregon); founded 1923. Lumber mills and food-processing and aluminum plants.

Longworth, Nicholas, 1869–1931, U.S. Representative (1903–13, 1915–31). Speaker of House (1925–31). Married Alice Lee Roosevelt, daughter of Pres. Theodore Roosevelt, at White House (1906).

Longwy (lôwē'), town (pop. 12,064), Meurthe-et-Moselle dept., NE France. It is an industrial center of Lorraine iron-mining dist.

Lönnrot, Elias (ĕlē'äs lûn'rōōt), 1802–84, Finnish philologist, compiler of the KALEVALA, Finnish national epic. From 1828 he traveled through Finland, Lapland, and NW Russia, collecting fragments of the epic (pub. 1835, 1849).

Lookout, Cape, E N.C., headland at meeting of Core and Shackelford banks, SW of Cape Hatteras; has lighthouse.

Lookout Mountain, town (pop. 1,675), E Tenn., near Chattanooga. On Lookout Mt. (2,126 ft. high, extending into Ga., Ala.), scene of Civil War battle in CHATTANOOGA CAMPAIGN; partly in Chickamauga and Chattanooga Natl. Military Park. Limestone caves, cable railway, observatory, and museum are here.

loom, frame or machine used for weaving. Has a beam,

on which warp threads are wound; heddles (rods or cords), each with an eye through which a warp thread is drawn; the harness, a frame which operates to form a shed for insertion of weft threads between warp threads; the reed, which pushes each new weft row against the finished cloth; and a beam to hold the roll of finished fabric. Hand looms operated by foot treadles were forerunners of the power loom patented 1785 by Edmund Cartwright. The Jacquard loom, invented by J. M. Jacquard and perfected by 1804, made it possible to weave any design.

loon, migratory aquatic bird of colder parts of N Hemisphere, found in fresh and salt water. It is a swift flier and a strong swimmer and adept diver. Common North American loon or great northern diver is black and white bird (c.32 in. long).

Loos, Adolf (ä'dôlf lōs'), 1870–1933, Austrian architect. Influenced development of functional style.

Loos (lô-ôs'), town (pop. 3,170), Pas-de-Calais dept., N France. In World War I it was recaptured by British forces from the Germans with tremendous losses (Oct., 1915).

Lope de Rueda (lō'pä dā rōōā'dhä), 1510?–1565, Spanish dramatist, author of comedies, farces, and *pasos* (a dramatic form created by him), precursor of the Golden Age of Spanish literature.

Lope de Vega (Carpio), Felix (fā'lēks lō'pä dā vā'gä), 1562–1635, Spanish dramatic poet, a chief figure of the Golden Age of Spanish literature. His many plays range from tragedy to farce and are notable for warmth of feeling, wit, highly dramatic effects, and character portrayal. His disregard of the classic unities freed the drama and had much influence on other writers. He also wrote epics, lyric poetry, and tales.

López, Francisco Solano (fränsē'skō sōlä'nō lō'päs), 1826?–1870, president of Paraguay (1862–70). Succeeded his father, Carlos Antonio López (president, 1844–62). Ambitious and arrogant, Francisco brought on a war with Argentina, Brazil, and Uruguay (see TRIPLE ALLIANCE, WAR OF THE), in which he was killed. Considered by some Latin Americans as champion of rights of small nations against aggression of more powerful neighbors.

López, Narciso (närsē'sō), 1798?–1851, Spanish American soldier, b. Venezuela. When his plan for a Cuban revolution against Spain was discovered, he fled to U.S. (1848). Captured and executed in later filibustering expedition to Cuba.

López de Legaspi, Miguel (mēgěl' lō'päth dā lāgä'spē), d. 1572, Spanish navigator. Led expedition which conquered Philippines (1563–70). His conquest was accomplished largely by peaceful means. Founded modern Manila (1571).

López de Mendoza, Iñigo, marqués de Santillana: see SANTILLANA.

López y Fuentes, Gregorio (grägō'rēō lō'päs ē fwän'tās), 1895–, Mexican novelist, poet, and journalist, known for realistic novels on centuries-long oppression of Indians (e.g., *El Indio* (1935).

Lop Nor: see LOB NOR.

loquat (lō'kwŏt), small ornamental evergreen tree (*Eriobotrya japonica*), native to China. It is grown in S U.S. for its small fragrant white flowers and pear-shaped fruits eaten fresh or used in preserves.

Lorain, city (pop. 51,202), W Ohio, on L. Erie at mouth of Black R. and W of Cleveland; settled 1807. Ore-shipping port with ship-building; mfg. of iron and steel, chemicals, and clothing; commercial fisheries and sandstone quarries.

Loras College: see DUBUQUE, Iowa.

Lorca, Federico García: see GARCÍA LORCA.

Lords, House of: see PARLIAMENT.

Lord's Prayer or **Our Father,** the principal Christian prayer, taught by Jesus to his disciples. Mat. 6.9–13; Luke 11.2–4. English versions vary. Roman Catholics do not add the doxology ("For thine is the kingdom," etc.) which is used by most Protestants. Prayer is called, in Latin, Pater or Pater Noster.

Lord's Supper, Protestant sacrament of the EUCHARIST. REFORMATION leaders rejected transubstantiation but retained belief in the sacrament as mystically uniting believers and Christ. Lutherans held that there is a change by which the body and blood of Christ becomes really present in the bread and wine: the extreme view of ZWINGLI was that communion was purely symbolic. Calvinists imputed a spiritual meaning only to the words of institution; this has been the prevailing Protestant view. The communion service, usually short, varies widely among Protestants. It always involves both bread and wine; this was a crucial point with the Hussites. Quakers reject the sacrament altogether.

Lorelei (lô'rŭlī), cliff, 433 ft. high, W Germany, overlooking dangerous narrows of the Rhine, about midway between Coblenz and Bingen. Heine's poem *Die Lorelei* tells legend of a fairy who lived here and lured sailors to their death by her singing. Another legend places the Nibelungs' hoard here.

Lorentz, Hendrick Antoon (hěn'drück än'tōn lō'rěnts), 1853–1928, Dutch physicist, pioneer in formulating relations between electricity, magnetism, light. One of first to postulate concept of electrons. Shared 1902 Nobel Prize for explanation of Zeeman effect (change in spectrum lines in magnetic field).

Lorentz, Pare (pâr' lôrents'), 1905–, American film director. Director of U.S. Film Service (1938–40), he produced such documentary films as *The Plow That Broke the Plains* (1936), *The River* (1937).

Lorenzetti (lōrāntsět'tē), two Sienese painters, brothers, who introduced naturalism into Sienese art. They were **Pietro Lorenzetti** (pyā'trō), c.1280–1348, and **Ambrogio Lorenzetti** (ämbrō'jō), d. 1348?. Both were influenced by Giovanni Pisano. Many of their religious paintings are in churches in Siena.

Lorenzini, Carlo: see COLLODI, CARLO.

Lorenzo, Fiorenzo di: see FIORENZO DI LORENZO.

Lorenzo di Credi (lōrän'tsō dē krā'dē), 1459–1537, Florentine painter and sculptor, who was greatly influenced by Leonardo da Vinci.

Lorenzo di Pietro (dē pyā'trō), c.1412–1480, Sienese painter and sculptor, called Il Vecchietta.

Lorenzo Monaco (mō'näkō), c.1370–1425?, Florentine painter, a Camaldolite monk. Real name was Piero di Giovanni. His work has features of Sienese school and of Giotto.

Loreto (lŭrě'tō), small town, central Italy. Has shrine of Holy House of the Virgin in Nazareth, said to have been brought here through the air by angels in 13th cent. A church built around the house is rich in works of art.

Loretto Heights College: see DENVER, Colo.

Loria, Roger of: see ROGER OF LORIA.

Lorient (lôryä'), town (pop. 10,764; 1936 pop. 40,753), Morbihan dept., NW France; port and naval station on the Atlantic. Founded 1664. A German submarine base in World War II, it was heavily bombed by Allies but held out until end of European war.

Loris-Melikov, Mikhail Tarielovich (mēkhüyěl' tŭryěl'-uvīch lô'rīs-mě'lyīkŭf), 1825–88, Russian general and statesman, of Armenian descent. Was created a count for his services in Russo-Turkish War of 1877–78. As minister of the interior (1880–84) he promoted liberal reforms, which were voided after Alexander II's assassination.

Lorme, Marion de: see DELORME, MARION.

Lorrain, Claude: see CLAUDE LORRAIN.

Lorraine (lùrän', lô–, Fr. lôrĕn'), Ger. *Lothringen*, region and former province, E France, in Moselle, Meurthe-et-Moselle, Meuse, and Vosges depts.; historic cap. Nancy. Crossed by Meuse and Moselle rivers and by Vosges mts., it is a generally hilly, agr., and pastoral region. Its iron fields, among the largest in Europe, depend largely on German Ruhr coal. Except in Moselle dept. (cap. METZ), where German is largely spoken, Lorraine is predominantly French-speaking. A remnant of the kingdom of LOTHARINGIA,

Lorraine after 10th cent. became a duchy of the Holy Roman Empire. The independent bishoprics of Metz, Toul, and Verdun were annexed to France 1552. The duchy itself was united with Bar (see BAR-LE-DUC) in 1431 through the accession of RENÉ of Anjou as duke. Charles the Bold of Burgundy seized Lorraine but was defeated and slain at Nancy by Duke René II and his Swiss allies. In the 16th cent. the GUISE family, a branch of the house of Lorraine, gained great influence in France. Occupied by France in the Thirty Years War, Lorraine was recovered in 1697 by Leopold I. His heir Francis married Maria-Theresa of Austria and as Emperor Francis I founded the house of HAPSBURG-LORRAINE. By an arrangement (1735) with Louis XV of France, he exchanged Lorraine for Tuscany; Lorraine was given to Louis's father-in-law, STANISLAUS I of Poland, upon whose death it was to pass to France. Stanislaus died in 1766, and Lorraine became French. In 1871 Moselle dept. was ceded to Germany, as a result of the Franco-Prussian War, and united with ALSACE to form the imperial territory of Alsace-Lorraine. It was restored to France in 1918 but was again briefly annexed to Germany in World War II. Lorraine suffered heavily in both world wars: Verdun was a center of fighting in 1916–18; Metz and the Vosges in 1944.

Lorris, Guillaume de: see GUILLAUME DE LORRIS.

Los Alamos (lŏs ăl'ùmōs), community (pop. 9,934; alt. 7,500 ft.), N. N.Mex., near Rio Grande and NW of Santa Fe. First atomic bomb was made here and tested (July 16, 1945) at Alamogordo air base.

Los Angeles (lŏs ăng'gùlùs, ăn'jùlùs, –lēz), city (pop. 1,970,358), S Calif., on Pacific coast; founded 1781. Site visited 1769 by Gaspar de Portolá. Several times cap. of Alta California, it was cattle ranching center under Spanish and Mexicans. Taken by U.S. forces 1846. Expanded with railroads (1876, 1885), discovery of oil (1890s), motion pictures (early 20th cent.), and aircraft mfg. (early 1920s). A major port, rail, and air center, it is tourist mecca and motion picture cap. of world. Also a radio and television center, it has other industries including mfg. of aircraft and food (esp. citrus fruits), metal, wood, and chemical products. Oil fields are near. Large increase in pop. since World War II. It has absorbed HOLLYWOOD, Encino, Tujunga, Venice, Van Nuys, and other towns. Incorporated cities in metropolitan area (with over 29,000 pop.) include Alhambra, Beverly Hills, Burbank, Glendale, Huntington Park, Inglewood, Long Beach, Pasadena, Pomona, Santa Ana, Santa Monica, and South Gate. International airport at Culver City. Seat of Univ. of SOUTHERN CALIFORNIA, Univ. of CALIFORNIA at Los Angeles, Occidental Col. (coed.; 1887), Loyola Univ. of Los Angeles (R.C.; mainly for men; 1865), and George Pepperdine Col. (coed.; 1937). Water comes from Colorado and Owens rivers and Mono Basin, and Hoover Dam supplies power.

Lossing, Benson John (lŏ'sĭng), 1813–91, American historian and wood engraver, known for illustrated books on American Revolution and Civil War.

Lost Battalion, popular name given to eight American units of 77th Division, numbering c.600 men, which were cut off by German forces in World War I after the launching of an American attack in Argonne Forest in early Oct., 1918. Some 400 men perished before units were rescued.

Lost Dauphin (dô'fĭn). The obscure circumstances of the death of Louis XVII of France made it possible for impostors to claim that they were the "Lost Dauphin"—i.e., Louis XVII. In the U.S., Eleazer WILLIAMS was the most important claimant. There were even rumors that J. J. Audubon was the Lost Dauphin.

lost tribes, 10 Jewish tribes transported to Assyria after the conquest of Israel. Conjecture has linked them with, among other groups, the Hindus, the English, and American Indians.

Lot, nephew of Abraham. A good man, he was warned by an angel to leave the doomed Sodom. His wife looked back and was turned into pillar of salt. Gen. 11–14; 19.

Lot (lôt), department (2,018 sq. mi.; pop. 154,897), SW France, in Quercy; cap. Cahors. The **Lot** river, 300 mi. long, rising in the Cévennes mts., flows W through Quercy and joins the Garonne near Agen.

Lot-et-Garonne (lôt'-ā-gärôn'), department (2,079 sq. mi.; pop. 265,449), SW France; cap. Agen.

Lothair (lōthâr'), emperors and German kings. **Lothair I,** 795–855, was associated in power with his father, LOUIS I, from 817 and succeeded him as emperor in 840, with the E part of the Carolingian empire as his share. His attempt to gain sole rule over the empire was checked by his brothers Charles (later Emperor CHARLES II) and LOUIS THE GERMAN, who defeated him at Fontenoy (841) and in 843 forced on him the Treaty of VERDUN. His remaining lands were divided on his death among his sons, the main shares falling to Emperor Louis II and to Lothair, king of Lotharingia. **Lothair II** (the Saxon), 1075–1137, duke of Saxony from 1106, was elected German king to succeed Henry V (1125). With the help of his son-in-law, HENRY THE PROUD, he defeated the antiking Frederick of Hohenstaufen and Frederick's brother Conrad (who was to succeed him as Conrad III). He was crowned emperor at Rome in 1133. Lothair was active in the conversion of NE Germany to Christianity.

Lothair, 941–86, French king (954–86). Tried unsuccessfully to take Lorraine from Emperor Otto II.

Lothair, d. 869, king of LOTHARINGIA (855–69).

Lotharingia (lōthŭrĭn'jù). The Treaty of VERDUN (843) divided the Carolingian empire into three parts, the central portion falling to Emperor Lothair I. Of that portion, the N part was inherited in 855 by Lothair's second son, also named Lothair, whose kingdom was named Lotharingia. It comprised, roughly, the modern Netherlands, Belgium, Luxembourg, NW Germany, Alsace, and Lorraine (the name *Lorraine* is derived from Lotharingia). This was in turn divided by the Treaty of MERSEN (870) between the E Frankish and W Frankish kingdoms (i.e., Germany and France). Emperor Henry I gained control over all Lotharingia; Otto I in 959 divided it into the duchies of Lower Lorraine (in the N) and Upper Lorraine (S). In Upper Lorraine the ducal title continued until 1766 in what came to be known simply as the duchy of LORRAINE, a relatively small area. In Lower Lorraine, the ducal title soon disappeared, and many fiefs emerged, notably Brabant, Bouillon, Limburg, Jülich, Cleves, Berg, Hainaut, and the bishopric of Liége.

Lothians, the (lŏ'dhēùnz), division of Scotland, including East Lothian, West Lothian, and Midlothian. Ancient Lothian was part of Northumbria.

Loti, Pierre (pyĕr' lôtē'), pseud. of Julien Viaud, 1850–1923, French author, a navy officer. His novels *Pêcheur d'Islande* (1886; Eng. tr., *An Iceland Fisherman*) and *Ramuntcho* (1897; Eng. tr., 1897) and his travel book *Vers Ispahan* (1904) are among his best-known works, noted for accurate exotic settings, sobriety of style, and romantic pessimism.

Lotophagi: see LOTUS-EATERS.

Lötschberg Railway (lûch'bĕrk), Swiss electrical railroad crossing Bernese Alps from Thun to Brig. **Lötschberg Tunnel** (9 mi. long; max. alt. 4,078 ft.) carries it under Lötschen Pass.

Lotto, Lorenzo (lōrän'tsō lôt'tō), c.1480–1556, Venetian painter, known for sensitive portraits.

lotus, name for certain water plants. The true Egyptian lotus (*Nymphaea*) is a blue or white WATER LILY and a national emblem of Egypt. The Indian lotus or sacred bean (*Nelumbo nucifera*) is an aquatic plant with large pink flowers; its seed pods resemble a sprinkling-can nozzle. The blossom is symbolic in the religion and art of India. American lotus (*Nelumbo lutea*) has yellow flowers.

lotus-eaters or **Lotophagi** (lōtŏ'fûjĭ), people on N coast of Africa who lived on lotus, which caused forgetfulness and indolence. Some of Odysseus' men ate lotus and had to be dragged back to ships.

Lotze, Rudolph Hermann (lŏ'tsŭ), 1817–81, German philosopher. Conceding that the physical world is governed by mechanical laws, he explained relation and development in the universe as functions of a world mind. His medical studies were pioneer efforts in modern scientific psychology.

Loubet, Émile (āmēl' lōōbā'), 1838–1929, president of France (1899–1906). Granted pardon to Dreyfus. During his term Franco-British Entente Cordiale began.

Loudon, Gideon Ernst, Freiherr von: see LAUDON.

Loudon (lou'dŭn), town (pop. 3,567), E Tenn., SW of Knoxville near Fort Loudon Dam, at junction of Tennessee and Little Tennessee rivers. Site of Fort Loudon (1756, fell to Cherokee 1760) near.

loudspeaker or **speaker,** device translating audiofrequency electric currents into audible sound. A diaphragm (a stiff paper cone or metal disk) which reproduces sound by molecular disturbance is attached to small coil movable in response to current of driving amplifier. One type with great power has no diaphragm but includes compressor for supplying air to horn through valve which modifies air stream.

Louis, Saint: see LOUIS IX, king of France.

Louis, emperors. Louis I or **Louis the Pious,** Fr. *Louis le Débonnaire,* 778–840, son of Charlemagne. Became king of Aquitaine 781; coemperor with his father 813; sole emperor 814. In 817 he took his son LOTHAIR I as coemperor and gave Aquitaine and Bavaria to his sons PEPIN I and LOUIS THE GERMAN. His attempts at creating a kingdom for Charles, his son by second marriage (later Emperor CHARLES II), led to rebellions by his other sons, notably in 829–30 and 833. Abandoned by his troops, he was defeated near Colmar (833; battle of the "Field of Lies," Ger. *Lügenfeld*). However, the sons fell out among themselves and Louis was restored to power. He died while trying to uphold a new division of the empire, between Lothair and Charles. The raids of the Norsemen were intensified during his weak reign. **Louis II,** d. 875, was the son of Lothair I, who made him king of Italy (844) and whom he succeeded as emperor (855). His power in Italy was curbed by the independent Lombard dukes and by the Arab invasion. After the death of his brother LOTHAIR (869), he claimed Lotharingia, but the Treaty of MERSEN (870) divided it between his uncles Charles the Bald (who later succeeded him as Charles II) and Louis the German. **Louis IV** or **Louis the Bavarian,** 1287?–1347, duke of Upper Bavaria, was elected German king in 1314 to succeed Henry VII. A minority faction elected Frederick the Fair of Hapsburg, whom Louis defeated and captured at Mühlberg (1322). From 1324 to his death Louis struggled against the papacy. On the theory, evolved by MARSILIUS OF PADUA, that princes owed their rule to the will of the people, he had himself crowned emperor by the "representatives of the Roman people" (1328) and in 1338 claimed that the imperial title could be conferred by the electors without papal confirmation. By marriage and investiture he sought to add Brandenburg, Tyrol, and Holland to the Wittelsbach family possessions, but none of these acquisitions proved permanent. In 1346 Pope Clement VII declared him deposed and secured the election of Charles IV. Louis was successfully resisting his rival when he died in a hunting accident.

Louis, kings of Bavaria. **Louis I,** 1786–1868, son of Maximilian I, reigned 1825–48. A lavish patron, he made Munich a center of the arts. He was at first a liberal, but his later turn toward reaction and his scandalous liaison with Lola MONTEZ led to his enforced abdication in favor of his son Maximilian II. **Louis II,** 1845–86, son of Maximilian II, reigned 1864–86. Handsome, gifted, liberal, romantic, he also displayed a prodigality and eccentricity which eventually turned into incurable insanity. He spent a fortune on his friend Richard Wagner, who held great in-

fluence over him. Confined after 1866 at his fantastic château on L. Starnberg, he drowned himself, forcing his physician to share his death. His brother Otto I, who succeeded him, was also insane. **Louis III,** 1845–1921, succeeded his father Luitpold as regent for Otto I (1912); proclaimed himself king 1913; was forced to abdicate 1918.

Louis, Frankish kings and kings of France.

Carolingian dynasty. **Louis I:** see LOUIS I, emperor. **Louis II** (the Stammerer), 846–79, son of Emperor Charles II, reigned in France 877–79. His succession was shared by his sons Carloman and **Louis III,** c.863–882, who routed the Normans at Saucourt (881). **Louis IV** (Louis d'Outre-Mer), 921–54, son of Charles III (the Simple), spent his youth in exile in England; was recalled and made king in 936 by the nobles under the leadership of Hugh the Great. His energy and independence displeased Hugh, who made war on him but was forced to submit in 950. **Louis V** (the Sluggard), c.967–987, last Carolingian, reigned 986–87; was succeeded by Hugh Capet.

Capetian dynasty, direct line. **Louis VI** (the Fat), 1081–1137, reigned 1108–37. Laid groundwork for unified monarchy by increasing royal domain, destroying castles of robber barons, favoring Church and burgher class. Was chronically at war with Henry I of England, whose inroads from Normandy he checked. His son **Louis VII** (the Young), c.1120–1180 (reigned 1137–80), continued centralizing policy and took part in Second Crusade (1147–49). His divorce from ELEANOR OF AQUITAINE (1152) and her marriage to Henry II of England gave English a foothold in SW France and led to recurrent warfare. His grandson **Louis VIII,** 1187–1226 (reigned 1223–26), invaded England (1216) but was defeated at Lincoln (1217). Resuming the Albigensian Crusade (1226), he conquered Languedoc. His son **Louis IX** or **Saint Louis,** 1214–70, began his reign in 1226 under the regency of his mother, BLANCHE OF CASTILE. In 1241–43 he secured submission of Poitou, repulsed an English invasion, and defeated RAYMOND VII of Toulouse. He led the Seventh Crusade to Egypt (1248), was defeated and captured at El Mansura (1250), and, after being ransomed, remained in the Holy Land until 1254. Another crusade, against Tunis, ended with his death of the plague soon after his landing. His reign was for France a period of peace, prosperity, and progress. He stamped out private warfare, simplified administration, improved the distribution of taxes, and extended the right of appealing to the crown to all cases. The great Gothic cathedrals were largely built during his reign, as was SAINTE-CHAPELLE in Paris. Embodying the ideals of a Christian monarch, he was canonized in 1297. Feast: Aug. 25. **Louis X,** Fr. *Louis le Hutin* [the quarrelsome], 1289–1316 (reigned 1314–16), was dominated by his uncle, Charles of Valois.

Valois dynasty. **Louis XI,** 1423–83, reigned 1461–83. As dauphin he joined several conspiracies against his father, Charles VII, but after his accession he devoted himself to creating a new, national state, based on the central power of the crown. This goal he achieved, despite the military superiority of his enemies the great nobles, by dint of stubbornness, skillful and unscrupulous diplomacy, and bribery. The League of the Public Weal, formed 1465 and headed by CHARLES THE BOLD of Burgundy and FRANCIS II of Brittany, forced him to grant concessions which he violated soon afterward. A new coalition was formed against him in 1467. Louis forced the Peace of Ancenis on Francis of Brittany (1468) but was outfoxed for once by Charles the Bold, who lured him to Péronne for an interview and then refused to let him go until Louis had helped him suppress the revolt of Liége, which Louis himself had stirred up. After Charles's death (1477) Louis seized part of the inheritance of MARY OF BURGUNDY—Burgundy, Picardy, Artois, and Franche-Comté. Louis tended toward autocratic rule and chose his advisers among men of humble origin. Though he revoked the PRAGMATIC SANCTION OF BOURGES and practiced a superstitious brand of piety that bordered on mania, he intervened freely in church matters. He dreaded assassination and died in virtual self-imprisonment at the castle of Plessis-les-Tours. **Louis XII,** 1462–1515, called "father of the people," son of Charles d'OR-LÉANS, succeeded his cousin Charles VIII in 1498 and married Charles's widow, ANNE OF BRITTANY. He resumed the ITALIAN WARS (1499) but was expelled from Italy by the HOLY LEAGUE (1513).

Bourbon dynasty. **Louis XIII,** 1601–43, son of Henry IV, began his reign in 1610 under the regency of his mother, MARIE DE' MEDICI. He married ANNE OF AUSTRIA (1615). In 1617 he procured the murder of CONCINI and exiled his mother, but in 1622 he was reconciled with her and in 1624 he entrusted the government to her protégé, Cardinal RICHELIEU. The Cardinal and his successor, MAZARIN, dominated the rest of his reign. His son, **Louis XIV,** 1638–1715, called "Roi Soleil" (Sun King) and "the Great," brought the monarchy to its zenith. His long reign (1643–1715) began under the regency of his mother, Anne of Austria, and was dominated by MAZARIN until 1661. Chief events of that period were the French victory in the THIRTY YEARS WAR, the FRONDE, and the Peace of the PYRENEES with Spain (1659), which resulted in Louis's marriage with Marie Thérèse of Austria. The period 1661–83 was one of administrative and economic reform, in which COLBERT played the leading part. France became an absolute monarchy, epitomized by Louis's apocryphal remark, *L'état, c'est moi* [I am the state]. The administration passed from the nobles into the hands of loyal civil servants. Commerce, industry, naval power, and colonies were expanded along the principles of MER-CANTILISM. Louis's quest for supremacy in Europe began with the War of DEVOLUTION and the third of the DUTCH WARS, which netted him Franche-Comté and part of Flanders. In the following 10 years he seized, on various pretexts, several border cities, notably Strasbourg (1681). Colbert's death (1683) gave LOUVOIS increased influence, but after 1691 Louis ceased to take advice from his ministers. The period 1683–1715 was marked by large-scale foreign wars, caused chiefly by European fears of Louis's aggressive designs (see GRAND ALLIANCE, WAR OF THE; SPANISH SUCCESSION, WAR OF THE). These wars brought France no gains but exhausted its resources. The persecution of the HUGUENOTS after the revocation of the Edict of NANTES (1685) depopulated entire provinces. Louis's GALLICANISM caused a violent quarrel with the papacy (1673–93); Louis had to give in. He ruthlessly suppressed JANSENISM. Among his mistresses, Mlle de LA VALLIÈRE and Mme de MONTESPAN were the most influential; in 1684 he secretly married Mme de MAINTENON. The cent. of Louis XIV is the great classical age of French culture; Pascal, Corneille, Molière, Racine were among the foremost names of his reign. Louis himself was a generous and discerning patron. The pomp and etiquette surrounding his life at VERSAILLES symbolized the almost divine dignity to which he had raised the office of king. His great-grandson, **Louis XV,** 1710–74, succeeded him under the regency of Philippe II d'ORLÉANS. Cardinal FLEURY guided his policies after 1726, and his mistress, Mme de POMPADOUR, from 1743 to her death (1764). His queen, MARIE LESZCZYNSKA, and his last mistress, Mme DU BARRY, held no political influence. Louis's participation in the War of the POLISH SUC-CESSION, the War of the AUSTRIAN SUCCESSION, and the SEVEN YEARS WAR cost France its colonial empire. The extravagance, corruption, immorality, and inefficiency of his court ruined the treasury and prepared the French Revolution while the philosophers of the ENLIGHTENMENT helped to undermine the established order. The saying, *Après moi le déluge* [after

me, the flood], though wrongly attributed to Louis XV, aptly sums up his irresponsible rule. His grandson and successor, **Louis XVI,** 1754–93, was ill equipped to deal with the problems he inherited. Shy, well-intentioned, stupid, and phlegmatic, he preferred hunting and his locksmith's workshop to his royal duties. What popularity he had was offset by the unpopularity of his pleasure-loving queen, MARIE ANTOINETTE. The intrigues of the queen, of the chief minister, Maurepas, and of the court faction led to the dismissal of his ablest ministers—TURGOT (1776) and NECKER (1781). French intervention in the American Revolution brought the treasury to the brink of bankruptcy; in 1788 Louis recalled Necker, in 1789 he opened the STATES-GENERAL: the FRENCH REVOLUTION entered its first phase. Swayed alternately by his horror of violence and the rash advice of his queen and courtiers, he ended by letting events take their course. In June, 1791, he and his family attempted to flee abroad in disguise but were stopped at Varennes and brought back to Paris. Louis made a sincere attempt at fulfilling the few duties left him under the constitution of 1791, but the suspicion of treason hung over the royal couple, and when France suffered reverses early in the French Revolutionary Wars, this suspicion was naturally increased. The royal family was imprisoned in the Temple (Aug., 1792) and the monarchy was abolished. Tried for treason by the Convention, the king was sentenced to death by a vote of 387 to 334. He was guillotined Jan. 21, 1793, facing death with steadfast courage. His son, **Louis XVII,** 1785–1795?, was imprisoned from 1792 to his death but was proclaimed king in 1793 by the French royalists in exile. The brutality of his jailer, Antoine Simon, hastened the death of the delicate child. The rumor that he actually was rescued and that another child was substituted for him, though impossible to disprove, deserves extreme skepticism; it inspired several impostors to exploit the legend of a LOST DAUPHIN. **Louis XVIII,** 1755–1824, brother of Louis XVI, was known as count of Provence until his proclamation as king by the émigrés (1795). He had fled abroad in 1791, was hunted through Europe by Napoleon I, but was placed on the French throne in 1814 by the victorious allies with the help of TALLEYRAND. He sought to conciliate the former revolutionists and granted a liberal constitutional charter. Forced to flee during the HUNDRED DAYS, he returned after Napoleon's defeat at Waterloo (1815). After the assassination of his nephew, the duc de Berry (1820), the ultraroyalists, led by his brother (later CHARLES X), triumphed over the moderate policy of Louis and his minister Decazes. The new and ultrareactionary VIL-LÈLE ministry curtailed the franchise and curbed civil liberties and continued this course under Charles X.

Louis, kings of Hungary. **Louis I** (the Great), 1326–82, succeeded his father Charles I in Hungary (1342) and his uncle Casimir III as king of Poland (1370). He conquered Dalmatia from Venice; was recognized as overlord by the princes of Serbia, Walachia, Moldavia, and Bulgaria; campaigned successfully against the Turks; and brought the power of Hungary to its greatest height. Two expeditions to avenge the murder of his brother Andrew at the court of JOANNA I of Naples ended in a truce with Joanna (1352). Louis fostered art and learning and introduced the Italian Renaissance into Hungary. He provided for his succession by marrying his daughter Mary to Sigismund of Luxemburg (later Emperor SIGISMUND) and his daughter JADWIGA to Ladislaus Jagiello of Lithuania (later LADISLAUS II of Poland). **Louis II,** 1506–26, succeeded his father Uladislaus II as king of Hungary and Bohemia (1516). He was slain and his army was destroyed by the Turks in the battle of MOHACS. The crowns of Hungary and Bohemia passed to Louis's brother-in-law, Ferdinand of Austria (later Emperor Ferdinand I).

Louis, titular kings of Naples, dukes of Anjou, and

counts of Provence (see ANGEVIN dynasty). **Louis I,** 1339–84, second son of John II of France, was a great-great-grandson of Charles II of Naples. In 1380 JOANNA I of Naples adopted him as heir, repudiating her first choice, Charles of Durazzo. Charles, however, conquered Naples and was crowned king as CHARLES III (1381). Louis died while trying to expel his rival. Backed by the papacy and France, his heirs sought to make good their claim, but without lasting effect. His son, **Louis II,** 1377–1417, warred against Charles III and LANCELOT. **Louis III,** 1403–34, son of Louis II, invaded Naples in 1420. Queen JOANNA II called Alfonso V of Aragon to her aid and made him her heir, but after quarreling with Alfonso she adopted Louis instead (1423). Louis had conquered most of the kingdom when he died, leaving his claim to his brother RENÉ.

Louis I, 1838–89, king of Portugal (1861–89).

Louis, Joe (Joseph Louis Barrow) (lōō'ĭs), 1914–, American boxer. Won (1937) heavyweight championship by knocking out James J. Braddock. When he first retired (1949) from ring, he had defended his title 24 times, scoring 21 knockouts. Attempted to regain crown, but was defeated (1950) by Ezzard Charles, knocked out (1951) by Rocky Marciano.

Louis, Pierre Charles Alexandre (pyĕr' shärl älĕksä'drü lwē'), 1787–1872, French physician. Introduced use of statistics in medicine. Noted for research on tuberculosis and typhoid fever.

Louisburg (lōō'ĭsbûrg), town (pop. 1,120), E Cape Breton Isl., N.S., Canada, SE of Sydney. Just SW was site of French fort Louisbourg, built 1720–40, guarding entrance to Gulf of St. Lawrence. Port became naval and fishing base. Captured by force of New Englanders 1745, but returned to France 1748. Taken by British 1758, it became Wolfe's base for operations against Quebec (1759). Razed by British 1760. Site now Louisbourg Natl. Historic Park (340 acres; 1928).

Louise, 1776–1810, queen of Prussia, consort of Frederick William III; a princess of Mecklenburg-Strelitz. Her patriotic bearing in the Napoleonic Wars won her great popularity. In 1807 she humiliated herself in vain at Tilsit before Napoleon, begging him to lighten the peace terms for Prussia.

Louise, Lake, 1½ mi. long, alt. 5,680 ft., SW Alta., Canada, in Banff Natl. Park. Resort noted for mountain peaks and snow fields. Discovered 1880.

Louise of Savoy, 1476–1531, mother of Francis I of France, during whose absences she acted as regent. Negotiated Treaty of Cambrai (1529).

Louisiade Archipelago (lōōē"zēăd'), comprising c.10 volcanic islands and numerous coral reefs, SW Pacific, part of Territory of Papua. Battle of Coral Sea (1942) was fought near by.

Louisiana, state (50,820 sq. mi.; pop. 2,683,516), S U.S.; admitted 1812 as 18th state (slaveholding); cap. BATON ROUGE. Bordered on S by Gulf of Mexico, partly on E by Mississippi R. Low country on Gulf coastal plains and Mississippi alluvial plain; low hills in N. Major cities are NEW ORLEANS, SHREVEPORT, MONROE, ALEXANDRIA, LAKE CHARLES. Waterways include RED RIVER, OUACHITA, ATCHAFALAYA, CALCASIEU rivers; TECHE, MACON, LAFOURCHE bayous. PONTCHARTRAIN is largest lake. INTRACOASTAL WATERWAY traverses marshes. Produces rice, sugar cane, furs, oil, natural gas, sulphur, salt, cotton, truck, potatoes, livestock, fish. Main industries based on processing these products. Visited by Spanish 1541–42; claimed for France by La Salle in 1682. NATCHITOCHES oldest town (1714). MISSISSIPPI SCHEME of John Law brought large settlement. La. W of Mississippi R. ceded to Spain (1762), E of river to England (1763). French settlers arrived from ACADIA. Spanish La. retroceded to France 1800; went to U.S. in LOUISIANA PURCHASE (1803). Settlement of WEST FLORIDA CONTROVERSY extended area. Andrew Jackson defeated British at battle of New Orleans (1815).

Progress came from cotton gin, new sugar-refining methods, steamboat. Joined Confederacy 1861. Adm. Farragut captured New Orleans (1862); Grant's Vicksburg campaign left only W La. to South. Suffered much in Reconstruction. Politics colorful (esp. governorship of Huey P. LONG). Economy has changed through fall of plantations, rise of farm tenancy, discovery of oil and gas.

Louisiana, city (pop. 4,389), NE Mo., on the Mississippi below Hannibal. Ammonia plant was converted to study and produce synthetic fuels.

Louisiana Purchase. Pres. Jefferson, fearing the results of French occupation of New Orleans, instructed Robert R. Livingston, U.S. minister to France, to attempt to purchase New Orleans and West Florida from France. Napoleon, to whom Louisiana was of diminishing importance, permitted his ministers to open negotiations for sale of all of Louisiana. Purchase, in which James Monroe participated, was accomplished at a price of about $15,000,000; made effective by a treaty dated April 30, 1803, and ratified by U.S. on Oct. 21, 1803. Boundaries were not settled for several years (see WEST FLORIDA CONTROVERSY). From Louisiana Purchase, which more than doubled size of U.S., were carved all or part of 13 states.

Louisiana State University and Agricultural and Mechanical College, at Baton Rouge; land-grant, state supported, coed.; chartered 1853, opened 1860, moved 1869, became university 1870, and absorbed Agricultural and Mechanical Col. 1877. W. T. Sherman was first head. Has medical center in New Orleans, and Audubon Sugar School. Greatly expanded during Huey Long's regime.

Louis Napoleon: see NAPOLEON III.

Louis period styles, 1610–1793, a series of modes of interior decoration in France. Louis XIII period (1610–43) was transition from the baroque to classical dignity of Louis XIV style (1643–1715), marked by extensive use of colorful tapestries, rich hangings, murals, and large mirrors. Furniture was made of ebony or covered with silver, gilt, or lacquer, and was scaled to huge proportions of rooms. REGENCE STYLE (1715–23) was transition to intimate gaiety of Louis XV style (1723–74) with its free curves, smaller rooms, and use of chinoiserie and ROCOCO ornament. Classical revival of Louis XVI style (1774–93) brought return of straight lines, symmetry, and proportions in wall treatment and furniture. See ill., p. 356.

Louis Philippe (lwē' fēlēp'), 1773–1850, king of the French (1830–48); son of Philippe Égalité (see ORLÉANS, LOUIS PHILIPPE JOSEPH, DUC D'). Deserted French army 1793; lived in England and U.S. until Bourbon Restoration. As duke of Orléans, he was prominent in liberal opposition to Charles X, after whose overthrow (see JULY REVOLUTION) he was chosen "king of the French." As king, he affected bourgeois manners, symbolized by his eternal umbrella, and became known as the "citizen king." His reign, the "July Monarchy," gave business its fullest opportunities and was marked by colonial expansion (the conquest of Algeria) and the effects of the Industrial Revolution. It was an era of peace and uninhibited money making. The constitutional charter of 1814 was liberalized but continued to exclude the non-propertied from the polls. The growth of the industrial proletariat and its inhuman living conditions led to the rise of radical doctrines (e.g., of Karl Marx and Louis Blanc). In the arts, romanticism reacted against the dull conventionality of the era. Against growing opposition, the king and his successive cabinets resorted to reactionary measures. GUIZOT was the leading political figure after 1840; THIERS passed to the liberal opposition. A systematic campaign for electoral reform helped to precipitate the FEBRUARY REVOLUTION of 1848. Louis Philippe abdicated and went to England. His supporters and those of his descendants were called Orléanists (see ORLÉANS, family), as opposed to legitimists (adherents of the senior branch of the Bourbon dynasty).

Louis the Bavarian: see LOUIS IV, emperor.

Louis the Child, 893–911, German king (899–911), son of Emperor Arnulf and last of German line of Carolingians.

Louis the German, c.804–876, East Frankish king; son of Emperor LOUIS I, who gave him Bavaria in 817. In the conflict between his brother LOTHAIR I and his father, Louis sided now with the one, now with the other. After his father's death (840), he joined forces with his half-brother Charles the Bald (later Emperor CHARLES II) against Lothair, whom they defeated at Fontenoy (841) and forced to accept the Treaty of VERDUN (843), which made Germany and France separate kingdoms. Louis later campaigned against Charles (858–59, 875), but the two agreed on partitioning Lotharingia in the Treaty of MERSEN (870). Louis's succession was divided among his sons Louis the Younger, Charles the Fat (later Emperor Charles III), and Carloman.

Louis the Pious: see LOUIS I, emperor.

Louis the Stammerer: see LOUIS II, king of France.

Louis the Younger, d. 882, German king, ruler (876–82) over Saxony, Franconia, and Thuringia; son of LOUIS THE GERMAN. Shared succession with his brothers CARLOMAN (d. 880) and Charles the Fat (later Emperor CHARLES III).

Louisville. 1 (lōō′ĭsvĭl) City (pop. 2,231), E Ga., SW of Augusta and on Ogeechee R. Laid out 1786 as prospective cap. of Ga. State buildings completed 1795. Seat of government until 1804. **2** (lōō′ĕvĭl) City (pop. 369,129), N Ky., SW of Cincinnati at Falls of the Ohio (power); laid out 1773 and settled after G. R. Clark built fort 1778. Fort Nelson built by Clark 1782. Union base in Civil War, it grew as river, then as rail shipping point. State's largest city, it is port and industrial, financial, and market center. Has railroad shops, distilleries, and meat, tobacco, oil, and food processing plants. Seat of Univ. of Louisville (city supported; coed.; opened as medical institute 1837, chartered as university 1846) with Speed Scientific School and Louisville Municipal Col. for Negroes; and Nazareth Col. (R.C.; for women; 1920). Here are Churchill Downs (Kentucky Derby race track), grave of G. R. Clark, and (near by) home and tomb of Zachary Taylor. **3** (lōō′ĭsvĭl) City (pop. 5,282), E central Miss., SW of Columbus, in timber and farm area.

Louisville, University of: see LOUISVILLE, Ky.

Loup, river formed in E central Nebr. by junction of North Loup R., 212 mi. long, and Middle Loup R., 221 mi. long. Flows 68 mi. E to Platte R. at Columbus. Used in power project.

Lourdes (lōōrd, lōōrdz, Fr. lōōrd), town (pop. 12,421), Hautes-Pyrénées dept., SW France. Near-by grotto, where Our Lady of Lourdes appeared to St. BERNADETTE in 1858, is visited by up to a million pilgrims a year seeking miraculous cures.

Lourenço Marques (lōrĕn′sō mär′kĕs), city (pop. 93,-516), cap. of Mozambique; port on Delagoa Bay. Named for Lourenço Marques, Portuguese trader who explored area in 1544. Chief exports include coal and livestock products from South Africa.

louse, name both for a bloodsucking and for a chewing or biting insect. Both groups are small wingless insects. Bloodsuckers have piercing, sucking mouth parts, are external parasites of man and other mammals. The biting or chewing lice attack birds, including poultry, some mammals; they feed on epidermal scales, hairs, feathers, dried blood; usually associated with uncleanliness. See *ill.*, p. 469.

Louth (louth, loudh), maritime county (317 sq. mi.; pop. 66,194), Ireland, in Leinster; co. town Dundalk. Smallest Irish county, its chief occupations are dairying and fishing. Has some linen mfg.

Louvain (lōōvăn′, Fr. lōōvĕ′), Flemish *Leuven,* city (pop. 37,188), Brabant prov., central Belgium, on

Dyle R. Brewing industry. Was cap. of Brabant until 15th cent. Louvain is an episcopal see and has one of world's leading Catholic universities (founded 1426). The university library, with unique collections, was destroyed in World War I, rebuilt with funds from U.S., and destroyed again in World War II. The Gothic city hall (1447–63) was also damaged.

L'Ouverture, Toussaint: see TOUSSAINT L'OUVERTURE.

Louvois, Michel Le Tellier, marquis de (mēshĕl′ lŭ tĕlyä′ märkĕ′ dù lōōvwä′), 1639–91, French minister of war under Louis XIV. Introduced completely modernized military system which made French army the strongest in Europe and long served as universal model. Gaining much influence after death of Colbert (1683), he was largely responsible for the ruthless execution of the revocation of the Edict of Nantes (1685) and for the devastation of the Palatinate (1689).

Louvre (lōō′vûr), art museum, Paris. Built 1204 by Philip II as fortress-palace, reconstructed after 1541, and converted into national museum by Napoleon. Among its treasures are Leonardo's *Mona Lisa* and the sculpture *Victory of Samothrace.*

Louÿs, Pierre (pyĕr′ lwē′), 1870–1925, French novelist and poet. Noted for novel *Aphrodite* (1896) and poems *Chansons de Bilitis* (1894).

love bird: see PARAKEET.

love-in-a-mist, annual plant (*Nigella damascena*) with wispy blue or white flowers and finely cut foliage. Seeds of *N. sativa,* called black cumin, have been used in the Old World for seasoning.

Lovejoy, Elijah Parish, 1802–37, American abolitionist. Edited *Observer* at Alton, Ill. Killed defending press against mob, Nov. 7, 1837. His martyrdom advanced abolitionist cause. His brother, **Owen Lovejoy,** 1811–64, witness of killing, took up cause and became leader of Ill. abolitionists.

Lovejoy, Ill.: see BROOKLYN.

Lovelace, Richard, 1618–57, English poet, one of CAVALIER POETS. A royalist, he was imprisoned by Commonwealth in 1648. His first and chief work, *Lucasta: Epodes, Odes, Sonnets, Songs, &c.* (1649), includes well-known lyrics "To Althea from Prison" and "To Lucasta, Going to the Wars."

Lovelock, city (pop. 1,604), W Nev., on Humboldt R. Center of Humboldt project (1935–36).

Low, David (lō), 1891–, British political cartoonist, b. New Zealand. Comments perceptively on national and international affairs. Created "Colonel Blimp," symbolizing the British ultraconservative.

Low, Seth, 1850–1916, American political reformer, president of Columbia Univ. (1889–1901). Mayor of New York city (1901–3); reformed police and education departments, reorganized city finances.

Low, W(ill) H(icok), 1853–1932, American painter, an early exponent of the plein-air school.

Low Archipelago: see TUAMOTU ISLANDS.

Low Church: see ENGLAND, CHURCH OF.

Low Countries, region of NW Europe comprising the NETHERLANDS, BELGIUM, and the grand duchy of LUXEMBOURG. The name is a political and historic rather than a geographic concept. See also FLANDERS; BRABANT; HOLLAND; NETHERLANDS, AUSTRIAN and SPANISH.

Lowell, distinguished American family of Mass. **Francis Cabot Lowell,** 1775–1817, a pioneer in textile manufacture, was the chief mover in building at Waltham, Mass., the first U.S. factory to perform all operations needed to convert raw cotton into cloth. Lowell, Mass., was named for him. His nephew, **James Russell Lowell,** 1819–91, was an outstanding poet of the 19th cent. His poetry ranges from the didactic (e.g., *The Vision of Sir Launfal,* 1848) to the satiric (notably in the *Biglow Papers,* in Yankee dialect, collected as books 1848, 1867) and acutely critical (*A Fable for Critics,* 1848). He was professor of French and Spanish at Harvard (1856–86), editor of several periodicals (notably the *Atlantic Monthly,*

1857–61; the *North American Review*, 1864–72), and an essayist. He served also as minister at Madrid (1877–80) and London (1880–85) and did much to gain European respect for American letters and customs. Of a later generation of the family two brothers and a sister were especially well known. **Percival Lowell,** 1855–1916, was an astronomer, an authority on the planet Mars, and founder (1894) of Lowell Observatory, Flagstaff, Ariz. **Abbott Lawrence Lowell,** 1856–1943, was professor of political science and later (1909–33), president of Harvard. There he modified the elective system, set up general examinations in their major fields for B.A. candidates, and instituted the tutorial system—all with a view to increasing general education and decreasing specialization for undergraduates. **Amy Lowell,** 1874–1925, was a poet. After writing conventional poetry in *A Dome of Many-coloured Glass* (1912), she joined the IMAGISTS and attracted much interest with her free verse and polyphonic prose (as in *Sword Blades and Poppy Seed*, 1914; *Can Grande's Castle*, 1918; *What's o'Clock*, 1925). She wrote a life of Keats (1925).

Lowell, city (pop. 97,249), NE Mass., on Merrimack R. at junction with Concord R. and NNW of Boston; settled 1653. Became great textile center after mills were built 1822; mfg. also of electrical and leather products. Has Lowell Textile Inst. (coed.; 1895). Whistler's birthplace preserved.

Lower Austria, Ger. *Niederösterreich*, province (7,097 sq. mi.; pop. 1,249,610), NE Austria. Though outside its boundaries, Vienna is provincial cap. Over half of Austrian industry centers in Vienna and Wiener Neustadt basins; there is oil near Zistersdorf. Most of province is hilly and agr. area. History is that of Austria.

Lower Avon: see AVON 1, river, England.

Lower California, Span. *Baja California*, peninsula, c.760 mi. long, and 30–150 mi. wide, NW Mexico, separating Gulf of California from Pacific. Politically divided into N territory (27,655 sq. mi.; pop. 226,-871; cap. Mexicali) and S territory (27,979 sq. mi.; pop. 60,495; cap. La Paz). Most of land is semiarid and undeveloped but there is copper, silver, and gold mining and some pearl fishing. Agua Caliente and Tijuana are resorts in N territory.

Lower Canada: see QUEBEC, province.

Lower Saxony, Ger. *Niedersachsen*, German state (18,-231 sq. mi.; pop. 6,795,128), NW Germany; cap. Hanover. Formed 1946 in British zone of occupation, it includes former Prussian prov. of HANOVER and former states of BRUNSWICK, OLDENBURG, and SCHAUMBURG-LIPPE. Area has had no historic unity since 1180, when Emperor Frederick I broke up duchy of Henry the Lion of Saxony. Name continued as geographic expression and designated (16th cent.–1806) an imperial circle of Holy Roman Empire. Lower Saxony joined Federal Republic of [West] Germany in 1949.

Lowestoft (lō′stôft, –stûf), municipal borough (pop. 42,837), Suffolk East, England; fishing port, yachting center, and resort. Lighthouse marks most easterly point of England. Lowestoft ware, fine bone china, was made here 1757–1802.

Lowie, Robert Harry, 1883–, American anthropologist, b. Vienna. An authority on North American Indians, he contributed much to anthropological theory.

Loyalists, in American Revolution, colonials who adhered to British cause. Most numerous among propertied class, clergy, and officeholders under crown. Strongest in far southern and Middle Atlantic colonies. Fighting sometimes led to civil war with raids and reprisals. Many fled to British-held lands. Patriots confiscated many Loyalist estates.

Loyalty Islands, coral group (800 sq. mi.; pop. 11,854), S Pacific, 60 mi. E of NEW CALEDONIA, of which they are a dependency. Chief export is copra.

Loyang (lō′yäng′), city (pop. 77,159), NW Honan prov., China. Agr. and stock-raising center. Was cap. of Chou dynasty (770–255 B.C.) and Eastern Han dynasty (c.100 A.D.). Continued intermittently to be imperial residence until 13th cent. Nationalist government briefly moved here from Nanking in 1932. Called Honan until 1913.

Loyola, Ignatius of: see IGNATIUS OF LOYOLA, SAINT.

Loyola University (loiō′lū). 1 Mainly at Chicago; Jesuit, partly coed.; chartered and opened 1870 as St. Ignatius Col., renamed 1909. Includes a liberal-arts college at West Baden Springs, Ind. Has large collection of writings on the Jesuits. 2 See NEW ORLEANS, La. 3 Loyola University of Los Angeles: see LOS ANGELES, Calif.

Lozère (lôzěr′), department (2,000 sq. mi.; pop. 90,-523), S France, in Languedoc; cap. Mende.

Lu, chemical symbol of the element LUTETIUM.

Lualaba: see CONGO, river.

Luanda (lōōän′dù), city (pop. 66,932), cap. of Angola; port on the Atlantic; founded 1575. Center of slave traffic to Brazil, 17th–18th cent. Formerly called Loanda.

Lubbock, city (pop. 71,747), NW Texas, S of Amarillo on Llano Estacado; founded 1891. Processes and ships cotton, grain, poultry, dairy products, cattle, and oil. Seat of Texas Technological Col. (coed.; 1923).

Lubec (lōō′běk), resort and fishing town (pop. 2,973), SE Maine, on PASSAMAQUODDY BAY S of Eastport. WEST QUODDY HEAD is SE.

Lübeck (lōō′běk, Ger. lü′běk), city (pop. 237,860), Schleswig-Holstein, N Germany; a major Baltic seaport on mouth of Trave R. Produces machinery, textiles, marzipan. Its third city charter, granted 1158 by Henry the Lion, was copied by many N German cities. A free imperial city from 1226, Lübeck under its merchant aristocracy rose to leadership of the HANSEATIC LEAGUE, whose diets met here until 1630. Occupied by the French 1806–13, it joined in 1815 the German Confederation as a free Hanseatic city, a status it retained until 1937, when it was inc. into Schleswig-Holstein prov. of Prussia. Despite damage received in World War II, the inner city remains a monument of medieval N German architecture. There are several fine Gothic churches (13th and 14th cent.), old patrician residences, and the Holstentor, a famous city gate flanked by two towers (15th cent.). Thomas Mann, born in Lübeck, describes the city in his *Buddenbrooks*. The city was not part of the former bishopric of Lübeck, whose rulers resided from c.1300 at near-by Eutin. Territorial princes of the Holy Roman Empire, the bishops accepted the Reformation (16th cent.). The prince-bishopric passed to a branch of the Danish house of Holstein-Gottorp, which in 1773 also acquired the duchy of Oldenburg. Secularized in 1803, it became a district of Oldenburg but was transferred to Schleswig-Holstein in 1937.

Lubitsch, Ernst (ěrnst′ lōō′bĭch), 1892–1947, German film director; in U.S. after 1922. Noted for such films as *Design for Living* and *Ninotchka*.

Lublin (lōō′blēn), city (pop. c.111,000), E Poland. Trade and mfg. center. One of oldest Polish towns, it was the scene of the diet which united Poland with Lithuania (1569). It passed to Austria 1795, to Russia 1815. Seat of temporary Polish Socialist government (1918) and of provisional Polish government after liberation by Soviet forces in 1944. The latter was broadened by Yalta Conference (Feb., 1945) to include members of London cabinet of Polish government in exile and recognized by Potsdam Conference (Aug., 1945) as sole Polish authority. Catholic university of Lublin was founded 1918.

lubrication, introduction of a substance (lubricant) between contact surfaces of moving parts to reduce friction. Unlubricated surfaces produce dry or solid friction, resulting in injury by abrasion and in generation of heat causing one part to "seize" the other because of unequal expansion, or to develop (in metals) "hot points" which may cause welding of metals. Lubrication aims to produce thin-film or (better) fluid-film friction. In thin-film friction, boundary layers of the lubricant tend to be absorbed by contact surfaces thus producing slipperiness and separation which prevent intermolecular attraction between surfaces. Thin-film friction usually occurs with heavy loads, slow speeds, or intermittent action. In fluid or thick-film friction, moving surfaces form separative pressure film which carries load. Excessively thick fluid film increases internal friction in fluid causing power loss. Lubricants, usually a fat or oil, grease, or slippery solid, are obtained largely from petroleum or shale oil. Machinery requires controllable, varied lubricators, ranging from drop-feed and wick-feed types to collar devices and bath-oiling and splash-oiling arrangements.

Lucan (Marcus Annaeus Lucanus) (lū′kŭn), A.D. 39– A.D. 65, Latin poet. Forced to kill himself for plotting against Nero. Ten books of his epic *Pharsalia* (on civil war between Caesar and Pompey) survive.

Lucania (lūkā′nēŭ), anc. region of S Italy between Gulf of Taranto and Tyrrhenian Sea; now in Campania and Basilicata. Italic tribes and Greek colonists were subjected by Rome (3d cent. B.C.). Chief cities were Heraclea and Paestum.

Lucas van Leyden (lü′käs vän lī′dŭn), 1494–1533, Dutch painter and engraver, whose real name was Lucas Jacobsz. His realistic and dramatic pictures represent the beginning of Dutch genre painting. Also depicted biblical scenes.

Lucca (lŏok′kä), city (pop. 32,896), Tuscany, central Italy, near Tyrrhenian Sea. Trade center for olive oil and wine; tobacco mfg. A Roman town, it became (6th cent.) cap. of a Lombard duchy and (12th cent.) seat of a free commune, later a prosperous republic. It was a major medieval banking center and famous for its velvets and damasks. Save for short periods under tyrants, notably CASTRACANI, and foreign rule, republic was independent until Napoleon I made it a principality in 1805. It became part of duchy of Parma in 1817, of grand duchy of Tuscany in 1847. Annexed by Sardinia 1860. Height of economic and artistic flower came 12th–15th cent., when the cathedral and churches of San Frediano and San Michele were built.

Lucerne (lŏosûrn′), Ger. *Luzern,* canton (576 sq. mi.; pop. 223,409), central Switzerland. Agr., pastoral, and forested. Population is mainly German-speaking and Catholic. One of FOUR FOREST CANTONS, its history is that of its cap., **Lucerne** (pop. 60,365), which grew up around an 8th-cent. monastery. It became a Hapsburg possession in 1291 but joined Swiss Confederation 1332 and gained full freedom 1386. Chief town of the SONDERBUND 1845–47. Thorvaldsen's Lion of Lucerne monument (1820–21) memorializes SWISS GUARDS. City has 14th–15th cent. covered bridges and 8th-cent. church (Hofkirche). There are machine and printing industries. A summer resort, Lucerne is on **Lake of Lucerne**, Ger. *Vierwaldstättersee* (area 44 sq. mi.), noted for scenery. Lake borders cantons of Lucerne, Uri, Schwyz, and Unterwalden. Reuss R. flows through it.

lucerne: see ALFALFA.

Lucian, fl. 2d cent., Greek prose writer. Wrote nearly 80 works, known for their wit and vigorous satire. Most outstanding are his dialogues (*Dialogues of the Gods, Dialogues of the Dead,* etc.) satirizing ancient mythology and contemporary philosophy. *The True History* parodied incredible adventure stories.

Lucifer (lū′sĭfŭr) [Latin,= light-bearing], the planet Venus as the morning star. In Isaiah 14.12, Lucifer refers to king of Babylon, but was misunderstood to mean the fallen angel. Hence term became a name for SATAN. Name in Greek was Phosphorus.

Lucilius, Caius (kā′ŭs lūsī′lēŭs), c.180–102? B.C., Latin poet. Founder of Latin satire.

Lucioni, Luigi (lwē′jē lŏochō′nē), 1900–, American painter, b. Italy. Paints still life, landscapes, and por-

traits in polished style, accurate drawing, clear color.

Luck, Ukraine: see LUTSK.

Luckner, Felix, Graf von (fā′lĭks gräf′ fŭn lŏok′nŭr), 1886–, German naval hero of World War I. In command of the commerce raider *Seeadler* he destroyed $25,000,000 worth of Allied shipping before his capture (1918). Was nicknamed "Sea Devil."

Lucknow (lŭk′nou), city (pop. 387,177) SW Uttar Pradesh, India, on Gumti R. Was cap. of nawabs of Oudh, 1775–1856. During Sepoy Rebellion, British garrison and colony were besieged here, July–Nov., 1857. City retaken 1858 by Sir Colin Campbell. Seat of Lucknow Univ. Rail and industrial center.

Lucrece (lūkrēs′) or **Lucretia** (lūkrē′shŭ), in Roman legend, virtuous matron. Victim of rape by Sextus, son of Tarquinius Superbus, she begged her husband to avenge her and stabbed herself. The ensuing revolt drove the TARQUINS from Rome.

Lucretius (Titus Lucretius Carus) (lūkrē′shŭs), c.99 B.C.–c.55 B.C., Roman poet. His one celebrated work, *De rerum natura* [*On the Nature of Things*], in beautiful hexameter verse, sets forth arguments founded upon Epicurean philosophy. It urges man not to fear the gods or death, since "man is lord of himself." His proof, based on an atomic theory (not the same as modern atomic theory), states that the universe came into being through the workings of natural laws in the combining of atoms.

Lucullus (Lucius Licinius Lucullus Ponticus) (lūkŭ′lŭs), c.110–56 B.C., Roman general. A faithful follower of Sulla in the Social War, he was given offices and became successful commander against MITHRIDATES VI of Pontus. Attempts to reform Roman administration in Asia made him unpopular, and he was replaced by Pompey. In retirement Lucullus was known for showy elegance of life.

Ludendorff, Erich (ā′rĭkh lŏo′dŭndôrf), 1865–1937, German general. As chief of staff to HINDENBURG during World War I he was largely responsible for the victories credited to his superior. He later took part in ultranationalist movements, notably in Munich "beer-hall putsch" of HITLER (1923). With his second wife, Dr. Mathilde Ludendorff, he founded an "Aryan" cult, wrote cranky pamphlets.

Ludington, city (pop. 9,506), N Mich., harbor on L. Michigan at mouth of Pere Marquette R. Resort with fishing and some mfg. Monument marks Father Marquette's first burial place.

Ludlow, Roger, fl. 1590–1664, one of founders of Conn., b. England. Founded Fairfield in 1639. Completed first codification of Conn. laws (1650).

Ludlow (lŭd′lō), municipal borough (pop. 6,455), Shropshire, England. Has old houses and ruins of 11th cent. castle. Butler wrote *Hudibras* here.

Ludlow. 1 City (pop. 6,374), N Ky., on Ohio R. Suburb of Covington and Cincinnati. Rail center with mfg. of furniture and machinery. **2** Town (pop. 8,660), S Mass., NE of Springfield; settled c.1750. Jute and flax products.

Ludwig. For German rulers thus named, see LOUIS.

Ludwig, Emil (ā′mēl lŏot′vĭkh), 1881–1948, German author. Among his translated popular humanized biographies are *Goethe* (1920), *Napoleon* (1924), *Bismarck* (1926), and *The Son of Man* (1928; a life of Jesus).

Ludwig, Karl (kärl′), 1816–95, German physiologist, famous as professor and head of physiological institute at Univ. of Leipzig.

Ludwigshafen (lŏot′vĭkhs-hä′fŭn), city (pop. 122,329), Rhineland-Palatinate, W Germany, on the Rhine. An important transshipment point, it has a large chemical industry and mfg. of machinery and automobiles. Heavily damaged in World War II.

Lufkin, city (pop. 15,135), E Texas, ENE of Houston; founded 1882. Center for lumbering, newsprint mfg. (from native pine), woodworking. Also has farm products, foundries, and livestock.

Lugano (lŏogä′nō), town (pop. 17,718), Ticino canton,

S Switzerland. A scenic summer resort, it is on **Lake of Lugano**, Ital. *Lago di Lugano* or *Ceresio* (area c.19 sq. mi.), which lies both in Switzerland and in Italy.

Lugansk, Ukraine: see VOROSHILOVGRAD.

Lugo (lōō'gō), city (pop. 21,115), cap. of Lugo prov., NW Spain, in Galicia, on Miño R. Agr. center. Has Roman walls and 12th-cent. cathedral.

Luini, Bernardino (bārnärdē'nō lōōē'nē), c.1480–1532, Italian painter, influenced by Leonardo; known for graceful female figures.

Luitpold (lōō'ītpôlt), 1821–1912, regent of Bavaria (1886–1912). Ruled for his insane nephews LOUIS II and OTTO I.

Luke, Saint, Gentile physician, friend and companion of St. Paul and St. Mark. Since 2d cent. regarded as author of the Gospel according to St. Luke and the Acts of the Apostles. Acts 20; 21; Col. 4.14; 2 Tim. 4.11. His symbol: an ox. Feast: Oct. 28.

Luke, Gospel according to Saint, book of New Testament. It gives a unique account of Jesus' birth, tells of His ministry, and ends with the passion and resurrection. Verses 9.51–18.14 mainly unparalleled in other Gospels; contain many favorite passages. See also SYNOPTIC GOSPELS.

Lukeman, (Henry) Augustus, 1871–1935, American sculptor of historical monuments. Completed the gigantic sculptures on Stone Mt., Ga., started by Gutzon Borglum.

Luks, George (lōōks), 1867–1933, American portrait and genre painter. A member of The Eight.

Lule (lü'lü), Swed. *Lule älv,* river rising in N Sweden and flowing 280 mi. from Lapland mts. to the Baltic at Lulea. Its potential power, partly utilized at PORJUS, exceeds 2,000,000 hp.

Lulea (lü'lüō"), Swed. *Luleå,* city (pop. 22,514), co. seat of Norrbotten co., N Sweden, port (ice-bound in winter) on Gulf of Bothnia at mouth of Lule R. Exports include Lapland iron ore, timber, and reindeer hides. There are iron smelting and pulp milling.

Lull, Ramon (rämōn' lōōl'), or **Raymond Lully,** c.1236–1315, Catalan philosopher. Turning to religion in 1266, he became a Franciscan and longed to convert Islam. His study of Arabic and Moslem culture enriched his teaching (in France and Majorca), and he went to Africa and the East. His works (notably *Ars major*) argue that all articles of faith can be demonstrated by logic; set forth an elaborate system of symbols; and express profound mysticism. Later generations supposed him a magician.

Lull, Richard Swann, 1867–, American paleontologist. He taught at Yale (1906–36) and was director of Peabody Museum (1922–36). He was editor of the *American Journal of Science* (1933–49) and author of *Organic Evolution* (1917; rev. ed. 1948).

Lully, Jean Baptiste (zhä' bäptēst' lülē'), 1632–87, French composer, b. Italy. In 1653 he became chamber composer and conductor to Louis XIV. He composed many ballets to plays of Molière and others but is best known for his operas. Among them are *Alceste* (1674), *Cadmus et Hermione* (1673), *Amadis* (1684), and *Armide* (1686). He created a style which held the French operatic stage until the advent of Gluck.

Lully, Raymond: see LULL, RAMON.

lumber, name used in U.S. and Canada for timber which has been cut into boards. In U.S. it was one of first industries; Maine was the leading early producer but later Oregon, Wash., and Calif. assumed the lead and southern states became increasingly important. Logging (felling and preparation of timber for shipment to sawmills) was a frontier industry. Stories and legends of feats of the lumberjack are a colorful chapter in American folklore.

Lumberton, town (pop. 9,186), S N.C., on Lumber R., and S of Fayetteville. Processes tobacco, textiles, and lumber.

Lumière, Louis Jean (lümyĕr'), 1864–1948, and **Auguste Marie Louis Nicholas Lumière,** 1862–, French inventors, brothers. Invented (1895) the cinematograph, first mechanism to project moving pictures on a screen where they could be seen by an audience.

luminescence: see FLUORESCENCE; PHOSPHORESCENCE.

Luna, Alvaro de (älvä'rō dä lōō'nä), 1388?–1453, constable of Castile. As favorite of John II he virtually ruled kingdom until the queen's enmity led to his execution.

Luna, Pedro de, 1328–1423, Spanish cardinal, antipope as Benedict XIII (1394–1417; see SCHISM, GREAT). He was a supporter of ROBERT OF GENEVA and was elected to succeed him. As France shifted allegiance from and to the Avignon papacy, Benedict's position shifted. He was finally deposed at the Council of CONSTANCE (1417), but refused to accept the election of MARTIN V.

Lunacharsky, Anatoli Vasilyevich (ŭnùtô'lyē vŭsē'lyŭvīch lōōnŭchär'skē), 1875–1933, Russian revolutionist, dramatist, and poet. As commissar of education (1917–29) he greatly encouraged the Soviet theater. Three of his plays are available in English (*Three Plays,* 1923).

lunacy: see INSANITY.

lunar caustic: see SILVER.

Lund (lŭnd), city (pop. 33,954), Malmohus co., S Sweden, NE of Malmo. It is a university town and publishing center. University was founded 1666 by Charles XI. City was mentioned c.920 in the sagas. It became an archbishop's see in 11th cent. and a Lutheran bishopric in 1536. In 1658 it passed from Denmark to Sweden. There is a 10th-cent. cathedral.

Lundy's Lane, locality just W of Niagara Falls, scene of stubborn engagement of War of 1812, fought July 25, 1814. American forces pushing into Canada encountered British troops. After night-long fight against superior numbers, Americans withdrew to Fort Erie. Both sides had heavy casualties.

Lüneburg (lü'nŭbōōrk), city (pop. 58,269), Lower Saxony, NW Germany, on Ilmenau R. Salt- and chemical works. It was long cap. of dukes of Brunswick-Lüneburg (see HANOVER). Important member of Hanseatic League. Late Gothic in character as exemplified in huge city hall (12th–18th cent.) and gabled houses. Has salt springs and mud baths. **Lüneburger Heide** (lü'nŭbōōrgŭr hī'dù), a vast heath, lies between Elbe and Aller rivers; sheep raising.

Lunéville (lünāvēl'), town (pop. 19,065), Meurthe-et-Moselle dept., NE France, on Meurthe R. Faïence industry. Treaty signed here 1801 between France and Austria substantially renewed terms of Treaty of CAMPO FORMIO. Palace (18th cent.), damaged in World War II, was residence of STANISLAUS I.

lungs, respiratory organs of air-breathing vertebrates. In humans two lungs invested with membranes (pleura) lie in chest cavity. Carbon dioxide and oxygen are interchanged in air cells. See *ill.,* p. 595.

Lunt, Alfred, 1893–, American actor; husband of Lynn FONTANNE with whom he has acted since 1924.

lupine or **lupin,** annual or perennial leguminous plant, of genus *Lupinus,* sometimes grown for forage and cover crop, but mostly for ornament in North America. Varieties of *Lupinus perennis* bear spikes of richly colored bonnet-shaped blooms. Others include tree lupine (*L. arborescens*) and BLUEBONNET.

Luray (lōōrā'), tourist town (pop. 2,731), N Va., in Shenandoah Valley SW of Front Royal. Hq. of Shenandoah Natl. Park. Here are **Luray Caverns,** limestone caves known for beauty of formations.

Luria, Isaac ben Solomon (lōō'rēù), 1534–72, Jewish cabalist, called Ari, b. Jerusalem; leader of a large circle of mystics. Also spelled Loria.

Lusatia (lōōsā'shù), Ger. *Lausitz,* Pol. *Łużyce,* region (pop. c.1,000,000), E Germany, bounded by Lusatian Mts. in S and by Oder R. in E. Chief towns: Bautzen, Görlitz, Sagan, Zittau. Region consists of Upper Lusatia, in NE Saxony, and Lower Lusatia, in S Brandenburg and Lower Silesia. Lusatian Neisse R. separates Russian-occupied and Polish-administered parts of E Germany. Agr. and heavily forested, Lusatia also produces textiles and lignite. Lusatians (also called Sorbs) are descended from Slavic WENDS; some, as in SPREE FOREST, still speak Wendish. Region was colonized by Germans in 10th cent., frequently changed masters. Saxon from 1635 to 1815, when larger part went to Prussia.

Lüshun, China: see PORT ARTHUR.

Lusiads, The: see CAMÕES, LUÍS DE.

Lusignan (lüzēnyä'), French noble family. It was prominent in the Crusades and ruled Cyprus 1192–1489. Its ancestral castle, in Poitou, was built according to legend by the fair MELUSINE. Guy of Lusignan (d. 1194) married Sibylla, sister of Baldwin IV of Jerusalem, and was chosen king of Jerusalem on the death of Baldwin V (1186). Defeated and captured at Hattin by Saladin in 1187, he was released in 1188 and began the siege of Acre, which was taken in 1191 with the help of Richard I of England and Philip II of France (Third Crusade). After Sibylla's death (1190), Guy's right to the throne was contested by CONRAD of Montferrat, who had Philip II's support. Guy abdicated 1192 but was invested as king of Cyprus by Richard I. Cyprus continued under Guy's brother AMALRIC II and his descendants. A branch of the family also ruled Lesser Armenia (Cilicia) 1342–75, and the family listed the kingships of Jerusalem and Armenia among its sonorous but largely empty titles. Cyprus flourished under Lusignan rule and was a center of French medieval culture, but it declined after 1370, becoming dependent on Venice, Genoa, and Egypt. The rule of Caterina CORNARO ended with outright annexation by Venice (1489).

Lusin (loo'sin'),1881–1936, Chinese author. Known primarily for his brilliant political essays, although he first won fame for his short stories. Complete works are translated into English.

Lusitania (lūsītä'nēu), Roman province in Iberian peninsula, including modern central Portgual and much of W Spain. It was inhabited by the Lusitani, tribes subdued by Rome only after death of their leader, Viriatus, in 139 B.C. Old identification of ancestors of the Portuguese with the Lusitanians is now largely ignored.

Lusitania, liner under British registration sunk without warning off Irish coast by German submarine on May 7, 1915. Of more than 1,000 lost, 114 were American citizens. Incident had much to do with preparing way for U.S. entry into World War I.

lusterware: see POTTERY.

lute: see STRINGED INSTRUMENTS.

Lutetia, Roman name of PARIS, France.

lutetium (loote'shēum), rare element (symbol = Lu; see also ELEMENT, table); metal of rare earths.

Luther, Hans (häns' loo'tùr), 1879–, German statesman. As finance minister (1923–24) he helped Schacht stabilize currency. Later was chancellor (1925–26), president of Reichsbank (1930–33), German ambassador to U.S. (1933–37).

Luther, Martin, 1483–1546, German leader of Protestant Reformation. By 1505 he had completed master's examination at Univ. of Erfurt and began study of law. Instead, he entered monastery of Augustine friars, was ordained priest in 1507, and was assigned to the Univ. of Wittenberg. Through his study and thought he became convinced that sinner's hope lay entirely in grace of God and redemption by Christ, accepted through faith. In 1510, on mission to Rome, he was shocked by spiritual laxity in high church circles. Returning to Wittenberg, he formulated plans for reformation of church doctrine and practices. In 1517 he protested dispensation of INDULGENCE then being granted by Johann TETZEL. In challenge he posted his historic 95 theses on door of castle church. These aroused ire of church authorities. At Augsburg in 1518 Luther refused to recant and stood openly against certain doctrines. He further stirred ire of Roman Church in supporting new nationalism with German state control of German church. When a

papal bull of condemnation came, Luther burned it publicly. In 1521 formal excommunication was pronounced, and he was summoned before Diet of Worms. When an edict demanded his seizure, he took refuge in the Wartburg. There he translated New Testament into German and began the translation of entire Bible that was to be a great force in molding the German language. He returned to Wittenberg and there remained for rest of his life. His opposition to the Peasants' War (1524–25) cost him some popularity, but he was generally revered. In 1525 he married a former nun, Katharina von Bora, who bore him six children. Under his sanction Philipp Melanchthon wrote and presented Augsburg Confession at Diet of Augsburg (1530). Luther had many controversies, esp. with Zwingli and later with Calvin over LORD'S SUPPER, which divided Protestants into the Lutheran Church and Reformed Churches. He was active in building up competent education system and wrote widely on church matters. The religious faith based on his teachings is **Lutheranism.** Luther had conservative attitude, as distinguished from views of Reformed (Calvinistic) communions. The principal statements of faith were collected in the BOOK OF CONCORD (1580), fundamental doctrine being justification by faith. Baptism was counted necessary but no form was specified, and no uniform liturgy was required. In general a synodical form of organization was set up, but unity of the church is unity of doctrine rather than of structure. In Germany, Lutheranism has always been in close association with political life. Lutheran Church is estab. church of Denmark, Iceland, Sweden, Norway, and Finland. In North America, Lutherans formed first congregation in 1638 at Fort Christina (Wilmington, Del.); second on Manhattan in 1648. In 18th cent. exiles from Palatinate estab. German Lutheran churches in N.Y., Pa., Del., Md., and South. In 1748 Heinrich Melchior MÜHLENBERG formed in Pa. the first synod.

Luther College: see DECORAH, Iowa.

Luton (loo'tùn), municipal borough (pop. 110,370), Bedfordshire, England. Center of straw-plaiting industry, estab. here in time of James I.

Lutsk (lootsk), Pol. Łuck, city (1931 pop. 35,700), W Ukraine, on Styr R. Agr. market center. The seat of the princes of VOLHYNIA in Middle Ages, it passed to Russia 1795, reverted to Poland 1921, was ceded to Russia 1945.

Lutter am Barenberge (loo'tùr äm bä'rùnbërgù), town (pop. 2,547), central Germany, near Brunswick. Here in 1626 Tilly defeated Christian IV of Denmark in the Thirty Years War.

Lutyens, Sir Edward Landseer (lü'chùnz, lü'tyùnz), 1869–1944, English architect. Planned New Delhi, India; designed Cenotaph in London.

Lützelberger, Hans (häns' lü'tsùlboorgùr), d. 1526, German wood engraver, also called Hans Franck. Executed *Dance of Death* designs of Holbein, the younger.

Lützen (lüt'sùn), town (pop. 5,739), Saxony-Anhalt, E Germany, SW of Leipzig. In Thirty Years War Gustavus II of Sweden defeated Wallenstein here in 1632, but fell in the battle. In 1813 Napoleon I defeated Russian and Prussian forces at near-by Grossgörschen.

Luxembourg, François Henri, duc de (fräswä' ärĕ' dük dü lüksäboor'), 1628–95, marshal of France. He distinguished himself in all the wars of Louis XIV, especially in the War of the Grand Alliance (victorious at Fleurus, 1690; Steenkerke, 1692; Neerwinden, 1693).

Luxembourg or **Luxemburg** (both: lük'sùmbùrg), grand duchy (999 sq. mi.; pop. 290,992), W Europe, bordering on Belgium, Germany, and France; cap. Luxembourg. It includes the S Ardennes mts. and part of the Luxembourg-Lorraine iron-mining basin. Luxembourg ranks sixth among the steel-producing countries of Europe (not counting USSR). It formed a customs union with Belgium in 1922 and joined the

BENELUX bloc in 1947. A constitutional monarchy, it has a bicameral legislature. Catholicism is the prevailing religion. French is the official, German the literary language, but a Low German dialect is widely spoken. The county of Luxembourg (originally Lützelburg) emerged (10th cent.) as one of the largest fiefs of the Holy Roman Empire, but it was gradually whittled down by its neighbors to its present size. Its counts also ruled the Holy Roman Empire and Bohemia 1308–1437. Raised to a duchy by Emperor Charles IV, Luxembourg continued under a cadet line. (A distant collateral line also played a prominent role in French history.) Conquered by Philip the Good of Burgundy in 1443, the duchy passed after 1482 to the Hapsburgs and became part of the Spanish, after 1714 Austrian, Netherlands (see NETHERLANDS, AUSTRIAN AND SPANISH). The Congress of Vienna (1814–15) made it a grand duchy, member of the German Confederation but in personal union with the Netherlands. Luxembourg shared in the Belgian revolt of 1830. After much wrangling, Belgium in 1839 received the larger part of the grand duchy—i.e., the present LUXEMBOURG prov. of Belgium. The rest continued as member of the German Confederation until 1866 and under the kings of the Netherlands until 1890, when Wilhelmina acceded in the Netherlands and Duke Adolf of NASSAU became grand duke of Luxembourg. His successors were his daughters Marie Adelaide (abdicated 1919) and Charlotte (married Prince Felix of Bourbon-Parma). Neutral Luxembourg was occupied by the Germans in World War I (1914–18) and in World War II (1940–44), when Grand Duchess Charlotte fled with her government to London. Luxembourg joined in the Five-Power Pact with England, France, Belgium, and the Netherlands (1948) and in the North Atlantic Treaty (1949).

Luxembourg, province (1,706 sq. mi.; pop. 213,917), SE Belgium, in the Ardennes; cap. Arlon. Cattle raising. Steel mfg. in S. Population is mostly French-speaking but includes large German minority. Province was detached from grand duchy of LUXEMBOURG in 1839.

Luxembourg or **Luxemburg,** city (pop. 61,996), cap. of grand duchy of Luxembourg, on Alzette R. Has picturesque houses, 16th-cent. grand ducal palace. Was strongly fortified until 1867. Became hq. of European Coal and Steel Community (see SCHUMAN PLAN) 1952.

Luxembourg Palace, in Paris, France, was built 1615–20 in Renaissance style for Marie de' Medici by Salomon de Brosse. Houses French council of the Republic (formerly senate). Was used for the peace conference of 1946. Luxembourg gardens are famous.

Luxemburg, Rosa (rō'zä lŏŏk'sŭmbŏŏrk), 1870?–1919, German revolutionist, b. Russian Poland. A brilliant writer and orator, she rose to leading position in Social Democratic party and, with Karl LIEBKNECHT, founded SPARTACUS PARTY in World War I. After her release from protective custody in 1918 she helped to transform Spartacists into German Communist party. Arrested in the Spartacist uprising of 1919, she and Liebknecht were murdered by soldiers who were taking them to prison.

Luxemburg, grand duchy and city: see LUXEMBOURG.

Luxeuil (lüksü'yù), former abbey, at Luxeuil-les-Bains, Haute-Saône dept., E France. Founded 590 by St. Columban (whose rule was soon replaced by St. Benedict's), it became a major center of early medieval learning. Its abbots came to rank as princes of Holy Roman Empire. Abolished in French Revolution.

Luxor (lŏŏk'sôr), town (pop. 24,118), central Egypt, on the Nile. Near Karnak, it occupies part of site of THEBES. Chief ruin is temple of Luxor, built in reign of Amenhotep III as temple to Amon.

Luynes, Charles d'Albert, duc de (shärl' dälbĕr' dük' dù lüĕn'), 1578–1621, constable of France, favorite of Louis XIII. With Louis's collaboration he planned assassination of CONCINI (1617), exiled Marie de'

Medici, and became chief minister, with great power.

Luzán, Ignacio de (ēgnä'thyō dä lŏŏthän'), 1702–54, Spanish scholar and critic, author of *La poética* (1737), statement of the rules of neoclassical poetry.

Luzern, Switzerland: see LUCERNE.

Luzerne (lŏŏzûrn'), borough (pop. 6,176), NE Pa., near Wilkes-Barre. Anthracite mining.

Luzon (lŏŏzŏn'), island (40,420 sq. mi.; pop. 7,374,798), largest and most important of Philippine Isls. Manila, cap. of republic, is on SW coast. Paralleling part of E coast is the mountain range Sierra Madre. Mt. Mayon and Mt. Taal in S are active volcanoes. Produces sugar cane, rice, cotton, hemp, and tobacco. Limited mining of gold, iron, copper, and manganese. Inhabited mainly by Ilocanos and Tagalogs. Invaded Dec. 10, 1941, by the Japanese; Allied forces made last stand on BATAAN and CORREGIDOR. U.S. and guerrilla forces regained the island early in 1945.

Luzzatto, Moses Hayyim (hä'yēm lŏŏt-tsät'tō), 1707–47, Hebrew poet and playwright, a leader in the renaissance of Hebrew literature. Wrote allegorical *Glory to the Righteous.*

Lvov, Prince Georgi Yevgenyevich (gēôr'gē yĭvgä'nyù-vĭch lyùvôf'), 1861–1925, Russian liberal statesman. After abdication of Nicholas II (Feb., 1917) he headed provisional government. Resigned July, 1917; succeeded by Kerensky.

Lvov (lyùvôf'), Ger. *Lemberg,* Pol. *Lwów,* city (1931 pop. 316,177), W Ukraine, in N foothills of Carpathians. Transportation and industrial center (machinery, textiles, chemicals, oil refining). Seat of a university (founded 1658). Founded c.1250 by a prince of Galicia, Lvov soon grew to commercial importance on Vienna-Kiev route and was a major Polish stronghold against attacks from E. After first Polish partition (1772), Lvov became cap. of Austrian Galicia. Lost and retaken by Austria in World War I (1914, 1915), it was taken by Poland in 1919 and confirmed in Polish possession by Treaty of Riga (1921). It was annexed to USSR in 1939 and formally ceded by Poland in 1945. During German occupation in World War II (1941–44) most of its 100,000 Jewish inhabitants were exterminated. Among historic buildings are a 16th-cent. palace and three cathedrals (two dating from 14th cent.).

Lyautey, Louis Hubert Gonzalve (lwē' übĕr' gôzälv' lyōtā'), 1854–1934, marshal of France. As French resident general in Morocco (1912–16, 1917–25), he proved an extremely able colonial administrator and may be said to have created modern Morocco.

lycanthropy (līkăn'thrùpē) [from Gr.,= wolf-man]. Belief that person can by witchcraft or magic take on form and nature of animal is widespread in time and space. Most common is belief in the werewolf, person who changes into a wolf and eats human flesh, then returns to human form. The morbid desire to eat human flesh, characteristic of certain psychoses, is also called lycanthropy.

lyceum, association providing lectures and entertainments. The first organization of Josiah HOLBROOK grew into Natl. American Lyceum, for 40 years a powerful force in adult education, social discussion, and political reform. Movement waned after Civil War, but was succeeded by CHAUTAUQUA MOVEMENT.

Lycomedes (līkŏ'mùdēz), in Greek legend, king of Skyros, who killed Theseus.

Lycurgus (līkûr'gùs), legendary reformer of Spartan constitution (said to be of 7th cent. B.C.).

Lydda (lĭ'dù, Arabic *Ludd,* city (pop. over 10,000), central Israel, SE of Tel Aviv; just N is Israel's chief international airport. City mentioned in Old Testament as Lod. Lydda was the scene of Peter's healing of the paralytic (Acts 9.32). It was occupied by Crusaders in 1099, destroyed by Saladin in 1191, and rebuilt by Richard Cœur de Lion. City is the traditional birthplace of St. George.

lyddite: see PICRIC ACID.

Lydgate, John (lĭd'gāt), c.1370–c.1450, prolific English poet, a monk. He was a pedestrian imitator of Chaucer (as in *The Fall of Princes*, c.1430).

Lydia, Christian convert at whose home in Philippi Paul stayed. Acts 16.14–40.

Lydia, anc. country, W Asia Minor; cap. Sardis. Flourished from time of King Gyges (seized power 687 B.C.) to that of King CROESUS (defeated by Persians before 540 B.C.). Its wealth was proverbial.

lye, name for several substances strongly alkaline in solution. In U.S. it commonly indicates sodium hydroxide, which is used in making hard soaps, in textile manufacture, canning industry, leather tanning, petroleum refining. It causes destruction of animal tissues.

Lyell, Sir Charles (lī′ŭl), 1797–1875, English geologist. He did much to popularize the theory of UNIFORMISM, first proposed by James Hutton, and was author of many works on geology.

Lyly or **Lilly, John** (lĭl′ē), 1554?–1606, English prose writer and dramatist. He is remembered chiefly for *Euphues* (published as *Euphues; or the Anatomy of Wit*, 1578, and *Euphues and His England*, 1580), a popular didactic novel written in highly ornamented euphuistic style, stressing alliteration, learned allusion, and antithesis.

lymphatic system (lĭmfă′tĭk), system of vessels and nodes through which lymph is conveyed in the body. Lymph, derived chiefly from blood plasma, filters through capillary walls and serves as exchange medium between blood and body cells. Small lymph vessels unite into two main channels emptying into veins. Trapping of bacteria in lymph nodes prevents their passage into blood.

Lynaker, Thomas: see LINACRE, THOMAS.

Lynbrook, residential village (pop. 17,314), SE N.Y., on SW Long Isl.; settled before Revolution. Mfg. of sportswear, machinery, metal products.

Lynch, Charles, 1736–96, American Revolutionary soldier. Term "lynch law" may be derived from his name. Presided over extralegal court in Bedford co., Va., which summarily punished Loyalists.

Lynch, village (pop. 440), N Nebr., between Missouri and Niobrara rivers. Excavation of near-by prehistoric settlements was begun in 1936.

Lynchburg, city (pop. 47,727), S Va., on James R., in Blue Ridge foothills; settled 1757. Trade center and tobacco market, it has mfg. of shoes, textiles, and clothing. Confederate supply base in Civil War; resisted Union assault 1864. Seat of RANDOLPH-MACON WOMAN'S COLLEGE and Lynchburg Col. Near by is Sweet Briar Col. (nonsectarian; for women; opened 1906) which stresses individualized education and honors work; in 1948 began sponsoring junior-year-in-France plan.

lynching, extralegal infliction of capital punishment by a self-constituted group. Though origin of the word is unknown, there are various explanations, one of the most popular being that it is derived from the extralegal court (1780) of Col. Charles Lynch, a Revolutionary soldier. American pioneers, in settlements where law had not yet been established, tended to punish by lynching such crimes as horse stealing and rape. In the South during the reconstruction, there was considerable resort to lynching, particularly by the Ku Klux Klan, when Negroes were accused of serious crimes against whites. Lynching today is very rare, although Southern legislators still block antilynching bills on the grounds of Federal interference in state matters.

Lynd, Robert Staughton, 1892–, American sociologist, b. New Albany, Ind. With his wife, Helen Merrell Lynd, he made a noted sociological study of Muncie, Ind., published (1929) as *Middletown: a Study in Contemporary American Culture*.

Lyndhurst. 1 Township (pop. 19,980), NE N.J., near Rutherford. Machinery, metal products, clothing. **2** City (pop. 7,359), NE Ohio, E suburb of Cleveland.

Lyndsay, Sir David: see LINDSAY, SIR DAVID.

Lynn, Norfolk, England: see KING'S LYNN.

Lynn, city (pop. 99,738), E Mass., on Massachusetts Bay arm and NE of Boston; settled 1629. Mfg. of shoes, electrical appliances, and machinery.

Lynn Canal, N arm of Chatham Strait and Stephens Passage, 90 mi. long, SE Alaska, extending to Skagway. Navigable throughout. Thrusts N between mountains to inlets of Chilkoot and Chilkat rivers. Provides sea lane to Haines, Chilkoot, and Skagway.

Lynn Regis, Norfolk, England: see KING'S LYNN.

Lynwood, city (pop. 25,823), S Calif., adjacent to Los Angeles. Metal products and chemicals.

lynx (lĭngks), short-tailed mammal (*Lynx* or *Felis*) with soft, thick black-marked beige to gray fur and tufted ears. Common or northern lynx of Europe found in Alps, Scandinavia, N Russia; some races in Asia. American species are BOBCAT and Canada lynx.

Lyon, Mary, 1797–1849, American educator. In 1837 she founded what is now Mt. Holyoke Col. at SOUTH HADLEY, Mass.

Lyon, Matthew, 1750–1822, American politician and pioneer, b. Ireland. Founded Fair Haven, Vt. (1783). Able exponent of frontier views as Congressman from Vt. (1797–1801) and Ky. (1803–11).

Lyonesse (lī′ŭnĕs″), region W of Cornwall, now sunk 40 fathoms under sea. In Celtic legend, home of Tristram and of the Lady of Lyones.

Lyons, Joseph Aloysius, 1879–1939, Australian prime minister (1932–39). Helped form United Australia party. Restored solvency in depression.

Lyons (lī′ŭnz), Fr. *Lyon* (lyŏ), city (pop. 439,861), cap. of Rhône dept., E central France; a port at confluence of Rhone and Saône rivers. A leading silk and rayon center of Europe, it also has chemical, electrical, and metallurgical industries. Seat of a stock exchange (founded 1506, oldest in France) and of a university (founded 1808). Founded 43 B.C. as Roman colony (Lugdunum), it became chief city of Gaul and a cradle of Christianity. Its archbishops exercised temporal rule until c.1307, when Philip IV inc. Lyonnais region and its cap., Lyons, into royal domain. WALDENSES emerged here in 12th cent. Lyons was devastated 1793 in reprisal for a counterrevolutionary insurrection. Invention of Jacquard loom helped to restore prosperity. Generally modern, city has preserved old quarter around Cathedral of St. John (12th–14th cent.). Birthplace of emperors Claudius and Caracalla, St. Ambrose, Ampère.

Lyons, Councils of, 13th and 14th ecumenical councils of the Roman Catholic Church. **1** 1245, convened by INNOCENT IV. Deposed Emperor FREDERICK II, who paid no heed. **2** 1274, summoned by Gregory X to discuss the Holy Land, remove schism of East and West, and reform the Church. Reunion of Constantinople and Rome, previously proposed by Emperor Michael VIII, was proclaimed and then ignored. Among the clerical reforms was establishment of the conclave.

lyre: see STRINGED INSTRUMENTS.

lyre bird, Australian bird; the tail plumage of the male when spread out resembles a lyre. The lyre is fully developed in fourth year. Both sexes have brown plumage. They are poor fliers.

lyric, in ancient Greece, a short poem accompanied by a musical instrument, usually a lyre. Word often refers to songlike quality of poetry; as opposed to narrative or dramatic poetry it refers to any short poem (sonnet, ode, song, elegy) expressing a personal emotion. Sappho, Alcaeus, and Pindar wrote Greek lyrics. Latin lyrics of Catullus and Horace were followed by Christian hymns, folk songs, and troubadour songs of Middle Ages. Lyric has been a major form of poets in English literature.

Lys (lēs), Flemish *Leie*, river, 135 mi. long, NE France and Belgium, flowing NE past Armentières and Courtrai into Scheldt at Ghent. Scene of heavy fighting in World War I.

Lysander (līsăn′dŭr), d. 395 B.C., Spartan naval commander, diplomat, credited with capture of Athenian fleet (405 B.C.) and with submission of Athens (404 B.C.) that ended the PELOPONNESIAN WAR.

Lysenko, Trofim Denisovich (lĭsĕng′kō, Rus. trŭfēm′ dyĭnyē′sŭvĭch lĭsyĕn′kŭ), 1898–, Russian agronomist, leader of Soviet school of genetics opposing theories accepted by most geneticists. He supports doctrine of inheritance of characteristics acquired through environmental influence.

Lysias (lĭ′sēŭs), c.459–c.380 B.C., Greek orator. One of the best Greek prose writers. His oration against Eratosthenes is a model of Greek oratory.

Lysimachus (lĭsĭ′mŭkŭs), c.355 B.C.–281 B.C., general of Alexander the Great. After Alexander's death, he took Thrace and fought vigorously in the wars of the DIADOCHI, gaining W Asia Minor after the defeat of ANTIGONUS I (314 B.C.). Lysimachus was defeated and killed at Magnesia ad Sipylum, ending his war with Seleucus.

Lysippus (lĭsĭ′pŭs), 4th cent. B.C., Greek sculptor, head of Sicyon school. Largely originated Hellenistic style of sculpture. He modified proportions of the human figure set by the canon of Polyctetus. Copies of his bronzes include the APOXYOMENUS (Vatican). Said to have produced 1,500 works.

Lytton, Baron, and **earl of:** see BULWER-LYTTON.

M′. Names beginning thus are entered as if spelled Mac-. See the article MAC.

Maas, Nicolaas: see MAES, NICOLAAS.

Maas, Dutch and Flemish name for MEUSE river.

Maastricht (mäs′trĭkht″), municipality (pop. 74,449), cap. of Limburg prov., SE Netherlands, on the Meuse and the Albert Canal system; formerly spelled Maestricht. Transportation center; mfg. of textiles, ceramics, glass, chemicals. Dating from Roman times, it belonged to domain of early Frankish kings, later passed to dukes of LIMBURG. The Spanish under Farnese captured it from the Dutch rebels in 1579 and massacred many inhabitants, but the Dutch recovered it in 1632 and were confirmed in its possession in 1648. A strategic fortress, it repeatedly fell into French hands, notably in 1673 and 1794. Cathedral of St. Servatius, founded 6th cent., is oldest church in Netherlands.

Mabillon, Jean (zhä′ mäbēyō′), 1632–1707, French scholar. His *De re diplomatica* (1681, 1704) first used critical method in authenticating documents.

Mabinogion (mäbĭnō′gēŭn) [Welsh plural of *Mabinogi* = youthful career], collection of medieval Welsh stories from manuscripts called the *White Book of Rhydderch* and the *Red Book of Hergest*. First four tales are *The Four Branches of the Mabinogi*. Other tales show Welsh versions of tales that were to become part of Arthurian legend. A famous English translation was made by Lady Charlotte Guest.

Mabuse, Jan de (yän′ dü mäbüz′), c.1478–c.1533, Flemish painter. Real name was Jan Gossaert or Gossart. Influenced by work of Italian masters.

Mac, Mc, or M′ [Irish,= son], element in names derived from Irish and Scottish Gaelic patronymics. In most such names second element was a forename; others included titles or epithets. It is untrue that some forms of the prefix are more typically Scottish or Irish. In this book all names beginning with any of the three forms are alphabeted as Mac-.

macadam road, constructed of compacted layers of small stones. Introduced c.1815, it superseded dirt roads in Europe and U.S. and revolutionized road transportation. Earlier water-bound macadam (small compacted stones sprinkled with stone dust and water, then rolled) largely replaced by bituminous macadam (bituminous surface is spread over macadam, often not sprinkled).

McAdoo, William Gibbs (mă′kŭdōō), 1863–1941, American political leader, U.S. Secretary of the Treasury (1913–18). Prominent Democratic contender for presidency in 1920 and 1924. U.S. Senator from Calif. (1933–39). His second wife was a daughter of Woodrow Wilson.

McAfee, Mildred Helen (mă′kŭfē), 1900–, American educator. She was president of Wellesley Col., 1936–48, and director of the WAVES, 1942–46.

McAlester (mŭkăl′ĭstŭr), city (pop. 17,878), SE Okla., ESE of Oklahoma City; settled c.1870. Trade center for agr. area with cotton gins and food processing plants. Coal mines, oil wells. Former Choctaw cap.

Macalester College: see SAINT PAUL, Minn.

McAllen, city (pop. 20,067), S Texas, WNW of Brownsville; settled 1904. Has food-processing and chemical plants and oil refineries. Winter resort.

McAllister, (Samuel) Ward, 1827–95, American social leader. Designated the Four Hundred members of "true" N.Y. society (1892).

Macao or **Macau** (mŭkou′), Portuguese colony (6 sq. mi.; pop. 374,737), SE China, on estuary of Canton R. Portuguese settlement was begun 1557; present holdings confirmed by treaty with China 1887. Colony consists of **Macao** city (pop. 312,717), on Macao isl., and 3 offshore islets. City was leading port for China's foreign trade until rise of Hong Kong in 19th cent. Now derives much revenue from smuggling and gambling interests.

macaque: see MONKEY.

macaroni, generic name for shaped and dried doughs prepared from flour (usually semolina, a durum wheat flour) and water. Similar pastes probably originated in Asia and reached Europe in 13th cent. Varieties include tubes, ribbons, elbows, cords (spaghetti), fine strands (vermicelli). Noodles, usually flat ribbons, contain eggs. All may be stored dry and are prepared for eating by boiling.

MacArthur, Arthur, 1845–1912, American general. Served in Civil War and Spanish-American War. Military governor of Philippines (1900–1901). His son, **Douglas MacArthur,** 1880–, is also a general. Fought in France during World War I. Chief of staff 1930–35. Commanded U.S. armed forces in Far East during World War II. Promoted general of the army ("five-star general") in 1944. Directed Allied occupation of Japan after war. Dismissed by Pres. Truman in 1951 in dispute over China policy. Became chairman of Remington Rand, Inc. in 1952.

Macassar or **Makassar** (both: mùkă′sùr), town (pop. 84,855), E Indonesia, on SW Celebes isl. Exports coffee, teak, spices, and copra. In World War II, in Macassar Strait (between Borneo and Celebes) the Japanese were defeated in a naval battle.

Macau, China: see MACAO.

Macaulay, Thomas Babington, 1800–1859, English historian and author. Had a distinguished career in Parliament and in India (1834–38). In 1857 made Baron Macaulay of Rothley. His major work was *The History of England from the Accession of James the Second* (5 vols., 1849–61), noted for colorful and dramatic presentation of facts and events from a Whig point of view. His poetry, in *Lays of Ancient Rome* (1842), was very popular.

macaw (mùkô′), name of several species of parrot family, native to Central and South America. They are large and colorful and have long tails and large hooked beaks.

Macbeth, d. 1057, king of Scotland (1040–57). A commander for Duncan I, he defeated and slew Duncan and took his kingdom. Was defeated and killed by Malcolm III. Subject of Shakspere's *Macbeth.*

Maccabees (măk′ùbēz), also called Hasmoneans or Asmoneans, Jewish family of the 2d and 1st cent. B.C. which led in opposition to Syrian dominance and Hellenizing tendencies and in the restoration of Jewish political and religious life. Resisting desecration of the Temple, Mattathias, a priest, killed a Syrian officer; he fled with his five sons and began a guerrilla warfare. On his death (166 B.C.) the leadership passed to his son Judas Maccabeus, from whose surname the family name is derived. Judas resisted a Syrian army and renewed Jewish religious life by rededicating the Temple; the feast of Hannukah celebrates this event. Judas was killed in 161 B.C. opposing the conquering army of Bacchides; his brother and successor Jonathan was slain in 143 B.C. Under the last brother, Simon, recognized as civil ruler and high priest, Palestine enjoyed peace. Simon was murdered by his son-in-law (135 B.C.); Simon's son John Hyrcanus gained the leadership in the ensuing strife, and ruled until his death (105? B.C.). John's grandson, John Hyrcanus II, a high priest, acquired temporal rule upon the death of his mother, Salome Alexandra; his brother Aristobulus II revolted, and a civil war followed. Rome intervened and captured Jerusalem (63 B.C.). With the execution of Hyrcanus II for treason (30 B.C.), the family ceased to exist. Their influence continued, however, in opposition to Romanization. Best sources for the family history are **Maccabees,** in Western Canon, last two books of Old Testament; placed in Apocrypha in AV. 1 Maccabees begins with the rebellion of Mattathias and ends with murder of Simon. 2 Maccabees emphasizes religious rather than historical issues with accounts of martyrdom of Jews resisting Hellenization. It is composed in self-deprecatory, witty style (e.g., 2.23–32; 4.40; 5.21). There are other books of Maccabees among the PSEUDEPIGRAPHA.

Maccabees, Feast of the: see HANUKKAH.

McCarthy, Joseph R(aymond), 1909–, U.S. Senator from Wis. (1947–), a Republican. Known for vigorous attacks on many as Communists and subversives.

M'Carthy, Justin, 1830–1912, British historian, novelist, and journalist. Works include *Dear Lady Disdain* (1875) and *A History of Our Own Times* (1879–1905). His son, **Justin Huntly M'Carthy,** 1860–1936, wrote the novel *If I Were King* (1901), on which the musical *The Vagabond King* was based.

McClellan, George Brinton, 1826–85, Union general in Civil War. Commander, Dept. of the Ohio (1861); cleared western Va. of Confederate troops. Briefly commander in chief. Commanded Army of the Potomac (1862); he failed in PENINSULAR CAMPAIGN but checked R. E. Lee in ANTIETAM CAMPAIGN. Relieved

of command in Nov., 1862. He was a leader in criticizing Lincoln as Democratic nominee for President in 1864.

McClernand, John Alexander, 1812–1900, Union general in Civil War. Commanded river expedition in Vicksburg campaign (1863); later led 13th Corps in Grant's successful advance on Vicksburg.

Macclesfield (măk′ùlzfēld), municipal borough (pop. 35,981), Cheshire, England. Silk mfg. center of England, it also has tanning and papermaking.

McClintock, Sir Francis Leopold, 1819–1907, British arctic explorer. Participated in several expeditions seeking lost Franklin party. Discovered and mapped Prince Patrick Isl. Commanded Lady Franklin's expedition (1857–59); found records disclosing Franklin's fate.

McCloskey, John, 1810–85, American cardinal, archbishop of New York after 1864, principal builder of St. Patrick's Cathedral.

McClure, Alexander Kelly, 1828–1909, American journalist and political leader. Early Republican, supported Lincoln; a leader of Liberal Republican party in 1872. Founded Philadelphia *Times* in 1875.

McClure, Sir Robert John Le Mesurier, 1807–73, British arctic explorer. Commanded one of two ships seeking Franklin party in W Arctic Archipelago (1850–53). Discovered McClure Strait. First proved existence of Northwest Passage.

McClure, S(amuel) S(idney), 1857–1949, American editor, publisher, b. Ireland; emigrated to U.S. as a boy. Founded (1893) and edited *McClure's Magazine,* notable for "muckraking" attacks on the evils of big business and economic and political corruption.

McComb, city (pop. 10,401), SW Miss., SSW of Jackson near La. line; founded c.1857. Mfg. and trade center for cotton and truck area. Railroad shops.

McConnelsville, village (pop. 1,941), NE Ohio on Muskingum R. and SE of Zanesville. Council Rock, with Indian pictographs, near by.

McCook, Alexander McDowell, 1831–1903, Union general in Civil War. Fought ably at Perryville (1862). Routed at Murfreesboro and Chickamauga; relieved of command in Oct., 1863, later exonerated.

McCook, city (pop. 7,678), S Nebr., on Republican R. near Kansas line. Trade and processing center in grain and livestock area. Has railroad shops.

McCormack, John, 1884–1945, Irish-American tenor. He sang principally in concert and for phonograph records and became widely beloved, especially for the singing of simple sentimental songs.

McCormick, Cyrus Hall, 1809–84, inventor of the reaper, first demonstrated in 1831 and patented in 1834. The Chicago factory was built in 1847; by 1851 McCormick's reaper was known in England and soon after throughout Europe. Although other reapers were introduced, McCormick, through his unusual business ability, kept his in the running. His nephew, **Robert Sanderson McCormick,** 1849–1919, was first American ambassador to Austria-Hungary (1902). Married daughter of Joseph MEDILL. His son, **Joseph Medill McCormick,** 1877–1925, managed Chicago *Tribune* after 1907, was U.S. Representative (1917–19) and U.S. Senator (1919–25). His wife, **Ruth Hanna McCormick,** 1880–1945, daughter of Mark Hanna, served in U.S. Congress (1929–31). Another son of R. S. McCormick was **Robert R(utherford) McCormick,** 1880–, who gained sole ownership of Chicago *Tribune.* He attracted attention by attacks on U.S. participation in world affairs.

McCoy, Isaac, 1784–1846, American missionary among the Indians. As a Federal agent after 1830, he supervised removal of Wabash valley tribes to places chosen by him in Kansas and Okla.

MacCracken, Henry Mitchell, 1840–1918, American educator. After 1884 he was vice chancellor of what is now New York Univ. and chancellor there 1891–1910. The University Heights campus was acquired and the medical school merged with Bellevue Hospital Medical Col. during his administration. One of his sons, **Henry Noble MacCracken**, 1880–, was president of Vassar Col., 1915–46.

McCrae, John, 1872–1918, Canadian poet. His famous poem, "In Flanders Fields," was written under fire in World War I.

McCullers, Carson, 1917–, American novelist, b. Ga., author of evocative psychological studies, principally set in the South (e.g., *The Heart Is a Lonely Hunter*, 1940; *The Member of the Wedding*, 1946).

McCulloch, Hugh (mŭkŭ′lŭ), 1808–95, U.S. Secretary of the Treasury (1865–69, 1884–85). Favored severe deflation in Pres. Johnson's administration.

McCulloch vs. Maryland, case, decided 1819 by U.S. Supreme Court. Involved control of currency. Md. opposed U.S. branch bank in Baltimore. Decision upheld supremacy of Federal government over states.

Macdhui, Ben, Scotland: see BEN MACDHUI.

Macdonald, Alexandre, 1765–1840, marshal of France, of Scottish descent. Fought in French Revolutionary and Napoleonic wars; was created duke of Taranto for his distinguished conduct at Wagram (1809).

Macdonald, Flora, 1722–90, Scottish Jacobite heroine. Aided Charles Edward Stuart to escape to the Continent after his defeat (1746) at Culloden Moor. Commemorated in Highland legend and poetry.

Macdonald, George, 1824–1905, Scottish novelist and poet, known for tales of rural Scotland (e.g., *Robert Falconer*, 1867), narrative poem *Within and Without* (1855), and especially his juvenile classic *At the Back of the North Wind* (1871).

Macdonald, Sir John Alexander, 1815–91, Canadian statesman, first premier of Dominion of Canada, b. Glasgow. Became premier in 1847. Dominant figure in promoting union of provinces. Forced to resign when PACIFIC SCANDAL broke (1873). Returned as premier in 1878.

MacDonald, (James) Ramsay, 1866–1937, British statesman. A founder of Labour party, he was its leader in House of Commons (1911–14) until discredited for pacifist stand. First Labour prime minister (1924), he was defeated for supposed pro-Communism on issue of Zinoviev letter. Premier of second Labour cabinet (1929), he accepted post of prime minister in Conservative dominated National government (1931). This act and his policy of economic nationalism caused him to be repudiated by Labour party.

McDonald, Ranald, 1824–94, American adventurer. Reared in Pacific Northwest. Reached Japan in 1848; imprisoned and subjected to ordeals, but because of his courage he was released in 1849.

Macdonough, Thomas (mŭkdŏ′nŭ), 1783–1825, American naval officer. Commanded L. Champlain fleet in War of 1812. His flagship, *Saratoga*, defeated the *Confiance* in significant naval battle (1814).

McDougall, Alexander, 1731–86, American Revolutionary patriot and general, b. Scotland. Helped form Sons of Liberty in N.Y. Served through Revolution.

McDougall, William, 1871–1938, American psychologist, b. England. He pioneered in physiological and social psychology and was noted for biological approach to problems of psychology.

MacDowell, Edward A(lexander), 1861–1908, American composer. His chief works are four piano sonatas, the *Indian Suite* for orchestra, two piano concertos, and numerous smaller works, including the popular *Woodland Sketches* (including "To a Wild Rose," "To a Water Lily") for piano. His widow, Marian Nevins MacDowell, founded the MacDowell Colony for composers, artists, and writers at Peterborough, N.H.

McDowell, Ephraim, 1771–1830, American pioneer surgeon. In 1809 he made surgical history by performing the first ovariotomy (removal of an ovary). Known also for skill in lithotomy.

McDowell, Irvin, 1818–85, Union general in Civil War. Commanded at first battle of BULL RUN and led

Pope's 3d Corps in second battle (1862). Shared blame for defeat; removed from command.

mace: see NUTMEG.

Macedon (mă′sŭdŏn), anc. country of the Balkan peninsula, roughly equivalent at its height to modern Macedonia. In the 7th cent. B.C. a state under Greek rulers began to develop. This PHILIP II with well-trained armies and well-organized administration made the master state of Greece after victory at Chaeronea (338 B.C.). His brilliant son, ALEXANDER THE GREAT, carried victory even to the limits of the known world and incidentally, with it, HELLENISTIC CIVILIZATION. After his death (323 B.C.) his successors (the DIADOCHI) broke up the empire by incessant wars, in which Macedon suffered. The drain of manpower for armies and the ruinous battles weakened the country, which was frequently under control of Epirus. ANTIGONUS II restored Macedon, but PHILIP V was defeated by Rome in the Macedonian Wars (215–205 B.C., 200–194 B.C.), and matters went worse under Perseus, who lost the Third Macedonian War (171–168 B.C.). After a pretender, Andriscus, tried to assert independence, Macedon became the first Roman province, Macedonia (146 B.C.).

Macedonia (măsŭdō′nēŭ), region of SE Euurope, in the Balkan Peninsula, extending N from the Aegean Sea between Epirus and Thrace. Roughly corresponding to ancient MACEDON, it is predominantly mountainous, pastoral, and agr. Tobacco is an important crop. Politically, the region is divided into Greek Macedonia (13,380 sq. mi.; pop. 1,754,092; cap. Salonica), the Yugoslav autonomous republic of Macedonia (10,229 sq. mi.; pop. 1,152,054; cap. Skoplje), and Bulgarian Macedonia (pop. 252,258). In the Middle Ages, the Byzantine emperors had an uneasy hold over Macedonia, which repeatedly was the prey of invaders, notably the Bulgars. It was conquered by Stephen Dushan of Serbia in the 14th cent. and, after his death, by the Ottoman Turks. Macedonia became a patchwork of religions and nationalities—Christians, Moslems, Jews; Serbs, Bulgars, Greeks, Turks. When the Ottoman Empire began to break up in the 19th cent., Macedonia was claimed by Greece, Serbia, and Bulgaria. The Treaty of SAN STEFANO gave the major share (incl. the coast) to Bulgaria, but the Congress of BERLIN restored direct Turkish rule (1878). Secret terrorist organizations (*komitadjis*), working to free Macedonia from the Turks, were supported by Bulgaria, which gained a large share of Macedonia in the First Balkan War (1912–13). In the Second Balkan War (1913), Greece and Serbia defeated Bulgaria and obtained approximately the present boundaries. Population exchanges after 1923 resulted in the replacement of most of the Bulgarian and Turkish elements in Greek Macedonia by Greek refugees from Asia Minor. Nevertheless, Bulgaria continued to agitate for a greater share of Macedonia. Border incidents, terrorism, and mutual accusations of violations of minority rights created an explosive situation. In World War II all Macedonia was briefly held by Bulgaria (1941–44), but the peace treaty of 1947 restored the former boundaries.

Maceió (măsāō′), city (pop. 102,301), NE Brazil, cap. of Alagoas state; an Atlantic port. Area produces cotton and sugar; city has some factories.

MacEwen, Sir William (mŭkū′ŭn), 1848–1924, Scottish surgeon, especially noted for surgery of brain and spinal cord.

McFee, Henry Lee, 1886–1953, American painter. Early work was influenced by cubism and expressionism; later style was naturalistic.

McFee, William, 1881–, Anglo-American author, a marine engineer, b. London; in U.S. after 1911. Wrote novels and sketches of nautical life (e.g., *Casuals of the Sea*, 1916).

Macgillicuddy's Reeks (mŭgĭ′lŭkŭ″dēz rēks′), mountains of Co. Kerry, Ireland, near Lakes of Killarney. They include Carrantuohill (3,414 ft.), the highest peak in Ireland, and other peaks over 3,000 ft. high.

McGillivray, Alexander (mŭgĭ'lĭvrā), 1759–93, Indian chief. Son of a Scots trader and his French-Creek wife. Allied Creeks with the Spanish in 1784; attacked American frontier settlements. Signed treaty with U.S. (1790), but later repudiated it.

McGill University: see MONTREAL, Que.

McGrath, J(ames) Howard (mŭgrath'), 1903–, U.S. Attorney General (1949–52). Resigned during controversy over investigation of Justice Dept.

McGraw, John J(oseph), 1873–1934, American baseball manager. Led N.Y. Giants to 10 pennants 1904–5, 1911–13, 1917, 1921–24) and three world series victories (1905, 1921–22).

MacGregor, Robert: see ROB ROY.

McGregor, town (pop. 1,138), NE Iowa, on the Mississippi almost opposite mouth of Wisconsin R. Annual American School of Wild Life Protection sessions. Effigy Mounds Natl. Monument is near by.

McGuffey, William Holmes (mŭgŭ'fē), 1800–1873, American educator. He compiled the six McGuffey Eclectic Readers (1836–57), used for nearly two generations, with estimated sales of 122,000,000 copies.

Machado, Antonio (mächä'dhō), 1875–1939, Spanish lyric poet, author of *Soledades* (1903; brooding and evocative poems on nature and man) and other volumes, collaborator with his brother, Manuel Machado (1874–1947), in plays, both original and translated.

Machado, Gerardo (härär'dō mächä'dhō), 1871–1939, president of Cuba (1925–33). Began his regime with interest in material and social reform. Became dictatorial and instituted bloody terrorism of secret police. U.S. finally intervened, and Machado was forced to flee. Died in Miami Beach, Fla.

Machado de Assis, Joaquim Maria (zhwäkēm' mŭrē'ŭ mŭshä'dō dù äsēzh'), 1839–1908, Brazilian realist novelist. Pictures of Brazilian social conditions in *Iaiá Garcia* (1878), *Memórias postumas de Braz Cubas* (1881), *Quincas Barba* (1891), and *Dom Casmurro* (1900) show psychological insight and are highlighted by ironic humor. Considered by many Brazil's greatest writer.

Machen, Arthur (mă'kùn), 1863–1947, British author of bizarre romances (e.g., *The Great God Pan*, 1894; *The Three Impostors*, 1895; *The Hill of Dreams*, 1907) and essays, all notable for exquisite style.

McHenry, James, 1753–1816, American statesman. In Continental Congress (1783–86). U.S. Secretary of War (1797–1800); followed leadership of Alexander Hamilton. Fort McHenry named for him.

McHenry, Fort, former U.S. military post in Baltimore, Md., now a national monument and historic shrine (estab. 1939). Fort's defense against British bombardment (Sept. 13–14, 1814) inspired Francis Scott Key to compose the STAR-SPANGLED BANNER.

Machias (mùchī'ùs), town (pop. 2,063), SE Maine, on Machias R.; settled 1763. Burnham Tavern (1770), historical museum, has mementos of "first naval battle of the Revolution." This was the capture of a British ship in June, 1775, off **Machiasport** town (pop. 781), at head of Machias Bay and E of Machias.

Machiavelli, Niccolò (nēk-kōlō' mäkyävĕl'lē), 1469–1527, Italian author and statesman, an outstanding figure of the Renaissance; b. Florence. Playing a leading role under the Florentine republic (1492–1512), he was sent on diplomatic missions to France, to the pope, and to the emperor. As secretary of the republican council from 1506 he organized an efficient citizens' militia. The restoration of the Medici in 1512 forced his retirement to his country estate, where he wrote his chief works. His most famous book, *The Prince*, has made his name a symbol of political unscrupulousness. Actually, it is neither moral nor immoral, but is instead the first objective, scientific analysis of the methods by which political power is obtained and kept. Its complete detachment lends the book an air of cynicism but contributes to its lucid

brilliance. Its influence even to most recent times is incalculable. Machiavelli's personal preference seems to have been for the republican form of government. He also was an ardent champion of Italian unity. In his *Discourses on the First Ten Books of Livy* he expounded the first modern general theory of politics; his *History of Florence* with its scientific approach opened a new era in history writing. He also wrote poems and plays, notably the ribald comedy *Mandragola*.

machine. Term commonly used for complicated assembly of parts operating together to do work. It is applied technically to any device increasing intensity of applied force, changing direction of force, or changing one form of motion or energy into another. Thus the lever, pulley, inclined plane, screw, and wheel and axle are simple machines. Mechanical advantage of a machine is ratio between the resistance or load and the force applied to overcome it. Since some force is required to overcome friction this ratio does not hold exactly, so mechanical advantage is calculated as ratio between the distance the force applied moves and the distance the resistance moves. Efficiency of a machine is degree in percentage to which machine accomplishes the work it is capable theoretically of doing if there were no friction. Complex machines are complicated combinations of the simple machines. Certain machines used to transform some other form of energy (e.g., heat) into mechanical energy are known as engines. See also HYDRAULIC MACHINE; *ill.*, p. 619.

machine gun, firearm discharging rifle bullets with great rapidity, utilizing for firing either the power of recoil or the explosion gases as the gun is fired. Developed almost exclusively by American inventors (including R. J. Gatling and J. M. Browning). First used in the Franco-Prussian War, it was employed extensively in World War I.

Machpelah (măkpē'lù), cave bought by Abraham for family tomb. Gen. 23; 25.9,10; 49.29–32; 50.13.

Machu Picchu (mä'chōō pēk'chōō), fortress city of anc. Incas, Peru, c.50 mi. NW of Cuzco. May have been home of the Inca prior to migration to Cuzco, as well as last stronghold after Spanish conquest.

McIntosh, Millicent Carey, 1898–, American educator, dean of Barnard Col. after 1947 and president after 1952.

McIntyre, James Francis Aloysius, 1886–, American cardinal. Roman Catholic auxiliary bishop of New York (1940–48) and archbishop of Los Angeles (after 1948), he was made cardinal 1953.

Macip or Masip, Vicente Juan (vēthän'tä hwän' mäthēp', mäsēp'), c.1500–1579, Spanish painter, who was strongly influenced by Italian art. Also called Juan de Juanes and Vicente Joanes.

MacIver, Robert M(orrison) (mùkē'vùr), 1882–, Scottish sociologist, at Columbia Univ. after 1927. His works include *Society: Its Structure and Changes* (1931) and *The Web of Government* (1947).

Mack, Connie (Cornelius McGillicuddy), 1862–, American baseball manager. Managed Philadelphia Athletics (1901–1950) to nine pennants (1902, 1905, 1910–11, 1913–14, 1929–31) and five world series (1910–11, 1913, 1929–30).

McKay, Claude (mùkā'), 1890–1948, American Negro author, b. Jamaica, British West Indies. His works include poetry (e.g., *Harlem Shadows*, 1922), novels (e.g., *Home to Harlem*, 1927), and an autobiography (*A Long Way from Home*, 1937).

McKay, Donald, 1810–80, American shipbuilder, b. Nova Scotia. From his Boston shipyard came sleek, swift clippers, some of the most beautiful ships ever upon the sea. Among them were the *Flying Cloud*, the *Sovereign of the Seas*, the *Great Republic*, and the *Glory of the Seas*.

McKay, Douglas, 1893–, U.S. Secretary of the Interior (1953–). Governor of Oregon (1949–52).

Mackay, John William (mă'kē), 1831–1902, American financier, b. Ireland. Made fortune in Nev. silver mines. Formed the Postal Telegraph Cable Co. 1886).

MacKaye, Percy (mŭkī'), 1875–, American author, b. New York city. Wrote long poems, plays, and collected Ky. mountain folklore.

McKeesport, city (pop. 51,502), SW Pa., on Monongahela R. at mouth of Youghiogheny R. and SE of Pittsburgh; settled 1755. Mfg. of iron and steel products and tin plate. Braddock's camp and crossing are marked with tablets. Was armament center in World War II.

McKees Rocks, borough (pop. 16,241), SW Pa., NW of Pittsburgh; settled c.1764. Mfg. of steel products and chemicals; bituminous coal mining.

Mackensen, August von (ou'gŏost fŭn mä'künzün), 1849–1945, German field marshal. In World War I he defeated the Russians in the battle of the MASURIAN LAKES (1915); occupied Rumania (1917). Later was active as a monarchist leader.

Mackenzie, Sir Alexander, 1764?–1820, Canadian fur trader and explorer, b. Scotland. Supervised Athabaska fur district. Followed then unknown Mackenzie R. to Arctic Ocean (1789). Completed first overland journey across North America N of Mexico (1793).

Mackenzie, Alexander, 1822–92, Canadian statesman, b. Scotland. First Liberal prime minister of dominion (1873–78).

Mackenzie, Henry, 1745–1831, Scottish novelist, best known for *The Man of Feeling* (1771).

Mackenzie, Sir William, 1849–1923, Canadian railroad builder and financier. Helped organize and build Canadian Northern Railway.

Mackenzie, William Lyon, 1795–1861, Canadian journalist and insurgent leader, b. Scotland. As publisher of *Colonial Advocate* (1824–34) he attacked Family Compact. Founded the *Constitution* as a Reform party organ (1836). Enraged by policies of Sir F. B. Head and by defeat of Reform party, MacKenzie and a group of insurgents attempted to seize Toronto (1837), but rebellion was quickly put down. He escaped to U.S., set up provisional government on Navy Isl. in Niagara R. Later imprisoned for 18 months by U.S. for violating neutrality laws (see CAROLINE AFFAIR). Returned to Canada 1849.

Mackenzie, provisional district: see NORTHWEST TERRITORIES, Canada.

Mackenzie, river of NW Canada, with its basin between the Rockies (W) and the Laurentian Plateau (E), flowing N and NNW to the Arctic Ocean. The Mackenzie proper is 1,120 mi. long, flowing between Great Slave L. and the Arctic Ocean. Mackenzie R. system includes Great Slave R. (between Great Slave L. and L. Athabaska), and Peace and Athabaska rivers, chief headstreams. Together they form a continuous stream 2,514 mi. long (second longest in North America), navigable for c.2,000 mi. with only one portage. Delta at mouth is 80–100 mi. wide. Long important in fur trading. Recently oil fields and mineral resources have been developed. Valley has regular air service. Named for Sir Alexander Mackenzie, who explored it 1789.

Mackenzie King, William Lyon: see KING, WILLIAM LYON MACKENZIE.

mackerel, spiny-finned fish related to tuna and bluefish. It is spindle shaped, has a deeply forked tail and a series of small, spiny finlets on dorsal and ventral sides between dorsal and ventral fins and tail. Common mackerel (*Scomber scombrus*), c.12 in. long, travels in schools. It spawns in deep waters, swims to coastal waters in spring, and returns to deep waters in autumn. Spanish mackerel and frigate mackerel are related forms.

McKim, Charles Follen, 1847–1909, American architect, who belonged to firm of McKim, Mead, and White, which handled many important commissions. Favored classic architecture and its Renaissance derivatives. A founder and first president of American Academy in Rome.

Mackinac (mă'kĭnô″), strait between peninsula of Upper Mich. and Lower Mich., separating L. Huron and L. Michigan. Name is shortening of Michilimackinac. Early used as gathering place for nomadic Indians. Important trading center and military post in New France. Passed into British control 1761. Garrison massacred by Indians 1763. Treaty of Ghent gave it permanently to U.S. ownership. Long the chief center of operations for American Fur Co. Lost importance in 1840s as fur trade declined.

Mackinaw City, resort village (pop. 970), N Mich., on S shore of Straits of Mackinac. Rebuilt stockade of French Fort Michilimackinac is here.

McKinley, William, 1843–1901, 24th President of the United States (1897–1901). A Republican U.S. Representative from Ohio (1877–91), he sponsored highly protective McKinley Tariff Act. Governor of Ohio (1892–96). The skill of M. A. HANNA and a gold-standard party platform elected him President in 1896. Trouble with Spain ended in the SPANISH-AMERICAN WAR, McKinley asking Congress for the declaration though Spain had hinted at concessions to avoid war. After victory, he demanded Philippine Isls. for U.S. Signed bill to annex Hawaii; supported Open Door policy in China. Advanced interests of American commerce. Currency Act of 1900 consolidated gold-standard policy. Reelected in 1900, he was shot down at Buffalo, N.Y., on Sept. 6, 1901, by Leon Czolgosz; died on Sept. 14.

McKinley, Mount (20,270 ft.), S central Alaska, in Alaska range, in Mount McKinley Natl. Park. Highest peak in North America. First climbed by Hudson Stuck 1913.

McKinney, city (pop. 10,560), N Texas, NNE of Dallas; founded 1842. Handles cotton, grains (esp. corn), pecans, truck, and textiles.

Maclaurin, Colin, 1698–1746, Scottish mathematician, philosopher, authority on fluxional calculus.

MacLeish, Archibald (mŭklēsh'), 1892–, American poet, notable for technical innovation and proficiency. His early poems were highly personal; his later work speaks of social responsibility. Among his volumes are *Conquistador* (1932) and *The Fall of the City* 1937; radio verse drama). He was the head of the Library of Congress 1939–44.

MacLennan, Hugh, 1907–, Canadian novelist, author of *Two Solitudes* (1945), *The Precipice* (1948).

Macleod, Fiona: see SHARP, WILLIAM.

Macleod, John James Rickard (mŭkloud'), 1876–1935, Scottish physiologist. He shared 1923 Nobel Prize in Physiology and Medicine for work on use of insulin in treating diabetes.

Maclise, Daniel (mŭklēs'), 1806–70, British portrait and historical painter, b. Ireland.

McLoughlin, John (mŭklŏk'lĭn), 1784–1857, fur trader in Oregon, b. Canada. Hudson's Bay Co. man in Columbia R. country (1824–46). Controlled Indians, expanded trade, aided settlers.

Maclure, William, 1763–1840, American geologist, b. Scotland. In his early business career in London he made a fortune. He visited America in 1782 and 1796 and on his third visit undertook an extensive survey. His *Observations on the Geology of the United States* (1809; 2d ed., 1817) and the accompanying geologic map marked an epoch in American geological history.

MacMahon, Marie Edmé Patrice de (märē' ĕdmä' pätrēs' dü mäkmäō'), 1808–93, marshal of France, president of France (1873–79), duke of Magenta; of Irish ancestry. Fought in Crimean War; defeated Austrians at Magenta (1859); held a command in Franco-Prussian War; aided in suppression of Commune of Paris (1871). Chosen president of France by the royalist majority of the National Assembly, he sought to restore the Bourbons but failed. In 1875 France received a republican constitution. MacMahon's persistent habit of appointing royalist cabinets despite the clear republican majority in parliament eventually forced his resignation. Jules Grévy succeeded him.

McMaster, John Bach, 1852–1932, American historian.

Known for *History of the People of the United States* (8 vols., 1883–1913; Vol. IX, 1927).

McMaster University: see HAMILTON, Ont.

MacMillan, Donald B(axter), 1874–, American arctic explorer. Made ethnological studies of Labrador Eskimo (1911, 1912). Led Greenland expedition (1913–17) and subsequent arctic expeditions, collecting varied scientific data and specimens. Made extensive air surveys (1944).

McMillan, Edwin Mattison, 1907–, American physicist. Shared 1951 Nobel Prize in Chemistry for discoveries in chemistry of elements having atomic number greater than that of uranium. He is codiscoverer of neptunium (element 93) and plutonium (element 94); known also for work on microwave radar and on sonar. Associated with Univ. of California from 1932.

McMinnville. 1 City (pop. 6,635), NW Oregon, SW of Portland. Trade center in lumber, wheat, dairy area. Seat of Linfield Col. (Baptist; coed.; 1857). **2** Town (pop. 7,577), central Tenn., ESE of Nashville. Mfg. of wood, marble products, shoes, and hosiery. Here are tree nurseries.

MacMonnies, Frederick William (mùkmŏ′nēz), 1863–1937, American sculptor of monuments. His *Civic Virtue* (formerly in City Hall Park, New York) was the subject of much controversy.

McMurrough, Dermot: see DERMOT MCMURROUGH.

McNaughton, Andrew George Latta (mùknô′tùn), 1887–, Canadian engineer and army officer. Became president of Canadian Natl. Research Council in 1935. During World War II he commanded Canadian forces in Great Britain. Delegate to Security Council of UN (1948–49).

MacNeice, Louis (mùknēs′), 1907–, British poet. He joined "Oxford revolt" against formal language, and his three volumes of collections (1940, 1945, 1948) show his connection with Auden, Spender, and T. S. Eliot. Among his translations are *Agamemnon* (1936) and *Faust* (1951).

MacNeil, Hermon Atkins, 1866–1947, American sculptor, best known for his Indians and pioneers.

Macomb (mùkōm′), city (pop. 10,592), W Ill., SSW of Galesburg; laid out 1831. Trade and industrial center in farm and coal area. Mfg. of clay and metal products.

Macon, Nathaniel (mā′kùn), 1758–1837, American statesman. U.S. Representative (1791–1815; speaker of the House 1801–7) and Senator (1815–28) from N.C. A staunch Jeffersonian.

Mâcon (mäkŏ′), town (pop. 18,221), cap. of Saône-et-Loire dept., E central France, on Saône R. Famous for red Burgundy wine. Birthplace of Lamartine.

Macon (mā′kùn), city (pop. 70,252), central Ga., at head of navigation on Ocmulgee R. and SE of Atlanta. Fort Hawkins settled on E bank of river 1806; Macon, laid out 1823 on W bank, annexed Newtown (Fort Hawkins) 1829. Industrial and shipping center for extensive farm area (cotton, truck, livestock), it has textile and lumber mills. Clay products are made, and foods processed. Seat of Wesleyan Col. (for women; 1836) and Mercer Univ. (Baptist; coed.; 1833). Sidney Lanier's birthplace is preserved. Ocmulgee Natl. Monument is near.

Macon, Bayou (bī′ō mā′kùn, bī′ōō), rising in SE Ark. and flowing S to Tensas R. in NE La. Was haunt of the James brothers.

Macpherson, James, 1736–96, Scottish poet. His epics *Fingal* (1761) and *Temora* (1763), purportedly translations from Irish bard Ossian, were widely translated in Europe and influenced romantic movement. Later investigation proved them to be based on Gaelic myths but written by Macpherson himself.

McPherson, city (pop. 8,689), central Kansas, NNE of Hutchinson and on old Santa Fe trail. Refines and ships oil and mills flour.

Macready, William Charles (mùkrē′dē), 1793–1873, English actor and manager. Won fame as Richard III (1819). Managed Covent Garden (1837–39) and Drury Lane (1841–43). Appeared in U.S. in 1826, 1843 and

1847 when the Astor Place riot (instigated by Edwin FORREST supporters) occurred.

McReynolds, James Clark (mùkrē′nùldz), 1862–1946, U.S. Attorney General (1913–14), Associate Justice of U.S. Supreme Court (1914–41). Strict constructionist; a key figure in F. D. Roosevelt's unsuccessful attack on Supreme Court.

Macrobius (mùkrō′bēùs), fl. c.400, Latin writer, philosopher. His seven-book dialogue, *Saturnalia*, is a source of quotations from early writers.

Macy, Anne Sullivan, 1866–1936, American educator, teacher and companion of Helen KELLER after 1887. As a child she learned manual alphabet at Perkins Inst., where she was sent because of eye trouble.

Madagascar (mădùgä′skûr), island (227,602 sq. mi.; pop. c.4,153,000), in Indian Ocean, separated from Africa by Mozambique Channel; overseas territory of French Union. Coffee (chief export) is grown in uplands between fertile coastal plain and forested mountains in interior. Main ports are Tamatave, linked by rail with Tananarive (chief town), and Majunga. Natives are Malagasy (a Malay stock). Discovered 1500 by Portuguese explorers. Brought under French control, 1885–1905. In World War II, island was under Vichy government until 1942, when it was occupied by British troops. A former colony, it became an overseas territory in 1946, with representation in French parliament.

Madariaga, Salvador de (sälvädhōr′ dä mädhryä′gä), 1886–, Spanish essayist and internationalist. He held posts in the League of Nations and the diplomatic service, but is best known for historical studies (e.g., of Columbus and Cortés) and essays on national psychologies (e.g., *The Genius of Spain*, 1928, originally in English; *Ingleses, franceses, españoles*, 1928).

Madawaska, river, S Ont., Canada, rising in Algonquin Provincial Park and flowing 250 mi. E to Ottawa R. W of Ottawa.

madder, Old World dye plant (*Rubia tinctorum*) with whorled leaves and small yellow flowers. Alizarin, the source of such pigments as madder purple and madder orange, was obtained from its fleshy roots from ancient times; it is now made synthetically.

Madeira (mùdā′rù), river, formed by junction of Beni and Mamoré on Bolivian-Brazilian border. With Mamoré it forms greatest tributary of Amazon.

Madeira Islands (mùdēr′ù, mùdä′rù), archipelago (c.300 sq. mi.; pop. 269,179), far off Moroccan coast in the Atlantic, forming Funchal dist. of Portugal; cap. Funchal. Though they were known as early as the 14th cent., their discovery is traditionally credited to explorers under orders of Prince Henry the Navigator, 1418–19. They comprise the uninhabited Desert and Savage island groups, Porto Santo Isl., and Madeira, largest of the archipelago. Madeira is noted for its beautiful mountains and valleys; its mild climate, which makes it a favorite health resort; its wine; and its embroidery industry.

Madera (mùdä′rù), city (pop. 10,497), central Calif., NW of Fresno in San Joaquin Valley; laid out 1876. Produces wood, wine, canned foods, cotton. Served by Madera Canal of CENTRAL VALLEY project.

Madero, Francisco Indalecio (fränsē′skō ēndälä′syō mädhä′rō), 1873–1913, Mexican statesman, president of Mexico (1911–13). A champion of democracy and social reform, he was the leader of the great revolution against Díaz (1910), but in his own administration he could not control the various revolutionary forces which had been unleashed. Overthrown by Huerta, Madero was arrested and shot, allegedly in an attempt to escape.

Madhya Bharat (mäd′yù bŭ′rùt), state (46,710 sq. mi.; pop. 7,941,642), W central India; winter cap. Lashkar, summer cap. Indore. Includes former princely states of Indore and Gwalior.

Madhya Pradesh (mäd′yù prä′dĭsh), state (130,323 sq. mi.; pop. 21,327,898), central India; cap. Nagpur. Formerly called Central Provs. and Berar. Rich agr.

SMALL CAPITALS = cross references. Pronunciation key on inside end pages. Abbreviations: p. 2.

area, with dense forests and large deposits of manganese and coal. Cotton-textile mfg.

Madison, James, 1751–1836, 4th President of the United States (1809–17), b. Va. Member of Continental Congress (1780–83, 1787–88). Worked successfully to have FEDERAL CONSTITUTIONAL CONVENTION called in 1787, and was chief drafter of the Constitution. Fought for its adoption by contributing to FEDERALIST PAPERS. As U.S. Congressman from Va. (1789–97) he strongly advocated first ten amendments to Constitution, steadfastly supported Thomas Jefferson. Prepared Virginia resolutions (see KENTUCKY AND VIRGINIA RESOLUTIONS) protesting Alien and Sedition Acts. U.S. Secretary of State (1801–9). Jefferson's choice as his successor. WAR OF 1812, chief event of Madison's administration, proved difficult. New Englanders at Hartford Convention resisted "Mr. Madison's War"; British burned the White House in Sept., 1814. After the war Madison encouraged the new nationalism. In retirement he lived quietly with his wife, **Dolly Madison,** 1768–1849, who had been official hostess for Jefferson and her husband and who was noted for the magnificence of her entertaining as well as for charm, tact, and grace.

Madison. 1 Village (pop. 7,963), SW Ill., on the Mississippi and adjoining Granite City. Railroad yards. Mfg. of steel products. **2** City (pop. 7,506), SE Ind., on Ohio R. and NE of Louisville, Ky. Tobacco market; mfg. of texiles. **3** Residential borough (pop. 10,417), NE N.J., SE of Morristown; settled 1685. Rose-growing center. Sayre House (1745) was Wayne's hq. Seat of Drew Univ. (Methodist; mainly for men; opened 1867); includes Brothers Col. (since 1928). **4** City (pop. 5,153), SE S.Dak., NW of Sioux Falls. Farm trade center and resort near lakes. **5** City (pop. 96,056), state cap., S Wis., on isthmus between lakes Monona and Mendota, in Four Lakes group; founded 1836. Chosen territorial cap. before settlement. State's second largest city and trade, mfg. (machinery, electrical equipment), and cultural center of dairy region. City of many parks. Seat of Univ. of WISCONSIN.

Madison, river rising in Yellowstone Natl. Park, NW Wyo., and flowing 183 mi. N through Mont. to Jefferson and Gallatin rivers, forming the Missouri.

Madison, Mount: see PRESIDENTIAL RANGE.

Madisonville, city (pop. 11,132), W Ky., ENE of Paducah, in farm, timber, and oil area; settled 1807. Tobacco market.

Madoc or **Madog,** fl. 1170?, quasi-historical Welsh prince; discoverer of America in Welsh legend.

Madoera, Indonesia: see MADURA.

Madras (mŭdräs'), state (127,768 sq. mi.; pop. 56,952,-332), S India, including Laccadive Isls. Coromandel and Malabar coasts are its most fertile areas. Textile mfg. is important. Colonies were estab. here by the Portuguese in 16th cent., and by the Dutch, French, and British in 17th cent. By 1801 the British had become supreme in the area. **Madras,** city (pop. 777,481), on Coromandel Coast, is state cap. and main port; founded 1639 by the British. Textile and mfg. center. Seat of Madras Univ. Near by is Mt. St. Thomas, traditional site of martyrdom (A.D. 68) of Thomas the apostle.

Madrazo (mädrä'thō), family of Spanish painters, leaders of the academic school. Eminent members included **José de Madrazo y Agudo,** 1781–1859, and his grandson **Raimundo de Madrazo y Garreta,** 1841–1920.

Madre de Dios (mädrä' dä dyōs'), river, c.700 mi. long, rising in Andes of SE Peru and flowing NE through Bolivia to Beni R. Forests of the Madre de Dios valley formerly exploited for rubber.

Madrid (mŭdrĭd', Span. mädhrēdh'), city (pop. 1,088,-647), cap. of Spain, in New Castile, on the Manzanares. Chief communications center of Spain; rivaled only by Barcelona in commercial and industrial importance. Archiepiscopal see; seat of university (transferred from ALCALÁ DE HENARES 1836). Originally a Moorish fortress, Madrid fell to Castile in 1083 but

became the Spanish cap. only in 1561. It expanded under the Bourbons in the 18th cent., when the royal palace, the world-famous PRADO Mus., and other fine buildings were erected. In May, 1808, a popular uprising against French occupation was bloodily suppressed. In the civil war of 1936–39, Madrid under the command of Gen. José Miaja resisted 29 months of siege by the Insurgents but surrendered in March, 1939. Madrid is essentially a modern city. Its W suburbs, particularly the modern Ciudad Universitaria [university city], were heavily damaged during the siege.

madrigal. The Italian madrigal of the 14th cent. was a poetic form consisting of from one to four stanzas of three iambic pentameters each, followed by two rhymed lines in a contrasting meter. Subject matter was usually pastoral or amatory. Composers of the period made contrapuntal two- and three-voice settings of the madrigal. The number of voices was later increased to four or five. Brought into England in the late 16th cent., the madrigal came to mean an unaccompanied part song. Outstanding English madrigalists were William Byrd, Thomas Morley, and Orlando Gibbons.

madroña (mŭdrōn'yŭ), broad-leaved evergreen tree or shrub (*Arbutus menziesi*) native to W coast of U.S. It has white flowers followed by showy red berries.

Madura or **Madoera** (both: mädōō'rä), island (1,762 sq. mi.; pop. 1,858,183), Indonesia, near Java. Has chalky soil. Chief products are salt and fish.

Maecenas (Caius Cilnius Maecenas) (mĭsē'nŭs, mē–), d. 8 B.C., Roman statesman and patron of letters under Augustus. His famous literary circle included Horace, Vergil, Propertius. His name is the symbol of the wealthy benefactor of the arts.

Maelstrom (māl'strŭm), Nor. *Malstrøm,* narrow sound in Lofoten isls., NW Norway, just S of Moskenes isl. Its powerful tidal currents create a dangerous whirlpool, and its name is used for all fatal whirlpools.

Maerlant, Jacob van (mär'länt), c.1235–c.1300, Flemish poet, earliest important figure of Dutch literature. Wrote lyric poems, chivalric verse romances, and long didactic poems.

Maes or **Maas, Nicolaas** (nē'kōläs mäs'), 1632–93, Dutch genre and portrait painter. Was influenced first by Rembrandt, later by Van Dyck.

Maestricht, Netherlands: see MAASTRICHT.

Maeterlinck, Maurice (mōrēs' mätĕr'lēk'), 1862–1949, Belgian author who wrote in French. He was considered the representative dramatist of the SYMBOLISTS. His works, mystical and metaphysical, include critical essays, the zoological study *The Life of the Bee* (1901), and the famous dramas *Pelléas et Mélisande* (1892), *Monna Vanna* (1902), and *The Blue Bird* (1909). He won the 1911 Nobel Prize in Literature and was created a count by King Albert.

Mafeking (mä'fĭkĭng), town (pop. 5,864), N Cape Prov., South Africa; extraterritorial cap. of Bechuanaland protectorate. In South African War British forces under Lord Baden-Powell were besieged here by Boer forces, Oct. 12, 1899–May 17, 1900.

Mafia (mä'fēä) name of organized bands of Sicilian brigands in 19th and 20th cent. They lacked the hierarchic organization of the CAMORRA; each band operated on its own. As an institution, the Mafia dates from feudal times, when lords hired brigands to guard their estates and in exchange afforded them protection from the royal authority. Political corruption gave the Mafia tremendous influence until its suppression by Mussolini. Emigrants brought it to the U.S. (esp. to La.).

Magallanes, Chile: see PUNTA ARENAS.

magazine: see PERIODICAL.

Magazine, Mount: see OUACHITA MOUNTAINS.

Magdala (mäg'dŭlŭ), place on shore of Sea of Galilee. Mat. 15.39; sometimes given as Magadan; traditional home of Mary Magdalen. Identified with Mejdel, a hamlet on W shore.

Magdalen: see MARY MAGDALEN.

Magdalena (mägdhälä′nä), river, over 1,000 mi. long, rising in SW Colombia and flowing N to Caribbean near Barranquilla. Discovered (1501) by Bastidas, is republic's natural avenue of communication, but navigation is difficult because of rapids and sand bars. Explored by Jiménez de Quesada (1536).

Magdalen College: see OXFORD UNIVERSITY.

Magdalene College: see CAMBRIDGE UNIVERSITY.

Magdalen Islands (măg′dúlŭn), group of nine main islands and numerous islets (102 sq. mi.; pop. 9,999), in Gulf of St. Lawrence, E Que., Canada, N of Prince Edward Isl. Discovered 1534 by Cartier. Fishing and sealing.

Magdeburg (mäk′dùbŏork), city (1939 pop. 336,838; 1946 pop. 236,326), Saxony-Anhalt, E central Germany, on the Elbe. Inland port; mfg. center (machinery, paper, textiles, beet sugar). Became archiepiscopal see 968. The archbishops later ruled a vast territory as princes of the Holy Roman Empire and granted the city a charter (1188) which gave it self-rule and exempted it from all duties save rent payments; this "Magdeburg Law" was copied by hundreds of Central European towns. Magdeburg prospered as a member of the Hanseatic League, accepted the Reformation 1524, and became a stronghold of Lutheranism. In 1561–63 the archbishop, a prince of the house of Brandenburg, also went over to Protestantism; members of his family continued (with dubious legality) to rule the archbishopric as administrators. In the Thirty Years War the imperials under Tilly stormed Magdeburg after a long siege (1630–31). In the ensuing sack, which Tilly vainly sought to halt, the city burned down and c.20,000 people (half the pop.) perished. The Peace of Westphalia (1648) provided for the transfer of the former archbishopric to Brandenburg. Magdeburg became an important Prussian fortress and (1816) the cap. of the former Saxony prov. of Prussia. More than half the city was destroyed in World War II. Birthplace of GUERICKE, inventor of the Magdeburg hemispheres, and of Baron von Steuben.

Magellan, Ferdinand (mùjĕ′lŭn), c.1480–1521, Portuguese navigator. Received Spanish support in proposal to reach the Moluccas by W route. Sailed (1519) with five vessels; crossed from Atlantic to Pacific by strait named for him. Killed by Philippine natives. Only one ship completed first voyage around world (1522). Voyage proved roundness of earth, revolutionized ideas of relative proportion of land and water, revealed Americas as new world, distinct from Asia.

Magellan, Strait of, c.350 mi. long and 2½–15 mi. wide, separating South America from Tierra del Fuego. But for a few miles at W end which pass through Argentina, straits are in Chile. Discovered by Magellan (1520). Were important to sailing ships before Panama Canal was built. Open city on strait is Punta Arenas.

Magendie, François (fräswä′ mäzhädē′), 1783–1855, French physician, pioneer in experimental physiology.

Magenta (mäjän′tä), town (pop. 10,470), Lombardy, N Italy, near Milan. Here in 1859 the French and Sardinians defeated the Austrians. MacMahon, who commanded the French, was created duke of Magenta.

magenta: see FUCHSINE.

Maggiore, Lago (lä′gō mäd-jō′rä), or **Verbano** (vĕr-bä′nō), lake, area 82 sq. mi., c.40 mi. long, in the Alpine foothills of N Italy and S Switzerland. It is formed by the Ticino R. Stresa (Italy) and Locarno (Switzerland) are among its many resorts. The Borromean Isls., near Stresa, include Isola Bella, with the Borromeo Palace (now museum) and gardens.

Magi (mā′jī), priestly caste of anc. Persia, reputedly possessed of "magic" powers. After Zoroaster's death Magian priests headed Zoroastrianism; the greatest was Saena. See WISE MEN OF THE EAST.

magic [from Persian priests, *Magi*], practice of manipulating course of nature by supernatural means. Its aim (use and changing of nature) approximates that of science, an outgrowth of magic. It is allied to religion, but whereas religion reverences and worships supernatural beings, magic seeks to control supernatural forces to a desired end. This is done by means of verbal or written pronouncements, wearing of an amulet, or by imitative acts (e.g., agr. fertility rites based on analogy between plant and human generation). Almost all ancient peoples practiced magic. Christian Church has always combated black (i.e., malevolent) magic. Those who practiced it were considered sorcerers and witches. Many present-day superstitions are remnants of pagan magic, and belief in its powers is still extant. See YOGA.

magic lantern: see STEREOPTICON.

magic square, square divided into parts with letters or numbers inscribed therein which, whether read horizontally, vertically, or diagonally, spells same word or gives same sum. Such squares in ancient times were thought to have magic powers.

Maginot Line (mă′zhīnō), system of fortifications along E frontier of France, extending from the Swiss to the Belgian border. Started by André Maginot (1877–1932), French war minister in 1929–30. It proved useless as the Germans flanked it in 1940.

Magliabechi, Antonio (mälyäbä′kē), 1633–1714, Italian librarian and scholar. Appointed (1673) court librarian by Cosimo III de' Medici, grand duke of Tuscany, to whom he bequeathed his library, which now forms part of National Library of Florence.

Magna Carta or **Magna Charta,** the most important instrument of English constitutional history, issued by King John at Runnymede, under compulsion by the barons, in 1215. Purpose of original charter was to insure feudal rights and guarantee that king could not encroach on baronial privileges. Provisions also guaranteed freedom of church and customs of towns; protections of rights of subjects and communities (which king could be compelled to observe); and words later to be interpreted as guarantees of trial by jury and habeas corpus. John repudiated charter as a grant made under coercion, was released from its observance by pope, and civil war broke out. Later reissues of charter had significant omissions; remaining clauses came to be known as Great Charter or Charter of Liberties. Later it became symbol of supremacy of constitution over king.

Magna Graecia (măg′nú grē′shù) [Latin,= great Greece], collective term for Greek colonies in S Italy, founded mostly in 8th cent. B.C., on both coasts S of Bay of Naples and Gulf of Taranto. These city-states did not thrive as did those of closely related Greek Sicily and declined badly after 500 B.C. Cumae, Tarentum, Heraclea, and Crotona were among them. They early brought Romans in contact with Greek culture.

magnalium (măgnä′lēùm), alloy of aluminum and magnesium (c.5%). Lighter and more workable than aluminum, it is used in making metal mirrors and scientific instruments.

Magnesia, two anc. towns of Lydia, now W Turkey, so called because settled by Magnetes of E Thessaly. Magnesia ad Maeandrum (SE of Smyrna) was later colonized by Ionians and given by the Persian king to Themistocles, who died there. Magnesia ad Sipylum was on the Hermus R. at the foot of Mt. Sipylus, NE of Smyrna; scene of Roman victory over Antiochus III (190 B.C.).

magnesia (măgnē′zhù), magnesium oxide. Because of high melting point and low heat conductivity it is used to line electric furnaces, make firebricks, cover hot pipes, etc. Suspension in water is milk of magnesia, an antacid and laxative.

magnesite (măg′nùsīt), a magnesium carbonate mineral, white, yellow, or gray. It is mixed with magnesium chloride to make oxychloride cement; also used in making firebrick, Epsom salts, face powder.

magnesium (măgnē′sēùm), active metallic element (symbol = Mg; see also ELEMENT, table), silver white, ductile, malleable. Sometimes included as metal of alkaline earths. Forms many compounds. It burns brilliantly in air and is used in making signal lights and fireworks. It also is used in medicine, in photography, and in alloys with aluminum. It is present in some glass, in soil (as salts), in chlorophyll. A strip of the metal is used as a fuse in thermite process.

magnet: see MAGNETISM.

magnetic poles. The earth, like any magnet (see MAGNETISM), has two magnetic poles—surface points where magnetic force is vertically downwards (dipping needle stands at 90°) and where horizontal compass is useless. North magnetic pole was placed (1948) at lat. 73° N, long. 100° W; south magnetic pole is at present near lat. 70° S, long. 148° E.

magnetism, property of attracting iron, probably first observed in a form of magnetite called lodestone which is called a natural magnet. Artificial magnets are substances that acquire magnetism after special treatment, e.g., by rubbing or stroking a bar of iron or steel with a strong magnet or by laying the piece of metal parallel to a magnet and tapping it gently (this is magnetic induction). An ELECTROMAGNET can be made by winding around a soft iron bar or core a coil of insulated wire carrying an electric current. When a suspended steel bar magnet can move freely it comes to rest in a general N–S direction, because of the magnetic effect of the earth; end of the bar pointing in northerly direction is N-seeking pole and opposite end is S-seeking pole. Like poles (i.e., N and N or S and S) repel each other while unlike attract. Magnetism of a magnet is concentrated in region of its poles, a condition termed polarity. Area in which magnetism is active is called magnetic field of force. Theoretically, the flow of magnetic force is through a continuous path (closed circuit), the direction of flow being from N-seeking pole outward through lines of force (lines through which magnetism appears to act) to S-seeking pole and from there through body of magnet to N-seeking pole. Strength of magnetic field is measured according to number of lines of force crossing unit area (e.g., 1 sq. cm.). One theory of nature of magnetism holds that it is a property of molecules and depends on their arrangement in body of magnet; another states that magnetism is caused by movement of electrons in the atom. Contributors to knowledge of magnetism include William Gilbert, C. A. de Coulomb, C. F. Gauss, A. M. Ampère, Oersted, Michael Faraday, Joseph Henry, Harold Pender, J. C. Maxwell, and J. J. Thomson. The study of **terrestrial magnetism** is based on assumption that earth is a gigantic magnet. Compass needles do not point directly to N and S geographical poles of earth because magnetic and geographical poles do not coincide. Deviation of compass needle from geographic N–S direction is called declination. Magnetic poles are not fixed so declination at given point varies. Isogonic lines drawn on map indicate points on earth's surface where declination is same. If magnetic needle is mounted so it is free to move it does not remain horizontal at all points on earth's surface; this deviation is called dip or inclination. At magnetic poles needle is vertical, at magnetic equator no dip is observable. Among those who contributed to study of terrestrial magnetism are William Gilbert, Alexander von Humboldt, Gauss, Johann von Lamont, and L. A. Bauer.

magnetite (măg′nŭtīt), lustrous black magnetic iron oxide, an important iron ore, occurring in crystals, masses, and loose sand. A variety known as lodestone shows magnetic polarity.

magnifying glass: see MICROSCOPE.

Magnitogorsk (mŭgnyē″tŭgôrsk′), city (pop. c.200,000), RSFSR, on Ural R. Planned 1929, it grew rapidly into the chief metallurgical center of the USSR. Industries are based on high-grade magnetite mined in Magnitaya Mt. (on which city is built), iron ore and alloys from Urals, coal from Karaganda and Kuznetsk Basin.

magnitude, in astronomy, term denoting brightness of celestial object. Ptolemy's scale of six gradations, in which first magnitude was assigned to brightest stars, was later systematized and extended by estab. of ratio of brightness (2.51) between any two successive magnitudes. A star c.2.51 times as bright as standard first magnitude star is of zero magnitude; still greater brightness is expressed by negative numbers.

Magnolia, city (pop. 6,918), SW Ark., near La. line. Processes oil, cotton, and lumber.

magnolia, handsome deciduous or evergreen tree or shrub (*Magnolia*) native to North and Central America and Asia. The southern magnolia or bull bay (*Magnolia grandiflora*) has huge white flowers. The lily or saucer magnolia (*M. liliflora* or *M. purpurea*), with rose flowers in early spring, is hardy in U.S. Other magnolias include the sweet bay (*M. virginiana*) and the cucumber tree (*M. acuminata*).

Magnus, Norwegian kings. **Magnus I** (the Good), 1024–47, son of St. Olaf, succeeded the deposed Sweyn as king of Norway in 1035; in 1042 he succeeded HARTHACANUTE in Denmark. A rebellion in Denmark kept him from asserting his claim to England. After 1046 he was forced to share his throne with his uncle and successor, Harold III. **Magnus VI** (the Law Mender), 1238–80, king of Norway (1263–80), made peace with Scotland by ceding the Hebrides and Isle of Man (1266). He revised the law code (1274), introducing the concept that crime is an offense against the state rather than against the individual and making the throne the source of justice. He also gave increased freedom to the cities; fixed the royal succession; created a new royal council and nobility; made a concordat with the Church. **Magnus VII,** 1316–73, king of Norway (1319–43, by succession) and of Sweden (1319–64, by election). Neglecting Norway in favor of Sweden, he was forced in 1343 to abdicate as king of Norway in favor of his son Haakon VI but exercised a nominal regency until 1355. In Sweden he was forced from the throne (1356–59) by his rebellious son Eric (d. 1359) and in 1361 had to accept Haakon as joint king. Magnus and Haakon in 1363 concluded an alliance with Waldemar IV of Denmark against the Hanseatic League; Haakon married Waldemar's daughter MARGARET. This Danish alliance was unpopular with the Swedes, who in 1364 deposed both Magnus and Haakon and chose Albert of Mecklenburg as king. Magnus was imprisoned 1365–71 and spent his last years in Norway.

Magog, in Bible: see GOG.

Magog (mā′gŏg), town (pop. 12,423), S Que., Canada, SW of Sherbrooke and on L. Memphremagog; founded by Loyalists after 1776. Resort and trade center with textile mills, woodworking, and dairying.

magpie, bird of crow family, c.20 in. long. American or black-billed magpie has black, iridescent plumage except for white abdomen and wing patches. It makes huge, domed nests in trees.

Magruder, John Bankhead, 1810–71, Confederate general. Successfully held off McClellan at Yorktown (1862). Recaptured Galveston, Texas (1863).

Magyars (mŏd′yärz, măg′yärz), the people of Hungary. They belong to the Finno-Ugric language family. Originally nomadic, they migrated c.460 from the Urals to N Caucasia, where they came in close contact with Turkic peoples; from them they learned agr. and borrowed their political and military organization. In the 9th cent. the PETCHENEGS forced them W; led by ARPAD, the Magyars settled in Hungary c.895. Ferocious mounted warriors, they conquered Moravia and penetrated deep into Germany but were checked by Emperor Otto I at the Lechfeld (955). With St. STEPHEN, who introduced Christianity, the history of Hungary begins.

Mahabharata (mŭhä′bä′rŭtŭ), great Sanskrit epic of India, composed 200 B.C.–A.D. 200 by bardic poets and later revised by philosophical writers. Its 110,000 couplets of 16-syllable lines tell of a fabulous dynastic struggle in kingdom of Hastinapur. Contains BHA-GAVAD-GITA.

Mahan, Alfred Thayer (mùhăn'), 1840–1914, American writer on naval affairs. His books, such as *The Influence of Sea Power upon History* (1890), had wide influence. Related naval affairs to international politics and economics.

Mahanoy City (mähùnoi'), borough (pop. 10,934), E Pa., NE of Pottsville; settled 1859. Anthracite mining; mfg. of textiles and beer.

Mahdi [Arabic = divine guide] (mä'dē), in Islam, title of the IMAM, the man who will arise at end of the world as leader of faithful. Despite canonical saying and Sunnite belief that "There is no Mahdi but Jesus," Shiism periodically gives rise to men claiming to be the Mahdi. Perhaps most prominent of these was **Mohammed Ahmed**, 1848–85, in Anglo-Egyptian Sudan. He led a rebellion in 1881 against Anglo-Egyptian rule, but died soon after capturing Khartoum. His followers, the **Mahdists,** were decisively defeated in 1898 by Anglo-Egyptian army under Lord Kitchener.

Mahican Indians (mùhē'kùn), confederacy of North American tribes of Algonquian linguistic stock, occupying the banks of the upper Hudson in 17th cent. They warred with the Mohawk, who with the aid of Dutch arms subdued them. Most of them were driven to join the Delaware Indians or seek protection of the Iroquois Confederacy. One remnant became the Christianized Stockbridge Indians. The name Mohican is applied to the whole group and to the E branch of the group, the MOHEGAN INDIANS.

Mahler, Gustav (mä'lùr), 1860–1911, Austrian composer, conductor of the Imperial Opera, Vienna, 1897–1907. From 1908 to 1911 he conducted both the Metropolitan Opera, New York, and the Philharmonic Symphony. His works include nine symphonies (some with chorus) and the song cycle *Das Lied von der Erde* (for solo voices, chorus, and orchestra).

Mahmud II (mämoōd', mä'moōd), 1784–1839, Ottoman sultan (1808–39). A vigorous reformer, he destroyed the JANIZARIES (1826); began "westernization" of Turkey. He could not prevent the loss of GREECE and fought unsuccessfully against MOHAMMED ALI of Egypt. His son Abdu-l-Mejid succeeded him.

mahogany, valuable hardwood obtained chiefly from the West Indian or Spanish mahogany tree (*Swietenia mahogani*) native to the West Indies and S Fla. The wood, golden brown to dark, rich, red brown, is hard and close-grained, and valued for furniture. African mahogany is obtained from *Khaya ivorensis*.

Mahone, William (mùhōn'), 1826–95, Confederate general and Va. politician. Fought chiefly in campaigns in N Va. U.S. Senator (1881–87). He controlled Va. politics for several years.

Mahoning (mùhō'nĭng), river rising in NE Ohio near Alliance and flowing c.90 mi. N then SE past Youngstown into Pa. to Shenango R., forming Beaver R. Berlin Dam (1943) is for flood control and power.

Mahrattas or **Marathas** (both: mùrä'tùz), Marathi-speaking people of W central India. Led by Sivaji, they conquered much territory in 17th cent. and by mid-18th cent. had displaced Mogul empire as leading power in India. Subdued 1818 by the British. Mahratta cap. was Poona.

Mährisch Ostrau, Czechoslovakia: see MORAVSKA OSTRAVA.

Mai, Angelo (än'jälō mī'), 1782–1854, Italian philologist, cardinal (from 1838) of the Roman Church. He discovered manuscript of Cicero's *De republica.*

Maia (mä'ù, mī'ù). **1** In Greek religion, one of Pleiades; daughter of Atlas and nymph Pleione and mother of Hermes by Zeus. **2** In Roman religion, goddess of spring and fertility (month of May named for her).

Maiden Castle, anc. fortress, Dorsetshire, England. Finest earthwork in British Isles, c.115 acres in area. Excavations show occupation c.2000 B.C.

maidenhair fern, delicate fern (*Adiantum*) mostly native to tropics and grown as a pot plant. *Adiantum*

pedatum is native to the North American woodlands.

Maidstone (mäd'stùn), municipal borough (pop. 54,-026), co. seat of Kent, England. Has hospital (founded 1260 for pilgrims to Canterbury) and archbishops' palace. Birthplace of William Hazlitt.

Maidu Indians (mī'doō), North American tribes of Penutian linguistic stock, located in early 19th cent. on E tributaries of Sacramento river. Their culture was typical of California area with brush shelters, acorn gathering, and a spirit cult.

Maikop (mīkôp'), city (pop. 67,302), Krasnodar Territory, RSFSR, at N foot of Greater Caucasus. Maikop oil fields are SW, connected by pipe line with refineries at Krasnodar and Black Sea port of Tuapse. Occupied 1942–43 by Germans in World War II.

mail: see POSTAL SERVICE.

Maillol, Aristide (ärēstēd' mäyôl'), 1861–1944, French sculptor. A neoclassicist, he is best known for his simple, massive figures of women.

Maimonides (mīmō'nĭdēz), called Rambam, 1135–1204, rabbi, physician, philosopher, b. Córdoba, Spain; d. Cairo. He attempted to codify the Jewish oral law in the Mishna Torah [copy of the Law]. Foremost among his many other writings is the *Moreh Nebukim* (Eng. tr., *Guide for the Perplexed,* 1919), in which he elucidated baffling religious and metaphysical problems; it has profoundly influenced Jewish and Christian religious thinkers.

Main (män, Ger. mīn), river, 307 mi. long, central and W Germany, formed in N Bavaria by two affluents (Red and White Main) and flowing W past Bamberg, Schweinfurt, Würzburg, and Frankfurt into the Rhine opposite Mainz. Navigable from Bamberg; connected by canal with the Danube.

Maine, Sir Henry James Sumner, 1822–88, English jurist and historian. Known for work on history of laws as history of civilization. Books include *Ancient Law* (1861; new ed., 1931).

Maine (män, Fr. měn), region and former province, NW France, in Sarthe and Mayenne depts.; historic cap. Le Mans. Watered by Mayenne, Loir, and Sarthe rivers, it is largely agr. Stock raising (horses) in Perche hills. A county from the 10th cent., later a duchy, it shared the history of ANJOU after 1110, was inc. into royal domain 1481. Several later royal princes were titular dukes of Maine.

Maine, state (33,215 sq. mi.; pop. 913,774), NE U.S.; admitted 1820 as 23d state (free); cap. AUGUSTA. PORTLAND, LEWISTON, BANGOR other important cities. Bounded S by the Atlantic; Saint John and Saint Croix rivers form part of boundary with New Brunswick. Many rivers (e.g., PENOBSCOT, KENNEBEC, ANDROSCOGGIN, Saco), lakes (MOOSEHEAD LAKE is largest), mountains (KATAHDIN is highest), islands (MOUNT DESERT ISLAND is largest). Mfg. of wood products, textiles, shoes; farming (potatoes quite important, grains, fruits, dairy, and poultry); lumbering; fishing; mining; tourism. Champlain estab. short-lived colony at mouth of the St. Croix (1604–5). Further French development prevented by Sir Samuel Argall (1613). Settlements attempted by Sir Ferdinando GORGES. Later came under control of Mass. (1659). Strength of troublesome Indians broken in Queen Anne's War. Set up as admiralty district of Mass. in 1775. Turned from commerce to industry through disturbances of Embargo Act of 1807 and War of 1812. Admitted as state through MISSOURI COMPROMISE. NORTHEAST BOUNDARY DISPUTE ended by WEBSTER-ASHBURTON TREATY of 1842. Mainly Republican state since Civil War. First state to have prohibition law (1851–1934). Hydro-electric power developed in 20th cent. but restricted to state. The trend toward industrialization and urbanization has been strong in recent times.

Maine, short river, W France, formed just N of Angers by the confluence of the Sarthe and Mayenne rivers and flowing S into the Loire.

Maine, U.S. battleship, center of a serious international incident in 1898. In Havana harbor on Feb. 15 a mysterious explosion occurred, and the *Maine* sank with a loss of 260 men. Separate U.S. and Spanish inquiries reached differing conclusions as to cause of explosion; neither inquiry fixed responsibility. "Remember the Maine" became an American catchword in SPANISH-AMERICAN WAR.

Maine, University of: see ORONO.

Maine-et-Loire (měn"-ā-lwär'), department (2,787 sq. mi.; pop. 496,068), NW France, in Anjou; cap. Angers.

Mainland. 1 Island, Orkney Isls., Scotland: see POMONA. 2 Island (pop. 15,172), 55 mi. long and 20 mi. wide, off N Scotland, largest of Shetland Isls. Has Lerwick, county town of the Shetlands.

Maintenon, Françoise d'Aubigné, marquise de (frāswäz' dōbēnyā' märkēz' dù mētŭnõ'), 1635–1719, second wife of Louis XIV of France; granddaughter of T. A. d'AUBIGNÉ. Born in France and baptized a Catholic, she spent her childhood in Martinique and was brought up a Protestant. After her father's death she and her mother returned to France, where they lived in great poverty. She was converted to Catholicism and became very devout. At 16 she married the poet SCARRON (d. 1660), through whom she entered Parisian society, and after his death she was appointed governess for the children of Mme de MONTESPAN, whom she gradually replaced in the king's affections. Louis XIV created her a marquise, but in all likelihood she resisted his advances until a year after the queen's death, when the king married her in a secret morganatic ceremony (1684). Her influence was largely responsible for the austere and somewhat hypocritical tone of the court, but she probably had little weight in political matters. In her later years she gave much attention to the school of Saint-Cyr (see SAINT-CYR-L'ÉCOLE).

Mainz (mīnts), city (pop. 87,046), cap. of Rhineland-Palatinate, W Germany, on the Rhine opposite mouth of the Main. Its French name, Mayence, is sometimes also used in English. River port; trade center (Rhine wines); mfg. (chemicals, machinery). University (1477–1816; reconstituted 1946 as Johannes Gutenberg Univ.). The Roman Maguntiacum, Mainz became (8th cent.) an archiepiscopal see under St. BONIFACE. Later archbishops acquired territories on both sides of the Rhine and Main. They ranked first among the ELECTORS, crowned the German kings, and were archchancellors of the Holy Roman Empire. Under their rule Mainz flourished commercially and culturally. GUTENBERG made it the first printing center. Mainz was occupied by the French in 1792 and ceded to them in 1797; the archbishopric was secularized and reduced to a diocese in 1803. The Congress of Vienna in 1815 gave Mainz along with Rhenish HESSE to the grand duchy of Hesse-Darmstadt. More than half destroyed in World War II, Mainz was assigned in 1945 to the French zone of occupation, but the suburbs E of the Rhine passed to Hesse (U.S. zone). The Romanesque cathedral (consecrated 1009), the Renaissance electoral palace, and other historic buildings were heavily damaged.

Maipú (mīpōō'), battlefield, central Chile, a few mi. S of Santiago. Victory of San Martín here (1818) assured Chilean independence from Spain and made possible the liberating expedition to Peru.

Maisonneuve, Paul de Chomedey, sieur de (shômdā' syûr' dù māzŏnûv'), c.1612–1676, founder (1642) and first governor of Montreal, Canada, b. France.

Maistre, Joseph de (zhôzěf' dù mě'strù), 1754?–1821, French writer, b. Savoy. Was Sardinian ambassador to St. Petersburg 1803–17. Detesting 18th-cent. rationalism, he developed with great logical skill his idea that the world should be one, under the absolute spiritual rule of the pope (*Du pape*, 1819; *Les Soirées de Saint-Pétersbourg*, 1821). His brother **Xavier de Maistre** (zävyā'), 1763–1852, served in the Russian army. He wrote *Voyage autour de ma chambre* (1794), a witty peregrination from object to object

in his room, allowing each to call up recollections. *Le Lépreux de la cité d'Aoste* [the leper of Aosta] (1811) is a remarkable portrayal of Christian resignation.

Maitland, Frederic William, 1850–1906, English legal historian. Major work is *The History of English Law before the Time of Edward I* (2 vols., 1895), written with Sir Frederick Pollock.

Maitland, John: see LAUDERDALE, JOHN MAITLAND, DUKE OF.

Maitland, William (Maitland of Lethington), 1528?–1573, Scottish statesman. Secretary of State to Mary Queen of Scots, he sought to effect union of Scotland and England. Abandoned Mary after her marriage to Bothwell, but later became leader of her party.

maize: see CORN.

Majano, Benedetto da: see BENEDETTO DA MAJANO.

Majdanek (mīdä'něk), extermination camp (see CONCENTRATION CAMP), Poland, near Lublin, estab. and operated by the Germans in World War II. About 1,500,000 persons (mostly Jews) were killed in its gas chambers.

majolica: see POTTERY.

Majorca (mùjôr'kù), Span. *Mallorca,* Mediterranean island (1,405 sq. mi.; pop. 327,102), Spain, largest of BALEARIC ISLANDS; cap. Palma. Its scenery and mild climate make it a popular resort. Agr., hog and sheep raising, fruit growing; mining (lead, marble, copper). Majorca became a kingdom in 1276 under a branch of the house of Aragon. It comprised the Balearic Isls., Roussillon, and several fiefs in S France; its cap. was Perpignan. In 1343 Peter IV of Aragon reunited the kingdom with Aragon. In the Spanish civil war of 1936–39 Majorca early passed to the Insurgent side.

Majorian (mùjô'rēun), d. 461, West Roman emperor (457–61). RICIMER raised him to power but, finding him too vigorous and independent, slew him in battle. Majorian's expedition against Gaiseric (460) was unsuccessful. He enacted laws to protect the people from excessive taxes.

Majuba Hill (mùjōō'bù), NW Natal, South Africa, in Drakensberg range. Here in 1881 a British force was routed by Boer troops under Joubert.

Makassar, Indonesia: see MACASSAR.

Makemie, Francis (mùkě'mē), 1658–1708, American clergyman, called founder of Presbyterianism in America, b. Ireland. As missionary he organized churches (c.1682) in Md. and first presbytery (1706) in Pa.

Makeyevka (mùkyä'ùfkù), city (pop. 240,145), SE Ukraine, in Donets Basin. Major metallurgical and coal-mining center.

Makhachkala (mùkhäch"kŭlä'), city (pop. 86,847), cap. of Dagestan ASSR, SE European RSFSR; a Caspian seaport. Its oil refineries are linked by pipe line with the Grozny fields. Formerly called Petrovsk.

Makin: see GILBERT ISLANDS.

Malabar Coast (mă'lùbär), SW coast of India from Goa to S tip of peninsula at Cape Comorin. Bounded inland by Western Ghats. Fertile area.

Malacca (mùlǎ'kù), city (pop. 54,507), cap. of Settlement of Malacca (633 sq. mi.; pop. 258,508), Malaya, on SW coast of Malay Peninsula. On Strait of Malacca, which links Indian Ocean with South China Sea. Founded c.1400, it became a rich trade center of SE Asia. In 15th cent., kings of Malacca extended their power over much of Malay Peninsula and Sumatra and introduced Islam into Malay world. Seized 1511 by Portuguese under Afonso de Albuquerque. Held by Dutch from 1641 to 1824, when it was ceded to Britain. Declined with rise of Singapore.

Malachi (mă'lùkī), **Malachias** (–kī'ùs), or **Malachy** (mă'lùkē), last book of Old Testament in AV. Author is otherwise unknown. Book is chiefly concerned with the neglect of the Law and foreign marriages among the people, ending with prediction of a messiah.

malachite (mă'lùkīt), green mineral, carbonate of copper, occurring as crystals or in masses. An important copper ore, it is used also as a gem, for various ornaments, and is ground to make pigment. Found in U.S., Cuba, Chile, Russia, Rhodesia, Australia.

Malachy, Saint (mă′lŭkē), 1095–1148, Irish churchman, successively abbot of Bangor, bishop of Connor, archbishop of Armagh, and bishop of Down. Reformed the Irish church, making it conform to the plan of the Church on the Continent. Friend of Bernard of Clairvaux. Feast: Nov. 23.

Maladetta Mountains (mälădĕ′tä), Span. *Montes Malditos*, massif of central Pyrenees, Spain, near French border. Pyrenees reach highest point here in Pico de ANETO.

Málaga (mä′lägä), city (pop. 208,344), cap. of Málaga prov., S Spain, in Andalusia; a Mediterranean port and winter resort. Exports sweet Malaga wine, fruit, fish, olive oil. Was founded by Phoenicians. Taken by the Moors in 711, it flourished later as chief port of the Moorish kingdom of Granada until its fall (1487) to Ferdinand and Isabella. Has cathedral (begun 16th cent.), ruins of Moorish alcazar, and an imposing cathedral, the Gibralfaro.

Malakhov (mŭlä′khŭf), hill just E of Sevastopol, RSFSR, S Crimea. Stronghold during Crimean War; stormed by French (1855) after long siege.

Malan, Daniel F(rançois) (mälän′), 1874–, prime minister of Union of South Africa (1948–), leader of Nationalist party. A determined advocate of *apartheid* (racial segregation) and of white supremacy. Returned to power by 1953 elections.

Malaparte, Curzio (mäläpär′tä), pseud. of Curzio Suckert, 1898–, Italian writer. He both defended and criticized Fascism. His works include *Kaputt* (Eng. tr., 1946) and *The Skin* (Eng. tr., 1952).

Malaren (mĕ′lärŭn) or **Malar**, Swed. *Mälaren*, lake, area 440 sq. mi., E Sweden. Extends c.70 mi. W from Stockholm, which is on strait connecting it with Baltic Sea. On its shores and islands are resorts and castles, e.g., Skokloster and Gripsholm.

malaria, infectious febrile disease caused by certain protozoa (genus *Plasmodium*), transmitted by anopheles mosquito. Three main types are benign and malignant tertian, in which chills occur every 48 hr.; and quartan, with chills every 72 hr. Shaking chills coincide with release of microorganisms from red blood cells. Drugs specific against malaria include quinine and atabrine. See *ill.*, p. 633.

Malartic (mälärtĕk′), town (pop. 5,983), W Que., Canada, W of Val d'Or, in Rouyn mining area.

Malaspina (mălŭspē′nŭ), glacier, 1,500 sq. mi., SE Alaska, on Gulf of Alaska and S of Mt. St. Elias.

Malaspina, volcano: see CANLAON, MOUNT.

Malatesta (mälätĕs′tä), Italian family which ruled RIMINI 13th–15th cent. Most famous were Giovanni Malatesta, husband of FRANCESCA DA RIMINI, and Sigismondo Pandolfo Malatesta (1417–68), a typical Renaissance ruler, who built the Malatesta temple in Rimini.

Malatya (mälätē′ä), anc. *Melitene*, city (pop. 49,077), E central Turkey, in Armenia, at E foot of Taurus mts. Cotton milling; agr. trade center. Was an important city of ancient Cappadocia.

Malay: see MALAYAN.

Malaya (mŭlā′ŭ), federation (50,600 sq. mi.; pop. 5,226,549), in S part of Malay Peninsula; cap. Kuala Lumpur. Comprises two British settlements (PENANG and MALACCA) and nine British-protected states. European influence in Malaya dates from 1511, when Malacca fell to the Portuguese. The Dutch followed in 1641 and controlled Malacca area until Napoleonic Wars, after which the British became dominant in the area. In 1895 Perak, Selangor, Negri Sembilan, and Pahang were formed into Federated Malay States. In 1909 Siam lost Kedah, Kelantan, Perlis, and Trengganu to the British, who combined Johore with these areas to form Unfederated Malay States. Malaya was occupied by the Japanese throughout most of World War II. In 1946 the British estab. Malayan Union,

comprising all Malaya except Singapore, and dissolved STRAITS SETTLEMENTS. In 1948 union was reorganized as Federation of Malaya, under British high commissioner. Political unrest led to war (begun 1948) between Malayan guerrillas and British troops.

Malayalam (mä″lŭyä′lŭm), language of the Dravidian family. See LANGUAGE (table).

Malayan (mŭlā′ŭn) or **Malay** (mā′lā), one of a population of some 100,000,000 inhabitants of SE Asia and adjacent islands. Term *Indonesian* is used both synonymously with Malayan and for people of interior districts. Physical appearance is generally Mongoloid; the many languages or dialects form a group of the Malayo-Polynesian languages.

Malay Archipelago or **Malaysia**, great island group, SE of Asia, in Indian and Pacific oceans, comprising Indonesia and the Philippines.

Malay language, one of the chief languages of the Malayo-Polynesian family. See LANGUAGE (table).

Malay Peninsula (mŭlā′), southern extremity of continent of Asia, between Indian Ocean and Strait of Malacca on W and South China Sea on E. Stretches south for c.400 mi. from Isthmus of Kra (its narrowest point) to Singapore. N part forms part of Thailand; S part is occupied by Federation of Malaya. Mountain range (rising to c.7,000 ft.) forms backbone of peninsula. Largely jungle. Area is one of world's leading producers of tin and rubber.

Malaysia: see MALAY ARCHIPELAGO.

Malazgirt, Turkey: see MANZIKERT.

Malbaie, La: see MURRAY BAY.

Malbork, former East Prussia: see MARIENBURG.

Malcolm III (Malcolm Canmore), d.1093, king of Scotland (1054–93), son of Duncan I and successor of MACBETH. His frequent wars with England insured independence of his kingdom and made possible church reforms of his wife, St. MARGARET OF SCOTLAND.

Malden, residential and industrial city (pop. 59,804), E Mass., N suburb of Boston; settled 1640. Metal products, rubber footwear, and chemicals.

Malditos, Montes: see MALADETTA MOUNTAINS.

Maldive Islands (mǎl′dīv), republic (c.115 sq. mi.; pop. 82,068), comprising a group of atolls in Indian Ocean, SW of Ceylon; under British protection. Inhabitants are mainly Moslem. Formerly a sultanate, the islands became a republic on Jan. 1, 1953.

Maldon (môl′–), municipal borough (pop. 9,721), Essex, England. Leader of East Saxons, Byrhtnoth, killed here (991) in battle celebrated in one of last Anglo-Saxon heroic poems.

Mâle, Émile (ämĕl′ mäl′), 1862–, French art historian, authority on medieval sculpture.

Malebranche, Nicolas (mälbräsh′), 1638–1715, French Cartesian philosopher. Laid greater stress on dualism of mind and matter in doctrine of occasionalism, maintaining that interaction between the two is impossible.

Malenkov, Georgi Maksimilianovich (gēôr′gē mäksē-mīlyä′nŭvich mälyĕnkôf′), 1901–, Russian premier (1953–). A favorite of Stalin, he rose to secretary of the central committee of the Communist party; directed war production in World War II; became deputy premier 1946; became premier after Stalin's death in 1953.

Malesherbes, Chrétien Guillaume de Lamoignon de (krätyĕ′ gēyôm′ dü lämwänyō′ dü mälzĕrb′), 1721–94, French magistrate and statesman, twice minister under Louis XVI (1774–76, 1787–88). Undertook Louis XVI's defense in king's trial (1792). Was guillotined as a royalist.

Malherbe, François de (fräswä′ dü mälĕrb′), c.1558–1628, French poet and critic. His poetry was cold and official, but his insistence on objectivity, clarity, and perfection of form influenced the classical ideal in French literature.

Malheur (mŭlŏor′), river, E Oregon, rising in Blue Mts. and flowing c.165 mi. NE to Snake R. at Ontario. Used in Vale irrigation project.

Malibran, Maria (mälēbrä′), 1808–36, operatic contralto, b. Paris; pupil of her father, Manuel GARCÍA. One of the most popular singers of her day.

Malibu Beach (măl'ĭbōō), beach resort, S Calif., W of Los Angeles. Has many film stars' homes.

malice, in law, intent to violate the law of crimes or torts to injure another. It need not involve malignancy but may be simply inferred from reckless or wanton acts. Malice aforethought (i.e., deliberate intent) is a technical element of murder.

Malines (mŭlēn', mŭlēnz', Fr. mälēn'), Flemish *Mechelen,* city (pop. 60,740), Antwerp prov., N Belgium, on Dyle R. In English it is also known as Mechlin. Famous for exquisite lace formerly made here; now has textile mills. Archiepiscopal see since 1561, it is seat of primate of Belgium. Cathedral of St. Rombaut (13th cent.) has famous carillon and contains Van Dyck's *Crucifixion.* Other landmarks are archiepiscopal palace and city hall (14th cent.). Birthplace of Frans Hals.

Malinowski, Bronislaw (brŏnē'slôf mälĭnôf'skē), 1884–1942, Polish-English anthropologist. One of founders of functionalist school in social anthropology. He made intensive studies of Trobriand primitives.

Malipiero, Gian Francesco (jän' fränchä'skō mälēpyä'-rō), 1882–, Italian composer, editor of works of Monteverdi, and researcher in early Italian music. His own works include songs, choral and orchestral works, and operas (e.g., *Giulio Cesare,* 1936).

Mallarmé, Stéphane (stäfän' mälärmä'), 1842–98, French poet, leader of the SYMBOLISTS. He held that poetry should express the transcendental and correspond most closely to music. He disregarded syntax and was often hermetic. Though hardly popular (he earned a meager living by teaching English), he was the center of a brilliant literary group, gathered every Tuesday evening at his flat, and he influenced all modern French writing.

malleability, property of metal describing extent to which it can be hammered, beaten, pressed, or rolled into thin sheets. Metals vary in this respect; gold is most malleable metal. Temperature and impurities affect malleability.

Mallorca, Balearic island: see MAJORCA.

mallow, white- or pink-flowered annual or perennial plants of genus *Malva.* The pink-flowered marsh mallow (*Althaea officinalis*) is found in swamps of E U.S. The rose mallow is hibiscus.

Malmaison (mälmāzō'), château at Rueil-Malmaison, a W suburb of Paris, France. Was residence of Bonaparte 1800–1803 and of Empress Josephine 1809–14. Napoleonic museum.

Malmédy (mälmādē'), town (pop. 5,569), Liége prov., SE Belgium, near German border. Treaty of Versailles transferred it from Prussia to Belgium (see EUPEN).

Malmesbury (mämz'bŭrē), municipal borough (pop. 2,509), Wiltshire, England. Site of magnificent abbey founded in 7th. cent.

Malmo (mäl'mō), Swed. *Malmö,* maritime industrial city (pop. 192,498), co. seat of Malmohus co., SE Sweden, on the Oresund opposite Copenhagen. It has shipyards, machine shops, textile mills, sugar refineries, and tobacco, rubber, and chemical plants. Founded 12th cent., it was major herring port during Hanseatic period. Until annexed by Sweden as part of SKANE in 1658, it was under Denmark. Bothwell was a prisoner in Malmo castle (built 1537).

Maloja (mälō'yä), pass, Grisons canton, Switzerland, leading from Engadine Valley to Italy.

Malolos (mälō'lōs), municipality (pop. 33,384), on SW Luzon, Philippines, NW of Manila. Short-lived revolutionary capital was set up here in 1898 under Emilio Aguinaldo.

Malone, Dumas (dōōmä' mŭlōn'), 1892–, American historian and editor, professor of history at Columbia Univ. (1945–). Editor in chief of *Dictionary of American Biography* (1931–36). Undertook later a four-volume work on Jefferson.

Malone, Edmund, 1741–1812, Irish Shaksperian scholar, noted as exposer of Shaksperian forgeries of Wil-

liam IRELAND (1796). He published editions of Shakspere (1790) and Dryden (1800).

Malone (mŭlōn'), village (pop. 9,501), N N.Y., on Salmon R. near Quebec line. Mfg. of metal powders, clothing, paper, and furniture. FENIAN MOVEMENT members gathered here to attack Canada 1866.

Malory, Sir Thomas, d. 1471, English author of *Morte d'Arthur,* last medieval English treatment of ARTHURIAN LEGEND. The long romance is notable for heroic tone and vigorous prose style.

Malpighi, Marcello (märchěl'lō mälpē'gē), 1628–94, Italian anatomist, pioneer microscopist. His observation of blood in capillaries completed proof of circulation theory.

Malplaquet (mälpläkä'), village, Nord dept., N France. Here in 1709 Marlborough and Eugene of Savoy defeated the Fench.

Malraux, André (ädrä' mälrō'), 1895–, French author. Profoundly concerned with the problems of freedom and revolution, he took an active part in the Chinese civil war (1925–27), on the side of the Kuomintang, and in the Spanish civil war of 1936–39, on the Loyalist side. From these experiences came two of the most powerful social novels of his time—*La Condition Humaine* (1933; Eng. tr., *Man's Fate*) and *L'Espoir* (1938; Eng. tr., *Man's Hope*). His *Psychology of Art* (1947; Eng. tr., 2 vols., 1949) has an entirely novel approach to esthetics. Malraux, though early associated with Communism, in 1947 became Gen. Charles de Gaulle's propaganda chief.

malt, a partly germinated grain (usually barley) dried and cured for use in brewing. Rich in carbohydrates and protein, it has nutritional value.

Malta (môl'tù), British colony (total area 122 sq. mi.; total pop. 305,991) in the Mediterranean S of Sicily, comprising islands of Malta (95 sq. mi.), Gozo, and Comino; cap. Valletta. Group sometimes called the Maltese Isls. Has belonged to Phoenicians, Greeks, Carthaginians, Romans, and Saracens. Given (1530) to KNIGHTS HOSPITALERS who held it until surrender to Napoleon in 1798. Annexed by British in 1814. Valletta is chief British Mediterranean naval and military base. Malta suffered over 2,000 air raids in World War II; entire pop. awarded decoration for bravery by George VI in 1942. The 1947 constitution gave limited self-government. British naval dockyards chief source of employment. St. Paul shipwrecked here.

Malta, city (pop. 2,095), N Mont., on Milk R. and E of Havre. Chief town of Milk R. project.

Malta, Knights of: see KNIGHTS HOSPITALERS.

Malta fever: see BRUCELLOSIS.

Maltese Islands: see MALTA.

Malthus, Thomas Robert (mäl'thùs), 1766–1834, English economist, pioneer in modern population study. In *An Essay on the Principle of Population* (1798; rev. ed., 1803), he contended that poverty is unavoidable because population increases by geometrical ratio and the means of subsistence by arithmetical ratio. He believed that the only preventive checks to growth of population were war, famine, disease, and "moral restraint" (see BIRTH CONTROL). Subsequent POPULATION trends have outmoded much of his analysis.

maltose (môl'tōs) or **malt sugar,** carbohydrate with same chemical formula as sucrose; results from action of an enzyme on starch.

Malvern (môl'vùrn, mô'–), urban district (pop. 21,681), Worcestershire, England. Medicinal springs make it a favorite watering place. Annual dramatic festival begun in 1928 as tribute to G. B. Shaw.

Malvern, city (pop. 8,072), S central Ark., SE of Hot Springs. Mfg. of wood products, brick, chemicals, shoes, and cotton. Aluminum plant near.

Malverne, residential village (pop. 8,086), SE N.Y., on SW Long Isl. ESE of Jamaica.

Malvern Hills, range of hills, c.9 mi. long, on the Worcestershire-Herefordshire border, England.

Malvern Hill: see SEVEN DAYS BATTLES.

Mamaroneck (mùmä'rùněk), residential village (pop.

15,016), SE N.Y., on Long Isl. Sound near New Rochelle; settled 1661. Food, wood, metal products.

Mamelukes (măʹmŭlooks) [Arabic,= slaves], originally slaves brought to Egypt by Fatimite caliphs in 10th cent. and by later Ayyubite sultans and trained as soldiers. Many were freed and rose to high rank. In 1250 the Mameluke emir Eibek killed last Ayyubite ruler and proclaimed himself sultan. For c.250 years Egypt was ruled by Mamelukes, who at one time controlled much of Asia Minor. Their two dynasties were Bahrites (1250–1382), chiefly Turks and Mongols, and Burjites (1382–1517), chiefly Circassians. They retained high posts even after Turkish conquest of Egypt (1517). Their rebellion against the Turks was put down by Napoleon in 1798, and in 1811 their power was totally destroyed by Mohammed Ali.

Mamison or **Mamisson** (both: mŭmēsônʹ), pass, 9,550 ft. high, USSR, in Greater Caucasus, on border between Georgian SSR and RSFSR. Crossed by Ossetian Military Road; links Ardon and Rion river valleys.

mammal, warm-blooded animal of highest vertebrate class, Mammalia. Female has glands that secrete milk to nourish young. In most, the body is hairy. The heart is four-chambered and a diaphragm separates thorax from abdomen. Young of higher mammals are fed prenatally through placenta and are born alive except among egg-laying monotremes. Orders include Carnivora (flesh-eaters); Cetacea (e.g., whale); Rodentia (see RODENT); Perissodactyla and Artiodactyla (both hoofed mammals); and primate order (incl. man).

mammon, Aramaic term meaning riches, retained in New Testament Greek. Mat. 6.24; Luke 16.9,11,13.

mammoth, extinct elephant which ranged over parts of Eurasia and North America during Pleistocene epoch. Shoulder height of imperial mammoth was c.13½ ft.; of woolly variety 9 ft. Whole specimens have been found preserved by freezing in Siberia.

Mammoth Cave National Park: see NATIONAL PARKS AND MONUMENTS (table).

Mammoth Hot Springs, Wyo., hq. of Yellowstone Natl. Park (see NATIONAL PARKS AND MONUMENTS, table).

Mamoré (mämôräʹ), river, c.600 mi. long, Bolivia, formed by tributaries in Andes and plains of central Bolivia. Flows N to Brazil forming small section of Brazil-Bolivia border. Joins Beni to form Madeira.

Mamun (mämoonʹ), 786–833, 7th ABBASID caliph (813–33), son of HARUN-AL-RASHID. Belonged to a rationalistic sect of Islam. Arts and sciences flourished under his reign.

man: see ANTHROPOLOGY; MAN, PRIMITIVE; ANATOMY; PHYSIOLOGY. See ill., p. 595.

Man, Isle of, island (221 sq. mi.; pop. 55,213), Great Britain, in Irish Sea; cap. Douglas. Scenery and mild climate make it a resort. Has varied agr., dairying, fishing, and quarrying. Formerly held by Norway, Scotland, and earls of Derby, it has been under British crown since 1827. Manx language is now little spoken.

man, primitive, or early man. Millions of human beings of forms transitional between the apelike and the contemporary man lived in the Pleistocene period. There arose then roughly three types. The most primitive men, *Pithecanthropus* (Java ape man) and *Sinanthropus* (Peking man), both probably variants of *Homo erectus*, showed modern and archaic physical features. They were capable of speech, used fire, and lived in bands. Neanderthaloid man (*Homo neanderthalensis*) was found in association with Mousterian culture and ranged from Europe to Africa and central Asia. Among the earliest confirmed representatives of *Homo sapiens* is Cro-Magnon man, although many believe that *Homo sapiens* existed before the disappearance of Neanderthal man. Evidence from Mt. Carmel suggests that modern man may be a mixture of Neanderthal and other types, such as Cro-Magnon. An even more complicated mixture of traits has been found in fossils such as those of the Solo man of Java, which present a mosaic of traits of *Pithecanthropus*, Nean-

derthal, and *Homo sapiens*. Whatever the origin of *Homo sapiens*, many hold it probable that he is in part the result of crossing with other types, which took place whenever early men in their wanderings came in contact.

Managua (mänäʹgwä), city (pop. 104,444), W Nicaragua; cap and largest city of Nicaragua, on S shore of L. Managua. Made permanent cap. (1855) as compromise to end feud between Granada and León. U.S. marines stationed here, 1912–25, 1926–33.

Manáos, Brazil: see MANAUS.

Manasquan (mănʹŭskwän), Atlantic resort borough (pop. 3,178), E N.J., SSW of Asbury Park.

Manassas, town (pop. 1,804), N Va., WSW of Alexandria. Civil War battles of BULL RUN, fought near by, sometimes called battles of Manassas.

Manasseh (mŭnăʹsē) or **Manasses** (–sŭs). **1** Son of Joseph and ancestor of one of the 12 tribes of Israel. Tribe settled both E and W of Jordan R. Gen. 41.51; Num. 26.28–34; Deut. 3.13; Joshua 17; 2 Kings 10.33; 1 Chron. 2.21–23; 5.25–26; 7.14–19; Rev. 7.6. **2** Died c.643 B.C., king of Judah (c.698–c.643 B.C.). Denounced in Bible as one of Judah's worst kings, he later reformed. 2 Kings 21; 2 Chron. 33; Mat. 1.10. The Prayer of Manasses, one of the PSEUDEPIGRAPHA, placed in Apocrypha in AV, is a penitential psalm ascribed to the repentant king.

manatee (mănŭtēʹ), herbivorous aquatic mammal (*Trichechus*) allied to dugong. Its oil, flesh, and hide are used by man.

Manaus (mŭnäʹŭs, Port. mŭnooshʹ), city (pop. 110,678), cap. of Amazonas state, NW Brazil, on left bank of Rio Negro near junction with Amazon. Though more than 900 mi. inland, Manaus is large port for ocean-going vessels. Founded in late 17th cent., it thrived during wild rubber boom, is now metropolis of all upper Amazon. Formerly Manáos.

Mancha, La (lä mänʹchä), region of central Spain, in New Castile; a high, barren plateau. Made famous by DON QUIXOTE, whose home was in a village of La Mancha.

Manche (mäsh) [Fr. name for English Channel], department (2,295 sq. mi.; pop. 435,432), NW France, in Normandy; cap. Saint-Lô. Includes COTENTIN peninsula, Cherbourg, Mont-Saint-Michel.

Manchester (mănʹchŭstŭr), city (pop. 703,175), Lancashire, England, on Irwell, Medlock, Irk and Tib rivers; center of England's most densely populated area and world's foremost cotton city. MANCHESTER SHIP CANAL makes city a seaport. Artificial-silk industry balanced losses in cotton after World War I. Relics have been found of Roman origin. Mentioned in Domesday Book. Has long led in liberal reform movements. Scene of PETERLOO MASSACRE in 1819. Manchester *Guardian* dates from 1821. Site of Victoria Univ. (1846), Cooperative Col. (1919), two art galleries and libraries. Home of Hallé Orchestra. Suffered heavy bomb damage in World War II.

Manchester. 1 Town (pop. 34,116), central Conn., E of Hartford; settled c.1672. Textiles, metal goods. **2** City (pop. 82,732), S N.H., on Merrimack R. between Concord and Nashua; settled 1722. First (1846) and largest city in state. Great Amoskeag (ămʹŭskĕg) cotton textile mills (power from Amoskeag Falls) closed Sept., 1935. Amoskeag Industries, Inc. (citizens' organization) bought the property in Sept., 1936, and sold or leased its parts to various concerns. Textiles, shoes, machinery, building materials, and luggage. Seat of St. Anselm's Col. Grenier Air Force Base was built 1941. **3** Resort town (pop. 2,425), SW Vt., N of Bennington and E of Mt. Equinox.

Manchester school, group of English economists of the 19th cent., led by William Cobden and John Bright. Chief tenets were FREE TRADE and LAISSEZ FAIRE.

Manchester Ship Canal, 35½ mi. long; connecting Manchester, England, with the Mersey estuary above Birkenhead. Opened in 1894.

Manchester terrier: see TERRIER.

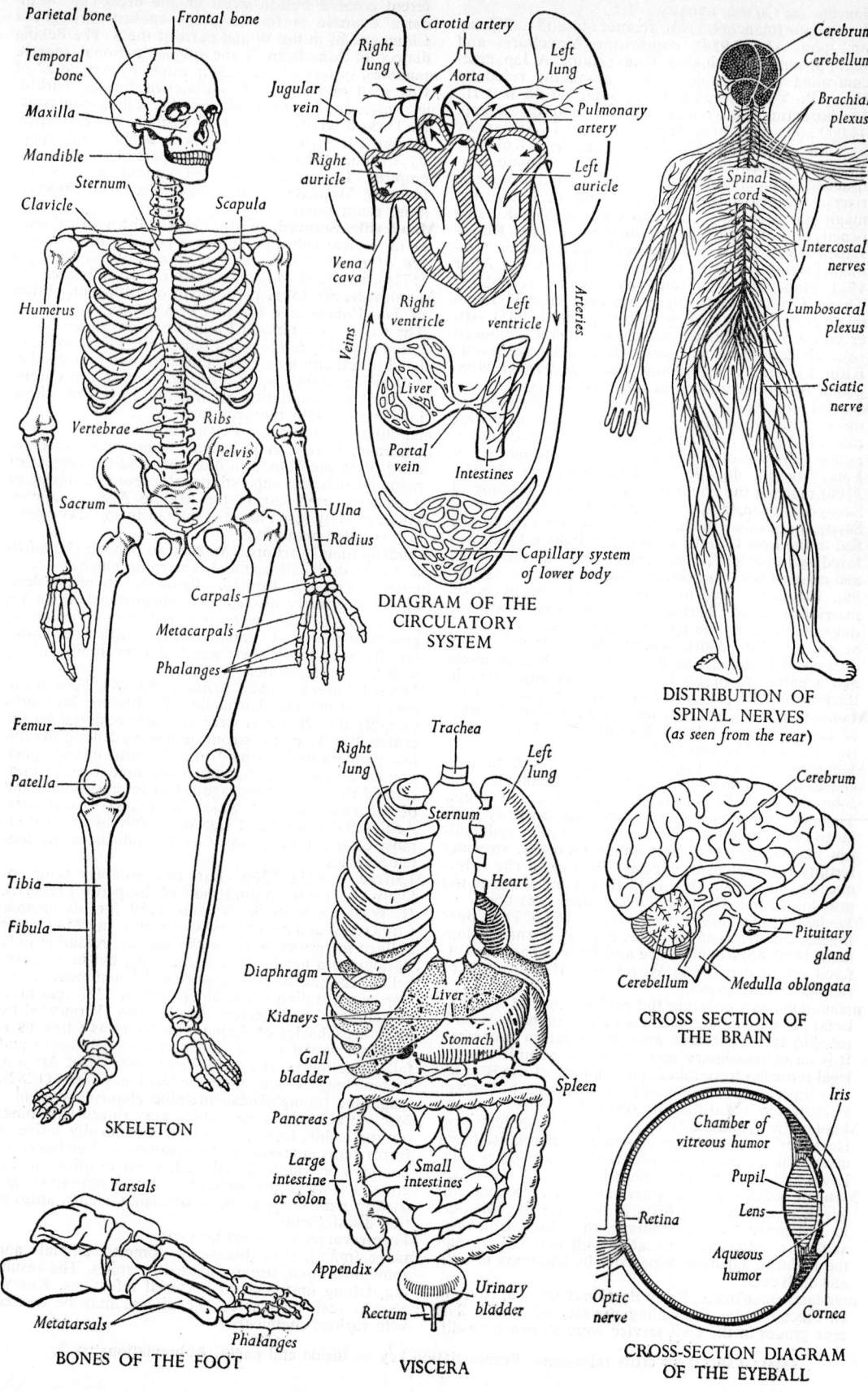

SKELETON

Parietal bone
Frontal bone
Temporal bone
Maxilla
Mandible
Sternum
Clavicle
Scapula
Humerus
Vertebrae
Ribs
Pelvis
Sacrum
Ulna
Radius
Carpals
Metacarpals
Phalanges
Femur
Patella
Tibia
Fibula

DIAGRAM OF THE CIRCULATORY SYSTEM

Right lung
Carotid artery
Left lung
Aorta
Jugular vein
Pulmonary artery
Right auricle
Left auricle
Vena cava
Right ventricle
Left ventricle
Veins
Arteries
Liver
Portal vein
Intestines
Capillary system of lower body

DISTRIBUTION OF SPINAL NERVES
(as seen from the rear)

Cerebrum
Cerebellum
Brachial plexus
Spinal cord
Intercostal nerves
Lumbosacral plexus
Sciatic nerve

VISCERA

Trachea
Right lung
Left lung
Sternum
Heart
Diaphragm
Liver
Kidneys
Stomach
Gall bladder
Spleen
Pancreas
Large intestine or colon
Small intestines
Appendix
Rectum
Urinary bladder

CROSS SECTION OF THE BRAIN

Cerebrum
Pituitary gland
Cerebellum
Medulla oblongata

BONES OF THE FOOT

Tarsals
Metatarsals
Phalanges

CROSS-SECTION DIAGRAM OF THE EYEBALL

Iris
Chamber of vitreous humor
Pupil
Lens
Retina
Aqueous humor
Optic nerve
Cornea

Manchu: see CH'ING, dynasty.

Manchukuo (mănchōō'kwō), former state (512,766 sq. mi.; pop. 43,233,954), comprising Manchuria and Jehol prov.; cap. Hsinking (Changchun). A Japanese-controlled puppet state, it was nominally ruled by Henry Pu Yi. Restored to China after World War II.

Manchuria (mănchōō'rēù), region (585,000 sq. mi.; pop. 44,000,000), NE China. Separated from USSR largely by Amur, Argun, and Ussuri rivers and from Korea by Yalu and Tumen rivers. Its great central plain, surrounded by mountains, is drained by Liao and Sungari rivers. Agr. (soybeans, kaoliang, grain), lumbering; major mines (mostly iron and coal) in SW. Russian penetration of Manchuria began c.1900. After Russo-Japanese War (1904–5) Japan replaced Russia as dominant foreign power in region (see LIAOTUNG). After 1911 Manchuria was ruled by war lords, notably Chang Tso-lin. Occupying entire area in 1931 Japan set up puppet state of MANCHUKUO (expired 1945). After World War II Manchuria came under Communist rule; divided into 6 provinces (Heilungkiang, JEHOL, Kirin, Liaosi, LIAOTUNG, Sungkiang) and Inner Mongolian Autonomous Region (see MONGOLIA).

Mancini (mănchē'nē), family name of five sisters, nieces of Cardinal Mazarin. Born in Rome, they were called to France by their uncle. Laure (1636–57) married a grandson of Henry IV and was the mother of Louis Joseph, duc de Vendôme. Olympe (1639?–1708) married the count of Soissons, of the house of Savoy-Carignan, and was the mother of Eugene of Savoy. Implicated in the POISON AFFAIR (1680), she fled to the Low Countries. Marie (c.1640–c.1715) was loved by Louis XIV, but Mazarin broke up the liaison and married her to a Prince Colonna. Hortense (1646–99), Mazarin's favorite and most beautiful niece, married Armand Charles de la Porte, who was made duke of Mazarin. She left him and became a favorite at the English court. Marie Anne (1649?–1714), duchess of Bouillon, was the center of a literary circle and a patroness of La Fontaine. Also implicated in the Poison Affair, she was banished from court (1680).

Manco Capac (mäng'kō käpäk'). **1** Legendary founder of Inca dynasty of Peru. **2** Died 1544, last of Inca rulers; son of Huayna Capac.

Mandaeans (măndē'ùnz), small religious sect in Iran and Iraq, also known as Christians of St. John (i.e., St. John the Baptist), Nasoreans, Sabaeans, and Subbi. Their rite preserves ancient beliefs: an astrology similar to the Babylonian; an emanation system and dualism like GNOSTICISM, but, unlike Gnostics, stressing fertility rather than asceticism. Their chief rite is frequent baptism, and they hold that living water is the principle of life. The Ginza Rba is their holy book.

Mandalay (măn"dùlā'), town (pop. 163,527), Upper Burma, on Irrawaddy R. Was cap. of Burmese kingdom, 1860–85. Royal palace and famous pagodas suffered severe damage in World War II. Terminus of rail line from Rangoon.

mandamus, writ ordering the performance of a ministerial act (i.e., an act which a person or body is obligated by law to perform, without descretion or choice). It is an extraordinary remedy, not used unless usual legal remedies have failed. One sample of use is order by a superior court compelling a lower court to accept a suit which it had illegally refused.

Mandan (măn'dăn), city (pop. 7,298), S N.Dak., on Heart and Missouri rivers opposite Bismarck. Railroad division point; distribution center for grain, dairy area. Lewis and Clark wintered here 1804–5.

Mandan Indians, North American tribe of Siouan linguistic stock, living in historic times on the Missouri R. Sedentary "village" Indians, they lived from agr. and were culturally associated with the Arikara and the Hidatsa. Virtually wiped out by smallpox in 18th and 19th cent.

mandarin (măn'dùrĭn) [from Port. mandar = to govern], an official under the Ch'ing dynasty of China. The nine grades in the civil service were shown by a dif-

ferent colored button worn on the dress cap. Mandarin Chinese is the language spoken throughout China except in the W and parts of the S. The Peking dialect of Mandarin is the official national speech.

mandates, system of trusteeship estab. by Article 22 of Covenant of League of Nations for former Turkish territories and German colonies. Areas in three classes: A, Turkish territories, with provisional independence; B, German African colonies, with commercial equality; C, other German colonies, as part of mandatories' empires. League administered system through 11-member Mandates Commission. See also TRUSTEESHIP, TERRITORIAL.

Mandeville, Bernard, 1670–1733, English satirical writer on ethical subjects, known especially for The Fable of the Bees; or, Private Vices, Public Benefits (1714), an attack on social restraint of individuals.

Mandeville, Sir John, pseudonym of 14th-cent. author of The Voiage and Travaile of Sir John Mandeville. The writer calls himself Englishman. Work first composed probably in Liége in French (c.1371), soon translated into many languages. Purporting to be record of author's travels through Jerusalem and rest of Orient, the book is compilation of authentic travels of others, interspersed with fantastic lore.

mandolin: see STRINGED INSTRUMENTS.

mandrake, European perennial (Mandragora officinarum) often mentioned in literature and the subject of many legends and superstitions. Its root, the source of a narcotic used during the Middle Ages as a pain killer, crudely resembles the human form. MAY APPLE is also called mandrake.

mandrill, mainly arboreal W African baboon (Mandrillus) with short tail, red and blue rump patches.

manes (mā'nēz), in Roman religion, spirits of the dead taken collectively, also called euphemistically di manes [good gods]. They were placated with offerings at graves of the dead. Later identified with di parentes [family ancestors], they watched over family along with lares and penates. See LARVAE.

Manet, Édouard (ädwär' mänä'), 1832–83, French impressionist painter. Throughout his lifetime his works (notably the Olympia) were violently attacked by the critics. But he had a strong following among his fellow painters and a friend in Zola, who lost his position on a newspaper for defending him. Usually considered the greatest protagonist of impressionism and of plein-air painting, which he helped to originate. Achieved dramatic and vigorous paintings with the utmost economy of means. Greatly influenced his contemporaries.

Manfred, c.1232–1266, last Hohenstaufen king of Sicily (1258–66); natural son of Emperor Frederick II. Was regent in Sicily after 1250 for his brother CONRAD IV and his nephew CONRADIN. In 1254 he was obliged to restore Sicily to the papacy, retaining only Taranto as a fief held from the pope, but he soon rebelled, conquered S Italy and Sicily, assumed leadership of all Italian Ghibellines, and in 1258 had himself crowned at Palermo. Pope Urban IV retorted by investing Charles of Anjou with Sicily as CHARLES I. Manfred was defeated by Charles at Benevento and fell in the battle. His son-in-law, Peter III of Aragon, became king of Sicily after the Sicilian Vespers (1282).

manganese (măng'gùnēs), metallic element (symbol = Mn; see also ELEMENT, table), gray tinged with pink, not malleable, harder than iron. Chemically active, it forms many compounds. Does not occur free but compounds are widely distributed. Used in alloys to increase hardness; it is present in steel. Compounds are used in paints, dry cells, as oxidizing agents, antiseptics, disinfectants.

Mangareva: see GAMBIER ISLANDS.

mange (mānj), skin disease of domestic animals and sometimes man, usually caused by mites. The resulting itching may lead to bacterial infections. Known also as scab or scabies, the disease may be treated with various chemicals.

Mangin, Charles (shärl′ mäzhě′), 1866–1925, French general. Served in Sudan and North Africa; was prominent in defense of Verdun.

mango, evergreen tree (*Mangifera indica*) native to Asia and long grown in the tropics for its large, delicious fruit which has yellow-red skin and golden flesh. It is now cultivated in Fla. and Calif.

mangrove (măng′grōv), tropical evergreen tree which produces stiltlike aerial roots from the trunk. The American mangrove (*Rhizophora mangle*) is abundant along shores and in brackish marshes in S Fla., Mexico, West Indies, Central and South America.

Manhasset (mănhăs′ĭt), suburban village (1940 pop. 5,099), on N shore of Long Isl., SE N.Y., near the head of Manhasset Bay and E of Great Neck.

Manhattan. 1 City (pop. 19,056), NE Kansas, WNW of Topeka near junction of Big Blue and Kansas rivers; founded 1854. Trade and processing center of agr. and grazing area. Seat of KANSAS STATE COLLEGE OF AGRICULTURE AND APPLIED SCIENCE. **2** Borough (land area 22 sq. mi.; pop. 1,960,101) of NEW YORK city, SE N.Y., coextensive with New York co. Composed chiefly of Manhattan isl. (c.12 mi. long and 2 mi. wide at greatest width), but also including islands in East R. and in New York Bay (GOVERNORS ISLAND; ELLIS ISLAND; Bedloe's Isl., with Statue of Liberty); bounded on W by Hudson R., NE and N by Harlem R. and Spuyten Duyvil Creek. Many bridges, tunnels, ferries link it to the other boroughs and to N.J. DUTCH WEST INDIA COMPANY bought Manhattan from Manhattan Indians in 1626 for trinkets worth $24; first known as NEW AMSTERDAM, it became New York under the English 1664; its boundaries were those of New York city until 1874, when several Westchester co. communities were inc. into city; became a New York city borough 1898. Commercial, cultural, financial heart of the city, with extensive and diversified mfg., tremendous wholesale and retail trade, major distributing facilities (rail, ship, truck), banking and finance establishments. Here are METROPOLITAN MUSEUM OF ART, AMERICAN MUSEUM OF NATURAL HISTORY, MUSEUM OF MODERN ART; hq. of NEW YORK PUBLIC LIBRARY; numerous theaters (theatrical center of the country) and institutions of music, COLUMBIA UNIVERSITY, parts of College of the City of NEW YORK and of NEW YORK UNIVERSITY, NEW SCHOOL FOR SOCIAL RESEARCH, JUILLIARD SCHOOL OF MUSIC, theological seminaries and medical schools, COOPER UNION; Trinity Church (chartered 1697), SAINT PATRICK'S CATHEDRAL, Cathedral of SAINT JOHN THE DIVINE, Riverside Church, Temple Emanu-El. Famous areas: HARLEM, GREENWICH VILLAGE, the BOWERY; streets: BROADWAY, FIFTH AVENUE, WALL STREET; parks: the BATTERY, CENTRAL PARK, Fort Tryon Park (with the Cloisters). Some of the much-visited buildings are: Empire State Building, Rockefeller Center, Jumel Mansion, and UN hq.

Manhattan Beach, resort and residential city (pop. 17,-330), S Calif., SW of Los Angeles.

Manhattan College: see BRONX, THE, N.Y.

Manhattan Indians, North American tribe of Algonquian linguistic stock, occupying in early 17th cent. N Manhattan isl. and near-by areas. The Dutch bought the island from them in 1626 and then practically destroyed them in wars of 1640–45.

Manheim, borough (pop. 4,246), SE Pa., NW of Lancaster. Munitions center in Revolution. Here H. W. Steigel produced first flint glass in U.S.

manic-depressive psychosis, functional disorder involving mania or depression or fluctuation between the two. Manic patient is exalted, extravagant, distracted, tends toward moral laxness, antisocial behavior. Depressive patient has pathological melancholia, ideas of unworthiness, sin, suicide. Recovery is likely but danger of recurrence always remains. Shock therapy may shorten depressive phase. Predisposition may be hereditary.

Manichaeism (mă′nĭkēĭzùm) or **Manichaeanism** (mă-nĭkē′ūnĭzùm), religion founded by a 3d-cent. Persian named Mani, who announced himself a prophet in 242, was driven into exile under Zoroastrian pressure, and finally after his return was flayed to death. His religion, however, spread over the Roman Empire and Asia. The influence of Buddhism and Gnosticism was strong, and Manichaeism took the dualism of ZOROASTRIANISM, spiritualizing the struggle between light and dark into warfare between good and evil. The teaching was strongly ascetic, and the "elect" or "perfect" practiced strict celibacy and austerity; they were assured of immediate happiness after death. The lower "auditors" or "hearers," laymen, could marry once but were called on to restrict sensual pleasures; they might hope to be reborn among the elect. This widespread religion was successfully opposed by Christianity and died out as a dynamic faith c.500, though it was later revived among Paulicians, Bogomils, Cathari, and Albigenses.

Manich Depression, RSFSR: see MANYCH DEPRESSION.

Manicouagan (mänĭkwä′gùn), river, rising in E central Que., Canada, and flowing S c.310 mi. to St. Lawrence R. SW of Baie Comeau.

Manihiki (mänĭhē′kē), atoll (pop. 435), S Pacific, E of Samoa. Discovered 1822 by Americans; placed under New Zealand Cook Isls. administration, 1901.

Manila (mùnĭ′lù), city (pop. 983,906), cap. and chief port of Philippines, on SW Luzon, on Manila Bay. Divided into two sections by navigable Pasig R. Here are Malacañan Palace (presidential mansion), Univ. of Santo Tomás, Univ. of the Philippines, Natl. Univ., and Philippine Women's Univ. In 1571 a Spanish colony was estab. here by López de Legaspi. Early in World War II, city was heavily bombed by the Japanese; Intramuros (old walled city) was destroyed.

Manila Bay, inlet of South China Sea, in SW Luzon, Philippines. At entrance is Corregidor isl. In Spanish-American War, Spanish fleet was destroyed here by Adm. George Dewey.

Manila hemp, important cordage fiber obtained from the abacá or Manila hemp plant (*Musa textilis*), a close relative of the banana. Leafstalks yield the strong fibers, the finer being used in fabrics, the coarse in ropes, matting twine, and paper.

Manin, Daniele (dänyä′lä mänēn′), 1804–57, Italian patriot. Became head of Venetian republic when Venice rebelled against Austrian rule (1848) and organized resistance to a long siege by the Austrians. After the Venetian surrender (Aug., 1849), he went into exile at Paris.

Manipur (mŭnĭpŏor′), state (8,620 sq. mi.; pop. 512,-069), NE India; cap. Imphal. Lies in heavily forested Manipur Hills. Invaded 1944 by Japan.

Manistee (mănĭstē′), city (pop. 8,642), N Mich., on L. Michigan at mouth of Manistee R. and W of Cadillac, in fruit region. Resort, shipping, and industrial center with salt plants.

Manistique (mănĭstēk′), resort city (pop. 5,086), E Upper Peninsula, N Mich., on L. Michigan at mouth of Manistique R. Shipping and fishing center with lumbering and mfg. of wood products.

manito (mă′nĭtō), name used among Indians of Algonquian linguistic stock to describe supernatural power permeating all things, equated by some missionaries and romanticists with the Christian God.

Manitoba (mănĭtō′bù), province (219,723 sq. mi., with water surface 246,512 sq. mi.; pop. 776,541) W central Canada; cap. WINNIPEG. Easternmost of the Prairie Provs., it has large uninhabited tundra in N, wooded lake area in central part (largest lakes are WINNIPEG, Manitoba, WINNIPEGOSIS), and broad farmlands in S. Other large cities are SAINT BONIFACE and BRANDON. Major rivers are Red, Assiniboine, Churchill, and Nelson. Agr. (wheat, other grains, potatoes) main occupation, supplemented by lumbering, mining (copper, gold, zinc, silver, cadmium), and fur farming. Area chartered to Hudson's Bay Co. 1670 as part of Rupert's Land. Competition from French fur traders died out after 1763. Agr. settlement made in Red R. valley by Lord SELKIRK 1812. Dominion bought land between Ont. and B.C. from Hudson's Bay Co. 1869. Purchase unsuccessfully resisted in Red River insurrection led by Louis RIEL. Province created 1870 embracing small area S of L. Winnipeg, enlarged 1881, and extended to Hudson Bay 1912. Outlet to grain markets through Great Lakes achieved when railroads reached Winnipeg, now a major world grain center. Railroad to CHURCHILL on Hudson Bay, completed 1929, opened short sea route eastward. Winnipeg district suffered disastrous floods 1950.

Manitoba, University of: see WINNIPEG, Man.

Manitoulin Islands (mănŭtoōʹlĭn), archipelago made up of three large and several smaller islands, separating N part of L. Huron from North Channel and from NW Georgian Bay. Manitoulin Isl. (80 mi. long, 2–32 mi. wide), largest lake island in world, encloses over 100 lakes and has rugged coast. Drummond Isl. (c.20 mi. long, 11 mi. wide) belongs to Mich., the rest to Ontario. Resorts and fishing.

Manitou Springs, Colo.: see COLORADO SPRINGS.

Manitowoc (măʺnĭtŭwŏkʹ), city (pop. 27,598), E Wis., on L. Michigan at mouth of Manitowoc R. and N of Sheboygan. North West Co. estab. trading post here 1795; permanently settled 1837. Fishing industry gave way to shipbuilding in 1860s. Metal goods.

Maniu, Iuliu (yoōʹlyoō mänyoōʹ), 1873–1951?, Rumanian politician, leader of Peasant party. Premier 1928–30, 1932–33. A liberal, he was tried for treason in 1947 by the Communist regime and sentenced to life imprisonment.

Manizales (mänēsäʹlĕs), city (pop. 51,025), W central Colombia in Andes; founded c.1846; commercial and agr. center, especially of coffee.

Mankato (măn-kāʹtō), city (pop. 18,809), S Minn., on Minnesota R. and SW of Minneapolis; platted 1852. Center of dairy, farm, and quarry area, with mfg. of agr. equipment and food products. Sibley Park was site of Camp Lincoln, where over 300 Sioux were held after 1862 uprising.

Manley, Mary de la Rivière, 1663–1724, English author. Among her works, often scurrilous, most famous is the prose romance *New Atlantis* (1709–10).

Manlius Capitolinus, Marcus (kăʺpĭtŭlīʹnŭs), d. 384? B.C., Roman consul (392 B.C.), Took refuge in the Capitol when Rome was taken by the Gauls (c.389 B.C.); aroused by cackling geese at night, he repulsed the Gauls from the hill. Later impeached for treason and thrown from the Tarpeian Rock. His kinsman **Titus Manlius Imperiosus Torquatus,** 4th cent. B.C., fought the Gauls (361 B.C.), killing one of their leaders in single combat and taking his torque (hence name Torquatus). He subjugated the Latins (340 B.C.) and killed his own son for engaging the enemy against his orders.

Mann (män), family of German writers. **Heinrich Mann** (hīnʹrĭkh), 1871–1950, wrote the novels *Professor Unrat* (Eng. trs., *The Blue Angel,* 1932, *Small Town Tyrant,* 1944); *The Little Town* (1909); the trilogy *Das Kaiserreich* (1917–25; Eng. tr., *The Patrioteer,* 1921, *The Poor,* 1917, and *The Chief,* 1925); and a biography of Henry IV of France (1935–38). He wrote with romantic passion and fierce satire. His brother, **Thomas Mann** (tōʹmäs), 1875–, is one of the outstanding literary figures of the 20th cent. His first novel, *Buddenbrooks* (1900; Eng. tr., 1924), brought him fame. His shorter works were collected in *Stories of Three Decades* (1936). These reflected his preoccupation with the proximity of art to neurosis, the artist's longing for death, the affinity of genius to disease, and the problem of the artist's position in a bourgeois society—themes which appear, too, in the novel *The Magic Mountain* (1924; Eng. tr., 1927), perhaps his masterpiece. In his tetralogy on the biblical story of Joseph (1933–43), however, the gloomy turbulence of his early work is replaced by a somewhat idyllic but profound study of the mythological and psychological.

In 1948 appeared *Dr. Faustus,* in 1951 *The Holy Sinner.* Thomas Mann's political essays denouncing fascism are published in *Order of the Day* (1942); his literary essays are collected as *Essays of Three Decades* (1947). He left Germany in 1933 and later (1936) came to the U.S., returning to Europe in 1952. He received the 1929 Nobel Prize in Literature. His son, **Klaus Mann** (klous), 1906–49, was a novelist, essayist, and playwright. His works include *Alexander: a Novel of Utopia* (1929; Eng. tr., 1930); *Pathetic Symphony* (1936; Eng. tr., 1948); and *Turning Point* (1942).

Mann, Horace (măn), 1796–1859, American educator. Became a member of Mass legislature in 1827 and secretary of state board of education in 1837. He won much note for his reforms in reorganizing the school system, with improvement in buildings and equipment as well as in quality of instruction and in the training and salaries of teachers.

Mann, James Robert, 1856–1922, U.S. Representative from Ill. (1897–1922). Author (1910) of **Mann Act,** also known as White Slave Act, which forbade, under heavy penalties, transportation of women from one state to another for immoral purposes.

Mann, Thomas, and **Klaus Mann:** see MANN, family.

manna, in Bible, flaky, white edible substance provided by God for the Hebrews in the wilderness. It fell on the ground, was baked or stewed, and had a sweet taste. Ex. 16; Num. 11.7,8; Joshua 5.12. Many botanical definitions of manna have been proposed. Christians have compared the symbol to the body of Christ in the sacrament of communion.

Mann Act: see MANN, JAMES ROBERT.

Mannerheim, Baron Carl Gustav Emil (kärlʹ gŭʹstäv äʹmĭl mäʹnŭrhäm), 1867–1951, Finnish field marshal. Rose to rank of general in tsarist army. A hero of Finland's liberation, he was regent of the new republic in 1919. He commanded Finnish forces in the Finnish-Russian War of 1939–40 and again 1941–44. President of Finland 1944–46. The **Mannerheim Line,** a fortified line of defense across the Karelian Isthmus, was planned by him. It was taken by the Russians in 1940 and was dismantled.

Mannheim, Karl (kärlʹ mänʹhīm), 1893–1947, Austro-Hungarian sociologist. Taught in Germany and at Univ. of London. His *Ideology and Utopia* (1929) treats of social beliefs and thought.

Mannheim (mänʹhīm), city (pop. 244,000), Württemberg-Baden, W Germany, on the Rhine opposite Ludwigshafen and at mouth of the Neckar. Inland port; industrial center (machinery, precision instruments, chemicals). Chartered 1606; became residence of electors palatine (see PALATINATE) 1720. The famous Mannheim orchestra ranked first among European orchestras in 18th cent. and greatly influenced symphonic writing (notably Mozart's). Schiller began his career at the Mannheim theater (1782–83). Mannheim passed to Baden in 1803. It was largely destroyed in World War II. The electoral palace and the regularly laid-out baroque buildings of the inner city were heavily damaged or destroyed.

Manning, Henry Edward, 1808–92, English cardinal. Educated at Oxford, he became an Anglican pastor, but under the influence of the OXFORD MOVEMENT he followed J. H. NEWMAN and W. G. WARD into the Roman Catholic Church (1851), in which he was later ordained. He strongly advocated social reforms, tried to improve prison conditions, and fought for the rights of workingmen. After he had succeeded Wiseman as archbishop of Westminster (1865) he was influential in the labor movement, and in 1889 he supported the London dock strike, then single-handedly settled it. He opposed Catholic participation in Anglican universities, thus coming in conflict with Newman, with whom he later disagreed violently on the enunciation of papal infallibility, which Manning favored.

Manning, William Thomas, 1866–1949, American Episcopal bishop of N.Y. (1921–46). He greatly forwarded work on Cathedral of St. John the Divine.

SMALL CAPITALS = cross references. Pronunciation key on inside end pages. Abbreviations: **p. 2.**

Manoel, name of Portuguese rulers: see MANUEL.

manorial system or **seignorial system** (sēnyô'rēul), economic-social system in which peasants of medieval Europe held lands they tilled. Fundamental basis was holding of lands from lord (Fr. *seigneur*) of estate in return for fixed dues in kind, money, and services. System was allied with FEUDALISM, but was not feudal as it had no connection with fief. It flourished 11th to 15th cent. and declined with wide growth of towns and of capitalistic commerce which broke down small unit, the manor, and built up larger units. System was based on division of land into self-sufficient estates—great domains. Such domain was held by a lord, who might be king, ecclesiastical lord, baron, or any lesser noble. Land was in his holding, not given to man who tilled it but only loaned in return for dues and services. Peasant was either a SERF, who was bound to lord, or VILLEIN, who was not personally bound but held land by fixed payment. Domain was divided into arable land, meadow, woodland, and waste. Arable land was held by peasant, meadow in common, and woodland by lord. Manor was also administrative and political unit, with manorial courts, and unit for raising of taxes and for public improvements.

Man o' War, 1917–47, American race horse by Fair Play out of Mahubah, owned by Samuel Riddle after 1918. "Big Red" raced only as two-year-old and three-year-old, won 20 of 21 races, set five world records. Only loss was to horse named Upset at Saratoga, 1919. Became leading sire of all time.

Manresa (mänrä'sä), city (pop. 34,075), NE Spain, in Catalonia. Cotton and silk mfg. The grotto where St. Ignatius used to pray during his stay at Manresa (1522–23) is now a place of pilgrimage.

Mans, Le (lü mä'), city (pop. 90,693), cap. of Sarthe dept., NW France, on the Sarthe; historic cap. of Maine. Metallurgy. Dates from pre-Roman times. Its cathedral (11th–13th cent.), partly Romanesque, partly Gothic, is noted for its daring system of flying buttresses and contains the tomb of Queen Berengaria of England.

Mansart or **Mansard, François** (both: fräswä' mäsär'), 1598–1666, French architect, whose works are fine examples of French classical design. His Church of Val-de-Grâce, Paris, may have influenced Wren's design of St. Paul's Cathedral, London. His pupil and grandnephew, **Jules Hardouin Mansart** (zhül' ärdwē'), c.1646–1708, designed Grand Trianon (Versailles), Place Vendôme (Paris), and Dôme des Invalides. The family name is applied to a type of roof (*ill.,* p. 447).

Mansfeld, Peter Ernst, Graf von (pä'tùr ĕrnst' gräf' fün mäns'fĕlt), 1580?–1626, German nobleman, commander of a mercenary force in the Thirty Years War. He fought, with varying success, on the Protestant side in the service of Frederick the Winter King and, later, in Dutch and English pay. Wallenstein routed him at Dessau (1626).

Mansfield, Katherine, 1888–1923, British short-story writer, whose real name was Kathleen Beauchamp; wife of John Middleton MURRY. Her stories (as in *The Garden Party,* 1922) show techniques that strongly influenced later writers.

Mansfield, Richard, 1854–1907, American actor. A success in *Beau Brummel* (1890), *Cyrano de Bergerac* (1898), he was also among first to do Shaw in U.S.

Mansfield. 1 Town (pop. 10,008), NE Conn., N of Willimantic; settled c.1692. Includes Storrs village, main seat of Univ. of Connecticut (land-grant; state supported; coed.); chartered and opened 1881 as Storrs Agricultural School, it became a college 1893, Connecticut Agricultural Col. 1899, a university 1939. **2** Town (pop. 4,440), NW La., S of Shreveport. Confederate victory at Sabine Crossroads (Apr. 8, 1864) commemorated by near-by park. **3** Town (pop. 7,184), SE Mass., SSW of Boston. Machine parts. **4** City (pop. 43,564), N central Ohio, WSW of Akron; laid out 1808. Mfg. of electrical appliances and steel and brass products.

Mansfield, Mount: see GREEN MOUNTAINS.

Manship, Paul, 1885–, American sculptor. Often inspired by classical mythology for his subjects.

manslaughter, homicide without justification or excuse, distinguished from murder by absence of malice aforethought. The crime is usually by statute divided into degrees (e.g., voluntary manslaughter, an intentional killing committed in the heat of passion provoked by the victim; involuntary manslaughter, an unintentional killing resulting from a minor crime such as rioting or reckless driving.

Mansur (mänsoor') or **Al Mansur,** d. 775, 2d ABBASID caliph (754–75); brother and successor of Abu-l-Abbas. Founded Baghdad in 762.

Mansur or **Al-Mansur,** 914–1002, Moslem regent of Córdoba, known in Spanish as Almanzor. Acting in name of Hisham II, he extended power of Omayyad caliphs throughout Moslem Spain. Gave up premiership in 991, but held actual power until his death.

Mansura, El (ĕl mänsoo'rù), town (pop. 102,519), N Egypt, on the Nile. Here in 1250 the Crusaders led by Louis IX were defeated by the Mamelukes.

Mantegna, Andrea (ändrä'ä mäntä'nyä), 1431–1506, Italian painter of Paduan school. Married the daughter of Jacopo Bellini. Worked under patronage of the Gonzagas of Mantua. Strongly influenced by the antique, he was a master of anatomy and perspective. Works include *Holy Family* (Metropolitan Mus.), *Parnassus,* and *Triumph of Virtue* (both in Louvre).

Mantell, Robert Bruce (män"tĕl'), 1854–1928, British-American actor. Made debut 1876, formed company 1905. Excelled in Shakspere and melodrama.

Mantinea (män"tĭnē'ù), city of anc. Arcadia, Greece. Here Thebes defeated Sparta and Epaminondas was killed (362 B.C.).

mantis (män'tĭs), member of insect group usually considered a family (Mantidae) of order Orthoptera, found in most warm countries. Body is elongated and bears two pairs of wings. Mantis holds forelegs as though praying. Female often eats its smaller mate. Young hatch as wingless nymphs. See *ill.,* p. 469.

Mantua (män'choou, –toou), Ital. *Mantova,* city (pop. 36,489), Lombardy, N Italy, on the Mincio R. An Etruscan and later a Roman city, it became a free commune (12th cent.). The GONZAGA family gained power in 1328 and made Mantua a flourishing center of Renaissance culture. A duchy from 1530, it was contested after 1627 between the Nevers branch of the Gonzaga family (backed by France) and the Guastalla branch (backed by Spain). The Nevers branch won and held Mantua until its extinction (1708), when the duchy was annexed by Austria. After a period of French control (1797–1814), the strategic fortress reverted to Austria, which ceded it to Italy in 1866. Among the architectural treasures of Mantua are the Gonzaga palace (13th–18th cent.), with frescoes by Mantegna; the Palazzo del Te, created by Giulio Romano; the Church of Sant' Andrea, designed by Alberti; and the city hall (begun 1250). Vergil was born near Mantua.

Manu (mä'noo), in Hindu legend, a divinely inspired lawgiver. The Laws of Manu, compiled (probably between 200 B.C. and A.D. 200 from diverse ancient sources, govern Brahman ritual and daily life.

Manua (mänoo'ä), district (pop. 2,597), American Samoa, comprising Tau, Ofu, and Olosega islands; annexed 1899 by U.S. Cradle of their race, according to Samoan tradition.

Manuel, Byzantine emperors. **Manuel I** (Manuel Comnenus), c.1120–1180, succeeded his father John II in 1143. When the Second Crusade (1147–49) devastated his territories, he made a truce with the Seljuk Turks, thus leaving them free to defeat the Crusaders. His later diplomacy supported Pope Alexander III against Emperor Frederick I and aimed at the reunion of the Eastern and Western empires and churches. His crushing defeat by the Turks at Myriocephalon put an end to his ambitions (1176). He favored foreigners at his court and encouraged the settlement of Genoese, Pisan, and Venetian colonies at Constantinople. **Manuel II** (Manuel Palaeologus), 1348?–1425. During his reign (1391–1425) the Turks reduced the empire to Constantinople and its environs. Tamerlane's victory over Bajazet (1402) saved Constantinople from Turkish capture.

Manuel, kings of Portugal. **Manuel I,** 1469–1521, reigned 1495–1521. Under him Portugal reached the zenith of its colonial and commercial power, owing to such explorers as Vasco da GAMA and CABRAL and such commanders as Francisco de ALMEIDA and Alfonso de ALBUQUERQUE. Manuel reluctantly undertook measures for forcible conversion of the Jews (1496–97), causing many to emigrate, and he set a trend toward royal absolutism. **Manuel II,** 1889–1932, succeeded his father Charles I in 1908. In 1910 he was dethroned and a republic was estab. He spent his exile in England.

manure, any material used as fertilizer, especially barnyard manure. Green manure is a crop plowed under to improve soils.

manuscript, a handwritten work as distinguished from printing or typescript. Oldest manuscripts were on PAPYRUS; earliest extant dates probably to c.3500 B.C. Later PARCHMENT was much used (important parchment scrolls of Old Testament books written in 2d and 3d cent. B.C. were found in 1947 in Palestine). The science of dealing with old manuscripts, paleography, is highly technical; manuscripts are carefully compared to determine their age, history, and relationship to other manuscripts. Those of the Middle Ages were often illuminated in colors on vellum, a variety of parchment. PAPER was invented in China in 2d cent. A.D., but not known in Europe until 12th cent. Printed book dates from 15th cent. After that point manuscripts are of more importance for literary criticism than for other knowledge. See BOOK.

Manutius, Aldus: see ALDUS MANUTIUS.

Manville, borough (pop. 8,597), N central N.J., SW of Bound Brook. Asbestos products, textiles.

Manx (măngks), language of the Celtic subfamily of Indo-European languages. See LANGUAGE (table).

Manych Depression (mä′nĭch), lowland, SE European RSFSR, between the Lower Don and the Caspian Sea. It is drained by the Western Manych R., c.200 mi. long, a tributary of the Don, and by the Eastern Manych R., which flows c.100 mi. E to a system of salt lakes and marshes c.75 mi. W of the Caspian Sea. A canal linking the Don and the Caspian has been projected. Also spelled Manich.

Manzala, Egypt: see MENZALEH.

Manzanares (mänthänä′rĕs), river, c.55 mi. long, central Spain. Flows S past Madrid to the Jarama, a tributary of the Tagus.

Manzikert (măn′zĭkûrt), Turkish *Malazgirt,* village of E Turkey. Here in 1071 the Seljuk Turks under Alp Arslan routed and captured Emperor ROMANUS IV, thus gaining control of most of Asia Minor.

Manzoni, Alessandro (äles-sän′drō mändzō′nē), 1785– 1873, Italian author. The famous romantic novel *I promessi sposi* (1825–26; Eng. tr., *The Betrothed,* 1828), established him as a chief figure in Italian literature. He also wrote plays, notable religious poetry in *Inni sacri* (1812–22), and an ode, *Cinque Maggio* (1821), inspired by Napoleon's death.

Maori: see NEW ZEALAND.

Mao Tse-tung (mou′ dzŭ-dŏong′), 1893–, leader and a founder of Chinese Communist party. Chairman of central government council of Chinese People's Republic (estab. 1949).

Map, Walter, c.1140–c.1210, British writer and churchman, author of *De nugis curialium* (1181?–1193?), a Latin prose collection of legends, anecdotes, and court gossip told with wit and satire. Name also Mapes.

map, conventionalized picture of earth's surface pattern drawn on flat surface. Physical features, political or cultural features, or both, may be emphasized. Each point on map corresponds to geographic position in terms of a definite SCALE and PROJECTION. Cartography (i.e., map making) antedates art of writing. Present system was estab. by Greeks, especially Ptolemy, whose underestimation of earth's size was uncorrected until Mercator's age. Arabs carried on work, especially Idrisi (12th cent.). Rediscovery of Ptolemy's *Geographia,* invention of printing and engraving, and great voyages of discovery caused renaissance of cartography (c.1500). After 1750 many European governments undertook systematic mapping of their countries. In U.S. the Geological Survey (estab. 1879) has mapped much of the country. At Internatl. Geographical Congress meetings (1890, 1909, 1913) Albrecht Penck presented plans for a world map at uniform scale; work is only partly completed. Aerial photography is a valuable aid in map making.

maple, ornamental and useful tree of genus *Acer,* native to the N Hemisphere. Maples have deeply cut or lobed leaves. Sugar maple (*Acer saccharum*) furnishes bird's-eye and curly maple prized by cabinetmakers. Other North American species include red or swamp maple (*A. rubrum*), with red or orange foliage in autumn, and the fast-growing silver maple (*A. saccharinum*). The Norway maple (*A. platanoides*) is a European native while the small kinds with purple or red leaves are native to Japan. **Maple syrup** is the sap obtained chiefly from the sugar and black maple in early spring. Once a staple sweetening, its use is now mainly for confectionery and flavoring.

Maplewood. 1 Suburban city (pop. 13,416), E Mo., W of St. Louis; settled c.1865. **2** Suburban township (pop. 25,201), NE N.J., W of Newark. Map publishing.

map projection: see PROJECTION.

maquis (mäkē′), the brush country of Corsica; hence, the robber bands who hid out in the brush and, in World War II, the underground resistance in France under German occupation. Supplied with weapons parachuted by Allied planes, the *maquis* was organized into the FFI (French Forces of the Interior), which helped in the liberation of France (1944).

Mar, earls of. John Erskine, 1st earl of Mar, d. 1572, was regent of Scotland and had custody of young king James VI. His son, **John Erskine, 2d earl of Mar,** 1556 –1634, seized control of James VI in 1578. Later negotiated question of James's succession to English throne. **John Erskine, 6th earl of Mar,** 1675–1732, was Scottish leader of Jacobites. Played a leading part in promoting union of Scotland with England. His rebellion (1715) on behalf of Old Pretender failed and he fled to France.

marabou, large African bird of stork family. It has long legs, and a huge bill, is 4–5 ft. tall, with a 10-ft. wing spread. Adjutant bird of India is of same genus; their names are sometimes interchanged. Its elongated tail feathers were once popular as trimming in ladies' clothing.

Marabouts (mä′rŭbōōts) [Arabic,= devotee hermit], Berber Moslem sect which spread from NW Africa to Spain (11th–12th cent.). Venerated as saints, prophets, the Marabouts live in monasteries or attached to mosques.

Maracaibo (märäkī′bō), port (pop. 233,488), NW Venezuela, second largest city of Venezuela, at outlet of L. Maracaibo. Founded 1571, it was sacked five times by buccaneers in 17th cent. Foreign interests (British, Dutch, U.S.) in exploiting vast oil resources have brought about improvement in health conditions of city. Besides oil, exports include coffee, cacao, sugar, hardwoods.

Maracaibo, Lake, area c.5,000 sq. mi., NW Venezuela; discovered 1499 by Vespucci. Surrounding area is largely unexplored agriculturally, but since 1918 production of petroleum has been a vital activity here. Lake is major artery of communication for products, but the channel connecting it with Gulf of Venezuela is in places only 11 ft. deep, and goods must be transshipped at Maracaibo.

Marajó (märŭzhô'), island (c.150 mi. long and c.100 mi. wide; pop. 124,312), N Brazil, in mouth of Amazon, dividing river into Amazon proper and Pará R.

Maranhão (märänyä'ō), state (129,270 sq. mi.; pop. 1,600,396), NE Brazil; cap. São Luis. Fronts on Atlantic in N and has low, hot coastal plain where most of population lives. Babassu nuts (processed for vegetable oil) are important product. In S, in fertile valleys, cotton, sugar, rice, and tobacco are grown. French settled here in 1612 but were displaced by Portuguese (1615).

Marañón (märänyōn'), river, a headstream of the Amazon, rising in central Peru, flowing NNE through Andes almost to Ecuador, then NE and E to Ucayali R. Often considered part of Amazon proper. Descended by Ursúa (1560).

maraschino (mä"rŭskē'nō), liqueur prepared from a sour cherry of Dalmatia. **Maraschino cherry** is the name given to cherries preserved in maraschino or in imitation syrup.

Marat, Jean Paul (zhä' pôl' märä'), 1743–93, French revolutionist, b. Switzerland. A physician and scientist, he turned toward politics in 1789, founding the journal *L'Ami du peuple* [the friend of the people], in which he attacked everybody in power with vicious virulence. After its suppression, he published the paper secretly. His articles were instrumental in the overthrow of the monarchy (Sept., 1792). Elected to the Convention, he was a leader of the extremist CORDELIERS and waged deadly war on the GIRONDISTS. A skin disease forced him to spend much of his time in a warm bath. He was in his bath when Charlotte CORDAY stabbed him to death.

Marathas: see MAHRATTAS.

Marathi (mŭrä'tē), language of the Indic group of the Indo-Iranian subfamily of Indo-European languages. See LANGUAGE (table).

Marathon (mär'ŭthŏn), village and plain, anc. Greece, NE of Athens. Here the Athenians defeated the Persians in 490 B.C. (see PERSIAN WARS). A runner was sent to bear news of the victory to Athens, and from his run is derived the name of the **marathon race**, a long-distance run standardized (1908) as 26 mi. and 385 yd. It was first included in the Olympic games in 1896.

Marble, Alice, 1913–, American tennis player. U.S. women's singles champion (1936, 1938–40).

marble, limestone composed of calcite or dolomite crystals, this structure resulting from extreme metamorphism. Sometimes is snow white, but color varies widely because of impurities, which add greatly to beauty of stone when polished. Used for statuary, monuments, public buildings. Found in British Isles, Belgium, France, Germany, Italy, Greece, U.S. Finest U.S. marble comes from Vt., though other states are important producers.

Marblehead, town (pop. 13,765), NE Mass., on the coast NE of Boston; settled 1629. Long-time fishing port; resort since 19th cent.; yachting center. Has Revolutionary Fort Sewall and graves of many Revolutionary soldiers.

marbling, process of coloring sides, edges, or end papers of books to suggest marble patterns. Colors are arranged on a liquid surface to which book surfaces are applied. In tree marbling, in which the effect suggests a tree trunk and branches, liquid colors are run over a surface bent to form a trough.

Marburg (mär'bŏork) or **Marburg an der Lahn** (än dĕr län'), city (pop. 39,256), Hesse, W Germany, in former Electoral Hesse, on the Lahn R. Its medieval castle, which dominates the picturesque city, was the residence of the landgraves of Hesse 13th–17th cent. Philip of Hesse founded (1527) its famous Protestant university. In 1529 LUTHER and ZWINGLI met at the castle in the Marburg Colloquy, sponsored by Philip, but reached no agreement. St. Elizabeth of Hungary is buried in the fine Gothic church dedicated to her; in 1946 she came into profane company when the bodies of Hindenburg and of Frederick William I and Frederick II of Prussia were transferred here.

Marburg, Yugoslavia: see MARIBOR.

Marbury vs. Madison, case, decided 1803 by U.S. Supreme Court. Involved one of Pres. John Adams's "midnight appointments" which new administration failed to carry through. The opinion, written by Chief Justice John Marshall, was first Supreme Court decision authorizing all courts to review constitutionality of legislation.

Marc, Franz (fränts' märk'), 1880–1916, German postimpressionist painter. Evolved a style dominated by colorful crystallike patterns.

Marc Antony, Roman general: see ANTONY.

Marcel, Étienne (ätyĕn' märsĕl'), d. 1358, French popular leader; merchants' provost of Paris. He won from the dauphin (later Charles V) enormous concessions to the States-General (*Grande Ordonnance*, 1357). Charles soon revoked his concessions; Marcel, in alliance with Charles II of Navarre, was preparing Paris for resistance to the dauphin when he was assassinated.

Marcellus, Marcus Claudius (märsĕl'ŭs), c.268–208 B.C., Roman consul. In the Second Punic War he besieged Syracuse and captured it (212 B.C.); he also took Capua from the Carthaginians (211). Plutarch wrote his biography.

March, earls of: see MORTIMER, family.

March, river, Czechoslovakia: see MORAVA.

March: see MONTH.

Marche (märsh), region and former province, central France, in Creuse and Haute-Vienne depts.; part of the Massif Central. Towns: Guéret, Aubusson. Agr., sheep raising. A border fief (march) of old Aquitaine, it passed to Lusignan family in 13th cent. and later to the house of Bourbon. Was annexed to royal domain 1527.

Marches, the, Ital. *Marche,* region (3,744 sq. mi.; pop. 1,278,071), central Italy, between Apennines and Mediterranean; cap. Ancona. Agr., vineyards. Region was included in Pepin's donation to the popes, but after the 10th cent. the emperors granted fiefs in the area (the marches of Ancona, Fermo, and Camerino), while several cities (e.g., Urbino, Pesaro) were ruled by local dynasties. Reconquest by the popes was completed 16th–17th cent.; Marches formed part of Papal States until their annexation (1860) by Sardinia.

Marchfeld (märkh'fĕlt"), strategic plain, Lower Austria, NE of Vienna, between Danube and Morava (Ger. *March*) rivers. Here OTTOCAR II of Bohemia defeated Bela IV of Hungary (1260); Rudolf I defeated Ottocar II (1278); and Archduke Charles of Austria defeated Napoleon I (battle of Aspern, 1809, followed by Napoleon's victory at Wagram).

Marcian (mär'shŭn), c.390–457, East Roman emperor (450–57). Convoked Council of CHALCEDON (451). Refused to pay tribute to ATTILA.

Marcion (mär'shŭn), fl. 144, founder of Marcionites, first great heresy to rival Catholicism. Taught a dualism like that of GNOSTICISM and rejected the God of the Old Testament entirely. Stressed ascetic practices and influenced Manichaeism, which finally absorbed Marcionism.

Marconi, Guglielmo, Marchese (gōōlyĕl'mō märkä'-zä märkō'nē), 1874–1937, Italian physicist. Shared 1909 Nobel Prize in Physics for development of wireless telegraphy. His achievement based on earlier work on electromagnetic waves. Transmitted long-wave signals in 1895, transatlantic signals in 1901.

Marco Polo: see POLO, MARCO.

Marcos de Niza (mär'kōs dä nē'sä), c.1495–1558, missionary explorer in Spanish North America; a Franciscan friar who served in Peru, Guatemala, and Mexico. Headed expedition (1539) into territory N of present Sonora in search of rich Indian cities about which Cabeza de Vaca reported to Viceroy Antonio de Mendoza. The friar's stories of fabulous Seven Cities of Cíbola confirmed Cabeza de Vaca's stories, but were proved wrong by the expedition of Coronado (1540).

Marcus Aurelius (mär′kŭs ôrē′lēŭs), 121–180, Roman emperor (161–180) and Stoic philosopher; nephew of Faustina, wife of Antoninus Pius, who adopted him; husband of Faustina, daughter of Antoninus. Succeeded with Lucius Verus in 161, became sole emperor 169. Devoted himself to defending the empire and was successful. He is, however, best remembered for his philosophic *Meditations,* notable for epigrammatic, classic expression.

Marcus Hook, borough (pop. 3,843), SE Pa., on Delaware R. and SW of Philadelphia. Oil refining. Was rendezvous of Blackbeard and other pirates.

Marcus Island, volcanic island, area 1 sq. mi., W Pacific, 700 nautical mi. E of Bonin Isls. Discovered 1896 by Japanese; annexed 1899 by Japan. Had naval and air bases in World War II. Under U.S. military rule since end of war.

Marcy, William Learned, 1786–1857, American statesman. U.S. Senator from N.Y. (1831–32). Term "spoils system" supposedly originated from speech of his defending practice. U.S. Secretary of War (1845–49); U.S. Secretary of State (1853–57).

Marcy, Mount: see ADIRONDACK MOUNTAINS.

Mar del Plata (mär′ dhĕl plä′tä), city (pop. 114,729), Buenos Aires prov., Argentina; fashionable Atlantic coast resort.

Mardi Gras (mär′dē grä′), French name for Shrove Tuesday. As last day before Lent, it was occasion for merrymaking in Middle Ages. Many cities (e.g., New Orleans, Rio de Janeiro, Nice, and Cologne) preserve the custom and now hold elaborate carnivals for several days before Mardi Gras itself.

Marduk: see BABYLONIAN RELIGION.

Maree, Loch (lŏkh mŭrē′), lake (13½ mi. long and 2 mi. wide), Ross and Cromarty co., Scotland.

Mare Island: see VALLEJO, Calif.

Marengo (mùrĕng′gō), village, Piedmont, NW Italy. Scene of famous victory of French under Bonaparte over Austrians under Melas (June 14, 1800).

Margaret, 1353–1412, queen of Denmark, Norway, and Sweden; daughter of Waldemar IV of Denmark. Married to Haakon VI of Norway in 1363, she ruled as regent for her son Olaf (in Denmark from 1375; in Norway after Haakon's death, 1380). After Olaf's death (1387), she defeated the Swedish king, Albert of Mecklenburg (1389) and persuaded the Danish, Norwegian, and Swedish diets to accept her grandnephew, Eric of Pomerania, as king. He was crowned at Kalmar, and the KALMAR UNION of the three kingdoms was drawn up (1397). Eric was actually a puppet king; Margaret remained the real ruler. She governed autocratically and sought to consolidate and centralize her vast empire.

Margaret (Rose), 1930–, British princess, daughter of George VI and only sister of Elizabeth II.

Margaret Maid of Norway, 1283–90, queen of Scotland (1286–90), daughter of Eric II of Norway and granddaughter of Alexander III of Scotland. Her death led to great civil war of Scotland over succession.

Margaret Mary, Saint, 1647–90, French nun, promoter of the cult of the Sacred Heart in the Roman Catholic Church. Her family name was Alacoque. Canonized 1920. Feast: Oct. 17.

Margaret Maultasch (moul′täsh) [Ger.,= pocket mouth], 1318–69, countess of Tyrol (1335–63). After a turbulent reign, in the course of which she divorced one husband and buried another, she abdicated and left Tyrol to the Hapsburgs. In popular legend she is known as the Ugly Duchess, a woman of great evil power. Her portrait was Tenniel's model for the "duchess" in *Alice in Wonderland.*

Margaret of Angoulême: see MARGARET OF NAVARRE.

Margaret of Anjou (än′jōō), 1430?–1482, queen consort of HENRY VI of England. Became highly unpopular by her autocratic rule through the feeble king. Struggle between followers of Richard, duke of York, and king's supporters grew into Wars of the ROSES

(1455). Eventually captured (1471), she returned to France and died in poverty.

Margaret of Austria, 1480–1530, daughter of Emperor Maximilian I and Mary of Burgundy. She was regent of the Netherlands and guardian of her nephew, the later Emperor Charles V, 1507–15. After 1518 she again governed the Netherlands for Charles and was one of his most influential advisers. She ruled with wisdom and moderation. In 1529 she negotiated the Treaty of CAMBRAI.

Margaret of Navarre or **Margaret of Angoulême** (ăgōōläm′), 1492–1549, queen of Navarre; sister of Francis I of France. Her second husband was Henri d'Albret, titular king of Navarre. She was a patron of Marot and Rabelais and wrote the *Heptameron* (72 stories in Boccaccio's manner), a classic of French Renaissance literature.

Margaret of Parma, 1522–86, natural daughter of Emperor Charles V. She became duchess of Parma by marriage to Ottavio Farnese (1538) and governed the Netherlands 1559–67 for her half-brother, Philip II of Spain. Following a conciliatory policy, she secured the recall of the unpopular Cardinal GRANVELLE (1564) but was firm toward the Flemish national party and its leaders, Count Egmont and William the Silent. In 1567 ALBA arrived at Brussels to put down opposition by force. Margaret, opposing Alba's harsh policy, resigned.

Margaret of Scotland, Saint, d. 1093, queen of Scotland; wife of MALCOLM III and sister of Edgar Atheling. Promoted church reform and founded new monasteries, creating a pro-English trend in Scotland.

Margaret of Valois (välwä′), 1553–1615, queen of France and Navarre, daughter of Henry II; called Queen Margot. Married Henry of Navarre (later HENRY IV of France) 1572; the wedding was the prelude to the massacre of SAINT BARTHOLOMEW'S DAY. Her intrigues and notorious immorality caused her banishment from Paris (1583) and, after she attempted an armed rebellion, her confinement at the castle of Usson (1587–1605). Her marriage was annulled 1599, and she later was permitted to return to Paris. At Usson she assembled a prominent literary circle. Her memoirs, letters, and other writings show considerable talent.

Margaret Tudor, 1489–1541, queen of James IV of Scotland, daughter of Henry VII and sister of Henry VIII of England. After James's death she married Archibald Douglas, 6th earl of Angus. Played large part in Scottish politics, her affiliations varying with her personal interest.

margarine (mär′jŭrēn), artificial butter, an emulsified blend of edible vegetable oils or animal fats. In U.S., most margarine is made from refined cottonseed and soybean oils, churned, usually with milk, salted, and sometimes colored yellow. Commonly fortified with vitamin A, it is similar to butter in composition and in nutritional qualities. Oleomargarine is its legal designation in U.S.

Margarita (märgärē′tä), island (43 mi. long, 22 mi. wide), off coast of N Venezuela. Discovered (1498) by Columbus, was important pearl fishing center. With surrounding islands forms state of Nueva Esparta, of which La Asunción (pop. 4,502), is cap.

Margate (mär′gĭt), municipal borough (pop. 42,487), Isle of Thanet, Kent, England; seaport and resort.

Margelan (mŭrgyĭlän′), city (pop. 44,327), Uzbek SSR, in Fergana Valley. Silk mfg. since 10th cent.

Marggraf, Andreas Sigismund (ändrā′äs zē′gĭsmōont märk′gräf), 1709–82, German pioneer in analytical chemistry. He isolated zinc, improved method of producing phosphorus, discovered beet sugar.

margin, an amount of cash placed with a broker for speculation in securities. It forms a percentage of the money involved, the broker supplying the balance. By the Securities Exchange Act (1934) the Federal Reserve Board can control speculation by fixing the percentage of the margin.

marginal unit, in economics, the last unit of a given commodity that an owner will sell and a purchaser will buy. It is said to have marginal utility. Marginal land is land that barely repays the cost of labor and capital applied to its cultivation.

marguerite, daisylike perennial (*Chrysanthemum frutescens*) of Canary Isls. It is grown in pots by florists. Paris daisy is another name.

Maria (mürē′ù), queens of Portugal. **Maria I,** 1734–1816, daughter of Joseph I, was married to her uncle, who became joint ruler with her as Peter III (1777). They began their reign with the dismissal of POMBAL. After Peter's death (1786) she ruled alone, but by 1792 she had become insane, and her son (later John VI) assumed the regency. **Maria II** (Maria da Gloria), 1819–53, became queen in 1826, when her father abdicated the Portuguese throne to become emperor of Brazil as PEDRO I. She was betrothed to her uncle, Dom MIGUEL, who deposed her in 1828. Maria was taken to England but regained her throne in 1834, after the victory of the liberal forces, led by her father and assisted by England. The rest of her reign was marked by chronic revolutions. Her second husband, Ferdinand of Saxe-Coburg, ruled jointly with her as Ferdinand II after 1837; her son Louis I succeeded her.

Maria Christina, 1806–78, queen of Spain, fourth consort of Ferdinand VII. Her regency (1833–40) for her daughter ISABELLA II was troubled by the revolt of the CARLISTS and was overthrown by ESPARTERO. She later regained much influence at her daughter's court.

Maria Christina, 1858–1929, queen of Spain, consort of Alfonso XII. During her regency (1885–1902) for her son Alfonso XIII, Spain lost the Spanish-American War.

María Luisa (lwē′sä), 1751–1819, queen of Spain, consort of CHARLES IV. Dissolute and domineering, she, with her lover GODOY, controlled the government. She shared her husband's internment (1808–14).

Mariamne (mārēäm′nē), d. 29 B.C., one of Herod the Great's 10 wives, greatly loved by him. After false accusations by Herod's sister, Herod had her murdered.

Mariana, Juan de (hwän′ dä märyä′nä), 1536?–1623?, Spanish historian, political philosopher. Known for *Historiae de rebus Hispaniae* and *De rege et regis institutione*, which condoned tyrannicide.

Marianao (märyänä′ō), city (pop. 120,163), NW Cuba; practically a suburb of Havana.

Marianas Islands (märēä′näs), island group (370 sq. mi.; pop. c.29,700), W Pacific, 1,500 mi. E of Philippines, extending in 500-mi. chain from N to S. Chief islands are GUAM, Saipan, and Tinian. Sugar cane, coffee, and coconuts are produced. Inhabited by Japanese, Chamorros, and Micronesians. Discovered 1521 by Magellan, group was named the Marianas by Spanish Jesuits arriving in 1668. A Spanish possession, 1668–1898, group was sold to Germany in 1899, except Guam, which became U.S. possession. Japan occupied German islands 1914, received mandate 1922, claimed them as possession 1935. Captured 1944 by U.S. forces. In 1947, group (exclusive of Guam) was included in U.S. Trust Territory of the Pacific Isls. under UN trusteeship.

Marianna, city (pop. 5,845), NW Fla., NW of Tallahassee. Lumber mills and limestone quarries.

Marianske Lazne, Czechoslovakia: see MARIENBAD.

Maria Theresa, Ger. *Maria Theresia,* 1717–80, empress as consort of FRANCIS I (reigned 1745–65), queen of Bohemia and Hungary (1740–80); daughter of Emperor Charles VI. She succeeded to the Hapsburg lands under the PRAGMATIC SANCTION but had to defend her rights in the War of the AUSTRIAN SUCCESSION (1740–48) and the SEVEN YEARS WAR (1756–63). She lost most of Silesia to Prussia but won S Poland in the Polish partition of 1772, which she signed with tears while helping herself generously. With her chancellor, KAUNITZ, she governed ably and shrewdly; her reign was an era of prosperity. Though conservative

and devoutly Catholic, she cooperated in agrarian and other reforms with her son, JOSEPH II, with whom she shared her power after he became emperor in 1765. A model wife and mother (of 16 children) and a kindhearted ruler, she was very popular. During her reign Vienna became, with Gluck and Mozart, the foremost musical center of Europe.

Mari Autonomous Soviet Socialist Republic (mä′rē), administrative division (8,900 sq. mi.; pop. 579,456), E central European RSFSR, in middle Volga valley; cap. Ioshkar-Ola. Forests; agr. The Mari (over half of pop.), formerly called Cheremiss, are a Finnic people. The rest of the inhabitants are mostly Russians. Dominated by the Eastern Bulgars 9th–12th cent., later by the Golden Horde, the region was conquered by Ivan IV in 1552.

Maribor (mä′rĭbôr), Ger. *Marburg,* city (pop. 66,498), Slovenia, N Yugoslavia, on Drava R. Mfg. center (cars, textiles, leather, chemicals). Belonged to Styria (Austria) until 1919. Has Gothic cathedral (R.C.), Renaissance city hall.

Marie, 1875–1938, queen of Rumania, consort of Ferdinand I; daughter of Alfred, duke of Edinburgh and of Saxe-Coburg-Gotha (a son of Victoria of England). She helped to bring Rumania into the Allied camp in World War I; served as Red Cross nurse. She traveled widely, visiting U.S. in 1926. Wrote novels and autobiography (in English).

Marie Antoinette (ăntùnĕt′, ătwänĕt′), 1755–93, queen of France, consort of Louis XVI; daughter of Emperor Francis I and Maria Theresa. Distrusted because of her Austrian origin and finding in Louis a most inadequate husband, the beautiful young queen threw herself into a life of pleasure and careless extravagance. She probably had no share in the Affair of the DIAMOND NECKLACE, but this and other scandals, as well as the greed of her favorites, increased her unpopularity. She contributed to the dismissal of Turgot (1776), was hostile to Necker's economy measures, and showed little understanding of the problems of her time. The famous solution to the bread famine —"Let them eat cake"—is, however, unjustly attributed to her. After the birth of her first son she became more sedate and responsible. She probably had little influence on the king's policy during the first two years of the FRENCH REVOLUTION. After 1791, when the royal couple had failed in its attempted flight, the king's apathy forced her to conduct negotiations with MIRABEAU and BARNAVE. At the same time, she secretly urged Austrian intervention, and it is generally held that she betrayed the French campaign plans for 1792 to the enemy. She was imprisoned in the Temple and, after Louis's execution, in the Conciergerie. Convicted of treason, she was guillotined Oct. 16. The brutality to which she was subjected during her last months (particularly the sadistic pleasure her jailers took in informing her of the mistreatment of her child, LOUIS XVII) and the unfairness of her trial dwarf any of the faults she thus expiated. She faced her martyrdom with noble and heroic firmness.

Marie Byrd Land, Antarctic area, E of Ross Shelf Ice and Ross Sea and S of Amundsen Sea. Discovered and claimed for U.S. by Richard E. Byrd 1929.

Marie Caroline, 1752–1814, queen of the Two Sicilies, consort of Ferdinand I; daughter of Empress Maria Theresa. With her favorites, Sir John ACTON and Emma, Lady HAMILTON, she was a center of intrigues.

Marie de France (dù fräs′), fl. 1185, French poet who lived in England. She wrote a dozen lais, based on Celtic sources, with love as main theme.

Marie de' Medici (mĕd′ĭchē), 1573–1642, queen of France; daughter of Francesco de' Medici, grand duke of Tuscany. Became second wife of Henry IV in 1600 and was regent for her son Louis XIII after Henry's assassination (1610). With her favorite CONCINI she dissipated the treasury and adopted a pro-Hapsburg policy. Though banished after Concini's murder (1617), she was reconciled to her son in 1622. In 1630 her former favorite, Cardinal RICHELIEU, had her exiled from court; in 1631 she fled to the Netherlands, never to return. She was the mother of Queen Henrietta Maria of England.

Marie Leszczynska (lĕshchĭn'skŭ), 1703–68, queen of France; daughter of STANISLAUS I of Poland. Married Louis XV 1725; bore him 10 children.

Marie Louise, 1791–1847, empress of the French; daughter of Emperor Francis I of Austria. She was married to NAPOLEON I in 1810, bore him a son (see NAPOLEON II), and abandoned him in 1814. The Congress of Vienna made her duchess of Parma, Piacenza, and Guastalla, which she ruled ineptly from 1816 till her death. In 1821 she married, morganatically, her lover Count Neipperg. After his death she married another Austrian count, Bombelles.

Marienbad (märĕ'ŭnbät), Czech *Mariánské Lázně,* spa (pop. 6,027), NW Bohemia, Czechoslovakia. Has noted mineral springs and baths.

Marienburg (märĕ'ŭnbo͞ork), Pol. *Malbork,* town (pop. 10,017), former East Prussia; transferred to Polish administration 1945. Founded 1274 by Teutonic Knights; became seat of their grand master 1309; was sold to Poland 1457; passed to Prussia 1772. Its Gothic castle (14th cent.; restored 19th cent.) is a magnificent example of German secular medieval architecture.

Marie Thérèse of Austria (märĕ' tärĕz'), 1638–83, queen of France, consort of Louis XIV; daughter of Philip IV of Spain. Her marriage (1660) had been stipulated in the Peace of the Pyrenees. Louis neglected her for a series of mistresses.

Marietta (mârēĕt'ŭ). **1** City (pop. 20,687), NW Ga., NW of Atlanta. Mfg. of hosiery, furniture, prefabricated houses, and aircraft. A national cemetery is here. Just W is Kennesaw Mt. Natl. Battlefield Park, commemorating a Union defeat 1864. **2** City (pop. 16,006), SE Ohio, at junction of Muskingum and Ohio rivers. First permanent settlement in Old Northwest, founded 1788 among mound builders' earthworks by Ohio Company of Associates. Grew as shipbuilding and shipping center for agr. area. Now has mfg. of metal products and chemicals. Seat of Marietta Col. (coed.; 1835). Intercollegiate regatta held here 1950 and 1951. Preserved are Gen. Putnam's house (in Campus Martius Memorial State Mus.) and land office.

Mariette, Auguste Édouard (märyĕt'), 1821–81, French Egyptologist. Directed excavations in pyramid fields.

Marignano, battle of, 1515, victory of Francis I of France and his Venetian allies over the Swiss. One of the bloodiest engagements of the Italian Wars, it was fought near Marignano (now Melegnano), a town SE of Milan. As a result, Massimiliano Sforza lost Milan to the French and the Swiss gave up further military ventures.

marigold, widely grown annual (*Tagetes*) with colorful yellow, orange, or maroon and gold flowers. The large-flowered African and smaller French types are derived from native Mexican species. Marsh marigold and pot marigold (*Calendula*) are unrelated.

marihuana: see MARIJUANA.

Mariinsk System (mürĕ'ĭnsk), inland navigation route, NW European RSFSR, linking the Neva R. with the Volga at Shcherbakov by way of several lesser rivers and several canals. It makes possible uninterrupted navigation from the Baltic to the Caspian Sea and is also connected with the Northern Dvina and thus with the White Sea.

marijuana or **marihuana** (both: märŭwä'nŭ, –hwä'nŭ, mä–), habit-forming drug obtained from HEMP plant. Effects combine excitation and depression. Sale illicit.

Marin, John (mä'rĭn), 1870–, American landscape painter, best known as a water-colorist.

marine biology, study of plants and animals of the sea and their relationship to each other and their environment. Marine organisms may be grouped by mode of life as nekton (swimming, freely migrating animals), plankton (floating, drifting plants or animals), and

benthos (plants or animals living on sea bottom, including sessile forms, creeping organisms, burrowing animals). Distribution depends on chemical and physical properties, circulation, and light penetration of sea water; plants exist only to c.300 ft. See also OCEANOGRAPHY.

marine engine has heavier construction than engine for land use. So-called reduction gearing, enabling high-speed engine operation (for economy) and low propeller speed (for efficiency), developed with the steam turbine. Also used are reciprocating steam engine, Diesel engine, and gasoline engine. See *ill.,* p. 303.

marine insurance: see INSURANCE.

marines, troops usually having ranks comparable to those of the army and serving on board warships or in conjunction with naval operations. The Continental Marines, established in 1775, fought in the American Revolution. The present U.S. Marine Corps was created by Congress in 1798. It was incorporated into the Navy in 1947 as a complete operating unit.

Marinette (märĭnĕt'), city (pop. 14,178), NE Wis., on Green Bay at mouth of Menominee R. (bridged to Menominee, Mich.). Fisheries, dairy plants, and paper mills.

Marinetti, Filippo Tommaso (fēlēp'pō tōmmä'zō märĕnĕt'tē), 1876–1944, Italian author, founder of futurism, a movement to glorify the dynamic character of the 20th-cent. machine age, together with war and danger; an early advocate of Fascism.

Marino, Giovanni Battista (jōvän'nē bät-tē'stä märĕ'nō), 1569–1625, Italian poet, noted for elaborately florid style, called *marinismo,* which influenced literature of several countries.

Marion, Francis, c.1732–1795, American partisan leader in Revolution. Organized cavalry troop (1780) which conducted guerrilla warfare against British in S.C. Known as the Swamp Fox.

Marion. 1 City (pop. 10,459), S Ill., NNE of Cairo. Mining and shipping center in agr. (fruit, grain) and coal area. **2** City (pop. 30,081), E central Ind., NNW of Muncie; settled 1826. Farm trade center near gas and oil fields. Mfg. of glass and metal products and paper. **3** City (pop. 5,916), E central Iowa, just NE of Cedar Rapids. Railroad division point. **4** City (pop. 33,817), central Ohio, N of Columbus; laid out 1821. Rail and agr. trade center with mfg. of steam shovels, farm and road-construction machinery, and metal products. Home of W. G. Harding now a museum. **5** Town (pop. 6,834), E.S.C., E of Florence. Lumbering, farming, and cotton processing. **6** Town (pop. 6,982), SW Va., in Holston R. valley. Lumber, grain, and textile milling, and limestone quarrying. Near by are White Top Mt. (with annual music festival) and Mt. Rogers.

Marion, Fort: see SAINT AUGUSTINE, Fla.

marionette: see PUPPET.

Mariposa (mä"rĭpō'zù), town, central Calif. A boom town of the Mother Lode in the gold rush, it is today a gateway to Yosemite Natl. Park.

Mariposa lily, bulbous plant of genus *Calochortus* with tuliplike flowers in spring. It is native to the U.S. and is also called butterfly tulip.

Maris (mä'rĭs), three Dutch painters, who were brothers. Jacob or Jakob Maris, 1837–99, the most famous, produced some of finest landscape paintings of The Hague school. Matthew or Matthijs Maris, 1839–1917, and William or Willem Maris, 1844–1910, are also best known for their landscapes.

Maritain, Jacques (märētĕ'), 1882–, French neo-Thomist philosopher. Converted to Catholicism in 1916, he broadened the teachings of St. Thomas Aquinas and applied them to various fields of modern life, as in *An Introduction to Philosophy* (1923–30), *True Humanism* (1938), and *Christianity and Democracy* (1944).

Maritime Commission, United States, estab. 1936 by Congress. Replaced U.S. Shipping Board. Designed to develop a merchant fleet capable of serving as a naval and military auxiliary in time of war or national emergency, and to provide essential shipping service at all times.

maritime law, system of law concerning navigation and overseas commerce. Agreements between states on shipping began in ancient days and created a body of customs and usages which in the late Middle Ages was incorporated under influence of Roman laws into such collections as the *Consolato del Mare, The Law of Oléron,* and the English *Black Book of the Admiralty.* In England admiralty courts grew up but were more and more restricted until abolished in 1873. In the U.S. maritime cases (except for collision at sea) are under Federal jurisdiction.

Maritime Provinces, the Atlantic seaboard provinces of NOVA SCOTIA, NEW BRUNSWICK, and PRINCE EDWARD ISLAND in E CANADA. As part of New France this region was called ACADIA. Before Canadian confederation (1867) these provinces were politically distinct from Canada proper.

Maritime Territory, Rus. *Primorski Krai,* administrative division (64,900 sq. mi.; pop. c.1,475,000), RSFSR, between Manchuria and Sea of Japan; cap. Vladivostok. Has densely wooded coastal range rich in minerals (lead, zinc, tin, molybdenum). Coal mines in S. Important fisheries on coast. Population is Russian and Ukrainian with Korean, Chinese, and Mongol minorities. For history, see FAR EASTERN TERRITORY.

Maritsa (märē′tsä), river, c.300 mi. long, rising in Bulgaria and flowing SE and S, partly along Greek-Turkish border, into the Aegean Sea. Plovdiv and Adrianople lie on its course.

Maritzburg, South Africa: see PIETERMARITZBURG.

Mariupol, Ukraine: see ZHDANOV.

Marius, Caius, c.155 B.C.–86 B.C., Roman general, a plebeian. He was seven times consul and won a reputation in wars against Jugurtha (under Quintus Metellus and then as sole commander) and against the Germans. The rival of SULLA, he was reputed to be the friend of the people. When Sulla got the command against Mithridates VI, Marius fled, but returned to seize Rome with the help of CINNA, and butchered his opponents. Civil war followed, and Sulla triumphed with much bloodshed. Julius Caesar, nephew of Marius' wife, was much influenced by him.

Marivaux, Pierre de (pyĕr′ dù märēvō′), 1688–1763, French dramatist. His love comedies—e.g., *Le Jeu de l'amour et du hazard* (1730), *Le Legs* (1736), *Les Fausses Confidences* (1737)—are remarkable for extreme psychological refinement and for a lightness and simplicity bordering on artificiality.

marjoram: see SWEET MARJORAM.

Mark, Saint, friend and companion of St. Peter, St. Paul, and St. Luke; since 2d cent. regarded as author of the Gospel according to St. Mark. His full name was John Mark. His mother is thought to have owned house where Last Supper was held. Acts 12.12,25; 13.5; 15.37–39; Col. 4.10,11; Philemon 24; 2 Tim. 4.11; 1 Peter 5.13. He is the patron of Venice. His symbol is a lion. Feast: April 25.

Mark, Gospel according to Saint, book of New Testament, shortest and simplest of the Gospels. Only Gospel to have no passage unparalleled in another Gospel; many critics hold that it was the first composed. It narrates the life of Jesus from his baptism by John the Baptist to the passion and resurrection. See also SYNOPTIC GOSPELS.

Markham, Sir Clements Robert, 1830–1916, English geographer and writer. Directed India Office geographical work (1867–77). Authority on Inca civilization. Wrote biographies, books of his travels.

Markham, Edwin, 1852–1940, American poet, noted for "The Man with a Hoe" (1899).

Markiewicz, Con(stance Georgine Gore-Booth), Countess (märkyä′vĭts), 1884?–1927, Irish patriot. Sentenced to death for her part in the 1916 rebellion, she was later released. Served in the Sinn Fein parliament

(1918–22) and also in the Dáil Éireann (1923–27).

Markova, Alicia (märkō′vù, mär′kùvù), 1910–, English ballet dancer, whose real name is Lilian Alicia Marks. She combines ethereal quality with strong technique; her most famous role is Giselle.

marl, a clay soil mixed with carbonate of lime, sometimes shells of minute invertebrates. Valued as dressing and fertilizer, for correcting soil acidity and making it lighter.

Marlboro, city (pop. 15,756), E Mass., W of Boston. Mfg. of shoes, lamps, paper, metal products.

Marlborough, John Churchill, 1st duke of (märl′bùrù), 1650–1722, English general and statesman, one of greatest military commanders of history. Under James II he crushed the rebellion of the duke of Monmouth. Supported William III against James II; later gave secret aid to Jacobites. Won countless victories in War of SPANISH SUCCESSION. His wife, Sarah Jennings (1660–1744), was influential friend of Queen ANNE (in whose reign his power was greatest). With GODOLPHIN he turned to the Whigs who favored the war. The Whigs fell in 1711, and he and his wife were dismissed. On accession of George I in 1714 he again commanded the army.

Marlborough, municipal borough (pop. 4,556), Wiltshire, England. Marlborough Col. (built 1843) has grounds said to contain body of Merlin, of Arthurian Legend.

Marlborough House, in London, on Pall Mall. Built 1710 by Wren for duchess of Marlborough. Residence of dowager Queen Mary.

Marlin, city (pop. 7,099), E central Texas, SE of Waco and near Brazos R. Resort with mineral springs (ships mineral crystals) and hospitals.

Marlowe, Christopher, 1564–93, English dramatist and poet. Leader of a "radical" group, he was accused of atheism and blasphemy, and possibly a plot led to his being stabbed to death by a drinking companion. For dramatic power and development of blank verse into most expressive English meter, he is regarded as greatest Elizabethan playwright next to Shakspere. Among his powerful poetic dramas are *Tamburlaine* (c.1587), *Dr. Faustus* (c.1588), *The Jew of Malta* (c.1589), and *Edward II* (c.1592).

Marlowe, Julia, 1865?–1950, American actress, b. England, whose real name was Sarah Frances Frost. Played Shaksperian roles (e.g., Juliet) opposite her second husband, E. H. SOTHERN.

marmalade (mär′mùlād), a thick, tart preserve of fruit pulp (often citrus) similar to jam.

Marmara or **Marmora, Sea of,** anc. *Propontis,* area c.4,300 sq. mi., between Europe and Asia; connected with the Black Sea through the BOSPORUS and with the Mediterranean through the DARDANELLES. Its shores belong entirely to Turkey.

Mármol, José (hōsā′ mär′mōl), 1817–71, Argentine romantic writer. He was exiled to Montevideo because of opposition to Rosas. His novel *Amalia* (1851–55) depicts the tyranny of Rosas.

Marmont, Auguste Frédéric Louis Viesse de (ōgüst′ frädärēk′ lwē′vyĕs′ dù märmō′), 1774–1852, marshal of France. For his part in the battle of Wagram (1809) Napoleon made him duke of Ragusa and governor of Illyria. Succeeding Masséna in the Peninsular War, he was defeated at Salamanca (1812). In 1814 he made a convention with the allies which made Napoleon's military position hopeless. He supported the Bourbon restoration.

Marmora, Sea of: see MARMARA, SEA OF.

marmoset (mär′mùzĕt), small arboreal monkey (*Callithrix*) of Central and South America. It is squirrel-size and has a long, hairy tail and clawed feet.

marmot (mär′mùt), rodent (*Marmota*) allied to squirrel. It has a stout body, rounded ears, strong digging claws, and coarse fur, chiefly brown (often white-tipped). Lives in burrows and hibernates. Chiefly Old World marmot skins used in fur trade. See also WOODCHUCK.

Marmousets (märmōozā') [Fr.,= little fellows], ministers of Charles V of France, so called by the royal princes because of their humble origin. CLISSON was the most prominent. They again held power under Charles VI, 1388–92.

Marne (märn), department (3,168 sq. mi.; pop. 386,-926), NE France, in Champagne; cap. Châlons-sur-Marne. Rheims is the chief city. Named for the **Marne** river, 325 mi long, which rises in the Langres Plateau and flows W past Châlons, Épernay, and Château-Thierry to join the Seine near Paris. The two **battles of the Marne** in World War I were both crucial. In the first (Sept. 6–9, 1914), the German advance on Paris seemed assured when, for reasons that are still debated, William II called it off. A notable incident of this battle was the dispatch of the French "taxicab" army by Gen. GALLIENI. In the second battle (July, 1918), the last great German offensive was decisively repulsed; U.S. troops took a prominent part.

Marne, Haute: see HAUTE-MARNE.

Marnix, Philip van (fē'lĭp vän mär'nĭks), 1540–98, Flemish patriot, lord of Sainte-Aldegonde. A Calvinist, he was leader in the struggle for independence from Spain and a supporter of William the Silent. Wrote *Wilhelmus van Nassauwe,* national anthem of the Netherlands.

Maronites (mă'rŭnīts), Arabic-speaking Christian community in Lebanon (like Melchites and Syrian Catholics) in communion with the pope. Their liturgy (in Syriac) is of Antiochene type with Latin imitations. Head is called patriarch of Antioch. Priests are allowed to marry. In 19th cent. massacres of Maronites by Druses brought intervention of France, which obtained modern hold on Syria.

Maros, river, Rumania: see MURES.

Maros Vasarhely, Rumania: see TARGUL-MURES.

Marot, Clément (klämä' märö'), 1496?–1544, French court poet, author of graceful rondeaux, ballades, epigrams. Translated Psalms into French verse.

Marprelate controversy (mär'prĕ"lĭt), 16th-cent. English religious argument. Under pseudonym of Martin Marprelate seven Puritan pamphlets appeared (1588–89), satirizing Church of England authoritarianism and starting flood of literature from both factions.

Marquand, J(ohn) P(hillips) (märkwänd'), 1893–, American novelist. Spent his boyhood in Newburyport, Mass. Among his many novels are *The Late George Apley* (1937), *H. M. Pulham, Esq.* (1941), *Point of No Return* (1949), "Mr. Moto" adventure stories.

Marquesas Islands (märkā'säs), volcanic group of 11 islands, S Pacific, c.740 mi. NE of Tahiti. Included in FRENCH ESTABLISHMENTS IN OCEANIA. Chief islands are Nuku Hiva and Hiva Oa. Islands are fertile and mountainous. Exports include copra, tobacco, and vanilla. S cluster of islands was discovered 1595 by a Spaniard; N cluster in 1791 by an American. Commodore David Porter persuaded natives to agree to annexation to U.S. in 1813, but Congress took no action. Ceded 1842 to France. Of all Polynesian peoples, Marquesans suffered greatest decline from European diseases. Grave of Gauguin on Hiva Oa.

Marquette, Jacques (zhäk' märkĕt'), 1637–75, French missionary and explorer in North America, a Jesuit priest. With Louis JOLLIET he estab. existence of waterway from the St. Lawrence to Gulf of Mexico in voyage down the Mississippi.

Marquette (märkĕt'), city (pop. 17,202), W Upper Peninsula, N Mich., on L. Superior. Iron ore shipping point and center of mining, lumbering, farming, and resort area, it has mfg. of foundry and wood products and chemicals.

Marquette University: see MILWAUKEE, Wis.

Marquis, Don(ald Robert Perry) (mär'kwĭs), 1878–1937, American columnist, whose mild and hilarious social satire is expressed through his characters "The Old Soak," "archy," a cockroach, and "mehitabel," a cat.

Marrakesh (märä'kĕsh), commercial city (pop. 238,-237), French Morocco. Founded 1062 by Yusuf ibn Tashufin as cap. of Almoravides. Noted landmark is 220-ft. tower of Koutoubya mosque (completed 1195). City was formerly starting point for Trans-Saharan caravans. Renowned for fine leather goods.

marram grass: see BEACH GRASS.

marriage, union of persons of opposite sex as husband and wife, forming new family, sanctioned by custom and religion. Marriage is generally initiated by rite combining words and symbolic acts, dramatizing and making public the new relationship. Where group is divided into clans, the individual is required to marry outside his clan, a practice known as exogamy. At same time, he must marry within his tribe, a practice known as endogamy; in small tribes, this results in inbreeding. Monogamy is dominant form of marriage in all groups, even where polygamy is permitted. Of variant forms of marriage, polygyny, or marriage of one man to more than one wife, is more frequent than polyandry, the marriage of one woman to more than one husband. In polygynous unions, usually one chief wife ranks above the others. The custom of levirate marriage, practiced by the ancient Hebrews, required that a man marry his deceased brother's wife. Throughout history and in many lands today the parents of the bride and groom customarily negotiate marriage, often binding it with property exchange. In Christian countries, the Church exercises close supervision over marriage, but civil marriage is now permitted in most countries.

Marryat, Frederick (mär'ēăt) 1792–1848, English novelist. Long naval service gave Captain Marryat material for tales of sea adventure (e.g., *Frank Mildmay,* 1829; *Mr. Midshipman Easy,* 1836). *Masterman Ready* (1841–42) is a story for children.

Mars (märz), in Roman religion, god of war. The father of Romulus, he occupied, next to Jupiter, the highest place in Roman religion. In early times he was probably god of fertility. He had many temples in Rome. Festivals to him were held in March (named for him). Identified with Greek Ares.

Mars, in astronomy, PLANET revolving (with its two satellites) around sun in orbit next outside that of earth. Mean distance from sun is c.141,540,000 mi.; period of revolution c.1.88 years; mean diameter c.4,216 mi. Surface is dull red or orange; greenish areas near equator are believed to be vegetation. Tilt of axis (24°50') results in seasons nearly twice as long as on earth; polar white spots increase and diminish with seasonal regularity. Network of dark lines called canals, reported 1877 by Schiaparelli, are regarded by some astronomers as work of intelligent beings. Temperatures believed to range from 80°F. to −130°F. See *ill.,* p. 927.

Marsala (märsä'lä), seaport (pop. 24,650), Sicily, Italy, on Cape Boeo, westernmost point of the island; anc. LILYBAEUM. Noted for sweet wine. Here in 1860 Garibaldi began conquest of Two Sicilies.

Marseillaise (märsùläz'), French national anthem, written and composed by ROUGET DE LISLE; originally called *Chant de guerre de l'armée du Rhin.* Became known as the *Marseillaise* because it was sung by soldiers from Marseilles as they marched on the Tuileries (Aug. 10, 1792).

Marseilles (märsälz'), Fr. *Marseille* (märsä'yù), city (pop. 551,640), cap. of Bouches-du-Rhône dept., SE France; second largest city and chief Mediterranean port of France. Its port is connected with the Rhone by the Rove Tunnel, a 4½ mi. underground canal (opened 1927). Mfg. of soap, chemicals, machinery; shipbuilding. Settled by Greeks c.600 B.C., ancient Massilia later became an ally of Rome, which annexed it 49 B.C. Sharing the history of Provence, it passed to the French crown 1486. The 19th cent. brought great commercial expansion. A gleaming white city rising in a semicircle from the sea, Marseilles is famous for its beauty. The slums of the port section, long famous for its vice, crime, and exotic mixture of races, were razed by the Germans in World War II. Much of the waterfront was gutted by Allied guns in the landing of Aug., 1944. Part of Aix-en-Provence Univ. is now at Marseilles.

Marsh, Othniel Charles, 1831–99, American paleontologist, first professor of paleontology at Yale, also curator of the Peabody Museum. Served with U.S. Geological Survey on many expeditions to West, and made large collection of fossil vertebrates, now at Yale and National Museum. His discoveries influenced teaching of evolution.

Marsh, Reginald, 1898–, American painter, b. Paris. Often depicts Manhattan street life.

marsh: see SWAMP.

Marshal, William: see PEMBROKE, WILLIAM MARSHAL, 1ST EARL OF.

Marshall, Alfred, 1842–1924, English economist. His systemization of classical economic theories laid foundation of neoclassical school of economics. Developed theory of marginal utility. Principal work: *Principles of Economics* (1890).

Marshall, George C(atlett), 1880–, American army officer and statesman, chief of staff (1939–45) and Secretary of State (1947–49). Became general of the army ("five-star general") in 1944. Integrated EUROPEAN RECOVERY PROGRAM (called Marshall plan).

Marshall, James Wilson, 1810–85, American pioneer, discoverer of gold in Calif. Discovery launched famous gold rush of 1849.

Marshall, John, 1755–1835, fourth Chief Justice of U.S. Supreme Court (1801–35). Raised prestige and power of Supreme Court and molded Constitution by breadth and wisdom of his interpretations—achievements made despite bitter quarrels with Jefferson and later Presidents. Made indisputable the right of Supreme Court to review Federal and state laws and pronounce final judgment on their constitutionality. Viewed the Constitution both as a precise document setting forth specific powers and as a living instrument which should be broadly interpreted to give Federal government means to act effectively within its limited sphere. In general he opposed states' rights doctrines, and there were many criticisms advanced against him.

Marshall. 1 City (pop. 5,777), S Mich., on Kalamazoo R. and near Battle Creek. Mfg. of metal products. **2** City (pop. 5,923), SW Minn., WNW of Mankato. Farm and dairy trade center. **3** City (pop. 8,850), N central Mo., N of Sedalia, in farm area. Mfg. of shoes. **4** City (pop. 22,327), E Texas, WNW of Shreveport, La.; settled 1838. Processes and ships truck, cotton, oil, lumber, bricks, dairy products, carbon, and cottonseed oil.

Marshall College: see HUNTINGTON, W.Va.

Marshall Islands, archipelago (70 sq. mi.; pop. 10,223), central Pacific, 2,595 nautical mi. N of Auckland, New Zealand. Comprises 34 atolls and coral islands, of which KWAJALEIN is the most important. Inhabited by Micronesians, who produce copra for export. Discovered 1526 by the Spanish; visited 1788 by Captains Gilbert and Marshall. Was German protectorate, 1885–1914. Occupied in 1914 by Japan, who received mandate 1922 and claimed sovereignty over group in 1935. Captured 1944 by U.S. forces. Included in 1947 in U.S. Trust Territory of the Pacific Isls. under UN trusteeship. Bikini atoll was site of atom-bomb test in 1946.

Marshall Plan: see EUROPEAN RECOVERY PROGRAM.

Marshalltown, city (pop. 19,821), central Iowa, on Iowa R. and NE of Des Moines; settled 1851. Industrial, trade, and rail center with meat packing and mfg. of metal products.

Marshalsea (mär'shŭlsē), former prison in London, closed in 1842. Setting of Dickens' *Little Dorrit.*

Marshfield. 1 City, Oregon: see COOS BAY. **2** City (pop. 12,394), central Wis., SE of Eau Claire; settled 1868. Dairy products.

marsh gas: see METHANE.

marsh mallow: see MALLOW.

marsh marigold, spring-blooming perennial (*Caltha*) of north temperate zone, found in wet places. Common marsh marigold (*Caltha palustris*) or cowslip has rounded glossy leaves and shining yellow flowers similar to buttercups.

Marsh's test, chemical test for arsenic and antimony discovered by James Marsh (1789–1846), English chemist. The unknown is treated with zinc, which combines with arsenic to form arsine; this is burned in air and deposits on a cold plate an "arsenic mirror" that is soluble in sodium hypochlorite. In test for antimony, stibine is formed and "mirror" is insoluble in sodium hypochlorite.

Marsilius of Padua (märsĭ'lēŭs, pä'dūù), d. c.1342, Italian political theorist, supporter of Emperor LOUIS IV, for whom he wrote his great work, the *Defensor Pacis.* This work holds that the power of the state and the power of the church derive equally from the people. The church should be limited solely to worship, and governing powers of the pope Marsilius held to be self-arrogated. These views caused great scandal at the time.

Marston, John, 1576–1634, English satirist and dramatist. Wrote tragedies *Antonio and Mellida* and *Antonio's Revenge* (both 1602), *The Malcontent* (1604; with John Webster), and *Eastward Ho!* (1605; with Ben Jonson and George Chapman).

Marston Moor, W. Riding of Yorkshire, England. Battle fought here (July 2, 1644) gave parliamentarians a decisive victory over royalists.

marsupial (märsoō'pēul, –sū'–), member of order of pouched mammals, found chiefly in Australia. In most, the female lacks a true placenta. Young are born in undeveloped state. The kangaroo and the opossum are marsupials.

Marsyas (mär'sēŭs), in Greek mythology, Phrygian satyr. Skilled in use of Athena's flute, he challenged lyre-playing Apollo to a contest. The Muses favored Apollo, who flayed Marsyas. A river, called for him the Marsyas, sprang from his blood or from tears of his mourners.

marten, carnivorous, largely arboreal mammal (*Martes*) of weasel family, found in North America, Europe, central Asia. Well known are the American marten (or pine marten), FISHER, Siberian SABLE.

Martens, Frederick (mär'tĕns), Rus. *Feodor Feodorovich Martens,* 1845–1909, Russian authority on international law, professor at Univ. of St. Petersburg (1871–1905). Influenced Russian diplomacy; laid base for Hague Conferences; hoped for a world community based on common standard of civilization.

Martens, Georg Friedrich von, 1756–1821, German authority on international law, professor at Göttingen (1784–89), state councilor of Westphalia (1808–13), representative of Hanover at the Frankfurt diet (1816–21). Wrote a monumental comparative study of modern law and commenced an enormous collection of treaties.

Martha, friend of Jesus, sister of Mary and Lazarus of Bethany. Luke 10.38–42; John 11.1–46; 12.1–9. Concerned mainly with her duties, she is the symbol of the active, as against the contemplative, life.

Martha's Vineyard, island in the Atlantic, off SE Mass.; 20 mi. long and 10 mi. wide; separated from Elizabeth Isls. and Cape Cod by Vineyard Sound. Gosnold visited here 1602; settled 1642. Includes towns of EDGARTOWN, GAY HEAD, OAK BLUFFS, Tisbury (including VINEYARD HAVEN village). Whaling and fishing were important, but island is now mainly resort. Boat and air connections with mainland.

Martí, José (hōsā' märtē'), 1853–95, Cuban writer and leader of movement for independence; outstanding poet and one of greatest prose writers of Hispanic America. Exiled at age of 16 because of revolutionary activities, he continued his efforts for independence in Spain, Mexico, Guatemala, Venezuela, New York.

Supported himself by contributing articles to New York *Sun* and Buenos Aires *Nacion*. Returned to Cuba in 1895 and died at battle of Dos Ríos.

Martial (Marcus Valerius Martialis) (mär'shŭl), A.D. c.40–c.104, Roman writer. His witty, original verse became the model for the modern epigram.

Martianus, Capella: see CAPELLA, MARTIANUS.

Martignac, Jean Baptiste Gay, vicomte de (zhä' bäptēst' gā' vēkōt' dü märtēnyäk'), 1778–1832, French statesman under Charles X. His ministry (1827–29) proposed liberal reforms but was overthrown by the ultraroyalists. Polignac succeeded him.

Martin, Saint, c.316–397?, bishop of Tours. While yet a heathen, he gave his cloak to a beggar. After conversion he went (c.360) to St. Hilary of Poitiers and built himself a hermitage. Acclaimed bishop against his will (371). Feast: Nov. 11. St. Martin's summer (mid-Nov.) named for him.

Martin I, Saint, d. 655, pope (649–55). Defying Emperor Constans II, he summoned a council that condemned MONOTHELETISM. The emperor had him imprisoned, then banished to the Crimea. Feast: Nov. 12.

Martin IV, d. 1285, pope (1281–85), a Frenchman. He supported the efforts of Charles of Anjou to restore the Latin Kingdom of Constantinople, thus alienating the Eastern Church. After the SICILIAN VESPERS, he turned all his power against Aragon.

Martin V, 1368–1431, pope (1417–31), a Roman named Oddone Colonna. The conclave of the Council of CONSTANCE chose him as pope to end the Great SCHISM. He rehabilitated Rome and papal power, restoring Church unity. He rejected the conciliar theory popular at Constance, but did follow the wishes of that council in calling a new one at Pavia (1423). This was ineffective and Martin summoned another to meet at Basel in 1431. He was opposed by Antipope Benedict XIII (Pedro de LUNA) and later by Antipope Clement VIII (Gil Sánchez Múñoz). Martin prevailed.

Martin, Archer John Porter, 1910–, English biochemist. Shared 1952 Nobel Prize in Chemistry for discovery of partition chromatography, a new method for separating compounds in chemical analysis.

Martin, Homer Dodge, 1836–97, American landscape painter. Influenced by Barbizon school.

martin, name used chiefly for certain swallows—European martin, bank swallow or sand martin of Europe and North America, American purple martin (destroys insects and chases crows).

Martin du Gard, Roger (rôzhä' märtē' dü gär'), 1881–, French novelist, author of *Les Thibault* (8 vols., 1922–40; Eng. tr., *The World of the Thibaults*), in which he dissects the conflicting strata and beliefs of modern French society. Was awarded 1937 Nobel Prize in Literature.

Martineau, Harriet (mär'tĭnō), 1802–76, English writer. Interested in reform, she advocated, in turn, Unitarianism, abolition, mesmerism, and positivism. Among her many works are *Illustrations of Political Economy* (9 vols., 1832–34); *Society in America* (1837), written after a tour of the U.S.; and a free translation (1853) of Comte's *Cours de philosophie positive*.

Martinelli, Giovanni (jōvän'nē märtēnĕl'lē), 1885–, Italian-American operatic tenor. Appeared at the Metropolitan Opera, New York, 1913–46.

Martinez (märtē'nùs), city (pop. 8,268), W Calif., on Suisun Bay and NNE of Oakland. Oil refining, copper smelting, wine making, and fishing. Reservoir here is end of Contra Costa Canal.

Martínez de Campos, Arsenio (ärsän'yō märtē'nĕth dä käm'pōs), 1831–1900, Spanish general. Brought Carlist Wars and Cuban Ten Years War to an end; was premier 1879. Sent to Cuba in 1895, he was criticized for leniency toward the insurgents and was replaced by Weyler.

Martínez de la Rosa, Francisco (fränthē'skō märtēnäth dä lä rō'sä), 1787–1862, Spanish romantic dramatist, poet, novelist, historian.

Martínez Ruiz, José (hōsä' märtē'näth rōōēth'), 1873–, pseud. Azorín (äsōrēn'), Spanish essayist, novelist, and dramatist of the Generation of 1898, noted for descriptive and psychological essays and penetrating literary criticism.

Martínez Sierra, Gregorio (grägō'rēō märtē'näth syĕ'rä), 1881–1947, Spanish dramatist, novelist, poet, widely known for drama *The Cradle Song* (1911).

Martini, Simone (sēmō'nä märtē'nē), or **Simone di Martino,** c.1283–1344, a leader of Sienese school of painting; master of delicate, sinuous line.

Martinique (märtĭnēk'), overseas dept. of the French Republic (427 sq. mi.; pop. 261,595), in Windward Isls., West Indies; cap. FORT-DU-FRANCE. Discovered by Columbus, 1502, it was colonized by French under Esnambuc from 1635. Sugar cane, introduced from Brazil in 1654, is principal crop. Rum is a major export. Island is subject to tidal waves, earthquakes, volcanic eruptions (most disastrous of which was that of Pelée, 1902.).

Martino, Simone di: see MARTINI, SIMONE.

Martinsburg, city (pop. 15,621), in E Panhandle of W.Va., SW of Hagerstown; chartered 1778. Mfg. of textiles, hosiery, and wood products. Belle Boyd, Confederate spy, lived and was imprisoned here. Near-by Bunker Hill, settled c.1729, is oldest recorded settlement in W.Va.

Martins Ferry, city (pop. 13,220), E Ohio, on Ohio R. opposite Wheeling, W.Va.; settled 1785 as Norristown. Has coal mining and mfg. of steel. Birthplace of W. D. Howells.

Martinsville. 1 City (pop. 5,991), S central Ind., on White R. and SW of Indianapolis. Health resort with artesian springs. **2** City (pop. 17,251), SW Va., WNW of Danville in Blue Ridge foothills; founded 1793. Center of agr. area. Mfg. of furniture and textiles.

Martinu, Bohuslav (bô'hōōsläf märtĭnōō), 1890–, Czech composer; came to the U.S. in 1941. He has written symphonies, operas, a Concerto Grosso, and *Memorial to Lidice* (1943) for orchestra.

Martiny, Philip (märtē'nē), 1858–1927, American sculptor, b. Alsace. Decorations for public buildings.

Marvel, Ik, pseud. of **Donald Grant Mitchell,** 1822–1908, American author. Sentimental essays in *Reveries of a Bachelor* (1850) and *Dream Life* (1851) were long popular.

Marvell, Andrew, 1621–78, English poet, best known for lyrics, such as "The Garden," "To His Coy Mistress," and for his "Horatian Ode" to Cromwell.

Marwar, India: see JODHPUR.

Marx, Karl, 1818–83, German social philosopher and radical leader, the chief theorist of modern socialism. Took (1842) a Ph.D. degree at Jena. In Paris (1843) he began his lifelong association with Friedrich ENGELS, with whom, in 1848, he published the *Communist Manifesto*, a basic formulation of MARXISM. From 1850 until his death he lived in London. Here he founded (1864) the International Workingmen's Association (see INTERNATIONAL, FIRST) and wrote his monumental work *Das Kapital* (Vol. I, 1867; Vols. II and III, posthumously ed. by Engels, 1885–94), a book which has exerted an incalculable influence on modern world. Most modern forms of SOCIALISM and COMMUNISM are derived from his dynamic theory of social change. He adapted Hegel's dialectical method to his own materialistic position to produce theory of DIALECTICAL MATERIALISM.

Marx, Wilhelm (vĭl'hĕlm), 1863–1946, chancellor of Germany (1923–24, 1926–28); head of Catholic Center party. Accepted Dawes Plan (1924). Was defeated by Hindenburg in presidential elections (1925).

Marx Brothers, a team of American comedians. They are Julius (1895–), called Groucho; Arthur (1893–), called Harpo; and Leonard (1891–), called Chico. Originally in vaudeville and on the stage, they have been popular in moving pictures since 1929.

Marxism, economic-political system named for Karl MARX. It is also known as economic or materialistic determinism, scientific (as opposed to utopian) socialism, and DIALECTICAL MATERIALISM. Virtually all modern socialist and communist thought is directly based on Marxism. Marx and Friedrich ENGELS published in 1848 the *Communist Manifesto*, in which the fundamental assumptions of the system were set forth. It was asserted that "the history of all hitherto existing society is the history of class struggles." Every social order based on class division contains the germs of its own destruction, until the emergence of a classless society. The modern social struggle is between the bourgeoisie (i.e., the capitalist class) and the nonpropertied proletariat. In *Das Kapital*, Marx developed his theory that the value of the commodities consumed by a worker is less than the value of the commodities he produces; the difference, called surplus value, represents the profit of the capitalist. Marx prophesied that the proletariat would become the ruling class and centralize production in the hands of the state, which would, in its turn, "wither away." To hurry along this inevitable process, revolution was to be used if necessary.

Mary, the Virgin, mother of Jesus, the principal saint, called Our Lady. Her name in Hebrew is Miriam. The New Testament tells much of her, though the principal stress is upon the annunciation to her by Gabriel that she was to bear the Savior and upon the actual birth of Jesus. She was married to Joseph, a carpenter of Nazareth, and she was a cousin of Elizabeth, mother of John the Baptist. She played some part in Jesus' public life, notably in the miracle at Cana, and she stood at the foot of the Cross when her Son was crucified. She was honored from early days in Christianity, and tradition has supplied other details of her life: that her parents were St. Joachim and St. Anne; that she was presented and dedicated at the Temple as a virgin; that she was later protected chastely by St. Joseph; and that after the death of Jesus she was cared for by St. John the Divine. Mary is the object of the highest veneration in the Orthodox and the Roman Catholic Church because of her unique position doctrinally defined as Mother of God; expressly, however, she is not the object of worship, which is restricted to God alone. The Roman Catholic Church has other important dogmas concerning the Virgin, among them that she was born without original sin (doctrine of the Immaculate Conception); that she remained a virgin throughout her life (the "brethren of the Lord" in the Bible being construed to mean only kinsmen); that she was "assumed" directly into heaven in the body (doctrine of the Assumption). Most Catholics express their veneration and love for her by daily recitation of the Ave Maria and frequent saying of the rosary, and there are many other prayers and hymns in her honor. Besides these ordinary attentions she is also specially venerated under various aspects—some derived from titles (as Our Lady Queen of Heaven; Our Lady Star of the Sea or Stella Maris), some from events of her life (as Our Lady of the Immaculate Conception; Our Lady of Sorrows), some from miraculous events or visions associated with her (see CZESTOCHOWA; GUADALUPE HIDALGO; LOURDES; FÁTIMA). Every Saturday and the month of May are devoted to her, and she has many special feasts, among them: Dec. 8, the Immaculate Conception (important in U.S., because Our Lady in her Immaculate Conception is patron of U.S.); Feb. 2, the Purification of Our Lady (Candlemas); March 25, the Annunciation (Lady Day); Aug. 15, the Assumption (principal of her feasts); Sept. 8, the Birthday of Our Lady. Though Protestant churches generally discarded veneration of Mary, she is revered especially by "high-church" groups in the Anglican and Episcopal churches, respected (particularly at Christmas) in nonevangelical churches, and disregarded in extreme evangelical churches. Stories concerning her rejected in all Western churches appear in the PSEUDEPIGRAPHA.

Mary, queens of England. Mary I, 1516–58, queen 1553–58, was the daughter of HENRY VIII and KATHARINE OF ARAGON. After her parents' divorce Mary was forced to acknowledge herself as illegitimate and to repudiate Catholic Church. Pope absolved her from these statements, and she remained loyal to her faith. Succeeded her brother, Edward VI, after an unsuccessful attempt was made to put Lady Jane Grey on the throne. Her marriage in 1554 to PHILIP II of Spain and consequent Spanish alliance were unpopular. Papal authority was reestab. in 1554. Religious persecutions and loss of Calais increased popular hatred of "Bloody Mary." **Mary II,** 1662–94, queen 1689–94, was the daughter of James II and Anne Hyde. Reared as Protestant, she married William of Orange in 1677. Was joint sovereign with him (see WILLIAM III) after Glorious Revolution of 1688, but ruled only during his absences.

Mary, 1867–1953, queen consort of George V and mother of Edward VIII and George VI of England.

Mary, in Bible. 1 Mary, the Virgin. **2** MARY MAGDALEN. **3** One of those to stand at foot of the Cross. Possibly the mother of James the Less; also identified as sister of Mary, the Virgin. Mat. 27.56, 61; Mark 15.40,47; 16.1; Luke 24.10; John 19.25. **4** Sister of Lazarus and Martha of Bethany. Her greatest happiness was to sit at Jesus' feet and listen to his teachings. Luke 10.38–42; John 11.1–46; 12.1–9. Some identify her with Mary Magdalen.

Mary, Turkmen SSR: see MERV.

Mary Baldwin College: see STAUNTON, Va.

Maryknoll (mâ′rĕnōl), place, SE N.Y., near Ossining, hq. of Catholic Foreign Mission Society of America; estab. 1911. Here priests ("Maryknoll Fathers") are trained for foreign missions.

Maryland, state (10,577 sq. mi.; pop. 2,343,001), E U.S.; one of Thirteen Colonies; cap. ANNAPOLIS; metropolis BALTIMORE. Bordered largely by POTOMAC R. on W and SW; partly by the Atlantic on E. CHESAPEAKE BAY separates E shore from main part of state. Farming (poultry, tobacco, truck, dairy products, cattle, fine horses); fishing; processing of produce and sea food. Mfg. of steel, ships, transportation equipment, chemicals, textiles; refines oil, sugar. William Claiborne set up trading post on Kent Isl. 1631. Territory under proprietorship of the Calverts 1632–89. Attempt to achieve religious freedom (esp. for Catholics) was opposed by encroaching Puritans. Supported American Revolution. Remained in Union during Civil War, though torn between two loyalties. Industry prospered after war. Remains true border state (reflected in differences between tidewater and upland Md.).

Maryland, University of, at College Park and Baltimore (with Maryland State Col. at PRINCESS ANNE); land-grant and state supported, coed.; chartered and opened 1807 as Col. of Medicine of Maryland, became university 1812. Has absorbed Maryland Agricultural Col., Baltimore Dental Col. (1840; first U.S. dental school), and several law and pharmacy schools.

Marylebone, Saint (sŭnt mâ′rĕlŭbŏn′), metropolitan borough (pop. 75,764) of NW London, England. Includes zoological and botanical gardens, B.B.C. studios, Mme Tussaud's waxworks, Harley St. (a center of medical practice), and London's chief shopping district.

Mary Magdalen or **Mary Magdalene** (both: măg′dŭlŭn; formerly môd′lŭn, hence *maudlin*, i.e., tearful), woman cured of madness by Jesus; one of those who waited at the Cross and among the first to see the risen Jesus. Mat. 27.56,61; 28; Mark 15.47; 16; Luke 8.2; 24; John 19.25; 20. Traditionally identified with the reformed prostitute who anointed Jesus' feet (Luke 2.36–50), she has become the symbol of the penitent, hence the word *Magdalen*. Also identified with Mary of Bethany. Widely venerated among Christians. Feast: July 22.

Marymount College: see TARRYTOWN, N.Y.

Mary of Burgundy, 1457–82, daughter of CHARLES THE BOLD, whose death in 1477 left her the richest heiress in Europe. Louis XI of France immediately attacked her inheritance, seizing Burgundy and Picardy and threatening the Low Countries and Franche-Comté. To win her subjects' support, Mary issued, at Ghent, the Great Privilege, which restored the former liberties of Flanders, Brabant, Hainaut, and Holland. In the same year (1477) she married her ally, Maximilian of Austria (later Emperor MAXIMILIAN I), who defeated the French at Guinegate (1479). Mary's untimely death in a riding accident left her son Philip (later PHILIP I of Castile) as heir and thus transferred the Low Countries to Hapsburg control. Troubles in the Netherlands forced Maximilian to ratify (1483) the Treaty of ARRAS, which gave Franche-Comté and Artois to France (ceded back by France 1493).

Mary of England (Mary Tudor), 1496–1533, queen consort of Louis XII of France, daughter of Henry VII of England. After death of Louis (1515) she married Charles Brandon, duke of Suffolk.

Mary of Guise (gēz), 1515–60, queen of Scotland, wife of James V and mother of Mary Queen of Scots. After James's death (1542) she sought to bring France and Scotland together. As regent (after 1554), she married her daughter to the French dauphin and brought in French troops to oppose the Protestant and pro-English party.

Mary of Modena (mŏ′dĭnù), 1658–1718, queen of James II of England. As a devout Catholic she was unpopular in England. Birth of her son (a Catholic heir) was a cause of revolution of 1688.

Mary Queen of Scots (Mary Stuart), 1542–87, only child of James V of Scotland and MARY OF GUISE. She was sent by her mother to France, where she grew up and married (1558) Francis II. After his death in 1560, she returned to Scotland as queen in 1561. Despite harsh attacks from John Knox, she refused to abandon her Catholicism and her charm and intelligence won many over. To reinforce her claim to succeed ELIZABETH on the English throne, she married (1565) her English cousin Lord DARNLEY. Soon despised by Mary, he joined a conspiracy of Protestant nobles who murdered her trusted counselor, David RIZZIO. Mary, however, talked Darnley over and escaped to loyal nobles. Her son, James I, was born soon after. At this period she fell in love with earl of BOTHWELL. Darnley, disliked by everyone, was murdered in 1567. Bothwell, widely suspected of the murder, was acquitted and married Mary. Outraged Scots flew to arms. Mary surrendered at Carberry Hill, abdicated, and named earl of Murray as regent. She escaped (1586) and gathered a large force, but was defeated by Murray and fled to England. Although welcomed by Elizabeth, she became a prisoner. In prison she became involved in several ill-starred plots with English Catholics, the Spanish, the French, and others. Finally confirmed her son's kingship (1583) but was denied liberty. In 1586 a plot to murder Elizabeth was reported. Charged with being an accomplice, Mary was tried and beheaded in 1587. Deeply religious in her later years, Mary's conduct at trial and execution gained much admiration. A clear-cut decision about her guilt is made difficult by web of intrigue surrounding both the murder of Darnley and the plot against Elizabeth.

Marysville, city (pop. 7,826), N central Calif., at confluence of Yuba and Feather rivers, N of Sacramento. Fruitgrowing center.

Maryville. 1 City (pop. 6,834), NW Mo., N of St. Joseph, in livestock (esp. hogs) area. **2** City (pop. 7,742), E Tenn., S of Knoxville, in fruitgrowing area. Lumbering and textile mfg. Has log cabin where Sam Houston taught.

Mary Washington College: see VIRGINIA, UNIVERSITY OF.

Masaccio (mäzät′chō), 1401–1428?, Florentine painter,

pioneer of Italian Renaissance. Real name was Tommaso Guidi. His frescoes (esp. those in Brancacci Chapel of Church of Santa Maria del Carmine, Florence) were studied by such painters as Michelangelo and Raphael. Began new era of painting by expert use of perspective and by naturalistic treatment of figures and landscape.

Masaniello (mäzänyĕl′lō), 1620?–1647, Neapolitan revolutionist, whose original name was Tommaso Aniello; a fisherman. He led a rebellion against increased taxation (1647) but came to terms with the viceroy, who promised reforms and made him captain general. The title went to Masaniello's head; he was killed by his own supporters.

Masaryk, Thomas Garrigue (gùrēg′ mä′särĭk), 1850–1937, chief founder and first president (1919–35) of Czechoslovakia, b. Moravia. Taught philosophy at Prague Univ.; married Charlotte Garrigue, an American. Leading the Czech independence party from 1907, he headed (with BENES) the Czechoslovak national council at Paris during World War I and was acclaimed president of the new republic in Nov., 1918 (reelected 1920, 1927, 1934). He resigned because of his age in 1935 and was succeeded by Benes. An ardent liberal and democrat, he was revered by the great majority of the people but was attacked by extremists of all sorts. Among his writings translated into English are *Spirit of Russia* (1919), *The Making of a State* (1927), *Ideals of Humanity* (1938), *Modern Man and Religion* (1938). His son **Jan Masaryk** (yän), 1886–1948, became (1940) foreign minister of the Czechoslovak government in exile at London during World War II. He kept that post after his government's return to Prague (1945) until his death, shortly after the Communist coup d'état of Feb., 1948. He was a liberal but advocated cooperation with Russia. According to the official account of his death, he committed suicide by leaping from a window, but the exact circumstances remain subject to speculation.

Mascagni, Pietro (pyä′trō mäskä′nyē), 1863–1945, Italian composer of operas (e.g., *L'amico Fritz, Iris*, and the popular *Cavalleria rusticana*).

Mascara (mä′skùrù), city (pop. 26,086), NW Algeria, SE of Oran. Became headquarters of Abdu-l-Kadir in 1832; occupied by the French in 1841. A market center, noted for its white wine.

Mascarene Islands (mäskürēn′), in Indian Ocean, E of Madagascar. Include MAURITIUS, RÉUNION, and RODRIGUEZ.

Masefield, John, 1878–, English poet laureate (after 1930). A boyhood spent at sea was basis for first poems, *Salt-Water Ballads* (1902), containing "Sea Fever" and "Cargoes." First long narrative poem, *The Everlasting Mercy* (1911), won him fame. Of later poetry best known are *The Widow in the Bye Street* (1912) and *Dauber* (1913). Author also of novels (e.g., *Sard Harker,* 1924), plays, books for boys, and sketches.

Masereel, Frans (fräns′ mäsäräl′), 1889–, Belgian painter and illustrator of books. Famous for woodcuts expressing miseries of men.

Masham, Abigail, Lady, d. 1734, favorite of Queen Anne of England. Power behind the throne, she gave influence to her kinsman, Robert Harley, until they quarreled in 1714; then to Henry St. John.

Masinissa (mäsĭnĭ′sù), c.238–149 B.C., king of Numidia. Joined Romans (206 B.C.) in the Second Punic War and led cavalry in victory at Zama. When Carthage began to revive, he attacked Carthaginian territory and brought on the Third Punic War. Also Masinissa.

mask, artificial face or head covering used as disguise or protection, fashioned of many kinds of materials. Medicinal, religious, protective masks have been used by many primitive peoples. Theatrical masks have appeared in Japanese *no* dramas, Chinese temple dramas, in Greek and Roman theaters, Italian commedia dell'arte, medieval miracle plays, in modern

German expressionist drama, and in Eugene O'Neill's work. Death masks date from ancient times. See also MASQUE.

Maskat, Arabia: see MUSCAT.

Maskelyne, Nevil (nĕ'vŭl mă'skŭlīn), 1732–1811, English astronomer. Estab. *Nautical Almanac* (1766). He was astronomer royal from 1765.

Masolino da Panicale (mäzōlē'nō dä pänēkä'lä), 1383–c.1447, Florentine painter, whose real name was Tommaso di Christoforo Fini. Works represent transition between tradition estab. by Giotto and later techniques involving perspective and chiaroscuro. His frescoes in Brancacci chapel were continued by his pupil Masaccio, completed by Filippino Lippi.

Mason, George, 1725–92, American statesman. Drew up Virginia Declaration of Rights. Member of Federal Constitutional Convention (1787). A Bill of Rights he forwarded formed basis for first ten amendments to U.S. Constitution. His grandson, **James Murray Mason,** 1798–1871, was U.S. Senator from Va. (1847–61) and Confederate diplomat. Appointed Confederate commissioner to England (1861), he was seized en route and interned at Boston (see TRENT AFFAIR).

Mason, John, 1586–1635, founder of New Hampshire, b. England. Received land grant 1629. Claims to land by heirs led to litigation and favorable settlement. Rights sold in 1746 to 12 Portsmouth men, Masonian Proprietors, who issued permits to settle.

Mason and Slidell Affair: see TRENT AFFAIR.

Mason City, city (pop. 27,980), N central Iowa, NW of Waterloo; settled 1853 by Masons. Rail, trade, and industrial center of agr. area with mfg. of food and clay products.

Mason-Dixon line, boundary between Pa. and Md. (lat. 39° 43′ 26.3″ N), surveyed by English astronomers Charles Mason and Jeremiah Dixon in 1763–67 to settle boundary dispute. Term popularly used to distinguish South from North.

Masonian Proprietors: see MASON, JOHN.

Masonic orders: see FREEMASONRY.

Masora (mŭsō'rŭ) [Heb.,= tradition], collection of critical annotations made by Hebrew scholars called Masoretes to establish the text of the Old Testament. Since the Hebrew alphabet has no vowels, the Masoretes had to formulate rules for an accurate reading of each verse. They evolved two systems of vowels: the Tiberian (now in use), consisting of curves, dots, and dashes, which can be traced to the 7th cent., and the Babylonian, a more complicated system of earlier origin. The language of the Masora is mostly Aramaic; many scholars contributed to the work, which ceased c.1425.

Masovia (mŭsō'vēŭ), Pol. *Mazowsze,* historic region, central Poland; cap. Warsaw. Became duchy under one of four branches of PIAST dynasty in 1138; was annexed by Polish crown 1526.

Maspero, Gaston (gästō' mäspŭrō'), 1846–1916, French Egyptologist. Founded French School of Oriental Archaeology at Cairo, did valuable work at Luxor and Karnak, and wrote several well-known works on ancient history.

Masquat, Arabia: see MUSCAT.

masque or **mask** (both: măsk), form of dramatic entertainment, usually mythological or allegorical in form, popular in early 17th-cent. England. Popularity at court resulted in masques becoming elaborate spectacles emphasizing costumes, scenery, dancing, and music. Ben Jonson wrote many masques.

masquerade. Now usually a fancy dress or costume ball in which guests wear half-face masks, masquerades originally accompanied religious festivals such as Greek Bacchanalia, Roman Saturnalia, and Purim feast of the Jews. Masquerade balls were introduced into England from France in 16th cent.

Mass [Latin,= dismissal], in the Roman Catholic Church and also among Anglo-Catholics, the primary religious service, a performance of the sacrament of the EUCHARIST. In most, but not all, Roman Catholic churches the Mass is said in Latin according to the liturgy of the city of Rome. The service is the same all over the world, though minor variant "uses" are permitted to certain groups (e.g., the Dominican order). Some parts of the text of the Mass are invariable; these make up the "ordinary." Other parts change with the occasion and the day; these prayers are "proper" to the occasion. The Mass may be merely read by the priest (Low Mass) or it may be an elaborate ritual, a solemn, or High, Mass, with a priest, deacon, and subdeacon (usually also priests) and choir. In a sung Mass, some portions are chanted solo at the altar with choral response, some portions are merely read, and nine hymns are sung by the choir. Of these nine, four are "proper": the introit, the anthem after the epistle, the offertory, and the communion; their texts are rendered in plain song. The other five are "ordinary"—*Kyrie eleison, Gloria in excelsis* (omitted in penitential seasons), creed, *Sanctus,* and *Agnus Dei*—and are the portions for which musical settings have been written by many composers (including Palestrina, Bach, Mozart, Beethoven, and Verdi). The central portion of the Mass is the eucharistic prayer, the canon, which is read rapidly and inaudibly. Some of the other prayers are read audibly, some silently.

mass, in physics, quantity of matter in a body without regard to volume or pull of gravity. "Weight" is measurement of force of gravity and depends on where measurement is made; mass is constant and this is sometimes called standard weight. Local weight divided by local acceleration of gravity multiplied by standard acceleration of gravity equals mass. According to theory of relativity, mass is not constant; both inertia and mass are held to increase as velocity approaches that of light.

Massa (mäs'sä), city (pop. 12,508), Tuscany, central Italy, near Tyrrhenian Sea. Marble quarries. From 15th to 19th cent., it was the cap. of the small principality (later duchy) of Massa and Carrara, ruled by the Malaspina and Cybo-Malaspina families. In 1829 the duchy passed, through marriage, to the house of Austria-Este (dukes of Modena); in 1859 it was united with Sardinia. Has 15th-cent. castle and cathedral.

Massachusetts, state (8,257 sq. mi.; pop. 4,690,514), NE U.S.; one of Thirteen Colonies; cap. BOSTON. Other cities are WORCESTER, SPRINGFIELD, FALL RIVER, CAMBRIDGE, NEW BEDFORD, SOMERVILLE, LOWELL, LYNN. Bounded E and S by the Atlantic. To E is coastal plain (with CAPE COD); W are uplands and BERKSHIRE HILLS, split by Connecticut R. valley. Mfg. of electrical supplies, textiles, shoes, ships, metal and rubber products; also food processing, printing, and publishing. Farming yields corn, potatoes, cranberries, poultry, truck, dairy products. Fishing important. MAYFLOWER brought PILGRIMS to PLYMOUTH 1620. PLYMOUTH COLONY developed under William BRADFORD. SALEM (1626) became center for Puritan MASSACHUSETTS BAY COMPANY. John Winthrop brought over large Puritan group, founded Boston (1630). Colony became a theocracy. Education emphasized early. Member of NEW ENGLAND CONFEDERATION. Difficulties with England (NAVIGATION ACTS, STAMP ACT, TOWNSHEND ACTS) preceded BOSTON MASSACRE and BOSTON TEA PARTY and precipitated American Revolution (see LEXINGTON AND CONCORD, BATTLES OF, and BUNKER HILL, BATTLE OF). Postwar depression caused violence in SHAYS'S REBELLION (1786). Dissatisfaction with EMBARGO ACT OF 1807 and War of 1812 led to HARTFORD CONVENTION. Decline of shipping caused rise of industry. Leaders of thought arose (see UNITARIANISM, TRANSCENDENTALISM). Union vigorously supported in Civil War. Increased industrialism brought struggle of labor unions for recognition. Two world wars expanded industries.

Massachusetts, University of: see AMHERST.

Massachusetts Bay, inlet of the Atlantic, where Mass. coast curves inward. Extends from Cape Ann to Cape

Cod. Boston Bay and Cape Cod Bay are arms of it.

Massachusetts Bay Company, English chartered company, organized (1628) with grant of land between Charles and Merrimac rivers, extending W to "the South Sea." Puritan leaders estab. colony at present site of Boston as religious and political refuge. Attempts by Sir Ferdinando GORGES to annul claims were unsuccessful. Company and colony were synonymous until company ceased to exist in 1684.

Massachusetts Institute of Technology, at Cambridge; nonsectarian, land-grant, mainly for men; chartered 1861, opened 1865 by W. B. Rogers in Boston, moved to Cambridge 1916. Leading technical school of university grade with first school of architecture in U.S. Pioneered in various forms of engineering. Conducts combination course with group of liberal arts colleges. Has nautical museums and important technical library.

Massachusetts State Teachers College: see FRAMINGHAM.

Massasoit (măsŭsoit'), c.1580–1661, chief of the Wampanoag Indians. Signed treaty with Pilgrims (1621) which he faithfully observed. His son, Metacomet, became famous as King PHILIP.

Massawa (mŭsä'wŭ), city (pop. c.25,000), Eritrea; port on Red Sea; market for pearls. Was cap. of Eritrea 1885–97. Allied base in World War II.

Masséna, André (ädrä' mäsänä'), 1758–1817, marshal of France under Napoleon I, who created him duke of Rivoli (1808) and prince of Essling (1810). Helped win battle of Rivoli (1797); defeated Korsakov at Zurich (1799); took part in victories of Essling and Wagram (1809). His failure in the Peninsular War has been blamed on his colleagues' lack of cooperation. He supported Louis XVIII in 1814; remained neutral during Hundred Days (1815).

Massena (mŭsē'nŭ), village (pop. 13,137), N N.Y., near St. Lawrence R. and NE of Ogdensburg, in dairy area; settled 1790. Large aluminum plant. Near by is Roosevelt Internatl. Bridge (1934).

Massenet, Jules (zhül' mäsĕnā'), 1842–1912, French composer. He wrote oratorios, songs, and orchestral suites, but is best known for his operas (e.g., *Le Cid, Manon, Hérodiade,* and *Werther*).

Massif Central (mäsēf' säträl'), great mountainous plateau (average alt. c.2,650 ft.) covering most of central France. Its core is the volcanic mass of the AUVERGNE mts. (Puy de Sancy, 6,187 ft. high), and it comprises the *causses* of QUERCY and ROUERGUE and the CÉVENNES mts. Sheep raising, dairying, cattle raising; agr. in valleys. Coal mines. Clermont-Ferrand, Le Creusot, Saint-Étienne are industrial centers.

Massilia, anc. city in Gaul: see MARSEILLES.

Massillon, city (pop. 29,594), NE Ohio, on Tuscarawas R. and W of Canton; settled 1812. Coal shipping point with mfg. of steel and aluminum products and clothing. Has a state mental hospital.

Massine, Léonide (läônēd' mäsēn'), 1896–, Russian ballet dancer and choreographer. Works include *Gaité parisienne* and *The Three-cornered Hat.*

Massinger, Philip, 1583–1640, English dramatist. Wrote tragedy *Duke of Milan* (1618) and satirical comedies *A New Way to Pay Old Debts* (1625) and *The City Madam* (1632). Collaborated with John Fletcher, Dekker, and possibly with Shakspere (in *King Henry VIII*).

Massive, Mount: see SAWATCH MOUNTAINS.

Massys, Matsys, Messys, or **Metsys, Quentin** (kvĕn'tĭn mäsīs', mätsīs', mĕ–, mĕt–), c.1466–1530, Flemish painter. Though influenced by Italian Renaissance, he retained intimacy and color of earlier Flemish art. His sons, **Jan Massys,** c.1509–1575, and **Cornelis Massys,** d. c.1580, were also painters.

Masters, Edgar Lee, 1879–1950, American poet, known for *Spoon River Anthology* (1915), a volume of free-verse "epitaphs," picturing the secret lives of people in the small-town Midwest. Also wrote a caustic biography of Lincoln.

mastodon (măs'tŭdŏn"), extinct mammal from which elephants probably developed. Earliest known forms

associated with Oligocene epoch in Africa were c.4½ ft. in height. Their descendants, the size of large elephants, spread over Eurasia and North America, persisting into the Pleistocene epoch.

mastoid (mă'stoid) or **mastoid process,** cone-shaped portion of temporal bone behind ear. Infection of mastoid cells (mastoiditis) is serious since brain and large blood vessels of neck may become involved.

Masudi (mäsoo'dē), d. 956, Arabian historian, geographer, and philosopher, b. Baghdad. His *Muruj adh-Dhahab* is a history of the universe from creation to A.D. 947. Traveled in many lands.

Masulipatam (mŭsoo"lŭpŭ'tŭm) or **Bandar** (bŭn'dŭr), city (pop. 59,146), NE Madras, India; port on Bay of Bengal. First major British trading post in India was founded here in 1611. Cloth mfg.

Masuria (mŭzoo'rēŭ), Pol. *Mazury,* S region of former East Prussia, transferred to Polish administration 1945; chief city Lyck. Lakes, forests. The **Masurian Lakes** were the scene of heavy fighting in World War I. After Samsonov's defeat at TANNENBERG, the Russians under Rennenkampf were driven by the Germans under Mackensen into the lake country and lost 125,000 men. A second Russian drive into East Prussia was repulsed in Feb., 1915.

masurium: see TECHNETIUM.

Matabele (mätŭbē'lē), Bantu-speaking tribe of W Southern Rhodesia. Founded 1823 when a Zulu general fled with some followers into what is now Transvaal and began attacking surrounding tribes and white settlers. Suppressed 1896 by the British.

Matagorda Bay (mătŭgôr'dù), Gulf of Mexico inlet, S Texas, protected by Matagorda Peninsula. Probably visited 1685 by LaSalle. Lavaca Bay is arm. Has small ports. Matagorda Isl. is sand bar at entrance of San Antonio Bay.

Mata Hari (mä'tù hä'rē), 1876–1917, Dutch-Indonesian dancer and spy in German service during World War I. Her real name was Margaretha Geertruida Zelle. In 1917 she was executed by the French.

Matamoros, Mariano (märyä'nō mätämō'rōs), d. 1814, Mexican revolutionist in war against Spain, a priest.

Matamoros (mätämō'rōs), city (pop. 7,961), Tamaulipas, NE Mexico, on Rio Grande, near mouth, opposite Brownsville, Texas.

Matane (mŭtän'), town (pop. 6,345), E Que., Canada, on St. Lawrence R., NW Gaspé Peninsula, ENE of Rimouski. Lumbering center and pulpwood port.

Matanuska Valley (mătŭnoo'skŭ), region, S Alaska, W of Chugach Mts. and crossed by Matanuska R. Agr. area with coal deposits and timber stands. U.S. government resettled farmers from Middle Western drought area here 1935.

Matanzas (mätän'säs), port (pop. 54,844), W Cuba, E of Havana. Has sugar refineries, tanneries, fertilizer plants. Once a pirate haven.

Matanzas, Fort: see SAINT AUGUSTINE, Fla.

Matapan, Cape (mä'tŭpän"), anc. *Taenarum* or *Tainaron,* S extremity of Greek mainland and of the Peloponnesus, projecting into Ionian Sea. British won naval victory (1941) off cape over Italians in World War II.

Matapedia, Lake (mätŭpē'dēù), E Que., Canada, 14 mi. long, 2 mi. wide, at base of Gaspé Peninsula.

match. Friction match devised 1827 in England. Phosphorus match invented 1831 in France. Nontoxic chemicals are used in modern match. In safety match, invented 1855 in Sweden, oxidizing agent on tip is ignited by striking on special material on matchbox.

mate (mä'tā), **yerba mate** (yĕr'bä), or **Paraguay tea,** evergreen tree (*Ilex paraguariensis*) and the tea brewed from its leaves since ancient times by South American Indians. The tea, high in caffeine, is popular in much of South America. The gourd cups in which it is made are also called mate.

materialism, any philosophical system maintaining that the final reality of the universe is matter; opposed to idealism. Notable materialists in the ancient world were DEMOCRITUS, the Stoics, and the Epicureans. Materialism again became prominent in the 17th cent. with GASSENDI and Thomas HOBBES and in the 18th cent. with the philosophers of the Enlightenment. Various types of materialist philosophy gained wide following in the 19th and 20th cent. In common use, materialism means devotion to money and worldly things, to the exclusion of spiritual and intellectual values.

materials, strength of: see STRENGTH OF MATERIALS.

mathematics, study of numerical quantities and their relationships, of spatial quantities and their relationships, and of various abstractions of such relationships. The chief branches studied in school and college are ARITHMETIC (numerical quantities); ALGEBRA and theory of numbers (whole numbers only), which are arithmetical abstractions; GEOMETRY (spatial quantities); TRIGONOMETRY; and CALCULUS. All mathematical method is closely founded on logic, and mathematics has from ancient times been related to philosophy and to science (calculus is fundamental in important aspects of modern physics).

Mather, Richard (mä'dhŭr), 1596–1669, British Puritan clergyman in North America. His son, **Increase Mather,** 1639–1723, was a Puritan pastor in Boston (1664–1723). A conservative upholder of Puritan theocracy, he opposed Sir Edmund Andros and supported Sir William PHIPS. His son, **Cotton Mather,** 1663–1728, clergyman and writer, assisted his father and succeeded him as pastor. His religious writings had wide influence. Remembered for his part in Salem witch trials of 1692. A promoter of learning, he was also a power in the state.

Mathew, Theobald, 1790–1856, Irish social worker, a Capuchin priest called "the apostle of temperance." He took and persuaded others to take a pledge of total abstinence. Worked for social welfare.

Mathews, Shailer, 1863–1941, American theologian, educator, and author. Taught history and theology at Univ. of Chicago (1894–1933) where he was dean (1908–33) of divinity school.

Mathewson, Christopher (Christy Mathewson), 1880–1925, American baseball pitcher. A right-hander, he won 373 major-league games. Won 30 or more games each of three consecutive seasons (1903–05); pitched three shutout victories in 1905 world series; won 37 games in 1908.

Mathura, India: see MUTTRA.

Matilda, Saint: see HENRY I, German king.

Matilda or Maud, 1102–67, queen of England, daughter of Henry I. First married to Emperor Henry V, after his death (1125) she married Geoffrey IV. At her father's death (1135) her cousin STEPHEN took the throne. In 1139 Matilda and her half-brother Robert, earl of Gloucester, challenged Stephen. She was made "lady of the English" in 1141 but soon dethroned. Withdrew (1148) in favor of her son, Henry II.

Matilda, 1046–1115, countess of Tuscany. Ruled larger part of central Italy. At her castle at CANOSSA Henry IV humiliated himself before Gregory VII (1077). She made a will bequeathing her alodial lands to the Holy See, but there are indications that she later changed it in favor of Emperor Henry V. Henry, at any rate, seized her lands in 1116. The dispute over her lands continued under later emperors and popes, while the Tuscan cities themselves achieved independence.

Matisse, Henri (ärē' mätēs'), 1869–, French painter and sculptor, the outstanding representative of FAUVISM. Renounced academic style, developing instead along a postimpressionist line of brighter, simpler design. His travels in Morocco inspired decorative canvases in which bold patterns of lines and flowers serve as background for odalisques. Other works include still lifes and interiors. Uses large surfaces of pure color and reduces aerial perspective to a minimum. Designed the chapel Ste Marie du Rosaire at Vence, near Nice, France.

Mato Grosso (mä'tō grô'sù), state (487,479 sq. mi.; pop. 528,451), central and W Brazil; cap. CUIABÁ. Other

chief city is Corumbá. Borders Bolivia on W, Paraguay on SW and S. Drained to N by tributaries of Amazon and to S by the Paraguay and Paraná. Cattle raising is principal occupation, but farms are being opened. First explored and settled by gold seekers but mineral resources are still largely undeveloped.

matriarchy (mā'trēär"kē), society (or aspects of a society) having its social base in the mother, rather than the father. In many societies lineage is traced only through the mother, and the mother determines the place of residence and rules family conduct. Sometimes the mother's brother has more authority over the family than the father. Opposite is patriarchy.

Matsuoka, Yosuke (yō'skĕ mätsōō'ōkù), 1880–1946, Japanese statesman. Graduate of Univ. of Oregon law school. In 1932 he led Japanese delegation out of League of Nations. Foreign minister in Konoye cabinet, 1940–41. After World War II indicted as war criminal but death prevented trial.

Matsys, Quentin: see MASSYS, QUENTIN.

Mattagami Lake (mùtä'gùmē), 88 sq. mi., W Que., Canada, N of Val d'Or.

Mattathias, father of the MACCABEES. 1 Mac. 2.

Matteawan: see BEACON, N.Y.

Matteotti, Giacomo (jä'kōmō mät-tāôt'tē), 1885–1924, Italian Socialist leader, outstanding opponent of the early Fascist regime. His murder by Fascist hirelings marked the actual beginning of Mussolini's complete dictatorship.

matter, anything that occupies space, has weight and mass, and exhibits such properties as INERTIA, ELASTICITY, impenetrability. Law of conservation of matter states it can neither be created nor destroyed. Kinetic molecular theory holds that matter is composed of many minute particles (see MOLECULE) in constant vibratory motion. Change from any of three states of matter (gas, liquid, solid) to another is physical change and does not alter molecule. Atomic theory is concerned with nature and internal structure of molecules. CHEMICAL REACTION is change in which matter is broken down into atoms, then recombined into molecules. Recent work has shown that TRANSMUTATION OF ELEMENTS is possible. Matter is divided into living and nonliving.

Matterhorn (mä'tùrhôrn), Fr. *Mont Cervin,* Ital. *Monte Cervino,* peak, 14,701 ft. high, on Swiss-Italian border, SW of Zermatt. First scaled 1865 by Edward Whymper. Near-by **Matterjoch** (mä'tùryôkh) or Théodule is a pass linking Italy with Switzerland.

Matthew, Saint, one of the Twelve Apostles, a publican of Capernaum. Also called Levi. Mat. 9.9–13; 10.3; Mark 2.14; Luke 5.27,29. Since 2d cent. regarded as author of the Gospel according to St. Matthew. His symbol: a young man or an angel. Feast: Sept. 21.

Matthew, Gospel according to Saint, first book of New Testament, traditionally ascribed to Matthew the Apostle. It gives unique account of Jesus' birth, tells of His ministry, and ends with the Passion and Resurrection. See also SYNOPTIC GOSPELS.

Matthew of Paris or **Matthew Paris,** d. 1259, English historian, monk of St. Albans and historiographer of the convent. His *Chronica majora,* a history of world, is valuable source book.

Matthew of Westminster, imaginary author of English chronicle in Latin, *Flores historium,* written by several monks, including Matthew of Paris.

Matthew Paris: see MATTHEW OF PARIS.

Matthews, (James) Brander, 1852–1929, American authority on the drama. Taught at Columbia 1891–1924.

Matthias, Saint, apostle chosen by lot to replace Judas Iscariot. Acts 1.23–26. Feast: Feb. 24.

Matthias, 1557–1619, German emperor (1612–19). After negotiating the Peace of Vienna (1606) with BOCSKAY, he had himself proclaimed head of the house of Hapsburg, in view of the incapacity of his brother, Emperor RUDOLF II. He forced Rudolf to yield him the rule of Hungary, Austria, and Moravia in 1608 and that of Bohemia in 1611; in 1612 he succeeded him as emperor. Influenced by Melchoir, Cardinal Klesl (or Khlesl), he sought a compromise between Catholics and Protestants. Matthias had his son FERDINAND II crowned king of Bohemia in 1617 and of Hungary in 1618. His lack of resolution in the face of the Bohemian rising of 1618 caused Germany to drift into the THIRTY YEARS WAR.

Matthias Corvinus (kôrvī'nùs), 1443?–1490, king of Hungary (1458–90); son of John HUNYADI and successor of Ladislaus V. He fought successfully against the Turks and, with papal blessing, made war on his father-in-law, GEORGE OF PODEBRAD, king of Bohemia. He conquered Moravia, Silesia, and Lusatia and in 1469 took the title king of Bohemia. The struggle continued until 1478, when Ladislaus II of Bohemia (later also ULADISLAUS II of Hungary) made a compromise peace that allowed Matthias to retain his title and conquests during his lifetime. In 1482 Matthias attacked Emperor Frederick III, from whom he conquered most of Austria (incl. Vienna, 1485); all his conquests reverted to their former rulers after his death. A true Renaissance despot, Matthias was warlike, harsh, and grasping but a generous patron of art and learning. He founded the famous Corvina library at Buda.

Mattoon (măt"toon'), city (pop. 17,547), E central Ill., SE of Decatur. Trade, industrial, rail center of agr. (corn, soybeans, broom-corn) area. Mfg. of wood products and Diesel engines.

Mattson, Henry Elis, 1887–, American landscape painter, b. Sweden.

matzoth (mät'sù, mät'sōth) [Heb.,= unleavened], bread made without leaven. Eaten by Jews during PASSOVER.

Mauclerc, Pierre: see PETER I, duke of Brittany.

Maud: see MATILDA, queen of England.

Maugham, W(illiam) Somerset (môm), 1874–, English novelist, playwright, and short-story writer. His most famous novel is *Of Human Bondage* (1915). Other well-known works are novel *The Moon and Sixpence* (1919); short story "Miss Thompson," dramatized as *Rain;* satire *Cakes and Ale* (1930); novel *The Razor's Edge* (1944); and play *The Constant Wife* (1927).

Maui (mou'ē), island (728 sq. mi.; pop. 40,103), second largest of Hawaiian Isls. Consists of two mountain masses, constituting E and W peninsulas, connected by an isthmus. HALEAKALA is highest peak. Has cattle ranches and sugar and pineapple plantations. Chief port is Lahaina.

Maumee (mômē'), city (pop. 5,548), NW Ohio, on Maumee R. and SW of Toledo. Fort Miami, last of several military or trading posts on this site, was surrendered by British after War of 1812.

Maumee, river formed at Fort Wayne, NE Ind., by St. Joseph and St. Marys rivers. Flows c.130 mi. NE past Toledo, Ohio, to L. Erie.

Mauna Kea (mou'nù kā'ù), mountain, 13,784 ft. high, on Hawaii, T.H.; world's highest island mountain.

Mauna Loa (mou'nù lō'ù), mountain, 13,675 ft. high, on Hawaii, T.H. Its many craters include KILAUEA and MOKUAWEOWEO.

Maupassant, Guy de (gē' dù mōpäsä'), 1850–93, French author. He wrote some 300 short stories, some of which are unsurpassed in style, craftsmanship, and psychological realism. Among them are "Boule de Suif" ("Tallow Ball"), "La Ficelle," ("The Piece of String"), and "Miss Harriet." "The Necklace," his most popular story, is hardly representative of his best work. Among his novels are *Une Vie* (1883; Eng. tr., *A Life*) and *Bel Ami* (1885). Maupassant, greatly influenced by Flaubert, in turn influenced modern short-story writing. He went mad in 1891.

Maupeou, René Nicolas de (rùnä' nēkôlä' dù mōpoo'), 1714–92, chancellor of France (1768–74). Dissolved PARLEMENT of Paris and provincial parlements; substituted a new parlement and a system of superior courts (1771). Strove to abolish sale of offices. His high-handed methods made him unpopular. Louis XVI dismissed him, restored parlements (1774).

Maupertuis, Pierre Louis Moreau de (pyĕr' lwĕ' môrō' dù mōpĕrtüĕ'), 1698–1758, French mathematician, astronomer, and author of works on astronomy, cosmology, and biology. His work on Newton's theory won him membership in Royal Society of London (1728); he headed expedition to Lapland (1736–37) where he confirmed Newton's theory of flattening of earth at poles.

Maurepas, Jean Frédéric Phélippeaux, comte de (zhä' frädärĕk' fālēpō' kôt' dù môrùpä'), 1701–81, French statesman. His hostility to Mme de Pompadour caused his dismissal from the ministry in 1749. Appointed minister of state (1774), he caused the dismissal of Turgot (1776) and of Necker (1781); supported alliance with American colonies.

Mauretania (môrĭtä'nyù), region in N Africa in Roman times, vaguely W of Numidia. In 2d cent. B.C. Bocchus, father-in-law of Jugurtha of Numidia, built the kingdom of Mauretania (in present N Morocco and W Algeria). Augustus put Juba II on the throne (25 B.C.). Later revolts caused Claudius to make the region two Roman provinces, but native chiefs were never wholly subdued.

Mauriac, François (fräswä' mōryäk'), 1885–, French novelist, author of *The Desert of Love* (1925; Eng. tr., 1929), *Thérèse Desqueyroux* (1927; Eng. tr., 1928), *Vipers' Tangle* (1932; Eng., 1933), and other novels which place him among the foremost Catholic writers of his time. Received 1952 Nobel Prize in Literature.

Maurice (mô'rĭs), c.539–602, Byzantine emperor (582–602). Restored KHOSRU II in Persia (591). Was murdered by the usurper Phocas.

Maurice, 1521–53, duke (1541–47) and elector (1547–53) of Saxony. He joined, then abandoned, the SCHMALKALDIC LEAGUE and was rewarded (1547) by Emperor Charles V with the rank of elector and with Electoral Saxony (both taken from his cousin, John Frederick I). He then formed a league against Charles, secured French aid, and negotiated the Treaty of PASSAU (1552), whereupon he turned about once more and made war on his ex-ally, Albert Alcibiades of Brandenburg-Kulmbach. He fell in battle.

Maurice of Nassau, 1567–1625, prince of Orange (1618–25), stadholder of Holland and Zeeland (1584–1625) and of Utrecht, Gelderland and Overijssel (1589–1625). He succeeded his father, William the Silent, as leader of the United Provs. in the struggle for independence from Spain. From his elder brother, Philip William, he inherited the principality of Orange. After a successful campaign on land and sea he concluded (1609) a 12-year truce with Spain, thus virtually establishing Dutch independence. To his chief adviser, OLDENBARNEVELDT, was due the great expansion of Dutch trade in the East. In the struggle between strict Calvinists and REMONSTRANTS, Maurice sided with the Calvinists and countenanced Oldenbarneveldt's execution. His brother Frederick Henry succeeded him.

Maurice of Saxony: see MAURICE (1521–53) and SAXE, MAURICE, COMTE DE (1696–1750).

Mauritania (môrĭtä'nẽù), French overseas territory (c.449,800 sq. mi.; pop. 497,000), NW French West Africa, on the Atlantic. Its cap., Saint-Louis, is in Senegal. Mainly desert. Became a French protectorate in 1903 and an overseas territory in 1946.

Mauritius (môrĭ'shẽùs), island (720 sq. mi.; pop. 419,-185), in Indian Ocean, one of Mascarene Isls. With Rodriguez and outlying dependencies it forms a British colony; cap. Port Louis. Sugar is main crop and export. Discovered 1507 by the Portuguese, occupied 1638–1710 by the Dutch, and settled 1721 by the French, who named it Ile de France. La Bourdonnais was governor, 1735–46. Island was captured 1810 by the British. Abolition of slavery in British Empire (1834) caused influx of laborers from India, who now outnumber the native Negroes.

Maurocordatos, Alexander: see MAVROCORDATOS.

Maurois, André (ädrä' môrwä'), 1885–, French author.

Noted for novel *The Silence of Colonel Bramble* (1918; Eng. tr., 1920) and for biographies of Shelley (*Ariel*, 1923), Byron, Disraeli, Chateaubriand, Washington, and others.

Maurras, Charles (shärl′ môräs′), 1868–1952, French author and critic. Edited the royalist daily *Action française*. Sentenced (1945) to life imprisonment for collaboration with Germans in World War II, he was released shortly before his death.

Maury, Matthew Fontaine (mô′rē), 1806–73, American hydrographer, a naval officer. Made valuable charts of the Atlantic. His *Physical Geography of the Sea* (1885) was first classic of modern oceanography.

Maurya (mou′ùryù), Indian dynasty, 325–184 B.C., founded by SANDRACOTTUS (Chandragupta). ASOKA, his grandson, united nearly all India and Afghanistan. Substituted Buddhism for Hinduism and began a golden age of arts and public works.

mausoleum (môsủlē′ủm), a tomb, especially one of some size and elaborateness, so called from sepulcher of that name at Halicarnassus, Asia Minor, erected c.352 B.C. for Mausolus of Caria. One of seven wonders of the ancient world, it was a white marble structure, richly decorated by Scopas and other sculptors, probably including Praxiteles. A famous Roman mausoleum is that of Hadrian, now called CASTEL SANT′ ANGELO. Most celebrated of mausoleums built under Mogul emperors of India is TAJ MAHAL.

Mausolus (môsō′lùs), d. 353 B.C., Persian satrap, ruler of Caria and Rhodes. After his death, his wife erected the mausoleum at Halicarnassus.

maverick (măv′rĭck), in cowboy terminology, an unbranded yearling calf or any older animal not bearing the owner's mark. Formerly such an animal became the property of the first person to brand it.

Mavrocordatos or Maurocordatos, Alexander (both: măv″rôkôr-dhä′tôs), 1791–1865, Greek statesman. Drafted declaration of Greek independence (1821). Later, as president of national assembly, he opposed pro-Russian policy of Demetrios Ypsilanti and Capo d'Istria. Was premier under King Otto after 1831.

Maxen (mäk′sùn), village, Saxony, E Germany, S of Dresden. Here, in Seven Years War, a Prussian army surrendered to Daun 1759.

Maxentius (măksĕn′shùs), d. 312, Roman emperor in Italy and Africa; son of MAXIMIAN. After CONSTANTIUS I died (306) he was aided by his father in making his claim to the throne good, opposing Severus, Galerius, and CONSTANTINE I. Ultimately Constantine defeated him in the decisive battle of Milvian Bridge (312).

Maxim, family of inventors and munition makers. **Sir Hiram Stevens Maxim,** 1840–1916, b. Sangerville, Maine, moved to England, where he invented (1884) the Maxim machine gun. His other inventions include explosives and a heavier-than-air airplane. His brother, **Hudson Maxim,** 1853–1927, b. Orneville, Maine, remained in the U.S. He was a chemist and developed a number of explosives. **Hiram Percy Maxim,** 1869–1936, b. Brooklyn, N.Y., was the son of Sir Hiram. He, too, remained in the U.S. He invented an automobile and a silencer for explosive weapons. Perhaps more useful inventions of his were silencers for gasoline engines.

Maximian (măksĭ′mēùn), d. 310, Roman emperor. Was made subemperor in 285 and ruled jointly with Diocletian (286–305). Both emperors abdicated in 305 in favor of CONSTANTIUS I and GALERIUS, but the death of Constantius (306) caused a complicated struggle for power. Maximian at first aided his son MAXENTIUS, defeating Severus in Italy and gaining the support of CONSTANTINE I (who married his daughter Fausta). Later he fell out with Maxentius and fled to Constantine. He revolted in 310 and was forced to commit suicide.

Maximilian, emperors and German kings. **Maximilian I,** 1459–1519. His father, Emperor Frederick III, secured his election as king in 1486 and delegated most of his powers to him. Sole ruler after Frederick's death (1493), he was never crowned emperor by the pope but in 1508 took the title emperor-elect, which was also assumed by his successors (see HOLY ROMAN EMPIRE). His marriage to MARY OF BURGUNDY (1477) brought the Low Countries and Franche-Comté to the house of Austria but involved him in war with France, as did his marriage by proxy to ANNE OF BRITTANY (1490). The Treaty of Senlis (1493) restored Artois and Franche-Comté, which he had lost to France in the Treaty of ARRAS of 1482, to his family possessions. In the same year he married a niece of Ludovico Sforza, who paid him a huge dowry and whom he invested as duke of Milan. This third marriage, and his difficulties with Venice, involved him in the ITALIAN WARS, which drained his funds and made him dependent on loans from the FUGGER family. He gained nothing in Italy and was equally unsuccessful in his favorite project of a crusade against the Turks. His reign was marked by attempts at constitutional reforms of the Holy Roman Empire; by the ascendency of the towns (notably the SWABIAN LEAGUE, which he favored) and of the merchant classes; by the flowering of German art and humanism (he was a patron of Dürer and Ulrich von Hutten); and by the beginning of the Reformation. His dynastic policy secured for his grandsons CHARLES V and FERDINAND I one of the largest successions in history—the Low Countries, the Spanish empire, Austria, Bohemia, and Hungary. Maximilian, because of his chivalrous and slightly quixotic disposition, has been called the last of the knights. **Maximilian II,** 1527–76, son of Ferdinand I, was crowned German king and king of Bohemia in 1562 and king of Hungary in 1563; in 1564 he succeeded his father as emperor-elect. He probably sympathized with Lutheranism and granted considerable religious freedom, while at the same time encouraging the Catholic Reform. In 1568 he made a truce with Turkey by which he agreed to pay tribute to the sultan for his share of Hungary. He died while preparing to invade Poland, where he had been elected king by a minority of the nobles, the majority having chosen Stephen Bathory.

Maximilian, 1832–67, emperor of Mexico (1864–67); brother of Austrian Emperor Francis Joseph. When Mexican conservatives sought aid of Napoleon III in founding a Mexican empire, Maximilian was persuaded to accept the crown. When he and his wife, Carlotta, arrived in Mexico (1864), they found most of Mexico hostile to them and loyal to Benito Juárez. Maximilian's tenure rested solely on French soldiers, and when Napoleon III was compelled to withdraw these (1866–67), the flimsy fabric of Mexico's empire dissolved. Carlotta went to Europe to seek aid. Maximilian took personal command of his forces, was captured, and was shot (1867). Carlotta went mad but survived Maximilian 60 years.

Maximilian, electors and kings of Bavaria. **Maximilian I,** 1573–1651, duke of Bavaria from 1597, founded the Catholic League (1609) and headed it in the THIRTY YEARS WAR. He was rewarded by Emperor Ferdinand II for his aid against Frederick the Winter King with the rank of elector (see ELECTORS) and with the Upper Palatinate (1623). He secured Wallenstein's dismissal in 1630. **Maximilian I,** 1756–1825, king of Bavaria (1806–25), acceded in 1795 as duke of PALATINATE-Zweibrücken and in 1799 as elector of Bavaria. His alliance with Napoleon I earned him vast territorial increases (1805), the royal title (1806), and leadership over the CONFEDERATION OF THE RHINE. He passed over to the allies just before the battle of Leipzig (1813). With his minister Montgelas he carried out important social reforms and granted a liberal constitution (1818). His grandson, King **Maximilian II,** 1811–64, succeeded his father LOUIS I in 1848. He was a liberal and a patron of art and learning. His son Louis II succeeded him.

Maximilian, prince of Baden (Max of Baden), 1867–

Maximin 1929, chancellor of Germany (Oct.–Nov., 1918). Began to negotiate for an armistice with the Allies of World War I; surrendered government to Friedrich Ebert after Emperor William II's flight.

Maximin (măk'simĭn), name of two Roman emperors. **1** Died 238, ruled 235–38. A Thracian soldier of great physical strength, he was chosen emperor at Mainz by rebels against ALEXANDER SEVERUS. He warred successfully against the Germans, but was overthrown by Gordian I. **2** Died 313, proclaimed himself emperor 308 in opposition to Licinius and was powerful after the death of Galerius (310), but allied himself with Maxentius, was defeated by Licinius, and was superseded by Constantine I. Called also Maximin Daia.

Maximus, d. 388, Roman emperor of the West (383–88), after murdering GRATIAN to get the throne. Defeated Valentinian II in Italy (387), but was beaten and put to death by Theodosius.

Max-Müller, Friedrich: see MÜLLER, MAX.

Max of Baden: see MAXIMILLIAN, PRINCE OF BADEN.

Maxwell, James Clerk (klärk), 1831–79, Scottish physicist. Developed theory of electromagnetic field on mathematical basis; said electricity and magnetic energy travel in transverse waves and light waves are of this nature. Studied heat, kinetic theory of gases, color and color blindness. Unit of magnetic flux, the maxwell, is named for him.

May, Thomas, 1595–1650, English translator and poet. Known for translations of *Virgil's Georgics* (1628), and *Selected Epigrams of Martial* (1629).

May: see MONTH.

May, Cape: see CAPE MAY.

Maya (mä'yä, mī'ù), American Indians, mostly in Yucatan peninsula and Chiapas in Mexico, in Guatemala, and in W Honduras. Mayan languages (see LANGUAGE, table) are spoken in this area and in a few isolated spots elsewhere. Theirs was one of the greatest of pre-Columbian civilizations; although archaeologists have learned much about it from early Spanish writings and 20th-cent. excavations, much remains to be discovered. Sylvanus G. Morley divides their early history into three periods—Pre-Maya (2500 B.C.?–A.D. 317), Old Empire (317–987), and New Empire (987–1697)—*empire* being merely a convenient term, since government was by city-states. In the late Pre-Maya came invention of the calendar, hieroglyphic writing, and beginning of stone architecture. The Old Empire saw territorial and cultural consolidation and flowering of architecture in cities (Copán, Quiriguá, Palenque). For reasons still unknown these cities were abandoned, and the New Empire was based on new cities founded after migration (CHICHÉN ITZÁ, Mayapán, Uxmal). Mexican influence was strong because of migration or invasion. The last part of this period was dominated by civil wars and the Spanish conquest under the elder and younger Francisco de MONTEJO. In the city-states the hereditary chieftain, the priests, and the nobility held power. Outstanding achievements of the Maya were their highly accurate calendar; their massive architecture, notable for harmony and rich decoration; their knowledge of mathematics; and their development of writing.

Mayagüez (mīägwäs'), city (pop. 87,307), W Puerto Rico; a port on Mona Passage; center of fertile agr. region. Colleges of agr. and mechanical arts of Univ. of Puerto Rico are here.

Mayakovsky, Vladimir (vlüdyě'mĭr mī'ükôf'skē), 1893–1930, Russian poet. Leader of the futuristic school, he became the chief spokesman in verse of the revolution. Died by suicide.

May apple, North American woodland perennial (*Podophyllum peltatum*) with large lobed leaves and solitary white flowers in spring, followed by an edible berry. The roots yield a drug. It is also called mandrake.

May beetle: see JUNE BEETLE.

May Day, first day of May. Celebration probably originated in spring festivals of goddesses of fertility of India and Egypt. In medieval England the chief feature of the celebration was dancing around Maypole. This custom survives for exhibition purposes in England and U.S. In 1889 Second Socialist International designated May Day as holiday for radical labor, and it is very important day in USSR.

Mayence, Germany: see MAINZ.

Mayenne, Charles de Lorraine, duc de (shärl' dù lôrěn' dük' dù mäyěn'), 1554–1611, French Catholic general. Succeeded his brother Henri, 3d duc de Guise, as head of LEAGUE. In 1596 he broke with his Spanish allies; made peace with King Henry IV.

Mayenne (mäyěn'), department (2,012 sq. mi.; pop. 256, 317), NW France, in Maine; cap. Laval.

Mayer, Tobias (tōbē'äs mī'ùr), 1723–62, German astronomer and mathematician, noted for his lunar tables (1752) and zodiacal star catalogue.

Mayerling (mī'ùrlĭng), village, Lower Austria, SW of Vienna. Here, in a hunting lodge, Archduke RUDOLF and Maria Vetsera met their death (1889).

Mayfair, fashionable residential area of W London, England. Includes Berkeley and Grosvenor Squares.

Mayfield, city (pop. 8,990), SW Ky., S of Paducah in farm, clay, and timber area. Tobacco and mule market and trade, and industrial center of agr. area. Cemetery has curious Woolridge monuments.

Mayfield Heights, residential city (pop. 5,807), NE Ohio, E of Cleveland.

Mayflower: see TRAILING ARBUTUS.

Mayflower, ship which in 1620 brought Pilgrims from England to New England. After two-month voyage land was sighted in Nov., and settlement was estab. at Plymouth, Mass. Group signed agreement for government of colony known as **Mayflower Compact.** Society of Mayflower Descendants (estab. 1894) is for proved descendants of *Mayflower* passengers.

Maynard (mā'nùrd), town (pop. 6,978), E Mass., near Concord.

Maynooth (mā'nōŏth, mānōōth'), town (pop. 572), Co. Kildare, Ireland. Seat of St. Patrick's Col., chief Irish institution for training Catholic clergy.

Mayo, Charles Horace (mā'ō), 1865–1939, American surgeon, specialist in goiter and cataract. With his brother, **William James Mayo,** 1861–1939, specialist in abdominal surgery, he developed **Mayo Clinic** from small clinic opened 1889 by their father in Rochester, Minn. They estab. 1915 Mayo Foundation for Medical Education and Research at Univ. of Minnesota.

Mayo (mā'ō), county (2,084 sq. mi.; pop. 148,120), W Ireland, in Connaught; co. town Castlebar. Mountainous in W, it has many lakes and deeply indented coastline. Oats and potatoes are grown and livestock is raised. Population is dwindling.

maypop: see PASSIONFLOWER.

Maysville, city (pop. 8,632), N Ky., on Ohio R. (bridged) and SE of Covington. Transportation, trade and industrial center with distilleries and tobacco and metal-products plants. Here Daniel Boone had tavern and U. S. Grant went to school. Site of Simon Kenton's trading post near by.

Maywood. 1 Residential and industrial city (pop. 13,292), S Calif., SSE of Los Angeles; founded 1920. Auto-assembling, steel, food-processing plants. **2** Residential village (pop. 27,473), NE Ill., W suburb of Chicago and on Des Plaines R., in industrial area. **3** Residential borough (pop. 8,667), NE N.J., near Hackensack, inc. 1894.

Mazarin, Jules (zhül' mäzärē'), 1602–61, Italian cardinal, chief minister of Louis XIII and Louis XIV of France. His original name was Giulio Mazarini. Served in papal army; was papal nuncio to France 1634–36; entered French service as protégé of Cardinal Richelieu, whom he succeeded 1642. Though never ordained a priest, he was made cardinal in 1641. He completely dominated the regent, ANNE OF AUSTRIA, to whom he may have been secretly married. Though he won excellent terms for France in the Peace of WESTPHALIA (1648), his financial abuses and dictatorial, centralizing policy provoked the troubles of the FRONDE. His victory over the Fronde (1653) and the Peace of the PYRENEES with Spain (1659) marked the triumph of his dip'omacy.

Mazarin Bible (mă'zŭrĭn), probably the first book printed by Gutenberg and from movable types at Mainz, 1456. Its folio pages of two columns of 42 lines each were in gothic type and hand-illuminated. A copy was first rediscovered in Cardinal Mazarin's library. One of the finest printed books, it is also called the Gutenberg or 42-line Bible.

Mazatlán (mäsätlän'), city (pop. 32,117), Sinaloa, NW Mexico; a port on the Pacific. Spanish colonial trade with Philippines began development of port.

Mazeppa (mŭzě'pŭ), 1644?–1709, hetman of Cossacks in Ukraine. Joined Charles XII of Sweden against Peter I of Russia, died a refugee in Turkey. Byron's poem *Mazeppa* relates how the husband of young Mazeppa's Polish mistress tied him naked to a horse, which was driven into the steppes.

Mazo, Juan Bautista Martínez del (hwän' boutēs'tä märtē'nĕth dĕl mä'thō), c.1612–1667, Spanish landscape and portrait painter. Was son-in-law of Velázquez, with whom he often collaborated.

Mazzini, Giuseppe (jōōzĕp'pä mät-sē'nē), 1805–72, Italian patriot and revolutionist, a key figure of the RISORGIMENTO. After 1831 he spent most of his life in exile, chiefly in London. In books and periodicals he expounded his revolutionary doctrine, advocating a unified Italian republic as his aim and direct popular action as the means. His writings, imbued with highest idealism, are also distinguished for style. Mazzini took direct part in the revolution of Milan (1848), in the Roman republic of 1849, and in other ventures. His ideas clashed with those of CAVOUR, who eventually won out.

Mc–. Names beginning thus are entered as if spelled Mac–. See the article MAC.

Mdina, Malta: see CITTÀ VECCHIA.

Mead, George Herbert (mēd), 1863–1931, American philosopher, proponent of "social behaviorism."

Mead, Margaret, 1901–, American anthropologist. She contributed toward enlarging scope of anthropology through work on relation of culture to personality. Perhaps the most widely known of her works is *Coming of Age in Samoa* (1928).

Mead, William Rutherford, 1846–1928, American architect; partner in firm of McKim, Mead, and White.

mead, alcoholic beverage fermented of honey and water, sometimes spiced. Known in ancient times.

Mead, Lake: see HOOVER DAM.

Meade, George Gordon, 1815–72, Union general in Civil War. Distinguished in Seven Days battles, at Antietam, Fredericksburg, Chancellorsville. Commanded Army of Potomac from 1863; at Gettysburg he won greatest battle of war. His sound generalship in Wilderness campaign aided final victory.

meadow beauty, rose-flowered perennial (*Rhexia virginica*) native to moist fields in E North America.

meadow lark, North American bird of blackbird family, with black-and-brown streaked coat, yellow breast with black crescent. It nests in grass.

meadow saffron, hardy Old World crocuslike plant of genus *Colchicum* most species of which bloom in autumn. Corms and seeds of *Colchicum autumnale* yield COLCHICINE.

meadowsweet, hardy perennial of genus *Filipendula* with large clusters of small flowers. Common species in North America are the native pink-flowered queen of the prairie and the Eurasian white queen of the meadow.

Meadville, city (pop. 18,972), NW Pa., S of Erie; settled c.1788. Trade center in agr. area with mfg. of zippers, rayon, and metal products. Seat of Allegheny Col. (coed.; 1816).

Meagher, Thomas Francis (mär), 1823–67, Irish revolutionist and Union general in Civil War, b. Ireland. Aided Irish rebellion of 1848; escaped to New York city in 1852. Organized and led "Irish Brigade" that fought with Army of Potomac through Chancellorsville in the Civil War.

mean, in statistics, a type of average. Arithmetic mean of a group of numbers equals their sum divided by their number; geometric mean is square root of product of the quantities.

Meany, George, 1894–, American labor leader, president of American Federation of Labor (1952–). A.F. of L. secretary-treasurer 1940–52.

Meares, John (mērz), 1756?–1809, British naval officer, explorer, and trader. Explored coast of Alaska. Built trading post on NOOTKA SOUND (1788).

measles (rubeola), contagious epidemic disease caused by virus. Incubation period c.10 days. Attended by fever and by rash beginning on face and neck. Attack usually gives lifelong immunity. German measles (rubella) is similar but milder. Incubation period 10–21 days. Attack does not give immunity. Reported as harmful to embryo when contracted by mother in early pregnancy.

measures: see WEIGHTS AND MEASURES.

meat, the flesh of animals, especially of cattle, sheep, lambs, and swine, intended for food. Although sometimes used in distinction from game, poultry, and fish, the term may also apply to all animal flesh. Meat contains chiefly water, protein, and fat, with some minerals; it is almost entirely utilized by the body. Lean and fat flesh of a carcass and certain glands and organs (heart, liver, kidneys, tongue, tripe, brains, sweetbreads) are edible. Cooking softens tissue, coagulates blood and albumen, destroys undesirable organisms in meat, and imparts flavor.

Meath (mēth, mēdh), county (903 sq. mi.; pop. 66,232), E Ireland, in Leinster; co. town Trim. Farming and cattle raising are important. Long considered a fifth province of Ireland. TARA was seat of the high kings of Ireland.

meat packing, one of the largest modern industries, in its present form dates from the introduction of refrigeration, first used for a railroad shipment in 1870. It includes the operation of large central plants (such as those for which Chicago is known) for buying, inspecting, slaughtering, and preparing animals for food; utilization of by-products for many purposes; and the distribution of meat by means of refrigerated warehouses, railroad cars, and steamships. Federal laws prescribe examination of animals slaughtered for interstate trade or export.

Meaux (mō), city (pop. 13,030), Seine-et-Marne dept., N France, on Marne R.; chief city of Brie. Has cathedral (12th–16th cent.) with tomb of Bossuet, who was bishop of Meaux.

Mecca (mĕ'kù), city (pop. 90,000), cap. of Hejaz, Saudi Arabia, c.50 mi. from its port, Jidda. Birthplace of MOHAMMED the Prophet; holiest city of Islam. Called Macoraba by Ptolemy, city was ancient center of commerce and a holy place of Arab sects before rise of Islam. Mohammed's flight (the hegira) from Mecca in 622 is beginning of Moslem era. City was captured by Mohammed in 630. Sacked in 930 by the Karmathians, captured in 1517 by Ottoman Turks, and held 1803–13 by the Wahabis. In 1916 it became cap. of Husein ibn Ali, who overthrew Turkish rule and made himself king of the Hejaz; he was ousted by Ibn Saud in 1924. Here is the great mosque, the Haram, enclosing the KAABA (chief goal of Moslem pilgrimages), near which is the holy well, the Zemzen. Trade depends almost wholly on pilgrims. Though then banned to unbelievers, city was visited in 19th cent. by Richard Burton and other non-Moslems in disguise.

mechanical advantage: see MACHINE.

mechanics, branch of physics concerned with action of forces upon bodies (solids, liquids, or gases). Science of mechanics treats primarily of motion, of effects of forces applied to bodies in motion (kinetics) and motion alone (kinematics) without considering causes, such as mass and force. Kinetics and kinematics are sometimes classed together under dynamics; statics is a branch treating of bodies in equilibrium and of the forces holding them in that state. Mechanics of liquids deals with hydrostatics (bodies of liquids in equilibrium), hydrodynamics (motion of liquids and principles involved), and hydraulics (application of these principles to machines). Mechanics of gases (pneumatics) is concerned largely with pressure exerted by atmosphere and with physical properties of gases in general. See *ills.*, pp. 303, 619.

Mechanicsburg, borough (pop. 6,786), S Pa., WSW of Harrisburg. Mfg. of clothing and metal products.

Mechanicsville: see SEVEN DAYS BATTLES.

Mechanicville, city (pop. 7,385), E N.Y., N of Albany, on the Hudson and on the Barge Canal. Railroad shops. Clothing, knit goods; food, paper products.

mechanized warfare, in the broadest sense, modern mobile attack and defense depending upon machines, particularly those powered by gasoline engines. Such warfare centers around use of the tank and the armored vehicle, with support and supply from motorized columns and airplanes. The tank and the automobile, already used in World War I, presaged the full potential of mechanized warfare as displayed by the Germans in World War II. The Allies quickly countered by building up mechanized units of their own and evolving an effective defense technique based on the use of artillery and aircraft.

Mechelen or **Mechlin,** Belgium: see MALINES.

Mechnikov, Ilya Ilyich: see METCHNIKOFF, ÉLIE.

Mecklenburg (Ger. mĕ′klŭnbŏŏrk), state (8,856 sq. mi.; pop. 2,139,640), [East] German Democratic Republic, on Baltic Sea; cap. Schwerin. Has fertile agr. plain, forests, lakes. Cities of Rostock, Wismar, Stralsund were long important as Hanseatic ports. Settled by Slavic Wends in 6th cent., region was Christianized and colonized by Germans in 12th cent. Its Wendish princes were raised to dukes of Holy Roman Empire in 1348. In 1628 Mecklenburg was awarded to Wallenstein, its conqueror, but in 1632 it reverted to its old dynasty. In 1701 began the division of the territory into two duchies (after 1815, grand duchies)—Mecklenburg-Schwerin and Mecklenburg-Strelitz. Both sided with Prussia in Austro-Prussian War (1866) and joined the German Empire in 1871. Grand dukes were deposed 1918. In 1934 both Mecklenburgs were united as a single state, and after 1945, when Mecklenburg came under Russian occupation, the state was enlarged by the addition of Hither Pomerania (minus Stettin).

Mecklenburg Declaration of Independence, allegedly proclaimed at Charlotte, N.C., by citizens of Mecklenburg co., May 20, 1775. Widely regarded as spurious document. Anti-British resolutions actually adopted May 31, 1775, do not mention independence.

Medea (mēdē′ù), in Greek mythology, princess of Colchis, famous for her knowledge of sorcery. She aided Jason, against will of her father, Aeëtes, to gain Golden Fleece, and fled with him, killing her brother to detain her father. When Jason later wished to marry Creusa, Medea sent her a magic wedding gown which burned her to death. Medea then killed her own children by Jason and went to Athens where she married Aegeus.

Medellín (mādhāyēn′), city. (pop. 143,952; alt. c.5,000 ft.), W central Colombia; founded 1675. The leading industrial center of republic, Medellín also exports coffee (introduced after 1918).

Medes, anc. people of Asia Minor: see MEDIA.

Medford. 1 City (pop. 66,113), E Mass., N suburb of Boston, on Mystic R.; settled 1630. Paper boxes, metal products, chemicals. Main seat of Tufts Col. (nonsectarian; for men and women; chartered 1852, opened 1855 by Universalists); cooperates with Harvard in Crane (theology) and Fletcher (law, diplomacy) schools, and with other colleges; has some divisions at Boston. **2** City (pop. 17,305), SW Oregon, W of Klamath Falls; founded 1883. Processing and ship-

ping center in agr. (dairy, fruit, truck) and lumbering region. Fishing and hunting area, Crater Lake Natl. Park, Oregon Caves Natl. Monument are near.

Media (mē′dèù), anc. country of W Asia, in region now in W Iran and S Azerbaijan SSR; cap. Ecbatana. It is said that a dynasty founded by Arbaces ruled until Cyrus the Great forcibly annexed it to Persia. The inhabitants were the Medes, who were supposed to be learned in astronomy and the magic arts.

Media, borough (pop. 5,726), SE Pa., W of Philadelphia. Near-by Providence Meetinghouse (1664) has graves of many William Penn followers.

median (mē′dèun), in statistics, a type of average. In a group of numbers, as many of the numbers are larger than the median as are smaller.

Medici (mě′dĭchē, Ital. mā′dēchē), Italian family which directed the destinies of FLORENCE (and, after 1569, of TUSCANY) from the 15th cent. to 1737. Their rise from obscurity to immense wealth as merchants and bankers marked the triumph of the capitalist class over guild merchants and artisans. Until 1532 the democratic constitution of Florence was outwardly upheld, but the Medici exerted actual control over the government (except when exiled, 1494–1512, 1527–30) without holding any permanent official position. They are perhaps best remembered as patrons of the RENAISSANCE. Under their usually tolerant rule Florence rivaled ancient Athens. The first important member and common ancestor of the senior and junior lines of the family was Giovanni di Bicci de' Medici (1360–1429). Below follows an account of the principal members of both lines, in chronological order.

Senior line. **Cosimo de' Medici** (kō′zēmō), 1389–1464, son of Giovanni di Bicci, was first of his family to rule Florence. Banished 1433, he returned 1434 and with support of the people became the acknowledged leading citizen of the republic. He vastly expanded the family's banking business and, despite lavish charities and patronage, doubled his fortune. In Florence, he made his power as little felt as possible; in foreign policy, he sought a balance of power among Italian states. Founded Medici Library and academy for Greek studies (headed by Ficino); protected major artists of his time. His son, **Piero de' Medici** (pyā′rō), 1416–69, nicknamed Il Gottoso [the gouty], succeeded as head of family. He put down a plot against his life but allowed conspirators to go free (1466). His son and successor, **Lorenzo de' Medici** (lōrän′tsō), 1449–92, called Lorenzo il Magnifico, was a towering figure of the Renaissance. An astute politician, generous patron, and able scholar and poet, he showed little success as a business man; lavish public entertainments made him popular but drained his funds. In 1478 took place the PAZZI CONSPIRACY, in which Lorenzo's brother Giuliano de' Medici was killed; Lorenzo was merely wounded and the plot collapsed. Resulting warfare with Pope Sixtus IV ended in 1481. Lorenzo allowed his enemy SAVONAROLA to preach freely. His second son, **Giovanni de' Medici** (jōvän′nē), became pope (see LEO X); his oldest son and successor, **Piero de' Medici,** 1471–1503, was expelled from Florence in 1494 by the republicans, led by Savonarola, during the invasion of Italy by Charles VIII of France. In 1512 Piero's youngest brother, **Giuliano de' Medici** (jōōlyä′nō), 1479–1516, reentered Florence with the help of the Holy League. He became duke of Nemours by marriage (1515). After his death, control over Florence was exercised by Leo X through Piero's son **Lorenzo de' Medici,** 1492–1519, whom Leo also made duke of Urbino (1516). Giuliano's and Lorenzo's statues by Michelangelo adorn their tombs in the Church of San Lorenzo, Florence. Lorenzo's daughter was CATHERINE DE' MEDICI, queen of France. After Lorenzo's death his cousin **Giulio de' Medici** (see Pope CLEMENT VII) took control of Florence. Elected pope (1523), he continued to rule through Giuliano's illegitimate son, **Ippolito de' Medici** (ēp-pō′lētō), 1509–35, whom he made a cardinal in 1531, and through

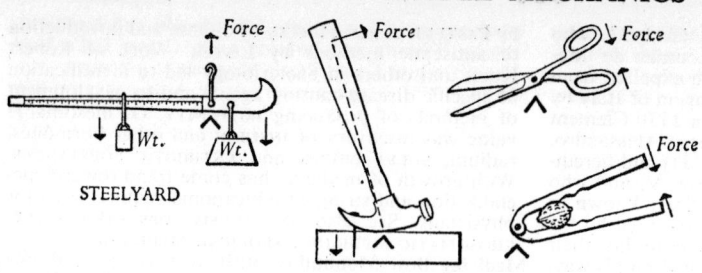

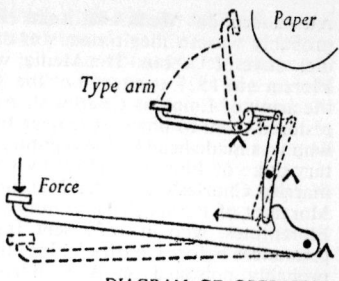

LEVER The moments (= force x distance) around the fulcrum, ∧, are equal.

STEELYARD

DIAGRAM OF OPERATION OF A TYPEWRITER KEY

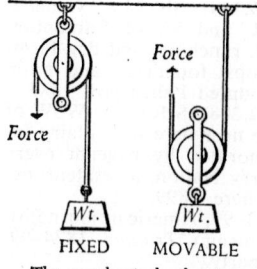

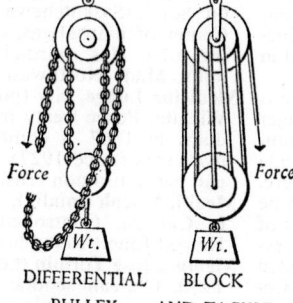

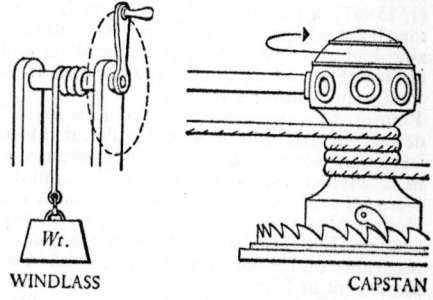

FIXED **MOVABLE**

The mechanical advantage of the movable pulley pictured above is twice that of the fixed.

PULLEY

DIFFERENTIAL PULLEY **BLOCK AND TACKLE**

Systems of pulleys give even greater mechanical advantage.

WINDLASS **CAPSTAN**

WHEEL AND AXLE

The amount of force required is proportional to the radii of wheel and axle.

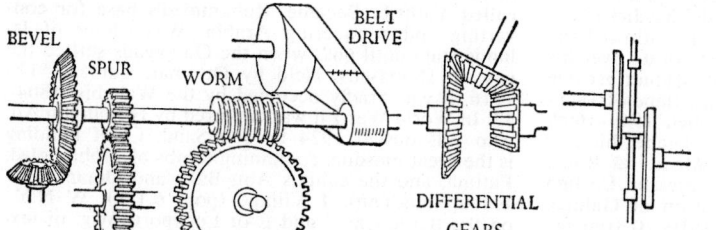

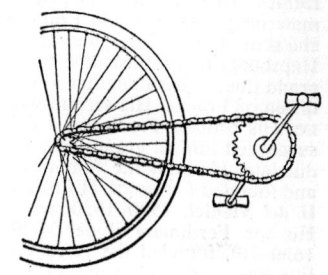

GEARS

Gears are derived from the wheel-and-axle principle. They are used to change the direction of applied force, to change one kind of motion into another, or to alter ratios and hence power.

SCREW

A screw is essentially an inclined plane wrapped around a cylinder.

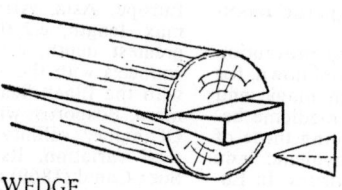

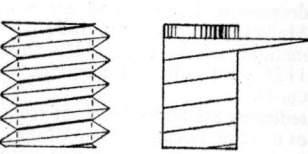

INCLINED PLANE

The mechanical advantage is determined by the height and length of the incline.

WEDGE

A wedge is a double inclined plane.

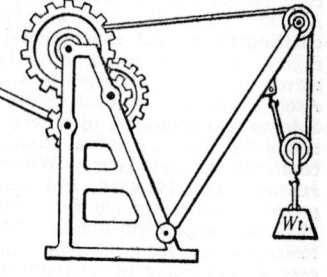

JACK **MECHANIC'S VISE**

SIMPLE DEVICES UTILIZING SCREWS

ARCHIMEDES' SCREW

An early device for lifting water.

SIMPLE CRANE

This is essentially a combination of levers, pulleys, and gears.

Alessandro de' Medici (äles-sän'drō), 1511–37, who probably was an illegitimate son of Lorenzo de' Medici, duke of Urbino. The Medici were expelled from Florence in 1527 as a result of the invasion of Italy by the army of Emperor Charles V, but in 1530 Clement restored them to power. Clement favored Alessandro, who was made head of the republic (1531) and hereditary duke of Florence (1532) by Charles V, and who married Charles's daughter Margaret (later known as Margaret of Parma). His tyranny was resented by the Florentines, who in 1535 sent Ippolito to lay their grievances before Charles V. Ippolito died on his way, probably poisoned on Alessandro's orders. He had been a lavish patron of literature. Two years later Alessandro was murdered by Lorenzino de' Medici (1515–47), a member of the younger line and his former boon companion. The republican uprising Lorenzino had anticipated did not materialize, and the succession fell to Cosimo I. Lorenzino was assassinated in Venice on Cosimo's orders.

Younger line and grand dukes of Tuscany. This line is descended from **Lorenzo de' Medici**, d. 1440, younger son of Giovanni di Bicci. His great-grandson **Giovanni de' Medici**, 1498–1526, called Giovanni delle Bande Nere [of the black bands], was a famous condottiere. He fought in the service of Leo X, on whose death he acquired his nickname because of the black stripes of mourning on his banners. He continued in papal service, except in 1525, when he fought and was wounded on the side of Francis I of France. His older son, **Cosimo I de' Medici**, 1519–74, succeeded Alessandro as duke of Florence (1537), assumed absolute authority, acquired Siena (1555), and in 1569 was raised to grand duke by Pope Pius V. Under his able, though ruthless, rule Florence reached its highest political and material power. His son **Francesco de' Medici** (fränchä'skō), 1541–87, reigned 1574–87. He allowed the Hapsburgs to establish a virtual protectorate over his grand duchy. His daughter MARIE DE' MEDICI became queen of France. His second wife was Bianca CAPELLO. His brother **Ferdinand I de' Medici**, 1549–1609, succeeded him as grand duke after resigning his cardinalate. He built the famous Villa Medici at Rome and founded LEGHORN. His son and successor, **Cosimo II de' Medici**, 1590–1620, was a patron of Galileo. His son **Ferdinand II de' Medici**, 1610–70 (reigned 1620–70), founded the Accademia del Cimento, first European academy of natural sciences (1657). His son **Cosimo III de' Medici**, 1642–1723, reigned 1670–1723. His government was one of bigoted and corrupt despotism. His son and successor, **Gian Gastone de' Medici** (jän' gästō'nä), 1671–1737, was the last male member of the family. His succession was settled in 1735 on Francis of Lorraine (later Emperor FRANCIS I).

medicine, art and science of treatment and prevention of disease. Because origin of disease was unknown, for centuries its treatment was coupled with magic and superstition. More scientific practice of medicine began in ancient Asiatic civilizations including those of Mesopotamia. Israel later formulated hygienic laws and Arabs contributed to knowledge of drugs. In Europe, progress can be traced through Greek school of ASCLEPIADES OF BITHYNIA and HIPPOCRATES. GALEN contributed original experimental work and encouraged dissection. Remnants of early learning were preserved during Middle Ages by Christian Church and Arab physicians. Medical school estab. 9th cent. at Salerno was prototype of others. Work of VESALIUS stimulated more accurate anatomical studies. Valuable contributions made later by William HARVEY, Edward JENNER, John HUNTER, and many others. Medical progress was hampered for centuries by refusal of physicians to perform SURGERY. Bloodletting was common practice from ancient times until late 18th cent. Development of HOMEOPATHY influenced revolt against prescription of large doses of drugs. Mortality declined sharply during 19th cent. after formulation by PASTEUR of germ theory of disease and introduction of antiseptic methods by LISTER. Work of Robert KOCH and others in bacteriology led to identification of specific disease-causing agents and to development of methods of producing IMMUNITY. Of inestimable value was discovery of INSULIN and other hormones, radium, SULFA DRUGS, and ANTIBIOTIC SUBSTANCES. With growth of medicine has come trend toward specialization and stringent educational requirements for physicians. See also ANESTHESIA; OBSTETRICS; PSYCHOSOMATIC MEDICINE; TROPICAL MEDICINE.

Medicine Bow Mountains, outlying E range of Rocky Mts. extending S from town of Medicine Bow, Wyo., NW of Laramie, to Cameron Pass, Colo. Medicine Bow Peak is 12,005 ft. high.

Medicine Hat, city (pop. 16,364), SE Alta., Canada, on South Saskatchewan R. and SE of Edmonton. Center of natural-gas, coal, ranching, and dry farming area. Has railroad shops, foundries, and grain mills. Made Northwest Mounted Police post 1882.

Medicine Lodge, city (pop. 2,288), S Kansas, WSW of Wichita. Peace treaty made near here with Plains Indians in 1867 is commemorated by pageant every five years (since 1927). Carry Nation, a resident, began her antisaloon crusade here, 1899.

Medill, Joseph (mùdîl'), 1823–99, American journalist, b. Canada. Controlled Chicago *Tribune* 1874–99. Helped found Republican party.

Medina, José Toribio (hōsä' tōrē'byō mādhē'nä), 1852–1930, Chilean scholar. His numerous works cover vast range of learning: history, biography, bibliography, archaeology, journalism.

Medina (mîdē'nä), city (pop. 12,000), Hejaz, Saudi Arabia; sacred city of Islam, second only to Mecca. Situated in an oasis. Before the HEGIRA (622), it was called Yathrib. Became Mohammed's base for converting and conquering Arabia. Was center of Islamic state until 662, when the Omayyads shifted the cap. to Damascus. Held by Ottoman Turks, 1517–1916, it was briefly occupied by the Wahabis, 1804–12. In World War I it was captured by Husein ibn Ali, who was ousted 1924 by Ibn Saud. Chief building is the great mosque, containing tombs of Mohammed, Fatima, and the caliphs Abu Bakr and Oman.

Medina (mùdî'nù). **1** Village (pop. 6,179), W N.Y., on the Barge Canal and E of Lockport. Mfg. of textiles, canned foods, furniture, and iron products. **2** City (pop. 5,097), N Ohio, NW of Akron. Mfg. of apiary supplies and toys.

Medina Sidonia, Alonso Pérez de Guzmán, duque de (mādhē'nä sēdhō'nyä), 1550–1615, commander of Spanish ARMADA.

Mediterranean Sea, largest inland sea, surrounded by Europe, Asia, Africa. Area is c.1,145,000 sq. mi.; max. length, c.2,300 mi.; max. width, c.1,200 mi.; greatest depth, c.14,435 ft., off Cape Matapan. It connects with the Atlantic by the Strait of Gibraltar; with the Black Sea by the Dardanelles, Sea of Marmara, Bosporus; with the Red Sea by the Suez Canal. Of higher salinity than the Atlantic, it has little tidal variation. Its shores are chiefly mountainous. Suez Canal (1869) reestab. its ancient commercial and strategic military importance. European civilization was born on the shores of the Mediterranean, which encompassed the civilized world in ancient and medieval times.

medlar, small, deciduous tree (*Mespilus germanica*) of the rose family, with white or pink flowers. Native to Europe and Asia, it has long been grown in Europe for its apple-shaped fruit.

Médoc (mādôk'), district of Bordeaux wine region, on W bank of Gironde R.; chief town Pauillac. Vineyards include Château Lafite, Château Margaux.

Medusa (mîdū'zù), in Greek mythology, most famous of the three GORGON monsters. Once beautiful, she offended Athena, who made her so hideous that all who looked on her were turned to stone. Perseus slew her and gave her head to Athena. It still kept its petrifying power, and Athena used it on her aegis.

Medway, river of SE England, flowing 70 mi. from two headstreams in Sussex and Surrey to the Thames.

meerschaum (mēr'shôm) [Ger.,= sea foam], a mineral, hydrous magnesium silicate, resembling white clay, chiefly used for making tobacco pipes. Soft and easily carved before drying. Tobacco smoke stains it a rich brown. Main source Asia Minor.

Meerut (mē'rŭt), city (pop. 169,290), NW Uttar Pradesh, India; trade center. Scene of one of first major outbreaks of Sepoy Rebellion (1857).

megalithic monuments (mĕgŭlĭ'thĭk), huge, simple stone structures, found especially along coast of W Europe. Earliest date from 2d millennium B.C.

Mégantic (mügăn'tĭk, Fr. māgătĕk') or **Lac Mégantic,** town (pop. 6,164), SE Que., Canada, on L. Mégantic, ENE of Sherbrooke. Rail center.

Megara (mē'gŭrŭ, mē'gärä), town (pop. 13,360), central Greece, on site of anc. town of Megara, cap. of small dist. of Megaris. Dorians made it wealthy by maritime trade. After Persian Wars Athenian aid was summoned against the Corinthians (459 B.C.), but later expulsion of Athenians helped to provoke the Peloponnesian War.

megatherium (mĕgŭthēr'ēùm), extinct ground sloth widely distributed in North and South America during the Pleistocene. It attained a length of 18 ft. and had massive hind legs and tail.

Megiddo, anc. city, Palestine, on S edge of plain of Esdraelon. Archaeological remains found here date back to c.2000 B.C. Many important battles were fought at Megiddo; here Deborah defeated Sisera, and Josiah was killed. Plain called Megiddon in Zech. 12.11. See also ARMAGEDDON.

Mehemet. For persons thus named, see MOHAMMED.

Meiggs, Henry (mĕgz), 1811–77, American promoter and railroad contractor. One of most spectacular railroad builders in South America.

Meigs, Fort, founded (Feb., 1813) in War of 1812 by Gen. W. H. Harrison on Maumee R., near present Perrysburg, Ohio, across river from British Fort Miami. British attacks (esp. in May and July, 1813) failed to take this "Gibraltar of the West."

Meiji (mā'jē), reign name of Emperor MUTSUHITO of Japan. Meiji restoration (1868) was revolution in Japanese government won by overthrowing Tokugawa Shogunate and returning full power to emperor. Revolt was precipitated by shogun's submission to foreign demands (1854), enmity of powerful clans, and general discontent. Shogun surrendered 1868 to emperor after brief civil war. Crushing of Satsuma rebellion (1877) against new government ensured supremacy of imperial government led by reform groups favoring Westernization. Feudalism abolished; land held by great clans nationalized; new constitution adopted 1889.

Meiklejohn, Alexander (mĭ'kŭljŏn), 1872–, American educator, president of Amherst Col., 1912–24, professor of philosophy at Univ. of Wisconsin (1926–38) and chairman of Experimental Col. (1927–32).

Meiningen (mĭ'nĭng-ùn), city (pop. 23,700), Thuringia, central Germany, on Werra R. Cap. of duchy of Saxe-Meiningen 1680–1918. Ducal theater and orchestra enjoyed world reputation in late 19th cent.

Meinong, Alexius (mĭ'nŏng), 1853–1920, Austrian philosopher and psychologist; pupil of BRENTANO and a founder of first psychological laboratory in Austria.

Meissen (mĭ'sùn), city (pop. 48,348), Saxony, E Germany, on the Elbe. Famous since 1710 for porcelain ware, known as "Dresden" china in English. Became 965 seat of margraviate of Meissen, where WETTIN dynasty of SAXONY originated.

Meissonier, Jean Louis Ernest (zhā' lwē' ĕrnĕst' mäsônyä'), 1815–91, French painter of genre and battle scenes having much accurate detail.

Meissonier, Juste Aurèle (zhüst' ōrĕl'), 1693?–1750, French goldsmith and decorator to Louis XV. He is

generally considered to be originator of ROCOCO style.

meistersinger (mī'stùr–) [Ger.,= mastersinger], member of one of the musical and poetic guilds which flourished in Germany from 14th to 16th cent., succeeding the MINNESINGER. Wagner's *Die Meistersinger von Nürnberg* faithfully represents the guild practices. Hans SACHS was the greatest meistersinger.

Meitner, Lise (lē'zù mīt'nùr), 1878–, Austrian-Swedish physicist, mathematician, codiscover of protactinium. She made studies of disintegration products of radium, thorium, and actinium, and of action of beta rays. Her work on bombardment of uranium nucleus contributed to atomic bomb.

Meknès (mĕknĕs'), city (pop. 159,811), French Morocco; trade center on fertile plateau. Founded in 11th cent. as Almohade fort. Near by is palace built in 17th cent. by Sultan Ismail.

Mekong (mākŏng'), river of SE Asia, c.2,600 mi. long. Rises in Tibet and flows SE through Yünnan prov., China, and Indo-China to South China Sea. Forms vast delta (great rice-growing area) in Cochin China.

Melanchthon, 1497–1560, German scholar and humanist and after Luther chief figure of Lutheran Reformation; original name Philipp Schwarzerd. His *Loci communes* (1521) presented and explained principles of Reformation, and he was liaison between Luther and the humanists, often representing him at conferences. He wrote the Augsburg Confession (1530).

Melanesia (mĕlùnē'zhù), one of three main divisions of Pacific islands, in S and SW Pacific, S of equator. Includes the Solomons, New Hebrides, New Caledonia, Bismarck Archipelago, and Admiralty and Fiji isls. People are largely of Negroid stock; their languages are Malayo-Polynesian (see LANGUAGE, table).

Melba, Dame Nellie, 1861?–1931, Australian soprano, whose original name was Helen Porter Mitchell. She sang at Covent Garden, 1888–1926, and at the Metropolitan Opera, New York, 1893–1910.

Melbourne, William Lamb, 2d Viscount (mĕl'bùrn), 1779–1848, English Whig statesman. Prime minister (1834, 1835–41), he taught statecraft to young Queen Victoria. Did not promote the many reforms made during his administration. His wife, **Caroline Lamb, Viscountess Melbourne,** 1785–1828, is better remembered for her love affair with Lord Byron than for the minor novels she wrote.

Melbourne (mĕl'bùrn), city (pop. 99,861; metropolitan pop. 1,226,409), cap. of Victoria, Australia, port on Yarra R. near its mouth on Hobson's Bay (N arm of Port Phillip Bay). Was first commonwealth cap. (1901–27). Known as Dootigala when settled in 1835; renamed in 1837 for the British prime minister. Commercial center with mfg. of textiles and machinery. Exports wheat, meat, and wool. Seat of Univ. of Melbourne (1854), Conservatorium of Music (1910), and Natl. Art Gall. (1904). Royal mint is here. Many suburbs are seaside resorts.

Melchers, Gari (gâ'rē mĕl'chùrz), 1860–1932, American figure, genre, and portrait painter.

Melchior: see WISE MEN OF THE EAST.

Melchior, Lauritz (lou'rĭts mĕl'kêôr), 1890–, Danish heroic tenor. Sang at the Bayreuth Festivals, 1925–31; at the Metropolitan Opera, New York, 1926–50.

Melchites (mĕl'kīts) [royalists, from Syriac,= king], Christian community of Syria, Jordan, Palestine, Egypt, and America. In communion with the pope, they have a Byzantine rite (in Arabic), and their head is called patriarch of Antioch. They are distinct from Maronites and Syrian Catholics. Also Melkites.

Melchizedek or **Melchisedec** (both mĕlkĭ'–), king of Salem and "priest of the most high God" who blessed Abraham. Gen. 14.18–20. Later regarded as typifying priesthood of the Messiah. Ps. 110.4; Heb. 5–7.

Melcombe Regis: see WEYMOUTH AND MELCOMBE REGIS.

Meleager (mĕlēā'jùr), hero in Greek mythology. At

his birth it was prophesied that he would die when a certain log in the fire burned, so his mother hid that log. He was an Argonaut and later led CALY-DONIAN HUNT. To Atalanta, whom he loved, he gave the Calydonian boar's skin. When his brothers objected, he slew them. Then his mother threw the hidden log on the fire, and Meleager died when it was burned.

Melfi (mĕl'fē), city (pop. 14,190), Basilicata, S Italy. Noted for its wine. Cap. of Norman county of Apulia in 11th cent. Emperor Frederick II promulgated here his code, the Constitutions of Melfi or the Liber Augustalis.

Melilla (mālē'lyä), city (pop. 94,319), on Mediterranean coast of Spanish Morocco. Held by Spain since 1497, it is governed as part of Spanish province of Málaga. A port, with exports of iron ore.

Melitene, Turkey: see MALATYA.

Melitopol (mālyĕtô'pùl), city (pop. 75,735), S Ukraine. Heavy machinery, food products. Was recovered 1943 from the Germans after bloody battle.

Melk or **Mölk** (both: mĕlk), town (pop. 3,139), Lower Austria, on the Danube. Earliest residence of Austrian rulers. Its splendid Benedictine abbey, founded 1089, has a library containing a rich collection of ancient manuscripts and incunabula.

Mellon, Andrew (William), 1855–1937, American financier, industrialist, and public official. President of Mellon Natl. Bank, Pittsburgh. Held large interests in many key American industries (notably aluminum). U.S. Secretary of the Treasury (1921–31); reduced national debt. NATIONAL GALLERY OF ART resulted from his benefactions.

melodrama, originally a spoken text with musical background, as in Greek drama. Popular in 18th cent. (e.g., works of Pietro Metastasio). Action was generally romantic, violent; virtue usually triumphed. Term later used for plays having overdrawn characters, smashing climaxes, and great appeal to sentiment, with or without music.

melon, trailing annual vine (*Cucumis melo*), native to Asia, and its fruit, an important market crop in the U.S. where growing seasons are long. Varieties include muskmelons, which have soft rind and netted surface and are often called cantaloupe (although true cantaloupe is a hard-shelled Mediterranean variety), and the winter types—casaba, honeydew, and Persian. See also WATERMELON.

Melos (mē'lŏs), Aegean island (61 sq. mi.; pop. 6,045), Greece, in the Cyclades; also known as Milo. Flourished as center of Aegean civilization (Early Minoan period, after 3000 B.C.). Resistance to Athenian imperialism led to massacre of population (416 B.C.). Famous Venus of Milo (now in Louvre, Paris), was discovered here in 1820.

Melozzo da Forlì (mālôt'tsō dä fôrlē'), 1438–94, Umbrian painter, a pioneer in bold foreshortening.

Melpomene, Muse of tragedy: see MUSES.

Melrose, burgh (pop. 2,146), Roxburghshire, Scotland. Site of one of Scotland's finest ruins—Melrose Abbey, founded in 1136 and now owned by the nation. Abbey, described in Scott's *Lay of the Last Minstrel*, contains the heart of Robert the Bruce.

Melrose, city (pop. 26,988), E Mass., N of Boston; settled c.1629. Home furnishings.

Melrose Park, residential village (pop. 13,366), NE Ill., W suburb of Chicago, in industrial area.

melting point, temperature at which substance changes from solid to liquid; under standard pressure, each solid·has specific melting point. When heat is applied, temperature rises until liquefaction begins and no further rise occurs until substance is entirely liquefied. Heat needed to change one gram of substance from solid to liquid at melting point is latent heat of fusion. Usually melting and freezing points of substance are the same.

Melton Mowbray (mōb'rē), urban district (pop. 14,052), Leicestershire, England. Known for pork pies and Stilton cheese, it is also known as a fox-hunting center.

Melun (mülü'), town (pop. 15,128), cap. of Seine-et-Marne dept., N France. Was an early Capetian residence. Near by is Chateau of Vaux, built for Nicolas Fouquet.

Mélusine (mālüzēn') or **Melusina** (mĕlyoōsē'nä), in French legend, water sprite who married a mortal. She built fairy castle from which Lusignan is said to be derived. At times she was a mermaid, and when her husband discovered this, she left him.

Melville, Andrew, 1545–1622, Scottish religious reformer. As rector (after 1590) of St. Andrews, he reorganized Scottish universities. Successor to John Knox, he molded Scottish church, introducing presbyterian system, and fought for its independence.

Melville, George Wallace, 1841–1912, American naval engineer and arctic explorer. Led only surviving boat of De Long expedition (1879). Noted for role in modernization of U.S. navy.

Melville, Herman, 1819–91, American author. Experience aboard the whaler *Acushnet,* and ashore in the Marquesas (among the cannibalistic Typees) and in Tahiti gave him the background of the sea and far places for his novels such as *Typee: a Peep at Polynesian Life* (1846), *Omoo: a Narrative of Adventures in the South Seas* (1847), and *Mardi and a Voyage Thither* (1849). His masterpiece is generally considered to be *Moby-Dick; or, The Whale* (1851), a powerful and symbolic work of idealistic but bitter philosophy. Among his other works are *Pierre* (1852); *Piazza Tales* (short stories, 1856); poems, notably *Clarel* (1876); and another novel, *Billy Budd, Foretopman* (first published 1924). Melville died an obscure customs official and achieved a major position long after his death.

Melville, Lake, 120 mi. long, up to 25 mi. wide, SE Labrador. Receives Hamilton R. in Goose Bay and reaches the Atlantic through Hamilton Inlet.

Melville Bay, broad indentation of W coast of Greenland, opening SW into Baffin Bay.

Melville Island, 200 mi. long, 30–130 mi. wide, W Franklin dist., Northwest Territories, Canada, in Arctic Ocean. Largest (c.16,503 sq. mi.) of Parry Isls., separated from Victoria Isl. by Viscount Melville Sound. Discovered 1819 by Sir W. E. Parry.

Melville Island, area 2,400 sq. mi., in Timor Sea, off N coast of Australia; aboriginal reservation. Here was made first British settlement in the Northern Territory (1824–28).

Melville Sound: see VISCOUNT MELVILLE SOUND.

Melvindale, residential city (pop. 9,483), SE Mich., SW suburb of Detroit.

Memel (mā'mùl), Lithuanian *Klaipeda,* Rus. *Klaypeda,* city (pop. 41,297), W Lithuania; a Baltic port on the Kurisches Haff. Founded 1252 by the Teutonic Knights, it belonged to Prussia until 1919, when the Treaty of Versailles placed Memel and surrounding territory (1,026 sq. mi.; 1941 pop. 134,034) under French administration. The territory was forcibly occupied by Lithuania 1923; became an autonomous region of Lithuania 1924; was returned to Germany (under threat of war) 1939; reverted to Lithuania 1945. For **Memel** river, see NIEMEN.

Memling or **Memlinc, Hans** (häns' mĕm'lĭng, –lĭngk), c.1430–1494, Flemish religious painter; follower of the Van Eycks and of Van der Weyden. Name is sometimes spelled Hemling.

Memnon (mĕm'nŏn), in Greek mythology, king of Ethiopia; son of Tithonus and Eos. He fought for Troy against the Greeks, and, though killed by Achilles, was made immortal by Zeus to please Eos.

Memorial Day or **Decoration Day.** In U.S., now the day for decorating graves of all American soldiers; inaugurated 1868 to honor Civil War veterans. Celebrated in the North on May 30, in the South on April 26, May 10, or June 3.

memory, term indicating ability to retain and to recall images of objects or situations of past experience. Memories affecting personality often can be recalled only through hypnosis or psychoanalysis. Learning ability also affects memory. Experiments show that rate of forgetting is highest at first; rapid learners retain better than slow learners; things consistent with intellectual bias and emotional needs are best remembered. Attempts to establish a physical basis for memory have been hypothetical and subject to question.

Memphis (měm'fĭs), cap. of the Old Kingdom of anc. Egypt (c.3400–c.2445 B.C.), at apex of Nile delta near Cairo; founded by MENES. Across the Nile are the pyramids, extending to Gizeh.

Memphis, city (pop. 396,000), SW Tenn., on bluffs above the Mississippi at Wolf R. mouth; planned 1819. De Soto may have crossed river here; La Salle's Fort Prudhomme may have been here. Site disputed by British, French, Spanish in 18th cent. U.S. built fort here 1797. Fell to Union navy under elder C. H. Davis, June 6, 1862; served as Federal base for rest of Civil War. River port and rail center (with shops), it is a cotton, lumber, and livestock market. Mfg. of cottonseed products, feeds, wire, rubber, and chemicals. Has TVA power. Seat of Southwestern at Memphis (Presbyterian; coed.; 1875) and Univ. of TENNESSEE divisions. Has museums, art gallery, parks, and holds annual cotton carnival. Beale St. made famous by W. C. HANDY.

Memphremagog, Lake (měm"frŭmā'gŏg), 30 mi. long and up to 4 mi. wide, mainly in S Que., partly in N Vt. Newport, Vt., and Magog, Que., are on lake.

Menahem (mě'nŭhěm), d. c.737 B.C., king of Israel (c.749–c.737 B.C.). A general of the army, he murdered Shallum for the throne. Gave tribute to the Assyrians. 2 Kings 15.13–22.

Menai Strait (mě'nī), channel of Irish Sea, between Anglesey Isl. and Caernarvonshire, N Wales.

Menander (mĭnăn'dŭr), 342?–291? B.C., Greek poet of the New Comedy. Only fragments remain of his plays, which were imitated by Plautus and Terence and through them influenced 17th-cent. comedy.

Menasha (mŭnă'shŭ), city (pop. 12,385), E Wis., on L. Winnebago opposite Neenah and on Fox R.; settled before 1850. Mfg. of paper and wood products. Region visited by early French explorers.

Mencius (měn'shŭs), Mandarin *Meng-tse*, 371?–288? B.C., Chinese sage. He believed man was innately good, not selfish, but man will be free to do good only if he has the peace of mind which follows from material well-being. Rulers must ensure such security or be deposed. *The Book of Mencius* is a classic commentary on doctrines of CONFUCIUS.

Mencken, H(enry) L(ouis), 1880–, American editor, author, and critic. A journalist in Baltimore (notably on *Sun* papers) after 1906, he later with George Jean Nathan edited *Smart Set* (1914–23). As founder (1924) and editor of *American Mercury* (1925–33), Mencken attacked American complacency and bourgeois customs. He also wrote on American speech in *The American Language* (1919; 4th ed., 1936; later supplements).

Mendel, Gregor Johann (grä'gôr yō'hän měn'dŭl), 1822–84, Austrian scientist and Roman Catholic priest. In his experiments, chiefly with garden peas, he carried on systematic cross-breeding and kept records of many offspring over several generations, on the basis of which he formulated principles of heredity. **Mendelism** is system of heredity based on his conclusions (Mendel's laws) which state that separate characters are inherited independently of one another; each reproductive cell receives only one of a pair of alternative factors existing in other body cells; and some factors are dominant over others. See also GENETICS; HEREDITY.

Mendelejeff, Dmitri Ivanovich (měndŭlā'ŭf, Rus. dùmē'trē ēvä'nùvĭch myĭndyĭlyä'ŭf), 1834–1907, Russian chemist. He developed concept of PERIODIC LAW of classification of elements; predicted properties of

elements then unknown; studied nature of solutions and expansion of liquids.

Mendele mocher sforim (měn'dùlù môkh'ùr sfô'rĭm), pseud. of **Sholem (or Solomon) Yakob Abramovich,** 1836–1917, Yiddish novelist, b. Russia. His style greatly influenced later writers.

Mendelism: see MENDEL, GREGOR JOHANN.

Mendelsohn, Erich (ā'rĭkh měn'dùlzōn), 1887–, German architect, an exponent of German expressionism. His Potsdam observatory (1927) was highly original structure suggestive of sculpture. Has worked in England and Palestine; moved to U.S. in 1941.

Mendelssohn, (Jakob Ludwig) Felix (měn'dùlsùn), 1809–47, German composer. He conducted in Düsseldorf, Leipzig, and London. His compositions include the Overture to *A Midsummer Night's Dream* (written when he was 17); five symphonies, of which the Scotch, Italian, and Reformation symphonies are best known; the E Minor violin concerto; *The Hebrides,* concert overture; and two oratorios, *St. Paul* and *Elijah.* His father changed the family name to Mendelssohn-Bartholdy, a form seldom used.

Mendelssohn, Moses, 1729–86, German-Jewish philosopher, a leader in the movement for cultural assimilation. His philosophical writings, which anticipated the aesthetics of Kant and J. C. F. von Schiller, include *Philosophische Gesprache* (1755) and *Phädon* (1767).

Mendès, Catulle (kätül' mēděs'), 1841–1909, French poet, critic, and novelist; one of the PARNASSIANS.

Mendip Hills, range of hills, c.23 mi. long and 6 mi. wide, Somerset, England. They contain many caves and beautiful gorges, notably near Cheddar.

Mendocino, Cape (měndùsē'nō), promontory, westernmost point of Calif., N of San Francisco.

Mendota (měndō'tù). **1** City (pop. 5,129), N Ill., N of La Salle. Processing, shipping center in agr. area. Mfg. of tools and machinery. **2** Village, SE Minn., just S of St. Paul at junction of Minnesota R. with the Mississippi. First permanent white settlement in state, it was known before 1819, but settlement dates from 1834. Some old houses restored.

Mendoza, Antonio de (äntō'nyō dä' mändō'thä), 1490?–1552, Spanish conquistador, first viceroy of New Spain (1535–40) and viceroy of Peru (1551–52). He alleviated the misery of the Indians, encouraged education, brought first printing press to America, quelled numerous revolts, pushed exploration into N. Was called "the good viceroy."

Mendoza, Diego Hurtado de: see HURTADO DE MENDOZA, DIEGO.

Mendoza, Iñigo López de: see SANTILLANA, IÑIGO LÓPEZ DE MENDOZA, MARQUÉS DE.

Mendoza, Pedro de (pä'dhrō), b. 1501 or 1502, d. 1537, Spanish conquistador, first *adelantado* of Río de la Plata (present Argentina). Founded Buenos Aires (1536), but attacks by Indians made place untenable. Mendoza, returning to Spain, died at sea.

Mendoza (měndō'sä), city (pop. 97,496), cap. of Mendoza prov., metropolis of W Argentina, in an oasis irrigated by Mendoza R.; founded (1561) by Pedro del Castillo. The wine industry is controlled by large Italian population. Oil exploitation is increasing.

Menelaus (měnŭlā'ùs), in Greek mythology, king of Sparta; husband of Helen, father of Hermione, and younger brother of Agamemnon. When Paris abducted Helen to Troy, the other Greeks joined Menelaus in Trojan War. Afterward Helen rejoined him in Sparta.

Menelik II (mě'nùlĭk), 1844–1913, emperor of Ethiopia after 1889. After the death of Emperor Theodore II (1868) he conquered most of the country with Italy's aid and seized the throne. Signed a treaty (1889) with Italy which made Ethiopia a protectorate. His denunciation of the Treaty provoked Italian invasion (1895–96). Ousting the invaders he forced Italy's recognition of Ethiopia's freedom. Made efforts to centralize and modernize his country.

Mene, Mene, Tekel, Upharsin (mē'nē, tē'–, ūfär'–), in Bible, riddle written on wall by mysterious hand at Belshazzar's feast. Daniel translated it as "to number, to number, to weigh, to divide" and interpreted it to mean the fall of Babylon. Dan. 5.5–29.

Menéndez de Avilés, Pedro (pā'dhrō mänēn'dĕth dä ävēlēs'), 1519–74, Spanish naval officer and colonizer. Massacred French settlement of Fort Caroline under René de LAUDONNIÈRE; also killed group under Jean RIBAUT. Founded St. Augustine, Fla., in 1565.

Menéndez y Pelayo, Marcelino (märthälē'nō mänēn'dĕth ē pälä'yō), 1856–1912, Spanish literary historian and critic.

Menes (mē'nēz), fl. 3400? B.C., first ruler of the Old Kingdom, anc. EGYPT; reputed to have united N and S kingdoms and to have founded Memphis.

Menger, Karl (mĕng'ùr), 1840–1921, Austrian economist, a founder of the Austrian school of economics. Taught at Univ. of Vienna 1873–1903. He advanced the theory of marginal utility.

Mengs, Anton Raphael (än'tōn rä'fäĕl mĕngs'), 1728–79, German historical and portrait painter, b. Bohemia. Did some of best work in Spain.

Meng-tse: see MENCIUS.

menhaden (mĕnhā'dùn), fish related to shad and herring, found from Nova Scotia to Brazil. It is a source of oil, poultry feed, and fertilizer.

meningitis (mĕnĭnjī'tĭs), inflammation of meninges (membranes of brain and spinal cord). Commonly results from infection by any of several organisms. Called cerebrospinal meningitis when both brain and spinal cord are affected. See *ill.,* p. 633.

Menken, Adah Isaacs, 1835–68, American actress, whose real name was Dolores Adios Fuertes. Noted for unconventionality, she caused a sensation in *Mazeppa.*

Menkure (mĕnkōō'rä), fl. 2800? B.C., king of anc. Egypt, successor of Khafre, IV dynasty. Built third pyramid at Gizeh.

Menlo Park. 1 Residential city (pop. 13,587), W Calif., S of San Francisco. **2** Village, NE N.J., NE of New Brunswick. Memorial tower commemorates T. A. Edison, whose workshops were here 1876–87.

Menninger, Karl A(ugustus) (mĕ'nĭnjùr), 1893–, and **William C(laire) Menninger,** 1899–, American psychiatrists, brothers. Karl and his father founded the Menninger Clinic, Topeka, Kansas (1920), and were joined by William (1926). The Menninger Foundation (1941) is a psychiatric center. After World War II, Karl helped found the Winter Veterans' Administration Hospital, center of world's largest psychiatric training program. He wrote *The Human Mind* (1930).

Mennonites, Protestant sect arising among Swiss Anabaptists; first called Swiss Brethren, renamed for Menno Simons. In Zurich, group seceded (1523–25) from state church, rejecting its authority and also infant baptism. They were nonresistants, and refused to take oaths; took Bible as sole rule of faith and retained only two sacraments, baptism and Lord's Supper. Sect spread to Russia, France, and Holland, where Dordrecht Confession was issued in 1632. In America, Mennonites settled (1683) at Germantown, Pa., and are found mainly in Pa., Ohio, and Middle West. The Amish are among the numerous Mennonite bodies.

Menno Simons (mĕ'nō sē'mōns), 1496?–1561, Dutch religious reformer, leader in Holland and Germany of moderate Anabaptists, later called Mennonites.

Menominee (mùnŏm'ùnē), city (pop. 11,151), W Upper Peninsula, N Mich., on Green Bay at mouth of Menominee R. (bridged to Marinette, Wis.); settled c.1840. Fishing port with mfg. of paper and wood products and machinery. Resort.

Menominee, river formed by union of Brule and Michigamme rivers above Iron Mountain, W Upper Peninsula, N Mich. Flows S c.118 mi. into Green Bay at Menominee, forming part of Wis.-Mich. line. Hydroelectric power.

Menominee Indians, North American tribe of Algonquian linguistic stock, in 17th–19th cent., a sedentary people of Eastern Woodlands area, inhabiting Wis. and Mich. They depended on wild rice for subsistence and fought bitter wars for control of rice areas. In 1854 settled on reservation in Wis.

Menomonie (mùnŏm'ùnē), city (pop. 8,245), W Wis., NW of Eau Claire and on Red Cedar R. Mfg. and trade center of dairy area.

menopause (mĕ'nùpôz), period of normal cessation of menstruation, also called change of life and climacteric. Results from gradual slowing of ovarian activity. Commonly occurs between ages of 45–50.

Menorca, Spain: see MINORCA.

Menotti, Gian-Carlo (jän'-kär'lō mänôt'tē), 1911–, American composer, b. Italy. His outstanding works are the operas *Amelia Goes to the Ball* (1937); *The Old Maid and the Thief* (1939); *The Medium* (1946); *The Telephone* (1947); *The Consul* (1950); and *Amahl and the Night Visitors* (1951).

Menshevism: see BOLSHEVISM AND MENSHEVISM.

Menshikov, Aleksandr Danilovich (ŭlyĭksän'dùr dŭnyē'lùvĭch mĕn'shĭkùf), 1672–1729, Russian field marshal and statesman. Of lowly origin, he was Peter the Great's boon companion, later became his chief adviser, and was made a prince. He ably carried out Peter's reforms. On Peter's death, he helped place Catherine I on the throne and was the chief power during her reign.

menstruation, flow of blood from uterus, occurring in women from puberty to menopause usually in 28-day cycles. Controlled by hormones secreted by certain endocrine glands; associated with release of ovum from ovary, after which cells lining uterus increase. Unless conception occurs, egg and sloughed cells are discharged with flow of blood.

mental age: see INTELLIGENCE.

mental hygiene, science of promoting mental health and preventing mental disease through psychiatry and psychology. Reformers in 19th cent. roused periodic waves of interest in problems of the insane, but mental hygiene movement as such resulted directly from Clifford W. Beers's *A Mind That Found Itself* (1908), describing his experiences in asylums. The Natl. Committee for Mental Hygiene was founded 1909. The mental hygiene movement, supported by noted individuals, was spread through U.S. by state organizations. An Internatl. Committee was formed 1930. In U.S. the movement won wide reforms in institutional care, estab. child-guidance clinics, spread information through publications, e.g., *Mental Hygiene,* published quarterly from 1917.

mental tests, standard tests for studying psychological traits or special abilities (as opposed to INTELLIGENCE TESTS). Schools use aptitude and achievement tests to compare ability and actual accomplishment; business administrators use tests for special talents and motor skills to learn potential capacities of applicants. Psychoanalysis gave rise to "projective" tests based on individual's tendency to project unconscious attitudes into ambiguous situations. Hermann Rorschach used 10 standardized inkblots, had patient tell what he saw. Henry A. Murray's Thematic Apperception Test uses a standard series of pictures about which stories must be told. Lipot Szondi used photographs of 48 mentally disturbed or sexually perverted people; a given number of those liked and those disliked must be chosen. Other projective tests are word-association, finger painting, and draw-a-man tests.

Mentana (mäntä'nä), village NE of Rome, Italy, where GARIBALDI was defeated by French and papal troops (1867).

Menton (mätõn'), town (pop. 11,079), Alpes-Maritimes dept., SE France, at Italian border; resort on the Riviera. A plebiscite transferred it from Sardinia to France in 1860.

Mentor (mĕn'tùr, –tôr"), in Greek mythology, friend of Odysseus and tutor of Telemachus. His name is proverbial for a faithful and wise adviser.

Mentor, village (pop. 2,383), NE Ohio, near L. Erie and NE of Cleveland. Garfield was living here when he was elected President.

Menuhin, Yehudi (yŭhōō'dē měn'ūĭn), 1916–, American violinist, b. U.S., of Russian parents. Made his debut at seven; later studied with Adolph Busch and Enesco. He returned to the concert stage a mature artist and in the first rank of violinists.

Menzaleh or **Manzala** (both: měnzä'lù), lagoon, area 660 sq. mi., Egypt, partly separated from the Mediterranean by narrow spit (site of Port Said).

Menzel, Adolph Friedrich Erdmann von (měn'tsùl), 1815–1905, German historical painter.

Menzies, Robert Gordon, 1894–, Australian statesman; prime minister 1939–41, 1949–.

Mephibosheth (mě"fībō'–), Jonathan's lame son, to whom King David restored Saul's lands. David thus fulfilled his vow of friendship made with Jonathan that was to include each other's children. 2 Sam. 4.4; 9; 16.1,4; 19.24. Also Merib-baal.

Mephistopheles (měfĭstŏf'ùlēz), in the German FAUST legend, the personification of the devil.

Merab, daughter of Saul promised to David but married to another man instead. 1 Sam. 18.17–19. Called MICHAL (probably by textual error) at 2 Sam. 21.8.

Merano (märä'nō), Ger. **Meran,** city (pop. 22,575), Trentino-Alto Adige, N Italy; Alpine resort.

mercantilism (mûr'kùntīlĭzùm), important economic policy in Western Europe from 1500 until the Industrial Revolution and the advent of laissez-faire ideas. Mercantilist nations, identifying money with wealth, sought to obtain bullion by increased manufactures and exports, taxation of imports, and state colonial exploitation. State control was a vital part of the process. British mercantilism flourished under Henry VIII, Elizabeth, and Cromwell. Chief French exponent was Jean COLBERT.

Mercator, Gerardus (jùrär'dùs mûrkā'tùr, mùr–), Latin form of real name, **Gerhard Kremer** (gā'rärt krā'mùr), 1512–94, Flemish geographer, mathematician, cartographer. His first map using PROJECTION named for him appeared 1569.

Merced (mùrsĕd'), city (pop. 15,278), central Calif., NW of Fresno. Tourist and farm center in San Joaquin Valley. Yosemite Natl. Park is NE.

Mercedes (mûrsā'dēz), city (pop. 10,081), S Texas, WNW of Brownsville; founded 1907. Packing and processing of citrus fruits and vegetables; some meat packing.

mercerizing, process of treating cotton textiles with sodium hydroxide and drying under tension to produce greater strength and luster. Developed by John Mercer, English chemist, in mid-19th cent.

Mercer University: see MACON, Ga.

Merchants Adventurers, English trading company in Low Countries and German free cities in 16th and 17th cent. Derived from GUILD system and forerunner of CHARTERED COMPANIES, it operated in cloth market of Netherlands and greatly influenced English foreign trade. Dissolved in Napoleonic Wars.

Mercia, kingdom of (mûr'shù), in Anglo-Saxon England, consisting generally of the region of the Midlands. Settled by Angles c.500. Overlordship extended over all S England by Penda and Wulfhere. After death of Offa (796), it gradually was taken over by Wessex. Part of it was later included in the Danelaw (886).

Mercier, Désiré Joseph (dāzērā' zhōzěf' mârsēā'), 1851–1926, Belgian cardinal. As professor of philosophy at Louvain, he became a leader in 20th-cent. revival of Thomistic scholasticism. Made Roman Catholic archbishop of Malines (1906) and cardinal (1907), he did much to promote social welfare. In World War I, Mercier was the fearless spokesman of the Belgians when the country was under German conquest.

Mercury, Roman equivalent of HERMES.

Mercury, in astronomy, PLANET revolving in orbit nearest sun. Its mean distance from sun is c.35,960,000 mi.

Period of revolution c.88 days, probably same as period of rotation on axis. Same side believed always toward sun; probably has no atmosphere. Passes through phases similar to moon's. Transits across sun's disk occur at intervals of 7–13 years in November and 13–46 years in May. See *ill.,* p. 927.

mercury or **quicksilver,** silvery, liquid metallic element (symbol = Hg [Lat. *hydroargyrus*]; see also ELEMENT, table). It forms mercurous and mercuric compounds. Forms special alloy (AMALGAM) with other metals. Used in barometer because of great weight and in thermometer because of equal expansion per degree rise in temperature. Occurs free to limited extent. Chief ore is cinnabar. Mercury-arc lamp is fused quartz tube with confined mercury; when current is passed through, metal vaporizes, giving greenish-blue luminescence.

Mer de Glace (měr" dù gläs') [Fr.,= sea of ice], glacier, 3½ mi. long, E France, on N slope of Mont Blanc, near Chamonix.

Meredith, George, 1828–1909, English novelist and poet. First gaining notice with *The Ordeal of Richard Feverel* (1859), he wrote a series of novels notable for psychological insight and close inspection of the relationship of the individual and social events; among them are *Evan Harrington* (1860), *Rhoda Fleming* (1865), *The Egoist* (1879), *The Tragic Comedians* (1880), *Diana of the Crossways* (1885), and *Lord Ormont and His Aminta* (1894). His poetry, dealing with the same themes, includes a well-known sequence "Modern Love" and individual poems such as "Love in the Valley" and "Lucifer in Starlight." His critical essay, "On . . . the Comic Spirit," has been much admired.

Meredith, Owen: see BULWER-LYTTON, EDWARD R.

Merezhkovsky, Dmitri Sergeyevich (dùmē'trē sīrgā'üvĭch mârĭshkôf'skē), 1865–1941, Russian author and religious philosopher. Parts of his trilogy *Christ and Antichrist* (1896–1905) were very popular in English —*Julian the Apostate, The Death of the Gods, The Romance of Leonardo da Vinci.* He went into exile in 1918.

Mergenthaler, Ottmar (ôt'mär měr'gùnta"lùr), 1854–99, American inventor of the LINOTYPE, b. Germany.

Merian, Matthäus (mätē'ōōs mä'rēän), the elder, 1593–1650, Swiss engraver. Settled c.1623 in Frankfurt-am-Main. Etchings include *Dance of Death* and Bible illustrations. His son, **Matthäus Merian,** the younger, 1621–87, was a portrait and historical painter; his daughter, **Maria Sibylla Merian,** 1647–1717, was a naturalist and painter of insects and flowers.

Mérida (mā'rēdhä), city (pop. 96,852), cap. of Yucatan, SE Mexico, in NW part of Yucatan peninsula; founded 1542 on site of ruined Mayan city. Tourist attractions are near-by Chichén Itzá and Uxmal.

Mérida (mā'rēdhä), city (pop. 22,440), SW Spain, in Estremadura, on Guadiana R. A Roman colony, it became cap. of Lusitania. Roman remains (e.g., bridge, triumphal arch) are among most important in Spain. Prospered under Moors, 713–1228.

Meriden (mě'rĭdùn), city (pop. 44,088), S central Conn., SW of Hartford; settled 1661. Mfg. of silverware (since 18th cent.), electrical equipment, and precision goods.

Meridian. 1 Village (pop. 1,810), SW Idaho, W of Boise, in Boise project. **2** City (pop. 41,893), E Miss., E of Jackson near Ala. line; founded c.1854. Trade, shipping, and industrial center for farm, livestock and lumber area. Temporary cap. 1863. Destroyed by Sherman, Feb., 1864.

meridian, imaginary line drawn on earth's surface from pole to pole, cutting equator and all parallels at a right angle. International agreement (1884) designated the Greenwich meridian as zero or prime meridian; other meridians are measured E and W to 180° longitude.

Mérimée, Prosper (prôspěr' mārēmā'), 1803–70, French author. He is best known for his short novels *Colomba* (1840) and *Carmen* (1845; basis of Bizet's opera), in which he treats his romantic themes in concise, lucid style and with psychological realism.

Merino sheep: see SHEEP.

Merionethshire (mĕrēō'nŭthshĭr) or **Merioneth,** county (660 sq. mi.; pop. 41,456), N Wales; co. seat Dolgelley. Mountainous region with poor soil, it draws wealth from manganese, slate, and limestone deposits. Beautiful scenery attracts tourists. One of the last areas to submit to English influence, a large percentage of population speak Welsh.

Meriwether Lewis National Monument: see NATIONAL PARKS AND MONUMENTS (table).

Merlin: see ARTHURIAN LEGEND.

Mermaid Tavern, in Elizabethan London, where Shakspere, Ben Jonson, and their friends often met.

Merneptah (mĕrnĕp'tä), d. c.1215 B.C., king of anc. Egypt. Succeeded his father, RAMSES II, in 1225. His reign started decline of dynasty XIX.

Merodach (mĕ'rōdăk), biblical form of the god Marduk of Babylon. Jer. 50.2.

Merodach-baladan (–bă'lŭdăn) [Assyrian,= Marduk has given a son], fl. 721 B.C., Chaldaean prince. Sargon of Assyria drove him from Babylon (c.710). In 705 B.C., on Sargon's death, he returned.

Merom, Waters of: see BAHR EL-HULEH.

Merope (mĕ'rŭpē), in Greek mythology. **1** One of the Pleiades; daughter of Atlas and nymph Pleione. One legend calls her the lost Pleiad. **2** Daughter of Oenopion. She was loved by ORION.

Merovingians (mĕr"ōvĭn'jŭnz), dynasty of Frankish kings, descended from the semilegendary Meroveus, chief of the Salian FRANKS, whose grandson CLOVIS I founded the Frankish monarchy (481). Clovis's kingdom was divided among his descendants into kingdoms of AUSTRASIA, NEUSTRIA, AQUITAINE, BURGUNDY, Paris, and Orléans; these were often combined and at times reunited under a sole ruler (under Clotaire I, 558–61; Clotaire II, 613–c.622; Dagobert I, 630–33). Before Dagobert, chronic warfare among the kingdoms was the rule; Dagobert's successors, the "idle kings," left government to mayors of the palace, the CAROLINGIANS. In 751 Pepin the Short deposed Childeric III, the last Merovingian, and became king.

Merrill, city (pop. 8,951), central Wis., at junction of Wisconsin and Prairie rivers and N of Wausau. Mfg. of paper and furniture. Near by are Grandfather Falls of Wisconsin R.

Merrimac: see MONITOR AND MERRIMAC.

Merrimack, river formed in S central N.H., at Franklin, by junction of Pemigewasset and Winnipesaukee rivers. Flows S into NE Mass., then NE to the Atlantic below Newburyport; c.110 mi. long. Furnishes power to mfg. centers.

Merritt Island, c.30 mi. long and up to 7 mi. wide, E Fla. Separated from mainland on W by Indian R. and from Cape Canaveral by Banana R. Citrus fruit.

Merry Mount: see MORTON, THOMAS.

Merseburg (mĕr'zŭbŏŏrk), city (pop. 33,978), Saxony-Anhalt, E central Germany, on the Saale. Lignite mining; industries (steel, paper, machinery, chemicals). Bishopric of Merseburg, founded 968, was secularized 1561 and passed to Saxony. City was seat of dukes of Saxe-Merseburg 1656–1738; passed to Prussia 1815. Its many ancient buildings were largely destroyed in World War II.

Mersen, Treaty of, 870, signed by CHARLES II (the Bald) of the W Franks (i.e., France) and LOUIS THE GERMAN, at Mersen (Dutch *Meersen*), now in Netherlands. It divided LOTHARINGIA between France (which received, roughly, the Low Countries and Lorraine) and Germany (which received Alsace and left bank of Lower Rhine).

Mersey (mûr'zē), river of England, flowing 70 mi. between Lancashire and Cheshire, from Stockport to Irish Sea NW of Liverpool. Estuary, 16 mi. long and 2 mi. wide, is navigable for ocean-going liners. River is of great commercial importance.

Merthyr Tydfil (mûr'thŭr tĭd'vĭl), county borough (pop.

61,093), Glamorganshire, Wales. In center of great coal field, it has iron and steel works.

Merton, Thomas (mûr'tŭn), 1915–, American religious writer and poet, b. France, a Trappist monk since 1941. His works include poetry (e.g., *Figures for an Apocalypse,* 1947), devotional books (e.g., *Seeds of Contemplation,* 1949), and well-known autobiographical volumes (e.g., *The Seven Storey Mountain,* 1948).

Merton, Walter de, d. 1277, English bishop, founder of Merton Col., Oxford. In 1264 he obtained charter of incorporation and estab. at Malden, Surrey, a "House of Scholars," later transferred to Oxford. This marks beginning of collegiate system of education. Merton became model for other colleges.

Merton College: see OXFORD UNIVERSITY.

Merv (myĕrf), anc. city in large oasis of Kara Kum desert, Turkmen SSR, on Murgab R. As Margiana it was cap. of a N province of ancient Persia. A center of medieval Islamic culture, it was conquered from Uzbeks by Russia in 1884. Near old Merv (now called Bairam-Ali) there grew a new Merv (pop. 37,100), renamed Mary in 1937. Textile mfg.

Merwede, river, Netherlands: see MEUSE.

Meryon, Charles (shärl' mĕryō'), 1821–68, French etcher, known for poetic series of etchings of old sections of Paris.

Mesa (mā'sù), city (pop. 16,790), S central Ariz., in SALT RIVER VALLEY; founded 1878 by Mormons. Univ. of Arizona experimental farm is here.

mesa (mā'sù) [Span.,= table], name given in SW U.S. to a small, isolated tableland or a flat-topped hill, with at least two steep, often perpendicular, sides. Picturesque; often deep red or yellow. Less precipitous, smaller formations are buttes.

Mesabi (mùsä'bē), range of low hills, NE Minn., known as iron range. Richest of three iron ranges: Vermilion (NE Minn., between Vermilion L. and Ely; first ore shipped 1884), Mesabi (between Grand Rapids and Aurora; Hibbing and Virginia are centers; first ore shipped 1892), and Cuyuna (central Minn., between Brainerd and Aitkin; first ore shipped 1911). Leonidas Merritt, with brothers, discovered Mesabi iron 1887, estab. claims to area, organized company to exploit ore 1890. John D. Rockefeller took over 1893. Mesabi ore in horizontal layers mined by open-pit method. Ores of other ranges in vertical strata, less accessible. Most of ore shipped from Duluth.

Mesa Verde National Park: see NATIONAL PARKS AND MONUMENTS (table).

mescal (mĕskäl'), Mexican spirituous liquor, usually obtained by distilling a liquid made from leaves, juicy stalk, and roots of certain species of agave (maguey). Name is sometimes given to liquor distilled from agave sap which, fermented, is pulque and also to drug obtained from peyote.

Mesdag, Hendrik Willem (hĕn'drĭk vī'lùm mĕs'däkh), 1831–1915, Dutch marine painter. Mesdag Mus., The Hague, is his gift to the nation.

Mesha (mĕ'–), king of Moab, contemporary of Ahab. 2 Kings 3. Composed inscription on Moabite Stone.

Meshach (mĕ'–), one of the THREE HOLY CHILDREN.

Meshed (mĕsh'hĕd), city (pop. 167,471), NE Iran; a leading center of Shiite pilgrimage. Site of 9th-cent. shrine of the Imam Riza. Located near the USSR and Afghanistan frontiers, it assumed strategic importance after late 19th cent.

Mesilla (māsĕ'yä), historic village (pop. 1,264), SW N.Mex., on Rio Grande and S of Las Cruces; settled c.1850. It was a central station on overland mail route. Changed hands several times in Civil War; proclaimed cap. of new Confederate territory. Mesilla Valley came to U.S. under Gadsden Purchase (1853).

Mesmer, Friedrich (or **Franz**) **Anton** (mĕz'mùr), 1733?–1815, German physician. He developed a system of treatment through hypnotism known as mesmerism.

mesmerism: see HYPNOTISM.

Mesolonghi, Greece: see MISSOLONGHI.

meson (mĕ'zŏn) or **mesotron** (mĕ'zŭtrŏn), nuclear particle intermediate in mass between electron and proton. Positive, negative, and neutral mesons are identified. Most have life span of few millionths of second; yield energy on disintegration.

Mesopotamia (mĕ″sùpùtä′mēù) [Gr.,= between rivers], region of W Asia, around the lower Tigris and the lower Euphrates, now in Iraq. The heart of it was a plain, rendered fertile in ancient times by canals. This "cradle of civilization" saw the rise of city-states older than Egypt—Eridu, Ur, Lagash, Akkad, Babylon. Civilization as early as the 4th millennium B.C. flowered into the empires of BABYLONIA and ASSYRIA. It declined later but was still important in the Byzantine Empire. Hulagu Khan and his Mongols laid the area waste in A.D. 1298, and it is today largely arid and barren, but enriched by oil wells.

mesotron: see MESON.

Mesozoic era (mĕsùzŏ′ĭk), one of the grand divisions of geologic time (the fourth if Archeozoic and Proterozoic are considered separately, i.e., not combined as pre-Cambrian). In North America, the land, especially the Appalachian region, was in general elevated and subject to erosion; much of the West was often submerged as geosynclines (enormous downfolds) were formed. Mesozoic life was dominated by reptiles. Dinosaurs were numerous in the TRIASSIC, were more abundant during the JURASSIC and CRETACEOUS, but most forms became extinct when violent disturbances brought the era to an end. See also GEOLOGY, table.

mesquite (mĭskēt′), leguminous spiny shrub (*Prosopis glandulosa*). It is native to arid and chaparral regions of SW U.S. Fruit pods have edible pulp. Other species are in South America, Asia, Africa.

Messalina (Valeria Messalina) (mĕsùlī′nù), d. A.D. 48, corrupt Roman empress, wife of CLAUDIUS I, who had her killed after a serious scandal.

Messenia (mĕsē′nēù), anc. region of Peloponnesus, SW Greece. A Messenian city, Pylos, an early center of Mycenaean culture. Held subject by Sparta after c.700 B.C., Messenia revolted several times and was freed from Spartan control when Thebes defeated Sparta at Leuctra (371 B.C.).

Messiaen, Olivier (ôlēvyä′ mĕsyĕ′), 1908–, French organist, composer of religious music, and teacher. Some of his works are based on scale formulas of his own invention. His compositions include *L'Ascension,* for orchestra; a symphony, *Turangalia; Le Banquet céleste,* for organ; and Masses and songs.

Messiah (mùsī′ù) or **Messias** (mùsī′ùs) [Heb.,= anointed], in Judaism, a righteous man who will be sent by God to restore Israel. The idea developed among the Jews in their adversity. Jesus Christ considered himself and is considered by Christians to be the promised Messiah to whom the Old Testament pointed. The Christian ideal of the Messiah is fundamentally different from the Jewish conception in the aspect of suffering; the common idea of Jesus' time was that the Messiah should reign in glory on earth.

Messina (mäsē′nä), Mediterranean port (pop. 192,051), NE Sicily, Italy; one of the large commercial centers of the island. Founded (8th cent. B.C.) by Greeks as Zancle, it later was called Messana. Roman intervention to protect Messina from Syracuse brought on (264 B.C.) the Punic Wars. Messina was later a wealthy city under the Roman Empire and throughout the Middle Ages, but declined somewhat later. It was conquered (1860) by Garibaldi in his Sicilian campaign. The city suffered a severe earthquake in 1908 and was rebuilt. It is on the **Strait of Messina,** c.20 mi. long, 2–10 mi. wide, which separates the Italian peninsula from Sicily and connects the Ionian and Tyrrhenian seas. Its currents and whirlpools gave rise to legends on danger to sailors (see SCYLLA).

Messys, Quentin: see MASSYS, QUENTIN.

mestizo (mĕstē′sō) [Span.,= mixture], person of mixed race. In Latin American countries, descendants of Spanish or Portuguese and Indians.

Mestrovic, Ivan (ē′vän mĕsh′trōvĭch), 1883–, Yugoslav sculptor. His style is a modern adaptation of archaic Greek sculpture and Byzantine tradition. Often treats religious subjects.

metabolism (mùtā′bùlĭzùm), sum of chemical processes resulting in growth, production of body heat and energy, and maintenance of vital functions. Basal metabolism represents minimum energy needed to maintain normal temperature of body at rest.

metal, chemical ELEMENT with characteristic metallic luster, ability to conduct heat and electricity, capacity to form positive ION. About two thirds of known elements are metallic. They differ in hardness, ductility, malleability, tensile strength, density, melting point; definite line between metals and nonmetals cannot be drawn. Chromium is hardest metal; softest is cesium. Silver is best electric conductor; copper, gold, aluminum follow. All metals are relatively good heat conductors. They can be arranged in order of activity in electromotive or replacement series. In general, any metal will replace in compounds any other metal, or hydrogen, which it precedes in the series and will be replaced by any which it follows. Metals fall into groups according to PERIODIC LAW; certain similar elements fall into families, e.g., alkali metals, alkaline earth metals, RARE EARTHS. Metals differ from nonmetals chemically in forming positive ions, basic oxides, and hydroxides. Many metals corrode on exposure to moist air, i.e., enter into chemical reaction which results in formation of new compound. Metals are combined with nonmetals in salts. When mixed in definite amount, metals form alloys. Some metals occur uncombined, most are combined in ores. For uses of specific metals and their compounds, see separate articles.

metallurgy (mĕ′tùlûr″jē), branch of chemistry concerned with extraction of metals from their ores. Processes used depend upon chemical nature of ore to be treated and properties of metal to be extracted. If metal occurs uncombined chemically in sand or rock, mechanical methods alone sometimes produce relatively pure metal. Finely divided waste material is washed away or separated by gravity; rock is crushed and heated until metal fuses and separates. Other processes involve use of a flux—material that will combine with waste when heat is applied—to form a lighter mass called slag which floats and can be skimmed off. Gold and silver are sometimes treated with mercury in which they dissolve, forming an amalgam. CYANIDE PROCESS is also used for extraction of gold and silver. Generally chemical rather than mechanical processes must be used since most metals occur in nature in chemical compounds. Treatment of ore by heat is smelting. Oxides are heated with reducing agent, e.g., carbon in the form of coke or coal; waste, called gangue, mixed with ore is removed by a flux. Sulphide ore is commonly roasted (heated in air) to form metal oxide, which is then reduced. Carbonate ore is heated, oxide of metal formed and then reduced with carbon. Some active metals, e.g., aluminum, barium, calcium, magnesium, potassium, and sodium, are prepared by electrolysis. Flotation process can be used for many ores; it involves adding a chemical to pulverized ore, forming a froth when air is added to mixture, brushing off wet ore which rises to surface, and filtering out mineral.

metamorphic rocks: see ROCK.

metamorphism (mĕ′tùmôr′fĭzùm), in geology, processes bringing about profound changes in rock. Causes include heat, infiltration of liquids or gases, thrust or pull of earth movements, weight of overlying rocks, or (most commonly) the combination of two or more of these. Schist, gneiss, marble, and slate are common metamorphic rocks.

metaphor (mĕ′tùfûr, –fôr) [Gr.,= transfer] and **simile** (sĭ′mùlē) [Latin,= likeness], in rhetoric, two figures of speech. In metaphor, an object belonging to one class of things is referred to as if it belonged to another class, either explicitly ("All the world's a dream") or by implication (referring to a beloved woman as "a rose without a thorn"). In simile, an object is explicitly compared to another object ("My love is like a red, red rose").

metaphysical poets, group of English poets of the 17th cent. Their primary subject was the relation of God and man; their poetry was marked by unusual figures —blending passion and logic—termed metaphysical conceits. The poems show intellectual wit and subtle argument. Chief metaphysical poets were Donne, Traherne, George Herbert, Crashaw, and Henry Vaughan.

Metastasio, Pietro (pyä'trō mätästä'zēō), pseud. of Pietro Bonaventura Trapassi, 1698–1782, Italian author of melodramas, used as librettos for operas by many composers, including Hasse, Handel, Haydn, Mozart, and Gluck. Long court poet at Vienna, Metastasio exercised much influence on 18th-cent. opera.

Metaurus (mĭtô'rus), river of central Italy, flowing into the Adriatic. On its banks Romans defeated Carthaginians under Hasdrubal 207 B.C.

Metaxas, John (mä'täksäs"), 1871–1941, Greek general and royalist politician. As premier (1936–41) he governed dictatorially. He successfully directed Greek resistance against Italy after 1940.

Metcalf, Willard Leroy (mĕt'kăf), 1858–1925, American landscape painter. Taught at Cooper Union and Art Students League, New York.

Metcalfe, Charles Theophilus Metcalfe, 1st Baron, 1785–1846, British colonial administrator, b. India. After a long career in the Indian civil service he was governor general of Canada 1843–45.

Metchnikoff, Élie (mĕch'nĭkôf), Rus. *Ilya Ilyich Mechnikov,* 1845–1916, Russian biologist. Developed theory that certain white corpuscles (phagocytes) ingest and destroy bacteria. Shared 1908 Nobel Prize in Physiology and Medicine for work on immunity. Associated with Pasteur Inst., Paris.

Metellus (mĕtĕ'lus), distinguished anc. Roman family. **Quintus Caecilius Metellus Macedonicus** (măsĭdŏ'nĭkus), d. 115 B.C., conquered Macedonia (148 B.C.) and pacified Greece (146). His nephew **Quintus Caecilius Metellus Numidicus** (nūmĭ'dĭkus), d. 91? B.C., led the senatorial party. As consul (109 B.C.) he conducted the Numidian War against Jugurtha. Fought against MARIUS and Saturninus and was exiled (100). His son, **Quintus Caecilius Metellus Pius** (pī'us), d. c.63 B.C., continued his father's opposition to Marius. In 89 B.C. he fought in the Social War; in the civil war he defended Rome against Marius and CINNA. Joining SULLA in 83, he defeated the Marians and became consul (80 B.C.). In Spain he warred against Sertorius. For his adoptive son, **Quintus Caecilius Metellus Pius Scipio,** see SCIPIO.

meteor (mē'tēur), one of the small bodies entering earth's atmosphere from space and becoming incandescent partly because of collisions of emitted atoms and air molecules. Estimated to become visible at height of 60–90 mi. and to move at average velocity of c.26 mi. per second. Called shooting or falling star if no brighter than zero-magnitude star; fireball or bolide if very large or brighter. If it reaches earth, it is called a METEORITE. Meteor showers are common at certain times of year at intervals coinciding with comet periods; appear to proceed from certain constellations.

Meteor Crater: see WINSLOW, Ariz.

meteorite (mē'tēurīt), METEOR that reaches earth's surface. Those called siderites are composed of metal; aerolites, of stone; siderolites, of metal and stone. Their surface, liquefied by heat and pressure resulting from rapid passage through atmosphere, forms crust as friction finally reduces velocity. Velocity of giant meteorites is so great that impact with earth results in penetration beneath ground, accompanied by compression, heating, vaporization, and expansion of gases which may cause explosion shattering meteorite and carving crater in ground. Meteorites have been discovered in most parts of world.

meteorology (mē"tēurŏl'ŭjē), science of atmosphere with its associated phenomena, WEATHER. Dates from 5th cent. B.C. Progress as a science began with development of physics and basic instruments (wind vane, 1500; thermometer, c.1593; mercurial barometer, 1643).

methane (mĕ'thān), commonly called marsh gas, a colorless, odorless gas. Burns in air, explosive when mixed with air. Formed by decomposition of organic matter in swamps and marshes, it is chief component of natural gas and fire damp. It is used as a fuel and illuminant and in treating steel. It consists of one carbon atom and four hydrogens, and is the first member of saturated hydrocarbon series, **methane or paraffin series.** Other members have same relation between number of carbons and hydrogens. They are common compounds occurring in benzine, gasoline, kerosene, paraffin. Substances considered derivatives include chloroform, methyl alcohol, ethyl alcohol, formaldehyde, acetic acid.

methanol: see METHYL ALCOHOL.

Methodism, doctrine, polity, and worship of Protestant denominations originating in England under John WESLEY. He and his brother Charles, George WHITEFIELD, and others formed group at Oxford in 1729. Their resolve to conduct lives and study by "rule and method" won them name Methodists. Followers preached in houses, barns, and open fields. Lay preachers were trained and given "circuits," and a system of itinerancy began. First annual conference in 1744 adopted Articles of Religion, based largely on Thirty-nine Articles though stress was put on repentance, faith, sanctification, and full, free salvation. Whitefield could not agree to this doctrine and became leader of Calvinistic Methodists. Main body adopted constitution 1784, formally separated from Church of England 1791, and organized Wesleyan Methodist Church. In America real beginning of Methodism was in N.Y. under preaching of Philip Embury (c.1766). In 1771 Francis ASBURY brought about rapid spread of Methodism, with first conference in 1773. In 1784 Methodist Episcopal Church was formed, with Asbury and Thomas Coke as bishops. As in England the church divided into many branches. Issue of slavery separated Methodist Episcopal Church South (1845) from main body. But in 1939 these two, with Methodist Protestant Church, united as Methodist Church.

Methodius, Saint: see CYRIL AND METHODIUS, SAINTS.

Methuen, (mĭthōō'un), town (pop. 24,477), NE Mass., near N.H. line NW of Lawrence; settled c.1642. Mfg. of worsteds, yarn, and wooden heels.

Methuselah (mĕthū'–), son of Enoch, known for the length of his life: according to Bible, he lived 969 years. Gen. 5.21. Mathusala: Luke 3.37.

methyl (mē'thĭl), organic radical with one carbon, three hydrogen atoms; name derived from methane. Has never been isolated but is in many compounds.

methyl alcohol, methanol (mē'thŭnōl), or **wood alcohol,** colorless, poisonous, liquid alcohol, inflammable, miscible with water. Used as organic solvent, in making formaldehyde, as denaturant. Prepared by destructive distillation of wood or by synthetic process with combination of carbon monoxide and hydrogen.

methylbenzene: see TOLUENE.

metric system, system of weights and measurements worked out in France and adopted by many nations. Based on meter (theoretically $\frac{1}{10,000,000}$ of distance from equator to pole, measured on earth's surface; legally, the length of platinum bar kept in Paris). Surface unit is the are (100 sq. meters); volume unit, the liter (cube of $\frac{1}{10}$ meter); weight unit, the gram (theoretical weight of distilled water filling cube with edges of $\frac{1}{100}$ meter). Weights or measures larger or smaller than meter are related to these units by a decimal system (e.g., kilometer equals 1,000 meters, etc.). For equivalents of metric denominations, see WEIGHTS AND MEASURES (table).

Metropolis (mǐtrŏ'pŭlǐs), city (pop. 6,093), S Ill., on Ohio R. and E of Cairo, in farm and timber area. State park here has site of Fort Ascension (later Fort Massac) estab. by French 1757; later held by British and Americans. Clark landed here 1778 at start of his Illinois campaign. Kincaid Indian mounds are in the general area.

Metropolitan Museum of Art, New York city, founded 1870. Opened 1880 on present site in Central Park facing Fifth Ave. Building owned by city, which provides upkeep; supported mainly by private endowment and membership dues. Admission is free. Outstanding features include European paintings, medieval art (part of which is in the CLOISTERS), Egyptian and American wings, and Costume Inst. (containing costumes from all over the world).

Metropolitan Opera Company, term used in referring collectively to organizations which have produced opera at the Metropolitan Opera House, New York. The house was built by members of New York society who could not be accommodated with boxes at the Acad. of Music. The first presentation, on Oct. 22, 1883, was Gounod's *Faust*. Devastated by fire in 1892, the opera house was rebuilt and taken over by the Metropolitan Opera and Real Estate Co. The management became known as the Metropolitan Opera Co. for the first time in 1908. The gradual transference from private to public ownership, with performances underwritten by public subscription, was completed when the Metropolitan Opera Association, Inc. (formed 1932 to replace the Metropolitan Opera Co.) bought the opera house (1940) from the Metropolitan Opera and Real Estate Co. Among the Metropolitan's directors have been Leopold Damrosch, Maurice Grau, Heinrich Conrad, Gatti-Casazza, Edward Johnson, and Rudolph Bing. The world's greatest singers and conductors have contributed to its rich traditions and glamorous legend.

Metsu or **Metzu, Gabriel** (both: gä'brēĕl mĕt'sü), 1630?–1667, Dutch genre painter, b. Leiden. Worked mainly in Amsterdam.

Metsys, Quentin: see MASSYS, QUENTIN.

Metternich, Clemens, Fürst von (klā'mĕns fürst' fŭn mĕ'tŭrnĭkh), 1773–1859, Austrian statesman, b. Coblenz, Germany. As minister of foreign affairs from 1809, he negotiated the marriage of MARIE LOUISE to Napoleon I (1810) and an alliance with France (1812), but in 1813, after attempting to mediate between Napoleon and the Allies, he joined the Allied camp. At the Congress of Vienna (1814–15) he sought a general balance of power, opposed Russian and Prussian expansion in Poland and Saxony, and secured a dominant place for Austria in the GERMAN CONFEDERATION. A dominating figure of the HOLY ALLIANCE, Metternich based his extreme conservatism on the theory that peace and order could be secured by an immutable maintenance of the *status quo.* Espionage, censorship, and armed repression of liberal movements were essential features of his policy, and the era 1815–48 has been called the Age of Metternich. Ousted by the Revolution of 1848, he returned to Vienna in 1851. He was created a prince in 1818.

Metuchen (mǔtŭ'chǔn), borough (pop. 9,879), NE N.J., NE of New Brunswick. Auto assembly plant; mfg. of chemicals and insulation products.

Metz (mĕts, Fr. mĕs), city (pop. 65,472), cap. of Moselle dept., NE France, on the Moselle; a cultural and commercial center of LORRAINE. An early episcopal see, it became the cap. of AUSTRASIA (6th cent.). Bishops ruled considerable territory as fief of Holy Roman Empire, but the city itself became a free imperial city in 12th cent. Metz was annexed to France in 1552 after a sort of plebiscite. In the Franco-Prussian War, Marshal Bazaine capitulated with 180,000 men after a two-month siege (1870). Annexed to Germany 1871–1918, Metz was a center of pro-French sentiment. In World War II it was liberated from German occupation by U.S. troops after heavy fighting for its outer fortifications (1944). The city retains many medieval buildings, notably its Gothic cathedral.

Metzu, Gabriel: see METSU, GABRIEL.

Meudon (mûdõ'), town (pop. 20,106), Seine-et-Oise dept., N France. Astrophysics dept. of Paris Observatory is in a pavilion of 17th-cent château. Rabelais was curate of Meudon.

Meun, Jean de: see JEAN DE MEUN.

Meunier, Constantin (kõstătĕ' mûnyā'), 1831–1905, Belgian sculptor and painter. Chiefly concerned with expressing dignity of the worker. Masterpiece is unfinished *Monument to Labor* (Brussels).

Meurthe (mûrt), river, 105 mi. long, E France, in Lorraine. Rises in the Vosges and flows NW to the Moselle just N of Nancy.

Meurthe-et-Moselle (mûr'tāmôzĕl'), department (2,039 sq. mi.; pop. 528,805), NE France, in Lorraine; cap. Nancy.

Meuse (mûz), department (2,410 sq. mi.; pop. 188,786), NE France, in Lorraine; cap. Bar-le-Duc.

Meuse (mûz, Fr. mûz), Dutch and Flemish *Maas*, river, c.560 mi. long, traversing NE France, S Belgium, and the Netherlands. It flows N from Langres Plateau, winds E through an industrial and mining region centered on Liège (Belgium), turns N into the Netherlands at Maastricht, swings W, and branches out to form a common delta with the Rhine. Bergsche Maas branch flows into a North Sea inlet S of Dordrecht. Maas branch flows NW to join the WAAL in forming the Merwede, which bifurcates into the Lower Merwede and the New Merwede. Latter forms the Hollandschdiep, a North Sea estuary. A branch of the Lower Merwede is the Old Meuse. The New Meuse is a continuation of the LEK. The Meuse is linked with Antwerp by ALBERT CANAL, with Dutch ports by intricate system of waterways. A strategic line of defense, valley has often been a battleground.

Mewar, India: see UDAIPUR.

Mexia (mùhā'ù), city (pop. 6,627), E central Texas, ENE of Waco. Processing center of oil and cotton area.

Mexicali (mĕksĭkä'lē), city (pop. 18,775), cap. of N district of Lower California, Mexico; farm center in IMPERIAL VALLEY.

Mexican art. The massive classic art of ancient Mayan and Aztec civilizations has influenced later artistic developments of Mexico. Highly developed arts are also identified with the pre-Aztec civilization of the Toltec. Unique medium of early Mexican art was feather painting (feathers gummed against a background to make a picture). European art (esp. painting) was introduced after Spanish conquest of Mexico. In 17th and 18th cent. natives became adept at religious oil painting and wax modeling, adding mellowness and richness of color to Spanish styles. Baltásar de Echave, the elder, who is considered the first great Mexican artist, founded the first native school (1609). Notable 18th-cent. artists included José Ibarra and Miguel Cabrera; outstanding in late 19th and early 20th cent. were José María Velasco and José Guadalupe. Since the 1910 revolution, mural painting to express social themes has become important, with Diego Rivera, José Orozco, and David Alfaro Siqueiros among its chief exponents. A noted abstract painter is Rufino Tamayo. Wood sculpture and folk arts (e.g., weaving, pottery making, silverwork) have long flourished. For Mexican architecture, see SPANISH COLONIAL ARCHITECTURE.

Mexican hairless dog: see TOY DOG.

Mexican War, 1846–48, fought by U.S. and Mexico. While immediate cause was annexation of Texas (Dec., 1845), other factors disturbed peaceful relations. American citizens had long-standing claims against Mexico; many wished acquisition of Calif. After admission of Texas into Union, Pres. Polk sent John Slidell to offer assumption of American claims by his government in return for boundary adjustment and to purchase Calif. and N.Mex. Mexico declined to negotiate. War was supported by imperialists and by those who wished to see slaveholding territory extended. In March, 1846, Gen Zachary TAYLOR occupied Point Isabel, at mouth of the Rio Grande. To the Mexicans, who claimed the Nueces as the boundary, this was an act of aggression. After Mexican crossing of the Rio Grande and shelling of Fort Brown (then Fort Taylor), U.S. declared war, May 12, 1846. Santa Fe was taken by S. W. KEARNY; Calif. exchanged Mexican for American rule. American victories preceded drawn battle with forces under SANTA ANNA at Buena Vista, Feb., 1847. Supported by naval task force, Winfield SCOTT took Veracruz, then began drive on Mexico city. Following the storming of Chapultepec, American troops entered Mexico city, Sept. 14, 1847, remaining until peace was restored. Treaty of GUADALUPE HIDALGO was ratified by U.S. Senate on March 10, 1848.

Mexico (měk′sĭkō), Span. *México* or *Méjico* (both: mě′-hēkō), republic (760,373 sq. mi.; pop. 25,581,250), North America, between U.S. and Central America; cap. Mexico city. Administratively divided into 28 states, 3 territories, and Federal District. States are (see individual articles): Aguascalientes, Campeche, Chiapas, Chihuahua, Coahuila, Colima, Durango, Guanajuato, Guerrero, Hidalgo, Jalisco, Mexico, Michoacán, Morelos, Nayarit, Nuevo León, Oaxaca, Puebla, Querétaro, San Luis Potosí, Sinaloa, Sonora, Tabasco, Tamaulipas, Tlaxcala, Veracruz, Yucatan, Zacatecas. Territories are Lower California (two) and Quintana Roo. Much of Mexico is mountainous (see SIERRA MADRE) with narrow, hot coastal plains and high central plateau transversed by E–W range with lofty volcanoes (e.g., Popocatepetl, Ixtacihuatl, Orizaba, Paricutín). Acapulco and Mazatlán are harbors on the Pacific; Tampico and Veracruz on the Gulf of Mexico. The Laguna District, an irrigated area in N, is agriculturally productive, but most of N is desert and semiarid with stockraising the principal occupation. Population is mostly on central plateau with principal cities located there—MEXICO city, GUADALAJARA, MONTERREY, PUEBLA; in them are most industries, except for oil industry on E coast, mining in the mountains, and many home crafts (pottery, baskets, weaving). Climate varies with altitude; although Mexico lies mostly in tropical zone, it has hot, temperate, and cool areas. Agr. products vary with the climate (tropical fruits, rubber, chicle, sugar cane, cacao, corn, wheat, tobacco, cotton). The country was the seat of highly developed ancient Indian civilizations; MAYA, TOLTEC, AZTEC, Mixtec, and Zapotec. Early visits to coast had been made by Fernández de Córdoba, 1517, and Grijalva, 1518, and soon Spanish conquest was accomplished under Cortés after 1519. In 1528 the first *audiencia* was set up, and the viceroyalty of New Spain under Antonio de Mendoza was estab. in 1535. Most of present Mexico and former Spanish holdings in present U.S. (from Ga. and Fla. to Calif.) were occupied in 16th and 17th cent. Population developed slowly into three groups—white, mestizo, Indian—who did not coalesce easily in spite of efforts of some able administrators and churchmen (e.g., ZUMÁRRAGA; the two Luis de VELASCO). Friction between these groups, plus dissatisfaction with the political power of the Church and with the Spanish mercantilist system which drained Mexico of its mineral wealth all helped bring about the rebellion against Spain led by the priest Hidalgo y Costilla, who issued the *grito de Dolores* on Sept. 16, 1811. Independence was finally achieved in 1821, with the establishment of a short-lived empire under Agustín de Iturbide. A period of selfish strife among leaders (notably SANTA ANNA) brought a series of presidents for the next several decades, with land problems and other social evils going unsolved. In 1836, Texas successfully revolted against Mexico, and in 1845, when the U.S. accepted Texas as a state, the Mexican War ensued. A democratic reform movement was led by Benito Juárez and resulted in the constitution of 1857. The conservatives sought aid abroad, and with the help of French sol-

diers were able to make Maximilian emperor of Mexico (1864–67). Juárez opposed the empire and at its fall again ruled Mexico but was unable to put his reforms into effect. Porfirio Díaz became president in 1876 and continued as dictator of Mexico until 1910. His regime was marked by material development, increase in foreign investments, and growth of national wealth but social conditions steadily worsened and education stagnated. A revolution, led by Francisco I. Madero in 1910, succeeded. Madero, however, proved incapable of accomplishing reforms, and another period of civil war followed under such leaders as Huerta, Carranza, Zapata, Villa (whose troubles with the U.S. brought on a U.S. expedition into Mexico, 1916), Obregon, and De la Huerta. A reform constitution was adopted in 1917, still the basic constitution of Mexico. Under it mineral wealth was expropriated from foreign owners. Politically CALLES was long dominant. With the inauguration of Lázaro Cardenas (1934) a vigorous program of social, educational, and industrial reforms was instituted which has continued to the present. The building of the Inter-American Highway greatly increased the number of U.S. tourists. Mexico declared war on the Axis powers in 1942; in 1945, the Inter-American Conference on the Problems of War and Peace met in Mexico city and drew up the Act of Chapultepec (see PAN AMERICANISM). Later presidents are: Manuel Ávila Camacho (1940–46), Miguel Alemán (1946–52), Adolfo Ruiz Cortines (1952–).

Mexico, state (8,268 sq. mi.; pop. 1,317,303), central Mexico; cap. TOLUCA. State encircles the Federal District except on the S. A range of high mountains (N–S) lies between Toluca and Mexico city, but most of the state lies in the flat Valley of Mexico. Mining, agr., and stock raising are chief activities; mfg. includes processing of agr. and dairy products, making of textiles, baskets, glassware, pottery, bricks.

Mexico, city (pop. 1,448,422; alt. 7,800 ft.), central Mexico, cap. and largest city of Mexico, in SW part of Valley of Mexico near S end of plateau of Anáhuac on site of former L. Texcoco. The volcanoes of Popocatepetl and Ixtacihuatl are near by. The climate is cool, dry (with rainy season late May–early Sept.), and healthful. The city fans out from a central plaza (called the Zócalo) where the cathedral and Natl. Palace are located to the sprawling suburbs (called *colonias*). Near-by places of interest include Xochimilco, Guadalupe Hidalgo, and pyramids of Teotihuacán. Architecturally the city is a mixture of buildings of various styles—Spanish colonial, 19th-cent. French, starkly modern. The Natl. Univ. (founded in 16th cent.), which until Nov., 1952, was scattered throughout the city, has been consolidated in a completely modern University City in a suburb. Many of the public buildings have murals by Diego Rivera, Orozco, and Siqueiros. The city's chief problems have from its beginning been its drainage system and a potable water supply. Many of its finest buildings (notably the Palace of Fine Arts) are sinking as a result of the drying of the old lake bed. The completion in 1951 of a $26,000,000 project bringing water from L. Lerma has solved the water-supply problem. From the time that Cortés built a city where the Aztec capital, TENOCHTITLÁN, had stood throughout the Spanish regime, the brief empires of Iturbide and Maximilian, and the republic of Mexico, it has been not only the political capital but the financial and cultural center of the nation. Recent industrial developments plus a tourist trade mounting since completion of the Inter-American highway has brought increasing prosperity.

Mexico, city (pop. 11,623), central Mo., NE of Columbia, in farm area; laid out 1836. Raises saddle horses. Has mfg. of firebrick and shoes.

Mexico, Gulf of, arm of Atlantic Ocean, 700,000 sq. mi., 1,000 mi. E–W, 800 mi. N–S; bordered N by U.S., SW by Mexico; opens to Atlantic through Florida Straits (Gulf Stream exit) N of Cuba, to Caribbean through Yucatan Channel S of Cuba. Deepest part

(Sigsbee Deep) 12,714 ft. Shore line mostly low, sandy, marshy. Main ports are Tampico and Veracruz in Mexico; Corpus Christi, Galveston, Houston, Mobile, New Orleans, and Pensacola in U.S.; and Havana in Cuba. Receives Mississippi, Sabine, Brazos, Colorado (of Texas), and Rio Grande rivers. Has oil deposits.

Meyer, Adolf (ä'dôlf mī'ùr), 1866–1950, American psychiatrist, b. Switzerland. He suggested term "mental hygiene" and was active in the movement in U.S. His system, psychobiology, considered each patient's problem in light of his total personality.

Meyer, Conrad Ferdinand (kôn'rät fĕr'dēnänt mī'ùr), 1825–98, Swiss poet and novelist, one of the foremost stylists in modern German literature. His short novels are usually laid in the Renaissance period.

Meyer, Lothar (lōtär' mī'ùr), 1830–95, German chemist. Contributed to development of PERIODIC LAW; evolved atomic volume curve.

Meyerbeer, Giacomo (jäkō'mō mī'yùrbâr), 1791–1864, German composer, of Jewish ancestry, whose real name was Jakob Liebmann Beer. He wrote in many forms, but his greatest success was in opera—*Robert le Diable, Les Huguenots, Le Prophète, L'Africaine,* and *Dinorah.*

Meyerhof, Otto (ô'tō mī'ùrhōf), 1884–1951, German physiologist. Shared 1922 Nobel Prize in Physiology and Medicine for work on cellular oxidation and transformation of lactic acid in muscles.

Meynell, Alice (Thompson) (mě'nùl), 1847–1922, English poet and essayist on Roman Catholic themes. Her poems, variously published, were collected in 1923.

Mézières (māzyĕr'), town (pop. 7,898), cap. of Ardennes dept., NE France, on the Meuse opposite Charleville, its twin city. Its capture (1918) by the Allies marked last major battle of World War I.

Mg, chemical symbol of the element MAGNESIUM.

Miami. 1 Town (pop. 4,329), E Ariz., near GLOBE, in mining area; copper-smelting center. 2 City (pop. 249,276), SE Fla., on Biscayne Bay at mouth of Miami R. Largest city in state and one of leading resorts (esp. in winter) of E U.S., with extensive recreational facilities. Air transportation center, with a number of air bases (private and governmental) and important connections with Latin America. Handles coastal and foreign shipping. Greater Miami includes Miami, MIAMI BEACH, CORAL GABLES, and HIALEAH. Settled in 1870s near site of a Seminole War post, Fort Dallas. H. M. Flagler made it a rail terminus in 1896, dredged the harbor, and began city's development as a resort. Greatest growth came during land boom of 1920s. A Seminole Indian village is at Musa Isle. 3 City (pop. 11,801), NE Okla., on Neosho R. Center for lead, zinc, cattle, and farm area.

Miami, Fort: see FORT WAYNE, Ind.; SAINT JOSEPH, Mich.; MAUMEE, Ohio.

Miami, Great and **Little,** rivers: see GREAT MIAMI.

Miami, University of: see CORAL GABLES, Fla.

Miami Beach, city (pop. 46,282), SE Fla., part of Greater Miami, on island between Biscayne Bay (crossed by causeways) and the Atlantic. Developed slowly until 1920s. Popular resort.

Miamisburg, city (pop. 6,329), SW Ohio, on Great Miami R. and SW of Dayton, in state's leading tobacco area. Near by is large Indian mound.

Miami Shores. 1 Village (pop. 5,086), SE Fla. Separated 1932 from Miami. 2 Former name of NORTH MIAMI, Fla.

Miami Springs, town (pop. 5,108), SE Fla., NW suburb of Miami.

Miami University: see OXFORD, Ohio.

Miaskovsky, Nikolai (Yakovlevich) (nyĭkùlī' myŭskôf'skē), 1881–1950, Russian composer of symphonies and chamber, piano, and vocal music.

mica (mī'kù), name for group of minerals, silicates of aluminum and potassium. Mica splits into thin, elastic sheets; occurs in granites, gneiss, schist. Common varieties are muscovite (usually colorless) and biotite

(black). Sheet mica is used in many ways, e.g., as insulating material, to make diaphragms for phonographs, loud-speakers, etc.; it is ground for use in fancy paints and for various ornamental purposes. Chief sources are India and Brazil.

Micah or **Micheas** (mīkē'–), book of Old Testament. The prophet Micah, a contemporary of Isaiah (fl. 710 B.C.), foretold doom of Judah and Israel. Messianic prophecy in 5.2–6 is famous. Mat. 2.6; John 7.42.

Michael [Heb.,= Who is like God?], archangel, who appears in Bible as prince or warrior. Dan. 10.13,21; 12.1; Jude 9; Rev. 12.7. In Christian tradition he is the conqueror of Satan and carries a sword and has appeared at various times to humans (e.g., to Joan of Arc). His chief feast, called Michaelmas, is Sept. 29.

Michael, Byzantine emperors. **Michael I** (Michael Rhangabe), d. c.845, reigned 811–13. Recalled Theodore of Studium from exile. Was deposed after being routed by Bulgars. **Michael II** (the Stammerer), d. 829, a Phrygian, helped Leo V to power after Michael I's deposition. He became emperor in 820 after his supporters had murdered Leo. The controversy over ICONOCLASM, which he favored over orthodoxy, was ended during the minority of his grandson, **Michael III** (the Drunkard), 839–67, who reigned 842–67. The iconoclasts were overthrown, the PAULICIANS persecuted. Addicted to drink and debauches, Michael left the government to his uncle, the Caesar Bardas, whose able administration was marked by the missions of SS. CYRIL AND METHODIUS. Michael's boon companion Basil had Bardas murdered in 866, murdered Michael in 867, and became emperor as BASIL I. **Michael VIII,** 1224–82, first of the Palaeologus dynasty, became emperor of Nicaea in 1259 by first sharing, then usurping, the throne of John IV, whom he had blinded and imprisoned. In 1261 he recovered Constantinople by an ingenious stratagem (his soldiers entered at night through an unused aqueduct). Thus the Latin Empire fell and the Byzantine Empire was restored. The rest of his life was spent in struggle with the Seljuk Turks and with CHARLES I of Naples. To win papal support against Charles he negotiated for union of the Eastern and Western Churches (see LYONS, SECOND COUNCIL OF), but eventually failed. He helped to prepare the SICILIAN VESPERS, which broke Charles's power. An able scholar, he left an interesting autobiography.

Michael (Michael Romanov), 1596–1645, tsar of Russia (1613–45), founder of ROMANOV dynasty. His election ended Time of Troubles (see DMITRI).

Michael, 1921–, king of Rumania. His father, Prince Carol (later CAROL II), having renounced the succession, he became king in 1927 under a regency. In 1930 Carol returned to be recognized as king, but on Carol's abdication in 1940 Michael became king again. He overthrew the dictatorship of ANTONESCU in 1944 and made an armistice with the Allies. In 1947 his Communist-dominated government forced him to abdicate. In exile, he married Princess Anne of Bourbon-Parma.

Michael (Michael Obrenovich), 1823–68, prince of Serbia. Succeeded his brother Milan 1839. His attempts at reform led to his deposition in 1842. Alexander Karageorgevich became prince, but in 1858 Michael's father MILOSH was restored. On Milosh's death (1860) Michael became prince again. He modernized his country and prepared its complete liberation from Turkish vassalage. He was murdered by members of the Karageorgevich faction.

Michaelmas: see MICHAEL, archangel.

Michaelmas daisy: see ASTER.

Michael the Brave, d. 1601, prince of Walachia (1593–1601). After ordering a general massacre of the Turks in Walachia, he forced the sultan to grant him virtual independence (1596) and conquered Transylvania (1599) and Moldavia (1600). His dealings with the imperial court of Vienna were marked by duplicity on both sides and ended with his assassination by an imperial agent. His empire fell apart on his death.

Michal (mī'kŭl), daughter of Saul, wife of David. 1 Sam. 18.20; 19.12; 2 Sam. 6.16. See MERAB.

Micheas (mīkē'ŭs), variant of MICAH.

Michelangelo (Buonarroti) (mīkŭlăn'jŭlō, Ital. mēkälän'jälō bwônär-rō'tē), 1475–1564, Italian artist, one of the greatest figures of Italian Renaissance and of world art history, b. Caprese, Tuscany. Studied in Florence with Domenico Ghirlandaio and at art school held in Medici gardens. Lived two years of his youth in palace of Lorenzo de' Medici, where he met the humanists Pico della Mirandola and Politian. Worked in Rome (1496–1501) and carved *Bacchus* (Bargello, Florence) and *Pietà* (St. Peter's, Rome). Returning to Florence (1501), he was commissioned by the city to execute the giant *David* (Academy, Florence). Called to Rome in 1505 to execute tomb for Pope Julius II, but major interruptions, such as work on ceiling of SISTINE CHAPEL (1508–12), kept the project uncompleted for c.30 years; most significant work on it includes colossal *Moses* (San Pietro in Vincoli, Rome). Worked 1520–34 on Medici chapel (Florence), in which he achieved unity of sculpture and architecture. In 1529 he assisted as engineer in defense of Florence. After suppression of Florentine freedom he again went to Rome. Sonnets written in this period were inspired by the young nobleman Tommaso Cavalieri and the poetess Vittoria Colonna. Painted the *Last Judgment* (Sistine Chapel) 1534–41 and executed frescoes for Pauline Chapel (Vatican) 1541–50. In 1546 he became chief architect of St. Peter's. *Pietà* in Florence cathedral shows tendency toward the spiritual in his old age.

Michelet, Jules (zhül' mēshŭlā'), 1798–1874, French writer, greatest historian of romantic school. Major work *Histoire de France* (many vols., 1833–67).

Michelozzi, Michelozzo (mēkälôt'tsō mēkälôt'tsē), 1396 –1472, Italian architect and sculptor. With Brunelleschi he shared leadership in establishing Renaissance style. Built Riccardi Palace and Medici Chapel in Santa Croce (both in Florence).

Michelson, Albert Abraham (mī'kŭlsŭn), 1852–1931, American physicist. He won 1907 Nobel Prize and is known especially for his determination of velocity of light and experimental studies of ether drift which contributed to theory of relativity.

Michener, James A(lbert), 1907–, American author. His works include *Tales of the South Pacific* (1947; later made into the musical play *South Pacific*), *The Fires of Spring* (1949), *Return to Paradise* (1951), and *The Voice of Asia* (1951).

Michigan, state (57,022 sq. mi.; pop. 6,371,766), N U.S., in Great Lakes region; admitted 1837 as 26th state (free); cap. LANSING. Other cities are DETROIT, GRAND RAPIDS, FLINT, DEARBORN, PONTIAC. In two parts, Upper Peninsula and Lower Peninsula, separated by Straits of Mackinac. Farming (dairying, grains, fruits, potatoes, livestock); mining (iron, copper, oil, salt); fishing; lumbering. Mfg. of motor vehicles and parts, steel, machinery, food products, airplanes, furniture, paper; printing and publishing. First explored and settled by French; important fur-trading center. Taken by English in French and Indian Wars. Passed to U.S. after American Revolution. In British hands in War of 1812 until W. H. Harrison in battle of the Thames and O. H. Perry in battle of L. Erie restored American prestige. Period of economic expansion preceded Civil War; Mich. supported Union. Farmer discontent in late 19th cent. brought legislation for agrarian improvement. 20th cent. has seen rise of automobile industry (esp. under Henry FORD). Labor unions gained, not without conflicts, in 1930s–40s. World War II saw great industrial expansion.

Michigan, Lake, 22,400 sq. mi., 307 mi. long, 118 mi. wide, 923 ft. deep; third largest of Great Lakes, 579.79 ft. above sea level. Mich. is E and N, Ill. and Wis. W, and Ind. S. Empties NE into L. Huron. Linked with Mississippi R. by Illinois Waterway. Ports to N are icebound four months a year. Much shipping is done despite abrupt, fierce storms. Shore cities include Michigan City and Gary, Ind.; Chicago, Evanston, and Waukegan, Ill.; Kenosha, Racine, Milwaukee, Manitowoc, and Two Rivers, Wis.; Escanaba, Manistee, Ludington, Muskegon, Grand Haven, and Benton Harbor, Mich. Green Bay is largest arm. Discovered 1934 by Jean Nicolet.

Michigan, University of, at Ann Arbor, state supported, coed. Chartered 1817 as Catholepistemiad (or University) of Michigania, rechartered 1821 and 1837; opened as school in Detroit 1817, reopened as college in Ann Arbor 1841. Has noted library and museums and observatories in Ann Arbor, in South Africa, and near Detroit.

Michigan City, city (pop. 28,395), NW Ind., on L. Michigan ENE of Gary; settled 1830. Summer resort. Mfg. of furniture, Pullman cars.

Michigan State College of Agriculture and Applied Science, at East Lansing; with land-grant support, coed.; chartered 1855, opened 1857 as first state agricultural college, renamed 1925. Has courses in police administration.

Michilimackinac: see MACKINAC.

Michoacán (mēchōäkän'), state (23,202 sq. mi.; pop. 1,412,830), W Mexico; cap. MORELIA. Extends from the Pacific to the central plateau, with wide variation in topography, climate, and soil. Mining is chief occupation in mountains (Sierra Madre Occidental and E-W volcanic chain). Fine cabinet wood and dyewoods come from forests. Agr. dominates state; sugar cane, coffee, vanilla, tobacco, cereals. Of interest to tourists are L. PATZCUARO, L. CHAPALA, PARACUTÍN (volcano), TARASCAN INDIANS.

Michurin, Ivan Vladimirovich (ēvän' vlŭdyē'mīrŭvĭch mēchoō'rĭn), 1855–1935, Russian horticulturist. His theory that hereditary changes can be induced by grafting and that acquired characters are inherited was elaborated by T. D. Lysenko and his followers and was officially supported (1948) by Soviet Central Committee.

Mickiewicz, Adam (mětskyē'vĭch), 1798–1855, greatest romantic poet of Poland. Arrested (1823) for activities in secret patriotic societies, he was deported to Russia, whence he fled (1829). He taught literature in Paris after 1840 and died in Constantinople, where he was organizing a Polish legion against Russia. His chief works (all tr. into English) are the epic poems *Pan Tadeusz* (1834) and *Konrad Wallenrod* (1825–28) and the dramatic poem *Forefather's Eve* (1823).

Micon (mī'kŏn), fl. c.460 B.C., Greek painter and sculptor. Collaborated with Polygnotus in painting the *Battle of Marathon* in Stoa Poecile, Athens.

microbiology: see BIOLOGY.

Micronesia (mīkrōnē'zhŭ), one of three main divisions of Pacific islands, in W Pacific, N of equator. Includes the Carolines, Marshalls, Marianas, and Gilbert Isls. Inhabitants stem from Negroid and Mongoloid stock and speak Malayo-Polynesian languages (see LANGUAGE, table).

microphone (mī'krŭfōn), device converting acoustic energy of sound waves into electrical energy waves, used to record, broadcast, and amplify sound. Early types based on fact of resistance varying inversely with pressure holding electrical contacts together. Other common types generate audio voltages responding to pressure of sound; crystal type uses piezoelectric effect of Rochelle salt crystals. Ribbon or velocity type and moving coil or dynamic type both use Faraday electromagnetic induction principle.

microscope, optical instrument used to increase apparent size of object. Magnifying glass, a double convex LENS, is simple microscope. When object is placed within focal length of double convex lens, a virtual IMAGE is produced which is erect and larger than object; magnification is expressed in diameters. Compound microscope is two or more such lenses fixed in hollow metal tube; tube can be raised or lowered. Object is magnified by lower lens, image of object by upper. It is used to examine unicellular organisms,

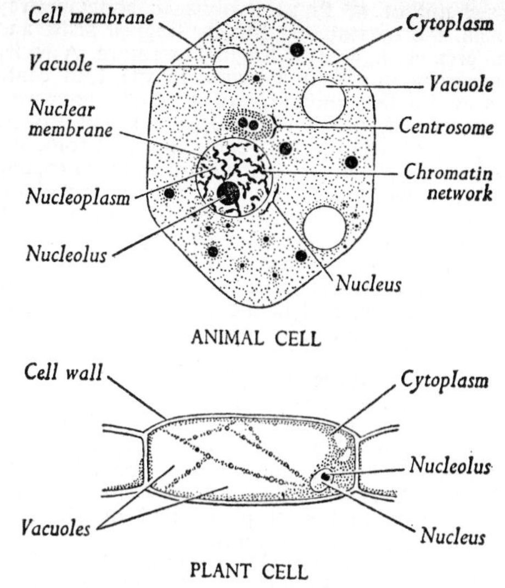

DIAGRAM OF CELL STRUCTURES

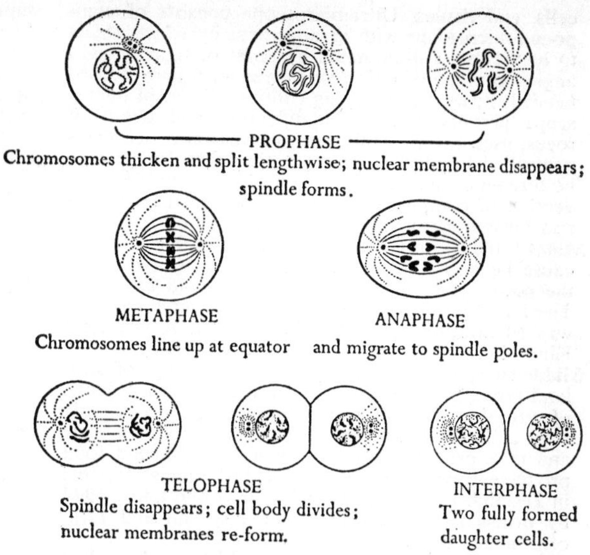

ANIMAL CELL

Cell membrane
Vacuole
Nuclear membrane
Nucleoplasm
Nucleolus
Cytoplasm
Vacuole
Centrosome
Chromatin network
Nucleus

PLANT CELL

Cell wall
Vacuoles
Cytoplasm
Nucleolus
Nucleus

STAGES IN MITOTIC CELL DIVISION

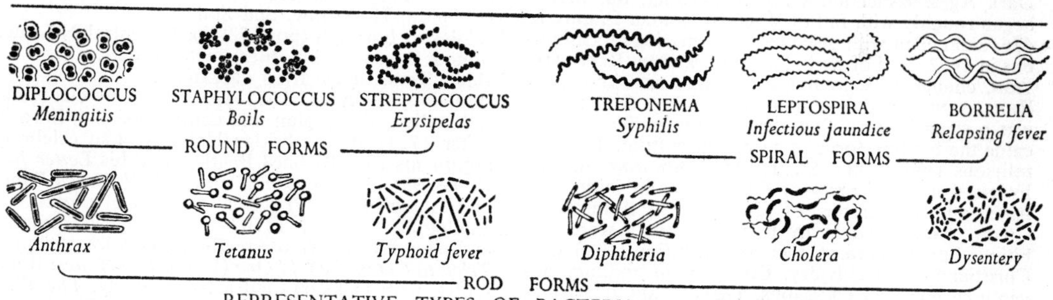

PROPHASE
Chromosomes thicken and split lengthwise; nuclear membrane disappears; spindle forms.

METAPHASE
Chromosomes line up at equator

ANAPHASE
and migrate to spindle poles.

TELOPHASE
Spindle disappears; cell body divides; nuclear membranes re-form.

INTERPHASE
Two fully formed daughter cells.

REPRESENTATIVE TYPES OF BACTERIA (Magnification x c.1500)

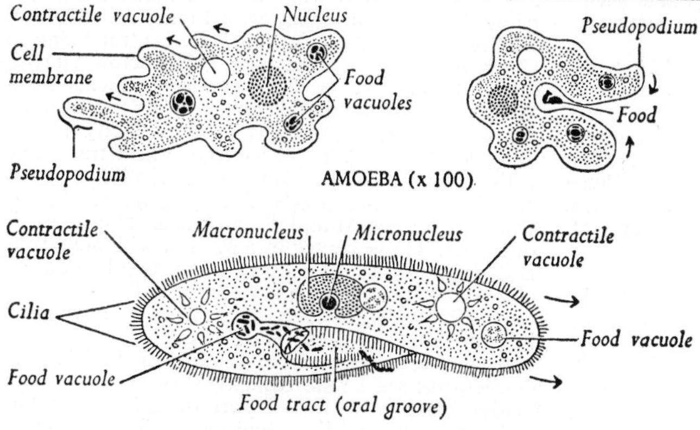

ROUND FORMS

DIPLOCOCCUS
Meningitis

STAPHYLOCOCCUS
Boils

STREPTOCOCCUS
Erysipelas

SPIRAL FORMS

TREPONEMA
Syphilis

LEPTOSPIRA
Infectious jaundice

BORRELIA
Relapsing fever

ROD FORMS

Anthrax

Tetanus

Typhoid fever

Diphtheria

Cholera

Dysentery

TWO OF THE SIMPLEST ANIMALS: PROTOZOA

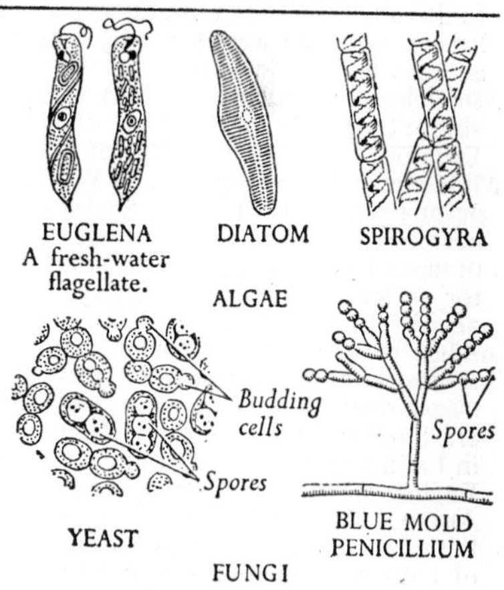

AMOEBA (x 100)

Contractile vacuole
Cell membrane
Pseudopodium
Nucleus
Food vacuoles
Pseudopodium
Food

THE PARAMECIUM (x c.450) HAS DEFINITE FORM

Contractile vacuole
Cilia
Food vacuole
Macronucleus
Micronucleus
Contractile vacuole
Food vacuole
Food tract (oral groove)

SIMPLE PLANTS

EUGLENA
A fresh-water flagellate.

DIATOM

SPIROGYRA

ALGAE

YEAST
Budding cells
Spores

FUNGI

BLUE MOLD
PENICILLIUM
Spores

BLOOD CELLS

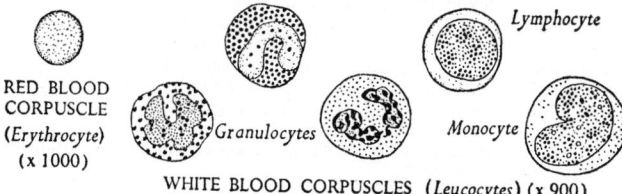

RED BLOOD CORPUSCLE (Erythrocyte) (x 1000)

Granulocytes

Lymphocyte

Monocyte

WHITE BLOOD CORPUSCLES (Leucocytes) (x 900)

These do not divide, but are formed by body organs.

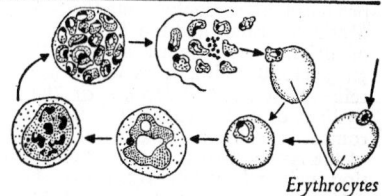

Erythrocytes

Series showing erythrocyte being invaded by malaria parasite.

cells, and tissues. Ultramicroscope consists of compound microscope with arrangement by which object to be viewed is illuminated by point of light at right angles to plane of objective (lower lens) and focused beneath it; used in studying colloids. Electron microscope permits greater magnification and depth of focus; uses instead of light rays a stream of electrons controlled by electric or magnetic fields. Image may be thrown on fluorescent screen or photographed. Invention of compound microscope ascribed to Zacharias Janssen c.1590 and to Galileo 1609 or 1610.

Midas (mī'dŭs), in Greek legend, king of Phrygia. Because he befriended Silenus, Dionysus granted him the power of turning everything into gold by touch. Tired of his gift when even food became gold, he washed away the power in Pactolus R. A historical King Midas of Phrygia lived in 8th cent. B.C.

Middelburg, municipality (pop. 20,605), cap. of Zeeland prov., SW Netherlands, on Walcheren isl., NNE of Flushing. It flourished commercially in Middle Ages and belonged to Hanseatic League. Now a trade and mfg. center, it produces wood, metal, and food products. It was captured 1574 as last Spanish fortress in Zeeland. Flooded in World War II and taken 1944 by British troops, but 15th-cent. city hall and 12th-cent. abbey remain.

Middle Ages, period in W European history, also called Dark Ages. Exact dates are misleading, but period began roughly with fall of Western Roman Empire in 476, and ended with discovery of America by Columbus in 1492. End of period also marked by REFORMATION, change in scholarship and fine arts known as RENAISSANCE, and invention of printing. Christianity was a struggling religion early in the period but became the binding force of medieval culture. Through religious leaders like St. THOMAS AQUINAS and St. FRANCIS of Assisi unity of Europe was in faith, doctrine, and institutions of Christianity. Empires of CHARLEMAGNE and HOLY ROMAN EMPIRE were ambitious but insecure. A secular institution allied with Christianity was chivalry. Conspicuous military adventures included CRUSADES. GOTHIC ARCHITECTURE was originated and carried to highest development. In literature, masters were DANTE and CHAUCER. Secular organizations were typically local (see FEUDALISM), artisans banded in GUILDS.

Middleboro, town (pop. 10,164), including Middleboro village (pop. 5,889), SE Mass., between Plymouth and Taunton; settled 1660. Mfg. of shoes.

Middlebury, town (pop. 4,778), W Vt., S of Burlington; permanently settled 1783. Sheldon Art Mus. (1829) has colonial collections. Seat of **Middlebury College** (nonsectarian; coed.; 1800); holds noted conference for writers and foreign-language summer schools at near-by Bread Loaf.

middle class: see BOURGEOISIE.

Middle English literature, 1100–1500, literature in transitional dialects between Anglo-Saxon and modern English. Much writing in England at the time was in Latin and in Anglo-Norman (French). Until c.1250 English works were mostly religious (e.g., in prose, ANCREN RIWLE; in verse, An Orison of Our Lady), but there also appeared some secular works (e.g., Brut of LAYAMON; OWL AND THE NIGHTINGALE; SUMER IS ICUMEN IN, rhymed lyric for a love song). Writing in Anglo-Norman, the language of the upper classes, produced more sophisticated works such as lais by Marie de France and the Tristan romance by Thomas of Britain. As English became the ascendant language (1250–1350), many works were composed, both religious (e.g., The Debate of the Body and Soul; writings of mystic Richard Rolle) and secular, mainly romances—some adapted from French such as those of the ARTHURIAN LEGEND, others from English tradition such as HAVELOK THE DANE. The last half of the 14th cent. saw the apex of Middle English in the works of the anonymous poet of The PEARL and SIR GAWAIN AND THE GREEN KNIGHT; William LANGLAND,

supposed author of PIERS PLOWMAN; and Geoffrey CHAUCER, the outstanding Middle English artist and one of greatest figures of English literature. A lesser contemporary was John GOWER. In the 15th cent., numerous English imitators of Chaucer appeared, such as John LYDGATE, King JAMES I and Robert HENRYSON. Also in the 15th cent. appeared some excellent anonymous poetry in the carol and BALLAD, and English medieval drama reached a peak in the Wakefield mystery cycle (see MIRACLE PLAY) and the morality Everyman. Expressive, flexible English prose developed in the translation of the Bible by John PURVEY, in popular translations like the Voiage of Sir John MANDEVILLE, and in the vigorous narrative of the Morte d'Arthur of Sir Thomas MALORY.

Middlesboro, city (pop. 14,482), S Ky., in the Cumberlands at point where Ky., Tenn., and Va. meet; founded 1889. Resort and center of mining and agr. area, has metal and wood products. Cumberland Gap, Pinnacle Mt., and Cudjo's Cave are near by.

Middlesbrough (–brŭ), county borough (pop. 147,336), N. Riding of Yorkshire, England, on Tees R. estuary. Has great iron and steel plants and metallurgical schools, libraries, and museums.

Middlesex, inland county (232 sq. mi.; pop. 2,268,776), S central England, within Greater London area. Residential suburb traversed by main traffic routes. Towns include Brentford, Harrow, Tottenham, Uxbridge, Hampton, Hounslow, and Staines.

Middlesex, borough (pop. 5,943), N central N.J., near Bound Brook. Paint, tiles, metal products.

Middle Temple: see INNS OF COURT.

Middleton, Conyers, 1683–1750, English clergyman, rationalistic theologian and controversialist; librarian (after 1721) at Cambridge Univ. He had celebrated arguments with Richard Bentley, and his Letter from Rome, Showing an Exact Conformity between Popery and Paganism (1729) roused a storm of protest.

Middleton, Thomas, 1570?–1627, English dramatist and pamphleteer. Wrote realistic comedies, such as A Trick to Catch the Old One (1608), The Honest Whore (1604; with Dekker), and a tragicomedy, The Witch (1617). His most powerful tragedies were The Changeling and Women Beware Women (both c.1623). His pamphlets show intimacy with London's underworld.

Middletown. 1 City (pop. 29,711), central Conn., on Connecticut R. (bridged here 1938) below Hartford; settled 1650. Textiles, metal goods, chemicals. Seat of Wesleyan Univ. (liberal arts college; nonsectarian; for men); opened 1831 by Methodists. **2** City (pop. 22,586), SE N.Y. SW of Newburgh. Farm trade center with railroad shops, foundries; clothing, textiles, chemicals, leather goods. **3** City (pop. 33,695), SW Ohio, on Great Miami R. and near Hamilton; laid out 1802. Trade center in agr. area with steel-rolling and paper mills; mfg. of clothing, textiles, and machinery. **4** Borough (pop. 9,184), SE Pa., on Susquehanna R. and SE of Harrisburg. Mfg. of stoves, clothing, and shoes. **5** Resort town (pop. 7,382), SE R.I., between Newport and Portsmouth on Rhode Isl.

Middletown: see LYND, ROBERT STAUGHTON.

Middle West or **Midwest**, part of U.S. about Great Lakes and upper Mississippi valley. This vague term is sometimes applied to all of N U.S. between the Alleghenies and the Rockies, but more often to only Ohio, Ind., Ill., Mich., Wis., Minn., Iowa, Mo., Kansas, and Nebr. The Dakotas may be included, and even Prairie Provs. of Canada. Some of world's richest farm land, it is known for corn and hogs and wheat. Has huge industries, such as mfg. of cars and tires. Popularly conservative, isolationist, Protestant, "American," the region actually has a variety of creeds and peoples. The region has a distinctive dialect of English.

Midgard [Norse,= middle court], in Norse mythology, the earth.

Midhat Pasha (mĭd-hät' pä'shä), 1822–84, Turkish statesman. Leader of the reforming party that deposed

Abdu-l-Aziz (1876), he framed the first Turkish constitution but was soon dismissed by Abdu-l-Hamid II and was later strangled.

Midi, Pic du, France: see PIC DU MIDI.

Midianites (mĭ'dēŭn–), enemies of the Hebrews who were defeated by Gideon. Gen. 25.2; 37.28,36; Ex. 3.1; Num. 31.1–9; Judges 6–8.

Midland, town (pop. 7,206), S Ont., Canada, on E Georgian Bay and W of Toronto. Port with government coal dock, textile mills, and mfg. of machinery. Near by is shrine to Jesuit martyrs.

Midland. 1 City (pop. 14,285), S Mich., at junction of Pine, Chippewa, and Tittabawassee rivers W of Bay City. Early lumber town, developed after 1890 by Dow Chemical Co. Oil, coal, and salt in area. **2** Borough (pop. 6,491), W Pa., on Ohio R. and NW of Pittsburgh. Mfg. of steel, machinery, and coke. Has shipyard and railroad shops. **3** City (pop. 21,713), W Texas, on S border of Llano Estacado, WNW of San Angelo; settled 1885. Oil company offices and plants (fields at Odessa). Cattle shipping and cotton ginning.

Midland Park, borough (pop. 5,164), NE N.J., N of Paterson. Textiles.

Midlands, region of central England. Includes the counties of Bedford, Buckingham, Derby, Leicester, Northampton, Nottingham, Rutland, and Warwick.

Midlothian (mĭdlō'dhēŭn), formerly **Edinburghshire,** county (366 sq. mi.; pop. 565,746), E central Scotland. County town is EDINBURGH, cap. of Scotland. Mainly agr. region (market gardening, stock raising, and dairying), it also has fishing and mfg. (paper, whisky, and ironware). Leith and Granton are shipbuilding centers.

Midrash (mĭd'răsh) [Heb.,= investigation], a homiletical interpretation of the Scriptures by Jewish rabbis since A.D. c.200. It is incorporated in the Mishna of the TALMUD, and, like the Gemara, contains elements of both HALAKAH and haggada. Midrashim were compiled for many books of the Bible.

midsummer day, feast of the nativity of St. John the Baptist, June 24. The preceding night is **midsummer night** or St. John's Eve, and because it comes near the solstice, it is in many parts of Europe connected with magic. Great bonfires are built and there is merrymaking. Emphasis on love and lovers on this night undoubtedly reflects old fertility rites.

Midway, group (2 sq. mi.; pop. 437) comprising Sand and Eastern islands with surrounding atoll, central Pacific, c.1,150 mi. NW of Honolulu. U.S. discovery (1859); annexed 1867. Cable station (1903), and civil (1935) and military (1941) air base. Scene (June 5–6, 1942) of **battle of Midway,** a decisive U.S. victory in World War II. Fought entirely with aircraft, it caused destruction of a Japanese battle fleet, crippling of Japanese navy, and end of Pacific invasion threat.

Midwest: see MIDDLE WEST.

Midwest City, residential town (pop. 10,166), central Okla., Oklahoma City suburb.

midwifery: see OBSTETRICS.

Mieris (mē'rĭs), family of Dutch genre and portrait painters of Leiden. **Frans van Mieris,** 1635–81, the most important, excelled in faithful rendering of texture. His sons and pupils were **Jan van Mieris,** 1660–90, and **Willem van Mieris,** 1662–1747.

Miës van der Rohe, Ludwig (lōōt'vĭkh mē'ĕs vän dĕr rō'ù), 1886–, German-American architect. Headed the BAUHAUS, 1932–33. In 1938 became director of Armour Inst. (now Illinois Inst. of Technology).

Mifflin, Thomas, 1744–1800, American Revolutionary general and politician. Rose to be quartermaster general. President of Continental Congress (1783–84). Governor of Pa. (1790–99).

Mignard, Pierre (pyĕr' mēnyär'), 1610–95, French painter. Lived many years in Italy and did portraits of two popes. In France he served Louis XIV.

mignonette (mĭnyŭnĕt'), Old World annual (*Reseda odorata*) with small sweetly fragrant flowers of white, yellowish, or greenish.

migraine (mī'grān, mĭgrān'), intense headache usually recurring periodically. Pain, commonly arising in one temple, results from expansion of arteries in neck and brain and is often attended by visual disturbances, vertigo, and nausea.

migration, movement of people into new and usually distant areas. Migrations, which played an important part in the peopling of the world, have been due to physical changes (e.g., glaciers) or economic, political, or religious pressure. Internal migration is exemplified by population shift from country to city. See IMMIGRATION; MIGRATORY LABOR.

migration of animals, movements of animals in large numbers from one place to another. Sporadic migrations are made by the LEMMING, the locust or migratory grasshopper, and the army worm. Many butterflies undertake seasonal migrations. SALMON migrate from salt water to fresh water to breed, and the freshwater EEL breeds in the Atlantic Ocean SE of Bermuda. Sea turtles return to land to lay eggs. In Africa, game animals migrate to avoid drought. Regular seasonal migrations are best exemplified by birds, but the causes of these flights are not fully understood. Various theories attribute migration to climatic changes and glacial movements in geologic time, to failure of food supply and temperature changes, and to need for avoiding overcrowding at breeding season. Many agree, however, that migration probably results from an environmental stimulus and an allied physiological one. Experiments made by William Rowan with juncos and other birds support the theory that the chief external stimulus is variation in day length (with resulting variation in amount of activity) causing enlargement of reproductive organs, and the internal stimulus is the production of a hormone by the reproductive organs. Especially long migrations are made by the arctic TERN and golden PLOVER.

migratory labor (mī'grŭtô″rē), workers such as those who follow crops from place to place, or urban dwellers who seek seasonal employment on the land. In the 1930s, many farmers of the plains states—perhaps as many as 3,000,000 in all—became migrants because of drought. In wartime, migratory workers travel about to jobs in war plants.

Miguel (mēgĕl'), 1802–66, Portuguese prince; younger brother of PEDRO I of Brazil. In 1826 he became guardian of Pedro's daughter MARIA II, to whom he was betrothed, but in 1828 he accepted the crown for himself from the Cortes. Supported by the reactionary factions, he fought against the liberal forces commanded by Pedro I, who had English support (1832–34). Defeated, he left Portugal. Later Miguelist uprisings against Maria II all failed.

Mikhailovich, Draja or **Dragoliub** (drä'zhä mēhī'lôvĭch, drä'gôlyōōb″), 1893?–1946, Yugoslav soldier. In World War II he led Serbian guerrilla forces (*chetniks*) in successful operations against the Axis armies; was promoted to general and appointed war minister by Yugoslav government in exile. He soon clashed with the partisans of Marshal TITO, who accused him of collaborating with the Axis. In 1944 his dwindling forces lost Allied support, and he was reluctantly dismissed by his king. He was captured, tried for treason at Belgrade, and executed despite world-wide protests against the irregularity of his conviction.

Mikulov, Czechoslovakia: see NIKOLSBURG.

Milan (Milan Obrenovich) (mĭ'län), 1854–1901, prince (1868–82) and king (1882–89) of Serbia. Declared war on Turkey (1876; see RUSSO-TURKISH WARS); secured recognition of full independence of Serbia at Congress of Berlin (1878); took title king (1882). After proclaiming a liberal constitution (1889), he abdicated in favor of his son Alexander.

Milan (mĭlăn', mĭ'lùn), Ital. *Milano,* city (pop. 1,068,-079), cap. of Lombardy, N Italy. Chief industrial and commercial city of Italy; produces textiles, machinery, chemicals; leading European silk market; publishing center (esp. of music). Has a Catholic university (founded 1921), a state university (founded 1924);

world-famous opera house (Teatro alla Scala); art gallery (Brera palace). Of Celtic origin, Milan (Latin *Mediolanum*) served as cap. of the late Western Empire. Twice destroyed in barbarian invasions (c.450, 539), it became a free commune in 12th cent. and, despite its destruction by Emperor Frederick I (1163), emerged as leading city of the LOMBARD LEAGUE. In the 13th cent. Milan lost its republican liberties. The VISCONTI family took control in 1277 and was succeeded in 1450 by the SFORZA. Made a duchy in 1395, Milan became one of the chief Italian states (comprising most of LOMBARDY) and a brilliant center of the Renaissance. The duchy repeatedly changed hands in the ITALIAN WARS and passed to Spain in 1535, to Austria in 1713. Bonaparte took Milan in 1796 and made it the cap. of the Cisalpine Republic (1797) and of the kingdom of Italy (1805–14). Restored to Austria in 1815, Milan briefly expelled its foreign masters in 1848. It was ceded to Sardinia in 1859. Heavily damaged in World War II, it was rebuilt along modern lines. Its best-known building is the Gothic cathedral (begun 1386, finished 1813), with its elaborate lacework in stone. Among other landmarks are a Romanesque church, founded 386 and dedicated to St. AMBROSE, the great bishop of Milan; Santa Maria delle Grazie, with a refectory containing Leonardo da Vinci's *Last Supper;* and the imposing Sforza castle, designed by Leonardo and Bramante.

Milan (mī'lùn), village (pop. 846), N Ohio, SE of Sandusky. Birthplace of T. A. Edison.

Milan Decree, 1807, issued by Napoleon I to enforce CONTINENTAL SYSTEM. Authorized French warships and privateers to capture neutral vessels sailing from British-held territory.

mildew, fungus disease of plants which dwarfs and distorts growth. Powdery mildew, which grows on the leaf surfaces of many plants, forms a gray or white coating. Dusting with sulphur is a control. Other mildews attack leather, fabrics, and paper.

Miles, Nelson Appleton, 1839–1925, American army officer. Served in Civil War and later in Indian campaigns. Commanded troops in Pullman strike (1894). Commander in chief of army (1895–1903).

Miles City, city (pop. 9,243), SE Mont., on Yellowstone R. Grew up around Fort Keogh (1877). Makes saddles and leather goods. Ships wool and livestock.

Miletus (mīlē'tùs), anc. seaport, W Asia Minor, in Caria, near Samos. Occupied by the Greeks in settlement of the Aegean (c.1000 B.C.), it became a principal city of Ionia. Led in colonization and took the lead in revolt against Persia (499 B.C.).

milfoil: see YARROW.

Milford. 1 Town (pop. 26,870), SW Conn., at mouth of Housatonic R. on Long Isl. Sound E of Bridgeport; settled 1639. Has resorts and yacht harbor. Produces oysters, truck, dairy products, and metal goods. **2** City (pop. 5,179), S central Del., S of Frederica. Trade center for truck farms. **3** Town (pop. 15,442), including Milford village (pop. 14,396), S Mass., SE of Worcester; settled 1662. Mfg. of shoes and metal products.

Milford Haven, urban district (pop. 11,717), Pembrokeshire, Wales, on N side of Milford Haven Bay; one of Britain's chief fishing ports.

Milhaud, Darius (däryüs' mēyō'), 1892–, French composer, now teaching in the U.S. He often combines simple diatonic melodies in polytonal counterpoint, producing a highly dissonant effect. His compositions include operas (e.g., *Christophe Colombe;* ballets (e.g., *Le Bœuf sur le toit; or, The Nothing Doing Bar*); concertos; orchestral works (e.g., *Suite Française*); and chamber music.

Military Academy, United States: see UNITED STATES MILITARY ACADEMY.

militia, military force of volunteers, formed on permanent basis for use only in emergencies. An early example was Anglo-Saxon *fyrd*. In the 19th cent. various states of the United States had their militias,

which participated in all the wars of that cent. They were superseded, in 1903, by the National Guard. Militia troops in U.S. lost importance when conscription was introduced in World War I.

Miliukov, Pavel Nikolayevich: see MILYUKOV.

Milk, river, 729 mi. long, rising in NW Mont. and flowing N into Alberta, E and S into Mont., then SE to the Missouri below Fort Peck Dam. Milk R. project irrigates c.140,000 acres, also using St. Mary R. Fresno Dam is 111 ft. high, 2,070 ft. long.

milk, glandular secretion from breast or udders of animals that suckle their young. In addition to cow's milk, man has used milk from the mare, goat, ewe, camel, ass, zebra, reindeer, and llama. Milk, the best source of calcium, contains most of the vitamins, especially vitamin A, and is a nearly complete food for infants and valuable in the diet of adults. Milk of Jersey and Guernsey cows is especially rich in fat. Skim milk, fat free, is low in vitamin A. Milk may be partially evaporated (canned milk) or dried as a powder; sweetened evaporated milk is known as condensed milk. Malted milk is a dried mixture of milk and mash of barley malt and wheat flour. DAIRYING is subject to Federal, state, and local laws. PASTEURIZATION checks bacterial growth.

milk snake: see KING SNAKE.

milk sugar: see LACTOSE.

milkweed, tall New World perennial plant of genus *Asclepias* found in swamps and open fields. The plants usually have milky sap and clusters of small flowers, purple in the common milkweed (*Asclepias syriaca*); the fruit pods enclose the many seeds, each of which bears a tuft of silk.

Milky Way system or **Galaxy** (gă'lùksē), system of stars and nebulae. Comprises c.30 thousand million stars in the form of a disk; greatest diameter is c.100,000 light-years; thickness c.10–16 thousand light-years. Solar system is c.30,000 light-years from center. Position of earth permits observation of numerous stars appearing to form white pathway commonly called Milky Way.

Mill, James, 1773–1836, British philosopher, b. Scotland. In London he wrote and edited periodicals. His *History of India* (1817) won him a position at India House. Became an associate of Bentham and one of the leaders in utilitarian thought. His son, **John Stuart Mill,** 1806–73, developed the theories of utilitarianism, tempering them with humanitarianism, and even reflected some agreement with socialism. He insisted upon the method of empiricism as the source of all knowledge. His *Essay on Liberty* (1859) is one of the most celebrated documents of political economy. He stressed that pleasure (considered as the basic motivating force by utilitarians) should be measured by quality as well as quantity. He pushed many political and social reforms and had direct influence on events as well as a profound, indirect influence on subsequent economists and philosophers. Among his works are *System of Logic* (1843), *Principles of Political Economy* (1848), *Utilitarianism* (1863), *Auguste Comte and Positivism* (1865), and a famous autobiography (1873).

Millais, Sir John Everett (mĭlā'), 1829–96, English painter, a leading member of PRE-RAPHAELITES. Was a close friend of Ruskin.

Millay, Edna St. Vincent, 1892–1950, American lyric poet. She first attracted notice with "Renascence" (1912), and later gained a large audience with her volumes—*A Few Figs from Thistles* (1920), *Second April* (1921), *The Ballad of the Harp Weaver* (1922; later in *The Harp-Weaver and Other Poems,* 1923). She also wrote dramatic verse, as in *Aria da Capo* (1920); *The King's Henchman* (1927; libretto for opera); *The Murder of Lidice* (1942; for radio). Her sonnets (in various vols. and in *Fatal Interview,* 1931) are much admired.

Millburn, residential township (pop. 14,560), NE N.J., W of Newark; settled c.1725. Includes Short Hills.

Millbury, town (pop. 8,347), S Mass., S of Worcester. Mfg. of textiles and metal products.

Milledgeville, city (pop. 8,835), cental Ga., on Oconee R. and NE of Macon. Laid out 1803 as site of state cap., it was seat of government 1804–67. Processing center for cotton and clay area. Here are Georgia State Col. for Women (1889) and many fine old classic revival houses.

Mille Lacs Lake (mĭl″ lăk′), 18 mi. long, 14 mi. wide, E central Minn., N of Minneapolis. Visited 1679 by Sieur Duluth. Hennepin and companions Indian captives here 1680. Tourist and sport center.

millepede: see MILLIPEDE.

Miller, Arthur, 1915–, American dramatist, author of *All My Sons* (1947), *Death of a Salesman* (1949).

Miller, Cincinnatus Heine (or **Hiner**): see MILLER, JOAQUIN.

Miller, Henry, 1860–1926, American actor-manager, b. London. Appeared with Modjeska and the Boucicault troupe. Became a star (1897) in his own play *Heartsease* and thereafter was his own manager.

Miller, Joaquin (wäkēn′), pseud. of **Cincinnatus Heine** (or **Hiner**) **Miller,** 1839?–1913, American poet, who lived on the Pacific Northwest frontier. His best-known volume is *Songs of the Sierras* (1871), and his best-known poem is "Columbus."

Miller, Joe, 1684–1738, English popular comedian. He did not actually write the collection of puns and trite witticisms called *Joe Miller's Jests,* but the publisher John Mottley put his name on it.

Miller, Kenneth Hayes, 1876–1952, American painter and teacher, associated with New York School of Art and Art Students League.

Miller, Samuel Freeman, 1816–90, Associate Justice of U.S. Supreme Court (1862–90). Concerned with general welfare, practical application of law.

Miller, William, 1782–1849, American founder (1845) of Second ADVENTISTS, often called Millerites. From 1831 he prophesied second coming of Christ in 1843, then set date in 1844.

Millerand, Alexandre (älĕksä′drŭ mēlrä′), 1859–1943, French politician. At first a Socialist, after World War I an ardent nationalist and rightist, he was premier in 1920 and president of France 1920–24.

Milles, Carl (mĭl′lŭs), 1875–, Swedish sculptor, a follower of Rodin. His work consists mainly of large linear human figures (e.g., statues in Rockefeller Center, New York).

Millet, Jean François (zhä′ fräswä′ mēlā′), 1814–75, French painter, an outstanding member of Barbizon school. His *Gleaners* and *Angelus* are in the Louvre.

millet (mĭl′lŭt), popular name for certain grasses and cereals including the common or hog millet (*Panicum miliaceum*) and foxtail millet (*Setaria italica*). Hog millet has been grown since ancient times for human food and forage. In North America the foxtail millet is a fodder plant.

Milligan, ex parte, case decided by the U.S. Supreme Court in 1866 in which the suspension (1863) of habeas corpus by Lincoln in the military arrest and trial of a civilian was voided, the court ruling that civilians might be tried by military tribunal only if because of invasion or disorder the civil courts cannot function to give them justice.

Millikan, Robert Andrews (mĭl′ĭkŭn), 1868–, American physicist and educator. Won 1923 Nobel Prize for measurement of charge on electron and work on photoelectric effect. Made important studies of cosmic rays, X rays, physical and electrical constants. He was associated with Univ. of Chicago (1896–1921) and California Inst. of Technology (1921–45).

milling. Wheat and other grains were originally ground into flour by pounding between two stones. This led to the mortar and pestle, superseded by the quern, in which grain placed on one millstone was ground by revolving an upper stone. This device was adapted to animal, wind, or water power. Windmills became widespread in Europe after the Crusades. Steam power

and improvements in machinery came with the Industrial Revolution. Modern grinding processes involve about 180 operations. Processing centers for grains and other materials are called mills.

Millinocket, town (pop. 5,890), central Maine, on a branch of Penobscot R. SE of Millinocket L. Paper mills (built 1899–1900).

millipede or **millepede** (both: mĭl′lŭpēd), wormlike segmented arthropod, somewhat similar to centipede but body is more cylindrical and legs more numerous. Feeds on plants (some injure crops) and decaying vegetation.

Mills, Ogden L(ivingston), 1884–1937, American political leader. U.S. Congressman from N.Y. (1921–27); noted as fiscal expert. Secretary of the Treasury (Feb., 1932–March, 1933).

Mills, Robert, 1781–1855, American architect of the classic revival period. As official architect of public buildings in Washington, D.C., he designed the Washington Monument (1836), which was executed without the base originally intended for it.

Mills College: see OAKLAND, Calif.

Millspaugh, A(rthur) C(hester) (mĭlz′pô), 1883–, American political scientist. Served as financial adviser to Iran (1922–27, 1943–45) and Haiti (1927–29). Staff member of Brookings Inst. (1929–42, 1946–48). Author of works on political science.

Millvale, borough (pop. 7,287), SW Pa., on Allegheny R. opposite Pittsburgh. Mfg. of metal products and boxes; meat packing.

Mill Valley, residential town (pop. 7,331), W Calif., N of San Francisco and at foot of Mt. Tamalpais. Near by is Muir Woods Natl. Monument.

Millville, city (pop. 16,041), S N.J., E of Bridgeton; settled 1756. Farm trade center (poultry, truck, fruit). River fisheries. Mfg. of glass, textiles, and cast iron.

Milmore, Martin, 1844–83, American sculptor, b. Ireland. Known for monumental sculpture and for portrait busts.

Milne, A(lan) A(lexander) (mĭln), 1882–, English dramatist and humorous writer for children; assistant editor of *Punch* (1906–14). His novel, *The Red House Mystery* (1921), is a classic of its genre. His books of verse for children include *When We Were Very Young* (1924) and *Now We Are Six* (1927), and children's stories are in *Winnie-the-Pooh* (1926). Among his successful comedies are *Mr. Pim Passes By* (1919) and *The Dover Road* (1922).

Milnes, Richard Monckton: see HOUGHTON, RICHARD MONCKTON MILNES, 1st BARON.

Milo (mī′lō) or **Milon** (mī′lŏn), fl. 500 B.C., athlete of anc. Greece. Many times a victor in wrestling at Olympic and Pythian games.

Milo (Titus Annius Papianus Milo), 95 B.C.–47 B.C., Roman partisan leader. As tribune (57), he recalled Cicero from exile. A gang hired by him fought the gang of P. CLODIUS and kept Rome in an uproar. POMPEY was appointed sole consul to restore order, and Milo was exiled. Joining a revolt, he was defeated and killed.

Milo (mī′lō), town (pop. 2,898), central Maine, NNW of Bangor, serving Schoodic, Seboois, Sebec lakes.

Milosh (Milosh Obrenovich) (mī′lôsh), 1780–1860, prince of Serbia (1817–39, 1858–60), founder of OBRENOVICH dynasty. An illiterate shepherd, he fought the Turks under KARAGEORGE, later his rival. In 1815 he led a successful rebellion; in 1817, after killing Karageorge, he took the title prince of Serbia (confirmed 1830 by the sultan, who remained his sovereign) and ruled tyrannically. Forced to abdicate in 1839, he was recalled in 1858.

Miltiades (mĭltī′ŭdēz), d. 489 B.C., Athenian general in the PERSIAN WARS. In 490 he defeated the Persians at Marathon, then force-marched 20 mi. to Athens and successfully defended the city from attack by sea.

Milton, John, 1608–74, English poet. Educated at St. Paul's School and Christ's College, Cambridge, he early prepared to be a poet. His early work includes

"On the Morning of Christ's Nativity" (1629), "L'Allegro," "Il Penseroso," the masque *Comus* (1634), and the elegy "Lycidas" (1638). He traveled on Continent (1638–40), chiefly in Italy. Growing trouble in England drew him home to support the Puritan cause. He wrote prose pamphlets on church government (e.g., *Of Reformation in England*, 1641) and later issued tracts defending the imprisonment and execution of Charles I (notably, *The Tenure of Kings and Magistrates*, 1649). In 1643 he had married Mary Powell, who soon left him, but later returned. He wrote four tracts on divorce. In 1644 appeared his *Areopagitica*, an eminent defense of freedom of the press. He was Latin secretary in Cromwell's government and its chief defender in several notable tracts. His arduous duties brought on complete blindness—the best known of his distinguished sonnets is the poignant "On His Blindness." At the Restoration (1660) Milton was fined and driven into retirement. It was then that he dictated his epics *Paradise Lost* (1667) and *Paradise Regained* (1671), In the first he recounts the story of Satan's rebellion against God and of Adam and Eve with the stated intention to "justify the ways of God to men." In the second he tells the story of Christ's temptation. *Paradise Lost* is one of the world's greatest epics. Its sonorous blank verse is unsurpassed in English. Among other works written at the close of his life is *Samson Agonistes* (1671), a distinguished drama on the classic Greek model. While much of Milton's work is representative of the Puritan age, it is also supremely universal and timeless.

Milton. 1 Village (pop. 8,232), SW Ill. **2** Town (pop. 22,395), E Mass., S of Boston; settled 1636. Food products. Here is Harvard's Blue Hill meteorological observatory. **3** Borough (pop. 8,578), E Pa., on West Branch of Susquehanna R. and S of Williamsport. Mfg. of metal products and clothing.

Milvian Bridge, over the Tiber, near Rome. Here Constantine I saw the cross in the sky presaging victory; defeated Maxentius to become sole ruler of the West (312). Also Mulvian Bridge.

Milwaukee (mĭlwô′kē), city (pop. 637,932), SE Wis., N of Chicago and at point where Milwaukee, Menomonee, and Kinnickinnic rivers join to enter L. Michigan. Largest city in Wis. and shipping center with good harbor, it is famous for brewing and meat packing. Missionaries here in late 17th cent.; North West Co. estab. trading post 1795; and Solomon JUNEAU came 1818. Several settlements in area merged after 1835 as Milwaukee village. After 1848 German refugees, including Carl SCHURZ, spurred growth. Socialists influential here. Seat of Milwaukee-Downer Col. (nonsectarian; for women; opened 1848, chartered 1851) and Marquette Univ. (R.C.; coed.; chartered 1864, opened 1881, became university 1907).

Milwaukie, city (pop. 5,253), NW Oregon, on Willamette R. just S of Portland. Trees from Iowa started state's cherry industry here in 1847.

Milyukov or **Miliukov, Pavel Nikolayevich** (pä′vĭl nyĭkŭlī′ŭvĭch mēlyōōkôf′), 1859–1943, Russian statesman and historian. As foreign minister (Feb.–May, 1917) he made himself unpopular by insisting on carrying out obligations to Russia's World War I allies. Author of *Outlines of Russian Culture* (Eng. tr., 3 vols., 1942).

Mimico (mĭ′mĭkō), SW suburb of Toronto (pop. 11,342), S Ont., Canada, on L. Ontario.

mimicry, in biology, an organism's advantageous resemblance to another of different species or to feature of environment (this is usually called PROTECTIVE COLORATION). Mimicry is often observed among insects. In theory of H. W. Bates, through natural selection an edible insect (for example) acquires deceptive resemblance to inedible insect, thus escaping aggressor; this occurs only if no radical changes in structure required. Animals may also mimic prey or an animal feared by others.

mimosa, leguminous woody or herbaceous plant of genus *Mimosa*, native to tropical America, with feathery foliage and rounded flower clusters, similar to acacia. The sensitive plant (*Mimosa pudica*) has leaves which fold up when touched.

minaret (mĭnŭrĕt′), small tower used in Moslem architecture. A part of most mosques, it has one or more projecting balconies, from which the muezzin chants his summons to prayer. Early minarets (7th–12th cent.) are square with little adornment; those after 12th cent. are slender and richly decorated.

Minas de Ríotinto, Spain: see RÍO TINTO.

Minas Gerais (mē′nŭs zhŭrīsh′) [Port.,= various mines], state (224,701 sq. mi.; pop. 7,839,792), E Brazil; cap., BELO HORIZONTE. Inland state on central plateau cut off from coast by mountain escarpment, has largest known iron reserves in world; also deposits of manganese, diamonds, gold, and semiprecious stones. Gold was first discovered 1698. Old cap., Ouro Prêto, was important colonial city. Late in 18th cent. Minas was center of literary group and here in 1788 Tiradentes led an abortive revolt against Portuguese government. Today Minas is second most populous state in Brazil. Besides mining, agr. and cattle breeding are important.

Minch or **North Minch,** strait, 25 to 35 mi. wide, separating Lewis with Harris Isl., Outer Hebrides, from mainland of Scotland. Little Minch separates Skye from neighboring Outer Hebrides.

Mincio (mēn′chō), river of Lombardy, N Italy. Called Sarca R. before entering L. Garda; from there the Mincio flows c.40 mi., past Mantua, to the Po. Sarca-Garda-Mincio line, marking natural border between Lombardy and Venetia, was long of strategic importance.

mind: see PSYCHOLOGY.

Mindanao (mĭndŭnä′ō), island (36,536 sq. mi.; pop. 1,828,071), second largest of Philippine Isls.; NE of Borneo. Off its NE coast in Philippine Sea is Mindanao Deep (35,400 ft.). Mainly mountainous, rising to 9,690 ft. at Mt. Apo. Has large W peninsula (site of Zamboanga). The navigable Mindanao, 200 mi. long, is largest river. Products include hemp, rice, corn, and coffee. Many of the natives are Moros, whose religion is Islam.

Minden (mĭn′dŭn), city (pop. 40,811), North Rhine-Westphalia, NW Germany; a port at junction of Ems-Weser and Weser-Elbe canals. An episcopal see from c.800, it joined the Hanseatic League (13th cent.) and accepted the Reformation (1530). The secularized bishopric passed to Brandenburg in 1648. Scene of English-Hanoverian victory over French (1759). Cathedral (11th–13th cent.) and city hall (13th–17th cent.) were destroyed in World War II.

Minden, city (pop. 9,787), NW La., NE of Shreveport. Trade center of agr. area with cotton gins and cottonseed mills. Oil wells near.

Mindoro (mĭndô′rō), island (3,758 sq. mi.; pop. 116,988), Philippines, SW of Luzon. Coal is mined, and rice and coconuts are grown.

mind reading: see TELEPATHY.

Mindszenty, Joseph (mĭnd′sĕntē), 1892–, Hungarian cardinal, archbishop of Esztergom, Catholic primate of Hungary. Imprisoned for his anti-German attitude in World War II, he later opposed the Communist regime and was arrested on charges of treason in 1948. At his sensational trial he pleaded guilty to fantastic charges and was sentenced to life imprisonment. It is widely held in the free world that his confessions were extorted either by drugs or by extreme moral pressure.

mine, in warfare, explosive weapon used in land and sea operations. The submarine mine is used against ships; it consists of a watertight case enclosing an explosive charge, and its use dates back to the 16th cent. There are controlled mines (connected by electric cable to a shore station and detonated from there) and contact mines (detonated electrically or mechanically upon contact with an outside body). Land mines were sown over wide areas (mine fields) in World War

I and World War II by defenders as well as attackers.

Mineola (mĭnē̄ō'lŭ), village (pop. 14,831), SE N.Y., on W Long Isl. Commercial center with repair and service shops for near-by U.S. Mitchel Air Force Base.

mineral, inorganic substance occurring in nature, having definite chemical composition and physical properties, and often a typical crystalline form. (Some organic substances are included.) A few minerals are elements (e.g., carbon, gold, mercury), but most are compounds. Rocks are usually mixtures of minerals, lacking the definite chemical formula which characterizes their mineral constituents.

mineral water, water flowing from hot or cold springs, containing dissolved mineral salts and often charged with gases. Many people believe in the curative powers of such waters.

Mineral Wells, city (pop. 7,801), N Texas, near Brazos R. and W of Fort Worth. Health resort. Has sericulture and mfg. of mineral crystals and hosiery. Near are Camp Wolters and L. Mineral Wells reservoir in Trinity R. system.

Minersville, borough (pop. 7,783), E Pa., NNW of Pottsville. Coal mining and mfg. of clothing.

Minerva, in Roman religion, goddess of learning and handicrafts. Identified with Greek ATHENA.

Ming (mĭng), dynasty of China, 1368–1644. Founded by Chu Yüan-chang, a former Buddhist monk, who expelled the Mongols from China. Empire at its height extended from Burma to Korea. Despite Ming opposition to foreign trade, European settlements were made at Macao and Canton. Era marked by literary achievements and renowned for fine porcelain.

Mingan Islands (mĭng'gŭn), group of 15 small islands and many islets, E Que., Canada, N of Anticosti Isl., in Mingan Passage of St. Lawrence R. Discovered by Cartier 1535.

Mingrelia (mĭn-grē'lĕŭ), region, W Georgian SSR, a lowland bordering on Black Sea; main port Poti. Produces tea and grapes. The COLCHIS of the ancients, later a vassal principality of Ottoman Empire, it was annexed by Russia 1803.

Minho (mē'nyō), Span. *Miño,* river rising in NW Spain and flowing c.210 mi. S and SW to the Atlantic. Forms Spanish-Portuguese border. It gives its name to the northernmost province (1,868 sq. mi.; pop. 741,510) of Portugal; cap. Braga.

Minidoka project, S Idaho, in Snake R. valley, for irrigation. Minidoka Dam (built 1909; forms L. Walcott near Rupert) and AMERICAN FALLS Dam (built 1927; collects water for privately irrigated lands) impound Snake R. Project serves an area around Minidoka and Burley and another near Gooding and Shoshone. Jackson L., Wyo., stores water.

minimum wage, lowest wage permitted in an industry, government, or other organization, introduced first in New Zealand in 1894. Aim is to assure wage earners a minimally decent standard of living. First held unconstitutional in U.S., the minimum wage was established by 1938 Fair Labor Standards Act. In 1949 the minimum wage was set at $.75 an hour.

mining, the extraction of ores or other mineral resources from the earth. Deposits are worked from the surface or from underground. Placer mining involves no excavating; gold and diamonds which accumulate in stream beds are washed out by panning, sluicing, hydraulic nozzles, dredging. In open-pit mining, ore is dug at the surface. Deep mines require vertical shafts with horizontal tunnels.

minister, in diplomacy: see DIPLOMATIC SERVICE and EXTERRITORIALITY.

Minitari Indians: see HIDATSA INDIANS.

mink, semiaquatic mammal (*Mustela*) of weasel family, found in N Hemisphere. American mink has slender, arched body, bushy tail. Valued for rich brown fur. Secretes acrid musk.

Minkowski, Hermann (hĕr'män mĭn-kôfskē), 1864–1909, Russian mathematician. He contributed to development of theory of numbers and evolved a four-dimensional geometry credited with influencing formulation of geometrical expression of general theory of relativity.

Minneapolis (mĭ"nēä'pŭlĭs). **1** City (pop. 1,801), N central Kansas, N of Salina. Rock City, area of curious eroded geological formations, is near. **2** City (pop. 521,718), E Minn., largest city in state, on both sides of the Mississippi at Falls of St. Anthony and adjoining its Twin City, St. Paul; settled c.1847 on site of Fort SNELLING (1819). Twin Cities are financial, industrial, and commercial center of large agr. area. Minneapolis has flour mills, dairy products plants, and mfg. (machinery, agr. equipment, clothing). Here are many lakes and parks, and Univ. of MINNESOTA.

Minneapolis Symphony Orchestra, founded 1903. Among its conductors have been Eugene Ormandy (1931–36); Dimitri Mitropoulous (1936–49), and Antal Dorati.

Minnehaha Falls (mĭ"nĕhä'hä") [traditionally Indian,= laughing water], over 50 ft. high, in SE Minneapolis, in Minnehaha Creek, which flows from L. Minnetonka to the Mississippi. Included in public park. Name immortalized in Longfellow's *Hiawatha.*

minnesinger (mĭ'nĕsĭng"ŭr), in German literature, a singer of *Minne* (romantic love), corresponding to the TROUBADOUR of S France. Minnesingers flourished in the 12th and 13th cent. Greatest were Walther von der Vogelweide and Wolfram von Eschenbach.

Minnesota, state (84,068 sq. mi.; pop. 2,982,483), N U.S., in Great Lakes region; admitted 1858 as 32d state (free); cap. SAINT PAUL. Other cities are MINNEAPOLIS, DULUTH. Bounded E by L. Superior, St. Croix R. and Mississippi R., NW by Red R. Watershed for three river systems: Hudson Bay, Great Lakes–St. Lawrence, Mississippi-Missouri. State of lakes, prairies (esp. S), some highlands. Farming (grains, livestock, dairying, truck); mining (iron, granite, limestone); lumbering. Food, meat processing; mfg. of machinery, paper, chemicals; printing and publishing. French and British fur traders gave way to American Fur Co. E part included in NORTHWEST TERRITORY, W part joined by Louisiana Purchase. Became territory in 1849. Lumbering was major industry. Big Soo Canal opened waterway to E. Sioux uprising during and after Civil War. Farmer discontent in late 19th cent. expressed in GRANGER MOVEMENT. State is leader in use of cooperatives. Mfg. stimulated by World War II.

Minnesota, river, 332 mi. long, rising in Big Stone L. at W boundary of Minnesota and flowing SE to Mankato, then NE to the Mississippi at Mendota. As St. Peter or St. Pierre R. was explorers' and fur traders' route. Follows valley of prehistoric River Warren, outlet of L. Agassiz.

Minnesota, University of, mainly at Minneapolis; landgrant, state supported, coed.; chartered 1851 and 1868, opened as university 1869. Has two-year General Col. Includes school of medicine (for affiliated foundation, see MAYO, CHARLES H.) and branches at St. Paul and Duluth. Library has Scandinavian collection. In General Col., through extension work, effort has been made to raise general cultural level.

Minnetonka, Lake (mĭ"nĭtŏng'kŭ), 10 mi. long, E Minn., just W of Minneapolis. Outlet is Minnehaha Creek. Resorts on shore.

minnow, name for certain fish of carp family. In Europe, refers chiefly to small form, *Phoxinus phoxinus;* in America, chiefly to many small minnows of same family. Squawfish or Sacramento pike (c.3 ft.) is largest in U.S.

Miño, river: see MINHO.

Minoan civilization, period of anc. culture in AEGEAN CIVILIZATION. Named for King Minos of Crete and covered Bronze Age (3000–1200 B.C.). Our archaeological knowledge, derived from palace at CNOSSUS, shows it developed from simple culture with pictographic writing into high culture with linear writing. It declined in last period as cultural center passed to Troy and Greek mainland.

Mino da Fiesole (mē'nō dä fyä'zōlä) or **Mino di Giovanni** (dē jōvän'nē), 1431–84, Florentine sculptor of the early Renaissance. Produced many tombs.

Minorca (mĭnôr'kù), Span. *Menorca*, island (271 sq. mi.; pop. 43,025), Spain, in W Mediterranean, second largest of BALEARIC ISLANDS; chief city Port Mahon. Products include cereals, wine, olive oil, and flax. Stock raising. Has many megalithic monuments. Minorca shared history of Balearic Isls. until 1708; frequently changed hands in 18th cent. (British, 1708–56; French, 1756–63; British, 1763–82; occupied by French and Spanish, 1782; recovered by England, 1798; definitively awarded to Spain, 1802). Was held by Loyalists in Spanish civil war until 1939.

minority, in international law, population group with a characteristic culture and a sense of identity living in a state where another culture group is dominant. Religious minorities were known from earliest times, but it was only with the rise of nationalism at the beginning of the 19th cent. that the question of ethnic minorities became a burning one in Europe. Nationalist aspirations frequently led to suppression of minorities, and the situation led to many international clashes when a minority group was supported by, or stirred up by, their fellows in another state (as the Slavs in Austria-Hungary before World War I, the Sudeten Germans in Czechoslovakia in the 1930s). Minorities may, however, face problems that are social rather than political (e.g., Negroes in the U.S.), or they may be linked with similar minorities in other states largely by resistance to oppression (e.g., Jewish minorities facing the forces of anti-Semitism in various states of the Western world).

Minos (mī'nŏs, –nùs), in Greek myth, king of Crete; son of Zeus and Europa and father of Ariadne and Phaedra. His wife also bore the MINOTAUR. There was presumably a historical King Minos of Crete, after whom is named archaic MINOAN CIVILIZATION.

Minot, George Richards (mī'nùt), 1885–1950, American physician and pathologist. Shared 1934 Nobel Prize in Physiology and Medicine for research on value of liver in treating pernicious anemia.

Minot (mī'nùt), city (pop. 22,032), NW N.Dak., on Souris R. and NNW of Bismarck; settled 1886. Rail, trade, and distribution center for agr. (esp. wheat) area; food processing; lignite mining.

Minotaur (mī'nùtôr), monstrous offspring of Pasiphaë and a bull, with head of bull and body of man. Minos, husband of Pasiphaë, had Daedalus build Labyrinth to keep the monster. Theseus killed him.

Minseito (mēn"sä'tō), Japanese political party. First formed in 1881 by Okuma as the Kaishinto. Chief rival of SEIYUKAI from 1927 to 1932. Was loosely tied to Mitsubishi interests.

Minsk (Rus. mēnsk), city (pop. 238,772), cap. of Belorussia. Industrial center (cars, tractors, textiles, wood products). Was cap. of a principality conquered 1326 by Lithuania. Passed to Russia 1793. In Middle Ages, Minsk became one of largest Jewish centers of Eastern Europe. Virtually destroyed in World War II by Germans, who held it 1941–44. Jews were exterminated.

minstrel, professional secular musician of the Middle Ages, especially one of unusual talent who was attached to a court to play or sing the songs of the TROUBADOUR or TROUVÈRE. Term indicated a higher social class than the jongleur. In the 19th and early 20th cent., NEGRO MINSTREL shows were very popular in the U.S.

mint, name for a plant family, Labiatae, a group characterized by square stems, aromatic foliage, and often showy flowers. Among the members of the family are catnip, thyme, bee balm, and lavender. The name is used more specifically for plants of the genus *Mentha* of the same family, e.g., PEPPERMINT and SPEARMINT.

mint julep: see JULEP.

Minton, English family of potters. **Thomas Minton,** 1765–1836, founded a small pottery at Stoke-on-Trent and created the famous WILLOW-PATTERN WARE. His son **Herbert Minton,** 1793–1858, developed the firm and made it famous.

Minturnae (mĭntùr'nē), anc. town, Latium, Italy; near modern Minturno. Founded by the Aurunci or Ausones, it became a flourishing Roman colony (295 B.C.). It guarded the Appian Way bridge over the Liris R.

minuet (mĭnūet'), French dance in 3–4 meter, introduced (1650) at Louis XIV's court. Popular during 17th–18th cent. Left a definite imprint on the era's music (e.g., works of Haydn and Mozart).

Minuit, Peter (mĭn'ūĭt), c.1580–1638, first director general of New Netherland (1626–31). Purchased Manhattan from Indians. Helped found NEW SWEDEN (1638).

Minya Konka (mĭn'yù kŏng'kù), peak, 24,900 ft. high, Sikang prov., China, in Tahsüeh Mts. Climbed 1932 by American expedition.

Miocene epoch (mī'ùsēn), third epoch of the Tertiary period of geologic time. The Atlantic and Gulf coasts and the Great Valley of Calif. were extensively submerged. Mid-Miocene saw uplift of Cascades and Coast Ranges, with accompanying volcanic activity. Cool climate increased grass areas at expense of forests. Mammalian life was marked by further development of the horse. Mastodons, weasels, camels, cats, and others appeared. See also GEOLOGY, table.

Miquelon (mī'kùlŏn, Fr. mēkùlō'), two islands (area 83 sq. mi.), and adjacent island group of St. Pierre (10 sq. mi.), constituting territory of the French Union, S of N.F., Canada; pop. c.4,354; cap. St. Pierre. Nearness to Grand Banks makes islands important fishing base. Settled by French c.1660, taken several times by British. In French possession since early 19th cent.

Mirabeau, Victor Riquetti, marquis de (vēktôr' rēkētē' märkē' dù mēräbō'), 1715–89, French leader of the PHYSIOCRATS, father of the statesman and revolutionist, **Honoré Gabriel Riquetti, comte de Mirabeau** (ōnôrä' gäbrēēl', kōt'), 1749–91. The younger Mirabeau's life before 1789 was a series of wild excesses. He was repeatedly jailed on request of his father, with whom he carried on a long public quarrel. Though noble, he was elected a delegate of the third estate for the STATES GENERAL of 1789, where his formidable eloquence made him a leading figure. His aim was to create a constitutional monarchy; when events took a radical turn late in 1789, Mirabeau came to a secret understanding with the king and queen in order to save the monarchy. His moderate policy was attacked by the Jacobins, but he died just before his dealings with the court were discovered.

miracle, departure from the usual course of nature attributed to supernatural interposition. Adherents of the principal monotheistic religions—Judaism, Christianity, and Islam—have generally agreed in explaining miracles by the omnipotence of one God, the Creator, alone able to interrupt the operation of nature or to allow miracles to be wrought through man by delegating that power to a particular person. The miracle of the Resurrection has always been considered the central fact of Christianity, and the Virgin Birth is usually called a miracle. Among the many miracles of Jesus recorded in the Gospels were raising the dead, casting out demons, healing of the blind, lame, and sick, and performing awesome acts such as stilling the storm, walking on the water, feeding the multitude with a few loaves and fishes, and turning water into wine. The New Testament also records miracles done by apostles. Every age of Christianity has had miracles supposedly performed. They are especially associated with saints' bodies and relics and with shrines. The Roman Catholic Church requires rigid attestation of miracles before canonization, but does not officially require belief in miracles other than those in the Bible and those officially incorporated into dogma. Protestants generally reject miracles except those in the Bible. There are also several instances of miracles in the Old Testament (e.g., Elijah being fed by the ravens).

miracle play or **mystery play**, medieval form of drama, developed (10th–16th cent.) from small scenes added to mass at Christmas and Easter. Simple, dramatic presentation of religious stories originally in Latin, miracle plays later were done in French, English, or German. As plays lengthened and audiences grew they were performed outside churches. This increased realism, humor, and secularism. Moralities (e.g., *Everyman*) were 15th cent. offshoots. The PASSION PLAY is the chief modern example of the miracle play.

mirage (mǐräzh'), optical illusion that causes person to see what appears to be a real object where none is. Can be explained by facts that light rays undergo REFRACTION when passing from medium of one density into another of different density and combined surfaces of two such media act like mirror under certain conditions and cause REFLECTION of light rays. Since density of air varies at different temperatures, mirage is formed when light rays pass through layers of air of different densities and when they are reflected as they strike line of adjacent surfaces at extremely oblique angles. Fata morgana (fä'tä môrgä'nä) is a form of mirage, especially evident at Strait of Messina, in which images of objects are seen suspended over object or in water.

Miranda, Francisco de (fränse'skō dä mērän'dä), 1750–1816, Venezuelan revolutionist, b. Caracas. Imbued with ideas gained in American Revolution and French Revolutionary wars, he became apostle of Venezuelan liberty. Led in preliminary stages of struggle for independence but when he surrendered to Spanish (1812), Bolívar imprisoned him. Later Spanish seized him and kept him imprisoned for rest of his life.

Miranda, Francisco de Sá de: see SÁ DE MIRANDA, FRANCISCO DE.

Mirandola, Giovanni Pico della: see PICO.

Miriam, sister of Moses and Aaron, who watched over the baby Moses in the bulrushes and led the women in song by the Red Sea. Later stricken with leprosy for defying Moses. Ex. 2.4–8; 15.20,21; Num. 12. Miriam and Mary are forms of the same original name.

Miró, Joan (hwän' mērō'), 1893–, Catalan surrealist painter; early went to Paris. He uses brilliant color, free forms with geometric lines.

mirror. REFLECTION of light is such that clear-cut reproductions of objects are formed when light rays from object fall on certain surfaces; such a surface is called a mirror and IMAGE of object is a reproduction. Mirrors usually are plate glass with one surface coated to serve as reflecting surface. Junction of reflecting surface and glass is mirror line. Plane mirror is one with flat surface; image is almost exactly like object, illusion of perspective is created. Image appears to be behind mirror, but is at mirror line. Image is virtual and same size as object and appears to be same distance behind mirror as object is in front of it. Exactness of image depends on quality and condition of mirror. In concave mirror center of reflecting surface is farther from object than are edges. Center of imaginary sphere of which it is part is center of curvature. Line through center of curvature and mid-point of mirror is principal axis; principal focus is point halfway between center of curvature and vertex. Size, nature, and position of image depend on position of object in relation to principal focus and center of curvature. In convex mirror image is always smaller than object, erect, and virtual. Mirrors are used in interior decoration, in microscopes to reflect light, in astronomical telescope.

Mirzapur (mēr'zäpoor"), city (pop. 70,944), SE Uttar Pradesh, India, on Ganges R. Has noted temple to Kali, consort of Siva. Trade center.

Misael (mǐ'säul), one of the THREE HOLY CHILDREN.

miscarriage: see ABORTION.

miscegenation (mǐ"sǐjǐnä'shǔn), the interbreeding of persons of different racial types. It is now believed

that only ill effects are those resulting from social disapproval of mixed unions.

misdemeanor, a minor crime, distinguished from a felony. In the U.S., a misdemeanor is usually punishable summarily by fine and imprisonment for less than a year. Conviction for a misdemeanor does not cancel citizenship or subject an alien to deportation.

Miseno, Cape (mēzä'nō), S Italy, at NW end of Bay of Naples. Was site of Roman naval station founded by Augustus.

Miserere (mǐzǔrěr'ē), the 51st (or 50th) Psalm, beginning, "Miserere mei, Deus (Have mercy upon me, O God)"; one of the penitential psalms. Palestrina and Allegri are among those who have written music for it.

Mishael (mǐ'shäul), one of the THREE HOLY CHILDREN.

Mishawaka (mǐshǔwô'kǔ), city (pop. 32,913), N Ind., on St. Joseph R. and near South Bend; settled c.1830. Mfg. of clothing, rubber, plastic goods, and metal products.

Mishna: see MIDRASH; TALMUD.

Miskolc (mǐsh'kôlts), city (pop. 77,362), NE Hungary, on Sajo R. Has large iron and steel mills.

Mission, city (pop. 10,765), S Texas, WNW of Brownsville, founded 1908 near extant Spanish chapel (1824). Packs and cans citrus fruits (esp. grapefruit) and vegetables. Annual Citrus Fiesta.

Missionary Ridge: see CHATTANOOGA CAMPAIGN.

missions, name of organizations that extend religious teaching, at home or abroad, and of efforts to disseminate Christian religion. History of church from beginning has been history of missions, which spread Christianity through Asia Minor into Europe by way of Greece and Rome. The following centuries saw notable missionary labors in Scotland, Ireland, Central Europe, and among Northmen, reaching into Iceland and Greenland. St. PATRICK, St. AUGUSTINE, and St. BONIFACE are great names of the large era. In 16th cent. missionaries took part in exploration and colonization of America, especially the Jesuits and the Franciscans. In colonial days Roger WILLIAMS and John ELIOT did notable work among Indians, as did Moravian Church. In the 19th cent. missionary work was intense in Africa and Asia and continues so today; it has been graced by such diverse figures as David LIVINGSTONE and Albert SCHWEITZER.

Mississippi, state (47,420 sq. mi.; pop. 2,178,914), S U.S.; admitted 1817 as 20th state (slaveholding); cap. JACKSON. Other cities are MERIDIAN, VICKSBURG, HATTIESBURG, GREENVILLE, LAUREL, BILOXI, NATCHEZ, GULFPORT. Bordered W mostly by MISSISSIPPI R., partly by Pearl R.; S by Gulf of Mexico (with MISSISSIPPI SOUND). Mostly in Gulf coastal plain. Between Mississippi R. and Yazoo R., from Memphis to Vicksburg, is Yazoo Basin or the Delta. Farming (cotton, grains, tung nuts, dairying, livestock, sugar cane, truck); mfg. of wood products, textiles; food processing. Mining (oil, natural gas, clay); lumbering; fishing; coast resorts. Settled by French 1699. Area disputed in WEST FLORIDA CONTROVERSY. High price for cotton and land boom brought settlers. Seceded from Union 1861: saw Civil War action at battle of SHILOH and in VICKSBURG CAMPAIGN. Suffered in Reconstruction. Share-cropping system rose after war. Plagued with race problem. Illiteracy problem has largely declined. Recent industrial growth helped by TVA, community subsidization.

Mississippi, river, c.2,350 mi. long, principal river of U.S., "main stem" of system draining area of 1,244,-000 sq. mi. in 31 states and two Canadian provinces. Rises in N Minn. near L. Itasca and flows S across Minn., past Wis., Ill., Iowa, Ky., Mo., Tenn., Ark., and La. to Gulf of Mexico. Navigable S of Falls of St. Anthony at Minneapolis. Sediment deposits from delta crossed by river's several mouths. Chief tributaries include Ohio, Missouri, Arkansas, and Red rivers. St. Louis, Mo., is largest river city. Levee building against floods began at New Orleans under the French 1717; flood control act of 1928, following flood of 1927, brought great engineering program to the river and its tributaries. Indians made much use of river. La Salle traveled it to mouth and claimed region for France 1682. Spanish followed French control of river 1762. Louisiana Purchase (1803) ended international wrangling and schemes for new nations. Thereafter valley began democratic settlement; river and ports became centers for westward migration. Steamboats, especially after 1830s, marked zenith of river life. Civil War victories (as at ISLAND NO. 10 and in VICKSBURG CAMPAIGN) led to Union gaining control of river and cutting off Confederacy from supply bases W. Following war and with coming of railroads, ports deteriorated. River traffic still heavy, but no longer vital.

Mississippi, University of: see OXFORD.

Mississippian period: see CARBONIFEROUS PERIOD.

Mississippi Scheme, plan formulated by John LAW for colonization and commercial exploitation of Mississippi valley for French. Overspeculation and haste brought collapse of plan, but number of settlers was increased.

Mississippi Sound, arm of Gulf of Mexico, c.80 mi. long, 7–15 mi. wide, separated from the Gulf by islands and sand bars. Extends from L. Borgne (La.) on W, E to Mobile Bay. Washes Miss. and parts of Ala. and La. Bay St. Louis, Pass Christian, Gulfport, Biloxi, Pascagoula, Miss., on Sound.

Mississippi State College: see STARKVILLE.

Mississippi State College for Women: see COLUMBUS.

Missolonghi (mĭsŭlông′gē) or **Mesolonghi** (mĕsŭ–), Gr. *Mesolongion,* town (pop. 10,565), W central Greece; a port on an inlet of Gulf of Patras. Major stronghold of Greek insurgents in Greek War of Independence, was besieged by the Turks in 1822 and 1825–26. Lord Byron died here in 1824.

Missoula (mĭzŏo′lŭ), city (pop. 22,485), W Mont., on Clark Fork (here called the Missoula) near mouth of Bitterroot R. Estab. 1865 at present site. Growth aided by railroads. Commercial and industrial point in mining and agr. region. Food-processing plants. Seat of Montana State Univ. (see Univ. of MONTANA). Fort Missoula (1877) is near.

Missouri, state (69,270 sq. mi.; pop. 3,954,653), central U.S.; admitted 1821 as 24th state (slaveholding) under MISSOURI COMPROMISE; cap. JEFFERSON CITY. Cities are SAINT LOUIS, KANSAS CITY, SPRINGFIELD, SAINT JOSEPH. Bounded E by MISSISSIPPI R., partly NW by MISSOURI R. Prairie land to N; S are OZARK MOUNTAINS; part of Great Plains are in SW; Mississippi flood plains in SE. Mfg. of shoes, food and grain products, beer, chemicals; meat packing; printing and publishing. Farming (corn, livestock, grains, potatoes, fruit, cotton); mining (lead, zinc, coal, limestone, granite, marble, fire clay, glass sand). French worked lead deposits, estab. fur trade; founded SAINTE GENEVIEVE 1732, St. Louis 1764. Went to U.S. in Louisiana Purchase (1803). Territory estab. 1812. Stayed with Union in Civil War. Some fighting in Mo., notably guerrilla warfare (esp. under W. C. QUANTRILL). Postwar confusion marked by some violence (e.g., Jesse JAMES). Steamboat traffic declined as railroads grew. Industry developed. Political position enhanced by election of H. S. TRUMAN, native son, to presidency. It is hoped that eventually the MISSOURI RIVER BASIN PROJECT will help agr.

Missouri, river, 2,714 mi. long, longest river of U.S. and chief tributary of the Mississippi, formed where Gallatin, Madison, and Red Rock–Jefferson (main headstream of the Missouri) rivers join in SW Mont. at Three Forks. Flows SE across N.Dak. and S.Dak., past E Nebr. and parts of E Kansas and W Iowa, through Mo. to the Mississippi c.17 mi. above St. Louis. Tributaries include Milk, Yellowstone, and Platte rivers. Largest river city is Kansas City. U.S. MISSOURI RIVER BASIN PROJECT is planned. River a trade artery for Indians; lower river familiar to fur traders after 1762. Lewis and Clark opened up mountain country 1804–6 and area became well known

with fur trade of mountain men in 1820s and 1830s. Steamboats became important. In 1840s and 1850s, the Missouri and the Platte were part of route to Oregon and Calif.; Mormon route to Utah. Before and after Civil War river traffic boomed, but railroads caused decline. River now important for power and irrigation.

Missouri, University of, mainly at Columbia; landgrant, state supported, coed.; chartered 1839, opened 1841; oldest state university W of the Mississippi. Includes schools of journalism (1908; oldest in world) and, at Rolla, mines and metallurgy.

Missouri Compromise, 1820–21, measures passed by U.S. Congress to end first of a series of crises concerning extension of slavery into national territory. Provided that Maine would enter Union as free state, Mo. as slave state; prohibited slavery elsewhere in Louisiana Purchase N of 36°30′, a proviso which held until 1854, when KANSAS-NEBRASKA BILL repealed Missouri Compromise.

Missouri river basin project, plan advanced 1944 for coordinated development and control of the Missouri and its basin lands. States chiefly involved are Mont., Colo., Wyo., N.Dak., S.Dak., Nebr., Kansas, and Mo. For the plan Flood Control Act of 1944 authorized over 100 dams, reservoirs, and levees intended to irrigate c.5,500,000 acres, control floods, improve navigation, restore surface and ground water, and develop hydroelectric power. Project will also conserve wildlife and abate stream pollution. Committee of federal and state representatives estab. 1945 to help advance the scheme, which will ultimately include existing projects such as those of NORTH PLATTE and SOUTH PLATTE rivers, and control other tributaries. Kanopolis Dam on Smoky Hill R. was first unit of the project completed (1948).

Mistassini (mĭstŭsē′nē), river, central Que., Canada, flowing c.200 mi. S, then SE to L. St. John. W is **Lake Mistassini** which drains W to James Bay.

Misti, El (ĕl mē′stē), volcano, 19,166 ft. high, S Peru, near Arequipa. With a perfect, snow-capped cone, it is apparently significant in Inca religion and has figured in many Peruvian legends and poems.

mistletoe, evergreen plant with white berries, parasitic on many trees and shrubs. The European mistletoe of literature, sacred to the druids, is *Viscum album.* The mistletoe of American holiday markets is of the genus *Phoradendron.*

Mistral, Frédéric (frädärĕk′ mĕsträl′), 1830–1914, French Provençal poet, leader of the Felibrige movement promoting Provençal as a literary language. His best-known work is the verse romance *Mirèio* (1859; Eng. tr., 1867). Shared 1904 Nobel Prize in Literature with Echegaray.

Mistral, Gabriela (gäbrēä′lä mĕsträl′), 1889–, Chilean poet, whose real name is Lucila Godoy Alcayaga. An educator of note, she also served in diplomatic posts and in League of Nations. Her poems are simple and fluently lyrical. She was awarded the 1943 Nobel Prize in Literature.

Mitau, Latvia: see JELGAVA.

Mitchell, Donald Grant: see MARVEL, IK.

Mitchell, Margaret, 1900?–1949, American novelist. Her one novel, *Gone with the Wind* (1936), dealt with the Civil War and Reconstruction periods. Both the book and the motion picture version (1939) were enormously popular.

Mitchell, S(ilas) Weir, 1829–1914, American physician and author. Pioneered in applying psychology to medicine. Also wrote historical romances (*Hugh Wynne, Free Quaker,* 1896) and psychological studies (*Constance Trescot,* 1905).

Mitchell, Wesley C(lair), 1874–1948, American economist, author of *Business Cycles.* With evidence from behaviorist psychology, attacked orthodox economics.

Mitchell, William Lendrum, 1879–1936, American general, advocate of large, independent air force. "Billy" Mitchell's criticisms led to court-martial in 1926.

Mitchell. 1 City (pop. 3,245), SW Ind., S of Bedford. Near-by state park has caves and a restored pioneer village. **2** City (pop. 12,123), SE S.Dak., near James R. and L. Mitchell, WNW of Sioux Falls; platted 1879. Trade and processing center for agr., dairy, and livestock area. Seat of Dakota Wesleyan Univ. (Methodist; coed.; 1885). Holds annual agr. festival in Corn Palace.

Mitchell, Mount, peak, 6,684 ft., W N.C., in Black Mts. NE of Asheville; highest peak of E U.S.

Mitchill, Samuel Latham, 1764–1831, American scientist. An educator of note, he taught at Columbia (1792–1801) and College of Physicians and Surgeons (1807–26) and in 1826 helped found Rutgers Medical Col. (no longer in existence). He introduced chemical nomenclature of Lavoisier and was a pioneer in research in mineralogy, geology, and zoology. Served in N.Y. state assembly (1791, 1798, 1810), in U.S. House of Representatives (1801–4, 1810–13), and U.S. Senate (1804–9).

mite, small, often microscopic, arachnid of tick order, of world-wide distribution. Itch mite burrows into skin of humans and other mammals. Other mites attack vegetation and infest stored foods.

Mitford, Mary Russell, 1787–1855, English writer, noted for rural sketches in *Our Village* (1824–32).

Mithra (mĭ'thrù) [Old Persian,= friend], anc. cultic god of Iran and India. Originally a minor figure of Zoroastrianism, he became in 5th cent. B.C. chief Persian god. Extension of his cult into Mesopotamia and Armenia made it a world-wide religion, **Mithraism** (mĭ'-thrùĭzùm). It was one of great religions of Roman Empire, more general in 2d cent. A.D. than Christianity. Its central myth was story of Mithra's slaying of a sacred bull in a grotto. Its ethics were rigorous, loyalty was inculcated, and fasting and continence were prescribed. A mystery-faith, it had sacramental forms, e.g., baptism, and the sacred banquet. Mithraism was long in dying out.

Mithridates VI or **Mithradates VI** (Eupator) (mĭthrĭdā'tēz; ū'pùtôr), c.131 B.C.–63 B.C., king of anc. Pontus, called Mithridates the Great. Rival expansion of territories brought him into war with Rome. In the First Mithridatic War (88–84 B.C.) he conquered all Asia Minor and defied SULLA in Greece. In 85 he was defeated in both spheres. In the Second War (83–81 B.C.) he defeated the Romans. In the Third War (74–63 B.C.) Lucullus defeated Mithridates, and POMPEY drove the king into the Crimea, where he had himself killed by a slave.

Mitilini, Greece: see MYTILENE.

Mitla (mēt'lä) [Nahuatl,= abode of the dead], religious center of the Zapotec, near Oaxaca, SW Mexico.

mitosis (mītō'sĭs), in growth of plants and animals, method of division of the nucleus of a cell, characteristic of body (somatic) cells as distinguished from sex cells (gametes). Process varies, but generally may be divided into four or five stages that are continuous. In prophase chromatin material in the nucleus of the cell thickens and forms chromosomes, which split lengthwise; the nuclear membrane disappears, and a spindle-shaped structure forms (this forming is sometimes considered a separate phase, the prometaphase). In metaphase the chromosomes move to the equator of the spindle. During anaphase, the two halves of each chromosome separate, and all draw into two groups around poles of the spindle. In telophase, nuclear membrane forms around each group, and thus two nuclei are complete, each with same number of chromosomes as original nucleus. Usually the cell then splits into two, one for each nucleus. In sex cells of animals and plants that reproduce by union of two cells, a further process, called meiosis, occurs as the sex cells mature. Complex changes take place in stages similar to those of mitosis, but in meiosis the number of chromosomes is reduced by half (reduction division); when egg and sperm nuclei unite in fertilization the normal number of chromosomes for the species is restored.

The new individual develops by mitotic divisions of the fertilized egg. See *ill.,* p. 633.

Mitre, Bartolomé (bär"tōlōmā' mē'trä), 1821–1906, Argentine statesman, general, and author, president of Argentina (1862–68). Forced into exile by Rosas, he had colorful career as journalist and soldier in Uruguay, Bolivia, Peru, and Chile. Aided Urquiza in overthrow of Rosas (1852), then warred with Urquiza. National political unity was achieved and reforms were initiated during his presidency. Founded newspaper *La Nación* (Buenos Aires) and wrote works on history.

Mitropoulos, Dimitri (dēmēt'rē mētrô'pōolôs), 1896?–, American conductor, b. Greece. Conductor of the Minneapolis Symphony Orchestra (1937–46), he became in 1949 associate conductor of the New York Philharmonic and permanent conductor in 1950. He is known as a champion of contemporary music.

Mitscherlich, Eilhard (īl'härt mĭ'chùrlĭkh), 1794–1863, German chemist. Discovered principle of ISOMORPHISM, worked on compounds of phosphorus and arsenic, discovered nitrobenzene and some acids.

Mitsubishi: see ZAIBATSU.

Mitsui: see ZAIBATSU.

Mitylene, Greece: see MYTILENE.

Miya-jima, Japan: see ITSUKU-SHIMA.

Mizpah or **Mizpeh** (mĭz'pù) [Heb.,= watch tower]. **1** See GALEED. **2** Meeting place of anc. Hebrews on important occasions. Judges 20.1; 21.1,5,8; 1 Sam. 7.5.

Mjosa (myû'sä), Nor. *Mjøsa,* lake, area 141 sq. mi., depth 1,453 ft., SE Norway; largest in Norway. It is drained by a tributary of the Glomma. Lillehammer, Gjovik, and Hamar are on its shores.

Mn, chemical symbol of the element MANGANESE.

Mnemosyne (nēmŏ'sĭnē, –zĭnē) [Gr.,= memory], Greek personification of memory; daughter of Uranus and Gaea and mother of the nine MUSES by Zeus.

Mnesicles (nē'sĭklēz), 5th cent. B.C., Greek architect. Designed the PROPYLAEA and possibly the ERECHTHEUM on the Acropolis at Athens.

Mo, chemical symbol of the element MOLYBDENUM.

moa (mō'ù), extinct flightless New Zealand bird, related to kiwi, emu, cassowary, and ostrich.

Moab (mō'ăb), anc. nation in hilly region E of Dead Sea, sporadically at war with the Hebrews. Moabites traditionally descended from Lot; language on MOABITE STONE almost the same as biblical Hebrew. Gen. 19.37; Num. 22–24; Judges 3; 2 Kings 3; Isa. 15–16; Jer. 48; Ezek. 25; Amos 2; Zeph. 2.

Moab, town (pop. 1,274), E Utah, on Colorado R. Near by are Arches Natl. Monument and vanadium and uranium mines.

Moabite stone, erected by Mesha of Moab, who composed the inscription (850 B.C.) on it to commemorate a victory in his revolt against Israel. Discovered 1868 at Dibon; fragments are in the Louvre.

Moallakat: see MUALLAQAT.

mob, in psychology, a group of people, strongly interacting, their conduct dominated by suggestion and emotion, not reason. Crowds, lacking intense mob emotionality, may become mobs in stress or danger. Fervent or hysterical leaders can drive crowds to mob heroism or extreme brutality. In mobs, individuals are in heightened, almost hypnotic state of suggestibility and lose normally controlling inhibitions. See also SOCIAL PSYCHOLOGY.

Moberg, Vilhelm (vĭl'hĕlm mōō'bĕryù), 1898–, Swedish novelist and dramatist. His novels (e.g., *Ride This Night!* 1941; *The Emigrants,* 1950) often deal with lives of small farmers.

Moberly (mō'bùrlē), city (pop. 13,115), N central Mo., NNW of Columbia; laid out 1866. In area of coal and fire-clay deposits, it has rail shops and light mfg.

Mobile (mōbēl'), city (pop. 129,009), SW Ala., at mouth of Mobile R. (crossed by Bankhead Tunnel, 1941) on MOBILE BAY. Only seaport in state; has large South American trade. Processes and ships food, lumber, cotton, naval stores, paper; ships iron, steel products.

Shipbuilding; mfg. of asbestos, chemicals. Founded 1710 by sieur de Bienville; cap. of La. 1710–19. Ceded to Britain 1763, taken by Spain 1780, by U.S. 1813. Rebel ships ran Federal blockade from here in Civil War, until Adm. Farragut's victory (1864). Captured by Gen. CANBY, 1865. In 1937, second free port in U.S. estab. here. Has cathedral (R.C.), ante-bellum homes, U.S. marine hospital. Spring Hill Col. (Jesuit; for men; 1831) is near. Annual Mardi Gras (from 1704), Azalea Trail Festival (from 1929).

Mobile, river in SW Ala. formed by junction of Alabama and Tombigbee rivers. Flows c.45 mi. S to Mobile. Here it enters **Mobile Bay,** a Gulf of Mexico arm, c.35 mi. long from the Gulf to mouth of river and 8–18 mi. wide. Ship channel enters Gulf between Mobile Point and Dauphin Isl. Battle won here on Aug. 5, 1864, by Adm. FARRAGUT.

moccasin flower: see LADY'S SLIPPER.

Mocha (mō′kù), town (pop. 600), Yemen, SW Arabia; a port on Red Sea. Formerly noted for coffee export. Declined in 19th cent. with rise of Aden.

mockingbird, North American songbird of catbird and brown thrasher family, allied to thrushes and wrens. Noted for melodious song and as mimic.

mock orange or **syringa,** deciduous shrub of genus *Philadelphus,* native to Eurasia and North America. Their fragrant white flowers blooming in late spring are similar to orange blossoms. *Syringa* is the generic name for the unrelated lilac.

Moctezuma: see MONTEZUMA.

mode, in grammar: see MOOD.

mode, in music, any pattern of arrangement of the tones and half-tones of a scale. Modes are not scales; they vary in patterns of tones and half-tones. This can best be understood by considering the white keys of the piano. One mode can be represented by the series of white keys from D to D, whereas another would be from F to F, and so on. The pattern of whole and half-tones from D to D would thus be 1, ½, 1, 1, 1, ½, 1; from F to F it would be 1, 1, 1, ½, 1, 1, ½. A melody composed within one mode, if transferred to another, would be completely changed. The use of modes evolved from the highly developed modal system of ancient Greece. In medieval plain song, there were eight modes, four called authentic, four plagal, each authentic mode having a corresponding plagal one (later, after 1547, there were 12). The difference between an authentic mode and its plagal is in range. For example, the authentic mode (D–D) has as its plagal A–A, but there is an authentic mode A–A that has as its plagal E–E. If, in a piece of music written in the D mode, the melody fell between D and D, the mode would be authentic; if between A and A, the mode would be plagal.

mode, in statistics, an infrequently used type of average. In a group of numbers, the mode is the number occurring most frequently.

Model Parliament: see PARLIAMENT.

Modena (mô′dänä), city (pop. 50,451), Emilia-Romagna, N central Italy, on Aemilian Way. Agr. center. Free commune from 12th cent. Passed to ESTE family 1288; became a duchy 1452. Has 12th-cent. Romanesque cathedral and fine art collections.

modern art: see ABSTRACT ART; CUBISM; DADA; FAUVISM; FUTURISM; IMPRESSIONISM; POSTIMPRESSIONISM.

modernism, in religion, movement to reconcile developments of 19th-cent. science and philosophy with historic Christianity. It arose from evident disparity between Darwin's theory of evolution and old literal interpretation of Genesis and was influenced by attempts to read Darwinian principles into history of civilization. Its general trait was to reject belief in supernatural, and to consider Church as only a human society. Ideas were opposed by fundamentalists in 1920s and by Anglican groups. In the Roman Catholic Church a similar movement headed by Loisy was declared heretical by the pope (1907).

modernismo (mōdhĕrnē′smō), movement in Spanish lit-

erature, beginning in Latin America in late 19th cent. with poetry of José Martí. It was marked by conscious artistry in choosing images, portraying color, and creating subtle word music. The subject matter of modernist poetry is exotic, remote, and escapist (swans, princesses, Japanese landscape). The best-known modernist in both poetry and prose was Rubén DARÍO.

Modestinus, Herennius (hùrĕ′nēùs mŏdùstī′nùs), fl. c.250 B.C., Roman jurist, much cited in the Corpus Juris Civilis.

Modesto (mŏdĕ′stō), city (pop. 17,389), central Calif., SE of Stockton and on Tuolumne R.; founded 1870. Processing and trade center for fruit, poultry, and dairy products of San Joaquin Valley.

Modigliani, Amedeo (ämädä′ō mōdēlyä′nē), 1884–1920, Italian painter. Studied in Florence but early went to Paris, where his sculptures were influenced by cubism and Negro art. In paintings he used distortion for emotional effect. Recognized only by leading artists during short life; died in poverty.

Modjeska, Helena (mùjĕ′skù), 1844–1909, Polish actress; in U.S. after 1877. Considered among greatest tragic actresses of her time in *Adrienne Lecouvreur, Doll's House,* and plays of Shakspere.

Modoc Indians (mō′dŏk), North American tribe of Lutuamian linguistic stock, in early 19th cent. in SW Oregon and N Calif. Their culture was almost identical with that of KLAMATH INDIANS, their kinsmen. Trouble between the Modoc and early American settlers ended when a group of Modoc under Captain Jack left the reservation in 1870, defended themselves in lava beds of N Calif., murdered Gen. Edward R. S. Canby and another U.S. mediator, and were finally defeated. The tribe was dispersed.

Modred, Sir: see ARTHURIAN LEGEND.

modulation, in music, changing from one key to another in a composition. Among devices used to make this transition smooth to the ear is using a chord common to both the old and new keys as a pivot. If there is no common chord between the two keys, a passage may have to move through several keys before the desired modulation has been effected smoothly. In enharmonic modulation, a chord of the old key is simply changed in notation (e.g., A sharp becomes B flat) and is then considered a chord of the new key.

Moe, Jorgen Engebretsen, Nor. *Jørgen Engebretsen Moe* (yûr′gùn ĕng′ùbrĕtsùn mō′ù), 1813–82, Norwegian folklorist and poet, bishop of Kristiansand.

Moesia (mē′shù), anc. region SE Europe. Organized as Roman prov. (A.D. 44) including, roughly, modern Serbia (Upper Moesia) and Bulgaria (Lower Moesia).

Mofaddaliyat (mōfä″dälēät′) or **Mufaddaliyat** (mōō–), great Arabic anthology compiled by Al Mufaddal of Kufa (d. c.775). Contains 126 poems by 67 authors of Golden Age of Arabic poetry (500–650).

Moffat Tunnel: see FRONT RANGE.

Mogilev (mùgēlyôf′), city (pop. 99,440), E Belorussia. It is an industrial and transportation center on the Dnieper.

Mogollon Plateau (mōgōyōn′), tableland, c.7,000–8,000 ft. high, E central Ariz., S of Winslow. Mogollon Rim, its rugged S escarpment, is sometimes called Mogollon Mts. Not directly linked to Mogollon Mts. of W N.Mex.

Mogul (mō′gùl) or **Mughal** (mōōgùl′), Moslem empire of India, 1526–1857. Founded by BABER, who claimed descent from the Mongol conqueror Jenghiz Khan. Its greatest rulers were AKBAR, SHAH JEHAN, and AURANGZEB. Disintegrated in 18th cent. under blows of Sikhs and Mahrattas, but the British maintained puppet emperor until 1857. Empire's lasting achievements were in art (see MOSLEM ART AND ARCHITECTURE).

Mohacs, Hung. *Mohács* (mô′häch), city (pop. 18,355), S Hungary, on the Danube. Here, on Aug. 29, 1526, Louis II of Hungary was disastrously defeated by Suleiman I of Turkey. The king and nearly the entire Hungarian army were killed. Louis's defeat, which laid Hungary open to Turkish domination, was partly caused by the probably deliberate failure of John Zapolya to join Louis with his Transylvanian contingent. In 1687 Charles V of Lorraine routed the Turks on the same battlefield.

mohair, hair of the Angora goat or a fabric made from it alone or combined with other fibers.

Mohammed (mōhŏ'mĭd, mōhă'mĭd) [Arabic,= praised], 570?–632, the Prophet of ISLAM, founder of one of the world's great religions, b. Mecca. Born into the tribe of Koreish, which ruled Mecca, he married Khadija, a wealthy widow. After he was 40 he had visions that were to be collected and recorded in the KORAN; these were the basis of the new religion, which made little headway in Mecca, though he converted Ali, who married Mohammed's daughter Fatima, and Abu Bakr. A plot to murder him led to his flight (the HEGIRA) in 622 to Yathrib (now Medina). From this event Islam counts its dates. At Medina he built a theocratic state, from which the great Mohammedan empire was to grow. He fought with Mecca, but in 630 it fell to him without a fight. His sayings are the law of Islam, together with the Koran. In later life he had many wives, notably Ayesha. Name also Mahomet, Muhammad, and other forms (e.g., Mehemet).

Mohammed, Ottoman sultans. **Mohammed II** (the Conqueror), 1429–81, reigned 1451–81. He completed the conquest of the Byzantine Empire by storming Constantinople after a 50-day siege (1453). He also conquered most of the Balkan Peninsula but was checked at Belgrade by Hunyadi, in Albania by Scanderbeg, and in Rhodes by the Knights Hospitalers. In Asia, he conquered Karamania and Trebizond. He captured Otranto, in Italy (1480), but the expedition had no results. The true founder of the Ottoman Empire, he was outstanding as a commander, an administrator, and a scholar. **Mohammed IV,** 1641–92, reigned 1648–87. His army, driven back from the siege of Vienna (1683), was routed at Mohacs (1687), and he was deposed. **Mohammed V,** 1844–1918, succeeded to the throne in 1909, the Young Turk revolution having deposed his brother, Abdu-l-Hamid II. ENVER PASHA held the actual control. His reign was a series of disasters: the loss of Tripoli to Italy (1911–12); the BALKAN WARS (1912–13); and the defeat of Turkey in World War I. Turkey capitulated to the Allies soon after the accession of his brother, **Mohammed VI,** 1861–1926, who accepted the Treaty of SÈVRES and ruled as a puppet of the Allies. He was overthrown and exiled in 1922 by Kemal ATATURK. His cousin Abdul-l-Mejid succeeded him as caliph, but in 1924 the caliphate was abolished, and all Ottoman princes were exiled.

Mohammed Ahmed: see MAHDI.

Mohammed Ali, 1769–1849, pasha (governor) of Egypt after 1805. In 1811 he dealt final blow to power of the MAMELUKES. With his son IBRAHIM PASHA, he defended the Turkish sultan (his nominal overlord) in campaigns in Arabia and in Greece, where he scored successes until his defeat in battle of NAVARINO. When the sultan denied him the governorship of Syria, he turned against him and marched into Syria (1833). His revolt, begun 1839 in Asia Minor, was checked by opposition of European powers. By way of compromise, Abdul-l-Mejid, the sultan, made governorship hereditary in Mohammed's line. Present royal family of Egypt is descended from him.

Mohammedan and **Mohammedanism:** see ISLAM.

Mohammed ibn Tumart (ĭ'bün tōōmärt'), c.1080–1128?, Berber Moslem leader, founder of the ALMOHADES.

Mohammed Reza Shah Pahlevi (rēzä' shä' pä'lüvē), 1919–, shah of Iran. In 1941 he succeeded his father, Reza Shah Pahlevi. Visited U.S. in 1949. Launched liberal Seven-Year Plan for economic development of country. His reign has seen rise of leftist Tudeh party and nationalization of oil industry. He clashed with Premier Mossadegh in 1953.

Mohave, river and desert: see MOJAVE.

Mohave Indians (mōhä'vē), North American tribe of Yuman linguistic stock, formerly on Ariz. and Calif. banks of Colorado R. Practiced semisedentary agr.

Mohawk, river, largest tributary of the Hudson, rising in central N.Y. and flowing c.140 mi. S and SE, past Rome, Utica, Amsterdam, Schenectady, to the Hudson at Cohoes. Paralleled by the Barge Canal from Rome to its mouth. ERIE CANAL (1825) also followed it. Beautiful, fertile valley was scene of many battles in French and Indian War and in Revolution; important route in western migration.

Mohawk Indians: see IROQUOIS CONFEDERACY.

Mohawk Trail. 1 Old road in N.Y. following Mohawk R., important as route for settlers emigrating W. **2** Motor highway across N Mass. from Greenfield to North Adams.

Mohegan Indians, North American tribe, also called Mohican, the E branch of the MAHICAN INDIANS. In SW Conn. in the 17th cent. they joined with the Pequot, but later Uncas rebelled against Pequot rule and formed a band generally known as the Mohegan. This band in alliance with the English became very powerful, but as white settlement increased the Indians declined and died out on a reservation in Conn.

Mohenjo-Daro (mōhĕn'jō-dä'rō), archaeological site in Sind, W Pakistan, near Indus R. Gave its name to **Mohenjo-Daro civilization** or **Indus civilization,** revealed by finds here and at Harappa, 400 mi. NE, in S Punjab near Ravi R. It was an urban culture resembling that of Sumer, which existed at same time (3d millennium B.C.). Cotton textiles and burnt modern-type brick were used. Quasi-pictographic writing, as yet undeciphered, is apparently related to that of Sumer, to Brahmi alphabet of India and to South Arabian alphabet. Shift of river course caused decline of Mohenjo-Daro.

Mohican Indians: see MAHICAN INDIANS; MOHEGAN INDIANS.

Mohl, Hugo von (hōō'gō fün mōl'), 1805–72, German botanist. An expert on microscopy, he is noted for research on nature of protoplasm and chlorophyll and on physiology of higher plants; laid foundation for later work on structure of palms and cycads.

Moholy-Nagy, Laszlo (lä'slō môhoi-nŏ'dyü), 1895–1946, Hungarian painter and designer. A founder of constructivism. Taught at BAUHAUS in Germany and later at its offshoot, the Chicago Inst. of Design.

Moisie (mwäzē'), river of E Que., Canada, rising near Labrador border and flowing 210 mi. S to St. Lawrence R. Near mouth is Moisie village.

Moissan, Henri (ärē' mwäsä'), 1852–1907, French chemist. Won 1906 Nobel Prize for isolating fluorine and inventing an electric-arc furnace.

Moivre, Abraham de (äbrä-äm' dü mwä'vrü), 1667–1754, French-English mathematician. He assisted Royal Society in deciding between Newton and Leibniz as prior inventor of differential calculus. Contributed to trigonometry and law of probabilities.

Mojave (mōhä'vē), river of S Calif. rising in San Bernardino Mts. and flowing c.100 mi. N and NE, mostly underground, to disappear in Mojave Desert. Also spelled Mohave.

Mojave Desert, c.15,000 sq. mi. of barren mountains and flat desert valleys in S Calif., S of the Sierra Nevada and N of the San Gabriel and San Bernardino Mts. Supports mining (silver, gold, tungsten, iron), granite quarrying, and chemical extraction (borax, potash, salt). Its lakes are usually dry. Mojave R is in S part. Death Valley is to N.

Moji (mō'jē), industrial city (pop. 109,567), N Kyushu, Japan; port on Shimonoseki Strait. Tunnel connects it with Shimonoseki on Honshu.

Moki Indians: see HOPI INDIANS.

Mokuaweoweo (mōkōō'üwä'ōwä'ō), active volcano, on Hawaii, T.H., on summit of Mauna Loa. Crater is 3.7 mi. long, 1.7 mi. wide, and 800 ft. deep.

molasses, viscid residue separated from cane sugar during crystallization process. The least-refined grade, blackstrap, used in stock feed, alcohol manufacture, and for human food. Greater refining produces lighter grades with more sugar; they are used as food and to make rum.

Molay, Jacques de (zhäk' dù mōlā'), 1243?–1314, last grand master of the KNIGHTS TEMPLARS. Summoned to France in 1306, he was tried for heresy by an inquisitorial court, confessed under torture, and was burned when he recanted.

mold, name for certain multicellular fungi, generally saprophytic. One of the commonest is the black bread mold (*Rhizopus nigricans*). Species of *Penicillium* are useful in the preparation of certain cheeses. PENICILLIN and other antibiotics are obtained from certain molds. Some molds cause mildew, ringworm, and other diseases. See *ill.,* p. 633.

Moldau (môl'dou), Czech *Vltava,* longest river in Czechoslovakia, rising in Bohemian Forest, and flowing 267 mi. N past Prague into the Elbe.

Moldavia (môldă'vēū), historic province (c.14,700 sq. mi.; pop. 2,598,258), E Rumania, between the Carpathians (W) and the Pruth R. (E); cap. Jassy. Galati, on the Danube, is the chief port. A fertile plain drained by Sereth R., it is the granary of Rumania. Region formed part of Roman Dacia. After many foreign invasions, Moldavia became a principality under native rulers (14th cent.); it then also included BUKOVINA and BESSARABIA. The princes ruled despotically; the boyars (great landowners) reduced rural population to serfdom. Moldavia reached its height under Stephen the Great, but after his death (1504) became tributary to Turkey. Early in 18th cent. the native princes were replaced by governors (hospodars) mostly Greek PHANARIOTS, appointed by the sultans. Their rule ended 1822 after the Greek insurrection instigated by Alexander YPSILANTI, and native hospodars were appointed. The Treaty of ADRIANOPLE (1829) made Moldavia a virtual Russian protectorate, but in 1856 the Congress of Paris guaranteed the independence—under nominal Turkish overlordship—of the two Danubian Principalities (Walachia and Moldavia). With the accession (1859) of Alexander John Cuza as prince of both principalities, the history of modern Rumania began.

Moldavian Soviet Socialist Republic, constituent republic (c.13,000 sq. mi.; pop. c.2,660,000) of the USSR, in SE Europe, separated from Rumania by the Pruth R.; cap. Kishinev. Population is mostly Moldavian (i.e., Rumanian-speaking), with Russian, Jewish, Ukrainian, and Bulgarian minorities. The republic, which corresponds to the larger part of BESSARABIA, was estab. 1940, after Rumania had ceded Bessarabia back to Russia.

Molde Fjord (môl'dù, mô'lù), inlet (60 mi. long) of North Sea, W Norway. Town of Molde (pop. 3,774), tourist center, is on N bank overlooking the Dovrefjell. Famous Romsdal Fjord is an arm.

mole, in chemistry: see MOLECULAR WEIGHT.

mole, in zoology, small insectivorous burrowing mammal belonging to various genera found in Europe, Asia, North America. Moles have soft, thick, gray or brown fur; pointed muzzle; small, weak eyes; no external ears; strong forelimbs, digging claws.

Molech or **Moloch** (both mō'lùk), Canaanitish god of fire, to whom children were offered in sacrifice. Shrine was at Tophet in valley of Hinnom. Solomon and Ahaz are said to have introduced this worship. Lev. 18.21; 20.2; 1 Kings 11.7; 2 Kings 23.10; Jer. 32.35.

molecular weight (mùlē'kyōolùr), relative weight of MOLECULE of substance compared with a standard. Can be calculated from FORMULA by adding relative weights (ATOMIC WEIGHT) of atoms in molecule. Molecular weights can be determined by various methods in laboratory; are important in chemical analysis. Gram-molecular weight (or mole) of substance is often used, i.e., weight in grams equal numerically to molecular weight of substance.

molecule (mŏl'ùkūl), smallest particle into which sub-

stance can be divided without changing properties. Molecules are in constant, vibratory motion; state or form in which matter appears (liquid, solid, or gas) depends on velocity of molecules and distance between them. In general, when heat is applied to substance, molecules vibrate faster and move farther apart; at constant pressure this causes expansion. When heat is withdrawn contraction occurs. If heat is added continuously, the velocity of molecules becomes so great that change of state occurs. Pressure also affects molecular state of substance. Molecules are made up of atoms either of same kind or of two or more kinds; substances differ according to structure and composition of their molecules. Molecules of different substances differ in size, weight, structure. Molecular structure is affected in chemical action.

Molière, Jean Baptiste Poquelin (zhā' bäptēst' pôkùlē' môlyěr'), 1622–73, French dramatist and actor, one of the world's greatest comic authors. Originally named Poquelin and son of a prosperous merchant in Paris, he early joined the BÉJART company of actors. After touring the provinces, the company was estab. in Paris (1658); in 1665 it became the King's Troupe and in 1680 the COMÉDIE FRANÇAISE. In Louis XIV, Molière found a generous patron and a protector against his many enemies. The genius of Molière is equally apparent in his broad farces (such as *Le Médecin malgré lui,* 1666; *Les Fourberies de Scapin,* 1671) and in his great comedies of character, in which he ridicules a vice or a type of excess by caricaturing a person incarnating it. Among these timeless satires are *L'Avare* (1668)—the miser; *Le Bourgeois gentilhomme* (1670)—the parvenu; *Les Femmes savantes* (1672)—bluestockings; *Le Malade imaginaire* (1673)—the hypochondriac; and *Tartuffe* (1664)—the religious hypocrite. In *Le Misanthrope* (1666), perhaps his greatest play, the chief character is psychologically more complex, the plot less conventional, as is also the case in *L'École des femmes* (1663). Both these plays probably caricature Molière himself. *Amphytrion* (1668) is Molière's most poetic and one of his funniest works. There are many English translations.

Molina, Luis (lwēs' mōlē'nä), 1535–1600, Spanish Jesuit. His *Concordia* (1589) set forth a doctrine since called Molinism in an attempt to reconcile the dogma of God's grace and that of man's free will. The theology of Francisco SUÁREZ was an effort at compromise between Thomism and Molinism.

Molina, Tirso de: see TIRSO DE MOLINA.

Moline (mōlēn'), city (pop. 37,397), NW Ill., on the Mississippi (bridged); platted 1843. Forms, with ROCK ISLAND, EAST MOLINE, and DAVENPORT, Iowa, an economic unit called Quad Cities. Transportation, trade, and industrial center; coal fields near by. Mfg. of farm equipment and machinery, wood and metal products. John DEERE moved here 1847.

Molinos, Miguel de (mēgěl' dä mōlē'nōs), 1640–97, Spanish mystic, founder of QUIETISM. His *Guida spirituale* (1675) detailed perfection as complete contemplative passivity of soul. He was condemned by the Inquisition (1687) and died in prison.

Molise, region of Italy: see ABRUZZI E MOLISE.

Mölk, Austria: see MELK.

mollusk (mō'lùsk), chiefly aquatic, invertebrate animal of phylum Mollusca. It has a soft, unsegmented body with the under part usually forming a muscular foot. Many forms have an external shell, some have an internal one, a few have no shell. Classes include gastropods, e.g., snail, slug; cephalopods, e.g., squid; and bivalves, e.g., clam, oyster, mussel.

Mollwitz (môl'vĭts), village near Breslau, Lower Silesia, where Frederick II of Prussia defeated Austrians in 1741. Battle proved superiority of modern infantry over cavalry.

Molly Maguires (mùgwī'ùrz), secret organization of Irishmen in coal districts of Scranton, Pa., c.1865–75. An attempt to combat oppressive industrial and living conditions, it often resorted to murdering the police, who were controlled by the mine owners. A strike was organized in 1875, but the organization's power was finally broken by the spying activity of the Pinkerton agency on behalf of the industrialists. Twenty miners were hanged.

Molnar, Ferenc (fĕ'rĕnts môl'när), 1878–1952, Hungarian dramatist and novelist. His plays, very successful in the U.S., include *Liliom, The Swan, The Guardsman,* and *The Play's the Thing.*

Moloch, in Bible: see MOLECH.

Molokai (mō'lōkī'), island (259 sq. mi.; pop. 5,280), one of Hawaiian Isls. Cattle, pineapples. On N coast is Kalaupapa Settlement (leper colony, estab. 1860), where Father DAMIEN worked and died.

Molotov, Vyacheslav Mikhailovich (vyĕ"chīsläf' mēkhī'lŭvĭch mô'lŭtŭf), 1890–, Russian statesman whose real name is Skriabin. Chairman of council of people's commissars (i.e., premier) 1930–41; vice premier from 1941; foreign minister 1939–49, 1953–. Negotiated Russo-German nonaggression pact (1939). Was outstanding Russian spokesman in world affairs during World War II and postwar years.

Molotov, city (pop. c.450,000), RSFSR, on Kama R., in W foothills of the Urals; named Perm until 1940. Major inland port and transportation center; produces pig iron, machinery, chemicals, wood products. Has numerous cultural institutions.

molting, periodic shedding and renewal of outer skin or skeleton, fur, or feathers of animal. In birds, the number and completeness of molts varies; loss and replacement of feathers is usually gradual, in sequence. Invertebrates, e.g., insects and crabs, with outer skeletons shed them periodically to permit growth. Snakes shed skins; mammals change from heavy winter to light summer coat, and some change color.

Moltke, Helmuth, Graf von (hĕl'mōōt gräf' fŭn môlt'kŭ), 1800–1891, Prussian field marshal. Served in Danish army before 1822, in Turkish army 1835–39. As chief of the general staff from 1858 he shaped the modern Prussian army and was the chief architect of the Prussian victories in the Danish, Austro-Prussian, and Franco-Prussian wars. Resigned 1888. His nephew **Helmuth von Moltke,** 1848–1916, succeeded SCHLIEFFEN as chief of staff in 1906. Shortly before the outbreak of World War I he modified and weakened Schlieffen's famous plan.

Moluccas (mŭlŭ'kŭz) or **Spice Islands,** island group (c.32,300 sq. mi.; pop. 560,000), Indonesia, between Celebes and New Guinea. Includes HALMAHERA, CERAM, AMBOINA, and TERNATE. Discovered in early 16th cent. by the Portuguese; taken in 17th cent. by the Dutch, who monopolized clove trade.

molybdenite (mŭlĭb'dŭnīt), a mineral, molybdenum disulphide, blue gray, with metallic luster and greasy feel. An important ore of molybdenum, found in Saxony, Bohemia, England, Australia, U.S.

molybdenum (mŭlĭb'dŭnŭm), rare, silvery metallic element (symbol = Mo; see also ELEMENT, table). Has luster, can be drawn into wires and thin sheets. Combines with various substances. Does not occur uncombined; ores are widely but sparingly distributed. Used to make alloy steel, in radio-tube grids and filaments, and in electrodes.

Mombasa (mômbä'sŭ), city (pop. 84,746), Kenya, port on Indian Ocean, on Mombasa Isl. and near-by mainland area. An early center of Arab trade, it was visited 1498 by Vasco da Gama. Held by Portuguese until 1698, when it was recaptured by Arabs. Later became part of Zanzibar sultanate and passed to Great Britain c.1880. Ships coffee, cotton, and tin (from Uganda).

momentum (mōmĕn'tŭm), term commonly used to indicate force or power that moving body exerts to maintain its motion. In mechanics it is defined as the quantity of motion of the body, specifically the product of its mass and velocity. An external force acting on a body or system of bodies causes change in momentum of the body. Impulse of a force (i.e., product of force

and time in which it acts) upon a body is measured by change in momentum. If no external force acts on body in motion or a system of bodies there is no change in momentum, even though there is, in some cases, internal disturbance of the system; this conclusion is known as principle of conservation of momentum.

Mommsen, Theodor (tā'ōdōr môm'sŭn), 1817–1903, Germany historian. Major work *History of Rome* (vols I–III, 1854–56; Vol. V, 1885). Received 1902 Nobel Prize in Literature.

Momus or **Momos** (both: mō'mŭs), in Greek myth, personification of mockery and rebuke; son of Night.

Monaca (mŏn'ŭkŭ), borough (pop. 7,415), W Pa., on Ohio R. and NW of Pittsburgh. Mfg. of glass and metal products.

Monaco, Lorenzo: see LORENZO MONACO.

Monaco (mŭnä'kō, mŏ'nŭkō), principality (c.370 acres; pop. c.20,000), on the Mediterranean, an enclave within SE France. Consists of three adjoining sections: Monaco (cap.), La Condamine (business dist.), and MONTE CARLO. Its beautiful situation and its famous gambling casino make it one of the most fashionable Riviera resorts. Reigning prince: Rainier III. Casino, privately managed as concession, supplies most of state revenue. Only c.2,000 inhabitants are Monegasque subjects; these are barred from gambling. Principality has customs union with France; its currency is interchangeable with French. Monaco was ruled by Genoese Grimaldi family from 13th cent.; in 1731 the French Matignon family succeeded to principality by marriage; it adopted the name Grimaldi. Monaco was under Spanish protection from 1524, under French protection from 1641, under Sardinian protection 1815–61. By treaty of 1918, succession to the throne must be approved by the French government.

monad: see BRUNO, GIORDANO; LEIBNIZ, G. W.

Monadhliath Mountains (mō'nŭlē'ŭ), Inverness-shire, Scotland, between the Spey valley and Loch Ness.

Monadnock (mŭnäd'nŏk), isolated peak, 3,165 ft. high, SW N.H., NW of Jaffrey.

Monaghan (mŏ'nŭgŭn), inland county (498 sq. mi.; pop. 57,215), Ireland, in Ulster; co. town Monaghan. Primarily an agr. area. Much livestock is raised.

Monahans (mŏn'ŭhăns), city (pop. 6,311), W Texas, N of Pecos R. Processes oil, gasoline, carbon black, and cottonseed products. Chemical plant near by.

monarchianism (mōnär'kēŭnĭzŭm) [Gr.,= belief in the rule of one], concept of God, holding his sole authority even over Christ and the Holy Spirit. Its characteristic tenet, that God the Father and Jesus Christ are one person, was developed as ADOPTIONISM and as philosophy of SABELLIUS.

monasticism, organized life in common in a retreat from worldly life for religious purposes. Men who belong to these communities are monks and their establishments are monasteries; communities of women are commonly called convents and their inhabitants nuns. The monastic life is known to most great religions—Buddhism (incl. Lamaism), Jainism, and Islam, as well as Christianity. In Christianity it arose from movement to seek voluntary seclusion of a hermit's life. In the Eastern Orthodox Church monks still have cenobitic (i.e., hermitlike but lived in common) practices. The usual rules are those of St. Basil the Great (see BASILIAN MONKS). In the West communal life has been the usual form of monasticism since the time of St. Benedict. The Benedictine abbeys under his rule were the preservers of Roman civilization in the period of chaos from the 6th to the 10th cent. and were the source of later learning. In the Roman Catholic Church there are many orders of monks and nuns, including the friars—FRANCISCANS, DOMINICANS, and CARMELITES. Some are entirely secluded (enclosed) but most are devoted to teaching, charity, or missionary work. The Jesuits (see JESUS, SOCIETY OF) and the Christian Brothers are typical of modern monastic effort. In the Reformation many monasteries were destroyed, and in general Protestantism has not fostered the ascetic ideal of monasticism.

Monastir, Yugoslavia: see BITOLJ.

monazite (mŏ′nŭzīt), one of the rare earths and the chief source of thorium and cerium. Brown or reddish with resinous luster, translucent to opaque. Occurs with granites and gneisses but more commonly in river and beach sands derived from monazite-bearing rocks.

Moncenisio, Italian name for Mont CENIS.

Monck, Charles Stanley, 4th **Viscount,** 1819–94, governor general of Canada (1861–68).

Monck or **Monk, George,** 1st **duke of Albemarle,** 1608–70, English soldier and politician. Lieutenant-general under Cromwell, he subdued the Scots in 1651. In 1660 he supported the Stuarts, raised an army, and persuaded Parliament to dissolve itself. On his advice Charles II issued Declaration of Breda and the Restoration was effected.

Moncks Corner, town (pop. 1,818), SE S.C., N of Charleston, on Cooper R. near Santee-Cooper hydroelectric and navigation project.

Monckton Milnes, Richard: see HOUGHTON, RICHARD MONCKTON MILNES, 1ST BARON.

Moncton, city (pop. 27,334), SE N.B., on Petitcodiac R. and NE of St. John. Industrial and transportation center in lumbering and farming area. Settled by French, who were followed (1763) by Germans from Pennsylvania.

Monday: see WEEK.

Mondrian, Piet (pēt′ môn′drēän), 1872–1944, Dutch painter. Influenced by cubists, he developed a geometric, nonobjective style called neoplasticism. Influenced Bauhaus movement. Generally used only primary colors; typical compositions have only vertical and horizontal lines at 90° angles.

monel metal (mōnĕl′), silver white alloy of copper and nickel (c.⅓ copper, ⅔ nickel) with small amount of other metals. It is strong, resists acid corrosion, holds bright finish.

Monessen (mùnĕs′ŭn), city (pop. 17,896), SW Pa., on Monongahela R. and S of Pittsburgh; laid out 1897. Steel and iron works.

Monet, Claude (klōd′ mônā′), 1840–1926, French impressionist landscape painter. With Sisley and Berthe Morisot he organized the exhibition of 1875, which the critics derisively called impressionist, after the title of one of his pictures, *Impression: soleil levant.* Lived in extreme poverty until 1883 when he gained some recognition. A leader in plein-air painting, he eliminated black and brown and achieved light effects by means of broken color.

Moneta, Ernesto Teodoro (mōnā′tä), 1833–1918, Italian pacifist, president (1906) of the International Peace Congress in Milan. Awarded 1907 Nobel Peace Prize.

monetary union, agreement among nations to unify currency values, stabilizing currencies or arriving at a common currency. Best-known monetary unions are the Latin Monetary Union (formed 1865) and the Scandinavian union (1873). The Bretton Woods agreements of 1944 planned the International Monetary Fund.

money, term involving two concepts—the abstract units of value and the means of payment. Many ancient communities took cattle as their standard of value but made payments with manageable objects. Similarly the Code of Hammurabi indicated that silver was used for both purposes. A great variety of objects have served as money, e.g., shells, tobacco, and dried fish. Precious metals, because of their durability, convenience, and high intrinsic value, are preferred. However, the intrinsic value of the object being used as money is no longer important. (State coinage, said to have originated in Lydia in 7th cent. B.C., enabled governments to issue coins whose nominal value exceeded their value as metals.) Paper currency, much in use for the past 300 years, is usually backed by some

standard commodity of intrinsic value into which it may be converted upon demand. U.S. currency was based on BIMETALLISM during most of the 19th cent., and on a full gold standard from 1900 to 1933. Since the 1934 Gold Reserve Act, the U.S. has been on a modified gold standard of value, but gold is no longer used as a medium of exchange. Today the favored means of payment is the bank check, rather than coin or currency.

Monferrato, Italy: see MONTFERRAT.

Monge, Gaspard, comte de Péluse (gäspär′ mōzh′ kōt′ dü pālüz′), 1746–1818, French mathematician and physicist. His geometrical researches laid foundations of modern descriptive geometry.

Mongolia (mŏn-gō′lĕŭ), Asiatic region (1,000,000 sq. mi.; pop. 3,500,000), lying roughly between Sinkiang prov., China, on W and Manchuria on E, between Siberia on N and Great Wall of China on S. Comprises Mongolian People's Republic (Outer Mongolia) and Inner Mongolia (Chahar, Suiyuan, Ningsia provs., China). Mainly a high plateau with Gobi desert in central part. Exports include wool, cloth, and hides. Jenghiz Khan conquered Mongolia c.1205 and led Mongols in creating a great empire. China took Inner Mongolia c.1635. In late 17th cent. she subjugated Outer Mongolia; it broke away in 1921 to become in 1924 **Mongolian People's Republic** (615,000 sq. mi.; pop. 1,000,000). Closely allied to USSR, the republic (comprising over half of Mongolia) remained unrecognized by China until 1945. In 1949 Chinese Communists joined most of N Inner Mongolia to parts of Manchuria to form **Inner Mongolian Autonomous Region** (230,000 sq. mi.; pop. 2,000,000).

Mongolian languages: see LANGUAGE (table).

Mongolian People's Republic: see MONGOLIA.

Mongolism: see FEEBLE-MINDEDNESS.

Mongols (mŏng′gŭlz), Asiatic people, numbering c.3,-000,000 and distributed mainly in Mongolia, N and W Manchuria, and Buryat-Mongol ASSR in USSR. Group includes KALMUCKS. Mainly a pastoral people adhering to Lamaism. Mongol hordes, especially those which conquered Russia and penetrated Europe, included large elements of Turkic and other peoples; these became known collectively as TATARS. Mongols established YÜAN dynasty in China, khanate of GOLDEN HORDE in Russia, and other khanates in Turkistan and Persia.

mongoose (mŏn′gōōs), small carnivorous mammal related to civet, found chiefly in India, SE Asia, Africa. Indian mongoose (*Herpestes*) is agile and slender, has brownish-gray fur, and is c.30 in. long, including tail. It kills venomous snakes and rats.

Monhegan (mŏnhĕ′gĭn), resort island, 10 mi. off coast of S Maine near Bristol. Battle between *Boxer* and *Enterprise* fought offshore, 1813.

monitor, type of warship used in Civil War; named from *Monitor,* built by John Ericsson for Union navy, launched 1862. Characterized by revolving turret carrying two 11-in. guns. Deck was only 18 in. above water. Heavily sheathed in iron. This vessel was involved in the famous drawn battle of **Monitor and Merrimac.** The *Merrimac* was a frigate, scuttled by the Union, raised by the Confederates and made into an ironclad, the *Virginia.* The battle between the two ironclads in Hampton Roads, March 9, 1862, altered naval warfare.

monitorial system, method of elementary education devised by Joseph Lancaster and Andrew Bell to make maximum use of limited facilities to furnish schooling to the poor. Sometimes called Lancasterian system. All pupils met in one room; there the teacher instructed the monitors, the older and better students, and these taught the other pupils.

Moniz, Egas (ā′gŭsh mō′nĕsh), 1874–, Portuguese physician. Shared 1949 Nobel Prize in Physiology and Medicine for developing prefrontal lobotomy (brain operation used in treating certain mental disorders). Author of many medical works.

Monk, George: see MONCK, GEORGE, 1ST DUKE OF ALBEMARLE.

monk: see MONASTICISM.

monkey, mammal of primate order. Old World monkeys include the family of true monkeys (e.g., macaque, baboon, and langur) and the APE family. Man is often classed in a third family. In these the nasal septum is narrow; nostrils are directed down; there are 32 teeth. New World monkeys and marmosets are arboreal; the nose is flat; nostrils are directed sidewise; usually there are 36 teeth.

Mon-Khmer languages (mŏn'-kŭmâr'), group of Austro-Asiatic languages scattered over SE Asia. They include Mon or Talaing (Burma), Khmer or Cambodian (Thailand and S Indo-China), and Cham (Indo-China).

monkshood: see ACONITE.

Monmouth, James Scott, duke of (mŏn'mŭth), 1649–85, claimant to English throne, natural son of Charles II. After Popish Plot agitation (1678) supporters of Protestant succession championed him as King's heir. After accession of James II (1685) he landed in England and raised a small force. Was defeated, captured, and beheaded.

Monmouth, England: see MONMOUTHSHIRE.

Monmouth, city (pop. 10,193), W Ill., W of Galesburg; laid out 1831. Center for livestock, farm, and clay area. Mfg. of clay and metal products. Seat of Monmouth Col.

Monmouth, battle of, in American Revolution, June 28, 1778, near Monmouth Courthouse (now Freehold, N.J.). Attack on British suddenly turned into retreat by Charles LEE. Arrival of Washington and Steuben prevented American rout; British escaped.

Monmouthshire (mŏn'mŭth-shĭr) or **Monmouth,** border county (546 sq. mi.; pop. 424,647), W England. Low, fertile land in Wye valley, rising to hills in N and NW. Has grazing, farming, and fruit growing, but large coal and iron deposits are area's main importance. Sometimes considered as part of Wales. Many inhabitants speak Welsh. County town is **Monmouth,** municipal borough (pop. 5,432), a market town.

Monnier, Henry (ärē' mônyā'), 1799–1877, French lithographer and writer of satiric sketches and plays, creator of characters pillorying the French bourgeoisie, notably with Mme Gibou and M. Joseph Prudhomme.

Monocacy (mŭnŏ'kŭsē), river rising in S Pa. and crossing Md. to join the Potomac S of Frederick, Md. Just E of Frederick was fought Civil War battle, July 9, 1864. Although defeated, Gen. Lew Wallace delayed Confederate move on Washington.

Monongahela (mŭnŏng"gŭhē'lŭ), city (pop. 8,922), SW Pa., on Monongahela R. and S of Pittsburgh. Mfg. of metal products and chemicals. Center in Whisky Rebellion.

Monongahela, river formed in N W.Va. Flows 128 mi. N into SW Pa. and joins Allegheny R. at Pittsburgh to form Ohio R.

Monophysitism (mŭnŏ'fĭsĭ"tĭzŭm), heresy of 5th and 6th cent. continuing the principles of EUTYCHES, opposing NESTORIANISM. It challenged the orthodox creed of Chalcedon by saying that Jesus Christ had only one nature. In the East, the emperor invalidated (c.476) the Council of CHALCEDON and after several attempts at compromise which satisfied neither side, the pope excommunicated the East. By the 6th cent. Monophysitism dominated Syria, Egypt, and Armenia, and after alternate periods of imperial favor and suppression, a permanent schism set in (by 600) and the COPTIC, JACOBITE, and ARMENIAN churches were established. See also MONOTHELETISM.

monopoly (mŭnŏ'pŭlē), virtually complete control of the supply of a product, forcing consumers to purchase at whatever price the owner fixes. Government monopolies, such as the postal system, are often operated in the public interest, and socialism advocates the extension of this principle to all basic industries. Monopolies may be constructed by controlling the entire production and marketing of a product (see CARTEL), or by forming corporation mergers or agreements to restrain competition (see TRUST). In the U.S. antitrust laws act to curb private monopolies.

Monotheletism or **Monothelitism** (mŭnŏ'thĭlĭtĭ"zŭm), 7th-cent. heresy condemned by Third Council of CONSTANTINOPLE (680). It declared that Christ had two natures but operated with one will and was adopted by HERACLIUS I as imperial compromise between MONOPHYSITISM and orthodoxy. Vehemently opposed by Rome, it died out after 680 except among Syrian MARONITES.

monotype (mŏ'nŭtĭp) [Greek *mono* = one], a machine invented by Tolbert Lanston (patented 1887) for casting and setting type for printing. Monotype makes each character separately, assembling as in hand composition. Keyboard unit punches holes in a roll of paper, which is used in casting unit to govern casting and assembling of type.

Monreale (mōnrāä'lā), town (pop. 14,340), NW Sicily, Italy, near Palermo. Has famous cathedral (founded 1174) with Byzantine mosaics.

Monro, Harold, 1879–1932, English poet. Founded periodicals *Poetry Review* (1911) and *Chapbook* (1919–25), which influenced the poetry of his day. His *Collected Poems* appeared in 1933.

Monroe, Harriet, 1860–1936, American editor, critic, poet, founder (1912) and long editor of influential *Poetry: a Magazine of Verse* in Chicago.

Monroe, James, 1758–1831, 5th President of the United States (1817–25), b. Va. Foundation of his political career was friendship that resulted from his studying law (1780–83) under Thomas Jefferson. As U.S. Senator (1790–94) he violently assailed Federalists. Served on diplomatic missions to France, Spain, and England. U.S. Secretary of State (1811–17), Secretary of War (1814–15). His two administrations as President have been known as the "era of good feeling." Florida question and boundary question with Canada were resolved; the settlement of Liberia took place with his approval; struggle over slavery question was met by MISSOURI COMPROMISE; MONROE DOCTRINE was announced.

Monroe. 1 City (pop. 38,572), N La., on Ouachita R., in agr. and natural gas area; settled c.1785 as Fort Miro. Mfg. of carbon black, chemicals, and lumber, paper, meat, cotton, and cottonseed products. **2** City (pop. 21,467), SE Mich., on L. Erie at mouth of Raisin R. and SW of Detroit; settled c.1780. Shipping point for agr. area with nurseries and mfg. of paper and metal products. Limestone quarries near. Scene of Raisin R. massacre (1813), and "Toledo War" (see TOLEDO, Ohio). Home of G. A. Custer. **3** City (pop. 10,140), S N.C., SE of Charlotte, settled 1751. Trade and mfg. center for agr. and timber area. **4** City (pop. 7,037), S Wis., SW of Madison, in dairy region. Population largely of Swiss descent. Cheese center with annual cheese fair.

Monroe, Fort, at Old Point Comfort, Va., commanding entrance to Chesapeake Bay and Hampton Roads. Held by Union in Civil War; prison (1865–67) of Jefferson Davis. Hq. U.S. army field forces 1946.

Monroe, Mount: see PRESIDENTIAL RANGE.

Monroe Doctrine, dual principle of American foreign policy enunciated in Pres. Monroe's message to Congress, 1823. Doctrine grew out of two diplomatic problems: minor clash with Russia concerning NW coast of North America, and fear that European governments commonly called Holy Alliance would seek to regain Latin American states that had recently revolted from Spain. The British foreign minister, Canning, wanted to send a joint Anglo-American note to powers of the Holy Alliance, but J. Q. Adams insisted on U.S. acting alone and drafted the doctrine. Two main points: no new colonization in the Americas, no European interference in American nations. Though never recognized in international law, it was several times invoked with success. As imperialistic tendencies appeared in U.S., doctrine came to be viewed with suspicion by Latin American countries as protecting U.S. hegemony, a suspicion heightened by the "corollary" of Theodore Roosevelt saying that fear of European intervention in an ill-conducted Latin American country would justify U.S. intervention. Feeling against the doctrine decreased in the 1920s and disappeared with Roosevelt's "good neighbor" policy.

Monrovia (mŭnrō'vēù) [for Pres. James Monroe], city (pop. c.12,000), cap. of Liberia; port on the Atlantic. Founded 1822 by American Colonization Society as haven for ex-slaves from U.S. In World War II its harbor was vastly improved by U.S.

Monrovia, city (pop. 20,186), S Calif., NE of Los Angeles; laid out 1886. Growing and packing of citrus fruit.

Mons (mŏnz, Fr. mōs), Flemish *Bergen,* city (pop. 25,-684), cap. of Hainaut prov., SW Belgium, at junction of Condé-Mons Canal and Canal du Centre, it is processing and shipping center for Borinage coal-mining dist. Became seat of counts of Hainaut in 9th cent. It was repeatedly attacked in wars of 16th, 17th, and 18th cent., and in World War I was scene of first British-German battle (1914). Among the buildings preserved are a 12th-cent. castle chapel and a 15th-cent. town hall.

Monsalvat or **Monserrat,** Spain: see MONTSERRAT.

Monson, town (pop. 6,125), S Mass., E of Springfield. Here are granite quarries and textile mills.

monsoon (mŏnsōōn'), a wind changing direction with season. Monsoons are most notable in India, where they bring heavy rains, but they appear also in Iberian peninsula, Africa, Australia, and China.

Mont, (Karel Maria) Pol(ydoor) de (mŏ'), 1857–1931, Flemish poet and critic. Curator (1904–19) of the museum of fine arts in Antwerp, he defended modern tendencies in art, and forwarded the Flemish literary revival. Author of lyrics and short stories.

Montagna, Bartolomeo (bärtōlōmä'ō mōntä'nyä), c.1450–1523, Italian religious painter, founder of school of Vicenza.

Montagnards: see MOUNTAIN, THE.

Montagu, Charles: see HALIFAX, CHARLES MONTAGU, EARL OF.

Montagu, John: see SANDWICH, JOHN MONTAGU, 4TH EARL OF.

Montagu, Lady Mary Wortley, 1689–1762, English wit and letter writer. Her letters, notably a series from Turkey, where her husband was ambassador 1716–18, were witty and informative. Pope, once her friend, later bitterly satirized her.

Montague, town (pop. 7,812), N Mass., SE of Greenfield. Has large hydroelectric plant. Includes Turners Falls village (pop. 5,179), site of first dam across Connecticut R.

Montaigne, Michel Eyquem, seigneur de (mōntän', Fr. mēshĕl' äkĕm' sänyûr' dù mōtĕn'yù), 1533–92, French author. He was a magistrate until 1570 and mayor of Bordeaux (1581–85), but after 1571 he lived mostly in a rural retreat, aloof from the religious and political troubles of his time. His *Essais* (1st ed., 1580; 1st complete ed., 1595) are considered the finest examples of the essay ever wrritten; their influence on European literature is incalculable. In them, Montaigne reveals himself intimately and fully, digressing on a wide variety of subjects, in a style unsurpassed in wisdom, directness, expressive imagery, vigor, charm, and ironic humor. The "Apologie de Raimond Sebond," longest of the essays, states most fully his philosophy of skepticism.

Montale, Eugenio (āōōjä'nyō mōntä'lä), 1896–, Italian modernist poet, author of volumes *Ossi de seppia* (1925) and *Le occasioni* (1940); often compared to T. S. Eliot.

Montalembert, Charles Forbes René de Tryon, comte de (mōtäläbĕr'), 1810–70, French orator and writer. A collaborator with Lacordaire and Lamennais in the Catholic liberal movement and in editing *L'Avenir,*

he submitted to papal condemnation of the journal. He used his oratorical powers to oppose Napoleon III in the early years of the empire. He accepted the dogma of papal infallibility, which he had contested earlier. His *Monks of the West* (7 vols., 1860–77) is still a standard (though incomplete) work.

Montana, state (146,316 sq. mi.; pop. 591,024), NW U.S.; admitted 1889 as 41st state; cap. HELENA. Other cities are BUTTE, GREAT FALLS, BILLINGS. BITTERROOT RANGE to W, Great Plains in E. YELLOWSTONE main river. Mining (copper, silver, gold, zinc, lead, manganese, sapphires, natural gas, oil, coal). Farming (wheat, potatoes, corn, livestock, fruits, sugar beets). Mfg. based on processing of resources. Tourism (e.g., Glacier Natl. Park). Area opened after Louisiana Purchase. Fur trade estab. Discovery of gold (1860s), silver (1875), and copper (c.1880), as well as growth of ranching, brought settlers. G. A. CUSTER wiped out by Sioux at Little Bighorn R. in 1876. Anaconda controls state's copper. Drought in 20th cent. brought irrigation, Federal water power projects. World War II put large demands on copper industry.

Montana, University of, state system of higher education constituted 1913, with hq. at Helena. Its six units include Montana State Univ. (coed.; chartered 1893) at Missoula, Montana State Col. (1893) at Bozeman, Montana School of Mines (1893) at Butte.

Montañes, Juan Martínez (mōntän'yĕs), c.1568–1649, Spanish sculptor, famous for polychrome figures in wood. Work is best seen in Seville.

Montanism (mŏn'tùnīzùm), enthusiastic Christian movement in 2d cent., led by Montanus and two prophetesses of Phrygia. It stressed ecstatic prophecy and severe asceticism in immediate expectation of Judgment Day. Montanists believed that a Christian fallen from grace could not be redeemed. By c.220 Montanism had died as a sect.

Montargis (mōtärzhē'), town (pop. 13,529), Loiret dept., N central France. Agr. market. Has kept medieval aspect. The celebrated legend of the dog of Montargis, which may have some basis in fact, tells of the murder, near Montargis, of Aubry de Montdidier, a courtier of Charles V, by one Macaire (c.1371). Aubry's dog showed such animosity toward Macaire that the king ordered a trial by combat between the dog and Macaire, armed with a cudgel. The dog won; Macaire confessed and was hanged.

Montauban (mōtōbä'), city (pop. 23,016), cap. of Tarn-et-Garonne dept., S France, on Tarn R. Textile mills. Was a stronghold of Albigenses in 13th cent., of Huguenots in 16th cent. Birthplace of Ingres, whose work is richly represented in cathedral and museum.

Montauk Point, N.Y.: see LONG ISLAND.

Mont Blanc (mō blä'), Alpine massif on Franco-Italian border. It rises to 15,781 ft. (in France), highest point of the Alps. Mer de Glace, largest of its numerous glaciers, flows into Chamonix valley. First ascended 1786.

Montcalm, Louis Joseph de (mōntkäm'), 1712–59, French general. Sent (1756) to defend Canada in French and Indian War. Captured Fort Ontario (1756), Fort William Henry (1757), and withstood strong attack on Ticonderoga (1758). Defended Quebec against a siege by Gen. James Wolfe until British strategy effected an open engagement on Plains of Abraham. English won (Sept. 13, 1759), but both Montcalm and Wolfe were killed.

Montclair, residential town (pop. 43,927), NE N.J., NNW of Newark; settled 1669. Has art museum containing works of Inness, who lived here.

Mont-Dore (mō-dôr'), town (pop. 2,165), Puy-de-Dôme dept., central France. Thermal station and winter sports center. It lies at foot of the Puy de Sancy, highest peak of Mont-Dore mountain group of Auvergne (6,187 ft.).

Monte Albán (mōn'tä älbän'), anc. city of the Zapotec in Oaxaca, SW Mexico; seat of advanced culture c.200 B.C.–A.D. 1521. Excavation begun in 1931 revealed vast treasure of jewelry and elaborate carvings.

Montebello (mŏntĭbĕ′lō), city (pop. 21,735), S Calif., SE of Los Angeles. Oil wells; truck and flower farms.

Monte Carlo (mŏn″tē kär′lō), town (pop. 7,967), principality of Monaco, on the Riviera. It is one of the world's most famous gambling resorts.

Monte Cassino (mŏn′tä käs-sē′nō), famous monastery on a hill, 1,702 ft. high, overlooking town of Cassino, Latium, central Italy. Abbey, founded c.529 by St. Benedict of Nursia, was a great center of Christian learning and piety; its influence on European civilization is immeasurable. It was destroyed by the Lombards in 581; by the Arabs in 883; by earthquake in 1349; by Allied aerial bombardment in 1944, the German garrison having used the abbey as fortress. Most of valuable manuscripts of library had been removed to safety.

Montecatini (mŏn″täkätē′nē), town (pop. 8,292), Tuscany, central Italy. Health resort.

Monte Cristo (mŏn′tē krĭ′stō), small Italian island in Tyrrhenian Sea, made famous by Dumas père's novel, *The Count of Monte Cristo.*

Montecucculi or **Montecuccoli, Raimondo, conte di** (rīmōn′dō kōn′tä dē mōn′täkōok′kōōlē, –kōlē), 1609–81, Italian field marshal in imperial service. Fought in Thirty Years War; defeated Turks at Szent-Gotthard, Hungary (1664).

Montefiore, Sir Moses Haim (mŏn″tĭfēō′rē), 1784–1885, British-Jewish philanthropist, b. Leghorn. He worked to alleviate discriminatory practices against Jews and was influential in preparing the way for political Zionism.

Montego Bay (mŏntē′gō), port (pop. 11,547), on NW Jamaica, British West Indies; winter resort.

Montejo, Francisco de (fränthē′skō dä mōntä′hō), b. c.1473 or c.1479, d. c.1548, Spanish conquistador. Commissioned to conquer the Maya of Yucatán, he made two unsuccessful attempts, one from the E (1527–28), and one from W (1531–35). His son of the same name finally subdued the Maya (1546).

Montemayor, Jorge de (hôr′hä dä mōn″tämäyôr′), c.1520–1561, Spanish poet and novelist, author of pastoral novel *Diana* (1559?).

Montemezzi, Italo (ē′tälō mōntämĕt′tsē), 1875–1952, Italian composer of operas (e.g., *L'amore dei tre re,* 1913, and *La nave,* 1918).

Montenegro (mŏn″tŭnē′grō), Serbo-Croatian *Crna Gora,* autonomous republic (5,343 sq. mi.; pop. 376,573), SW Yugoslavia, bordering on Adriatic and on Albania; cap. Titograd. Mountainous, difficult of access, it has forests and pastures (sheep and goat raising) and some agr. in the Zeta R. valley and near L. of Scutari. The Montenegrin people are Serbs, mostly of Eastern Orthodox faith. The region formed the semi-independent principality of Zeta in 14th-cent. Serbia. After the Serbian defeat at Kossovo (1389), Montenegro for five centuries resisted all Turkish attempts at subjugation. The Turks did, however, control part of the present republic, and Venice held the coast, including Kotor. From 1516 to 1851 Montenegro was ruled by the prince-bishops (called *vladikas*) of Cetinje. Danilo I (reigned 1696–1735) made the episcopal succession hereditary from uncle to nephew (the bishops being barred from marrying) and initiated (1715) the traditional alliance with Russia. Danilo II (reigned 1851–60) secularized the principality, transferring his spiritual functions to an archbishop; his successor Nicholas I secured recognition of Montenegrin independence (1878) and proclaimed himself king (1910). Montenegro gained some territory in the Balkan Wars (1912–13); in World War I it invaded Albania and declared war on Austria but was occupied by Austro-German forces 1915–18. In Nov., 1918, the king having been deposed, Montenegro was united with Serbia. It gained autonomy and some additional coastal territory under the 1946 constitution of Yugoslavia.

Monterey (mŏntŭrā′), city (pop. 16,205), W Calif., on Monterey Bay and S of San Francisco. Resort and home of artists and authors. Bay named 1602 by Sebastián Vizcaino. In 1770 Gaspar de Portolá estab. a presidio (now U.S. army post) and Junípero Serra, a mission. Intermittent cap. of Alta Calif. 1775–1846. Taken by U.S. navy 1846. State constitutional convention met here 1849. State's first theater (1844) and first brick building (1847) stand. Sardine fisheries and canneries. Fruit and vegetable canneries.

Monterey Park, residential city (pop. 20,395), S Calif., E of Los Angeles; founded 1910.

Monterrey (mōntĕrā′), city (pop. 186,092), cap. of Nuevo León, NE Mexico; third largest city of Mexico (after Mexico city and Guadalajara); founded 16th cent. Except for Mexico city, the most important industrial city in country (and a popular resort on Inter-American Highway), it has mfg. of beer, paper, flour, cotton goods, iron and steel, furniture, textiles, cigars, bricks, and glass and metal goods. City is regarded as evidence of Mexico's potential ability to develop a balanced economy.

Montespan, Françoise Athénaïs, marquise de (fräswäz′ ätänäēs′ märkēz′ dù mōtùspä′), 1641–1707, mistress of Louis XIV of France. Succeeded Mlle de la Vallière and was followed by Mme de Maintenon in king's favor.

Montesquieu, Charles de Secondat, baron de la Brède et de (shärl′ dù sùkŏdä′ bärō′ dù lä brĕd′ ä dù mōtùskyû′), 1689–1755, French political philosopher; a high magistrate at Bordeaux. His *Persian Letters* (1721; Eng. tr., 1730), a satire of European society, is one of the world's masterpieces of irony. *Reflections on the Causes of the Grandeur and Declension of the Romans* (1734; Eng. tr., 1734) presents, in a few lapidary and luminous pages, a philosophy of history akin to that of Vico. His most influential work was *The Spirit of the Laws* (1748; Eng. tr., 1750), a scientific study of comparative government. Its theory of checks and balances found its way into the U.S. Constitution. Its analysis of geographic and economic factors in the origin of laws, its wise emphasis on the complexity of the subject, and its caution against ready-made utopias have influenced several later schools of political thought.

Montessori, Maria (märē′ä mōntĕs-sō′rē), 1870–1952, Italian educator and physician; first woman to receive medical degree in Italy (1894). Her method for education of preschool children features development of initiative through individual freedom of action, improvement of sense perception, and development of coordination.

Monteux, Pierre (pyĕr′ mōtû′), 1875–, French-American conductor. As conductor (1911–14) of Diaghilev's Ballet Russe, he conducted premières of ballets of Stravinsky, Ravel, and Debussy. He conducted various U.S. orchestras including the Boston Symphony (1919–24), and the San Francisco (1935–51).

Montevallo (mŏntĭvă′lō), town (pop. 2,150), central Ala., S of Birmingham. Seat of Alabama Col. (state; for women; 1893).

Monteverdi, Claudio (klou′dyō mōntävĕr′dē), 1567–1643, Italian composer, first great name in operatic history. His bold experiments in instrumentation contributed to the development of the modern orchestra. His best-known operas are *Orfeo* and *L'incoronazione de Poppea.* He also wrote religious music and madrigals.

Montevideo (mŏntùvĭ′dēō), city (pop. 5,459), W Minn., on Minnesota R. and NW of Granite Falls, in agr. area. Near-by Camp Release State Park commemorates release in 1862 of 269 white captives of Sioux.

Montevideo (mōntävēdhä′ō), city (pop. 750,000), Uruguay, cap. and largest city of Uruguay. On the Río de la Plata, it is one of major ports of South America. Founded (1726) because of rival colonial expansion of Portuguese and Spanish, it has seen much strife and in 19th cent. was besieged many times by warring factions. Today it is a beautiful modern city, governmental, financial, and commercial focus of nation. The national university is here.

Monte Vista (mŏn'tĭ vĭs'tù), city (pop. 3,272; alt. c.7,500 ft.), S Colo., in San Luis Valley on Rio Grande. Near by are Picture Rocks (with pictographs), dude ranches, potato farms, gold and silver mines.

Montez, Lola (mŏn'tĕz, mŏntĕz'), 1818?–1861, Irish dancer and adventuress whose real name was Gilbert. Her sensational success was due to beauty rather than artistry. She became official mistress of LOUIS I of Bavaria, who made her a countess, and virtually ruled Bavaria until her banishment in 1848. She died in poverty in the U.S.

Montezuma (mŏntùzōō'mù) or **Moctezuma** (mŏktāsōō'-mä), 1480?–1520, Aztec ruler (1502–20). Reign was marked by incessant warfare and unrest among subject peoples, facilitating conquest by Hernán Cortés. Montezuma vacillated in his policy towards Spanish and was killed in later fighting between Spanish and Aztecs.

Montezuma Castle National Monument: see NATIONAL PARKS AND MONUMENTS (table).

Montferrat (mŏntfùrăt', –rät'), Ital. *Monferrato*, historic region of Piedmont, NW Italy, S of the Po. Has noted vineyards. A marquisate after 10th cent., with Casale as cap. after 1435, it passed to GONZAGA family of Mantua in 1536. Savoy invaded Montferrat in 1612, and in 1631 part of the marquisate was assigned to Savoy, the remainder in 1713.

Montfort, Simon de (mŏnt'fûrt, Fr. mōfôr'), c.1160–1218, French nobleman, leader of the crusade against the ALBIGENSES. Combining religious fanaticism with ruthless ambition, he laid waste S France. After his victory at MURET he was proclaimed (1215) lord of Toulouse and Montauban. In 1217 Raymond VI of Toulouse recovered some of his lands, and Simon fell fighting him. Through his mother, Simon claimed the earldom of Leicester. He was the father of **Simon de Montfort,** c.1208–1265, earl of Leicester, leader of revolt against HENRY III of England. In 1258 he was active in forcing king to accept the PROVISION OF OXFORD. In 1260 he broke with Henry. He assumed leadership in BARONS' WAR. In 1264 fierce civil war broke out. After victory at Lewes Montfort became master of England. The Great Parliament he summoned in 1265 was one of most important in history of Parliament in that he called representatives from boroughs and towns, as well as knights from each shire. The wars were resumed and Montfort was defeated and killed at Evesham.

Montgolfier, Joseph Michel (zhôzĕf' mĕshĕl' mōgôlfyä'), 1740–1810, and **Jacques Étienne Montgolfier** (zhäk ätyĕn'), 1745–99, French inventors (brothers) of first practical balloon, demonstrated 1783.

Montgomery, Bernard Law, 1st Viscount Montgomery of Alamein, 1887–, British field marshal. Became idol of British public in World War II after victory at ALAMEIN (1942). Field commander of all ground forces in invasion of Normandy. Headed British occupation forces in Germany 1945–46. Chief of imperial general staff 1946–49. In 1951 he was made deputy supreme commander of NATO.

Montgomery, Lucy Maud, 1874–1942, Canadian novelist. Her first novel, *Anne of Green Gables* (1908), and its sequels have been popular stories for girls.

Montgomery, Richard, 1738?–1775, American Revolutionary general, b. Ireland. Commanded Montreal expedition in QUEBEC CAMPAIGN. Killed in assault on Quebec.

Montgomery, county, Wales: see MONTGOMERYSHIRE.

Montgomery, city (pop. 106,525), state cap. (since 1846), SE central Ala., on Alabama R. (navigable here), in Black Belt; settled 1817. Rail center; cotton, livestock, dairy market; mfg. of textiles, fertilizer, cottonseed and lumber products; food (esp. meat) packing. First cap. of CONFEDERACY (1861). Fell to Union troops, 1865. Seat of Huntingdon Col. (Methodist; for women; 1854). Has "First White House of

the Confederacy." Maxwell and Gunter air force bases are near.

Montgomeryshire (mùntgŭ'mùrēshĭr) or **Montgomery,** border county (797 sq. mi.; pop. 45,989), Wales; co. town Montgomery. Hilly region, devoted mostly to pasturage and farming. Important in medieval times as fortified border district.

month, period of passage of MOON through its phases, usually reckoned at c.29 or 30 days. Months of the CALENDAR are roughly equated to phases of the moon. Some calendars (e.g., the Moslem) are based on this calculation, and feast days change seasons. Names in West and birthstones are: *January* [from Janus], garnet; *February* [from Latin,= expiatory, because of rites in February], amethyst; *March* [from Mars], aquamarine and bloodstone; *April,* diamond; *May,* emerald; *June* [from gens (clan) *Junius*], pearl, alexandrite, moonstone; *July* [from Julius Caesar], ruby; *August* [from Augustus], peridot and sardonyx; *September* [from Latin,= seven], sapphire; *October* [eight], opal and tourmaline; *November* [nine], topaz; *December* [ten] turquoise and zircon.

Montherlant, Henry de (ärē' dù mōtĕrlä'), 1896–, French author. His novels, glorifying force and the masculine ego, include *Les Bestiaires* (1926; Eng. tr., *The Bullfighters,* 1927) and the tetralogy *Les Jeunes Filles* (1936–40; Eng. tr., 2 vols., 1937–40).

Monti, Vincenzo (vēnchän'tsō mōn'tē), 1754–1828, Italian poet, known chiefly for his epic *Bassvilliana* (1793) and for translations of Homer.

Monticelli, Adolphe (ädôlf' mōtēsĕlē'), 1824–86, French painter. Represented in Lille and Marseilles.

Monticello (mŏntĭsĕl'ō), resort village (pop. 4,223), SE N.Y., in hills NW of Middletown.

Monticello, estate, central Va., SE of Charlottesville, home (for 56 yrs.) and burial place of Thomas Jefferson, who designed mansion. Building materials prepared on estate and construction done largely by Jefferson's slaves. Mansion begun 1770, occupied 1772. Early example of American classic revival, it is owned by Thomas Jefferson Memorial Foundation. Near by is "Ash Lawn," Monroe's home.

Montluçon (mōlüsō'), town (pop. 45,535), Allier dept., central France, on Cher R. Metallurgical center. Has 15th–16th cent. houses, castle of dukes of Bourbon.

Montmagny (mōmänyē'), town (pop. 5,844), SE Que., Canada, on St. Lawrence R. and ENE of Quebec. Silk and rayon mills and woodworking.

Montmartre (mōmär'trù), hill in Paris, France, topped by Church of SACRÉ-CŒUR, on right bank of the Seine; highest point of Paris. Ancient quarter was long a favorite residence of bohemian world and is famous for its night life.

Montmorency (mōnt"mùren'sē, Fr. mōmôräsē'), French noble family. Most notable members were: **Mathieu, baron de Montmorency** (mätyü' bärō' dù), d. 1230, constable of France, called the Great Constable. Took part in battle of Bouvines (1214); fought Albigenses (1226). **Anne, duc de Montmorency** (än' dük' dù), 1493?–1567, constable of France. Captured with Francis I at Pavia (1525), he helped negotiate Francis's release and received governorship of Languedoc, which remained in his family until 1632. He took Metz from the Spanish (1552); was captured at Saint-Quentin (1557); sided with Guises in Wars of Religion; was killed in siege of Paris. His son, **Henri, duc de Montmorency** (ärē'), 1534–1614, marshal and constable of France, was known as count of Damville before 1579. Though a zealous Catholic, he was led by the murder of his relative COLIGNY to advocate a conciliatory policy toward the Huguenots. He adhered to Henry of Navarre in 1589.

Montmorency (mōnt"mùren'sē), village (pop. 5,817), S Que., Canada, on St. Lawrence R. and NE of Quebec. Power for Quebec and area is furnished by plant here at Montmorency Falls on Montmorency R. which flows from the Laurentian Mts. to the St. Lawrence R.

Montparnasse (mŏpärnäs'), quarter of Paris, France, on left bank of the Seine. Its noted cafés are centers of Parisian artistic and intellectual life.

Mont Pelée: see PELÉE.

Montpelier (mŏntpēl'yŭr), city (pop. 8,599), state cap. (since 1805), central Vt. on Winooski R. and NW of Barre; settled 1787. Produces granite, textiles, wood products, and machinery. Has supreme court with Vermont Historical Society Coll.

Montpelier, estate, central Va., NNW of Richmond; home of James Madison, built c.1760, now privately owned. Madison and his wife buried near by.

Montpellier (mŏpĕlyä'), city (pop. 80,673), cap. of Hérault dept., S France, near the Mediterranean; trade center for wines and brandy. A fief under counts of Toulouse after 8th cent., it passed in 13th cent. to kings of Majorca, from whom Philip VI of France bought it in 1349. It was a Huguenot center taken by Louis XIII in 1622. Its university was founded 1289. Famous faculty of medicine is traced to 10th cent.

Montpensier, Louise d'Orléans, duchesse de (lwēz' dôrlää düshĕs' dù mŏpäsyä'), 1627–93, French princess, called La Grande Mademoiselle; daughter of Gaston d'Orléans. A leader of the FRONDE, she relieved Orléans at the head of her troops and opened the gates of Paris to Condé's retreating soldiers (1652). Her love affair and secret marriage with LAUZUN ended in separation.

Montreal (mŏntrēôl'), city (pop. 1,021,520), S Que., Canada, on Montreal Isl. in St. Lawrence R. at foot of Mt. Royal. Largest city in Canada and its commercial, financial, and industrial center, it has excellent harbor at head of navigation on St. Lawrence R. and direct connections to Great Lakes via Lachine Canal. Major transshipment point with large grain elevators and cold-storage warehouses and mfg. of steel products, railroad equipment, machinery, paper, pulp, leather, and clothing. Visitors are attracted by its foreign air and many old buildings. Seat of McGill Univ. (nonsectarian, coed.; opened 1829), noted for graduate work in the physical sciences; and the **University of Montreal** (French language; R.C., pontifical; coed.). Site visited by Cartier (1535) and Champlain (1603). Settled 1642, it became a fur trade center. Fortified 1725, taken by British 1760, and briefly held by American forces 1775. Cap. of Upper Canada 1844–49. Population remains largely French.

Montreal North, N suburb of Montreal (pop. 14,081), S Que., Canada, on Montreal Isl.

Montreux (mŏtrŭ'), name of the adjacent communes of Montreux-Châtelard, Planches, and Veytaux (combined pop. 17,424), Vaud canton, SW Switzerland, on NE bank of L. of Geneva. Resort; chocolate mfg.

Montreux Convention, 1936, international agreement permitting Turkey to refortify DARDANELLES. Ratified by all signers of Treaty of Lausanne of 1923 except Italy.

Montrose, James Graham, 5th earl and 1st marquess of, 1612–50, Scottish nobleman, soldier. Leader in Bishops' Wars, he then supported Charles I from fear of a Presbyterian oligarchy. With highland troops he defeated Presbyterian army six times 1644–45. After king's defeat at Naseby he was unable to unite Scottish royalists and was finally hanged.

Montrose, city (pop. 4,964), SW Colo., on Uncompahgre R. and SE of Grand Junction. Near by are carnotite deposits (source of radium, uranium) and Black Canyon of the Gunnison Natl. Monument.

Monts, Pierre du Guast, comte de (pyĕr' dü gwäst' kŏt' dù mŏ'), c.1560–c.1630, French colonizer in North America, called the sieur de Monts. Patron of Samuel de Champlain. Planted first French colony in Canada at Port Royal (present Annapolis Royal) in 1605.

Mont-Saint-Michel (mŏ-sä-mēshĕl'), rocky isle (pop. 149) in English Channel, NW France, 1 mi. off Norman coast; accessible by land at low tide and connected with mainland by causeway. The cone-shaped rock is girt by medieval walls and towers; above rise the clustered buildings of the village and the celebrated Benedictine abbey, crowned by the abbey church. Abbey was founded 708 by Aubert, bishop of Auvranches, according to directions received from Archangel Michael in a vision. The six abbatial buildings facing the sea form unit called La Merveille (built 1203–28), one of the great treasures of Gothic architecture. In the Hundred Years War the abbey was successful in repulsing all English attempts to capture it.

Montserrat (mŏntsùrăt'), island (c.37 sq. mi.; pop. 14,-333), British West Indies; a presidency of Leeward Isls. colony; discovered by Columbus 1493.

Montserrat or **Monserrat** (both: mŏn"sùrăt', mŏnt"–), mountain of NE Spain, NW of Barcelona, rising abruptly to 4,054 ft. from a plain. Half-way up is a celebrated Benedictine monastery, a major shrine of pilgrimage. Only ruins are left of old monastery (11th cent.); new monastery dates from 19th cent. The Renaissance church contains black wooden image of the Virgin, carved, according to tradition, by St. Luke. In the Middle Ages the mountain, also called Monsalvat, was thought to have been the site of the castle of the Holy GRAIL. At Montserrat, St. Ignatius of Loyola vowed himself to the religious life.

Monza (mŏn'tsä), city (pop. 58,503), Lombardy, N Italy. Textile and machinery mfg. Has automobile races. Its cathedral (founded 6th cent.) contains iron crown of Lombardy, said to have been made from nails of Christ's cross. Charlemagne, Charles V, Napoleon I, and other emperors were crowned with it as kings of Italy.

mood or **mode,** in Latin INFLECTION, one of four major sets of forms of verbs. Three of them cross with the category of person and are subdivided by tenses: indicative (used normally), imperative (in commands), and subjunctive (in certain kinds of subordinated constructions). Fourth set, the infinitive, is nonpersonal. These names of moods are often used for similar categories in other languages.

Moodus, village in East Haddam town, S Conn., SE of Middletown. "Moodus noises," underground rumblings, are thought to be caused by minor earthquakes.

Moody, Dwight L(yman), 1837–99, American evangelist; associated after 1870 with Ira D. Sankey in evangelistic tours in U.S. and Great Britain. Founded Northfield Seminary (1879), Mt. Hermon School (1881), mission school (1889), now Moody Bible Inst.

Moody, Helen Wills: see WILLS, HELEN NEWINGTON.

Moody, William Vaughn, 1869–1910, American lyric poet and dramatist. Vigorous liberal and philosophic verse in *The Masque of Judgment* (1900) and *Poems* (1901). Best-known prose play is *The Great Divide* (1909; originally, *A Sabine Woman,* 1906).

moon, earth's only SATELLITE (diameter c.2,160 mi.). Earth-moon system revolves about sun in orbit of center of combined mass (c.2,900 mi. from earth's center). Moon revolves about earth in elliptical orbit; mean distance between their centers is 238,857 mi. Because moon's periods of rotation on axis and revolution about earth are equal, same side of moon is always toward earth but about 59% of its surface comes into view in a month owing to librations (rocking movements) of the moon. On the surface appear plains, mountains, craters. Apparent changes of shape result from variation in amount of visible surface as position changes relative to earth and sun. New moon phase occurs when moon is between earth and sun; full moon, when earth is between sun and moon. Month is measured by moon's revolution. Sidereal month, interval between recurrence of conjunction with any given star, averages c.27⅓ days. Synodic month, time required to bring moon again into same position relative to sun (e.g., interval from one new moon to next), averages c.29½ days. Difference results from earth's rotation, which brings earth forward in path around sun, making moon appear to move westward. Its revolution about earth makes moon seem to move eastward relative to constellations; because this apparent eastward movement is more rapid than that of sun, moon rises on an average 50½ min. later each night. See also ECLIPSE. See ill., p. 927.

Moon, Mountains of the: see RUWENZORI.

Mooney, Thomas J., 1883–1942, American labor agitator. Convicted of a bomb killing in 1916, he was sentenced to death. His case aroused international interest because of a wide belief in his innocence. In 1918 his sentence was commuted to life imprisonment, and in 1939 he was pardoned.

moonflower, tropical American night-blooming vine (*Calonyction aculeatum*) with white, fragrant flowers, similar to the morning-glory.

moonstone, variety of feldspar used as a gem. It has a milky bluish sheen.

Moore, Clement Clarke, 1779–1863, American poet, grad. Columbia, 1798. He is remembered for his "Visit from St. Nicholas" (1823), beginning " 'Twas the night before Christmas." A biblical scholar, he compiled Greek and Hebrew lexicon (1809).

Moore, George, 1852–1933, Irish novelist, noted for his brilliant style. His poetry and novels (e.g., *Esther Waters,* 1894) have been much admired, as have *Brook Kerith* (1916; on the life of Christ), *Héloïse and Abélard* (1921), and autobiographical works.

Moore, George Edward, 1873–, English philosopher; a neorealist opponent of idealism.

Moore, Henry, 1898–, English sculptor. His works are notable for balancing of mass with vacant spaces that emphasize three-dimensionality. Commissioned by British government in 1940 to make series of drawings in underground bomb shelters.

Moore, Sir John, 1761–1809, British general. Noted for brilliant retreat and victory (in which he was killed) at Coruña, Spain, in Peninsular War.

Moore, John Bassett, 1860–1947, American authority on international law. Was Assistant Secretary of State (1898) and represented the U.S. in various international affairs. Compiled many documents in international law.

Moore, Marianne, 1887–, American poet, acting editor of *Dial* (1925–29). Her precise, witty verse is distinguished by impeccably crisp style. Among her volumes are *Poems* (1921) and *Selected Poems* (1935).

Moore, Thomas, 1779–1852, Irish poet, best known for *Irish Melodies,* songs published 1808–34, including such favorites as "Believe Me if All Those Endearing Young Charms" and "Oft in the Stilly Night." His poetic romance *Lalla Rookh* (1817) was popular. He was Byron's close friend and biographer.

Moores Creek National Military Park: see NATIONAL PARKS AND MONUMENTS (table).

Moorestown, residential township (pop. 9,123), SW N.J., E of Camden. Has several 18th-cent. houses.

Mooresville, textile-mill town (pop. 7,121), W central N.C., N of Charlotte.

Moorhead, city (pop. 14,870), NW Minn., on Red R. opposite Fargo, N.Dak. Ships grain, potatoes, and dairy products. Seat of Concordia Col. (Evangelical Lutheran; coed.; 1891).

Moorish art and architecture: see MOSLEM ART AND ARCHITECTURE.

Moors, nomadic people of N Africa, once inhabitants of Mauretania. Converted to Islam in 8th cent., and became fanatic Moslems. Crossed into Spain in 711 and easily overran crumbling Visigothic kingdom of RODERICK. Spreading beyond Pyrenees into France, they were turned back at Tours by CHARLES MARTEL 732. Moors made TOLEDO, CÓRDOBA, and SEVILLE centers of learning and culture, but never had a strong central government. Christian reconquest of Spain began with recovery of Toledo (1085) by Alfonso VI, king of Leon and Castile, and ended with recovery of Granada by Ferdinand and Isabella in 1492. Moors were driven from Spain, leaving contributions to W

Europe in art, architecture, medicine, science, and learning well-nigh incalculable.

moose, largest of deer family (*Alce*), found in Canada, Alaska, N U.S. Two species: the American and the larger Alaska or Kenai moose. The moose has a heavy brown body, lighter-colored legs, and flattened, usually palmately branched antlers. Old World species is called ELK.

Moose Factory, trading post, NE Ont., Canada, on island in Moose R. near James Bay. Estab. 1671, destroyed c.1696, rebuilt 1730.

Moosehead Lake, 35 mi. long and 10 mi. wide, area 120 sq. mi., W Maine, N of Augusta. Largest lake in Maine. Center of resort region. Steamers link shore points. Source of Kennebec R.

Moose Jaw, city (pop. 24,355), S Sask., Canada, W of Regina. Railroad and trade center with oil refineries, grain elevators, stockyards, and flour, lumber, and woolen mills.

moraine (mürän', mō–), rock waste carried and deposited by a glacier. The great ice sheets of the Pleistocene left terminal moraines extending across North America and Europe.

Morales, Luis de (lwēs' dā mōrä'lĕs), c.1509–1586, Spanish painter of intense and melancholy religious works. Lived and worked in Badajoz.

morality play: see MIRACLE PLAY.

morals: see ETHICS.

Moran, Edward, 1829–1901, American painter of marine and historical subjects, b. England. Settled in U.S. in 1844. His brothers **Thomas Moran,** 1837–1926, and **Peter Moran,** 1841–1914, both painted landscapes; his sons **Edward Percy Moran,** 1862–1935, and **John Léon Moran,** 1864–1941, were genre painters.

Morat (môrä'), Ger. *Murten,* town (pop. 2,405), Fribourg canton, W Switzerland, on L. Morat. Swiss defeated CHARLES THE BOLD here 1476.

Moratín, Leandro Fernández de: see FERNÁNDEZ DE MORATÍN, LEANDRO.

Morava (mô'rävä), Ger. *March,* river, 227 mi. long, Czechoslovakia and Austria, rising in Sudetes and flowing generally S past Olmütz into the Danube near Bratislava. See also MARCHFELD.

Moravia, Alberto (älbĕr'tō mōrä'vyä), 1907–, Italian novelist, whose real name is Alberto Pincherle. Of his grimly realistic novels, best known is *The Woman of Rome* (1947).

Moravia (mürà'vēů, mō–), Czech *Morava,* Ger. *Mähren,* region, central Czechoslovakia. Chief cities: BRNO, OLMÜTZ, MORAVSKA, OSTRAVA, ZLIN. With Czech SILESIA, it formed until 1949 a single province (10,350 sq. mi.; pop. 3,134,614), now united with BOHEMIA. Drained by the Morava R., it is a hilly, fertile agr. region and has important industries (textiles, machinery, coal, metallurgy, shoes). The Moravians, a branch of W Slavs, settled here c.6th cent. By the 9th cent. their dukes ruled an empire including Bohemia, Silesia, S Poland, and N Hungary; Christianity was introduced 863 by SS CYRIL AND METHODIUS. The empire broke up in the 10th cent. and fell to the Magyars. After Emperor Otto I's victory over the Magyars (955), Moravia became a march of the Holy Roman Empire. From the 11th cent. it was in effect a crownland of the kingdom of Bohemia, with which it passed under Hapsburg rule in 1526 and became part of Czechoslavakia in 1918. The Moravian towns were largely Germanized after the 13th cent., while the rural population remained Czech. As a result of the Munich Pact (1938), Germany annexed Czech Silesia and part of Moravia. From 1939 to 1945 Bohemia and Moravia were a German "protectorate," but after World War II the pre-1938 boundaries were restored and most of the German-speaking population was expelled.

Moravia, resort village (pop. 1,480), W central N.Y., near Owasco L. and SW of Syracuse. Millard Fillmore was born near here.

Moravian Church, Renewed Church of the Brethren, or Unitas Fratrum, evangelical communion; the adherents are called United Brethren or Herrnhuters. Arose (1457) among followers of John Huss as Church of the Brotherhood. Consecration of a bishop (1467) caused break with Church of Rome. Persecution drove the Brethren from Bohemia. In 1722 a group took refuge in Saxony, at Herrnhut on estate of Graf von ZINZENDORF. Missionary effort carried movement to West Indies, North and South America, Asia, and Africa. In Pa., Bethlehem, Nazareth, and Lititz were founded c.1740 and became center of faith in America. Church has modified episcopacy and simple ritual.

Moravian College and **Moravian College for Women:** see BETHLEHEM, Pa.

Moravska Ostrava (mô′räfskä ô′strävä), Ger. *Mährisch Ostrau,* city (pop. 116,225), NE Moravia, Czechoslovakia; industrial center of coal-mining region. With several other adjacent communities, it forms Greater Ostrava (pop. c.180,000). Has iron and steel mills and produces rolling stock, machinery, ship and bridge parts, chemicals.

Moray, Scottish name: see MURRAY.

Moray Firth (mŭ′rē, –rā), inlet of North Sea, NE Scotland. Extends from Kinnairds Head, Aberdeenshire, to Duncansbay Head, Caithness.

Morayshire (mŭ′rēshĭr) or **Elginshire** (ĕl′gĭn-shĭr), maritime county (477 sq. mi.; pop. 48,211), NE Scotland; co. town Elgin. Interior hills devoted to grazing; coastal plain is heavily cultivated. Region saw much strife among early Picts.

Morbihan (môrbēä′), department (2,739 sq. mi.; pop. 506,884), NW France, in Brittany; cap. Vannes.

mordant (môr′dŭnt), substance used to make fast certain dyes on cloth. Either the mordant or colloid produced by it adheres to fiber, attracts and fixes an oppositely charged colloidal dye, forming an insoluble precipitate (a lake). Acid mordants are used with basic dyes and vice versa. Certain dyes not requiring mordant are made more vivid with it.

Mordecai (môr″dēkā′ī), guardian and uncle of ESTHER.

Mordred, Sir: see ARTHURIAN LEGEND.

Mordvinian Autonomous Soviet Socialist Republic (môrdvĭ′nēŭn), autonomous republic (10,080 sq. mi.; pop. 1,188,598), central European RSFSR, in uplands W of the Middle Volga; cap. Saransk. Primarily agr., it also has mineral resources (oil shale, peat, phosphorite). Population is 55% Russian, 40% Mordvinian, a Finnic people which adopted Russian culture and Greek Orthodox religion from Russian colonies estab. here in 16th cent.

More, Sir Anthony: see MORO, ANTONIO.

More, Hannah, 1745–1833, English author, a noted bluestocking. A founder of Religious Tract Society (1799). Her novel *Coelebs in Search of a Wife* (1808) was very popular in her day.

More, Paul Elmer, 1864–1937, American editor, essayist, and critic, a leader of "new humanists" and an authority on Greek philosophy. Edited the *Nation.* Chief works are *Shelburne Essays* (11 vols., 1904–21) and *The Greek Tradition* (5 vols., 1921–31).

More, Sir Thomas (St. Thomas More), 1478–1535, author of UTOPIA, English statesman and humanist, saint and martyr in the Roman Catholic Church. Rose in the favor of Henry VIII to become lord chancellor 1529, but he disapproved the king's divorce from Katharine of Aragon and retired in 1532. He was cleared of charges connected with Elizabeth BARTON, but he refused to subscribe to Act of Supremacy. He was imprisoned and finally beheaded on charge of treason. Canonized 1935. Feast: July 6.

Morea, Greece: see PELOPONNESUS.

Moréas, Jean (zhä′ môrääs′), 1856–1910, French poet, b. Athens. His name was originally Papadiamantopoulos. First a symbolist (*Les Syrtes,* 1884), he gradually turned to classic style, as in *Stances* (1899–1901) and in the drama *Iphigénie* (1903).

Moreau, Gustave (güstäv′ môrō′), 1826–98, French painter, known for his pictures of the weird and mystical. His house in Paris is now a state-owned museum of art.

Moreau, Jean Victor (zhä′ vēktôr′), 1763–1813, French general in FRENCH REVOLUTIONARY WARS. Won decisive victory over Austrians at Hohenlinden (1800). Opposed Napoleon, who exiled him. In 1813 he served with allies against Napoleon, was killed in battle.

Moreau (mŭrō′), river rising in NW S.Dak. and flowing 289 mi. E to the Missouri. Used in Missouri R. basin project.

Morehead City, resort and fishing town (pop. 5,144), E N.C., on Newport R. opposite Beaufort.

Morelia (môrā′lyä), city (pop. 44,304; alt. 6,187 ft.), cap. of Michoacán, W Mexico; founded as Valladolid (1541) by Viceroy Antonio de Mendoza. Chief manufactures are shawls, hats, flour, cotton goods, soap, beer, cigars, cigarettes, wine. Iturbide and Morelos y Pavón were born here.

Morelos (y Pavón), José María (hōsā′ märē′ä môrā′lōs ē pävōn′), 1765–1815, Mexican leader in the revolution against Spain, national hero. A liberal priest, he joined the revolution (1810), conducted a brilliant campaign in S, was elected generalissimo with chief executive's powers (1813). Captured by Iturbide's forces, he was shot.

Morelos (môrā′lōs), state (1,917 sq. mi.; pop. 268,-863), central Mexico; cap. and chief city CUERNAVACA. Mountainous, with broad semiarid valleys opening to the S, state is chiefly agr. State named in honor of Morelos y Pavón. Depredations of Zapata and regime of Carranza caused almost irreparable damage to sugar industry and agr. productivity.

Morenci (mŭren′sē), town (pop. 6,541), E Ariz., near N. Mex. line, on hillside around copper mines.

Moretto, Il (ēl môrĕt′tō), c.1498–1554, Italian painter of portraits and religious subjects, whose real name was Alessandro Bonvicino. Leading painter of Brescian school, teacher of Moroni. Influenced by the Venetians but developed own style, marked by cool and luminous coloring.

Morgagni, Giovanni Battista (jōvän′nē bättē′stä môrgä′nyē), 1682–1771, Italian anatomist, noted for studies of effect of disease on body.

Morgan, American family of financiers and philanthropists. **Junius Spencer Morgan,** 1813–90, headed international banking enterprise which handled most of British funds invested in U.S. His son, **J(ohn) Pierpont Morgan,** 1837–1913, built family fortunes into a colossal financial and industrial empire. Increased his railroad holdings. Formed in 1901 U.S. Steel Corp., first billion-dollar corporation in world. Subject to much criticism and held as popular symbol of wealth. He dispensed numerous philanthropies and was a renowned art collector. **J(ohn) Pierpont Morgan,** 1867–1943, became active head of house of Morgan when his father died in 1913. Helped finance World War I. Like his father, he disliked publicity; continued philanthropies. His sister, **Anne Morgan,** 1873–1952, a leading feminist, was devoted to philanthropic and civic organizations.

Morgan, Daniel, 1736–1802, American Revolutionary general. Captured in attack on Quebec. Exchanged 1776. Took part in Saratoga campaign. Defeated British at Cowpens, S.C. (1780).

Morgan, Sir Henry, 1635?–1688, British buccaneer. Led Barbadoes pirates c.1666, but was later given British authority for his exploits. Knighted as a hero (1674). Made lieutenant governor of Jamaica.

Morgan, John Hunt, 1825–64, Confederate general. Noted for daring raids in Civil War; most famous one in 1863 through Ky., Ind., and Ohio.

Morgan, J(ohn) Pierpont, and **Junius Spencer Morgan:** see MORGAN, family.

Morgan, Justin: see JUSTIN MORGAN.

Morgan, Lewis H(enry), 1818–81, American anthropologist. Originally a lawyer, he became interested in N.Y. Indians and wrote notable report on Iroquois League. His concern with social organization and social evolution was shown in his *Ancient Society* (1877) and other works.

Morgan, Thomas Hunt, 1866–1945, American zoologist. Won 1933 Nobel Prize in Physiology and Medicine for theory that hereditary unit characters are dependent upon certain factors, or genes, in the chromosome, the behavior of which he studied and mapped.

Morgan, resort city (pop. 1,064), N Utah, on Weber R. and SE of Ogden. Trade center in Weber R. project. Also Morgan City.

Morgan City, city (pop. 9,759), S La., port on Atchafalaya R. at Berwick Bay. Handles oil, sulphur, chemicals, and shells, and has shipyards and sea food processing and shipping.

Morgan le Fay: see ARTHURIAN LEGEND.

Morgan Library: see PIERPONT MORGAN LIBRARY.

Morganton, town (pop. 8,311), W N.C., ENE of Asheville. Mfg. of textiles, hosiery, furniture, and leather products.

Morgantown, city (pop. 25,525), N W.Va., on Monongahela R. and S of Pittsburgh; settled 1767. Coal-mining center with mfg. of glass and chemicals. Seat of West Virginia Univ. (land-grant; state supported; coed.; opened 1867).

Morgarten (mȯr′gärtŭn), mountain slope, central Switzerland, c.5 mi. N of Schwyz. Here in 1315 a small Swiss force decisively defeated the Austrians, thus paving the way for Swiss independence.

Morgenstern, Christian (krĭs′tyän mȯr′gŭnshtĕrn), 1871–1914, German poet-philosopher. Though influenced by mysticism and theosophy, he is best known for his whimsical humor. *Galgenlieder* (1905) and *Palmström* (1910) are volumes of grotesque verse. *Ich und du* (1911) contains love lyrics.

Morgenthau, Henry (mȯr′gŭnthô), 1856–1946, American banker, diplomat, and philanthropist, b. Germany. Ambassador to Turkey (1913–16). Raised funds for Near East relief (1919–21); later directed resettlement of Greek refugees. An incorporator of Red Cross in U.S. His son, **Henry Morgenthau, Jr.,** 1891–, was Secretary of the Treasury (1934–45). Supervised huge sale of government bonds, advocated international monetary stabilization. Authored famous plan for reconverting German industries to agr. and the service trades.

Moriah (mōrī′ŭ), place where Abraham was to sacrifice Isaac. Gen. 22.2. May be same as Mt. Moriah.

Moriah, Mount, biblical name of hill of E Jerusalem; site of Solomon's Temple. 2 Chron. 3.1.

Moriscos (mŏrĭs′kōz), Spanish Moors converted to Christianity after Christian reconquest of Spain. Moslems were generally tolerated before 1492, but later faced the choice of conversion or expulsion. Many converts secretly continued to practice Islam. Growing intolerance led to Moorish uprisings, which were severely suppressed (1500–1502, 1568–71). In 1609 all Moriscos were expelled from Spain. This inhuman measure also had evil consequences for Spain's economy.

Morison, Samuel Eliot, 1887–, American historian. Works include *Admiral of the Ocean Sea* (1942), biography of Christopher Columbus which won Pulitzer Prize 1943; official *Tercentennial History of Harvard College and University* (3 vols., 1930–36); and, by U.S. appointment, official *History of United States Naval Operations in World War II* (5 of 14 projected vols., 1947–).

Morison, Stanley, 1889–, English typographer and journalist; typographical consultant to Cambridge Univ. Press, English Monotype Corp., and the London *Times* (1929–44). He became editor of *The Times Literary Supplement* in 1945.

Morisot, Berthe (bĕrt′ mȯrēzō′), 1841–95, French impressionist painter. She was influenced by Manet,

then Monet. Typical is *La Toilette* (Art Inst., Chicago).

Morland, George, 1763–1804, English genre and landscape painter; pupil of his father, Henry Morland (c.1730–1797), a portrait painter. Produced over 4,000 pictures. His masterpiece, *Interior of a Stable,* is in Natl. Gall., London.

Morley, Christopher, 1890–, American novelist and familiar essayist, a founder and editor (1924–40) of the *Saturday Review of Literature.* His novels and studies, usually in a light vein, include *Parnassus on Wheels* (1917), *Where the Blue Begins* (1922), and *Kitty Foyle* (1939).

Morley, John, 1838–1923, English statesman and man of letters. Edited *Fortnightly Review* 1867–83. Secretary of state for India 1905–10; lord president of the council 1910–14. Author of a number of fine biographies.

Morley, Sylvanus Griswold, 1883–1948, American archaeologist. Specialist in Middle American archaeology and in Maya hieroglyphics.

Morley, Thomas, b. 1557 or 1558, d. 1603, English composer, noted mainly for his madrigals and settings of Shakspere's songs. He also wrote anthems, services, Latin motets, and a treatise on theory.

Mormons, popular name of members of Church of Jesus Christ of LATTER-DAY SAINTS, founded by Joseph SMITH after golden tablets of Book of Mormon had been revealed to him at Palmyra, N.Y. He gathered followers rapidly and in 1831 estab. group at Kirtland, Ohio. Conflict with "Gentile" neighbors in Mo. caused them to move to a new Zion at Nauvoo, Ill., but again hostility arose, culminating in mob murder in 1846 of Smith and his brother Hyrum. Mormons went W and settled (1847) in valley of Great Salt Lake. After many hardships they, under Brigham Young's brilliant guidance, created a self-sustaining economy and weathered trouble with neighbors as well as with U.S. government. Young's announcement of doctrine of plural marriage caused Congress to pass anti-polygamy laws and prevented admission of Utah as state until 1896, after Pres. Wilford Woodruff in 1890 accepted laws as binding in secular life.

Mornay, Philippe de, seigneur du Plessis-Marly (fēlēp′ dü mȯrnä′ sänyûr′ dü plĕsē′-märlē′), 1549–1623, French Protestant leader and apologist in the Wars of Religion.

morning-glory, annual or perennial plant, usually climbing, of genus *Ipomoea.* Its funnel-shaped flowers (variously colored) open in the morning.

Morny, Charles, duc de (shärl′ dük′ dü mȯrnē′), 1811–65, French statesman; natural son of Hortense de Beauharnais and Joseph, comte de Flahaut (a natural son of Talleyrand). Helped place his half-brother Napoleon III on throne; played important role in Second Empire.

Moro [Span.,= Moor], one of a group of Moslem natives of Mindanao and Sulu Archipelago in Philippines and of Borneo, who were converted in great missionary extension of Islam from India in 15th and 16th cent. Not ethnically or linguistically units, they are of largely Malayan stock. Have long maintained enmity toward Christian Filipinos. Chief occupation is agriculture; industries are cloth weaving, pottery making, boatbuilding, metal crafts.

Moro, Antonio (äntō′nyō mō′rō), c.1512–c.1575, Flemish portraitist, court painter to the Hapsburgs; also called Sir Anthony More. Visited Spain, Portugal, and England (where he painted Mary Tudor).

Morocco (mȯrō′kō), sultanate (c.160,000 sq. mi.; pop. 9,850,000), N Africa, on the Mediterranean and the Atlantic. Bordered by Spanish Sahara (S) and by Algeria (S and E). Nominally ruled by the sultan, who is mainly important as religious leader of the Moslems. Politically divided into three parts: French Morocco (c.151,000 sq. mi.; pop. 8,617,387), a protectorate and since 1946 an associated state of the French Union, with cap. at RABAT; Spanish Morocco (c.7,600 sq. mi.; pop. 1,082,009), a protectorate (roughly coextensive with the RIF), with cap. at TETUÁN; and the international zone of TANGIER. Coastal enclaves directly governed by Spain are CEUTA, MELILLA, and IFNI. Population is concentrated on coastal plains, where grains, citrus fruit, olives, and grapes are grown. Atlas Mts. occupy central Morocco and contain valuable mineral resources (esp. phosphates, shipped mainly from CASABLANCA). The area was roughly coextensive with ancient Roman district of MAURETANIA. Islam was brought by the Arabs, who first invaded Morocco in 683. Independent state was first estab. 788; Moroccan power reached its height under the great Berber dynasties of the ALMORAVIDES and the ALMOHADES. European encroachments began 1415 with Portuguese capture of Ceuta and subsequent seizure of most of the main ports. Decline of Portuguese influence began with their defeat by the Moors at the battle of ALCAZARQUIVIR (1578). The Alouites, the present ruling house, came to power in 1660, succeeding the Saadian or first Sherifian dynasty. Like the other BARBARY STATES, Morocco was a pirate base 17th–19th cent. In 19th cent. its strategic and economic importance excited the interest of European powers, and an explosive situation was soon created by intense rivalry. A temporary settlement was reached by Algeciras Conference (1906), which assured protection of German investments and gave France and Spain authority to police Morocco. But peace was soon broken by several clashes, notably the AGADIR incident. In 1911 Germany agreed to a French protectorate in Morocco in exchange for French territory in Africa. French and Spanish protectorates were estab. 1912. In World War II, French Morocco remained loyal to the Vichy regime after fall of France (1940). Allied forces landed at major ports on Nov. 8, 1942, and on Nov. 11 all resistance ended. After the war an independence movement won the active support of Sultan Sidi Mohammed, but it was firmly opposed by France and Spain.

Morone (mōrō'nā), name of two Italian religious painters of Veronese school. **Domenico Morone,** b. c.1442, d. after 1517, and his son, **Francesco Morone,** 1471–1529, were both influenced by Mantegna.

Moroni, Giovanni Battista (jōvän'nē bät-tē'stä mōrō'nē), c.1525–1578, portrait painter of Brescian school; pupil of Il Moretto. Works have much force.

moronity: see FEEBLE-MINDEDNESS.

Moronobu (Moronobu Hishigawa) (mōrō'nōbōo), fl. 1659–95, Japanese genre artist; pioneer in use of wood block for book illustration and popular sheet prints. Illustrated book of etiquette and feminine hygiene.

Morpheus (môr'fēūs, môr'fūs) [Gr.,= shaper], in Greek and Roman mythology, god of dreams; son of Sleep. He brought dreams of human forms.

morphine, derivative of OPIUM.

Morphy, Paul Charles (môr'fē), 1837–84, American chess player. At 21 he was acknowledged the greatest player in world. After 1859 mental instability ended his chess play.

morrice dance: see MORRIS DANCE.

Morrill, Justin Smith (mŏ'rŭl), 1810–98, U.S. Representative (1855–67) and Senator (1867–98) from Vt. Best known for Morrill Act (1862), which provided for granting of public lands for establishment of educational institutions.

Morrilton, city (pop. 5,483), W central Ark., on Arkansas R., in livestock and cotton area. Has cotton mill, sawmill, and meat-packing plant.

Morris, family of American landowners and statesmen. **Richard Morris,** d. 1672, purchased land from Dutch in what became N.Y. His son, **Lewis Morris,** 1671–1746, first governor of N.J. (1738–46) after its separation from N.Y., became first lord of N.Y. family manor, called Morrisania, in 1697. His namesake and grandson, **Lewis Morris,** 1726–98, signer of the Dec-

laration of Independence, was prominent in N.Y. affairs before and after American Revolution. His half brother, **Gouverneur Morris** (gŭvŭrnēr', –nōōr'), 1752–1816, aided the patriot cause in American Revolution, assisted in handling finances of new government (1781–85), and helped write the Constitution.

Morris, Robert, 1734–1806, American banker, "financier of American Revolution," signer of Declaration of Independence, b. England. Superintendent of finance (1781–84). Founded national bank.

Morris, William, 1834–96, English artist, writer, printer, and socialist. Studied painting with D. G. Rossetti and was influenced by Ruskin and Burne-Jones. In 1861 he estab. Morris and Company, whose furnishings and art objects refreshed Victorian taste. He indirectly sponsored the arts and crafts movement by using medieval craft techniques in his factory. Study of the medieval also influenced his verse tales—*The Earthly Paradise* (3 vols., 1868–70) and the epic poem *Sigurd the Volsung* (1876). He spent his last 20 years working for socialism, writing *A Dream of John Ball* (1888), *News from Nowhere* (1891), and *Socialism: Its Growth and Outcome* (1893). His last artistic venture was the improvement of printing through the Kelmscott Press.

Morris, city (pop. 6,926), NE Ill., on Illinois R. and SW of Chicago, in coal and clay area. Shipping center with paper and leather products.

Morris Brown College: see ATLANTA, Ga.

morris dance or **morrice dance,** rustic dance of N England, derived from country festivals (e.g., May Day) as early as 15th cent. Main dancers were Robin Hood, Maid Marian, hobbyhorse, and fool.

Morris Island: see CHARLESTON, S.C.

Morris Jesup, Cape, northernmost land point in the world, N Greenland, in Peary Land. At lat. 83°39'N, it is 440 mi. from North Pole.

Morrison, Herbert Stanley, 1888–, British statesman. Home secretary and minister of home security 1940–45. In Labour government he was lord president of privy council and leader in House of Commons (1945–51) and foreign secretary (1951).

Morrison Cave State Park, SW Mont., on Jefferson R. and SE of Butte. Large limestone cave was in former Lewis and Clark Cavern Natl. Monument.

Morristown. 1 Residential town (pop. 17,124), N N.J., WNW of Newark; settled c.1710. Mfg. of electrical and metal products, clothing, and paving materials; greenhouses. Washington made Morristown his winter hq. (1776–77, 1779–80) during the Revolution. Morristown Natl. Historical Park (see NATIONAL PARKS AND MONUMENTS, table) is here. Town's old buildings include Jabez Campfield House where Alexander Hamilton courted Elizabeth Schuyler 1779–80. S. F. B. Morse and Alfred Vail worked here. Near by is Seeing Eye establishment for training dogs. **2** Town (pop. 13,019), E Tenn., ENE of Knoxville, settled 1783. Dairy, poultry, and tobacco center. Cherokee Dam on Holston R. and Douglas Dam on French Broad R. are near by.

Morrisville, borough (pop. 6,787), SE Pa., on Delaware R. opposite Trenton, N.J. Washington had hq. here, Dec. 8–14, 1776. Near by is Pennsbury, William Penn's manor (reconstructed 1946). Here is one of largest steel plants in nation.

Morro Castle (mô'rō), three forts in West Indies: (1) at entrance of harbor of Havana, Cuba, erected 1589; (2) at entrance of harbor of Santiago de Cuba, taken by American forces in Spanish-American War, 1898; (3) on harbor of San Juan, Puerto Rico.

Morrow, Dwight W(hitney), 1873–1931, American diplomat. Ambassador to Mexico (1927–30).

Morse, Jedidiah, 1761–1826, American Congregational clergyman. Opposed Unitarianism. Wrote series of geography textbooks that were widely used. His son, **Samuel Finley Breese Morse,** 1791–1872, was an inventor and artist. In portrait painting especially he gained considerable reputation and was a founder of the National Academy of Design (1825). He invented the electric telegraph, devised MORSE CODE, and experimented with submarine cable telegraphy. His brother, **Sidney Edwards Morse,** 1794–1871, was a journalist, inventor, and geographer. With a brother, R. C. Morse, he founded (1823) the *New-York Observer.* Coinventor (c.1839) of cerography, method of making stereotype plates; perfected the bathometer (1866). Edited and wrote geography textbooks.

Morse code [for S. F. B. Morse], an arbitrary set of signals used on TELEGRAPH. International code is a simplified form used in radio telegraphy. American Morse differs from international in 11 letters, in all numerals except numeral 4, and in punctuation. Unit of code is *dot,* representing a very brief depression of telegraph key; *dash* is three times as long. Message is translated through combination of dots and dashes representing letters, numbers, punctuation, and pauses between letters and words.

mortar, in warfare, field piece which fires projectiles at a high trajectory; mostly used by infantry because of ease of handling and emplacement.

Mortimer, English noble family. **Roger de Mortimer, 1st earl of March,** 1287?–1330, opposed EDWARD II and the Despensers in wars of 1321–22. Escaped to France where Queen ISABELLA became his mistress. They invaded England and forced Edward II to abdicate (1326). Virtually ruled England until EDWARD III had him seized, tried, and executed. His great-grandson, **Edmund de Mortimer, 3d earl of March** and **1st earl of Ulster,** 1351–81, married Philippa, granddaughter of Edward III. This marriage led to claim to throne by house of YORK. His son, **Roger de Mortimer, 4th earl of March** and **2d earl of Ulster,** 1374–98, was proclaimed heir presumptive by Richard II in 1385. He was killed fighting in Ireland. His son, **Edmund de Mortimer, 5th earl of March** and **3d earl of Ulster,** 1391–1425, succeeded his father as heir presumptive to the throne. Imprisoned (1399) after the revolution of Henry IV, he was released by Henry V (1413) and served in the French Wars. His death ended the male line. He refused to aid plots to put him on the throne, including those of his uncle, **Sir Edmund de Mortimer,** 1376–1409?. Allied himself with Owen Glendower and the Percy family against Henry IV.

mortmain [Fr.,= dead hand] (môrt'mān"), ownership of land by religious, charitable, or business corporation. As imperishable legal entity such body can hold and increase property to detriment of state in taxes and other dues. In 13th cent. Church holdings led to conflict between Church and state; by 19th cent. rights were greatly restricted. Business corporations have generally been freed from restrictions.

Morton, James Douglas, 4th earl of, d. 1581, regent of Scotland (1572–78). A principal in murder of David Rizzio, he was later convicted and beheaded for his part in the murder of Lord Darnley.

Morton, Sarah Wentworth, 1759–1846, American poet, long reputed the author of the first American novel, *The Power of Sympathy* (1789), now generally credited to William Hill BROWN.

Morton, Thomas, fl. 1622–47, British trader and adventurer. Pilgrims, disliking him for his "scandalous" revelry at Merry Mount and his rival trade with the Indians, arrested him and sent him to England.

Morton, William Thomas Green, 1819–68, American dentist and physician. Demonstrated ether anesthesia (1846) at Massachusetts General Hospital.

mosaic (mōzā'ĭk), art of producing surface ornament by inlaying colored pieces of marble, glass, tile, or other material. In Italy and the Roman colonies floor patterns were produced both by large slabs of marble in contrasting colors and by small marble tesserae or cubes. Tessera floors varied from simple geometrical patterns in black and white to huge designs of figures or animals. Glass mosaics were used to decorate walls of ancient basilicas. The craft reached perfection in 6th cent. at Byzantium (Constantinople), where gold mosaics were extensively used to decorate Hagia Sophia. In the West, Ravenna became the center of Byzantine mosaic, 5th–6th cent. Revival of the art in Italy, 11th–13th cent., produced such beautiful mural works as those of St. Mark's Church, Venice. Rise of fresco decoration in early 14th cent. in Italy caused decline of mosaic. Modern workers use ancient system (setting each piece by hand in the damp cement mortar) as well as a new method of fastening the tesserae with glue on a paper cartoon drawn in reverse and then transferring to the mortar.

Mosby, John Singleton (mōz'bē), 1833–1916, Confederate partisan leader. His Partisan Rangers raided Union cavalry, communications, and supplies. Famous feat was capture of E. H. Stoughton at Fairfax Courthouse in 1863.

Moscow (mŏ'skou, mŏ'skō), Rus. *Moskva,* city (125 sq. mi.; pop. c.5,100,000), cap. of USSR and of RSFSR, in central European Russia and on the Moskva R. It is the largest city and the largest industrial concentration of the USSR, producing 15% of the total Soviet output (steel, machinery, automobiles, aircraft, rolling stock, chemicals, textiles); a major transportation and communications center; hq. of the Communist party. Has Lomonosov Univ. (founded 1755); Soviet Acad. of Sciences; numerous technical schools; several famous theaters, notably the Moscow Art Theatre and the Bolshoi Theater (opera and ballet); Tretyakov art gallery and other museums. See of the patriarch of the Russian Orthodox Church. First mentioned 1147, Moscow was made c.1271 the seat of a principality under Daniel, son of Grand Duke Alexander Nevsky of Vladimir-Suzdal. Moscow rose to commercial importance. In the 14th cent. the grand dukes of Vladimir made it their cap. and took the title grand dukes of Moscow or Muscovy. IVAN III and VASILY III enlarged the state, which under them became identical with Great RUSSIA. Moscow was twice burned by the Tatars (1381, 1572), was briefly held by the Poles in the Time of Troubles (liberated by a volunteer army under Prince Pozharski, 1612), and was occupied by Napoleon I in Sept., 1812. A few days later, a fire broke out, burned the entire city except its few stone buildings, and forced the French to begin their disastrous retreat. It probably was started accidentally by French looters. From 1713 to 1918 St. Petersburg superseded Moscow as cap. of Russia. Moscow doubled its population between World Wars I and II and underwent considerable modernization. A subway system was opened 1935; huge housing projects were undertaken. Construction of the Palace of the Soviets (planned to reach 1,300 ft. in height) was interrupted by World War II, when Moscow nearly was captured by a two-pronged German drive (Dec., 1941). The heart of Moscow is Red Square, which contains the 16th-cent. Cathedral of St. Basil, one of the most imposing and exuberant examples of Russian architecture, and the mausoleum of Lenin and Stalin. Red Square abuts on one side on the KREMLIN, the nerve center of the Soviet Union, and on the other side on the old Kitaigorod [Chinatown] dist., once the merchant quarter and now the site of many public buildings. Moscow is surrounded by a belt of large parks and of suburbs.

Moscow (mŏs'kō), city (pop. 10,593), NW Idaho, at Wash. line N of Lewiston; founded 1871. Shipping and processing center for wheat area. Seat of Univ. of Idaho (land-grant, state supported; coed.; opened 1892); pioneered in student-cooperative living.

Moscow Art Theatre, world-famous Russian repertory theater founded (1898) by STANISLAVSKY and Nemirovich-Danchenko. Greatly influenced theaters throughout the world (esp. by Chekhov productions).

Moscow Conferences, four meetings (1941–45) at Moscow. At first (Sept.–Oct., 1941) Great Britain and U.S. planned lend-lease aid to Russia. At second

(Oct., 1943) Britain, U.S., and USSR pledged formation of UN. At third (Oct., 1944) Churchill and Stalin made agreements respecting Poland, Bulgaria, and Yugoslavia. For fourth conference (Dec., 1945), see FOREIGN MINISTERS, COUNCIL OF.

Moseley, Henry Gwyn Jeffreys (mōz'lē), 1887–1915, English physicist. His brilliant research led to his arrangement of chemical elements according to atomic numbers; this resolved the few discrepancies inherent in Mendelejeff's system (see PERIODIC LAW). Moseley was killed at Gallipoli in World War I.

Moselle (mōzĕl'), department (2,405 sq. mi.; pop. 622,- 145), NE France, in LORRAINE; cap. Metz.

Moselle (mōzĕl'), Ger. *Mosel*, river, 320 mi. long, E France and W Germany, rising in Vosges mts. and flowing N past Épinal, Toul, and Metz, then along German-Luxembourg frontier, past Trier, and into the Rhine at Coblenz. German section of valley has many old castles and celebrated vineyards.

Moses (mō'–), lawgiver of Israel, the prophet who led his people out of bondage in Egypt to edge of Canaan, the Promised Land. Through Moses, God gave the Ten Commandments, the criminal code, and liturgical law to the people; these are called Mosaic Law. Moses' story, including his dramatic rescue from the bulrushes and his divine calling at the burning bush is told in the books of Exodus, Leviticus, Numbers, and Deuteronomy. Authorship of these and Genesis (collectively the Pentateuch) ascribed to him. Moses mentioned throughout Bible. Among the PSEU-DEPIGRAPHA is the Assumption of Moses.

Moses, Anna Mary Robertson, 1860–, American painter known as Grandma Moses. A farmer's wife, she began painting in her 70's; her so-called American primitives depict scenes of farm life.

Moskva (mūskvä'), river, 315 mi. long, central European RSFSR, flowing E, past Moscow, into Oka R. Connected with the Volga by Moscow Canal (80 mi. long), below which it is navigable (April–Nov.).

Moslem: see ISLAM.

Moslem art and architecture. The art which the no-madic Moslems brought to the lands around the Mediterranean in the 7th cent. was purely ornamental and lacked a definite building style. Local styles, mainly Christian (i.e., Syrian, Byzantine, or Coptic), were used as a basis on which to display surface decorations, chiefly of geometrical design. In 7th and 8th cent. great mosques were built, including those at Cairo, Damascus, and Córdoba. In 11th and 12th cent. Egypt became the center of architectural activity; here a distinctive tomb mosque was developed and elaborate minarets were built. The same period saw flowering of Moorish style in Spain, chief examples of which are the GIRALDA tower and palace of ALHAMBRA. Spanish art subsequent to expulsion (1492) of Moors continued to reflect Moorish influence (see MUDEJAR). Persian art evolved a distinctive MOSQUE type (e.g., Blue Mosque at Tabriz, 1437–68) and dominated native traditions in India to produce such structures as the TAJ MAHAL. The Turks added Moslem surface adornment to Byzantine architecture; their greatest architect in the style was SINAN. In all Moslem styles the arch (see *ill.*, p. 47) occurs in many variations: pointed, multifoil, ogee, and horseshoe; interior ornamentation includes ceramic wainscots and stucco wall carvings. In minor arts (e.g., metalwork, pottery making, rug weaving), as in architecture, the emphasis is on ornament, which is based on the arabesque, intertwined bands, and the flowing Arabic script.

Moslem League, political organization of India, founded 1906. Led by JINNAH after 1934. In 1940 it demanded creation of PAKISTAN, opposed by INDIAN NATIONAL CONGRESS. Won most of the Moslem vote in 1946 elections and forced the acceptance of separate Moslem state in 1947.

Mosley, Sir Oswald (Ernald), 1896–, British fascist leader. Organized (1932) the British Union of Fas-

cists. Interned 1940–43. After World War II he attempted to revive the movement.

mosque (mŏsk), building for worship used by the Moslem faith. Certain mosques, called madrasahs, also serve as theological schools. Essential elements of mosque design are the *maksoura* (prayer hall with the *mihrab* or prayer niche, which indicates direction of Mecca); the *dikka* (platform for services) near which is the mimbar or pulpit; and a large court with minarets at its corners, a central fountain, and arcaded porticoes. First domical mosque was that of Omar at Jerusalem, built 687, but such mosques were not commonly built until about 13th cent. Moorish school produced the huge mosque at Córdoba, Spain (built 8th–10th cent.). Persian mosques are characterized by pointed bulbous domes and gorgeous tile decoration. Turkish school converted Byzantine architecture to Islamic uses, making a notable model of HAGIA SOPHIA; another superb monument achieved at Constantinople was mosque of Suleiman, built 1550–57 by the architect Sinan. Indian school retained bulbous domes and round minarets of Persian school but used stone and marble for exteriors rather than traditional Persian tile sheathing. Under the Moguls were built such magnificent mosques as Pearl Mosque at Agra.

mosquito (mŭskē'tō), insect of fly family, of almost world-wide distribution. Female pierces skin, injects own salivary fluid, sucks blood of humans and many animals. Usually lays eggs in stagnant water. Yellow fever, malaria, and other diseases are transmitted by bite of certain species. See *ill.*, p. 469.

Mosquito Coast, Span., *Mosquitia* (mōskētē'ä), region, never exactly delimited, c.40 mi. wide extending from San Juan R. in Nicaragua N along coast into NE Honduras. Name is derived from Mosquito Indians in area over whom Great Britain estab. protective kingdom at Bluefields (1678). British seized San Juan del Norte in 1848, causing Nicaraguan and U.S. protest, and expansion was checked by Clayton-Bulwer Treaty. In 1860 autonomy of Mosquito Kingdom was secured by a treaty between Nicaragua and Great Britain, but in 1894 it was forcibly incorporated into Nicaragua. N part is still claimed by Honduras.

Moss (môs), city (pop. 17,415), co. seat of Ostfold co., SE Norway, on E shore of Oslo Fjord. Shipyards, sawmills, foundries; seaside resort. Personal union of Sweden and Norway was signed here Aug. 14, 1814.

moss, small primitive plant of class Musci of world-wide distribution. Usually characterized by tufted growth, mosses are often evergreen and some are creeping, others erect. One moss, SPHAGNUM, is a source of peat. Club moss, reindeer moss, Spanish moss, and flowering moss or pyxie, are unrelated.

Mossadegh, Mohammed (mōsädĕkh'), 1880–, Iranian statesman, leader of National Front party; premier (1951–). His nationalizing of the British-owned oil industry in 1951 led to a break in diplomatic relations with Great Britain and international repercussions. Received dictatorial powers from the Majlis, 1952–53. In trying to do away with the limited power of the shah he was opposed by the powerful Moslem leader, speaker of the Majlis, Ayatollah Kashani.

Mostar (mô'stär), city (pop. 23,239), Yugoslavia; chief city of Hercegovina.

most-favored-nation clause, provision in commercial treaties that the signatory will enjoy benefits equal to those accorded to any other state. Clauses may be unilateral (i.e., only one of the signatories receives favored treatment) or bilateral. Many Asiatic countries were bound to Western nations by unilateral clauses, but in recent years such clauses have usually been bilateral.

Mosul (mō'sul, mōsōōl'), city (pop. 203,273), N Iraq, on Tigris R., opposite ruins of Nineveh and S of Tepe Gawra. After c.750 it was chief center of N Mesopotamia. Occupied by British in 1918, formally renounced by Turkey in 1926. Inhabited mainly by Arabs. Once known for fine cotton goods called muslins from its name. Near by are large oil fields.

motet, name given to an important musical form of the 13th cent. and to a different form which originated in the Renaissance. The medieval motet was usually a three-voice composition arranged in a brief re-iterated rhythmic pattern. Each part had a separate text; sometimes both French and Latin, and sacred and secular subject matter were mingled in one motet. The second voice was called *motetus* [from Fr. *mot* = word], hence the term motet. The Renaissance motet had a single Latin text, with four to six voices, and was free from 13th-cent. rhythmic rigidity. The peak of this form is reached in the six motets of Bach. Since his time, the term motet has been applied to almost any kind of sacred choral polyphony but usually refers to the unaccompanied Latin motets used in the Roman Catholic Church.

moth, any of insect group comprising with BUTTERFLY group the order Lepidoptera. See also CLOTHES MOTH; CODLING MOTH; CUTWORM; GYPSY MOTH; SILKWORM.

Mother Lode, belt of gold-bearing quartz, central Calif., E of Sacramento and San Joaquin rivers and W of the Sierra Nevada. Sometimes limited to strip c.70 mi. long and 1–6½ mi. wide, running NW from Mariposa. Discovery of placer gold on South Fork of American R. led to 1848 rush.

mother-of-pearl or **nacre** (nā′kùr), iridescent substance secreted by mantle and lining shells of some mollusks, e.g., pearl oyster, pearl mussel, abalone.

Motherwell and Wishaw (wī′shô), burgh (pop. 68,137), Lanarkshire, Scotland. In coal and iron region, it has important steel industry and other mfg.

motion. A body in act of changing its position relative to another body is said to be in motion relative to that body. Thus passenger in moving car, though at rest in relation to car, is in motion relative to earth; bodies in motion on earth are also in motion relative to ether through which earth is moving (if ether is considered stationary or moving at velocity other than that of earth). Newton's **laws of motion:** (1) a body remains in a state of rest or of uniform motion in a straight line unless compelled by some external force acting upon it to change that state; (2) a change in momentum is proportional to the force causing the change and takes place in the direction in which the force is acting, or the increase or decrease in velocity is proportional to the force; and (3) to every action there is an equal and opposite reaction. These laws and that of universal gravitation continued to serve as basic principles of dynamics, maintaining their importance through times of discovery and hypothesis which led to Einstein's theory of relativity.

motion pictures: see MOVING PICTURES.

Motley, John Lothrop, 1814–77, American historian and diplomat. Known for *The Rise of the Dutch Republic* (3 vols., 1856) and *The Life and Death of John of Barneveld* (1874). Served as minister to Austria (1861–67) and to Great Britain (1869–70).

Moton, Robert Russa (mō′tùn), 1867–1940, American Negro educator. He was commandant (1890–1915) of Hampton Inst. and afterwards principal of Tuskegee Inst., from which he retired as president in 1935. He received Harmon (1930) and Spingarn (1932) awards.

motor, electric, machine which transforms electrical energy into mechanical energy. Its function reverses that of generator, but is based on same general principal. Usually it consists of a fixed cylindrical frame with copper conductors wound through iron parts to produce a magnetic field of force (see MAGNETISM) inside, where the ARMATURE revolves about a shaft held by the frame and connects with driving gear. Interaction between magnetic poles (the fields of force) makes armature rotate and turn gear. Electric motors are classified according to type of electric current by which they are driven as direct-current (DC) or alternating-current (AC) motors. The universal motor can be used with either direct or alternating

current and is used to drive small portable machines.

Mott, John Raleigh, 1865–, American official of Y.M.C.A. Shared Nobel Peace Prize with Emily Balch in 1946.

Mott, Lucretia (Coffin), 1793–1880, American feminist and reformer. Organized Female Anti-Slavery Society, and her home was a station on Underground Railroad. Refusal of London antislavery convention (1840) to admit women led her and Elizabeth Cady Stanton to organize (1848) first woman's rights convention.

Mott, Valentine, 1785–1865, American surgeon, especially noted for skill in ligating arteries and for bone surgery.

Moulins (mōōlẽ′), city (pop. 20,832), cap. of Allier dept., central France, on Allier R.; historic cap. of Bourbonnais. Ironworks; tanneries. Among its historic and artistic treasures are a famous 15th-cent. tryptich, in the cathedral; the former convent of the Order of Visitation, founded 1616 by St. Jane Frances de Chantal (who died here); the ruined castle of the dukes of Bourbon; and the Renaissance pavilion of Anne de Beaujeu.

Moulmein (mōōlmān′), town (pop. 65,506), S Lower Burma; port on Salween R. mouth. Was chief town of British Burma, 1826–52. Exports rice and teak.

Moultrie, William (mōōl′trē), 1731–1805, American Revolutionary general. Defense of fort on Sullivans Isl. (later named Fort Moultrie) prevented fall of Charleston in 1776.

Moultrie (mōl′trē), city (pop. 11,639), SW Ga., on Ochlockonee R. and SE of Albany. Tobacco market. Mfg. of cotton goods, meat packing, food canning.

Moultrie, Fort, on Sullivans Isl., at harbor of Charleston, S.C. Figured in action that started Civil War (see SUMTER, FORT). Held by Confederates till evacuation of Charleston in Feb., 1865.

Mound, village (pop. 2,061), E Minn., on L. Minnetonka and W of Minneapolis. Resort in farm area.

Mound Bayou, town (pop. 1,328), NW Miss., NNE of Greenville in farm area; founded 1887. All-Negro self-governing community.

mound builders, in American archaeology, peoples who built mounds in area from Wis. to Gulf of Mexico and from Mississippi R. to Appalachian Mts. All were sedentary farmers in villages, but were unconnected politically. Mounds vary in size (some being more than 100 acres) and purpose (tumuli; foundations for buildings; fortresses; temples). Mound builders supposed to be ancestors of Indians.

Mound City, city (pop. 2,167), S Ill., on the Ohio and near Cairo. Important Union naval base during Civil War; Civil War shipyard still used. National cemetery near by.

Mound City Group National Monument: see NATIONAL PARKS AND MONUMENTS (table); MOUND BUILDERS.

Moundsville, city (pop. 14,772), in N Panhandle of W.Va., on Ohio R. and S of Wheeling; organized 1865. Mfg. of glass and enamel ware; coal mining.

Moundville, town (pop. 901), W Ala., SW of Birmingham and on Black Warrior R., near state monument noted for numerous large Indian mounds.

Mount, William Sidney, 1807–68, American painter, noted for humorous scenes of country life.

Mountain, the, in the French Revolution, deputies of extreme left, who sat on the raised seats in the National Convention. Among the *Montagnards* were the JACOBINS and CORDELIERS; they ruled France during REIGN OF TERROR (1793–94). See also PLAIN, THE.

mountain, a high land mass with little level ground at its summit. Some mountains are isolated but usually they occur in a group or range—either a single complex ridge or a series of related ridges. Mountain system is a group of ranges closely related in form and origin; chain is a group of systems occupying same general region; cordillera, zone, or belt is complex of ranges, systems, and chains occupying a whole area of a continent. Some mountains are remains of plateaus dissected by erosion; others are either volcanic cones or intrusions of igneous rock forming domes. Fault-block mountains are formed by raising huge blocks of earth's surface relative to neighboring blocks. All great mountain chains are either fold mountains or complex structures in the forming of which folding, faulting, and igneous activity have been involved; most have been uplifted vertically after folding occurred. Ultimate causes of earth movements resulting in mountain building are not definitely known. Some doubt has been cast on long-accepted idea that earth movements are adjustments of crust to shrinking interior. More recent is hypothesis that earth movements are isostatic, i.e., adjustments which keep weights of sections of earth's crust approximately equal.

Mountainair, village (pop. 1,418; alt. c.6,550 ft.), central N.Mex., SSE of Albuquerque. Pueblo ruins, Gran Quivira natl. and state monuments are near.

mountain ash, name for hardy ornamental trees and shrubs of genus *Sorbus,* native to the N Hemisphere. They have showy clusters of red berrylike fruits. The European species (*Sorbus aucuparia*) is also called rowan tree.

Mountain-Badakhshan (–bŭdŭkhshän′), Rus. *Gorno-Badakhshan,* autonomous *oblast* or region (23,600 sq. mi.; pop. c.50,000), SE Tadzhik SSR, in the PAMIR; cap. Khorog. Borders E on China, S and W on Afghanistan, and is separated from Pakistan by narrow Afghan strip. Livestock raising, wheat growing. Population is mainly Tadzhik with some Kirghiz tribes. Despite Afghan claims and British opposition, Russia annexed the region in late 19th cent.

Mountain Brook, town (pop. 8,359), N central Ala., S suburb of Birmingham.

mountain goat: see ROCKY MOUNTAIN GOAT.

Mountain-Karabakh (–kŭrŭbäkh′), Rus. *Nagorno-Karabakh,* autonomous *oblast* or region (1,700 sq. mi.; pop. c.130,000), SW Azerbaijan SSR, on E slopes of the Lesser Caucasus; cap. Stepanakert. Forest and agr.; produces cotton and silk. Population is largely Armenian.

mountain laurel, ornamental evergreen shrub (*Kalmia latifolia*) native to E North America. It is not a true laurel. In spring it bears lovely clusters of pink or white flowers. It requires an acid soil.

mountain lion: see PUMA.

Mountain Meadows, small valley, c.3 mi. long and c.¼ mi. wide, extreme SW Utah, c.300 mi. SSW of Salt Lake City. In Sept., 1857, some 140 emigrants bound for Calif. were massacred here by a group under the fanatical Mormon, J. D. Lee, at a time when Mormons bitterly resented coming of U.S. troops. Lee was later executed.

mountain men, trappers and traders who made the area of Rocky Mts. in U.S. familiar to the public. Tough and self-reliant, they were members of loose companies. Guided expeditions, also led wagon trains of settlers to Oregon.

mountain sheep: see BIGHORN.

Mountains of the Moon: see RUWENZORI.

Mountain View, village (pop. 2,880), S Alaska, just E of Anchorage.

Mountain View, city (pop. 6,563), W Calif., SE of San Francisco. Fruit canning and packing.

Mount Airy, town (pop. 7,192), N N.C., NW of Winston-Salem in Blue Ridge foothills. Produces granite, textiles, and furniture.

Mount Allison University: see SACKVILLE, N.B.

Mountbatten, family: see also BATTENBERG.

Mountbatten, Louis (Francis Albert Victor Nicholas), 1st Earl Mountbatten of Burma (mountbä′tŭn), 1900–, British admiral, great-grandson of Queen Victoria. In World War II he directed Commando raids on Norway and France and Allied operations against the Japanese in Burma in 1943. Last British viceroy of India (1947). Became NATO naval commander in the Mediterranean in 1952.

Mountbatten, Philip: see EDINBURGH, PHILIP MOUNTBATTEN, DUKE OF.

Mount Carmel. 1 City (pop. 8,732), SE Ill., on Wabash R. below Vincennes, Ind. Trade and industrial center in agr. area. Mfg. of electronic and sports equipment. **2** Borough (pop. 14,222), E Pa., E of Sunbury; laid out 1835. Anthracite mining.

Mount Clemens, city (pop. 17,027), SE Mich., NE of Detroit and on Clinton R. near its mouth on L. St. Clair; settled c.1798. Health resort with mineral springs and mfg. of metal products and pottery. Has Selfridge Field, U.S. air base.

Mount Desert Island (dĭzûrt′), off coast of S Maine, in Frenchman Bay SE of Bangor; almost divided by Somes Sound into E and W halves (each c.10 mi. long, 5 mi. wide). Champlain landed here and named island, 1604. Jesuit mission estab. 1613. French claims were relinquished 1713. First settlement made c.1762. Area is mountainous and wooded, with lakes, trout streams, and beaches. Resort development began mid-19th cent. On island are Mt. Desert town (pop. 1,776), including Northeast Harbor and Seal Harbor villages, and BAR HARBOR. Marine biological laboratory near Bar Harbor. E half of island includes most of Acadia Natl. Park (see NATIONAL PARKS AND MONUMENTS, table).

Mount Edgecumbe, village (pop. 1,147), SE Alaska, on S Kruzof Isl., at foot of Mt. Edgecumbe.

Mount Healthy, city (pop. 5,533), SW Ohio, N suburb of Cincinnati. Mfg. of clothing.

Mount Holly, village (pop. 8,206), W N.J., E of Camden. Farm trade center; textiles. Has Friends' meetinghouse (1775), courthouse (1796), firehouse (1752), Stephen Girard's home (1777), and John Woolman Memorial Bldg. (1771).

Mount Holyoke College: see SOUTH HADLEY, Mass.

Mount Kisco, residential village (pop. 5,907), SE N.Y., N of White Plains.

Mount McKinley National Park: see NATIONAL PARKS AND MONUMENTS (table).

Mount of Olives: see OLIVES, MOUNT OF.

Mount Pleasant. 1 City (pop. 5,843), SE Iowa, NW of Burlington. Limestone quarries near by. **2** City (pop. 11,393), S Mich., W of Bay City and on Chippewa R.; settled before 1860. Processes oil, sugar, and dairy products. **3** Borough (pop. 5,883), SW Pa., SE of Pittsburgh. Mfg. of glass and coke; coal mining. **4** Town (pop. 2,931), central Tenn., SSW of Nashville. Meriwether Lewis Natl. Monument is near by. **5** City (pop. 6,342), E Texas, SE of Paris. City has cottonseed milling, woodworking, oil refining, and lumbering. **6** City (pop. 2,030), central Utah, S of Provo, in Sanpete project (sheep, alfalfa).

Mount Rainier (rā′nŭr), town (pop. 10,989), W central Md., suburb NE of Washington, D.C.

Mount Rainier National Park: see NATIONAL PARKS AND MONUMENTS (table).

Mount Robson Provincial Park, 803 sq. mi., E B.C., Canada, in Rocky Mts., W of Jasper, Alta. In the park is Mt. Robson (12,972 ft. high), highest peak in the Canadian Rockies.

Mount Rushmore National Memorial: see RUSHMORE, MOUNT.

Mount Stephen, George Stephen, 1st Baron, 1829–1921, Canadian financier and railroad builder, b. Scotland. Became president of bank of Montreal in 1876. Helped to construct Canadian Pacific Railway; its president 1881–88.

Mount Sterling, city (pop. 5,294), N central Ky., E of Lexington in bluegrass region. Trade center of livestock and farm area. Sacked by Gen. J. H. Morgan in Civil War. Indian mounds near by.

Mount Union College: see ALLIANCE, Ohio.

Mount Vernon. 1 City (pop. 15,600), S Ill., SE of Centralia. Trade and rail center for farm, coal, and oil area. Mfg. of freight cars and apparel. **2** City (pop. 6,150), SW Ind., on Ohio R. near junction with Wabash R. and W of Evansville. Trade center for farm area. Prehistoric remains found near by. **3** Town (pop. 2,320), E Iowa, ESE of Cedar Rapids. Seat of Cornell Col. (Methodist; coed.; 1853). **4** Town (pop. 1,106), central Ky., S of Lexington and on old Wilderness Road. Langford House (1790) served as Indian fort. Great Saltpeter Caves near by were Civil War mines. **5** City (pop. 71,899), SE N.Y., just N of the Bronx; settled 1664, separated from Eastchester 1892. Oil-distributing center with mfg. of dies, machinery, silverware, electrical equipment, chemicals, and rubber and food products. Here is St. Paul's Church Natl. Historic Site. **6** City (pop. 12,185), central Ohio, NE of Columbus; laid out 1805. Farm trade center with mfg. of engines and paperboard products. **7** City (pop. 5,230), NW Wash., on Skagit R. Processes farm and dairy products.

Mount Vernon, national shrine, N Va., overlooking Potomac R. near Alexandria; home of George Washington from 1747 to his death. Land patented 1674, house built 1743, Washington inherited estate 1754. Mansion (restored after Washington's notes) is wood structure with Georgian design and with columned portico. Has fine gardens and outbuildings. Tomb (built 1831–37) holds remains of George and Martha Washington.

Mourne Mountains (môrn), in S part of Co. Down, N. Ireland. Highest peak is Slieve Donard, 2,796 ft.

mouse, name for various small rodents of all continents. House mouse (*Mus musculus*) is believed to have evolved from wild mice of central Asia. It damages grains and other food, leather, and other materials. Sometimes produces 5–8 litters per year.

Moussorgsky, Modest (Petrovich) (mŭdyĕst' mōōsôrg'skē), 1839–81, Russian composer. His masterpiece, the opera *Boris Godunov*, was later revised by Rimsky-Korsakov. Outstanding are his piano suite, *Pictures at an Exhibition* (later orchestrated by Ravel) and *Night on Bald Mountain*, for orchestra.

mouth, oral cavity forming beginning of digestive tract. It is divided by teeth and gums into outer vestibule and mouth cavity proper. Roof is formed by hard and soft palates; tongue rests on floor. Teeth prepare food for digestion which begins in mouth by action of SALIVA.

mouth organ: see HARMONICA **1.**

moving pictures, motion pictures, or **cinema** (sĭ'nŭmŭ), a series of pictures produced by projecting on a screen the images in a film. These images are photographs of objects at successive instants of motion projected so rapidly that the eye perceives them as in continuous motion. Work on such serial photographs began in the 1870s and was furthered by inventions of Thomas A. Edison and the Lumière brothers. Projection on screens replaced penny arcade peep-shows. As the novelty decreased, longer pictures were gradually made. Improved techniques and subjects were introduced (esp. by Georges Méliés and Edwin S. Porter). D. W. GRIFFITH set the general structure of the form as it is known today. Hollywood, Calif., became the center of the industry. Early anonymity of actors gave way (largely because of such personalities as Mary Pickford and Charles Chaplin) to the star system in which actors dwarfed producers. In 1926 sound effects and music were successfully used; dialogue was introduced in Al Jolson's *Jazz Singer* (1927). Color films were successful after the development (c.1932) of the Technicolor process. Besides dramatic films there are such special types as the ANIMATED CARTOON, the newsreel (dating from 1909, one of the earliest film types), and the documentary film. The making of so-called three-dimensional films, using either the principle of the stereoscope with special glasses or projection upon a large curved screen, was begun on a wide scale in 1952.

Mowbray, Thomas: see NORFOLK, THOMAS MOWBRAY, 1ST DUKE OF.

Mozambique (mō″zŭmbēk') or **Portuguese East Africa,** Portuguese colony (297,731 sq. mi.; pop. 5,732,767),

SE Africa, on Indian Ocean; cap. Lourenço Marques. Lowlands are in coastal areas, savanna highlands in interior. Coal, gold, and mica are mined. Exports include copra, sugar, cashew nuts, and sisal. Settling in early 16th cent., the Portuguese carried on a flourishing slave trade until slavery was abolished here in 1878. Ruled by an appointed governor.

Mozarabs (mōză'rŭbz), community of independent Christians under the rule of the Moors in medieval Spain; under a local ruler (count) responsible to Moslem caliph. Maintained their own hierarchy under the archbishop of Toledo; used Visigothic, not Moslem, canon law. Their liturgy, called the Mozarabic rite, was like that of ancient Gaul. Chief centers: Toledo, Seville, Córdoba.

Mozart, Wolfgang Amadeus (vŭl'gäng ämädā'ōōs mō'tsärt), 1756–91, Austrian composer, b. Salzburg. Under the tutelage of his father, Leopold Mozart (court musician to the archbishop of Salzburg), the boy became a child prodigy at the harpsichord, violin, and organ, and appeared at court and in aristocratic circles throughout Europe. He tried long to secure a suitable position and finally was appointed to succeed Gluck as imperial chamber musician and court composer in 1787; nevertheless he died in poverty. He wrote in all forms—Masses and other church music (he was feverishly trying to finish his Requiem Mass when he died); vocal music; instrumental pieces (e.g., the popular *Eine kleine Nachtmusik*); chamber music (his string quartets rank with the greatest); sonatas; and concertos (25 for piano; others for violin, flute, horn, and other instruments). Opera was perhaps his greatest interest. Among his operas are *Idomeneo* (1781); *The Marriage of Figaro* (1786); *Don Giovanni* (1787); *Così fan tutte* (1790); and *Die Zauberflöte* (The Magic Flute, 1791). He wrote many symphonies; the last three, generally considered his best—No. 39 in E flat, No. 40 in G minor, and No. 41 (called the Jupiter) in C—were written in 1788 in the space of three months. A catalogue of Mozart's works was made by Ludwig von Köchel (pub. 1862; revised by Alfred Einstein, 1937). Works are usually identified by their numbers in this list.

Mtskhet (ŭmtskhyĕt') or **Mtskheta** (mŭtskhyĕ'tŭ), town (pop. over 2,000), Georgian SSR, NW of Tiflis and on Kura R. Cap. of Georgia to 5th cent. Has 15th-cent. cathedral, with tombs of Georgian rulers.

Muallaqat (mōōä″läkät') or **Moallakat** (mō–), Arabic anthology compiled by Hammad al Rawiya (d. c.775). Its seven odes, some written by greatest Arabic poets, reflect pre-Islamic Bedouin life.

Muawiya (mōōä'wēä), d. 680, first OMAYYAD caliph, b. Mecca. Became secretary to Mohammed the Prophet. Served Omar as governor of Syria. Opposed ALI and helped depose HASAN, Ali's son. As caliph he unified the Moslem empire by his statesmanship.

mucilage (mū'sŭ'ij), thick glutinous fluid related to natural gums. It is secreted by certain plants, e.g., marsh mallow, flax, some seaweeds (agar contains mucilage). Functions of mucilage in plant include checking loss of water, aiding seed dispersal, serving as food reserve. Used in medicine as emollient and demulcent. Is used also as adhesive.

Mudania or **Mudanya** (both: mōōdä'nyä), town (pop. 5,624), NW Turkey, on Asiatic shore of Sea of Marmara; port for near-by Bursa.

Mudd, Samuel Alexander, 1833–83, Confederate sympathizer, physician in Md., who on April 15, 1865, set broken leg of Lincoln's assassin, J. W. Booth. Sentenced to life imprisonment; pardoned 1869.

Mudejar (mōō-dhä'här), name given to the Moors in Spain converted to Christianity and to style of Spanish architecture and decoration, strongly influenced by Moorish taste, which developed after Christian reconquest. Elements of Mohammedan art were used in architecture, and ornamental work was marked by Oriental emphasis on geometrical effect.

Mueller, Paul Herman (poul hĕr'män mü'lŭr), 1899–,

Swiss research chemist. Won 1948 Nobel Prize in Physiology and Medicine for discovery of insecticidal powers of DDT (1939).

Mufaddaliyat: see MOFADDALIYAT.

mufti (mŭf'tē), in Moslem law, attorney who writes opinions (*futwas*) on legal subjects. The *futwas* were binding only in fields of marriage, divorce, and inheritance. The Grand Mufti of Constantinople was (until 1924) head of Moslem religious administration in Turkey. For the mufti of Jerusalem, see HUSSEINI. The term mufti, meaning civilian dress of military or naval man, is derived from the apparel of the attorney.

Mughal: see MOGUL, empire of India.

mugwumps (mŭg'wŭmps"), in U.S. history, slang term applied to Republicans who in 1884 deserted their party nominee, J. G. Blaine, to vote for Grover Cleveland, Democratic nominee.

Muhammad: see MOHAMMED.

Mühlberg (mül'bĕrk), town (pop. 4,466), Saxony-Anhalt, E Germany, where Emperor Charles V defeated the SCHMALKALDIC LEAGUE (1547).

Mühlenberg, Heinrich Melchior (hīn'rīkh mĕl'khêôr mü'lŭnbĕrk), 1711–87, American Lutheran clergyman, b. Germany; came to Pa. 1742. He became leader of all Lutherans in colonies, and formed first synod (1748). His eldest son, **John Peter Gabriel Muhlenberg** (mū'lŭnbûrg), 1746–1807, was Lutheran clergyman, Revolutionary officer, and legislator, serving three terms in the House of Representatives. **Frederick Augustus Conrad Muhlenberg,** 1750–1801, second son of Heinrich, was pastor of churches in Pa. and of Christ Church, New York city (1773–76). He was a delegate (1779–80) to the Continental Congress and member (1789–97) of the House of Representatives, twice as speaker. Heinrich's great-grandson, **William Augustus Muhlenberg,** 1796–1877, was an Episcopal clergyman, hymn writer, and philanthropist; rector of the Church of Holy Communion, New York city; and founder (1858) of St. Luke's Hospital. Among his hymns is *I Would Not Live Alway.*

Muhlenberg College: see ALLENTOWN, Pa.

Mühlhausen (mülhou'zùn), city (pop. 48,013), Thuringia, central Germany, on Unstrut R. Mfg. center of electrical equipment and sewing machines. It was dominated during Peasants' War by Thomas MÜNZER, executed here 1525. Free imperial city 1251–1803. Awarded to Prussia 1815. Transferred to Thuringia after 1945.

Muich-Dhui, Ben, Scotland: see BEN MACDHUI.

Muir, Alexander, 1830–1906, Canadian song writer, b. Scotland. Wrote *The Maple Leaf Forever* (1867), regarded by many as national hymn of Canada.

Muir, John, 1838–1914, American naturalist, b. Scotland. Came to U.S. in 1849 and settled in Calif. in 1868. Muir Woods National Monument was named for him in recognition of his efforts as conservationist and crusader for national parks. He wrote a number of books on his travels in the U.S. He discovered Muir glacier (Alaska) and journeyed also to Russia, India, Australia.

Muir Glacier, area 350 sq. mi., SE Alaska, in Glacier Bay Natl. Monument, SW of Skagway. Explored 1880 by John Muir.

Muir Woods National Monument: see NATIONAL PARKS AND MONUMENTS (table).

Mukachevo (mōō'kächĕvô), Czech *Mukačevo,* Hung. *Munkács,* city (pop. 26,123), W Ukraine, in Ruthenia. Trade center.

Mukden (mōōk'dùn, mōōk'dùn), Chinese *Shenyang,* city (pop. 1,120,918), cap. Manchuria, in, but independent of, Liaotung prov. Political and economic center of Manchuria. Aircraft plants, textile mills. Cap. of Manchu emperors, 1625–44. Russia began development of Mukden in c.1900; her interests were taken over by Japan after Russo-Japanese War. During early phase of Chinese republic, city was seat of war lords, notably Chang Tso-lin.

mulberry, deciduous tree of genus *Morus,* native to N

Hemisphere, with blackberrylike fruit. White mulberry (*Morus alba*) has been grown in China since early times for the leaves, used to feed silkworms. Other plants called mulberry include French mulberry (*Callicarpa americana*) with violet berries, and the paper mulberry (*Broussonetia papyrifera*).

mule, the sterile hybrid of jackass and mare. The hybrid of stallion and jennet is sometimes called mule but more often hinny. Mules, generally larger and more spirited than asses, are tough, sure-footed and are favored over horses as pack animals.

Mulhacén (mōōläthän'), highest peak (11,411 ft.) of Spain, in the Sierra Nevada.

Mülhausen, France: see MULHOUSE.

Mülheim (mül'hīm) or **Mülheim an der Ruhr** (än dĕr rōōr'), city (pop. 148,606), North Rhine-Westphalia, NW Germany, adjoining Essen; an industrial center of RUHR dist.

Mulholland, John, 1898–, American magician. Gifted as a boy, he has become one of most celebrated of stage performers of magic. He also has written on magic and on spiritism.

Mulhouse (mülōōz'), Ger. *Mülhausen,* city (pop. 85,-956), Haut-Rhin dept., E France, in Alsace, on Ill R. and Rhone-Rhine Canal. Textile mills, chemical (esp. potash) plants, and metalworks. Free imperial city from 13th cent. and an allied member of Swiss Confederation from 1515. Voted union with France in 1798. Damaged in World War II.

Mull, island (224,324 acres; pop. 2,903) of Inner Hebrides, off W Scotland, in Argyllshire. Mountainous, it has a deeply indented and picturesque coastline. Chief occupation is grazing.

Mullan, John, 1830–1909, American army officer, pioneer road builder. Built military road from Fort Benton, Mont., to Walla Walla, Wash. (1858–62); helped open up country to miners and settlers.

mullein, Old World herbaceous plant (*Verbascum*), chiefly biennial. Common mullein (*Verbascum thapsus*), with woolly leaves and a tall spike of yellow blooms, grows along roadsides and in fields in North America. Moth mullein (*V. blattaria*) is smaller and has cream-colored flowers.

Müller, Hermann (hĕr'män mü'lùr), 1876–1931, chancellor of Germany (1920, 1928–30), a Social Democrat. As foreign minister in 1919 he signed the Treaty of Versailles.

Muller, Hermann Joseph (mü'lùr), 1890–, American geneticist and educator. Won 1946 Nobel Prize in Physiology and Medicine for discoveries regarding hereditary changes or mutations produced by X rays.

Müller, Johannes: see REGIOMONTANUS.

Müller, Johannes Peter (yōhä'nùs pā'tùr mü'lùr), 1801–58, German physiologist and anatomist. Famed as teacher, researcher, and author of work on human physiology (1833–40).

Müller, Wilhelm (vïl'hĕlm), 1794–1827, German lyric poet. The song cycles *Die schöne Müllerin* (1823) and *Winterreise* (1827) by Franz SCHUBERT are set to his lyrics. He was the father of **Max Müller** (Friedrich Maximilian Müller or Friedrich Max-Müller), 1823–1900, German philologist and Orientalist. He popularized philology and mythology. His greatest work was *Sacred Books of the East* (51 vols.; begun 1875), translations of Oriental religious writings.

Mull of Galloway (gă'lùwä), headland, Wigtownshire, Scotland; southernmost point of Scotland.

Mulock, Dinah Maria (mü'lŏk), later **Mrs. Craik,** 1826–87, English didactic novelist, known for her *John Halifax, Gentleman* (1856) and a children's classic *The Little Lame Prince* (1875).

Mulroy Bay, inlet of the Atlantic, 12 mi. long, indenting N coast of Ireland, in Co. Donegal.

Multan (mōōltän'), city (pop. 190,000), S Punjab, W Pakistan. Dates from time of Alexander the Great. Mfg. of steel products.

multiplication, a basic process in arithmetic and algebra, in which a number or numerical quantity is increased by taking it a certain number of times. Multiplicand is the number acted upon; multiplier, the number showing the times the multiplicand is to be taken; product is result. The symbol of the operation is × or · and, in algebra, simple juxtaposition (e.g., xy means x × y).

Multscher, Hans (mōōl'chŭr), fl. 1427–67, noted German sculptor and painter of Swabian school of Ulm.

Mumford, Lewis, 1895–, American author and critic. His major views are set forth in a trilogy *Techniques and Civilization* (1934), *The Culture of Cities* (1938), and *The Condition of Man* (1944). Other works include *Herman Melville* (1929), *Conduct of Life* (1951), and *Art and Technics* (1952). He edited *Roots of Contemporary American Architecture* (1952).

mummy, corpse preserved by embalming. Mummification seems related to belief in life after death, the body being preserved so that soul may return to it.

mumps, epidemic disease caused by virus. Marked by swelling and pain in parotid and other salivary glands. Incubation period 12–26 days. Attack usually gives lifelong immunity.

Mun, Albert, comte de (älbĕr' kŏt' dü mü'), 1841–1914, French Catholic leader. Advocated social reform and organized Catholic workers' associations.

Münch, Charles (münsh'), 1891–, French conductor; conductor of the Paris Conservatoire orchestra, 1938–46. In 1949 he succeeded Koussevitsky as conductor of the Boston symphony orchestra.

Munch, Edvard (ĕd'värt mōōngk'), 1863–1944, Norwegian painter. Studied in Paris under Bonnat. His work, which shows influence of neo-impressionism, is highly original in color and design and full of psychological suggestion.

Munchausen, Baron (mŭnchô'zŭn, –chou'zŭn), Ger. *Karl Friedrich Hieronymus, Baron von Münchhausen,* 1720–97, German cavalry officer whose tales of his incredible adventures in Russia became classics. Written and published (1785) in English by Rudolf Erich Raspe, they were put into German by G. A. Bürger.

München, Bavaria: see MUNICH.

München Gladbach (mün'khŭn glät'bäkh), city (pop. 122,388), North Rhine-Westphalia, NW Germany. Center of Rhenish cotton textile industry.

Münchhausen: see MUNCHAUSEN, BARON.

Muncie, city (pop. 58,470), E Ind., on White R and NE of Indianapolis; platted 1827. Rail and trade center of agr. area with mfg. of glass and metal products, dairying, and meat packing. Original of "Middletown" in sociological research of R. S. and Helen M. Lynd.

Mundelein, George William (mŭn'dŭlīn), 1872–1939, Roman Catholic archbishop of Chicago (after 1915); made cardinal (1924). He criticized Nazism severely. Mundelein was active in social work.

Munhall, borough (pop. 16,437), SW Pa., on Monongahela R. and ESE of Pittsburgh. Has large steel works; scene of Homestead strike.

Munich (mū'nĭk), Ger. *München,* city (pop. 831,017), cap. of Bavaria and of Upper Bavaria, on Isar R. and at foot of Bavarian Alps. A commercial, industrial, and cultural center, it produces machinery, chemicals, precision instruments. Brewing and printing also are important industries. Archiepiscopal see. University, founded 1472 at INGOLSTADT, was transferred to Munich 1826. Academy of fine arts has long been of international importance. Chartered 1158 and cap. of Bavaria from 1255, Munich did not expand until 19th cent., when the art-loving kings of Bavaria built it up as a "modern Athens." It was the scene of Hitler's "beer-hall putsch" of 1923 and later became his party hq. Nearly half of the handsome city was destroyed in World War II, including the Glyptothek and the Old and New Pinakothek, which were among the world's foremost art museums (most of their contents were saved). The 15th-cent. Liebfrauenkirche [Church of Our Lady], chief landmark of Munich, and the royal palace were heavily damaged. Undamaged were the Propyläen, a monumental gate on the palace square,

and St. Michael's Church, one of the finest German baroque churches. Near Munich is the famous château of NYMPHENBURG.

Munich Pact, Sept. 29–30, 1938, agreement signed at Munich, Bavaria, by Hitler for Germany, Mussolini for Italy, Neville Chamberlain for Great Britain, Édouard Daladier for France, and their respective foreign ministers. It permitted the immediate occupation by Germany of large parts of CZECHOSLOVAKIA. Czechoslovakia itself was not consulted in the negotiations, nor was the USSR, although it had promised to assist Czechoslovakia if France did likewise. The events leading up to the pact began in the summer, when Hitler openly began to support the agitation of German nationalists in Czechoslovakia, particularly in the SUDETES, for self-rule. The Czech government offered a compromise, but Hitler kept increasing his demands; by Sept., war seemed imminent. At this point Prime Minister Chamberlain, meeting Hitler at Berchtesgaden, yielded to Hitler's demand for annexation of some border areas. France, though pledged by treaty to support Czechoslovakia, followed suit, and Czechoslovakia accepted. At a second meeting, at Bad Godesberg, Hitler vastly increased his demands, and Chamberlain rejected them. War seemed certain, when Mussolini proposed a meeting at Munich. There, within a few hours, France and England yielded to Hitler. Czechoslovakia gave in; Pres. Benes resigned; and Chamberlain, back in London, announced that he had won "peace in our time." The plebiscites stipulated by the pact never took place. On the basis of a provision for Polish and Hungarian minorities, Poland and Hungary seized, respectively, the TESCHEN dist. and S Slovakia. Finally, in March, 1939, Czecho-Slovakia, as the truncated state was called, was dissolved by Hitler. The Munich Pact, which marked the height of Western appeasement policy toward Hitler, is believed by some to have delayed World War II by a year, while others believe that a firmer stand in 1938 might have forestalled war.

municipal government: see CITY GOVERNMENT.

municipal home rule: see HOME RULE, MUNICIPAL.

municipal ownership: see PUBLIC OWNERSHIP.

Munising (mū'nĭsĭng), city (pop. 4,339), N Upper Peninsula, N Mich., on Munising Bay of L. Superior and SE of Marquette. Scenic resort center touched by lake steamers.

Munk, Kaj (kī' mōōngk'), 1898–1944, Danish playwright, a clergyman. His dramas, all with a strong ethical slant, include *The Word* (1932) and *Niels Ebbesen* (1943). An opponent of the Nazi invaders, he was murdered by Germans or Danish Nazi sympathizers.

Munkacs, Ukraine: see MUKACHEVO.

Munkacsy, Michael (mōōn'kächĭ), 1844–1900, Hungarian genre and historical painter, whose real name was Michael Lieb. His *Christ before Pilate* has been widely reproduced.

Munn vs. Illinois, case decided by U.S. Supreme Court in 1876. Munn had been found guilty in 1872 of violating Ill. state laws providing for fixing of max. charges for storage of grain. Court upheld constitutionality of Granger laws (see GRANGER MOVEMENT), maintaining that regulation of business devoted to public use was a matter of public interest.

Muñoz Marín, Luis (lwēs' mōō'nyōs märēn'), 1898–, Puerto Rican liberal leader and journalist. Organized (1938) and headed Popular Democratic party, whose slogan "Bread, Land, and Liberty" won large peasant following. In 1948 won first election for governorship of Puerto Rico.

Munro, Dana Carlton, 1866–1933, American educator and historian. Professor (1915–33) of medieval history at Princeton. An authority on Crusades, he worked wholly from contemporary sources, wrote and edited many books on medieval civilization.

Munro, Hector Hugh, pseud. Saki (sä'kē), 1870–1916,

British author, b. Burma of Scottish parents; killed in World War I. A journalist, he gained immortality by his short stories, notable for dryly brilliant style, sharp wit, and sparkling imagination. He also wrote novels (e.g., *The Unbearable Bassington*, 1912) and letters.

Munsey, Frank Andrew, 1854–1925, American publisher. In 1882 he began publishing career with magazine *Argosy, Munsey's Magazine* (1889), and others. In 1891 he entered newspaper field, buying and selling papers, and after 1916 he controlled such papers as New York *Press, Sun, Herald, Tribune, Mail,* and *Evening Telegram.*

Münster, Sebastian (mün'stûr), 1489–1552, German scholar and geographer. His geography, *Cosmographia universalis* (1544), was standard for over a century.

Munster (mŭn'stûr), province (9,317 sq. mi.; pop. 917,-306), SW Ireland, largest of the four provinces. Includes Clare, Cork, Kerry, Limerick, Tipperary, and Waterford counties. Was an ancient kingdom.

Münster (mün'stûr), city (pop. 119,788), North Rhine-Westphalia, NW Germany; a port on Dortmund-Ems Canal. Machinery and hardware mfg. Founded an episcopal see c.800, Münster was the scene of the theocratic experiment of JOHN OF LEIDEN in 1533–35 and of the signing of the Treaty of Münster (1648; see WESTPHALIA, PEACE OF). The prince-bishopric of Münster, which included a large part of Westphalia, was secularized in 1803. Münster was famous for its many fine medieval buildings until its virtual destruction in World War II. University was chartered 1773, restored 1902.

Muntenia, Rumania: see WALACHIA.

Munthe, Axel (mŭn'tü), 1857–1949, Swedish physician and writer; lived for many years on Capri. Wrote (in English) *The Story of San Michele* (1929).

Münzer, Thomas (tō'mäs mün'tsûr), c.1489–1525, German Anabaptist, leader in Reformation. An associate of Luther in 1519, he diverged as his political and social beliefs grew more radical. He advocated simple, godly, communistic society, which was realized briefly in communistic theocracy at Mülhausen.

Muonio, river: see TORNE.

Murad or **Amurath,** Ottoman sultans. **Murad I,** 1326?–1389, reigned 1362?–1389. Took Adrianople (1361) and forced Byzantine Empire to pay tribute (1373). Was killed just before victory at KOSSOVO. **Murad II,** 1403–51, reigned 1421–51. Seized Salonica from the Venetians (1430); defeated Christian army at Varna (1444). Basically of peaceful disposition, he was a patron of poetry and learning. **Murad IV,** 1612?–1640, last of the warrior-sultans, reigned 1623–40. Recovered Baghdad from Persia (1638); ordered death of his brother Bajazet (subject of Racine's tragedy, *Bajazet*). His strength and severity were prodigious. **Murad V,** 1840–1904, who was insane, reigned briefly in 1876. Was dominated by Midhat Pasha.

Murano (mōōrä'nō), town (pop. 6,368), Venetia, NE Italy, on small islands in Venetian lagoon. Center of Venetian glass industry since 13th cent. Has a Venetian-Byzantine church (7th–12th cent.).

Murasaki Shikibu (mùrä"kē shkē'bōō), b. c.978, Japanese novelist. Lady Murasaki is celebrated for *Genji-Monogatari* [tale of Genji].

Murat, Joachim (zhôäshē' mürä'), 1767–1815, marshal of France, king of Naples. Helped Bonaparte in coup d'état of 18 Brumaire; married Caroline BONAPARTE (1800); became grand duke of Berg 1806; succeeded Joseph Bonaparte as king of Naples 1808. A brilliant cavalry leader, he played a major part in all Napoleonic campaigns. In 1813 he saved his throne by an agreement with Austria, but he lost it in 1815 by rejoining Napoleon during Hundred Days. Was captured and shot in attempt to regain Naples. His son, **Achille Murat** (äshēl'), 1801–47, American author, came to U.S. in 1823 and settled in Fla. Wrote works praising U.S. democracy.

Muratori, Ludovico Antonio (lōōdōvē'kō äntō'nyō mōōrätō'rē), 1672–1750, Italian scholar, a priest. Edited collections of historical documents, the *Rerum Italicarum scriptores* (1723–38) and *Antiquitates Italicae medii aevi* (1738–42), and discovered early list of New Testament books.

Murchison, Sir Roderick Impey (mûr'kĭsùn), 1792–1871, British geologist. He investigated unclassified strata below Old Red Sandstone and as a result established the Silurian system. Later, with Adam Sedgwick, he established the Devonian.

Murcia (mûr'shŭ, mōōr–, Span. mōōr'thyä), region (10,-108 sq. mi.; pop. 1,094,173), SE Spain, on the Mediterranean. Dry and hot, but irrigated garden areas and Segura R. valley yield fruits and vegetables. Hemp, esparto, and minerals (lead-silver ore, iron, zinc) are exported. Silk culture is traditional occupation. Carthaginians founded here Cartago Nova (now Cartagena) in 3d cent. B.C. Taken in 8th cent. by Moors, who made it independent kingdom of Murcia in 11th cent. Became 1243 a vassal of Castile, which in 1266 annexed it outright. Cap. of the Moorish kingdom was **Murcia** city (pop. 60,113), on Segura R. Has silk mills and food-processing plants. Gothic cathedral (14th–15th cent.), with rococo façade, and episcopal palace are landmarks. University was founded 1915.

murder, criminal HOMICIDE, distinguished usually from MANSLAUGHTER in having the element of MALICE aforethought. Likewise a killing incidentally committed in the course of a felony (e.g., rape or robbery) is murder. Some statutes set different degrees of murder; in these murder in the first degree generally is a calculated act of slaying receiving the severest penalty (normally capital punishment).

Mures (mōō'rĕsh), Hung. *Maros,* river, 550 mi. long, rising in Carpathians in Rumania and flowing W into Hungary to join the Theiss at Szeged.

Muret (mürä'), small town of S France, near Toulouse. Here in 1213 Simon de Montfort decisively defeated RAYMOND VI of Toulouse and PETER II of Aragon in the Albigensian Crusade.

Murfree, Mary Noailles: see CRADDOCK, CHARLES EGBERT.

Murfreesboro. 1 Town, SW Ark., near Little Missouri R. and near only U.S. diamond mine (now closed). **2** City (pop. 13,052), central Tenn., on Stones R. and SE of Nashville. Shipping, processing, and trade center of dairy, grain, and timber area. State cap. 1819–25. Andrew Jackson and T. H. Benton practiced here. Scene of Civil War battle of Murfreesboro (or Stones River) fought Dec. 31–Jan. 2, 1863. This Union victory marked by Stones River Natl. Military Park.

Murger, Henri (ärē' mürzhĕr'), 1822–61, French author of *Scènes de la vie de bohème* (serially, 1845–49), basis of Puccini's opera *La Bohème.*

muriatic acid: see HYDROCHLORIC ACID.

Murillo, Bartolomé Estéban (myōōrĭ'lō), 1617?–1682, Spanish painter, b. Seville. Famous for religious pictures of a sweet charm and for paintings of street urchins. Early in his career he visited Madrid (1642–45), where he was befriended by Velázquez. Born a poor orphan but ended his days as favorite painter of Seville. His paintings of the *Assumption* are among his most renowned work.

Murmansk (mōōr'mŭnsk), city (pop. 117,054), N European RSFSR, on NW Kola Peninsula; an ice-free port on Kola Gulf of Barents Sea. Largest city within Arctic Circle. Founded 1915 and connected with Leningrad by railroad in 1916, it was strategically important in both world wars for supplies to Russia from Western Allies. During civil war it was occupied (1918–20) by Allied interventionist forces.

Murom (mōō'rùm), city (1926 pop. 22,607), central European RSFSR, on Oka R.; machinery mfg. One of oldest Russian cities (founded 864).

Murphy, Frank, 1893–1949, Associate Justice of U.S. Supreme Court (1940–49). Known for liberal opinions.

Murphy, John Benjamin, 1857–1916, American surgeon. Contributed new techniques especially in surgery of blood vessels, digestive system, and chest.

Murphy, William Parry, 1892–, American physician. Shared 1934 Nobel Prize in Physiology and Medicine for work on liver treatment of pernicious anemia.

Murphy, town (pop. 2,433), W N.C., in Nantahala Natl. Forest near Ga. line.

Murphysboro, city (pop. 9,241), S Ill., on Big Muddy R. and N of Cairo. Center for dairy and coal area. Mfg. of clothing, food and metal products. Has memorial to J. A. Logan, born here.

Murray, (George) Gilbert (Aimé), 1866–, British classical scholar, best known as a translator of Greek drama.

Murray, James, 1722–94, British general, first civil governor of Canada (1764–68), b. Scotland. His efforts to protect French Canadians paved way for Quebec Act (1774) and earned him enmity of many of the English.

Murray, Sir James Augustus Henry, 1837–1915, English lexicographer, editor (from 1879) of the *New English Dictionary* (the *Oxford English Dictionary*).

Murray or Moray, James Stuart, 1st earl of (both: mŭ′rē), 1531?–1570, natural son of James V and half brother of MARY QUEEN OF SCOTS. An adviser to Mary, he became regent after her abdication. Largely responsible for success of Scottish Reformation.

Murray, John, 1741–1815, founder of Universalist church in America, b. England; emigrated 1770. He was pastor (after 1779) of the Independent Church of Christ, Gloucester, Mass., and (after 1793) of the Universalist Society of Boston.

Murray, Sir John, 1841–1914, British oceanographer and marine naturalist, noted for his deep-sea observations, b. Canada.

Murray, Nicholas, 1803–61, Presbyterian clergyman, b. Ireland; after 1834 pastor at Elizabeth, N.J. Nicholas Murray Butler was his grandson.

Murray, Philip, 1886–1952, American labor leader, b. Scotland. Headed C.I.O. steel workers' organizing campaign (1936). President of C.I.O. (1940–52) and of United Steel Workers of America (1942–52).

Murray. 1 City (pop. 6,035), SW Ky., SE of Paducah and near Tenn. line, in tobacco and livestock area. **2** City (pop. 9,006), N central Utah, S of Salt Lake City, in irrigated farm area. Lead smelter.

Murray, principal river of Australia, rising in SE New South Wales in Australian Alps and flowing W to encounter Bay in South Australia. Forms 1,200 mi. of Victoria–New South Wales border. Total length, including the DARLING (main tributary), is 2,310 mi. Important primarily for irrigation; has Hume Reservoir (70 sq. mi.), largest in Australia.

Murray Bay, village (pop. 2,324), S Que., resort on N shore of the St. Lawrence at mouth of Murray (or Malbaie) R., NE of Quebec. Called also La Malbaie.

Murrieta, Joaquín (hwäkēn′ mōōryä′tä), 1829?–1853, Calif. bandit, b. Mexico.

Murry, J(ohn) Middleton, 1889–, English author and critic. His works include *Fyodor Dostoevsky* (1916), *Keats and Shakespeare* (1925), and *William Blake* (1933). He wrote a valuable biography of his wife, Katherine Mansfield (1933), and edited her work. Also wrote a biography of his friend, D. H. Lawrence (1931).

Murten, Switzerland: see MORAT.

Musa Dag or Musa Dagh (both: mōō′sù däg′), peak, 4,445 ft. high, S Turkey, rising from the Mediterranean W of Antioch. Heroic stand of Armenians against Turks here in World War I is immortalized in Werfel's *Forty Days of Musa Dagh.*

Muscat, Maskat, or Masqat (all: mŭ′skăt), city (pop. 4,200), cap. of Oman, SE Arabia; port on Gulf of Oman. Held by Portugal from 1508 to 1648, when it fell to Persian princes. Became cap. of Oman 1741.

Muscatine (mŭskùtēn′), city (pop. 19,041), SE Iowa, on the Mississippi below Davenport; settled 1833. Mfg. of pearl buttons and metal and food products. Near-by Muscatine Isl. noted for fine melons.

muscle, contractile body tissue. Skeletal (striated) muscles controlled by will, constitute red flesh. Plain (unstriated) muscles (in alimentary canal and vessel walls) and heart muscles are controlled by autonomic nervous system.

Muscle Shoals, town (pop. 1,937), NW Ala., on Tennessee R. opposite Florence. Here, rapids (Muscle Shoals) formerly extended 37 mi. upstream, had 134-ft. drop, were unnavigable. Canalized in 1830s (unsuccessfully) by Ala. and in 1890 by army engineers. Finally submerged by Wilson and Wheeler dams, units of the TENNESSEE VALLEY AUTHORITY, which bought unused U.S. nitrate works (1916) in 1933. TVA made Muscle Shoals the center of experimental development of phosphate and nitrate fertilizers, animal foods. Various products (e.g., synthetic rubber) made in chemical works.

muscovite: see MICA.

Muscovy: see Moscow.

Muscovy Company (mŭ′skùvē) or **Russia Company,** first major English joint-stock trading company, chartered 1555. Sent out trading and exploring expeditions to Russia and Asia. Its ventures ended in 1615.

Muses [Gr., whence also *music*], nine Greek goddesses, patrons of arts and sciences; daughters of Zeus and Mnemosyne. Calliope (kùlī′ōpē) was Muse of epic poetry and eloquence; Euterpe (ūtûr′pē), of music or of lyric poetry; Erato (ĕr′ùtō), of the poetry of love; Polyhymnia (pŏlēhĭm′nēù), of oratory and sacred poetry; Clio (klī′ō), of history; Melpomene (mĕlpŏm′ĭnē), of tragedy; Thalia (thălī′ù), of comedy; Terpsichore (tûrpsĭk′ùrē), of choral song and dance; Urania, of astronomy. Apollo was their leader. Their worship originated among the Thracians, and they are connected with the Pierian spring, fountain of AGANIPPE, and Mt. Ida.

Museum of Fine Arts, Boston, chartered and inc. 1870, after a decision by Boston Athenaeum, Harvard Univ., and Massachusetts Inst. of Technology to combine their separate collections. First building was opened 1876, the present one in 1909. Supported by private endowments and contributions. Most notable of its collections is that of Chinese and Japanese art. Egyptian wing and collection of John Singer Sargent's paintings are also important.

Museum of Modern Art, New York city, estab. 1929. Its founders included Mrs. John D. Rockefeller and Lillie P. Bliss. Permanent building was erected 1939 on ground donated by the Rockefellers. Among its facilities are a reference library and film library. Privately supported.

mushroom, fleshy fungus with a dome-shaped cap which has spore-bearing gills on its under surface. Mushrooms, especially inedible and poisonous ones, are often called toadstools. One of the most poisonous is the deadly amanita or death angel (*Amanita phalloides*). The common edible meadow mushroom (*Agaricus campestris*) is raised commercially from spawn (prepared material containing the rootlike mycelium of the mushroom). For subterranean mushrooms, see TRUFFLE.

musical glasses: see HARMONICA **2.**

musical notation, the visual symbols used to indicate musical sounds. Early Western music was written in neumes (probably derived from grammatical accent marks) which indicated only the outline of a melody and reminded the singer of a melody previously learned by ear. By the end of the 12th cent., the staff, perfected by Guido d'Arezzo, was in use. Guido placed letters on certain lines to indicate their pitch and thereby also the pitch of the remaining lines and spaces. These letters evolved into the clef signs used today. Differences in coloring (with red and black ink) and in shape (square or diamond) were used to indicate the time-value of a note. Stems and flags were added, and time signatures eventually replaced coloration in indicating note value. In 15th cent., the shape of notes became round, as it is today. Key signatures developed early, sharps and flats assuming their present shapes by the end of the 17th cent. The five-line

GREEK LYRE

REBEC
17th Century

ALTO RECORDER
German 18th Century

BOW

FLUTE

TRUMPET

HUNTING HORN
English c.1700

OBOE

CLARINET

LUTE
17th Century

GUITAR

TROMBONE

FRENCH HORN

60

50

40

30

20

10

Inches

VIOLIN

BASS
CLARINET

CELLO

VIOLA

ENGLISH
HORN

BASSOON

TUBA

STRINGS

WOODWINDS

BRASSES

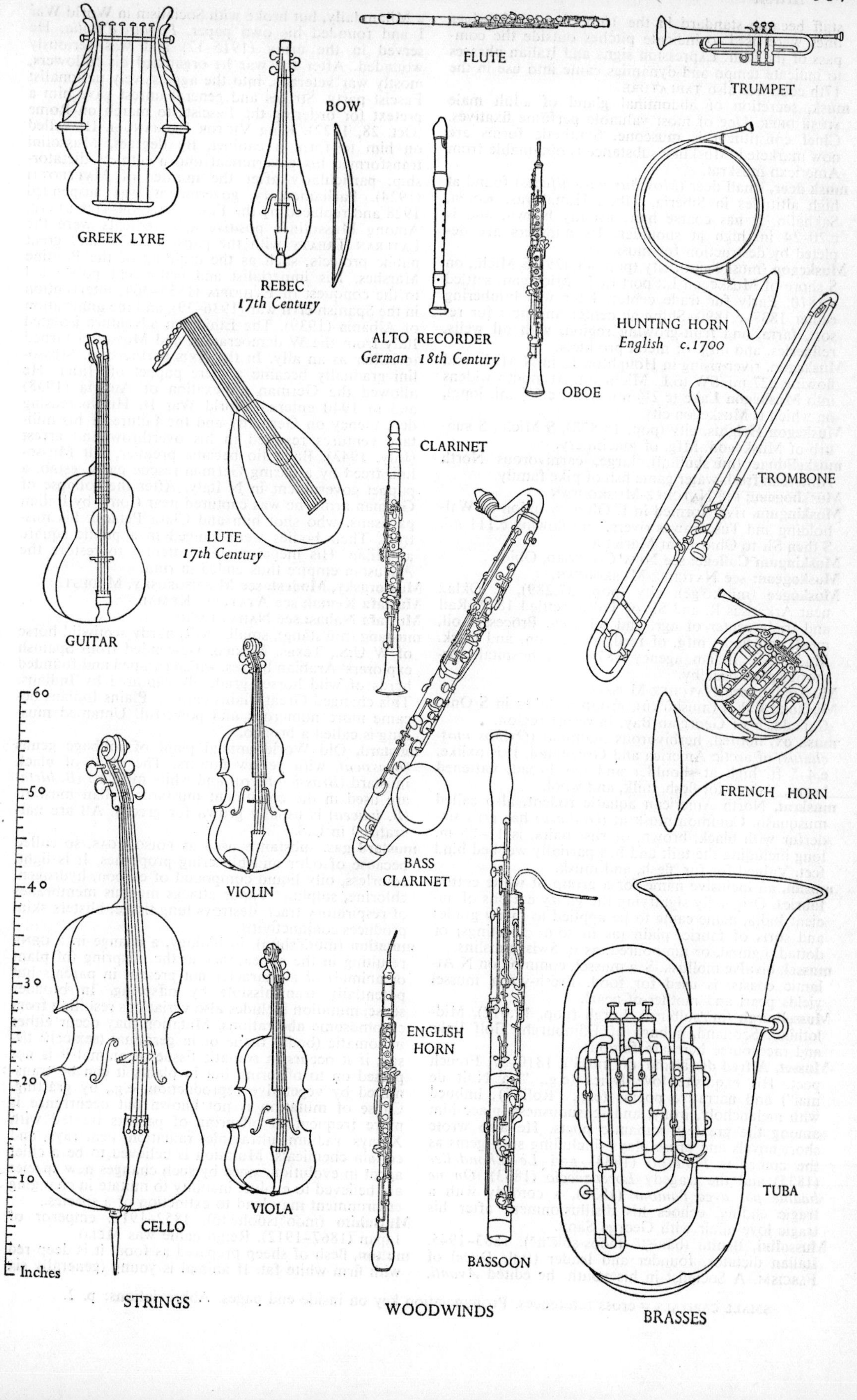

staff became standard in the 16th cent., and ledger lines were used to indicate pitches outside the compass of the staff. Expression signs and Italian phrases to indicate tempo and dynamics came into use in the 17th cent. See also TABLATURE.

musk, secretion of abdominal gland of adult male MUSK DEER. One of most valuable perfume fixatives. Chief constituent is muscone. Synthetic forms are now marketed. Musklike substance is obtainable from American muskrat.

musk deer, small deer (*Moschus moschiferus*) found at high altitudes in Siberia, Tibet, Himalayas, Korea, Sakhalin. It has coarse hair, usually brown, and is c.20–24 in. high at shoulder. Its numbers are depleted by destruction for musk.

Muskegon (mŭskē′gŭn), city (pop. 48,429), S Mich., on S shore of Muskegon L.; port of L. Michigan; settled c.1810. Early fur trade center, later was lumbering center 1837–c.1890. Shipping center and port for resort, farm, and fruit-growing region, with oil wells, refineries, and mfg. of metal products.

Muskegon, river rising in Houghton L. in N Mich. and flowing 227 mi. SW to L. Michigan. At mouth widens into **Muskegon Lake** (c.2½ mi. wide, c.5½ mi. long), on which is Muskegon city.

Muskegon Heights, city (pop. 18,828), S Mich., S suburb of Muskegon. Mfg. of machinery.

muskellunge (mŭ′skŭlŭnj), large, carnivorous North American fresh-water game fish of pike family.

Muskhogean: see NATCHEZ-MUSKOGEAN.

Muskingum, river formed in E Ohio by union of Walholding and Tuscarawas rivers, and flowing c.111 mi. S then SE to Ohio R. at Marietta.

Muskingum College: see NEW CONCORD, Ohio.

Muskogean: see NATCHEZ-MUSKOGEAN.

Muskogee (mŭskō′gē), city (pop. 37,289), E Okla., near Arkansas R. and SE of Tulsa; settled 1872. Rail and trade center of agr. and oil area. Processes oil, meat, and flour; mfg. of feed, glass, iron, and brick. Made U.S. Indian agency 1874. VA hospital, memorial park near by.

Muskogian: see NATCHEZ-MUSKOGEAN.

Muskoka Lakes (mŭskō′kŭ), group of lakes in S Ont., Canada, E of Georgian Bay, in resort region.

musk ox, hoofed, herbivorous mammal (*Ovibos moschatus*) of arctic America and Greenland. It is oxlike, c.4–5 ft. high at shoulder and has broad, flattened horns. Valued for flesh, milk, and wool.

muskrat, North American aquatic rodent, also called musquash. Common muskrat (*Ondatra*) has gray underfur with black, brown, or rust hairs; is 17–25 in. long including the tail; and has partially webbed hind feet. Valued for fur, flesh, and musk.

muslin, an inclusive name for a group of white cotton fabrics. Originally signifying the gauzy cottons of ancient India, name came to be applied to many grades and sorts of fabric, plain (as in some sheetings) or dotted, figured, or tamboured, as in Swiss muslins.

mussel, bivalve mollusk. Sea mussel, common on N Atlantic coasts, is used for food. Fresh-water mussel yields pearl and mother-of-pearl.

Musselburgh (mŭ′sŭlbŭrŭ), burgh (pop. 17,012), Midlothian, Scotland, suburb of Edinburgh. Golf links and racecourse here are famous.

Musset, Alfred de (ălfrĕd′ dŭ mŭsā′), 1810–57, French poet. His exquisite love lyrics (e.g., "La Nuit de mai") and narrative poems (e.g., "Rollo"), imbued with melancholy, irony, and sensuousness, place him among the greatest romantic poets. He also wrote short novels and prose plays—including such gems as the comedies *Fantasio* (1833) and *Le Chandelier* (1835) and the tragedy *Lorenzaccio* (1833). *On ne badine pas avec l'amour* (1836), a comedy with a tragic ending, echoes his disillusionment after his tragic love affair with George Sand.

Mussolini, Benito (bānē′tō mōōs-sōlē′nē), 1883–1945, Italian dictator, founder and leader (Ital. *Duce*) of FASCISM. A Socialist in his youth, he edited *Avanti,* a Milan daily, but broke with Socialism in World War I and founded his own paper, *Popolo d'Italia.* He served in the army (1915–17) and was seriously wounded. After the war he organized his followers, mostly war veterans, into the aggressively nationalist Fascist party. Strikes and general unrest gave him a pretext for ordering the Fascists to march on Rome (Oct. 28, 1922). King VICTOR EMMANUEL III called on him to form a cabinet. By degrees, Mussolini transformed his government into a ruthless dictatorship, particularly after the murder of MATTEOTTI (1924). Parliamentary government was suspended 1928 and replaced by the Fascist CORPORATIVE STATE. Among Mussolini's positive achievements were the LATERAN TREATY with the papacy (1929) and great public projects, such as the draining of the Pontine Marshes. His imperialist and belligerent policy led to the conquest of ETHIOPIA (1935–36), intervention in the Spanish civil war (1936–39), and the annexation of Albania (1939). The Ethiopian adventure isolated Italy from the W democracies, and Mussolini turned to Hitler as an ally. In the AXIS partnership, Mussolini gradually became a mere puppet of Hitler. He allowed the German annexation of Austria (1938) and in 1940 entered World War II. His increasing dependency on Germany and the failure of his military ventures resulted in his overthrow and arrest (July, 1943). Badoglio became premier, but Mussolini, freed by a daring German rescue party, estab. a puppet government in N Italy. After the collapse of German arms, he was captured near Como by Italian partisans, who shot him and Clara Petacci, his mistress. Their bodies were hanged in a public square at Milan. His megalomaniac attempt to restore the Augustan empire thus ended in ruin.

Mussorgsky, Modest: see MOUSSORGSKY, MODEST.

Mustafa Kemal: see ATATURK, KEMAL.

Mustafa Nahas: see NAHAS PASHA.

mustang (mŭ′stăng), small, swift, hardy semiwild horse of W U.S., Texas, Mexico. Descended from Spanish explorers' Arabian horses, which escaped and founded herds of wild horses gradually captured by Indians. This changed Great Plains culture; Plains Indians became more numerous and powerful. Untamed mustang is called a bronco.

mustard, Old World annual plant of cabbage genus (*Brassica*), with yellow flowers. The seeds of black mustard (*Brassica nigra*) and white mustard (*B. hirta*) are used in the condiment mustard. Indian mustard (*B. juncea*) is usually grown for greens. All are naturalized in U.S.

mustard gas, substance used as POISON GAS, so called because of odor and blistering properties. It is light, colorless, oily liquid compound of carbon, hydrogen, chlorine, sulphur. Vapor attacks mucous membranes of respiratory tract, destroys lung tissue, blisters skin, produces conjunctivitis.

mutation (mūtā′shŭn), in biology, a change in a GENE resulting in the appearance in the offspring (of plant or animal) of a character not present in parents but potentially transmissible by offspring. In broader sense, mutation includes also variations resulting from chromosome aberrations. Mutation may occur either in somatic (body) tissue or in germinal (sex-cell) tissue; if it occurs in somatic tissue of animal it is not passed on to offspring but in plants it can be transmitted by vegetative reproduction, e.g., by grafting. Cause of mutation is not known but occurrence is more frequent in offspring of parents treated with X rays, radium, ultraviolet radiation, heat rays, and certain chemicals. Mutation is believed to be a chief agent in evolution, since by such changes new species are believed to evolve; inability to mutate in changing environment may lead to extinction of a species.

Mutsuhito (mōō″tsōōhē′tō), 1852–1912, emperor of Japan (1867–1912). Reign name was MEIJI.

mutton, flesh of sheep prepared as food; it is deep red with firm white fat. If animal is young (generally six weeks to three months old), it is known as lamb; this flesh is preferred in U.S.

Muttra or Mathura (both: mŭ′trù), city (pop. 80,532), W Uttar Pradesh, India, on Jumna R. Traditional birthplace of Krishna, it attracts Hindu pilgrims. Rich in archaeological remains.

Mutual Security Program. Mutual Security Act of 1951, passed by U.S. Congress, estab. Mutual Security Agency to replace ECA as administrator of economic aid to foreign countries and to coordinate economic, military, and technical aid programs. In 1953 Harold E. Stassen succeeded W. Averell Harriman as director of program.

Muybridge, Eadweard (ĕd′wùrd mī′brǐj), 1830–1904, English photographer and student of animal locomotion. After experimentation (1872) in photographing moving objects for U.S. government he was engaged by Leland Stanford to record, with succession of cameras, the movements of a horse. Invented (1881) zoopraxiscope, which projected animated pictures on a screen, a forerunner of moving picture.

MVD: see SECRET POLICE.

Mycenae (mīsē′nē), anc. city, Argolis, Greece; significant as center of Mycenaean civilization.

Mycenaean civilization (mīsēnē′ùn), type of anc. AEGEAN CIVILIZATION known from excavations at Mycenae. Undertaken by Heinrich Schliemann and others after 1876, these helped rewrite history of Greece. Locale was inhabited 3000 B.C., but not by Greeks. In period of city's greatness (c.1600 B.C.) people were Achaeans, an offshoot of Greek family. Architecture of fortress-palace and tombs was massive. People had close relations with Crete, and early culture paralleled Minoan civilization except that Mycenaeans were illiterate. After c.1300 B.C., invasion of Greeks from North led to decline and end of civilization by 900 B.C. Excavations have given new value to *Iliad* and *Odyssey* as sources of information on a phase of Mycenaean civilization.

My Country, 'Tis of Thee: see AMERICA, hymn.

Myers, Gustavus, 1872–1942, American historian. In muckraking era of American literature, wrote exposés such as *History of Tammany Hall* (1901) and *History of the Great American Fortunes* (3 vols., 1910).

Myitkyina (myĭt′chĭnä), town (pop. 7,328), cap. of Kachin state, N Upper Burma, on Irrawaddy R. Trade center on Ledo Road. In World War II it fell to Allies in Aug., 1944, after 78-day siege.

Mylae (mī′lē), anc. port, N Sicily, now Milazzo. Here in 260 B.C. the Romans won a naval victory over Carthage in First Punic War. Here also Agrippa defeated Sextus Pompeius, the pirate ruler (36 B.C.).

myopia: see NEARSIGHTEDNESS.

Myrdal, Gunnar (gŭ′när mēr′däl), 1898–, Swedish economist, sociologist, and public official. Adviser to Swedish government on economic and social policy 1933–38. Made a study (1938–42) for the Carnegie Corp. of the American Negro problem; wrote *The American Dilemma* (1944). Secretary of Commerce of Sweden 1945–47. Executive secretary of UN Economic Commission for Europe (1947–).

Myrmidons (mûr′mĭdùnz, –dōnz″), anc. Greek tribe of Thessaly; in Homer, the warriors of Achilles, descendants of ants changed into men by Zeus to serve his son Aeacus.

Myron (mī′rùn), 5th cent. B.C., Greek sculptor, reputedly a pupil of Ageladas. His works have perished, but two of them are known by copies, the DISCOBOLUS and *Athena and Marsyas* (Rome).

myrrh (mûr), name for small thorny tree of genus *Commiphora* of E Africa and Arabia, and the gum resins yielded by various species. Bitter or herabol myrrh, used medicinally, is obtained from *Commiphora myrrha*. In the Bible (Mat. 2.11) myrrh is associated with frankincense. A European herb, sweet cicely, is also called myrrh.

myrtle. The classic myrtle is a shrub (*Myrtus communis*), native to Mediterranean regions. It has small, shiny, aromatic leaves, white or rosy flowers, blackish berries. Periwinkle is also called myrtle.

Myrtle Beach, beach-resort town (pop. 3,345), E S.C., on coast SE of Conway.

Mysore (mīsôr′), state (29,458 sq. mi.; pop. 9,071,678), S India; cap. Bangalore. Formerly a princely state. Its large tea, coffee, rubber, and spice plantations are mainly in W Ghats. Produces nearly all India's gold; iron ore and manganese are also mined. Steel and textile mills, aircraft plants. Old Mysore dynasty, overthrown 1761 by Hyder Ali, was restored in 1799, when his son, Tippoo Sahib, was defeated by the British. Joined free state of India in 1947. **Mysore,** city (pop. 150,540), is seat of the maharaja and a mfg. center. Wide streets and many parks make it a "garden city." Maharaja's throne is said to rival Peacock Throne of Delhi. Part of Univ. of Mysore is here.

mysteries, in Greek religion, term used for certain secret cults. Conventional religions of Greece and Rome were mainly for state and family and only secondarily for the individual, who therefore sought an emotional religion that would fulfill his desire for salvation and immortality. This the mysteries supplied. Though they were highly secret, we know the four stages through which the initiate passed—purification rites, teaching of mystic knowledge, sacred drama (core of mystery), and garlanding of the initiate to signify his union with deity. Since mystery deities, e.g., Demeter, Persephone, and Dionysus, were fertility gods, origin of mysteries may have been FERTILITY RITES. Most important Greek cults were Eleusinian and Orphic mysteries. All Roman mysteries were importations—e.g., Isis cult, which came from Egypt as fertility cult but became ascetic religion glorifying continence and chastity.

mystery play: see MIRACLE PLAY.

mystery story: see DETECTIVE STORY.

Mystic, Conn.: see STONINGTON.

mysticism, in its proper meaning, practice of uniting oneself with the Deity or other unifying principle of life, linked with religion; in a more popular sense any sort of nonrational belief. It is a term much used to refer to the religious in India, who are, technically, quietists. The aim of Christian mysticism is union with God, and in the literature of mysticism several stages have been distinguished. Visions may or may not accompany mystical practices. Some of the great Christian mystics have been St. Augustine, St. Gregory I, St. Hildegard of Bingen, Hugh of Saint Victor, Jacopone da Todi, St. Thomas Aquinas, Ramon Lull, Nicholas of Cusa, St. Catherine of Siena, St. John of the Cross, St. Theresa of Ávila, and St. Theresa of Lisieux. Among Protestants the Society of Friends (the Quakers) have been vigorous in promoting mysticism. In Judaism the CABALA has been important, and the modern Hasidim are mystics. In Islam, Sufism was the most important mystic expression.

myth [Gr.], in its usual sense, traditional story concerning supernatural events and gods. It differs from legends or sagas, which record human doings, and from fairy tales or fables, invented to amuse or to teach. Association of myth and religion is close, and religious rites often rehearse events of a myth. Myths combine religious purpose with an explanatory one (i.e., mythmaker tries to interpret nature by personification). In 4th cent. B.C. Euhemerus called myths exaggerated adventures of real people. Modern investigation of myths began with Max MÜLLER, who considered them linguistic corruptions. The allegorical interpretation is that myths were invented to point out truth but later were taken literally; the theological, that they are foreshadowings of Scriptures or corruptions of them. Sir James Frazier, in *The Golden Bough,* stated that all myths originally were linked with idea of fertility in nature. Most anthropologists now do not believe in one general theory for all myths, but in specific explanation for myths of a single people. Myths have been widely used in literature—both those that are borrowed from old religions and those reshaped for the writer's own purpose.

Mytilene (mĭtĭlē'nē), chief city (pop. 27,125) on Lesbos isl., Greece; a port on Aegean Sea opposite Asia Minor. Sometimes spelled Mitylene or Mitilini. The name is also occasionally applied to whole island of Lesbos.

Mzab (mùzäb'), group of Saharan oases in central Algeria. Settled in 11th cent. by members of a heretic Moslem sect. Mzabites are still a closely-knit cultural group. Chief center is Ghardaïa.

N, chemical symbol of the element NITROGEN.

Na, chemical symbol of the element SODIUM.

Naaman (nā'ùmùn), Syrian captain whom Elisha cured of leprosy. 2 Kings 5.

Nabal (nā'bùl) [Heb.,= fool], man who resisted David's attempts at extortion. David's anger was appeased by the charm of ABIGAIL, Nabal's wife. 1 Sam. 25.

Nablus (näbloos'), town (est. pop. 24,660), Palestine, N of Jerusalem. Here was the Hebrew city SHECHEM, rebuilt by Hadrian and called Neapolis. Near by are reputed sites of Joseph's tomb and Jacob's well. Long the cap. of Samaria, it still has a small colony of SAMARITANS. Populated mainly by Moslems, city is now in territory claimed by Jordan.

Nabonidus (năbùnī'dùs), d. 538? B.C., last king of the Chaldaean dynasty of Babylon. Not of Nebuchadnezzar's family, he may have usurped the throne. His kingdom fell to Cyrus of Persia c.538 B.C. Bible calls last king of Babylonia BELSHAZZAR.

Naboth (nā'-), man who refused to sell his vineyard to Ahab and was put to death. Elijah cursed Ahab for this action. 1 Kings 21; 2 Kings 9.21–37.

Nabuco, Joaquim (zhwäkēm' nùboo'kù), 1849–1910, Brazilian writer and statesman, strongest single force in abolition of slavery in Brazil.

Nacogdoches (nă"kùdō'chĭs), city (pop. 12,327), E Texas, NE of Houston. Spanish mission founded here 1716; settled 1779. Eastern bastion of Spanish against French. Twice seized (1812, 1819) by U.S. filibusters after Louisiana Purchase. Aided rebels in Texas Revolution 1835–36. Long-time cotton center with sawmills and food and oil processing. Has Old Stone Fort (replica of Spanish colonial presidio) at S. F. Austin State Col.

Nadab (nā'-), **1** Aaron's son, a priest, died with Abihu for offering "strange fire"; exact nature of crime not clear. Ex. 6.23; 24; 28; Lev. 10; Num. 3.1–4; 26.61; 1 Chron. 6.3; 24.1–2. **2** Died c.909 B.C., king of Israel (c.910–c.909 B.C.), succeeded Jeroboam I. Murdered by Baasha. 1 Kings 15.25–31.

Nadelman, Elie, 1882–1946, Polish-American sculptor, b. Warsaw. Worked in wood and metal.

Nadir Shah or **Nader Shah** (both: nä'dēr shä'), 1688–1747, shah of Iran (1736–47), founder of Afshar dynasty. Won power under Safavid dynasty by his victories over the Afghans and the Turks. Became shah when Safavid line came to an end. Successfully invaded India in 1739, carrying off vast treasure, notably Koh-i-noor diamond and Peacock Throne. His conquests restored limits of Iran to what they had been under the Sassanidae.

Näfels (nā'fùls), village of Glarus canton, E Switzerland. Scene of Swiss victory over Austrians (1388).

Nagasaki (nägä'säkē), city (pop. 198,642), W Kyushu, Japan; port on Nagasaki Bay. Shipyards, fisheries. Was early Christian center. First Japanese port to receive Western trade, it was opened 1560 to Holland, 1854 to U.S., and 1858 to other Western powers. In World War II it was target (Aug. 9, 1945) of second atomic bomb.

Nagorno-Karabakh, Azerbaijan SSR: see MOUNTAIN-KARABAKH.

Nagoya (nä"gō'yä), industrial city (pop. 853,085), central Honshu, Japan; port on Ise Bay. Engineering works, chemical plants, textile mills. Seat of Nagoya Imperial Univ. and a Shinto shrine founded in 2d cent. Castle here was built 1612 by Ieyasu.

Nagpur (näg'poor), city (pop. 301,957), cap. of Madhya Pradesh, India. Was cap. of Mahratta kingdom of Nagpur, 1743–1817. Rail and textile mfg. center. Seat of Nagpur Univ.

Naguib, Mohammed (nägēb'), 1901–, Egyptian general. Led the coup which deposed Farouk in 1952 and assumed direct control as premier. With the long-range dictatorial powers granted him by the cabinet he began land reform and a purge of corruption in government. Settled the problem of ANGLO-EGYPTIAN SUDAN by treaty with Great Britain 1953.

Nagyszeben, Rumania: see SIBIU.

Nagyszombat, Czechoslovakia: see TRNAVA.

Nagyvarad, Rumania: see ORADEA.

Naha (nä'hä), port town (pop. 44,779), on Okinawa isl., in Ryukyu Isls.; headquarters of U.S. military governor of the Ryukyus since Aug., 1945.

Nahas Pasha (Mustafa Nahas) (nähäs' päshä'), 1876–, Egyptian political leader. Succeeded Zaghlul Pasha as head of WAFD party and was chief negotiator of Anglo-Egyptian treaty (1936) which set Egypt free. Lost his enormous power after Gen. Naguib took control of the government in Sept., 1952.

Nahuatlan (nä'wŏt"lùn), group of languages of Uto-Aztecan linguistic stock. See LANGUAGE, table.

Nahum (nā'ùm), book of Old Testament. Written in poetry, it is a prophecy of doom against Nineveh, which fell in 612 B.C. Identity of prophet unknown.

Naidu, Sarojini (sùrō'jìnē nĭ'doo), 1879–1949, Indian poet and political leader. Became first woman president of Indian Natl. Congress in 1925. Her poetry, written in English, deals romantically with Indian themes.

Nain (nā'ĭn), village SE of Nazareth where Jesus raised a widow's son from the dead. Luke 7.11.

Nairnshire (nârn'shĭr, –shùr), or **Nairn,** county (163 sq. mi.; pop. 8,719), N Scotland; co. town Nairn. Land, rising inland from coast, is used mostly for cattle grazing. Cawdor Castle, traditional scene of Duncan's murder by Macbeth, is here.

Nairobi (nīrō'bē), town (pop. 118,976; alt. c.5,450 ft.), cap. of Kenya; founded 1899. Rebuilt c.1920 on modern town plan. Ships coffee and sisal by rail to Mombasa, its port.

Naismith, James (nā'smĭth), 1861–1939, American ath-

SMALL CAPITALS = cross references. Pronunciation key on inside end pages. Abbreviations: p. 2.

letic director. Originated (1891), with help of Luther H. Gulick, basketball as gymnasium sport.

Najaf, Iraq: see NEJEF.

Nájera (nä'härä), city (pop. 2,994), NW Spain, in New Castile. Here Peter the Cruel and Edward the Black Prince defeated Henry of Trastamara and Du Guesclin (1367).

Nakhichevan Autonomous Soviet Socialist Republic (nŭkhēchĭvän'yù), autonomous republic (2,100 sq. mi.; pop. c.130,000), Azerbaijan SSR, bordering S on Iran. Irrigated lowlands produce cotton, tobacco, rice, wheat. Winegrowing and sericulture in foothills. Population is 80% Azerbaijani Turks and 15% Armenians. The cap. is Nakhichevan (1926 pop. 10,296), near Aras R. An Armenian trade center in 15th cent., it was ceded to Russia by Persia in 1828. Has Greek, Roman, and medieval ruins.

Nalchik (näl'chĭk), city (pop. 47,993), cap. of Kabardian ASSR, RSFSR, on N slope of the Greater Caucasus. Health and tourist resort.

Namaqualand (nùmä'kwùländ), coastal region of SW Africa. Inhabited by Namaquas, a Hottentot tribe numbering c.25,000.

Nampa (năm'pù), city (pop. 16,185), SW Idaho, W of Boise; estab. 1885. Processing and shipping center of rich farm and dairy area in BOISE PROJECT.

Namur (nùmoõr', Fr. nämür'), province (1,413 sq. mi.; pop. 357,774), S Belgium, crossed by Meuse R. and Ardennes plateau. Has stone quarries, coal and iron ore, glass and cutlery mfg. Population is mostly French-speaking (see WALLOONS). Province was formed by combining former county of Namur with parts of Hainaut and of former bishopric of Liége. The cap. is Namur (pop. 31,637), at confluence of the Meuse and the Sambre. Produces leather and metal goods. Episcopal see. County of Namur was bought by Philip the Good of Burgundy in 1421; later shared history of Austrian and Spanish Netherlands. A strategic fortress, city was taken by French 1692, retaken by Dutch 1695, garrisoned by Dutch under Barrier Treaties of 1709, 1713, and 1715. Annexed to France 1792–1814. New citadel dates from 19th cent. City was heavily bombed in World War II.

Nanaimo (nùnī'mō), city (pop. 7,196), on the Strait of Georgia, Vancouver Isl., SW B.C., Canada, NNW of Victoria. Coal port with herring fleet, and center of farm and lumbering region.

Nana Sahib (nä'nä sä'hĭb), b. c.1821, a leader of Sepoy Rebellion; adopted son of last peshwa (hereditary chief) of the Mahrattas. Responsible for massacre of British colony at Cawnpore.

Nanchang (nän'jäng'), commercial city (pop. 266,651), cap. Kiangsi prov., China; port on Kan R. delta on Poyang L. Has university and medical college.

Nancy (Fr. näsē'), city (pop. 108,131), cap. of Meurthe-et-Moselle dept., NE France, on Meurthe R. and Marne-Rhine Canal; historic cap. and cultural and commercial center of LORRAINE. Charles the Bold of Burgundy was defeated and killed here in 1477 by René II of Lorraine and his Swiss allies. A model of 18th-cent. urban planning, the center of modern Nancy was largely built up under STANISLAUS I. Particularly noteworthy are Place Stanislas, Place de la Carrière, the cathedral (1703–42), and the ducal palace (1502–44). University was founded 1854.

Nanda Devi (nŭn'dù dā'vē), mountain, c.25,650 ft. high, N Uttar Pradesh, India, in Himalayas. Climbed 1936 by Anglo-American expedition.

Nanga Parbat (nŭng'gù pûr'bùt), peak, 26,660 ft. high, W Kashmir, in Himalayas. Several attempts to climb it have ended in disaster.

Nanking (năn'kĭng', nän'jĭng'), city (pop. 1,084,995), in, but independent of, Kiangsu prov., China, on Yangtze R. Political and literary center; seat of several universities. Site of Sun Yat-sen memorial. Has textile mfg. Was cap. of Ming dynasty from 1368 to 1421. Treaty signed here 1842 ended Opium War and opened China to foreign trade. In Taiping Rebel-

lion it was held by rebels 1853–64. Served briefly as seat of Sun Yat-sen's provisional presidency (1912). Was cap. of Nationalist government from 1928 to 1937 (when government moved temporarily to Chungking), and from 1945 to 1949, when it fell to Communists. Japanese surrender was signed here Sept., 1945.

Nansen, Fridtjof (frĭt'yôf), 1861–1930, Norwegian arctic explorer, scientist, statesman, and humanitarian. Planned to reach North Pole by drifting with ice in special crush-resistant ship, *Fram.* Never reached pole, but gained much valuable new arctic information and international fame. First Norwegian minister to Great Britain (1906–8). Directed international commission for sea study; made several scientific voyages (1910–14). Noted for service in Russian famine and work in war prisoner repatriation. Awarded Nobel Peace Prize 1922.

Nantes (nănts, Fr. nät), city (pop. 187,259), cap. of Loire-Inférieure dept., W France; a shipping center on Loire R. and largest city of Brittany. Its ocean port is at SAINT-NAZAIRE. Shipbuilding; metallurgy; rail yards. Has castle of dukes of Brittany and 15th-cent. cathedral, with ducal tombs. Was severely bombed in World War II. In 1793 some 3,000–5,000 royalist troops of the VENDÉE were massacred at Nantes, largely by drowning, by the French revolutionists (*noyades*).

Nantes, Edict of, 1598, issued by Henry IV of France at end of Wars of Religion to define the rights of French Protestants (see HUGUENOTS). It granted liberty of conscience and the right of private worship to all; liberty of public worship wherever it had been previously granted; royal subsidies to Protestant schools; and the right for Protestants to fortify and garrison c.200 cities. The last provision, intended to serve as guarantee of the other rights, created a state within the state—a condition incompatible with the policies of Richelieu, Mazarin, and Louis XIV. The fall of La Rochelle (1628) ended the Protestants' political privileges. Louis XIV's anti-Protestant measures culminated in the revocation of the edict (1685). His promise to respect private worship was not kept. Though the edict of revocation forbade Protestants to leave France, many thousands fled to escape persecution, leaving several provinces almost depopulated. Louis's measure contributed to the political isolation and economic decline of France.

Nanticoke (năn'tĭkōk), city (pop. 20,160), NE Pa., on Susquehanna R. below Wilkes-Barre. Mfg. of rayon and nylon yarn and cigars; anthracite mining.

Nantucket (năntŭ'kĭt), island in the Atlantic, 14 mi. long and 3½ mi. wide, c. 25 mi. S of Cape Cod, Mass., across Nantucket Sound; separated on W from Martha's Vineyard by Muskeget Channel. Visited 1602 by Gosnold; settled after 1659. Nantucket and small adjacent islands comprise Nantucket town (pop. 3,484). One of the chief whaling towns until c.1850; became summer resort and artists' colony. Has whaling museum in old sperm-candle factory. Nantucket village (pop. 2,901), trade center with fine harbor, is on N coast. Siasconset or Sconset (both: skŏn'sĭt) is summer resort on the Atlantic (E). First U.S. lightship station (1856) is off Nantucket.

Nanty Glo (năn'tē glō), borough (pop. 5,425), SE Pa., NE of Johnstown. Bituminous coal mining.

Nanuet (nănūĕt'), village (1940 pop. 2,057), SE N.Y., W of Nyack. Has Internatl. Shrine of St. Anthony.

Naomi (nāō'mē), Ruth's mother-in-law. Ruth 1.19,20.

Napa (nä'pù), city (pop. 13,579), W Calif., on Napa R. and N of Oakland; settled 1840. Ships fruit, dairy products, and poultry. Produces wine, clothing, and leather goods, and processes fruit.

Naperville (nā'pùrvĭl), city (pop. 7,013), NE Ill., E of Aurora, in farm area. Mfg. of cheese and furniture. Seat of North Central Col.

Naphtali (năf'tùlī), son of Jacob, ancestor of one of the 12 tribes of Israel. Tribe settled NW of Sea of

Galilee. Gen. 30.7; 46.24; 49.21. Nephthalim: Mat. 4.13,15; Rev. 7.6.

naphtha (năf'thů, năp'–), colorless, volatile, inflammable liquid mixture of hydrocarbons obtained from fractional distillation of petroleum, wood, and coal tar. Used as organic solvent, in making varnish and soap, as cleaning fluid.

naphthalene (năf'thůlēn, năp'–), colorless, crystalline solid with pungent odor. A coal-tar derivative, it is used in dyes, insecticides, solvents.

naphthol (năf'thŏl, năp'–), either of two crystalline derivatives of naphthalene with same chemical formula but differing in atomic arrangement. They show antiseptic properties and are used also to make some dyes.

Napier, John (nā'pēr, nŭpēr'), 1550–1617, Scottish mathematician. Invented logarithm and wrote an original work containing the first logarithmic table and first use of the word *logarithm*. He invented various methods of abbreviating arithmetical calculations, including Napier's rods or bones (a sort of abacus) based on multiples of numbers. He introduced the decimal point in writing numbers.

Naples, Ital. *Napoli*, city (pop. 739,349; with suburbs 865,913), cap. of Campania, S Italy. Italy's second largest port, it lies at base and on slopes of hills rising from Bay of Naples (dominated by Mt. Vesuvius), and occupies one of most beautiful sites of Europe. Mfg. of food, metal, and leather products; also textiles and chemicals. Famed for its songs and festivals. Old Santa Lucia quarter is characteristic of the once rampant slums. An ancient Greek colony mentioned as Parthenope and Neapolis, Naples was conquered 4th cent. B.C. by Romans, by Byzantines in 6th cent. A.D. It was an independent duchy from 8th cent. until Roger II added it to kingdom of Sicily in 1139. After Sicilian Vespers (1282) Italian peninsula S of the Papal States became kingdom of Naples (see separate article), annexed to Sardinia in 1860. City suffered tremendous damage in World War II from both Allies and Germans. Among innumerable churches (most of them restored in baroque style in 17th and 18th cent.) is Cathedral of St. Januarius, where are two vials of the saint's blood, said to liquefy miraculously twice a year. Other landmarks include several medieval castles, the national museum (Farnese collection and objects excavated at Pompeii and Herculaneum), the San Carlo Opera (opened 1737), the university (founded 1224), and a fine aquarium.

Naples, kingdom of, former state, S Italy, comprising present Abruzzi e Molise, Apulia, Basilicata, Calabria, and Campania; cap. Naples. Conquered by the Normans under Robert Guiscard and his successors (11th–12th cent.), it became part of the kingdom of Sicily, which passed to the Angevin dynasty in 1266. The Sicilian Vespers (1282) resulted in the expulsion of the Angevins from Sicily proper; the Angevin possessions on the mainland, which they held in fief from the pope, became known as the kingdom of Naples. The 14th and 15th cent. were marked by recurrent warfare between the Neapolitan Angevins and the Aragonese kings of Sicily. After 1380, a long struggle for the succession in Naples broke out between two rival branches of the Angevin dynasty (see Charles, kings of Naples; Joanna, queens of Naples; Lancelot; Louis, kings of Naples; René). In 1442 Alfonso V of Aragon conquered Naples, and in 1443 the pope invested him as king. After Alfonso's death, Naples continued under a branch of the Aragonese dynasty, while the Angevin claim was inherited by Charles VIII of France. Charles's brief occupation of Naples (1495) started off the Italian Wars, which in 1504–5 resulted in the union of Naples with the crown of Aragon. Under the Spanish viceroys the kingdom sank into misery and backwardness, with ruthless exploitation by the crown and the great landowners. The effects of these conditions is still acutely felt, S Italy remaining one of the poorest regions of Europe. Naples was transferred to Austria by the Peace of Utrecht (1713) but was reconquered by the Spanish in the War of Polish Succession. From 1759 Naples and Sicily were ruled as separate kingdoms by a branch of the Spanish Bourbons (see Bourbon-Sicily). The Bourbons were briefly expelled in 1799 (see Parthenopean Republic) and again in 1806–15, when Napoleon I gave the kingdom first to his brother Joseph Bonaparte (1806–8), then to his marshal Joachim Murat. After the Bourbon restoration Naples and Sicily were united into the single kingdom of the Two Sicilies, which in 1860 fell to Sardinia as Italy was being unified.

Napo (nä'pō), river, more than 550 mi. long, rising in N Ecuador and flowing SE into Peru, where it joins Amazon. First explored by Orellana (1540) and later by Teixeira (1638).

Napoleon I, 1769–1821, emperor of the French, b. Ajaccio, Corsica; son of Carlo and Letizia Bonaparte. Attended military schools in Brienne and Paris. In 1793 the Bonaparte family, who had supported French interests against Paoli, fled Corsica. Having attracted notice at the capture of Toulon (1793), Napoleon was promoted brigadier general. In 1795 his determined action in the Vendémiaire uprising made him the man of the hour. In command of the Italian campaign of 1796–97 (see French Revolutionary Wars) he transformed his demoralized, starving troops into an invincible army and, after the victories of Lodi, Arcole, and Rivoli, negotiated the Treaty of Campo Formio with Austria. His plan to strike at England through India led to his expedition to Egypt (1798), where he won the battle of the Pyramids but lost his fleet at Aboukir. News of French reverses in Italy and political instability in France determined him to return to France, leaving Kléber in charge at Cairo. The coup d'état of 18 Brumaire (1799), engineered by Sieyès, overthrew the Directory and estab. the Consulate, with Napoleon as First Consul. By a series of energetic measures Napoleon halted inflation, made peace with the Church (see Concordat of 1801), began a new legal code (see Code Napoléon), and, after crossing the Saint Bernard, defeated the Austrians at Marengo (1800). The treaties of Lunéville (1801) and Amiens (1802) brought brief peace; in 1803 England again declared war on France. Elected consul for life in 1802, Napoleon had himself proclaimed emperor of the French in 1804 and king of Italy in 1805. He was crowned at Notre Dame cathedral by Pope Pius VII (Dec. 2, 1804). The new constitution was soon curtailed. In 1805, the Third Coalition (England, Austria, Russia, and Sweden, joined 1806 by Prussia) was formed. Napoleon defeated Austria at Austerlitz (1805); Prussia at Jena (1806); Russia at Friedland (1806); the Peace of Tilsit (1807) left Napoleon master of the Continent. Peace with Sweden (1808) left only England in the field. Defeated at sea at Trafalgar (1805), Napoleon resolved upon economic warfare against England (see Continental System). The map of Europe was remade, with Napoleon controlling a much-enlarged France and Italy as emperor-king; Germany, as protector of the Confederation of the Rhine; Switzerland, as "Mediator"; Holland, through his brother Jérôme Bonaparte; Naples, through his brother Joseph Bonaparte and, after 1808 (when he made Joseph king of Spain), through his brother-in-law Joachim Murat. Austria's attempt to renew warfare was crushed at Wagram (1809), and in 1810, after annulling his marriage with Josephine, he married Archduchess Marie Louise of Austria. Meanwhile, the Peninsular War in Spain (1808–14) and the Continental System showed up the weaknesses of his empire. In 1812, at the head of the *Grande Armée* (500,000 French and auxiliary troops), Napoleon attacked Russia, his only remaining rival on the Continent. He entered Moscow (Sept. 14), but after the Moscow fire was forced to order a retreat by his lack of supplies and winter quarters (Oct. 19). The Russians, who until then had avoided battles and practiced a scorched-earth policy, now began to harry his army. After the passage of the BEREZINA, the retreat became a rout; the *Grande Armée* was annihilated. Napoleon hastened to Paris to raise a new army. A new coalition (Russia, Prussia, England, Sweden, and—after Aug., 1813—Austria) came into existence, defeated Napoleon at LEIPZIG, and pursued him into France. On April 12, 1814, Napoleon abdicated. He was exiled to Elba, which the allies gave him as sovereign principality. His victors were still deliberating at the Congress of Vienna when Napoleon, with a handful of followers, landed in France (March 1, 1815). Once more France rallied to him; LOUIS XVIII fled. Napoleon's rule of the Hundred Days ended disastrously in the WATERLOO CAMPAIGN. After his second abdication he surrendered to a British warship, hoping to find asylum in England, but was taken to SAINT HELENA, where he spent his dreary exile dictating memoirs. He died of cancer. His body, brought back to France in 1840, is entombed under the dome of the Invalides, Paris. Napoleon's personality and achievements remain subject to extreme controversy, but of his exceptional genius and tremendous impact on modern history there is no doubt. For the peace settlements following the Napoleonic Wars, see PARIS, TREATY OF, 1814 and 1815; VIENNA, CONGRESS OF.

Napoleon II, 1811–32, son of Napoleon I and of Marie Louise. Held titles king of Rome (1811–14), prince of Parma (1814–18), and duke of Reichstadt (1818–32). Napoleon I abdicated in his favor in 1815, but he never ruled, spending his life as virtual prisoner in Vienna, where he died of tuberculosis. The pitiful life of the "Eaglet" is the subject of Rostand's drama *L'Aiglon.*

Napoleon III (Louis Napoleon Bonaparte), 1808–73, emperor of the French (1852–70); son of Louis BONAPARTE, king of Holland, and of Hortense de BEAUHARNAIS; nephew of Napoleon I. His youth was spent in Switzerland, Germany, and England. Two early attempts (1836, 1840) at having himself proclaimed emperor in France failed dismally. He was sentenced to life imprisonment (1840), escaped to England (1846), returned to France after the Revolution of 1848, and, posing as champion of law, order, and democracy, was elected president of the republic (Dec., 1848). Increasingly dictatorial, he dissolved the legislative assembly by a coup d'état (Dec. 2, 1851), brutally suppressed a workers' uprising, and gained dictatorial power under the constitution of Jan., 1852. In Nov., 1852, a plebiscite confirmed his new title, emperor of the French. The internal history of the "Second Empire" falls into three periods. Until 1860 Napoleon ruled as absolute dictator; in 1860–67 he sought to regain some of his popularity by lifting restrictions on civil liberties and widening the powers of the legislative assembly; the years 1867–70 are known as the Liberal Empire, in which the opposition gained great power under such leaders as Jules Favre, Émile Ollivier, and Adolphe THIERS. The entire period was one of material progress, industrial expansion, and imperialistic ventures (e.g., acquisition of Cochin China, construction of Suez Canal, intervention in MEXICO). French participation (1854–56) in the CRIMEAN WAR restored French military prestige. In Italian affairs, Napoleon intervened decisively. In 1849 French forces restored Pope Pius IX on his throne; in 1859, following up the PLOMBIÈRES agreement, he joined Sardinia in making war on Austria. After his Pyrrhic victory of SOLFERINO, Napoleon concluded the separate peace of VILLAFRANCA DI VERONA, which considerably antagonized the Italians. His virtual protectorate over the Papal States delayed their incorporation into Italy until 1870. Napoleon's ill-advised confidence in his military strength contributed to the outbreak (1870) of the FRANCO-PRUSSIAN WAR. He took the field in person and was captured at Sedan. A bloodless revolution in Paris declared him de-

posed; in 1871 he went into exile in England. His wife, Empress EUGÉNIE, bore him a son, who fell in British service.

Napoleon, city (pop. 5,335), NW Ohio, on Maumee R. and SW of Toledo, in agr. area.

Napoleonic Wars, 1803–15: see NAPOLEON I.

Nara (nä′rä), city (pop. 82,399), S Honshu, Japan; anc. cultural and religious center. Was first permanent cap. (710–84) of Japan. Here is 7th-cent. Buddhist temple, Horyu-ji, oldest in Japan. Imperial Mus. has art treasures of Nara period.

Narbada (nŭrbŭ′dù), river, c.775 mi. long, central India. Sacred to Hindus.

Narbonne (närbôn′), city (pop. 26,301), Aude dept., S France, near the Mediterranean. The first Roman colony (estab. 118 B.C.) in Transalpine Gaul, it became the cap. of Narbonensis prov. and an early archiepiscopal see. It reached great prosperity and independence in the Middle Ages, but the silting up of its port and the expulsion (13th cent.) of its large Jewish population caused its decline. Has a splendid cathedral and 13th-cent. archiepiscopal palace (now city hall).

Narcissus (närsĭ′sùs), in Greek myth, beautiful youth who refused all love, even that of Echo. He fell in love with his own image in a pool and, pining away, died for love of himself.

narcissus, spring-blooming, bulbous plant of Old World genus *Narcissus.* Some species are also called daffodils, especially the yellow trumpet-shaped types. The common daffodil is *Narcissus pseudo-narcissus.* Poet's narcissus (*N. poeticus*) has fragrant white flowers with a red crown. The jonquil (*N. jonquilla*) has fragrant yellow flowers. The Chinese sacred lily and paper white narcissus (varieties of *N. tazetta*) are not hardy in cold regions.

narcotics (närkŏ′tĭks), substances producing stupor that eventually becomes coma and may be fatal. They are used in medicine to relieve pain (anodynes) or produce sleep (hypnotics). Chief narcotics are opium and its derivatives. Illicit traffic is fought by U.S. Bureau of Narcotics and United Nations commission estab. 1946.

Narew (nä′rĕf), Rus. *Narev,* river, 245 mi. long, rising in Byelorussian SSR and flowing W into the Vistula near Warsaw, Poland. Navigable in part.

Nariño, Antonio (äntō′nyō närē′nyō), 1767–1823, Colombian revolutionist. A liberal intellectual, he was one of first South Americans to foment revolution against Spain and argue for independence. Imprisoned for translating and distributing copies of *The Declaration of the Rights of Man* (1795), he escaped to Europe. Later he returned to South America to help in revolution.

Naroda, peak, RSFSR: see URALS.

Narragansett (nărügăn′sĕt), town (pop. 2,288), S R.I., on W shore of Narragansett Bay. Includes Point Judith promontory and resort, and Narragansett Pier resort (pop. 1,247), near 18th-cent. pier.

Narragansett Bay, arm of the Atlantic, 30 mi. long and 3–12 mi. wide, deeply indenting R.I. state. Its many inlets provided harbors advantageous to colonial trade, later to resort development. Providence is on arm at head of bay, RHODE ISLAND at entrance; also contains Conanicut and Prudence isls.

Narragansett Indians, North American tribe of Algonquian linguistic stock, occupying most of R.I. in the 17th cent. Their chief, Canonicus, sold land to Roger Williams. They sided with the settlers in the Pequot War but in King Philip's War were decimated by the whites in the Swamp Fight (1675).

Narragansett Pier, R.I.: see NARRAGANSETT.

Narrows, the: see NEW YORK BAY.

Narses (när′sēz), c.478–c.573, Roman general under Justinian I. The rival and successor of BELISARIUS in Italy, he became exarch at Ravenna after defeating (552) the Ostrogoth TOTILA.

Narva (när′vù), city (pop. 23,512), NE Estonia, on Narva R. Textile and machinery mfg.; sawmills.

Narvaez Founded by Danes 1223; passed to Livonian Knights 1346; was member of Hanseatic League. After dissolution of Livonian Order (1581) it was contested between Russia and Sweden. In 1700 Charles XII of Sweden, with inferior forces, routed Peter I of Russia at Narva, but in 1704 Peter took the city, which remained Russian to 1919. The Narva, river, 47 mi. long, flows from L. Peipus into the Gulf of Finland, forming border between RSFSR and Estonia. Furnishes power to Narva city.

Narváez, Pánfilo de (pän'fēlō dä närvä'ĕth), c.1470–1528, Spanish conquistador. After an unsuccessful attempt in Mexico to make Cortés submit to the authority of the governor of Cuba, he was commissioned to conquer and settle Florida. In 1528 he reached Florida, sent his ships on to Mexico, and led his men inland in search of gold. Disappointed and harassed by Indians, they returned to coast, built crude vessels, and set out for Mexico. All save Cabeza de Vaca and three companions were lost.

Narváez, Ramón María (rämōn' märē'ä närvä'ĕth), 1800–1868, Spanish soldier and statesman; created duque de Valencia 1845. He helped to overthrow Espartero (1843) and was several times premier under Isabella II. His policy was reactionary.

Narvik (när'vĭk), town (pop. 10,281), Nordland co., NW Norway, port on Ofoten Fjord opposite Lofoten isls. Founded 1887 as Atlantic port (ice-free) for Kiruna (Sweden) iron ore. German-held 1940–45, except for brief Allied occupation, May 28–June 9, 1940.

Naryn, river, USSR: see Syr Darya.

Nasby, Petroleum V., pseud. of David Ross Locke, 1833–88, American journalist. In the Civil War, Locke aided the Union cause with satiric letters in his newspapers, supposed to be by a stupid, prejudiced, proslavery man, the Rev. Petroleum Vesuvius Nasby.

Naseby (nāz'bē), village, Northamptonshire, England. Parliamentarians defeated royalists in a decisive battle near here in 1645.

Nash, John, 1752–1835, English architect, who initiated neoclassic Regency style. Famous for achievements in town planning, notably his design for Regent St. in London with its graceful Quadrant.

Nash, Ogden, 1902–, American humorous poet, noted especially for skilled versification and cleverly outrageous rhymes.

Nash, Richard (Beau Nash), 1674–1762, English dandy; master of ceremonies and society leader at Bath.

Nashe or **Nash, Thomas,** 1567–1601, English satirist and pamphleteer. Wrote moralizing satire, violently attacked the Puritans in the Marprelate controversy, and then engaged triumphantly in a scurrilous pamphlet battle with Richard and Gabriel Harvey. His whole life was stormy. He is best remembered for a novel foreshadowing Defoe's work—*The Unfortunate Traveler; or, The Life of Jack Wilton* (1594). With Marlowe he wrote a tragedy, *Dido, Queen of Carthage.*

Nashoba (näshō'bù), former community, SW Tenn., on Wolf R. and near Memphis. Founded 1825 by Frances Wright and others as place to educate Negro slaves for freedom. Plan unsuccessful due to poor management, sickness, and hostility of outsiders. Abandoned 1829–30.

Nashua, city (pop. 34,669), S N.H., at junction of Nashua and Merrimack rivers near Mass. line; settled c.1655. Threatened closing in 1948 of largest textile mill resulted in its sale to citizens' group, which arranged immediate partial operation and eventual full use of the plants. Mfg. of textiles, shoes, wood products, tools, hardware, and machinery.

Nashville. 1 Town (pop. 526), S central Ind., E of Bloomington. Beautiful scenery attracts tourists. Has art gallery and several resident painters. **2** City (pop. 174,307), state cap. (since 1843), central Tenn., on Cumberland R.; founded 1780 at N end of Natchez Trace. Grew as cotton center, river port, and rail focus. Abandoned in Civil War to Federals under D. C. Buell after fall of Fort Donelson, Feb. 16, 1862. J. B. Hood

beaten by Union Gen. G. H. Thomas here, Dec. 15–16, 1864. Port, shipping, industrial, and educational center. Mfg. of food and tobacco products, shoes, rayon, aircraft, and cellophane; printing and publishing houses, railroad shops. Seat of Vanderbilt University, Fisk University, and Meharry Medical Col. (Negro; coed.; 1876). Points of interest include capitol, J. K. Polk tomb, war memorial building, and old churches and houses. Near the Hermitage.

Nasik (nä'sĭk), city (pop. 55,524), N Bombay, India. Linked with legend of Rama, it is a holy place of Hindu pilgrimage.

Nassau (nä'sô, Ger. nä'sou), former duchy, W Germany, N and E of Main and Rhine rivers, since 1945 comprised in Hesse; historic cap. Wiesbaden. Agr. and forested region, famous for Rhine wines (Rüdesheim, Johannisberg) and spas (Bad Homburg, Bad Ems). Duchy takes name from small town of Nassau, on Lahn R., where a count of Laurenburg, ancestor of counts of Nassau, built his castle in 12th cent. In 1255 the dynasty split into two main lines. (1) Walramian line, founded by Count Walram II, ruled Nassau (raised to a duchy 1806) until 1866, when it was annexed by Prussia as a result of Austro-Prussian War. With former Electoral Hesse, Nassau formed Hesse-Nassau prov. of Prussia 1866–1945. In 1890 Duke Adolf of Nassau succeeded to grand duchy of Luxembourg, which continues under Nassau dynasty. (2) The Ottonian line, descended from Walram's younger brother Otto, acquired lordship of Breda, Netherlands, in 15th cent. and rose to prominence with William the Silent, who inherited principality of Orange in S France and became stadholder of Netherlands. His great-grandson, William III of Orange, became king of England; at his death (1702), the title prince of Orange passed to collateral branch of Nassau-Dietz, which, as house of Orange, has ruled the Netherlands from 1747.

Nassau (nä'sô), city (pop. 29,391), cap. of Bahama Isls.; port on New Providence. Rendezvous for pirates, notably Blackbeard in 18th cent., it is now the commercial and social center of colony and a tourist resort.

Nast, Thomas, 1840–1902, American political cartoonist, b. Germany. His work exerted great influence on politics of New York city. Created the tiger, elephant, and donkey as symbols of Tammany Hall, Republican party, and Democratic party.

nasturtium (nùstûr'shùm), dwarf or climbing plant (*Tropaeolum majus*), native to tropical America, widely used as U.S. garden plant, with spurred single or double flowers in shades of red, yellow, and orange. Sometimes the seeds are pickled and used as capers, and leaves and flowers are added to salads.

Natal (nùtäl'), province (35,284 sq. mi.; pop. 2,202,392), E South Africa, on Indian Ocean; cap. Pietermaritzburg; chief town Durban. Sugar and tobacco are grown along the coast, and much coal is mined in interior highlands. The Boers on their trek reached Natal in 1837 and after defeating the Zulus founded republic of Natal (1838). In 1843 the British annexed Natal, which became crown colony in 1856 and absorbed Zululand in 1897. Became province of South Africa in 1910.

Natal (nùtäl'), city (pop. 97,736), cap. of Rio Grande do Norte state, NE Brazil; port just above mouth of Potengi R. Far out on NE bulge of Brazil and only 2,000 mi. from towns in Africa, it was important as an airport in World War II.

Natchez (nä'chĭz), city (pop. 22,740), SW Miss., on bluffs above Mississippi R. Trade, shipping and processing center for cotton and livestock area. Founded 1716 by Bienville as Fort Rosalie; wiped out by Natchez Indians 1729. Passed to England (1763), Spain (1779), U.S. (1798). Cap. of Territory of Miss. 1798–1802. Location on Natchez Trace and Mississippi R. brought prosperity. Taken by Federals 1863. Fine colonial and ante-bellum homes shown during annual spring festival.

Natchez Indians, North American tribe of Natchez-Muskogean linguistic stock, living in SW Miss. in the 17th cent. They warred on the French settlers and massacred many at Fort Rosalie (1729). The French retaliated and scattered the tribe.

Natchez-Muskogean (mŭskō'gĕŭn), linguistic family of North American Indians. Among the languages it included were Natchez, Alibamu, Choctaw, Chickasaw, and Creek. Muskogean also appears as Muskhogean and Muskogian.

Natchez Trace, road from Natchez, Miss., to Nashville, Tenn., very important from 1780s to 1830s. Grew from Indian trails. First used only northward (flat-boats used only southward); used both ways with U.S. expansion SW. Made post road 1800, improved by army. Jackson used it to New Orleans in War of 1812 and in Indian campaigns. Declined with rise of steamboat. Natchez Trace Parkway (estab. 1934, 450 mi.) commemorates, generally follows it.

Natchitoches (nă'kĭtŏsh), city (pop. 9,914), NW La., near Red R. and N of Shreveport. Oldest city in La., founded 1715 by French as military and trading post. Produces, processes, and ships cotton.

Nathan (nā'–), prophet in time of David and Solomon. He denounced David for marrying Bathsheba. Later his advice saved the kingdom for Solomon. 2 Sam. 7; 12; 1 Kings 1; 1 Chron. 29.29; 2 Chron. 9.29.

Nathan, George Jean, 1882–, American editor and critic. He was an editor with H. L. Mencken on *Smart Set* (1914–23) and the *American Mercury* (1924–30), but is chiefly noted for the exacting standards and violent expression in his criticism of the drama.

Nathanael (nùthă'–), one of the Twelve Apostles. John 1.45–51; 21.2. Identified with BARTHOLOMEW.

Natick (nā'tĭk), town (pop. 19,838), E Mass., W of Boston. Shoes. Founded in 1651 as a "praying Indian" village by John ELIOT.

Nation, Carry, 1846–1911, American temperance agitator. Convinced of divine appointment, she began breaking up saloons with a hatchet in 1900.

National Academy of Design, society of American painters, sculptors, and engravers, with hq. on upper Fifth Ave., New York city; estab. 1825, inc. 1828. Founders included S. F. B. Morse, Asher B. Durand, and Daniel Huntington. Operates tuition-free school.

National Archives, estab. 1934 by U.S. Congress for preservation of Federal government records.

national bank, in the U.S., bank of a class estab. by Congress in 1863–64. These banks were required to invest in U.S. bonds and were then authorized to issue their notes as currency, up to 90% of the value of their bonds. All national banks are now members of the FEDERAL RESERVE SYSTEM, whose notes gradually replaced those of the national banks after 1913.

National City, residential and industrial city (pop. 26,-832), S Calif., on San Diego Bay SW of San Diego. Produces refined oil and citrus fruit by-products.

National Council of the Churches of Christ in the United States of America, interdenominational organization composed of some 25 Protestant and 4 Eastern Orthodox bodies, founded 1950. It is not a governing body, but promotes general spiritual welfare through various activities.

national debt: see DEBT, PUBLIC.

national forests in 42 states of U.S., Alaska, and Puerto Rico now total over 220,000,000 acres. Federal government also owns c.4,500,000 acres of forest lands in national parks and monuments, over 8,000,000 in Indian reservations. Administered by Forest Service of Dept. of Agriculture, which does research on forest fires, tree diseases and pests, lumber products, land drainage, correct harvesting.

National Gallery, London, one of permanent art collections of Great Britain. Its building in Trafalgar Square was built 1832–38. Especially rich in Italian paintings of 15th and 16th cent.

National Gallery of Art, Washington, D.C., a bureau of the Smithsonian Inst., estab. 1937 by act of Congress.

Funds for the building (designed by John Russell Pope and opened in 1941) and his own collection were given by Andrew W. Mellon. Other art donors included Samuel H. Kress and Joseph E. Widener. Rich in Italian and French painting.

nationalism, political and social philosophy in which good of nation is paramount. Word used loosely and mostly in derogatory sense implying excessive zeal for national welfare and advancement. Though exact definition is impossible, nationalism is characterized by patriotism, and by faith in political and cultural values of a nation and in its destiny. Extreme nationalism arose in 19th cent. and has led to many clashes within and between countries. Many see nationalism as a divisive force in the world; others point to its invigorating effect on peoples.

National Labor Relations Board (NLRB), set up under the National Labor Relations Act of 1935 (also known as the Wagner Act) which affirms labor's right to organize and bargain collectively. Its principal function is to investigate charges of (and to render decisions on) unfair labor practices by employers, but with the passage (1947) of the Taft-Hartley Act, the NLRB's field was extended to cover complaints filed by employers against unions.

national parks and monuments. The Natl. Park Service, a bureau of U.S. Dept. of Interior, was estab. 1916 to correlate administration of national parks and monuments then under the charge of the department. In 1933 its trusteeship was extended to include certain areas hitherto under the jurisdiction of other government departments; by 1950 it was administering some 182 areas. In addition to those listed in NATIONAL PARKS AND MONUMENTS table (see pp. 676–79), the Natl. Park Service has charge of certain national cemeteries, parkways, and capital parks and also has responsibilities toward certain national recreational areas and historic sites not owned by the government. National parks may be estab. only by Congress; the President may designate national monuments.

National Recovery Administration, 1933–36, U.S. administrative bureau estab. under Natl. Industrial Recovery Act, designed to encourage industrial recovery and combat widespread unemployment. NRA head was H. S. Johnson; emblem was Blue Eagle. Over 500 compulsory fair-practice codes were adopted for various industries. U.S. Supreme Court decision of May, 1935, voided code system, made NRA ineffective. Many of its labor provisions were reenacted in later legislation (e.g., WAGES AND HOURS ACT).

National Republican party, in U.S. history, short-lived political organization opposed to Andrew Jackson. Formed after Jackson victory in 1828 by wealthier classes and others fearing his radical ideas. Nominated Henry Clay in 1831. By 1836 party had united with other groups to form WHIG PARTY.

National Road, authorized by Congress 1806, begun 1815. Great highway of Western migration. First section (Cumberland road), from Cumberland to Wheeling, opened in 1818. Turned over to states, which collected tolls for maintenance, road eventually ran to St. Louis. Present U.S. Highway 40 follows its route closely.

National Socialism, ideology of the National Socialist German Workers' party (abbreviated in German as NSDAP) in GERMANY. It became the program of the totalitarian dictatorship of Adolf HITLER, 1933–45. (The term *Nazi* was a derisive abbreviation of National Socialist.) The program, formulated by Hitler in *Mein Kampf* (1923) and based in part on the pseudo-scientific speculations of Alfred ROSENBERG, drew on such diverse sources as Gobineau's and H. S. Chamberlain's racial theories; Lassallean socialism; Italian FASCISM; GEOPOLITICS; and some of Nietzsche's ideas. It appealed to the masses of defeated Germany through hysterical nationalism and ANTI-SEMITISM, resentment of the Treaty of Versailles, and certain anti-capitalist features; it also found support among capi-

NATIONAL PARKS

Name	Location	Date Estab.	Area (acres)	Special Characteristics
Acadia	S Maine	1919	28,545.62	Mountain and coast scenery. See MOUNT DESERT ISLAND.
Big Bend	W Texas	1944	692,304.70	Canyons and desert plain.
Bryce Canyon	SW Utah	1928	36,010.38	Box canyon with fantastic and beautifully colored walls.
Carlsbad Caverns	SE N.Mex.	1930	45,526.59	Great limestone caverns.
Crater Lake	SW Oregon	1902	160,290.33	Very blue lake in crater.
Everglades	S Fla.	1947	1,100,173.00	Saw-grass prairies and mangrove forests. See EVERGLADES.
Glacier	NW Mont.	1910	998,415.93	Rocky Mt. region of glaciers, forests, and lakes.
Grand Canyon	NW Ariz.	1919	645,295.91	Tremendous gorge of the Colorado river, remarkable for formations and coloring.
Grand Teton	NW Wyo.	1929	95,360.46	Most scenic portion of the Teton Range.
Great Smoky Mountains	W N.C., E Tenn.	1930	505,173.79	Wild, beautiful area. See GREAT SMOKY MOUNTAINS.
Hawaii	T.H.	1916	176,456.60	Volcanic region, with two active volcanoes.
Hot Springs	SW central Ark.	1921	1,019.13	Mineral hot springs.
Isle Royale	N Mich.	1940	133,838.51	Forested island, the largest in Lake Superior, with moose herd.
Kings Canyon	E Calif.	1940	453,064.82	Beautiful Kings river canyons; sequoias.
Lassen Volcanic	N Calif.	1916	103,429.28	Mt. Lassen, only active volcano in United States proper.
Mammoth Cave	S Ky.	1936	50,695.73	Underground passages with beautiful limestone formations.
Mesa Verde	SW Colo.	1906	51,017.87	Well-preserved prehistoric cliff dwellings.
Mount McKinley	Central Alaska	1917	1,939,319.04	Highest peak in North America, 20,300 ft. high; glaciers.
Mount Rainier	SW central Wash.	1899	241,571.09	Some 26 active glaciers.
Olympic	NW Wash.	1938	840,838.69	Rain forests and glaciers. See OLYMPIC MOUNTAINS.
Platt	S Okla.	1906	911.97	Sulphur and other cold mineral springs.
Rocky Mountain	N central Colo.	1915	253,131.45	Many snow-capped peaks over 10,000 ft. high.
Sequoia	Central Calif.	1890	385,099.79	Groves of giant sequoias; Mt. Whitney; Kern river canyon.
Shenandoah	N Va.	1935	193,472.98	Forested mountains of the Blue Ridge; Skyline Drive.
Wind Cave	SW S.Dak.	1903	26,576.15	Limestone caverns in the Black Hills.
Yellowstone	Wyo., Mont., Idaho	1872	2,213,206.55	Geysers, Yellowstone canyon, falls, great wildlife sanctuary.
Yosemite	Central Calif.	1890	757,000.62	Beautiful mountain region with Yosemite Valley.
Zion	SW Utah	1919	94,241.06	Multicolored gorge in desert and canyon region.

NATIONAL HISTORICAL PARKS

Name	Location	Date Estab.	Area (acres)	Special Characteristics
Abraham Lincoln	Central Ky. near Hodgenville	1939	116.50	Traditional birthplace cabin on site of Lincoln's birthplace.
Chalmette	SE La.	1939	69.61	Part of scene of battle of New Orleans in War of 1812.
Colonial	SE Va.	1936	7,134.60	Historic Yorktown, Jamestown, Williamsburg, and Cape Henry.
Morristown	N N.J.	1933	958.37	Washington's headquarters. See MORRISTOWN.
Saratoga	E N.Y.	1948	2,113.59	Scene of American victory over British in American Revolution. See SARATOGA CAMPAIGN.

NATIONAL MONUMENTS

Name	Location	Date Estab.	Area (acres)	Special Characteristics
Ackia Battleground	NE Miss.	1938	49.15	See TUPELO.
Andrew Johnson	NE Tenn. in Greenville	1942	17.08	President Johnson's home, tailor shop, and grave.
Appomattox Court House	Central Va.	1940	968.25	Scene of Lee's surrender to Grant. See APPOMATTOX.
Arches	E Utah near Moab	1929	33,929.94	Giant arches formed by erosion.
Aztec Ruins	NW N.Mex. near Farmington	1923	27.14	Ruins of 12th-century Indian town.

NATIONAL MONUMENTS (continued)

Name	Location	Date Estab.	Area (acres)	Special Characteristics
Badlands	SW S.Dak.	1939	123,052.46	See BADLANDS.
Bandelier	N N.Mex. near Santa Fe	1916	27,048.89	Ruins of prehistoric Indian homes.
Big Hole Battlefield	SW Mont.	1910	200.00	Scene of attack by U.S. soldiers on Chief JOSEPH.
Black Canyon of the Gunnison	SW Colo. near Montrose	1933	13,176.02	Deep, narrow canyon of the Gunnison river.
Cabrillo	S Calif. on San Diego Bay	1913	0.50	Memorial to Juan Rodríguez Cabrillo.
Canyon de Chelly	NE Ariz.	1931	83,840.00	Red sandstone canyons with many cliff dwellings.
Capitol Reef	S Utah	1937	33,068.74	20-mile-long sandstone cliff.
Capulin Mountain	NE N.Mex. E of Raton	1916	680.42	Huge cinder cone of recently extinct volcano.
Casa Grande	S Ariz. E of Casa Grande	1918	472.50	Casa Grande [big house] in ruins of prehistoric villages.
Castillo de San Marcos	NE Fla.	1924	18.51	Old masonry fort. See SAINT AUGUSTINE.
Castle Pinckney	SE S.C.	1924	3.50	Part of the early defenses of Charleston harbor.
Cedar Breaks	SW Utah near Cedar City	1933	6,172.20	Amphitheater (2,000 ft. deep) formed by erosion.
Chaco Canyon	NW N.Mex. S of Farmington	1907	21,239.95	Important Indian ruins.
Channel Islands	Off S Calif.	1938	26,819.26 (land and water area)	Including Santa Barbara and Anacapa islands; fossils; sea lions.
Chiricahua	SE Ariz.	1924	10,529.80	Curious rock formations—pillars, balanced rocks, fantastic figures.
Colorado	W Colo. near Grand Junction	1911	18,120.55	Huge monoliths, curious products of erosion.
Craters of the Moon	S Idaho	1924	47,210.67	Volcanic cones, craters, fissure lava flows.
Custer Battlefield	S Mont. near Hardin	1946	765.34	Site of Custer massacre. See LITTLE BIGHORN, river.
Death Valley	SE Calif., S Nev.	1933	1,860,138.31	Lowest land area in North America with distinctive desert vegetation.
Devil Postpile	Central Calif., SE of Yosemite	1911	798.46	Basaltic columns, some 60 ft. high.
Devils Tower	NE Wyo.	1906	1,193.91	Volcanic rock tower, rising c.1,280 ft. from Belle Fourche river bed.
Dinosaur	NE Utah, NW Colo., near Vernal, Utah	1915	190,798.49	Rich fossil quarries in fine condition; area of great scientific interest.
Effigy Mounds	NE Iowa	1949	1,000.00	Indian mounds in bird and animal shapes.
El Morro	W N.Mex.	1906	240.00	Sandstone monolith, with inscriptions of Spanish explorers and early American emigrants.
Fort Frederica	Off SE Ga.	1945	74.53	Ruins of fort built by James Oglethorpe. See SEA ISLANDS.
Fort Jefferson	Off S Fla.	1935	86.82	Building of this fort began in 1846. See DRY TORTUGAS.
Fort Laramie	E Wyo. SE of Casper	1938	214.41	Buildings of old fort on the Oregon Trail.
Fort McHenry	N Md.	1939	47.64	Birthplace of the *Star-spangled Banner*. See McHENRY, FORT.
Fort Marion				See SAINT AUGUSTINE.
Fort Matanzas	NE Fla.	1924	227.76	Spanish fort. See SAINT AUGUSTINE.
Fort Pulaski	SE Ga.	1924	5,427.39	Fort on Cockspur Island. See PULASKI, FORT.
Fort Sumter	SE S.C. at Charleston	1948	2.40	Scene of engagement which opened the Civil War. See SUMTER, FORT.
Fossil Cycad	SW S.Dak. near Hot Springs	1922	320.00	Area in Black Hills containing fossilized plants.
George Washington Birthplace	E Va. near Fredericksburg	1930	393.68	Estate and reconstructed mansion. See WAKEFIELD.
Gila Cliff Dwellings	SW N.Mex. near Silver City	1907	160.00	Well-preserved cliff dwellings in 150-foot cliff.
Glacier Bay	SE Alaska	1925	2,297,734.10	Tidewater glaciers.

NATIONAL MONUMENTS (continued)

Name	Location	Date Estab.	Area (acres)	Special Characteristics
Grand Canyon	NW Ariz.	1932	196,051.00	Part of Grand Canyon including Torowcap Point.
Gran Quivira	Central N.Mex. near Mountainair	1909	450.94	Ruins of Spanish mission and Indian pueblos.
Great Sand Dunes	S Colo. SW of Alamosa	1932	35,908.19	Large, high sand dunes in Sangre de Cristo Mts.
Holy Cross	W central Colo.	1929	1,392.00	Snow-filled crevasses, forming a cross.
Homestead	SE Nebr. near Beatrice	1939	162.73	Site of first farm claimed under Homestead Act of 1862.
Hovenweep	SE Utah, SW Colo. near Blanding, Utah	1923	299.34	Four groups of prehistoric pueblos and cliff dwellings.
Jewel Cave	SW S.Dak. near Hot Springs	1908	1,274.56	Limestone caves, chambers connected by narrow galleries, in Black Hills.
Joshua Tree	SE Calif. near Indio	1936	695,221.64	Stand of the rare Joshua trees, a species of yucca.
Katmai	S Alaska	1918	2,697,590.00	Volcanic area, with the Valley of Ten Thousand Smokes.
Lava Beds	N Calif. NE of Mt. Shasta	1925	46,027.56	Examples of volcanic activity; scene of Modoc Indian war.
Lehman Caves	E Nev. near Ely	1922	640.00	Gray and white limestone caves; stalactites.
Meriwether Lewis	Central Tenn. near Hohenwald	1925	300.00	Grave of the leader of the Lewis and Clark expedition.
Montezuma Castle	Central Ariz. S of Flagstaff	1906	738.09	Well-preserved cliff dwellings.
Mound City Group	S central Ohio near Chillicothe	1923	57.00	Prehistoric Indian mounds.
Muir Woods	W Calif. near Mill Valley	1908	424.56	Grove of redwoods.
Natural Bridges	SE Utah near Blanding	1908	2,649.70	Three sandstone bridges, one 222 ft. high, with 261-foot span.
Navajo	NE Ariz.	1909	360.00	Ruins of several large cliff dwellings.
Ocmulgee	Central Ga. near Macon	1936	683.48	Remains of mounds and prehistoric towns.
Old Kasaan	SE Alaska	1916	38.00	Site of abandoned Haida Indian village.
Oregon Caves	SW Oregon S of Grants Pass	1909	480.00	Limestone caverns of beauty and variety.
Organ Pipe Cactus	S Ariz. W of Tucson	1937	328,161.73	Organ pipe cactus and other desert growth unique to the region.
Perry's Victory Memorial	N Ohio NW of Sandusky	1936	14.25	Site of Oliver H. Perry's victory in War of 1812 at Put in Bay.
Petrified Forest	E Ariz. E of Holbrook	1906	85,303.63	Petrified logs from Triassic period; part of the Painted Desert.
Pinnacles	S Calif. S of Hollister	1908	12,817.77	Rock spires 500–1,200 ft. high; caves.
Pipe Spring	NW Ariz. near the Grand Canyon	1923	40.00	Spring first visited by Mormons; old fort; in Kaibab Indian Reservation.
Pipestone	SW Minn. near Pipestone	1937	115.60	Quarry here was source for Indian peace pipes.
Rainbow Bridge	S Utah	1910	160.00	Pink sandstone arch, 309 ft. high.
Saguaro	SE Ariz. near Tucson	1933	53,669.24	Saguaro, other cacti, and varied desert growth.
Scotts Bluff	W Nebr. near Scottsbluff	1919	2,196.44	Landmark on the Oregon Trail.
Shoshone Cavern	NW Wyo. near Cody	1909	212.37	Big cave with encrustations of crystals.
Sitka	SE Alaska near Sitka	1910	57.00	Site of an Indian defeat by the Russian settlers.
Statue of Liberty	SE N.Y.	1924	10.38	See LIBERTY, STATUE OF.
Sunset Crater	N Ariz. near Flagstaff	1930	3,040.00	Red, yellow, and orange volcanic crater; ice caves; lava flows.

NATIONAL MONUMENTS (continued)

Name	Location	Date Estab.	Area (acres)	Special Characteristics
Timpanogos Cave	N central Utah near Salt Lake City	1922	250.00	Limestone cavern on Mt. Timpanogos.
Tonto	S central Ariz. near Roosevelt Dam	1907	1,120.00	Two well-preserved cliff dwellings at junction of Tonto Creek and Salt river.
Tumacacori	S Ariz. N of Nogales	1908	10.00	Mission founded by Eusebio F. KINO, rebuilt by Franciscans.
Tuzigoot	Central Ariz. near Clarksdale	1939	42.67	Excavated Indian ruins.
Verendrye	NW N.Dak.	1917	253.04	Commemorates Vérendrye's explorations.
Walnut Canyon	N Ariz. near Flagstaff	1915	1,641.62	Cliff dwellings.
Wheeler	SW Colo.	1908	300.00	Pinnacles and gorges, carved by volcanic action and erosion.
White Sands	S central N.Mex. near Alamogordo	1933	140,247.04	Wind-drifted gypsum sands; dunes 10–60 ft. high.
Whitman	SE Wash. near Walla Walla	1940	45.84	Site of mission of Marcus WHITMAN.
Wupatki	N Ariz. N of Flagstaff	1924	35,013.03	Several prehistoric pueblos.
Yucca House	SW Colo. near Cortez	1919	9.60	Remains of prehistoric Indian village.
Zion	SW Utah	1937	33,920.75	Examples of geologic phenomena; Hurricane Fault and colorful Kolob Canyon.

NATIONAL MILITARY PARKS

Name	Location	Date Estab.	Area (acres)	Special Characteristics
Chickamauga and Chattanooga	NW Ga., E Tenn.	1890	8,127.16	See CHATTANOOGA.
Fort Donelson	N Tenn.	1928	102.54	See DONELSON, FORT.
Fredericksburg and Spotsylvania County Battlefields Memorial	N Va.	1927	2,420.71	See FREDERICKSBURG, Va.
Gettysburg	S Pa.	1895	2,534.11	See GETTYSBURG, Pa.
Guilford Courthouse	Central N.C. near Greensboro	1917	148.83	Battle in Carolina campaign of American Revolution.
Kings Mountain	N S.C.	1931	4,012.00	See KINGS MOUNTAIN.
Moores Creek	SE N.C. near Wilmington	1926	30.00	Battlefield in the American Revolution.
Petersburg	SE Va.	1926	1,531.02	See PETERSBURG, Va.
Shiloh	S Tenn.	1894	3,729.26	See SAVANNAH, Tenn.
Stones River	Central Tenn.	1927	323.86	See MURFREESBORO, Tenn.
Vicksburg	W Miss.	1899	1,323.56	See VICKSBURG, Miss.

NATIONAL MEMORIAL PARK

Name	Location	Date Estab.	Area (acres)	Special Characteristics
Theodore Roosevelt	SW N.Dak.	1947	58,341.26	Part of Roosevelt's Elkhorn ranch; Badlands along Little Missouri river.

NATIONAL BATTLEFIELD PARKS

Name	Location	Date Estab.	Area (acres)	Special Characteristics
Kennesaw Mountain	NW Ga. near Marietta	1947	3,094.21	Union defeat in Atlanta campaign.
Richmond	E Va.	1944	684.44	See RICHMOND, Va.

talists and industrialists, who hoped to use it as a tool against German Social Democracy and as a bulwark against Communism. The basic principles of its ideology were the superiority of the Nordic or Aryan "master race," which was to be led by a supreme, infallible *Führer* [leader] to victory over its internal and external enemies—notably the Jews and Communists, who were credited with a plot to enslave the world. All German-speaking peoples were to be united in a single empire (the "Third Reich"), which was to last 1,000 years, and to rule the inferior races. The emotional appeal of these theories was immense and received impetus from skillful propaganda, mass meetings, and uniformed militias—the brown-shirted SA (*Sturmabteilung,* or storm troops) and the black SS (*Schutzstaffel,* or security echelon; originally Hitler's bodyguard). The party symbol was the swastika. After Hitler took power, the NSDAP became the sole legal party and the chief instrument of his policy. Its rule of brutality and terror led, after the outbreak of World War II, to the slaughter of millions (see CONCENTRATION CAMP; WAR CRIMES), and it eventually fell under the complete control of its own SECRET POLICE. The NSDAP had affiliates in other countries (esp. Austria and Czechoslovakia).

National Trust, British association to preserve for the nation places of natural beauty or buildings of architectural or historic interest; founded 1894. May either acquire land inalienably or protect private property by special covenant.

National University, at Manila; founded 1900 as Colegio Filipino, inc. 1921 under present name. First nonsectarian university in the Philippines.

National Youth Administration, 1935–44, estab. by U.S. Congress. At first purpose was to find part-time work for unemployed youths; emphasis later shifted to training youths for war work.

NATO: see NORTH ATLANTIC TREATY.

Nattier, Jean Marc (zhä' märk' nätyä'), 1685–1766, fashionable French portrait painter at court of Louis XV.

Natural Bridge, village, western Va., SW of Lexington. Natural Bridge over Cedar Creek (arch 215 ft. high, span 90 ft.) is W. Once owned by Thomas Jefferson.

Natural Bridges National Monument: see NATIONAL PARKS AND MONUMENTS (table).

natural gas, mixture of gases obtained from the earth and widely used as fuel. Composition varies, but is chiefly methane. It is commonly associated with production of petroleum, but also occurs far from oil fields. Pipe lines, some more than 1,000 mi. long, carry the fuel to industrial centers. Largest U.S. producers are Texas, Okla., Calif., La., W.Va. Some gasoline is obtained from natural gas.

natural resources, conservation of: see CONSERVATION OF NATURAL RESOURCES.

natural rights, theory holding that man is born with inalienable rights; known to Greeks, developed by Rousseau and Jefferson.

Naugatuck (nô'gŭtŭk"), borough (pop. 17,455), SW Conn., on Naugatuck R. below Waterbury; settled 1702. Rubber center (Goodyear estab. plant here, 1843). Metal and plastic products and chemicals.

Naugatuck, river rising in NW Conn., flowing c.65 mi. S, past mfg. centers, to Housatonic R. at Derby.

Nauheim, Germany: see BAD NAUHEIM.

Naumburg (noum'boork), city (pop. 41,379), Saxony-Anhalt, E central Germany, on Saale R. It is famed for its cathedral (13th–14th cent.), which has fine German Gothic sculptures.

Naupaktos (nôpǎk'tŭs), Ital. *Lepanto,* town (pop. 5,494), W central Greece; a port on Gulf of Corinth. Important Athenian naval base in Peloponnesian War. It passed to Venice 1407, to Turkey 1499, and was again held by Venice 1687–99. Naval battle of LEPANTO took place here (1571).

Nauplia (nô'plēu), Gr. *Nauplion,* port town (pop. 7,960), S Greece, on E coast of Peloponnesus. First cap. of independent Greece, 1830–34 (succeeded by Athens).

Nauru (näōō'rōō), atoll (8 sq. mi.; pop. 2,855), central Pacific. Discovered 1798 by the British. Annexed 1888 by Germany, it was occupied in World War I by Australians, who won mandate over it in 1920. Came under UN trusteeship in 1947, held jointly by Great Britain, Australia, New Zealand. Occupied throughout World War II by Japanese. Important for rich phosphate deposits.

Naushon, island, Mass.: see ELIZABETH ISLANDS.

Nausicaä (nôsǐ'käü), in the *Odyssey,* princess of Phaeacia, who led shipwrecked Odysseus to her father's court and helped entertain him.

nautilus (nô'tŭlŭs), either of two types of mollusk. One genus (*Nautilus*) is represented by pearly or chambered nautilus of S Pacific; habit of secreting shell in successive "chambers" is celebrated in poem by O. W. Holmes. Paper nautilus or argonaut (*Argonauta*) is found in most warm waters.

Nauvoo (nôvōō'), city (pop. 1,242), W Ill., on the Mississippi and N of Keokuk, Iowa; settled shortly after 1830 as Commerce, occupied and renamed 1839 by MORMONS under Joseph SMITH. Pop. reached c.20,000 under Mormons. After Smith's death, 1844, group left for Utah (1846). French communist colony (the Icarians) under Étienne CABET was here 1849–56. Smith's house still stands.

Navaho Indians or **Navajo Indians** (both: nä'vŭhō), North American tribe of Athapascan linguistic stock. A nomadic tribe of the Southwest, they lived in earth-covered lodges in winter, brush shelters in summer. Sheep were introduced in the early 17th cent. and the Navaho became primarily sheep raisers. Warlike, they raided the Pueblo Indians, and they resisted the whites until Kit Carson subdued them by killing their sheep (1863–64). Many Navaho were imprisoned until 1868, when they were given a reservation in NE Ariz., NW N.Mex., and SE Utah. Their turquoise and silver jewelry and their textiles (esp. blankets) are popular among whites.

Navajo National Monument: see NATIONAL PARKS AND MONUMENTS (table).

Naval Academy, United States: see UNITED STATES NAVAL ACADEMY.

naval conferences, international assemblies to consider rules of naval warfare, limitation of armaments, and related topics. *London Naval Conference* (1908–9), with delegates of 10 naval powers, convened to reach agreement on establishment of International Prize Court. Adopted Declaration of London, which, though unratified, influenced international law. Pres. Harding called *Washington Conference* (1921–22) to consider naval matters in Pacific. Attended by Great Britain, Japan, Italy, France, U.S., China, Netherlands, Portugal, and Belgium. Several treaties resulted. A Five-Power Treaty—Britain, U.S., Japan, France, Italy—estab. tonnage ratio, especially in capital ships and aircraft carriers. Another five-power treaty governed submarines. In Four-Power Pact France, Japan, Britain, and U.S. agreed to respect one another's rights in Pacific. Treaties were to stand until Dec. 31, 1936. Two Nine-Power treaties guaranteed independence and integrity of China. *Geneva Conference* of 1927 and *London Conference* of 1930 failed to limit armaments, though a new ratio was estab. In 1934 Japan declared intention to terminate Washington Conference treaty, and withdrew from *London Conference* of 1935. All attempts of other powers to limit armaments failed in part. With outbreak of war in 1939, treaties were completely abandoned.

Navarino, battle of (nävärē'nō), 1827, naval battle in Greek War of Independence, resulting from Turkey's refusal to accept an armistice demanded by England, France, and Russia. Egyptian fleet of MOHAMMED ALI, anchored at Pylos (then called Navarino), was defenseless against allied attack; its destruction influenced Egypt's withdrawal from Greek war in 1828.

Navarre (nŭvär'), Span. *Navarra,* province (4,024 sq.

mi.; pop. 369,618), N Spain, bordering on France, between W Pyrenees and Ebro R.; cap. Pamplona. Pastures, vineyards, cattle raising. Sparsely populated. Population is largely of Basque stock (see BASQUES). The Basque kingdom of Navarre (founded 824 as kingdom of Pamplona) expanded quickly and reached its zenith under SANCHO III, who ruled over nearly all Christian Spain (1000–1035). On his death, Navarre went to his son García. The kingdom then also comprised the Basque Provs. and, N of the Pyrenees, the district of Lower Navarre (now in France). The crown passed, by inheritance and marriage, to the counts of Champagne (1234), the kings of France (1305), the counts of Évreux (1349), JOHN II of Aragon (1425), the counts of FOIX (1479), and the lords of ALBRET (1494), from whom it devolved upon HENRY IV of France and his Bourbon successors until Louis XVI. In fact, however, Ferdinand V of Aragon seized all but Lower Navarre in 1512 and thus brought it to Spain. The Spanish kings carried the title kings of Navarre until 1833, when Navarre sided with the Carlists.

Navarrete, Juan Fernández (nävärä′tä), 1526–79, Spanish religious painter, court painter to Philip II. Influenced by the Venetians.

Navarro, Madame de: see ANDERSON, MARY A.

Navas de Tolosa (nä′väs dä tōlō′sä), town (pop. 1,134), S Spain, in Andalusia. Here in 1212 Alfonso VIII of Castile routed the Moors.

Navasota (nä′vŭsō′tŭ), city (pop. 5,188), E central Texas, near confluence of Navasota and Brazos rivers and NW of Houston. Shipping and processing center for cotton and lumber area. Has statue of LaSalle, allegedly killed near by.

Navigation Acts, in British colonial history, name given to parliamentary Acts of Trade. An outgrowth of MERCANTILISM, they were caused by threat to English navigators of rise of Dutch carrying trade. First Navigation Act (1660) aimed to bar foreigners from English trade; to regulate plantation trade; to give England the monopoly of certain colonial produce. In 1663 shipment from English ports was required of all foreign goods for American plantations. Last important act was the Act to Prevent Frauds and Abuses of 1696. Contention that the American revolution partly derives from the Acts is questionable. More adverse effects were felt in Ireland, Scotland, and the Channel Isls. Acts were repealed in 1849.

Navigators' Islands: see SAMOA.

Navy, United States Department of the, estab. 1798 by act of Congress as a separate department headed by Secretary of the Navy. Functioned as separate department until 1947, when it was incorporated in Natl. Military Establishment; in 1949 became a division of U.S. Dept. of Defense.

Navy Island, S Canada, in Niagara R., just above Niagara Falls. Here W. L. MACKENZIE estab. hq. in rebellion of 1837.

Naxos (näk′sŏs, Gr. näk′sôs), island (169 sq. mi.; pop. 20,132), off S Greece, in Aegean Sea, largest and most important of the CYCLADES. Exports a noted white wine and other agr. products. In legend Theseus abandoned ARIADNE here.

Nayarit (näyärēt′), state (10,547 sq. mi.; pop. 292,343), W Mexico, on the Pacific; cap., TEPIC. Volcanic soil, heavy rains, and variation in altitude cause variety of agr. produce. Forest and mineral wealth on mainland and on Las TRES MARÍAS isls. are almost unexploited. Separated from Jalisco as territory 1884, it became a state 1917.

Nazarenes (nä′zŭrēnz), group of German artists of early 19th cent. who worked in Rome and tried to revive Christian art. Exerted much influence in Germany. Inspired by early Italian painters, they worked from imagination and not from nature. Members included J. F. Overbeck, Philipp Veit, and Peter von Cornelius. Were at one time called Pre-Raphaelites, but little of their work links them to later English group.

Nazareth (nă′–), town (pop. over 20,000), N Israel. Here Jesus lived before beginning his ministry. It is a pilgrimage center with many shrines and churches.

Nazareth, borough (pop. 5,830), E Pa., NW of Easton. Mfg. of clothing and cement.

Nazareth College: see LOUISVILLE, Ky.; ROCHESTER, N.Y.

Nazarite, in Bible, man dedicated to the service of Jehovah by various vows, either his own or those of his parents, (e.g., to abstain from wine, not to cut his hair). Samson was a Nazarite. Num. 6.1–21; Judges 13.4,5.

Naze, the, Norway: see LINDESNES.

Nazi: see NATIONAL SOCIALISM.

Nazimova, Alla (nŭzĭ′mŭvŭ), 1879–1945, Russian-American actress. Studied with Stanislavsky. In U.S. after 1905, she was memorable in Ibsen roles and in *Mourning Becomes Electra* (1931–32).

Nb, chemical symbol of the element NIOBIUM.

Nd, chemical symbol of the element NEODYMIUM.

Ne, chemical symbol of the element NEON.

Neagh, Lough (lŏkh nä), lake, 18 mi. long and 11 mi. wide, N. Ireland, in Counties Armagh, Tyrone, Londonderry, Antrim, and Down. Largest fresh-water body in British Isles, it has fine fisheries.

Neanderthal (nēän′dŭrtäl″), small valley, W Germany, E of Düsseldorf. Here in 1856 skeletal remains of the so-called Neanderthal man were discovered (see MAN, PRIMITIVE).

Neapolis (nēä′pŭlĭs) [Gr.,= new city], name of many anc. Greek and Roman cities (e.g., Naples, Italy).

Nearchus (nēär′kŭs), fl. 324 B.C., Macedonian general. Commanded Alexander's fleet in voyage from India up Persian coast to Susa (325–324 B.C.).

Near Islands: see ALEUTIAN ISLANDS.

nearsightedness or **myopia** (mīō′pēŭ), sight defect resulting when light rays focus in front of retina. It is caused by abnormal length of eyeball from front to back or by distortion of lens.

neat's-foot oil, yellow, almost odorless oil obtained by boiling feet of cattle. It is used as a lubricant and in leather dressing.

Nebo, Mount, summit of Pisgah ridge from which Moses viewed Canaan, the Promised Land. Deut. 34.1.

Nebraska, state (76,653 sq. mi.; pop. 1,325,510), central U.S., in GREAT PLAINS; admitted 1867 as 37th state; cap. LINCOLN. OMAHA largest city. Bounded NE and E by MISSOURI R. PLATTE R. important. Plains rise to tableland in W. Agr. of grains (esp. wheat, corn), sugar beets; raising of livestock. Industries based on these products. Part of Louisiana Purchase (1803). Scene of fur-trading activities. First permanent settlement BELLEVUE (c.1823). Made territory under KANSAS-NEBRASKA BILL (1854). Land boom in 1860s. Ranchers opposed the coming of homesteaders who opened farms despite severe winter and droughts. Hard times caused farmers to support the GRANGER MOVEMENT and POPULIST PARTY in late 19th cent. Depression of 1930s was severe, but food demands of World War II, soil conservation, agr. experimentation have revived agr.

Nebraska, University of, mainly at Lincoln; land-grant, state supported; coed.; chartered 1869, opened 1871.

Nebraska City, city (pop. 6,872), SE Nebr., on Missouri R. and E of Lincoln. Processes livestock, grain, truck, and dairy products.

Nebraska Wesleyan University: see LINCOLN.

Nebuchadnezzar (nĕ″byŭkŭdnĕ′zŭr; nĕ″bŭ–), d. 562 B.C., king of Babylonia (c.605–562 B.C.); son of Nabopolassar. In his father's reign he defeated the Egyptians under NECHO (605). In 597 B.C. he quelled revolt of Judah and set Zedekiah on throne. Putting down a new revolt, he took king and nobles captive, thus beginning the Captivity. Under Nebuchadnezzar Babylonia flourished and Babylon became magnificent. Also Nebuchadrezzar, Nebuchodonosor.

nebula (nĕ′byōōlŭ), in astronomy, a cloudlike mass, usually luminous. Within our Galaxy exist planetary nebulae, each a central star with shell of gaseous material; bright diffuse nebulae; and dark diffuse nebulae (masses of opaque particles). Luminosity of galactic nebulae attributed to reflection from, and radiation excited by, associated stars. Extragalactic nebulae are star systems (most of them spiral) similar to our Galaxy. Their apparent recession from earth supports expanding universe theory.

nebular hypothesis, theory of origin of solar system to which Laplace gave scientific form. Postulates that solar system was once a vast rotating mass of hot nebulous matter contracting as it cooled and increasing its speed of rotation; that centrifugal force caused successive rings to be detached, the smaller revolving more rapidly; that from each ring evolved a planet. Theory now held untenable because each ring would tend to form many small bodies rather than planets and momentum of planetary rotation is too great relative to that of sun.

Necessity, Fort, entrenched camp at Great Meadows (near present Uniontown, Pa.), site of defeat of George Washington and Va. militia by French in 1754. Grave of Gen. Braddock is near Fort Necessity Natl. Battlefield Site.

Necho (nē'kō), 609–593 B.C., king of anc. Egypt, of XXVI dynasty; son of PSAMTIK. After fall of Nineveh (612) he took Palestine and Syria after battle of Megiddo. His empire fell when Nebuchadnezzar came W. Necho met him at Carchemish, was beaten (605) and returned to Egypt.

Neckar (nĕ'kär), river, 228 mi. long, SW Germany, rising in Black Forest and flowing N and W through Württemberg and Baden, past Tübingen, Esslingen, Stuttgart, Heilbronn, and Heidelberg, to join the Rhine at Mannheim. Navigable from Stuttgart. Celebrated for its scenic charm.

Necker, Jacques (zhäk' nĕkĕr'), 1732–1804, French banker and financial expert, b. Geneva, Switzerland. After the fall of TURGOT, whose free-trade policy he had criticized, he became director of the treasury (1776) and director general of finances (1777). He sought to limit the growing national debt by stringent economies, which made him unpopular with the court. He resigned in 1781, after making public the financial situation in his *Compte rendu,* and retired to Coppet, his Swiss estate. In 1788, when France was on the verge of bankruptcy, Louis XVI recalled him and made him minister of state. Necker gained immense popularity by recommending the calling of the STATES-GENERAL. When the court party secured his dismissal, the populace stormed the Bastille (July 14, 1789) and forced his reinstatement. He resigned in 1790 and retired to Coppet. His wife, **Suzanne (Curchod) Necker,** 1739–94, wrote on various subjects, notably *Réflexions sur le divorce* (1794). Her salon was very influential. Their daughter was Mme de Staël.

nectarine: see PEACH.

Needham (nē'dùm), residential town (pop. 16,313), E Mass., WSW of Boston; settled 1680. Mfg. of knit goods, elastic goods and surgical, dental instruments.

Needles, city (pop. 4,051), SE Calif., on Colorado R. near Hoover Dam. Mojave Indian trade center.

Neenah (nē'nù), city (pop. 12,437), E Wis., on L. Winnebago opposite MENASHA; settled 1835. Wood and metal products are made.

Neer, Aert van der (ärt' vän dĕr när'), 1603–77, Dutch landscape painter. Excelled in painting light effects (e.g., moonlight scenes and sunsets). His son, **Eglan Hendrik van der Neer,** c.1635–1703, is noted for his paintings of luxurious interiors, hunting scenes, and biblical subjects.

Neerwinden (närvĭn'dùn), village SE of Louvain, Belgium. Here in 1693 the French under Luxembourg defeated William III of England, and in 1793 the Austrians defeated the French under Dumouriez.

negative, in PHOTOGRAPHY, a film after developing and fixing. It is so named because light and dark areas of image are reversed. Developing is done in darkness; fixing process stops further reduction of silver salts. Metallic silver and gelatin form the image. A positive is produced from negative by printing, i.e., placing negative between light source and sensitive paper. After exposure to light the sensitive paper is treated chemically and "print" is washed and dried.

Negaunee, (nĭgô'nē), city (pop. 6,472), W Upper Peninsula, N Mich., on Marquette iron range near Ishpeming. Resort. Iron discovered here 1844.

Negev (nĕ'gĕv) or **Negeb** (–gĕb), semidesert region (c.4,700 sq. mi.), S Israel, between the Mediterranean and Gulf of Aqaba. Borders on Egypt (W) and on Jordan (E). Today its only town is Beersheba, but in ancient times it had several prosperous cities. Comprises over a third of Israeli territory. Plans have been made to open it up to agr. and settlement. Scene of fighting between Egyptian and Israeli forces, 1948.

Negoiul (nĕgoi'ōōl) or **Negoi** (nĕgoi'), peak, 8,361 ft. high, Rumania; highest of Transylvanian Alps.

Negri, Ada (ä'dä nä'grē), 1870–1945, Italian writer, known for her love lyrics and an autobiographical novel, *Morning Star* (1921).

Negri Sembilan: see MALAYA.

Negro, member of any of several groups of peoples, characterized physically by black or dark brown skin, wooly hair, broad flat nose, prominent eyes with yellowish cornea, thick lips, and prognathous jaw. Term most properly applied to tribes of central and W Africa. Negroid peoples include Negrillo and Negrito (see PYGMY). Negroes in Africa generally have crude form of agr. and simple handicrafts; religion is generally form of ANIMISM. Negroes once invaded Egypt, and various Negro kingdoms flourished in N Africa. Begun in 15th cent., slave trade from Africa was profitable European enterprise by 17th cent. Negroes entered the Americas by 1501. First Negroes in present U.S. came to Va. in 1619. Tobacco planting increased Negro slavery in South. Although Northern colonies also had slaves, after American Revolution slavery there gradually declined. Large-scale production of cotton in South, spurred by invention of cotton gin in 1793, greatly increased slavery. Life of slaves on cotton plantations was often harsh. Slavery became important political issue in MISSOURI COMPROMISE (1820) and KANSAS-NEBRASKA BILL (1854). EMANCIPATION PROCLAMATION technically freed slaves of Confederacy. Difficult problem of adjustment after Civil War met by FREEDMEN'S BUREAU and Republican RECONSTRUCTION program, countered by KU KLUX KLAN organization of Southerners. Share-cropping system left Negro in economically poor position, and Southern states maintained "white supremacy" through enactment of segregation and poll tax laws. Wide Negro migration to North sometimes resulted in race riots. Negroes fought in both World Wars, made cultural contributions to American life, and widened scope of activities in public life, but questions of economic and political discrimination still pose a problem in U.S.

Negro, Rio (rē'ō nä'grō), river of N Brazil, one of chief tributaries of Amazon and a primary commercial channel. Originates as Guainía in Colombia. A natural canal connects it with Orinoco. There are many other rivers named Rio Negro (Span., Río Negro).

Negro minstrel, white entertainer in Negro make-up. T. D. Rice gave first blackface performance (song-and-dance act *Jim Crow*) c.1828. After 1846 Christy's minstrels (see CHRISTY, E. P.) set minstrel show pattern with interlocutor and two end men telling jokes as well as chorus and soloists to sing. After 1870, vaudeville, films, and radio eclipsed minstrel shows.

Negropont, Greece: see CHALCIS; EUBOEA.

Negros (nä'grōs), island (4,905 sq. mi.; pop. 1,218,710), one of Visayan Isls., in Philippines. Mainly mountainous. Products include sugar cane, rice, and hemp. Silliman Univ. (1901) is at Dumaguete on SE coast. Negritos inhabit interior.

Nehemiah (nē″ûmī′ù), central figure of book of Nehemiah: see EZRA.

Nehru, Jawaharlal (jùwähùrläl′ nē′rōo), 1889–, Indian statesman, b. Allahabad, educated at Harrow and Cambridge. Admitted to the bar in 1912. After massacre of Amritsar (1919) he joined in struggle for India's freedom. Headed Indian Natl. Congress several times after 1929. His advocacy of industrialization and socialization was opposed by Gandhi, whose ideal was an agrarian society. Spent most of the period 1930–36 in jail for conducting civil disobedience campaigns. In World War II he was again imprisoned for opposing aid to the British, who refused to free India immediately. With creation of new state of India in 1947 he became its prime minister and continued to hold that office after elections of 1952. Wrote several books, including *Glimpses of World History* (1936) and the autobiography, *Toward Freedom.*

Neilson, William Allan (nēl′sùn), 1869–1946, American educator, a Shaksperian scholar. He was president of Smith Col., 1917–39, and editor in chief of second edition (1934) of *Webster's New International Dictionary.*

Neisse (nī′sù), two rivers of Silesia; tributaries of the Oder. The **Glatzer Neisse** (glä′tsùr), 120 mi. long, rises in the Sudetes and winds NE past Glatz. The **Lausitzer Neisse** (lou″zī″tsùr) or **Lusatian Neisse** (lōosä′shùn), Czech *Lužická Nisa,* 140 mi. long, is farther W. Rising in Czechoslovakia, it flows N across the Sudetes and Lusatia, past Gorlitz, and forms the border between the [East] German Democratic Republic and Polish-administered Germany.

Nejd (nĕjd), former emirate, N central Arabia, now forming a province of SAUDI ARABIA. It is mainly a plateau with oasis in E part; RIAD is chief city. The WAHABI leader, Ibn Saud, conquered the Nejd from Turkey, 1900–1912.

Nejef (nĕ′jĕf) or **Najaf** (nä′jäf), town, central Iraq; pilgrimage center for Shiite Moslems. Tomb of Ali, son-in-law of Mohammed, is here.

Nekhtnebf (nĕkt″nĕ′bùf), Gr. *Nectanebos,* name of two kings of anc. Egypt. **Nekhtnebf I** (reigned 379–361 B.C.) founded the XXIX dynasty. Resisted a Persian invasion successfully. Built splendid temples. **Nekhtnebf II** (reigned 359–343 B.C.) was the son of a viceroy. He overthrew the son of Nekhtnebf I. He also was a builder. Beat off one Persian invasion but was defeated in another.

Nekrasov, Nikolai Alekseyevich (nyĭkùlī′ ùlyĭksyä′ĭvĭch nyĭkrä′sùf), 1821–77, Russian poet and publicist. The driving force of his life was to improve social conditions—especially the lot of the peasant—in Russia. This theme permeates his literary journal, *Contemporary* (1846–66), as well as his lyrics and narrative poems. *Who Is Happy in Russia?* (1873) is a satirical portrait of Russia under serfdom.

Nelson, (John) Byron (Jr.), 1912–, American golfer. Won U.S. Natl. Open title 1939, P.G.A. title 1940.

Nelson, Horatio Nelson, Viscount, 1758–1805, English naval hero. Won fame in FRENCH REVOLUTIONARY WARS. His destruction of French fleet at Aboukir (1798) ended Napoleon I's plan of conquest in the East. While assisting king of Sicily, he prolonged his stay in Naples because of the presence there of his mistress, Lady HAMILTON. Defeated the Danes at Copenhagen (1801). Destroyed combined French and Spanish fleets off Cape TRAFALGAR (1805), but was killed in action.

Nelson, William Rockhill, 1841–1915, American journalist. Launched Kansas City *Evening Star* in 1880. His editorship gained national attention.

Nelson, city (pop. 6,772), SE B.C., Canada, on Kootenay R. and N of Spokane, Wash. Railroad and mining center.

Nelson, river, N Man., Canada, rising at N end of L. Winnipeg and flowing 400 mi. NE to Hudson Bay at Port Nelson. Mouth discovered by Sir Thomas Button 1612. Was fur trade route.

Nemacolin's Path (nĕ′mùkō″lĭnz), Indian trail between Potomac and Monongahela rivers, going from site of present Cumberland, Md., to mouth of Redstone Creek (where Brownsville, Pa., now stands). Route of George Washington's first Western expedition and of Gen. Braddock's expedition. National Road was built on same route.

Neman, Russian name of NIEMEN, river.

Nemea (nē′mēù), anc. city, N Argolis, Greece. At the temple of Zeus were held the Nemean games (begun 573 B.C.), one of four Panhellenic festivals.

Nemean lion (nĭmē′ùn, nē′mēùn), beast of Nemea, invulnerable to weapons. HERCULES strangled it.

Nemesis (nĕm′ĭsĭs), Greek personification of law and order as avenging itself on the violator.

Nemi, Lake (nā′mē), small crater lake, Latium, central Italy. Here are the sacred wood and ruins of a famous temple of Diana. Two pleasure ships of Emperor Caligula, at lake's bottom for almost 2,000 years, were raised 1930–31.

Nemours (nùmōor′), town (pop. 5,336), Seine-et-Marne dept., N France. Was cap. of a duchy held in fief by house of Armagnac until 16th cent. and later given in appanage to various princely houses. Du Pont family of Delaware originated here.

Nemunas, Lithuanian name of NIEMEN, river.

Nenets National Okrug (nyĕ′nyĭts), administrative division (67,300 sq. mi.; pop. c.30,000), NE European RSFSR. Inhabitants are chiefly Nentsy—formerly and still generally known as SAMOYEDES.

Nennius, fl. 796, Welsh writer, to whom is ascribed the *Historia Britonum,* important because it records early British legends, especially about King Arthur.

neoclassicism. In English literature, Restoration and 18th-cent. period is often called Age of Neoclassicism or Age of Reason: classical learning, ancient literary "rules," reason, and common sense were preferred to enthusiasm and uncontrolled imagination. In architecture, see CLASSIC REVIVAL.

neodymium (nē″ōdĭ′mēùm), rare metallic element of rare earths (symbol = Nd; see also ELEMENT, table). Used in some yellow-green glassware and goggles.

Neolithic period (nēùlĭ′thĭk, nēō–) or **New Stone Age,** period of industrial development following the Paleolithic period or Old Stone Age, and characterized by new sources of food supply and use of polished stone tools. Pottery making, carpentry, and weaving emerged. Domestic animals and agr. appeared, and no new important species of animals have since been added to those domesticated in this period.

neon, rare gaseous element (symbol = Ne; see also ELEMENT, table), colorless, odorless, tasteless, chemically inert. Produces reddish orange glow when confined in glass tube through which electric current passes; used in electric advertising signs and airplane beacons.

Neoplatonism (nē″ōplä′tùnĭzùm), last of the great Greco-Roman pagan philosophies, so called because it was to some extent a return to Platonic doctrines with rejection of Stoic and Epicurean teachings. Though it was foreshadowed by many, notably Philo, Neoplatonism was founded by PLOTINUS in the 3d cent. The system was antimaterialistic and mystical. Neoplatonists believed that there is an utterly transcendent One or Unity (the great Cause and Principle), from whom everything in the universe proceeds by a process of emanations: the divine Mind emanates from the One, the world soul from the divine Mind; below that in scale come particular souls and finally material things. The fundamental idea of the connection of the individual soul with the One was to be paralleled in Christian mysticism. Plotinus' chief followers were Porphyry, Iamblichus, Proclus, and Hypatia. Emperor Julian was Neoplatonic. Justinian in 529 banned pagan schools, and Neoplatonism itself soon disappeared, but its influence continued through the Middle Ages.

Neoptolemus (nē″ōptō′lĭmùs), in Greek legend, son of

Achilles and Deidamia; husband of Hermione (daughter of Menelaus and Helen). Brave but cruel, he killed Priam at the altar of Zeus in the Trojan War. After the war Andromache and Helenus were his slaves. Also called Pyrrhus.

Neo-Pythagoreanism (nē'ō-pǐthă″gùrē'ùnǐzùm), philosophical and religious movement of 2d cent. and 1st cent. B.C., centering at Alexandria and based on revival of mystical doctrines derived from teachings of Pythagoras. Neo-Pythagoreans stressed sacrifices and miracles and held certain rarefied beliefs (objective reality of numbers, transmigration of souls, oneness of all in Divinity) without a well-developed mysticism. The movement lost out in rivalry with Neoplatonism. Its chief leader was Apollonius of Tyana.

Neosho (nēō'shō), city (pop. 5,790), SW Mo., SSE of Joplin, in an Ozark farm and resort area. Pro-Confederate convention passed ineffective ordinance of secession here in 1862.

Neosho, river, c.460 mi. long, rising in E central Kansas and flowing SE into Okla., where it is chiefly known as Grand R., then S to the Arkansas near Muskogee. In Okla., GRAND RIVER DAM is SE of Vinita, and Fort Gibson Dam is NNE of FORT GIBSON.

NEP: see NEW ECONOMIC POLICY.

Nepal (nùpôl'), kingdom (c.56,000 sq. mi.; pop. 6,283,-649), S central Asia, between India and Tibet; cap. Katmandu. In N is main section of Himalayas, including Mt. Everest. Nepal Valley (where rice, wheat, and fruits are produced) is the only densely populated area. Trades almost exclusively with India and Tibet. The Nepalese are mainly Hindus, with Buddhists forming a minority; they speak Tibeto-Burman languages. Since 18th cent. Nepal has been dominated by the GURKHA. In 1792 it first entered into treaty relations with the British, who recognized its full sovereignty in treaty of 1923. Ruled by premier belonging to Rana family until 1951, when successful revolts gave power to the king, who had formerly been a mere figurehead.

Nepos, Cornelius (nē'pŏs), c.100 B.C.–c.25 B.C., Roman historian, known for his biographies.

Neptune, in Roman religion, anc. god of water. Probably an indigenous god of fertility, he was later identified with Greek POSEIDON, god of sea.

Neptune, N.J.: see OCEAN GROVE.

Neptune, in astronomy, eighth PLANET in order from sun. With atmosphere and two satellites, it revolves about sun in c.164.8 years at mean distance of c.2,793,-400,000 mi. Mean diameter c.31,000 mi., rotation period c.15.8 hr. Discovery (1846) resulted from independent computations by J. C. Adams and U. J. J. Leverrier. See ill., p. 927.

neptunium, chemical element (symbol = Np; atomic no. = 93), discovered in 1940 by E. M. McMillan and P. H. Abelson by means of the cyclotron at Univ. of California.

Nerchinsk (nyĕr'chǐnsk), city (pop. c.15,300), RSFSR, in SE Siberia, on Trans-Siberian RR. Formerly a place of exile. By Treaty of Nerchinsk (1689) Russia conceded Far Eastern Siberia to China.

Nernst, Walther (väl'tùr nĕrnst'), 1864–1941, German physicist and chemist. Worked on osmotic pressure, ionization, electroacoustics, astrophysics. Won 1920 Nobel Prize for work in thermodynamics and behavior of matter at temperatures approaching absolute zero.

Nero (Claudius Caesar) (nē'rō), A.D. 37–A.D. 68, Roman emperor (A.D. 54–A.D. 68), son of AGRIPPINA II, who persuaded CLAUDIUS I to adopt Nero. When Claudius died, Nero succeeded; when his mother, losing control of her son, intrigued in favor of Claudius' son Britannicus, Britannicus died, probably poisoned at Nero's order. The brutal behavior that has made the emperor's name a byword came, however, after he was under the influence of POPPAEA SABINA, whom he later married. He murdered his mother and later his wife (Octavia). Rumor blamed him for the great fire of Rome (A.D. 64), but he accused the

Christians of setting it and began the first persecution. A plot against him the next year caused him to begin a bloody series of violent deaths (including those of Seneca and Poppaea), which bred new revolts. When one was proving successful he committed suicide. He greatly fancied himself as a poet and an artist and said when he was dying, "What an artist the world is losing in me!"

Neruda, Jan (yän' nĕ'rōōdä), 1834–91, Czech essayist and poet. Noted for a collection of tales, *Stories from Mala Strana* (1878), and lyric poetry which has been compared to Heine's for its clarity and simplicity. Of his dramas, *Francesca da Rimini* (1860) is best known.

Neruda, Pablo (pä'blō närōō'dhä), pseud. of Naftali Ricardo Reyes, 1904–, Chilean surrealist poet, notable for bold experiments in verse.

Nerva (Marcus Cocceius Nerva) (nûr'vù), A.D. c.30–98, Roman emperor (A.D. 96–98), chosen by the senate on the death of DOMITIAN. Unassuming and mild, he aided the poor and tolerated the Christians. Unable to manage the Praetorian guard, he adopted TRAJAN and turned over rule to him.

Nerval, Gérard de (zhärär' dù nĕrväl'), pseud. of Gérard Labrunie, 1808–55, French author. He translated Goethe's *Faust* (1828), wrote fantastic short stories, travel sketches, and poems. His life ended in madness and suicide.

Nervo, Amado (ämä'dhō nĕr'vō), 1870–1919, Mexican poet, a leader of *modernismo.* Most of his verses deal with his inward world where he sought peace from torments without.

nervous system, system comprising nerves and nerve tissue of animal body and concerned with coordination and control of other systems and organs. In human it consists of central nervous system (BRAIN and SPINAL CORD); peripheral nervous system (nerve fibers connecting receptors, or sense organs, with effectors, or muscles and glands); and autonomic nervous system (nerves and ganglia, or groups of nerve cells, regulating actions, not under control of will, of the smooth muscle tissue of digestive and circulatory systems and the secretory action of glands). Portions of autonomic system, usually functioning antagonistically, are parasympathetic system (including fibers arising in midbrain and sacral region) and sympathetic system (including fibers arising in thoracic and lumbar region of spinal cord, a chain of ganglia on either side of cord, and plexuses composed of ganglia and fibers). Unit of structure is neuron, or nerve cell, typically a nucleated cell body with one or more branching processes (dendrons or dendrites) and a single sheathed process (axon). Sensory, or afferent, fibers carry impulse from receptor to central system; motor, or efferent, fibers transmit impulse to effector. A nerve consists of fibers, either of one type or mixed, bound together with connective tissue. Human body has 12 pairs of cranial nerves, 31 pairs of spinal nerves. Reflex arc is pathway from receptor over sensory fibers to central system and thence over motor fibers to effector. Reflex action, not under voluntary control, results from stimulation of a sensory nerve. Conditioned reflex, acquired through association of particular stimulus with specific result, is basis of habit formation and learning. See ill., p. 595.

Nesiotes: see CRITIUS AND NESIOTES.

Ness, Loch (lŏkh), lake (c.24 mi. long; c.1 mi. wide), Inverness-shire, Scotland, part of Caledonian Canal along Great Glen. Very deep, it is overhung by mountains. A "monster," 40–50 ft. long, has supposedly been seen in the loch.

Nesselrode, Karl Robert, Count (nĕ'sùlrōd), 1780–1862, Russian statesman of German descent. b. Lisbon. Guided Russian foreign policy 1816–56.

Nessus (nĕ'sùs), in Greek legend, centaur who carried travelers across the river Evenus. He tried to abduct Deianira, but Hercules shot him with a poisoned arrow. Dying, he gave his bloody robe to Deianira, telling her to give it to her husband, Hercules, when his love waned. She did, and the poisoned robe ("the shirt of Nessus") killed Hercules.

nest, refuge in which animal lays eggs or gives birth to young and where young pass their helpless period. Many birds and certain insects, fish, reptiles, and mammals build nests. Among birds, male selects territory and female usually selects site and does most of construction of nest; factors in choice of site are access to food, protection from elements, and concealment from enemies. Among some birds, the male assists the female with incubation. Many birds lay eggs on ground and build no nest. See *ill.*, p. 105.

Nestor (nĕ′stŭr), in Greek mythology, wise king of Pylos; husband of Eurydice and father of Antilochus. He took part in Argonaut expedition and Calydonian hunt and, when very old, in the Trojan War.

Nestorianism, heresy advanced by Nestorius, 5th-cent. patriarch of Constantinople. Its chief point was objection to calling the Virgin Mary the Mother of God, saying that she bore him as a man. Cyril of Alexandria opposed this view, and the Councils of Ephesus (431), Chalcedon (451), and Constantinople (553) clarified the orthodox position that the two natures of Jesus Christ (divine and human) are inseparably joined in one person and partake of one divine substance. The clergy of Antioch briefly stayed out of communion with Alexandria, but only the Persian church upheld Nestorius to the end. It became a separate Christian community, the **Nestorian Church,** which now has some members in Iraq, Iran, and Malabar, India (as well as a few in the U.S.). The liturgy (in Syriac) is probably Antiochene; the rite is called Chaldean or East Syrian, and the Church is sometimes called the Assyrian Church. They uphold Nestorius' teaching on the title of the Virgin, but otherwise their doctrines have little connection with Nestorius. The Church was spread across the East from the 7th to the 10th cent. Also using the Chaldean rite are the Chaldean Catholics, who have been separated from the Nestorian Church since the 16th cent. and are in communion with the pope. The Nestorians were subject to persecution by Chinese, Hindus, and Moslems, and in the 19th and early 20th cent. were the object of massacres by Kurds and Turks.

Nestroy, Johann Nepomuk (yō′hän nä′pōmŏŏk nĕs′-troi), 1801–62, Austrian dramatist and actor. Known for his farce *Lumpacivagabundus* (1833) and for his parodies of the romantic drama.

Netcong, resort borough (pop. 2,284), NW N.J., near L. Musconetcong. It has a transoceanic radiotelephone station.

Netherlands, Dutch *Nederland* or *Nederlanden,* kingdom (12,868 sq. mi.; with water surface, incl. IJSSEL-MEER, 15,765 sq. mi.; pop. 9,625,499), NW Europe, on the North Sea, bordering on Belgium (S) and Germany (E). It is also known in unofficial usage as Holland. Chief cities: AMSTERDAM (constitutional cap.), The HAGUE (*de facto* cap.), ROTTERDAM, UTRECHT, HAARLEM. There are 11 provinces, with considerable self-governing power. The coastal provinces, largely won from the sea by centuries of toil, are NORTH HOLLAND, SOUTH HOLLAND, ZEELAND, UTRECHT, GELDERLAND, OVERIJSSEL, FRIESLAND, GRONINGEN. The inland provinces are NORTH BRA-BANT, LIMBURG, DRENTHE. The country's wealth is derived from commerce (world's fourth largest merchant marine), industry (textiles, machinery, processed foods, electrical equipment, chemicals), dairying (esp. cheese), cattle raising, truck gardening, flower growing, and fishing. There are coal mines, and Dutch interests control much of the world's petroleum and tin production (in the former Dutch colonies in IN-DONESIA). Colonies: see WEST INDIES; GUIANA, DUTCH. Transit trade owes its volume to canal system which interconnects the main rivers (Scheldt, Meuse, Waal, Rhine) and links them with the waterways of Germany and Belgium. The Netherlands is a hereditary monarchy with a bicameral legislature (States-General).

Succession is settled on house of Orange (see NASSAU). Protestants outnumber Catholics by c.500,000; all religions receive state subsidies. In Roman times the region was settled by Germanic Batavi (W of Rhine) and Frisians (E of Rhine). It passed under Frankish rule (5th–8th cent.) and later to the Holy Roman Empire. The counts of HOLLAND were the most powerful lords of the region, which in the 15th cent. passed to the dukes of BURGUNDY and after 1482 to the house of Hapsburg. Emperor Charles V in 1555 made all the LOW COUNTRIES (incl. modern Netherlands) over to his son, Philip II of Spain. Philip's attempt to introduce the Spanish Inquisition and to abolish self-government led to a general uprising, led by WILLIAM THE SILENT, prince of Orange. Spain recovered the S provinces (i.e., modern Belgium; see NETHERLANDS, AUSTRIAN AND SPANISH), but Holland and the other six N provinces drew together in 1579 (Union of Utrecht) and declared their independence (1581). The struggle with Spain continued, except for a 12-year truce (1609–21) and became part of the Thirty Years War. In 1648 the independence of the United Provs. was formally recognized. The 17th cent. was the golden age of the Netherlands. Through the Dutch EAST INDIA COMPANY and DUTCH WEST INDIA COMPANY the Dutch gained a vast colonial empire and captured most of the world's carrying trade. Jewish and Huguenot refugees contributed to the prosperity and cultural life. The rule of the house of Orange (through the office of stadholder) was repeatedly interrupted by the republican party until 1747, when the stadholderate was made hereditary. After the DUTCH WARS against England and France and the wars of the GRAND ALLIANCE and the SPANISH SUC-CESSION, the Netherlands emerged as strong as ever, but in the 18th cent. it lost its trade supremacy to England. Occupied by the French revolutionary armies in 1794, the Netherlands became the BATAVIAN RE-PUBLIC (1795), was made a kingdom under Louis BONAPARTE (1806), and was annexed to France (1810). The Congress of Vienna (1814–15) united the former United Provs. with the former Austrian Netherlands (i.e., Belgium) as a single kingdom. BELGIUM seceded 1830. Neutral in World War I, the Netherlands was invaded, without warning, by German forces in World War II. During the German occupation (1940–45) the Netherlands suffered heavily. Nearly all of its 112,000 Jews were exterminated. The Dutch government fled abroad, and Dutch forces continued to fight alongside the Allies against Germany and Japan. Postwar recovery was speedy, but early in 1953 the country suffered one of the worst disasters in its history when a North Sea storm flooded one third of its area. A charter member of the UN, the Netherlands joined the BENELUX union and the European Recovery Program (1947) as well as the North Atlantic Treaty (1949). Kings and ruling queens of the Netherlands from 1815: WILLIAM I; WILLIAM II; WILLIAM III; WILHELMINA; JULIANA.

Netherlands, Austrian and Spanish, that part of the LOW COUNTRIES which remained in possession of the house of Austria after the secession of the United Provs. (1581). The death of MARY OF BURGUNDY (1482) brought Flanders, Brabant, Artois, Hainaut, Luxembourg, Limburg, Holland, and Zeeland to the Hapsburgs; Emperor Charles V added Utrecht, Gelderland, Overijssel, Friesland, and Drenthe. His successor, PHILIP II of Spain, attempted to stamp out Protestantism and to curtail the powers of the provincial estates (assemblies). The cruel measures of the duke of ALBA provoked a general uprising, led by WILLIAM THE SILENT of Orange. By 1585 Alessandro FARNESE had reconquered the S provinces (i.e., roughly, modern Belgium and Luxembourg) for Spain, but the seven N provinces were definitely lost (see NETH-ERLANDS). Protestantism was extirpated in the Spanish Netherlands. In the wars of the 17th cent., Spain lost several border areas to the United Provs. and to

France. The remainder passed to the Austrian branch of the Hapsburgs by the Peace of Utrecht (1714). The reforms introduced by Emperor Joseph II met Catholic and conservative resistance and led to a declaration of independence (1789). Austrian control was peaceably restored in 1790, but in 1794 the country was conquered by the French revolutionary armies. It was formally ceded to France 1797 and incorporated with the kingdom of the Netherlands 1815. For later history, see BELGIUM; LUXEMBOURG.

Netherlands East Indies: see INDONESIA.

Netherlands New Guinea: see NEW GUINEA.

Netherlands West Indies: see CURAÇAO.

Nethersole, Dame Olga (nĕ'dhùrsōl), 1870–1951, English actress. Won fame in England and U.S. in *Camille, Sapho,* and *The Second Mrs. Tanqueray.*

Néthou, Pic de: see ANETO, PICO DE.

Netley, village, Hampshire, England; site of one of chief military hospitals in England.

nettle, weedy annual or perennial plant of genus *Urtica,* native to the Old World, with stinging hairs which sometimes cause a rash. In some places nettles have been used medicinally and for food and fiber. Horse nettle is a nightshade.

Neuber, (Friederike) Karoline (kärōlĕ'nù noi'bùr), 1697–1760, German actress-manager. With her husband, Johann Neuber, she managed a company (after 1727) and was its leading actress in Racine, Corneille, Molière dramas (translated by J. C. Gottsched) presented for the first time in Germany.

Neuchâtel (nûshätĕl'), Ger. *Neuenburg,* canton (309 sq. mi.; pop. 127,205), W Switzerland, in Jura mts. Cattle raising, dairying, wine growing. Watchmaking (notably at Le Locle and La Chaux-de-Fonds). Population is mainly French-speaking and Protestant. A county of the Holy Roman Empire, Neuchâtel was allied with the Swiss Confederation from the 15th cent. It became an independent principality in 1648. In 1707 the kings of Prussia succeeded the house of Orléans-Longueville as princes of Neuchâtel. Their rule was interrupted 1806–13 by that of Marshal Berthier. Neuchâtel, though still a principality, became a Swiss canton in 1815. The monarchy was overthrown in 1848; in 1857, after some complications, the king of Prussia renounced his claim to the principality. The cap., **Neuchâtel** (pop. 23,799), has a cathedral, an old castle, and a university. It lies on the **Lake of Neuchâtel,** 24 mi. long, 4–5 mi. wide, which is surrounded by fine vineyards.

Neuilly-sur-Seine (nûyĕ'-sür-sĕn'), residential suburb (pop. 58,658) of Paris, France, near Bois de Boulogne. Here in 1919 was signed the **Treaty of Neuilly,** between Bulgaria and the Allies of World War I. Bulgaria ceded part of W Thrace to Greece and some border areas to Yugoslavia. S Dobruja was confirmed in Rumanian possession.

neuralgia (nŏŏräl'jù, nyŏŏ–), paroxysmal pain along course of peripheral sensory nerve or its branches. Varieties are distinguished according to part affected (e.g., facial, intercostal) or according to cause (e.g., syphilitic neuralgia).

neuritis (nŏŏrī'tĭs, nyŏŏ–), degenerative change in nerve fibers. Causes include deficiency in vitamins (esp. B_1 and B_6), injury, disease, toxic substances, and pressure.

neurosis, functional mental disorder whose symptoms result from compromise between gratification of and defense against libidinal impulses. Neurosis causes persistent fatigue, intellectual constriction, feelings of alienation, reactions disproportionate to stimuli, somatic disorders (see PSYCHOSOMATIC MEDICINE). Normality, neurosis, and PSYCHOSIS differ only quantitatively. FREUD attributed psychoneurosis (neurosis of mental origin) to frustration of infantile sexual drives (e.g., OEDIPUS COMPLEX) in first six years when ego is weak, fears censure; unsolved infantile conflicts appear under later stress as neurotic symptoms. Alfred ADLER, JUNG, Karen HORNEY, H. S. SULLIVAN, deviated from Freud. Social anthropologists have shown that behavior neurotic in one culture is normal in others.

Neusatz, Yugoslavia: see NOVI SAD.

Neuse (nūs), river rising N N.C. in piedmont near Va. line and flowing SE c.300 mi. to Pamlico Bay.

Neusiedler Lake (noi'zĕdlùn), Ger. *Neusiedlersee,* Hung. *Fertö tó,* E Austria and W Hungary; c.20 mi. long. Chateau of ESTERHAZY family is at S end.

Neustrelitz (noi"shträ'lĭts), town (pop. 24,692), Mecklenburg, N Germany. Founded 1733 as cap. of Mecklenburg-Strelitz. Damaged in World War II.

Neustria (nūs'trēù), Frankish kingdom (6th–8th cent.), in France N of the Loire; cap. Soissons. For history, see MEROVINGIANS.

neutrality, in international law, status of a nation refraining from entry into war between other states and holding impartial attitude. At start of conflict nonbelligerent state issues proclamation of neutrality to explain its position. This serves also to warn own nationals it will not protect them if they commit unneutral acts. Proclamation commits nation to strict impartiality in relations with warring states, and obligates belligerents to respect neutral territory and territorial waters.

Neutrality Act, passed by U.S. Congress in 1935. Designed to keep U.S. out of possible European war by banning shipment of war materials to belligerents at the discretion of the President. Later revisions and the LEND-LEASE policy made act practically inoperative even before Pearl Harbor.

neutralization, chemical process which involves mixing and reacting of acid and basic solutions. Commonly refers to reaction between active acid and active base to form salt and water. Hydrogen (H) ion of acid and hydroxyl (OH) ion of base come together to form water (HOH). The salt is made of metallic element of base and element or radical (other than H) of acid. Heat produced is heat of neutralization. Process is important in determining concentration of acids in solution, in industrial processes, in removing excess acids.

Neutral Nation, group of North American Indians of Iroquoian linguistic stock, living in the 17th cent. on N shore of L. Erie; so called because they were at first neutral in Iroquois-Huron wars. When remnants of the Huron joined the Neutral Nation (1649) the Iroquois virtually wiped out the group.

neutron (nū'trŏn), nuclear particle of matter of minute size, with no charge. Some believe it consists of a proton and an electron held together. Bombardment of some elements with neutrons produces nuclear changes. See also ATOMIC ENERGY. See *ill.,* p. 773.

Neva (nē'vù), river, 46 mi. long, RSFSR, connecting L. Ladoga with Gulf of Finland at LENINGRAD. Linked by canal with Volga R. and White Sea.

Nevada (nùvă'dù, nùvä'dù), state (109,802 sq. mi.; pop. 160,083), W U.S.; admitted 1864 as 36th state; cap. CARSON CITY. Main cities are RENO, LAS VEGAS. Lies in GREAT BASIN, with the Sierra Nevada on W border. Most rivers (including HUMBOLDT) have no sea outlet. Mining main industry (silver, gold, copper, zinc, tungsten, mercury); also ranching, farming. Tourist trade important (esp. gambling and divorce centers of Reno and Las Vegas). Area not well known until explorations of J. C. FRÉMONT (1843–45). Part of Utah Territory (1850); estab. separately (1861) after Mormon difficulties with government, gold and silver strikes (see COMSTOCK LODE). Statehood rushed to aid passage of Thirteenth Amendment. Mining dominates state, but changes in price of minerals often shake economy. Atomic-weapons testing ground, U.S. Air Force bombing range NW of Las Vegas.

Nevada (nùvä'dù), city (pop. 8,009), SW Mo., W of Joplin. Shipping center for farm, oil, asphalt, coal area.

Nevada, University of: see RENO.

Nevers (nùvĕr'), city (pop. 32,246), cap. of Nièvre dept., central France, on the Loire at mouth of the Nièvre. Pottery and china mfg. Has ducal palace (15th–16th cent.), Romanesque Church of St. Étienne (11th cent.), and cathedral (13th–16th cent.). The county of Nevers was inherited in 1384 by the house of Burgundy, was raised to a duchy in 1539, and later passed to a cadet line of the GONZAGA family. Annexed to the royal domain in 1669, the duchy became the Nivernais prov. of France, an agr., stock-raising region. The ducal title, purchased by Cardinal Mazarin 1659, remained in his family.

Neville (nĕ'vĭl), English noble family. One of the most powerful in country, they shared control of N with the Percy family. **Ralph Neville, 1st earl of Westmorland,** 1364–1425, was married to half-sister of Henry IV. Supported Henry against Richard II and helped put down Percy revolts in 1403 and 1405. His daughter Cicely was mother of Edward IV and Richard III. His grandson, **Richard Neville, earl of Warwick,** 1428–71, was chief baronial figure in Wars of the ROSES. By marriage he inherited huge Beauchamp estates. Fought for Yorkists and was principal man in early reign of EDWARD IV. After king's marriage (1464) to Elizabeth Woodville, Warwick began to intrigue with duke of Clarence and fled to France. Invaded England (1470) and restored Henry VI. Edward secured aid from Burgundy and Warwick was defeated and slain in battle of Barnet.

Nevin, Ethelbert (Woodbridge), 1862–1901, American composer and pianist. He wrote popular songs, notably *My Rosary,* and composed a setting of Eugene Field's *Little Boy Blue.* Of his piano works, perhaps *Narcissus* is best known.

Nevins, Allan, 1890–, American historian. Author and editor of many works on American scene. Twice won Pulitzer Prize for biography: with *Grover Cleveland* (1932) and *Hamilton Fish* (1936). *Ordeal of the Union* (2 vols., 1947) and *The Emergence of Lincoln* (2 vols., 1950) comprise history of years 1847–61.

Nevis, Ben, Scotland: see BEN NEVIS.

New Albany, city (pop. 29,346), SE Ind., on Ohio R. opposite Louisville, Ky.; settled c.1800. Mfg. of wood products and auto parts.

New Alesund: see SPITSBERGEN.

New Amsterdam, early name of NEW YORK city. Dutch colony (1625–64), cap. of NEW NETHERLAND.

New Archangel, Alaska: see SITKA.

Newark, Ont.: see NIAGARA-ON-THE-LAKE.

Newark. 1 (nōō'ärk″, nü'–) Town (pop. 6,713), NW Del., SW of Marshallton; settled before 1700. Vulcanized fiber and packaged food. Seat of Univ. of Delaware (land-grant, state supported; coed.), which dates from a Pa. Presbyterian school, founded 1743 and moved to Newark 1765. Chartered 1769 by the Penns as Newark Acad., it became a college 1833 and was called Delaware Col. 1843–1921. **2** (nōō'ürk, nü'–) City (pop. 438,776), NE N.J., on Passaic R. and Newark Bay, and W of lower Manhattan; settled from Conn. by Treat and others 1666. Largest city in N.J.; important industrial, transshipping, and commercial metropolis. Port Newark and Newark Airport (1929) are administered by Port of New York Authority. Rapid industrial growth of 19th cent. spurred by improved rail and water transportation. Jewelry industry began 1801 and insurance 1810; celluloid first made here 1872 by J. W. Hyatt. Diverse mfg. (electrical equipment, machinery, wire and metal products, paper and leather goods, chemicals, paint, fountain pens) and meat packing. Seat of Newark Colleges of RUTGERS UNIVERSITY, Newark Col. of Engineering (state, city supported; mainly for men; opened 1919). Has Plume House (c.1710; probably city's oldest house); Trinity Cathedral (1810); Sacred Heart Cathedral (begun 1898); First Presbyterian Church (1791); Newark Public Library (1888), developed mainly by J. C. DANA, who founded Newark Mus. 1909; statue of Lincoln (in front of courthouse) and *Wars of America* (1926; in Military Park), both by Borglum. Birthplace of Aaron Burr and Stephen Crane. **3** Village (pop. 10,295), W central N.Y., on the Barge Canal and SE of Rochester. Nurseries; mfg.

of paper, chemicals, and metal products. **4** City (pop. 34,275), central Ohio, on Licking R. and E of Columbus; plotted 1801. Trade center for agr. area. Mfg. of wire and cables and electrical equipment. Has many Indian mounds.

New Bedford, city (pop. 109,189), SE Mass., on harbor at mouth of Acushnet R. on Buzzards Bay; settled 1640. Nearly destroyed by British in Revolution. World's greatest whaling port (first whaler fitted out 1755) until mid-19th cent. Then cotton mfg. grew; mfg. also of electrical equipment, tools, rubber goods, glass, and machinery. Has Jonathan Bourne whaling museum. Seamen's Bethel (1832) is a scene in Melville's *Moby Dick.*

New Bern, city (pop. 15,812), E N.C., port and trading center at junction of Neuse and Trent rivers; settled (1710) by Swiss. Early colonial cap., seat of first provincial convention 1774. Has Tyrone Palace, capitol, and governor's mansion. Taken by Union troops, March, 1862.

Newberry, Walter Loomis, 1804–68, American merchant and banker. His numerous philanthropies include the **Newberry Library** in Chicago, an internationally known free reference library, specializing in history, literature, music, philology.

Newberry. 1 Village (pop. 2,802), E Upper Peninsula, N Mich., between Sault Ste Marie and Munising. Resort hq. for Tahquamenon Falls. **2** Town (pop. 7,546), N central S.C., NW of Columbia, in farm and dairy area. Mfg. of cotton goods and mattresses.

Newberry Library: see NEWBERRY, WALTER LOOMIS.

Newbery, John, 1713–67, English author and first publisher of children's books. Possibly wrote *The History of Little Goody Two-Shoes* (1765). Newbery medal (for children's book) estab. in his honor in 1922.

New Braunfels (broun'fŭlz), city (pop. 12,210), S central Texas, on Guadalupe R. and NE of San Antonio; settled 1845 by Germans. Beauty of Comal R. makes city a resort. It has power plants and mfg. of clothing, textiles, furniture, and flour. Near by is Landa Park.

New Brighton, borough (pop. 9,535), W Pa., NW of Pittsburgh. Mfg. of clay and metal products and machinery. Merrick library and museum is here.

New Britain, industrial city (pop. 73,726), central Conn., SW of Hartford; settled 1686–90. Metalworking (esp. tin, brass) center since early 18th cent., it is known as the Hardware City.

New Britain, volcanic island (14,600 sq. mi.; pop. c.80,-000), SW Pacific, largest of BISMARCK ARCHIPELAGO. Mountainous, with active volcanoes and hot springs. In NE is Rabaul, which was key Japanese naval base, 1942–44.

New Brunswick, province (27,473 sq. mi.; with water surface 27,985 sq. mi.; pop. 515,697), E Canada; cap. FREDERICTON. A Maritime Prov., its coastline on the Gulf of St. Lawrence (E) and the Bay of Fundy (S) provides excellent fishing and shipping facilities. The rolling countryside is marked by ridges, lakes, and navigable rivers (St. John, St. Croix, Miramichi). Lumbering, paper milling, and allied industries (operated largely by hydroelectric power) are main activities. Fuel resources include much untapped water power, coal, gas, and oil. Fertile river valleys and reclaimed marshlands support dairying and agr. (grains, potatoes, berries, fruit). Abundant fish and game exist. Seaside towns and islands (e.g., GRAND MANAN and CAMPOBELLO) are summer resorts. Trade flows through ports of SAINT JOHN and MONCTON, implemented by railroad connections throughout the province, E to N.S., and W to Que. Province visited by Cabots 1497. First settlement was at mouth of the St. Croix by de Monts and Champlain 1604. During the early period when both France and England claimed the area, all of N.S. and N.B. was called ACADIA by the French and Nova Scotia by the English. British control gained by the Peace of Utrecht (1713–14) and Acadians forcibly expelled. New Brunswick became separate colony 1784 after United Empire

Loyalists sought haven here. Responsible government granted 1849. Accepted confederation with other provinces to form dominion of Canada 1867.

New Brunswick, city (pop. 38,811), E N.J. on Raritan R. at E terminus of old Delaware and Raritan Canal and SW of Newark; settled 1681. Grew as commercial and grain-shipping center. British troops quartered here in Revolution; Washington stopped here 1776. Industry (rubber, chemicals, textiles) began in 19th cent.; medical- and surgical-supply factory opened 1886; mfg. also of machinery and motor vehicles. Seat of RUTGERS UNIVERSITY and affiliated New Jersey Col. for Women and New Jersey State Col. of Agriculture. U.S. Camp Kilmer is near. Joyce Kilmer's birthplace and several pre-Revolutionary houses are preserved.

New Brunswick, University of: see FREDERICTON.

Newburgh, city (pop. 31,956), SE N.Y., on W bank of the Hudson opposite Beacon; settled 1709 by Palatines, resettled 1752 by English and Scotch. Mfg. of textiles, rugs, and machinery. Former whaling town, now deepwater port. Hasbrouck House was Washington's hq., April, 1782–Aug., 1783. Continental Army was disbanded here.

Newburyport, city (pop. 14,111), NE Mass., on Merrimack R. just above its mouth; settled 1635. Former shipping, whaling, and shipbuilding center. Mfg. of shoes, silverware, and electrical supplies. Birthplace of W. L. Garrison.

New Caledonia, volcanic island (8,548 sq. mi.; pop. c.48,000), SW Pacific, on California–New Zealand air route. Has important mining industry (esp. nickel and chrome). Coffee is chief crop. Natives are blend of Melanesian and Polynesian; indentured laborers are Javanese and Tonkinese. Discovered 1774 by Capt. Cook. Claimed 1835 by the French, who used it 1864–94 as penal colony. In World War II island was Free French; occupied 1942 by U.S. forces to prevent Japanese invasion. Chief town, Nouméa, is cap. of French overseas territory of **New Caledonia** (9,401 sq. mi.; pop. c.60,000), which comprises New Caledonia isl., Loyalty Isls., and several small islands.

New Canaan, residential town (pop. 8,001), SW Conn., NE of Stamford; settled c.1700.

New Castile, Spain: see CASTILE.

Newcastle, Thomas Pelham-Holles, duke of, 1693–1768, English politician. Prime minister 1754–56, his weak policy in Seven Years War caused his fall. Nominal head of Pitt-Newcastle administration 1757–62.

Newcastle, William Cavendish, duke of, 1592–1676, English soldier and politician. Gave financial aid (nearly £1,000,000 in all) and military aid to royalist cause in Puritan Revolution.

Newcastle, city (pop. 127,138), New South Wales, Australia, on Port Hunter (Newcastle Harbour); center of largest coal-mining area in Australia. Founded 1797. Exports coal, wheat, and wool.

New Castle. 1 City (pop. 5,396), NE Del., on Delaware R. and S of Wilmington. Rayon, steel, aircraft. Stuyvesant built Fort Casimir near here, 1651. Successively held by Swedes, Dutch, English. Cap. of Three Lower Counties-on-the-Delaware, 1704–77. **2** City (pop. 18,271), E Ind., on Big Blue R. and S of Muncie; founded c.1820. Trade and distribution center in farm area. Mfg. of metal products. Birthplace of Wilbur Wright near by. **3** Town (pop. 583), SE N.H., on island in Portsmouth harbor (bridged to mainland). Has ruins of Fort Constitution, seized by colonists 1774. **4** City (pop. 48,834), W Pa., on Shenango R. and NNW of Pittsburgh; settled 1798. Mfg. of tin plates, metal products, and pottery. Near by is Cascade Park, summer amusement center.

Newcastle, city (pop. 3,395), NE Wyo., SW of Black Hills, in region of caves, canyons, and lakes. Ships livestock, lumber, oil products, and bentonite.

Newcastle-on-Tyne or **Newcastle-upon-Tyne,** county borough (pop. 291,723), co. seat of Northumberland, England, on Tyne R. Called Monkchester until the Conquest because of its many monastic settlements. Renamed for castle, built in 1080. Has Col. of Medicine and Armstrong Col. of Science, both affiliated with Univ. of Durham. Has great coal-shipping industry and is one of England's chief shipbuilding centers. Suffered severe depression in 1920s.

Newcastle-under-Lyme, municipal borough (pop. 70,028), Staffordshire, England, in the Potteries area. Has coal mines, potteries, and other industries.

New Church: see NEW JERUSALEM, CHURCH OF THE.

New College: see OXFORD UNIVERSITY.

Newcomb, Simon, 1835–1909, American astronomer, an authority on moon's motion. He constructed standard planetary system tables. He was known also as mathematician.

Newcomb College: see TULANE UNIVERSITY.

Newcomen, Thomas (nūkŭ′mŭn), 1663–1729, English inventor of early atmospheric steam engine similar to that patented (1698) by Thomas Savery. In partnership with Savery he later developed improved steam engine used to pump water.

New Concord, village (pop. 1,797), central Ohio, E of Zanesville. Seat of Muskingum Col. (Presbyterian; coed.; 1836).

New Cumberland, borough (pop. 6,204), S Pa., on Susquehanna R. opposite Harrisburg. Mfg. of textiles, hosiery, and tobacco products.

New Deal, expression commonly adopted to describe reform legislation enacted under F. D. Roosevelt's administration. U.S. Congress in special session (1933) enacted laws designed to combat the economic depression and to institute long-range social and economic reforms; set up many emergency organizations (e.g., NATIONAL RECOVERY ADMINISTRATION), some longterm organizations (e.g., TENNESSEE VALLEY AUTHORITY). Later Democratic Congresses expanded and modified these laws (e.g., SOCIAL SECURITY). Following adverse Supreme Court decisions, the President tried unsuccessfully to reorganize the Court (1937). New Deal, which had been especially supported by agrarian, liberal, and labor groups, was increasingly criticized, but most New Deal legislation was still intact after World War II.

New Delhi, India: see DELHI.

New Economic Policy (NEP), program for economic reconstruction of war-torn Russia, adopted by Lenin 1921. A temporary measure, it enlisted aid of non-Communists by restoring a limited system of private enterprise. Having accomplished its purpose, it was replaced in 1928 by the Five Year Plan.

New England, name applied to region comprising six states of NE U.S.—Maine, N.H., Vt., Mass., R.I., Conn. Region was so named in 17th cent. because of its resemblance to English coast. Partly cut off from rest of U.S. by Appalachian Mts. on W; land slopes gradually toward Atlantic Ocean and Long Isl. Sound. Connecticut R. is only large river. Generally rather barren soil encouraged development of commerce and fisheries along deeply indented coast line. Great shipbuilding center during era of wooden ships. Chief center of events leading to American Revolution; scene of Revolution's opening engagements. Threatened secession in War of 1812. Growth of mfg. (esp. cotton textiles) was rapid thereafter; region is now highly industrialized. It has long led in literary and educational activities. Geographic and early political conditions developed type known as Yankee—resourceful, thrifty, generous, self-governing.

New England Confederation, union for "mutual safety and welfare" formed in 1643 by colonies of Mass. Bay, Plymouth, Conn., and New Haven. Weakened by rivalry of colonies and advisory nature of league. Confederation declined after 1664 except for activity in King Philip's War.

New England Conservatory of Music: see BOSTON.

New England Primer, American schoolbook, first published before 1690; compiled by Benjamin Harris. Some 2,000,000 were sold during 18th cent.

New Forest, anc. royal hunting ground, Hampshire, England. Made a forest under William I. Since 1877 it has been a national park of 92,400 acres.

Newfoundland (nū"fŭndländ', nū'fŭndländ"), island and easternmost province with LABRADOR as a dependency (excluding Lab., 42,734 sq. mi.; pop. 353,526), E Canada, in Atlantic Ocean at mouth of Gulf of St. Lawrence; cap. SAINT JOHN'S. Steep rocky cliffs edge a thousand inlets, with many islands offshore. The wooded plateau of the interior is broken by lakes and marshes where fur-bearing animals, waterfowl, and fish are abundant. Hydroelectric power is used for mfg. (paper, pulpwood) and mining (copper, gypsum, iron, zinc). Agr. is limited and much food must be imported. Fishing, particularly at the GRAND BANKS, dominates the economy. Population, concentrated on Avalon Peninsula, is predominantly of Irish and British extraction. N.F. is Britain's senior colony, discovered by Cabot 1497 and formally claimed 1583 by Sir Humphrey Gilbert. France contested this claim until the Peace of Utrecht (1713–14) gave sovereignty to England, with France maintaining special fishing rights to 1904. N.F. was awarded jurisdiction over Lab. 1763–64 and again in 1809. Representative government estab. 1832 and responsible government 1855. Islanders rejected entry into Canada in 1869 and were refused it in 1890s because of their precarious financial position. In World War I the island over-extended its economy and sought aid from a commission from the United Kingdom. The Amulree Report was issued, responsible government was suspended (1934), and a commission appointed to administer the government. During World War II N.F. became an important Canadian and U.S. air and radio base. The Atlantic Charter was signed in Newfoundland waters 1941. Voted for union with Canada 1948.

Newfoundland dog: see SHEEP DOGS.

New France: see CANADA.

Newgate (nū'gĭt), former London prison, dating from 12th cent. Scene of efforts to improve prison conditions. Outside executions held here until 1868. Torn down in 1902.

New Georgia: see SOLOMON ISLANDS.

New Glasgow, town (pop. 9,933), N N.S., Canada, port on East R. and NE of Halifax, in coal region. Mfg. of steel products, boilers, and bricks.

New Goa, Portuguese India: see GOA.

New Granada (grŭnä'dù), former Spanish colony, N South America, which included at its greatest extent modern Colombia, Ecuador, Panama, and Venezuela. It was for a time (18th–early 19th cent.) a viceroyalty.

New Guinea (gĭ'nē) or **Papua** (pă'pūù, pä'pōōä), island (c.304,200 sq. mi.; pop. 1,500,000), except for Greenland largest in world, separated from N Australia by Torres Strait and Arafura Sea. Separated into Netherlands (or Dutch) New Guinea (W), Territory of Papua (SE), and Territory of New Guinea (NE). Island is c.1,500 mi. long and 400 mi. wide. Largely tropical jungle with vast mountain ranges rising to more than 16,000 ft. Inhabited by Melanesians, Negritos, and Papuans. Fauna is like that of Australia and consists mainly of marsupials and monotremes. Chief product is copra. Gold is mined in E area. Visited early 16th cent. by Spanish and Portuguese explorers, who were followed 17th–18th cent. by the Dutch, English, and Germans. In World War II island was invaded 1942 by Japan and gallantly defended by small Allied force based at Port Moresby. Wholly regained by Allies July, 1944.

New Guinea, Territory of (93,000 sq. mi.; pop. c.725,-000), SW Pacific. Includes NE New Guinea, BISMARCK ARCHIPELAGO, and two of Solomon Isls. (Buka and Bougainville). Territory belonged to Germany from 1884 to 1914, when it was occupied by Australian forces. Mandated 1920 to Australia, which won UN trusteeship over it in 1947.

New Hampshire, state (9,304 sq. mi.; pop. 533,242), NE U.S.; one of Thirteen Colonies; cap. CONCORD.

MANCHESTER is largest city. Hilly, wooded section with lakes except for rolling seaboard in SE. Connecticut R. forms W boundary. Mfg. of shoes, paper and wood products, cotton and woolen goods, machinery; farming (poultry, dairying, potatoes, apples); lumbering; fishing; mining (granite, feldspar, mica); resorts. To N are WHITE MOUNTAINS, PRESIDENTIAL RANGE. In S are isolated peaks ("monadnocks"). MERRIMACK R. much used for power. Patent for region given to John MASON in 1620s. After boundary disputes, royal colony estab. 1679. Further difficulties arose over NEW HAMPSHIRE GRANTS. Cast ninth, and deciding, vote in ratification of U.S. Constitution. DARTMOUTH COLLEGE CASE argued successfully by famous native son, Daniel WEBSTER. Pres. Franklin Pierce was born here. Republican party came into power after Civil War, has usually stayed there since. Conservation measures, water-power projects added in 20th cent. Trend away from one-industry towns, toward broader economy since depression of 1930s.

New Hampshire, University of: see DURHAM.

New Hampshire Grants, early name for present Vt., given because most early settlers came in under land grants from Benning Wentworth, governor of N.H. Conflict over boundary with N.Y. led to organizing of GREEN MOUNTAIN BOYS and to violence.

New Harmony, town (pop. 1,360), SW Ind., on Wabash R. and WNW of Evansville; founded 1815. Settled by HARMONY SOCIETY under George Rapp; holdings sold 1825 to Robert OWEN, who estab. communistic colony. Colony existed until 1828. Many Rappite buildings remain.

New Haven, city (pop. 164,443), S Conn., on harbor on Long Isl. Sound. Founded 1637–38 as strict Puritan theocracy, it joined Conn. colony in 1664 and was joint cap. with Hartford 1701–1875. Raided by British in Revolution, blockaded in War of 1812. Was important sealing port in late 18th and early 19th cent. Now second largest Conn. city and an industrial center, it has mfg. of firearms, clocks, locks, toys, sewing machines, tools, and elevators; railroad shops. Seat of YALE UNIVERSITY. City centers on the old green, with three graceful early 19th-cent. churches. Has sandstone cliffs—West Rock, with Judges' Cave in which 2 regicides hid, and East Rock.

New Hebrides (hĕ'brĭdēz), island group (c.5,700 sq. mi.; pop. 44,750), S Pacific. Principal islands are Espiritu Santo (largest) and Efate (site of Vila, cap. of condominium). Mountainous and in malarial area. Natives are Melanesians. Products include copra, coffee, and mother-of-pearl. Discovered 1606 by the Portuguese. Governed jointly by Great Britain and France since 1887. In World War II, group supported the Free French.

New Hope, borough (pop. 1,066), SE Pa., on Delaware R. and NW of Trenton. Artist colony with old stone farmhouses.

New Hyde Park, residential village (pop. 7,349), on NW Long Isl., SE N.Y., near Mineola.

New Iberia (ībēr'ēù), city (pop. 16,467), S La., on Bayou Teche; settled c.1779 by Spanish. Processes sugar cane, rice, vegetables, and sea food. Oil fields and salt mines (Avery Isl.) are near. Has fine plantation house.

Newington, town (pop. 9,110), central Conn., near Hartford; settled in late 17th cent.

New Ireland, volcanic island (3,340 sq. mi.; pop. c.19,-000), SW Pacific, in BISMARCK ARCHIPELAGO. Formerly called New Mecklenburg.

New Jersey, state (7,522 sq. mi.; pop. 4,835,329), E U.S.; one of Thirteen Colonies; cap. TRENTON. Other main cities are NEWARK, JERSEY CITY, CAMDEN, PATERSON; ELIZABETH. Bounded S and W by Delaware R. and Delaware Bay; E by Hudson R., New York Bay, Atlantic Ocean. Industry concentrated mainly in Triassic lowlands region; coastal plains in S have farms, ocean resorts. Highly developed transportation system. Mfg. of chemicals, food products, textiles, machinery, rubber and leather goods, plastics; also dyeing, shipbuilding, printing and publishing. Has refineries, copper smelting plants. Farming (truck, poultry, dairying); mining (zinc, marl, clay). Resort center. First settled by Dutch and Swedes. Area seized by English in 1664. W N.J. granted to Lord John Berkeley, E N.J. to Sir George CARTERET. Period marked by confusion over land claims; rule reverted to crown in 1702. Important center in American Revolution (e.g., battles of Trenton, PRINCETON, and MONMOUTH). Third state to ratify Constitution. Next 50 years brought enormous expansion, change from agr. to industry. Woodrow Wilson sponsored reform movement as governor (1910–12). Production soared during World War II. Adopted new constitution in 1947.

New Jersey College for Women: see RUTGERS UNIVERSITY.

New Jersey Turnpike, part of N.J. highway system extending 115 mi. NE from Deepwater on Delaware R. to Ridgefield Park, near the Hudson; toll road.

New Jerusalem, Church of the, or **New Church,** religious body estab. by followers of SWEDENBORG. First congregation founded in London (1788), general conference in 1789. In U.S. teachings were introduced (1784) by James Glen. New Church society formed (1792) in Baltimore with general convention in 1817. In 1890 separatists estab. group named (1897) General Church of the New Jerusalem. Polity is modified episcopacy, with much freedom in local societies.

New Kensington, city (pop. 25,146), SW Pa., on Allegheny R. and NNE of Pittsburgh; laid out 1891. Has large aluminum plant and mfg. of magnesium sheets and glass products.

New Lanark, Scotland: see LANARK.

Newlands, Francis Griffith, 1848–1917, U.S. Representative from Nev. (1893–1903); U.S. Senator (1903–17). Wrote Reclamation Act of 1902 and Newlands Act of 1913 concerning labor problems.

Newlands project, irrigation and power development, W. Nev.; estab. 1903–8. Includes two dams on the Carson (Carson River, 1905; Lahontan, 1915) and two on the Truckee (Derby, 1905; Lake Tahoe, 1913).

New London, city (pop. 30,551), SE Conn., on harbor at Thames R. mouth on Long Isl. Sound; laid out 1646 by John Winthrop. Mfg. of metal goods and machinery. Maritime center, with U.S. coast guard academy (1932). U.S. submarine base is across river at Groton. Privateering port in Revolution, it was partly burned by Benedict Arnold in 1781. Blockaded in War of 1812. Flourished as shipbuilding and whaling port in 19th cent. Has New London Lighthouse (1760). Seat of Connecticut Col. for women (nonsectarian; chartered 1911, opened 1915). Annual Yale-Harvard boat races here.

New Madrid, city (pop. 2,726), SE Mo., on the Mississippi and SW of Cairo, Ill.; laid out 1789 by George Morgan. In Civil War, Federals captured it before taking ISLAND No. 10 (1862).

Newman, John Henry, 1801–90, English cardinal, one of the leaders in the OXFORD MOVEMENT, an eminent writer. Deeply religious from early youth, he was ordained in the Church of England (1824) and became tutor at Oriel Col. (1826) and vicar of St. Mary's, Oxford (1827). In 1832 he resigned his tutorship and went on a Mediterranean tour. While on this journey he wrote many hymns, including *Lead, Kindly Light.* On his return he threw himself into the religious discussion begun by KEBLE, began (1833) his influential series of *Tracts for the Times,* and offered guidance to the Oxford movement. Reading an article by WISEMAN turned his thoughts to Roman Catholicism, and his *Tract 90* (1841) outraged Anglicans by attempting to demonstrate that the Thirty-nine Articles were consistent with Catholicism. His conversion continued and he was received in the Roman Catholic Church in 1845, went to Rome and joined the Oratorians, and returned to England (1847), where he finally founded an Oratory at Edgbaston (near Birmingham). He was one of the most influential English Catholics of all time, both through his personal activities and his writing. His *Idea of a University Defined* (1873) grew out of a much earlier abortive attempt to found a Catholic university, stressing moral training. His *Apologia pro Vita Sua,* begun in 1864 to answer Charles Kingsley's slurs at the Roman Catholic clergy, is a masterpiece of religious autobiography. His many essays are models of lucid prose. He and another English Catholic leader, Henry Edward MANNING, disagreed on many matters, especially education, and their quarrel reached a height when Newman opposed enunciation of the dogma of papal infallibility (but not the dogma itself). The dust later settled, and Newman, made a cardinal in 1879, was universally revered at the time of his death.

Newmarket, town (pop. 5,356), S Ont., Canada, on Holland R. and N of Toronto. Here are tanneries, dairies, and furniture factories.

Newmarket, urban district (pop. 10,184), Suffolk West, England; racing center since early 17th cent.

New Market, town, N Va., in Shenandoah Valley, NE of Staunton. In Civil War battle here Union forces were defeated (May 15, 1864). Near by are limestone caverns.

New Mexico, state (121,511 sq. mi.; pop. 681,187), SW U.S.; admitted 1912 as 47th state; cap. SANTA FE. ALBUQUERQUE largest city. Main rivers are RIO GRANDE, SAN JUAN, PECOS. Grazing lands broken by mountain ranges, canyons, deserts, mesas. Cattle, sheep raising; agr. (grains, beans, potatoes, apples); mining (potash, copper, petroleum, natural gas, coal, lead, zinc). Spanish settlements destroyed by Apache revolt (1676) and by Pueblo uprising (1680). Diego de Vargas reestab. Spanish dominance in 1692. Became Mexican province 1821. Opening of SANTA FE TRAIL brought U.S. settlement. Went to U.S. after MEXICAN WAR. Occupied by Confederate troops, then by Union forces in Civil War. Indian warfare largely ended with surrender of Geronimo in 1886. Cattlemen opposed farmers and sheepherders. Atomic research laboratory at LOS ALAMOS, testing ground at ALAMOGORDO. Climate, natural and historic sights make N.Mex. a resort and health center.

New Mexico, University of: see ALBUQUERQUE.

New Mexico College of Agriculture and Mechanic Arts: see LAS CRUCES.

New Milford. 1 Town (pop. 5,799), W Conn., on Housatonic R. and N of Danbury. Has Canterbury School for boys. Mfg. of metal products and textiles. **2** Residential borough (pop. 6,006), NE N.J., N of Hackensack.

Newnan, city (pop. 8,218), W Ga., SW of Atlanta. Livestock market. Has textile and lumber mills.

New Netherland, territory included in indefinite commercial grant by Holland to Dutch West India Co. in 1621. Principal settlement after 1625 was at New Amsterdam (later New York city), purchased from Indians. Territory taken by English in 1664.

Newnham College (nū'nùm), affiliated with Cambridge Univ.; for women. Organized 1873, it has been a college since 1875. In 1881 some privileges of the university were open to women; degrees have been given only since 1921.

New Orleans (ôr'lēunz), city (pop. 570,445), SE La., on great bend of the Mississippi (Huey P. Long Bridge here), 170 mi. from its mouth by water; on subtropical lowlands protected by levees; near L. Pontchartrain. Largest city of the South, it is a major U.S. port of entry. Imports include coffee, sugar, bananas; exports include lumber, petroleum products, machinery. Has coastwise traffic (esp. on Intracoastal Waterway) and heavy rail and air traffic. Mfg. of twine, furniture, construction materials, and foodstuffs; sugar refining. Platted 1718 by sieur de Bienville. Ceded to Spain 1762 and back to France briefly before Louisiana Purchase 1803. French-Creole influence still felt. Andrew Jackson defeated British here, Jan. 8, 1815, in War of 1812. City became wealthy through cotton and slave trade and entered lavish period. Then as now, Negroes comprise large segment, contributing to exotic flavor. Golden era ended with fall of city (1862) to Adm. D. G. FARRAGUT in Civil War and subsequent occupation by B. F. BUTLER. Colorful past, old buildings of French Quarter (Vieux Carré), superb food, and famous Mardi Gras festival draw visitors, artists, and writers. Has parks, museums (esp. Isaac Delgado Mus. of Art), symphony, opera. Seat of TULANE UNIVERSITY; Loyola Univ. (R.C., Jesuit, partly coed.; opened 1911, chartered 1912, successor to Loyola Col., 1904, and Col. of Immaculate Conception, 1849); Dillard Univ., for Negroes (coed., chartered 1930, opened 1935; named for J. H. Dillard); and Xavier Univ. (R.C.; coed.; 1915).

New Philadelphia, city (pop. 12,948), E central Ohio, on Tuscarawas R. and S of Canton; founded 1804. Mfg. of machinery, clay products, and enamelware.

Newport, Christopher, 1565?–1617, English mariner. Commanded several early expeditions to Virginia, bringing colonists to Jamestown 1607–8.

Newport. 1 Municipal borough (pop. 20,426), cap. of Isle of Wight, England. **2** County borough (pop. 105,-285), Monmouthshire, England, on Usk R. Has extensive docks and is one of Great Britain's chief coal and iron exporting points.

Newport. 1 City (pop. 6,254), NE Ark., on White R. Rail and trade center for agr. (notably pecans) area. Mfg. of button blanks. **2** City (pop. 31,044), N Ky., on Ohio R. opposite Cincinnati and at mouth of Licking R. opposite Covington; laid out 1791, annexed Clifton 1935. Mfg. of metal products. Fort Thomas near by. **3** Town (pop. 2,190), S central Maine, on Sebasticook L. W of Bangor. Fishing resort. **4** Town (pop. 5,131), SW N.H., E of Claremont. Mfg. of shoes and woolens. **5** Resort city (pop. 37,564), on SW RHODE ISLAND, SE R.I.; settled 1639 by William CODDINGTON. Newport and Portsmouth (united 1640) joined Providence and Warwick 1654. Newport was joint cap. of R.I. with Providence until 1900. Shipbuilding (after 1646) and "triangular trade" in rum, Negro slaves, molasses brought colonial prosperity. British occupation temporarily ruined town's economy (1776–79). Haven for refugees—Friends, Jews, Seventh-Day Baptists—in 17th cent. Since 19th cent. it has been fashionable resort of the very rich. Holds polo, tennis, boating meets. Has Trinity Church (1726; Episcopal), Touro Synagogue (1763; oldest in U.S.; national historic site since 1946), Redwood Library (1747), brick market house or city hall (1760), old colony house or statehouse (1739). Old Stone Mill is thought to be either Benedict Arnold's gristmill or a Norse relic. Near by are U.S. Fort Adams, naval training station, naval war college, torpedo and coast guard stations. **6** Town (pop. 3,892), E Tenn., on Pigeon R. and E of Knoxville. Near John Sevier Preserve and Great Smoky Mountains Natl. Park. **7** Resort city (pop. 5,217), N Vt., on L. Memphremagog; settled 1793. Important gateway between Canada and U.S.

Newport Beach, resort city (pop. 12,120), S Calif., SE of Long Beach and on landlocked Newport Bay.

Newport News, city (pop. 42,358), SE Va., a port of HAMPTON ROADS with harbor at mouth of James R.; settled 1611. A shipping center, with dry docks and shipbuilding plants, it has railroad shops and mfg. of paper, machinery, and foundry products. Terminus of Chesapeake and Ohio RR since 1880.

New Richmond, village (pop. 1,960), SW Ohio, on Ohio R. and SE of Cincinnati. Just S at Point Pleasant is birthplace of U. S. Grant.

New River, rising in W N.C. and flowing c.320 mi. NE, N through SW Va. into W.Va. to form the Kanawha with Gauley R. Impounded by Bluestone Dam near Hinton, W.Va.

New Rochelle (rōshĕl'), city (pop. 59,725), SE N.Y., on Long Isl. Sound and E of Mt. Vernon; settled 1688 by Huguenots. Yachting, fishing center; mfg. of plumbing and heating equipment, surgical dressings. Here is Thomas Paine's house and memorial. Seat of Col. of New Rochelle (R.C.; for women; 1904).

news agency, local, national, international, or technical agency which gathers and distributes news. Major U.S. agencies are Associated Press (AP); United Press Associations (UP), the Scripps-Howard agency; and Internatl. News Service (INS), the Hearst agency. They employ reporters and have exchange agreements. Foreign agencies include Reuters (London), Agence Havas (Paris), Wolff Agency (Berlin), Tass (USSR). Most European agencies are government controlled or subsidized.

New Salem, restored historic village, central Ill., NW of Springfield and on Sangamon R. Lincoln's home was here 1831–37. Site now state park. Settled 1828, declined rapidly after 1839. Small museum has pioneer relics.

New Sarum, Wiltshire, England: see SALISBURY.

New School for Social Research, in Manhattan borough of New York city; nonsectarian, coed.; opened 1919 for adult education. Founders included C. A. Beard, John Dewey, J. H. Robinson, Thorstein Veblen, Alvin Johnson. Its divisions include graduate faculty of political and social science (formerly called Univ. in Exile).

New Shoreham, R.I.: see BLOCK ISLAND.

New Siberian Islands, archipelago, 11,000 sq. mi., between Laptev and East Siberian seas of Arctic Ocean, belonging to Yakut Autonomous SSR, RSFSR. Includes Anjou, Lyakhov and DeLong groups. Sparsely settled, ice and snow covered, with scanty tundra.

New Smyrna Beach (smûr'nù), resort city (pop. 5,775), NE Fla., S of Daytona Beach and on coastal lagoon. Fishing, shrimping, citrus-fruit-packing, and rail center. Has ruins of Spanish Franciscan mission (1696). Recolonized 1767, abandoned 1776, and resettled c.1803.

New South Wales, state (309,433 sq. mi.; pop. 2,985,-464), SE Australia; cap. SYDNEY. The Pacific is on E, Tasman Sea on SE, Victoria on S, South Australia on W, and Queensland on N. Area was visited 1770 by Capt. James Cook, who proclaimed British sovereignty over E coast of Australia. Original colony of New South Wales included Tasmania, South Australia, Victoria, Queensland, Northern Territory, and New Zealand. These territories were made separate colonies 1825–63. State has temperate climate. Murray R. waters much of S area. Rich mineral resources include coal, gold, iron, copper, silver, and lead. Exports of wool, meat, wheat, and coal are important. Within the state is AUSTRALIAN CAPITAL TERRITORY.

New Spain, Spanish viceroyalty in North America, created 1535 under Antonio de MENDOZA. Included present republic of Mexico, but indefinite N boundaries varied with decline of Spanish influence.

newspaper, publication issued periodically, usually daily or weekly, to convey news. Modern newspaper arose in 17th cent. with widespread use of printing. First English newspaper was Nathaniel Butter's *Weekly Newes* (1622–41). First French newspaper was the *Gazette* (founded 1631). In 18th cent. many journals of high literary merit were published; in 19th cent. newspapers began to reach the masses. Today newspapers range from the sober *Times* of London and the New York *Times* to tabloid newspapers of a sensational nature.

Newstead Abbey (nū'stĭd, –stĕd), Nottinghamshire, England, by Sherwood Forest. Founded (1170) by Henry II to atone for the murder of Thomas à Becket. Byron inherited the estate (1798); later sold it.

New Stone Age: see NEOLITHIC PERIOD.

New Sweden, Swedish colony (1638–55) on Delaware R., including parts of present Pa., N.J., and Del. Tinicum Isl. became cap. in 1643. Colony captured by Peter STUYVESANT for Dutch (1655).

newt, name for certain tailed amphibians smaller than related salamander. Common spotted newt (pond newt or red eft), is found in E U.S., parts of W U.S., and

Canada. Gill-breathing larva emerges as land animal that matures in two to three years, then lives in water, rising to surface for air.

New Territories: see HONG KONG.

New Testament, the distinctively Christian portion of the Bible, consisting of 27 books dating from earliest Christian times. There are four biographies of Jesus called Gospels: MATTHEW, MARK, LUKE, and JOHN; a history of missionary activity, the ACTS OF THE APOSTLES; 21 letters or epistles named either for their addressee or for their author: ROMANS, 1 and 2 CORINTHIANS, GALATIANS, EPHESIANS, PHILIPPIANS, COLOSSIANS, 1 and 2 THESSALONIANS, 1 and 2 TIMOTHY, TITUS, PHILEMON, HEBREWS, JAMES, 1 and 2 PETER, 1, 2, and 3 JOHN, and JUDE; and finally a prophecy, the REVELATION or Apocalypse. All these are now accepted as canon by all major Christian churches. Other books considered canonical by many but finally rejected were the epistles of St. Ignatius and St. Clement and the Shepherd of Hermas. For other gospels, epistles, and prophecies, see PSEUDEPIGRAPHA.

New Thought, philosophico-religious movement based on "creative power of constructive thinking." Originating in healing practices of P. P. Quimby and mental science of W. F. Evans, Swedenborgian minister, it has evolved into optimistic philosophy of life. Name was adopted in 1890s, first annual convention held 1894. Internatl. New Thought Alliance was formed 1914. Unlike Christian Science, New Thought accepts existence of matter, but only as expression of mind. Central idea is that man is spirit or mind and by thought can so mold body and circumstances as to achieve his desires.

Newton, Sir Charles Thomas, 1816–94, English archaeologist. Discovered site of Halicarnassus. Keeper of Greek and Roman antiquities, British Mus. (1861–85).

Newton, Sir Isaac, 1642–1727, English physicist, philosopher. In his experiments on light he used the prism to break white light into colors of spectrum and recombined the colors to form white light; invented a reflecting telescope. He formulated the law of GRAVITATION and laws of MOTION.

Newton, John, 1725–1807, English clergyman and hymn writer. Curate of Olney, Buckinghamshire (from 1764). With William Cowper he published *Olney Hymns* (1779).

Newton. 1 City (pop. 11,723), central Iowa, ENE of Des Moines; settled 1846. Washing machines. **2** City (pop. 11,590), S central Kansas, N of Wichita; founded 1871. Boomed as cattle town (1871–73), when it was railhead for Chisholm Trail. In early 1870s German Mennonites from Russia brought seed for what became first hard winter wheat in Kansas. Now railway division point in grain area. Bethel Col. is near. **3** City (pop. 81,994), E Mass., on Charles R. and W of Boston; settled before 1640. City is aggregate of chiefly residential villages, but has mfg. of radio supplies, textiles, paper and rubber goods, and machinery. **4** Town (pop. 5,781), NW N.J., NW of Morristown. Dairy center. Near by is Little Flower Monastery (Benedictine). **5** Town (pop. 6,039), W central N.C., NW of Charlotte. Mfg. of furniture and textiles.

New Toronto, W suburb of Toronto (pop. 11,194), S Ont., Canada, on L. Ontario. Rubber and tire mfg.

Newtown, town (pop. 7,448), SW Conn., N of Bridgeport. Mfg. of rubber, plastic, paper, and wire products.

New Ulm (ŭlm), city (pop. 9,348), S Minn., on Minnesota R. and NW of Mankato. Farm trade center with dairy products. Harbored refugees, defended by C. E. Flandrau, in 1862 Sioux uprising.

New Waterford, town (pop. 10,423), NE N.S., Canada, on NE Cape Breton Isl., NE of Sydney. Coal-mining center and fishing port.

New Westminster, city (pop. 28,639), SW B.C., Canada, on Fraser R. and ESE of Vancouver; founded 1859 as Queensborough. Major year-round port and base of Fraser R. fishing fleet. Varied industries include oil refining, processing of food and lumber, and distilling.

Seat of Columbia and St. Louis colleges. Was cap. of B.C. until union of B.C. with the former crown colony of Vancouver Isl.

New Windsor, Berkshire, England: see WINDSOR.

New York, state (47,576 sq. mi.; pop. 14,830,192), E U.S.; one of Thirteen Colonies; cap. ALBANY. NEW YORK city, BUFFALO, ROCHESTER, SYRACUSE, YONKERS, UTICA, SCHENECTADY are other chief cities. Bounded NE by L. Champlain; SE by LONG ISLAND SOUND, Atlantic Ocean; W by L. Erie, NIAGARA R. (with NIAGARA FALLS), L. Ontario; N by St. Lawrence R. Main waterways are HUDSON R., MOHAWK R., NEW YORK STATE BARGE CANAL. CATSKILL MOUNTAINS are in SE, ADIRONDACK MOUNTAINS in N. FINGER LAKES are in W hill country. Mfg. of clothing, machinery, metal products, textiles, chemicals, paper, electrical and scientific equipment; printing and publishing; food processing. Farming (dairying, fruits, truck, grains); mining (natural gas, oil, lead, zinc, salt, talc, limestone); fishing; tourism. IROQUOIS CONFEDERACY dominated area before white man. Dutch West India Co. (on claims of Henry HUDSON) founded NEW NETHERLAND; English (on claims of John CABOT) seized area from Peter STUYVESANT in 1664, renaming region New York. Scene of much fighting in American Revolution (see CROWN POINT; LONG ISLAND, BATTLE OF; SARATOGA CAMPAIGN). New Yorkers such as Alexander HAMILTON, John JAY, and Gouverneur MORRIS were important political figures after Revolution. Old landed families, such as LIVINGSTON family, retained much power, but the ERIE CANAL (1825) gave impetus to early industrialization. New York city grew to be nation's metropolis, and conflict in "Empire State" between city and rural "upstate" appeared. Albany regency controlled politics 1820s to 1840s. Great industrial growth after Civil War brought political corruption (e.g., activities of W. M. TWEED, Roscoe CONKLING, and T. C. PLATT). Reform movements and social improvement measures were carried out in late 19th and early 20th cent. Election of Thomas E. Dewey in 1942 brought Republican party back to power after Democratic governorships of Alfred E. Smith, F. D. Roosevelt, and Herbert H. Lehman.

New York, city (area with water surface c.365 sq. mi.; land only, 299; pop. 7,891,957), SE N.Y., largest city in U.S., on NEW YORK BAY at mouth of HUDSON R. Comprised of five boroughs, each coextensive with a county: MANHATTAN, the BRONX, QUEENS, BROOKLYN, Richmond (see STATEN ISLAND). The metropolitan area (1952 census, preliminary total pop. 12,831,914) includes industrial and residential parts of SE N.Y. and NE N.J. Many bridges and tunnels link the boroughs. With a magnificent natural harbor and over 500 mi. of water front, New York is largest port in the world. Extensive industries, chiefly consumer goods, are led by mfg. of clothing, textiles; printing and publishing; food and metal processing. Leading U.S. commercial (since 1840) and financial (stock exchange founded 1792) metropolis, it is a world center of banking (Bank of New York founded 1784 under Alexander Hamilton) and trade. With its vast array of cultural and educational resources, famous shops and restaurants, places of entertainment, striking architecture, colorful national neighborhoods, and rich historic background, New York is almost unparalleled. Began with settlement (NEW AMSTERDAM) made by Dutch on Manhattan isl. in 1625. British seized control 1664. Though divided in its loyalties, Washington's troops defended city until after battle of LONG ISLAND in Revolution. State cap. until 1797, first U.S. cap. under the Constitution (1789–90); Pres. Washington was inaugurated here. Until 1874, when portions of Westchester co. were annexed, city's boundaries were confined to present-day Manhattan. Charter of 1898 set up five boroughs of Greater New York. Flatiron Bldg., first skyscraper, completed 1902; first subway, 1904. Many planning and administrative bodies (e.g., PORT OF NEW YORK AUTHORITY, 1921; Municipal Housing Authority, 1934) have been set up to cope with problems of the vast metropolis. Seat of permanent UN hq.

New York, College of the City of, system organized 1929, including Brooklyn Col., at Flatbush, Brooklyn (coed.; opened 1930 by merging branches of City Col. and Hunter Col.); City Col., in Manhattan (mainly for men; chartered 1847; opened 1849, through Townsend Harris's efforts, as Free Acad.; granted degrees after 1854), with Lewisohn Stadium (summer musical performances); Hunter Col., in Manhattan and the Bronx (first free college for women; opened 1870 as Normal Col., chartered 1888, renamed 1914); and Queens Col. at Flushing, Queens (coed.; opened 1937).

New York, State University of, founded by N.Y. state legislature in 1948. Consists of colleges, technical institutes, and professional schools in different parts of the state, administered by single board of 15 trustees.

New York, University of the State of, unique organization which oversees all educational activities in state; chartered 1784. Board of regents (1894) heads state education department and determines policy subject to N.Y. legislature.

New York Bay, Atlantic arm, at junction of Hudson and East rivers, opening SE to the Atlantic between Sandy Hook, N.J., and Rockaway Point, N.Y. Its Upper and Lower bays are connected by the Narrows (a strait c.3 mi. long, 1 mi. wide), which separates Staten Isl. from Brooklyn. Upper Bay, c.6 mi. in diameter, is joined to Newark Bay by Kill Van Kull (bridged 1931 between Staten Isl. and Bayonne, N.J.) and to Long Isl. Sound by East R. Extensive port facilities on N.J., Manhattan, Brooklyn shores (see PORT OF NEW YORK AUTHORITY). Islands include Ellis, Governors, Bedloes. Lower Bay joined to Newark Bay by Arthur Kill. Ambrose Channel (called Anchorage in Upper Bay) leads to piers of New York harbor; Buttermilk Channel leads into East R.

New York Central Railroad. In 1853 many small N.Y. state railroads were consolidated into New York Central Railroad Co. to connect Albany with Buffalo. A series of mergers by Cornelius VANDERBILT after 1866 connected New York and Buffalo. Many subsequent mergers extended line. By 1930 New York Central was one of leading railroads connecting Eastern seaboard cities with those of Midwest.

New York International Airport: see QUEENS.

New York, New Haven, and Hartford Railroad, incorporated 1872 as a consolidation of New York and New Haven RR (opened 1849) with Hartford and New Haven RR (completed 1839). Railroad's holdings were vastly expanded after 1903. Line went bankrupt in 1934, but later under new management recovered and prospered after 1940.

New York Philharmonic-Symphony Orchestra, formed 1928 when the New York Philharmonic Society (founded 1842) merged with the New York Symphony (founded 1878). Arturo Toscanini, who had been a conductor of the Philharmonic Society since 1926, continued as conductor of the Philharmonic-Symphony until 1936. Among the many conductors who have contributed to the orchestra's development are Toscanini, Leopold and Walter Damrosch, Willem Mengelberg, Bruno Walter, and Dimitri Mitropoulos, its present conductor.

New York Public Library, free library supported by private endowments and gifts and by New York city, chartered 1895. John Jacob Astor endowed (1848) a reference library opened 1854. J. G. COGSWELL was first superintendent (1848–61). James Lenox endowed the Lenox Library (chartered 1870; opened 1876). The will of S. J. Tilden estab. (1886) the Tilden Trust (chartered 1887) for maintenance of a free reading room. These three were combined in 1895. J. S. BILLINGS was appointed first director. In 1897 New York city agreed to build and equip a central building on Fifth Ave. at 42d St. and to provide for its maintenance and repair. It was designed by Thomas Hastings and J. M. Carrère and completed in 1911. A cir-

culation department was formed by the absorption (1901) of the 11 branches of the New York Free Circulating Library founded 1878. In 1901 Andrew Carnegie gave more than $5,000,000 for buildings for circulation branches provided the city would give land and maintenance. The circulating department also absorbed several independently endowed circulating libraries including the Harlem Library, the Washington Heights Library, the Aguilar Free Library (Jewish; four branches), and the Cathedral Library (Roman Catholic; five branches). The department in 1952 had 70 branches in the boroughs of Manhattan, the Bronx, and Richmond; Queens and Brooklyn have independent systems. The central library also has an art gallery and a library for the blind. The library has especially fine collections on Americana, art, economics, folklore, music, Negro history and literature, New York city, and Semitic languages.

New York School of Social Work: see COLUMBIA UNIVERSITY.

New York State Barge Canal, 525 mi. long, traversing N.Y. and connecting Great Lakes with Hudson R. and L. Champlain. Begun 1905, completed 1918. Modification and improvement of Erie Canal. The 12-foot deep Barge Canal has 310-foot electrically operated locks, accommodates 2,000-ton vessels.

New York State College of Forestry: see SYRACUSE UNIVERSITY.

New York University, at University Heights in the Bronx and Washington Square in Manhattan, New York city; private, nonsectarian, mainly coed.; opened 1832 as Univ. of the City of New York; renamed 1896. Much expanded under Chancellor H. M. MacCracken 1891–1910. Has large evening and graduate classes. Its medical school absorbed Bellevue Hospital Medical Col. 1898. HALL OF FAME is in Bronx.

New Zealand, British dominion (103,416 sq. mi.; pop. 1,702,298), in the S Pacific; cap. WELLINGTON. Comprises NORTH ISLAND (site of Auckland, largest city and chief port), SOUTH ISLAND, STEWART ISLAND, and Chatham Isls. Cook Isls. are most important of the dependencies; Western Samoa is under New Zealand trusteeship. Islands are known for variety and beauty of scenery. Flora includes kauri pine and giant tree ferns. Among fauna are the kiwi and tuatara (survivor of a prehistoric order of reptiles); there are no land snakes. Over 90% of Maoris, the Polynesian natives, live on North Isl. Maori art (esp. wood carvings) is famous. Chief exports are dairy products, meat, wool, and kauri gum. Islands were discovered 1642 by A. J. Tasman and visited 1769 by Capt. James Cook. First missionary arrived 1814. Colony became a dependency of New South Wales in 1840, a separate British colony 1841, and a dominion 1907. Treaty of Waitangi (1840) guaranteed natives full possession of their land in exchange for admission of British settlers, but their hostility brought bloody conflict, 1854–64. Extensive social welfare program is notable—New Zealand was first to adopt noncontributory old-age pensions (1898). Began program of socialized medicine 1941. A governor general represents the British crown. Parliament is bicameral.

Nexo, Martin Andersen: see ANDERSEN NEXO.

Ney, Elisabeth or **Elisabet** (nī), 1833–1907, German-American sculptor, b. Germany. Made busts of Garibaldi, Bismarck, S. F. Austin, Samuel Houston.

Ney, Michel (mēshĕl' nā'), 1769–1815, marshal of France, b. Saarlouis; called by Napoleon I "the bravest of the brave." Covered retreat from Moscow (1812); was created duke of Elchingen and prince of the Moskowa by Napoleon and raised to peerage by Louis XVIII, whom he supported after Napoleon's abdication. On Napoleon's return from Elba he promised the king that he would bring Napoleon to Paris in a cage, but he changed his mind and joined forces with the emperor. After Waterloo, where he commanded the Old Guard, he was tried for treason and shot on orders of the house of peers.

Nez Percé Indians (nā″ pùrsā′, nĕz″ pûrs′) [Fr.,= pierced nose], North American tribe, also called Sahaptin, of Shahaptin linguistic stock, occupying in the early 19th cent. a region in W Idaho, NE Oregon, and SE Wash. After introduction of the horse (c.1700) they added some Plains customs (notably buffalo hunting) to their original fishing and root-gathering culture. Gold rushes in the 1860s and '70s caused the uprising led by Chief Joseph (1877). A few Nez Percé are on Colville reservation in Wash., most on an Idaho reservation.

Ni, chemical symbol of the element NICKEL.

niacin: see VITAMINS.

Niagara, Ont.: see NIAGARA-ON-THE-LAKE.

Niagara, river, c.34 mi. long, issuing from L. Erie between Buffalo, N.Y., and Fort Erie, Ont. It flows N, forming international line, around Grand Isl. and over Niagara Falls to L. Ontario. Navigable c.20 mi. above falls and again 7 mi. before entering L. Ontario. N.Y. State Barge Canal enters river at Tonawanda, N.Y. In Ont., Welland Canal is lake-freighter route around falls. Many bridges cross the Niagara.

Niagara, Fort, post on E side of Niagara R. Strategic spot in fur trade. Captured by British from French in 1759. Surrendered to U.S. in 1796, but held by British in War of 1812.

Niagara Falls, city (pop. 22,874), S Ont., Canada, on Niagara R. (bridged) opposite Niagara Falls, N.Y. and overlooking Niagara Falls. Port of entry, hydroelectric and industrial center. Queen Victoria Park extends between city and river.

Niagara Falls, city (pop. 90,872), W N.Y., on Niagara R. (bridged to Niagara Falls city, Ont.) and NW of Buffalo; settled after 1800. Power from falls here is widely distributed. Mfg. of chemicals, paper, abrasives, cereals, and metal products. Tourist trade long an important industry. Has Niagara Falls Mus. (historical, natural-history collections). Niagara Univ. (R.C.; partly coed.; 1856) is near.

Niagara Falls, in Niagara R., W N.Y. and S Ont., famous natural wonder of North America and important source of hydroelectric power. Falls are on international line, between Niagara Falls, N.Y., and Niagara Falls, Ont. Goat Isl. splits cataract into American Falls (c.165 ft. high, c.1,000 ft. wide) and Canadian or Horseshoe Falls (c.155 ft. high, c.2,500 ft. wide). Behind American Falls is Cave of the Winds, natural chamber made by water action. Recession of the crest (now lessening) has formed narrow gorge, with Whirlpool Rapids, below the falls. Here is Rainbow Bridge (1941) between U.S. and Canada. The two governments control appearance of the area, largely in parks. Colored lights illuminate falls at night. Diversion of water for power is internationally controlled; weirs divert some flow above Canadian Falls to supplement shallower American Falls. Regional collections are in Niagara Falls Mus., Niagara Falls, N.Y.

Niagara-on-the-Lake or **Niagara,** town (pop. 2,108), S Ont., Canada, on L. Ontario at mouth of Niagara R.; settled 1780 by Loyalists. As Newark was cap. of Upper Canada 1792–96. Fort George built here in 1790s. Taken by Americans in 1813 but retaken by British in same year.

Nibelungen, Niebelungen (both: nē′bùlŏŏng″ùn), or **Nibelungs,** in Germanic myth and literature, an evil family possessing an accursed magic hoard of gold. The **Nibelungenlied** (–lēt″) [Ger.,= song of the Nibelungen] is a long Middle High German epic composed by an Austrian or S German poet c.1160. Siegfried obtains the Nibelung hoard, marries Kriemhild, and procures for King Gunther, her brother, the Icelandic maiden Brunhild, who contrives Siegfried's death at the hands of Hagen. Hagen buries the treasure in the Rhine. Kriemhild marries Etzel (Attila the Hun) and contrives to avenge Siegfried's death; out of the final slaughter only Etzel and a few others survive. **Der Ring des Nibelungen** (dĕr rĭng dĕs) [Ger.,= the ring of the Nibelung] is an operatic tetralogy by Richard Wagner (*Das Rheingold, Die Walküre, Siegfried,* and *Die Götterdämmerung*). Elements from the *Nibelungenlied* are used, although most of the legends are Icelandic, mainly from the VOLSUNGASAGA.

Nicaea (nīsē′ù), anc. city of Asia Minor; founded 4th cent B.C. A flourishing trade center under Roman rule, it was the seat of two church councils (325, 787) and remained prominent through the Middle Ages. It was captured by the Crusaders in 1097. It became in 1204 the center of the **empire of Nicaea,** one of the Greek states founded after the Fourth Crusade that had broken up the Byzantine Empire. Its rulers defeated the Seljuk Turks in the S, warred successfully against the Latin Empire, and in 1261 Emperor MICHAEL VIII recaptured Constantinople and restored the Byzantine Empire.

Nicaea, Councils of. 1 325, first ecumenical council, convened by Constantine I to deal with the problems raised by ARIANISM. The chief figures were Arius himself and his opponent, St. ATHANASIUS. The council adopted a simple baptismal creed presented by Eusebius of Caesarea, in which the word *homoousion* [consubstantial] was used of the Son and the Father, thus ruling out the Arian doctrine of the Trinity. It was adopted by all the bishops except two. It was not, however, the misnamed Nicene Creed (see CREED). **2** 787, seventh ecumenical council, convened by Empress Irene. Opposing ICONOCLASM, it decreed that images ought to be venerated (not worshiped) and restored them to the churches.

Nicanor (nīkā′–), one of the seven deacons. Acts 6.5.

Nicaragua (nīkúrä′gwä), republic (57,145 sq. mi.; pop. 1,053,189), Central America; cap. MANAGUA. To the N and NW lies Honduras; to the E, the Caribbean; to the S, Costa Rica; to the SW, the Pacific. The highlands of the NW produce cattle and gold; the Caribbean coast (see MOSQUITO COAST) produces hardwoods and bananas. The real productive wealth of the country, however, lies between the Pacific and the lakes—L. Managua and L. Nicaragua—in a narrow volcanic belt, where most of the mestizo population is concentrated. From Corinto are shipped coffee, cotton, and sugar. The Spanish under Gil González de Ávila defeated the Indian cacique, Nicarao, in 1522, and Fernández de Córdoba founded LEÓN and GRANADA in 1524. León became the political and intellectual capital, and Granada the stronghold of aristocracy. Because of constant strife between the two, Managua was founded as compromise capital in 1855. After gaining independence from Spain in 1821, Nicaragua was briefly part of Iturbide's empire, and from 1823 to 1838 it was a member of the CENTRAL AMERICAN FEDERATION. Since then, the nation's history has been one of almost continual internal strife and foreign controversy—with Great Britain over control of Mosquito Coast and Bay Isls., and with the U.S. over rights to transisthmian route and financial matters. The vigorous government of José Santos Zelaya (1894–1909) was met with U.S. hostility. Later, U.S. marines were stationed in Nicaragua from 1912 to 1925 and again from 1926 to 1933. Anastacio Somoza emerged as the strong man of Nicaragua in 1936 and dominated the political scene after that time, although opposed by the head of the Conservative party, Emiliano Chamorro, and bitterly criticized by liberals the world over. Prolonged political strife has slowed down Nicaragua's development, but the Inter-American Highway has opened up parts of the NW highlands, and the W section has railroads and roads.

Nicaragua, Lake, area 3,100 sq. mi., SW Nicaragua, largest between Great Lakes and Peru. It forms a vital part of long-proposed Nicaragua Canal.

Nicaragua Canal, proposed waterway between the Atlantic and the Pacific, which would use the San Juan R. and L. Nicaragua and would shorten water route between New York and San Francisco by 500 mi. Plans for it from early 19th cent. were abandoned when the Panama route was chosen but were later revived and led to Bryan-Chamorro Treaty (1916) by which Nicaragua gave U.S. a canal option and naval bases. The Central American Court of Justice upheld protests that rights of Costa Rica and Honduras were infringed, and when U.S. and Nicaragua ignored the ruling, ill feeling resulted and the court was eventually dissolved.

Niccoli, Niccolò de' (nĕk-kōlô′ dā nĕk′kōlē), 1363–1437, Italian humanist. The Laurentian Library of Florence began with his collection of manuscripts.

Nice (nēs), Ital. *Nizza*, city (pop. 181,984), Alpes-Maritimes dept., SE France. The most famous resort on the French Riviera, it also is a center of the perfumery industry. It probably originated with the Greek colony of Nicaea (estab. 5th cent. B.C.). Ceded to France by Sardinia in 1796, it was restored to Sardinia in 1814, and ceded again to France in 1860, after a plebiscite.

Nicene Creed: see CREED.

Nicephorus, Saint (nīsĕ′fūrŭs), 758?–829?, patriarch of Constantinople (806–15), Byzantine historian, theologian, opponent of ICONOCLASM.

Nicephorus, Byzantine emperors. **Nicephorus I,** d. 811, deposed and succeeded Empress IRENE (802). His assertion of imperial authority over the Church was opposed by THEODORE OF STUDIUM. **Nicephorus II** (Nicephorus Phocas), c.913–969, usurped the throne in 963, after marrying Theophano, widow of Romanus II. Oppressive taxation and anticlerical legislation made him unpopular. He was murdered by his wife's lover, who became John I.

Nicholas, Saint, 4th cent., bishop of Myra, Asia Minor; patron of boys, of sailors, of Greece and Sicily; also called St. Nicholas of Bari (Italy) because his relics, when stolen, were taken there. In the Netherlands and elsewhere, his feast (Dec. 6) is a children's holiday. The English in New York accepted him from the Dutch, made him Santa Claus.

Nicholas I, Saint, c.825–867, pope (858–67). He set many precedents (e.g., right of a bishop to appeal to the pope over his superior's head) and forced Lothair of Lotharingia to reinstate his wife. Nicholas also challenged the right of PHOTIUS to occupy the see of Constantinople and tried to have St. Ignatius restored.

Nicholas III, d. 1280, pope (1277–80), a Roman named Giovanni Gaetano Orsini. As cardinal he was notable as diplomatic agent for earlier popes. He set out to free the papacy from civil interference, got Rudolf I to give up control over the Romagna, and thwarted the ambitions of Charles I, king of Naples, to dominate central Italy. Called the founder of the Vatican. Dante denounced Nicholas as a nepotist.

Nicholas V, antipope (1328–30): see RAINALDUCCI.

Nicholas V, 1397–1455, pope (1447–55), an Italian named Tommaso Parentucelli. He consolidated the close of the Great Schism by concluding with Frederick III the Concordat of Vienna (1448), which undid much of the work of the Council of BASEL. He made the repentant antipope, Felix V (Amadeus VIII), a cardinal. Nicholas was a learned man and a patron of learning.

Nicholas, emperors and tsars of Russia. **Nicholas I,** 1796–1855, succeeded his brother Alexander I in 1825. The confused circumstances of his accession (his elder brother Constantine had secretly renounced the succession in 1823) made possible the DECEMBRIST CONSPIRACY, which he crushed. He ruled despotically according to his motto, "Orthodoxy, autocracy, national unity," and strove to control national life through censorship and secret police. He suppressed the Polish uprising (1830–31) and abrogated the Polish constitution; aided Austria in suppressing the Hungarian republic (1849); and through his aggressive militarism invited the CRIMEAN WAR, which ended disastrously soon after his death. His great-grandson **Nicholas II,** 1868–1918, son and successor of Alexander III, was last of the Russian emperors

(reigned 1894–1917). Against growing revolutionary and terroristic agitation and liberal opposition he stoutly upheld the autocratic principle. His efforts for international peace (see HAGUE CONFERENCES) did not keep Russia from becoming embroiled in the RUSSO-JAPANESE WAR (1904–5). Its humiliating outcome resulted in the violent outbreaks known as the Revolution of 1905. In Jan., 1905, a crowd of workers who had come to petition the tsar peacefully were fired upon before the Winter Palace; this "Bloody Sunday" proved fateful. After the general strike of Oct., 1905, Count WITTE induced Nicholas to sign a manifesto promising civil liberties and representative government. Nicholas, however, soon replaced Witte with STOLYPIN and curtailed the DUMA. In World War I, he personally took the field in 1915, leaving Empress ALEXANDRA FEODOROVNA in charge. The influence of RASPUTIN over the imperial household became intolerable and undermined Nicholas's authority; after Rasputin's murder (1916) he ceased in effect to reign. Forced to abdicate in March, 1917, by the RUSSIAN REVOLUTION, he was imprisoned first at Tsarskoye Selo palace, then at Tobolsk, and was shot with his family by the soviets in a cellar at Ekaterinburg (now Sverdlovsk) on July 16, 1918.

Nicholas I, 1841–1921, king of Montenegro. Acceded as prince in 1860; changed his title to king in 1910; was deposed 1918 because of his opposition to union of Montenegro with Serbia. King "Nikita" married his five beautiful daughters to Peter I of Serbia, Victor Emmanuel III of Italy, Grand Dukes Nicholas and Peter of Russia, and a prince of Battenberg.

Nicholas of Cusa (kū′zŭ), 1401?–1464, German churchman, humanist, and mystic. Made a cardinal (1448), he tried to reform monasteries all over the Holy Roman Empire (1451–52). A Renaissance man, he wrote much on classics. He was first to expose the False Decretals.

Nicholls, Francis Redding Tillou, 1834–1912, governor of La. (1877–80, 1888–92). Involved in disputed state and presidential election returns of 1876. Destroyed La. state lottery.

Nicholson, Francis, 1655–1728, British colonial administrator. Lieutenant governor of New York, he fled (1689) during revolt of Jacob Leisler. Commanded (1709–10) expedition against Port Royal, N.S. Governor of Maryland (1694–98), Virginia (1698–1705), Nova Scotia (1713), and South Carolina (1720–25).

Nicias (nĭ′shĕŭs), d. 413 B.C., Athenian statesman. In the Peloponnesian War he arranged the truce called the Peace of Nicias (421 B.C.). Opposed the scheme of Alcibiades for an expedition to Syracuse but was chosen as one of its commanders. By his indecision and his superstition (he refused to retreat in time because of an eclipse of the moon) he brought the expedition to ruin. He was killed in the retreat.

nickel, lustrous, silver-white metallic element (symbol = Ni; see also ELEMENT, table). It is malleable, ductile, hard; takes high polish. Resembles iron in magnetic properties and chemical activity. Forms nickelous (valence = 2) and nickelic (valence = 3) compounds. Compounds are used in nickel plating; element is used in alloys to add strength, ductility, resistance to corrosion and heat. Occurs in a number of minerals and in meteorites.

nickel silver: see GERMAN SILVER.

Nicobar Islands: see ANDAMAN AND NICOBAR ISLANDS.

Nicodemus (nĭ″kŭdē′–), a prominent Pharisee who visited Jesus at night and later helped to bury Jesus. John 3.1–21; 7.50,51; 19.39–42. Among the PSEUDEPIGRAPHA is a Gospel of Nicodemus.

Nicolai, Otto (nĕ′kōlī), 1810–49, German composer and conductor. His masterpiece was the comic opera *The Merry Wives of Windsor.*

Nicola Pisano: see PISANO, NICOLA.

Nicolas (nĭ′–), one of the seven deacons. Acts 6.5.

Nicolay, John George (nĭ′kŭlā), 1832–1901, American

biographer. He and John Hay, who had both been secretaries to Lincoln, brought out in 1890 authorized biography, *Abraham Lincoln: a History* (10 vols.).

Nicolet, Jean (zhä′ nĕkôlä′), 1598?–1642, French explorer in Old Northwest. Explored L. Michigan, Green Bay, and Fox R. in 1634.

Nicolle, Charles (shärl′ nēkôl′), 1866–1936, French physician and microbiologist. Won 1928 Nobel Prize in Physiology and Medicine for work on transmission of typhus.

Nicollet, Joseph Nicolas (zhôzĕf′ nēkôlä′ nēkôlä′), 1786–1843, French mathematician and astronomer, explorer in America. Led expedition seeking source of the Mississippi (1836–37); went on government surveying expedition up the Missouri (1838–39).

Nicolls, Richard, 1624–72, first English governor of New York (1664–68). Seized colony from Dutch.

Nicol prism (nǐ′kŭl), optical device, consisting of crystal of calcite or Iceland spar cut at angle into two pieces and joined together again. Beam of light entering prism undergoes double refraction; one part undergoes total reflection, other passes on through crystal. Used in POLARIZATION OF LIGHT.

Nicolson, Harold, 1886–, English biographer and historian, a diplomat and a member of Parliament. Wrote skillful, sympathetic biographies of Verlaine (1921), Tennyson (1923), Byron (1924), Swinburne (1926), and others; *Peacemaking, 1919* (1933) and *The Congress of Vienna* (1946).

Nicomedia (nĭkōmē′dēŭ), anc. city of NW Asia Minor, on the site of modern Izmit, Turkey; cap. of Bithynia. Goths sacked it in A.D. 258. Diocletian chose it as E capital, but it was soon superseded by Constantinople.

Nicosia (nĭkŭsē′ŭ), Gr. *Levkosia,* city (pop. 34,485), cap. of Cyprus. Also called Lefkosha (Turkish). Agr. trade center, it also has mfg. of brandy, cigarettes, and leather. Was residence (after 1192) of Lusignan kings of Cyprus.

nicotiana (nĭkō″shēä′nŭ), annual or perennial plant of genus *Nicotiana,* chiefly native to tropical America. The fragrant, tubular flowers (often white, yellow, or purple) usually open at night. Commercial TOBACCO is obtained from the leaves of *Nicotiana tabacum.*

nicotine, colorless oily liquid alkaloid with pungent odor and biting taste. Occurs in leaves of tobacco. Very poisonous; used as insecticide.

nicotinic acid: see VITAMINS.

Nicoya, Gulf of (nēkō′yä), Pacific inlet, Central America, between Nicoya Peninsula and NW mainland of Costa Rica.

Nidaros, Norway: see TRONDHEIM.

Nidwalden, Switzerland: see UNTERWALDEN.

Niebelungen: see NIBELUNGEN.

Niebuhr, Barthold Georg (bär′tôlt gā′ôrk nē′bōōr), 1776–1831, German historian. His history of Rome (3 vols., 1811–32; Eng. tr., 1828–42) inaugurated modern scientific historical method.

Niebuhr, Reinhold (rĭn′hōld nē′bōōr), 1892–, American theologian; teacher at Union Theological Seminary after 1928. A liberal in politics, theologically he has stressed sinful man's dependence upon the goodness of God. His works include *The Nature and Destiny of Man* (Vol. I, 1941; Vol. II, 1943), *Faith and History* (1949), *The Irony of American History* (1952).

Niel, Adolphe (ädôlf′ nyĕl′), 1802–69, marshal of France; minister of war 1867–69. His program of far-seeing military reforms was halted by his death.

Niemcewicz, Julian Ursyn (yōōl′yän ōōr′sin nyĕmtsĕ′vĕch), 1757–1841, Polish writer and patriot. Served in 1794 insurrection under Kosciusko (whom he later accompanied to U.S.); held high posts under duchy of Warsaw (1807–13); took part in 1831 insurrection; died in exile. His works include historical and political plays, novels, and epics.

Niemen (nē′mŭn, Pol. nyĕ′mĕn), Ger. *Memel,* Lithu-

anian *Nemunas,* Rus. *Neman,* river, 597 mi. long, rising in Belorussia and flowing W through Lithuania and along former East Prussian border, past Kaunas and Tilsit, into the Baltic Sea at Memel. It is partly navigable.

Niemeyer, John Henry (nē′mīŭr), 1839–1932, American painter and teacher, b. Germany. Taught at the Yale school of fine arts, 1871–1908.

Niemoeller or **Niemöller, Martin** (both: mär′tĕn nē′mŭlŭr), 1892–, German Protestant churchman. Originally a National Socialist, he fought neopaganism of Hitler regime and "German Christian Church." Imprisoned 1938; liberated by Allies 1945.

Nietzsche, Friedrich Wilhelm (nē′chŭ), 1844–1900, German philosopher. His brilliance was early apparent and he was made professor of philology at Basel in 1869, but increasing ill health and nervous afflictions made him give up the post in 1879 and in 1889 he became hopelessly insane. His works have a poetic and passionate grandeur and show a morbid sensitivity; they have attracted many readers and are capable of widely varying interpretation. The best-known is *Thus Spake Zarathustra* (1883, 1891), which condemns traditional Christian morality as the code of the slavish masses and preaches the superiority of the morality of the masters (the natural aristocrats), which arises from the will to power. The will of man must create the superman, who would be beyond good and evil and would by his own power destroy decadent democracy. Essentially poetic and symbolic, the book is obscure. Other well-known works are *The Birth of Tragedy* (1872) and *Beyond Good and Evil* (1886).

Nièvre (nyĕ′vrŭ), department (2,659 sq. mi.; pop. 248,-559), central France, in Nivernais; cap. Nevers.

Niger (nī′jŭr), overseas territory (449,400 sq. mi.; pop. c.1,873,000), French West Africa; cap. Niamey. Mainly desert in N; in SW are fertile areas along Nigeria border and Niger R. Stock raising.

Niger, river, c.2,600 mi. long, in French West Africa and Nigeria. Empties into Gulf of Guinea through 200-mi. delta in Nigeria. Has little economic value. First explored by Mungo Park.

Nigeria (nījēr′ēŭ), British colony and protectorate (372,-674 sq. mi.; est. pop. 24,000,000), W Africa, on Gulf of Guinea; cap. Lagos. Includes British CAMEROONS. Named for Niger R., which crosses it. Has desert in N, savannas in central highlands, and rain forests in S. Main ports are Lagos and Port Harcourt. Exports include goatskins, palm oil, tin, peanuts, and cacao. British rule began 1861 with annexation of Lagos, then a notorious slave depot, and was extended 1885–1906 to include entire territory. Appointed governor is assisted by legislative council with native majority.

night-blooming cereus (sēr′ēŭs), name for various plants (chiefly of genera *Hylocereus* and *Selenicereus*) of the cactus family, which bloom at night. They are mostly climbing or sprawling plants with large flowers, usually lasting one night.

nighthawk or **bull bat,** North American bird of goatsucker family, related to whippoorwill. Eastern nighthawk has mottled brown, gray, black plumage, with white wing, throat, and (in male) tail bands.

Nightingale, Florence, 1820–1910, English hospital administrator and reformer of nurses' training. In 1884 she began visiting hospitals and studying methods of training. In Crimean War she organized (1854) hospital unit of 38 nurses, estab. hospitals at Scutari and Balaklava, and operated them against bitter opposition. Founded (1860) Nightingale School and Home for training nurses, at St. Thomas's Hospital, London. Known as the "Lady of the Lamp."

nightingale, migratory bird of thrush family. Common nightingale of England and W Europe is c.6½ in. long, reddish brown above, grayish white underneath. It is noted for song during breeding season. Winters in Africa. For nightingale in mythology see PHILOMELA.

nightshade, any plant of the widely distributed genus

Solanum, with star-shaped flowers and showy berries. Many have poisonous qualities, e.g., juice from wilted leaves of the deadly nightshade (*Solanum nigrum*). The orange-fruited Jerusalem cherry (*S. pseudo-capsicum*) is grown in pots. Potato and eggplant are also of the genus *Solanum.*

nihilism (nī'ŭlīzùm), a theory, held mainly by Russian revolutionists under the tsarist regime, that existing economic and social institutions had to be destroyed, whatever the succeeding situation might prove to be. Direct action, such as assassination and arson, was characteristic. Nihilists' constructive programs, which were relatively moderate, included establishment of a parliamentary government.

Niigata (nē'gätä), industrial city (pop. 204,477), NW Honshu, Japan, on Sea of Japan. Main port for W Honshu; ships oil, machinery, textiles.

Niihau (nē'hou), island (72 sq. mi.; pop. 222), Hawaiian Isls.; privately owned. Cattle grazing.

Nijinsky, Vaslav (vŭsläf' nyĭzhēn'skē), 1890–1950, Russian ballet dancer. Won fame (e.g., in *Petrouchka, The Afternoon of a Faun, The Spectre of the Rose*) as one of the world's greatest dancers. His career was cut short (1919) by insanity.

Nijmegen (nī'mä"khùn), Ger. *Nimwegen,* Fr. *Nimègue,* municipality (pop. 106,523), Gelderland prov., E Netherlands, on Waal R. and near German border; chartered 1184. It is a railroad junction and inland shipping center, with mfg. of electrical equipment, machinery, and clothing. Treaty of Nijmegen was signed here, 1678–79 (see DUTCH WARS). Allied airborne troops wrested Nijmegen from Germans in Sept., 1944. Landmarks include remains of palace built by Charlemagne, 13th-cent. church, 16th-cent. city hall, and 17th-cent. weighhouse. Formerly also spelled Nimegen, Nymegen, and Nymwegen.

Nike (nī'kē), in Greek mythology, daughter of Pallas and Styx. She presided over all contests, including war, and so was goddess of victory; identified with Roman Victoria. Of many portrayals in art, most famous is *Victory* (or *Nike*) *of Samothrace* (Louvre).

Nikko (nĕk'kō), town (pop. 27,931), central Honshu, Japan; tourist resort and religious center. Splendid 17th-cent. shrine houses tomb of Ieyasu.

Nikolayev (nyĭkŭlī'ŭf), city (pop. 167,108), SW Ukraine, on the Southern Bug. Major Black Sea port with shipyards, flour mills. Founded 1784.

Nikolayevsk or **Nikolayevsk-on-Amur** (nyĭkŭlī'ŭfsk), city (pop. over 50,000), Khabarovsk Territory, RSFSR, in Far Eastern Siberia; port on the Amur. Center of fishing, gold-mining, fur-hunting area.

Nikolsburg (nē'kôlsbŏŏrk), Czech *Mikulov,* town (pop. 5,220), Moravia, Czechoslovakia, near Austrian border. Three important treaties were signed here: 1621, between Gabriel Bethlen, who renounced Hungarian crown, and Emperor Ferdinand II; 1805, armistice between France and Austria, followed by Treaty of PRESSBURG; 1866, armistice between Prussia and Austria (see AUSTRO-PRUSSIAN WAR).

Nikon (nē'kŏn), 1605–81, Russian churchman, patriarch of the Russian Orthodox Church (1652–66). His sweeping reforms, accomplished without state interference, rejuvenated the Church but awakened much opposition. The Raskolniki (Old Believers) became an opposition sect and were reinforced by such heterodox groups as the Dukhobors. Nikon was deposed by Tsar Alexis, but his reforms lasted.

Nikopol (nēkô'pôl), town (pop. 5,409), N Bulgaria, on the Danube opposite Rumania. Scene of major Turkish victory, under Bajazet I, over a Christian army led by Sigismund of Hungary (later Emperor Sigismund) in 1396. It laid the Balkans open to Turkish conquest.

Nikopol (nyĭkô'pùl), city (pop. 57,841), S central Ukraine, on the Dnieper. Industrial center of large manganese-mining area.

Nile, great river of Africa. One of the world's longest rivers, it flows c.4,150 mi. from its ultimate head-

stream (the Kagera, which rises near border between Tanganyika and Ruanda-Urundi) to the Mediterranean. Drains c.1,100,000 sq. mi. The Nile proper, formed by junction of the BLUE NILE and the WHITE NILE at Khartoum (in Anglo-Egyptian Sudan) is c.1,875 mi. long. Below Cairo in Egypt, it enters its delta, which it crosses chiefly through Damietta and Rosetta channels. Between Khartoum and Aswan, the Nile drops 935 ft. in a series of six rapids (called cataracts). The river's periodic floods are due to abundant waters of the Blue Nile, fed by heavy rains of monsoon season in Ethiopia. The source of the Blue Nile, L. Tana, was discovered c.1770 by James Bruce; that of the White Nile, L. Victoria, by John Speke in 1858. Attempts to harness the flood-waters date back to 4000 B.C. Today, Nile waters are stored in several reservoirs (e.g., ASWAN), and agr. is no longer dependent on annual floods alone.

Nile, battle of the: see ABOUKIR.

Niles, Hezekiah, 1777–1839, American journalist, founder (1811) of *Niles' Weekly Register.*

Niles. 1 City (pop. 13,145), SW Mich., on St. Joseph R. and N of South Bend, Ind. Permanently settled 1827 on site of Jesuit mission (1690) and French Fort St. Joseph (1697; successively occupied by French, British, Indians, Spanish). Center of agr. area with mfg. of metal, wood, and leather products. **2** City (pop. 16,773), NE Ohio, on Mahoning R., near Warren; settled 1806. Iron and steel mills. Birthplace of William McKinley (memorial).

Niles Center, Ill.: see SKOKIE.

Nimègue or **Nimeguen,** Netherlands: see NIJMEGEN.

Nîmes (nēm), city (pop. 75,398), cap. of Gard dept., S France. Trades in wines and fruits. Its Roman remains include the great arena (still used), Maison Carrée (a perfectly preserved temple of 1st or 2d cent. A.D.), and temple of Diana (2d cent.). Near by is Pont du Gard, a Roman aqueduct.

Nimitz, Chester W(illiam) (nī'mĭts), 1885–, American admiral. Commanded Pacific Fleet throughout World War II. Made admiral of fleet ("five-star admiral") 1944. Chief of naval operations (1945–47).

Nimrod, mighty hunter. Gen. 10.8; 1 Chron. 1.10.

Nimwegen, Netherlands: see NIJMEGEN.

ninebark, hardy, ornamental, deciduous shrub (*Physocarpus*), chiefly native to North America. The shrubs have shreddy bark and clusters of small white or pinkish flowers in the spring.

Nine-Power Treaty: see NAVAL CONFERENCES.

Nineveh (nī'nùvù), capital of anc. ASSYRIA, on the Tigris, opposite modern Mosul, Iraq. Reached its full glory under SENNACHERIB and ASSUR-BANI-PAL. Fell in 612 B.C. to the Medes and Chaldaean Babylonians, and the Assyrian Empire came to an end.

Ning-hsia, China: see NINGSIA.

Ninghsien, China: see NINGPO.

Ningpo (nĭng'bŭ'), commercial city (pop. 210,377), NE Chekiang prov., China, on Yung R. Became a treaty port in 1842. Formerly called Ninghsien.

Ningsia or **Ning-hsia** (both: nĭng'shyä'), province (100,-000 sq. mi.; pop. 750,000), NW China, largely in Inner Mongolia; cap. Yinchwan. Region divided into fertile Yellow R. valley and Alashan Desert. Wool weaving, fur processing.

Niobe (nī'ōbē), in Greek legend, queen of Thebes. Because she boasted of her children (accounts vary from 12 to 20) to LETO, Apollo and Artemis killed them all. Niobe became a stone image of sorrow.

niobium (nīō'bēùm), steel-gray lustrous metallic element (symbol = Nb; see also ELEMENT, table). It is malleable and ductile and can be welded; reacts with nonmetals at high temperatures. Used in vacuum tubes and to make stainless steel and cutting tools. Columbium (Cb) was formerly an alternate name.

Niobrara (nīùbrâ'rù), river rising in E Wyo. and flowing 431 mi. across N Nebr. to Missouri R. on NE line. Box Butte Dam, SW of Rushville, Nebr., is in Mirage Flats project.

SMALL CAPITALS = cross references. Pronunciation key on inside end pages. Abbreviations: p. 2.

Niort (nyôr), town (pop. 29,068), cap. of Deux-Sèvres dept., W France. Glove mfg. Two towers of the old fortress (12th–13th cent.) and several Renaissance buildings are preserved.

Nipigon Lake (nǐ′pǐgŏn), 66 mi. long, 46 mi. wide, W central Ont., Canada, NE of Port Arthur. Has many islands. Drains S into L. Superior via Nipigon R.

Nipissing, Lake (nǐ′pǐsǐng), S Ont., Canada, between Ottawa R. and L. Huron, extending W from North Bay city. It drains WSW to Georgian Bay via the French R.

Nippur (nǐpŏor′), city of anc. Mesopotamia, on the Euphrates; a Sumerian city-state of great antiquity, seat of the worship of the god En-lil.

nirvana: see BUDDHISM.

Nis or **Nish** (nēsh), Serbo-Croatian *Niš*, city (pop. 50,-962), S Serbia, Yugoslavia. Railroad center; iron and tobacco mfg. Birthplace of Constantine the Great. The city was held by the Turks from c.1386 to 1878, but with several interludes when Christians captured it. It has a medieval fortress.

Nishapur (nēshäpŏor′), town (pop. 24,270), NE Iran, on site of anc. city built by the Sassanidae. Omar Khayyam was born and buried here. Near by are valuable turquoise mines.

Nishinomiya (nē″shēnō′mēä), manufacturing city (pop. 108,893), S Honshu, Japan, on Osaka Bay. Seat of Kobe Women's Col.

niter: see SALTPETER.

Niterói (nētŭroi′), city (pop. 174,535), cap. of Rio de Janeiro state, SE Brazil, on Guanabara Bay; primarily a residential suburb of near-by Rio de Janeiro.

niton: see RADON.

nitrate (nī′trāt), either a salt or an ester of nitric acid, a compound with the nitrate radical (NO_3). Nearly all metallic nitrates are water soluble and therefore are widely used—to make explosives, as fertilizers, in fireworks, and in medicine. Nitrates in soil are source of nitrogen needed by plants for growth.

nitric acid (nī′trǐk), corrosive, colorless liquid which gives off choking fumes in air. It is a good conductor of electricity, ionizes readily, is a strong oxidizing agent, and reacts with metals, oxides, and hydroxides to form nitrates. Used to make explosives, dyes, some organic compounds. Aqua regia is mixture of one part nitric acid, three parts sulphuric; it dissolves gold and platinum.

nitrifying bacteria: see NITROGEN-FIXING BACTERIA.

nitrobenzene (nī″trōbĕn″zēn′), poisonous, yellow, oily liquid. It is used in making some soaps, perfumes, and aniline.

nitrogen (nī′trŭjŭn), colorless, odorless, tasteless gaseous element (symbol = N; see also ELEMENT, table). Does not burn or support combustion; is relatively inactive; combines with some active metals and oxygen. It is a constituent of ammonia, nitric acid, many explosives, proteins. It forms c.⅘ of earth's atmosphere and is present in all living matter and its compounds are therefore essential to life. It is used in electric-light bulbs, thermometers, certain industrial processes, and fertilizers. **Nitrogen cycle,** the continuous course of nitrogen in nature. Nitrogen compounds are stored in plants which animals use for food. Nitrogen enters into other compounds in body of animal; animal waste matter with high nitrogen content passes into soil or sea. Certain bacteria convert these new compounds into forms which can be utilized by plants and then transformed into form usable by animals. Cycle is thus completed. **Nitrogen fixation** refers to extraction of nitrogen from the atmosphere and its combination with other elements to form compounds. Commercially it is accomplished by various processes, e.g., the arc process for preparing nitric acid, cyanamide process used in producing ammonia, and Haber process in which ammonia is synthesized by direct combination of nitrogen and hydrogen. In nature, nitrogen-fixing bacteria accomplish nitrogen fixation.

nitrogen-fixing bacteria and nitrifying bacteria (nī′trŭ-fī″ĭng), bacteria which convert nitrogen into forms usable by higher plants. Nitrogen, essential to all protoplasm formation, is constantly depleted in soil by plants, making restoration vital. Nitrogen-fixing bacteria live in soil or in nodules on roots of leguminous plants (e.g., alfalfa, peas, beans, clover, lupine, soybeans); they convert nitrogen in atmosphere or from other sources into forms usable by plants. Nitrifying bacteria convert nitrogen compounds from decayed organic material of soil into forms that plants can use.

nitroglycerin (nī″trōglǐ′sŭrǐn), very explosive, heavy, colorless, oily liquid. It is an ester of glycerin and nitric acid and is more accurately called glyceryl trinitrate. Very sensitive to slight shocks, it is usually mixed with glycerin to form blasting gelatin or used as DYNAMITE. It is used also to make smokeless powder, and in medicine.

nitrous oxide: see LAUGHING GAS.

Nitti, Francesco Saverio (fränchä′skō sävä′rēō nēt′tē), 1868–1953, Italian premier (1919–20). A liberal, he was exiled during Fascist period.

Nivernais, French province: see NEVERS.

Nixon, Richard M(ilhous), 1913–, Vice President of the United States (1953–). U.S. Senator from Calif. (1951–53); known for investigation of Communists.

Niza, Marcos de: see MARCOS DE NIZA.

Nizhni Novgorod, RSFSR: see GORKI.

Nizhni Tagil (nyĕzh′nyē tŭgēl′), city (pop. c.250,000), RSFSR, in central Urals. Metallurgical center.

Nizza, Italian name of NICE, France.

NKVD: see SECRET POLICE.

no: see JAPANESE DRAMA.

Noah (nō′ù) [Heb.,= rest] or **Noe** (nō′ē), builder of the ARK that saved human and animal life from the DELUGE. Noah's sons, Shem, Ham, and Japheth, are ancestors of the races of mankind as divided in Bible. Gen. 6–10; 1 Chron. 1.4; Ezek. 14.14,20; Mat. 24.37; Luke 3.36; 17.26; Heb. 11.7.

Noailles, Maurice, duc de (mōrēs′ dük′ dü nōī′yù), 1678–1766, marshal of France. Commanded in War of the Austrian Succession.

Nobel, Alfred Bernhard (äl′frĕd bĕrn′härd nōbĕl′), 1833–96, Swedish chemist and inventor. In 1863 patented mixture of nitroglycerine and gunpowder, in 1866 dynamite. Bequeathed fund for annual awards in physics, chemistry, physiology and medicine, and literature, and for promotion of international peace. Nobel Prizes are awarded on international basis by board named by Nobel, with hq. in Stockholm. See NOBEL PRIZES (table).

Nobile, Umberto (nō′bēlä), 1885–, Italian aeronautical engineer and arctic explorer. Designed and piloted dirigible, *Norge,* in Amundsen-Ellsworth flight over North Pole (1926). Commanded another polar dirigible flight in 1928; ship crashed on return. Technical adviser for airship construction in USSR (1931–36).

Noblesville, city (pop. 6,567), central Ind., NNE of Indianapolis. Mfg. of wood and rubber products. Breeds draft horses.

Nobunaga (Nobunaga Oda) (nōbŏonä′gä), 1534–82, Japanese military commander. Became virtual dictator in 1568 despite continued existence of Ashikaga shogunate. Crushed rival feudal barons and laid basis for country's unification, later completed by former lieutenants, Hideyoshi and Ieyasu.

Nod, Land of, in Bible, refuge of Cain. Gen. 4.16.

Noe (nō′ē), variant of NOAH.

Noé, Amédée, comte de: see CHAM.

Nogales (nōgä′läs), town (pop. 13,866), Sonora, NW Mexico, contiguous to Nogales, Ariz. Derives its importance chiefly from international trade.

Nogales (nōgä′lǐs), city (pop. 6,153), S Ariz., adjoining Nogales, Mexico. Port of entry in rich mining and ranching area. To N are Tumacacori (1696; now a national monument) and Guevavi (1692; in ruins), missions founded by Father Kino, and the ruins of Tubac (1752), pioneer Spanish settlement.

Year	Peace	Chemistry	Physics	Physiology and Medicine	Literature
1901	J. H. Dunant Frédéric Passy	J. H. van't Hoff	W. C. Roentgen	E. A. von Behring	R. F. A. Sully-Prudhomme
1902	Élie Ducommun C. A. Gobat	Emil Fischer	H. A. Lorentz Pieter Zeeman	Sir Ronald Ross	Theodor Mommsen
1903	Sir William R. Cremer	S. A. Arrhenius	A. H. Becquerel Pierre Curie Marie S. Curie	N. R. Finsen	Bjornstjerne Bjornson
1904	Institute of International Law	Sir William Ramsey	J. W. S. Rayleigh	Ivan P. Pavlov	Frédéric Mistral José Echegaray
1905	Baroness Bertha von Suttner	Adolf von Baeyer	Philipp Lenard	Robert Koch	Henryk Sienkiewicz
1906	Theodore Roosevelt	Henri Moissan	Sir Joseph Thomson	Camillo Golgi S. Ramón y Cajal	Giosuè Carducci
1907	E. T. Moneta Louis Renault	Eduard Buchner	A. A. Michelson	C. L. A. Laveran	Rudyard Kipling
1908	K. P. Arnoldson Fredrik Bajer	Sir Ernest Rutherford	Gabriel Lippman	Paul Ehrlich Élie Metchnikoff	R. C. Eucken
1909	Auguste Beernaert P. H. B. Estournelles de Constant	Wilhelm Ostwald	Guglielmo Marconi C. F. Braun	Emil T. Kocher	Selma Lagerlof
1910	International Peace Bureau	Otto Wallach	J. D. van der Waals	Albrecht Kossel	P. J. L. Heyse
1911	T. M. C. Asser A. H. Fried	Marie S. Curie	Wilhelm Wien	Allvar Gullstrand	Maurice Maeterlinck
1912	Elihu Root	Victor Grignard Paul Sabatier	N. G. Dalen	Alexis Carrel	Gerhart Hauptmann
1913	Henri La Fontaine	Alfred Werner	Heike Kamerlingh Onnes	C. R. Richet	Sir Rabindranath Tagore
1914		T. W. Richards	Max von Laue	Robert Barany	
1915		Richard Willstätter	Sir William H. Bragg Sir William L. Bragg		Romain Rolland
1916					Verner von Heidenstam
1917	International Red Cross		C. G. Barkla		K. A. Gjellerup Henrik Pontoppidan
1918		Fritz Haber	Max Planck		
1919	Woodrow Wilson		Johannes Stark	Jules Bordet	C. F. G. Spitteler
1920	Léon Bourgeois	Walther Nernst	C. E. Guillaume	August Krogh	Knut Hamsun
1921	Hjalmar Branting C. L. Lange	Frederick Soddy	Albert Einstein		Anatole France
1922	Fridtjof Nansen	F. W. Aston	N. H. D. Bohr	A. V. Hill Otto Meyerhof	Jacinto Benavente y Martínez
1923		Fritz Pregl	Robert A. Millikan	Sir Frederick G. Banting J. J. R. Macleod	W. B. Yeats
1924			K. M. G. Siegbahn	Willem Einthoven	L. S. Reymont
1925	Sir Joseph Austen Chamberlain Charles G. Dawes	Richard Zsigmondy	James Franck Gustav Hertz		G. B. Shaw
1926	Aristide Briand Gustav Stresemann	Theodor Svedberg	J. B. Perrin	Johannes Fibiger	Grazia Deledda
1927	F. É. Buisson Ludwig Quidde	Heinrich Wieland	A. H. Compton C. T. R. Wilson	Julius Wagner-Jauregg	Henri Bergson
1928		Adolf Windaus	Sir Owen W. Richardson	C. J. H. Nicolle	Sigrid Undset
1929	Frank B. Kellogg	Sir Arthur Harden Hans von Euler-Chelpin	L. V. Broglie	Christian Eijkman Sir Frederick G. Hopkins	Thomas Mann
1930	Nathan Soderblom	Hans Fischer	Sir Chandrasekhara V. Raman	Karl Landsteiner	Sinclair Lewis
1931	Jane Addams Nicholas Murray Butler	Carl Bosch Friedrich Bergius		Otto H. Warburg	E. A. Karlfeldt
1932		Irving Langmuir	Werner Heisenberg	E. D. Adrian Sir Charles Sherrington	John Galsworthy

NOBEL PRIZES (continued)

Year	Peace	Chemistry	Physics	Physiology and Medicine	Literature
1933	Sir Norman Angell		P. A. M. Dirac Erwin Schrödinger	Thomas H. Morgan	I. A. Bunin
1934	Arthur Henderson	Harold C. Urey		G. H. Whipple G. R. Minot W. P. Murphy	Luigi Pirandello
1935	Carl von Ossietzky	Frédéric Joliot-Curie Irène Joliot-Curie	Sir James Chadwick	Hans Spemann	
1936	Carlos Saavedra Lamas	P. J. W. Debye	C. D. Anderson V. F. Hess	Sir Henry H. Dale Otto Loewi	Eugene O'Neill
1937	E. A. R. Cecil, Viscount	Sir Walter N. Haworth Paul Karrer	C. J. Davisson Sir George P. Thomson	Albert von Szent-Gyorgyi	Roger Martin du Gard
1938	Nansen International Office for Refugees		Enrico Fermi		Pearl S. Buck
1939		Adolf Butenandt Leopold Ruzicka	E. O. Lawrence	Gerhard Domagk	F. E. Sillanpää
1940					
1941					
1942					
1943		Georg von Hevesy	Otto Stern	E. A. Doisy Henrik Dam	
1944	International Red Cross	Otto Hahn	I. I. Rabi	Joseph Erlanger H. S. Gasser	J. V. Jensen
1945	Cordell Hull	A. I. Virtanen	Wolfgang Pauli	Sir Alexander Fleming E. B. Chain Sir Howard W. Florey	Gabriela Mistral
1946	J. R. Mott Emily G. Balch	J. B. Sumner J. H. Northrop W. M. Stanley	P. W. Bridgman	H. J. Muller	Hermann Hesse
1947	American Friends Service Committee and Friends Service Council	Sir Robert Robinson	Sir Edward V. Appleton	C. F. Cori Gerty T. Cori B. A. Houssay	André Gide
1948		Arne Tiselius	P. M. S. Blackett	Paul H. Mueller	T. S. Eliot
1949	John Boyd Orr, Baron	W. F. Giauque	Hideki Yukawa	W. R. Hess Egas Moniz	William Faulkner
1950	R. J. Bunche	Otto Diels Kurt Alder	C. F. Powell	P. S. Hench E. C. Kendall Tadeus Reichstein	Bertrand Russell
1951	Leon Jouhaux	G. T. Seaborg E. M. McMillan	J. D. Cockcroft E. T. S. Walton	Max Theiler	P. F. Lagerkvist
1952		Archer Martin Richard Synge	Felix Bloch E. M. Purcell	S. A. Waksman	François Mauriac

Nogi, Maresuke, Count (märĕs′kä nō′gē), 1849–1912, Japanese general and hero of Russo-Japanese War.

Noguchi, Hideyo (hēdā′ō nōgōō′chē), 1876–1928, Japanese bacteriologist, on staff of Rockefeller Inst. from 1904. Worked on yellow fever, smallpox, snake venoms, and diagnosis of syphilis.

Noguchi, Isamu, 1904–, American sculptor, known for stylized portraits and abstractions. Studied in New York and Paris (under Brancusi). His father, **Yone Noguchi,** 1875–1947, was a Japanese poet, who also wrote critical essays in English.

Nola (nō′lä), town (pop. 10,733), Campania, S Italy. It was a flourishing Roman colony influenced by Greek culture. Augustus died here A.D. 14.

Nolde, Emil (ā′mĕl nōl′dŭ), 1867–, German expressionist painter. Draws subject matter from nature (seascapes, flower gardens) and the supernatural.

Nolichucky (nō″lĭchŭ′kē), river rising in Blue Ridge in W N.C. and flowing c.150 mi. NW into Tenn. and W to French Broad R. (Douglas Reservoir) near Newport. Power dam near Greeneville.

Nome (nōm), city (pop. 1,876), W Alaska, on Norton Sound on S side of Seward Peninsula; estab. 1899 with discovery of gold. Had c.30,000 population by summer of 1900, but many died or left because of arctic hardships. Dredge mining introduced later. Trade, supply, and tourist center for NW Alaska and center of Eskimo handicrafts; fur farming and fishing. Annual fair and dog race. Airport; steamer to Seattle (May–Nov.). Cape Nome is SE.

nominative: see CASE.

Nomura, Kichisaburo (kēchēsäbōōrō′ nō′mōō″rä), 1877–, Japanese admiral and diplomat. Commanded fighting at Shanghai in 1932. Sent to U.S. in 1940 as ambassador. He conducted Washington negotiations (1941) cut short by Japanese attack on Pearl Harbor.

nonconformists, those who refuse to comply with rules of discipline or doctrine of an estab. church. Term applied especially to Protestant dissenters from the Church of England, a group arising soon after the Reformation. The Act of Uniformity (1662), making episcopal ordination compulsory, made a split inevitable. Term *dissenter* came into use with Toleration Act (1689).

nonjurors [from Latin,= not swearing], the English and Scottish clergymen who refused to break allegiance to James II and take oath to William III in 1689. Five bishops were deprived of their sees in 1690. James II in exile appointed bishops. Nonjuring episcopal succession lasted until 1805 although the Scots actually submitted in 1788.

nonmetal, chemical ELEMENT distinguished from METAL in appearing as negative ion or in negative radical and in that its oxide yields an acid. Nonmetal may be solid, liquid, or gas. Some nonmetals form crystals. All lack metallic luster. They vary in hardness and are poor conductors of heat and electricity. Most do not occur free, but exist in numerous relatively abundant compounds.

Nonpartisan League, organization of business farmers formed by A. C. Townley in N.Dak. in 1915. Subsequently expanded into Wis. and other Western states. Set out to improve farm business conditions by legislation; endorsed, sometimes nominated candidates. Though strongly opposed, it had permanent effects on legislation in some states.

Nootka Indians (nŏŏt′kù), North American tribe, of Wakashan linguistic stock, living on W coast of Vancouver Isl. Name is also given generally to the Aht Confederacy, including more than 20 tribes. They fish for salmon and live in long wooden houses.

Nootka Sound, harbor on W coast of Vancouver Isl., B.C., Canada, lying between it and Nootka Isl. First visited by Juan Pérez 1774. Fort built here by John Meares 1788. Its seizure by the Spanish 1789 led to controversy with Great Britain. Agreement in Nootka Convention (1790) opened N Pacific coast to British settlement.

Noranda, city (pop. 9,672), W Que., Canada, N of Rouyn. Gold, copper, and zinc mining center.

Nord (nôr), department (2,229 sq. mi.; pop. 1,917,452), N France, bordering on North Sea and Belgium; cap. Lille, chief port Dunkirk. Occupying French Flanders and Hainaut, it is a traditional battleground and a vital industrial region (coal mines).

Nordenskjold, Nils Adolf Erik, Baron (nŏŏr′dùnshûld), 1832–1901, Swedish geologist and arctic explorer, first to navigate Northeast Passage (1878–79), b. Finland. Commanded series of mapping and scientific expeditions to Spitsbergen and Greenland.

Norderney (nôr′dùrnī′), island (9 sq. mi.; pop. 6,452), off N Germany, in North Sea, one of East Frisian Isls.; a popular bathing resort.

Nord Fjord (nôr′ fyôr″), inlet, 70 mi. long, Sogn og Fjordane co., W Norway; Norway's third largest fjord. The JOSTEDALSBREEN is just S.

Nordhoff, Charles, 1830–1901, American journalist and author of books on the sea and on politics, b. Germany. Some of his works were edited by his grandson, **Charles Nordhoff,** 1887–1947, who also wrote with James Norman Hall *Mutiny on the Bounty* (1932) and other works.

Nordkyn, Cape: see NORTH CAPE.

Nördlingen (nûrt′lĭngùn), town (pop. 13,268), W Bavaria. Free imperial city 1217–1803. In the Thirty Years War, the imperialist victory here (1634) was a major cause for direct French intervention in 1635. In 1645 Nördlingen was the scene of a French victory. The town has kept much architecture of the 14th–15th cent.

Nore (nôr), river of Ireland, flowing 70 mi. from Co. Tipperary to the Barrow N of New Ross.

Nore, the, sandbank in the Thames estuary, England. Name also given to anchorage in the estuary, scene of a famous mutiny in the British fleet in 1797.

Norfolk, dukes of (Howard line): see HOWARD, family.

Norfolk, Hugh Bigod, 1st earl of (bī′gŏd, nôr′fùk), d. 1177, English nobleman. Supported Stephen (1135) and later (1153) Henry II. When he unsuccessfully rebelled against Henry (1173), his lands were seized.

Norfolk, Thomas Mowbray, 1st duke of, c.1366–1399, English statesman. With the Lords Appellants, he

drove out the king's favorites (1387) and virtually ruled until Richard II regained control (1389) but retained king's favor. Banished for life after a dispute with earl of Hereford (later Henry IV).

Norfolk (nôr′fùk), maritime county (2,053 sq. mi.; pop. 546,550), E England; co. town Norwich. Region of flat, fertile farmlands. Cereals, root crops, cattle and poultry breeding, and fishing are important. Has many prehistoric remains.

Norfolk (nôr′fôk). **1** Resort town (pop. 1,572), NW Conn., in Litchfield Hills. Annual Litchfield county choral concerts began here 1899. **2** (nôr′fùk) City (pop. 11,335), NE Nebr., on Elkhorn R. and NW of Omaha; settled 1866. Rail and trade center in grain and livestock area. **3** City (pop. 213,513), SE Va., on Elizabeth R. and HAMPTON ROADS; founded 1682. Port with superior natural harbor, it is a major E coast naval installation (hq. of Atlantic fleet). Shipping of food products, seafood, lumber. Mfg. of textiles, fertilizers, and metal products. Town burned in Revolution; commerce ruined by embargo of 1807. Notable are St. Paul's Church (1739), Fort Norfolk (1794), and Myers House (1791). Near by are resort areas and historic sites.

Norfolk Island (nôr′fùk), island (13 sq. mi.; pop. 1,231), S Pacific, belonging to Australia. Discovered 1774 by Capt. James Cook. In 1856 some descendants of *Bounty* mutineers were moved here from Pitcairn Isl. Known for pine trees, scenic island thrives as a resort.

Noricum (nŏ′rĭkùm), province of the Roman Empire, occupying modern Austria S of the Danube and W of Vienna. Conquered 16 B.C.–A.D. 14, it was Roman until the 6th cent.

Normal, town (pop. 9,772), central Ill., adjacent to Bloomington. Has canneries. Illinois State Normal Univ. is here.

Norman, city (pop. 27,006), central Okla., SE of Oklahoma City; settled 1889. Center of agr. area. Seat of Univ. of OKLAHOMA.

Norman architecture, name applied to the buildings erected by the Normans in all lands under their rule. Norman buildings in England and France (built 1066–1154) were Romanesque, with massive proportions, sparsely adorned masonry, and use of round arch. Dormitory and refectory of Westminster Abbey are earliest extant Norman work in England. Of the many English cathedrals commenced by the Normans, Durham (begun 1093) is considered the finest. In both England and Normandy church plans were cruciform, with square tower over crossing of nave and transepts. In Sicily, the large Norman cathedrals of Cefalù, Palermo, and Monreale were commenced after 1130. They are in composite style incorporating domes and pointed arches of Saracens, wood roofs and geometric ornament of Normans, and interior mosaic decorations of Byzantine-Greek artisans.

Norman Conquest, conquest of England after defeat in 1066 of Harold by William, duke of Normandy (WILLIAM I). Intercourse with Europe in politics and trade grew and sped England's rise as major European power. Life and property became more secure, and ecclesiastical jurisdiction increased. To English judicial system was added jury system. General survey of the country was compiled in DOMESDAY BOOK. Cause of learning was enhanced (e.g., by Lanfranc and Anselm). ENGLISH LANGUAGE was superseded by French as language of culture and was much influenced by French. Norman architecture and new methods of warfare were also introduced.

Normandy (nôr′mùndē), Fr. *Normandie,* former province, N France, on English Channel, in Seine-Inférieure, Eure, Calvados, Manche, and Orne depts.; historic cap. Rouen. Rich agr. region; dairying, cattle raising, apple orchards. Important fisheries; shipping (at Le Havre and Cherbourg). Many seaside resorts (e.g., Dieppe, Deauville). The region is named for its conquerors, the NORSEMEN or Normans, to whose leader ROLLO it was given as a duchy in 911 by

Charles III (the Simple) of France. The Normans accepted Christianity and soon adopted French speech and customs but kept their taste for adventure and conquest. In 1066 Duke William II conquered England, where he became king as WILLIAM I. About the same time Norman adventurers conquered S Italy and Sicily (see ROBERT GUISCARD; ROGER I). Normandy itself was wrested from Duke ROBERT II by his brother, HENRY I of England, in 1106; in 1144, it was conquered by GEOFFREY of Anjou. Geoffrey's son, Henry Plantagenet, became duke of Normandy 1151 and king of England 1154 (see HENRY II); thus the ANGEVIN dynasty was estab. in England. Recovered for France by Philip II (1204), Normandy was devastated in the Hundred Years War, when England conquered it once again (1415). It was definitively restored to France in 1450. In World War II Normandy was the scene of the Allied invasion of the Continent (operation "Overlord," June 6, 1944), directed by Gen. Eisenhower. In the subsequent Normandy campaign the Cotentin peninsula (U.S. sector) and the Caen area (British sector) were devastated in heavy fighting. Capture of Saint-Lô (July 18) by U.S. forces cut off the German force under Rommel. The British, after taking Caen (July 19), were stalled but resumed their offensive in Aug. and captured Falaise Aug. 16. Nearly an entire German army was caught in the "Falaise pocket" between U.S. and British forces, and the rest of France was liberated in the following weeks.

Norman Isles: see CHANNEL ISLANDS.

Normans: see NORMANDY; NORSEMEN.

Norns, in Germanic mythology, the FATES, who spun and wove web of life. There were three—URTH (past), Verthandi (present), and Skuld (future).

Norrbotten (nôr′bôtůn), Swed. *Norrbottens län,* northernmost and largest county (40,750 sq. mi.; pop. 241,-602) of Sweden, bordering on Gulf of Bothnia, Finland, and Norway; cap. Lulea. It comprises historic Norrbotten prov. and larger part of Lappland prov. Its economy is based on cattle, sheep, and reindeer herds; hay; and iron ore (see KIRUNA). The KEBNEKAISE peak is here.

Norris, (Benjamin) Frank(lin), 1870–1902, American novelist, known for his powerful *Epic of Wheat,* a planned trilogy, including *The Octopus* (1901), *The Pit* (1903), and *The Wolf* (unfinished). A brother, **Charles G(ilman) Norris,** 1881–1945, wrote analytical novels of American life such as *Brass* (1921). His wife, Kathleen Norris (1880–), is known for her many romantic novels.

Norris, George William, 1861–1944, U.S. Representative (1903–13) and Senator (1913–43) from Nebr. Fearless, liberal Republican; secured reform of House rules (1910). Became an independent (1936). Author of Twentieth Amendment to Constitution, father of bills creating TVA.

Norris Dam: see TENNESSEE VALLEY AUTHORITY.

Norristown, borough (pop. 38,126), SE Pa., NW of Philadelphia and on Schuylkill R., near E end of Pa. Turnpike; settled 1784. Agr. shipping center with mfg. of machinery, metal products, and asbestos. Most populous independent borough in U.S.

Norrkoping, Swed. *Norrköping* (nôr′chû″pǐng), city (pop. 84,939), Ostergotland co., SE Sweden, a Baltic port. Sweden's chief textile center, it also produces paper, lumber, and ships. Burned 1719 by Russians, but its 16th-cent. castle remains.

Norrland: see SWEDEN.

Norse language, language of Norway or of Iceland at any period, a branch of Germanic subfamily of Indo-European languages. Sagas are written in Old Norse. See LANGUAGE (table).

Norse literature: see OLD NORSE LITERATURE.

Norsemen, Northmen, or **Normans,** Scandinavian VIKINGS who raided the coasts of continental Europe, particularly of France, in the 9th–10th cent. They were known as Danes in England, as Varangians in

Russia. Their sudden appearance was caused partly by overpopulation in Scandinavia, partly by the measures taken by HAROLD I of Norway against the independent nobles. Norse raiders began to sail up French rivers c.843, repeatedly sacked Paris and Rouen, and threatened, with rapacious destructiveness, to plunge France back into barbarism. They estab. settlements at the river mouths and in 911 received the duchy of NORMANDY.

Norse religion: see GERMANIC RELIGION.

North, Christopher, pseud. of **John Wilson,** 1785–1854, Scottish author of critical articles in *Blackwood's Magazine* and (with J. G. Lockhart and others) of *Noctes Ambrosianae,* a potpourri of humorous sketches and verse.

North, Frederick, 2d **earl of Guilford** and 8th **Baron North,** 1732–92, English statesman, known as Lord North. Prime minister (1770–82) during the American Revolution, he supported George III's policies.

North, Sir Thomas, 1535?–1601?, English translator of Plutarch's *Lives.*

North Adams, city (pop. 21,567), NW Mass., in the Berkshires, on Hoosic R. near W termini of Hoosac Tunnel and Mohawk Trail; settled c.1737. Electrical goods, textiles, paper. Mt. Greylock in SW.

North Africa, campaigns in. Italy's entrance into World War II (June 10, 1940) made North Africa an active theater in which the ultimate prize was control of the Mediterranean. Fighting began in Sept., 1940, after the swift Italian conquest of British Somaliland. The great desert war took place (except in final phases) along Libya-Egypt coast, where the level terrain provided poor defensive positions; success or failure hinged on speed in amassing armored and air strength. In Sept., 1940, Italian forces (under Graziani) from Libya penetrated c.60 mi. into Egypt, but a British surprise attack led by Wavell (Dec. 9, 1940) all but destroyed Italian army in a 500-mi. pursuit back into Libya. But the Italians were quickly reinforced by Rommel's Afrika Korps, and in March, 1941, they drove the British back to the Egyptian border, bypassing the strong Australian garrison at TOBRUK. Rommel was forced back into Libya in Nov., 1941, by a British counterattack led by Auchinleck. When Rommel struck back, May 26, 1942, the British suffered a crushing defeat and were driven c.250 mi. into Egypt, where they dug in along a 35-mi. line from ALAMEIN to Qattara Depression, only c.70 mi. W of Alexandria. Commanded by Montgomery, they withstood German attacks while reinforcements (esp. tanks and planes from U.S.) poured in. Montgomery's decisive thrust of Oct. 23, 1942, sent Axis troops through Libya into Tunisia on one of the longest sustained retreats in history. Allied troops under Eisenhower landed in Morocco and Algeria in Nov., 1942, and pushed toward Tunisia. Axis troops were compressed in a diminishing pocket in Tunisia between Eisenhower's forces on W, British 8th Army on E, Free French forces on S, and Allied planes and ships in the Mediterranean. After bitter fighting (notably at KASSERINE PASS) Axis forces in North Africa capitulated on May 12, 1943. Meanwhile, the Allies had won E Africa—British and Italian Somaliland had fallen by Feb., 1941, Eritrea and Ethiopia had been conquered by Nov., 1942.

Northallerton, urban district (pop. 6,087), cap. of North Riding of Yorkshire, England; a trade center. Battle of the Standard, between English and Scots, fought near here in 1138.

North America, N continent of Western Hemisphere; including ALASKA, CANADA, UNITED STATES, MEXICO; area c.8,000,000 sq. mi.; pop. c.200,000,000. Central America, generally considered S part of North America, is separated from South America by Isthmus of Panama. Continent is roughly triangular in shape, narrowest toward S. Offshore are Greenland (northernmost region of Western Hemisphere) and the West Indies. Highest point is Mt. McKINLEY (Alaska); low-

CAPITAL CITIES are designated by CAPITAL AND SMALL CAPITAL type

est, DEATH VALLEY (Calif.). Vast central plain, c.1,500 mi. wide, separates E coastal plain and mountain systems (LAURENTIAN MOUNTAINS, ADIRONDACK MOUNTAINS, APPALACHIAN MOUNTAINS) from extensive, high, rugged mountains of W (COAST RANGES and ROCKY MOUNTAINS, with GREAT BASIN between). Central plain drained by great river systems: the MISSISSIPPI, MISSOURI, SASKATCHEWAN, MACKENZIE and SAINT LAWRENCE (with GREAT LAKES). Other great rivers are the YUKON, COLUMBIA, COLORADO, and RIO GRANDE. Continental temperatures reach great extremes. Rainfall abundant along parts of coast, deficient in parts of interior. Mountainous E and W have heavily forested areas; N are the BARREN GROUNDS; central part is main agr. region; and large desert areas are SW. Generally fertile soil provides some of world's largest wheat, cotton, and grazing areas. Continent has extensive mineral resources. Present population consists chiefly of descendants of Europeans, together with Negroes, Asiatics, and remnants of aboriginal INDIANS.

Northampton, Henry Howard, earl of: see HOWARD, family.

Northampton, England: see NORTHAMPTONSHIRE.

Northampton. 1 City (pop. 29,063), W Mass., on Connecticut R. above Springfield. Mfg. of hosiery, brushes, and cutlery. Seat of SMITH COLLEGE. The Northampton Association of Education and Industry, communistic settlement, was here 1842–46. **2** Borough (pop. 9,332), E Pa., N of Allentown. Mfg. of cement and textiles.

Northamptonshire (nôrthămp'tùnshĭr) or **North Hants** (hănts), inland county (914 sq. mi.; pop. 359,550), central England. Soke of PETERBOROUGH, separate administrative county, is in NE. Agr. county devoted to sheep and cattle pasturage, it has long been a center of boot and shoe mfg. The county town is **Northampton,** county borough (pop. 104,429), on the Nene. Was important settlement of Angles and Danes. Has one of four round churches in England. An Eleanor Cross (ELEANOR OF CASTILE) is near by. Shoemaking is the chief industry.

North Andover, town (pop. 8,485), NE Mass., on Merrimack R. and just E of Lawrence. Textiles.

North Arlington, borough (pop. 15,970), NE N.J., NE of Newark. Metal, plastic, and rubber products.

North Atlantic Drift, warm ocean current in northern Atlantic Ocean, a continuation of the GULF STREAM. It tempers climate of Western and N Europe.

North Atlantic Treaty, defensive alliance signed in 1949 by the U.S., Canada, Great Britain, France, the Netherlands, Belgium, Luxembourg, Italy, Norway, Denmark, Iceland, and Portugal. Greece and Turkey were admitted in 1951. North Atlantic Treaty Organization (NATO) consists of a supreme council, a staff headed by a secretary general (Lord Hastings Ismay, appointed 1952), and military hq. under a supreme commander (Gen. Dwight Eisenhower, 1950–52; Gen. Matthew Ridgway, 1952–). Treaty, set up as a regional alliance under the Charter of the United Nations, is to be renewed in 10 years.

North Attleboro, town (pop. 12,146), SE Mass., at R.I. line; settled 1669. Mfg. of jewelry (since 18th cent.), silverware, and foundry products.

North Australia: see NORTHERN TERRITORY.

North Battleford, city (pop. 7,473), W Sask., Canada, on North Saskatchewan R. at mouth of Battle R., NW of Saskatoon and opposite Battleford. Trade center for W Sask.

North Bay, city (pop. 17,944), S Ont., Canada, on L. Nipissing and N of Toronto. Rail center in lumber and mining area and outfitting point for hunting and fishing region.

North Bend, city (pop. 6,099), SW Oregon, on Coos Bay. Lumber mills and fisheries.

North Bergen, suburban township (pop. 41,560), NE N.J., NE of Jersey City. Mfg. of ink, electrical equipment, radio parts, clothing, and metal goods.

North Borneo or **British North Borneo,** British colony (29,307 sq. mi.; est. pop. 330,000), NE BORNEO; cap. Jesselton. Was protectorate until 1946. Here is Mt. Kinabalu, highest peak of Borneo. Products include rubber and timber.

North Brabant (brübănt'), Dutch *Noordbrabant,* province (1,894 sq. mi.; pop. 1,180,133), S Netherlands; cap. 's Hertogenbosch. Agr. in N; heathland in S. Textile mfg.; electrical appliances (notably at Eindhoven). Shared history of BRABANT until 1648, when Spain ceded it to the United Provs.

North Braddock, borough (pop. 14,724), SW Pa., ESE suburb of Pittsburgh. Mfg. of steel.

Northbridge, town (pop. 10,476), S Mass., SE of Worcester; settled 1704. Includes Whitinsville village (pop. 5,662), with mfg. of textiles.

North Canadian, river rising in NE N.Mex. and flowing E into Okla. Panhandle, SE through Oklahoma City, to South Canadian R. near junction with Arkansas R. in E Okla. With Wolf Creek tributary, it is in Arkansas R. basin project.

North Cape, N Norway, near N end of Mageroy isl., Finnmark co., NE of Hammerfest. At lat. 71°10'N, it is northernmost important point of Europe. Tourist steamers call here. Cape Nordkyn (nôr'chün) or Kinnarodden (chĭ'närô"dùn), at lat. 71°8'N, on Barents Sea, is northernmost point on mainland.

North Carolina, state (52,712 sq. mi.; pop. 4,061,929), SE U.S.; one of Thirteen Colonies; cap. RALEIGH. Other cities include CHARLOTTE, WINSTON-SALEM, GREENSBORO, DURHAM, ASHEVILLE, WILMINGTON. Bordered E by the Atlantic (tidewater region), with capes HATTERAS, FEAR, LOOKOUT. Coastal plains rise to fall line and piedmont area. W are the BLUE RIDGE and GREAT SMOKY MOUNTAINS. Mt. MITCHELL (6,684 ft.) highest point E of Mississippi R. Rivers include Catawba (WATEREE), Yadkin (PEE DEE), TAR, ROANOKE, NEUSE, CAPE FEAR RIVER. Farming (tobacco, cotton, peanuts, corn, dairying); minerals (granite, mica, feldspar); fishing. Mfg. of tobacco products, textiles, clothing, paper, fertilizer, aluminum. Ralegh's colonies at ROANOKE ISLAND (1580s) failed; Va. colonists estab. settlements beginning 1653. Made royal colony (1729) after dissatisfaction with proprietors. Farmers organized REGULATOR MOVEMENT (1768); it was suppressed in 1771. MECKLENBURG DECLARATION OF INDEPENDENCE allegedly proclaimed in May, 1775. Invaded in Revolution in CAROLINA CAMPAIGN (1780–81). Tidewater planter aristocracy dominated government until 1830s. Seceded from Union after Lincoln called for troops. Tobacco mfg. grew with introduction of cigarette-making machinery in 1880s. Farm tenancy system dominated agr. Since World War I state government has followed policy of consolidation and centralization.

North Carolina, Agricultural and Technical College of: see GREENSBORO.

North Carolina, University of, at Chapel Hill; state supported; partly coed.; chartered 1789, first to open as state university 1795. Consolidated Univ. of North Carolina includes State Col. of Agriculture and Engineering (Raleigh; coed., 1887), Woman's Col. (Greensboro, 1891). Has planetarium, art gallery, folk theater, folklore council, and press.

North Channel, strait between Northern Ireland and Scotland, connecting Irish Sea with the Atlantic.

North Chicago, city (pop. 8,628), NE Ill., N of Chicago on L. Michigan, adjoining Waukegan. Mfg. of metal products. Steel strike (1937) here led to Supreme Court ruling (1939) made sit-down strikes illegal. Great Lakes Naval Training Station near by.

Northcliffe, Alfred Charles William Harmsworth, Viscount, 1865–1922, British journalist. With his brother Harold, later Viscount Rothermere, he formed the world's largest newspaper combine, the Amalgamated Press. In 1896 he founded the *Daily Mail,* and in 1903 the *Daily Mirror.* In 1908 he bought *The Times* and gave it new life. His activities revolutionized journalism and influenced war policies as well as political affairs. He was made viscount in 1917.

North Conway, N.H.: see CONWAY.

North Dakota, state (70,665 sq. mi.; pop. 619,636), N central U.S.; admitted 1889 as 39th state; cap. BISMARCK. Other cities are FARGO and GRAND FORKS. Bounded E by RED RIVER OF THE NORTH. Crossed by MISSOURI R. Central lowlands in E, hills and Badlands in W. Farming grains (esp. wheat), livestock, dairying. Processing of these products. Deposits of lignite, clay, bentonite. Explorations began 1738 with VÉRENDRYE. U.S. got NW N.Dak. in Louisiana Purchase (1803), SE half from Great Britain (1818). Fur trade dominated region for over half a century. Dakota Territory organized 1861. Indian warfare disturbed region in 1860s and 1870s. Wheat fields, homesteading, railroad building brought settlers. Struggle between farmers and corporate interests dominated politics in late 19th cent. Drought of 1930s brought about irrigation, power developments. Additional improvement is proposed in MISSOURI RIVER BASIN PROJECT.

North Dakota, University of: see GRAND FORKS.

North Dakota Agricultural College: see FARGO.

North Downs, England: see DOWNS, THE, chalk hills.

Northeast Boundary Dispute, controversy between U.S. and Great Britain concerning Maine-New Brunswick boundary. Treaty of 1783 had described NE U.S. boundary as a line drawn due N from source of St. Croix R. to highlands dividing the Atlantic and St. Lawrence tributaries and along those highlands to NW head of Connecticut R. Disputes over that definition lasted almost 60 years. In 1839 dispute led to so-called AROOSTOOK WAR. WEBSTER-ASHBURTON TREATY ended controversy.

Northeast Harbor, Maine: see MOUNT DESERT ISLAND.

North East Land, island: see SPITSBERGEN.

Northeast Passage, passage from North Sea to the Pacific. Sought notably by William Barentz (16th cent.), Henry Hudson (17th cent.), Vitus Bering (18th cent.). First successful navigation by N. A. E. Nordenskjold of Sweden (1878–79). Passage has become regular shipping route for Siberian ports, navigable from June to Sept.

Northern Dvina, RSFSR: see DVINA.

Northern Ireland, administrative unit (5,238 sq. mi.; pop. 1,370,709) of United Kingdom; cap. Belfast. Estab. by Government of Ireland Act of 1920, Ireland (often called ULSTER) comprises six counties of Armagh, Down, Antrim, Londonderry, Tyrone, and Fermanagh, with county boroughs of Belfast and Londonderry. Republic of IRELAND refuses to recognize division as valid. N Ireland, represented in British Parliament by 12 members, has large degree of self-government. History began in early 17th cent. when British confiscated much of land and "planted" it with Scotch and English settlers. Rift between two parts came with Gladstone's proposed first HOME RULE Bill (1886). Protestant North feared domination by southern Catholic majority. By World War I civil war was a danger. Bill of 1920 set up separate parliaments for N and S Ireland. Growing Catholic minority now threatens Protestant hegemony. Land is mountainous; farming is the main industry. Area is famous for its fine linens. Heavier industry is concentrated in and around Belfast, one of chief ports of British Isles.

Northern Land, RSFSR: see SEVERNAYA ZEMLYA.

northern lights: see AURORA BOREALIS.

Northern Pacific Railway, American railway system, chartered 1864. Construction began in 1870. Jay COOKE first managed enterprise. After financial contest with E. H. Harriman, group under J. J. Hill and J. P. Morgan secured control. Line extends from Duluth and St. Paul, Minn., to Seattle, Wash., and Portland, Oregon; operating several branch systems, it controls nearly 6,900 mi. of trackage. Numerous traffic connections give it access to L. Superior, Gulf of Mexico, Pacific Ocean.

Northern Rhodesia (rōdē′zhù), British protectorate (292,323 sq. mi.; est. pop. 1,565,547), S central Africa; cap. Lusaka. On high plateau with generally healthful climate. Chief crops are corn, tobacco, and coffee. Copper is leading export. Livingstone first came on missionary journeys in 1851; traveled through Barotseland (in W part) and in 1855 discovered Victoria Falls. In 1891 the British made Barotseland a protectorate. British control over area was estab. 1891–94 by ousting Arab slave traders. Governed as part of RHODESIA until 1911. Controlled by British South Africa Co. until 1924, when direct British rule was estab. with appointed governor aided by executive and legislative councils.

Northern Territories, British protectorate (30,600 sq. mi.; pop. 1,077,138), N Gold Coast, W Africa; cap. Tamale. Stock raising and cotton growing.

Northern Territory (523,620 sq. mi.; pop. 10,866), N Australia, on Timor and Arafura seas; cap. Darwin. Originally a part of New South Wales, it later belonged to South Australia. In 1911 it came under direct control of federal government; divided 1926 into North Australia and Central Australia, reunited 1931. First explored by Leichhardt (1844–45). Climate is tropical, with monsoon season. Sparse population is composed mainly of aborigines, who occupy 15 reservations. Discovery of uranium ore has boosted area's economic development.

Northern War, 1700–1721, conflict arising from the desire of Sweden's neighbors to break Swedish supremacy in N Europe. In 1699 PETER I of Russia, FREDERICK IV of Denmark, and AUGUSTUS II of Poland and Saxony allied themselves against CHARLES XII of Sweden. Hostilities opened in 1700. Against immense odds, the young Swedish king quickly forced Denmark out of the war and routed Peter at Narva (1700); took Warsaw and Cracow (1702); had STANISLAUS I elected king of Poland (1704); and forced Augustus to renounce Poland and his alliance with Russia (Treaty of Altranstädt, 1706). In 1707 Charles invaded the Ukraine with the help of MAZEPPA. Utterly defeated by Peter at Poltava (1709), he found asylum in Turkey and induced the sultan to declare war on Russia (1710). When Peter bought off Turkey in the Peace of the Pruth (1711), Charles's position became untenable. Nevertheless, he stubbornly stayed on in Turkey until 1714. Meanwhile Augustus reconquered Poland; Peter completed the conquest of Swedish Livonia, Ingermanland, and Karelia; and Denmark resumed warfare in alliance with Hanover and Prussia. Undaunted, Charles invaded Norway but was fatally shot in 1718. By the treaties of Stockholm and Frederiksborg (1719–20) Sweden made peace with all the allies but Russia, ceding the duchies of Verden and Bremen to Hanover and part of W Pomerania to Prussia. By the Treaty of Nystad (1721), Sweden ceded Livonia, Ingermanland, and part of Karelia to Russia. Russia became a major European power.

Northfield. 1 Town (pop. 2,246), N Mass., on Connecticut R. and NE of Greenfield. Birthplace of D. L. Moody, founder of Northfield Seminary (now Northfield School) for girls and Mt. Hermon School for boys; he started summer religious conferences. First youth hostel in U.S. opened here 1934. **2** City (pop. 7,487), SE Minn., S of St. Paul, in farm area. Seat of Carleton Col. (coed.; 1866) and Saint Olaf Col. (Lutheran; coed.; opened by Norwegians as school 1875, became college 1886, chartered 1889). Jesse James gang tried to rob bank here, Sept. 7, 1876. **3** Town (pop. 4,314), central Vt., SW of Montpelier. Includes Northfield village (pop. 2,262). Town is seat of Norwich Univ. (state military college, but privately controlled; for men; founded 1819, opened 1820 at Norwich, became university 1834, moved to Northfield 1866).

North German Confederation, alliance of 22 German states N of Main R., under Prussian leadership, which replaced the GERMAN CONFEDERATION, destroyed by the Austro-Prussian War (1866). The S German states, though excluded, were closely bound to it through membership in the ZOLLVEREIN. Constitution, prepared by Bismarck, provided for federal council and diet (Reichstag); king of Prussia was the president. In 1871 this constitution, with some modification, was adopted by the German Empire.

North Hants, England: see NORTHAMPTONSHIRE.

North Haven, town (pop. 9,444), S Conn., N of New Haven. Mfg. of bricks and hardware.

North Holland, Dutch *Noordholland*, province (1,017 sq. mi.; pop. 1,774,273), NW Netherlands; cap. Haarlem; largest city Amsterdam. A peninsula between the North Sea and the Ijsselmeer, it is a lowland drained by numerous small rivers and canals and protected by dikes. Agr., cattle raising, dairying, flower growing, fishing. Famed for its many windmills, drawbridges, tulip fields. For history, see HOLLAND.

North Island (44,281 sq. mi.; pop. 1,146,292), New Zealand, separated from South Isl. by Cook Strait. Chief towns are Wellington (cap. of New Zealand) and Auckland. Irregularly shaped with long NW peninsula. Has volcanic peaks and many hot springs. Drained mainly by Waikato R., which rises in L. Taupo.

North Kingstown (kĭng'stùn), town (pop. 14,810), S R.I., on Narragansett Bay S of Providence; settled 1641. Birthplace of Gilbert Stuart. Mfg. of woolens and elastic braid. Includes old Wickford resort (pop. 2,437) and Quonset Point (kwŏn'sĭt), site of Northeastern Naval Air Station (1941).

North Little Rock, city (pop. 44,097), central Ark., on Arkansas R. opposite LITTLE ROCK; settled c.1856, annexed Levy 1946. It has railroad shops, stockyards, and processing plants for timber-creosoting and cottonseed oil.

Northmen: see NORSEMEN.

North Miami, town (pop. 10,734), SE Fla., near Miami; renamed 1931 from Miami Shores.

North Minch, Scotland: see MINCH.

North Olmsted, city (pop. 6,604), NE Ohio, W suburb of Cleveland. Makes machine tools.

North Ossetia, RSFSR: see OSSETIA.

North Platte (plăt), city (pop. 15,433), central Nebr., at junction of North Platte and South Platte rivers; laid out 1866. In irrigated grain and livestock area, it is a Great Plains shipping point on transcontinental rail and air lines.

North Platte, river rising in N Colo. and flowing 680 mi. in great bend through Wyo. and across W Nebr. to join the South Platte and form the Platte. Has 27 major reservoirs. Dams include Kingsley Dam at OGALLALA, Nebr., those of Kendrick project at CASPER, Wyo., and of North Platte project.

North Platte project, developed by U.S. in North Platte valley in W Nebr. and E Wyo. Irrigates 237,000 acres and supplies some 175,000 privately developed acres. Guernsey Reservoir is created by Guernsey Dam (105 ft. high) in North Platte R. and is fed by Pathfinder Reservoir, made by Pathfinder Dam (214 ft. high), and by three small reservoirs near Scottsbluff. On project are Glendo Reservoir, Whalen Diversion Dam, and Guernsey Dam and Lingle power plants. Main activities in area are agr. and livestock raising. Serves Bridgeport, Bayard, Minatare, Scottsbluff, Mitchell, and Gering, Nebr., and Torrington, Wyo.

North Pole, northern end of earth's axis, lat. 90° and long. 0°. It is distinguished from the north magnetic pole. R. E. Peary reached the North Pole (1909). See also ARCTIC REGIONS.

North Providence, textile town (pop. 13,927), NE R.I., NW of Providence.

North Rhine–Westphalia (–wĕstfāl'yu), Ger. *Nordrhein-Westfalen*, German state (13,157 sq. mi.; pop. 13,147,-066), NW Germany; cap. DÜSSELDORF. Formed 1947 in British zone of occupation, it includes the former Prussian WESTPHALIA prov. and RHINE PROVINCE and

the former state of Lippe. With the RUHR and the Rhenish industrial dists., it is one of the world's greatest centers of heavy industries. Joined Federal Republic of [West] Germany 1949.

North Riding: see YORKSHIRE, England.

North River, N.Y.: see HUDSON, river.

Northrop, John Howard, 1891–, American biochemist. He shared 1946 Nobel Prize in Chemistry for work on enzymes and viruses.

North Saskatchewan: see SASKATCHEWAN, river.

North Schleswig, Denmark: see SCHLESWIG.

North Sea, part of the Atlantic (c.600 mi. long) between British Isles and NW Central Europe. 400 mi. at widest, it narrows to Strait of Dover. Has many shallows. Largest is Dogger Bank, between England and Denmark, a center of the North Sea fisheries.

North Smithfield, textile town (pop. 5,726), N R.I., at Mass. line and NW of Providence.

North Star: see POLESTAR.

North Sydney, town (pop. 7,354), NE Cape Breton Isl., N.S., Canada, on Sydney Harbour, NW of Sydney. Coal-shipping port and winter fishing base.

North Tarrytown, residential village (pop. 8,740), SE N.Y., on E bank of Hudson R. near Tarrytown. Has Castle Philipse (see PHILIPSE MANOR) and Dutch Reformed Church (c.1697), where Washington Irving is buried, in Sleepy Hollow, the setting for his story, "Legend of Sleepy Hollow." John André's capture here revealed Benedict Arnold's treachery. Near by are Rockefeller estates.

North Tonawanda (tŏnùwŏn'dù), city (pop. 24,731), W N.Y., on Niagara R., at W end of the Barge Canal; settled 1808. Lumber port; mfg. of iron, steel, wood products, boats, paper, and musical instruments.

Northumberland, earls of: see PERCY, family.

Northumberland, John Dudley, duke of, c.1502–1553, English statesman. Helped estab. Edward SEYMOUR as protector of EDWARD VI, later deposed (1549) and executed him. Posed as a Protestant and persuaded dying Edward to name Lady Jane Grey as successor. Deserted by his army, he was executed for treason.

Northumberland, border county (2,019 sq. mi.; pop. 798,175), N England; co. town Newcastle-on-Tyne. Has rugged coastline, with high moorlands and fertile valleys in the interior. Oats, barley, and turnips are grown; sheep grazing is important. There are great coal deposits in SE. Newcastle is major coal-shipping port and a shipbuilding and industrial center.

Northumbria, kingdom of (nôrthùm'brĕù), one of the Anglo-Saxon heptarchy, England. Originally it comprised kingdoms of Bernicia and Deira, settled by invading Angles c.500. United by Aethelfrith. Edwin estab. Northumbrian supremacy, which declined as that of MERCIA increased. 8th and early 9th cent. saw golden age of Church and culture. Invading Danes occupied S Northumbria and Angles had to acknowledge (920) Edward the Elder of Wessex as overking.

North Vancouver, city (pop. 15,687), SE B.C., Canada, on Burrard Inlet of Strait of Georgia, opposite Vancouver (bridge, ferry). Port and fishing base with shipbuilding, lumbering, and woodworking.

Northwest Boundary Dispute: see SAN JUAN BOUNDARY DISPUTE.

North West Company, organized 1787 by Montreal merchants and fur traders as rival of HUDSON'S BAY COMPANY. Extended fur trade W. Explorers such as Sir Alexander MACKENZIE and David THOMPSON were North West Co. men. Company pushed business into territory of U.S. American post, Astoria, was purchased by company in 1813. Rivalry with Hudson's Bay Co. reached peak in quarrel over RED RIVER SETTLEMENT; two companies were forced to unite in 1821.

Northwestern University, at Evanston and Chicago, Ill., coed.; chartered 1851, opened 1855 by Methodists. In 1873 absorbed Evanston Col. for Ladies (opened 1871), headed by Frances Willard, with which

Northwestern Female Col. (opened 1855) had merged.

North-West Frontier Province (41,057 sq. mi.; pop. 5,699,000), W Pakistan; cap. Peshawar. Mostly mountainous, with caravan trade via Khyber Pass. Main occupations are agr. and livestock raising. In ancient times area belonged to Persian empire; today most inhabitants speak Pushtu, an Iranian language. Islam was introduced in 11th cent. by Afghan invaders. Under Sikh control from 1818 to 1849, when area was taken by the British. Areas bordering on Afghanistan are inhabited by Moslem tribes, which have long resisted outside authority.

Northwest Mounted Police: see ROYAL CANADIAN MOUNTED POLICE.

Northwest Ordinance: see ORDINANCE OF 1787.

Northwest Passage, route sought through American continent to South Sea for commercial purposes. Spurred exploration in the 16th and 17th cent. Later scientific expeditions estab. existence of a passage through icy seas N of the continent; this was traversed 1903–6.

Northwest Territories, region (1,304,903 sq. mi.; pop. 16,004), NW Canada, W of Hudson Bay, E of Yukon, N of lat. 60°N. Includes islands of Hudson Bay, Hudson Strait, and James Bay. Area is divided into three provisional districts: Keewatin, W of Hudson Bay; Mackenzie, E of Yukon; and Franklin, N and including the Arctic Archipelago. Most development has been in Mackenzie dist. Fur trading is extensive. Although vast mineral resources remain untapped, oil is produced at Fort Norman, gold at Yellowknife, copper from Coppermine R. area, and pitchblende and uranium on Great Bear L. Here are two of world's largest lakes, GREAT BEAR and GREAT SLAVE, which drain into Arctic Ocean via Mackenzie R. Much of Keewatin dist. is part of the BARREN GROUNDS and here, as in Franklin dist., fur trapping is the major occupation. Franklin dist. is a game preserve. Region's transport and travel is largely by air. Henry Hudson opened the gateway to the area 1610. After that Hudson's Bay Co. sponsored many explorations and opened trading posts. Area was known as RUPERT'S LAND until it was ceded to Canada by HUDSON'S BAY CO. 1870, then including Man., Sask., Alta., and parts of B.C. and Que. The S border of 60°N was estab. 1912. Government of the territories, enforced by the Royal Canadian Mounted Police, is under a commissioner and council.

Northwest Territory, first national territory of U.S., comprising geographical region generally known as Old Northwest. This area about the Great Lakes and between the Ohio and the Mississippi included present states of Ohio, Ind., Ill., Mich., Wis., and part of Minn. French control here began with exploring and trading in early 17th cent. By the Treaty of Paris (1763), which ended FRENCH AND INDIAN WARS, British obtained Canada and Old Northwest. G. R. CLARK led expedition against British in American Revolution. Treaty of Paris (1783), ending Revolution, declared Old Northwest within U.S. boundaries. Cession of all lands to U.S. government by 1786 ended strife among states over rival claims. ORDINANCE OF 1787 set up machinery for organization of territories and admission of states. OHIO COMPANY OF ASSOCIATES was most active force in early colonization. JAY'S TREATY and subsequent negotiations smoothed out some British-American difficulties, but British influence remained strong among the Indians. Quarrel over Northwest was a chief cause of War of 1812. Treaty of Ghent (1814) irrevocably settled region upon U.S.

Northwich, urban district (pop. 17,480), Cheshire, England; center of England's salt industry.

Norton, Caroline (Elizabeth Sarah Sheridan), 1808–77, English author; granddaughter of R. B. Sheridan. She became the subject of notoriety when her husband, suing for divorce, accused her of an affair with Lord Melbourne. She wrote vigorously to improve the status of women and to better working conditions, especially for children.

Norton, Charles Eliot, 1827–1908, American scholar; an influential professor of history of art at Harvard (1875–98); an editor of the *North American Review* and a founder of the *Nation.* Translated Dante and edited poems of John Donne, as well as letters of Carlyle, Emerson, Lowell, and Ruskin.

Norton, town (pop. 4,401), SE Mass., NW of Taunton. Seat of Wheaton Col. (nonsectarian; for women; opened 1835, chartered as pioneer female seminary 1837, organized by Mary Lyon, became college 1912).

Norton Sound, 130 mi. long, inlet of Bering Sea, on W coast of Alaska, S of Seward Peninsula. Nome is on N shore; Yukon R. enters sea on S side. Explored by Capt. James Cook 1778.

Norumbega (nôrŭmbĕ′gù), region or city on E coast of North America, possibly mythical, used on 16th–17th cent. maps. Location and identity uncertain.

Norwalk. 1 City (pop. 49,460), SW Conn., on harbor on Long Isl. Sound SW of Bridgeport; settled 1649. Mfg. of hats, textiles, hardware, and machinery. Includes South Norwalk (annexed 1913; rail junction), Silvermine (artists' colony), other villages, and offshore islands. **2** City (pop. 9,775), N Ohio, SSE of Sandusky. Mfg. of wood and rubber goods.

Norway, Nor. *Norge,* kingdom (119,240 sq. mi.; with water surface 125,182 sq. mi.; pop. 3,156,950), N Europe, occupying the mountainous W part of the Scandinavian peninsula. Largest cities: Oslo (cap.), Bergen, Trondheim, Stavanger. Overseas possessions: SPITSBERGEN and Jan Mayen (Arctic Ocean); Bouvet and Peter I isls. (S Atlantic). Extending from the SKAGERRAK NE to NORTH CAPE, Norway has a W coastline c.2,100 mi. long, fringed with islands (incl. LOFOTEN) and deeply indented by fjords. Its land borders are with Sweden (W) and Finland and USSR (N). Land rises precipitously from coast to high plateaus (e.g., DOVREFJELL); culminates at 8,098 ft. in JOTUNHEIM range. Only 4% of land is under cultivation. Climate is mild because of North Atlantic Drift. Chief natural resources are timber (covers c.25% of Norway) minerals (pyrites, copper, iron), hydroelectric power. Fishing (cod, herring, mackerel) and whaling provide chief exports. Other important industries: pulp and paper milling, electrochemistry, electrometallurgy. Merchant fleet ranks third in world. The population, predominantly Lutheran, is concentrated in S. LAPPS and Finns predominate in N. Norway is a constitutional monarchy, with legislative powers vested in the STORTING. Reigning king: HAAKON VII. The several petty kingdoms of Norway were united (872) by HAROLD I in the age of the VIKINGS. (See also NORSEMEN; ICELAND.) OLAF II (reigned 1015–28) estab. Christianity. He was driven out by CANUTE, but his son MAGNUS I was restored on the Norwegian throne 1035. After a period of anarchy, King SVERRE defeated the nobles (1201) and centralized royal power. Medieval Norway reached its flowering under MAGNUS VI and HAAKON IV (13th cent.) but soon declined when the HANSEATIC LEAGUE monopolized its trade. It ceased to exist as a separate kingdom in the 14th cent. Under Queen MARGARET its crown was permanently united with that of DENMARK (1397); Danish governors ruled Norway until 1814, when Denmark ceded the kingdom to Sweden. Norway attempted to set itself up as a separate kingdom but was forced to accept union with Sweden in 1815. It did, however, retain its separate constitution of 1814. Late in 19th cent. the Liberal leader, Johan SVERDRUP, obtained concessions from Sweden, but Sweden refused to grant Norway a separate consular service and flag. This, among other issues, led the Storting to declare the union dissolved. Sweden acquiesced; Haakon VII was chosen king of Norway. The late 19th and early 20th cent. saw a large-scale emigration of Norwegians to the U.S. Norway was neutral in World War I. In World War II Germany invaded Norway without warning (April, 1940). Norwegian troops briefly resisted, but French and British aid was inadequate. The government continued the war from abroad, bringing the Norwegian merchant fleet to the Allies. The attempts of QUISLING to enlist the people in his collaboration with the German authorities failed utterly. Russian troops entered N Norway late in 1944; the rest of the country remained under German occupation until May, 1945. A charter member of the UN, Norway also joined the European Recovery Program (1947) and North Atlantic Treaty (1949).

Norway, resort town (pop. 3,811), SW Maine, NW of Auburn. Mfg. of wooden articles, shoes, moccasins, and equipment for winter sports.

Norwegian language, either of two slightly different North Germanic standard languages. Dano-Norwegian or Rigsmaal is Oslo dialect of standard Danish, which was official until 20th cent. Landsmaal is a standardization of Norwegian dialects, introduced by Ivar AASEN. See LANGUAGE (table).

Norwegian Sea, name of that part of the Atlantic NW of Norway between Greenland Sea and North Sea.

Norwich (nŏr'ĭj, –rĭch), county borough (pop. 121,-226), co. seat of Norfolk, England. In 11th cent. it ranked with London, York, and Bristol in ecclesiastical and commercial importance. Has many ancient churches and buildings, including 11th-cent. cathedral. Saw much early fighting, and twice suffered Black Death. A grain market, it has varied mfg.

Norwich. 1 (nŏr'wĭch, nŏ'rĭch), Industrial city (pop. 23,429) in Norwich town (pop. 37,633), SE Conn., at head of Thames R. estuary. Mfg. of metal and leather goods, textiles, and chemicals. Pewter making began here 1730. Has art gallery, with art school. **2** (nôr'wĭch), City (pop. 8,816), S central N.Y., on Chenango R. and NE of Binghamton. Mfg. of pharmaceuticals, dairy goods, and machinery.

Norwich University: see NORTHFIELD, Vt.

Norwood. 1 Town (pop. 16,636), E Mass., SW of Boston; settled 1678. Printing and tanning. **2** City (pop. 35,001), SW Ohio, suburb of Cincinnati; settled as Sharpsburg in early 19th cent. Mfg. of automobiles, electrical and metal goods. **3** Borough (pop. 5,246), SE Pa., SW suburb of Philadelphia.

Noske, Gustav (gōōs'täf nôs'kŭ), 1868–1946, German politician, a Social Democrat. As minister of defense (1919–20), he ruthlessly suppressed SPARTACUS PARTY and other radical uprisings.

Nostradamus (nŏs"trŭdā'mŭs), Fr. *Michel de Nostredame,* 1503–66, French astrologer and physician. His obscure rhymed prophecies (*Centuries,* 1555) have enjoyed popularity for centuries.

Notker Labeo (lā'bēō), c.950–1022, German monk, teacher at St. Gall, a founder of German literature. He translated Boethius, Aristotle, Capella, and Gregory I into Old High German.

Notre Dame, University of (nō"tûr dām'), at Notre Dame, Ind., N of South Bend; Holy Cross Fathers, mainly for men; chartered and opened 1844. Knute ROCKNE was a famous football coach here.

Notre Dame de Paris (nô'trũ däm' dũ pärē'), cathedral church on Île de la Cité, Paris. Site was originally occupied by Roman temple and later by two Christian churches, which were demolished by Maurice de Sully in order to erect the cathedral. Construction began 1163, finished c.1230. Spires of original design were never added to the twin towers. In French Revolution rioters destroyed sculptures of W façade. Under Viollet-le-Duc restorations were begun 1845. In Notre Dame, Gothic forms are clearly dominant, with few traces of Romanesque design.

Notre Dame Mountains, continuation of Green Mts. of Vt., c.3,500 ft. high, SE and E Que., Canada, extending NE to St. Lawrence R. below Quebec and E into the Gaspé Peninsula where they are continued by Shickshock Mts.

Nott, Eliphalet (ĭlĭ'fŭlĭt nŏt'), 1773–1866, American educator, clergyman, and inventor. He was president

of Union Col., 1804–66. Among his inventions was first anthracite coal base-burner stove.

Nottaway (nŏ'tũwā), river of W Que., Canada, rising in Mattagami L. Flows c.400 mi. NW to James Bay.

Nottingham, Charles Howard, 1st earl of: see HOWARD, family.

Nottinghamshire (nŏ'tĭng-ũmshĭr) or **Nottingham,** inland county (844 sq. mi.; pop. 841,083), central England. In S are upland moors, the Wolds, bordering low-lying fertile land. Sherwood Forest, scene of Robin Hood legends, includes the Dukeries, area noted for fine estates. Dairying and cereal crops are important. Coal fields are along W border. Textiles, bicycles, and motors are manufactured. The county town is **Nottingham** (nŏ'tĭng-ũm), county borough (pop. 306,008), on the Trent. Was an important Danish borough in 9th cent. In 1642 standard of Charles I was raised here, marking start of civil war. Site of a Catholic cathedral and Univ. Col. Manufactures include cotton and silk goods. Traditional birthplace of Robin Hood.

Notus (nō'tŭs), in Greek mythology, personification of the south wind, bringer of fog and sickness.

Nouméa (nōōmē'ũ, nōōmää'), port town (pop. 11,-108), New Caledonia; cap. of French colony of New Caledonia. Airline base on Calif.–New Zealand route. Exports nickel, chrome, and copra. Had U.S. air base in World War II. Name is sometimes spelled Numea.

nova: see VARIABLE STAR.

Novalis (nōvä'lĭs), pseud. of **Friedrich von Hardenberg** (frē'drĭkh fūn här'dũnbĕrk), 1772–1801, German poet, one of the most extreme and most gifted romanticists. His works include the unfinished novel *Heinrich von Ofterdingen,* the deeply religious *Hymnen an die Nacht* [hymns to the night] (1800; Eng. tr., 1948), and *Christendom or Europe* (1826; Eng. tr., 1844), an exposition of his Catholicism.

Novara (nōvä'rä), city (pop. 52,269), Piedmont, N Italy. Chemical plants; rice, flour, and textile mills. Produces Gorgonzola cheese. The Swiss defeated the French here in 1513, and in 1849 the Austrians defeated the Sardinians.

Nova Scotia (nō'vũ skō'shũ), province (20,743 sq. mi.; with water surface 21,068 sq. mi.; pop. 642,584), E Canada; cap. HALIFAX. Other large cities are SYDNEY, GLACE BAY, DARTMOUTH, TRURO, and NEW WATERFORD. Fisheries operate out of numerous bays and inlets on Atlantic Ocean (E, S, W) and Gulf of St. Lawrence and Northumberland Strait (NE, N). Hills, lakes, and streams nourish lumber and woodworking industry, and river valleys and reclaimed lowlands provide grain, fruit, and dairy products. Fine railroad and highway system serves province and encourages tourism, while sailing, fishing, and hunting attract sportsmen. Province settled by French as ACADIA, with Port Royal estab. 1605. British bitterly contested French claims and were awarded the area now in provinces of N.S. (excluding Cape Breton Isl.) and N.B. by Treaty of Utrecht (1713–14). Hostilities continued to 1763, during which time the British expelled many Acadians. Prince Edwards Isl. was annexed 1763, but made separate colony 1769. Cape Breton Isl. was united with N.S. 1763–84 and reunited 1820. Became first colony to achieve responsible government 1848 and accepted Canadian confederation 1867.

Novatian (nōvā'shũn), fl. 250, Roman priest, antipope (after 251) in opposition to St. Cornelius. He espoused MONTANISM and won some following, but later the Church generally, led by St. Cyprian of Carthage, recognized Cornelius. Novatian's successors continued to have their own hierarchy until in the 4th cent. they were merged with DONATISM. Novatian wrote *On the Trinity* and other works.

Novaya Zemlya (nŏ"vĭū zĭmlyä') [Rus.,= new land], archipelago (c.35,000 sq. mi.; pop. c.400), N European RSFSR, in Arctic Ocean between Barents and Kara seas. Ice-covered in N; mountainous in central section; tundra lowlands in S. Inhabitants, the Nentsy (formerly SAMOYEDES), subsist on hunting and fishing. Mineral deposits include copper, lead, zinc, pyrite.

Novels: see CORPUS JURIS CIVILIS.

November: see MONTH.

Novgorod (nôv′gŭrŭt), city (1926 pop. 32,764), W European RSFSR, on Volkhov R. near L. Ilmen. One of oldest Russian cities, it was a major commercial center of medieval Europe. Here RURIK is said to have founded the Russian state (862). A dependency of Kiev, Novgorod became the cap. of an independent republic in the 12th cent. It was governed by a popular assembly, which elected the dukes. Situated on the great trade route to the Volga valley, it became one of the four chief foreign centers of the HANSEATIC LEAGUE, extended its rule over all N Russia and several colonies, and reached its peak in the 14th cent., with a population of c.400,000. Its colorful splendor in that period has inspired much of Russian art and folklore. Novgorod fell to Moscow in 1478; in 1570 Ivan the Terrible laid it waste to punish it for suspected treachery and abolished its last remaining liberties. It was called the "museum city" for its magnificent architectural monuments until World War II, when it suffered heavily during German occupation (1941–44). Chief among its losses was the 12th-cent. KREMLIN, which included the Cathedral of St. Sophia (founded 1045).

Novibazar, Yugoslavia: see NOVI PAZAR.

Novikov, Nikolai Ivanovich (nyĭkŭlī′ ēvä′nŭvĭch nô′-vēkŭf), 1744–1818, Russian publicist, an advocate of Enlightenment. Catherine II suspended his satirical journal *The Drone* in 1774 for attacking serfdom. Later his press, which published books for popular education, was closed down, and he was imprisoned for several years.

Novi Pazar (nô″vĕ päzär′), town (pop. 12,196), W Serbia, Yugoslavia. The Turkish sanjak (district) of Novibazar (an older spelling) was occupied by Austrian troops 1889–1908; passed to Serbia 1913.

Novi Sad (säd), Ger. *Neusatz,* Hung. *Újvidék,* city (pop. 77,127), N Serbia, Yugoslavia, on the Danube; cap. of Vojvodina. Flour-milling center. Orthodox metropolitan see. Though it belonged to Hungary until 1920, it was the center of Serbian cultural revival in 18th and early 19th cent.

Novocherkassk (nô″vŭchŭrkäsk′), city (pop. 81,286), S European RSFSR, near Don R. Mfg. of locomotives, machinery, explosives; lumber mills, distilleries. Founded 1865 as headquarters of Don Cossacks, it has former hetman's palace.

Novorossisk or **Novorossiisk** (nô″vŭrŭsēsk′), city (pop. 95,280), W Krasnodar Territory, S European RSFSR; a major Black Sea port. It has petroleum refineries, machinery plants, shipyards. Founded 1838. Was occupied by Germans 1942–43.

Novosibirsk (nŭvŭsēbērsk′), city (pop. c.750,000), RSFSR, in S central Siberia, on upper Ob R. and on Trans-Siberian RR. Founded 1893 as Novonikolayevsk (renamed 1925), it grew rapidly (partly because of proximity of KUZNETSK BASIN) into cultural, transportation, and industrial center of Asiatic Russia. Produces heavy machinery, steel, textiles.

Noyes, Alfred, 1880–, English poet. His poems, chiefly narrative and traditional in form, include *Drake* (1908; an epic); *Tales of the Mermaid Tavern* (1912); and *The Torch Bearers* (1922–30; a trilogy on science). Familiar short poems are "The Barrel-Organ" and "The Highwayman." Works also include criticism, biography, novels, and an account of his conversion to Roman Catholicism.

Noyes, John Humphrey, 1811–86, American reformer, founder of the ONEIDA COMMUNITY. He taught "perfectionism," doctrine that man's innate sinlessness could be regained through communion with Christ.

Noyon (nwäyô′), city (pop. 5,900), Oise dept., N France. Here in 768 Charlemagne was crowned king of the Franks. Cathedral of Notre Dame (12th–13th cent.)

and the birthplace of John Calvin are preserved here.

Np, chemical symbol of element NEPTUNIUM.

Nubia (nū′bēŭ), anc. country, NE Africa. Extended from First Cataract of the Nile (near Aswan, Egypt) to Khartoum in Anglo-Egyptian Sudan. In 8th cent. B.C. the Nubians estab. the short-lived XXV dynasty in Egypt. A Negro tribe, the Nobatae, settled in Nubia in 3d cent. and formed a powerful kingdom. Converted to Christianity in 6th cent., the kingdom long resisted Moslem encroachment but finally collapsed in 1366. The area was conquered in 19th cent. by Mohammed Ali of Egypt.

Nuevo Laredo (nwä′vō lärä′dhō), city (pop. 28,872), Tamaulipas, NE Mexico, across Rio Grande from Laredo, Texas. The N terminus of the Inter-American Highway, it is a center of international trade in an agr. and stock-raising region.

Nuevo León (nwä′vō lāōn′), state (25,136 sq. mi.; pop. 743,297), NE Mexico; cap. MONTERREY. S and W parts of state are traversed by Sierra Madre Oriental and extreme W portion lies in semiarid basin lands of N Mexico, which are cultivable under irrigation. Mining is chief industry, and refining ores has helped make Monterrey a booming industrial city.

nullification, in U.S. history, doctrine expounded by advocates of extreme STATES' RIGHTS. Held states have right to declare null and void and to set aside in practice any Federal law which violates their voluntary compact embodied in U.S. Constitution. KENTUCKY AND VIRGINIA RESOLUTIONS gave first notable expression to doctrine. After tariff act of 1832 John C. CALHOUN brought about ordinance of nullification passed by S.C. legislature. U.S. FORCE BILL was a result. Following passage of compromise tariff (1833), S.C. rescinded ordinance nullifying tariff acts, but passed new ordinance nullifying force bill. Issue not pressed further until doctrine of SECESSION was brought to fore.

Numantia (nōōmän′shŭ), anc. settlement, Spain, near the Duero. After repeated attacks it was finally captured (133 B.C.) by Scipio Aemilianus after an eight-month siege.

Numa Pompilius (nū′–, –pĭl′–), legendary king of Rome, successor to Romulus. To him was ascribed origin of Roman ceremonial law and religious rites.

number, in arithmetic, indicates count (or sum) of group of objects or their positions in an ordered list. Count is indicated by cardinal numbers, position by ordinal numbers. System of cardinal numbers consisting only of natural numbers (positive whole numbers) has been extended from time to time to include new types of numbers as concept of quantity became more complicated. Negative numbers and zero were added, forming with natural numbers the group called integers, which, with fractions added, comprise rational numbers. Rational plus irrational numbers (such as $\sqrt{2}$, $\sqrt[3]{4}$) form real number system. Imaginary and complex numbers (i.e., numbers involving $\sqrt{-1}$) set a precedent for many further modern extensions. See also DECIMAL SYSTEM.

number, in grammar, class (see GENDER) referring to distinctions of number. In English, nouns are said to be singular or plural. Some languages (e.g., anc. Greek and Arabic) have singular, dual, and plural numbers. *Individual* vs. *collective* is the number distinction in still other languages.

Numbers, book of Old Testament, 4th of five books of Law (the Pentateuch or Torah), ascribed by tradition to Moses. It continues the history (begun in Exodus) of the Hebrews' journey from Egypt to Canaan, the Promised Land; contains two censuses, whence the title; and tells of the rise of Joshua as leader.

numbers, theory of, branch of mathematics concerned with higher arithmetic in which properties of integers only are studied. A prime number has no factors other than itself and 1. One of the important theorems states that every composite integer can be expressed as the product of primes and only one combination of primes (disregarding order). Divisibility, another topic in theory of numbers, is related to concept of prime numbers. Also important is theory of congruences, a generalization of idea of classification of numbers into odd and even.

Numea, New Caledonia: see NOUMÉA.

Numidia (nūmĭ'dĕu), anc. country, NW Africa, very roughly the modern Algeria. Part of Carthaginian empire until in the Punic Wars, MASINISSA sided with Rome and gained independence (201 B.C.). Numidia flourished until JUGURTHA engaged in a fatal war with Rome. Juba II was restored as prince subject to Rome (1st cent. A.D.), and Numidia survived Vandal invasion (5th cent.) but declined after Arabs came (8th cent.).

nun: see MONASTICISM.

Nun'Álvares Pereira: see PEREIRA, NUN'ÁLVARES.

Nuneaton (nūnē'tùn), municipal borough (pop. 54,408), Warwickshire, England. George Eliot, born here, used town in several of her novels. Has varied mfg. There are coal mines in the vicinity.

Núñez Cabeza de Vaca, Álvar: see CABEZA DE VACA.

Núñez Vela, Blasco (blä'skō nōō'nyäs vä'lä), d. 1546, first viceroy of Peru (1544–46). Sent by Charles V to enforce the New Laws, he met tremendous opposition which ended when he was arrested by *audiencia*. Put aboard ship for return to Spain, he escaped, returned to Peru but was defeated by Gonzalo Pizarro, and was put to death.

Nunivak (nōō'nĭvăk), island, 56 mi. long, off W Alaska, in Bering Sea; discovered 1821. Treeless and fogbound with primitive native culture. Reindeer and musk ox recently introduced.

Nureddin (nōō'rĕdĕn'), 1118–74, ruler of Syria (1145–74). Fought with BALDWIN III of Jerusalem. Gained control of Egypt through his lieutenant Shirkuh (predecessor of Saladin), who defeated Amalric I.

Nuremberg (nyōō'rùmbûrg), Ger. *Nürnberg*, city (pop. 360,017), Middle Franconia, N Bavaria, on Pegnitz R. Mfg. center (machinery, precision instruments, chemicals; breweries; toys, gingerbread). A free imperial city 1219–1803, it was independent from the burgraviate of Nuremberg, which comprised a large part of Franconia and was ruled by the Hohenzollern family from 1192. A major trade center, the city reached its flower in the 15th and 16th cent., when it was the center of the German Renaissance (birthplace of Albrecht Dürer, Hans Sachs, Peter Vischer, Veit Stoss, Michael Wolgemut; center of MEISTERSINGER; early printing center). First pocket watches ("Nuremberg eggs") were made here. Nuremberg early accepted the Reformation. By the religious Peace of Nuremberg (1532) the Protestants won important concessions. City declined after Thirty Years War; passed to Bavaria 1806; became industrial center. First German railroad (Nuremberg-Fürth) was opened 1835. Under Hitler, Nuremberg was the scene of the National Socialist party congresses. The Nuremberg Laws (1935) deprived German Jews of civic rights, forbade intermarriage between Jews and "Aryans." In World War II Nuremberg, as a major production center for airplane, submarine, and tank engines, was heavily bombed by the Allies. Its old section, once a marvel of Gothic and Renaissance architecture, was gutted, though many famous landmarks escaped total destruction—e.g., Church of St. Sebaldus, burgraves' castle, city hall, Dürer's house. In 1945–46 Nuremberg was the scene of the first international WAR-CRIMES trial.

Nurmi, Paavo (pä'vō nōōr'mē), 1897–, Finnish track star. Between 1920 and 1932 he set 20 world running records, won six Olympic titles at distances from 1,500 meters to 10,000 meters.

Nürnberg, Bavaria: see NUREMBERG.

nursery school, educational institution for children from two to four years old, designed to promote their social adjustment. The first nursery schools were opened in London in 1907. Pioneers in nursery school

work in U.S. were State Univ. of Iowa; Teachers Col., Columbia Univ.; and Smith and Vassar. Most such schools in U.S. are privately owned.

nursing, care of sick. Practiced by women outside of own homes since early Christian era. Training was encouraged by St. Vincent de Paul in 17th cent. First hospital training school estab. 1836 at Kaiserswerth, Germany. Here Florence Nightingale studied. School she established at St. Thomas's Hospital, London, was pattern for other schools of nursing. Legislation regulating practice of nursing was initiated in 20th cent. and nursing education began to be improved and expanded in scope to meet modern needs.

nut, a dry one-seeded fruit which does not open in maturity, e.g., acorn, chestnut, filbert, and hazelnut. Commonly the word is used also for any seed or fruit with an edible kernel surrounded by a hard or brittle covering, including the ALMOND, BRAZIL NUT, CASHEW, COCONUT, LITCHI, PEANUT, PECAN, and WALNUT.

nuthatch (nŭt'hăch), name for various Old and New World small birds related to titmouse and creeper.

Nutley, town (pop. 26,992), NE N.J., N of Newark. Mfg. of chemicals, metal products, drugs, paper.

nutmeg, the seed, a valuable spice, of an evergreen tree (*Myristica fragrans*), also called nutmeg, and native to the Moluccas. The seeds are sold whole or ground. Mace, also a spice, is derived from the seed covering. Both seed and covering yield an oil used in medicine and cosmetics.

nutria (nōō'trĕu, nū'–), large aquatic South American rodent (*Myocastor*) introduced into S U.S. Valued for beaverlike fur.

nutrition (nūtrĭ'shùn), term generally used to include various processes concerned with the securing, digestion, and utilization of food substances. Plants containing green pigment chlorophyll can synthesize their food in process called PHOTOSYNTHESIS. Parasitic nutrition (see PARASITE) is characteristic of some plants and animals. Scientific research in nutrition has made great strides in recent years. Human nutrition is subject of vital importance to individual and to communities and nations. Importance of the daily DIET in helping to maintain good physical as well as mental health is recognized. Discoveries of value of VITAMINS in preventing deficiency diseases and in contributing to optimum health are significant. Good nutritional status depends on normal functioning of digestive, circulatory, excretory, and other systems and demands that food intake be chosen to include essential nutrients (vitamins, proteins, carbohydrates, fats, and minerals) and that calorie value be considered in relation to energy output. Food intake of too high calorie value results in overweight and sometimes in obesity, which, like underweight, indicates faulty nutrition. Ratio of height to weight is not an adequate indication of whether a child or an adult is well nourished; other factors include condition of skin, eyes, hair, subcutaneous fat, muscles, skeletal structures, and the posture.

Nuttall, Thomas, 1786–1859, American naturalist, b. England; pioneer paleontologist; curator of Harvard botanical garden (1822–32); author of *Travels into the Arkansa Territory* (1821).

Nutting, Mary Adelaide, 1858–1948, American teacher of nursing, authority on history of nursing.

Nuuanu Pali: see KOOLAU RANGE.

Nyack (nī'ăk), residential village (pop. 5,889), SE N.Y., on W bank of Hudson R. opposite Tarrytown. Leather goods, organs, sewing machines. Hook Mt. section of Palisades Interstate Park is just N.

Nyasa, Lake (nīä'sù), 360 mi. long, 15–50 mi. wide, E Africa, between Nyasaland on W and Tanganyika and Mozambique on E; southernmost of Africa's great lakes. Discovered c.1616 by Portuguese explorers, rediscovered 1859 by Livingstone.

Nyasaland, British protectorate (37,374 sq. mi.; pop. 2,314,000), E Africa; cap. Zomba. Bordered on E by L. Nyasa and on W by Northern Rhodesia. Lies in

Great Rift Valley, flanked by high plateaus. Chief exports are tobacco, tea, cotton, and sisal. Visited 17th–18th cent. by Portuguese explorers. Rediscovered 1859 by Livingstone, it became British protectorate in 1891. Ruled by appointed governor aided by executive and legislative councils.

Nyborg (nü'bôr), town (pop. 10,775), Fyn isl., Denmark, on Great Belt. Has shipyards and textile mills. It was important medieval fort and trade center.

Nye, Edgar Wilson (nī), known as **Bill Nye**, 1850–96, American humorist. His comments and yarns are collected in a number of volumes.

Nykobing, Dan. *Nykøbing* (nü'kû"bǐng), name of several places in Denmark, especially a city (pop. 17,192) on Falster isl. It is a Baltic port, with sugar refineries, shipyards, and fishing fleet. Ruins of 12th-cent. castle and a Gothic church remain. Lutheran espiscopal see.

Nykoping, Swed. *Nyköping* (nü'chû"pǐng), Baltic port (pop. 20,447), co. seat of Sodermanland co., SE Sweden. It has mfg. of furniture, textiles, and autos. There remain 13th-cent. castle ruins and 17th-cent. town hall, though city burned 1665 and 1719.

nylon, synthetic material derived from coal, air, and water. Strong, elastic, resistant to abrasion and chemicals, and low in moisture absorbency, it can be permanently set by heat. It is manufactured as filaments (for hosiery and textiles), and in sheets and molded shapes. Introduced after 10 years of research by E. I. du Pont de Nemours & Co. in 1938.

Nymegen, Netherlands: see NIJMEGEN.

Nymphenburg (nüm'fŭnboŏrk), suburb of Munich, Bavaria. Has magnificent royal château and park (begun 1664); famous china manufacture (founded 1761).

Nymwegen, Netherlands: see NIJMEGEN.

Nyssa (nǐ'sủ), town (pop. 2,525), E Oregon, on the Snake near OWYHEE R. mouth and NW of Boise, Idaho. Market for Owyhee, Vale, and Boise projects.

Nystad, Treaty of, 1721: see NORTHERN WAR.

O, chemical symbol of the element OXYGEN.

Oahu (oä'hoō), island (589 sq. mi.; pop. 353,020), third largest but most important of Hawaiian Isls. On SE shore is HONOLULU (territorial cap.), near which is famous beach of Waikiki. A vital defense area, with PEARL HARBOR naval base and military posts. Landscape is dominated by Waianae and KOOLAU ranges. Manoa Valley is site of Univ. of Hawaii. Rural areas produce pineapples, sugar cane.

oak, deciduous or evergreen tree and shrub of the genus *Quercus* including about 300 species widely distributed in the north temperate zone. Oaks have long been valued for their durable wood. The bark of some is used in tanning and medicine; that of the cork oak (*Quercus suber*) supplies the cork of commerce. Group known as black or red oaks (e.g., scarlet, black or yellow, pin, and laurel oaks) have leaves or leaf lobes usually bristle-tipped and acorns mature in two years. White oaks (e.g., the white, bur, post, holly, cork, and live oaks) have leaves or leaf lobes not bristle-tipped and mostly rounded, and acorns mature in one year.

Oak Bluffs, resort town (pop. 1,521), on NE Martha's Vineyard, SE Mass. Has summer theater.

Oakdale, city (pop. 5,598), SW La., near Calcasieu R. and SW of Alexandria, in timber and agr. area.

Oak Island, S N.S., Canada, in Mahone Bay. Reputed hiding place of Captain Kidd's treasure.

Oakland. 1 City (pop. 384,575), W Calif., on E side of San Francisco Bay; founded 1850. Port and industrial center. Has oil refineries, shipyards, railroad shops, and lumber mills. Processes fruits and produces automobiles, glass, beer, wine, chemicals, and building materials. City rises inland to 1,550 ft. in Berkeley Hills (residential section). Connected by San Francisco–Oakland Bay Bridge (1936) and several tunnels with near-by cities. Seat of Mills Col. (nonsectarian, mainly for women; opened 1852 as a seminary; chartered 1885 as a college, it was first woman's college in Far West). St. Mary's Col. (R.C.; for men; 1863) is near. **2** Town (pop. 1,640), NW Md., SW of Cumberland. Resort hq. near Backbone Mt.

Oak Lawn, residential village (pop. 8,751), NE Ill., near Chicago. Nurseries, truck farms.

Oakley, Annie, 1860–1926, American markswoman, performer with Buffalo Bill's Wild West Show.

Oakmont, borough (pop. 7,264), SW Pa., on Allegheny R., NE suburb of Pittsburgh. National tournaments have been held on golf links here.

Oak Park. 1 Residential village (pop. 63,259), NE Ill., adjoining Chicago; settled 1833. One of largest communities with village form of government. Mfg. of food and metal products. Has many houses designed by F. L. Wright, who lived here. **2** City (pop. 5,267), SE Mich., NW suburb of Detroit.

Oak Ridge, area (pop. 30,229), E Tenn., on Black Oak Ridge and Clinch R. near Clinton. Chosen 1942 as site for "Manhattan District" atom bomb project (called Clinton Engineer Works before). Existence and purpose secret until July, 1945. Transferred from U.S. Corps of Engineers to Atomic Energy Commission, Dec. 31, 1946. Has Oak Ridge Natl. Laboratory (formerly Clinton Natl. Laboratory) for nuclear research. Plants make radioactive isotopes for medical, industrial use and U-235 (may be used in atomic bombs). Has Oak Ridge Inst. of Nuclear Studies (1948; 14 member univs.).

Oakville, town (pop. 6,910), S Ont., Canada, on L. Ontario and SW of Toronto. Port with boatbuilding, woodworking, and mfg. of automobiles.

oasis (oā'sǐs, ō'ŭsǐs), fertile area in deserts, found where moisture is enough for growth of vegetation. Water comes to surface in springs or is collected and retained in mountain hollows. Irrigation is used to create oases, e.g., S Israel (Negev). Oases range from ponds with date palms to important centers of caravan trade with extensive agr.

Oates, Titus, 1649–1705, English conspirator. Invented (1678) the story of the Popish plot, a Jesuit-guided plan to assassinate Charles II. In ensuing frenzy many Catholics were persecuted and killed.

oats, hardy grasses, mostly annual, of genus *Avena,* grown for grain, forage, and hay. In North America and the British Isles, oatmeal is a popular breakfast cereal. Oats are much used for horse feed. Common species is *Avena sativa*.

Oaxaca (wähä'kä), state (36,375 sq. mi.; pop. 1,444,-929), S Mexico, on the Pacific and its inlet, Gulf of Tehuantepec. Benito Juárez and Porfirio Díaz were born here. Mountainous with deep tortuous valleys in S, it has broad, semiarid valleys and plateaus in N. Agr. and stock raising are important. Mixtec and Zapotec Indians predominate in the population. Has two famous archaeological sites: Mitla and Monte Alban. The capital, **Oaxaca** (pop. 29,306), is most important city in S Mexico. It lies in a long, broad valley. Noted for handwrought gold and silver filigree, pottery, and serapes.

Ob (Rus. ôp), river, 2,113 mi. long, RSFSR, in W Siberia, formed by junction of Biya and Katun rivers in Altai region and flowing generally N past Novosibirsk into Ob Bay, an estuary (c.500 mi. long, 35–50 mi. wide) of the Kara Sea. The Irtysh is its main tributary. The Ob is an important trade route, though frozen for six months of the year.

Obadiah (ō"bŭdï'ù) or **Abdias** (ăbdï'ùs), book of Old Testament. The prophet, otherwise unknown, calls down doom on Edom and predicts triumph for Israel.

Obaidallah: see FATIMITE.

Oban (ō'bùn), burgh (pop. 6,227), Argyllshire, Scotland, on Firth of Lorne; port and seaside resort. Scene of annual Argyllshire Highland Gathering.

obbligato (ōblēgä'tō) [Ital.,= obliged], in music, originally a term by which a composer indicated that a certain part was indispensable to the music. Misunderstanding of the term, however, resulted in a reversal of its meaning; when a violin part, for example, is added to a song it is called a violin obbligato, meaning that it is a superfluous ornament and unnecessary to the music.

Obed (ō'–), son of Ruth and grandfather of David. Ruth 4.21,22; 1 Chron. 2.12; Mat. 1.5; Luke 3.32.

obelisk (ō'bùlĭsk), a slender four-sided tapering monument, usually hewn of single piece of stone, with pointed or pyramidal top. Among ancient Egyptians these monoliths, commonly of red granite, were dedicated to the sun god. On each of four sides were hieroglyphs, giving names and titles of the Pharaoh. Some obelisks date as far back as IV dynasty (c.2900–c.2750 B.C.). Of those still standing in Egypt, one is at Heliopolis and two at Karnak. Many have been taken to other countries, notably one depicting reign of Ramses II, now in Place de la Concorde, Paris, and CLEOPATRA'S NEEDLES in London and New York.

Oberammergau (ō"bùrä'mùrgou), village (pop. 5,101), Upper Bavaria, in Bavarian Alps near Garmisch-Partenkirchen. PASSION PLAY here attracts tourists.

Oberhausen (ō'bùrhou"zùn), city (pop. 202,343), North Rhine–Westphalia, NW Germany; an industrial center of RUHR dist.

Oberholtzer, Ellis Paxson (ō'bùrhōlt"sùr), 1868–1936, American historian, author of *A History of the United States since the Civil War* (5 vols., 1917–37).

Oberland, Bernese: see BERN.

Oberlin (ō'bùrlĭn), village (pop. 7,062), N Ohio, S of Lorain. Most of Oberlin College (nonsectarian; coed.; opened 1833) is here. Pioneered in coeducation; was abolitionist center in Civil War and one of first colleges to admit Negroes. Alumni and students sponsor Oberlin-in-China. Oberlin theology, a modified form of Calvinism, was developed by early theological faculty members of the college.

Oberon (ō'bùrön), in literature of Western Europe, fairy king, husband of Titania. He appears in Middle French *Huon de Bordeaux*, probable source for Chaucer, Spenser, and Shakspere.

obesity (ōbē'sĭtē, ōbĕ'–), excessive accumulation of fat in body. Usually it results from excess food intake. Certain obese persons have low rate of metabolism associated with glandular disturbances.

oboe: see WIND INSTRUMENTS.

Obregón, Álvaro (äl'värō ōbrāgōn'), 1880–1928, Mexican general and president (1920–24). He supported Madero in the revolution against Porfirio Díaz (1911) and by a coup was made president in 1920. His administration saw the educational reforms of Vasconcelos. Obregón was reelected president in 1928 but was assassinated before taking office.

Obrenovich (ōbrĕ'nùvĭch), family name of princes MILOSH and MICHAEL and kings MILAN and ALEXANDER of Serbia. The dynasty, in constant feud with the KARAGEORGEVICH family, ruled 1817–42, 1858–1903.

O'Brien, William, 1852–1928, Irish journalist and political leader. His paper *United Ireland* championed agrarian cause. Helped shape Wyndham Land Act (1903) to solve Irish Land Question.

O'Brien, William Smith, 1803–64, Irish revolutionary. Follower of Daniel O'Connell in nationalist struggle, he seceded from him and helped to organize abortive revolt of 1848.

observatory, building or institution for observation and recording of astronomical, meteorological, magnetic, or seismological phenomena. Term is chiefly applied to astronomical observatories. The earliest on record estab. c.300 B.C. at Alexandria. Early notable observatory in Europe estab. by Tycho Brahe (1584) on island of Ven. Application of telescope to astronomical use by Galileo stimulated founding of observatories by rulers, individuals, and institutions. National observatories include Royal Observatory (1675), Greenwich, England; Paris Observatory (1667–71); UNITED STATES NAVAL OBSERVATORY. Observatories with important refracting telescopes include Yerkes Observatory (40 in.), Univ. of Chicago, at Williams Bay, Wis.; Lick Observatory (36 in.), Univ. of California, on Mt. Hamilton; Allegheny Observatory (30 in.), Univ. of Pittsburgh; Leander McCormick Observatory (26 in.), Univ. of Virginia; Lowell Observatory (24 in.), Flagstaff, Ariz. Noted for great reflecting telescopes are Mt. Palomar Observatory (200 in.), California Inst. of Technology, near Pasadena; Mt. Wilson Observatory (100 in.), Carnegie Inst., at Mt. Wilson, Calif.; McDonald Observatory (82 in.), Univ. of Texas, at Mt. Locke, Texas; David Dunlap Observatory (74 in.), Univ. of Toronto; Dominion Astrophysical Observatory (73 in.), Victoria, British Columbia.

obsidian (ōbsĭ'dēùn), a lava resembling black glass. The fine texture results from very rapid cooling. Primitive people used it for stone tools and weapons.

obstetrics (ōbstĕ'trĭks), branch of medicine dealing with pregnancy and labor. Care during labor was originally known as midwifery and was in hands of women. Began to pass to physicians in 16th cent. Use of forceps was introduced in 17th cent. Anesthesia during labor was first used by Sir J. Y. Simpson. Incidence of puerperal fever was reduced by methods of Semmelweis and Lister.

Obwalden, Switzerland: see UNTERWALDEN.

Ocala (ōkä'lù), city (pop. 11,741), N central Fla., W of L. George. Processes and ships fruit, limestone, phosphate, and lumber. Grew around Fort King (protection against the Seminoles 1827–43), near site of Indian village visited by De Soto, 1639. SILVER SPRINGS is near.

O'Casey, Sean (shôn' ōkä'sē), 1884–, Irish dramatist, noted playwright of Abbey Theatre. Well-known plays are *Juno and the Paycock* (1924), *The Plough and the Stars* (1926), and *Within the Gates* (1934). His autobiographical works, including *Inishfallen, Fare Thee Well* (1949) and *Rose and Crown* (1952), depict his early life, with anticapitalist slant and impeccable prose.

Occam, William of: see WILLIAM OF OCCAM.

Occidental College: see LOS ANGELES, Calif.

occultism, belief in supernatural sciences or powers, such as magic, astrology, alchemy, theosophy, and spiritism—for purpose of enlarging man's powers, protecting him from evil forces, or predicting future. All the so-called natural sciences were partly occult in origin, and scientists were suspect because of secrecy.

occupational diseases, illnesses contracted through working conditions. They result from extrahazardous conditions; work under abnormal air pressures (see CAISSON DISEASE); handling or breathing fumes of poisonous substances including lead, phosphorus, mercury compounds, and silica dust (see SILICOSIS); exposure to radioactive substances and release of atomic energy. Preventive legislation dates from Factory Act of 1802 in England. In U.S., workmen's compensation acts cover many occupational illnesses.

occupational therapy, any form of activity devised to aid recovery from disease and adjustment to living. It is essential in treating mental disorders or paralysis. Was used in ancient Greece and Egypt. Natl. Association of Occupational Therapists formed in U.S. 1917.

ocean, connected mass of water which covers c.71% of earth's surface. Arbitrarily delimited into the Pacific, Atlantic, and Indian oceans; popular usage also distinguishes the Arctic and the Antarctic. Oceans retain heat; currents and winds distribute it. Air temperatures over oceans vary little from that of the water. Ocean waters shift constantly. Currents move masses of water; in waves particles of water oscillate, hardly change position except when carried forward by crest of breakers. Friction of water and wind probably causes surface waves. Average ocean depth is c.12,-500 ft. Pressure increases by one atmosphere (15 lb. per sq. ft.) for 33 ft. of depth. Greatest known depth (35,400 ft.) is in the Pacific off Mindanao. Sea-water density increases with coldness and salinity (average salinity is c.3%). Sea water is believed to have in solution all chemical elements; chlorine, sodium, sulphur, magnesium are most common. Distribution of marine life varies with temperature, salinity, pressure, light.

Ocean City. 1 Resort town (pop. 1,234), SE Md., on Atlantic Ocean. Game-fishing port. **2** Atlantic resort city (pop. 6,040), SE N.J., SW of Atlantic City. Fishing, boatbuilding.

ocean currents, progressive movements of ocean waters. Density currents are chief circulators of ocean waters. Hot equatorial waters expand; higher sea level causes surface flow poleward, but trade winds force water masses westward. Waters flow along the western shores of the Atlantic and the Pacific—clockwise in N Hemisphere, counterclockwise in S Hemisphere, due to earth's rotation (e.g., GULF STREAM and JAPAN CURRENT). The currents cool gradually; their higher salinity (from evaporation in hot latitudes) makes them denser than adjacent waters of equal temperature, causes them to sink and displaced waters to rise. Masses of poleward-flowing water result in compensating surface currents of less saline water (partly from melting ice) that flow from subpolar to temperate regions (e.g., Labrador Current). Pressure from added mass of equatorial waters causes an equatorward drift of bottom water that completes circulatory cycle by welling up in equatorial zones to replace water carried poleward. Wind affects rate and direction of density currents, also causes wind currents. By friction on sea's surface, wind causes surface drift, each moving layer affecting next underlying layer. Currents are classed as streams (well defined, relatively fast, 2–4 mi. per hr.), drifts (slow), or creeps (barely perceptible). Flow of ocean currents effects a transfer of heat globally that modifies climate of lands receiving sea winds and influences distribution of marine life. For tidal currents, see TIDE.

Ocean Grove, Atlantic resort village (pop. 3,806) in Neptune township (pop. 13,613), E N.J., S of Asbury Park; founded 1869, owned and controlled by Methodist camp meeting association. Has tent city and auditorium for summer camp meetings.

Oceania (ōshēä′nēŭ, -ā′nēŭ) or **Oceanica** (ōshēä′nĭkŭ), collective name for Pacific islands, sometimes including Australasia and Malaysia. Usually considered as synonymous with South Sea Isls.

Ocean Island, phosphate island (2.2 sq. mi.; pop. 2,060), central Pacific. Formerly the cap. of British colony of Gilbert and Ellice Isls. Discovered 1804 by British, annexed 1915. Occupied by Japanese 1942–45. Formerly called Banaba.

Ocean Island, T.H.: see KURE ISLAND.

oceanography (ō″shŭnŏ′grŭfē), study of the sea. It integrates marine applications of geography, geology, physics, chemistry, and biology and draws upon astronomy and meteorology. Sometimes term is restricted to study of topography and sediments of ocean basins and shores and characteristics and dynamics of ocean waters, but MARINE BIOLOGY is also usually included. Term *oceanography* dates from CHALLENGER EXPEDITION (1872–76) and became current through expedition reports. The science is important to shipping, fisheries, laying of telegraph cables, climatological studies. Many ocean phenomena (e.g., waves, currents) are not fully explained.

Oceanport, borough (pop. 7,588), E N.J., NW of Long Branch. Near by is U.S. Fort Monmouth.

Oceanside, city (pop. 18,377), S Calif., N of San Diego. Beach resort and agr. trade center. San Luis Rey Mission (1798) is near.

Ocean Springs, Miss.: see BILOXI, Miss.

Oceanus (ōsē′ŭnŭs), in Greek mythology. **1** Circular stream flowing round edge of earth, source of rivers. **2** Personification of this stream; a Titan, son of Uranus and Gaea.

ocelot (ō′sŭlŭt), New World cat (*Felis*) ranging from S Texas to South America. Fur is tawny to gray with variable pattern of black spots, streaks, rings.

Ochakov (ŭchä′kŭf), city (pop. over 10,000), SW Ukraine; a Black Sea port. Its fall (1788) as a Turkish fortress was a decisive Russian victory.

ocher (ō′kŭr), mixture of hydrated iron oxide and clay used as pigment, the colors ranging from yellow to red. It is produced in U.S., France, Italy.

Ochil Hills (ō′khĭl), range, c.25 mi. long, in Perth, Clackmannan, Kinross, and Fife Counties, Scotland. They have valuable mineral deposits.

Ochino, Bernardino (bärnärdē′nō ōkē′nō), 1487–1564, Italian religious reformer. A Capuchin friar, he accepted belief in justification by faith alone and gave his life to forwarding of Protestantism.

Ochrida or **Okhrida** (both: ō′krĭdŭ), Serbo-Croatian *Ohrid*, town (pop. 11,419), Macedonia, SW Yugoslavia, on rock above L. Ochrida. An important trading town under Roman rule, it flourished as cultural and political cap. of Bulgaria in 10th cent. A.D. Among its many ancient churches are cathedrals of St. Sophia (founded 9th cent.) and of St. Clement (1299). **Lake Ochrida,** area 134 sq. mi., forms part of Yugoslav-Albanian border.

Ochs, Adolph S. (ōks), 1858–1935, American newspaper publisher. He became publisher of the Chattanooga *Times* in 1878. In 1896 he acquired the New York *Times* and brought it to national eminence.

Ockham, William of: see WILLIAM OF OCCAM.

Ocmulgee (ōkmŭl′gē), river formed in NW Ga., SE of Atlanta. Flows c.255 mi. SSE to join Oconee R. and form Altamaha R.

Ocmulgee National Monument: see NATIONAL PARKS AND MONUMENTS (table).

O Come, All Ye Faithful: see ADESTE FIDELES.

Oconee (ōkō′nē), river rising in N Ga., NE of Atlanta and flowing 282 mi. SSE to join Ocmulgee R. and form Altamaha R.

O'Connell, Daniel, 1775–1847, Irish political leader. Founded (1823) the powerful Catholic Association whose pressure led to Catholic Emancipation Act of 1829. Urged repeal of union with Great Britain and worked to solve Irish Land Question.

O'Connor, Rory or **Roderick,** 1116?–1198, last high king of Ireland. King of Connaught after 1156, he seized (1166) the high kingship. Dermot McMurrough brought in the English against O'Connor, who was forced to submit (1175) as a vassal to Henry II.

O'Connor, T(homas) P(ower), 1848–1929, Irish journalist and nationalist, known as Tay Pay O'Connor. Member of Parliament after 1880, he supported Parnell until 1891. Founded many newspapers (e.g., *T.P.'s Weekly*) in London. Worked for Home Rule.

Oconomowoc (ŏkŏn'ŭmō̄wŏk"), city (pop. 5,345), SE Wis., W of Milwaukee. Resort in lake and mineral-spring area with processing of foodstuffs.

Oconto (ŏkŏn'tō), city (pop. 5,055), NE Wis., on W shore of Green Bay and at mouth of Oconto R. Lumber products. First church erected specifically for Christian Science worship was built here 1886.

Octavia (ŏktā'vēŭ). **1** Died 11 B.C., sister of AUGUSTUS and wife of Marc ANTONY. Helped keep peace between them until Antony deserted her for Cleopatra. **2** A.D. 42–A.D. 62, daughter of Claudius I. She was the wife of NERO, who deserted her for Poppaea; later on false charges he had Octavia put to death.

Octavian and **Octavius:** see AUGUSTUS.

October: see MONTH.

octopus (ŏk'tŭpŭs), cephalopod mollusk, also called devilfish, found in temperate and tropical waters. It has a pouch-shaped body, eight arms, each bearing two rows of suction disks, and no shell. Ink sac darkens water in case of danger. Span of arms from tip to tip ranges from few feet to more than 20 ft. Poisonous saliva paralyzes prey.

Oda Nobunaga: see NOBUNAGA.

ode, originally, in Greek, a poem sung to musical accompaniment. Odes of Sappho, Alcaeus, and Anacreon are for a single voice. Pindar's choral odes are formal, elaborate, passionate; Horace's Latin odes are personal, simple, controlled. Odes were revived in France most successfully by Ronsard (16th cent.). Horace's odes influenced 17th-cent. English poets, although Milton shows Pindaric influence, and Cowley and Dryden tried to imitate Pindar in poems for public occasions. Odes of romantic and later poets tend to be more free in form and subject matter.

Odenathus, Septimius (sĕptĭ'mēŭs ŏdĭnā'thŭs), d. 267, king of PALMYRA. He cooperated with Rome and made his state powerful. He and his eldest son were murdered, possibly through machination of his second wife, ZENOBIA, who brought Palmyra to ruin.

Ödenburg, Hungary: see SOPRON.

Odense (ō'dhŭnsŭ), city (pop. 100,940), port on N Fyn isl., Denmark. Lutheran episcopal see. Many industries (shipyards, canneries; machinery, rubber, tobacco, textiles, sugar, and glass factories). Has 14th-cent. cathedral. Birthplace of Hans Christian Andersen.

Oder (ō'dŭr), Czech and Pol. *Odra,* river, 563 mi. long, rising in Moravia, Czechoslovakia, and flowing N through Silesia, Brandenburg, and Pomerania into the Baltic at Stettin. Breslau and Frankfurt-an-der-Oder lie on its course. From its junction with the Lausitzer Neisse it forms the boundary line between Russian-occupied Germany and the former German territory placed under Polish administration in 1945. Navigable from Ratibor, it is linked by canals with the Spree, Elbe, and Vistula.

Odessa (ōdĕ'sŭ, Rus. ŭdyĕ'sŭ), city (pop. 604,223), SW Ukraine, on Black Sea. It is one of the chief ports of the USSR, an industrial center (machinery, chemicals, petroleum, flour), and a cultural center (university, technical schools, famous opera house and conservatory). Founded in late 18th cent. on site of an ancient Greek colony (Odessos or Ordyssos), it soon became the chief Russian grain-exporting center. Severe pogroms, following the mutiny on the battleship *Potemkin* at Odessa (1905), caused large-scale emigration of the Jews (then c.35% of pop.). Between 1918 and its final fall to the Red Army in 1920, Odessa was successively occupied by the Central Powers, the French, the Ukrainians, the Reds, and the Whites. In World War II it was occupied by the Rumanians (1941–43) and suffered much destruction; 280,000 civilians, mostly Jews, are said to have been massacred or deported.

Odessa (ōdĕ'sŭ), city (pop. 29,495), W Texas, WNW of San Angelo; founded 1881. Oil center with refineries, carbon-black plant, and oiling supplies. Meteor crater near. Region has potash.

Odets, Clifford (ōdĕts'), 1906–, American dramatist. Among his plays (mostly concerned with social problems) are *Waiting for Lefty, Awake and Sing* (both 1935), and *Golden Boy* (1937).

Odin, Norse name for chief Germanic god, WODEN.

Odo, French king: see EUDES.

Odoacer (ŏdōā'sŭr) or **Odovacar** (ōdōvā'kŭr), c.435–493, German conqueror of the West Roman Empire; chieftain of the Heruli, a people allied to the Goths. He and his soldiers were mercenaries in Roman service, but in 476 the Heruli rebelled and proclaimed him king. Odoacer defeated the general ORESTES, took Ravenna, deposed ROMULUS AUGUSTULUS (last Roman Emperor of the West until Charlemagne), and was recognized in authority over Italy by the Eastern emperor Zeno. The year 476 is the conventional date of the fall of West Rome; in fact, chaos had prevailed for some time before, and Roman administration continued to function under Odoacer. In 488 Zeno sent THEODORIC THE GREAT, king of the Ostrogoths, into Italy to expel Odoacer. After several defeats, Odoacer in 493 agreed to share his authority with Theodoric, who then invited him to a banquet and had him murdered.

O'Donnell, Leopoldo (lāōpōl'dō ōdhō'nĕl), 1809–67, Spanish general and statesman, of Irish descent. As premier (1856–57, 1858–63, 1865–66) he followed a relatively liberal policy; restored the old constitution (1856); and commanded in the Spanish campaign in Morocco (1859–60), for which he was created duque de Tetuán.

Odovacar: see ODOACER.

O'Dwyer, William (ōdwī'ŭr), 1890–, American public official, b. Ireland. Mayor of New York city (1946–50), U.S. ambassador to Mexico (1950–52).

Odysseus (ōdĭs'ŭs, ōdĭ'sēŭs), Latin *Ulysses* (ūlĭ'sēz), in Greek mythology, king of Ithaca. He was husband of Penelope and father of Telemachus. A Greek leader in Trojan War, he was famed for cunning strategy and wisdom. Afterward he wandered for 10 years before returning home. The story of his wanderings and regaining of his kingdom is told in the **Odyssey** (ŏ'dĭsē), Homeric Greek epic in 24 books.

Oecolampadius, Johannes (jōhă'nĕz ē"kŭlămpā'dēŭs), 1482–1531, German reformer, associate of ZWINGLI in Reformation in Switzerland.

Oedipus (ĕ'dĭpŭs, ē'–), hero in Greek mythology. When it was foretold that he would kill his father, Laius, king of Thebes, and marry his mother, Jocasta, baby Oedipus was exposed on Mt. Cithaeron, but he was saved and raised by king of Corinth. On learning of the prophecy when grown, and ignorant of his real parentage, he fled from Corinth to Thebes. En route, he met and quarreled with Laius and killed him. He won Jocasta by answering riddle of the Sphinx. When, after many years, he learned the truth, he blinded himself, and Jocasta committed suicide. CREON, Jocasta's brother, became king. Oedipus died in peace at Colonus, but his unwitting sin still cursed Thebes and his children (see SEVEN AGAINST THEBES). Legend has been used often in literature, music, and art and gives name to the **Oedipus complex** (ĕ'dĭpŭs), psychological condition, especially evident between ages of four and five, in which boys love mothers intensely, hate fathers; girls, the reverse (Electra complex). Freudians hold that if complex is not worked out in childhood or by PSYCHOANALYSIS, adult relationships are determined by feelings in the original situation.

Oehlenschläger, Adam Gottlob (û'lŭnshlägŭr), 1779–1850, Danish author of poems and dramas dealing with Scandinavian history.

Oelwein (ōl'wīn), city (pop. 7,858), NE Iowa, NE of Waterloo, in farm and livestock area.

Oenone (ēnō'nē), in Greek legend, nymph loved by

Paris, who deserted her for Helen. When he was later wounded, she refused to use her healing powers to heal him, but on hearing of his death she killed herself.

Oersted, Hans Christian (häns' krĭs'tyän ûr'stĭdh), 1777–1851, Danish physicist and chemist. His work estab. a relationship between magnetism and electricity; he was first to isolate aluminum.

O'Faoláin Seán (shôn' ōfā'län), 1900–, Irish writer, interpreter of Ireland through biographies, travel books, historical writing, short stories, and novels.

Offa (ŏf'ŭ), d. 796, king of Mercia (757–96). Gradually asserted his overlordship in Kent and Sussex, also ruled East Anglia. Signed (796) with Charlemagne the first recorded English commercial treaty. Built OFFA'S DYKE in late 8th cent.

Offaly (ŏf'ŭlē), formerly **King's**, county (771 sq. mi.; pop. 53,686), central Ireland, in Leinster; co. town Tullamore. Mostly flat, covered largely by Bog of Allen, it has Slieve Bloom mts. in S. Agr. and livestock breeding are main occupations. Clonmacnoise has ruins of an early religious center.

Offa's Dyke, entrenchment along England-Wales border. Built in 8th cent. by Offa, king of Mercia, as a barrier against the Welsh. Paralleled at a distance of c.2 mi. by Watt's Dyke.

Offenbach, Jacques (ŏf'ŭnbŏk), 1819–80, French composer, b. Cologne. Creator of the French operetta and composer of over 100, e.g., *Orphée aux enfers, La Vie parisienne, La Belle Hélène*. His one serious opera, *The Tales of Hoffman*, was his masterpiece.

Office of Price Administration (OPA), estab. April, 1941, by executive order as Office of Price Administration and Civilian Supply and renamed Aug., 1941. Fixed consumer prices, rent ceilings; rationed scarce consumer goods. After World War II rationing ended, and price controls were gradually abolished. Rent-control functions were transferred to Office of the Housing Expediter in May, 1947. In 1950 the Office of Price Stabilization was created under Economic Stabilization Agency; discontinued 1953.

Office of Strategic Services (OSS), secret agency of U.S., created 1942 for purpose of obtaining information about enemy nations and of sabotaging their war potential and morale. Headed by W. H. Donovan. In 1945 Pres. Truman transferred the research and analysis branch to Dept. of State and the rest to War Dept.

offset: see PRINTING.

O'Flaherty, Liam (lē'ŭm ōflä'hŭrtē), 1896–, Irish novelist. One of his realistic, psychological works, *The Informer* (1925), gained awards both as fiction and as a film. He has also written notable short shories and autobiographical works.

Og (ŏg), giant king of Bashan conquered by the Israelites. Deut. 3.1–13.

Ogaden (ōgä'dän), arid region, SE Ethiopia, bordering British Somaliland and Italian Somaliland. A clash between Italian and Ethiopian troops at village of Wal-wal in 1934 helped to precipitate Italo-Ethiopian War.

Ogallala (ōgŭlä'lū), city (pop. 3,456), W central Nebr., on South Platte R. and W of North Platte city. Kingsley Dam (162 ft. high, 10,700 ft. long; earthen; completed 1941) in North Platte R. is near.

Ogata, Korin: see KORIN.

Ogden, city (pop. 57,112), N Utah, at junction of Ogden and Weber rivers and N of Salt Lake City; founded on trading-post site by Mormons after 1847. Important intermountain rail junction. Processes and ships fruit, grain, livestock of irrigated area. Seat of Weber Col. Mt. Ogden (9,592 ft.), ski center, and Ogden Canyon, recreational area, are near.

Ogden, river rising in N Utah in Wasatch Range and flowing c.35 mi. S to Weber R. at Ogden. Used for c.100 days for irrigation.

Ogdensburg city (pop. 16,166), N N.Y., on St. Lawrence R. and NE of Watertown; settled 1749. Ships grain and lumber; mfg. of paper, wood, and metal products. Here is Remington Art Memorial.

ogham (ŏ'gŭm, ŏ'ŭm), anc. alphabet of the British Isles (esp. Ireland), used in early Christian era for gravestone inscriptions. Language is local Celtic. Key is given in Irish manuscripts.

Ogier the Dane (ō'jēur, ōzhyä'), in the chansons de geste, a paladin who rebelled against Charlemagne. William Morris uses story in *The Earthly Paradise.*

Oglethorpe, James Edward (ō'gŭlthôrp), 1696–1785, English general, founder of Ga. Estab. colony (1733) as refuge for imprisoned debtors. His defeat of Spanish in 1742 assured English control of area.

Oglethorpe University: see ATLANTA, Ga.

OGPU: see SECRET POLICE.

Ogunquit, Maine: see WELLS.

O'Higgins, Bernardo (bĕrnär'dhō ōē'gēns), 1776–1842, Chilean revolutionist and dictator, b. Chillán; natural son of Ambrosio O'Higgins, an Irish-born Spanish colonial administrator. Bernardo took part in early uprisings in Chile, was forced to flee to Argentina, returned with San Martín's victorious army, and became supreme director of Chile (1818). His reform movements were opposed, and he was exiled to Peru (1823).

Ohio, state (41,288 sq. mi.; pop. 7,946,627), NE central U.S.; admitted 1803 as 17th state (free); cap. COLUMBUS. Other cities are CLEVELAND, CINCINNATI, TOLEDO, DAYTON, AKRON, YOUNGSTOWN, CANTON. Bordered S and SE by OHIO R., partly N by L. Erie. Generally level. Iron and steel mills; mfg. of machinery, motor vehicles and parts, rubber products, metal goods, paper, foodstuffs, clothing, chemicals, cement, glass. Mining coal, clay products, lime, rock salt, natural gas, oil. Agr. of grains, fruit, truck; dairying, livestock. Activities of OHIO COMPANY helped pave way for last of French and Indian Wars, in which English won land from French. QUEBEC ACT (1774) sought to make territory a dependency of Canada. Passed to U.S. after Revolution. Trouble over claims to land by old states ended with dropping of all (see WESTERN RESERVE) and adoption of ORDINANCE OF 1787. OHIO COMPANY OF ASSOCIATES promoted development. Anthony WAYNE defeated Indians at Fallen Timbers (1794). Became territory in 1799. Supported Union in Civil War despite activity of COPPERHEADS. Mfg. expanded after war. Big business and politics became entwined as in relations of Mark HANNA and McKinley. Labor strife marked 1930s. World War II brought great industrial prosperity. Flood-control measures increased in 20th cent.

Ohio, river, 981 mi. long, E central U.S., formed by confluence of Allegheny R. and Monongahela R. at Pittsburgh, Pa. Flows NW then generally SW as state line between Ohio–W.Va., Ohio–Ky., Ind.–Ky., and Ill.–Ky., entering the Mississippi at Cairo, Ill., as its chief E tributary. Drains a highly populated and productive area, receiving as its major tributaries the Muskingum, Scioto, Great Miami, and Wabash from the N, and the Kanawha, Big Sandy, Licking, Kentucky, Green, Cumberland, and Tennessee from the S. Important cities on its route include Pittsburgh, Cincinnati, Wheeling, W.Va., Evansville, Ind., and Louisville and Paducah, Ky. Water control system reduces the danger of floods, provides hydroelectric power, and extends navigation. Used by Indians, then French, was a focus of conflict in the French and Indian Wars. After the Revolution it became a route of westward migration. A temporary set-back after the Erie Canal opening was compensated for by the success of steamboats. The Ohio remains an important channel of freight transport despite the inroads of railroads.

Ohio Company, organization formed in 1748 to extend Va. settlements W into Ohio valley. Rivalry with French claims helped cause final French and Indian War. This and the Revolution blocked company plans.

Ohio Company of Associates, organization for purchase and settlement of lands on Ohio R., founded at Boston, Mass., in 1786. Negotiations by Manasseh Cutler with Congress in 1787 resulted in company's gaining right to purchase 1,500,000 acres at junction of the Ohio and Muskingum rivers. Settlement of company's grant began in April, 1788, at town of Marietta.

Ohio State University, at Columbus; land-grant supported, coed.; chartered 1870, opened 1873 as Ohio Agricultural and Mechanical Col., renamed 1878. There are various research bureaus, experiment stations, and clinics. The university also has the Ohio Biological Survey and a radio station and owns large telescope with Ohio Wesleyan Univ.

Ohio University: see ATHENS.

Ohio Wesleyan University: see DELAWARE, Ohio.

Ohm, Georg Simon (gā´ôrk zē´môn ōm´), 1787–1854, German physicist. Formulated **Ohm's law:** V (volts) = A (amperes) × R (resistance in ohms), or E (electromotive force or volts) = I (current) × R. The **ohm,** unit of electrical resistance, was named in his honor. International ohm is resistance offered to flow of unwavering electric current by column of mercury at 0°C., 106.3 cm. long, constant in cross section, with mass of 14.4521 g.

Ohrid, Yugoslavia: see OCHRIDA.

Oil City, city (pop. 19,581), NW Pa., on Allegheny R. and NNE of Pittsburgh; laid out c.1860. Oil center since discovery of oil at near-by Titusville 1859, it has mfg. of oil equipment.

Oildale, village (pop. 16,615), S central Calif., oil-field center N of Bakersfield, across Kern R.

oil of vitriol: see SULPHURIC ACID.

oils, term commonly used for greasy, fluid substances, generally viscous liquids, insoluble in water, soluble in ether and alcohol and inflammable. Petroleum and its products are classified as mineral oils. **Fatty oils** or **fixed oils** are obtained from animals and plants and are carbon-hydrogen-oxygen compounds. There is no real difference between them and fats (see FATS AND OILS). Depending on ability to absorb oxygen when exposed to atmosphere and form skinlike layer over surface, they are classed as drying and nondrying oils. **Essential oils** or **volatile oils** occur in plants and to them certain plants owe their characteristic odor, flavor, or other properties. They are used in perfumes, flavorings, medicine. In general they are complex mixtures of various chemicals, differing from fixed oils in being volatile.

Oise (wäz), department (2,273 sq. mi.; pop. 396,724), N France, in Île-de-France and Picardy; cap. Beauvais. It is drained by the **Oise** river, 186 mi. long, rising in the Ardennes mts., Belgium, and flowing SW into N France to the Seine NW of Paris.

Oisin: see OSSIAN.

Ojibwa Indians (ōjĭb´wù), North American tribes of Algonquian linguistic stock, commonly also called Chippewa, occupying the shores of L. Superior in the 17th cent. With French firearms they drove the Fox from N Wis., drove the Sioux to the W, penetrating to N.Dak., and conquered the peninsula between L. Huron and L. Erie from the Iroquois. By the mid-18th cent. they were very powerful. Except for the most westerly (Plains Ojibwa) they had an Eastern woodlands culture, with agr. supporting fishing and hunting and with their usual dwelling the wigwam. They had picture writing connected with religious rites of their Midewin society. They fought on the side of the French in the French and Indian Wars and on the side of the British in the War of 1812. Later they were settled on reservations in Mich., Wis., Minn., and N.Dak. Also Chippeway, Ojibway.

Oka (ùkä´), rivers of RSFSR. **1** In central European RSFSR. Rises S of Orel and flows 918 mi., N, E, and NE to the Volga at Gorki. Navigable for 550 mi. **2** In S central Siberia. Rises in Sayan Mts. and flows 500 mi. N to the Angara.

Okanagan Lake (ōkùnä´gùn), 69 mi. long and 2–4 mi. wide, S B.C., Canada. Drained S by Okanogan R. to Osoyoos L.

Okanogan (ōkùnä´gùn), town (pop. 2,013), N central Wash., on Okanogan R. and near site of first American settlement in Wash. Territory.

Okayama (ōkä´yämù), city (pop. 140,631), SW Honshu,

Japan. Railroad and mfg. center (porcelain ware, cotton textiles). Medical university.

Okeechobee, Lake (ō´´kēchō´bē), S central Fla., N of the EVERGLADES; second largest fresh-water lake wholly in U.S. It is c.35 mi. long, 30 mi. wide, and 15 ft. deep and covers c.750 sq. mi. Most important canals of Everglades reclamation project are those of Okeechobee Waterway. Drained lands around lake yield winter vegetables and sugar cane. Grasslands W of lake support cattle raising. Levees built after hurricane of 1926. Resort and commercial fisheries.

O'Keeffe, Georgia, 1887–, American painter, known for her enlarged and stylized flower studies.

Okefenokee Swamp (ō´´kùfùnōk´, –nō´kē), c.45 mi. long, 30 mi. wide, NE Ga. and N Fla. Main part of Okefenokee Wildlife Refuge. One of most primitive swamps in U.S., has varied wildlife; drained by Suwanee and St. Marys rivers. Abundant timber is too expensive to bring out.

Okhotsk, Sea of (ôkŏtsk´), NW arm of the Pacific, W of Kamchatka Peninsula and Kurile Isls. Connected with Sea of Japan on SW by Tatar and La Pérouse straits. N part is icebound during much of year.

Okhrida, Yugoslavia: see OCHRIDA.

Okinawa (ō´´kĭnä´wä), volcanic island (467 sq. mi.; pop. 517,634), SW Pacific; largest of Okinawa Isls. in Ryukyu chain. Mountainous with dense vegetation. Produces sugar cane. NAHA is chief city and port. Scene of last great U.S. amphibious campaign (April 1–June 25, 1945) in World War II. Ie-jima (islet off W coast) was also a battleground.

Oklahoma, state (69,283 sq. mi.; pop. 2,233,351), SW U.S.; admitted 1907 as 46th state; cap. OKLAHOMA CITY. TULSA other large city. Bounded S by RED RIVER. Great Plains in W, broken by Black Mesa in Panhandle and by Wichita Mts. in SW. Mostly prairie in E, with Ozark Mts. in NE, Ouachita Mts. in SE. Great oil state, also natural gas, lead, zinc, gypsum. Farming (wheat, corn, cotton, grain sorghums, oats, livestock). Petroleum refining, mfg. of flour, grain products, cotton goods, packed meat. Scene of several Indian cultures before early Spanish exploration. Set aside for FIVE CIVILIZED TRIBES after Louisiana Purchase in what became INDIAN TERRITORY. These groups sided with Confederacy in Civil War; as punishment they lost W part of territory. Advent of railroads and desire for grazing land for cattle brought white settlers. April 22, 1889, saw first land run for legal settlement. Oklahoma Territory organized in 1890. DAWES COMMISSION divided tribal lands of Indian Territory; two territories combined into state. Suffered seriously from drought in 1930s; irrigation and conservation measures brought back degree of prosperity.

Oklahoma, University of, mainly at Norman; state supported, coed.; chartered 1890, opened 1892. Law and medical schools are in Oklahoma City. Has radio station and university press.

Oklahoma Agricultural and Mechanical College, at Stillwater; land-grant and state supported, coed.; chartered 1890, opened 1891.

Oklahoma City, city (pop. 243,504), state cap., central Okla., on North Canadian R.; settled 1889, made cap. 1910. Industrial, commercial, and distribution center for oil and agr. area. Mfg. of oil equipment, flour, and metal and wood products. Has civic center, capitol, historical society building, and air base.

Oklawaha (ŏklùwô´hô), river, c.140 mi. long, rising in central Fla. lake system. Flows N, receiving waters of SILVER SPRINGS, then E to St. Johns R. S of Palatka.

Okmulgee (ŏk´´mŭl´gē), city (pop. 18,317), E central Okla., SE of Tulsa; settled c.1899 on site of Creek town. Trade center of oil and agr. area. Oil, glass, cotton, and food processing. Old Creek council house and L. Okmulgee near by.

okra or **gumbo,** African plant (*Hibiscus esculentus*) grown for its mucilaginous seed pods, eaten as a vegetable and used to thicken gumbo soups.

Okubo, Toshimichi (tō"shēmē'chē ō'kōobō), 1832?–1878, Japanese statesman. After Meiji restoration he became chief figure in new government and influenced Westernization of Japan. Opposed fellow clansmen in Satsuma rebellion (1877) against imperial government.

Okuma, Shigenobu, Marquis (shēgä'nōbōo ō'kōomä), 1838–1922, Japanese statesman. Founder of a reform party (Kaishinto), forerunner of Minseito; agitated for parliamentary government. Favored working with zaibatsu to strengthen Japan's industry. In second premiership (1914–16), Japan entered World War I, seized Kiaochow, and presented China with Twenty-one Demands.

Olaf (ō'läf), kings of Norway. **Olaf I** (Olaf Tryggvason), c.963–1000, reigned 995–1000. He undertook conversion of Norway to Christianity—by force and by persuasion. **Olaf II** (Saint Olaf), c.995–1030, also a convert, reigned 1015–28. He completed the Christianization of Norway but failed in attempt to unify his kingdom. An insurrection in favor of CANUTE of England and Denmark forced him to flee abroad (1028). He returned in 1030 to seek his throne but was defeated and slain at Stiklestad. Patron saint of Norway. Feast: July 29.

Olaf, 1903–, crown prince of Norway; son of Haakon VII. Supreme commander of Norwegian forces (1944–45) in World War II.

Oland (û'länd), Swed. *Öland,* Baltic island, area 520 sq. mi., SE Sweden, separated from mainland by Kalmar Sound; chief town Borgholm. Agr., cattle raising; quarrying. Has summer resorts and Stone Age monuments.

Olathe (ōlā'thē), city (pop. 5,593), E Kansas, SW of Kansas City. Agr. trade center on Old Santa Fe Trail and near Oregon Trail.

Olcott, Chauncey, 1860–1932, American actor and singer. Developed (after 1893) a type of drama featuring his own ballads (e.g., *My Wild Irish Rose*).

old-age pension: see PENSION; SOCIAL SECURITY.

Old Castile, Spain: see CASTILE.

Oldcastle, Sir John, d.1417, English leader of LOLLARDS and martyr. Performed military service for Henry IV and was a friend of Henry V. Condemned (1413) for heresy, he escaped and was active in plots until his capture and execution. He was known as "the good Lord Cobham" (he had married into the Cobham family). See also FALSTAFF.

Old Catholics, Christian church estab. (1874) by Germans who rejected the decrees of the Vatican Council (notably papal infallibility). Leader of the movement, Döllinger, had not intended to found a new church, but the break with the Roman Catholics was complete. A Dutch Jansenist bishop consecrated the first Old Catholic bishop. The Roman ritual is retained in German, priests are allowed to marry, confession is optional.

Old Dominion, name for state of Va., probably derived from phrase (found in old documents) "the colony and dominion of Virginia."

Oldenbarneveldt, Jan van (yän' vän' ôl'dûnbär'nùvĕlt), 1547–1619, Dutch statesman. Aided William the Silent; later helped concentrate military power in hands of MAURICE OF NASSAU. As permanent advocate of Holland from 1586, he controlled civil affairs of United Provs.; expanded Dutch commercial empire; sided with States-General against nobles and house of Orange. His adherence to the Remonstrants gave his enemies a pretext for securing his death sentence as a traitor, without a shred of evidence.

Oldenburg (ôl'dùnbŏork), former German state, now a district (2,085 sq. mi.; pop. 812,371) of Lower Saxony, NW Germany, on the North Sea. Largely a marshy lowland, it has fertile agr. districts; cattle and horse breeding; peat bogs. Counts of Oldenburg came into prominence in 12th cent. The accession of Count Christian as king of Denmark (see CHRISTIAN I) in 1448 gave the house of Oldenburg international importance. The main line ruled Denmark until 1863

and was succeeded by its offshoot, the line of Schleswig-Holstein-Sonderburg-Glücksburg; another offshoot, the ducal line of Holstein-Gottorp, ruled Sweden 1751–1818 and merged with the Russian Romanov dynasty in the person of Peter III. Oldenburg itself was ruled by a younger line 1448–1667, then passed to the main (i.e., Danish) line. In 1773 Christian VII ceded Oldenburg to Grand Duke (later Emperor) Paul of Russia, in exchange for Paul's claim to part of Schleswig. Paul, in turn, ceded Oldenburg to his great-uncle, Frederick Augustus of Holstein-Gottorp, bishop of Lübeck. Oldenburg was annexed to France 1806–13, was made a grand duchy in 1815 under Frederick Augustus' nephew, and continued a grand duchy to 1918. It joined the German Empire (1871) and the Weimar Republic (1919) and was incorporated into Lower Saxony 1946. Two distant districts—Birkenfeld and the former bishopric of LÜBECK —were ruled by Oldenburg from 1815. Annexed by Prussia in 1937, they passed after World War II to, respectively, Rhineland-Palatinate and Schleswig-Holstein. The cap., **Oldenburg** (pop. 121,643), is a commercial center with varied mfg. Has Renaissance castle.

Old English: see TYPE; ENGLISH LANGUAGE; ANGLO-SAXON LITERATURE.

old English sheep dog: see SHEEP DOGS.

Old Forge, borough (pop. 9,749), NE Pa., SW of Scranton and on Lackawanna R. Anthracite mining.

Oldham, county borough (pop. 121,212), Lancashire, England; chief cotton-spinning center of county.

Old Hickory, industrial village (1940 pop. 5,993), N central Tenn., on Cumberland R. and NNE of Nashville. Owned by E. I. du Pont de Nemours and Co., town produces rayon, cellophane, and chemicals.

Old Hundred: see DOXOLOGY.

Old Ironsides: see CONSTITUTION, ship.

Old Kasaan National Monument: see NATIONAL PARKS AND MONUMENTS (table).

Old Man of the Mountain: see ASSASSIN.

Old Man of the Mountain: see FRANCONIA MOUNTAINS.

Old Norse literature, the literature of the Northmen, almost entirely medieval ICELANDIC LITERATURE. Its best-known form, the saga, was, however, borrowed from the Celts and was probably first used by Vikings in the British Isles. The golden period of Old Norse was in the 11th, 12th, and early 13th cent. The poets, called scalds, composed for recitation, not reading; metrical rules were strictly observed; phrases were ingenious. As time went on strict form and ingenuity deadened scaldic verse, and a new type of rhymed verse appeared (used chiefly to translate foreign romances). Norse prose developed in remarkably limpid, forceful style as in the works of the historian Ari Thorgilsson and the celebrated SNORRI STURLUSON. See also EDDA.

Old Northwest: see NORTHWEST TERRITORY.

Old Orchard Beach, resort town (pop. 4,707), SW Maine, on the coast SSW of Portland.

Old Point Comfort, resort, SE Va., on Chesapeake Bay at entrance to Hampton Roads. Here is U.S. Fort MONROE.

Old Red Sandstone, series of sandstones and shales deposited in parts of Wales, Scotland, and England in the Devonian period. It is largely a fresh-water formation, with many well-preserved fossils.

Old Sarum (sâr'ùm), site of ancient city, Wiltshire, England, N of New Sarum or Salisbury. Excavations have shown remains of ancient British, Roman and Saxon settlements. Parts of the cathedral were used in building Salisbury cathedral. Declined after removal of the see to New Sarum in 1220.

Old Saybrook, resort town (pop. 2,499), S Conn., at Connecticut R. mouth on Long Isl. Sound.

Old Stone Age: see PALEOLITHIC PERIOD.

Old Testament, the older portion of the Bible, of Jewish authorship. It consists of a varying number of books given in varying order. Traditional Jewish grouping is as follows: (1) the Torah or Law, consisting of the five books of the Pentateuch, i.e., Genesis,

Exodus, Leviticus, Numbers, and Deuteronomy; (2) the Prophets—Joshua, Judges, 1 and 2 Samuel, 1 and 2 Kings, Isaiah, Jeremiah, Ezekiel, and the minor prophets; (3) the Writings (Hagiographa)—Psalms, Proverbs, Job, Song of Solomon, Ruth, Lamentations, Ecclesiastes, Esther, Daniel, Ezra and Nehemiah together, and Chronicles. This order and canon dates back to Hebrew source called the Masoretic text (see MASORA). The Old Testament first used in the Christian church was not derived from Masoretic text, but from a Greek translation of c.3d cent. B.C. called the Septuagint. The number and order of books in the Septuagint differs from that of the Masoretic. The Latin Bible which found its official form in the Vulgate of St. Jerome largely agreed with the list of books of the Septuagint. The Vulgate was the form accepted by the Western Church; its order is called Western canon. At the Reformation, English Protestants denied canonical standing to those books of the Old Testament which appeared in Western canon but not in the Masoretic text. These are called deutero-canonical books and are described as suitable for instruction but not divinely inspired. To set them clearly apart from works considered inspired, the AV (Authorized Version or King James Version) translators put them together in an appendix to the Old Testament which they called the APOCRYPHA. Thus, AV canon became like the Masoretic, but retained the Western order. Difference between Western canon and AV can be seen by comparing King James Version with the Douay version (representing Western canon). The following are the books of the Old Testament according to AV; the names in parentheses are the usual names in Douay when it differs from that used in AV, names in italics are those appearing in Douay and not in AV: Genesis, Exodus, Leviticus, Numbers, Deuteronomy, Joshua (Josue), Judges, Ruth, 1 and 2 Samuel (1 and 2 Kings), 1 and 2 Kings (3 and 4 Kings), 1 and 2 Chronicles (1 and 2 Paralipomenon), Ezra (1 Esdras), Nehemiah (2 Esdras), *Tobias, Judith*, Esther, Job, Psalms, Proverbs, Ecclesiastes, Song of Solomon (Canticle of Canticles), *Wisdom, Ecclesiasticus*, Isaiah (Isaias), Jeremiah (Jeremias), Lamentations, *Baruch*, Ezekiel (Ezechiel), Daniel, Hosea (Osee), Joel, Amos, Obadiah (Abdias), Jonah (Jonas), Micah (Micaeus), Nahum, Habakkuk (Habacuc), Zephaniah (Sophonias), Haggai (Aggeus), Zechariah (Zecharias), Malachi (Malachias), *1 and 2 Maccabees.*

Old Town, city (pop. 8,261), S central Maine, on Penobscot R. above Bangor; settled 1774. Mfg. of canoes, shoes, paper, and woolens. Penobscot Indian reservation is on island. Maine's first railroad connected Old Town with Bangor (1836).

Olean (ō'lēăn″), city (pop. 22,884), W N.Y., SE of Buffalo and on Allegheny R. near Pa. line; settled 1804. Oil-storage center. Mfg. of carbon black, clothing, chemicals, and metal goods.

oleander (ōlēăn'dŭr), Old World evergreen shrub of genus *Nerium* with white, pink, or red flowers. Used as a hedge in warm regions; elsewhere a pot plant.

Oleg (ō'lĕg), d. 912, semilegendary Varangian ruler of Russia, possibly b. Norway. Succeeded his father, Rurik, 879; took KIEV from Khazars 882.

Olenek (ŭlyĭnyôk′), river, 1,345 mi. long, rising in central Siberia, RSFSR, and flowing E and N into Laptev Sea. Navigable for c.500 mi.

oleomargarine: see MARGARINE.

Oléron (ōlärō′), island (68 sq. mi.; pop. 12,820), W France, in Bay of Biscay; chief town Saint-Pierre. Oyster beds. Law of Oléron, a maritime code, was promulgated by Louis IX.

Olga, Saint, d. 969?, duchess of Kiev, widow of Igor (d. 945), regent (945–57) for her son, Svyatoslav. She promoted Christianity in Russia.

Oligocene epoch (ŏ'lĭgōsēn″), third epoch of the Cenozoic period of geologic time (second if Paleocene and Eocene are classed as one). More of North America was dry land than in the preceding Eocene. Archaic

mammals of the Paleocene had vanished and were replaced by true carnivores (dogs, cats, saber-tooth cats), beavers, mice, rabbits, squirrels. The horse was developing. Giant hogs and camels were other new arrivals.

Oliva, Peace of (ōlē'vù), 1660, treaty signed at Oliva (now a suburb of Danzig) by Poland and Sweden. John II of Poland renounced claim to Swedish crown and confirmed Sweden in possession of N Livonia. Frederick William, elector of Brandenburg, was recognized in full sovereignty over Prussia but in turn confirmed West Prussia as Polish.

Olivares, Gaspar de Guzmán, conde de (gäspär′ dä gōōthmän′ kōn'dä dä ōlēvä'räs), 1587–1645, chief minister of Philip IV of Spain from 1621 to 1643. Hardworking and honest, he cleaned up corruption at court but involved Spain in Thirty Years War, levied oppressive taxation to finance campaigns, and pursued a centralizing policy which caused several insurrections and led to secession of Portugal (1640). He was a patron of Rubens, Velázquez, Murillo, and Lope de Vega.

olive, small evergreen tree (*Olea europaea*), native to Mediterranean region and cultivated from prehistoric times for its fruit (the olive), which is eaten pickled green or ripe and is the source of OLIVE OIL. In Calif. the olive has been of commercial importance since c.1890. The olive branch has been the symbol of peace since before Christian times.

Olive Hill, town (pop. 1,351), E Ky., WSW of Ashland. Near are Carter and Cascade caves and several natural bridges.

olive oil, clear, bland, usually yellowish oil expressed from the olive. Best grade (virgin oil) comes from slightly unripe fruit, peeled and gently pressed; this pulp, repeatedly pressed, then yields oil of inferior quality, as do fully ripe or imperfect olives. Technical oil, for industrial uses, is yielded after extraction of edible grades. Countries in Mediterranean region are chief exporters.

Olives, Mount of, or **Olivet,** ridge E of Jerusalem, frequently visited by Jesus. Garden of Gethsemane is on W slope. 2 Sam. 15.30; Mat. 21.1; Acts 1.12.

Olivet College (ŏ'lĭvĕt), at Olivet, Mich.; coeducational, founded 1844.

Olivier, Sir Laurence (Kerr) (ōlĭ'vĕŭr), 1907–, English actor and director. His notable films include *Henry V* and *Hamlet.* A director (after 1944) of the Old Vic company, he won acclaim for such productions as *Oedipus* and *Uncle Vanya.*

Ollivier, Émile (āmēl′ ôlēvyä′), 1825–1913, French statesman. A leader of liberal opposition to Napoleon III; after 1863 a supporter of Napoleon's "Liberal Empire." Made premier in 1869, he was dismissed after outbreak of Franco-Prussian War (1870).

Olmedo, José Joaquín (hōsā′ hwäkēn′ ōlmä'dhō), 1780?–1847, Ecuadorian poet. He and Bello and Heredia are considered the three outstanding poets of revolutionary period in Spanish America.

Olmsted, Frederick Law, 1822–1903, American landscape architect, noted as planner of city parks, notably Central Park, New York city, and Jackson Park, Chicago. Also wrote books about the South. His son, **Frederick Law Olmsted,** 1870–, is also a landscape architect and city planner.

Olmütz (ôl'müts), Czech *Olomouc,* city (pop. 58,617), Moravia, Czechoslovakia, on the Morava. Varied mfg.; breweries. Archiepiscopal see. The Treaty of Olmütz (1850), between Austria and Prussia, dissolved the German Union (under Prussian presidency) and restored the German Confederation (under Austrian leadership). Prussia smarted under the "humiliation of Olmütz" until its victory over Austria in 1866. Olmütz has a 12th-cent. cathedral and a 13th-cent. city hall.

Olney, Jesse (ŏl'nē), 1798–1872, American geographer. His *Practical System of Modern Geography* (1828) was standard text with wide influence.

Olney, Richard, 1835–1917, American statesman. U.S. Attorney General (1893–95); U.S. Secretary of State

(1895–97). Took part in negotiations over Venezuela Boundary Dispute.

Olney (ŏl'nē, ō'nē), village, Buckinghamshire, England. Home (1767–86) of William Cowper, who with John Newton wrote *Olney Hymns*, is now a museum.

Olney (ŏl'nē), city (pop. 8,612), SE Ill., W of Vincennes, Ind. Center of farm and timber area. Mfg. of shoes and flour.

Olomouc, Czechoslovakia: see OLMÜTZ.

Olsztyn, East Prussia: see ALLENSTEIN.

Oltenia, Rumania: see WALACHIA.

Olustee (ōlŭ'stē), village, N Fla., on Ocean Pond E of Lake City. Site of most important Civil War battle (Feb. 20, 1864) fought in Fla. Federal defeat saved supplies of interior Fla. for the Confederacy.

Olympia (ōlĭm'pēu), city (pop. 15,819), state cap., W Wash., at S end of Puget Sound; founded 1850. Made territorial cap. 1853. Ships and processes lumber, fish, food products. Farm machinery and canning equipment. Was end of a branch of Oregon Trail.

Olympia, small plain of Elis, anc. Greece, near Alpheus R. From earliest times it was a center of worship of Zeus and scene of the Olympic games. Excavation here revealed the great temple which contained celebrated statue of Zeus by Phidias—one of the Seven Wonders of the World.

Olympiad, four-year chronological unit of anc. Greece, each beginning with OLYMPIC GAMES. First Olympiad was reckoned from 776 B.C.

Olympian, in Greek religion, one of 12 major gods, who lived on Mt. Olympus. Zeus, father, ruled over Hera, his sister and wife; Athena, Hebe, Artemis, and Aphrodite, his daughters; Hermes, Ares, Apollo, and Hephaestus, his sons; Hestia, his elder sister; and Poseidon, his brother. Their sanctuary was Olympia, in Elis, where Olympic games were held in their honor.

Olympias, d. 316 B.C., wife of Philip II of Macedon and mother of Alexander the Great. After Alexander's death tried to seize Macedon, but was defeated and killed by Cassander.

Olympic games, principal athletic meeting of ancient Greece, held in summer once every four years at Olympia in honor of Olympian Zeus. According to tradition, games began 776 B.C., were discontinued by Emperor Theodosius I of Rome at end of 4th cent. A.D. Games were first confined to running. Later, pentathlon, boxing, chariot racing, other sports were introduced. Modern revival of Olympic games began (1896) at Athens.

Olympic Mountains, part of Coast Ranges, NW Wash., S of Juan de Fuca Strait and W of Puget Sound. Rise to 7,954 ft. in Mt. Olympus, center of **Olympic National Park** (see NATIONAL PARKS AND MONUMENTS, table).

Olympus (ōlĭm'pŭs), mountain range, 25 mi. long, N Greece, between Thessaly and Macedonia and near Aegean coast. Its summit (9,570 ft.), highest point in Greece, was in Greek religion the home of the OLYMPIAN gods. Later the name Olympus was applied to heavenly palace of the gods.

Olympus, Mount: see CYPRUS; OLYMPIC MOUNTAINS; OLYMPUS (Greece).

Olynthus (ōlĭn'thŭs), city of anc. Greece, on Chalcidice peninsula. Headed Chalcidian League and opposed Athens and Sparta. Olynthus at first was allied with Philip II against Athens, then asked Athenian aid against Philip. Demosthenes in the Olynthiac orations pleaded for Athenians to send the aid. Philip razed the city (348 B.C.).

Olyphant (ŏ'lĭfŭnt), borough (pop. 7,047), NE Pa., on Lackawanna R. and NE of Scranton. Coal mines, silk mill, and iron foundries.

Omaha (ō'mŭhä), city (pop. 251,117), E Nebr., largest city in state, on the Missouri opposite Council Bluffs, Iowa. Founded 1854 with opening of Nebr. Territory. Grew as river port and supply point for pioneers, but great expansion came after arrival of Union Pacific RR (1865). Territorial cap. 1855–67. Transportation, shipping, and industrial center, it is served by railroads, transcontinental air lines, bus lines, and highways. Has oil refineries, lead smelters, grain elevators, and meat-packing plants; mfg. of farm implements, flour, and dairy products. Seat of Creighton Univ. (Jesuit; for men; opened 1878; includes Univ. Col. for women), Univ. of Nebraska medical school, Municipal Univ. of Omaha, and Joslyn Memorial (1931). Fort Omaha (1868) and Boys Town are near.

Omaha Indians, North American tribe of Siouan linguistic stock. Probably emigrated with the Ponca from the Ohio valley to Iowa, then to the Niobrara R. Separated from the Ponca and went up the Missouri, but after a smallpox epidemic (1802) they moved to NE Nebr. Sold lands W of the Missouri in 1854 and settled in Dakota co., Nebr. Sold part of their reservation to the U.S. in 1865 and in 1882 got right to own land individually. They had a typical Plains culture.

Oman, Sir Charles William Chadwick (ō'mŭn), 1860–1946, British historian, authority on military history. His many works include exhaustive *History of the Peninsular War* (7 vols., 1902–30).

Oman (ōmän', ō'män), sultanate (c.82,000 sq. mi.; est. pop. 550,000), SE Arabia; cap. Muscat. Officially called Oman and Muscat. Mainly a narrow coastal plain (along Gulf of Oman and Arabian Sea), backed by hills and sandy interior plateau. Dates are main export. Occupied 1508 by the Portuguese, who controlled much of coastal area until mid-17th cent. Present royal line was founded 1741 by Ahmed ibn Said of Yemen. In early 19th cent. Oman was most powerful state of Arabia, controlling ZANZIBAR and coastal areas of Persia and Baluchistan. Today its only possession outside Arabia is Gwadar in Baluchistan. Bound to Britain by treaty.

Omar, c.581–644, 2d caliph. Converted to Islam by 618, he succeeded ABU BAKR (634). In his reign Islam became imperial power by many conquests. Omar created the administrative system.

Omar Khayyam (kīäm'), fl. 11th cent., Persian poet and mathematician. His fame as mathematician and astronomer has been eclipsed by popularity of his *Rubáiyát,* epigrammatic verse quatrains, which became widely known after 1859 through Edward FITZGERALD's paraphrased translation. Other translations in English and other languages have been made.

Omayyad (ōmä'yäd), Arabian dynasty of caliphs, founded in 7th cent. by MUAWIYA. Islam was united by the 5th caliph, ABDU-L-MALIK. The Omayyad cap. was usually Damascus until 750, when Marwan II (14th caliph) was defeated in battle by the ABBASID clan, who then massacred the Omayyad family. One member escaped to Spain, where he estab. himself over the Moors as ABDU-R-RAHMAN I, emir of Córdoba, in 756. In 10th cent. the emirate became a caliphate. The brilliant civilization created by the dynasty reached its peak under Abdu-r-Rahman III, and in late 10th cent. Al MANSUR put almost all Spain under Omayyad rule. The caliphate survived until 1031; it included most of Moslem Spain.

Omdurman (ōmdûrmän'), city (pop. 125,300), central Anglo-Egyptian Sudan, on the Nile near Khartoum; largest city of the Sudan. Became headquarters of the Mahdi in 1884. Captured 1898 by Kitchener. City trades in cotton, grain, and livestock.

Omei (ō'mä'), peak, 9,957 ft. high, SW Szechwan prov., China, near Loshan. On its slopes are many temples and monasteries.

Omphale (ŏm'fŭlē), in Greek legend, queen of Lydia. To expiate for murder of his son, Hercules had to serve her for three years. She made him wear women's clothes and spin, while she wore his lion's skin and carried his club.

Omri (ŏm'rī), d. c.874 B.C., king of Israel (c.885–c.874 B.C.). When ZIMRI murdered King Elah, Omri, a general in Elah's army, seized the throne for himself. He moved the capital to Samaria, making it Israel's chief city. Name mentioned on Moabite stone. Succeeded by his son Ahab. 1 Kings 16.16–28; 20.34.

Omsk (ômsk), city (pop. c.450,000), RSFSR, in W Siberia, on confluence of Om and Irtysh and on Trans-Siberian RR. Transportation and industrial center (machinery, locomotives, rolling stock, cars, lumber). Has several scientific institutes. Became administrative center of Siberia 1824; industrialization began under Soviet regime.

Omuta (ō'mōōtä), industrial city (pop. 166,438), W Kyushu, Japan; coal-shipping port on Amakusa Sea.

Onan (ō'nŭn), Judah's son whose wickedness was punished by sudden death. Gen. 38.

Oñate, Juan de (hwän' dā ōnyä'tä), d. c.1624?, Spanish explorer in Southwest. Conquered and settled New Mexico in 1598. Led search for Quivira (1601). Explored Colorado R.

Oncken, Hermann (hĕr'män ông'kùn), 1869–1946, German historian. Works on political and diplomatic history include *Napoleon III and the Rhine* (1926; Eng. tr., 1928) and *Nation und Geschichte* (1935).

Oncken, Wilhelm (vĭl'hĕlm), 1838–1905, German historian. Edited cooperative history, *Allgemeine Geschichte in Einzeldarstellungen* (45 vols., 1879–93), to which he contributed three major studies.

Onega (ōnē'gù, ōnä'gù), river, N European RSFSR, rising in L. Lacha and flowing 252 mi. N into Onega Gulf of White Sea. **Lake Onega**, area c.3,800 sq. mi., S Karelo-Finnish SSR and NW European RSFSR, Europe's second largest lake (140 mi. long, 50 mi. wide, max. depth 400 ft.). Receives Vytegra R. in S and drains through Svir R. in SW to L. Ladoga. Baltic–White Sea Canal has its S terminus at Povenets. Petrozavodsk is chief city and port on the lake (frozen Nov.–May). **Onega Canal**, 45 mi. long, part of MARIINSK SYSTEM, runs parallel to S shore of the lake and joins Svir and Vytegra rivers.

Oneida (ōnī'dù), city (pop. 11,325), central N.Y., E of Syracuse and SE of Oneida L. Several industries, notably silverware, introduced by **Oneida Community**, religious communistic society estab. here 1848 by J. H. NOYES and reorganized 1881 as stock company.

Oneida Indians: see IROQUOIS CONFEDERACY.

Oneida Lake, 20 mi. long and 1–5 mi. wide, central N.Y., NE of Syracuse. Resorts. The Barge Canal links E end with Mohawk R. and from W end follows Oneida R., which joins Seneca R. to form Oswego R.

O'Neill, Eugene (Gladstone), 1888–, American dramatist. Son of a well-known actor, James O'Neill, he knew the stage before he became a seaman, a prospector, and a newspaperman. He studied briefly under George Pierce Baker, and his career began with association with the Provincetown Players in 1916. A number of short plays came before *Beyond the Horizon* (1920), first in a succession of plays generally viewed as the best written in the U.S. Among them are *The Emperor Jones* (1920), *Anna Christie* (1921), *The Hairy Ape* (1922), *Desire under the Elms* (1924), *The Great God Brown* (1926), *Strange Interlude* (1928), *Mourning Becomes Electra* (1931; a trilogy expressing the Electra story in modern terms; generally considered his masterpiece), *Ah, Wilderness!* (1933; his only comedy), and *The Iceman Cometh* (1946). His plays are notable for symbol in stage effects and words (e.g., the beating of tom-toms in *The Emperor Jones* and masks in *The Great God Brown*) and for their brooding philosophical and psychological studies of modern man.

O'Neill, Hugh: see TYRONE, HUGH O'NEILL, 2D EARL OF.

O'Neill, Margaret, c.1796–1879, wife of J. H. EATON. Peggy O'Neill was snubbed socially because of her alleged intimacy with Maj. Eaton before their marriage and because of her humble birth. Attempt of Pres. Jackson to insure her place in society almost disrupted cabinet and worsened his relations with Vice Pres. J. C. Calhoun, whose wife was a social leader.

O'Neill, Owen Roe, 1590?–1649, Irish rebel. Nephew

of earl of Tyrone, he left Ireland after "flight of the earls" in 1607. Spent 30 years in Spanish army. Returned to Ireland (1642); became leader of his clan; led Catholic faction against the English.

O'Neill, Shane, c.1530–67, Irish chieftain. Fought with his father over his succession. Refused to acknowledge Elizabeth, but submitted in 1564. Carried on tribal warfare and was murdered.

Oneonta (ōnēōn'tù), city (pop. 13,564), E central N.Y., on Susquehanna R. and NE of Binghamton; settled c.1780. Railroad shops; clothing, gloves, and flour.

onion, biennial bulbous plant (*Allium cepa*) of lily family, native to W Asia but widely grown elsewhere for its edible bulbs. Plants are grown from seeds, "sets" (seedlings arrested in development by being ripened off early in the season), bulb division (as in multiplier onions), and "tops" (small bulbs which form in place of seed on some varieties). There are red, yellow, and white varieties; the Spanish and Bermuda types are large and mild. See *ill.*, p. 783.

Onkelos (ông'kùlōs), reputed author (c.100–130) of the Targum Onkelos, standard Aramaic translation of the Pentateuch according to the Talmud.

Onnes, Heike Kamerlingh: see KAMERLINGH ONNES, HEIKE.

Onondaga Indians: see IROQUOIS CONFEDERACY.

Onondaga Lake (ōnùndä'gù), 5 mi. long and 1 mi. wide, central N.Y., extending NW from Syracuse. Bought by state from Indians for salt resources 1795.

Ontario (ôntâ'rēō), province (363,282 sq. mi., with water surface 412,582 sq. mi.; pop. 4,597,542), central Canada; cap. TORONTO. Other large cities are OTTAWA (cap. of Canada), HAMILTON, WINDSOR and LONDON. Bounded N and NE by Hudson and James Bays, S by the Great Lakes. NW Ont. is part of the LAURENTIAN PLATEAU, a mineral-rich forested region threaded by lakes and rivers where trapping is main activity. Mining (nickel, gold, silver, copper) is important in central Ont., which also attracts sportsmen and vacationists. Old Ontario (the S peninsula hemmed in by the Great Lakes) is the center of population and economic development. Access to raw materials and hydroelectric power encourages mfg. of machinery and other iron and steel products and varied consumer goods. Diverse agr. is intensive. Its geographical position makes Ont. the focus of E–W trade and distribution is facilitated by fine ports, railroads, and highways. Area first visited by Champlain 1615, and French posts were soon estab. England gained control 1763 and in 1774 the region became part of Quebec province. An influx of UNITED EMPIRE LOYALISTS 1784 led to the formation of Upper Canada (W of Ottawa R.). York (now Toronto), the cap., was burned in War of 1812. Internal dissension between the FAMILY COMPACT and reformers under W. L. MACKENZIE led to the rebellion of 1837. The insurgents were quickly repulsed but the movement for responsible government, under the more moderate leadership of ROBERT BALDWIN, gained strength. The Act of Union (1840) uniting Upper and Lower Canada proved unsuccessful and in 1867 confederation was achieved and Ont. became a province of the new dominion. In 1912 the province was enlarged by part of the Keewatin dist. of Northwest Territories. Politically Ont. fluctuates between the Liberal and Conservative parties, with considerable strength in the CO-OPERATIVE COMMONWEALTH FEDERATION. Because of its population and economic importance, Ontario's politics are a major factor in Canadian government.

Ontario. 1 City (pop. 22,872), S Calif., E of Los Angeles; founded 1882. Processes citrus fruits, olives, and wine. Mfg. of electrical equipment and aircraft parts. **2** City (pop. 4,465), E Oregon, on Snake R. at mouth of Malheur R. A center in OWYHEE project. Gateway to Oregon cattle country.

Ontario, Lake, 193 mi. long and 53 mi. wide, smallest and most easterly of the Great Lakes, lying between province of Ontario and N.Y. Connected with L. Erie,

L. Huron, Hudson R., and Ottawa by various canals. Fed chiefly by Niagara R. and drained NE by St. Lawrence R. Major ports are Hamilton, Toronto, Cobourg, and Kingston, Canada; Rochester and Oswego, N.Y. Étienne Brulé was first white man to see lake 1615, and Champlain visited (also 1615).

onyx (ŏ′nĭks), variety of quartz showing parallel and regular color bands. The black and white specimens are used for cameos.

OPA: see OFFICE OF PRICE ADMINISTRATION.

opal (ō′pŭl), gem characterized by remarkable play of colors (opalescence). Opals have wide color range, including orange-red (fire opal). Main sources: Czechoslovakia, Australia, Honduras, Nevada, Mexico.

Opava, Czechoslovakia: see TROPPAU.

Opelika (ōpŭlī′kủ), city (pop. 12,295), E Ala., ENE of Montgomery near Chattahoochee R., in farm area; settled 1836. Has textile plants.

Opelousas (ōpŭlōō′sủs), city (pop. 11,659), S central La., W of Baton Rouge; founded 1765. Temporary state cap. during Civil War. Processes and ships cotton, rice, sugar cane and truck.

Open Door, maintenance in area of equal commercial and industrial rights for all nations. Notable example was policy in treaties with China after OPIUM WAR (1839–42). Policy was made effective for China through efforts of John Hay in 1899 and was confirmed after the BOXER REBELLION (1900). Japan in 1915 flouted it by presenting the TWENTY-ONE DEMANDS, but the Nine-Power Treaty after the Washington Conference (1921–22) guaranteed China's integrity and reaffirmed principle of Open Door, which lasted until World War II. Then recognition of China's absolute sovereignty ended Open Door policy.

open shop: see CLOSED SHOP AND OPEN SHOP.

Opéra (ôpärä′), chief opera house of Paris on Place de l'Opéra on right bank of the Seine. Designed by Garnier and built 1863–75. Its ornate grand staircase is famous.

opera, drama set to music. Although its antecedents date from the lyric theater of ancient Greece, true opera was a creation of the baroque in Italy. First opera on record (although the music is lost) is *Dafne* (1597) by Jacopo Peri; opera's first real master was Monteverdi; first public opera house was opened in Venice in 1637. A definite opera style emerged wherein the aria and virtuoso soloist became more important than the recitative and chorus. Early operas took their plots from mythology; later comedy and parody became popular. In the late 17th cent., the dramatically unified, three-act *opera seria* was created in an effort to purge opera of irrelevant episodes, bombast, and mechanical contrivances then so prevalent. Distinguished from *opera seria* were *opéra comique,* which meant any opera—regardless of subject matter —that had spoken dialogue, and *opera buffa,* which did not have spoken dialogue. After the French Revolution, spectacular and melodramatic operas became popular, evolving into 19th-cent. grand opera with its emphasis on historical subjects, religious elements, and violent passions (as in operas of Meyerbeer). Outstanding among opera composers are Gluck, Mozart, Verdi, Wagner, and Puccini.

operetta, type of theatrical presentation with a frivolous, sentimental story (often employing satire) and both spoken dialogue and much light, pleasant music. It developed from *opéra comique.* Noted operetta composers have been Offenbach, Johann Strauss the younger, Gilbert and Sullivan, Victor Herbert, and Sigmund Romberg.

Ophion (ŏf′ĭŭn), in Greek legend, Titan who ruled the world before Cronus. His wife was Eurynome.

Ophir (ō′fủr), in Bible, seaport or region from which ships of Solomon brought gold and also gems, ivory, apes, and peacocks. Variously identified with India, Ceylon, Malay Peninsula, Africa, and Arabia.

Opitz, Martin (mär′tēn ō′pĭts), 1597–1639, German poet, critic, metrical reformer. Known for his trans-

lations and writings on poetry, especially the *Buch von der deutschen Poeterey* [book on German poetry] (1624).

opium (ō′pēŭm), bitter dried juice from unripe capsules of opium poppy. Contains alkaloids including morphine (of which heroin is a derivative) and codeine, valuable drugs but, like opium, habit-forming NARCOTICS. Laudanum is a tincture of opium. Opium addiction is a serious problem especially in Orient.

Opium War, 1839–42, struggle between Great Britain and China. The British had long wanted China to end restrictions on foreign trade; they found pretext for war (which they easily won) when China banned import of opium in 1839 and destroyed British-owned opium stored at Canton. Treaty of Nanking (1842) opened ports of Canton, Shanghai, Amoy, Foochow, and Ningpo to British trade and ceded Hong Kong to Britain.

Oporto (ủpôr′tō, ō–), Port. *Pôrto,* city (pop. 279,738), Douro Litoral prov., NW Portugal, on Douro R. Second city of Portugal and an important port, with its harbor at near-by Leixões on the Atlantic, it exports its famous port wine (since 17th cent.). Textile mfg. Traditionally founded c.138 B.C. by Romans as Cale (later Portus Cale). Henry of Burgundy secured the title duke of Portucalense in 11th cent., and thus Oporto gave its name to the future kingdom. It was ruled by its bishops until after the Cortes of Leiria (1254), when kings estab. control. First city to revolt in the Peninsular War, it was retaken by the French but liberated 1809 by Wellington. Suffered siege in 1832 in Miguelist Wars.

opossum (pŏ′sŭm, ủpŏ′sŭm), MARSUPIAL of South America and U.S. Virginia opossum (*Didelphis*) of U.S. somewhat resembles a large rat, has a white face, ordered grayish fur, a nearly naked prehensile tail (the opossum can sleep while hanging head down), and is nocturnal and largely arboreal. Practice of lying absolutely still when frightened gives rise to term "playing 'possum."

Opp, city (pop. 5,240), E Ala., near Fla. line, in pine and farm area.

Oppeln (ô′pủln), Pol. *Opole,* city (1939 pop. 52,977; 1946 pop. 27,666), Upper Silesia, on Oder R.; since 1945 under Polish administration. Seat of dukes of Oppeln, of PIAST dynasty, 1163–1532. Duchy passed 1532 to the Hapsburgs and 1742 to Prussia.

Oppenheimer, J. Robert (ŏ′pŭnhī″mủr), 1904–, American physicist. He was director of atomic-energy research project at Los Alamos, N.Mex. (1942–45). He later became chairman of general advisory committee of U.S. Atomic Energy Commission and director of the Inst. for Advanced Study, Princeton, N.J.

Opper, Frederick Burr, 1857–1937, American cartoonist and illustrator of books.

Ops (ŏps), in Roman religion, goddess of fertility; wife of Saturn and mother of Jupiter. As goddess of sowing and reaping she was known as Consiva. Identified with Greek Rhea.

Optic, Oliver, pseud. of William Taylor Adams, 1822– 97, American juvenile writer. His 116 books combine exciting tales with wholesome instruction.

optics, a branch of physics, the study of LIGHT. Physical optics is concerned with the nature and properties of light; physiological, with role of light in VISION; geometrical, with geometry of REFLECTION and REFRACTION of light as encountered in study of the MIRROR and the LENS.

optometry (ŏptŏm′ủtrē), science of detecting and correcting, usually with spectacles, certain nonpathological ocular defects. Word came into use 1903, with establishment of American Optometric Association. Legislation regulating practice of optometry was enacted in 20th cent.

oracle, in Greek religion, response given by a god to a human question; term also used commonly to refer to institution itself. Oracles were fixed in a locality, and each represented a god (e.g., Zeus at Dodona and

Apollo at Delphi). Some oracles were uttered by persons entranced, some were heard in rustling of leaves, and some came in dreams. Priests or priestesses, who were greatly respected, interpreted oracles. The Delphic oracle, the most influential, was chiefly interested in preserving piety and in extending Greek colonies.

Oradea (orä'dyä) or **Oradea-Mare** (–mä'rĕ), Ger. *Grosswardein*, Hung. *Nagyvárad*, city (pop. 82,282), W Rumania, on Rapid Koros R. Commercial center of grape-growing area. Episcopal see. Ceded by Hungary to Rumania after World War I, though population is about half Magyar.

Oraefajokull, Icelandic *Öræfajökull* (û'rīväyû"kütùl), highest mountain (6,952 ft.) of Iceland, rising from VATNAJOKULL ice field near SE coast.

Oraibi (orī'bē), Indian pueblo on a mesa c.100 mi. N of Winslow, Ariz.; built c.1150. A mission estab. here (1629) was destroyed in the revolt of 1680. Long the most important pueblo of the Hopi, it declined because of economic troubles and internal quarrels.

Oran (ōrän', ōrän'), city (pop. 244,594), NW Algeria; port on the Mediterranean, chief French naval base in N Africa. Founded in 10th cent. by Moorish Andalusian traders. Alternately under Spanish and Turkish rule, 16th–18th cent. Occupied 1831 by the French. Old quarter has casbah and 18th-cent. mosque. City's rise dates from late 19th cent., when port facilities (here and in adjacent Mers-el-Kebir) were improved. In Nov., 1942, Oran was a key landing area of Allied invasion forces.

Orange (Fr. ô'räzh'), city (pop. 8,145), Vaucluse dept., SE France, near Avignon. Its fine Roman amphitheater is still in use. In 11th cent. it became the cap. of a county, later the principality of Orange, which in 1544 passed to William the Silent of the house of NASSAU. Orange was conquered for France by Louis XIV, but the title remained with the Dutch princes of Orange. House of Orange is the reigning dynasty of the Netherlands.

Orange. 1 City (pop. 10,027), S Calif., SE of Los Angeles; founded 1868. Processes citrus fruits. **2** Town (pop. 5,894), N Mass., E of Greenfield. Mfg. of metal goods, shoes, and clothing. **3** Industrial city (pop. 38,-037), NE N.J., W suburb of Newark and New York city; settled c.1675. Mfg. of clothing, chemicals, metal products. Orange, East Orange, South Orange, West Orange, and Maplewood known as "The Oranges," a suburban unit. **4** City (pop. 21,174), SE Texas, on Sabine R. and E. of Beaumont; founded 1836. Deepwater port (channel to Gulf) shipping oil, lumber, and food. Has paper mills, nylon and salt plants, shipyards, and rail shops. **5** Town (pop. 2,571), central Va., NE of Charlottesville. MONTPELIER is near by.

orange, citrus fruit, the most important fresh fruit of international commerce, native to tropical Asia. Trees bearing the sweet orange (*Citrus sinensis*) were estab. in Fla. by 1600 and in Calif. about 175 years later; its varieties are now the most important commercially. The sour or Seville orange (*C. aurantium*) is grown in U.S. chiefly for understock; the fruits are used, mostly in Europe, for marmalade. The trifoliate orange (*Poncirus trifoliata*), a hardier species, is also used as an understock. Orange trees begin to bear when three years old and flowers and fruits may appear throughout the year. The tangerine is a variety of the high-quality king orange (*C. nobilis*). Hybrids include the citrange (result of crossing trifoliate orange and a sweet orange variety) and tangelo (obtained by crossing tangerine and grapefruit).

Orangeburg, city (pop. 15,322), central S.C., SSE of Columbia on North Fork of Edisto R.; settled c.1735. Mfg. of cotton, timber and food products. Seat of South Carolina State Agricultural and Mechanical Col. (Negro; land grant; coed.; 1896).

Orange Free State, province (49,647 sq. mi.; pop. 879,-071), E central South Africa; cap. Bloemfontein. Bounded by Orange R. (S) and Vaal R. (N). Mainly a plateau. Major crops are wheat and corn. Diamonds, gold, and coal are mined. Settled 1835–48 by Boers, who created free republic, 1854. Annexed 1902 by the British. Joined Union of South Africa 1910.

Orangemen, members of the Loyal Orange Institution, an Irish society in province of Ulster. Estab. 1795 to maintain Protestant ascendancy. Name taken from family of William III of England.

Orange Mountains: see WATCHUNG MOUNTAINS.

Orange River, c.1,300 mi. long, South Africa. Near its mouth are extensive diamond deposits.

orangutan (ōräng'ōōtän) or **orangoutang** (–tăng), anthropoid ape (genus *Pongo* or *Simia*) of swampy coastal forests of Borneo and Sumatra. It is intelligent and teachable. Walks on all fours or swings through trees. It has shaggy, reddish hair, and the adult male is c.5 ft. high and weighs c.250 lb.

Oranienbaum, RSFSR: see LOMONOSOV.

Oranienburg (ōrä'nyünbŏōrk), town (pop. 18,633), Brandenburg, N Germany, on the Havel. Site of one of first concentration camps of Nazi regime.

oratorio, musical form employing chorus, orchestra (or organ), and soloists, usually having a sacred libretto and always performed without stage action or scenery. It developed in the late 16th and early 17th cent. and reached its peak in works of Bach, Handel, Haydn, and Mendelssohn.

oratory, the art of eloquent speech. In ancient Greece and Rome oratory was part of rhetoric (composition and delivery of speeches) and was important in public and private life. Aristotle and Quintilian discussed theory of rhetoric; subject, with definite rules and models, was emphasized in education of Middle Ages and Renaissance, though generally confined to the Church. With development of parliaments in 18th cent., great political orators appeared. Recently, especially with advent of radio, oratory has become less grandiloquent, more conversational, as in "fireside chats" of Pres. F. D. Roosevelt. Term *oratory* has given way to *public speaking*.

Oratory, Congregation of the, Roman Catholic secular priests organized locally according to the rule of St. PHILIP NERI. J. H. NEWMAN introduced the order in England.

orbit, in astronomy, path described by one heavenly body in its revolution about another whose attracting force controls the orbit. Position of a planet at a given time can be computed by using KEPLER'S LAWS and allowing for deviations from elliptic orbit if certain numerical elements of orbit are known. These include the maior axis; eccentricity; inclination (angle of plane of planet's orbit to ECLIPTIC); longitudes of perihelion and of ascending node (one of two points of intersection of planes of planet and earth); and date when planet passes a determinate part of orbit, e.g., perihelion. Orbits of most comets are nearly parabolic, those of satellites, nearly circular. See *ill.*, p. 927.

Orcagna (ōrkä'nyä) or **Arcagnolo** (ärkä'nyōlō), c.1308–1368, Florentine artist, whose real name was Andrea di Cione. Studied sculpture with Andrea Pisano. His marble tabernacle at Or San Michele, Florence, is an Italian Gothic masterpiece. In fresco painting he was a follower of Giotto.

orchestra. As composers began to develop an instrumental style as distinct from a vocal style and as orchestral music became valued for its own sake and was freed from subservience to vocal music, the orchestra began its long, slow period of development. The baroque period was the beginning. Until then, instruments that played in ensemble were members of one family rather than a blend of the different sonorities of the orchestra. The center of the baroque orchestra was a keyboard instrument (usually the harpsichord). Artistic need and the development of instruments themselves are interweaving factors influencing the make-up of the orchestra. First of modern instruments to be fully developed and assume dominance of the orchestra was the violin and its family. As the various wind and percussion instruments were introduced and more strings were added to balance them, the keyboard instrument (though often still present) was no longer needed to fill in the harmony. The 19th century saw the completion of the modern symphony orchestra—often augmented to extremes by composers such as Richard Strauss and Mahler. Instruments most often found in the modern orchestra are strings (violin, viola, cello, bass, harp); winds (piccolo, flute, oboe, clarinet, bassoon, contrabassoon, English horn, French horn, trumpet, trombone, tuba); and tympani and percussion instruments. See *ill.*, p. 667.

orchid (ôr'kĭd), flowering plant of orchid family, containing c.500 genera, most abundant in the tropics. Many have curiously shaped and beautifully colored flowers. An orchid may be an air plant or a terrestrial form, e.g., the hardy North American species, including LADY'S-SLIPPER and orchis.

Orcus: see HELL.

ordeal, anc. legal custom allied to divination. By it appeal was made to divine authority to decide guilt or innocence of one accused, or to choose between disputants. It persisted in W Europe until trial by JURY became common. Forms varied from ordeal by fire or by water to drawing lots. Trial by battle or by combat was recognized form in Middle Ages. DUEL has also been recognized form based on idea that God would favor cause of righteous.

Order of American Knights: see KNIGHTS OF THE GOLDEN CIRCLE.

orders, holy. In the Roman Catholic and Eastern churches the clergy are empowered to undertake their sacred duties by receiving holy orders in a sacrament called order (the ceremony is called ordination or in the case of bishops, consecration). There are three orders—bishop, priest, and deacon. Priests and bishops have double functions, liturgical and administrative; a deacon is only an assistant. The bishop may confer all sacraments, the priest all except confirmation and holy orders. A priest may head a parish, a bishop heads a diocese made up of a number of parishes. An archbishop is the bishop of an important center; he may have a province (made up of several dioceses) assigned to him, but his authority over other bishops is not strong. A patriarch is an archbishop with several provinces. In the Roman Catholic Church all bishops are ruled by the pope because he is the bishop of Rome. There are priests who are in monastic orders and do not usually head parishes; these are the regular clergy. Those who do not belong to orders are called secular clergy.

orders in council, in British government. **1** An order given by the king on advice of all or some of members of his privy council, without prior consent of parliament. First so named in 18th cent. Most commonly used in emergencies. Most notable use was blockade of Europe and system of embargoes after 1806 as an answer to Napoleon's Continental System. **2** Administrative orders, issued on authority of a parliamentary act, to carry out the act's provisions. Corresponds to "executive order" in U.S.

orders of architecture: see DORIC ORDER; IONIC ORDER; CORINTHIAN ORDER.

Ordinance of 1787, adopted by Congress of Confederation for government of Western territories ceded to U.S. by the states. Frequently called Northwest Ordinance; it created Northwest Territory in region N of the Ohio. Provided for admission of states from the territory; prohibited slavery there. Ordinance was most significant achievement of Congress under Articles of Confederation.

Ordovician period (ôrdŭvĭ'shùn), second period of the Paleozoic era of geologic time. Shallow seas flooded much of N Eurasia and North America. Low elevation of solid land restricted erosion, so that limestone formations are more characteristic than sandstone and shale. The seas were rich in invertebrate life, trilobites being very numerous. A few fishlike vertebrates made their appearance.

ore, mineral carrying enough metal to make its extraction profitable. Ores usually occur in concentrated deposits, classed as primary and secondary. Primary ores may be formed at the same time as the enclosing rock or later by filling of fissures. Chief types are sulphides and oxides. Secondary ores result chiefly from weathering of primary deposits.

Orebro (ûrùbrōō'), Swed. *Örebro,* city (pop. 66,548), co. seat of Orebro co., central Sweden, on Hjalmaren L. Shoe mfg. The national diet meeting at Orebro in 1810 elected Bernadotte king of Sweden as Charles XIV. Has 13th-cent. church and castle.

Oregon, state (96,981 sq. mi.; pop. 1,521,341), NW U.S.; admitted 1859 as 33d state (free); cap. SALEM. PORTLAND largest city. Bordered partly N by COLUMBIA R., partly E by Snake R., W by Pacific Ocean. Varies from coast-mountain-valley region (W) to upland plateau (E). GREAT BASIN wastelands in SE. CASCADE RANGE runs N–S. Agr. of fruits, grains, nuts, truck; livestock, dairying, poultry; lumbering, fishing. Processing of agr. and forest resources; mfg. of lumbering and agr. equipment, chemicals; publishing. Some mining of gold, silver, copper, manganese. U.S. claim to region estab. by Robert GRAY (1792). J. J. Astor estab. fur-trading post at ASTORIA in 1811. U.S.–Great Britain ruled jointly 1818–46, when 49th parallel was made international boundary. Oregon Territory created 1848 (N part made Washington Territory 1853). Settlers arrived over OREGON TRAIL. Indians subdued by 1880. Lumbering and agr. prospered with completion of railroads; population increased. Columbia Valley Authority project brought much development of industries and farming lands, but its merits have been disputed.

Oregon, city (pop. 3,205), N Ill., on Rock R. and below Rockford. Near by is Eagle's Nest Art Colony, founded 1898 by Lorado Taft and others; has Taft's *Black Hawk* statue.

Oregon, name sometimes applied to COLUMBIA R. in early days of American settlement in its valley.

Oregon, University of: see EUGENE.

Oregon Caves National Monument: see NATIONAL PARKS AND MONUMENTS (table).

Oregon City, city (pop. 7,682), NW Oregon, at falls of Willamette R. and S of Portland, in fruit and dairy area; platted 1842 by John McLoughlin of Hudson's Bay Co., who later lost his claims to American immigrants. Territorial cap. until 1851. Had first newspaper (*Oregon Spectator,* 1846) W of Missouri R. Has paper, pulp, and wool mills.

Oregon grape, evergreen shrub (*Mahonia aquifolium*) of NW North America. Formerly considered a barberry, it has hollylike leaflets, yellow flowers, and showy grapelike clusters of edible blue berries.

Oregon State College: see CORVALLIS.

Oregon Trail, overland emigrant trail in U.S. from Missouri R. to Columbia R. country. Pioneers by wagon train did not, however, follow any single narrow route. Independence and Westport (now in Kansas City) were favorite starting points. Pioneers starting from Independence followed same route as SANTA FE TRAIL for some 40 mi. Trail's "end" shifted as settlement spread. Mountain men were chiefly responsible for making route known. First genuine emigrant train was that led by John Bidwell in 1841, which turned off on what was to be California Trail. First emigrant train to reach Oregon was led by Elijah White in 1842. Trail was used for many years. See also OVERLAND TRAIL.

Orel (ôrĕl'), city (pop. 110,567), central European RSFSR, on Oka R. Important industrial transportation center of a fertile agr. region. During World War II it was held by the Germans 1941–43 and was the scene of heavy fighting.

Orellana, Francisco de (fränthē'skō dā ōrĕlyä'nä), d. c.1546, Spanish explorer of Amazon R. Took part in conquest of Peru and was with Gonzalo Pizarro on expedition into interior of South America (begun

1538). At Napo R. his detachment was separated from expedition and he went down Amazon, arriving at the mouth 1541. His tales of female warriors gave the river its name. A later attempt to return up river took him to his death.

Orem (ô′rŭm), town (pop. 8,351), N central Utah, near Utah L. and N of Provo. Served by Provo R. project. Vegetable canning. Steel plant near.

Ore Mountains: see ERZGEBIRGE.

Orenburg, RSFSR: see CHKALOV.

Orestes (ôrĕ′stēz), in Greek mythology, prince of Mycenae; only son of Agamemnon and Clytemnestra. When his mother and Aegisthus murdered Agamemnon, she sent boy away for fear of his vengeance. He later returned and joined his sister Electra in killing his mother and her lover. The Erinyes then persecuted him until he reached Athens, where he was tried and acquitted by the Areopagus. To complete his purification, he brought sacred image of Artemis from Tauris. There he found his sister Iphigenia.

Orestes, d. 476, Roman general. Raised his son ROMULUS AUGUSTULUS to the throne (475); was defeated and slain by ODOACER at Piacenza.

Oresund (ûrŭsŭnd′) or **the Sound,** Scandinavian *Öresund* and *Øresund,* sound, 87 mi. long, between Sweden and Denmark, connecting Kattegat with Baltic Sea. Narrowest place (2½ mi.) is between Halsinborg and Elsinore.

Orford, Robert Walpole, 1st earl of: see WALPOLE, ROBERT, 1ST EARL OF ORFORD.

organ, musical wind instrument in which sound is produced by one or more ranks (or rows) of pipes and which has a mechanically produced wind supply. Modern organ pipes vary in size from 64 ft. to less than an inch. The several keyboards of the organ which are played with the hands are called manuals. The projecting knobs (called stops), usually both to the left and to the right of the keyboard, operate wooden sliders which pass under the mouths of a rank of pipes and can keep a particular rank out of action or "stopped." The pedals of the organ do not have the same function as those of a piano but are rather like another keyboard, played with the feet. The entire assembly of keyboards and stops is called the console. The organ has existed, in crude form, since ancient times. Organs of the Middle Ages already had several rows or ranks of pipes; these were all diapasons, those pipes whose timbre is characteristic of the organ alone. The keyboard was a creation of the 13th cent.; reed pipes and stops with timbres imitative of other instruments (e.g., the flute) were added in the late 15th and early 16th cent. Organ building reached its peak during the baroque era, and then declined. In the 19th cent., the increased use of stops imitative of orchestral tone and the overuse of the swell and crescendo led to the obscuring of the diapason pipes. The early 20th cent. saw the electrifying of mechanical parts, thus continuing the trend toward monstrous size and overwhelming power. Under the leadership of Albert Schweitzer and others, however, interest in the organ of the baroque era has revived.

Organization of American States, international organ created at Bogotá, Colombia (1948), by agreement of the 21 American republics. Treaty ratified 1951.

Organ Pipe Cactus National Monument: see NATIONAL PARKS AND MONUMENTS (table).

Orgetorix (ôrgĕ′tŭrĭks), d. 60? B.C., Helvetian leader. Planned a migration of the Helvetii across Gaul, but plan was discovered. He died soon after, but his people undertook the migration, bringing on the GALLIC WARS.

Oriel College: see OXFORD UNIVERSITY.

Origen (ô′rĭjĭn), 185?–254?, Christian philosopher, b. Egypt. He taught with great acclaim in Alexandria and then in Caesarea. Edited the Bible in six parallel Hebrew and Greek versions (the *Hexapla*) and wrote many works. Among them was his theological *De principiis* and his polemical *Contra Celsum.*

Orillia (ôrĭ′lēŭ), town (pop. 12,110), S Ont., Canada, on L. Couchiching and N of Toronto. Resort with boatbuilding, woodworking, and flour milling. Was home of Stephen Leacock.

Orinoco (ôrŭnô′kō), river rising in Guiana Highlands and flowing NW to Colombia, then N to Apure and E to Atlantic. Most of course is in Venezuela. One of largest South American rivers, its estimated length is from 1,200 to 1,700 mi. Navigable for most of length, it is joined to Amazon system by natural channel of Casiquiare and the Rio Negro. Chief port is CIUDAD BOLÍVAR. Probably discovered by Columbus (1498), explored by Lope de Aguirre (1560), and centuries later by Alexander von Humboldt. The origin of river in mountain wilderness, sought by several expeditions, was finally determined in 1951.

oriole (ôr′ēōl), name for various Old and New World perching birds. European orioles are allied to crows; golden oriole, orange-yellow with black wings and tail, ranges from England to Siberia and winters in Africa. Related species include mango bird of India. American orioles, called hangnests, are of blackbird and meadowlark family. Best known is Baltimore oriole; plumage of male is black and orange. See *ill.,* p. 105.

Orion (ôrī′ŭn), in Greek mythology, gigantic Boeotian hunter. He loved Merope but violated her and was blinded by her father. His eyes were healed by the sun's rays. At death he became a constellation, of which Orion's belt is a part.

Orissa (ŭrĭ′sŭ), state (59,869 sq. mi.; pop. 14,644,293), W India; cap. Bhubaneswar. Mainly hilly with fertile coastal strip. Major iron-ore deposits are mined in N. Except for Munda-speaking aborigines in interior, inhabitants speak Oriya language. Conquered 1803 by the British. Absorbed 24 former princely states in reorganization of 1948–49.

Orizaba (ōrēsä′bä), city (pop. 47,910), Veracruz, E Mexico, in a fertile valley surrounded by wooded hills; a popular resort and agr. center. Development of water power has made it an important mfg. city.

Orizaba, peak, 18,700 ft. high, E Mexico, on Veracruz-Puebla border. A snow-capped inactive volcano, it is the highest point in Mexico.

Orkhon (ôr′kôn), river, c.700 mi. long, rising in Khangai mts., NW Mongolian People's Republic, and flowing NE to Selenga R. just S of boundary with USSR. **Orkhon Inscriptions,** dating from 8th cent., were found near river's lower course. They comprise minor Chinese texts and oldest known material in a Turkic language.

Orkney, county (376 sq. mi.; pop. 21,258), NE Scotland, consisting of **Orkney Islands** or **Orkneys,** archipelago c.50 mi. long, made up of 90 islands. Less than a third are inhabited. Largest, Pomona or Mainland, has county town, Kirkwall. Except for Hoy, they are mostly low, rocky, and treeless. Fishing and farming are main occupations. Belonged to Norway 865–1468. Scapa Flow is naval base.

Orland, town (pop. 2,067), N Calif., NNW of Sacramento. Hq. of an irrigation project (1910). Three dams supply water from a Sacramento R. tributary.

Orlando: see ROLAND.

Orlando, Vittorio Emmanuele (vēt-tō′rēō āmänwā′lā ōrlän′dō), 1860–1952, Italian premier (1917–19). One of "Big Four" at Paris Peace Conference of 1919, he failed to secure, largely because of Wilson's opposition, the territorial gains promised Italy in the Secret Treaty of London (1915). In protest, he left the conference (April–May) and resigned soon afterward. He opposed Fascism; after its fall in 1943 he served as elder statesman.

Orlando (ôrlän′dō), city (pop. 52,367), central Fla., SE of L. Apopka; settled near Fort Gatlin (1837–48). Largest inland city in Fla. Trade, processing, and shipping center for citrus fruits, lumber, and naval stores. Mfg. of machinery.

Orléans (ôrlää′), name of two branches of the French royal line; derived their name from the duchy of Orléans, held in appanage by various princes of the blood. *Valois-Orléans.* This branch was founded by **Louis, duc d'Orléans**, 1372–1407, brother of King Charles VI. His murder by John the Fearless of Burgundy caused the civil war between ARMAGNACS AND BURGUNDIANS. His son **Charles, duc d'Orléans**, 1391–1465, was captured by the English at Agincourt (1415) and remained captive until 1440. He was a fine poet; his court at Blois was a center of literary life. His son became king as LOUIS XII (last of the line). *Bourbon-Orléans.* **Gaston, duc d'Orléans**, 1608–60, younger brother of Louis XIII, was the first Bourbon duke of Orléans. He conspired against Richelieu but won his pardon by betraying his associates (e.g., CINQ MARS), and he played a leading part in the FRONDE (as did his daughter, Mlle de MONTPENSIER). He had no male issue. The present house of Bourbon-Orléans began with **Philippe I, duc d'Orléans**, 1640–1701, brother of Louis XIV. His first wife was HENRIETTA OF ENGLAND; his second wife, Elizabeth Charlotte of Bavaria. A notorious libertine, he was excluded from state affairs. His son **Philippe II, duc d'Orléans**, 1674–1723, was regent for Louis XV. Cynical, debauched, and dictatorial, he set the tone for the licentiousness of the regency period. He was responsible for the rise of John LAW. The ambitions of the regent and his descendants brought them in conflict with the ruling house. His great-grandson, **Louis Philippe Joseph, duc d'Orléans**, 1747–93, supported the French Revolution, helped the Jacobins into power, and changed his name to Philippe Égalité. A member of the Convention, he voted for the execution of Louis XVI but was guillotined soon afterward on the charge of aspiring to the crown. His son was King LOUIS PHILIPPE (reigned 1830–48). Louis Philippe's grandson, **Louis Philippe Albert d'Orléans, comte de Paris**, 1838–94, went to the U.S. after 1848 and fought in the Civil War under McClellan. Back in France in 1871, he renounced his claim to the throne in favor of the legitimist pretender, Henri de CHAMBORD (1873). After Chambord's death (1883), he became head of the entire house of Bourbon. He wrote *Workingmen's Associations in England* (1869) and *History of the Civil War in America* (Eng. tr., 4 vols. 1875–88), a standard work of military history. He was succeeded as pretender by his son, **Louis Philippe Robert, duc d'Orléans**, 1869–1926, who spent his life in England and in the Indian army; by his nephew, **Jean d'Orléans, duc de Guise**, 1874–1940; and by the duc de Guise's son **Henri Robert Ferdinand d'Orléans, comte de Paris**, 1908–.

Orléans (ôr'lĕŭnz, Fr. ôrlää'), city (pop. 64,755), cap. of Loiret dept., N central France, on the Loire. Clothes mfg.; food processing. Dating from Roman times, it became (6th cent.) the cap. of a Frankish kingdom which in 7th cent. was united with Neustria. With surrounding Orléanais prov., Orléans was part of the original royal domain of the Capetians and was given at times in appanage to members of the royal family (dukes of Orléans). The siege by the English in 1428–29 threatened to bring all France under English rule until the appearance of JOAN OF ARC. After Joan had taken several of the English forts, the English lifted the siege, and the tide of the Hundred Years War was turned. The city, including Sainte-Croix cathedral and Joan of Arc museum, suffered severe damage in World War II.

Orléans, Ile d' (ēl" dôrlää'), or **Orléans Island** (20 mi. long, 5 mi. wide), S Que., Canada, in St. Lawrence R. and NE of Quebec; settled 1651 by French. Site of one of Wolfe's camps 1759. Highway bridge built to mainland 1935.

Orlon, trade name for synthetic fiber developed by E. I. du Pont de Nemours & Co. It is made from natural gas, oxygen, and atmospheric nitrogen and is resistant to sunlight, moisture, alkalis, acids, and to attacks by fungus diseases and insects.

Orlov, Aleksey Grigoryevich, Count (ŭlyĭksyā' grĭgôr'-yŭvĭch ŭrlôf'), 1737–1808, Russian nobleman. He took part in the conspiracy which placed Catherine II on the throne and probably murdered PETER III. Leader of the conspiracy was his brother, **Count Grigori Grigoryevich Orlov** (grĭgô'rē), 1734–83, a favorite of Catherine II. He later held high posts but had little political influence.

Ormandy, Eugene (ôr'mŭndē), 1899–, American conductor, b. Budapest. Conductor of the Minneapolis Symphony Orchestra, 1931–36. In 1936 he became conductor of the Philadelphia Symphony Orchestra.

Ormond, city (pop. 3,418), NE Fla., N of Daytona Beach. Ormond Beach, across Halifax R. (lagoon), has part of Daytona Beach speedway and former winter home of J. D. Rockefeller.

Ormonde, dukes and earls of: see BUTLER, family.

Ormuz, Iran: see HORMUZ.

Orne (ôrn), department (2,372 sq. mi.; pop. 273,181), N France, in Normandy; cap. Alençon.

Orono (ô'rŭnō), town (pop. 7,504), S Maine, on Penobscot R. above Bangor; settled c.1775. Mfg. of wood products. Seat of Univ. of Maine (land-grant, state supported; coed.); chartered 1865 as Maine State Col. of Agriculture and the Mechanic Arts, opened 1868, and renamed 1897.

Orontes (ōrŏn'tēs), river, c.240 mi. long, SW Asia. Rises in Lebanon and flows through Syria and Turkey to the Mediterranean near Antioch. On its banks are Antioch, Homs, Hama, and other centers dating from ancient times.

Orosius, Paulus (ōrō'shĕŭs), c.385–420, Iberian historian and theologian, a priest; friend and disciple of St. Augustine. In Africa he completed *Seven Books of History against the Pagans*, a work of universal history, demonstrating how events proved the truth of Biblical prophecies.

Oroville (ô'rōvĭl), city (pop. 5,387), N Calif., N of Sacramento and on Feather R.; settled 1849 as gold camp. Center of an olive and orchard region. Feather River Canyon and Feather Falls are near.

Orozco, José Clemente (hōsā' klāmän'tā ōrō'skō), 1883–1949, Mexican mural and genre painter. With Rivera he led the Mexican renaissance. Deals mainly with social themes in starkly simple style.

Orpah (ôr'pù), sister-in-law of Ruth. Ruth 1.4,14.

Orpen, Sir William, 1878–1931, British portrait and genre painter, b. Ireland.

Orpheus (ôr'fēŭs, ôr'fūs), in Greek mythology, celebrated Thracian bard, the beautiful music of whose lyre charmed even trees and rocks. He was son of Calliope by Apollo or Oeagrus. After Argonaut expedition, he married the nymph Eurydice. When she was killed by a snake, he sought her in Hades, where the gods, charmed by his music, freed her on condition that he not look at her before they reached earth. He disobeyed and she vanished. This myth has been popular as an operatic libretto. Orpheus is considered founder of Orphism.

Orphic Mysteries (ôr'fĭk), secret religious rites in worship of Dionysus. These were based on myth of Dionysus Zagreus. Zagreus, son of Zeus and Persephone, was devoured by Titans to please the jealous Hera. Zeus destroyed Titans by lightning, and from their ashes sprang the race of men, who were now part evil (Titan) and part divine (Zagreus). Zeus swallowed Zagreus' heart and from it was born the new Dionysus Zagreus. Thus initiate to cult had to eat raw flesh to achieve union with god. Poems purported to have been written by Orpheus in 6th cent. B.C. were basis of Greek mystery religion Orphism. This explained good and evil in men by myth of Dionysus Zagreus, and it taught importance of pure moral and ritual life for immortality.

Orr, John Boyd Orr, 1st Baron, 1880–, British nutritionist and agr. scientist. Won 1949 Nobel Peace Prize. Contributed to science of nutrition and solution of world food problems.

Orrefors (ôrùfôrs', –fôsh'), village, SE Sweden; famous

for its fine glassware, which is known over the world.

Orrery, Roger Boyle, 1st earl of: see BOYLE.

orrisroot: see IRIS.

Orrville, city (pop. 5,153), NE Ohio, NE of Wooster, in agr. area. Mfg. of food and dairy products.

Orsini (ōrsē'nē), Roman family which included Popes Celestine III, Nicholas III, Benedict XIII. Rose in 13th cent. Rivalry between Guelph Orsini and Ghibelline Colonna families often plunged Rome into anarchy. Members were made princes of Holy Roman Empire in 17th cent.

Orsk (ôrsk), city (pop. c.100,000), E European RSFSR, on Ural R. Metallurgical plants, oil refineries.

Ortegal, Cape (ôrtăgäl'), NW Spain, in Galicia, on Atlantic coast; SW limit of Bay of Biscay.

Ortega y Gasset, José (hōsā' ôrtā'gä ē gäsĕt'), 1883–, Spanish essayist and philosopher; long a professor of metaphysics at Madrid. Wrote much on Spanish and other national cultures and held (notably in *The Revolt of the Masses*, 1930) that an intellectual minority should direct the masses to prevent chaos.

Ortelius, Abraham (ôrtē'lyùs), 1527–98, Flemish geographer, of German origin. Noted for his atlas, *Theatrum orbis terrarum* (1570).

Orthez (ôrtĕz'), town (pop. 4,609), Basses-Pyrénées dept., SW France; former cap. of Béarn. Here Wellington defeated the French under Soult (1814).

Orthodox Eastern Church, community of Christian churches, independent but mutually recognized; originating in E Europe and SW Asia through a split with the Western Church. They agree in accepting the decrees of the first seven ecumenical councils and in rejecting the authority of the bishop of Rome (the pope). Orthodox and Roman Catholics view each other as schismatic, but consider the Nestorian, Coptic, Jacobite, and Armenian churches as heretical. There were differences within the whole church in early days, but the split between E and W began only in the 5th cent. and became definite only with the challenge to papal authority by Photius (9th cent.) and the condemnation of the patriarch of Constantinople by Pope Leo IX (1054). The Crusades embittered feelings, and many attempts at reunion since that time have been unsuccessful. There is considerable variation of practice between the two. Thus in the Eastern Church the liturgy is always sung and is not usually celebrated daily as in the West, and communion is given with a spoon. Parish priests are usually married; monks and bishops are not. The relationship of the various churches of the E community is complex and even terms vary greatly. Thus the term *Greek Church* may be used very loosely, though it is best confined to the patriarchate of Constantinople, the Church of Greece (dating from the Greek War of Independence), and churches using the Byzantine rite (liturgy in Greek). There are six other national churches, the most ancient being the Church of Cyprus and for centuries by far the most important being the Russian Orthodox Church. This was headed at first by the metropolitan of Kiev, under Constantinople; the see was moved to Moscow and a patriarchate was set up in 1589. The rite is in Old Slavonic. Peter I abolished this (1721) and set up a synod. In general the relations of church and state were very close and influence was mutual. Perhaps the greatest single early event in the Church was the reform movement under Nikon. In the Russian Revolution the Church suffered greatly and went into an eclipse. The patriarchate (just revived in 1917) lapsed in 1925, but a new patriarch was appointed in 1943. Relation of the Church to the Communist state appeared to be highly intimate. As Communist influence spread after World War II it greatly weakened the Orthodox Churches of Bulgaria, Yugoslavia, Rumania, Finland, and Poland (these last two founded only after World War I).

Ortles (ôrt'läs), Ger. *Ortler,* Alpine group, Trentino–Alto Adige, N Italy, rising to 12,792 ft.

Orton, Edward, 1829–99, American geologist and educator. He served as professor and president at Antioch and at Ohio Agricultural and Mechanical Col. (later Ohio State Univ.). From 1869 he was affiliated with Ohio geological survey; he made important studies of natural gas and petroleum.

Oruro (ōrōō'rō), city (pop. 52,600), W Bolivia; founded 1595 to exploit near-by silver deposits. Declined in importance as silver production declined in 19th cent., but with exploitation of other minerals (notably tin), it grew again and is third largest city in Bolivia.

Orvieto (ôrvyā'tō), town (pop. 8,883), Umbria, central Italy, on a rocky hill; probable site of the Etruscan VOLSINII. Near by are remains of an Etruscan necropolis. Cathedral, begun 1290 to commemorate miracle of BOLSENA and completed in 16th cent., has black and white marble façade. Its chapel was frescoed by Fra Angelico and Luca Signorelli.

Orwell, George, pseud. of Eric Blair, 1903–50, English satirist. His hatred of authoritarianism and fears for loss of individual liberty are shown in his novels *Animal Farm* (1946) and *Nineteen Eighty-Four* (1949).

Os, chemical symbol of the element OSMIUM.

Osage, river formed in W Mo. by Marais des Cygnes and Little Osage rivers. Winds c.250 mi. NE to the Missouri below Jefferson City. Impounded by BAGNELL DAM, it forms L. of the OZARKS.

Osage Indians (ō'sāj, ōsāj'), North American tribe of Siouan linguistic stock, once living in the Ohio valley, but removed by 1673 to the Osage R. in Mo. They were a typical Plains tribe. Early they allied themselves with the French. They were moved to a reservation in N central Okla., which turned out to be rich in oil land.

Osage orange, deciduous spiny tree (*Maclura pomifera*) native to Ark. and Texas, useful as a hedge. It has inedible orangelike fruits. The flexible, durable wood was a favorite bow wood of the Osage Indians.

Osaka (ō'säkä), city (pop. 1,559,310), S Honshu, Japan; port on Osaka Bay. Second largest city and chief commercial center of Japan; focal point of industrial belt. Seat of Osaka Imperial Univ. and Kansai Univ. Has Buddhist temple founded in 6th cent. Noted for puppet theater. As Naniwa, city was 4th-cent. cap. of Japan. Seat of Hideyoshi in 16th cent.

O Salutaris Hostia (săl"ūtā'rĭs, sä'lōōtä'rĭs) [Latin,= O saving victim], hymn to the Host, one of two hymns regularly sung at the exposition in Benediction of the Blessed Sacrament in the Roman Catholic Church. The other hymn is *Tantum ergo. O Salutaris* is the last two stanzas of a Corpus Christi hymn, probably written by St. Thomas Aquinas.

Osawatomie (ō"sùwŏ'tùmē), city (pop. 4,347), E Kansas, SSW of Kansas City. Once a station on the Underground Railroad, it has cabin where John Brown lived in 1856. Monument commemorates raid in which five of Brown's men were killed.

Osborn, Henry Fairfield, 1857–1935, American geologist. He was distinguished as teacher at Princeton and Columbia, as member of the U.S. Geological Survey, and for his long association with the American Mus. of Natural History (president 1908–33). His son, **Fairfield Osborn,** 1887–, became a naturalist and a conservationist.

Osborne, Dorothy, later **Lady Temple** (ŏz'bùrn), 1627–95, English letter writer. Letters to Sir William Temple (pub. 1888) clearly portray her period.

Osborne, Thomas Mott, 1859–1926, American prison reformer. Became a voluntary prisoner in Auburn, N.Y., penitentiary to investigate conditions and wrote *Within Prison Walls* (1914). As warden of Sing Sing (1914–15) instituted a system of self-government. Argued that prisons should educate, not punish.

Osborne House, a residence of Queen Victoria (who died here in 1901) near East Cowes, Isle of Wight.

Oscan, language of the Italic subfamily of the Indo-European languages. See LANGUAGE (table).

Oscar, Swedish kings. **Oscar I,** 1799–1859, king of

Sweden and Norway (1844–59); son of Charles XIV (Bernadotte). **Oscar II,** 1829–1907, succeeded his father Charles XV as king of Sweden and Norway in 1872 but lost Norway when it severed its union with Sweden (1905).

Osceola (ŏsēō'lù, ō–), c.1800–1838, leader of SEMINOLE INDIANS. Also called Powell, surname of his supposed white father. Led fight against U.S. troops (1835–37).

oscillator (ŏ'sĭlātûr), in electronics, circuit producing alternating audio-frequency or radio-frequency voltage. In transmitters, it generates carrier wave; in receivers, is used in SUPERHETERODYNE and superregenerative circuits and in heterodyne method of receiving unmodulated code transmission.

Osee (ōsē'), variant of HOSEA.

Ösel, Estonia: see SAARE.

Osgood, Herbert Levi, 1855–1918, American historian. Author *The American Colonies in the Seventeenth Century* (3 vols., 1904–7) and *The American Colonies in the Eighteenth Century* (4 vols., 1924).

Osh (ŏsh), city (pop. 33,315), Kirghiz SSR, in Fergana Valley. A major silk production center for the last thousand years, it is one of the oldest cities of central Asia. Has Oriental and Russian sections.

Oshawa (ŏ'shùwù), city (pop. 41,545), S Ont., Canada, on L. Ontario and ENE of Toronto. Has mfg. of automobiles, steel products, and woolen goods.

Oshkosh (ŏsh'kŏsh"), city (pop. 41,084), E Wis., on L. Winnebago where Upper Fox R. enters; settled 1836. Father Allouez visited site 1670; French fur-trading post estab. early 19th cent. Resort center with mfg. of woodwork, machinery, and clothing.

osier: see WILLOW.

Osijek (ō'sēyěk), Ger. *Esseg,* Hung. *Eszék,* city (pop. 50,398), NE Croatia, Yugoslavia; a port on Drava R. and chief city of Slavonia. Varied mfg.

Osiris (ōsī'rĭs), in Egyptian religion, god of the underworld. In a famous myth he was son of Keb (Earth) and Nut (Sky), husband of ISIS, and father of HORUS. He was slain by his evil brother Set (Night). Osiris was identified with forces of fertility, e.g., the sun and the Nile. He was also the creative force giving life to seeds and thus was linked with doctrine of immortality, a potent force in Egyptian life. The trio of Osiris, Isis, and Horus were long important in Egypt, and were later worshiped in Greece and Rome.

Oskaloosa (ŏskùlōō'sù), city (pop. 11,124), SE Iowa, ESE of Des Moines; settled 1843 by Quakers. Center of livestock, farm, and coal area with mfg. of food, clay, and metal products, and music publishing. Annual Quaker meeting.

Osler, Sir William (ō'slùr), 1849–1919, Canadian physician, renowned also as teacher and medical historian. Associated with Johns Hopkins Univ. (1889–1904) and Oxford (from 1905). Author of *The Principles and Practice of Medicine* (1892; 16th ed., 1947).

Oslo (ŏs'lō, ŏz'lō, Nor. ōōs'lōō), cap. and largest city of Norway, coterminous with Oslo co. (175 sq. mi.; pop. 417,238), SE Norway, at head of Oslo Fjord, a large inlet of the Skagerrak. Norway's commercial, industrial, and intellectual center; seat of a university (founded 1811), of a Lutheran bishop, and of Nobel Inst. Its busy harbor is kept ice free. Metalworking; mfg. of chemicals, clothing, paper and food products; brewing. Founded 1050 by Harold III, Oslo came under Hanseatic dominance in 14th cent. Rebuilt by Christian IV after destructive fire of 1624, it was called Christiania (or Kristiania) from then until 1925. It was under German occupation 1940–45. Built on modern lines, Oslo has fostered contemporary art in public projects, e.g., sculptures of VIGELAND in Frogner Park and new city hall (1950). Planned residential sections have eliminated slums. Points of interest include royal palace, the Storting (parliament), Folk Mus., ruins of Oslo's first cathedral (St. Hallvard), Akerskirke (12th-cent. church), and Akershus fortress (13th cent.).

Osman, caliph: see OTHMAN.

Osman I (ŏz'mùn, ŏsmän') or **Othman I** (ŏth'mùn, ŏthmän'), 1259–1326, leader of the Osmanli or Ottoman TURKS, who were named for him. Founded Ottoman dynasty (see OTTOMAN EMPIRE).

Osmeña, Sergio (sĕr'hēō ōsmā'nyä), 1878–, Filipino statesman. President 1944–46. Returned to Philippines with U.S. invasion forces in Oct., 1944.

osmium (ŏz'mēùm), metallic element (symbol = Os; see also ELEMENT, table). It has highest specific gravity of the elements, is hard to fuse, not affected by ordinary acids. Member of group of platinum metals.

osmosis (ŏsmō'sĭs), selective passage of fluids through semipermeable substance or membrane. Makes possible the absorption of water by plant roots and, in animals, passage of digested foods through walls of digestive tract into blood stream. Tendency is for less dense material to pass through membrane toward more dense material; water generally moves from place where its molecules are more numerous to where they are less so. Osmotic pressure develops as result of differences in concentrations of substance on opposite sides of membrane; it increases with heat.

Osnabrück (ŏz'nùbrōōk, Ger. ôs''näbrük'), city (pop. 108,900), Lower Saxony, NW Germany, on Hase R., linked by canal with Ems-Weser Canal. Inland port; industrial center (iron, steel, machinery, textiles, paper). Became episcopal see 8th cent.; later joined Hanseatic League; accepted Reformation 1543. For the treaty signed here 1648, see WESTPHALIA, PEACE OF. Under treaty of 1648, bishopric alternated between Catholics and Lutherans. It was secularized 1803, but Catholic diocese was restored 1858. Osnabrück passed to Hanover 1815 and shared its subsequent history. Much of its fine Gothic architecture was destroyed in World War II.

Osorno (ōsôr'nō), city (pop. 22,772), S central Chile, in the heart of the lake district. Founded 1558, it was destroyed by Araucanian Indians and was reestab. in 1776. It had large German immigration in latter half of 19th cent. and is a modern progressive city.

osprey (ŏs'prē), bird of prey found in most parts of world. American osprey or fish hawk is usually seen near large bodies of fresh or salt water. It has long, angular wings and white under parts.

Ossa, mountain, Greece: see PELION.

Ossetia (ōsē'shù), region, RSFSR and Georgian SSR, in central Greater Caucasus. On N slope is North Ossetian ASSR (3,550 sq. mi.; pop. c.450,000), RSFSR; cap. Dzhaudzhikau (formerly Vladikavkaz). On S slope is South Ossetian Autonomous Oblast [region] (1,500 sq. mi.; pop. c.116,000), Georgian SSR; cap. Stalinir. Ossetia produces fruit, wine, grain, cotton, lumber, and livestock. Silver, lead, and zinc are mined in N Ossetia. The Ossetians are an ancient people speaking an Iranian language. They are Moslem in N and Eastern Orthodox in S.

Ossian (ŏsh'ùn) or **Oisin** (ûshēn'), legendary Gaelic poet, supposed author of poems and tales about the exploits of his father, FINN MAC CUMHAIL, hero of the 3d cent. In 18th cent. James MACPHERSON produced forged "Ossianic" poems.

Ossietzky, Carl von (fũn ôsyĕt'skē), 1898–1938, German pacifist. Coeditor of antimilitaristic weekly *Weltbühne,* he led German peace movement after World War I, was imprisoned 1931–32, and held in a concentration camp 1933–36. The award to Ossietzky of the 1935 Nobel Peace Prize was sharply protested by the Nazi regime.

Ossining (ŏ'sùnĭng), village (pop. 16,098), SE N.Y., on Hudson R. and near Tarrytown; settled c.1750, named Sing Sing 1813–1901. Mfg. of machinery, clothing, wire, and paper goods. Seat of Sing Sing state prison, where T. M. OSBORNE and L. E. LAWES introduced notable reforms.

Ossipee (ŏ'sĭpē), resort town (pop. 1,412), E N.H., on Ossipee L. and E of L. Winnipesaukee. Whittier summered here.

Ossory, Thomas Butler, earl of: see BUTLER, family.

Ossory, anc. kingdom of Ireland, including Co. Kilkenny and parts of Co. Offaly and Co. Laoighise.

Ostade, Adriaen van (ä'drēän vän ô'städù), 1610–85, Dutch painter of everyday scenes of village life. Studied with Frans Hals. His brother **Isaac van Ostade,** 1621–49, was a landscape painter.

Ostend (ôstĕnd'), Flemish *Oostende,* Fr. *Ostende,* city (pop. 50,225), West Flanders prov., N Belgium; a port and resort on North Sea. Has large fishing fleet. Fortified 1583, it heroically resisted a Spanish siege (1601–4) but eventually surrendered. It was a German submarine base in World War I; in 1918 the British, in a daring raid, partially sealed off the harbors of Ostend and Zeebrugge by sinking ships at their entrances. Again used by the Germans in World War II, Ostend suffered some damage.

Ostend Manifesto, document drawn up in Oct., 1854, at Ostend, Belgium, by James Buchanan, American minister to Great Britain, J. Y. Mason, minister to France, and Pierre Soulé, minister to Spain. Outlined value of Cuba to U.S.; implied that if Spain refused to sell, U.S. might consider taking island by force. Widely denounced, manifesto was immediately repudiated by Secretary of State W. L. Marcy for U.S. government.

osteopathy (ôstēō'pùthē), system of therapy emphasizing manipulation, founded 1874 by A. T. Still. Based on principle that most ailments result from "structural derangement" of body. Osteopaths may usually prescribe drugs and perform surgery.

Ostergotland (ü'stùryût''länd), Swed. *Östergötlands län,* county and historic province (4,266 sq. mi.; pop. 347,-996), SE Sweden, E of Vattern L.; cap. Linköping. Agr., stock raising, lumbering, mining (iron, zinc).

Ostia (ô'stēù), anc. city, Italy, at the mouth of the Tiber. Founded (4th cent. B.C.) as protection for Rome, it became Rome's port. Declined after 3d cent. A.D.

Ostrava, Czechoslovakia: see MORAVSKA OSTRAVA.

ostrich (ô'strĭch), flightless bird of Africa and parts of SW Asia, allied to rhea, emu, moa. Largest of living birds. Head, neck, and thighs are scantily feathered; long, white plumes from wings and tail of male were formerly in great demand for trimming millinery, etc.

Ostrogoths (ô'strŭgŏths") or **East Goths,** division of the Goths, one of chief groups of anc. German peoples. Descended, according to unproved tradition, from the Gotar of S SWEDEN, the Goths by the 3d cent. A.D. were settled in region N of the Black Sea. They split into two divisions in the 4th cent. The VISIGOTHS, under pressure of the HUNS, moved W; the Ostrogoths were subjected by the Huns and served in their army. On Attila's death (453), they settled in Pannonia (modern Hungary) as allies of East Rome. In 493 their king THEODORIC THE GREAT, after conquering Italy from ODOACER, set up the Ostrogothic kingdom of Italy. The murder of his daughter AMALASUNTHA (535) gave Emperor Justinian I the pretext for reconquering Italy through his generals BELISARIUS and NARSES. Narses' victory over TOTILA (552) ended the kingdom of the Ostrogoths, who soon lost their ethnic identity. Although they had largely preserved Roman law and institutions, the Ostrogoths had clung to their Arian religion.

Ostroleka (ôstrôwĕ'kä), Pol. *Ostroleka,* Rus. *Ostrolenka,* town (pop. 9,279), Poland, on Narew R. Russians defeated Polish insurgents here in 1831.

Ostrovsky, Aleksandr Nikolayevich (ülyĭksän'dùr nyĭkùlì'ùvĭch üstrôf'skē), 1823–86, Russian dramatist. Most of his plays deal critically with the merchant and petty-official class. His chief plays, among which *The Storm* (1880) is best known, have been translated into English.

Ostrovsky, Nikolai Alekseyevich (nyĭkùlì' ülĭksyä'ĭvĭch), 1904–37, Russian novelist. *How the Steel Was Tempered* (1936; Eng. tr., *The Making of a Hero*), an autobiographical tale of the civil war, was one of the most popular of all the novels of Soviet literature.

Ostwald, Wilhelm (vĭl'hĕlm ôst'vält), 1853–1932, German chemist. Won 1909 Nobel Prize for work on catalysis and research on fundamental principles of equilibrium and rates of reaction. Invented **Ostwald process** for making nitric acid by oxidation of ammonia. Did outstanding research on color.

Oswego (ôswē'gō), city (pop. 22,647), N N.Y., on L. Ontario at Oswego R. mouth and NW of Syracuse, at N end of the Barge Canal; founded 1722 by English. Important lake port with mfg. of machinery, textiles, and matches. Early fur-trading post. Present Fort Ontario (1755) held alternately by French and British in colonial wars.

Oswego, river formed in central N.Y. by confluence of Oneida and Seneca rivers. Flows c. 23 mi. NW to L. Ontario at Oswego. Part of the Barge Canal.

Oswego tea or **bee balm,** aromatic perennial plant (*Monarda didyma*) of the mint family with showy heads of scarlet or salmon flowers. Indians and colonists made tea from the leaves.

Oswiecim (ôshfyĕ'chēm), Ger. *Auschwitz,* town (pop. 6,708), S Poland, E of Cracow. Here in World War II the Germans maintained a concentration camp where c.4,000,000 inmates, mostly Jews, were exterminated by gas, phenol injections, shooting, hanging, hunger, and disease.

Oswy or **Oswiu** (both: ôz'wē), d. 671, king of Northumbria. Continued conversion of England to Christianity and called Synod of WHITBY.

Otaru (ôtä'rōō), city (pop. 164,934), SW Hokkaido, Japan; chief coal-shipping port of island.

Othman (ôth'mùn, ōth'män) or **Osman** (ŏz'mùn), c.574–656, 3d caliph (644–56); son-in-law of Mohammed; of OMAYYAD family.

Othman I, Turkish leader: see OSMAN I.

Otho, Marcus Salvius (ô'thō), A.D. 32–A.D. 69, Roman emperor (A.D. 69). His wife, Poppaea Sabina, became NERO's mistress. He joined Galba against Nero, killed Galba, and was briefly emperor until defeated by Vitellius.

Otis, Elisha Graves, 1811–61, American inventor. From his invention (1854) of a device to prevent fall of hoisting machinery, he developed first passenger elevator (1857). Invention made feasible the building of skyscrapers and Otis's company became great industrial enterprise.

Otis, James, 1725–83, American colonial orator and patriot. Led radical wing of colonial opposition to British measures. Proposed Stamp Act Congress.

Oto Indians (ô'tō), North American tribe of Siouan linguistic stock, once a part of the Winnebago nation N of the Great Lakes, later in S Minn., then on the Platte R. In 1880–82 they migrated to Okla. They had a typical Plains culture. Also Otto.

Otranto (ôträn'tō, Ital. ô'träntō), town (pop. 2,507), Apulia, S Italy. Until its destruction by the Turks in 1480 it was a flourishing port on the Strait of Otranto, which connects the Adriatic with the Ionian Sea between Italy and Albania.

Otsego Lake (ôtsē'gō), 8 mi. long, E central N.Y., SE of Utica, in resort area. Susquehanna R. issues from S end at Cooperstown.

ottava rima: see PENTAMETER.

Ottawa (ô'tùwù), city (pop. 202,045), cap. of Canada, SE Ont., Canada, on Ottawa R. (bridge) opposite Hull, Que., WSW of Montreal. Industries include paper milling, woodworking, and watchmaking. Rideau Canal separates city into upper and lower sections. Parks and drives line canal and river banks. Founded 1827 and called Bytown until 1854. Became cap. of Canada in 1858 and cap. of the dominion in 1867. Places of interest include Parliament buildings, Natl. Victoria Mus., Natl. Art Gall., Royal Mint, Anglican and R.C. cathedrals, dominion observatory, and Rideau Hall (residence of governor general). Seat of Univ. of Ottawa (bilingual; R.C., pontifical; coed.; estab. 1848).

Ottawa. 1 City (pop. 16,957), N Ill., at junction of Illinois and Fox rivers; laid out 1830, settled 1832 after Black Hawk War. Coal mines, clay and sand pits in area. Mfg. of food, glass, and clay products and farm machinery. Scene of first Lincoln-Douglas debate 1858. Near by is Starved Rock. **2** City (pop. 10,081), E Kansas, SE of Topeka. Settled 1832 by Ottawa Indians, who moved to Okla. 1867. Baptist mission estab. 1837. Trade center for grain and poultry area.

Ottawa, river of Ont. and Que., Canada, 696 mi. long, largest tributary of the St. Lawrence. Rises in W Que. NE of North Bay and flows W, then SE to the St. Lawrence above Montreal forming the Ont.-Que. line for much of its length. Lower course has several expansions. Numerous rapids furnish hydroelectric power. Connects with L. Ontario by Rideau Canal system. Valley explored by Champlain 1613–15. As Grand R. it was important highway for fur traders, explorers, and missionaries.

Ottawa Indians, North American tribe of Algonquian linguistic stock, in the 17th cent. on Manitoulin Isl. in L. Huron and on the shores of Georgian Bay. Allied themselves with the French and were forced by the Iroquois to move to the W Great Lakes region. Under French protection they returned to Manitoulin (1670), later joined the Huron. Pontiac was an Ottawa Indian.

otter (ŏ′tŭr), aquatic carnivorous mammal of weasel family, found on all continents except Australia. North American otter has slender body, c.3½–4½ ft. long including heavy tail, a flat head, and webbed hind feet. The fur is valuable. **Sea otter** (*Enhydra*) of N Pacific is larger, heavier; swims on back. Hunted for fur, it is now protected in Alaskan waters.

Otter, Peaks of, two peaks, western Va., in Blue Ridge Mts., W of Lynchburg; 4,001 and 3,875 ft. high.

Otterbein, Philip William, 1726–1813, German-American clergyman, a founder of United Brethren in Christ. Missionary in America for German Reformed Church in 1752. With Martin Boehm he carried on evangelistic work in Pa. and Md. and helped lay foundation (1789) for new church. He was bishop in 1800.

Otterbein College: see WESTERVILLE, Ohio.

Otto, emperors and German kings. **Otto I** or **Otto the Great,** 912–73, succeeded his father Henry I as German king in 936. He defeated the rebellious nobles, led by Duke Eberhard of Franconia, at Andernach (939); interfered in French affairs (940–50); and invaded Italy (951). His pretext for that last move was the appeal addressed to him by Adelaide or Adelheid, widow of King Hugh of Italy, who was about to be forced into marriage with the son of BERENGAR II. Otto forced Berengar to become his vassal, took the title king of the Lombards, married Adelaide, and returned to Germany. Another rebellion, led by CONRAD THE RED of Lorraine, broke up under the threat of invasion by the Magyars, whom Otto routed at the Lechfeld (955). Meanwhile Berengar II had resumed his aggressions. Pope JOHN XII appealed to Otto, who entered Rome and was crowned emperor by the pope (962). This union of Germany and Italy under the imperial crown created the HOLY ROMAN EMPIRE; it also began the long struggle between emperors and popes, as Otto's subsequent struggle with John XII and the Romans shows. Otto's reign saw the expansion and growing commercial prosperity of the German towns. He was succeeded as German king by his son **Otto II,** 955–83. He married the Byzantine princess Theophano (972) and in 980 was crowned emperor at Rome. Successful in putting down internal rebellions and in checking Danish and Bohemian inroads (974–77), he was disastrously defeated by the Arabs in Calabria (982). His son **Otto III,** 980–1002, was elected German king just before Otto II's death. The regency was held by his mother Theophano and later by his grandmother Adelaide. In 996 he estab. his cousin Bruno as Pope Gregory V; in 999 he made his tutor Gerbert pope as SYLVESTER II. Crowned emperor in 996, he keenly felt his high position as scion of both the Eastern and Western imperial houses. He resided at Rome after 998 and seriously set about acting like an ancient Roman emperor, which made him unpopular both in Germany and in Italy. In 1001 a Roman mob forced him to flee to Sicily, where he died. **Otto IV,** 1182?–1218, second son of HENRY THE LION of Saxony, was chosen antiking to PHILIP OF SWABIA in 1198, was reelected king after Philip's death in 1208, and was crowned emperor at Rome in 1209. Though he had acknowledged the papacy's rights to the Papal States and Sicily in 1208, he later disregarded his commitments, seized the lands of MATILDA of Tuscany (1210), and invaded Apulia. Pope INNOCENT III excommunicated him, and part of the German nobles rebelled and elected Frederick of Hohenstaufen (later Emperor FREDERICK II) as king. In the ensuing war Otto was supported by his uncle, King John of England, but was defeated at Bouvines by Philip II of France (1214). He was deposed in 1215 and retired to Saxony.

Otto I, 1848–1916, king of Bavaria (1886–1913); brother of Louis II. Incurably insane from 1872. His uncle Luitpold was regent 1886–1912; Luitpold's son, regent from 1912, deposed Otto and became king as Louis III.

Otto I, 1815–67, first king of the Hellenes (1832–62); second son of Louis I of Bavaria. Was placed on Greek throne by Great Powers. An uprising forced him to adopt a constitution (1843). Was deposed 1862.

Otto, 1912–, Austrian archduke and pretender to the Austro-Hungarian throne; son of Emperor Charles I and Empress Zita.

Otto, Nikolaus August nē′kōlous ou′gŏost ô′tō), 1832–91, German engineer. He was coinventor (1867) of an internal-combustion engine and devised (1876) four-stroke Otto cycle widely adopted for motors.

Ottocar, kings of Bohemia, of the PREMYSL dynasty. **Ottocar I,** d. 1230, became duke of Bohemia in 1197 and in 1198 was given the title king by Philip of Swabia. His grandson **Ottocar II,** d. 1278, reigned 1253–78. By marriage, conquest, and diplomacy he acquired Austria (1251), Styria (1260), and Carinthia, Carniola, and Istria (1269). In Bohemia, he encouraged the growth of the towns and sought to reduce the power of the nobles. His ambition was to act as arbiter of the Holy Roman Empire, but the election in 1273 of Rudolf of Hapsburg (see RUDOLF I) as German king proved Ottocar's undoing. Having contested Rudolf's election, he was declared forfeit of his dominions (1274), and in 1276 he was forced to surrender all but Bohemia and Moravia to Rudolf. A new war with Rudolf ended with Ottocar's defeat and death on the MARCHFELD, scene of Ottocar's earlier victory over Bela IV of Hungary.

Otto Indians: see OTO INDIANS.

Ottoman Empire (ŏ′tŭmùn), greatest of Moslem states, formed (14th–16th cent.) in Near East by the Ottoman or Osmanli TURKS after the breakdown of the Seljuk empire. It was also called Turkey, but modern Turkey formed only a part of it. The Ottoman state emerged and expanded under OSMAN I (founder of the empire's dynasty), MURAD I, and BAJAZET I at the expense of the Byzantine Empire, Bulgaria, and Serbia. After their victories at BURSA (1326), KOSSOVO (1389), and NIKOPOL (1396), the Turks were only temporarily checked by TAMERLANE (1402). In 1453 MOHAMMED II conquered CONSTANTINOPLE and became heir to the Byzantine Empire. The Ottoman Empire reached its height in the 16th cent. under SELIM I, who assumed the CALIPHATE after his victories in Syria and Egypt (1516–17), and under SULEIMAN I (the Magnificent). Algiers, most of Greece and Hungary, and much of Persia and Arabia had come under Turkish rule; Transylvania, Walachia, and Moldavia had become tributary principalities. However, in every respect Turkey remained a medieval state, with its Byzantine-Asiatic despotic system mitigated only by observance of Moslem law. Decline began with Suleiman's death. Militarily, the first setback was the naval defeat at LEPANTO (1571), but the decisive blow was the repulse of the Turkish siege of Vienna (1683), followed 1699 by the Treaty of KARLOWITZ. Political decay set in—e.g., the JANIZARIES made and unmade sultans; corruption and bribery were raised to a system of administration. The breakup of the state was accelerated by the RUSSO-TURKISH WARS of the 18th cent. After the Greek War of Independence the fate of the "Sick Man of Europe" became a major European concern; the Western Powers feared Russian expansion (see EASTERN QUESTION) and loss of their investments in Turkey, which in a series of treaties, called capitulations, had virtually surrendered its economic independence to them. Civil reforms were attempted. MIDHAT PASHA framed a constitution (1876), but ABDU-L-HAMID II soon abolished it. In 1908 the Young Turks, a reformist and nationalist movement, forced the restoration of the constitution, but the dissolution of the empire was beyond remedy. With much of its territory already lost, most of remaining European Turkey went in the BALKAN WARS (1912–13). ENVER PASHA, leader of the Young Turks, assumed dictatorial powers in 1913. In World War I Turkey was allied with Germany. Turkish troops were successful in the GALLIPOLI CAMPAIGN (1915), but in 1918 all resistance collapsed, and the Treaty of SÈVRES confirmed the dissolution of the empire. With the overthrow of the last sultan by Ataturk (1922) the history of modern TURKEY began.

Otto of Freising (frī'zǐng), d. 1158, German chronicler, bishop of Freising. Wrote world history to 1146, *The Two Cities*, a most valuable source book.

Otto the Great: see OTTO I, emperor.

Ottumwa (ŏtŭm'wŭ), city (pop. 33,631), SE Iowa, on Des Moines R. and SE of Des Moines; settled 1843. Rail and industrial center of farm and coal area with mfg. of food and metal products.

Otway, Thomas, 1652–85, English dramatist. His plays *The Orphan* (1680) and *Venice Preserved* (1682) reach highest point of pathetic tragedy in Restoration drama. His genius lay in portraying heights of passion and love and depths of misery and despair.

Ötztal Alps (ûts'täl), mountain group, Tyrol, W Austria, S of the Inn. Wildspitze (12,379 ft.) is highest peak in Tyrol.

Ouachita (wŏ'shĭtô''), river rising in W Ark. in Ouachita Mts. and flowing c.605 mi. SE into NE La., becoming part of Red R. system. Partially navigable. Lakes Hamilton and Catherine were created by Carpenter (1931) and Remmel (1924) dams.

Ouachita Mountains, range S of Arkansas R., extending from central Ark. into SE Okla., and rising to 2,800 ft. in Mt. Magazine. Several public parks and forest reservations in region.

Ouchy, Switzerland: see LAUSANNE.

Oud, J(acobus) J(ohannes) P(ieter) (out'), 1890–, Dutch architect, who influenced growth of modern architecture. Associated with Mondrian.

Oude Maas, Dutch name of Old MEUSE, river.

Oudenarde (ōō'dŭnärd, ou'–), Fr. *Audenarde,* town (pop. 6,567), East Flanders prov., NW Belgium, on the Scheldt. Here Marlborough and Eugene of Savoy defeated the French under Vendôme (1708).

Oudh, province, India: see UTTAR PRADESH.

Oudjda, French Morocco: see OUJDA.

Oudry, Jean Baptiste (zhä' bätēst' ōōdrē'), 1686–1755, French animal painter, who served Louis XV. Illustrated La Fontaine's *Fables.*

Ouessant, French island: see USHANT.

Ouida (wē'dŭ), pseud. of Louise de la Ramée (dù lä rùmä'), 1839–1908, English writer of sentimental romantic novels (e.g., *Under Two Flags,* 1867; *A Dog of Flanders,* 1872).

Oujda or Oudjda (both: ōōjdä'), city (pop. 88,658), NE French Morocco, near Algerian border; founded 10th cent. Under French rule since 1907. Important rail junction and trade center.

Oulu (ō'lōō), Swed. *Uleåborg,* city (pop. 38,703), NW Finland; a Baltic seaport on Gulf of Bothnia and at mouth of Oulu R. Shipyards; lumber and cellulose mfg. City grew around castle which was founded by Swedes in 1375.

Ouray (ōōrā', yōōrā'), city (pop. 1,089; alt. c.7,800 ft.), SW Colo., on Uncompahgre R. Health resort.

Ourcq (ōōrk), river, 50 mi. long, N France, a tributary of the Marne. Crosses CHÂTEAU-THIERRY battlefield of World War I.

Our Father: see LORD'S PRAYER.

Ourique (ōrēk'), town (pop. 1,378), SE Portugal, in Alentejo, S of Beja. According to tradition, it was the scene of the great victory of Alfonso I of Portugal over the Moors (1139); actually, battle took place elsewhere, probably near Santarém.

Ouro Prêto (ō'rōō prā'tōō) [Port.,= black gold], city (pop. 8,819), in Minas Gerais state, E Brazil, in mountains SE of Belo Horizonte. An important gold-mining center in 18th cent., is now almost a ghost city; with its former grandeur it is kept as a national museum.

Ouse (ōōz), rivers in England. **1** Also called **Great Ouse.** Flows 156 mi., through six counties, from Oxfordshire to the Wash. **2** Sussex, flows 30 mi. to English Channel at Newhaven. **3** Yorkshire, formed by confluence of Ure and Swale rivers NW of York; flows 45 mi. to join Trent R. and form the Humber.

Outardes (ōō'tärd'), river of E central Que., Canada, rising in Otish Mts. and flowing 300 mi. S to St. Lawrence R. SW of Baie Comeau.

Outer Hebrides, Scotland: see HEBRIDES.

Outer Mongolia: see MONGOLIA.

Outremont (ōōtrŭmô'), city (pop. 30,057), S Que., Canada, on Montreal Isl., NW suburb of Montreal.

ovary (ō'vŭrē), female reproductive gland in which eggs (ova) are formed. In humans and higher vertebrates there are two ovaries, one on each side of uterus. These secrete hormones which function in control of menstruation and mammary gland development. From puberty successive eggs mature; one is released about every 28 days.

ovenbird, name in North America for a bird of wood warbler family, whose nests resemble Dutch ovens. In South America, it is name for several species of thrush-like birds.

Overbeck, Johann Friedrich (yō'hän frē'drĭkh ō'vŭrbĕk), 1789–1869, German religious painter, a member of the NAZARENES.

Overbury, Sir Thomas, 1581–1613, English author of verse and informal essays. Among his works are a poem, *A Wife* (1614), and sketches called "characters," describing types and individuals. He was murdered in prison; his former friend, Robert Carr, earl of Somerset, and Carr's wife were convicted of the crime but pardoned by the king's favor.

Overijssel (ō'vŭrī'sùl), province (1,254.6 sq. mi.; pop. 638,797), NE Netherlands, between the Ijsselmeer (W) and Germany (E); cap. Zwolle. Drained by Ijssel R. and several canals. Stock raising, dairying, textiles, machinery. Under bishops of Utrecht in Middle Ages, it was sold to Emperor Charles V in 1527. Joined Union of Utrecht 1579. It is also spelled Overyssel.

Overland Trail, name given to several trails of westward migration in U.S. Sometimes used to mean all trails W from the Missouri to the Pacific and sometimes for central trails only. Particularly, term is applied to southern alternate route of Oregon Trail. Term also particularly applied to a route to Calif. going W from Fort Bridger.

overture, instrumental music written as an introduction to a stage work or oratorio. The early opera overture was simply a piece of symphonic music; in Gluck's time, it began to foreshadow what was to come in the opera. By the 19th cent. it was often just a potpourri of the opera's tunes. The concert overture is a separate work. Those of Mendelssohn, Beethoven, and Brahms are especially popular.

Overyssel, Netherlands: see OVERIJSSEL.

Ovid (Publius Ovidius Naso) (ŏ'vĭd), 43 B.C.–A.D. 18, Latin poet, always popular for his imaginative and facile verse. His poems, which reflect his ideal of poetry as the ministry of pleasure, fall into three groups —erotic poems (notably the *Art of Love,* in masterful elegiacs), mythological poems (notably *Metamorphoses,* his greatest work, in hexameters), and poems of exile (he was mysteriously exiled in A.D. 8 to a Black Sea outpost, where he died).

Oviedo (ōvyā'dhō), city (pop. 51,410), cap. of Asturias, N Spain, near iron-mining dist. of Cantabrian Mts. Armaments factories; chemical plants; distilleries. Flourished in 9th cent. as cap. of Asturian kings. Has famous cathedral (begun 1388) and Cámara Santa (9th and 11th cent.), containing cathedral's relics and treasures. University was founded 1604.

Ovoca: see AVOCA, river.

ovum, in biology, female sexual cell produced in ovary. In higher animals it is larger than male sexual cell (sperm) because of stored food and it is nonmotile. Before fertilization ovum undergoes maturation divisions; these include reduction division (meiosis; see MITOSIS) by which chromosomes are reduced to one half number normally present in cells. Union of mature ovum and sperm (fertilization) results in single cell with full number of chromosomes. Successive cell divisions result in development of new individual. Reproductive cells undergo similar processes in plants. Term *egg* commonly is used also for complex structure such as bird's egg, in which yolk is ovum swollen by stored food and rest of egg is secreted in oviduct. Development from unfertilized ovum is called PARTHENOGENESIS.

Owasco Lake: see FINGER LAKES.

Owatonna (ōwŭtŏ'nù), city (pop. 10,191), SE Minn., S of St. Paul; settled in early 1850s. Center for farm region with mineral springs. Produces dairy products and farm equipment.

Owego (ōwē'gō), village (pop. 5,350), S N.Y., on Susquehanna R. and W of Binghamton. Shoes, furniture.

Owen, John, 1616–83, English Puritan divine and theologian. At Oxford he became Presbyterian, but later was Congregationalist. In civil war he supported Parliament. Later made dean of Christ Church, Oxford (1651) and vice chancellor of university (1652).

Owen, Robert, 1771–1858, British social reformer and socialist, pioneer in the cooperative movement. A successful cotton manufacturer of New Lanark, Scotland, he reconstructed the community into a model industrial town, with nonprofitmaking stores and, for the time, excellent working conditions. The Factory Act of 1819 was instigated by him. He estab. (1825) the ill-fated community of NEW HARMONY, Ind., promoted the Natl. Equitable Labor Exchange and other cooperative societies trading goods for labor, and assisted the trade-union movement. His son, **Robert Dale Owen,** 1801–77, became a social reformer in the U.S. At NEW HARMONY he met Frances WRIGHT, with whom he estab. (1829) the New York *Free Enquirer.* In 1830 he advocated birth control publicly for the first time in America. He was a member of Congress, favored emancipation of slaves, helped found the Smithsonian Inst., and served as minister to Naples.

Owen, Ruth Bryan, 1885–, U.S. minister to Denmark (1933–36); daughter of W. J. Bryan. First woman minister of U.S. Married Reginald Owen in 1910; later married Boerge Rohde of Danish army.

Owen Glendower (glĕn'dou"ùr, glĕndou'ùr), 1359?–1416?, Welsh leader. Allied with the Percy family, he led revolt against Henry IV. Recognized as prince of Wales by Scotland and France. Weakened by military failures, he disappeared into the mountains.

Owens, Jesse, 1915–, American Negro track star. At 1936 Olympic games at Berlin he equaled world record (10.3 sec.) in 100-meter race, set new records in 200-meter race (20.7 sec.), broad jump (26 ft. 5²¹⁄₆₄ in.).

Owens, river, E Calif., rising in the Sierra Nevada SE of Yosemite Natl. Park and flowing c.120 mi. SSE,

nominally to enter Owens L. (now nearly dry), near Mt. Whitney. At point above lake, aqueduct diverts most of river's water to Los Angeles.

Owensboro, city (pop. 33,651), W Ky., on Ohio R. and SW of Louisville; settled c.1800. Center of agr., oil, coal, and tobacco area with mfg. of electrical equipment, foodstuffs, and whisky.

Owen Sound, city (pop. 16,423), S Ont., Canada, on Owen Sound of Georgian Bay and NW of Toronto. Port and railroad terminal in farm region.

Owen Stanley Range, on SE New Guinea, containing Mt. Victoria (13,240 ft.), highest peak of Territory of Papua. Japanese attempt in 1942 to reach Port Moresby through mountain pass was checked by Allies.

owl, chiefly nocturnal bird of prey found in most parts of world; related to nighthawk and whippoorwill. Order of owls is divided into barn owl family (those with heart-shaped faces) and family including all other species.

Owl and the Nightingale, The, Middle English poem written c.1200, probably by a Nicholas de Guildford of Dorsetshire. It is a humorous debate between the birds as to their respective merits.

Owosso (ōwŏ'sō), city (pop. 15,948), S Mich., on Shiawassee R. and NE of Lansing; settled c.1835. Mfg. of machinery. Here are Indian relics and birthplace of T. E. Dewey.

Owyhee (ōwī'ē), river rising in SW Idaho, N Nev., SE Oregon, and flowing 170 mi. NE across SE Oregon to Snake R. near Nyssa. Owyhee power and irrigation project (estab. 1928), W of the Snake, improves 82,000 acres in Oregon near Owyhee R. mouth, and 30,500 acres in SW Idaho near Homedale; is contiguous with BOISE PROJECT and project at Vale. Owyhee Dam, SW of Nyssa, is 417 ft. high, 833 ft. long, forms reservoir 48 mi. long.

oxalic acid (ŏksä'lĭk), strong, poisonous, organic acid, a colorless crystalline solid with a sour taste. It is present (usually in harmless quantities) in many plants either as the acid or in the form of some of its many salts. It is used in bleaching, in printing cloth, and removing stains.

oxalis (ŏk'sùlĭs) or **wood sorrel,** low-growing plant of genus *Oxalis,* widely distributed. Most species have cloverlike leaves, dainty flowers, and tuberous roots, sometimes used for food in South America. The European wood sorrel (*Oxalis acetosella*) is one of the plants identified as the SHAMROCK.

oxbow lake, stagnant lake formed in old bed when river cuts through the neck of a meander or loop.

Oxenstierna, Count Axel Gustavsson (ŏk'sùnstûr"nù, Swed. äk'sùl gŭs'täfsôn ōōk'sùnshĕr"nä), 1583–1654, chancellor of Sweden (1612–54), a leading figure in the THIRTY YEARS WAR. During the reign of GUSTAVUS II he controlled the administration, organized the territories conquered by his king, and proved a successful diplomat. Though originally opposed to Sweden's entry into the Thirty Years War, he directed the war in Germany after Gustavus's death (1632) and secured open French intervention (1636). He virtually ruled Sweden during the minority of CHRISTINA (1632–44); instituted far-reaching reforms; and centralized the administration. He often clashed with the queen but opposed her abdication (1654).

Oxford, Edward de Vere, 17th earl of, 1550–1604, English poet, supposed by a few to have written Shakspere's plays.

Oxford, Robert Harley, 1st earl of: see HARLEY.

Oxford, county, England: see OXFORDSHIRE.

Oxford, Latin *Oxonia,* city (pop. 98,675), co. seat of Oxfordshire, England, on the Thames or Isis R. Site of OXFORD UNIVERSITY. Was royalist capital in civil wars. Historic buildings (other than colleges) include Radcliffe Observatory, Sheldonian Theatre (Wren), and old churches and inns. Has important automobile mfg. at suburb Cowley and Iffley.

Oxford. 1 Town (pop. 5,851), S Mass., SSW of Worcester. Mfg. of wooden boxes and woolens. **2** City pop. 3,956), N central Miss., SE of Memphis, Tenn. Seat of Univ. of Mississippi (state supported; coed.; 1844; liberal arts college). Home of William Faulkner. **3** Town (pop. 6,685), N N.C., N of Raleigh. Markets tobacco and has mfg. of yarn and furniture. **4** City (pop. 6,944), SW Ohio, NW of Hamilton. Seat of Miami Univ. (state supported; coed.; chartered 1809, opened 1824; W. H. McGuffey taught here), and Western Col. (for women; 1853).

Oxford, Provisions of: see PROVISIONS OF OXFORD.

Oxford and Asquith, Herbert Henry Asquith, 1st earl of, 1852–1928, British statesman. Prime minister 1908–16, he saw triumphs of LIBERAL PARTY. Social-insurance program was started after power of House of Lords was broken. Attempts were made to establish Irish Home Rule. World War I brought his downfall in favor of David Lloyd George. His second wife, **Margot (Tennant) Asquith, countess of Oxford and Asquith,** 1864–1945, was noted for her wit. Author of a frank autobiography, a novel, and several volumes of personal reminiscences.

Oxford Group: see BUCHMAN, FRANK N. D.

Oxford movement, known first as Tractarian movement, an attempt to revitalize Established Church. It began in Oriel Col., Oxford, among spiritual leaders, notably J. H. NEWMAN, John KEBLE, and R. H. Froude. Keble, whose *Christian Year* had appeared in 1827, preached in July, 1833, a sermon *On the National Apostasy,* which Newman considered the start of the movement. Newman, with Keble and E. B. PUSEY, launched a series of pamphlets, *Tracts for the Times,* which preached Anglicanism as *via media* between Catholicism and evangelicalism. Newman was chief defending advocate. Pusey stressed observance of ritual, earning for the movement the name of "Puseyism." Newman's *Tract 90* on Thirty-nine Articles was counted "perilous to the peace of the Church" and brought series to an end (1841). The movement lost valuable supporters, among them Newman, in secession to the Church of Rome in 1842. This trend was checked by Pusey, whose leadership effected firm organization. Movement eventually spread into Scotland and Wales and overseas. Clergy made changes such as intoning sermons, wearing vestments in chancel, and facing east while praying. Hence group became known as "ritualists," and also as Anglo-Catholics.

Oxfordshire or **Oxford,** inland county (748 sq. mi.; pop. 275,765), S central England. County town is Oxford, seat of the university and an automobile mfg. center. Mostly flat terrain, drained by the Thames (or Isis, the local name). Farming is chief occupation. Blenheim Palace is at Woodstock.

Oxford University, Oxford, England, one of the two ancient English universities. Began in early 12th cent. Residential college system (see CAMBRIDGE UNIVERSITY) began in 1264 with Merton Col. A center of learning throughout Middle Ages, the medieval college maintained (and still does) almost complete autonomy within the university. The colleges are University (1249), Balliol (1263), Merton (1264), St. Edmund Hall (1269), Exeter (1314), Oriel (1326), Queen's (1340), New (1379), Lincoln (1427), All Souls (1437), Magdalen (1458; pronounced môd'-lĭn), Brasenose (1509; pronounced brāz'nōz), Corpus Christi (1516), Christ Church (1546), Trinity (1554), St. John's (1555), Jesus (1571), Wadham (1610, charter received 1612), Pembroke (1624), Worcester (1714), Keble (1871) and Hertford (1874). Women's colleges are Lady Margaret Hall (1878), Somerville (1879), St. Hugh's (1886), and St. Hilda's (1893). Oxford has eleven faculties and has led in the classics, theology, and political science. Oxford Union is world's most famous debating club. Ashmolean Mus. and BODLEIAN LIBRARY are notable. Instruction is by lectures and tutorial system. Cecil J. RHODES left large sum for scholarships.

oxidation and reduction. Originally oxidation indicated reaction in which oxygen and some other substance combined; reduction, the removal of oxygen from substance. Rapid oxidation is COMBUSTION. Terms were later redefined on basis of electron theory: when substance loses electrons and increases positive valence, this is termed oxidation and substance causing it is an oxidizing agent. Also, when substance gains electrons and increases its negative valence, it is said to be reduced and the substance causing this change is a reducing agent. Oxygen need not be involved in either reaction. When oxidation of a substance occurs, it is accompanied by reduction of another substance.

oxide (ŏk'sīd), compound of oxygen and some other elemental substance. Oxygen combines directly with many other elements; these binary compounds (composed of two substances) occur abundantly and widely distributed in nature. Monoxides, dioxides, and trioxides are named according to number of oxygen atoms in molecule. Oxides may be acidic or basic oxides or anhydrides. Oxides of metals may be acidic, basic, neutral, or amphoteric (i.e., react with both acids and bases). Inert gases do not form oxides; halogens and inactive metals do not combine directly with oxygen, but oxides can be formed by indirect methods.

Oxnam, G(arfield) Bromley, 1891–, American Methodist bishop; president (1928–36) of DePauw Univ. Bishop of Omaha (1936–39), of Boston (1939–44), of New York (1944); a president of the World Council of Churches.

Oxnard, city (pop. 26,353), S Calif., near coast and WNW of Los Angeles; founded 1898. Processes beet sugar, fruit, and oil. Mfg. of implements.

Oxonia, Latin name of OXFORD, England.

Oxus: see AMU DARYA.

oxyacetylene flame (ŏk"sēŭsĕt'ŭlēn), Acetylene flame is hot and luminous, combines with oxygen to liberate enormous amount of heat. **Oxyacetylene torch** is designed to supply proper amount of oxygen to acetylene flame. It is used in cutting steel and in welding various metals.

oxygen, colorless, odorless, tasteless gaseous element (symbol = O; see also ELEMENT, table). It is heavier than air, slightly soluble in water, and a poor conductor; it supports combustion but does not burn. Active and important chemically, it is involved in OXIDATION, COMBUSTION, RESPIRATION, rusting, and corrosion. It is the most abundant element, forms many compounds, and is present in all living things (since it is a constituent of protoplasm) and in the atmosphere. OZONE is an allotropic form. **Heavy oxygen** is name for two isotopes of oxygen of mass 17 and 18.

Oxyrhynchus (ŏk"sīrĭng'kŭs), place, Upper Egypt, near the Fayum where in 1896–97, 1906–7 a great number of papyri were found, mostly Roman and Byzantine.

oyster, edible mollusk (*Ostrea*) found in beds in coastal waters of most temperate regions. Shell consists of two unequal valves with rough outer surface. Sexes in some species are separate, in others united in one individual. Each female lays 5–50 million eggs, larva swims about before attaching itself to rough surface. Pearl oyster is of another family.

Oyster Bay, town (pop. 66,930), SE N.Y. on arm of Long Island Sound and W of Huntington. Includes resort and residential villages, e.g., Oyster Bay (pop. 5,215). Oyster industry is important. Park and bird sanctuary are memorials to Theodore Roosevelt, whose home was "Sagamore Hill."

Ozaki, Yukio (yōō'kyō ōzä'kē), 1859–, Japanese statesman, the outstanding liberal of modern Japan. Helped form the Kaishinto (reform party); joined Seiyukai party in 1900. Fought for universal manhood suffrage. After 1931 he was almost alone in protest against Japanese militarism in China.

Ozanam, Antoine Frédéric (ätwän' frādārēk' ōzänäm'), 1813–53, French Catholic scholar. A leader of 19th-cent. Catholic social thought, and a founder of the St. Vincent de Paul Society (1833), he also wrote notable works on early medieval history and on medieval literature and thought.

Ozark (ō′zärk), city (pop. 5,238), SE Ala., NW of Dothan, in diversified farm area.

Ozark Mountains, dissected plateau, c.50,000 sq. mi., chiefly in Mo., but partly in Ark., Okla., and Kansas, lying between Arkansas and Missouri rivers. Averaging 2,000 ft. in altitude, plateau slopes gently into the plains: BOSTON MOUNTAINS are highest, most rugged sector. Minerals (lead, zinc) are present; there is some fruit growing. Scenery, forests, and mineral springs make region a resort.

Ozarks, Lake of the, central Mo. Created by BAGNELL DAM in Osage R., it is c.130 mi. long and of irregular shape. The lake offers numerous recreation facilities.

ozocerite (ōzō′kŭrīt, –sŭrīt), waxy solid mixture of hydrocarbons, a mineral wax occurring in rock deposits. Used as substitute for beeswax; adulterant; in making candles, hard-rubber substitutes, and polishes; and in electrotyping.

ozone (ō′zōn), allotropic form of oxygen with molecule consisting of three oxygen atoms. It is an unstable, bluish gas with a fresh penetrating odor, more active than oxygen and one and one-half times as heavy. It is formed when an electrical discharge passes through oxygen and is present in air after electrical storms. It is used as a bleach and in purifying water and air.

P, chemical symbol of the element PHOSPHORUS.

Pa, chemical symbol of the element PROTACTINIUM.

Pacher, Michael (mĭkh′äĕl pä′khŭr), c.1435–1498, German religious painter and wood carver; native of the Tyrol. Famous for grand altarpiece at Sankt Wolfgang, Austria.

Pachuca (pächoo′kä), city (pop. 53,345), cap. of Hidalgo, central Mexico; founded (1534) on site of anc. Toltec city. Region has richest silver deposits in Mexico, mined since Aztec days.

Pacific, College of the: see STOCKTON, Calif.

Pacific, War of the, 1879–84, war between Chile and allied nations, Peru and Bolivia. Trouble began when in 1879 the president of Bolivia rescinded the contract that had given a Chilean company the right to exploit nitrate deposits in Atacama prov. Chile took port of Antofagasta, and war was declared. Peru, bound by a defensive alliance to Bolivia, became involved. Chile was victorious, and separate treaties were signed—Treaty of Ancón (1883) between Peru and Chile and a truce (1884) and final treaty (1904) between Chile and Bolivia. Chile acquired from Bolivia, prov. of Atacama (now Antofagasta) and from Peru, control of provs. of Tacna and Arica (See TACNA-ARICA CONTROVERSY).

Pacific Grove, residential and resort city (pop. 9,623), W Calif., on Monterey Bay. Has Hopkins Marine Laboratory of Stanford Univ.

Pacific Islands, Trust Territory of the (685 sq. mi.; pop. 53,900), consisting of CAROLINE ISLANDS, MARSHALL ISLANDS, MARIANAS ISLANDS, held by U.S. under UN trusteeship (since 1947).

Pacific Ocean, largest ocean, c.70,000,000 sq. mi.; max. length, c.7,000 mi.; greatest width, c.11,000 mi. Named by Magellan (1520). Its numerous islands are concentrated in S and W. The deepest ocean, its average depth is c.14,000 ft.; greatest known ocean depth (35,-400 ft.) is off Mindanao. Chief Pacific currents are N and S equatorial, East Australian, Humboldt (or Peru), Japan and California currents; West Wind and North Pacific drifts. Recognition of the Pacific as distinct from the Atlantic dates from Balboa's discovery of its eastern shore (1513). In 16th cent. supremacy in Pacific area was shared by Spain and Portugal; English, Dutch foothold was estab. in 17th cent.;

French, Russian in 18th; German, Japanese, and U.S. in 19th cent. Desire to exploit Pacific commerce was a factor in U.S. westward expansion. Area has great strategic importance.

Pacific scandal, 1873, a major event in Canadian political history. Charges were made that Conservative administration of Sir J. A. Macdonald had accepted campaign funds from Sir Hugh Allan in return for promise to award his syndicate contract to build Canadian Pacific Railway. Government was forced to resign, and Conservative party was badly defeated in ensuing elections.

pacifism (pă′sĭfĭzŭm), advocacy of suppression of war by individual or collective obstruction of militarism. Although complete, enduring peace is goal of all pacifists, methods differ. Some oppose international war, but advocate revolution for suppressed nationalities; others countenance defensive but not offensive war; still others oppose all war, but accept police force; a few believe in no coercive, disciplinary force at all. Line is often drawn between advocates of absolute peace, pacifists, and those who would prevent war by international cooperation, internationalists (SEE PEACE CONGRESSES). In all peace movements religion has been potent force, on basis that willful taking of human life is evil. Strong pacifistic elements exist in Eastern religions and in Christianity, later sects of which like Quakers, Moravians, and Dukhobors advocate nonresistance. Humanitarian and economic motives have also played a part. Peace associations and movements have been numerous in 19th and 20th cent. Award of Nobel Peace Prize has encouraged pacifist thought, as have life and teachings of Mohandas K. GANDHI in India. Among many groups working for peace are Carnegie Endowment for Internatl. Peace, Women's Internatl. League for Peace and Freedom, World Peace Foundation, Natl. Council for Prevention of War, and Natl. Peace Foundation (London).

packing industry: see MEAT PACKING.

Pactolus (păktō′lŭs), small river of anc. Lydia, W central Asia Minor (now Turkey). Famous for gold washed from its sands.

paddlefish, scaleless, fresh-water fish of Mississippi valley. It is also called duckbill because of long paddle-shaped snout. Sometimes is 6 ft. long and over 150 lb.

Paderborn (pä"dürbôrn'), city (pop. 40,440), North Rhine–Westphalia, NW Germany, in Westphalia. Archiepiscopal see (since 1930). Became episcopal see c.800. Under Holy Roman Empire prince-bishops ruled large area until secularization (1803). City, once famed for medieval and baroque architecture, was largely destroyed in World War II.

Paderewski, Ignace Jan (pädŭrĕf'skē), 1860–1941, Polish pianist and statesman. His world-wide popularity exceeded that of any pianist since Liszt; he made his American debut in 1891. He represented Poland at the Versailles peace table (1919) and was for 10 months premier of a coalition ministry. In addition to his famous Minuet in G, he composed two symphonies, a piano concerto, and an opera, *Manon*.

Padilla, Juan de (hwän' dä pädhē'lyä), c.1490–1521, Spanish revolutionary leader in the war of the *comunidades* [municipalities] against Emperor Charles V (1520–21). Rising against Charles's oppressive taxation, Toledo, Segovia, and other Castilian cities demanded severe limitations on the royal power, and together formed a provisional government under the Santa Junta, but the movement soon degenerated into class warfare. Padilla's army was defeated at Villalar (1521), and he was executed.

Padua (pä'dūŭ), Ital. *Padova*, city (pop. 90,325), Venetia, NE Italy. Commercial and transportation center. The ancient Patavium, it has flourished since Roman times and won its greatest fame through its university (founded 1222), which had the first anatomy hall in Europe and where Galileo taught. It was a free city (12th–14th cent., except during rule of EZZELINO DA ROMANO); passed to the Carrara family in 1318; became Venetian in 1405. Among its art treasures are the Capella degli Scrovegni, with frescoes by Giotto; the 13th-cent. basilica, with the tomb of St. Anthony of Padua; the 13th-cent. Eremitani church, with frescoes by Mantegna; and the equestrian statue of Gattamelatta, by Donatello.

Paducah (pùdū'kù, –dōō'kù), city (pop. 32,828), SW Ky., on Ohio R. (bridged) at mouth of Tennessee R.; settled 1821 as Pekin, laid out and renamed 1827. Taken (1861) by Grant in Civil War, and raided unsuccessfully by Forrest in 1864. Important tobacco market and shipping center for agr. and mining area, it has mfg. of shoes, machinery, and chemicals. Irvin S. Cobb was born and lived here. Atomic Energy Commission plant to W.

Paean (pē'ŭn), in Greek mythology, divine physician of Olympic gods. Later an epithet for Apollo as healer, it came to be a hymn of praise or a prayer for safety or deliverance.

Paeonius (pēō'nĕŭs), fl. 5th cent. B.C., Greek sculptor of Thrace. His statue of Nike (Victory) is at Olympia.

Páez, José Antonio (hōsā' äntō'nyō pä'äs), 1790–1873, Venezuelan revolutionist, president (1831–35, 1839–43), supreme dictator (1861–63). A powerful *caudillo*, he assisted Bolívar in gaining Venezuelan independence from Spain but later disrupted Bolívar's dream of a large republic and made Venezuela a separate nation. Died in exile.

Pagan (pùgän'), ruined city, Upper Burma, on Irrawaddy R. Was cap. of a Burmese dynasty from 11th cent. to 1287. Has imposing temple ruins.

Paganini, Niccolo (nēkōlō' pägänē'nē), 1782–1840, Italian violinist, whose virtuosity became a legend. Among his compositions are the 24 caprices for solo violin (Brahms and Rachmaninov wrote variations on one of them), his Concerto in D, and the often-performed *Perpetual Motion*.

Page, Thomas Nelson, 1853–1922, American novelist and diplomat, author of romantic stories and novels of the Old South, such as *In Ole Virginia* (1887) and *Red Rock* (1898). He was ambassador to Italy from 1913 to 1919.

Page, Walter Hines, 1855–1918, American journalist, editor of periodicals, and diplomat; U.S. ambassador to Great Britain (1913–18).

pageant, semidramatic spectacle, generally held outdoors and performed by local talent. Usually elaborates an event in the history of a locality, e.g., the Coventry pageant depicting Lady Godiva's story. Processional spectacles (e.g., New Orleans Mardi Gras) are also termed pageants.

Paget, Sir James (pa'jĭt), 1814–99, British surgeon and pathologist, authority on bone diseases.

pagoda, name given in the East to tower-like buildings which are generally part of a temple or monastery group and serve as shrines. Those of India are chiefly pyramidal structures of masonry, tapering to a point and adorned with carving and sculptures. In China the pagoda, derived from India, is usually octagonal in plan and built (usually of brick) in superimposed stories, decreasing in size toward the top. In Japan the pagodas were introduced from China with Buddhism. Built of wood, they are usually square in plan and five stories high, each with its projecting roof.

Pagopago (päng'ōpäng'ō), village (pop. 1,610), SE Tutuila, American Samoa; ceded to U.S. 1872 as naval and coaling station. Only port of call in American Samoa; landlocked harbor. Wireless station, naval hospital. Also Pangopango.

Pagosa Springs (pùgō'sù), resort town (pop. 1,379; alt. 7,077 ft.), SW Colo., on San Juan R. Hot Springs. Chimney Rock ruins (cliff dwellings) to W.

Pahang: see MALAYA.

Pahlavi language (pä'lùvē") or **Pehlevi language** (pä'lùvē"), a Middle Iranian language of Indo-Iranian subfamily of Indo-European languages. It was used in Middle Ages. See LANGUAGE (table).

Pahlevi: see REZA SHAH PAHLEVI; MOHAMMED REZA SHAH PAHLEVI.

Pahlevi (pälŭvē'), city (pop. 37,511), N Iran; chief Iranian port on Caspian Sea. Naval base. Formerly called Enzeli.

pain, sensation arising usually from excessive stimulation of nerve endings. Stimulus is carried by nerve fibers to centers of consciousness in brain.

Paine, Albert Bigelow, 1861–1937, American biographer and writer of juvenile stories; an editor of *St. Nicholas* (1899–1909). Friend and literary executor of Mark Twain, he wrote authorized biography (3 vols., 1912) and edited author's letters (1917), autobiography (1924), and notebook (1935).

Paine, Thomas, 1737–1809, American political theorist and writer, b. England; came to America 1774. His *Common Sense* (Jan., 1776) hastened Declaration of Independence, and his pamphlet series *The American Crisis* heartened patriots in the Revolution. In London after 1787, he defended French Revolution in *The Rights of Man* (2 parts, 1791, 1792). Prosecuted for attacks on English institutions, he fled (1792) to Paris, where he was a member of the Convention, was imprisoned (1793) for anti-Jacobinism. His deistic *Age of Reason* (2 parts, 1794, 1795) and his venomous *Letter to Washington* (1796) alienated many, and led to ostracism in U.S. on his return in 1802.

Paine College: see AUGUSTA, Ga.

Painesville, city (pop. 14,432), NE Ohio, on Grand R. and NE of Cleveland; laid out c.1805. Trade center for agr. area. Seat of Lake Erie Col.

Painlevé, Paul (pôl' pēlùvā'), 1863–1933, French statesman and mathematician. Briefly premier in 1917, he emerged in 1924 as leader, with Herriot, of the "left cartel" (a moderate group); was premier again in 1925; later held various cabinet posts. His chief importance was as a mathematician (he made valuable contributions in field of differential equations) and as a scientist.

painted cup: see INDIAN PAINTBRUSH.

Painted Desert, vividly colored badlands on E bank of Little Colorado R., N Ariz., extending SE from Grand Canyon to Petrified Forest.

Paisley (pāz'lē), burgh (pop. 93,704), Renfrewshire, Scotland. Has cotton thread, textile, and varied mfg. Famous Paisley shawl is no longer made.

Paiute Indians (pīŏŏt'), North American tribes of Uto-Aztecan linguistic stock, in SW Utah, NW Ariz., SE Calif., and S Nev. Two groups are distinguished: N Paiute (which some say are properly Paviosto), warlike people who opposed white miners and settlers in the 1860s and joined the Bannock in the war of 1878 (often called Snake Indians); S Paiute (often called the Digger Indians, from their digging for roots to supplement a sparse diet from hunting and fishing). Wovoka, leader of the ghost dance religion, was a Paiute.

Pakistan (pă'kĭstăn"), dominion (365,907 sq. mi.; pop. 75,687,000) of British Commonwealth of Nations, S Asia; cap. Karachi. Consists of two parts separated by c.900 mi. of territory belonging to INDIA. W part is on Arabian Sea and borders Iran and Afghanistan on W; includes Baluchistan, North-West Frontier Prov., and Punjab. Region is partly desert with broad alluvial plains watered by Indus R. E Pakistan (coextensive with East Bengal prov.) is on Bay of Bengal and borders Burma on SE. Dominion's principal cities are Karachi and Lahore; main ports Karachi (W) and Chittagong (E), shipping jute, tea, and cotton. Pakistan was formed 1947 out of predominantly Moslem areas of India, mainly through efforts of Mohamed Ali JINNAH and MOSLEM LEAGUE. Foreign affairs were dominated by KASHMIR dispute with India and by trouble with rebellious Pathan tribes in regions about the border of Afghanistan.

Palacio Valdés, Armando (ärmän'dō pälä'thyō väldäs'), 1853–1938, Spanish novelist and critic, author of realistic novels (e.g., *Marta y María*, 1883; *José*, 1885).

Palacky, Frantisek (frän'tyĭshĕk pä'lätskĕ), 1798–1876, Czech national leader and historian. His *Geschichte Böhmens* (Ger., 5 vols., 1836–67; Czech, 5 vols., 1848–67) influenced national consciousness.

Palaemon (pŭlē'mŏn), Greek sea-god, protector of ships. Isthmian games were celebrated in his honor.

palaeo–, for words beginning thus: see PALEO–.

Palaeologus (pălēŏ'lŭgŭs), Greek dynasty ruling Byzantine Empire 1261–1453. Included Michael VIII, Andronicus III, John V, John VI, Andronicus IV, Manuel II, John VII, John VIII, Constantine XI. Were humane, erudite; helped revive Hellenism.

Palafox, José de (hōsā' dā päläfōkh'), 1776?–1847, Spanish general in Peninsular War. Celebrated for his heroic defense of SARAGOSSA (1808–9) with an improvised garrison of citizens and peasants. Was created duke of Saragossa 1834.

Palafox y Mendoza, Juan de (hwän' dā päläfōkh' ē mändō'thä), 1600–1659, Spanish churchman, administrator in Mexico. Was made bishop of Puebla and visitor general of New Spain (1640). Named viceroy ad interim (1642). Ruled vigorously, corrected financial abuses, but quarrels with Jesuits forced him to flee to Spain (1649).

Palamas, Kostes (kôstēs' pälämäs'), 1859–1943, Greek poet; secretary of Univ. of Athens (1897–1943). Except for his early work, he wrote in vernacular Greek. His works include *Life Unshakable* (1904) and *The Twelve Speeches of the Gypsy* (1907).

Palamedes (pălŭmē'dēz), in Greek mythology, crafty Greek hero in Trojan War. He was credited with invention of measures, scales, dice, discus, alphabet, and lighthouses.

Palatinate (pŭlă'tĭnĭt), Ger. *Pfalz*, two regions of Germany, historically but not geographically related. The **Rhenish** or **Lower Palatinate** (Ger. *Rheinpfalz* or *Niederpfalz*), often called simply the Palatinate, extends W from the Rhine to France and the Saar Territory; cap. Neustadt an der Haardt. Other cities: Ludwigshafen, Speyer. Agr.; famous vineyards. Bavarian until 1945, it became a district (2,111 sq. mi.; pop. 1,047,844) of RHINELAND-PALATINATE in 1946. The **Upper Palatinate** (Ger. *Oberpfalz*), a province (3,724 sq. mi.; pop. 896,520) of Bavaria, is separated in E from Czechoslovakia by the Bohemian Forest; cap. REGENSBURG. Agr.

History. The name Palatinate is derived from the office of count palatine, a title of Roman origin. In 1214 the Rhenish Palatinate (then comprising parts of Baden and Hesse, but not the bishopric of SPEYER) passed to the Bavarian WITTELSBACH dynasty, which also acquired the present Upper Palatinate. After the 14th cent., the senior Wittelsbach line held the two palatinates, the junior line ruled Bavaria. The rank of ELECTORS was permanently assigned to senior line 1356; Rhenish Palatinate hence was known as Electoral Palatinate (Ger. *Kurpfalz*). After extinction of direct line, it passed to successive junior branches—the Protestant branch of Simmern (1559) and the Catholic branches of Neuburg (1685), Sulzbach (1742), and Birkenfeld-Zweibrücken (1799). Mannheim replaced Heidelberg as cap. 1720. The election (1619) and defeat (1620) of Elector Frederick V as king of Bohemia (see FREDERICK THE WINTER KING) led to transfer of Upper Palatinate and of electoral vote to Bavaria, but in 1648 a new vote was created for Frederick's successor. Ravaged in the Thirty Years War, the Palatinate was systematically devastated by the French in the War of the Grand Alliance (1688–89). Extinction of Bavarian Wittelsbach line (1777) and accession of Duke Maximilian of Zweibrücken (1799) reunited all Wittelsbach lands under single ruler—but France had annexed all lands W of the Rhine, and in 1803 Maximilian ceded the palatine lands E of the Rhine to Baden, Hesse, and Nassau. In 1815 Maximilian (king of a much-enlarged Bavaria since 1806) received the territory forming present Rhenish Palatinate, which remained Bavarian until 1945.

Palatka (pŭlăt'kŭ), city (pop. 9,176), NE Fla., port on St. Johns R. and S of Jacksonville. Founded 1821 as trading post, it was site of military post in Seminole War. Processes wood, sea food, and citrus fruits. Noted for azalea gardens.

Palau (pälou'), island group (188 sq. mi.; pop. 5,900), W Pacific, in W Caroline Isls. Includes four volcanic islands and many coral islets. Phosphate and bauxite are produced. Was major Japanese naval base in World War II. Name is sometimes spelled Pelew.

Palawan (pälä'wän), island (4,550 sq. mi.; pop. 43,813), Philippine Isls., N of Borneo and between Sulu and South China seas. Rice, corn, tobacco, copra. Populated by Moros. Has U.S. naval air base. Puerto Princesa is on E coast.

Pale, in Irish history, area around Dublin under English rule. Term first used 14th cent. An English Pale centered around Calais until 1558, another in Scotland in 16th cent. In Russia, Pale was region where Jews might live, estab. in first partition of Poland and existing until Revolution of 1917.

Palembang (pälĕmbäng'), city (pop. 108,145), on SE Sumatra, Indonesia; port on Musi R. and largest city on island. Trade center for area producing rubber and oil. Cap. of Hindu-Indonesian kingdom in 8th cent.

Palenque (päleng'kä), anc. city of the Maya in Chiapas, S Mexico. Its architectural elegance shows the high degree of skill the Maya attained.

Paleocene epoch: see EOCENE EPOCH.

paleography (pälēŏ'grŭfē) [Gr.,= early writing], term sometimes meaning all study and interpretation of old ways of recording language, but in a narrower sense excluding epigraphy (study of inscriptions). Letters made with a stylus, brush, or pen favor curved lines and tend to become cursive. In Western European ways of writing, letters of all kinds are derived from capital letters of Roman inscriptions. From these "square" capitals developed less severe "rustic" capitals and uncial letters (with more curves). Capitals and uncials are called majuscules, lower-case letters minuscules. Lower-case letters became estab. in Alcuin's school at Tours in Charlemagne's time. The black letter, sometimes called Gothic, is no longer in common use except for German language; it developed from efforts at ornateness. In type, italic letters were introduced by Aldus Manutius. Experts in hand-writing can often assign a place and a date to a document of earlier times (for a simple example, Spencerian script denotes 19th cent.), and they can sometimes even identify a particular writer and dis-tinguish forgeries from authentic documents.

paleolith (pā′lēŭlĭth), crude implement of flint or other hard stone shaped by chipping, found in caves which served primitive man as shelters and in old gravel beds. Their great antiquity is proved by association with the remains of extinct animals.

Paleolithic period (pā″lēŭlĭ′thĭk, –lēō, pă″–) or **Old Stone Age,** earliest and longest period of human his-tory, approximately coextensive with Pleistocene geo-logic epoch. It is usually divided into lower Paleo-lithic—generally subdivided into Pre-Chellean, Ab-bevillain (or Chellean), Acheulian, and Mousterian (sometimes considered middle Paleolithic); and upper Paleolithic—embracing Aurignacian, Solutrean, and Magdalenian phases. Early Paleolithic humans prob-ably were nomadic hunters and food gatherers who sought shelter in caves and had knowledge of fire. Characteristic tool of lower Paleolithic was *coup de poing* or hand axe, shaped on a central core or rock mass. Flake implements were fashioned from struck-off fragments. Neanderthal man, a cave dweller of Mousterian times, made carefully shaped flake tools. Sculpture and painting probably had their beginning in the caves and rock shelters of these times. Through-out upper Paleolithic lived Cro-Magnon man gen-erally considered a race of modern man (*Homo sapiens*). Caves and rock shelters housed man in Aurignacian and Magdalenian times; CAVE ART reached its height in Magdalenian period. Bone de-vices including needles appeared in upper Paleolithic. Long, slender flint blades struck from a core were feature of the period. Magdalenian blade industries derived from upper Aurignacian. Relatively brief ap-pearance of Solutrean culture, with its fine lance points and blades, was perhaps an invasion from Iran. By close of the Paleolithic, agriculture and domesticated animals, both features of Neolithic, were about to appear.

paleontology (pā″lēŭntŏ′lŭjē, pā″lēŏn–), science of the life of past geologic time as studied through the FOS-SIL, which serves as the most important means of cor-relating the ages of rock strata.

Paleozoic era (pā″lēŭzō′ĭk), third grand division of geo-logic time. In North America two great geosynclines (downfolds) were main physical features—the Appa-lachian and the Cordilleran geosynclines. The rhythm of Cambrian, Ordovician, and Silurian periods of the era was alternating submergence and uplift. In the Carboniferous began major disturbances which con-tinued in Permian and brought Paleozoic to a close. Early Paleozoic was rich in marine invertebrate life. Amphibians appeared in the Devonian period, and rep-tiles in the Carboniferous; in this period plant life reached its climax. See also GEOLOGY, table.

Palermo (pŭlûr′mō, Ital. pälĕr′mō), city (pop. 339,497; with suburbs 411,879), cap. and largest city and port of Sicily, at the edge of the Conca d'Oro, a fertile plain on the NW coast. Exports citrus fruit and wine. Founded (probably by Phoenicians) between 8th and 6th cent. B.C., it later was a Carthaginian military base until its conquest by Rome (254–253 B.C.). It was under Byzantine rule A.D. 535–831, then fell to the Arabs, and was conquered 1072 by the Normans, who made it the cap. of Sicily. Its cultural and economic flowering began under the Arabs and reached its peak under Emperor Frederick II (13th cent.). The SICILIAN VESPERS began at Palermo (1282). The city is rich in architecture; Byzantine, Arabic, and Norman influ-ences are blended in many of its churches and palaces. There was much damage in World War II. University was founded 1805.

Palermo stone, diorite stone engraved probably in

28th cent. B.C. with earliest extant annals, a list of kings of anc. Egypt. Part of it is in Palermo, Italy, part in Cairo, Egypt.

Palestine [ultimately from Philistine], country on E shore of the Mediterranean. This article covers the region's history up to the formation of ISRAEL in 1948. In the Bible, Palestine is called Canaan before the in-vasion of Joshua. It is the Holy Land, of the Jews as having been promised them by God, of Christians because it was the home of Christ, and of Moslems as heirs of Jews and Christians. Places of pilgrimage include Jerusalem, Bethlehem, Nazareth, and He-bron. Its boundaries, never long constant, have always included the region between the Mediterranean and Jordan R., bordering SW on Egypt. Comprises three zones (E-W): the depression (part of Great Rift Val-ley) in which lie Jordan R. and Dead Sea; a steep ridge (running from GALILEE through SAMARIA) and the mountains of JUDAEA; and a narrow coastal plain. Detailed history begins with the Hebrews (see JEWS). By 1000 B.C. the Hebrew kingdom, consolidated by Saul and David, was well estab. at Jerusalem. After the reign of Solomon the kingdom fell into two states, Israel and Judah, which were destroyed by Assyria and Babylonia. The Persian-sponsored autonomous Jewish community, subsequently estab. at Jerusalem, was perhaps the foundation of the modern Jewish people. Palestine was conquered in 4th cent. B.C. by Alexander the Great, but eventually the Jews re-volted under the MACCABEES, who set up a new state in 141 B.C.; this yielded to Rome after 70 years. Palestine of the time of Christ had puppet kings in the Herods (see HEROD) who never succeeded in reconciling Jews and Romans. To quell a revolt the Romans destroyed the Temple in A.D. 70 and ex-pelled the Jews from Judaea. With Constantine I, Palestine became a center of Christian pilgrimage; under Justinian, the country flourished. But after 640 when it came under Moslem rule, the country declined, its land wasting into barrenness. In 9th cent., when Palestine passed to Egypt, the Fatimite rulers provoked the CRUSADES by destroying the Church of the Holy Sepulcher and molesting pilgrims. The Latin Kingdom of Jerusalem, estab. 1099 by the Crusaders, lasted less than 100 years. The next rulers of Palestine were the Mamelukes, who ruled until 1516, when Ottoman Turks took over. Jewish colonization from Europe began c.1870, but ZIONISM entered the field only in early 20th cent. In 1920 the British, who had won the area in World War I, acquired Palestine and Trans-Jordan (now JORDAN) as mandates; they desig-nated Palestine for the establishment of a Jewish na-tional home, but with due regard for rights of non-Jewish Palestinians. There followed (esp. in '30s) Jewish-Arab clashes resulting from Arab resentment of Jewish immigration and land purchases. The Brit-ish White Paper of 1939 revealed plans for an inde-pendent, predominantly Arab state, which would be closed to Jewish immigration after 1944. Political tensions were eased by World War II, in which all parties cooperated with the British, but at war's end enmity flared into open conflict, out of which the state of Israel was forged.

Palestine (pă′lŭstēn), city (pop. 12,503), E Texas, N of Houston; settled 1846. Center of oil and agr. area, has railroad shops and large salt dome.

Palestrina, Giovanni Pierluigi da (jōvän′nē pyĕrlōōē′jē pä′lāstrē′nä), c.1525–1594, Italian composer. Con-ducted choirs of the Sistine Chapel, St. John Lateran, and Julian Chapel at the Vatican. Composer mostly of religious choral music—motets and Masses, of which the *Missa Papae Marcelli* is best known. He is often called "the first Catholic Church musician."

Paley, William, 1743–1805, English theologian. Wrote *Principles of Moral and Political Philosophy* (1785), an 18th-cent. statement of utilitarianism, and *A View of the Evidences of Christianity* (1794).

Palgrave, Francis Turner, 1824–97, English poet and

anthologist. Edited *The Golden Treasury of the Best Songs and Lyrical Poems in the English Language* (1861; a notable anthology).

Pali (päʹlē), dead language of Indic group of Indo-Iranian subfamily of Indo-European languages; a dialect of Sanskrit. Pali literature was the sacred literature of Buddhism, written 5th cent.–3d cent. B.C. The canon is the *Tipitaka* [threefold basket], consisting of *Vinayapitaka* [basket of discipline], *Suttapitaka* [basket of teaching] and *Abhidhammapitaka* [basket of metaphysics]. Commentaries in Pali still written in Ceylon, Burma, and Siam.

Palikao, Charles Guillaume Cousin-Montauban, comte de (shärlʹ gēyōmʹ kōōzēʹ-mōtōbäʹ kōtʹ dù pälēkäōʹ), 1796–1878, French general. Commanded French forces in China (1860); created count after victory at Palichiao, near Peking. His premiership (1870) ended with fall of Second Empire after battle of Sedan.

Pali literature (päʹlē), sacred literature of Buddhism. Written 483–250 B.C., the canon is called the *Tipitaka* [threefold basket]. Divided into three parts: monastic rules; statement of tenets, plus a miscellany of speeches and dialogues of Buddha and his disciples, lives of the saints, poems, and fables; and an analytical elaboration of doctrine. Pali (a dialect of Sanskrit) died out in India but was brought 2d cent. B.C. to Ceylon, where it has been studied up to present day. Also used to some extent in Burma and Siam as language of literature and religion.

Palisades, bluffs along W bank of the Hudson, NE N.J. and SE N.Y., from N of Jersey City, N.J., to vicinity of Piermont, N.Y.; general alt. 350–550 ft. The Palisades, rising vertically from near the river's edge, are a margin of a sill of diabase, slowly cooled; probably uplift and faulting occurred at close of Triassic period. Much of the most scenic section, between Fort Lee, N.J., and Newburgh, N.Y., is in **Palisades Interstate Park,** with summer and winter sports facilities. Notable points are BEAR MOUNTAIN and STORM KING.

Palisades Park, residential borough (pop. 9,635), NE N.J., adjoining Fort Lee. Amusement park.

Palissy, Bernard (bĕrnärʹ pälēsēʹ), c.1510–c.1589, French potter. Created pottery with smooth glazes in richly colored enamels. Noted for pieces decorated with reptiles, insects, and plants.

Palladio, Andrea (ändräʹä päl-läʹdēō), 1518–80, Italian architect of the Renaissance, b. Vicenza. Known for formal, grandiose designs based on Roman style. Designed San Giorgio Maggiore in Venice. Palladian style imported into England in 17th cent. by Inigo Jones was closely followed by architects of Georgian period. Palladio's famous treatise, which appeared 1713 as *The Four Books of Architecture,* was widely influential. Much imitated "Palladian motive" consists of arches supported on minor columns and framed between larger columns.

Palladium (pùläʹdēùm) [Gr.,= belonging to Pallas], in Greek and Roman religion, anc. sacred image of Pallas Athena. It was guardian of the safety of a city. Palladium of Troy protected the city until Diomed and Odysseus stole it. Only then did Troy fall.

palladium (pùläʹdēùm), rare, silver-white, lustrous metallic element (symbol = Pd; see also ELEMENT, table), strongly resistant to corrosion. A member of the platinum group of metals, it occurs in ores of this metal. It can absorb great quantities of hydrogen. It is used for plating and in alloys with gold and platinum.

pallah: see IMPALA.

Pallas (päʹlùs), in Greek mythology. **1** Name given to Athena. **2** Giant killed by Athena. **3** Titan; son of Creus, husband of Styx, and father of Nike.

Pall Mall (pĕl mĕlʹ, päl mälʹ), street in W London. Originally constructed by Charles II for playing the game pall-mall. Here are St. James's Palace, Marlborough House, and a number of clubs.

palm, evergreen treelike, bushy, or climbing plant of the family Palmaceae, native mostly to tropics but with some representatives in warm temperate regions. Most palms have a tall, woody, unbranched stem with a crown of compound leaves. The COCONUT, the DATE, and the SAGO palm are important commercially. Carnauba wax is obtained from the leaves of a South American palm (*Copernicia cerifera*). Other palms include the royal palm (*Roystonea*) and PALMETTO palm. **Palm oil** is yellowish orange to brownish red fat pressed from fibrous flesh of fruit of the African oil palm (*Elaeis guineensis*). Palm-kernel oil is a white oil obtained from the endosperm.

Palma, Jacopo (yäʹkōpō pälʹmä), c.1480–1528, Venetian painter, called Palma Vecchio. Known for idyllic landscape backgrounds and female portraits.

Palma, Ricardo (rēkärʹdhō pälʹmä), 1833–1919, Peruvian writer, known chiefly for sketches of colonial days of Peru (*Tradiciones peruanes*).

Palma or **Palma de Mallorca** (pälʹmä dä mälyôrʹkä), seaport (pop. 97,009), cap. of Majorca isl., chief city of Balearic Islands, Spain. Has Gothic cathedral (founded 1229), remains of Moorish castle, 15th-cent. Lonja (exchange). Near by is former royal castle of Bellver (14th cent.).

Palm Beach, town (pop. 3,886), SE Fla., on an island between the Atlantic and L. Worth (lagoon bridged to West Palm Beach). With H. M. Flagler's arriving 1893, it began development as wealthy, exclusive resort.

Palmer, A(lexander) Mitchell, 1872–1936, U.S. Attorney General (1919–21). Ardently prosecuted those suspected of disloyalty to U.S..

Palmer, Nathaniel Brown, 1799–1877, American sea captain. First sighted PALMER PENINSULA on whaling voyage (1820–21).

Palmer, Samuel, 1805–81, English etcher and landscape painter, a follower of William Blake.

Palmer, town (pop. 9,533), S Mass., ENE of Springfield; settled 1716. Metal goods.

Palmer Archipelago, Antarctic island group off NW Palmer Peninsula. Discovered 1898 by Adrien de Gerlache. Sometimes called Antarctic Archipelago.

Palmer Peninsula, Antarctica, c.800 mi. long; tip is 650 mi. from Cape Horn. Mostly mountainous, covered with shelf ice; W coast washed by Weddell Sea. Discovered 1820 by N. B. Palmer. Claimed by British as Graham Land (or Graham Coast), a Falkland Island dependency, and by Chile and Argentina as O'Higgins Land.

Palmerston, Henry John Temple, 3d **Viscount**, 1784–1865, English statesman. As foreign minister (1830–41) he pursued a liberal policy (e.g., aided Belgian independence). Twice prime minister (1855–58, 1859–65), he prosecuted Crimean War, aided Italian independence, and dealt with Sepoy Rebellion. His reckless diplomacy advanced British prestige.

Palmerton, borough (pop. 6,646), E Pa., on Lehigh R. and NNW of Allentown. Zinc refining.

palmetto palm or **palmetto** (pälmĕʹtō), palm tree of genus *Sabal*, native to the W Hemisphere. The young head of leaves of the cabbage palmetto (*Sabal palmetto*), native to the SE U.S., is edible. The wood is used for piles, and the leaves for thatch.

palmitin (pälʹmùtĭn), name for any fat that is ester of palmitic acid and glycerin but generally refers to the tripalmitate. Occurs in most FATS AND OILS.

palm oil: see PALM.

Palms, Isle of, resort island, SE S.C., E of Charleston.

Palm Springs, desert resort city (pop. 7,660), S Calif., in Coachella Valley near San Jacinto Peak and E of Los Angeles.

Palmyra (pälmīʹrù), anc. city of central Syria, NE of Damascus, traditionally founded by Solomon and called in the Bible Tadmor. A trade center, it grew to political importance after the Romans had established control and a local family the Septimii ruled. The greatest of these, Septimius ODENATHUS defeated the Persians for Emperor Gallienus and made Palmyra an enormous autonomous state (including Syria, Mesopotamia, and E Armenia). His widow, ZENOBIA, conquered Egypt and most of Asia Minor, but her ambition brought a Roman expedition (A.D. 272), which humbled and partly ruined Palmyra. It declined and after a sack by Tamerlane disappeared.

Palmyra. 1 Borough (pop. 5,802), SW N.J., on Delaware R. (bridged 1929), above Camden. Metal products. **2** Village (pop. 3,034), W central N.Y., SE of Rochester. Joseph Smith lived here and published Book of Mormon here. **3** Borough (pop. 5,910), SE Pa., E of Harrisburg. Limestone quarrying and mfg. of textiles.

Palmyra, atoll (pop. 32), comprising 55 islets, c.1,105 mi. SSW of Honolulu, central Pacific. Included in city and county of Honolulu. Discovered 1802 by Americans and annexed 1912; naval base authorized 1939. Privately owned.

Palo Alto (pä"lō äl'tō), residential city (pop. 25,475), W Calif., SSE of San Francisco; founded 1891. Seat of STANFORD UNIVERSITY.

Palo Alto (pä"lō äl'tō), locality not far from Brownsville, Texas, where first battle of Mexican War was fought, May 8, 1846. U.S. troops under Gen. Zachary Taylor won victory.

Palomar, Mount (pä'lōmär), 6,126 ft. high, S Calif., NE of San Diego. Site of Mt. Palomar Observatory, with 200-in. reflecting telescope, operated by California Inst. of Technology and Carnegie Inst.

Palomino de Castro y Velasco, Acislo Antonio (pälō-mē'nō dä käs'trō ē välä'skō), 1653–1726, Spanish painter and writer on art, called the Spanish Vasari.

palsy: see PARALYSIS.

Pamir (pùmēr', pä–) or **Pamirs,** mountainous region, central Asia. Mainly in Tadzhik SSR and Mountain Badakhshan; extends also into China and Afghanistan. Mt. Stalin (24,590 ft.) is highest in USSR.

Pamlico Sound (păm'lĭkō), 80 mi. long, E N.C., separated from Atlantic Ocean by islands and sand bars ending to E in Cape Hatteras. Receives Pamlico (see TAR) and Neuse rivers.

Pampa (păm'pù), city (pop. 16,583), N Texas, ENE of Amarillo. Shipping center in cattle and wheat area, it has oil refineries and carbon-black plants.

pampas (păm'pùz), wide, treeless grassy plains in S South America, particularly in Argentina, Uruguay, and Paraguay. In central and N Argentina, the **Pampa** (c.250,000 sq. mi.) has given Argentina wealth from cattle raising, agr., and dairying; industries based on them—meat packing, milling, and processing of dairy products; and traditional character from early gauchos and later S European immigrants.

pampas grass, tall South American grass (*Cortaderia*). Common pampas grass (*Cortaderia selloana*) is a perennial with clusters of long narrow leaf blades. Plants bearing female flowers are most ornamental.

Pampeluna, Spain: see PAMPLONA.

Pamplona (pämplō'nä), city (pop. 45,885), cap. of Spanish Navarre, N Spain, at foot of Pyrenees. Communications center; iron and lead works; linen mfg. The Basque kingdom of Pamplona, founded 824, was the nucleus of NAVARRE. Made a stronghold by Philip II, Pamplona is still surrounded by old walls. An older spelling is Pampeluna.

Pan, in Greek religion, pastoral god of fertility. Worshiped chiefly in Arcadia. He was portrayed as merry, ugly man with horns, beard, tail, and goat's feet. All his myths deal with amorous affairs: e.g., his unsuccessful pursuit of the nymph Syrinx, who became a reed, which Pan plays in memory of her. He was later identified with Greek Dionysus and Roman Faunus, both gods of fertility.

Pana (pä'nù), city (pop. 6,178), S central Ill., SE of Springfield. Shipping center in farm and coal area. Rose-growing industry.

Panama (pä'nŭmä"), Span. Panamá (pänämä"), republic (29,128 sq. mi., including PANAMA CANAL ZONE; pop. 801,290), Latin America, occupying the Isthmus of Panama which forms connecting link between Central and South America; cap. PANAMA city. Panama has

an extreme length of c.385 mi. and varies from c.32 to 113 mi. in width. In the W there is a range of mountains of volcanic origin; the middle of the country about the Panama Canal is lower; and in the E it rises again. Soil is of volcanic origin and fertile; vast forest reserves are unexploited. Subsistence crops are grown on upland savannas. Main exports are bananas, abaca, cacao, rubber, and mahogany. Population is divided into whites, mestizos (about two thirds of population), Indians, and Negroes. Panama city and COLÓN have grown because of their strategic world position rather than their relation with the hinterland. Roman Catholicism is prevailing religion, and Spanish the official language. Rodrigo de Bastidas discovered the coast (1501) and Columbus anchored there (1502), but not until 1513 when BALBOA took control of region and made his famous trip across isthmus to discover Pacific did the area become important—then mainly as a channel of trade. The immense wealth carried through the port of Portobelo attracted raids of British buccaneers 16th through 18th cent. Panama was a part of viceroyalty of Peru until 1740 when it was transferred to New Granada. After independence from Spain it became a part of Colombia. When the goldfields in California were discovered, interest in the long-discussed canal across the isthmus was revived in the U.S. The project ultimately led in 1903 to a Panamanian revolt against Colombia and—with assistance from the U.S.—independence was gained and the Panama Canal built. The U.S. was generally criticized throughout the world and in 1921 agreed to pay to Colombia $25,-000,000 as redress for the loss of Panama. One immediate benefit to Panama of the revolution was eradication of yellow fever and improved sanitation in the country. Panama has taken an active part in Pan-Americanism and is a member of UN. Internal politics have been stormy with frequent changes in administration; Arnulfo Arias became a dominant figure in 1931.

Panama, city (pop. 127,874), central Panama, cap. and largest city of Panama, on the Gulf of Panama. Founded 1519 by Pedro Arias de Ávila, it flourished during colonial times as Pacific port for transshipment of Andean riches to Spain. Construction of the Panama Canal brought prosperity, and American sanitary measures have made it a healthful city. Univ. of Panama is here.

Panama Canal, waterway across Isthmus of Panama, connecting the Atlantic and Pacific oceans, built by U.S. (1904–14) on territory leased in perpetuity from republic of Panama. Canal, running S and SE from Limón Bay at Colón on the Atlantic to the Bay of Panama at Balboa on the Pacific, is 40.27 mi. long from shore to shore, 50.72 mi. long between channel entrances. Min. depth is 41 ft. Passage, aided by several sets of locks, takes 7 to 8 hr. There was rivalry with Great Britain over proposed canal (see CLAYTON-BULWER TREATY and HAY-PAUNCEFOTE TREATY). Interest also developed in alternate route, NICARAGUA CANAL. Negotiations with Colombia led to abortive HAY-HERRÁN TREATY (1903). By Hay–Bunau-Varilla Treaty of 1903, the new republic of Panama granted U.S., in return for an initial cash payment of $10,000,-000 and a stipulated annuity, exclusive control of a canal zone in perpetuity, other sites necessary for defense, and sanitary control of Panama city and Colón. Actual construction, headed by G. W. Goethals, took seven years; eradication of malaria and yellow fever was a notable achievement. In 1921 U.S. paid Colombia $25,000,000 in damages.

Panama Canal Zone, administrative area (552.8 sq. mi.) of U.S., extending 5 mi. on either side of Panama Canal, bounded by the Caribbean on N, the Pacific on S, and Panama on E and W. Administered by a governor appointed by U.S. CRISTOBAL, BALBOA, ANCON are chief towns.

Panama City, city (pop. 25,814), NW Fla., on St. Andrews Bay and E of Pensacola. Gulf resort. Processes lumber and paper. Fishing.

Pan American Highway, projected system of roads, 15,714 mi. long, to link nations of W Hemisphere.

Pan-Americanism, movement towards commercial, social, economic, military, and political cooperation among the 21 republics of North, Central, and South America. The struggle for independence from Spain after 1810 evoked a sense of unity among the Latin American nations and the U.S. was looked on as a model. In 1820 Henry Clay set forth principles for Pan-Americanism, but soon afterwards the Monroe Doctrine was declared and became a source of irritation to the Latin American countries as they believed it to be only a mask for U.S. imperialistic ambition. An early limited attempt at union (see CENTRAL AMERICAN FEDERATION) failed, and national rivalries and wars split the Latin American republics. An attempt by Simón Bolívar to assemble a Pan-American conference in 1826 failed, and it was not until 1889–90 that the first of the Pan-American Conferences (or Congresses) was held at Washington. Subsequent meetings were at Mexico city (1901–2), Rio de Janeiro (1906), Buenos Aires (1910), Santiago (1923), Havana (1928), Montevideo (1933), Lima (1938), and Bogotá (1948). Their achievements include treaties for arbitration of disputes and adjustment of tariffs, establishment of Pan American Union, codification of international law, acceptance of peace machinery, and creation of scientific and social agencies. F. D. Roosevelt was responsible for the "Good Neighbor" policy which bettered relations between U.S. and Latin America. Most of the republics supported or actively participated in World War II on the side of the Allies. Further evidence of cooperation, friendliness, and interdependence are the Inter-American Conferences—Buenos Aires, 1936; Mexico city, 1945; Rio de Janeiro, 1947—and the formation of the ORGANIZATION OF AMERICAN STATES, 1948.

Pan American Union, international agency founded April 14, 1890, at first Pan-American Conference; name adopted 1910. The day of its founding is Pan-American Day.

Panamint Range (pă'nŭmĭnt), SE Calif., near Nev. line. Rugged mountains between Death (E) and Panamint valleys. Altitudes range from c.6,000 ft. to 11,145 ft. in Telescope Peak.

Panay (pänī'), island (4,446 sq. mi.; pop. 1,291,548), one of Visayan Isls., in Philippine Isls.; NW of Negros. Rice, coconuts, citrus fruit, copper, manganese. Horses are bred in mountainous interior. Chief town is Iloilo.

Panchatantra (pän"chŭtän'trŭ), chief Sanskrit collection of animal fables, probably compiled before A.D. 500. Bidpai is the supposed author. The Buddhistic prose fables are interspersed with wise sayings in verse.

pancreas (păn'krēŭs, păng'–), gland found in most vertebrates and lying in abdominal cavity. In man it secretes fluid (containing digestive enzymes) which flows via bile duct into small intestine. Scattered cell groups (islands of Langerhans) in the pancreas produce hormone INSULIN. See *ill.*, p. 595.

panda (păn'dŭ). Lesser panda or cat bear (*Ailurus*) resembles raccoon, but has longer body and tail, more rounded head. Its fur is rust to deep chestnut, black on under parts, legs, and ears, with dark eye patches on white face. Found in Himalayas; a Chinese subspecies is in Yunnan, Szechwan, N Burma. Giant panda (*Ailuropoda*) lives in Szechwan, Kansu, at 6,000–14,000 ft. altitudes. Its bearlike body is chiefly white, with dark limbs and shoulders, and black ears and eye patches. Feeds on bamboo shoots.

Pandarus (păn'dŭrŭs), in Greek mythology, the Trojan who broke the truce by wounding Menelaus. He was killed by Diomed. Another Pandarus was the go-between in the story of Troilus and Cressida.

Pandects: see CORPUS JURIS CIVILIS.

Pandit, Vijaya Lakshmi (vĭjī'ŭ läk'shmē pŭn'dĭt), 1900–, Indian diplomat; sister of Jawaharlal Nehru. Active in Indian Natl. Congress since 1920s, she was first woman in India to hold ministerial office (1937). Madame Pandit was ambassador to USSR 1947–49 and to U.S. 1949–51. Headed Indian delegation to UN for first time in 1946; reappointed 1952.

Pandora (păn"dô'rŭ) [Gr.,= all gifts], in Greek mythology, first woman on earth. Zeus ordered her creation as vengeance on man and sent her as wife to Prometheus' brother, Epimetheus, with box that he forbade her to open. She disobeyed and loosed all evils attending man. Only Hope stayed inside.

Pange lingua (păn'jä lĭng'gwä) [Latin,= sing, O tongue], Corpus Christi hymn of the Roman Catholic Church, written by St. Thomas Aquinas; used in honor of the Sacrament. The last two stanzas, called, as a separate hymn, *Tantum ergo* (tän'tŏŏm âr'gō), are sung at Benediction of the Blessed Sacrament.

Pangim, Portuguese India: see GOA.

Pangnirtung (păng"nŭrtŭng'), trading post, E Baffin Isl., Northwest Territories, Canada, on N side of Cumberland Sound; estab. 1921. Here are radio and meteorological station, mounted police post, and medical center for Baffin Bay with hospital.

pangolin (păng-gō'lĭn), toothless insectivorous mammal (*Manis*) of Asia and Africa, probably related to South American anteater. It has heavy scales on head, upper part and sides of body, and on tail; hairs are on under parts and scattered among scales.

Pangopango: see PAGOPAGO.

panic, sudden and widespread loss of confidence in the soundness of financial institutions. There is a general rush to convert assets into money, resulting in numerous bank failures and bankruptcies. A panic often occurs at the end of a period of prosperity, thereby coinciding with a "crash" or economic crisis. Among severe U.S. panics were that of 1837, the panic on "Black Friday," Sept. 19, 1873, and the stock-market crash of Oct., 1929.

Panipat (pä'nēpŭt"), town (pop. 37,837), E Punjab, India. Here in 1526 Baber won decisive victory over Delhi Sultanate.

Panizzi, Sir Anthony (pänēt'sē), 1797–1879, British librarian, b. Italy. He was chief librarian (1856–67) at British Mus. library. His 91 rules (1839) became basis of the museum's catalogue. Enforced act requiring deposition at the museum of copies of books copyrighted in Great Britain.

Panjabi (pŭnjä'bē), language of Indic group of Indo-Iranian subfamily of Indo-European languages. See LANGUAGE (table).

Pankhurst, Emmeline (Goulden) (păngk'hûrst), 1857–1928, English woman-suffragist, leader of militant movement. Organized (1905) Women's Social and Political Union; its methods invited arrest and imprisonment. In 1928, after voting rights were granted to women, she stood for Parliament as a Conservative. Her daughters, **Christabel Pankhurst,** 1880–, educated for law but barred by her sex, and **Sylvia Pankhurst,** 1882–, shared her activities in promoting woman suffrage.

Panmunjom (păn"mŏŏnjŏm, pän–), village, central Korea, S of 38th parallel, 6 mi. SE of Kaesong. Scene of truce talks, Oct., 1951–Oct., 1952, and of prisoner exchange, April, 1953.

Pannonia (pănō'nēŭ), anc. Roman province, S and W of the Danube. The natives, identified by Romans with the Illyrians, were subjugated by A.D. 9, and the territory was held by Rome until after 395.

pansy, garden flower (*Viola tricolor hortensis*), closely related to the violet, also called heartsease. Probably one of the plants longest cultivated.

Pantaloon (păntŭlōōn'), stock *commedia dell' arte* character, a mean miserly old man in pantaloons.

Pantelleria (pän"tāl-lārē'ä), volcanic island (32 sq. mi.; pop. 9,306), in the Mediterranean between Sicily and Africa. Was a strategic Italian military and air base;

capitulated to Allies after severe bombing (1943).

pantheism (păn'thēīzùm), belief that God is in all things and all things are in God: God and the universe are identical. There are wide variations in the belief, depending largely on whether it is based principally on religious mysticism (e.g., in Hinduism), poetic appreciation of nature, or philosophical logic (e.g., in teachings of Spinoza). Varieties of pantheism have been known from early times and persistently crop up in the history of thought.

pantheon (păn'thēŏn', –thēùn) [Gr.,= of all gods], term applied originally to a temple to all the gods and now to a building dedicated to a nation's illustrious dead. The **Pantheon** at Rome was built by Agrippa in 27 B.C. and rebuilt in 2d cent. by Hadrian. Converted in 609 into a Christian church. The **Panthéon** (pätäõ') in Paris was designed by J. G. Soufflot and built 1764–81; now a mausoleum for illustrious Frenchmen.

panther, name applied to LEOPARD and less correctly to PUMA and other large cats.

pantomime (păn'tùmīm) [Gr.,= all in mimic], silent drama using movement, gesture, and facial expression. Dates from ancient times and is seen in primitive cultures. Traditional pantomime characters (e.g., Harlequin, Columbine) originated in 16th cent. COMMEDIA DELL' ARTE. English pantomime is pageant rather than pantomime. Charles Chaplin was a great pantomime actor in silent films in America.

Pánuco (pä'nōōkō), river rising in San Luis Potosí, N central Mexico, flowing generally E to Gulf of Mexico near Tampico. Drains much of central plateau and, by artificial means, Valley of Mexico.

Panza, Sancho: see DON QUIXOTE DE LA MANCHA.

Paoli, Pasquale (päskwä'lä pä'ōlē), 1725–1807, Corsican patriot. Headed Corsican insurrection against Genoa (1755); president of Corsica 1755–69. In 1768 Genoa sold its rights to Corsica to France. Defeated by the French (1769), Paoli fled to England, but in 1791 Louis XVI appointed him governor of Corsica. Opposed to the radical turn of the French Revolution, Paoli proclaimed Corsica independent and called on British aid. With help of Admiral Hood, he defeated the French (1794), but instead of declaring independence, the Corsican assembly made the island a British protectorate. Paoli was recalled to England in 1795. In 1796 the Corsicans drove out the English with French help.

papacy (pā'pùsē), office of the pope, head of the ROMAN CATHOLIC CHURCH. According to the belief of that Church he is, as bishop of Rome, successor to St. Peter, the first bishop of Rome and the chief of the Apostles and the representative (vicar or vicegerent) of Christ; hence, the pope is the head of Christendom. This is the theory of Petrine supremacy. It is not held by other churches; some interpret early assertions of papal dignity as expressing a position of honor only, others deny all papal claims whatever. This question of papal supremacy was the chief cause of division between the Roman Catholic Church and the ORTHODOX EASTERN CHURCH, and Protestant churches since the Reformation reject all papal claims of any sort. In the Roman Catholic Church, however, the belief, held from earlier times, that the pope is infallible when speaking *ex cathedra* (i.e., as solemn official head of the Church) on matters of faith and morals was made into dogma at the Vatican Council in 1870. Early popes (e.g., Clement I) asserted rights to guide the Church, and with the decline of the Roman Empire in the W the pope became an important political leader. Such men as Julius I, Innocent I, Leo I, Gregory I, and Martin I enhanced the position of the pope not only by leadership but also by promoting missionary efforts, thus tying the expanding Church more closely to the Holy See (the papal seat at Rome). Conflict with lay rulers ensued, and the popes struggled with some, allied themselves with others. PEPIN THE SHORT by his Donation made the pope the lord of a large area, and down to modern

times the pope was secular ruler of the Papal States as well as religious ruler. This fact caused many difficulties, but more came from the contest between lay rulers (notably the emperor, head of the Holy Roman Empire, and the kings of France and England, and, later, of Spain) and the pope over their relative spheres of influence. The more ambitious emperors and kings tried to control all affairs of the Church in their dominions, the more extreme of the popes claimed overlordship over all princes. The 10th cent. was the low point for the papacy; the office was bought and sold in a game of corrupt Roman politics. After the reforms of Gregory VII in the 11th cent., however, the popes had great prestige, and by the end of the 12th cent. Innocent III was trying with some success to assert his claims as arbiter of all lay affairs. By the 14th cent. a new period began when Philip IV of France defied Boniface VIII, and France secured control of the Church. The papal see was moved by Clement V to Avignon, and it remained there from 1309 to 1378; this is the "Babylonian captivity" of the pope. His return to Rome brought on the Great SCHISM (1378–1417), in which there were two or three rival popes, a contest ended by the Council of Constance. Since that time there has been no schism in the papacy, though there was a brief and unsuccessful effort to make the general Church council superior to the pope. In the 15th cent. the popes generally devoted themselves to worldly rule in Italy, to patronizing Renaissance art, and to forwarding their family fortunes. Upon this spiritual apathy fell the REFORMATION, but it was some time before the popes realized that the Protestant leaders had really broken Christendom. Reform within the Church followed election of Paul III (see REFORM, CATHOLIC). Spiritual leadership of the papacy was reasserted, but unfortunately the contest with the Catholic rulers of the empire, Spain, and France grew more pronounced. In the 18th cent. the papacy seemed doomed to be subordinated to lay rulers, but with the overthrow of the absolutist states in the late 18th and early 19th cent. the pope was enabled to reassert his rule within the Church. Even the loss of the Papal States (1870) proved in the end to be a boon (see LATERAN TREATY) since it made the pope perforce a purely ecclesiastic ruler. He governs the tiny Vatican state (see VATICAN), where he has his court, the Curia Romana, under the direction of his officers (see CARDINAL). The following is a list of the popes. The date of election is given rather than that of consecration. Before St. Victor I dates may err by one year. Official lists no longer number the popes in sequence. St. Peter, d. 67?; St. Linus, 67?–76?; St. Cletus or Anacletus, 76?–88?; St. Clement I, 88?–97?; St. Evaristus, 97?–105?; St. Alexander I, 105?–115?; St. Sixtus I, 115?–125?; St. Telesphorus, 125?–136?; St. Hyginus, 136?–140?; St. Pius I, 140?–155?; St. Anicetus, 155?–166?; St. Soter, 166?–175?; St. Eleutherius, 175?–189?; St. Victor I, 189–99; St. Zephyrinus, 199–217; St. Calixtus I, 217–222 (antipope, St. Hippolytus, 217–35); St. Urban I, 222–30; St. Pontian, 230–35; St. Anterus, 235–36; St. Fabian, 236–50; St. Cornelius, 251–53 (antipope, Novatian, 251); St. Lucius I, 253–54; St. Stephen I, 254–57; St. Sixtus II, 257–58; St. Dionysius, 259–68; St. Felix I, 269–74; St. Eutychian, 275–83; St. Caius, 283–96; St. Marcellinus, 296–304; St. Marcellus I, 308–9; St. Eusebius, 309 or 310; St. Miltiades or Melchiades, 311–14; St. Sylvester I, 314–35; St. Marcus, 336; St. Julius I, 337–52; Liberius, 352–66 (antipope, Felix II, 355–65); St. Damasus I, 366–84 (antipope, Ursinus, 366–67); St. Siricius, 384–99; St. Anastasius I, 399–401; St. Innocent I, 401–17; St. Zosimus, 417–18; St. Boniface I, 418–22 (antipope, Eulalius, 418–19); St. Celestine I, 422–32; St. Sixtus III, 432–40; St. Leo I, 440–61; St. Hilary, 461–68; St. Simplicius, 468–83; St. Felix III (II), 483–92; St. Gelasius I, 492–96; Anastasius II, 496–98; St. Symmachus, 498–514 (antipope, Lawrence, 498, 501–5); St. Hormisdas,

514–23; St. John I, 523–26; St. Felix IV (III), 526–30; Boniface II, 530–32 (pope or antipope, Dioscurus, 530); John II, 533–35; St. Agapetus I, 535–36; St. Silverius, 536–37; Vigilius, 537–55; Pelagius I, 556–61; John III, 561–74; Benedict I, 575–79; Pelagius II, 579–90; St. Gregory I, 590–604; Sabinianus, 604–6; Boniface III, 607; St. Boniface IV, 608–15; St. Deusdedit or Adeodatus I, 615–18; Boniface V, 619–25; Honorius I, 625–38; Severinus, 640; John IV, 640–42; Theodore I, 642–49; St. Martin I, 649–55; St. Eugene I, 654–57; St. Vitalian, 657–72; Adeodatus II, 672–76; Donus, 676–78; St. Agathon, 678–81; St. Leo II, 682–83; St. Benedict II, 684–85; John V, 685–86; Conon, 686–87 (antipopes: Theodore, 687; Paschal, 687); St. Sergius I, 687–701; John VI, 701–5; John VII, 705–7; Sisinnius, 708; Constantine, 708–15; St. Gregory II, 715–31; St. Gregory III, 731–41; St. Zacharias, 741–52; Stephen II, 752 (never consecrated); Stephen III (II), 752–57; St. Paul I, 757–67 (antipopes: Constantine, 767–69; Philip, 768); Stephen IV (III), 768–72; Adrian I, 772–95; St. Leo III, 795–816; Stephen V (IV), 816–17; St. Paschal I, 817–24; Eugene II, 824–27; Valentine, 827; Gregory IV, 827–44 (antipope, John, 844); Sergius II, 844–47; St. Leo IV, 847–55; Benedict III, 855–58 (antipope, Anastasius, 855); St. Nicholas I, 858–67; Adrian II, 867–72; John VIII, 872–82; Marinus I, 882–84; St. Adrian III, 884–85; Stephen VI (V), 885–91; Formosus, 891–96; Boniface VI, 896; Stephen VII (VI), 896–97; Romanus, 897; Theodore II, 897; John IX, 898–900; Benedict IV, 900–903; Leo V, 903 (antipope, Christopher, 903–4); Sergius III, 904–11; Anastasius III, 911–13; Lando, 913–14; John X, 914–28; Leo VI, 928; Stephen VIII (VII), 928–31; John XI, 931–35; Leo VII, 936–39; Stephen IX (VIII), 939–42; Marinus II, 942–46; Agapetus II, 946–55; John XII, 955–64; Leo VIII, 963–65, or Benedict V, 964–66 (one of these was an antipope); John XIII, 965–72; Benedict VI, 973–74 (antipope, Boniface VII, 974, 984–85); Benedict VII, 974–83; John XIV, 983–84; John XV, 985–96; Gregory V, 996–99 (antipope, John XVI, 997–98); Sylvester II, 999–1003; John XVII, 1003; John XVIII, 1004–9; Sergius IV, 1009–12; Benedict VIII, 1012–24 (antipope, Gregory, 1012); John XIX, 1024–32; Benedict IX, 1032–44, 1045, 1047–48 (popes or antipopes: Sylvester III, 1045; Gregory VI, 1045–46; Clement II, 1046–47); Damasus II, 1048; St. Leo IX, 1049–54; Victor II, 1055–57; Stephen X (IX), 1057–58 (antipope, Benedict X, 1058–59); Nicholas II, 1059–61; Alexander II, 1061–73 (antipope, Honorius II, 1061–72); St. Gregory VII, 1073–85 (antipope, Clement III, 1080–1100); Victor III, 1086–87; Urban II, 1088–99; Paschal II, 1099–1118 (antipopes: Theodoric, 1100; Albert, 1102; Sylvester IV, 1105–11); Gelasius II, 1118–19 (antipope, Gregory VIII, 1118–21); Calixtus II, 1119–24; Honorius II, 1124–30 (antipope, Celestine II, 1124); Innocent II, 1130–43 (antipopes: Anacletus II, 1130–38; Victor IV, 1138); Celestine II, 1143–44; Lucius II, 1144–45; Eugene III, 1145–53; Anastasius IV, 1153–54; Adrian IV, 1154–59; Alexander III, 1159–81 (antipopes: Victor IV, 1159–64; Paschal III, 1164–68; Calixtus III, 1168–78; Innocent III, 1179–80); Lucius III, 1181–85; Urban III, 1185–87; Gregory VIII, 1187; Clement III, 1187–91; Celestine III, 1191–98; Innocent III, 1198–1216; Honorius III, 1216–27; Gregory IX, 1227–41; Celestine IV, 1241; Innocent IV, 1243–54; Alexander IV, 1254–61; Urban IV, 1261–64; Clement IV, 1265–68; Gregory X, 1271–76; Innocent V, 1276; Adrian V, 1276; John XXI, 1276–77; Nicholas III, 1277–80; Martin IV, 1281–85; Honorius IV, 1285–87; Nicholas IV, 1288–92; St. Celestine V, 1294; Boniface VIII, 1294–1303; Benedict XI, 1303–4; Clement V, 1305–14; John XXII, 1316–34 (antipope, Nicholas V, 1328–30; Benedict XII,1334–42; Clement VI, 1342–52; Innocent VI, 1352–62; Urban V, 1362–70; Gregory XI, 1370–78; Urban VI, 1378–89; Boniface IX, 1389–1404; Innocent VII,

1404–6; Gregory XII, 1406–15 (Avignon succession of antipopes: Clement VII, 1378–94; Benedict XIII, 1394–1423; Clement VIII, 1423–29; Benedict XIV, 1425–30; Pisan succession of antipopes: Alexander V, 1409–10; John XXIII, 1410–15); Martin V, 1417–31; Eugene IV, 1431–47 (antipope, Felix V, 1439–49); Nicholas V, 1447–55; Calixtus III, 1455–58; Pius II, 1458–64; Paul II, 1464–71; Sixtus IV, 1471–84; Innocent VIII, 1484–92; Alexander VI, 1492–1503; Pius III, 1503; Julius II, 1503–13; Leo X, 1513–21; Adrian VI, 1522–23; Clement VII, 1523–34; Paul III, 1534–49; Julius III, 1550–55; Marcellus II, 1555; Paul IV, 1555–59; Pius IV, 1559–65; St. Pius V, 1566–72; Gregory XIII, 1572–85; Sixtus V, 1585–90; Urban VII, 1590; Gregory XIV, 1590–91; Innocent IX, 1591; Clement VIII, 1592–1605; Leo XI 1605; Paul V, 1605–21; Gregory XV, 1621–23; Urban VIII, 1623–44; Innocent X, 1644–55; Alexander VII, 1655–67; Clement IX, 1667–69; Clement X, 1670–76; Innocent XI, 1676–89; Alexander VIII, 1689–91; Innocent XII, 1691–1700; Clement XI, 1700–1721; Innocent XIII, 1721–24; Benedict XIII, 1724–30; Clement XII, 1730–40; Benedict XIV, 1740–58; Clement XIII, 1758–69; Clement XIV, 1769–74; Pius VI, 1775–99; Pius VII, 1800–1823; Leo XII, 1823–29; Pius VIII, 1829–30; Gregory XVI, 1831–46; Pius IX, 1846–78; Leo XIII, 1878–1903; Pius X, 1903–14; Benedict XV, 1914–22; Pius XI, 1922–39; Pius XII, 1939–.

Papal States, former independent territory under temporal rule of the popes; cap. Rome. Also called States of the Church and Pontifical States, they extended across the Italian peninsula from the Adriatic Sea and the lower Po (N) to the Tyrrhenian Sea (S) and included Latium, Umbria, the Marches, Emilia, and Romagna. The states had their origin in land endowments given to the popes in the 4th cent.—the "Patrimony of St. Peter"—in Italy, Sicily, and Sardinia. The popes gradually lost their more distant lands, but in the duchy of Rome their power grew and made Rome independent of the Eastern emperors. Pepin the Short's donation of RAVENNA and the PENTAPOLIS to the papacy (754; confirmed by Charlemagne 774) and the forged Donation of CONSTANTINE gave the popes claims of overlordship over central and S Italy, Sicily, and Sardinia, but they did not give them effective control. The bequest of Countess MATILDA of Tuscany (1115) resulted in a long struggle between emperors and popes over Matilda's lands; in the 14th cent. the emperors renounced their claims to the duchy of Spoleto, the ROMAGNA, and the March of Ancona. However, the free communes and petty tyrants of these regions long resisted papal domination, while the "Babylonian Captivity" of the popes in Avignon and the Great Schism (1309–1420) threw the Papal States into chaos. Actual control by the papacy of its states began in the 16th cent. under JULIUS II. After the French invasion of 1796 the Papal States were curtailed, occupied, and twice abolished, but they were fully restored and placed under Austrian protection by the Congress of Vienna (1814–15). PIUS IX granted a constitution but revoked it after the Revolution of 1848–49. During the RISORGIMENTO, the Papal States lost Bologna, the Romagna, the Marches, and Umbria to Sardinia (1860), but French intervention prevented their total absorption until the fall of Napoleon III (1870), when Victor Emmanuel II annexed Rome. The popes refused to recognize their loss of temporal power, and in 1929 they received full sovereignty over VATICAN CITY by the Lateran Treaty.

papaw tree or **pawpaw,** deciduous tree (*Asimina triloba*), native E of Mississippi. It has purple flowers and fleshy fruits with custardlike edible pulp.

papaya (pŭpī'ū), palmlike tropical American tree (*Carica papaya*). It bears edible yellow fruits which yield a juice containing the enzyme papain.

Papeete (päpä-ā'tä), port town (pop. 12,428), on Tahiti, S Pacific; cap. of French Establishments in Oceania and of Tahiti.

Papen, Franz von (fränts' fūn pä'pùn), 1879–, German politician. His implication in sabotage plots as military attaché in Washington caused U.S. to request his recall (1915). In 1932 he succeeded Brüning as chancellor of Germany, heading a conservative cabinet. His actions soon afterward led to his expulsion from his party (the Catholic Center). He resigned when he could not secure a working majority in the Reichstag; Schleicher succeeded him. Early in 1933 his behind-the-scenes maneuvers were instrumental in bringing about Hitler's appointment as chancellor. Under Hitler, he served as ambassador to Austria and to Turkey. At the war-crimes trial he was acquitted (1946).

paper, thin sheet or layer made from vegetable fiber (commonly wood pulp) and used in some 14,000 products. Papermaking is said to have originated c.105 in China and spread via Samarkand and N Africa to Spain (c.1150), thence through Europe, and in 1690 to American colonies. Fiber, mixed with water, is reduced mechanically or chemically to pulp introduced into mesh mold, then pressed and dried. Watermark is made by design attached to mold. Dipping molds were superseded by machine forming continuous web invented 1798 in France by Nicolas Robert and improved in England by Henry and Sealy Fourdrinier. In modern Fourdrinier machine, pulp is poured on endless wire-mesh belt edged with deckle strips, then pressed between revolving rolls and carried over series of drying rolls. Paper is modified for various purposes by sizing or other materials added to pulp or used as coating.

Paphlagonia (pǎ"flùgō'nēù), anc. region, N Asia Minor, on the Black Sea, famous for timber, horses, and mules. Greeks colonized the coast.

Paphos (pā'fŏs), two anc. cities, SW Cyprus. The first, founded by Phoenicians, was center of the worship of Astarte or Aphrodite. The second was cap. of Cyprus in Roman times.

Papineau, Louis Joseph (päpēnō'), 1786–1871, French Canadian political leader and insurgent. Speaker of legislative assembly of Lower Canada (1815–37). Leader of Reform party. Believing British government in Canada unfair to French Canadians, he inflamed some of his followers, the *Patriotes,* to open rebellion in 1837. Took no part in uprising but fled to U.S. Returned to Canada c.1845.

Papini, Giovanni (jōvän'nē päpē'nē), 1881–, Italian writer. *Un uomo finito* (1912) was his first success. After embracing Catholicism, he wrote the famous *Life of Christ* (1921) and *Dante vivo* (1933).

Papinian (pùpī'nēùn), d. 212, Roman jurist, one of the greatest figures of Roman law. He was a friend of Septimius Severus, but was put to death by Caracalla, son of Septimius Severus.

Pappus (pǎ'pùs), fl. c.300, Greek mathematician of Alexandria whose works (which recorded and enlarged those of his predecessors) stimulated 17th-cent. revival of geometry. Descartes expounded several of his theorems.

Papua: see NEW GUINEA.

Papua, Territory of (pä'pūù), area (90,540 sq. mi.; pop. 373,000), belonging to Australia and including SE NEW GUINEA and near-by islands; cap. Port Moresby. Became British protectorate 1884. Annexed to Great Britain as British New Guinea. Governed by Australia since 1906.

papyrus (pùpī'rùs), sedge (*Cyperus papyrus*). Ancient Egyptians used roots as fuel, pith as food, and stem for boats, cloth, twine, and sheets of writing material. This writing material, also called papyrus, was made from slices of the sedge laid side by side in two layers at right angles, pressed together with adhesive, glued end to end, and rolled on rods to form manuscripts.

Pará (pùrä'), state (469,778 sq. mi.; pop. 1,142,846), N Brazil, in lower Amazon basin, S of the Guianas; cap., BELÉM. A hot, humid region, not extensively developed. Chief products: rubber, hardwoods, Brazil nuts, medicinal plants.

Pará, river, c.200 mi. long, E Brazil. Actually is SE arm of Amazon, divided from rest of river by Marajó isl. Great port of Belém is on right bank.

parable, in Bible. Term used in the Gospels for a short narrative illustrating a moral or for a figurative statement. There are a few parables in the Old Testament, e.g., the ewe lamb (2 Sam. 12.1–4). Among the many parables told by Jesus were: the Good Samaritan (Luke 10.29–37); the prodigal son (Luke 15.11–32); the sower (Mat. 13.3–9,18–23; Mark 4.3–9; 14–20; Luke 8.4–15); the Pharisee and the publican (Luke 18.9–14); the lost sheep (Mat. 18.11–14); the rich man (Dives) and Lazarus (Luke 16.19–31).

parabola (pùrã'bùlù), plane curve such that distances from any point on it to fixed point (focus) and fixed line (directrix) are equal; also a conic section cut by plane parallel to one element of cone. Axis of parabola is line through focus perpendicular to directrix; vertex is point in which axis intersects curve; latus rectum is chord through focus perpendicular to axis.

Paracelsus, Philippus Aureolus (fīlī'pùs ôrēō'lùs pärù-sĕl'sùs), 1493?–1541, Swiss physician, alchemist, and chemist. He promoted use of specific remedies and was author of many medical and occult works. Real name was Theophrastus Bombastus von Hohenheim.

parachute (pǎ'rùshoōt), umbrellalike device designed to slow descent of body falling through air and permit safe landing on surface. Jean Pierre Blanchard claimed invention (1785). Jacques Garnerin made first successful descent (from balloon, 1797). Modern designs for carrying aviators and cargo.

Paraclete (pǎ'rùklēt) [Gr.,= advocate], title of the Holy Ghost, often translated as "Comforter" or "Advocate." John 14.16,26; 15.26; 16.7; 1 John 2.1.

Paradise, name sometimes used for Garden of Eden or synonymously with HEAVEN. It originally was a Persian word meaning park or garden. Many ancient peoples had myths about a place where man lived in a state of bliss until he lost it through sinning. With the beginning of the Messianic concept in late Jewish thought came the hope of regaining this earthly bliss, and Paradise became identified with the promised Messianic kingdom. In some Christian thought, Paradise is regarded as a state of bliss secondary to heaven itself; the souls of certain righteous dwell free from pain and punishment in this place but are denied seeing God face to face.

paraffin or **paraffine** (both: pǎ'rùfĭn), colorless, odorless, tasteless mineral wax, a mixture of hydrocarbons, chiefly of methane series. It is used in making candles, tapers, and paper matches, in sizing and waterproofing, and in sealing jams and jellies.

Paragould (pǎ'rùgoōld), city (pop. 9,668), NE Ark., near St. Francis R. Railroad shops. Processes wood, cotton, and food.

Paraguay (pǎ'rùgwā, Span. pärägwī'), republic (157,047 sq. mi.; pop. 1,259,826), SE South America; cap. ASUNCIÓN. Paraguay has no seacoast and is surrounded by Bolivia, Brazil, and Argentina. The E part, where most of population lives, lies between the Paraguay and Paraná rivers. To the W of the Paraguay R. lies the Chaco, largely uninhabited and unexploited, although there is some cattle raising, quebracho is found in the forests, and petroleum has been discovered. Agr. products in the E are cotton, tobacco, citrus fruits, and *mate* (Paraguayan tea). Industries include meat packing, the extraction of petitgrain from wild oranges (Paraguay furnishes most of world's supply) and manufacture of rum, molasses, and alcohol. Chief cities besides Asunción are Villarica, Concepción, and Encarnación. Population is largely a homogeneous mixture of Spanish and Guaraní strains, and the Paraguayans are almost all bilingual. German, Italian, and French immigration have added new elements to the distinctive civilization of Paraguay, which has arts and crafts showing the varied strains. In music, the *guarania* is a notable form of modern music and the handmade lace, called *nanduti,* is exquisite. The established religion is Roman Catholic, but other faiths are tolerated and Mennonite settlements were founded before and during World War II. Asunción was founded in 1536 or 1537, and it was from here that Buenos Aires was re-established and many of the Argentine cities were founded. It was through the forceful rule of Hernando Árias de Saavedra (called Hernandárias) that Paraguay's virtual independence from the Spanish administrators in Buenos Aires and Peru was established. Also in his regime the Jesuit missions, which played such an important part in Paraguayan culture from the late 16th cent. to the 18th, were founded. Independence from Spain came with Argentina's successful revolution (1810); the next year Paraguay quietly overthrew the colonial officials, and in 1814, the first of the three great dictators who were to mold Paraguay came into power (José Gaspar Rodríguez Francia, Carlos Antonio López, and Francisco Solano López). During the rule of F. S. López a war was fought against the combined forces of Brazil, Argentina, and Uruguay (1865–70; see Triple Alliance, War of the). The disastrous effects of that war were slow to disappear, and political confusion was added to economic depression. Decades later, as the country was slowly recovering, it was plunged again into war with Bolivia over the boundary in the Chaco (1932–35). This time Paraguay emerged victorious but exhausted. A rapid succession of governments ensued, with Higinio Morínigo's regime lasting the longest (1940–48).

Paraguay, river, c.1,300 mi. long, rising in Mato Grosso state, W Brazil, with headstreams in E Bolivia. Flows S, marking border between Brazil and Paraguay, divides Paraguayan Chaco from E Paraguay, and forms boundary between Argentina and Paraguay; is important in Río de la Plata system.

Paraguay tea: see MATE.

Paraíba or **Parahiba** (both: pärŭē′bù), state (21,730 sq. mi.; pop. 1,730,784), NE Brazil; cap., Joâo Pessoa, on the Atlantic. Primarily cotton growing area with some copper and tin mining. Settled by Portuguese (1584).

Paraíba or **Paraíba do Sul** (dōō sōol), river, c.600 mi. long, rising W of Rio de Janeiro, SE Brazil. Flows SW to a point near São Paulo, then NE to the Atlantic. Valley produces rice, sugar cane, livestock.

parakeet or **parrakeet** (pä′rükēt), any of various small parrots of Australia, Polynesia, Asia, Africa. Carolina parakeet of E and S U.S. believed extinct. Shell (or zebra) parakeet is a green cage bird with yellow head, grayish green wings with black markings, and a long narrow blue and black tail. It is sometimes called love bird but true love birds are African and have short wide tails and short bodies.

Paralipomenon: see CHRONICLES.

paralysis or **palsy** (pôl′zē), loss of motion or sensation resulting from lesion in brain, spinal cord, nerves, or muscles and caused by injury, poison, or disease. Types include general; hemiplegia (on one side); paraplegia (on both sides at one level); *paralysis agitans* or Parkinson's disease, accompanied by tremor; cerebral palsy, usually caused by lesion in brain motor tissue resulting from birth injury.

Paramaribo (pä″rūmä′rībō), city (pop. 76,466), cap. of Dutch Guiana, port on Surinam R. Founded 1650 as cap. of a new English colony. Leading exports today are rum, coffee, timber, and bauxite.

Paramus (pùrä′mùs), residential borough (pop. 6,268), NE N.J., NE of Paterson. Truck farming.

Paran (pä′rän), wilderness, probably S of Beersheba. Ishmael settled here.

Paraná (päränä′), state (77,717 sq. mi.; pop. 2,149,509), S Brazil, between Paraná R. and Atlantic; cap., Curitiba. Grows coffee, cotton, fruit. Population includes Italians, Germans, and Slavs.

Paraná, city (pop. 84,153), cap. of Entre Rios prov., NE Argentina, port on Paraná R. Center of grain and cattle district. Founded 1730, it was cap. of Argentine confederation (1853–61).

Paraná, river, c.2,050 mi. long, formed in S Brazil by junction of Paranaíba and Rio Grande. Flows S and W to confluence with Paraguay and then S and E through N section of Argentina to join Uruguay R. at head of Río de la Plata. Principal ports are: Posadas, Corrientes, Santa Fe, Paraná, Rosario.

Paranaíba (pä″rünäē′bù), river, c.500 mi. long, rising in W Minas Gerais state, E central Brazil, and flowing W to join Rio Grande in forming Paraná.

paranoia (pä″rùnoi′ù), type of psychosis characterized by persistent, logically reasoned delusions, especially of persecution or grandeur. True paranoia is rare; often paranoid reactions are caused by schizophrenia. Recovery is considered unlikely.

parapsychology: see PSYCHICAL RESEARCH.

Para rubber tree (pùrä′), large tree (*Hevea brasiliensis*), native to South America and a member of the spurge family. The most important source of natural RUBBER, it is widely grown in tropical regions. Latex, the milky juice from which rubber is made, is obtained by tapping the tree's trunk at regular intervals, beginning after the fifth to seventh year.

parasite (pä′rùsīt), plant or animal which, at some stage of existence, obtains nourishment from another living organism, called its host. Includes many disease-causing bacteria, protozoans, and worms; fungi, e.g., rust, smut; and insects, e.g., flea, louse. A saprophyte obtains nourishment from organic matter, not from a living host; mushrooms and Indian pipe are examples of saprophytes.

Paray-le-Monial (pärä′-lù-mônyäl′), town (pop. 6,240), Saône-et-Loire dept., E central France. It is a major place of pilgrimage, where St. Margaret Mary founded the cult of the Sacred Heart (17th cent.).

Parca (pär′kù), Roman goddess of childbirth. Her name pluralized (Parcae) was applied to FATES.

parcel post, system of package delivery, established on an international basis in 1878. The U.S. delayed organizing domestic parcel post service until 1913; rural parcel-post routes were established in 1919. Packages are limited to 70 lb. and to 100 in. for girth and length combined.

parchment, untanned animal skins, dehaired, stretched, and rubbed with chalk and pumice. Name is a corruption of Pergamum where it was prepared c.2d cent. B.C. It slowly superseded papyrus and was used for the handwritten copies of books until the advent of printing. Superseded by paper.

Pardo Bazán, Emilia, condesa de (ämē′lyä kōndä′sä dä pär′dhō bäthän′), 1852–1921, Spanish novelist and critic. She wrote *La cuestión palpitante* (1883; in defense of Zola's naturalism), regional novels of Galicia, and other works.

Paré, Ambroise (äbrwäz′ pärä′), c.1510–1590, French army surgeon, known for advancing humane methods of treating wounds.

parent education, movement to help parents' understanding of child life. Carried on through adult education and parent-teacher associations. Child Study Association (1888) and Natl. Congress of Parents and Teachers (1897) are active in field.

Pareto, Vilfredo (vēlfrä′dō pärä′tō), 1848–1923, Italian economist and sociologist. He applied mathematics to economic theory and sought to differentiate rational and nonrational factors in social action and the cyclical rise and fall of governing elite groups. Italian Fascist ideology utilized some of his theories. His chief work (1916) was translated (1935) as *Mind and Society.*

Paria, Gulf of (pär′yä), between mainland of Venezuela and island of Trinidad.

Parian marble: see PAROS.

Paricutín (pärēkōotēn′), volcano, c.8,200 ft. high, Michoacán, W central Mexico. Erupting from a level field in 1943, it grew c.800 ft. before it became quiescent in 1952.

Parini, Giuseppe (jōōzĕp′pä pärĕ′nē), 1729–99, Italian poet, a priest; author of the satiric masterpiece, *Il* *giorno* [the day] (1763–1801), a mock-didactic poem about a young nobleman's daily life.

Paris or **Alexander,** in Greek legend, Trojan prince; son of Priam and Hecuba. Because of a prophecy that he would destroy Troy, his parents exposed him, but he was saved and grew up as a shepherd. His elopement with HELEN caused the Trojan War.

Paris, Matthew: see MATTHEW OF PARIS.

Paris (păʹrĭs), town (pop. 5,249), S Ont., Canada, on Grand R. and W of Hamilton. Woolen mill center.

Paris (păʹrĭs, Fr. pärēʹ), city (pop. 2,691,473), cap. of France, on the Seine; Greater Paris, with industrial and residential suburbs, virtually covers all Seine dept. (pop. 4,775,711). Largest city and industrial center of France; transport and communications center of W Europe (large river port, seven major railroad stations, two airports); world center of fashions and luxury goods; probably world's greatest tourist center. Archiepiscopal see. Intellectually and artistically, Paris led the W world in the 17th–19th cent. and in some respects retains a unique position ("city of light"). Among its many cultural institutions are the university (see SORBONNE), French Academy, Pasteur Institute, École des Beaux Arts, Conservatoire, Comédie Française, Opéra, and LOUVRE. Divided into 20 *arrondissements* [boroughs], Paris is governed by a municipal council. N of the Seine extends the right bank, center of fashions and business. Here are the great boulevards and some of the world's most celebrated thoroughfares (the CHAMPS ÉLYSÉES, from the ARC DE TRIOMPHE to the Place de la Concorde; Rue de la Paix; Place Vendôme); here also are the Bois de Boulogne and MONTMARTRE, topped by the Church of Sacré-Cœur. On the left bank are the Old Latin Quarter, for centuries the preserve of the university; MONTPARNASSE; the LUXEMBOURG PALACE; many governmental buildings; the Hôtel des Invalides and its domed church (tomb of Napoleon I); and the EIFFEL TOWER. The historic core of Paris is the Île de la Cité, a small island occupied in part by the Palais de Justice (incl. SAINTE CHAPELLE), the city hall, and the Cathedral of NOTRE DAME DE PARIS. A fishing hamlet at the time of Caesar's conquest, ancient Lutetia Parisiorum soon grew into an important Roman town. It became (5th cent. A.D.) a cap. of the Merovingian kings but was devastated by Norse raids in 9th cent. With the accession (987) of Hugh Capet, count of Paris, as king of France, Paris became the national cap. It flowered as a medieval commercial center and as the fountainhead of scholasticism but suffered severely during the Hundred Years War (English occupation 1420–36). Throughout its history, Paris displayed a rebellious and independent spirt—as in the civil troubles under Étienne Marcel (1358), its resistance to Henry IV (1589–93), the first Fronde (1648–49), the revolutions of 1789, 1830, and 1848, the German siege of 1870–71, and the COMMUNE OF PARIS of 1871. Most of modern Paris was planned in the 19th cent. by HAUSSMANN. Occupied by the Germans in 1940, Paris was liberated Aug. 25, 1944, by U.S., French, and Parisian resistance forces. Its industrial districts suffered considerable bomb damage.

Paris (păʹrĭs). **1** City (pop. 9,460), E Ill., NW of Terre Haute, Ind. Rail center in farm and coal area. Mfg. of brooms, shoes, and metal products. **2** City (pop. 6,912), N Ky., NE of Lexington, on South Fork of Licking R. in bluegrass country. Tobacco and bluegrass-seed market. One of first distilleries in state (1790) here; whisky from region called bourbon after county. **3** City (pop. 8,826), W Tenn., near Ky. line, in farm, clay, and timber area. Railroad shops, cotton gins; mfg. of cosmetics and pottery. **4** City (pop. 21,643), E Texas, NE of Dallas. Processing and shipping center for agr. area, it has woodworking, flour and cottonseed oil milling, and meat packing.

Paris, Commune of: see COMMUNE OF PARIS.

Paris, Congress of, 1856, conference held by representatives of France, Great Britain, Turkey, Sardinia, Russia, Austria, and Prussia to negotiate the peace after the CRIMEAN WAR. In the Treaty of Paris (March 30, 1856) Russia agreed to neutralization of Black Sea; the Danubian principalities (Moldavia and Walachia, after 1859 called RUMANIA) became semi-independent states under nominal Turkish suzerainty; Russian-Turkish boundary in Asia was restored to pre-war status. Turkey became a member of the European concert. Provisions were altered (1878) by Treaty of SAN STEFANO and Congress of BERLIN. The Congress also issued the **Declaration of Paris,** an agreement concerning the rules of maritime warfare. Its four principles were: privateering was no longer legal; a neutral flag would protect the goods of an enemy, except for contraband of war; neutral goods, except for such contraband, would not be liable to capture when under the enemy's flag; a blockade would be binding only if it prevented access to the coast of the enemy. The U.S. refused to accept the declaration, but later followed its principles.

Paris, Pact of: see KELLOGG-BRIAND PACT.

Paris, Treaty of, name given to several important treaties signed in or near Paris. **1763,** treaty signed by England, France, and Spain, ending (with Peace of HUBERTUSBURG) the SEVEN YEARS WAR. France lost Canada and possessions E of Mississippi R. to England and ceded W Louisiana to its ally, Spain, in compensation for Florida, which Spain lost to England. In India, France recovered its posts but was forbidden to maintain troops or build forts in Bengal. Treaty laid foundation of British colonial supremacy. **1783,** treaties ending war of AMERICAN REVOLUTION. (1) U.S. treaty with England (negotiated, for U.S., by John Adams, Benjamin Franklin, and John Jay) fixed boundaries of U.S. and settled other problems arising out of severance of U.S. from Britain. (2) Anglo-French treaty generally restored mutual status quo as of 1763. (3) Anglo-Spanish treaty restored Floridas and Minorca to Spain; England kept Gibraltar. (4) Anglo-Dutch treaty (ratified 1784) awarded several Dutch colonies to Britain. **1814,** treaty between France and the principal allies (England, Russia, Austria, Prussia) after Napoleon's first abdication. Reduced France to boundaries of 1792. France paid no indemnities. England returned most French colonies to France but kept Malta. A general conference was called to settle all other territorial questions (see VIENNA, CONGRESS OF). Leniency of treaty was due chiefly to skill of TALLEYRAND. **1815,** between France and the allies after Napoleon's return and defeat at Waterloo. Reduced France to 1790 boundaries; exacted heavy indemnity; provided for five-year occupation of NE France; ratified Final Act of Congress of Vienna. Simultaneously, QUADRUPLE ALLIANCE was renewed. **1856:** see PARIS, CONGRESS OF. **1898:** see SPANISH-AMERICAN WAR. **1919–20:** see Treaties of VERSAILLES, SAINT-GERMAIN, NEUILLY, TRIANON, and SÈVRES. **1947:** see ITALY; RUMANIA; HUNGARY; BULGARIA; FINLAND.

Paris green, highly poisonous compound containing arsenic and copper. Used as insecticide and fungicide.

Paris Peace Conference, 1919: see VERSAILLES, TREATY OF.

Park, Mungo, 1771–1806, Scottish explorer in Africa. Explored course of Niger R. Drowned when natives attacked party.

Park, William Hallock, 1863–1939, American bacteriologist, known for work in public health and preventive medicine. Author of standard works in field.

Park College, at Parkville, Mo., NW of Kansas City; coed.; opened 1875, chartered 1879 by Presbyterians. School industries operated by students.

Parker, Alton B(rooks), 1852–1926, American jurist, U.S. Democratic presidential candidate (1904). Noted for liberal decisions in labor cases.

Parker, Dorothy, 1893–, American short-story and verse writer, best known for sardonic, humorous light verse and stories of social satire.

Parker, Francis Wayland, 1837–1902, American educator. He was superintendent of schools in Quincy, Mass., 1875–80, and there originated "Quincy movement," emphasizing learning by doing, socialized activities, teaching of science, and informal instruction. He was founder and principal (1899–1901) of part of Univ. of Chicago's school of education.

Parker, Sir Gilbert, 1862–1932, Canadian novelist. Many of his novels and collections of tales deal with material from Canadian history.

Parker, Sir Hyde, 1739–1807, British admiral. In American Revolution he broke North River defenses at New York city in 1776. Horatio Nelson's refusal to obey his cease-fire signal at Copenhagen victory (1801) is famous incident in naval history.

Parker, Lottie Blair, 1858?–1937, American playwright, author of melodrama *Way Down East* (1898).

Parker, Matthew, 1504–75, English prelate. Archbishop of Canterbury after 1559, he revised (1562) Thirty-nine Articles and supervised (1563–68) preparation of Bishops' Bible.

Parker, Theodore, 1810–60, American theologian and social reformer. As Unitarian pastor in Boston, he set forth views in *Discourse of Matters Pertaining to Religion* (1842) then thought radical but later accepted. He was a transcendentalist and contributor to the *Dial,* a lyceum lecturer, and a leader in antislavery and prison-reform activities.

Parker Dam, 320 ft. high, 856 ft. long, at Ariz.-Calif. line, in Colorado R.; completed 1938. Used for water supply, power, irrigation.

Parkersburg, city (pop. 29,684), NW W.Va., SSW of Wheeling and at junction of little Kanawha and Ohio rivers; settled 1785. Shipping center for oil, gas, and coal region with mfg. of rayon, implements, oil-well equipment. Near by in the Ohio is Blennerhasset Isl.

Parkhurst, Charles Henry, 1842–1933, American clergyman and reformer, pastor (1880–1918) of Madison Square Presbyterian Church, New York city. As president after 1891 of Society for Prevention of Crime, he instigated investigation of Tammany by Lexow committee.

Parkman, Francis, 1823–93, American historian. On basis of travel and study in W U.S. (1846) he wrote famous work, *The Oregon Trail* (1849). Also wrote studies of early Northwest and Canada, notably *Pioneers of France in the New World* (1865), *The Discovery of the Great West* (1869), *The Old Régime in Canada* (1874), *A Half-Century of Conflict* (1892).

Park Range, part of Rocky Mts., central Colo. and S Wyo., N from Colorado R. Gore Range is SE part, Sierra Madre (Wyo.) is NW extension. Mt. Lincoln (14,284 ft.) is highest point.

Park Ridge, residential city (pop. 16,602), NE Ill., NW suburb of Chicago.

parlement (Fr. pärlŭmä'), in French history, the chief judiciary body until 1789. There were (as of 1789) 14 provincial parlements and the Parlement of Paris, which had superior authority. Growing out of the feudal Curia Regis, the Parlement of Paris began its separate existence under Louis IX (13th cent.) and grew into an extremely elaborate organization. Its political power rested on the fact that it registered royal edicts, which thereby became law, and it repeatedly challenged royal authority, notably in the first FRONDE. It was abolished (1771–74) by Chancellor MAUPEOU, whose attempted judicial reform failed largely for lack of new magistrates to replace the old ones. The defiance of the parlements when Loménie de Brienne proposed fiscal reforms (1787–88) led to the calling of the States-General (1789) and the beginning of the French Revolution.

Parley, Peter: see GOODRICH, SAMUEL GRISWOLD.

Parliament, legislative assembly of Great Britain and British Empire. Has come to be the actual sovereign rather than the king, whose authority is nominal. Consists technically of the king, House of Commons, and House of Lords. Membership in Lords is heredi-tary (except for the Anglican bishops) for peers of England, Ireland, and Scotland; since 1911 its powers have been slight. The power of Commons lies in its control of finances. An elective body of 625 members (506 for England, Wales and Monmouth 36, Scotland 71, N. Ireland 12), it is presided over by the speaker, elected from party in power. The two-party system is feature of English parliamentary government. The majority party chooses executive head (the prime minister) and must call general election if unable to get support on major issues. Unlike the U.S. system the government executive branch is in effect a committee of the legislature. Parliament drew from many ancient institutions. Its first modern developments were in 13th cent. King's feudal court of Curia Regis produced the House of Lords (so-named in Henry VIII's reign). Irregular assemblies of other social elements of the state grew into the House of Commons. Until early 14th cent. judicial issues prevailed over financial. Attempts of the barons to win support led to the Mad Parliament at Oxford (1258) and Parliament of Simon de MONTFORT (1265). Edward I's Model Parliament (1295) set a precedent for future development. Familiar parliamentary features did not appear until transfer of taxation control from king to Parliament (1340) and soon to Commons. Power to withhold financial grants enabled Parliament to force the king's acceptance of national petitions, which were gradually supplanted by bills enacted by Commons, Lords, and king. Under the Tudors the king used Parliament as his instrument. Its claim to actual sovereignty became the issue of the PURITAN REVOLUTION. Petition of Right presented (1628) to Charles I demanded recognition of sole authority to levy taxes. The Long Parliament (1640–49) opposed the king in the civil war. After control by Oliver Cromwell, the Restoration returned Parliament to power. The Glorious Revolution affirmed its permanent sovereignty (1688). The appearance of parties led to parliamentary control of the ministries. Representation was limited to the propertied upper classes until democratic agitation and Chartism led to REFORM BILLS (1832, 1867) and finally to universal suffrage (1918). House of Lords was stripped of power by Parliament Act of 1911. Parliament is housed in Westminster Palace.

parliamentary law, rules under which deliberative bodies conduct their proceedings. Based on the practice of the English Parliament (largely conventional, rather than statutory) and including practices from the U.S. congressional bodies, they have been codified in H. M. Robert's *Rules of Order* (1876), the usually accepted authority, though the presiding officers of the British and U.S. legislative bodies are the respective interpreters of parliamentary law.

Parma (pär'mä), city (pop. 65,126), Emilia-Romagna, N central Italy, on Aemilian way. Agr. market; silk mfg. A Roman colony after 183 B.C., it became a free commune in 12th cent.; annexed to Papal States 16th cent. In 1545 Pope Paul III created the duchy of Parma and Piacenza for his son Pierluigi Farnese. The duchy continued under the FARNESE family till 1731, when it passed to the Spanish Bourbons. The cadet line of BOURBON-PARMA began 1748. The duchy was annexed to France 1802; awarded to MARIE LOUISE 1815; restored to Bourbons 1847; annexed to Sardinia 1860. Parma is rich in works of Correggio (frescoes in Convent of St. Paul and in Romanesque cathedral). Among notable buildings are the baptistery (13th cent.) and the wooden Farnese Theater (built 1618; damaged in World War II). University dates from 1502. Region is noted for Parmesan cheese.

Parma, city (pop. 28,897), NE Ohio, S suburb of Cleveland; inc. 1925.

Parmenas (pär'–), one of the seven deacons. Acts 6.5.

Parmenides (pärmĕn'ĭdēz), b. c.514 B.C., Greek philosopher of the ELEATIC SCHOOL. He believed in the unity of existence and held that "being" is eternal reality, change an illusion.

Parmenion (pärmē'nēun), d. 330 B.C., Macedonian general under Philip II and Alexander the Great, prominent in Alexander's Persian battles. A plot against Alexander in 330 B.C. seemed to implicate Parmenion's son Philotas, who under torture accused his father. Alexander had both killed.

Parmigiano (pärmējä'nō) or **Parmigianino** (–jänē'nō), 1503–40, Italian painter, whose real name was Francesco Mazzola, b. Parma. Influenced by Correggio and Raphael. Best-known picture is *Cupid Making a Bow* (Vienna). Credited with introducing etching into Italy.

Parnaíba (pärnäē'bù), river, c.750 mi. long, rising in NE Brazil. Flows N to Atlantic near town of Parnaíba (pop. 30,900), which is shipping point for river valley.

Parnassians (pärnä'shùnz), group of 19th-cent. French poets, named for their journal *Parnasse contemporain* (1866–76) and including Leconte de Lisle, Banville, Sully-Prudhomme, and Heredia. In reaction against romanticism, they stood for rigid forms and careful workmanship.

Parnassus (pärnä'sùs), mountain, more than 8,000 ft. high, SW Phocis, Greece, sacred to Apollo, Dionysus, and the Muses; therefore a symbol of the apex of literature, art, and culture. The Castalian fountain was on its slopes. Here the Pythian games were held. At the foot lay Delphi.

Parnell, Charles Stewart, 1846–91, Irish nationalist leader. United diverse elements of Irish patriots. Elected to British parliament in 1875, he used filibusters to stress gravity of Irish problem. His agitation on the IRISH LAND QUESTION led to increased crime against landlords and he was arrested. Released after issuing popular no-rent manifesto from jail. Formed an alliance with Gladstone who introduced (1886) first HOME RULE Bill. Named co-respondent in divorce suit (1889), he lost his political influence, and died a broken man.

Parnell, Thomas, 1679–1718, British poet. He was a friend of Pope and Swift, and his verse (e.g., "The Hermit") was praised by Johnson and Goldsmith.

Paros (pâ'rŏs, Gr. pä'rôs), Aegean island (77 sq. mi.; pop. 8,993), Greece; one of the Cyclades. Famed for quarries of Parian marble, used by sculptors from 6th cent. B.C. After Persian Wars, Paros was taken into Athenian confederacy. The Parian Chronicle, found here, consists of two marble fragments of a great inscription relating events 1581 B.C.–263 B.C. The larger is at Oxford, the other at Paros.

Parowan (pă'rùwăn"), city (pop. 1,455), SW Utah, NE of Cedar City. Nominal territorial cap. 1858–59.

Parr, Catherine, 1512–48, queen consort; sixth wife of Henry VIII of England. Served as queen regent in 1544. After Henry's death in 1547 she married Baron Seymour of Sudeley.

parrakeet: see PARAKEET.

Parran, Thomas (pä'rŭn), 1892–, American surgeon general (1936–48). Launched campaign against venereal diseases (1937). Wrote *Shadow on the Land* (1937).

Parrhasius (pùrä'shēus), fl. c.400 B.C., Greek painter. Reputedly the first painter to create figures with correct proportions and a sense of contour.

Parrington, Vernon L(ouis), 1871–1929, American educator and literary critic, author of *Main Currents in American Thought* (3 vols., 1927–30).

Parrish, Maxfield, 1870–, American illustrator and mural decorator. His brilliant colors (esp. blue) are characteristic.

Parris Island: see SEA ISLANDS.

parrot, name for certain members of order of birds (Psittaciformes) which includes PARAKEET, COCKATOO, and MACAW, occurring chiefly in tropics and subtropics of both hemispheres. In parrots the bill is strong and hooked; the feet have four toes. Many species learn to speak by imitation. See *ill.*, p. 105.

parrot fever: see PSITTACOSIS.

Parry, Sir William Edward, 1790–1855, British arctic explorer and rear admiral. Served in and commanded several expeditions seeking Northwest Passage. All were unsuccessful but informative.

Parry Islands, archipelago off N Canada, in Arctic Ocean; part of Franklin dist., Northwest Territories. Discovered by Sir W. E. Parry 1819–20.

Parry Sound, town (pop. 5,183), S Ont., Canada, on Parry Sound (inlet of Georgian Bay), NNW of Toronto. Resort with railroad shops, lumbering, and woodworking.

Parsees: see PARSIS.

Parsifal (pär'sĭfäl), figure of ARTHURIAN LEGEND, also known as Sir Percivale, who is in turn a later form of a hero (also identified as Gawain) of Celtic myth. CHRESTIEN DE TROYES first wrote the story of the hero's quest for the Holy GRAIL; WOLFRAM VON ESCHENBACH's *Parzival*, considered one of the greatest medieval poems, became the basis for Wagner's music drama *Parsifal*.

Parsis or Parsees (both: pär'sēz), religious community of India (esp. Bombay) practicing Zoroastrianism. They say they reverence, but do not worship, fire. The dead are exposed in "towers of silence," where vultures devour them. Parsis are important in cotton and steel industries. They stress education.

parsley, Old World aromatic herb (*Petroselinum crispum*). Its curly leaves are used as a garnish and in salads.

Parsnip, river rising in central B.C., Canada, and flowing 150 mi. NW to join Finlay R. and form Peace R. Became important fur-trade route after discovery by Sir Alexander Mackenzie in 1793.

parsnip, Old World vegetable plant (*Pastinaca sativa*), with edible fleshy roots.

Parsons, William: see ROSSE, WILLIAM PARSONS, 3d EARL OF.

Parsons, city (pop. 14,750), SE Kansas, W of Pittsburg; laid out 1870. Ships grain and dairy products.

parthenogenesis (pär"thŭnōjĕn'ùsĭs), in biology, form of reproduction in which egg (female sexual cell) develops without fertilization (i.e., without union with sperm cell). It is considered sexual reproduction because the cell is an ovum, undergoing maturation as do other ova; in some cases it may develop whether fertilized or unfertilized. Eggs of several invertebrates yield to artificial parthenogenesis by mechanical or chemical stimulation.

Parthenon (pär'thŭnŏn) [Gr.,= the virgin's place], temple to Athena, built 447–432 B.C. on the ACROPOLIS at Athens; a masterpiece of Greek architecture. Its architects were Ictinus and Callicrates; Phidias supervised the sculpture. Has 8 Doric columns at front and rear and 17 along the two sides. Within the building, at W end of nave, stood the 40-ft. high *Athena Parthenos*. Friezes representing procession regularly held in homage to Athena formed a continuous band of sculpture around the building; of the 525 ft. of the frieze 335 ft. still exist (see ELGIN MARBLES). In 6th cent. the temple became a Christian church and later a mosque (with addition of a minaret). Used for storing gunpowder by the Turks in 1687, center section was destroyed by an explosion. Recognition of its beauty began 18th cent.; reconstruction work has continued up to the present.

Parthenopean Republic (pär"thŭnōpē'ùn) [from Parthenope, anc. name of Naples], Jan.–June, 1799, set up in Naples by liberal leaders, under French auspices, after flight of Bourbon king. After military reverses in N Italy forced the French to evacuate, Naples fell to Cardinal RUFFO and Admiral Nelson.

Parthia (pär'thĕù), anc. country of Asia, SE of the Caspian Sea, with heart of the region in modern Khurasan. The Parthians, of Scythian origin, were famous horsemen and archers in the Assyrian and Persian empires. Under Arsaces in 250 B.C. they shook off the rule of the Seleucids and estab. their own empire, which in the 1st cent. B.C. extended into India. They defeated the Romans under Crassus in 53 B.C., but they suffered defeat by the Romans 39–38 B.C. and began to decline. In A.D. 226 Ardashir I overthrew the Parthians finally and estab. the Sassanian empire. The expression "a Parthian shot" came from the Parthian ruse of pretending to flee in order to shoot arrows more successfully.

partridge, name used for various henlike birds including ruffed grouse and bobwhite. True partridges are native to Old World; common European partridge has been introduced in parts of North America.

partridgeberry, small evergreen plant (*Mitchella repens*) of North American woods. Also known as squawberry and twinberry, it has white flowers borne in pairs and red berries which last all winter.

Parzifal: see PARSIFAL.

Pasadena (păs″sude′nu). 1 Residential and resort city, (pop. 104,577), S Calif., NE of Los Angeles between San Gabriel Mts. and San Rafael Hills; founded 1874. Scene of annual Tournament of Roses and of East-West football game (Jan. 1) in Rose Bowl. Here are California Inst. of Technology (nonsectarian; for men; opened 1891), a technical school of university grade, which cooperates in Mt. Palomar and Mt. Wilson observatories; Pasadena Col. (Nazarene; coed.; 1901); playhouse; and Busch Gardens. 2 Town (pop. 22,483), S Texas, SE of Houston. Has oil refining and paper milling.

Pasargadae (pusär′gude), anc. Persian city, NE of Persepolis, cap. under Cyrus the Great.

Pascagoula (păskugoo′lu), city (pop. 10,805), SE Miss., port on Mississippi Sound at mouth of Pascagoula R.; grew around "Old Spanish Fort" 1718. Resort; pecan, fishing, and boatbuilding center. Has U.S. dry docks and coast guard base.

Pascal, Blaise (blĕz′ păskäl′), 1623–62, French scientist and religious philosopher. His family embraced Jansenism, and Pascal himself lived for a time at Port-Royal and wrote the ironic *Provincial Letters* (1656) in defense of Jansenism. His religious writings, collected in *Pensées* (1670), are profoundly mystical and extremely pure in literary style. His scientific work was wide: he laid the foundation for the modern theory of probabilities, invented the mathematical triangle (Pascal's triangle), discovered the properties of the cycloid, advanced differential calculus, and formulated Pascal's law.

Pascal's law [for Blaise Pascal] states that pressure applied to confined fluid at any point is transmitted undiminished through fluid in all directions and acts upon every part of confining vessel at right angles to its interior surfaces and equally on equal areas.

Paschal II (pă′skul), d. 1118, pope (1099–1118), a Cluniac monk and member of the reform group of Gregory VII. In his reign Philip I of France was reconciled with the Church, St. Anselm triumphed in England, and Emperor Henry IV was deposed, but Henry V invaded Italy (1110), seized the pope and made him surrender the papal position on investiture. Paschal later repudiated this surrender to force. Succeeded by Gelasius II. Also Pascal.

Pasco (păs′kō), city (pop. 10,228), SE Wash., near junction of Columbia and Snake rivers. Farm trade center and rail junction. Boomed in World War II by atomic project near Richland.

Pascoli, Giovanni (jōvän′nē pä′skōlē), 1855–1912, Italian poet. He wrote thoughtful idyllic verse.

Pas-de-Calais (pä-du-kälä′), department (2,607 sq. mi.; pop. 1,168,545), N France, on Strait of Dover (Fr. *Pas de Calais*); cap. Arras.

Pashitch, Nikola (nē′kôlä pä′shĭch), Serbo-Croatian *Pašić*, 1846–1926, Serbian statesman. He controlled Serbia from 1903 to his death and was repeatedly premier. His pro-Russian, anti-Austrian policy was a factor leading to World War I. In 1917 he negotiated the union of Serbia, Croatia, and Slovenia (see YUGOSLAVIA).

Pasiphaë (pusi′fäē), in Greek legend, wife of Minos and mother of Ariadne and Phaedra. When Poseidon gave

Minos a bull for sacrifice, Minos kept it for himself. Poseidon aroused a passion for the bull in Pasiphaë, who bore the monstrous Minotaur.

Paso Robles (pä′sō rō′bulz, pä′sō rō′blĕs), resort city (pop. 4,835), S Calif., on Salinas R. and N of San Luis Obispo. Has hot springs.

pasqueflower (păsk–), wild flower (*Anemone patens*) of North American prairie regions, with open bluish flowers followed by silvery heads of feathery seeds. Its European counterpart (*A. pulsatilla*) is a spring garden flower.

Passaic (pusā′ĭk, pusäk′), city (pop. 57,702), NE N.J., on Passaic R. and N of Newark; settled 1678 by Dutch traders as Acquackanonk. Developed industrially in late 19th cent.; textile and metal-products center. Famous strike here (1926), against wage cut, involved right of free assembly.

Passaic, river, c.80 mi. long, rising SW of Morristown, N.J., and winding S, then N to Paterson (c.70–ft. falls), then S again to Newark Bay. Power aided industrial growth of many towns in NE N.J.

Passamaquoddy Bay (păsumukwō′dē), inlet of Bay of Fundy, between Maine and N.B., at mouth of St. Croix R. Most of it (including Campobello island) is in Canada. Towns on the bay are St. Andrews and St. George (N.B.), Lubec (at entrance) and Eastport (Maine). Hydroelectric project (also called Quoddy project), begun 1935 with PWA funds to harness heavy tides (18-ft. average range) in U.S. sector, was suspended after Congress refused funds (1936).

Passarowitz, Treaty of (päsä′rōvĭts), 1718, signed at Pozarevac (Ger. *Passarowitz*), Yugoslavia, between Turkey and Holy Roman Empire and Venice. In war of 1714–18 the Turks had defeated the Venetians in Greece and Crete and the imperials had defeated the Turks in the Balkans. In the treaty, Turkey lost the Banat of Temesvar and N Serbia (incl. Belgrade) to Emperor Charles VI but gained all Venetian possessions in the Peloponnesus and on Crete.

Passau (pä′sou), city (pop. 34,338), Lower Bavaria, on Austrian border; a port on confluence of Danube and Inn rivers. Textile and machinery mfg. Seat of prince-bishopric till 1803. Has fine Gothic and baroque architecture. By Treaty of Passau (1552) King Ferdinand I (representing Emperor Charles V) secured agreement of the Protestant princes to submit the religious question to a diet; the Peace of AUGSBURG resulted (1555).

Passchendale, formerly **Passchendaele** (both: pä′sundä″lu), small town near Ypres, Belgium. In World War I it was carried by the British after heavy losses (1917); retaken by the Germans (1918).

Pass Christian (păs″ krĭs″chēän′), resort city (pop. 3,383), SE Miss., on Mississippi Sound.

passenger pigeon, extinct E North American wild pigeon, abundant until late 19th cent. In form and color it resembled the smaller mourning dove.

passionflower, chiefly tropical American vine of genus *Passiflora*. The most common North American species, *Passiflora incarnata*, native from Va. to Texas, has purple and white flowers and edible fruits called maypops. Others are grown in the tropics and in greenhouses in northern regions.

Passion play, genre of miracle play about Jesus' suffering and death—surviving from Middle Ages into modern times. First given in Latin, by 15th cent. they were entirely in German. Chief surviving Passion play is that at Oberammergau, Bavaria.

passive: see VOICE.

Passover, Jewish festival celebrating the deliverance of the Israelites from bondage in Egypt. The observance begins on the evening of the 14th of Nisan (first month of the religious calendar, corresponding to March-April) and lasts seven days. The narrative of the Exodus is recited at the ceremonial evening meals (called Seders) which are served during the first and second nights of the festival. Only unleavened bread (matzoth) may be eaten during the seven days of

Passover, in memory of the fact that the Jews, hastening from Egypt, had no time to leaven their bread. The Christian feast of Easter is calculated from the Pasch or Passover.

Passy, Frédéric (päse'), 1822–1912, French internationalist. Abandoned law for journalism and study of economics and the problems of peace. He founded (1867) a French society to promote international arbitration and (with Sir William R. Cremer) the Interparliamentary Union of Arbitration. Wrote much on peace. Awarded, with J. H. Dunant, the first (1901) Nobel Peace Prize.

Pasternak, Boris Leonidovich (bŭrēs' lyä"ŭnyē'dŭvĭch pŭstyïrnäk'), 1890–, Russian poet. Began as futurist, but his talent transcends classification. His work includes two narrative poems (*Spektorsky*, 1926; *The Year 1905*, 1927). See his *Collected Prose Works* (Eng. tr., 1945); *Selected Poems* (Eng. tr., 1947).

Pasteur, Louis (pästŭr'), 1822–95, French chemist. Through his experiments with bacteria he exploded the myth of spontaneous generation. His work on wine, vinegar, and beer led to PASTEURIZATION. He solved the problems of control of silkworm disease and chicken cholera. He developed the technique of vaccination against anthrax and extended it to hydrophobia. **Pasteur Institute,** opened in Paris in 1888, includes clinic for treatment of hydrophobia and teaching and research center for work on virulent and contagious diseases. Pasteur Institutes have been estab. in other countries.

pasteurization (păs"chŏorĭzā'shŭn), method of treating foods, especially milk, to make them free from disease-causing bacteria. Milk is heated to c.145° F. for 30 min., then cooled rapidly.

Pasto (pä'stō), city (pop. 27,564), SW Colombia; founded 1539. It was a royalist city in revolution against Spain. Volcano El Pasto is near by.

Paston Letters, collection of personal and business correspondence of Paston family of Norfolk and others, 1422–1509; indispensable source for history and customs of England at close of Middle Ages.

Pastor, Tony, c.1837–1908, American theater manager. Opened his first theater in 1861. Introduced many performers who became famous; made vaudeville suitable for a mixed audience.

pastoral (pä'stŭrŭl), literary work in which shepherd life is presented in conventionalized manner. Contrasts pure simplicity of shepherd life to corrupt artificiality of court and city. Many subjects have been presented in pastoral setting. Theocritus, 3d cent. B.C., wrote first pastoral poetry recorded, and delineated the Daphnis, Lycidas, Corydon, and Amaryllis of pastoral convention. Vergil's *Bucolics* (37 B.C.) present unrealistic characters and landscape (Arcadia); allegorical scenes celebrate Roman greatness, prophesy a golden age. Renaissance saw great revival of pastoral eclogue. Milton's "Lycidas" (1637) is most famous pastoral elegy in English. Except for Shelley's *Adonais* (1821) and Matthew Arnold's *Thyrsis* (1866), 19th and 20th cent. poets rarely use conventions of Vergil and Theocritus.

pastry, general name for foods made wholly or partly of paste, which is composed of flour, liquid (milk, water, or beaten egg), and shortening; best-known form is pie crust. Name is also given to small fancy sweets ("French pastry") and bunlike Danish pastry.

Patagonia (pătŭgō'nēŭ), region primarily in S Argentina, S of Río Colorado and E of Andes, but including extreme SE Chile and N TIERRA DEL FUEGO. Patagonia, except for S plains, subandean region, and Andes, is vast semiarid grassy plateau, terminating in cliffs along Atlantic. In W are large lakes fed by Andean glaciers. (Nahuel Huapí National Park, estab. 1934, is resort area here.) Sheep raising is principal industry in Patagonia, although oil production around Comodoro Rivadavia is of great importance. The coast, probably first visited by Vespucci (1501), was explored by Magellan (1520). Area not perma-

nently settled until late in 19th cent. Has more than half Argentina's territory but sparse population.

Patan (pä'tŭn), city (pop. 104,928), Nepal, near Katmandu. Has ancient Buddhist temples.

Patapsco (pŭtăp'skō), river rising in N Md. Flows c.65 mi. SE to Chesapeake Bay SE of Baltimore.

Patay (pätä'), village (pop. 1,313), Loiret dept., N central France, NW of Orléans. Here Joan of Arc defeated the English in 1429.

Patchogue (pä'chäg"), resort and fishing village (pop. 7,361), SE N.Y., on S shore (Great South Bay) of Long Isl.

patchouli (păch'ŏolē), fragrant shrubby plant (*Pogostemon heyneanus*) of India. It yields an essential oil, used in the perfume patchouli.

Patel, Vallabhbhai (vŭ'lŭbī pŭtĕl'), 1876–1950, Indian statesman. As deputy prime minister of India (1947), he directed the integration of the numerous princely states into the new political structure.

Patenier, Joachim de: see PATINIR, JOACHIM DE.

Pater, Walter (Horatio) (pä'tŭr), 1839–94, English essayist and critic, long at Brasenose Col., Oxford. He was the leader of a movement stressing the moral importance of artistic perfection, urging that literature should "burn with a hard, gemlike flame." His own writing is superb in precision and clarity. Among his works are *Studies in the History of the Renaissance* (1873), *Marius the Epicurean* (1885; his masterpiece), *Imaginary Portraits* (1887), and *Plato and Platonism* (1893).

Pater Noster: see LORD'S PRAYER.

Paterson, William, 1658–1719, British financier, adviser to William III, and projector (1691) of the Bank of England. He also promoted (1695) the ill-fated DARIEN SCHEME. Advocated union of Scotland and England.

Paterson, William, 1745–1806, American statesman, b. Ireland. Set forth the New Jersey or small-state plan in Federal Constitutional Convention. U.S. Senator (1789–90).

Paterson, city (pop. 139,336), NE N.J., at Passaic R. falls and N of Newark; founded 1791 by Alexander Hamilton. Water power used for cotton spinning after 1794. Important silk industry started 1839; first loom for silk fabric built here 1842. Industry characterized by many small "family" shops; has had numerous strikes, notably in 1912–13, 1933, 1936. City devastated by fire, flood, and tornado, 1902. In World War II nylon, rubber, aircraft, and metal industries employed many former silk workers. Public library designed by Henry Bacon.

Patiala and East Punjab States Union (pŭtēä'lŭ, pŭnjäb'), state (10,099 sq. mi.; pop. 3,468,631), NW India; cap. Patiala. A center of Sikh population. Formed 1948 by merging eight former princely states. Name often abbreviated as Pepsu.

Patinir, Patenier, or **Patiner, Joachim de** (all: yō'äkhīm dŭ pätīnēr'), c.1485–1524, first Flemish painter to subordinate figures to landscape.

Patiño, Simón Ituri (sēmōn' ētōo'rē pätē'nyō), 1886–1947, Bolivian capitalist, owner of tin mines and other enterprises in Bolivia. His fortune was considered one of largest in world.

Patmore, Coventry (Kersey Dighton), 1823–96, English poet, associated with the Pre-Raphaelites. *The Angel in the House* (1854–63) is on married love, *The Unknown Eros* (1877) is a series of odes on his conversion to Catholicism.

Patmos (păt'mŏs), Aegean island (13 sq. mi.; pop. 2,428), Greece, off SW Asia Minor, in the Dodecanese. St. John the Divine wrote the Revelation here.

Patna (pŭt'nŭ), city (pop. 196,415), cap. of Bihar, India, on the Ganges. As Pataliputra, it was cap. of Maghada kingdom in 6th cent. B.C. Univ. of Patna opened 1917. Cotton mills.

Patras (pŭträs', pä'trŭs), Gr. *Patrai*, city (pop. 88,414), Greece, in N Peloponnesus; a port near head of Gulf of Patras, which connects Gulf of Corinth with the

Ionian Sea. Commercial and industrial center (exports currants, olive oil, wine, citrus fruit). In antiquity, Patras was a member of both Achaean Leagues. Was held by Venice in 15th cent.; later passed to Turkey, but was again held by Venice 1687–1715. Destroyed 1821 in Greek War of Independence, it was rebuilt.

patriarch (pā'trēärk) [Gr.,= head of a family], revered male head of a kinship group; in the Bible, one of the antediluvian progenitors of the race or one of the ancestors of the Jews (Abraham, Isaac, Jacob, the sons of Jacob). The name, therefore, came to be used as a high title in Christian churches, especially E churches. Original patriarchates were those of Alexandria, Antioch, and Rome (the bishop—not patriarch—of Rome; the pope). To these were added Constantinople (chief prelate of the Byzantine Empire) and Jerusalem. The triumph of heresies created new churches, many headed by patriarchs. In the Russian Church a patriarch of Moscow was set up (1589), abolished by Peter I (1721), reestab. 1917 (see ORTHODOX EASTERN CHURCH).

patriarchy (pā'trēär"kē), term, meaning "father right," used to designate certain features of family or kinship group ruled by father or eldest male. In patriarchal family, succession is in male line, the patriarch's name, property, and authority passing to sons. Patriarchal family is strongly developed among nomads of Asia and in Africa, China, and Japan, and in ancient times was firmly estab. in Palestine, Greece, and Rome.

Patrick, Saint, c.385–461, Christian missionary, called the Apostle of Ireland. His life is shrouded in legend, and even the dates of birth and death are obscure. He is said to have been born in Britain and enslaved by the Irish until, in response to a voice, he escaped and went to Gaul. Later he studied at Auxerre and went as missionary to Ireland, where he converted many. In 441 he went to Rome and received the pallium from the pope. Later he was archbishop of Armagh. When he retired (457) Ireland was Christian. He wrote much, including his *Confessions* and probably *The Lorica of St. Patrick* (called also *The Cry of the Deer*). Buried at Downpatrick. Feast: March 17.

Patrimony of Saint Peter: see PAPAL STATES.

patristic literature, writings of the Christian Church Fathers in the first few centuries of the Christian era. They are in Greek and in Latin. Early writings are principally apologetics, addressed to pagans or to Christians in disagreement with the author. Later they were more devoted to larger theological works, sermons, and exegesis of Scripture. Among the many authors are St. Clement I, St. Ignatius of Antioch, St. Justin Martyr, Origen, Tertullian, St. Cyprian, Eusebius of Caesarea, St. Gregory Nazianzen, St. Basil the Great, St. John Chrysostom, St. Ambrose, St. Jerome, St. Gregory I, St. John of Damascus. The 3d-cent. writers are called the ante-Nicene Fathers, the later ones post-Nicene.

Patroclus (pŭtrō'klŭs), in Greek legend (esp. in the *Iliad*), hero of the Trojan War, intimate friend of Achilles. When Patroclus was slain fighting in his place, Achilles returned to battle and slew Hector. Thus Patroclus' excursion is crux of the epic.

Patrons of Husbandry: see GRANGER MOVEMENT.

Patterson, family of American journalists. **Robert Wilson Patterson**, 1850–1910, was editor-in-chief of the Chicago *Tribune* (1899–1910). He married daughter of the owner, Joseph MEDILL. His son, **Joseph Medill Patterson**, 1879–1946, was coeditor of the *Tribune* (1914–25) with his cousin, R. R. McCORMICK. Founded New York *Daily News*, first successful tabloid in country, in 1919. His sister, **Eleanor Medill Patterson**, 1884–1948, merged Washington newspapers to form *Times-Herald* (1939). "Cissy" Patterson became well known for her spectacular news presentation.

Patterson, Elizabeth, 1785–1879, American wife of Jérôme Bonaparte, and celebrated beauty. Marriage performed in 1803 was annulled by Napoleon in 1806.

Patterson, Robert Porter, 1891–1952, U.S. Secretary of War (1945–47). Designed unification of armed forces under single establishment.

Patti, Adelina (pä'tē), 1843–1919, coloratura soprano, b. Madrid of Italian parents. She made her debut in New York in 1859 and eventually became the most popular and most highly paid singer of her day.

Patton, George S(mith), Jr., 1885–1945, American general. As commander of 3d Army he spearheaded the spectacular final thrusts of U.S. forces in Europe in World War II.

Pátzcuaro (pät'skwärō), lake, Michoacán, W Mexico; popular resort area. Town of Pátzcuaro (pop. 9,557) is primarily Tarascan fishing settlement.

Patzinaks: see PETCHENEGS.

Pau (pō), city (pop. 40,604), cap. of Basses-Pyrénées dept., SW France; a tourist center at foot of the Pyrenees. It was the cap. of Béarn and the residence of the kings of Navarre. Birthplace of Henry IV.

Paul, Saint, d. A.D. 67?, the apostle to the Gentiles, one of the greatest figures in the history of the Christian Church, b. Tarsus. He was a Jew, originally named Saul, a tentmaker by trade, and a Roman citizen. Educated in Jerusalem, he was a zealous Jewish nationalist. To trace the course of his life minutely is difficult. The chief sources are the Acts of the Apostles and the EPISTLES attributed to Paul himself. These Epistles are recognized as masterpieces of world literature as well as fountainheads of Christian doctrine. Of them several are undoubtedly by him (Romans, 1 and 2 Corinthians, 1 Thessalonians, Philemon), two are accepted by all but a few as his (Ephesians, 2 Thessalonians), three are considered by many to be in their present form later (1 and 2 Timothy, Titus), and one is usually said not to have been written by Paul, though possibly at his request (Hebrews). Paul's first contact with the Christians was his approving presence at the martyrdom of St. Stephen. Soon afterward (A.D. 35?) he was on his way to Damascus to help suppress Christianity there, when he was halted by a blinding light and a Voice asking, "Why persecutest thou me?" Thus was he converted to Christianity. Saul turned Paul was the greatest of all early Christian missionaries. With different companions he went about the Near East and the Greek world, making conversions, setting up churches, and ever moving on to spread the Gospel. In Jerusalem (A.D. 57) he was arrested for provoking a riot and imprisoned two years before being sent to Rome, where he was again imprisoned (A.D. 60–62) before being cleared of all charges. He was apparently martyred in the persecution under Nero, traditionally by beheading and traditionally on the same day that Peter was killed. They are commemorated together on June 29; the conversion of St. Paul is celebrated on Jan. 25.

Paul III, 1468–1549, pope (1534–49), a Roman named Alessandro Farnese. His election ushered in the Catholic REFORM. After long preparation the Council of TRENT began in 1545. He favored the reform party and encouraged the new Society of Jesus. Paul created the modern Congregation of the Holy Office (see INQUISITION 3). He also was an art patron, founded the Farnese Palace, and had Michelangelo decorate the Sistine Chapel.

Paul IV, 1476–1559, pope (1555–59), a Neapolitan named Gian Pietro Carafa. A strict ascetic monk and a rigid reformer, he did much to purify the clergy and to do away with papal worldliness and nepotism. His rigidity brought him into conflict with all the Catholic monarchs, even Mary Tudor.

Paul V, 1552–1621, pope (1605–21), a Roman named Camillo Borghese, an expert in canon law. He tried to reassert all the lay powers the pope had ever enjoyed, but he was defeated in a quarrel with Venice that ended in 1607 and did not fare well in arguments with the French and English kings. He built the Villa

Borghese and was responsible for a lovely chapel in the Church of Santa Maria Maggiore.

Paul I, 1754–1801, emperor and tsar of Russia (1796–1801); son and successor of Catherine II. He joined in the Second Coalition against France but withdrew in the same year (1799; see FRENCH REVOLUTIONARY WARS) and concluded the Northern Convention with Sweden, Denmark and Prussia, aimed against British rules on neutral shipping (1800). His insanity, which often was violent, became apparent, and a conspiracy was formed to force his abdication. When Paul refused, the conspirators, crazed by fear, strangled him. His son and successor, Alexander I, was a party to the plot but was blameless in the murder.

Paul, 1901–, king of the Hellenes (1947–); brother and successor of George II.

Paul, Jean: see RICHTER, JOHANN PAUL FRIEDRICH.

Paulding, James Kirke, 1779–1860, American author, Secretary of the Navy under Van Buren. He collaborated with Washington Irving in producing *Salmagundi*, wrote the satirical *John Bull in America* (1825), tales, novels (e.g., *Koningsmarke*, 1823; *The Dutchman's Fireside*, 1831), and a life of Washington.

Pauli, Wolfgang (vŏlf'gäng pou'lē), 1900–, Austrian physicist. Won 1945 Nobel Prize for discovery of exclusion principle, according to which no two electrons in atom may be in same quantum state.

Paulicians (pôlĭ'shŭnz), Christian heretical sect holding obscure tenets. Almost certainly they were dualists and they may have taken doctrines from Manichaeism. They rejected sacraments, images, and much of the Bible. They had arisen by the 4th cent., and some believe them to have been a survival of primitive Christianity. They were strong in the Byzantine Empire by the 7th cent. and though put down in the time of Michael III they persisted in Thrace. In Bulgaria they joined the Bogomils.

Paulist Fathers, order of Roman Catholic priests (in full, Society of Missionary Priests of St. Paul the Apostle); founded 1858 by Isaac HECKER primarily for the purpose of converting Americans.

Paul Knutson (nōōt'sŭn, kŭnōōt'sŭn), fl. 1354–64, Norse leader, alleged to have explored America.

Paullus, Aemilius, c.229–169 B.C., Roman general, consul (182 B.C., 168 B.C.). He defeated Perseus of Macedon at Pydna (168 B.C.) and made Macedon a Roman province. Also Paulus.

Paul of Aegina (ējī'nù), 7th cent.?, Greek physician, author of influential treatise on surgery. Known also as Paulus Aegineta.

Paul of Samosata (sùmō'sùtù), fl. 260–72, Syrian theologian, who enjoyed the favor of Zenobia of Palmyra. He denied the doctrine of the Trinity. His teachings influenced Arius, Nestorius, and, possibly, the Paulicians.

Paulsboro, borough (pop. 7,842), SW N.J., near Delaware R. and SW of Camden. Fortified in the Revolution. Oil refineries, chemical plants.

Pauls Valley, city (pop. 6,896), S central Okla., on Washita R. and SW of Ada, in rich agr. area. Oil industries.

Paul the Deacon, c.725–799?, Lombard historian, also called Paulus Diaconus. Chief work is history of Lombards in 6th, 7th, and 8th cent.

Paulus (pô'lùs), fl. c.200, Roman Jurist.

Paulus, Aemilius: see PAULLUS, AEMILIUS.

Paulus Diaconus: see PAUL THE DEACON.

Paulus Hook, N.J.: see JERSEY CITY.

Paumotu: see TUAMOTU ISLANDS.

Pausanias (pôsā'nēùs), d. c.470 B.C., Spartan general, victor at the battle of Plataea in the Persian Wars. Twice he was accused of treason to Sparta, the second time taking refuge in a temple, where he starved to death.

Pausanias, fl. A.D. 174, traveler and geographer, probably b. Lydia. His *Description of Greece* is valuable source on ancient Greek topography, monuments, and legends.

Pausias (pô'shēùs), fl. 1st half of 4th cent. B.C., Greek painter, famous for decorative works. *A Sacrifice* is preserved in Pompey's temple, Rome.

pavement, wearing surface of road, street, or sidewalk. Paving surfaces include concrete, penetration macadam, bituminous-mixed macadam, sheet asphalt, bituminous concrete, and brick, wood, or stone-block pavements. Subgrade must be shaped and rolled; concrete road slab is commonly used as foundation. Both foundation and surface should be crowned or sloped for shedding of water and, if concrete, provided with expansion joints. Concrete is often reinforced with steel mesh or bars. ROMAN ROADS were noted for durable paving; cobblestones were common from Middle Ages to 19th cent.; MACADAM ROAD was popular in 19th cent.

Pavia (pävē'ä), city (pop. 40,208), Lombardy, N Italy, on Ticino R. near its confluence with the Po. It was the cap. of the Lombard and Carolingian kingdoms of Italy; became a free commune 12th cent.; fell to VISCONTI family 1359; shared later history of Lombardy. In 1525 Emperor Charles V defeated and captured Francis I of France near Pavia. Its celebrated law school, founded 11th cent., became a university 1361. The most notable building is the celebrated CERTOSA DI PAVIA.

Pavlov, Ivan Petrovich (ēvän' pētrô'vĭch päv'lùf), 1849–1936, Russian physiologist, pioneer in study of conditioned reflexes. Won 1904 Nobel Prize in Physiology and Medicine for work on digestive glands.

Pavlova, Anna Matveyevna (pävlô'vù), 1882–1931, Russian ballet dancer, famed for classic technique and ethereal quality. After European tours she made U.S. debut in 1910. Excelled in *Giselle* and in *The Dying Swan* (composed for her by Fokine).

Pavlovsk (päv'lùfsk), city (pop. over 10,000), RSFSR, near Leningrad. Formerly a summer residence of St. Petersburg nobility.

Pawcatuck, Conn.: see STONINGTON.

Pawhuska (pôhŭ'skù), city (pop. 5,331), NE Okla., NW of Tulsa, in oil, agr., and stock area. Osage Indian cap.; has tribal museum.

Pawling, village (pop. 1,430), E N.Y., SE of Poughkeepsie, in hilly country; settled c.1740 by Quakers. Trinity-Pawling School for boys is here.

Pawnee Indians (pônē'), North American tribe of Caddoan linguistic stock, possibly once living in Texas, but by the time of Coronado's visit (1541) apparently in the Platte R. valley. Later they extended their territory to the Republican R. and the Niobrara R. Though fierce fighters against the Cheyenne, they were friendly to the U.S. and helped protect the builders of the Union Pacific. Put on a reservation in present Okla. in 1876. Also spelled Pani.

pawpaw: see PAPAW TREE.

Pawtucket (pùtŭ'kĕt), industrial city (pop. 81,436), NE R.I., on Blackstone R. at Pawtucket Falls. Area deeded to Roger Williams 1638; city was in Mass. until 1862. Mfg. of textiles, electrical equipment, machinery; metal, paper, wood products. Samuel Slater built first successful water-power cotton mill in U.S. here 1790; Slater mill (1793) now museum. Narragansett race track is in Pawtucket and East Providence.

Pax, in Roman religion, goddess of Peace.

Payette (pāĕt'), city (pop. 4,032), W Idaho, near junction of Payette R. and Snake R. Serves BOISE PROJECT and Vale project, Oregon.

Payette, river rising in mountains of W Idaho and flowing c.70 mi. S and W to Snake R. near Payette; used in BOISE PROJECT.

Payne, John Howard, 1791–1852, American actor and playwright, famous for song *Home, Sweet Home*, in his opera, *Clari, the Maid of Milan* (London, 1823).

Payne-Aldrich Tariff Act, 1909, passed by U.S. Congress. Sponsored by Rep. Sereno E. Payne and Sen. Nelson W. Aldrich. Less aggressively protectionist than McKinley Tariff Act of 1890 and Dingley Act of 1897. Adopted principle of max. and min. tariffs for compelling concessions from other countries.

Paysandú (pīsändoo'), city (pop. 46,000), cap. of Paysandú dept., W Uruguay, port on Uruguay R., founded 1772. In rich stock raising and farming region, it is at head of ocean navigation.

Payson, city (pop. 3,998), N central Utah, near Utah L.; served by STRAWBERRY VALLEY PROJECT.

Pazmany, Peter, Hung. *Pázmány* (päz'mänyu), 1570–1637, Hungarian cardinal. A convert from Calvinism, he entered the Society of Jesus, became primate of Hungary, and, without coercion, won a large part of his people back to Catholicism. He founded a university at Trnava (later transferred to Budapest) and wrote many literary works.

Pazzi conspiracy (pät'tsē), 1478, against Lorenzo and Giuliano de' MEDICI to end family's hegemony in Florence. Largely carried out by the Pazzi family, it had the support of Pope SIXTUS IV. During Mass in cathedral, Giuliano was stabbed to death while Lorenzo escaped. Conspirators were killed; the Medici remained in power.

Pb, chemical symbol of the element LEAD.

Pd, chemical symbol of the element PALLADIUM.

pea, annual climbing leguminous plant (*Pisum sativum*), with edible pod-borne seeds high in protein, grown in home gardens and commercially for canning. The plants are used for forage. Split peas are obtained from the field pea (*P. arvense*). The CHICK-PEA and SWEET PEA belong to other genera.

Peabody, Elizabeth Palmer, 1804–94, American educator, lecturer, and reformer. With her sister Mary (wife of Horace Mann) she estab. school near Boston. After its failure she turned to writing history textbooks and lecturing. Her path crossed those of most of great New Englanders of her day, and her bookshop in Boston (1840–49) was a literary center. She also did some publishing: notably the *Dial,* pamphlets of Anti-Slavery Society, and some of Hawthorne's early works. In 1861 she opened one of first kindergartens in U.S., and she later estab. first kindergarten training school in U.S.

Peabody, Endicott, 1857–1944, American educator, founder of Groton School, Groton, Mass., in 1884.

Peabody, Francis Greenwood, 1847–1936, American Unitarian theologian; pastor (1874–80) of First Parish Church, Cambridge; teacher (1881–1913) at Harvard.

Peabody, George, 1795–1869, American financier and philanthropist. Became prosperous broker in London. Numerous philanthropies include Peabody Education Fund, given to promote education in the South.

Peabody, city (pop. 22,645), NE Mass., adjoining W Salem. Tanning (since early 18th cent.).

Peace, river of N B.C., Canada, formed by union of Parsnip and Finlay rivers. Flows E into Alta., then N and ENE to Great Slave R. near L. Athabaska. Was fur-trade route. Settlement in fertile valley dates from early 20th cent. Length 1,054 mi. to head of Finlay R.

peace congresses. Although PACIFISM is almost as old as war, organized efforts to outlaw war began in middle of 19th cent. Term "peace congress" applies to meetings of diplomats to end specific wars by acceptable treaties, and to convenings of internationalists to prevent future wars. International peace efforts have in general followed five lines: international arbitration; a league of nations or international authority; codification of international law by tribunal such as WORLD COURT or INTERNATIONAL COURT OF JUSTICE; sanctions or international coercion of state adjudged in wrong; and disarmament. First international peace congress met in London 1843, followed by series of conferences and Universal Peace Congress in London 1851. Agitation for peace was stopped for many years by Crimean War, then by American Civil War, but after Franco-Prussian War (1870–71) efforts were renewed. Important Paris Congress met in 1878, first Pan-American Conference in

1889. The First Hague Conference estab. the Permanent Court of Arbitration (1899). Again all peace efforts were interrupted by World War I, but from Versailles Treaty were born LEAGUE OF NATIONS and World Court. Between two world wars NAVAL CONFERENCES were held at Washington and at London; with DISARMAMENT CONFERENCE and other meetings, they led to KELLOGG-BRIAND PACT and LOCARNO PACT. Horrors of World War II intensified world-wide peace movements, with much hope and determination that UNITED NATIONS would succeed where the League had failed.

peach, fruit tree (*Prunus persica*) with decorative pink blossoms and a juicy, fine-flavored stone fruit. Native to China, it is an important fruit of temperate climates. The Elberta is the chief commercial variety. Purple-leaved and double-flowering forms are grown for ornament. The nectarine is a smooth-skinned variety of peach (*P. persica nectarina*) cultivated from early times.

Peacock, Thomas Love, 1785–1866, English novelist and poet. His rather eccentric novels blend satire and extravagant romance, with lyrics interspersed. They include *Headlong Hall* (1816), *Melincourt* (1817), *Nightmare Abbey* (1818), *Crotchet Castle* (1831), and *Gryll Grange* (1860).

peacock, large forest bird of pheasant family. Male is the peacock; female is peahen. Common peacock is found in India and Ceylon, the Burmese or Javan peacock in Indo-China. Male displays during courtship the green and gold erectile tail marked by eyelike spots.

Peacock Throne: see DELHI.

Peak, the, tableland c.30 mi. long and 22 mi. wide, Derbyshire, England, forming S extremity of Pennine Chain. Highest point is Kinderscout (2,088 ft.).

Peaks of Otter: see OTTER, PEAKS OF.

Peale, Charles Willson, 1741–1827, American portrait painter. Studied under J. S. Copley and Benjamin West. Painted earliest known portrait of Washington (1772; Washington and Lee Univ.). Succeeded Copley as most popular portrait painter in U.S. His brother, **James Peale,** 1749–1831, painted landscapes and miniature portraits. Of his 11 children, three became painters—**Raphaelle Peale,** 1774–1825, who painted still lifes; **Titian Peale,** 1799–1885, who did portraits; and **Rembrandt Peale,** 1778–1860, who was a portrait and historical painter.

peanut, annual leguminous plant (*Arachis hypogaea*), and its edible seeds, usually two to a pod. Native to South America, it is an important crop in S U.S. The seeds are eaten fresh or roasted, used in confectionery, and yield an oil, peanut butter, and other products. The plants are used for forage. Goober and groundnut are other names.

pear, fruit tree of genus *Pyrus* (closely related to the apple), and its fruit, grown for canning as well as for eating fresh. Most varieties come from two species, the common European pear (*Pyrus communis*) and the Oriental pear (*P. pyrifolia*). Leading varieties in the U.S. include Bartlett, Kieffer, Seckel, Anjou, Bosc, and Comice.

Pea Ridge, chain of hills, NW Ark., where Civil War battle of Pea Ridge (or Elkhorn Tavern) was fought March 6–8, 1862. Strongly entrenched Union army defeated Confederate attack.

Pearl, river, China: see CANTON, river.

Pearl, river, rising in E central Miss. and flowing 485 mi. SW and S to L. Borgne, Gulf of Mexico inlet. Forms Miss.–La. boundary for 116 mi.

Pearl, The, one of four anonymous alliterative poems composed c.1370–90 in West Midland dialect by a gifted Middle English poet. *The Pearl* is usually explained as an allegorical elegy for the poet's little daughter. *Patience* and *Cleanness* or *Purity* teach those virtues. *Sir Gawain and the Green Knight,* one of greatest medieval romances, recounts the adventures of Gawain, one of King Arthur's knights.

pearl, secretion of certain mollusks used as a gem. It is formed of the same organic material as the mollusk shell, usually with a grain of sand or a parasite as nucleus. Pearls occur in various shapes and colors. Main sources are pearl oyster and the fresh-water mussel. Cultured pearls are produced by inserting a bead in the mantle of pearl oyster.

Pearl Harbor, U.S. naval base, S Oahu, T.H. A key naval base with installations and anchorages around 10 sq. mi. of navigable water. Air bases at Fords Isl. and Barbers Point. In area are also army, air force, and marine bases (e.g., Hickham Field, Ewa). U.S. gained coaling and repair station here 1887; it became naval station 1900. The base was strengthened, especially after signing of Axis Pact (1940). Japanese attack on Pearl Harbor, Dec. 7, 1941, severely damaged installations and plunged U.S. into World War II. Charges of negligence on part of those responsible for base's defense resulted in a commission accusing (1942) Gen. W. C. Short and Adm. H. E. Kimmel of dereliction of duty. Army and navy announced (1944) that no grounds existed for court-martial. A congressional committee report (1946) found Pres. Roosevelt blameless, absolved Kimmel and Short, but censured War Dept. and Dept. of the Navy.

pearl millet, annual grass (*Pennisetum glaucum*) of the E Hemisphere, grown from anc. times for food. It has spikes of white grains Indian millet is another name.

Pearse, Patrick Henry, 1879–1916, Irish educator and patriot. Active in Gaelic League. Leader of Irish forces in Easter Rebellion (1916), he was shot.

Pearson, Sir Cyril Arthur, 1866–1921, English publisher. He founded and directed the London *Daily Express* (1900), as well as several periodicals. His own sight failed, and he founded St. Dunstan's for soldiers blinded in World War I.

Pearson, Karl, 1857–1936, English scientist. He applied statistical methods to biological problems, a science he called biometry.

Peary, Robert E(dwin) (pēr'ē), 1856–1920, American arctic explorer, discoverer of North Pole. Led several expeditions to Greenland. Made various attempts to reach North Pole before success on April 6, 1909. Although challenged by prior claim of F. A. COOK, Peary's achievement was recognized and later verified scientifically. In 1891–92 and later he explored **Peary Land,** peninsula, N Greenland, in Arctic Ocean. Mountainous, fertile area, free of inland icecap, it terminates in Cape Morris Jessup, northernmost arctic land point yet discovered.

Peasants' War, 1524–26, general rising of the peasants in central and S Germany against increased exploitation by the nobles, introduction of Roman law (which interpreted peasant status as servile), and progressive encroachments on their rights. Peasants' demands were listed in 12 Articles of Memmingen (1525). The revolt was partly religious in spirit. Zwingli encouraged it, and the Anabaptist Thomas MÜNZER led it in Thuringia, but Luther's savage condemnation of the rebels was a major factor in their defeat. Despite their able leadership by Florian Geyer, Götz von BERLICHINGEN, and other discontented nobles, the peasants were routed by the princes and the SWABIAN LEAGUE (1525). The peasants' few acts of atrocity were far surpassed by the victors. In Tyrol, the peasants won some concessions in 1526, but in general the peasants' defeat prolonged serfdom in Germany for nearly three centuries and stunted democratic development.

peat, carbonized, decayed vegetation, found in bogs of the temperate zone. Formed by slow decay of plants, e.g., sedges, reeds, rushes, and mosses, it is an early stage in the formation of coal. Two types of commercial peat are peat moss, derived from SPHAGNUM, and fuel peat.

peat moss: see SPHAGNUM.

pecan (pĭkän', pīkän', pē'kăn), tree (*Carya illinoensis* or *C. pecan*), a species of hickory, native from S Ill. to Texas and Mexico. The most important North American nut-bearing tree, it yields nuts used as table delicacies, in ice creams, and in confectionery.

peccary (pĕ'kŭrē), piglike mammal (*Tayassu*). Collared peccary or javelina is found in parts of Ariz., N.Mex., Texas, and S to Patagonia; white-lipped peccary found from central Mexico to Paraguay. Peccaries fight viciously with their tusks.

Pechenga (pyĕ'chĭn-gù), Finnish *Petsamo,* town (pop. over 2,000), N European RSFSR, on inlet of Barents Sea and near Norwegian border. Nickel mines near by. Ceded by Russia to Finland 1920; retroceded to USSR 1944 (confirmed 1947).

Pechora (pyĭchô'rù), river, N European RSFSR, rising in N Urals and flowing 1,110 mi. N into Pechora Bay (inlet of Barents Sea). Navigable for 470 mi. in summer, for 1,040 mi. in freshets of spring and autumn. Pechora coal basin extends E from river's middle course.

Peck, Annie Smith, 1850–1935, American mountain climber. First American to reach (1908) summit (22,-205 ft.) of Huascarán in Peru.

Pecos (pā'kùs), city (pop. 8,054), W Texas, on Pecos R. (irrigation). Trade and shipping center of cattle, agr., and oil region.

Pecos, river rising in N N.Mex. near the Truchas peaks and flowing 926 mi. S and SE across N.Mex. and Texas to the Rio Grande above Del Rio. Dams in N.Mex. serve Carlsbad project. Federal bill (1949) settled interstate disputes over water use. Pecos State Monument, near Pecos, N.Mex., encloses ruins of Pecos pueblo, mighty in Coronado's time.

Pecs, Hung. *Pécs* (pāch), Ger. *Fünfkirchen,* city (pop. 73,000), SW Hungary, in a coal-mining region. Produces tobacco, leather goods, vegetable oil. Seat of first Hungarian university (1367).

pectin, any of a group of amorphous, complex carbohydrates occurring in ripe fruits and some vegetables. Pectin content causes jellying when fruit of proper acidity and sugar are cooked together for jelly or jam. Commercial preparations may be used if fruit is low in pectin. Pectin also has medical uses (e.g., in treating sores and in slowing the rate of absorbing certain drugs).

Peculiar People, small Protestant sect founded in London, 1838, also known as Plumstead peculiars. Relying on prayer, they refused medical aid.

Pedrarias: see ARIAS DE ÁVILA, PEDRO.

Pedro I (pā'drō), 1798–1834, first emperor of Brazil (1822–31), son of John VI of Portugal. Growing up in Brazil after royal family fled Portugal before Napoleon's conquering French, he remained as regent of Brazil when King John returned to Portugal (1821). Heeding Brazilian advisers, Dom Pedro issued, Sept. 7, 1822, the *grito de Ipiranga,* making Brazil a separate empire. Abdicated 1831. Succeeded to Portuguese throne (1826), abdicated in favor of his daughter, Maria, and after 1831 assisted in securing rule for her. In Brazil he was succeeded by his son, **Pedro II,** 1825–91, emperor (1831–89). His long reign was period of internal peace and material progress. He was personally popular, but events worked against him, and in 1889 while he was in Europe, a revolution established a republic. Pedro did not return.

Pedro. For Spanish and Portuguese rulers thus named, see PETER.

Peeblesshire (pē'bùlz-shĭr), **Peebles,** or **Tweeddale,** county (347 sq. mi.; pop. 15,226), S central Scotland, co. town Peebles. Mainly a hilly pastoral region, it has little arable land.

Pee Dee, river rising in W N.C. in Blue Ridge and flowing 435 mi. SE to Winyah Bay, S.C. Called the Yadkin in central N.C.

Peekskill, city (pop. 17,731), SE N.Y., on E bank of Hudson R. (bridged NW to Bear Mt.) and N of Ossining, in farm and resort area. Mfg. of food products, alcohol, jewelry, and textiles.

Peel, Sir Robert, 1788–1850, English statesman. As home secretary he secured passage (1829) of a Catholic Emancipation bill (which he had earlier opposed) and estab. (1829) London police force. Sought to form a conservative party favorable to general reforms. Abandonment of custom duties and repeal of the corn laws during his second premiership (1841–46) split the party.

peewee: see PEWEE.

Pegasus (pĕ'gŭsŭs), in Greek legend, immortal winged horse; offspring of Poseidon and Medusa. He was faithful companion of Bellerophon. His hoof print made the spring of Hippocrene (sacred to the Muses), which gave gift of song to those who drank of it. His name is given to a constellation.

Pegram, George Braxton (pē'grŭm), 1876–, American physicist, educator. Demonstrated transmutation of elements by splitting atom with slow neutrons; in 1939 announced successful splitting of uranium atom. He was associated with Columbia Univ. from 1900.

Pegu (pĕgōō'), city (pop. 21,712), Lower Burma, on Pegu R. and on Rangoon-Mandalay railroad. Was cap. of Burma in 16th cent.

Péguy, Charles (shärl' pāgē'), 1873–1914, French author. A Socialist, he later became imbued with Catholic mysticism and (though usually at odds with the Church) became one of the foremost modern Catholic writers. He took a part in the Dreyfus Affair (on Dreyfus's side) and continued his fiery polemics against social injustice. His poetry gains power from his original, chantlike verse, as in *Le Mystère de la charité de Jeanne d'Arc* (1910; Eng. tr. by Julian Green, 1950). He fell in World War I.

Peham, artists: see BEHAM.

Pehlevi language: see PAHLAVI LANGUAGE.

Peiping, China: see PEKING.

Peipus, Lake (pī'pŭs), Estonian *Peipsi Järv*, Rus. *Chudskoye Ozero*, lake, area c.1,400 sq. mi., NE Europe, between Estonia and RSFSR. It empties through Narva R. into Gulf of Finland. Connected by 15-mi.–long strait with L. PSKOV.

Peirce, Charles Sanders, 1839–1914, American philosopher. He considered the meaning of an idea to lie in an examination of consequences to which idea would lead. From him William James adopted term PRAGMATISM. Works of Josiah Royce and John Dewey reflect Peirce's influence.

Peirce, Waldo, 1884–, American painter. Worked in France, Spain, Tunis, and Algiers, 1919–30.

Peisistratus, tyrant of Athens: see PISISTRATUS.

Pekah (pē'kŭ), d. c.730 B.C., king of Israel (c.736–c.730 B.C.). Murdered Pekahiah for the throne. Lost part of his kingdom to Assyria. 2 Kings 15.26–16.9.

Pekahiah (pē"kŭhī'ŭ), d. c.736 B.C., king of Israel (c.737–c.736 B.C.). Murdered by Pekah, one of his generals, who seized the throne. 2 Kings 15.26–16.9.

Pekalongan (pĕ"kälông'gän), town (pop. 65,982), on N Java, Indonesia; port on Java Sea. Exports sugar, rubber, and tea.

Pekin (pē'kĭn), city (pop. 21,858), central Ill., on Illinois R. and S of Peoria; settled 1829. Shipping and industrial center in farm and coal area. Mfg. of food and leather products.

Peking (pē'kĭng') or **Peiping** (pā'pĭng'), city (pop. 1,603,-324), Hopeh prov., cap. of People's Republic of China. Cultural center; seat of several universities and national library. Consists of Outer or Chinese City (walled 15th cent.) and Inner or Tartar City (walled 16th cent.). Latter contains Forbidden City (formerly emperor's residence), Imperial City, and Legation Quarter (which contained foreign concessions 1860–1946). At near-by Chowkowtien were discovered the bones of Peking man (*Sinanthropus pekingensis*). First known city to have existed on Peking's site was Chi of Chou dynasty. In 13th cent. Kublai Khan's cap., called Cambuluc, was built here. As Peking, the city was cap. of China from 15th cent. to 1928 with one brief break in early Ming period. City was renamed Peiping in 1928 when Nationalists moved cap. to Nanking. Occupied 1937–45 by the Japanese. In

1949 it became cap. of Chinese Communists, who restored historical name of Peking.

Pekingese or **Pekinese:** see TOY DOGS.

Peking man: see MAN, PRIMITIVE.

Pelagianism (pŭlā'jŭnĭzŭm), 5th-cent. Christian heretical sect, deriving its name from a monk and theologian, Pelagius (c.355–c.425). He rejected the teaching of St. Augustine on predestination and grace, calling them pessimistic. In his preaching in N Africa and Palestine Pelagius maintained that a child is born innocent (without original sin) and therefore need not be baptized. He argued that grace consists of the natural attributes in man that lead him to God—reason, free will, understanding of the gospel. Anyone could thus enter Heaven, even the pagans. This challenged the whole function of the Church and the sacraments. St. Augustine and St. Jerome fought Pelagianism vigorously, and it was condemned at the Council of Ephesus (431). A modified doctrine, Semi-Pelagianism, continued popular in France and the British Isles into the 6th cent.; this accepted all of Augustine's views except those of predestination. This was condemned at the Council of Orange (529).

Pelasgians (pĭlăz'jēŭnz), name meaning aboriginal, non-Greek inhabitants of Greece; possibly the builders of Mycenaean civilization.

Pele (pā'lā), Hawaiian goddess of the volcano. Her traditional home is Halemaumau, fire pit of Kilauea crater on Hawaii isl.

Pelée (pŭlā'), volcano, 4,429 ft. high, on N Martinique, French West Indies; erupted 1792, 1851, 1902. Last eruption killed c.40,000 people, and a thick deposit of volcanic ash left area a wasteland.

Peleus (pē'lūs, pē'lēŭs), in Greek mythology, king of the Myrmidons; father of Achilles by the nymph Thetis. He took part in Calydonian hunt and Argonaut expedition. All the gods were invited to his wedding except Eris. In revenge she sent the APPLE OF DISCORD.

Pelew, Caroline Isls.: see PALAU.

Pelias, uncle of JASON.

pelican (pĕ'lĭkŭn), large, gregarious bird of warm regions, allied to cormorant and gannet. Upper mandible is hooked, lower one has pouch to hold fish; feet are webbed. Great white, eastern brown, and California brown pelicans are found in U.S. See *ill.*, p. 105.

Pelican Rapids, village (pop. 1,676), W Minn., N of Fergus Falls and on Pelican R. "Minnesota man," human skeleton believed prehistoric, was found near by, 1932.

Pelion (pē'lēŭn), mountain, 5,252 ft. high, N Greece, in E Thessaly, near Aegean coast. In ancient legend, giants known as the Aloadae tried to storm heaven and overthrow the gods by piling Mt. Ossa on Olympus and Pelion on Ossa. They were killed by Apollo.

pellagra (pŭlā'grŭ, pŭlā'grŭ), disease resulting from diet deficient in vitamin B complex constituents, especially niacin. The disease is attended by reddening of parts of body and by gastrointestinal and nervous disturbances.

Pelletier, Pierre Joseph (pyĕr' zhôzĕf' pĕlŭtyā'), 1788–1842, French chemist; codiscoverer of quinine, strychnine, brucine, and other alkaloids.

Pellico, Silvio (sēl'vyō pĕl'lēkō), 1789–1854, Italian author of dramatic poetry (e.g. *Francesca da Rimini*, 1815) and of *Le mie prigioni* (1832), a moving account of his life as a political prisoner.

Pelly, river of S central Yukon, rising W of Mackenzie Mts. and flowing 330 mi. WNW to join Lewes R. and form Yukon R. at Fort Selkirk. Receives Ross and Macmillan rivers.

Pelopidas (pĭlŏ'pĭdŭs), d. 364 B.C., Theban general. Recovered Thebes from Spartans (379 B.C.) and later won victories over Sparta (e.g., at Leuctra, 371 B.C.). With Epaminondas he successfully invaded the Peloponnesus (370–369 B.C.). Captured on expedition to Macedonia (368 B.C.), he was rescued by Epaminondas.

Peloponnesian League: see SPARTA.

Peloponnesian War (pĕ″lŭpŭnē′zhŭn), 431–404 B.C., struggle in anc. Greece between Athens and Sparta, long-standing rivals. The war began with a contest between Athens and Corinth (Sparta's ally) over dependencies. In 431 a Spartan army first invaded Attica, but Athens and its port, Piraeus, were walled and resisted. The Athenian fleet raided Spartan allies and was victorious off Naupactus. Though plague wiped out a quarter of the Athenians and Pericles died, Athens was still able to maintain itself and refused a Spartan bid for peace. The tide began to turn when the Spartan Brasidas led a brilliant campaign that ended with a decisive victory at Amphipolis (424). The Athenian leader, Nicias, arranged a peace that was little more than a truce, and soon the brilliant Athenian general Alcibiades was aiding a revolt of Spartan allies. He also forwarded the plan for an Athenian expedition against Syracuse but was charged with sacrilege; the expedition was led by Nicias to disastrous loss (413). Alcibiades going over to Sparta helped create a Spartan fleet. Though he returned to Athenian service and won victories over the Spartans (notably at Cyzicus, 410), the rise of Lysander as Spartan leader prepared the end of the war. With a new fleet he won at Notium (407?) and, despite an Athenian victory at Arginusae, sealed the fate of Athens by crushing the Athenian navy under Conon at Aegospotamos (405) and taking the proud city itself by land and sea attack. After its surrender in 404 Athens was never to regain its old glory. Sparta was briefly mistress of Greece.

Peloponnesus (pĕ″lŭpŭnē′sŭs) or **Morea** (mōrē′ŭ), southernmost region of continental Greece. Morea, its medieval name, was used until recently, when its classic name was restored. A mountainous peninsula between the Ionian and Aegean seas, it extends c.140 mi. S from the Isthmus of Corinth to Cape Matapan. Patras, Corinth, Kalamata, and Nauplia are its chief cities and ports. It produces currants, grapes, tobacco, and olives but lacks grain crops. Sheep and goat raising; silk-culture; fishing. Industries are little developed. In ancient times, the chief political divisions were Elis, Achaea, Argolis, Corinth, Arcadia, and Lacedaemonia (comprising Messenia and Laconia). Sparta, Corinth, Argos, and Megalopolis were among chief cities. SPARTA long had hegemony over peninsula (except over Achaea and Argos). Its power was broken by Thebes and Macedon in 4th cent. B.C. Conquered by Rome (146 B.C.), the Peloponnesus became a Roman, later a Byzantine, province. After A.D. 1204 the VILLEHARDOUIN family (followed by other foreign rulers) held the whole peninsula except several ports, which went to Venice. Byzantine control, restored by 1432, was replaced by Turkish rule in 1460. Venice held parts of Morea at various times between 15th cent. and 1718.

Pelops (pē′lŏps), in Greek myth, son of Tantalus. He won Hippodamia by defeating her father in a race, in which he bribed charioteer. Later, rather than pay him, he drowned the charioteer, who cursed Pelops' seed. Peloponnesus was named for him.

pelota (pālō′tä), name for several Spanish ball games, generally played with rackets. Originated in the Basque provinces. Best known in U.S. is the game of jai alai (hī′ älī). Jai alai, one of fastest of sports, is scored on same general principles as handball.

Pelotas (pĕlō′täsh), city (pop. 79,649), S Rio Grande do Sul state, SE Brazil, port on lagoon SSW of Pôrto Alegre; leading meat-packing and exporting center.

Pemaquid, peninsula: see BRISTOL, Maine.

Pemba (pĕm′bù), island (380 sq. mi.; pop. c.100,000), off E Africa, in Indian Ocean; part of Zanzibar protectorate. Formerly a slave market, it now has a large trade in cloves.

Pembina (pĕm′bēnù), city (pop. 640), extreme NE N.Dak., at junction of Pembina and Red rivers. Trading post here in 1797; first settlers came 1812. Became state's first permanent settlement 1819. Base for early buffalo hunts.

Pembroke, Mary Herbert, countess of, 1561–1621, sister of Sir Philip Sidney and patroness of poets (including Spenser and Jonson). Her son, **William Herbert, 3d earl of Pembroke,** 1580–1630, was a patron of letters. He is one of those suggested as "Mr. W. H." of dedication of Shakspere's sonnets. Pembroke Col., Oxford, is named for him.

Pembroke, Richard de Clare, 2d earl of, d. 1176, English nobleman, known as Richard Strongbow. Went to Ireland (1170) to aid Dermot McMurrough and recoup his fortune. Subdued much of E Ireland.

Pembroke, William Marshal, 1st earl of, d. 1219, English nobleman. As regent for Henry III he repelled invasion of Louis VIII of France.

Pembroke, county, Wales: see PEMBROKESHIRE.

Pembroke, town (pop. 12,704), S Ont., Canada, WNW of Ottawa and on Ottawa R. Has pulp, paper, wool, lumber, flour mills. Gateway to Algonquin Prov. Park.

Pembroke College: see BROWN UNIVERSITY; OXFORD UNIVERSITY; CAMBRIDGE UNIVERSITY.

Pembrokeshire (pĕm′brŏŏk-shĭr) or **Pembroke,** maritime county (614 sq. mi.; pop. 90,896), SW Wales; co. town Pembroke. Largely agr. region of rolling hills and fertile valleys, it has metal deposits. SAINT DAVID's has noted cathedral.

pemmican, a travel food of North American Indians. Lean meat, sun dried, was pulverized and packed with melted fat, and sometimes dried berries, into rawhide bags. Fish was also used in the Northwest.

pen, pointed writing implement for applying ink or similar material. Reeds frayed at end were used in antiquity; quills were introduced in Middle Ages. Metal slip-in nib came into common use after 1828; fountain pen, in 1880s. Ball-point pen, introduced c.1944, is tipped by ball bearing which rolls gelatinous ink onto paper.

Penal Laws (pē′nŭl), general term for oppressive legislation against Catholics of England and Ireland. Begun under Henry VIII, they were inspired as much by political and economic fear as by religious hatred. Plots against Elizabeth and the Gunpowder Plot inflamed anti-Catholic feeling. Stuart attempts to soften the laws were a factor in the Puritan Revolution, and the laws became connected with efforts to limit power of the crown. TEST ACT (1673) kept Catholics from holding office. Act of SETTLEMENT (1701) excluded Catholics from the throne. Small number of Catholics in England and Scotland made laws unimportant after failure of Jacobite rebellions (1745). In Ireland, however, most of the population was Catholic. Laws there made harsher in 1695 for purpose of strengthening English possession of land. Made so strict that many left country and Protestants aided in evasion. The laws were repealed and conditions remedied by long process of CATHOLIC EMANCIPATION.

penance, SACRAMENT of the Roman Catholic Church. By it the penitent is absolved of his sins by his confessor, to whom he recites verbally the serious sins he has committed since his last confession or since his baptism. The confessor must be a priest or bishop, the person receiving the sacrament must be truly sorry and determined to amend his life. The confessor inflicts a penance as punishment for guilt (usually recital of stipulated prayers), and the penitent must, of course, make restitution for any injuries done to others. The confessor acts only as instrument of God, not with any powers of his own right, and he may not reveal what is told him in confession. Every Roman Catholic must receive the sacrament of penance once a year.

Penang (pùnăng′), settlement (400 sq. mi.; pop. 473,-227), NW MALAYA, on Straits of Malacca; cap. George Town. Consists of Penang isl. (110 sq. mi.) and Province Wellesley (290 sq. mi.), a strip on Malay Peninsula facing the island. Chief products are rubber and tin. Chinese greatly outnumber Malays and Indians. Britain has held Penang isl. since 1786 and Province Wellesley since 1791. Penang was one of STRAITS SETTLEMENTS, 1826–1946.

penates, household gods: see LARES AND PENATES.

Penck, Albrecht (äl'brĕkht pĕngk'), 1858–1945, German geographer and geologist. Noted for glaciation study, pioneer classification of land forms, development of modern regional geography.

Penda, d. 655, king of Mercia (632–55). A great fighter, he extended his power over Wessex and East Anglia. Killed fighting Oswy of Northumbria.

Pend d'Oreille Indians (pŏn"dūrā'), North American tribe of Salishan linguistic stock. Together with the Kalispel (from whom they cannot well be distinguished), they occupied NW Mont., N Idaho, and NE Wash. in early 19th cent. Today on reservations in Mont. and Wash.

Pendergast, Thomas Joseph, 1873–1945, American political boss. Kansas City, Mo., and Mo. state Democratic leader. Convicted in 1939 of income-tax evasions.

Pendleton, Edmund (pĕn'dŭltùn), 1721–1803, American Revolutionary patriot and Va. jurist. His great-grandnephew, **George Hunt Pendleton,** 1825–89, was U.S. Representative from Ohio (1857–65) and U.S. Senator (1879–85). Secured legislation introducing competitive examinations in CIVIL SERVICE.

Pendleton, city (pop. 11,774), NE Oregon, on Umatilla R. and SW of Walla Walla, Wash.; founded 1869 on old Oregon Trail. Ships wheat, sheep, and cattle. Flour and woolen mills; leather goods. Indians from near-by reservation take part in annual Pendleton Roundup.

Pend Oreille (pŏn"dūrā') [Fr.,= ear ornament], river, 119 mi. long, N Idaho, rising in Pend Oreille L. and flowing W, NW into Wash., joining Columbia R. in Canada near border (see CLARK FORK). **Pend Oreille Lake,** c.40 mi. long, N Idaho; state's largest lake. Fed by Clark Fork. Noted for beauty.

Pendragon, Uther: see ARTHURIAN LEGEND.

pendulum, a weight suspended from fixed point so that it can vibrate in arc determined by its momentum and the force of gravity. Galileo found each swing of a pendulum to be of equal duration. Christiaan Huygens determined relation between length of pendulum and vibration time and in 1673 applied pendulum control to clocks. Pendulum is used to control other mechanisms, measure intensity of gravity, register direction of earthquakes, demonstrate rotation of earth (1851 by J. B. L. Foucault in Paris).

Penelope (pùnĕ'lùpē), in Greek legend, queen of Ithaca; faithful wife of Odysseus. In the *Odyssey,* while Odysseus was away, she was beset by suitors. To evade them she said she would decide after weaving Laertes' shroud, then unraveled each night each day's work. Her plan was discovered and she agreed to marry the one who could bend Odysseus' bow, but none could. Odysseus, returning disguised as a beggar, bent the bow, was reunited with Penelope, and slew the suitors.

Peneus (pìnē'ùs), river, 135 mi. long, N Greece, in Thessaly, rising in Pindus mts. and flowing E past Larissa, through valley of Tempe to Aegean Sea.

Penfield, Edward, 1866–1925, American illustrator, originator of the colored poster in America.

penguin (pĕng'gwĭn, pĕn'–), flightless, web-footed, swimming and diving bird of S Hemisphere from Galapagos Isls. to antarctic regions. It has a white breast and gray or gray-blue back. On land it usually walks upright.

penicillin (pĕ"nĭsī'lĭn), antibiotic secreted by certain strains of the mold *Penicillium notatum.* Discovered by Sir Alexander Fleming; its antibacterial powers and nontoxicity to humans estab. 1941 by Florey, Chain, and others.

Penikese Island: see ELIZABETH ISLANDS.

Peninsular campaign, April–July, 1862, of Civil War. Attempt of G. B. McClellan to take Richmond, Va.,

via peninsula between York and James rivers. J. E. Johnston withdrew Confederate forces from Yorktown (May 3), fighting rear-guard action. Norfolk also abandoned (May 10). Two retreats opened both rivers to Union gunboats, which were repulsed, however, at Drewrys Bluff (9 mi. S of Richmond). Union army spread across Chickahominy R., but Stonewall Jackson's brilliant campaign in Shenandoah Valley diverted Irvin McDowell's Army of the Rappahannock, and heavy rains menaced Union communications. On May 31–June 1 Johnston and James Longstreet attacked at Fair Oaks or Seven Pines; Federals held ground. R. E. Lee took command and withdrew to Richmond. His offensive in SEVEN DAYS BATTLES closed campaign with Southern victory.

Peninsular War, 1808–14, fought by France in Iberian Peninsula against the British (with Spanish and Portuguese volunteer forces). Background: Spain, having become dependent on Napoleon I, agreed to French occupation of Portugal (1807). In March, 1808, a palace revolution deposed the pro-French CHARLES IV and put his son FERDINAND VII on Spanish throne, thus giving Napoleon a pretext for occupying Madrid and other Spanish cities. An uprising in Madrid was bloodily suppressed by the French (May 2); Charles IV and Ferdinand VII were both lured into France and forced to abdicate; Napoleon's brother Joseph Bonaparte was proclaimed king of Spain (June 15). The Spanish and Portuguese rose in revolt. Military operations: Spanish insurrectionists forced French to abandon Madrid and the siege of SARAGOSSA, while a British expeditionary force under Arthur Wellesley (later duke of WELLINGTON) landed in Portugal and defeated Junot's French forces at Vimeiro (Aug. 21, 1808). By the Convention of Cintra, Junot surrendered Lisbon and agreed to evacuation of his troops. The British under Sir John MOORE now invaded Spain, where Napoleon personally took the field with 200,000 troops. The conflict thus grew into a major war. Napoleon stormed Madrid; Lannes took Saragossa; Soult pursued Moore's forces into Galicia and forced them to evacuate (Dec., 1808–Jan., 1809). These French successes were offset by Wellington after April, 1809. He drove the French out of Portugal and defeated them at Talavera (1809); repulsed them at Bussaco (1810); prevented the junction of Soult's and Masséna's forces (battles of Fuentes de Oñoro and Albuera, 1811); and, by then in supreme command, routed King Joseph and Jourdan at Vitoria (1813) and invaded France. He had reached Toulouse (1814), when Napoleon's abdication ended the war.

Penitentes (pĕnĭtĕn'tēz), secret lay order in SW U.S. (esp. N.Mex.), arising originally from the third order of the Franciscans. They are notorious for practicing flagellation in Holy Week (ending with a crucifixion). Though condemned (1889) by the Roman Catholic Church, the rites persist somewhat.

penitentiary: see PRISON.

Penitent Thief: see Good Thief.

Penn, Sir William, 1621–70, British admiral. Fought in the Dutch Wars and captured Jamaica. Father of **William Penn,** 1644–1718, English Quaker, founder of Pennsylvania. Laid out Philadelphia in 1682. Estab. liberal government in colony.

Pennamite Wars, conflicts between Pa. and Conn. settlers over claims to WYOMING VALLEY.

Pennell, Joseph (pĕ'nùl), 1860–1926, American illustrator, etcher, lithographer; one of the foremost American graphic artists. Treated mainly landscapes and architectural views. Influenced by Whistler.

Pennine Chain (pĕ'nīn), long hill range ("backbone of England"), extending from the Cheviot Hills to the Peak in NW Derbyshire. Consists of a series of upland blocks separated by transverse river valleys. Cross Fell (2,930 ft.) is highest peak.

Pennsauken (pĕnsô'kìn), township (pop. 22,767), SW N.J., near Camden. Bricks, terra cotta, beer.

Penns Grove, residential borough (pop. 6,669), SW

N.J., on the Delaware R. opposite Wilmington, Del.

Pennsylvania, state (45,333 sq. mi.; pop. 10,498,012), NE U.S.; one of Thirteen Colonies; cap. HARRISBURG. Main cities are PHILADELPHIA, PITTSBURGH, ERIE, ALLENTOWN, SCRANTON, READING. Bounded E by Delaware R. (Atlantic Ocean outlet). Country of mountains, hills, valleys but for L. Erie coastal plains (NW). Drained by Delaware, Susquehanna, Allegheny, Monongahela rivers (last two form the Ohio at Pittsburgh). Mines coal, oil, natural gas, limestone, slate; mfg. of steel, iron, textiles, petroleum products, machinery, electrical goods, metal and food products. Farming (dairying, poultry, grains, tobacco, fruits, vegetables), fishing. William PENN secured proprietary rights in 1681 (few settlements before by Swedes and Dutch), added Lower Counties (Del.) in 1682. Colony designed around liberal principles. Penn signed good-will treaty with Indians. Active in American Revolution (see BRANDYWINE, GERMANTOWN, VALLEY FORGE). Benjamin FRANKLIN one of leaders in revolutionary movement. Philadelphia was important center of activities—scene of First and Second Continental Congresses, signing of Declaration of Independence, drafting of Federal Constitution. Surged forward after war; national capital 1790–1800. Boundary disputes settled (see WYOMING VALLEY). Economic dislocation expressed in WHISKY REBELLION (1794), Fries Rebellion of 1798 (see FRIES, JOHN). Active for Union in Civil War (see GETTYSBURG CAMPAIGN, CHAMBERSBURG). Post-war industry boomed. Labor troubles appeared in activities of MOLLY MAGUIRES, HOMESTEAD strike of 1892. Simon CAMERON built powerful political machine for Republicans. High degree of regional individuality has been retained by some groups, e.g., PENNSYLVANIA DUTCH.

Pennsylvania, University of, in Philadelphia; nonsectarian, private, for men and women; planned 1740 as charity school, opened 1751 as academy with Benjamin Franklin as chief founder, chartered 1755 as college, reorganized 1779 as university. Pioneer in secular education in the colonies; had first university medical and business schools in U.S. Pennsylvania School of Social Work is affiliated.

Pennsylvania Academy of the Fine Arts, at Philadelphia, estab. 1805, inc. 1806. An outgrowth of the Columbianum, which held first art exhibition in U.S. (1794). Present building was erected 1876 to house academy's art collection, notable for early and modern American paintings and 19th-cent. European paintings. Privately supported. Connected with oldest art school in U.S.

Pennsylvania Dutch, name popularly but erroneously applied to the descendants of Germans who settled in Pa. (esp. in Northampton, Berks, Lancaster, Lehigh, Lebanon, and York counties). Most of the original settlers belonged to religious sects persecuted in Europe—Mennonites, Dunkards, Moravians, Amish. Germantown was founded in 1683, but the large immigration came from the Palatinate after 1710. Most of the Germans became prosperous farmers, and over the decades they preserved their religious customs, dress, and language (a blend of several dialects, with some High German and English; see LANGUAGE, table) to a remarkable degree. A considerable body of Pennsylvanian German literature was written. Pennsylvania German folk art (e.g., in pottery, barns, illuminated writing) has attracted much attention in recent years.

Pennsylvania Museum of Art: see PHILADELPHIA MUSEUM OF ART.

Pennsylvanian period: see CARBONIFEROUS PERIOD.

Pennsylvania Railroad. Incorporated in 1846 by act of Pa. legislature. Company completed in 1854 a single-track line between Philadelphia and Pittsburgh. In 1857 company purchased many railroads owned and operated by state of Pa. Railroad rapidly extended operations between Atlantic seaboard and Mississippi R. and between Great Lakes and Ohio R.

Pennsylvania State College: see STATE COLLEGE.

Penn Yan (pĕn" yăn'), village (pop. 5,481), W central N.Y., in FINGER LAKES region, on Keuka L. Mfg. of wines, fruit juices, machinery, baskets. Near by is Keuka Col. (Baptist; for women; 1888). Jemima WILKINSON lived near by.

pennyroyal, name for two similar plants of the mint family, true or European pennyroyal (*Mentha pulegium*) and American or mock pennyroyal (*Hedeoma pulegioides*). Both have small bluish flowers in the leaf axils and both yield a pungent oil.

Penobscot (pŭnŏb'skŭt), river, 350 mi. long (from head of longest branch), formed in central Maine. Its headstreams are the outlets of many lakes. Flows S, past Old Town and Bangor (head of navigation), to Penobscot Bay. Furnishes power for pulp and paper mills. Upper course is favorite canoe route. Chief freight is lumber.

Penobscot Bay, islanded inlet of the Atlantic, S Maine, at Penobscot R. mouth. Shores lined with summer resorts. Bay entered by Martin Pring, 1603; Champlain ascended the river, 1604. Long Anglo-French dispute over area. Chief French port was Castine.

Penobscot Indians, North American tribe of Algonquian linguistic stock, occupying the region around the Penobscot R. in 17th cent. They were the largest tribe of the Abnaki Confederacy. They were friendly with the French until they changed allegiance to the British in 1749.

Penrhyn (pĕn'rĭn) or **Tongareva** (tŏng"gŭrĕ'vù), atoll in S Pacific belonging to New Zealand. Discovered 1788 by the British. Exports copra and pearl shells.

Penrose, Boies (boiz'), 1860–1921, U.S. Senator from Pa. (1897–1921) and Republican state boss.

Penry, John, 1559–93, British Puritan author, an instigator of MARPRELATE CONTROVERSY. With others he issued (1588–89), under name Martin Marprelate, seven pamphlets attacking Church of England.

Pensacola (pĕnsŭkō'lù), city (pop. 43,479), extreme NW Fla., on fine natural harbor on Pensacola Bay. Shipping, fishing, and wood-processing center, it also has shipyards and seafood canneries. Nylon plant near by. Site of a major U.S. naval air station (estab. 1914). Spanish settlement, 1559–61; recolonized by Spanish in 1698, and Fort San Carlos erected on Santa Rosa Isl., across the bay. Shuttled between Spain and France, 1719–63. British held it until 1783, when it was formally returned to Spain (Bernardo de Gálvez had captured it, 1781). British base (though city still Spanish) in War of 1812. Captured by Andrew Jackson in 1814 and 1818. U.S. took formal possession 1821. Held alternately by Federals and Confederates in Civil War, though Fort PICKENS remained Federal throughout. Fort Barrancas is only garrisoned fort here now. Has ruins of forts Barrancas (old), San Carlos (1780s), Pickens, and McRae (1830s).

Pensacola Bay, inlet of Gulf of Mexico, c.13 mi. long and 2½ mi. wide, NW Fla. Pensacola city is c.7 mi. from the entrance (protected by peninsula and Santa Rosa Isl.). Receives Escambia R.

Pensacola Dam: see GRAND RIVER DAM.

pension, originally a gratuity to persons favored by the sovereign, to soldiers, and, later, to superannuated public servants. The idea of extending old-age protection to all persons appeared in 19th-cent. Germany and was developed in the U.S. in 1935 as a form of SOCIAL SECURITY. Many corporations and groups give supplementary pensions to their workers. The usual method is through group insurance, to which the employee contributes as well as employer or government.

penstemon: see BEARDTONGUE.

pentameter (pĕntă'mùtur), in prosody, a line scanning in five feet. Iambic pentameter is great English meter. Chaucer used seven iambic pentameters rhyming *ababbcc*; as he pronounced a final short *e*, his pentameters often ended in an 11th unstressed syllable.

When final *e* disappeared from speech, the pentameter became strict; as heroic couplet it was prominent in poetry of 17th and 18th cent., notably that of Dryden and Pope. Blank verse—unrhymed iambic pentameters—has been used in great dramatic and epic verse from Shakspere and Milton to the present. Renaissance England borrowed the ottava rima (eight iambic pentameters rhyming *ababacc* of Ariosto and Tasso; Spenser added to it an alexandrine (a line of six iambic feet) rhyming with the last pentameter. The sonnet is a notable use of iambic pentameter.

Pentapolis (pĕntá′pŭlĭs) [Gr.,= five cities], any group of five cities. One such was the combination of the cities of Cyrenaica (Apollonia, Arsinoë, Berenice, Cyrene, Ptolemais), so called from the 4th cent. B.C. to 7th cent. A.D. Another was that of five cities on the Adriatic coast of Italy (Rimini, Ancona, Fano, Pesaro, Senigallia), important as a group 5th–11th cent. A.D., largely as outposts of Byzantine culture.

Pentateuch (pĕn′tūtŭk) [Gr.,= five books], the first five books of Old Testament, the books of the Law.

Pentecost (pĕn′tŭkôst) [Gr.,= fiftieth], important Jewish and Christian feasts. In Jewish calendar it comes 50 days after Passover and marks the closing of the Palestinian harvest, a period of 49 days or seven weeks. Called in Bible the Feast of Weeks, Feast of Harvest, or Feast of Firstfruits; 50th day is Feast of Pentecost, in Hebrew *Shabuot*. Also known as anniversary of the giving of the Law; this aspect stressed in modern Judaism. See Ex. 23.16; 34.18–26; Lev. 23.15–22; Num. 28.26; Deut. 16.9–12; 2 Chron. 8.13. In Christian calendar Pentecost falls on seventh Sunday after Easter. On the Pentecost after the resurrection of Jesus (i.e., 50 days from the Passover in which He was crucified), the spirit of the Holy Ghost descended upon his followers (Acts 2). The Christian feast commemorates this event and has always been solemnly observed by the Church as her birthday and as the feast of the Holy Ghost. Anciently converts were baptized at this time; from white garments worn by them comes Whitsunday, an English name for Pentecost. The great Latin hymns *Veni Creator Spiritus* and *Veni Sancte Spiritus* were composed for Pentecost.

Penthesilea (pĕn″thĕsŭlē′û), in Greek mythology, queen of the Amazons. She joined the Trojans in the Trojan War and was killed by Achilles.

Penticton, city (pop. 10,548), S B.C., Canada, on Okanagan R. at S end of Okanagan L. Fruit-growing center with canning and packing plants. Resort.

Pentland Firth (pĕnt′lŭnd fûrth′), channel 6½–8 mi. wide and c.14 mi. long, separating the Orkneys from mainland of Scotland.

Penuel (pēnū′ûl) [Heb.,= face of God], place by Jabbok R. where Jacob wrestled with the angel.

Penza (pyĕn′zŭ), city (pop. 157,145), E central RSFSR, on Sura R., in a fertile black-earth district. Machinery mfg. and food processing.

Penzance (pĕnzăns′), municipal borough (pop. 20,648), Cornwall, England, NE of Lands End. Fishing center and resort, it is a port for the Scilly Isls.

peony, hardy perennial plant of genus *Paeonia*, prized for the large handsome flowers in spring. Herbaceous peonies have single or double, often fragrant, flowers in white, red, or pink. Tree peonies, with woody stems, are less commonly grown. Both kinds, chiefly native to Asia and Europe, have been venerated in China and Japan.

People's Charter: see CHARTISM.

People's party: see POPULIST PARTY.

Peoria (pēō′rĕu), city (pop. 111,856), central Ill., on Illinois R. where it widens into L. Peoria. Second largest city in Ill. Trade and shipping center in agr. (esp. grain) and coal area. Mfg. of agr. equipment and food products. Oil refining. Distilling center. La Salle estab. Fort Creve Coeur in area 1680; it became trading post 1691 and was abandoned in Revolution. Fort Clark (1813) was nucleus of American settlement, 1818. Lincoln made speech on slavery here 1854. Seat of Bradley Univ. (coed.; 1896).

Pepi (pā′pē), name of two kings of anc. Egypt, of the VI dynasty. **Pepi I** ruled c.2595–c.2571 B.C. His son, **Pepi II,** ruled supposedly for more than 90 years (c.2567–c.2473) in an area of prosperity. He took expeditions into Nubia.

Pepin (pĕ′pĭn) or **Pippin** (pĭ′–), Frankish mayors of the palace and kings. **Pepin of Landen,** d.639?, helped CLOTAIRE II of Neustria in conquest of Austrasia (613), which he later governed for Dagobert I as mayor of the palace. Out of the marriage of his daughter with the son of Arnulf, bishop of Metz, arose the Carolingian dynasty. His grandson, **Pepin of Héristal,** d. c.714, ruled Austrasia and Neustria as mayor of the palace, the Merovingian dynasty retaining nominal kingship. He was father of CHARLES MARTEL and grandfather of **Pepin the Short,** c.714–768, who became mayor in 741. In 751, with the consent of Pope Zacharias, he forced the last Merovingian king, Childeric III, into a monastery and had himself proclaimed king of the Franks. He defended Rome against the Lombards (754, 756), from whom he wrested Ravenna and other cities. These he ceded to the pope, laying the foundation for the Papal States. He was the father of Charlemagne. His great-grandson **Pepin I,** d. 838, son of Emperor LOUIS I, was king of Aquitaine (817–38). He joined in the rebellions of 830 and 833 against his father but each time helped restore him.

Pepin, Lake (pē′pĭn), widening of the Mississippi, 21 mi. long, 3 mi. wide, SE Minn., SE of Red Wing.

pepper, name for pungent fruit of several plants, used as condiments and in medicine. True or black pepper (*Piper nigrum*) is a perennial shrub native to East Indies; black and white pepper are prepared from its dried berries. Red peppers, eaten green or ripe as a vegetable or pickled, used as condiments, and in medicine, are various species of the genus *Capsicum*, either annuals or biennials. Well-known kinds are the pimento and the sweet or bell pepper. Cayenne pepper, very sharp, is made from a species perennial in the tropics. Paprika is prepared from a milder kind. Pungent "chili" pepper is used in Mexican food and in pepper sauces.

peppergrass, widely distributed herbs of genus *Lepidium*, especially garden cress (*Lepidium sativum*), sometimes used in salads.

pepperidge: see BLACK GUM.

peppermint, aromatic European perennial herb (*Mentha piperita*), naturalized in the U.S. It is a typical MINT, grown commercially for the oil and its derivative menthol.

Pepperrell, Sir William, 1696–1759, American colonial military commander. Led land forces at capture of Louisburg (1745) in French and Indian Wars. First native American to be created baronet.

pepper tree, ornamental resinous evergreen tree (*Schinus*) native to Peru but widely grown in mild climates. The California pepper tree (*Schinus molle*) has panicles of greenish flowers followed by rose berrylike fruits, sometimes used as a substitute for pepper.

pepsin: see STOMACH.

Pepusch, John Christopher (pā′pōosh), 1667–1752, German musician; lived in London after 1700. Composed the overture and arranged the rest of the music for John Gay's *The Beggar's Opera* (1728).

Pepys, Samuel (pēps), 1633–1703, English diarist. A diligent naval official, he rose to be secretary to the admiralty (1672–79, 1684–89). In 1684 he also became president of the Royal Society. In retirement after the accession of William III, he wrote his *Memoirs . . . of the Royal Navy* (1690). His famous diary, in cipher, left with his books to Magdalene Col., Cambridge, was deciphered and was first published in 1825. It is an intimate record of his daily domestic, social, and political life from 1660 to 1669 and furnishes a graphic picture of social life and manners and court morals of the Restoration period.

Pequot Indians (pē'kwŏt), North American tribe of Algonquian linguistic stock. They had a culture typical of the E Woodlands area. Originally united with the Mohegan, they moved S to the Conn. coast in 17th cent. There by murdering John Oldham they brought on the Pequot War (1637), which ended with dispersal of the tribe.

Pera, Turkey: see ISTANBUL.

Peraea (pērē'ù), in Roman times, region E of Jordan R. It is the Gilead of the Old Testament.

Perak: see MALAYA.

Percé Rock (pèrsā'), E Que., Canada, in the Atlantic off E Gaspé Peninsula opposite Percé village. A bird sanctuary and tourist attraction, it is 1,420 ft. long, 300 ft. wide, 290 ft. high.

perch, small, beautifully colored, fresh-water game fish of Europe, Asia, North America. It is typical of large family of spiny-finned fishes. Maximum weight is c.5 lb. It is an excellent food fish.

Percier, Charles (shärl' pèrsyā'), 1764–1838, French architect. He and Pierre FONTAINE were official architects under Napoleon. They worked as partners on Louvre and Tuileries palaces. Their influence on interior decoration of Empire period was enormous. They also collaborated on books on architecture.

Percivale, Sir, knight of King Arthur's court: see ARTHURIAN LEGEND; PARSIFAL.

percussion instruments, in music, those instruments whose sound is usually produced by a blow from a mallet or stick. There are many varieties of percussion instruments, but those discussed in this article are most often found today in a symphony orchestra. Scientifically, percussion instruments are classified as idiophones (those made of a substance, such as wood or metal, which vibrates when struck) and membranophones (those whose sound producing agent is a stretched skin); musically, they are considered as to whether or not they can be tuned to produce a sound of definite pitch. The only drums which can be tuned are kettledrums (also called timpani), kettle-shaped metal vessels over which a membrane (the drumhead) is stretched; they are tuned by adjusting tension of the head. The celesta (sĭlĕ'stù), a keyboard instrument whose set of steel bars are struck by hammers operated from the keyboard, has a range of 4 octaves upward from middle C. The glockenspiel, a set of steel plates played by hand with two little hammers, and the XYLOPHONE also produce tones of definite pitch. The snare drum has two drumheads; across one of them are stretched several strings (called snares) that cause a rattling sound of indefinite pitch when the opposite head is struck. The bass drum, the largest drum used; the cymbals, a pair of metal discs which are sounded by being struck together; the gong; the tambourine, a single drumhead stretched over a wooden frame with metal plates or jingles in the frame; and the triangle, made of steel and struck with a small steel stick, are all of indefinite pitch.

Percy, English noble family. **Henry Percy, 1st earl of Northumberland,** 1342–1408, received earldom from Richard II. Banished by Richard in 1398, he was instrumental in securing crown for Henry IV. Took part in family rebellion of 1403, but submitted. Later fled to France, made attempt to invade England (1408), and was killed at Branham Moor. His son, **Sir Henry Percy,** 1366–1403, called Hotspur, was active against the Scots. Fought battles of Otterburn (1388) and Humbledon Hill (1402). Quarreled with Henry IV and plotted to crown Edmund Mortimer, 5th earl of March. Plot is treated in Shakspere's *Henry IV.* Killed at battle of Shrewsbury. His uncle, **Thomas Percy, earl of Worcester,** c.1344–1403, fought against France and Spain and served as a diplomat under Richard II. Later supported Henry IV. Joining his brother and nephew in 1403 revolt, he was captured at Shrewsbury and executed. **Henry Percy, 4th earl of Northumberland,** 1446–89, served Yorkish king Ed-

ward IV after imprisonment following death of his Lancastrian father, the 3d earl. Withheld aid from Richard III in favor of Henry VII. **Thomas Percy, 7th earl of Northumberland,** 1528–72, defended Scottish border for Mary I. Under Elizabeth, he plotted (1569) to release Mary Queen of Scots and restore Catholicism. Led unsuccessful revolt and was beheaded. **Algernon Percy, 10th earl of Northumberland,** 1602–68, was lord high admiral of England. Commanded Charles I's expedition against Scotland. Disagreement with king's policy led him to support Parliament, giving it control of fleet.

Percy, Thomas, 1729–1811, English antiquary, a churchman. His collection of English and Scottish ballads, *Reliques of Ancient English Poetry* (3 vols., 1765), aroused interest in earlier literary forms.

Perdiccas (pùrdĭ'kùs), d. 321 B.C., Macedonian general under Philip II and Alexander the Great. Regent after the death of Alexander (323 B.C.), he failed to hold the empire together and was defeated in the wars of the Diadochi by Ptolemy I.

Pereda, José María de (hōsā' märē'ä dā pārā'dhä), 1833–1906, Spanish novelist. Wrote stories of his native Santander.

Pereira, Nun'Alvares (noōn'äl'vùrĭsh pèrā'rù), 1360–1431, Portuguese hero, called the Great Constable. He was the friend, counselor, and general of JOHN I, who largely owed him the victory at Aljubarrota (1385) and his throne. From the union of his daughter with a natural son of John I the house of Braganza is descended.

Perekop, Isthmus of (pèrĭkôp'), c.20 mi. long and 4–15 mi. wide, USSR, connecting Crimea with mainland and separating Gulf of Perekop (an arm of Black Sea) from Sivash Sea (an inlet of Sea of Azov).

perennial, a plant that lives for more than two years in contrast to an ANNUAL and BIENNIAL. Perennials are either herbaceous (surviving winter chiefly by rootstocks), e.g., iris and chrysanthemum, or woody (surviving by roots, stems, and sometimes, leaves), e.g., most trees and shrubs. Some perennials act as annuals outside their natural habitat.

Peretz, Isaac Loeb (lōb' pě'rĕts), 1851–1915, Yiddish-Hebrew playwright and poet, b. Poland. His work is imbued with the spirit of his people and an understanding of Jewish life.

Pérez, Antonio (äntō'nyō pä'räth), b. between 1534 and 1540, d. 1611, Spanish nobleman, confidential adviser of Philip II and lover of the princess of ÉBOLI. His ruin was brought about by his arrest (1579) for the murder of John of Austria's secretary. He was prosecuted on various charges until in 1590 he escaped to Saragossa, where he placed himself in the hands of the authorities of his native Aragon and openly accused the king of having procured the murder. The people of Aragon, jealous of their privileges, sided with Pérez; an uprising was crushed in 1591, and Pérez fled abroad.

Pérez de Ayala, Ramón (rämōn' pä'räth dä äyä'lä), 1881–, Spanish poet, novelist, and essayist. His poetry's chief theme is nature (e.g., in *La paz del sendero* and *El sendero innumerable*). One of his novels is *The Fox's Paw* (1912), the story of his courtship of his American wife.

Pérez Galdós, Benito (bānē'tō pä'räth gäldōs'), 1843–1920, Spanish novelist and dramatist. Wrote *Episodios nacionales,* 46 novels on 19th-cent. Spain; other novels, including *Doña Perfecta* (1876), *Gloria* (1877), and *Marianela* (1878).

Perez-uzza or **Perez-uzzah** (both: pě'rĕz-ŭz'ù) [Heb.= breach of Uzzah], name given to threshing floor where Uzzah touched the ark and died. 2 Sam. 6.6–8; 1 Chron. 13.9–11. Previously called Chidon or Nachon.

perfume, aroma produced by essential oils of plants and synthetic aromatics. Used from antiquity. Modern perfumes are commonly blends of natural and synthetic scents and fixatives which add pungency and equalize vaporization of ingredients. Ingredients are combined with alcohol for liquid scents, with fatty base for many cosmetics.

Pergamum (pûr'gŭmŭm), anc. city of Asia Minor (now Turkey) on the Caicus R. An independent kingdom, it flourished as a brilliant center of Hellenistic culture 3d–2d cent. B.C., particularly notable for sculpture and for a large library (with books on parchment, which takes its name from the city). Attalus III (d. 133 B.C.) bequeathed Pergamum to Rome. Also Pergamos, Pergamus, Pergamon.

Pergolesi, Giovanni (Battista) (jōvän'nē pĕrgōlā'zĕ), 1710–36, Italian composer. His *La serva padrona* (1733) became the model for *opera buffa*. He is also known for his *Stabat Mater*.

Peri, Jacopo (yä'kōpō pā'rē), 1561–c.1633, Italian composer. With Caccini, he wrote *Dafne* (c.1597), the earliest opera on record, and *Euridice* (1600), the earliest opera whose music is extant.

Periander (pĕ'rēăn"dûr), d. 585 B.C., tyrant of Corinth, one of the Seven Wise Men of Greece.

Peribonca, river of central Que., Canada, rising in Otish Mts. and flowing 300 mi. S to L. St. John.

Pericles (pĕ'rĭklēz), c.495–429 B.C., Athenian statesman, of the distinguished family of the Alcmaeonidae. Well educated and interested in the arts, he was determined to make Athens a center of culture as well as a political power. Under his leadership Athens reached her zenith: the Delian League was powerful, Athens was beautiful, rich, and increasingly democratic. Peace was made with Persia in 448 B.C. after the death of Pericles' rival, Cimon, and the Peloponnesian War did not begin until 431 B.C. The new war and a disastrous plague brought Pericles' deposition. He was later reinstated, but died soon afterward. Aspasia was his mistress, Alcibiades his ward.

Périer, Casimir Pierre (käzēmēr' pyĕr' pĕryä'), 1777–1832, French banker and statesman. He played a large part in the overthrow of Charles X and served as premier (1831–32) under Louis Philippe. Conservative, he sought to repress republicanism, failed to send aid to the Polish revolutionists, but helped Belgium gain its independence. His descendants took the name Casimir-Perier.

Périgord (pārēgôr'), region and former county, SW France; historic cap. Périgueux. Consists of arid limestone plateaus cut by fertile valleys. Truffles and goose liver pâté are major exports. County, estab. 9th cent., was wrested from English rule c.1370, passed to house of Bourbon, and was inc. into royal domain after 1589.

Périgueux (pārēgû'), city (pop. 37,287), cap. of Dordogne dept., SW France; historic cap. of Périgord. Has 12th-cent. cathedral and basilica.

Perim (pārēm'), island (5 sq. mi.; pop. 360), belonging to British colony of Aden; off SW coast of Arabia. Formerly a coaling station.

periodical, publication issued at regular intervals, usually distinguished from the newspaper in purporting to express authors' and editors' points of view instead of recounting current news, also by the frequency of its publication. The term *periodical* applies to journals, literary reviews, and fiction magazines; term *magazine* is usually limited to periodicals designed primarily for entertainment. A list of contemporary periodicals may be found in the annual *N. W. Ayer & Son's Directory*.

periodic law. J. W. Döbereiner (1829) arranged a number of elements in groups of three (triads) on basis of physical and chemical properties; element lying between the other two had properties that were intermediate, and ATOMIC WEIGHT that was average of other two. J. A. R. Newlands discovered (1863–65) that when elements are listed in order of increasing atomic wt., starting with the second, the 8th and 16th elements following a given element are similar in properties. Because of counting by groups of eight, this is known as law of octaves. About the same time, A. E. B. de Chancourtois arranged elements in

one continuous order by atomic wts. In 1869 Mendelejeff stated periodic law: properties of chemical elements are periodic functions of their atomic wt., i.e., a definite relationship is seen in periodic occurrence of similar properties in certain elements when all are arranged according to increasing atomic wt. Lothar Meyer drew same conclusion independently; pointed out relation between atomic volume of elements (ratio of atomic wt. to specific gravity). Arrangement of elements showed a number of spaces into which no known element would fit; Mendelejeff said these indicated undiscovered elements and predicted the atomic wts. and properties of these elements with great accuracy. Not all elements fall in positions corresponding correctly to properties. This was corrected by work of Henry Gwyn Jeffreys Moseley which led to statement of new periodic law. In this system the elements are arranged in order of decreasing wave length of X-ray spectra. Order is almost the same as that by atomic wt. Elements are numbered according to position they occupy; this number, the atomic number, indicates the number of positive charges on nucleus and the number of extranuclear electrons, number and arrangement of which are believed to determine the properties of the element. New periodic law states that properties of elements are a function of their atomic numbers. Tabulation consists of nine vertical columns (groups) and a number of horizontal columns (periods).

Peripatetics (pĕ"rŭpŭtĕ'tĭks) [from Gr.,= walking about; from Aristotle's method of teaching], followers of Aristotle. Theophrastus and Strato of Lampsacus were later leaders of the school, which concerned itself with interpreting Aristotle.

periscope (pĕ'rĭskōp), device for viewing objects out of line of vision or concealed by intervening body. Essential parts are prisms, mirrors, tube, lenses, and eyepiece. Image received in one mirror is reflected through tube with its lenses to a mirror visible to the viewer.

peritonitis (pĕ"rĭtŭnī'tĭs), inflammation of peritoneum, the membranous tissue lining abdominal cavity and enclosing many organs. Causes include perforation of gastrointestinal tract, ruptured appendix, abdominal surgery, abortion, primary infection. Causative agents are usually bacteria.

periwinkle (pe'rŭwing"kŭl), small mollusk with conical, spiral shell, found in temperate and cold waters.

periwinkle, plant of Old World genus *Vinca*, especially the common periwinkle or myrtle (*Vinca minor*), a trailing ground cover for shade. It has evergreen leaves and blue flowers.

Perkins, Charles Callahan, 1823–86, American art critic, whose writings had great influence on development of American art. Illustrated his *Italian Sculptors* (1868) with his own etchings.

Perkins, Frances, 1882–, U.S. Secretary of Labor (1933–45), first U.S. woman cabinet member.

Perkins Institution and Massachusetts School for the Blind, at Watertown, Mass., chartered 1829, opened 1832 in South Boston, as New England Asylum for the Blind, given present name 1877, moved 1912. S. G. Howe was first director. Laura BRIDGMAN and Anne Sullivan MACY were pupils.

Perkin Warbeck: see WARBECK, PERKIN.

Perlis: see MALAYA.

Perm, RSFSR: see MOLOTOV.

Permanent Court of Arbitration: see HAGUE TRIBUNAL.

Permanent Court of International Justice: see WORLD COURT.

Permian period (pûr'mĕun), sixth and last period of the Paleozoic era of geologic time. It saw climax of the changes in the earth's surface begun in Carboniferous, which together with extremes of cold and aridity resulted in extinction of some marine animals and some plants; aridity is proved by extensive salt and gypsum deposits. A long marine submergence occurred during early Permian in SW U.S., with deposits of sandstones and limestones up to 6,000 ft. thick. Also submerged was the Cordilleran area, where red sediments were laid down. In Upper Permian practically all of North America was above sea level and Appalachian Mts. were thrust up. Plant and animal life in general transitional between that of Paleozoic and Mesozoic. See also GEOLOGY, table.

Pernambuco (pĕr″nŭmbōō′kō), state (37,458 sq. mi.; pop. 3,430,630), NE Brazil, extending inland from the Atlantic; cap., RECIFE. First European settlement made here in 1530s; occupied by Dutch, 1630–54; scene of several revolts in early 19th cent. Stockraising and agr. region.

Perón, Juan (Domingo) (hwän′ dōmēng′gō pärōn′), 1895–, president of Argentina (1946–). Rose to prominence as one of the officers in the "colonels' group" that overthrew government of Ramón Castillo in 1943, and he thereafter dominated Argentine politics. Perón developed a large following among the working class while he was secretary of labor and social welfare. His dictatorship, supported by a combination of labor and conservatives, has sought to maintain a highly nationalistic economy. He married (1945) Eva Duarte de Perón (d. 1952), who was largely responsible for his release from prison when in 1945 he was temporarily divested of his offices, and she thereafter played a spectacular part in his government.

Péronne (pärôn′), town (pop. 3,669), Somme dept., N France, on Somme R. Here in 1468 took place the "interview" between LOUIS XI of France and Charles the Bold of Burgundy.

Pérouse, Jean François de Galaup, comte de la: see LA PÉROUSE.

Perov, Vasily Grigoryevich (vŭsē′lyē grĭgôr′yùvĭch pyĭrôf′), 1833–82, Russian painter, leader of Russian realists. Best known for scenes of peasant life.

peroxide of hydrogen: see HYDROGEN PEROXIDE.

Perpignan (pĕrpēnyä′), city (pop. 64,358), cap. of Pyrénées-Orientales dept., S France, near Spanish border and the Mediterranean. Trades in fruit and wine. Was cap. of Spanish kingdom of Majorca and, after 1642, of Roussillon prov. (France). Has 14th-cent. Loge (merchants' exchange), Gothic cathedral (14th–16th cent.), and royal castle (13th–15th cent.).

Perrault, Charles (shärl′ pĕrō′), 1628–1703, French poet. Author of *Histoires ou contes du temps passé* (1697), which gave classic form to the stories of Bluebeard, Sleeping Beauty, Cinderella, and other fairy tales. He opposed Boileau and the ancients in the "quarrel of the ancients and the moderns." His brother **Claude Perrault** (klōd), 1613–88, French architect and scientist, designed famous east façade (Colonnade) of the Louvre.

Perrers, Alice (pĕr′ùrz), d. 1400, mistress of EDWARD III of England, over whom she had great power.

Perrin, Jean Baptiste (zhã bätēst′ pĕrē′), 1870–1942, French physicist. Won 1926 Nobel Prize for work on discontinuous structure of matter and discovery of equilibrium of sedimentation.

Perry, Bliss, 1860–, American educator, author, and editor; professor of English at Williams, Princeton, and Harvard; editor of *Atlantic Monthly* (1899–1909). Works include biographies of Whitman, Whittier, and R. H. Dana; critical works and selections; and his autobiography, *And Gladly Teach* (1935).

Perry, Frederick John, 1909–, English tennis player. Won U.S. singles title (1933–34, 1936), British singles crown (1934–36), many other amateur championships. Professional singles champion, 1938 and 1941.

Perry, Matthew Calbraith, 1794–1858, American naval officer. In 1853–54 he visited Japan with a fleet; concluded treaty guaranteeing protection for shipwrecked U.S. seamen, right to buy coal, opening of ports of Shimoda and Hakodate to U.S. trade. His brother, **Oliver Hazard Perry,** 1785–1819, was also an American naval officer. During War of 1812 he secured British surrender in battle of L. Erie (Sept. 10, 1813). His report—"We have met the enemy and

they are ours"—has become familiar to Americans.

Perry, Ralph Barton, 1876–, American philosopher, long a professor at Harvard. Edited the works of William James and wrote *The Thought and Character of William James* (1935), *The New Realism* (1912).

Perry. 1 City (pop. 6,174), central Iowa, near Raccoon R. and NW of Des Moines. Center of farm area. **2** City (pop. 5,137), N central Okla., NE of Oklahoma City, in farm area.

Perrysburg, village (pop. 4,006), NW Ohio, on Maumee R., S suburb of Toledo. Monument near by marks site of Fort MEIGS.

Perry's Victory and International Peace Memorial National Monument: see NATIONAL PARKS AND MONUMENTS (table).

Perryton, city (pop. 4,417), N Texas, NE of Amarillo near Okla. line. Shipping, mfg. center for wheat area.

Perryville, town (pop. 660), central Ky., W of Danville, SW of Lexington. Near by is site of battle (Oct. 8, 1862) between Bragg's Confederates and Buell's Federals which, though called indecisive, ended Bragg's invasion of Ky. Natl. cemetery in area.

Perse, Saint-Jean: see LÉGER, ALEXIS SAINT-LÉGER.

Persephone (pùrsē′fùnē), Latin *Proserpine* (prō′sùrpĭn), or *Proserpina* (prōsûr′pĭnù), in Greek religion, goddess of fertility; daughter of Zeus and Demeter and wife of Hades, ruler of the underworld. He stole her, but Demeter induced gods to let her return to earth for eight months of each year. She had to remain in the underworld four months because Hades had tricked her into eating four pomegranate seeds. On her return to earth plants blossomed anew. She personified birth and decay of vegetation. As queen of the underworld she was a stern woman, but as daughter of Demeter, a lovely young maiden with horn of plenty as her symbol.

Persepolis (pùrsē′pùlĭs) [Gr.,= city of Persia], anc. city of Persia, NE of present Shiraz; ceremonial (but not administrative) cap. of the Persian empire under Darius and successors. It has been excavated. The area was inhabited as early as 4000 B.C.

Perseus (pûr′sūs, –sēus), in Greek mythology, hero; son of Zeus and Danaë and grandson of Acrisius. Told by an oracle that Perseus would kill him, Acrisius set him and Danaë afloat in a chest, but King Polydectes rescued them. Later, because Perseus was an obstacle to his love for Danaë, the king sent him to get Medusa's head, expecting him to die. However, aided by the gods he slew MEDUSA. When Atlas refused him help in his flight from the Gorgons, Perseus used Medusa's head to turn him into a stone mountain. He killed Polydectes and, with his mother and wife (ANDROMEDA), went to ARGOS. Here in a discus contest he killed his grandfather, thus fulfilling the prophecy. The statue *Perseus* by Benvenuto Cellini is in Florence. A N constellation is named for him.

Perseus, c.212–166 B.C., last king of Macedon (179–168 B.C.), son and successor of Philip V. His vigorous and anti-Roman policy brought on the Third Macedonian War (171–168), and the Roman general L. Aemilius Paullus thoroughly defeated Perseus at Pydna (168).

Pershing, John J(oseph) (pûr′shĭng), 1860–1948, American general, commander in chief of American Expeditionary Force in World War I.

Persia, old alternate name for the Asiatic country IRAN, in which anc. Persian Empire had its core. Early Persians were presumably a nomadic tribe who filtered down at an unknown time through the Caucasus to Iranian plateau. By 7th cent. B.C. they were estab. in present region of Fars, which then belonged to Assyrian Empire. Persian rulers were early associated with the Medes, who created a strong state in 7th cent. B.C. CYRUS THE GREAT (first of the Achaemenidae) made himself ruler of MEDIA in mid-6th cent. B.C. and by rapid conquest estab. the great Persian Empire. From the beginning the Persians built on foundations of earlier states, borrowing political structure of Assyria and arts of Babylonia and Egypt. Country was beset by dynastic troubles, concerning first the claims of CAMBYSES and later those of DARIUS I. Under Darius a highly efficient centralized system of administration was organized and Persian rule was extended E into modern Afghanistan and NW India and as far N as the Danube. Although the Greeks revolted successfully in PERSIAN WARS, Persian influence continued strong in Greece. After mid-5th cent., however, signs of decay began to appear. The state was weakened by dynastic troubles (notably the rebellion of CYRUS THE YOUNGER against ARTAXERXES II), increasing power of the satraps (regional governors), and successful revolt of Egypt. Finally, ALEXANDER THE GREAT routed the Persians on the Granicus in 334 B.C., and in 331 the battle of Gaugamela destroyed the Achaemenid empire. After Alexander's death most of Persia fell to the Seleucids, who, though they introduced a fruitful Hellenistic culture, were unable to maintain control. Parthia, which broke away in mid-3d cent. B.C., became a kind of successor to the old Persian Empire, and came to rival Rome. Its decline was followed by establishment of new empire in A.D. c.226 under the SASSANIDAE. This magnificent state flourished until 641 or 642, when invading Arabs took the cap., Ctesiphon. Islam replaced Zoroastrianism, and the caliphate made Persia part of a larger pattern, from which modern Iran later emerged.

Persian art and architecture. Ancient pottery, cult figurines, and bronzes already embody Persian feeling for decorative motifs. Artistic culture, to which Zoroastrian cult contributed bases for symbolism, arose in Achaemenidae period (c.550–330 B.C.). The great columned palaces set on high terraces at Pasargadae and Persepolis reveal distinctive sense of space and scale. Persepolitan columns were slenderer and more closely fluted than those of Greece, and their bases were often bell shaped. In sculpture, stylization is subtly combined with realism; typical is the *Frieze of Archers* (Louvre), done in molded and enameled brick. Outstanding among minor arts is exquisite metalwork (esp. gold and silver ornaments). For 500 years after the conquest by Alexander the Great, Persian art was strongly influenced by Hellenistic and Roman motifs. Under the Sassanidae (c.226–c.640) there was a revival of native aesthetic feeling. Enormous palaces were built, richly decorated in stucco. Painting was encouraged, especially by Mani, founder of Manichaeism and himself a painter. A favorite motif was the *simurgh*, a beast with head of an animal and body of a bird. In 7th cent. there was gradual merging of Persian and Islamic cultures (see MOSQUE). Great Mosque at Isfahan, one of world's great architectural monuments, was built during high period of Persian art (11th–12th cent.). With the invasion (1220) of Jenghiz Khan, Chinese influence became important. The arts of book illumination, mosaic faience, and tile marquetry developed throughout 14th cent. Dynasty estab. by Tamerlane (14th–15th cent.) saw another flowering of Persian culture. Miniature painting emerged, stressing intense colors and economy of line, harmonized in a deliberately flat decorative pattern. Earliest extant carpets, unsurpassed in beauty of design and material, date from early 16th cent., when native Persian dynasty was restored. European influences, which began operating in 17th cent., have tended to debase rather than invigorate native art.

Persian Gulf, arm of Arabian Sea, between Iran and Arabia. Connected with Gulf of Oman by Strait of Ormuz. Major oil-shipping lane.

Persian language, Iranian language of Indo-Iranian subfamily of Indo-European languages. See LANGUAGE (table).

Persian literature. Among its most ancient examples is the literature of ZOROASTRIANISM. After overthrow of the Sassanidae by the Arabs (7th cent. A.D.), new religion of Islam became dominant theme and many notable works in Arabic were written by Persian authors. In 9th cent., Persian re-emerged as literary language and was given new luster by the great poet FIRDAUSI and OMAR KHAYYAM. The period 13th–15th cent. saw flowering of mystic poetry of SUFISM (see FERID ED-DIN ATTAR, RUMI, SADI, and HAFIZ). The mass of Persian writings after 15th cent. is almost entirely untranslated.

Persian lynx: see CARACAL.

Persian Wars, 500–449 B.C., contest of Greek city-states and the Persian Empire. The war started with the revolt of Ionian Greek cities on the coast of Asia Minor against the rule of Darius I. Athens and Eretria aided them, but the Persians crushed the revolt (494 B.C.). Darius then set out to punish Athens and Eretria and annex all Greece. The first Persian expedition (492 B.C.) ended when a storm crippled the Persian fleet. A second (490 B.C.) destroyed Eretria and set out for Athens but was defeated at Marathon by a smaller Athenian force (aided by some men from Plataea) under the brilliant Miltiades. The Spartans, sent to aid, arrived the day after the battle. Darius was planning a gigantic third expedition when he died, and his son, Xerxes I, undertook it (480 B.C.). His vast army was held back by a small group headed by Leonidas of Sparta at Thermopylae, where the Greeks died to a man. Athens under Themistocles made no attempt to defend the city but crushed the Persian fleet off Salamis. Xerxes returned to Persia, leaving in Greece an army under Mardonius, who was decisively defeated at Plataea (479 B.C.) by Greeks under the Spartan Pausanias, with Athenian troops led by Aristides. The Athenian fleet also won a victory at Mycale. Though the wars dragged on for many years, the Greek cities were then free, and the great period of Greek history was begun.

persimmon, name for several trees of genus *Diospyros* and their fleshy orange fruits. The common native persimmon of the U.S. (*Diospyros virginiana*) bears fruit of good flavor but too soft to market. The Japanese persimmon (*D. kaki*) is grown commercially in S U.S. and Calif. for its large red fruits.

Persius (Aulus Persius Flaccus) (pûr′shēŭs), A.D. 34–A.D. 62, Roman satirical poet. His six satires preach Stoic morality, censure vice of Rome.

personnel management: see INDUSTRIAL MANAGEMENT.

Perth, county, Scotland: see PERTHSHIRE.

Perth, city (pop. 98,890; metropolitan pop. 272,528), cap. of Western Australia, on estuary of Swan R.; founded 1829. Commercial and cultural center of the state. Its port is Fremantle. Univ. of Western Australia is at near-by Crawley.

Perth, town (pop. 5,034), S Ont., Canada, SW of Ottawa. Textile mills and woodworking.

Perth, burgh (pop. 40,466), co. seat of Perthshire, Scotland, on the Tay. Cap. of Scotland until murder here of James I in 1437. Battle of two clans here (1396) is told in Scott's *Fair Maid of Perth*. Has General Prison for Scotland (estab. 1812). Has mfg. of carpets, textiles, and farm machinery.

Perth Amboy, city (pop. 41,330), NE N.J., on harbor at Raritan R. mouth on Arthur Kill (Outerbridge Crossing to Staten Isl., 1928); settled 1683. Cap. of East Jersey 1686–1702; then, until 1790, alternate cap. with Burlington of united Jerseys. Grew as coal-shipping center after becoming tidewater terminal of Lehigh Valley RR 1876. Shipyards, drydocks, oil refineries; mfg. of metal and clay (from local deposits) products, plastics, and chemicals. Here are mansion of Gov. William Franklin, used as a British hq. in Revolution; St. Peter's Church (1722); and Parker Castle (1723).

Perthshire or **Perth,** inland county (2,493 sq. mi.; pop. 128,072), central Scotland; co. town Perth. Mountainous region with many lochs, wild forests, and moors. Agr. and grazing are main industries. Scottish kings were long crowned at Scone.

SMALL CAPITALS = cross references. Pronunciation key on inside end pages. Abbreviations: p. 2.

Pertz, Georg Heinrich (pĕrts), 1795–1876, German historian, first editor (1823–74) of *Monumenta Germaniae historica*.

Peru (pûrōō'), Span. *Perú*, republic (514,059 sq. mi.; pop. 8,277,031). W South America; cap. LIMA. The chief port is CALLAO. Stretching from the Pacific on the W across the Andes and down to the rain forests of the W Amazon basin on the E, Peru has a wide variety of climate and topography. The E country is well-watered by the Ucayali and Marañón; great resources largely unexploited. Its population is largely Indian. The Andes in Peru fan out in E and W ranges, the W range including the lofty volcanoes, Huascarán and El Misti. Between these two cordilleras lie the upland basins of the altiplano (more than 10,000 ft. above sea level)—cold, windy, and generally barren, though around L. Titicaca (which Peru shares with Bolivia) some foodstuff is raised and there is grazing land for llamas, sheep. The Inca capital, Cuzco, is on the altiplano. Chief industry in the mountains is mining (gold, silver, copper, lead, zinc, bismuth). Along the Pacific for 1,400 mi. stretches desert land, where agr. (mostly cotton and sugarcane) depends on irrigation from streams from the mountains. Off the coast lie the Peruvian Lobos and Chincha islands which yield GUANO, rich in nitrate and an excellent fertilizer. Petroleum resources in the NW are proving an important source of income. Industrial activities include ore reduction, oil refining, and cotton and woolen textile mills. Transportation is one of Peru's chief problems, as few railroads or highways have been built over the mountains. Air transport now supplements the railroads and roads that were built with much difficulty. Indians account for about half the population; the remainder is largely mestizo, with some Orientals and Europeans. The prevailing religion is Roman Catholic. Education is free, but illiteracy rate is high. The Univ. of San Marcos at Lima is one of oldest institutions of higher learning in America. The Spanish Conquest began in 1532 when Francisco Pizarro with a small band of adventurers landed on coast and with bold audacity and the use of firearms (which the Indians had never seen) undertook the overthrow of the INCA empire; he captured the ruler, ATAHUALPA, and treacherously executed him. Expeditions of conquest went out from the conquered Inca capital into present Ecuador and Chile and although the conquistadors fought against each other for power and spoils, they stood together in their mistreatment of the Indians. The New Laws, which were intended to do away with many of the wrongs done to the Indians, were never enforced in Peru, which early became a viceroyalty. Francisco de Toledo arrived in 1569, and through his superior administration a pattern was set for a functioning government throughout the colonial period. There was an abortive uprising in Cuzco against the Spanish regime in 1813, but independence did not come to Peru until after SAN MARTÍN, and, later, BOLÍVAR arrived to assist. At the battles of Junín and Ayacucho, Spanish forces were defeated (1826). Efforts to form Bolivia and Peru into one state failed, and after 1839 they went their separate ways. Dictatorships and revolts came in succession, and a disastrous war in 1879 (see PACIFIC, WAR OF THE) slowed the material advancement of Peru (see also TACNA-ARICA CONTROVERSY). Foreign influence and holdings have been detrimental to the economy. After World War I, APRA, a political party under the leadership of Víctor Raúl Haya de la Torre, was organized with a program of radical reform in the government and betterment of conditions among the Indians. Though it has never been in power, it has continued to play an important role in Peruvian political life.

Peru (pûrōō'). **1** City (pop. 8,653), N Ill., on Illinois R. (bridged) adjoining La Salle. Processes zinc in agr. and coal area. **2** City (pop. 13,308), N Ind., on Wabash R. and E of Logansport in farm area; laid out

1825. Electrical equipment. Has winter quarters for circuses and historical museum.

Perugia (pārōō'jä), city (pop. 31,839), cap. of Umbria, central Italy, on hill overlooking Tiber valley. Agr. center; chocolate mfg. Inhabited by Umbrians and Etruscans before it fell to Rome 3d cent. B.C. Became free commune in 12th cent. A.D., with hegemony over other Umbrian cities. Was annexed to Papal States 1540. Seat of Umbrian school of painting (13th–16th cent.), which reached its zenith with Perugino and Pinturicchio. Perugino's frescoes decorate the Cambio [exchange]. Other noted buildings include cathedral (14th–15th cent.), town hall (13th cent.), and Church of Sant' Angelo (5th or 6th cent.). There are medieval quarters; the city walls are Etruscan, Roman, and medieval. University may be traced to 13th cent.; it now holds special courses for foreign students.

Perugino (pārōōjē'nō), c.1445–1523?, Umbrian painter, b. near Perugia. Real name was Pietro di Cristoforo Vannucci. Was a fellow pupil of Leonardo da Vinci in Verrocchio's studio in Florence. Called to Rome in 1480 by Pope Sixtus IV to paint in Sistine Chapel; of his four frescoes for the chapel only one remains. Spent productive last period mainly in Perugia, where he had many pupils, notably Raphael. His many religious paintings, which include *The Annunciation* (Natl. Gall. of Art, Washington, D.C.), are noted for their grace and tenderness.

Peruzzi, Baldassare (bäldäs-sä'rä pārōōt'tse), 1481–1536, Italian architect of the Renaissance. Designed Massimo Palace in Rome and assisted Bramante in plan for St. Peter's.

Pesaro (pā'zärō), city (pop. 24,163), the Marches, central Italy; a Mediterranean port. A city of the PENTAPOLIS, it was ruled 13th–17th cent. by the Malatesta, Sforza, and Della Rovere families and passed to Papal States in 1631. Has rich collection of ceramics, manufactured here since 15th cent. Birthplace of Rossini.

Pescadores (pĕskûdō'rûz), Chinese *P'eng-hu*, island group (49 sq. mi.; pop. 66,843) between Formosa and mainland of China. Comprises 64 islands. Named in 16th cent. by the Portuguese. Ceded 1895 to Japan, restored 1945 to China. Held in early 1953 by Nationalists.

Pesellino, Il (ĕl pāzĕl-lē'nō), 1422–57, Florentine painter, whose real name was Francesco di Stefano; grandson and pupil of Giuliano Giuochi, called Pesello. Famous for animal paintings and for *cassone* pictures (decorative panels for chests). Assisted Fra Lippo Lippi in painting of altarpieces.

Peshawar (pûshä'wûr), city (pop. 114,000), cap. of North-West Frontier Prov., W Pakistan, near Khyber Pass; trade center. Ancient Buddhist center. The British captured it (1848) in Afghan Wars.

Pest, Hungary: see BUDAPEST.

Pestalozzi, Johann Heinrich (yō'hän hīn'rĭkh pĕ"stälôt'se), 1746–1827, Swiss educational reformer. He conducted school for poor children, 1769–98. From 1805 to 1825 he was director of an experimental institute at Yverdon. Pestalozzi's theory stresses a pedagogical method corresponding to natural order of individual development and of concrete experiences. His theory and methods laid foundation for modern elementary education.

Pestszenterzsebet (pĕsht'sĕntĕr"zhäbĕt), industrial city (pop. 76,876), N central Hungary, near Budapest. Petroleum refineries; iron and steel plants. Former name is Erzsebetfalva.

Pétain, Henri Philippe (ärē' fēlēp' pātĕ'), 1856–1951, marshal of France. Halted Germans at VERDUN in World War I; brought joint French-Spanish campaign against ABD-EL-KRIM to victorious end (1926); ambassador to Spain 1939–40. In World War II, France being on the brink of collapse, he succeeded Reynaud as premier and concluded armistice with Germany (June, 1940). A rump parliament suspended the republican constitution (July), and Pétain took office as "chief of state" at Vichy (see VICHY GOVERNMENT). After 1942, when LAVAL took power, Pétain became a mere figurehead. He was tried for treason after the war and sentenced to death (1945), but Gen. de Gaulle commuted the sentence to life imprisonment. The impartiality of the court has been widely questioned, and the extent of his collaboration with Germany is still under debate.

Petaluma (pĕtŭloō'mù), city (pop. 10,315), W Calif., N of San Francisco; founded 1852. Center of large poultry and egg industry.

Petchenegs (pĕchùnĕgz') or **Patzinaks** (pätsīnäks'), nomadic people of Turkic family. Advanced from Ural region into lower Danube area in A.D. c.880, ousting the Magyars. Besieged Kiev in 968 and killed the Kievan duke Sviatoslav. Twice threatened Constantinople (934, c.1075). Defeated 1091 by Emperor Alexius I.

Petén (pātän'), region (c.15,000 sq. mi.), mostly in N Guatemala. Sparsely populated today, it was once center of the Old Empire of the Maya and has many ruins (e.g., Tikal, Uaxactún). A region of heavy rains and many lakes, it has largely undeveloped resources.

Peter, Saint [Gr. *Petros* as tr. of Aramaic *Cephas* = rock, nickname given him by Jesus], d. A.D. 67?, disciple of Jesus, listed first in the Gospels, called Prince of the Apostles. His original name was Simon; he was a native of Bethsaida; and he and his brother, St. Andrew, were fishermen when called to follow Jesus. He was generally considered as leader and spokesman of the Twelve Apostles. He was, with James and John, at the transfiguration. When Judas came to betray Jesus, Peter drew his sword in defense. Later the same night Peter denied being of Jesus' following. After the Resurrection Jesus appeared and charged Peter to "feed my sheep." The first part of the Acts of the Apostles tells of Peter acting as leader. Sources of the 2d cent. say he left Antioch for Rome and headed the local church there. He is said to have been martyred at the time of Nero, traditionally on the same day as St. Paul and traditionally by being crucified head downward. The Vatican hill has been since early times considered the place of his martyrdom, and St. Peter's Church houses his tomb, one of the great shrines of the Roman Catholic Church. Recent archaeological discoveries seem to show that from earliest Christian times Christians believed this to be the tomb of Peter. There is an old tradition that Peter helped write the Gospel of Mark. Many critics hold that the epistles of Peter are falsely attributed to him. Roman Catholics believe that the bishop of Rome (the pope) is supreme in the Church as successor to Peter. This is the doctrine of the Petrine supremacy, based principally on Mat. 16.13–20 and John 21.15–25 (see PAPACY). Probably because he is represented with keys, he is popularly considered the gatekeeper of Heaven. Besides the feast of St. Peter and St. Paul (June 29), there are three feasts of St. Peter in the West: St. Peter's Chains (Lammas Day), Aug. 1; St. Peter's Chair, Jan. 18; St. Peter's Chair at Antioch, Feb. 22.

Peter, emperors and tsars of Russia. Peter I or **Peter the Great,** 1672–1725, founder of the modern Russian state; son of Tsar Alexis by his second wife. He became tsar in 1682 jointly with his half-brother IVAN V under the regency of their sister SOPHIA ALEKSEYEVNA. He was brought up in virtual exile and utter neglect, but in 1689 he overthrew Sophia with the help of some loyal troops and began his personal rule. Ivan died 1696. "Westernization" and expansion toward the Baltic and the Black Sea were the fixed objects of Peter's policies. After taking Azov from the Turks (1696), he toured W Europe (1697–98), studying European industrial techniques and even working, for a time, as ship's carpenter in Holland. Recalled to Russia by the news of a military revolt, he punished his enemies with characteristic sadism. In the NORTHERN

WAR (1700–1721) he won access to the Baltic; in 1713 he shifted his cap. from Moscow to this "window of Europe," where he built St. Petersburg (see LENINGRAD). His conquests in the S, from Turkey and Persia, were less permanent. Peter's internal reforms were thorough. He introduced universal taxation; created a new nobility of civil and military officers and a new administration; reformed the calendar and the alphabet; founded hospitals, medical schools, and fire departments; encouraged private industries, trade expansion, and exploration (notably Vitus Bering); emancipated women from servile status; estab. government control over monastic estates; abolished the patriarchate of Moscow and replaced it by a holy synod, headed by the tsar himself; and even ordered his subjects to shave their beards and wear Western garments. On the other hand, he made the serfs virtual slaves of the landowners. In 1721 Peter took the title emperor; in 1722 he declared the choice of a successor dependent on the sovereign's will; in 1724 he made his second wife, CATHERINE I, joint empress. The conservative opposition and clergy saw Peter as the Antichrist. His own son Alexis joined the opposition, was tortured, and died in prison (1718). Of bearlike constitution, Peter was capable of stupendous orgies as well as utmost self-discipline and devotion to work. Ruthless in his demands on others, he did not spare himself. His genius was undoubtedly tinged with madness. He has been regarded by posterity with horror and with adulation. **Peter II,** 1715–30, grandson of Peter I, succeeded Catherine I in 1727 under a regency. During his reign MENSHIKOV fell from power and the reactionary nobility took over. Empress Anna succeeded him. **Peter III,** 1728–62, son of Peter I's daughter Anna and of Charles Frederick, dispossessed duke of Holstein-Gottorp, succeeded his aunt Elizabeth in 1762. An admirer of Frederick II of Prussia, he took Russia out of the SEVEN YEARS WAR. In 1744 he had married Sophia of Anhalt-Zerbst, better known as CATHERINE II. Debauched and half insane, he was unfit to rule. A conspiracy headed by the ORLOV brothers forced Peter to abdicate and proclaimed Catherine sole ruler. A few days later Peter died in mysterious circumstances, presumably assassinated.

Peter, kings of Aragon and counts of Barcelona. Peter II, 1174–1213, reigned 1196–1213. Helped Alfonso VIII of Castile defeat the Moors at Navas de Tolosa (1212). When Simon de Montfort, leader of the Albigensian Crusade, refused Pope Innocent III's command to do homage to Peter for his conquests, Peter joined Raymond VI of Toulouse against the crusaders. His defeat and death at Muret ended Catalan influence in S France. **Peter III,** 1239?–1285, succeeded his father James I in 1276. From his marriage to Constance, daughter of MANFRED of Sicily, the house of Aragon derived its claims to SICILY and Naples. After the SICILIAN VESPERS he was offered the crown of Sicily, and he took possession of the island in 1282. Pope Martin IV thereupon excommunicated him and, jointly with the French, organized a crusade against him, but the invaders were repulsed by Peter and defeated at sea by ROGER OF LORIA. **Peter IV** (the Ceremonious), 1319?–1387, reigned 1336–87. Recovered Majorca (1343–44); won overlordship over Athens (1381).

Peter, kings of Portugal. Peter I, 1320–67, reigned 1357–67. Before his accession he married a Castilian noblewoman but fell violently in love with her lady in waiting, Inés de CASTRO. In 1355 Inés was murdered, with the complicity of his father, Alfonso IV. Peter, after a brief rebellion, was forced to pardon the murderers, but when he became king he had two of them hunted down and had their hearts drawn out. He was known as Peter the Severe, the Justiciar, and the Cruel. **Peter II,** 1648–1706, forced his brother ALFONSO VI to abdicate in 1667, and married Alfonso's queen after having her marriage annulled. He ruled as regent 1667–83 and as king 1683–1706. Chief event of his reign was signing of Methuen Treaty with England (1703). **Peter III,** 1717–86, married his niece, MARIA I, and ruled jointly with her.

Peter, kings of Serbia and Yugoslavia. **Peter I,** 1844–1921, son of Prince ALEXANDER Karageorgevich. Spent his youth in exile. Called to throne in 1903, after assassination of King ALEXANDER (Alexander Obrenovich), he ruled ably, with PASHITCH the dominating figure of his reign. In 1918 he was chosen to rule the kingdom of the Serbs, Croats, and Slovenes (later known as Yugoslavia). His son and successor Alexander was regent for the ailing king from 1914. **Peter II,** 1923–, became king of Yugoslavia on the murder of his father, Alexander (1934). The regent, his cousin Prince Paul, was overthrown early in 1941 after signing an agreement with the Axis Powers. Peter's personal rule began with the German invasion of Yugoslavia. He fled to England, where he headed the government in exile. In 1945 the Yugoslav assembly, dominated by Marshal Tito, proclaimed a republic and deposed Peter, who remained in exile.

Peter I (Peter Mauclerc), d. 1250, duke of Brittany (1213–37), count of Dreux. A grandson of Louis VI of France, he became duke by marrying Constance, sister and heiress of Arthur I of Brittany. His quarrels with the clergy earned him his excommunication (1217) and his nickname Mauclerc. He took part in several rebellions of nobles, but later did penance by going on crusade (1248–50).

Peter, epistles of New Testament, called 1 and 2 Peter, traditionally ascribed to St. Peter. 1 Peter, early to be accepted as canonical, discusses the duties of Christians, encourages those facing persecution. 2 Peter, one of the last of New Testament books to be considered canonical, warns of heresies, ends with a reminder of the Second Coming.

Peter, Apocalypse of: see PSEUDEPIGRAPHA.

Peterborough, city (pop. 38,272), S Ont., Canada, NE of Toronto and at falls on Otonabee R. Connected via Trent Canal with L. Ontario and L. Huron. Rail center with mfg. of textiles and machinery.

Peterborough, municipal borough (pop. 53,412), Northamptonshire, England, co. seat of administrative co. of Soke of Peterborough. Rail, engineering, and farm trade center, it has varied mfg. Has an impressive cathedral, a bishop's palace, and ruins of a great Benedictine abbey (founded 655).

Peterborough or **Peterboro,** town (pop. 2,556), S N.H., between Keene and Nashua. Seat of an artists' colony, planned by Edward MACDOWELL and founded (1907) and sustained by his widow. Has first free tax-supported library in U.S. (1833).

Peter Damian, Saint (dā'mēun), 1007?–1072, Italian reformer, Doctor of the Church. He was a member of the reform party of Hildebrand (Gregory VII) and was violent in attacking simony, concubinage, and other abuses among the clergy. His *Gomorrhianus* is a violent denunciation of such wrong-doing. Feast: Feb. 23.

Peter des Roches (dā rōsh'), d. 1238, English churchman and statesman. Bishop of Winchester, he was guardian of young Henry III (1216). Waged prolonged struggle for power with Hubert de Burgh.

Peter Gonzalez, Saint (gŏnzä'lĭs), 1190–1246, Spanish Dominican priest. Worked among mariners and became confused as patron of sailors with St. Elmo, a 4th-cent. martyr, who was also a patron of sailors (recalled in the name of St. Elmo's fire). Peter has not been canonized.

Peterhead (pētŭrhĕd'), burgh (pop. 12,765), Aberdeenshire, Scotland; herring fishing center. James Edward Stuart landed here secretly in 1715.

Peterhof (pē'tŭrhŏf), city (pop. 28,000), RSFSR, on Gulf of Finland, SW of Leningrad. Founded 1711 by Peter I; became summer residence of the tsars. Includes Great Palace (built 1715) and vast parks, famous for their fountains and cascades. Sacked by the Germans in World War II, it was afterwards re-

stored. Name was Russianized to Petrodvorets 1944.

Peterhouse College: see CAMBRIDGE UNIVERSITY.

Peter Lombard, Latin *Petrus Lombardus,* c.1100–c.1160, Italian theologian, archbishop of Paris. Studied at Bologna, Rheims, and Paris. His *Sentences,* largely a compilation of the opinions of theologians (sometimes conflicting), has been widely used. His doctrine on the sacraments was made official by the Council of Trent.

Peterloo massacre, public disturbance in St. Peter's field, Manchester, England, Aug. 16, 1819. Crowd of 60,000 men, women, and children, petitioning for corn laws repeal and reform of Parliament, were charged by cavalry. Caused great indignation.

Peter Martyr: see ANGHIERA, PIETRO MARTIRE D'; VERMIGLI, PIETRO MARTIRE.

Petersburg, town (pop. 1,619), on Mitkof Isl., in Alexander Archipelago, SE Alaska. Population largely Scandinavian. Fishing and lumbering. Univ. of Alaska has experimental fur farm here.

Petersburg. 1 City (pop. 2,325), central Ill., on Sangamon R. and NNW of Springfield. Has grave of Ann Rutledge. Near by is New Salem. **2** City (pop. 35,054), SE Va., port on Appomattox R., S of Richmond. Important shipping point in agr. (peanuts, tobacco) area, it has mfg. of luggage and clothing. Fort Henry built here 1646. In Revolution city taken by British (1781); from here Cornwallis initiated campaign which ended at Yorktown. In Civil War Petersburg withstood assault by Grant's forces (June, 1864), but was under partial siege until city fell in April, 1865. Petersburg Natl. Military Park commemorates battle. Seat of Virginia State Col. Points of interest include Blandford Church (1735) and Cemetery (with Confederate dead), Golden Ball Tavern (c.1750), Center Hill Mansion (1825), "Battersea" (18th cent.), Wallace-Seward House (Grant and Lincoln conferred here after Lee's retreat).

Peter the Cruel, 1334–69, king of Castile and Leon (1350–69). He punished a rebellion fomented by his half-brothers by having two of them murdered in 1358. His surviving half-brother, Henry of Trastamara, obtained the help of Aragon and of DU GUESCLIN, defeated Peter, who fled, and was crowned as HENRY II (1366). In 1367 Peter, aided by EDWARD THE BLACK PRINCE, defeated Henry and Du Guesclin at Nájera, but in 1369 he was defeated and slain at Montiel. His daughter Constance married John of Gaunt; his daughter Isabella married Edmund, duke of York.

Peter the Great: see PETER I, emperor and tsar.

Peter the Hermit, c.1050–1115, French preacher. He promoted the First Crusade and led one of the bands of Crusaders, arriving at Constantinople in 1096. Returned to Europe after taking of Jerusalem. His importance has been much exaggerated.

Petition of Right, 1628, sent by English Parliament to Charles I. Secured recognition of four principles—no taxes without consent of Parliament; no imprisonment without cause; no quartering of soldiers on citizenry; no martial law in peacetime.

Petit Nord Peninsula: see GREAT NORTHERN PENINSULA.

Petitot, Jean (pütētō'), 1607–91, French painter of portraits in enamel, b. Switzerland. Patronized by Charles I of England and Louis XIV. His son and successor, **Jean Louis Petitot,** 1652–c.1730, served Charles II.

Petofi, Alexander (pĕ'tûfē), Hung. *Petöfi,* 1822–49, Hungarian poet and patriot, killed in the Hungarian revolutionary war. Author of exquisite lyrics, several epics, and the national poem "Up, Magyar."

Petoskey (pētō'skē), resort city (pop. 6,468), N Mich., on Little Traverse Bay, in agr. area. Limestone quarrying and mfg. of Portland cement.

Petra (pē'trù), anc. city of Jordan, near the foot of Mt. Hor, on the Wadi Musa; cap. of Edomites and Nabataeans. It declined in late Roman times, was conquered by the Moslems (7th cent.), and had a Crusaders' citadel (12th cent.). Called by J. W. Burgon poetically, "A rose-red city half as old as time."

Petrarch (pē'trärk) or **Francesco Petrarca** (fränchä'skō päträr'kä), 1304–74, Italian poet, surpassed in Italian literature by Dante alone. First and greatest of all humanists, he hunted manuscripts, refined his Latin style, even Latinized his name, in an effort to revive the spirit of antiquity. In Rome (1341) he was crowned with the poet's laurel. Proud of his Latin epic *Africa*, he is honored instead for his Italian *Trionfi* and for the great songs and sonnets of his *Canzoniere* [song book], telling of his love for Laura, in life and death.

petrel (pĕ'trŭl), sea bird belonging to order of tube-nosed swimmers, which includes albatross and shear-water. Diving petrels are unlike birds of S Hemisphere.

Petrie, Sir (William Matthew) Flinders (pē'trē), 1853–1942, English archaeologist, noted Egyptologist. Made many outstanding discoveries in excavating ancient remains in Egypt and Palestine.

petrifaction: see FOSSIL.

Petrified Forest National Monument: see NATIONAL PARKS AND MONUMENTS (table).

Petrillo, James Caesar (pĕtrĭ'lō, pĭ–), 1892–, American labor leader, president of the American Federation of Musicians (1940–).

Petrodvorets, RSFSR: see PETERHOF.

Petrograd, RSFSR: see LENINGRAD.

petrolatum (pĕtrŭlā'tŭm), colorless to yellow-white hy-drocarbon from petroleum. Semisolid form is used in ointments and for lubrication; refined liquid is mineral oil—a laxative.

petroleum, name applied to an oily, inflammable liquid, usually dark brown or greenish in hue, but sometimes black or even colorless. It is rather widely found in the upper strata of the earth and is generally believed to be of organic origin. Known throughout historic times, petroleum was early used for coating walls and the hulls of ships, as a fire weapon, and sometimes in lamps. The real age of petroleum began with the de-velopment of the gasoline engine, and modern civiliza-tion is heavily dependent on petroleum for motive power, lubrication, fuel, dyes, drugs, and many syn-thetics. Crude petroleum is refined by a process known as fractional distillation. It is based upon the fact that the different components of petroleum have different boiling points and can, therefore, be separated from one another by heating the crude oil to successively higher temperatures and collecting the portions that boil off within certain temperature ranges. These por-tions are known as fractions. Gasoline, benzine, naph-tha, and kerosene are important fractions. To meet the great demand for gasoline another process, called cracking, is used; in this the heavier molecules are broken down by heat, pressure, and the use of catalysts into the lighter ones that make up gasoline. Leading producers of petroleum are the U.S. (chiefly Texas, Calif., La., Okla., and Kansas), the USSR, Venezuela, and Iran.

petrology (pĕtrŏ'lŭjē), branch of geology concerned with origin, structure, and properties of rock.

Petronius (pĭtrō'nēŭs), d. c.66, Roman satirist, called Petronius Arbiter, known for his profligate love of luxury. When he lost Nero's favor, he opened his veins and made even dying leisurely, playing host at a feast. The fragments (notably *Trimalchio's Dinner*) of his *Satyricon* that remain are vivid studies in col-loquial language of life and manners.

Petropavlovsk or **Petropavlovsk-Kamchatski** (pyĕtrŭ-pävʹlŭfsk-kŭmchät'skĕ), city (pop. over 20,000), Kha-barovsk Territory, RSFSR, on SE coast of Kamchatka peninsula and on Avacha Bay of Pacific Ocean. Naval base and port (ice-free nine months a year).

Petrópolis (pùtrô'pùlĭsh), city (pop. 61,843), Rio de Janeiro state, SE Brazil, situated in hills just N of Rio de Janeiro. Colonized by German immigrants (1845). Fashionable resort and industrial city.

Petrov, Yevgeny Petrovich (yĭvgä'nyĕ pĕtrô'vĭch pĕtrôf'), pseud. of Y. P. Katayev, 1903–43, Russian author, collaborator of I. A. ILF.

Petsamo, RSFSR: see PECHENGA.

Pettit, Edison, 1890–, American astronomer, noted for research in physics of the sun.

petunia, South American flowering plant of genus *Petunia*. Petunias are grown as annuals and are prized for their funnel-shaped flowers, often fragrant, and of various colors.

Peutinger, Konrad (kôn'rät poi'tĭng-ùr), 1465–1547, German humanist and antiquarian. He owned the *Peutinger Table,* ancient chart showing plan of mili-tary roads of Roman Empire radiating from Rome. It is probably a 13th-cent. copy of a 3d-cent. original.

Pevensey (pĕv'ŭnzē), village, Sussex East, England, near Hastings. Landing place of William I, it was a "mem-ber" of the CINQUE PORTS.

pewee or **peewee** (pē'wē), small American woodland bird of flycatcher family, related to phoebe.

pewter, name applied to various silver-white alloys con-sisting chiefly of tin. Pewters vary with the percentage of tin used and with the nature of the added material. Lead imparts a bluish tinge and increases malleability; antimony adds whiteness and hardness; other metals often added include copper, bismuth, and zinc. Pewter is shaped by casting, hammering, or lathe spinning on a mold, and may be variously decorated. It was early used in the Far East. In the West it was the chief tableware until superseded by china. Pewter making was an important activity in colonial America.

peyote (pāō'tē), Aztec *peyotl,* a spineless cactus (*Lopho-phora williamsi*) producing a drug used by Indians in N Mexico and the SW U.S. The mushroom-shaped plant tops are eaten or made into a beverage; the drug causes nausea and hallucinations but the general ef-fect is a feeling of well-being.

Pflüger, Eduard (ā'dŏōärt pflü'gùr), 1829–1910, Ger-man experimental physiologist. Showed that respira-tion occurs in tissues, not in lungs or blood.

pH, symbol of hydrogen-ion concentration: see ION.

Phaeacia (fēā'shù), in Greek mythology, island of Scheria (location unknown). In Books VI–XIII of the *Odyssey,* a place where Odysseus was shipwrecked.

Phaedra (fē'drù), in Greek legend, daughter of Minos and Pasiphaë, wife of Theseus. Her advances were re-jected by her stepson, Hippolytus, and she brought about his death.

Phaëthon (fā'ùthùn, –tùn) or **Phaëton,** in Greek my-thology, son of HELIOS and the nymph Clymene. He once tried to drive his father's chariot but could not control the horses. Falling, it dried the earth of Libyan Desert.

phagocyte: see WHITE CORPUSCLE.

phalanx, anc. Greek formation of infantry. The soldiers formed a solid block of 8 or 16 rows that could sweep through the more dispersed ranks of the enemy. Orig-inally used by Spartans, developed by Epaminondas, and brought to its height by Alexander. The phalanx became obsolete after its weaknesses (poor maneuvera-bility and lack of protection of the right because shields were carried on the left arms) were dem-onstrated in battle with the Romans, notably at Pydna (168 B.C.).

Phaleron (fùlēr'ùn) or **Phalerum** (–ùm), port of ancient Athens, Greece, on Bay of Phaleron, an inlet of the Saronic Gulf of Aegean Sea. Was superseded in 5th cent. B.C. by Piraeus.

phallicism, worship of reproductive powers of nature as symbolized by male generative organ. Its aim was to increase tribe, flocks, and crops, and it was part of fertility rites of many peoples, often incorporated into existing religions.

Phanariots or **Fanariots** (both: fùnä'rēùts), in the Otto-man Empire, the Greeks of Constantinople; so called for their quarter, Phanar. In the 18th and 19th cent., Phanariots held high positions in the Greek Orthodox Church, as Turkish governors of Moldavia and Wala-chia, and as chief dragomans [interpreters] of the Porte. Their rule was often corrupt. Many Phanariots joined the fight for Greek independence in the 1820s and played a vital role in later Greek politics and cultural life.

Pharaoh (fâ′rō, –rē̄ō, fā′–) [Heb., from Egyptian,= the great house], biblical title of kings of Egypt.

Pharisees (fā′rĭsēz), one of two great Jewish religious parties that arose within the synagogue (the opponents were the Sadducees) after the Maccabees had freed their people from Syrian oppression. The Hasidim aimed to keep all that was Jewish set apart and thus undefiled; the extremists among them were known as Pharisees. Basing all upon the Law, the Pharisees insisted upon the strictest observance of the ordinances of Judaism, in all aspects of life. The active period of Pharisaism, which was influential in the development of orthodox Judaism, extended to A.D. c.135.

pharmacopoeia (fär″mŭkŭpē′ủ), authoritative list of drugs, describing their properties, use, dosage, and tests of purity. First U.S. national pharmacopoeia issued 1820; periodically revised. Became legal standard 1906.

pharmacy (fär′mủsē), practice of preparing and dispensing medicines and also a place used for these purposes. Practice separated from that of medicine in 18th cent. First U.S. pharmacy school founded in Philadelphia 1821. Study of pharmacy became a four-year course in U.S. in 1932.

Pharos (fâ′rŏs), peninsula at Alexandria, Egypt. Originally an offshore island, it was joined to mainland by a mole built by order of Alexander the Great. Here was the lighthouse completed c.280 B.C. by Ptolemy II which was one of Seven Wonders of the World; destroyed 14th cent. by earthquake.

Pharpar (fär′pǔr), river of Damascus. 2 Kings 5.12. The other river of Damascus was the ABANA.

Pharr (fär), city (pop. 8,690), S Texas, WNW of Brownsville. Packs and ships fruit and vegetables.

Pharsala (fär′sälä), anc. city, Thessaly, Greece. Near here in 48 B.C. Caesar routed Pompey.

pheasant (fĕ′zǔnt), Old World game bird. It has a wattled head and long tail, and the male has brilliant plumage. Many hybrids of English, Chinese ring-necked, and Japanese pheasants exist. Hybrid ring-necked pheasant is common in E U.S.

Pheidias: see PHIDIAS.

Pheidippides (fīdĭ′pĭdēz), fl. 490 B.C., Athenian courier said to have run 150 mi. in two days to ask Spartan help against the Persians.

Phenicia: see PHOENICIA.

Phenix City, city (pop. 23,305), E Ala., on Chattahoochee R. opposite Columbus, Ga. Cotton, bricks.

phenol: see CARBOLIC ACID.

phenolphthalein (fē″nŏlthă′lēn), white, crystalline compound of carbon, hydrogen, and oxygen. Used as indicator because it turns red when added to solution of alkali; used also as a laxative.

Phi Beta Kappa, oldest Greek-letter society in U.S., founded 1776 at Col. of William and Mary, Williamsburg, Va. It became a scholarship honor society.

Phidias or **Pheidias** (both: fī′dēǔs), c.500–c.432 B.C., Greek sculptor, considered the greatest artist of anc. Greece. No extant original can be definitely ascribed to him; his fame rests mainly on estimates and descriptions of ancient writers and on his influence on all later sculpture. His greatest works were ATHENA PARTHENOS at Athens and *Zeus* (one of Seven Wonders of the World) at Olympia. According to tradition he supervised the sculpture for the great works on the Acropolis.

Philadelphia, city (pop. 2,071,605), SE Pa., on Delaware R. at mouth of Schuylkill R. Largest city in Pa. and third largest in nation, it is one of chief U.S. ports and a great commercial, industrial, and cultural center. Important industries are oil refining, metalworking, printing and publishing, and shipbuilding. Mfg. of petroleum-derived chemicals, railroad cars, and textiles. Has large navy yard, U.S. mint, and U.S. arsenals. Swedes settled here in 17th cent. In 1682 William PENN founded the "City of Brotherly Love" as a

Quaker colony. It quickly became a major colonial center. Had first magazine (1741) and first daily newspaper (1784) in America. In Revolution Philadelphia was American cap. except during British occupation, Oct., 1777 to July, 1778; and was cap. of U.S. 1790–1800 and state cap. to 1799. Well-known residential sections are Chestnut Hill and Germantown. "Main Line," on Pennsylvania RR, is a wealthy outlying area. City has Pennsylvania Acad. of Fine Arts (1805). PHILADELPHIA MUSEUM OF ART, PHILADELPHIA ORCHESTRA, American Philosophical Society (organized by Benjamin Franklin), FRANKLIN INSTITUTE, Univ. of PENNSYLVANIA, TEMPLE UNIVERSITY, Drexel Inst. of Technology (nonsectarian; coed.; opened 1892), Girard Col. (see GIRARD, STEPHEN), Curtis Inst. of Music (coed.; founded 1924; on scholarship basis), HAHNEMANN MEDICAL COLLEGE, and Woman's Medical Col. of Pennsylvania (1850). Historic shrines include INDEPENDENCE HALL (houses LIBERTY BELL), Congress Hall, Carpenters Hall (where first Continental Congress met), Betsy Ross House, and Gloria Dei (Old Swedes') Church. Fairmount Park, one of world's largest, includes Rodin Mus. and Robin Hood Dell.

Philadelphia Museum of Art, estab. 1875, chartered 1876; called Pennsylvania Mus. of Art until 1938. Occupied its present building (city owned) in 1928. Most notable of its many fine collections is that of European old masters. Museum is connected with School of Industrial Art (estab. 1877) and Textile Inst. (estab. 1883).

Philadelphia Orchestra, founded 1900. Under the leadership of Leopold Stokowski 1912–36, and of Eugene Ormandy from 1936, it became world famous.

Philae (fī′lē), island, S Egypt, in the Nile above Aswan Dam. Submerged during most of the year. Site of temple to Isis, built by early Ptolemies.

Philaret or **Filaret, Vasily Drosdov** (vŭsē′lyē drŭsdôf′ fēlŭrĕt′), 1782–1867, Russian prelate, metropolitan of Moscow. Wrote the standard catechism and supposedly drafted the Edict of Emancipation for Alexander II (1861).

Philemon (fĭlē′–) [Gr.,= loving], epistle of New Testament, written by St. Paul to Philemon, a Christian, whose runaway slave had joined Paul. Paul sent the slave home, carrying this letter urging Philemon to show Christian mercy to the fugitive.

Philemon and Baucis (bô′sĭs), in Greek legend. Zeus and Hermes were refused food and shelter by all except this couple, who survived flood sent to destroy their unkind neighbors. They later died together and became trees.

Philip, Saint [Gr.,= lover of horses], one of the Twelve Apostles. Mat. 10.3; John 1.43–51; 6.5,7; 12.21,22; Acts 1.3. Feast: May 1.

Philip, Saint, one of the seven deacons. He converted the eunuch of Queen Candace of Ethiopia. Also called St. Philip the Evangelist and St. Philip the Deacon. Acts 6.5; 8.25–40; 21.8–10. Feast: June 6.

Philip (the Arabian), 204?–249, Roman emperor (244–49). He brought about the murder of Gordian III. Made peace with Persia, celebrated the millennium of Rome with splendor (248). Decius with rebel troops killed Philip in battle.

Philip, kings of France. Philip I, 1052–1108, reigned 1060–1108. **Philip II** or **Philip Augustus,** 1165–1223, reigned 1180–1223. One of greatest French medieval kings, he doubled size of royal domain; consolidated royal power at expense of feudalism; created advisory council (to replace hereditary offices) and a royal court of justice with wide powers. Repeatedly at war with England, he supported ARTHUR I of Brittany against King John, whom he forced to surrender Normandy, Brittany, Anjou, Maine, and Touraine (1204). His victory at BOUVINES (1214) estab. France as leading power; his campaigns against the ALBIGENSES (1215, 1219) prepared annexation of S France. Philip joined in the Third Crusade in 1190 but after a quarrel with RICHARD I of England returned to France (1191). His reign saw the virtual disappearance of serfdom, the growing prosperity of the cities and the merchant class, and the building of the great cathedrals. **Philip III** (the Bold), 1245–85, son of St. Louis, reigned 1270–85. Annexed county of Toulouse to royal domain (1271). Died while campaigning in Spain and was succeeded by his son **Philip IV** (the Fair), 1268–1314. His first quarrel with Pope BONIFACE VIII grew out of his attempt to perpetuate an emergency tax of the clergy. When Philip forbade the export of precious metals, thus depriving the pope of revenues, Boniface capitulated (1297). In 1301 the quarrel was revived by the arrest of Bishop SAISSET. While Philip called the first STATES-GENERAL to justify his course, Boniface issued the bull *Unam sanctam* (1302). Philip countered by having his troops seize the pope at Anagni (1303) and later estab. French control over the papacy through the election of CLEMENT V, who transferred his see to Avignon. He replenished his treasury by persecuting the KNIGHTS TEMPLARS, the Jews, and the Lombard bankers, whose wealth he confiscated, and by debasing the coinage. His war with Edward I of England over possession of Guienne (1294–97) ended with Philip conceding Guienne to Edward. His attempt to control Flanders ended with the French rout at Courtrai (BATTLE OF THE SPURS, 1302). He was the father of Louis X and of **Philip V** (the Tall), c.1294–1322. On Louis X's death (1316), Philip became regent for his nephew John I, who died in infancy (1317); declaring the SALIC LAW to govern the French succession, he proclaimed himself king. His reign was notable for his administrative reforms. Although he suppressed fanatical anti-Jewish outbreaks (1321), he confiscated the Jews' property. **Philip VI**, 1293–1350, son of CHARLES OF VALOIS, was the first Valois king of France. He succeeded his cousin Charles IV in 1328, invoking the SALIC LAW to set aside Charles's daughter and Charles's nephew, EDWARD III of England. In the same year, by his victory at Cassel, he reinstated the count of Flanders, whom the rebellious Flemings had deposed. The HUNDRED YEARS WAR began in 1337. Defeated at Crécy (1346), Philip made a truce (1347) which lasted till after his death. His son John II succeeded him.

Philip, kings of anc. Macedon. **Philip II**, 382–336 B.C., reigned 359–336 B.C. after seizing the throne. He reorganized and trained the army and set out to expand his kingdom by conquest and diplomacy. Took over the gold mines of Thrace and the Chalcidice by 348. Despite the thunderings of Demosthenes, Philip continued to build his power. He crushed Athens and Thebes at Chaeronea (338) and was master of Greece. He was planning an expedition against Persia when he was killed (possibly by his wife Olympias). His son, Alexander the Great, carried conquest further. **Philip V**, 238–179 B.C., reigned 221–179 B.C.; son of Demetrius II, successor of Antigonus III. He interfered successfully in Greece and tried to take Illyria from Rome. In the First Macedonian War with Rome (215–205 B.C.) he managed to hold his own, but in the Second (200–197 B.C.) he was decisively defeated by Flaminius at Cynoscephalae (197 B.C.). His son was Perseus.

Philip, Spanish kings. **Philip I** (the Handsome), 1478–1506, king of Castile (1506); son of Emperor Maximilian I and of MARY OF BURGUNDY, whose possessions in the Low Countries he inherited in 1482. Was kept a virtual prisoner of city of Ghent until 1493, when he became nominal governor of the Netherlands under his father's guardianship. He married Queen JOANNA of Castile and became joint king in 1506. He was the first Hapsburg ruler in Spain and the father of Emperor CHARLES V. **Philip II**, 1527–98, became king of Spain, Naples, and Sicily on the abdication of his father Charles V (1556). Previously, he had received the Low Countries, Franche-Comté, and Milan. After the death of his first wife, Mary of Portugal, he married MARY I of England, but he left

England in 1555 after failing to obtain his coronation there. He continued his father's war against France and at the Treaty of CATEAU-CAMBRÉSIS (1559) made Spain the chief power of Europe. Though repeatedly at odds with the papacy, he was a fanatic Catholic. To secure absolute power and to stamp out heresy became his immutable aims. The Spanish INQUISITION reached its height during his reign, and its attempted introduction into the Low Countries led to the rebellion of the NETHERLANDS and the loss of the Dutch provinces. In 1580, when Henry I of Portugal died without issue, Philip claimed the succession, seized Portugal, and was recognized as king by the Portuguese Cortes. The aid given by England to the Dutch rebels and the raid by Sir Francis Drake on the port of Cádiz (1587) determined Philip to fit out the Invincible ARMADA for an invasion of England (1588). The destruction of the Armada made British seapower supreme. Philip also aided the Catholic LEAGUE in the French Wars of Religion, ultimately without success. His chief colonial conquest was that of the PHILIPPINE ISLANDS. Despite the tremendous influx of American gold, Philip's wars necessitated increasing tax burdens. His reign, however, saw a short-lived economic prosperity. His coldness, cruel fanaticism, and tyrannical attention to detail are well-known. His third wife, Elizabeth of Valois, and his unfortunate son Don CARLOS died in 1568. His fourth wife, Anne of Austria (daughter of Emperor Maximilian II) gave birth to his successor, **Philip III**, 1578–1621, king of Spain, Sicily, Naples, and Portugal (1598–1621). He left the actual government to Francisco de LERMA. Peace was made with England (1604), and a truce with the United Provs. (1609), but in 1620 Spain entered the Thirty Years War. Philip's bigotry was a factor in the expulsion of the MORISCOS (1609). His reign was a glorious period of Spanish civilization—the age of Cervantes, Lope de Vega, and El Greco. He was succeeded by his son, **Philip IV**, 1605–65, who lost PORTUGAL in 1640. His reign was a period of decline and was dominated until 1643 by OLIVARES. The Peace of the PYRENEES with France (1659) was humiliating for Spain. His son Charles II succeeded him. **Philip V**, 1683–1746, first Bourbon king of Spain (1700–1746), was a grandson of Louis XIV. CHARLES II of Spain designated him as his successor. Louis XIV, by accepting the Spanish throne for his grandson, set off the War of the SPANISH SUCCESSION (1701–14), which greatly reduced Spanish power (see UTRECHT, PEACE OF). Weak and mentally unbalanced, he was dominated by women—first by the princesse des URSINS, who made French influence paramount, then by his queen, ELIZABETH FARNESE, who in turn was dominated by Cardinal ALBERONI. Alberoni's attempt to regain the Spanish possessions in Italy led to the QUADRUPLE ALLIANCE of 1718, to which Spain had to submit (1720). The dynastic interests of the Bourbon family involved Spain in the Wars of the POLISH SUCCESSION and the AUSTRIAN SUCCESSION. His son Ferdinand VI succeeded him.

Philip, duke of Edinburgh: see EDINBURGH.

Philip (King Philip), d. 1676, Indian leader in most important Indian war of New England, chief of Wampanoag Indians; son of Massasoit. Hostility of Indians over forced land cessions, aided by execution of three Indians for murder by English, led to **King Philip's War**, 1675–76. Attacks on border settlements involved New England colonies and several Indian tribes. War, costly to colonists, brought end of fur trade and virtual end of tribal Indian life in S New England.

Philip Augustus: see PHILIP II, king of France.

Philip Neri, Saint (nā′rē), 1515–95, Italian priest. As a layman and later as a priest (after 1551) he worked among the poor of Rome, especially among men and boys. He founded a community of secular priests, which became the Oratory, and his oratories at San Girolamo in Rome and San Giovanni were very influential. Besides revivifying the faith of many, he also extended the use of the vernacular in services. Feast: May 26.

Philip of Hesse (Philip the Magnanimous), 1504–67, landgrave of Hesse (1509–67), champion of the Reformation. After vainly trying to reconcile Zwingli and Luther, he signed the Lutheran Augsburg Confession. He formed the SCHMALKALDIC LEAGUE (1531) and after its defeat at Mühlberg was held prisoner by Emperor Charles V (1547–52).

Philip of Swabia, c.1177–1208, German king (1198–1208); brother of Henry VI. On Henry's death (1197) he sought to secure the succession of his infant nephew, the later Emperor FREDERICK II, but he finally agreed to his own election. A minority of princes chose OTTO IV as antiking. The resulting warfare between the Ghibelline and the Guelphic rivals ended 1206 in Philip's favor, but Philip's murder by a private enemy eventually placed Otto on the throne. It is widely held that Philip was instrumental in diverting the Fourth Crusade in order to restore his father-in-law, ISAAC II of Byzantium.

Philippe Égalité: see ORLÉANS, LOUIS PHILIPPE JOSEPH, DUC D' (under ORLÉANS, family).

Philippeville (fēlēpvēl'), city (pop. 40,647), NE Algeria; port on the Mediterranean and outlet for Constantine. Founded 1838 by the French on site of Carthaginian colony.

Philippi (fĭlĭ'pī), anc. city of Macedonia founded (358? B.C.) by Philip II. Near here Octavian (Augustus) and Antony defeated Brutus and Cassius (42 B.C.). Paul addressed his epistle to the Philippians to the church recently estab. here.

Philippians, epistle of New Testament, written by St. Paul to Christians of Philippi (Macedonia). Letter contains eloquent lines on humility, on Christian joy and fear, and on renunciation for Christ.

Philippics (fĭlĭ'pĭks), three denunciatory orations against Philip II of Macedon by DEMOSTHENES. Cicero's polemics against Marc Antony are also called Philippics.

Philippine Islands (fĭ'lĭpēn), group of some 7,000 islands and rocks off SE Asia, in Malay Archipelago, constituting republic of the Philippines (total land area 114,830 sq. mi.; 1948 pop. 19,234,182). QUEZON CITY, near metropolis of MANILA, on LUZON, is cap.; there are 51 provinces. Largest island is Luzon (40,420 sq. mi.). Most of the islands are of volcanic origin; only c.400 are permanently inhabited. Mountain ranges traverse larger islands; Mt. Apo (9,690 ft.) on MINDANAO is highest peak. Of the many navigable rivers, CAGAYAN on Luzon is largest. The Philippines are entirely within the tropical zone; monsoons bring heavy rainfalls. Economy is predominantly agr.; rice and corn cover largest areas; sugar and copra are among principal exports. Islands have one of world's great stands of commercial timber, abound in mineral resources. Vast majority of inhabitants belong to Malay group, are known as Filipinos. Tagalog is basis of new national language; many Filipinos speak English. Ferdinand MAGELLAN led first Europeans to visit here (1521). Spanish conquest began in 1564, with arrival of Miguel LÓPEZ DE LEGASPI. Religious orders became increasingly powerful as Spanish Empire waned. Opposition to this power furthered sentiment for independence in 19th cent. in movement led by José RIZAL. Following SPANISH-AMERICAN WAR islands were transferred to U.S. control; Emilio AGUINALDO led insurrection. With inauguration of M. L. QUEZON as president (Nov. 15, 1935), Commonwealth of the Philippines was formally estab. After a ten-year transition period complete independence was to be estab. on July 4, 1946. War came in 1941 with Japanese attack; after fall of CORREGIDOR, Japanese occupied islands. U.S. forces, under Gen. Douglas MacArthur, liberated islands in 1944–45. Independence came as scheduled in 1946, but long-term U.S. trading rights and provisions for U.S. bases were granted.

Philippines, University of the, mainly at Manila; coed.,

state controlled; founded 1908. There are an agr. college at Laguna and junior colleges at Vigan and Cebu.

Philips, Ambrose, 1675?–1749, English author. His pastoral poems provoked Pope's ridicule and a famous quarrel. Wrote play *The Distrest Mother* (1712), from Racine, and estab. periodical *Freethinker* (1718).

Philips, John, 1676–1709, English poet, known for use of blank verse, as in *The Splendid Shilling* (1705), and for his turn to interest in nature, as in *Cyder* (1708).

Philipse Manor or **Philipsburgh Manor**, SE N.Y., colonial estate of Frederick Philipse, confirmed by royal charter in 1693, between Hudson (W) and Bronx rivers and between what are now North Tarrytown (N) and Yonkers. Manor hall (c. 1682) at Yonkers, now state-owned, has historical collections. Castle Philipse (c.1683) at North Tarrytown has been restored as a museum of colonial Dutch life.

Philip the Bold, king of France: see PHILIP III.

Philip the Bold, 1342–1404, duke of Burgundy (1363–1404) and count of Flanders (1384–1404); younger son of John II of France. His father invested him with Burgundy; his marriage with Margaret, heiress of Flanders, brought him the succession to Flanders after his victory over Philip van ARTEVELDE (1382). He virtually ruled France as regent during the minority of Charles VI (1380–88). After the outbreak of the king's madness began Philip's struggle for power with the king's brother, Louis, duc d'ORLÉANS. His son, JOHN THE FEARLESS, inherited the quarrel.

Philip the Fair, king of France: see PHILIP IV.

Philip the Good, 1396–1467, duke of Burgundy and count of Flanders (1419–67); son of JOHN THE FEARLESS. Through marriage, treaty, conquest, and purchase, he acquired Hainaut, Holland, Zeeland, Friesland, Brabant, Limburg, Namur, Luxembourg, and Liége—i.e., the entire Low Countries. Supporting England in the Hundred Years War, he sponsored the Treaty of TROYES (1420) and helped estab. English rule in France; in 1435, however, he changed sides by concluding the Treaty of Arras with Charles VII of France. He later supported the PRAGUERIE rebellion against Charles and gave asylum to the dauphin (later LOUIS XI). His court was the most splendid in W Europe. His son Charles the Bold succeeded him.

Philip the Handsome, king of Castile: see PHILIP I, Spanish king.

Philip the Tall, king of France: see PHILIP V.

Philistia (fĭlĭs'tyù), anc. region of SW Palestine reaching to the Mediterranean. The five chief cities, Gaza, Ashkelon, Ashdod, Ekron, and Gath, formed a confederacy. In Bible the great Hebrew antagonists of the Philistines are Samson, Saul, and David. Philistines later paid tribute to Assyria; were assimilated by various Semitic races.

Phillips, Stephen, 1868–1915, English poet and dramatist. His works include the poetic dramas *Paolo and Francesca* (1900) and *Herod* (1901).

Phillips, Wendell, 1811–84, American reformer and orator. Fought for many unpopular causes. Prominent as an abolitionist. His oratorical style was easy, colloquial.

Phillips Academy: see ANDOVER, Mass.

Phillipsburg, industrial town (pop. 18,919), NW N.J., on Delaware R. (bridged) opposite Easton, Pa.; settled 1739. Peter Cooper introduced Bessemer process here 1856. Mfg. of metal products, chemicals, cement, and textiles.

Phillips Exeter Academy: see EXETER, N.H.

Philo (fī'lō) or **Philo Judaeus** (jŏōdē'ùs), c.20 B.C.–A.D. c.50, Alexandrian Jewish philosopher. He took the Mosaic law as the foundation of philosophy, but he held that God had created the world indirectly through his potencies and attributes. All beings between the perfection of God and imperfect, finite matter have their unity in, and proceed from, the divine Logos. These teachings had a profound influence on Jewish and Christian writers.

Philoctetes (fĭlŏktēʹtēz), in Greek mythology, king of Malians. He inherited bow and poisonous arrows of his friend Hercules. Oracle said that Troy could not be taken without these weapons. Though ill, Philoctetes was taken to Troy, where he was healed and where he then killed Paris.

philology [Gr.,= love of the word], study of texts (esp. to establish correct ones). In 19th cent. term was extended to include comparative study of languages. Later the word LINGUISTICS was applied to scientific study of language (including comparative linguistics), and philology fell back into its old restricted use.

Philomela (fĭlōmēʹlù), in Greek myth, sister of Procne. Tereus, Thracian king, married Procne, then hid her and married Philomela, whose tongue he cut out to silence her. The gods changed them all into birds. Philomela became the nightingale, and her name is used as in poetic references to that bird (as in Milton and Keats).

philosopher's stone: see ALCHEMY.

Philostratus (Flavius Philostratus) (fĭlŏʹstrùtùs), fl. c.217, Greek Sophist, called the Athenian, author of *Lives of the Sophists.*

Phinehas or **Phinees** (both: fĭʹnēùs). **1** Grandson of Aaron. His swift punishment of two sinners made his name a symbol of holy indignation. Ex. 6.25; Num. 25; 31.6; Joshua 22.13; 24.33; Judges 20.28; 1 Chron. 6.4,50; 9.20; Ezra 7.5; Ps. 106.30; 1 Mac. 2.26,54. **2** Son of Eli who, with his brother Hophni, met death because of sacrileges. 1 Sam. 1–4.

Phippsburg, town (pop. 1,134), including Popham Beach resort, SW Maine, at Kennebec R. mouth and S of Bath. Site of Fort St. George (1607), a Plymouth Co. colony led by George Popham, destroyed by Indians, and resettled c.1737.

Phips, Sir William, 1651–95, American colonial governor. Became first royal governor of Mass. in 1692 through support of Increase MATHER.

Phiz: see BROWNE, HABLOT KNIGHT.

phlogiston theory (flōjĭʹstŏn) of combustion; propounded by J. J. Becher and G. E. Stahl. It stated that phlogiston is present in all materials that burn and is given off during burning. It was widely supported until Lavoisier showed true nature of combustion.

phlox (flŏks), annual or perennial plant of genus *Phlox,* native to North America and widely cultivated. They range in size from the tall, showy border types with masses of fragrant flowers, to the creeping moss pink (*Phlox subulata*). The annuals are mostly derived from a Texan native, *P. drummondi.*

Phocis (fōʹsĭs), anc. state, central Greece, N of the Gulf of Corinth. Included Mt. Parnassus and particularly Delphi, which after the Sacred War of c.596 B.C. was put in control of a council of states. With Athenian help Phocis regained it in 457 B.C. Later Phocis was under Theban control; an attempt to regain independence led to the Sacred War of 356–346 B.C., in which Philip II of Macedon triumphed.

Phocylides (fùsĭʹlĭdēz), fl. early 6th cent. B.C., Greek gnomic poet. His moral epigrams exist in fragments.

Phoebe (fēʹbē), in Greek mythology. **1** Daughter of Gaea, mother of Leto, and grandmother of Artemis. **2** Name of Artemis as goddess of the moon.

phoebe, small migratory bird of flycatcher family of North America. Eastern phoebe or water pewee is brownish gray above, gray and yellow below.

Phoebus: see APOLLO.

Phoenicia (fĭnēʹshù, fĭnĭʹshù), territory of Phoenician civilization. Area of Tyre and Sidon, coast of present Lebanon. Also spelled Phenice, Phenicia.

Phoenician civilization. Early in history in Middle East, people speaking Semitic language moved westward and occupied coast of E Mediterranean. By 1250 B.C. Phoenicians were well estab. as navigators and traders. Organized politically into city-states, they later estab. outposts, notably Utica and Carthage. They sailed and traded all over Mediterranean and even into Atlantic. They made glass and metal articles, and were skilled weavers, dyers, and architects. Greatest contribution was alphabet, an idea adopted by Greeks. Rise of Persians and Greeks destroyed their maritime power, and Hellenistic culture finally eliminated last traces of Phoenician civilization.

Phoenix (fēʹnĭks), city (pop. 106,818), state cap., S central Ariz., on Salt R.; founded 1867. Largest city in state. Sunny winter and health resort, it has opulent hotels and homes. Commercial and processing center for rich SALT RIVER VALLEY (irrigated farming), it also serves surrounding desert and mountains (mining, ranching). Succeeded Prescott as territorial cap., 1889. Has Heard (prehistoric relics) and Arizona museums, La Ciudad (Indian pueblo ruins), U.S. Indian school. Near by are South Mt. Park, with active gold mine, and Frank Lloyd Wright's "Taliesin West." Annual rodeo in Feb.

phoenix (fēʹnĭks), fabulous bird of Egyptian legend. When it became 500 years old, it burned itself on a pyre. From its ashes another phoenix arose. As symbol of death and resurrection it has been favorite metaphor in pagan and Christian literature.

Phoenix Islands, group of eight coral islands (11 sq. mi.; pop. 984), central Pacific. CANTON ISLAND and Enderbury Isl. are under Anglo-American control; other islands belong to British colony of Gilbert and Ellice Islands. Group produces copra. Formerly worked for guano.

Phoenixville, borough (pop. 12,932), SE Pa., on Schuylkill R. and NW of Philadelphia; settled 1720. Near by is Valley Forge. Most western point of British advance in Pa. in Revolution (1777). Ironworks, meat packing plants, and textile mills.

phonetics and **phonemics,** system of sounds of language, studied from two basic points of view. Phonetics is study of sounds of language according to their production in the vocal organs (articulatory phonetics) or their effect on the ear (acoustic phonetics). All phonetics is interrelated because human articulatory and auditory mechanisms are uniform. Systems of phonetic writing are aimed at transcribing accurately any sequence of speech sounds; most famous is International Phonetic Alphabet. Phonemics of a language is study of its phonemes and their arrangement. A phoneme is a group of variants of a speech sound, where the phonetic differences (including features of accent, pitch, intonation) are nonsignificant to the hearer-speaker. The sounds grouped in one phoneme of a particular language may in other languages be so distinct (significant) as to form separate phonemes.

phonograph, a device for reproducing sound waves already recorded in a spiral groove on a cylinder or disk. In 1877 Thomas A. Edison built the first such machine, using a wax cylinder. Disks were introduced by Emil Berliner in 1887. Capabilities of the machine were limited until electrical recording devices were developed (1925). A late innovation (1948) was the long playing record, made to revolve at a slower speed. This improved the quality of the sound and increased the amount of material that could be put on one disk. The "juke box," a coin-operated phonograph capable of playing by automatic selection up to 100 records, has a history which dates from the early part of the century and the coin-operated machines of the penny arcade.

phosphate, salt of phosphoric acid. Calcium phosphate is the most abundant and important. Acid calcium phosphate for fertilizers is prepared from it. Trisodium phosphate is used as a cleaner and in water softening, disodium salt in medicine. Acid phosphate of sodium is used in some baking powders.

phosphorescence (fŏsfùrĕʹsùns) or **luminescence** (lōomĭnĕʹsùns), in general sense, property of emitting light without perceptible heat. It is believed to result from motion of electrons and is classified according to nature of motion. Chemiluminescence is produced by chemical reactions, electroluminescence by electrical discharges, triboluminescence by rubbing or crushing crystals. It is also caused by absorption of radiant energy by certain substances; if it ceases when radiation stops it is called fluorescence; it is phosphorescence if it continues. Bioluminescence is luminescence emitted by living organism, e.g., luminous bacteria, glowworms, fireflies, and many deep-sea fish.

phosphoric acid (fŏsfôʹrĭk). Three phosphoric acids are known, all derived from phosphorus pentoxide by addition of water. Metaphosphoric acid results from addition of one water molecule to one of pentoxide; pyro- of two; ortho- of three. Orthophosphoric acid is the common form; it appears as a crystalline solid and thick liquid. It is used in the laboratory and in medicine in form of salts.

phosphorus (fŏsʹfûrŭs), nonmetallic chemical element (symbol = P; see also ELEMENT, table). Shows ALLOTROPY, appears in three forms. White phosphorus is a poisonous waxy solid, which ignites spontaneously in air and glows in dark at low temperatures. Red phosphorus is a dull, reddish brown crystalline powder, less active than the white form, and nonpoisonous. Black phosphorus is also known. Phosphorus does not occur free but is found abundantly in some compounds, e.g., calcium phosphate. The element is a constituent of protoplasm and therefore essential to life. It is used in fertilizers, in making matches, in smoke screens, in rodent poisons, and in certain alloys. White (or yellow) phosphorus melts at 44°C., boils at c.280°C.; red sublimes when heated under atmospheric pressure and under excess pressure melts at 550°–600°C.

Photius (fōʹshŭs), c.820–892?, Greek churchman and theologian. He was a learned professor at the Univ. of Constantinople and president of the imperial chancellery under Michael III. Photius was in favor of treating the iconoclasts leniently, and when St. Ignatius of Constantinople was forced from the office of patriarch of Constantinople (858) Photius was rushed through ordination and made patriarch. Pope Nicholas I refused to recognize him. Photius called a synod that questioned some Latin customs, including the right of the pope to pass on election of patriarch. Under Basil I, Ignatius was patriarch again, and Photius was condemned at the Fourth Council of Constantinople; but Photius was restored on the death of Ignatius (877) and recognized by Pope John VIII. On the accession of Leo VI (886) Photius was forced to resign. He died in exile. The split of East and West is conventionally reckoned from this schism, though the significance can be easily exaggerated.

photoelectric cell or **phototube**, electron tube in which one of two electrodes emits electrons as a result of irradiation by visible light, ultraviolet, or infrared rays. Main types are highly evacuated or vacuum tube and gas tube, containing inert gas; form varies with purpose. Current is slight so battery is connected with tube so that anode is made positive and attracts electrons. Cell is integral part of "electric eye" devices which can act as switches to operate electrical devices when light reaches cell and to stop operation when light disappears. As phototube, the cell is used in sound-reproducing and television apparatus. See *ill.*, p. 293.

photoengraving, photomechanical process used in printing (notably for illustrations). A photograph of the subject to be reproduced is recorded on a sensitized metal plate which is then etched in an acid bath. For line cuts (solid black and white subjects) photoengravings are done on zinc. Half-tone cuts are photographed through a screen; the copper plate used is thus sensitized in a dotted pattern, larger dots creating darker areas, smaller dots, high lights.

photogrammetry: see AERIAL PHOTOGRAPHY.

photography, science and art concerned with forming and fixing an image on a film or a plate made sensitive to light. Earliest known form is camera obscura (see CAMERA) described by Leonardo da Vinci but generally credited to Giambattista della Porta. Development of light-sensitive surface which would retain an image stemmed from discovery (1727) that light causes darkening of silver salts. Thomas Wedgwood, Sir Humphry Davy, and others contributed to extending knowledge of silver salts. Sir John Herschel discovered hyposulphites (1819) and pointed out value of sodium hyposulphite as fixative for silver chloride when daguerreotypy became known (1839). Joseph Nicephore Niepce is generally credited with making first photograph (probably in 1822) by exposure of a light-sensitive surface within a camera. Niepce and later his son Isidore worked with Louis J. M. Daguerre on improving methods. Daguerre discovered (1837) principle of making daguerreotypes, which won popularity. Coloring of daguerreotypes was probably practiced by 1840. Tintypes also became popular in 19th cent. W. H. F. Talbot introduced practical method of photography in which negative image was formed within camera on light-sensitive paper from which positive images or prints could be made; he called his later modifications calotype and afterward talbotype process. Although others, too, claim the discovery, F. S. Archer is usually credited with making practicable the wet collodion process (1851) which replaced earlier photographic methods. Mathew B. Brady made notable photographs of Civil War scenes by wet collodion process. Eadweard Muybridge made early action photographs. Stereoscopic photography (see STEREOSCOPE) was popular in second half of 19th cent. Twin-lens cameras were developed for taking the pictures. Their use has been revived recently. By 1850s photography had begun to develop into an art. Among those who contributed to its development are H. P. Robinson, O. G. Rejlander, P. H. Emerson, Alfred Stieglitz, E. J. Steichen, Charles Sheeler, Paul Strand, Edward Weston, and C. H. White. Jacob Riis made early photographs of slum areas; later Dorothea Lange and Margaret Bourke-White depicted the lot of itinerant agricultural workers. Berenice Abbott became known especially for her scenes of life in New York city and her portraits. Photography became important, also, as a means of preserving a record of events; for illustrating books, periodicals, newspapers, and advertising matter; for documentary material; for teaching, e.g., in medical education and certain manual skills; for decorative purposes, e.g., photomurals. This growth was in part made possible by improvement in photographic equipment. The introduction of roll film by George Eastman in 1884 freed the photographer from the difficulties of coping with the fragile plates and bulky equipment used in wet and dry collodion plate methods. Daylight-loading roll-film camera came into use in 1891. Film made with varying degrees of sensitivity and for special purposes was developed for use in the box, folding, miniature, and other styles of cameras. Color film that required only one exposure and could be used in ordinary cameras (commonly the 35-millimeter size) was introduced in 1935; the processed film forms transparencies which can be projected in color on a screen and from which enlarged color prints can be made. Another type of color film became available (1942) in most ordinary camera sizes; this forms negatives that show a reversal of color and of light and shade, and color prints can be made from them. The cost of a camera depends to a great extent upon the quality of the lens. Modern lenses are designed to prevent astigmatism and the better ones to avoid chromatic and spherical aberration and other defects. One system for indicating diaphragm opening (size of which determines amount of light permitted to pass through lens) is F number system, in which F number represents ratio of focal length to effective diameter of lens. Methods of using cameras and of developing and printing and principles of composition are given in many books on photography.

photometry (fōtŏʹmŭtrē), branch of physics dealing

with measurement of intensity of a light source, such as a lamp. Measuring instruments (photometers) make possible the comparison of unknown light intensity with known intensity. Experiments show that as light source moves away from surface it illuminates, illumination decreases in inverse proportion to square of distance. Commonly, electric-light intensity is given in candle power, intensity of illumination in foot-candles.

photosphere (fō'tusfēr"), layer of gases beneath sun's chromosphere. Its incandescent gases, reaching temperature of c.6000° C., are so bright as to be seen as the sun's apparent surface.

photosynthesis (fō"tōsĭn'thŭsĭs), process in which green plants utilize energy of sunlight to make carbohydrates from carbon dioxide and water. All animal and plant life are ultimately dependent upon it for food and oxygen. All plant forms containing the essential green pigment (see CHLOROPHYLL) are capable of photosynthesis; this process occurs only where chlorophyll is present. Oxygen is liberated in the process.

phototube: see PHOTOELECTRIC CELL.

Phrixus (frĭk'sŭs), in Greek mythology. He was carried over the Hellespont to Colchis by the ram with the GOLDEN FLEECE.

Phrygia (frĭ'jēŭ), anc. region of central Asia Minor, now in central Turkey. The Phrygians apparently came here from Europe c.1200 B.C. Little is known of their history. After 700 Lydia dominated the area. Later invaded by Gauls, then ruled by Pergamum and by Rome.

Phrynichus (frĭ'nĭkŭs), fl. c.512–476 B.C., Athenian tragedian, by some ancients considered the founder of tragedy. The painful theme of his *The Taking of Miletus* so moved the audience that he was fined.

Phuket (pōō'kĭt), island, area c.200 sq. mi., off W coast of Malay Peninsula, belonging to Thailand. Chief town (pop. 18,759) is also called Phuket; chief tinmining center of Thailand. Malay name, Ujong Salang, was corrupted by early European voyagers to Junkceylon.

Phumiphon (pōōm'ĭpŏn"), 1927–, king of Thailand (1950–). Succeeded Ananda, his elder brother, who died mysteriously in 1946. A regency exercised the royal power until Phumiphon ascended the throne.

Phyfe, Duncan (fīf), c.1768–1854, American cabinetmaker, b. Scotland. During most productive period (until 1820) he was influenced by the Adam brothers, Hepplewhite, Sheraton, and French Directoire and Consulate styles. Designs of early period are marked by simple ornament and decorative motifs such as the lyre and the acanthus; those of last period tended to be heavy and overornamented. Used mainly solid mahogany but also satinwood, maple, and rosewood. See *ill.*, p. 356.

phylacteries (fĭlăk'tŭrēz) [Gr.,= safeguard], two small leather boxes worn during prayers by orthodox Jews after the age of 13 years. Each box contains strips of parchment inscribed with verses from the Scriptures: Ex. 13.1–10; 13.11–16; Deut. 6.4–9; 11.13–21. One box is fastened to the forehead and the other to the left arm. They are intended to serve as a reminder of the constant presence of God. They are not worn on the Sabbath or holy days.

phylloxera (fĭlŏk'sŭrŭ, fĭlŭksēr'ŭ), small greenish insect, classed with aphids or with closely related group. Many phylloxeras produce galls on deciduous trees. Best-known is grape phylloxera, *Phylloxera vitifoliae*, harmful pest of W U.S. and Europe.

physical geography: see GEOGRAPHY.

physical therapy (thĕ'rŭpē) or **physiotherapy** (fĭ"zēō–), treatment of disease with the aid of physical agents including radiation, light, heat, water, massage, and exercise.

Physick, Philip Syng, 1768–1837, pioneer American surgeon, first professor of surgery at Univ. of Pennsylvania (1805–19).

physics, science dealing with matter and energy and the relations between them. In addition to its major objective, the rational explanation of natural phenomena, it seeks quantitative definition of these phenomena. Its various branches include HEAT, MECHANICS, SOUND, MAGNETISM, ELECTRICITY. With discovery that matter is fundamentally electrical, higher physics and chemistry have become closely interrelated. Biophysics is concerned with the physical analysis of biological behavior, determination of effects of physical agents on biological material, and application of physical techniques to biological measurements.

physiocrats (fĭ'zēŭkrăts"), 18th-cent. French thinkers who evolved the first complete system of economics. Founder of the group was François QUESNAY; his most ardent disciple was Victor de Mirabeau. Quesnay held that all wealth originated with the land and that agriculture alone would multiply wealth. Laissez faire was necessary if the total economic process, based on agriculture, were to follow its natural course. Taxation was to be on land alone—an argument not without charm for industrialists. Physiocracy influenced Turgot and Joseph II and, even more profoundly, Adam SMITH and Henry GEORGE, but today it is a dead doctrine.

physiology (fĭzēō'lŭjē), study of normal functioning of plants and animals and of activities by which life is maintained and transmitted. Includes vital activities of cells, tissues, organs, and systems (e.g., circulatory, nervous) and, in plants, also photosynthesis and transpiration.

physiotherapy: see PHYSICAL THERAPY.

pi, in mathematics, ratio of circumference of circle to its diameter (symbol is π). Ratio is same for all circles (c.3.1416). It is important in such advanced mathematics as continued fractions, periodic functions, and logarithms of imaginary numbers.

Piacenza (pyächĕn'tsä), city (pop. 49,527), Emilia-Romagna, N central Italy, on Po R. Agr. center. Formed part of duchy of PARMA and Piacenza 1545–1860. Has several fine churches.

piano or **pianoforte,** keyboard musical instrument, historically the youngest member of its family which includes the DULCIMER, the clavichord, the harpsichord, the spinet, and the virginal. The basic difference between the clavichord and harpsichord is that the strings of the clavichord are struck with hammers (called tangents), whereas the strings of the harpsichord are plucked by quills. Both instruments reached the height of their popularity between the 16th and 18th cent. The clavichord consists of a small, rectangular wooden box containing a sounding board and strings running parallel to the keyboard. The tone, which can be modified by the touch of the performer, is expressive but faint. The harpsichord of the 15th cent. was wing-shaped (similar to today's grand piano), but the square harpsichord, with strings at right angles to the keyboard, was more common in the 16th cent. Varying the touch in harpsichord playing does not alter the quality or volume of tone. The spinet and virginal are similar to the harpsichord in that their strings are plucked. The terms *spinet* and *virginal,* interchangeable until the 17th cent., were sometimes used indiscriminately to designate any harpsichord. The spinet is generally distinguished by its wing-shaped case and strings at a 45° angle to the keyboard in contrast to the virginal's rectangular case and strings parallel to the keyboard. A keyboard instrument was needed that would combine the brilliance of the harpsichord with the expressiveness of the clavichord. Bartolomeo Cristofori, a Florentine harpsichord maker, is given credit for making the first piano in 1709. He called his instrument *gravicembalo col piano e forte.* In the piano, like the clavichord, the strings are struck with a hammer. The design of the piano's case and the arrangement of strings was taken from the harpsichord. Because of its great capabilities (further increased by technical developments of the 19th cent.), the piano displaced the clavichord and harpsichord and steadily evolved into the concert grand of today. In the 19th cent. appeared the upright piano and the small oblong piano called the spinet. Mozart and Haydn were the first major composers to write for the piano; with the works of Beethoven, Chopin, Schumann, and Liszt, the piano became the outstanding solo instrument.

Piast (pyäst), first dynasty of Polish dukes and kings. Duke Mieszko I (962–92) introduced Christianity and began unification of Poland. BOLESLAUS I, his son, was crowned king 1025. The law of succession introduced by Boleslaus III (1102–38), which provided for the rotation of the crown among four branches of the family, destroyed Polish unity until CASIMIR II and LADISLAUS I restored the royal authority. The dynasty died out in Poland proper with Casimir III (1370) and was succeeded by the JAGIELLO dynasty. In SILESIA, members of the Piast dynasty ruled several principalities (after 1335 under Bohemian overlordship)—the duchy of Oppeln until 1532 and the principalities of Brieg and Liegnitz until 1675.

Piatigorsky, Gregor (pyätigôr'skē), 1903–, Russian-American cellist and teacher. First cellist with the Berlin Philharmonic in 1923, he became a solo cellist in 1928 and came to the U.S. in 1929.

Piauí (pyouē'), state (97,261 sq. mi.; pop. 1,064,438), NE Brazil, on E bank of Parnaíba R.; cap. TERESINA. Extensive livestock grazing. Exports include oilseeds, babassu nuts, cotton, tobacco, rubber.

Piave (pyä'vä), river, 137 mi. long, flowing through Venetia, N Italy, to the Adriatic. In World War I Italians entrenched here withstood Austrian attacks from 1917 until Austrian rout by Allies in 1918.

Piazzi, Giuseppe (jōōzĕp'pä pyät'tsē), 1746–1826, Italian astronomer, a Theatine priest. Discovered first asteroid (Ceres; 1801). Made star catalogue.

Picard, Jean (zhä' pēkär'), 1620–82, French astronomer, first to measure accurately the length of one-degree arc of earth's surface.

Picardy (pĭ'kûrdē), Fr. *Picardie*, region and former province, N France, in Somme, Aisne, Oise, and Pas-de-Calais depts. and bordering on English Channel and Belgium; historic cap. Amiens. Other cities: Abbeville, Calais, Boulogne-sur-Mer. Agr.; textile mfg. Name was first used in 13th cent. to designate fiefs added to royal domain by Philip II.

Picasso, Pablo (Ruiz y) (pä'blō pēkä'sō), 1881–, Spanish painter, b. Malaga. Studied in Barcelona and in Paris (after 1900), where he remained and associated with Derain, Bracque, and Matisse. His "blue" and "rose" periods (1901–6), named for dominant colors of the paintings, tended to be conventional. Influenced by Iberian sculpture, Negro masks, and the art of Cézanne, he began c.1906 to create compositions in angular planes, painting such works as *Les Demoiselles d'Avignon* and the portrait of Gertrude Stein (Metropolitan Mus.). By 1909 his dissection of forms developed into the style known as CUBISM. There followed a neoclassical period in '20s. A new period of powerful expression was climaxed (1937) by the mural *Guernica*, a dramatic response to agonies of Spanish civil war. He continued to produce paintings and sculptures, working as always in many styles simultaneously. Much of his later output has been in pottery. The dove he drew for Communist-sponsored Congress of Partisans of Peace (1949) became famous as a political symbol.

Picayune (pĭkûyōōn'), city (pop. 6,707), S Miss., near Pearl R. and NE of New Orleans. Processing and shipping tung products and naval stores.

Piccadilly (pĭk"ûdĭl'ē), famous street of shops, hotels, and clubs in W London, extending from Piccadilly Circus to Hyde Park Corner.

Piccard, Auguste (ōgüst' pēkär'), 1884–, Belgian physicist. Ascended into stratosphere in balloons to study cosmic rays; in 1932 ascended to c.55,500 ft. After 1938 made undersea dives with bathysphere. His twin brother, **Jean Piccard** (zhä), 1884–, American citizen from 1931, chemist and aeronautical engineer on

Univ. of Minnesota faculty, also made stratosphere balloon ascents.

Piccinni or **Piccini, Niccolò** (both: pēchē'nē), 1728–1800, Italian composer of over 100 operas, of which *La buona figliuola* was most successful. Opponents to the opera reforms of GLUCK made Piccinni their unwilling champion.

Piccirilli (pēt-chērē'lē), family of Italian-American marble cutters and sculptors. Workshop in Bronx, New York, is widely known. Came to U.S. in 1888.

piccolo: see WIND INSTRUMENTS.

Piccolomini, Enea Silvio de': see PIUS II.

Piccolomini, Octavio (ōktä'vyō pēk-kōlô'mēnē), 1599–1656, Italian general in imperial service during Thirty Years War. Supported conspiracy against WALLENSTEIN.

Pic du Midi (pēk' dü mēdē'), two peaks of Pyrenees, S France—**Pic du Midi de Bigorre** (dù bēgôr'), 9,439 ft. high, in central Pyrenees; **Pic du Midi d'Ossau** (dôsō'), 9,465 ft. high, in W Pyrenees.

Pickens, Andrew, 1739–1817, American Revolutionary partisan leader. Formed armed band to harass British in S.C. His grandson, **Francis Wilkinson Pickens,** 1805–69, was governor of S.C. (1860–62) when that state seceded.

Pickens, Fort, fortification on W end of Santa Rosa Isl. at entrance to Pensacola Bay, Fla. Occupied and held by Union throughout Civil War.

pickerel (pĭ'krŭl, pĭ'kûrŭl), name for various small fish of pike family. Eastern or common and barred pickerel are in fresh waters of E U.S.

Pickering, Edward Charles (pĭ'kûrĭng), 1846–1919, American astronomer and physicist, pioneer in photographic photometry and spectroscopy. His brother **William Henry Pickering,** 1858–1938, also a noted astronomer, predicted discovery and location of Pluto, discovered ninth satellite of Saturn, added to knowledge of Mars, other planets, and moon.

Pickering, Timothy, 1745–1829, American Revolutionary general and statesman. Quartermaster general (1780–85). U.S. Secretary of State (1795–1800); dismissed by Pres. John Adams. U.S. Senator (1803–11). A strong Federalist.

picketing, act of guarding a place of work affected by a strike in order to discourage patronage and often to prevent strikebreakers (scabs) from taking over the strikers' jobs. Has also been used by political movements to influence legislation.

Pickett, George Edward, 1825–75, Confederate general. Best known for "Pickett's charge" in Gettysburg campaign (July 3, 1863), a heroic effort ending in virtual annihilation of his division. Defeated at Five Forks (April 1, 1865).

Pickford, Mary, 1893–, American film actress, whose real name is Gladys Smith. Known as "America's Sweetheart" for simple, sentimental roles (e.g., in *Poor Little Rich Girl, Daddy Long Legs*).

pickle, name for fruits and vegetables preserved in vinegar, often with spices or sugar or both. Many materials and combinations have been used in many lands; perhaps best known in U.S. is the cucumber pickle, either sweet or flavored with dill. In a wider sense, a pickle is a preservative liquid, such as brine for meat, brandy for fruit.

Pico della Mirandola, Giovanni, Conte (jōvän'nē kōn'tä pē'kō dĕl'lä mērän'dōlä), 1463–94, Italian humanist, renowned for youthful brilliance and learning. He was interested in science and magic.

Picquart, Georges (zhôrzh' pēkär'), 1854–1914, French officer. As chief of intelligence in 1895 he discovered the evidence which eventually exonerated Capt. Dreyfus (see DREYFUS AFFAIR). In reprisal for disclosing the evidence he was dismissed, but he was later reinstated and served as war minister.

picric acid (pĭ'krĭk), explosive, pale yellow, bitter tasting crystalline solid compound of carbon, hydrogen, oxygen, and nitrogen; also called trinitrophenol. It reacts with metals to form explosive salts; explodes

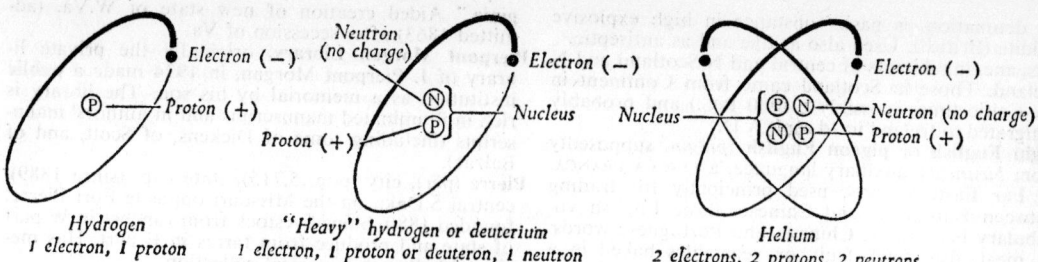

Hydrogen
1 electron, 1 proton

"Heavy" hydrogen or deuterium
1 electron, 1 proton or deuteron, 1 neutron

Helium
2 electrons, 2 protons, 2 neutrons

DIAGRAMMATIC REPRESENTATION OF SIMPLE NUCLEI

(These are conventional diagrams; actually the electron orbits are not precisely determined geometric curves.)

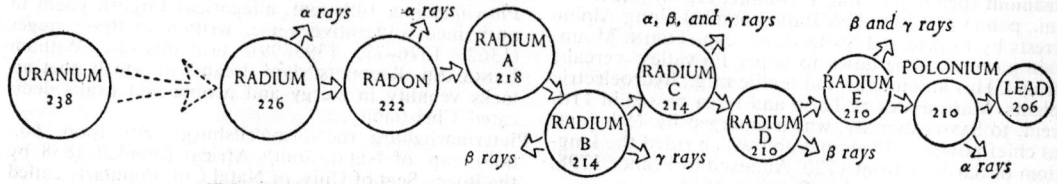

SPONTANEOUS DISINTEGRATION OF RADIOACTIVE ELEMENTS

Energy is released in the form of α rays (helium ion), β rays (electrons), and γ rays (X rays)

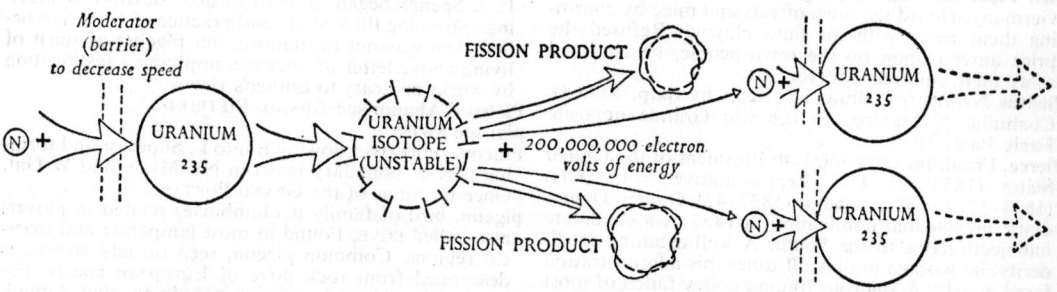

NUCLEAR FISSION RESULTING FROM HITTING URANIUM-235 WITH NEUTRON BULLETS

The released neutrons at the right contribute to a "chain reaction" with other uranium atoms. U-235 is a scarce isotope; uranium ore contains U-235 and U-238 in proportion c.1:140.

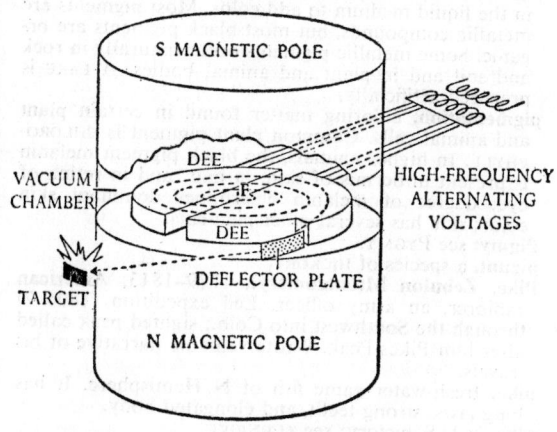

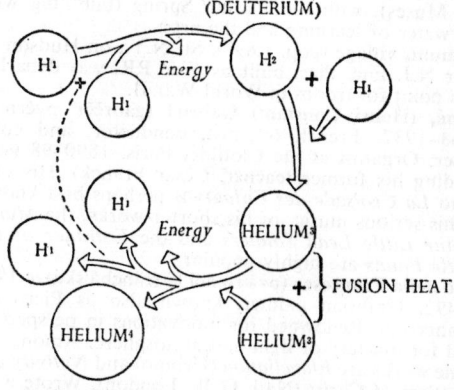

PROTON-PROTON CYCLE TAKING PLACE IN THE SUN

DIAGRAM OF A CYCLOTRON USED IN NUCLEAR RESEARCH

Protons or deuterons produced at a source F rotate within the dee spaces, between the poles of a heavy magnet. They are accelerated by the alternating current every time they cross the gap. When their velocity is great enough they pass out of the dee, rebound from the deflector plate, and bombard the target.

During this continuous cycle vast amounts of energy (heat, light, ultraviolet rays) are given off. The H-bomb employs a similar principle. Whereas the energy of the A-bomb is derived from *fission* of a heavy atom, here energy is released when light hydrogen nuclei *fuse* to form a helium nucleus. The reaction is thermonuclear, since it takes place only at temperatures of some 15-20 million degrees C. In the H-bomb this temperature is provided by a preceding A-type explosion.

on detonation; is basic substance in high explosive lyddite (British). Used also as dye and as antiseptic.

Picts, anc. inhabitants of central and N Scotland and N Ireland. Those in Scotland came from Continent in pre-Celtic times (possibly c.1000 B.C.) and probably emigrated to Ireland in 2d cent. A.D.

pidgin English or **pigeon English** [*pidgin,* supposedly from *business*], auxiliary language, a LINGUA FRANCA, of Far Eastern ports, used principally for trading between Europeans and Chinese. Basic English vocabulary has Malay, Chinese, and Portuguese words.

pie, meat, fish, fowl, fruit, or vegetables baked in a crust of pastry. Pies were known to Romans, and were common in England by 14th cent.; mince pie early became a festive Christmas dish. Early Americans evolved new kinds, including pumpkin pie.

Piedmont (pēd'mŏnt), Ital. *Piemonte,* region (9,817 sq. mi.; pop. 3,418,300), NW Italy, bounded along Alpine crests by France and Switzerland; cap. TURIN. Mountain pastures slope down to upper Po valley (cereals, fruits). Has automobile and textile mfg.; hydroelectric plants. Marquisates of Turin and Ivrea passed in 11th cent. to SAVOY dynasty, which emerged by 15th cent. as chief power in Piedmont and which ruled the kingdom of Sardinia from 1720. Annexed to France 1798, Piedmont was restored to Sardinia 1814.

Piedmont, residential city (pop. 10,132), W Calif., surrounded by Oakland.

Pied Piper of Hamelin, legendary figure of Hameln, Germany. He rid the town of rats and mice by charming them away with his flute playing. Refused the price agreed upon by the townspeople, he charmed away their children in revenge.

Piedras Negras (pyā'dhräs nā'gräs), city (pop. 15,663), Coahuila, N Mexico, on the Rio Grande opposite Eagle Pass, Texas.

Pierce, Franklin, 1804–69, 14th President of the United States (1853–57). U.S. Representative from N.H. (1833–37) and U.S. Senator (1837–42). Gained Democratic presidential nomination in 1852 as a candidate unobjectionable to the South. A well-meaning mediocrity, he worked in difficult times; his administration fared poorly. A vigorous foreign policy failed of most of its objectives. Domestically, GADSDEN PURCHASE was made, but plans for transcontinental railroad fell through; KANSAS-NEBRASKA BILL brought on explosive sectional difficulties.

Pieria (pīēr'ēū), region of anc. Macedonia, including Mt. Olympus and Mt. Pierus (sacred to Orpheus and the Muses), with the Pierian Spring (bubbling with the water of learning and the arts).

Piermont, village (pop. 1,897), SE N.Y., on Hudson R. near N.J. line. Pier, built by Erie RR, was debarkation point for troops in World War II.

Pierné, (Henri Constant) Gabriel (gäbrēēl' pyĕrnä'), 1863–1937, French organist, conductor, and composer. Organist at Ste Clotilde, Paris, 1890–98 (succeeding his former teacher, César Franck). His oratorio *La Croisade des Enfants* is perhaps best known of his serious music; of his shorter works, the *March of the Little Lead Soldiers* and the *Entrance of the Little Fauns* are highly popular.

Piero della Francesca (pyä'rō dĕl'lä fränchā'skä), c.1420 –1492, Umbrian painter, known also as Piero de' Franceschi. Renowned for innovations in perspective and for mastery of light and atmosphere. Among notable works are *Flagellation* (Urbino) and *Nativity* and *Baptism of Christ* (Natl. Gall., London). Wrote a remarkable treatise on geometry.

Piero di Cosimo (dē kŏ'zēmō), 1462–1521, Florentine painter, whose real name was Piero di Lorenzo. Adopted the name of his master, Cosimo Rosseli, whom he assisted in decorating Sistine Chapel. Famed for landscape backgrounds of his mythological and religious pictures. Influenced in later years by Leonardo da Vinci.

Pierpont, Francis Harrison, 1814–99, Civil War leader of Union government in Va., "father of West Vir-

ginia." Aided creation of new state of W.Va. (admitted 1863) after secession of Va.

Pierpont Morgan Library, originally the private library of J. Pierpont Morgan, in 1924 made a public institution as a memorial by his son. The library is rich in illuminated manuscripts and in authors' manuscripts (including some of Dickens, of Scott, and of Balzac).

Pierre (pēr), city (pop. 5,715), state cap. (since 1889), central S.Dak., on the Missouri opposite Fort Pierre; founded 1880. Ships livestock from ranches in W part of state and produce from farms in E part. Has memorial hall with historical collection.

Pierrot (pē'ûrō) [Fr.,= little Peter], French pantomime character, a buffoon in a large tunic, whose face is painted white.

Piers Plowman (pērz). *The Vision Concerning Piers Plowman* is a 14th-cent. allegorical English poem in unrhymed alliterative verse, written in three stages (1362, 1376–77, 1393–99), probably by William LANGLAND. Recounts vivid dreams in which poet attacks venality in clergy and people and exalts dedicated Christianity.

Pietermaritzburg (pē"tûrmä'rītsbûrg), city (pop. 60,-609), cap. of Natal, South Africa; founded 1838 by the Boers. Seat of Univ. of Natal Col. Popularly called Maritzburg.

Pietism, movement in Lutheran Church in 17th and 18th cent. to combat settled, intellectual attitude. P. J. Spener began in 1670 to hold devotional meetings, stressing Bible study and practice of Christian belief. Aim was not Puritanism, but placing of spirit of living above letter of doctrine, implying a justification by works contrary to Luther's views.

Pietro d'Abano: see ABANO, PIETRO D'.

pig: see SWINE.

Pigeon, short river flowing E into L. Superior and forming part of boundary between NE Minn. and W Ont. Once terminus of the GRAND PORTAGE.

pigeon, bird of family (Columbidae) related to plover; also called DOVE. Found in most temperate and tropical regions. Common pigeon, seen on city streets, is descended from rock dove of European coasts. Favorite domesticated varieties include Jacobin, fantail, tumbler, pouter, carrier, homing pigeon. Young are fed on "pigeon's milk" from parents' crops.

pigeon English: see PIDGIN ENGLISH.

pig iron: see IRON.

pigment, in paint, powdered substance which is mixed in the liquid medium to add color. Most pigments are metallic compounds, but most black pigments are organic. Some metallic pigments occur naturally in rock and soil and in plant and animal bodies. A LAKE is prepared artificially.

pigmentation, coloring matter found in certain plant and animal cells. Common plant pigment is CHLOROPHYLL. In higher animals, the black pigment melanin is present in dermis of skin, in hair, and in retina of eye; degree of melanin determines dominant skin color; skin has several other pigments.

Pigmy: see PYGMY.

pignut, a species of HICKORY.

Pike, Zebulon M(ontgomery), 1779–1813, American explorer, an army officer. Led expedition (1806–7) through the Southwest into Colo.; sighted peak called after him Pikes Peak. Wrote valuable narrative of his travels.

pike, fresh-water game fish of N Hemisphere. It has long jaws, strong teeth, and elongated body.

pike, in U.S. history: see TURNPIKE.

Pikes Peak, 14,110 ft. high, central Colo., in S part of Front Range; discovered 1806 by Z. M. PIKE. Best known and most conspicuous peak in the Rockies. Colorado Springs is stands on edge of Great Plains. Colorado Springs is at E base. Railroad, highway to snow-covered top.

Pikeville, town (pop. 5,154), E Ky., in Cumberlands on Levisa Fork, in coal and timber region.

Pilate: see PONTIUS PILATE.

Pilcomayo (pēlkōmä'yō), river rising in the Bolivian Andes E of L. Poopó and flowing 700 mi. SE across Chaco to Paraguay R. near Asunción. In Chaco it is boundary between Argentina and Paraguay.

pile, post of timber, steel, or concrete for supporting a structure. Vertical piles or bearing piles (most common form) generally are needed for foundations of bridges, docks, piers, and buildings. Wooden piles are usually shaped for driving, sometimes tipped with iron. Concrete piles are of two types, precast and cast in place.

piles, in medicine: see HEMORRHOIDS.

pilgrim, one who travels to a shrine out of religious motives. Pilgrimages are a feature of many cultures. Jews made annual pilgrimage to Jerusalem at Passover. Moslems make pilgrimage to Mecca. Protection of Holy Places in Palestine was the aim of the Crusades. Since 1300 the popes have set aside Holy Years for special pilgrimages to Rome. Modern Western shrines of the Roman Catholic church include Loreto, Santiago de Compostela, Lourdes, and Fátima. Canterbury was an important shrine in the Middle Ages. In the New World well-known shrines are Ste Anne de Beaupré and Guadalupe Hidalgo.

Pilgrimage of Grace, 1536, rising of Roman Catholics in N England to protest against the abolition of papal supremacy and the confiscation of the monarchy. The significant part of the movement was led by Robert Aske in Yorkshire; he and his many followers reopened monasteries at York and moved on to Doncaster. But met by representatives of Henry VIII who offered them general pardon and a Parliament to be held in a year, they dispersed. Aske went to London and was received well. In 1537 Francis Bigod led a new rising at Beverly. Although Aske and other leaders of the Pilgrimage had tried to prevent this new move, they were arrested, tried, and executed with Bigod.

Pilgrims, in American history, founders of PLYMOUTH COLONY in Mass. Nucleus of group was English separatists who had moved to Holland in 1607–8. Obtained charter from London Co. and, with help of London merchants, sailed in MAYFLOWER in 1620.

Pillars of Hercules (hûr'kyŏolēz), promontories at Gibraltar in Europe and at Ceuta in Africa, at E end of Strait of Gibraltar.

Pillnitz, Declaration of, 1791, statement issued at Castle of Pillnitz, Saxony, by Emperor Leopold II and Frederick William II of Prussia. Its call on the European powers to restore Louis XVI to his full authority as king of France helped to bring on the FRENCH REVOLUTIONARY WARS.

Pillow, Gideon Johnson, 1806–78, American general. Commanded in Mexican War. Confederate general in Civil War; suspended from command because of his conduct in escaping from Fort Donelson before Confederate surrender (1862).

Pillow, Fort, Civil War fortification on Mississippi R., c.40 mi. N of Memphis, built by G. J. Pillow in 1862. Taken by Union in 1862, it was captured by N. B. Forrest in 1864.

Pilnyak, Boris (bürēs' pēlnyäk'), pseud. of Boris Andreyevich Vogau, 1894–, Russian author. Among his works are *The Naked Year* (1922; Eng. tr., 1928), *Mahogany* (1927), and *The Volga Falls into the Caspian Sea* (1930; Eng. tr., 1931)—novels on revolutionary and postrevolutionary Russia—and *OK* (1932), an unflattering report on a trip to the U.S. His antiurbanism and his criticism of mechanized society brought him into suspicion with Communist critics.

Piloty, Karl von (kärl' fŭn pēlō'tē), 1826–86, German historical painter, an influential teacher.

Pilsen (pĭl'sŭn), Czech *Plzeň*, city (pop. 103,767), NW Bohemia, Czechoslovakia. Famous for its beer. Has huge Skoda works, producing locomotives, cars, armaments. City was a center of Catholicism in Hussite Wars and withstood many sieges (15th cent.).

Pilsudski, Joseph (pĭlsŏod'skē), 1867–1935, Polish marshal and statesman. Originally a Socialist, he was repeatedly exiled and imprisoned by Russian authorities. In World War I he commanded Polish forces under Austrian sponsorship, but toward the war's end he quarrelled with the Central Powers and was interned. Released in Nov., 1918, he proclaimed an independent Polish republic, with himself as chief of state. His campaign against Russia (aimed at restoring E frontier of 1772) ended victoriously with the Treaty of RIGA (1921). He retired to private life in 1922 but in 1926 overthrew the government by a coup d'état and from then to his death governed as virtual dictator.

Pima Indians (pē'mù), North American tribe of Uto-Aztecan linguistic stock, in S Ariz. Visited early by Spanish missionaries, they were friendly to the whites. They were hostile to the Apache. They farm with use of irrigation and are noted for basketry.

pimento, name for tree which bears ALLSPICE berry and also for a large sweet Spanish PEPPER.

Pimlico (pĭm'lĭkō), district of W London, England.

pimpernel (pĭm'pûrnĕl), Old World flowering plant of genus *Anagallis*. Scarlet pimpernel (*Anagallis arvensis*) has red (sometimes white or blue) starlike flowers which remain open only in sunshine.

Pinchot, Gifford (gĭ'fûrd pĭn'chō), 1865–1946, American forester and public official. Served in division of forestry, U.S. Dept. of Agriculture (1898–1910). Member of many conservation commissions. Governor of Pa. (1923–27, 1931–35).

Pinckney, Charles, 1757–1824, American statesman, governor of S.C. (1789–92, 1796–98, 1806–8). As minister to Spain (1801–5) he failed to gain cession of Fla. to U.S. His cousin, **Charles Cotesworth Pinckney,** 1746–1825, participated in mission which led to XYZ AFFAIR. C. C. Pinckney's brother, **Thomas Pinckney,** 1750–1828, served as envoy extraordinary to Spain (1794–95). Negotiated treaty with Spain (1795).

pincushion flower: see SCABIOSA.

Pindar (pĭn'dùr), 518?–c.438 B.C., generally regarded as greatest Greek lyric poet. Wrote chiefly choral lyrics; developed triumphal ode or epinicion, celebrating athletic victories but usually invoking a myth. Extant are 44 complete odes and numerous fragments. His style is marked by high-flown diction, intricate word order, and religious tone. The **Pindaric ode** (pĭndä'rĭk) is a verse form used especially in England in 17th and early 18th cent., based on incorrect understanding of Pindar's metrics. Form, originated (1656) by COWLEY, and used by Dryden, Pope, and Swift, was irregular and of grandiose diction.

Pindus (pĭn'dùs), Gr. *Pindos*, mountain range, 100 mi. long, NW and W central Greece, along border of Thessaly and Epirus. Rises to 8,650 ft.

pine, coniferous pyramidal tree of genus *Pinus*, represented by c.80 species in the N Hemisphere. The needlelike leaves (1–12 in. long) are produced singly or in clusters up to five; they remain on the branch from two to ten years. Staminate and pistillate cones are borne on the same tree. Pine nuts are the edible seeds of various species, e.g., the Colorado pine nut or piñon tree (*Pinus cembroides edulis*). The white pine (*P. strobus*) of E North America is a valuable timber tree. Species with similar straight-grained, soft wood containing little resin include the western white pine (*P. monticola*), the lodgepole pine (*P. contorta latifolia*), and the sugar pine (*P. lambertiana*). Yellow or pitch pines have harder, more resinous wood. These include the longleaf pine (*P. palustris*), a source of turpentine and other naval stores; the red or Norway pine (*P. resinosa*); and the shortleaf pine (*P. echinata*). In European forests the Scotch pine (*P. sylvestris*) is one of the chief coniferous trees.

pineal gland (pĭ'nēùl), small cone-shaped body on roof of brain. In man, its glandular tissue begins to become fibrous at age of about seven. Function not definitely known. Gland is rudimentary in vertebrates from fish to mammals.

pineapple, herbaceous perennial (*Ananas comosus*) of tropical America, and its spiny delicious fruit. Cuba, Puerto Rico, and Hawaii lead in commercial production of the fruit, the juice and flesh of which are canned in large quantities. A fiber from the spiny leaves is made into piña or pineapple cloth in the Philippines.

Pine Barrens, coastal plain region (area c.3,000 sq. mi.) of S and SE N.J. Region of sandy soils and swamp-edged streams; supports pine stands and tracts of cranberries and blueberries.

Pine Bluff, city (pop. 37,162), SE central Ark., on Arkansas R. and SE of Little Rock; settled 1819. Rail and market center for agr. area. Cotton and lumber processing; chemical mfg.; stockyards. Seat of Arkansas Agricultural, Mechanical, and Normal Col. (Negro; coed.; chartered 1873).

Pinehurst, winter resort (pop. 1,016), central N.C., SW of Raleigh. Golf courses and horse-training facilities.

Pinel, Philippe (fēlēp' pēnĕl'), 1745–1826, French physician. He advocated humane treatment of the insane, empirical study of mental disease. He stressed the role of the passions in mental disease, kept well-documented case histories for research.

Pinero, Sir Arthur Wing (pĭnēr'ō), 1855–1934, English dramatist. Wrote realistic "problem" plays such as *The Second Mrs. Tanqueray* (1893), *The Notorious Mrs. Ebbsmith* (1895), and *Mid-Channel* (1909) and the farce *Trelawny of the Wells* (1898).

Pines, Isle of, Span. *Isla de Pinos*, island (1,182 sq. mi.; pop. 9,812), off SW Cuba. Discovered by Columbus (1494), it was used as penal colony and rendezvous for buccaneers. Claimed by U.S. citizens but confirmed as belonging to Cuba (1925). Popular tourist resort. Chief products are tobacco, fruits, vegetables.

Pineville. 1 Town (pop. 3,890), S Ky., on Cumberland R. near Cumberland Gap. Resort, holds annual laurel festival. **2** Town (pop. 6,423), central La., on Red R. opposite Alexandria. Mfg. of stone monuments and wood products. U.S. Camp Beauregard and U.S. veterans' hospital near. **3** Town (pop. 1,373), S N.C., at S.C. line, S of Charlotte. J. K. Polk born near by.

ping pong: see TABLE TENNIS.

Pingyuan (pĭng'yüän'), province (18,000 sq. mi.; pop. 13,000,000), N central China; cap. Sinsiang. Formed 1949 from sections of Honan, Hopeh, and Shantung provs. Lies on level plain drained by Yellow, Tsin, and Wei rivers. Wheat, millet, and kaoliang are grown. Coal mines.

pink or **dianthus,** Old World annual and perennial plant (*Dianthus*) with spicily fragrant flowers. The grass pink (*Dianthus plumarius*) and maiden pink (*D. deltoides*) are popular species. See also CARNATION and SWEET WILLIAM.

Pinkerton, Allan, 1819–84, American detective, founder of the Pinkerton National Detective Agency, which solved train robberies, acted as a Union spy service in the Civil War, broke up the MOLLY MAGUIRES, and was active in the 1892 Homestead strike; its methods (particularly its use of labor spies) have been bitterly attacked by unions.

pinkeye: see CONJUNCTIVITIS.

Pinkie, battlefield E of Edinburgh, Scotland. Scene of a victory (1547) by English over larger Scottish force. The Scots, fearing that Princess Mary (later Mary Queen of Scots) would be forced to marry Edward VI, then sent her to France.

Pinnacles National Monument: see NATIONAL PARKS AND MONUMENTS (table).

Pinocchio: see COLLODI, CARLO.

pinochle (pē'nŭ"kŭl), card game played by two, three, or four players, with a deck of 48 cards. Types include auction (most popular), two-handed, and partnership pinochle. Probably originated in Europe in 19th cent.; later became very popular in the U.S.

piñon: see PINE.

Pinsk (pĭnsk, Rus. pēnsk), city (1931 pop. 31,913), W Belorussia, in Pripet Marshes. Varied mfg. Ceded to USSR by Poland 1945. Until World War II majority of inhabitants were Jews; they were virtually exterminated during German occupation.

Pinski, David (pĭn'skē), 1872–, Yiddish novelist and playwright. Among his successful plays are *The Treasure,* and *King David and His Wives.*

Pinturicchio (pēntoōrēk'kyō) or **Pintoricchio** (pēntō-) [Ital.,= little painter], c.1454–1513, Umbrian painter, influenced by Perugino. Real name was Bernardino di Betto. Known for frescoes depicting life of Pius II in cathedral library at Siena.

Pinza, Ezio (āts'yō pēn'tsä), 1892 or 1895–, Italian-American basso; with the Metropolitan Opera, New York, 1926–48. He has been especially successful in *Don Giovanni* and *Boris Godunov.* In 1949 he appeared in the musical comedy *South Pacific.*

Pinzón, Martín Alonso (märtēn' älōn'sō pēnthōn'), d. 1493, Spanish navigator. Commander of *Pinta* on Columbus's first voyage to New World (1492). Died soon after return to Spain. His younger brother, **Francisco Martín Pinzón** (fränthē'skō), fl. 1492, was master of *Pinta.* Youngest brother, **Vicente Yáñez Pinzón** (vēthän'tä yä'nyäth), fl. 1492–1509, commanded *Niña* on Columbus's expedition. Returning to New World (1500), he discovered mouth of Amazon R.; was made governor of Puerto Rico (1505); explored the coasts of Yucatan, Honduras, and Venezuela with Solís (1508–9).

Piombo, Sebastiano del: see SEBASTIANO DEL PIOMBO.

Piozzi, Madame: see THRALE, HESTER LYNCH.

pipal: see BO TREE.

pipe, tubular structure used to carry liquids or gases, as structural material, and for electrical wiring conduits. Pipe materials include metal, the most commonly used; fireclay, for drains; fiber, chiefly for chemicals; cement and concrete, for large water pipes. Cast iron is extensively used for gas and water mains. **Pipe lines** convey water, petroleum products, and natural gas over long distances from source to refinery or point of consumption. U.S. government financed construction (completed 1943) of "Big Inch" pipe line for carrying crude oil and "Little Big Inch" for carrying petroleum products from Texas to New York and Philadelphia areas.

pipe rolls, old records of crown revenue and expenditures of England. Dating from 1131, they are invaluable source of social history. Not completely replaced by modern accounting methods until 1833.

Pipe Spring National Monument: see NATIONAL PARKS AND MONUMENTS (table).

Pipestone, city (pop. 5,269), SW Minn., near S.Dak. line, in agr. area. Near by are pipestone quarries used by Indians, seen by Catlin 1836; made part of Pipestone Natl. Monument (115.6 acres) 1937.

pipestone, dull red clay stone, used by Indians in making ceremonial pipes, and found in Canada, the Dakotas, and Minn. Also called catlinite, after George Catlin, who lived many years among Indians.

Pippin, Frankish rulers: see PEPIN.

Piqua (pĭ'kwā), city (pop. 17,447), W Ohio, on Great Miami R. and N of Dayton; settled 1797 as Washington. Mfg. of fabrics and machinery.

piracy, robbery committed on high seas by force of arms, comparable to brigandage on land. Distinguished from PRIVATEERING in that pirate holds no commission; is not under national flag, and attacks vessels of all nations; he is highwayman of seas. Piracy flourished in Mediterranean until Great Britain, Netherlands, and U.S. wiped out Barbary pirates in 1815–16. English buccaneers of SPANISH MAIN pillaged Spanish American coast settlements and returned to England to share spoils and receive pardon. Piracy was destroyed in West Indies by David Porter in 1825. In long history of piracy are many famous names, such as Sir Francis Drake, Sir John Hawkins, and Henry Morgan. Other well-known pirates were Jean Laffite, Edward Teach (Blackbeard), and semi-mythical Capt. Kidd.

Piraeus (pīrē'ŭs), Gr. *Peiraieus* or *Piraieus,* city (pop. 184,802), E central Greece, on the Saronic Gulf; port of Athens and largest port of Greece. Built c.450 B.C., it was linked with Athens by the Long Walls, two parallel walls c.5 mi. long (built 461–456 B.C.; destroyed by Spartans 404 B.C., rebuilt 393 B.C.). After Sulla destroyed the arsenal and fortifications in 86 B.C., Piraeus sank into insignificance until the 19th cent. It was heavily bombed in World War II.

Pirandello, Luigi (lwē'jē pērändĕl'lō), 1867–1936, Italian dramatist. He wrote many short stories and novels, but is famous for his plays, among them *Six Characters in Search of an Author* (1921), *Right You Are if You Think So* (1917), and *As You Desire Me* (1930). Awarded the 1934 Nobel Prize in Literature.

Piranesi, Giovanni Battista (jōvän'nē bät-tē'stä pē"-ränä'zē), or **Giambattista Piranesi** (jäm"–), 1720–78, Italian engraver. Made numerous copperplates of buildings in Rome.

Pirate Coast, Arabia: see TRUCIAL OMAN.

Pirenne, Henri (ārē' pērĕn'), 1862–1935, Belgian historian. Chief works are *History of Belgium* (Eng. tr., 7 vols., 1899–1932), *Belgian Democracy* (Eng. tr., 1915), and *Medieval Cities* (Eng. tr., 1925).

Pisa (pē'sä), city (pop. 49,471), Tuscany, central Italy, on Arno R. and near Tyrrhenian Sea. By late 11th cent. Pisa was a powerful maritime republic, but its naval power was crushed by Genoa in 1284. Ghibelline Pisa defended its independence against Guelphic Florence until 1406. It was the seat of a school of sculpture (13th–14th cent.), founded by Nicola Pisano. Galileo, born here, was a student and teacher at the university (founded 14th cent.). Many of Pisa's architectural treasures suffered in World War II, but the old cathedral, the baptistery, and the famous leaning tower (180 ft. high; 14 ft. out of perpendicular) were only slightly damaged.

Pisa, Council of, 1409, council of the Roman Catholic Church, summoned to end the Great SCHISM. Supporters of both GREGORY XII and Benedict XIII (Pedro de LUNA) agreed to depose both men as heretical and schismatic. They chose a new pope with the result that there were three claimants, not two. At Pisa the theory that councils are superior to the pope in the Church was put forward. This was to appear again at the Councils of Constance and Basel.

Pisan, Christine de (krēstēn' dù pēzä'), b. 1364, d. between 1429 and 1431, French poet, b. Italy. One of the first professional woman writers, she is esteemed for her lyric poems, concerned mostly with love and chivalry.

Pisanello (pēzänĕl'lō), c.1395–1455?, Italian artist of the early Renaissance. Also called Vittore Pisano, but real name was Antonio Pisano. His medals are valued as historic memorials of the period. Famed also for animal drawings. Most of his paintings have perished.

Pisano, Andrea (ändrā'ä pēzä'nō), c.1270–c.1348, Italian sculptor, also called Andrea da Pontedera. Considered the founder of Florentine school of sculpture. Strongly influenced by Giotto, whom he succeeded as director of the work on Florence cathedral; made first bronze doors (depicting life of John the Baptist) for the baptistery (1336). Also directed work on façade of Orvieto cathedral.

Pisano, Nicola (nēkô'lä), b. c.1220, d. between 1278 and 1287, Italian sculptor and architect, founder of new school of sculpture which combined Gothic and classic elements. Made marble pulpit for Pisa baptistery c.1260. In creating pulpit for Siena cathedral and great fountain for Perugia he was assisted by his son, **Giovanni Pisano,** b. 1245, d. after 1314. Giovanni also carved a pulpit for Sant' Andrea, Pistoia, his masterpiece, and designed cloisters of the Pisa *camposanto* and façade of Siena cathedral.

Pisano, Vittore: see PISANELLO.

Piscataqua, river: see SALMON FALLS RIVER.

Pisces (pī'sēz) [Latin,= fishes], 12th sign of ZODIAC.

Pisgah (pĭz'gù), mountain ridge, N central Jordan, E of N end of Dead Sea. Its summit identified with biblical Mt. NEBO.

Pisistratus (pīsĭs'trùtùs), c.605–527 B.C., tyrant of Athens. Apparently gained popularity by liberal laws. He pushed the hegemony of Athens over Ionian cities. Twice exiled by his rivals, the Alcmaeonidae and the aristocracy, he nevertheless left a strong state to his sons, Hippias and Hipparchus. Also Peisistratus.

Piso (pī'sō), name of a Roman family. **Lucius Calpurnius Piso Caesoninus,** d. after 43 B.C., as consul helped banish Cicero (58 B.C.). Cicero attacked him bitterly. His daughter married Julius Caesar. **Caius Calpurnius Piso,** d. A.D. 65, a patron of literature, was discovered in a plot against Nero and killed himself.

Pissarro, Camille (kämē'yù pēsärō'), 1830–1903, French impressionist painter. The Barbizon school influenced his early work; later he allied himself with the impressionists, painting chiefly street scenes of Paris and London. Achieved light effects by use of broken color.

pistachio (pĭstä'shēō), tree (*Pistacia vera*), native to the Orient and Mediterranean region, and its greenish seeds. The seeds, known as pistachio nuts, are eaten salted or used in confections. Other species include the TEREBINTH; the Chinese pistachio (*P. chinensis*), grown in Fla. and Calif. for ornament; and *P. lentiscus,* a source of mastic and an oil.

Pistoia (pēstô'yä), city (pop. 29,532), Tuscany, central Italy, at foot of the Appennines. A free commune in 12th and 13th cent., it came under Florentine rule in 14th cent. The Ospedale del Ceppo has a frieze by Giovanni della Robbia. There are several fine churches. Pistols, first made here (16th cent.), were named after Pistoia.

pistol, small firearm designed for use with one hand. First manufactured in the 16th cent. in Pistoia, Italy (hence the name pistol). The early pistol (short-barreled and with heavy butts) was superseded by the revolver (carrying ammunition in a revolving drum) and the automatic pistol (with ammunition in a clip inside the stock).

Piston, Walter, 1894–, American composer; pupil of Nadia Boulanger. Among his works are three symphonies, concertos, chamber music, the *Suite for Orchestra,* and the ballet, *The Incredible Flutist.*

Pitcairn, borough (pop. 5,857), SW Pa., E suburb of Pittsburgh. Railroad shops and brickworks.

Pitcairn Island, volcanic island (2 sq. mi.; pop. 126), S Pacific, belonging to Great Britain. Discovered 1767 by Adm. Philip Carteret. Natives are descendants of mutineers of the BOUNTY and their Tahitian wives who settled here 1790. Colony was discovered 1808 by Americans. Overpopulation caused removal of part of colony to NORFOLK ISLAND.

pitch, in music, the position of a TONE in the musical scale, determined by the number of vibrations per second of the sound and today designated by a letter name. Present-day standard of pitch is an A (the A above middle C) of 440 vibrations per second (in the U.S.) or of 435 vibrations per second (in Europe). Other tones vibrate less frequently if below A, more frequently if above. The upper note of an octave has twice as many vibrations per second as the lower note.

pitch: see TAR AND PITCH.

pitchblende (pĭch'blĕnd"), dark, lustrous, amorphous mineral, a source of radium, uranium, polonium, and plutonium. Uranium yield is 50–80%. Occurs in small quantities throughout the world; Canadian Great Lakes, Belgian Congo, and Czechoslovakia are major sources.

Pitcher, Molly, c.1754–1832, American Revolutionary heroine; real name was Mary Ludwig Hays or Heis. Carried water for soldiers at battle of Monmouth (1778), thus earning sobriquet.

pitcher plant, insectivorous flowering plant with leaves adapted for trapping insects. Each leaf forms a "pitcher" that usually holds liquid. The common pitcher plant of North America is *Sarracenia pur-*

purea, native to bogs from Labrador to Fla. and Iowa. The California pitcher plant (*Darlingtonia californica*) resembles *Sarracenia.* Oriental pitcher plants (*Nepenthes*) are sometimes cultivated. See *ill.,* p. 783.

Pitch Lake: see TRINIDAD AND TOBAGO.

pith, plant tissue, chiefly a region of food storage, composed of relatively large cells loosely fitted together. Present in the center of the stem of certain herbaceous and woody plants (becoming much reduced in trees as woody tissue grows). In Orient rice paper has been made from pith of certain shrubs.

Pithecanthropus: see MAN, PRIMITIVE.

Pitman, Sir Isaac, 1813–97, English deviser of a shorthand system based on phonetic rather than orthographic principles (in *Stenographic Soundhand,* 1837); this became one of most-used systems in the world. His brother, **Benn Pitman,** 1822–1910, and Stephen P. Andrews introduced Pitman system to U.S.

Pitman, borough (pop. 6,960), SW N.J., S of Camden; settled 1871 as site of Methodist camp meetings.

Pitt, William, 1st **earl of Chatham** (chă′tùm), 1708–78, English statesman. His criticism of War of the Austrian Succession led to downfall (1742) of Robert Walpole. By denouncing government policy in Seven Years War he became head of coalition government in 1757. Shrewd policy led to defeat of French in India and Canada. Broke with Whigs over American colonies. Urged conciliation, then any settlement short of independence. Forced to retire by mental disorder (1768). Known as the Great Commoner for his insistence on constitutional rights. His second son, **William Pitt,** 1759–1806, was prime minister (1783–1801) under George III. Estab. the custom of general elections. A liberal Tory, his policies included new taxes to cut national debt, reforms in India and Canada, and parliamentary reform. French Revolutionary and Napoleonic Wars doomed these policies. Financial support of allies led to monetary crisis. Military coalitions against France failed on land. Using bribery to achieve union with Ireland, he resigned on king's veto of CATHOLIC EMANCIPATION. Recalled 1804, but defeat at Austerlitz was the death blow to his political career.

Pitt, Fort: see DUQUESNE, FORT.

Pittsburg. 1 Industrial city (pop. 12,763), W Calif., at junction of Sacramento and San Joaquin rivers. Steelworks and canneries (fish, fruit). **2** City (pop. 19,341), SE Kansas, near Mo. line; founded 1872 in mining area. Mfg. of coal by-products and food products.

Pittsburgh, city (pop. 676,806), SW Pa., at point where Allegheny and Monongahela rivers join to form the Ohio. One of main U.S. industrial centers, city is in rich coal, gas, and oil region. Large part of nation's iron and steel produced here. Fine port and rail facilities ship diverse goods, including coke, aluminum, and petroleum products, tin plate, and electrical equipment. A 17th-cent. fur-trading post supplanted an Indian village here, and itself gave way to French Fort DUQUESNE in 1754. Taken by British and renamed Fort Pitt. Village around fort settled 1755. City grew with development of coal and iron resources and because of its position on E–W transportation arteries. Here are Carnegie Mus.; Carnegie Library; Buhl Planetarium; Duquesne Univ. (R.C.; coed.; 1878); an atomic-energy research laboratory; CARNEGIE INSTITUTE OF TECHNOLOGY. The **University of Pittsburgh** (nonsectarian, private, coed.; opened 1787) includes Mellon Inst. of Industrial Research.

Pittsburg Landing: see SHILOH, BATTLE OF.

Pittsfield, city (pop. 53,348), W Mass., on branches of Housatonic R.; settled 1752. Metropolis of the Berkshires. Mfg. of electrical machinery, woolen goods, paper, metal products. "Arrowhead" was Herman Melville's home, 1850–63.

Pittston, city (pop. 15,012), NE Pa., on Susquehanna R. and NE of Wilkes-Barre; settled 1770. Mfg. of textile and metal products; coal mining.

pituitary gland (pĭtū′ĭtĕ″rē), small, round three-lobed organ attached to base of brain; it is a ductless, or endocrine, gland. Anterior lobe produces hormones regulating growth, development of sexual characteristics, and lactation. Posterior lobe hormones affect blood pressure, kidney function, and certain muscles.

Pius II (pī′ŭs), 1405–64, pope (1458–64), a Sienese named Enea Silvio de' Piccolomini. At the Council of Basel he supported the theory that the council should be superior to the pope in the Church and was later at the court of Antipope Felix V (Amadeus VIII of Savoy). Piccolomini was a humanist and court poet and an official under Emperor Frederick III before he was converted to a holy life (1445), became a priest (1446), bishop of Trieste (1447), bishop of Siena (1450), and a cardinal (1456). As pope he tried in vain to unite Europe against the Turks, struggled with Louis XI of France, and continued opposition to George of Podebrad. Wrote many works, one autobiographical.

Pius IV, 1499–1565, pope (1559–65), a Milanese named Giovan Angelo de' Medici. He convened the last session of the Council of TRENT. His chief aid was his nephew, St. Charles Borromeo.

Pius V, Saint, 1504–72, pope (1566–72), an Italian named Michele Ghislieri, a Dominican. He put the decrees of the Council of Trent into vigorous effect, took a firm tone in declaring Elizabeth I of England deposed, and by uniting with Spain and Venice against the Turks helped bring about Don John of Austria's victory at Lepanto. Pius was a leading figure of the Catholic Reform. Feast: May 5.

Pius VI, 1717–99, pope (1775–99), an Italian named G. Angelo Braschi. Early in his reign he tried in vain to stop the efforts of Emperor Joseph II to "reform" the Church by suppressing monasteries and taking over control. Later even more serious trouble came with the French Revolution. Pius forbade the French clergy (1791) to take oath under the new Civil Constitution of the clergy. Later he sided with the anti-French coalition, and Napoleon attacked the Papal States. Pius was forced (1797) to cede Avignon, Venaissin, Ferrara, Bologna, and the Romagna to the French and pay them a large indemnity. After a French general was murdered in Rome, the French set up a republic (1798) and took Pius to Siena, then to Turin. He died at Valence.

Pius VII, 1740–1823, pope (1800–1823), an Italian named Barnaba Chiaramonti. Succeeded Pius VI in the midst of trouble with the French. He and Napoleon signed the CONCORDAT OF 1801, but when Napoleon's Organic Articles virtually rescinded much of it Pius would not accept them. Napoleon made Pius come to Paris to consecrate him as emperor; the French took Rome (1808) and the Papal States (1809); when Pius excommunicated the enemies of the Holy See, he was taken prisoner, moved to Fontainebleau, and forced to sign a new concordat. This humiliation Pius bore with stolid dignity. As Napoleon's star fell, Pius disavowed the enforced contract, recovered the Papal States, and set about restoring the Church. He reconstituted the Society of Jesus. His secretary was the able Ercole Consalvi, who regained the Papal States at the Congress of Vienna.

Pius IX, 1792–1878, pope (1846–78), an Italian named Giovanni M. Mastai Ferretti. In 1848 revolutionary rioting drove him from Rome to Gaeta and from a liberal policy in the Papal States to ruling, after his return to Rome, with the support of Napoleon III's soldiers. He opposed the Italian nationalists. In 1870, when the Italians entered Rome, Pius retired to the Vatican and refused to treat with the new kingdom, thus creating the Roman Question (not settled until the Lateran Treaty). He also had difficulties in Germany in the KULTURKAMPF. His encyclical *Quanta Cura* (1864) denounced errors of modernism. He declared the dogma of the Immaculate Conception of the Virgin an article of faith (1854) and summoned the Vatican Council, which enunciated the doctrine of papal infallibility. Sometimes called in English by Italian form, *Pio Nono*.

Pius X, 1835–1914, pope (1903–14), an Italian named Giuseppe Sarto. He had an invigorating effect upon the Church, and his firm resistance to the anticlerical laws on church property and education in France (1904) was supported by all French Catholics. In the decree *Lamentabili* and the encyclical *Pascendi* (1907) he opposed modernism in the Church. He was notable for his love of the common people.

Pius XI, 1857–1939, pope (1922–39), an Italian named Achille Ratti. Before becoming pope he was legate and then nuncio to Poland and archbishop of Milan. As pope he sought friendly relations with all powers. The Lateran Treaty (1929) ended the quarrel between Church and state in Italy, but Pius expressed his strong disapproval of Fascist methods in a letter *Non abbiamo bisogno* (1931). A concordat with Germany (1933) was flouted by the Nazis; the pope in a powerful encyclical (*Mit brennender Sorge,* 1937) denounced the tenets of National Socialism. He also issued the statement *On Atheistic Communism.* Pius opposed nationalism, racism, and anti-Semitism. His criticism of laissez-faire capitalism in the encyclical *Quadragesimo anno* (1931; forty years after Leo XIII's plea on the subject) urged social reform. He also stressed the part to be played by lay people in all things religious and the recognition of the rights of Eastern Catholics and of native cultures. His chief assistants were the cardinals Pietro Gasparri and Eugenio Pacelli (Pius XII).

Pius XII, 1876–, pope (1939–), an Italian named Eugenio Pacelli. As a cardinal under Pius XI, he had much experience in diplomatic affairs, and international questions occupied much of his pontificate. Before, during, and after World War II he preached the blessings of peace and tried to alleviate the sufferings of prisoners and, later, of displaced persons. He early opposed the use of atomic energy in warfare and urged international accord. He continued Pius XI's opposition to laissez-faire capitalism. The contest between Catholicism and atheistic Communism became a burning issue in Italian politics, and the pope asked Catholics to oppose Communism but refused to approve a "crusade." In 1946 the pope created some 32 new cardinals from 22 nations; in Jan., 1953, he elevated 24 more cardinals, bringing the college to its maximum of 70. He proclaimed 1950 a Holy Year, and in that year enunciated the doctrine of the Assumption of the Virgin Mary as a Catholic dogma.

Piute Indians: see PAIUTE INDIANS.

Pi y Margall, Francisco (fränthē'skō pē' ē märgäl'), 1824–1901, Spanish liberal statesman, journalist, and author. Was president of first Spanish republic (1873). As deputy in the Cortes after Bourbon restoration he advocated federalism.

Pizarro, Francisco (fränthē'skō pēthä'rō), c.1476–1541, Spanish conquistador, conqueror of Peru, b. Trujillo, Spain. Accompanied Ojeda to Colombia (1510) and Balboa in discovery of Pacific. Hearing of wealth of the Inca, Pizarro formed partnership with Almagro and Fernando de Luque (a priest who secured funds) and made several expeditions S. In 1532 he landed at Tumbes and ascended Andes to Cajamarca where he met the Inca, ATAHUALPA, and professing friendship at first, seized and killed him. With conquest of Peru assured, he founded new settlements (among them, Lima) and allotted lands and Indians to his followers. He sent Almagro, whom he had cheated several times, to conquer Chile. When Almagro returned empty-handed, Pizarro had him put to death. By alienating Almagro's followers, he paved way for his own assassination (1541). His brother, **Gonzalo Pizarro** (gônthä'lō), c.1506–1548, assisted in conquest of Peru. Commanded disastrous expedition down Napo. On his return, he learned of Francisco's assassination and offered to help the crown's representative but was refused. Led revolt against viceroy when New Laws to protect Indians were enforced. When the laws were revoked, his followers disbanded and he was beheaded. Another brother, **Juan Pizarro** (hwän), d. 1536, aided in conquest of Peru. Killed leading attack on Indian fortress, Sacsahuaman. A half brother, **Hernando Pizarro** (ērnän'dō), fl. 1530–60, also took part in conquest. He returned to Spain to advance fortunes of family at court (at expense of Almagro). Back in Peru, he fought against and defeated Almagro. In 1539, he returned to Spain to argue case of Pizarros but was imprisoned for 20 years.

Place, Francis, 1771–1854, English radical reformer. Active in the trade-union movement, he secured repeal (1824) of Combination Acts of 1799–1800. An early Chartist leader, he helped draft "People's Charter," the primary document of the Chartist movement.

placenta (plüsĕn'tü) or **afterbirth,** thick, disk-shaped mass connected with fetus by umbilical cord. Made up of tissue from mother and embryo. Permits mutual passage of components of blood, but blood itself does not mingle. Expelled after BIRTH.

Placentia Bay, Atlantic inlet, SE N.F., Canada, between Burin and Avalon peninsulas. Has been a naval base since 1622. In World War II U.S. estab. naval and air base at Argentia, on E shore.

placer mining: see MINING.

Placerville, city (pop. 3,749), N central Calif., ENE of Sacramento. Boomed with 1848 discovery of gold at near-by Coloma. Gateway to sierra resorts.

Placid, Lake, N.Y.: see LAKE PLACID village.

Placidia, Roman empress: see GALLA PLACIDIA.

plague (plāg), infectious epidemic disease carried by fleas infected through biting diseased animals, especially rats. Types include bubonic, marked by swellings (buboes) of lymph nodes; pneumonic, affecting lungs; and septicemic, infecting blood. Probably only pneumonic plague spreads from person to person; other types are eradicated by destroying infected animals. Causative agent of plague, a rod-shaped bacterium, discovered independently by Kitasato and Yersin during 1894 epidemic in China. Catastrophic European epidemic (Black Death) began in Constantinople 1347. Great London plague 1665.

plagues of Egypt, in Bible, 10 disasters brought upon Egypt by God through Moses because Pharaoh refused to free the Hebrews. Story told in Exodus 7.19–12.36. Among plagues: Egyptian waters turning into blood, swarms of insects, an epidemic of boils. Finally when death struck the firstborn of all of Egypt—both man and beast—from Pharaoh's palace to the rudest hut—the terrified ruler allowed the children of Israel to leave Egypt. The first Passover was observed on the night of the last plague.

plaice (plās), edible flatfish of N European seas.

plaid (plăd), long shawl or wrap of woolen cloth, usually with checks or tartan figures; part of the Highland costume. Tartan plaids have designs of colored crossbars; each Scottish clan has its distinctive pattern. Today, term sometimes signifies merely a pattern, as a plaid gingham.

Plain, the, in French history, the independent members of the National Convention during the French Revolution; occupied lower benches of the chamber. Though forming a majority, the Plain was a leaderless mass, easily dominated by the radical MOUNTAIN.

plain, large area of level or nearly level land. Plains have different names in different countries and climates, including tundra, steppe, prairie, pampas, savanna, llanos. Causes of formation include erosive action of water, glaciation, draining of a lake, deposition of sediment, and uplift of continental shelf or part of ocean floor.

plain chant: see PLAIN SONG.

Plainfield. 1 Town (pop. 8,071), E Conn., E of Willimantic; settled c.1690. Textiles and wood products. **2** City (pop. 42,366), NE N.J., near Watchung Mts., SW of Newark; settled 1684 by Friends. Mfg. of trucks, printing machinery, and concrete products.

Has Martine house (1717), Drake house (1746), and Friends' Meetinghouse (1788).

Plains of Abraham: see ABRAHAM, PLAINS OF.

plain song or **plain chant,** unison vocal music of the church, particularly the Roman Catholic Church. Texts of plain song are taken from the Mass, the Bible, and hymns. Term often used synonymously with Gregorian chant although, in a broad sense, the chant of the Orthodox Eastern Church, as well as that of the four main Western rites—Ambrosian, Roman, Mozarabic, and Gallician—is considered plain song. Gregorian chant underwent its greatest development and codification in the 7th cent. after the reign of Gregory I. In the Middle Ages polyphony largely supplanted plain song, and distortions crept into its performance in succeeding centuries. In the 19th cent. the Benedictine monks of Solesmes undertook years of research to restore Gregorian chant to its original form and to establish its proper rhythm. The tonality of Gregorian chant derives from eight modes (see MODE). Its rhythm stems from that inherent in the text, whether prose or verse.

Plainview, city (pop. 14,044), NW Texas, SW of Amarillo on Llano Estacado; founded 1886. Processes and ships grains, cotton, truck, and dairy products.

Plainville, town (pop. 9,994), central Conn., SW of Hartford. Metal goods.

Planck, Max (mäks plängk), 1858–1947, German physicist. Won 1918 Nobel Prize for evolving QUANTUM THEORY in thermodynamics.

plane, in geometry, flat surface of infinite extent but no thickness. It is defined as surface containing all of any straight line with two of its points on the surface. Any three points, a point and line, or two parallel lines determine a plane.

planet (plă′nĭt), opaque, spherical body, revolving counterclockwise about sun and shining by reflected sunlight. Term [Gr.,= wanderer] was given by Greeks to heavenly bodies that changed position relative to constellations; believing earth to be central heavenly body, they included moon and sun as well as planets visible to unaided eye. Copernicus showed sun to be center of SOLAR SYSTEM and moon a satellite of earth. KEPLER'S LAWS of planetary motion state that orbit of a planet is ellipse. Order of orbits of large planets outward from sun is MERCURY, VENUS, EARTH, MARS, JUPITER, SATURN, URANUS, NEPTUNE, PLUTO. Orbits of minor planets (see ASTEROID) lie between orbits of Mars and Jupiter. See ill., p. 927.

planetarium (plănŭtâ′rēŭm), name used both for projecting device or model portraying heavenly bodies and for theaterlike chamber with hemispherical ceiling upon which celestial phenomena are reproduced by optical projection. Juxtaposition and movements of lights reproduce panorama of sky. Notable chamber planetaria include Hayden Planetarium, New York city; Adler Planetarium, Chicago; Fels Planetarium (of Franklin Inst.), Philadelphia; Planetarium Theatre of Griffith Observatory, Los Angeles; Buhl Planetarium, Pittsburgh; Morehead Planetarium, Chapel Hill, N.C.; Montevideo has planetarium made in U.S.

planetesimal hypothesis (plănŭtĕ′sŭmŭl), theory of origin of planets developed after 1900 by T. C. Chamberlin and F. R. Moulton. Assumes that in distant past attractive force of star passing close to sun raised tidal bulges on sun's fluid mass. Materials ejected from bulges by sun's eruptions, affected by cross-pull of moving star, were set to moving in elliptical orbits. Small masses solidified into planetesimals; the larger of these swept in the smaller, forming planets. Theory accepted with modifications (e.g., TIDAL THEORY) by many scientists.

planetoid: see ASTEROID.

plane tree, deciduous tree of genus *Platanus* of temperate regions. The loose bark scales off causing a mottled appearance. The American plane (*Platanus occidentalis*), also known as sycamore and buttonwood (from the hard brown seed balls), has hard wood used for furniture. The London plane (*P. acerifolia*) is common in cities of E U.S.

plankton: see MARINE BIOLOGY.

plant, organism of vegetable kingdom as contrasted with one of animal kingdom. It may be as small and simple as one of the algae or complex as a tree. Plants perform PHOTOSYNTHESIS and are therefore ultimate source of food, and probably of most of oxygen, for all animals. For growth, plants need light, water, oxygen, carbon dioxide, varying amounts of nitrogen, phosphorus, potassium, sulphur, magnesium, calcium, and iron, and small amounts of other elements. Organic matter from plants of past ages is found in coal and probably in petroleum. Plants are divided into four large groups or phyla: spermatophytes or seed plants (conifers and flowering plants); the pteridophytes (ferns, club mosses, and horsetails); the bryophytes (mosses and liverworts); and the thallophytes (algae, fungi, lichens, and bacteria). Each group is further divided into classes, orders, families, genera, species, and varieties. BOTANY is scientific study of plants; ECOLOGY, study of their relation to environment; HORTICULTURE, their cultivation for food and decoration. See ill., p. 783.

Plantagenet, English royal house: see ANGEVIN.

plantain (plăn′tĭn), name for plants of genus *Plantago*, chiefly annual or perennial weeds. The mucilaginous seeds of an Old World species (*Plantago psyllium*) are imported as psyllium seed for use as a laxative. Tropical plantain is a BANANA.

Plant City, city (pop. 9,230), W central Fla., E of Tampa. Processes and ships fruit (esp. strawberries) and vegetables. Produces phosphates.

Plantin, Christophe (plătē′), 1514–89, leading printer of his time. He began (1555) printing in Antwerp, and his shop continued until 1867.

plant louse: see APHID.

Planudes Maximus (plŭnū′dēz), c.1260–c.1330, Greek scholar, also known as Maximus Planudes, a learned monk. His edition of the *Greek Anthology* was long standard.

Plaquemine (plă′kŭmĭn), town (pop. 5,747), SE La., near the Mississippi and S of Baton Rouge. Government locks connect Bayou Plaquemine and Intracoastal Waterway with the Mississippi. U.S. waterfowl refuge (1936) is near.

Plassey (plă′sē), village, S West Bengal, India. Clive's defeat of Nawab of Bengal here in 1757 helped establish British rule in NE India.

plaster of Paris: see GYPSUM.

plastics, name for organic derivatives of resin, cellulose, and protein that can be shaped by applying heat, pressure, or both. Celluloid was discovered c.1869, but plastics did not come into industrial use until after Bakelite was produced c.1907. Plastics are either thermoplastic, i.e., they soften again and again at high temperatures, or thermosetting, i.e., they become infusible, insoluble mass at high temperatures. According to substance from which they are derived plastics are further grouped as phenolic, urea, cellulose, acrylic, polystyrene, or vinyl. Almost any color or shape, and many combinations of hardness, durability, elasticity, and resistance to heat, cold, and acid can be obtained. Endless variety of plastic products has become available.

Plata, Río de la (rē′ō dä lä plä′tä), estuary, SE South America, formed by Paraná R. and Uruguay R. It is c.120 mi. wide at mouth on Atlantic, decreasing to c.20 mi. near head. Focal point of one of great river systems; its ports are Buenos Aires and Montevideo. Discovered by Juan Díaz de Solís (1516), explored by Magellan (1520) and by Sebastian Cabot (1526–29). First settlement on its banks was made at Buenos Aires by Pedro de Mendoza (1536).

Plataea (plŭtē′ŭ), anc. city, S Boeotia, Greece. For aid to Athens at Marathon (490 B.C.), it was destroyed by Xerxes I of Persia (480). In 479 B.C. the Greeks under Pausanias defeated the Persians here. In the

Peloponnesian War it was besieged (429–427), taken, and sacked by Spartans.

plateau (plă″tō′), level elevated portion of the earth's surface, with lower land on at least one side. Causes of formation include earth movements, great lava flows, erosion of adjacent lands.

plate mark: see HALLMARK.

Platen, August, Graf von (ou′gŏost gräf′ fŭn plä′tŭn), 1796–1835, German poet. His sonnets and odes express his tormented inner life in forms of classical perfection.

plating, application of coat of metal to metallic or other object for decoration, protection against corrosion, or increased wearing qualities. Art of gilding was practiced in early Egypt, Greece, and Rome; was much used during Renaissance and in Orient in all periods. Production of Sheffield plate and GALVANIZING of iron started in 18th cent. Plating by dipping, fusing, and soldering has been largely replaced by electrolysis methods. Term *electroplating* refers to electrolytic deposition of decorative or protective coats, and *electroforming* to formation of metallic objects by deposition of metal on temporary cores and to coating of electrically negative casts or molds called electrotypes, used for reproducing printers' type, engravings, medals.

platinite: see GUILLAUME, CHARLES ÉDOUARD.

platinum, grayish white metallic element (symbol = Pt; see also ELEMENT, table), malleable, ductile, and chemically inactive. Because of its resistance to corrosion, it is used in alloys for making laboratory utensils, electric wires and contact points, standard weights, and foils. It acts as a strong catalytic agent. It is used in dentistry, in photography, and in making jewelry. Most important alloys are those with iridium. In nature it is found chiefly alloyed with other metals.

Plato (plā′tō), 427?–347? B.C., Greek philosopher, one of the most influential thinkers of all time. Born of a good Athenian family, he studied under Socrates, who appears as chief speaker in all Plato's early writings. Plato traveled, stayed for a time in Syracuse, and on returning to Athens founded the ACADEMY, where he taught for the rest of his life (with two more brief visits to Syracuse). His philosophy is expressed in his dialogues. These, because of their beauty of style as well as their depth and range of thought, are outstanding masterpieces of world literature. Among them, besides the early defense of Socrates in the *Apology,* are *Charmides, Crito, Protagoras, Ion, Phaedrus, Gorgias, Meno, Theaetetus, Sophist, Parmenides, Symposium, Phaedo, Philebus, Republic* (perhaps the most celebrated; a demonstration of justice by picturing the ideal state), *Timaeus, Critias,* and *Laws.* They cover many subjects with richness and complexity. Primarily, however, Platonism, based on his teachings, stressed the importance of the idea, the general form, as the basis of true reality, permanent and sure behind all appearances. Knowledge is, when true, eternal and unchangeable. By the logical process of dialectic general ideas may be obtained through induction and may be classified. The supreme Idea is the Idea of the Good. He also suggested that there is a world soul and postulated a Demiurge, creator of the physical universe. He believed the rational soul to be immortal. Virtue consists in the harmony of the soul with the universe of Ideas, attained by man when reason governs his conduct. The cardinal virtues are justice, temperance, courage, and wisdom. The world of Platonism is a world of order, and all disorder is evil. Hence the best state is one ruled by a man who is a philosopher as well as a ruler; in it each class and each person has his assigned place. In the Platonic views of literature and art, the love of ideal beauty leads to the Idea of the Good, hence, anything that merely pictures the physical world is generally rejected. The Platonic teachings and the doctrines of Plato's pupil, Aristotle, are still much alive in the world of today.

Platt, Charles Adams, 1861–1933, American architect, inspired by Italian and Georgian traditions. Designed Freer Gall. of Art, Washington, D.C.

Platt, Orville Hitchcock, 1827–1905, U.S. Senator from Conn. (1879–1905). Framed **Platt Amendment.** A rider attached to Army Appropriations Bill of 1901, it stipulated conditions for American intervention in Cuban affairs. Incorporated in permanent treaty between U.S. and Cuba; revoked in 1934.

Platt, Thomas Collier, 1833–1910, American politician. U.S. Representative from N.Y. (1873–77); U.S. Senator (1881, 1897–1909). Powerful Republican politician; largely responsible for election of Theodore Roosevelt as governor of N.Y. (1898).

Platt Amendment: see PLATT, ORVILLE HITCHCOCK.

Plattdeutsch, Low German. See LANGUAGE (table).

Platte (plăt), river formed in S central Nebr. by junction of North Platte and South Platte rivers. Flows 310 mi. E to Missouri R. S of Omaha. Used for power and irrigation.

Plattensee, Hungary: see BALATON.

Platteville (plăt′vĭl), city (pop. 5,751), SW Wis., SW of Madison and on Little Platte R. Lead- and zinc-mining and dairying center. In near-by state park is restored Wis. territorial capitol (1836).

Platt National Park: see NATIONAL PARKS AND MONUMENTS (table).

Plattsburg, city (pop. 17,738), NE N.Y., on L. Champlain at mouth of Saranac R.; laid out 1784. Agr. and Adirondack-resort trade center, with paper mills. Military training camps, estab. in World War I, were closed in 1946 and the barracks converted for use by Champlain Col., a state emergency college for veterans and now part of State Univ. of New York. British invasion from Canada repulsed near by (Sept., 1814) by Thomas MACDONOUGH and Alexander Macomb.

platypus (plă′tŭpŭs), semiaquatic Australian egg-laying mammal (*Ornithorhynchus*), of order Monotremata (most primitive living mammals); also called duckbill. Considered a link between mammals and reptiles. It has thick, brown fur and the head, trunk, and tail are broad and flattened. The muzzle is shaped like a duck's bill, the feet are webbed, and the heel bears a spur connected with a poison gland. Adult male is c.2 ft. long.

Plauen (plou′ŭn), city (pop. 84,778), Saxony, E Germany, at NW foot of the Erzgebirge. Textile-mfg. center since 15th cent.; machinery, electrical appliances, leather. Ancient buildings include former castle of Teutonic Knights (1224).

Plautus (Titus Maccius Plautus) (plô′tŭs), c.254–184 B.C., Roman comic poet. His 21 surviving plays (adapted from Greek New Comedy), vigorous portrayals of middle- and lower-class life, are governed by a genius for situation and coarse humor and have characteristic stock figures. His influence on later European literature was enormous.

playing cards. There is evidence that playing cards were used in the ancient world, but they were probably first known to Europeans in 14th cent. Present-day variety of hearts, diamonds, clubs, and spades adopted in France in 16th cent. Modern deck consists of 52 cards.

Pleasantville. 1 Residential city (pop. 11,938), SE N.J., near Atlantic City. Farm products. **2** Residential village (pop. 4,861), SE N.Y., N of White Plains. Publishing.

plebiscite (plĕ′bĭsīt) [Latin,= popular decree], vote of the people on a question submitted to them, as in a referendum. Plebiscites may be taken on ordinary legislation, on national constitutions, and to decide the national allegiance of a population.

Plehve, Vyacheslav Konstantinovich (vyĕ″chĭsläf′ kŭnstŭntyĕ′nŭvĭch plyĕ′vyĭ), 1864–1904, Russian statesman. An ultrareactionary, he controlled police from 1881; was minister of interior 1902–4. Sought to divert popular discontent by Jewish pogroms, Russo-Japanese War. Assassinated.

Pleiad (plē′ăd) [from Pleiades], group of seven tragic poets of Alexandria under Ptolemy II, c.280 B.C. It gave its name to the **Pléiade** (plāyäd′), a group of French poets formed c.1553 for the purpose of purifying and enriching the French language and of creating a modern French literature equal to any other. The group cultivated classical forms and the sonnet. Led by RONSARD and DU BELLAY, it also included Remy Belleau, Antoine de Baïf, Estienne Jodelle, Pontus de Tyard, and Jean Daurat.

Pleiades (plē′ŭdēz, plī′–), in Greek mythology, seven daughters of Atlas and the nymph Pleione, attendants of Artemis. They became stars.

Pleistocene epoch (plī′stŭsēn), last epoch of the Cenozoic period of geologic time, notable as the great ice age and for being coextensive with human evolution. The ice came south at least four times, alternating with warmer periods of retreat. At their maximum, ice sheets covered Antarctica, large portions of Europe, North and South America, and parts of Asia. In America ice radiated from two main centers, the Keewatin, W and NW of Hudson Bay, and the Labrador, E of James Bay. Characteristic Pleistocene mammals included four types of elephants, true horses, sabertooth cats, giant wolves, sloths, armadillos, bisons, camels, pigs, and man. See also NEOLITHIC PERIOD; PALEOLITHIC PERIOD; GEOLOGY, table.

Plekhanov, Georgi Valentinovich (gĕôr′gē vŭlyĭntyĕ′nŭvĭch plyĭkhä′nŭf), 1857–1918, Russian revolutionist and Marxist social philosopher. Lived abroad 1882–1917; collaborated with Lenin until 1903. His view that Russia was not ripe for socialism before capitalism and industrialization had sufficiently progressed was adopted by the Mensheviks (see BOLSHEVISM AND MENSHEVISM). Also wrote on relationship between art and economics.

plesiosaurus (plē″sēŭsô′rŭs), marine reptile which existed in the Mesozoic era. It had a small head, long neck, broad body, and paddlelike legs, and in total length ranged from c.10–60 ft.

Plessisville (plĕ′sēvĭl), village (pop. 5,094), S Que., Canada, on Becancour R. and SW of Quebec.

pleurisy (plŏo′rĭsē), inflammation of pleurae (serous membranes), causing friction between pleurae covering lungs and those lining chest wall.

pleurisy root: see BUTTERFLY WEED.

Plevna (plĕv′nù), Bulgarian *Pleven*, city (pop. 38,997), N Bulgaria. Agr. center; mfg. of textiles, foodstuffs, machinery. Famous for its stubborn defense by Turks in Russo-Turkish War of 1877–78; its fall (1877) caused Turks to demand armistice.

Plimsoll, Samuel (plĭm′sùl), 1824–98, English reformer. Because he secured legislation to limit loading of ships, the compulsory load line is called Plimsoll line.

Pliny the Elder (Caius Plinius Secundus) (plī′nē), A.D. 23–79, Roman naturalist. His one remaining work is the encyclopedic *Natural History*, in 37 books, a prodigious collection of secondhand information. His nephew and ward was **Pliny the Younger** (Caius Plinius Caecilius Secundus), A.D. 62?–c.113, orator and statesman, who became consul in 100. His letters mirror Roman life.

Pliocene epoch (plī′ŭsēn), fifth epoch of the Cenozoic period of geologic time (fourth if Paleocene is not considered a separate epoch). Continental outlines of North America were much as at present. Close of the epoch was marked by uplift of Cascades, Rockies, Colorado plateau, and Appalachians; there was volcanic activity in W North America. Pliocene sea covered parts of NW Europe; Vesuvius, Etna, and other volcanoes were active; mountain building included folding and thrusting of Alps. Cool climate foreshadowed the ice age. See also GEOLOGY, table.

Plock (plôtsk), Pol. *Płock*, city (pop. 28,508), central Poland, on the Vistula. Agr. market center; metal and electrical industries. Was residence of medieval dukes of Masovia. Passed to Prussia 1793, to Russia 1815, to Poland 1921.

Ploesti (plô′yĕsht′), city (pop. 95,632), S central Rumania, in Walachia. Chief center of Rumanian petroleum industry and of the important Ploesti oil region.

Plombières (plôbyĕr′), spa in Vosges dept., E France. Scene of agreement (1858) between Napoleon III and Cavour calling for French military aid to kingdom of Sardinia in exchange for Nice and Savoy.

Plotinus (plōtī′nŭs), c.205–207, Egyptian philosopher, for a time at Alexandria, later at Rome; chief philosopher of NEOPLATONISM. His pupil Porphyry preserved his works.

plough: see PLOW.

Plovdiv (plôv′dĭf), city (pop. 125,440), central Bulgaria, on the Maritsa. Commercial center with varied mfg. Was founded as Philippopolis by Philip II of Macedon (341 B.C.); became cap. of Thrace under Roman rule and of Eastern RUMELIA in 19th cent.

plover (plŭ′vùr), small shore bird of Old and New Worlds, related to gulls. It has a plump body, short neck and tail, rather long legs, and long, pointed wings. Nonstop flights of over 2,000 mi. are often made by eastern American golden plover (on autumn migration from arctic and Canadian breeding grounds to Nova Scotia, thence over the Atlantic to South America) and by Pacific golden plover, which breeds in Alaska and Siberia and winters in Hawaiian Isls.

plow or **plough**, implement to turn or break up soil. Probably originated in Bronze Age as single piece of wood drawn by man. Later was drawn by draught animals and in 20th cent. often by tractor. The share or point was early made of iron or steel and moldboard was often faced with metal. John Deere and Leonard Andrus led in introducing steel moldboard (c.1837).

Plücker, Julius (yōō′lyōōs plü′kùr), 1801–68, German mathematician, physicist. Known for work in analytical geometry, magnetic properties, spectroscopy (first to suggest lines in spectrum of element were peculiar to that element); originated line geometry.

plum, low wide-spreading tree and its edible fruit, classed as a drupe, comprising many species of *Prunus*, widely grown in temperate zones. The plum has been grown from ancient times, perhaps longer than any fruit except the apple. Many plums, including the greengage and Damson types, as well as prune varieties, are derived from the common plum (*Prunus domestica*), probably of Asiatic origin but long cultivated in Europe and the U.S. Of more than 100 species, about 30 are native to North America, including the beach plum (*P. maritima*) found along the E coast. Double-flowered varieties, often with red or purple foliage, are used in landscaping, especially in Japan.

plumbing, portion of water supply and sewage inside buildings. Modern water-supply piping, usually of brass, is concealed within walls or partitions; exposed piping under fixtures usually is chromium-plated brass or nickel. Waste and soil piping must be impervious to gas and water and there should be no corners where filth may collect. Water-sealed trap usually separates fixture and piping.

Plumptre, Edward Hayes (plŭmp′trē), 1821–91, English clergyman and classical scholar; chaplain (1847–68) and professor (1853–81) at King's Col., London. A reviser (1869–74) of Old Testament, an author, and translator of Sophocles, Aeschylus, and Dante.

Plutarch (plōo′tärk), A.D. 46?–c.120, Greek biographer and essayist. His great work is the *Parallel Lives*, 46 paired Greek and Roman biographies and 4 single biographies. Using anecdotes, he vividly portrays character and its moral implications. His dignity, narrative charm, and ethical insight have made him widely read and loved. His *Moralia*, dialogues and essays on ethical, literary, and historical subjects, also have great charm.

Pluto [Gr.,= rich], in Greek religion, god of the underworld. Also called Hades and, by the Romans, Dis. He ruled HELL with his wife, PERSEPHONE.

Pluto, in astronomy, ninth major PLANET in order of distance from sun. Revolves about sun at mean dis-

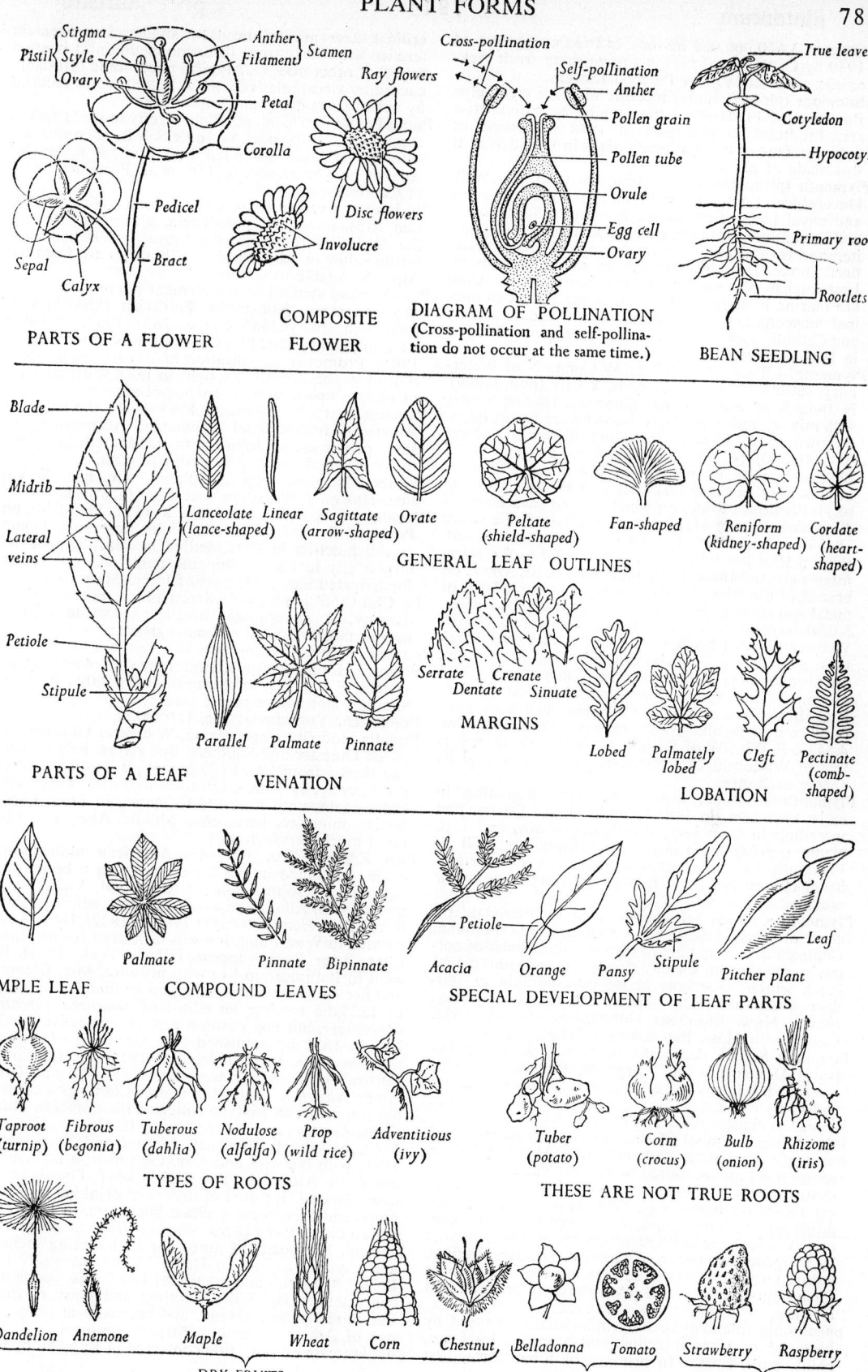

PARTS OF A FLOWER

Stigma, Pistil, Style, Ovary, Anther, Filament, Stamen, Petal, Corolla, Pedicel, Sepal, Calyx, Bract

COMPOSITE FLOWER

Ray flowers, Disc flowers, Involucre

DIAGRAM OF POLLINATION
(Cross-pollination and self-pollination do not occur at the same time.)

Cross-pollination, Self-pollination, Anther, Pollen grain, Pollen tube, Ovule, Egg cell, Ovary

BEAN SEEDLING

True leaves, Cotyledon, Hypocotyl, Primary root, Rootlets

PARTS OF A LEAF

Blade, Midrib, Lateral veins, Petiole, Stipule

GENERAL LEAF OUTLINES

Lanceolate (lance-shaped), Linear, Sagittate (arrow-shaped), Ovate, Peltate (shield-shaped), Fan-shaped, Reniform (kidney-shaped), Cordate (heart-shaped)

VENATION

Parallel, Palmate, Pinnate

MARGINS

Serrate, Dentate, Crenate, Sinuate

LOBATION

Lobed, Palmately lobed, Cleft, Pectinate (comb-shaped)

SIMPLE LEAF

COMPOUND LEAVES

Palmate, Pinnate, Bipinnate

SPECIAL DEVELOPMENT OF LEAF PARTS

Petiole, Acacia, Orange, Pansy, Stipule, Pitcher plant, Leaf

TYPES OF ROOTS

Taproot (turnip), Fibrous (begonia), Tuberous (dahlia), Nodulose (alfalfa), Prop (wild rice), Adventitious (ivy)

THESE ARE NOT TRUE ROOTS

Tuber (potato), Corm (crocus), Bulb (onion), Rhizome (iris)

DRY FRUITS

Dandelion, Anemone, Maple, Wheat, Corn, Chestnut

FLESHY FRUITS

Belladonna, Tomato

AGGREGATE FRUITS

Strawberry, Raspberry

TYPES OF FRUITS

tance of 3,670,000,000 mi. in c.248 years. Discovered 1930 by C. W. Tombaugh while working from reckonings made in 1914 by Percival Lowell.

plutonium (plōōtō′nēŭm), metallic element (symbol = Pu; see also ELEMENT, table) exhibiting RADIOACTIVITY. Produced in cyclotron in 1940 by fission of uranium. One of three atomic bombs in World War II was made of plutonium.

Plymouth (plĭ′mŭth), county borough (pop. 208,985), Devonshire, England, on Plymouth Sound. Seaport and naval base, it comprises Plymouth, Stonehouse, and Devonport. Has important trade in minerals, granite, marble, and fish. Was rendezvous of anti-armada fleet. Drake, Hawkins, and Ralegh set out from here. Last English port touched by *Mayflower*. Noteworthy are marine biological laboratories, aquarium, municipal museum and Athenaeum, several old churches, and Catholic cathedral. Sections of city were destroyed in 1941 bombing.

Plymouth. 1 Town (pop. 6,771), W Conn., N of Waterbury; settled 1728. Metal goods. 2 City (pop. 6,704), N Ind., S of South Bend. Shipping, trading center with mfg. of metal products. Near by are resort lakes. 3 Town (pop. 13,608), including Plymouth village (pop. 10,540), SE Mass., on Plymouth Bay and SE of Boston. Site of 1st permanent European settlement in New England (see PILGRIMS and PLYMOUTH COLONY). Plymouth Rock, on which legend says Pilgrims disembarked from *Mayflower* in 1620, is shrine (since 1880 on original site). Leyden St. was the 1st laid out. Pilgrim Hall has relics. *Natl. Monument to the Forefathers* erected 1889. 4 City (pop. 6,637), SE Mich., on branch of the River Rouge and W of Detroit. Mfg. of metal and rubber products. 5 Winter-resort town (pop. 3,039), central N.H., S of Franconia Notch. Daniel Webster pleaded his first case here. Nathaniel Hawthorne died here. 6 Borough (pop. 13,021), NE Pa., on Susquehanna R. and SW of Wilkes-Barre. Coal mining. 7 Town (pop. 348), S central Vt., SE of Rutland. Birthplace of Calvin Coolidge, who took oath of office near by and whose grave is here. 8 City (pop. 4,543), E Wis., W of Sheboygan. Cheese center, it is seat of Wisconsin Cheesemakers' Association and its cheese exchange.

Plymouth Brethren, evangelical sect originating in early 19th cent. in Ireland under J. N. Darby, and spreading to Continent, British dominions, and U.S. Name derived from association formed c.1830 at Plymouth, England. Sect was reaction against formality of church practices; it has no set organization or ordained ministers.

Plymouth Colony, settlement made by PILGRIMS on coast of Mass. (1620), after sailing in MAYFLOWER. Compact drawn up aboard ship remained basis of colony's government. Colony slowly expanded after first harsh winter, especially under governorship of William BRADFORD. Developed into quasi-theocracy. Joined NEW ENGLAND CONFEDERATION in 1643. United with Mass. Bay colony in 1691.

Plymouth Sound, deep inlet of English Channel, between Devonshire and Cornwall, England. Famous roadstead, it forms bay c.3 mi. broad. Receives Tamar and Plym rivers.

Plzen, Czechoslovakia: see PILSEN.

Pm, chemical symbol of element PROMETHIUM.

pneumatic appliances and tools (nōōmă′tĭk, nū–) use compressed air as source of power. Pneumatic tools include percussion tools, which employ a piston striking successive blows, e.g., pneumatic hammers, rock drills; and reciprocating-motor-driven tools, in which tool is held by spindle revolved by gearing actuated by reciprocating piston, e.g., drills, grinders, buffers, hoists. Other pneumatic devices are air lifts, chucks for holding work or tool, blowguns, air brushes, and air guns.

pneumonia (nūmō′nyŭ), lung inflammation caused by bacterial or virus infection and attended by fever, chills, pain, cough. In primary or lobar form, first critical days are followed by sudden improvement (crisis). Secondary form (bronchopneumonia) is often sequel of other disease. Atypical pneumonia (probably caused by virus) relatively mild. Fatalities are reduced by use of sulfa drugs and antibiotics.

Pnom Penh (nŏm″pĕn′, pŭnōōm″–), city (pop. 110,639), cap. of Cambodia; port on Tonle Sap R. at confluence with the Mekong. Founded 14th cent., it succeeded Angkor as Khmer cap. in 15th cent. Permanent cap. of Cambodia since 1867.

Po, longest river of Italy, 405 mi. long, rising in Cottian Alps, flowing E past Turin, and emptying into the Adriatic through a delta. Forms widest and most fertile valley in Italy. Its chief tributaries are from the Alps. Navigable to Casale.

Po, chemical symbol of the element POLONIUM.

Pobyedonostzev, Konstantin Petrovich (kŭnstŭntyēn′ pĕtrō′vĭch pŭbyĕdŭnôs′tsyĭf), 1827–1907, Russian statesman and jurist. Procurator of holy synod (1880–1905). Promoted Russification of minorities, persecution of nonconformists; sought to raise spiritual level of clergy; opposed Western liberalism.

Pocahontas (pōkŭhŏn′tŭs), c.1595–1617, daughter of American Indian chief Powhatan. Authenticity of story of her saving John Smith is disputed. Marriage to John ROLFE estab. peace with English.

Pocahontas, town (pop. 2,410), SW Va., near W.Va. line. Has only exhibition coal mine in world.

Pocatello (pōkŭtĕ′lō), city (pop. 26,131), SE Idaho, on Portneuf R., near American Falls Reservoir. Begun as rail junction in 1882, settled in 1887–88. Second largest city in Idaho. Shipping point and rail center for irrigated agr. area. Seat of Idaho State Col.

Po Chü-i (bô′ jōō-ē′), 772–846, Chinese poet of T'ang dynasty. A government official, he wrote c.3,000 poems, mostly topical and quite short.

pocket gopher: see GOPHER.

Pocono Mountains (pō′kŭnō), range of Appalachian system, E Pa., NW of Stroudsburg; c.2,000 ft. high. Summer and winter resort area.

Podgorica, Yugoslavia: see TITOGRAD.

Podolia (pōdō′lyŭ), agr. region, W central Ukraine, between Dniester and Southern Bug rivers. Part of Kievan Russia from 10th to 13th cent., it was later ruled, successively, by Tatars, Lithuanians, Poles, Turks, and Poles again, until it passed to Russia in 1793. Large Jewish minority, here since Middle Ages, has suffered much persecution.

Poe, Edgar Allan, 1809–49, American author and critic. Orphaned in 1812, he was given a home and educated by John Allan, of Richmond, Va. After a quarrel with Allan, Poe went to Boston, where he published *Tamerlane and Other Poems* (1827). He was appointed to West Point, but was dismissed for breaking rules. After *Poems* appeared (New York, 1831), he went to Baltimore to live with his aunt, Mrs. Clemm, and her daughter Virginia, whom he married in 1836. In 1835 he became an editor of *Southern Literary Messenger,* but lost position through excessive drinking. In 1838 he published *The Narrative of Arthur Gordon Pym.* In Philadelphia (1838–44), he edited Burton's *Gentleman's Magazine* (1839–40) and *Graham's Magazine* (1841–42), winning fame as a caustic but just critic. In 1840 he collected his stories in *Tales of the Grotesque and Arabesque.* In New York after 1844, he edited *Broadway Journal* and lived, after 1846, with his wife and Mrs. Clemm in a cottage at Fordham. After Mrs. Poe died in 1847, Poe returned to Richmond. He died of excessive drinking in Baltimore, ending a career brilliant but tragic. In 1845 *The Raven and Other Poems* won him fame at home and abroad. His poetry is noted for its haunting melody and rhythm, as in "To Helen," "The Raven," "The Bells," "Israfel," and "Annabel Lee." His stories are characterized by skillful plotting and unity of tone. Poe is recognized abroad, and belatedly at home, as one of America's greatest literary geniuses.

poet laureate (lô′rēĭt), title conferred in England by the king on a poet, whose duty it becomes to write commemorative odes and verse. Ben Jonson held an analogous position in 1617, but Dryden first had the actual title in 1670. His successors have included Southey, Wordsworth, Tennyson, Bridges, and Masefield.

Poggio Bracciolini, Gian Francesco (jän' fränchä'skō pŏd'jō brät"chōlē'nē), 1380–1459, Italian humanist. Best known for his tales *Facetiae* (1474) and for scholarly quarrels.

pogrom (pŏ'grŭm, pōgrŏm'), Russian word, originally connoting a riot, but later meaning attacks on Jews in Russia. The tsarist regime sought to divert upon the Jews the revolutionary anger of the masses. Pogroms were especially serious in 1881–82 and 1903–21.

Pohai, China: see CHIHLI, GULF OF.

poi, fermented, sticky food paste of the Pacific islands, made by pounding the roasted roots of the taro.

Poincaré, Jules Henri (zhül ārē' pwĕkärä'), 1854–1912, French mathematician, physicist. One of greatest mathematicians of his age, he enlarged field of mathematical physics by research on theory of functions (esp. automorphic, Fuchsian, Abelian functions) and did notable work on differential equations and astronomical theory of orbits.

Poincaré, Raymond (rāmō'), 1860–1934, French statesman; cousin of Jules Poincaré. He was president of the republic 1913–20; premier 1912, 1922–24, 1926–29. A conservative and ardent nationalist, he called for harsh punishment of Germany after World War I; ordered occupation of the RUHR in 1923; secured stabilization of currency in 1928.

poinciana, royal (poinsēā'nù, –ā'nù), name for a tropical leguminous tree (*Delonix regia*) native to Madagascar, and known also as peacock flower. It is widely grown in many warm regions for its vivid clusters of scarlet flowers. The fruits are long pods (6 in.–c.2 ft.). There is also a genus *Poinciana*, chiefly of tropical America, a shrub or small tree with bright orange or yellow flowers.

poinsettia (poinsĕt'ù, –sĕt'ēù), ornamental shrub (*Euphorbia pulcherrima*), native to tropical America. It has small true flowers in the center of a rosette of red bracts. It is much used as a pot plant especially for Christmas decoration.

Point Barrow, northernmost point of Alaska, on Arctic Ocean. Discovered 1826 by F. W. Beechey. Prominent in arctic exploration and aviation. Naval station estab. 1944; navigation open 2–3 months a year. Barrow village in SW, with weather station, airfield, school, hospital, and monument to Will Rogers and Wiley Post, killed in airplane crash here (1935).

Pointe aux Trembles (pwĕtōträ'blù), residential town (pop. 8,241), S Que., Canada, on St. Lawrence R. and NNE of Montreal.

Pointe Claire (point klâr', Fr., pwĕt klĕr'), residential town (pop. 8,753), S Que., Canada, on S shore of Montreal Isl., SW suburb of Montreal.

pointer: see HUNTING DOGS.

Point Grey, W suburb of Vancouver, SW B.C., Canada. Site of the Univ. of British Columbia.

Point Judith, R.I.: see NARRAGANSETT.

Point Pleasant. 1 Atlantic resort borough (pop. 4,009), E N.J., S of Asbury Park; settled 1850. **2** City (pop. 4,596), W W.Va., on Ohio R. at mouth of Kanawha R. In battle of Point Pleasant (1774) frontiersmen defeated Indians.

Point Roberts, summer resort, NW Wash., on Strait of Georgia, at tip of peninsula extending S from British Columbia and separated from Wash. mainland by Boundary Bay. Salmon fishing. Reachable by land only from Canada.

Poiré, Emmanuel: see CARAN D'ACHE.

poison, agent which may produce chemically an injurious or deadly effect when introduced into organism in sufficient quantity. Poisons are classed as irritant, corrosive, or systemic. Call doctor when poisoning is suspected. If poison has been swallowed, several glasses of water should usually be given immediately

to dilute poison. Avoid use of emetics for corrosive poisons. Treat patient for shock if necessary. Give artificial respiration if breathing fails and for gas poisoning. See also CARBON MONOXIDE; FOOD POISONING; LEAD POISONING; POISON IVY; SNAKE BITE.

Poison Affair, scandal involving various prominent persons at the court of Louis XIV, beginning with the trial and execution (1676) of the Marquise de Brinvilliers, who had confessed to poisoning her father and brother. Her trial attracted attention to other "mysterious" deaths. Parisian society had been indulging in a fad for séances, fortunetelling, and love potions. When the quack practitioners (some may also have sold poisons) were arrested, they revealed the names of high-ranking clients. A celebrated case was that of La Voisin (or Catherine Monvoisin), midwife and fortuneteller, whose clientèle included Mme de Montespan, two nieces of Cardinal Mazarin, Marshal Luxembourg, and Racine. No formal charges were made nor was any evidence found against any of these, but La Voisin, after a sensational trial, was burned as a sorceress (1680). A special court, the *chambre ardente* [burning court] was estab. to judge poison and witchcraft cases; the poison epidemic subsided. Although indulging in less hysteria and judicial irregularities, the Affair was symptomatic of witchcraft trials then prevalent in Europe and New England.

poison gas, name for substances used in warfare because of poisonous or corrosive nature. Some are gases at ordinary temperatures but commonly they are liquids or solids that vaporize. CHLORINE was first used by Germans; difficulties of use led to development of others. Phosgene was used in shells; like chlorine, it affects lungs. MUSTARD GAS and lewisite attack skin; TEAR GAS affects eyes. See also CHEMICAL WARFARE.

poison ivy, native woody vine or shrub (*Rhus radicans, R. toxicodendron,* or *Toxicodendron radicans*) and the skin irritation it causes. The flowers are small, greenish clusters and the fruits are berrylike. The leaves, composed of three leaflets, may have entire or lobed margins. Plants with wavy-margined leaves are often called poison oak. The poison toxicodendrol, which causes itching and blistering, is present in all plant parts, and the irritation may result from touching the plant itself or from contact with clothes, tools, animals, smoke, etc., contaminated by the poison. Washing with an alkaline, nonoily soap after exposure may help prevent the skin irritation.

Poisson, Siméon Denis (sēmäō' dùnē' pwäsō'), 1781–1840, French mathematician and physicist. Known for work in many fields, especially definite integrals, but his chief interest was in applications of mathematics to physics (esp. electrostatics and magnetism).

Poitiers, Diane de: see DIANE DE POITIERS.

Poitiers (pwätyā'), city (pop. 41,279), cap. of Vienne dept., W France; historic cap. of POITOU. Dating from pre-Roman times, it was an early episcopal see and a residence of the Visigothic kings (until its capture by Clovis I, 507). In 732 Charles Martel routed the Saracens between Poitiers and Tours; in 1356 John II was defeated and captured at Poitiers by Edward the Black Prince. The scene of many other historic events, Poitiers has retained a Roman amphitheater and many magnificent churches and residences dating from the 4th cent. to the Renaissance. University was founded 1432.

Poitou (pwätōō'), region and former province, W France, on Atlantic coast, in Vendée, Deux-Sèvres, and Vienne depts.; historic cap. Poitiers. The Vendée is largely pasture land; Upper Poitou is a rich agr. region. Counts of Poitou took the title dukes of AQUITAINE in 9th cent. With Aquitaine, Poitou passed to England 1152; was recovered by Philip II of France 1204; ceded to England 1360; and recovered for France by Du Guesclin c.1370.

poker, card game, believed to have been first played in U.S. on Mississippi river steamboats. Two basic forms are draw and stud poker, many variations in-

---

SMALL CAPITALS = cross references. Pronunciation key on inside end pages. Abbreviations: p. 2.

clude high-low poker, seven-card stud poker, "spit in the ocean."

pokeweed, tall perennial herb (*Phytolacca americana*) native to North America and naturalized in Europe. It has dark, flattened berries containing a red juice. Young shoots of the plant are eaten but the roots are poisonous.

Pola (pō′lä), Serbo-Croatian *Pula,* city (pop. 22,714), Croatia, NW Yugoslavia: an Adriatic seaport near S tip of Istria. A Venetian possession from 1148, it passed to Austria 1797 and became a major naval base. Was transferred to Italy 1919; to Yugoslavia 1947. Has well-preserved Roman amphitheater, triumphal arch, and temple.

Poland, Pol. *Polska,* republic (120,359 sq. mi.; pop. 24,976,926, incl. former German territories placed under Polish administration in 1945), E central Europe, between the Baltic Sea (N) and the Carpathian mts. (S); cap. Warsaw. It is mostly a lowland but rises to 8,210 ft. in the Tatra group of the Carpathians. Chief rivers: Vistula, Oder, Warta, Western Bug. Largest cities: Warsaw, Lodz, Cracow, Poznan (Poland proper); Breslau, Danzig (formerly German). Largely agr. and forested, Poland also has important coal and ore mines (esp. in KATOWICE area); large salt deposits; some petroleum. Chief industries: metallurgy, textiles. Majority religion: Roman Catholicism. The Slavic Poles were united (10th cent.) by the PIAST dynasty. The early Piasts vastly increased their domains, but the kingdom split in 1138 and was fully reunited only in 1320. The TEUTONIC KNIGHTS, defeated at Tannenberg (1410), accepted Polish overlordship in 1466. In 1370 the crown passed to Louis I of Hungary. His daughter Jadwiga married the grand duke of LITHUANIA, who as LADISLAUS II of Poland founded the JAGIELLO dynasty (1386–1572). The Polish-Lithuanian state, mightiest of E Europe, was fully merged in 1569 (Union of Lublin). Under the Jagiellos, Poland reached its political and cultural zenith. At the same time, under pressure of the gentry, the kings conceded extraordinary powers to the diet; any single deputy to the *sejm* (lower house) could dissolve the diet. This practice (*liberum veto*) was recklessly applied after 1572, when Poland became a "royal republic," with the entire nobility taking part in the royal elections. STEPHEN BATHORY and the VASA kings (1587–1668) were involved in bitter struggles with Russia and Sweden. Poland, though preserved by the miracle of CZESTOCHOWA, lost much territory in the treaties of OLIVA and ANDRUSOV. JOHN III briefly restored Polish prestige, but with the accession (1697) of the electors of Saxony as kings of Poland, national independence was virtually lost (see AUGUSTUS II; AUGUSTUS III; NORTHERN WAR; POLISH SUCCESSION, WAR OF THE). STANISLAUS II, elected 1764, maintained himself only through Russian aid and in 1772 had to cede vast areas to Russia, Austria, and Prussia (first Partition of Poland). He attempted a constitutional reform (1791), but the second partition (1793, between Russia and Prussia) and, after Kosciusko's unsuccessful uprising, the third partition (1795, among Russia, Prussia, and Austria) took Poland off the map of Europe. Napoleon I sponsored the duchy of Warsaw (1807–13), a buffer state under the king of Saxony. The Congress of Vienna (1814–15) gave WEST PRUSSIA and POZNAN prov. to Prussia and GALICIA to Austria; made CRACOW a separate republic (annexed by Austria, 1846); and created a kingdom of Poland (cap. Warsaw), in personal union with Russia but with its own constitution ("Congress-Poland"). The defeat of a general insurrection in Congress-Poland (1830–31) led to suspension of its constitution; another insurrection (1863) was followed by intense Russification, parallelled in German Poland by Bismarck's Germanization program. Austrian Poland kept considerable autonomy. Polish dreams of national rebirth materialized in World War I. A Polish republic was proclaimed by PILSUDSKI (1918). Its W and S bound-

aries were fixed at, approximately, those of 1772 (see POLISH CORRIDOR; SILESIA). Polish insistence on restoration of its 1772 border in the E led to war with Russia (1920–21). The Treaty of RIGA gave Poland most of its claims; moreover, Poland seized VILNA from Lithuania. A third of Poland's population consisted of minorities—Germans, Ukrainians, Belorussians, Jews—whose treatment was not always equitable. In 1926 Pilsudski assumed virtual dictatorship, continued after his death (1935) by the "colonels' clique," a military junta. On Sept. 1, 1939, Poland having rejected German demands for DANZIG, Hitler attacked Poland and began WORLD WAR II. On Sept. 17, Soviet troops invaded from the E. Polish resistance, though gallant, was soon crushed. Germany annexed W Poland, Russia the E; the central portion ("Government General") was placed under German occupation. When Germany attacked the USSR (1941) all Poland came under German occupation. Though all Poles suffered cruelly, none fared worse than the Jews, nearly all of whom (c.3,000,000) were exterminated. Polish forces under a government in exile continued to fight alongside the Allies. In Poland itself there arose an effective underground army. Polish charges regarding the KATYN massacre, Russian demands for cession of E Poland, and the creation of a Russian-sponsored provisional Polish government at LUBLIN created a tense situation. Early in 1945 all Poland was in Russian hands, and the YALTA CONFERENCE prepared Allied recognition of a somewhat broadened Lublin government. The Polish-Russian border was shifted considerably W, while the POTSDAM CONFERENCE transferred large parts of E Germany to Polish administration, pending a general peace treaty. Most of the German population was expelled. By 1947 Communists and left-wing Socialists had gained full control of the government. Poland became a "people's democracy" within the Soviet orbit.

Poland, town (pop. 1,503), including Poland Spring resort (mineral water), SW Maine, W of Auburn. Mansion House inn dates from 1797.

polar bear, large white or cream-colored bear (*Thalarctos*) of arctic regions. It has a relatively small head and neck. It is a strong swimmer and the hairy soles facilitate walking on ice. Fish, seal, and other animals form its food. Probably does not hibernate. Cubs are born in burrows in ice and drifted snow.

polar exploration: see ARCTIC REGIONS and ANTARCTICA.

polar front, in meteorology, surface separating cold polar air masses of north and warmer air masses of lower latitudes.

polarimeter: see POLARIZATION OF LIGHT.

Polaris: see POLESTAR.

polariscope: see POLARIZATION OF LIGHT.

polarization of light. Certain crystals cause double REFRACTION, i.e., separate an entering light ray into two parts, one passing through with ordinary refraction, the other (extraordinary ray) bent farther from original direction; each emerging part is said to be polarized. Ordinary light vibrates in all planes perpendicular to line of travel; polarized light vibrates in one plane or circularly or elliptically. A single polarized ray can be produced by a crystal that absorbs the ordinary ray or by a NICOL PRISM. Certain organic substances (called optically active) rotate polarized light either to right or left. Rotation direction can be determined by polariscope; amount, by polarimeter.

polar regions: see ARCTIC REGIONS and ANTARCTICA.

Polasek, Albin (pôl′ä′shĕk), 1879–, American sculptor of busts and memorials, b. Czechoslovakia.

Pole, English noble family. **Michael de la Pole, 1st earl of Suffolk,** d. 1389, was trusted adviser and chancellor of Richard II. His grandson, **William de la Pole,** 4th earl and 1st duke of Suffolk, 1396–1450, had great power under Henry VI (whose marriage he arranged). Accused of treason for his efforts to secure peace in

France, he was exiled and murdered. His son, **John de la Pole, 2d duke of Suffolk,** 1442–91, married Edward IV's sister. His son, **John de la Pole, earl of Lincoln,** c.1464–1487, had claim to throne by Richard III. Joined Lambert Simnel's revolt and was killed. His brother, **Edmund de la Pole, earl of Suffolk,** c.1472–1513, aspired to the throne. Captured and long imprisoned, he was executed by Henry VIII.

Pole, Reginald, 1500–1558, English churchman, archbishop of Canterbury (1556–58), a cardinal. He remained Catholic when Henry VIII broke with the papacy and spent much time in Rome. After Mary was made queen Cardinal Pole was sent as papal legate to England, but plans to restore Catholicism there failed. Died the same day as Mary.

polecat (pōl'kăt"), mammal (*Mustela*) of Europe and Asia, allied to ferret, weasel, marten (not closely to skunk). Destroys poultry. Scent gland emits fetid odor. Fur of European polecat is called fitch.

poles, magnetic: see MAGNETIC POLES; MAGNETISM.

polestar, conspicuous star nearest north celestial pole; also called North Star. Star holding position at present is Polaris (Alpha of constellation Ursa Minor or Little Dipper) which lies c.1°9' from pole; its light power is c.47 times that of sun. Alpha Draconis was polestar c.2300 B.C.; Vega will hold position in c.12,000 years.

police, agents concerned with enforcement of law, order, and public protection. In many countries they have a political function (see SECRET POLICE). European police forces are centralized; U.S. ones are mostly under local control. SCOTLAND YARD was reorganized (1829) under the police system laid out by Sir Robert Peel. In the U.S. regular police forces followed the establishment (1844) of the New York city organization. There is no regular Federal force except the FBI for detection.

police dog: see SHEEP DOGS.

police power, in law, right of a government to make laws necessary for health, morals, and welfare of the populace. In the U.S. it has been defined by Supreme Court as power of the states to enact such laws even if they contravene literal terms of the Constitution. Doctrine first stated by John Marshall; broadened by Roger B. Taney. Concept became of great importance after passage of Fourteenth Amendment. Supreme Court gradually evolved an attitude tolerant toward economic regulation by the states.

Polignac, Jules Armand, prince de (zhül' ärmä' prēs' dü pôlēnyäk'), 1780–1847, French premier (1829–30), an ultraroyalist and reactionary. In March, 1830, the chamber of deputies demanded his dismissal. Instead, Charles X dissolved the chamber. When the new elections again produced a liberal majority, Polignac issued the July ordinances, which dissolved the new chamber even before it met, estab. a new electoral law, and ended freedom of the press. This precipitated the JULY REVOLUTION. Arrested in 1830, Polignac was amnestied in 1836 and withdrew to England.

Poling, Daniel A(lfred), 1884–, American clergyman, editor, and author. Pastor of Marble Collegiate Church, New York city (1923–30) and of Baptist Temple, Philadelphia (1936–48), he became (1948) chaplain of Chapel of Four Chaplains, Philadelphia. Editor of *Christian Herald* and *Christian Endeavor World.*

poliomyelitis (pō"lēōmī"ŭlī'tĭs, pŏ–) or **infantile paralysis,** inflammation of gray matter of spinal cord, caused by virus. In a minority of cases, motor nerve paralysis causes atrophy of groups of muscles. Physical therapy is preferred treatment. Chilling and overfatigue increase susceptibility.

Polish Corridor, strip of territory along the lower Vistula, separating East Prussia from rest of Germany, which was given to Poland by the Treaty of Versailles (1919) to provide it with an outlet to the Baltic Sea. Once part of Polish POMERANIA, Polish Corridor had a large German minority and was cause of chronic Polish-German friction. Failure of negotiations over return of Free City of DANZIG and creation of extraterritorial German corridor across Polish Corridor produced the immediate cause of the German invasion of Poland and World War II.

Polish language, one of the Slavonic subfamily of Indo-European languages. See LANGUAGE (table).

Polish Succession, War of the, 1733–35, European war which broke out of the death of Augustus II of Poland. STANISLAUS I, who sought to regain his throne, was elected by a majority of Polish nobles and was backed by France (later also by Spain and Sardinia). Augustus's son, elected by a minority as AUGUSTUS III, was backed by Emperor Charles VI and by Russia. Stanislaus was defeated in 1734, but fighting continued along the Rhine and in Italy, for reasons which had nothing to do with Poland. By the Treaty of Vienna (1735; ratified 1738) a general settlement was reached: Augustus kept Poland; Stanislaus received LORRAINE; Francis of Lorraine was promised succession of TUSCANY; Austria ceded Naples and Sicily to Spain; Spain ceded to Austria its claim to Parma; Sardinia received nothing, lost nothing, exchanged nothing.

Politian (pōlĭ'shùn), Ital. *Poliziano,* surname of **Angelo Ambrogini,** 1454–94, Italian poet and humanist. His *Orfeo* (1471) marks the transition from sacred to profane drama, and *Stanze per la giostra* (1475–76) are descriptive lyric masterpieces hardly surpassed by Ariosto or Tasso.

political science, the science of the nature of the state and of government. Its considerations include such subjects as the nature of sovereignty, international law, colonial government, and constitutions.

Polk, James K(nox) (pōk), 1795–1849, 11th President of the United States (1845–49). U.S. Representative from Tenn. (1825–39), speaker of the House (1835–39). A leading Jacksonian Democrat. As President he ably managed MEXICAN WAR. Achieved reduction of tariff, reestablishment of INDEPENDENT TREASURY SYSTEM, settlement of dispute over Oregon, acquisition of Calif. Few Presidents have equalled his record of attaining specific, stated aims; few have worked harder.

Polk, Leonidas, 1806–64, Protestant Episcopal bishop and Confederate general. Bishop of La. (1841–61). A founder of Univ. of the South, Sewanee, Tenn. (1857). Fought at Shiloh, Murfreesboro, in Chattanooga campaign. Killed at Pine Mountain, Ga.

Pollaiuolo (pōl-läyoō-ō'lō), family of Florentine artists. **Jacopo Pollaiuolo** (yä'kōpō) was a noted 15th-cent. goldsmith. His son and pupil, **Antonio Pollaiuolo,** 1429?–1498, is said to have been first artist to study anatomy by dissection. Famous for drawings and paintings with active, muscular figures, as in *Labors of Hercules* (Uffizi). Executed bronze tomb of Sixtus IV in Rome (1484) and monument to Innocent VIII in St. Peter's, aided by his brother **Piero Pollaiuolo** (pyä'rō), 1443–96, who also collaborated with him on many paintings. Their nephew, **Simone del Pollaiuolo** (sēmō'nä dĕl), 1457–1508, was an architect. Worked mainly in Florence, where he finished the Strozzi Palace. Nicknamed Il Cronaca.

polled shorthorn cattle: see CATTLE.

pollination, the transfer of pollen from the stamen to the pistil of the same or another flower. Pollen grains, microscopic grains invisible to the naked eye except in quantity, are borne, usually as a yellow powder, on the stamens within the corolla of a flower. Insects, wind, and hummingbirds serve to transfer pollen. Self-pollination is usually prevented in flowers by adaptations to insure cross-pollination, believed to make for stronger offspring. After pollination, the pollen grain germinates and produces a tube which grows down through the pistil of the flower to the embryo sac; one of the sperm nuclei formed from living matter within the pollen grain fuses, in the act of fertilization, with the ovum or egg lying in the embryo sac. See *ill.,* p. 783.

Pollock, Sir Frederick (pŏ'lŭk), 1845–1937, English

jurist, professor of jurisprudence (1887–1903), judge of the admiralty court of the Cinque Ports. Wrote much on law, including *The History of English Law* (1895; with F. W. Maitland). His correspondence with Justice O. W. Holmes has been published (1941).

Pollonarrua or **Polonnaruwa** (both: pŏ″lŭnŭrōō′ŭ), ruined anc. city, E central Ceylon. Was cap. of Ceylon in 8th cent. Has impressive ruins of Buddhist temples.

poll tax, in U.S. history, a tax levied by a state on its voters, usually ranging from $1 to $5. Many otherwise eligible voters, particularly in the South, have thus been disfranchised. Though some southern states have passed legislation forbidding poll taxes (North Carolina in 1920, Louisiana in 1934, Florida in 1937, and Georgia in 1945), efforts to enact a Federal anti-poll-tax law have failed.

Pollux, Greek hero: see CASTOR AND POLLUX.

Polo, Marco, 1254?–1324?, Venetian traveler in China. Accompanied father and uncle on Eastern expedition (1271). Reached Cambuluc (Peiping) in 1275; Marco became Kublai Khan's favorite and his agent. Traveled widely. Returned to Venice in 1295. Later dictated account of his experiences—chief Renaissance source of information on East.

polo, game played on horseback by teams of four on field 200 by 300 yd. Said to have originated in Persia. Revived in India in 19th cent., it became popular with British officers stationed there, spread to other countries. Introduced in England 1869, in U.S. 1876.

polonium (pŭlō′nēŭm), element similar to radium (symbol = Po; see also ELEMENT, table) exhibiting RADIO-ACTIVITY. See *ill.,* p. 773.

Polonnaruwa, Ceylon: see POLLONARRUA.

Polovtsi, Russian name of the CUMANS.

Polson (pōl′sŭn), resort city (pop. 2,280), NW Mont., on Flathead L.

Poltava (pŭlta′vŭ), city (pop. 130,305), E central Ukraine; agr. center. Near here Peter I routed Charles XII of Sweden in 1709.

polyandry: see MARRIAGE.

Polybius (pōlĭ′bēŭs), 203? B.C.–c.120 B.C., Greek historian. In Rome, under patronage of the Scipios, he wrote great universal history, covering Mediterranean world of 220–146 B.C. Of 40 books, first five are intact, with large fragments of others.

Polycarp, Saint (pŏ′lĭkärp), A.D. c.70–156?, Greek bishop of Smyrna, Father of the Church; author of an *Epistle to the Philippians* (said by some to be two letters). Said to have died a martyr in Rome. Feast: Jan. 26.

Polycletus (pŏlĭklē′tŭs) or **Polyclitus** (–klī′tŭs), two Greek sculptors of school of Argos. **Polycletus,** the elder, fl. c.450–c.420 B.C., was a contemporary of Phidias. Famous for his *Doryphorus* or *Spear-Bearer* (a copy is in Naples), which embodied his ideal of physical perfection. None of his originals exists today. **Polycletus,** the younger, worked in 4th cent. B.C. and was also a sculptor of athletes.

Polydorus: see LAOCOÖN.

Polyglot Bible (pŏ′lēglŏt), a Bible in which different versions, often in different languages, are given in parallel columns. Origen's HEXAPLA is most famous anc. example. Most elaborate of modern Polyglot Bibles is the London, or Walton's, Polyglot (1657), containing Hebrew, Greek, Syriac, Ethiopic, Arabic, and Persian texts.

Polyhymnia: see MUSES.

polymerization (pŏ″lĭmŭrĭzā′shŭn), joining of a number of molecules of same kind to form one larger molecule. Two compounds having molecules so related are called polymers.

Polynesia (pŏlĭnē′zhŭ) [Gr.,= many islands], one of three main divisions of Pacific isls., in central and S Pacific. Includes Hawaiian Isls., Samoa, Tonga, islands of French Establishments in Oceania, and, ethnologically, New Zealand. Languages are Malayo-Polynesian (see LANGUAGE, table).

Polynesian languages or **Malayo-Polynesian languages:** see LANGUAGE (table).

Polynices (–nī′sēz), in Greek legend, leader of the SEVEN AGAINST THEBES; son of Oedipus, brother of Eteocles and Antigone, and nephew of CREON. Polynices and Eteocles killed each other in battle.

polyp (pŏ′lĭp), elongated or hydroid form of various coelenterates (jellyfish and relatives). Alternation of generations between polyp and jellyfish or medusa stage is common. Coral animal and sea anemone are polyp forms.

Polyphemus (pŏlĭfē′mŭs), in Greek mythology, a Cyclops or one-eyed giant; son of Poseidon. In the *Odyssey,* Odysseus was captured by him but escaped by blinding him.

polyphony (pŭlĭ′fŭnĭ), music whose texture is formed by the interweaving of several more or less independent melodic lines. Term practically synonymous with COUNTERPOINT. Contrasting terms are homophony (one part dominates while others serve only a harmonic function) and monody (a single melodic line, for example, plain song). The 16th cent. was the great age of polyphony. With the gradual acceptance of tonality, polyphonic music adopted a style more dependent on harmony, evolving into the homophonic music of the 19th cent. Some 20th-cent. music recalls medieval and Renaissance polyphony.

Pombal, Sebastião José de Carvalho e Melo, marquês de (sĕbästyä′ō zhōōzā′ dŭ kärvä′lyō ē mĕ′lō märkäs′ dŭ pômbäl′), 1699–1782, Portuguese statesman. As secretary of state for foreign affairs and war he ruled Portugal under king Joseph for 26 years (1750–77). Absolutist and anticlerical, he crushed all opposition, expelled the Jesuits, curbed the Inquisition, reformed the schools and the army, fostered agr. and industry, built up Brazil, and reconstructed Lisbon after earthquake of 1755. Maria I dismissed and exiled him.

pomegranate (pŭm′grä″nĭt, pŏm′–), handsome, thorny shrub or small tree (*Punica granatum*) native to S Asia and its fruit, about the size of an apple with hard yellowish to purple rind. It has shining leaves and showy red-orange flowers. Grenadine syrup is made from the red pulp of the fruits. Commercial orchards are found in Ariz. and Calif. Pomegranate connected with legend of PERSEPHONE.

pomelo: see GRAPEFRUIT.

Pomerania (pŏmŭrā′nēŭ), Ger. *Pommern,* former Prussian province (14,830 sq. mi.; 1939 pop. 2,393,844; cap. Stettin), N Germany, on the Baltic Sea. Agr. lowland; forests, lakes; fishing. Inhabited by Slavic tribes by the 10th cent., Pomerania became a duchy 11th cent.; was Christianized and passed under Polish overlordship 12th cent. By 1181 it had split into two principalities. (1) The E part, including DANZIG, continued separately as Pomerelia (Ger. *Pommerellen,* Pol. *Pomorze*). Annexed by Poland 1295, it was ceded to the TEUTONIC KNIGHTS 1308; reverted to Poland 1466; was ceded to Prussia in the partitions of Poland (1772, 1793). Part of WEST PRUSSIA prov. till 1919, Pomerelia was partitioned by the Treaty of Versailles: the larger part became Polish; Danzig became a free city; the rest remained Prussian. (2) The W part, or Pomerania proper, became a duchy of the Holy Roman Empire. It was occupied (1628), with the consent of its last native duke, Bogislav XIV, by Wallenstein in the Thirty Years War. The resistance of STRALSUND precipitated Swedish intervention. The Peace of Westphalia (1648) gave W or Hither Pomerania (incl. Stettin and Stralsund) to Sweden; E or Farther Pomerania went to Brandenburg-Prussia, which in 1720 also acquired the E half, and in 1815 the whole, of Swedish Pomerania. While Pomerelia was largely Polish-speaking and Catholic, Pomerania had long been thoroughly Germanized and Protestant. The Potsdam Conference of 1945 assigned Pomerania E of the Oder (incl. Stettin) to Polish administration, pending a peace treaty with Germany. Danzig and the rest of Pomerelia, after German annexation in World War II, reverted to Poland. Pomerania W of the Oder became part of Mecklenburg.

Pomeranian dog: see TOY DOG.

Pomerelia: see POMERANIA.

Pommerellen and **Pommern:** see POMERANIA.

Pomona (pùmō'nù), Roman goddess, protectress of fruit trees.

Pomona (pùmō'nù), city (pop. 35,405), S Calif., E of Los Angeles; laid out 1875. Packs and ships citrus fruit, refines oil, produces metal and paper products.

Pomona (pùmō'nù, pō–) or **Mainland,** island (c.189 sq. mi.; pop. 13,352), off N Scotland, largest of Orkney Isls. Kirkwall (cap.) is here. Irregular coastline is indented by Kirkwall Bay and Scapa Flow. Interior has hills, lakes, and fertile valleys.

Pomona College: see CLAREMONT, Calif.

Pomorze: see POMERANIA.

Pompadour, Antoinette Poisson, marquise de (pŏm'-pùdôr, Fr. ätwänĕt' pwäsō' märkēz' dù pōpädoōr'), 1721–64, mistress of Louis XV of France from 1745 to her death. Of humble origin, she rose through her beauty, intelligence, and ambition to become virtual ruler of France. Her foreign policy was responsible for the French alliance with Austria, which involved France in the Seven Years War. She was a lavish patron to artists and writers.

Pompano (pŏm'pùnō), city (pop. 5,682), SE Fla., on Atlantic coast N of Fort Lauderdale. Packs vegetables.

Pompeii (pŏmpā'), ruined Roman city, S Italy, at the foot of Mt. Vesuvius, near Naples. A Samnite city long before it became Roman (1st cent. B.C.), it was a flourishing port and wealthy resort when it was injured (A.D. 63) by earthquake and buried (A.D. 79) by an eruption of Vesuvius. Volcanic ashes and cinders preserved the ruins, which were rediscovered in 1748 and have been since much excavated.

Pompeius, Sextus (sĕk'stùs pŏmpā'ùs), d. 35 B.C., Roman commander; son of Pompey the Great. After his father's defeat, he warred against Caesar from Spain until 44 B.C. Later outlawed, he seized Sicily and stopped grain ships from reaching Rome—a practice he resumed against Octavian (Augustus). He won two battles with the aid of storms, but was later defeated, captured, and killed.

Pompey (Cneius Pompeius Magnus; Pompey the Great) (pŏm'pē), 106 B.C.–48 B.C., Roman general. Fought for Sulla successfully, then (76 B.C.) forwarded Roman conquest in Spain and with great severity broke up the last of the revolt of Spartacus (72 B.C.). He served as consul before undertaking successfully to rid the Mediterranean of pirates and to defeat Mithridates VI of Pontus (65 B.C.). Back in Rome, he met opposition from extremists in the senate and was driven into combination with his rival and the senate's enemy, Julius CAESAR. He, Caesar, and Crassus formed the First Triumvirate (60 B.C.). The rivalry would not down, and though peace was kept while Pompey's wife, Julia, who was Caesar's daughter, lived, the two men became open enemies later. Pompey took measures against Clodius, supporting MILO, and went over to the senate and became consul (52 B.C.). Later senate measures against Caesar and for Pompey caused Caesar to cross the Rubicon and begin the civil war (49 B.C.). Pompey was defeated at Pharsala (48 B.C.) and fled to Egypt, where he was assassinated by one of his soldiers.

Pomponazzi, Pietro (pōmpōnät'tsē), 1462–1525, Italian philosopher, a humanist who attacked scholasticism, argued that the soul was mortal (*De immortalitate,* 1516).

Ponape (pō'näpä), volcanic island (129 sq. mi.; pop. 5,735), W Pacific, E Caroline Isls. Has deposits of bauxite and iron. Produces copra and dried bonito. Site of Japanese air base in World War II.

Ponca City, city (pop. 20,180), N Okla., near Arkansas R.; founded 1893. Trade and mfg. center for agr. and oil area with grain elevators, refineries, and food processing plants.

Ponce (pōn'sä), city (pop. 99,429), S Puerto Rico. Second largest city on island, it is thriving port and center of agr. area.

Ponce de León, Juan (Span. hwän' pōn'thä dä lāōn'), c.1460–1521, Spanish explorer. Made fortune as governor of Puerto Rico (1509–12). Discovered Fla. in 1513, explored coast. Legend of fountain of youth he supposedly sought has been discredited. Mortally wounded by Indians in later colonization expedition to Fla.

Poncelet, Jean Victor (zhä' vēktôr' pōslä'), 1788–1867, French mathematician, army engineer. He evolved basis of modern form of projective geometry.

Ponchielli, Amilcare (ämēlkä'rä pōngkyĕl'lē), 1834–86, Italian composer of the opera *La Gioconda,* containing the popular ballet, *The Dance of the Hours.*

Pond, Peter, 1740–1807, American fur trader, explorer of Old Northwest. Best known for his maps of country covered in voyages.

Pondichéry (pōdēshärē') or **Pondicherry** (pŏndĭchĕ'rē), French settlement (112 sq. mi.; pop. 222,572), on Bay of Bengal, adjacent to Madras state, India. Territorial limits were estab. 1815. The town **Pondichéry** (pop. 59,835) is cap. of French India. Acquired 1674, it fell three times to the British in 18th cent.

pond lily, coarse aquatic plant of genus *Nuphar* of north temperate zone; also called cow lily and spatterdock. It has yellow cup-shaped flowers and erect or floating leaves.

pondweed, weedy aquatic plant (*Potamogeton*), with both narrow, grasslike, submerged leaves and stouter floating ones.

Poniatowski (pônyätôf'skē), Polish noble family Stanislaus Augustus Poniatowski was king of Poland (see STANISLAUS II). His nephew, **Prince Jozef Anton Poniatowski,** 1763–1813, Polish general, fought the Russians under Kosciusko (1794); commanded Polish forces under Napoleon in campaigns of 1809 and 1812. He committed suicide after battle of Leipzig.

Pons, Lily, 1904–, French-American coloratura soprano. First appeared at the Metropolitan Opera, New York, 1930. Her many successes include *Lakmé, La Fille du regiment,* and *Lucia di Lammermoor.*

Ponselle, Rosa (pōnzĕl'), 1894–, American soprano. With the Metropolitan Opera, New York, 1918–37; she made her debut singing opposite Caruso in Verdi's *La forza del destino.*

Ponsonby, Sir Henry (Frederick) (pŭn'sùnbē), 1825–95, English administrator, private secretary to Queen Victoria (1870–95). His son **Sir Frederick Ponsonby,** 1867–1935, served in the households of Victoria, Edward VII, and George V. Author of *Recollections of Three Reigns* (1951). Created Baron Sysonby 1935.

Pontchartrain, Lake (pōn'chùrtrān), shallow lake, 41 mi. long, 25 mi. wide, SE La., N of New Orleans. Connected with L. Maurepas, the Mississippi, and Gulf of Mexico (through L. Borgne). Crossed by bridge (10 mi. long) at narrow eastern end. Has many small resorts.

Pont du Gard (pō' dü gär'), perfectly preserved Roman aqueduct (c.900 ft. long, c.160 ft. high), built 19 B.C. across Gard R. near Remoulins, S France, to supply Nîmes with water. Has three tiers of arches (lowest in use as road bridge).

Pontefract (pōn'tĭfrăct, pŭm'frĭt), municipal borough (pop. 23,173), West Riding of Yorkshire, England. Had 11th-cent. castle where Richard II died (1400); dismantled in 1649.

Pontiac, Indian chief: see PONTIAC'S REBELLION.

Pontiac (pōn'tēăk). **1** City (pop. 8,990), NE central Ill., on Vermilion R. and NE of Bloomington. Trade, rail, industrial center in agr. and coal area. **2** City (pop. 73,681), SE Mich., on Clinton R. and NW of Detroit, in agr., lake, and resort area; founded 1818. Carriage making, important in 1880s, gave way to automobile industry. Also has mfg. of rubber, metalwork, and other products contributing to the automobile industry.

Pontiac's Rebellion or **Pontiac's Conspiracy,** 1763–66,

Indian uprising against British after close of French and Indian Wars, so called after one of its leaders, Pontiac (d. 1769), Ottawa Indian chief. Resistance was aroused by English assumption of ownership to Indian lands. Pontiac led siege of Detroit. Many outposts were destroyed before an offensive campaign by the English brought treaties of peace.

Ponticus, Aquila: see AQUILA PONTICUS.

Pontine Marshes (pŏn'tĭn, –tīn), low-lying region, S Latium, central Italy, between Tyrrhenian Sea and Apennine foothills. Populated and fertile in antiquity; later abandoned because of malaria. Though repeatedly begun, drainage of marshlands was completed only under Mussolini.

Pontius Pilate (pŏn'shŭs pī'–), fl. A.D. 26, Roman procurator of Judaea (A.D. c.26–A.D. c.36?). To satisfy the people, he condemned Jesus to death. Mat. 27; John 18.28–19.42. According to tradition, Pilate committed suicide. The Acts of Pilate, one of the PSEUDEPIGRAPHA, is part of Gospel of Nicodemus.

pontoon (pŏn'tŭn, pŏntōōn'), flat-bottomed boat or other floating unit for building bridges, raising sunken ships, and the like. Barrels or casks, open boats, and enclosed watertight compartments of wood, metal, concrete, canvas, or rubber have been used in pontoon bridges. Floating foundation units are joined and anchored, and roadway is laid across them. Most frequent use is in warfare. Darius I built pontoon bridges across Bosporus and Danube in war against Scythians; his son Xerxes I built bridge of boats across Hellespont in war against Greece. U.S. army experimented with rubber pontoons from 1846 on. In 1941 collapsible rubber fabric floats were adopted and steel treadways made roadway; navy introduced light welded steel box pontoons for making ship-to-shore bridges, docks, or causeways and, with addition of motor, for use as self-propelled barges. For raising sunken ships, watertight cylinders filled with water are made fast to vessel and then emptied by compressed air. Hydroplane landing floats are a form of pontoon. See *ill.,* p. 131.

Pontoppidan, Henrik (pôntô'pĭdän), 1857–1943, Danish novelist, who in books such as *The Kingdom of the Dead* (1912–16) and *Man's Heaven* (1927) attacked materialism. Shared 1917 Nobel Prize in Literature with Gjellerup.

Pontormo, Jacopo da (yä'kōpō dä pōntōr'mō), 1494–1557?, Florentine painter, whose real name was Jacopo Carucci or Carrucci. Imitated Michelangelo in later period.

Pontus, anc. country, NE Asia Minor, on Black Sea coast. It grew important in the 4th cent. B.C. as an independent kingdom and continued to wax until King MITHRIDATES VI controlled Asia Minor and the Crimea and threatened Roman power in Greece. He was defeated by the Romans under Pompey (65 B.C.). An attempt by a later king, Pharnaces II, to increase the greatness of Pontus was ended by Julius Caesar at Zela (47 B.C.).

poodle, medium-sized and small dog of superior intelligence. Depending upon their size poodles are classed as standard, miniature, or toy poodles. The standard poodle measures c.15 in. or more at the shoulder; the miniature, well under 15 in.; and the toy poodle weighs less than 12 lb. The curly coat of poodles grows profusely and is clipped in several rather fantastic styles; it is solid in color, often black or silver, but sometimes white, blue, cream, apricot, or red.

pool: see BILLIARDS.

Poole, Ernest, 1880–1950, American writer. His novels include *The Harbor* (1915) and *His Family* (1917).

Poole, William Frederick, 1821–94, American librarian and bibliographer. He compiled the first general index to periodicals in the U.S., *Poole's Index to Periodical Literature* (1848; later to become *Reader's Guide to Periodical Literature*).

Poole, municipal borough (pop. 82,958), Dorsetshire, England, on N side of Poole Harbour, an inlet of

English Channel. A naval supply station and seaplane base, it has a considerable coastal trade.

Poona (pōō'nù), commercial city (pop. 298,001), central Bombay, India. Was center of Mahratta empire in 18th cent. Has pleasant climate; formerly a favorite residential area of British officials.

Poopó (pō''ōpō'), salt lake, area 970 sq. mi., c.8 ft. deep, alt. 12,106 ft., on plateau of E Bolivia. No outlet except in time of flood.

Poor, Henry Varnum, 1888–, American painter of still lifes, portraits, and landscapes.

poor law, legislation relating to public assistance for the poor. In 1601 England passed a poor relief act that recognized the state's obligation to the needy; poorhouses, supported by local levies, grouped the aged, sick, and insane together; work relief for the ablebodied was emphasized. From c.1700 workhouses were established. In late 18th cent. home relief became customary. Laws in 1834 placed relief under national supervision; a liberalized poor law was passed in 1927. In U.S., where poor-relief statutes of the different states were based on English poor law, uniform relief on a national scale was introduced in 20th cent. See also SOCIAL SECURITY.

poor-man's-orchid: see BUTTERFLY FLOWER.

Pope, Alexander, 1688–1744, English poet. Son of a prosperous linen draper, he early began study of poetry and literary criticism. In 1711 appeared his *Essay on Criticism,* a poem outlining contemporary critical tastes and standards. In 1713 he published *Windsor Forest,* and in 1714 *The Rape of the Lock,* a mock-heroic satire based on an incident in high society. In 1717 he issued a volume of poetry, including "Elegy to the Memory of an Unfortunate Lady" and "Eloisa to Abelard." In 1720 appeared his translation of the *Iliad,* and in 1725–26 the *Odyssey,* both tremendous literary and financial successes. At famous estate at Twickenham he edited Shakspere (1725). This work was adversely criticized by Lewis Theobald, who drew down on his head Pope's *Dunciad* (1728), a comprehensive satire on literary dullness of the time. Between 1732 and 1734 Pope composed *An Essay on Man,* a poetical defense of deism. He also wrote a series of epistles in verse, *Moral Essays* (1731–35), and ethical satires (1733–38), including the celebrated "Epistle to Dr. Arbuthnot." Pope's important poetry is in the heroic couplet, and only Dryden rivals him in the use of it.

Pope, John, 1822–92, Union general in Civil War. Captured ISLAND No. 10. Removed from command after defeat at second battle of BULL RUN (1862).

Pope, John Russell, 1874–1937, American architect, whose work was inspired by classic styles. Designed National Gall. of Art, Washington, D.C.

pope: see PAPACY.

Popham, George (pŏ'pùm), c.1550–1608, early American colonist, b. England. Estab. short-lived colony (1607–8) at mouth of Kennebec R., Maine.

Popham Beach, Maine: see PHIPPSBURG.

Popish Plot: see OATES, TITUS.

Poplar, city (pop. 1,169), NE Mont., on Missouri R. at mouth of Poplar R. Has Indian agency. Chief GALL surrendered here.

poplar, deciduous fast-growing tree of genus *Populus.* The Lombardy poplar is a variety of the Eurasian black poplar (*Populus nigra*). Some poplars, especially those with cottony seed coverings, are called cottonwoods, e.g., the eastern cottonwood (*P. deltoides*); others include ASPEN and BALM OF GILEAD.

Poplar Bluff, city (pop. 15,064), SE Mo., in Ozark foothills, on Black R. near Ark. line; founded 1850. Center of a farm and resort area, it has railroad shops and mfg. of shoes and wood products. Wappapello Dam is near.

Popocatepetl (pōpùkă'tùpĕtùl, pōpō''kätä'pùtùl) [Aztec,= smoking mountain], volcano, 17,887 ft. high, central Mexico, on border between Puebla and Mexico states. Perpetually snow-capped, it has large crater with practically pure sulphur deposits, partially exploited. Dormant since 1702.

Popol Vuh (pōpōl′ vōō′), [Quiché,= collection of the council], sacred book of Quiché Indians, containing their cosmogony, religion, mythology, migratory traditions, and history. Original was destroyed by Pedro de Alvarado, but it was rewritten soon after. Content and style reveal high level of learning.

Poppaea Sabina (pōpē′u sùbī′nù), d. A.D. 65, mistress and later wife of NERO (her third husband). She is said to have influenced him to evil. He finally had her killed, but the legend that he kicked her to death is probably false.

poppy, annual, biennial, or perennial plant of genus *Papaver,* mostly native to the Old World, cultivated for the brilliant but short-lived flowers. Well known are the Oriental poppy, Iceland poppy, and Shirley poppy. OPIUM, and poppy or maw seed (not narcotic) used to flavor rolls, are obtained from the opium poppy (*Papaver somniferum*). The poppy of "Flanders Field" is the European red corn poppy (*P. rhoeas*).

population. The world contains roughly 2,000,000,000 people, over half of whom are in Asia, a fourth in Europe, and an eighth in the Americas. From the time of the Industrial Revolution, European population has quadrupled, but is now becoming stabilized, due to such factors as BIRTH CONTROL. Overpopulation is still a serious threat to many countries, particularly in Asia. See MALTHUS, EUGENICS.

Populist party. After Panic of 1873 farmers of Middle West and South grew poorer, while financial-industrial group in the East grew wealthier. Farmers blamed management of currency. GREENBACK PARTY accomplished little. Advocating government ownership of railways and free coinage of silver, Populist party was formed in 1891. Party convention of 1892 adopted platform calling for these and other reforms (e.g., graduated income tax); J. B. Weaver, Populist presidential candidate, polled over 1,041,000 votes. Helped by the eloquence of W. J. BRYAN, Democratic party captured bulk of Populist votes in 1896. Period of rising farm prices thereafter brought about dissolution of party.

porcelain: see POTTERY.

Porcupine, gold-mining district: see TIMMINS, Ont.

Porcupine, river, N Yukon and NE Alaska, rising N of Dawson and flowing 525 mi. NE then W to enter Yukon R. at Fort Yukon in NE Alaska. Discovered 1842 by John Bell.

porcupine (pôr′kyùpīn), heavy, short-legged, slow-moving rodent, with erectile barbed quills. Old World forms are chiefly terrestrial. New World porcupines, of a different family, are partly arboreal. North American porcupine belongs to genus *Erethizon.*

Porcupine Mountains, NW Upper Peninsula, N Mich., near L. Superior, with highest point (2,023 ft.) in state.

porgy (pôr′gē), name for several fishes of Sparidae family found in warm coastal seas of the Americas and Europe.

Porjus (pôr′yùs), cataract, c.170 ft. high, in Stora Lule R., N Sweden. Supplies power to Sweden's second largest hydroelectric plant, which operates Lapland RR, iron mines at Kiruna and Gallivare, and iron smelters and electrochemical plants.

pork, the flesh of swine prepared as food, either fresh, cured (as ham, bacon), or in other products. Lard, the refined fat, is used as shortening. Pork must be thoroughly cooked to prevent TRICHINOSIS.

Porkkala (pôrk′kälä), small peninsula in Gulf of Finland. Leased (1947) by Finland to Russia for 50 years as naval base.

Porphyry (pôr′fùrē), 233–c.304, Greek Neoplatonic philosopher, disciple and editor of Plotinus.

porphyry (pôr′fùrē), igneous rock composed of large crystals embedded in matrix or ground mass. This texture indicates its two states of solidification.

porpoise (pôr′pùs), blunt-nosed sea mammal (*Phocaena*), order Cetacea, allied to whale. Travels in

schools, appearing chiefly in N Atlantic and N Pacific.

Porpora, Niccolò Antonio (pôr′pōrä), b. 1686, d. 1766 or 1767, Italian composer and outstanding voice teacher. His best compositions were cantatas for harpsichord and voice. He taught all the greatest singers of the 18th cent., including Farinelli.

Porrentruy (pôrätrüě′), town (pop. 6,121), Bern canton, NW Switzerland, in Bernese Jura. Watch mfg. Was a residence of prince-bishops of Basel 1528–1792; their territory passed to Bern 1815.

Porsena, Lars: see LARS PORSENA.

Porson, Richard, 1759–1808, English classical scholar. He created a sensation by supporting Edward Gibbon in declaring that John 1.7 was spurious. Noted for his textual criticism of Greek drama and for his grasp of metrical principles of Greek poetry. Translated Euripides.

port, fortified wine made in Portugal from grapes grown in the Douro valley. Blending and the length and manner of storage determine whether vintage, ruby, tawny, crusted, or white port is produced.

Porta, Giacomo della (jä′kōmō dĕl′lä pôr′tä), c.1540–1602, Italian architect. Completed some works by Vignola and Michelangelo, such as dome of St. Peter's and Farnese Palace.

Port Adelaide, city (pop. 33,382), South Australia, on inlet of Gulf St. Vincent; the state's chief port and wool-trading center.

Portage (pôr′tìj), city (pop. 7,334), central Wis., on Wisconsin R. Portage here (now ship canal) between Wisconsin and Fox rivers first used by Jolliet and Father Marquette 1673. Town is farm trade center. Has site of Fort Winnebago (1828) and restored Indian Agency House (1832). Birthplace of Zona Gale and F. J. Turner.

Portage Lake, inlet of Keweenaw Bay, c.20 mi. long and 2 mi. wide, N Mich. Once connected to L. Superior by portage across Keweenaw peninsula; passage now made by a ship canal.

Portage la Prairie (pôr″tìj lù prä′rē), city (pop. 8,511), S Man., Canada, near Assiniboine R. and W of Winnipeg. Center of wheat-growing region. Near site of Fort La Reine, built 1738 by Vérendrye.

Port Alberni, city (pop. 7,845), on S central Vancouver Isl., SW B.C., Canada, NW of Victoria. Inland port and lumbering and fishing center at head of Alberni Canal.

Portales (pôrtă′lìs), city (pop. 8,112), E N.Mex., near Texas line. Trade center of irrigated truck-farm and grazing area.

Port Angeles (ăn′jùlùs), port city (pop. 11,233), NW Wash., on Juan de Fuca Strait opposite Victoria, British Columbia. Fish, lumber, cellulose, dairy, and paper products. Hq. for Olympic Natl. Park.

Port Apra, Guam: see APRA HARBOR.

Port Arthur, city (pop. 31,161), W Ont., Canada, on NW shore of L. Superior and NE of Duluth, Minn. With its twin city, Fort William, is major grain and iron shipping center with grain elevators, shipyards, and paper, pulp, and lumber mills. Tourist center for hunting and fishing area.

Port Arthur, Chinese *Lüshun,* city (pop. 27,241), S Manchuria, on LIAOTUNG peninsula; naval base on Yellow Sea. Included in Kwantung leased territory 1898–1945. Became joint Sino-Soviet naval base and headquarters of Port Arthur–Dairen administrative district in 1945.

Port Arthur, city (pop. 57,530), SE Texas, on Sabine L. and SE of Beaumont; founded 1895. Oil discovered 1901 at near-by Spindletop. Oil port and rail focus on Sabine-Neches Canal and Intracoastal Waterway. Has refineries, foundries, shipyards, chemical plants and railroad shops.

Port-au-Prince (pôrt-ù-prĭns′), city (commune pop. 195,672), S Haiti, cap. of republic, at head of the Gulf of Gonaïves. Founded in 1749 by French sugar planters moving southward; replaced Cap-Haïtien as capital in 1770. Ships half of Haiti's exports.

Port Chester, residential village (pop. 23,970), SE N.Y., at Conn. line and on Long Isl. Sound. Electric razors, food products, hardware, machinery.

Port Clinton, city (pop. 5,541), N Ohio, on L. Erie W of Sandusky and at mouth of Portage R. Mfg. of auto parts and boats. Near by is Camp Perry.

Port Colborne, town (pop. 8,275), S Ont., Canada, on L. Erie, S of St. Catharines; port at S end of Welland Ship Canal. Nickel-refining center with iron smelters, cereal mills, and grain elevators.

Port Elizabeth, city (pop. 133,400), S Cape Prov., South Africa, on Algoa Bay of Indian Ocean. Developed after 1873, when railroad to Kimberley was completed. Exports wool, mohair, and diamonds.

Porter, Cole, 1893–, American composer of musical comedies. His lyrics, which he writes himself, are known for their wit and sophistication. Among his many successes are *Night and Day* (his most famous song) from *The Gay Divorce* (1932); *You're the Top,* from *Anything Goes* (1934); *My Heart Belongs to Daddy,* from *Leave It to Me* (1938); *Begin the Beguine,* from *Jubilee* (1935); *In the Still of the Night,* from *Rosalie* (1937).

Porter, David, 1780–1843, American naval officer. Achieved greatest success as commander of *Essex* in War of 1812. His son, **David Dixon Porter,** 1813–91, was also a naval officer. Next to D. G. Farragut, he was outstanding Union naval commander in Civil War. Appointed full admiral in 1870.

Porter, Horace, 1837–1921, American soldier and diplomat. Aide-de-camp to Gen. Grant (1864–65). Amended DRAGO DOCTRINE to provide arbitration for collection of contract debts (1907).

Porter, Katherine Anne, 1894–, American author. Short stories, notable for purity of style, are collected in *Flowering Judas* (1930), *Pale Horse, Pale Rider* (1939), and *The Leaning Tower* (1944). Essays are in *The Days Before* (1952).

Porter, Noah, 1811–92, American educator and philosopher. At Yale he became professor of philosophy (1846) and was president 1871–86. He edited revised editions of Webster's dictionary (1864, 1890).

Porter, William Sydney: see HENRY, O.

Porterville, city (pop. 6,904), S central Calif., SE of Fresno. Fruit-packing center.

Port Gibson, town (pop. 2,920), SW Miss., near Mississippi R. and S of Vicksburg. Civil War battle fought here in Vicksburg campaign. Near by is Alcorn Agricultural and Mechanical Col. (Negro; land-grant; coed.; 1871).

Port Glasgow, burgh (pop. 21,612), Renfrewshire, Scotland, on S shore of Firth of Clyde. Founded as port for Glasgow before that city was accessible to large ships. Has a large graving dock.

Port Hope, town (pop. 6,548), S Ont., Canada, on L. Ontario and E of Toronto. Summer resort and radium-refining center.

Port Hudson, village, SE La., on E bank of the Mississippi, 20 mi. N of Baton Rouge. Fortified 1862 by Confederates, it was surrendered to N. P. Banks in July, 1863.

Port Huron (hyōō'rŭn), city (pop. 35,725), E Mich., at junction of St. Clair R. with Black R. and at foot of L. Huron; settled 1686 as French fort. Grew in 1800s with lumbering. Rail and water shipping center, it has shipyards, railroad shops, grain elevators, and mfg. of metal products, cement, and paper. Connected by bridge and tunnel with Ontario.

Portinari, Cândido (kän'dēdō pōrtēnä're), 1903–, Brazilian painter, known for his frescoes.

Port Isabel, fishing resort (pop. 2,372), S Texas, on Intracoastal Waterway and NE of Brownsville. Was American supply base in Mexican War.

Port Jefferson, resort and residential village (pop. 3,296), SE N.Y., on Long Island Sound (ferry) opposite Bridgeport, Conn.

Port Jervis, city (pop. 9,372), SE N.Y., on Delaware R. and near point where N.Y., N.J., and Pa. meet. Rail

center. Mfg. of textiles, glass, concrete, silverware.

Portland, William Bentinck, 1st earl of, 1649–1709, Dutch statesman in England; William III's most trusted adviser. Negotiated treaty of Ryswick with France and the unpopular Partition Treaties.

Portland, urban district (pop. 11,324), Dorsetshire, England. On Isle of Portland, a rocky peninsula composed of limestone which has long been used for building. Scene of some of Hardy's works.

Portland. 1 Town (pop. 5,186), central Conn., on Connecticut R. (bridged to Middletown); settled c.1690. Sandstone is quarried. Mfg. of metal products. **2** City (pop. 7,064), E Ind., NE of Muncie. Mfg. of vehicle parts. **3** City (pop. 77,634), SW Maine, on harbor on Casco Bay; settled 1632, set off from Falmouth town 1786. Almost destroyed by British in 1775 and by great fire, 1866. State cap. 1820–31. Largest city and commercial center of Maine, it serves large farm, lumber, paper-milling, fishing, and resort region. Mfg. of paper, cellulose, shoes, wood products, steel, and explosives. Maine's first newspaper, Falmouth *Gazette,* was published here 1785. Has birthplace and home of Longfellow. Was important U.S. naval base and shipping center in World War II. **4** City (pop. 373,628), NW Oregon, on Willamette R. near its mouth in Columbia R.; laid out 1845. Grew fast after 1850 as supply point for Calif. gold fields, after 1883, when railroad came, 1897–1900 during Alaska gold rush. Largest city in state and its major fresh-water port served by oceangoing vessels, with shipyards and mfg. of furniture, paper, and food, wool, and lumber products. Partly flooded by Columbia R., May, 1948. Seat of Univ. of Portland (R.C.; for men; 1901); Reed Col. (nonsectarian; coed.; 1911), which pioneered in progressive and individualized education; Univ. of Oregon medical and dental schools. Holds Pacific International Livestock Exposition and a rose festival annually.

Portland vase, a funerary urn, probably of 1st cent. B.C., known also as the Barberini vase. Made of violet-blue glass overlaid with opaque white glass with cameo relief. Found in ancient tomb near Rome in 17th cent., it was placed in library of Barberini Palace. Bought by duchess of Portland in late 18th cent. and by British Mus. in 1945.

Port Lavaca (lŭvä'kŭ), city (pop. 5,599), S Texas, on Lavaca Bay and SE of San Antonio; founded 1815, destroyed 1840 by Comanches. Deepwater port with refineries, cotton gins, and fish-processing plants. Near by is an aluminum plant. Connected with Intracoastal Waterway.

Port Moresby (môrz'bē), town (pop. 1,300), on SE New Guinea, cap. of Territory of Papua; port on Fairfax Harbor. In World War II chief Allied base on island was here.

Port Neches (nĕ'chĭz), city (pop. 5,448), SE Texas, on Neches R. below Beaumont. Port on Sabine-Neches Canal, it processes and ships oil, synthetic rubber, and chemicals.

Porto, Portugal: see OPORTO.

Pôrto Alegre (pôr'tō ŭlä'grŭ), city (pop. 381,964), cap. of Rio Grande do Sul state, SE Brazil; port at N end of Lagoa dos Patos; founded in 1742 by immigrants from Azores. Population increased since 19th cent. by Germans and Italians. Shipping center for agr. and pastoral hinterland.

Portobelo (pôr"tōbĕ'lō), town (pop. 573), Panama; port on Caribbean coast. Visited by Columbus; founded 1597; became an important colonial port often attacked by British buccaneers. Also Porto Bello, Puerto Bello.

Portoferraio (pôr'tōfĕr-rä'yō), seaport (pop. 7,682), Elba isl., Italy. Ships iron. While sovereign of Elba, Napoleon I lived here (1814–15).

Port of New York Authority, self-sustaining public corporation, estab. 1921 by N.Y. and N.J. to administer and develop terminal and transportation facilities of the New York city port area (771-mi. water front). Manages George Washington Bridge; Holland and Lincoln tunnels; LaGuardia, New York Internatl., Teterboro, and Newark airports.

Port of Spain, town (pop. 92,793), on Trinidad, cap. of Trinidad and Tobago, on fine harbor of Gulf of Paria opposite Venezuela. Transference of bauxite from British and Dutch Guiana and iron ore from Venezuela is made here from coastal and river steamers to ocean-going vessels.

Portolá, Gaspar de (gäspär' dä pôrtölä'), fl. 1734–84, Spanish explorer in Far West. Extended Spanish control up Pacific coast to Monterey (1769–70).

Port Phillip Bay, large inlet of Bass Strait, S Victoria, Australia. Its N arm, Hobson's Bay, is site of Port Melbourne.

Port Pirie (pĭ'rē), city (pop. 12,019), South Australia; port at base of Yorke Peninsula, on inlet of Spencer Gulf. Smelting works for silver-lead mines at Broken Hill, ENE of Port Pirie.

Port Radium or **Eldorado Mines,** arctic village, Mackenzie dist., Northwest Territories, Canada, on Great Bear L. Pitchblende and uranium mining center. Site of government radio and meteorological station and Royal Canadian Mounted Police post. Mines taken over by Canadian government 1944.

Port Republic, village, NW Va., at junction of North and South rivers, which form the South Fork of Shenandoah R. Scene of battle in Stonewall Jackson's Shenandoah Valley campaign (1862), a Confederate victory.

Port Royal, N.S.: see ANNAPOLIS ROYAL.

Port-Royal (pôr'-rwäyäl'), former abbey for women, c.17 mi. W of Paris, founded 1204 as Benedictine, later Cistercian. Its importance came after its abbess, Angélique ARNAULD, began a reform in 1608. In 1626 the abbey was moved to Paris, becoming Port-Royal-de-Paris and the prime center of JANSENISM. The old buildings, Port-Royal-des-Champs, were used as a retreat for men and after 1638 for successful classes for boys. When the Church repudiated Jansenism, Port-Royal-des-Champs was suppressed (1704) and the buildings razed (1710). The nuns were expelled from Port-Royal-de-Paris.

Port Royal Island, c.13 mi. long, 7 mi. wide, S S.C., at head of Port Royal Sound, one of SEA ISLANDS. Resort with fishing and farming.

Port Said (sīd, säd, säēd'), city (pop. 178,432), NE Egypt, on the Mediterranean at entrance to Suez Canal. Founded 1859 by builders of canal and named for Said Pasha, then khedive of Egypt. Important coaling station. On its outer pier is a massive statue of Ferdinand de Lesseps.

Portsmouth, Louise Renée de Kéroualle, duchess of (kārōöäl', pôrts'mŭth), 1649–1734, French mistress of Charles II of England. Exerted great influence in favor of France after 1671. Hated in England, she lived mainly in France after Charles's death.

Portsmouth, county borough (pop. 233,464), on Portsea Isl., Hampshire, England, at entrance to Portsmouth Harbour; chief naval base of Great Britain. Includes Portsea (over 300 acres of dockyards), Southsea (resort), and Portsmouth (garrison town). Cathedral of Thomas à Becket dates from 12th cent. H.M.S. *Victory,* Nelson's flagship at Trafalgar, is a museum. City and harbor were bombed 1940–41.

Portsmouth. 1 City (pop. 18,830), SE N.H., on harbor at Piscataqua R. mouth (bridged) opposite Kittery, Maine. A lumbering and fishing base was estab. at near-by Odiorne's Point 1623. Portsmouth was made a town by Mass. 1653. Provincial cap. of N.H. until Revolution. Shipbuilding began early. U.S. Naval Base (estab. 1800), located on islands linked together and to Kittery by bridges, was ceded to U.S. government by Kittery. Treaty of Portsmouth signed here 1905. City is commercial center for agr. and resort area and only N.H. seaport. It is rich in 18th- and early 19th-cent. homes (many preserved by historical societies). Richard Jackson House (1664) is restored.

First N.H. newspaper, *New Hampshire Gazette,* was published here. Daniel Webster was a resident. **2** City (pop. 36,798), S Ohio, on Ohio R. at mouth of Scioto R. and S of Columbus; laid out 1803. Industrial and railroad center with mfg. of steel and iron products and shoes. **3** Resort and residential town (pop. 6,578), on N RHODE ISLAND, SE R.I., connected with Bristol by Mt. Hope Bridge; includes Prudence Isl.; founded 1638. Colony's first general assembly met here, 1647. Colonial fishing and shipping center. Scene of battle of R.I., 1778. **4** City (pop. 30,039), SE Va., on Elizabeth R. opposite Norfolk; laid out 1750. A port of HAMPTON ROADS, seat of Norfolk Navy Yard. Rail and shipping center with food processing and mfg. of paving materials, fertilizer, and knit goods. Landing base for British in American Revolution. In Civil War navy yard was burned and evacuated by Federals (1861) and occupied by Confederates; retaken by Union forces 1862. Places of interest are Trinity Church (1762), U.S. naval hospital (1827–30), and late-18th-cent. houses.

Portsmouth, Treaty of, 1905, ending Russo-Japanese War, signed at Portsmouth Naval Base, N.H. Achieved through good offices of Theodore Roosevelt. Japan secured Russian evacuation of S Manchuria; cession of S section of Manchurian RR; "paramount" interests in Korea; S half of Sakhalin; and ownership of Russian lease of Liaotung peninsula.

Port Sudan (sōōdän'), city (pop. 47,450), NE Anglo-Egyptian Sudan; port on Red Sea; founded 1906. Chief port of entry into the Sudan.

Port Talbot (tôl'bŭt), municipal borough (pop. 44,024), Glamorganshire, Wales. Export point for coal and mineral industries of the Avon valley.

Port Tobacco, village, SW Md., on inlet of Potomac R. Was important port until harbor silted up. Near by are old manor houses. Jesuit missionaries bought land here in 1649 which order still maintains. Indian name was Potopaco.

Port Townsend, city (pop. 6,888), NW Wash., at entrance to Puget Sound. Ships lumber, coal, fish.

Portugal (pôr'chŭgŭl), republic (35,409 sq. mi.; pop. 8,490,455, incl. MADEIRA ISLANDS and AZORES), W Europe; cap. LISBON. Continental Portugal, in W part of Iberian Peninsula, borders on the Atlantic (W and S) and on Spain (E and N). Largely mountainous, it is crossed by the Tagus, Douro, and Minho rivers. Their fertile valleys and the coastal plains support agr. and vineyards (port wine is a major export). Mountains have cork oak forests, pastures (sheep, cattle, horses); olive groves on lower slopes. Fishing and canning (sardines, tuna) are major industries. Large transit and tourist trade. Continental Portugal's six historic provinces (now redistributed into 11 provinces) are ALENTEJO (cap. ÉVORA), ALGARVE (cap. FARO), BEIRA (cap. COIMBRA), Entre Douro e MINHO (cap. BRAGA; chief port OPORTO), ESTREMADURA (cap. Lisbon), and TRÁS-OS-MONTES (cap. BRAGANÇA). For Portuguese colonies, see ANGOLA; CAPE VERDE ISLANDS; MACAO; MOZAMBIQUE; PORTUGUESE GUINEA; PORTUGUESE INDIA; SÃO TOMÉ AND PRINCIPE; TIMOR. Roman Catholicism is predominant religion. Constitution of 1933 made Portugal a CORPORATIVE STATE, with a corporative chamber (representing industries and professions) alongside national assembly. The state is nominally headed by a president, but as of 1953 Premier Antonio de Oliveira SALAZAR held virtual dictatorial power. Part of modern Portugal coincides with ancient LUSITANIA; its conquest by Rome became final only under Augustus. The region was thoroughly Romanized but fell to the Germanic Suebi and VISIGOTHS (5th cent. A.D.) and to the Moors (711). Portugal as a state was born (11th cent.) as a result of the Christian reconquest. Ferdinand I of Castile took Coimbra (1064); his son Alfonso VI made HENRY OF BURGUNDY count of Coimbra (1095?), a title later changed to count of Portucalense (so called for the land port–i.e., toll station–at the old city of

Cale). Henry's son styled himself king as ALFONSO I (1139) and conquered Lisbon with aid of foreign crusaders (1147). The next 250 years saw Portuguese expansion at expense of the Moors (completed by conquest of Algarve, 1249); the development of the towns, of agr., and Portuguese culture, particularly under kings ALFONSO III and DINIZ; the chronic struggle of the crown against nobles and Church; and unceasing dynastic wars with the Spanish kingdoms, notably with Castile in the reign (1367–83) of FERDINAND I. Ferdinand's succession would have passed to Castile but for the leadership of Nun'Álvares PEREIRA, who defeated the Castilians at Aljubarrota (1385) and estab. JOHN I, founder of the AVIZ dynasty, on the throne. John's son, Prince HENRY THE NAVIGATOR, laid the foundation of the Portuguese empire. Explorers and naval commanders such as Da GAMA, CABRAL, Francisco de ALMEIDA, and ALBUQUERQUE made Portugal the world's leading commercial nation, dominating the East Indian and the African slave trade and owning colonies in Africa, South America (see BRAZIL), and Asia. The zenith was reached under MANUEL I and JOHN III (15th–16th cent.), but depopulation (through colonization and expulsion of the Jews) and neglect of agr. brought rapid decline. The reign of SEBASTIAN ended in the disaster of his African campaign (1578). In 1580 the house of Aviz died out, and Philip II of Spain, nephew of John III, made good his claim to Portugal by force of arms. Under Spanish rule, Portugal lost most of its empire to the Dutch. In 1640 the Portuguese threw off the Spanish yoke; JOHN IV, first king of the BRAGANZA dynasty, cemented Portugal's traditional alliance with England in 1654. Royal absolutism reached its height in the 18th cent. under John V and Joseph. The reforms of POMBAL, Joseph's minister, revitalized Portuguese economy. On the losing side in the French Revolutionary Wars, Portugal made peace in 1801 but was occupied by the French in 1807. Portuguese patriots fought heroically in the PENINSULAR WAR while the royal family was safely in Brazil. In 1822 Brazil became a separate empire under PEDRO I. JOHN VI continued as king of Portugal, but his death (1826) opened the vexed question of his succession. In the Miguelist Wars, MARIA II, backed by the liberals, eventually won out over her uncle MIGUEL (1834). Her and her successors' reigns (see FERDINAND II; CHARLES I; MANUEL II) were a chaotic era of coups and dictatorships, ending with Manuel's abdication and the establishment of a republic (1910). Political troubles continued under the republic until in 1926 Gen. CARMONA estab. his dictatorship. After 1928 Salazar held power. His financial efficiency considerably improved Portugal's economy, though at the expense of democratic rights. Portugal sided with the Allies in World War I; was neutral in World War II; joined the North Atlantic Treaty 1949.

Portuguese East Africa: see MOZAMBIQUE.

Portuguese Guinea (gǐ'nē), colony (13,948 sq. mi.; pop. 351,089), W Africa, on the Atlantic; cap. Bissau. An enclave in French West Africa, it includes Bijagós Isls. off Geba R. estuary. Exports rice, palm oil, and copra. Discovered by the Portuguese in mid-15th cent. Boundaries were estab. 1886.

Portuguese India, colony (1,538 sq. mi.; pop. 624,177), comprising DAMAO, GOA, and DIU.

Portuguese language, Romance language of Italic subfamily of Indo-European languages. See LANGUAGE (table).

Portuguese West Africa: see ANGOLA.

portulaca (pôr"tŭlăk'ù), fleshy annual plant (*Portulaca grandiflora*), native to Brazil. It is widely grown for its bright flowers. Also called rose moss or purslane.

Port Washington, resort and residential village (1940 pop. 10,509), on N shore of Long Isl., SE N.Y., NNW of Mineola. Shellfishing; mfg. of machinery, and concrete products.

Posada, José Guadalupe (pōsä'dhä), 1852–1913, Mexican artist, who strongly influenced the generation of Orozco and Rivera. Produced thousands of prints which were sold cheaply to the masses.

Posadas (pōsä'dhäs), city (pop. 37,588), NE Argentina, port on upper Paraná R. Center of mate industry; tobacco, grains, fruit also grown.

Poseidon (pōsī'dùn), in Greek religion, sea-god, protector of all waters; son of Cronus and Rhea, husband of Amphitrite, and father of Pegasus, Orion, Polyphemus, and other giants and monsters. Horse was his gift to man. He bore the TRIDENT, with which he caused storms. Identified with Roman Neptune.

Posen, Poland: see POZNAN.

positive, in photography: see NEGATIVE.

positivism (pŏ'zĭtĭvĭzm), any philosophical system which rejects metaphysics and maintains that knowledge is founded exclusively on sense experience and the positive sciences. The term is applied specifically to the thought of Auguste COMTE.

positron (pŏ'zĭtrŏn"), positively charged, short-lived particle with same mass as electron.

Post, Emily (Price), 1873–, American authority on etiquette. Her famous book *Etiquette* (1922) has had a number of editions. In the field of interior decoration she is known for *The Personality of a House* (1930).

Post, Wiley, 1900–1935, American aviator. Made round-the-world flights (in 1931, with Harold Gatty; in 1933, alone). Killed in crash near Point Barrow, Alaska, on flight with Will Rogers.

postage stamp, government stamp affixed to mail to indicate payment of postage. Adopted in England in 1839, custom spread throughout the world by 1850. First U.S. official issue was in 1847. Special stamps include air-mail, special-delivery, and postage-due stamps.

postal savings bank, government savings bank operated through local post offices. First established in England in 1861, in U.S. in 1910.

postal service, arrangement for delivering letters, packages, and periodicals. Courier systems for government use existed under the Persian Empire. Britain's postal service, an outgrowth of royal courier routes, was estab. finally in 1657 and penny postage (see POSTAGE STAMP) was begun in 1839. The U.S. system was derived from the colonial service established by England. In the U.S. postage stamps were first used 1847, registered mail 1855, city delivery 1863, money orders 1864, penny post cards 1873, special delivery 1885, rural delivery 1896, postal savings 1910, parcel post 1913. The pony express operated across the continent, 1860–61, rail service was instituted in 1862, AIR MAIL in 1918. The Universal Postal Union was established after the International Postal Convention of 1874.

postimpressionism, term applied to the work of various French painters of the late 19th cent. who wished to apply certain features of IMPRESSIONISM to a more subjective art. Group included Cézanne, Van Gogh, and Gauguin.

Postojna (pô'stoinä), Ger. *Adelsberg*, Ital. *Postumia*, resort town (pop. 3,651), Slovenia, N Yugoslavia, in the KARST. Famous for its stalactite caves (largest in Europe). Was ceded by Italy 1947.

Postumia, Yugoslavia: see POSTOJNA.

potash, name for certain potassium compounds, particularly potassium carbonate, a white crystalline substance when pure. Originally obtained from wood ashes or from residue left in pots after burning plants in them, it is now usually prepared from potassium chloride. It is used to make other potassium compounds, hard glass, and soap, and as a fertilizer. Caustic potash is potassium hydroxide, a strong alkali.

potassium (pùtă'sēùm), active, silver-white, soft metallic element (symbol = K; see also ELEMENT, table). It is so active that it must be kept submerged in oil, out of contact with air. The metal has no commercial value but its compounds are used widely. It reacts violently with water to form potassium hydroxide; combines directly with many nonmetallic elements. It is not found free but occurs in many compounds.

potato, perennial plant (*Solanum tuberosum*) and its swollen underground stem, a tuber, a widely used staple food in temperate climates. The plant belongs to the nightshade family and is probably native to the Andes; it is believed that it was introduced into Spain from Peru in the 16th cent. By the mid-18th cent. it had reached even remote parts of Europe. It became the major food in Ireland (it is often called the Irish potato); a crop failure from blight in 1846 caused famine resulting in death, disease, and emigration. Potatoes contain c.78% water and are a source of carbohydrates (c.18%, mostly starch), iron, and vitamins (esp. vitamin C, much of which is lost by long boiling of peeled potatoes). A potato plant, which needs rich soil high in potash, may produce five tubers. Propagation is by planting pieces of tubers bearing two or three eyes. Plants sometimes produce yellow-green fruits containing seeds. The Colorado potato beetle is the worst pest. See *ill.,* p. 783.

potato bug: see COLORADO POTATO BEETLE.

Potawatami Indians (pŏ″tŭwŏ′tŭmē), North American tribe of Algonquian linguistic stock, closely related to the Ojibwa and Ottawa. In the early 17th cent. they were at Green Bay but later moved to the S end of L. Michigan and expanded E. They supported the French against the British, supported Pontiac, opposed the expansion of the U.S., and sided with the British in the War of 1812. They later retreated W to Iowa and Kansas, and a large group was moved (1868) to Okla. where they took lands individually. Others are on reservations in Kansas, Mich., Wis., and Okla. and in Canada. Also Pottawatomi, Pottawatami.

Potchefstroom (pŏ′chŭfstrōm, –strōōm), town (pop. 27,-205), SW Transvaal, South Africa; founded 1838. Was first cap. of Transvaal (1838–60). Has college connected with Univ. of South Africa.

Potemkin, Grigori Aleksandrovich (grĭgô′rē ŭlyĭksän′-drŭvĭch pŭtyôm′kĭn), 1739–91, Russian field marshal, favorite and adviser of Catherine II, to whom he was perhaps secretly married. Played important part in annexation of Crimea (1783); was created prince and governor of new province, which he administered ably despite his personal eccentricities. The allegation that he had sham villages built to impress Catherine is probably false.

Potenza (pōtĕn′tsä), city (pop. 18,872), cap. of Basilicata, S Italy, in the Apennines.

pothole, deep round hole in bedrock along a stream, usually near falls or rapids, formed by erosive action of whirling water which carries rock debris.

Potidaea (pōtĭdē′ù), anc. city, NE Greece, in Chalcidice. With Corinthian help it attempted to defy Athens and leave the Delian League in 432 B.C., thus providing one immediate cause of the Peloponnesian War. Philip II is said to have destroyed it. Later Cassander rebuilt it as Cassandreia.

Potiphar (pŏ′tĭfûr), Joseph's high-ranking Egyptian master whose wife falsely accused Joseph. Gen. 39.

Poti-pherah (pōtĭ′fûrù), priest of On and father of Joseph's wife Asenath. Gen. 41.45,50; 46.20.

pot marigold: see CALENDULA.

Potomac (pùtō′mùk), river formed SE of Cumberland, Md., and flowing generally SE 285 mi. to Chesapeake Bay. Part of boundary between Md.-W.Va., Md.-Va., and Va.-D.C. Tidal and navigable for large ships to Washington (there bridged); just upstream are Great Falls of the Potomac. Receives the Shenandoah at Harpers Ferry, W.Va. Noted for its beauty and historical associations. Mt. Vernon is on Va. shore below Washington.

Potosí (pōtōse′), city (pop. 43,700), S Bolivia; founded c.1545 at foot of one of world's richest ore mountains. In Andes at height of 13,780 ft., it is one of highest cities in world. For first 50 years Potosí pro-

duced vast amounts of silver, but because of rigorous living conditions, population declined until recent technological developments have revived commerce. Tin, wolfram, and copper also mined.

Potosi (pùtō′sē), city (pop. 2,359), E Mo., SW of St. Louis. Center of a barite-mining area, with zinc, iron, and limestone deposits. Grew with development of lead mines by Moses Austin in 1790s.

Potsdam (pôts′däm), city (pop. 113,568), cap. of Brandenburg, E Germany, on the Havel, near Berlin. Primarily residential. Has moving picture industry (at suburb of Babelsberg); observatory of Univ. of Berlin; astrophysical observatory. Chartered 14th cent.; became electoral residence in 17th cent., later royal residence. Frederick II of Prussia rebuilt the Town Palace and built SANS SOUCI and the New Palace. The Garrison Church (built 1731–35) was destroyed in World War II. Potsdam was the scene of the POTS-DAM CONFERENCE of 1945.

Potsdam, village (pop. 7,491), N N.Y., E of Ogdensburg. Mfg. of paper and cheese. Seat of Clarkson Col. of Technology (for men; 1896).

Potsdam Conference, meeting (July 17–Aug. 2, 1945) of principal Allies in World War II (U.S., USSR, and Great Britain) to supplement, clarify, and implement agreements reached at YALTA CONFERENCE. Present were Pres. Truman, Premier Stalin, and Prime Minister Churchill (later replaced by C. R. Attlee), and their foreign ministers. So-called Potsdam Agreement gave chief authority in Germany to American, Russian, British, and French military commanders in respective zones of occupation (see GERMANY) and to four-power Allied Control Council. It abolished former military and political power in Germany and called for punishment of war criminals, controlled education to foster democratic ideals, restored local self-government with close supervision, and controlled German economy and production. Allies further agreed to transfer former German territory E of Neisse and Oder rivers to Polish and Russian administration pending peace treaty. Rift between USSR and Western powers caused agreement to fail.

Pott, Percivall, 1714–88, English surgeon. He wrote classic descriptions of an ankle fracture and a spine deformity (both known by his name), of hernia, and other conditions.

Pottawatami Indians or **Pottawatomi Indians:** see POTA-WATAMI INDIANS.

Potter, Alonzo, 1800–1865, American Episcopal bishop. As bishop of Pa. (1845–65), he founded in Philadelphia an Episcopal hospital and a divinity school. His son, **Henry Codman Potter,** 1835–1908, was bishop coadjutor of New York (after 1883), bishop after 1887. Initiated first stages of Cathedral of St. John the Divine.

Potter, Beatrix (Mrs. William Heelis), 1866–1943, English author and illustrator of over 25 children's books, such as *The Tale of Peter Rabbit* (1902).

Potter, Edward Clark, 1857–1923, American sculptor of animals. Produced equestrian statuary in collaboration with Daniel Chester French.

Potter, Henry Codman: see POTTER, ALONZO.

Potter, Paul or **Paulus,** 1625–54, Dutch animal painter, noted for simplicity and naturalism of his works. Worked mainly in Delft and The Hague.

Potteries, the, district, c.9 mi. long and 3 mi. wide, Staffordshire, England, in the Trent valley. Densely populated, it has been a center of pottery making since the 16th cent. Includes STOKE-ON-TRENT. Region is "Five Towns" of Arnold Bennett's works.

potter's field: see ACELDAMA.

pottery embraces all the baked clay wares of the ceramics field, from coarse, unglazed, and crudely painted earthenware, through the glazed but heavy faïence and stoneware, to the crowning achievements of the art—porcelain and lusterware. The process for all these is essentially the same: the clay is shaped by building (piece by piece) or is thrown upon a potter's wheel which spins the clay as the hands give it form; it is then slowly dried; and finally it is fired in a kiln which brings it to a permanent hardness. Temperatures of firing vary, reaching as much as 2500° F. for hard porcelain. To give the pottery finish, a vitreous coating called a glaze is often fired on the clay. Glazes may be transparent, white, or colored and of many kinds (e.g., alkaline, lead, felspar) to suit the nature of the pottery. Variations in these techniques produce the many different kinds of pottery. Earthenware is fired at a relatively low temperature so that the clay does not vitrify; stoneware is fired at a high temperature, but unlike porcelain, it is heavy and opaque. On stoneware a salt glaze is produced by putting salt in the fires at the proper time. Porcelain is known for its delicate translucence. After the first firing, body and glaze are fired together at a very high temperature. Lusterware has an overglaze finish containing copper or silver which gives it an iridescence as well as luster. The film producing this effect is applied over the glaze, and the ware receives a third firing. Majolica (or maiolica) is an enameled and decorated faïence of Spain and Italy. The clay object is first fired, given a coating of tin enamel, refired, then decorated in brilliant colors and fired again. Pottery is one of the most enduring materials known to man and is in most places the oldest art. Archaic and later examples are of value as historical and literary records; Assyrian and Babylonian writings have been inscribed upon clay tablets and perpetuated as pottery, many ancient wares are decorated with human and animal figures and portray dress, customs, and events of the times. The Egyptians, Persians, and Greeks all had highly developed forms of pottery. Porcelain probably originated in 14th-cent. China. European wares of the Middle Ages were crudely fashioned and coarsely glazed; Chinese porcelain was a luxury of the wealthy. European imitation of the Chinese art began in the 17th and 18th cent. Since then many places throughout the world have lent their names to potteries which have become famous—Sèvres and Limoges china in France, Cologne and Dresden ware in Germany, delftware in Holland, and the English potteries of Staffordshire, Lambeth (Doulton ware), Bow, Chelsea, Lowestoft, Worcester, Derby, Wedgwood, Minton, and Spode.

Pottstown, borough (pop. 22,589), SE Pa., on Schuylkill R. and NW of Philadelphia; settled 1775. Mfg. of steel and rubber products. First ironworks in state estab. here 1716.

Pottsville, city (pop. 23,640), E Pa., on Schuylkill R. and NW of Reading; settled c.1780. Anthracite mining center with mfg. of clothing, aluminum and steel products. Rallying place for Molly Maguires, who were tried here 1877. Seat of branch of Pennsylvania State Col.

Poughkeepsie (pŭkĭp'sē), city (pop. 41,023), E N.Y., on E bank of Hudson R. (Mid-Hudson Bridge to Highland); settled 1687 by Dutch. Agr. trade center; mfg. of ball bearings, cream separators, business machines, hardware. VASSAR COLLEGE is at adjacent Arlington village (pop. 5,374). Intercollegiate Rowing Regatta held here 1895–1950. Has Van Kleeck Homestead (1702). Federal Constitution ratified here 1788.

Poulenc, Francis (pōōläk'), 1899–, French composer and pianist. Among his numerous works are concertos and short pieces for piano, chamber music, ballets, and songs.

Poulsen, Valdemar (väl'dùmär poul'sùn), 1869–1942, Danish electrical engineer. Invented telegraphone (electromagnetic telephone-conversation recorder) and high-frequency Poulsen arc used in radio.

poultry, domestic birds raised for food (eggs or meat). The chief poultry bird is the chicken, once a jungle fowl in SW Asia, and domesticated over 3,000 years ago. There are over 100 varieties, including egg, meat, and dual-purpose breeds, classed according to their place of origin. Popular American breeds include Plymouth Rocks, Rhode Island Reds, and New Hampshires—all dual-purpose breeds. An outstanding European breed raised in the U.S. for egg production is the Leghorn. Among chickens raised for ornament and other uses are the small Bantam and the Game (formerly bred for cockfighting). Commercial poultry raising is a large-scale enterprise which often includes raising chickens in mechanized indoor batteries with each bird in a separate compartment, and artificial hatching of eggs in an incubator. See also DUCK; GOOSE; GUINEA FOWL; PHEASANT; PIGEON; TURKEY.

Pound, Ezra (Loomis), 1885–, American poet. Led poetic movement of IMAGISTS, later turned to VORTICISM. Works include *Cathay* (1915; from Chinese) and *Umbra* (1920; from Latin). His later work was in series of *Cantos* (1925–48; including *Pisan Cantos*), brilliant, erudite, allusive poems woven of scraps from many literatures. His controversial work has had much influence. Much criticized for his Fascist activity in Italy in World War II. Later put in mental hospital.

Pound, Roscoe, 1870–, American jurist, professor (1910–17) and dean (1916–36) of Harvard Law School; author of influential works on jurisprudence.

Poussin, Nicolas (nēkôlä' pōōsē'), 1594–1665, French classical painter, b. Normandy. Spent most of his life in Rome, where he first won recognition. During brief stay in Paris (1640–43) he served Louis XIII and Richelieu. Famous for discipline and intellectuality of his compositions (e.g., *Shepherds in Arcadia* in Louvre). Influenced many French painters, notably Claude Lorrain and Cézanne.

Powder, river rising in N Wyo. and flowing 486 mi. NE into Mont. to join Yellowstone R. near Terry.

powder, substance composed of finely granulated particles. In special sense word is applied to powdered propellent explosives, e.g., GUNPOWDER, and to powders that produce bright light when ignited. In 19th cent. various smokeless powders began to supersede gunpowder. In 1864 Edward Schultze, Prussian artillery captain, invented a smokeless powder (probably first successful kind) known after 1870 as Schultze powder and made chiefly of nitrocellulose; used in shotguns, blank cartridges, hand grenades, and in igniting propellent powder used in artillery. Paul Vieille invented (1885) *poudre* B (nitrocotton and ether-alcohol) for rifles. Ballistite (nitrocotton gelatinized by nitroglycerine) was later added to the growing list of powders by Alfred Nobel. Cordite, another smokeless powder, invented (1889) by Sir F. A. Abel and Sir James Dewar, contained highly nitrated guncotton and nitroglycerine blended by means of acetone. Indurite, invented (1891) by C. E. Monroe, is made from guncotton colloided with nitrobenzine.

Powderly, Terence Vincent, 1849–1924, American labor leader. Joined (1874) KNIGHTS OF LABOR, which he led (1879–93) during its greatest strength.

Powell, Cecil Frank, 1903–, English physicist. Won 1950 Nobel Prize for developing photographic method for studying atomic nucleus and for discoveries regarding the nuclear particles called mesons.

Powell, John Wesley, 1834–1902, American geologist and ethnologist, noted for his explorations of W U.S. While making a survey of the Colorado R. he led a party by boat through the Grand Canyon. He was instrumental in founding U.S. Geological Survey; served as director (1881–94).

Powell, town (pop. 3,804), NW Wyo. Hq. of SHOSHONE PROJECT. Fossil beds in area.

power, defined as energy made capable of doing work. In mechanics, capacity is measured by units of accomplishment correlated with time. Commonly used is the horsepower unit (550 foot-pounds per second; a foot-pound is ability to lift a pound one foot). In engineering, power is energy of all kinds taking the form of mechanical or electrical energy. The simple water wheel, rotated by falling or swiftly flowing water, has given way to the modern turbine linked to electric generators, for the production of hydroelectric power. Hydroelectric plants in U.S. include those at Boulder Dam, Grand Coulee Dam, and Hoover Dam in the Central Valley Project. Energy of fuel is converted to mechanical energy in INTERNAL-COMBUSTION ENGINE and STEAM ENGINE. In various devices power is transmitted by means of belt, rope, and chain drives, by gears or shafts, by pipes (steam and compressed air), and wires (electrical currents). Potential source is atomic, or nuclear, energy. See *ills.*, pp. 303, 619.

Powers, Hiram, 1805–73, American sculptor, who was extremely popular in his day. His *Greek Slave* (1843) was renowned in Europe and America. Worked mainly in Florence.

Powhatan (pou″ŭtän′), d. 1618, American Indian chief of Powhatan tribe in Va.; father of POCAHONTAS. He extended dominion of **Powhatan Confederacy,** group of tribes extending along coast and up rivers of tidewater Va. Indian attacks after Powhatan's death led to bloody reprisals by English. Confederacy yielded much territory in 1646 and disappeared after 1722.

Pownal, town (pop. 1,453), SW Vt., S of Bennington. J. A. Garfield and C. A. Arthur taught here. Scene of land-grant strife between N.Y. and N.H.

Pownall, Thomas (pou′nŭl), 1722–1805, English statesman and colonial governor of Mass. (1757–59). Urged stronger union of colonies with mother country. Member of Parliament (1767–1780).

Powys, John Cowper (pō′ĭs), 1872–, English author and lecturer. His works include novels (e.g., *Wolf Solent,* 1929), poetry, essays and criticism (e.g., *The Enjoyment of Literature,* 1938), and autobiography. His brother, **Theodore Francis Powys,** 1875–, wrote novels (e.g., *Black Bryony,* 1923) and short stories. Another brother, **Llewelyn Powys,** 1884–1939, was also an author. His works include novels (e.g., *Love and Death,* 1939), essays and sketches (e.g., *Earth Memories,* 1938), and autobiography.

Poyang (pō′yäng), shallow lake, area 1,070 sq. mi., N Kiangsi prov., China. Connected with Yangtze R. by Hukow Canal.

Poynings, Sir Edward, 1459–1521, English statesman. Lord deputy of Ireland 1494–96, he had enacted (1494) **Poynings's Law,** providing that English privy council must assent to calling of Irish Parliament and to any of its legislation. Henry Grattan procured its repeal in 1782.

Poznan, Pol. *Poznań* (pôz′nänyù), Ger. *Posen,* city (pop. 267,978), W Poland, on Warta R. Commercial center. See of Catholic primate of Poland since 1821 (when it was transferred from Gniezno). It became (10th cent.) the first Polish episcopal see and was a nucleus of the Polish state. Passed to Prussia in second Polish partition (1793); was included in duchy of Warsaw 1807; reverted to Prussia 1815; to Poland 1919. Was heavily bombed in World War II. University was founded 1919. Poznan prov. includes sections of Brandenburg, Pomerania, and Lower Silesia, placed under Polish administration in 1945.

Pozsony, Czechoslovakia: see BRATISLAVA.

Pozzo di Borgo, Carlo Andrea (kär′lō ändrā′ä pôt′tsō dē bôr′gō), 1764–1842, Russian diplomat, b. Corsica. Supported British occupation of Corsica (1794); superseded Paoli in authority. An exile after French reconquest, he entered Russian service (1804), promoted Russian opposition to Napoleon I, and served as ambassador to France after 1814.

Pr, chemical symbol of the element PRASEODYMIUM.

Prado (prä′dō), national Spanish museum of painting and sculpture, on Paseo del Prado, Madrid. Begun by Juan Villanueva under Charles III and finished 1830 under Ferdinand VII. Has priceless masterpieces of Spanish, Flemish, and Venetian schools.

Praetorians (prētô′rēŭnz), bodyguard of the Roman emperors, formally organized in the time of Augustus from the troop that had guarded the general commanding in Rome. They attended the emperor everywhere, had special privileges, and, in times of trouble, chose many of the emperors. Constantine I disbanded them (312).

Praetorius, Michael (prētô′rēŭs), 1571–1621, German composer and musicologist, whose name originally was Schultheiss. Chiefly known today for his *Syntagma musicum* (3 vols.), which minutely describes the musical practices and instruments of his day.

pragmatic sanction (prăgmă′tĭk), decision of state dealing with a matter of great importance and having force of fundamental law. The **Pragmatic Sanction of Bourges,** issued by Charles VII of France in 1438, limited papal authority over Church in France and estab. liberty of Gallican Church (see GALLICANISM). It was revoked by Louis XI (1461). The **Pragmatic Sanction** of 1713, issued by Emperor Charles VI, altered the HAPSBURG family law. In absence of a male heir, it reserved succession to all Hapsburg lands (but not to the elective imperial dignity) to MARIA THERESA. Charles obtained, after much labor, the adherence to the Pragmatic Sanction of most European powers and of the local diets of the various Hapsburg lands. However, at his death several monarchs challenged Maria Theresa's rights to succession—notably Augustus III of Poland and Saxony and Elector Charles Albert of Bavaria (later Emperor Charles VII), both of whom had married nieces of Charles VI. The War of the AUSTRIAN SUCCESSION resulted.

pragmatism (prăg′mùtĭzùm), any system of philosophy in which it is held that the truth of a proposition must be measured by its correspondence with experimental results and by its practical outcome. Thus in pragmatism any metaphysical significance of thought is discarded, and all methods supposedly leading to truth through deduction from a priori grounds are rejected. Pragmatists hold that truth is modified as discoveries are made and that truth evolves, being relative to time, place, and purpose. Most pragmatists hold that in ethics knowledge which contributes to human values is real and that values inhere in the means as much as in the end. These principles are generally said to have been first developed formally by C. S. PEIRCE. William JAMES advanced them greatly, and they have had great force in philosophy since (as in the instrumentalism of John DEWEY).

Prague (präg, prāg), Czech *Praha,* Ger. *Prag,* city (pop. 922,284), cap. of Czechoslovakia and of Bohemia, on the Moldau. Commercial and industrial center (machinery, foodstuffs); archiepiscopal see. A castle from the 9th cent., it was chartered 1232 and settled by German colonists. Under Emperor Charles IV it became one of the most splendid cities of Europe. The reforms preached by John Huss led to civil troubles; in 1419 the first Defenestration of Prague (see WENCESLAUS, emperor) touched off the Hussite Wars. The second Defenestration of Prague took place in 1618, when the Protestant Czech nobles threw two royal councilors and the secretary of the royal council of Bohemia out of the windows of Hradcany Castle. Nobody was hurt, but the event marked the outbreak of the THIRTY YEARS WAR, which resulted in the total subjection of Bohemia to Austrian rule. Until 1860 German was the sole official language. The cap. of Czechoslovakia from 1918, Prague was occupied by the Germans 1939–45 but suffered very little war damage. On the W bank of the Moldau are the imposing Hradcany Castle, formerly the royal, now the presidential residence (14th–18th cent.); the Gothic Cathedral of St. Vitus, with the tombs of St. Wenceslaus and of several kings and emperors; the 18th-cent. archiepiscopal palace; the baroque Church of Our Lady of Victory, with the miraculous statuette of the Infant Jesus of Prague; several magnificent baroque palaces (Waldstein, Schwarzenberg, Czernin); and the quaint Alchemists' or Golden Lane. Among the 12 bridges the most famous is Charles Bridge (14th cent.).

On the E bank are the university and the Gothic Old Town Hall and Tyn Cathedral; the business district, with Wenceslaus Square; and the ancient Visehrad quarter. The **University of Prague** (Charles Univ.) was founded 1348 by Charles IV. Its faculty was organized in four "nations"—Czech, Saxon, Bavarian, Polish. In 1409, by the Decree of Kutna Hora, Emperor Wenceslaus gave the Czech "nation" preponderance in the voting procedure, thus making possible the election of Huss as rector; the Germans left and founded the Univ. of Leipzig. In the Hussite Wars, Charles Univ. was the stronghold of the Utraquists. It was Germanized after 1620, but in 1882 two branches were organized—Charles Univ. (Czech) and Ferdinand Univ. (German). In 1939–45 the Czech university was suppressed; in 1945 the German university was abolished.

Prague, Peace of, 1635: see THIRTY YEARS WAR.

Prague, Treaty of, 1866: see AUSTRO-PRUSSIAN WAR.

Praguerie (prägürē'), 1440, revolt of great feudal lords against Charles VII of France; so called by allusion to Hussite uprising in Prague. The dauphin (later Louis XI) was among rebels, who received support from Philip the Good of Burgundy. Charles suppressed the revolt, but treated the rebels leniently.

Praha, Czechoslovakia: see PRAGUE.

prairie chicken, American game bird of GROUSE family. Found in parts of Canada; on Great Plains; in Texas and La.

prairie dog, North American rodent (*Cynomys*) of squirrel family. The short fur is brownish or buff, whitish on the under parts; plump body is 12–15 in. long. Prairie dogs live in burrows grouped in colonies.

Prairie du Chien (prâ'rē dù shēn'), city (pop. 5,392), SW Wis., on the Mississippi just above mouth of Wisconsin R. Fox-Wisconsin river route from Great Lakes reached the Mississippi here, and here Nicolas Perrot built Fort St. Nicolas 1686. War of 1812 fort here changed hands, burned. Town grew around American Fur Co. post; later was important river port. Fort Crawford built here 1816. Dr. William Beaumont conducted his experiments there. Site of fort now has museum.

Prairie Grove, town (pop. 939), NW Ark, SW of Fayetteville. Civil War battle here (Dec. 7, 1862) resulted in Confederate defeat, thus strengthening Union hold in NW Ark.

Prairie Provinces, see: MANITOBA; SASKATCHEWAN; ALBERTA.

prairies, generally level, originally grass-covered and treeless plains of U.S., stretching from W Ohio through Ind., Ill., and Iowa to Great Plains region. Prairie belt also extends into N Mo., S Mich., Wis., and Minn., E N.Dak. and S.Dak., and S Canada. With rich prairie soil, area is one of most productive regions of U.S.

prairie schooner, wagon covered with white canvas, almost universally used in migration across plains of W U.S. Commonly it was a farm wagon with top drawn in at ends and drawn by two or four horses or by oxen. Often traveled in wagon train.

prairie wolf: see COYOTE.

Praise, Ky.: see ELKHORN CITY.

Prajadhipok (prùchä'tïpôk), 1893–1941, king of THAILAND (1925–35). Constitutional limits placed on the royal power led to his abdication.

Prakrit (prä'krĭt) [Sanskrit;= common], any of several languages of Indic group of Indo-Iranian subfamily of Indo-European languages. See LANGUAGE (table).

Prakrit literature is mostly devoted to JAINISM, but it also includes secular literature and lyric poetry. The sacred texts (*Siddhanta* or *Agama*) of the two main sects of the Jains are written in three types of Prakrit: Ardha-Magadhi, Maharastri, and Savraseni. In Sanskrit drama, Prakrit was often used as the speech of the common people.

Prasad, Rajendra (rùjĕn'drù prùsäd'), 1884–, first president of India (1950–); educated at Univ. of Allahabad.

Admitted to the bar, 1911. Headed Indian Natl. Congress four times. Presided 1948–49 over drafting of Indian constitution. Reelected 1952.

praseodymium (prä"zēōdĭ'mēum), rare metallic element of rare earths (symbol = Pr; see also ELEMENT, table). Its salts are used to color glass.

Pratt, Charles, 1st Earl Camden, 1714–94, English jurist, lord Chancellor (1766–70). Declared the prosecution of John Wilkes illegal. Denounced British policy toward American colonists.

Pratt, Edwin John, 1883–, Canadian poet. With *Titans* (1926) he broke away from romantic tradition of Canadian poetry. *Dunkirk* (1941) is considered one of the best poems of World War II.

Pratt, Orson, 1811–81, Mormon apostle. Appointed (1835) missionary abroad. In Utah, he was after 1847 influential member of assembly. His brother, **Parley Parker Pratt,** 1807–57, was also apostle (1835) and missionary in England. He helped frame constitution of state of Deseret and devised a Mormon alphabet.

Pratt, city (pop. 7,523), S Kansas, W of Wichita. Shipping center for wheat area.

Pratt Institute, at Brooklyn, New York city; nonsectarian, coed; chartered and opened 1887. Has schools of architecture, art, engineering, home economics, and library science.

prawn, decapod crustacean closely allied to shrimp, found in temperate and tropical, salt and fresh waters.

Praxiteles (prăksĭ'tùlēz), fl. c.370–c.330 B.C., most famous of the Attic sculptors. His *Hermes with the Infant Dionysius* is the only undisputed extant original by an ancient master. A copy of his *Aphrodite of Cnidus* is in the Vatican. He was unsurpassed as a worker in marble.

Prayer, Book of Common: see BOOK OF COMMON PRAYER.

praying mantis: see MANTIS.

Preble, Edward (prĕ'bùl), 1761–1807, American naval officer. Commanded a squadron in war against Barbary States (see TRIPOLITAN WAR).

Pre-Cambrian: see ARCHEOZOIC ERA; PROTEROZOIC ERA.

precession of the equinoxes (prēsĕ'shùn), progression of equinoctial points (see EQUINOX) whereby each point reaches a given meridian progressively sooner than a given star in successive passages. The motion results in completion of a cone figure by earth's axis in c.25,800 years and in westward movement of vernal equinox along ZODIAC.

precipitation, in chemistry, reaction in which an insoluble substance is formed when some specific reagent is added to a solution. Colloids can be precipitated by addition of strong electrolyte. Precipitation is believed to result from neutralizing effect of ions with charge opposite to that of suspended particles.

predestination, Christian theological doctrine regarding question of free will. Fundamental dilemma is whether man is free to take responsibility for actions or whether his choice is controlled. Christian predestination is based on two assumptions—that God's plan is absolute and that God elects or condemns men to salvation or damnation. John Calvin formulated doctrine of absolute predestination, expressed later in Westminster Confession and in Westminster Larger Catechism. Less extreme forms exist in many Christian systems, such as Luther's.

Preemption Act, passed in 1841 by U.S. Congress in response to demands of Western states that squatters be allowed to preempt lands. Permitted settlers to locate a claim of 160 acres and after six months of residence to purchase it from the government for as low as $1.25 an acre. After passage of HOMESTEAD ACT (1862), value of preemption declined. Preemption act repealed in 1891.

Pregl, Fritz (frĭts' prä'gùl), 1869–1930, Austrian physiologist and chemist. Won 1923 Nobel Prize in Chemistry for work on quantitative organic microanalysis.

pregnancy or **gestation** (jĕstä'shùn), period between fertilization of ovum and birth. Duration in humans is c.280 days. Chief early symptom is cessation of menstruation. Tests for pregnancy are based on changes in certain animals injected with urine from pregnant woman. Fetal heart beat and movements are detectable by end of fifth month. Disorders include ABORTION and toxemia. See also PRENATAL CARE.

prehistoric man: see MAN, PRIMITIVE.

premier: see PRIME MINISTER.

Premysl, Czech *Přemysl* (pshĕ'mĭsùl), earliest dynasty of Bohemia, founded 8th cent. by the semilegendary peasant Premysl, whom the Bohemian princess Libussa chose as husband. Best-known among early Premysl dukes of Bohemia is St. WENCESLAUS ("Good King Wenceslaus"). The title king became hereditary with OTTOCAR I (1198). His successors were WENCESLAUS I, OTTOCAR II, WENCESLAUS II, and WENCESLAUS III, on whose death in 1306 John of Luxemburg succeeded.

prenatal care (prē"nā'tùl), medical attention given expectant mother during PREGNANCY. Comprises thorough examination, blood and urine tests, and periodic checks of mother and of growth of embryo. Suitable regimen is set up; pregnancy diet, usually high in protein, calcium, iron, and vitamins, may be enriched to counteract anemia and vitamin deficiencies.

Prendergast, Maurice (Brazil), 1859–1924, American painter, a member of The Eight. Used small dots of colors to create landscapes with tapestry effect.

Pre-Raphaelites (prē"-rä'fĕ͞ulīts"), brotherhood of British painters and poets formed 1848 in protest against prevailing standards of British art. Chief founders were ROSSETTI, Holman Hunt, and John Millais. So called because they found inspiration in work of Italian painters prior to Raphael. Also influenced by Ford Madox Brown and by the NAZARENES. Defended by Ruskin and attracted such followers as Burne-Jones, G. F. Watts, and William Morris. Movement died out before end of 19th cent.

Presbyterianism, system of church polity based on government by series of courts composed of clerical and lay presbyters. It stands between episcopacy and Congregationalism. Presbyters or elders manage spiritual conduct of church; deacons and trustees, temporal affairs. Court of congregation is session; next higher is synod; highest is general assembly, with supervisory power over denomination. Presiding officer is moderator. Presbyterian churches are direct heirs of CALVINISM in doctrine and polity. They believe in Bible as sole rule of faith and in sacraments of baptism and Lord's Supper. Presbyterianism organized in British Isles uses Westminster Confession of Faith and Luther's Catechisms. By mid-16th cent. system was strong in England and esp. in Scotland under John KNOX. Divisions of Church of Scotland were Cameronians or Covenanters, Associate Synod, "Burghers," and Free Church of Scotland. Irish Presbyterianism is largely confined to Northern Ireland. Welsh Presbyterianism is represented by Calvinistic Methodist Church. In America Francis Makemie, Irish missionary, set up first presbytery at Philadelphia 1706; synod was formed 1716. Main body today is Presbyterian Church in U.S.A. Other bodies include Presbyterian Church in the U.S., Cumberland Presbyterian Church, Orthodox Presbyterian Church, and United Presbyterian Church of North America.

Prescott, William Hickling, 1796–1859, American historian. Known especially for *History of the Conquest of Mexico* (1843) and *The Conquest of Peru* (1847). He wrote in style that made history live.

Prescott, town (pop. 3,518), SE Ont., Canada, on St. Lawrence R. and S of Ottawa, opposite Ogdensburg, N.Y. Fort Wellington, now a museum, was built in War of 1812. At near-by Windmill Point, British repulsed large American force 1814.

Prescott, city (pop. 6,764), central Ariz., in mountains NNW of Phoenix. Built near Fort Whipple (now a VA hospital) in 1864, was territorial cap. 1865–67 and 1877–89. Center for mining (e.g., copper), ranching; health and summer resort. Has annual Frontier Days rodeo and reenactment of Indian ceremonials.

president, in modern republics, the chief executive and therefore highest officer in a government. Powers vary greatly in different countries; status ranges from largely honorific (e.g., in France) to dictatorial (as sporadically occurs in many Latin American countries). In U.S., President has been delegated substantial powers by Constitution, amplified by statutes. He serves a four-year term, taking office on Jan. 20 (according to Twentieth Amendment); must be 35 years old, a native of U.S., 14 years a resident within U.S. F. D. Roosevelt in 1940 broke the precedent of no third term estab. by Washington. See ELECTORAL COLLEGE. For a list of U.S. Presidents, see UNITED STATES.

Presidential Range, group of the White Mts., N N.H. Includes mounts WASHINGTON (6,288 ft.), Adams (5,798 ft), Jefferson (5,715 ft.), Clay (5,532 ft.), Monroe (5,385 ft.), and Madison (5,363 ft.).

Prespa, Lake (prĕ'spä), area 112 sq. mi., in SW Yugoslavia, NW Greece, and E Albania. Underground channels connect it with L. Ochrida.

Presque Isle (prĕskīl'), city (pop. 9,954), NE Maine, N of Houlton. Trade and shipping center of Aroostook valley (potatoes). Site of U.S. air base (1941).

press, freedom of the. Pervasive censorship was estab. by Church and state in Europe soon after the advent of printing. In post-Reformation England, monopolies were granted to a few printers by the crown, licensing of all publications before printing was required (1534–1695), criticism of government was made a felony, and until the 1770s publishing of parliamentary debates was closely restricted. Compulsory stamp duties on newspapers were rescinded by 1855; truth became admissible as defense in libel cases in 1868. The First Amendment to U.S. Constitution forbade Congress to make laws abridging freedom of the press; this was made binding on the states by judicial interpretation of Fourteenth Amendment (1868). ALIEN AND SEDITION ACTS (1798) were first serious threat to this guarantee. During World War I government censorship was widely enforced for the first time. After 1919 the Supreme Court used a "clear and present danger" test–to determine whether the words would induce acts that Congress had a right to prevent. During World War II an effective Office of Censorship operated (1941–45). In dictatorships, governments control the press; in a free-enterprise system, freedom of the press may be eclipsed by consolidation and monopolization of press by limited private interests.

Pressburg, German name of BRATISLAVA, Czechoslovakia. The **Treaty of Pressburg,** 1805, restored peace between France and Austria after Napoleon's victory at Austerlitz. Austria ceded Venetia to Napoleon (in his quality as king of Italy); Tyrol and Vorarlberg to Bavaria; and its Swabian holdings to Württemberg and Baden. Salzburg was annexed to Austria.

pressure, in mechanics, FORCE acting upon unit area of surface of a body, distinct from total force applied to the body. Atmospheric pressure is c.15 lb. per square inch at sea level. It is measured by a BAROMETER. Term "pressure gauge" is commonly used for other pressure-measuring instruments. Pressure variations are accompanied by observable changes in boiling point and melting point of materials.

Prester John (prĕs'tùr) [Mid. Eng. *prester* = priest], legendary Christian monarch of a vast, wealthy empire in Asia or Africa. The legend appeared in the 12th cent. and may have been based on Ethiopia or some Nestorian kingdom.

Preston, town (pop. 7,619), S Ont., Canada, on Grand R. and ESE of Kitchener. Resort with sulphur springs and flour and woolen mills.

Preston, county borough (pop. 119,243), Lancashire, England. A center of cotton mfg., it has harbor with extensive docks. A guild-merchant festival is held every 20 years. Scene of a Cromwell victory (1648) and Jacobite surrender (1715).

SMALL CAPITALS = cross references. Pronunciation key on inside end pages. Abbreviations: p. 2.

Prestonpans, burgh (pop. 2,907), East Lothian, Scotland. Scene of a famous rout (1745) of forces under Sir John Cope by the Jacobites.

Prestwick, burgh (pop. 11,386), Ayrshire, Scotland; a resort. A large airport, built in World War II, is now a civil airport.

Pretoria (prĭtô′rēù), city (pop. 168,058), S central Transvaal; administrative cap. of South Africa and cap. of Transvaal prov. Founded 1855 and named for Andries Pretorius. Seat of Univ. of Pretoria. Has steel mills and railroad workshops.

Pretorius, Andries Wilhelmus Jacobus (prĭtô′rēùs), 1799–1853, Boer leader. Helped create the nucleus of South African Republic estab. 1853 in the Transvaal. City of Pretoria was named for him. His son **Martinus Wessel Pretorius,** 1818?–1901, was first president of South African Republic in the Transvaal (1857–71) and concurrently president of Orange Free State (1859–63).

Prevost, Sir George (prĕ′vō), 1767–1816, English general, governor in chief of Canada (1811–15). Commanded British forces in Canada in War of 1812; blamed for retreat at Sackets Harbor (1813) and defeat at Plattsburg (1814).

Prévost, Marcel (märsĕl′ prăvō′), 1862–1941, French novelist. His best-known novel is Les Demi-Vierges (1894; Eng. tr., 1895).

Prévost d'Exiles, Antoine François (ätwän′ fräswä′ prăvō′ dāgzēl′), known as **Abbé Prévost,** 1697–1763, French author. He entered the Benedictine order in 1720; fled in 1727; led an adventurous life as a journalist in England, Holland, and Germany; later was readmitted into the order and died as a prior. Of his innumerable writings, only the novel Manon Lescaut (1732), his masterpiece, is still widely read. It served as basis for the operas Manon, by Massenet, and Manon Lescaut, by Puccini.

Priam (prī′ùm), in Greek legend, Trojan king; husband of Hecuba and father of Hector, Paris, Troilus, Cassandra, and others. Killed in Trojan War.

Priapus (prīā′pùs), in Greek religion, god of the countryside, associated with phallicism. Represented as very ugly. Priapic rites were orgiastic.

Pribilof Islands (prĭ′bĭlôf″), group of four islands off SW Alaska, in Bering Sea and N of Aleutian Isls. Visited and named 1786 by Russian navigator, Gerasim Pribilof. Residents are Aleuts and few U.S. government representatives. Important seal breeding ground. To prevent extinction of seals, U.S., Great Britain, Japan, and Russia in 1911 settled BERING SEA FUR-SEAL CONTROVERSY by giving U.S. right to enforce its provisions. Japan withdrew 1941. Under protection, seal herd has greatly increased. Aleuts make living by processing seal and fox furs.

Price, Sterling, 1809–67, Confederate general. Helped defeat Union forces at Wilson Creek, Mo. (1861), but his campaign in Miss. (Oct., 1862) was unsuccessful. His defeat at Westport, Mo. (1864), marked last Confederate thrust in Far West.

Price, city (pop. 6,010), E central Utah, on Price R. Coal-mining center in irrigated agr. area.

Prichard, industrial city (pop. 19,014), SW Ala., N suburb of Mobile. Meat packing; canning.

prickly ash, deciduous shrub or tree (Zanthoxylum americanum) of E North America with prickly twigs, foliage similar to that of the ash, small flower clusters, and red pods with black seeds.

prickly pear, jointed flat-stemmed cactus plant of genus Opuntia, often spiny, and with colorful edible fruits. Some are grown as hedge plants in Mexico and Calif. and as pot plants farther north. Prickly pears known as Indian fig (Opuntia ficus-indica) and tuna (O. tuna) are grown in warm regions; the fruits, stems, and seeds yield various food products.

Pride, Thomas, d. 1658, English soldier in Puritan Revolution. Carried out (1648) **Pride's Purge,** excluding Presbyterians from Parliament as royalists. Remaining Rump Parliament tried Charles I.

Priestley, J(ohn) B(oynton), 1894–, English author, best known for novels (e.g., The Good Companions, 1929; Angel Pavement, 1930) and plays (e.g., Laburnum Grove, 1933).

Priestley, Joseph, 1733–1804, English theologian and scientist. He prepared for Presbyterian ministry, but gradually adopted Unitarian views. He founded the Theological Repository. He opposed orthodox doctrines and some government policies. Because of his sympathy with the French Revolution his home and scientific materials were destroyed and he emigrated to the U.S. 1794. In his History of Electricity (1767) he explained the rings (Priestley's rings) formed by discharge on metallic surface. He produced oxygen, but did not realize importance of discovery.

Prim, Juan (hwän′ prĕm′), 1814–70, Spanish general and politician. Supported Isabella II against Carlists; fought in Morocco (1859–60) and Mexico (1861–62). Held high offices under Isabella but was repeatedly exiled by his rivals; took a major part in Isabella's overthrow (1868). Was assassinated.

primary, in U.S., a preliminary election in which a party candidate is nominated directly by the voters. Resulted from demand to eliminate evils of nomination by party conventions. Primary was first used in local elections in 1868; in 1903 Gov. R. M. La Follette secured in Wis. a direct primary law for nomination of state-wide candidates. By 1917 all but four states had enacted primary laws. Some states extend primary principle to national party conventions by electing state delegates who reflect popular preference for presidential candidates. U.S. Congress has power to regulate primaries for Federal candidates.

primate (prī′māt, –mĭt), animal of highest order of mammals, the Primates (as order pronounced prīmā′-tēz). Includes APE, LEMUR, MONKEY, MAN. Subdivisions are controversial.

Primaticcio, Francesco (fränchä′skō prēmätĕt′chō), 1504–70, Italian artist. Influenced by Giulio Romano and Corregio. Helped extend influence of Italian art in France mainly through his frescoes and stucco work at Fontainebleau.

prime minister or **premier** (prē′mēùr, prùmēr′, prĕm′-yùr), the chief member of a responsible cabinet, as in England. He is in effect the leader of his party, he appoints the ministry, and makes government policy.

primitive man: see MAN, PRIMITIVE.

Primitive Methodist Church, group which seceded from Wesleyan Methodist Church in England under William Clowes and Hugh Bourne. Merged (1932) with Wesleyan and United Methodists. Branch estab. in U.S. c.1830.

Primo de Rivera, Miguel (mēgĕl′ prē′mō dā rēvä′rä), 1870–1930, Spanish general and dictator (1923–30). His reactionary rule was supported by Alfonso XIII but was overthrown when part of the army joined the Socialist, liberal, and Catalan separatist opposition. His son José Antonio, founder of the FALANGE, was executed by the Loyalists in the civil war (1936).

primogeniture (prī″mōjĕn′ĭchùr), in law, rule of inheritance whereby land descends to oldest son. Under feudal system, primogeniture governed land held in military tenure; disinherited younger sons in knight service. When payment of a tax supplanted military service, need for primogeniture lessened, but the custom continued in England.

Primrose, William, 1904–, Scottish-American violist, generally regarded as the world's outstanding solo violist.

primrose, low herbaceous perennial of genus Primula, of north temperate zone, with spring-blooming flowers of various colors borne in heads or umbels. Primroses are grown in rock gardens, borders, or indoors in pots. In England a yellow species (Primula veris) is called cowslip.

Prince, Thomas, 1687–1758, American clergyman and historian; copastor from 1718 of Old South Church, Boston. Best known for Chronological History of New

England (2 vols., 1736, 1755), covering years 1602–33.

Prince Albert, city (pop. 17,149), central Sask., Canada, on North Saskatchewan R. and NNE of Saskatoon; founded 1866. Trade center in fur-trapping, lumbering, and ranch area. Gateway to Prince Albert Natl. Park (NW). Hq. of Royal Canadian Mounted Police for central and N Sask.

Prince Albert National Park, 1,496 sq. mi., central Sask., Canada, NW of Prince Albert; estab. 1927. Largely wooded parklands with many lakes. Animal sanctuary. Hq. at Waskesiu, on L. Waskesiu.

Prince Edward Island, province and island (2,184 sq. mi.; 145 mi. long, 5–35 mi. wide; pop. 98,429), E Canada, in Gulf of St. Lawrence, off Nova Scotia and New Brunswick; cap. CHARLOTTETOWN. One of the Maritime Provs. Although the most densely populated Canadian province, SUMMERSIDE is the only other city. Along N shore is Prince Edward Natl. Park (estab. 1936). Farming and stock raising provide more than half of the island's income. Fisheries and fox-fur farms are important. Mfg. is limited to food processing. Discovered by Cartier 1534 and first settled by Acadians, it was annexed to Nova Scotia 1763, and became a separate colony 1769. Lord Selkirk settled impoverished Scottish colonists here 1803 and the population is largely descended from this group. Responsible government was estab. 1851 and confederation with Canada accepted 1873.

Prince George, city (pop. 4,703), central B.C., Canada, on Fraser R. at mouth of the Nechako and N of Vancouver. Railroad division point; center of lumbering, mining, and ranching region. Fort George, fur-trading post, estab. here 1807.

Prince of Wales, Cape, westernmost point of North America, NW Alaska, on Bering Strait, opposite East Cape (Cape Dezhnev) in Siberia.

Prince of Wales Island, area 2,231 sq. mi., off SE Alaska. Largest island of Alexander Archipelago; 135 mi. long, 45 mi. wide. Densely wooded. On E coast is Old Kasaan Natl. Monument.

Prince of Wales Island, area 13,736 sq. mi., Franklin dist., Northwest Territories, in the Arctic Ocean. Magnetic pole located here in 1948.

Prince Rupert, city (pop. 8,546), W B.C., Canada, on Kaien Isl. in Chatham Sound, near mouth of Skeena R. Highway and railroad terminus with fish processing plants and cellulose factory; year-round port serves wide area. A major supply base for U.S. forces in Alaska during World War II.

Princess Anne, town (pop. 1,407), Eastern Shore, Md., SW of Salisbury. Seat of Maryland State Col., formerly Princess Anne Col. (coed.; for Negroes), a branch of Univ. of Maryland.

Princeton. 1 City (pop. 5,765), N Ill., N of Peoria, in coal, nursery, and farm area. Mfg. of clay products, vinegar, and sealing wax. **2** City (pop. 7,673), SW Ind., N of Evansville. Trade and rail center with oil refining and mfg. of paint brushes and clocks. **3** City (pop. 5,388), W Ky., between Cumberland and Tradewater rivers and E of Paducah. Rail point shipping tobacco, livestock, farm goods, clothing, and fluor spar. **4** Borough (pop. 12,230), W N.J., NE of Trenton; settled 1696 by Friends. Residential and educational center; mfg. prohibited within borough limits. Washington defeated British here on Jan. 3, 1777, but Gen. Hugh Mercer was mortally wounded. Nassau Hall (of Princeton Univ.) served as barracks for British and colonial troops, and meeting place of Continental Congress, June–Nov., 1783. Seat of PRINCETON UNIVERSITY, INSTITUTE FOR ADVANCED STUDY, Princeton Theological Seminary (Presbyterian; for men; founded 1812), Rockefeller Inst. for Medical Research. Includes Palmer Square (civic center on Nassau St., with Colonial-style buildings), Bainbridge birthplace (now public library), battle monument (by F. W. MacMonnies), and "Morven" (1701; Richard Stockton's home and Cornwallis's hq.). **5** City (pop. 8,279), S W.Va., NE of Bluefield. Trade center of agr. and coal area.

Princeton University, at Princeton, N.J.; nonsectarian, for men; chartered 1746 and 1748 as Col. of New Jersey by Presbyterians, renamed 1896. Opened at Elizabethtown (now Elizabeth) (see DICKINSON, JONATHAN) and moved to Newark 1747, to Princeton 1756. An administrative feature which led trend toward more individualized college instruction was the preceptorial system introduced by Woodrow Wilson as president. Other distinguished presidents have been Jonathan Edwards, Witherspoon, McCosh, Hibben. Princeton's special schools include: public and international affairs, architecture, and engineering; has various research bureaus and museums and a university press (1905). Shares many of the resources of the Inst. for Advanced Study. Notable buildings include Nassau Hall (1756), Cleveland Tower, Fine Hall, Frick Laboratory, and Harvey S. Firestone Memorial Library.

Prince William Sound, large, irregular, islanded inlet of Gulf of Alaska, S. Alaska, S of Chugach Mts. Good harbors; access to interior by highway, railroad. Fishing and some mining. Valdez (NE) and Cordova (E) are ports.

Principe, Africa: see SÃO TOMÉ AND PRINCIPE.

Principia, The: see ALTON, Ill.

printing. For the early history of printing and its introduction to Europe, see TYPE. After Johann Gutenberg's first work at Mainz, the art spread rapidly over the Continent. By 1476 it had been brought to England by William Caxton; by 1539 a press had been set up in New Spain (Mexico). In the region now the U.S., printing first appeared with the work of Stephen and Matthew DAYE. The mechanical processes of printing changed little between the 15th and 19th centuries. In 1810 Friedrich König applied steam power to printing; in 1846–47 Richard March Hoe designed a rotary press in which the types were arranged on a cylinder; in 1866 a press using curved stereotype plates was patented in England; late in the 19th cent. typesetting machines were invented. In recent years photographic processes have been much used to produce books from typewritten (or drawn) copy, and very recently the application of electronics to typesetting has been proved practical. Printing in relief (with type projecting above the surface of the plate) continues to be the most widely used process, but two other kinds of printing have been developed. For intaglio printing—as in etchings and engravings—the design to be printed is cut into the surface of the plate, and the paper receives an impression from the incised design filled with ink. Gravure processes are of the intaglio kind; in photogravure the plates are made photographically. Planographic printing is done from a flat surface. The original process of this sort was lithography, in which a drawing is made with greasy crayon on a specially prepared flat stone. The stone is rolled with water, then with greasy ink. The ink adheres only to the crayon drawing, and is then transferred to the paper. The basic process has been much refined and altered. In offset printing, the inked plate transfers the impression to a rubber roller, which in turn carries the ink to the paper. Collotype plates employ a gelatin surface on which the printing image has been obtained by exposure to light. PHOTOENGRAVING is widely used, especially for illustrations. See also Ben DAY.

Prior, Matthew, 1664–1721, English poet and diplomat. Noted as a wit, he wrote, with Charles Montagu, *The City Mouse and the Country Mouse* (1687), a parody of Dryden's *The Hind and the Panther*. He also wrote pleasant "society verse" and two satiric poems and served as envoy to draw up the Peace of Utrecht.

Pripet (prī'pĕt), Pol. *Prypeć,* Rus. *Pripyat,* river, c.500 mi. long, Belorussia, flowing E into the Dnieper. The **Pripet Marshes** are a forested, swampy area (c.33,500 sq. mi.) extending S from the Pripet and its affluents. A natural defense barrier, the marshes were a battlefield in World War I, but they were bypassed by the Germans in 1941.

SMALL CAPITALS = cross references. Pronunciation key on inside end pages. Abbreviations: p. 2.

Priscian (Priscianus Caesariensis) (prĭ'shùn), fl. 500, Latin grammarian. Among his extant works is *Commentarii grammatici*, long a standard grammar and basis of the work of Rabanus Maurus.

Priscilla or **Prisca**, wife of Aquila, a Jew living in Rome. They were friendly to Paul.

prism: see SPECTRUM.

prison, place of detention for the punishment and reform of convicts. At the end of the 18th cent., when it had become the chief mode of punishment, a reform movement (led by BECCARIA in Italy and John Howard in England) improved some of the unspeakable prison conditions. Reform in the U.S. began in Philadelphia (1790) and Auburn, N.Y. In the 19th cent. reform was led by Elizabeth Fry and Dorothea L. Dix. British (especially Irish) influences led to the practice of parole. There is a growing tendency to regard the aim of imprisonment as regeneration, with constructive labor policies and social readjustment, but such notoriously brutal forms as chain gangs still exist. There are now usually separate institutions for the insane, sick, minor offenders, and the young.

prisoners of war. The first international convention on prisoners of war was signed at the Hague Peace Conference of 1899 and broadened in 1907. The rules proved to be insufficient in World War I, and the Internatl. Red Cross proposed a new code which was signed at Geneva, Switzerland, in 1929. This Geneva Convention is still in effect. Provides that prisoner need divulge only name and rank, is entitled to food and medical care, has right to exchange correspondence and receive parcels, must obey military discipline, and may attempt escape at his own risk. Detention camps should be open to inspection by a neutral power. Nations which do not adhere to (and hence are not bound by) the Geneva Convention include USSR and Communist China.

Pritchett, Henry Smith (prĭ'chĭt), 1857–1939, American astronomer and educator. Among his posts after 1878 were superintendent of U.S. Coast and Geodetic Survey and president of Massachusetts Inst. of Technology. He was president of Carnegie Foundation for the Advancement of Teaching, 1906–30.

privateering, former usage of war permitting privately owned war vessels (privateers) under government commission to capture enemy shipping. Great era was 1692–1814. After defeat of French fleet in 1692, France commissioned privateers to prey on English shipping. In American Revolution and in War of 1812 American privateersmen (notably Stephen Decatur) took hundreds of prizes. The system was subject to much abuse later as a mask for piracy, and it was abolished by Declaration of Paris (1856).

privet (prĭv'ĭt), Old World evergreen or deciduous shrub or small tree (*Ligustrum*). The common privet (*Ligustrum vulgare*) and California privet (*L. ovalifolium*) are hedge plants.

Prix de Rome, Grand (grã' prē' dù rōm'), prize awarded by French government, through competitive examination, to students of fine arts (including music). Instituted 1666 by Louis XIV. Award involves four years' study in Rome and exemption from military service. Open to those between ages of 15 and 20 who have done required work at École des Beaux-Arts and elsewhere.

prize fighting: see BOXING.

probability, in mathematics, a precisely defined value indicating chance of (or odds for) occurrence of a given event. Sometimes it is defined as ratio of number of ways event can happen to total ways in which it can or cannot happen. Where this is undeterminable, it is then defined as limiting value of a sequence of ratios of number of successes (occurrences of event) to number of trials, as number of trials is increased indefinitely. Blaise Pascal developed theory of probability c.1654.

Probus, d. 282, Roman emperor (276–82), a commander under Valerian and successor to M. Claudius Tacitus. He did much to restore order in the empire before his troops mutinied and killed him.

procedure, in law, body of formal rules that must be observed to obtain legal redress and satisfaction of claims through the courts. It does not include evidence but does embrace all other matters concerning legal actions and is the means for enforcing the rights determined by the substantive law. Criminal procedure concerns the forms of enforcing criminal law by public prosecution. Civil procedure concerns the enforcement of a civil claim by private action before the court, begun by the plaintiff's having a process (e.g., a summons) served upon the defendant, which gives a court jurisdiction over the case. In early common law an action could be brought only if it conformed closely to a writ ("no writ, no right"). This situation stimulated the growth of equity. In the 19th cent., however, technical intricacy of law procedure caused too many cases to hinge on technicalities of procedural detail. In New York the civil code in 1848 abolished the distinction of law and equity and made the cause of the action the procedural cornerstone. A similar reform was accomplished in Great Britain by the Judicature Acts of 1875. Today procedure in most American states is based on codes, as that in civil-law countries has been since early times. The guarantee of proper procedure ("due process") is included in the Constitution of the U.S.

Prochorus (prŏ'kùrùs), one of the seven deacons. Acts 6.5. Traditionally bishop of Nicodemia.

Procida, John of: see JOHN OF PROCIDA.

Procne, wife of Tereus and sister of PHILOMELA.

Procopius (prōkō'pēùs), d. 562?, Byzantine historian. Chief works are *Procopius' History of His Own Time* and *Secret History of Procopius*. His authorship of the latter has been questioned.

Procopius the Great, d. 1434, Czech Hussite leader, called Prokop; a married priest. Becoming chief of the radical TABORITES (c.1425), he defeated the Saxons at Usti-nad-Labem (1426); invaded Hungary, Silesia, Saxony, Thuringia (1426–30); and as chief commander of Czech forces routed an anti-Hussite crusade at Domazlice (1431). He continued hostilities even after peace negotiations were under way at Council of Basel, and rejected the Compactata, to which the UTRAQUISTS (moderate wing of Hussites) had agreed. Utraquist and Catholic Bohemian forces now united against the Taborites, whom they crushed at Lipany (1434). Procopius fell in the battle, as did his ally **Procopius the Little** (Prokupek), leader of the Orphans, a radical group close to the Taborites.

Procrustes (prōkrŭ'stēz) [Gr.,= stretcher], in Greek legend. He forced guests to lie on either a very long or a very short bed and fitted them to beds either by stretching them or by cutting off their legs.

Procter, Bryan Waller: see CORNWALL, BARRY.

Proctor, town (pop. 1,917), W Vt., NW of Rutland. Vermont Marble Co. was developed here.

prodigal son, parable of Jesus illustrating heaven's welcome of the repentant sinner. Luke 15.11–32.

producer gas, fuel gas consisting chiefly of carbon monoxide and nitrogen (60%). It has low heating value but it can be made with cheap fuel.

progressive education, modern movement, based on idea of learning by doing. Developed in Europe by Froebel, Pestalozzi, and Montessori and in U.S. by F. W. Parker and John Dewey. Postulates are that child learns best in situations involving self-interest, and that modes of behavior are learned most easily by actual performance; hence education must be reconstruction of life experiences directed by child without authoritarian control. Notable experiments in U.S. have been Dewey's project method, used at his Laboratory School in Chicago (1896–1904); Dalton (Mass.) plan (1919), which subdivides traditional curriculum into contract units for individual pupils; and Winnetka (Ill.) plan (1919), which follows Dalton plan but uses cooperative methods and socialized activities. Many conventional schools now add an activities program to supply values of progressive education.

Progressive party, in U.S. history, name of three different political organizations. In 1912 the Republican national convention renominated W. H. TAFT, whereupon supporters of Theodore ROOSEVELT organized Progressive party (Bull Moose party), nominated Roosevelt for President. Progressive platform called for lower tariff, political and social reforms. In the election Roosevelt received 88 electoral and 4,000,000 popular votes, faring better than Taft. Party maintained its organization until 1916, when most Progressives supported Republican ticket. In 1924 another Progressive party nominated R. M. LA FOLLETTE for President. Program, supported by most non-Communist left-wing groups, called for social and economic reforms. La Follette won only 13 electoral votes of Wis., polled nearly 5,000,000 popular votes. Party continued strong in Wis. until 1938, dissolved in 1946. Third Progressive party, organized as challenge to Democratic party, nominated H. A. WALLACE for President in 1948. It was endorsed to some degree by Communist party, which was said by many to control it. Its candidates won no electoral votes, only slightly more than 1,000,000 popular votes.

prohibition, legal method of controlling the manufacture and sale of alcoholic beverages, the extreme of regulatory LIQUOR LAWS. TEMPERANCE MOVEMENTS, especially the ANTI-SALOON LEAGUE and the PROHIBITION PARTY, became increasingly militant in the U.S. during the 19th cent. After World War I, national prohibition became law by the Eighteenth Amendment to the Constitution. In spite of the strict VOLSTEAD ACT, law enforcement proved impossible. It was a period of bootlegging and unparalleled drinking. In 1933, prohibition was repealed by the Twenty-first Amendment. A number of states, counties, and divisions maintain full or partial prohibition under local option.

Prohibition party, in U.S. history, minor political party formed in 1869 primarily for legislative prohibition of the manufacture, transportation, and sale of alcoholic beverages. Since 1872 party has offered candidates in every presidential election. Other reform planks were adopted over the years. Peak of popular support came in 1892 with 271,000 votes. Party split in 1896 over currency issue. Institution of PROHIBITION by Eighteenth Amendment and its later repeal greatly weakened party.

projection or **map projection.** Only a globe can represent earth's surface features correctly with reference to area, shape, scale, and directions. Projection from a globe to flat map causes distortion of some of these characteristics. A grid or net of two intersecting systems of lines corresponding to parallels and meridians must be drawn on plane surface. Some projections (equidistant) aim to keep correct distances in all directions from center of map; other projections show areas (equal-area) or shapes (conformal) equal to those on globe of the same scale. Projections are cylindrical, conical, or azimuthal in geometric origin. Mercator's projection, first published in 1569 and widely used, has parallels and meridians as straight lines, intersecting at right angles, with all parallels as long as the equator; high latitudes are badly distorted. It is of great value in navigation.

Prokofiev, Sergei (Sergeyevich) (syĭrgā′prōkôf′ēĕf), 1891–1953, Russian composer. His music is often witty and satirical, ranging from the harsh and energetic to the lyrical. Among his compositions are symphonies (including the popular Classical Symphony); concertos for piano and for violin; operas (e.g., *Love for Three Oranges*); orchestral suites (e.g., *Lieutenant Kije*); an orchestral fairy tale, *Peter and the Wolf*; chamber music; and ballets. He toured the U.S. and Europe several times, both as a pianist and as a conductor, but in later years remained in the USSR.

proletariat (prōlŭtâ′rēŭt), in socialist theory, the class of exploited wage earners who depend on their labor for their existence. In ancient Rome, a proletarian was a citizen without property or assured income. Marxist theory holds that the proletariat must take power from the capitalist class in order to create a classless society.

Prometheus (prōmē′thēŭs) [Gr.,= forethought], in Greek religion, a Titan. He gave fire and arts to mankind. Zeus punished him for this by chaining him to a mountain where a vulture devoured his liver. He was freed by Hercules. This is the theme of Aeschylus' *Prometheus Bound.* Shelly wrote *Prometheus Unbound* on theme of mankind's deliverance.

promethium (prōmē′thēŭm), rare metallic element of rare earths (symbol = Pm; see also ELEMENT, table). Its existence was predicted in early 20th cent.; discovery reported in 1926, but definite identification not made until 1945. Illinium was a former name.

prominences: see CHROMOSPHERE.

pronghorn or **prongbuck,** North American hoofed mammal of SW U.S., Mexico. Called antelope but is only living member of different family (Antilocapridae). Usually the back is reddish brown; the under parts, neck bands, and rump patch are white. The horns have a bony core with a horny covering, shed annually.

propaganda (prŏpŭgăn′dù) [from Latin *de propaganda fide* = for the propagation of the faith], method of creating an attitude toward some person, organization, or ideal by the influencing of opinion. It may be religious, social, cultural, or political. It may be effected by all media of communication and by the arts. The Congregation of the Propaganda (see CARDINAL) and Protestant missionary boards (see MISSIONS) are disseminators of religious propaganda. All the warring countries found it necessary to estab. departments of propaganda, often called information services. Nazi Germany's was particularly effective. Dissemination of propaganda is one of the chief activities of COMMUNISM.

propagation of plants is commonly effected by seeds and spores. Such vegetative means as CUTTING, layering, root or tuber division, and GRAFTING are also used, especially with plants not breeding true from seed.

Propertius, Sextus (sĕk′stŭs prōpûr′shŭs), c.50 B.C.–c.16 B.C., Roman elegiac poet of the circle of Maecenas. His poems are mostly love lyrics to his mistress, Cynthia.

property, things of economic value to which ownership rights are applicable. Realty (or real estate or real property) is distinguished from personalty (or personal property). Realty is chiefly land and improvements built thereupon. Personal property is chiefly movable objects, whose distribution the owner may determine by WILL, gift, or sale. Realty in medieval society was the basis of wealth and was controlled in many ways to protect society, while ownership of personalty, considered unimportant, was almost unfettered. Gradually, personalty grew to be the economic mainstay of a large class, and the law of realty tended to be assimilated to that of personalty. See PUBLIC OWNERSHIP.

prophet [Gr.,= foreteller], in Bible, religious leader of Israel. The Major Prophets are Isaiah, Jeremiah, Ezekiel, and Daniel. The Minor Prophets are Hosea, Joel, Amos, Obadiah, Jonah, Micah, Nahum, Habbakuk, Zephaniah, Haggai, Zechariah, and Malachi. All have Old Testament books ascribed to them. Title also given to other biblical persons, e.g., Moses, Elijah, Elisha, and Nathan. In the writings of the prophets monotheism receives its most eloquent support. From earliest times they were studied for revelations of the future, especially of the Messiah to come. It is part of traditional Christian belief that the Holy Ghost "spoke through the prophets" (Nicene Creed), who foretold the life and passion of Christ. In New Testament, the term *prophecy* is used of enthusiastic, and presumably inspired, utterance. At times this sort of prophecy has played a dubious role in the history of Christianity, but there have been orthodox Christian preachers and mystics who have spoken and acted like prophets, e.g., St. Vincent Ferrer and St. Catherine of Siena. In some forms of Protestantism prophecy is essential, e.g., Quakerism. Emanuel Swedenborg and Joseph Smith are examples of prophets with a Protestant background. Outside Christianity, Islam recognizes Mohammed as the last and greatest of prophets. Men and women who interpret for a divine power have existed in the religions and cults of the world since ancient times.

proportion, in mathematics, the equality of two ratios. Two pairs of quantities a,b and c,d, are in proportion if their ratios a/b and c/d are equal (i.e., if equation $a/b/ = c/d$ is true). Product of means (b,c) equals product of extremes (a,d); this rule is result of algebraic operation.

propylaeum (prŏpĭlē'ŭm), in Greek architecture, a monumental roofed entrance to a sacred enclosure or group of buildings. An outstanding example is the **Propylaea,** built (477–432 B.C.) on the Acropolis at Athens by Mnesicles.

Proserpina or **Proserpine:** see PERSEPHONE.

prospecting, the search for mineral deposits suitable for mining. Modern prospecting employs sampling and analysis of deposits; geophysical methods, using the dipping needle (to measure variations in earth's magnetic attraction), torsion balance (to measure variations in gravitational pull), and seismograph; electrical methods, using instruments (galvanometer, potentiometer) to indicate relative conductivity between points on earth; and, in searching for radioactive materials, the Geiger counter. In spotting outcrops of metals airplanes are used.

prostate gland (prŏ'stāt), small muscular and glandular organ in male situated at beginning of urethra and neck of bladder. Its alkaline secretion aids motility of sperm.

prostitution, act of offering oneself for sexual intercourse for mercenary purpose. In ancient times prostitution had religious connotations—intercourse with temple maidens was an act of worship of the temple deity. In the Middle Ages prostitution flourished, but serious efforts were made to control it after an epidemic of venereal disease in the 16th cent. Paris began to register prostitutes in 1785. Cooperation on an international scale to stamp out the white-slave traffic began with a London congress in 1899. The League of Nations set up (1919) a fact-gathering body, and in 1921 a Geneva conference set up a committee whose work was assumed (1946) by the UN. By 1930, 30 countries had no system of licensing houses of prostitution. Until 1945 France registered prostitutes, but in 1946 passed a bill suppressing prostitution. In the U.S. no serious efforts were made to curtail prostitution until the passage (1910) of the Mann Act (forbidding interstate transportation of women for immoral purposes). The May Act (July, 1941) makes it a Federal offense to practice prostitution in designated military neighborhoods. In all states except Ariz. and Nev. it is a crime to keep a house of prostitution.

protactinium (prŏ"tăktĭ'nĕŭm), rare radioactive element (symbol = Pa; see also ELEMENT, table), precursor of actinium. Formerly called protoactinium.

Protagoras (prŏtă'gŭrŭs), c.480–c.410 B.C., Greek Sophist of Abdera. He taught at Athens but was compelled to flee when charged with agnosticism. He originated the saying, "Man is the measure of all things." One of Plato's dialogues uses his name.

protection, regulation of imports and exports in order to shield domestic industries from foreign competition. The usual method is to impose duties on imports (see CUSTOMS). England abandoned protection for FREE TRADE c.1860, but returned to it between World Wars I and II. The U.S. has always followed a protectionist policy.

protective coloration, color or color pattern of animal affording it protection. Resemblance to features of native habitat is achieved by color similarity supplemented by various effects, e.g., pattern of deepened and softened shades to counteract light and shadow contrasts, irregular color contrasts to distract predatory eye from mass beneath, and dappled and barred patterns to blend with leaves, water, or other features of habitat. Protective coloration includes resemblance and MIMICRY.

Protectorate, in English history, the name given to the English government 1653–59. After civil war (see PURITAN REVOLUTION) the Rump Parliament was ended by Oliver CROMWELL. The army made him lord protector of commonwealth of England, Ireland, and Scotland, to rule with Parliament of one house. Was virtual dictator. Laws were puritanical, and the army collected taxes. Peace was made in first of Dutch Wars; English sea power used against Spain. Cromwell became hereditary protector after refusing crown in 1657. Resignation of his successor, Richard Cromwell, led to restoration of the monarchy.

proteins (prō'tēĭnz, –tēnz), class of complex substances forming essential part of protoplasm. Their presence in cells and tissue is essential to life—they serve as nitrogen source, aid in tissue building, are source of energy. Most are insoluble in water; those that are soluble form colloidal solutions. Carbon, hydrogen, oxygen, nitrogen are always present; other elements sometimes occur. Molecules are very large and are made up of amino acids; nature of protein depends on nature and number of amino acids in molecule. Simple proteins yield only amino acids or derivatives on hydrolysis; examples are albumins, glutelins, globulins, etc. Conjugated proteins are composed of proteins combined with one or more other compounds; e.g., nucleoproteins, glycoproteins, chromo-proteins, etc. Derived proteins (peptones, proteoses, peptides) are intermediate products of protein decomposition.

Proterozoic era (prŏ"tŭrŭzō'ĭk, prō"–), second grand division of geologic time, the Archeozoic being first. The two eras are often called Pre-Cambrian time. Following the Archeozoic there was prolonged erosion, when sediments of the Huronian system were deposited. The Mesabi iron ores (in Minn.) are late Huronian. The Keweenawan was a period of great volcanic activity and was followed by upthrusting of mountains, and later by long erosion. Though many forms of primitive life probably existed, the Proterozoic is poorly represented by fossils. The Pre-Cambrian eras are believed to have lasted c.500 million years each. See also GEOLOGY, table.

Protestant Episcopal Church: see EPISCOPAL CHURCH, PROTESTANT.

Protestantism, religious movement originating with REFORMATION, and principles underlying it. Name Protestant, used in many senses, broadly applies to Christians not belonging to Roman Catholic Church or to an Eastern church. Protestantism embodies conceptions of liberty in secular as well as religious matters, of private judgment and religious toleration, as against tradition and authority. Essence is responsibility of individual to God alone and not to Church. For some major tendencies of Protestantism see ADVENTISTS; ANABAPTISTS; BAPTISTS; CALVINISM; CONGREGATIONALISM; FUNDAMENTALISM; LUTHERANISM; METHODISM; MODERNISM; PRESBYTERIANISM; PURITANISM; UNITARIANISM.

Protestant Union. 1 In German history, defensive alliance of German Protestant states, founded 1608 by Elector Palatine Frederick IV; also known as Evangelical League. It opposed the attempt of the imperial government to impose an exact fulfillment of the Peace of Augsburg of 1555, which provided for restoration of all former church lands appropriated by Protestant princes after 1552. Weak from the start, the Protestant Union never really became operative and went out of existence in 1621. **2** In French history, the alliance (1573–74) of Huguenot cities, districts, and nobles in the Wars of Religion.

Proteus (prō'tĕŭs, –tūs), in Greek legend, old man of

the sea. Could change into any shape, but if seized and held, he would foretell the future.

Protevangelium of James: see PSEUDEPIGRAPHA.

protoactinium: see PROTACTINIUM.

protocol (prō′tŭkŏl), diplomatic term referring usually to a more or less informal written document. Examples are the minutes of international conferences, preliminary agreements which lead to a treaty, and agreements which do not need ratification. Diplomatic protocol is the code of courtesy governing conduct of diplomatic service. Term is sometimes applied to agreement similar to a treaty. Thus, the Geneva Protocol of 1924, adopted by the League of Nations, made aggressive warfare an international crime. British refusal to adhere to it kept the protocol from coming into force.

Protogenes (prōtŏ′jŭnēz), fl. c.300 B.C., Greek painter, considered second only to Apelles by the ancients. His works included decorations for the Propylaea, Athens.

proton, term for single positive (+) unit charge of electricity believed to form nucleus of hydrogen ATOM. Hydrogen ion or proton is believed to be fundamental positively charged unit of the atom. See *ill.,* p. 773.

protoplasm (prō′tŭplăzŭm), fundamental material of which all living things are composed. It exists in all living plants and animals in units called cells, and is enclosed by thin surface (called plasma membrane) which controls passage of materials in and out of cell. Protoplasm is composed of water (70–90% by weight), protein (c.15%), fatty substances (c.3%), carbohydrates (less than 1%), and inorganic salts (c.1%). The elements carbon, oxygen, hydrogen, and nitrogen make up c.99% of protoplasm; sulphur, phosphorus, potassium, iron, and magnesium are also present. In both plant and animal cells the protoplasm consists of a more dense portion forming the nucleus (rounded or ovoid) and a less dense portion, the cytoplasm (this forms bulk of cell in animal cells and in plant cells is usually found in rather thin layers or strands). Since it is living material, protoplasm exhibits the properties associated with life, i.e., capacity to respond to environmental influences and ability to perform physiological functions. See *ill.,* p. 633.

Protopopov, Aleksandr Dmitreyevich (ŭlyĭksän′dŭr dümē′trĕŭvĭch prŭtŭpô′pŭf), 1866–1918, Russian landowner and statesman. A trusted friend of Nicholas II and of Rasputin and an extreme reactionary, he was minister of the interior from 1916 until his fall in February Revolution of 1917. He was executed.

protozoa (prōtŭzō′ŭ), phylum of microscopic one-celled animals. Most are solitary, a few are colonial. Majority are aquatic species of salt and fresh water, found on surface and at great depths, at sea level and high altitudes; some live in damp sand and moss. Many are parasitic. Phylum is usually divided into four classes: Sarcodina, Mastigophora, Infusoria, and Sporozoa. Reproduction in various forms is by fission, conjugation, budding, and spore formation. See also AMOEBA and FORAMINIFERA. See *ill.,* p. 633.

Proudhon, Pierre Joseph (pyěr′ zhôzěf′ prōodô′), 1809–65, French social theorist. He achieved prominence through his pamphlet, *What Is Property?* (1840; Eng. tr., 1876), a condemnation of the abuses of private property. He sought a society of loosely federated groups, in which the government might become unnecessary. He believed in the moral responsibility of the individual rather than in any system authoritatively imposed.

Proust, Joseph Louis (zhôzěf′ lwē′ prōost′), 1754–1826, French chemist. He discovered grape sugar. Was establisher of law of definite proportions (Proust's law) which states that in any compound the elements are present in a fixed proportion by weight.

Proust, Marcel (märsěl′ prōost′), 1871–1922, French novelist. As a youth he sought the company of fashionable and intellectual society, but after 1905 he retired almost completely and began work on his semiautobiographical cyclic novel *À la recherche du temps perdu* (16 vols., 1913–27; Eng. tr., *Remembrance of Things Past,* 1922–32). His complicated style seeks by total recall to recapture the minutest psychological and sensory detail, and his work succeeds in recreating a past society with the illusion of complete objectiveness. His influence on later novelists is incalculable.

Prout, William, 1785–1850, English chemist and physician. He demonstrated presence of free hydrochloric acid in gastric juice. Prout's hypothesis: atomic weights of elements are multiples of that of hydrogen and elements are formed by condensation or grouping of hydrogen atoms.

Prouts Neck, Maine: see SCARBORO.

Provençal (prôväsäl′), *langue d'oc* dialect of SE France. A Romance language (see LANGUAGE, table) developed by troubadours of Provence, it became the standard literary idiom of S France in the Middle Ages. It enjoyed a literary revival commencing in mid-19th cent., and a group of seven poets, including Frédéric Mistral, formed the Felibrige to introduce standard Provençal, but French remains the standard language.

Provence (prôväs′), former province, SE France, in Var, Bouches-du-Rhône, Vaucluse, Basses-Alpes, and Alpes-Maritimes depts. Chief cities: MARSEILLES, NICE, TOULON, AVIGNON, AIX-EN-PROVENCE, ARLES. Region borders on Mediterranean in S (see RIVIERA), on Rhone R. (W), and on Italy (E). Rhone valley and S slopes of Maritime Alps produce wine, silk, fruits, olives, flowers, vegetables. Cattle raising (esp. on CAMARGUE). Interior is rugged and largely unproductive. Large tourist trade. Coast was settled after 600 B.C. by Greeks and Phoenicians. Romans estab. colonies 2d cent. B.C. and made the region their first transalpine province (hence its name). Provence fell to the Visigoths (5th cent. A.D.), the Franks (6th cent.), and, briefly, to the Arabs (8th cent.). In 879 Count Boso of Arles estab. the kingdom of Provence, which in 933 was joined with Transjurane Burgundy to form the kingdom of ARLES. The county of Provence, which later emerged as a nominal fief of the Holy Roman Empire, passed by marriage from the house of Aragon to the ANGEVIN dynasty of Naples (1246). After the Angevins' extinction it fell to the French crown (1486). ORANGE was added 1672; Avignon and the Comtat VENAISSIN 1791; Nice and Menton 1860.

Proverbs, book of Old Testament. It is a collection of sayings, many of them moral maxims, mostly ascribed by tradition to Solomon. Book is an early example of wisdom literature popular among Jews of postexilic times (see WISDOM).

Providence, city (pop. 248,674), state cap., NE R.I., on harbor receiving Seekonk and other rivers at head of Providence R., arm of Narragansett Bay. Largest city in R.I. Port and industrial center noted for silverware (since 1831) and jewelry; mfg. also of textiles, machine tools, hardware, watches, oil products, chemicals, plastics. Roger WILLIAMS secured title to site from Narragansett chiefs after his exile from Mass. 1636; named it in gratitude for "God's merciful providence." Prosperity came with 18th-cent. foreign trade. After Revolution the Brown brothers played leading role in town's growth and industrial development. Became sole state cap. in 1900 (Newport had been joint cap.). Has many historic structures—e.g., old colony house or statehouse (1762), old market house (1773)—and Roger Williams Park (over 450 acres). Seat of BROWN UNIVERSITY, Providence Col. (R.C., Dominican; for men; 1919), R.I. School of Design (1877).

Provincetown, town (pop. 3,795), SE Mass., on N Cape Cod, on harbor on Cape Cod Bay; Pilgrims landed here 1620; permanently settled c.1700. Has Pilgrim Memorial (1910). Whaling, saltmaking, rumrunning, smuggling were once important. Fishing is still staple industry, but town gained fame as resort (esp. for artists) in 20th cent. Provincetown Players pioneered in Little Theater movement.

Province Wellesley, Malaya: see PENANG.

Provisions of Oxford, 1258, a scheme of governmental reform forced upon Henry III of England by his barons. Drawn up by Simon de Montfort, it provided for an advisory council and tried to limit taxing power. Repudiation (1261) of the agreement by King Henry III led to Barons' War (1263–67).

Provo (prō′vō), city (pop. 28,937), N central Utah, on Provo R. near Utah L., at base of Wasatch Range and SSE of Salt Lake City; settled 1849 by Mormons. Grew as shipping center of mining (silver, lead, copper, gold) and agr. area. Now a rail, trade, industrial hub. Water supply supplemented by Provo R. project. Large steel plant at near-by Geneva. Seat of BRIGHAM YOUNG UNIVERSITY. Provo Peak (11,054 ft.) and Mt. Timpanogos (12,008 ft.) are near.

Provo, river rising in NE Utah in Uinta Mts. and flowing c.70 mi. SW, past Provo, to Utah L. Project begun in 1930s to rehabilitate and expand early irrigation facilities. Water from the Weber (via canal) and the Duchesne (via mountain tunnel) feeds into Provo R. to irrigate Utah Valley and supply local towns and Salt Lake City (via 41-mi. Salt Lake Aqueduct).

Provoost, Samuel (prō′vōst), 1742–1815, first Episcopal bishop of N.Y. after 1786; chaplain to Continental Congress (1785) and U.S. Senate (1789).

Prud'hon, Pierre Paul (prüdō′), 1758–1823, French painter. Noted for subtle use of light and shade. Portrait of Empress Josephine is in the Louvre.

prune, a dried PLUM, especially varieties of *Prunus domestica.* After falling from tree, plums are dipped in lye solution to prevent fermentation and are then dried in the sun or in kilns.

pruning, removing parts of plants, especially woody ones, to increase flower or fruit production or to control shape or dimensions. It is also practiced to prolong a plant's survival by cutting off diseased portions or to induce vigorous branching growth. Pruning roots and top parts proportionally is done when trees and shrubs are transplanted. There is no set rule for the best time of year to prune plants.

Prussia (prù′shù), Ger. *Preussen,* former German state (113,410 sq. mi.; 1933 pop. 39,934,011); cap. Berlin. It occupied, roughly, the N half of GERMANY, with nearly two thirds of the total German population, and led Germany politically and economically. Its historic roots were the electorate of BRANDENBURG and the duchy of Prussia, united as a kingdom in 1701 under the HOHENZOLLERN dynasty. Originally, Prussia was the region along the Baltic Sea between the Niemen and Vistula rivers–i.e., the later EAST PRUSSIA. Its pagan population (of the Baltic language group) was largely exterminated in the 13th cent. by the TEUTONIC KNIGHTS, who made Prussia their domain. In 1525 their grand master ALBERT OF BRANDENBURG embraced Protestantism and transformed the domain into a hereditary duchy under Polish overlordship. The duchy passed, by inheritance, to the electors of Brandenburg (1618), who shook off Polish overlordship in 1660. In 1701 Elector Frederick III had himself crowned king of Prussia as Frederick I. Under his successors FREDERICK WILLIAM I and FREDERICK II (the Great), Prussia rose to a European power and threatened Austrian leadership in Germany. In the War of the AUSTRIAN SUCCESSION (1740–48) Prussia won most of SILESIA; in the SEVEN YEARS WAR (1756–63) it defeated a formidable coalition; in the Polish partitions (1772, 1793, 1795) it gained WEST PRUSSIA prov. and W Poland. The reigns (1786–1840) of Frederick William II and Frederick William III saw the French Revolutionary and Napoleonic Wars. Defeated, Prussia withdrew from the First Coalition against France in 1795 but joined the Third Coalition in 1806, was routed at Jena, and accepted the harsh Treaty of TILSIT (1807). Yet, at the same time, under the leadership of Freiherr vom STEIN, K. A. von HARDENBERG, Wilhelm von HUMBOLDT, and SCHARNHORST, a series of drastic social, cultural, and military

reforms prepared the rebirth of Prussian greatness. Joining the allies in 1813, Prussian forces under BLÜCHER were decisive in Napoleon's defeat. The Congress of Vienna (1814–15) gave Prussia the RHINE PROVINCE, WESTPHALIA, half of SAXONY, Swedish POMERANIA, West Prussia, and W Poland (incl. Poznan). In the GERMAN CONFEDERATION Prussia was overshadowed by Metternich's Austria, but it led in forming the ZOLLVEREIN. FREDERICK WILLIAM IV put down the Revolution of 1848 and yielded to Austria in the Treaty of OLMÜTZ (1850). WILLIAM I, his successor, entrusted the government to BISMARCK, who brought Prussia to its ultimate triumph. The war on Denmark (1864; see SCHLESWIG-HOLSTEIN) served as prelude to the AUSTRO-PRUSSIAN WAR of 1866, which excluded Austria from German affairs, brought Schleswig-Holstein, HANOVER, Electoral HESSE, NASSAU, and FRANKFURT to Prussia, and resulted in creation of the NORTH GERMAN CONFEDERATION. The FRANCO-PRUSSIAN WAR led to the formation of a German Empire, with the king of Prussia as emperor (1871). The history of Prussia became essentially that of Germany. Prussia retained its constitution of 1850, which reserved the vote to the propertied classes, until the overthrow of the monarchy in 1918; it joined the Weimar Republic in 1919. As a result of World War I it lost most of West Prussia, Prussian Poland, and parts of Silesia to Poland (temporarily reannexed 1939–45). After World War II, Prussia was redivided into several new states (see GERMANY). It was formally dissolved by the Allied Control Council in 1947.

Prussian blue, pigment used for laundry bluing, dyeing, making inks and paints.

prussic acid: see HYDROCYANIC ACID.

Pruth or **Prut** (prōot), river, 530 mi. long, USSR and Rumania, rising in Carpathians and flowing generally SE (forming border between Moldavian SSR and Rumania) into the Danube at Galati. By the Peace of the Pruth (1711) Peter I of Russia restored Azov to the Turks.

Prynne, William (prĭn), 1600–1669, English political figure and pamphleteer, an extreme Puritan. Imprisoned (1634), he was released (1640) by Long Parliament. Opposed Presbyterians, Independents; disputed with John Milton. Expelled from Parliament in Pride's Purge, he attacked the Commonwealth and was imprisoned (1650–53). Worked for Stuart cause.

Przhevalsky, Nikolai Mikhailovich (pŭrzhĭväl′skē), 1839–88, Russian explorer in Asia. First Westerner to explore systematically mountainous region of W China and E Tibet. Credited with discovering Lob Nor and Altyn Tagh range.

Przhevalsky's horse: see TARPAN.

Przybyszewski, Stanislaus (pshĭbĭshĕf′skē), 1868–1927, Polish author. Wrote in Polish and German. His philosophy repudiates reason, exalts intuition. His works include the drama *For Happiness* (1912; Eng. tr., 1912) and the novel *Homo Sapiens* (1898; Eng. tr., 1915).

Psalmanazar, George (săl″mùnä′zùr), 1679?–1763, English literary impostor, whose real name is unknown. He posed as Formosan Christian convert and wrote fraudulent books on Formosa. Exposed and disgraced in 1706.

Psalms (sämz) or **Psalter** (sôl′tùr), book of Old Testament, a collection of 150 poetic pieces, the hymnal par excellence of Judaism and Christendom. Many of the poems traditionally ascribed to David. Different versions vary in dividing individual psalms, thus making citation of number and verse confusing. Hebrew, AV, and RV texts use one numbering; other versions, such as Douay, use another, as follows: AV Pss. 1–8 = Douay 1–8; AV 9–10 = Douay 9; AV 11–113 = Douay 10–112; AV 114–115 = Douay 113; AV 116 = Douay 114–115; AV 117–146 = Douay 116–145; AV 147 = Douay 146–147; AV 148–150 = Douay 148–150. The poems vary in tone and subject.

Some are called penitential psalms, e.g., 51 (called, from opening word in Latin, Miserere), 130 (De profundis). Others express the poet's awareness of the presence of God, e.g., 23. (Numbers cited above are those of AV.) The Psalms have been translated into more languages and into greater varieties of form than any other part of the Old Testament.

Psalms of Solomon: see PSEUDEPIGRAPHA.

Psalter: see PSALMS.

Psaltery: see STRINGED INSTRUMENTS.

Psamtik (säm′tĭk, säm′–), d. 609 B.C., king of anc. Egypt (663–609 B.C.), founder of the XXVI dynasty; son of Necho, lord of Saïs. Viceroy of Lower Egypt under Assur-bani-pal, he shook off the Assyrian yoke and became master of the whole country. His son was the Pharaoh Necho.

pseudepigrapha (sū″dĭpĭ′grŭfŭ) [Gr.,= things falsely ascribed], uncanonical writings of a biblical type, usually of spurious date and authorship. Pseudepigrapha of Jewish origin were composed 200 B.C.–A.D. 200. They are usually named after some great Hebrew leader or seer to give them an air of authenticity and are generally apocalyptic in nature, describing the Day of Judgment and foretelling the coming of the Messiah. Other books are romantic embroideries of biblical stories and religious histories of the world. Among Jewish pseudepigrapha are: the Ethiopic Book of Enoch; the Secrets of Enoch; the Testaments of the Twelve Patriarchs (i.e., the sons of Jacob); the Assumption of Moses; the Sibylline Oracles; the Apocalypse of Baruch; Books of Adam and Eve, Joseph and Asenath, Jannes and Jambres; the Psalms of Solomon; the Book of Jubilees or Little Genesis; the Book of Biblical Antiquities; and 3, 4, and 5 Maccabees. Three pseudepigrapha are placed in the APOCRYPHA of AV: 3 and 4 Esdras and the Prayer of Manasses. Christian pseudepigrapha were composed A.D. 50–A.D. 400. Many of them were written to support various heresies, or, in sincere but misguided piety, to surround the life story of Jesus with glamorous legend. Nearly all the apostles have apocalypses, gospels, and acts ascribed to them. Some roughly follow canonical writings; others contain accounts of alleged miracles of a sensational and even violent nature and attribute fantastic words and deeds to Jesus, Mary, and others. Among these many books are: the Apocalypse of Peter; the Shepherd of Hermas; the Ascension of Isaiah; the Gospel of Nicodemus (containing the Acts of Pilate and the Harrowing of Hell); Gospels according to the Hebrews, the Egyptians, Thomas, Judas Iscariot, and the Twelve; the Protevangelium of James; the Arabic Gospel of the Infancy of Jesus; and spurious epistles ascribed to Jesus (Epistles of Abgar), Barnabas, Paul, Clement, Ignatius, and others. Certain other epistles of Ignatius, Clement, and Polycarp are considered genuine (actually written by these men) but not canonical (of divine inspiration). Probably genuine are the DIDACHE and Apostolic CONSTITUTIONS. For canonical writings, see OLD TESTAMENT; NEW TESTAMENT.

Pseudo-Dionysius: see DIONYSIUS THE AREOPAGITE, SAINT.

psittacosis (sĭtŭkō′sĭs) or **parrot fever,** contagious disease of certain birds (esp. parrot family) probably caused by virus. Transmissible to man.

Pskov (pŭskôf′), city (pop. 59,898), W European RSFSR, near S end of L. Pskov (sometimes considered S part of L. PEIPUS). Machinery and linen mfg. One of oldest Russian cities, it became (14th cent.) a democratic city state and flourishing commercial center. Annexed by Moscow 1510. Scene of Nicholas II's abdication (1917). Damaged in World War II. Inner walled city contains famous kremlin (12th–16th cent.).

Psyche (sī′kē), [Gr.,= breath, soul, spirit], in Greek literature, personification of human soul. Legend says Cupid (or Eros) loved her but forbade her to look at him. When she disobeyed, he left her, but she became immortal and was united with him forever.

psychiatry (sŭkī′ŭtrē, sī–), branch of medicine dealing with diagnosis and treatment of mental disorders. Organized attempt to study or treat mental ills, to improve institutional conditions, began with Philippe PINEL. Humanitarian reformers of 19th cent. fought for legislation (see MENTAL HYGIENE) while scientists sought underlying causes of mental and nervous disorders. Emil Kraepelin was first to delineate PSYCHOSIS; FREUD turned attention to patient's behavior and emotional history, initiated PSYCHOANALYSIS. SHOCK THERAPY, PSYCHOTHERAPY, new methods of psychosurgery, PSYCHOSOMATIC MEDICINE, are used to treat mental and some apparently physical ills.

psychical research or **parapsychology,** study of mental phenomena not explainable by accepted principles of science. Society for Psychical Research, founded 1882 in London, first used the scientific method for this study, dissociating psychical phenomena from spiritualism and superstition and making careful investigations of mediums. Best known work done by American Society for Psychical Research is that of J. B. Rhine of Duke Univ. in extrasensory perception and in psychokinesis (mental influence over matter). Increasing interest in psychical research is shown by fellowships at Cambridge and Harvard and laboratory at Univ. of Gröningen.

psychoanalysis (sī′kōŭnă′lŭsĭs), name given by Freud to a system of psychopathology and therapeutic procedure for treating NEUROSIS. FREUD saw the UNCONSCIOUS as dynamic, an area of great psychic activity affecting all action but operating from repressed material that resists recall. Therefore he made conscious recognition of forgotten scenes, especially by free association, the basis of therapy; dreams were also a key to the unconscious. Therapy also depended on transference. Freud and his followers introduced a vast body of theory, with emphasis on two oppositional instincts—the destructive (aggressive or hostile) death instinct and the constructive sexual instinct. An ideal adjustment neutralizes the overt primitive expression of each, but damming up of instinctual energies is a factor in causing neurosis. Freud believed that in the emotionally mature person much of the libidinal energy could be deflected by sublimation from its unconscious sexual aim to nonsexual, socially useful goals. Psychoanalysts believe that the ego has available, besides repression and sublimation, other means (see DEFENSE MECHANISM) of protecting itself against the demands of the id (the reservoir, deep in the mind, of instinctual drives). After 1906 Freud was joined by others, among them JUNG and Alfred ADLER, both of whom later parted from him. In the 1920s Freudian psychoanalysis was challenged by Otto RANK, Sandor Ferenczi, Wilhelm Reich; in the 1930s by Karen HORNEY, Erich Fromm, and H. S. SULLIVAN, a group emphasizing social and cultural factors in neurosis and, in therapy, stressing the interpersonal aspect of the analyst-patient relationship.

psychology, the science of the mind. Psychologists do not agree upon any one definition of mind, some considering it almost synonymous with soul and therefore a thing apart from the body, others tying mind closely with brain, making each a function of the other. Generally modern psychology is defined as the science that studies all interactions between living organisms and environment, thus avoiding the mechanistic approach of strict behaviorism as well as the extreme idealism of philosophy. Although psychology is close to the biological, physical, and social sciences, it remains a specific science since no complete explanation of individual behavior can be given solely in the terms of any other one science. Its important concepts (i.e., of emotions, instincts, consciousness, and the intelligence) are therefore described in terms of their relationship to the behavior of the individual as a whole. Aristotle's *De anima* is considered the first great psychological work. Modern psychology grew from work of Hobbes (17th cent.). Emphasis in the

psychoneurosis

19th cent. on experimental methods led to the work of J. M. Charcot and Pierre Janet; the theory of evolution led to dynamic psychology, as of William James. Sigmund Freud laid the basis of PSYCHOANALYSIS and widened the scope of psychology. GESTALT psychology and BEHAVIORISM greatly influenced 20th-cent. thought. Applied psychology is adapted to industry and commerce.

psychoneurosis: see NEUROSIS.

psychosis (sīkō'sĭs), mental disease involving emotional disturbances that prevent realistic adjustment to environment. Symptoms may include hallucinations, delusions, severe deviation of mood, lack or inappropriateness of apparent emotional response, severe distortion of judgment. The term INSANITY is applied to those psychoses where moral judgment is considered impaired. Organic psychoses are caused by structural damage of brain; functional psychoses show no observable organic damage. Psychoanalysts emphasize the role of emotional conflicts. New techniques of psychosurgery and SHOCK THERAPY are useful in treating certain psychoses.

psychosomatic medicine (sī"kōsōmǎ'tĭk) treats emotional disturbances, often unconscious, manifested as physical disorders. Treatment usually involves a medical regimen and some PSYCHOTHERAPY. Freud's theories, Adolf Meyer's psychobiology, W. B. Cannon's research on physiological effects of acute emotion, were reinforced psychosomatics. Stomach ulcer, heart diseases, rheumatics, asthma, endocrine disorders, are sometimes treated by psychosomatics.

psychotherapy, treatment of mental disorders by psychological methods. Freudian psychoanalysis was the first systematized form. When this seems inadvisable or unwarranted, direction, support, suggestion, and often occupational therapy, are used to help patients function more efficiently without awareness of unconscious motives of behavior.

psyllium seed: see PLANTAIN.

Pt, chemical symbol of the element PLATINUM.

ptarmigan (tär'mĭgŭn), northern game bird of grouse family. The legs are almost completely feathered. Seasonal changes in plumage result in protective coloration all year.

pterodactyl (tĕrŭdăk'tĭl), extinct flying reptile of the Mesozoic, not related to birds or mammals. Pterodactyls ranged in size from very small up to a flying dragon with wingspread of more than 20 ft.

Ptolemy (tŏ'lŭmē), kings of the Macedonian, Lagid, or XXXI dynasty of anc. Egypt. **Ptolemy I** (Soter), d. 283 B.C., was a general of Alexander the Great and in the wars of the DIADOCHI estab. himself as king of Egypt (304 B.C.), the defeat of Antigonus making his position firm. Founded the library at Alexandria. His son, **Ptolemy II** (Philadelphus), c.308–246? B.C., reigned 283?–246? B.C. Warred against Antiochus II of Syria until he married his daughter Berenice to Antiochus. Helped Rome in the First Punic War. His son, **Ptolemy III** (Euergetes), d. 222? B.C., reigned 246?–222? B.C. Plunged into war with Syria to aid his sister Berenice, but she and her son were murdered before he arrived. Controlled coasts of Asia Minor and E Greece. His son, **Ptolemy IV** (Philopator), d. 204? B.C., reigned 222?–204? B.C. Defeated Antiochus III at Raphia (217) but saw Egyptian administration decline. It declined even more under his son, **Ptolemy V** (Epiphanes), d. 181? B.C., who reigned 204?–181? B.C. Civil wars and invasions weakened Egypt. His son, **Ptolemy VI** (Philometor), d. 145 B.C., reigned 181?–145 B.C., but was first under the regency of his mother, Cleopatra, then was forced after defeat by Antiochus IV of Syria (170 B.C.) to share the reign with his wife, Cleopatra (also his sister), and his brother **Ptolemy VII** (Physcon), d. 117? B.C., who reigned alone after 145. He had his nephew put to death and married his sister-in-law (also his sister), Cleopatra, whom he repudiated to marry her daugh-

ter, also Cleopatra. The elder Cleopatra briefly drove him from the throne. His son, **Ptolemy VIII** (Lathyrus), d. 81 B.C., reigned 117?–107, 89–81 B.C. His mother, the younger Cleopatra, made him accept as coruler his brother, **Ptolemy IX** (Alexander), d. 89? B.C., who drove his brother from the throne in 107. He was defeated by a revolt in Alexandria (89 B.C.). His son, **Ptolemy X** (Alexander), d. 80 B.C., under Roman pressure married his stepmother Cleopatra Berenice (daughter of Ptolemy VIII). He ruled jointly with her, then murdered her and was in turn killed by the angry Alexandrians. **Ptolemy XI** (Auletes), d. 51 B.C., was the illegitimate son of Ptolemy VIII. He succeeded Ptolemy X, was ousted by the Alexandrians (58 B.C.), but got Roman aid of Pompey and Aulus Gabinius (to whom he paid vast sums) and was restored in 55 B.C. He made the Roman senate executor of his will and Pompey guardian of his elder son, **Ptolemy XII,** 61?–47 B.C., who was overshadowed by his wife and sister, the famous Cleopatra. Trouble arose, and Ptolemy was defeated. After he drowned in the Nile, Cleopatra married her younger brother, **Ptolemy XIII,** d. 44 B.C. He was joint ruler with her until she had him murdered. **Ptolemy XIV** (Caesarion), 47–30 B.C., was the son of Cleopatra and (almost certainly) Julius Caesar. He was joint ruler with his mother. After she and Antony was defeated, Octavian (Augustus) had Caesarion put to death.

Ptolemy (Claudius Ptolemaeus), fl. 127 to 141 or 151, Greco-Egyptian astronomer, mathematician, and geographer. He systematized, recorded, and added to data and doctrines known to Alexandrian scientists. His *Almagest,* widely translated and influential in Europe until superseded by findings of Copernicus, presented Ptolemaic system of astronomy, based chiefly on concepts of Hipparchus, which represented spherical earth as stationary center of universe, with sun and other heavenly bodies revolving about it.

ptomaine poisoning: see FOOD POISONING.

public health, field of medicine and hygiene dealing with disease prevention and health promotion. Activities are carried on chiefly by federal, state, and local public health and education services and by private agencies. Public health work includes regulation of sanitation and communicable diseases (see SOCIAL HYGIENE); collection of vital statistics; promotion of health education, school and industrial hygiene, and maternal and child health.

public land, in U.S. history, land owned by Federal government but not reserved for any special purpose, e.g., for a park. Settlement was encouraged by selling tracts of 160 acres or more (see HOMESTEAD ACT). Vast tracts were given railroads and land-grant colleges. To insure CONSERVATION OF NATURAL RESOURCES public lands were withdrawn from sale in late 19th cent. In New Deal period public domain was increased by purchase of barren lands. Public land sometimes called land in public domain, term also applied to products or operations on which copyright or patent protection has lapsed or was not taken out.

public ownership, government ownership of lands, streets, utilities, and other enterprises. The theory that all land and resources belong to the people and therefore to the government is very ancient and from it comes the doctrine of eminent domain. Until the policy of laissez faire in the 18th cent. emphasized capitalistic activity, public ownership was unquestioned. Public ownership is to be distinguished from government control of private enterprises. Examples of U.S. public ownership are the Panama Canal, the atomic energy development, and TVA.

Public Works Administration (PWA), government organ estab. 1933 by U.S. Congress as Federal Administration of Public Works. Administered construction of various public works, made loans to states and municipalities for similar projects. H. L. Ickes headed it 1933–39. Virtually liquidated by Jan. 1, 1947.

publishing, in the broadest sense, making some information publicly known; generally as the term is used today, the issuing of printed materials (books, pamphlets, periodicals, and the like). Publishing is not easily distinguished from the allied occupations of printing and bookselling, since these all may overlap. Properly, publishing may be said to be primarily the service of preparing the work of an author in the most suitable form and presenting it in the most efficient manner to the widest possible audience for that particular work (through dealers or directly). The dissemination of books in manuscript form and for sale was known in ancient Greece and was an organized business in the Roman Empire. In the Middle Ages manuscript reproduction was wholly in the hands of the monks, and publication as such ceased. It was revived somewhat in the Renaissance, but it was only with the introduction into Europe of movable TYPE in the middle of the 15th cent. that large-scale reproduction of written material was possible. Printing spread rapidly, its growth encouraged somewhat by the religious quarrels following the Reformation, when polemical works were numerous. The beginning of separation of publishing from printing appeared early. It is commonly said that the first great publishing house was that of the Elzevir family, which began publishing books in 1583. The true distinction between printer, publisher, and seller of printed materials did not, however, become sharp until the 19th cent., and in many cases the lines between them are still blurred.

Puccini, Giacomo (jä′kōmō pŏōt-chē′nē), 1858–1924, Italian operatic composer. His outstanding operas are *Manon Lescaut* (1893); *La Bohème* (1896); *La Tosca* (1900); *Madame Butterfly* (1904); *Turandot* (completed by Franco Alfano); and *The Girl of the Golden West* (1910), based on Belasco's play.

Puck (pŭk), in Germanic folklore, generic name for a minor order of devils, sprites, goblins, or demons. In *Piers Plowman* the name (spelled *pouke*) signifies the devil. Shakspere was first to identify Puck as a merry attractive elf.

Puebla (pwä′blä), state (13,126 sq. mi.; pop. 1,595,920), E central Mexico. Extremely mountainous with Sierra Madre Oriental in N and volcanic belt across center, with three highest peaks of Mexico—Orizaba, Popocatepetl, and Ixtacihuatl—on its borders. NE section is on humid coastal plain of Gulf of Mexico. Agr., stock raising, and mining are important. **Puebla,** the capital (pop. 138,491), is commercial center of state. Founded 1535, it is today noted for cotton mills, onyx quarries, pottery, fine tiles. Cathedral, constructed between 1552 and 1649, is one of finest in Mexico.

Pueblo (pwē′blō, pūē′blō), city (pop. 63,685), S central Colo., on Arkansas R. (levee-controlled) in foothills of the Rockies. Z. M. Pike visited area in 1806. Here were a trading post (1842) and a Mormon settlement (1846–47). Pueblo City laid out 1860. Second largest city in Colo., it is a shipping and industrial center for livestock and irrigated farm area. Mfg. of many metal products and building materials, oil refining, and meat packing.

Pueblo Indians, North American people, in SW U.S., living in stone or adobe community houses, comprising villages called pueblos. Their ancestors came into this area, succeeding the BASKET MAKERS, who had already developed agr. The newcomers advanced in civilization but later had to retreat from predatory tribes and became CLIFF DWELLERS. This period ended A.D. c.1300 after a severe drought and invasions of the Navaho and the Apache. The Pueblos had by the time of the Spanish conquest of Mexico developed the highest Indian civilization N of Mexico, and the Zuni pueblos were apparently the originals of the mythical Seven Cities of Cibola that attracted Spanish interest. Coronado's party in 1540 began Spanish penetration; missions were founded by 1580 and Spanish colonies in 1598. The Pueblos were hostile and finally in 1680 rose and drove the Spanish out. In 1692 the Spanish

reconquered the territory, and since that time the Pueblos have generally lived in peace. They are noted for rich, polychrome pottery, for baskets, and for textiles. Their public religious ceremonies attract tourists annually. They are divided into four linguistic families—Tanoan (11 pueblos, incl. Taos, Isleta, Jemez, San Juan, San Ildefonso, and the Hopi pueblo of Hano), Western Keresan (Acoma and Laguna), Eastern Keresan (San Felipe, Santa Ana, Sia, Cochiti, and Santo Domingo), and Hopi.

puerperal fever (pūūr′pūrŭl), acute disease of genital tract caused by septic infection contracted during childbirth, usually from failure to use aseptic methods. Early advocates of prevention by cleanliness include Semmelweis and Oliver Wendell Holmes.

Puerto Montt (pwĕr′tō mōnt′), city (pop. 18,688), S central Chile, port on the Pacific; founded 1853. S terminus of railroad and starting point for navigation through inland waterways. Near-by hills, lakes, and fjords make city a popular resort. Sheep raising and fishing are major commercial activities.

Puerto Rico (pwĕr′tō rē′kō), formerly Porto Rico, island (3,425 sq. mi.; pop. 2,210,703), smallest and most easterly of Greater Antilles, in West Indies. It is coextensive with the Commonwealth of Puerto Rico; cap. and largest city, SAN JUAN. Other important cities are Ponce and Mayagüez. The island is crossed by mountain ranges and has short rivers, unnavigable but useful for irrigation and hydroelectric power. The climate is mildly tropical; the fertile soil supports one of the densest populations of a purely agr. area in the world. Sugar is its major product, but the Puerto Rican government is working out a program of diversification (coffee, tobacco, tropical fruits, winter vegetables) in order to help solve the economic problems caused by a one-crop economy. Processing of sugar (mills, refineries, distilleries) is the main industry. Puerto Rican needlework is distinctive and popular in U.S. The people are descended from Spanish colonists, with an admixture of Indian and African strains. The language is Spanish, the religion predominantly Roman Catholic. The island, called by the natives Boriquén or Borinquén, was visited by Columbus in 1493. It was first settled by Ponce de León in 1508. Caparra, the first settlement, was replaced by San Juan, 4 mi. away, in 1521. The Indians—of Arawak stock—were soon wiped out, and Negro slaves were imported to work on plantations (slavery was abolished in 1873). In 1898, during the Spanish-American War, U.S. troops landed; with little difficulty, military occupation was accomplished. In the Treaty of Paris, Puerto Rico was ceded outright to U.S. There has been a progressive development toward self-rule in the island; now the governor is elected by the people (Luis Muñoz Marín was the first, 1948), there is an elected commissioner in U.S. Congress, and the Puerto Ricans have U.S. citizenship. In 1952, it ceased to be a colonial possession and became a "Free Commonwealth" and the way lay open for statehood in the U.S. Health and sanitary conditions and educational facilities have improved with U.S. occupation, but a one-crop economy, absentee ownership, and overpopulation still plague the island. Emigration to continental U.S. became very heavy after World War II.

Puerto Rico, University of, mainly at Río Piedras, near San Juan; coed.; founded 1903. Agr. and mechanical college at Mayagüez, school of tropical medicine at San Juan.

Pueyrredón, Juan Martín de (hwän′ märtēn′ dä pwāïrrä-dōn′), 1776–1850, Argentine general, supreme director of United Provs. of La Plata (1816–19). With Liniers resisted invasion of Buenos Aires by British (1806). Took important part in revolutionary government (1810–18). When unitarian constitution was rejected, Pueyrredón resigned.

Pufendorf, Samuel, Freiherr von (pōō′fŭndôrf), 1632–94, German jurist and historian, writer on international law. He considered the law of nations a part of natural rights. Wrote *Elementa jurisprudentiae universalis* (1661) and *De jure naturae et gentium* (1672). Also wrote a historical work on the Holy Roman Empire.

puffball or **smokeball,** fungus with a globular spore-bearing body, usually stalkless, common in meadows and woods. None are poisonous and most are edible when young. When mature, they emit their dustlike spores like puffs of smoke.

puffin, swimming and diving bird of N Atlantic, N Pacific, and arctic regions, related to auk. It has short legs, a dumpy body, and large bill.

Pugachev, Yemelyan Ivanovich (yĭmĭlyän' ēvä'nŭvĭch poōgŭchôf'), d. 1775, Russian rebel leader. An illiterate Don Cossack, he claimed to be PETER III. Became figurehead of formidable peasant revolt (1773–75), seized large parts of E Russia, proclaimed abolition of serfdom. He was betrayed, captured, and beheaded.

Puget, Pierre (püzhā'), 1622–94, French sculptor and painter. Spent most of his life in S France and Italy. His famous statue of St. Sebastian is in Genoa. Well represented in the Louvre.

Puget Sound (pū'jĭt), NW Wash., connected with the Pacific by Juan de Fuca Strait and extending c.100 mi. S from the strait to Olympia. Navigable, it serves rich industrial and agr. region. Seattle, Tacoma, and Everett are on E shore, Port Townsend at entrance. Explored by George Vancouver 1792.

Puget Sound, College of: see TACOMA, Wash.

Pugin, Augustus Charles (pū'jĭn), English writer on medieval architecture, b. France. He and his son, **Augustus Welby Northmore Pugin,** 1812–52, who was an eminent architect, were important for their prominent role in the Gothic revival.

Pula, Yugoslavia: see POLA.

Pulaski, Casimir (kǎ'sĭmēr pŭlä'skē), c.1748–1779, Polish military commander in American Revolution. Organized cavalry unit in 1778. Mortally wounded in attack on Savannah.

Pulaski (pŭlä'skē). **1** Town (pop. 5,762), S Tenn., SSW of Nashville. Trade, processing, and shipping for farm area. Ku Klux Klan organized here 1865. **2** Town (pop. 9,202), SW Va., SW of Roanoke. Trade and processing center of agr., lumber, mining area.

Pulaski, Fort (pŭlä'skē), fortification on Cockspur Isl., SE Ga., at mouth of Savannah R. Constructed 1829–47. Seized Jan., 1861, by Confederates, retaken by Union force under Q. A. Gillmore, April 11, 1862. Fort Pulaski Natl. Monument (estab. 1924) now includes all Cockspur Isl.

Pulci, Luigi (lwē'jē poōl'chē), 1432–84, Italian poet; protégé of Lorenzo de' Medici and author of *Morgante maggiore* (1460–70), a mock-heroic poem.

Pulitzer, Joseph (poō'lĭtsŭr, pū'–), 1847–1911, American newspaper owner, b. Hungary; in U.S. after 1864. He was a journalist under Carl Schurz in St. Louis and in 1878 became successful owner-publisher of the *Post-Dispatch.* In 1883 he bought the New York *World* and built it up aggressively, adding in 1887 the *Evening World.* Outstripped in popular appeal by Hearst's *Journal,* his papers became more conservative after 1900. In 1931 the *Evening World* was merged with the New York *Telegram.* Pulitzer left funds to found the School of Journalism at Columbia Univ. Since 1917 **Pulitzer Prizes** have been awarded annually for achievements in American journalism and letters. There are seven awards in specific fields of journalism; in letters, for fiction, drama, history, biography, poetry, and musical composition. In addition, there are four traveling scholarships given each year.

pulley, simple machine consisting of sheave (wheel with grooved rim in which rope can run) and block (frame in which wheel turns freely on axle). Fixed pulley has frame attached to rigid support; movable pulley frame is free to move. One block may contain several wheels. No mechanical advantage is ob-

tained by single fixed pulley; single movable pulley has mechanical advantage of 2 (i.e., given weight, or resistance, can be balanced by a force, or effort, of one half that amount). By combinations of fixed and movable pulleys, a small effort can overcome a large resistance; amount of work done is not increased, since the effort applied moves through a greater distance than the load. See *ill.,* p. 619.

Pullman, George Mortimer (poōl'mùn), 1831–97, American industrialist. Founded Pullman Palace Car Co. in 1867.

Pullman. 1 Former city, part (since 1889) of Chicago, Ill. Founded 1880 by G. M. Pullman as model community for workers of his sleeping-car company. Strike over wage cuts (May–July, 1894) here resulted in jail for E. V. DEBS, president of American Railway Union, and a complaint from Ill. governor J. P. ALTGELD because Pres. Cleveland quelled strike with U.S. troops. **2** City (pop. 12,022), SE Wash., near Idaho line, in grain, livestock, poultry area; founded 1884. Seat of State Col. of Washington (land-grant, state supported; coed.; opened 1892).

pulque (poōl'kā), Mexican spirituous liquor made by fermenting sap of maguey (see AGAVE).

pulse, alternate expansion and contraction of artery walls as heart action causes changes in arterial blood volume. Normal rate at rest is about 70–80 pulsations a minute in adults.

puma (pū'mù), New World predatory cat (*Felis*), variously called cougar, mountain lion, catamount, panther. Ranges from Canada to Patagonia. Northerly puma reddish to grayish brown above; adult male is 7–8 ft. long. Tropical races are smaller and redder.

pumice (pū'mĭs), volcanic glass permeated with bubbles. Used as abrasive, included in many scouring materials. Lipari Isls. off Italy are chief source.

pump, device for lifting fluid or varying fluid pressure. Atmospheric pressure limits lift of suction pump to c.34 ft. Variation of pressure inside cylinder and attached pipe of pump is basic to its operation. Other types include reciprocating pumps, centrifugal and force pumps, and air lift. Rotary pump employs the screw principle.

pumpkin, vinelike tender annual (*Cucurbita pepo*), of unknown origin, and its large yellow edible fruit. The name pumpkin is often used interchangeably with squash. It was among the fruits of the first Thanksgiving and has been a favorite pie filling of autumn festivities ever since. Its shell is the Jack-o'-lantern of Halloween.

puna (poō'nä) [South American], high plateau region between ridges of Andes in Peru and Bolivia. Icy wind sweeping plateaus also called *puna.*

Punch and Judy, English puppet play, popular with children. Probably originated in *commedia dell' arte.* Punch is cruel and boastful, his wife Judy faithless and obstreperous.

Punchbowl, hill, 498 ft. high, Honolulu, T.H. In bowl-like extinct crater at summit is Natl. Cemetery of the Pacific for World War II dead.

punctuation, device of using special arbitrary marks other than letters in written material. These marks supplement the spelling by giving some indication of tone, accent, pauses, and relationships that are significant in the use of a language but are not shown by letters alone. In English, punctuation particularly represents the intonations. Marks commonly used are the comma, the semicolon, the period, full stop, or point, the exclamation point, the interrogation point or question mark, the colon, quotation marks, and the dash. With the increase of silent as opposed to vocal reading other marks have come into use, such as the apostrophe (marking an omission or a possessive case), square brackets (secondary parentheses), and the hyphen (to indicate a more or less intimate joining of two words). Today punctuation is properly used only when it makes the meaning clear to the eye; arbitrary rules that reached an elaborate point in the 19th cent. have lost some of their force. In other Western languages the same signs and a few others are used, but each language has its own system of punctuation, since marks are actually arbitrary and conventional symbols gaining their meaning only from use.

Punic language, language of Carthage, belonging to Canaanite group of Semitic languages. See LANGUAGE (table).

Punic Wars, series of three contests between Rome and Carthage for dominance of the Mediterranean. When they began Carthage was a great power dominating NW Africa and the islands and commerce of the W Mediterranean. When they ended Carthage was a ruin and Rome the greatest power W of China. The **First Punic War,** 264–241 B.C., began when Messana called on both Rome and Carthage for help in a quarrel with Syracuse. The Carthaginians arrived first and arranged a peace, but the Romans ejected them and took E Sicily. The Roman fleet won at Mylae (260) and off Cape Economus (256), but a Roman expedition to Africa failed. Hamilcar Barca kept the Romans from taking Lilybaeum, but a new Roman victory at sea off the Aegadian Isles (241) caused Carthage to ask for peace. Rome now had Sicily and (contrary to the treaty) set out to conquer Sardinia and Corsica. When the Carthaginians under HANNIBAL took Saguntum (Sagunto) in Spain (219), Rome declared war. The **Second Punic** (or Hannibalic) **War,** 218–201 B.C., was the most celebrated of the three. It was marked by Hannibal's invasion of Italy and success there (against Fabius and others) until the failure of supplies and the defeat of his brother Hasdrubal on the Metaurus (207) made his attempt hopeless. He returned to Africa to defend Carthage against SCIPIO AFRICANUS MAJOR, but failed in the battle of Zama (202). Carthage surrendered its Spanish province and its war fleet and did not recover. Nevertheless CATO THE ELDER long agitated for complete destruction of Carthage and the **Third Punic War,** 149–146 B.C., originated when Rome charged Carthage with technical breach of the treaty by resisting the aggression of Rome's ally Masinissa. Carthage was blockaded but did not surrender. SCIPIO AFRICANUS MINOR conquered it and razed it.

punishment: see CAPITAL PUNISHMENT; CORPORAL PUNISHMENT; CRIMINAL LAW; PRISON.

Punjab (pŭn"jäb') [Sanskrit,= five rivers], region of NW India and W Pakistan, lying between Indus and Jumna rivers. Mainly a level plain irrigated by Jhelum, Chenab, Ravi, Sutlej, and Beas rivers. Region was probably seat of earliest Aryan settlements in India. Occupied 326 B.C. by Alexander the Great and later by Maurya empire. Moslems occupied W Punjab by 8th cent. and implanted Islam but failed to dislodge Hinduism as dominant religion in E Punjab, which they conquered (12th cent.). Sikhs rose to power in late 18th cent. as Mogul empire declined. Twice defeated in battle, they lost the area to the British in 1849. Punjab was divided 1947 between Pakistan and India on basis of concentrations of Moslem and Hindu population. Indian state of Punjab (37,428 sq. mi.; pop. 12,638,111) was originally called East Punjab; cap. Simla. First known as West Punjab, Pakistan's province (62,987 sq. mi.; pop. 18,814,000) is also called Punjab; cap. Lahore.

Punta Arenas (pōōn'tä ärä'näs) [Span.,= sandy point], city (pop. 24,706), cap. of Magallanes prov., S Chile. Only city on Strait of Magellan and world's southernmost city. Founded 1847 to maintain Chile's claim to strait. Exports Patagonian wool and mutton.

Punxsutawney (pŭngksŭtô'nē), industrial borough (pop. 8,969), W Pa., NE of Pittsburgh. Coal mining.

pupa (pū'pù), third stage in life of insect undergoing complete metamorphosis (egg, larva, pupa, adult). Complete metamorphosis is characteristic of members of orders Coleoptera (beetles), Diptera (flies, mosquitoes, gnats, etc.), Lepidoptera (moths, butterflies). Some pupae are active, but most are enclosed in a

hard covering and are quiescent. Butterfly pupa case is called chrysalis. Most moth pupae are covered by cocoon, often silk secreted by larva. See *ill.*, p. 469.

Pupin, Michael (Idvorsky) (pūpēn') 1858–1935, American physicist and inventor, b. in the present Yugoslavia. He came to U.S. in 1874 and from 1889 was associated with Columbia Univ. Known for researches in X ray, for invention of many electrical devices used in telegraphy and telephony, and for Pulitzer Prize-winning autobiography (1923).

puppet, small figure of man or animal performing on miniature stage, manipulated by unseen operator who also speaks the dialogue. Distinction is made between marionettes (moved by strings or wire from above) and puppets (in which operator's hand is concealed in doll's costume). Puppet show is so ancient that it is impossible to tell where it first appeared. In Europe (16th–18th cent.) great writers and composers created works for puppets.

Purbeck, Isle of, peninsular district, c.12 mi. long and 8 mi. wide, Dorsetshire, England. Noted for production of Purbeck marble and china clay.

Purcell, Edward Mills, 1912–, American physicist. Shared 1952 Nobel Prize for development of a new method of measuring magnetic fields in atomic nuclei. Associated with Harvard from 1938.

Purcell, Henry (pûr'sùl), 1659–95, English composer; organist at Westminster Abbey, 1679–95. Among his many stage works are *The Fairy Queen* (based on Shakspere's *Midsummer Night's Dream*) and his music for Dryden's *King Arthur. Dido and Aeneas* (1689) is his only opera in the modern sense. He also wrote anthems, instrumental music, and secular songs.

Purchas, Samuel (pûr'chùs, –kùs), 1577–1626, English clergyman and compiler of travel books. Wrote *Purchas His Pilgrimage* (1613) and compiled famous *Hakluytus Posthumus; or, Purchas His Pilgrims* (1625).

Purdue University (pûrdū'), at Lafayette, Ind.; land-grant, state supported; coed.; chartered 1865, opened 1874. Known for large engineering schools. Has public safety institute.

pure-food laws: see FOOD ADULTERATION.

purgatory, in the teaching of the Roman Catholic Church, the state after death in which the soul destined for heaven is purged of all taint of unpunished or unrepented minor sins. Souls in purgatory may be aided by the prayers of the living (one form of prayer is the requiem Mass).

Puri (pōō'rē), town (pop. 41,055), E Orissa, India, on Bay of Bengal. A center of cult of Juggernaut (or Jagannath), a form of Krishna avatar (incarnation) of Vishnu. In annual festival, god's image is mounted on huge cart and dragged by pilgrims through main street. Contrary to common belief, festival rite does not require pilgrims to hurl themselves under the cart wheels.

Purim (pyōō'rĭm, pōō'–) [Heb.,= lots], Jewish festival which commemorates the deliverance of the Persian Jews from a massacre (Esther 3.7; 9.24,26). It is celebrated on the 14th and 15th of Adar, the sixth month in the Jewish calendar, and is a day of joy.

Puritanism, a composite of social, political, ethical, and theological ideas in English and American Protestantism. It originated in reign of Elizabeth as a movement for reform in state church, intended to do away with ritual, vestments, and hierarchical organization. At first there was no quarrel over doctrine and no plan for secession. But by 1567 a group in London was worshiping after the pattern of Geneva. Gradually, congregation by congregation, they tended to become separatists, Presbyterians, and Independents (later Congregationalists), joined in Calvinistic opposition to the Church of England. But when their cause triumphed in the PURITAN REVOLUTION they fell to quarreling among themselves. The Restoration ended the brief Puritan dominance, and by the end of the 17th cent. Puritanism ceased as an organized movement. The early settlements in New England were Puritan in origin, and the spirit of Puritanism long persisted there. The Puritan ideal of society was a theocracy, with powerful ministers and absolute control of individual conduct. The family was the fortress of godliness, and life was to be lived in strict obedience to detailed laws of God as read in the Bible. The term today is used generally to refer only to repressive aspects.

Puritan Revolution, usual name for the conflict between English kings JAMES I (1603–25) and CHARLES I (1625–49) and the large middle-class parliamentary party. To the religious issue of Puritanism and episcopacy was added the conflict between king's divine-right claims and Parliament's desire to govern, with legal rights instead of favors from the king. James I's need for money made him temporize with Parliament. Sir Edward Coke upheld its rights; was dismissed by the king. Sir Francis Bacon upheld royal prerogative; was impeached by Parliament. James's last Parliament directed him how to use its financial grant. Charles I proved more intractable. Parliament tried by every means to limit his powers; withheld grant till he signed PETITION OF RIGHT. Charles still levied forced taxes and dissolved Parliament for its further opposition. He governed alone for 11 years; recalled Parliament for financial needs of Bishops' Wars. In the Grand Remonstrance, Parliament recited the evils of Charles's reign. By a militia bill it tried to gather an army. King also organized an army and refused Parliament's final 19 demands. His attempt to seize five members of Commons made civil war inevitable. Both sides bid for popular support. Charles was aided by the nobles, Anglicans, and Catholics; Parliament by the trading and artisan classes and by the Scotch Covenanters (after it accepted the Solemn League and Covenant). After first indecisive campaign, victories of Oliver CROMWELL at Marston Moor and Naseby led to king's surrender (1645) and end of first civil war. His escape caused second civil war (1647); it failed quickly. PRIDE'S PURGE expelled from Parliament all those opposed to the army. The remainder sentenced and beheaded Charles for treason (1649). A quasi-democratic Commonwealth was followed by Cromwell's domination in the PROTECTORATE. The Puritan Revolution assured emergence of the middle class, aided religious toleration, and settled contest between king and Parliament. Results confirmed by the glorious Revolution of 1688.

Purkinje, Johannes Evangelista (yōhä′nŭs ā″väng-gälĭs′tä pŏŏr′kĭnyä), 1787–1869, Czech physiologist. He contributed to microscope technique, study of tissues, and embryology.

purslane, weedy, fleshy annual (*Portulaca oleracea*), also known as pussley. In the Old World it has been used as a potherb.

Purus (pŏŏrŏŏs′), river, c.2,100 mi. long, rising in E Peru. Flows generally NE across Brazil into Amazon well above Manaus.

Purvey, John, c.1354–c.1421, English scholar. In support of LOLLARDRY he completed the first thorough translation of the Bible into English (c.1395).

Purvits, Vilhelms (vĭl′hĕlms pŏŏr′vĭts), 1872–, Latvian landscape painter. As director of Latvian museums he was among the first to introduce modern Western art into E Europe.

Pusan (pŏŏ′sän), city (pop. 473,619), S Korea, on Korea Strait; largest port of Korea. In 1950 it became chief UN supply port in Korean war.

Pusey, Edward Bouverie, 1800–1882, English clergyman, leader in OXFORD MOVEMENT, known also as Puseyism. He was regius professor of Hebrew at Oxford, with canonry of Christ Church. His sermon "The Rule of Faith" (1851) checked secessions to Roman Church, caused in part by controversy over church government.

Pushkin, Aleksandr Sergeyevich (ŭlyĭksän′dŭr sĭrgä′-ŭvĭch pŏŏsh′kĭn), 1799–1837, greatest of Russian poets. He came of an old Russian family, but a great-grandfather was Hannibal, the Negro general of Peter I. His best-known works include the drama *Boris Godunov* (1831) and *Eugene Onegin* (1831), a novel of manners in verse, his masterpiece. Other works are the fairy romance *Russlan and Ludmilla* (1820), the poems *The Prisoner of the Caucasus* (1821), *The Fountains of Bakchiserai* (1822), and *The Gypsies* (1823–24), written under Byron's influence; the historical poems *Poltava* (1828) and *The Bronze Horseman* (1833); *The Golden Cockerel* (1833), a folktale; and *The Queen of Spades* (1834), a short story. He died in a duel.

Pushkin, city (pop. over 50,000), RSFSR, S of Leningrad. Founded under Peter I as Tsarskoye Selo; renamed Detskoye Selo in 1920s and Pushkin 1937. Amid large parks are baroque summer palace of Catherine II and classic summer palace of Alexander I, which were partially destroyed in World War II.

Pushtu (pŭsh′tŏŏ), language of Afghanistan, belonging to Iranian group of Indo-Iranian subfamily of Indo-European languages. Also called Afghan. See LANGUAGE (table).

pussy willow: see WILLOW.

Puszta (pŏŏ′stä), grazing lands which once covered a large part of Hungarian plain and were used for extensive cattle raising. Irrigation and drainage have caused disappearance of the Puszta except in a small district near Debrecen.

Puteoli (pūtē′ŭlī), anc. city of Campania, Italy; founded c.520 B.C. by Greeks. A wealthy port in Roman times, it was destroyed by Germans in 5th cent. A.D. Modern Pozzuoli is near.

Put in Bay, harbor of South Bass Isl., N Ohio, in L. Erie NW of Sandusky. At Put in Bay village, resort on bay, is Perry's Victory and Internatl. Peace Memorial Natl. Monument.

Putnam, Amelia Earhart: see EARHART, AMELIA.

Putnam, George Palmer, 1814–72, American publisher; grandnephew of Israel Putnam. Founder (1848) of G. P. Putnam's Sons; owner of *Putnam's Magazine* (estab. 1853). A founder and honorary superintendent of Metropolitan Mus. of Art. A son, **George Haven Putnam,** 1844–1930, succeeded his father in 1872 as head of the firm. He served in the Civil War, was active in civil and social causes, and wrote many books. Another son, **Herbert Putnam,** 1861–, was Librarian of Congress (1899–1938). **George Palmer Putnam,** 1887–1950, a grandson of the founder, served the firm as treasurer (1919–30). He was also an explorer, and author of a biography of his wife, Amelia Earhart (1939).

Putnam, Israel, 1718–90, American Revolutionary general. A farmer, he left plow in furrow to join patriot forces. Commanded at Long Island (1776).

Putnam, Rufus, 1738–1824, American Revolutionary general, a founder of Ohio Company of Associates. Laid out Marietta, Ohio (1788).

Putnam, textile city (pop. 8,181) in Putnam town (pop. 9,304), NE Conn., NE of Willimantic; settled 1693.

Putney, district of SW London, England, on the S side of the Thames. Swinburne and William Pitt lived here. Putney Heath was the scene of duels.

Putney, town (pop. 1,019), SE Vt., N of Brattleboro, on Connecticut R. Has Putney School (progressive; coed; 1935). J. H. NOYES formed first of his three Perfectionist societies here, 1839.

Putrid Sea, RSFSR: see SIVASH SEA.

Putumayo (pŏŏtŏŏmä′yō), river, c.1,000 mi. long, formed by tributaries rising in Colombian Andes, flowing SE to Amazon. Marks part of boundary of Colombia with Ecuador and Peru. Called Içá in Brazil. In wild-rubber boom an investigation showed shocking working conditions in area.

Puvis de Chavannes, Pierre (pyĕr′ püvĕs′ dü shävän′), 1824–98, French mural painter. Studied with the romanticists (notably Delacroix), but his work is classical in inspiration.

Puy, Le (lü püē′), city (pop. 18,347), cap. of Haute-Loire dept., S central France. Has old lace industry. An episcopal see from 6th cent., it became the cap. of the medieval county of Velay (part of Aquitaine; inc. into Languedoc 15th cent.). Its shrine to the Virgin has been a major goal of pilgrimage since the 10th cent. The old part of the city lies at the foot of a bare rock nearly 500 ft. high, capped by the 50-ft. bronze statue of the Virgin (erected 1860). It has a daringly constructed cathedral (12th cent.) and many Gothic buildings. Atop a lesser, needle-shaped rock is the Romanesque Church of St. Michel d'Aiguilhe.

Puyallup (pūā′lüp), city (pop. 10,010), W Wash., on Puyallup R. and E of Tacoma; settled 1877. Berries, bulbs, truck, and wood products. Canneries.

Puy-de-Dôme (püē′-dü-dōm′), department (3,095 sq. mi.; pop. 478,876), S central France, in Auvergne; cap. Clermont-Ferrand. Named for the **Puy de Dôme**, an extinct volcano near Clermont, 4,806 ft. high. Here in 1648 Florence Périer, following instructions of his brother-in-law Blaise Pascal, conducted historic experiment which confirmed Torricelli's theory on air pressure.

Puy de Sancy, France: see MONT-DORE.

Pu Yi, Henry (pōō′ē), 1905–, last emperor (1908–12) of China, who ruled as Hsüan T'ung. Abdication in 1912 ended Ch'ing dynasty. In 1934 he became emperor of Japanese puppet state of MANCHUKUO. Testified in 1946 at war-crimes trial that he had been the unwilling tool of Japanese militarists.

Pyatigorsk (pyïtyēgôrsk′), city (pop. 62,875), S Stavropol Territory, RSFSR, in N Caucasus. Health resort, with hot sulphur springs and mud baths.

Pydna (pĭd′nü), anc. town, S Macedonia, near the Gulf of Salonica. Here Romans under Aemilius Paullus defeated Perseus, king of Macedon (168 B.C.).

Pye, John, 1782–1874, English engraver, founder of modern landscape engraving.

Pygmalion (pĭgmāl′yün), in Greek mythology, king of Cyprus and sculptor of GALATEA.

Pygmy or **Pigmy**, any of various populations of short stature scattered from Africa to New Guinea. African Pygmies, often called Negrillos, average less than 5 ft. in height; are lighter in color than Negroids among whom they live and whose languages they speak. Far Eastern Pygmies, sometimes called Negritos, include Aetas of Philippines, Semangs of Malay Peninsula, and several other small groups from Andaman Isls. eastward; there is pygmy admixture in populations of Malaya and Melanesia. In this area the Pygmies average c.5 ft. tall, have thick lips, very dark skin, scant body hair and woolly head hair.

Pyle, Howard, 1853–1911, American illustrator and writer of tales of chivalry and adventure, such as *The Merry Adventures of Robin Hood of Great Renown* (1883).

Pylos (pī′lŏs), harbor of anc. Messenia, Greece; a center of Mycenaean civilization (13th cent. B.C.). A town, formerly known as Navarino, now as Pylos, is on the S shore of the Bay of Pylos. In the bay Athenians beat Spartans in 425 B.C., and British, French, and Russian ships defeated Egyptians in battle of Navarino (1827) in Greek War for independence.

Pym, John (pĭm), 1583?–1643, English Puritan leader in Parliament. Leader in both Short and Long Parliaments, he opposed the royalist party of Charles I's reign. One of five members of Commons that Charles tried to arrest. Arranged alliance with Scots after signing (1642) the Covenant.

Pynchon, William (pĭn′chŭn), c.1590–1662, American colonist and theologian, b. England. Settled Springfield, Mass., in 1636. Denounced as heretic.

Pynson, Richard (pĭn′sŭn), d. 1530, English printer, b. Normandy, supposedly the most skillful printer in England at his time.

Pyongyang (pyŭng′yäng′), industrial city (pop. 342,551), N Korea; cap. of People's Republic of Korea. According to legend it was founded 1122 B.C. by the Chinese sage Ki-tze. Invaded by the Japanese in 1592, 1894, and 1904. After World War II it was hq. of Russian occupation zone.

pyorrhea (pīŭrē′ü), a discharge of pus. Term is used commonly for alveolar pyorrhea, or Riggs's disease, a disease of bony supporting structure of teeth, described by an American dentist, John M. Riggs.

pyramid. The pyramids in Egypt are square in plan with triangular sides meeting at a point. The pyramid was evolved in period of IV dynasty (2900 B.C.). Each monarch built his own pyramid to preserve his mummified body for eternity; its building required measureless time and labor. Sepulchral chamber, excavated from rock on which pyramid is built, lies deep beneath structure. Great Pyramid of Khufu or Cheops at Gizeh, one of Seven Wonders of the World, is largest pyramid ever built; covering 13 acres, it was originally 768 ft. square and 482 ft. high. Though the pyramids were usually built of rough limestone blocks, many were of mud bricks with stone casing. Pyramidal structures were also built by Assyrians and by the Maya of Central America and Mexico. Assyrian ziggurat was square in plan and built up in receding terraces formed by ramp winding around sides and leading to temple chamber at top. Maya pyramids were also topped by ritual chambers. The **battle of the Pyramids** was a notable victory won by Napoleon over the Mamelukes in Egypt (July, 1798) which gave him brief control over Egypt until Nelson destroyed his fleet at Aboukir, Aug., 1798.

Pyramid Lake, c.30 mi. long and c.10 mi. wide, W Nev., NNE of Reno in Pyramid Lake Indian Reservation. Remnant of ancient L. Lahontan. Discovered 1844 by J. C. Frémont. Receives Truckee R.

Pyramus and Thisbe (pī′rümüs, thïz′bē), in classic legend, youth and maiden of Babylon. At their trysting place Thisbe fled from a lion, dropping her mantle. Pyramus found the bloodied mantle and, thinking her dead, killed himself. Thisbe, on returning, killed herself with his sword. White fruit of the mulberry tree, stained by Pyramus' blood, was red ever after.

Pyrenees (pī′rünēz), mountain chain, SW Europe, separating Iberian Peninsula from European mainland and France from Spain. Extending c.270 mi. from Bay of Biscay (W) to the Mediterranean (E), it rises to 11,168 ft. in the Pico de Aneto (Spain). The French slopes, much steeper than the Spanish, have many resorts (e.g., Pau, Tarbes) and celebrated sights (e.g., the Cirque de GAVARNIE). The Pyrenees are rich in timber, pastures, hydroelectric power. Stock raising and agr. are chief occupations. In the W, the population is largely of Basque stock. Among the passes, which are high and difficult, the Col de Perthus and Roncesvalles are the best known. The chief rail lines skirt the mountains in the W and E. Wedged between France and Spain, in the E Pyrenees, is the republic of Andorra.

Pyrénées, Hautes and **Basses**, France: see HAUTES-PYRÉNÉES; BASSES-PYRÉNÉES.

Pyrenees, Peace of the, 1659, peace treaty between France and Spain, which had remained at war after Peace of Westphalia (1648). Franco-Spanish border was fixed at Pyrenees; Spain ceded Roussillon and parts of Flanders to France; Louis XIV was to marry Marie Thérèse, daughter of Philip IV of Spain.

Pyrénées-Orientales (pēränā′-zôryätäl′), department (1,600 sq. mi.; pop. 228,776), S France, virtually identical with ROUSSILLON; cap. Perpignan.

pyrethrum (pīrē′thrŭm), hardy perennial (*Chrysanthemum coccineum*), also called painted daisy, with lacy foliage and red, pink, or white daisies in late spring. It is one of the species from which the insecticide pyrethrum is derived.

pyridine (pī′rĭdēn), colorless liquid with putrid odor. It is chemically stable and somewhat like benzene in structure. Used as solvent, denaturant, antiseptic.

pyrite (pī′rīt), widely distributed pale brass-yellow mineral, iron bisulphide. Sometimes called "fool's gold," it often does contain gold. Used as source of sulphur in manufacture of sulphuric acid.

Pyrmont (pĭrmônt′) or **Bad Pyrmont** (bät′), town (pop. 16,534), Lower Saxony, W Germany. Noted spa. Former small principality of Pyrmont was united with WALDECK.

pyrogallol (pī″rōgă′lŏl) or **pyrogallic acid** (–lĭk), colorless, crystalline phenol with biting taste. It is used as developing agent in photography and in ointments.

pyroligneous acid (pī″rōlĭg′nēus), dark liquid mixture of acetic acid and wood alcohol obtained by destructive distillation of wood. It is a source of acetic acid.

pyrotechnics (pī″rōtĕk′nĭks), science and art of making and using fireworks. Gunpowder was used in fireworks in 9th cent. by Chinese, who brought the art to high stage of development. Many combustibles, explosives, and combinations are used for displays. Fireworks are also used as signal devices.

pyroxene (pī′rōksēn), name given to a group of widely distributed rock minerals, metasilicates of magnesium, iron, and calcium, often with aluminum, sodium, lithium, manganese, or zinc.

pyroxylin (pīrŏk′sĭlĭn), highly inflammable, cottonlike mixture of lower cellulose nitrates made by treating cellulose with nitric acid. It is used to make celluloid, collodion, and paints.

Pyrrha: see DEUCALION.

Pyrrho (pĭ′rō), c.360–270 B.C., Greek philosopher, much respected at Elis and Athens; called the father of skepticism.

Pyrrhus (pĭ′rūs), c.318–272 B.C., king of Epirus (295–272 B.C.). He gained the throne with the aid of Ptolemy I and invaded Macedon but was driven out by Lysimachus (283 B.C.). Leading an expedition to Italy to aid the Tarentines, he had a large force and some elephants and defeated the Romans at Heraclea (280 B.C.). He beat them again at Asculum (279 B.C.) but with such heavy casualties that he said, "One more

such victory and I am lost"—this was the "Pyrrhic victory." He was defeated at Beneventum (275 B.C.), but regained prestige by defeating Antigonus II of Macedon (273 B.C.). He was killed in Argos by a falling roof tile.

Pythagoras (pĭthă′gŭrŭs), c.582–c.507 B.C., Greek philosopher, b. Samos. At Crotona he founded a religious brotherhood, which borrowed the idea of transmigration of souls from Orphism and practiced purification rites to get release from reincarnations. The Pythagoreans believed that the essence of all things was number and that all relationships could be expressed numerically. This view led them to discover the numerical relationship of tones in music and to some knowledge of later Euclidean geometry. They considered the earth as a planet revolving about a fixed point ("the hearth of the universe"). They took part in politics, and their opposition to accepted religion caused them to be persecuted from existence in Magna Graecia. See NEO-PYTHAGOREANISM.

Pythagoras of Rhegium (rē′jŭm), 5th cent. B.C., Greek sculptor. His works formed part of transition from archaic style to that of the masters.

Pythia (pĭ′thēŭ), in Greek religion, priestess of the oracle at DELPHI. Pythian games, held every four years at Delphi, included musical, literary, and athletic contests. Twelve of Pindar's odes honoring winners of games are called Pythian odes.

Pythias: see DAMON AND PYTHIAS.

python (pī′thŏn″, pī′thŭn), nonvenomous snake, found chiefly in tropical Africa, Asia, East Indies, Australia. It climbs and swims expertly. Most pythons are egg layers. They kill prey by constrictor force of body muscles.

pyxie, low evergreen plant (*Pyxidanthera barbulata*) of pine barrens of E U.S. It has pink or white flowers in the spring. Other names are flowering moss and pine barren beauty.

"Q": see QUILLER-COUCH, SIR ARTHUR THOMAS.

Qatar (kä′tär), sheikdom (4,000 sq. mi.; pop. 20,000), Arabia, on peninsula projecting into Persian Gulf; cap. Doha. Largely barren. Oil fields, fisheries. Closely bound to Britain by treaty.

Qazvin, Iran: see KAZVIN.

Qom, Iran: see KUM.

Quabbin Reservoir (kwŏ′bĭn), covers 39.4 sq. mi. in Swift R. valley, central Mass., NE of Springfield; completed 1937. Water flows to WACHUSETT RESERVOIR through Quabbin Aqueduct (24.6 mi. long).

quack grass, Old World perennial grass (*Agropyron repens*), widely distributed and a troublesome weed in the U.S. It has creeping, yellowish rootstalks.

quadrant (kwŏ′drŭnt). **1** Instrument for measuring angular altitudes, generally consisting of graduated arc of 90° or more, an index arm, and a sighting arrangement with plumb line or spirit level. Superseded by sextant. **2** Heavy casting for turning ship's rudder. **3** Fourth part of a circle, i.e., area bounded by an arc and two radii drawn at right angles to each other.

quadrivium: see LIBERAL ARTS.

Quadruple Alliance, several European alliances. That

of 1718 (England, France, Austria, Netherlands) forced Spain, by military intervention, to give up in 1720 Sicily and Sardinia, which it had seized in violation of the Peace of Utrecht. The Quadruple Alliance of 1814 (England, Austria, Russia, Prussia) was formed at Chaumont, France, to strengthen the coalition against Napoleon I. Renewed at Paris in 1815, it aimed at cooperation among the Great Powers for peace and the preservation of the status quo, but it came to be dominated by the spirit of the HOLY ALLIANCE. It was joined in 1818 by France. The congresses at Aachen (1818), Troppau (1820), Laibach (1821), and Verona (1822) were held under its provisions. The withdrawal of England (1822) effectively ended the alliance.

quagga (kwă′gŭ), extinct African mammal of genus *Equus,* which includes horse, ass, zebra. Hunted for its skin, it was exterminated in 19th cent.

Quai d'Orsay (kā dôrsā′), quay on left bank of the Seine, in Paris, France. The French foreign ministry, which is situated on it, is often referred to as the Quai d'Orsay.

quail, name for various small game birds of Old and

New Worlds. Originally the name referred to common Old World quail. New World birds sometimes called quail include bobwhite, mountain or plumed quail (or partridge), Gambel's quail, California and valley quails. Quails eat insects and weed seeds.

quaker-ladies: see BLUET.

Quakers: see FRIENDS, SOCIETY OF.

Quakertown, borough (pop. 5,673), SE Pa., N of Philadelphia. Mfg. of clothing and luggage. Has a Quaker meetinghouse (1802).

quaking grass, name for annual or perennial grasses of genus *Briza,* with graceful seed panicles which vibrate in a breeze.

Quanah (kwä'nù), city (pop. 4,589), N Texas, WNW of Wichita Falls. Center of agr. (wheat) area; has mfg. of gypsum products. Annual Texas-Okla. Wolf Hunt held near by.

Quantico (kwŏn'tĭkō), town (pop. 1,240), N. Va., on Potomac R. below Washington, D.C. Here is an important U.S. Marine Corps base.

Quantrill, William (Clarke) (kwŏn'trĭl), 1837–65, Confederate guerrilla leader. Known for Civil War raids in Mo. and Kansas; notably brutal one at Lawrence, Kansas, in 1863.

quantum theory, theory concerning emission and absorption, by atomic and subatomic particles, of light and energy. In 1900 Max Planck hypothesized that energy transfer is discontinuous and involves unit of energy (quantum), which is a function $(q = hv)$ of Planck's constant $(h;$ value c.6.6×10^{-27} erg-second) and of radiation frequency of particle (v). Einstein postulated (1905) comparable light quanta (photons). Quantum theory as extended by Niels Bohr and others to atomic structure held inconsistencies. Reorganization initiated c.1923 by Louis de Broglie's suggestion that matter has dual aspects and that electrons be regarded not only as individual particles but also as associated in wave systems. Mathematical formulations (wave mechanics) of theory were developed independently by Schrödinger and Heisenberg and were amalgamated 1927 by P. A. M. Dirac. This new form became basis of modern quantum mechanics which has revolutionized methods of dealing with atomic phenomena and undermined concept of causality in physics because theory cannot as yet predict behavior of individual particles but considers statistically large numbers of particles.

Quapaw Indians (kwô'pô), North American tribe of Siouan linguistic stock, living when visited by Hernando De Soto (1540) on the W bank of the Mississippi N of the Arkansas R.; called also the Arkansas. They are now in Okla.

quarantine (kwŏ'rŭntēn), limitation of movement imposed upon humans and animals for time just beyond incubation period of disease to which they may have been exposed. Public health regulations require physician's report of cases of certain diseases; posting of warning notices; disinfection. Quarantine originated in 12th cent. in Venice, where 40-day offshore wait was required of ships.

Quarnero, Gulf of (kwärnā'rō), arm of Adriatic Sea, between Istria and Dalmatia.

quarrying (kwŏ'rēing), removing rock from a natural deposit. Methods employed depend on nature and location of stone and uses intended. Nonshattering rock can be blasted. Soft varieties are channeled by power drills; in some cases by wire saws.

quartz (kwôrts), one of the commonest and most important rock-forming minerals, silicon dioxide or silica. It may be transparent, translucent, or opaque; it varies widely in color and often forms hexagonal crystals (if colorless these are called rock crystal). Among the varieties of quartz are amethyst, cat's-eye, flint, and chalcedony, including such colored varieties as carnelian, agate, jasper, onyx, and sardonyx.

quartzite, tough rock composed of firmly cemented quartz grains. Usually a metamorphosed sandstone.

Quaternary period, name originally given to the second period of the Cenozoic era of geologic time, the Tertiary being the first. Many geologists tend to abandon these divisions as unjustified, and use the term Cenozoic both for era and period.

Quay, Matthew Stanley (kwā), 1833–1904, American political leader. Boss of state Republican machine in Pa. U.S. Senator (1887–99, 1901–4).

Quebec (kwēbĕk'), Fr. *Québec* (kābĕk'), province (523,-860 sq. mi.; with water surface 594,860 sq. mi.; pop. 4,055,681), E Canada; cap. QUEBEC. Other cities are MONTREAL, VERDUN, SHERBROOKE, TROIS RIVIÈRES, and HULL. Bounded N by Hudson Strait and Ungava Bay, W by James and Hudson bays, SE by Gulf of St. Lawrence. The N LAURENTIAN PLATEAU, well-forested and rich in minerals (iron, gold, silver, copper, zinc), is largely uninhabited and undeveloped. The St. Lawrence R. cuts NW–SE through S part of the province. Industrial, commercial, and agr. life is centered in St. Lawrence Valley (S). Lumbering is extensive and feeds pulpwood and paper mfg. Other industries include metal smelting, textile milling, and mfg. of shoes, industrial equipment, and consumer goods. ARVIDA leads world aluminum production. Quebec is first in Canada in water power and second in total value of production. Served by many lakes and rivers. SE the GASPÉ PENINSULA, a region of small coastal fishing and farming villages, extends into the Gulf of St. Lawrence. Tourist trade is important. Province early became center of French colonization in America. Cartier landed on the Gaspé 1634. Champlain founded trading post on the site of Quebec 1608, and soon exploring, trading and missionary expeditions radiated from this center. In 1663 chartered fur trade ended and royal government of New France was estab. Struggle for control between France and England in FRENCH AND INDIAN WARS ended with establishment of British control (1763) after Wolfe's defeat of Montcalm on the Plains of ABRAHAM. England sought to pacify French Canadians in the QUEBEC ACT of 1774 which guaranteed civil liberties and the retention of customs and institutions. The Constitutional Act of 1791 introduced representative government and Quebec became Lower Canada. Resentment against arbitrary rule resulted in the revolution of 1837 under Louis PAPINEAU. In 1840 Lower and Upper (Ontario) Canada were joined under the Act of Union and in 1849 responsible government was instituted. With the BRITISH NORTH AMERICA ACT (1867) Canadian federation was achieved and Quebec again became a province. A dual school system was set up to meet the needs of a pop. three quarters French-Canadian and predominantly Catholic. The conflict between French and British cultures continues to hamper Canadian unity.

Quebec, city (pop. 164,016), provincial cap., S Que., Canada, on St. Lawrence R. at mouth of St. Charles R. and NE of Montreal. Cultural and tourist center of French Canada, divided into Lower Town (on river front) and Upper Town (on Cape Diamond, bluff 300 ft. above river). Dufferin Terrace, a promenade, extends 1,400 ft. along bluff. Seaport trading extensively in wheat and fur. Tanning, brewing, and mfg. of paper, metal products, shoes, clothing, and bricks. Visited 1535 by Cartier; Champlain estab. colony in Lower Town 1608. Held by the British 1629–32. Made cap. of New France 1663. Unsuccessfully attacked by the British 1690 and 1711, it finally fell when Wolfe defeated Montcalm on the Plains of ABRAHAM 1759. Became cap. of Lower Canada 1791; after the Union of Upper and Lower Canada was cap. 1851–55, 1859–65. Population largely French-speaking. Points of interest include the Citadel, Basilica, Chapel of Notre-Dame-des-Victoires, Quebec seminary, Kent House, Parliament buildings, and remains of early fortifications. Seat of Laval Univ. (R.C.; partly coed.; chartered 1852, outgrowth of seminary estab. 1663 by Bishop Laval).

Quebec Act, 1774, passed by British Parliament to institute permanent administration in Canada. Allowed political and legal concessions and gave French Canadians religious freedom. Considered one of IN-TOLERABLE ACTS because it nullified many Western claims of coast colonies.

Quebec campaign, 1775–76, of American Revolution. Expedition sent to Canada to protect frontier from Indians and to persuade Canada to join revolt against England. Richard Montgomery captured Montreal, Nov., 1775, and aided Benedict Arnold in unsuccessful assault on Quebec, Dec., 1775. Americans were pushed back to Crown Point in spring.

Quebec Conference, two meetings held in World War II. First (Aug., 1943), attended by Pres. F. D. Roosevelt, Prime Ministers Churchill and Mackenzie King, and Foreign Minister Soong. Created China-Burma-India theater of operations, approved plans for landing in France. Second meeting (Sept., 1944), attended by Roosevelt and Churchill and military aides, dealt with broad strategy of war.

quebracho (kābrä′chō), name for South American hardwood trees of various genera and their wood. Wood of both the red quebracho (*Schinopsis*) and the white quebracho (*Aspidosperma*) is used in construction. The red quebracho also yields tannin. Both are sources of medicinal substances.

Quedlinburg (kväd′lēnbŏŏrk), city (pop. 35,142), Saxony-Anhalt, E central Germany, at foot of lower Harz. Walled 922 by Henry I. He and his wife, St. Mathilda (who with Otto I founded famous convent here in 936), are buried in castle church. Castle, church, and convent (secularized 1803) were built 10th–14th cent.

Queen Anne's lace: see WILD CARROT.

Queen Anne's War: see FRENCH AND INDIAN WARS.

Queen Charlotte Islands, archipelago of c.150 islands off coast of W B.C., Canada. Main islands are Graham and Moresby. Haida Indians form bulk of population. Valuable timber and fishing resources. First visited 1774 by Juan Pérez.

Queens, borough (land area 108 sq. mi.; pop. 1,550,-849) of NEW YORK city, SE N.Y., at W end of Long Isl. adjoining Brooklyn borough. Separated from Manhattan and the Bronx by East R. (many bridges, e.g., Queensboro Bridge, built 1909, which stimulated borough's greatest growth; and tunnel connections); on S is Jamaica Bay, separated from the Atlantic by Rockaway peninsula (c.12 mi. long; resorts and commuters' communities). First settled by Dutch 1635; old Queens co. estab. 1683; divided in 1898 into Queens and Nassau counties, when Queens also became a New York city borough (largest in area). Mainly residential as in communities of Flushing, with Flushing Meadows park (site of New York World's Fair in 1939–40, later site of General Assembly meetings of the UN) and Queens Col. (see NEW YORK, COLLEGE OF THE CITY OF); and Forest Hills (has West Side Tennis Club where national and international matches are held). Heavily industrialized in area of Long Island City (shipping facilities on East R.; rail yards; consumer commodities); also at Astoria and Jamaica (important railroad transfer point, with extensive business and residential sections). Has two municipal airports, both administered by Port of New York Authority—LaGuardia (lŭgwär′dēŭ) (558 acres; opened 1939) and New York International. Airport (4,900 acres; opened 1948; sometimes called Idlewild). Here are Jamaica and Aqueduct race tracks.

Queensberry, James Douglas, 2d duke of, 1662–1711, Scottish statesman. One of the first Scots to favor William III. Worked for Scottish-English union.

Queensberry, John Sholto Douglas, 8th marquess of, 1844–1900, English nobleman, originator of rules which govern modern boxing. Drafted (1865), with aid of Arthur Chambers, Queensberry rules, superseding London prize-ring rules introduced (1743) by Jack Broughton.

Queens' College: see CAMBRIDGE UNIVERSITY.

Queen's College: see OXFORD UNIVERSITY.

Queens College: see CHARLOTTE, N.C.; QUEENS, New York city borough.

Queensland, state (670,500 sq. mi.; pop. 1,106,269), NE Australia; cap. Brisbane. Bounded on E by Coral Sea and the Pacific, on S by New South Wales, and on W by Northern Territory. Most of its coast line is sheltered by Great Barrier Reef. Moreton Bay area (where Capt. James Cook landed 1770) was used for penal settlement, 1824–43. Queensland became a British colony in 1859 and a state of Commonwealth of Australia in 1901. Roughly half of state is tropical, with rainfall ranging from 5 in. in SW desert to 160 in. in NE jungle area. Great Dividing Range separates fertile coast from interior plains. Great Artesian Basin (376,000 sq. mi.) in interior provides water for large stock-raising area. Main products are sugar cane, cotton, wheat, and fruits.

Queensland, University of: see BRISBANE, Australia.

Queenston Heights, S Ont., Canada, on Niagara peninsula and N of Niagara Falls. Battle of Queenston Heights fought here in War of 1812.

Queenstown, Co. Cork, Ireland: see CÓBH.

Queen's University: see KINGSTON, Ont.

Quellinus or **Quellin, Artus** (är′tŭs kvĕlē′nŭs, kvĕ′lĭn), 1609–68, Flemish sculptor, follower of Rubens tradition in sculpture. Notable for his decorations of royal palace of Amsterdam.

Quemoy (kĭmoi′), island (pop. 49,485), in Formosa Strait, off the coast of Fukien prov., China, 15 mi. E of Amoy. Held by Nationalists after Communist conquest of China (1949).

Quental, Antero de (äntĕ′rō dù kĕntäl′), 1842–91, Portuguese poet, notable for restrained, finely fashioned *Odas modernas* (1865) and *Sonetos* (1881).

Quercia, Jacopo della (yä′kōpō dĕl′lä kwĕr′chä), c.1374–1438, Italian sculptor. Called Jacopo della Fonte for his Gaia Fountain (Siena). Masterpiece is central doorway of San Petronio (Bologna).

Quercy (kĕrsē′), region and former county, S Central France in Lot and Tarn-et-Garonne depts; historic cap. Cahors. Consists of arid limestone plateaus (*causses*) and fertile river valleys. Sheep raising.

Querétaro (kārā′tärō), state (4,432 sq. mi.; pop. 282,-608), central Mexico, on central plateau; cap. Querétaro (pop. 33,629). Mountainous in N with valleys and plains in S. Famous for opals, it also produces silver, iron, tin, mercury. Agr. products include sugar cane, cotton, tobacco, grains. Indians were conquered 1531, but territory was not colonized until 1550; became state 1824.

Quesnay, François (fräswä′ kĕnā′), 1694–1774, French economist, founder of the physiocratic school (see PHYSIOCRATS). He wrote *Tableau économique* [economic table] (1758).

Quesnel, Pasquier (päskyä′ kĕnĕl′), 1634–1719, French priest. His editions of the works of Leo I and of the New Testament were condemned for JANSENISM.

Quetta (kwĕ′tù), town (pop. 82,000), cap. of Baluchistan, W Pakistan, on trade route (via Bolan Pass) between Afghanistan and Indus valley.

quetzal (kĕtsäl′) or **quezal** (kĕsäl′), bird of high-altitude rain forests of Central America and Mexico. It is iridescent green above, crimson below, and has streamerlike tail coverts and crested head. Revered by Maya and Aztec. It is national emblem of Guatemala.

Quetzalcoatl (kĕt″sälkōä′tùl) [Nahuatl,= feathered serpent], anc. god and legendary ruler of Toltec in Mexico. As god, represented goodness and light in combat with darkness and evil. As culture hero and ruler, he was credited with discovery of maize, the arts, science, and the calendar. When culture hero disappeared on E coast of Mexico A.D. c.1000, he left promise to return. Some Aztec viewed later Spanish invaders as returning hosts of Quetzalcoatl. In poetic sense, plumed serpent is symbol of Mexico.

Quevedo y Villegas, Francisco Gómez de (fränthē′skō gō′mäth dä kävä′dhō ē vēlyä′gäs), 1580–1645, Spanish satirist, novelist, and poet, one of the greatest writers of the Golden Age.

quezal: see QUETZAL.

Quezaltenango (käsältänäng'gō), city (pop. 27,782), SW Guatemala; metropolis of W highlands; second city of Guatemala. Center of fertile area producing coffee, sugar cane, cacao, grains, and tropical fruits. Mfg. has increased with development of hydroelectric power.

Quezon, Manuel Luis (mänwĕl' lwēs' kā'sōn), 1878–1944, Filipino statesman. As president of Philippine senate (1916–35) he ardently crusaded for independence. First president of Commonwealth of the Philippines (1935–44); loyal friend of U.S.

Quezon City (kā'sōn), city (1948 pop. 107,977), central Luzon, P.I., near Manila. Replaced Manila as cap. of republic, July, 1948.

Quiberon (kēbrō'), peninsula of Brittany, Morbihan dept., NW France, in Bay of Biscay. Here in 1795 c.3,000 Royalists were landed by British ships in hope of reviving Vendée uprising. Failure resulted in capitulation of the invaders, of whom c.800 were shot. **Quiberon Bay** was scene of British naval victory over France 1759.

Quichua (kēch'wä), linguistic family of W South America whose member languages are spoken in the plateaus of Peru, Ecuador, much of Bolivia, and NW Argentina. Official language of Inca empire was of this family. See LANGUAGE (table).

quicklime: see LIME.

quicksilver: see MERCURY.

Quidde, Ludwig (loot'vĭkh kvĭ'dù), 1858–1941, German pacifist and historian. Imprisoned for *Caligula* (1894), portrait of Emperor William II. Supported League of Nations; shared 1927 Nobel Peace Prize.

quietism, extreme form of mysticism proposed by Miguel de Molinos and more moderately by Fénelon and Madame Guyon. Its essence is passivity of soul before God for sake of achieving unity with Him. This involves abandonment of effort, reason, emotion, sacraments, even of prayer. Fundamental principle is common in Oriental religions.

Quill, Michael J(oseph), 1905–, American labor leader, president of Transport Workers Union of America, affiliated (1937) with the CIO, of which he is a leading figure.

Quiller-Couch, Sir Arthur Thomas (kwĭl'ùr-kōōch"), pseud. **Q,** 1863–1944, English man of letters; professor of English at Cambridge after 1912. Wrote novels of Cornwall and essays; edited many anthologies, including *Oxford Book of English Verse* (1900) and *Oxford Book of English Prose* (1923).

Quilmes (kēl'mäs), city (pop. 115,113), E Argentina, 11 mi. S of Buenos Aires and on Río de la Plata. Summer resort and industrial city.

quilting, antique form of needlework in which two layers of fabric are sewn together over an interlining. Quilting has been long used for adding warmth to clothing in N Asia and Europe. It has been a distinctive type of American needlework, used since colonial days chiefly for bed coverings.

Quimby, Phineas Parkhurst, 1802–66, American mental healer and mesmerist. He had many followers. The extent of his influence on Mary Baker Eddy and on Christian Science is a subject of much controversy.

Quimper (kĕpĕr'), town (pop. 17,722), cap. of Finistère dept., NW France; a fishing port on an inlet of the Atlantic. It is famous for its pottery.

Quinault, Philippe (fēlēp' kēnō'), 1635–88, French dramatist. Best known for his opera librettos, for which Lully wrote the music. *Armide* (1686) is considered his masterpiece.

quince, shrub or small tree (*Cydonia oblonga*) of rose family, native to Asia but widely grown elsewhere, and its stemless, fuzzy yellow fruits. The fruits, which follow white or pink flowers, are fragrant but astringent and chiefly used in jelly. For ornamental quinces, see FLOWERING QUINCE.

Quincy, Josiah (kwĭn'zē), 1744–75, American Revolutionary patriot. Opposed British colonial policies through writings. His son, **Josiah Quincy,** 1772–1864, was a Federalist leader in U.S. Congress (1805–13) and president of Harvard (1829–45).

Quincy. 1 City (pop. 6,505), NW Fla., near Ga. line NW of Tallahassee. Fuller's earth and tobacco. **2** City (pop. 41,450), W Ill., on the Mississippi and W of Springfield; settled 1822. Has good harbor, was important mid-19th cent. river port. Industrial and distributing center for agr. area. Mfg. of machinery, flour, and furniture. Scene of several pro-slavery-abolitionist struggles. **3** Industrial city (pop. 83,835), E Mass., on Boston Bay SE of Boston. T. MORTON ran trading post here 1625–27; town settled 1634. Granite quarrying (since 1750); shipbuilding; mfg. of metal and rubber products, chemicals. John and John Quincy Adams are buried in Old South Temple; their home is a national historic site (since 1946). For Quincy movement in education, see PARKER, F. W.

quinine (kwī'nīn", kwīnēn'), bitter alkaloid derived chiefly from cinchona bark. Used in treating malaria and allaying fever and pain. Isolated 1820; synthesized 1944. Excess dosage or continuous use may result in poisoning (cinchonism).

Quintana Roo (kēntä'nä rō'ō), territory (19,630 sq. mi.; pop. 26,996), SE Mexico, on Caribbean; cap. Chetumal (pop. 4,672). Occupies most of E half of Yucatan peninsula, population mostly Maya. Has been little explored; climate is hot, rainfall heavy.

Quintanilla, Luis (lwēs' kēntänē'lyä), 1895–, Spanish painter. Known for scenes of popular life in mildly satirical vein. Settled in U.S. in 1942.

Quintero, Serafín Álvarez, and **Joaquín Álvarez Quintero:** see ÁLVAREZ QUINTERO.

Quintilian (Marcus Fabius Quintilianus) (kwĭntĭ'lyùn), A.D. c.35–A.D. c.95, Roman rhetorician, known for his beautiful Latin style. His *Institutio oratoria,* a 12-book survey of rhetoric, also has acute comments on the great writers.

Quirino, Elpidio (ĕlpē'dhyō kērē'nō), 1890–, Filipino statesman. Long an aide to Manuel Quezon, he was elected first vice president of independent Philippine republic in 1946, president in 1949.

Quirinus (kwĭr'īnùs), in Roman religion, name of ROMULUS as a god. The Quirinalia honored him.

Quiroga, Juan Facundo (hwän' fäkōōn'dhō kērō'gä), 1790–1835, Argentine *caudillo.* A zealous advocate of federalism, he rejected unitarian constitution of 1826 and participated in civil strife that followed. Was assassinated. Sarmiento's *Facundo* is study of him and his era.

Quisling, Vidkun (kwĭz'lĭng, Nor. vĭd'kōōn kvĭs'lĭng), 1887–1945, Norwegian fascist leader. Founded Nasjonal Samling [national unity] party (1933); assisted German invasion of Norway (1940); was premier (1940, 1942–45) under German occupation. After the war convicted of high treason and shot. His name became a common noun meaning traitor.

Quitman, John Anthony, 1798–1858, American general in Mexican War and statesman. Fought at Monterrey, Veracruz, and Chapultepec. U.S. Representative from Miss. (1855–58).

Quito (kē'tō), city (pop. 212,873), cap. of Ecuador and second largest city. Educational, cultural, and political center. A Quito Indian settlement, it was captured by the Inca shortly before conquest by Benalcázar (1534). In 1563 it became seat of *audiencia.* Presidency of Quito was shifted between viceroyalty of Peru and New Granada. Freed from Spain by Sucre (1822).

Quivira (kēvē'rä), fabulous land sought by CORONADO and others. Site uncertain but probably in Kansas. Name finally (and quite erroneously) settled on Gran Quivira Natl. Monument, N.Mex.

Quixote, Don: see DON QUIXOTE DE LA MANCHA.

Qum, Iran: see KUM.

Quonset Point, R.I.: see NORTH KINGSTOWN.

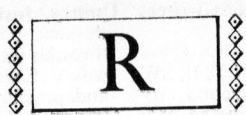

Ra (rä), Egyptian sun-god. His worship centered at Heliopolis but later became widespread. The obelisk was his chief symbol. His worship was later joined with that of Amon. Also Re (rä).

Ra, chemical symbol of the element RADIUM.

Raabe, Wilhelm (vĭl'hĕlm rä'bŭ), pseud. Jakob Corvinus, 1831–1910, German novelist. His novels include *Die Chronik der Sperlingsgasse* (1857) and *Der Hungerpastor* (1864; Eng. tr. 1885).

Raasay (rä'zā), island, off NW Scotland, in Inverness-shire, one of the Inner Hebrides.

Rabat (räbät'), city (pop. 161,416), French Morocco; port on the Atlantic at mouth of Bon Regreg. Seat of French resident general and sultan's residence. Old walled town was founded 12th cent. by Abdu-l-Mumin. Was stronghold of corsairs, 17th–18th cent. Exports agr. products. Textile mfg.

Rabaul: see NEW BRITAIN, Bismarck Archipelago.

rabbi (răb'bī) [Heb.,= my master or my teacher], in the U.S., the title of a Jewish minister. He is called *rav* [great] among certain Jews in Eastern Europe, where the word *rabbi* is used only for a scholar or teacher. The title originated among the Palestinian Jews. The modern rabbi serves to expound Judaism and act as a leader of Israel.

Rabbi Ben Ezra: see IBN EZRA, ABRAHAM BEN MEIR.

rabbit, herbivorous mammal of hare family (Leporidae). Some species mature at six months and bear four litters a year. Species of genus *Sylvilagus* (e.g., cotton-tail, marsh, and swamp rabbits) are found from U.S. to N South America. Domesticated breeds are varieties of European rabbit (*Oryctolagus*). Fur is known as cony or coney. Some fur is used in making felt.

rabbit fever: see TULAREMIA.

Rabboni (răbō'nī) [Heb.,= my great master], title of respect addressed to Jesus. John 20.16.

Rabelais, François (rä'bŭlä', Fr. fräswä' räblä'), c.1490–1553, French author of the satirical romances *Gargantua* and *Pantagruel.* A Benedictine monk, he took a medical degree at Montpellier (1530), where he later also taught (1537–39). It was during his stay at Lyons (1532–34) that Rabelais wrote the first two books of his history of the giant Gargantua and his son Pantagruel. The third and fourth books followed in 1546–52; the fifth book (of doubtful authorship) was published 1562. Under its burlesque humor, sometimes ribald, this masterpiece conceals serious discussions of education, politics, and philosophy. The breadth of Rabelais's learning, his zest for living, and his humanistic outlook are evident. Primarily, the work is a satire against the vulgarity and abuses of society. Its verbal virtuosity has been approximated in the classic 17th-cent. translation by Sir Thomas Urquhart (Books I–III) and Pierre Motteux (Books IV–V). After the death of his patron, King Francis I, Rabelais spent his last years as curate at Meudon.

Rabi, Isidor Isaac (rŏ'bē), 1898–, American physicist, b. Austria. Known for work in magnetism, molecular beams, and quantum mechanics. Discovered and measured radiations of atoms. Won 1944 Nobel Prize.

rabies: see HYDROPHOBIA.

Rabinowitz, Solomon or **Shalom:** see ALEICHEM, SHOLOM.

raccoon (răkōōn'), New World mammal (*Procyon*) related to kinkajou and panda. It is c.2½–3 ft. long, has brown and black hair, a black-masked, pointed face, and a black-ringed bushy tail. It often nests in trees.

race, obsolete division of humanity based on such physical criteria as skin color and hair texture. Concept of race had great vogue in 19th cent., when such divisions as Alpine, Aryan, Caucasian, Nordic, etc., were freely referred to. Although lack of scientific foundation of concept has been demonstrated, notion of race continues potent in 20th cent. Chief arguments against race concept are that multiple origins of man have not been proven; that population movement, and hence interbreeding, has been constant since man's beginning; and that no pure stocks exist, populations grading into each other with respect to the physical criteria that are supposed to distinguish one alleged race from another. Long isolation, rather than original purity, is held to account for relative distinctiveness of such stocks as the Eskimo and Japanese.

Race, Cape, SE tip of Avalon Peninsula, SE N.F., Canada. Has lighthouse and radio direction-finding station.

Raceland, city (pop. 1,001), E Ky., on Ohio R. and near Ashland. Has noted race track.

Rachel [Heb.,= ewe], Jacob's favorite wife, mother of Joseph and Benjamin, daughter of Laban. Although Jacob had been promised Rachel in marriage if he worked seven years for Laban, at the end of that time he was tricked into marrying Leah, her older sister. Jacob then had to serve Laban another seven years for Rachel. Gen. 29–33; 35; Mat. 2.18.

Rachel (räshĕl'), 1821–58, stage name of Elisa or Elizabeth Félix, French actress. Queen of the French stage in tragic roles, she was notable in works of Racine (esp. *Phèdre*) and Corneille.

Rachmaninov, Sergei (Vasilyevich) (syĭrgä' räkhmä'nēnôf), 1873–1943, Russian pianist, composer, and conductor. The romanticism and lyricism of his music owes much to his friend Tchaikovsky. Outstanding are his Second Piano Concerto; his Second Symphony; *Rhapsody on a Theme of Paganini,* for piano and orchestra; a tone poem, *The Isle of the Dead;* and his piano preludes in C sharp minor and G minor.

Racine, Jean (zhä' räsēn'), 1639–99, French dramatist, foremost representative of modern classic tragedy. His third play, *Andromaque* (1667), gave him Corneille's place as leading dramatist and won him the protection of Louis XIV. His next six tragedies were all masterpieces: *Britannicus* (1669), *Bérénice* (1670), *Bajazet* (1672), *Mithridate* (1673), *Iphigénie en Aulide* (1674), and *Phèdre* (1677). Representing French classicism at its perfection, they are unsurpassed in nobility and simplicity of diction, musicality of verse, psychological insight, and dramatic construction. His only comedy, *Les Plaideurs* (1668), wittily satirizes the law courts. After a concerted attack on *Phèdre,* Racine gave up the theater, but Mme de Maintenon persuaded him to write two more plays for performance at her school at Saint-Cyr—*Esther* (1689) and *Athalie* (1691). Based on biblical themes, these two tragedies contain notable innovations, particularly the use of choruses, and rank among his best. Racine is generally considered the greatest of French dramatists.

Racine (rùsēn'), industrial city (pop. 71,193), SE Wis., on L. Michigan at mouth of Root R. and S of Milwaukee; settled 1834. Site known to French explorers and fur traders. Industrial growth came with harbor improvement and railroad. Mfg. of farm machinery, waxes and polishes, and paints and varnishes.

racing. Earliest Olympic Games consisted of foot races only. In Roman era chariot racing was favorite pastime. Organized horse racing under saddle dates from 12th cent. in England. After 1830, introduction of racing sulky led to harness racing. Automobile rac-

SMALL CAPITALS = cross references. Pronunciation key on inside end pages. Abbreviations: p. 2,

818

ing, boat racing, bicycle racing, dog racing also popular in U.S.

Rackham, Arthur (rä'kŭm), 1867–1939, English artist, known for illustrations for children's books.

Racovian Catechism: see SOCINIANISM.

racquets (rä'kĭts), game played by two or four persons on court 60 ft. by 30 ft., surrounded by three walls 30 ft. high and backwall 15 ft. high. Originated in 18th cent. England, probably in debtors' prison, but was soon taken up by wealthy classes.

radar (rā'där), radio detecting and ranging device used to locate planes and ships and to bomb precisely. Consists of short-wave radio transmitter; wave-concentrating, beam-directing antenna, which receives beam reflected back upon hitting an object; receiver; and indicator (usually cathode-ray tubes that act as radar screen). Target found by revolving antenna to direction of strongest echo or by synchronizing cathode beam to revolve on screen in conjunction with antenna so as to show target bearing. Reception time lag of two antennae varying in height gives target altitude.

Radburn, N.J.: see FAIR LAWN.

Radcliffe, Ann (Ward), 1764–1823, English novelist, author of stories of mystery and intrigue, such as *The Mysteries of Udolpho* (1794).

Radcliffe College: see HARVARD UNIVERSITY.

Radetzky, Joseph, Graf (yō'zĕf gräf rädĕt'skē), 1766–1858, Austrian field marshal. Routed Sardinians at Custozza (1848) and Novara (1849).

Radford, city (pop. 9,026), SW Va., WSW of Roanoke. Mfg. of foundry products and textiles; railroad shops. Near by are Claytor L. and hydroelectric dam.

radiation, emission of energy by matter and its transfer through space; sunlight is best-known form. Invisible radiation also occurs; ultraviolet rays range in wave length from 0.10–0.4 microns; X rays are still shorter, as are gamma rays of RADIOACTIVITY. Radio waves and infrared are longer than light. All these waves travel through space at c.186,000 mi. per second. Radiometer detects radiant energy. See *ill.*, p. 773.

radiator (rā'dēā"tùr). Radiators of hot-water heating systems in buildings are usually constructed in sections which can be joined for required radiating surface, and are made of cast iron, steel, brass, or copper. Heating efficiency is reduced by covering radiator with screens, shelves, and even certain paints. Coil radiators set in walls or ceilings are essentially long steam pipes. Automobile radiator is part of cooling system.

radical, in chemistry, elements which are grouped together in same proportion by weight in different compounds and act as units in many reactions. Common radicals are hydroxyl, sulphate, ammonium, carbonate, chlorate, nitrate, phosphate. Carboxyl group (COOH) is characteristic of organic acids.

radio. Growing from studies of electromagnetic waves, radiotelegraphy demonstrated by Marconi in 1895. Radiotelephony (transmission of speech and music) began with invention of diode rectifier tube, 1904, and triode amplifier tube, 1906. FACSIMILE, TELEVISION, RADAR developed later. Transmitter, through antenna, emits magnetic field inducing voltage in any receiver within radiation area; voltage (carrier wave) generated by oscillator is amplified and combined, by amplitude modulation or FREQUENCY MODULATION, with amplified audio-frequency microphone signal. Receiver selects, amplifies desired carrier (see SUPERHETERODYNE); detects or demodulates; LOUDSPEAKER transforms signal into sound. See *ill.*, p. 293.

radioactivity, property shown by certain elements, e.g., actinium, polonium, plutonium, radium, thorium, and uranium that involves emission of special types of RADIATION. It is a property of the atom of the element. Radiation is of three kinds: alpha, beta, and gamma rays. Alpha rays are positive particles, helium nuclei, hurled from atom; have lower velocity, smaller penetrating power than other radiations; direction is slightly changed by magnetic field. Beta rays are elec-

trons (negative charges); faster than alpha rays; their direction is changed markedly by magnetic field. Gamma rays have greatest penetrating power; velocity almost that of light; direction not changed by magnetic field. Atoms of radioactive elements are not stable; disintegration proceeds at definite rate (each element has a definite "life"). Disintegration cannot be changed by known means. Elements of lower atomic weights are produced from those with higher one; final result is nonradioactive element; series is called disintegration series. For example, disintegration of uranium yields ionium and this yields radium which also disintegrates; lead is end product of uranium series. See also ISOTOPE. See *ill.*, p. 773.

radio beacon, radio transmitting station to aid plane and ship navigation. Airport radio-range signals, known as A (. –) and N (– .), transmitted in alternate quadrants produce overlap zones or beams in which only a steady hum can be received; zones coincide with standard flight approaches to field. Pilot follows beam in to cone of silence over beacon. Very high frequency (VHF) beacon is omnidirectional; distance-measuring equipment (DME) used. Fan and Z markers give vertical, horizontal orientation.

Radio City: see ROCKEFELLER CENTER.

radio frequency. Electromagnetic waves with periods or cycles suitable for use in wireless communication have radio frequency. They carry the lower frequency audio waves from the microphone.

radiometer (rā"dēō'mùtùr), instrument for detecting radiant energy and measuring its intensity. Within vacuum bulb are two delicate crossed bars free to rotate about the top of vertical support; each bar end has upright metal vane with one polished side, one blackened (energy-absorbent) side. Radiant energy absorbed by blackened side heats vane, increases activity of air molecules left within bulb, and sets all vanes moving. Speed of rotating vanes indicates intensity of radiant energy.

radiotherapy (rā"dēōthē'rùpē), treatment by means of radiation. Chief agents are X RAY; penetrating gamma rays given off by radium salts and radon and used to treat growths; and beta rays from radium salts, used for superficial conditions.

radish, annual or biennial vegetable (*Raphanus sativus*) of mustard family with tuberlike root used in spring salads and as a garnish. In one variety, the rat-tailed radish, the long seed pods are eaten raw or pickled.

Radisson, Pierre Esprit (pyĕr' ĕsprē' rädēsō'), c.1632–1710, French explorer and fur trader in North America. In 1659–60 he went as far W as present Minn. with his brother-in-law, Médard Chouart, sieur des Groseilliers. Largely responsible for formation of Hudson's Bay Co.

radium, lustrous, white, radioactive element (symbol = Ra; see also ELEMENT, table). Corrodes on exposure to air; resembles calcium in chemical activity. Bromide is usual commercial form. RADIOACTIVITY high for salts and metal. Element is derived indirectly from disintegration of URANIUM. Disintegrates to yield RADON; this disintegrates, producing in order radium A, B, C, D, E, F (polonium), and G (uranium lead). Present in ores in minute amounts; difficult to extract. Used in treating cancer, in making luminous paints and varnishes. Mme Curie isolated it from pitchblende (1910). See *ill.*, p. 773.

radium emanation: see RADON.

Radnorshire (räd'nùr-shĭr) or **Radnor,** border county (471 sq. mi.; pop. 19,998), E central Wales; co. town New Radnor. Terrain, mostly hilly, includes Forest of Radnor (moorland 2,000 ft. high). Sheep and cattle raising is chief occupation. Sparsely populated region, it has no large towns and no mfg.

Radom (rä'dôm), city (pop. 69,455), central Poland, S of Warsaw. Mfg. of clothes, metal products. One of oldest Polish towns, it was seat of Polish diets (14th–16th cent.). Passed to Austria 1795; to Russia 1815; reverted to Poland 1919.

radon (rā′dŏn), **radium emanation,** or **niton** (nī′tŏn), gaseous, radioactive element (symbol = Rn; see also ELEMENT, table). It is an inert gas derived from disintegration of RADIUM; yields radium A. See *ill.,* p. 773.

Raeburn, Sir Henry (rā′bûrn), 1756–1823, Scottish portrait painter. Rose from humble beginnings as son of a miller. Worked in Edinburgh, where he enjoyed much popularity. His frank likenesses of Scottish celebrities have a quality of intimacy.

Rafa or **Rafah** (both: rä′fä), anc. *Raphia,* village, on border of Egypt and Palestine. Here in 217 B.C. Ptolemy IV defeated Antiochus III. Under Egyptian control since 1948.

raffia, fiber obtained from large leaves of the raffia palm (*Raphia*) of Madagascar. The tan-colored fiber is easily dyed and is exported for such uses as weaving baskets, hats, and mats, and tying up plants which need support.

Raffles, Sir Thomas Stamford Bingley, 1781–1826, English East Indian administrator. Lieutenant governor of Java 1811–15, he reduced power of native princes and made reforms in taxation and land tenure. Secured Singapore for East India Company 1819.

Rages (rā′jēz) or **Rhagae** (rā′jē), city of Persia prominent in anc. and medieval days. It was on an important trade route. Religious dissension damaged the city in 1186 and the Mongols destroyed more of it in 1220. Also Ray, Rei, and Rey.

ragged robin, perennial plant (*Lychnis floscuculi*) native to Europe and Asia but naturalized in E North America. It has clusters of pink or red flowers with deeply cleft petals.

Ragnarok (räg′närûk″) [Norse,= history of the gods], in the *Elder Edda,* a conception of the end of heaven, earth, and hell.

Ragusa, Yugoslavia: see DUBROVNIK.

ragweed, weedy American annual plant of genus *Ambrosia* with soft, lobed leaves and inconspicuous flowers. Pollen of the common ragweed (*Ambrosia artemisifolia*) is a chief cause of hay fever.

Rahab (rā′hăb), woman of Jericho who aided Joshua's spies, thus saving herself and family from destruction. Joshua 2. May be same as Rachab of Mat. 1.5.

Rahway (rô′wā), city (pop. 21,290), NE N.J., SW of Newark; settled c.1720 from Elizabeth. Mfg. of pharmaceuticals, lubricating oil, chemicals, cereals, metal and rubber goods.

Raiatea: see SOCIETY ISLANDS.

Raikes, Robert (rāks), 1735–1811, English philanthropist. His school held on Sunday for poor children (after 1780) was basis for Sunday-school system.

railroad or **railway.** The first railroads were horse-drawn wagons on wooden rails used in England to haul coal and ore in 17th and 18th cent. Iron rails replaced wooden ones in 18th cent. when inventors in England, France, and the U.S. experimented with steam locomotives. Among these inventors were Oliver EVANS, James WATT, and Richard Trevithick, who in 1801 perfected a steam locomotive capable of pulling a heavy load. Famous early locomotives were the *Stourbridge Lion,* imported from England, the first locomotive to run on any American railway; the *Rocket,* invented in 1829 by George STEPHENSON; and the *Tom Thumb,* built by Peter COOPER, which made a successful run in 1830. Major cities on the Atlantic coast became nerve centers for many short railroads, while inland points were readily connected with one another. Soon railroads were undermining the commercial value of the turnpike and canal. The Civil War gave great impetus to railroads which aided in the transportation of troops and supplies. The first transcontinental railroad was the Union Pacific, completed 1869. The great railway financiers, among them Cornelius Vanderbilt (who consolidated the New York Central Railroad) Jay Gould, Daniel Drew, James Fisk, and others were accused of acting with complete disregard for the American public. One of the greatest financial battles was fought by James J. HILL and Edward H. Harriman. The GRANGER MOVEMENT protested the rebate and other abuses. The 1880s saw the creation of the INTERSTATE COMMERCE COMMISSION, which sought to fix adequate controls upon railroads, and the adoption of a standard gauge (4 ft. 8½ in. between rails). Labor became a potent force with the organization of the four independent brotherhoods in the late 19th cent. After World War I, railroads in part met the increasing competition of bus, automobile, and airplane by measures for increasing safety and comfort. Outstanding railroads in the U.S. not previously mentioned include the Pennsylvania, the Baltimore and Ohio, the Erie, the Northern Pacific, the Southern Pacific, and the Santa Fe. Among other well-integrated systems are those of England, the European continent, India, and Japan. Of world importance are the Baghdad, Chinese Eastern, and Transandine railways, and the Trans-Caspian and Trans-Siberian railroads, all serving large areas.

Raimondi, Marcantonio (märkäntō′nyō rīmōn′dē), b. c.1480, d. before c.1534, Italian copperplate engraver of works by Dürer and Raphael.

rain, precipitation formed by further condensing of cloud moisture. Drops grow by coalescing on impact and by condensation on their surface of moisture in air as they fall. Evaporation begins as drops leave cloud, rate depending on lower-air warmth, dryness. Rain a primary climatic element; great factor in distribution of plant and animal life. Annual rainfall varies from less than 2 in. in arid DESERT to 400 in. in Khasi hills, Assam, India, and on windward slopes of Hawaiian mountains. Controlling factors in earth's rain distribution: converging-ascending air-flow belts (e.g., the doldrums), air temperature, moisture-bearing winds, ocean currents, distance inland from coast, mountain ranges. Ascending air cools, forms cloud, and causes rain. Descending air belts (horse latitudes) mark great deserts.

Rainalducci, Pietro (pyä′trō rīnäldōōt′chē), d. 1333, Italian churchman, antipope as Nicholas V, a Franciscan. When Emperor Louis IV declared Pope John XXII (at Avignon) deposed for heresy, he set up Pietro instead (at Rome) in 1328. Finding his position untenable, Pietro gave up the office in 1330 and was held in honorable captivity at Avignon.

rainbow, arc with colors of SPECTRUM that appears in sky, opposite sun, when sun shines through water droplets. The sun, observer's eye, and center of arc must be in line. Bow is caused by reflection and refraction of sun's rays. Sometimes two bows are seen, one paler than and outside of the primary bow. Symbolizes God's promise of mercy to man after the flood (Gen. 9.13).

Rainbow Bridge National Monument: see NATIONAL PARKS AND MONUMENTS (table).

Rainbow Division, nickname of 42d Division of U.S. army in World War I. First American combat division to arrive in France, it fought through several campaigns, suffered heavy losses.

Rainier, Mount (rūnēr′, rā′–), 14,508 ft. high, SW central Wash., in Mt. Rainier Natl. Park (see NATIONAL PARKS AND MONUMENTS, table). Snow-crowned volcanic peak with 26 glaciers and heavily forested lower slopes. Highest point in Wash. and in CASCADE RANGE.

Rain-in-the-Face, d. 1905, North American Indian chief, leader of the Sioux. A commander at annihilation of G. A. Custer's force on Little Bighorn R. in Mont., June 25, 1876.

Rainy Lake, c.60 mi. long, W Ont., lying partly on Minn.-Ont. boundary, in wooded area with many islands. Outlet, **Rainy River,** flows W 85 mi. along international line to L. of the Woods.

Rais, Gilles de: see RETZ, GILLES DE LAVAL, SEIGNEUR DE.

Raisin, river rising in S Mich. and flowing c.115 mi. E to L. Erie at Monroe. Scene of defeat in War of 1812 of U.S. troops by British and Indians and subsequent massacre (Jan. 22, 1813) of remaining Americans by Indians.

raisin, dried fruit of certain varieties of grapevines of the European type (*Vitis vinifera*). Production is limited to regions with a long, hot growing season, since grapes must stay on vines until fully mature and are then dried, usually in the sun. Most seedless raisins, especially in Calif., are produced from the Sultanina or Thompson seedless grape, known in international trade as the Sultana; a different kind, produced in Calif., is known there as the Sultana. The Muscat is a flavorful variety, commonly sold in clusters for table use. Raisins of sharp flavor and firm texture are often called currants. Raisins are valuable nutritionally because of their sugar, mineral (esp. iron), and vitamin A and B content.

Rajagopalachari, Chakravarti (chŭkrŭvär′tē rä″jŭgō-pä″lŭchä′rē), 1879–, Indian nationalist. Joined Indian Natl. Congress in 1919. In World War II he broke with the Congress because he favored support of British war effort, but rejoined it after the war. Was last governor general of India (1948–50). Became minister of home affairs, 1951.

Rajasthan (rä′jüstän), state (128,424 sq. mi.; pop. 15,-297,979), NW India; cap. Jaipur. Formed 1948–50 largely by merging princely states (notably Bikaner and Jaipur) formerly making up region of Rajputana. Partly desert. Agr. area in E part produces grains and cotton. Region was settled 7th cent. by the Rajputs, who resisted Moslem invasion until 16th cent., when Mogul rule was estab. In 19th cent. the British ousted Mahratta invaders and assumed protection of Leo princely states.

Rajasthani (rä′jüstä′nē), a language of Indic group of Indo-Iranian subfamily of Indo-European languages. See LANGUAGE (table).

Rajputana, India: see RAJASTHAN.

Rajputs (räj′pŏots), a people, numbering c.650,000, mostly in Rajasthan, India. They are of the warrior caste and claim divine origin. Dominant in Rajputana since 7th cent.

Rakoczy, Hung. *Rákóczy* (rä′kôtsĭ), noble Hungarian family, princes of TRANSYLVANIA. **Sigismund Rakoczy**, 1544–1608, succeeded Stephen Bocskay as prince 1607. His son **George I Rakoczy**, 1591–1648 (reigned 1630–48), made war on Emperor Ferdinand III and forced him to grant religious freedom to Hungary (Peace of Linz, 1645). His son **George II Rakoczy**, 1621–60, succeeded his father as prince but was deposed 1657 after unsuccessfully invading Poland. His son **Francis I Rakoczy**, 1645–76, claimed succession but never was recognized as prince. Conspired with his father-in-law, Peter ZRINYI, against Emperor Leopold I. His son **Francis II Rakoczy**, 1676–1735, led Hungarian uprising against Hapsburgs in 1703; was elected "ruling prince" of Hungary 1704; secured aid of Louis XIV. Defeated in 1708 and 1710, the Hungarians made peace with the emperor 1711, but Rakoczy refused to accept treaty, fled abroad, and died an exile in Turkey. He is a national hero of Hungary. The Rakoczy March, named for him, was composed 1809 by John Bihari but may be based on an older tune; Berlioz and Liszt made use of it.

Ralegh or Raleigh, Sir Walter (both: rô′lē, rä′–), 1552?–1618, English statesman and man of letters. A favorite of Queen Elizabeth, he was involved in rivalry with the earl of Essex. Originated colonizing expeditions to America (see ROANOKE ISLAND); introduced potatoes and tobacco to England. Associated with poetic group called "school of night" which gained a reputation for atheism. In 1595 Ralegh made first expedition up Orinoco R. His fortunes fell with James I's accession. He was convicted of treason on slim evidence and imprisoned in Tower. Released (1616) to make another voyage to the Orinoco. On his return he was executed under the original sentence for treason. His writings include poetry and political and philosophical works.

Raleigh (rô′lē), city (pop. 65,679), state cap., central N.C. Selected as state cap. 1788, laid out 1792. Taken by Sherman in Civil War, April 14, 1865. Cottonseed-oil and lumber mills; printing, publishing; tobacco market. Birthplace of Andrew Johnson. Seat of Meredith Col. (Baptist; women; 1891), State Col. of Agriculture and Engineering of Univ. of NORTH CAROLINA, Shaw Univ. (Negro; Baptist; coed.; 1865), and St. Augustine's Col. (Negro; Episcopal; coed.; 1867).

Raleigh, Fort: see ROANOKE ISLAND.

Rama, hero: see RAMAYANA.

Ramadan (rämädän′, rä″mŭdän′), in ISLAM, ninth month of the year, when Moslems fast strictly during daylight. It commemorates the first revelation of the Koran. Because the Islamic calendar is lunar, Ramadan falls in different seasons.

Ramah (rä′mŭ), traditional burial place of Rachel, an important outpost N of Jerusalem.

Ramakrishna (rä″mŭkrĭsh′nŭ), 1836–86, Hindu mystic. Advocating active benevolence rather than quietism, he believed all religions equally valid forms needed (except by mystics) to approach the Eternal. He won many followers, even in the West.

Raman, Sir Chandrasekhara Venkata (chŭn′drŭsĕkä′rŭ vĕng′kŭtŭ rä′mŭn), 1888–, Indian physicist. Won 1930 Nobel Prize for research on diffusion of light and discovery of **Raman effect:** produced when part of beam of monochromatic light is scattered in passing through transparent medium; light is changed in wave length (mainly increased) and in frequency (mainly decreased).

Ramapo Mountains (räm′ŭpō″), forested range of the Appalachians, NE N.J. and SE N.Y. Hiking trails.

Ramayana (rämä′yŭnŭ) [story of Rama], great Sanskrit epic of India, perhaps written in 2d cent. B.C. In c.43,000 couplets of 16-syllable lines, it tells the adventures of Rama, heir to kingdom of Ajodhya, who, with his half brothers, collectively made up an avatar (incarnation) of the god Vishnu.

Rambam: see MAIMONIDES.

Rambaud, Alfred Nicolas (älfrĕd′ nēkôlä′ räbō′), 1842–1905, French historian and politician. Minister of public instruction (1896–98). Author of Byzantine history, notably *L'Empire grec au dixième siècle* (1870) and *Études sur l'histoire Byzantine* (1912).

Rambouillet, Catherine de Vivonne, marquise de (kä-trēn′ dù vēvôn′ märkĕz′ dù räbōōyä′), 1588–1665, famous Frenchwoman, whose salon exercised deep influence on French literature. Her circle included Mme de Sévigné, Mme de La Fayette, Corneille, Balzac, Richelieu, Malherbe, Bossuet, Scarron, La Rochefoucauld. The preciosity made fashionable by her salon later degenerated into extravagance and was much ridiculed by Molière.

Rambouillet (räbōōyä′), town (pop. 6,531), Seine-et-Oise dept., N France, S of Paris. Château is summer residence of French presidents. Vast Forest of Rambouillet is used for official hunting parties.

Rameau, Jean Philippe (rämō′), 1683–1764, French composer and theorist. His compositions include harpsichord suites and operas (e.g., *Castor et Pollux*). His treatises on harmony, in which he introduced the doctrine of inversions of chords (i.e., E-G-C and G-C-E are the same chord as C-E-G), are the basis of musical theory today.

Ramée, Pierre de la: see RAMUS, PETRUS.

Rameses or Ramesses: see RAMSES.

ramie (räm′ē), tall perennial plant (*Boehmeria nivea*), also called China grass, long grown in the Far East for its fiber, obtained from the bast. It has been made into underwear, paper, and in the Orient, grass cloth and other fabrics.

Ramillies (rä′mĭlēz, Fr. rämēyē′), village near Namur, Belgium. Scene of brilliant victory of allies under Marlborough over French under Villeroi (1706).

Ramiro I (rämē′rō), d. 1063, first king of Aragon (1035–63), natural son of Sancho III of Navarre. Annexed Sobrarbe and Ribagorza and fought the Moors.

Ramón y Cajal, Santiago (säntyä′gō rämōn′ ē kähäl′), 1852–1934, Spanish histologist. Shared 1906 Nobel Prize in Physiology and Medicine for work on structure of nervous system.

Ramos, João de Deus (zhwä′ō dù dā′ōōsh rä′mōōsh), 1830–96, Portuguese poet; author of *Campo de flores* (1893; a collection of lyrics in the popular idiom).

Ramoth-Gilead (rā′mŏth-gĭ′lēäd) or **Ramoth in Gilead**, anc. town, E of Jordan R., named by Joshua as city of refuge. Site of Ahab's last battle.

Ramsay, Allan, 1686–1758, Scottish poet, major figure in revival of vernacular poetry; best known for his pastoral comedy *The Gentle Shepherd* (1725).

Ramsay, Sir William, 1852–1916, Scottish chemist. Discovered helium; was codiscoverer of argon, krypton, neon, xenon; worked on radium emanation. Won 1904 Nobel Prize for this work.

Ramsden, Jesse, 1735–1800, English optician and mechanician, noted for mathematical instruments.

Ramses (răm′sēz), **Rameses** (răm′ŭsēz″, rùmē′sēs), or **Ramesses** (răm′ŭsēz″), kings of anc. Egypt of XIX and XX dynasties. **Ramses I,** d. 1314 B.C., was successor to Harmhab. He began the hypostyle at Karnak. His grandson, **Ramses II,** d. 1225 B.C., was the son of SETI I but not the heir. He usurped the throne and in his long reign (1292–1225 B.C.) brought Egypt to unprecedented splendor. The empire stretched from S Syria to the fourth cataract of the Nile, and social life was very luxurious for the upper classes. Ramses left many monuments, completing the temple at Karnak and building a mortuary temple at Thebes and the great rock temple at Abu-Simbel. He long warred on the Hittites. He was succeeded by Merneptah. Anarchy later was ended by **Ramses III,** d. 1167 B.C., who reigned c.1198–1167 B.C., second king of the XX dynasty. He warred successfully in Libya and Syria. The great luxury of his reign, particularly the riches of the temples and nobles, presaged the decay that followed. Toward the end of his reign his wife Tiy conspired unsuccessfully against him.

Ramsey (răm′zē), market town (pop. 5,772), Huntingdonshire, England. Ramsey Abbey was founded in 10th cent. Property later held by Cromwell family.

Ramsgate (rămz′gĭt), municipal borough (pop. 35,748) on Isle of Thanet, Kent, England; a resort and seaport. Victoria lived here as a princess. Near-by Ebbsfleet was landing place of St. Augustine and, traditionally, of Hengist and Horsa. Site of a Jewish college founded by Montefiore.

Ramus, Petrus (pē′trùs rä′mùs), Fr. *Pierre de la Ramée*, 1515–72, French humanist. After 1551 taught rhetoric and philosophy at the Collège de France, but having become Protestant had to flee to Germany. Returned and was killed in the massacre of St. Bartholomew's Day. He tried to develop a logic to supersede Aristotle's and encouraged skeptical thought.

Ramusio, Giambattista (jäm″bät-tē′stä rämōō′zyō), 1485–1557, Italian editor and compiler. Known for his *Delle navigationi e viaggi,* collection of geographical accounts of explorations.

Ramuz, Charles Ferdinand (shärl′ fĕrdēnä′ rämü′), 1878–1947, Swiss novelist, who wrote in French. His novels, dealing with simple people faced with elemental nature, include *The Reign of the Evil One* (1917; Eng. tr., 1922) and *Derborence* (1935; Eng. tr., *When the Mountain Fell,* 1947).

Rancagua (rängkä′gwä), city (pop. 29,442), central Chile, S of Santiago; founded 1743 in fertile valley of Andean foothills. Although one of Chile's largest copper mines is near by, city has developed primarily as agr. center. Here in 1814 revolutionary forces resisted a siege and escaped.

Rand, the, South Africa: see WITWATERSRAND.

Randers (rä′nùrs), city (pop. 40,098), E Jutland, Denmark; a port on Randers Fjord (inlet of the Kattegat) and at mouth of Guden R. Varied mfg. Important trade center in Middle Ages.

Randolph, Edmund (răn′dŏlf), 1753–1813, American statesman. At Federal Constitutional Convention (1787) he presented Virginia or Randolph Plan, favoring large states. U.S. Attorney General (1789–94); U.S. Secretary of State (1794–95). His uncle, **Peyton,** U.S. Secretary of State (1794–95). His uncle, **Peyton,**

Randolph, c.1721–1775, was first president of Continental Congress (1774) and was active in patriot cause in Va. before American Revolution.

Randolph, Edward, c.1632–1703, British colonial agent. Attacked legality of Mass. Bay charter.

Randolph, John, 1773–1833, American statesman, known as John Randolph of Roanoke. U.S. Representative (1799–1813, 1815–17, 1819–25, 1827–29) and U.S. Senator (1825–27) from Va. Known for sharp, biting tongue; opposed Madison and Northern Democrats, War of 1812, Missouri Compromise.

Randolph, Peyton: see RANDOLPH, EDMUND.

Randolph, town (pop. 9,982), E Mass., S of Boston; settled c.1710. Food products.

Randolph-Macon College, at Ashland, Va.; Methodist, for men; chartered 1830, opened 1832 at Boydton, moved 1868, named for John Randolph and Nathaniel Macon. Same board controls **Randolph-Macon Woman's College** (1893) at Lynchburg.

Rand School of Social Science, in New York City; opened 1906; a socialist institution but not officially connected with the Socialist party. Classes scheduled to suit needs of working people.

Randwick, municipality (pop. 100,931), New South Wales, Australia, just SE of Sydney, in metropolitan area. Large race track is here.

Ranelagh (rä′nĭlù), former amusement resort in Chelsea, London. Founded (1742) on the estate of the earl of Ranelagh, it was closed in 1803 or 1804.

Rangabe (rägäbä′) or **Rhangavis, Alexandros Rizos** (älĕk′sändrôs rē′zôs räng″gävēs′), 1810–92, Greek scholar, author, and diplomat. Was prominent in Greek classicist revival. Particularly notable as dramatist, he wrote in classic Greek.

range, grazing land of large area in W U.S. and Canada, formerly unfenced public land, now chiefly privately owned. Rights to the grazing on unfenced land in the national forests are purchased.

Rangeley, town (pop. 1,228), W Maine, NNW of Rumford and on Rangeley L. (7 mi. long), one of a group of lakes in Maine and N.H. Hq. of famous fishing and hunting region.

Rangoon (răng″gōōn′), city (pop. 500,800), cap. and chief port of Burma, on Rangoon R., near its mouth on Gulf of Martaban. Modernized after 1852, when British rule was estab. Exports rice, oil, and teak. Site of the famous Shwe Dagon Pagoda and a university (founded 1920). In World War II it was occupied 1942–45 by the Japanese and was severely damaged by bombing.

Ranjit Singh (rùn′jĭt sĭng′), 1780–1839, Sikh ruler, who conquered the Punjab and Kashmir. After Second Sikh War (1848–49) his domain fell to the British.

Rank, Otto (ō′tō rängk), 1884–1939, Austrian psychoanalyst, an early pupil of Freud. He used Freudian techniques to interpret myths, but differed from Freud in that he regarded the birth trauma (rather than Oedipus complex) as chief cause of neurosis.

Ranke, Leopold von (lä′ōpôlt fün räng′kù), 1795–1886, German historian. Known as father of modern objective historical school, through teaching and writing he influenced generation of historians. In writings he ranged over all European nations; collected works fill 54 volumes (1867–90). Culminating work was *Weltgeschichte* (9 vols., 1881–88).

Rankin, borough (pop. 6,941), SW Pa., ESE of Pittsburgh. Mfg. of steel.

Rannoch, Loch (lŏkh rä′nùkh), lake, c.9½ mi. long and 1 mi. wide, Perthshire, Scotland.

Ransom, John Crowe, 1888–, American poet and critic. His verse includes *Selected Poems* (1945).

Ranters, adherents of antinomian movement in England during Commonwealth. Teaching was pantheistic. Individuals were given freedom of thought. In 19th cent. Primitive Methodists were called Ranters.

Rantoul (răn"tōōl'), village (pop. 6,387), E Ill., N of Champaign, in farm area. Chanute Air Force Base is here.

Raoul (räōōl'), d. 936, French king (923–36), duke of Burgundy. Was elected king to succeed his father-in-law, Robert I. Established his authority over claims of Charles III (the Simple).

Raoult's law (räōōlz') states that lowering of vapor pressure of a solvent is proportional to concentration (molar) of substance dissolved. Formulated by François Marie Raoult (1830–1901), French chemist.

Rapallo (räpäl'-lō), resort town (pop. 6,766), Liguria, NW Italy, on the Riviera. For the **Treaty of Rapallo** of 1920, see FIUME. The **Treaty of Rapallo** of 1922 was an agreement signed by Germany and the USSR during but independently of the Conference of GENOA. Germany accorded the Soviet government its first *de jure* recognition; both signatories mutually canceled all pre-war debts and war claims; extensive trade agreements were made.

rape, annual or biennial plant (*Brassica napus*) related to the cabbage and grown chiefly for forage in North America. The seed yields an oil and is used in birdseed mixtures.

rape, in law, crime of sexual intercourse with a woman (other than one's wife) without her consent. A woman is deemed legally incapable of consent if insane, feebleminded, or below the age set by statute as the age of consent. Failure on the part of the woman to resist—unless resistance would be obviously useless—usually is considered to imply consent.

Raphael (rä'fēul, rä'–) [Heb.,= God heals], archangel. Prominent in book of TOBIT as companion of Tobias, healer of Tobit, and rescuer of Sara. Feast: Oct. 24. Appears in Milton's *Paradise Lost.*

Raphael, Ital. *Raffaello Santi* or *Raffaello Sanzio,* 1483–1520, Italian painter, one of the greatest artists of the Renaissance, b. Urbino. His father, Giovanni Santi, was court painter and poet to duke of Urbino. In c.1500 Raphael entered the workshop of Perugino, whose influence is seen in coloring and graceful composition of such early works as *The Three Graces* (Chantilly) and the *Sposalizio* (Brera, Milan). In Florence (1504–8) he painted *The Entombment* (Rome) and the many famous Madonnas, whose landscape backgrounds reflect influence of Leonardo and Massaccio. From 1508 until his death he worked in Rome, where he succeeded Bramante as chief architect of St. Peter's (1514). Here his mature style benefited from Michelangelo's influence. For his patron, Leo X, he made a survey of ancient Rome showing the chief monuments. His many works for the Vatican include 10 tapestries with themes from Acts of the Apostles for the Sistine Chapel and the great mural *School of Athens* for the Stanza della Segnatura. Also of the Roman period are the *Sistine Madonna* (perhaps his best-known work), named after the Church of San Sisto, Piacenza, and the superb portraits of Baldassare Castiglione (Louvre) and Pope Leo X (Pitti Palace, Florence).

Raphia: see RAFA, Egypt.

Rapidan, river rising in N Va., in Blue Ridge mts., and flowing SW then NE to the Rappahannock.

Rapid City, city (pop. 25,310), SW S.Dak., near Black Hills, SE of Lead; founded 1876 after gold discovered. Trade center for gold and silver mines, farms, and dairies. Seat of South Dakota School of Mines and Technology (state supported; mainly for men; opened 1887), with collection of prehistoric fossils in Dinosaur Park. Near-by Deerfield Dam (1947) is in Rapid valley project.

Rapido (rä'pēdō), short river, S central Italy. Joins Liri below Cassino. In World War II, Allied attempt to outflank Cassino by crossing the Rapido resulted in heavy losses, particularly to U.S. troops (Jan., 1944).

Rappahannock, river rising in N Va., on E slope of

Blue Ridge E of Front Royal, and flowing SW 212 mi. to Chesapeake Bay. Navigable to Fredericksburg. Much Civil War fighting took place along river.

rare earths, group of rare, vari-colored, earthy, mineral substances (oxides of certain metals). Originally were thought to be elements, but later metals were obtained from them. These **metals of the rare earths** have a valence of 3; atomic nos. range from 57 to 71; are obtained only in small amounts.

Raritan (rä'rĭtŭn), town (pop. 5,131), N central N.J., on Raritan R. and near Somerville.

Raritan, river, N central N.J., formed by branches W of Raritan and flowing c.35 mi, generally SE, past New Brunswick, to Raritan Bay (arm of Lower New York Bay) between Perth Amboy and South Amboy. Connected with Delaware R. by old Delaware and Raritan Canal.

Rarotonga: see COOK ISLANDS.

Rashi (rä'shē), 1040–1105, Jewish scholar, b. France; author of important commentaries on the Talmud and the Pentateuch. Real name Rabbi Solomon bar Isaac.

Rasis, Persian physician: see RHAZES.

Rask, Rasmus Christian (räs'mōōs krĭs'tyän räsk), 1787–1832, Danish philologist. He published perhaps the first usable Anglo-Saxon and Icelandic grammars (translated into English), and did valuable work on relationship of the Indo-European languages.

Rasmussen, Knud Johan Victor (räs'mōōsŭn), 1879–1933, Danish arctic explorer and ethnologist, authority on Greenland Eskimo. Sought confirmation of theory that Eskimo and North American Indian are of same Asian stock. First to traverse Northwest Passage by dog sled.

raspberry, prickly deciduous shrub of genus *Rubus* which includes other brambles, and the red, purple, or black fruits. In North America most cultivated red raspberries are derived from *Rubus idaeus strigosus.* Blackcap raspberries are varieties of *R. occidentalis,* also native to North America. Purple varieties are hybrids of these and European species.

Rasputin, Grigori Yefimovich (grĭgô'rē yĭfē'mŭvĭch rŭspōō'tyĭn), 1872–1916, Russian monk, notorious figure at court of Nicholas II. An illiterate peasant and debauchee, he gained complete control over imperial couple through his miraculous "cure" of the hemophilic tsarevich, exerted sinister influence over politics and appointments, and was suspected of pro-German sympathies in World War I. Assassinated by group of noblemen headed by Prince Yussupov.

Rassam, Hormuzd (hôrmōōzd' räsäm'), 1826–1910, Turkish archaeologist. In Assyria and Babylonia he discovered the palace of Assur-bani-pal and the site of Sippar.

Rastatt (rä'shtät), town (pop. 16,551), S Baden, SW Germany. For Treaty of Rastatt (1714), see UTRECHT, PEACE OF.

Rastrelli, Bartolomeo Francesco, Conte (rästrĕl'lē) 1700–1771, Italian architect, important in development of St. Petersburg (now Leningrad). Designed Winter Palace and Stroganov Palace.

rat, rodent of global distribution. Brown house rat (*Rattus norvegicus*) and black house rat (*R. rattus*) of Asia spread to Europe and New World. Rats cause huge property losses, spread typhus, bubonic plague, rat-bite fever, tularemia, and rabies.

ratchet and pawl, mechanical device generally used to permit motion in one direction only. Ratchet (toothed wheel) is arranged with pawl (lever with catch) so that pawl moves smoothly over teeth in one direction but catches teeth if reversed.

rath (rä, räth), hill fort protected by earthworks, used by anc. Irish as retreat in time of danger. Many remain throughout Ireland (esp. at Tara).

Rathenau, Walter (väl'tŭr rä'tŭnou), 1867–1922, German industrialist and statesman. As minister of reconstruction (1921) and foreign minister (1922) he made sincere attempts to meet German reparations obligations. A Jew, he was assassinated by nationalist fanatics. His idealistic social philosophy found expression in several writings.

Rathlin (răth′lĭn), island (3,564 acres; pop. 245), off N. Ireland, in Co. Antrim. St. Columba founded a church here in 6th cent.

Ratibor (rä′tēbôr), Pol. *Racibórz*, city (1939 pop. 50,-004; 1946 pop. 19,605), Upper Silesia, on Oder R.; transferred to Polish administration 1945. Mfg. of precision instruments, textiles, chemicals. Cap. of principality founded in 13th cent., it passed to Austria 1526, to Prussia 1745. Raised to a titular duchy 1840.

ratio. Ratio of two quantities (in terms of same unit) is fraction with first quantity as numerator and second as denominator.

rationalism (ră′shŭnŭlĭzŭm) [Latin,= belonging to reason], any philosophic theory assigning first place to reason in attainment of knowledge, from that of Plato to idealists of today. The term is most commonly applied to the 18th-cent. philosophers who attacked religion by rejecting all claims based on faith or revelation. Rationalism may also be opposed to EMPIRICISM, if the rationalist argues that truth may be obtained by reasoning from "self-evident" premises; empiricism rejects such premises.

Ratisbon, Bavaria: see REGENSBURG.

Rat Islands: see ALEUTIAN ISLANDS.

Raton (ră″tōon′), city (pop. 8,241; alt. 6,400 ft.), NE N.Mex., near Colo. line; settled in 1870s on Santa Fe Trail. Resort and trade center in coal and livestock area. Capulin Mt. Natl. Monument, Folsom (see FOLSOM CULTURE), and Raton Pass (7,834 ft.) are near by.

rattan (rătăn′), name for certain climbing palms of genera *Calamus* and *Daemonorops* of tropical Asia from which the rattan cane of commerce is obtained. The cane, flexible and strong, is split for use in wickerwork, baskets, and chair seats.

rattlesnake, poisonous New World snake of pit viper family. Head is widened at base; "rattle" (series of dried, hollow segments making whirring sound if shaken) is at end of tail. Well known are timber, diamondback (largest), western diamondback, and prairie rattlesnakes.

Ratzel, Friedrich (frĕ′drĭkh rät′sŭl), 1844–1904, German geographer. Pioneered in development of anthropogeography and emphasized effects of physical environment on human activity.

Rauschenbusch, Walter, 1861–1918, American Baptist clergyman; professor of church history (after 1902) at Rochester Theological Seminary. Wrote influential books on social interpretation of Christianity.

Ravaillac, François (fräswä′ räväyäk′), 1578–1610, assassin of Henry IV of France; a religious fanatic. Was drawn and quartered.

Ravel, Maurice (rävĕl′), 1875–1937, French composer. His music, subtle and lucid, often combines exotic materials with classic form. His works for piano include the suite *Le Tombeau de Couperin, Pavane pour une infante défunte, Ma Mère l'Oye, Valse nobles et sentimentales*, and two concertos; for orchestra, *Daphnis et Chloé, La Valse, Rhapsodie Espagnole*, and the popular *Bolero*.

raven, large glossy black bird of crow family, native to N Eurasia and North America. It can be tamed and learns to imitate words. Is primarily a scavenger.

Ravenna (rävĕn′nä), city (pop. 31,251), Emilia-Romagna, N central Italy, near the Po delta and Adriatic Sea. Augustus made its port, Classis, a major Roman naval station. Cap. of West Roman Empire from 402, Ravenna was after 476 the seat of Odoacer and Theodoric the Great; after 540 the seat of the Byzantine exarchs (governors) of Italy. The Lombards seized it in 751 but lost it to Pepin the Short, who deeded it to the pope (754; see PAPAL STATES). Ruled by the Da Polenta family 13th–15th cent., then briefly by Venice, it passed under the effective control of the popes only in 1509. Ravenna is famous for its Roman and Byzantine buildings—mausoleums of Galla Placidia and Theodoric; octagonal baptistery (earlier a Roman bath); churches of San Vitale, Sant' Apollinare Nuovo, and Sant' Apollinare in Classe. These contain unique mosaics of the 5th and 6th cent. Dante's tomb is at Ravenna.

Ravenna, city (pop. 9,857), NE Ohio, NE of Akron. Mfg. of rubber goods, yarn, and textiles.

Ravensberg (rä′vŭnsbĕrk), former county, NW Germany, in Westphalia, NW of Lippe. Passed to count of Berg 1346, to duke of Jülich 1348, to duke of Cleves 1524, to Brandenburg 1614.

Rawalpindi (räwŭlpĭn′dē), city (pop. 243,000), Punjab prov., W Pakistan; mfg. and trade center. Formerly British military hq. in the Punjab. Liaquat Ali Khan was assassinated here in 1952.

Rawlings, Marjorie Kinnan, 1896–, American author, writing usually of Florida backwoods. Novel *The Yearling* (1938) very popular.

Rawlins, city (pop. 7,415; alt. 6,755 ft.), S Wyo., WNW of Laramie. Oil, coal, and livestock center.

Rawlinson, Sir Henry Creswicke, 1810–95, English Orientalist and administrator. He investigated the inscription, in Persian CUNEIFORM, of Darius I at BEHISTUN. From 1865 to 1868 he sat in Parliament, and after that was a member of the India council.

ray, marine fish related to shark. It has a flat, disklike body and wide, fleshy, pectoral fins. Sting rays can inflict wound with saw-toothed tail spine. Devilfish or manta is a gigantic warm-water ray.

ray, in physics, narrow pencil of light or other radiation that proceeds through space in straight line from source. See also COSMIC RAYS; INFRARED RAYS; ULTRA-VIOLET RAY; X RAY.

Rayburn, Sam(uel Taliaferro), 1882–, U.S. Congressman (1913–) from Texas. Democratic speaker of the House (1940–46, 1949–53), he had the longest record in that office.

Rayleigh, John William Strutt, 3d Baron (rā′lē), 1842–1919, English physicist. Won 1904 Nobel Prize. Known for research in sound, light, codiscovery of argon, determinations of electrical units, application of Boyle's law to gases at low pressures.

Raymond, counts of TOULOUSE. **Raymond IV**, d. 1105?, a leader in the First Crusade. Refused oath of fealty to Alexius I; quarreled with BOHEMOND over possession of Antioch; laid siege to Tripoli, later made into a county by his descendants. **Raymond VI**, d. 1222, was repeatedly excommunicated for support he gave to the ALBIGENSES. Attacked by Simon de MONTFORT, he received aid of PETER II of Aragon but was defeated at Muret (1213). His attempts to regain his lands from Montfort were continued by his son and successor, **Raymond VII**, 1197–1249. In 1229 Raymond VII was forced to sign a treaty which transferred most of S France to the French crown—partly through immediate cession, partly through the marriage of his daughter to Alphonse of Poitiers (a brother of Louis IX of France), who eventually inherited Toulouse. Raymond permitted establishment of the INQUISITION (1233).

Raymond, c.1140–1187, count of Tripoli (1152–87); great-great-grandson of Raymond IV of Toulouse. Regent for BALDWIN IV and Baldwin V during the last years of the Latin Kingdom of Jerusalem; allied himself with SALADIN when Guy of LUSIGNAN succeeded Baldwin V. After a reconciliation, he fought on Christian side at Hattin (1187), where Jerusalem fell to the Moslems.

Raymond Berengar IV (bĕ′rŭngär), d. 1162, count of Barcelona (1131–62). By his marriage to Petronella, daughter and heir of Ramiro II of Aragon, Catalonia and Aragon were united.

Raymondville, city (pop. 9,136), S Texas, NNW of Brownsville. Trade and shipping center for agr. area with some oil. Tourist trade.

Rayne, town (pop. 6,485), SW La., SW of Baton Rouge. Mills rice and ships frogs.

rayon (rā'ŏn"), synthetic fibers made from CELLULOSE and the fabrics woven from them. Rayon is produced by dissolving cellulose (from wood pulp or cotton linters) in chemicals, then forcing it through minute holes so that filaments, hardened either in liquid or warm air, are formed. Filaments are then either twisted into thread or cut into lengths and spun. Spun rayon can be made to simulate wool, linen, or cotton. Methods of manufacturing rayon include the nitro-cellulose process, developed in 1880s and no longer important; the VISCOSE PROCESS, discovered in 1892; the cuprammonium process, yielding very fine, strong yarn; and the acetate process, originated in England in 1918, which produces an acetate derivative of cellulose rather than the regenerated cellulose of the other types. Rayon yarns with new properties are constantly being developed, as are such substances as cellulose substitutes for sponge rubber, acetate fillers for nonshatterable glass, and flexible grease-proof and moistureproof sheets such as CELLOPHANE.

Razin, Stenka (stĕng'kä rä'zēn), d. 1671, ataman (leader) of Don Cossacks, celebrated in song and legend. Aided by peasants and local tribes, he rebelled against tsar (1670), took lower and middle Volga region, but was ultimately defeated and beheaded.

Rb, chemical symbol of the element RUBIDIUM.

Ré (rā), island (33 sq. mi.; pop. 7,908), off La Rochelle, W France, in Bay of Biscay; formerly also spelled Rhé. Citadel, built by Vauban (1681), is now a penitentiary.

Re, chemical symbol of the element RHENIUM.

reaction, chemical: see CHEMICAL REACTION.

Read, Opie (Percival), 1852–1939, American author, editor of the humorous *Arkansas Traveler,* author of robust novels (e.g., *A Kentucky Colonel,* 1889).

Read, Thomas Buchanan, 1822–72, American poet and artist, author of the poem, "Sheridan's Ride."

Reade, Charles, 1814–84, English novelist. Wrote propagandist novels in favor of various causes, but is remembered for his great medieval romance, *The Cloister and the Hearth* (1861).

Reading, Rufus Daniel Isaacs, 1st marquess of (rĕ'dǐng), 1860–1935, British statesman. A successful lawyer, he became (1910) attorney general. Accused of buying American Marconi Corp. stock while government was negotiating with the firm, he was cleared. Was lord chief justice (1913–21), viceroy of India (1921–26), and foreign secretary (1931).

Reading (rĕ'dǐng), county borough (pop. 114,176), co. town of Berkshire, England. History dates from 871. Univ. of Reading (1926) has noted departments of agr. and dairying. Oscar Wilde wrote *Ballad of Reading Gaol* while in prison here. Town was Aldbrickham of Hardy's *Jude the Obscure.*

Reading (rĕ'dǐng). **1** Town (pop. 14,006), NE Mass., N of Boston; settled 1639. Photographic supplies, stoves. **2** City (pop. 7,836), SW Ohio, N of Cincinnati. Lithographing, mfg. of chemicals. **3** City (pop. 109,320), SE Pa., on Schuylkill R. and NW of Philadelphia; laid out 1748. Important commercial and industrial center of Pennsylvania Dutch region with railroad shops and mfg. of aluminum, steel, and brass products. Provided cannon for Revolution. Seat of Albright Col.

real estate: see PROPERTY.

realism, in literature, the attempt to describe life without idealization. In 19th-cent. France it became a conscious literary movement opposing romanticism; novelists (e.g., Flaubert, in *Madame Bovary*) presented the sordid and trivial as well as the noble and dramatic. Flaubert also insisted that stories exclude the writer's reactions. Naturalism, as exemplified by Émile Zola, advocated a thorough, dispassionate inquiry into all aspects of society. Some recent novelists, reacting to an overemphasis on facts as such, tried to reach the underlying meaning of the facts. With diverse 20th-cent. interpretations, term *realism* has lost much of its meaning although it is still a major literary force.

real property: see PROPERTY.

reaper, machine for reaping grain. A practical reaper for field work was introduced 1831 by C. H. McCormick. Marsh harvester, patented 1858, carried driver and two men to bind grain. Reaper improvements include self-binder and combine which also threshes grain.

Réaumur, René Antoine Ferchault de (rā'ùmyŏor, Fr. rùnä' ätwän' fĕrshō' dù räōmür'), 1683–1757, French physicist and naturalist. Invented a thermometer (1731), studied expansion, improved iron manufacture, isolated gastric juice of birds, studied and wrote six-volume study of insects.

rebate, in U.S. history, a return of part of the transportation charges formerly given by railroads to favored shippers. Railroad rebates are now prohibited by laws (e.g., Elkins Act of 1903) and penalized by the Interstate Commerce Commission.

rebec or **rebeck** (rē'bĕk), medieval stringed musical instrument, played with a bow. It usually had three strings. Although popular with amateurs, it was never considered of concert caliber. See *ill.,* p. 667.

Rebecca or **Rebekah** (both: rēbĕ'kù) [Heb.,= noose], wife of Isaac, mother of Jacob and Esau. Helped Jacob to secure the birthright that should have been Esau's. Gen. 24–27; 49.31; Rom. 9.10.

Récamier, Juliette (zhülyĕt' räkämyä'), 1777–1849, French beauty and social figure. From Consulate through July Monarchy, Mme Récamier's salon was meeting place of political and literary figures, among them Mme de Staël, Sainte-Beuve, Constant, and Chateaubriand, to whom she devoted her later years.

Recared (rĕ'kùrĕd), d. 601, Visigothic king in Spain (586–601). His conversion to Catholicism brought about conversion of Arian Visigoths.

Receswinth (rĕ'kùswǐnth), d. 672, Visigothic king in Spain (653–72). Either he or his father Chindaswinth revoked the Breviary of Alaric, and he completed a new code, called *Forum Judicum,* which combined German and Roman law and was the basis of Spanish medieval law.

Rechabites (rē'kùbīts), in Bible, a clan given to asceticism, similar to the NAZARITES. Jer. 35.

Recife (rùsē'fù) [Port.,= reef], city (pop. 522,466), cap. of Pernambuco state, NE Brazil; port on the Atlantic. City lies partly on mainland, partly on island. Exports great quantities of hinterland's products—sugar, rum, fruits, hides, cotton, lumber. Founded in 1530s by Portuguese.

reciprocity, commercial agreement whereby nations grant each other mutual privileges. In Germany, the ZOLLVEREIN was based on reciprocity, and reciprocity has been part of the U.S. tariff policy since 1880. In European countries, reciprocity usually involves the MOST-FAVORED-NATION CLAUSE, but American treaties ordinarily do not make reference to a third state.

recitative (rĕ"sǐtùtēv'), musical declamation for solo voice, used in opera and oratorio for dialogue and narration. Its development at end of the 16th cent. contributed to the rise of opera, since it enabled words to be clearly understood and the rhythms of natural speech to be followed. Musical accompaniment to recitative ranges from a few occasional chords to the complete molding of music and text used by Wagner.

Reclamation, United States Bureau of, agency set up in Dept. of the Interior under Reclamation Act of 1902. Its purpose is to encourage and promote irrigation of lands in arid and semiarid regions of the West by examination, survey, and construction of irrigation works. CAREY LAND ACT (1894) rendered governmental help to reclamation schemes. Attention focused sharply on conservation of natural resources in time of Theodore Roosevelt. Interest in reclamation quickened after drought of late '20s and early '30s; program was linked with flood control and development of power.

reclamation of land, practice of making unproductive

land productive, by IRRIGATION, drainage, flood control, improvement of physical condition of soil, and by checking EROSION. U.S. Bureau of Reclamation relies mostly on irrigation and flood control.

Reclus, Jean Jacques Élisée (ālēzā′ rŭklü′), 1830–1905, French geographer. Chief among his many valuable works was *Nouvelle Géographie universelle* (20 vols., 1876–94).

recognition, political action acknowledging that a new state is qualified to assume its responsibilities under international law. Three varieties exist: recognition of the formation of a new state; recognition of the establishment of a new political regime; and recognition of belligerency. When a nation recognizes belligerency, it offends the state against which the rebellion is directed.

Reconstruction. During Civil War, Pres. Lincoln launched a moderate restoration program in areas of Confederacy occupied by Union armies. Congressional radicals opposed his plan. His successor, Andrew JOHNSON, adopted a plan much like Lincoln's. By end of 1865 every ex-Confederate state except Texas had fulfilled President's requirements for restoration of civil government. Control of white over Negro, however, seemed to have been resumed. Whites refused to enfranchise the blacks; black codes (laws defining new status of emancipated Negroes) were generally severe. Republican party ascendancy depended on Negro suffrage. Rep. Thaddeus STEVENS and Sen. Charles SUMNER led Congressional movement to make Reconstruction dependent on civil rights for Negro. Radicals won 1866 election; on March 2, 1867, Congress enacted Reconstruction Act, which, supplemented by later acts, divided the South (except Tenn.) into five military districts, in which authority of army commander was supreme. House impeached Johnson for defiance of TENURE OF OFFICE ACT, scuttled his program. South was reduced to degradation, with state governments falling to CARPETBAGGERS and scalawags. Aided by FREEDMEN'S BUREAU and UNION LEAGUE CLUBS, they shamelessly manipulated Negro votes, terrorized communities with Negro troops. In some districts anarchy and crime ruled; KU KLUX KLAN appeared. Its own corruption broke down the carpetbagger governmental structure. By 1876 only Fla., S.C., La. remained under Republican domination. Following disputed national election of that year year, all Federal troops were withdrawn from the South; home rule was restored. Social and economic rehabilitation began years later.

Reconstruction Finance Corporation (RFC), U.S. government organ, created 1932. Originally designed to facilitate economic activity in the depression by making loans, it later helped finance World War II. Removed from Dept. of Commerce control in 1945. In 1948 its life was extended to 1956, but its lending powers were sharply curtailed.

recorder: see WIND INSTRUMENTS.

Red Bank, borough (pop. 12,743), E N.J., on Navesink estuary and NE of Long Branch. Resort and distributing center; mfg. of clothing, machinery, boats. Albert Brisbane helped estab. Fourierist community near here 1843. U.S. Fort Monmouth is S.

redbird: see CARDINAL.

redbreast: see ROBIN.

redbud or **Judas tree,** names for handsome leguminous trees and shrubs of genus *Cercis,* with rose or white flowers in spring. The common redbud (*Cercis canadensis*) is native to E North America.

red bug, name for various red insects. Apple red bug is reddish black hemipterous insect; in nymph stage, it attacks leaves and fruits of certain trees. Cotton red bug discolors fiber in cotton seeds. See also CHIGGER.

Red Cloud, 1822–1909, North American Indian chief, leader of the Oglala Sioux. Led massacre of party under William J. FETTERMAN (1866).

Red Cloud, city (pop. 1,744), S Nebr., on Republican R. Childhood home of Willa Cather.

Red Cross, international organization for the alleviation of human suffering and the promotion of public health; estab. at Geneva convention of 1864, largely through the efforts of J. H. Dunant, a Swiss. A red cross on a white background—the Swiss flag with its colors reversed—is its symbol. There are self-governing Red Cross societies in 68 countries, and two international groups. The American Natl. Red Cross was organized (1881) by Clara BARTON. It is supported entirely by voluntary contributions.

Red Deer, city (pop. 7,575), S central Alta., Canada, on Red Deer R. and S of Edmonton. Trade center in agr. area. Oil refineries, grain elevators.

Red Deer, river of S Alta., Canada, rising in Banff Natl. Park and flowing 385 mi. NE, S, SE, and S across Alta. to South Saskatchewan R.

Redding. 1 City (pop. 10,256), N Calif., on Sacramento R. near Shasta Dam. Trade and processing center for lumbering, gold and copper mining, and fruitgrowing region. Gateway to mountain hunting and fishing regions. Lassen Volcanic Natl. Park is near. **2** Town (pop. 2,037), SW Conn., NW of Bridgeport. Mark Twain summered here. Israel Putnam Memorial Campground commemorates winter of 1778–79.

Redfield, William C., 1789–1857, American scientist. Developed theory of rotary motion of hurricanes. An organizer (1848) and first president of American Association for the Advancement of Science.

Redfield, resort city (pop. 2,655), NE S.Dak., S of Aberdeen. Game-bird hunting.

Redi, Francesco (fränchā′skō rā′dē), 1626?–1698?, Italian naturalist, poet, and court physician to dukes of Tuscany. He helped to disprove theory of spontaneous generation through controlled experiments which showed that certain living organisms, notably maggots in rotting meat, arose only by reproduction of like living things. His chief poetical work was a dithyrambic ode, *Bacchus in Tuscany* (1685; Eng. tr., 1825).

Redlands, city (pop. 18,429), S Calif., in San Bernardino Valley E of Los Angeles. Ships oranges. Seat of Univ. of Redlands (Baptist; coed.; 1907).

red lead, red powdery lead tetroxide (also called minium). Used in making storage batteries, glass, red pigments, and red paint.

Red Lion, borough (pop. 5,119), SE Pa., near York. German customs preserved here.

Redmond, John Edward, 1856–1918, Irish political leader. Head (after 1890) of Parnellite faction in Parliament, he became (1900) chairman of combined Irish party. Supported Home Rule bills; opposed exclusion of Ulster. Rebellion of 1916 was a blow to him; his influence waned with rise of the revolutionary Sinn Fein.

Red Oak, city (pop. 6,526), SW Iowa, on East Nishnabotna R. and SE of Council Bluffs, in farm area. Printing of art calendars.

Redon, Odilon (ôdēlô′ rŭdô′), 1840–1916, French painter. Depicted mystical subjects and flowers.

Redondo Beach (rĭdŏn′dō), resort and residential city (pop. 25,226), S Calif., SSW of Los Angeles.

Red River, chief river of Tonkin, c.730 mi. long, rising in Yunnan prov., China, and flowing SE through Tonkin to South China Sea. Near head of delta is Hanoi.

Red River. 1 River, 1,300 mi. long, southernmost of large Mississippi R. tributaries. Rises near Amarillo in Texas Panhandle and flows ESE between Texas and Okla., and Texas and Ark., then S and SE through La. to ATCHAFALAYA R. and Mississippi R. Has DENISON DAM and reclamation project on North Fork near Altus, Okla. Shipping important for a time; still navigable for small ships to above Shreveport. Many lakes and bayous along lower course; reservoirs planned as flood control measures. Expedition under Gen. N. P. Banks and Adm. Porter went up river (1864) in Civil War to open way to Texas, but was defeated at Sabine Crossroads. **2** Or **Red River of the North,** river formed

SMALL CAPITALS = cross references. Pronunciation key on inside end pages. Abbreviations: p. 2.

in N.Dak. N of L. Traverse by junction of Bois de Sioux and Otter Tail rivers and flowing 533 mi. N between Minn. and N.Dak. and through Manitoba to L. Winnipeg. Drains principal spring-wheat area of U.S. Chief tributary is Assiniboine R.

Red River Rebellion: see RIEL, LOUIS.

Red River Settlement, agr. colony in present Man., N.Dak., and Minn., promoted by Thomas Douglas, 5th earl of SELKIRK. He desired to assist dispossessed and impoverished of Scotland and N Ireland. He secured sufficient financial interest in Hudson's Bay Co. to obtain grant of land called Assiniboia. Settlement was strongly opposed by fur traders, mainly from North West Co. A small group of Scotch and Irish attempted to start a colony (1812), but North West Co. men persuaded settlers to desert. In 1816, when colony was restored, settlers were attacked and some 22 killed in massacre of Seven Oaks. Selkirk seized Fort William, a North West Co. post. In court action that ensued Selkirk was impoverished and union between North West Co. and Hudson's Bay Co. furthered.

Red Sea, anc. *Sinus Arabicus,* narrow sea, c.1,500 mi. long, between Africa and Arabia, in Great Rift Valley; important shipping lane linking Europe and Asia. Connected with the Mediterranean by Suez Canal and with Gulf of Aden by the strait Bab el Mandeb. Its N arms, Gulf of Aqaba and Gulf of Suez, enclose Sinai peninsula. The Bible in telling of Red Sea crossing by the Israelites probably intended the Gulf of Suez.

Red Springs, town (pop. 2,245), S N.C., SW of Fayetteville. Flora Macdonald Col. (Presbyterian; women; 1896) is here.

reduction: see OXIDATION AND REDUCTION.

Red Wing, city (pop. 10,645), SE Minn., at head of L. Pepin; settled 1852. Farm trade center with mfg. of pottery and dairy products. Swiss mission to Indians here 1836–40.

redwood: see SEQUOIA.

Redwood City, city (pop. 25,544), W Calif., SSE of San Francisco. Grows and ships chrysanthemums. Has tanning, food canning, and mfg. of rubber goods.

Reed, John, 1887–1920, American journalist and radical. Attached to radical magazine the *Masses* after 1913. *Ten Days That Shook the World* is his eyewitness account of the Russian Revolution. Buried at the Kremlin.

Reed, Thomas Brackett, 1839–1902, American legislator. U.S. Representative from Maine (1877–99). As speaker of House (1889–91, 1895–99) he used his power to aid orthodox Republican legislation.

Reed, Walter, 1851–1902, American army surgeon, head of Havana commission for study of YELLOW FEVER (1900). Washington, D.C., medical center and army hospital were named for him.

reed, name for several grasses. The common reed (*Phragmites communis*) is a tall grass which has been used for thatching and, in SW U.S., for adobe huts. The giant reed (*Arundo donax*) is sometimes used in reed musical instruments.

Reed College: see PORTLAND, Oregon.

reed instruments: see WIND INSTRUMENTS.

reed mace: see CATTAIL.

Reelfoot Lake, c.20 mi. long, W Tenn., near Mississippi R. and Ky. line. Formed 1811–12 by earthquakes; filled with river water. In Reelfoot L. Fish and Game Preserve.

Reese, Lizette Woodworth, 1856–1935, American poet, noted for lyric treatment of nature. *A Wayside Lute* (1909) includes her best-known poem, "Tears."

Reeve, Tapping, 1744–1823, American lawyer and jurist. Had famous law school at Litchfield, Conn.

referendum: see INITIATIVE AND REFERENDUM.

refining includes processes of metallurgy, separation of petroleum into its products, purification of sugars and other substances. Nature of process varies according to material involved, value of end product, degree of purity required, etc. Electrolysis is much used for metals: BLAST FURNACE and REVERBERATORY FURNACE for copper and iron particularly; and amalgamation process and CYANIDE PROCESS for chemical refining of metals. Sugar refining involves adding lime in some form, filtration, evaporation, and crystallization.

reflection occurs when light ray or sound wave strikes surface and is thrown back into medium through which it has come. Principles are similar for light and sound since both travel in straight lines and are wave phenomena. Objects are visible because of light reflected from their surfaces; their color depends on ability to reflect light of certain wave length. Smooth surfaces give regular reflection; rough or uneven surfaces give diffuse reflection. Total reflection is seen when light passing from one medium to less dense one reaches one of surfaces and is thrown back into denser medium again; this occurs when light strikes at an oblique angle greater than a certain degree up to which refraction (not reflection) takes place. Internal reflection accounts in part for rainbow and mirage. Reflection of sound waves causes ECHO. Heat and other forms of radiant energy also are reflected.

reflex action: see NERVOUS SYSTEM.

Reform, Catholic, 16th-cent. reformation within the Roman Catholic Church. Frequently called the Counter Reformation by Protestants, but Catholics object to the term on the grounds that reform had begun within the Church before the first rumblings of the Reformation and that Protestantism, with its aim of destroying the old Church organization, is entirely different from the Counter Reform with its aim of removing abuses within the organization. Those abuses were mainly simony (buying and selling of church offices and favors and even sometimes of purely spiritual things, such as indulgences), worldliness and corruption of the higher clergy, ignorance on the part of the lower clergy, and general apathy toward doctrinal matters and care of the faithful. Some, such as St. Catherine of Siena, had cried out against such abuses in the 14th cent., but quarrels within the Church (notably the Great SCHISM), the heavy hand of kings and princes, and the entrenched position of rich, worldly, and powerful prelates prevented reform; thus Nicholas of Cusa had in 1451 been unable to reform the German church against the opposition of the bishops. The tide of the Renaissance had washed worldly corruption as well as artistic sensibility into the papal court. The reform began with a small group at Rome, with Cardinal Carafa (later Paul IV) and Cardinal CAJETAN at its center, in the late 15th cent. They were supported from abroad by such humanists as Erasmus, St. Thomas More, and Cardinal Jiménez. The first major effort failed with the failure of the Fifth Lateran Council, but reformers were growing in number and forming new orders (Theatines, 1524; Capuchins, 1525) to carry the gospel to the common people just as the storm of the Reformation was breaking. Emperor Charles V helped the reform not only by encouragement but by the sack of Rome by his soldiers (1527), an event that stirred even the most complacent cardinals. In 1534 PAUL III became pope. St. IGNATIUS OF LOYOLA and the Society of JESUS began their work. In 1545 after long delay and preparation the Council of TRENT was convened. This council was the central feature of the Reform under Paul III, Julius III and Pius IV. PAUL IV reformed the papacy itself and instituted the quasi-monastic air that has prevailed at the Vatican since. The council ended in 1563, but its gains were consolidated under St. Pius V, Gregory XIII, and Sixtus V. Simony was uprooted, worship was standardized, the administration of the Church was reorganized, educational requirements for priests were set, the moral life of all the clergy came under scrutiny. The new spirit breathing in the Church was shown by St. Charles Borromeo, St. Philip Neri, St. Theresa of Ávila and St. John of the Cross in Spain, St. Francis of Sales and St. Vincent de Paul in France, the Jesuit missionaries in England (e.g., Edmund Campion, Robert Parsons).

Reformation, religious revolution in Western Europe in 16th cent. beginning as reform movement in Catholic Church, but evolving into doctrines of Protestantism. There had long been outcries against abuses in Church. In 14th cent. John Wyclif had led dissident movement; this was followed by larger reform group of John Huss in Bohemia. Movement was stimulated by growth of Renaissance humanism with its questioning of authority. It was also hastened by invention of printing. In secular affairs conflict between the Church and state (and more particularly in Germany, conflict of princes and emperor), rise of commerce and the middle class were factors. The Reformation itself began when Martin Luther, stirred by Johann Tetzel's campaign for dispensing indulgences, on Oct. 31, 1517, posted his 95 theses on the church door in Wittenberg. Open attack upon doctrines and authority of Church came soon. His defiance of pope led in 1520 to open breach with Church, which Diet of Worms failed to heal. Luther's doctrine of justification by faith alone instead of by sacraments, good works, and mediation of Church, and his insistence on reading Bible gave individual a greater responsibility for his own salvation. The new faith met widespread acceptance, and revolt spread rapidly in Germany and beyond. Quarrel with Church and the emperor was long and bitter, unresolved by Diets of Speyer (1526, 1529) and Diet of Augsburg (1530). A temporary and ineffective settlement, the Augsburg Interim (1548) was followed by the more stable Peace of Augsburg (1555) but conflict went on later. Within Protestant movement many differences arose, as in doctrinal arguments on the Lord's Supper, debated inconclusively at Colloquy of Marburg (1529) by Luther and Melanchthon with Oecolampadius and Zwingli. Radical social and religious ideas were spread by the Anabaptists, and such leaders as Carlstadt, Thomas Münzer, and John of Leiden. Most important of all, in 1536 Geneva became the center for teachings of John Calvin, greatest theologian of Reformation. His influence was enormous. In France, Huguenots, fired by his doctrine, resisted Catholic majority until Henry IV issued Edict of Nantes in 1598. Calvinism superseded Lutheranism in Netherlands. It conquered Scotland through victory of John Knox over Mary Queen of Scots. Both Calvinism and Lutheranism came into conflict with Evangelicalism. In England, Henry VIII signed the Act of Supremacy (1534), rejecting papal control and creating Church of England. But Calvinistic and Evangelical thought were strong in England and influenced course of Reformation there, notably in Puritanism. On the Continent, divisions in Protestant churches served to forward counterrevolution within Catholic Church with some recovery of lost ground. The Peace of Westphalia (1648) brought stabilization after the exhaustion of war. This marks the end of the period of the Reformation, but Protestantism, born of it, has been a basic force in the Western world to the present day.

Reform Bills, in English history, name given to five measures liberalizing representation in House of Commons. System had not changed after time of Elizabeth despite population shifts and rise of new social classes in Industrial Revolution. Corruption and sale of seats flourished. **Reform Bill of 1832,** passed by Earl Grey's Whig ministry, redistributed seats in interest of larger communities; gave franchise to middle-class men. **Reform Bill of 1867,** enacted by Benjamin Disraeli, gave franchise to workingmen in the towns; more than doubled electorate. **Reform Bill of 1884,** passed by William Gladstone, reduced rural qualifications; added 2,000,000 voters. Last two bills (1918, 1928) are usually called REPRESENTATION OF THE PEOPLE ACTS.

Reformed churches, in general sense, all Protestant churches stemming from Reformation; in particular, those having origin in Calvinism, as distinct from those that are Lutheran or Evangelical.

Reformed Church in America, better known as Dutch Reformed Church, founded in colonial times by Dutch Protestant settlers. Reformed Church in Holland grew in 16th cent. from Calvinistic Reformation. In 1571 the synod at Emden adopted presbyterian polity and formulated liturgical worship, with Belgic Confession of Faith (1561) and Heidelberg Catechism (1563). In America, congregation was formed in New Amsterdam in 1628. In 1754 assembly declared itself independent of Classis of Amsterdam. In 1766 charter was secured for Queens Col. (now Rutgers Univ.). In 1792 constitution was adopted; name became official 1867.

Reformed Church in the United States: see EVANGELICAL AND REFORMED CHURCH.

Reformed Episcopal Church, formed 1873 by group who withdrew from Protestant Episcopal Church because of ritualistic dissensions.

Reformed Presbyterianism: see CAMERON, RICHARD.

refraction, in physics, bending of light ray, sound wave, or heat ray away from original direction when passing from medium of one density into that of another. No bending occurs if the ray enters surface at right angles. Light travels with greater velocity in some media than in others; front of wave is flat and at right angles to direction it is following; e.g., when light traveling through air strikes glass at oblique angle, under part of ray entering glass first is slowed first and turns from original direction; upper part follows same direction as lower part. When passing from less to more dense medium, ray is bent toward normal (perpendicular to surface). A constant ratio exists between the velocities of light in two given media. This ratio is called index of refraction or refractive index for the two media.

refrigeration, the act of drawing heat away from solids or liquids to lower their temperatures, generally for purposes of preservation. Most systems of refrigeration are based on the principle that heat is absorbed from the surrounding area when a solid is liquefied (ice melting), or a liquid changed into gas, or when compressed air is permitted to expand. Ammonia, carbon dioxide, and sulphur dioxide are widely used as refrigerants. These become, in a constantly alternating evaporation and condensation process, part of a sealed system kept in motion through electricity or gas apparatus. For example, an electric motor is used to exert pressure on ammonia before it moves into the coils of the refrigeration compartment. As the ammonia changes to its gaseous form heat is drawn to the coils. The motor then acts to compress the gas issuing from the coils, rendering it liquid for its passage back into the coils. A development of the preservation of foods by refrigeration is preparation of frozen foods.

Refugio (rĭfū'ēō), town (pop. 4,666), S Texas, on Mission R. and NNE of Corpus Christi; settled 1829. Previously estab. Spanish mission moved here 1795. Taken by Mexicans in Texas Revolution, 1836, and again briefly in invasion of 1842. Bells of present R.C. church, from original mission, were taken and returned by Mexicans.

regatta (rĭgä'tù), series of rowing or other boating races. Royal Henley Regatta, most famous race for eight-oared boats, is held annually on the Thames. First was held 1839. In U.S., Poughkeepsie Regatta was held annually 1895–1949; since 1950 it has been held at other sites.

Regence style (rē'jŭns), in French architecture and decoration, was prevalent during regency (1715–23) of Philippe II, duc d'Orléans. Retaining the restraint and symmetry of Louis XIV style, it introduced curved lines and intricate motifs (e.g., shells) that were to be developed later in rococo design. Leaders in creating the style were Boulle, Cressent, J. A. Meissonier, Boucher, and Watteau.

Regency, in British history, the last nine years (1811–

20) of reign of George III when, due to his periodic insanity, government was conducted in name of Prince of Wales (later George IV). The rise of Tories like Lord Castlereagh accompanied reform agitation of such men as Jeremy Bentham and William Cobbett. Social color was given by gay and dissolute group around the prince regent. There was a flowering of arts, letters, and architecture.

Regency style, in English architecture, flourished during regency and reign of George IV (1811–30) and was represented mainly by John NASH. Stucco was widely used. Effect of simplicity was achieved by flat painted surfaces, elegant Greek ornament, glazed casement doors, and flat, partitioned bay windows. Balconies (popular for first time in England) were usually supported by slender columns or brackets. Characteristic buildings are town houses on Regent's Park terraces.

Regensburg (rā'gŭnzbûrg, rä'gŭnsbŏŏrk), city (pop. 116,997), cap. of Upper Palatinate, E Bavaria, on the Danube; in English, also known as Ratisbon. River port; mfg. center (precision instruments; printing; brewing). Was important Roman frontier station (Regina Castra); became episcopal see 739; free imperial city 1245–1803; permanent seat of diet of Holy Roman Empire 1663–1803. Flourished as medieval trade center; accepted Reformation 16th cent.; passed to Bavaria 1810. Last diet (1801–3) prepared liquidation of Holy Roman Empire. Its final resolution (tersely named *Reichsdeputationshauptschluss*) secularized the ecclesiastic principalities and "mediatized" most of the petty princes—gave their lands to the larger states but left them their titles. Though severely bombed in World War II, city retains its fine medieval cathedral, churches, and city hall.

Reger, Max (rā'gùr), 1873–1916, German composer, pianist, and conductor. His complicated technique has kept his music from becoming generally popular. His best-known works are for organ. He also wrote a symphony, sonatas, concertos, and chamber music.

Reggio di Calabria (rĕd'jō dē kälä'brēä), city (pop. 60,-342), cap. of Calabria, S Italy, on Strait of Messina.

Reggio nell' Emilia (nĕl' lämē'lyä), city (pop. 49,069), Emilia-Romagna, N central Italy, on Aemilian Way. Agr. trade center. Passed to Este family 1289 and became part of duchy of Modena. Birthplace of Ariosto.

regicides (rĕ'jīsīdz) [Latin,= king-killers], name given to judges and court officers responsible for trial and execution of Charles I of England. After Restoration (1660) 10 regicides were condemned to death and 25 to life imprisonment. Some escaped.

Regina (rĭjī'nù), city (pop. 71.319), provincial cap., S Sask., Canada, SE of Saskatoon; founded 1882. Principal trade and rail center of province with stockyards, oil refineries, and auto-assembly, meat-packing, woodworking, and printing plants. Western hq. of Canadian Royal Mounted Police. Cap. of Northwest Territories 1883–1905.

Regiomontanus (rē"jēōmŏn"tā'nùs), 1436–76, German astronomer and mathematician; original name Johannes Müller. Improved instruments and methods of observation and calculation.

Régnier, Henri de (ārē' dù ränyä'), 1864–1936, French poet, a leader of the young SYMBOLISTS.

Regulator movement, organized (1768) by small farmers of W N.C. to protest oppressive local government. Unjust taxation and extortion by officials were chief grievances. Unable to secure legal relief, they resorted to violence. Routed in battle by militia, May 16, 1771; leaders were executed and movement collapsed.

Regulus, Marcus Atilius (rĕ'gyōōlùs), d. c.250 B.C., Roman general. After some successes in the First Punic War he led an expedition to Africa that ended in his defeat and capture. It is said that he was sent with Carthaginian envoys to seek peace but instead bravely urged the senate to go on with the war and to refuse exchange of prisoners. He honored his parole, returned to Carthage, and was tortured to death.

rehabilitation, in therapy, restoration of maximum physical, mental, and vocational capacities to handicapped persons. It sometimes requires services of physician, surgeon, psychologist, physiotherapist, and social worker; vocational guidance; training for new work or to restore skills. Rehabilitation achieved notable success in the course of World War II.

Rehan, Ada (rē'ùn), 1860–1916, American actress, whose real name was Crehan, b. Ireland. In Daly's company 1879–99, she co-starred with John Drew in French, German, and Shaksperian comedies.

Rehnskiold or **Rehnskjold, Karl Gustaf,** Swed. *Rehnskiöld* (rän'shûld"), 1651–1722, Swedish field marshal under Charles XII. Won important victories in Poland during Northern War but was outnumbered, defeated, and captured at Poltava (1709), where the wounded king had delegated the command to him.

Rehoboam (rē"ùbō'ùm), d. c.914 B.C., Hebrew king (c.932–c.914 B.C.), son of Solomon. Under him the northern tribes revolted and formed a new kingdom under Jeroboam I, retaining the name Israel. Only Judah and part of Benjamin remained loyal to Rehoboam; these formed a kingdom in the S called Judah. 1 Kings 11.43–12.24; 14.21–31; 2 Chron. 9.31–12.16.

Rehoboth Beach (rĭhō'bùth), Atlantic resort town (pop. 1,794), SE Del., SE of Lewes.

Reichenbach Falls (rī'khùnbäkh), cataract, Bern canton, Switzerland, where the Reichenbach joins Aar R. Name is familiar to readers of A. Conan Doyle. Has hydroelectric project.

Reichenberg, Czechoslovakia: see LIBEREC.

Reichstadt, Napoleon, duke of: see NAPOLEON II.

Reichstag (rīkhs'täk). **1** The DIET of the Holy Roman Empire (until 1806). **2** The lower chamber of the federal parliament of Germany, 1871–1945. The upper chamber, called Bundesrat in imperial Germany (1871–1918) and Reichsrat under the Weimar Republic (1919–34), represented the member states, whereas the Reichstag was elected by direct suffrage and represented the country at large. When Hitler became chancellor (Jan., 1933), he lacked an absolute majority in the Reichstag. As a result, Pres. Hindenburg ordered new elections (as was his constitutional right). On Feb. 27 a carefully planned fire broke out in the Reichstag building in Berlin. Hitler immediately accused the Communists of setting the fire; yet, despite his terrorist measures, the elections of March 5 still gave him no absolute majority. Only after he had expelled the 81 Communist deputies from the Reichstag could he muster a majority to vote him dictatorial powers (March 23). The sensational Reichstag fire trial ended with the conviction and beheading of Marinus van der Lubbe (1933). The other defendants, all Communists (incl. Georgi Dimitrov and Ernst Torgler), were acquitted. It is almost certain that the fire was actually instigated by the Nazis, notably Goering, who used Van der Lubbe as their tool. Under the Hitler regime, only the National Socialist Party was represented in the Reichstag, which was summoned merely to ratify major government decisions. The Reichsrat was abolished 1934. After 1949 the Reichstag was replaced in W Germany by a federal diet or Bundestag, in E Germany by a "people's chamber" (1949).

Reichstein, Tadeus, 1897–, Swiss chemist. Shared 1950 Nobel Prize in Physiology and Medicine for work on the chemistry of the hormone cortisone and other secretions of the adrenal glands.

Reid, (Thomas) Mayne, 1818–83, British novelist. Came to the U.S. in 1840 and had adventures reflected in his stories for boys.

Reid, Robert, 1862–1929, American figure and mural painter, a noted teacher.

Reid, Thomas, 1710–96, Scottish philosopher, teacher at King's College, Aberdeen, and Univ. of Glasgow. The leader of the common-sense school, he held that we know the objects of the external world directly and in their true sense because such knowledge is self-evident. He based morality on conscience, the intuitive moral sense.

Reid, Whitelaw, 1837–1912, American journalist and diplomat. Distinguished himself as Civil War correspondent of Cincinnati *Gazette.* Made managing editor of New York *Tribune* (1868), he later gained full control. Was minister to France (1889–92), ambassador to England (1905–12).

Reidsville, city (pop. 11,708), N N.C., NNE of Greensboro; settled c.1815. Cigarette mfg. center.

Reigate (rī′gĭt), municipal borough (pop. 42,234), Surrey, England; residential suburb of London. Has vestiges of an old castle with caves beneath it.

Reign of Terror, 1793–94, culminating phase of the FRENCH REVOLUTION, when France was under the dictatorship of the Committee of Public Safety (incl. ROBESPIERRE, COUTHON, SAINT-JUST, Lazare CARNOT). Its measures were aimed at routing out counterrevolutionary elements (Law of Suspects, carried out by Committee of General Security and by Revolutionary Tribunal, brought c.2,500 persons to the guillotine); at raising new armies by universal conscription; and at preventing run-away inflation through maximum price and wage laws. After ousting the GIRONDISTS, the JACOBINS held the sole power; Robespierre's purges of his own party (e.g., of DANTON and HÉBERT) eventually goaded the Convention into overthrowing his dictatorship (9 THERMIDOR).

Reims, France: see RHEIMS.

Reinach, Salomon (sälômō′ rĕnäk′), 1858–1932, French archaeologist, one of first to relate archaeology and anthropology. Wrote history of religion, *Orpheus* (1909; rev. Eng. ed., 1933), and history of art, *Apollo* (1904; rev. Eng. ed., 1935).

reindeer, gregarious, migratory mammal (*Rangifer*) of deer family, found in arctic and subarctic regions. Both sexes have antlers. Reindeer was early domesticated from CARIBOU and provides meat, milk, clothing, and transportation.

Reindeer Lake, 2,444 sq. mi., NE Sask. and NW Man., Canada. Many islands. Outlet is Reindeer R.

reindeer moss, low-growing LICHEN (*Cladonia rangiferina*) of arctic regions, a chief food of reindeer and caribou.

Reinhardt, Max (mäks′ rīn′härt), 1873–1943, Austrian theatrical director, whose real name was Goldmann. A great innovator, he was a master of spectacle. Made Salzburg Festivals a world theatrical center after World War I. Forced to flee Germany (1933), he became a U.S. citizen in 1940.

Réjane (räzhän′), 1857–1920, stage name of Gabrielle Réju, French actress. Versatile and vivacious, she appeared notably in Sardou's *Mme Sans-Gêne.*

relativity, theory in physics, introduced by Einstein, which discards the concept of time and space as absolute entities and views them as relative to moving frames of reference. Einstein enunciated (1905) the special relativity theory. Included among its assertions and consequences are the propositions that the maximum velocity attainable is that of light; that mass appears to increase with velocity; that mass and energy are equivalent and interchangeable; that events which appear simultaneous to observer in one system may not seem so to observer in another system and that both may be correct since absolute time cannot be measured and must therefore be excluded from physical reasoning. Physical realities cannot be visualized, but may be represented mathematically in a four-dimensional geometry of space time. Einstein extended the theory into a general theory (completed c.1916) applicable also to systems in nonuniform motion. This recognizes the equivalence of gravitation and inertia and asserts that material bodies produce curvatures in space that form a gravitational field. In 1950 Einstein presented a unified field theory, as yet unevaluated, which applies also to subatomic and electromagnetic phenomena.

Religion, Wars of, 1562–98, series of civil wars in France. Ostensibly a struggle between Protestants (see HUGUENOTS) and Catholics, the wars were also a contest for power between the crown and the great nobles and among the nobles themselves for control of the king. The Catholics were led by the GUISE family; foremost Protestant leaders were, successively, Louis I de CONDÉ, Gaspard de COLIGNY, and Henry of Navarre (after 1589 HENRY IV of France). A third party, the *Politiques* (moderate Catholics) sided with the Protestants, while CATHERINE DE' MEDICI and her sons CHARLES IX and HENRY III vainly sought to estab. a balance of power. The wars were marked by fanatic cruelty on both sides. The first three wars (1562–63, 1567–68, 1568–70) ended favorably for the Protestants. The massacre of SAINT BARTHOLOMEW'S DAY started off the fourth war (1572–73). The fifth war (1574–76) ended with the Edict of Beaulieu, granting freedom of worship throughout France except in Paris. The Catholics now formed the LEAGUE. After a sixth war (1577), the Edict of Beaulieu was confirmed, but Henry failed to carry it out. The seventh war (1580) was inconsequential, but in 1585 Henry of Navarre's nomination as heir presumptive to Henry III precipitated the War of the Three Henrys (see HENRY III; HENRY IV; Henri, 3d duc de GUISE). After Henry IV's accession (1589), the League invoked Spanish aid. Henry defeated the League and entered Paris in 1594. The Treaty of VERVINS with Spain and the Edict of NANTES restored peace in 1598.

relocation center, in U.S. history. War Relocation Authority, created March, 1942, enabled army to move all persons of Japanese ancestry from defined area on West Coast to ten relocation centers in Western states. After July, 1943, loyal persons were released to live anywhere except in proscribed area. Many young men left centers to serve in the army. In Dec., 1944, mass exclusion orders were revoked. War Relocation Authority was terminated 1946.

Remarque, Erich Maria (ā′rĭkh märē′ä rümärk′), 1897–, German novelist. His fame rests mainly on his first novel, *All Quiet on the Western Front* (1929), a bitter antiwar story. He fled the Nazis and became an American citizen in 1947.

Rembrandt (Harmenszoon van Rijn or **Ryn)** (rĕm′bränt, –bränt), 1606–69, celebrated Dutch painter and etcher, b. Leiden. In 1631 he moved to Amsterdam, where he became the most popular painter of his day. In 1634 he married the wealthy Saskia van Uylenburgh, who bore him four children, only one of whom, Titus, survived. To this period belong such canvases as *Portrait of an Old Woman* (Natl. Gall., London), which show the golden tone and bold brushwork of his most characteristic work. After Saskia's death in 1642, he painted the *Sortie of the Banning Cocq Company* (Rijks Mus.), which brought his downfall as a popular portraitist. It was derisively called *The Night Watch* because of its departure from convention in focusing strong light only on a few central figures, leaving the others in shadow. Declared bankrupt in 1657, he was supported in his last years by Titus and his housekeeper, Hendrickje Stoffles. Many fine self-portraits were done in his last period of poverty and retirement. The famous *Lesson in Anatomy* (the Hague) was painted in his early period. In addition to c.700 paintings, he produced a vast number of superb etchings.

Remington, Eliphalet (ĭlĭ′fŭlĭt), 1793–1861, American inventor and gunsmith. His firearms factory, estab. c.1828, at Ilion, N.Y., was expanded 1856 to make agr. implements. Directed after 1861 by his son **Philo Remington,** 1816–89. He became a pioneer typewriter manufacturer after 1873.

Remington, Frederic, 1861–1909, American sculptor and painter of subjects drawn from life in the West.

Remonstrants, Dutch Protestants, adherents to ideas of Jacobus Arminius, known later as Arminianism. Under Simon Episcopius they practiced modified Calvinism as set forth in the "Remonstrance." Synod of Dort (1618–19) condemned the Remonstrants, but ban was lifted in 1625. Group was recognized 1795 as independent church.

Remscheid (rĕm′shīt), industrial city (pop. 102,929), North Rhine-Westphalia, W Germany, on the Wupper, adjoining Solingen and Wuppertal. Tool and toolmachines; steel; textiles. Heavily damaged in World War II.

Remus, in Roman legend, twin of ROMULUS.

Renaissance (rĕnùsäns′, –zäns′) [Fr.,= rebirth], period of transition from medieval to modern times. Though term may denote chronological period (14th–16th cent.), it more often designates cultural and intellectual currents that began in 14th cent. in Italy, where it reached highest flower in 15th and 16th cent. From Italy Renaissance spread to France, Spain, Germany, Low Countries, England, and rest of Europe. Italian Renaissance culminated under patronage of MEDICI at Florence, of SFORZA at Milan, of Renaissance popes at Rome, of ESTE at Ferrara, and of GONZAGA at Mantua. Important figures of Italian Renaissance were LEONARDO DA VINCI, MICHELANGELO, GUICCIARDINI, and MACHIAVELLI. Other great figures of period were ERASMUS, RABELAIS, and MONTAIGNE. Period had far-reaching influence in art and architecture and in formation of modern mind.

Renaissance architecture. The 15th-cent. rebirth of classic architecture in Italy ended the supremacy of the Gothic style. Façades and interiors, rather than structure, became the important elements. Three periods of the Italian Renaissance can be seen: early (c.1420–c.1500), with its chief centers at Florence (its birthplace), Milan, and Venice; high, or classic (c.1500–c.1580), with Rome as the center; and late, or BAROQUE and ROCOCO (c.1580–c.1780). The great designers of the early period were Brunelleschi, Alberti, and Bramante. The second period began roughly with Bramante's later works, notably SAINT PETER'S CHURCH, which made full use of the classical orders of architecture and show a deeper understanding of the monumental Roman works of the classic period. To bigness of scale the baroque architects (notably BERNINI) of the last period added a theatrical character, giving the classic details a bold sense of movement. Introduced into France, the style passed through three general phases: early (c.1490–c.1547), in which Renaissance details were mingled with Gothic elements; classical (c.1547–c.1610), in which the LOUVRE was begun; and the LOUIS PERIOD STYLES (c.1610–1793). In the 16th cent. the style was adopted in Germany, Spain, and England (where Inigo JONES became its chief exponent).

Renaissance art was the natural outgrowth of the new humanism which replaced medieval thought. Based on classic forms, it developed first and most fully in Italy. The period saw the important development of perspective and of modeling in light and shadow, which replaced the medieval over-all brightness. Italian Renaissance developed three periods (see RENAISSANCE ARCHITECTURE). Florence was the great center of many Renaissance masters, including Giotto, Fra Angelico, Leonardo da Vinci, Botticelli, and Michelangelo. Siena, Venice, Rome (where Raphael did much of his work), and other Italian cities also developed important schools. With Charles VIII's expedition to Naples, Renaissance influences penetrated into France. Francis I imported Italian artists, and Henry II's marriage to Catherine de' Medici strengthened Italian prestige. Renaissance France was most active in the minor arts (esp. glass and miniature painting). Filtering into Spain in late 15th cent. the style assumed a definitely native character in the early 16th cent. Under Renaissance influences the Low Countries produced such masters as the Van Eyck brothers, Roger van der Weyden, and Rubens. The Renaissance spirit had relatively little effect on the contemporary art of England and Germany.

Renan, Ernest (ĕrnĕst′ rŭnä′), 1823–92, French historian and critic, apostle of the scientific approach to history, religion, and literature. Among his best-known works are *L'Avenir de la science* (1890) and *Life of Jesus* (Vol. I of *The History of the Origins of Christianity,* 8 vols., 1863–83).

Renault, Louis (lwē′ rŭnō′), 1843–1918, French jurist, professor of international law at Univ. of Paris. Sat on Hague Tribunal, helped advance international arbitration. Shared 1907 Nobel Peace Prize with E. T. Moneta.

René (rŭnä′), 1409–80, titular king of Naples, of the ANGEVIN dynasty; younger son of Louis II. By marriage, he became count of Bar and duke of Lorraine. In 1434 he inherited Anjou and Provence from his brother, LOUIS III of Naples, and was adopted as heir by Queen JOANNA II of Naples (d. 1435). He was defeated (1438) by his rival claimant, Alfonso V of Aragon, and retired to Angers, later to Tarascon, where he devoted himself to poetry, painting, and pastoral games, bringing medieval Provençal culture to a last flowering. He made Lorraine and Bar over to his son John in 1452 and left Anjou to Louis XI of France. Provence and his claim to Naples passed first to his nephew Charles, duke of Maine (d. 1486), then to the French crown. His daughter, Margaret of Anjou, married Henry VI of England.

Renewed Church of the Brethren: see MORAVIAN CHURCH.

Renfrew (rĕn′frŏŏ), town (pop. 7,360), S Ont., Canada, on Bonnechere R. and W of Ottawa. Woolen mills, wood works, mfg. of metal products.

Renfrewshire or **Renfrew,** county (227 sq. mi.; pop. 324,652), SW Scotland, on the Clyde estuary. One of smallest but most populous Scottish counties, it is a hilly region with rich mineral deposits. Important industrial area, it has mfg. (sugar, chemicals, textiles, and whisky; coal mining, shipbuilding, and shale quarrying. County town is **Renfrew,** burgh (pop. 17,-093), one of oldest Clyde R. ports and site of Glasgow's airport.

Reni, Guido: see GUIDO RENI.

Rennes (rĕn), city (pop. 102,617), cap. of Ille-et-Vilaine dept., NW France, on Ille and Vilaine rivers; historic cap. of Brittany. Varied mfg.; archiepiscopal see; university (founded 1735). Seat of a powerful provincial parlement before French Revolution. Damaged in World War II. Notable buildings include 17th-cent. palace of justice, 18th-cent. cathedral.

rennet (rĕ′nĭt), substance containing rennin, an enzyme that curdles milk. It is obtained from stomachs of young milk-feeding mammals and is made and sold commercially. It is used in making cheese. Heat interferes with its action.

Reno, city (pop. 32,497), W Nev., on Truckee R. near L. Tahoe. Site was camping place on Donner Pass route to Calif. in pioneer days. Town laid out as Reno in 1868 when railroad came. Largest city in Nev., it is shipping center for cattle, minerals, and farm produce. Crisp climate, resort facilities, legalized gambling, and quick and easy divorces keep Reno prosperous. Has annual rodeo. Seat of Univ. of Nevada (land-grant, state supported; coed.; opened 1874), which includes Mackay School of Mines.

Renoir, Pierre Auguste (rŭnwär′), 1841–1919, French painter, an outstanding master of the French school. Began working at age of 13 as decorator of porcelain in a Paris factory. In 1862 he entered Gleyre's art school, where he met Cézanne, Monet, and Sisley. Lived in extreme poverty until 1870, when portrait commissions brought him some prosperity. After 1890 he lived in Provence. Especially famous for pictures of women and children and for nude figure compositions, all characterized by lyrical quality, lovely color, and rhythmic line. He is often grouped with the postimpressionists.

Renouvier, Charles Bernard (rŭnōōvyä′), 1815–1903, French philosopher. He tried to meld some of the ideas of Comte's positivism and Kant's idealism (though he rejected Kant's doctrines of the unknowable and the infinite).

Rensselaer (rĕnsŭlēr', rĕn'sŭlŭr), city (pop. 10,856), E N.Y., on E bank of Hudson R. (bridged) opposite Albany; settled by Dutch in 17th cent. Mfg. of textile products and chemicals. *Yankee Doodle* was supposedly written at Fort Crailo.

Rensselaer Polytechnic Institute, at Troy, N.Y.; nonsectarian, for men; founded 1824 by Stephen Van Rensselaer, opened 1825, chartered 1826 to give degrees. University courses in architecture, business administration, engineering, science. Pioneer technical school. Granted first U.S. engineering degrees (1835).

rent, in law, the amount that a tenant is required to pay for use of another's property. In economics, however, it has a broader, more complex meaning—any income or yield from an object capable of producing wealth (e.g., land, tools, machinery). Early English writers on economics (16th–18th cent.) used the word also to mean interest on a loan. Modern rent doctrine began with the physiocrats and Adam Smith. There have been many and contradictory theories.

Renton, city (pop. 16,039), W Wash., near L. Washington, SE of Seattle. Produces aircraft, coal, clay products, timber, poultry, and truck.

Renwick, James, 1818–95, American architect, who designed St. Patrick's Cathedral, New York.

reparations, payments imposed by victorious on defeated nations as indemnity for material losses in war. After World War I, a reparations commission fixed the sum to be paid by Germany to the Allies (excluding the U.S., which waived its claims) at 132,000,000,000 gold marks, partly payable in kind. When Germany fell behind in its payments, the Allies took the stand that they could not honor their WAR DEBTS to the U.S.—a view not shared by the U.S. Attempted solutions to the problem were the Dawes Plan (1924), by which Germany received a foreign loan and undertook to pay 1,000,000,000 gold marks yearly in reparations; and the Young Plan (1929), which eased the annuities, sought to secure their payment by mortgaging the German state railways, and estab. Bank for Internatl. Settlements at Basel. The economic world crisis led in 1931 to a one-year moratorium on all intergovernmental debts, proposed by Pres. Hoover; reparations payments were never resumed. In World War II the principles of reparation payments by Germany were worked out in the Yalta and Potsdam conferences (1945). The USSR was to receive 50%, of which 15% was to go to Poland; Great Britain and the U.S. were to distribute the rest among the other claimants. Payments were to be effected through removal of assets and equipment. Soviet authorities dismantled German industries on a large scale (as they also did with Austrian and Manchurian plants); in W Germany, Allied measures to collect reparations were fitful. Disagreement over the settlement of reparations was a factor in the split between the USSR and the Western Powers. Reparations varying from $125,000,000 to $360,000,000 were also imposed on Bulgaria, Finland, Hungary, Italy, and Rumania; the U.S., France, and Britain claimed no part of these.

repartimiento (räpärtēmyĕn'tō), a Spanish system of distribution of lands, goods, and services of conquered peoples to conquerors. Introduced in Spanish America at beginning of conquest, system became core of peonage in New Spain and *mita* in Peru. See also ENCOMIENDA.

replacement series: see METAL.

Repplier, Agnes (rĕ'plēr), 1855–1950, American essayist, noted for scholarly, keen, and witty social criticism. Also wrote biographies, historical studies.

Representation of the People Acts, enacted by British Parliament to extend the franchise reform begun by REFORM BILLS. **Representation of the People Act of 1918** gave vote to most men of 21 or over; to women

over 30. **Representation of the People Act of 1928** gave vote to all women on same terms as men. Later acts of 1948 and 1949 made minor changes.

Representatives, House of: see CONGRESS OF THE UNITED STATES.

reproduction, a fundamental function of all living things, the production of new individuals by other individuals. Varies widely in method and complexity; two main types are asexual (production of offspring by one individual) and sexual (involving two individuals). Asexual reproduction is common in plants, but in animals is found only in some lower organisms. Simplest form of process is division (fission) of single cell, followed by reorganization of material in each part. Sexual type involves union of two cells to form a third cell capable of developing into new organism; if two cells are of like nature, it is called conjugation; if unlike, it is FERTILIZATION. Sexual cells in higher animals and plants are distinguished as OVUM and SPERM.

reptile (rĕp'tŭl, –tīl), member of the class of cold-blooded and lung-breathing vertebrate animals called Reptilia, ranking higher than amphibians and lower than birds and mammals. Reptiles are covered by scales, bony plates, or horny shells. Probably appeared in Carboniferous era.

Repton, town and parish (pop. 1,518), Derbyshire, England; site of Repton School (1557) for boys.

republic, a sovereign state ruled by representatives of a widely inclusive electorate. The U.S. exemplifies a federal republic whose central government is restricted in power. In the French republic, power is centralized, and constituent regions are permitted to perform only limited functions.

Republican, river, 422 mi. long, formed in S Nebr. and flowing E across Nebr. and SE across Kansas to join Smoky Hill R. and form the Kansas at Junction City. Included in several units of the Missouri river basin project.

Republican party, in U.S. history, name first used by Thomas Jefferson's party, later called Democratic Republican party or, simply, Democratic party. Name reappeared when the Republican party of today was founded in 1854. Party opposed extension of slavery. Election of Abraham Lincoln, Republican candidate, in 1860, brought about secession of Southern states. Republican radicals (e.g., Thaddeus STEVENS) opposed Andrew Johnson's moderate RECONSTRUCTION program. Their excesses under Pres. Grant and the open scandals of his administration created a new schism (see LIBERAL REPUBLICAN PARTY). In disputed election of 1876 Republican candidate R. B. Hayes was successful, but Republican domination of the South and radical rule of party ended with that election. The MUGWUMPS illustrated the lack of real issues between Republicans and Democrats in period after 1876. Party became champion of gold standard and conservative economic doctrines in late 19th cent. Many party INSURGENTS supported Theodore ROOSEVELT and the new PROGRESSIVE PARTY in 1912. Republican opposition was a large factor in defeating peace program of Democrat Woodrow Wilson. Republicans were blamed for disastrous economic depression that began in the administration of Herbert HOOVER. Led by Sen. A. H. Vandenberg, party joined Democratic administration in a bipartisan foreign policy after World War II. Victory in 1952 of party candidate, Dwight D. Eisenhower, returned presidency to Republican hands after 20 years of Democratic rule.

requiem (rĕ'kwēŭm) [Latin,= rest; from the first words of the introit, "Eternal rest grant unto them"], proper MASS for the souls of the dead, performed on All Souls' Day, at funerals, and in other Masses for the dead. The sequence is the DIES IRAE. Vestments are black. Among modern musical settings for the Mass are those of Mozart and Verdi.

Resaca de la Palma (räsä'kä dä lä päl'mä), valley, an

abandoned bed of the Rio Grande, N of Brownsville, Texas, where second battle of Mexican War was fought, May 9, 1846. U.S. forces under Gen. Zachary Taylor won victory.

reservoir (rĕ′zŭrvôr, –vwär), storage tank for water or a wholly or partly artificial lake for water supply. Use of dam to preserve water for irrigation arose in ancient times. In building reservoirs for water supply, factors to be considered include all aspects of CATCH-MENT AREA. Some reservoirs are built to insure water supply for hydroelectric plants, to aid flood control, or to maintain water level for navigation (esp. on canals).

residence: see DOMICILE.

resin (rĕ′zĭn), any of a class of amorphous solids, yellowish to brown in color, tasteless and odorless or slightly aromatic, translucent and sometimes transparent, brittle, and inflammable. Chemical composition varies but all contain carbon, hydrogen, oxygen. There are many kinds, classified by source or qualities. Natural resins are found as exudations from trees or from insects or as fossils. Among the natural resins are copaiba, turpentine, benzoin, Canada balsam, dragon's blood, frankincense, mastic. Resins are used mostly in varnish, shellac, lacquer; medicines; material for molded articles; electric insulators; phonograph records; radio parts. Synthetic resins (see PLASTICS) are used in varnishes and for great variety of molded articles.

resorcinol (rĭzôr′sĭnōl) or **resorcin** (–sĭn), colorless, sweetish, crystalline substance made from benzene. Used to make dyes and medicines.

Respighi, Ottorino (ôt″tōrē′nō räspē′gē), 1879–1936, Italian composer. His outstanding works are the romantic tone poems *The Fountains of Rome, The Pines of Rome,* and *Roman Festivals.* He also wrote operas, suites, songs, and chamber music.

respiration, process by which air enters plant or animal body, oxygen is absorbed by cells in which oxidation occurs, and carbon dioxide and water are expelled. In man, combined action of inspiration and expiration occurs about 18 times per minute when body is at rest. Blood absorbs oxygen in lungs and distributes it through body.

respiratory tract, air passages consisting of nasal passages, pharynx, larynx, windpipe, two bronchi with terminal branches (bronchioles) connecting with air sacs in lungs. See *ill.,* p. 595.

restaurant, an establishment serving food to the public. In inns of 16th-cent. England, a common table served all comers; such dining rooms, early called "ordinaries," became popular gathering places, particularly in London. The name restaurant was first used c.1765 for a Paris place serving light ("restoring") dishes. Delmonico's, opened c.1834, was New York city's first modern restaurant, as distinct from inns. Peculiar to U.S. is the self-service cafeteria.

Restif de la Bretonne, Nicolas Edme (nēkôlä′ ĕd′mù rĕstēf′ dù lä brütôn′), 1734–1806, French author of some 250 novels, mostly based on incidents of his own rather libertine life and characterized by detailed realism. *Le Paysan perverti* (1775) is among the best-known.

Restigouche (rĕstĭgōōsh′), river, E Canada, rising in NW N.B. and flowing 130 mi. NE, ENE to Chaleur Bay at Dalhousie. Lower course is Que.–N.B. line.

Restoration, in English history, the reestab. of monarchy on accession (1660) of CHARLES II. Period extends to fall of JAMES II in 1688. Death of Oliver Cromwell was followed by reaction against Puritan and military control in favor of recall of exiled king. After his return power went first to earl of Clarendon, then to the Cabal. All remaining military republicans and Quakers were persecuted; militant Anglicanism was restored. Unwillingness of both kings to accept financial dependence on Parliament was one cause of James II's deposition in Glorious Revolution. Period was marked by advance in colonization and trade,

by Dutch Wars, by birth of Whig and Tory parties, by opposition to Catholics, and by the revival of drama and poetry.

Restoration, in French history, the period from abdication of Napoleon I (1814) to July Revolution (1830). Includes reigns of LOUIS XVIII (interrupted by HUNDRED DAYS) and of CHARLES X.

resurrection [from Latin,= arising again], arising again from death to life. In Christian theology, the resurrection of Jesus from the tomb (celebrated at Easter) to dwell on earth 40 days before ascending to heaven is a cornerstone of Christian experience. It guaranteed His mission and promised the resurrection of all men. The doctrine of the resurrection of the body has been variously interpreted. Most Christians hold that on Judgment Day the souls of men will be rejoined with their risen (but glorified and incorruptible) bodies. Myths of resurrection of gods and heroes are common in pagan mythologies and are often associated with the change of seasons (see FERTILITY RITES).

resurrectionists: see BODY SNATCHING.

Reszke, Jean de (jän dù rĕ′skē), 1850–1925, Polish operatic tenor and teacher; known for both lyric and Wagnerian roles. He was leading tenor of the Metropolitan Opera, New York, 1891–1901. His brother, **Edouard de Reszke,** 1855–1917, was a leading bass at the Metropolitan Opera, 1891–1903.

Rethel (rùtĕl′), town (pop. 4,482), Ardennes dept., N France, on Aisne R. Scene of heavy fighting in both world wars. The county of Rethel, held by the house of Burgundy from 1384 and by the cadet branch of Burgundy-Nevers from 1477, was raised to a duchy in 1581 and passed, by marriage, to the Nevers branch of the Gonzaga family. The Mazarin family bought the ducal title in 1663 from the Gonzagas.

retriever: see HUNTING DOGS.

Retz or Rais, Gilles de Laval, seigneur de (zhĕl′ dù lävál′ sānyûr′ dù rĕts′, rĕs′), 1404–40, marshal of France in Hundred Years War. Rumors of satanic doings at his castle led to trial. He confessed to kidnaping, torturing, and killing over 100 children and was executed. Gilles de Retz is supposed by some to be the original of Bluebeard.

Retz, Paul de Gondi, Cardinal de (pôl′ dù gōdē′, dù rĕts′), 1613–79, French cardinal and politician. Was prominent in the FRONDE. His memoirs (1717; Eng. tr., 4 vols., 1723) are among classics of French literature.

Reuben (rōō′bŭn) [Heb.,= behold a son!], Jacob's eldest son, ancestor of one of the 12 tribes of Israel. Tribe settled E of Jordan R. and near the Dead Sea. Gen. 29.32; 35.22; 37; 42.22,37; 46.8; 49.3,4; Num. 1.20,21; 2.10; 26.5–10; 32.37; Joshua 22; 1 Chron. 5.26.

Reuchlin, Johann (yō′hän roikh′lùn), 1455–1522, German humanist, a scholar of Greek and Hebrew. His *Rudimenta Hebraica* (1506) was first Hebrew grammar written by a Christian. When a converted Jew, Johann Pfefferkorn, advocated destruction of all Hebrew books, Reuchlin suggested in return that only those Hebrew books which calumniated Christianity should be suppressed, and that the Jews should be required to furnish books for universities, with two chairs of Hebrew learning to be set up in every university in Germany. In struggle that developed between humanists supporting Reuchlin and clericals supporting Pfefferkorn, Reuchlin was victorious.

Réunion (rāünyō′), island (970 sq. mi.; pop. 242,067), of Mascarene group, in Indian Ocean, an overseas department of France; cap. Saint-Denis. Settled c.1646 by the French and held by the British in Napoleonic Wars. Volcanic and mountainous. Exports sugar and rum. Formerly called Bourbon.

Reuss (rois), two former principalities in E Thuringia, central Germany. House of Reuss dates from 12th cent. Two branches emerged—Reuss Older Line, which held princely rank from 1778 and which had cap. at Greiz, and Reuss Younger Line, which held princely rank from 1806 and had cap. at Gera. Rule was abdicated 1918, and both territories became part of Thuringia 1920.

Reuss (rois), river, 99 mi. long, central Switzerland. Flows N from St. Gotthard Pass, through L. of Lucerne, then joins Aar R.

Reuter, Paul Julius (roi'tŭr), 1816–99, founder of Reuter's Telegraph Co., b. Germany.

Reuther, Walter (Philip) (rōō'thŭr), 1907–, American labor leader, president of United Automobile Workers of America (1946–), president of C.I.O. (1952–). Important anti-Communist liberal spokesman.

Reval, Estonia: see TALLINN.

Revelation or **Apocalypse** (ŭpŏ'kŭlĭps), last book of New Testament, traditionally ascribed to St. John the Disciple. Book is a mysterious prophetic work full of visions of God and the New Jerusalem and dramatic portrayals of the triumph of good over evil. One immediate purpose of Revelation was to encourage Christians faced with martyrdom. Whether the author intended a deeper and more esoteric meaning is greatly debated. The veiled symbolism (e.g., the beast with the number 666, recurrence of the number seven) has been subject to cabalistic explanations in every period of Christian history.

Revelstoke, city (pop. 2,917), SE B.C., Canada, on Columbia R. at mouth of Illecillewaet R. and E of Kamloops. Center of mining and lumbering area, outfitting point for sportsmen and tourists, and gateway to Mt. Revelstoke Natl. Park.

reverberatory furnace, furnace used for separating metal from ore and in refining some metals. Differs from blast furnace chiefly in having separate compartments for burning fuel and for treating material. Used in producing wrought iron from pig and lead from its sulphide ores, and in refining copper.

Revere, Paul, 1735–1818, American Revolutionary patriot. He was a silversmith, designer, and printer. Took part in Boston Tea Party. Remembered for ride, April 18, 1775, to warn Mass. countryside of advance of British soldiers.

Revere, suburban city (pop. 36,763), E Mass., on the coast NE of Boston; settled c.1630; named for Paul Revere. Optical goods, processed foods. Includes Revere Beach, popular resort.

Revillagigedo Island (rŭvĭ'lügŭgĕ'dō), area, 1,120 sq. mi., off SE Alaska, in Alexander Archipelago, E of Prince of Wales Isl. Ketchikan is chief town.

Revillagigedo Islands (rāvĕ'yä-hēhä'dō), archipelago (320 sq. mi.), belonging to Colima, Mexico, in the Pacific, c.400 mi. W of mainland. A new volcano erupted here in 1952.

revival, religious, renewal of religious faith and service in church, community, or district. It is often marked by intense fervor in spiritual expression. Christian revivals began c.1737 in England and Europe with the evangelistic preaching of John and Charles Wesley and George Whitefield. In America simultaneously Great Awakening occurred. Revivals were common on frontier, often in form of a CAMP MEETING. Preeminent figure in modern revivalism was Dwight L. Moody, who with singing evangelist Ira D. Sankey moved audiences for 25 years. Other notable revivalists were Billy Sunday, Gipsy Smith, Aimee Semple McPherson.

revolver, a pistol with a revolving cylinder capable of firing several shots without reloading. An early type appeared in the 16th cent., but usable revolvers were introduced only early in the 19th cent. The first to become a standard weapon was that made by Samuel COLT. The "six-shooter" is said to have civilized the "Wild West."

revue (rĭvū'), stage presentation, originally a light, satirical commentary on current events. Developed, especially in England and U.S., as musical shows (e.g., Ziegfeld's *Follies*) notable for extravagant staging and the display of feminine beauty.

Reyes, Alfonso (älfŏn'sō rā'ās), 1889–, Mexican writer,

notable especially for his superb poetical prose style.

Reykjavik (rā'kyŭvĭk), Icelandic *Reykjavík,* city (pop. 54,707), cap. of Iceland, on Faxa Fjord, SW Iceland; founded 874, chartered 1786. It is Iceland's chief port and fishing and fish-processing center; a Lutheran episcopal see; and seat of a university (founded 1911). At Keflavik (to W) is international airfield, built by U.S. Army in World War II. Hot-water supply system (completed 1945) uses natural hot springs.

Reymont, Ladislaus (Stanislaus) (rā'mônt), Pol. *Władisław Stanisław Reymont,* 1867–1925, Polish novelist. His best-known work is *The Peasants* (4 vols., 1902–9; Eng. tr., 1924–25). Was awarded 1924 Nobel Prize in Literature.

Reynard the Fox (rĕ'nŭrd, rā'närd), hero of medieval beast epics, fables that satirize the upper classes and the clergy. The type of story probably originated in Alsace and Lorraine, but versions of Reynard stories occur in Low German, Dutch and Flemish, High German, Latin, French, and English. There is much dispute as to priority of the versions. Caxton's *Historie of Reynart the Foxe* (1481) was translated from Flemish.

Reynaud, Paul (pôl' rānō'), 1878–, French minister of finance (1938–40) and premier (1940); a conservative. When Marshal Pétain insisted on concluding armistice, Reynaud resigned. One of defendants at RIOM trial, he was imprisoned by Germans until 1945.

Reynolds, Sir Joshua, 1723–92, celebrated English portrait painter. His career was advanced by his social gifts no less than his artistic talent; the wide circle he entertained included the great literary figures of the day, and he was known for his eloquence as first president of the Royal Acad. Employing assistants, he painted c.2,000 portraits and historical paintings. His works are notable for richness of color; in design he surpassed his rivals Gainsborough and Romney. One of his masterpieces, *Mrs. Siddons as the Tragic Muse,* is in the Huntington Gall., San Marino, Calif.

Reza Shah Pahlevi (rĕ'zä shä' pälävĕ'), 1877–1944, shah of Iran (1925–41). Headed a coup d'état in 1921 and assumed full dictatorial power in 1925 as first of Pahlevi dynasty. Deposed and succeeded by his son, Mohammed Reza Shah. Name is also written Riza Shah Pahlavi.

Rh, chemical symbol of the element RHODIUM.

Rhaetia (rĕ'shŭ), anc. Roman province including parts of S Bavaria, Tyrol, and E Switzerland; annexed by the Romans c.15 B.C.; cap. Augusta Vindelicorum (Augsburg).

Rhaeto-Romanic (rĕ'tō-rōmä'nĭk), generic name for several Romance dialects spoken in Switzerland and small bordering areas. They include Romansh, an official Swiss language, Ladin, and Fruili or Friouli. See LANGUAGE (table).

Rhagae: see RAGES.

Rhangavis, Alexandros Rizos: see RANGABE.

Rhazes (rā'zēz) or **Rasis** (rā'sĭs, –zĭs), c.860–c.925, Persian physician. Author of influential works including medical text, *Almansor,* and encyclopedia, *Liber continens.*

Rhé, island, France: see RÉ.

Rhea (rĕ'ū), in Greek religion, Titaness, Great Mother of the Gods; daughter of Uranus and Gaea, sister and wife of Cronus, and mother of Zeus, Poseidon, Demeter, Hera, Pluto, and Hestia. Her worship was associated with fertility rites. Identified with Cybele in Crete, with Ops in Rome.

Rhea Silvia, mother of ROMULUS and Remus.

Rhee, Syngman (sĭng'män rē), 1875–, president of Republic of Korea in S Korea (1948–). Reelected 1952.

Rhegium (rĕ'jĕŭm), anc. city, S Italy, on the Strait of Messina, today Reggio di Calabria. Founded in the 8th cent. B.C. by Greeks, it was powerful until destroyed by Dionysius the Elder of Syracuse (386 B.C.). It was also important under the Romans as Rhegium Julium.

Rheims (rēmz), Fr. *Reims* (rēs), city (pop. 106,081),

Marne dept., NE France. Archiepiscopal see from 8th cent.; seat of university (founded 1547). Center of French champagne industry since 18th cent. Clovis I was crowned here king of the Franks (496), and Rheims was the traditional place of coronation of the kings of France. Most famous coronation, in present cathedral, was that of Charles VII, with Joan of Arc standing by his side (1429). The cathedral, a treasure of Gothic architecture, was begun by Robert de Coucy in 1211. Partly destroyed in World War I by German shells, it was restored (except for its irreplaceable stained-glass windows) and reopened in 1938. On May 7, 1945, German emissaries signed Germany's unconditional surrender at Allied hq. in Rheims.

Rhenish Palatinate: see PALATINATE.

rhenium (rē'nēŭm) or **dvi-manganese** (dvī"măng'gŭnēs), heavy, silvery, metallic element (symbol = Re; see also ELEMENT, table).

rheostat (rē'ŭstăt), device using varying resistance to control electrical equipment. Metallic type is wire-wound insulated cylinder in contact with an arm movable one way to decrease windings and lessen resistance, other way to increase windings and resistance. Other types are carbon and electrolytic rheostats.

rhetoric: see ORATORY.

Rhett, Robert Barnwell, 1800–1876, American secessionist. A leading "fire-eater" at Nashville Convention of 1850; member of S.C. secession convention of 1860.

rheumatic fever: see RHEUMATISM.

rheumatism (rōō'mŭtĭzŭm), term applied to painful conditions of muscle, bone, joint, or nerve. Associated diseases include arthritis, bursitis, neuritis, lumbago, sciatica, gout. Some forms are relieved by Cortisone, derived from adrenal gland cortex. Rheumatic fever is an acute disease marked by migratory arthritis and often affecting heart.

Rh factor, factor in blood of c.85% of population. Discovered 1940 in blood of rhesus monkey by Landsteiner and A. S. Wiener. Introduction of Rh positive blood by blood transfusion induces forming of antibodies in Rh negative recipient; these may cause fatal reaction if Rh factor is introduced by second transfusion. Factor passing from blood of Rh positive fetus to blood of negative mother may cause antibody formation in maternal blood. If such antibodies enter fetal blood the child may have a critical disease.

Rhine (rīn), Dutch *Rijn,* Fr. *Rhin,* Ger. *Rhein,* river of Europe, c.820 mi. long, formed in E Switzerland by the junction of two headstreams (Vorder-Rhein, Hinter-Rhein). After traversing the L. of Constance it turns W, passes Schaffhausen, where it falls in a cataract, and forms Swiss-German border to Basel (head of steamship navigation). At Basel it turns N, forming French-German border, passes Strasbourg, and fully enters German territory below Karlsruhe. Continuing N (past Speyer, Mannheim, Ludwigshafen, Worms, Mainz, Wiesbaden, Coblenz, Bonn, Cologne, and Duisburg), it enters the Netherlands and divides into two branches—the WAAL and the Lower Rhine. The latter in turn fans out into the IJSSEL, the LEK, and the Old Rhine, which enters the North Sea below Leiden. The Waal and Lek link the Rhine with the Meuse estuary and the port of Rotterdam; the Rhine-Herne and Dortmund-Ems canals, with the Ruhr dist. and the German port of Emden. Other canals: Rhine-Marne Canal, Rhine-Rhone Canal (long but unimportant), Rhine-Main-Danube Canal (incomplete). Among tributaries are the Aar, Neckar, Main, Moselle, Ruhr, and Wupper. Section between Mainz and Bonn is particularly famous for its idyllic landscape, noble vineyards, ruined castles, and legendary landmarks (e.g., LORELEI; DRACHENFELS). The Rhenish Slate Mts., through which it winds here, include the Taunus and EIFEL. The industrial RUHR, WUPPER, and DÜSSELDORF dists. make the Rhine the chief

commercial river of Europe (coal, iron, grain). An international navigation commission, estab. 1919, resumed functioning after World War II (hq. Strasbourg).

Rhine, Confederation of the: see CONFEDERATION OF THE RHINE.

Rhineland (rīn'lănd), Ger. *Rheinland.* **1** Alternate name of the former RHINE PROVINCE of Prussia. **2** Region of W Germany, along the Rhine, comprising Rhine Prov., Rhenish Palatinate, and parts of Hesse and Baden. Under the Treaty of Versailles (1919) the Allies were to occupy parts of the region for 5–15 years, and Germany was forbidden to build fortifications or maintain troop concentrations W of a line running 50 km. E of the Rhine. U.S. troops, first of the occupation forces to withdraw, were replaced by the French. The entire RUHR dist. was occupied by French and Belgian troops in 1923–25. Last French troops left Rhineland in 1930, five years ahead of time. Although Germany had reaffirmed the demilitarization of the Rhineland in the Locarno Pact (1925), Hitler in 1936 began its remilitarization. The Siegfried Line, a formidable defense system, was penetrated by the Allies in World War II after heavy fighting (1944–45).

Rhinelander, city (pop. 8,774), N Wis., on Wisconsin R. and NW of Green Bay, in lake and dairy region. Trade center for resort area with mfg. of wood products.

Rhineland-Palatinate (pŭlă'tĭnĭt"), Ger. *Rheinland-Pfalz,* German state (7,666 sq. mi.; pop. 2,993,652), W Germany, W of the Rhine; cap. Mainz. Formed 1946 in French zone of occupation, it includes S part of former RHINE PROVINCE (with Trier and Coblenz), the Rhenish PALATINATE, and Rhenish HESSE. Produces Rhine wines. Has many spas (e.g., Bad Ems). Joined Federal Republic of [West] Germany 1949.

Rhine Province, Ger. *Rheinprovinz,* former Prussian province (9,451 sq. mi.; 1939 pop. 7,915,830), W Germany, bordering on the Netherlands, Belgium, and Luxembourg; also known as Rhenish Prussia and as Rhineland. Contained historic cities of AACHEN and COLOGNE; part of the industrial RUHR dist.; the industrial centers of DÜSSELDORF, WUPPERTAL, and SOLINGEN; and the MOSELLE wine dist., with Coblenz (former provincial cap.). Earliest acquisition by the house of Brandenburg-Prussia in this part of Germany was the duchy of CLEVES (1614). The remainder (incl. former bishoprics of Cologne and TRIER and former duchies of JÜLICH and BERG) was awarded to Prussia by the Congress of Vienna (1814–15). The Rhine Prov. was vital in the industrialization of Germany. Strongly Roman Catholic, it played a major part in the Kulturkampf. The Treaty of Versailles (1919) deprived it of the Saar Territory and of Eupen and Malmédy. After World War II the province was partitioned among British-occupied NORTH RHINE-WESTPHALIA and French-occupied RHINELAND-PALATINATE. See also RHINELAND.

rhinoceros (rīnŏ'sŭrŭs), massive herbivorous ungulate mammal, of Africa, India, SE Asia, with thick skin, often deeply folded. African black rhinoceros (*Diceros*) and white rhinoceros (*Ceratotherium* or *Diceros*) have two nasal horns. Indian and Javan rhinoceroses (*Rhinoceros*) have one nasal horn.

rhizome (rī'zōm), fleshy, creeping rootstock, actually an underground stem. Among plants that can be propagated by dividing or cutting up their rhizomes are iris, ginger, and trillium. See *ill.,* p. 783.

Rhode Island, state (1,058 sq. mi.; pop. 791,896), NE U.S.; one of Thirteen Colonies; cap. PROVIDENCE. Smallest, most densely inhabited state. Bordered on S by Atlantic Ocean. Takes name from largest island in NARRAGANSETT BAY. Rolling land cut by short, swift streams. Mfg. of textiles, machine tools, jewelry, silverware, rubber goods; some mining; some farming, especially poultry. Roger WILLIAMS estab. Providence (1636). Anne HUTCHINSON and other Puritan

SMALL CAPITALS = cross references. Pronunciation key on inside end pages. Abbreviations: p. 2.

exiles founded PORTSMOUTH (1638). Royal charter of 1663 reaffirmed religious freedom. NEWPORT occupied by British forces (1776–79) in American Revolution. Textile mfg. advanced by Samuel SLATER and Moses BROWN in late 18th cent. Suffrage extended after rebellion of Thomas W. DORR (1842). Mill owners dominated political and economic life until well into 20th cent. Recently new, diversified industries have been introduced.

Rhode Island, island, c.15 mi. long and 3½ mi. wide, S R.I., at entrance to Narragansett Bay. Largest island in state. Site of NEWPORT, Middletown, PORTSMOUTH. Known to Indians and early colonials as Aquidneck, named Rhode Isl. 1644.

Rhode Island, University of, and **Rhode Island State College:** see SOUTH KINGSTOWN.

Rhoden, Ausser and **Inner,** Switzerland: see APPENZELL.

Rhodes, Cecil (John), 1853–1902, British statesman and capitalist. Made fortune in South Africa by monopoly of Kimberley diamond production. Persuaded Britain to annex Bechuanaland in 1881. Formed British South Africa Co. to exploit mining concessions. Prime minister and virtual dictator of Cape Colony 1890–96, he conspired to seize Transvaal; forced to resign after raid of Sir Leander Jameson. Developed Rhodesia. Left fortune to public service, including Rhodes Scholarships (32 for U.S.; others for Germany and British colonies).

Rhodes, James Ford, 1848–1927, American historian. Major work was *History of the United States from the Compromise of 1850* (7 vols., 1893–1906). His *History of the Civil War, 1861–1865* (1917) won him 1918 Pulitzer Prize in history.

Rhodes (rōdz), Gr. *Rhodos,* Aegean island (542 sq. mi.; pop. 55,181), Greece, off SW Asia Minor, largest of the Dodecanese; cap. Rhodes (pop. 21,694), on NE coast. Mountainous in the interior, the island has a fertile coastal strip. Fishing; sponge diving. Population is 11% Italian. Settled by Dorians before 1000 B.C., Rhodes reached its height as a commercial power and a center of culture in the 4th–3d cent. B.C. The COLOSSUS OF RHODES was one of the wonders of the world. After its decline, Rhodes became an ally of Rome. Involved in the civil wars, it was seized and sacked by Cassius 43 B.C. At that period, Rhodes had a famous school of rhetoric, where Caesar studied. Captured from the Byzantines in the Fourth Crusade (1204), Rhodes passed to various lords. In 1309 the KNIGHTS HOSPITALERS took it from the Seljuk Turks; after defending the island for 50 years against the Ottoman sultans, the knights capitulated to Suleiman I on Jan. 1, 1523. It was taken from Turkey by Italy 1912; ceded to Greece 1947.

Rhodes, Knights of: see KNIGHTS HOSPITALERS.

Rhodesia (rōdē′zhù), region of Africa, comprising NORTHERN RHODESIA and SOUTHERN RHODESIA. Named 1894 for Cecil RHODES, who took it for British South Africa Co. in 1888. Divided in 1923.

rhodium (rō′dēùm), hard, gray-white, metallic element (symbol = Rh; see also ELEMENT, table). Alloyed with platinum it is used to make thermocouples for measuring high temperatures; alone it is used to plate reflecting surfaces and to prevent tarnish of metals.

rhododendron (rō″dùdĕn′drùn), evergreen or deciduous flowering shrub of genus *Rhododendron,* widely distributed, especially in mountainous regions. Azaleas, once considered a separate genus, are rhododendrons with largely deciduous foliage and funnel-shaped flowers, in contrast to the mostly evergreen leaves and bell-shaped flowers of rhododendrons. Both types are much used as ornamentals; many tender azaleas are grown as house plants. All require an acid, woodsy soil. American species include the rose bay (*Rhododendron maximum*), the Carolina rhododendron (*R. catawbiense*), the flame azalea (*R. calendulceum*), the fragrant swamp honeysuckle (*R. viscosum*), and the pinxter flower (*R. nudiflorum*).

Rhodope (rŏ′dùpē), mountain range of Balkan Peninsula, in S Bulgaria and NE Greece. Extends E from Struma R. to the Maritsa, rising to 9,596 ft. in the Musala (Bulgaria).

Rhoecus (rē′kùs), 6th cent. B.C., Greek sculptor. Helped improve methods of casting bronze statues.

Rhondda (rŏn′dù), urban district (pop. 111,357), Glamorganshire, Wales, on Rhondda R. Lower Rhondda valley is the great coal-mining region of S Wales.

Rhône (rōn), department (1,104 sq. mi.; pop. 918,866), E central France; cap. Lyons.

Rhone, Fr. *Rhône* (both: rōn), river, 505 mi. long, Switzerland and SE France. Springing from Rhone glacier in the upper Valais (Switzerland), it flows W and passes through L. of Geneva, then enters France and receives the Saône at Lyons, where it becomes navigable. Flowing S, it separates at Arles into two branches which enclose Camargue isl. and enter the Mediterranean W of Marseilles. These branches are silted up, but the Rove Tunnel, a 4.4-mi. underground channel, connects the Rhone with Marseilles (opened 1927). The fertile Rhone valley, cradle of Provençal culture, is covered with fine vineyards, orchards, olive groves, and vegetable gardens. In the S silkworms are raised. A large project for making the Rhone navigable up to Geneva and for exploiting its huge power potential is under way. The Génissiat Dam and hydroelectric plant, one of the world's largest, c.20 mi. S of Geneva, was inaugurated in 1948. A related Swiss project would link the L. of Geneva with the Rhine.

Rhône, Bouches du, France: see BOUCHES-DU-RHÔNE.

rhubarb, hardy large-leaved perennial plant (*Rheum rhaponticum*), also called pieplant. Its fleshy leafstalks are used in pies and sauces, especially in spring. Leaf blades are poisonous.

rhyme or **rime,** a literary artifice used in versification. Used in oldest extant Oriental poetry, but rare among ancient Greeks and Romans; began to develop when classical quantitative meters gave way to accentual meters. Alliteration and assonance used to be called rhyme; now, however, words are said to rhyme only when their final accented syllables sound alike. For proper rhyme, vowels and succeeding consonants must agree, but preceding consonants must differ. Words rhyme only when accented on the same syllable. Single or masculine rhyme is of one syllable or ends in a consonant with no mute *e* following; when rhymes are of two syllables or when they are not accented on last syllable or end in final mute *e,* they are called double or feminine rhymes.

rhythm, the element of music concerned with the relative duration of tones and with the stress or accent placed on certain tones. The practice of using a recurrent rhythm pattern throughout a composition began in the late 12th cent. and led to dividing a work into units of equal time value called measures. One 20th-cent. trend is to use several different rhythm patterns at the same time.

Riad, Riyad, or **Riyadh** (all: rēäd′), city (pop. 80,000), cap. (with Mecca) of Saudi Arabia and cap. of the Nejd; in an oasis. Center of Wahabi movement in Islam since early 19th cent.

Rialto (rēäl′tō), originally island and oldest quarter of Venice, Italy. Name is now applied to Rialto bridge, built 1588–91, a single marble arch with shop-lined arcades.

Ribalta, Francisco (fränthē′skō rēbäl′tä), c.1555–1628, Spanish religious painter, a pioneer in Spain in the use of dramatic light and shade. Taught Ribera.

Ribaut or **Ribault, Jean** (both: zhä′ rēbō′), c.1520–1565, French mariner and colonizer in Fla. Estab. unsuccessful colony on present Parris Isl., S.C. (1562). Killed in massacre by Pedro MENÉNDEZ DE AVILÉS on coast S of St. Augustine.

Ribbentrop, Joachim von (yō′äkhĭm fŭn rĭ′bùntrôp), 1893–1946, German foreign minister under Hitler (1938–45), influential in forming German-Soviet pact of 1939. Was hanged as war criminal.

Ribble, river of England. Flows 75 mi. SW from the Pennines in Yorkshire to the Irish Sea.

Ribera, Jusepe, José or **Giuseppe** (hŏŏsä′pä rēbä′rä, hōsä′, jŏŏzĕp′pä), c.1590–c.1652, Spanish painter. Studied in Valencia with Ribalta. Lived mainly in Naples where he enjoyed great prestige and influence as court painter to the Spanish viceroy. Famous for austere, realistic figures in strong light and shade against a dark background. His style reflects influence of Caravaggio.

Rib Mountain, 1,940 ft. high, central Wis., quartzite outcrop near Wausau. Summit is state park. Winter sports.

riboflavin: see VITAMINS.

Ricardo, David (rĭkär′dō), 1772–1823, British economist. He held that wages cannot rise above the lowest level necessary for subsistence, and that the value (not the price) of goods is measured by the amount of labor involved in their production. Greatly influenced radical economists. His chief work was *Principles of Economics and Taxation* (1817).

Ricci, Matteo (mät-tä′ō rēt′chē), 1552–1610, Italian Jesuit missionary. In China after 1582 he won much Chinese respect for Christianity and sent back to Europe valuable reports on Chinese life.

Rice, Elmer, 1892–, American dramatist. Plays include *On Trial* (1914), *The Adding Machine* (1923), *Street Scene* (1929), *Counsellor-at-Law* (1931), and *Dream Girl* (1945).

rice, cereal grass (*Oryza sativa*), native to deltas of great Asiatic rivers (Ganges, Tigris, Yangtze, and Euphrates), and cultivated mainly in tropical and subtropical areas. The plant is an annual grass, 2–4 ft. tall, with round, jointed stem, long, pointed leaves, and seeds borne in a dense head on separate stalks. Much rice is grown on lowlands which can be flooded when desirable; terraced hillsides irrigated by means of pumps are also used in both Orient and Occident. Primitive methods are still used in much of the Orient but in W countries cutting and threshing are usually done by machines. The threshed rice is known as paddy (rice fields are also called paddy fields or rice paddies) and is covered by a brown hull or coating which is removed before marketing. This is done in the Orient mainly by flailing, treading, or working in a mortar, though machinery is being introduced; in the U.S. a special mill is used. After husking, grains are usually polished and become white and glistening. Brown rice (without the bran layer removed) has much greater food value since brown coating and germ are rich in B-complex vitamins and minerals. Rice is rich in starch but low in protein and fat; combined with meat, oil, cheese, or soybean sauces it is a valuable food. In the Orient the fine, soft straw is plaited for hats and shoes. Broken grain is used in making laundry starch and also by distillers. Arrack is a distilled liquor sometimes prepared from a rice infusion; in Japan the beverage sake is brewed from rice. Important rice-producing countries are China, India, Japan, Indo-China, Java, Egypt, Brazil, U.S. (esp. La., Texas, Ark., Calif., S.C.).

Rice Institute, at Houston, Texas; non-sectarian, coed.; chartered 1891, endowed by W. M. Rice, opened 1912. University courses with no tuition fees.

Rice Lake, city (pop. 6,898), NW Wis., NW of Eau Claire and on Rice L. and Red Cedar R. Farm and resort center.

Rich, Edmund: see EDMUND, SAINT.

Rich, John, 1692–1761, English pantomime actor and originator of pantomime in England. Unexcelled as Harlequin, he imported pantomime in annual productions 1717–60. Built Covent Garden theater (1732).

Richard, kings of England. **Richard I, Richard Cœur de Lion** (kŭr″ dü lē′ŭn), or **Richard Lion-Heart,** 1157–99, was king of England (1189–99), duke of Aquitaine and Normandy, and count of Anjou. Warred against his father, Henry II, as ally of his mother, Eleanor of Aquitaine. Went (1190) on Third Crusade

with PHILIP II of France, who afterwards plotted with Richard's brother JOHN to divide England. Richard, on his way home, was imprisoned by Leopold II, who surrendered him to Emperor Henry VI. Was released by huge ransom and surrender of England, which was returned as a fief. Fought Philip in France, was killed in minor engagement. Although seldom in England, his personal qualities have made him an English symbol of chivalry. **Richard II,** 1367–1400, king of England 1377–99, was son of Edward the Black Prince. In peasant uprising under Wat Tyler in 1381 young king met insurgents and won their allegiance. Asserted his independence as ruler 1383. In struggle for power party of barons led by Thomas of Woodstock, earl of Gloucester, dismissed (1388) Richard's favorites. Richard had Gloucester murdered 1397. Richard's cousin, Henry of Bolingbroke, returned to England in his absence, forced him to abdicate, and was crowned HENRY IV (1399). Richard was imprisoned and died in Pontefract Castle. His reign was outstanding in literary and ecclesiastical history of England. Subject of Shakspere's *Richard II*. **Richard III,** 1452–85, king 1483–85, was brother of Edward IV. Gained control of his nephew, young EDWARD V, and had himself named king. Murder of Edward in Tower (1483) led to unsuccessful rebellion of Henry Stafford. Earl of Richmond landed in England (1485), Richard was killed at Bosworth Field, and Richmond became HENRY VII. Death of Richard, last Yorkist king, ended Wars of the Roses. Subject of Shakspere's *Richard III*.

Richard, earl of Cornwall, 1209–72, titular king of the Romans (see HOLY ROMAN EMPIRE). Brother of Henry III of England, he became Henry's adviser and acted as regent in king's absence. Wanted to be emperor and was elected king of the Germans (1257) but never ruled all of the country.

Richard Cœur de Lion: see RICHARD I, of England.

Richard de Bury (bĕr′ē), 1287–1345, English bibliophile, and bishop of Durham. *Philobiblon* describes his experiences as book collector.

Richard Lion-Heart: see RICHARD I, of England.

Richards, Laura E(lizabeth Howe), 1850–1943, American writer of children's books, notably *Captain January* (1890).

Richards, Theodore William, 1868–1928, American chemist. Won 1914 Nobel Prize for determining atomic weights of many elements.

Richardson, Dorothy M., 1882–, English novelist, author of *Pilgrimage* (12 vols., 1915–38). She introduced as a narrative method "interior monologue"—akin to "stream of consciousness."

Richardson, Henry Handel, pseud. of Henrietta Richardson Robertson, 1870–1946, Australian novelist. Abandoned music for writing. Her major work is the trilogy *The Fortunes of Richard Mahony* (1930).

Richardson, Henry Hobson, 1838–86, American architect, noted exponent of Romanesque design. Finest work is Trinity Church in Boston (1872–77).

Richardson, John, 1796–1852, first Canadian novelist to write in English. Wrote frontier romances.

Richardson, Sir Owen Willans, 1879–, English physicist. Won 1928 Nobel Prize for researches on electrons and establishment of Richardson's law of motions of electrons emanating from hot bodies.

Richardson, Samuel, 1689–1761, English novelist. At 50 a prosperous printer, he conceived idea of a moral novel in letter form, and wrote *Pamela; or, Virtue Rewarded* (4 vols., 1740–41). Similar works followed: *Clarissa; or, The History of a Young Lady* (7 vols., 1747–48) and *The History of Sir Charles Grandison* (7 vols., 1753–54). These realistic, sentimental stories were immensely popular. Richardson ranks as one of the great inventors of the novel.

Richelieu, Armand Jean du Plessis, duc de (ärmä′ zhä′ dü plĕsē′ dük′ dü rēshülyü′), 1585–1642, French prelate and statesman; commonly known as Cardinal Richelieu. Became bishop of Luçon 1607; secretary of state 1616; cardinal 1622; chief minister to Louis

XIII 1624. Though he owed his rise to the regent, MARIE DE' MEDICI, he turned against her, reversed her pro-Hapsburg policy, had her exiled in 1630, and governed as virtual dictator until his death. The founder of French absolutism, he broke the power of the HUGUENOTS (capture of La Rochelle, 1628; Peace of Alais, 1629) and kept the recalcitrant great nobles under control, rigorously suppressing their ceaseless conspiracies. He intervened in the THIRTY YEARS WAR —indirectly at first, by subsidizing Sweden (1631), then by active participation on the Protestant side (from 1635). He encouraged trade with India and Canada, but his reckless expenditures and taxation depleted the treasury and made him highly unpopular. Founder of the French Academy, he also wrote literary works.

Richelieu (rǐ'shŭlōō), river, issuing from N end of L. Champlain and flowing c.75 mi. N across S Quebec to St. Lawrence R. at Sorel. Link in waterway between Hudson R. and St. Lawrence R. Discovered 1609 by Champlain; was route of early explorers.

Richet, Charles Robert (shärl' rōbĕr' rĕshā'), 1850–1935, French physiologist. Won 1913 Nobel Prize in Physiology and Medicine for work on body sensitivity to alien proteins (anaphylaxis).

Richland, village (pop. 21,809), SE central Wash., on Columbia R. and E of Yakima. Built 1943–45 to house workers of Hanford Works, U.S. atomic-energy research and production plant.

Richmond, municipal borough (pop. 41,945), Surrey, England, on Thames R. Site of Palace of Sheen (where many sovereigns lived), a large deer park, and Kew Observatory. Inn of the Star and Garter, which figures in Scott's works, was torn down in 1919.

Richmond. 1 City (pop. 99,545), W Calif., across the bay from San Francisco. Settled on Spanish ranch site when railroad came, 1899. Deep-water port with oil refining, railroad shops, foundries, metal-products and chemical plants, and canneries. Its shipyards were active in World War II. **2** City (pop. 39,539), E Ind., near Ohio line E of Indianapolis; settled 1806. Trade center of farm area. Mfg. of machinery. Earlham College is at adjacent Earlham. **3** City (pop. 10,268), central Ky., SSE of Lexington; settled 1784. Confederates won first Ky. victory near by (Aug. 30, 1862). Tobacco, livestock, corn, clothing, and concrete products. **4** New York city borough: see STATEN ISLAND. **5** City (pop. 230,310), state cap., E Va., port on James R. at head of navigation. State's largest city, it is a cultural, financial, commercial, and industrial center of the South. A great tobacco marketing and processing center, it has mfg. of synthetic textiles, paper, fertilizer, and metal goods. Settled 1637 as trading post, town was projected 1733 by Col. William Byrd and made state cap. 1779. Pillaged by British 1781. As cap. of CONFEDERACY in Civil War, it was constant objective of Union forces. Seriously threatened in PENINSULAR CAMPAIGN of 1862 (saved in SEVEN DAYS BATTLES) and again in Wilderness campaign (1864), the city fell and was burned, April 3, 1865, at end of Grant's campaign (see PETERSBURG). Richmond Battlefield Natl. Park includes battlefields in and near city. Seat of Richmond Professional Inst. of the Col. of WILLIAM AND MARY, Medical Col. of Virginia, and Univ. of Richmond (Baptist; coed.; 1832). Points of interest include capitol (begun 1785), Washington Monument, White House of the Confederacy, St. John's Church (1741), Poe Foundation (city's oldest building, c.1686), John Marshall's house (1793), and Virginia Mus. of Fine Arts.

Richmond and Derby, Margaret Beaufort, countess of: see BEAUFORT, MARGARET.

Richter, Johann Paul Friedrich (yō'hän poul' frē'drĭkh rĭkh'tŭr), pseud. **Jean Paul** (zhä pōl'), 1763–1825, German author. His fantasies *Quintus Fixlein* (1796; Eng. tr. by Carlyle, 1827) and *Siebenkäs* (1796–97; Eng. tr., 1845), influenced by Laurence Sterne, won him a wide vogue.

Richwood, city (pop. 5,321), S W.Va., on Cherry R. Lumber mills, limestone quarries, coal mines.

Ricimer (rī'sĭmŭr), d. 472, Roman general of German birth. Won naval victory over Vandals and deposed Emperor Avitus (456). Thereafter was real ruler of Italy, making and deposing several puppet emperors, among them MAJORIAN.

Rickenbacker, Edward Vernon (rĭ'kŭnbă"kŭr), 1890–, American aviator. Awarded Congressional Medal of Honor and Croix de Guerre in World War I. Eddie Rickenbacker became (1938) Eastern Airlines president. Adrift 27 days on Pacific after World War II plane crash.

rickets (rĭ'kĭts) (rachitis), deficiency disease of infancy and childhood affecting calcium metabolism and resulting in softening of bone structure and consequent bone deformities. Prevented and treated by adequate intake of vitamin D, calcium, and phosphorus.

Ricketts, Charles, 1866–1931, British artist, b. Geneva. As designer-manager of Vale Press (1896–1904), he contributed greatly to fine bookmaking.

Rickman, Thomas, 1776–1841, English architect, important in the Gothic revival. Wrote first systematic treatise on English medieval period (1817).

Rideau Canal (rēdō', rē'dō), SE Ont., Canada, extends 126 mi. between Ottawa R. (at Ottawa) and L. Ontario (at Kingston). Built 1826–32 to connect St. Lawrence R. to L. Ontario without exposure to American attack. Now popular recreation area.

Ridgefield. 1 Residential town (pop. 4,356), SW Conn., at N.Y. line. Has fine homes. Scene of Revolutionary battle on April 27, 1777. **2** Borough (pop. 8,312), NE N.J., E of Rutherford.

Ridgefield Park, residential village (pop. 11,993), NE N.J., NW of Ridgefield. N end of N.J. Turnpike.

Ridgewood, residential village (pop. 17,481), NE N.J., NNE of Paterson.

Ridgway, Matthew B(unker), 1895–, American general. Commanded 82d Airborne Div. in World War II (1942–44). UN and U.S. commander in Japan, Korea, and Far East (1951–52). Replaced Dwight D. Eisenhower as supreme commander of Allied powers in Europe in 1952.

Ridgway, borough (pop. 6,244), NW Pa., S of Bradford. Mfg. of electrical products.

Riding, East, North, West: see YORKSHIRE, England.

Riding Mountain National Park, 1,148 sq. mi., SW Man., Canada, S of Dauphin, W of L. Manitoba; estab. 1929. Recreation area and big game preserve.

Ridley, Nicholas, 1500?–1555, English prelate and Protestant martyr; bishop of Rochester (after 1547), of London (from 1550). Under Mary Tudor, excommunicated (1553) as heretic. Convicted at second trial (1555) and, with Latimer, burned at stake at Oxford.

Riel, Louis (rēēl'), 1844–85, Canadian insurgent. In 1869–70 he led rebels of Red R. settlements and headed provisional government of their founding. His followers felt that transfer of Hudson's Bay Co. territory to Canada threatened their land rights. Rebellion collapsed without bloodshed. In 1884 **Riel's Rebellion** occurred when he led a group in Saskatchewan bent on securing land titles. Riel was captured, tried for treason, and hanged.

Riemann, Georg Friedrich Bernhard (gā'ôrk frē'drĭkh bĕrn'härt rē'män), 1826–66, German mathematician. Contributions include work on theory of functions of complex variables and method of representing them on coincident planes or sheets (Riemann's surfaces). He laid foundations of Riemannian geometry (non-Euclidian geometry system representing elliptic space).

Rienzi or **Rienzo, Cola di** (kō'lä dē rēĕn'tsē, rēĕn'tsō), 1313?–1354, Roman popular leader and humanist. Made papal notary by Clement VI at Avignon, he returned to Rome and in 1347 assumed, with popular support, wide dictatorial powers, styling himself tribune of the sacred Roman republic. His dream was to create a popular Italian state, unified under Roman leadership. Rienzi quickly lost Clement's support and was forced to leave Rome after a tumult (1347), but Clement's successor, Innocent VI, restored him to favor and sent him to Italy with ALBORNOZ. Made senator of Rome, Rienzi entered the city in triumph (1353), but his violent and arbitrary rule soon ended with his murder. Subject of an early opera by Richard Wagner.

Riesener, Jean Henri (rē'zùnùr), 1734–1806, French cabinetmaker, b. Germany; one of artists who helped form Louis XVI style.

Riesengebirge (rē'zùngúbǐr'gù) or **Giant Mountains,** Czech. *Krkonše,* Pol. *Karkonosze,* range along border of Bohemia (Czechoslovakia) and Silesia; a part of the Sudetes. Highest peak, Schneekoppe, rises 5,258 ft. on Czech-Silesian border. There are many spas and resorts.

Rievaulx (rē'vōz, rǐv'ùz), village, North Riding of Yorkshire, England. Has ruins of Rievaulx Abbey.

Rif or **Riff,** mountainous region on Mediterranean coast of Spanish Morocco. Berber tribes here were unsubdued until 1926, when joint French-Spanish campaign defeated their leader, Abd-el-Krim.

rifle, firearm with the bore spirally grooved to impart a spinning motion to the bullet. The rifle's history goes back to the 15th cent. but its widespread use dates from the settling of the woodland regions of the present E U.S. in the 18th cent. Early muzzle-loading weapons were succeeded by breech-loading rifles (used in the Civil War). The model 1903 Springfield armory rifle was long standard. The semi-automatic Garand rifle, a self-loading, clip-fed, gas-operated shoulder weapon, was much used in World War II. The principle of grooving or "rifling" the inner surface of the barrel is used also in artillery and pistols.

Riga (rē'gù), city (pop. 392,926), cap. of Latvia, on the mouth of the Western Dvina and on the Gulf of Riga (an E inlet of the Baltic Sea). A major seaport (though frozen Dec.–Jan.); mfg. center (machinery, precision instruments, food products, paper, textiles); cultural center (university, founded 1919; academy of fine arts; conservatory of music). Founded 1201, Riga was the base from which the LIVONIAN KNIGHTS conquered the Baltic coast. It joined the Hanseatic League 1282 and accepted the Reformation; its culture was German. Riga passed to Poland 1582; to Sweden 1621; to Russia 1710 (officially ceded 1721). Became cap. of independent Latvia 1919; of Latvian SSR 1940. Was occupied by the Germans in both world wars (1917–19; 1941–44). Its old section, or Hansa town, was damaged in World War II. It contains many fine medieval buildings—castle, Lutheran cathedral, Church of St. Peter. Across the Dvina is industrial Jelgava. The **Treaty of Riga** of **1920,** between the USSR and Latvia, confirmed Latvian independence. The Treaty of Riga of **1921,** between the USSR and Poland, fixed the Russo-Polish frontier. It awarded Poland large parts of Belorussia and the Ukraine. Was superseded by Polish-Russian treaty of 1945.

Rigaud, Hyacinthe (rēgō'), 1659–1743, French portrait painter, b. Perpignan, of Spanish ancestry. Sitters included most of the notables of the day.

rigging, wire, rope, and chain supporting and operating the masts, yards, booms, and sails of a ship. The shrouds are mast supports, crossing ropes ratlines. Footropes are hung from stirrups to help the crew furl the sails. Running rigging includes the ropes, blocks, and other apparatus needed to operate the yards, booms, gaffs, and sails, to raise and lower boats, and to handle cargo. For the chief simple types of rigging, see *ill.,* p. 865.

Riggs, Lynn, 1899–, American dramatist, known especially for *Green Grow the Lilacs* (produced 1931; basis for musical comedy, *Oklahoma!*).

Rights, Bill of: see BILL OF RIGHTS.

Rights of Man: see DECLARATION OF THE RIGHTS OF MAN.

Rigsdag (rǐks'dä), national parliament of Denmark.

Consists of an upper house (Landsting) and a lower house (Folketing).

Rigsmaal: see NORWEGIAN LANGUAGE.

Riis, Jacob August (rēs), 1849–1914, Danish-American journalist and philanthropist. He wrote and lectured in behalf of slum clearance in New York. His first book, *How the Other Half Lives* (1890), began lifelong association with Theodore Roosevelt in civic betterment. *The Making of an American* (1901) is autobiographical.

Rijeka-Susak, Yugoslavia: see FIUME.

Rijks Museum or **Ryks Museum** (both: rīks'), at Amsterdam, opened 1885. Has the outstanding collection of Dutch master paintings, notably those of Rembrandt.

Rijswijk, Netherlands: see RYSWICK, TREATY OF.

Riksdag (rēks'däg, rēks'tä), national parliament of Sweden. Upper house is elected by county and city councils, lower house by direct universal suffrage. Except in matter of taxation, king has right (rarely used) to absolute veto on legislation.

Riley, James Whitcomb, 1849–1916, American poet, b. Indiana. As the "Hoosier poet" he wrote homely, appealing poems such as "Little Orphant Annie" and "The Raggedy Man." Collections include *Rhymes of Childhood* (1890) and *An Old Sweetheart of Mine* (1902).

Riley, Fort, U.S. military post, estab. in 1852 on Kansas R. near Junction City, Kansas, to protect travelers on Santa Fe Trail from Indian attacks. Today it maintains permanent garrison for training field artillery, cavalry, and other units.

Rilke, Rainer Maria (rī'nùr märē'ä rǐl'kù), 1875–1926, German lyric poet, b. Prague. His peculiar blending of impressionism and mysticism was first recognized with *Das Buch der Bilder* (1902; enlarged ed., 1906). Though his poetry collections became more popular and he won wide popularity with the prose ballad *The Tale of the Love and Death of Cornet Christopher Rilke* (1906; Eng. tr., 1932), his stature as a major poet of his time developed only after his death. His later poetry—*Duinese Elegies* (1923; Eng. tr., 1930, 1939) and *Sonnets to Orpheus* (1923; Eng. tr., 1936)—was profound and austere.

Rimbaud, Arthur (ärtür' rēbō'), 1854–91, French poet, precursor of the SYMBOLISTS and usually classed with the DECADENTS. He stopped writing at 19. His poems, noted for a hallucinatory, dreamworld quality, include "Le Bateau ivre." *Une Saison en enfer* (1873) is his adolescent memoirs. A close, tempestuous relationship with VERLAINE was followed by a life of adventure in Ethiopia.

rime: see RHYME.

Rimini (rē'mēnē), anc. *Ariminium,* city (pop. 31,505), Emilia-Romagna, N central Italy; an Adriatic port and bathing resort. At junction of Flaminian and Aemilian Ways, it had strategic importance in Roman days; was a member of the Pentapolis under Byzantine rule. It was included in Pepin's donation to the pope (754). MALATESTA family seized power in 1295 and later conquered neighboring cities. Papal possession became effective in 1509. City was heavily damaged in World War II; the famous Malatesta temple (a 13th-cent. church rebuilt by Sigismondo Malatesta, c.1450), one of the finest Renaissance buildings, was partly destroyed.

Rimmer, William, 1816–79, American sculptor. His knowledge of anatomy (gained from his medical studies) is apparent in his few surviving works (e.g., *The Dying Centaur,* Metropolitan Mus.).

Rimmon (rǐ'mùn), Syrian god. 2 Kings 5.18.

Rimouski (rǐmōō'skē), town (pop. 11,565), E Que., Canada, on St. Lawrence R. at mouth of Rimouski R. and NE of Quebec. Lumbering, woodworking.

Rimsky-Korsakov, Nicolai (Andreyevich) (nyǐkŭlī rǐm'skē-kôr'sùkôf), 1844–1908, Russian composer; one of the Five (see BALAKIREV). The subjects of his operas are chiefly drawn from Russian history or legend—

Le Coq d'Or, The Snow Maiden, The Maid of Pskov (also known as *Ivan the Terrible*). He also wrote the orchestral suite *Scheherezade;* three symphonies; the *Russian Easter* overture, and the well-known *Flight of the Bumblebee.* He was a master of orchestral color and often arranged works of other composers (e.g., Moussorgsky's *Boris Godunov* and parts of Borodin's *Prince Igor.*

rinderpest (rĭn'dûrpĕst"), communicable virus disease of cattle, endemic to Russia, central Asia, and Africa; also called cattle plague. It is unknown in U.S. and Canada. High fever, chills, mouth and udder eruptions, and labored breathing are characteristic; disease is usually fatal. A preventive vaccine was discovered during World War II.

Rinehart, Mary Roberts, 1876–, American novelist and dramatist. Known especially for mystery novels, such as *The Circular Staircase* (1908; dramatized by her and Avery Hopwood, 1920, as *The Bat*) and *The Man in Lower Ten* (1909), and for her humorous "Tish" stories.

Rinehart, William Henry, 1825–74, American sculptor. His masterpiece, *Clytie,* is in Peabody Inst., Baltimore, along with casts of many of his works.

Ringwood, borough (pop. 1,752), N N.J., in Ramapo Mts. near N.Y. line. Iron mines developed after 1764; munitions made in Revolution. Ringwood Manor State Park has historic manor house, now a museum.

ringworm (tinea), fungus infection of skin marked by reddish, disk-shaped areas. Interdigital ringworm is often called athlete's foot.

Río and **Rio,** respectively Spanish and Portuguese terms for river. For those not listed here, see under second element of name—e.g., for Rio Amazonas, see AMAZON.

Rio de Janeiro (rē'ō dù jùnâ'rō), state (16,443 sq. mi.; pop. 2,326,201), SE Brazil, on the Atlantic; cap. Niterói. Encloses but does not include Federal District (with city of Rio de Janeiro). Escarpment divides area into coastal lowland, central hill section, and fertile Paraíba R. valley in west. Is leading industrial region.

Rio de Janeiro, city (pop. 2,335,931), colloquially Rio; cap. of Brazil on Guanabara Bay of Atlantic, in Federal District. Beautiful harbor is surrounded by landmarks—Sugar Loaf Mt.; Corcovado peak, on which stands huge statue of Christ; crescent-shaped beaches—notably, Copacabana. City handles much of Brazil's trade, exporting coffee, iron ore, manganese, meat, cotton, hides. Varied manufactures include glass, textiles, household appliances, chemicals, trucks. Has botanical garden (founded 1808), and many fine public buildings and educational institutions. Area was visited by Portuguese explorers, Jan., 1502 (whence name meaning January River). French Huguenots estab. colony here (1555) but were driven out (1567) by Mem de Sá. Replaced Bahia as capital of Brazil (1763).

Río de Oro: see SPANISH SAHARA.

Rio Grande (rē'ō gränd', rē'ō grän'dē), river, c.1,800 mi. long, rising in San Juan Mts. of SW Colo. Flows S through middle of N.Mex., then SE as Texas-Mexico line, empties into Gulf of Mexico at Brownsville, Texas, and Matamoros, Mexico. Coronado saw its Indian pueblos and irrigation 1540. Elephant Butte Dam, near Hot Springs, N.Mex., serves large area. Irrigation continues downstream, aids citrus-truck region near mouth (Rio Grande Valley). U.S.-Mexico pact of 1945 provided new projects. In Mexico: Río Bravo del Norte.

Rio Grande de Cagayan, P.I.: see CAGAYAN.

Rio Grande do Norte (rē'ō grän'dù dōō nôr'tù), state (20,482 sq. mi.; pop. 983,572), NE Brazil, on the Atlantic; cap. NATAL. Has valuable mineral resources. Sugar cane is widely grown. First European settlement 1599. Dutch occupied area briefly in 17th cent.

Rio Grande do Sul (rē'ō grän'dù dōō sōōl'), state (109,-066 sq. mi.; pop. 4,213,316), S Brazil; cap. PÔRTO

ALEGRE. Southernmost state of Brazil, it is leading stock-raising and meat-processing state and most important producer of wheat and wine. First European settlement made by Jesuits in 17th cent. Many German and Italian farmers immigrated to area. **Rio Grande do Sul,** city (pop. 64,241), is in S part of state, on Lagoa dos Patos; an important port.

Riom (rēō'), town (pop. 10,420), Puy-de-Dôme dept., S central France. Here in 1942 the VICHY GOVERNMENT tried several French political and military leaders (incl. Léon Blum and Édouard Daladier) for having plunged France into World War II unprepared. The trial was indefinitely postponed when the defendants produced evidence detrimental to their accusers.

Río Muni: see SPANISH GUINEA.

Rion (rēôn'), anc. *Phasis,* river, 180 mi. long, rising in the Caucasus in W Georgian SSR and flowing S and W past Kutais into Black Sea at Poti. Upper course used for hydroelectric power.

Río Piedras (pyä'dhräs), town (pop. 132,438), NE Puerto Rico. Seat of Univ. of Puerto Rico.

Río Tinto, Ríotinto (rē'ōtĕn'tō), or **Minas de Ríotinto** (mē'näs dā), town (pop. 2,727), SW Spain, in Andalusia. Center of rich copper-mining region.

Riouw Archipelago (rē'ou, rē'ō), island group (2,279 sq. mi.; pop. 77,149), Indonesia, at entrance to Strait of Malacca. Important bauxite and tin mines on Bintan isl.

Ripley, George, 1802–80, American literary critic and author. A Unitarian minister, he was a noted transcendentalist and wrote for *Dial.* Left ministry (1841) to found BROOK FARM. Later he became an influential literary critic on New York *Tribune.*

Ripley, village (pop. 1,792), SW Ohio, SE of Cincinnati. Here is Rankin Home, said to be original of Underground Railroad station where Eliza of *Uncle Tom's Cabin* found refuge.

Ripon (rĭ'pùn), municipal borough (pop. 9,464), West Riding of Yorkshire, England. St. Cuthbert founded monastery here c.660. Present minster dates from 12th–15th cent. Treaty signed here (1640) ended second of Bishops' Wars.

Ripon, (rĭ'pùn), city (pop. 5,619), central Wis., NW of Fond du Lac; settled 1844 as Ceresco, a Fourierist community. Birthplace of Carrie C. Catt. Seat of Ripon Col. (coed.; 1851).

Rip Van Winkle, name of character and story by Washington IRVING, in *The Sketch Book of Geoffrey Crayon, Gent.* (first pub. serially, 1819–20). It tells of a man who slept 20 years.

Risorgimento (rēsôr"jēmĕn'tō) [Ital.,= resurgence], in Italian history, the period of national unification (c.1815–1870). After the French Revolution and Napoleon had disappointed Italian hopes of unity and independence, the Congress of Vienna in 1814–15 again divided ITALY into several states, of which only SARDINIA was free of Austrian influence or domination. Uprisings of secret patriotic societies (e.g., the CARBONARI) were suppressed by the Italian rulers with the sanction of the HOLY ALLIANCE, but the movement toward unity could not be stopped. There were three main parties—a republican, anticlerical group, led by MAZZINI; a conservative group, advocating a confederation under the presidency of the pope; and a middle-of-the-road group, which favored unification under the house of Savoy (i.e., the kings of Sardinia). This last group, led by CAVOUR, eventually won out. Revolutions flared up throughout Italy in 1848–49 but were suppressed by Austria. Sardinian forces, who twice came to the rebels' aid, were defeated at Custozza (1848) and Novara (1849). In Rome, French troops restored PIUS IX. Cavour's diplomacy secured the alliance of France (see PLOMBIÈRES) for Sardinia's war of 1859 against Austria. The French and Sardinians won costly victories at Magenta and Solferino, but the preliminary peace of VILLAFRANCA DI VERONA disappointed Sardinia's ambitions by giving it only Lombardy. In 1860 Sardinia annexed Tuscany, Parma, Modena, and Romagna, then joined in the campaign of GARIBALDI, annexing Umbria and the Marches while Garibaldi's volunteers were conquering the Two Sicilies. In 1861 VICTOR EMMANUEL II was proclaimed king of united Italy. Venetia came to Italy after the Austro-Prussian War (1866). The remnant of the Papal States—Rome and Latium—remained under French protection until 1870, when it was annexed by Italy.

Ristori, Adelaide (rēstō´rē), 1822–1906, Italian actress. A tragedienne, she won fame in Europe and U.S. in familiar Italian roles, classical French drama, and as Lady Macbeth and Medea.

Ritter, Karl, 1779–1859, German geographer, a founder of modern human geography. His major work was *Die Erdkunde* (2d ed., 19 vols., 1822–59).

river, stream of running fresh water larger than a brook or creek. Runoff after precipitation flows downward by the shortest and steepest course in depressions formed by intersecting slopes. Runoff may join in a stream that deepens its bed by erosion; it becomes permanent when it cuts deeply enough to be fed by subsurface water. Sea level is the ultimate base level, but floor of lake or basin into which stream flows may become local and temporary base level. A river's discharge depends on the cross-section area of its channel and on its velocity (governed by water volume, bed slope, and channel shape). Rivers modify topography by erosion and by deposition. Young streams have steep-sided valleys, steep gradients, and irregularities in the bed; mature streams have valleys with wide floors and flaring sides, advanced headward erosion by tributaries, and a more smoothly graded bed; the old stream has graded its course to base level and runs through a peneplain.

Rivera, Diego (dēā´gō rēvā´rä), 1886–, Mexican painter. Worked in Europe 1907–9, 1912–21; became friendly with Cézanne and Picasso and with Russian communists. Believing that art should express "new order of things" through mass medium of murals in public buildings, he became a sort of prophet to peasants and workers. Visited Moscow 1927–28. Through his influence Trotzky was allowed to enter Mexico. Several of his murals depict the life, history, and problems of Mexico. A mural for Rockefeller Center, New York, was rejected because it contained a portrait of Lenin.

Rivera, Primo de: see PRIMO DE RIVERA, MIGUEL.

River Brethren, Christian group originating 1770 in E Pa. among Swiss Mennonites settled along Susquehanna R. Sect probably took name from practice of baptism in river. In 1843 conservative group in York co. withdrew as Old Order or Yorker Brethren. Main body became Brethren in Christ. They are like Dunkards in church practices, dress, and customs.

Riverdale. 1 Village (pop. 5,840), NE Ill., just S of Chicago. Rail center with steel plant. **2** Town (pop. 5,530), W central Md., suburb of Washington, D.C.

River Edge, borough (pop. 9,204), NE N.J., on Hackensack R. and E of Paterson.

River Forest, residential village (pop. 10,283), NE Ill., W suburb of Chicago; settled 1836.

Riverhead, town (pop. 9,973), on E Long Isl., SE N.Y., on Peconic Bay. Fishing center in farm area (potatoes, truck).

Riverina (rĭ″vûrē´nù), rural administrative district (26,-560 sq. mi.; pop. 83,000), S New South Wales, Australia, between Lachlan and Murray rivers.

River Junction: see CHATTAHOOCHEE, Fla.

River Oaks, city (pop. 7,097), N Texas, NW suburb of Fort Worth. Formerly Castleberry.

River Rouge (rōōzh´), city (pop. 20,549), SE Mich., on Detroit R. at mouth of the River Rouge, next to S Detroit. Grew in 1920s with expansion of Ford Motor Co. in area.

Riverside, town (pop. 9,214), S Ont., Canada, on Detroit R., E suburb of Windsor.

Riverside. 1 Residential and resort city (pop. 46,764), S Calif., E of Los Angeles. Citrus center where navel orange was introduced in 1873. Annual Easter sunrise services are held on Mt. Rubidoux, site of huge cross to Father Junípero Serra. March Field (U.S.) is near. **2** Residential village (pop. 9,153), NE Ill., W suburb of Chicago. Designed as model suburb by F. L. Olmsted and Calvert Vaux. **3** Village (pop. 7,199), SW N.J., on Delaware R. above Camden. Mfg. of watch cases, clothing, roller skates, metal products, textiles.

Riverton, town (pop. 4,142), W central Wyo., where Wind and Popo Agie rivers form Bighorn R. Served by Riverton project.

Riviera (rĭvēâ´rù), coastal strip between Alps and N Apennines and the Mediterranean, extending from La Spezia (Italy) to Hyères (France). French Riviera is also called Côte d'Azur. Celebrated for scenery, mild climate, vegetation; dotted with resorts: Rapallo, San Remo (Italy); Nice, Monte Carlo, Cannes (Côte d'Azur).

Rivière du Loup (rēvyĕr´ dü lōō´), city (pop. 9,425), E Que., Canada, on St. Lawrence R. at mouth of Rivière du Loup and NE of Quebec. Resort, tourist, and trade center with railroad shops, lumbering, and woodworking.

Rivoli (rē´vōlē), village, Venetia, NE Italy, on Adige R., near Verona. Scene of decisive victory of French under Bonaparte over Austrians (1797).

Riyad or **Riyadh,** Arabia: see RIAD.

Rizal, José (hōsä´ rēsäl´), 1861–96, Philippine patriot and author, a physician. His first novel, *Noli me tangere* (1886), attacking Spanish administration and the religious orders in Philippines, brought about his exile in 1887. Arrested and returned to Manila in 1896, he was executed as instigator of insurrection.

Riza Shah Pahlavi: see REZA SHAH PAHLEVI.

Rizzio, David (rĭt´sēō), 1535?–1566, favorite of MARY QUEEN OF SCOTS. A Piedmontese musician, he became Mary's secretary. Jealous nobles persuaded Lord Darnley that Rizzio was Mary's lover and, with Darnley's aid, murdered him in Mary's presence.

Rjukan (rēōō´kän), village (pop. 5,460), S Norway, on the Rjukanfoss, a waterfall (983 ft. high) of Mane R. Its hydroelectric and nitrogen-fixation plants were destroyed by Allied bombings 1943. Has heavy-water plant.

Rn, chemical symbol of the element RADON.

road. History of roads is related to centralizing of populations in powerful cities, which they served for military purposes and for collection of supplies and tribute. In Persia between 500 and 400 B.C., the capital, Susa, had roads leading to every province. Greeks, opposed to centralization, built few roads. Famous ROMAN ROADS were surfaced with large stone slabs; parts of them are still serviceable. From fall of Rome to 19th cent., European roads were generally neglected, although in France there were some good military roads. Development of MACADAM ROAD was important to Industrial Revolution. Inca empire had fine roads. North American Indians used chiefly footpaths and waterways. With stagecoaches came TURNPIKE and the NATIONAL ROAD but canal and railroad took precedence until automobile again made road paramount and U.S. highways became complex system. Road-building is now a major branch of engineering.

road runner, cuckoo found in cactus country of W U.S. and parts of Mexico. It flies with ease but more often runs over ground, with head down.

Roanoke. 1 City (pop. 5,392), E Ala., near Ga. line SE of Anniston, in farm area. **2** City (pop. 91,921), SW Va., on Roanoke R., between Blue Ridge and Allegheny Mts., S gateway to Shenandoah Valley; founded 1834. Center of agr., coal, and lumber area. Mfg. of iron and steel products, textiles, and chemicals. Near by is Hollins Col. (nonsectarian; for women; 1842).

Roanoke, river rising in SW Va. and flowing 410 mi.

SE to Albemarle Sound, N.C. Flood-control and power projects under way.

Roanoke Island, NE N.C., off coast in Croatan Sound between Albemarle and Pamlico sounds. Manteo (pop. 635) is chief town. Island is 12 mi. long, averages 3 mi. in width; fishing main industry. Site of unsuccessful colonies organized by Sir Walter Ralegh in 1585 and 1587. Discovery of stone tablets in 1930s, supposedly recording history of "lost colony," would seem to dispel CROATAN theory of second colony's disappearance. Fort Raleigh Natl. Historic Site estab. 1941.

Roanoke Rapids, city (pop. 8,156), N N.C., on Roanoke R. and NNE of Rocky Mount. Textile and paper mills.

Robber Synod: see EUTYCHES.

robbery, felonious taking of property from a person against his will by threatening or committing force or violence. The threat may be against his property or against someone else rather than his own person. If there is no use of force or fear, the crime is not robbery but larceny; if force or fear is used to get the consent of the victim the crime is extortion.

Robbia, Italian sculptors: see DELLA ROBBIA.

Robbins, village (pop. 4,766), NE Ill., near Chicago; an all-Negro community.

Robbinsdale, city (pop. 11,289), E Minn., NW suburb of Minneapolis.

Robert, kings of France. **Robert I,** c.865–923, younger brother of Eudes, led rebellion against Charles III (the Simple) and was crowned 922 but was soon killed in battle. His son-in-law Raoul succeeded him. **Robert II** (the Pious), c.970–1031, son of Hugh Capet, reigned 996–1031. Sought to strengthen royal power, with moderate success. Henry I succeeded him.

Robert, kings of Scotland. **Robert I** or **Robert the Bruce,** 1274–1329, king 1306–29, led in the struggle for national independence. Defeated at Methven after defying Edward I by being crowned (1306) at Scone. Legend says Bruce learned courage and hope while in hiding from watching a spider spinning its web. Defeated Edward II at Bannockburn in 1314. Bruce's title to throne was recognized by Treaty of Northampton in 1328. By his skill and courage he delivered Scotland from English control. **Robert II,** 1316–90, king 1371–90, was founder of STUART dynasty. Various of his sons acted as guardian during most of his reign. Scots fought off English invasions and won great victory at Otterburn in 1388. His eldest son, **Robert III,** c.1340–1406, king 1390–1406, was an invalid. Real power held by his brother Robert Stuart, duke of Albany.

Robert, dukes of Normandy. **Robert I** (the Magnificent), d. 1035, reigned 1027–35; often identified with ROBERT THE DEVIL. Designated his natural son, William the Conqueror, as successor. **Robert II** or **Robert Curthose,** c.1054–1134, succeeded his father, William I of England, as duke of Normandy in 1087. Warred against WILLIAM II and HENRY I of England, whose throne he claimed. Henry defeated him at Tinchebrai (1106) and imprisoned him in England.

Robert, Henry Martyn, 1837–1923, American military engineer. During Civil War he worked as engineer on defenses of Washington, Philadelphia, and New England coast. From 1867 to 1895 he was in charge of river, harbor, and coast improvements of Pacific and Gulf coasts, Great Lakes, and Long Isl. Sound. He is more widely known for his *Pocket Manual of Rules of Order for Deliberative Assemblies* (1876).

Robert Bruce: see ROBERT I, king of Scotland.

Robert College, at Istanbul, opened 1863 with funds contributed by Christopher R. Robert and other Americans for education of Turkish men.

Robert Curthose: see ROBERT II, duke of Normandy.

Robert Grosseteste: see GROSSETESTE, ROBERT.

Robert Guiscard (gĕskär'), c.1015–1085, Norman conqueror of S Italy; son of Tancred de Hauteville, a Norman nobleman. His brothers William Iron Arm,

Drogo, and Humphrey preceded him to Italy. Humphrey in 1053 forced the pope to invest him with Apulia and all other S Italian lands the Normans had acquired or were to acquire from the Byzantines and the Arabs. Robert, succeeding Humphrey in 1057, completed the conquest of S Italy while his brother ROGER I took Sicily from the Arabs. In 1081, Robert began his expedition against the Byzantine Empire. He took Corfu and defeated Alexius I but returned in 1083 to aid Pope GREGORY VII against Emperor Henry IV. He briefly held and sacked Rome (1084). Expelled again by Henry's forces, he resumed his campaign in the E and died of fever on Cephalonia. His possessions in S Italy, after passing to his son and grandson, were annexed by Roger II of Sicily.

Robert of Courtenay (kôrt'nē, kŏŏrtùnà'), d. 1228, Latin emperor of Constantinople (1221–28). His empire was reduced to city of Constantinople.

Robert of Geneva, d. 1394, Genevan churchman, antipope as Clement VII. After the death of Gregory XI, who had returned the papacy from Avignon to Rome, the cardinals elected URBAN VI (1378) but shortly reconsidered and elected Robert instead. He fled to Avignon, and the Great SCHISM was begun. Robert was succeeded as antipope by Pedro de Luna.

Roberts, Sir Charles George Douglas, 1860–1943, Canadian author. He influenced other Canadian poets of "Confederation school" with his nature lyrics and idyls. Wrote tales of wildlife, a popular *History of Canada* (1897).

Roberts, Elizabeth Madox, 1885–1941, American poet and novelist, known for stories of her native Kentucky (e.g., *The Time of Man,* 1946; *The Great Meadow,* 1930), with faithful lyric renditions of regional speech. Her lyrics and ballads (in *Song in the Meadow,* 1940) have been much admired.

Roberts, Frederick Sleigh, 1st **Earl Roberts of Kandahar** (kăndŭhär'), 1832–1914, British field marshal. Forced Afghans to accept British demands in 1879. Commanded all Indian forces 1885–93. Was commander in chief in SOUTH AFRICAN WAR 1899–1900.

Roberts, Kenneth L(ewis), 1885–, American author of historical novels, including the series *Chronicles of Arundel.* Also well known are *Northwest Passage* (1937), *Oliver Wiswell* (1940), and *Lydia Bailey* (1946).

Roberts, Owen J(osephus), 1875–, American jurist, Associate Justice of U.S. Supreme Court (1930–45).

Robertson, James, 1742–1814, American frontiersman, a founder of Tenn. Founded Nashville (1780); primarily responsible for its survival.

Robertson, Thomas William, 1829–71, English author of superficial realistic comedies (e.g., *Caste,* 1867).

Robert the Bruce: see ROBERT I, king of Scotland.

Robert the Devil, hero of medieval legend, who was sold to the devil by his mother, did penance, and purified himself. Often identified with Robert I of Normandy.

Robeson, Paul (rōb'sùn), 1898–, American Negro actor and singer. Roles in O'Neill's *Emperor Jones* and *All God's Chillun Got Wings* preceded his wide fame as a singer. Appeared later in *Showboat, Othello, Hairy Ape,* and films. A controversial figure because of leftist political affiliations.

Robespierre, Maximilien (rōbz'pēēr, –pēr, Fr. mäksē-mēlyē' rôbĕspyēr'), 1758–94, French revolutionist. Practiced law at Arras; was elected to States-General of 1789 and to Convention (1792); slowly rose to leadership of JACOBINS and took part in destruction of GIRONDISTS. It was his entry into the Committee of Public Safety (July, 1793) that raised him to the first rank. The REIGN OF TERROR enabled him to remove his chief rivals (notably HÉBERT, DANTON, and DESMOULINS) and to attempt the realization of his dogmatic version of J. J. Rousseau's theories. With his lieutenants SAINT-JUST and COUTHON he initiated the horrors of the Great Terror. The Law of 22 Prairial (June 10, 1794) made the Revolutionary Tribunal supreme. By establishing the worship of the Supreme Being, Robespierre even sought to impose his deism as state religion. On 9 THERMIDOR (July 27), when Saint-Just was about to demand the heads of another installment of "traitors," the Convention at last rallied in self-defense. In face of the Convention's dramatic uprising, Robespierre was surprisingly timid and undecided. He was summarily tried and guillotined with several followers (July 28). Robespierre's fanatic devotion to virtue, which earned him the epithet "The Incorruptible," has never been questioned, but in other respects he has veen variously appraised as a maniac, a self-seeking dictator, and an idealistic champion of social revolution.

robin or **robin redbreast,** Old World name for small bird of warbler family. In New World it is name for migratory bird of thrush family; eastern American robin is c.10 in. long, with brownish-olive head, back, and tail, black-barred white throat, and chestnut red breast.

Robin Hood, legendary outlaw of medieval England. With Little John (his chief archer), Friar Tuck, Maid Marian, and his band, he lived in Sherwood Forest and robbed the rich to help the poor.

Robinson, Boardman, 1876–1952, American painter, b. Canada. Cartoonist for newspapers and periodicals, 1907–24. Murals in Rockefeller Center, N.Y.

Robinson, Charles, 1818–94, first governor of state of Kansas (1861–63), b. Mass. EMIGRANT AID COMPANY agent, thrice elected territorial governor; opposed by proslavery forces.

Robinson, E(dwin) A(rlington), 1869–1935, American poet, b. Maine. Early work appeared in *The Torrent and the Night Before* (1896) and *The Children of the Night* (1897). After a courageous struggle he won long-delayed fame with *The Man against the Sky* (1916). Longer poems include *Avon's Harvest* (1921), *Cavender's House* (1929), and Arthurian romances. His somber, ironic analysis of character is shown in such poems as "Flammonde," "Miniver Cheevy," and "Ben Jonson Entertains a Man from Stratford." Robinson wrote in traditional metrical forms, often in colloquial language, and always with strong emotional power.

Robinson, Jackie (Jack Roosevelt Robinson), 1919–, American baseball infielder, first Negro to play in major leagues. Won (1949) National League batting title, named most valuable player in league.

Robinson, James Harvey, 1863–1936, American historian. Through writings and teaching he stressed "new history," i.e., social and scientific rather than purely political, and influenced study and teaching of history. Works include *The New History* (1912) and *The Mind in the Making* (1921).

Robinson, John, 1576?–1625, English nonconformist pastor of Pilgrim Fathers in Holland. He led separatist group from Scrooby, England, to Amsterdam (1608), and to Leiden (1609). He encouraged but did not join emigration (1620) to America.

Robinson, Lennox, 1886–, Irish dramatist, connected with Abbey Theatre. His dramas of Irish life include *The Dreamers* (1915), *The Lost Leader* (1918), *The Whiteheaded Boy* (1920), and *The Far-off Hills* (1928).

Robinson, Ray, 1921–, American boxer, whose real name is Walker Smith. Considered one of the greatest boxers of his time, "Sugar Ray" was welterweight champion 1946–51, middleweight champion 1951–52. Retired (1952) after unsuccessful try for light heavyweight title.

Robinson, Sir Robert, 1886–, English biochemist. Worked on structures of vegetable substances, synthesis of hormones, plant pigments; won 1947 Nobel Prize in Chemistry.

Robinson, city (pop. 6,407), E Ill., NNW of Vincennes, Ind., in oil and farm area. Mfg. of china, pottery, and glycerin.

Robinson Crusoe, character created by Daniel DEFOE in his story (1719) of a castaway on a desert island, suggested in part by adventures of Alexander Selkirk, a Scottish sailor.

Robinson-Patman Act, 1936, passed by U.S. Congress to supplement CLAYTON ANTI-TRUST ACT. Designed to protect independent retailer from chain-store competition.

robot (rō'bŭt, rŏ'bŭt), mechanical device designed to perform actions or work generally performed by humans. Karel Capek, Czech dramatist, used the expression in his play *R. U. R. (Rossum's Universal Robots),* to describe artificial workers with human form and intelligence, but devoid of feelings. Terms *automaton* and *robot* are both commonly used for devices supplanting a human in given task of some complexity. Examples include many electronic devices for industrial functions, automatic pilot which keeps plane on course, electronic calculators, and robot bombs or "buzz-bombs" used against England by Germany in World War II.

Rob Roy [Scottish Gaelic,= red Rob], 1671–1734, Scottish freebooter, whose real name was Robert MacGregor. Known by Sir Walter Scott's novel *Rob Roy.* An outlaw, he pillaged and burned (with aid of his clan). Pardoned (1727) after voluntary submission. Also used his maternal name of Campbell.

Robsart, Amy (rŏb'särt), 1532?–1560, maiden name of wife of Robert Dudley, earl of Leicester. She was found dead and it was rumoured that Dudley had arranged her death. Mystery has never been cleared up. Story figures in Scott's *Kenilworth.*

Robson, Mount: see MOUNT ROBSON PROVINCIAL PARK.

Robstown, city (pop. 8,278), S Texas, W of Corpus Christi. Processing and shipping center for oil and agr. area.

Roca, Julio Argentino (hōō'lyō ärhäntē'nō rô'kä), 1843–1914, Argentine general and statesman, president of republic (1880–86, 1898–1904). Drove Patagonian Indians beyond Río Negro (1878–79), thus opening vast territory for colonization. Accomplishments during his administrations include federalization of Buenos Aires, great material expansion, settlement of boundary dispute between Chile and Argentina (see CHRIST OF THE ANDES), and formulation of DRAGO DOCTRINE.

Roca, Cape (rô'kü), W Portugal, near Lisbon, on the Atlantic; western extremity of Europe.

Rochambeau, Jean Baptiste Donatien de Vimeur, comte de (zhä' bätēst' dônäsyē' dù vĕmûr', kôt' dù rôshäbō'), 1725–1807, marshal of France. Landed in 1780 at Newport, R.I., with 6,000 regulars to aid American Revolution. Joined Washington on the Hudson 1781. Planned YORKTOWN CAMPAIGN with Washington. In 1792 he resigned command of Northern Army in French Revolutionary Wars; was imprisoned during Reign of Terror. His son **Donatien Marie Joseph de Vimeur, vicomte de Rochambeau** (märē' zhôzĕf', vēkôt'), 1750–1813, fought in American Revolution; quelled Negro revolt on the island of Haiti (1793); fell at Leipzig.

Rochdale (rŏch'dāl), county borough (pop. 87,734), Lancashire, England. Has mfg. of cotton and woolen goods. Birthplace of John Bright.

Rochdale Society of Equitable Pioneers, one of the first consumers' cooperatives, founded 1844 in Rochdale, England. Laid down basic tenets of the coOPERATIVE.

Rochefort (rôshfôr') or **Rochefort-sur-Mer** (–sür-mēr'), fishing port (pop. 22,930), Charente-Maritime dept., W France, on Charente R. near Bay of Biscay. Was founded 1666 and fortified by Vauban. Its important arsenal and shipyards were severely damaged in World War II.

Rochelle (rōshĕl'), city (pop. 5,449), N Ill., S of Rockford. Center of farm area.

Rochelle, La (lä rôshĕl'), city (pop. 45,864), cap. of Charente-Maritime dept., W France; an Atlantic port. Fishing; canning; shipbuilding. Chartered 12th cent., it became a major port of medieval France. The last stronghold of the HUGUENOTS, it fell to Richelieu's forces after a 14-month siege (1627–28). La Rochelle prospered again as chief trade center with Canada (17th–18th cent.). La Palisse, its chief port (c.3 mi. from city) was a German submarine base in World War II. The picturesque old city escaped war damage.

Rochelle salt, sodium potassium tartrate, first made in Rochelle, France (1672). Used in Seidlitz powders and FEHLING'S SOLUTION.

Rochester, John Wilmot, 2d earl of (rŏ'chĭstŭr), 1647?–1680, English poet and courtier, remembered for his witty satires and occasional lyrics.

Rochester (rŏ'chĭstŭr), municipal borough (pop. 43,-899), Kent, England. Norman wall (12 ft. thick) surrounds ruins of 12th-cent castle. Dickens's home, "Gadshill Place," is near by.

Rochester (rŏ'chě"stŭr, rŏ'chĭstŭr). **1** City (pop. 29,-885), SE Minn., SSE of St. Paul; settled 1854. Farm trade center. Seat of Mayo Clinic, founded 1889 by Dr. W. W. Mayo, with sons C. H. MAYO, and W. J. Mayo. Large transient population because of medical center. **2** City (pop. 13,776), SE N.H., on Salmon Falls R. and NW of Dover; settled 1728. Mfg. of woolens, shoes, and wood products. **3** City (pop. 332,488), W N.Y., at Genesee R. mouth on L. Ontario and E of Buffalo; permanent settlement began 1812. State's third-largest city and a major lake port. Mfg. of photographic and optical goods, clothing, precision instruments, business machines, chemicals; extensive nurseries. Has Philharmonic, civic, and Eastman orchestras; Mus. of Arts and Sciences, Memorial Art Gall., Rundel Memorial Building; Highland Park (lilacs). Seat of Nazareth Col. (R.C.; for women; 1924); Univ. of Rochester (nonsectarian; private; coed.; chartered and opened 1850 by Baptists), which is especially known for Eastman School of Music (1918; Howard Hanson became director 1924), school of medicine and dentistry, courses in engineering, optics, physics. Susan B. Anthony and Frederick Douglass lived here. George EASTMAN was prominent in city's modern growth. **4** Borough (pop. 7,197), W Pa., at union of Ohio and Beaver rivers and NW of Pittsburgh. Mfg. of abrasives and food products.

rock, solid matter composed of one or more minerals forming the earth's crust. Rocks are divided into three major classes: igneous rocks are formed by cooling of molten material from earth's interior (e.g., granite, obsidian, basalt, pumice); sedimentary rocks, often called stratified rock (see STRATIFICATION), are consolidated fragments of older rocks (forming shale, sandstone, conglomerate), or lime rocks made of cemented shells or calcium carbonate precipitated out of solution (e.g., limestone); metamorphic rocks have been changed by heat and pressure (slate, schist, gneiss, marble, quartzite).

Rockaway peninsula: see QUEENS.

Rockefeller, John D(avison), 1839–1937, American industrialist and philanthropist. By strict economy, mergers with competitors, and ruthless crushing of opponents his Standard Oil Co. dominated U.S. oil-refining industry. Founded Univ. of Chicago (1892). Other philanthropies, amounting to some $500,000,-000, included Rockefeller Foundation, estab. in 1913 to promote public health and to further science. His son, **John D(avison) Rockefeller, Jr.,** 1874–, took over active management of his father's interests in 1911, engaged in numerous philanthropies, founded ROCKEFELLER CENTER. His son, **Nelson Aldrich Rockefeller,** 1908–, served as Coordinator of Inter-American Affairs in U.S. Dept. of State (1940–45). J. D. Rockefeller's brother, **William Rockefeller,** 1841–1922, was associated with Standard Oil Co. His vast resources built up Natl. City Bank of New York.

Rockefeller Center, in central Manhattan, New York city, between 48th and 51st streets and Fifth Ave. and the Ave. of the Americas; built 1931–39. Comprises 14 buildings, including a 70-story skyscraper and a radio and entertainment section (Radio City).

Rockefeller Foundation, founded 1913 by John D. Rockefeller with an endowment of $150,000,000. Its expressed purpose is to promote the well-being of mankind throughout the world.

Rockefeller Institute for Medical Research, philanthropic organization (founded 1901) for study of nature, cause, and treatment of diseases of humans, animals, and plants. Maintains laboratories and hospital in New York city.

rocket, name for several plants of mustard family. Sweet or dame's rocket (*Hesperis matronalis*) is an Old World biennial, naturalized in North America, with fragrant white to purple flowers. Rocket salad (*Eruca sativa*), the roquette of Europe, is a coarse plant, with creamy flowers; it is used in salads.

rocket, projectile propelled by force within itself. It is set in motion by reaction of rapid stream of gas escaping through vents. Rockets were used in Asia before discovery of gunpowder and have been widely used in festive and military activities; in World War II they became basis of various explosive projectiles (e.g., "buzz-bombs" or German V-2 weapons). Rockets provide motive force for skyrockets, airplane rockets, "bazookas," plane catapults, and the like. See *ill.*, p. 19.

Rock Falls, city (pop. 7,983), NW Ill., on Rock R. opposite Sterling, in farm area. Mfg. of farm machinery.

Rockford, city (pop. 92,927), N Ill., on both banks of Rock R. (power dam) near Wis. line; founded 1834. Industrial, shipping, trade center in grain, dairy, and livestock area. Mfg. of knit goods, furniture, and metal products. Seat of Rockford Col. Near by is U.S. Camp Grant.

rock garden, garden among natural rock formations or rocks artificially arranged, with deep soil pockets to accommodate the long roots of plants. Alpine plants, low herbaceous plants, and dwarf shrubs are suitable.

Rockhampton (rŏkhămp'tŭn), city (pop. 34,988), Queensland, Australia, on Fitzroy R. near its mouth on the Pacific; founded 1858. Chief port for pastoral and mining regions of central Queensland.

Rock Hill, city (pop. 24,502), N S.C., SSW of Charlotte, N.C. Textile mills. Seat of Winthrop Col. (state supported; for women; 1886).

Rockingham, Charles Watson-Wentworth, 2d marquess of, 1730–82, English Whig statesman. His coalition government (1765–66) saw repeal of Stamp Act and attempted conciliation with America. His second ministry (1782) saw repeal of Poynings's Law.

Rockingham, town (pop. 5,499), SE Vt., on Connecticut R. N. of Brattleboro. Includes industrial village of Bellows Falls (pop. 3,881); mfg. of paper since 1802. Navigation canal, said to have been first to be undertaken in U.S., was built around falls here (1792–1802), and rebuilt as part of hydroelectric power project (1926–28).

Rock Island, city (pop. 48,710), NW Ill., on the Mississippi. Forms, with MOLINE, EAST MOLINE (Ill.), and DAVENPORT (Iowa), an economic unit called Quad Cities. Rail, industrial, trade, and insurance center. Mfg. of metal products, electrical and heating equipment, and clothing. George DAVENPORT built house (1833) on fortified island, which had been important in Black Hawk War. Now site of U.S. arsenal. Seat of Augustana Col. and Theological Seminary (see SIOUX FALLS, S.Dak.), noted choir.

Rockland. 1 City (pop. 9,234), S Maine, on harbor on Penobscot Bay. Fishing, trading, and resort center. Ships lime from its quarries. **2** Town (pop. 8,960), SE Mass., SE of Boston; settled 1673. Shoes.

Rockne, Knute (Kenneth) (rŏk'nē), 1888–1931, American football coach. From 1918 through 1930 his Notre Dame teams won 105, lost 12, tied 5, were undefeated, untied five seasons (1919–20, 1924, 1929–30).

Rockport. 1 City (pop. 2,493), SW Ind., on Ohio R. and E of Evansville. Has Lincoln Pioneer Village, memorial with reconstructed homes. **2** Town (pop. 4,231), NE Mass., on Cape Ann; resort and artists' colony.

3 City (pop. 2,266), S Texas, on Aransas Bay and NE of Corpus Christi. Resort with fisheries.

Rock River, c.285 mi. long, rising in S Wis. and flowing S and SW through NW Ill. to the Mississippi near Rock Island. Irrigates fertile farm area.

rock salt: see SALT.

Rock Springs, city (pop. 10,857; alt. c.6,270 ft), SW Wyo., on Bitter Creek; estab. in 1860s. Trade center in livestock and coal area with hunting and fishing supplies. Polyglot population holds annual Internat. Night.

Rockville. 1 City (pop. 8,016) in agr. Vernon town (pop. 10,115; settled c.1726), N Conn., NE of Hartford; chartered 1889. Textiles. **2** Town (pop. 6,934), W central Md., NNW of Washington, D.C. Near by are Clara Barton's house and testing laboratory of Navy Dept.

Rockville Centre, residential village (22,362), on SW Long Isl., SE N.Y., S of Hempstead. Machinery, lighting fixtures, metal and rubber products.

Rockwall, city (pop. 1,501), N Texas, near East Fork of Trinity R. and NE of Dallas. Named for geological formation that looks man-made.

Rockwell, Norman, 1894–, American illustrator, best known for magazine covers.

Rocky Hill, town (pop. 5,108), central Conn., on Connecticut R. below Hartford. Rayon yarn.

Rocky Mount, city (pop. 27,697), E N.C., on Tar R. and ENE of Raleigh. Processes and markets tobacco and cotton.

Rocky Mountain College: see BILLINGS, Mont.

Rocky Mountain goat, goatlike mammal (*Oreamnos*) of Rocky Mts. of Alaska, Canada, NW U.S. Not a true goat, it is related to the antelope and chamois. It has a white coat and the male stands c.3 ft. high at the humped shoulder.

Rocky Mountain House, town (pop. 1,147), S central Alta., Canada, at foot of Rocky Mts., on North Saskatchewan R. Founded 1799 as fur-trading post.

Rocky Mountain National Park: see NATIONAL PARKS AND MONUMENTS (table).

Rocky Mountains, longest and highest mountain system of North America, composed of many complex systems, extending S from N Alaska through W Canada and into SW U.S. Alaska has the BROOKS RANGE; Canadian portion includes CARIBOO MOUNTAINS, SELKIRK MOUNTAINS. Section at boundary between British Columbia and Alberta is called Canadian Rockies. In U.S. the Rocky Mts. across portions of Wash., Idaho, Mont., Utah, Wyo., and Colo. and end in N N.Mex. Include WIND RIVER RANGE, TETON RANGE, FRONT RANGE. E the system rises from the GREAT PLAINS; W the GREAT BASIN and other depressions separate it from the Coast Ranges. Continental Divide follows crests of the Rockies, source of great river systems (e.g., the Yukon, the Missouri). The Rockies, geologically young, are chiefly a granite and gneiss mass with occasional evidence of volcanic action. System has some glaciers, many peaks over 14,000 ft. (e.g., Pikes Peak, Colo.). Gold, silver, copper, lead, and coal are found; extensive farming and grazing regions. Many national parks in Canada and U.S. For early travelers' routes, see OREGON TRAIL and OVERLAND TRAIL. Early explorations included LEWIS AND CLARK EXPEDITION and those of Z. M. PIKE, J. C. FRÉMONT, and the MOUNTAIN MEN.

Rocky Mountain sheep: see BIGHORN.

Rocky Mountain spotted fever, acute infectious disease transmitted by bite of certain ticks. Caused by rickettsia (forms intermediate between viruses and bacteria). Fatalities among livestock and humans are reduced by use of serum and preventive vaccine.

Rocky River, city (pop. 11,237), NE Ohio, on L. Erie at mouth of Rocky R., W suburb of Cleveland.

rococo (rŭkō′kō, rō–), style in architecture, especially in interiors and the decorative arts, which originated in France under Louis XV in early 18th cent. A more delicate offshoot of the BAROQUE, it made use of such forms as shells, scrolls, and flowers in room decorations and furniture. The craze for Chinese art added bizarre motives to the style and produced decorative work known as *chinoiserie*. The style spread to other countries (esp. Germany and Austria); in England it had a marked influence on the furniture of Chippendale.

rococo, in music, an offshoot of the baroque, less formal and more graceful in style; began in France. Its chief medium was keyboard music, its greatest composer François Couperin (1668–1733).

Rocroi (rôkrōōä′), village, Ardennes dept., N France, where French under Louis II de Condé decisively defeated the Spanish (1643).

rodent, member of largest order of mammals, Rodentia, with teeth fitted for gnawing and chewing. The enlarged upper and lower incisor teeth grow throughout life. In size, rodents range from harvest mouse (4½–7 in. long, including tail) to CAPYBARA (c.4 ft. long). Among the rodents are chipmunk, squirrel, rat, beaver, porcupine, guinea pig, chinchilla. Hare and rabbit are now usually placed in another family.

Roderick (rŏ′dŭrĭk), d. 713?, last Visigothic king in Spain (710–713?). Was defeated by the Moslems under TARIK (711). Subject of many legends.

Rodez (rôdĕz′), city (pop. 16,366), cap. of Aveyron dept., S France; historic cap. of Rouergue.

Rodgers, John, 1773–1838, American naval officer. Served in Tripolitan War. His defeat of British vessel, the *Little Belt*, was an incident leading to War of 1812. Saw distinguished service in war.

Rodgers, Richard, 1902–, American composer of musical comedies. He collaborated with lyricist Lorenz Hart (1895–1943) in many successes, e.g., *The Girl Friend* (1926); *A Connecticut Yankee* (1927), containing the song *My Heart Stood Still; Babes in Arms* (1937); and *The Boys from Syracuse* (1938), containing *Falling in Love with Love*. Rodgers's collaboration with Oscar Hammerstein 2d began with *Oklahoma!* (1943) and was continued in *Carousel* (1945), *South Pacific* (1949), and *The King and I* (1951).

Rodin, Auguste (ōgüst′ rōdĕ′), 1840–1917, French sculptor. Began art studies at age of 14, while working for an ornament maker; later worked for architectural sculptors. In Salon of 1877 he exhibited a nude male figure for which he was praised by some, while others accused him of having cast from life. Upshot was that he gained official support; the government gave him a studio in Paris, where he worked the rest of his life. Considered the most important sculptor of his time, he produced works that are both realistic and poetic. Most famous works include *The Thinker* (Paris) and *Adam and Eve* (Metropolitan Mus.). Rodin museums in Paris and Philadelphia.

Rodney, George Brydges Rodney, 1st Baron, 1719–92, British admiral. His defeat (1782) of French fleet under De Grasse in West Indies led to better peace terms with French after American Revolution.

Rodó, José Enrique (hōsā′ ānrē′kā rôdō′), 1872–1917, Uruguayan essayist, literary and social critic, and moralist. His *Ariel* (1900) calls on Latin America to resist materialism of U.S.

Rodriguez (rōdrē′gŭs), island (40 sq. mi.; pop. 11,885), of Mascarene group, in Indian Ocean. Belongs to British colony of Mauritius. Discovered 1645 by the Portuguese, taken 1810 by the British.

Roe, E(dward) P(ayson), 1838–88, American clergyman, author of moralistic novels, e.g., *Barriers Burned Away* (1872) and *The Opening of a Chestnut Burr* (1874).

Roebling, John Augustus (rō′blĭng) 1806–69, German-American engineer, b. Mulhouse. In 1831 he came to U.S. He was a pioneer in the use and manufacture of steel cable and in building steel suspension bridges. His ambitious Brooklyn Bridge project was scarcely begun when injuries suffered in an accident while directing the work caused his death. Thereafter the construction was in charge of his son, **Washington**

Augustus Roebling, 1837–1926, who had aided his father in earlier work. Because he worked underground so much he was stricken (1872) with caisson disease, but despite invalidism he directed the project until the bridge was opened to traffic (1883).

Roemer, Olaus: see RÖMER, OLAUS.

Roentgen or **Röntgen, Wilhelm Conrad** (rĕnt'gïn, Ger. vïl'hĕlm kôn'rät rûnt'gùn), 1845–1923, German physicist. Won 1901 Nobel Prize for discovery of X ray.

Roentgen ray: see X RAY.

Roerich, Nicholas (Konstantin) (rûr'ïkh), 1874–1947, Russian painter and archaeologist. Associated with Moscow Art Theater and Diaghilev ballet. Spent five years exploring the Himalayas. Roerich Mus. (N.Y.) founded 1921 in his honor.

Rogation Days, in the Roman Catholic Church, four days set apart for solemn processions to invoke God's mercy: April 25 (the Major Rogation), three days before Ascension Day (Minor Rogations). Processions are a Christian adaptation of Roman pagan custom.

Roger, Norman rulers of Sicily. **Roger I,** c.1031–1101, joined with his brother ROBERT GUISCARD in the conquest of Apulia and Calabria from Byzantium and of Sicily from the Arabs (1057–91). Robert made him count of Sicily and Calabria (1072). His son and successor, **Roger II,** c.1097–1154, conquered Apulia and Salerno (1127), despite opposition of Pope Innocent II, and was crowned king of Sicily by Antipope Anacletus II (1130). Innocent eventually yielded and invested Roger with the lands he already possessed. Roger estab. a strong central administration. His brilliant court at Palermo was a center of arts, letters, and sciences.

Roger de Coverley (dù kŭ'vùrlē) or **Roger of Coverley,** old English country dance and tune, resembling Virginia reel. Sir Roger de Coverley, literary figure in *Spectator* (1711), is introduced as a descendant of the originator of the dance.

Roger of Loria or **Lauria,** c.1245–1304, Sicilian admiral in service of Peter III and James II, kings of Aragon and Sicily. As commander of the Aragonese fleet during the struggle between the house of Aragon and the Angevin dynasty for possession of Sicily, he repeatedly defeated the Angevins.

Rogers, Bruce, 1870–, American book designer. As printing adviser to Cambridge Univ. Press, Harvard Univ. Press, and special commercial houses, he did much to advance fine book design.

Rogers, John, 1500?–1555, English Protestant martyr. First a Catholic priest, he became Protestant 1535. Using name of Thomas Matthew, he helped prepare second Coverdale Bible. Under Queen Mary he was imprisoned in 1554, tried, and burned as heretic at Smithfield.

Rogers, John, 1829–1904, American sculptor. An early clay group, *The Slave Auction,* was publicized by the abolitionists. Many "Rogers groups" were reproduced in quantity by machine.

Rogers, Lindsay, 1891–, American political scientist; teacher at Columbia Univ. after 1920.

Rogers, Robert, 1731–95, American frontiersman. Headed famous company of frontier rangers in last of French and Indian Wars. Commanded post at Mackinac (1765–68), sent out expedition of Jonathan CARVER, and was arrested on charges of conspiracy. Joined Loyalists in American Revolution. Often reviled for drunkenness and dishonesty.

Rogers, Will(iam Penn Adair), 1879–1935, American humorist. The "cowboy philosopher" was known for his salty comments, on the stage, in motion pictures, and in newspapers, on the passing show.

Rogers, Mount, peak, 5,720 ft. high, SW Va., near Tenn.–N.C. line; highest point in state.

Roger van der Weyden: see WEYDEN, ROGER VAN DER.

Roget, Peter Mark (rō'zhā, rōzhā'), 1779–1869, English lexicographer, a physician. Successive editions of his *Thesaurus of English Words and Phrases* (1852) remain standard reference books.

Rogue, river, SW Oregon, rising in Cascade Range N of Crater L. and flowing c.200 mi. SW and W, through fruitgrowing area, to the Pacific near Calif. line.

Rohan, Édouard, prince de (ādwär' prĕs' dù rôâ'), 1734–1803, French cardinal, archbishop of Strasbourg, grand almoner of Louis XVI. His anti-Austrian attitude earned him the hatred of Marie Antoinette. In his eagerness to gain the queen's favor he fell victim to a confidence game—the inglorious Affair of the DIAMOND NECKLACE. Though acquitted (1780), he was disgraced.

Rohan, Henri, duc de (ārē' dük'), 1579–1638, French Protestant general. Led Huguenot resistance against Richelieu, notably in 1627–29, but was chosen in 1635 by Richelieu to command French forces in the Grisons. Treachery forced his retreat in 1637. He joined the Protestant forces in Germany and fell at Rheinfelden.

Rohde, Ruth Bryan: see OWEN, RUTH BRYAN.

Rojas, Fernando de (fĕrnän'dō dā rō'häs), 1465?–1526?, Spanish novelist. See CELESTINA, LA.

Rojas Zorrilla, Francisco de (fränthē'skō dā rō'häs thōrē'lyä), 1607–48, Spanish dramatist, author of farces exaggerating peculiarities of characters.

Rokitansky, Karl (kärl rōkïtän'skē), 1804–78, Austrian pathologist. He wrote valuable descriptions of diseases based on post-mortem examinations.

Roland, d. 778, French hero of medieval legend and of the 11th-cent. epic, *La Chanson de Roland.* The historic Roland, prefect of the Breton march, was among the slain when the rear guard of Charlemagne's army, returning from Spain, was ambushed by the Basques in the Pyrenees. Legend changes the Basques into Saracens, locates the action at Roncesvalles, and vastly exaggerates the importance of both the event and its hero. The skillful characterization of its main protagonists and its simple, moving poetry make the epic one of the best-loved masterpieces of medieval literature. Roland also appears in other chansons of the Charlemagne cycle. As Orlando, he is transformed beyond recognition in the epics of BOIARDO and ARIOSTO.

Roland de la Platière, Jean Marie (zhã' märē' rôlä' dù lä plätyĕr'), 1734–93, and **Manon (Phlipon) Roland de la Platière** (Mme Roland) (mänō' flēpō'), 1754–93, French revolutionists; husband and wife. Mme Roland, imbued with classical ideals and with Rousseau's philosophy, made her house the intellectual center of the GIRONDISTS. Her husband, an inspector general of commerce before the Revolution, was strongly influenced by her and became minister of the interior in the Girondist ministry of 1792. When the Girondists fell, Mme Roland was arrested; she walked to the guillotine crying out, "O Liberty, what crimes are committed in your name!" Her husband, who had fled Paris, committed suicide upon hearing her fate.

Rolfe, John (rŏlf), 1585–1622, English colonist in Va. Introduced regular cultivation of tobacco (1612). Married POCAHONTAS.

Rolla (rŏ'lù). **1** City (pop. 9,354), S central Mo., SE of Jefferson City, in a farm, timber, clay, and pyrite area of the Ozarks. Seat of Univ. of Missouri school of mines and metallurgy. **2** City (pop. 1,176), N N.Dak., near Canadian border and NNW of Devils Lake. Hq. for International Peace Garden.

Rolland, Romain (rômē' rôlä'), 1866–1944, French author. He wrote biographies of Beethoven (1903), Michelangelo (1905), Tolstoy (1911), and Gandhi (1924). His magnum opus is the 10-vol. novel *Jean-Christophe* (1904–12; Eng. tr., 1910–13). *The Wolves* (1898) is his best-known play. He received the 1915 Nobel Prize in Literature. His pacifism, reflected in *Above the Battle* (1915) led to self-imposed exile in Switzerland until 1938. His chief works have been translated into English.

roller skating: see SKATING.

Rollins College, at Winter Park, Fla.; nonsectarian, coed.; founded 1884 by Congregationalists, chartered

1885. Stresses conference plan and individualized curriculum. Has Inter-American Center.

Rollo (rŏ'lō), c.860–c.932, leader of Norman pirates. By Treaty of Saint-Clair-sur-Epte (911) Charles III of France gave him in fief the territory which became the duchy of Normandy. In return, he accepted Christianity. Was direct ancestor of William the Conqueror.

Rolvaag, Ole (Edvart) (ō'lü ĕd'värt rōl'väg), 1876–1931, Norwegian-American novelist, known for his *Giants in the Earth* (1927) and other powerful realistic novels of Norwegian pioneers in Northwest.

Romagna (rōmä'nyä), historic region, N central Italy, on the Adriatic, now part of EMILIA-ROMAGNA. Contains RAVENNA, RIMINI, and independent republic of SAN MARINO. Under Byzantine rule 540–751, region was donated to papacy by Pepin the Short (754) and Charlemagne (774) but was claimed by later emperors. The rise of free communes and of petty tyrants prevented effective control by either emperors or popes. Cesare BORGIA, created duke of Romagna by Pope Alexander VI (1501), made himself master of the region. His downfall resulted in the effective incorporation of Romagna with the PAPAL STATES.

Romains, Jules (jhül' rômĕ'), 1885–, French novelist, whose real name is Louis Farigoule. Principal work is the cycle *Men of Good Will* (27 vols., 1932–46; Eng. tr., 13 vols., 1933–46). His plays include *Cromedeyre-le-Vieil* (1920) and the farce *Doctor Knock* (1923; Eng. tr. 1925). Elected to the French Academy 1946.

roman: see TYPE.

Roman architecture. First inspired by Greek buildings of S Italy and Sicily, it later borrowed from Greece itself and the Hellenistic East. From the Etruscans came the true arch, vault, and dome. Introducing the use of concrete after 2d cent. B.C., the Romans developed revolutionary structural forms, in which the arch eventually came to be the chief structural element, with the columns serving merely as buttresses or for decoration. Of early Rome and of the republic (c.500 B.C.–27 B.C.) the aqueducts outside Rome are the most impressive remains. The main examples of Roman architecture belong to the period between 100 B.C. and A.D. 300. Though unfired brick was used in all periods, under the empire baked bricks became popular as a facing for concrete walls. From early times stucco was used as a finish for important buildings. Vaults were highly developed; types included the barrel vault, cross or groined vault, and dome and semi-dome (see *ill.,* p. 47). Roman architecture reached its climax under Trajan (A.D. 98–A.D. 117). In all periods splendor and utility were the Roman ideals, as opposed to the subtle refinements of the Greeks. Civic planning resulted in the series of great fora created to extend the area of the Old Roman Forum (see FORUM). Most important among the buildings developed by the Romans were basilicas, baths, amphitheaters, and triumphal arches. A type of Roman dwelling was the luxurious country home or villa.

Roman art. Early Etruscan art, though strongly influenced by that of archaic Greece, reveals a native feeling for bold decorative color effects and exuberance of spirit. From c.400 B.C. the vitality of the earlier art gave way to imitation of Greek classical models. Romano-Etruscan art between 300 B.C. and 100 B.C. with its imitation of early Etruscan as well as Greek forms throws light on the eclecticism of Roman taste. In the Augustan period (30 B.C.–A.D. 14) there was an attempt to combine realism with the Greek feeling for idealization and abstract harmony of forms; subsequent decades produced magnificent portrait busts, notable for psychological penetration. From the time of Trajan (A.D. 98–A.D. 117) the influence of the Egyptian or Near Eastern illustrative tradition became important and is reflected in such works as the spiral band of narrative reliefs on Trajan's Column (Rome). Under Hadrian (117–38) there was a reversion to idealization, but the later assimilation of Oriental influence (211–337) encouraged a tendency

toward abstraction. Roman painting, like sculpture, was strongly influenced by the art of Greece. The few extant paintings (e.g., murals at Pompeii) suggest that the art was mainly one of interior decoration. In general the Roman minor arts (esp. cameos, metalwork, pottery, glassware) tended to emphasize richness of materials and ornamentation.

Roman Catholic Church, Christian church headed by the pope, the bishop of Rome, whose primacy is based on his claim as successor to St. Peter (the "Petrine supremacy"; see PAPACY). The term "Roman Catholic Church" dates only from the 19th cent., but is now in common use among English-speaking people; the use of the term "Roman Church" for the whole Church is, however, unfortunate, since it means when used officially the archdiocese of Rome. There are at least some adherents in most of the countries of the world, and the claim that there are, in all, hundreds of millions of Catholics is probably true, though no actual census has been made. The vast majority belong to the Roman rite, i.e., have a liturgy said in Latin and follow the usages of the church at Rome. Even in the West, however, there are variant rites with somewhat different usages (e.g., the Ambrosian rite, the Dominican rite, the Mozarabic rite). In the East there are groups in communion with the pope that have other rites—Byzantine, W Syrian or Antiochene, E Syrian or Chaldean, Alexandrian, and Armenian. Some of the adherents to these have left other churches to accept communion with the pope. (For information on some of these Eastern groups, see ARMENIAN CHURCH; JACOBITE CHURCH; MARONITES; NESTORIAN CHURCH.) All members of the Church accept the gospel of Christ as handed down, uncontaminated, by the Church. They accept the teachings of the Bible together with the interpretations placed upon those teachings by the Church. Central to Catholic belief is the doctrine that God conveys his grace direct to man through the sacraments (see SACRAMENT). The EUCHARIST is the center of Catholic worship, which may have much pomp and color (see MASS). Emphasis is laid on oneness and wholeness of the whole Christian body, which includes the dead as well as the living, the Virgin Mary and other saints in heaven, the souls in PURGATORY, and struggling mortals on earth. Many traits of Catholic life are more conspicuous to non-Catholics than essential to the Catholic faith (e.g., many ceremonies, the use of incense, eating fish on Friday). The sense of solidarity and the grace given by the sacraments rather heightens than lessens the burden put upon the individual, who must act according to the dictates of his conscience and be judged (as he believes) by God according to his motives in acting. The integrated structure of the Church from the parish priests through the bishops to the pope is impressive (see ORDERS, HOLY). The heart of the Church is in the papal court at VATICAN City in Rome, where matters of central administration are handled by papal officials, Offices, and commissions (see CARDINAL). The Church strives for spiritual universality. Outside the secular organization of the Church are the orders of regular priests, brothers, and nuns, who are part of the body of the Church (see MONASTICISM). In early centuries of the Christian era the Christian body was one, though split by numerous heresies, which withered away as they were opposed by the organized strength of ecumenical councils and by the popes, who gained increasing power in the West despite some faltering (see PAPACY). The contest between the pope on the one hand and lay rulers on the other over ecclesiastic and lay power was a dominant theme of the Middle Ages. Mingled with this were recurrent reforms within the Church, notably the Cluniac reform (10th–11th cent.) and the reform led by Gregory VII (11th cent.). The 12th cent. saw the great effort of the CRUSADES, the purging influence of Bernard of Clairvaux, and the codification of CANON LAW by Gratian. The 13th cent. was marked by the development of SCHOLASTICISM and the flowering of the Church. The new orders of friars, DOMINICANS and FRANCISCANS, had much to do with this. The pope was in eclipse in the "Babylonian captivity" of the papacy (1309–78), and the Church was rocked later by the Great SCHISM. Reform stagnated, and most churchmen were involved in politics and worldliness—a tendency increased by the Renaissance. Some moves had been made for internal reform, before the REFORMATION in the 16th cent. brought revolt and the break-up of the Church. The Catholic REFORM, especially through the Council of TRENT, purified the Church of many abuses, but the papacy was still beset by the demands of "Catholic princes" until the late 18th cent. The overthrow of despotism released the Church soon afterward, and in the 19th cent. the reign of Pius IX saw the loss of the PAPAL STATES (a blessing in disguise) and also enunciation of the doctrine of papal infallibility in matters of faith and doctrine. The Church in the 19th and 20th cent. has had as one of its great problems adjustment to modern political and social conditions, under the leadership of such men as Leo XIII, Pius XI, and Pius XII. The Church in America was founded first by Spanish and French missionaries, but in the English-speaking colonies may fairly be said to have begun with John Carroll, first bishop (1790).

romance [O.Fr.,= something written in popular languages, i.e., Romance language]. The *roman* of Middle Ages in Europe was a chivalric and romantic narrative. It was lengthened into *roman d'adventure*, or romance of love and adventure, from which the modern romance derives.

Romance languages or **Romanic languages**, group of Italic languages of Indo-European family. See LANGUAGE (table).

Roman de la Rose, Le (lù rōmä' dù lä rōz'), French poem of 22,000 lines in two parts. The first, written c.1237 by Guillaume de Lorris, is an allegory on the psychology of love, often subtle and charming. The second, written in 1275–80 by Jean de Meun, is wholly different in its satirical tone and seems to typify the medieval bourgeois spirit as against Guillaume's courtly ideals. Chaucer translated the first 1,700 lines of the *Roman* (or *Romaunt*).

Roman Empire: see ROME; BYZANTINE EMPIRE; HOLY ROMAN EMPIRE.

Romanesque architecture (rōmŭnĕsk'), style which prevailed throughout Europe, 11th–13th cent.; influenced chiefly by buildings of the Roman Empire. In early Middle Ages the artistic revival fostered by monasteries resulted in the building of many churches and abbeys. From about 11th cent. to middle of 15th, the great evolution progressed from the Romanesque with its round arch to the pointed arch of the Gothic. Notable in Romanesque style was the return to masonry vaulting which after the decline of Roman building had been ignored. Unlike the Roman type, however, the Romanesque vault was built of blocks of cut stone, and not of brick and concrete. The attempt to create a vaulted style forced a steady progression in technique; the vital problem of interrelating vaults, supports, and abutments (for receiving the pressure of arches and vaults), was ultimately solved by the creation of the stone skeleton (exemplified by the abbey church of St. Denis, France). An adequate framework for carrying the weight of the vault surface was provided by the groined vault (see *ill.,* p. 47), supported by upright shafts. Early Romanesque churches followed the general plan of the Christian basilica, but those after c.1050 show the advance toward the more complex Gothic plan. NORMAN ARCHITECTURE was based on the Romanesque style.

Romanesque art developed roughly from 500 to 1200, the period of transition from Roman to Gothic. Roman and Byzantine elements remained more or less dominant though blended with Eastern influences (esp.

Persian and Mesopotamian). Barbaric vigor was lent by Celtic and Lombard elements. Sculpture was developed as decoration for Romanesque buildings, such dramatic scenes as the *Last Judgment* being used to enrich the portals of churches. Silverwork, bronze casting, mosaic work, needlework (notably BAYEUX TAPESTRY), and other crafts flourished during the period. In painting there was no marked development, but Romanesque artists excelled in the decoration of manuscripts, the most brilliant school being produced in 7th-cent. Ireland.

Romania: see RUMANIA.

Romanic languages: see ROMANCE LANGUAGES.

Roman law, system of law developed in the republic of Rome, the Roman Empire, and the Byzantine Empire. Highly formalistic in the beginning, it developed from the Law of the Twelve Tables (450 B.C.?) to the THEODOSIAN CODE (A.D. 438), and in the time of Justinian I was compiled by Tribonian and others in the CORPUS JURIS CIVILIS, probably the most influential code of law ever made. The clarity, completeness, and systematic construction of Roman law made it admirably adaptable. It was continued in the GERMANIC LAWS and CANON LAW and persisted as well itself. In the 12th and 13th cent. there was a return to the study of original Roman law, spreading from the center of the law school of Bologna (with such masters as Irnerius and Accursius). It is the base of the legal systems of continental Europe (see CIVIL LAW). In English-speaking countries COMMON LAW has been dominant, but Roman law entered through EQUITY and has greatly affected all statute law.

Romano, Giulio: see GIULIO ROMANO.

Romanov (rō'mùnôf), ruling dynasty of Russia, 1613–1917. Ivan IV's first wife was Anastasia Romanov. Her grandnephew MICHAEL was chosen tsar in 1613. In the following list of Michael's successors, the names of rulers not descended from Michael are placed within brackets.
Descendants through males (1645–1730): ALEXIS, FEODOR III, IVAN V, PETER I, [CATHERINE I], PETER II. *Descendants through females* (1730–1917): ANNA, IVAN VI (deposed, later murdered), ELIZABETH, PETER III (deposed, probably murdered), [CATHERINE II], PAUL I (murdered), ALEXANDER I, NICHOLAS I, ALEXANDER II (assassinated), ALEXANDER III, NICHOLAS II (executed). Members of the Romanov family who escaped execution by the Bolsheviks fled abroad. Grand Duke Cyril (1876–1938), a grandson of Alexander II, was succeeded as pretender by his son Vladimir (b. 1917).

Roman religion. The indigenous Italic religion, nucleus of Roman religion, was animistic. The spirits in natural objects were thought to control human destiny and were placated to secure peace between men and gods. In early period, when Italy was dotted with small agr. groups, family and household were basic religious units. To perpetuate the family, for household safety, for an abundant harvest, and for protection from spirits of the dead the Romans made offerings, prayed, and took part in festivals. In performing these religious functions head of the family acted as the priest. Presumably as families coalesced into tribes and then into a state, family cult and ritual became the basis of state cult and ritual. Early Rome honored the gods of war and justice—Jupiter, Mars, and Quirinus. The Romans adopted many foreign gods—e.g., in 7th cent. B.C., Minerva from Etruscans and in 3d to 1st cent., Greek gods and Oriental cults (e.g., Isis). At end of the republic there were in general three religions in Rome—the old religion of the countryside, the Greco-Roman religion of upper classes, and Oriental cult-worship. Emperor Augustus tried to revive old religious ways because public morality was at a low ebb when he came to the throne, but Roman religion finally degenerated into Oriental emperor-worship. With loss of family and tribal worship the individual Roman sought a more dramatic, emotional, and optimistic religion that would satisfy his yearnings. This was religious soil in which Christianity took root.

Roman roads, network of hard-surfaced roads built to connect the city of Rome with the outposts of Roman control. They were built usually in four layers, the top one of hard stones, concrete, or pebbles set in mortar. They were remarkably durable, and many are in part still used today. The first great highway was the APPIAN WAY. Other famous roads included: the Praenestine Way (short, SE from Rome to present Palestrina); the Latin Way (S from Rome to Capua, to join Appian Way); three routes to the N and the Alps—the Flaminian Way, the Aurelian Way, and the Aemilian Way (an extension of the Flaminian); two routes across the Appenines—Salanian Way and Valerian Way. In Britain, Romans used old routes and built new ones for military purposes; notable were Icknield Street (pre-Roman), Watling Street, Ermine Street, Fosse Way.

Romans, epistle of New Testament, written by St. Paul to Christians at Rome. Subject treated is central in Paul's teaching, justification by faith (i.e., that salvation must be achieved through faith). The love and mercy of God extend to all mankind. It is for the individual to claim this love and mercy by accepting the gospel of Jesus Christ and His sacrifice on the Cross. Romans is claimed as an authority by various theologians; thus, Lutheran and Roman Catholic interpretations of justification, diametrically opposed, both depend on this epistle.

Romansh: see RHAETO-ROMANIC.

romanticism, a movement in the arts variously defined as a return to nature, exaltation of emotion and the senses over the intellect, and revolt against 18th-cent. rationalism. J. J. Rousseau had proposed that man is good by nature but corrupted by society; early romanticists idealized the "noble savage," peasants, children, and emphasized the individual. The romantic movement influenced 19th-cent. writers in every country and found expression in historical novels, tales of fantasy and horror, romances of love and adventure, as well as in poetry; although no longer a literary movement, it remains influential and controversial. In painting, romanticism was the chief 19th-cent. movement. Classic forms and rules were avoided; the emotional and spiritual were emphasized; themes were drawn from simpler or less civilized ways of living. Its major, and international, phase was landscape painting, which emphasized intimate and spiritual in nature. Musical romanticism emphasized feeling and dealt freely with form. Romanticism as the spirit of a work of art may be present in any age and can be found notably in Middle Ages and early baroque. See CLASSICISM.

Romanus (rōmā′nùs), Byzantine emperors. **Romanus I,** d. 948, usurped throne of Constantine VII (919–44). Issued laws to protect peasant and military holdings from absorption into great landed states. **Romanus II,** 939–63, reigned 959–63. With his wife Theophano, a former courtesan, he probably poisoned his father, Constantine VII. On his death Theophano married his successor, Nicephorus II. **Romanus III,** d. 1034, became emperor by marrying Zoë. His generous aid to victims of plague and earthquake and his building mania depleted the treasury. Took Edessa from Saracens (1031). Michael IV, who probably murdered him, succeeded him as emperor and husband. **Romanus IV,** d. 1071, reigned 1067–71. Was routed by the Seljuks at MANZIKERT (1071).

Romany (rŏ′mùnē, rō′–), the GYPSY language, member of Indic group of Indo-Iranian subfamily of Indo-European languages. See LANGUAGE (table).

Romberg, Sigmund, 1887–1951, Hungarian-American composer of operettas; came to U.S. in 1910. Among his successes were *Maytime* (1917), *The Student Prince* (1924), *The Desert Song* (1926), *Blossom Time* (1926), and *The New Moon* (1927).

Rome, Ital. *Roma,* city (1948 est. pop. 1,613,660), central Italy near the W coast, on both sides of the Tiber R.; cap. of Rome prov., Latium, and Italy; see of the pope, who resides in VATICAN City. The "Eternal City," it has long been a cultural, artistic, and religious center (called also the Holy City).

Rome before Augustus. Founded on the E bank of the Tiber, Rome was originally a trading and meeting ground of Latins, Sabines, and Etruscans. City-states were merged and grew to cover seven hills (Palatine, Capitoline, Quirinal, Viminal, Esquiline, Caelian, Aventine) as well as other hills and plains (e.g., the Martian Fields or *Campus Martius*). Tradition says it was founded by ROMULUS in 753 B.C. Tradition also tells of kings of the TARQUIN family. Probably the young city was under Etruscan rule until c.500 B.C. Then began the rule of the Roman republic, which was not a democracy, but a state governed by the patrician class (with increasing concessions to the lower-class plebs) and later by the senate. The ruling magistrates were the consuls. Gradually the city asserted hegemony over the neighboring Latin states, then over surrounding peoples (e.g., the Samnites). Though sacked by the Gauls in 390 B.C., Rome continued its climb to greatness and was by the 3d cent. A.D. a land power strong enough to challenge CARTHAGE in the PUNIC WARS. Success crowned Roman ambitions, and Rome became undisputed mistress of the W Mediterranean by 201 B.C. Then came the spread of power to the E, the defeat of Philip V of Macedon and Antiochus III of Syria and the humbling of Egypt by 168 B.C. The spread of Roman influence, however, benefited only the senatorial class and the *equites* (knights). Class dissension grew, and agrarian laws were adopted to pacify the masses while slave revolts were ruthlessly put down (as in Sicily, c.136–c.131, 104–c.101 B.C.). The attempted reforms of the GRACCHI came to nothing. Yet despite discontent, Rome continued its march. The Social War (90 B.C.–88 B.C.) forced Rome to widen the privileges of citizenship to other Italians. The contest between the people and the conservative rulers came to a head in the bloody struggle between MARIUS and SULLA in civil war. The result was only to make division between the senatorial and popular parties more pronounced. POMPEY secured the Roman power in the E and Julius CAESAR spread it in the W by his GALLIC WARS. The two had been temporarily joined with the rich CRASSUS in the First Triumvirate (60 B.C.), but rivalry brought out Pompey as leader of the senatorial party, Caesar as leader of the popular party. Civil war between them ended with the victory of Caesar at Pharsala (48 B.C.). Caesar then governed until he was assassinated (44 B.C.) and introduced the golden age of Roman culture and the beginnings of the empire.

The Roman Empire. Out of the anarchy following Caesar's murder came his adopted son, AUGUSTUS, who aided ANTONY in destroying the murderers of Caesar, then defeated Antony at Actium (31 B.C.). He actually estab. the Roman Empire and created the atmosphere for the golden age of Latin literature and Roman art and architecture, notable for spacious nobility and sound engineering skill (seen also in aqueducts, roads, and other projects). The Romans also were notable for developing administrative techniques to control the vast empire, which expanded under TIBERIUS, CALIGULA, and CLAUDIUS I to stretch from Britain to the Orient, the largest unified state the West has known. In the reign of NERO (A.D. 54–A.D. 68) occurred the great fire of Rome; rebuilding made the city more beautiful. At this time Christianity first began to assume importance, which was to grow through the centuries of the empire. After Nero's death there was a brief struggle (see GALBA; OTHO; VITELLIUS) before VESPASIAN (A.D. 69–A.D. 79) estab. the Flavian line. TITUS, DOMITIAN, and NERVA preceded TRAJAN, an able administrator. Un-

---

der HADRIAN the Romans drew back the frontiers of empire slightly, but within the borders were peace and prosperity. The empire was thriving and continued to do so under ANTONINUS PIUS and MARCUS AURELIUS. It is conventional to date the beginning of the wavering decline with COMMODUS (180–92), but, the process was slow and such emperors as Septimius SEVERUS and CARACALLA were able to assert themselves, as did CLAUDIUS II and AURELIAN. The reign of DIOCLETIAN (283–305) marked the division of the empire into East and West, a split deepened when CONSTANTINE I moved the capital to Constantinople. He granted tolerance (313) to the Christians, and the church grew, despite such setbacks as the revival of paganism under Julian the Apostate. German invaders were pounding at the borders and gaining some successes before THEODOSIUS strengthened Roman power. The West was now weakened as the BYZANTINE EMPIRE emerged. Rome was sacked by the Ostrogoths under ALARIC I (410), taken by GAISERIC (455), and saved from ATTILA only by the efforts of Pope Leo I. The state disintegrated, and it is customary to say that the Roman Empire in the West ended when ODOACER deposed the last emperor, Romulus Augustulus, in 476.

Medieval Rome. With the disappearance of the Roman Empire the city lost importance, suffering severely in wars of Germans and Byzantines. Yet it cradled a new institution, the PAPACY, and held the memory of the Roman commune. Popes such as GREGORY I (reigned 590–604) made Rome once more a notable city and helped shake off the burdensome but ineffective rule of Byzantine exarchs of Ravenna. Rome reasserted itself as capital of the PAPAL STATES and as center of Christianity. Even sack by the Arabs (846) and the unhappy days of the 10th cent., when great families (such as the Orsini and Colonna) controlled city and papacy, did not extinguish the light of Rome. German kings came there to be crowned emperor. Reforms in the Church by GREGORY VII had little effect on the city; he died in exile after Emperor Henry IV had taken Rome (1083), and the expedition of Normans under Robert Guiscard to aid him led only to the sack of Rome (1084). Later the commune was revived, and Arnold of Brescia set up communal government (1144–45). This was put down. A republic followed, under papal patronage, but civil strife was vigorous between GUELPHS AND GHIBELLINES. In the "Babylonian captivity" of the papacy (1309–78) Rome was desolate and disturbed. Cola di RIENZI attempted (1347) to revive the old Roman institutions, but failed. Only after the Great SCHISM was ended and Pope MARTIN V estab. himself in Rome (1420) did Rome reach stability.

Renaissance and Modern Rome. The popes who ruled Rome in the Renaissance were paradoxically responsible for moral decay in the clergy and the beautification of the city by such artists as Bramante, Michelangelo, Raphael, and Domenico Fontana. The political activities of the pope led to the sack of Rome by the soldiers of Emperor Charles V (1527). The Catholic REFORM cleansed the papal court and made the city prosperous as well as rather strictly noble in mien. Artistically the baroque style flowered in the creations of Bernini, and Rome has post-Renaissance as well as Renaissance monuments. The city became more than ever a center of world civilization. In 1796, Pope Pius VI bought a truce with the soldiers of Napoleon Bonaparte and surrendered Roman art treasures to the French. In 1798 the French occupied Rome and declared it a republic. Trouble between the pope and the French emperor continued until 1814 when papal rule was restored. Pope Pius IX (reigned 1846–78) granted a liberal constitution, but was nevertheless driven from Rome, which became a republic under Mazzini. French troops restored the pope and kept him in power until the fall of Napoleon III. In 1871 the troops of a uniting Italy

took the city and made it the capital. The pope refused to recognize his loss of temporal sovereignty, and it was only with the LATERAN TREATY of 1929 that the Roman Question was solved; at that time the pope relinquished sovereignty over all but Vatican City. Rome of today has expanded greatly but retains its great monuments of the past. Among them are the Forum and the Colosseum, the Lateran, St. Peter's Church and other great churches (St. Mary Major, St. Lawrence without the Walls, St. Paul's without the Walls, St. Peter in Chains), and graceful palaces and villas (e.g., Farnese Palace, Farnesina, Villa Borghese). The immense riches of art and its religious importance make Rome one of the most-visited cities of the world. It is also an immense center of commerce and has varied and flourishing industries (e.g., printing, publishing, mfg. of machinery, and motion pictures).

Rome. 1 City (pop. 29,615), NW Ga., at confluence of Etowah and Oostanaula rivers and NW of Atlanta; founded 1834 on a Cherokee village site. Mfg. of textile goods, machinery, and furniture; meat packing. Sherman destroyed city's industrial facilities in Nov., 1864. Shorter Col. (Baptist; for women; 1873) is here. Mountain schools, founded by Martha M. BERRY, are near. **2** Industrial city (pop. 41,682), central N.Y., on Mohawk R. and the Barge Canal and NW of Utica; laid out c.1786. Copper and brass-working center; mfg. of wire products, machinery, heating and cooling equipment, textiles. Building of Erie Canal (begun here 1817) stimulated city's growth.

Römer, Olaus or **Ole** (ōlä′ŏōs, ō′lü rû′mùr), 1644–1710, Danish astronomer. Noted for discovery that light travels, not instantaneously, but at definite speed. Name also appears as Roemer.

Romford (rŭm′–), municipal borough (pop. 87,991), Essex, England; a market town. Was cap. of Saxon royal lands called "Liberty of Havering-atte-Bower."

Romilly, Sir Samuel (rŏ′mĭlē), 1757–1818, English law reformer. He heartily approved the French Revolution in *Letters Containing an Account of the Late Revolution in France* (1792). His *Thoughts on Executive Justice* (1786) developed the humane views of Beccaria on punishment of criminals.

Rommel, Erwin (ĕr′vēn rô′mùl), 1891–1944, German field marshal. Commanded in North African desert warfare 1941–43. His initial successes were turned into defeat after ALAMEIN (1942). He commanded German forces in N France in 1944. It is said that he was ordered to take poison for his alleged part in the plot on Hitler's life. Known as the "desert fox," Rommel is considered one of the most brilliant generals of World War II.

Romney, George (rŏm′nē), 1734–1802, English portrait painter, b. Lancashire. In 1762 he went to London, where he estab. a fashionable practice and soon rivaled Reynolds. His best portraits (esp. those of women) rank among finest of English school. A notable portrait of Lady Hamilton as a bacchante is in National Gall., London.

Romsdal (rōōms′däl″), valley of Rauma R., central Norway. Piercing Dovrefjell mts., it leads through the Kringen pass to central and SE Norway. Weird outlines of peaks have inspired many legends.

Romulo, Carlos P(ena) (rō′mūlō, Span. kär′lōs pā′nä rō′mōōlō), 1900–, Filipino statesman. Became a delegate to UN in 1945; president of UN General Assembly in 1949. Appointed ambassador to U.S. in 1951.

Romulus (rŏm′ūlŭs), in Roman legend, founder of Rome. He and his twin, Remus, were sons of Mars and Rhea Silvia, daughter of Numitor, king of Alba Longa. Amulius, usurper of Numitor's throne, cast them adrift on the Tiber but they were suckled by a she-wolf and reared by a shepherd. When grown, they slew Amulius and restored throne to Numitor. Then they founded a new city (traditionally c.753 B.C.), but quarreled, and Remus was slain. To get wives, Romulus led rape of Sabine women. He estab.

a constitution. After disappearing he was worshiped as Quirinus.

Romulus Augustulus (ŏgŭs'tūlŭs), d. after 476, last West Roman emperor (475–76); son of ORESTES. Was captured, deposed, and pensioned off by ODOACER.

Roncesvalles (rōn"thāsvä'lyäs), Fr. *Roncevaux* (rōsŭvō'), pass in W Pyrenees between Spain and France; traditionally the scene of death of ROLAND.

Ronkonkoma, Lake (rŏngkŏng'kŭmŭ), central Long Isl., SE N.Y., SE of Smithtown; resort.

Ronsard, Pierre de (pyĕr' dù rōsär'), 1525–1585, French poet and courtier; leader of the PLÉIADE. A prolific writer in all forms, he excelled in love poetry (e.g., *Sonnets pour Hélène*, 1578). Among his patriotic poems are the epic fragment, *La Franciade* (1572) and two powerful appeals to the French people in which he deplores the Wars of Religion—*Discours des misères de ce temps* and *Remontrances au peuple de France* (both 1582).

Röntgen, Wilhelm Conrad: see ROENTGEN.

Röntgen ray: see X RAY.

rook (rŏŏk), common European bird of crow family, slightly smaller than American crow. Rooks nest in large colonies.

Rookwood pottery, American artware made in Cincinnati. Known for superior glazes and wide range of rich colors.

Roon, Albrecht, Graf von (äl'brĕkht gräf fŭn rōn'), 1803–79, Prussian field marshal. As minister of war 1859–73) he reorganized the Prussian army, making possible the success of Prussia in the Danish, Austro-Prussian, and Franco-Prussian wars.

Roosebeke (rō'zŭbä"kŭ), modern Flemish *Rozebeke*, village, East Flanders, Belgium. French victory here over Philip van ARTEVELDE (1382) restored Flanders to its count, Louis de Maële, and prepared succession of Louis's son-in-law, PHILIP THE BOLD.

Roosevelt, Franklin Delano (dĕ'lŭnō rō'zŭvŭlt), 1882–1945, 31st President of the United States, b. Hyde Park, N.Y. U.S. Assistant Secretary of the Navy (1913 –20). Democratic vice presidential candidate in 1920. Stricken with poliomyelitis in 1921, he recovered partial use of his legs by unremitting effort. Later he estab. a foundation at WARM SPRINGS, Ga., for poliomyelitis victims. Governor of N.Y. (1929–33). Inaugurated President at height of crisis (1933), he promptly declared a general bank holiday. NEW DEAL was born. Government agencies were set up to revive economy by vast expenditures of public money, by developing natural resources, by offering work to unemployed. Following reelection in 1936, Roosevelt encountered increasing opposition. Supreme Court declared several New Deal measures invalid. Attempted reorganization of Supreme Court in 1937 failed. Attempt to "purge" New Deal opponents in Congress also failed. In foreign affairs, Roosevelt furthered "good neighbor" policy toward Latin America. Reelected to unprecedented third term in 1940, he helped align U.S. more and more with Britain, while first peacetime selective service act came into being. Following U.S. entry into World War II, his diplomatic duties were heavy. During his fourth administration he engaged in international conferences (see CASABLANCA CONFERENCE; QUEBEC CONFERENCE; TEHERAN CONFERENCE; YALTA CONFERENCE); labored for perpetual peace through UNITED NATIONS. Died suddenly; buried at Hyde Park. His character and achievements are still hotly argued. His wife, **(Anna) Eleanor Roosevelt**, 1884–, a niece of Theodore Roosevelt and a distant cousin of F. D. Roosevelt, has worked for social betterment as lecturer, newspaper columnist, world-wide traveler. A U.S. delegate to UN (1945–52), she was made chairman of Commission on Human Rights in 1946.

Roosevelt, Theodore, 1858–1919, 25th President of the United States (1901–9), b. New York city. His health was delicate in childhood; his determination to rebuild his strength later had a marked effect on his char-

acter. U.S. Assistant Secretary of the Navy (1897–98), he resigned to organize the ROUGH RIDERS. He was a popular hero when he returned from Cuba. Governor of N.Y. (1899–1900). U.S. Vice President (1901), succeeding to presidency on death of McKinley. Vigorously championed rights of "little man," denounced "malefactors of great wealth." Engaged in "trust busting" under terms of Sherman Anti-Trust Act; brought about progressive reforms not so much directed at abolition of "big business" as at its regulation. Followed policy of conservation of natural resources. Claimed that U.S. had direct interest and some police power in foreign affairs of Latin American countries; this "big stick" policy awoke great indignation in Latin America. Promoted "dollar diplomacy" in the Caribbean area; sought to keep OPEN DOOR in China; mediated to end Russo-Japanese War. His hand-picked successor was W. H. TAFT, but, as candidate of PROGRESSIVE PARTY, Roosevelt ran against Taft in 1912. Engaged in hunting and exploring expeditions throughout his career; also wrote many books dealing with history, hunting, wildlife, politics.

Roosevelt, river, c.400 mi. long, W Brazil, rising in E Guaporé territory and flowing N across NW Mato Grosso and SE Amazonas. Called River of Doubt until explored by Theodore Roosevelt.

Roosevelt Dam: see SALT RIVER VALLEY.

Roosevelt Lake: see GRAND COULEE DAM.

Root, Elihu, 1845–1937, American statesman. U.S. Secretary of War (1899–1904); U.S. Secretary of State (1905–9); U.S. Senator from N.Y. (1909–15). One of the greatest of internationalists. Awarded 1912 Nobel Peace Prize.

Root, John Wellborn, 1850–91, American architect. Worked with James Renwick and D. H. Burnham. Developed a Romanesque type of ornament.

root, in botany, the descending axis of a plant, usually underground. Its function is to absorb water and food from the soil and to provide support. Bulbs, corms, rhizomes, and some tubers, although found underground, are actually stem structures. Taproot (long main root) is edible in carrot, parsnip, radish, and other root crops. An epiphyte is a plant without soil roots. See *ill.*, p. 783.

root, in mathematics. If a quantity is multiplied by itself a given number of times, the product is a power of that quantity, and that quantity is a root. Second root is called square root; third root is cube root.

Rops, Félicien (fălēsyē' rôps'), 1833–98, Belgian artist, of Hungarian descent. Worked mainly in Paris, where he became known as an illustrator. Also produced many etchings and lithographs.

Rorschach Test: see MENTAL TESTS.

Rosa, Salvator (sälvätōr' rō'zä), 1615–73, Neapolitan painter, famous for vigorous landscapes and spirited battlepieces. Worked in Rome and Florence (under patronage of the Medici). Known also as a satiric poet.

Rosa, Monte (mōn"tä rō'zä), mountain group on Swiss-Italian border. Highest peak, Dufourspitze, 15,203 ft., is also highest point in Switzerland.

Rosalie, Fort: see NATCHEZ.

Rosamond, fl. c.570, Lombard queen. She supposedly had her husband, King Alboin, murdered after he had forced her to drink from a cup made from the skull of her father, whom Alboin had slain. She married her accomplice Helmechis, but later regretted it and offered him a poisoned drink. Helmechis drank half and forced her to swallow the rest. The pretty story was used by Swinburne and by Alfieri in two tragedies.

Rosamond, d. 1176?, mistress of Henry II of England, known as the "fair Rosamond." There is much legendary material by medieval chroniclers concerning her supposed murder by Eleanor of Aquitaine.

Rosario, city (pop. 467,937), Santa Fe prov., E central Argentina, port on Paraná R., on E margin of Pampa. Second largest city in Argentina, it is primarily an export-import center for central and N provinces.

Rosas, Juan Manuel de (hwän' mänwĕl' dā rō'säs),

1793–1877, Argentine dictator, governor of Buenos Aires prov. (1829–32, 1835–52). In 1820 he began his political career by leading his well-trained gaucho troops in support of conservatives and federalism. Soon became governor of Buenos Aires and temporarily but with sanguinary thoroughness destroyed unitarian cause. Surrendered office (1832) but maintained prestige by successful expedition against Indians. Returning to office (1835) he soon assumed dictatorship over most of Argentina. Instituted régime of terror. Finally, because of foreign difficulties and economic crisis, a revolt, led by Urquiza and backed by Brazil and Uruguay, succeeded, and he fled to England, where he lived until his death.

Roscius, Quintus (kwĭn′tŭs rŏ′shŭs), c.126 B.C.–62 B.C., greatest Roman actor of his day.

Roscommon (rŏskŏ′mŭn), inland county (951 sq. mi.; pop. 72,510), N central Ireland, in Connaught; co. town Roscommon. Low-lying region with many lakes and bogs, it is an agr. county.

rose, wild and cultivated plant and its flower, a favorite all over the world since prehistoric times. There are many hundreds of species and varieties, ranging from tiny rock garden forms to large shrub or climbing types, with single or double flowers often fragrant, in white, yellow, and shades of red and pink. Among the old species are the damask rose and the cabbage or hundred-leaved rose, cultivated in Europe for attar of roses. Famous roses of England include the white rose, emblem of the house of York, the red rose of the house of Lancaster in the Wars of the Roses, and the variegated red and white rose, now called the York and Lancaster. Hybridization, resulting in the rambler, tea, and hybrid tea, began when the East India Company's ships brought new everblooming roses from the Orient.

Rosebery, Archibald Philip Primrose, 5th earl of (rōz′-bŭrē), 1847–1929, English statesman. Prime minister 1894–95, he split Liberal party by advocating a form of imperial federation. Was leader of Liberal imperialist division of party 1895–1905.

Rosebud, river of SE Mont., tributary of the Yellowstone. Also called Rosebud Creek. On its banks Indians under Crazy Horse defeated U.S. troops under Gen. George Crook in June, 1876.

Roseburg, city (pop. 8,390), SW Oregon, S of Eugene and on Umpqua R.; settled c. 1851. Rail and trade center with fruit canneries and lumber mills.

Rosecrans, William Starke, 1818–98, Union general in Civil War. Victor at Iuka and Corinth (1862). Commanded Army of the Cumberland, victor at Murfreesboro. In CHATTANOOGA CAMPAIGN, defeated at Chickamauga, relieved of command.

Roselle (rōzĕl′), borough (pop. 17,681), NE N.J., near Elizabeth. Mfg. of machinery, metal products.

Roselle Park, borough (pop. 11,537), NE N.J., near Roselle. Mfg. of rugs, machinery, oil burners.

rosemary, evergreen shrub (*Rosmarinus officinalis*) of Mediterranean region, widely grown for its aromatic leaves used for seasoning and perfume.

Rosemont, village, SE Pa., seat of Rosemont Col. (R.C.) for women; 1921).

Rosenberg, Alfred (äl′frät rō′zŭnbĕrk), 1893–1946, German National Socialist leader, b. Estonia. His book *Der Mythus des 20 Jahrhunderts* [the myth of the 20th cent.] (1930) supplied Hitler with the spurious philosophical and scientific basis for his racist doctrine. As minister for the occupied Eastern territories after 1941 he was responsible for German atrocities in the Baltic states and Russia. He was hanged after conviction at Nuremberg war crimes trial.

Rosenberg, city (pop. 6,210), S Texas, near Brazos R. and SW of Houston. Market and shipping center for agr. area with cotton ginning and some oil.

Rosenthal, Moriz (mō′rĭts rō′zŭntäl), 1862–1946, Polish pianist; pupil of Liszt. His American debut was in 1888 with Fritz Kreisler. He was considered one of the greatest pianists of his time.

Rosenwald, Julius (rō′zŭnwôld), 1862–1932, American merchant and philanthropist. In 1917 he estab. Julius Rosenwald Fund, used mainly to found rural schools for Negroes. He also gave to Jewish relief in the Near East and to Y.M.C.A. and Y.W.C.A.

rose of Jericho, name for certain desert plants (esp. *Anastatica hierochuntica*), of Asia Minor, sometimes called resurrection plants. Their branches curl up when dry and unfold when moist.

Rose of Lima, Saint, 1586–1617, Peruvian Dominican nun, noted for austerities; first saint of the New World to be canonized (1671). Feast: Aug. 30.

rose of Sharon, ornamental Asiatic shrub (*Hibiscus syriacus*), also called shrubby althea. It has white, rose, or purple, single or double flowers resembling those of the hollyhock.

Roses, Wars of the, name given to struggle for the throne of England 1455–84 between houses of LANCASTER (whose badge was a red rose) and YORK (whose badge was a white rose). Lancastrians had held the throne since the deposition of Richard II (1399). HENRY VI was controlled by his queen, MARGARET OF ANJOU, and by William de la Pole, duke of Suffolk, and Edmund Beaufort, duke of Somerset. They were opposed by Richard, duke of York, who gained support from popular unrest over losses in France and corruption at court. Suffolk was banished and murdered in 1450. York was made protector during insanity of king 1453–54. Yorkists won first battle of St. Albans (1455). After a period of comparative quiet, Yorkists captured Henry at battle of Northampton (1460) and arranged compromise whereby Richard would succeed Henry. Queen (whose son would be disinherited) raised an army and slew York at battle of Wakefield (1460). Richard NEVILLE, earl of Warwick, became real leader of Yorkist party. Margaret defeated Warwick and rescued Henry (1461) but Richard's son meanwhile had entered London and been crowned as EDWARD IV. Lancastrians were repeatedly defeated, Margaret fled to France, and Henry was imprisoned (1465). Warwick and Edward quarreled over king's marriage (1464) and Warwick intrigued with George, duke of Clarence. They fled to France (1470). Warwick and Margaret were reconciled, and he returned to England and restored Henry. Edward secured aid and regained the throne (1471). Warwick was killed and Henry soon died. Edward was succeeded (1483) by his 12-year-old son, EDWARD V. The boy's uncle gained control, had himself made king as RICHARD III, and had young Edward murdered. Henry Stafford, duke of Buckingham, unsuccessfully revolted in 1483. Lancastrian claimant, Henry Tudor, landed in England and defeated Richard at Bosworth Field (1485). Became king as HENRY VII and united the two houses by marrying Edward IV's daughter. Wars ended feudalism in England because they so weakened the nobles that they could not contest rise of the monarchy under the Tudors.

Rosetsu (Nagasawa) (rō′sĕtsōō), 1755–99, Japanese painter of landscapes with amusing animals.

Rosetta (rōzĕ′tŭ), Arabic *Rashid,* city (pop. 24,094), Egypt, near Rosetta mouth of the Nile. **Rosetta stone,** a basalt slab inscribed by priests of Ptolemy V in hieroglyphic, demotic, and Greek, was found near here by troops of Napoleon in 1799. Captured 1801 by British, it is now in British Mus. It gave Champollion and others key to Egyptian HIEROGLYPHIC.

Roseville. 1 City (pop. 8,723), N central Calif., NE of Sacramento. Fruit-shipping center. **2** Residential village (pop. 15,816), SE Mich., NE suburb of Detroit. Sheet metal plant.

rosewood, name for ornamental heartwood of several tropical trees of Brazil. Brazilian rosewood or jacaranda, from *Dalbergia nigra,* fragrant and purpleblack, has long been used whole or in veneers for piano castings, cabinetwork, and tools. Other rosewoods include East Indian and Honduras rosewood.

Rosh ha-Shanah (hŭ-shä′nŭ) [Heb.,= head of the year],

the Jewish New Year, observed on the first two days of the seventh month, Tishri, occurring usually in Sept. Considered days of judgment, they are spent in prayer. A trumpet (shofar—a ram's horn) is sounded during the religious ceremonies. Various other spellings, e.g., Rosh-ha-Shonah.

Rosicrucians, esoteric groups, all claiming origin in ancient Egypt. Secret learning deals with occult symbols —rosy cross, swastika, pyramid—and cabalistic writings. American Rosicrucians follow theosophical doctrines. Rosicrucian Order has hq. in San Jose, Calif.; Rosicrucian Brotherhood, in Quakertown, Pa.; Society of Rosicrucians, in New York city.

rosin (rŏz'ĭn), solid residue from crude turpentine after oil of turpentine is distilled off; also called colophony. It is hard, brittle, translucent, tasteless, pale yellow or amber; color and appearance depend on crude turpentine used and method of preparation. Used to make soaps, varnishes, paints, sealing wax; for treating violin bows; in pharmacy.

Roskilde (rôs'kĭlŭ), city (pop. 26,355), E Zealand, Denmark, W of Copenhagen; a port on Roskilde Fjord (inlet of the Kattegat). Fishing; varied mfg. It was the cap. of Denmark until 1443; ecclesiastical cap. until 1536. Many Danish kings are buried in magnificent cathedral (11th–12th cent.). By Treaty of Roskilde (1658) Denmark ceded lands in Sweden to CHARLES X of Sweden.

Roslyn (rŏz'lĭn), village (pop. 1,612), on NW Long Isl., SE N.Y., N of Mineola. William Cullen Bryant's home ("Cedarmere") and grave are here.

Ross, Betsy (Elizabeth Griscom Ross), 1752–1836, American flagmaker. Story that she designed and made first American national flag now generally discredited.

Ross, Sir John, 1777–1856, British arctic explorer and rear admiral. Sought Northwest Passage. Discovered Boothia Peninsula, Gulf of Boothia, and King William Isl. Accompanied on voyages by his nephew, **Sir James Clark Ross,** 1800–1862, also a rear admiral. Discovered Ross Isl. in command of expedition to Antarctica (1839–43); also discovered Victoria Land.

Ross, John, called in Cherokee *Kooweskoowe* (kōō"-wĭs"kōōwē'), 1790–1866, Indian chief, of mixed Scottish and Cherokee (one eighth) blood. Led Cherokee journey to present Okla. (1838–39). Chief, united Cherokee nation (1839–66).

Ross, Sir Ronald, 1857–1932, English physician, authority on tropical medicine. Won 1912 Nobel Prize in Physiology and Medicine for work on transmission of malaria.

Rossa, O'Donovan, 1831–1915, Irish rebel, whose original name was Jeremiah O'Donovan. Edited a Fenian newspaper. Convicted of treason, he was released (1871) and emigrated to New York.

Ross and Cromarty (krŏ'mŭrtē), maritime county (3,089 sq. mi.; pop. 60,503), N Scotland; co. town Dingwall. Includes Lewis and other islands. Mainly a mountainous region with fertile strip along E coast, grazing and fishing are main occupations.

Rossbach (rôs'bäkh), village, Saxony-Anhalt, E central Germany, near Weimar. Here in 1757 Frederick II of Prussia defeated the imperials and French under Soubise in one of his most brilliant victories.

Rosse, William Parsons, 3d **earl of** (rôs), 1800–1867, British astronomer. Noted for construction of telescope reflectors and for observations of nebulae.

Rosselli, Cosimo (kô'zēmō rōs-sĕl'lē), 1439–1507, Florentine painter. Painted *The Last Supper* for Sistine Chapel, Vatican.

Rossellino, Bernardo (bĕrnär'dō rōs-sĕl-lē'nō), 1409–64, Florentine architect, whose real name was Bernardo di Matteo di Domenico Gambarelli. Built Rucellai Palace in Florence. His most famous sculpture is tomb of Leonardo Bruni in Santa Croce, Florence. His brother, **Antonio Rossellino,** 1427–c.1478, was also a celebrated sculptor.

Rossetti, Gabriele (gäbrēä'lä rŏs-sĕt'tē), 1783–1854, Italian author of patriotic verse; a political exile in England after 1824. His son, **Dante Gabriel Rossetti** (dăn'tē gā'brēŭl), 1828–82, was an English Pre-Raphaelite painter and poet. With W. Holman Hunt, Millais, and others he formed brotherhood of PRE-RAPHA-ELITES (1848). In their journal, the *Germ,* edited by his brother William Michael Rossetti (1829–1919), appeared his poem "The Blessed Damozel." In 1860 he married his model, Elizabeth Siddal, who died in 1862. In his grief Rossetti buried with her the manuscript of his poems, later recovered. His *Poems* (1870) and *Ballads and Sonnets* (1881) contain the great sonnet sequence "The House of Life" and the ballad "Sister Helen." Among his best-known paintings are *Beata Beatrix, The Blessed Damozel,* and a triptych, *Francesca and Paolo.* His sister **Christina (Georgina) Rossetti,** 1830–94, was also a poet, with a true lyric gift. Some of her poems appeared in the *Germ.* Very religious, she spent last years as a recluse, and her poetry is usually religious, often melancholy. Her works include *Goblin Market and Other Poems* (1862), *The Prince's Progress* (1866), and *Sing-Song* (1872).

Rossini, Gioacchino (Antonio) (jōäk-kē'nō rôs-ē'nē), 1792–1868, Italian operatic composer. His *Barber of Seville* is a masterpiece of comic opera. Selections from his *La gazza Ladra* [the silken ladder], *L'italiana in Algeri, Semiramide,* and *William Tell* are popular.

Ross Sea, large Antarctic inlet of Pacific Ocean, E of Victoria Land. Its southern extension is Ross Shelf Ice or Barrier, between Marie Byrd Land and Victoria Land. Indented by Bay of Whales, site of Little America. Discovered by Sir James Clark Ross 1839–43.

Rostand, Edmond (ĕdmô' rôstä'), 1868–1918, French poet and dramatist. Best-known for the dramas *Cyrano de Bergerac* (1897) and *L'Aiglon* (1900) and the barnyard fable *Chantecler* (1910).

Rostock (rŏs'tŏk), city (pop. 114,869), Mecklenburg, NE Germany, on Baltic Sea. Port with petroleum tank installations and shipyards. Mfg. of machinery and chemicals. University was founded 1419. City was important in Hanseatic League. Heavily damaged by World War II air raids.

Rostov (rŏ'stŏv). **1** Or **Rostov-on-Don,** Rus. *Rostov-na-Donu,* city (pop. 510,253), S European RSFSR; a major port and rail hub on the Don c.25 mi. above its mouth on Sea of Azov. Produces machinery, sheet metal, autos, rolling stock, ships, textiles, and leather goods. Founded 1761 as fortress, it became a major grain-export center in 19th cent. Twice held (1941, 1942–43) by Germans in their drive on the Caucasus in World War II, and heavily damaged. **2** City (1926 pop. 20,864), N Central European RSFSR, NE of Moscow. One of oldest Russian cities (founded 864), it was cap. (from 10th cent.) of a principality which passed to Moscow in 1474. Its old kremlin contains Uspenski Cathedral (1214).

Rostovtzeff, Michael Ivanovich (rŏstŏv'tsĕf), 1870–, American historian, b. Kiev; an authority on the history of the ancient world.

Roswell, city (pop. 25,738), SE N.Mex., on Rio Hondo in Pecos valley; settled 1869. Resort; trade center in livestock and irrigated farm area, with oil wells and potash mines. Ships wool, processes food, refines oil, distills cottonseed oil. Carlsbad Caverns Natl. Park is c.100 mi. S.

Roswitha: see HROSWITHA.

Rotary International, organization of business and professional men, founded 1905. Supports charities and encourages international friendship.

rotation of crops, agr. practice of varying crops in a planned series to conserve and enrich soil and to eradicate weeds, insects, plant diseases.

rotenone: see INSECTICIDE.

Rothenburg ob der Tauber (rō'tŭnbŏŏrk ôp dĕr tou'bŭr), town (pop. 11,223), Middle Franconia, W Bavaria, on Tauber R. Founded in 11th cent., it almost completely preserves its medieval appearance; encircling walls date from 14th–15th cent.

Rothenstein, Sir William (rŏ'thŭnstīn), 1872–1945, English portrait painter and writer.

Rothermere, Harold Sidney Harmsworth, 1st Viscount (rŏ'dhùrmēr), 1868–1940, English publisher; financial wizard of publishing firm headed by his brother, Viscount NORTHCLIFFE. Founded (1915) *Sunday Pictorial;* gained control of newspaper empire after his brother's death. Though earlier friendly to fascism, he supported British cause valiantly in World War II.

Rothesay (rŏth'sē, –sā), burgh (pop. 10,145), county town of Buteshire, Scotland, on Bute Isl.; a resort. Has hq. of Royal Northern Yacht Club.

Rothschild (rŏth'chīld, Ger. rŏt'shīlt), prominent international family of bankers. **Mayer Amschel Rothschild** (mī'ùr äm'shùl), 1743–1812, son of a small Jewish money-changer in Frankfurt, Germany, rendered great services as financial agent of the landgraves of Hesse-Kassel and laid the foundation of the family fortune. Of his five sons, the oldest continued the business in Frankfurt. The other four estab. branches in Vienna, London, Naples, and Paris. All five were created barons by Francis I of Austria (1822), a title which continues in the family. Ablest of the brothers was **Nathan Meyer Rothschild**, 1777–1836, who opened the London branch in 1805. As agent of the British government in the Napoleonic Wars, he was of vital help in Napoleon's ultimate defeat. Under his guidance and that of his son, **Baron Lionel Nathan de Rothschild**, 1808–79, the family gained immense power by floating loans to various countries, but the family's virtual monopoly on these transactions was soon broken, and its wealth also declined. Members of the family were prominent as philanthropists, patrons of the arts, sportsmen, writers, physicians.

rotogravure: see PRINTING.

Rotorua (rōtùrōō'ù), borough (pop. 7,512), on N North Isl., New Zealand; health resort in Hot Springs Dist.

Rotten Row, track in Hyde Park, London, for horseback riders. The origin of the name is unknown.

Rotterdam (rŏ'tùrdăm", Dutch rôtùrdäm'), municipality (pop. 646,248), South Holland prov., W Netherlands, on the Nieuwe Maas near its mouth on the North Sea. Largest port and second largest city of Netherlands; accessible to ocean-going vessels through New Waterway (constructed 1866–90). Connected by waterways with the Rhineland-Ruhr industrial area of Germany, it has a huge volume of transit trade, with Antwerp its only rival on continental Europe. It has large shipyards, petroleum refineries, and mfg. of chemicals, machinery, and food products. Chartered 1328, it grew to major importance only in the 19th cent. In World War II, Rotterdam suffered a most destructive aerial bombardment, even though it had capitulated to the Germans several hours earlier (May 14, 1940). The old city center (incl. house where Erasmus was born) was obliterated.

Roty, Louis Oscar (lwē' ôskär' rôtē'), 1846–1911, eminent French medalist.

Roualt, Georges (zhôrzh' rōō-ō'), 1871–, French painter. Studied under Gustave Moreau and was a fauvist in his early period. His characteristic works have rough conventionalized forms and movingly portray injustice and human suffering. Recurrent subjects are clowns, corrupt judges, passion of Christ, and misery of war.

Roubaix (rōōbā'), city (pop. 98,834), Nord dept., N France. Center of French wool industry.

Rouen (rōōä'), city (pop. 101,187), cap. of Seine-Inférieure dept., N France, on the Seine near its mouth; historic cap. of Normandy. Major port. Cotton mfg. Archiepiscopal see since 5th cent. Held by English 1419–49 during Hundred Years War; scene of burning of Joan of Arc (1431). Seat of a provincial parlement (1499–1789) and proverbial breeding place of lawyers. Though heavily damaged in World War II, Rouen remains famous for its magnificent Gothic architecture—Cathedral of Notre Dame (13th–15th

cent., with two strikingly different towers; damaged); churches of St. Maclou (15th–16th cent.; damaged) and St. Ouen (begun 14th cent.; intact); palace of justice (15th–16th cent.; damaged). Birthplace of Corneille and Flaubert.

Rouergue (rōōĕrg'), region and former county, S France, in Aveyron dept.; historic cap. Rodez. Part of Massif Central, it has eroded limestone plateaus (*causses*), used for sheep raising (Roquefort cheese). Agr. in valleys. A Bourbon family possession, it was inc. into Guyenne prov. 1589.

Rouge (rōōzh'), river rising in S Mich. and winding c.30 mi. S and SE to Detroit R. at River Rouge city.

Rouget de Lisle, Claude Joseph (rōōzhā' dù lēl'), 1760–1836, French poet, musician, and army officer. He wrote the words and music of the MARSEILLAISE as a marching song for his soldiers. Although the song later was associated with the Revolution, he himself was a royalist and barely escaped the guillotine.

Rough Riders, name popularly given to 1st Regiment of U.S. Cavalry Volunteers in Spanish-American War. Recruited largely by Theodore Roosevelt, lieutenant colonel in regiment. Exploits, especially at San Juan Hill, were highly publicized.

roulette (rōōlĕt'), game of chance popular at Monte Carlo and other gambling resorts. Dates from late 18th cent.

Roumelia: see RUMELIA.

Round Table: see ARTHURIAN LEGEND.

Round Tops: see GETTYSBURG CAMPAIGN.

roup (rōōp), infectious disease of poultry, causing inflammation of mucous membranes of air passages and of eyes. Argyrol is used in treatment.

Rourke, Constance, 1885–1941, American writer of works on social history (e.g., *American Humor,* 1931) and biographies of American figures.

Rouses Point (rou'sīz), village (pop. 2,001), extreme NE N.Y., on L. Champlain. On the Que. line, it is a port of entry.

Rousseau, Henri (ārē' rōōsō'), 1844–1910, French painter, self-taught. Called Le Douanier from his profession as customs official. Known for jungle scenes painted in exotic colors.

Rousseau, Jean Jacques (zhä' zhäk'), 1712–78, French philosopher, b. Geneva. His wandering and troubled life was made tolerable by patrons and friends—notably Mme de Warens (his mistress as well as protector), Mme d'Épinay, the duc de Luxembourg, Diderot, and other Encyclopedists. His daring statements got him into trouble with authorities at Paris and Geneva and he had to seek asylum in the 1760s in Bern canton and then (1765) with David Hume in England. With Hume as with Diderot and other friends he quarreled bitterly, for his mind darkened with paranoiac ideas as he grew older, and he thought all were in a gigantic plot against him—including his common-law wife, Thérèse Le Vasseur (who may or may not have borne him five children, put into foundling homes, according to his account). Rousseau probably had more influence in shaping romanticism and later thought than any other man of the 18th cent. His important works include an essay contending that man is good by nature and corrupted by civilization; another essay, *Discours sur l'origine de l'inégalité des hommes* (1754); a didactic novel, *La Nouvelle Héloïse* (1761); *Le Contrat social* (1762); a novel on education, *Émile* (1762); and draft constitutions for Corsica and Poland—neither put in effect. His ideas were too complex for a brief summary, but some of them that had great effect were these. "Natural man" was a pure animal, neither good nor bad. Equality between men disappeared with the introduction of property, agriculture, and industries. Laws were instituted to preserve the inequality of oppressor and oppressed. Men may, however, enter into a social contract among themselves to set up a government (monarchic, aristocratic, or democratic), but holding the sovereignty inalienably among the people as a whole. The aim of government and education is to offset the corrupting influence of institutions. The child should be allowed to develop without interference. These ideas are also reflected in Rousseau's *Confessions,* one of the most celebrated autobiographical works ever written. This shows also in full the romantic sensibility and love of nature that was to dominate literature in the 19th cent. Rousseau was also a self-taught authority on musical theory and a composer.

Rousseau, Théodore (täŏdôr'), 1812–67, French landscape painter of the Barbizon school.

Roussel, Albert (rōōsĕl'), 1869–1937, French composer. His music is romantic and impressionistic; later works show the influence of polytonality. His compositions include the orchestral-choral *Evocations; Padmavati* (which adapts Hindu scales and story to 18th-cent. opera-ballet technique); symphonies; piano pieces; and chamber music.

Roussillon (rōōsēyô'), region and former province, S France, on Spanish border, in Pyrénées-Orientales dept.; historic cap. Perpignan. Conquered by the Franks from the Arabs in the 8th cent., it later was held by the house of Aragon and by Spain. It was ceded by Spain to France in 1659.

Rouvray, battle of: see HERRINGS, BATTLE OF THE.

Roux, (Pierre Paul) Émile (āmĕl' rōō'), 1853–1933, French bacteriologist and physician. Contributed to study of diphtheria and syphilis. Director of Pasteur Institute (1904–18).

Roux, Wilhelm (vĭl'hĕlm), 1850–1924, German anatomist, a founder of experimental embryology.

Rouyn (rōō'ĭn, Fr. rōōĕ'), city (pop. 14,633), W Que., Canada, on Osisko L. and S of Noranda. Gold, copper, and zinc mining center.

Rowe, Nicholas (rō), 1674–1718, English dramatist, author of tragedies (e.g., *Jane Shore,* 1714). Also edited Shakspere (1709). Made poet laureate in 1715.

rowing. Boats propelled by oars were used in ancient times for both war and commerce. Rowing is now mainly a sport. Most famous annual crew race, between Oxford and Cambridge, was first held at Henley, in 1839.

Rowlandson, Thomas, 1756–1827, English caricaturist, known for humorous commentary on social life. Notable work is series of drawings *Tour of Dr. Syntax* (3 vols., 1812–21).

Rowley, William, 1585?–1642?, English playwright and actor, best known for plays written with Thomas Middleton (e.g., *The Changeling,* presented 1623).

Rowson, Susanna Haswell (rou'sŭn), 1762–1824, American author, actress, and teacher; author of the novel *Charlotte Temple* (1791).

Roxana (rŏksă'nù) or **Roxane** (rŏksă'nē), d. 311 B.C., Bactrian (Persian) princess, wife of Alexander the Great. After his death, she and Alexander's posthumous son, Alexander Aegeus, were imprisoned by Cassander and finally killed.

Roxas, Manuel (mänwĕl' rô'häs), 1892–1948, Filipino statesman. Supporting Japanese-sponsored government during World War II, he is said to have aided Filipino underground at same time. First president of Philippine republic (1946–48).

Roxburghshire (rŏks'bŭrŭshĭr) or **Roxburgh,** border county (666 sq. mi.; pop. 45,562), S Scotland; co. town Jedburgh. Has Cheviot Hills in S. Drained by the Teviot and the Tweed, county is often called Teviotdale. Main occupation is sheep grazing.

Roxelana: see SULEIMAN I.

Royal Academy of Arts, London, in Burlington House; founded 1769 by George III at suggestion of Sir William Chambers and Benjamin West. Sir Joshua Reynolds was first president. Has two yearly exhibitions, one of old masters and one of contemporary art. Membership is fixed at 40.

Royal Canadian Mounted Police, constabulary organized (1873) as Northwest Mounted Police to bring law and order to Canadian Far West and especially to prevent Indian disorders. Present name acquired 1920. Enforces dominion law throughout Canada.

Royal Gorge: see ARKANSAS, river.

Royal Highlanders: see BLACK WATCH.

Royal Leamington Spa, England: see LEAMINGTON.

Royal Oak, residential city (pop. 46,898), SE Mich., NW suburb of Detroit; settled c.1820. Mfg. of tools, abrasives, paint, and mattresses.

royal poinciana: see POINCIANA, ROYAL.

Royal Society, first incorporated in 1662, in 1663 and again in 1669 chartered as Royal Society of London for Improving Natural Knowledge. Founded by learned men who met for scientific discussion, especially in physical sciences. Government-subsidized, it stimulates research and advises government. Publishes its *Proceedings* and *The Philosophical Transactions.*

Royce, Josiah (rois), 1855–1916, American philosopher, a teacher at Univ. of Calif. (1878–82) and later at Harvard. The foremost American idealist, he held that the world exists only in so far as beings with minds know it and that the finite self knows truth only because the individual mind is part of the world-mind. Among his works are *The Spirit of Modern Philosophy* (1892), *The World and the Individual* (1900–1901), and *The Philosophy of Loyalty* (1908).

Rozebeke, Belgium: see ROOSEBEKE.

RSFSR: see RUSSIAN SOVIET FEDERATED SOCIALIST REPUBLIC.

Ru, chemical symbol of the element RUTHENIUM.

Ruanda-Urundi (rōōän'dä-ōōrōōn'dē), UN trust territory (20,575 sq. mi.; pop. 3,889,058), E Africa, under Belgian administration; cap. Usumbura. Bordered on N by Uganda, on E by Tanganyika, and on W by Belgian Congo and L. Tanganyika. Lies on a plateau. Cotton, coffee, tobacco, and sisal are grown; tin and gold are mined. Belonged to German East Africa 1899–1917. After World War I it became a mandate under Belgium; status was changed to that of UN trust territory in 1946.

Ruapehu (rōōupä'hōō), extinct volcanic peak, 9,175 ft. high, on central North Isl., New Zealand; island's highest mountain. Skiing center.

Rub al Khali (rōōb' äl khä'lē), great desert, 250,000 sq. mi., S Arabia. Relatively unexplored.

rubber, hydrocarbon obtained from milky secretion (latex) of various plants. Its elasticity, toughness, impermeability, adhesiveness, and electrical resistance make it useful as adhesive, coating, fiber, molding compound, and electrical insulator. Over 95% is obtained from PARA RUBBER TREE. Some latex (treated to prevent coagulation) is shipped to manufacturing centers but more is exported as crude rubber rolled into sheets from slabs of coagulated latex. For use in most products rubber is ground; dissolved; compounded with fillers, pigments, plasticizers, and other ingredients; sheeted, extruded in various shapes, molded, or applied as coating; then vulcanized. Uncoagulated latex may be extruded as thread, coated on other materials, or beaten to a foam (sponge rubber). Over one half of world supply is used by U.S., chiefly for tires and inner tubes; U.S. manufacturing center is Akron, Ohio. Early use of rubber by Indians of South and Central America was recorded by Spanish in 16th cent. First factory estab. 1811 in Vienna. In 1823 Charles Macintosh developed practical waterproofing process; in 1839 Charles Goodyear invented VULCANIZATION process which revolutionized rubber industry. See also RUBBER, SYNTHETIC.

rubber, synthetic. Various rubberlike commercial products are generally known as synthetic rubber, but no synthetic substance completely identical with natural rubber in chemical and elastic properties has yet been produced. Basic materials from which most synthetic rubbers are derived are the hydrocarbon substances (e.g., petroleum, alcohol, coal tar, natural gas, and acetylene). Rubberlike qualities are obtained by polymerization (i.e., linking molecules of the basic substances into long chains) or sometimes by a process of condensation. Natural rubber is superior to synthetic rubber in that it is easier to process, usually has greater elasticity (and keeps it even at low temperatures), and resists tearing; synthetic rubbers, however, are less affected by oils, solvents, sunlight, heat, and acids, and are less permeable to gases and liquids. In the U.S., butadiene (a hydrocarbon derived from ethyl alcohol or petroleum) is the basis of many leading synthetic rubber materials; among these are GR-S (general-purpose rubber, styrene; the type produced in largest quantities during World War II), Perbunan (formerly Buna N), Hycar (Ameripol), and Chemigum. Other commercially important synthetics include Butyl rubber and neoprene (successfully produced in U.S. from c.1931). The term *elastics* is sometimes used in preference to "synthetic rubber" and the term *elastomer* has been accepted by many for synthetic rubber material.

rubber plant or **India rubber tree**, a large tree (*Ficus elastica*) in its native Asia, but elsewhere grown as a pot plant. It has long, leathery, evergreen leaves.

Rubens, Peter Paul (roo'bŭnz), 1577–1640, foremost painter of the Flemish school. After spending eight years in the service of the duke of Mantua, he returned to Antwerp in 1608 and won immediate success. Besieged with commissions, he organized a workshop of skilled apprentices, who did much of the work on the larger works (esp. allegorical paintings and altarpieces), although he himself made the designs and added the finishing touches. He did many paintings for the Spanish and French courts, notably a series of 24 paintings of the life of Marie de' Medici (Louvre). Entering diplomatic service in 1626, after the death of his wife, Isabella Brant, he went on a mission to Spain in 1628; here he met Velázquez and painted the royal family. In London, where he was knighted, he painted the ceiling at Whitehall. Returning to Antwerp in 1630 he married the young beauty Helen Fourment, who became the subject of some of his masterpieces. Equally skillful in all fields of painting, Rubens was one of the most popular and prolific artists of all time. Over 2,000 paintings are attributed to his studio. The works of his mature period are lustily painted in bright, clear colors with a pervading luminosity. Among his masterpieces are the *Descent from the Cross* (cathedral, Antwerp) and *Venus and Adonis* (Metropolitan Mus.).

Rubicon (roo'bĭkŏn), stream that in days of early Rome divided Gaul from Italy; not certainly identified. In 49 B.C. Caesar led his army across it, defying the Roman senate and commencing civil war. He is reported to have said, "The die is cast." Hence to cross the Rubicon is to take an irrevocable step.

rubidium (roobĭ'dēŭm), rare, silver-white, soft metallic element (symbol = Rb; see also ELEMENT, table). It is an alkali metal and very active; resembles potassium in activity; not found free.

Rubinstein, Anton (Grigoryevich) (roo'bĭnstīn), 1829–94, Russian virtuoso pianist and composer, founder (1862) of the St. Petersburg Conservatory. His concertos, symphonies, and operas were successful in his lifetime, but his *Kamennoi-Ostrov* is his best-known work today. His brother, **Nicholas (Grigoryevich) Rubinstein**, 1835–81, a pianist and teacher, founded (1864) the Moscow Conservatory.

Rubinstein, Artur, 1886–, Polish-American piano virtuoso. First appeared in the U.S. in 1906, but it was after his third appearance here, in 1937, that he achieved his greatest acclaim.

ruby, precious stone, variety of red corundum, classed among the most valuable of gems. Found in Burma, Siam, and Ceylon.

Rückert, Friedrich (frē'drĭkh rü'kŭrt), 1788–1866, German Orientalist and lyric poet.

Ruckstull, Frederick Wellington (rŭk'stŭl"), 1853–1942, American sculptor, b. Alsace. Principal founder of the Natl. Sculpture Society (1893).

rudbeckia: see BLACK-EYED SUSAN; GOLDEN GLOW.

Rude, François (fräswä' rüd'), 1784–1855, French sculptor. Works include the patriotic group, *Le Départ*, on Arc de Triomphe, Paris.

Rüdesheim (rü'dŭs-hīm), town (pop. 5,736), Hesse, W Germany, on the Rhine, in famous wine district.

Rudolf (roo'dŏlf), emperors and German kings. **Rudolf I** (Rudolf of Hapsburg), 1218–91, count of Hapsburg, was elected king in 1273 after a lawless interregnum of 20 years. He sought friendly relations with the papacy and tried, with moderate success, to stamp out feudal warfare and the robber barons. His victories over OTTOCAR II of Bohemia (1276, 1278) enabled him to confiscate Austria, Styria, and Carniola, which he bestowed in 1282 on his sons. It was thus that the Hapsburg family began its rise to world empire. **Rudolf II**, 1552–1612, son of Emperor Maximilian II, was crowned king of Hungary (1572) and Bohemia (1575) before succeeding his father as emperor (1576). Mentally unbalanced, he had to delegate his imperial power to his brother MATTHIAS (1606), to whom he also ceded Hungary, Moravia, and Austria (1608) and, finally, Bohemia (1611). Remembered for his passionate—if misguided—interest in science, he called Kepler and Tycho Brahe to his court at Prague and locked up alchemists, under orders to make gold, in the little houses of Golden Lane.

Rudolf, 1858–89, Austrian archduke, crown prince of Austria and Hungary; only son of Emperor Francis Joseph and Empress Elizabeth. Was found shot dead, with his mistress, Baroness Maria Vetsera, at Mayerling. Supposedly a double suicide, their deaths remain a mystery.

Rudolf, Lake, 180 mi. long, 10–30 mi. wide, NW Kenya, in Great Rift Valley. Has no outlet.

rue (roo), aromatic woody herb of genus *Ruta*. Common rue, *Ruta graveolans*, has green-yellow flowers and blue-green, bitter leaves. In medieval times it was used as a drug.

Rueda, Lope de: see LOPE DE RUEDA.

Ruef, Abraham (Abe Ruef) (roof'), 1865–1936, American political boss in San Francisco. Sentenced to 14-year prison term (1909) after sensational trial for bribery and extortion.

Ruffin, Edmund (rŭ'fĭn), 1794–1865, American agriculturist, a Southern "FIRE-EATER." He was a pioneer in soil chemistry. An ardent supporter of states' rights and secession, on April 12, 1861, he was allowed to fire first shot against Fort Sumter. After Lee surrendered, he committed suicide.

Ruffo, Fabrizio (fäbrē'tsēō roof'fō), 1744–1827, Italian cardinal. Led royal Neapolitan army against PARTHENOPEAN REPUBLIC and obtained capitulation of Naples by promising full pardon (June, 1799). Admiral Nelson peremptorily revoked Ruffo's terms, had CARACCIOLO executed on his flagship, and permitted a general massacre of the rebels.

Rufinus (roofī'nŭs), d. 395, Roman statesman. As minister to Theodosius I he made himself hated for his rapacity. After the accession of Arcadius he virtually ruled the Eastern Empire, but his ambitions led to his murder by Gothic mercenaries, perhaps on the instigation of Stilicho.

rug: see CARPET AND RUGS.

Rugby, urban district (pop. 45,418), Warwickshire, England. Important railroad junction and engineering center. Chiefly known as seat of great public school, Rugby School (1567). Became famous in 19th cent. under headmastership of Thomas Arnold. *Tom Brown's School Days* by Thomas Hughes deals with Rugby life. Rugby football originated here 1823.

rugby, game which originated (1823) on playing fields of Rugby in England. Has many characteristics of soccer and American football. Field about 160 yd. long, 75 yd. wide. Team consists of 15 men. No substitutions permitted.

Rügen (rü'gŭn), Baltic island (358 sq. mi.; pop. 89,306), Pomerania, NE Germany; connected by a dam with

Stralsund, on mainland. Agr., fishing; seaside resorts. Conquered by Denmark 1168; passed to Pomerania 1325, to Prussia 1815. Was incorporated with Russian-occupied Mecklenburg 1945.

Ruhr (rŏor), river, 145 mi. long, NW Germany, a right (E) tributary of the Rhine, which it joins at Duisburg. Its lower course is the S limit of the **Ruhr** district (c.2,000 sq. mi.; pop. c.4,000,000) of North Rhine-Westphalia, one of the world's densest and most important industrial concentrations. Its huge anthracite basin provides coal for its own heavy industries (steel, machinery, chemicals) and for the industries of other countries. An almost continuous urbanized district, it comprises such cities as Essen, Dortmund, Gelsenkirchen, Bochum, and Duisburg and is linked by waterways with the ports of Rotterdam and Emden. After World War I the Ruhr dist. was occupied by French and Belgian troops (1923–25), on the ground that Germany had defaulted on reparations payment. Germany in turn stopped all payments; a passive resistance movement in the Ruhr led to severe reprisals by the occupation authorities. After Stresemann became chancellor (Aug., 1923), passive resistance ceased and Germany sought to fulfill its treaty obligations punctiliously. German acceptance of the Dawes Plan prepared the evacuation of the occupation forces. In World War II the Ruhr dist., being the chief arsenal of the Axis forces, was devastated by Allied air raids. Postwar reconstruction was spectacularly speedy. In 1949 an international authority for the Ruhr was set up, with hq. at Düsseldorf (members: Belgium, Federal Republic of [West] Germany, France, Great Britain, Luxembourg, Netherlands, U.S.). The economic interdependence of the Ruhr and the industries of neighboring countries—notably of Ruhr coal and Lorraine iron ore—was a basic factor in the establishment in 1952 of the European Coal and Steel Community (see SCHUMAN PLAN).

Ruisdael or **Ruysdael, Jacob van** (both: yä'kōp vän rois'däl), c.1628–1682, Dutch painter, most celebrated of the Dutch landscapists. His somber landscapes (usually with overcast skies) were painted from memory and imagination. Rembrandt's influence is seen in the impressive light effects of his mature work.

Ruiz, Juan (hwän' rŏoēth'), 1283?–1350?, Spanish poet, archpriest of Hita. Wrote *Libro de buen amor,* satire of medieval life.

rum, spirituous liquor distilled from molasses dissolved in the lees of a previous distillation, then fermented. Inferior rum is made in other ways. Deep brown color of some rums comes from long storage and addition of caramel.

Rumania (rŏomä'nēu) or **Romania** (rōmä'nēu), republic (91,700 sq. mi.; pop. 15,872,624), SE Europe; cap. Bucharest. Bounded by the USSR, the Black Sea, Bulgaria, Yugoslavia, and Hungary, it is crossed by the CARPATHIANS and the lower Danube. Its chief regions are low-lying WALACHIA, MOLDAVIA, and N DOBRUJA; mountainous TRANSYLVANIA and S BUKOVINA; and, geographically part of the Hungarian Plain, Crisana-Maramures (with Arad and Oradea) and the BANAT of Timisoara. Chief cities: Bucharest, Cluj, Jassy, Timisoara. Ports: Galati, Constanta. Primarily agr., Rumania is a major producer of wheat and corn. Other products are timber, wine, fruit, processed foods. Sheep and cattle raising. Important petroleum industry in Ploesti area. Majority of population belongs to Orthodox Eastern Church. There are large Magyar and German minorities; also Jews, Roman Catholics, Protestants, Moslems. Corresponding, roughly, to the Roman province of DACIA, Rumania has retained its Latin tongue despite centuries of invasions and foreign rule. The history of Rumania before 1856 is that of the principalities of Moldavia and Walachia. The Congress of Paris (1856) gave these virtual independence under nominal Turkish overlordship. In 1861 they were united as the principality of Rumania under Alexander John CUZA (de-

posed 1866). Cuza's successor was CAROL I. Rumania joined Russia in its war on Turkey (1877); obtained full independence at the Congress of Berlin (1878); and was proclaimed a kingdom in 1881. It won S Dobruja from Bulgaria in the second Balkan War (1913) and joined (1916) the Allies in World War I. The treaties of Saint-Germain (1919) and Trianon (1920) awarded it Transylvania, the E Banat, Crisana-Maramures, and Bukovina. Rumania's annexation of BESSARABIA from Russia (1918) was never recognized by the USSR. To safeguard its acquisitions, Rumania entered the LITTLE ENTENTE (1921). Internal history is one of chronic violence, turmoil, and corruption. The wretched lot of the peasantry was somewhat improved by agrarian reforms after 1917, but inequality of wealth remained extreme. After World War I, electoral laws were constantly revised in favor of the party in power; in 1927 the death of King Ferdinand threw the succession in confusion (see MICHAEL; CAROL II). Violence increased in the 1930s with the rise of the IRON GUARD. In 1938 Carol II assumed dictatorial powers, and in 1940 he joined the AXIS as a neutral partner. Russian and German pressure forced Rumania to cede N Bukovina and Bessarabia to the USSR; S Dobruja to Bulgaria; and part of Transylvania and other border lands to Hungary (1940). Soon afterward, Ion ANTONESCU seized power, exiled Carol, restored Michael as king, and began his dictatorship (1940–44). Rumania declared war on the USSR (1941). By the Treaty of Paris of 1947 Rumania recovered its lost territories except N Bukovina, Bessarabia, and S Dobruja. A Communist-led government came into power in 1945, forced Michael to abdicate in 1947, and made Rumania a "people's republic" in 1948. Suppressing all opposition, it nationalized industries and resources (giving the USSR virtual control over its production).

Rumanian language, Romance language, belonging to Italic subfamily of Indo-European languages. See LANGUAGE (table).

Rumelia or **Roumelia** (both: rŏomē'lēu), former administrative region of the Ottoman Empire, comprising most of S Balkan Peninsula; cap. Sofia (until 1878). The Congress of Berlin (1878) made N Bulgaria a principality under nominal Turkish overlordship; S Bulgaria, or **Eastern Rumelia,** became an autonomous province. In 1885 Bulgaria annexed Eastern Rumelia. Serbia, which also claimed the area, made war but was defeated (1886). Turkey tacitly consented to the annexation.

Rumford, Benjamin Thompson, Count, 1753–1814, American-British scientist and administrator. He was born in Mass. and went to England in 1776. Later he served the elector of Bavaria as administrator and in 1791 was created count of Holy Roman Empire. His title was from town Rumford (later Concord), N.H., where his wife was born. He reorganized the army in Bavaria and introduced sociological reforms there and in England and Ireland. He made contributions to methods of heating, lighting, and cooking and introduced a scientific theory of heat.

Rumford, town (pop. 9,954), including Rumford village (pop. 7,888), W Maine, at Androscoggin R. falls and NW of Augusta. Paper mills. Winter sports.

Rumi, Jalal ed-Din (jŭläl' ŭdēn' rŏo'mē), 1207–73, Persian poet. A major Sufist poet; his lyrics express mystic thought in finely wrought symbols.

rummy, card game played by two to six players with an ordinary deck. Variations include knock rummy, gin rummy (very popular in U.S. in early 1940s), contract rummy, continental rummy, and five-hundred rummy. Canasta (kùnä'stù) [fr. Span.,= basket], another variation, is played with two decks of cards plus four jokers.

Rump Parliament: see PRIDE'S PURGE.

Rumsey, James (rŭm'zē), 1743–92, American inventor of a steamship tried out on the Potomac in 1787.

Rumson, resort borough (pop. 4,044), E N.J., near the

Atlantic, S of Sandy Hook; estate and boating center.

Runcorn, urban district (pop. 23,933), Cheshire, England, on the Mersey, at terminus of Manchester Ship Canal and Bridgewater Canal. It is a tanning and mfg. subport of Manchester.

Rundstedt, Gerd von (gĕrt' fŭn rōŏnt'shtĕt), 1875–1953, German field marshal in World War II. Commanded German forces in West (1944–45). Defeated in Normandy campaign and in BATTLE OF THE BULGE, he was replaced by Kesselring.

Runeberg, Johan Ludvig (yōō'hän lŭd'vĭg rü'nùbĕryù), 1804–77, Finnish national poet. His works include an epic, *The Elkhunters* (1832), and long romances based on Scandinavian legend and history, such as *King Ejalar* (1844) and *The Tales of Ensign Stal* (1848; from it the Finnish national anthem is taken). He wrote in Swedish.

runes (rōōnz), anc. Germanic alphabet, adapted to carving inscriptions on wood. Probably first used by East Goths (c.300) and suggested by a Greek cursive script. There were two alphabets, one of 16 signs, the other of 24 (the 16, plus 8). In historical times runes were used in England and Scandinavia, in parts of Sweden after the Middle Ages.

Runnymede or **Runnimede** (rŭ'nĭmēd), meadow near London, England. Either here or on near-by Charter Isl., King John accepted the Magna Carta in 1215.

Rupert, 1352–1410, German king and emperor-elect (1400–1410), elector palatine. Chosen to succeed the deposed Emperor WENCESLAUS, he never was able to impose his authority.

Rupert, Prince, 1619–82, son of Frederick the Winter King and Elizabeth of Bohemia; grandson of James I of England. After fighting for the Dutch in the Thirty Years War, he went to England (1641) to assist Charles I in the civil wars. He was successful until his defeat at Marston Moor (1644). Returning to England after the Restoration, he served Charles II as admiral in the Dutch Wars and took part in colonial schemes, notably in ventures of the Hudson's Bay Co.

Rupert, city (pop. 3,098), S Idaho, NE of Burley near Snake R., in Minidoka project.

Rupert, river of W Que., Canada, issuing from L. Mistassini and flowing 380 mi. W to James Bay.

Rupert House, village and oldest Hudson's Bay Co. furtrading post, W Que., Canada, on Rupert R., E of its mouth on James Bay; founded 1668 as Fort Charles. Captured 1686 by French and alternately held by French and English to 1713.

Rupert's Land, Canadian territory held 1670–1869 by Hudson's Bay Co., named for Prince Rupert, company's first governor. Region comprised drainage basin of Hudson Bay. Land was transferred to Canada in 1869 for £300,000, but certain blocks of land were retained.

rupture: see HERNIA.

Rural Electrification Administration (REA), created in 1935 as independent U.S. bureau, reorganized 1939 as a division of Dept. of Agriculture. Its loan system provides farms with cheap electricity.

Rurik (rōō'rĭk), d. 879, reputed founder of Russia. Supposedly led a band of VARANGIANS who settled in Novgorod 862. His heirs ruled RUSSIA till 1598.

Ruse (rōō'sĕ), city (pop. 53,420), NE Bulgaria, on the Danube. Communications center. Mfg. of machinery, textiles, tobacco. It is noted for its mosques and ruins of medieval fortress.

Rush, Benjamin, 1745?–1813, American physician, signer of Declaration of Independence. Estab. first free dispensary in U.S. at Philadelphia (1786). Taught medical theory and practice at Univ. of Pennsylvania; made notable contributions to psychiatry. His son, **Richard Rush,** 1780–1859, was temporarily U.S. Secretary of State (1817), minister to Great Britain (1817–25). Helped negotiate RUSH-BAGOT CONVENTION. Obtained Smithson bequest for establishment of the Smithsonian Inst.

Rush, William, 1756–1833, American sculptor, whose

wood carvings and clay models were famous in his day. His wooden statue of Washington is in Independence Hall, Philadelphia.

rush, name for various tall grasslike plants with hollow stems. The common or bog rush (*Juncus effusus*) grows in moist places and has been used for basketwork and mats. Others include the BULRUSH, wood rush (*Luzula*), Dutch or scouring rush (*Equisetum hyemale*), and sweet rush or flag (*Acorus calamus*).

Rush-Bagot Convention (băg'ŭt), 1817, agreement between U.S. and Great Britain concerning Canadian border. Consisted of exchange of notes by U.S. Acting Secretary of State Richard Rush and Charles Bagot, British minister in Washington. Provided for practical disarmament of U.S.-Canadian frontier. Set precedent for pacific settlement of all Anglo-American difficulties and inaugurated policy of strict peace between U.S. and Canada.

Rush Medical College: see ILLINOIS, UNIVERSITY OF.

Rushmore, Mount, SW S.Dak., in Mt. Rushmore Natl. Memorial (1,220.32 acres; estab. 1929, completed 1941) and in Black Hills. On it are carved Gutzon Borglum's huge busts of presidents Washington, Jefferson, Lincoln, and Theodore Roosevelt.

Rushville, city (pop. 6,761), E Ind., ESE of Indianapolis. Farm trade center with wood products.

Rusk, town (pop. 6,598), E Texas, E of Palestine. Center for truck, dairy, lumber, and oil area. Near by is a steel plant.

Ruskin, John, 1819–1900, English author and critic. Spurred by wealthy evangelical parents, he ardently studied painting and continued education at Oxford. His first work, *Modern Painters* (5 vols., 1843–60), begun as a defense of the painter J. M. W. Turner, developed the principle that art is based on national and individual integrity and morality. *The Seven Lamps of Architecture* (1849) and *The Stones of Venice* (1851–53) applied the same principle to architecture. After 1860 Ruskin turned increasingly to attacking economic and social evils and proposing reforms, in *Munera Pulveris* (1862–63), *Sesame and Lilies* (1865), *The Crown of Wild Olive* (1866), *Time and Tide* (1867), and *Fors Clavigera* (1871–84). Last work was autobiographical *Praeterita* (1885–89).

Russell, English noble family. First appeared prominently in reign of Henry VIII with rise of **John Russell,** 1st **earl of Bedford,** 1486?–1555, who helped to arrange marriage of Mary I to Philip II of Spain. He gained great wealth and lands that are still in the family. His son, **Francis Russell, 2d earl of Bedford,** c.1527–1585, was influential under Elizabeth. **Francis Russell, 4th earl of Bedford,** 1593–1641, was the most important opponent of Charles I in House of Lords. His son, **William Russell, 5th earl and 1st duke of Bedford,** 1613–1700, fought on alternate sides in civil war. His son, **Lord William Russell,** 1639–83, joined the opposition under Charles II. Was executed for supposed complicity in the RYE HOUSE PLOT. **John Russell,** 4th duke of Bedford, 1710–71, attacked Robert Walpole and succeeded him in government. His grandson, **Francis Russell, 5th duke of Bedford,** 1765–1802, by his criticism of Edmund Burke's pension, elicited Burke's *Letter to a Noble Lord* (1796). His nephew was **John Russell, 1st Earl Russell,** 1792–1878, a statesman. Gave name to the newly formed Liberal party. Supported Catholic Emancipation; helped introduce the Reform Bill of 1832. Twice prime minister (1846–52, 1865–66), he forced the resignation (1851) of Palmerston, his foreign secretary, for recognizing Louis Napoleon's coup d'état in France without authorization. As foreign secretary (1860–65) he advocated English neutrality during American Civil War and worked for liberation of Italy. His grandson, **Bertrand (Arthur William) Russell, 3d Earl Russell,** 1872–, is a philosopher and mathematician. With A. N. Whitehead he wrote *Principia Mathematica* (1910–13), a pioneer work in symbolic logic. A realist, his object has been to give philosophy a scientific basis. As social thinker he stresses creative activity of man, which he calls the principle of growth. Won Nobel Prize in Literature for 1950. The Bedford title is now held by **Hastings William Sackville Russell,** 12th **duke of Bedford,** 1888–.

Russell, Bertrand: see RUSSELL, family.

Russell, George William, pseud. **A. E.,** 1867–1935, Irish poet. An active nationalist, a famous conversationalist, and a convincing lecturer, he worked for agricultural cooperatives. He was a mystic and theosophist, and his poetry (as in *The Candle of Vision,* 1918; *Selected Poems,* 1935) is noted for religious tone and melody. Also known as a landscape painter.

Russell, Hastings William Sackville, 12th **duke of Bedford:** see RUSSELL, family.

Russell, Henry Norris, 1877–, American astronomer, propounder of theory of stellar evolution based on spectroscopic studies.

Russell, James Earl, 1864–1945, American educator. As professor of education and dean at Teachers Col., Columbia Univ. after 1897, he developed it into a leading professional college. He became dean emeritus in 1927, but taught until 1931. His son, **William Fletcher Russell,** 1890–, succeeded him as dean in 1927, becoming president in 1949.

Russell, John, dukes and earls of Bedford; Earl Russell: see RUSSELL, family.

Russell, Lillian, 1861–1922, American actress and singer, whose real name was Helen Louise Leonard. Famous for her beauty and talent in light opera.

Russell, William, 5th **earl and** 1st **duke of Bedford,** and **Lord William Russell:** see RUSSELL, family.

Russell, city (pop. 6,483), central Kansas, W of Salina near Smoky Hill R., in oil region.

Russell Sage College: see TROY, N.Y.

Russellville. 1 City (pop. 6,012), NW Ala., S of Florence, in cotton, grain, and iron area. **2** City (pop. 8,166), NW central Ark., near Arkansas R., in area yielding coal, natural gas, lumber, and farm products.

Russia, Rus. *Rossiya,* name commonly applied to the UNION OF SOVIET SOCIALIST REPUBLICS, of which Great Russia (see RUSSIAN SOVIET FEDERATED SOCIALIST REPUBLIC) is the chief constituent member. Historically—as used in this article—the term refers to the Russian state before the revolution of 1917. *Medieval Russia.* From earliest times the steppes of S Russia and the Volga basin attracted invaders. The SCYTHIANS were replaced by the SARMATIANS (3d cent. B.C.), who in turn made way for the Goths, Huns, Avars, KHAZARS, and E BULGARS (3d cent. A.D.–8th cent. A.D.). By the 9th cent. the E SLAVS, ancestors of the Russians, were estab. in the W and were rapidly expanding. In the S, they were subject to the Khazar empire. The foundation of the Russian state is traditionally credited to RURIK, leader of a band of Scandinavian traders (see VARANGIANS), who estab. himself at NOVGOROD in 862. His successors united the E Slavs, freed them from Khazar rule, took KIEV (882). Duke SVIATOSLAV crushed the Khazar empire and extended the borders of Kievan Russia to the Caucasus and the Balkans. VLADIMIR I estab. the Orthodox Eastern Church as state religion (c.989). The cultural tie with Byzantium and the civilizing and unifying influence of the Church kept medieval Russia alive despite its political disunity. In 1154 the Kievan empire broke up into several principalities, ruled by branches of the house of Rurik. Perpetual warfare among the princes and the raids of the CUMANS caused large-scale migration to the NE, where VLADIMIR became the new center. In 1237–40 the Mongols (commonly called TATARS) subjugated Russia, estab. the empire of the GOLDEN HORDE in the S and E, and forced the Russian princes to pay tribute. W Russia (incl. BELORUSSIA and the UKRAINE but not the merchant republics of Novgorod and Pskov) was absorbed by LITHUANIA. From the ruins of old Russia there rose in the 14th cent. a new powerful state, patterned in its auto-

cratic organization on the Mongol model and destined to lead Russia on the road of empire. This was the grand duchy of Moscow, which under IVAN III shook off the Tatar yoke (1480) and under IVAN IV (the Terrible) controlled much of present European Russia and began to penetrate SIBERIA (1581). Ivan IV imposed his autocratic regime on all his conquests and changed his title from grand duke of Moscow to tsar of all Russia. With his son, Feodor I, the Rurik dynasty ended (1598). The reign of Boris GODUNOV (1598–1605) and the ensuing "Time of Troubles" was a turbulent period of false pretenders (see DMITRI) and of Polish invasion, but the election of Michael Romanov as tsar restored order in 1613. The march of conquest was resumed.

Growth of Empire. The Russian ambition to gain access to the sea and the weakening of Russia's principal neighbors—Poland, Sweden, Turkey, Persia—furthered the continuous expansion of Russia's frontiers, notably in the NORTHERN WAR (1700–1721); the RUSSO-TURKISH WARS of the 18th–19th cent.; the partions of POLAND of 1772, 1793, and 1795; and the annexations of the CRIMEA (1783), FINLAND (1809), BESSARABIA (1812), and the Caucasus (Georgia, 1801; parts of Armenia and Azerbaijan, 1813, 1828; Circassia, 1829–64). Russian aggrandizement at the expense of Turkey created the EASTERN QUESTION and met the firm opposition of the Western Powers in the CRIMEAN WAR (1853–56) and at the Congress of BERLIN (1878). Russian colonists reached the Pacific Ocean by 1640 and went on to ALASKA in the 18th cent. Central Asia (i.e., the present Turkmen, Uzbek, Tadzhik, Kirghiz, and Kazakh SSRs) and the Far Eastern Territory were annexed in the mid-19th cent., but further expansion in Asia was checked by the RUSSO-JAPANESE WAR of 1904–5.

Rise and fall of autocracy. Russia in the 17th cent. was still a medieval, semi-Oriental state. In the 18th cent., particularly under PETER I and CATHERINE II, it was transformed into a European power. It was this enforced "Westernization" that brought absolutism to its peak. To make Russia a modern state, Peter had to crush the opposition of the nobles or boyars (on whom he foisted a new nobility of officers and civil servants) and of the Church, which he made subservient to the state. To compensate the nobles, he gave them increasing rights over their serfs. Serfdom began in Russia in the 15th cent. and reached its peak in 1785, when Catherine II gave the serfs the status of chattels. One third of the nation became enslaved to the landowning aristocracy. By shifting his cap. to St. Petersburg and taking the title emperor, Peter I emphasized the Western character of the new Russia. The mass of the people, however, were little touched by Westernization, whereas many of the nobles and the educated classes began to absorb European liberal ideals along with European customs. This trend became marked in the late 18th cent. The early liberalism of ALEXANDER I and the patriotic fervor generated by the War of 1812 against NAPOLEON I offered an opportunity for reform, but after 1815 Alexander turned to a thoroughly reactionary policy, continued by NICHOLAS I. Alongside the liberal, constitutionalist opposition there rose groups of radical terrorists—nihilists, anarchists, and, ultimately, Marxists. ALEXANDER II, a liberal, abolished serfdom in 1861 (see EMANCIPATION, EDICT OF) but failed to create a land-owning peasantry. His assassination (1881) by revolutionists opened a reign of terror under ALEXANDER III. Russia became a thorough police state. Under NICHOLAS II the Russo-Japanese War revealed the weakness of the régime and led to the RUSSIAN REVOLUTION of 1905. A parliamentary constitution was granted (see DUMA). The ministries of WITTE and STOLYPIN were marked by industrial expansion and land reform, but the régime as a whole quickly regained its authoritarian character. Its foreign policy, notably its support of Slavic nationalism in central Europe and the Balkans, brought Russia into conflict with Austria-Hungary and Germany, led to its alliance with France and England (see TRIPLE ALLIANCE AND TRIPLE ENTENTE), and eventually drew it into WORLD WAR I (1914). Russian reverses and economic suffering were both cause and occasion for the February Revolution of 1917, which overthrew the tsarist régime and which in turn was superseded by the Communist October Revolution (see RUSSIAN REVOLUTION). Though old Russia ceased to exist, its problems and trends were carried over into the new Soviet Russia. For a list of Russian rulers 1613–1917, see ROMANOV.

Russia Company: see MUSCOVY COMPANY.

Russian Church: see ORTHODOX EASTERN CHURCH.

Russian language, language of Slavic subfamily of Indo-European languages. See LANGUAGE (table).

Russian Revolution. For a brief sketch of conditions leading to the revolutions of 1905 and 1917, see RUSSIA. Discontent with tsarist autocracy was nearly universal—among the land-hungry peasantry, the new industrial proletariat, the lower ranks of the armed forces, the frustrated intelligentsia, the oppressed national and religious minorities, and a large segment of the bourgeoisie and aristocracy. Among opposition groups the most important were the moderate Constitutional Democrats, the Socialist Revolutionaries (mostly peasants and intelligentsia), and the Marxist Social Democrats (split into BOLSHEVISM AND MENSHEVISM). In 1905, as Russia was losing the RUSSO-JAPANESE WAR, discontent flared up in a series of strikes and mutinies, collectively known as the Revolution of 1905. Its only results were the granting of civil rights and the establishment of a parliament (see DUMA), but these concessions were soon curtailed by STOLYPIN. Russian reverses in World War I and the reactionary policy of NICHOLAS II brought the situation to a head in March, 1917 (in old-style calendar February; hence, "February Revolution"). The striking Petrograd workers seized the capital while the Duma defied Nicholas's order to dissolve and set up a provisional government under Prince LVOV. The emperor abdicated March 15. Lvov's decision to continue the war clashed with the Socialists' demand for immediate peace, propagated by workers', peasants', and soldiers' councils (see SOVIET) and particularly by the Bolsheviks under the leadership of LENIN. Though outnumbered by Socialist Revolutionaries and Mensheviks at the first all-Russian soviet congress (June, 1917), Lenin staged an unsuccessful uprising at Petrograd (July). Lvov resigned, and KERENSKY organized a moderate Socialist cabinet. Kerensky's vacillation and his unpopularity both with right and left enabled the Bolsheviks to seize power in Petrograd (Nov. 7, 1917; "October Revolution" according to old-style calendar). A council of people's commissars, headed by Lenin and approved by the second soviet congress, immediately decreed the abolition of private land ownership, set up a "dictatorship of the proletariat"— actually, of the Communist party, as the Bolsheviks came to be called—and began a reign of terror against all opposition. Peace negotiations led to the humiliating Treaty of BREST-LITOVSK (March, 1918). The Bolsheviks had extended their authority over Moscow and a large part of European Russia, but elsewhere they faced the resistance of the anti-Bolshevik parties, whose supporters ranged from Socialist Revolutionaries to tsarists. The resulting civil war lasted till 1920 and was complicated by foreign intervention. The main areas of warfare between "Reds" and "Whites" were: S Russia and the Caucasus, where KORNILOV, DENIKIN, and P. N. WRANGEL commanded, in turn, the White forces; the UKRAINE, where Germany, France, and Poland intervened; the N, where British, French, and U.S. forces held Murmansk and Archangel, 1918–19; the Baltic states, where a White army and German free corps battled the Reds; and Siberia, where KOLCHAK set up his government and where the Japanese held Vladivostok until 1922. The

organizing genius of the Red Army was TROTSKY; its victory, however, was largely due to bad cooperation among the White Commanders. By the end of 1920 the last White troops evacuated the Crimea. Russia recognized the independence of Finland and the Baltic republics and made peace with Poland (see RIGA, TREATY OF) but recovered all other territories save Bessarabia. In 1922 the USSR was organized and the stringent "War Communism" was replaced by the NEW ECONOMIC POLICY, designed to put the starving, devastated country back on its feet.

Russian Soviet Federated Socialist Republic (RSFSR), chief constituent republic (6,533,600 sq. mi.; pop. c.111,000,000) of the USSR; cap. Moscow. Extending W-E from the Baltic Sea to the Pacific Ocean and N-S from the Arctic to the Black and Caspian seas and the Caucasus, Altai, and Sayan mts., it comprises 76% of the area and 58% of the population of the USSR. The Asiatic part of the RSFSR (4,922,800 sq. mi.; pop. c.19,500,000, excluding the URALS) is commonly known as Siberia. Although 74% of the population are Great Russians, there are many non-Slavic groups, 12 of which form autonomous republics— BASHKIR ASSR, BURYAT-MONGOL ASSR, CHUVASH ASSR, DAGESTAN, KABARDIAN ASSR, KOMI ASSR, MARI ASSR, MORDVINIAN ASSR, N OSSETIA, TATAR ASSR, UDMURT ASSR, YAKUT ASSR. Other large administrative divisions include ALTAI, KHABAROVSK, KRASNODAR, KRASNOYARSK, MARITIME, and STAVROPOL Territories. The RSFSR possesses the chief industrial and mining areas of the Soviet Union and exerts a dominant influence over Soviet life. For history, geography, and economy, see RUSSIA; SIBERIA; UNION OF SOVIET SOCIALIST REPUBLICS.

Russian wolfhound: see HOUND.

Russo-Japanese War, 1904–5, imperialistic conflict which grew out of rival designs of Russia and Japan on Manchuria and Korea. Russia had penetrated these areas and refused to negotiate with Japan for their division into spheres of influence. Without declaring war, Japan attacked Port Arthur and bottled up the Russian fleet. In 1905 the Japanese captured Port Arthur, defeated the Russians at Mukden, and destroyed a Russian fleet at Tsushima. Peace was made through the mediation of U.S. Pres. Theodore Roosevelt (see PORTSMOUTH, TREATY OF). The war helped bring on the Russian Revolution of 1905 and made Japan a world power.

Russo-Turkish Wars, 1696–1878, series of campaigns in which Russia expanded at the expense of the decaying Ottoman Empire. The Black Sea was Russia's original goal. Peter I took Azov in 1696 but lost it again in the Peace of the Pruth (1711; see NORTHERN WAR). In the war of 1736–39 Russia recaptured Azov and occupied Moldavia but had to give up its gains after its ally, Austria, made a separate peace. The Treaty of KUCHUK KAINARJI, which ended Catherine II's first Turkish war (1768–74), gave Russia a voice in Turkish affairs and prepared the annexation of CRIMEA and the S Ukraine (1783). This treaty and a secret plan for partioning the Ottoman Empire between Russia and Austria alarmed the Western Powers and created the explosive EASTERN QUESTION. Catherine's second war (1787–92), ending with the Treaty of Jassy, gave Russia the SW Ukraine, with Odessa; the war of 1806–12 gave it BESSARABIA; the war of 1828–29, linked with the Greek War of Independence, brought Russian power in the Near East to a peak (see ADRIANOPLE, TREATY OF) and completed the conquest of the Caucasus. (The Persian parts of the Caucasus fell to Russia by the treaties of Gulistan, 1813, and Turkamanchai, 1828.) In the CRIMEAN WAR (1853–56) Turkey found allies in Britain and France. The Congress of PARIS (1856) was a severe setback for Russia, but another opportunity for extending Russian influence to the Balkan peninsula came with the anti-Turkish uprising in Bulgaria, Bosnia, and Hercegovina (1875). Serbia and Montenegro, on Russian instigation, joined the rebels, and in 1877 Russia and Rumania declared war on Turkey. The fall of PLEVNA was followed by the Treaty of SAN STEFANO (1878), which revised the map so drastically in favor of Russia and Bulgaria that the European powers called a conference to review its terms (see BERLIN, CONGRESS OF).

rust, name for various fungi which parasitize plants, forming brown or rusty patches of spores on the host. Some live entirely on one plant; others (e.g., cedar rust of juniper and apple and stem rust of wheat and barberry) require two or more different plants to complete their life cycles.

rusting of metals is essentially OXIDATION. Rust is formed by combination of metal with atmospheric oxygen; when iron is exposed to moist air, reddish brown substance forms on surface; this flakes off and process continues on new surface. For protection against rust, certain paints, layers of other metals, and oil are used.

Ruston, town (pop. 10,372), N La., E of Shreveport; estab. c.1884. Center of agr. and dairying area. Seat of Louisiana Polytechnic Inst.

rutabaga: see TURNIP.

Rutebeuf (rütbûf'), fl. 1254–85, French poet. Wrote an early miracle play, *Le Miracle de Théophile*, fabliaux, and satires.

Rutgers University, mainly at New Brunswick, N.J.; undenominational, with land-grant, state, and private support, for men and women. Chartered 1776 as Queens Col. by George III in response to petition of leaders of Dutch Reformed Church; opened 1771 as 8th colonial college. Name changed 1825 to honor Henry Rutgers (1745–1830), Revolutionary captain. In 1864 Rutgers Scientific School became State Col. for the Benefit of Agriculture and the Mechanic Arts; name changed to State Univ. of N.J. 1917. Entire institution became Rutgers Univ. 1924, and in 1945, State Univ. of New Jersey. A branch, New Jersey Col. for Women, estab. 1918. Univ. of Newark (chartered 1933) became Newark Colleges of Rutgers Univ. 1946.

Ruth, George Herman (Babe Ruth), 1895–1948, American baseball player. As left-handed Boston Red Sox pitcher (1914–19), he won 87, lost 44 games. Sold (1920) to N.Y. Yankees, where he became star outfielder. Set many slugging records, including most home runs in one season (60 in 1927), most home runs in major-league play (714).

Ruth, book of Old Testament. Story, one of most popular in Bible, tells of Ruth, a Moabite widow, who refused to desert her Jewish mother-in-law, Naomi. Together they returned to Naomi's home in Bethlehem. There Ruth married Boaz, a wealthy kinsman. Ruth and Boaz are ancestors of David.

Ruthenia, (rŏŏthē'nèü) [Latin,= Russia], in medieval usage, Russia in general. In later usage, the term *Ruthenians* was used in the Austro-Hungarian Monarchy to designate the Ukrainian population of the NE Carpathians (i.e., in Poland, Hungary, and Bukovina). There was no difference between Ukrainians and Ruthenians except a religious distinction: the Eastern Orthodox Ruthenians outside Russia had entered into union with the Roman Church (1596 in Poland; 1649 in Hungary) and belonged to the Ruthenian Uniate Church of the Eastern Rite; in the Russian Ukraine, the Greek Orthodox Church was fully restored in the 17th cent. The Hungarian part of Ruthenia became in 1919 the easternmost province of Czechoslovakia (Carpathian Russia or Carpathian Ukraine, Czech *Podkarpatská Rus;* 4,890 sq. mi.; pop. c.900,000; cap. Uzhgorod). A thousand years of feudal exploitation had made it one of Europe's most backward areas. Annexed by Hungary 1939 and recovered by Czechoslovakia 1944, it was ceded to the USSR 1945. Along with SE Poland and N Bukovina, it was incorporated with the Ukrainian SSR. Under Soviet pressure the Uniate Church seceded from Rome and united with the Russian Orthodox Church.

ruthenium (rŏŏthē'nèüm), rare, gray-white metallic element (symbol = Ru; see also ELEMENT, table). Is in platinum group of metals and occurs chiefly in platinum ores.

Rutherford, Daniel (rŭ'dhûrfûrd), 1749–1819, Scottish physician, botanist, and chemist; uncle of Sir Walter Scott. Discovered nitrogen (1772).

Rutherford, Ernest Rutherford, 1st Baron, 1871–1937, British physicist. Won 1908 Nobel Prize in chemistry for research in radioactivity. Contributed greatly to knowledge of structure of atom.

Rutherford, residential suburban borough (pop. 17,-411), NE N.J., NE of Newark. Seat of Fairleigh Dickinson Col. (coed.; 1942). Dye works; mfg. of metal products, and asphalt.

Ruthven (rǐ'vùn, rŏŏth'vùn), noble family of Scotland. **Patrick Ruthven, 3d lord of Ruthven,** 1520?–1566, was privy councilor to Mary Queen of Scots. Aided in murder of Rizzio, as did his son, **William Ruthven, 4th lord of Ruthven and 1st earl of Gowrie,** 1541?–1584. Beheaded for treason as head of confederated nobles who captured James VI in "raid of Ruthven" in 1582. His two sons, **John Ruthven, 3d earl of Gowrie and 6th lord of Ruthven,** 1578?–1600, and **Alexander Ruthven,** 1580?–1600, were killed for making an attempt on king's person in mysterious Gowrie conspiracy. Descended in collateral line, **Patrick Ruthven,** 1573?–1651, supported Charles I in Scotland and England. Was general in chief of royalist forces 1643–44.

rutile (rŏŏ'tēl), a mineral, one of three forms of titanium dioxide. Crystals are tetragonal. Mineral typically brownish red, found in igneous rock.

Rutland or **Rutlandshire** (rŭt'lùndshĭr), inland county (151 sq. mi.; pop. 20,510), central England; co. town Oakham. Smallest of English shires, it has rolling terrain devoted to agr.

Rutland, city (pop. 17,659), W Vt., N of Bennington and surrounded by separate Rutland town (pop. 1,416); settled 1770. Second-largest Vt. city, it is rail center with mfg. of metal products, tools, machinery, and scales. Marble no longer quarried here, though quarrying flourished after c.1845.

Rutlandshire, England: see RUTLAND, county.

Rutledge, Ann, 1813?–1835, American heroine of romantic story concerning Abraham Lincoln. Her sudden death grieved Lincoln deeply; from this one known fact W. H. Herndon wove story of Lincoln's alleged great love for the girl. Actually, Ann was engaged to Lincoln's friend, John McNamar.

Rutledge, John, 1739–1800, American jurist and statesman. Member of Continental Congress (1774–76, 1782–83). Associate Justice of U.S. Supreme Court (1789–91); nominated Chief Justice in 1795, but Senate refused to confirm appointment.

Rütli (rüt'lē) or **Grütli** (grüt'lē), meadow, Uri canton, Switzerland, on shore of L. of Lucerne. Here, according to legend of William TELL, representatives of Uri, Schwyz, and Unterwalden met 1307 to swear the **Rütli Oath,** on which Swiss freedom was founded. The 19th-cent. discovery of a written alliance of the cantons, dated Aug. 1, 1291, reduced historic importance of Rütli meeting.

Ruwenzori (rŏŏ"wünzō'rè), mountain range, central Africa, on Uganda–Belgian Congo border. Highest peaks are Mt. Margherita (16,795 ft.) and Mt. Alexandra (16,750 ft.). The range may be the "Mountains of the Moon," supposed by the ancients to be the source of the Nile.

Ruxton, George Frederick, 1820–48, English traveler and author. His *Adventures in Mexico and the Rocky Mountains* (1847) and *Life in the Far West* (1849) are valuable works on the U.S. frontier.

Ruysbroeck, John, Dutch *Jan van Ruusbroec* (rois'-brŏŏk), 1293–1381, Brabantine mystic, a Roman Catholic Augustinian monk. Wrote mystical treatises and also by his counsel aided such men as Tauler and Gerard Groote.

Ruysdael, Jacob van: see RUISDAEL, JACOB VAN.

Ruyter, Michiel Adriaanszoon de (mēkhēl′ ä′drēänsōn″ dü roi′tür), 1607–76, Dutch admiral. Served under Tromp in first of DUTCH WARS (1652–54). Captured English holdings on Gold and Guinea coasts in Second Dutch War (1664–67); saved Dutch fleet after defeat at North Foreland 1666; burned English ships in the Medway 1667. Led Dutch fleet with Tromp in Third Dutch War (1672–78), saving Dutch ports from attack 1672. Killed at Messina.

Ruzicka, Leopold (lā′ōpôlt rōō′tsĭkä), 1887–, Swiss chemist. Shared 1939 Nobel Prize for production of androsterone and testosterone from sterols.

RV, the Revised Version of the BIBLE.

Ryan, Loch (lŏkh rī′ún), long narrow inlet (9 mi. long; c.1½ mi. wide), Wigtownshire, Scotland, at S entrance to Firth of Clyde. Has good harbor.

Ryazan (ryūzän′yü), city (pop. 95,358), central European RSFSR, on Oka R. Agr.-processing center. Became cap. of Ryazan principality when Mongols destroyed Old Ryazan (1237); was annexed by Moscow 1520. Has picturesque medieval churches and a kremlin wall (1209). In World War II German advance on Moscow was stopped just short of Ryazan.

Rybinsk, RSFSR: see SHCHERBAKOV.

Rydberg, Abraham Viktor (ä′brähäm vĭk′tôr rüd′bēryü), 1828–95, Swedish philosopher, lyric poet, and novelist.

Ryder, Albert Pinkham, 1847–1917, American painter. Moonlight and the sea are predominant in his work. Was a recluse during much of his life.

Rye, municipal borough (pop. 4,511), Sussex East, England, near the Channel. One of towns added to CINQUE PORTS, it had good trade until sea receded in 19th cent. A resort of writers and artists. Henry James lived here for some years.

Rye. 1 Coast-resort town (pop. 1,982), SE N.H., S of Portsmouth; settled 1623 at Odiorne's Point. Includes Rye Beach village. **2** Residential and resort city (pop. 11,721), SE N.Y., on Long Isl. Sound SW of Port Chester.

rye, staple grain crop (*Secale cereale*), widely cultivated, especially in Central and N Europe. It can be grown profitably on soil too poor for wheat. Rye is grown for flour, for making whisky and gin, and for livestock feed. Is attacked by fungus ergot.

rye grass, short-lived perennial grass used for pasturage and temporary lawns. Italian rye grass (*Lolium multiflorum*) and English or perennial rye grass (*L. perenne*) are both grown in the U.S.

Rye House Plot, conspiracy (1683) to assassinate Charles II of England and his brother (later James II) on the London road by Rumbold's Rye House in Essex. They did not make the journey; the plot was revealed.

Ryerson, (Adolphus) Egerton, 1803–82, Canadian clergyman and educator. He attacked John Strachan on questions of clergy reserves and church control of education. A founder and first president (1841) of Victoria Col., Cobourg (later Victoria Univ.).

Rykov, Aleksey Ivanovich (ŭlyĭksyä′ ēvä′nŭvĭch rē′kôf), 1881–1938, Russian revolutionist. A chief lieutenant of Lenin, after whose death he supported Stalin against Trotsky and became chairman of council of commissars (i.e., Soviet premier). Accused 1930 of "rightist deviation," he recanted (1931) but was implicated (1936) in party purge trials. Pleaded guilty and was executed.

Ryks Museum: see RIJKS MUSEUM.

Rymer, Thomas, 1641–1713, English critic and historiographer. A fanatically hostile critic of drama, he excoriated Shakspere's *Othello* in *A Short View of Tragedy* (1692). He began a compilation of many documents of England's international relations, 1101–1654, in *Foedera*.

Ryswick, Treaty of, 1697, ending War of the GRAND ALLIANCE; signed at Rijswijk (formerly Ryswick), near The Hague, Netherlands. France had to surrender most conquests made after 1679, except Strasbourg; Netherlands obtained commercial concessions; independence of Savoy was recognized; William III was acknowledged king of England.

Ryukyu Islands (rēōō′kyōō), archipelago (1,803 sq. mi.; pop. 759,683), extreme W Pacific, between Formosa and Kyushu, Japan. Chain extends 650 mi.; includes Amami Isls., Okinawa Isls., and Sakishima Isls. Sugar cane, pineapples, and bananas are grown. Group constituted ancient kingdom which became tributary to China in 14th cent. and also to Japan in 17th cent. Japan won full control 1874. Governed by U.S. since Aug., 1945.

S, chemical symbol of the element SULPHUR.

Sá, Mem de (män′ dü sä′), d. 1572, Portuguese colonial official, governor general of Brazil (1557?–1572). After driving French away from Guanabara Bay (1567), he estab. city of Rio de Janeiro there.

Saadi: see SADI.

Saadia ben Joseph al-Fayumi (sä′dëä, älfīōō′mē), 892?–942, Jewish scholar, b. Egypt. Laid the foundation of Hebrew grammar in *Book of Language*. Wrote great philosophical work, *The Book of Beliefs and Opinions* (Eng. tr., 1948).

Saale (zä′lü), river, 265 mi. long, E central Germany, rising in NE Bavaria and flowing N through Thuringia and former Saxony-Anhalt to join the Elbe SE of Magdeburg. Also called Saxonian or Thuringian Saale,

to distinguish it from the Franconian **Saale,** 84 mi. long, which flows SW from the Thuringian forest into the Main.

Saar, region: see SAAR TERRITORY.

Saar (zär), Fr. *Sarre,* river, 150 mi. long, rising in Vosges mts., E France, and flowing generally N to join the Moselle SW of Trier, Germany. Forms part of border between France and Saar Territory.

Saarbrücken (zär″brü′kún), Fr. *Sarrebruck,* city (pop. 89,700), cap. of Saar Territory, on Saar R. Industrial center (steel, machinery). Was cap. of county of Saarbrücken (a dependency of Nassau) 1381–1793. Heavily damaged in World War II.

Saare (sä′rä), Estonian *Saaremaa,* Ger. and Swed. *Ösel,* Baltic island, 1,046 sq. mi., Estonia, across entrance to Gulf of Riga; chief town Kuressaare. Dairy farming; stock raising.

Saarinen, Eliel (ĕ′lēĕl sä′rĭnĕn), 1873–1950, Finnish architect and city planner, a noted exponent of the modern school. Settled 1923 in U.S.

Saar Territory or **Saar,** Fr. *Sarre,* region (988 sq. mi.; pop. 904,040), W Europe, between Germany and France; cap. Saarbrücken. A hilly region, drained by the Saar R., it has important coal mines and is intensely industrialized (coal, steel). Population is German-speaking and mostly Catholic. The territory was created by the Treaty of Versailles (1919) from parts of the Rhenish Palatinate and the Prussian Rhine Prov. and was administered by France, under League of Nations supervision, pending a plebiscite to be held in 1935. France also received the right to exploit the Saar coal fields until that date. The 1935 plebiscite gave an overwhelming majority in favor of reunion with Germany, but after World War II (in which the region suffered much destruction) the territory was placed under French occupation and was again detached from Germany. It obtained an autonomous government and in 1948 entered into a customs union with France. In 1950 France obtained a 50-year lease on the Saar coal mines. German claims to the Saar are a serious factor in Franco-German relations.

Saavedra Lamas, Carlos (kär′lōs sävä′dhrä lä′mäs), 1880–, Argentine statesman. Promoted League of Nations; drew up anti-war pact (1932); helped to end war in Chaco. Received 1936 Nobel Peace Prize.

Saba: see SHEBA.

Sabaeans: see SHEBA.

Sabaoth (sä′bāōth, säbā′ŭth) [Heb.,= armies], Hebrew term used in New Testament (Romans 9.29; James 5.4) and in Christian hymns (e.g., *Sanctus* and *Te Deum*) as a title of God. Translated in Old Testament as "Lord of Hosts" (Isa. 1.9).

Sabatier, Paul (pôl′ säbätyä′), 1854–1941, French chemist. Shared 1912 Nobel Prize for method of hydrogenating organic compounds in presence of metallic catalysts.

Sabbatai Zevi (säbätī′ zä′vē), 1626–76, Jewish mystic and self-proclaimed Messiah, founder of the Sabbatean sect. Embraced Islam when taken by Turks, 1666.

Sabbatarians, strict observers of Sunday as Sabbath (e.g., Lord's Day Alliance of the U.S.); also observers of Saturday as Sabbath, such as Seventh-Day Adventists and Seventh-Day Baptists.

Sabbath [Heb.,= repose], last day of the week (Saturday), observed as a holy day of rest by Jews since immemorial time. Early Christians observed the first day of the week in commemoration of the Resurrection, and Sunday became the Christian Sabbath, though some sects (e.g., Seventh-Day Baptists) have reverted to Saturday. Friday is the holy day in Islam.

Sabeans: see SHEBA.

Sabellius, fl. 215, Christian theologian. Went from N Africa to Rome where he taught a variety of MONARCHIANISM. Held the doctrine of the "economic Trinity" with God one indivisible substance appearing successively as Father, Son, and Holy Spirit. He was excommunicated (220). Term **Sabellianism** came later to be given to all sorts of speculative doctrines related to monarchianism.

Sabin, Joseph (sä′bĭn), 1821–81, American bibliographer, b. England; compiler of *A Dictionary of Books Relating to America* (begun in 1868; after his death continued by others).

Sabine (sä″bēn′), river rising in prairies NE of Dallas, Texas, and flowing E and SE across Texas, then turning S to form part of Texas-La. line. Broadens near mouth making Sabine L. (c.17 mi. long, 7 mi. wide), then through Sabine Pass to Gulf of Mexico. Passes Port Arthur and Orange. Sabine-Neches Canal leads to Beaumont.

Sabines (sä′bīnz), anc. people of central Italy, in Sabine Hills, NE of Rome. From the earliest days there was always a Sabine element in Rome (the legend of the womanless followers of Romulus abducting Sabine women is a fictional explanation of this). They warred with Rome, but by the 3d cent. B.C. were completely amalgamated with the Romans.

sable (sä′bŭl), carnivorous mammal (*Martes zibellina*) of N Eurasia. Fur is thick, usually brown or black mixed with gray or brown; is highly valued in fur trade. American sable is a marten.

Sable, Cape, S Fla., southernmost extremity of U.S. mainland.

Sable Island, 30 mi. long, 2 mi. wide, in the Atlantic off SE N.S., Canada, ESE of Halifax. Exposed part of extensive sand shoal, it is a major hazard to navigation. Has lighthouse, lifesaving station, and radio beacon.

Sacajawea (sä″kŭjŭwē′ŭ, sŭkä″–), **Sacagawea** (–gŭwē′ŭ), or **Sakakawea** (–kŭwē′ŭ), fl. 1804–6, Indian woman guide on LEWIS AND CLARK EXPEDITION. Generally called in English the Bird Woman.

Sac and Fox Indians, North American tribes of Algonquian linguistic stock. They were driven out of the Saginaw Bay region in the 17th cent. and settled in NE Wis. as allies. They were warlike, and the French by 1730 had practically exterminated the Fox tribe. The remnants amalgamated with the Sac and after defeating the Illinois moved into Ill. A fraudulent treaty of 1804 would have compelled them to move W of the Mississippi. They resisted but were finally induced to Iowa (1831). The next year they returned E of the river, and the BLACK HAWK WAR began. Defeated they moved W, finally settling on reservations in Iowa, Kansas, and Okla. Sac is also written Sauk.

saccharin (sä′kŭrĭn), very sweet, white, crystalline coaltar product prepared from toluene. Has no nutritive value, but its sodium salt used in sweetening food for those who cannot eat sugar.

Sacchetti, Franco (fräng′kō säk-kĕt′tē), c.1330–1400, Italian author of *Trecento novelle* (1388–95), an imitation of Boccaccio's *Decameron.*

Sacco-Vanzetti Case (sä′kō-vänzĕ′tē), case involving trial and conviction (1921) of Nicola Sacco and Bartolomeo Vanzetti for murder and robbery at Braintree, Mass. Many believed conviction had been influenced by the men's reputation as radicals. After much evidence had been discredited but denial of a new trial upheld, public outcry forced review of case. Advisory group to governor upheld judicial procedure. Execution took place Aug. 22, 1927. The two men are widely regarded as martyrs.

Sacheverell, Henry (sŭshĕ′vŭrŭl), 1674?–1724, English clergyman. Tried for seditious libel for attacking the Whig government in sermons, he was convicted (1710) but given a light sentence. Case created a furore and humiliated the Whigs.

Sachs, Hans (häns′ zäks′), 1494–1576, German MEISTERSINGER, leading poet of the school at Nuremberg; a shoemaker. A prodigious writer, he is best known for the poem *The Nightingale of Wittenberg,* the *Schwänke* or verse anecdotes, and his Shrovetide plays. Figures as a principal character in Wagner's opera *Die Meistersinger.*

Sac Indians: see SAC AND FOX INDIANS.

Sackets Harbor, village (pop. 1,247), N N.Y., at E end of L. Ontario W of Watertown; settled c.1801. Important naval base in War of 1812.

Sackville, Charles, 6th earl of Dorset, 1638–1706, English poet and courtier. Wrote witty epigrams, short pieces, and songs (notably *To All You Ladies Now at Land*).

Sackville, Thomas, 1st earl of Dorset, 1536–1608, English statesman and poet. Served under Elizabeth and James I. Author (with Thomas Norton) of *Gorboduc* (1562), considered earliest English tragedy.

Sackville, town (pop. 2,873), SE N.B., Canada, near head of Chignecto Bay and SE of Moncton. Surrounding Tantramar marshes were reclaimed by early French settlers. Seat of Mount Allison Univ. (United Church; coed.; 1858).

Sackville-West, V(ictoria Mary), 1892–, English poet and novelist; wife of Harold Nicolson. Poetry includes *The Land* (1926). Best-known novels are *The Edwardians* (1930) and *All Passion Spent* (1931).

Saco (sô′kō), city (pop. 10,324), SW Maine, at Saco R. falls opposite Biddeford; settled 1631. Mfg. of textiles, textile machinery, shoes. Seat of first legislative and judicial "court" in Maine (1640).

Saco, river rising in N central N.H. and flowing c.105 mi. SE, crossing SW Maine, to the Atlantic below Biddeford.

sacrament, in Christianity, one of certain ceremonial observances held to be instituted by Christ when on earth. Roman Catholics and the Orthodox have seven sacraments: the EUCHARIST, baptism, confirmation, penance (the forgiveness of sins), matrimony, order (see ORDERS, HOLY), and extreme unction (anointing of those in danger of death). They hold that these actually bestow grace. Protestants generally (though not universally) all accept the Eucharist and baptism and hold these to be merely symbols of grace.

Sacramento (săkrŭmĕn′tō), city (pop. 137,572), state cap. (since 1854), central Calif., at junction of Sacramento and American rivers; founded 1848 at settlement of New Helvetia (owned by J. A. SUTTER). Gold discovery in 1848 at near-by Sutter's Mill boomed colony to pop. of 10,000. City became terminus of first railroad in Calif. in 1856, W terminus of pony express in 1860, and terminus of first transcontinental railroad in 1869. Now a shipping and rail center for agr., lumbering, mining, and recreational area. Vegetable and fruit canneries, meat- and poultry-packing plants, sugar refineries, and metal products factories. Here are Sutter's Fort (1840; restored) and Crocker Art Gall.

Sacramento, river, 382 mi. long, rising in N Calif. near Mt. Shasta and flowing SW to Suisun Bay, a San Francisco Bay arm. Receives Pit, Feather, and American rivers. San Joaquin R. forms delta with it near its mouth. Navigable 256 mi. upstream at high water. Valley prospered with 1848 gold strike here. CENTRAL VALLEY project units in river include SHASTA DAM and Keswick Dam.

Sacré-Coeur (săkrā-kûr′), basilica in Paris, dedicated to the Sacred Heart of Jesus; famous landmark in Montmartre. Designed by Paul Labadie in Byzantine-Romanesque style, with a 267–ft. high bell tower. Built 1875–1914 by subscriptions as a votive offering after Franco-Prussian War; consecrated after World War I.

Sadducees (să′jŏosēz, să′dyŏo–), sect of Jews of the time of Jesus which accepted only the five books of the Law and rejected all it thought was not taught therein, e.g., immortality and the resurrection.

Sade, Donatien Alphonse Francois, comte de (dônăsyē′ älfôs′ fräswä kôt′ dù säd′), 1740–1814, French author; known as the marquis de Sade. His scandalous conduct caused his imprisonment for many years in the Bastille. He took part in the French Revolution, later was confined in the insane asylum of Charenton. His novels, such as *Justine* (1791) and *Histoire de Juliette* (6 vols., 1797), are notorious for their obscenities but had great influence on later writers; their literary merit is still subject to controversy. Sade gave his name to the perversion known as sadism.

Sá de Miranda, Francisco de (fränsēsh′kō dù sä′ dù mēran′dä), d. 1558, Portuguese writer. He introduced Italian Renaissance style in Portugal. His *Estrangeiros* and *Vilhalpandos* became models for classical drama. He also wrote in Spanish.

Sadi or **Saadi** (both: sä′dē), 1184–1291, Persian poet, a Sufi writer of great power. His masterpiece, *Gulistan* (1258), combines prose and poetry.

Sadowa (zädō′vä), Czech *Sadová* (sä′dôvä), village, E Bohemia, Czechoslovakia, near Hradec Kralove (Ger. *Königgrätz*). Austria suffered its decisive defeat here in Austro-Prussian War (1866).

Safarik, Pavel Josef, Czech *Šafařík* (pä′vĕl yô′zĕf shä′-far-zhĕk), 1795–1861, Slovak antiquarian, scholar, critic, journalist. Author of *History of Slavic Language and Literature* (in German, 1826; free Eng. tr., 1850) and of *Slavonic Antiquities* (1837), a pioneering work in modern Slavonic studies.

saffron, name for the autumn-flowering white or lilac crocus (*Crocus sativus*), and for its dried stigmas also called saffron, long used for coloring, flavoring, perfume, and medicine.

Saffron Walden, municipal borough (pop. 6,825), Essex, England; agr. market. Named for saffron crocus, grown here 14th–18th cent.

saga (sä′gù), in Old Norse literature, epic in prose or verse centering about a legendary or historical figure. Composed in 11th–13th cent. Among them are the *Heimskringla* and the *Starlunga Saga* by Snorri Sturluson, the *Laxdæla,* the *Njala,* and the *Frithjof* by Esaias Tegner.

Sagan (zä′gän), Pol. *Żagán,* town (1939 pop. 22,770; 1946 pop. 4,359), Lower Silesia, on Bober R.; under Polish administration since 1945. Textile mfg. Was seat of a principality 1274–1472. Passed to Saxony 1472, to Austria 1547, to Prussia 1745. Wallenstein was created duke of Sagan 1628. Title was later held by French Talleyrand family.

Sagasta, Práxedes Mateo (präk′sädhäs mätä′ō sägä′stä), 1825–1903, Spanish statesman. Founded Liberal party (1880). Was five times premier between 1871 and 1903. Unable to handle the situation in Cuba, he was generally blamed for the disastrous outcome of the Spanish-American War (1898).

Sage, Russell, 1816–1906, American financier. His wife, **Margaret Olivia Slocum Sage,** 1828–1918, undertook distribution of his fortune. Russell Sage Foundation, estab. 1907 in New York city, is concerned with improvement of social and living conditions in U.S.

sage, herb or shrub of genus *Salvia* of the mint family. Common in herb gardens is *Salvia officinalis,* with blue or white flowers and grayish aromatic foliage used as a seasoning. Clary salvia (*S. sclarea*), with pink flowers, is also planted in herb gardens. Some sages, especially the scarlet sage (*S. splendens*), are grown for ornament. Most sages are good honey plants.

sagebrush, deciduous shrub of genus *Artemisia,* abundant in W North America. Common sagebrush (*Artemisia tridentata*) has silvery gray leaves; it is important as forage on cattle ranges.

sage grouse, sage hen, sage cock, or **cock of the plains,** large grouse of W North America. Plumage is chiefly mottled brown, black, and gray.

Saghalien: see SAKHALIN.

Sag Harbor, resort village (pop. 2,373), on E Long Isl., SE N.Y., on Gardiners Bay; settled 1720–30. Has Whalers' Church and Whalers' Mus. (commemorates 19th-cent. importance as whaling port), first custom-house in N.Y.

Saginaw, city (pop. 92,918), S Mich., on Saginaw R. and S of Bay City; settled c.1816. Here Lewis Cass arranged treaty with Indians (1819) which ceded much of Mich. to U.S. Lumbering followed fur trade but declined after 1890. In agr. area with coal, oil, and salt deposits. Mfg. of auto parts, machinery, graphite, and wood products.

Saginaw, river formed near Saginaw in S Mich. and flowing c.22 mi. NNE to Saginaw Bay near Bay City. With headstreams and tributaries, river drains large lower Mich. area.

Saginaw Bay, arm of L. Huron, c.60 mi. long, 15–25 mi. wide, N Mich. Bay City is at head, near mouth of Saginaw R.

Sagittarius (săjĭtä′rēùs) [Latin,= the archer], ninth sign of ZODIAC.

sago (sä′gō), edible starch extracted from pithlike center of several East Indian palms (chiefly of genus *Metroxylon*) or palmlike plants. It is an important item of food and is exported for use in puddings and in stiffening textiles. The wild sago or coontie yields Florida arrowroot.

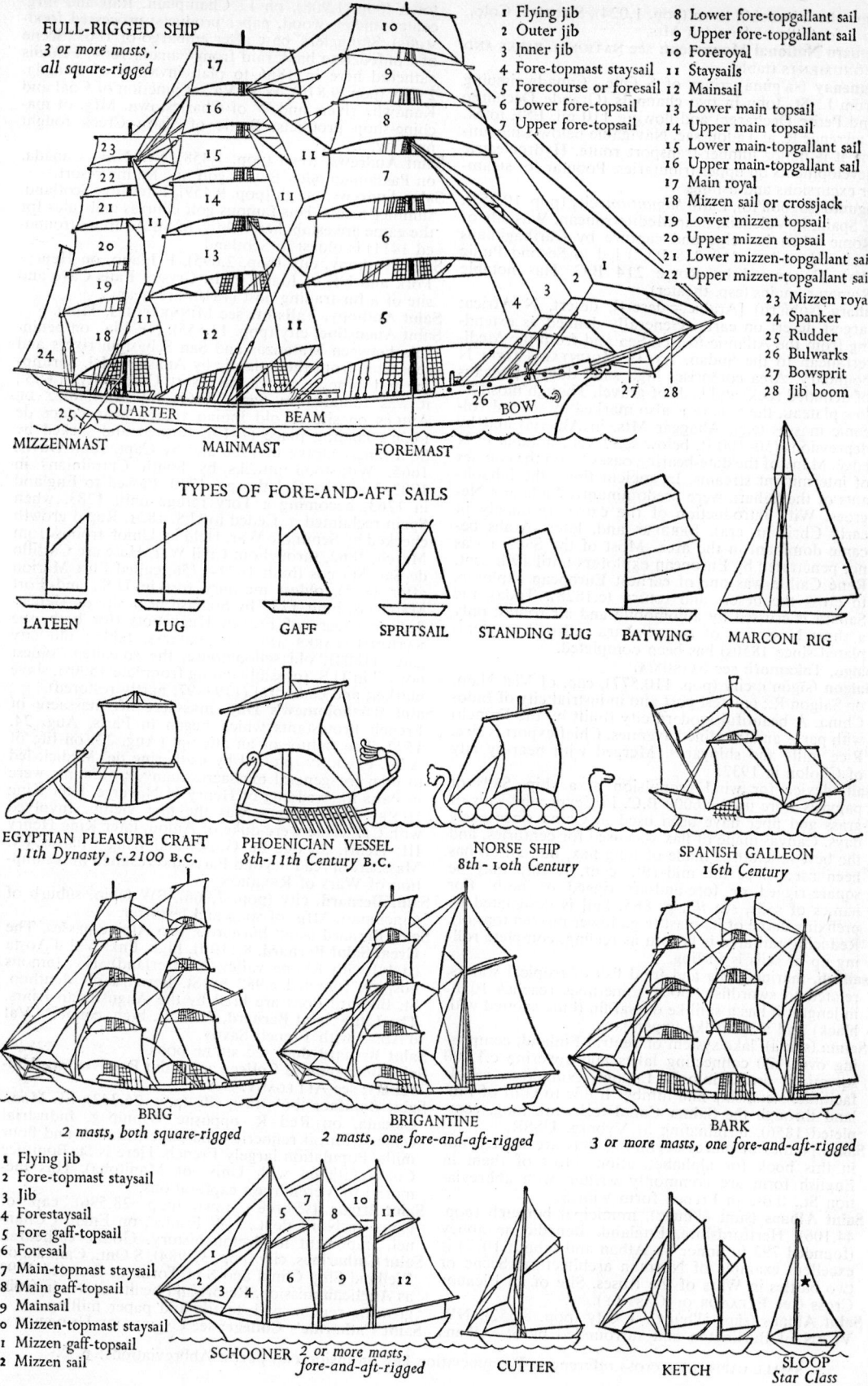

FULL-RIGGED SHIP
3 or more masts, all square-rigged

1 Flying jib
2 Outer jib
3 Inner jib
4 Fore-topmast staysail
5 Forecourse or foresail
6 Lower fore-topsail
7 Upper fore-topsail
8 Lower fore-topgallant sail
9 Upper fore-topgallant sail
10 Foreroyal
11 Staysails
12 Mainsail
13 Lower main topsail
14 Upper main topsail
15 Lower main-topgallant sail
16 Upper main-topgallant sail
17 Main royal
18 Mizzen sail or crossjack
19 Lower mizzen topsail
20 Upper mizzen topsail
21 Lower mizzen-topgallant sail
22 Upper mizzen-topgallant sail
23 Mizzen royal
24 Spanker
25 Rudder
26 Bulwarks
27 Bowsprit
28 Jib boom

QUARTER BEAM BOW

MIZZENMAST MAINMAST FOREMAST

TYPES OF FORE-AND-AFT SAILS

LATEEN LUG GAFF SPRITSAIL STANDING LUG BATWING MARCONI RIG

EGYPTIAN PLEASURE CRAFT
11th Dynasty, c.2100 B.C.

PHOENICIAN VESSEL
8th-11th Century B.C.

NORSE SHIP
8th-10th Century

SPANISH GALLEON
16th Century

BRIG
2 masts, both square-rigged

BRIGANTINE
2 masts, one fore-and-aft-rigged

BARK
3 or more masts, one fore-and-aft-rigged

1 Flying jib
2 Fore-topmast staysail
3 Jib
4 Forestaysail
5 Fore gaff-topsail
6 Foresail
7 Main-topmast staysail
8 Main gaff-topsail
9 Mainsail
10 Mizzen-topmast staysail
11 Mizzen gaff-topsail
12 Mizzen sail

SCHOONER *2 or more masts, fore-and-aft-rigged*

CUTTER KETCH SLOOP
Star Class

Saguache (sŭwŏch′), town (pop. 1,024), S central Colo., in S foothills of Sawatch Mts.

Saguaro National Monument: see NATIONAL PARKS AND MONUMENTS (table).

Saguenay (sä′gŭnā), river of S Que., Canada, issuing from L. St. John in two channels (Grande Décharge and Petite Décharge) and flowing 110 mi. ESE to St. Lawrence R. at Tadoussac. Navigable below Chicoutimi, it is major lumber-transport route. Hydroelectric developments on upper tributaries. Popular for steamer excursions and fishing.

Sagunto (sägōon′tō), Latin *Saguntum*, city (pop. 10,352), E Spain, in Valencia, near Mediterranean. Was ally of Rome when its seige and capture by Carthaginians under Hannibal (219–218 B.C.) led to Second Punic War. Conquered by Rome 214 B.C. Has notable Roman remains (esp. theater).

Sahara (sŭhâ′rủ) [Arabic,= desert], desert, N Africa; largest desert on earth. Generally defined as extending from the Atlantic to Red Sea and from the Mediterranean to the Sudan. ATLAS MOUNTAINS form N boundary. Area comprises high sand dunes, plateaus of denuded rock, and beds of gravel. Though mostly a low plateau, the Sahara is also marked by several volcanic masses (e.g., Ahaggar Mts. in Algeria) and by depressions (50–100 ft. below sea level), notably in N edge. Many of the date-bearing oases lie on the courses of intermittent streams. In ancient times the inhabitants of the Sahara were predominantly Sudanese Negroes. With introduction of the camel (probably in early Christian era), BERBERS and, later, Arabs became dominant in the area. Most of the Sahara was not penetrated by European explorers until 19th cent. René Caillié was one of earliest European explorers to cross the desert and return (c.1828). Today the Sahara is crossed by automobile and air routes; only a short N section of trans-Sahara railroad (contemplated since 1850s) has been completed.

Saigo, Takamori: see SATSUMA.

Saigon (sīgŏn′), city (pop. 110,577), cap. of Viet Nam, on Saigon R.; greatest port and industrial city of Indo-China. A beautiful modern city (built by the French) with parks and tree-lined avenues. Chief export is rice. Rice mills and shipyards. Merged with near-by city of Cholon in 1932.

sail, device for wind propulsion of a ship. Sails of papyrus were used c.6000 B.C. in Egypt, and sails of grass and fiber have been used in China since early days. Canvas made of flax was used for centuries, and the best sailcloth is made of long flax, but cotton has been used since the mid-19th cent. A ship may be square-rigged or fore-and-aft rigged or both. For names of sails, see *ill.,* p. 865. Sail is designated by prefixing name of its mast (e.g., lower mizzen topsail). Reducing sail area is known as reefing; complete rolling up of sails is furling.

sailfish, marine game and food fish of tropical waters, related to swordfish. Body sometimes reaches 10 ft. in length; it has a saillike dorsal fin (blue spotted with black) and a spearlike upper jaw.

Saima (sī′mä), lake system of central Finland, comprising over 120 connecting lakes and covering c.1,700 sq. mi. It drains into L. Ladoga. Numerous canals facilitate steamship and lumber traffic to Gulf of Finland through the **Saima Canal** (c.36 mi. long, completed 1856), terminating at Vyborg, USSR.

Saint. Names of places beginning thus are written out in this book for alphabetization. Most of them in English form are commonly written with abbreviation St., those in French form with S.

Saint Albans (sǔnt ôl′bǔnz), municipal borough (pop. 44,106), Hertfordshire, England. Benedictine abbey (founded 793 to honor St. Alban and rebuilt 1077) is excellent example of Norman architecture. Scene of two battles in Wars of the Roses. Site of an Eleanor Cross (see ELEANOR OF CASTILE).

Saint Albans (sānt âl′bǔnz). **1** City (pop. 8,552), NW Vt., N of Burlington and surrounded by St. Albans

town (pop. 1,908), on L. Champlain. Rail and mfg. center (metal, wood, paper products; processed foodstuffs; Smugglers' base after embargo of 1807. Scene of Confederate bank raid from Canada 1864. Fenians gathered here in 1866 to plan invasion of Canada. **2** City (pop. 9,870), W W.Va., at junction of Coal and Kanawha rivers and W of Charlestown. Mfg. of machine-shop products. Battle of Scary Creek fought near by, 1861.

Saint Andrews, town (pop. 1,458), SW N.B., Canada, on Passamaquoddy Bay; a golf and fishing resort.

Saint Andrews, burgh (pop. 9,459), Fifeshire, Scotland; summer resort. Has famous golf courses and rules for the game are estab. here. Univ. of St. Andrews (founded 1411) is oldest in Scotland.

Saint Anthony, city (pop. 2,695), E Idaho, on Henrys Fork and NE of Idaho Falls. Crystal Falls Cave and site of a fur-trading post (1810) are near.

Saint Anthony, Falls of: see MINNEAPOLIS, Minn.

Saint Augustine, city (pop. 13,555), NE Fla., on peninsula between Matanzas and San Sebastian rivers and separated from the Atlantic by Anastasia Isl. Shrimping and shipping center and resort. Oldest city in U.S., it was founded in Sept., 1565, by MENÉNDEZ DE AVILÉS on site of old Indian village near Ponce de León's landing place (1513). Burned and sacked by Sir Francis Drake in 1586 and by Capt. John Davis, 1665. Withstood attacks by South Carolinians in 1702–3 and by Oglethorpe, 1740. Passed to England in 1763, becoming a Tory refuge until 1783, when Spain reclaimed it. Ceded to U.S. 1821. Rapid growth checked by Seminole War. Held by Union troops from March, 1862, throughout Civil War. Here are Castillo de San Marcos (built 1672–1756; called Fort Marion after 1825), oldest masonry fort in U.S., and Fort Matanzas, built 1737 by Spanish near site of Menéndez's massacre of French Huguenots (for both, see NATIONAL PARKS AND MONUMENTS, table); old city gates (1804); old schoolhouse, the so-called "oldest house" in U.S. (possibly dating from late 1500s); slave market; and cathedral (1793–97; partly restored).

Saint Bartholomew's Day, massacre of, massacre of French Protestants which began in Paris, Aug. 24, 1572. The failure of an attempt (Aug. 22) on life of Adm. COLIGNY, plotted by Catherine de' Medici, led to plan for general massacre (many Protestants were in Paris for wedding of Henry of Navarre, later King HENRY IV). Coligny was the first victim. Involved with Catherine were duke of Anjou, later King Henry III; Henri, 3d duc de Guise; and King Charles IX. Massacre spread beyond Paris and resulted in resumption of Wars of RELIGION.

Saint Bernard, city (pop. 7,066), SW Ohio, suburb of Cincinnati. Mfg. of soap and fertilizer.

Saint Bernard (sānt′ bǔrnärd′), two Alpine passes. The **Great Saint Bernard,** 8,110 ft. high, links Val d'Aosta (Italy) with Rhone valley (Switzerland). Has famous hospice, founded c.982 by St. Bernard of Menthon. St. Bernard dogs are bred by the Augustinian friars. The **Little Saint Bernard,** 7,178 ft. high, connects Val d'Aosta with French Savoy.

Saint Bernard dog: see SHEEP DOGS.

Saint Bonaventure College and **Saint Bonaventure University:** see ALLEGANY, N.Y.

Saint Boniface (bŏ′nĭfās), city (pop. 26,342), SE Man., Canada, on Red R. opposite Winnipeg. Industrial center with oil refineries and paper, lumber and flour mills. Population largely French. Here is St. Boniface Col. (affiliated with Univ. of Manitoba). Has memorial to Vérendrye's explorations.

Saint-Brieuc (sĕ-brêû′), town (pop. 28,596), cap. of Côtes-du-Nord dept., NW France, on English Channel. Important in Breton history. Gothic cathedral.

Saint Catharines, city (pop. 37,984), S Ont., Canada, on Welland Ship Canal and S of Toronto; founded 1792 as Anglican mission. Resort and health center in fruit-growing region, with textile and paper milling.

Saint Catharine's College: see CAMBRIDGE UNIVERSITY.

Saint Charles. 1 City (pop. 6,709), NE Ill., W of Chicago and on Fox R. Residential and industrial center in farm area. **2** City (pop. 14,314), E Mo., on Missouri R. and NW of St. Louis. Settled 1769 by French traders, it was earliest permanent white settlement on the Missouri. Trading post and starting point westward on Boone's Lick Trail. Was state cap. to 1826. Now a farm center, with mfg. of metal products. Seat of Lindenwood Col. for Women.

Saint Christopher: see SAINT KITTS.

St. Clair, Arthur, 1734–1818, American general, b. Scotland. Fought in American Revolution; abandoned Ticonderoga to British in 1777. First governor (1787–1802) of Northwest Territory. Defeated by Indians under Little Turtle in 1791.

Saint Clair, borough (pop. 5,856), E Pa., N of Pottsville. Coal and textiles.

Saint Clair, Lake, c.27 mi. long, 24 mi. wide, between S Ontario and SE Mich. Joined to L. Erie by Detroit R. and to L. Huron by St. Clair R.

Saint Clair Shores, residential village (pop. 19,823), SE Mich., on L. St. Clair and NE of Detroit.

Saint-Cloud (sĕ-klōō′), town (pop. 17,101), Seine-et-Oise dept., N France, on Seine R.; W suburb of Paris. Palace (built 1572; destroyed by fire 1870) was scene of Napoleon's proclamation as emperor (1804).

Saint Cloud (sănt kloud′), city (pop. 28,410), central Minn., on the Mississippi and NW of Minneapolis, in farm area; settled 1852. Granite quarrying and finishing and mfg. of wood and metal products.

Saint Croix: see VIRGIN ISLANDS OF THE UNITED STATES.

Saint Croix (sănt kroi′). **1** River rising in the Chiputneticook Lakes on Maine-N.B. border and flowing 75 mi. S and E, past Calais, Maine, to Passamaquoddy Bay, forming international boundary. **2** River rising in N Wis. lake region and flowing 164 mi. SW, then S, through L. St. Croix to the Mississippi at Prescott, Wis. Forms part of Wis.-Minn. boundary.

Saint Croix Falls, village (pop. 1,065), NW Wis., on St. Croix R. Park has Old Man of the Dalles and other rock formations.

Saint-Cyr-l'École (sĕ-sēr′-lākôl′), town (pop. 4,288), Seine-et-Oise dept., France, near Versailles. Mme de Maintenon estab. here famous girls' school (1684). Building later housed Saint-Cyr military academy (estab. by Napoleon 1808; the "West Point" of France).

Saint David's, village, Pembrokeshire, Wales. Cathedral (12th cent.) is most famous one in Wales. Was for centuries one of most important places of pilgrimage in Great Britain. **St. David's Head,** NW of village, is most westerly point of Wales.

St. Denis, Ruth (sănt dĕ′nĭs), 1880–, American dancer, whose real name is Dennis. Founded Denishawn School with husband Ted Shawn. A dance pioneer, she has also trained many famous dancers.

Saint-Denis (sănt-dĕ′nĭs, Fr. sĕ-dŭnē′), town (pop. 68,-595), Seine dept., N France; a N suburb of Paris. Metalworks; chemical plants. Town grew around a Benedictine abbey, founded 626 at tomb of St. Denis, patron saint of France, which played prominent part in French medieval history. Its basilica (12th–13th cent.) deeply influenced evolution of Gothic architecture. In it are tombs of the kings of France.

Saint-Dié (sĕ-dyä′), city (pop. 11,423), Vosges dept., E France, on Meurthe R. Grew around monastery founded in 7th cent. In 1944 retreating German troops destroyed most of the city, including cathedral and Gothic cloisters. Here in 1507 was printed the *Cosmographiae introductio,* first book to refer to newly discovered continent as America.

Sainte Agathe des Monts (sĕtägät″ dä mŏ′), town (pop. 5,169), S Que., Canada, on North R. and NW of Montreal. Health and ski resort.

Sainte Anne de Beaupré (sănt ăn′ dù bōprä′, Fr. sĕtän″), village and pilgrim resort (pop. 1,827), S Que., Canada, on St. Lawrence R. and NE of Quebec. Noted shrine here estab. 1620 by shipwrecked sailors. Chapel built 1658, church 1876; magnificently rebuilt after 1922 fire.

Sainte Anne de Bellevue (sĕtän″ dù bĕl′vü), town (pop. 3,342), S Que., on Montreal isl. Has lumbering and publishing. In fur-trading days town was point of departure for canoes going west. Thomas Moore's "Canadian Boat Song" mentions it. Seat of Macdonald Col., a branch of McGill Univ.

Sainte-Beuve, Charles Augustin (shärl′ ōgüstĕ′ sĕt-bûv′), 1804–69, French literary historian and critic. Much of his vast critical output is gathered under the title *Causeries du lundi* (1851–70; Eng. tr., *Monday Chats,* 1877). His *Port-Royal* (1840–60) places him among the greatest modern critics and cultural historians.

Sainte-Chapelle (sĕt-shäpĕl′), former chapel, Paris, part of Palais de Justice. Built 1242–48 by order of Louis IX, it is one of purest jewels of medieval art. Magnificent stained glass windows, separated only by buttresses, form walls of the upper chapel (there is also a lower chapel and a spire).

Saint Edmund Hall: see OXFORD UNIVERSITY.

Sainte Geneviève (sănt jĕ′nùvēv), city (pop. 3,992), E Mo., on the Mississippi below St. Louis. Earliest permanent white settlement in Mo., it was founded before 1750 as French trading post.

Saint Elias, Mount, 18,008 ft. high, on Yukon-Alaska border in **St. Elias Mountains,** section of the Coast Ranges. Highest peak Mt. LOGAN.

Saint Elmo's fire, luminous electrical discharge into atmosphere from projecting or elevated object. Usually observed as brushlike, fiery jets. Occurs when atmosphere is charged and electrical potential strong enough to cause discharge is created between object and air.

Saintes (sĕt), town (pop. 20,711), Charente-Maritime dept., W France, on Charente R.; historic cap. of Saintonge. Trade center for grain and spirits. Has well-preserved Roman remains.

Sainte Thérèse (sĕt′ tärĕz′), town (pop. 7,038), S Que., Canada, WNW of Montreal. Mfg. of furniture.

Saint-Étienne (sĕtätyĕn′), industrial city (pop. 156,315), cap. of Loire dept., E central France, in a mining district (coal, iron). Produces steel, machinery, arms, textiles.

Saint-Évremond, Charles de (shärl′ dù sĕtävrùmŏ′), 1616?–1703, French author and soldier. Was a political exile from France after 1659; buried in Westminster Abbey. His free-thinking skepticism is revealed in his *Comédie des académistes* and in his acute critical essays.

Saint Exupéry, Antoine de (ätwän′ dù sĕtĕgzüpārē′), 1900–1944, French author and aviator. *Night Flight* (1931; Eng. tr., 1932), *Wind, Sand, and Stars* (1939), and *Flight to Arras* (1942), all based on his own flying experiences, and the fantasy *The Little Prince* (1943) are works imbued with poetry, introspection, and deep thought. He was reported missing in action in 1944.

Saint Francis, river rising in SE Mo. hills and flowing c.470 mi. S through Ark. to join the Mississippi above Helena. Forms part of Ark.-Mo. line.

Saint Francis Indians, group of Abnaki Indians, attacked by Robert Rogers and his Rangers (1759).

Saint Francis Xavier University: see ANTIGONISH, N.S.

Saint Gall (sănt gôl′), Ger. *Sankt Gallen,* canton (777 sq. mi.; pop. 308,483), NE Switzerland. Largely mountainous, it borders on L. of Constance and on the Rhine and entirely surrounds Appenzell canton. Population is German-speaking. Has noted silk, cotton, and embroidery mfg., especially in its cap., **Saint Gall** (pop. 67,865). The early history of St. Gall is that of its former Benedictine abbey, which originated in a cell built c.614 by St. Gall, an Irish missionary and companion of St. Columban. An abbey from 8th cent., it became a major center of early medieval learning, where invaluable classic manuscripts were copied and preserved. Its abbots, who ruled present St. Gall and APPENZELL cantons, were made princes of Holy Roman empire in 1204. The town of St. Gall joined the Swiss Confederation in 1454, and in 1457 bought its freedom from the prince-abbot. While the territory ruled by the abbot remained Catholic, the town became Protestant—a source of civil strife until 1718. The abbey was secularized in 1798 and its domains, together with the town, became a canton in 1803. The present abbey buildings date from the 18th cent.; former abbey church became cathedral in 1846. Library has important medieval manuscripts.

Saint-Gaudens, Augustus (sănt-gô′dŭnz), 1848–1907, foremost American sculptor of his time, b. Dublin, Ireland. Best known for public monuments (e.g., statue of Gen. Sherman at entrance to Central Park, New York). Also created portrait plaques and low reliefs. His brother, **Louis Saint-Gaudens,** 1854–1913, was also a sculptor.

Saint George, town (pop. c.1,500), on St. George's isl., Bermuda; cap. of Bermuda until Hamilton was selected in 1815.

Saint George, city (pop. 4,562), extreme SW Utah, in Virgin R. valley. Former cotton center, now tourist center. Has Mormon temple and tabernacle.

Saint George's, town (pop. 5,772), cap. of Grenada, British West Indies; administrative hq. of Grenada and Windward Isls. colony.

Saint George's Channel, sea arm, c.100 mi. long and 50–95 mi. wide, linking the Atlantic and the Irish Sea. It separates SE Ireland from Wales.

Saint-Germain, Treaty of (sĕ-zhĕrmĕ′). Several treaties were signed at Saint-Germain-en-Laye, France. Treaty of **1570** ended first phase of Wars of RELIGION. Treaty of **1679,** between France and Brandenburg at end of Third Dutch War, forced Elector Frederick William to restore most of his conquests to Sweden. Treaty of **1919,** between Austria and Allies of World War I, dissolved Austro-Hungarian Monarchy; reduced AUSTRIA to its present size; awarded the rest of the former Austrian Empire to the new states of Poland, Czechoslovakia, and Yugoslavia (whose independence was recognized) and to Italy and Rumania; prohibited political or economic union of Austria with Germany (see ANSCHLUSS). The U.S. did not ratify the treaty because it contained the Covenant of the League of Nations.

Saint-Germain-des-Prés (sĕ-zhĕrmĕ″-dā-prā′), historic abbey and church of Paris, founded 6th cent. Present Romanesque church dates from early 11th cent. Only ruins of once powerful abbey remain (it was destroyed in French Revolution), but 16th-cent. Renaissance palace of abbots stands near by.

Saint-Germain-en-Laye (sĕ-zhĕrmĕ″nä-lā′), town (pop. 20,028), Seine-et-Oise dept., N France; a W suburb of Paris. Renaissance château (now museum) was chief royal residence from Francis I to Louis XIII; birthplace of Louis XIV.

Saint Gotthard (sănt gŏ′thŭrd), Alpine group, S central Switzerland, crossed by the **Saint Gotthard Pass,** 6,929 feet high, used since 13th cent. Road was built 1820–30. The **Saint Gotthard Tunnel** (length 9.3 mi.; maximum alt. 3,786 ft.) was constructed 1872–80 and is used by St. Gotthard RR., which links N and S Switzerland.

Saint Helena (hŭlē′nŭ), British island (47 sq. mi.; pop. 4,748), in the Atlantic, 1,200 mi. W of Africa; cap. Jamestown. A British crown colony since 1834, it now includes Ascension and Tristan da Cunha. Best known as place of Napoleon's exile 1815–21.

Saint Helena Island (sănt hĕ′lŭnŭ), c.15 mi. long, 3–5 mi. wide, S S.C., between St. Helena and Port Royal sounds, one of largest SEA ISLANDS. Discovered early 16th cent. by Spanish. Inhabited by Negro descendants of sea-island plantation slaves. Gullah (Sea Island Negro dialect) spoken. Farming.

Saint Helens, county borough (pop. 110,276), Lancashire, England. Center of glass mfg. in England, it also has iron and copper foundries, chemical and soap factories, and potteries.

Saint Helier (sănt hĕl′yŭr), town (pop. 25,360), cap. of Jersey, Channel Isls. Resort and export point of local produce. Scene of a battle (1781) when the French tried unsuccessfully to regain Jersey. Victoria Col. was founded in 1852.

Saint Hilda's College: see OXFORD UNIVERSITY.

Saint Hugh's College: see OXFORD UNIVERSITY.

Saint Hyacinthe (sănt hī′ŭsĭnth, Fr. sĕtyäsĕt′), city (pop. 20,236), S Que., Canada, on Yamaska R. and ENE of Montreal. Hosiery and textile mills.

Saint Ignace (sănt′ ĭg′nŭs), resort city (pop. 2,946), E Upper Peninsula, N Mich., on Straits of Mackinac. Here are early French fort (restored 1938), and grave of Père Marquette.

Saint Ives (sŭnt īvz′), municipal borough (pop. 9,037), Cornwall, England, on St. Ives Bay. Fishing town and resort, it has a noted artists' colony.

Saint James's Palace, in London, on St. James's St. and fronting on Pall Mall. Henry VIII built palace and park about it. Royal residence from 1697 until Victoria's time, it is now occasionally used. British court is still called the Court of St. James's.

Saint Jean, Que.: see SAINT JOHNS.

Saint-Jean-de-Luz (sĕ-zhä″-dù-lüz′), town (pop. 8,848), Basses-Pyrénées dept., SW France. Fishing port and beach resort on Bay of Biscay.

Saint Jérôme (sĕ zhärōm′), city (pop. 17,685), S Que., Canada, on North R. and NW of Montreal. Mfg. center with woolen and paper mills. Scene of annual passion play.

St. John, Henry, Viscount Bolingbroke (sĭn′jŭn, bŏ′-lĭngbrŏŏk), 1678–1751, English statesman. As Tory secretary of state (1710–14) under Robert HARLEY he intrigued to end unpopular War of Spanish Succession and tried to weaken Whigs by laws against dissenters. Gradually supplanted Harley, who was dismissed (1714). For intriguing with the Old Pretender he was dismissed by George I and attainted by Parliament after flight to France. Helped plan Jacobite rising of 1715. After leaving Jacobite cause he was pardoned (1723). Organized opposition to Robert Walpole. A lucid writer and great orator, he reflected low moral standard of politics in his time. Friend of Pope and of Voltaire.

Saint John, city (pop. 50,779), S N.B., Canada, at mouth of St. John R. on Bay of Fundy. Major year-round port with extensive shipping connections. Provincial center with important fishing industry and mfg. of cotton goods, sugar, pulpwood and metal products. Fort estab. here 1631–35. Contested by French and British until British control estab. 1758. United Empire Loyalists built settlement (called Parr Town) here 1783; renamed 1785. Much of old city destroyed by fire 1877.

Saint John, Virgin Islands: see VIRGIN ISLANDS OF THE UNITED STATES.

Saint John, river, c.400 mi. long, rising in N Maine and flowing NE to N.B., then SE below Edmundston to Bay of Fundy at St. John. Forms Maine-N.B. line for 75 mi. At Grand Falls drops 75 ft. in great cataract, soon drops 50 ft. more in rapids through mile-long gorge. At mouth, within St. John city, are Reversing Falls Rapids, caused by Bay of Fundy tides which force river to reverse flow at high tide. River discovered by Champlain and Monts on St. John the Baptist's Day 1604. Navigable to Fredericton for vessels of 120 tons.

Saint John, Lake, area 375 sq. mi., S Que., Canada, NNW of Quebec, drained by Saguenay R.

Saint John of Jerusalem, Knights of: see KNIGHTS HOSPITALERS.

Saint John's, town (pop. 10,965), cap. of Leeward Isls. colony and Antigua presidency, British West Indies, port on Antigua isl.

Saint John's, city (pop. 52,873), provincial cap., SE N.F., Canada, on NE coast of Avalon Peninsula; estab. early 16th cent. Center of provincial life, with shipping connections with U.S., Canada, and Great Britain and rail connections with W coast of island. Base of fishing fleet with many industries connected with fishing. Control fluctuated between French and British until British authority was estab. 1763. Naval base in Revolution and War of 1812. Here Marconi heard first transatlantic wireless message 1901, and from here first nonstop transatlantic flight was made 1919. In World War II U.S. army and naval base and Canadian air base were estab. N of city.

Saint Johns or **Saint Jean** (sē zhä'), city (pop. 19,305), S Que., Canada, on Richelieu R. and SE of Montreal. Silk, paper, and hosiery mills. Fort built here 1666, rebuilt 1749, was captured by American forces 1775, and retaken by British and used as supply base. Terminal of first railroad from Laprairie 1836.

Saint Johns, river rising in swamps of SE Fla. Flows c.300 mi. N, forming eight lakes, and turns E at Jacksonville to enter the Atlantic 28 mi. away. Receives many streams, notably the Oklawaha. Navigable for 200 mi.

St.-John's-bread: see CAROB.

Saint Johnsbury, town (pop. 9,292), including St. Johnsbury village (7,370), NE Vt., NE of Montpelier; settled 1786. Has famous maple-sugar industry. Mfg. of scales and farm implements; granite works. Platform scales invented here. Seat of St. Johnsbury Acad. (1842).

Saint John's College: see CAMBRIDGE UNIVERSITY; OXFORD UNIVERSITY.

Saint John's College: see ANNAPOLIS, Md.

Saint John's University: see BROOKLYN, N.Y.

Saint John's Wood, residential district of NW London, England. Many artists have lived here. Lord's Cricket Ground is hq. of Marylebone Cricket Club, authority for rules of the game.

Saint-John's-wort, widely distributed herbaceous or woody plant of genus *Hypericum,* usually with yellow flowers. Common European St.-John's-wort (*Hypericum perforatum*) is naturalized in North America.

Saint John the Divine, Cathedral of, New York city. Charter for building was granted 1873 to Episcopal diocese. Building began 1892, and crypt was opened for worship 1899. Entire length of cathedral was opened 1941. In 1911 plans were changed from Romanesque to Gothic, with adoption of design by Ralph Adams Cram.

Saint Joseph. 1 City (pop. 10,223), SW Mich., on L. Michigan at mouth of St. Joseph R. opposite BENTON HARBOR; settled permanently c.1830 on site of Fort Miami (built 1679 by LA SALLE). Resort and port, it is trade center for fruit growing region with metal products. **2** City (pop. 78,588), NW Mo., on bluffs above the Missouri and NNW of Kansas City; laid out c.1843 on site of trading post (1826). Was E terminus of pony express from 1860. Now a huge livestock and grain market, it has meat-packing and grain-processing plants and railroad shops. The home of Jesse James is here.

Saint Joseph, river rising near Hillsdale, Mich., and flowing c.210 mi. W, past South Bend, Ind., to L. Michigan between St. Joseph and Benton Harbor, Mich. Important route for Indians and early travelers.

Saint Joseph d'Alma (sē zhôzĕf" dälmä'), town (pop. 7,975), S Que., Canada, on Saguenay R. and WNW of Chicoutimi. Wool carding and lumbering.

Saint Jovite (sē zhôvĕt'), village (pop. 1,453), S Que.; a skiing resort in the Laurentians.

Saint-Just, Louis de (lwē' dŭ zhüst'), 1767–94, French revolutionist, known as the "archangel of the Revolution." During the REIGN OF TERROR (1793–94) he and Couthon were the chief aides of Robespierre. He believed fanatically in the possibility of a perfect state, based on Spartan virtue. He fell with Robespierre on 9 THERMIDOR and was guillotined the next day.

Saint Kitts or **Saint Christopher,** island (68 sq. mi.; pop. 28,818), British West Indies, in Leeward Isls. With Nevis and smaller islands makes up St. Kitts–Nevis presidency; cap. BASSETERRE. Discovered by Columbus (1492); long disputed by British and French; awarded to Great Britain (1713).

Saint Lambert, residential city (pop. 8,615), S Que., Canada, on St. Lawrence R. opposite Montreal.

St. Laurent, Louis Stephen (sē lôrä'), 1882–, Canadian prime minister (1948–).

Saint Laurent (sē lôrä'), town (pop. 20,426), S Que., Canada, on Montreal isl., W suburb of Montreal.

Saint Lawrence, a principal river of North America, linking Great Lakes to Gulf of St. Lawrence to form waterway c.2,350 mi. long from W end of L. Superior to the Atlantic. River proper issues from NE end of L. Ontario and flows 774 mi. NE to its mouth (c.90 mi. wide), N of Cape Gaspé. Tidal below Quebec city. Forms c.114 mi. of international boundary between N.Y. and Ont. Between Kingston and Brockville, Ont., are scenic Thousand Isls. L. St. Francis, L. St. Louis, L. St. Peter are widened sections. Montreal is head of ocean-going navigation, but canals make entire river navigable by smaller vessels. Important source of hydroelectric power. A S tributary is Richelieu R. (link to L. Champlain and Hudson R.). GREAT LAKES-SAINT LAWRENCE SEAWAY AND POWER PROJECT has long been discussed. River visited by Jacques CARTIER 1534–35. River system long used by explorers, fur traders, and missionaries. Valley taken by British from French 1763. River became international boundary 1783.

Saint Lawrence, Gulf of, large bay of the Atlantic, SE Canada, at mouth of St. Lawrence R. between N.S. (S), Newfoundland (E), Que. (N), and N.B. and Gaspé Peninsula (W). Chaleur Bay is W inlet. Strait of Belle Isle, Cabot Strait, and Strait of Canso lead to the Atlantic. Ice-free mid-April to early Dec., it has important fishing grounds, especially cod.

Saint Lawrence Island, 90 mi. long, 8–22 mi. wide, off W Alaska, in Bering Sea. Barren and snow-covered. Natives engage in whaling, fox trapping. Discovered 1728 by Vitus Bering. Primitive Eskimo culture interests anthropologists.

Saint Lawrence Islands National Park, 189.4 acres, S Ont., Canada, in the THOUSAND ISLANDS; estab. 1914. Contains 13 Canadian islands and some adjacent mainland.

Saint Lawrence University: see CANTON, N.Y.

St. Leger, Barry (sĭl'ŭnjür, sänt" lĕj'ŭr), 1737–89, British officer in American Revolution. Laid siege to Fort Stanwix in SARATOGA CAMPAIGN.

Saint-Lô (sē-lō'), town (pop. 5,190), cap. of Manche dept., NW France, in Normandy. It was partially destroyed in 1944, when its capture by U.S. troops (July 18) cut off German forces under Rommel.

Saint Louis (sānt loō'ĭs), city (pop. 856,796), E Mo., largest city in state and eighth largest in U.S., on W bank of the Mississippi below mouth of the Missouri. Post chosen and built by Pierre LACLEDE and R. A. CHOUTEAU, 1763–64. Transferred to Spain 1770 and later returned to France, it was acquired by U.S. in LOUISIANA PURCHASE. Mainly French into 19th cent., it received Germans after 1850. Gateway to the Missouri and West for fur traders and explorers. Became great river port after W migration following War of 1812. Union base in Civil War, it had industrial expansion after that war. Great traffic handler, it is a livestock, agr., fur, and lumber market, and a financial and cultural center. Has food processing, brewing, distilling, and mfg. of chemicals, apparel, transportation equipment, and metal, oil, wood, and coal products. Here are SAINT LOUIS UNIVERSITY, WASHINGTON UNIVERSITY, and Jefferson Natl. Expansion Memorial (historic buildings). Near by is Jefferson Barracks, military base.

Saint Louis Park, village (pop. 22,644), E Minn., SW suburb of Minneapolis; settled 1853. Produces ice cream and tools.

Saint Louis University, mainly at St. Louis, Mo.; R.C. (Jesuit), for men and women; opened 1818, oldest college W of the Mississippi, chartered as a university 1832. Includes University Col.; Webster Col. (at WEBSTER GROVES); Parks Col. of Aeronautical Technology (at East St. Louis, Ill.); and Inst. of Geophysical Technology.

Saint Lucia (sănt lōō′shū), island (233 sq. mi.; pop. 70,-113), British West Indies, part of Windward Isls.; cap. CASTRIES. British attempts to settle it in early 17th cent. met with fierce resistance from Carib Indians. French and British contested ownership until 1803, when British gained control. U.S. obtained 99-year lease for naval base here (1940).

Saint-Malo (sē-mälō′), town (pop. 10,873), Ille-et-Vilaine dept., NW France, built 9th cent. on a rocky promontory in English Channel. Its prosperity as a port dates from 16th cent. Famed old ramparts, Gothic and Renaissance cathedral, and 17th-cent. houses here were damaged in World War II, particularly in 11-day siege of the citadel constructed by the Germans on a harbor island (Aug., 1944).

Saint Mark's Church, Venice. Originally a Romanesque church, built in 9th cent. and destroyed by fire in 976. Rebuilt c.1071 with help of Byzantine architects. Façade received Gothic additions in 15th cent. Its plan is a Greek cross, with a dome over the center and one over each arm of the cross; each dome is covered with mosaics on a golden background. Over the main entrance are the Four Horses of St. Mark's in gilded bronze. Originally in Rome, they were moved to Constantinople, Venice, and Paris (by Napoleon in 1797); in 1815 they were returned to Venice by Francis I of Austria.

Saint Martin, island (33 sq. mi.), West Indies, in Leeward Isls. Divided since 1648 between Dutch in S part (pop. 1,600) and French in N (pop. 6,786).

Saint Martin's-in-the-Fields, church in London, on Trafalgar Square. Built 1722–26, it has a Corinthian portico and elaborate spire. Crypt is open all night for use of homeless.

Saint Martinville, historic town (pop. 4,614), S La., on Bayou Teche; first settled c.1760 by French. Conflicting French groups came (royalists, republicans, Acadians); also Spanish. Quiet French town today. Alleged site of Evangeline romance, it has Longfellow-Evangeline state park.

Saint Marylebone, London: see MARYLEBONE, SAINT.

Saint Marys. 1 City (pop. 1,201), NE Kansas, on Kansas R. and WNW of Topeka; laid out 1866. One of oldest Kansas towns, it was site (1847–48) of Catholic mission to Potawatami Indians. **2** City (pop. 6,208), W Ohio, on St. Marys R. and SW of Lima. Trade center for Grand L. resort area. **3** Borough (pop. 7,846), NW Pa., on Elk Creek and E of Ridgway. Mfg. of carbon and clay products and electrical equipment.

Saint Marys. 1 River rising in Okefenokee Swamp, SE Ga., and flowing with south bend 175 mi. E to Cumberland Sound, arm of the Atlantic. Forms part of Ga.-Fla. line. **2** River, c.63 mi. long, flowing SE from L. Superior to L. Huron and forming part of international boundary. On river are cities of Sault Ste Marie, Mich. and Ont.; canals with five locks bypass falls here.

Saint Mary's City, first town settled (1634) in Md., on St. Mary's R., S Md. Leonard Calvert's colonists built Fort St. George on site of Indian village. Was provincial cap. 1676–94.

Saint Mary's College: see OAKLAND, Calif.; SOUTH BEND, Ind.

Saint Mary's Loch (lŏkh), lake, Selkirkshire, Scotland. Sir Walter Scott celebrates its beauty.

Saint Maurice (Fr. sē môrēs′), river, S Que., Canada, rising in Laurentian Mts. and flowing 325 mi. SE and S to St. Lawrence R. at Trois Rivières.

Saint Michaels, resort town (pop. 1,470), Eastern Shore, Md., NNW of Cambridge. Oyster-dredging center. Historic house (c.1670) still stands.

Saint Michel (sē mēshĕl′) or **Cote Saint Michel** (kōt′), town (pop. 10,539), S Que., Canada, on Montreal isl., N suburb of Montreal.

Saint Michel, Mont: see MONT-SAINT-MICHEL.

Saint-Mihiel (sē-mēēl′), town (pop. 4,134), Meuse dept.,

NE France, on the Meuse. Captured 1914 by Germans, recovered 1918 in one of most important American actions of the war. Gothic Church of St. Étienne contains sculptures by Ligier Richier.

Saint Moritz (sänt mō′rĭts), Ger. *Sankt Moritz,* resort (resident pop. 2,418), Upper Engadine, Grisons canton, Switzerland, on L. of St. Moritz. Winter sports center; mineral springs.

Saint-Nazaire (sē-näzĕr′), town (1936 pop. 37,710; 1946 pop. 4,408), Loire Inférieure dept., W France, at mouth of the Loire on the Bay of Biscay. As port of Nantes, it had, until its destruction by Allied bombing in 1943, the largest shipyards in France. Chief German submarine base in World War II. German garrison resisted Allied siege 1944–45.

Saint Olaf College: see NORTHFIELD, Minn.

Saint-Omer (sētômĕr′), city (pop. 15,785), Pas-de-Calais dept., N France. Gothic Basilica of Notre Dame (13th–14th cent.) is rich in works of art.

Saintonge (sētōzh′), region and former province, W France, in Charente-Maritime dept., on Atlantic at mouth of the Gironde; historic cap. Saintes. Cognac mfg. A subfief of Aquitaine, it passed to the French crown 1372.

Saint Patrick's Cathedral, New York city, on Fifth Av., largest Roman Catholic church in U.S. Designed in Gothic style by James Renwick. Begun 1858, dedicated 1879. Built of marble, it has 12 side chapels and a chime of 19 bells.

Saint Patrick's Purgatory, place where St. Patrick had a vision of purgatory, traditionally located on little Station Isl. in Lough Derg, SE Donegal, Ireland. Place of pilgrimage since Middle Ages though location is not accepted by modern scholars.

Saint Paul, city (pop. 311,349), state cap. (since 1858), E Minn., on the Mississippi at mouth of Minnesota R. and adjoining Minneapolis. Permanent white settlement in area began with establishment of MENDOTA fur-trading post and Fort Snelling; traders, lumbermen, settlers made homes here. Took name 1841 from St. Paul's Church. Settlers came from east after treaties with Indians opened land to settlement, lumbering; increased by immigrants, many of them Irish, and German Catholics (Bishop IRELAND long their leader). City became territorial cap. 1849. Location of St. Paul and Minneapolis at head of navigation of the Mississippi made Twin Cities metropolis of large area. St. Paul became center of railroad empire of James J. HILL. Second largest city of state, it has printing, publishing, meat packing, and automobile assembling. *Pioneer Press* (1849) is one of oldest papers in Middle West. Seat of Hamline Univ. (Methodist; coed.; 1854), Macalester Col. (coed.; 1874), Col. of St. Thomas (R.C.; for men; 1885), and Col. of St. Catherine.

Saint Paul's Cathedral, London, at the head of Ludgate Hill; masterpiece of Sir Christopher Wren. Built 1675–1710 on site of a 13th-cent. church which was badly ruined by the great fire of London (1666) and was demolished 1668. Wren's original design, in the shape of a Greek cross, was modified to provide the long nave and choir of the traditional medieval plan. The crossing is covered by a great dome, which rises impressively above a colonnaded drum. Bombed in World War II; the E end with altar and chapel behind it and roof and floor of N transept were destroyed.

Saint Paul's School, London, England, noted public school. Founded 1512 in St. Paul's churchyard. Mainly a day school with a few boarders, it is now in Kensington. Milton and Pepys were pupils.

Saint Peter, city (pop. 7,754), S Minn., on Minnesota R. and N of Mankato. Farm trade center. Seat of Gustavus Adolphus Col. (Lutheran; coed.; 1862). Traverse des Sioux, near site of St. Peter, was scene of treaty with Sioux in 1851.

Saint Peter Port, town and parish (pop. 16,720), cap. of Guernsey, Channel Isls. Exports vegetables, fruits, and flowers. Victor Hugo lived here 1856–70. Elizabeth Col. for boys was established here in 1563.

Saint Petersburg, Russia: see LENINGRAD.

Saint Petersburg, city (pop. 96,738), W Fla., on Pinellas peninsula in Tampa Bay (Gandy Bridge to Tampa); settled in mid-19th cent., but really estab. c.1876. Ships fish, fruit, and vegetables. Has yacht basin, municipal pier, alligator farm, Indian shell mounds, and U.S. coast guard base. A veterans' hospital is near. Winter training ground of big-league baseball teams.

Saint Peter's Church, Rome, principal and largest Christian church in the world. Built on site of Nero's circus and of a 4th-cent. basilica. Original design for the present church was by Bernardo Rossellino, but little was done until c.1503, when Julius II selected Bramante's Greek-cross plan with a central dome. After Bramante's death (1514) several architects, including Raphael, directed the work but accomplished little. In 1546 Michelangelo was made chief architect; disregarding recommended changes, he returned to Bramante's original plan. He designed the great dome and finished part of it. His successor, Vignola, built the secondary domes, and Giacomo della Porta and Domenico Fontana completed the central dome after Michelangelo's drawings, 1573–90. The dome, 404 ft. high from the pavement, has an interior diameter of 137 ft. Beneath it is the high altar, covered by Bernini's bronze baldachin, 95 ft. high. At this altar only the pope may read Mass. Beneath it is the crypt containing St. Peter's tomb. Church plan was transformed 1605 into a Latin cross with addition of a long nave by Carlo Maderna. The church was dedicated 1626 by Urban VIII. The forecourt and majestic elliptical piazza bounded by colonnades were created 1629–67 by Bernini.

Saint-Pierre, Jacques Henri Bernardin de: see BERNARDIN DE SAINT-PIERRE, JACQUES HENRI.

Saint Pierre, island: see MIQUELON.

Saint-Quentin (sănt-kwĕn'tĭn, Fr. sĕ-kätĕ'), city (pop. 46,876), Aisne dept., N France, on the Somme. Textile mfg. Its capture by Emmanuel Philibert of Savoy (1557) was a major Spanish victory. It was the center of heavy fighting in World War I and was virtually destroyed, but its fine Gothic collegiate church and city hall survived.

Saint Regis (sānt' rē'jĭs), settlement of Catholic Iroquois, on the S bank of the St. Lawrence, partly in Que.; partly in N.Y.; founded c.1755.

Saint-Saëns, (Charles) Camille (kämēy' sĕ-säs'), 1835–1921, French composer. He is known for his symphonies; the opera, *Samson et Dalila;* the *Introduction and Rondo Capriccioso,* for violin and orchestra; the piano concertos in G minor and C minor; and symphonic poems, notably *Omphale's Spinning Wheel* and *Danse macabre.*

Saintsbury, George (Edward Bateman), 1845–1933, English critic, authority on French and English literature. Wrote histories, special studies, and biographies of Dryden, Scott, Arnold, and Thackeray.

Saint-Simon, Claude Henri de Rouvroy, comte de (klōd' ärē dù rōōvrwä' kôt' dù sĕ-sēmô'), 1760–1825, French social philosopher. His writings foreshadow socialism, European federation, and the positivism of Comte. His pupils constructed system of **Saint-Simonianism** (sănt sīmô'nĕŭnĭzm), calling for public control of means of production, abolition of inheritance rights, and gradual emancipation of women.

Saint-Simon, Louis de Rouvroy, duc de (lwē', dük'), 1675–1755, French courtier, author of memoirs on the court of Louis XIV (first pub. 1788; complete ed., 41 vols., 1879–1928; abridged Eng. tr., 4 vols., 1899). A monument of French literature, the memoirs are remarkable for his psychological observations and brilliant sketches. Saint-Simon's arrogance, petulant resentments (particularly against the king), and hatred of the rising bourgeoisie give his work both a strong bias and an intensely personal flavor.

Saint Simons Island: see SEA ISLANDS.

Saint Sophia: see HAGIA SOPHIA.

Saint Stephen, town (pop. 3,769), SW N.B., Canada, on St. Croix R. and W of St. John. Opposite is Calais, Maine, connected by international bridge. Two towns cooperate in providing public services. Founded by Loyalists after Revolution.

Saint Stephens, hamlet, SW Ala., on Tombigbee R. and N of Mobile. First Ala. territorial legislature met here (1818) on site of Spanish fort (1789; became U.S. possession by demarcation line of 1798) and on site of U.S. trading post (1803).

Saint Thomas, city (pop. 18,173), S Ont., Canada, near L. Erie and S of London. Trade center in farm and orchard district with railroad shops, foundries, and lumber mills.

Saint Thomas: see VIRGIN ISLANDS.

Saint Thomas, College of: see SAINT PAUL, Minn.

Saint-Tropez (sĕ-trôpĕz'), town (pop. 3,171), Var dept., SE France; a resort on French Riviera.

Saint Vincent, island (133 sq. mi.; pop. 57,168), British West Indies; cap. KINGSTOWN. British and French contested ownership until 1783, when it was restored to British. Eruption of SOUFRIÈRE caused much damage in 1902.

Saint Vincent, Cape, Port. *Cabo de São Vicente,* SW extremity of Portugal. In 1797 the British under Jervis defeated a Spanish fleet near by.

Saint Vincent, Gulf, large inlet of Indian Ocean, South Australia, E of Yorke Peninsula. Port Adelaide on E shore.

Saint Vitus's dance: see CHOREA.

Saionji, Kimmochi, Prince (kĕm'mō'chē sīōn'jē), 1850–1940, Japanese statesman, member of old court nobility and supporter of Meiji restoration. With Prince Ito he visited Europe in 1882 to study foreign governments. Prime minister 1906–8, 1911–12. Officially retired 1914, but as genro [elder statesman] he exerted great influence until his death.

Saipan: see MARIANAS ISLANDS.

Saisset, Bernard (bĕrnär' sĕsä'), d. 1314, French churchman, bishop of Pamiers. His arrest in 1301 by PHILIP IV on the charge of inciting rebellion sparked the struggle between Philip and Pope BONIFACE VIII. He later was allowed to go to Rome and recovered his see in 1308.

Sakai (säkī'), industrial city (pop. 194,048), S Honshu, Japan, on Osaka Bay.

Sakakawea: see SACAJAWEA.

sake (sä'kē), chief alcoholic beverage of Japan. Yellowish and somewhat sherrylike, it is made by fermenting rice.

Sakhalin (sä'kúlēn") or **Saghalien** (sä'gúlēn'), Jap. *Karafuto,* island (29,700 sq. mi.; pop. c.500,000), RSFSR, off the coast of Siberia, between Sea of Okhotsk and Sea of Japan. Mainly mountainous. Lumbering, coal mining, herring fishing; agr. is limited by severe climate. Colonized by Russia and Japan 18th–19th cent. Under joint control until 1905, when Treaty of Portsmouth gave Japan the S half of the island. After World War II Japanese territory was given to USSR in accordance with agreement at Yalta Conference.

Saki, pseud.: see MUNRO, HECTOR HUGH.

Sakonnet, R.I.: see LITTLE COMPTON.

Sakuntala: see KALIDASA.

Saladin (să'lŭdĭn), 1137?–1193, Moslem warrior and sultan of Egypt, the great opponent of the Crusaders; b. Mesopotamia, of Kurdish descent. Lived for 10 years in Damascus at the court of NUREDDIN, where he became known for his knowledge of Sunnite theology. Went with his uncle, Shirkuh, a lieutenant of Nureddin, on campaigns against the Fatimite rulers of Egypt. Shirkuh became vizier there and on his death (1169) was succeeded by Saladin. After Nureddin's death Saladin made himself sultan of Egypt, thus beginning the Ayyubite dynasty. He extended his domain W into what is now Tunisia and E into Yemen, Palestine, and Syria. With a large force of Moslems of various groups (collectively called Saracens by the Christians) he defeated the Crusaders (see CRU-SADES) in 1187 in the great battle of Hattin (near Tiberias), which led to his capture of Jerusalem. His celebrated encounter with Richard I of England came during the Third Crusade (1189), which failed to recover the Holy City. Saladin is said to have been respected by the Christians for his chivalry and generosity. A man of culture, he encouraged literature and learning.

Salamanca (sälùmäng'kù, Span. sälämäng'kä), city (pop. 71,725), W Spain, in Leon, on Tormez R. Conquered 1085 from the Moors, it became world-famous after foundation (c.1230) of its university, which made Arabic philosophy available to Western world. In late Middle Ages and Renaissance city was center of Spanish cultural life and fountainhead of Spanish theology. Among notable sights are the Plaza Mayor (fine colonnaded square); 12th-cent. Gothic cathedral, adjoined by new cathedral (1513–1733); university building (15th cent.); several splendid palaces (e.g., Casa de las Conchas).

Salamanca (sälùmäng'kù), city (pop. 8,861), W N.Y., on Allegheny R. and S of Buffalo, in Allegany Indian Reservation. Farm trade center; mfg. of furniture, dairy products, metal goods, textiles.

salamander (să'lùmän'dùr), tailed amphibian with small, weak legs, related to newt. Regenerates lost limbs or tail. Many are gregarious at breeding time. Larvae breathe by means of gills. Giant salamander of China and Japan is 3–5 ft. long. Salamander was portrayed in legends as unharmed by flames.

Salamis (să'lùmĭs), island, E Greece, in the Gulf of Aegina. Off its shore the Greek fleet decisively defeated the Persians in 480 B.C.

sal ammoniac (săl ùmō'nēăk), ammonium chloride, a white crystalline substance with biting taste. Used in dry cells, metals for soldering, smoke screens, ammonia, and in medicine.

Salazar, Antonio de Oliveira (äntô'nyō dù ōlēvä'rù sùläzär'), 1889–, Portuguese statesman. Taught economics at Univ. of Coimbra; was appointed finance minister in 1926 and again in 1928; premier and dictator from 1932. Through his reforms he put Portugal's chaotic finances on a stable footing, and in 1933 he devised the constitution of the *Novo Estado* [new state], a CORPORATIVE STATE influenced by the social principles expressed in the encyclicals of Pope Leo XIII. The attempt in 1945 to institute a democratic party system came to nought.

Salem (sä'lùm) [Heb.,= peace], in Bible. **1** Unidentified kingdom of Melchizedek. Gen. 14.18; Heb. 7.1,2. May be Jerusalem. **2** Abbreviation for Jerusalem. Ps. 76.2.

Salem. 1 City (pop. 6,159), S central Ill., NE of Centralia, in coal, oil, timber, agr. area. Railroad shops. Mfg. of clothing. Birthplace of W. J. Bryan. **2** City (pop. 41,880), NE Mass., NE of Boston; settled 1626. Witchcraft trials of 1692 held here (SEWALL was a judge). A leading port from colonial times until mid-19th cent.; harbor is now silted up. Salem Maritime Natl. Historic Site preserves waterfront area. City rich in fine old mansions, some of them designed by McIntire. Hawthorne was surveyor of the port, 1846–49; his birthplace (17th cent.) and House of the Seven Gables are preserved. Essex Inst. and Peabody marine museum are here. Mfg. of electrical supplies, textiles, shoes, machinery. **3** City (pop. 9,050), SW N.J., near Delaware R., NW of Bridgeton; settled 1675 by Friends; first permanent English settlement in Delaware valley. Farm market center with mfg. of glass, linoleum; canneries. Has Alexander Grant House (1721; contains co. historical society collections) and Friends' meetinghouse (1772). **4** City (pop. 12,754), NE Ohio, SW of Youngstown; laid out 1806 by Friends. Early abolitionist center and station on Underground RR. Has mfg. of machinery and metal products. **5** City (pop. 43,140), state cap. (since 1859), NW Oregon, on Willamette R. and SSW of Portland; founded 1841 by Jason Lee. Territorial cap. after

1851. Processes fruit, grain, flax, hops, livestock, meat, lumber, linen, paper, and woolens. Seat of Willamette Univ. (coed.; opened 1844 as Oregon Inst.; chartered, renamed 1853), oldest institution of higher learning in Far West. **6** Town (pop. 6,823), SW Va., on Roanoke R. and W of Roanoke. Seat of Roanoke Col. Mfg. of textiles.

Salerno (sùlûr'nō, Ital. säler'nō), city (pop. 41,925), Campania, S Italy; a port on inlet of Tyrrhenian Sea. Part of duchy of Benevento after 6th cent., it became (9th cent.) an independent principality, which fell to the Normans in 1076. Was scene of fierce battle (Sept., 1943) between Allied landing forces and Germans, who retreated towards Naples. Its famous medical school, founded 9th cent., reached its peak in 12th cent., and closed 1817. Cathedral has 11th-cent. bronze doors and ancient mosaics.

Salford (sōl'fùrd, sôl'–), county borough (pop. 178,036), Lancashire, England. Textile center, it shares mfg. and commercial activities of Manchester.

Salic law (sä'lĭk), rule of succession in certain noble families of Europe, forbidding females and those descended in the female line to succeed to titles or offices in the family. It is so called on the mistaken supposition that it was part of the law of the Salian Franks. The rule has been of much importance at several crucial points in history. It was maintained by the Valois and the Bourbons in France (notably in accession of Philip V and Philip VI of France) and was taken to Spain by Philip V of Spain. There in the 19th cent. it was rescinded to allow the succession of Isabella II, and her opponents led the Carlist Wars. Another line observing this law was the Guelph; therefore Queen Victoria of England did not succeed to the rule in Hanover.

salicylic acid (sălĭsĭ'lĭk), white, crystalline, odorless, organic acid with a sweet taste. Used as food preservative since it inhibits bacterial growth. The acetate (aspirin) and salicylates are used as antipyretics, antiseptics, in treatment of rheumatism and other ailments. Methyl salicylate is used as flavoring and in liniments. Acid is used in making dyes.

Salida (sùlī'dù), city (pop. 4,553; alt. 7,050 ft.), central Colo., on Arkansas R. Resort near hot springs. Trade center for quarries, farms, mines.

Salina (sùlī'nù). **1** City (pop. 26,176), central Kansas, near junction of Saline and Smoky Hill rivers; platted 1858. Trade and distribution center for winter wheat and livestock area, it produces flour and farm implements. **2** Town (pop. 905), NE Okla., on Grand R. and ENE of Tulsa. Settled on site of first Okla. trading post, founded early 19th cent. by J. P. CHOUTEAU.

Salinas, Pedro (pä'dhrō säle'näs), 1892–1951, Spanish lyric poet and critic; in the U.S. after 1936.

Salinas (sùle'nùs), city (pop. 18,319), W Calif., SSE of San Francisco; settled 1856. Shipping and processing center for truck (esp. lettuce) and livestock valley. At edge is East Salinas (1933; pop. c.5,000), migratory farm camp.

Salinas, river rising in S Calif., in Santa Lucia Mts. E of San Luis Obispo, and flowing c.150 mi. NW (partly underground) past Salinas, to Monterey Bay.

Saline (sùlēn'), partly navigable river rising in Ouachita Mts., W Ark., and flowing c.300 mi. S to Ouachita R. in S Ark.

Salisbury, John of: see JOHN OF SALISBURY.

Salisbury, Robert Arthur Talbot Gascoyne-Cecil, 3d **marquess of** (sōlz'bùrē), 1830–1903, British Conservative statesman and diplomat. Foreign secretary under Disraeli, his "Salisbury Circular" led to Congress of Berlin (1878). Prime minister three times (1885; 1886–92; 1895–1902), he was his own foreign minister. Maintained peaceful relations with major powers and achieved some domestic reforms.

Salisbury, Robert Cecil, 1st earl of, 1563?–1612, English statesman, son of Baron Burghley. Succeeded (1598) his father as chief minister to Elizabeth. Prepared (after fall of earl of Essex) the peaceful accession of James I to English throne. Responsible for administration until his death.

Salisbury (sôlz'–) or **New Sarum** (sâr'ùm), municipal borough (pop. 32,910), co. town of Wiltshire, England. Bishopric moved here from OLD SARUM in 1220. Great cathedral, with highest spire in England (404 ft.), was built 1220–60. Noteworthy are 13th-cent. churches and bishops' palace. Town is the Melchester of Thomas Hardy's Wessex novels.

Salisbury (sôlz'–), city (pop. 53,211), cap. of Southern Rhodesia, in gold-mining area; founded 1890.

Salisbury. 1 Resort town (pop. 3,132), extreme NW Conn., in Taconic Mts.; settled c.1720. Includes Bear Mt., 2,355 ft., highest peak in state, and Lakeville, a resort center, on L. Wononskopomuc; seat of Hotchkiss School for boys. **2** City (pop. 15,141), Eastern Shore, Md., at head of Wicimico R.; settled 1732. Trade center for much of Eastern Shore, it has mfg. of clothing, tools, pumps, and boats. **3** City (pop. 20,-102), W central N.C., NNE of Charlotte in piedmont; settled 1751. Textile mills and granite quarries. Here are Salisbury Natl. Cemetery and Livingstone Col. (Negro; Methodist Episcopal Zion; coed.; 1879).

Salisbury Plain, chalk plateau, 300 sq. mi., Wiltshire, England, NW of Salisbury. Site of many ancient monuments, of which STONEHENGE is most famous. Important training ground for British army.

Salishan (sä'lĭshùn, sä'–), linguistic stock of North American Indians of NW U.S. and British Columbia, Canada. It includes the Flathead (also called Salish), Pend d'Oreille, Okanogan, Puyallup, Spokan, Coeur d'Alene, Bella Coola, and others. See LANGUAGE (table).

saliva (sùlī'vù), alkaline fluid containing digestive enzyme (ptyalin) that converts starch to sugar. Secreted by salivary glands and carried by ducts into mouth.

Sallust (Caius Sallustius Crispus) (sä'lùst), 86 B.C.–c.34 B.C., Roman historian. Chief work *Bellum Catilinarium* or *Catilina,* on conspiracy of Catiline.

Salmasius, Claudius (klô'dēùs sälmä'shùs), 1588–1653, French humanist and philologist. Knew Hebrew, Persian and Arabic as well as Latin and Greek. Wrote many learned works. Also wrote in support of the Stuarts a book upholding divine right of monarchy, which brought a dissenting reply from John Milton. He discovered the Greek anthology of Cephalas at Heidelberg in 1606.

Salmon (sä'mùn), river, c.425 mi. long, rising in central Idaho in Sawtooth and Salmon River Mts. and flowing NE (joined at Salmon by Lemhi R.), W (joined by Middle and South forks), then N to Snake R. Has large salmon run. Lower gorge is impressive.

salmon, marine game fish which breeds in fresh water. N Atlantic salmon (*Salmo*) is nearly exterminated; some remain in rivers of Maine, E Canada, Europe, and near Labrador. Pacific coast salmon (*Oncorhynchus*) is taken from Monterey, Calif., to Nome, Alaska, and near Japan and Siberia. Over half of canned salmon comes from Alaska. At spawning time salmon migrate from the ocean, each species seeking the region where it hatched. Pacific salmon, most of which make long hazardous journey against current, falls, and rapids, die soon after eggs are laid and fertilized; Atlantic salmon return to sea. The young of both groups remain in fresh water for varying periods, then travel to salt water.

Salmon Falls River, rising in lakes around Maine-N.H. line, which it forms, and flowing SSE, past Dover, N.H., below which it is called Piscataqua R. (pĭskǎ'tùkwù), to the Atlantic at Portsmouth Harbor.

Salome (sùlō'mē). **1** Daughter of Herodias. Usually identified with the dancer who asked Herod Antipas for John the Baptist's head. Mark 6.16–28. **2** One of the women who stood at the foot of the cross and later visited the empty tomb. Mark 15.40; 16.1.

Salomon, Haym, 1740–85, American Revolutionary patriot and financier, b. Poland.

Salona (sùlō'nù), Latin *Salonae,* port of Dalmatia, on

the Adriatic. Here Diocletian built a magnificent palace, which in the 7th cent. became the core of Spalato (now Split, Yugoslavia).

Salonica, Salonika (both: sälùnē'kù), or **Saloniki** (sälùnē'kē), Gr. *Thessalonike* or *Thessaloniki,* city (pop. 216,138), cap. of Greek Macedonia, NE Greece, on Gulf of Salonica, an inlet of Aegean Sea, and at neck of Chalcidice Peninsula. Second largest Greek city, major port, mfg. center (textiles, cigarettes, leather goods, machine tools). University was opened 1926. Founded c.315 B.C.; flourished under Roman and Byzantine rules. Kingdom of Thessalonica, created 1204, comprised most of N and central Greece and was largest fief of Latin Empire of Constantinople but was recaptured by the Greeks in 1222. After changing hands several times, Salonica passed finally to Turkey in 1430, to Greece 1912. World War II inflicted much damage. Famous churches include that of Hagia Sophia (notable mosaics). Ruins include triumphal arch of Emperor Constantine. The **Salonica campaigns** of World War I began, after the fall of the VENIZELOS government, with the landing of an Allied force at Salonica for "peaceful blockade" of neutral Greece (1915). Allies estab. (1916) a rival Greek government under Venizelos at Salonica. This body declared war on Central Powers. After Allies began to invade central Greece, King CONSTANTINE abdicated (June, 1917). On the Macedonian front, Allied operations were stalled by disunity and, especially, by malaria, but in 1918 fresh forces were landed and pushed N under Gen. Franchet d'Esperey. Bulgaria fell Sept. 30; Serbia was recovered by Nov. 1; Rumania fell Nov. 10.

Salop, county, England: see SHROPSHIRE.

salsify: see GOATSBEARD.

Salt, Sir Titus, 1803–76, English textile manufacturer and inventor. Model manufacturing village, Saltaire, near Shipley, Yorkshire, estab. by him 1851. Invented machine for making worsted and process for spinning and weaving alpaca.

salt. 1 A common and widely used substance, sodium chloride. Soluble in water; in solution it is a conductor of electricity. Constitutes large proportion of all solid matter dissolved in sea water and inland salt lakes; also occurs as large deposits of rock salt. Obtained by mining, by dissolving it in water underground and pumping to surface, and by evaporation of sea water. Salt is chief source of sodium and its compounds, and a source of chlorine. It is used in making glass, pottery, textile dyes, soap, and in preservation of foods. It is important in diet of man and animals. **2** In chemistry, a compound with metal or metallic radical as positive ion and nonmetal or nonmetallic radical as negative ion. Normal salt has neither hydrogen nor hydroxyl ion; acid salts have hydrogen with another positive ion; basic salts have hydroxyl and another negative ion. Salts are named from elements composing them and acid from which they are derived. Salt with two elements has name of nonmetallic element with ending -ide, e.g., sodium chloride. Salts made of more than two elements derived from acids ending in -ic have ending -ate, e.g., carbonate, sulphate. Salts from -ous acids have ending -ite.

Salta (säl'tä), city (pop. 67,403), cap. of Salta prov., NW Argentina; founded 1582. Center of rich agr. and oil area.

Salten, Felix (fä'lĭks zäl'tùn), 1869–1945, Austrian novelist. Best known for his animal stories, notably *Bambi* (1923; Eng. tr., 1928).

Saltillo (sältē'yō), city (pop. 49,430), cap. of Coahuila, N Mexico; founded 1575. Primarily an agr. and mining community, it is also a rail center. Famous for woolen serapes.

Salt Lake City, city (pop. 182,121), state cap., N central Utah, on Jordan R., SE of Great Salt L., and at foot of Wasatch Range. Founded 1847 by Brigham YOUNG as cap. of MORMONS, it was state's leading city from beginning. Huge Temple (built 1853–93) and

Tabernacle (1867) at city's heart show that this is still City of the Saints. Utah's largest city; distributing and commercial center; transcontinental air and highway focus. Mfg. of steel, petroleum, iron products; food processing, saltmaking; ore smelters, stockyards. Ships farm produce of rich irrigated area. Seat of Univ. of UTAH. Outfitting point for Calif. gold rush. Fort Douglas founded here in 1862 by Gen. P. E. Connor. Center for many years of Mormon Church-U.S. government dispute.

Salto (säl'tō), city (pop. 44,000), cap. of Salto dept., NW Uruguay, on Uruguay R. across from Concordia, Argentina, its commercial rival. Extensive citrus fruit orchards and vineyards in environs.

Salton Sea, shallow saline lake, c.30 mi. long and 10 mi. wide, SE Calif., between IMPERIAL VALLEY (S) and Coachella Valley. Was salt-covered lowland called Salton Sink until flooded by Colorado R. (1905–7). Receives irrigation water to help counteract evaporation. Surface is 245 ft. below sea level.

saltpeter or **niter** (nī'tùr), naturally occurring potassium nitrate. Used to make explosives, fireworks, and matches, and as food preservative. **Chile saltpeter,** natural sodium nitrate (called *caliche* when impure) is used to make potassium nitrate, fertilizers, explosives, and nitric acid.

Salt River Valley, S central Ariz., irrigated region around lower Salt R., which flows 200 mi. WSW from near Mogollon Rim to Gila R. WSW of Phoenix. Early Indians and U.S. settlers used Salt R. for irrigation. Salt R. project (begun 1905) was first major undertaking under Federal reclamation act; chief dams are Roosevelt (c.280 ft. high; built 1906–11), Horse Mesa, Mormon Flat, Stewart Mountain, all in Salt R., Bartlett in Verde R. Valley is farm (truck, citrus, alfalfa, cotton) and winter resort area. Centers are PHOENIX, Mesa, Glendale, Tempe.

Saltus, Edgar (Evertson) (sôltùs), 1858–1921, American author. His works, combining violent plots and lavish descriptions, include novels (e.g., *The Pace That Kills,* 1889) and a history of the Roman emperors (*Imperial Purple,* 1892).

Saltville, town (pop. 2,678), SW Va., in Holston R. valley SW of Marion. Saltmaking began here 1788. Saltworks taken by Union forces and destroyed 1864; later re-established.

Saltykov, Mikhail Evgrafovich (mēkhŭyēl' yĭvgrä'fùvĭch sùltĭkôf'), pseud. of Nikolai E. Shchedrin, 1826–89, Russian author. His satirical *Fables* (1885; Eng. tr., 1931) attacked contemporary conditions in Aesopic language. His novel *The Golovlyov Family* (1876; Eng. tr., 1917) is a study of decaying gentry.

Saluafata (sä"lōòùfä'tù), U.S. naval station, NE Upolu isl., Western Samoa.

Saluda (sùlōō'dù), river rising in Blue Ridge of W S.C. and flowing c.145 mi. SE across piedmont to Broad R. (forming Congaree) at Columbia. Has Saluda (or Dreher Shoals) Dam (1930) forming L. Murray and Buzzard Roost Dam forming L. Greenwood.

Salvador (sälvädhôr") or **El Salvador,** republic, (13,-176 sq. mi.; pop. 1,858,656), Central America, on the Pacific; cap. SAN SALVADOR. Homogeneity of population (about 80% ladino or mestizo, less than 20% Indian) and uniformity of terrain have contributed to agr. prosperity. From W to E, Salvador is broken by two roughly parallel volcanic ranges; between them lie warm valleys with excellent grazing land for cattle. Dominant crop is coffee; indigo is produced in W. Communication is good, with Inter-American Highway extending the length of the country and railroads and highways leading out from the cap. to interior and coast. Throughout colonial period, Salvador was under captaincy general of Guatemala and after independence from Spain (1821) was briefly a part of Iturbide's empire and then a member of Central American Federation (1825–38). With development of coffeegrowing in second half of 19th cent. there was a phenomenal increase in population,

and today Salvador is one of Latin America's most densely populated countries. Other cities of importance besides San Salvador are La Libertad, La Union, and Acajutla on the coast and Santa Ana in highlands.

Salvador (sälvädôr'), city (pop. 395,993), cap. of Bahia state, E Brazil; a port on the Atlantic at entrance to Todos os Santos Bay. City formerly called Bahia. Founded by Tomé de Souza (1549), it was cap. of Portuguese possessions in America until 1763.

salvage, in maritime law, compensation the owner must pay for having his vessel or cargo saved from peril such as shipwreck and fire. Salvage is distributed by the court to the owner, the master, and the crew of the rescue ship according to fixed ratios.

Salvation Army, international body for religious and philanthropic work, chiefly among those not ordinarily under influence of Christian churches. It was started in London (1865) by William Booth (see BOOTH, family) as East London Revival Society or Christian Mission. It was in 1878 named Salvation Army and organized on military lines with ministers as officers and members as soldiers. By 1890 Army had spread to Continent, North America, Australia, and India. Work in U.S. began 1880 with branch in Pa. Evangeline Booth became commander of work in U.S. (1904) and general of international Army (1934). There is no formal creed, but belief is evangelical. Army operates various practical social projects throughout world.

Salvemini, Gaetano (gäätä'nō sälvämē'nē), 1873–, Italian historian. Became U.S. citizen in 1940. Chief works deal with contemporary history, particularly the Fascist period.

Salvian (säl'vēùn), 5th cent., Christian writer in Gaul, a renowned preacher and teacher of rhetoric. Wrote part of *De gubernatione Dei* and all of *Contra avaritiam.*

Salween (säl"wēn'), river, c.1,750 mi. long, rising in E Tibet. Flows through Yünnan prov., China, and Burma to Gulf of Martaban of Andaman Sea.

Salzburg (sôlz'bûrg, Ger. zälts'bōōrk), province (2,762 sq. mi.; pop. 324,117), W central Austria, in the Alps. Has large salt deposits and several small gold and copper mines. Includes part of SALZKAMMERGUT and has huge tourist trade. Its history is that of its cap., **Salzburg** (pop. 100,096), on the Salzach R. Its archbishops ruled the region as princes of the Holy Roman Empire from 1278 to 1802, when Salzburg passed to Austria. It was transferred to Bavaria 1809; reverted to Austria 1815. The city is world-famous for its Renaissance and baroque architecture—e.g., the cathedral, the archiepiscopal palace (*Residenz*), Mirabell castle and garden. The Hohensalzburg, an 11th-cent. fortress, dominates it from a hill. Of the university (founded 1623) only the theological faculty still exists. The birthplace of Mozart, Salzburg honors his memory by annual music and theatrical festivals. Its prosperity is largely due to the tourist trade.

Salzkammergut (zälts'kä"mùrgōōt"), Alpine resort area in Upper Austria, Styria, and Salzburg, Austria. Has beautiful mountain lakes (Sankt Wolfgangsee, Traunsee, Mondsee) and resorts (Ischl, Sankt Wolfgang, Hallstatt, Gmunden, Altaussee). Salt mines.

Samar (sä'mär), island (5,050 sq. mi.; pop. 470,678), one of Visayan Isls., P.I.; NE of Leyte. Lumbering, agr. (rice, hemp, corn), iron mining.

Samara, RSFSR: see KUIBYSHEV.

Samaria (sùmâ'rēù), anc. city, central Palestine, NW of Nablus (Shechem); site now occupied by Sebaste village. Samaria built by King Omri as cap. of Israel in early 9th cent. B.C.; fell in 722 B.C. to Assyria. Destroyed in 120 B.C. by John Hyrcanus; rebuilt by Herod the Great. Traditional burial place of John the Baptist. City gave its name to **Samaritans,** a sect recognizing only the Pentateuch of the Bible and rigidly adhering to its law. In Jesus' time a great enmity existed between them and the Jews, since each claimed to be the only true inheritors of Abraham and Moses; hence the choice of a Samaritan for Jesus' parable. Luke 10.30–37. A small group of Samaritans still live at Nablus. The Samaritan language is a type of Aramaic.

samarium (sùmâ'rēŭm), lustrous gray element (symbol = Sm; see also ELEMENT, table), a metal of the rare earths.

Samarkand (sămŭrkănd'), city (pop. 134,346), Uzbek SSR, on Trans-Caspian RR. Major cotton and silk center. One of oldest existing cities in the world and oldest of central Asia, it was built on site of Afrosiab (ruins extant), which dated from 3d or 4th millennium B.C., and was chief city of SOGDIANA. After conquest by Alexander the Great in 329 B.C. it became a meeting point of Western and Chinese cultures. Fell to Moslems early in 8th cent. A.D. and developed as a center of Arabic civilization. First paper mill outside China was estab. here 751. City continued to prosper as part of Khurasan (874–999) and of Khorezm. Though taken and devastated by Jenghiz Khan in 1220, Samarkand reached its greatest splendor as cap. of Tamerlane's empire in 14th cent. After breakup of Timurid empire (15th cent.), Samarkand region was ruled by Uzbeks until 1920 as part of emirate of BUKHARA, which came under Russian overlordship in 1868. Old Samarkand contains, among other remarkable monuments, Tamerlane's mausoleum and Bibi Khan mosque (now ruined).

Samarra (sämä'rä), town (pop. c.8,000), Iraq, on the Tigris. Seat of Abbasid caliphs from 836 to 876. Has a mosque sacred to Shiites.

Sambre (sä'brù), river, 120 mi. long, N France and SE Belgium, flowing NE to the Meuse at Namur. Scene of heavy fighting in World War I.

Samnites (săm'nīts), anc. people of central Italy, Oscan-speaking and perhaps related to the Sabines. Rome defeated them in the Samnite Wars (328 or 326–304 B.C., 298–290 B.C.), and they declined. They sided with Marius and were crushed by Sulla in 82 B.C. Their territory was called **Samnium**.

Samoa (sùmō'ù), island group, S Pacific, between Honolulu and Sydney. Has 10 principal and several uninhabited islands in 350 mi.-long chain. Formerly Navigators' Isls. Volcanic and mountainous, it has tropical trees (fern, coconut, hardwood, rubber) and tropical produce (copra, taro, fruits, cacao, yams). Discovered 1722 by Dutch. Savaii, Upolu, Apolima, Manono, and four uninhabited islands are known as **Territory of Western Samoa** (1,135 sq. mi.; pop. 68,197), under New Zealand trusteeship in UN. Rest of group is **American Samoa** (76 sq. mi.; pop. 18,602), consisting of TUTUILA, Aunuu, Manua group, Swains Isl., Rose Isl. PAGOPAGO is on Tutuila. Almost all land owned by Polynesians.

Samos (sä'mŏs), Aegean island (194 sq. mi.; pop. 56,-273), Greece, off W Asia Minor; one of the Sporades. Largely mountainous, it produces wine, tobacco, fruit. Colonized c.11th cent. B.C. by Ionian Greeks. Flourished under Polycrates (6th cent. B.C.). Anacreon and legendary Aesop lived here; birthplace of Pythagoras. Samian ware is ancient Roman pottery of a soft, deep red.

Samothrace (sä'mōthrās"), Gr. *Samothrake,* Aegean island, area 71 sq. mi., Greece, between mainland of Thrace and Gallipoli Peninsula. Mountainous. In ancient times it was the center of worship of the Cabiri. Winged *Nike* (or *Victory*) *of Samothrace* (now in Louvre, Paris) was erected here 306 B.C. Island was first stop in St. Paul's Macedonian itinerary. Ceded by Turkey to Greece 1913.

Samoyedes or **Samoyeds** (both: sămoi-ĕdz'), partly nomadic, partly settled agricultural tribes of N Siberia and the Taimyr Peninsula. They are also known as Nentsy. Samoyede language perhaps related to Finno-Ugric.

Sampson, William Thomas, 1840–1902, American naval officer. Commanded N Atlantic squadron in Span-

ish-American War. Laid down instructions for battle of Santiago, but the credit for victory went to W. S. SCHLEY.

Sampson, N.Y.: see FINGER LAKES.

Samson [Heb.,= sun], judge and hero of Israel, proverbial for his strength. Samson, a NAZARITE, owed his strength to his vow to God that he would never cut his hair. He was betrayed to his enemies the Philistines by Delilah. His revenge came when he pulled down the Philistine temple, crushing his enemies as well as himself. Judges 13–16.

Samsun (sämsōōn'), city (pop. 43,937), N Turkey; a Black Sea port. Tobacco-mfg. center; agr. market. The ancient Amisus, it was founded 6th cent. B.C. Important in Pontic and Roman empires. Fell to Ottoman Turks 14th cent.

Samuel, books of Old Testament, called 1 and 2 Samuel in AV, 1 and 2 Kings in Western canon. They are histories of Israel, chiefly covering the careers of Samuel, Saul, and David. Samuel, last and one of the greatest of Israel's judges, was, as a boy, dedicated to the service of God and grew up in the temple at Shiloh. He led his people against their Philistine oppressors. When an old man, and at divine behest, he anointed Saul as first king of Israel and later anointed David as Saul's successor.

samurai (sä"mōōrī'), members of aristocratic warrior class of feudal Japan; retainers of the daimyo. Followed BUSHIDO as code of conduct. Abolished as a class after Meiji restoration, but former samurai were leaders in building modern Japan.

Sana or **Sanaa:** see YEMEN.

San Angelo (săn ăn'jùlō), city (pop. 52,093), W Texas, at start of Concho R.; laid out 1869 beside border fort (still extant). Processes, markets, and ships wool, cotton, livestock, farm produce, and oil. Near by is L. Nasworthy, reservoir.

San Antonio (săn ăntō'nyù, –nēō), city (pop. 408,442), S central Texas, at source of San Antonio R. Spanish knew site long before mission and presidio were founded here 1718. Other missions followed 1720–31; San Fernando, now city's heart, founded 1731. Taken by Texans in Texas Revolution, Dec., 1835, and saw fall of the ALAMO, March, 1836. Group of Comanches killed 1840 in "council house fight." City taken by Mexicans 1842. Prospered as cowtown after Civil War and with coming of railroad. Port and rail focus, it ships cattle, cotton, truck, fruits, pecans, oil, and gas and processes food, oil, and metals. Mfg. of clay products and garments. Here are Fort Sam Houston (1865) and Brooks, Kelly, and Randolph airfields. Seat of Trinity Univ. (Presbyterian; coed.; 1869). History, climate and exotic atmosphere make it a resort.

San Augustine (săn ô'gùstēn), town (pop. 2,510), E Texas, on Ayish Canyon and ESE of Nacogdoches. Spanish mission estab. 1716, abandoned 1719, and refounded 1721. Presidio estab. 1756 for guarding French-Spanish border. All abandoned before American settlement began 1818. Large Negro population.

San Benito (săn bùnē'tō), city (pop. 13,271), S Texas, NW of Brownsville. Processes citrus fruit, vegetables, and cotton. Resort trade.

San Bernardino (săn bûrnùrdē'nō), city (pop. 63,058), S Calif., E of Los Angeles; laid out 1853. Rail and citrus-fruit center. Annual national orange show. Gateway to mountain and lake resort region.

San Bernardino Mountains, S Calif., extending c.55 mi. SE from Cajon Pass at E end of San Gabriel Mts. to N end of San Jacinto Mts. and rising to 11,485 ft. in Mt. San Gorgonio.

San Blas (sän bläs'), archipelago off NE coast of Panama, comprising c.332 islands. Also called Mulatas. Islanders mostly pure-blooded aborigines of Carib origin, protected by treaty with Panama.

Sanborn, Franklin Benjamin, 1831–1917, American author and philanthropist. Founded several welfare societies. Member of Emerson's group; wrote lives of Alcott, Emerson, W. E. Channing, Hawthorne, and Thoreau, as well as one of his friend John Brown.

San Bruno, residential city (pop. 12,478), W Calif., S of San Francisco. Ships truck and poultry.

San Buenaventura: see VENTURA, Calif.

San Carlos, residential city (pop. 14,371), W Calif., S of San Francisco. Flower shipping point.

Sánchez-Coello, Alonso: see COELLO, ALONSO SÁN-CHEZ.

Sancho III or **Sancho the Great** (sän'chō), c.965–1035, king of Navarre (1000–1035). He inherited Navarre and Aragon; conquered territories from the Moors; married heiress of Castile, Vizcaya, and Álava. His kingdom thus included most of Christian Spain, but at his death it was divided among his sons García (Navarre), Ferdinand I (Castile), Ramiro I (Aragon), and Gonzalo (Sobrarbe and Ribagorza).

Sancho Panza: see DON QUIXOTE DE LA MANCHA.

sanction, inducement to follow or abstain from a course of action. Legal sanction may be positive (reward) or negative (penalty). Word *sanctions* designated coercive measures of League of Nations to stop aggression, e.g., economic sanctions (1935) against Italy for invasion of Ethiopia. Powers of UN also include infliction of sanctions.

Sanctis, Francesco de: see DE SANCTIS, FRANCESCO.

Sanctorius (sängktô'rēŭs), Ital., *Santorio,* 1561–1636, Italian physiologist. Laid foundation for metabolism study through quantitative experiments.

Sanctus (also *Tersanctus*) [Latin,= holy], choral ending of the preface in Roman MASS. Parts of the short hymn are called the *Benedictus* and the *Hosanna.*

Sand, George (sänd, Fr. zhôrzh' sä'), pseud. of Aurore Dupin, baronne Dudevant, 1804–76, French novelist. Her grandmother was a natural daughter of Maurice, comte de Saxe. Divorced in 1836, she asserted her independence through her eccentric manners and a series of open liaisons—notably with Jules SANDEAU, Musset (whom she betrayed somewhat cynically), and Chopin (with whom her relations were tempestuous). She was, however, a devoted mother, and her unconventional conduct was motivated chiefly by her belief in equal rights for women. Her novels, which rank high in French fiction, are marked by deep love for nature and the soil and by moral idealism. They include *La Mare au diable* (1846; Eng. tr., *The Haunted Pool*), *Indiana* (1832), and *La Petite Fadette* (1848; Eng. tr., *Fanchon the Cricket*). *Elle et lui* (1858) is her version of her affair with Musset; *Un Hiver à Majorque* [a winter in Majorca] tells of her life with Chopin.

sand, mineral material occurring as loose grains, formed from weathering of rocks, and usually consisting in the main of quartz. Most extensive deposits are seen in deserts and on beaches. Uses include making brick, cement, glass, pottery; as an abrasive, and in filtering water.

sandalwood, name for several fragrant tropical woods, especially that of an evergreen semiparasitic tree, *Santalum album,* of India. The wood is made into various wares; the oil has been used in perfume since early days.

sandbur, weedy sandy-soil grass of genus *Cenchrus* with burlike seeds. Bur grass is another name.

Sandburg, Carl, 1878–, American poet and biographer, b. Ill. Life as a day laborer, soldier, secretary, and newspaperman influenced his poetry. It is frank, often slangy and vernacular in style, but sometimes impressionistic. Collected verses as in *Chicago Poems* (1916) and *The People, Yes* (1936) estab. him as an artist. His biography of Lincoln (6 vols., 1926–39) won acclaim. Also wrote children's poems and stories; a novel, *Remembrance Rock* (1948); autobiographical *Always the Young Strangers* (1953).

Sandeau, Jules (zhül' sädō'), 1811–83, French novelist. Collaborated with George SAND, who took her pen name from him.

Sanderson, village (pop. 2,047), W Texas, N of Rio Grande, on El Paso-Del Rio highway. Ships wool, mohair, and livestock.

sand fly, minute biting, bloodsucking, water-breeding fly, also called punkie and nosee-um.

Sandhurst, village, Berkshire, England; site of the Royal Military Col. (founded in 1802).

San Diego (săn dēā'gō), city (pop. 434,924), S Calif., port on fine natural harbor on E side of San Diego Bay. State's first permanent white settlement. Cabrillo entered bay 1542. Junípero Serra founded San Diego de Alcalá Mission 1769. Beach and fishing resort. Produces aircraft, and processes fish (esp. tuna), fruit, and dairy goods. Seat of important U.S. naval installations. Balboa Park contains points of scenic and historic interest. City's Old Town district has early adobe houses.

Sandomierz (sändô'myĕsh), town (pop. 8,357), S Poland, at confluence of Vistula and San rivers. Became cap. of a duchy 1139. A synod held here in 1570 united all Polish Protestants. Passed to Austria 1795; to Russia 1815; reverted to Poland 1919.

San Domingo, old form of SANTO DOMINGO.

sandpiper, small wading bird of Old and New Worlds, related to snipe and curlew. Has long bill and legs; plumage is usually streaked brown or gray above, lighter with streaks or spots below.

Sandpoint, resort city (pop. 4,265), N Idaho, on Pend Oreille L. (spanned here by 2-mi. bridge).

Sandracottus (săndrŭkŏ'tŭs), Greek name of **Chandragupta** (chändrŭgōōp'tŭ), d. c.298 B.C., Indian ruler, founder of MAURYA empire. Conquered the Magadha kingdom in c.320 B.C. and expelled the garrisons of Alexander the Great from NW India.

Sandringham (săn'drĭngŭm), village, Norfolk, England. Sandringham House (7,000 acres) was bought by Edward VII in 1861. George V died here (1936).

Sand Springs, industrial suburb (pop. 6,994) of Tulsa, NE Okla, on Arkansas R. Has memorial group by Lorado Taft.

sandstone, rock formed of sand grains cemented by iron oxide, calcium carbonate, quartz. Commonly gray, red, brown. Chief use is building material.

sandstorm, dry desert wind carrying sand or dust which often reduces visibility to zero, obscures sun. Called simoom or simoon in Arabia and N Africa.

Sandusky, city (pop. 29,375), N Ohio, W of Cleveland and on Sandusky Bay of L. Erie; laid out 1817 as Portland. Port and coal-shipping point with mfg. of paper products and communications equipment. Center of resort area.

Sandusky, river, c.120 mi. long, rising in N Ohio and flowing W, then N to Sandusky Bay of L. Erie.

Sandwich, Edward Montagu, 1st earl of (mŏn'tŭgū), 1625–72, English statesman and admiral. Served (1653–56) on Cromwell's council of state. Aided restoration of Charles II. Held high naval command in Dutch Wars. Killed in battle of Southwold Bay.

Sandwich, John Montagu, 4th earl of, 1718–92, English politician. Twice first lord of the admiralty, he used the navy for political ends. His mismanagement led largely to British failure in American Revolution. Sandwich (Hawaiian) Isls., were named for him, as was (supposedly) the sandwich.

Sandwich (săn'wĭch, săn'dwĭch), municipal borough (pop. 4,142), Kent, England. One of the Cinque Ports, it was chief naval and military port under Henry VII. Harbor is now silted up.

Sandwich, town (pop. 2,418), SE Mass., on W Cape Cod E of Bourne; settled 1637. Historical museum displays Sandwich glass (made here 1825–88).

Sandwich Islands: see HAWAIIAN ISLANDS.

Sandy Hook, peninsula, NE N.J., projecting c.5 mi. N toward New York city, between Sandy Hook Bay and the Atlantic. U.S. reservation with Fort Hancock at tip. Lighthouse (1763; 85 ft. high) is oldest in use in U.S. Hudson's men explored here 1609.

Sandys, Sir Edwin (săndz), 1561–1629, English statesman, leading promoter of the colony in Virginia. Won dislike of James I by speech (1614) denying doctrine of divine right. Leader of liberal faction in Virginia Co., he was responsible for many progressive features of company's rule. His brother, **George Sandys,** 1578–1644, was a traveler and poet. Wrote *Relation of a Journey* (1615) about his trip to Europe and Near East. While in Virginia (1621–31), he translated (1626) Ovid's *Metamorphoses.*

San Felipe (săn fĕ'lĭpē), town, S Texas, on Brazos R. and W of Houston. Founded 1823 as hq. of S. F. Austin's colony; Texans met here (1832, 1833, 1835), and it was burned in Texas Revolution. Declined in late 19th cent. Also called San Felipe de Austin.

San Felipe (săn" fūlĕ'pä), Indian pueblo village (1948 pop. 787), N central N.Mex., on Rio Grande and SW of Santa Fe; estab. in early 1700s. Semi-annual ceremonial dances. Keresan language.

San Fernando, city (pop. 12,992), S Calif., N of Los Angeles, in farm (citrus, truck) and oil region. San Fernando Valley entered by white men in 1769. Produced some gold after 1842. San Fernando Rey Mission (1797) is near.

Sanford. 1 City (pop. 11,935), E central Fla., on L. Monroe NE of Orlando. Resort and celery market. **2** Town (pop. 15,177), including Sanford village (pop. 11,094), SW Maine, SW of Portland. Mfg. of textiles (since mid-18th cent.). **3** Town (pop. 10,013), central N.C., SW of Raleigh. Tobacco, cotton, and clay products. Annexed Jonesboro 1947.

San Francisco, city (pop. 775,357), W Calif., on hilly peninsula between Pacific Ocean and SAN FRANCISCO BAY (connected by Golden Gate strait). Founded 1776 by Spanish as Yerba Buena, and taken by U.S. 1846, it became San Francisco 1847. Grew tremendously after 1848 gold rush. Ensuing period of lawlessness on BARBARY COAST saw rise of VIGILANTES. Linked with East by Pony Express (1860), then by Union Pacific RR (1869). Rebuilt rapidly after costly earthquake and fire of 1906. Panama Canal opening (celebrated with exposition, 1915) brought increased trade. Inter-city communication was improved, notably by SAN FRANCISCO-OAKLAND BAY BRIDGE (1936) and GOLDEN GATE BRIDGE (1937). Golden Gate International Exposition (1939–40) saw city largely industrialized. Recent historic events occurring here were drafting of UN Charter (1945) and signing of Japanese treaty (1951). One of most important U.S. ports, it is also a transportation and cultural center, key city of a great metropolitan area, and market for huge agr. and mining area. Besides oil refining, shipbuilding, and food processing, it has milling and processing of steel and iron and mfg. of machinery, chemicals, clothing, and wood and rubber products. Scenically beautiful, it has a reputation for individual charm. Among many points of interest are Market Street, Telegraph Hill, Opera House, Embarcadero, Chinatown (largest Chinese settlement outside Orient), wharves, bridges, and Mission Dolores (1782). Seat of Univ. of San Francisco (Jesuit; for men; 1855).

San Francisco Bay, 50 mi. long and 3–12 mi. wide, W Calif., entered between two peninsulas via Golden Gate strait. This natural harbor is one of best sheltered in the world. On S peninsula is San Francisco and on E shore are Alameda, Oakland, Berkeley, and Richmond. In bay are Alcatraz, Angel, and Yerba Buena islands. San Pablo Bay (N) and Suisun Bay are subsidiary waters. Sir Francis Drake entered bay 1579. Late 1700s brought Spanish explorations. **San Francisco-Oakland Bay Bridge,** built 1933–36, crosses bay to Yerba Buena Isl. where tunnel connects with spans to Oakland. Double-decked structure, it is 8¼ mi. long. See *ill.,* p. 131.

San Francisco Peaks, N Ariz., N of Flagstaff, consisting of Humphreys, 12,655 ft. (highest in Ariz.); Agassiz, 12,340 ft.; and Fremont, 11,940 ft.

San Gabriel, residential city (pop. 20,343), S Calif., E of Los Angeles. Spanish mission (1771).

San Gabriel Mountains, S Calif., E and NE of Los

Angeles, running c.60 mi. W from Cajon Pass, NNW of San Bernardino. Rises to 10,080 ft. in San Antonio Peak. Includes Mt. Wilson (5,710 ft. high), with observatory estab. 1904 and operated by Carnegie Inst. and California Inst. of Technology.

Sangallo (säng-gäl'lō), three Italian architects. **Giuliano da Sangallo** (jo͞olyä'nō), 1445–1516, worked on St. Peter's at Rome with Raphael and Fra Giocondo. His brother, **Antonio da Sangallo,** the elder, 1455–1534, built the domed church at Montepulchiano. Their nephew, **Antonio da Sangallo,** the younger, 1485–1546, designed Farnese Palace and Pauline Chapel (Vatican). Collaborated with Bramante.

Sangamon (săng'gŭmŭn), river, c.250 mi. long, rising in E central Ill., NE of Springfield. Flows SW to Decatur (dammed, forming L. Decatur), then W and NW to Illinois R. above Beardstown. Much of Lincoln's youth spent in its environs.

Sanger, Margaret (Higgins), 1883–, American leader in the BIRTH CONTROL movement. Organized first American (1921) and international (1925) birth control conferences; estab. many clinics.

Sanger, city (pop. 6,400), S central Calif., near Fresno in San Joaquin Valley. Packs raisins.

San Gimignano (sän jēmēnyä'nō), town (pop. 3,426), Tuscany, central Italy. With its city walls, palaces, and 13 towers, it has preserved its medieval aspect more than any other Italian town. It suffered some damage in World War II.

Sangre de Cristo Mountains (săng'grĕ dē krī'stō), part of Rocky Mts., including Sierra Blanca in S central Colo. (with Blanca Peak, 14,363 ft. high) and Truchas peaks in N.Mex.

Sanhedrin (să'nĭdrĭn, săn'hĭ–), Jewish legal and religious court in anc. Jerusalem. There probably were two Sanhedrins—one political and civil, the other purely religious. Both organizations perished with the destruction of the Temple.

San Ildefonso (săn" ēl"dŭfŏns'sō), Indian pueblo village (1948 pop. 174), N central N.Mex., on Rio Grande and NW of Santa Fe; present settlement estab. early 1700s. Tanoan language. Famous for fine pottery, paintings. Annual ceremonial dances.

San Ildefonso, Treaty of (sän ēldäfōn'sō), name of several treaties signed at village of San Ildefonso, central Spain, in the royal summer palace of La Granja. By the treaty of **1796** Spain became the ally of France in the French Revolutionary Wars. The treaty of **1800** (actually a draft, confirmed by later treaties in 1801 and 1802), restored Louisiana to France; prepared Louisiana Purchase of 1803.

sanitation: see HYGIENE; PLUMBING; PUBLIC HEALTH.

San Jacinto (săn jŭsĭn'tŭ), river rising E central Texas and flowing c.50 mi. S to Galveston Bay arm. Lower river used with Buffalo Bayou (tributary) for Houston ship channel. Monument to Sam Houston's defeat of Mexicans in final battle of Texas Revolution on river near Houston.

San Jacinto Mountains, range extending c.30 mi. SSE from S end of San Bernardino Mts. At N end, near Palm Springs, San Jacinto Peak or Mt. San Jacinto rises to 10,805 ft.

San Joaquin (săn wäkēn'), river, 317 mi. long, rising in E Calif., in the Sierra Nevada and flowing briefly W, then N through S part of CENTRAL VALLEY (San Joaquin Valley) to form delta with Sacramento R. near Suisun Bay, a San Francisco Bay arm. Receives many streams from Sierra Nevada. Rich irrigated agr. valley (see FRIANT DAM) includes independent Kings and Kern rivers. Chief centers are Bakersfield, Modesto, Merced, Fresno, and Stockton.

San José (sän hōsā'), city (pop. 86,909), W central Costa Rica, cap. and largest city of Costa Rica; founded c.1738. Center of economic, political, and social life of republic. University located here.

San Jose (sănŭsā', săn hōzā'), city (pop. 95,280), W Calif., SE of San Francisco; founded 1777. Meeting place of first state legislature (1849) and first state cap. (1849–51). Important canning and dried-fruit packing center in Santa Clara Valley. Annexed Willow Glen 1936. Mission San Jose de Guadalupe (1797) is near.

San Jose scale, scale insect introduced from China into San Jose, Calif. It spread over North American fruit-growing areas. Drains sap, attacks fruit of many trees. Covers bark with waxy scales it secretes, under which females remain for life. Some control possible with oil and lime sulphur sprays.

San Juan (sän hwän′), city (pop. 82,410), cap. of San Juan prov., W Argentina, on San Juan R.; founded 1562. Center of irrigated region, it also has mining and cattle raising.

San Juan, city (pop. 224,767), cap. and chief city of Puerto Rico, on NE coast; founded 1521. Grew in importance as West Indian port during 18th and 19th cent. and was scene of uprising (1885) against Spanish rule. Taken over by U.S. troops (Oct., 1898) in Spanish-American War. Points of interést include: El Morro castle (begun 1539), San Cristóbal castle (begun 1631), and La Fortaleza (begun 1529; now the governor's palace). Most of Univ. of Puerto Rico and School of Tropical Medicine are here.

San Juan (sän″ wän′), Indian pueblo village (1948 pop. 788), N N.Mex., on Rio Grande and NW of Santa Fe. State's first Spanish settlement made here in 1598 by Juan de Oñate. Popé, medicine man of San Juan, led Pueblo revolt of 1680. Tanoan language. Annual festival honors St. John the Baptist.

San Juan (sän hwän′), river, 108 mi. long, flowing from SE corner of L. Nicaragua to Caribbean. Lower course is boundary of Nicaragua and Costa Rica. Would be vital link in projected Nicaragua Canal.

San Juan (sän″ wän′), river, c.400 mi. long, rising in San Juan Mts. of SW Colo. and flowing SW into N.Mex., NW into Utah, and W to Colorado R. near Rainbow Bridge Natl. Monument.

San Juan Boundary Dispute, controversy between U.S. and Great Britain over U.S.–British Columbia boundary. Sometimes called Northwest Boundary Dispute. Difficulty arose from faulty wording of treaty settling Oregon question in 1846. Boundary line it set ran through middle of Juan de Fuca Strait. Strait, however, breaks into several channels; between two main ones lie San Juan Isls. Ownership of islands, especially San Juan itself, was disputed. Crisis loomed in 1859 when U.S. troops occupied San Juan Isl., but Gen. Winfield Scott arranged with British for joint occupation. Emperor William I of Germany arbitrated in 1872; decision gave archipelago to U.S.

San Juan Capistrano (sän″ wän″ kăpĭsträ′nō), town, S Calif., SE of Los Angeles. Junípero Serra estab. mission here 1776. Swallows said to return annually on March 19 and to depart on Oct. 23.

San Juan del Norte (sän hwä′ dĕl nôr′tä), town (pop. 307), E Nicaragua, a Caribbean port at N mouth of San Juan R. Occupied briefly by British after 1848 in effort to keep U.S. from building interoceanic canal. Also called Greytown.

San Juan Hill, E Cuba, near Santiago de Cuba; scene of battle in Spanish-American War (1898), in which Theodore Roosevelt and Rough Riders took part.

San Juan Islands (sän′ wän″), archipelago of 172 islands, NW Wash., E of Vancouver Isl., between Haro and Rosario straits; discovered c.1790 by Spanish. Awarded to U.S. 1872 after SAN JUAN BOUNDARY DISPUTE. San Juan, Orcas, Lopez are largest.

San Juan Mountains, in Rocky Mts., SW Colo. and NW N.Mex., W of San Luis Valley, S of Gunnison R. Rises to 14,306 ft. in Uncompahgre Peak, Colo.

Sankt Moritz, Switzerland: see SAINT MORITZ.

Sankt Wolfgang (zängkt vôlf′gäng), resort (pop. 2,640) in the Salzkammergut, Upper Austria, on L. of Sankt Wolfgang. Gothic church has altar carved by Michael Pacher.

San Leandro (sän lēän′drō), city (pop. 27,542), W Calif., adjoining Oakland, in truck and flower area. It has

canneries and automotive and metal-goods plants.

San Luis (sän lwēs′), city (pop. 25,147), cap. of San Luis prov., W central Argentina; founded c.1596. Oasis in arid region, in center of irrigated area; also has mining and cattle raising.

San Luis Obispo (sän lōō′ĭs ōbĭ′spō), city (pop. 14,180), S Calif., near San Luis Obispo Bay and NW of Los Angeles. Farm and oil center. San Luis Obispo de Tolosa Mission (1772) is now church.

San Luis Potosí (sän lwēs′ pōtōsē′), state (24,417 sq. mi.; pop. 855,336), N central Mexico. Most of state lies on E tablelands of central plateau. Although soil is fertile, agr. is economically unimportant because rainfall is light. Stock raising and mining are principal industries. Capital, **San Luis Potosí** (pop. 77,161), was founded 1576. Of strategic importance in colonial times and revolutionary period of 1910. Has smelters and factories (matches, candles, textiles, flour).

San Marcos (sän mär′kŭs), city (pop. 9,980), S central Texas, on San Marcos R. and SW of Austin. Resort with mfg. of cotton products, cottonseed oil, and clothing. Here are military air field and Southwest Texas State Teachers Col.

San Marcos, University of: see LIMA, PERU.

San Marino (sän märē′nō), independent republic (23 sq. mi.; pop. c.14,000), in the Apennines SW of Rimini, Italy. Agr., stockraising. Its independence dates from early Middle Ages. Government is exercised by two *reggenti* and a general council. Its picturesque cap., **San Marino,** stands on a rocky height and has kept part of medieval fortifications.

San Marino (sän mŭrē′nō), residential city (pop. 11,230), S Calif., near Pasadena. Seat of Henry E. Huntington Library and Art Gall.

San Martín, José de (hōsā dā sän märtēn′), 1778–1850, South American revolutionist. Returned to Argentina from Europe in 1812 to assist in revolution against Spain. Took command of insurgent army and accomplished the difficult feat of leading them across the Andean passes into Chile. Brought revolution to successful culmination in Chile at Chacabuco (1817) and Maipú (1818) and entered Peru. At a secret meeting at Guayaquil with Bolívar, who was entering Peru from the N, San Martin agreed to leave conquest of Peru to Bolívar and retired to private life.

San Mateo (sän mŭtä′ō), residential city (pop. 41,782), W Calif., S of San Francisco on San Francisco Bay, in flower and truck area; laid out 1863.

Sanmicheli, Michele (mēkā′lā sänmēkā′lē), 1484–1559, Italian architect and engineer. Built Grimani Palace, Venice, and Pompei Palace, Verona.

Sannazaro, Jacopo (yä′kōpō sän-nätsä′rō), 1458–1530, Italian author. His pastoral romance in prose and verse, *Arcadia* (1504), had great influence in Italian and European literature.

Sannikov Island (sä′nĭkôf), mythical island, N of New Siberian Islands, RSFSR. Reported by Russian explorer Sannikov 1810; existence disproved by 1937–40 expedition of Russian icebreaker *Sedov*.

San Pablo, city (pop. 14,476), W Calif., just N of Richmond near San Pablo Bay.

San Pedro (sän pē′drō) former city (est. 1940 pop. c.40,-000), S Calif.; laid out 1882, consolidated 1909 with Los Angeles. Important port for Los Angeles. Has shipyards, dry docks, fish canneries, and oil refineries. Santa Catalina Isl. is across San Pedro Channel. Bay discovered by Cabrillo 1542.

San Pedro Sula (sän pä′dhrō sōō′lä), city (pop. 22,116), NW Honduras, second largest city of country. It is, with Puerto Cortés, the chief port for banana and sugar plantations.

San Quentin, small peninsula in San Francisco Bay, W Calif. State prison here was begun 1852.

San Rafael (sän rŭfĕl′), residential city (pop. 13,848), W Calif., N of San Francisco. Seat of Mission San Rafael Arcángel (1817; restored).

San Remo (sän rä′mō), city (pop. 23,963), Liguria, NW Italy; a resort on the Riviera. Gambling casino.

San Salvador (sän sälvädhōr'), city (pop. 160,380), W central Salvador, cap. and largest city of Salvador. Founded early in 16th cent., it was for a time (1831–38) capital of Central American Federation. Suffers from recurrent and severe earthquakes.

San Salvador, name given by Columbus to one of Bahama Isls., first land discovered in the New World (Oct. 12, 1492). Long thought to have been what is now Cat Island, historians presently identify it with Watling or Watlings Island.

sans-culottes (sä-külōt') [French,= without knee breeches], term applied to lowest class in France during French Revolution, who wore long trousers. Jacobins identified themselves with sans-culottes.

San Sebastián (sän säbästyän'), seaport (pop. 89,276), cap. of Guipúzcoa prov., N Spain, in Basque Provs., on Bay of Biscay. Fashionable resort; former summer residence of Spanish court.

Sanskrit (săn'skrĭt) [Sanskrit,= perfect], classical standard language of India, of Indic group of Indo-Iranian subfamily of Indo-European languages (see LANGUAGE, table). Its earliest form, Vedic, is that of the VEDA. Sanskrit was spoken c.400 B.C. as standard court language, and Sanskrit remains are among oldest Indo-European documents. It was formerly supposed to be a "parent language."

Sanskrit literature, main body of the classical literature of India. It is generally divided into two main groups—writings in Vedic (c.1500–c.200 B.C.), the parent language of Sanskrit, and writings in classical Sanskrit (c.200 B.C.–A.D. c.1100). The early Vedic period produced the VEDA, the most sacred and ancient scriptures of Hinduism. The middle Vedic period produced the *Brahmanas,* which are prose commentaries relating the meaning of the Vedas to religious rites. Parts of the *Brahmanas* are theosophical treatises called *Aranyakas* [forest books], so named because they were meant to be studied in solitude. Late *Aranyakas* are the *Upanishads* (see VEDANTA). Both the Veda and the *Brahmanas* came to be called sruti [Sanskrit,= hearing, i.e., revealed], while all later works are called smitri [Sanskrit,= memory or tradition]. The *Sutras,* dealing with ritual and law, were written toward the end of the Vedic period and are the oldest source of Hindu law. Literature of the Sanskrit period is nearly all in verse. It began with the great epics, notably the MAHABHARATA and the RAMAYANA. The *Mahabharata,* which incorporates the *Bhagavad Gita,* also inspired the *Puranas,* a group of 18 epics. Although lyric poetry was chiefly erotic, many lyric poems were ethical in tone, stressing the vanity of worldly life. Sanskrit drama was an outgrowth of those hymns of the *Rig-Veda* which contain dialogue, and it borrowed stories from popular legend. A famous Sanskrit drama is the *Sakuntala* of KALIDASA. Sanskrit stories and fables (e.g., the PANCHATANTRA) contain stories within stories and thus have many levels to the narrative. Today, Sanskrit is chiefly used for academic exercise; modern INDIAN LITERATURE is mostly written in vernacular languages.

Sansovino, Jacopo (yä'kōpō sänsōvē'nō), 1486–1570, Italian sculptor and architect, whose real name was Tatti. Worked in Rome and Venice, where he built Library of St. Mark's.

Sans Souci (sä sōōsē') [Fr.,= without cares, content], palace built 1745–47 at Potsdam, Germany, by Frederick the Great. Executed by Knobelsdorff, but believed to have been designed by Frederick himself. The one-story palace is in a magnificent park.

San Stefano, Treaty of (sän stĕ'fänō), 1878, between Russia and Turkey, signed at village of San Stefano (now Yesilkoy), near Istanbul. Ending the last of the RUSSO-TURKISH WARS, it forced Turkey to cede parts of Armenia and the Dobruja to Russia; to recognize the independence of Rumania, Serbia, and Montenegro; and to make Bulgaria an autonomous principality including a large part of Macedonia. The tre-

mendous influence the treaty gave Russia in the Balkans caused the other great powers to obtain its revision at the Congress of BERLIN.

Santa Ana (sän'tä ä'nä), city (pop. 51,676), W Salvador. In warm, fertile valley, it is center of coffee, sugar, and cattle region. Santa Ana volcano is near by.

Santa Ana, city (pop. 45,533), S Calif., SE of Los Angeles, in Santa Ana valley; founded 1869. Beet sugar, canned fruits and vegetables, walnuts.

Santa Ana, Indian pueblo village (1948 pop. 294), central N.Mex., N of Albuquerque. Keresan language. Has Santa Ana de Alamillo church (1692).

Santa Anna, Antonio López de (äntō'nyō lō'päs dä sän'tä ä'nä), 1794–1876, Mexican general and politician, president of Mexico (1833–36, 1841–44, 1846–47, 1853–55). His political career was marked by opportunistic rather than fixed principles. First fought with royalist army in Mexico's struggle for independence, then supported ITURBIDE; turned against Iturbide; then opposed Guerrero and Bustamante, whom he had helped to power. His failure in crushing the revolution in Texas (1836) temporarily halted his political career, but his success in repulsing the French (1838) again brought him popularity. Failure in the Mexican War (1846) sent him into exile from which he returned to rule briefly as "perpetual dictator." He was exiled in 1855 when Benito Júarez came into power but was allowed to return to Mexico two years before his death.

Santa Barbara, residential and resort city (pop. 44,913), S Calif., on Santa Barbara Channel. Presidio founded 1782 and mission 1786 (present structure completed 1820). City retains some old Spanish flavor and is known for subtropical luxuriance of its flowers and fruit. Has museums of art and natural history. Holds annual historical fiesta.

Santa Barbara Islands, extending c.150 mi. along coast of S Calif. and separated from coast in N by Santa Barbara Channel. Anacapa Isl. and Santa Barbara Isl. are in Channel Isls. Natl. Monument. Include Santa Catalina (sän"tù kă"tùlē'nù) or Catalina Isl., 22 mi. long, off Long Beach. Discovered 1542 by Cabrillo. In 1919 William Wrigley bought and developed it as a pleasure resort. Avalon city (pop. 1,506) is center of this island's resort and sport activities. Has museums, aquarium, bird haven, and casino.

Santa Catalina or **Catalina Island:** see SANTA BARBARA ISLANDS.

Santa Catarina (sän'tù kätùrē'nù), state (36,435 sq. mi.; pop. 1,578,159), SE Brazil; cap. FLORIANÓPOLIS on Santa Catarina isl., just off coast. The mainland is between the Atlantic on E and Argentina on W. From coastal area, which has farming, state rises to tableland, where cattle and hogs are raised; in SE, coal is mined. Settled by Portuguese in 17th cent. Germans immigrated in 19th cent.

Santa Clara, city (pop. 14,178), W Calif., adjoining San Jose. Fruit and meat processing. Has Santa Clara de Asís Mission (1777; restored). Seat of Univ. of Santa Clara (R.C.; for men; 1851).

Santa Clara, Indian pueblo village (1948 pop. 579), N N.Mex., on Rio Grande and NW of Santa Fe; settled c.1700. Tanoan language. Distinctive black pottery is made. Annual St. Clare of Assisi feast. Near by are Puyé ruins of 15th-cent. pueblo.

Santa Claus: see NICHOLAS, SAINT.

Santa Cruz (sän'tä krōōs'), city (pop. 36,400), cap. of Santa Cruz dept., central Bolivia; founded 1557, reestab. at present site 1595 by settlers from Asunción, Paraguay. Center of agr. region and has potential importance; when railroad is completed, city will have access to the Pacific through Peru and to the Atlantic through Brazil.

Santa Cruz (sän'tù krōōz'), city (pop. 21,970), W Calif., on Monterey Bay, in area of fine beaches near Santa Cruz Mts. Fishing and fish canning.

Santa Cruz de Tenerife: see CANARY ISLANDS.

Santa Cruz Islands (sän'tù krōōz'), small volcanic group,

S Pacific, in SOLOMON ISLANDS. In 1942 Japanese relief of Guadalcanal was prevented by U.S. victory here.

Santa Fe (sän'tä fā'), city (pop. 168,791), cap. of Santa Fe prov., E central Argentina; river port near Paraná R., with which it is connected by canal. Founded (1573) by Juan de Garay, it has been important in Argentine history. On margin of Pampa, it is transshipping point for grain and meat.

Santa Fe (sän'tù fā'), city (pop. 27,998; alt. c.7,000 ft.), state cap., N N.Mex., between Pecos R. and Rio Grande. Second largest city in N.Mex., resort center with artists' and writers' colony, and shipping point for Indian wares, minerals (lead, zinc, coal, gold, silver), and farm products (fruit, potatoes). Founded c.1609 by Spanish under Oñate, it was Spanish-Indian trade center for over 200 years. Seat of government since its founding, it is oldest cap. city in U.S. Pueblo revolt of 1680 drove Spanish out for 12 years. Commerce with U.S. developed via Santa Fe Trail after Mexican freedom from Spain (1821). Gen. S. W. KEARNY took city for U.S. 1846. Railroad reached Lamy (station for Santa Fe), 16 mi. S, 1879. See of an archbishopric since 1875, city is a Roman Catholic center. Has San Miguel Mission Church (c.1636), Cathedral of St. Francis, and Palace of the Governors (over 300 years old). Near by are many Indian pueblos and Bandelier Natl. Monument.

Santa Fe Railroad. Chartered in Kansas as Atchison and Topeka Railroad in 1859. Formal name since 1895 is Atchison, Topeka & Santa Fe Railway Co. Made connection with city of Santa Fe in 1880. By early 1890s the Santa Fe became one of longest railroad systems in the world. Today its 13,000 mi. of trackage reach L. Michigan, Gulf of Mexico, the Rio Grande, and the Pacific.

Santa Fe Trail, important caravan route of W U.S., leading from W Mo. to Santa Fe, N.Mex. In Nov., 1821, William Becknell brought news that Mexico was free and that Santa Fe now welcomed trade; he organized trading party. Franklin was first outfitting point, succeeded by Westport (now part of Kansas City) and Independence. In 1850 a monthly stage line was estab. between Independence and Santa Fe. Coming of Atchison, Topeka, and Santa Fe RR in 1880 marked death of old trail. See also OREGON TRAIL.

Santa Maria, city (pop. 10,440), S Calif., near San Luis Obispo Bay. Has oil and beet-sugar refineries. Ships vegetables and flower seeds.

Santa Marta (sän'tä mär'tä), city (pop. 25,113), N Colombia; port on the Caribbean; founded by Bastidas (1525) on deep harbor surrounded by hills. Important in colonial times as seaport for Magdalena R., it was royalist center in revolution against Spain, but was finally liberated (1821). Today banana industry, operated by United Fruit Co., is most important on continent.

Santa Monica, resort and residential city (pop. 71,595), S Calif., W of Los Angeles and between Santa Monica Bay and Santa Monica Mts. Aircraft.

Santander, Francisco de Paula (fränsē'skō dā pou'lä säntändēr'), 1792–1840, Colombian revolutionist. Ably assisted Bolívar in revolution against Spain and afterwards as vice president of Colombia. A believer in constitutional government, he led federalist opposition to Bolívar and was banished (1828). After Bolívar's death and break up of Greater Colombia, Santander returned and served ably as president of New Granada (1832–36).

Santander (säntändēr'), city (pop. 84,971), cap. of Santander prov., N Spain, in Old Castile; a port on Bay of Biscay. Bathing resort. Has ironworks and shipyards.

Santa Paula, city (pop. 11,049), S Calif., NW of Los Angeles, in fruit and oil area.

Santaquin (săntùkēn'), city (pop. 1,214), N central Utah, S of Provo, in STRAWBERRY VALLEY PROJECT.

Santarém (säntùrän'), city (pop. 11,785), W Portugal, in Estremadura, on Tagus R. Agr. trade center. Taken from the Moors by Alfonso I (1147), it played an important part in Portuguese history. Old royal palace is now in ruins.

Santa Rita, village (pop. 2,135), SW N.Mex., near Silver City. Has large open-pit copper mines.

Santa Rosa, city (pop. 17,902), W Calif., N of San Francisco. Trade center for Sonoma Valley. Processes fruits and produces wines and shoes. Has home and gardens of Luther Burbank.

Santa Sophia: see HAGIA SOPHIA.

Santayana, George (säntäyä'nä), 1863–1952, American philosopher and poet, b. Madrid. He taught for many years at Harvard, but in 1912 returned to Europe, eventually settling in Italy, where he lived secluded in a convent. He rejected organized religion, but in his later works stressed the role of faith in the life of man—faith in the unknowable in a world entirely material. His broad views and his mastery of literary style gave him a large public even for such strictly philosophical works as *The Sense of Beauty* (1896), *The Life of Reason* (1905–6) and *The Realms of Being* (4 vols., 1927–40). A novel, *The Last Puritan* (1935), and his autobiography, *Persons and Places* (3 vols., 1944–53), gained more popular notice. Of his poems, his sonnets are best known.

Santee (säntē'), river formed by confluence of Congaree and Wateree rivers, central S.C., SE of Columbia. Flows 143 mi. to the Atlantic, S of Georgetown. Center of hydroelectric and navigation project (1942).

Santiago (säntēä'gō), city (pop. 1,161,633), central Chile, cap. of Chile and Santiago prov.; one of the largest cities in South America. Founded 1541 by Valdivia, it has been focal point of intellectual and cultural development of Chile; also the political, commercial, and financial heart of nation. National Univ. is here.

Santiago de Compostela (säntyä'gō dā kōmpōstä'lä), city (pop. 30,127), NW Spain, in Galicia. It has been one of chief Christian shrines of pilgrimage since the 9th cent., when a sanctuary was built here over the supposed tomb of the apostle St. James. Destroyed by the Moors (10th cent.), the earlier sanctuary was replaced by a Romanesque cathedral (11th–12th cent.), later transformed by baroque and plateresque additions. Here too are the Hospital Real (1501–11), built for accommodation of poor pilgrims, and a university (estab. 1501).

Santiago de Cuba (dā kōō'bä), city (pop. 118,266), SE Cuba. Founded in 1514 by Diego de Velásquez, it was for some time capital of Cuba. Exports mineral, agr., and wood products. In 1898 it played important part in Spanish-American War. With elimination of yellow fever, Santiago has become a fine modern port.

Santiago del Estero (dĕl ästä'rō), city (pop. 63,491), cap. of Santiago del Estero prov., N central Argentina. Founded 1553, it is center of cattle-raising and agr. region and popular health resort.

Santiago de los Caballeros (dā lōs käbäyä'rōs), city (pop. 56,192), N central Dominican Republic; commercial and agr. distributing point for the most densely populated part of republic.

Santillana, Iñigo López de Mendoza, marqués de (ēnyē'gō lō'päth dā mĕndō'thä märkäs' dā säntēlyä'nä), 1398–1458, chief Spanish poet and author of his era. Wrote first Spanish sonnets.

Santo Domingo (sän'tō dōmēng'gō), former Spanish colony on HISPANIOLA. Columbus discovered island in 1492 and left settlement there, but upon his return in 1493 settlers had vanished. He administered new colony until complaints of harsh rule caused his replacement by Bobadilla (1500), who in turn was replaced by Diego Columbus (1509). Finding no mineral wealth in quantity, settlers turned to farming with work done by Indians under *encomienda* system. No colonization of W part of island (present Haiti) being undertaken by Spanish, French planters began to settle there. Sugar cane was introduced in late 18th cent. and became dominant product. Spain ceded part of island to France 1697 and gave up whole island 1795.

Spanish colonists resisted French rule and—after Haiti gained independence—Haitian rule. (For later history of island, see HAITI; DOMINICAN REPUBLIC.) Seat of colonial administration was city of **Santo Domingo,** founded 1496, which is oldest continuously inhabited settlement in W Hemisphere. After hurricane of 1930, city was rebuilt and renamed TRUJILLO.

Santo Domingo, Indian pueblo (pop. 1,169), central N.Mex., on Rio Grande and SW of Santa Fe; present village founded c.1700. Eastern Keresan language. Farming, pottery making. Annual Green Corn dance.

santonin (săn'tŭnĭn), colorless, odorless, crystalline solid obtained from certain plants. It is used in medicines to expel worms and is poisonous in large doses.

Santos (săn'tŏosh), city (pop. 201,739, São Paulo state, SE Brazil, on small island in Atlantic, just off mainland, port for São Paulo (35 mi. inland); founded c.1545. World's greatest coffee port, also exports cotton, sugar, fruit, and meat.

Santos-Dumont, Alberto (săn'tŏs-dŏo'mŏnt), 1873–1932, Brazilian aeronaut. Pioneered in constructing and flying gasoline-motored airship (1898).

Santo Tomás, University of, at Manila, P.I.; R.C., coed.; founded 1611 by Dominicans.

São Francisco (sä'ŏ fränsĕsh'kŏo), river, c.1,800 mi. long, rising in SW Minas Gerais state, E Brazil, and flowing generally NE to Atlantic. Vast irrigation and hydroelectric project in its basin begun 1949.

São Luís (sä'ŏ lŏoĕsh'), city (pop. 81,432), cap. of Maranhão state, N Brazil, on São Luís isl., at mouth of Itapecuru R. Founded (1612) by French, captured (1615) by Portuguese. Exports cotton, babassu oil, sugar, balsam, and hides.

Saône (sōn), river, 267 mi. long, E France, rising in Vosges mts. and flowing S through Franche-Comté and Burgundy into the Rhone at Lyons.

Saône, Haute: see HAUTE-SAÔNE.

Saône-et-Loire (sōn"-ā-lwär'), department (3,331 sq. mi.; pop. 506,749), E central France, in Burgundy; cap. Mâcon.

São Paulo (sä'ŏ pou'lŏ), state (95,453 sq. mi.; pop. 9,242,610), SE Brazil; cap. São Paulo. State extends inland from the Atlantic to Paraná R. and is most populous and most important agr. and industrial state in Brazil. Coffee is dominant crop; vast quantities are exported from Santos. Development of coffee production and progressive agr. methods aided by immigration in 19th and 20th cent. Cattle are raised in many sections, and textile milling and processing and shipping agr. products important. Its cap., **São Paulo,** is a plateau city (pop. 2,227,512; alt. 2,700 ft.); commercial and industrial center of Brazil and one of most important Latin American cities. Transportation and shipping point for rich agr. hinterland, it has numerous factories (machinery, textiles, chemicals, automobiles, shoes, household appliances, cement, and processed foods). Educational institutions include Univ. of São Paulo, McKenzie Inst., police training school, and technical and professional schools. Founded 1554 by Jesuits, it became capital of area in 1681. Its residents are called *paulistas.*

São Tiago: see CAPE VERDE ISLANDS.

São Tomé and Principe (sã̄ō tŏomä', prēn'sēpä), islands in Gulf of Guinea, off coast of Africa, comprising a province (372 sq. mi.; pop. 60,159) of Portugal. Export cacao, coffee, and palm oil.

São Vicente, Cabo de: see SAINT VINCENT, CAPE.

sap, fluid of plants consisting of water, dissolved plant foods (esp. sugars, salts, and organic acids), and pigments. Sap water enters through root hairs by osmosis and is carried by vascular tissues (xylem or wood) to parts containing chlorophyll, usually the leaves. It is believed that sap ascent is caused by osmotic pull from higher sap concentrations in leaves after loss of water by transpiration and to some extent from osmotic pressure arising in the roots (esp. great in the spring). Maple sugar is made from the sap of the sugar maple. Other specialized plant fluids such as

the milky juice latex are sometimes called sap.

Sapir, Edward (sŭpēr'), 1884–1939, American linguist and anthropologist, b. Germany. Contributed greatly to development of descriptive linguistics.

Sapor, Persian kings: see SHAPUR.

Sapphira (sŭfī'rŭ), wife of ANANIAS 1.

sapphire (să'fīur), variety of transparent blue corundum, among the most valuable of gems. Found in Ceylon, Siam, Burma, India, Australia, Montana.

Sappho (să'fō), fl. early 6th cent. B.C., greatest early Greek lyric poet, b. Lesbos, an aristocrat. Her life is obscured by legend. Her verse, of which fragments survive, is the classic example of the "pure" love lyric, characterized by vehement expression of passion and perfect control of meter.

Sapporo (săp-pō'rō), city (pop. 259,602), SW Hokkaido, Japan; cap. and largest city of Hokkaido. Seat of Hokkaido Imperial Univ.

sapsucker, small North American woodpecker. Yellow-bellied sapsucker damages or kills trees because it girdles them with holes, eats inner tissue, drinks sap.

Sapulpa (sŭpŭl'pŭ), city (pop. 13,031), NE central Okla., SW of Tulsa. Trade center of agr. and oil region with mfg. of glass, clay products, and gasoline. Has U.S. Indian school.

Saracens, term used in the Middle Ages to mean Arabs and more generally Moslems. Strictly the term should have been applied only to the people of NW Arabia, but instead it finally came to be applied more particularly to the Seljuk Turks.

Saragossa (să"rügŏ'sù), Span. *Zaragoza,* city (pop. 205,-833), cap. of Saragossa prov. and of Aragon, NE Spain, on the Ebro. Communications and commercial center. Archiepiscopal see; seat of a university (founded 1474). The ancient Caesarea Augusta, it later was the cap. of a Moorish emirate (1017–1118). In the Peninsular War, Saragossa under the leadership of PALAFOX heroically repulsed the first French siege (1808) but surrendered after c.50,000 defenders had died in the second siege (1808–9). Many of the city's rich works of art show Moorish influence. There are two cathedrals—La Seo (12th–16th cent.), a former mosque, and El Pilar, with frescoes by Velázquez and Goya. Other monuments include Aljaferia castle (Moorish; later royal residence).

Sarah or **Sara** [Heb.,= princess], wife of Abraham, mother of Isaac. Her original name of Sarai was changed to Sarah when Abram became Abraham. Her jealousy drove HAGAR into the desert. Gen. 11.31-23.20; Rom. 4.19; 9.9; Heb. 11.11; 1 Peter 3.6.

Sarah Lawrence College: see EASTCHESTER, N.Y.

Sarajevo (să"rä'yĕvô), city (pop. 118,158), cap. of Bosnia and Hercegovina, central Yugoslavia, in Bosnia. Trade and railroad center; tobacco, carpet, and other mfg. See of Orthodox Eastern Metropolitan, Roman Catholic archbishop, and chief ulema of Yugoslav Moslems. Fell to Turkey 1429. Shared history of BOSNIA AND HERZEGOVINA after 1878. Assassination of Archduke FRANCIS FERDINAND here (June 28, 1914) was immediate cause of World War I. City has largely Moslem population.

Saranac Lake (să'rùnăk), village (pop. 6,913), N N.Y., SW of Plattsburg, in the Adirondacks on Flower L. and near Saranac Lakes. Health and year-round resort. Has tuberculosis sanatorium (1884) and research laboratory (1894) founded by E. L. Trudeau; Will Rogers Memorial Sanatorium (1930).

Saranac Lakes, N N.Y., three resort lakes in the Adirondacks. Upper (c.8 mi. long), Middle (c.2 mi. long), Lower (c.5 mi. long) lakes linked by Saranac R., which flows c.50 mi. NE to L. Champlain.

Sarasate, Pablo de (pä'blō dä säräsä'tä), 1844–1908, Spanish violin virtuoso. He wrote many brilliant violin pieces in a Spanish idiom (e.g., *Jota Aragonesa* and *Zigeunerweisen*).

Sarasota (să"rùsō'tù), city (pop. 18,896), SW Fla., on Sarasota Bay S of Tampa; settled c.1884 by Scotch. Winter resort. Packs and ships citrus fruit and vegetables (esp. celery). Fishing. The John and Mable Ringling Mus. of Art and winter hq. of Ringling Brothers–Barnum and Bailey Circus are here. Holds annual Sara de Sota pageant.

Saratoga campaign (să″rŭtŏ′gŭ), June–Oct., 1777, of American Revolution. British planned three-fold advance–S from Canada, N from New York city, and E along the Mohawk–to split colonies along the Hudson by meeting at Albany. Force advancing N never arrived at Albany. Barry St. Leger, coming E, besieged Fort Stanwix but retreated to Canada before Benedict Arnold's advance. John Burgoyne, coming from N, captured Ticonderoga, was beaten at Bennington, and halted near present Saratoga Springs. American forces, commanded by Horatio Gates, prevented break-through of British at Freeman's Farm and Bemis Heights; Burgoyne surrendered Oct. 17, 1777. Battle was first great American victory of war. Battlefield included in Saratoga Natl. Historical Park (estab. 1948).

Saratoga Springs, city (pop. 15,473), E N.Y., near Saratoga L., N of Albany. Health and pleasure resort with mineral springs; state-owned spa (1935) contains curative baths, Simon Baruch Research Inst. Bottles and ships springs' waters. Mfg. of chemicals, textiles, wallpaper. Horse racing after 1850. Seat of Skidmore Col. (nonsectarian; chiefly for women; men admitted 1946; chartered and opened 1911; chartered as a college 1922). Last battles of SARATOGA CAMPAIGN fought near by.

Saratov (sŭră′tŭf), city (pop. c.450,000), SE European RSFSR; a port on high right bank of the Volga. Major industrial center (machinery, chemicals, and textile plants; oil refineries; lumber mills; shipyards). Its important natural gas wells, discovered in World War II, were linked 1946 by pipe line with Moscow. Founded 1590 on left river bank; moved to present site 1674. University founded 1919.

Sarawak (sŭră′wŭk), British crown colony (47,071 sq. mi.; pop. 546,385), NW Borneo; cap. Kuching. Produces oil, rubber, rice, sago, and pepper. In 1841 sultan of Brunan ceded area to James Brooke, an Englishman, who became raja of independent state. As British protectorate (1888–1946) Sarawak was ruled by Brooke family. Occupied 1941–45 by Japanese. Became a colony in 1946.

Sarazen, Gene (să′rŭzŭn), 1901–, American golfer. Won U.S. Open (1922, 1932), British Open (1932), Professional Golfers Association (1922–23, 1933) and many other championships.

sarcoma (särkō′mŭ), malignant tumor composed of connective-type cells. Grows very large and spreads through tissues and along blood vessels and nerves.

Sardanapalus (särdŭnă′pŭlŭs), Assyrian monarch, who, after being besieged in Nineveh by the Medes for two years, burned his palace and himself. Some identify him with Assur-bani-pal.

sardine (särdēn′), name for various small fish canned with oil or sauce. True sardine is usually young pilchard (*Sardinia pilchardus*) of Mediterranean and warm Atlantic coastal waters. Young sprat and herring are also packed as sardines.

Sardinia (särdĭ′nĕŭ), Ital. *Sardegna*, island and autonomous region (9,302 sq. mi.; pop. 1,034,206), Italy, in the W Mediterranean; cap. Cagliari. The Strait of Bonifacio separates it from Corsica (N). Mostly mountainous (max. alt. 6,016 ft.), Sardinia has large pasture lands (horses, sheep, goats), minerals (zinc, lead, lignite), some agr., and important fisheries. Malaria and feudalism (abolished 1835) hampered its development until recent times, when reclamation projects were undertaken. Sardinia was settled by Carthaginians before its conquest by Rome (238 B.C.). It fell to the Vandals 5th cent. A.D.; was recovered by Byzantium 6th cent. The popes, however, claimed it as their patrimony (see PAPAL STATES) and acted as overlords. With their help, Sardinia repulsed Arab attacks (8th–11th cent.). Pisa and Genoa fought

through the 11th–14th cent. for supremacy over the island, but in the 14th cent. the pope bestowed it on the house of Aragon. Sardinia remained Spanish until 1713, when it passed to Austria by the Peace of Utrecht. Spain forcibly recovered it in 1717 but was obliged by the QUADRUPLE ALLIANCE to give it up (1720). It was then awarded to the duke of Savoy, who took the title king of Sardinia. The **kingdom of Sardinia** comprised SAVOY, PIEDMONT, NICE, Sardinia, and (after 1815) LIGURIA (incl. Genoa). Its cap. was Turin. Sardinia's defeat in the French Revolutionary Wars led to the annexation (1798–1814) of all its mainland possessions to France. Sardinia, especially under VICTOR EMMANUEL II, played the leading part in the Italian RISORGIMENTO. After annexing Lombardy (1859), Parma, Modena, and the N part of the Papal States (1860), and the Two Sicilies (1861), it became the kingdom of Italy. See also SAVOY, HOUSE OF.

Sardis (sär′dĭs), cap. of anc. Lydia, W Asia Minor. It was captured by the Persians with the conquest of Lydia. The city was finally destroyed by Tamerlane. Hittite inscriptions have been found here. Also Sardes.

Sardou, Victorien (vĕktôryē′ särdōō′), 1831–1908, French dramatist, author of some 70 popular plays ranging from light comedy to elaborate historical pieces. Best-known are *La Tosca* (1887; Eng. tr., 1925) and *Madame Sans-Gêne* (1893; Eng. tr., 1901).

Sargasso Sea (särgă′sō), part of N Atlantic Ocean, extending between West Indies and the Azores, from about lat. 20° N to lat. 35° N. Relatively still, it is the center of a swirl of ocean currents and is a rich field for marine biologists.

Sargent, John Singer, 1856–1925, American painter, b. Florence, Italy, of American parents. Educated in Europe. Spent early period in Paris, where first exhibit (1878) brought him recognition as a portraitist. In 1884 he moved to London, where he painted the portraits of American and English celebrities for which he is famous. Also produced many impressionistic landscapes in water color.

Sargon (sär′gŏn), fl. c.2800? B.C., king of Akkad or Agade in Mesopotamia. Conquered much territory and created a loose-knit empire. His dynasty seems to have spread Semitic and Sumerian civilization. Also Sharrukin.

Sargon, d. 705 B.C., king of Assyria (722–705 B.C.). He is supposed to have completed Shalmaneser's conquest of Samaria, and he certainly pushed conquests, taking Carchemish, subduing Babylon, and going E into Kurdistan. Won a great victory at Raphia (720). His palace of Dur Sharrukin (Khorsabad) was notably magnificent.

Sark, Fr. *Sercq* (sĕrk), island (2 sq. mi.; pop. 560), in English Channel, one of CHANNEL ISLANDS.

Sarmatia (särmā′shŭ), district about the lower Don R., occupied by the Sarmatians 3d cent. B.C.–2d cent. A.D. The area to which they were driven by the Germans, along the Danube and across the Carpathians, is also called Sarmatia. The **Sarmatians** were pastoral nomads related to the Scythians, whom they displaced in the Don region. Main divisions were Rhoxolani, Iazyges, and Alani. They spoke an Indo-Iranian language. They long warred against the Romans, then sought Roman help against the Germans, who forced them out.

Sarmiento, Domingo Faustino (dōmēng′gō foustē′nō särmyän′tō), 1811–88, Argentine statesman, educator, and author, president of republic (1868–74). Exiled as an opponent of Rosas, he was impressed in his travels with the educational system of the U.S. and after the downfall of Rosas (1852), he returned to Argentina and upon becoming president, effected educational reforms in Argentina patterned after U.S. school system. Best-known literary work is *Facundo*, a study of the *caudillo* as a type.

Sarnath (särnät′), archaeological site, SE Uttar Pradesh, India, near Benares. The deer park, traditional site where Buddha first preached, is located here.

Sarnia, city (pop. 34,697), S Ont., Canada, on St. Clair R., at S end of L. Huron opposite Port Huron, Mich. (connected by bridge, tunnel, and ferries); settled 1833 as The Rapids. Port and oil-refining center with steel, lumber, and flour mills.

Saronic Gulf (sŭrŏ'nĭk), inlet of Aegean Sea, W central Greece, bounded by Attica (NE), Isthmus of Corinth (N), Argolis peninsula (SW). Isthmian Canal connects it with Gulf of Corinth. Piraeus is among cities on Saronic Gulf, which also contains many islands (e.g., Aegina and Salamis). Also known as Gulf of Aegina.

Saroyan, William (sŭroi'ŭn), 1908–, American short-story writer and dramatist. Best known for short stories (e.g., those in *The Daring Young Man on the Flying Trapeze,* 1934) and semiautobiographical *My Name Is Aram* (1940). *The Time of Your Life* (1939) is his best-known play.

Sarre: see SAAR; SAAR TERRITORY.

Sarrebruck, Saar Territory: see SAARBRÜCKEN.

Sars, Michael (mēkäl' särs'), 1805–69, Norwegian biologist and pioneer in marine research.

sarsaparilla (särs"pŭrĭl'ù), name for various plants and the extract from their roots, used in medicine and beverages. True sarsaparilla is obtained from tropical species of *Smilax,* and a substitute from wild sarsaparilla (*Aralia nudicaulis*) of North America.

Sartain, John (särtān'), 1808–97, American engraver, b. London. In 1830 he came to U.S., where he pioneered in mezzotint engraving. His pupils included his daughter, **Emily Sartain,** 1841–1927, and two sons, **Samuel Sartain,** 1830–1906, and **William Sartain,** 1843–1924.

Sarthe (särt), department (2,411 sq. mi.; pop. 412,214), NW France, in Maine; cap. Le Mans. It is crossed by the **Sarthe** R., 175 mi. long, which joins with the Mayenne R., above Angers, to form the Maine R.

Sarto, Andrea del (ändrä'ä dĕl sär'tō), 1486–1531, Florentine painter, equally famous for his frescoes and his oils. His work is marked by sumptuous color and monumental composition. Notable paintings include *Madonna of the Harpies* (Uffizi) and *Holy Family* (Metropolitan Mus.).

Sartre, Jean Paul (zhä' pôl' sär'trù), 1905–, French philosopher and writer. Noted as originator of EXISTENTIALISM, expounded in *L'Être et le néant* (1943) and *Existentialism* (1946). Has written novels (e.g., *Nausea,* 1938; *Age of Reason,* 1945), and dramas (e.g., *The Flies,* 1943; *No Exit,* 1944; *The Respectful Prostitute,* 1946.

Sarum, England: see OLD SARUM; SALISBURY.

Sasanidae or **Sasanians:** see SASSANIDAE.

Sasebo (säsä'bō), city (pop. 175,233), W Kyushu, Japan; naval base on East China Sea.

Saskatchewan (sŭskă'chùwŭn), province (237,975 sq. mi.; with water surface 251,700 sq. mi.; pop. 831,-728), W Canada; cap. REGINA. Largest other cities are SASKATOON, MOOSE JAW, and PRINCE ALBERT. Abundant mineral resources, including pitchblende-yielding ore of high uranium content, are encouraging development in MACKENZIE R.–L. ATHABASKA area of N Sask. Parklands of central Sask. have large timber resources, much of it in PRINCE ALBERT NATIONAL PARK. Most settlement is S on prairies well-suited to large-scale mechanized farming (wheat, ranching, dairying). First explored by white men in late 17th cent. French fur-trading posts estab. in mid-18th cent. Later North West and Hudson's Bay companies operated here. Dominion bought territorial rights from Hudson's Bay Co. 1870, when area became part of Northwest Territories. Saw rebellion of Louis RIEL 1884–85. Farm settlement, aided by free land grants, followed arrival of Canadian Pacific RR 1882. Political experimentation under CO-OPERATIVE COMMONWEALTH FEDERATION has promoted farm and labor legislation.

Saskatchewan, river of W Canada, formed E of Prince Albert, Sask., by confluence of North Saskatchewan and South Saskatchewan rivers. Flows 340 mi. E to L. Winnipeg, Man. The North Saskatchewan rises at foot of Mt. Saskatchewan, SW Alta. flows E 760 mi. South Saskatchewan R. forms in S Alta. by confluence of Bow and Oldman rivers, flows 550 mi. (with the Bow 865 mi.) E then NE to junction with North Saskatchewan R. Was chief transportation route of old Northwest Territories before railroad.

Saskatchewan, University of: see SASKATOON.

Saskatoon, city (pop. 53,268), S central Sask., Canada, on South Saskatchewan R. and NW of Regina; laid out 1883. Mfg. and trade center for central and N Sask. with grain elevators, stockyards, breweries, and meat-packing, wood, and metal-working plants. Seat of Univ. of Saskatchewan (provincially supported; coed.; 1909).

sassafras (să'sùfrăs"), tree or shrub (*Sassafras albidum*) of E North America with entire, two- or three-lobed leaves. Bark from the roots is used to make sassafras tea and root beers.

Sassafras Mountain, peak, 3,560 ft. high, NW S.C., in the Blue Ridge. State's highest point.

Sassanidae (săsă'nĭdē), **Sassanids** (să'sùnĭdz), or **Sassanians** (săsā'nyùnz), last dynasty of native rulers to reign in Persia (A.D. c.226–c.640). Ctesiphon was its capital. The name (also spelled Sasanidae or Sasanian) derives from Sassan, an ancestor of dynasty's founder, ARDASHIR I. Sassanids were much occupied with wars, especially with Rome and Byzantium. Overthrown by the Arabs. Notable rulers were SHAPUR I, SHAPUR II, and KHOSRU II.

Sassoon, Siegfried (sùsōōn'), 1886–, English poet and novelist. After World War I he wrote powerful anti-war novels collected in *The Memoirs of George Sherston* (1937) and vigorous lyrics (in *Collected Poems,* 1949).

Satalia or **Satalieh:** see ANTALYA, Turkey.

Satan (sā'tùn) [Heb.,= adversary], in Judaism, Christianity, and Islam, the principle of evil conceived as a person. Also called the devil [from Gr.,= accuser]. Originally an angel, he rebelled against God and fell from heaven to eternal damnation. He presides over hell and is served by minor angels (called devils) who fell with him. To Satan is ascribed the origin of evil; he is the destroyer of souls and tempter of man to sin. He is the subject of much popular legend. Among literary representations of him are the Mephistopheles of Goethe's *Faust* and the Lucifer of Milton's *Paradise Lost.* Names and nicknames of Satan are legion, e.g., Abaddon, Apollyon, Dragon, Serpent, Lucifer, Asmodeus (see TOBIT), Beelzebub or Baalzebub, and Belial. Antichrist is not a proper name of Satan. There are many references in Bible to Satan: 1 Chron. 21.1; Job 1; 2; Zech. 3.2; Isa. 14.12; Mat. 4.1; 9.34; 10.25; 12.22–30; 13.13,39; 25.41; Mark 3.22–30; Luke 10.18; 11.14–26; John 8.44; 12.31; 14.30; 16.11; Acts 26.18; 2 Cor. 2.11; 4.4; 11.14; Eph. 2.2; 1 Thess. 3.5; Jude 6; and the book of REVELATION.

satellite (să'tùlīt), in astronomy, smaller celestial body revolving about a planet or star and shining only by reflected light. All planets except Mercury, Venus, and Pluto have one or more known satellites, most of them moving eastward in almost circular orbits, but a few having retrograde motion. Earth's only satellite, the moon, is largest in relation to its planet.

Satie, Erik (sätē'), 1866–1925, French composer. He rebelled against romanticism and impressionism in music and urged a return to simplicity in style. He gathered around himself a group of young composers —Poulenc, Honegger, Georges Auric (1899–), Louis Durey (1888–), Germaine Tailleferre (1892–), and Milhaud—who were to become known as *Les Six.* Satie himself wrote ballet and film music and piano pieces, including the popular *Gymnopédies.*

satin, lustrous fabric, usually silk, with the filling arranged so that practically nothing shows but warp.

First made in China, it was made in Europe after secrets of silk making were carried westward in the Middle Ages.

satinwood, hard, durable wood with satinlike sheen, used in cabinetmaking, especially in marquetry. East Indian or Ceylon satinwood, the heartwood of *Chloroxylon swietenia,* is used for furniture and veneers. West Indian satinwood, also called yellowwood, the wood of *Zanthoxylum* (or *Xanthoxylum*) *flavum,* is superior.

satire, term applied to any literary form, in prose or poetry, which ridicules situations, individuals, or ideas. Its purpose is to correct manners and morals through mockery, broad humor, sophisticated wit, harsh invective, parody, or gentle irony. It may be humorous or serious, but object is generally made to seem ridiculous rather than evil.

Satsuma (sätsoō'mä), peninsula, SW Kyushu, Japan. Was domain of powerful Satsuma clan and scene of Takamori Saigo's unsuccessful revolt (1877) against imperial government. Famous porcelain, Satsuma ware, made here.

Satterlee, Henry Yates, 1843–1908, American Episcopal bishop; first bishop of diocese of Washington D.C. (1896). Planned and began National or Washington Cathedral.

Satu-Mare (sä'too-mä're), Hung. *Szatmárnémeti* or *Szatmár,* city (pop. 46,519), NW Rumania, near Hungarian border. Commercial center; textile and machinery mfg. Population is c.60% Hungarian.

Saturday: see SABBATH; WEEK.

Saturn, in Roman religion, god of harvest; husband of Ops and father of Ceres. His festival was **Saturnalia;** work ceased, gifts were exchanged, and slaves could do as they pleased.

Saturn, in astronomy, planet sixth in order of distance from sun. Revolves about sun at mean distance of 886,120,000 mi. in c.30 years. Equatorial diameter is c.75,000 mi. Vaporous surface is indicated by latitudinal variations in rotation period (shortest at equator, c.10 hr. 14 min.). Has atmosphere and nine known satellites. Unique feature is system of rings composed of swarms of particles moving in individual orbits and encircling the planet in its equatorial plane. System comprises inner and outer bright rings separated by dark rift (Cassini's division) and a faint inner area (crape ring). Extreme diameter of ring system is c.172,000 mi.; thickness, 10–50 mi. See *ill.,* p. 927.

Saturnalia: see SATURN, in Roman religion.

satyr, in Greek mythology, one of a tribe of creatures inhabiting forests and mountains. A lesser deity of fertility and a follower of Dionysus, he was fond of revelry and mischief. He is pictured as a hairy little man, with tail and goatlike ears.

Saud, Ibn: see IBN SAUD.

Saudi Arabia (säoō'dē ūrä'bēu), kingdom (600,000 sq. mi.; pop. c.6,000,000), SW Asia, occupying most of Arabian peninsula. Its two capitals are RIAD and MECCA. Bounded on N by Jordan, Iraq, and Kuwait, on E by Persian Gulf, on W by Red Sea, and on S by the desert Rub al Khali. In the HEJAZ are the holy cities of Mecca and MEDINA. Basic economy is agr. and pastoral, but country's wealth lies in its oil industry, having perhaps the world's largest oil reserves. Arabian American Oil Co. (organized in Delaware) has held the oil concession since 1933. Saudi Arabia had its beginnings in 1925, when IBN SAUD, then king of the NEJD, formally annexed the Hejaz. His rule was recognized by Great Britain in 1927, and the name Saudi Arabia was adopted in 1932. Belongs to the UN and the Arab League.

Sauer, Christopher: see SOWER, CHRISTOPHER.

Saugus (sô'gŭs), town (pop. 17,162), NE Mass., N of Boston; settled before 1637. Saugus ironworks (1645) were first successful ones in the colonies.

Sauk Centre (sôk), city (pop. 3,140), central Minn., WNW of St. Cloud. Birthplace of Sinclair Lewis, who used it as model for town in *Main Street.*

Sauk Indians: see SAC AND FOX INDIANS.

Saul [Heb.,= asked for], fl. 1025 B.C., first king of the Hebrews. Saul was heroic in battle but proved himself unworthy of kingship by willful and foolish actions. He tried to destroy the rising star of David, his former protégé, who usurped his place, first in the hearts of the people and then on the throne itself. Adding to Saul's bitterness was the great friendship between his son Jonathan and David. Saul fell in battle on Mt. Gilboa. 1 Sam. 10–31.

Sault Sainte Marie (soō' sänt mûrē'), city (pop. 32,452), S Ont., Canada, on St. Marys R. opposite Sault Ste Marie, Mich. (connected by railroad bridge and ferry). Government canal and lock completed here 1895. Port with ore docks and steel, pulp, paper, and lumber mills. Tourist center and gateway to hunting and fishing region.

Sault Sainte Marie, city (pop. 17,912), E Upper Peninsula, N Mich., on St. Mary's R. opposite Sault Ste Marie, Ontario. Region named 1641 by French missionaries. Père Marquette estab. mission here 1668; this was followed by fur-trading posts. Fort Brady, built here after Lewis Cass negotiated treaty with Indians (1820), served until end of World War II. Present canals and locks link lakes Superior and Huron on Mich. side. City connected to Ont. by railroad bridge and ferry. Resort and shipping center with hydroelectric plants and mfg. of carbide, leather, and foundry products. Has U.S. Coast Guard station.

Saumur (sōmür'), town (pop. 14,885), Maine-et-Loire dept., W France, on Loire R. Noted for sparkling wine and for its cavalry school (estab. 18th cent.). Huguenot center in 16th–17th cent. Has early 12th-cent. church, 16th-cent. town hall. City was damaged in World War II.

Saurashtra (souräsh'trù), state (21,062 sq. mi.; pop. 4,136,005), W India; cap. Rajkot. Comprises major portion of Kathiawar peninsula.

sausage, food made of chopped meat, seasonings, and often other ingredients, usually packed into casings made of cleaned intestines or of cellulose, and sometimes pickled, smoked, or boiled. Over a hundred kinds are known; some, such as English black pudding, are of great antiquity. Popular in U.S. are frankfurters and wienerwursts, pork sausage, salami, and Bologna sausage.

Sausalito (sô"sülē'tù), residential city (pop. 4,828), W Calif., N of San Francisco across the Golden Gate. Shipyards built here in World War II.

Saussure, Horace Bénédict de (ôräs' bānādēkt' dù sōsür'), 1740–99, Swiss physicist and geologist. He made studies of the geology, meteorology, and botany of European mountain regions, particularly the Alps, which he described in his *Voyages dans les Alpes* (4 vols., 1779–96). His son, **Nicolas Théodore de Saussure** (nēkôlä' tāōdôr'), 1767–1845, was a chemist and plant physiologist, known especially for work on plant respiration and on fermentation.

Sava (sä'vä) or **Save** (säv), river, 583 mi. long, N Yugoslavia, rising in Julian Alps and flowing SE past Ljubljana and Zagreb into the Danube at Belgrade. Sava basin is fertile agr. region.

Savage, Richard, 1697?–1743, English poet. Now discredited story of his illegitimate noble descent and persecutions, set forth in a biography by Dr. Johnson, won him reputation his works did not merit.

Savage's Station: see SEVEN DAYS BATTLES.

Savaii (sävī'ē), volcanic island (703 sq. mi.; pop. 18,654), Western SAMOA, under New Zealand mandate; largest and most westerly of Samoan isls. Tuasivi is seat of resident commissioner.

Savanna (suvä'nù), city (pop. 5,058), NW Ill., on the Mississippi (bridged) above Clinton, Iowa. Trade and shipping center in rich agr. area.

Savannah. 1 City (pop. 119,638), SE Ga., port on Savannah R. near its mouth on the Atlantic. A major market for naval stores, it also has mfg. of pulp and paper, chemicals, and metal products; a sugar refinery; shipyards; seafood and truck canneries. Winter resort. Oldest and second largest city of Ga., founded 1733 by OGLETHORPE, it was colonial seat of government and later state cap. (1782–85). British captured and held it until Dec. 29, 1778, in the American Revolution. Trade grew after Revolution and War of 1812. The *Savannah,* first steamship to cross the Atlantic, sailed from here to Liverpool in 1819. Fort PULASKI, now a national monument, captured by Federals 1862, but city did not fall until Dec. 21, 1864, when Sherman ended his march to the sea here. Has Christ Episcopal Church (1838) and co-cathedral of St. John the Baptist (R.C.; 1876). **2** Town (pop. 1,698), S Tenn., on Tennessee R. and SE of Jackson. Nearby are Shiloh Natl. Military Park, Shiloh Natl. Cemetery (see SHILOH, BATTLE OF), and Pickwick Dam.

Savannah, river formed by confluence of Tugaloo and Seneca rivers, and forming part of Ga.-S.C. line. Flows 314 mi. SE to Tybee Sound, arm of the Atlantic. Has Clark Hill Dam.

Save, river, Yugoslavia: see SAVA.

Savigny, Friedrich Karl von (frē′drĭkh kärl′ fŭn sä′vĭnyē), 1779–1861, German jurist, teacher of Roman law at the Univ. of Berlin (1810–42). His works on Roman law are models of historical research.

Savile, Sir Henry (sä′vĭl), 1549–1622, English classical scholar and mathematician. He translated four books of Tacitus' history (1591), edited St. John Chrysostom (8 vols., 1610–13), and was a translator of the Bible under King James. At Oxford he founded chairs of geometry and astronomy.

Saville, Marshall Howard (sŭvĭl′), 1867–1935, American archaeologist, an authority on Mayan ruins.

Savoie (sävwä′), department (2,389 sq. mi.; pop. 235,939), E France, in SAVOY; cap. Chambéry.

Savoie, Haute: see HAUTE-SAVOIE.

Savo Island: see SOLOMON ISLANDS.

Savona (sävō′nä), city (pop. 57,354), Liguria, NW Italy; a Mediterranean port. Heavy industries.

Savonarola, Girolamo (jērō′lämō sävōnärō′lä), 1452–98, Italian religious reformer. A Dominican, he was sent to Florence, where his burning eloquence and direct attack on all sorts of moral laxity made him a popular preacher. He also foretold events, sometimes with success. When the Medici were exiled (1494), he became the virtual ruler of Florence, where he imposed a rigidly Puritan regime. Horrified at the immorality at the court of Pope Alexander VI, he allied Florence with Alexander's opponent, Charles VIII of France. Alexander silenced him, but he resumed preaching, and was excommunicated (1497). He then denounced Alexander. Matters reached a point of great tension, with rioting in Florence. City officials arrested him and put him to the torture. He was said to have confessed being a false prophet and was hanged.

Savoy, Prince Eugene of: see EUGENE OF SAVOY.

Savoy (sŭvoi′), Fr. *Savoie,* Alpine region, E France, bordering on Italy and Switzerland; historic cap. Chambéry. It is divided into Haute-Savoie dept. (cap. Annecy), with MONT BLANC and the S shore of L. of Geneva; and Savoie dept., with Chambéry and Aix-les-Bains. Dairying, agr., tourist trade. Conquered for Rome by Julius Caesar, Savoy later was part of the successive kingdoms of BURGUNDY and ARLES. It was split into many fiefs when the first counts of Savoy appeared in the 11th cent. Its history became that of the **house of Savoy,** which through conquest, exchange, and marriage acquired most of PIEDMONT (now Italy); the lower VALAIS, GENEVA, and VAUD (now Switzerland); BRESSE, Bugey, Gex, and NICE (now France). AMADEUS VIII took the title duke in 1416. By 1536 Savoy had lost its Swiss holdings. In that year Francis I of France occupied the rest of the duchy, which, however, was restored to EMMANUEL PHILIBERT in 1559. Turin replaced Chambéry as cap., but French remained the official lan-

guage. Later dukes took part in the major wars of the 17th–18th cent., repeatedly changing sides. The Peace of Utrecht (1713–14) gave them Sicily, which they exchanged for Sardinia in 1720. Thus the kingdom of SARDINIA came into existence. In 1831 the cadet line of Savoy-Carignano succeeded the senior line on the throne. The family had by now shifted its orientation from France to Italy. Under CHARLES ALBERT it identified itself with the Italian RISORGIMENTO, which led to the unification of Italy under his son VICTOR EMMANUEL II. Savoy itself, which is French-speaking, was annexed to France 1792, restored to Sardinia 1815, and again ceded to France 1860 (in return for French aid against Austria). Later kings of Italy of Savoy line were HUMBERT I, VICTOR EMMANUEL III, HUMBERT II (abdicated 1946).

Savoy, the, chapel in London, between the Strand and the Thames. Completed 1511, it is sole remaining part of palace built c.1245 by Peter of Savoy. Near by is the **Savoy Theatre,** built (1881) by D'Oyly Carte for Gilbert and Sullivan operas.

saw, cutting tool, usually with flat, toothed blade. Stone saws were used in Neolithic period. Types include circular saw; band saw, running like belt over two wheels; and cylinder or drum saw for making circular cut. Teeth usually are bent outward alternately in opposite directions to make cut wider than blade to eliminate binding.

Sawatch Mountains (sŭwŏch′), high range of Rocky Mts., W central Colo., extending c.110 mi. S from Eagle R. to near Saguache. Arkansas R. is on E, Elk Mts. on W. Includes three highest peaks of U.S. Rockies: Mt. Elbert, 14,431 ft.; Mt. Massive, 14,418 ft.; in Collegiate Range, Mt. Harvard, 14,399 ft.

sawfish, sharklike ray fish of most warm seas. It enters the Mississippi and rivers of Africa, India. Upper jaw has flat extension (up to 6 ft. long, 1 ft. wide) with row of strong, toothlike structures.

sawfly, insect of order Hymenoptera resembling wasp. Female saws with ovipositor into plant tissues to deposit eggs. Some species produce galls.

Sawtooth Mountains, central Idaho, NE of Boise. Castle Peak is 11,820 ft. high. Mt. Hyndman (12,078 ft.) and Ryan Peak (11,900 ft.) are in Pioneer Mts., sometimes considered part of Sawtooth Mts.

Sax, Charles Joseph (säks′), 1791–1865, Belgian maker of musical instruments. His son, **Adolphe (Antoine Joseph) Sax,** 1814–94, designed the saxhorn, the saxophone, and the saxotromba.

Saxe, Maurice, comte de (mōrēs′ kŏt′ dù säks′), 1696–1750, marshal of France; natural son of Augustus II of Poland and Saxony by Countess Königsmark. Entered French service 1720. A brilliant commander, he won the great victory at FONTENOY (1745). He wrote *Mes Rêveries* (1757), a remarkable work on the art of war.

Saxe-Altenburg (säks′-ăl′tùnbûrg), Ger. *Sachsen-Altenburg,* former duchy, central Germany; cap. Altenburg. A possession of WETTIN dynasty (Ernestine line), it passed to SAXE-GOTHA 1672; was separate duchy 1826–1918; was incorporated into Thuringia 1920.

Saxe-Coburg (-kō′bûrg), Ger. *Sachsen-Coburg,* former duchy, central Germany; cap. Coburg. A possession of WETTIN dynasty (Ernestine line), it was detached from SAXE-GOTHA 1679; passed to collateral branch of dukes of Saxe-Saalfeld 1699. In 1826 Ernest III of Saxe-Coburg gave Saalfeld to SAXE-MEININGEN, received Saxe-Gotha, and became Grand Duke ERNEST I of **Saxe-Coburg-Gotha** (-gō′thù). His brother was Leopold I, king of the Belgians; his younger son, Prince Albert, married Queen Victoria of England. The family was deposed 1918; Gotha was incorporated into Thuringia, Coburg into Bavaria.

Saxe-Eisenach: see SAXE-WEIMAR.

Saxe-Gotha (-gō′thù), Ger. *Sachsen-Gotha,* former duchy, Thuringia, central Germany; cap. Gotha. A possession of WETTIN dynasty (Ernestine line), it was united with Saxe-Altenburg 1672. In 1679, on the death of Duke Ernest the Pious, Gotha and Altenburg passed to Ernest's oldest son; Saxe-Coburg went to a younger son. The Saxe-Gotha line died out in 1825; Gotha passed to Saxe-Coburg in 1826, while Altenburg continued under a collateral branch.

Saxe-Meiningen (–mī′nĭng-ŭn), Ger. *Sachsen-Meiningen,* former duchy, central Germany; cap. MEININGEN. A possession of WETTIN dynasty (Ernestine line) it became a separate duchy in 17th cent. and in 1826 also received Saalfeld (see SAXE-COBURG). Last duke abdicated 1918. Joined state of Thuringia 1920.

Saxe-Saalfeld: see SAXE-COBURG.

Saxe-Weimar (–vī′mär), Ger. *Sachsen-Weimar,* former duchy, Thuringia, central Germany; cap. WEIMAR. When Saxony was redivided in 1547, the Ernestine line of WETTIN dynasty retained only its Thuringian possessions. These were divided among the sons of John Frederick, former elector of Saxony, into several duchies, of which Saxe-Weimar was the most important. The duchies were repeatedly redivided among the several collateral lines. In 1741 the duchy of Saxe-Eisenach (incl. Jena) was united with Saxe-Weimar, which thus became the duchy (after 1815, grand duchy) of **Saxe-Weimar-Eisenach** (–ī′zŭnäkh). Duke CHARLES AUGUSTUS, patron and friend of Goethe, had considerable political influence in the Napoleonic era. The last grand duke abdicated 1918; the grand duchy was incorporated into Thuringia 1920.

saxifrage (săk′sĭfrĭj), low, rock-loving perennial of genus *Saxifraga* with tufts or rosettes of leaves and clusters of small flowers in spring. Most species are prized for gardens, especially rock gardens, but the strawberry geranium (*Saxifraga sarmentosa*), also called mother-of-thousands, is commonly grown as a house plant.

Saxo Grammaticus (săk′sō grŭmă′tĭkŭs), fl. 1188–1201, Danish historian. Wrote *Gesta Danorum* in 16 books (Eng. tr., Books I–IX, 1894).

Saxons, Germanic people, first known to history in 2d cent. as living in area of Schleswig. In 3d and 4th cent. they spread into Roman territory, and in 5th cent. settled in N Gaul. They made many raids in SE Britain, finally settling there in 6th cent., and with Angles estab. Anglo-Saxon kingdoms such as Wessex. In Germany "Old Saxons" occupied NW area, and after Treaty of Verdun (843) formed core of section that was beginning of modern Germany.

Saxony (săk′sŭnē), Ger. *Sachsen,* name originally applied to the land inhabited in ancient and early medieval times by the SAXONS—i.e., roughly, present LOWER SAXONY, in NW Germany—and later given to several other political units. Late in the 9th cent. the first **duchy of Saxony,** comprising nearly all territory between the Elbe and the Rhine, emerged from the ruins of the Carolingian empire. In 919 Duke Henry I of Saxony was elected German king. His son, Emperor Otto I, founder of the Holy Roman Empire, bestowed Saxony on Hermann Billung (960). From the Billung dynasty the duchy passed (1137) to HENRY THE PROUD of Bavaria. His son, HENRY THE LION, was deprived of his duchies by Emperor Frederick I, who broke them up into smaller fiefs (1180). Henry's Guelphic descendants retained only BRUNSWICK (incl. the later kingdom of HANOVER). The ducal title of Saxony went to Bernard of Anhalt, a son of Albert the Bear of Brandenburg and founder of the Ascanian line of Saxon dukes. His dominions included ANHALT, LAUENBURG, and the country around WITTENBERG, which after 1260 were ruled by separate branches of the family. In 1356 the dukes of Saxe-Wittenberg received permanent rank of ELECTORS. Their territory, **Electoral Saxony,** along the middle Elbe, lay outside the original duchy, being part of the E march conquered from the Slavs. S of Electoral Saxony extended the margraviate of Meissen, ruled by the increasingly powerful house of WETTIN. The margraves acquired (13th–14th cent.)

most of THURINGIA and Lower LUSATIA, and in 1423 Margrave Frederick the Warlike also received Electoral Saxony. The Wettin lands were partitioned (1485) between two brothers—Ernest, founder of the Ernestine line of Wettin, received Electoral Saxony and most of Thuringia; Albert, founder of the Albertine line, received ducal rank and the Meissen territories (incl. Dresden and Leipzig). Electors FREDERICK III and JOHN FREDERICK I were Protestant leaders. After his defeat at Mühlberg (1547), John Frederick lost the electorate to Duke MAURICE of Saxony, of the Albertine line; the Ernestine line kept only Thuringia. Electoral Saxony changed sides several times in the Thirty Years War and was thoroughly devastated but received advantageous terms at the peace (1648). From 1697 to 1763 the electors of Saxony were also kings of Poland as AUGUSTUS II and AUGUSTUS III. Under them, Saxony reached its cultural flowering, but it declined politically, being caught between its powerful neighbors, Prussia and Austria (see AUSTRIAN SUCCESSION, WAR OF THE; SEVEN YEARS WAR). Saxony sided staunchly with France in the Napoleonic Wars; in 1806 it became the **kingdom of Saxony** under FREDERICK AUGUSTUS I. The king's loyalty to Napoleon cost him half his kingdom at the Congress of Vienna (1814–15). Defeated by Prussia in the AUSTRO-PRUSSIAN WAR of 1866, Saxony joined the North German Confederation and, in 1871, the German Empire. The last king of Saxony was deposed 1918, and in 1919 the country joined the Weimar Republic as the **state of Saxony** (6,561 sq. mi.; 1946 pop. 5,558,566), with DRESDEN its cap. Heavily industrialized (textiles, machinery), Saxony also has important mineral resources in the ERZGEBIRGE. LEIPZIG and CHEMNITZ are the chief commercial and mfg. centers. In 1949 the state joined the [East] German Democratic Republic. Most of the territories lost by Saxony in 1815 were merged with other Prussian possessions into the Prussian **province of Saxony** (9,853 sq. mi.; 1939 pop. 3,616,635), with Magdeburg its cap. This was united in 1946 with Anhalt to form the new state of SAXONY-ANHALT.

Saxony-Anhalt (–än′hält), Ger. *Sachsen-Anhalt,* state (9,515 sq. mi.; pop. 4,160,539), [East] German Democratic Republic; cap. Halle. Among other cities are Magdeburg, Dessau, Wittenberg, Eisleben. Formed 1946 in the Russian occupation zone from the former state of ANHALT and Prussian province of Saxony, it includes E part of HARZ mts. Its N section is largely agr. The state has important mineral resources (potash, coal, iron, copper) and industries (sugar, metallurgy, chemicals). It has no historic unity.

saxophone: see WIND INSTRUMENTS.

Say, Jean Baptiste (sā), 1767–1832, French economist. Reorganized and popularized theories of Adam Smith. Developed a theory of markets and concept of the entrepreneur.

Sayan Mountains (säyän′), central Asia, chiefly in RSFSR, in E Siberia. E Sayan Mts. rise to 11,453 ft., W Sayan Mts. to 9,180 ft. Yield gold, silver, lead, graphite, and coal.

Saybrook Platform: see CAMBRIDGE PLATFORM.

Saye and Sele, William Fiennes, 1st Viscount (fīnz, sā′ŭnsēl), 1582–1662, English statesman and promoter of colonization in America. A Puritan and leader in House of Lords against the king. Engaged (1630–44) in several colonization schemes (e.g., at Saybrook, Conn.). In Puritan Revolution, he pursued an independent course.

Sayers, Dorothy (Leigh) (sârz), 1893–, English writer of detective novels featuring the nobleman-detective Lord Peter Wimsey. Later devoted herself to religious poetry and prose.

Sayre, borough (pop. 7,735), NE Pa., NW of Towanda. Railroad shops. Mfg. of metal products.

Sayreville, borough (pop. 10,338), E N.J., on Raritan R., ESE of New Brunswick. Bricks, chemicals.

Sayville, resort village (pop. 4,251), on S Long Isl.,

SE N.Y., on Great South Bay. It is a yachting center.

Sazonov, Sergei Dmitreyevich (sĭrgā′ dùmē′trĕùvĭch sŭzô′nûf), 1861–1927, Russian foreign minister (1910–16). Urged Russian mobilization (July 29, 1914) at eve of World War I.

Sb, chemical symbol of the element ANTIMONY.

Sc, chemical symbol of the element SCANDIUM.

scabies (skă′bē-ēz, skă′bēz) or **itch,** contagious disease caused by penetration of skin by a mite. Occurs on hands and wrists, in armpit and groin, around anus.

scabiosa (skābēō′sù), annual or perennial plant (*Scabiosa*) native to Old World. It has lacy, flat-topped flowers in various colors. It is also called mourning bride, pincushion flower, and scabious.

Scaevola (sē′vôlù), Roman family name. **Caius Mucius Scaevola,** 6th cent.? B.C., legendary Roman hero. One story says that he tried to murder Lars Porsena, who was besieging Rome. Porsena condemned him to be burned at the stake, but when Scaevola thrust his hand into the flame and held it there Porsena was so impressed that he freed him and in face of such Roman courage gave up the siege. There are other stories of Porsena's change of heart. **Quintus Mucius Scaevola,** d. 82 B.C., was consul in 95 B.C. He and Crassus took citizenship away from many allies and helped bring on the Social War. He was pontifex maximus when he was killed in the proscription of Marius.

Scafell (skô′fĕl′) or **Scaw Fell,** mountain group, Cumberland, England, in Lake District. Includes Scafell (3,162 ft.), Scafell Pike (3,210 ft.; England's highest peak), Great End, and Lingmell.

Scala, Can Francesco della (kän′ fränchä′skō dĕl′lä skä′lä), or **Can Grande della Scala** (käng-grän′dä), 1291–1329, lord of Verona. As Ghibelline leader and imperial vicar, he fought the Guelphs and conquered a large part of Venetia (incl. Padua and Vicenza). He was a protector of Dante.

scalawags (skă′lùwăgz), opprobrious epithet used in the South after Civil War to describe native white Southerners who joined Republican party and aided RECONSTRUCTION program.

scalds: see BURNS.

scale, in cartography, ratio between distances on a map and those on earth's surface. Expressed numerically as a ratio or fraction; graphically, by recording mileage on a graduated line.

scale, in music, any series of tones arranged in rising or falling order of pitches. Since the 17th cent., the most common scale in Western music has been the diatonic scale which divides the octave into five whole tones and two half-tones as follows: major scale–1, 1, ½, 1, 1, 1, ½; minor scale–1, ½, 1, 1, ½, 1, 1. The pattern of tones and half-tones in a major or in a minor diatonic scale is always the same. The chromatic scale, which divides the octave into 12 equal half-tones, contains all the tonal material generally found in Western music. Since the end of the 19th cent., composers have experimented with whole-tone scales (C, D, E, F sharp, G sharp, A sharp) such as used by Debussy; five-tone scales (prevalent in Oriental music); quarter-tone scales (hence 24 tones in an octave and impossible on a modern keyboard instrument); and even up to 42-tone scales (which call for special instruments). See also EQUAL TEMPERAMENT; ATONALITY; TONE; and MODE.

scale, in weights and measures: see SCALES.

scale, in zoology, an outgrowth, bony or horny, of skin of animal. Scales characteristic of fish are bony. Teeth of vertebrates (from fish to man) are thought to be evolved from scales. Horny scales are found on most reptiles, on feet of birds, and on body of armadillo and pangolin. Some mammals have scales on the tail.

Scale Force, waterfall, c.120 ft. high, Cumberland, England, one of the finest of the Lake District.

scale insect, small sap-sucking insect of family Coccidae, destructive to many trees and greenhouse plants. Armored scale insects (e.g., cottony-cushion scale)

secrete protective wax covering; unarmored are protected by chitinized body wall. Ladybird beetle destroys scale insects.

scales, instrument for determining weight, generally for other than laboratory use. For the principles of operation of weighing devices see BALANCE. Platform scales, used for large objects, utilize a succession of multiplying levers which transmit weight to a beam or other registering device. Counter scales, used commercially, are largely of the beam type. Cylinder, drum, or barrel scales have their calibrations on a rotatable chart. A variety of scales are constructed for industrial uses in which continuous flow of material must be weighed.

Scaliger, Julius Caesar (skä′lĭjùr), 1484–1558, Italian philologist and physician in France. In his *De causis linguae Latinae* (1540) he analyzed Cicero's style and pointed out over 600 errors of his humanist predecessors. He wrote commentaries on medical and botanical works of Hippocrates, Theophrastus, and Aristotle and urged an improved classification of plants. His *Poetics* (1561) was important in creation of neoclassic principles. His son, **Joseph Justus Scaliger,** 1540–1609, was renowned for learning in mathematics, philosophy, languages, and critical methods. He did much work on the chronology of history. Was professor of philosophy at Geneva (1572–74), research professor at Leiden after 1593.

scallop (skŏ′lùp, skä′–), marine bivalve mollusk, with radially ridged shell, winged at side of hinge. Moves through water flapping shells. Adductor muscle (which closes shell) is edible.

scalping, taking the scalp of an enemy, a custom comparable to head-hunting. Formerly practiced in Europe, Asia, and Africa, as well as by some American Indians, who believed scalp bestowed on scalper some powers of the scalped enemy, dead or alive.

Scamander (skùmăn′dùr), anc. name of the Kucuk Menderes, a small river of NW Turkey, in Asia Minor. Flows W and NW from the Ida Mts. through the Troas into the Mediterranean.

scammony (skă′mùnē), twining plant (*Convolvulus scammonia*) of bindweed family, native to Asia Minor. Its taproot yields a resin used medicinally.

Scanderbeg (skăn′dùrbĕg), c.1404–1468, Albanian national hero, whose original name was George Castriota. Also known as Skanderbeg or Iskander Bey. Educated in the Moslem faith as a hostage of Sultan Murad II, he won the sultan's favor and was given a command with the title bey. In 1443 he fled home, abjured Islam, and proclaimed himself prince of Albania. He received Venetian support and was named captain general of an anti-Turkish Crusade by the pope (1457). Throughout his remaining years, he held out against the Turks—at the end virtually alone, in his fortress of Kroia. With his death, resistance collapsed.

Scandinavia, region of N Europe, comprising SWEDEN, NORWAY, and DENMARK and usually understood to include also FINLAND and ICELAND. The Scandinavian peninsula, occupied by Sweden and Norway, is washed by the Baltic Sea (E); the Kattegat, Skagerrak, and North Sea (S); the Atlantic Ocean (W); and the Arctic Ocean (N). Mountainous and indented by fjords in the W (Norway), it slopes down in the E and S (Sweden). Its N extremity is Cape Nordkyn. See articles on individual countries.

scandium (skăn′dēùm), metallic element of rare earths (symbol = Sc; see also ELEMENT, table). Occurs in compounds in rare minerals. Separation from its compounds is difficult.

Scania, Sweden: see SKANE.

Scapa Flow (skä′pù), area of water, c.15 mi. long and 8 mi. wide, in Orkney Isls., Scotland. Part of interned German fleet was scuttled here in 1919.

scarab (skă′rùb), name for certain members of a beetle family (Scarabaeidae), especially the dung beetle (*Scarabaeus sacer*), the Egyptian sacred scarab. Stone, metal, and faïence representations of beetle have long been used as symbols and seals.

Scaramouch (skă'rùmouch, –moŏsh), stock character in *commedia dell' arte,* a cowardly, boastful parody of grandiloquent Spanish don.

Scarboro or **Scarborough,** town (pop. 4,600), SW Maine, between Saco and Portland. Birthplace of Rufus King. Scarboro Beach and Prouts Neck resorts.

Scarborough, municipal borough (pop. 43,983), North Riding of Yorkshire, England; North Sea port and resort. Castle (12th cent.) was besieged many times. Has annual music festival and sports meet.

Scarlatti, Alessandro (skärlät'tē), b. 1658 or 1659, d. 1725, Italian composer. He developed the *aria de capo* and the Italian overture and wrote 115 operas, 200 Masses, and over 700 cantatas and oratorios. His son, **(Giuseppe) Domenico Scarlatti,** 1685–1757, was a harpsichord virtuoso and composed 545 sonatas mostly for that instrument.

scarlet fever (or scarlatina), acute communicable disease probably caused by a streptococcus. Attended by high fever, sore throat, skin eruption; early symptoms include vomiting or chills. Incubation period several hours to week. Attack usually gives permanent immunity. DICK TEST determines immunity.

scarp: see ESCARPMENT.

Scarpanto: see KARPATHOS.

Scarron, Paul (pôl' skärō'), 1610–60, French novelist, noted for his picaresque, burlesque style. His masterwork is *Le Romant comique* (1651). He was bedfast with paralysis most of his life. His wife, Françoise d'Aubigné, later became the marquise de MAINTENON.

Scarsdale, suburban village (pop. 13,156), SE N.Y., S of White Plains; settled c.1701.

Scaw Fell, mountain group, England: see SCAFELL.

Schacht, Hjalmar Horace Greeley (yäl'mär, skäkht'), 1877–, German banker and financial expert. President of the Reichsbank 1923–30, 1934–39; minister of economy 1934–37. Stabilized inflated currency (1924–25); elaborated intricate system of currency exchange controls and barter trade with foreign countries, thus helping German rearmament program under Hitler. A nationalist but not a Nazi, he took part in plot on Hitler's life (1944) and was placed in a concentration camp. He was acquitted at the Nuremberg war-crimes trial (1946).

Schadow, Johann Gottfried (yō'hän gôt'frēt shä'dō), 1764–1850, German sculptor of neoclassic school. His son **Rudolph Schadow,** 1786–1822, was also a sculptor. Another son, **Friedrich Wilhelm von Schadow-Godenhaus** (–gō'dùnhous), 1789–1862, was a religious and historical painter and one of the Nazarenes in Rome.

Schaff, Philip (shäf), 1819–93, biblical scholar and church historian in U.S., b. Switzerland. He was professor (after 1870) at Union Theological Seminary, and edited *Schaff-Herzog Encyclopedia of Religious Knowledge* (1882–84).

Schaffhausen (shäfhou'zùn), canton (115 sq. mi.; pop. 57,448), N Switzerland, on N bank of the Rhine. Consists of three unconnected agr. and forested areas, largely surrounded by German territory. Its cap., **Schaffhausen** (pop. 25,901), on the Rhine, was originally a Benedictine abbey (founded c.1050), whose 11th-cent. minster is preserved. Became a free imperial city c.1208 and joined Swiss Confederation 1501. Bombed by mistake in World War II by American aircraft. Hydroelectric works exploit falls near here on the Rhine for wool and metal goods mfg.

Scharnhorst, Gerhard von (gär'härt fŭn shärn'hôrst), 1755–1813, Prussian general. In charge of war ministry after Treaty of TILSIT (1807), he reorganized the army on a more democratic basis, cleverly evaded the treaty limitations on Prussia's armed strength, and created the army which in 1813–15 had a major share in Napoleon's downfall.

Schaulen, Lithuania: see SIAULIAI.

Schaumburg-Lippe (shoum'boörk-lǐ'pù), former state

(131 sq. mi.; 1939 pop. 53,195), W Germany, W of Hanover and E of Weser R.; cap. Bückeburg. After 1945 incorporated with British-occupied Lower Saxony. County of Schauenburg (as Schaumburg was originally called) occupied much of Westphalia in 12th cent. Counts held Holstein 1111–1459. In 1640 Schaumburg was divided among Brunswick-Lüneburg, Hesse-Kassel, and county of LIPPE. Principality of Schaumburg-Lippe was created 1790. Last prince abdicated 1918, and Schaumburg-Lippe joined Weimar Republic.

Scheele, Karl Wilhelm (kärl vǐl'hělm shä'lù), 1742–86, Swedish chemist. Prepared and studied oxygen; discovered nitrogen independently of Daniel Rutherford; was influential in discovery of manganese, barium, chlorine; isolated glycerin.

Scheer, Reinhard (rīn'härt shär'), 1863–1928, German admiral. Commanded in Battle of JUTLAND (1916).

Scheffer, Ary (ärē' shēfēr'), 1795–1858, Dutch painter in France. Best known for his religious paintings.

Scheffler, Johannes: see ANGELUS SILESIUS.

Scheherazade: see THOUSAND AND ONE NIGHTS.

Scheidemann, Philipp (fē'lǐp shī'dùmän), 1865–1939, first chancellor of German republic (1918–19), a Social Democrat. Resigned in protest over Treaty of Versailles.

Scheldt (skělt), Dutch and Flemish *Schelde,* Fr. *Escaut,* river, 270 mi. long, rising in N France and flowing NNE through Belgium, past Tournai, Ghent, and Antwerp, into the North Sea. Navigable for most of its course. The mouth forms estuary between Belgium and the Dutch islands of South Beveland and Walcheren. From 1648 until 1863 (except during Napoleonic period) the Netherlands possessed right to close the estuary, thus controlling Antwerp.

Schelling, Friedrich Wilhelm Joseph von (shě'lǐng), 1775–1854, German philosopher. He studied and taught at various universities (Tübingen, Leipzig, Jena, Würzburg, Erlangen) and lived at Munich before being called to the Univ. of Berlin (1841). He was early a collaborator of Fichte, and though they drew apart his philosophy started from a Fichtean base. He held that nature and mind cannot be separated, differing in force by degree, not in kind, with unity of mind and matter in the Absolute. He also argued that God takes part in the unfolding and development that is history and holds within Himself the limiting factors that define personality.

Schenectady (skùněk'tùdē), city (pop. 91,785), E N.Y., on Mohawk R. and the Barge Canal and NW of Albany; founded 1662. Center for mfg. of electrical equipment; athletic equipment; locomotive works. C. P. Steinmetz's home and laboratory are now a science museum. Seat of Union Col. (nonsectarian; for men; chartered and opened 1795), which pioneered in engineering courses; associated in Union Univ. (partly coed.; 1873) with Albany Medical Col. (1839), Albany Law School (1851), Albany Col. of Pharmacy (1881), and other schools.

scherzo (skěr'tsō) [Ital.,= joke], name given to several types of music, but chiefly one of a lively or facetious nature. Often appears as one of the movements of a symphony. Composers vary in their treatment of the scherzo, and often its humor is apparent only to the man who wrote it.

Scheveningen (skhä'vùnǐng"ùn), bathing resort, W Netherlands, on North Sea; forms part of The Hague.

Schiaparelli, Giovanni Virginio (jōvän'nē vērjē'nyō skyäpärěl'lē), 1835–1910, Italian astronomer. Discoveries include markings on Mars known as canals.

Schick test, skin test to determine susceptibility to diphtheria. Devised 1913 by **Bela Schick,** 1877–, Hungarian-born American pediatrician and allergist.

Schiedam (skhē"däm'), municipality (pop. 69,728), South Holland prov., W Netherlands, on the New Maas. Its gin is exported throughout the world.

Schiehallion (shǐhäl'yùn), mountain, 3,547 ft. high, Perthshire, Scotland, near Loch Rannoch.

Schiff, Jacob Henry (shĭf), 1847–1920, American banker and philanthropist, b. Germany. Head of Kuhn, Loeb and Co. in New York city after 1885. Endowed Jewish Theological Seminary.

Schiller, F(erdinand) C(anning) S(cott) (shĭ'lùr), 1864–1937, British philosopher, professor at Oxford (1897–1926) and at the Univ. of Southern California (1929–37). Called his pragmatic philosophy humanism, holding that "man is the measure of all things."

Schiller, Friedrich von (frē'drĭkh fùn shĭ'lùr), 1759–1805, German poet, dramatist, historian, and philosopher, b. Marbach, Württemberg. His first play, *Die Räuber* (1781), was a major STURM UND DRANG work. His many works include "An die Freude" (1785), the hymn to joy used by Beethoven in the Ninth Symphony; the drama *Don Carlos* (1787); historical studies, including one on the Thirty Years War (1793); the dramatic trilogy (1798–99) on Wallenstein, the last two parts translated by Coleridge as *Wallenstein* (1800); *Maria Stuart* (1800); *Die Jungfrau von Orleans* (1801); and *Wilhelm Tell* (1804; Eng. tr., 1825). A favorite among his many ballads is "The Song of the Bell." Schiller's friendship with Goethe is celebrated; his fruitful last years were spent in Weimar. One of the founders of German literature, second in his time only to Goethe. Strongly influenced by Kant, his idealism and hatred of tyranny were a powerful influence in modern German literature.

Schinkel, Karl Friedrich (kärl' frē'drĭkh shĭng'kùl), 1781–1841, German architect of the classical tradition. Built the imposing Old Mus. in Berlin.

Schipa, Tito (skē'pä), 1889–, Italian operatic tenor. He made his U.S. debut in 1919 with the Chicago Opera Co.; sang at the Metropolitan Opera, New York, 1932–35. He was a leading lyric tenor.

Schism, Great, split in the Roman Catholic Church, 1378–1417, After GREGORY XI had returned to Rome, ending the "Babylonian captivity" of the papacy. On his death (1378) the Roman mob brought pressure on the cardinals, who elected URBAN VI. He soon alienated all, and the cardinals declared his election null on the grounds of coercion and chose ROBERT OF GENEVA (Antipope Clement VII), who fled to Avignon. There he was succeeded in 1394 by Pedro de LUNA (Antipope Benedict XIII). In Rome, Urban was succeeded by Boniface IX, Innocent VII, and GREGORY XII. The two lines were completely divided. Theologians led by Pierre d'Ailly and John Gerson promoted the Council of PISA (1409), which advanced the theory of the superiority of councils to the pope but succeeded only in creating a third papal line (later represented by Baldassarre COSSA). The quarrel was ended at the Council of CONSTANCE with election of MARTIN V. One result of the schism was delay in beginning the Catholic Reform. Called also Schism of the West.

schist (shĭst), metamorphic rock having its minerals elongated and arranged in bands parallel to each other and to cleavage planes of the minerals. Common varieties are mica schist, chlorite schist, talc schist. Schists are abundant in Pre-Cambrian rocks. Schists split readily along their planes of schistosity, like slates along cleavage lines.

schizophrenia (skĭt'sùfrē'nēù), functional psychosis, characterized by faulty mental processes, unrealistic behavior, absorption in an inner world, and sometimes hallucinations. In 1896 Emil Kraepelin grouped various mental diseases under the heading of dementia praecox, using four subdivisions (simple, hebephrenic, catatonic, and paranoid). In 1911 Eugen Bleuler pronounced the disease curable, using the term *schizophrenia* (as emphasizing the splitting phenomena in the mind) to replace dementia praecox (which implied a hopeless outlook for cure). Patients are usually hospitalized; treatment may include psychosurgery or shock therapy as well as psychotherapy.

Schlegel, August Wilhelm von (ou'gŏŏst vĭl'hĕlm fùn shlā'gùl), 1767–1845, German author and scholar, a champion of romanticism. His excellent translations of Shakspere (1797–1810) were completed by others. He and his brother **Friedrich von Schlegel** (frēd'rĭkh), 1772–1829, founded and edited the influential periodical *Athenaeum*. Friedrich von Schlegel turned from literature to philosophy and the study of Sanskrit and of Hindu thought; in 1808 he joined the Catholic Church, in which he saw the union of Christian and romantic ideals. His wife, **Dorothea von Schlegel,** 1763–1839, daughter of Moses Mendelssohn, shared his conversion and was his literary assistant.

Schleicher, Kurt von (kŏŏrt' fùn shlī'khùr), 1882–1934, German general. Appointed chancellor of Germany in Dec., 1932, he vainly requested emergency powers to stem the Nazi tide. Upon his resignation, Hitler became chancellor (Jan., 1933). Schleicher and his wife were murdered by the Nazis in the "blood purge" of 1934.

Schleiden, Matthias Jakob (mätē'äs yä'kôp shlī'dùn), 1804–81, German botanist. A pioneer in development of cell theory, he showed plant tissues were composed of cells and emphasized importance of nucleus.

Schleiermacher, Friedrich Daniel Ernst (frē'drĭkh dä'nyĕl ernst' shlī'ùrmäkh'ùr), 1768–1834, German philosopher and Protestant theologian. Professor at Halle (1804–10) and Berlin (after 1810), he in *The Christian Faith* (1821–22) and other works sought to reconcile modern social theories and Evangelical religious beliefs.

Schlesinger, Arthur M(eier) (shlā'zĭng-gùr), 1888–, American historian, professor at Harvard. Special interest has been interpretation of social history, as in *The Rise of the City, 1878–1898* (1933). His son is **Arthur M(eier) Schlesinger, Jr.,** 1917–, historian, author of the Pulitzer Prize-winning *Age of Jackson* (1945), and associate professor at Harvard. He has vigorously defended liberal causes.

Schleswig (shlĕz'wĭg, Ger. shläs'vĭkh, Dan. *Slesvig,* former duchy, N Germany and S Denmark, in S Jutland. German Schleswig (part of Schleswig-Holstein), has Schleswig, Flensburg, and Husum as chief towns. Danish Schleswig or North Schleswig includes Sonderborg and Tondern. The duchy was created 1115 as a fief held directly from the kings of Denmark; it passed in 1386 to the counts of HOLSTEIN, and in 1460 to Christian I of Denmark. (For later history, see SCHLESWIG-HOLSTEIN.) The historic cap., **Schleswig** (pop. 36,668), is a port on an inlet of the Baltic Sea. Has Romanesque-Gothic cathedral (Lutheran); Gottorp or Gottorf castle (16th–17th cent.), former residence of dukes of Holstein-Gottorp.

Schleswig-Holstein (–hōl'stīn, Ger. –hôl'shtīn), German state (6,045 sq. mi.; pop. 2,593,617), N Germany, in S part and at base of the Jutland peninsula; cap. Kiel. A low-lying region between the North Sea and the Baltic (linked by Kiel Canal), it has fertile agr. land (cattle raising). In the center, heaths and moors predominate. It produces ships, machinery, processed foods. Population is Protestant. The state consists of the former duchies of SCHLESWIG (N of Eider R.), HOLSTEIN (S), and LAUENBURG (SW). Concerning the history of Schleswig-Holstein Lord Palmerston once stated that of the three men who had ever understood it, one was dead (Prince Albert), one was insane (a professor), and the third (Palmerston himself) had forgotten it. Both Schleswig and Holstein were inherited in 1460 by Christian I of Denmark. Schleswig was a fief held directly from the Danish crown; Holstein was held in fief from the Holy Roman Empire. Both duchies were connected with the Danish crown through personal union only and could not be incorporated into the Danish crownlands. In the 16th cent. the duchies underwent a complex subdivision. A "ducal portion" was conferred on a younger brother of King Christian III and on his descendants, the dukes of Holstein-Gottorp; a "royal portion" was ruled directly by the Danish kings; a "common portion" was ruled jointly by the Danish kings and the dukes of Holstein-Gottorp. Within the royal portion, the duchy of SONDERBORG was created in favor of King Frederick II's youngest brother; this Sonderborg branch in turn split into the Augustenburg line and the cadet Glücksburg line. As a result of the NORTHERN WAR (1700–1721) Duke Charles Frederick of Holstein-Gottorp, who had sided with Sweden, was dispossessed. His grandson, Grand Duke (later Emperor) Paul of Russia, renounced his claim to the ducal portion in exchange for OLDENBURG (1773). Thus both duchies were reunited under the Danish crown. The Congress of Vienna left status unchanged, except that the German Confederation replaced the Holy Roman Empire as suzerain over Holstein. The struggle between the German nationalists in the duchies and the Danish nationalists, who tried to impose the Danish constitution on them, flared into warfare in 1848. The German Confederation, particularly Prussia, gave military support to the rebellious duchies, but in 1850 peace was made on inconclusive terms. The London Conference of 1852 settled the succession of the childless Frederick VII on the Glücksburg line of the royal house; Denmark guaranteed the inseparability and autonomy of the duchies. However, in 1863 Christian IX signed a new constitution, which was to have force in Schleswig as well as in Denmark. On the ground that the London Protocol had been violated, Prussia and Austria declared war on Denmark, which was quickly defeated (1864). Austria favored the installation of the Augustenburg line in the duchies, but Prussia, under Bismarck's leadership, imposed the Treaty of Gastein (1865): Schleswig was to be administered by Prussia, Holstein by Austria. As Bismarck had anticipated, this solution led to friction with Austria, which in 1866 declared war on Prussia (see AUSTRO-PRUSSIAN WAR). Victorious Prussia annexed both duchies, which together with Lauenburg became a Prussian province. In 1920 a plebiscite restored Danish-speaking N Schleswig to Denmark. LÜBECK and the Lübeck dist. of Oldenburg were added to the province in 1937. Schleswig-Holstein became a state within the British occupation zone in 1946 and joined the Federal Republic of [West] Germany in 1949. The influx of displaced persons after World War II increased its population c.60%.

Schley, Winfield Scott (slī), 1839–1911, American naval officer. In command at battle of Santiago in Spanish-American War. Controversy over credit for victory arose between him and W. T. SAMPSON.

Schlieffen, Alfred, Graf von (äl'frät gräf' fün shlē'fün), 1833–1913, German field marshal, chief of the general staff 1891–1906. He developed the **Schlieffen plan,** based on Hannibal's tactics at Cannae. In case of war with France, an overwhelmingly strong right wing was to strike through the Low Countries, capture the Channel ports, and bear down on Paris from the W. Meanwhile a weak left wing was to draw out the French further S, along the Franco-German border. In World War I, the German command lacked the boldness to put all its strength into the right wing and thus ruined the plan. In World War II the plan was carried out successfully.

Schliemann, Heinrich (shlē'män), 1822–90, German archaeologist. Inspired by Homeric studies, he retired from business (1863) to find Troy and other Homeric sites. In 1871 he undertook at own expense excavations at Hissarlik, uncovering four superimposed towns. Made other notable excavations.

Schlüsselburg (shlü'sùlbōork), fortress, NW European RSFSR, E of Leningrad and on an island in L. Ladoga. Built 1323 by Novgorod, it fell to Sweden in 17th cent. but was recovered by Peter I in 1702. Used until 1917 for high-ranking and political prisoners. In World War II its recapture by Russians opened land route to besieged Leningrad (1943).

Schlüter, Andreas (ändrä'äs shlü'tür), 1664–1714, German baroque sculptor. Among his notable works in Berlin is the pulpit in the Marienkirche.

Schmalkalden (shmäl'käl"dùn), town (pop. 12,663), Thuringia, central Germany. Health resort; mineral springs. In its town hall (built 1419) was formed in 1531 the alliance of German Protestant princes and cities known as the **Schmalkaldic League** (shmälkäl'dĭk). It was led by Philip of Hesse and John Frederick I of Saxony. Emperor Charles V crushed the League in the Schmalkaldic War (1546–47) through his victory at Mühlberg.

Schmeling, Max, 1905–, German boxer. Won (1930) heavyweight championship when Jack Sharkey was disqualified for fouling, lost (1932) title when Sharkey defeated him in 15 rounds. First fighter to defeat Joe Louis, knocking him out (1936) in 12th round.

Schnabel, Artur (shnä'bùl), 1882–1951, Austrian pianist and teacher. He first toured the U.S., 1921–22. Best known for his interpretations of Beethoven's works. His own compositions, which are extremely modern, include his First Symphony and his Rhapsody for Orchestra.

Schnakenberg, Henry, 1892–, American painter, best known for naturalistic landscapes.

schnauzer: see TERRIER.

Schnitzler, Arthur (är'tŏōr shnĭts'lùr), 1862–1931, Austrian author. His works, distinguished by brilliance of style and acuteness of observation, mark the turn from romanticism to gloomy realism. They include the plays *Anatol* (1892), *Liebelei* (1895), and *Professor Bernhardi* (1912); several novels; and many short stories.

Schnorr von Carolsfeld, Julius (yōō'lyŏōs shnôr' fün kä'rôlsfĕlt), 1794–1872, German religious and historical painter.

Schoenbrunn Memorial State Park (shän'brun, –brōōn), E central Ohio, near New Philadelphia. Site of first town in Ohio, settled 1772, abandoned 1776; now being restored.

Schofield, John McAllister (skō'fĕld), 1831–1906, Union general in Civil War. Led Army of the Ohio in Atlanta campaign. Secretary of War (1868–69). Commander of U.S. army (1888–95).

Schofield Barracks, U.S. army military post (estab. 1909), central Oahu, T.H. WHEELER FIELD is at S edge.

scholasticism (skōläs'tĭsĭzùm), philosophical thought of medieval Christian Europe. It does not have the unity seemingly imputed to it by contemptuous later philosophers—an attitude still reflected in the popular mind, though medieval philosophy, reassessed in recent years, is now generally recognized as rich, varied, and subtle. Chief among the early sources were the writings of St. Augustine and other Church Fathers, and as learning revived in the 9th cent. it was tinted with Platonic and Neoplatonic thought. ERIGENA was one of the first to introduce speculative thought into medieval philosophy. By the 11th cent. the "schoolmen" (scholastics) were embarked on wide-ranging discussions. One major problem was that of the nature of universal concepts (i.e., the fundamental ideas of things, the idea of "chair" as opposed to an individual example). Some teachers, the realists, held that the basic forms had reality in and of themselves; others, the nominalists, claimed that the forms were only abstractions from particular examples. Another theme of argument was that concerning the place of reason and the place of faith in man's knowledge. Prominent among the earlier scholastics were St. ANSELM, ABELARD, WILLAM OF CHAMPEAUX, HUGH OF SAINT VICTOR, and PETER LOMBARD. As knowledge of Aristotle's work reached W Europe again through acquaintance with Arabian learning, scholasticism rose to its crest in the 13th cent. with the brilliant synthesis of Aristotelian rationalism and Christian thought. Robert GROSSETESTE and St. ALBERTUS MAGNUS preceded St. THOMAS AQUINAS, whose closely wrought system was one of the greatest achievements of European thought. His rationalism was opposed by several Franciscans, notably DUNS SCOTUS, St. BONAVENTURE, and WIL-

LIAM OF OCCAM, who stressed the necessity of faith and the weakness of reason in solving questions of theology. Both schools of thought persist in the Roman Catholic Church, though that of St. Thomas is dominant. The secular currents of the Renaissance and the growth of natural science caused scholasticism to decline and disappear.

Schomberg, Frederick Herman, 1st duke of (shŏm'bûrg), Ger. *Friedrich Hermann von Schönburg,* 1615–90, German soldier of fortune. Fought in Thirty Years War on Protestant side. Later commanded successfully in the service of Portugal (created conde de Mertola), France (created marshal of France and duke), and William III of Orange. He assisted William in the Glorious Revolution, was created duke in the English peerage (1688), and commanded the English forces in Ireland, where he won the battle of the Boyne, in which he was fatally wounded.

Schomburgk, Sir Robert Hermann (shŏm'bûrk) 1804–65, British explorer, b. Germany. Went on botanical and geographical expedition to British Guiana (1835). Surveyed that colony for British government (1841–43), outlining boundary important in subsequent boundary disputes with Venezuela.

Schön, Martin: see SCHONGAUER, MARTIN.

Schönbein, Christian Friedrich (krĭs'tyän frē'drĭkh shûn'bīn), 1799–1868, German chemist. Discovered ozone; developed guncotton and collodion.

Schönberg, Arnold (shûn'bĕrkh), 1874–1951, Austrian composer, in the U.S. after 1933. His early works, such as *Verklärte Nacht* (1899), are in the romantic tradition. In his first *Kammersymphonie* (1906), the use of chords built in fourths (C, F sharp, B flat) foreshadows his later use of atonality. Some of his vocal music (e.g., *Erwartung*) requires a special technique that is neither singing nor speaking. In 1914 he arrived at the 12-tone technique (see ATONALITY), which he first used explicitly in his *Serenade* (1924). Among his works are a violin concerto (1940); *Ode to Napoleon* (1944), to Byron's poem, for male reciter, piano, and string orchestra; and songs and piano pieces. Performances of his music offer great technical difficulties. Among pupils who follow his 12-tone technique are Alban Berg, Ernst Krenek, and Anton von Webern.

Schönbrunn (shûnbroōn'), former imperial palace in Vienna, Austria, built 18th cent. Park emulates Versailles. Heavily damaged in World War II. By **Peace of Schönbrunn,** 1809, imposed by Napoleon I, Austria temporarily lost W Galicia to duchy of Warsaw and Illyria to France.

Schongauer, Martin (mär'tĕn shōn'gou-ùr), c.1445–1491, German engraver, known also as Martin Schön. Worked in Colmar. Noted for engravings of religious subjects.

Schoodic Lake (skoō'dĭk), 9 mi. long, central Maine, SSW of Millinocket. Lumbering, hunting, fishing.

Schoolcraft, Henry Rowe, 1793–1864, American ethnologist, chief pioneer in study of the Indians.

schooner, fore-and-aft rigged sailing vessel, having two to seven masts. First designed by Capt. Andrew Robinson of Gloucester, Mass. (1713), it became a favorite craft in Newfoundland fisheries. See *ill.,* p. 865.

Schopenhauer, Arthur (är'toōr shō'pùnhou"ùr), 1788–1860, German philosopher. Studied at several German universities, traveled widely, and after 1831 lived mainly at Frankfurt-am-Main in seclusion. His philosophy of pessimism was presented with clarity and literary skill in books, of which *The World as Will and Idea* (1818) and *Will in Nature* (1836) are best known. He held that true reality is a blind impelling force, appearing in individual man as will. The constant mutual resistance of various wills causes strife, and the individual cannot satisfy the wants of his will and therefore lives in pain. The only escape is a negation of the will, but temporary escape can be found in science and art. Ethics rests only on sympathy for the pain of others.

Schouten, Willem Cornelis (vĭ'lùm kôrnā'lĭs skhou'tùn), 1567?–1625, Dutch navigator. Commanded expedition (1615) to evade Dutch East India Co. trade restrictions by finding new route to Pacific. Rounded and named Cape Horn (1616). Despite new route, Schouten was arrested and his ship was confiscated.

Schreckhörner (shrĕk'hûr"nùr), two peaks of Bernese Alps, Switzerland—Gross Schreckhorn, 13,390 ft.; Klein Schreckhorn, 11,474 ft.

Schreiner, Olive (shrī'nùr), pseud. Ralph Iron, 1855–1920, South African author and feminist, known for her novel *The Story of an African Farm* (1883). Her other works include an unfinished novel, *From Man to Man* (1926).

Schröder, Friedrich Ludwig (shrü'dùr), 1744–1816, German actor and dramatist. One of most famous tragic actors of his day, he translated Shakspere and other classics into German.

Schrödinger, Erwin (ĕr'vĭn shrü'dĭng-ùr), 1887–, Austrian physicist. Shared 1933 Nobel Prize for mathematical formulation of wave mechanics.

Schubert, Franz (Peter) (shoō'bùrt), 1797–1828, Austrian composer, foremost of the romantic movement. German lieder came to their fullest flower in his songs, especially his two great cycles, *Die schöne Müllerin* and *Die Winterreise.* The Quartet in D Minor (*Death and the Maiden*) and the Quintet in A (*The Trout*) are perhaps best known of his many chamber works. Among his symphonies are the B minor (the Unfinished Symphony) and the C major symphony. He also wrote overtures, Masses, and much piano music, including the *Moments musicaux.* Two of his most popular songs are the *Erlkönig* and his *Ave Maria.*

Schultze, Max Johann Sigismund (mäks yō'hän zēgĭs-moōnd shoōl'tsù), 1825–74, German biologist known for work on cell theory, protoplasm, protozoa.

Schumacher, Peder: see GRIFFENFELD, PEDER SCHUMACHER, COUNT.

Schuman, Robert (rōbĕr' shoōmä'), 1886–, French premier (1947–48) and foreign minister (1948–53), a member of the Catholic Mouvement Républicain Populaire (MRP). He proposed in 1950 the so-called **Schuman Plan,** which became effective in 1952 as the European Coal and Steel Community (members: France, Federal Republic of [West] Germany, Belgium, Netherlands, Luxembourg, Italy). The first practical step toward European unification, the ECSC has eliminated all restrictions, among the six member nations, on exports, imports, and currency exchange affecting coal, scrap iron, and iron ore. In 1953 the first international tax, a levy on coal and steel production in the member countries, took effect. The ECSC, with hq. at Luxembourg, thus has pooled the chief industrial resources of one of the world's most vital industrial areas, including the Ruhr coal basin and the Lorraine iron ore basin.

Schuman, William (shoō'mùn), 1910–, American composer. His music is contrapuntal and often suggests jazz rhythms. His chief works are his Third and his Fourth Symphony (both 1941); the ballet *Undertow* (1945); several suites; and chamber music.

Schumann, Robert (Alexander) (shoō'män), 1810–56, German romantic composer. He wrote many piano works, including *Papillons, Carnaval, Kinderszenen,* and *Kreisleriana,* and nearly 150 songs. His piano concerto in A Minor (1841–45), Spring Symphony (1841), Third, or Rhenish, Symphony (1850), and Fourth Symphony in D Minor (1841–51) and later chamber works are well known. He was a great personal friend of the young Brahms and championed his music. His last years were clouded by attacks of insanity, and he died in a sanitarium. His wife, **Clara (Wieck) Schumann,** 1819–96, was an outstanding pianist.

Schumann-Heink, Ernestine (shoō'mùn-hĭngk'), 1861–1936, American contralto, b. near Prague. She sang with the Metropolitan Opera, New York, 1899–1904.

Her concert tours won her the lasting affection of the public.

Schuman Plan: see SCHUMAN, ROBERT.

Schumpeter, Joseph Alois (yō'zěf ä'lōĕs shŏŏm'pā"tùr), 1883–1950, Austrian-American economist. Proposed theory of entrepreneur as the dynamic factor in disturbing business equilibrium.

Schurman, Jacob Gould (shûr'mùn), 1854–1942, American educator and diplomat. He was president (1892–1920) of Cornell Univ. and founder and editor of the *Philosophical Review*. He headed first U.S. Philippines Commission (1899) and served as minister to Greece (1912–13), envoy to China (1921–25), and ambassador to Germany (1925–30).

Schurz, Carl (shōŏrts), 1829–1906, American political leader, b. Germany. Civil War general of volunteers (1862–65). U.S. Senator from Mo. (1869–75); helped form LIBERAL REPUBLICAN PARTY. U.S. Secretary of the Interior (1877–81). Led MUGWUMPS in 1884. Edited various publications. Exercised wide influence through writings and speeches.

Schuschnigg, Kurt von (kŏŏrt' fŭn shōŏsh'nĭk), 1897–, chancellor of Austria (1934–38). Succeeded DOLLFUSS, under whom he had served as minister of justice. After 1936 he acted as virtual dictator. He resisted Hitler's attempts, through the large Nazi party of Austria, to unite Austria with Germany, but his situation became hopeless after he lost Mussolini's support (1937). Early in 1938 Hitler's pressure forced Schuschnigg to make concessions to the Nazis. In March, Schuschnigg called for a plebiscite on Austria's continued independence. Two days later (March 11) German troops occupied Austria. Schuschnigg resigned and was kept a prisoner until 1945. He settled in U.S. 1947.

Schütz, Heinrich (hīn'rĭkh shüts'), 1585–1672, German composer. His *Dafne* (no longer extant) is considered the first German opera. His chief works are *Seven Last Words of Christ on the Cross* and settings of the Passion as narrated in each of the Gospels. These works influenced Bach and Handel.

Schuyler, Philip John (skī'lùr), 1733–1804, American Revolutionary general. Command dispute between him and Horatio Gates in 1776 ended with Gates as commander of Saratoga campaign. Schuyler was court-martialed for negligence but acquitted.

Schuylerville, village (pop. 1,314), E N.Y., on W bank of Hudson R. and E of Saratoga Springs. Scene of Burgoyne's surrender in SARATOGA CAMPAIGN.

Schuylkill (skōŏl'kĭl", skōō'kùl), river rising in Schuylkill co., Pa., and flowing 130 mi. SE into Delaware R. at Philadelphia. Project to take anthracite from river started 1948.

Schuylkill Haven, borough (pop. 6,597), E Pa., on Schuylkill R. and SSE of Pottsville. Mfg. of shoes and clothing.

Schwab, Charles M(ichael) (shwäb), 1862–1939, American steel magnate. Made Bethlehem Steel Co. the leading manufacturer of war materials for Allies in World War I.

Schwabach (shvä'bäkh), town (pop. 19,448), Middle Franconia, W central Bavaria. Metalworking; lead processing. **Articles of Schwabach,** drawn up 1529, were used in drafting Augsburg Confession (1530).

Schwann, Theodor (tā'ōdŏr shvän'), 1810–82, German physiologist and histologist. Continued and amended work of Schleiden; showed cell to be basis of animal as well as of plant tissue.

Schwanthaler, Ludwig von (lōōt'vĭkh fŭn shvän'tälùr), 1802–48, German sculptor. Created sculptures for the Ruhmeshalle and other buildings in Munich. His portrait statue of Mozart is at Salzburg.

Schwarzenberg, Karl Philipp, Fürst zu (kärl' fē'lĭp fürst' tsōō shvär'tsŭnběrk), 1771–1820, Austrian field marshal. Commanded allied armies in campaign of 1813–14 against Napoleon. His nephew **Felix, Fürst zu Schwarzenberg** (fä'lĭks), 1800–1852, was Austrian prime minister 1848–52. He forced Emperor Ferdi-

nand's abdication (1848), suppressed the 1848 revolution throughout the empire, and restored Austrian leadership through the Treaty of OLMÜTZ.

Schwarzwald, Germany: see BLACK FOREST.

Schwatka, Frederick (shwŏt'kù), 1849–92, American explorer. On arctic expedition (1878–80) he unearthed evidence of fate of Sir John Franklin's party. Explored Alaska, Mexico, Southwest.

Schweinfurt (shvīn'fŏŏrt), city (pop. 45,901), Lower Franconia, NW Bavaria. Machine tools and dyes (Paris green is also called Schweinfurt green). Center of German ball-bearing industry in World War II. Heavily damaged in air raids of 1943–44.

Schweitzer, Albert (shvī'tsùr), 1875–, Alsatian philosopher, a physician and missionary in French Equatorial Africa. He is a scientist, humanitarian, theologian, and a skilled organist (also author of a biography of Bach and editor of his organ music). His works have attracted international attention.

Schwenkfeld, Kaspar von (kä'spär fŭn shvĕngk'fĕlt), 1490–1561, German religious reformer; a follower of Zwingli. His Anabaptist leanings caused enmity of Luther, and his books were banned. His followers, called Schwenkfeldians or Schwenkfelders, were persecuted and fled, some to America, where sect still exists in E Pa.

Schwerin, Kurt Christoph, Graf von (kŏŏrt' krĭs'tôf gräf' fŭn shvärēn'), 1684–1757, Prussian field marshal, b. Pomerania. Served under Charles XII of Sweden; entered Prussian service 1720; defeated Austrians at Mollwitz (1740); fell at Prague. He was one of Frederick II's ablest lieutenants.

Schwerin (shvärēn'), city (pop. 88,164), NE Germany, on L. of Schwerin. Center of agr. and dairying region. Bishopric, here since 1167, was secularized 1648 and passed to duke of Mecklenburg. City was cap. of Mecklenburg-Schwerin 1701–1934.

Schwyz (shvēts), canton (351 sq. mi.; pop. 71,246), Switzerland, one of FOUR FOREST CANTONS. Mountainous, forested, and pastoral region; large hydroelectric plants in N. German-speaking population. In 1274 Rudolf I of Hapsburg revoked charter granted by Emperor Frederick II in 1240. In protest, Schwyz concluded with Uri and Unterwalden the pact which became the basis for Swiss liberty (1291; see SWITZERLAND, which derives name from Schwyz). Schwyz joined Catholic SONDERBUND 1845. Its cap., **Schwyz** (pop. 10,192) has 16th-cent. town hall with historic paintings. Swiss federal archives here contain original pact of 1291.

Scilla (shĕl'lä), modern name of SCYLLA strait.

Scilly Islands (sĭl'ē), archipelago of over 150 isles off SW England. Many ships once wrecked on the rocky coasts, now marked by lighthouses. Five isles are inhabited, St. Mary's (has cap., Hugh Town), Tresco, St. Martin's, St. Agnes, and Bryher. Climate is mild and growing flowers for export is a leading occupation.

Scioto (sīō'tù), river, c.245 mi. long, rising in W Ohio and flowing E, then S, passing Columbus and Chillicothe, to enter Ohio R. at Portsmouth.

Scipio (sĭ'pēō), patrician family of anc. Rome, notable for love of learning as well as taking part in Roman warfare. **Cneius Cornelius Scipio Calvus** (nē'ùs), d. 211 B.C., was consul in 222 B.C. Sent to Spain (218 B.C.) in the Second Punic War to wreck the supply lines of Hannibal. He and his brother defeated Hasdrubal (215 B.C.) and captured Saguntum (212 B.C.), but both were killed in Spain. That brother, **Publius Cornelius Scipio,** d. c.211 B.C., had been consul in 218 B.C. He opposed Hannibal and was defeated at the Ticino and Trebia (218 B.C.) before going to Spain. His wife was the sister of Aemilius Paullus, and CORNELIA was their daughter. One of their sons was the greatest of the family, **Scipio Africanus Major** (Publius Cornelius Scipio Africanus) (ăfrĭkā'nùs), 234?–183 B.C., the conqueror of HANNIBAL. He was with his father at the Ticino (218 B.C.) and survived the disastrous defeat at Cannae (216 B.C.). After his father's death he was elected proconsul of Spain. There he showed his military genius; by 209 he had conquered Cartagena and in a few years had taken all of Spain. In 205 B.C. he was consul, but the senate denied him permission to take the war to Africa. He went to Sicily, where he drilled a volunteer army. In 204 B.C. he was permitted to go to Africa, where, after answering Hannibal's peace offers with impossible demands, he defeated the Carthaginians in the decisive battle of Zama (202 B.C.). Later he tried in vain to prevent the Romans from hounding Hannibal to death. His pride and position gained him jealous enemies, who brought him to trial on charges (probably false) of receiving bribes when he accompanied his brother on a campaign against Antiochus III in 190. Cato the Elder headed the party against him, and Scipio was saved only by his son-in-law, T. Sempronius Gracchus. He ordered that his body should not be buried in the ungrateful city. His eldest son adopted the son of Aemilius PAULLUS, who became **Scipio Africanus Minor** (Publius Cornelius Scipio Aemilianus Africanus Numantinus), c.185–129 B.C. He was a patron of literature and friend of Terence, Laelius, and Polybius. He had considerable military experience before he became consul (147 B.C.) in the Third Punic War. He went to Africa and destroyed Carthage utterly. Consul again in 134 B.C., he put down a rebellion in Spain, destroying Numantia. Though Tiberius Gracchus was his adoptive cousin and brother of Scipio's wife, he rejoiced openly at the murder of Gracchus and tried to destroy the Gracchan reforms. After a public denunciation of Gracchus he was himself murdered, possibly by his wife or his mother-in-law. His friendship with Laelius is celebrated in Cicero's *De amicitia*, and the *Dream of Scipio* in Cicero's *De republica* tells of an apparition of the greater Scipio to this Scipio. A kinsman, **Publius Cornelius Scipio Nasica Serapio** (nā'sĭkŭ sĭrā'pēō), d. c.132 B.C., had actually been a leader in the mob that murdered Tiberius Gracchus. He had to flee later to escape popular wrath. A descendant of his, **Quintus Caecilius Metellus Pius Scipio**, d. 46 B.C., was an ardent supporter of Pompey, who made him colleague in the consulship in 52 B.C. In the civil war he was a commander for Pompey at Pharsala, and after defeat went to Africa. Caesar defeated him at Thapsus, and he took to the sea to escape. About to be captured by Caesar's men, he committed suicide.

scissor-tailed flycatcher, bird of New World flycatcher family Tyrannidae. Male is gray with reddish patch at base of wing and shades of pinkish and orange-red in the gray; dark tail feathers are marked with white. Deeply forked tail is 7–10 in. long. Bird breeds chiefly in parts of Texas, Okla., Kansas, Nebr.; usually winters in Central America.

Scituate (sĭ'chŏŏwāt, –wĭt), resort town (pop. 5,993), SE Mass., on the coast SE of Boston; settled c.1630. Irish moss found here.

Scone (skōōn), parish (pop. 2,559), Perthshire, Scotland. Was royal residence of Scottish kings 1157–1488. Stone of Scone or CORONATION STONE is now in Westminster Abbey. Last coronation here was that of Charles II in 1651.

'Sconset, Mass: see NANTUCKET.

Scopas (skō'pŭs), Greek sculptor, fl. 4th cent. B.C., first to portray violent facial expressions.

Scopes trial, July, 1925, trial of public-school teacher John T. Scopes at Dayton, Tenn., for teaching Darwinian theory contrary to state statute. C. S. Darrow was a defense attorney, W. J. Bryan prosecuted. Convicted, Scopes was later released on a technicality.

scopolamine (skōpŏ'lŭmēn, –mĭn) or **hyoscine** (hī'ŭsēn, –sĭn), alkaloid drug obtained from plants of nightshade family. Acts as depressant of central nervous system; used as sedative.

scorbutus: see SCURVY.

Scoresby, William, 1789–1857, English arctic explorer and scientist. On yearly trips to Greenland (1803–22) he collected scientific data, giving special attention to terrestrial magnetism, a study he pursued further on visit to Australia (1856).

Scoresby Sound, inlet of E Greenland. Several of its branches extend c.150 mi. inland.

Scorpio (skôr'pēō) [Latin,= scorpion], eighth sign of ZODIAC.

scorpion (skôr'pēŭn), nocturnal arachnid, ½–8 in. long, of warm and tropical regions. With pincerlike claws attacks spiders and insects; paralyzes prey with poison injected by sharp, curved spine of post-abdomen. Sting of some is fatal to children.

Scot, Michael, c.1175–1232, medieval scholar. He supervised translations of Arabian works and of Aristotle into Latin, and in 1230 he introduced study of Aristotle at Oxford. He was also famous for occult learning and reputed miraculous powers. As a magician he figures in Dante's *Inferno*.

Scotia (skō'shù), Latin name for Scotland.

Scotland, northern part of Great Britain (30,405 sq. mi.; pop. 5,095,969), cap. EDINBURGH. Separated from England by Tweed and Liddell rivers, Cheviot Hills, and Solway Firth. It is 274 mi. long, 26–154 mi. wide. Irregular coastline with numerous lochs and firths (Moray, Tay, and Forth firths in E; Solway, Clyde, and Lorne firths in W) is 2,300 mi. long. In N are Orkney and Shetland isls.; W are Inner and Outer Hebrides, or Western Isles; SW are Arran and Bute isls. Scotland is divided into three physical regions: Highlands, central Lowlands, and southern uplands. Highlands (including Hebrides) are almost entirely mountainous and include highest point in Great Britain, Ben Nevis (4,406 ft.). Grampians are chief chain. Principal waterways are Dee, Don, Deveron, Spey, and Beauly rivers and Caledonian Canal. Central Lowlands, with general elevation of 500 ft., have many hill ridges and fine lakes. Here, on Clyde R., is Glasgow. In E are other mfg. towns. Coal and iron in this area have aided growth of heavy industry. Southern uplands, a slightly mountainous region of rolling moorlands, rise abruptly from Lowlands. Chief rivers are Nith, Cree, Ayr, and Tweed. Only c.25% of Scotland can be cultivated. Main crops are barley, oats, wheat, turnips, and beans. Chief occupations are mfg. of woolens, worsteds, linen, silk, whisky, beer, and paper, and sheep-raising and fisheries. Scotland, united with England since 1707, is represented in House of Commons and House of Lords. Secretary of state for Scotland is a cabinet member. Counties are Shetland, Orkney, Caithness, Sutherlandshire, Ross and Cromarty, Inverness-shire, Nairnshire, Morayshire, Banffshire, Aberdeenshire, Argyllshire, Perthshire, Angus, Buteshire, Kincardineshire, Dumbartonshire, Stirlingshire, Clackmannanshire, Kinross-shire, Fife, Renfrewshire, Ayrshire, Lanarkshire, West Lothian, Midlothian, East Lothian, Peebleshire, Wigtownshire, Kirkcudbrightshire, Berwick, Dumfriesshire, Selkirkshire, and Roxburghshire. Church of SCOTLAND, estab. 1560, is Presbyterian; was united (1929) with United Free Church (see SCOTLAND, FREE CHURCH OF). Universities are those of Edinburgh, Glasgow, Aberdeen, and St. Andrews. Scottish law is based on Roman rather than common law (as in England). For pre-Roman history of Scotland, see BRITAIN. Picts, here from beginning of historic times, with Gaels or Celts from Ireland kept Romans from penetrating far into Scotland or having much influence, despite Agricola's invasion of A.D. 80. St. Ninian introduced Christianity in 5th cent.; St. Columba landed it in 6th cent. In next century and a half, four kingdoms were estab.: Picts in N; Scots from Ireland; Britains from Strathclyde; and Northumbria, founded by Angles. Country was raided by Norsemen 8th–12th cent. Reign of MALCOLM III, who succeeded Macbeth (murderer of King Duncan), was long and peaceful. Peace with England came with marriage of King Edgar's sister

Maud to Henry I of England. Under David I, Scotland achieved stature of a nation. Alexander II and Alexander III pushed Norsemen out of Scotland. Alexander III's heiress, Margaret Maid of Norway, died a child and John de Baliol became king. Scotland's long relationship with France began in 13th cent.; they were allied against Edward I of England. Robert Bruce, crowned ROBERT I in 1306, defeated Edward II at Bannockburn 1314. In 1349 Black Death killed c.30% of the people. JAMES I was one of Scotland's most learned kings and best Chaucerian poets. His murder (1437) threw country into civil war for 100 years. Reformation was brought to Scotland by John KNOX. When MARY QUEEN OF SCOTS arrived from France, Catholicism had almost disappeared from Lowlands. Her struggle against Protestantism ended in loss of the throne, imprisonment in England, and execution. Her son succeeded Elizabeth as JAMES I of England, uniting the two crowns. The COVENANTERS resisted Charles I in BISHOPS' WARS (1639–40), and PURITAN REVOLUTION became civil war. Act of Union (1707) gave Scotland representation in Parliament of GREAT BRITAIN. JACOBITES tried unsuccessfully to destroy Union, economic results of which were favorable. As result of late 18th cent. and early 19th cent. inclosures, many Highlanders emigrated. By end of 18th cent. textile industry was pre-eminent. Commerce with British Empire led to growth of shipping, and Glasgow became great commercial center. By late 19th cent. coal and iron industries had taken lead in economy, and steamships were built at Clydeside. Concentration of heavy industry made Scotland important arsenal in both World Wars. Efforts to attract tourists include Edinburgh's festival of arts. There is still a nationalist movement which urges greater autonomy for Scotland.

Scotland, Church of, established church of Scotland. Under John KNOX Scottish reformers followed Calvinist teachings. After First Covenant (1557) Parliament abolished jurisdiction of Roman Church in Scotland in 1560. When it ratified *Second Book of Discipline* in 1592, it estab. Presbyterian polity and Calvinistic doctrine as recognized religion of Scotland. National Covenant was signed 1638; in 1643 the Solemn League and Covenant was signed in both England and Scotland. Westminster Confession was adopted 1647. Act of Settlement (1690) and union of England and Scotland (1707) ratified existence of Church of Scoland.

Scotland, Free Church of, formed 1843 by secession group from Church of Scotland, led by Thomas Chalmers, in dispute between church and state over patronage, and interference of the state. In 1900 main body of Free Church joined United Presbyterian Church as United Free Church of Scotland. In 1929 rejoined Church of Scotland.

Scotland Yard, short street in London which became hq. of metropolitan police in 1829. New hq. (New Scotland Yard) estab. 1890 on the Thames. The Criminal Investigation Department (CID), popularly known as "Scotland Yard," is part of it.

Scott, Cyril (Meir), 1879–, English impressionist composer of symphonies, operas, choral works, chamber music, songs, and piano pieces. He is also an author of books on musical and scientific subjects and occultism.

Scott, Sir George Gilbert, 1811–78, English architect, prominent in the Gothic revival. Designed Albert Memorial, London, and restored part of Westminster Abbey. His grandson, **Sir Giles Gilbert Scott,** 1880–, designed Liverpool Cathedral.

Scott, James Brown, 1866–1943, American authority on international law, b. Canada; dean of the law school at the Univ. of Southern California (1896–99) and the Univ. of Illinois (1899–1903) and professor at several other universities. Had many public posts concerned with international affairs.

Scott, John: see ELDON, JOHN SCOTT, 1ST EARL OF.

Scott, Robert Falcon, 1868–1912, British naval officer, antarctic explorer. Commanded expedition (1901–4) to explore Ross Sea region. Set forth in 1910 to seek South Pole. Reached it with four companions, Jan. 18, 1912, one month after Roald Amundsen. All died on return journey, but remains and records of epic journey were later recovered.

Scott, Sir Walter, 1771–1832, British novelist and poet. He studied at Univ. of Edinburgh and was called to the bar in 1792. In vacations he learned to know the Border countryside, and he collected folk songs in *Minstrelsy of the Scottish Border* (2 vols., 1802; 3 vols., 1803). This interest led to his *Lay of the Last Minstrel* (1805), *Marmion* (1808), and *The Lady of the Lake* (1810). Later narrative poems proving less popular, he turned to prose romances, among them *Waverley* (1814; beginning series called Waverley novels), *Guy Mannering* (1815), *The Heart of Midlothian* (1818), and *The Bride of Lammermoor* (1819). He was made baronet in 1820. *Ivanhoe* (1820) began the long series of romances of British history, such as *Kenilworth* (1821), *Quentin Durward* (1823), and *The Talisman* (1825). Scott now met financial reverses. He had bought Abbotsford in 1812, and he had invested heavily in the Ballantyne publishing house. When the firm failed in 1825, Scott heroically assumed its entire indebtedness. He wrote incessantly, and ruined his health, but the entire debt was paid off from the sale of his books after his death. In his ringing rhymes, such as "Lochinvar" and "Proud Maisie," and in his novels Scott recreated the heroic spirit of Scotland—and of England.

Scott, Winfield, 1786–1866, American general. A hero of War of 1812. His peacemaking talents were often useful to U.S., e.g., in Aroostook War (1839). From July, 1841, to Nov., 1861, he was supreme commander of U.S. army. In Mexican War he headed southern expedition; campaign was triumph for Scott's daring strategy and confirmed his reputation as a bold fighter. Made poor showing as Whig candidate for President in 1852. Although vain and pompous (he was called "Old Fuss and Feathers"), he was also generous and fair-minded. Greatest American general between Washington and Lee.

Scott City, city (pop. 3,204), W central Kansas, N of Garden City. To N are remains of an Indian pueblo.

Scottdale, borough (pop. 6,249), SW Pa., SE of Pittsburgh. Coal mining; mfg. of metal products.

Scotti, Antonio (skô′tē), 1868–1936, Italian baritone. He sang at the Metropolitan Opera, New York, 1899–1933, in such roles as Iago in *Otello*, Scarpia in *La Tosca*, and Hans Sachs in *Die Meistersinger*.

Scottish dialect, English dialect of the Lowlands, a modern form of Northumbrian Old English. Used in 11th-cent. courts, it became official language when Malcolm III abandoned Scottish Gaelic. History of Scottish grammar roughly parallels that of standard ENGLISH LANGUAGE, but in details of sound changes Scottish frequently differs from standard English, and in vocabulary it is more archaic than standard English. Oldest literary monument in Scottish dialect is *The Bruce* (14th cent.) by John Barbour. Following early great Scottish poets (Chaucerians such as James I) came a golden age in 15th and 16th cent., but thereafter Scottish declined as a literary medium (except for 18th-cent. revival by Allan Ramsay, Robert Burns, and others), and English has made continual inroads into the vernacular since early 17th cent. This fact may be explained by Stuart accession to English throne with loss of a Scottish national self-consciousness and use in Scotland of the English Bible.

Scottish Gaelic language and literature: see GAELIC; GAELIC LITERATURE.

Scottish terrier: see TERRIER.

Scottsbluff, city (pop. 12,858), W Nebr., on North Platte R., in Great Plains region near Wyo. line; settled after 1885. Trade center of irrigated agr. area, it produces beet sugar, flour, dairy products, and refined oil. Scotts

Bluff National Monument (see NATIONAL PARKS AND MONUMENTS, table) is across the river.

Scottsboro, city (pop. 4,731), NE Ala., near Tennessee R. at edge of Cumberland Plateau. Gave name to **Scottsboro Case.** On March 31, 1931, nine Negro boys were indicted on charges of having raped two white girls. After several trials and two U.S. Supreme Court reversals of conviction, five were convicted and sentenced (in Jan., 1936, and July, 1937) and four were acquitted. By Sept., 1946, all had been released except Haywood Patterson, the alleged ringleader; he escaped later (d. 1952 in Mich. prison). Northern liberals and radicals, charging anti-Negro bias in Ala., made the case a *cause célèbre*. Communists used it for propaganda purposes. The Scottsboro Defense Committee, for the most part representing liberal, non-Communist organizations, was largely responsible for ultimate freeing of the boys.

Scotus: see DUNS SCOTUS and ERIGENA, JOHN SCOTUS.

scouting: see BOY SCOUTS; GIRL SCOUTS.

Scranton, city (pop. 125,536), NE Pa., on Lackawanna R. and NW of New York city; settled late in 18th cent. Commercial and industrial center of anthracite region of NE Pa. with mfg. of textiles, clothing, and metal products.

screw, simple machine consisting of cylinder around which an inclined plane winds spirally. Mechanical advantage theoretically is ratio between circumference through which the end moves and pitch (distance between threads). Although, because of friction, the efficiency is small, screw devices such as jackscrew used to lift automobiles, houses, etc., are of great value because of enormous load raised by relatively small effort. See *ill.*, p. 619.

Scriabin, Aleksandr (Nikolayevich) (ŭlyĭksän'dŭr skrëä'bĭn), 1872–1915, Russian composer. A bold innovator, he introduced chords built in fourths (C–F sharp–B flat) instead of triads (C–E–G). His orchestral music includes his *Divine Poem* and *Prometheus: a Poem of Fire*, which calls for the play of colored lights upon a screen during the performance.

Scribe, Eugène (ûzhĕn' skrēb'), 1791–1861, French author of popular plays of every description and librettos for grand opera (notably for Auber, Meyerbeer, Boieldieu, Jacques Halévy). *Le Verre d'eau* is perhaps his best-known comedy.

scribe (skrīb), originally a Jewish scholar who knew the art of writing, later an official teacher of Jewish law. The work of the scribes developed into the Oral Law, as distinct from the Written Law of the Torah. The scribes lost their religious leadership in the 1st cent. A.D. and were followed by the Tannaim (plural of Tanna), scholars and teachers of the Oral Law who flourished between A.D. 10 and A.D. 220. The Mishna is the work of this group. They were succeeded by the Amoraim (c.200 to 350), who developed the Gemara of the Talmud. The period of the Geonim, who became the authoritative interpreters of the Old Testament and the Talmud, ended in 1038.

Scriblerus Club, English literary group formed (1713) to satirize "false tastes in learning." Members included Gay, Pope, Swift, and Arbuthnot, chief author of club's "Memoirs of . . . Martinus Scriblerus."

Scribner, Charles, 1821–71, American publisher. In 1846 founded publishing house which in 1878 became Charles Scribner's Sons. Founded in 1870 *Scribner's Monthly* (later *Century Magazine*). His son, **Charles Scribner,** 1854–1930, became head of firm in 1879; founded in 1887 *Scribner's Magazine.*

Scripps, Edward Wyllis, 1854–1926, American newspaper publisher. With brother George and M. A. McRae founded Scripps-McRae League, a powerful liberal, pro-labor newspaper chain. In 1907 estab. United Press Association, with R. W. Howard as manager (after 1908). After 1922 his son R. P. Scripps joined with Howard to control chain, now known as Scripps-Howard papers.

Scripps College: see CLAREMONT, Calif.

Scripps Institution of Oceanography: see LA JOLLA, Calif.

scrofula: see TUBERCULOSIS.

Scrooby, village, Nottinghamshire, England. Home of William Brewster, it was center of group later known as Pilgrims.

Scudder, Henry Martyn, 1822–95, American missionary, b. Ceylon; son of a missionary. He worked in India (1844–64) under American Board and Dutch Reformed Church. Missionary in Japan (1887–90).

Scudéry, Madeleine de (mädùlĕn' dù skùdārē'), 1607?–1701, French author of the romances *Artamène; ou, Le Grand Cyrus* (1649–53) and *Clélie* (1654–60). Despite their extreme preciosity, these foreshadowed in their analysis of sentiment and character the later French psychological novel.

scurvy (scorbutus), deficiency disease resulting from insufficient vitamin C (ascorbic acid) in diet. Attended by bleeding of gums, anemia, debility. Formerly common among sailors. May occur in babies after six months of age if diet lacks vitamin C.

scutage (skū'tĭj), feudal impost originating as a fine or cash impost in lieu of military service due by a vassal to a suzerain, especially to a king. Collected by kings for military expenses and other purposes. Impost resisted by barons, and in Magna Carta (1215) King John agreed to collect scutage only with counsel of barons. Growth of taxes after time of Edward III displaced scutage.

Scutari (skōō'tūrē), Albanian *Shkodër* or *Shkodra*, city (pop. 33,852), N Albania. Has textile, tobacco, and other mfg. An ancient Illyrian capital and a Roman colony (Scodra) from 168 B.C., it fell to the Serbs in 7th cent. A.D. Was seat of princes of Zeta (i.e., Montenegro) from 14th cent. to its fall to Turkey (1479). Though occupied by Montenegrin troops in the Balkan Wars (1913), it was assigned by the European powers to Albania. In World War I it was successively under Montenegrin, Austrian, and Allied occupation. Scutari lies on the SE end of **Lake Scutari,** part of which extends into Yugoslavia. Because of seasonal variations in depth, its area varies from 150 to 200 sq. mi. Abundant fishing.

Scutari or **Uskudar** (üskü'där), urban district (pop. 60,-722) of Istanbul, Turkey, on Asiatic side. Florence Nightingale worked in British military hospital here during Crimean War.

Scylla (sĭ'lù), in Greek mythology, sea nymph. Circe, her rival in love for Glaucus, made her a monster, who lived on a rock on Italian side of Strait of Messina. Opposite, on Sicilian side, was whirlpool of Charybdis. Odysseus passed safely through strait of Scylla and Charybdis (now called Scilla), as did Argonaut heroes.

Scyllis: see DIPOENUS AND SCYLLIS.

Scyros, Greek island: see SKYROS.

Scythia (sĭ'thēù), region of S Europe inhabited by the Scythians, varying in extent as their power grew or waned, but generally with its core on the N shore of the Black Sea about the lower Don and lower Dnieper and in the Crimea. The **Scythians** were nomadic and warlike horsemen, who were in the area by the 9th cent. B.C. They spoke an Indo-Iranian language. They traded with the Greeks and acted as Greek mercenaries. In the 7th cent. they invaded the Assyrian Empire and for a time held Palestine. Darius I led an expedition (c.512 B.C.) and Alexander the Great also led an expedition against them. In the 3d cent. B.C. they were replaced by their kinsmen, the Sarmatians.

Se, chemical symbol of the element SELENIUM.

sea, law of the: see MARITIME LAW.

sea anemone (ùnĕ'mùnē), marine invertebrate related to jellyfish and coral. It has a cylindrical body and stinging tentacles. Attaches to rock, shell, or seaweed in shallow water.

Seabees [from the initials of Construction Battalion], colloquial name for the U.S. Naval Construction Battalions of World War II. The first regiment was authorized in Dec., 1941. Force grew to c.250,000 men.

Seaborg, Glenn Theodore, 1912–, American chemist and physicist. Shared 1951 Nobel Prize in Chemistry for discoveries in chemistry of elements having atomic number greater than that of uranium. He is codiscoverer of plutonium (element 94), americium (element 95), curium (element 96), berkelium (element 97), and californium (element 98). Associated with Univ. of California from 1937, and with atomic bomb project (1942–46).

Sea Bright, summer-resort borough (pop. 999), NE N.J., between Shrewsbury R. and the Atlantic. In an estate area, it holds national and international tennis and polo matches.

Seabury, Samuel, 1729–96, American clergyman, first bishop of Protestant Episcopal Church. Consecrated in Scotland in 1784; became presiding bishop of Church in U.S. in 1789. His great-great-grandson, **Samuel Seabury,** 1873–, headed investigations in 1930–31 of New York city's magistrate courts and of New York city politics.

Seaford, town (pop. 3,087), SW Del., on Nanticoke R. Nylon-industry center.

sea horse, small warm-water fish (chiefly of genus *Hippocampus*). Elongated head and snout suggest appearance of horse. It swims weakly in upright position. Male has abdominal pouch in which eggs are carried until young hatch.

Sea Islands, chain of low islands along coast of S.C., Ga., and N Fla., between mouths of Santee and St. Johns rivers. Spanish, early in control, gave way to English. SAINT HELENA ISLAND and Port Royal Isl. (S.C.) had great cotton plantations in early 19th cent. Land divided among slaves by U.S. after Civil War. Carolina islands still largely inhabited by Negroes, who retain many old customs and dialects. Farming and fishing important. BEAUFORT (Port Royal Isl.) is main city. Parris Isl. has U.S. marine base. St. Simons, Sea, and Jekyll islands are Ga. resorts. St. Simons Isl. has ruins of Fort Frederica (now national monument), built 1736–54 by James Oglethorpe during English-Spanish struggle for SE U.S. Spanish defeated near by in battle of Bloody Marsh, July 7, 1742. Jekyll Isl. is state park. Cumberland Isl., Ga., largest (c.22 mi. long, 1–5 mi. wide), still mostly private.

seal, carnivorous aquatic mammal with front and hind flippers, found chiefly in cold regions. Suborder Pinnipedia (of order Carnivora) consists of three families: true, earless, or hair seals (Phocidae); eared fur seals and sea lions (Otariidae); walruses (Odobenidae). Alaskan fur seals winter from Alaska to N coast of Calif. and in spring migrate N to breeding grounds on Pribilof Isls.

Seal Harbor, Maine: see MOUNT DESERT ISLAND.

Seal Islands: see LOBOS ISLANDS.

Sealyham terrier: see TERRIER.

sea pink or **thrift,** perennial garden plant (*Armeria*), with papery, globe-shaped flower clusters and grass-like evergreen foliage. The sea lavenders (*Limonium*), also called sea pink, have panicles of dainty flowers. Plants of both genera are often called statice.

sea power. According to A. T. MAHAN, the naval strength which enables state to control part of sea and deny its use to enemy nations or to uphold its maritime rights in peace or war. Development of sea power dates from earliest history. By it Phoenicians controlled Mediterranean, and Athens defeated Persians at Salamis. Contributed to Rome's victory over Carthage and subsequent spread of empire. Italian city-states and HANSEATIC LEAGUE derived wealth from control of seas. Battle of LEPANTO (1571) ended Turkish naval power. Portugal built empire on seas, and Spain ruled the waves until the defeat of the Armada by England. Dutch gained importance through sea power. Great Britain vanquished France in 18th and 19th cent. to become mistress of seas. Sea power of U.S. increased rapidly from War of 1812 through Civil and Spanish-American wars. Bottling-up of German navy contributed to Allied victory in World War I. Despite growth of air power, necessity of navy in Pacific and in invasion of Europe in World War II pointed to its continuing importance. Naval forces have been of great value in atom-bomb experiments.

searchlight, device using lens and reflecting surface to direct a beam of light. After 1900 acetylene came into use as an illuminant and in 1916 Edison invented portable apparatus fed from batteries. Searchlights mounted on trucks and railroad cars came into use in World War I. In 1915 E. A. Sperry, American inventor, introduced high-intensity arc lamp. Revolving searchlights as beacons spaced along air routes have yielded to radio beacons. Use of powerful lights coordinated with anti-aircraft guns developed considerably in World War II.

Searcy (sûr′sē), city (pop. 6,024), N central Ark., NE of Little Rock, in strawberry area.

Searsport, resort town (pop. 1,457), S Maine, on Penobscot Bay. Has Penobscot Marine Mus. (1936).

Seaside. 1 Village (pop. 10,226), W Calif., on S shore of Monterey Bay. **2** Resort city (pop. 3,886), NW Oregon, on the Pacific and S of Astoria. Monument marks point sometimes considered end of Oregon Trail.

seasons, divisions of year characterized by variations in amount of heat received from sun. Variations depend on inclination of equator in plane of the ecliptic and on revolution of earth around the sun. The heat at a given point depends chiefly on the angle of the sun's rays and the daily duration of exposure to them. In temperate zones there are four well-defined seasons. In low latitudes and in certain areas (e.g., India) where oceans and winds especially affect seasonal changes, there are "wet" and "dry" seasons. See *ill.*, p. 927.

Seattle, city (pop. 467,491), W Wash., between Elliott Bay of Puget Sound and L. Washington, and between Olympic Mts. and Cascade Range; settled 1852 as lumber town. Grew after railroads came (1884) despite strikes, anti-Chinese riots, and fire of 1889. Boomed with Alaska gold rush (1897) and opening of Panama Canal (1914). Largest city in Wash., a metropolis of the Pacific Northwest. Great port and commercial center, with Alaskan and Far Eastern trade; has foreign trade zone (opened 1949). Mfg. of lumber, food products (fruit, fish, meat), aluminum, iron, steel, textiles. Important fur market. Hq. for fishing (esp. halibut) and pleasure boats. Great expansion brought by World War II (aircraft, shipbuilding) and new hydroelectric projects in region. Seat of Univ. of WASHINGTON, Seattle Univ. (Jesuit; coed.; 1898), Fort Lawton, and Sand Point Naval Air Station.

sea urchin, marine animal, like the starfish an echinoderm. Globular outer skeleton protects body. Irregular spines aid the tube feet in locomotion. In mouth region on underneath surface most forms have complex structure containing five sharp teeth. Sea urchins are scavengers.

seaweed, name for marine algae. Simple forms are of a single cell or a few cells, but higher forms have a disklike base and ribbonlike or leaflike frond of green, brown, or red. Few seaweeds grow below a depth of 150 ft. Some red seaweeds are eaten, especially in the Orient; commercial AGAR is obtained from a red alga. See also GULFWEED; IRISH MOSS; KELP.

Sebago Lake (sĭbā′gō), 12 mi. long and 1–8 mi. wide, SW Maine, NW of Portland, in resort area. Supplies Portland's water.

Sebastian, Saint, 3d cent.?, Roman martyr, said to have been beloved by Diocletian, who turned against him when he was converted to Christianity and had him killed with arrows. Feast: Jan. 20.

Sebastian, 1554–78, king of Portugal (1557–78). Was under regency of his grandmother 1557–62; under that of his uncle and successor, Henry, 1562–68. Fanatically religious, he led a great expedition against Moslems in Morocco but was defeated and slain in the battle of Alcazarquivir. His army was wiped out. A legend prophesying his return long persisted.

Sebastiano del Piombo (sābästyä′nō dĕl pyōm′bō), c.1485–1547, Venetian painter, whose real name was Sebastiano Luciani. So called because he held the office of *piombo* (keeper of papal seals). Influenced by Michelangelo.

Sebastopol, RSFSR: see SEVASTOPOL.

Sebec Lake (sē′bĭk), 11 mi. long and ½–3 mi. wide, central Maine, SE of Moosehead L. Noted for salmon and bass fishing.

Sebring (sē′brĭng), city (pop. 5,006), S central Fla., on L. Jackson, in citrus-fruit area.

Secaucus (sēkô′kŭs), town (pop. 9,750), NE N.J., N of Jersey City. Silk and metal products.

Secchi, (Pietro) Angelo (pyä′trō än′jälō sĕk′kē), 1818–78, Italian astronomer, a Jesuit priest, pioneer in classifying stars by their spectra.

secession, formal withdrawal from association by group discontented with decisions or actions of majority. Best-known example was withdrawal in 1860–61 of 11 Southern states from U.S. to form CONFEDERACY, which fought Civil War with Northern states. Central issue was question of STATES′ RIGHTS. Secessionists held Constitution was a compact between sovereign states, not paramount in power; hence they could legally secede from a voluntary union. Opponents held that Constitution created sovereign and inviolable union and that withdrawal was impossible. One course of action was NULLIFICATION movement. When Southern states felt threatened by election of Lincoln, they seceded.

Secession, War of: see CIVIL WAR.

Second Adventists: see ADVENTISTS.

Second Empire: see NAPOLEON III.

secretary bird, African bird of prey c.4 ft. high, with long legs, hooked beak, and black-feathered crest (like quill pens). Destroys reptiles and other animals.

secretion, in biology, substance formed by single cells or organ of animal or plant and performing special function or eliminated as waste. Secretions in man include external and internal secretions (see GLAND) and lubricants, e.g., synovial fluid in joints and tears. Wastes include urine and sweat.

secret police. Law enforcement has required in almost all organized societies a certain amount of secrecy, particularly in investigation of crime. Emergence of recognizable, uniformed police is probably more recent than secret bodies formed against external or internal attack. Generally secret police include all who operate without knowledge of a suspect that he is under investigation. In democracy, role of secret police usually ceases once investigation is closed. This limitation and right of offender to open trial and access to evidence against him are guarantees of individual freedom notable in countries which have adopted English and American systems. Secret police not bound by these conditions are endowed with authority superior to other law-enforcing agencies. They may investigate, apprehend, and sometimes judge a suspect and are responsible only to executive branch. A particular danger inherent in this type of secret police is that it may become a state within the state and ultimately overthrow the government, e.g., Nazi secret police under Heinrich Himmler. In 1933 the Gestapo was formed under Hermann Goering and in 1936 was combined with the SS (see NATIONAL SOCIALISM) under Himmler. He subordinated it to the *Sicherheitsdienst* or SD [security service]. This body, with its intricate ramifications and agents in all branches of government, eventually became so powerful as to make Himmler the real master of Germany. German crimes and atrocities in World War II were largely carried out by the SS and Gestapo. Secret police forces do not always have their roots in maintenance of security of the state. Such organizations as the VEHME of medieval Germany may be a spontaneous creation of a segment of the people to protect its interests. The institution has existed in most societies where a minority exercised uneasy rule over a majority. Sparta had secret police, and in Rome paid informers were employed. Venetian Inquisition saw early secret police organized along modern lines (see TEN, COUNCIL OF); also notable was the Oprichnina of Tsar IVAN IV. Russia saw organization of another secret police after Decembrist uprising of 1825. This group, like all others, worked with censorship to control not only subversive acts but even subversive thought. (This trend culminated in Japanese Thought Police in World War II.) After Russian Revolution of 1917, Soviets created own secret police, the dread Cheka. This was renamed OGPU or GPU [united department of political police] 1922, and was abolished 1934 to be absorbed by people's commissariat (later ministry) of internal affairs (NKVD, later MVD). Its responsibilities include detection of subversive elements, supervision of prison and labor camps, and "reeducation" of political offenders. Secret political police strengthened Mussolini's power in Italy.

secret society. Organization of almost universal occurrence and ancient origin. Typically, membership follows initiation rite involving pledge of secrecy, acceptance of obligations, and tests of worthiness. Candidate is then introduced to group's mysteries. Societies range from schools of tribal lore to FRATERNAL ORDERS. See also FREEMASONRY.

Securities and Exchange Commission (SEC), U.S. government agency created by Securities Exchange Act of 1934 to prevent unfair practices in the securities market. Administers government regulations on investments and supervises stock exchanges.

Security Council: see UNITED NATIONS.

Sedalia (sĭdā′lyù), city (pop. 20,354) W central Mo., ESE of Kansas City; laid out 1859. Center of a farm and limestone area. Has railroad shops and mfg. of disinfectants and food products.

Sedan (sĭdăn′, Fr. sùdä′), garrison town (pop. 12,987), Ardennes dept., NE France, on Meuse R. near Belgian border. Textile mfg. Until cession (1642) to France it was part of duchy of Bouillon. Served as a Protestant stronghold 16th–17th cent. It was scene in Franco-Prussian War of decisive French defeat and capture of Napoleon III (1870); in World War II of German breakthrough starting "battle of France" (1940).

sedge, name for grasslike and rushlike marsh plants of family Cyperaceae, of temperate and tropical regions. Some (species of *Carex, Cyperus,* and *Scirpus*) yield hay and can be woven into mats and chair seats.

Sedgemoor, moorland, Somerset, England. Site of duke of Monmouth's defeat in 1685 by James II.

Sedgwick, John, 1813–64, Union general in Civil War. Served with Army of the Potomac in the Peninsular, Antietam, and Wilderness campaigns.

sedimentary rock: see ROCK.

sedum (sē′dùm), succulent perennial plant of genus *Sedum,* also called stonecrop, often grown in rock gardens and borders. The creeping, yellow-flowered *Sedum acre* is naturalized from the Old World. The showy sedum (*S. spectabile*), white or rosy-flowered, is common in gardens.

seed, product of the fertilization of the ovum of a flower after POLLINATION. It is a many-celled structure borne within a fruit (see *ill.,* p. 783) and contains the embryo or young plant and stored food. Seeds are produced by the highest group of plants while those in lower orders (mosses and ferns) bear spores which are unicellular and contain no embryo. Seeds vary in size from the dustlike seed of some orchids to the huge seeds of a palm. Many seeds require a resting period before germination. A plant grown from seed may differ from its parent plant as a result of cross pollination or other causes.

Seeger, Alan, 1888–1916, American poet, famous for war poem "I Have a Rendezvous with Death," poignantly prophetic of his own death in action in 1916.

seeing-eye dog, trained to guide a blind person. Breeds used for this purpose include German shepherds, Doberman pinschers, and some bulldogs. At the Seeing

Eye, Inc., a school in Morristown, N.J., each dog is first trained alone, and then dog and master are trained together. Many blind people have gained new independence with a seeing-eye dog.

Seekonk, river: see BLACKSTONE, river.

Seeland, Denmark: see ZEALAND.

Seeley, Sir John Robert, 1834–95, English historian. Books include *Ecce Homo* (1865), a life of Christ; *The Expansion of England* (1883); and *Growth of British Policy* (1895).

Seelye, Julius Hawley (sē'lē), 1824–95, American clergyman, president (1876–90) of Amherst. Initiated first student self-government in America. His brother **Laurenus Clark Seelye,** 1837–1924, also a clergyman, in 1873 became first president of Smith Col., retiring in 1910.

sego lily (sē'gō), ornamental tuliplike white flower (*Calochortus nuttalli*), native to the W U.S.

Segonzac, André Dunoyer de (ädrä' dünwäyä' dü sügōzäk'), 1884–, French painter. His landscapes, still lifes, and nudes are done in highly simplified style.

Segovia, Andrés (ändräs' sägō'vyä), 1894–, Spanish virtuoso guitarist, most notable performer of his time. In transcriptions of early contrapuntal music he made the guitar a concert instrument.

Segovia (sägō'vyä), city (pop. 24,253), cap. of Segovia prov., central Spain, in Old Castile. Crowning the city are magnificent Gothic cathedral (1526–1616) and 14th-cent. alcazar, where Isabella I of Castile was proclaimed queen. Famous Roman aqueduct (c.900 yards long) is still in use.

Seguin (sŭgēn'), city (pop. 9,733), S central Texas, on Guadalupe R. and ENE of San Antonio; settled 1832 by Germans. Trade and processing center for cotton, farm, cattle, and oil area. River and near-by L. McQueeney attract visitors.

Seignobos, Charles (shärl' sānyōbō'), 1854–1942, French historian. Known for studies of French and European history and civilization, notably *The Feudal Régime* (Eng. tr., 1902; new ed., 1926).

seignorial system: see MANORIAL SYSTEM; FEUDALISM.

Seine (sān, Fr. sĕn), department (185 sq. mi.; pop. 4,775,711), N France, coextensive with Greater Paris (i.e., PARIS proper with its residential and industrial suburbs, the *banlieue*). Here is largest industrial concentration of population in France. Produces machinery, autos, airplanes, textiles, chemicals, and luxury goods.

Seine, river, 482 mi. long, N France. With its tributaries (e.g., Aube, Yonne, Marne, Oise) it drains entire Paris basin. Rising in Langres Plateau, it winds NW past Paris and Rouen to enter English Channel through a wide estuary (max. 6 mi.) at Le Havre. These three ports handle bulk of French river and ocean trade.

Seine-et-Marne (sĕn"-ā-märn'), department (2,290 sq. mi.; pop. 407,137), N France in Île-de-France; cap. Melun.

Seine-et-Oise (sĕn"-ā-wäz'), department (2,185 sq. mi.; pop. 1,414,910), N France, in Île-de-France; cap. Versailles.

Seine-Inférieure (sĕn"-ēfārēûr'), department (2,448 sq. mi.; pop. 846,131), N France, in Normandy; cap. Rouen.

Seir (sē'ûr), mountainous region, S Palestine, identical with EDOM. Frequently called Mt. Seir.

seismology (sīzmō'lŭjē, sīs–), scientific study of earthquakes. Instruments used are called seismographs, and the record, traced on a rotating drum, is the seismogram. From this graph information about the earthquake can be learned. An important commercial application is use of seismology in prospecting for petroleum. Earth tremors are caused by high explosive and the resulting waves recorded by the seismograph. Formations associated with oil can thus be located.

Seiyukai (sā'yōōkī'), Japanese political party, founded 1900. Derived from the Jiyuto, founded 1881. Ito was its first president, Saionji its second. First leader to form party cabinet (1918) on parliamentary principles was Takashi Hara. Seiyukai cabinets alternated 1927–32 with MINSEITO governments, with both having basically similar programs. After 1932, rising militarist power forced decline of political parties; all finally disbanded 1940 in favor of single government-sponsored party.

Sejanus, Lucius Aelius (sĭjā'nŭs), d. A.D. 31, Roman statesman, commander of the Praetorian guards, and a favorite of Tiberius, until he was suspected of plots and was put to death.

Sekia el Hamra: see SPANISH SAHARA.

Selangor: see MALAYA.

Selborne (sĕl'bôrn), village, Hampshire, England. Home of Gilbert White, author of *The Natural History and Antiquities of Selborne*. His grave is here.

Selden, John, 1584–1654, English jurist and scholar. Active in Parliament's struggle with crown, and in trial of George Villiers. One of most erudite men of his time, an authority in legal antiquarianism, he wrote *England's Epinomis, Jani Anglorum* (1610), and *Analecton Anglo-Britannicon* (1615).

selection. In Darwinism the mechanism of natural selection is considered of major importance in process of evolution. According to Darwin, because of various environmental factors (e.g., quantity of available food and water and conditions of temperature and pressure) and overproduction in animals and plants, a struggle for existence arises and only those best adapted to environment survive (survival of the fittest) and reproduce. In plant and animal breeding man practices artificial selection, choosing individuals best suited for his purpose.

selective service, in U.S. history. Although national military conscription was begun in 1863 in Civil War, Congress authorized release from service to anyone who furnished a satisfactory substitute and, at first, to those who paid $300. General conscription took place in World War I. First peacetime conscription in U.S. was undertaken in 1940. Following U.S. entry into World War II a new selective service act was passed. Selective service act of 1948 required all men from 18 through 25 to register, made men from 19 to 25 liable for induction for 21-month service; in 1951 the draft age was lowered to 18½, service period was raised to 24 months active service, 8 years in reserve.

Selene (sŭlē'nē) [Gr.,= moon], in Greek religion, moongoddess; identified with Artemis.

Selenga (sĕlĕng-gä'), river, c.750 mi. long, rising in Mongolian People's Republic and flowing through Buryat Mongol ASSR to L. Baikal. Orkhon is main tributary.

selenium (sŭlē'nēŭm), rare, nonmetallic element (symbol = Se; see also ELEMENT, table). It is allotropic, appearing in red powdery, red crystalline, and gray metallike forms; its conductivity increases with illumination, hence it has been used in some photoelectric tubes (see *ill.*, p. 293). It is used in rubber, red glass, enamels. Resembles sulphur in activity; rarely occurs uncombined in nature. In parts of U.S., livestock suffer from selenium poisoning caused by eating vegetation that has absorbed selenium from soil.

Seleucia (sŭlū'shŭ), anc. city of Mesopotamia on the Tigris below Baghdad. Founded by Seleucus I c.312 B.C., it replaced Babylon as chief city of region. Later the Parthians built Ctesiphon across the river. Seleucia was destroyed by Romans in A.D. 164.

Seleucus (sŭlū'kŭs), kings of anc. Syria of the Seleucid dynasty. **Seleucus I** (Nicator), d. 280 B.C., was a general of Alexander the Great and a leading figure in the wars of the DIADOCHI. He got Babylonia in the breakup of the empire and expanded his power E to the Indus. He joined the league against ANTIGONUS I and benefited from the battle of Ipsus (301 B.C.). Later gained more by defeating LYSIMACHUS (281 B.C.). **Seleucus II** (Callinicus), d. 226 B.C., was the son of ANTIOCHUS II. On his father's death he seized the throne, killing his stepmother, Berenice, and his infant half-brother before Berenice's brother, PTOL-

EMY III, could arrive with an army. A long war followed, as did civil wars, with loss of power. ANTIOCHUS III was his son.

Seligman, Edwin Robert Anderson (sĕ'lĭgmŭn), 1861–1939, American economist, professor at Columbia Univ. 1885–1931. Edited *Encyclopaedia of the Social Sciences* and advanced the economic interpretation of history.

Selim (sĕ'lĭm, sùlēm'), Ottoman sultans. **Selim I** (the Grim), 1467–1520, became sultan 1512 by deposing his father, Bajazet II, and killing his brothers. During his reign Turkey entered the height of its power. He defeated Shah Ismail of Persia (1514) and annexed Kurdistan. After his victory over the Mamelukes of Syria and Egypt (1516–17) he assumed the CALIPHATE for himself and his successors and took control over the holy cities, Mecca and Medina. A bloodthirsty despot, he ordered the massacre of 40,000 Shiites. His son Suleiman I succeeded him. **Selim II** (the Drunkard), c.1524–1574, son of Suleiman I, reigned 1566–74. Conquered Cyprus; recovered Morocco. His fleet was defeated at LEPANTO (1571). **Selim III**, 1761–1808, reigned 1789–1807. Concluded war with Russia by accepting humiliating Treaty of Jassy (1792), then set about to reform his empire with efficient zeal. He joined the anti-French coalition of 1798. His troops yielded Jaffa to Bonaparte but forced the French to retreat from Acre (1799). War with Russia broke out again in 1806, and in 1807 Selim was deposed by the rebellious Janizaries. He was strangled in prison.

Seljuks: see TURKS.

Selkirk, Alexander, 1676–1721, Scottish sailor, whose adventures suggested story of *Robinson Crusoe* (1719) to Daniel Defoe. Put ashore on one of the Juan Fernández Isls., he remained for over four years before rescue.

Selkirk, Thomas Douglas, 5th **earl of,** 1771–1820, Scottish philanthropist, founder of RED RIVER SETTLEMENT. To aid his impoverished countrymen he promoted a successful settlement on P.E.I., Canada (1803).

Selkirk, county, Scotland: see SELKIRKSHIRE.

Selkirk, town (pop. 6,218), SE Man., Canada, on Red R., NE of Winnipeg and S of L. Winnipeg. Center of RED RIVER SETTLEMENT, estab. 1812 by earl of Selkirk. Transships L. Winnipeg fish.

Selkirk Mountains, range of Rocky Mts., SE B.C., Canada, near Alta. border; extends NW 200 mi. from Idaho and Mont. borders.

Selkirkshire (sĕl'kûrkshĭr) or **Selkirk,** inland county (267 sq. mi.; pop. 21,724), S Scotland; co. town Selkirk. Region of rolling hills, sheep raising is the chief occupation. Associated with Sir Walter Scott and James Hogg. Saw much border warfare between England and Scotland.

Selma. 1 City (pop. 22,840), SW central Ala., on Alabama R. and W of Montgomery; settled 1816. Rail center in livestock and cotton area; processes foodstuffs, cotton, cottonseed oil, iron, lumber. Ravaged as Confederate supply base (1865). U.S. military aviation school (1941) is near. 2 City (pop. 5,964), central Calif., SE of Fresno in San Joaquin Valley. Area produces fruit, truck, and dairy products.

seltzer water, alkaline water, rich in salts, very popular in 19th cent. as beverage and medicine.

Selwyn College: see CAMBRIDGE UNIVERSITY.

Semarang (sùmä'räng), city (pop. 217,796), on N Java, Indonesia; port on Java Sea. Exports tobacco, sugar, copra, rubber, kapok, and coffee. Textile mills.

Sembrich, Marcella (sĕm'brĭk), 1858–1935, stage name of Praxede Marcelline Kochanska, Polish coloratura soprano. She appeared regularly at the Metropolitan Opera, New York, 1898–1909, and was outstanding as Violetta in *La Traviata.*

Semele (sĕ'mĭlē), in Greek religion; mother of Dionysus by Zeus. She asked Zeus to appear in his majesty, but when he did she died of terror. Dionysus later found her in Hades and took her to Olympus.

Seminole (sĕ'mĭnōl), city (pop. 11,863), central Okla., SE of Oklahoma City; settled 1890. Trade center for farm and oil region with refineries and carbon-black plant.

Seminole Indians, North American tribe of Natchez-Muskogean linguistic stock, originating when a group of Creek Indians separated from the main body in the early 18th cent. and settled in Fla. They absorbed remnants of the Apalachee and many runaway Negro slaves. They were hostile to the U.S., and in 1817–18 Andrew Jackson led a force into Spanish territory to punish them. By a treaty of 1832 they were bound to move W of the Mississippi, but many, led by Osceola, refused. The Seminole War began in 1835 and lasted until 1842, when the heroic resistance of the Seminole was beaten down. The American troops were led for a time by Richard Keith Call. Some remained in the Everglades, but most moved to Okla.

Semipalatinsk (syĭmē''pŭlä'tyĭnsk), city (pop. 109,779), E Kazakh SSR, on Irtysh R. and Turksib RR. Founded 1718 as Russian frontier post.

Semi-Pelagianism: see PELAGIANISM.

Semiramis (sĕmĭ'rùmĭs), in Assyrian mythology, queen of Assyria. Wife of King Ninus, she reigned 42 years after his death, and is said to have conquered Persia, Libya, and Ethiopia and to have founded Babylon and Nineveh. She was worshipped as a dove after her death. Sammuramat, who was regent of Assyria from 810 to 805 B.C., was probably historical figure behind this legend.

Semite, originally one believed to be descendant of Shem, son of Noah. Today term includes Arabs; Akkadians of ancient Babylon; Assyrians; Canaanites (Amorites, Moabites, Edomites, Ammonites, and Phoenicians); Aramaean tribes (including Hebrews); and large part of Ethiopians. These peoples are grouped as Semites chiefly because their languages were derived from common tongue, Semitic (see LANGUAGE, table). Original home probably was Arabia, whence they spread to Mesopotamia (see SUMER), E Mediterranean area (see PHOENICIAN CIVILIZATION), and Nile delta. These last formed basis of new nation and religion (see JEWS and JUDAISM).

Semitic languages (sùmĭ'tĭk), great linguistic family. See LANGUAGE (table).

Semmelweis, Ignaz Philipp (ĭg'näts fē'lĭp zē'mùlvĭs), 1818–65, Hungarian physician. A pioneer in use of antiseptic methods in obstetrics, he greatly reduced deaths from puerperal fever, which he recognized as infectious.

Semmering (zē'mùrĭng), resort region, E Austria, on border of Styria and Lower Austria. The Alps here are crossed by the **Semmering Pass,** 3,215 ft. high. Beneath the pass runs the world's oldest mountain railroad (built 1848–54).

Semmes, Raphael (sĕmz), 1809–77, American naval officer. In Civil War he served with Confederate navy, first on *Sumter,* then on *Alabama,* whose two-year cruise made him naval hero of Confederacy.

Sempach (zĕm'päkh), town (pop. 1,229), Lucerne canton, central Switzerland. Here the Swiss won a decisive victory over Austria in 1386, which legend credits to the self-sacrifice of Arnold von WINKELRIED.

Semper, Gottfried (gôt'frēt zĕm'pùr), 1803–79, German architect, an exponent of Italian Renaissance style.

Semple, Ellen Churchill, 1863–1932, American geographer. Helped develop study of anthropogeography.

Senancour, Étienne de (ātyĕn' dù sùnäkōōr'), 1770–1846, French author. Best known for his autobiographical epistolary novel *Obermann* (1804; Eng. tr., 1903), remarkable for its morbid melancholy.

Senate, United States: see CONGRESS OF THE UNITED STATES.

senate, Roman, governing council of the Roman republic. An outgrowth of the royal privy council, it gained immense power as Rome expanded in the 2d and 3d cent. B.C., sending out armies, making treaties, organizing the new domain. Membership in the senate was limited to ex-magistrates almost entirely from old families. Its tone tended to be reactionary. Yet there was no real challenge to its authority until the agitation of the Gracchi. This failed, but a popular party grew up to oppose the conservatives. MARIUS headed this but the popular party was thoroughly defeated by SULLA. The struggle was, however, resumed later with Julius CAESAR heading the popular group and POMPEY heading the senatorial party. Caesar triumphed (48 B.C.) and though he was assassinated the senate did not regain power. It was docile under AUGUSTUS and became a mere cipher in the later empire.

Sendai (sāndī'), city (pop. 293,816), N Honshu, Japan. Mfg. of silk textiles, lacquer ware, and sake. Seat of Tohoku Imperial Univ.

Sender, Ramón José (rämōn' hōsā' sānder'), 1902–, Spanish novelist. An active revolutionist, he has written works on social problems (e.g., *Seven Red Sundays*, 1932).

Seneca (Lucius Annaeus Seneca) (sĕ'nŭkù), c.3 B.C.–A.D. 65, Roman philosopher, dramatist, and statesman. Exiled by Claudius (A.D. 41), he was recalled to tutor Nero and became virtual ruler. Later in disfavor, he opened his veins; his death scene was considered remarkably noble by the Romans. He wrote Stoic essays on ethics and philosophy, but his nine tragedies (notably *Medea, Phaedra, Agamemnon, Oedipus*, and *Thyestes*), contrived but high-toned, were most influential in the Renaissance and in later European literature.

Seneca (sĕ'nŭkù), village (pop. c.1,500) N Ill., on Illinois R. and E of La Salle. Was World War II shipbuilding center with c.11,000 pop.

Seneca, river flowing ENE from Seneca L., W central N.Y., to Cayuga L. (this part in Barge Canal system), thence NE to join Oneida R. in forming Oswego R.

Seneca Falls, village (pop. 6,634), W central N.Y., on Seneca R. and E of Geneva. Machinery and metal goods. First woman's-rights convention in U.S., organized partly by Elizabeth Cady Stanton (who lived here), held here, 1848.

Seneca Indians: see IROQUOIS CONFEDERACY.

Seneca Lake, N.Y.: see FINGER LAKES.

Senefelder, Aloys (zā'nŭfĕl"dùr), 1771–1834, inventor of lithography (1796), b. Prague. Worked in Munich.

Seneff or **Seneffe** (sùnĕf'), town (pop. 3,270), Hainaut, Belgium, NW of Charleroi. Here the French under Louis II de Condé defeated the Dutch (1674).

Senegal (sĕ'nĭgôl), overseas territory (c.75,750 sq. mi.; pop. c.1,895,000), French West Africa, on the Atlantic; cap. Saint-Louis, chief city Dakar. Bordered on N by Senegal R. (c.1,000 mi. long). British colony of Gambia forms narrow enclave along Gambia R. Generally a flat region. Peanuts are chief crop and export. First explored by Portuguese in 15th cent. French occupation began 1854, and in 1895 Senegal became part of French West Africa.

senega snakeroot (sĕn'ĭgù), perennial wildflower (*Polygala senega*) with white blooms. Its roots, once used by Indians for snake bite, are source of drug senega.

Senigallia (sānēgäl'lyä), town (pop. 11,394), Marches, central Italy; a bathing resort on Adriatic. In 1502 Cesare Borgia had a number of his enemies treacherously slain in its castle.

Senlis (sälēs'), city (pop. 6,049), Oise dept., N France, NE of Paris. A royal residence from 6th cent. Church of Notre Dame is one of earliest Gothic structures (12th cent.). Here in 1493 Charles VIII signed treaty yielding Franche-Comté, Artois, and Charolais to Emperor Maximilian I.

senna, leguminous herb, shrub, or tree of genus *Cassia* most common in warm regions. Dried leaves of Alexandria senna (*Cassia acutifolia*) and Indian senna (*C. angustifolia*) are used medicinally.

Sennacherib (sĕnă'kùrĭb), d. 681 B.C., king of Assyria (705–681 B.C.). The son of Sargon, he spent his reign trying to maintain the empire. Defeated the Egyptians

(701) and prepared to take Jerusalem, but instead exacted only tribute. It is uncertain whether the destruction of his army took place at this time or later (Byron's "Destruction of Sennacherib" is based on 2 Chron. 32). He fought successfully in Babylonia and destroyed Babylon (c.689 B.C.). Built a magnificent palace at Nineveh. He was murdered, possibly by his sons. Esar-Haddon succeeded.

Sennett, Mack (sĕ'nĭt), 1884–, American film director and producer, whose real name was Michael Sinnott. His films (e.g., *Tillie's Punctured Romance*) were slapstick comedies with chases, custard pie wars, and Keystone cops. Starred Charles Chaplin, "Fatty" Arbuckle, and others.

Sens (säs), city (pop. 15,936), Yonne dept., N France. An archiepiscopal see, it has a famous 12th-cent. cathedral, one of the oldest Gothic monuments (slightly damaged in World War II). Sens was the scene of several ecclesiastic councils and of a massacre of Huguenots (1562) which rekindled the Wars of Religion.

sensitive plant: see MIMOSA.

Senta (sĕn'tä), Hung. *Zenta,* city (pop. 24,916), N Serbia, Yugoslavia. Here in 1697 Prince Eugene of Savoy won a decisive victory over the Turks.

sentence, in law, punishment inflicted by court order on a person convicted of crime. A sentence may consist of a fine or imprisonment (or both) or execution. The sentence imposed is often fixed by statute. If a person is convicted of more than one crime at his trial, sentences may run concurrently or consecutively. In some cases a sentence may be indeterminate, with a maximum and minimum term for imprisonment; if his behavior in prison is good, the convict may be freed on probation at any time after the end of his minimum term.

Sentinel Ridge, SW Wis., near Prairie du Chien, in Wyalusing State Park. Indian mounds.

Seoul (sā'ōol', sōl), Jap. *Keijo,* city (1949 pop. 1,446,-019), cap. of South Korean Republic. Was cap. of Korea from 1393 until the partition of the country after World War II. Here is Univ. of Seoul. Severely damaged 1950–51 in Korean War.

sepal: see CALYX.

separation, in law, either the voluntary agreement of a husband and wife to live apart or a partial dissolution of a marriage bond by court order. Unlike divorce, separation leaves the marriage bond intact and prohibits remarriage. Separation by court decree is called a divorce *a mensa et thora* [from bed and board]. Separation is more usual in states where divorce is hard to obtain.

separatists, in religion, groups that withdrew from Established Church in England. A 16th-cent. group were called Brownists after their leader, Robert Browne. Name Independents used in 17th cent. See CONGREGATIONALISM; PURITANISM.

separator, cream, dairy machine used to separate fresh milk into cream and skim milk. Design of the machine varies, but principle is that of centrifuge. The cream separator controls the amount of fat in the milk and lessens injury by bacterial action.

Sephardim, Jews descended from the Jews of Spain and Portugal. Some of their practices, notably pronunciation of Hebrew, differ from those of other Jews; Sephardic Hebrew is now the language of Israel.

Sepik (sā'pēk), river of NE New Guinea, 700 mi. long, emptying into Bismarck Sea.

Sepoy Rebellion (sē'poi), 1857–58, rebellion of native soldiers (sepoys) in Bengal army of East India Co. Many Indian princes, fearing confiscation of land by Gen. DALHOUSIE, may have encouraged unrest. The Bengalese soldiers (all Brahmins) resented the annexation in 1856 of Oudh, their homeland, and were further angered by issuing of cartridges coated with what they believed to be beef grease, the handling of which violated Hindu law. Revolt began at Berhampore, Feb., 1857, and soon raged over N central

SMALL CAPITALS = cross references. Pronunciation key on inside end pages. Abbreviations: p. 2.

India. Lucknow was besieged, and Cawnpore and Delhi were captured, with Nana Sahib massacring the entire British colony at Cawnpore. British reconquest was completed March, 1858. Rebellion led to many reforms, principally the transfer of rule from British East India Co. to the crown. Also called Indian Mutiny.

Seppänen, Unto Kalervo (ōōn′tō kä′lĕrvō sĕp′pănĕn), 1904–, Finnish writer of novels (e.g., *Sun and Storm*, 1931–34) and stories about Karelia.

September: see MONTH.

septicemia (sĕptĭsē′mĕṳ), serious form of blood poisoning in which blood stream is infected by both toxins and bacteria which multiply in the blood. It is commonly caused by streptococci and staphylococci. Blood poisoning in which only the toxins are absorbed into the blood is known as toxemia.

septic tank, sedimentation tank for sewage discharge, where it remains for periods of 8–24 hr. While oxygen is present, aerobic bacteria attack organic matter in sewage; when oxygen is exhausted, anaerobic bacteria attack it, causing it to disintegrate, liquefy, and give off gases.

Septimius Severus, Roman emperor: see SEVERUS.

Septuagint (sĕp′tū.ṳjĭnt) [Latin,=70], translation of Old Testament into Greek, made between 250 B.C. and c.100 B.C. Supposedly done in 72 days by 72 translators, hence its name. It includes the Apocrypha and some pseudepigrapha. This version used by Greek-speaking Christians such as St. Paul and is still used in the Greek church. Its symbol: LXX.

Séquard, Charles Édouard Brown-: see BROWN-SÉQUARD.

sequoia (sĭkwoi′ṳ), name for two huge, coniferous, evergreen trees of genus *Sequoia*. Once widespread in temperate regions of the N Hemisphere, only two species survive in a narrow strip near the Pacific coast of the U.S. The redwood (*Sequoia sempervirens*), growing from 100 to 340 ft. high, is the world's tallest tree. The big tree or giant sequoia (*S. gigantea* or *Sequoiadendron gigantea*) grows from 150 to 325 ft.; some specimens are believed to be 3,000 to 4,000 years old. Wood of both species is valued for outdoor building uses. China's "dawn redwood" (*Metasequoia*) is related.

Sequoia National Park: see NATIONAL PARKS AND MONUMENTS (table).

Sequoyah (sĭkwoi′ṳ), c.1770–1843, North American Indian leader, creator of the Cherokee syllabary. His "white" name was George Guess.

seraph (sĕ′rŭf), plural **seraphim,** kind of ANGEL; with cherubim, attendant upon God. According to Bible, seraphim have six wings. Isa. 6.2–6.

Serbia (sûr′bĕṳ), Serbo-Croatian *Srbija*, constituent republic (34,194 sq. mi.; pop. 6,523,224) of Yugoslavia, of which it occupies the E part; cap. Belgrade. Its NE section (incl. VOJVODINA prov.), acquired from Hungary in 1920, is part of the fertile Danubian plain; the rest is largely mountainous. Most of the population is agricultural. The Serbs are distinguished from the closely related Croats and Slovenes through their historic affiliation with the Eastern Orthodox Church, which also gave them the Cyrillic alphabet. They settled in the Balkan Peninsula in the 6th and 7th cent., under Byzantine overlordship; accepted Christianity 9th cent.; and formed an independent kingdom in 1217. Under STEPHEN DUSHAN medieval Serbia reached its greatest expansion (14th cent.), but it quickly declined. Its defeat at Kossovo (1389) made it tributary to Turkey, which in 1459 annexed it outright. Belgrade, then held by Hungary, fell to the Turks in 1521. Turkish rule was particularly oppressive in Serbia, but the weakening of the Ottoman Empire in the 18th cent. gave Serbia new hopes of independence. The uprising led by MILOSH Obrenovich was successful (1817); in 1828 the Sultan recognized Serbia as a vassal principality. Despite internal feuds (notably that of the OBRENOVICH and KARAGEORGE-

VICH factions), Serbia, largely with Russian backing, gained increasing independence and leadership of the S Slavs. The last Turkish troops left in 1867. In 1876 Serbia declared war on Turkey (see RUSSO-TURKISH WARS); in 1878 the Congress of Berlin, though disappointing its territorial claims, declared Serbia independent. In 1882 Prince MILAN proclaimed himself king. The opposition of Serbian ambitions to those of its neighbors led to war with Bulgaria over E RUMELIA in 1885 (which Bulgaria won), to the BALKAN WARS of 1912–13 (in which Serbia won), and, after the assassination of Archduke Francis Ferdinand by a Serb, to WORLD WAR I (1914). Though at first successful, Serbia was overrun by the Central Powers in 1915. Its troops and government were evacuated to Corfu, where in 1917 a S Slavic congress declared the union of Serbia, Croatia, Slovenia, and Montenegro under King PETER I of Serbia. The history of the new kingdom, which formally came into existence in 1918, is that of YUGOSLAVIA, as it was later called. In World War II a much-reduced Serbia was set up by the Axis powers in 1941 under a puppet government, but the Serbs continued guerrilla warfare. The Yugoslav constitution of 1945 made Serbia one of the federated republics of Yugoslavia and stripped it of Macedonia, Montenegro, and Bosnia and Hercegovina.

Serbo-Croat (–krō′ăt), language of S group of Slavic subfamily of Indo-European languages. See LANGUAGE (table).

serf. Serfdom was state of half freedom characteristic of peasant labor under FEUDALISM and MANORIAL SYSTEM. Distinguished from slavery by body of rights serf had and by strict group arrangement of serfdom. True serf was subject to labor service at will of his lord, but such matters came to be governed by custom and worked in set pattern. Although serfdom existed from earliest history, it developed in Middle Ages in France, Spain, and Italy, spread to Germany and in 15th cent. to Slavic lands. Developed separately in England after Norman Conquest, when most free villeins were depressed to serfdom, and disappeared before end of Middle Ages. In Hapsburg monarchy it was ended (1781) by Emperor Joseph II. In France it was swept away by French Revolution. It persisted in Russia until all serfs were freed in 1861 by Alexander II. Serfdom appeared and disappeared with feudalism in Japan, China, India, pre-Columbian Mexico, and elsewhere.

sergeanty: see SERJEANTY.

Sergiev or **Sergievski Posad,** RSFSR: see ZAGORSK.

series, in mathematics, a sum of several terms. An infinite series is a sum of infinitely many terms, the first several of which establish the pattern of formation for subsequent terms. Some infinite series converge toward a value called limit; i.e., the adding together of terms results in sums (called partial sums) that form a sequence of values approaching closer and closer the value called the limit. The series $\frac{1}{2} + \frac{1}{4} + \frac{1}{8} + \frac{1}{16}$ . . . converges to value 1 because partial sums form sequence $\frac{1}{2}, \frac{3}{4}, \frac{7}{8}, \frac{15}{16}$, ... Series such as $\frac{1}{2} + \frac{1}{3} + \frac{1}{4}$ . . . . do not converge.

Seringapatam (sûring″gṳpṳtäm′), town (pop. 7,678), S Mysore, India, on island in Cauvery R. Was cap. of Mysore, 17th–18th cent. Tippoo Sahib was killed here in British siege of 1799.

serjeanty or **sergeanty** (both: sär′jĕntē), type of TENURE in British FEUDALISM in which tenant held lands from king or overlord in return for service.

serpent, name applied to any crawling creature, chiefly to snake. Legends of sea serpents are unsubstantiated. In religion and art, serpent symbolizes Satan.

serpentine (sûr′pṳntēn, –tīn), a mineral, hydrous silicate of magnesium, usually some shade of green. Commercial asbestos is a fibrous variety. Massive varieties are used for interior decoration.

Serpent Mound State Park, S Ohio, NW of Portsmouth. Has prehistoric Indian mounds. Largest (c.1,330 ft. long) represents serpent swallowing egg.

Serra, Junípero (hōōnē'pärō sĕ'rä), 1713–84, Spanish Franciscan missionary in North America. Directed founding of many missions in Calif.

Sert, José María (hōsä' märē'ä sĕrt'), 1876–1945, Spanish painter, best known for his murals.

Sertorius, Quintus (sùrtô'rēùs), d. 72 B.C., Roman general, who became leader of the Lusitanians. He had been a supporter of Marius and fled to Africa to escape death at the hands of Sulla's party. Called to Spain by rebels in 80 B.C., he held off Roman armies sent against him until assassinated by one of his own men.

serum (sĕr'ùm), straw-colored fluid blood component which separates from corpuscles when clotting occurs. Immunity to certain communicable diseases is obtained for varying periods by introduction of serum containing specific antibodies. Human serum is sometimes used to counteract shock or loss of fluid.

Servetus, Michael (sùrvē'tùs), Span. *Miguel Serveto,* 1511–53, Spanish theologian and physician. He early came into contact with reformers in Germany and Switzerland, but his views on the Trinity were condemned by Catholics as well as Protestants. Fled to Lyons, where he edited Ptolemy's geography, and to Paris, where he studied medicine. He gained fame in medicine and was (1541–53) physician to the archbishop of Vienne. After he had a work on theology secretly printed (1553), the Inquisition moved against him. He escaped from prison and made for Italy but was seized on Calvin's order, tried, and burned at the stake. His doctrines are said to have anticipated Unitarianism.

Service, Robert W(illiam), 1876–, Canadian poet and novelist, b. England. He achieved considerable popularity with his works about the Yukon.

serviceberry: see SHADBUSH.

Servile Wars, in Roman history, three uprisings of slaves (134?–132? B.C., 104?–101? B.C., 73–71 B.C.). The first two took place in Sicily. The third was the famous uprising led by SPARTACUS in S Italy, eventually put down with great cruelty by Crassus and Pompey.

sesame (sĕs'ùmē), herb (*Sesamum indicum* or *S. orientale*) native to the tropics. It has long been grown for the seeds which are added to pastries; seeds yield the valuable benne oil, used in cooking and medicine, especially in India.

Sesostris (sĭsō'strĭs), kings of anc. Egypt of the XII dynasty. **Sesostris I,** d. 1935 B.C., was the son of Amenemhet I and coregent with him after 1980; sole ruler 1970–1938; coruler with his son Amenemhet II 1938–1935. He campaigned in the present Sudan. **Sesostris II,** d. 1887 B.C., was the son of Amenemhet II and coregent with him 1906–1903; sole ruler 1903–1887. His son **Sesostris III,** d. 1849 B.C., reigned 1887–1849. He put down the nobles, led an expedition to Syria, and set the S boundary of Egypt near present Wadi Halfa.

Sesshu (sĕs'shōō"), 1420–1506, Japanese painter and Buddhist priest, an outstanding figure in Japanese art. Famous for his murals and screen decorations. Visited China.

Sessions, Roger, 1896–, American composer and teacher. His works include incidental music (1923) for Andreyev's *Black Maskers;* choral preludes for organ; two symphonies (1926, 1946); a violin concerto (1931–35); a choral work, *Turn O Libertad* (1948); piano pieces; and a string quartet (1936).

Sestos (sĕ'stŏs), anc. town on the Thracian shore of the Hellespont, opposite Abydos. Xerxes crossed the Hellespont here on a bridge of boats. Scene of story of Hero and Leander.

Sète, formerly **Cette** (both: sĕt), town (pop. 29,914), Hérault dept., S France; a Mediterranean port.

Setesdal (sā'tùsdäl), narrow valley, S Norway, drained by Otra R. There are several lakes. Noted for its ancient dress, speech, customs, and handicrafts, which are still cultivated.

Seth, son of Adam and Eve, father of Enos. Gen. 4.25,–26; 5.3. Sheth: 1 Chron. 1.1.

Seti (sē'tī, sā'tē), kings of anc. Egypt of XIX dynasty. **Seti I,** d. 1292 B.C., succeeded his father Ramses I (c.1313 B.C.). Invaded Palestine and Syria; defeated the Libyans. Built temples and also a magnificent tomb at Abydos. Succeeded by Ramses II. **Seti II,** d. 1205 B.C., was the last king of the dynasty. Succeeded by Ramses III.

Seton, Elizabeth Ann (Bayley) (sē'tùn), 1774–1821, American Roman Catholic leader, called Mother Seton. She was the widow of a merchant William Seton before she was converted to Catholicism (1805). In 1808 she opened a school in Baltimore, later moved to Emmitsburg, Md., where she opened the first Catholic free school. She also founded St. Joseph's College for women and formed a community that adopted the rule of the Daughters of Charity (more commonly called Sisters of Charity). Her contribution to Catholic education in the U.S. was enormous.

Seton, Ernest Thompson, 1860–1946, American writer and artist, originally named Ernest Seton Thompson. Interpreted nature for boys and girls (as in *Wild Animals I Have Known,* 1898). Founded Woodcraft Indians, precursor of Boy Scouts.

Seton Hall University: see SOUTH ORANGE, N.J.

Seton Hill College: see GREENSBURG, Pa.

setter: see HUNTING DOGS.

Settignano, Desiderio da: see DESIDERIO DA SETTIGNANO.

Settlement, Act of, 1701, passed by English Parliament to provide that if William III and Princess (later Queen) Anne died without heirs, the succession should pass to members of house of HANOVER, if Protestants. From 1714 (George I) house of Hanover owes claim to this act. Prompted partly by fear of JACOBITES, further provisions, similar to those in Bill of Rights, limited king's power.

settlement house: see SOCIAL SETTLEMENT.

Setúbal (sùtōō'bäl), city (pop. 37,071), W Portugal, in Estremadura; a port on the Atlantic. Exports wine, fruit, cork. Fishing base.

Seurat, Georges (zhôrzh' sûrä'), 1859–91, French postimpressionist painter. Developed a technique of painting in dots of pure color, called pointillism, a refinement on the broken color of the impressionists. His masterpiece, *Un Dimanche à la Grande Jatte,* is at Art. Inst., Chicago.

Sevan (syĭvän'), mountain lake, area 546 sq. mi., central Armenian SSR. Fed by c.30 streams, but Zanga R. is only outlet. Sevan-Zanga hydroelectric project (begun 1930) has drained part of the lake. Formerly called Gokcha, its Turkish name.

Sevastopol (sĭvä'stùpōl"), city (pop. 111,946), RSFSR, in S Crimea; a major naval base and strategic stronghold on an inlet of Black Sea. Founded by Catherine II. In Crimean War, city heroically resisted besieging British, French, and Turks for 11 months. It was Wrangel's hq. during last stand of the "Whites" (1920) in Russian civil war. In World War II city was besieged for eight months by the Germans. Virtually destroyed, it fell July 3, 1942; recaptured May, 1944.

Seven against Thebes, in Greek legend, seven heroes—Polynices, Adrastus, Amphiaraüs, Hippomedon, Capaneus, Tydeus, and Parthenopaeus—who made war on ETEOCLES, who was king of Thebes, son of OEDIPUS, and brother of POLYNICES. Brothers killed each other, and only Adrastus survived. Ten years later the EPIGONI avenged their fathers, the Seven against Thebes.

Seven Churches in Asia, in Bible, churches addressed in Revelation 1–3. They are Ephesus, Smyrna, Pergamos, Thyatira, Sardis, Philadelphia, and Laodicea.

Seven Days battles, in Civil War, week of heavy fighting near Richmond, Va. (June 26–July 2, 1862). After battle of Fair Oaks in PENINSULAR CAMPAIGN, R. E. Lee moved to cut McClellan off from base at White House Landing. A. P. Hill attacked Union advance lines at Mechanicsville on June 26, was repulsed. Federals fell back to Gaines's Mill, where on June 27 a strong Confederate force was victor. As McClellan moved main force toward James R., Lee pursued and engaged him at Savage's Station on June 29 and at Frayser's Farm or Glendale on June 30 without stopping him. On July 1, Federals, posted on Malvern Hill, again repulsed attack, then withdrew to James R. Lee had suffered heavy losses, but he had saved Richmond.

Seven Pines: see PENINSULAR CAMPAIGN.

Seventh-day Adventists: see ADVENTISTS.

Seventh-Day Baptists, sect of Calvinistic Baptists, observing Saturday as Sabbath. First American group (1671) in R.I. In Pa., German group led by J. C. Beissel estab. (1728–33) EPHRATA.

Seven Weeks War: see AUSTRO-PRUSSIAN WAR.

Seven Wise Men of Greece. Arbitrary lists of wise men have drawn from among the best intellects of ancient Greece. A usual one is: Bias, Chilon, Cleobulus, Periander, Pittacus, Solon, and Thales.

Seven Wonders of the World, in anc. classifications were Great Pyramid of Khufu or all the pyramids with or without the Sphinx; Hanging Gardens of Babylon, with or without the walls; mausoleum at Halicarnassus; Artemision at Ephesus; Colossus of Rhodes; Olympian *Zeus,* statue by Phidias; and Pharos at Alexandria, or, instead, walls of Babylon.

Seven Years War, 1756–63, world-wide conflict fought in Europe, N America, and India between, on the one side, France, Austria, Russia, Saxony, Sweden, and (after 1762) Spain and, on the other side, Prussia, England, and Hanover. Two main issues were involved—(1) French-English colonial rivalry in America (see FRENCH AND INDIAN WARS) and in India (see CLIVE and DUPLEIX); (2) the struggle for supremacy in Germany between MARIA THERESA of Austria and FREDERICK II of Prussia. The years following the War of the AUSTRIAN SUCCESSION (ended 1748) were employed in maneuvering for alliances preparatory to a new test of strength. Hostilities were opened by Prussia invading Saxony (1756) and Bohemia (1757). Routed at Kolin, Frederick had to evacuate Bohemia but defeated the Austrians at Rossbach and Leuthen (late 1757) and the Russians at Zorndorf (1758). Nevertheless, his situation became nearly hopeless after his defeats at Kunersdorf and Maxen (1759). In 1760 the Russians briefly occupied Berlin. Frederick expelled them and defeated the Austrians at Torgau, but his final victory became assured only after the accession of Peter III of Russia, who made a separate peace with him (1762). Meanwhile England, after an inauspicious start, pushed the war vigorously under the leadership of William Pitt (1st earl of Chatham) and won victories at Krefeld, Minden, and Quiberon Bay in Europe; Louisburg and Quebec in America; and Plassey in India (1757–59). After protracted negotiations, peace was made at HUBERTUSBURG and at Paris (see PARIS, TREATY OF, 1763). The war confirmed Prussia's new rank as leading power and made England the world's chief colonial power, at the expense of France.

Severn, Joseph (sĕ'vŭrn), 1793–1879, English portrait painter. Best known as a devoted friend to Keats. Was consul at Rome, 1861–72.

Severn. 1 River rising in W Ont., Canada, and flowing 420 mi. NE to Hudson Bay. At mouth is Fort Severn, Hudson's Bay Co. trading post, estab. 1689. **2** River, S Ont., Canada, issuing from N end of L. Couchiching and flowing 20 mi. WNW to Georgian Bay. Forms part of inland waterway linking Georgian Bay with L. Ontario via Trent Canal.

Severn, one of principal rivers of England. Flows c.200 mi. from Plinlimmon, Wales, through great estuary, to Bristol Channel. Following a winding course, it borders or passes through Montgomery, Shropshire, Worcester, and Gloucester counties. Connected by canal with the Thames, Mersey, Trent, and other streams, it is an important transportation route.

Severnaya Zemlya (syĕ'vĭrnĭŭ zĭmlyä') [Rus.,= northern

land], archipelago, area 14,300 sq. mi., in Arctic Ocean, in Krasnoyarsk Territory, RSFSR, separating Kara and Laptev seas. Discovered 1913.

Severovostochny: Russian name of Cape CHELYUSKIN.

Severus or **Septimius Severus** (sĕptĭ'mĕŭs sĕvē'rŭs), 146–211, Roman emperor (193–211), b. Africa. He took the imperial throne by force, put down opponents, and reduced the empire to peace in Mesopotamia, Gaul, and Britain. He died at York. Did much to beautify Rome. Left the empire to his sons, but Caracalla took power.

Severus (Flavius Valerius Severus), d. 307, Roman emperor (306–7). In the struggle for power after the abdication of Diocletian and Maximian, he was proclaimed emperor by Galerius, but was captured at Ravenna by Maximian and was treacherously killed.

Sevier, John (sŭvēr'), 1745–1815, American frontiersman, governor of the State of Franklin (1784–88) and of Tenn. (1796–1801, 1803–9).

Sevier (sŭvēr'), river formed in SW Utah and flowing N through mountain canyons, then SW through desert to Sevier L.; 325 mi. long. Used for irrigation.

Sevierville (sŭvēr'vĭl), town (pop. 1,620), E Tenn., ESE of Knoxville. Near by are Great Smoky Mts. Natl. Park and Douglas Dam.

Sévigné, Marie de Rabutin-Chantal, marquise de (märē' dŭ räbütē'-shätäl' märkēz' dŭ sāvēnyä'), 1626–96, French noblewoman. Her correspondence (some 1,500 letters, mostly to her daughter, the comtesse de Grignan) are masterpieces of French prose. Their unaffected vivacity, whether she discusses personal, social, political, or literary news, makes them the most living account of the age of Louis XIV. Several English translations.

Seville (sŭvĭl', sĕ'vĭl), Span. *Sevilla,* city (pop. 270,126), cap. of Seville prov. and chief city of Andalusia, SW Spain. Connected with the Atlantic by Guadalquivir R. and by canal accessible to ocean-going vessels, it is a major port and industrial center, mfg. tobacco, ammunition, perfumes, textiles, and other goods. It is an archiepiscopal see and seat of a university (founded 1502). Important in Phoenician times, it was made cap. of Baetica prov. by the Romans. Continued to flourish under the Moors (from 712), when it was the seat (1023–91) of an independent emirate under the ABBADIDES, and under the Christians (from 1248), when it reached its greatest prosperity through its monopoly (until 1718) on trade with the New World. City was seat of a great school of painting to which Velázquez and Murillo belonged. Its Gothic cathedral (1401–1519), one of world's largest, includes Giralda tower and Court of Oranges (parts of a former mosque) and contains tomb of Columbus. It is adjoined by Moorish alcazar (14th cent.). Colombina library contains manuscripts by Columbus, and there are many notable churches and palaces.

Sèvres (sĕv'rŭ), town (pop. 15,112), Seine-et-Oise dept., N France; a SW suburb of Paris. Hq. of Internatl. Bureau of Weights and Standards. It is famous for producing **Sèvres ware,** delicate porcelain made by the royal (now national) potteries (estab. c.1740 by Louis XV at Vincennes, moved 1756 to Sèvres). The **Treaty of Sèvres,** 1920, restored peace after World War I between Mohammed VI of Turkey and the Allies (excluding Russia and the U.S.). It liquidated the Ottoman Empire, reducing Turkey to Anatolia in Asia and Constantinople, with environs, in Europe. Armenia was made a separate republic; Smyrna was placed under Greek administration pending a plebiscite; the Straits zone was internationalized; Allies were given virtual control over Turkish economy. The refusal of Kemal ATATURK to accept the treaty forced the Allies to negotiate another (see LAUSANNE, CONFERENCE OF).

sewage. Modern water-carriage sewerage systems for cities are conduits of iron, concrete, brick, stone, or earthenware through which sewage is dicharged from plumbing fixtures to house sewer and thence to street-sewer system. Sewage-treating methods include dilution, screening, tank treatment by sedimentation or precipitation, septic-tank treatment, broad irrigation, filtration, disinfection, and combinations of these methods. All rely on oxidation of organic matter and destruction of bacteria by chemicals or by burning.

Sewall, Samuel (sū′ùl), 1652–1730, American jurist, b. England. Repented part played in Salem witchcraft cases of 1692.

Sewanee: see SOUTH, UNIVERSITY OF THE.

Seward, William H(enry), 1801–72, American statesman. U.S. Senator from N.Y. (1849–61), prominent in troubled years before Civil War. As Lincoln's Secretary of State he sought to dominate policy, but President's ingenuity kept him in cabinet. In war period he was able statesman, handling adeptly such delicate matters as TRENT AFFAIR. He held his post under Andrew Johnson and supported Johnson's Reconstruction policy. Notable achievement was his far-sighted purchase of Alaska (1867), unappreciated at time and called "Seward's folly."

Seward, town (pop. 2,114), S Alaska, on E side of Kenai Peninsula, at head of Resurrection Bay. Founded 1902 as ocean terminus by surveyors for Alaska RR. Important supply center for Alaska interior. Major port of entry for U.S. troops and matériel in World War II.

Seward Peninsula, W Alaska, projecting c.200 mi. into Bering Sea, between Norton Sound and Kotzebue Sound, just below Arctic Circle. Mostly perpetually frozen tundra. Placer gold mining and trapping. Nome is on S coast.

Sewell, Anna (sū′ùl), 1820–78, English author. Her *Black Beauty* (1877), the story of a horse, is a children's classic.

Sewickley, residential borough (pop. 5,836), SW Pa., on Ohio R. and NW of Pittsburgh.

sewing machine. Devices for sewing mechanically were made in England (1790), France (1830 and later), and by Walter Hunt of New York city (1832), but the first successful machine was made by Elias HOWE in 1846. A. B. Wilson contributed improvements, as did Isaac M. SINGER, who coordinated previous attempts into the modern machine and began large-scale manufacturing. Both chain- and lock-stitch machines employ an eye-pointed needle; rising and falling rapidly, it pierces the material and casts a loop of thread to the under side of the seam. In the lock-stitch machine (the type of most domestic machines) a second loop of thread, fed from underneath, engages the loop to complete the stitch. In the chain stitch, the loop is held while the needle rises, the cloth is fed forward, and the needle descends again to engage the loop with the beginning of a second loop. Efficiency of household machines has been increased by electrification and an ever-increasing number of attachments. Power-driven specialized machines are used in industry.

sex, term used to refer both to the two groups distinguished as males and females and to anatomical and physiological characteristics associated with maleness and femaleness. Sex is associated with ability to produce special reproductive cells known as gametes (see REPRODUCTION). Among higher animals, i.e., the vertebrate animals, sexes are usually easily distinguishable by certain anatomical differences (e.g., structure of reproductive organs) and by secondary sexual characteristics (e.g., brightness of coloring of males in fish and birds, antlers of male deer, growth of beard and deepening of voice in human male). In higher plants there are male and female reproductive organs (see FLOWER). Sex is less easily distinguishable in simpler forms of plants and animals. Some animals are hermaphroditic, i.e., one individual produces both egg and sperm cells. In both plants and animals that form egg and sperm cells the union of two cells (see FERTILIZATION) results in formation of a fertilized egg or zygote from which new individual develops. Factors that determine sex of an individual vary and are not fully understood. In humans and some other

forms sex is believed to be determined by chance, depending upon the nature of the chromosome combinations resulting when egg and sperm unite.

sextant, instrument for finding geographical position by measuring the altitude of the sun or the stars; invented independently by Thomas Godfrey in the U.S. and John Hadley in England in 1731. It made maritime navigation much easier.

Seychelles (sāshĕlz′), British crown colony (156 sq. mi.; pop. 34,632), comprising c.30 volcanic islands in Indian Ocean, c.1,000 mi. E of Zanzibar; cap. Victoria, on Mahé (largest island). Occupied in 18th cent. by the French, who ceded it to the British in 1814. Copra, vanilla, cinnamon, and guano are exported. The inhabitants, of African-European descent, speak a French patois.

Seydlitz, Friedrich Wilhelm, Freiherr von (frē′drĭkh vĭl′hĕlm frē′hĕr fŭn zĭd′lĭts), 1721–73, Prussian general. Made cavalry a decisive weapon and took major part in all of Frederick II's chief victories.

Seyhan (sāhän′), anc. *Saurus,* river, 320 mi. long, Turkey. Flows SSW from Anti-Taurus mts. to the E Mediterranean. Also known as Sihun.

Seymour (sē′môr, sē′mùr), English noble family. **Jane Seymour,** 1509?–1537, was the third queen of Henry VIII. Her insistence on marriage was a cause of the trial of Anne Boleyn. She died after the birth of her son, Edward VI. Her brother, **Edward Seymour, duke of Somerset,** 1506?–1552, gained possession of young EDWARD VI on Henry VIII's death and was made protector of England. Wielded almost royal authority in making Protestant reforms. With Thomas Cranmer, he introduced (1549) Book of Common Prayer. He alienated Scots by laying waste SE Scotland. Ousted by duke of NORTHUMBERLAND, he was eventually beheaded. Of firm beliefs and great military ability, he was a practical leader of English Reformation. His brother, **Thomas Seymour, Baron Seymour of Sudeley** (sūd′lē), 1508?–1549, was lord high admiral of England. Tried to supplant his brother as the king's guardian. Secretly married (1547) Catherine Parr, the dowager queen. He was executed for treason.

Seymour, Horatio, 1810–86, American statesman. Governor of N.Y. (1853–55, 1863–65). Opposed Federal conscription. Democratic presidential candidate in 1868.

Seymour, Jane: see SEYMOUR, family.

Seymour. 1 Town (pop. 7,832), including Seymour village (pop. 5,342; metal products), SW Conn., on Naugatuck R. and NW of New Haven; settled c.1680. **2** City (pop. 9,629), SE Ind., S of Columbus. Mfg. of automobile parts, home appliances.

Seymour of Sudeley, Thomas Seymour, Baron: see SEYMOUR, family.

Sforza (sfôr′tsä), Italian family which ruled duchy of Milan 1450–1535. First prominent member was **Muzio Attendolo Sforza** (mōō′tsēō ät-tĕn′dōlō), 1369–1424, a great CONDOTTIERE. His natural son, **Francesco I Sforza** (fränchä′skō), 1401–66, was one of most powerful condottieri of his time. He married Bianca Maria, daughter of Duke Filippo Maria Visconti of Milan, after whose death he seized power and was proclaimed duke (1450). His eldest son and successor, **Galeazzo Maria Sforza** (gäläät′tsō märē′ä), 1444–76, a patron of the arts but a dissolute and cruel ruler, was murdered in a republican plot. The anticipated popular uprising did not materialize. His daughter Bianca Maria married Emperor Maximilian I; a natural daughter, **Caterina Sforza,** 1463?–1509, married Gerolamo Riario, lord of Imola and Forlì, after whose murder in 1488 she ruled both cities until she lost them to Cesare Borgia (1499). Her second husband was Giovanni de' Medici; to him she bore the famous condottiere Giovanni delle Bande Nere (see MEDICI). Galeazzo Maria's son **Gian Galeazzo Sforza** (jän′), 1468–94, succeeded him as duke in 1476 under the regency of his mother, Bona of Savoy. He was the father of Bona Sforza, queen of SIGISMUND I of Poland. His rule was usurped after 1480 by his paternal uncle, **Ludovico** or **Lodovico Sforza** (lōōdōvĕ′kō, lō-dōvĕ′kō), 1451–1508, called Ludovico il Moro (the Moor) because of his swarthy complexion. On Gian Galeazzo's death, Ludovico became duke. His alliance with Charles VIII of France was a factor in starting the ITALIAN WARS (1494). Ludovico turned against his French ally in 1495. In 1499 he lost his duchy to Louis XII of France, who claimed it as a great-grandson of Gian Galeazzo Visconti. He died a prisoner in France. With his wife, Beatrice d'Este, he is chiefly remembered as one of the most lavish princes of the Renaissance and as the patron of LEONARDO DA VINCI and Bramante. His son **Massimiliano Sforza** (mäs″sēmē-lyä′nō), 1491–1530, recovered Milan with Swiss help (1512) but had to surrender it to Francis I of France in 1515. He relinquished his title to the duchy to his brother **Francesco II Sforza**, 1495–1535, who entered in possession of Milan in 1522 with the help of Emperor Charles V. He died without issue; Milan, after a long contest between France and Spain, passed to Spain in 1559.

Sforza, Carlo, Conte (kär′lō, kōn′tä), 1872–1952, Italian foreign minister (1920–21; 1947–51). Led liberal opposition against Mussolini in the senate until 1927, when he went into exile. After Mussolini's fall (1943) he returned to Italy and played a major role in the overthrow of the monarchy.

's Gravenhage, Netherlands: see HAGUE, THE.

Shackleton, Sir Ernest Henry, 1874–1922, British antarctic explorer, b. Ireland. Member of Scott expedition (1901–4). Commanded south polar expedition (1907–9); located south magnetic pole; achieved important scientific results. Led perilous transantarctic expedition (1914–17). Died on expedition to study Enderby Land.

shad, N Atlantic fish of herring family. Flesh and roe of American shad are valued as food.

shadbush, Juneberry, or **serviceberry,** tree or shrub of genus *Amelanchier*, chiefly native to North America. The showy white flowers appear in early spring and are followed by edible, berrylike fruits.

shadow, relative darkness caused by interception of light waves by opaque mass. Factors involved are size and intensity of light source, proximity to opaque body, bulk of body, angle and distance of surface on which shadow appears. Complete shadow, where light is wholly interfered with, is called umbra. Penumbra is partial shadow.

Shadrach (shā′drăk), one of THREE HOLY CHILDREN.

Shadwell, Thomas, 1642?–1692, English poet and playwright, poet laureate 1688–92. Attacked Dryden in *The Medal of John Bayes* (1682) and was lampooned in Dryden's *Absalom and Achitophel* and *MacFlecknoe*.

Shafter, William Rufus, 1835–1906, American general. Commanded army invading Cuba in Spanish-American War. Received little credit for victories.

Shafter, Fort, military hq. of Hawaiian Dept., Oahu, T.H., NW of Honolulu. First post occupied (1907) after annexation by U.S.

Shaftesbury, Anthony Ashley Cooper, 1st earl of, 1621 –83, English statesman. Distrust of autocratic rule caused his support to fluctuate between Stuarts and parliamentarians. Helped restore Charles II, but urged leniency for the Regicides. Was member of the CABAL and opposed 1st earl of Clarendon. Anti-Catholic lord chancellor 1672–73, he supported TEST ACT and was dismissed. Promoted opposition to Danby, and on his fall became president of the council. Arrested (1681) for supporting claim to throne of duke of Monmouth, he fled to Holland 1682. His grandson, **Anthony Ashley Cooper, 3d earl of Shaftesbury,** 1671–1713, was a philosopher. Educated by John Locke. Held true morality to be a balance between egoism and altruism. Balance is made possible by a harmony between individual and society; man has innate instincts ("moral sense") to promote harmony. Most of his

essays were collected in *Characteristics of Men, Manners, Opinions, Times* (1711). **Anthony Ashley Cooper, 7th earl of Shaftesbury,** 1801–85, was a social reformer. In Parliament after 1826, he introduced legislation prohibiting employment of women and children in coal mines (1842), providing care for the insane (1845), and estab. 10-hour day for factory workers. Promoted building of model tenements.

Shah Jehan or **Shah Jahan** (both: shä′ jühän′), d. 1666, Mogul emperor (1628–58), who conquered much of S India. Built extensively in Delhi and Agra (noted for TAJ MAHAL). Deposed and imprisoned in 1658 by his son Aurangzeb.

Shaker Heights, residential city (pop. 28,222), NE Ohio, SE suburb of Cleveland; founded 1905.

Shakers, religious group self-styled "The United Society of Believers in Christ's Second Coming." Originated in 18th cent. in England as group called "Shaking Quakers" because of their tremblings during worship. Ann LEE, with eight followers, came (1774) to N.Y., settling (1776) at present Watervliet. Later communities were in N.Y., New England, Ky., Ohio, and Ind. After 1860 Shakerism declined. Shakers believed in strict separation of sexes and practiced communal ownership.

Shakespeare, William: see SHAKSPERE, WILLIAM.

Shakhty (shäkh′tē), city (pop. 155,081), S European RSFSR, NE of Rostov; major anthracite-mining center of Donets Basin.

Shakspere, Shakespeare, or **Shakspeare, William,** 1564–1616, greatest of English poets and dramatists, b. Stratford-on-Avon. Comparatively little is known of his life, and many theories concerning it have been advanced. He was fairly well educated and may have been a schoolmaster. In 1582 he married Anne Hathaway, and the couple may have had three children. As early as 1588 he had moved to London and linked his life with the stage, probably as an apprentice. About 1589 his first drama was produced—either *The Comedy of Errors* or the first part of *Henry VI.* He continued to produce plays in a steady stream until after his retirement to Stratford-on-Avon (c.1610) with a modest fortune. By 1593 he had Henry Wriothesley, earl of Southampton, as his patron. He was a member (1594–95) of the Lord Chamberlain's Men, later the King's Men of James I, and he seems to have been writer and actor for the group until his retirement. He was (1599) a partner in the Globe Theatre and (1609) in the Blackfriars Theatre. Most scholars accept some 38 plays as being by him, partially or totally. The chronology is very shaky, and indeed his authorship has been challenged—in earlier days by the proponents of Francis Bacon, in later days by proponents of the earl of Oxford as writer of all of them. Regardless of the name, Shakspere's plays show forth one of the towering geniuses of all time. They are sometimes divided, for the sake of convenience, into four groups. The first includes *The Comedy of Errors,* the three parts of *Henry VI, Titus Andronicus, The Two Gentlemen of Verona, Richard III, Love's Labour's Lost, The Taming of the Shrew,* and *King John.* Several of these are only dubiously of his authorship. The second period includes plays that are much surer, including most of his best comedies and chronicle plays—*Richard II, A Midsummer Night's Dream, The Merchant of Venice, Romeo and Juliet,* the two parts of *Henry IV, The Merry Wives of Windsor* (supposedly written at the behest of Queen Elizabeth I), *Much Ado about Nothing, Henry V, Julius Caesar, As You Like It,* and *Twelfth Night.* The third period saw the greatest of his tragedies and some of his light comedies—*Hamlet, Troilus and Cressida, All's Well That Ends Well, Measure for Measure, Othello, King Lear, Macbeth, Antony and Cleopatra, Timon of Athens, Coriolanus,* and *Pericles, Prince of Tyre.* The fourth period includes *Cymbeline, The Winter's Tale, The Tempest, Henry VIII,* and *The Two Noble Kinsmen.* Shakspere apparently was not the sole author of the first part of *Henry VI*, of *Timon of Athens*, and of *Pericles*. John FLETCHER was almost certainly the collaborator on *Henry VIII* and *The Two Noble Kinsmen*. The plays contain the richness of Shakspere's contribution to the world. Their poetry, at times majestic, at times lyric, at times surpassingly witty, has a beauty beyond comparison. Yet without the plays he would have been remembered for his sonnets (1593?–1596?), dedicated to a mysterious W. H., whose identity is much disputed. Other poems include *Venus and Adonis* (1593), *The Rape of Lucrece* (1594), *The Phoenix and the Turtle* (1601), and *The Passionate Pilgrim* (1599). It is doubtful whether he wrote *A Lover's Complaint* (1609), attributed to him. His genius transcends any specific accomplishments, but in many techniques he had a mastery that affected all followers, such as his perfection of the blank-verse line and his superlative development of the Renaissance tragedy.

shale (shāl), sedimentary rock formed by consolidation of mud or clay, having the property of splitting into thin layers parallel to bedding planes. Some shales are a potential source of petroleum.

shallot (shŭlŏt'), perennial plant (*Allium ascalonicum*), closely related to the onion. Its leaves and bulbs are similar to but milder than garlic.

Shallum (shăl'lŭm). **1** Died c.749 B.C., king of Israel for a month. He killed Zachariah for the throne and was himself killed by Menahem. 2 Kings 15.13–15. **2** King of Judah: see JEHOAHAZ.

Shalmaneser (shălmŭnē'zŭr), kings of anc. Assyria. **Shalmaneser I**, d. 1290 B.C., removed the capital from Assur to Calah and estab. a royal residence at Nineveh. **Shalmaneser III**, d. 825 B.C., had black obelisk inscribed with claims of victories in Syria and Palestine (including one over Ahab of Israel). Built a huge tower in Calah. **Shalmaneser V**, d. 722 B.C., attacked Hosea of Israel and captured Samaria.

shaman, a healer, priest, or magician, especially one capable of controlling or gaining aid of supernatural agencies. Term originally referred to this functionary in Siberian tribes and now extends to practitioners among all primitives. The American Indian medicine man performed same functions as the shaman and was usually a person of superior intellect and ability whose advice was sought by chiefs and elders. Shamans employ hypnotism, ventriloquism, sleight of hand, trancelike states, and other devices.

Shamokin (shŭmō'kĭn), borough (pop. 16,879), E Pa., ESE of Sunbury. Center in anthracite region; mfg. of textiles, clothing, and machinery.

Shamrock, city (pop. 3,322), N Texas, E of Amarillo in Panhandle. Has oil and gas refining.

shamrock, a plant with leaves of three leaflets which, according to legend, was used by St. Patrick to explain the doctrine of the Trinity. It is now the emblem of Ireland. In U.S., plants most often used as substitutes for shamrock are the white and hop clovers, black medic, and wood sorrel.

Shamyl (shä'mĭl), c.1798–1871, religious and political leader (imam) of Moslem mountaineers of E Caucasus in their Holy War against Russia (1834–59). Was captured 1859. Died in Mecca, where he was allowed to go 1870.

Shang (shäng) or **Yin**, dynasty of China. Varying dates given are c.1766–c.1122 B.C. and c.1523–c.1027 B.C. Empire comprised N China and part of Korea. Succeeded by Chou dynasty.

Shanghai (shäng'hī'), city (pop. 4,300,630), in, but independent of, Kiangsu prov., China; a great port on Whangpoo R. Largest city of China, it grew after 1842 when Treaty of Nanking opened it to foreign trade and ceded sections of it to foreign powers. Modern section of city is area formerly comprising Internatl. Settlement (estab. by Great Britain and U.S.) and French concession. Chief mfg. center of China; textile mills and food-processing plants. Seat of several universities, it ranks second to Peking as educational

center. Invaded 1932 by the Japanese; under Japanese occupation 1937–45. At end of World War II the entire city (including foreign holdings) was restored to Nationalists. Fell 1949 to Chinese Communists.

Shanhaikwan (shän'hī'gwän'), city (pop. 70,000), NE Hopeh prov., China, on Tientsin-Mukden RR. Strategic gateway to Manchuria, at easternmost end of Great Wall. Formerly called Linyü.

Shannon, principal river of Ireland. Rising in Co. Cavan, it flows mostly S c.220 mi. through several loughs to Limerick, where it turns W in broad estuary (c.70 mi. long) to the Atlantic. Between Limerick and Lough Derg is an important hydroelectric plant. River has valuable fisheries.

Shannontown, village (pop. 5,828), central S.C., S of Sumter. Woodworking plants.

Shansi (shän'shē'), province (50,000 sq. mi.; pop. 10,-000,000), N China; cap. Taiyüan. Bounded S by Yellow R. Mainly a plateau containing large deposits of coal. Crops include millet and wheat.

Shan State (shän), constituent unit (61,090 sq. mi.; pop. 1,699,585) of Union of Burma; cap. Lashio. Essentially a hilly plateau. The Shans, who are related to the Siamese, dominated N Burma 13th–16th cent. Came under British rule in 1885. In late 19th cent. area was split into c.30 petty states; most of these were merged 1922 to form Federated Shan States. Integrated 1948 as a single state within Union of Burma.

Shantung (shän'tŭng', shän'dŏong'), province (55,000 sq. mi.; pop. 36,000,000), E China, on peninsula in Yellow Sea; cap. Tsinan. Partly mountainous, partly on Yellow R. delta. Produces much coal. Chief crops are millet, wheat, kaoliang, peanuts, and cotton. Parts of province, WEIHAIWEI and KIAOCHOW, were formerly leased by Great Britain and Germany. Occupied by the Japanese 1937–45; fell to Chinese Communists 1948. A variety of silk is called shantung.

Shapiro, Karl (shŭpēr'ō), 1913–, American poet. Works include *V-Mail* (1944) and critical poem *Essay on Rime* (1945).

Shapley, Harlow (shăp'lē), 1885–, American astronomer. Noted for photometric and spectroscopic research and investigations of structure of universe.

Shapur I (shäpoor') or **Sapor I** (sä'pôr), d. 272, king of Persia (241–72), son and successor of Ardashir I, of Sassanid dynasty. His defeat of Valerian at Edessa (260) was a landmark in decline of Rome.

Shapur II or **Sapor II**, 309–79, king of Persia (309–79), of Sassanid dynasty, called Shapur the Great. Defeated the Romans under Constantius II and later under Julian. His reign saw great prosperity.

Sharaku (shä'räkōō), fl. 1794, Japanese color-print artist, known for portraits of *kabuki* actors.

share, in finance: see STOCK.

share cropping, system of farm tenancy common in the U.S. The system, which arose at the end of the Civil War, perpetuated system of having workers constantly devoted to cotton cultivation under rigid supervision. The cropper brings to the farm only his own and his family's labor while land, animals, and equipment are provided by the landowner, who also advances credit for living expenses. In return the cropper gets a share of the money realized; from this his debt to the landlord is deducted. Mechanization and reduction in cotton acreage have tended to reduce share cropping.

shark, member of fish group more primitive than bony fish, most abundant in warm seas. It has a cartilaginous skeleton; lacks scales and air bladder; dermal denticles roughen the body surface; toothed mouth is on ventral surface. Eats almost any animal food, including carrion and refuse. Length 2–50 ft.; larger species usually bear their young like mammals. See also DOGFISH.

Shark Island: see DRY TORTUGAS.

Sharon (shā'rŭn, shä'–), fertile plain of W Israel, between Samarian hills and the Mediterranean.

Sharon. 1 Town (pop. 1,889), NW Conn., in Taconic Mts. Noah Webster wrote his *Spelling Book* here. **2**

City (pop. 26,454), NW Pa., on Shenango R. near Ohio line; settled c.1800. Mfg. of steel, metal, and electrical products. **3** Town (pop. 470), E Vt., NE of Rutland. Birthplace of Joseph Smith, founder of Mormonism.

Sharon Springs, resort village, E central N.Y., NW of Albany. Sulphur springs used in hydrotherapy.

Sharp, James, 1618?–1679, Scottish divine. A Presbyterian minister, he supported conciliation with royalists. After Restoration he was made (1661) archbishop of St. Andrews and opposed Covenanters, a band of whom murdered him.

Sharp, William, pseud. **Fiona Macleod** (fē′nù mù-kloud′), 1855–1905, Scottish poet and literary biographer. Wrote poems, biographies, and novels under his own name, but verse, prose, and plays written under his pseudonym have greater misty and Celtic charm.

Sharpsburg. 1 Town (pop. 866), NW Md.: see AN-TIETAM CAMPAIGN. **2** Borough (pop. 7,296), SW Pa., on Allegheny R. and near Pittsburgh. Mfg. of hardware and chemicals.

Sharpsville, borough (pop. 5,414), NW Pa., on Shenango R. and near Sharon. Mfg. of metal products.

Shasta, Mount: see CASCADE RANGE.

Shasta Dam, N Calif., in Sacramento R. and near Redding; built 1938–45 for power, flood control, and navigation. It is huge unit (602 ft. high, 3,500 ft. long) in CENTRAL VALLEY project.

Shatt el Arab (shăt′ ĕl ä′räb), river, c.120 mi. long, formed by confluence of Tigris and Euphrates rivers. Flows through Iraq to Persian Gulf. Forms part of Iraq-Iran border.

Shaw, Anna Howard, 1847–1919, American woman-suffrage leader, b. England. Holder of a medical degree and a minister of the Methodist Protestant Church, she devoted herself after 1888 to woman-suffrage movement.

Shaw, George Bernard, 1856–1950, British dramatist, b. Dublin. He went to London, where he wrote five little-known novels. He became music critic (1888) for the *Star* and (1890) for the *World,* his lively music reviews showing his enthusiasm for Wagner. In 1895 he became dramatic critic for the *Saturday Review.* Long interested in economics and socialism, he was an early member of the FABIAN SOCIETY. Through Sidney and Beatrice Webb he met Charlotte Payne-Townshend, whom he married in 1898. His first collection of plays appeared in 1898 as *Plays Pleasant and Unpleasant,* and included "pleasant" *Candida* and *Arms and the Man* and "unpleasant" *Widowers' Houses* and *Mrs. Warren's Profession.* His major plays include *The Devil's Disciple* (written 1896); *Caesar and Cleopatra* (1899); *Captain Brassbound's Conversion* (written 1899), played in 1906 by Ellen Terry, with whom Shaw corresponded for years; *Man and Superman* (pub. 1903); *Major Barbara* (produced 1905); *The Doctor's Dilemma* (produced 1906); *Androcles and the Lion* (1911); *Pygmalion* (1912); *Heartbreak House* (produced 1920); *Back to Methuselah* (1924); and his masterpiece, *Saint Joan* (produced 1924). He was awarded the 1925 Nobel Prize in Literature. He also wrote essays on widely varying subjects, including *The Quintessence of Ibsenism* (1891) and *The Intelligent Woman's Guide to Socialism and Capitalism* (1928). His complete works were published in 1930–32 in 30 volumes. In his 60 years of literary and dramatic activity Shaw always expressed himself on all subjects with great frankness, sometimes with wisdom, but always with wit.

Shawangunk Mountain (shŏng′gùm, –gùngk), ridge of Appalachian system, SE N.Y., extending NE from junction with Kittatinny Mt. near N.J. border.

Shawano (shô′nō, shô′wùnō), city (pop. 5,894), NE Wis., on Wolf R. and NW of Green Bay. Farm trade center with wood products. Menominee Indian reservation is to the N.

Shawinigan Falls (shùwĭ′nĭgùn), city (pop. 26,903), S Que., Canada, on St. Maurice R. and NW of Trois Rivières. Falls (N) supply power for paper mills and other industries.

Shawnee (shô″nē′), city (pop. 22,948), central Okla., on North Canadian R. and SE of Oklahoma City. Trade, mfg., and rail center of agr. and oil area. Has U.S. Indian tuberculosis sanatorium.

Shawnee Indians, North American tribe of Algonquian linguistic stock. In mid-18th cent. they settled in Ohio and there took part in battles against the whites. The Treaty of Greenville forced them W, and they founded a village on the Tippecanoe in Ind. under command of the Shawnee Prophet and Tecumseh. This was the village destroyed by William Henry Harrison in the battle of Tippecanoe (1811). The Shawnee are living on reservations in Okla. Also Shawano.

Shawnee Prophet, 1768–1837, North American Indian of Shawnee tribe; twin brother of TECUMSEH. His Indian name was Tenskwatawa. Urged renunciation of white man's ways and return to Indian modes.

Shawneetown, city (pop. 1,917), SE Ill., on Ohio R. One of state's oldest towns, settled after 1800, laid out 1808. Important river port and commercial center in early 19th cent. First bank chartered in state preserved. After 1937 flood city moved few miles W to higher ground.

Shaw University: see RALEIGH, N.C.

Shays, Daniel (shāz) c.1747–1825, American soldier. Fought in Revolution. Led **Shays's Rebellion,** 1786–87, an armed insurrection in W Mass. Farmers showed economic discontent by rising against the merchants and the lawyers of the seaboard towns. Rebellion prevented sitting of courts. State troops routed rebels. Shays escaped, was later pardoned.

Shchedrin, Nikolai Evgrafovich: see SALTYKOV.

Shcherbakov (shchĕrbùkôf′), city (pop. 139,011), central European RSFSR. A major inland port and lumber center. Site of dam and hydroelectric station of Rybinsk Reservoir (area 1,800 sq. mi.), formed 1941 between the upper Volga and its left affluents (Mologa and Sheksna) as part of Mariinsk System. City was called Rybinsk until 1946.

Sheba (shē′bù), biblical name of region of S Arabia, including Yemen and the Hadramaut; also called Saba. Its inhabitants, Sabaeans or Sabeans, estab. an ancient culture there, as shown by inscriptions in a Semitic language. Legend said it was very wealthy. Its queen (called, in Moslem tradition, Balkis) visited Solomon (1 Kings 10). Sheba colonized Ethiopia, was later (6th cent. A.D.) under Ethiopian control.

Sheboygan (shĭboi′gùn), city (pop. 42,365), E Wis., on L. Michigan at mouth of Sheboygan R.; formed 1836 in site of North West Co. post (1795). Center of important dairy and cheese-making area. Liberal German refugees arrived in mid-19th cent.

Shechem (shē′kùm), one of the cities of refuge, central Palestine, N of Jerusalem; in modern Arabic NABLUS. Traditionally it is the site of Jacob's well and Joseph's tomb. Also Sichem and Sychem.

Sheeler, Charles, 1883–, American painter and photographer. Exhibited in Armory Show (1913).

Sheen, Fulton J(ohn), 1895–, American Roman Catholic clergyman, known for his radio broadcasts and his inspirational books (e.g., *Peace of Soul,* 1949). Made auxiliary bishop 1951.

sheep, wild and domesticated ruminant mammal of genus *Ovis,* of cattle family. The male is a ram (if castrated a wether), the female, a ewe, and their young are lambs. The wild BIGHORN has never been domesticated. Sheep are valued for wool, meat (mutton), and their skins. Cheese is made from the milk. Among leading breeds are the Karakul, prized for pelts used for coats and trimmings; the long-wool Cotswold; the Hampshire, hornless and black-faced, a leading breed in U.S. for market lambs; Merino, esteemed for fine wool; Shropshire and Southdown, producers of both mutton and wool. Colorado and Nebraska are important sheep-raising areas. The sheep was the literal and symbolic sacrifice in Judaism; hence in Christianity Jesus is called the Lamb of God.

sheep dogs. Various breeds of dogs which may be used in guarding or herding sheep or cattle. The name *sheep dog* forms part of the breed name of only certain dogs. These include the old English sheep dog, probably developed in 18th-cent. England for driving sheep and cattle to market and known by its long shaggy coat that covers the face as well as the body, and the Shetland sheep dog or "Sheltie" which greatly resembles the collie, but is 12–15 in. at the shoulder in contrast to the collie's 22–24 in. The collie, originally bred as a shepherd dog and recognized by its tapering nose, usually long hair, and abundant ruff, has become more of a show dog and a pet since the late 19th cent. The German shepherd dog, commonly called the police dog because of its extensive use in police work, has a long, straight back, plumed tail, and, when at attention, erect ears. Its stamina, intelligence, alertness, and loyalty make it an excellent war dog, watch dog, and seeing-eye dog. Two of the largest of all dogs (sometimes over 27 in. at the shoulder) are the St. Bernard (named after St. Bernard de Menthon, founder, c.982, of the well-known hospice in the Swiss Alps) and the Newfoundland. Although both may be used in guarding sheep, the St. Bernard is more famous for its Alpine rescue work, while the aquatic skill of the Newfoundland makes it an able saver of drowning persons. Both dogs have thick coats. The Newfoundland is usually black (sometimes with white markings) and has a domed forehead. The St. Bernard is red or brindle, with white; its wrinkled forehead gives it a morose expression.

Sheerness, urban district (pop. 15,727), on Isle of Sheppey, Kent, England. Seaport with government dockyards; much of town's industry depends upon the garrison. Another section is a resort.

Sheffield, county borough (pop. 512,834), West Riding of Yorkshire, England, on Don R.; a leading industrial center of England. Seat of cutlery mfg. since 14th cent.; silver and electroplate goods, tools, and heavy steel goods are also made. Mary Queen of Scots was imprisoned here 1569–84. Univ. of Sheffield (1905) has medical school and technical college. Mappin Art Galleries are noted. City was heavily bombed in 1940.

Sheffield, city (pop. 10,767), NW Ala., on Pickwick L. of Tennessee R. opposite Florence. Mfg. of aluminum products, ferroalloys, stoves, castings.

Sheherazade: see THOUSAND AND ONE NIGHTS.

Shelburne, William Petty Fitzmaurice, 2d earl of, 1737–1805, British statesman. Supported John Wilkes. Secretary of state under both William Pitts. Concluded Treaty of Paris (1783) giving independence to new U.S., but was driven from office by Tory-Whig coalition. Liberal but unpopular.

Shelby. 1 City (pop. 15,508), W N.C., W of Charlotte in the piedmont. Textile milling center. **2** City (pop. 7,971), N central Ohio, NW of Mansfield. Mfg. of steel tubing.

Shelbyville. 1 City (pop. 11,734), SE Ind., SE of Indianapolis; platted 1832. Farm trade center in Corn Belt. Mfg. of furniture. **2** Town (pop. 9,456), central Tenn., on Duck R. and SSE of Nashville. Mfg. of rubber goods and pencils. The Tennessee "walking horse" is bred in the area.

Sheldon, Charles Monroe, 1857–1946, American Congregational clergyman, author of the widely read religious novel, *In His Steps* (1896).

Shelekhov, Grigori Ivanovich (grĭgô′rē ēvä′nŭvĭch shĕ′lyĭkhŭf), 1747–95, Russian fur merchant. In 1784 he founded first permanent settlement in Alaska on Kodiak Isl.

shell, in zoology, hard outer covering secreted by animal. Usually refers to calcareous shells of many MOLLUSK species, but is also applied to the exoskeleton (outer skeleton) of crab and other crustaceans, and to the bony covering of turtle.

shellac (shŭlăk′), name for solution of LAC in alcohol or for the resin itself. It is orange to light yellow in color. Used as surface coating, spirit varnish, for stiffening, and in electrical insulation.

Shelley, Percy Bysshe, 1792–1822, English poet. Educated at Eton and Oxford, he was expelled from Oxford in 1811 because of his pamphlet *The Necessity of Atheism.* He then eloped to Scotland with his sister's schoolmate Harriet Westbrook. Three years later he eloped with Mary Wollstonecraft Godwin. The summer of 1816 was spent in Switzerland, where he began his friendship with Byron. Soon afterward, Harriet committed suicide, and Shelley married Mary Godwin. In 1818 they went to Italy, where he composed the greater part of his poetry. He was drowned on July 8, 1822, when sailing in the Bay of Lerici. His chief works include *Queen Mab* (1813); *Alastor* (1816); *The Revolt of Islam* (1817); *The Cenci* and *Prometheus Unbound* (both 1820), closet dramas; *Epipsychidion* (1821), praise of ideal love; and *Adonais* (1821), a threnody on the death of Keats. Shelley's political philosophy long inspired radical thinkers, but his reputation is based most firmly upon the fresh imagery and subtle melody of his inspired lyrics, such as "Ode to the West Wind," "To a Skylark," "The Indian Serenade," and "When the Lamp Is Shattered." His wife, **Mary (Wollstonecraft Godwin) Shelley,** 1797–1851, daughter of William Godwin and Mary Wollstonecraft, is remembered as a writer chiefly for her novel of terror, *Frankenstein* (1818).

shellfish, popular name for certain edible aquatic animals, including mollusks (e.g., oyster and clam) and crustaceans (e.g., crab, lobster, and shrimp).

Shelter Island, c.7 mi. long, between N and S peninsulas of Long Isl., SE N.Y. Summer resort.

Shelton. 1 City (pop. 12,694), SW Conn., on Housatonic R. and W of New Haven; settled 1697. Mfg. of textiles and metal products. **2** Lumber city (pop. 5,045), NW Wash., on a Puget Sound arm NW of Olympia. Oysters, lumber.

Shem, eldest son of Noah, ancestor of the Semites. Gen. 5.32; 7.13; 9.25–27; 11.10. Sem: Luke 3.36.

Shemya (shĕm′yŭ), island, 4 mi. long, off W Alaska, one of Aleutian Islands. U.S. air base estab. here in World War II.

Shenandoah (shĕnŭndō′ŭ). **1** City (pop. 6,938), SW Iowa, SE of Council Bluffs and on East Nishnabotna R. (power). Industrial center of agr. area. **2** Borough (pop. 15,704), E Pa., in Schuylkill anthracite region near Pottsville; settled 1835. Coal mining; mfg. of textiles.

Shenandoah, river formed in western Va. and flowing c.170 mi. N to the Potomac at Harpers Ferry, W.Va. Shenandoah Valley, site of much Civil War activity, figured in 1862 diversion of T. J. JACKSON, in GETTYSBURG CAMPAIGN (1863), in raid of J. A. Early (1864), and as retreat for Lee after Antietam campaign. Main Confederate supply source. Taken and ravaged by P. H. SHERIDAN 1864–65.

Shenandoah, ship: see CONFEDERATE CRUISERS.

Shenandoah National Park: see NATIONAL PARKS AND MONUMENTS (table).

Shenandoah Valley: see SHENANDOAH, river.

Shensi (shĕn′sē′), province (75,000 sq. mi.; pop. 10,000,000), N central China; cap. Sian. Bounded on E by Yellow R. Economic center of province is Wei R. valley. Major producer of oil, but rich coal deposits are largely untouched. Chief crops are wheat, millet, and kaoliang. Yenan (pop. 29,856) in N Shensi was center of Chinese Communists 1937–47.

Shenstone, William, 1714–63, English poet and landscape gardener, author of *The Schoolmistress* (1742).

Shenyang, Manchuria: see MUKDEN.

Sheol: see HELL.

shepherd dog: see SHEEP DOGS.

Shepherdstown, town (pop. 1,173), in E Panhandle of W.Va., on Potomac R. and SE of Martinsburg; settled 1762, one of oldest towns in state.

Sheppard, Jack, 1702–24, English criminal. Had short, spectacular career as thief, robber, and escape artist before he was hanged. His exploits became subject of many narratives and plays.

Sheppey, Isle of, Kent, England, in the Thames estuary. Largely flat with fertile soil. Vegetables, grain, and sheep are raised.

Sheraton, Thomas (shě'rŭtùn), 1751–1806, English designer of furniture. Wrote influential manuals of cabinetwork. His style is marked by simplicity, emphasis on straight lines, and preference for inlay decoration and classical motifs. See *ill.*, p. 356.

Sherborne (shûr'bŭrn), urban district (pop. 5,987), Dorsetshire, England. Site of Sherborne School (founded 1550), noted public school which has a library rich in musical scores.

Sherbrooke, city (pop. 50,543), SE Que., Canada, on St. Francis R. at mouth of Magog R. and E of Montreal. Trade center in agr. area with textile and knitting mills, foundries, and railroad shops.

Shere Ali (shēr' ä'lē, shâr'), 1825–79, emir of Afghanistan (1863–79), son of Dost Mohammed. His friendly relations with Russia led to second Afghan War (1878–80) with the British. Died in exile.

Sheridan, Philip Henry, 1831–88, Union general in Civil War. An outstanding cavalry leader, he gave brilliant support in many campaigns. Distinguished himself at Perryville (1862). In Chattanooga campaign 1863) he aided G. H. Thomas. Commander in Army of the Potomac (1864). Defeated J. E. B. Stuart at Yellow Tavern, J. A. Early at Winchester. Laid waste to Shenandoah Valley (1864). After victory at Five Forks (April 1, 1865) he cut off Lee's retreat at Appomattox Courthouse, forcing Lee's surrender.

Sheridan, Richard Brinsley, 1751–1816, British dramatist and politician. Director and part owner (1776) of the Drury Lane Theatre, he wrote many pieces (most enduring the comedies of manners, *The Rivals,* 1775, and *The School for Scandal,* 1777). In Parliament after 1780, he was among the most brilliant orators of his day, prominent in impeachment of Warren Hastings and defense of French Revolution.

Sheridan, city (pop. 11,500), N Wyo., E of Bighorn Mts., near Mont. line, in coal, cattle, farm, and dude-ranch area; settled 1878. Railroad division point; food processing (beet sugar, cereals). Annual rodeo. Near by are site of Fetterman massacre and replica of Fort Phil Kearny (1860s).

Sheriffmuir (shě'rĭfmyŏŏr"), battlefield in Perthshire, Scotland; scene of indecisive battle (1715) between Jacobites and forces of George I.

Sherman, John: see SHERMAN, WILLIAM TECUMSEH.

Sherman, Stuart P(ratt), 1881–1926, American critic and educator; professor of English at Univ. of Illinois (1907–24). An editor of *The Cambridge History of American Literature,* he wrote conservative critical works such as *Americans* (1922) and *The Main Stream* (1927).

Sherman, William Tecumseh, 1820–91, Union general in Civil War. Fought in Vicksburg and Chattanooga campaigns. Commander in the West, he launched ATLANTA CAMPAIGN (1864). City fell on Sept. 2, evacuation was ordered Sept. 9, and city was burned Nov. 15. Then with 60,000 men he marched through Ga., devastating country as he went. In Feb., 1865, he turned N through S.C., repeating destruction of country. He justified his actions on ground that in war it is necessary to break spirit of whole people to win victory. His brother, **John Sherman,** 1823–1900, was U.S. Representative from Ohio (1855–61) and U.S. Senator (1861–77, 1881–97). Gave his name to Sherman Anti-Trust Act and Sherman Silver Purchase Act. He was U.S. Secretary of the Treasury (1877–81), U.S. Secretary of State (1897–98).

Sherman, city (pop. 20,150), N Texas, near Red R. and NNE of Dallas; settled 1849. Highway and rail junction, it processes farm produce, grains, and cotton. Mfg. of textiles and machinery.

Sherman Anti-Trust Act, 1890, passed by U.S. Congress. Based on constitutional power of Congress to regulate interstate commerce, act declared illegal every contract, combination, or conspiracy in restraint of interstate and foreign trade. Supreme Court decisions reduced force of act for a decade. Pres. Theodore ROOSEVELT invoked it with some success. Pres. W. H. Taft employed act in 1911 to dissolve Standard Oil trust and American Tobacco Co. CLAYTON ANTI-TRUST ACT (1914) supplemented it. Anti-trust action was resumed under Pres. F. D. Roosevelt; further supplementing acts (e.g., ROBINSON-PATMAN ACT) were passed.

Sherman Silver Purchase Act, 1890, passed by U.S. Congress to supplant BLAND-ALLISON ACT. Required U.S. government to purchase nearly twice as much silver as before; added substantially to amount of money already in circulation. In operation it threatened to undermine U.S. Treasury's gold reserves. Act repealed in 1893.

Sherrington, Sir Charles Scott, 1857–1952, English physiologist, authority on nervous system. Shared 1932 Nobel Prize in Physiology and Medicine for research on function of neuron.

sherry, naturally dry, fortified wine (15 to 23 percent alcohol), originally made only from grapes grown in region of Jerez de la Frontera, Spain, but now also produced in the U.S. and Latin America. After long maturing, sherries are classed as *palma,* very dry; *raya,* full and rich; or *palo cortado,* intermediate. Blending and, in some cases, sweetening produce many varieties, ranging from dry cocktail wines to dessert types.

's Hertogenbosch (sĕr'tōkhŭnbôs'), Fr. *Bois-le-Duc,* municipality (pop. 53,208), cap. of North Brabant prov., S central Netherlands; chartered 1184. Mfg. center (electrical appliances, bicycles, food, tobacco). Heavily damaged in World War II.

Sherwood, Robert E(mmet), 1896–, American playwright. Among his many plays are *The Road to Rome* (1927), *The Petrified Forest* (1935), *Idiot's Delight* (1936), *Abe Lincoln in Illinois* (1938), and *There Shall Be No Night* (1940). Was director of overseas operations of Office of War Information and wrote speeches for F. D. Roosevelt. His memoir *Roosevelt and Hopkins* (1948) won popular notice.

Sherwood Forest, once a large royal forest, Nottinghamshire, England; famous as home of Robin Hood.

Sheshonk I (shē'shŏngk), d. c.924 B.C., king of anc. Egypt (c.945–c.924 B.C.). A commander of mercenaries, he took the throne when the line of Tanis died out and estab. Libyan (XXII) dynasty. Captured Gaza and presented it to Solomon. Later overran Palestine. Enlarged the Karnak temple. He is the biblical Shishak.

Shetland (shĕt'lŭnd) or **Zetland** (zĕt'–), county (550 sq. mi.; pop. 19,343) of Scotland, consisting of **Shetland Islands** or **Shetlands,** archipelago c.70 mi. long. Of some 100 islands, c.25% are inhabited. Mainland, longest island, has Lerwick, county seat and chief port. Surface is mostly low and rocky, with little good farm land. Oats and barley are chief crops, but fishing and cattle and sheep raising are more important. Knitted woolen goods are famous. The Shetland pony is bred here.

Shetland sheep dog: see SHEEP DOGS.

Shibboleth (shī'bōlĕth) [Heb.,= stream or ear of corn], password used by Gileadites to detect fugitive Ephraimites because Ephraimites, unable to pronounce *sh,* said "Sibboleth." Judges 12. Hence, *shibboleth* came to mean watchword, cant phrase of a particular party, meaningless standard of conformity.

Shickshock Mountains, E Que., Canada, range of Appalachian Mts. extending from Notre Dame Mts. c.100 mi. E-W near coast of Gaspé Peninsula. Rise to 4,160 ft. in Tabletop Mt. or Mt. Jacques Cartier.

Shidehara, Kijuro, Baron (shēdā'härä), 1872–1951, Japanese statesman, a career diplomat. Foreign minister 1929–31, premier Oct., 1945–May, 1946.

Shiel, Loch (lŏkh shēl'), lake, c.17 mi. long and 1 mi. wide, Inverness-shire, Scotland.

Shields, James, 1806–79, American soldier and statesman, b. Ireland. U.S. Senator from Ill. (1849–55), from Minn. (1858–59). In Civil War he fought in Shenandoah Valley (1862), was defeated at Port Republic. Resigned commission in 1863.

Shields, England: see SOUTH SHIELDS; TYNEMOUTH.

Shigatse (shēgät'sĕ), town (pop. c.14,000), SE Tibet, on tributary of Brahmaputra R. Near by is monastery of Tashilunpo (founded 1446), whose abbot is the powerful Panchen Lama.

Shiites (shē'ītz) [Arabic,= sectarian], the group of Moslems who split from the rest of ISLAM (see SUNNITES) by holding that Ali and his successors are divinely ordained caliphs (see CALIPHATE). Husein is considered by them a martyr. The nationalism of Persia helped build the sect, which accepts the idea of the hidden IMAM and of the MAHDI. These beliefs bred fanaticism, expressed in such sects as the FATIMITE believers and the ASSASSIN zealots. Shiism is the religion of Iran.

Shikoku (shĭkō'kŏō), island (c.6,860 sq. mi.; pop. 4,074,-708), Japan, S of Honshu, E of Kyushu, between Inland Sea and Philippine Sea. Smallest of major Japanese islands. Interior is mountainous and sparsely settled. Exports salt, copper, tobacco, lumber, fruit.

Shillelagh (shĭlā'lŭ), town, Co. Wicklow, Ireland. Ancient forest of Shillelagh gave name to the Irishman's oak or blackthorn cudgel, the shillelagh.

Shillington, borough (pop. 5,059), SE Pa., near Reading. Mfg. of building blocks and textiles.

Shiloh (shī'lō), in Bible, sanctuary where Ark of the Covenant rested after conquest of Canaan until it was captured by Philistines. Home of Eli and young Samuel.

Shiloh, battle of, April 6–7, 1862, also called battle of Pittsburg Landing, one of great battles of Civil War. Took name from Shiloh Church, meetinghouse c.3 mi. SSW of Pittsburg Landing, community in Tenn., 9 mi. S of Savannah, on W bank of Tennessee R. After victory at Fort Donelson, Grant moved up river for attack on Corinth, Miss. On April 6, A. S. Johnston and P. G. T. Beauregard made surprise attack, routing Federals; Johnston was killed. On next day Grant, with aid of D. C. Buell's Army of the Ohio, counterattacked. Outnumbered, Beauregard withdrew to Corinth; city was later abandoned to Federals. Shiloh, one of bloodiest and most controversial battles of war, was Union victory in that it led to later successful campaigns in West.

Shiloh National Military Park: see NATIONAL PARKS AND MONUMENTS (table).

Shimoda (shĭmō'dä), resort town (pop. 8,973), central Honshu, Japan, on Izu peninsula. First U.S. consulate, under Townsend Harris, opened here in 1856.

Shimonoseki (shē'mōnōsākē), industrial city (pop. 176,-666), extreme SW Honshu, Japan; port on Shimonoseki Strait. Connected by tunnel with Moji, Kyushu. Engineering works, shipyards, chemical plants, and fish canneries. Treaty of Shimonoseki ending First Chino-Japanese War signed here 1895.

Shimonoseki, Treaty of: see CHINO-JAPANESE WAR, FIRST.

Shinano (shĭnä'nō), river, 229 mi. long, central and N Honshu, Japan; longest in Japan.

Shinar (shī'när), in Bible, name for whole or part of Babylonia. Gen. 10.10; 11.2; 14.1; Isa. 11.11; Dan. 1.2; Zech. 5.11.

Shinn, Everett, 1876–, American muralist and magazine illustrator, a member of The EIGHT.

Shinto (shĭn'tō), religion of Japan, based on old animistic beliefs, modified by Buddhism and Confucianism, unsystematized, more a set of rituals and customs than an organized church. There are three compilations of beliefs and customs—the *Kojiki* (completed A.D. 712), the *Nihongi* (completed 720), the *Yengishiki* (10th cent.). The Kami in Shinto are supernatural beings, mostly beneficent. The sun-goddess gradually became much exalted and was held to be ancestress of the Japanese emperors (divine ancestry disavowed by Hirohito, 1946). Shinto worship consists primarily in prayer and food offerings.

ship, large craft for water transport. Homer's *Odyssey* and the legendary quest of Jason for the Golden Fleece hint that long voyages were common near the dawn of history. Ancient ships used oars, sails, or both, and the slow, heavier ships carried grain, while the oar-propelled Graeco-Roman trireme (later developed to the quinquireme) was the favored warship. Early medieval seafaring was marked by the appearance of the Nordic Vikings, whose fleet ships enabled them to forage French and English coasts; Alfred the Great's defense of England centered in the founding of a navy. Oar-and-sail driven Viking ships could make long voyages (e.g., Leif Ericsson's crossing to America). The Crusades, the tale of Marco Polo, the consequent desire for Eastern trade, and the activities of Prince Henry the Navigator introduced the great exploratory activity of the Renaissance, which was in a way capped by Columbus's discovery of the New World (1492). Sturdier, more refined vessels (bark, brig, clipper, and schooner) appeared later. The needs of warfare led to the men-of-war. Shipbuilding became a vital industry in Britain and America. The successful run of Fulton's *Clermont* on the Hudson R. (1807) began the era of the steamship, and in mid-19th cent. the first steel ships were built. Finally, the turbine and Diesel engine brought new speed and power to shipping. See *ill.*, p. 865.

Shipka (shĭp'kä), pass through Balkans, central Bulgaria, 4,166 ft. high.

Shippen, Margaret, 1760–1804, wife of Benedict Arnold, daughter of a prominent Philadelphia Tory. Her influence on her husband is much debated.

Shippensburg, borough (pop. 5,722), S Pa., SW of Carlisle. Mfg. of clothing and furniture.

Shipton, Mother, traditional English prophetess. Supposedly predicted great fire of London (1666).

shipworm, wormlike marine bivalve mollusk (*Teredo*). Makes cavities in wood damaging to ships and piers.

Shiraz (shēräz'), city (pop. 129,023), S central Iran; chief city of Fars region. Founded 7th cent., it was cap. of Persia 1750–94. Tombs of the great Persian poets Hafiz and Sadi are here. Founder of Babism was also a native of Shiraz.

Shirley, James, 1596–1666, English dramatist. He wrote some 40 plays, such as *The Lady of Pleasure* (1635) and *The Contention of Ajax and Ulysses* (1659; containing the dirge, "The glories of our blood and state").

Shirpurla: see LAGASH.

Shishak: see SHESHONK I.

Shittim, last camping place of the Hebrews before they entered Canaan. Num. 25; Joshua 2; 3.

shittim wood, of shittah tree, probably an acacia, used, according to Bible, to make Ark of the Covenant and furniture of the Tabernacle (Ex. 25.5).

Shiva: see HINDUISM.

Shizuoka (shĭzōō'ōkä), city (pop. 205,737), central Honshu, Japan; port on Suruga Bay. Known for tea and lacquer ware. Site of castle of last Tokugawa Shogun and Hodai-in, important Buddhist temple.

Shkodër or **Shkodra,** Albania: see SCUTARI.

shock, sudden depression of vital centers of nervous system. Causes include injury, surgery, certain drugs. Marked by pallor, rapid pulse and breathing, low temperature and blood pressure. Injury should be treated; patient must be kept warm and lying down.

shock therapy, in psychiatry, a treatment by chemical agents or electricity to improve or cure mental diseases, or to make the patient rational enough for psychotherapy. Its over-all value is disputed although electric shock has had notable success with depressive disorders, and metrazol and insulin have effected a few remissions of schizophrenia.

shoe, foot covering, commonly of leather and consisting of a sole and an upper. Sandal was probably earliest form. Probably the forerunner (15th cent.) of heeled shoe was the patten, raised on blocks and later attached to the upper. Early shoemakers worked at home or as itinerants. Industry was revolutionized by machine for stitching together soles and uppers, invented c.1858 by Lyman Blake and developed by Gordon McKay. Over 180 different machines are used in modern shoemaking.

shogun (shō'gŏon), title of military dictators who ruled Japan, 12th–19th cent. Title itself dates back to 794 and originally meant commander of imperial armies. Shogunate as system of government was estab. by Yoritomo and known as *bakufu* [literally, army hq.]. Emperor ruled only theoretically, with real power wielded by hereditary shogun. Minamoto family held shogunate 1192–1333; Ashikaga, 1338–1597; Tokugawa, 1603–1867. Overthrow of shogun brought Meiji restoration (1868) and birth of modern Japan.

Sholapur (shō'lŭpŏor), city (pop. 203,691), E Bombay, India; major cotton-milling center.

Sholokhov, Mikhail Aleksandrovich (mĕkhŭyĕl' ŭlyĭksän'drŭvĭch shô'lŭkhŭf), 1905–, Russian author, best known for his epic novel of the Don Cossacks, *The Silent Don* (1928–40; Eng. tr., *And Quiet Flows the Don,* 1934, and *The Don Flows Home to Sea,* 1940).

Sholom Aleichem: see ALEICHEM, SHOLOM.

shooting star, North American perennial wild flower (*Dodecatheon meadia*) of primrose family. Also called American primrose or cowslip, it bears a cluster of nodding flowers with white or lilac petals which flare backwards.

shooting star: see METEOR.

Shore, Jane, d.1527?, mistress of Edward IV of England, over whom she exerted great influence. Accused (1483) of sorcery by Richard III, placed in Tower, forced to do public penance as harlot.

Shoreditch, metropolitan borough (pop. 44,885), E London, England; center of furniture-making industry. London's first theater was built here c.1576. Suffered much bomb damage in World War II.

Shorewood, residential suburban village (pop. 16,199), SE Wis., on L. Michigan and Milwaukee R., adjoining N Milwaukee; settled c.1834.

short circuit occurs when current is deflected to path of less resistance. Term is often used for a broken electric circuit as when a fuse blows out or when connection wire in circuit is broken.

shorthand, any brief, rapid system of writing that may be used in transcribing or in recording the spoken word. Such systems, their characters based on letters of the alphabet, were used even in ancient times. Modern systems, frequently based on sound, date from 1558, when Timothy Bright published his symbols for words. Dozens of systems followed before 1837, when shorthand of Isaac Pitman appeared. Using geometric outlines, with shading and differences in slope and position on a given line, it is difficult to master but makes possible very great speed. J. R. Gregg published (1888) a popular system of business shorthand. Its outlines, curved and natural, with variations in length of line, call for a cursive motion, which promotes speed. Pitman and Gregg systems are widely used today.

Short Hills, N.J.: see MILLBURN.

shorthorn cattle: see CATTLE.

Shoshone (shōshō'nē), village (pop. 1,420), S Idaho, in MINIDOKA PROJECT and N of Twin Falls. Magic Dam (1907) in Big Wood R. is near. Gateway to Sun Valley and Sawtooth Mts.

Shoshone Cavern National Monument: see NATIONAL PARKS AND MONUMENTS (table).

Shoshone Falls, S Idaho, in Snake R., near Twin Falls. Shoshone Falls, once c.200 ft. high, are now reduced by irrigation projects upstream.

Shoshone Indians, North American tribe of Uto-Aztecan linguistic stock, living in the early 19th cent.

in SW Mont., W Wyo., S Idaho, and NE Nev. The E Shoshone were buffalo hunters, the W Shoshone did not have horses and hunted no buffalo; they lived on nuts and wild plants. They were sometimes called Snake Indians.

Shoshone project, NW Wyo., near Shoshone R. in Bighorn R. basin. Provides power and irrigation for 161,-654 acres. Has small dams, canals; Buffalo Bill Dam (largest) forms Shoshone Reservoir. Serves Cody and Powell.

Shostakovich, Dmitri (dyĭmē'trē shŏstŏkô'vĭch), 1906–, Russian composer. Notable among his nine symphonies are the First (1925), the Fifth (1937), and the Seventh (1942, composed during the siege of Leningrad). Other works include a satirical ballet, *The Golden Age* (1930); Twenty-four Preludes (1933), for piano; a piano concerto (1933); a piano quintet (1940); and other chamber works. The Soviet government has repudiated much of his music, including the opera *Lady Macbeth of Mzensk.*

shotgun, smooth-bore firearm designed for firing a number of small shot at short range. When the gun is fired, the shot spreads in a widening circle.

Shottery, village, Warwickshire, England, 1 mi. W of Stratford-on-Avon. Has cottage in which Shakspere's wife, Anne Hathaway, lived.

Shotwell, James T(homson)**,** 1874–, American historian. Active in national and international labor, peace, and historical conferences. Works include *War as an Instrument of National Policy* (1929) and *The Great Decision* (1944). An editor (1904–5) *Encyclopaedia Britannica.* Editor *Economic and Social History of the World War* (150 vols., 1919–29).

Shrapnel, Henry, 1761–1842, British general, inventor of the shrapnel shell, which is fired by a time fuse in mid-air and scatters shot and shell fragments over a wide area.

Shreve, Henry Miller, 1785–1851, American inventor of steamboats. His *Washington* opened the Mississippi and the Ohio to steam navigation.

Shreveport (shrēv'pôrt), city (pop. 127,206), NW La., on Red R. near Texas and Ark. borders; founded c.1834. Confederate cap. of La. 1863. Oil center processing cotton, glass, and lumber. Centenary Col. of Louisiana (Methodist; coed.; 1825) is here.

shrew (shrōō), insectivorous mammal, of family Soricidae, of North America and extreme N South America, Europe, and Asia. Related to mole. It has a musky odor. Common species of both hemispheres are of genus *Sorex.* Range in body length (including tail) is c.2½–6¼ in. Shrews are prodigious eaters and vicious fighters.

Shrewsbury, Charles Talbot, duke of, 1660–1718, English statesman. One of seven signers of invitation to William III to take throne in 1688. Regarded by king as his chief Whig minister, he was won to Tory cause by Robert Harley in 1706.

Shrewsbury (shrōz'būrē, shrōōz'–), municipal borough (pop. 44,926), co. seat of Shropshire, England. Ancient Saxon and Norman stronghold, it has much medieval atmosphere. Henry IV defeated (1403) Hotspur near by. Shrewsbury School founded 1551.

Shrewsbury, town (pop. 10,594), central Mass., NE of Worcester; settled 1722. Leather products.

shrike (shrīk) or **butcher bird,** bird of prey, chiefly of Old World but with two New World species (the northern and loggerhead shrikes). Certain shrikes impale prey on thorn or twig while tearing it apart.

shrimp, small marine crustacean, usually 1½–3 in. long, found along most coasts. Has 10 jointed legs and a translucent, flexible outer skeleton.

Shropshire (shrŏp'shĭr, –shŭr), border county (1,346 sq. mi.; pop. 289,844), W England; co. town Shrewsbury. Chiefly pastoral and agr., county has some coal mining. On the edge of Welsh Marches, it was scene of much strife and has ruins of medieval castles. County is sometimes called Salop.

Shropshire sheep: see SHEEP.

Shubun (shoō'boōn'), fl. early 15th cent., Chinese painter of Ming period. Naturalized c.1420 in Japan, where he founded Soga school of Ashikaga.

Shulamite (shoō'lümīt), character addressed in the Song of Solomon. Cant. 6.13.

Shumen (shoō'měn), city (pop. 31,169), NE Bulgaria. Trade and railroad center. Founded 927; strategic fortress during Turkish rule. Noted for Moslem architecture.

Shuster, George N(auman), 1894–, American educator and author. Dean and acting president of Hunter Col. 1939–40, he has been president since 1940. He was on editorial board of *Commonweal*, 1925–37. He became state commissioner for Bavaria (1950).

Si, chemical symbol of the element SILICON.

Sialkot (sēäl'kōt''), city (pop. 152,000), E Punjab prov., W Pakistan. Has 12th-cent. fortress. Mfg. of surgical instruments and sports goods.

Siam: see THAILAND.

Siam, Gulf of, arm of South China Sea, separating Malay Peninsula on W from Indo-China on E.

Siamese language, standard accepted speech of Thailand. Name sometimes includes all of Tai group of Indo-Chinese languages. The standard speech is also called Tai or Thai. See LANGUAGE (table).

Siamese twins, twins united by tissue. Term derived from male twins born in Siam (1811) and long exhibited in P. T. Barnum's circus.

Sian (sē'än', shē'än'), city (pop. 502,988), cap. Shensi prov., NW China; trade center. Was cap. of Han dynasty (206 B.C.–A.D. 220) and western cap. of Tang dynasty (618–906). Ancient center of foreign religious colonies; 8th-cent. Nestorian stone tablet is preserved. In 1936 Chang Hsueh-liang kidnapped Chiang Kai-shek here.

Siang (shyäng), river, c.715 mi. long, in Kwangsi and Hunan provs., China.

Siangtan (shyäng'tän'), city (pop. 82,589), NE Hunan prov., China; port on Siang R.

Siasconset, Mass.: see NANTUCKET.

Siauliai (shëou'lyī), Ger. *Schaulen*, Rus. *Shavli*, city (pop. 31,641), N Lithuania. Mfg. (shoes, textiles). Here Lithuanians defeated LIVONIAN KNIGHTS in 1236 and a German free corps in 1919.

Sibboleth: see SHIBBOLETH.

Sibelius, Jean (Julius Christian) (zhän' sĭbā'lyŭs), 1865–, Finnish composer. His orchestral works include tone poems on national subjects, such as *En Saga* (1892) and *Finlandia* (1900); *The Swan of Tuonela* (1893); *Valse triste;* a violin concerto (1903); and seven symphonies (1899–1924).

Sibenik, Serbo-Croatian *Šibenik* (shēbě'nĭk), town (pop. 16,015), Croatia, NW Yugoslavia; an Adriatic seaport. Chemical mfg. Its noted architecture (esp. its 15th-cent. cathedral) dates from its period under Venetian rule (1212–1797).

Siberia (sībē'rēŭ), Rus. *Sibir*, name commonly applied to the Asiatic part (c.5,000,000 sq. mi.; pop. c.20,-000,000) of the RSFSR. Occupying the N third of Asia, it stretches from the Urals to the Pacific, from the Arctic Ocean to Mongolia and Manchuria. Its four great vegetation belts are, from N to S: tundras; taiga; mixed forest belt; steppe. W Siberia, between Ural Mts. and Yenisei R., is a plain drained by the Ob and the Irtysh; it is agr. in the S and contains the KUZNETSK BASIN (coal) at the foot of the ALTAI. Largest cities: Novosibirsk, Omsk, Stalinsk. E Siberia, drained by the Lena, extends from the Yenisei to a huge mountain chain (Yablonovy, Stanovoi, Verkhoyansk, Kolyma, Anadir ranges) and contains L. Baikal. Largest cities (all in S): Krasnoyarsk, Irkutsk, Yakutsk, Ulan-Ude, Chita. The Far East comprises CHUKCHI PENINSULA, KAMCHATKA, and the MARITIME TERRITORY. Chief cities: Vladivostok, Khabarovsk, Komsomolsk. Nearly entire population (90% Russian) lives in S, mainly along the TRANS-SIBERIAN RAILROAD. Non-Russian groups include Turkic and Mongol peoples (S); Finno-Ugric peoples and Samoyedes

(NW and N); Chukchis and Kamchatkans (NE); Jews (in Birobidzhan); Tungus (center). Lumbering, fur-trapping, hunting, fishing, reindeer raising are the chief occupations in the thinly populated wilderness. Climate is extreme, ranging at Verkhoyansk from −92°F. to above 90°F. S central Siberia was the point of departure of the Huns, Mongols, and Manchus in their great conquests. Russian conquest of Siberia began 1581, when the Cossack YERMAK conquered the Tatar khanate of SIBIR. By 1640 the Cossacks reached the Pacific. By the Treaty of Nerchinsk (1689) Russia abandoned to China the FAR EASTERN TERRITORY (acquired by Russia 1858 and 1860). S Sakhalin Isl. and Kurile Isls. were annexed from Japan after World War II. Siberia was used as penal colony and place of exile from early 17th cent. Large-scale colonization began only with construction of Trans-Siberian RR; population was doubled between 1914 and 1946. During civil war of 1918–20 Siberia was held by the "Whites" under KOLCHAK; Vladivostok was occupied by Japanese till 1922. The tremendous industrial growth of Siberia dates from the first Five-Year Plan and was speeded during World War II. Siberian grain became a vital factor in Soviet economy; the Urals and W Siberia became the new center of Soviet heavy industries. These changes were carried out in part through forced resettlements and forced labor, particularly in the case of road and railroad construction projects and in the exploitation of the rich gold mines of the Aldan and Kolyma ranges.

Sibir (sībēr'), former city, SE of present Tobolsk, RSFSR; cap. of Tatar khanate of Sibir or Siberia. Was conquered by Ivan IV 1582.

Sibiu (sēbyoō'), Ger. *Hermannstadt*, Hung. *Nagyszeben*, city (pop. 60,602), central Rumania, in S Transylvania. Orthodox metropolitan see. Mfg. of machinery, textiles, foodstuffs. Founded 12th cent. by German colonists, it has preserved much of its German medieval character and has long been a cultural center of Transylvania.

sibyl, in Greek mythology, one of a group of prophetic old women. Most famous was Cumaean Sibyl, who sold to Tarquin the Sibylline Books, prophecies about Rome's destiny. Whatever their origin, they were kept at Rome until destroyed by fire in 83 B.C.

Sibylline Oracles: see PSEUDEPIGRAPHA.

Sicilian Vespers, 1282, rebellion of Sicily against King CHARLES I (Charles of Anjou), who had transferred his seat from Palermo to Naples and left Sicily to be governed by arrogant French officials. The general massacre of the French began at Palermo on Easter Monday and spread quickly through the island. It was probably prepared by John of Procida, agent of PETER III of Aragon, who also had negotiated for the support of Emperor Michael VIII against Charles. Peter was proclaimed king of Sicily by a federal assembly.

Sicily (sĭ'cĭlē), Ital. *Sicilia*, island and autonomous region (9,928 sq. mi.; pop. 4,000,078), Italy, separated from mainland by Strait of Messina; cap. Palermo. Largest and most populous Mediterranean island, it lies between the Ionian and Tyrrhenian seas, c.100 mi. N of Africa, and is roughly triangular in shape (hence its ancient name, Trinacria). Except for the fertile plain of Catania, it is mostly mountainous, culminating in Mt. ETNA. Agr., its main resource, is hampered by absentee ownership, primitive methods, lack of irrigation. Chief exports: grapes, olives, oranges; sulphur; fish. The ancient cities of Sicily were founded by Phoenicians (PALERMO), Carthaginians (LILYBAE-UM, TRAPANI), and Greeks (SYRACUSE; CATANIA; MESSINA; GELA; AGRIGENTO; HIMERA). Among the Greek city-states, Syracuse took the lead. Roman-Carthaginian rivalry in Sicily led to the PUNIC WARS and resulted (241 B.C.) in Sicily's becoming a Roman colony. Rome thoroughly exploited the island. Large estates and plantation slavery were introduced; slave revolts were cruelly suppressed (3d cent. B.C.). Sicily passed under Byzantine rule (6th cent. A.D.), then fell to the Arabs (9th cent.). Agr., commerce, and sciences flourished under the Arabs, who, however, were driven out by the Normans under ROGER I (11th cent.). ROGER II became the first king of Sicily (1130), under nominal overlordship of the pope. The marriage of Queen CONSTANCE to Emperor Henry VI brought the kingdom (incl. S Italy, with Naples) to the Hohenstaufen dynasty, which reached its apex with Emperor FREDERICK II (reigned 1197–1250). Frederick's successors (see CONRAD IV; MANFRED; CONRADIN) fought unsuccessfully against the popes; in 1266 Clement IV crowned Charles of Anjou (see CHARLES I of Naples) king of Sicily. Charles's unpopular rule was ended in Sicily by the SICILIAN VESPERS (1282). The island passed to the house of ARAGON; S Italy continued separately as the kingdom of NAPLES, which in 1442 also passed to Aragon. Ruled first by a branch of the Aragon dynasty, after 1409 by viceroys, Sicily deteriorated under its Spanish masters. The Peace of Utrecht gave Sicily to Savoy (1713), which in 1720 exchanged it with Austria for Sardinia. The War of the Polish Succession resulted in the transfer of Sicily and Naples to the Spanish Bourbons (1735). After 1759 the two kingdoms were ruled from Naples by a separate dynasty (see BOURBON-SICILY) and in 1816 they were united, despite Sicilian protests, into the kingdom of the TWO SICILIES. Rebellions against the Bourbon kings were ruthlessly suppressed (1820, 1848–49). After Sicily's conquest by GARIBALDI (1860), the island voted its union with Italy. In World War II it fell to the Allies after heavy fighting (July–Aug., 1943). It received self-rule in 1947.

Sickingen, Franz von (fränts' fün zǐ'kǐng-ùn), 1481–1523, German knight. Influenced by Ulrich von HUTTEN, he gave refuge to persecuted reformers at his castles and, with a private army, waged war against the ecclesiastic princes, aiming at secularization of their lands. He laid siege to Trier (1522), was placed under the ban of the empire, and after a long siege of his castle of Landstuhl was forced to capitulate and died of his wounds. His defeat symbolized the end of the power of German knighthood.

Sickles, Daniel Edgar, 1819–1914, American politician, Union general in Civil War. U.S. Congressman (1857–61, 1893–95). Fought in Peninsular, Antietam, and Gettysburg campaigns. Reconstruction commander in Carolinas (1865–67). Minister to Spain (1869–73).

Sicyon (sǐ'shēŏn), anc. city of Greece, in the Peloponnesus, just S of the Gulf of Corinth. Notable for its bronze work, it also had famous schools of painting and sculpture. It also was of some political importance, and briefly after the destruction of Corinth by the Romans (146 B.C.) was dominant in the region.

Siddons, Sarah Kemble, 1755–1831, English actress, most distinguished of the KEMBLE family. By her warm voice and majestic presence Mrs. Siddons won fame in such roles as Desdemona and Ophelia; she was unequalled as Lady Macbeth. Reynolds painted her portrait, *The Tragic Muse.*

Sidlaw Hills (sǐd'lô), range, E Scotland, extending NE from near Perth into Angus county.

Sidmouth, Henry Addington, Viscount, 1757–1844, English statesman. His ministry (1801–4) after William Pitt's resignation saw Treaty of Amiens with Napoleon 1802. As home secretary (1812–21) he incurred odium for repressive policy in face of hunger.

Sidney or **Sydney, Sir Philip,** 1554–86, English soldier, statesman, author, outstanding figure in Queen Elizabeth's brilliant court. His writings include unfinished *Arcadia* (1590), prose romance; *The Defense of Poesie* and *An Apology for Poetry* (both 1595), slightly different expositions of his critical tenets; *Astrophel and Stella* (1591), one of greatest English sonnet sequences, inspired by love for Penelope Devereux. He was a diplomat and an English foreign agent.

Sidney. 1 City (pop. 3,987), E Mont., in Yellowstone valley near N.Dak. line. Chief city of Lower Yellowstone project (estab. 1906). Beet sugar refining. **2** City (pop. 11,491), W Ohio, on Great Miami R. and N of Dayton; settled 1820. Machinery.

Sidney Sussex College: see CAMBRIDGE UNIVERSITY.

Sidon (sī'dùn), anc. Phoenician city, seaport on the Mediterranean, modern Saida, Lebanon. It was famed for purple dyes and glassware. Continued important through Roman times.

Sidra, Gulf of (sī'drù), arm of the Mediterranean, indenting coast of Libya.

Siegbahn, Karl Manne Georg (kärl' mä'nù yā'ôryù sēg'bän), 1886–, Swedish physicist. Won 1924 Nobel Prize for method for precise measurement of X-ray wave lengths.

Siegen, Ludwig von (fün zē'gùn), c.1609–1680, German engraver, b. Holland, inventor of mezzotint process of engraving.

Siegfried (sēg'frēd, Ger. zēk'frēt) or **Sigurd** (sǐ'gùrd), great ideal hero of Germanic mythology. In the NIBELUNGENLIED, he is conqueror of Brunhild. His role is similar when he appears as Sigurd (Icelandic form) in the VOLSUNGASAGA. In Wagner's opera *Siegfried,* he kills the dragon Fafnir, gains the ring, and wins Brünnehilde.

Siena (sēē'nù, Ital. syä'nä), city (pop. 36,064), Tuscany, central Italy, one of richest art cities in Italy. Produces wine and marble. Its university was estab. 13th cent. A free commune by 12th cent., it developed into a wealthy republic, but in 1555 it fell to Emperor Charles V and passed to the Medici of Florence. Sienese art reached its zenith 13th–15th cent. The Sienese school of painting included Duccio di Buoninsegna, Simone Martini, and Pietro and Ambrogio Lorenzetti. The main square of Siena (the Piazza del Campo) is one of the marvels of medieval architecture. Here the Palio festival, a horse race of medieval origin, is still held. The cathedral, one of finest examples of Italian Gothic, has elaborate marble façade. The adjoining Piccolomini Library is adorned with Pinturicchio's frescoes. Siena was birthplace of St. Catherine of Siena.

Sienkiewicz, Henryk (hĕn'rĭk shĕnkyĕ'vĭch), 1846–1916, Polish author. His novel of early Christianity, *Quo Vadis?* (1895; Eng. tr., 1896), had immense popular success. Among other novels is the trilogy *With Fire and Sword, The Deluge,* and *Pan Michael* (1883–88; Eng. tr., 1890–93), on 17th-cent. Poland's struggle for national existence. Won 1905 Nobel Prize in Literature.

Sierra, Justo (hōō'stō syĕ'rä), 1848–1912, Mexican educator and historian, largely responsible for intellectual renaissance in Mexico in early 20th cent.

Sierra Blanca (sēē'rù blăng'kù), village, W Texas. Rail junction in ranch region.

Sierra Blanca: see SANGRE DE CRISTO MOUNTAINS.

Sierra Leone (sēē'rù lēō'nē, lēōn'), British colony and protectorate (27,968 sq. mi.; pop. 1,858,275), W Africa, on the Atlantic; cap. Freetown. Colony consists mainly of small peninsula; area comprising protectorate has swamps, high savannas, and an arid plateau. Chief export crops are palm oil, cacao, and ginger. Iron, diamonds, and chromite are mined. Visited c.1462 by the Portuguese, who were followed by English slave traders. Settled in late 18th cent. by liberated slaves. Colony was created in 1808, protectorate in 1896.

Sierra Madre (sēē'rù mä'drä), city (pop. 7,273), S Calif., at foot of Mt. Wilson. Orange groves.

Sierra Madre (syĕ'rä mä'dhrä), chief mountain system of Mexico and greatest single geographic force in Mexican life. The **Sierra Madre Oriental** (ōryĕntäl') begins S of Rio Grande and runs 1,000 mi. roughly parallel to coast of Gulf of Mexico, ranging from 10 to 200 mi. inland. Reaches its highest elevation in ORIZABA peak (18,700 ft.), which belongs also to volcanic belt. This belt, which divides Mexico (E-W), also includes POPOCATEPETL and IXTACIHUATL. The **Sierra**

Madre Occidental (ōk″sēdēntäl′), parallels Pacific coast, extending SE from Ariz. The **Sierra Madre del Sur** (dĕl sōōr′) spreads over S Mexico between volcanic belt and Isthmus of Tehuantepec.

Sierra Madre, Rocky Mts.: see PARK RANGE.

Sierra Maestra (syĕ′rä määʹsträ), mountain range, SE Cuba, rising abruptly from coast; rich in minerals. Turquino (alt. 6,560 ft.) is highest peak.

Sierra Morena (syĕ′rä mōrä′nä), mountain range, SW Spain. Highest peak is at 4,340 ft.

Sierra Nevada (syĕ′rä nävä′dhä), chief mountain range of S Spain; c.60 mi. long. Highest peak of range and of Spain is Mulhacen (11,411 ft.).

Sierra Nevada (sēĕ′rü nüvä′dü), mountain range, E Calif., extending c.430 mi. NW from Tehachapi Pass, SE of Bakersfield, to gap S of LASSEN PEAK. E front has steep walls and rugged peaks; W face slopes into Sacramento and San Joaquin valleys. Mt. WHITNEY (14,495 ft.) is highest peak in U.S. (outside Alaska). Truckee Pass, N of Lake Tahoe, is best-known pass through the range. Snow-covered peaks feed W streams used for water power and irrigation in Calif. Range contains Yosemite, Sequoia, and Kings Canyon national parks.

Sierra Nevada de Mérida (syĕ′rä nävä′dhä dä mä′rēdhä), mountain range, NW Venezuela, spur of Andes, beginning at Colombian border and extending 200 mi. NE to the Caribbean. From 30 to 50 mi. wide, it has snow-capped peaks over 15,000 ft. high.

Sieyès, Emmanuel Joseph (ĕmänüĕl′ zhôzĕf′ syäĕs′), 1748–1836, French revolutionary pamphleteer and statesman; originally a priest. Played a leading part in States-General of 1789; edited DECLARATION OF RIGHTS OF MAN and constitution of 1791; led in Thermidorian reaction after Robespierre's fall (1794); entered the Directory in 1799 and conspired with Bonaparte in coup d'état of 18 BRUMAIRE. Lived in exile at Brussels after 1815.

Sigebert (sī′gübûrt), d. 575, Frankish king of Austrasia (561–75); husband of BRUNHILDA. When his brother, CHILPERIC I of Neustria, attacked Austrasia (573), Sigebert overran Neustria and was about to be proclaimed its king but was murdered by order of Chilperic's second wife, FREDEGUNDE.

Sigel, Franz (fränts′ sē′gŭl), 1824–1902, Union general in Civil War, b. Germany. Fought in Mo. and at second battle of Bull Run. Briefly commanded Dept. of West Virginia (1864).

sight: see VISION.

Sigismund (sī′jĭsmŭnd, sī′gĭs–), 1368–1437, emperor (crowned 1433) and German king. His marriage to Mary, daughter of Louis I of Hungary, brought him the Hungarian crown in 1387. He was elected German king in 1410, though his brother WENCESLAUS acknowledged his election only in 1411. Sigismund led a crusade against Bajazet I of Turkey, who routed him at Nikopol (1396). To heal the Great SCHISM, he joined with John XXIII in summoning the Council of CONSTANCE, where he also secured the condemnation and burning of John HUSS (although he had granted Huss a safe-conduct). When Wenceslaus died (1419) the Hussites bitterly opposed Sigismund's succession to the Bohemian crown. The HUSSITE WARS resulted. Sigismund had himself crowned at Prague (1420) but was repeatedly defeated and gained control over Bohemia only in 1436 through the aid of the UTRAQUISTS. His failure to keep his promises to the Czechs led to further disorders. The last emperor of the Luxemburg dynasty, he was succeeded by his son-in-law Albert II, a Hapsburg.

Sigismund, kings of Poland. **Sigismund I,** 1467–1548, reigned 1506–48. Estab. regular army and a fiscal system to maintain it; consented to double marriage contract arranged by his brother, ULADISLAUS II of Bohemia and Hungary (1515); accepted homage of ALBERT OF BRANDENBURG for duchy of Prussia (1525). He and his queen, Bona Sforza, fostered the Polish Renaissance culture, which began to flower during his

reign. Was succeeded by his son **Sigismund II** or **Sigismund Augustus,** 1520–72. His greatest accomplishment was the Union of Lublin (1569), which fused LITHUANIA and Poland into a single state. The dissolution of the Livonian Knights (1561) enabled him to acquire Courland and parts of Livonia, but he was drawn into war with Ivan IV of Russia, to whom he lost Polotsk (1563). He halted the growth of Protestantism by peaceful, tolerant means, introducing the Jesuits (1565) and favoring the Catholic Reform. Sigismund himself was an accomplished humanist and theologian. With his death the Jagiello dynasty was extinct in Poland. **Sigismund III,** 1566–1632, was the son of John III of Sweden and of Catherine, sister of Sigismund II of Poland. He was elected king of Poland in 1587, largely through the aid of Jan ZAMOJSKI; in 1592 he succeeded his father on the Swedish throne, but his staunch Catholicism brought him into conflict with his uncle (later CHARLES IX of Sweden), who defeated him at Stangebro (1598) and formally deposed him (1599). In 1621–29 he made war on his nephew, Gustavus II of Sweden, to whom he lost most of Livonia. He intervened in the Russian troubles which followed the appearance of the pretender DMITRI, but his army was expelled from Moscow and from Russia in 1612. His son Ladislaus IV succeeded him as king of Poland.

Siglufjord (sī′glōōfyôrd″), town (pop. 3,069), NE Iceland. Herring center.

Sigmaringen (zēk′märĭng″ün), town (pop. 6,158), Württemberg-Hohenzollern, S Germany, on the Danube; cap. of HOHENZOLLERN until 1945. Has 16th-cent. castle (rebuilt 19th cent.).

Signac, Paul (pôl′ sēnyäk′), 1863–1935, French postimpressionist painter, known for Parisian scenes.

Signal Hill: see LONG BEACH, Calif.

sign language, substitute for normal language, not including letter-for-letter signaling. Celebrated sign languages by use of the hands have been developed by deaf-mutes, by Trappist monks, who have a rule of silence, and by Plains Indians, where speakers of mutually unintelligible languages communicated freely. Many languages have conventionalized body gestures (e.g., nodding), and some of these are highly elaborated to accompany or supplement speech.

Signorelli, Luca (lōō′kä sēnyōrĕl′lē), 1441?–1523, Italian painter of Umbrian school. Worked with his master, Piero della Francesca, on frescoes in San Francesco, Arezzo. Introduced powerful treatment of anatomy, as in *End of the World* (Orvieto), which influenced Michelangelo. His paintings in the Vatican were later sacrificed to make way for some of Raphael's work.

Sigourney, Lydia (Huntley) (sī′gûrnē), 1791–1865, American sentimental poet ("the sweet singer of Hartford") and author of edifying children's books.

Sigurd, Icelandic form of SIEGFRIED.

Sigurdsson, Jon (yōn′ sī′khûrdhsōn), 1811–79, Icelandic statesman and historian. Leader in Copenhagen of Icelandic writers, scholars, and diplomats. Instrumental in securing constitution of Iceland (1874), and many reforms and institutions. President Icelandic Literary Society, he directed monumental studies in Icelandic history and literature, including *Diplomatarium Islandicum.*

Sikang (sē′käng′), province (90,000 sq. mi.; pop. 2,000,000), SW China; cap. Yaan. Bounded on W by Tibet. Consists mainly of high mountains, cut by gorges of Yangtze, Yalung, and other rivers. Stock raising and hunting. In 1950 part of W Sikang became the Tibetan Autonomous Dist. (60,000 sq. mi.; pop. 700,000), with cap. at Kangting.

Sikeston, city (pop. 11,640), SE Mo., in the Mississippi plain WSW of Cairo, Ill.; laid out 1860. Processes and ships cotton.

Sikhs (sēks), religious community of India and Pakistan, numbering c.5,500,000 persons, mainly in the Punjab. Religion was founded by Nanak (b. 1469), first guru [Hindustani,= teacher], who taught a mono-theistic creed and opposed maintenance of a priest-hood and the caste system. The 10th and last guru, Govind Singh (b. 1666), welded the Sikhs into a mili-tary community which adopted the caste practices and polytheistic beliefs typical of Hinduism. He intro-duced the customs of wearing turbans and never cut-ting the hair. Each Sikh in the warrior caste took the name Singh [lion]. Greatest leader in early 19th cent. was RANJIT SINGH. See SIKH WARS.

Sikh Wars. By a treaty with the British in 1809, the Sikhs had accepted the Sutlej R. as S boundary of their domain. Fearing British conquest, they crossed the river in 1845 to attack the enemy. Defeated in 1846, they were forced to accept a protectorate and to cede Kashmir. Resentment caused an uprising in 1848; this was quelled in 1849 and resulted in British annexa-tion of all Sikh territory.

Si-kiang, China: see WEST RIVER.

Sikkim (sĭ'kĭm), protectorate (2,745 sq. mi.; pop. 135,-646) of India; cap. Gangtok. In Himalayas between India and Tibet. Inhabitants are pastoral nomads who speak Tibeto-Burman languages. Hinduism has the most numerous adherents, although Buddhism is the state religion. Ruled since 17th cent. by rajas of Tibetan descent. Under British protection 1890–1947. India assumed control 1949.

silage: see ENSILAGE.

Silas, early Christian, companion of Paul. Acts 15.22–18.5. Probably same as Silvanus of 2 Cor. 1.19; 1 Thess. 1.1; 2 Thess. 1.1; 1 Peter 5.12.

Silenus (sīlē'nŭs), in Greek mythology, god of wine and fertility; son of Hermes. A jolly old man, he was friend and teacher of Dionysus.

Silesia (sīlē'zhŭ, sī–), Czech *Slezsko,* Ger. *Schlesien,* Pol. *Śląsk,* historic region, SE Germany, SW Poland, and N Czechoslovakia. Drained by the Oder, it is largely an agr. and forested lowland, except in the S, where it is occupied by the SUDETES. The S mountain-ous part is heavily industrialized, with coal, lignite, zinc, lead, and iron mines, steel mills, and textile mfg. Of its three political subdivisions, Czech Silesia, with Troppau as chief city, is much the smallest; it was part of Moravia and Silesia prov. until 1949, when the province was merged with Bohemia to form the Czech Lands. Polish Silesia consists of the KATOWICE industrial area and other former Prussian districts ceded to Poland in 1921 and of part of the former Austrian principality of TESCHEN. German Silesia (by far the largest part) was placed under Polish admin-istration in 1945. It consists of the former Prussian provinces of Upper Silesia (cap. OPPELN) and Lower Silesia (cap. BRESLAU). Together, Polish and Polish-administered Silesia have an area of c.15,400 sq. mi. and a population of 4,764,500. Settled by Slavic tribes A.D. c.500, Silesia was part of Poland by the 11th cent. After 1200 it fell into several minor principali-ties, ruled by branches of the Polish PIAST dynasty who in 1335 accepted the kings of Bohemia as over-lords. Most of Silesia became thoroughly Germanized. With the accession of the Hapsburgs on the Bohe-mian throne (1526), Silesia tended to become an Aus-trian province. The ducal title, along with the princi-palities of Brieg and Liegnitz, remained with the Piasts until their extinction in 1675, when they passed to the house of Austria. In 1740, on very shaky grounds, Frederick II of Prussia claimed parts of Silesia from Maria Theresa. The resulting Silesian Wars of 1740–42 and 1744–45 were part of the War of the AUSTRIAN SUCCESSION and ended in the cession of all but pres-ent Czech Silesia and Teschen to Prussia (treaties of Berlin and Dresden, 1742, 1745). Under the Treaty of Versailles, a plebiscite was held in 1921 which gave the predominantly Polish-speaking parts of Upper Silesia to Poland. After World War II the POTSDAM CONFERENCE allowed the transfer of German Silesia to Polish administration and the expulsion of the Ger-man population (in an "orderly and humane" manner)

from all Silesia, pending a general peace with Ger-many. A small section W of the Neisse was incor-porated with Saxony.

Silesian Wars: see AUSTRIAN SUCCESSION, WAR OF THE; SEVEN YEARS WAR.

Silesius, Angelus: see ANGELUS SILESIUS.

silica (sĭ'lĭkŭ), common name for silicon dioxide, widely and abundantly distributed. Occurs in many forms, e.g., in the different varieties of quartz, in sand, as a constituent of rocks, in the skeletal parts of certain animals and plants. It has many important uses, e.g., as an abrasive, in glass making, ceramics, and in prep-aration of Carborundum (silicon carbide).

silicate (sĭ'lĭkāt, –kĭt), compound containing silicon and oxygen combined with such metals as aluminum, barium, calcium, iron, magnesium, sodium, potassium. Silicates are widely distributed and include many familiar substances, e.g., asbestos, feldspar, talc, clay, emerald, garnet, beryl.

silicon (sĭ'lĭkŭn), nonmetallic element (symbol = Si; see also ELEMENT, table). Has two allotropic forms. Re-sembles carbon chemically. Very abundant, makes up large part of earth's crust; occurs in silica and silicates, but not uncombined. Used in making low-carbon steel, in alloys to add hardness and resistance to corrosion. Silicones, alternating chains of silicon and oxygen, are used to make silicone rubber, liquids used in hydraulic systems of airplanes, and varnishes.

silicon carbide, hard crystalline compound of silicon and carbon, used as an abrasive. Trade names include Carborundum and Crystolon.

silicosis (sĭlĭkō'sĭs), occupational disease caused by ex-cessive inhalation of rock dust or sand particles high in silica. Silica causes inflammation of lungs and growth of fibrous tissue; victims are susceptible to tuberculosis. National publicity resulted when work-ers constructing tunnel (begun 1929) at Gauley Bridge, W.Va., died from disease.

silk, fine, horny, translucent, yellowish fiber produced by the SILKWORM in making its cocoon. The silkworm of commerce is the larva of *Bombyx mori,* the mul-berry silkworm; wild silk, woven into Shantung or pongee, is produced by the tussah worm of India and China, a feeder on oaks. Silkworm culture and silk weaving began in remote ages in China and spread A.D. c.550 to Byzantium and thence over Europe and North Africa. In silk manufacture, the cocoon, after steaming or soaking to soften the gum that covers the fiber, is unwound, several strands of filament being reeled together to make a thread. A cocoon may yield 2,000–3,000 ft. of filament. Other steps in prepara-tion include doubling and twisting the thread to form yarn, removing the remaining gum, bleaching when needed, dyeing (in yarn or the piece), and sometimes weighting fabric by loading with metallic salts, as of tin. Silk is woven into innumerable fabrics, from airy gauzes to heavy plushes and velvets.

Silkeborg (sĭl'kŭbôr'), city (pop. 23,372), E central Jut-land, Denmark, on Guden R. Health resort among woods and lakes.

silkworm, larva of various moth species of Asia and Africa. Now raised for silk in most of temperate zone. Matures 32–38 days after hatching from tiny egg, then attaches self to twig to spin cocoon from secre-tion emitted from lip. See also SILK. See *ill.,* p. 469.

Sill, Edward Rowland, 1841–87, American poet, best known for two didactic lyrics—"The Fool's Prayer" and "Opportunity."

Sill, Fort, U.S. military reservation, estab. 1869 near Lawton, Okla. Reservation also used for Indians, and formerly fort was stronghold against Indian uprisings. Tribes trained in agr.; Geronimo, Satanta, and others imprisoned here. Lessened in importance until made field artillery school 1911. Two world wars made it important.

Sillanpää, Frans Eemil (fräns' ā'mĭl sĭl'lämpä"), 1888–, Finnish author of novels that are masterpieces of lyri-cal impressionism (e.g., *Meek Heritage,* 1919; *The*

Maid Silja, 1931). Awarded 1939 Nobel Prize in Literature.

Sillery (Fr. sēyûrē´), city (pop. 10,376), S Que., Canada, on St. Lawrence R., SW suburb of Quebec.

silo (sī´lō), watertight, airtight storage tank for ensilage, either pitlike or cylindrical in shape.

Siloam (sīlō´ŭm), pool, SE of Jerusalem, in Kidron valley. Connected with Virgin's Pool by 1,700-ft. tunnel; undated inscription (found 1880) describes digging of tunnel. Jesus put clay on a blind man's eye and told him to wash it off at Siloam, thus curing him. John 9.7. Also Shiloah and Siloah.

Siloam Springs (sī´lōm), city (pop. 3,270), NW Ark., in the Ozarks near Okla. line. Resort, with mineral springs. Baptist campgrounds here.

Silone, Ignazio (ēnyä´tsyō sēlō´nä), 1900–, Italian author, whose real name is Secondo Tranquilli. An anti-Fascist, he fled Italy in 1931 and returned in 1944. Well known are his novels *Fontamara* (1933) and *Pane e vino* (1937; Eng. tr., *Bread and Wine*, 1936).

silt, earth particles finer than sand but coarser than clay, produced by weathering. When consolidated into rock, silt becomes shale.

Silurian period (sīlōō´rēŭn), third period of the PALEOZOIC ERA of geologic time. Continents were about the same as in Ordovician period. In North America the main event was flooding of interior basin from north and deposition of Niagaran limestone, best seen at the falls. Desert conditions seem to have followed, with extensive salt deposits. Economic resources of Silurian strata include salt, iron ore, quartz sandstone. Primitive fish increased in the sea; on land, scorpions appeared, possibly the first animals to take oxygen from the air. See also GEOLOGY, table.

Silva, Antonio José da (äntô´nyō zhōōzä´ dä sēl´vù), 1705–39, Brazilian-Portuguese playwright; known as *o Judeo* [the Jew].

Silva, José Asunción (hōsä´ äsōōnsyōn´ sēl´vä), 1865–96, Colombian poet, one of creators of *modernismo*. Well known poem is "Nocturno III." Morbidly sensitive and pessimistic, he committed suicide at 31.

silver, metallic element (symbol = Ag; see also ELEMENT, table). It is nearly white, lustrous, soft, ductile, malleable, and a good conductor of heat and electricity. Chemically it is not active. At ordinary temperatures it unites with sulphur (tarnishes) to form the sulphide. Its halogen compounds are used in photography because of their light sensitivity. Silver nitrate is used in medicine either in solution or in fused sticklike form (lunar caustic); in indelible inks; for silvering mirrors; as a reagent. Occurs uncombined in ores; greatest amount is obtained in refining of lead and copper. Much silver is used in making coins and silver plate, utensils, jewelry, and other products.

Silver City, town (pop. 7,022) SW N.Mex., near Ariz. line. Trade and shipping point for mines (esp. copper), stock ranches, and irrigated farms. Health resort. Flourished as silver- and gold-mining camp in late 1800s. Near by is Gila Cliff Dwellings Natl. Monument.

silver nitrate: see SILVER.

Silver Purchase Act: see SHERMAN SILVER PURCHASE ACT.

Silver Springs, spring, N central Fla., E of Ocala, with outlet to Oklawaha R. Basin is 80 ft. deep; flow is c.25,000,000 gal. per hour.

Silvester: see SYLVESTER.

Silvretta, (sīlvrĕ´tù, Ger. zīlvrĕ´tä), Alpine group at Swiss-Austrian border. Highest peak is Piz Linard (11,200 ft.), in Grisons canton, Switzerland.

Simbirsk, RSFSR: see ULYANOVSK.

Simcoe, John Graves (sīm´kō), 1752–1806, British army officer, first governor of Upper Canada.

Simcoe, town (pop. 7,269), S Ont., Canada, on Lynn R. and SW of Hamilton. Center in agr. area with canneries and woolen and lumber mills.

Simcoe, Lake, 28 mi. long, 26 mi. wide, S Ont., Canada, N of Toronto. Drains N through L. Couchiching and

Severn R. to Georgian Bay, forming part of TRENT CANAL system. Resort area.

Simeon, tsars of Bulgaria. **Simeon I,** d. 927, reigned 893–927. An extremely warlike ruler, he twice threatened Constantinople (913, 924), conquered most of Serbia, and, with papal consent, took the title tsar. Under his rule the first Bulgarian empire reached its greatest power. Simeon also was an able scholar and fostered Old Slavonic literature. **Simeon II,** 1937–, succeeded his father Boris III in 1943, under a regency. He went into exile in 1946, when the monarchy was abolished.

Simeon. 1 Son of Jacob and ancestor of one of the 12 tribes of Israel. Tribe settled in S Palestine. Gen. 29.33; 34; 49.5–7; Joshua 19. **2** Devout man who blessed the infant Jesus at the Temple. Luke 2.21–34. In Acts 15.14 Simeon appears for Simon, referring to St. Peter.

Simeon Stylites, Saint (stīlī´tēz) [Gr.,= of a pillar], d. 459?, Syrian hermit, who lived many years on a platform atop a pillar. Feast: Jan. 5.

Simferopol (sēmfyîrô´pùl), city (pop. 142,678), cap. of Crimea, RSFSR, on Salgir R., in orchard, vineyard, and tobacco region. Food processing. It occupies site of an ancient Scythian cap. and of Greek colony Neapolis. Old part of city retains Oriental aspect.

simile: see METAPHOR.

Simla (sīm´lù), town (pop. 18,348; alt. 7,100 ft.) cap. of Himachal Pradesh, India; resort in Himalayas. Formerly summer cap. of India (1867–1947).

Simmons College: see BOSTON, Mass.

Simms, William Gilmore, 1806–70, American novelist; a prolific writer, best remembered for historical romances of S.C., such as *Guy Rivers* (1834), *The Yemassee,* and *The Partisan* (both 1835).

Simnel, Lambert (sīm´nùl), fl. 1486–1525, English impostor. Impersonating Edward, earl of Warwick (then confined in tower by Henry VII), he was, with Yorkist support, crowned at Dublin (1486) as Edward VI. Returning to England, he and supporters were defeated by royal forces. Simnel was pardoned.

Simois (sī´mōĭs), small river, NW Turkey; a tributary of the SCAMANDER. Scene of legendary events in siege of Troy.

Simon, in Bible. **1** One of the MACCABEES. **2** Or **Simon Peter:** see PETER, SAINT. **3** or **Saint Simon,** one of the Twelve Apostles. Called the Canaanite or Cananaean or Zelotes, terms which may mean he was a member of the ZEALOTS. Mat. 10.4; Mark 3.18; Luke 6.15; Acts 1.13. Feast: Oct. 28. **4** Leper in whose home a woman anointed Jesus' feet. He may have been father of Lazarus. **5** See SIMON OF CYRENE. **6** See SIMON MAGUS.

Simonides of Ceos (sīmŏ´nĭdēz, sē´ŏs), c.556–468? B.C., Greek lyric poet; rival of Pindar at Syracuse. Among the ancients a classic example of moderation in all things, he wrote masterful verse in an epigrammatic manner; two of his finest epitaphs are on Marathon and Thermopylae.

Simon Magus (mā´gŭs), Samaritan sorcerer who tried to buy spiritual power from the apostles, hence the term *simony.* Acts 8.9–24.

Simon of Cyrene (sīrē´nē), bystander forced to carry Jesus' cross. Mat. 27.32; Mark 15.21; Luke 23.26.

Simonov, Konstantin (kŭnstŭntyēn´ sē´mùnùf), 1915–, Russian author. Wrote *Days and Nights* (1945; Eng. tr., 1945), a novel on the defense of Stalingrad in World War II. His anti-American play *The Russian Question* (1947) won the Stalin Prize.

Simon Peter: see PETER, SAINT.

Simons, Walter (väl´tùr zē´mŏns), 1861–1937, German foreign minister (1920–21) and president of supreme court (1922–29). Outstanding authority on international law.

Simonson, Lee, 1888–, American scenic artist. Associated with Washington Square Players, 1915–17, and with Theatre Guild as director, 1919–40.

Simonstown (sī´mùnz-), town (pop. 7,315), SW Cape

Prov., South Africa, on the Atlantic; major British naval base (estab. 1814).

simoom or **simoon:** see SANDSTORM.

Simplon (sĭm'plŏn"; sĕplō'), pass, 6,589 ft. high, over Pennine Alps. Crossed by **Simplon Road,** built by Napoleon 1800–1806. Simplon RR passes through **Simplon Tunnel** (alt. 2,313 ft.), longest in world (12¼ mi.). Opened 1906, tunnel crosses Swiss-Italian border.

Simpson, Sir George, 1792–1860, governor of Hudson's Bay Co. in Canada and traveler, b. Scotland. Made famous "overland" trip around world (1841–42).

Simpson, Sir James Young, 1811–70, Scottish obstetrician, first to use general anesthetic in childbirth (1847).

Simpson College: see INDIANOLA, Iowa.

Sims, James Marion, 1813–83, American surgeon, specialist in diseases of women. Founded Woman's Hospital in New York city (1855).

Sims, William S(owden), 1858–1936, American admiral. In World War I he commanded American operations in European waters (1917–18).

Simsbury, town (pop. 4,822), Conn., NW of Hartford; settled 1660. Westminster School for boys and Ethel Walker School for girls are here.

Sin, wilderness through which the Israelites wandered after leaving Egypt. Ex. 16.1.

sin, in religion, unethical act in disobedience to a personal God. Among the ancient Jews there was besides personal sin the concept of national sin (usually idolatry). Except for original sin (which in Christian thought is the evil universally inherent in man since the fall of Adam, to be removed by baptism), Christians and Moslems have no idea of collective sin. Some Christians hold that all acts are good, indifferent, or sinful, others that there are no indifferent acts, only good or sinful. In Roman Catholic doctrine, a mortal sin is one committed with full knowledge and deliberate intent in a serious matter; others are venial. The seven deadly or capital sins are pride, covetousness, lust, anger, gluttony, envy, and sloth. The sins that cry out to heaven for vengeance are willful murder, the sin of Sodom, oppression of the poor, and defrauding a laborer of his wages. The "sin of angels" is pride.

Sinai (sī'nī, sī'nēī), triangular peninsula, E Egypt, extending from its broad base on the Mediterranean to Red Sea, whose two arms bound it on W (Gulf of Suez) and on E (Gulf of Aqaba). In S is Jebel Musa [Arabic,= mount of Moses] or Mt. Sinai. On its slope is the famed Greek Orthodox monastery of St. Catherine, founded c.250. Here in 19th cent. was found the Codex Sinaiticus, one of the oldest manuscripts of the New Testament. Produces manganese, iron, and oil.

Sinaia (sēnī'ä), town (pop. 6,531), S central Rumania, in Walachia. Health and winter sports resort in Transylvanian Alps. Former summer residence of Rumanian kings. One of two former royal palaces contains noted art collection.

Sinaloa (sēnälō'ä), state (22,582 sq. mi.; pop. 618,439), NW Mexico, on Gulf of California and the Pacific; cap. CULIACÁN. Various crops are produced on its fertile land, but mining of gold, silver, and copper is most important occupation. Has only one port of importance, MAZATLÁN. Culiacán was important in colonial period. Sinaloa and Sonora were made separate states in 1830.

Sinan (sĭnän'), 1489?–1578?, outstanding Moslem architect. Masterpieces are mosque of Selim I at Adrianople and mosque of Suleiman I at Istanbul.

Sinclair, May, 1865?–1946, English novelist. Wrote *The Divine Fire* (1904). *Mary Olivier* (1919) is among first examples of stream-of-consciousness technique.

Sinclair, Upton, 1878–, American novelist and socialist. His many novels voice social protest, as in *The Jungle* (1906) and *Boston* (1928). His social studies such as *The Brass Check* (1919) are impressive. Political adventure novels in "Lanny Budd" series, begun in 1940, have attracted wide audiences.

Sind (sĭnd) province (50,443 sq. mi.; pop. 4,619,000), W Pakistan, on Arabian Sea; cap. Hyderabad. Grain and fruit are grown in areas irrigated by the Indus. At MOHENJO-DARO in NW are remains of an ancient civilization. Sind was converted to Islam after its conquest by Arabs in 8th cent. Taken 1843 by the British, until 1937 administered as part of Bombay.

Sindhi (sĭn'dē), modern language of Indic group of Indo-Iranian subfamily of Indo-European languages. See LANGUAGE (table).

Sinding, Christian (sĭn'dĭng), 1856–1941, Norwegian composer of the opera *Der heilige Berg* [the holy mountain]; orchestral and chamber music; and piano pieces, including the popular *Rustle of Spring*.

Singapore (sĭng'gŭpôr), city (pop. 679,659), on Singapore island (217 sq. mi.; pop. 938,144), off S tip of Malay Peninsula. A great commercial center and major British naval base in Far East. Island was ceded 1824 to the British by sultan of Johore. A principal founder of modern city was T. Stamford RAFFLES. Development of Malaya under British rule made Singapore a leading port for export of tin and rubber. Inhabited mainly by Chinese. Although considered the key point in defense of SE Asia, island was quickly taken in final phase of Japan's Malaya campaign, Feb., 1945, in World War II. Part of the STRAITS SETTLEMENTS colony until 1946, it is now a crown colony, which includes Christmas Isl. in Indian Ocean.

Singer, Isaac Merrit, 1811–75, American inventor. In 1851 he patented a practical sewing machine and subsequently became a leading manufacturer. He later patented many improvements.

Singhalese (sĭng'gŭlēz) or **Sinhalese** (sĭn'hŭlēz), language of Ceylon, belonging to Indic group of Indo-Iranian subfamily of Indo-European languages. See LANGUAGE (table).

single tax, tax derived from economic rent. It is based on the doctrine that land is the source of all wealth. See PHYSIOCRATS and Henry GEORGE.

Sing Sing: see OSSINING, N.Y.

Sinhalese: see SINGHALESE.

Sinkiang (shĭn'jyäng'), province (700,000 sq. mi.; pop. 4,000,000) NW China; cap. Urumchi. Largest province of China. Bounded on S by Tibet and Kashmir, on W and NW by USSR. Roughly coextensive with Chinese Turkistan; consists of Dzungaria tableland and Taklamakan Desert. Dominant element in population is Turkic Uigurs. Products include cotton, silk, and grain. Region was ruled successively by Uigurs and Mongols before its annexation by China in 18th cent.

Sinn Fein (shĭn'fān') [Irish,= we, ourselves], Irish nationalistic movement which triumphed in establishment of Irish Free State (see IRELAND). Founded 1899 by Arthur GRIFFITH, advocate of an economically and politically self-sufficient Ireland. Started with passive resistance to British. After Home Rule Bill (1912) and tension between Ulster and S Ireland, it aided Patrick PEARSE in Easter Rebellion (1916). Suppression of rebellion and Ireland's military occupation aided Sinn Fein, under leadership of DE VALERA. It set up Irish assembly called DÁIL ÉIREANN which declared independence. The resulting disorders (extremists led by Michael Collins) were suppressed violently by British military irregulars known as Black and Tans. Continued resistance led to negotiations for Irish Free State. After period of civil war, De Valera became president 1932. With outlaw of Irish Republican Army, Sinn Fein virtually ended.

Sinnott, Edmund W(are) (sĭ'nŭt), 1888–, American botanist, known especially for research in plant morphology, morphogenesis, and genetics. After serving as professor of botany at Barnard, Columbia, and Yale he became director of the Sheffield Scientific School (1945) and dean of the graduate school (1950) at Yale.

Sino-Japanese War: see CHINO-JAPANESE WAR.

Sinope (sĭnō'pē), anc. city of Asia Minor, on the Black

Sea. Rose to commercial and political importance after 7th cent B.C. One of its exports, cinnabar, is named for Sinope. Sinope fell to kings of Pontus in 2d cent. B.C. and became their cap.; was taken by Romans under Lucullus in Third Mithridatic War (74–63 B.C.); reached a great prosperity under Roman and later under Byzantine rule; declined after its capture by Seljuk Turks (13th cent.). Modern Turkish town of Sinop (pop. 5,780) has excellent harbor but poor land communications.

Sintra, Portugal: see CINTRA.

Sinuiju (sĕn'ōō'ē'jōō), city (1944 pop. 118,414), N Korea, on Yalu R., opposite Antung, China.

Sion (sī'ùn), in Bible: see ZION; HERMON, MOUNT.

Sion (syō), Ger. *Sitten*, town (pop. 11,031), cap. of VALAIS canton, Switzerland, on the Rhone. Episcopal see since 6th cent. Hydroelectric station.

Siouan (sōō'ùn), linguistic family of North America. One of most widely distributed of American Indian stocks, Siouan stock includes languages spoken from Gulf of Mexico to Saskatchewan, mainly on Great Plains and W prairies. See LANGUAGE (table).

Sioux City, city (pop. 83,991), NW Iowa, at junction of Big Sioux and Floyd rivers with the Missouri; settled 1848. Second largest city of state, it is shipping, trade, and industrial center for agr. and livestock area. Has railroad shops and mfg. of food and clay products and machinery. Seat of Morningside Col.

Sioux Falls, city (pop. 52,696), SE S.Dak., on Big Sioux R. and N of Sioux City, Iowa; founded 1857, abandoned 1862, resettled 1865 when Fort Dakota was estab. Largest city in state, it is trade, industrial, and shipping center for agr. area; processes foodstuffs. Seat of Augustana Col. (Lutheran; coed.; opened 1860 as seminary in Chicago, chartered 1865; had various names and sites as it followed Norwegian pioneers W); a Swedish section split off and founded Augustana Col. and Theological Seminary (1869), at Rock Island, Ill.

Sioux Indians (sōō) or **Dakota Indians** (dùkō'tù), seven North American tribes of Siouan linguistic stock, the largest and most important being the Teton. They were driven (17th cent.) by the Ojibwa from the Great Lakes region to the N Great Plains and the prairies. They had a typical Plains culture, mainly dependent on the horse and the buffalo hunt. Their hostility to Americans grew as settlers came into their lands, and Little Crow led a band of Sioux in a massacre of whites in Minn. in 1862. The Sioux agreed (1867) to retire to a reservation. This was invaded by Black Hills gold prospectors, and in 1874 began the Sioux wars that were notably marked by the defeat of Custer (1876). The troubles did not fully end until the expedition under Nelson A. Miles (1890–91).

Siqueiros, David Alfaro (dävēdh' älfä'rō sēkā'rōs), 1898–, Mexican painter. Figured in revolutionary political movements. Best known for murals and frescoes, he uses his art as a means of social protest. Uses swirling brushwork and striking contrasts of light and dark.

Sirach (sī'rùk), father of the author of Ecclesiasticus, which is sometimes called Sirach.

Siren, in Greek mythology, one of three sea nymphs, whose sweet song lured men to shipwreck on rocky coast where they lived. Argonaut heroes were saved by music of Orpheus. Odysseus escaped by tying himself to the mast and stopping ears of his men.

Sir Roger de Coverley: see ROGER DE COVERLEY.

sisal hemp (sī'sùl), cordage fiber obtained from the leaves of the sisal hemp plant, a tropical agave (*Agave sisalana*). It is second only to Manila hemp in strength and value. Henequen, a fiber from *A. fourcroydes*, is also called sisal hemp, and is used to make binder twine, chiefly in Yucatan.

Sisera (sī'sùrù), Canaanite captain, defeated by Deborah and Barak, murdered by Jael. Judges 4.5.

Sisley, Alfred (älfrēd' sēslä'), 1839–99, French impressionist painter, b. Paris, of English parents. Known

for sunny landscapes, e.g., *The Banks of the Loing.*

Sismondi, Jean Charles Léonard Simonde de (zhä' shärl' lāônär' sēmôd' dù sēsmôdē'), 1773–1842, Swiss historian. Major work *History of the Italian Republics in the Middle Ages* (16 vols., 1809–18).

Sisters of Charity, name given several communities of Roman Catholic nuns devoted to work in schools, hospitals, and charitable institutions. Most of them stem from the work of the institute founded (1633) by St. VINCENT DE PAUL.

Sistine Chapel (sī'stēn), private chapel of the popes in Rome, one of the glories of the Vatican. Built 1473 for Pope Sixtus IV. Famous for its decorations, notably Michelangelo's frescoes of Old Testament scenes on vaulted ceiling and his *Last Judgment* on end wall. On side walls are frescoes by Perugino, Pinturicchio, Botticelli, and Ghirlandaio. Collection of illuminated music manuscripts is in archives of the choir.

Sisyphus (sī'sĭfùs), in Greek mythology, king of Corinth. Zeus, angered by his disrespect, condemned him to push a heavy rock up a steep hill forever.

Sitka (sĭt'kù), town (pop. 1,985), SE Alaska, on Baranof Isl., in Alexander Archipelago. Founded 1799 as New Archangel by Aleksandr Baranov. Destroyed by Indians 1802, rebuilt, renamed, and made Baranov's hq. 1804. U.S. officially took possession of Alaska from Russia here, 1867. Remained cap. of Alaska until 1900. Harbor dominated by Mt. Edgecumbe. Fishing, canning, and lumbering. Naval station since 1940. Has Sitka Natl. Monument and Russian Orthodox Cathedral of St. Michael (1844).

Sitka National Monument: see NATIONAL PARKS AND MONUMENTS (table).

Sitten, Switzerland: see SION.

Sitter, Willem de (vĭ'lùm dù sĭ'tùr), 1872–1934, Dutch astronomer and mathematician. Proposed theory of expanding universe.

Sitting Bull, d. 1890, Indian chief, Sioux leader in battle of the Little Bighorn, in which G. A. CUSTER and his force were killed.

Sitwell, Edith (sĭt'wùl), 1887–, English poet and critic. Her poetry is collected in *The Canticle of the Rose, 1917–1949* (1949). Her criticism includes *Aspects of Modern Poetry* (1934) and *A Poet's Notebook* (1943). She wrote *Twentieth Century Harlequinade* (1916) with her brother **Sir Osbert Sitwell,** 1892–, poet and novelist. Among his works are *Selected Poems* (1943); *Before the Bombardment* (1926), a novel; and his remarkable autobiographical family history in several volumes. Another brother, **Sacheverell Sitwell** (sùshĕ'vùrùl), 1900–, is also a poet and an art critic. His verse includes *Dr. Donne and Gargantua* (1930). He has also written histories of art, e.g., *The Gothick North* (1929), *British Architects and Craftsmen* (1945), and biographies.

Siva: see HINDUISM.

Sivas (sĭväs'), city (pop. 52,269), central Turkey, on the Kizil Irmak. Trade center. Cement and rug mfg. Copper mines near by. Known as Sebaste, Sebastia, or Cabira in ancient times. Here in 1919 Kemal Ataturk began nationalist revolution. Has many fine relics of medieval Moslem art.

Sivash Sea (sēväsh') or **Putrid Sea,** salt lagoon, area c.1,000 sq. mi., RSFSR, along NE coast of Crimea. Separated—except at Genichesk Strait—from Sea of Azov by Arabat land tongue, from Black Sea by Perekop Isthmus.

Siward (sū'ùrd), d. 1055, earl of Northumberland in England. Danish warrior, he probably came with Canute. Supported Edward the Confessor against Earl Godwin (1051); defeated (1054) Macbeth, Scottish king, for his nephew (later Malcolm III).

Sixtus IV, 1414–84, pope (1471–84), an Italian named Francesco della Rovere, a Franciscan. He struggled with Louis XI over control of the Church in France and Louis's attempts to interfere in Naples. A quarrel with Lorenzo de' Medici was embittered when a nephew of Sixtus led the PAZZI CONSPIRACY (1478), and Sixtus waged war on Florence. He consented to the establishment of the Spanish Inquisition. Although he was a politician and a nepotist, he was a good administrator. Founded the Sistine Chapel.

Sixtus V, 1521–90, pope (1585–90), an Italian named Felice Peretti, a Franciscan and a zealous preacher. He was sent to Spain to look into accusations against the archbishop of Toledo (1565) and there fell out with his companion, later Gregory XIII. Cardinal Peretti lived in retirement for a time, editing the works of St. Ambrose. He then succeeded Gregory, administered the Papal States and the Church well, and beautified Rome. He set the maximum number of cardinals at 70.

Sixtus of Bourbon-Parma, Prince, 1886–1934, son of Robert, last duke of Parma. Served in Belgian army in World War I. Served as intermediary for his brother-in-law, Charles I of Austria-Hungary, in Charles's secret quest for a separate peace (1917).

Sjaelland, Denmark: see ZEALAND.

Skagen (skä'gùn), town (pop. 6,446), N Jutland, Denmark; a port on the Kattegat. Fisheries. Also known in English as the Skaw.

Skagerrak (skä'gùrăk), strait, 80–90 mi. wide, between Norway and Denmark, stretching NE from North Sea and continued SE by the KATTEGAT. For battle of the Skagerrak, see JUTLAND, BATTLE OF.

Skagit (skä'jĭt), river, rising in Cascade Range, B.C., Canada, and flowing 163 mi. SW through Wash. to Puget Sound. Seattle owns three power dams (Diablo, Ross, Gorge) on upper Skagit.

Skagway (skăg'wā"), city (pop. 758), SE Alaska, at head of Lynn Canal and NNW of Juneau. At foot of White Pass, it was gateway to the Klondike in 1897–98 gold rush. Trade and tourist center and coastal terminus of White Pass and Yukon Railway.

Skanderbeg: see SCANDERBEG.

Skåne, Swed. Skåne (skō'nù), historic province of extreme S Sweden; chief city Malmo. Was held by Denmark until conquest by Charles X of Sweden (1658). Has prehistoric remains, medieval castles, manors.

Skaneateles, N.Y.: see FINGER LAKES.

skating, gliding on ice surface on skates. Earliest skates were made of bone. Iron skates introduced in 17th cent., steel skates first produced in 1850s. English books contain references to skating as early as 12th cent. **Roller skating,** gliding on smooth surface on skates with rollers or wheels, dates from 1860s. Ball-bearing skate wheel invented in 1880s.

Skaw, the, Denmark: see SKAGEN.

Skeat, W(alter) W(illiam), 1835–1912, English philologist. A scholar of Old English and Anglo-Saxon, he founded English Dialect Society in 1873. He edited many early English works.

Skeena (skē'nù), river of W B.C., Canada, rising in Stikine Mts. and flowing 360 mi. S and SW to Hecate Strait of the Pacific, SE of Prince Rupert.

skeleton, supporting or protective structure in animals. In invertebrate animals it is chiefly outside of body and is called an exoskeleton (e.g., shell of a clam); in vertebrates it is within the body and called an endoskeleton. In adult human, skeleton is a bony and cartilaginous framework of c.200 bones (plus 6 ear bones). Axial skeleton includes skull, SPINAL COLUMN, ribs (12 pairs), breast bone. Bones of arms and legs called appendicular skeleton. See ill., p. 595.

Skelton, John, 1460?–1529, English poet and clergyman, best known for satires largely against clergy, such as The Bowge of Court (1499), Colin Clout (1522), and Why Come Ye Not to Court? (c.1522). His short-lined, alliterative verses with insistent rhymes are called Skeltonics.

Skiddaw (skĭd'ô), mountain, 3,054 ft. high, Cumberland, England, in the Lake District near Keswick.

Skidmore College: see SARATOGA SPRINGS, N.Y.

skin, body covering composed of epidermis made up of layers of similar cells from which dried cells are shed, and underlayer or dermis containing blood capillaries, nerve endings, sweat glands, hair follicles, and sebaceous glands. Functions include protection, heat regulation, secretion, excretion, and sensation.

Skinner, Otis, 1858–1942, American actor. Was extremely popular in such plays as Kismet (1911) and Blood and Sand (1921) and in Shakspere. His daughter, **Cornelia Otis Skinner,** 1901–, is an actress and author, particularly noted for her monologues.

Skobelev, Mikhail Dmitreyevich (mēkhüyēl' dùmē'trēùvĭch skô'bĭlyĭf), 1843–82, Russian general. Led expedition to Kokand (1875–76) and march to Geok-Tepe (1881), which completed conquest of Turkistan.

Skokie (skō'kē), village (pop. 14,832), NE Ill., N suburb of Chicago; called Niles Center until 1940.

Skoplje (skôp'ùlyù), Macedonian Skopje, city (pop. 91,-557), cap. of Yugoslav Macedonia, S Yugoslavia, on Vardar R. Orthodox metropolitan see. University. Was scene of Stephen Dushan's coronation as tsar of Serbia (1346). Has medieval bridge, cathedral, mosques, and citadel; Oriental bazaar. Its Turkish name was Üsküb.

Skowhegan (skouhē'gĭn), town (pop. 7,422), including Skowhegan village (pop. 6,183), central Maine, on Kennebec R. above Waterville. Mfg. of textiles, shoes, and boats. Vacationist's supply point. Lakewood resort, with summer theater (1901), is near.

skull, bony framework of head, consisting of cranial bones and facial bones. In man, bones of cranium are occipital, parietal, temporal, frontal, ethmoid, sphenoid. Those of face are lachrymal, nasal, palatine, inferior turbinates, maxillary (upper jaw), malar (zygoma or cheek bones), vomer, and mandible (lower jaw). Brain is encased in bones of cranium and communicates with spinal cord through an opening (foramen magnum) at base of skull. Certain areas of cranial bones are not completely ossified at birth; these soft areas, called fontanels, close at different ages, but all are normally completely ossified by second year. See ill., p. 595.

skunk, carnivorous, nocturnal mammal of weasel family. Common or striped skunk (Mephitis) of U.S., N Mexico, and Canada has thick black fur and two white stripes on the back, and is c.2 ft. long including the bushy tail. It destroys insect pests. Protected by ability to spray offensive-smelling oily liquid from vents under tail.

skunk cabbage, early spring-blooming, rank-odored perennial (Symplocarpus foetidus) found in wet places in North America. Flower is enclosed in a low cowl-shaped dark red spathe. Yellow skunk cabbage of W U.S. (Lysichitum americanum) is similar.

Skutari, Turkey: see SCUTARI.

sky, apparent dome over earth, background of celestial bodies and atmospheric phenomena. Blue color results from selective scattering of light waves by minute particles of dust and vapor in atmosphere. Since shorter rays (blues) are scattered most readily, sky appears bluest when dust particles are few and small.

Skye (skī), island (with surrounding islets 428,998 acres; pop. 9,908), off NW Scotland, in Inverness-shire, one of Inner Hebrides. Has hilly terrain with many lochs. Sheep and cattle raising and fishing are main occupations. Cap. Portree.

Skye terrier: see TERRIER.

skylark, Old World bird famous for spirited song as it soars into air. Upper parts are brown streaked with black, and under parts are light with black streaks on breast. It is the subject of Shelley's "To a Skylark."

Skyros (skē'rôs, skī'rùs) or **Scyros** (sī'rùs), Aegean island (81 sq. mi.; pop. 3,395), Greece, E of Euboea; largest of N Cyclades. Marble quarries; fishing; sponge diving. In ancient legend, Thetis concealed her son Achilles here in woman's attire and Theseus was killed here. Rupert Brooke is buried on Skyros.

skyscraper, building of great height, constructed on a

steel skeleton, a purely modern and almost exclusively American type of structure. The birthplace of early skyscrapers was Chicago, where William Le Baron Jenney built the 10-story Home Insurance Bldg. (1883), generally considered to be the first skyscraper. In New York, the Flatiron Bldg. was built 1902, Metropolitan Life Insurance Tower 1909, and Woolworth Bldg. 1913. Tallest skyscraper in the world is EMPIRE STATE BUILDING.

skywriting, controlled emission of thick smoke by aircraft aloft to form message visible below. Engine heat turns light paraffin oil into white smoke exhausted under pressure, with added patented oil compound causing smoke particles to adhere. Invented by J. C. Savage of England (1922).

slaked lime: see LIME.

slander: see LIBEL AND SLANDER.

slang, novel, ostensibly careless, more or less humorous language. In colloquial standard English, slang has been a feature for more than a century, mainly consisting of faddish tricks of vocabulary. Yet some of the expressions have passed into ordinary vocabulary (e.g., "O.K.").

Slankamen (släng-kä'měn), village, N Serbia, Yugoslavia, where the imperials under Margrave Louis of Baden routed the Turks in 1691. Also known as Salem Kemen, Szalankemen.

slate, fine-grained gray-blue rock formed by metamorphism of shale. Splits into very thin layers presumably at right angles to metamorphic pressure; this slaty cleavage is parallel to longer axis of mineral particles. Better grades are used for roofing.

Slater, Samuel (slā'tùr), 1768–1835, American pioneer in cotton textile industry, b. England. At Providence, R.I., he reproduced from memory the machinery of Richard Arkwright (1790). Estab. mills in R.I. and elsewhere in New England.

Slaton (slā'tùn), city (pop. 5,036), NE Texas, SE of Lubbock on Llano Estacado. Rail division point processing grain and cotton.

Slaughterhouse Cases. In 1869 the La. legislature, chiefly to protect health of New Orleans residents, granted a 25-year monopoly to a slaughterhouse concern in that city. Other slaughterhouse operators brought suit, claiming they had been deprived of their property without due process of law in violation of Fourteenth Amendment. Justice S. F. Miller rendered U.S. Supreme Court majority decision against slaughterhouse operators in 1873. A conservative decision, it declared old police power of states intact and did not seize opportunity to extend Federal power.

Slave, river: see GREAT SLAVE LAKE.

Slave Coast, coast bordering Bight of Benin of Gulf of Guinea, W Africa. Main source of slaves from W Africa, 16th–18th cent.

Slave dynasty: see DELHI SULTANATE.

slavery. The institution of slavery has been known among peoples in all quarters of the world, not only among agriculturists but in other cultures (e.g., among American Indians and Asiatic nomads). Generally the ownership of human beings has been a form of private property, but there were examples of public slavery (e.g., temple slaves). Slavery was already well estab. before the first recorded days of history in Mesopotamia and Egypt. A large part of the population of the Greek city-states was servile. In Roman times arose a new type of slavery, what might be called the "plantation type," though there continued to be many house slaves and personal slaves. In the Middle Ages slavery continued in Europe but in diminishing form, since the manorial system largely replaced it with the semifreedom of serfdom. The discovery and conquest of the New World, however, created a slave trade on a world-wide scale after it was found that Negroes from Africa could be used on plantations in the warmer climates. The first ones were introduced into what is now the U.S. in 1619, and over the years slavery became "the peculiar institution" at the base of the plantation system in the South; it did not take lasting root in the North. The doctrines of the American and French revolutions implied the end of slavery, and the slaves in Haiti arose, ousted their masters, and were recognized as an independent nation by 1804. Many newly born Latin American nations banned slavery from their start. Humanitarianism played a part in abolition of the English slave trade (1807) and of slavery in the British West Indies (1833). In the U.S. antislavery sentiment rose in the North and was made a burning issue by the abolitionists. Most of the serious clashes in the period 1820–60 were between South and North and hinged on the question of extension of slavery to new territories. The matter did not end until Abraham Lincoln's EMANCIPATION PROCLAMATION (1863) and the North's victory in the Civil War freed the slaves. Emancipation in Brazil in 1888 virtually ended the institution in the New World. The Berlin Conference of 1885, the Brussels Act of 1890, and the activities of the League of Nations (particularly the convention of 1926) largely succeeded in banishing slavery from Asia and Africa.

Slavic (slă'vĭk, slä'–), subfamily of Indo-European languages. See LANGUAGE (table).

Slavonia (slŭvō'nēù), region, E Croatia, N Yugoslavia, between Drava and Sava rivers; cap. Osijek. Fertile agr. and forested lowland. Was ceded by Turkey to Hungary 1699; became Austrian crownland 1848; was restored to Hungarian crown and united with CROATIA 1868; part of Yugoslavia since 1918.

Slavonic (slŭvŏ'nĭk), subfamily of Indo-European languages. See LANGUAGE (table).

Slavs, large ethnic and linguistic group of peoples belonging to Indo-European linguistic family (see LANGUAGE, table). Classified usually in three main divisions. West Slavs include Poles, Czechs, Slovaks, and WENDS and other small groups in E Germany. East Slavs include Great Russians, Ukrainians (Little Russians), and White Russians (Belorussians). South Slavs include Serbs, Croats, Slovenes, Macedonians, and Bulgarians. Culturally all Slavs fall into two groups—those traditionally associated with Orthodox Eastern Church and those historically affiliated with Roman Catholic Church. Prominent in Slavic history is story of Russia's rise from separate states. Pan-Slavism has been powerful instrument of Russian expansion.

sleeping sickness, either of two diseases marked by somnolence or lethargy. One, *encephalitis lethargica* (ěnsě"fùlī'tĭs lěthär'jĭkù), is infectious and believed to be caused by a virus. The other, trypanosomiasis (trĭ"pùnōsōmī'ùsĭs, trĭ"–), is a disease of tropical Africa caused by a protozoan transmitted by tsetse fly.

Sleepy Hollow, N.Y.: see NORTH TARRYTOWN.

sleet, name for several forms of winter precipitation: small, hard, globular ice grains, differing in form and occurrence from hail; ice coating formed by freezing rain; rain and snow mingled.

Slesvig, Danish name of SCHLESWIG.

Slick, Sam: see HALIBURTON, THOMAS CHANDLER.

Slidell, John (slīděl', slī'dùl), 1793–1871, American politician and diplomat. U.S. Senator from La. (1853–61). Joined Confederacy, made commissioner to France. With J. M. Mason, figured in TRENT AFFAIR.

Slide Mountain: see CATSKILL MOUNTAINS.

slide rule, instrument for making numerical computations and readings by simple manipulations. Based on principle of logarithm, and on creation of logarithmic scale (1620), modern slide rule appeared in 1850. Three parts are stock, slide, and cursor (indicator). In one form of rule, stock consists of two parallel rules, each with scale on inner edge; slide is single rule, moving between them, with scales on outer edge. Cursor is glass square with hair line, movable along length of rule to aid in reading. On reverse side of slide rule are tables usable, in conjunction with scales, for determing sines, tangents, and logarithms. Calculating circle and calculating cylinder, for more complex calculations, are based on same principle.

Slieve Bloom (slēv), mountain range, 15 mi. long, central Ireland. Rises to 1,733 ft. at Arderin.

Sligo (slī′gō), maritime county (694 sq. mi.; pop. 62,-375), NW Ireland, in Connaught. Has irregular coastline and mountainous interior. Cattle raising and farming are chief occupations. County town is **Sligo,** urban district (pop. 12,920), seaport, fishing center.

Slipher, Vesto Melvin (slī′fŭr), 1875–, American astronomer, noted for spectroscopic research revealing rapid rotation and high velocities of nebulae.

Sloan, John, 1871–1952, American painter, a member of The EIGHT. Long a popular teacher at Art Students League. Painted realistic scenes of city life.

Sloane, Sir Hans (slōn), 1660–1753, British physician, naturalist. He was president of Royal College of Physicians (1719–35) and of Royal Society (1724–40). His collections of botanical specimens (some gathered in West Indies) and of books and manuscripts formed beginning of British Mus.

sloop, fore-and-aft rigged sailing vessel similar to the cutter, but with broader beam, center board and fixed bowsprit and a jibstay. The fast sloop-of-war, carrying 12 to 18 guns, used by the British navy in the mid-19th cent., resembled the later schooner. See *ill.,* p. 865.

sloth (slōth, slôth), arboreal mammal of tropical America. Eats, sleeps, and travels upside down clinging to branches. Three-toed (*Bradypus*) feeds on cecropia leaves, buds, and stems; two-toed sloth (*Choloepus*) has less restricted vegetarian diet.

Slovakia (slōvă′kēū), Slovak *Slovensko,* constituent state (18,902 sq. mi.; pop. 3,434,369) of Czechoslovakia, occupying E part of Czechoslovak republic; cap. Bratislava. Except for S section, which is part of the Hungarian Plain, it is traversed by the Carpathian mts., culminating in the TATRA. Agr., forests, pastures. Iron, copper, mercury, lead, gold, silver, lignite mines. Slovakia was part of Hungary from the early 10th cent. until 1918. Hungarian nobles owned most of land. Germans and Jews formed large part of urban population. Slovak national consciousness began to stir in 19th cent. Independence movement was backed by many Slovak emigrants in U.S. In World War I, Czech and Slovak leaders agreed on union of the two nations; CZECHOSLOVAKIA was proclaimed 1918; Treaty of Trianon (1920) estab. present boundary with Hungary, leaving a minority of over 1,000,000 Magyars in Slovakia. The minority problem was complicated by Slovak nationalist agitation for home rule and by friction between the intensely Catholic Slovaks and the anticlerical Prague government. After the MUNICH PACT of 1938 Slovakia ceded some territory to Hungary and became an autonomous state. The German seizure of Bohemia and Moravia (March, 1939) left Slovakia nominally independent under the dictatorship of the nationalist leader, Father Joseph Tiso. Actually a puppet of Germany, it entered World War II as an Axis partner but was occupied by Russian troops in 1944. Reunited to Czechoslovakia, it recovered its lost territories. The constitution of 1948 gave it its own legislature and cabinet, but in fact the Communist party seized all power. Exchange of the Magyar minority for Slovak minorities in Hungary began in 1945.

Slovenia (slōvě′nēū), autonomous republic (7,796 sq. mi.; pop. 1,389,084), NW Yugoslavia, bordering on Austria (N) and Italy (W); cap. Ljubljana. It includes most of the Julian Alps (highest point, TRIGLAV) and the KARST and is drained by the Drava and Sava. The Slovenes are Roman Catholics. Most of Slovenia was comprised in the Austrian crownlands of Carniola, Styria, and Carinthia until 1918, when the kingdom of the Serbs, Croats and Slovenes—later called Yugoslavia—was formed. After World War II, Slovenia received autonomous status and was awarded part of formerly Italian VENEZIA GIULIA.

Slowacki, Julius, Pol. *Juliusz Słowacki* (yŏōl′yōōsh swôvăts′kē), 1809–49, Polish romantic poet. Wrote historic dramas—e.g., *Mazeppa* (1834; Eng. tr., 1929); *Mary Stuart* (1830; Eng. tr. 1937)—and the allegorical prose epic *Anhelli* (1838; Eng. tr., 1930).

slug, name for a terrestrial mollusk similar to land snail and also for a marine sea slug of another mollusk order. Shell lacking or rudimentary. Terrestrial slug (*Limax*) is garden pest.

Sluis (slois) Fr. *L′Écluse,* town (pop. 1,615), Zeeland prov., SW Netherlands, on Scheldt estuary. Founded 13th cent. as subsidiary port of Bruges. Scene of English naval victory over French (1340) in Hundred Years War. Conquered by Dutch from Spanish in 1604. Formerly spelled Sluys.

Sluter, Claus (klous′ slü′tŭr), d. c.1406, Flemish sculptor, chief master of early Burgundian school. Famous for realistic and powerful works at Dijon.

Sluys, Netherlands: see SLUIS.

Sm, chemical symbol of the element SAMARIUM.

Smaland, Swed. *Småland* (smō′länd), historic province of S central Sweden; chief cities are Jonkoping and Kalmar.

small holding, term used in England for tract of agr. land larger than a cottage holding (three acres or less), but not too large to be cultivated by owner or tenant and his family. Maximum size was fixed by law at 50 acres. Unlike cottage holding, small holding is meant to provide a business capable of supporting family which farms it.

smallpox, infectious, contagious disease caused by a virus. Marked by red spots that form blisters and may leave scars (pocks). Attack usually gives permanent immunity. Disease can be wiped out by universal vaccination. Edward Jenner introduced vaccination with cowpox virus.

smaltite (smôl′tīt), opaque, white to gray mineral of pyrite group, a compound of cobalt and arsenic.

Smart, Christopher, 1722–71, English poet, author of cryptic poetry, such as *A Song to David* (1763, in biblical language; written in an asylum).

smartweed, annual species of genus *Polygonum* containing an acrid juice and bearing catkinlike pink flowers. Prince's-feather (*Polygonum orientale*) is often cultivated.

smell, sense by which odors are perceived. In man, organs of smell, olfactory cells in nasal cavity, receive at one end stimuli transmitted to brain by nerve fibers at other end. Smell long believed to be chemical; some evidence that infrared radiation is involved. Sense highly developed in certain animals in food getting and attracting mate.

smelt, small slender fish of north temperate waters, related to salmon. It is chiefly marine but many spawn in fresh waters; some are found in landlocked lakes. Adults average c.8 in. in length. Delicate flesh. Common American smelt of Atlantic coast is *Osmerus mordax.*

smelting, in metallurgy, any heat process for preparing a metal from its ores. Processes vary according to metal involved but are typified in use of BLAST FURNACE and REVERBERATORY FURNACE.

Smet, Pierre Jean de: see DE SMET, PIERRE JEAN.

Smetana, Friedrich, Czech *Bedřich Smetana* (smět′änä), 1824–84, Czech composer. Drawing on Czech folk music he created a national style. Of his eight operas only *The Bartered Bride* was successful outside his own country. He also wrote a symphonic cycle, *My Fatherland,* which contains the popular *Vltava (The Moldau);* and two string quartets, *From My Life.* He died both deaf and insane.

Smibert or **Smybert, John** (both: smī′bŭrt), 1688–1751, American portrait painter, b. Scotland. Among his subjects were George Berkeley and Jonathan Edwards. Practiced in Boston.

smilax (smī′lăks), South African twining vine (*Asparagus asparagoides*), commonly grown for greenery for florist trade. Greenbriers, prickly vines often weedy in parts of North America, belong to genus *Smilax*.

Smirke, Sir Robert, 1781–1867, English architect, a noted exponent of the classic revival. Designed main façade of British Mus. His brother, **Sydney Smirke,** 1793–1877, worked in the same style.

Smith, Adam, 1723–90, Scottish economist, author of *An Inquiry into the Nature and Causes of the Wealth of Nations* (1776). He postulated theory of division of labor, of laissez faire, and of value as a result of labor expended in the process of production. An opponent of mercantilism, he admitted that certain restrictions to free trade might be necessary. As an analyst of institutions and an influence on later economists he has perhaps never been surpassed.

Smith, Alfred E(manuel), 1873–1944, American political leader. Governor of N.Y. (1919–20, 1923–28); one of the most forceful in the history of the state. Accomplished many reforms. Democratic candidate for President in 1928.

Smith, Donald Alexander: see STRATHCONA AND MOUNT ROYAL, DONALD ALEXANDER SMITH, 1ST BARON.

Smith, Edmund Kirby, or **Edmund Kirby-Smith,** 1824–93, Confederate general. Commanded Trans-Mississippi Dept. (1863–65). Last general to surrender (May 26, 1865).

Smith, Gerrit, 1797–1874, American philanthropist and reformer. Aided various reforms (esp. temperance and abolition). Devoted friend of John Brown. Urged moderation toward South after Civil War.

Smith, Gipsy (Rodney), 1860–1947, British evangelist; son of a gypsy. He worked in Gen. Booth's Christian Mission, but later preached independently. From 1883 his evangelistic labors spanned England, Scotland, U.S., and Australia.

Smith, Henry John Stephen, 1826–83, British mathematician, known especially for work on theory of numbers and elliptic functions.

Smith, Horatio or **Horace,** 1779–1849, and **James Smith,** 1775–1839, English parodists, brothers. Wrote famous *Rejected Addresses* (1812), parodies of Wordsworth, Scott, Coleridge, and Byron.

Smith, Jedediah Strong, 1799–1831, American explorer, one of the greatest of the mountain men. He more than any other was breaker of trails to Calif. and Pacific Northwest.

Smith, John, 1580–1631, English colonist in America. Guided Jamestown settlement through periods of hardship. Supposedly saved from death by POCAHONTAS. Urged settlement of New England.

Smith, Joseph, 1805–44, American founder of Church of Jesus Christ of the Latter-Day Saints. In Palmyra, N.Y., in 1823, a vision revealed existence of secret records. When in 1827 their hiding place was made known to him, he unearthed golden tablets with sacred writing, which he translated as Book of Mormon. As prophet and seer he founded first church in 1830. Hostility of neighbors led him to move to Kirtland, Ohio, to Mo., and to Nauvoo, Ill. Disaffection grew, and trouble with non-Mormons led to arrest of Joseph and his brother Hyrum on charges of treason. On June 27, 1844, they were murdered by a mob at Carthage, Ill. His revelations, including one on plural marriage, were accepted as doctrine by the Mormons.

Smith, Kirby: see SMITH, EDMUND KIRBY.

Smith, Logan Pearsall, 1865–1946, Anglo-American author; b. N.J., in England after 1888. Wrote exquisite essays in *Trivia* (1902; with sequels), criticism in *On Reading Shakespeare* (1933) and *Milton and His Modern Critics* (1940).

Smith, Seba, 1792–1868, American editor and humorist. Editor of Portland (Maine) *Courier*, famous for humorous political letters signed "Major Jack Downing," later collected.

Smith, Sydney, 1771–1845, English clergyman, writer, and wit. With others he founded (1802) the *Edinburgh Review*. His "Peter Plymley" letters in defense

of Catholic Emancipation promoted religious toleration—an example of his defense of the oppressed.

Smith, Theobald, 1859–1934, American pathologist. Discovered cause of Texas cattle fever. Contributed much to preventive medicine.

Smith, Walter Bedell, 1895–, American general. Chief of staff (1942–45) to Dwight Eisenhower in World War II, he became ambassador to USSR (1946–49) and director of Central Intelligence Agency (1950–53). Appointed Undersecretary of State in 1953.

Smith, William Robertson, 1846–94, Scottish biblical scholar and encyclopedist. Ejected (1881) from professorship at Free Church college, Aberdeen, because of biblical articles written for *The Encyclopaedia Britannica*, he became an editor of that work, later (1887) editor in chief.

Smith College, at Northampton, Mass.; nonsectarian, for women; chartered 1871, opened 1875 through bequest of Sophia Smith. Pres. L. C. Seelye estab. high ideals of scholarship. Col. has school of architecture and landscape architecture at Cambridge, school for social work. Had pioneer music courses. Honors work is stressed. Conducted school for women naval officers in World War II.

Smithfield, district of central London, England. Site of the Central Meat Market. Formerly used for markets, fairs, jousts, and executions.

Smithfield. 1 Town (pop. 5,574), E central N.C., SE of Raleigh and on Neuse R. Cotton, tobacco. **2** Town (pop. 6,690), N R.I., NW of Providence, in agr. area. Textiles. **3** City (pop. 2,383), N Utah, in Cache Valley N of Logan. Near by is Newton Dam, started 1871 by Mormons, replaced 1946 by U.S. **4** Town (pop. 1,180), SE Va., NW of Portsmouth. Noted for its hams. Near by are St. Luke's Church (1632 or 1682; one of oldest Protestant churches in America), and Bacon's Castle (1655; house fortified during Bacon's Rebellion).

Smiths Falls, town (pop. 8,441), SE Ont., Canada, SW of Ottawa, on Rideau R. Rail and mfg. center.

Smithson, James, 1765?–1829, English founder of Smithsonian Inst., b. France. He was the illegitimate son of Sir Hugh Smithson and Elizabeth Macie. He wrote valuable scientific papers for Royal Society publications and *Annals of Philosophy*. His fortune was willed to the U.S. for establishment of Smithsonian Inst. for the "increase and diffusion of knowledge among men."

Smithsonian Institution (smĭthsō′nē̆un), estab. at Washington, D.C., by congressional act in 1846. Governing board of regents consists of Vice President of U.S., Chief Justice, three Senators, three Representatives, and six nonofficials. Secretary to the board is the executive officer of the Smithsonian and keeper of the U.S. National Mus. The Institution's activities embrace all branches of science relating to U.S., with special emphasis on scientific research. Under Smithsonian auspices are Bureau of American Ethnology, National Zoological Park, Astrophysical Observatory, Canal Zone Biological Area, National Air Mus., and U.S. National Mus. (including National Coll. of Fine Arts and Freer Gall. of Art).

smoke, visible gaseous product of incomplete combustion. Usually consists of carbon particles and tarry substances, or soot. Soft coal produces greatest amount; proper firing and equipment can eliminate much smoke. Smoke has caused much contamination in cities, and various means are used to reduce amount escaping into air, e.g., precipitation by electricity, sound waves, or chemicals. Among evils of smoke are interference with sunlight, disfiguring deposits on buildings, destructive chemical effects of acids in deposits, cost of cleaning off deposits, damaging effect on plant life and on animal respiratory systems. Smoke has been used as concealment in warfare (as smoke screens) at least since the late 17th cent. It is also used for a variety of sign language; particularly among the Indians of the W U.S.

Smoky, river of W Alta., Canada, rising in Jasper Natl. Park and flowing 245 mi. NNE to Peace R.

Smoky Hill River, rising in E Colo. and flowing c.560 mi. E across Kansas to join Republican R. and form Kansas R. at Junction City. Basin is in MISSOURI RIVER BASIN PROJECT. Kanopolis Dam, for flood control, completed 1948.

Smoky Mountains: see GREAT SMOKY MOUNTAINS.

Smolensk (smŏlĕnsk', smô–), city (pop. 156,677), W European RSFSR, on the Dnieper. Rail junction and industrial center (textiles, machinery, flour, lumber, spirits). Founded 882, it became a great medieval commercial center and the cap. of a principality which fell to Lithuania in 14th cent.; ceded to Russia 1667. Captured by Napoleon I in Aug., 1812. German-held (1941–43) in World War II and virtually razed by heavy fighting.

Smollett, Tobias (George), 1721–71, Scottish novelist. A naval surgeon, he turned to writing. His picaresque novels, realistic and vigorous in style, include *The Adventures of Roderick Random* (1748), *The Adventures of Peregrine Pickle* (1751), and *The Expedition of Humphry Clinker* (1771).

Smoot, Reed (smōot), 1862–1941, U.S. Senator from Utah (1903–33). First Mormon elected to Senate. Co-author of HAWLEY-SMOOT TARIFF ACT (1930).

smut, fungus disease of cereal plants which produces sootlike masses of spores on the host. Smuts lower vitality and may cause deformity. Among crops attacked are corn, oats, and wheat; stinking smut or bunt causes annual losses by spoiling wheat grain.

Smuts, Jan Christiaan, 1870–1950, South African statesman, soldier. Of Dutch stock, he gave up British citizenship after Jameson raid. Believed cooperation of Boers and British essential; was instrumental (with Louis Botha) in creation (1910) of Union of South Africa. Continuously held office in Botha's cabinet. Signed Treaty of Versailles (1918) protesting that its terms outraged Germany. Advocated League of Nations. Prime minister of South Africa 1919–24. In World War II he was again prime minister and held high place in British war councils; was active in organizing U.N.

Smybert, John: see SMIBERT, JOHN.

Smyrna (smûr'nù), Turkish *Izmir*, city (pop. 230,508), W Turkey; a port on the Bay of Smyrna of the Aegean Sea. Varied mfg. An early Ionian colony, it was rebuilt by Antigonus I (4th cent. B.C.) and became one of the largest and richest cities of Asia Minor under Roman and Byzantine rule. An early Christian center, it was one of the Seven Churches of Asia (Rev. 2–8). It was sacked by Tamerlane (1402) and fell in 1424 to the Ottoman Turks, who kept it until 1919, when it was occupied by Greek forces. The Treaty of SÈVRES (1920) placed the Smyrna region under Greek administration; it was nullified by the Treaty of Lausanne (1923), after the Turkish nationalists under Kemal Ataturk had driven the Greeks from Asia Minor in the campaign of 1920–22. The large Greek population of Smyrna was exchanged for Turkish minorities in Greece. With the loss of this prosperous, cultured element, Smyrna declined somewhat. It is one of the cities claiming to have given birth to Homer.

Smythe, Francis Sydney, 1901–49, English mountain climber. Climbed (1931) Kamet (25,447 ft.) in Garwhal Himalayas.

Sn, chemical symbol of the element TIN.

snail, gastropod mollusk with spiral shell. Thousands of species include land, fresh-water, and marine forms. Used for food, especially in Europe. Both sexes are represented in each individual.

Snake, river, c.1,000 mi. long, NW U.S., chief tributary (formerly, Lewis R. or Lewis Fork) of the Columbia. Rises in Yellowstone Natl. Park, NW Wyo., and flows S through Jackson L., S and W into Idaho, NW to be joined by Henrys Fork, then runs SW and NW across Idaho, bends into Oregon, turns N as

Idaho-Oregon and Idaho-Wash. line (receiving Boise, Salmon, other rivers), and flows W into Columbia R. near Pasco, Wash. Grand Canyon of the Snake (between Wallowa Mts., Oregon, and Seven Devils Mts., Idaho) is one of world's deepest; reaches maximum depth of 7,900 ft. Discovered 1805 by Lewis and Clark, the Snake aided expansion of NW U.S. Much used for irrigation privately (see TWIN FALLS), by U.S. in MINIDOKA PROJECT, BOISE PROJECT, and others. Major Idaho cities are in valley.

snake, reptile with elongated scaly body, limbless or with only traces of hind limbs, with forked retractile tongue, and recurved teeth. The eyes are covered by clear scales (instead of movable eyelids); there are no ears, and only one lung is developed. The skin is shed, usually several times a year. A snake moves by means of body muscles aided by elongated scales on abdomen and by ends of ribs. About 80% of the c.2,500 species are nonvenomous. Venom, produced by modified salivary glands, passes through a groove or bore in fangs into victim.

snake bite. Venom of poisonous snakes introduced by fangs. May injure nerves, blood vessels, or blood cells or cause hemorrhage. Treatment usually involves application of tourniquet between wound and heart; injection of antitoxin; cutting of wound to cause bleeding.

Snake Indians, popular name given to several tribes, notably the Shoshone and N Paiute.

snakeroot, name for several plants, including SENEGA SNAKEROOT and WHITE SNAKEROOT.

snapdragon, Old World perennial (*Antirrhinum majus*) grown as an annual in greenhouses and gardens. The handsome flower spikes come in various colors.

snare drum: see PERCUSSION INSTRUMENTS.

Snead, Sam(uel Jackson) (snēd), 1912–, American golfer. Won Professional Golfers Association (1942, 1949), British Open (1946) championships.

Snell or Snellius, Willebrord (vĭ'lùbrôrt snĕl', snĕ'lēus), 1591–1626, Dutch mathematician. Generally credited with discovery of law of refraction of light (1621).

Snelling, Fort, estab. 1819 on a bluff above the Mississippi at confluence of the Minnesota. Minneapolis later grew on fort reservation.

Snellius, Willebrord: see SNELL, WILLEBRORD.

snipe, wading bird of Old and New Worlds, related to woodcock. Plumage is usually brown, chestnut, and buff. Its long bill probes earth for insects and worms.

Snorri Sturluson (snô'rē stür'lùsôn), 1179–1241, Icelandic historian. His prose EDDA is a treatise on writing poetry and a compendium of Norse mythology. The *Heimskringla* is a series of biographies of Norse kings. Powerful in politics, he lost favor and was murdered.

snow, form of precipitation, hexagonal ice crystals, produced by condensation of vapor about a dust particle at below-freezing temperatures. Snowflakes usually consist of more than one crystal. Snowfall usually part of rainfall statistics (10 in. averages 1 in. rain).

snowball: see VIBURNUM.

snowberry, ornamental white-fruited shrub (*Symphoricarpos*), chiefly native to North America. The common snowberry (*Symphoricarpos albus*) has pink flowers and waxy berries.

Snowden, Philip Snowden, 1st Viscount, 1864–1937, British socialist statesman. Chancellor of exchequer in ministries of Ramsay MacDonald 1924, 1929. Advocate of free trade. Demanded increased German war reparations at Hague Convention 1929.

Snowdon, Welsh *Eryri*, mountain, 3,560 ft. high, Caernarvonshire, Wales; highest in Wales. Has five peaks, separated by passes. Railway to the summit. District (Snowdonia) has beautiful scenery.

snowdrop, hardy, low bulbous plant (*Galanthus nivalis*) of Old World. It has a single, nodding bell-shaped white flower in early spring.

snow-on-the-mountain: see SPURGE.

Snyder, town (pop. 12,010), NW Texas, NW of Sweetwater; settled 1876. Shipping and processing center for agr., oil, dairying, and livestock region.

Snyders, Frans (fräns' snī'dùrs), 1579–1657, Flemish painter of luminous still lifes and spirited animal compositions. Often collaborated with Rubens and Jordaens. Influenced mainly by Rubens.

Soane, Sir John (sōn), 1753–1837, English architect, a leader of the classic revival in England. Noted for his work on Bank of England.

soap, agent that cleanses by lowering surface tension of water, emulsifying grease, and adsorbing dirt into the foam. Results from reaction (saponification) of alkali and fat, forming metallic acid (soap) and glycerin. Made essentially by stirring alkali into heated fats or oils and adding salt to cause soap to form curds; these are usually churned and poured into frames, or, for hard-milled soaps, run over chilled rollers, scraped off, and shaped. Properties vary according to alkalis, fats, and fillers employed. Used in industry as paint driers, lubricating greases, and in other forms. Substitutes include certain plants (see SOAP PLANT) and soapless detergents (commonly sulfonated alcohols).

soap plant, any of various plants containing cleansing properties. The soapbark tree (*Quillaja saponaria*), the tropical American soapberry (*Sapindus*), the California soap plant (*Chlorogalum pomeridianum*), SOAPWORT (*Saponaria*), and species of agave, are among plants containing the lather-producing substance, saponin. The poisonous quality of saponin was used by Indians who caught fish by first stupefying them with plant bits thrown into pools.

soapstone or **steatite** (stē'ŭtīt), massive gray to green rock usually composed chiefly of talc. It is very soft, has soapy feel, is highly resistant to heat and acids. Used for laboratory equipment, sinks, laundry, tubs, electrical apparatus.

soapwort, perennial plant (*Saponaria officinalis*), grown in gardens in colonial America and now escaped along roads and railroads. It is also called bouncing Bet. It has pink or white flower clusters, and its leaves produce a cleansing lather.

Sobieski, John: see JOHN III, king of Poland.

soccer (sŏ'kùr), game played by teams of 11 men on grassy field preferably measuring 120 yd. by 15 yd. Name derived by usage from abbreviation of word *association*.

Sochi (sō'chē), city (pop. c.50,000), S Krasnodar Territory, SE European RSFSR; a port and health resort on the Black Sea.

social contract, agreement with which men are said to have abandoned the "state of nature" to form the society in which they now live. Theory of such a covenant, formulated by Hobbes and Locke, and expanded by Rousseau, had a strong effect on development of government responsibilities and the citizen's "natural rights" in a democracy.

Social Credit, economic plan, based on theories of Clifford H. Douglas. Central idea is that economic depressions are caused by maldistribution due to insufficient purchasing power. It was proposed to redistribute purchasing power by issuing dividends to every citizen. Scheme was adopted by a political party in Alta., Canada, led by William Aberhart, which won 1935 elections. Confederation government and courts disallowed attempts to tax banks and promote currency schemes. However, the party continued to win elections and after World War II it sponsored much social welfare legislation.

social hygiene deals with sex behavior relative to individual and social aspects of health. Stresses relation of VENEREAL DISEASE and poor sexual adjustment. Strives to improve sex education and to correct social ills resulting in such problems as sex crimes, prostitution, unmarried mothers.

socialism, general term for any economic doctrine that challenges sanctity of private property and favors its use for public welfare. In this sense it embraces great variety of economic theories, from those holding that only certain public utilities and natural resources should be owned by state, to thoroughgoing Marxian socialism, and, further, to edges of ANARCHISM. Industrial Revolution, first in British Isles in 18th cent. and later on Continent, created social and economic conditions that led intellectuals to plan reorganization. *Socialism* and *communism* emerged as terms, often used interchangeably, and movements were utopian. Thus in France, Étienne CABET and Charles FOURIER planned COMMUNISTIC SETTLEMENTS. In England, Robert OWEN and Thomas SPENCE were influential. American leaders were Albert BRISBANE and Bronson ALCOTT. A more practical leader in France was Louis BLANC. Marxian socialism appeared with *The Communist Manifesto* (1848) of Karl MARX and Friedrich ENGELS. CHRISTIAN SOCIALISM appeared in England under F. D. Maurice and Charles KINGSLEY. In Germany, Ferdinand LASSALLE, Wilhelm LIEBKNECHT, and August BEBEL prepared way for rise of Social Democratic parties under guidance of INTERNATIONAL. In Russia, PLEKHANOV founded Social Democratic party, which split between BOLSHEVISM AND MENSHEVISM. Similar parties gained strength on Continent between two world wars and after World War II. In England, FABIAN SOCIETY (leaders included G. B. SHAW and Sidney and Beatrice WEBB) led to establishment of Labour party. Socialist party in U.S. had as leaders Daniel DE LEON, E. V. DEBS, Morris HILLQUIT, and Norman THOMAS.

Socialist Labor party, in U.S. history, formed in 1870s. In 1880 it temporarily allied itself with Greenback party. Under Daniel DE LEON in 1890s, it advocated a syndicalist type of socialism. Party sharply declined after De Leon's opponents withdrew in 1899 to join Social Democratic party (see SOCIALIST PARTY).

Socialist party, in U.S. history, formed 1898 as Social Democratic party, redesignated Socialist party 1901. E. V. Debs was its candidate for President five times between 1900 and 1920; Morris HILLQUIT dominant figure of early period. After 1928 party was led by Norman THOMAS. Party's objectives are reformist, calling for evolutionary socialism.

socialization of medicine: see HEALTH INSURANCE.

social psychology, study of human relationships; the science in which experimental psychology, sociology, anthropology, and psychiatry meet. It is concerned with the influence of family, school, church, and economic and political background on the individual; the study of behavior patterns; the nature and forming of attitudes and ways of measuring and changing them; and the effects of interracial and international relations on the individual. Attempts have been made to adapt techniques of the physical and biological laboratory to the measuring and describing of human behavior.

social security, program of social insurance, brought about by government legislation, to protect wage earners and their dependents against major economic hazards. First adopted in Germany in the 1880s to forestall the program of the Socialists. Britain's Natl. Insurance Act of 1914 included sickness, unemployment, and old-age insurance (see PENSION). Social security did not reach the U.S. until 1935, when it became part of Roosevelt's New Deal program. It now covers approximately 46,000,000 people, but certain types of workers are still not covered, and HEALTH INSURANCE has not yet been added.

social settlement, institution in a poor and overcrowded area where resident workers improve conditions by promoting community cooperation and services. Among the famous settlement houses are Toynbee Hall (founded 1884 in London), Hull House (Chicago), and the Henry Street Settlement and Greenwich House (New York).

Social War, 90 B.C.–88 B.C., struggle of the Italian allies of Rome (the *socii*) to secure Roman citizenship promised them by the laws of M. Livius Drusus, but denied by the senate. A people called the Marsians were first to rise, and this is sometimes called the Marsic War. It ended only when L. Julius Caesar got a law passed giving citizenship to allies who had not joined the war or who laid down arms immediately.

social work, organized effort to aid needy or maladjusted individuals. Originally, churches and philanthropic groups sought to relieve poverty and distress of those "worthy of charity." In 1874 the Natl. Conference of Charities and Correction (later renamed Natl. Conference of Social Work) was organized in U.S. After 1930 the Federal government entered the field of social work, although private welfare funds are still raised (see COMMUNITY CHEST).

Society for the Prevention of Cruelty to Animals (S.P.C.A.). The English organization was founded 1824, the American 1866.

Society Islands (c.650 sq. mi.; pop. 42,129), S Pacific, part of FRENCH ESTABLISHMENTS IN OCEANIA. The 450-mi. chain comprises Windward Isls. (including TAHITI, site of the cap. Papeete) and Leeward Isls. (including Raiatea). Larger islands are mountainous and volcanic and produce copra, sugar, rum, mother-of-pearl, and phosphate. Natives are Polynesians. Discovered 1767 by the British; visited 1769 by Capt. James Cook and members of Royal Society, in whose honor the group was named. The French came in late 18th cent. and set up a protectorate in 1844. Group became a French colony in 1880.

Socinianism (sōsĭ'nēŭnĭzŭm), anti-Trinitarian religious system in 16th cent. based on ideas of Laelius and Faustus Socinus. It accepted rationalist doctrines and rejected belief in the Trinity; sometimes called Old Unitarianism. Basic ideas are in Racovian Catechism of 1605.

Socinus, Laelius (lē'lĕŭs sōsī'nŭs), originally **Lelio Sozzini,** 1525–62, Italian religious reformer. Lived in Switzerland from 1544. Never actually voiced anti-Trinitarian views, but from his writings his nephew, **Faustus Socinus** (fô'stŭs), originally **Fausto Sozzini,** 1539–1604, formulated doctrinal basis of Socinianism. In Poland (after 1579) he organized anti-Trinitarian groups into Polish Brethren.

sociology, the science of human groups or societies; the study of man in his collective aspect. An ancient philosophical study, it was first treated (1838) systematically by Auguste Comte. Herbert Spencer was also important in the founding of its principles.

Socorro (sōkô'rō), city (pop. 4,334), W central N.Mex., on Rio Grande and S of Albuquerque. On site of Piro pueblo, visited 1598 by Oñate. Part of Church of San Miguel dates from this period.

Socrates (sŏ'krŭtēz), 469–399 B.C., Greek philosopher of Athens, generally regarded as one of the wisest men of all time. At about 30 he dedicated himself to combat skepticism and arouse love of truth and virtue. He gathered about him a group of young men and instilled into them a love of inquiry that would lead to knowledge and justice. The Socratic method was to question someone, then show skillfully the inadequacy of the answer by further questions, all guiding toward a sounder answer. He said that his wisdom consisted in knowing that he knew nothing finally (the Socratic irony). Athenian conservatives, fearing new ideas, had him brought to trial for corrupting youth and introducing strange divinities. Condemned to die, he drank poison hemlock with noble calm and courage. He wrote nothing, and is known to us through the writings of his greatest pupil, Plato, and of Xenophon. His wife was XANTHIPPE.

soda, sodium carbonate, originally called soda ash. Forms alkaline solution on hydrolysis; obtained by LEBLANC PROCESS and SOLVAY PROCESS. Used in making glass, soap, caustic soda, enamel; as cleaning agent; as water softener. Baking soda is sodium bicarbonate; it is used in BAKING POWDER and in medicine and in the laboratory for neutralizing acids. Caustic soda is sodium hydroxide, also called lye.

Soda Springs, village (pop. 1,329), SE Idaho, near Bear R.; founded 1863. Its mineral springs (esp. Steamboat Spring) have drawn travelers since days of Oregon Trail. Area has phosphate deposits.

Soddy, Frederick (sŏ'dē), 1877–, English chemist. Won 1921 Nobel Prize for discovery (with others) of relationship between radioactive elements and parent compound that led to his theory of isotopes.

Soderberg, Hjalmar, Swed. *Söderberg* (yäl'mär sû'-dürbĕr"yû), 1869–1941, Swedish author of dramas, novels, and short stories depicting Stockholm life.

Soderblom, Nathan, Swed. *Söderblom* (nä'tän sû'dürblōōm), 1866–1931, archbishop of Uppsala, Sweden. Awarded 1930 Nobel Peace Prize.

Sodermanland, Swed. *Södermanland* (sû'dürmänländ"), historic province of E central Sweden, on the Baltic coast. It includes S part of Stockholm co. and Sodermanland co. Stockholm and Nykoping are the chief cities. Truck farming and dairying. Iron and steel industry at Eskilstuna.

sodium (sō'dēŭm), soft, silver-white, lustrous metallic element (symbol = Na; see also ELEMENT, table), a very active alkali metal. Oxidizes rapidly in air; must be kept under oil. Metallic sodium is of little commercial value. Sodium compounds are numerous and widely distributed and are used in chemical processes and in commercial preparation of other substances. Sodium hydroxide is used wherever cheap alkali is needed, e.g., in making soap. Compounds also occur in animal and plant cells.

sodium benzoate (bĕn'zōāt) or **benzoate of soda,** salt of benzoic acid, used as a preservative, but harmful except in small quantities.

Sodom (sŏ'dŭm), one of the Cities of the Plain destroyed by fire from heaven because of unnatural carnal wickedness. Others were Gomorrah, Admah, and Zeboiim; Zoar was spared. Gen. 10.19; 13; 14; 18; 19; Deut. 29.23; Amos 4.11; Mat. 10.15; Mark 6.11; 2 Peter 2.6; Jude 7. Sodoma: Rom. 9.29.

Sodoma, Il (ēl sô'dōmä), c.1477–1549, Italian painter, b. Lombardy. Real name was Giovanni Antonio Bazzi. His many frescoes in Siena and vicinity show influence of Leonardo da Vinci.

Soekarno: see SUKARNO.

Soerabaja, Indonesia: see SURABAYA.

Soerakarta, Indonesia: see SURAKARTA.

Soest (zōst), town (pop. 28,914), North Rhine-Westphalia, W Germany. The leading town of Westphalia in the later Middle Ages, it was comprised in the archbishopric of Cologne and later in the county of Mark (under dukes of Cleves) but enjoyed virtual independence. Passed to Brandenburg 1613. Heavy destruction in World War II included damage to many of its architectural treasures, notably the Romanesque cathedral (Patroklikirche, 10th cent.).

Sofia (sōfē'ŭ), city (pop. 366,925), cap. of Bulgaria, at the foot of the Balkans. Mfg. of machinery, chemicals, rubber, textiles, tobacco. Orthodox and Roman Catholic episcopal seees. University (founded 1889). The ancient Sardica, it was destroyed by the Huns (447) and restored by Justinian I (6th cent.). It was part of the first Bulgarian empire (9th–11th cent.), reverted to Byzantium, became part of the second Bulgarian empire in the 13th cent., passed to the Ottoman Empire 1386, and was the cap. of Turkish Rumelia until 1878, when it became the cap. of Bulgaria. It is largely a modern city.

Sogdiana (sŏgdēä'nŭ), part of anc. Persian Empire in central Asia between Oxus and Jaxartes rivers. Chief city was Samarkand.

Sogne Fjord (sông'nŭ fyôr"), inlet of Norwegian Sea, on W coast of Norway; longest (112 mi.) and deepest (4,081 ft.) fjord of Norway. Branches cut into the JOTUNHEIM and JOSTEDALSBREEN. The region is rich in Viking traditions and celebrated for its wild beauty.

Soho (sōhō', sŭ–), district of W London, England, noted for its French and Italian restaurants. Earlier a fashionable quarter, it was popular in the 19th cent. with writers and artists.

soil, substance in which most plants grow. It is made up of disintegrated rock, in the form of sand or clay, and organic matter (decaying vegetation), both in various stages of decomposition. Soils are acid, neutral, or alkaline (see ALKALI SOILS). Fertility may depend on texture, chemical composition, water supply, temperature and nature of subsoil. FERTILIZER may add to a soil's fertility, but unless the humus content is maintained, productivity will eventually decrease.

soilless gardening or **hydroponics,** growing of plants without soil in a medium (e.g., water, sand, gravel, or sawdust) to which nutrients have been added. Nutrient solutions must supply in correct balance nitrogen, phosphorus, potassium, and other essentials to plant growth normally found in soil. Light requirements of the crops must be satisfied. Though soilless gardening is still in an experimental stage, good results have been obtained commercially in producing tomatoes, carnations, roses, and gardenias.

Soissons (swäsŏ'), city (pop. 17,136), Aisne dept., N France, on Aisne R. Scene of decisive victory of CLOVIS I (486). Cap. of several Merovingian kings. Suffered severely in both world wars. Its cathedral (13th cent.) and its ancient abbey, where Thomas à Becket lived, were damaged.

Sojourner Truth: see TRUTH, SOJOURNER.

solan goose: see GANNET.

solar system, SUN and celestial bodies held in their orbits by its power of gravitation. Includes planets (see PLANET; ASTEROID), satellites, some comets and meteors. Theories of origin include NEBULAR HYPOTHESIS, PLANETESIMAL HYPOTHESIS, TIDAL THEORY.

solder (sŏ'dŭr), metal alloy used as a metallic cement. Type used depends on metals to be united. Soft solders are basically lead and tin and have low melting points; hard solders have high melting points and are of metal compounds suited for amalgamation with metals to be joined. When brass is used in the solder or when brass surfaces are to be joined, process is known as brazing, a name sometimes applied also to other hard soldering.

sole, name for several food fish of flatfish order. Most accurately refers to European sole (*Solea vulgaris*); American soles are small and bony. In U.S. flounder, cod, and haddock fillets are often sold as sole.

Solemn League and Covenant: see COVENANTERS.

Solent, the (sŏ'lŭnt), western part of channel between Isle of Wight and Hampshire, England.

Solesmes (sôlĕm'), famous Benedictine abbey, in Solesmes village, Sarthe dept., W France, on Sarthe R. Founded 1010 and enlarged in 19th cent. Led in revival of pure Gregorian chant.

Soleure, Switzerland: see SOLOTHURN.

solfège (sôlfĕzh') [Fr.] or **selfeggio** (sōlfĕd'jō) [Ital.], systems of musical training in vocalization and sight reading using the solmization syllables (do, re, mi, etc.) of Guido d'Arezzo. Term also used to mean training in various fundamentals of music.

Solferino (sôlfärē'nō), village NW of Mantua, N Italy. Scene (1859) of bloody battle between Austrians and allied French and Sardinians (combined casualties, c.30,000). No clear decision was won, but peace was made soon afterward at VILLAFRANCA DI VERONA. J. H. Dunant was present at battle, which inspired him to promote the Red Cross.

solid, one of three states of matter, a substance having both definite shape and volume. Some solids are crystalline, others noncrystalline. Molecules in solids are relatively closer together than in liquid or gas, cohesion between them is greater, and they move more slowly. Solid changes to liquid when temperature is raised to melting point; heat needed is heat of fusion. When substance passes from solid to gas without liquid stage it is sublimation; most substances pass through liquid phase.

Soliman, Ottoman sultans: see SULEIMAN.

Solingen (zō'lĭng-ùn), city (pop. 147,782), North Rhine-

Westphalia, W Germany, on the Wupper and adjoining Wuppertal and Remscheid. Its cutlery mfg. has been famous for centuries. City shared history of duchy of Berg.

Solís, Juan Díaz de (hwän dē'äth dä sōlēs'), d. 1516, Spanish navigator, discoverer of the Río de la Plata. After numerous voyages to New World, he was commissioned (1514) to seek passage between Atlantic and Pacific oceans. He entered estuary of the Río de la Plata (1516) and, landing on coast of present Uruguay, was killed by Indians.

Solnhofen (zō'lùnhō"fùn), village of Middle Franconia, W central Bavaria. Large quarries of lithographic stone near by have yielded fossils of the ARCHAEOPTERIX.

Solomon [Heb.,= peaceful], d. c.932 B.C., king of the Hebrews (c.972–c.932 B.C.), son of David. The bright side of his reign was characterized by peace, commercial expansion, and intensive building (e.g., the Temple at Jerusalem); the dark side by extravagance, heavy taxes, and rising discontent among the northern tribes. Several books of the Bible are traditionally ascribed to him: Proverbs, Ecclesiastes, Wisdom, and Song of Solomon. Among the PSEUDEPIGRAPHA is the Psalms of Solomon. Solomon is in popular legend the figure of the wise man and also the husband of many wives.

Solomon Islands, volcanic groups (16,000 sq. mi.; pop. 160,000), SW Pacific. Includes BOUGAINVILLE, GUADALCANAL, SANTA CRUZ ISLANDS, New Georgia, Choiseul, and Santa Isabela. Natives are Melanesians and Polynesians. Discovered 1567 by Spaniards. S and E Solomons were placed 1893–98 under British protectorate; N Solomons were transferred by treaty from Germany to Great Britain, 1900. Buka and Bougainville are governed separately by Australia as part of Territory of New Guinea. In World War II larger islands were occupied by the Japanese from early 1942 until 1943, when they were taken by Allied forces. Battle of Savo Isl. was only naval action lost by Allies.

Solomons, town, on Solomons Isl., S Md., in Patuxent R. Has fishing and yachting and is seat of Chesapeake Biological Laboratory.

Solomon's-seal, perennial spring-blooming plant of genus *Polygonatum*. Well-known wild flowers of North America, they have small, tubular greenish flowers attached along an arching stalk. False Solomon's-seal (*Smilacina*), a similar plant, has small white flowers in a terminal cluster.

Solon (sō'lùn), c.639–c.559 B.C., Athenian lawgiver. As archon in 594 B.C. he moved to protect the peasants of Attica from losing their farms to capitalists; threw open the assembly to all freemen; gave the Areopagus new powers; created a new Council of Four Hundred. His goal was a moderate democracy. Also a poet.

Solothurn (zō'lōtōōrn), Fr. *Soleure,* canton (306 sq. mi.; pop. 170,325), W Switzerland, mostly in the Jura mts. Agr. Population is mainly German-speaking and Catholic. History is that of its cap., Solothurn (pop. 16,745), on Aar R. Mfg. of electrical apparatus and watches. A free imperial city from 1218, it joined the Swiss Confederation in 1481. The French ambassadors who resided here until the French Revolution held very great power. Has a cathedral (see of bishop of Basel and Lugano) and has some charming medieval architecture.

Solovetski Islands (sùlùvyĕt'skē), archipelago, area c.150 sq. mi., N European RSFSR, in White Sea. On largest island is a 15th-cent. monastery, which became a dreaded place of exile for political prisoners under tsarist and Communist regimes.

Soloviev, Sergei Mikhailovich (sĭrgā' mĕkhī'lùvĭch sùlùvyôf'), 1820–79, Russian historian, author of the monumental *History of Russia* (29 vols., 1851–79, in Russian). His son, **Vladimir Sergeyevich Soloviev** (vlùdyē'mĕr sĭrgā'ùvĭch), 1853–1900, Russian religious philosopher and poet, urged synthesis of Eastern and

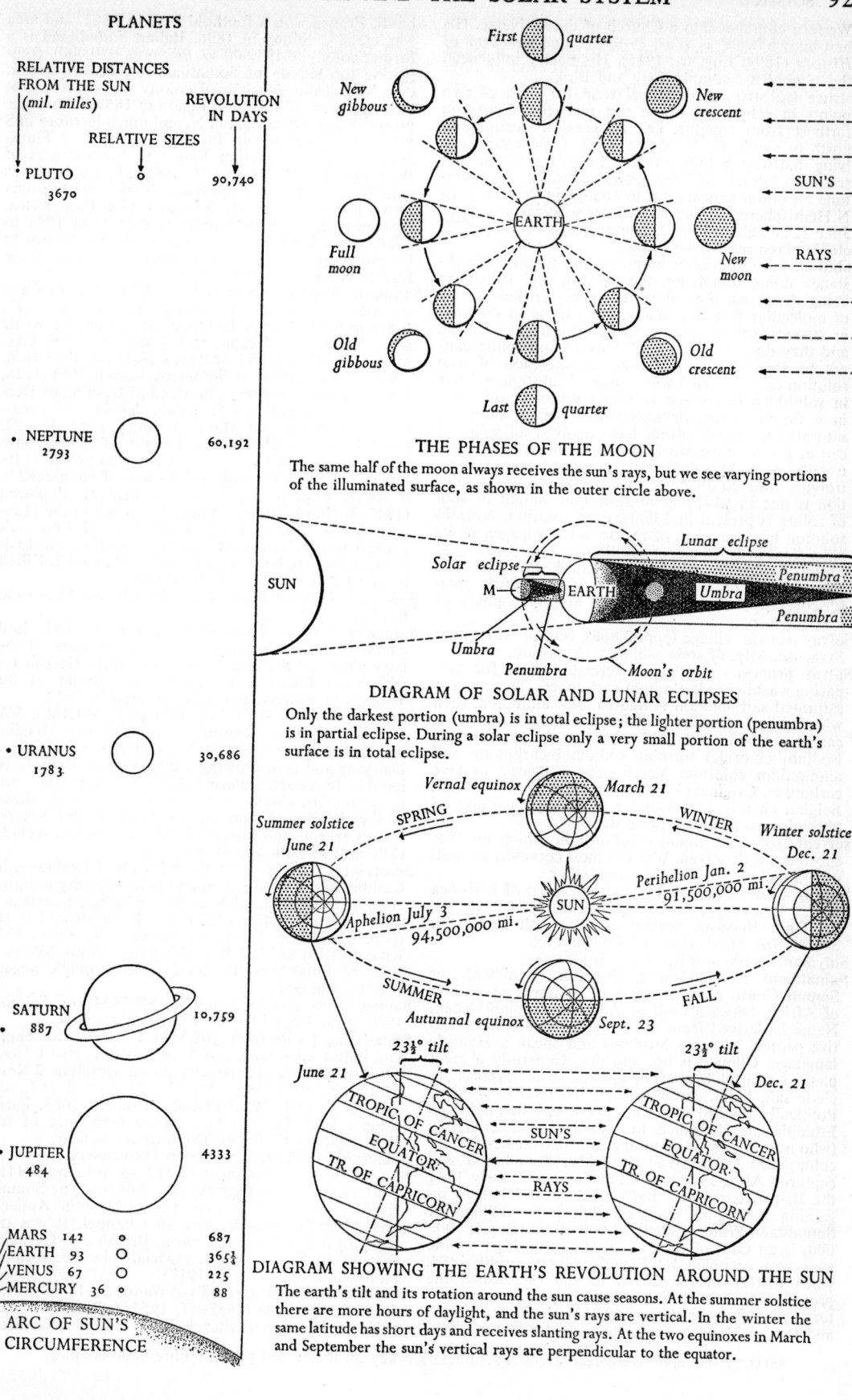

PLANETS

RELATIVE DISTANCES
FROM THE SUN
(mil. miles)

RELATIVE SIZES

REVOLUTION
IN DAYS

PLUTO   90,740
3670

NEPTUNE   60,192
2793

URANUS   30,686
1783

SATURN   10,759
887

JUPITER   4333
484

MARS   142   687
EARTH   93   365¼
VENUS   67   225
MERCURY   36   88

ARC OF SUN'S
CIRCUMFERENCE

First quarter

New gibbous

New crescent

Full moon

New moon

SUN'S

RAYS

Old gibbous

Old crescent

Last quarter

THE PHASES OF THE MOON

The same half of the moon always receives the sun's rays, but we see varying portions
of the illuminated surface, as shown in the outer circle above.

SUN

Solar eclipse

Lunar eclipse

Penumbra

M   EARTH   Umbra

Penumbra

Umbra

Penumbra   Moon's orbit

DIAGRAM OF SOLAR AND LUNAR ECLIPSES

Only the darkest portion (umbra) is in total eclipse; the lighter portion (penumbra)
is in partial eclipse. During a solar eclipse only a very small portion of the earth's
surface is in total eclipse.

Vernal equinox   March 21

Summer solstice   SPRING   WINTER   Winter solstice
June 21   Dec. 21

Perihelion Jan. 2
91,500,000 mi.

Aphelion July 3   SUN
94,500,000 mi.

SUMMER   FALL

Autumnal equinox   Sept. 23

23½° tilt   23½° tilt

June 21   Dec. 21

TROPIC OF CANCER   TROPIC OF CANCER

EQUATOR   SUN'S   EQUATOR

TR. OF CAPRICORN   RAYS   TR. OF CAPRICORN

DIAGRAM SHOWING THE EARTH'S REVOLUTION AROUND THE SUN

The earth's tilt and its rotation around the sun cause seasons. At the summer solstice
there are more hours of daylight, and the sun's rays are vertical. In the winter the
same latitude has short days and receives slanting rays. At the two equinoxes in March
and September the sun's vertical rays are perpendicular to the equator.

Western churches into a Church of the Universe. His best-known work is *War, Progress, and the End of History* (1899; Eng. tr., 1915). His poetry influenced the symbolists, notably Bely and Blok.

solstice (sŏl'stĭs), astronomical term for each of two points in ecliptic at which sun reaches its position farthest from equator, i.e., its greatest declination, north or south. Each solstice is 90° from equinoxes, lying halfway between them. In this position sun seems to "stand still" for several days, i.e., its noon-time elevation appears not to change in that time. In N Hemisphere summer and winter solstices are about June 22 and about Dec. 22 respectively. See *ill.*, p. 927.

soluble glass: see WATER GLASS.

solution. True solution is homogeneous mixture of substance doing dissolving, the solvent, and substance being dissolved, the solute. Particles are held to be of molecular fineness, smaller than those in COLLOID or SUSPENSION, invisible even under ultramicroscope, and they do not "settle out." Solvent and solute cannot be separated by filtration. Composition of true solution can be varied within limits. Substances differ in solubility in specific solvents; solubility of solid in a liquid usually increases with temperature. In saturated solution, solvent has dissolved all solute it can at given temperature. Boiling point of solvent is usually raised by solute, melting point lowered. Electrolytes undergo dissociation in solution. Molar solution is one in which gram-molecular weight or mol of solute is present in 1,000 c.c. of solution. Normal solution has one gram of replaceable hydrogen or its equivalent in 1,000 c.c. of solution.

Solutré (sŏlütra'), village, E central France, near Mâcon. Site of a burial place of prehistoric man (discovered 1867); gives name to Solutrean phase of Paleolithic period.

Solvay (sŏl'vā), village (pop. 7,868), central N.Y., near Syracuse. Mfg. of soda ash, salt, chinaware.

Solvay process (sŏl'vā), commercial process for preparing washing soda (sodium carbonate). Three steps: saturated salt solution is treated with ammonia, then with carbon dioxide, reaction yielding ammonium carbonate; ammonium bicarbonate reacts with salt (sodium chloride) forming sodium bicarbonate and ammonium chloride; bicarbonate is heated to give carbonate. Originated by Ernest Solvay (1838–1922), Belgian chemist and founder of Solvay institutes of physiology and sociology at Brussels.

solvent (sŏl'vŭnt), liquid substance in which another substance is dissolved. Water is most common solvent; others include alcohol, benzene, ether.

Solway Firth (sŏl'wā), inlet (c.40 mi. long) of Irish Sea at Esk R. estuary, separating NW England from SW Scotland. Receives several rivers. Firth figures in Scott's *Guy Mannering* and *Redgauntlet*.

Solyman, Ottoman sultans: see SULEIMAN.

Somaliland (sōmä'lēländ"), **Somalia** (sōmä'lēŭ), or **Somali Coast,** coastal region of easternmost section of Africa, between Gulf of Aden and Indian Ocean. Name is derived from the Somali, the dominant native people, who are Moslems and speak a Hamitic language. Climate is hot and dry. Generally a great plateau fringed by barren coastal strip. Exports include salt, hides, cotton, pearls, and mother-of-pearl. Politically divided into four parts, one belonging to Ethiopia, and the others to Britain, France, and Italy (who now has only temporary control over her former colony). In World War II, British Somaliland was captured Aug., 1940, by Italian forces. In early 1941 the British conquered Italian Somaliland before regaining their own territory. **British Somaliland** or **Somaliland Protectorate** (c.68,000 sq. mi.; pop. c.500,-000) is on Gulf of Aden; cap. Hargeisa. Most of the area was occupied by Egyptian forces until 1884, when British troops moved in and established the protectorate. **French Somaliland** is an overseas territory (c.8,500 sq. mi.; pop. 45,867) on Gulf of Aden and Bab el Mandeb (entrance to Red Sea); cap. Dji-

bouti. France won a foothold here in 1862, and area was made a colony in 1896. **Italian Somaliland** is a former colony (c.194,000 sq. mi.; pop. 970,000), comprising the section of Somaliland on Indian Ocean; cap. Mogadishu. Nucleus of colony was a small protectorate created in central region in 1889; later other protectorates were estab. in N, and much territory in S was ceded by Zanzibar. In 1925 Jubaland or Trans-Juba was detached from Kenya to become part of the Italian possession. In 1936 Italian Somaliland was combined with Somali-speaking districts of Ethiopia into a province of newly formed Italian East Africa. Area was under British military rule from 1941 to 1950, when the UN returned it to Italian control to be exercised until 1959, the provisional date of the former colony's independence.

Sombart, Werner (zôm'bärt), 1863–1941, German economist; professor at Univ. of Berlin after 1917. Influenced by Marx's historical approach, he wrote several analyses of capitalism. Later turned to German romanticism and accepted National Socialism.

Somers, John Somers or **Sommers, Baron,** 1651–1716, English jurist, statesman. Presided at framing of Declaration of Rights 1688. Estab. legality of accession of William and Mary. Attorney general 1692; lord chancellor 1697–1700. Leader of Whig Junto under Queen Anne until Tories came to power 1710.

Somerset, Edmund Beaufort, 2d duke of (sŭ'mùrsĕt"), d. 1455, English statesman and general. Replaced (1447) Richard, duke of York, in France in the Hundred Years War and (by 1453) lost all England's French territories except Calais. Leader of the Lancastrian faction, he was protected by Henry VI. Killed in first battle of Wars of the Roses.

Somerset, Edward Seymour, duke of: see SEYMOUR, family.

Somerset, Robert Carr, earl of, c.1589–1645, lord chamberlain of England. A favorite of James I, he later alienated the king by his arrogance. He and his wife were found guilty (1616) of murder of Sir Thomas OVERBURY, but were released in 1622.

Somerset, county (1,616 sq. mi.; pop. 551,188), SW England; co. town Taunton. Terrain includes Mendip, Exmoor, and Quantock Hills and fertile agr. valleys. Dairying and fruit-growing are important. Bath, fashionable 18th-cent. watering place, has important Roman remains. County is associated with King Alfred and with King Arthur legend. Glastonbury has religious legend and history. Famous churches include cathedral of Bath and Wells.

Somerset. 1 City (pop. 7,097), S Ky., S of Lexington in Cumberland foothills. Rail and industrial city in farm, coal, and timber area. Near by are national cemetery and Zollicoffer Memorial Park. **2** Residential town (pop. 8,566), SE Mass., on Taunton R. above Fall River; settled 1677. **3** Borough (pop. 5,936), SW Pa., ESE of Pittsburgh. Products include maple sugar, lumber, and coal.

Somersworth, city (pop. 6,927), SE N.H., on Salmon Falls R. and N of Dover. Electrical machinery.

Somerville. 1 City (pop. 102,351), E Mass., residential and industrial suburb just N of Boston; settled 1630. Food, paper, metal products; auto assembling. **2** Residential borough (pop. 11,571), N central N.J., on Raritan R. and SW of Plainfield; settled 1683. Farm trade center. Has Wallace House (residence of the Washingtons, 1778–79). Duke estate is near.

Somerville College: see OXFORD UNIVERSITY.

Somme (sôm), department (2,424 sq. mi.; pop. 441,-368), N France, in Picardy; cap. Amiens. The **Somme** river, 152 mi. long, flows past Saint-Quentin, Amiens, and Abbeville into the English Channel. It was the scene of heavy fighting between British and Germans throughout World War I, especially in the so-called battles of Somme (1916, 1917).

Somoza, Anastacio (änästa'syō sōmō'sä), 1896–, president of Nicaragua (1937–47; 1951–). Became virtual ruler of Nicaragua after a coup (1936). His dictatorial rule met bitter criticism of the Caribbean League and liberals throughout the world.

sonar (sō'när), naval device using sound waves for navigation and ranging. First used in World War II to detect enemy submarines, torpedoes, and mines. Usually the device operates by emitting its own sound waves which are reflected back by any object in their path; the sonar device receives the echo of the reflected waves and the echo is converted into an electric current and interpreted for range, speed, bearing, and nature of the target.

sonata (sùnä'tù), a form of instrumental composition which arose in the baroque period in Italy. The music of baroque sonatas was usually contrapuntal in texture; the rococo sonata had one outstanding melodic line and accompanying harmonic background. The classical sonata was developed by Haydn and Mozart; the first movement (and sometimes others) is in what is called **sonata form.** This form consists of an exposition of two (or more) contrasting themes, their development, and recapitulation. It is used in the string quartet, the symphony, and to some extent the concerto.

Sonderborg, Dan. *Sønderborg* (sû'nùrbôr), town (pop. 16,204), SE Jutland, Denmark; also known by its German name, Sonderburg. A port on the Als Sound, it also has textile and other mfg. It was part of SCHLESWIG until the 16th cent., when Christian III of Denmark created the duchy of Sonderburg for his younger son John, from whom the branch of Schleswig-Holstein-Sonderburg-Glücksburg (the present Danish royal line) is descended. Annexed to Prussia 1866; restored to Denmark by a plebiscite 1920.

Sonderbund (zôn'dùrbŏont) [Ger.,= separate league], 1845–47, defensive alliance of the Catholic cantons of Switzerland—Uri, Schwyz, Unterwalden, Lucerne, Valais, Fribourg, Zug—against the Radical party's anticlerical measures and program for closer federal union. The Radical majority in the federal diet declared the Sonderbund dissolved (1847) and dispatched a federal army under Gen. Dufour against the separatist forces. The Sonderbund's defeat in an almost bloodless campaign led to the adoption of a federal constitution (1848) and the expulsion of the Jesuits from Switzerland.

song, one of the most natural forms of musical expression, found in all cultures. In Western music, song is broadly classified as art song or folk song. Early art songs were those of the troubadour and meistersinger. The refined, lyrical *air de cour* of late 16th-cent. France provided inspiration for the *ayre* of early 17th-cent. English lutanists such as Thomas Campion and Thomas Morley. Outstanding among art songs is the German romantic lied of the 19th cent., in which the vocal line and piano accompaniment have equal musical significance. The style reached its peak in works of Schubert, Schumann, Brahms, and Hugo Wolf. All nations have contributed much to art-song literature, with perhaps the exception of Italy, where attention centered on the opera and the aria.

song, bird. Songs, call notes, and certain mechanical sounds constitute bird communication. Song, usually confined to male, is at its height in breeding season. It serves to announce selection of nesting place, warns away other males, and attracts females. Song is produced in syrinx at base of windpipe, is modified by larynx and tongue.

Song of Solomon, Song of Songs, or **Canticles,** book of Old Testament, written in form of a love poem, traditionally ascribed to Solomon. Accepted in Jewish and Christian canon as an allegory or parable of God's love for Israel, for the Church, and for the soul that loves Him.

sonnet, poem of 14 lines, usually in iambic pentameter, in definite rhyme scheme. The main types are the Italian (Petrarchan) sonnet, an octave and sestet rhyming *abbaabba cdecde,* and the Elizabethan (Shak-

sperian) sonnet, three quatrains and couplet rhyming *abab cdcd efef gg.* Essence of sonnet is unity of thought or idea.

Sonnino, Sidney, Barone (bärō'nä sōn-nē'nō), 1847–1922, Italian statesman and economist. Minister of finance 1893–96; premier (1906, 1909–10). As foreign minister in World War I he negotiated secret Treaty of London (1915), by which Italy joined Allies in return for promises of vast territorial gains. He and ORLANDO represented Italy at Paris Peace Conference (1919).

Sonoma (sùnō'mù), city (pop. 2,015), W Calif., N of San Francisco; founded 1835. J. C. FRÉMONT raised Bear Flag of Calif. republic here in 1846.

Sonora (sōnō'rä), state (70,484 sq. mi.; pop. 503,095), NW Mexico; cap. Hermosillo. On Gulf of California, S of Ariz., it is mountainous with vast desert stretches. Agr. by irrigation, cattle raising, and mining are chief occupations. Hermosillo, Guaymas, and Nogales (on Ariz. border) are principal cities. Spanish exploration of area was intensive after Coronado's expedition (1540). Originally part of Nueva Viscaya, it was later joined to Sinaloa. They were made separate states in 1830.

Sonora (sùnô'rù). **1** City (pop. 2,448), central Calif., E of Stockton, in famed Mother Lode gold-mining area. Site of Big Bonanza mine. **2** Ranch town (pop. 2,633), W Texas, S of San Angelo and on Dry Fork of Devils R.

Sons of Liberty, secret societies in American colonies, organized in protest against Stamp Act. In Civil War, name was adopted by KNIGHTS OF THE GOLDEN CIRCLE in 1864.

Sons of the American Revolution, national patriotic organization, founded in N.Y. in 1889 by union of Sons of Revolutionary Sires and certain members of the Society of the Sons of the Revolution. Membership is open to those whose ancestors saw active service in Revolutionary forces.

Soochow (sōō'jō), city (pop. 381,288), S Kiangsu prov., China, on Grand Canal, in scenic lake district. Textile mills. Dates from c.1000 B.C. Became treaty port 1896. Held 1937–45 by the Japanese. Formerly called Wuhsien.

Soong (sōōng), Chinese family prominent in public affairs. **Soong Yao-ju** or **Charles Jones Soong,** d. 1924, was a Methodist missionary and merchant in Shanghai. His son, **T. V. Soong,** 1894–, was educated at Harvard Univ. Ranked second to Chiang Kai-shek in Nationalist government, 1945–49. Left China 1949, resigned from Kuomintang to remain abroad (1950). Soong Yao-ju's three daughters all graduated from colleges in U.S. **Soong Ai-ling** (ī-lǐng'), 1888–, is wife of H. H. Kung. **Soong Ching-ling** (chǐng'-lǐng'), 1890–, married Sun Yat-sen, 1915. After his death (1925) she held high posts in Nationalist government; left it twice (1927, 1945) in protest against anti-Communist policy. In 1949 she became non-Communist member of central executive committee of Chinese People's Republic. **Soong Mei-ling** (mā'-lǐng'), 1896–, married Chiang Kai-shek, 1927. Addressed U.S. Congress 1943; again visited U.S. 1948 to seek aid for Nationalists. Joined husband on Formosa, 1950.

soot, black or brown deposit resulting from imperfect combustion of high-carbon fuel and consisting of amorphous carbon and tarry substances. Lampblack is fine soot used in making printer's and India ink.

Sophia (sōfī'ù, Ger. zōfē'ä), 1630–1714, electress of Hanover, consort of Elector Ernest Augustus; daughter of Frederick the Winter King and Elizabeth of Bohemia; granddaughter of James I of England. Through Act of SETTLEMENT (1701) her son succeeded to English throne as George I (1714).

Sophia, Santa: see HAGIA SOPHIA.

Sophia Alekseyevna (sō'fyù ùlyĭksyä'ĭvnù), 1657–1704, regent of Russia (1682–89). Ruled autocratically during minority of her brother IVAN V and her half-brother PETER I. Peter overthrew her after accusing her of plotting against his life and confined her to a convent (1689). In 1698, charging her with instigating a revolt of the Strelitsi (Moscow garrison), he forced her to take the veil.

Sophia Dorothea, 1666–1726, electress of Hanover, wife of Elector George Louis (later George I of England). Divorced (1694) for an alleged love affair, she was thereafter imprisoned.

sophist (sŏ'fĭst), in present usage, one who employs seemingly sound but fallacious arguments. Somewhat unfairly derived from the Greek Sophists, teachers who denied the possibility of reaching objective truth. Their chief function was to instill worldly wisdom in rich pupils. Socrates attacked them violently.

Sophocles (sŏ'fŭklēz), c.496–c.406 B.C., Greek tragic poet. Gained first dramatic triumph (over Aeschylus) in 468 B.C. and thereafter won first place about 20 times. He added a third actor, introduced scene painting, and abandoned the trilogy for the self-contained tragedy. His characters, on a more human level than those of Aeschylus, are governed in their fate more by their own faults than by the gods. Seven complete plays survive: *Ajax, Antigone, Oedipus Rex* or *Oedipus Tyrannus* (in which Greek dramatic irony reaches an apex; cited by Aristotle as a perfect example of tragedy), *Electra,* the *Trachiniae, Philoctetes,* and *Oedipus at Colonus.*

Sophonias (sŏ'fŭnī'ŭs), Greek form of ZEPHANIAH.

Sophonisba (sŏfŭnĭz'bŭ), 3d cent. B.C., Carthaginian lady, daughter of Hasdrubal, the brother of Hannibal. Legend (partly true) says she was betrothed to Masinissa before her father married her to Syphax of Numidia, who became an ally of Carthage. When he was defeated and slain by Masinissa (203 B.C.), the victor, to keep her from gracing a Roman triumph, sent her a bowl of poison to drink.

Sopron (shô'prôn), Ger. *Ödenburg,* city (pop. 42,255), W Hungary, in Hungarian section of BURGENLAND. An old cultural center, it has three 13th-cent. churches, a 15th-cent. palace, and a university.

Soracte (sōräk'tē), isolated mountain, 2,267 ft. high, central Italy, N of Rome. Celebrated by Vergil and Horace.

Soranus (sùrā'nùs), fl. 1st–2d cent., Greek physician. His treatise on obstetrics, diseases of women, and pediatrics influential until 16th cent.

Sorbonne (sôrbôn'), traditional name of the Univ. of Paris, France; more properly, the name of its first endowed college, founded by Robert de Sorbon (1201–74), chaplain of Louis IX, and opened c.1257. Because of its academic and theological reputation it gained precedence over earlier colleges at Paris; its doctors were often called upon to render decisions on important ecclesiastical and theological issues; its name was extended to the entire faculty of theology. The Univ. of Paris was thoroughly reorganized in the 19th cent., and the name Sorbonne is not official.

Sorbs: see WENDS.

Sordello (sôrdĕl'lō), 13th cent., Italian poet, author of Provençal verse; immortalized by a reference in Dante, subject of a poem by Browning.

Sorel, Agnès (änyĕs' sôrĕl'), c.1422–1450, mistress of Charles VII of France after 1444. Famed for her beauty and intelligence; had beneficial influence on king's policies. Unfounded rumor that she was poisoned was spread by enemies of Jacques CŒUR.

Sorel, Georges (zhôrzh'), 1847–1922, French social philosopher, author of *Reflections on Violence* (1908). Finding in democracy the triumph of mediocrity, he espoused syndicalism and the creation of a revolutionary elite. His views influenced Fascism.

Sorel, city (pop. 14,961), S Que., Canada, on St. Lawrence R. at mouth of Richelieu R. and NNE of Montreal. Grain shipping center with shipbuilding and iron and steel foundries. Fort Richelieu built here 1665.

sorghum, cornlike annual grass (*Sorghum vulgare*), widely cultivated in many varieties, and bearing grain in panicles. Sorghums are cultivated for forage and fodder and the grain is used for livestock feed. A molasses is obtained from sweet sorghum. Other varieties include milo, kaffir corn, broomcorn, Sudan grass, feterita, durra.

Sorokin, Pitirim Alexandrovitch (sōrō'kĭn), 1889–, Russian-American historian and sociologist. Banished by Bolsheviks, he came to U.S. 1923; naturalized 1930. Works include *Sociology of Revolution* (1925), *Social and Cultural Dynamics* (4 vols., 1937–41), and *Russia and the United States* (1944).

Sorolla y Bastida, Joaquín (hwäkēn' sōrō'lyä ē bästē'dhä), 1863–1923, Spanish painter of large figure compositions in full, glowing sunlight.

sorrel, name for several plants, especially DOCK and OXALIS.

Sorrento (sùrĕn'tō, Ital. sōr-rĕn'tō), town (pop. 7,031), Campania, S Italy; a famous resort on the Bay of Naples. Birthplace of Tasso.

Sosen (sōsän'), 1747–1821, Japanese painter, noted for animal paintings (esp. monkeys). His name literally means "monkey saint."

Sothern, Edward A(skew) (sŭ'dhùrn), 1826–81, English actor; in U.S. after 1852. Acted in such dramas as *Camille* and *Our American Cousin.* His son, **E(dward) H(ugh) Sothern,** 1859–1933, acted with Frohman's Lyceum company (1886–99) in such plays as *The Prisoner of Zenda* and *If I Were King.* Acted Shakspere almost exclusively after 1900, co-starring with Julia MARLOWE (whom he married in 1911).

Soto, Hernando de: see DE SOTO, HERNANDO.

Soufrière, volcano, 4,048 ft. high, on St. Vincent, British West Indies. Eruption in 1902 laid waste a third of island, killing more than 1,000 people.

soul, vital principle of a body, conceived as existing with it. Materialist philosophies deny its existence, pantheism denies that the soul can be individual. The concept on various levels (e.g., the idea of a world soul) is known in various religions and philosophies. Among many Christians it is considered the thinking life of man opposed to the material body. The scholastics distinguished among the rational soul of man, the animal soul of beasts, and the vegetative soul of plants, considering only the rational soul immortal. The question of the soul's immortality has been debated from Plato's time to ours. Some Eastern religions do not distinguish the soul of man from that of animals.

Soulé, Pierre (pyĕr' sōōlā'), 1801–70, American political leader and diplomat, b. France. U.S. Senator from La. (1847, 1849–53). Minister to Spain (1853–54); helped draft OSTEND MANIFESTO. Served in government of Confederacy (1863–64).

Soulouque, Faustin Élie (fōstē' ālē' sōōlōōk'), c.1785–1867, Negro emperor of Haiti (1849–59). An illiterate ex-slave, he became president (1847) and then declared himself emperor as Faustin I. Reign was corrupt and bloody.

Soult, Nicolas (nēkôlä' sōōlt'), 1769–1851, marshal of France; created duke of Dalmatia by Napoleon I (1808). Commanded in PENINSULAR WAR 1808–13. Minister of war under Louis XVIII (1814), but joined Napoleon in Hundred Days. Under Louis Philippe he again was minister of war (1830–34) and prime minister (1840–44).

Sound, the: see ORESUND.

sound, waves of vibratory motion radiating from a body moving to and fro so as to cause alternately in a given space a condensation and a rarefaction of molecules. Sound wave is longitudinal since vibration is along direction of wave. WAVE length depends on velocity in a given medium at a given temperature and on frequency of vibration of body causing sound. Sounds of frequencies of c.20–20,000 vibrations per second are considered audible to human ear. Sound is conducted best through dense media; will not pass through vacuum. Pitch is higher as frequency increases; sound is louder as vibration amplitude is greater; intensity decreases as distance from source increases. Sound waves can be reflected (see ECHO), refracted, or absorbed. See also INTERFERENCE; DOPPLER'S PRINCIPLE.

sound recording, process of converting acoustic energy of sound waves into electromechanical energy for inscription on various substances. In disk recording, sound-wave frequencies are converted into electrical voltages which vibrate a stylus, causing the stylus to cut into a soft disk revolving beneath it; the cuts (groovings) vary with the amplitude and frequency of the voltage. The soft disk serves as a mold for making a metal stamp from which more durable disks are pressed. In reproduction, as the disk revolves, a needle traverses the grooves and transmits the vibrations to a diaphragm; the vibrations of the diaphragm produce a voltage which is reconverted into sound waves and passed on to a loudspeaker. One device for reproducing recorded sound is the PHONOGRAPH. In wire or tape recording, disturbances in a magnetic field cause varying realignments of magnetic particles in the wire or tape passing through the field; when the wire is played back, the realignments redisturb the field and produce a voltage. Sound recordings for use with motion pictures are commonly made on film and interpret the acoustic characteristics of sound into photo or light characteristics.

sour gum: see BLACK GUM.

Souris (sŏŏ'rĭs), river, c.435 mi. long, rising in S Saskatchewan, looping into N.Dak., and entering Assiniboine R. in SW Manitoba.

Sousa, John Philip (sŏŏ'zù), 1854–1932, American bandmaster and composer. He was leader of the U.S. Marine Band from 1880 to 1892, when he formed his own band. In 1910–11 he and his band toured the world. He wrote c.100 marches, including *Semper fidelis, The Washington Post March, The Stars and Stripes Forever,* and comic operas, such as *El Capitan.*

Sousa, Martim Afonso de (märtēn' äfô'zō dù sō'zù), 1500?–1571?, Portuguese colonial administrator. Commissioned (1530) to drive French from Brazilian coast and to estab. colonies, he did both. He was true founder of Brazil.

South, the, region of U.S. embracing all of the southeast and part of the southwest. It includes, at the most, 14 states—Md., Va., N.C., S.C., Ga., Fla., Ky., Tenn., Ala., Miss., Ark., La., Okla., Texas. To many the region is restricted to 11 states below the Potomac which comprised the CONFEDERACY. The South has many distinctive areas. Whole region has greater humidity, more sunshine, less wind than other sections. Predominantly agr. economy led to introduction of NEGRO as source of cheap labor under institutions of plantation and SLAVERY. The MISSOURI COMPROMISE marked rise of Southern sectionalism, rooted in doctrine of STATES' RIGHTS. The Old South died in RECONSTRUCTION period after CIVIL WAR; increased industrialization came later. Agrarian revolt of late 19th cent. turned conservative Democrats out of power. Various Southern demagogues have achieved national attention (e.g., Huey LONG); so, too, has latter-day KU KLUX KLAN. The South has always had a strong regional literature.

South, University of the, called **Sewanee,** Sewanee, Tenn., on Cumberland Plateau and E of Winchester; Episcopal; for men; chartered 1858, opened 1868. Arts and sciences, theology, military academy. Publishes *Sewanee Review.*

South Africa, Union of, dominion (472,494 sq. mi.; pop. 11,418,349) of British Commonwealth of Nations; cap. Pretoria. Bounded on W by the Atlantic and on E by Indian Ocean. Comprises four provinces, CAPE OF GOOD HOPE, NATAL, ORANGE FREE STATE, and TRANSVAAL; administers SOUTH-WEST AFRICA. Basutoland is an enclave. Drakensburg mts. are in E, but country is mostly a plateau (2,000–6,000 ft. high). Climate is mild and dry. Crops include cereals, tobacco, cotton, peanuts, fruits, and sugar. Mineral wealth is enormous. Gold (mined mainly in WITWATERSRAND) makes up half of export volume. Other important minerals are diamonds (at Kimberley), coal, copper, iron, and manganese. Commerce, largely developed by Cecil RHODES, centers on JOHANNESBURG; major ports are CAPETOWN and DURBAN. First European to visit South Africa was the Portuguese Bartholomew Diaz (1488). Dutch East India Co. estab. first white settlement on the cape in 1652. In 1841 the British assumed control over the area. Boer settlers migrated N in 1830s to found republics of Transvaal, Orange Free State, and Natal. In latter half of 19th cent. the discovery of diamonds in Orange Free State and of gold in Transvaal brought numerous prospectors, mainly British, against whom the Boer governments took repressive measures. Mutual hostility exploded in SOUTH AFRICAN WAR (1899–1902). British victory was followed 1910 by establishment of Union of South Africa, but Boer population was recognized by retention of Roman-Dutch law and by making Afrikaans an official language along with English. Two main political parties developed: the Unionist, headed by J. C. SMUTS, who advocated cooperation between the Boer and British elements; and the Nationalist, which espoused Boer superiority and even opposed the country's entry into World War II. After the war, race relations became increasingly strained as the Nationalists, led by Daniel MALAN, sought to ensure white supremacy at all costs. The repressive Nationalist policy was violently opposed by the nonwhites, who comprise 8,000,000 Negroes, 300,000 immigrants from India, and 700,000 "Coloreds" or part-white persons (the only nonwhite group with the right to vote). In 1952 Malan clashed with the South African supreme court when he resorted to unconstitutional means in trying to disfranchise the "Coloreds."

South African War or **Boer War,** 1899–1902, war of the South African Republic (Transvaal) and Orange Free State against Great Britain. The Boers had long resented the British advance into S African territories, and the hostility was inflamed after the discovery of gold (1886) brought an influx of British prospectors. The Boer government denied these newcomers citizenship and taxed them heavily, despite British protests. The situation was aggravated in 1895 by the Jameson raid (see JAMESON, SIR LEANDER STARR), which was interpreted by S. J. P. KRUGER as a British plot to seize Transvaal and which led to the military alliance of Transvaal and Orange Free State (1896). The British brought in troops to defend what they considered their commercial rights. When they refused to withdraw, the Boer states declared war (Oct. 12, 1899). The large and well-equipped Boer forces won great victories, capturing Mafeking and besieging Kimberley and Ladysmith. But the tide turned in 1900, with the landing of heavy British reinforcements. Under the leadership of F. S. Roberts and Lord Kitchener the British occupied all the major cities and formally annexed the Boer states. The war was thought to be over, and Kitchener remained only for the mopping-up. The Boers, however, began guerrilla attacks, led by such men as Botha and Smuts. Kitchener struck back by interning Boer women and children and building chains of blockhouses to cut off large areas, while his troops combed the guerrilla country, section by section. Boer submission was formalized in the Treaty of Vereeniging (May 31, 1902). The bitterness caused by the war continues to affect political life in South Africa.

South Amboy, city (pop. 8,422), E N.J., on harbor at Raritan R. mouth (bridged) opposite Perth Amboy. Transships coal; makes clay products. Terminal (1832) of Camden and Amboy RR, state's first.

South America, continent (c.6,850,000 sq. mi.; pop. c.110,000,000), S continent of the W Hemisphere. Divided politically into 10 republics (ARGENTINA, BOLIVIA, BRAZIL, CHILE, COLOMBIA, ECUADOR, PARAGUAY, PERU, URUGUAY, and VENEZUELA) and three colonies

(British, Dutch, and French GUIANA). Geographical features include: the ANDES, range of mountains paralleling Pacific coast; great river systems emptying into Atlantic (N to S—MAGDALENA, ORINOCO, AMAZON, RÍO DE LA PLATA); GUIANA HIGHLANDS in Guiana and Venezuela; the PAMPA and frigid PATAGONIA; desert of ATACAMA in Chile; Lake TITICACA in Andes. See *map*, p. 933.

Southampton, Thomas Wriothesley, 1st earl of (rŏt′slē; rĭs′lē), 1505–50, lord chancellor of England. Noted for severity, he was dismissed by Edward Seymour. Later helped overthrow Seymour as protector. His grandson, **Henry Wriothesley, 3d earl of Southampton,** 1573–1624, was a patron of letters. He is best known as patron of William Shakspere. Sometimes thought to be man to whom sonnets are dedicated and by some thought to be author of Shakspere. Deeply involved in rebellion (1601) of Robert Devereux, earl of Essex, he was imprisoned by Elizabeth I. Restored to favor by James I. His son, **Thomas Wriothesley, 4th earl of Southampton,** 1607–67, was an adviser of Charles I. Opposed extreme policies of Strafford. Negotiated for king with Parliament (1643, 1645).

Southampton, county borough (pop. 178,326), Hampshire, England, at head of Southampton Water. Has large dockyards and is a major port. Was one of chief British military transport stations in both world wars. There are many ancient churches and buildings. Crusaders and Pilgrim Fathers embarked here. City has shipbuilding and varied mfg. Center of city was almost entirely destroyed by bombing in 1940. Administrative county of Southampton is mainland part of HAMPSHIRE.

Southampton, village (pop. 4,042), on SE Long Isl., SE N.Y. Summer resort with many fine estates. Here is Parrish Memorial Art Mus.

Southampton Insurrection, 1831, slave uprising in Va., led by Nat TURNER.

South Australia, state (380,070 sq. mi.; pop. 646,216), S Australia; cap. Adelaide. Bounded on N by Northern Territory, on S by Indian Ocean, on W by Western Australia, and on E by New South Wales and Victoria. Coastal area was visited 1627 by the Dutch. In 1836 South Australia became a British colony and in 1901 a state of the commonwealth. Included Northern Territory from 1863 to 1911, when it was transferred to federal government. Much of the state is wasteland, and population is largely concentrated in fertile SE area. Chief exports are pig lead, silver, wheat, wool, wine, and meat.

South Bakersfield, village (pop. 12,120), S central Calif., near Bakersfield.

South Bass Island: see PUT IN BAY.

South Bend, city (pop. 115,911), N Ind., on great bend of St. Joseph R. and ESE of Chicago; settled 1820 on site of French mission, trading post. Center for farming, dairying area. Mfg. of metal products, paint, paper, clothing. Univ. of NOTRE DAME and St. Mary's Col. (R.C.; for women; opened 1844, chartered 1851 at Bertrand, Mich., chartered 1853 by Indiana, moved 1855, became col. 1903) are near by.

South Boston, town (pop. 6,057), S Va., on Ran R. and ENE of Danville. Has important tobacco market.

South Bound Brook, industrial borough (pop. 2,905), N central N.J., on Raritan R. opposite Bound Brook. Von Steuben had hq. here 1778–79.

Southbridge, town (pop. 17,519), including Southbridge village (pop. 16,748), S Mass., SW of Worcester; settled 1730. Optical, textile, metal products.

South Carolina, state (31,055 sq. mi.; pop. 2,117,027), SE U.S.; one of Thirteen Colonies; cap. COLUMBIA. CHARLESTON, GREENVILLE, SPARTANBURG largest cities. Bounded on W and S by Savannah R., E by the Atlantic. Fall line separates coastal plain from piedmont. Blue Ridge in NW. Other rivers are PEE DEE, SANTEE, EDISTO. Cotton, tobacco, corn main agr. products; also grains, truck, fruit. Mining (clay, granite, gravel, limestone). Mfg. of cotton textiles main indus-

try; also lumbering, fishing. Short-lived Spanish and French settlements before English founded colony at Albemarle Point 1670 (moved to Charleston 1680). Indian and Spanish threats eventually removed. Became royal colony 1729. Rice and indigo were then main crops. In American Revolution British took Charleston in second attempt (1780). Ensuing CAROLINA CAMPAIGN forced British to retreat. First state to secede (Dec. 20, 1860) from Union; firing on Fort Sumter (see SUMTER, FORT) opened war. W. T. SHERMAN destroyed much of state in 1865. Suffered under Reconstruction. Soil erosion, high illiteracy rate, and discrimination are problems recently confronting state.

South Carolina, University of: see COLUMBIA.

South Carolina State Agricultural and Mechanical College: see ORANGEBURG.

South Charleston, town (pop. 16,686), W W.Va., on Kanawha R. and near Charleston; settled c.1900. Mfg. of chemicals; U.S. naval ordnance plant.

South China Sea, arm of the Pacific Ocean, between SE Asian mainland and Malay Archipelago.

Southcott, Joanna, 1750–1814, English religious visionary. Uneducated, she claimed (c.1792) the gift of prophecy and gained many followers.

South Dakota, state (77,047 sq. mi.; pop. 652,740), N central U.S.; admitted 1889 as 40th state; cap. PIERRE. Missouri R. bisects state. BLACK HILLS and BADLANDS are in SW. Agr. of grains (esp. corn, rye, wheat); dairying, livestock. Mining (gold, silver, feldspar, tantalum, lithium, limestone). Processes farm products; mfg. of farm implements and wood products. Land of SIOUX INDIANS. Dakota Territory estab. 1861. Immigrants came with railroad. Gold rush occurred in 1870s, continued despite trouble with Indians. DEADWOOD and LEAD had brief heyday. Boom stimulated settlement and cattle ranching. Hurt by recurrent droughts and depression of 1930s. Irrigation and power projects, erosion measures brought relief; proposed MISSOURI RIVER BASIN PROJECT would aid area.

South Dakota, University of: see VERMILLION.

South Dakota School of Mines and Technology: see RAPID CITY.

South Dakota State College of Agriculture and Mechanic Arts: see BROOKINGS.

Southdown sheep: see SHEEP.

South Downs: see DOWNS, THE, chalk hills.

Southend-on-Sea, county borough (pop. 151,830), Essex, England; popular seaside resort.

Southern Alps, mountain range, on South Isl., New Zealand, paralleling W coast and containing Mt. Cook (12,349 ft.), dominion's highest peak.

Southern California, University of, at Los Angeles; nonsectarian, private, coed.; chartered and opened 1880 by Methodists. Affiliates are Los Angeles Univ. of International Relations and dental college.

Southern Methodist University, at University Park, Texas (suburb of Dallas); coed.; chartered 1911, opened 1915. Has theater and history museums.

Southern Pacific Company, transportation system chartered in 1865 in Calif., reincorporated in Ky. in 1884 and in Del. in 1947. Built in S Calif. to provide Central Pacific RR with feeder lines and eventually to connect San Francisco and New Orleans. In 1884 the Southern Pacific and the Central Pacific were combined under Leland STANFORD and C. P. HUNTINGTON as a unit of interdependent systems. E. H. HARRIMAN expanded the railroads. In 1923 the Southern Pacific leased the Central Pacific RR's facilities. Also controls bus lines in Far West and a trucking service.

Southern Pines, winter resort (pop. 4,272), central N.C., SW of Raleigh. Mild climate; sports.

Southern Rhodesia (rōdē′zhù), British colony (150,333 sq. mi.; pop. 2,021,900), SE Africa; cap. Salisbury. Bordered on NW by Northern Rhodesia and on N and E by Mozambique. Mainly a high plateau. Gold, asbestos, coal, and chromite are mined; cotton, tobacco, peanuts, and wheat are grown. Stock raising and lumbering are also important. Originally

CAPITAL CITIES are designated by CAPITAL AND SMALL CAPITAL type

inhabited by the Mashona tribe, who were supplanted by the MATABELE. Occupied 1888 by the British. When RHODESIA was divided (1923), S Rhodesia became a colony ruled by an appointed governor. A legislative council is elected by white British subjects.

Southern University and Agricultural and Mechanical College: see BATON ROUGE, La.

South Euclid (ū'klĭd), city (pop. 15,432), NE Ohio, NE suburb of Cleveland. Seat of Notre Dame Col.

Southey, Robert (sou'dhē, sŭ'–), 1774–1843, English poet and historian. In 1803 he settled in the Lake District with Coleridge and Wordsworth. In 1813 he became poet laureate. His ambitious epics are little read; he is remembered rather for shorter poems (e.g., "The Battle of Blenheim" and "Inchcape Rock"). His prose includes a history of Brazil, a history of the Peninsular War (1823–32), and a masterly life of Nelson (1813).

South Gastonia (găstō'nĕù), village (pop. 6,465), S N.C., S of Gastonia. Post office name, Pinkney.

South Gate, city (pop. 51,116), S Calif., S of Los Angeles. Mfg. of furniture, building materials, tires, and chemicals.

South Georgia, island (c.1,450 sq. mi.; pop. c.700 during whaling season, c.250 at other times), S Atlantic, c.1,200 mi. E of Cape Horn. Capt. James Cook took possession for British in 1775. Included as dependency in British colony of Falkland Isls. Also claimed by Argentina.

South Hadley, town (pop. 10,145), W Mass., on Connecticut R. above Springfield; settled c.1660. Mfg. of paper. Seat of Mt. Holyoke Col. (hōl'yōk) (nonsectarian; for women; provides graduate work); chartered 1836, opened 1837 as Mt. Holyoke Female Seminary by Mary LYON, rechartered and renamed 1888 and 1893; model for many early women's schools.

South Haven, resort city (pop. 5,629), SW Mich., on L. Michigan at mouth of Black R. and N of Benton Harbor. Center of fruitgrowing area with fisheries and mfg. of pianos and organs.

South Holland, Dutch *Zuidholland,* province (1,085 sq. mi.; pop. 2,284,080), W Netherlands, on the North Sea; cap. The Hague. Other chief cities include Rotterdam and Leiden. Similar in character to NORTH HOLLAND, with which it was united until 1840 as HOLLAND.

Southington, village (pop. 5,955) in Southington town (pop. 13,061), central Conn., SW of Hartford; settled 1696. Mfg. of metal and wood products.

South Island (58,093 sq. mi.; pop. 556,006), New Zealand, larger of the dominion's two principal islands. SOUTHERN ALPS are dominant physical feature, with certain sections included in national parks. Wild SW area is mainly in Fiordland Natl. Park. Grain, timber, and sheep are chief products. Some coal and gold are mined in W. Christchurch and Dunedin are principal centers.

South Kingstown (kĭng'stŭn), town (pop. 10,148), S R.I., between Narragansett and Charlestown; settled 1641. Textiles. Narragansett Indians made final stand 1675 W of Kingston village in the town. Seat of Univ. of Rhode Island (land-grant; coed.); chartered 1888, opened as school 1890, became college of agriculture and mechanic arts 1892, named R.I. State Col. 1909, renamed 1950.

South Manchurian Railroad, trunk line between Changchun and Dairen. Originally part of Russian-built Chinese Eastern RR (with main section in N Manchuria), it was part of Japan's indemnity after Russo-Japanese War (1904–5). After World War II entire Manchurian rail system (renamed Chinese Changchun RR) passed to joint Soviet-Chinese control. The **South Manchurian Railroad Company** was main agency of Japanese penetration of Manchuria. It controlled all major economic activities (e.g., coal and iron mining, harbor improvements, and construction of towns).

South Milwaukee (mĭlwô'kē), city (pop. 12,855), SE Wis., on L. Michigan near Milwaukee; settled 1835. Mfg. of electrical equipment and machinery.

South Norfolk, city (pop. 10,434), SE Va., suburb of Norfolk. Has lumber milling.

South Norwalk, Conn.: see NORWALK.

Southold (south'hōld), town (pop. 11,632), on NE Long Isl., SE N.Y., on Long Isl. Sound; settled 1640. Includes resort village of Southold (pop. 1,027).

South Orange, residential suburban village (pop. 15,-230), NE N.J., W of Newark. Seat of Seton Hall Univ. (R.C.; men and women; 1856; became university on merging with John Marshall Col., 1950–51).

South Orkney Islands, group, S Atlantic, c.850 mi. ESE of Cape Horn. Claimed by British (1821) and included as dependencies of Falkland Isls. colony. Also claimed by Argentina.

South Ossetia, Georgian SSR: see OSSETIA.

South Pasadena (păsùdē'nù), residential city (pop. 16,-935), S Calif., between Pasadena and Los Angeles. Has citrus orchards and animal farms.

South Pass, valley (alt. c.7,550 ft.), SW Wyo., in Wind River Range of the Rockies. Used by pioneers crossing Continental Divide on Oregon Trail.

South Platte (plăt), river, c.450 mi. long, rising in Rocky Mts. in many branches which join in central Colo. Flows E and NE to Denver, then NE across Colo. to join North Platte R. in S central Nebr. and form the Platte. Basin has many private irrigation dams. Colo. section in COLORADO–BIG THOMPSON PROJECT; similar Blue–South Platte project planned.

South Pole, southern end of earth's axis, lat. 90° S and long. 0°. It is distinguished from the south magnetic pole. The South Pole was reached (1911) by Roald Amundsen. See also ANTARCTICA.

Southport, county borough (pop. 84,057), Lancashire, England; seaside resort. Has an observatory, art and technical schools, and a fine boulevard.

South Portland, city (pop. 21,866), SW Maine, across Fore R. from Portland. Has shipyards, foundries, and marine hardware plants. U.S. Fort Preble is here. Just S are U.S. Fort Williams and Portland Head Light, oldest lighthouse (1791) on Maine coast.

South River, borough (pop. 11,308), E N.J., SE of New Brunswick. Embroideries, clay products.

South Saint Paul, city (pop. 15,709), SE Minn., near St. Paul on the Mississippi. Stockyards, packing plants, tanneries, and foundries.

South San Francisco, city (pop. 19,351), W Calif., S of San Francisco. Has metalworking and meat-packing plants.

South Saskatchewan: see SASKATCHEWAN, river.

South Sea Bubble, popular name in England for speculation in the South Sea Co. formed (1711) by Robert Harley. Company assumed the national debt in return for annual payment by government plus a monopoly of British trade with islands of South Seas and South America. Fraudulent schemes resulted and the bubble burst (1720). Robert Walpole was made chancellor of the exchequer to restore company's credit.

South Shetland Islands, Antarctic archipelago off N Palmer Peninsula, in S Atlantic. Barren, snow-covered islands. Figured 1906–31 in whaling activity and later antarctic exploration. Discovered 1819 by an English mariner. Claimed by Great Britain, Argentina, and Chile.

South Shields, county borough (pop. 106,605), Durham, England, at mouth of the Tyne. North Shields, part of TYNEMOUTH, is opposite. Docks cover 50 acres. There is fishing and varied mfg.

South Victoria Land: see VICTORIA LAND.

Southwark (sŭdh'ùrk, south'wùrk), metropolitan borough (pop. 97,171), of S London, England. Also called "the Borough." Famous inns (including Tabard Inn) and Globe Theatre were here.

Southwell, Robert, 1561?–1595, English Jesuit poet and martyr. After ministering to oppressed English Catholics (1586–92), he was convicted and executed for treason. Wrote deeply religious poems (e.g., *St. Peter's Complaint* and *The Burning Babe*).

South-West Africa, territory (318,099 sq. mi.; pop.

384,627), SW Africa, on the Atlantic; cap. Windhoek. Bordered on N by Angola, on E by Bechuanaland, and on S and SE by South Africa. Mainly an arid plateau. Minerals worked include copper, tin, and gold. Chief export is karakul felt. Native population comprises several Bantu tribes. Area was visited 1486 by Bartholomew Diaz. Annexed 1892 by Germany; occupied in World War I by South African forces. Governed under a mandate from League of Nations by South Africa, which refused to make it a UN trust territory because of its intention of annexing it.

Southwestern at Memphis: see MEMPHIS, Tenn.

Southwestern College: see WINFIELD, Kansas.

Southwestern Louisiana Institute: see LAFAYETTE.

Southwestern University: see GEORGETOWN, Texas.

South Williamsport, borough (pop. 6,364), N central Pa., on West Branch of Susquehanna R. opposite Williamsport. Mfg. of furniture and hardware.

Southwold (south'wōld), municipal borough (pop. 2,473), Suffolk East, England; a resort. Battle of Southwold Bay or Sole Bay was fought (1672) by Dutch under De Ruyter and English and French under duke of York (later James II).

Southworth, E(mma) D(orothy) E(liza) N(evitte), 1819–99, American author of popular, romantic, melodramatic novels such as *The Hidden Hand* (1859).

sovereignty. A sovereign state is a free and independent state. In external relations it can send and receive ambassadors, make international agreements, and declare war and make peace. In internal relations it makes and enforces law of land, controls money and military power. Internal power may be exercised by individual (monarchy), class (oligarchy), or entire people (democracy). Tendency in modern practice has been to curb external powers of nation, especially in making of war, through League of Nations and through UN.

soviet (sō'vĕĕt') [Rus.,= council], primary unit in political organization of USSR. First revolutionary soviets were committees organized by the Socialists in 1905 among striking factory workers. Workers', peasants', and soldiers' soviets sprang up during RUSSIAN REVOLUTION of 1917. Bolshevik-dominated soviets overthrew the Kerensky government. Under constitution of the USSR, soviets form a hierarchy from rural councils to congress of soviets of Soviet Union (all elected by universal suffrage). In practice, they are subservient to the Communist party.

Sower or **Sauer, Christopher** (both: sō'ŭr, sou'ŭr), 1693–1758, American printer, b. Germany. His German Bible (1743) was the second Bible printed in America. His son, Christopher Sower, estab. the first type foundry in America (1772).

Soya Strait: see LA PÉROUSE STRAIT.

soybean, leguminous annual plant (*Glycine soja*), native to the Orient, where it has been grown for over 5,000 years. The beans are made into meal, oil, cheese, curds, or cake. Soybeans are now grown in the Occident, to some extent for food, but chiefly for soil improvement and forage; the oil has been used in manufacture of various products.

Sozzini, Lelio, and **Fausto Sozzini:** see SOCINUS.

Spa (spä), town (pop. 8,929), Liége prov., SE Belgium, in the Ardennes and near German border. Mineral springs and baths, frequented from 16th cent., have made it one of world's most fashionable watering places. Name now designates all similar health resorts. Spa Conference (1920) dealt with German reparations problem.

Spaak, Paul Henri (pôl' ärĕ' späk'), 1899–, Belgian foreign minister (1938–49) and twice premier (1938–39, 1947–49); a moderate Socialist. Presided over first UN Assembly (1946), Council for European Recovery (1948–49), and first consultative assembly of Council of Europe (1949).

Spaatz, Carl Andrew (spŏts), 1891–, American general, chief of staff of U.S. Air Force (1947–48).

space time, concept in physics which holds that time and space are indissolubly united. It was suggested by H. A. Lorentz. Einstein's special theory of relativity is partly based on this concept; the universe is described as a four-dimensional continuum in which events are located by three space coordinates and a time coordinate (fourth dimension).

spaghetti: see MACARONI.

Spain, Span. *España,* sovereign state (194,232 sq. mi.; pop. 27,909,009, incl. BALEARIC ISLANDS and CANARY ISLANDS), SW Europe; cap. MADRID. In Africa, Spain has Spanish West Africa, Spanish Guinea, and a protectorate over Spanish Morocco. Continental Spain occupies all the Iberian peninsula except Portugal and tiny Andorra. It stretches from the Pyrenees (boundary with France) and the Bay of Biscay in the N to the Strait of Gibraltar in the S. It has a long Mediterranean coast in the E and SE, Atlantic shores in the NW and the SW. Central Spain is a vast plateau, the *Meseta Central,* between the Cantabrian Mts. in the N and the Sierra Morena in the S. It is cut by mountains (notably the Sierra de Guadarrama) and river valleys (Duero, Tagus, Guadiana). N of the *Meseta* the Ebro flows to the Mediterranean. In the S the climate is subtropical; the great river is the Guadalquivir. Spanish products are mostly agr.—citrus fruit, olives, grapes (such wines as sherry and Malaga are well known), vegetables, cork, and cereals. Much of the soil of the *Meseta,* however, has been exhausted by sheep grazing and poor care. From the mountains come various minerals (e.g., copper, iron), and fishing is a major industry on the coasts. Industry has been developed particularly around Madrid, around Barcelona, and in the NW (Basque Provs.). Though there are strong elements of unity in Spain (e.g., Roman Catholicism is at least nominally almost universal), there are great regional variations. The standard language is Castilian Spanish, but there are dialects. In two regions (CATALONIA and the BASQUE PROVINCES) non-Spanish languages are spoken, and there have been many moves to autonomy or independence. Other regional divisions are more or less related to medieval kingdoms and historical provinces, among them: Andalusia, Aragon, Asturias, Old and New Castile, Estremadura, Galicia, Leon, Murcia, Navarre, Valencia (see articles on these for information on industries, cities, and history).

Spain before the Conquest of America. The Basques were in Spain in the Stone Age before the coming of the Iberians (who later amalgamated with invading Celts to become the Celt-Iberians). Phoenicians estab. trading posts in the S by the 11th cent. B.C., and later came Greek settlers and then the Carthaginians, who conquered most of Spain (3d cent. B.C.). Rome took it from them in the second of the PUNIC WARS (218–201 B.C.), completed conquest of most of the peninsula by 133 B.C. Spain was Romanized and integrated into the empire. Its Roman heritage was not lost even after the Germanic invasions, which began in A.D. 409. The Visigothic kings, who created a large state in the N and pushed to the S, kept Roman law (see ALARIC II) and much of Roman civilization. Christianity had been introduced early and survived. The Visigothic state was, however, weak, and collapsed when a Moslem army from N Africa defeated King Roderick (711). Thus began the rule of the Moslems, called in Spain the Moors. The emirate (later the Western caliphate) was estab. at Córdoba, and a rich civilization grew up, with prosperous cities, well-regulated agr. and industries, and flowering of architecture (as in the Alhambra at Granada) and learning (much knowledge of classic learning passed to W Europe through Spain). The Moors were, however, divided among themselves, not only with successive dynasties (ABBADIDES, ALMORAVIDES, ALMOHADES) but with local rivalry. They never controlled the N, where the kingdom of Asturias survived as the seed of the Christian conquest. Leon, Castile, and Aragon grew more powerful, and despite constant wars among themselves, dotted with temporary alliances with various Moorish rulers, the Spanish Christian states gradually conquered the Moors. A landmark was the Spanish victory at Navas de Tolosa (1212), but the last Moorish stronghold did not fall until 1492. By that time most of Spain had been united by the marriage of the rulers of Castile and Aragon, FERDINAND V and ISABELLA I. Their reign saw also the expulsion of the Jews from Spain (1492) and they later forced the Moors to accept Christianity (they were finally expelled). But the most important event of 1492 was the discovery of the New World by Christopher Columbus. This was the foundation of the Spanish Empire on which by the accession of Charles I (Emperor Charles V) in 1516 "the sun never set."

Golden Age and Decline. The reign of Charles's son, PHILIP II, saw Spain finally centralized (even Portugal was annexed in 1580, to become free again in 1640), the Spanish INQUISITION reached its height of terrible power, and wealth flowed in from Spanish lands in North and South America and the Philippines. Spanish literature and art flourished in the late 16th and the 17th cent. (the Golden Age). Economic and military decline, however, had set in, marked by the defeat of the Spanish Armada sent to conquer England (1588). Spanish warfare over Europe and connection with the Holy Roman Empire ultimately also worked to the ill of Spain. The Thirty Years War (1618–48) cost Spain territory and prestige. When the Hapsburg line disappeared, the War of the SPANISH SUCCESSION occurred (1701–14), costing Spain dearly and putting PHILIP V on the throne. Despite efforts at revival Spain stagnated, gradually sinking through numerous wars and treaties until humiliation by Napoleon, who forced the abdications of CHARLES IV and FERDINAND VII and in 1808 put his brother Joseph BONAPARTE (1808) on the throne. This caused a nationalist upsurge, and Spanish patriots played a part in the PENINSULAR WAR. In 1812 Ferdinand was restored to the throne.

Monarchists and Republicans. The Napoleonic invasion helped bring on the wars of independence in Latin America which had by 1825 stripped Spain of most of its empire (with Cuba, Puerto Rico, and the Philippines to be lost later in the SPANISH-AMERICAN WAR). In Spain itself conservatives and liberals struggled endlessly. Ferdinand's changing of the law of succession in favor of his daughter, ISABELLA II, brought on the first uprising of the Carlists (1836–39). Reactionary monarchists, constitutional monarchists, and republicans vied for power. Isabella had to abdicate (1868), as did her successor, Amadeus (1873). A brief republic (1873–74) was torn by new war. In 1876 Alfonso XII was put on the throne; he was succeeded by Alfonso XIII, who reigned until 1931. Spain was neutral in World War I. In 1923 a dictatorship was set up under PRIMO DE RIVERA, but republican opposition ended this (1930) and deposed the king (1931). A republic was set up. In 1936 a combination of radical parties won a majority, and there was an immediate military uprising. The bloody civil war was finally won by the Insurgents in 1939, and Francisco FRANCO set up a state on corporative lines. Fascistic Spain sympathized with the Axis in World War II but kept legal neutrality. The UN refused Spain membership. Long-drawn negotiations between the Franco government and Western powers had come to nothing by 1953. In 1947 Franco declared the country a monarchy, but no steps were taken to restore the Bourbons.

Spalato, Yugoslavia: see SPLIT.

Spalding, Albert, 1888–, American violinist. He made his New York debut 1908 and toured extensively. Wrote his autobiography, *Rise to Follow,* and a historical novel, *A Fiddle, a Sword, and a Lady.*

Spalding, Lyman, 1775–1821, American physician, founder of U.S. Pharmacopoeia (1820), a descriptive catalogue of approved therapeutic agents.

Spandau (shpän′dou), former town, since 1920 a W district (pop. 159,599) of Berlin, Germany, on Spree and Havel rivers. Mfg. of steel and electrical equipment. Its fortress became a political prison in 19th cent.

Spangenberg, August Gottlieb (ou′gōŏst gôt′lēp shpäng′ŭnbĕrk), 1704–92, a founder and bishop of Moravian Church in America, b. Prussia. After 1735 he founded settlements, churches, and schools in Ga., Pa., and N.C. He became bishop in 1744. One of his works was adopted as official Moravian doctrine.

spaniel, name of a large group of dogs, believed to have originated in Spain; records of existence date from 14th cent. In general, spaniels have silky coats (sometimes wavy or curled), relatively short legs, and long ears. Colors in land spaniels are greatly varied—solid colors include black, red, liver, gold, or cream; mixed colors include orange, lemon, liver, red, black, or mahogany, with white. Spaniels are all excellent in flushing game. Varieties include the clumber spaniel (weighing 50–60 lb.), the field and the springer spaniel (weighing 30–45 lb.), and the small cocker spaniel (weighing 18–24 lb.), widely popular as a pet. There are two breeds of water spaniel, the American and the Irish. The American breed, weighing from 28 to 45 lb., is a good swimmer and is useful as a retriever on land and in the water. It has a tightly curled coat of dark chocolate or liver color. The Irish water spaniel, the tallest member of the spaniel family (22–24 in. at shoulder), has a tightly curled coat of a solid liver color and a curly topknot.

Spanish Africa, name for Spanish possessions in Africa, i.e., Ifni, Spanish Guinea, Spanish Morocco, and Spanish Sahara.

Spanish America, Spanish-speaking countries of LATIN AMERICA (also called Hispanic America). Included are: Mexico, Central America (except British Honduras), South America (except Brazil and Guiana), Cuba, Dominican Republic, and Puerto Rico.

Spanish-American War, 1898, struggle of U.S. and Cuban revolutionists against Spain with chief object of liberating CUBA from Spanish control. Revolution broke out in Cuba in 1895, with heavy losses to American investments. U.S. government recognized strategic importance of Cuba to projected canal in Central America. War sentiment in U.S. rose with publication of a letter written by Spanish minister at Washington disparaging U.S. Pres. McKinley and with sinking of U.S. battleship MAINE. U.S. demanded Spain's withdrawal from Cuba; on April 24 Spain declared war. On May 1 a U.S. squadron under George DEWEY thoroughly defeated Spanish fleet at Manila, Philippine Isls. Spanish fleet at Santiago de Cuba was destroyed on July 3. U.S. troops secured surrender of Santiago. Armistice was signed on Aug. 12. Treaty of Paris, signed Dec. 10, 1898, freed Cuba (but under U.S. tutelage by Platt Amendment); ceded Puerto Rico and Guam to U.S.; surrendered the Philippines to U.S. for $20,000,000. Spanish Empire was practically dissolved. U.S. was entangled in Latin America in a new fashion and was tied more closely to course of Far Eastern events.

Spanish Armada: see ARMADA, SPANISH.

Spanish bayonet and **Spanish dagger:** see YUCCA.

Spanish colonial architecture flourished from 16th to late 18th cent. Though basically Spanish in style, it developed original features (esp. in Mexico and Peru). Intricate ornamentation was often used, as in the richly decorated portal of W façade of Santo Domingo cathedral (1521–41), earliest cathedral in America. But the chief characteristic of colonial building was simple, solid construction, as shown in Spanish missions of Calif. and Jesuit missions of Paraguay. In 16th-cent. Mexico the great builders were the Augustinian, Franciscan, and Dominican orders; they invented the open chapel, built with only three walls to speed construction. During most of 17th and 18th cent. the baroque style predominated, but simpler elements of early period were retained. A more conservative trend in Colombia kept the style severely simple. The baroque combined with native inventiveness to produce the ultra-baroque cathedral of Mexico city, with its strong light-and-shade patterns, richly carved columns, and violent contrasts of curves and angles. Central American buildings were generally provincial versions of the Mexican, but in Peru a rich architecture, more massive than the Mexican, was evolved, with wall surfaces divided into large compartments rather than covered with shallow carving as in Mexico. In S Peru and in Bolivia, Indian influence in ornament pervaded the basic European architectural forms. An invasion of neoclassicism ended the great days of Spanish colonial architecture.

Spanish Fork, city (pop. 5,230), N central Utah, S of Provo near Utah L.; processing center in irrigated region served by STRAWBERRY VALLEY PROJECT.

Spanish Guinea (gĭ′nē), colony (10,800 sq. mi.; pop. 170,582), W Africa, on Gulf of Guinea; cap. Santa Isabel on Fernando Po isl. Consists of mainland section, Río Muni (between French Cameroons and French Equatorial Africa) and several islands, of which Fernando Po is most important. Exports are cacao, palm oil, bananas, and coffee. Fernando Po was ceded by Portugal to Spain, 1778. Boundaries of Río Muni estab. 1885 by Treaty of Berlin.

Spanish language, language of Romance group of Italic subfamily of Indo-European languages. See LANGUAGE (table).

Spanish Main, mainland of Spanish America, particularly coast of South America from Isthmus of Panama to mouth of the Orinoco. From coast English buccaneers would attack Spanish treasure fleets sailing home from New World. Term now used to describe entire Caribbean area associated with piracy.

Spanish Morocco: see MOROCCO.

Spanish moss, fibrous gray air plant (*Tillandsia usneoides*) that hangs on trees of tropical America and the U.S. It belongs to the pineapple family.

Spanish Sahara, division (103,600 sq. mi.; pop. 37,000), Spanish West Africa, on the Atlantic; cap. Aiun. Comprises colony of Río de Oro (70,000 sq. mi.; pop. 24,000) and territory of Sekia el Hamra (32,000 sq. mi.; pop. 13,000).

Spanish Succession, War of the, 1701–14, general European war, fought for the succession to the Spanish empire after the death of Charles II, last Hapsburg king of Spain. Complicated negotiations regarding the succession of the childless king had been going on for years. By 1699 the chief claimants to the succession were Louis XIV of France, on behalf of his grandson Philip, a great-grandson of Philip IV of Spain; and Emperor Leopold I, as head of the Austrian house of Hapsburg, on behalf of his son Charles (later Emperor CHARLES VI). The reunion of the Austrian and Spanish Hapsburg dominions was unacceptable to England, France, and the United Provs. of the Netherlands; the union of France and Spain under the Bourbon dynasty was equally unacceptable to England, Austria, and the United Provs. In 1700 the dying Charles II named Philip his sole heir; Louis XIV accepted on behalf of his grandson, who became PHILIP V of Spain. England, the United Provs., and Austria allied themselves against France and were joined by most of the German states. Bavaria sided with France. Portugal and Savoy sided with France till 1703, then joined the allies. Military operations began in the Low Countries and Italy (1701) and became general in 1702. Of the French commanders, only VILLARS and L. J. de VENDÔME were a match to the great allied leaders—MARLBOROUGH and EUGENE OF SAVOY. However, despite such major allied victories as Blenheim and Gibraltar (1704), Oudenarde (1708), and Malplaquet (1709), the campaigns in Spain, Italy, and the Low Countries were indecisive, and England withdrew from the fighting in 1711. The war ended with the treaties of Utrecht, Rastatt, and Baden (1713–14; see UTRECHT, PEACE

OF), with England and the United Provs. the real winners. France had to compromise with Austria and was economically exhausted. In America, the conflict was known as Queen Anne's War (see FRENCH AND INDIAN WARS).

Spanish Town, city (pop. 12,007), S Jamaica, British West Indies. Was leading city of Jamaica until Kingston rose to prominence.

Sparks, Jared, 1789–1866, American historian, editor, and educator. Editor *North American Review* (1817–18, 1824–30). President Harvard (1849–53). Works include *The Writings of George Washington* (12 vols., 1834–37) and *Library of American Biography* (25 vols., 1834–48).

Sparks, city (pop. 8,203), W Nev., on Truckee R. just E of Reno. Rail hub in irrigated agr. area.

sparrow, name for various small Old and New World birds of finch family. Plumage is usually streaked brown and gray. Sparrows destroy weed seeds. English or house sparrow is not a true sparrow, but of weaver bird family.

Spars [from the motto "Semper Paratus"], Women's Reserve of U.S. Coast Guard Reserve, created Nov., 1942. In World War II Spars took over shore duty to release men for sea duty. Demobilized by June, 1946.

Sparta, city of anc. Greece, cap. of Laconia, chief city of the Peloponnesus, on the Eurotas R. The city-state was founded by Dorian conquerors of Laconia and Messenia and grew strong. In the 7th cent. B.C. it was a center of literature, but after 600 B.C. military arts were dominant, sons of the ruling class, Spartiates, were trained as soldiers, and the city was an armed camp. Below the warrior class were the perioeci (artisans and tradesmen) and helots (slaves attached to the land). Only Spartiates had legal and civil rights. The government was headed by two kings, but the board of five ephors held more governing power. Sparta took part in the PERSIAN WARS, and Spartans conducted themselves heroically at THERMOPYLAE (490) and also fought at Salamis (480) and, more gallantly, at Plataea under Pausanias (479). Sparta built the loose Peloponnesian League before 500 B.C. but made no effort to turn it into an empire. Sparta was the rival of Athens and was in the end involved in a ruinous war, the PELOPONNESIAN WAR (431–404 B.C.). Sparta emerged triumphant, but shortly was defeated by Thebans at Leuctra (371 B.C.). Sparta declined after conquest by Philip II of Macedon and disappeared altogether under Roman sway. Modern Sparta (pop. 9,700) was founded in the 19th cent. near ruins of the old city.

Sparta, city (pop. 5,893), W central Wis., NE of La Crosse and on La Crosse R., in agr. area. Creameries and tobacco warehouses.

Spartacus (spär′tŭkŭs), d. 71 B.C., Roman gladiator, leader of a slave revolt that was last and most important of the Servile Wars, b. Thrace. Escaped from gladiators' school at Capua, gathered many runaway slaves about him and in 72 B.C. dominated much of S Italy. Crassus and Pompey put down the revolt and crucified some 6,000 captured slaves.

Spartacus party or **Spartacists,** radical group of German Socialists, founded c.1916 and led by Karl LIEBKNECHT and Rosa LUXEMBURG. In December, 1918, it was officially transformed into the German Communist party. An outbreak and demonstration in Berlin (Jan., 1920) was suppressed by Gustav NOSKE.

Spartanburg, city (pop. 36,795), NW S.C., NW of Columbia; in piedmont; selected as co. seat 1785. Center of mill village area and important textile-milling center with railroad shops and mfg. of metal and lumber products and fertilizer. Supply point in Civil War. Seat of Converse Col. (nonsectarian; mainly women; 1889) and Textile Inst. Annual music festival.

spastic paralysis (spă′stĭk), condition characterized by muscle rigidity and exaggerated reflexes, generally resulting from injury to brain motor center. Causes include birth injuries and multiple sclerosis.

SMALL CAPITALS = cross references. Pronunciation key on inside end pages. Abbreviations: p. 2.

spatterdock: see POND LILY.

spavin (spă′vĭn), permanent deformity from bony enlargement on bones of hock joint in the horse. Probable cause is structural deformity aggravated by overweight and injury; lameness results.

Speaker, Tris(tram E.), 1883–, American baseball outfielder. Had lifetime major-league batting average of .344, was regarded as one of the best defensive outfielders in the American League.

spearmint, aromatic perennial mint (*Mentha spicata*), native to Old World but naturalized in U.S. It is a flavoring for chewing gum, medicine, candy.

species, in biology, a unit or category of classification lower than a genus and higher than a subspecies or variety. It is used for a plant or animal group in a genus possessing in common certain characters that distinguish the members as a group from other similar groups of the same genus. The species name is the second of the scientific names by which plants and animals are identified. In the case of the white oak, *Quercus alba*, the genus name is *Quercus* (oak) and the species is *alba* (white). Species names are usually descriptive of a characteristic, or are derived from the discoverer, the geographic area, or geologic period of the plant or animal.

specific gravity, pure number representing ratio of the mass or weight of a given volume of a substance and the given weight of an equal volume of another substance chosen as arbitrary standard. In metric system it is the same as DENSITY if water is taken as standard; but unlike density it is an abstract number. In English system density and specific gravity are not numerically the same. Methods of determining specific gravity vary as solid is more or less dense than water. It is calculated by dividing weight in air by loss of weight in water. HYDROMETER gives direct specific-gravity reading. Specific gravity of a gas is determined by comparing weight of one liter of gas with weight of equal volume of air or hydrogen as unity.

spectacles, device to protect eyes or improve vision. Convex lenses suggested 13th cent. by Roger Bacon; concave, used in 14th cent. Bifocals, with upper part for viewing distant objects and lower for near objects, invented by Benjamin Franklin. Trifocals later developed. Contact lenses, shaped to fit eye and worn under eyelid, first used 1887; popularity increased after 1930s because of improved grinding and fitting techniques.

Spectator, London daily journal (March, 1711–Dec., 1712) conducted by Richard Steele and Joseph Addison; successor to their *Tatler* (April, 1709–Jan., 1711). Written supposedly by members of a club, e.g., the famous Sir Roger de Coverley, but really by Addison and Steele. Consisted mainly of news, literary and theatrical essays, and criticisms of current follies and vices. Both papers greatly influenced public opinion and English journalism.

spectroscope (spĕk′trŭskōp), instrument used to produce spectra in SPECTRUM analysis. Usually consists of three hollow tubes mounted horizontally on disk supported by vertical shaft. One tube has slit at outer end and lens at inner end, which transforms light entering through slit into parallel rays. Another tube is telescope for observing spectrum formed. Third tube contains scale by which direct measurement of spectrum is made. Prism in center of disk disperses light entering tube through the slit and bends it into telescope for observation.

spectrum. When narrow beam of white light passes through prism, rays of colors of which it is composed are bent at different angles; they emerge as narrow band of color shading from red at one end to violet at other. This is a spectrum; process of breaking up the white light is DISPERSION. Spectrum also is produced by reflection from a grating ruled with fine lines. When such a band is unbroken it is a continuous spectrum; these are produced by incandescent solids. Characteristics displayed by spectra depend on nature of source. Presence of an element in a substance can be detected by examining with spectroscope the spectrum (called a line spectrum) produced by its incandescent vapor; each element can be identified by the appearance of one or more bright lines of characteristic color and in characteristic position in its spectrum. No two elements have the same spectral lines. An absorption spectrum is produced when light from one source passes through an incandescent gaseous substance; it has dark lines corresponding in position to bright lines which appear in spectrum of light source. Spectrum of sunlight shows dark lines called Fraunhofer lines. Kirchhoff explained these as caused by presence in sun's atmosphere of incandescent elements which absorb from sunlight passing through them those rays of light producing their characteristic spectra. Rays having photochemical effects, chiefly green, blue, and ultraviolet rays of sun's spectrum, are sometimes called actinic rays.

Spee, Maximilian, Graf von (gräf′ fŭn shpā′), 1861–1914, German admiral in World War I. Defeated English off Coronel but was defeated near Falkland Isls. and went down with his ship.

speech, freedom of, the right of citizens to voice opinions without interference, subject only to the laws against slander, profanity, and incitement to unlawful acts. Historically, the right has frequently been denied and it is usually curtailed somewhat even by democracies in wartime. Freedom of speech in the U.S. is guaranteed by the Bill of Rights and, as interpreted by the Supreme Court, by the Fourteenth Amendment, though the Supreme Court has justified restriction of free speech at the point where the spoken word creates "a clear and present danger."

speech defect, faulty speech such as stuttering, lisping, nasality, monopitch, mumbling, excessive sibilance, may result from improper training, psychological or neurological factors, or organic faults. Methods for eliminating or reducing defects include surgery, orthodontia, rhythmical and relaxing exercises, psychological aid, and clinical instruction in breathing, phrasing, and enunciation.

speedometer for automobiles utilizes flexible cable which, driven by drive gear, rotates permanent magnet and induces magnetic drag on drum held back by hairspring. As speed increases the magnetic force and drum movement increase. Numbers on drum rim indicate speed. Other speedometers use centrifugal force. Airplanes have air-speed indicators.

Speedway, town (pop. 5,498), central Ind., near Indianapolis. Has Indianapolis motor speedway.

speedwell or **veronica,** perennial flowering plant of genus *Veronica*. Veronicas vary from creeping types suitable for rock gardens to tall, bushy plants—all with showy flower spikes, usually blue. Closely related shrubby kinds are of genus *Hebe*.

Speer, Albert (äl′bĕrt shpär′), 1905–, German architect and National Socialist leader. For a time he was official architect of Nazi regime. In 1942 he succeeded the engineer Fritz Todt as minister for armaments, inheriting *Organisation Todt* (for building roads and defenses), important in German war machine. Indicted at Nuremberg Trial as a war criminal because of wide use of slave labor; sentenced 1946 to 20-year imprisonment.

Speicher, Eugene Edward (spī′kùr), 1883–, American portrait and landscape painter.

Speier, Germany: see SPEYER.

Speke, John Hanning (spēk), 1827–64, English explorer in Africa. Discovered L. Tanganyika in 1858 with Sir Richard Burton. Discovered Victoria Nyanza, later proved it was source of Victoria Nile.

Spellman, Francis J(oseph), 1889–, American Roman Catholic clergyman, made archbishop of New York (1939) and cardinal (1946).

Spemann, Hans (häns′ shpā′män), 1869–1941, German embryologist. Won 1935 Nobel Prize in Physiology and Medicine for research on cells.

Spence, Thomas (spĕns), 1750–1814, English agrarian socialist. Devised scheme of land tenure by parish, in which rent would be the only tax. Founded a society of Spenceans. Author of *The Real Rights of Man* (1775) and other pamphlets.

Spencer, Herbert, 1820–1903, English philosopher. He applied wide study of the natural sciences and psychology to philosophy, finding in the doctrine of evolution the unifying principle of knowledge and applying it to all phenomena. He did not deal with the "unknowable" (metaphysics and such scientific ideas as matter, space, time, motion, and force) but instead dealt only with those things which could be compared with and related to other things. Among his works are *First Principles* (1862), *The Principles of Biology* (1864–67), *The Principles of Psychology* (1855), *The Principles of Sociology* (1876–96), and *The Principles of Ethics* (1891).

Spencer, Platt Rogers, 1800–1864, American penman, originator of the style of handwriting known as Spencerian script.

Spencer. 1 City (pop. 7,446), NW Iowa, on Little Sioux R. and S of Spirit L., in agr. area. Has annual county fair. **2** Town (pop. 7,027), including Spencer village (pop. 5,259), central Mass., W of Worcester.

Spencer Gulf, inlet of Indian Ocean, indenting South Australia, between Eyre and Yorke peninsulas.

Spender, Stephen, 1909–, English poet and critic, educ. at Oxford. His poems (as in *Poems,* 1933) voiced social protest. Also wrote stories, a novel, works of criticism (e.g., *The Destructive Element,* 1935; *Life and the Poet,* 1942), a book on Germany (*European Witness,* 1946), and the autobiographical *World within in World* (1951).

Spener, Philipp Jakob (fē′lĭp yä′kôp shpā′nùr), 1635–1705, German theologian, founder of PIETISM. By organizing groups and by his writings he revivified religion through stress on Bible study, spiritual exercises, and good works. Made Halle (where he helped found the university) a center of his beliefs.

Spengler, Oswald (ôs′vält shpĕng′glùr), 1880–1936, German philosopher. His theory that every culture passes through a life cycle similar to that of human life is set forth in *The Decline of the West* (1918).

Spenser, Edmund, c.1552–1599, English poet. *The Shepheardes Calender* (1579) early marked him as gifted. He held a succession of minor civil offices in Ireland and after 1580 made his home there. Disappointment in getting court preferment was voiced in *Complaints* (1591) and *Colin Clouts Come Home Again* (1595). *Astrophel* is an elegy for Sir Philip Sidney; *Amoretti,* a sonnet sequence commemorating Spenser's courtship of Elizabeth Boyle; and *Epithalamion,* finest wedding poem in English, written for their marriage. All these appeared in 1595, followed by *Fowre Hymnes* (1596). His masterpiece, *The Faerie Queene* (Books I–III, 1590; I–VI, 1596), though unfinished, is one of the greatest English poems. A richly intricate allegory set in the kingdom of Gloriana (or Elizabeth), it expresses Spenser's moral, political, and religious beliefs. Spenser was a consummate artist in language, melody, and verse technique.

Speranski, Mikhail Mikhailovich (mēkhŭyĕl′ mēkhī′lùvĭch spyīrän′skĕ), 1772–1839, Russian minister of justice under Alexander I (1809–11). Drafted program of liberal reform, providing for emancipation of serfs and limited constitution, but fell from favor in 1812. Codified Russian law under Nicholas I.

sperm or **spermatozoon** (spûr″mùtùzō′ùn, –zō′ŏn), sexual cell formed in testis of male of humans and other higher animals. Smaller than ovum; whiplike process permits movement through fluid. As in OVUM, reduction division (reduction of number of chromosomes by one half) precedes process of FERTILIZATION as a result of which normal number is restored.

spermaceti (spûrmŭsĕ′tē), white, odorless, tasteless wax obtained chiefly from sperm whale. Used in ointments, cosmetics, candles, waterproofing.

sperm oil, liquid wax from blubber and oil cavity in head of sperm whale. It is clear pale yellow to brownish yellow. Formerly principally used for lamps, it today has several uses—as a machine lubricant, as a dressing for leather, and as a fat for soap.

Sperry, Elmer Ambrose, 1860–1930, American inventor of gyroscope, automatic ship steersman, gyrocompass, and numerous other electrical devices.

Spey (spā), river of Scotland. Flows 110 mi. NE from Inverness-shire highlands to Moray Firth. Rapid and unnavigable; valuable salmon fisheries.

Speyer (shpī′ùr), city (pop. 31,706), Rhineland-Palatinate, W Germany, on left bank of the Rhine; also called Spires in English; occasionally spelled Speier in German. Of pre-Roman origin, it became an episcopal see in 7th cent. and a free imperial city in 1111. Several imperial diets were held here, notably that of 1529, which granted toleration to Catholics in Lutheran states but not to Lutherans in Catholic states nor to Zwinglians and Anabaptists anywhere. The Protest of Speyer, signed by Elector John of Saxony, Landgrave Philip of Hesse, and other delegates who opposed this decision, gave the Protestants their name. Speyer was the seat of the imperial chamber of justice from 1527 until 1689, when the French devastated the city. Distinct from the city was the bishopric of Speyer, consisting of considerable territories held by the bishops as princes of the Holy Roman Empire. Both the city and the bishopric W of the Rhine were ceded to France in 1797 and were given to Bavaria in 1815. They were part of Rhenish Palatinate 1815–1945, Speyer being the cap. The episcopal lands E of the Rhine passed to Baden in 1803. Speyer has kept parts of its medieval walls. Its fine Romanesque cathedral (10th cent., several times restored) contains the tombs of eight emperors. An early printing center, the city was the home of John of Speyer.

Spezia, La (lä spā′tsyä), city (pop. 80,399), Liguria, NW Italy; a Mediterranean port on the Gulf of Spezia. Chief Italian naval station. Has arsenal, navigation school, shipyards, steel mills, oil refineries. Was heavily bombed in World War II.

sphagnum (sfăg′nùm) or **peat moss,** pale green, weak-stemmed bog plant of genus *Sphagnum,* economically the most valuable of any MOSS. Sphagnum mosses are the principle constituent of peat. In horticulture sphagnum is used as a mulch and as a packing material for plants being shipped.

sphalerite (sfă′lùrīt, sfā′–), mineral, zinc sulphide, usually with iron, manganese, cadmium, mercury. It is white when pure, but often is colored by slight impurities. It is the most important source of zinc. Found in Bohemia, Saxony, Cornwall, Japan, and U.S.

sphere, in geometry, three-dimensional analogue of circle (i.e., a solid with circle as its basic form). Term is applied to spherical surface, every point of which is same distance (radius) from fixed point (center) and also to volume enclosed by surface.

Sphinx (sfĭngks), in Greek mythology, a monster taken from Egyptian religion. She was a winged lion with a woman's head, who lived on a rock near Thebes. She asked of all a riddle and killed all who failed to answer. Oedipus solved it, and she leaped from the rock. Oedipus became king of Thebes. Egyptian sphinxes were recumbent figures, usually with men's heads. Most famous of all is the Great Sphinx of Gizeh (Egypt), a colossal figure carved from natural rock, guardian of the Nile valley.

spice, aromatic vegetable product used as a flavoring or condiment. Today, the term tends to be restricted to flavorings for food or drinks, although many spices have other commercial uses, e.g., in medicines, perfumes, incense, soap. Types include stimulating condiments (e.g., pepper), aromatics (cloves, cinnamon), and such sweet herbs as mint and marjoram. Spices are taken from part of plant richest in flavor (bark, stem, flower bud, fruit, seed, or leaf). They are commonly prepared as powder, but some are used as tinctures made from essential oils and others are used whole, as are many herbs. From ancient times, spices from the Far East were in great demand; after a lapse in trade in the early Middle Ages, the traffic grew greatly, especially after the Crusades. Later, the European demand was responsible for important explorations in search of new trade routes.

spicebush, ornamental and spicily fragrant shrub (*Lindera benzoin*) native to E North America. It bears small densely clustered yellow flowers in early spring followed by red berries which are sometimes used as a substitute for allspice.

Spice Islands, Indonesia: see MOLUCCAS.

spider, air-breathing arachnid, with body divided into two parts, four pairs of legs, usually four pairs of eyes, and without true jaws. Spinnerets under abdomen produce silk thread used for making webs and lines, encasing eggs, and lining retreats. Venom of black-widow spider is sometimes fatal.

spikenard (spīk'närd), name for several plants. The spikenard in the Bible was an aromatic ointment believed to be derived from *Nardostachys jatamansi*, of the valerian family. The American spikenard, or Indian root, is *Aralia racemosa,* with aromatic roots used medicinally.

Spillville, town (pop. 363), NE Iowa, on Turkey R. and SW of Decorah. Anton Dvorak composed (1893) part of symphony *From the New World* in this Czech community; his house became a clock museum.

spinach, annual vegetable plant (*Spinacia oleracea*) of Persian origin, long grown as a potherb. Its leaves are a dietary source of vitamins and iron.

spinal column, backbone, spine, or **vertebral column,** portion of vertebrate skeleton consisting of segments (vertebrae) united by cartilaginous disks and ligaments. Segments form a column supporting body and enclosing spinal cord. Human adult has 26 segments: 7 in neck; 12 in chest region; 5 in lumbar area; sacrum consisting of 5 fused vertebrae; coccyx, usually 4 fused bones. See *ill.,* p. 595.

spinal cord, whitish cord incased in spinal column and serving as pathway for impulses to and from brain and as system of reflex centers controlling activities of glands, organs, and muscles. Consists of central canal, layers of gray matter and of white matter, and three membranes. Along the spinal cord are 31 pairs of nerves. See *ill.,* p. 595.

Spinario (spinä'rēō), celebrated statue, probably of 1st cent. B.C., representing a boy pulling a thorn from his foot. Copies in Rome and London are possibly based on a work by Boethus.

Spinden, Herbert Joseph, 1879–, American anthropologist, authority on primitive cultures and Mayan calendar and chronology.

spine: see SPINAL COLUMN.

Spinello di Luca Spinelli (spēnĕl'lō dē lōō'kä spēnĕl'lē), c.1333–1410, Italian painter of the late Giotto school. Usually called Spinello Aretino.

spinet: see PIANO.

spinning, the drawing out, twisting, and winding of fibers into a continuous thread. Spinning was first done by holding fiber in one hand, twisting with the other; the earliest tools were the distaff, a stick on which fiber was wrapped, and the spindle, a shorter, weighted stick which was twirled to twist the thread. After the 14th cent., the spinning wheel, employing a spindle revolved by a belt passing over a wheel, came into use in Europe. Principal types were the great, or wool, wheel, with an intermittent action, and the flax, or Saxony wheel, a more elaborate mechanism operated by a treadle. In 18th-cent. England, improved looms stimulated spinning inventions. Notable were James Hargreaves's spinning jenny (c.1765), capable of spinning 8 to 11 threads at once, and Richard Arkwright's frame (1769), which eventually forced spinning into the factory. In 1779 Samuel Crompton combined the best features of these two devices into the mule spinning frame, the forerunner of the self-acting

mule used today for fine yarns. Coarser yarns are made on the ring frame, an elaboration of Arkwright's invention.

Spinoza, Baruch or **Benedict** (spĭnō'zù), 1632–77, Dutch philosopher. Because of independence of thought he was excommunicated (1656) from the Jewish group in which he was reared, but he continued to follow his own bent, earned his living as a lens grinder, and lived very quietly even when other philosophers broke his retirement by visiting him. He applied great learning to the building of his philosophic system. He unswervingly insisted that all existence is embraced in one substance—God (or Nature). Mind and matter, time, everything that appears is only a manifestation of the One. Evil exists only for finite minds and dissolves when seen as part of the whole. Man should try to adjust to the infinite plan, surrendering passion and accepting order, seeing events under the aspect of eternity. Spinoza favored democratic government.

spiraea or **spirea** (both: spīrē'ù), deciduous flowering shrub of genus *Spiraea* native to the N Hemisphere. Single or double small white or rose flowers are in rounded or spirelike clusters. Most common are the bridal wreath (*Spiraea prunifolia*) and the similar hybrid *S. vanhouttei.* Native to North America is the pink- or white-flowered *S. latifolia,* often called meadowsweet.

Spires, Germany: see SPEYER.

Spirit Lake, town (pop. 2,467), NW Iowa, near Minn. line. Tourist center between West Okoboji L. and Spirit L., largest glaciated lake in Iowa.

spirit level, instrument for determining direction of gravity. Position of a bubble in tube of alcohol, ether, or mixture of both indicates whether instrument is horizontal.

spiritual, in music, religious folk music. American Negro spirituals, long regarded as the spontaneous creation of the Negro, have been shown to be either adapted from, or inspired by, the spirituals of white Americans used in Southern camp and revival meetings throughout the 19th cent. Despite this, the distinctive quality and beauty of the Negro spiritual make it a major contribution to American music.

Spithead (spĭt'hĕd), eastern part of channel between Hampshire, England, and Isle of Wight. English defeated the French in battle here (1595). Scene of a famous fleet mutiny (1797).

Spitsbergen (spĭts'bûrgùn), archipelago, in Arctic Ocean, c.400 mi. N of Norwegian mainland, between lat. 76° and 81° N. With Bear Isl., farther S, it constitutes the Norwegian possession of Svalbard (23,979 sq. mi.; pop. 1,034, incl. 505 citizens of USSR). Chief island is West Spitsbergen (c.15,000 sq. mi.), which also has principal settlements (New Alesund, Longyear City). Other islands include North East Land, Hope Isl., King Charles Land, and Barents Isl. Chief wealth is coal. Islands were discovered by Vikings 12th cent., named Svalbard by them; rediscovered by Willem Barentz 1596. Henry Hudson reported good whaling here 1607; in 1618 Dutch limited own whaling operations to N Spitsbergen, leaving the rest to competitors. Russian fur traders began operations 18th cent.; Scandinavians followed. Islands were mapped late 19th cent. Conflicting claims to Spitsbergen were settled 1920 by international treaty (later ratified by Sweden, USSR, and others) which awarded archipelago to Norway, forbade military installations, and insured recognition of claims by other countries to parts of the coal fields. In 1941 the Allies of World War II set fires to the mines. German garrison was expelled by Norwegians in 1942, but in 1943 a German raid completed devastation of the mines. Demand by USSR for share in administration and defense of islands was rejected (1944).

Spitteler, Carl (kärl' shpī'tùlùr), 1845–1924, Swiss poet, author of the epics *Prometheus und Epimetheus* (1881; Eng. tr., 1931) and *Olympischer Frühling* [Olympian spring] (1900–1910). Was awarded 1919 Nobel Prize in Literature.

spitz dog: see CHOW.

Spitzka, Edward Charles (spĭts′kȯ), 1852–1914, American physician and psychiatrist. He pioneered in anatomical studies of the brain and in classification of mental disorders. His son, **Edward Anthony Spitzka,** 1876–1922, also a physician, made important studies of the human brain (esp. in criminals).

spleen, soft, purplish-red organ in upper part of abdominal cavity to left of stomach and close to diaphragm. Functions are not fully understood. It holds a reserve supply of blood which enters the circulation when need arises. Like other lymphoid tissue it produces lymphocytes; also it helps to destroy worn-out red corpuscles. Sometimes removal of the organ is necessary. See *ill.,* p. 595.

Split (splēt), Ital. *Spalato,* city (pop. 49,885), S Croatia, Yugoslavia; largest city of Dalmatia and a major Adriatic port. Tourist resort. Among its many Roman remains is the huge palace of Diocletian (who died here), begun in A.D. 295. Split became a city after the people of near-by Salona took refuge from the Avars in the palace (7th cent.). It became a Roman Catholic archiepiscopal see (episcopal see after 1820) and a flourishing medieval port. Contested between Hungary and Venice 13th–15th cent., it was under Venetian rule 1420–1797, then under Austrian rule until 1918. Cathedral and baptistery were originally Roman buildings; old walls and city hall date from Venetian period.

Splügen (shplü′gùn), Ital. *Spluga,* Alpine pass, 6,945 ft. high, on Swiss-Italian border, N of L. Como.

Spode, Josiah (spōd), 1754–1827, English potter at Stoke-on-Trent. Created the porcelain known as spode ware, a fine bone china similar to the French soft Sèvres ware.

spoils system, in U.S. history, practice of giving appointive offices to loyal members of party in power. First adopted on large scale by Andrew Jackson. Name supposedly derives from speech by W. L. MARCY. Corruption and inefficiency bred in system reached a peak in administration of U. S. Grant. Reaction helped bring about civil service reform; Civil Service Commission created in 1871. System has, however, continued for many Federal offices.

Spokane (spōkăn′), city (pop. 161,721), E Wash., at falls of Spokane R.; founded c.1872. Recovered rapidly from great fire of 1889. Trade and rail hub for "Inland Empire," a rich region yielding lumber, minerals, wheat, livestock, and fruit. Processes flour, meat, milk, oil, and lumber. Here are aluminum mills, machine and rail shops. Cultural center for the region. Seat of Gonzaga Univ. (Jesuit; mainly for men; 1887). Resorts in area.

Spokane, river, rising in Coeur d'Alene L., N Idaho, and flowing c.100 mi. W and NW through Wash. to Columbia R.

Spoleto (spōlā′tō), city (pop. 10,579), Umbria, central Italy. Of great antiquity, it was the cap. of a large duchy (founded by the Lombards about A.D. 570; under papal rule from 13th cent.). Has cathedral with fresco by Filippo Lippi; several churches with early mosaics and paintings; Roman remains.

sponge, animal of phylum Porifera (world-wide distribution; c.2,500 species). All but one family are marine forms. Live at all depths, usually in colonies attached to rocks or other surface. Usually classified by type of skeleton secreted by simple, jellylike body; some have skeleton with calcium carbonate crystals or glassy spicules, others have skeleton of spongin (chemically related to silk with no hard crystals) used as commercial bath sponge.

spontaneous combustion: see COMBUSTION.

spoonbill, large wading bird of Old and New Worlds related to ibis. With its long bill, like flattened spoon at end, it captures small aquatic animals. Roseate spoonbill has rosy pink plumage accentuated by the carmine of lesser wing coverts; range S North America to Argentina and Chile. See *ill.,* p. 105.

Sporades (spô′rùdēz), scattered islands in Aegean Sea, belonging to Greece. Grouped variously at different periods. N Sporades are generally understood to include Skyros and lesser islands off the coasts of Magnesia and Euboea, sometimes also Lemnos and Lesbos, off NW Asia Minor. S Sporades include Icaria, Samos, the Dodecanese, and Chios.

spore, term applied to a reproductive cell of certain plants (e.g., mosses, ferns) and protozoa (unicellular animals) and also to a resistant resting cell stage found especially among bacteria. Some spores develop into new organisms independently; others (called gametes) first unite with similar or dissimilar (male or female) cells. Organisms that form spores often reproduce also by fission or by budding. See *ill.,* p. 633.

spots and stains: see STAIN REMOVAL.

Spotswood, Alexander, 1676–1740, colonial governor of Va. (1710–22), b. Morocco. Encouraged settlement of frontier.

Spotsylvania, rural county, NE Va., between Rappahannock and North Anna rivers, formerly part of estate of Alexander Spotswood. In Civil War, scene of battles of Fredericksburg and Chancellorsville and of Spotsylvania Courthouse in WILDERNESS CAMPAIGN.

Spottiswoode, John, 1565–1639, Scottish prelate and church historian. Wrote *History of the Church of Scotland* (1655); advocated episcopacy in Church. For opposing King Charles I's attempt to impose Anglican liturgy he was excommunicated (1638). Also Spottiswood, Spotswood.

Spottiswoode, William, 1825–83, English mathematician and physicist. His elementary treatise on determinants (1851) was probably the first published.

sprat, European fish (*Clupea*) of herring family. Canned in Norway as sardines or anchovies.

Spray (sprā), village (pop. 5,542), N N.C., NNW of Reidsville, near Va. line. Mfg. of textiles.

Spree (shprā), river, c.250 mi. long, E Germany, rising in Lusatian Mts. of Saxony and flowing N and NW through Brandenburg and Berlin into the Havel. The picturesque **Spree Forest** (Ger. *Spreewald*), in Lower Lusatia, is a marshy region crisscrossed by small waterways which are the only traffic lanes connecting its villages. WENDS here have kept colorful traditions, local costumes.

Sprengel pump, device to produce partial vacuum by fall through tubes of liquid, usually mercury. It was important in early experiments for which production of vacuum was necessary and especially in development of X-ray tubes. Invented by Hermann J. P. Sprengel (1834–1906), German chemist and physicist who became naturalized British subject.

spring, natural flow of water from ground or rock. Hot springs occur when the water issues from great depths or is heated by volcanic force. Mineral springs have a high content of dissolved substances. See also ARTESIAN WELL; GEYSER; MINERAL WATER.

Springdale, city (pop. 5,835), NW Ark., in the Ozarks. Ships fruit; produces grape juice and wine.

springer spaniel: see SPANIEL.

Springfield. 1 City (pop. 81,628), state cap. (since 1839), central Ill., on Sangamon R. and SW of Chicago; settled 1818. Trade, industrial, and distribution center in agr. (Corn Belt) and coal area. Mfg. of farm machinery and food products. Abraham Lincoln lived and practiced here 1837–61; helped make city cap. He is buried here; his home is shrine. State historical society rich in Lincolniana. Birthplace of Vachel Lindsay. Near by are NEW SALEM, Camp Butler Natl. Cemetery. **2** Town (pop. 2,032), central Ky., SE of Louisville. Marriage certificate of Thomas Lincoln and Nancy Hanks in courthouse. Lincoln Homestead Park near by. **3** Industrial city (pop. 162,399), SW Mass., on Connecticut R. near Conn. line; settled 1636 by W. PYNCHON. Mfg. of electrical and other machinery, firearms, motorcycles, plastics. Was in

Shays's Rebellion (1786–87); station on Underground Railroad. U.S. armory here was founded by Washington. It has first American-made planetarium (1937). Saint-Gaudens's *Puritan* is in Merrick Park. Seat of Springfield and American Internatl. colleges. Annual Eastern States Fair is held at Storrowton, reconstructed colonial village. **4** City (pop. 66,731), SW Mo., in resort area of the Ozarks; laid out c.1835. Agr. and industrial center, it has railroad shops, stockyards, metal-working plants, and mfg. of clothing and food products. Seat of Drury Col. (Congregationalist; coed.; 1873). Battlefield (1861) of Wilson Creek is near by. **5** City (pop. 78,508), W central Ohio, on Mad R. and NE of Dayton; settled 1799. Mfg. of machinery, foundry and machine-shop products. Here is Wittenberg Col. (Lutheran; coed.; 1844). **6** City (pop. 10,-807), W Oregon, on Willamette R. just E of Eugene, in lumber, grain area. **7** City (pop. 6,506), N Tenn., N of Nashville. Tobacco market; mfg. of blankets. **8** Town (pop. 9,190), including industrial Springfield village (pop. 4,940), SE Vt., on Connecticut R. and SE of Rutland. Machinery and machine-tool factories have flourished since before 1900. Crown Point military road crossed this area.

Springhill, town (pop. 7,138), N N.S., SE of Amherst. Important coal-mining center.

Spring Hill College: see MOBILE, Ala.

Spring Valley, residential village (pop. 4,500), SE N.Y., W of Nyack. Summer resort.

Springville, city (pop. 6,475), N central Utah, S of Provo. Served by STRAWBERRY VALLEY PROJECT.

spruce, coniferous evergreen tree of the genus *Picea,* widely distributed in the N Hemisphere. Many species are grown as ornamentals; the wood, usually light, soft, and straight-grained, is important commercially. Best-known species of spruce include the Norway (*Picea abies*), white (*P. glauca* and *P. engelmanni*), Sitka (*P. sitchensis*), Colorado (*P. pungens*) and its variety, Colorado blue spruce.

Spruce Knob, mountain peak (4,860 ft.) of the Alleghenies, E W.Va.; highest point in state.

Spur, city (pop. 2,183), NW Texas, ESE of Lubbock on plain below Cap Rock escarpment. Processes and markets for cattle and agr. area.

spurge, name for any plant of genus *Euphorbia* and some related plants. Many are cactuslike succulents, with milky juice, often poisonous. Spurges have been used medicinally, others yield gums, oils, or dyes. Such spurges, as the green and white snow-on-the-mountain and poinsettia, are grown as ornamentals.

Spurgeon, Charles Haddon, 1834–92, English Baptist preacher. His popularity led to erection of Metropolitan Tabernacle, London, in 1861. His sermons (finally collected in 50 volumes) were widely read.

spurry, weedy annual plant with small white flowers. Field spurry (*Spergula sativa*) naturalized in U.S., is native to Europe where it is used for forage and binding sandy soils. Its seeds are edible and yield oil.

Spurs, Battle of the: see BATTLE OF THE SPURS.

Spuyten Duyvil Creek: see HARLEM RIVER.

Spyri, Johanna (yōhä′nä shpē′rē), 1827–1901, Swiss author of children's books, notably of *Heidi* (1880).

Squanto or **Tisquantum,** d. 1622, North American Indian of Pawtuxet tribe. Aided Plymouth colonists as interpreter and in their planting.

square, in geometry, figure bounded by four equal straight lines (sides) meeting at four points (vertices) to form four right angles. Opposite sides are parallel. Perimeter of a square is sum of its sides. Area is product of one side multiplied by itself or by any other side. In arithmetic, when a number is multiplied by itself product is called the square of that number. In algebra, an expression such as x^2 indicates that a quantity is multiplied by itself, the product being the square of that quantity.

squash, edible fruit of a vine of the same genus, *Cucurbita,* as the PUMPKIN. Summer squashes are of either the pattypan or long type and are used when young;

winter squashes, chiefly varieties of *Cucurbita maxima,* including the Hubbard and turban, called pumpkins in Europe, are hard-shelled, more flavorful, and may be kept over winter; third group contains varieties of *C. moschata,* including those called crookneck pumpkin and cheese pumpkin.

squash racquets, game played on four-walled court 16 ft. high by 18½ ft. wide by 32 ft. deep. Back wall usually measures 9 ft. In match play, usually 15 pts. win game, 2 of 3 games win match. Squash racquets probably originated in late 19th cent. from older game of RACQUETS.

squash tennis, game played on four-walled court similar to SQUASH RACQUETS court. Rule differences between squash tennis and squash racquets grew out of equipment differences. Livelier ball and heavier racquet in squash tennis emphasize hitting ball on carom.

squatter sovereignty, in U.S. history, doctrine under which slavery was permitted in territories, final question of its legal status being left to territorial settlers when they applied for statehood. First proposed in 1847, it was incorporated in COMPROMISE OF 1850 and KANSAS-NEBRASKA BILL. Its chief exponent, S. A. DOUGLAS, called it "popular sovereignty," but antislavery men contemptuously called it "squatter sovereignty."

squid, carnivorous marine mollusk with 10 arms bearing suction disks. It has a thickened mantle, and the shell is reduced to an internal horny plate; eyes highly developed. In danger, emits inky fluid.

Squier, Ephraim George (skwī′ŭr), 1821–88, American archaeologist and journalist. He worked on newspapers in New York and Ohio. His lifelong interest in archaeology and his many contributions to the field began with his study of prehistoric remains in Ohio and Mississippi valleys. Served as U.S. chargé d'affaires to republics of Central America (1849) and later as American commissioner to Peru.

squill, spring-blooming, low bulbous plant (*Scilla*) with dainty bell-shaped blooms, usually deep blue. The Siberian squill (*Scilla sibirica*) is a rock-garden favorite; the wood hyacinth (*S. nonscripta*) is the common bluebell of England. Bulbs of the sea squill or sea onion (*Urginea maritima*) are sold as white squill, a drug, and red squill, a rat poison.

squirrel, small rodent (chiefly of genus *Sciurus*) of North and South America, Europe, Asia, Africa. It has soft, thick fur and a bushy tail. Usually is diurnal and partly arboreal. Conceals winter food in ground or stumps. See also FLYING SQUIRREL and GROUND SQUIRREL.

Sr, chemical symbol of the element STRONTIUM.

Srinagar (srēnŭ′gŭr), city (pop. 209,595; alt. 5,227 ft.), summer cap. of Kashmir, on Jhelum R.; famed resort. Has many canals, and transportation is chiefly by boat. Textile mfg.

St. For placenames beginning thus, see SAINT and SANKT. Personal names beginning thus are filed as if spelled Saint. Persons recognized by the church as saints are under proper names (e.g., PAUL, SAINT).

Stabat Mater (stä′bät mä′tĕr), hymn of the Roman Catholic Church, a prayer meditating on the sorrows of the Virgin by the Cross; probably by Jacopone da Todi. It begins *Stabat mater dolorosa juxta crucem* [the sorrowful mother stood at the foot of the Cross]. It is the sequence for the Seven Sorrows of the Virgin and is much sung at Lenten services. Notable musical settings were composed by Josquin des Prés, Palestrina, Pergolesi, Haydn, Schubert, and Verdi.

Stabiae, Italy: see CASTELLAMMARE DI STABIA.

Staël, Germaine de (zhĕrmĕn′ dù stäl′), 1766–1817, French woman of letters; daughter of Jacques Necker. Her opposition to Napoleon caused her exile, first to her estate at Coppet, on the L. of Geneva, later to Russia and England. She wrote two successful novels —*Delphine* (1802) and *Corinne* (1807)—but her chief work is *De l'Allemagne* (1811), which tremendously influenced French literature through its enthusiasm

SMALL CAPITALS = cross references. Pronunciation key on inside end pages. Abbreviations: p. 2.

for German romanticism. Mme de Staël was the center of a brilliant circle which included Chateaubriand and Benjamin Constant.

Stafford, English noble family. **Humphrey Stafford, 1st duke of Buckingham,** 1402–60, fought in France in the Hundred Years War. Supported the Lancastrians in Wars of the Roses and was killed in battle. His grandson, **Henry Stafford, 2d duke of Buckingham,** 1454?–1483, was instrumental in having Richard III made king. Staged an unsuccessful revolt against Richard and was executed. His son, **Edward Stafford, 3d duke of Buckingham,** 1478–1521, was given high honors by Henry VIII. Henry actually was suspicious of Stafford and had him tried (1521) and executed for treason.

Stafford, William Howard, 1st Viscount: see HOWARD, family.

Stafford, county, England: see STAFFORDSHIRE.

Stafford, textile town (pop. 6,471), NE Conn., at Mass. line; settled 1719. Includes Stafford Springs borough (pop. 3,396), health resort (mineral springs).

Staffordshire (stă′fŭrdshĭr) or **Stafford,** inland county (1,154 sq. mi.; pop. 1,621,013), central England. Mainly industrial, it has POTTERIES district (china, glass, bricks, and pottery) in N and the BLACK COUNTRY (coal fields, foundries, and iron and steel mills) in S. County town is Stafford, municipal borough (pop. 40,275), a shoe-mfg. center. Birthplace of Izaak Walton.

Stafford Springs, Conn.: see STAFFORD.

stagecoach, public road conveyance carrying passengers. Operated from early 18th cent. Early coaches usually were drawn by four or six horses changed at stages along route; the coach traveled from 12 to 18 hr. a day, covering c.25 to 40 mi. Carried eight to fourteen passengers, baggage, and mail. Schedules and comfort were improved in England by competition from mail coaches. Heyday of stagecoach was early 19th cent.

stage design. Although painted scenery was used as early as 461 B.C., both Greek and Roman theaters required little or no scenery. Medieval mystery plays often had a single setting but used machinery for hoisting clouds and heavenly bodies. Traveling *commedia dell' arte* players introduced painted backdrops. These became generally used. In 20th cent., much experimental work has been done (e.g., by Gordon Craig). Such devices as improved lighting, revolving stages, raised platforms, and gauze curtains have been used effectively. Theater-in-the-round (i.e., stage in the center with audience on all four sides) has been adopted to some extent.

Stagg, Amos Alonzo, 1862–, American football coach, known as "grand old man of football." Coached at Univ. of Chicago (1892–1933), College of the Pacific (1933–46), Susquehanna Univ. (1947–).

Stagira (stŭjī′rŭ), anc. city on peninsula of Chalcidice, Macedonia, birthplace of Aristotle.

stained glass, in general, windows made of colored glass. Actually, staining is only one of the coloring methods used and the best medieval glass made little use of it. The true art of making stained glass reached its height in the 13th and 14th cent. Gothic glaziers used colored pot metal, i.e., glass colored with metallic oxides while in the melting pot, thus obtaining clear, transparent colors. Also used were white glass and flashed glass (glass to which a thin film of colored glass had been fused). For defining outlines and details, a brownish paint grisaille, made of powdered glass and iron oxide, was applied and then fired so as to fuse with the glass surface. A red-hot iron was used for cutting the glass to the required pieces and shapes. The pieces were then fitted into channeled lead strips, the strips soldered together at junction points, and the whole installed in a bracing framework of iron. In the 16th cent. the designs were painted on the glass with enamel paints and then fired. Thus the real art of stained glass was lost.

Romanticism and the Gothic revival of the 19th cent. reawakened interest in the study of glass as well as other medieval arts. William Morris and Burne-Jones designed windows of true medieval technique and spirit (e.g., at Birmingham Cathedral and at Christ Church, Oxford). John LA FARGE contributed to American stained glass. Famous stained glass windows of medieval days can still be seen in the cathedrals of Chartres, Le Mans, and elsewhere in France, and in York, Salisbury, and Lincoln, England.

Stainer, Sir John, 1840–1901, English composer, organist at St. Paul's Cathedral, London, and professor at the Royal Col. of Music; knighted 1888. He wrote much church music, including the cantatas *The Daughter of Jairus* and *The Crucifixion.* With W. A. Barrett he wrote *A Dictionary of Musical Terms* (1876).

stain removal, from fabrics. Prompt treatment may often prevent stains from penetrating fibers and may make the use of strong chemicals unnecessary. Certain fresh stains, especially grease spots, can be removed by applying an adsorbent, e.g., chalk, whiting, or corn meal. Many spots can be removed from fabrics which water does not injure by placing the fabric on a blotter or absorbent cloth, then sponging it with a damp cloth. Certain stains are removed only by the application of chemicals, which should be first tested on an inconspicuous part of the fabric. (*Caution.* Chemical cleaning fluids should not be used in a room where there is any open flame.) In rubbing spots, use a clean cloth and work toward the center of the spot using a circular motion. Solvents used for removing spots include alcohol, benzene, carbon tetrachloride, gasoline, naphtha, and turpentine. Bleaches include hydrogen peroxide (a mild agent that may be used on many colored fabrics), commercial chlorine bleaches (not advisable for silk or wool), Javelle water, oxalic acid, and potassium permanganate (this sometimes leaves a brownish spot removable with lemon juice, oxalic acid, or hydrogen peroxide; it is not safe for use on rayon). Bleaches are often applied with a medicine dropper to fabric stretched over a bowl of steaming water.

Note. Common causes of stains and methods of removing them from washable fabrics are listed below; certain of the methods suggested may be applied with care to non-washable fabrics.

Blood. Rinse in cold water; for stubborn stains add soap or ammonia to water and soak.

Chocolate and *cocoa.* Wash with soap or with borax and cold water.

Coffee (clear). Launder with soap or borax; remove remaining stain with potassium permanganate.

Coffee with cream. Wash with soap and cold water, then treat as for clear coffee.

Cream and *milk.* Rinse in cold water, adding a little ammonia if needed; then launder in hot, soapy water.

Egg. Scrape off excess, then use cold water, followed by hot soapy water.

Fruit juice. Pour boiling water over stain immediately; then use lemon juice and expose to sunlight.

Grass and *green foliage.* If not removed by laundering, use alcohol or a bleach, then rinse.

Gravy. Rinse in cold water; for stubborn stains add soap or ammonia to water and soak. If oily, follow with method for grease.

Grease, oil, and *wax.* Scrape off excess, then use one or more of the following methods: cover spot with chalk or other adsorbent; place blotting paper on both sides and apply hot iron; rinse in a grease solvent, e.g., gasoline or carbon tetrachloride; wash in hot, soapy water.

Gum. Remove excess with dull knife, soak in gasoline, kerosene, or carbon tetrachloride, then launder.

Ice Cream. Rinse in cool water, then follow with methods for removing chocolate, coffee, grease, fruit, or other stains.

Ink. Use commercial ink remover (consult directions on label); certain inks can be removed by soaking in cold water or milk, then laundering; bleaches are often effective.

Iodine. Soak in cold water or in very dilute ammonia solution, then launder.

Iron rust. See rust.

Lipstick. Rub lard into stain, scrape off excess, launder, then use bleach on remaining stain; or pour carbon tetrachloride on stain and blot.

Mildew. Launder, expose to sunlight; soak stubborn stains in milk or use bleach.

Milk. See cream.

Nail polish. Sponge with banana oil, then launder.

Oil. See grease.

Paint and varnish. Scrape off excess; many paint and varnish spots can be softened with turpentine or with lard, then laundered; alcohol is effective for certain paints.

Perspiration. Launder, then bleach and rinse or expose to sunlight.

Pitch, soot, and tar. Rub with lard, then launder; use gasoline, turpentine, or other solvent, if necessary.

Rust. Sprinkle with salt and lemon juice, expose to sunlight; or apply oxalic acid or very dilute hydrochloric acid with a dropper, rinse in hot water, using ammonia or borax to neutralize acid; or use commercial iron rust soap.

Scorch. Dampen and expose to sunlight.

Shoe polish. If polish contains turpentine, soak spot in turpentine, then launder; certain black liquid polishes can be removed with a bleach.

Soot. See pitch.

Stove polish. Rinse in gasoline or other solvent; launder.

Tar. See pitch.

Tea (clear). Rinse in boiling water; if stain remains, soak in borax, or apply potassium permanganate or oxalic acid, or use lemon juice and expose to sunlight.

Tea with milk. Wash with soap and cold water, then treat as for clear tea.

Varnish. See paint.

Vaseline. Remove with turpentine, then launder.

Water spots. Moisten evenly, then press while damp; or steam.

Wax. See grease.

Wine. Rinse in boiling water, then use bleach.

Stair, James Dalrymple, 1st Viscount, 1619–95, Scottish jurist. Prominent after the Restoration, he lost office in 1681, because of sympathy with Covenanters. Became lord advocate under William III. His son, **John Dalrymple, 1st earl of Stair,** 1648–1707, was joint secretary of state under William III. Dominated Scottish Parliament and promoted union with England. His son, **John Dalrymple, 2d earl of Stair,** 1673–1747, Scottish general and diplomat, fought under William III and was prominent in War of the Spanish Succession. Secured overthrow of Walpole in 1741.

Staked Plain: see LLANO ESTACADO.

Stakhanovism (stäkä′nŭvĭzm), movement begun in the USSR in 1935 to speed up industrial production by efficient working methods; named for Aleksey Stakhanov, a Donets Basin coal miner of fabulous efficiency. Stakhanovite workers receive higher pay and other privileges. Stakhanovism proved a successful incentive but is criticized outside the USSR as another form of the speed-up system.

stalactite (stŭlăk′tīt) **and stalagmite** (stŭlăg′mīt). A stalactite is an icicle-shaped mass of calcium carbonate hanging from the roof of a limestone cave, deposited by dripping ground water. A stalagmite forms under the stalactite, growing upward from cavern floor. If the two meet, a pillar is formed. Impurities cause color variations.

Stalin, Joseph Vissarionovich (stä′lĭn, Rus. vĭsŭryô′nŭvĭch stä′lyĭn), 1879–1953, Russian Communist dictator, b. Gori, Georgian SSR. His real name was Dzhugashvili; he called himself Stalin ["made of steel"] after joining the revolutionary movement. The son of a shoemaker, he became a Marxist while studying for the priesthood at Tiflis. He was expelled from the seminary 1899; joined the Bolshevik wing of the Social Democratic party; was arrested for the sixth time in 1913 and exiled for life to Siberia. Amnestied in 1917, he became people's commissar for nationalities in Lenin's cabinet after the October Revolution. His importance in the prerevolutionary underground and in the civil war of 1918–20 has been subject to much debate. In 1922 he was elected general secretary of the Communist party. After Lenin's death (1924) he assumed Lenin's succession jointly with KAMENEV and ZINOVIEV, but he secured in 1927 the expulsion of his two chief rivals—TROTSKY and Zinoviev—from the party, thus gaining sole leadership. Although he held no formal government office before 1941, he dictated Soviet policy as head of the Politburo of the Communist party. In 1928 he ended Lenin's NEW ECONOMIC POLICY and inaugurated the first FIVE-YEAR PLAN. Industrialization and collectivization were carried through at a tremendous cost in human life and liberty. Stalin emphasized the need for consolidating "Socialism in one country" rather than promoting world revolution, as Trotsky advocated. He made his dictatorship absolute by liquidating all opposition within the party in the "purge" trials of the 1930s— touched off by the murder of S. M. KIROV (1934). By 1938, "monolithic unity" was achieved. In 1941 Stalin took over the premiership from Molotov. Shortly after Hitler's attack on Russia, he also assumed military leadership (1941) and took the titles marshal (1943) and generalissimo (1945). At the TEHERAN CONFERENCE, YALTA CONFERENCE, and POTSDAM CONFERENCE he proved himself an astute diplomat. He continued to rule Russia with an iron fist until his death in March, 1953. He was succeeded as premier by MALENKOV. Usually hidden in the Kremlin, Stalin was both a remote figure and a subject of nearly unprecedented official adulation. His least utterances were accepted as party dogmas. Claiming to be the true interpreter of Leninism, Stalin in both his words and deeds created a version of Communism known as Stalinism and embraced by the majority of Communists the world over. To non-Stalinists, Stalinism represents the substitution of nationalism, despotism, and imperialist militarism for the internationalist, equalitarian, and pacifist ideals of earlier Communists. See also UNION OF SOVIET SOCIALIST REPUBLICS.

Stalin, formerly **Varna** (vär′nä), city (pop. 77,792), E Bulgaria; a major Black Sea port. Shipbuilding; textile and tobacco mfg. Seaside resort. University (founded 1920). Founded as Odessus by Greek colonists (6th cent. B.C.), it became a commercial center under Thracian, later under Roman and Byzantine, rule. In 1444 the Turks decisively defeated at Varna an army of Crusaders under Ladislaus III of Poland and Hungary. City was renamed 1949 to honor Joseph Stalin's 70th birthday.

Stalinabad (stä″lyĭnübät′), city (pop. c.110,000), cap. of Tadzhik SSR. Agr. and transportation center. Has textile mills, tanneries, machinery and tobacco plants, distilleries.

Stalingrad (stälyĭngrät′), city (pop. 445,476), SE European RSFSR; a port on the lower Volga. Leading industrial and commercial city in Volga region; important transshipment point and rail hub; a center of heavy industry (esp. steel mills, machinery works, oil refineries). Founded 1589 as a Russian stronghold (called Tsaritsyn until 1925). During Russian civil war it was defended against the Whites by Stalin and Voroshilov. City was virtually destroyed in one of the decisive battles of World War II. German army (including Italian, Hungarian, and Rumanian forces) attacked in Sept., 1942, with superior numbers, but was unable to overcome the desperate Russian stand. Soviet reinforcements, which arrived in Nov., finally forced surrender (Feb. 2, 1943) of the Axis forces, which had lost c.330,000 men. Russians then began a mighty drive W and remained generally on offensive till end of war. Rebuilding of city started immediately after liberation.

Stalino (stä'lyĭnŭ), industrial city (pop. 462,395), SE Ukraine, in the Donets Basin. Iron and steel mills; machinery works; nitrate and food-processing plants.

Stalin Peak, Czechoslovakia: see TATRA.

Stalin Peak, 24,590 ft., Tadzhik SSR, in the Pamir; highest in USSR. Formerly called Garmo Peak.

Stalinsk (stä'lyĭnsk), industrial city (pop. c.223,000), RSFSR, in S central Siberia, on Tom R. (head of navigation). It is the chief metallurgical center of Kuznetsk Basin.

Stallings, Laurence (stô'lĭngz), 1894–, American dramatist, best known for *What Price Glory* (1924), a successful war play written with Maxwell Anderson.

Stambul, Turkey: see ISTANBUL.

Stambuliski, Alexander, Bulgarian *Stamboliski* (stämbōlē'skĕ), 1879–1923, Bulgarian premier (1919–23), founder of the Radical Peasant party (1908). As virtual dictator after 1920, he carried out agrarian reforms and followed a conciliatory foreign policy. Was murdered in a nationalist coup d'état.

Stambulov, Stefan (stĕ'fän stämbōō'lôf), 1854–95, Bulgarian statesman, leader of National Liberal party. Organized revolution which put Ferdinand on throne (1887); was premier with dictatorial powers until 1894. Was assassinated.

Stamford, municipal borough (pop. 10,899), in Parts of Kesteven, Lincolnshire, England. Supposed site of defeat (449) of Picts and Scots by Saxons. Was one of Five Boroughs of the Danes.

Stamford. 1 City (pop. 74,293), SW Conn., on Long Isl. Sound SW of Norwalk; settled 1641. Many residents commute to New York city. Mfg. of metal goods, chemicals, and plastics. **2** City (pop. 5,819), W central Texas, NNW of Abilene. Trade and processing center for cotton and cattle area with oil and gas wells. Annual Texas Cowboy Reunion.

Stamford Bridge, village, East Riding of Yorkshire, England. King Harold here defeated Harold Hardrada (Harold III) and Tostig in 1066.

stammering: see STUTTERING.

Stamp Act, 1765, revenue law passed by English Parliament requiring publications and legal documents in the American colonies to bear a stamp. Act was strongly denounced. At **Stamp Act Congress,** which met Oct. 7, 1765, colonial delegates attacked law as unconstitutional because colonists were not represented in Parliament. Act repealed in 1766.

Standards, National Bureau of, in U.S. Dept. of Commerce, estab. 1901 for research in physics, mathematics, chemistry, and engineering. Determines national standards of weights and measures and advises government agencies about specifications for purchase of government supplies.

Standish, Miles or **Myles,** c.1584–1656, American colonist, b. England. Military leader of Plymouth Colony. A founder of Duxbury, Mass. Familiar as the disappointed suitor in Longfellow's poem.

standpatters, in U.S. history, term widely used early in 20th cent. to designate conservatives in Republican party as against INSURGENTS or progressive Republicans. Term derives from poker parlance.

Stanford, Leland (lē'lŭnd stăn'fûrd), 1824–93, American railroad builder, politician, and philanthropist. A founder and president (1863–93) of Central Pacific RR; also president of Southern Pacific Co. (1885–90). U.S. Senator from Calif. (1885–93). Founded Stanford University. His wife, **Jane Lathrop Stanford,** 1825–1905, continued to aid the university after his death.

Stanford University, mainly at Palo Alto, Calif.; nonsectarian, coed.; chartered 1885, opened 1891 by Leland and Jane L. STANFORD as Leland Stanford Jr. Univ. (still its legal name). Noted for research and graduate work, leadership in curriculum plans for major subjects, and independent study. Includes Hoover Library on War, Revolution, and Peace and

Hopkins Marine Laboratory at Pacific Grove, Calif.

Stanhope (stă'nŭp), English noble family. **James Stanhope, 1st Earl Stanhope,** 1673–1721, won victories as commander in chief of British forces in Spain (1708) in War of Spanish Succession. Was twice (1714–17, 1718–21) secretary of state under George I. His grandson, **Charles Stanhope, 3d Earl Stanhope,** 1753–1816, supported the younger William Pitt (whose sister he married) and opposed war with American colonies. Broke with Pitt over the French Revolution. His inventions include lenses and printing machines. His daughter, **Lady Hester (Lucy) Stanhope,** 1776–1839, was hostess and secretary for William Pitt. Traveled in Levant, adopting Eastern male dress. Settled as prophetess among the Druses of the Lebanon mts. The 3d Earl's grandson, **Philip Henry Stanhope, 5th Earl Stanhope,** 1805–75, was the author of several standard histories.

Stanhope, Philip Dormer: see CHESTERFIELD, PHILIP DORMER STANHOPE, 4TH EARL OF.

Stanhope, Philip Henry Stanhope, 5th Earl: see STANHOPE, family.

Stanislaus, kings of Poland. **Stanislaus I** (Stanislaus Leszczynski), 1677–1766, was elected king in 1704 through intervention of Charles XII of Sweden (see NORTHERN WAR). After Charles's defeat at Poltava (1709), he had to yield Poland to his rival, AUGUSTUS II, and retired to France. His daughter Marie Leszczynska married Louis XV, with whose help Stanislaus again sought the Polish throne in 1733 (see POLISH SUCCESSION, WAR OF THE). Defeated by AUGUSTUS III, he retained the title king and was given the duchy of LORRAINE. A man of culture and taste, he embellished Nancy and held a distinguished court at Lunéville. **Stanislaus II** (Stanislaus Augustus Poniatowski), 1732–98, was elected (1764) to succeed Augustus III. He was backed by Frederick II of Prussia and by Catherine II of Russia, whose lover he had been. Russian influence became paramount in Poland. An anti-Russian rebellion was crushed and was followed by the first partition of POLAND (1772). Stanislaus' subsequent attempts to revitalize the Polish state and his introduction of an efficient constitution (1791) brought about joint Russian and Prussian military intervention and the second partition (1793). Stanislaus took no firm stand in the KOSCIUSKO uprising of 1794, after the failure of which he lost his remaining lands in the third partition (1795). He went to live in Russia.

Stanislav (stŭnyĭsläf'), Pol. *Stanisławów,* city (1931 pop. 61,256), W Ukraine. Rail center; oil refineries; carpet mfg. Was Polish until 1772; Austrian 1772–1918; Polish 1919–39; formally ceded to USSR 1945.

Stanislavsky, Constantin (kŭnstŭntyēn' stŭnyĭsläf'skē), 1863–1938, stage name of Constantin Sergeyevich Alekseyev, Russian actor, director, and theatrical producer. Cofounder of MOSCOW ART THEATRE (1898). As its director he eliminated mechanical theatrical techniques, training actors to strive for inner interpretations of roles.

Stanisławow, Ukraine: see STANISLAV.

Stanley, Edward George Geoffrey Smith: see DERBY, EDWARD GEORGE GEOFFREY SMITH, 14TH EARL OF.

Stanley, Sir Henry Morton, 1841–1904, British explorer, a journalist. Sent to Africa by New York *Herald* (1871) to find David LIVINGSTONE. On expedition of 1879–84 he obtained territorial concessions which led to Belgian acquisition of Congo Free State. African expedition of 1887–88 led to land concessions for British.

Stanley, Wendell Meredith, 1904–, American biochemist. Shared 1946 Nobel Prize for isolation of crystalline forms of viruses.

Stanley, William, 1858–1916, American electrical engineer. Invented multiple system of alternating-current transmission; out of this grew modern system of light and power transmission.

Stanley Falls, cataracts of Lualaba R., NE Belgian Con-

go, extending 60 mi. between Stanleyville and Pon-
thierville. Total fall, c.200 ft.

Stanley Pool, lakelike expansion, area 320 sq. mi., of
Congo R. along border between Belgian Congo and
French Equatorial Africa. Discovered 1877 by Stan-
ley. On it are Leopoldville and Brazzaville.

Stanleyville, town (pop. 25,278), NE Belgian Congo;
port on the Congo R. On short rail line skirting Stanley Falls. Tourist center.

Stanovoi Range (stŭnŭvoi′), mountain chain, RSFSR,
in SE Siberia, extending c.450 mi. E from Olekma R.
and rising to 8,143 ft. Forms watershed between Lena
and Amur river basins.

Stans (stäns), town (pop. 3,449), cap. of Nidwalden half-
canton, Unterwalden, Switzerland.

Stanton, Edwin McMasters, 1814–69, American cabinet officer. Became Pres. Lincoln's Secretary of War
in Jan., 1862. Administered office with economy and
efficiency. A radical Republican, opposed to many of
Lincoln's policies, he continued under Andrew JOHN-
SON. Resisted Johnson's attempts to remove him; resigned 1868.

Stanton, Elizabeth Cady, 1815–1902, American reformer, a leader of woman-suffrage movement. With Lucretia Mott she organized (1848) first woman's rights
convention. Also closely associated with Susan B.
ANTHONY. President (1869–92) of woman-suffrage associations, she helped to compile a history of the
movement.

Stanwix, Fort, colonial outpost in N.Y., near site of
present city of Rome. Controlled principal route from
the Hudson to L. Ontario as trading center. Besieged
by British in American Revolution. Treaty between
Iroquois and U.S. signed here in 1784.

Stapleton, N.Y.: see STATEN ISLAND.

star, in astronomy, luminous globular mass of intensely
hot gases. Man distinguished in early times between
"fixed" stars and planets and identified groups of
stars (see CONSTELLATION) with mythological figures.
Actually stars are in rapid motion detectable only by
exacting observations over many years. Stars of our
Galaxy comprise MILKY WAY SYSTEM and include our
sun. Although similar in chemical composition, stars
vary in luminosity (see MAGNITUDE), temperature,
color, volume, density. Correlation between temperature and color is shown by classification into color
series (bluish white, white, yellowish white, yellow and
red stars) with temperatures decreasing from that of
the hottest bluish white stars (c.20,000°C. to 50,-
000°C.). Our sun is medium-sized yellow star, temperature c.6,000°C. Density ranges from over a ton per
cubic inch in certain dwarf white stars to density less
than one millionth that of sun in certain huge red
stars known as supergiants. LIGHT-YEAR is commonly
used to indicate vast stellar distances. Nearest stars,
other than sun, are c.4.3 light-years distant from earth.
Many apparently single stars have been discovered to
consist of two or more stars. Binary stars are double
stars revolving about same center of gravity. See also
CLUSTER; VARIABLE STAR.

starch, white, odorless, tasteless CARBOHYDRATE, important in functions of plants and animals. Produced
by PHOTOSYNTHESIS in green plants and stored. Animals obtain starch from plants; in animal body starch
is stored as GLYCOGEN. Digestion converts it to sucrose,
a source of energy. Test for presence of starch is blue-
black color produced on addition of iodine. Starch is
used for sizing paper and textiles, for stiffening, in
making dextrin. Cornstarch is used to make corn
syrup and glucose.

Star Chamber, anc. meeting place of king's councilors
in Westminster Palace, London, named for stars painted on ceiling. Originally used to curb powers of nobles, it became criminal court under Tudors. Abuses
of its power under James I and Charles I led to its
abolition in 1641. "Star Chamber proceedings" now
signifies acts of an arbitrary tribunal.

starfish, common marine echinoderm typically star-
shaped (five or more arms or rays radiate from a disk).
It has a spiny surface with calcareous plates embedded
in skin; moves by tube feet; c.1,000 known species.

Starhemberg, Ernst Rüdiger, Graf von (ěrnst′ rü′dĭgŭr
gräf′ fŭn shtä′rŭmběrk″), 1638–1701, Austrian field
marshal. Held Vienna with a small garrison in Turkish siege of 1683 until its relief by John III of Poland. His descendant, **Ernst Rüdiger von Starhemberg,**
1899–, Austrian politician, led the *Heimwehr,* a fascistic militia, supported Chancellor Dollfuss, and was
vice chancellor and security minister under Schuschnigg until 1936. In World War II he served in British
and Free French air forces.

Stark, Johannes (stärk, Ger. yōhä′nùs shtärk′), 1874–,
German physicist. Won 1919 Nobel Prize for discovery of Doppler effect in canal rays (positive particles produced in vacuum tube which pass through per-
forations in cathode) and broadening of spectrum lines
in electric field (Stark effect) which confirmed quantum theory.

Stark, John, 1728–1822, American Revolutionary commander. Repulsed attack by Gen. Burgoyne at Bennington in Saratoga campaign.

Starkville, city (pop. 7,107), E Miss., W of Columbus in
livestock and farm area. Near by is Mississippi State
Col. (land-grant; coed.; 1878).

Starling, Ernest Henry, 1866–1927, English physiologist, authority on nervous regulation of heart and circulation. He evolved (with Bayliss) hormone concept.

starling, European bird introduced into U.S. in 1890,
now common in parts of E U.S. Has iridescent black
plumage and long bill (yellow in spring and summer).
Destroys insects.

Star of Bethlehem, name for celestial body, probably
not a single star, in east which is related in the Gospel
led the Wise Men to Bethlehem (Mat. 2.1–10).

star-of-Bethlehem, low, spring-blooming bulbous plant
of the Mediterranean region. The common star-of-
Bethlehem (*Ornithogalum umbellatum*) has grasslike
leaves and clustered white starry flowers. Other species and some other flowers are also called star-of-
Bethlehem.

Starr, Belle, 1848–89, American outlaw, consort of notorious bandits of SW U.S. Original name was Myra
Belle Shirley.

star route, in U.S. postal service, surface route to post
offices not accessible by railroad or steamboat. U.S.
Postal Guide and maps once designated such an office
by an asterisk, hence the name. Private contracts to
carry mail over these routes are made with bonded
bidders. In April, 1881, Pres. Garfield dismissed Second Assistant Postmaster General T. W. Brady, suspected of having fraudulently increased compensation
of numerous star-route contractors, among them former Sen. S. W. Dorsey of Ark. Both narrowly escaped conviction in Pres. Arthur's administration.
Frauds, amounting to nearly $500,000, hastened civil
service reform.

Star-spangled Banner, The, American national anthem,
beginning, "Oh, say can you see." The words were
written by Francis Scott Key, an American lawyer
who, on a mission to recover a prisoner, was detained
by the British and forced to watch the bombardment
of Fort McHenry (Sept., 1814). The sight of the flag
still floating over the fort at dawn inspired Key's
verses. The tune, composed by John Stafford Smith
(1750–1836), was taken from an English song, *To
Anacreon in Heaven.* Song officially became national
anthem by a presidential order in 1916, confirmed by
Congress, 1931.

Starved Rock, cliff, 140 ft. high, N Ill., overlooking
Illinois R. between La Salle and Ottawa. Visited by
Jolliet and Père Marquette 1673, and by La Salle and
de Tonti 1679 (they completed fort here, 1682–83).
Legendary scene of starvation of Illinois band driven
here by Ottawa Indians in 18th cent. Vicinity was
hideout of brigands and outlaws in early 19th cent.
Now state park.

Stassen, Harold E(dward) (stä'sùn), 1907–, American statesman, president of Univ. of Pennsylvania (1948–53). Governor of Minn. (1939–43). Delegate to conference creating UN (1945). Became Mutual Security Director in 1953.

Stassfurt (shtäs'fŏŏrt), city (pop. 29,762), Saxony-Anhalt, E central Germany. Center of one of world's chief potash-mining areas. Produces chemicals and machinery.

State, United States Department of, executive department of Federal government responsible for determination and execution, under the President's direction, of American foreign policy. Estab. Sept., 1789, to replace Dept. of Foreign Affairs; oldest Federal department. Secretary of State is first ranking cabinet officer. Successive reorganizations of department culminated in 1909 reorganization, which gave department essentials of its present-day structure. At that time foreign policy and relations were reorganized along new geographical divisions—Western European, Near Eastern, Far Eastern, and Latin American. During Cordell Hull's administration (1933–44) changes were effected to meet rising tide of World War II. At close of the war the department's machinery was geared to dispense information to foreign nations, to estab. strict secrecy concerning its operation, to integrate foreign policy with the economic-aid programs, and to bring about effective liaison between U.S. and the UN.

State College, residential borough (pop. 17,227), central Pa., NW of Harrisburg. Seat of Pennsylvania State Col. (land-grant and state supported, coed.; opened 1859). Has forest school at Mont Alto, institute of animal nutrition, Ellen H. Richards Inst. for textile research, and five jr. branches.

state flowers. Each state of the U.S. has designated a floral emblem; the U.S. as a whole has none. The emblem of the Dist. of Columbia is the American Beauty rose; those of the states are: Ala., goldenrod; Ariz., saguaro; Ark., apple blossom; Calif., California poppy; Colo., blue-and-white columbine; Conn., mountain laurel; Del., peach blossom; Fla., orange blossom; Ga., Cherokee rose; Idaho, mock orange; Ill., violet; Ind., zinnia; Iowa, wild rose; Kansas, sunflower; Ky., goldenrod; La., magnolia; Maine, pine cone and tassel; Md., black-eyed Susan; Mass., trailing arbutus; Mich., apple blossom; Minn., lady's slipper; Miss., magnolia; Mo., hawthorn; Mont., bitterroot; Nebr., goldenrod; Nev., sagebrush; N.H., lilac; N.J., violet; N.Mex., yucca; N.Y., rose; N.C., daisy; N.Dak., wild rose; Ohio, red carnation; Okla., mistletoe; Oregon, Oregon grape; Pa., mountain laurel; R.I., violet; S.C., Carolina jasmine; S.Dak., pasqueflower; Tenn., iris; Texas, bluebonnet; Utah, sego lily; Vt., red clover; Va., dogwood; Wash., rhododendron; W.Va., rhododendron; Wis., violet; Wyo., Indian paintbrush.

Staten Island (57 sq. mi.; pop. 191,555), SE N.Y., in NEW YORK BAY, forming (with small adjacent islands) Richmond borough (since 1898) of NEW YORK city and Richmond co. of N.Y. state. N and W, bridges cross to N.J. over Kill Van Kull and Arthur Kill; ferries connect with Manhattan (NE) and Brooklyn. Generally residential, with some semirural sections and resort beaches (SE shore). Industries (shipbuilding and repairing, oil refining, lumber milling) mainly in N. Trade centers are St. George, Stapleton (site of first U.S. free port), Port Richmond. Staten Isl. visited by Henry Hudson 1609; permanent community estab. by 1661. Early buildings include Billopp (or Conference) House (built before 1688), where Lord Howe negotiated with Continentals in 1776; Church of St. Andrew (founded 1708); Garibaldi House (Italian liberator lived here in 1850s).

Statesboro, city (pop. 6,097), E Ga., NW of Savannah. Tobacco and livestock market; food processing.

States-General or **Estates-General. 1** In French history, national assembly in which the chief estates—clergy, nobility, and commons—were represented as separate bodies. It was comparable to the DIET of the Holy Roman Empire, to the old Spanish CORTES, and, in some respects, to the English PARLIAMENT, but it never developed the power and organization of these bodies. Originating in the king's council, or Curia Regis, the French States-General was first summoned in 1302 by Philip IV. Its powers were never clearly defined; its main function was to approve royal legislation. Its attempt, promoted by Étienne MARCEL, to secure wider authority collapsed in 1358. After the States-General of 1614, which accomplished nothing, no further meeting was called till 1789. There were, however, provincial estates in a number of provinces. The States-General of 1789 was called by Louis XVI as a last resort to solve the government's financial crisis (see FRENCH REVOLUTION). It first met on May 5, at Versailles, and it became immediately evident that the third estate (commons) and the liberals among the clergy and nobles intended to transform it from a consultative into a legislative assembly. The third estate (with 50% of total delegates) rejected the customary voting procedure (by estates) and insisted that balloting should proceed by head. In June, it and its sympathizers forced the issue by openly defying the king and declaring themselves the National Assembly. Louis XVI accepted the accomplished fact; the States-General ceased to exist; the Revolution began. **2** The name States-General also designates the two houses of parliament in the Netherlands, in which the upper house represents the provincial estates, the lower house the nation at large.

States of the Church: see PAPAL STATES.

states' rights, in U.S. history, an issue which has existed since the beginnings of national government. Tenth Amendment to U.S. Constitution says: "The powers not delegated to the United States by the Constitution, nor prohibited by it to the States, are reserved to the States respectively, or to the people." Controversy arose over interpretation of enumerated powers granted Federal government, which are not at all specific. Alexander Hamilton and Federalist party favored broad interpretation; Thomas Jefferson and his followers insisted that all powers not specifically granted Federal government be reserved to the states. KENTUCKY AND VIRGINIA RESOLUTIONS represent first formulation of states' rights school. Second important manifestation of states' rights occurred among Federalists of HARTFORD CONVENTION (1814). Opposition of S.C. to tariff acts of 1828 and 1832 caused state, guided by John C. CALHOUN, to pass its ordinance of NULLIFICATION. Proslavery forces soon backed a strong doctrine which ultimately led to SECESSION. Although today states' rights doctrine is usually associated with Southern wing of Democratic party, actually doctrine is not exclusive with any particular section or political party.

Statesville, city (pop. 16,901), W central N.C., SW of Winston-Salem, in piedmont; founded 1789. Mfg. of textiles, flour, and furniture.

static, radio reception noises unrelated to signal, usually from electrical discharges. Caused by atmospheric disturbances, electrical or motor-driven devices. Reduced by FREQUENCY MODULATION.

statice: see SEA PINK.

statistics, science of determining certain values representing tendencies indicated in large collection of observations or measurements. Statistical measures include: arithmetic MEAN; MEDIAN; MODE; standard deviation (measure of extent individual observations are scattered about mean). Important in statistical theory is sampling, an effort to determine for what larger group of individuals or characteristics the statistics of a smaller (sample) group would be representative and how representative it would be. This makes possible the applications of statistics to scientific and social research, insurance, finance, and various other fields.

Statius, Publius Papinius (stā'shùs), A.D. c.40–c.96, Latin epic poet. Surviving are 2 epics—the *Thebaid* and the *Achilleid* (incomplete)—and some minor poems.

Statuary Hall, National, in the Capitol, Washington, D.C. Formerly the chamber of U.S. Representatives 1807–57). In 1864 it was made a gallery for statues of distinguished Americans, each state being allowed two. Many have since been removed.

Statue of Liberty: see LIBERTY, STATUE OF.

statute, formal, written enactment by a legislature. Statute law is to be distinguished from COMMON LAW, which is derived from judicial decisions and custom. Statutes have been much used in common-law countries to meet new needs of changing society and economy, and therefore statute law has grown much. In nearly all European countries the law is statutory and covered by code.

Statute of Frauds: see CONTRACT.

Staunton (stăn′tŭn), city (pop. 19,927), western Va., in Shenandoah Valley WNW of Charlottesville; settled c.1738. Trade center in agr. area, it has mfg. of clothing, textiles, and furniture. Cap. of Northwest Territory 1738–70. Birthplace of Woodrow Wilson. Seat of Mary Baldwin Col. (for women; 1842).

Stavanger (stäväng′ur), city (pop. 50,320), SW Norway; a seaport on Stavanger Fjord. Shipbuilding; fish-canning. Gothic Cathedral of St. Swithin dates from 11th cent. Stavanger was one of first places taken by Germans in invasion of Norway (April 9, 1940).

Stavropol Territory (stä′vrŭpŭl), administrative division (2,950 sq. mi.; pop. c.1,500,000), S European RSFSR, extending N from main Caucasus range. Comprises MANYCH DEPRESSION (N), hilly Stavropol Plateau (center), and Pyatigorsk region, a major resort area. Irrigated since c.1945, territory now produces cereals, cotton, wine, fruit, vegetables. Population is Russian and Ukrainian, with seminomadic Turkmen and Nogai Tatar minorities. Cap. is **Stavropol** (pop. 85,100), agr. city on the plateau. It was an important base in Russian conquest of the Caucasus in 1830s.

Stead, W(illiam) T(homas) (stĕd), 1849–1912, English journalist, editor of *Pall Mall Gazette* (1883–89), founder of *Review of Reviews* (1890). Pioneered in modern journalistic methods and championed naval reform and social welfare. Lost life on *Titanic*.

Steamboat Springs, resort town (pop. 1,913; alt. 6,762 ft.), NW Colo., W of Park Range.

steam engine, machine to convert heat energy into mechanical energy. Expanding steam from boiler moves piston forward within cylinder. As expansive force ceases, piston is pressed back. Crank and flywheel convert total action into rotational motion which does work. Heron of Alexandria probably first harnessed steam, and many minds contributed to development of the steam engine; first practical solution came when James Watt patented his engine (1769). His separate condenser reduced fuel 75% and moved piston back as well as forward (reciprocal motion). Improvements he later introduced—governor, mercury steam gauge, and crank-flywheel mechanism—helped make steam engine the catalyst of the Industrial Revolution. Large-scale electrical generation has replaced steam engine as chief industrial power source. Steam TURBINE now provides most electrical power. See *ill.*, p. 303.

steamship, watercraft propelled by a steam engine or a steam turbine. In 1787 a steamboat built by James RUMSEY was demonstrated successfully. At the same time John FITCH was experimenting with building steamboats. Other Americans had worked with the problem (notably John Stevens) and the *Charlotte Dundas* was launched on the Forth and Clyde Canal (1803) before Robert FULTON successfully demonstrated his famous *Clermont* on the Hudson (1807). The first steamship to cross the Atlantic in 15 days was I. K. Brunel's *Great Western* (1838). The *Great Britain* was the first large iron steamship to use a screw propeller in Atlantic passage (1845). In the 1850s and 1860s the steamship began to supplant

the sailing ship—a triumph complete by 1900. The *Turbinia* was the first powered by a turbine (1897).

stearin (stē′urĭn), white, crystalline fat, an ester of stearic acid. Used in making soap, candles, and polishes, and in tanning.

steatite: see SOAPSTONE.

Stedman, Edmund Clarence, 1833–1908, American poet and critic, a Wall Street broker; a popular poet of his day and compiler of excellent anthologies.

steel, compound of iron and carbon with varying small amounts of other minerals. Steel-making processes include cementation process—heating two iron bars with charcoal to give them high carbon content, then fusing them; crucible process—receptacle of fire clay or graphite is charged with iron and charcoal and fired (various grades of fine steel are obtained by adding other components in small quantities); BESSEMER PROCESS; and open-hearth process. Open-hearth uses a regenerative furnace (type of reverberatory furnace) developed by Sir William Siemens c.1866. Pierre Martin with Siemens developed variation of process. Rolling mills shape steel for commercial use. Tensile strength of metal varies directly with carbon content. Alloy steels, now most widely used, contain one or more other minerals to give them special qualities; these include nickel (most widely used; nonmagnetic, has tensile strength but is not brittle), chromium (hard, strong, elastic), nickel-chromium (shock-resistant), and stainless (noncorrosive) steels. Most high-grade alloy steels are manufactured in electric furnace. U.S., USSR, and Great Britain lead in steel production.

Steele, Joel Dorman (stēl), 1836–86, American educator and textbook writer. Author of series of science texts which helped to popularize the subject.

Steele, Sir Richard, 1672–1729, English essayist and playwright. In 1709 he began famous journal *Tatler* and was soon joined by Joseph Addison. It was followed by the *Spectator* (1711–12), the *Guardian* (1713), and lesser papers. Perhaps the best known of many plays is *The Conscious Lovers* (1722). He became manager of Drury Lane Theatre in 1714, and that same year entered Parliament as a stalwart Whig. He was knighted in 1715. Plagued by financial troubles, he retired to Wales in 1724. Although impulsive and improvident, Steele was a man of engaging personality and charm, qualities reflected in his spontaneous and witty prose.

Steelton, borough (pop. 12,574), SE Pa., on Susquehanna R. below Harrisburg; settled 1865. Produces steel and limestone. First practical production of Bessemer steel in U.S. here 1867.

Steelyard, Merchants of the, German hanse or guild merchants (see HANSEATIC LEAGUE), residing at the Steelyard or German House, a separate walled community inside London, England. First Hanseatic merchants in England were licensed in 1157. Steelyard Merchants of Lübeck and Hamburg were chartered 1266 and gained wide privileges which made them highly unpopular. Queen Elizabeth I expelled the merchants and closed Steelyard 1597.

Steen, Jan (yän′ stān′), 1626–79, Dutch genre painter, b. Leiden. Studied in Utrecht and Haarlem. Largely humorous or moralistic, his works depict social life of his day. Favorite themes were scenes of revelry.

Steenkerke (stān′kĕr″kŭ), village near Mons, Belgium. Here in 1692 William III of England defeated the French under Marshal Luxembourg.

Stefansson, Vilhjalmur (vĭl′hyoulmŭr stē′fŭnsŭn), 1879–, arctic explorer, b. Canada, of Icelandic parents. Led several expeditions of exploration and of ethnological and archaeological investigation, successfully using Eskimo techniques of survival.

Steffens, (Joseph) Lincoln, 1866–1936, American editor and author. A magazine editor in muckraking era, he wrote exposés, collected in such works as *The Shame of the Cities* (1904) and *Upbuilders* (1909). Also wrote an illuminating autobiography (1931).

Stegosaurus (stĕgŭsô'rŭs), quadruped vegetarian dinosaur. It was c.20 ft. long, weighed c.10 tons, had short forelegs, two rows of upright bony plates on the back, and spines on the tail. Brain weighed c.2½ oz. Complete skeletons were found in the Jurassic of Colo. and Wyo.

Steichen, Edward (stī'kŭn), 1879–, American photographer and painter, b. Luxembourg. His early paintings are in various museums including the Metropolitan, and his work in photography has been widely exhibited. He was chief photographer for Condé Nast Publications (1923–38); in World War II he commanded U.S. navy photographic department.

Steilacoom (stī'lŭkŭm"), town (pop. 1,233), W Wash., on Puget Sound, S of Tacoma. State's oldest inc. town (1854), it has historic landmarks.

Stein, Charlotte von (shärlô'tŭ fŭn shtīn'), 1742–1827, German noblewoman, noted for her friendship with Goethe. After a separation from him, she wrote a tragedy, *Dido* (1794).

Stein, Gertrude (stīn), 1874–1946, American author, b. Pa. Through her salon and patronage of arts in Paris after 1903, she influenced many writers and artists. Her own writing is notable for repetitious, colloquially impressionistic style. She wrote stories, poems, a novel, art criticism, operas (notably *Four Saints in Three Acts* with music by Virgil Thomson, 1934), and several autobiographical works (esp. *The Autobiography of Alice B. Toklas*, 1933).

Stein, Karl, Freiherr vom und zum (kärl' frī'hĕr fŭm" ōont tsōom" shtīn'), 1757–1831, Prussian statesman and reformer. He was minister of commerce (1804–7) and premier (1807–8); was dismissed on pressure of Napoleon I; went to Russia and helped form Russo-Prussian alliance of 1813. Stein in 1807–8 abolished serfdom and all feudal class privileges or restrictions, began emancipation of Jews, abolished internal customs barriers, instituted local self-government. His reforms were continued by Hardenberg, Scharnhorst, and Humboldt and transformed Prussia into a modern state.

Steinach, Eugen (oigän' stī'näkh), 1861–1944, Austrian physiologist. Studied influence of sex glands and hormones in retarding senility.

Steinbeck, John (Ernst) (stīn'bĕk), 1902–, American author, known especially for realistic, compassionate novels of lowly people—*Tortilla Flat* (1935), *Of Mice and Men* (1937), *The Grapes of Wrath* (1939). Also wrote anti-Nazi fiction (both novel and play), *The Moon Is Down* (1942), a novel of Calif., *East of Eden* (1952), and several works of nonfiction.

Steiner, Jakob (yä'kôp shtī'nùr), 1796–1863, Swiss mathematician, a pioneer in synthetic geometry.

Steinmetz, Charles Proteus (stīn'mĕts), 1865–1923, American electrical engineer. Discovered law of hysteresis, making it possible to reduce loss of efficiency in electrical apparatus resulting from alternating magnetism; developed practical calculation method for alternating current; did valuable research on lightning and built generator for producing it artificially.

Stella, poetical name used by several writers for loved ones. Stella of the sonnets of Sir Philip SIDNEY was Penelope Devereaux. Stella who was the friend of Jonathan SWIFT was Esther Johnson.

Stellarton, town (pop. 5,575), N N.S., Canada, S of New Glasgow. Coal-mining center with railroad shops and mfg. of metal products.

Steller, Georg Wilhelm (gä'ôrk vīl'hĕlm shtĕ'lùr), 1709–46, German naturalist, whose name was originally Stöhler. Made extensive observations and collections as member of scientific staff of Vitus Bering's second expedition.

Stelvio Pass (stĕl'vyō), Alpine pass, 9,048 ft. high, N Italy, near Swiss border. It is crossed by the highest road in the Alps, connecting Valtellina and Engadine with Adige valley.

stem, part of a plant to which the leaves, roots, or floral parts are attached. The region at which a leaf is attached is called a node; the space between adjacent nodes is the internode. Stem transports food downward from leaves to roots and carries water and minerals upward to branches and leaves. Some plants have underground stems differentiated as bulbs, corms, tubers, or rhizomes. See *ill.,* p. 783.

Stenbock, Count Magnus (mäng'nùs stän'bôk), 1665–1717, Swedish field marshal; one of the ablest lieutenants of Charles XII.

Stendhal (stĕdäl'), pseud. of **Henri Beyle** (ärĕ' bāl'), 1783–1842, French author. He was an officer in Napoleon's army, later served as consul at Civitavecchia. Practically ignored in his lifetime, he produced such masterpieces as *The Red and the Black* (1830) and *The Charterhouse of Parma* (1839), which rank with the greatest novels of all times. His deep psychological insight, his dislike for lush romantic prose, and his sharp wit all combined to antagonize his contemporaries (except Balzac), but his greatness was recognized after his death. Most of his many other works and fragments were published posthumously.

Stentor (stĕn'tôr), Greek herald in the Trojan War. His voice was as loud as the voices of 50 men.

Stephan, Heinrich von (hīn'rïkh fŭn stĕ'fän), 1831–97, German statesman, chief founder of Universal Postal Union.

Stephanus, family of printers: see ESTIENNE.

Stephen, Saint (stĕ'vùn) [Gr.,= garland], first Christian martyr, stoned to death. One of the seven deacons. Acts 6; 7. Feasts: Dec. 26; Aug. 3.

Stephen, Saint, or **Stephen I,** 969–1038, duke (997–1001) and first king (1001–38) of Hungary, national hero of the Magyars, called the Apostle of Hungary. He continued the Christianization begun by his father, put down revolts of pagan nobles, and modeled his administration on that of German kings. The Hungarian state may be said to date from his time. The crown given him by Pope Sylvester II became the sacred symbol of Hungarian national existence. Feast: Sept. 2, but Hungarians celebrate Aug. 20 in his honor.

Stephen, 1097–1154, king of England (1135–54). He swore fealty to Henry I's daughter, MATILDA, but on Henry's death was proclaimed king. His long reign was constant struggle to maintain throne. He alienated clergy by threatening bishops who opposed him. Matilda, aided by her half-brother Robert, earl of GLOUCESTER, captured Stephen in 1141 and reigned briefly before Stephen regained throne. When his son Eustace died, Stephen was forced to name (1153) Matilda's son Henry (Henry II) as heir.

Stephen I, king of Hungary: see STEPHEN, SAINT (969–1038).

Stephen, George: see MOUNT STEPHEN, GEORGE STEPHEN, 1ST BARON.

Stephen, Sir Leslie, 1832–1904, English man of letters and philosopher; editor (1871–82) of the *Cornhill Magazine* and first editor (1882–91) of the *Dictionary of National Biography*. Works include *History of English Thought in the Eighteenth Century* (1876); biographies of Johnson, Pope, Swift, George Eliot; essays on mountain climbing. He was the father of Virginia Woolf.

Stephen Bathory (bä'tôrï), Hung. *Báthory István,* Pol. *Stefan Batory,* 1533–86, king of Poland (1575–86), prince of Transylvania (1571–75); married Anna, daughter of Sigismund II of Poland. He fought successfully against Ivan IV of Russia over Livonia, retaking Polotsk in 1582. His plan for subjugation of Russia and a Christian crusade against Turkey miscarried. Fostered Catholic Reform. His chancellor, Jan ZAMOJSKI, was a dominant figure of his reign.

Stephen Dushan (dōo'shän), Serbo-Croatian *Stefan Dušan,* c.1308–1355, king (1331–46) and tsar (1346–55) of Serbia. Ruthless and of unlimited ambitions, he conquered Bulgaria, Macedonia, Thessaly, Epirus; died while marching on Constantinople. Under him Serbia attained its greatest glory, but his empire disintegrated after his death.

Stephen Harding, Saint, d. 1134, English monastic reformer, founder of an abbey at Cîteaux (1098; see CISTERCIANS). Feasts: April 17, July 16.

Stephens, Alexander Hamilton, 1812–83, American statesman, vice president of Confederacy (1861–65). U.S. Congressman from Ga. (1843–59, 1873–82). Consistently opposed policies of Jefferson DAVIS. Early advocate of peace, commissioner to Hampton Roads Peace Conference.

Stephens, James, 1882–1950, Irish poet and novelist. Wrote many fanciful lyrics, but is perhaps best remembered for tales using Irish fairy lore or Irish legend, as in *The Crock of Gold* (1912).

Stephens, John Lloyd, 1805–52, American author of travel books (notably *Incidents of Travel in Central America, Chiapas, and Yucatan,* 1841; *Incidents of Travel in Yucatan,* 1843), an amateur archaeologist. Helped lay out Panama RR.

Stephens College: see COLUMBIA, MO.

Stephenson, George (stē′vŭnsŭn), 1781–1848, English engineer, a noted locomotive builder. He constructed (1814) a traveling engine or locomotive to haul coal from mines and in 1815 built first locomotive to use steam blast. His locomotive the *Rocket* bested the others in a contest in 1829 and was used on the Liverpool-Manchester Railway. He devised c.1815 a miner's safety lamp considered by some to have antedated the similar one invented by Sir Humphry Davy. His son **Robert Stephenson,** 1803–59, and a nephew, **George Robert Stephenson,** 1819–1905, were also railroad engineers.

Stephenville, city (pop. 7,155), N central Texas, on Bosque R. and SW of Fort Worth. Processing center in farm and dairy area.

Stepney (stĕp′nē), metropolitan borough (pop. 95,581), of E London. Industrial district, it was severely bombed in 1940–41. Includes Whitechapel, Limehouse, Wapping, and the Tower of London.

Stepniak, S. (styĭpnyäk′), pseud. of Sergei Mikhailovich Kravchinski, 1852–95, Russian revolutionist and author. He wrote *Underground Russia* (in Italian), *The Career of a Nihilist* (in English), and propaganda stories in disguise of fairy tales. He spent many years abroad, in exile.

steppe (stĕp), level, treeless plain of S and SE European RSFSR and of SW Asiatic USSR. Originally grassland; now largely under cultivation. Though the word is usually restricted to Russia, actually many of the world's most productive agr. districts are in steppe country—(e.g., U.S. prairies and Argentine Pampa).

stereopticon (stĕrĕŏp′tĭkŭn), improved form of magic lantern for throwing on screen a magnified image of a photograph, a drawing, a page of a book, or a microscopic slide. Moving pictures utilize principles applied in the stereopticon.

stereoscope (stĕ′rēŭskōp″), optical instrument that unites two similar pictures to give illusion of depth. In humans a mental image is composite of what the two eyes see separately from slightly different positions, thus giving the impression of depth. Stereoscope combines two photographs (taken from positions related approximately as positions of a person's two eyes) into a composite that has depth. Principle of stereoscope is applied in binocular field glasses and microscope.

sterility, inability to reproduce resulting from any of a number of causes, including impotence, glandular imbalance, production of defective sex cells, disease (e.g., gonorrhea), and emotional disturbances. In the female it sometimes is caused also by failure of the ovum (egg) to remain implanted on the uterine wall.

Sterling. 1 City (pop. 7,534), NE Colo., on South Platte R. Trade and shipping center for sugar-beet, grain, livestock region. A buffalo ranch is near. **2** City (pop. 12,817), NW Ill., on Rock R. (bridged) opposite Rock Falls, in farm and dairy area. Steel and oil products.

Stern, Daniel: see AGOULT, COMTESSE D'.

Stern, G(ladys) B(ronwyn), 1890–, English novelist,

author of a series about a Jewish family—*The Rakonitz Chronicles* (1932; later called *The Matriarch Chronicles,* 1936).

Stern, Otto, 1888–, American physicist, b. Germany. Won 1943 Nobel Prize for contributions to atomic-ray method and discovery of magnetic moment (force) of proton.

Sterne, Laurence, 1713–68, British author, b. Ireland. An Anglican clergyman, he published some sermons, but is remembered for his worldly writing, notably *The Life and Opinions of Tristram Shandy* (1759–67), a deliberately rambling, whimsical novel that ranks as one of the great works of English literature. Only a little less important is *A Sentimental Journey through France and Italy* (1768). Sterne started the great vogue of the sentimental novel, but none of his imitators approached his level of writing, his somewhat perverse wit, and his charm rising above his exaggerated and mock emotions.

Sterne, Maurice, 1877–, American painter and sculptor, b. Latvia. Still lifes, landscapes, figures.

Stesichorus (stĕsĭ′kŭrŭs), fl. c.600 B.C., Greek lyric poet. Legend says he invented the choral "heroic hymn" and the triad structure—strophe, antistrophe, epode—thenceforth much used.

stethoscope (stĕ′thŭskōp″), medical instrument used by physicians to auscultate (listen to) sounds in body. Especially valuable in diagnosing heart and lung conditions. Earliest form, invented by Laënnec, was a slender tube terminating in flanged opening placed against patient's body. Modern binaural type is composed of hollow cone connected by tubing to two earpieces.

Stetson, John Batterson, 1830–1906, American hat manufacturer.

Stettin (shtĕtēn′), Pol. *Szczecin,* city (1939 pop. 374,017; 1946 pop. 72,948), cap. of Pomerania; a major Baltic seaport at mouth of Oder R. and terminus of Berlin-Stettin Canal. Industrial center (shipyards; iron and coke works). Was seat of dukes of Pomerania until its transfer to Sweden (1648); passed to Prussia 1720; under French occupation 1806–13; heavily bombed in World War II. Although most of Stettin lies on W bank of the Oder, the Potsdam agreement of 1945 was interpreted by Poland as including Stettin in the German territory E of the Oder which was transferred to Polish administration. German population was expelled and replaced by Poles; Stettin was made cap. of a Polish province.

Stettinius, Edward R(eilly), Jr. (stŭtĭ′nēŭs), 1900–1949, American industrialist and statesman. Executive of General Motors (1926–34), chairman of board of U.S. Steel Corp. (1938–40). U.S. Secretary of State (1944–45). Resigned to serve as U.S. representative to UN (1945–46).

Steuben, Friedrich Wilhelm, Baron von (stū′bŭn), 1730–94, Prussian officer, general in American Revolution. Helped train Continental army.

Steubenville (stoō′bŭnvĭl), city (pop. 25,872), E Ohio, on Ohio R. and near Wheeling, W.Va.; laid out c.1797. Steel center in coal and clay region.

Stevens, John, 1749–1838, American inventor. He served in the American Revolution as treasurer of New Jersey, was later (1782–83) state surveyor, and played a major role in the establishment of the first U.S. patent laws. His interest in steamboat transportation led to his building (1806–8), with Nicholas J. Roosevelt, the *Phoenix,* a seagoing steamboat which later shuttled between Philadelphia and Trenton. After 1810 Stevens devoted himself to railroad activities; he received the first railroad charter in the U.S. and built a pioneer locomotive. His elder son, **Robert Livingston Stevens,** 1787–1856, was a mechanical engineer and inventor. He improved the construction of steamboats and also designed a rail (the American or Stevens rail) widely used in railroad track construction. Another son, **Edwin Augustus Stevens,** 1795–1868, invented the Stevens plow and was a pioneer builder of ironclad warships. He founded the STEVENS INSTITUTE OF TECHNOLOGY.

Stevens, Thaddeus, 1792–1868, U.S. Representative from Pa. (1849–53, 1859–68). A leader of radical Republican RECONSTRUCTION program; viewed Southern states as "conquered provinces." Proposed Fourteenth Amendment. He was both sincere in his devotion to Negro betterment and anxious to keep Republican party in power. He was a prime mover in impeaching Pres. Johnson.

Stevens, Wallace, 1879–, American poet, a successful insurance executive. His elegant, philosophic poems are collected in volumes such as *Harmonium* (1923), *Ideas of Order* (1935), *Owl's Clover* (1936), *The Man with the Blue Guitar and Other Poems* (1937), and *Transport to Summer* (1947).

Stevens Institute of Technology, at Hoboken, N.J.; nonsectarian, mainly for men; chartered 1870, opened 1871, engineering college of university grade. Gave first U.S. mechanical engineering degrees.

Stevenson, Adlai E(wing), 1835–1914, Vice President of the United States (1893–97). His grandson **Adlai E(wing) Stevenson,** 1900–, was governor of Ill. (1948–53) and Democratic candidate for President in 1952.

Stevenson, Robert Louis, 1850–94, British novelist, poet, and essayist. A lifelong victim of tuberculosis, he traveled much in search of health. In 1876 he began writing essays (collected in such volumes as *Virginibus Puerisque,* 1881). He wrote many short stories and travel books such as *Travels with a Donkey in the Cévennes* (1879). On a trip to California in 1879 he married, returning to Europe in 1880. His books, still avidly read, include such diverse works as *Treasure Island* (1883), *A Child's Garden of Verses* (1885), *Kidnapped* and *The Strange Case of Dr. Jekyll and Mr. Hyde* (both 1886). In 1887 he went to Saranac Lake, N.Y., where he began *The Master of Ballantrae* (1889). In 1889 he made an extensive tour of the South Seas and then settled down to write on his estate (Vailima) in Samoa. *Weir of Hermiston* (1896) and *St. Ives* (1897) were unfinished at his death.

Stevens Point, city (pop. 16,564), central Wis., on Wisconsin R. and S of Wausau; founded 1839. Wood products and fishing equipment.

Stewart, alternate form of the name STUART.

Stewart, William Morris, 1827–1909, American politician, a lawyer. U.S. Senator from Nev. (1864–75, 1887–1905). Sided with free-silver forces, but later returned to Republican party. Wrote Fifteenth Amendment to Constitution.

Stewart, river of central Yukon, rising in Mackenzie Mts. and flowing 320 mi. W to the Yukon S of Dawson. Used as transportation route for lead ore.

Stewart Island, volcanic island (c.660 sq. mi.; pop. 343), New Zealand, 20 mi. S of South Isl. Discovered 1808 by the British, who bought it from Maori natives in 1864. Summer resort.

Steyr (shtī'ûr), city (pop. 36,727), Upper Austria, on Enns and Steyr rivers. Automobile-mfg. center.

stibnite (stĭb'nīt), antimony trisulfide, gray with metallic luster. Important source of antimony.

stickleback, small fresh-water and marine fish of temperate and subarctic waters of N Hemisphere. Lacks true scales but often has plates along the sides; has spines on back. Male builds and guards nest in which a number of females lay eggs.

Stiegel, Henry William (stē'gŭl), 1729–85, American glass manufacturer, b. Germany. Produced ironwork before he turned to glassmaking, bringing European glassworkers to his plant at Manheim, Pa. Stiegel glass (in a variety of colors, such as light green, wine, amethyst, and blue) has become a collector's item.

Stieglitz, Alfred (stēg'lĭts), 1864–1946, American photographer and art exhibitor. Promoted photography as a fine art; edited photography magazines, 1892–1917. In 1905 he opened the famous gallery "291" at 291 Fifth Ave., New York, for exhibition of photographic art and introduced to America the works of Cézanne, Picasso, and other modern French masters.

Stifter, Adalbert (ä'dälbĕrt shtĭf'tûr), 1805–68, Austrian author, b. Bohemia. An outstanding stylist, he is best known for his tales and short novels, many of which appear in *Studien* (6 vols., 1840–45). One of these has been translated as *Rock Crystal* (1945).

Stikine (stĭkēn'), river rising in NW B.C., Canada, in Stikine Mts., and flowing 335 mi. in arc W and SW across SE Alaska to the Pacific N of Wrangell Isl. Navigable 130 mi. above mouth. Chief route to Cassiar mining region. Noted salmon stream.

Stikine Mountains, range of the Rocky Mts., NW B.C., Canada, extending 250 mi. NW-SE.

Stiklestad (stī'klŭstä"), site of battle (1030), on Trondheim Fjord, W Norway, where OLAF II was slain.

Stiles, Ezra, 1727–95, American theologian and educator. He was ordained in 1749 and tutored at Yale until 1855. After studying law, he returned to the ministry for 22 years. He was president and professor of ecclesiastical history at Yale after 1778.

Stilicho, Flavius (flā'vēŭs stī'līkō), d. 408, Roman general and statesman, of Vandal birth. Was chief general of Theodosius I; guardian of HONORIUS and regent of the West (395–408). He fought against Alaric I and other barbarian invaders. Arrested by Honorius on false accusations, he was executed.

Still, Andrew Taylor, 1828–1917, founder of OSTEOPATHY and school of osteopathy (1892) and author of works in field.

Stillwater. 1 City (pop. 7,674), E Minn., on St. Croix R. and NE of St. Paul. Former lumber center with mfg. of agr. equipment. In 1848 convention here drew up petition for territorial organization of Minn. **2** City (pop. 20,238), N central Okla., NNE of Oklahoma City; settled 1889. Industrial center of agr., livestock, and poultry area. Seat of OKLAHOMA AGRICULTURAL AND MECHANICAL COLLEGE.

Stilwell, Joseph W(arren), 1883–1946, American general, commander of Chinese troops, then of U.S. forces in China-Burma-India area (1942–44). His retreat and counterattack in Burma were masterly. His friction with Chiang Kai-shek caused his recall in 1944. Later commanded 10th Army on Okinawa (1945). Nicknamed "Vinegar Joe."

Stimson, Henry L(ewis), 1867–1950, American statesman. Secretary of War (1911–13) and Secretary of State (1929–33). Denounced Japanese invasion of Manchuria. Again Secretary of War (1940–45). Urged unification of U.S. armed forces (1944).

sting, organ of insects of order Hymenoptera (bees, many wasps, some ants) and of scorpions, used chiefly to paralyze or kill prey or enemy. In insects, it is found only in females and workers; venom secreted by glands is injected into victim.

Stirling, William Alexander, earl of, 1567?–1640, British poet, b. Scotland. Works include *Aurora* (1604), love poems; *Doomsday* (1614), 11,000-line epic; and *Four Monarchicke Tragedies* (1664–67), on Croesus, Darius, Alexander, and Julius Caesar.

Stirlingshire (stûr'lĭngshĭr) or **Stirling,** inland county (451 sq. mi.; pop. 187,432), central Scotland. Has a varied terrain of farm lands, bogs, pasture, and moorland. Falkirk (industrial center of county) produces iron, steel, textiles, and wool. Many decisive battles of Scottish history were fought in the county. County town is **Stirling,** burgh (pop. 26,960), which has varied industries. Castle long rivaled Edinburgh as royal residence. Mary Queen of Scots and James VI were crowned here. There are many ancient buildings and monuments.

stoat, European weasel (*Mustela erminea*). In north, male turns white (except for black-tipped tail) in winter; it is then known as ERMINE.

stock, in horticulture, annual, perennial, or biennial plant of Old World genus *Mathiola,* grown for spikes of fragrant, single or double blooms of various colors. Commonly cultivated are Brampton stock or gillyflower (*Mathiola incanis*) and night-blooming evening stock (*M. bicornis*). Virginia stock, without fragrance, belongs to genus *Malcomia*.

stock, in finance, an instrument certifying to shares in the ownership of a corporation. Preferred stock is entitled to fixed dividends, while common stock shares in the remainder of the profits. Holders of common stock may vote in the corporation's management.

Stockbridge, resort town (pop. 2,311), SW Mass., on Housatonic R., in the Berkshires S of Pittsfield. Has Berkshire Playhouse, a leading summer theater, and large art colony. Tanglewood estate is largely in Stockbridge, though near LENOX center. Birthplace of C. W. Field. Jonathan Edwards taught here.

stock exchange, organized market for stocks and bonds, in Europe called bourse. It is important to corporate capitalism because it facilitates financing of business. Certain of its practices are regulated by SECURITIES AND EXCHANGE COMMISSION.

Stockholm (stôk'hôlm"), city (pop. 745,936), cap. of Sweden, beautifully situated on L. Malaren and its outlet to the Baltic. Has large port, shipbuilding, mfg. of machinery, textiles, chemicals, rubber. Seat of a university (founded 1877) and cultural and artistic center. Founded 1255, it was an important Hanseatic trade center. In 1520 Christian II of Denmark proclaimed himself king of Sweden at Stockholm and ordered massacre of anti-Danish nobles. The massacre led to the successful uprising of Sweden under Gustavus Vasa, who became king as Gustavus I. Called the Venice of the North, Stockholm is built on several peninsulas and islands and is a model of modern urban planning. Its city hall, built 1923, is an impressive modern interpretation of the Scandinavian Renaissance style. A slumless city, Stockholm has many fine parks and cooperative residential districts. Staden isl. has retained much of its medieval and Renaissance architecture.

Stockmar, Christian Friedrich, Baron (krĭs'tyän frē'drĭkh bärōn' shtôk'mär), 1787–1863, Anglo-Belgian diplomat and courtier, b. Coburg, Germany, of Swedish parents. Unofficial adviser to Leopold I of the Belgians, Queen Victoria of England, and Prince Albert.

Stockport, county borough (pop. 141,660), partly in Cheshire, partly in Lancashire, England. Cotton-mfg. center, it also has varied mfg.

Stockton, Frank R(ichard), 1834–1902, American humorist, author of novels *Rudder Grange* (1879) and *The Casting Away of Mrs. Lecks and Mrs. Aleshine* (1886) and of many short stories (best known, "The Lady or the Tiger?").

Stockton, Robert Field, 1795–1866, American naval officer. Commanded Pacific squadron in Mexican War, aided in taking of Calif.

Stockton, city (pop. 70,853), central Calif., SE of San Francisco and on deepwater channel to San Joaquin R.; founded 1847. Supply point in gold-rush. Now an inland seaport and rail center, it ships farm produce of San Joaquin Valley. Produces lumber, farm machinery, flour, feeds, and canned goods. Seat of College of the Pacific (coed.; 1851).

Stockton-on-Tees (–tēz), municipal borough (pop. 74,-024), Durham, England. First important railroad in United Kingdom opened here in 1825. Has large shipbuilding industry.

Stoicism (stō'ĭsĭzŭm) [from the Stoa Poecile, in Athens], school of philosophy founded (c.200 B.C.) by Zeno of Citium and developed by his followers. Introduced into Rome in the 2d cent. B.C., it there attracted such notable followers as Seneca, Epictetus, and Marcus Aurelius. The Stoics held that all reality is material and that a universal working force (God) pervades everything. They sought "to live consistently with nature" and stressed putting aside passion, unjust thoughts, and indulgence in order to perform duty and gain true freedom.

Stoke-on-Trent, county borough (pop. 275,095), Staffordshire, England. Formed in 1910 of Hanley, Burs-lem, Tunstall, Longton, Fenton, and Stoke-upon-Trent and made a city in 1925. Center of Staffordshire pottery making, district is known as the Potteries or the "Five Towns."

Stoke Poges (pō'jĭs), village, Buckinghamshire, England, near Slough. Churchyard of St. Giles is generally held to be the scene of Gray's "Elegy."

Stoker, Bram, 1847–1912, British novelist, whose real first name was Abraham; author of *Dracula* (1897).

Stokes, Sir George Gabriel, 1819–1903, British mathematician and physicist. His researches developed modern theory of viscous fluids, revealed nature of fluorescence, made studies of chlorophyll.

Stokes, Isaac Newton Phelps, 1867–1944, American architect, housing expert, and historian.

Stokes, Whitley, 1830–1909, Irish scholar. A member of viceroy's council (1877–82) in India, he drafted Anglo-Indian civil and criminal codes. He is known for his translations of Celtic works.

Stokowski, Leopold (stŭkôf'skē), 1882–, American conductor, b. London, of Polish-Irish parentage. Was organist at St. Bartholomew's Church, New York, 1905–8; conductor of the Cincinnati Symphony, 1909–12. As the highly dramatic and vigorous conductor of the Philadelphia Orchestra (1912–36), he introduced much unfamiliar music. He conducted in several films.

Stolypin, Piotr Arkadevich (pyô'tŭr ŭrkä'dyĭvĭch stŭlĭ'pĭn), 1863–1911, Russian premier (1906–11). He fought the revolutionary movement by a régime of courts-martial; thousands were executed and exiled. His agrarian legislation facilitated the purchase of land by the peasants but was opposed by the leftist majority of the first DUMA, who favored expropriation of the large landowners. Stolypin dissolved the first two Dumas and secured a conservative majority in the third Duma by altering the election laws (1907). His Russification program for Finland was widely opposed. He was assassinated.

stomach, saclike portion of alimentary canal serving as temporary storage place for food. In humans, it is a pear-shaped organ lying below diaphragm and continuous in its upper portion with esophagus and in lower region with small intestine. Food is converted into semiliquid chyme by action of muscular walls and by gastric juice secreted by glands in stomach lining. Juice contains hydrochloric acid and enzymes rennin, which curdles milk, and pepsin, which acts on proteins in acid medium. Chyme is gradually sent by muscular action into the small intestine. See *ill.*, p. 595.

Stone, Harlan F(iske), 1872–1946, Chief Justice of U.S. Supreme Court (1942–46). Estab. reputation as Justice (from 1925) for vigorous minority opinions.

Stone, Lucy, 1818–93, American reformer, leader in woman suffrage and eloquent lecturer for Anti-Slavery Society. Married (1855) H. B. Blackwell, but kept own name (hence, Lucy Stone Leaguers, married women who keep their maiden names).

stone, in medicine: see CALCULUS.

Stone Age: see NEOLITHIC PERIOD; PALEOLITHIC PERIOD.

Stoneham (stō'nŭm), residential town (pop. 13,229), NE Mass., N of Boston; settled 1645.

Stonehenge (stōn'hĕnj"), group of standing stones on Salisbury Plain, Wiltshire, England, preeminent among MEGALITHIC MONUMENTS of British Isles. Enclosed by a circular ditch 300 ft. in diameter, stones are arranged in four series. Two outermost form circles; third is horseshoe shape; innermost is ovoid form. Outer circle is c.100 ft. in diameter. Some original uprights (up to 22 ft. high) remain. Within ovoid lies the "Altar Stone." Many explanations as to structure's purpose have been given. Excavations since 1920 indicate that it probably was a Bronze Age burying ground.

Stone Mountain, city (pop. 1,899), NW Ga., near Atlanta. Near by is partly completed **Stone Mountain Memorial** to Confederacy, carved into side of Stone Mt., an exposed granite dome.

Stones River National Military Park: see NATIONAL PARKS AND MONUMENTS (table).

stoneware: see POTTERY.

Stonington, town (pop. 11,801), extreme SE Conn., on Long Isl. Sound; settled 1649. Mfg. of textiles, machinery, tools. Includes Mystic village (pop. 2,266), former whaling port, now artists' resort; Pawcatuck village (pop. 5,269); and shore resorts.

Stony Brook, resort village (1940 pop. 768), on N shore of Long Isl., SE N.Y., near Port Jefferson. Restored (1941) to resemble 18th-cent. village.

Stony Point, village (pop. 1,438), SE N.Y., on Hudson R. and N of Nyack. Museum near by commemorates storming of Stony Point under Anthony Wayne in Revolution.

Stopes, Marie C(armichael) (stōps), 1880–, English eugenist, founder of first birth-control clinic in British Empire. She was author of books on eugenics, birth control, and paleobotany.

storage battery: see BATTERY, ELECTRIC.

Stor Fjord (stôr′ fyôr″), inlet of Norwegian Sea, on coast of SW Norway. Extends 70 mi. inland from Alesund. Wild and imposing in aspect. Most famous branch in Geiranger Fjord.

stork, large migratory wading bird related to heron. White and black wood ibis is only U.S. species. Many superstitions are connected with the stork, which is allowed to nest on house roofs in Europe (particularly the Low Countries). Said in some tales for children to bring babies from heaven. See *ill.,* p. 105.

Storm, Theodor (tā′ōdōr shtôrm′), 1817–88, German poet and writer of *Novellen.* Best known for *Immensee* (1851; Eng. tr., 1858) and *Aquis Submersus* (1876; Eng. tr., 1910). His work is imbued with melancholy and poetic realism.

Storm and Stress: see STURM UND DRANG.

Storm King, mountain, 1,355 ft. high, SE N.Y., in Palisades Interstate Park, overlooking Hudson R. near West Point.

Storm Lake, city (pop. 6,954), NW Iowa, on Storm L. W of Fort Dodge. Has meat and poultry packing.

Storrowton, Mass.: see SPRINGFIELD.

Storrs, Conn.: see MANSFIELD.

Storting (stôr′tĭng), parliament of Norway, elected by direct universal suffrage. It elects one fourth of its members to form the Lagting or upper house, the remainder constituting the lower house, or Odelsting.

Story, Joseph, 1779–1845, American jurist; Associate Justice of U.S. Supreme Court (1811–45). Story's decision in *Martin* vs. *Hunter's Lessee* (1816) estab. court's power to review issues of constitutional law raised in state cases. His legal texts have been important formative influences on American jurisprudence and legal education. His son, **William Wetmore Story,** 1819–95, was a sculptor, whose brilliant social gifts made his studio in Rome a social and artistic center. His classic figures were among the most admired sculptures of his day. Lived in Italy after 1856.

Stoss, Veit (fīt′ shtōs′), c.1445–1533, German wood carver. Worked in Cracow and in Nuremberg, where he did his best-known carving, the *Annunciation* for Church of St. Lorenz. Also worked in stone.

Stotsenburg, Fort, central Luzon, P.I. Main U.S. military base in Philippines. Clark Field is near.

Stoughton (stō′tŭn), town (pop. 11,146), E Mass., S of Boston; settled c.1713. Shoes, rubber products.

stove, heating and cooking device. Heating stoves of clay, tile, earthenware were used in Europe from Roman times. From late 15th cent. dates cast-iron stove, composed of iron plates; typical early form was walljamb five-plate box fueled from adjoining room. Five-plate stove was introduced in American colonies by settlers, but was superseded in the late 18th cent. by English 10-plate stove, standing free of wall and used also for cooking. Coal-burning ranges with removable lids were used for cooking from about middle of 19th cent. until displaced by modern appliances. Popular for heating was Franklin stove, invented 1743,

essentially a portable iron fireplace set into chimney.

Stow, John, 1525?–1605, English chronicler and antiquarian. Known for *Chronicles of England* (1580), better known as *Annales of England* (1592); and for immensely valuable *Survay of London* (1598).

Stowe, Harriet Beecher, 1811–96, American novelist; daughter of Lyman Beecher. Her interest in religious problems and social reforms was encouraged by her husband, Calvin E. Stowe, and she is remembered chiefly for *Uncle Tom's Cabin; or, Life among the Lowly* (serially 1851–52), an antislavery novel that was enormously popular. Dramatized, it was a stage success for many years. She also wrote another novel of slavery, *Dred* (1856), and novels of New England life (e.g., *The Pearl of Orr's Island,* 1862). She was also interested in other causes such as temperance and woman suffrage.

Stowe, town (pop. 1,720), N central Vt., NW of Montpelier and SE of Mt. Mansfield. Includes Stowe village (pop. 556), resort and winter sports center.

Strabo (strā′bō), b. c.63 B.C., d. after A.D. 21, Greek geographer and historian. His only extant work, a geography in 17 books, is a rich source of ancient knowledge of the world.

Strachan, John (strôn), 1778–1867, Canadian prelate, first Anglican bishop of Toronto (1839–67). An influential Conservative leader.

Strachey, (Giles) Lytton (strā′chē), 1880–1932, English biographer, known for keen, witty miniatures, in such works as *Eminent Victorians* (1918) and *Portraits in Miniature* (1931), and for longer biographies (e.g., *Queen Victoria,* 1921; *Elizabeth and Essex,* 1928).

Stradella, Alessandro (strädĕl′lä), c.1645–1682, Italian composer of oratorios, operas, cantatas, and *concerti grossi.* Many legends surround his life; one, that he was murdered at the behest of a Venetian nobleman, inspired an opera by Flotow.

Stradivari, Antonio (strädēvä′rē) or **Antonius Stradivarius,** 1644–1737, Italian violinmaker of Cremona; pupil of Niccolò Amati. His earliest extant label is dated 1666, and his last 1737; his finest work was done after 1700. He produced at least 1,116 instruments, including violas, cellos, viols, guitars, and mandolins. His artistry brought the violin to perfection; later craftsmen have tried to imitate his work. His son Francesco and Omobono Stradivari continued the craft after his death.

Strafford, Thomas Wentworth, 1st **earl of,** 1593–1641, English statesman. Lord deputy of Ireland 1632–39, he enforced rule of Charles I. To aid king in Bishops' Wars he advised severity against Scots. With Archbishop Laud he was king's chief adviser in 1639. Beheaded for alleged intention to use Irish soldiers against the British.

Straits: see DARDANELLES; BOSPORUS.

Straits Settlements, former British crown colony in Malaya. PENANG, MALACCA, and SINGAPORE were controlled as a unit by British East India Co., 1826–58, and briefly by the India Office. Colony was estab. 1867, dissolved 1946.

Stralsund (shträl′zŏont″), city (pop. 50,389), Mecklenburg, NE Germany; a seaport on an inlet of the Baltic Sea opposite Rügen isl. Shipyards; machinery plants; sugar refineries. Founded 1209, it became a leading member of the Hanseatic League but remained under the overlordship of the dukes of POMERANIA. By the Treaty of Stralsund (1370) with Waldemar IV of Denmark, the league won supremacy in the Baltic. Aided by Danish and later by Swedish troops, Stralsund withstood Wallenstein's siege (1628) in the Thirty Years War. It passed to Sweden (1648), to Prussia (1815), and to Mecklenburg (after World War II). Its rich medieval architecture suffered heavy war damage.

Strand, street of hotels, theaters, and office buildings in central London, running parallel with the Thames from Trafalgar Square to the Temple.

Strang, James Jesse (străng), 1813–56, American Mormon leader. Claimed succession to Joseph Smith. Ex-

Strasbourg

communicated, he organized colony in Wis., later (1847) estab. colony on Beaver Isl. in L. Michigan. Crowned King James in 1850, he ruled despotically. Died by assassination.

Strasbourg (străs'bûrg, Fr. sträzboōr'), Ger. *Strassburg*, city (pop. 167,149), cap. of Bas-Rhin dept., E France, on the Ill near its junction with the Rhine; cultural and commercial cap. of Alsace. Has a port on the Rhine, varied industries (leather, beer, goose liver *pâté*), and is the seat of a university (founded 1538) and of the Council of Europe. Its importance dates from Roman times. Its bishops ruled a considerable territory as princes of the Holy Roman Empire, but Strasbourg itself became a free imperial city (13th cent.), ruled by its guild corporations. Here medieval German literature reached its flower in Gottfried von Strassburg, and here Gutenberg may have invented the printing press. Strasbourg accepted the Reformation, in which it played an important part. Seized by Louis XIV in 1681, it shared the subsequent history of ALSACE and largely embraced French customs and speech. It was damaged in World War II, but its magnificent Catholic cathedral (built 1015–1439) was preserved.

Strasbourg, Oath of, 842, sworn by Charles the Bald and Louis the German in alliance against their brother Lothair I. The French version is the oldest known specimen of French.

Strasburg (strôz'bûrg), town (pop. 2,022), N Va., in Shenandoah Valley SSW of Winchester. Near by are Crystal Caverns, Hupp's Fort (c.1755), and Harmony Hall or Fort Bowman (c.1753).

Strassburg, France: see STRASBOURG.

Stratford, city (pop. 18,785), S Ont., Canada, on Avon R. and WSW of Toronto. Railroad shops and textile mills.

Stratford, town (pop. 33,428), SW Conn., at mouth of Housatonic R. on Long Isl. Sound near Bridgeport; settled 1639. Mfg. of asbestos and metal products.

Stratford, estate of the Lee family, SE Va., overlooking the Potomac, ESE of Fredericksburg. Stratford Hall, built 1716 by Thomas Lee, was birthplace of R. H. Lee, F. L. Lee, R. E. Lee; home of Henry Lee. Dedicated as national shrine 1935.

Stratford de Redcliffe, Stratford Canning, Viscount, 1786–1880, British diplomat. Aided internal reform in Turkey. Helped to bring on Crimean War by advising Turkish resistance to Russian demands.

Stratford-on-Avon or **Stratford-upon-Avon,** municipal borough (pop. 14,980), Warwickshire, England, on Upper Avon R. Market town, its fame is connected with Shakspere. He is buried in 14th-cent. Church of the Holy Trinity. Chief memorial is theater, scene of annual Shakspere festivals. Most buildings connected with him now belong to the nation.

Strathclyde (străth''klīd') and **Cumbria** (kŭm'brĕŭ), early medieval kingdom of Great Britain in what is now S Scotland and N England. One of four great British units after Anglo-Saxon invasion, it remained independent until 9th cent.

Strathcona and Mount Royal, Donald Alexander Smith, 1st Baron (străthkō'nù), 1820–1914, Canadian fur trader, financier, and railroad builder, b. Scotland. Governor of Hudson's Bay Co. (1889–1914). With others he acquired control of Great Northern lines (1878), and later was a leading member of company that completed Canadian Pacific (1885). Served as Canadian high commissioner in England (1896–1914).

Strathcona Provincial Park, 828 sq. mi., on central Vancouver Isl., SW B.C., Canada. Game sanctuary and recreation area.

Strathmore (străthmôr'), the "great valley" of Scotland, a plain c.100 mi. long and 5–10 mi. wide, largely in Perthshire and Angus.

stratification (strā''tĭfĭkā'shùn), division of sediments into parallel layers. Water tends to sort rock debris, depositing it according to weight, so coarser particles are dropped first. Sediments are thus graded horizontally and each distinct layer is called a stratum. Stratified rocks are classed as series if laid down during epochs of geologic time; as systems if deposited during periods.

stratosphere: see ATMOSPHERE.

Straus (strous), family of American merchants, public officials, and philanthropists. **Isidor Straus,** 1845–1912, b. Rhenish Bavaria, acquired ownership of R. H. Macy & Co. in New York city by 1896. Later he devoted his attention to philanthropy and reform. His brother, **Nathan Straus,** 1848–1931, b. Rhenish Bavaria, joined his brother in business and was also outstanding for philanthropy. Another brother, **Oscar S(olomon) Straus,** 1850–1926, b. Rhenish Bavaria, was a diplomat and author. Minister to Turkey (1887–89, 1898–1900). U.S. Secretary of Commerce and Labor (1906–9). His books include *Roger Williams* (1894). A son of Isidor Straus, **Jesse Isidor Straus,** 1872–1936, became president of R. H. Macy & Co. in 1919 and served as ambassador to France (1933–36). **Nathan Straus,** 1889–, son of Nathan Straus (1848–1931), headed U.S. Housing Authority (1937–42).

Straus, Oscar (strous), 1870–, Austrian composer. His best-known works are operettas, including *A Waltz Dream* (1907) and *The Chocolate Soldier* (1908; based on G. B. Shaw's *Arms and the Man*).

Strauss, family of Viennese musicians. **Johann Strauss,** 1804–49, composer and conductor, won fame during his lifetime with his waltzes but was surpassed by his son, **Johann Strauss,** 1825–99, composer and conductor, whose popularity reached fantastic heights. He wrote more than 400 waltzes, including *The Blue Danube* and *Tales from the Vienna Woods;* and operettas, including *Die Fledermaus* [the bat]. His brothers, **Josef Strauss,** 1827–70, and **Eduard Strauss,** 1835–1916, were also successful composers and conductors. Neither Oscar Straus nor Richard Strauss are related to this family.

Strauss, David Friedrich (dä'vēt frē'drĭkh shtrous), 1808–74, German theologian and philosopher. His *Das Leben Jesu* (2 vols., 1835–36; Eng. tr. by George Eliot, 1846) treated Gospel story as history.

Strauss, Eduard, Johann Strauss, Josef Strauss: see SRAUSS, family.

Strauss, Richard (Georg) (rīkh'ärt shtrous), 1864–1949, German composer and conductor. His music is characterized by rich harmonic and orchestral effects. His tone poems include *Don Juan* (1888), *Death and Transfiguration* (1889), *Till Eulenspiegel* (1894), *Thus Spake Zarathustra* (1895), *Don Quixote* (1897), and *Ein Heldenleben* (1898). His operas include *Salomé* (1905), *Elektra* (1909), and *Der Rosenkavalier* (1911); Hugo von Hofmannsthal was his librettist. Strauss also wrote lieder.

Stravinsky, Igor (Feodorovich) (strŭvĭn'skē), 1882–, Russian composer; became U.S. citizen 1945. His rhythms are often bold, his harmonies harshly dissonant. His most popular works are the ballets written during his association with Sergei Diaghilev—*The Fire Bird* (1910), *Petrouchka* (1911), and *Le Sacre du printemps* (1913). He has also written the opera-ballet *Histoire du soldat* (1918); the ballet *Le Baiser de la fée* (1928); the opera-oratorio *Oedipus Rex* (1926–27); *Symphonie de psaumes* (1930), for chorus and orchestra; and the opera *The Rake's Progress* (1951).

strawberry, low, white-flowered, herbaceous perennial of genus *Fragaria* and its fleshy, fragrant red fruit, an important commercial crop in U.S.

strawberry geranium: see SAXIFRAGE.

Strawberry Hill, western suburb of London, England, named for Horace Walpole's estate.

Strawberry valley project, N central Utah, developed 1906–13 by U.S. to irrigate lands S of Utah L. Strawberry R. water is diverted through Wasatch Range to Spanish Fork R. for use around Spanish Fork, Springville, Payson, and Santaquin.

strawflower, garden annual (*Helichrysum bracteatum*), an EVERLASTING, with papery blooms of various colors.

Streator (strē'tùr), city (pop. 16,469), N central Ill., on Vermilion R. and NE of Peoria; laid out 1863. Railroad shops. Mfg. of glass, clay, and metal products.

street cries, the imaginative, musical cries of itinerant vendors and workers of various sorts. The London cry "Who'll buy my sweet lavender?" provided a theme for Vaughan Williams's London Symphony. Few cries survive in cities such as London and New York, an exception being the ragpicker's "I cash clo'." Many picturesque cries exist among Negroes in the Southern U.S. (e.g., the cries of fish vendors and flower sellers used by Gershwin in *Porgy and Bess*).

Streicher, Julius (yōō'lyŏos shtrī'khûr), 1885–1946, German National Socialist leader. A sadistic pervert, he edited the pornographic and anti-Semitic periodical *Der Stürmer*, became *Gauleiter* of Franconia in 1933, and was hanged after conviction of crimes against humanity at Nuremberg war crimes trial.

strength of materials, measurement in engineering of capacity of steel, wood, concrete, and other materials to withstand stress and strain. Stress is internal force exerted by one part of a body upon adjoining part, while strain is deformation or change in dimension occasioned by stress. Materials are considered elastic in relation to applied stress if strain disappears after force is removed; elastic limit is stretch point beyond which material will not return to original form. In calculating dimensions of materials required for given functions, engineer uses working stresses that are ultimate strengths, or elastic limits, divided by a quantity called factor of safety. In laboratories static tests are run to determine a material's elastic limit, ductility, hardness, reaction to temperature change, and other qualities. Dynamic tests are those in which material is exposed to impact, vibration, fluctuating loads, fatigue, and other expected operating conditions. Polarized light, X rays, and miscroscopic examination are some means of testing materials.

streptococcus (strĕp″tŭkŏ'kŭs), genus of bacteria, spherical in shape and dividing by fission to form beadlike chains. Two major types are green-colony or viridans streptococci and hemolytic streptococci (producing substance which dissolves red blood cells). They include many disease-causing forms. See *ill.*, p. 633.

streptomycin: see ANTIBIOTIC SUBSTANCES.

Stresa (strā'zä), resort, Piedmont, N Italy, on Lago Maggiore. Here in 1935 England, France, and Italy held an inconclusive conference after Hitler announced the rearmament of Germany.

Stresemann, Gustav (gōōs'täf shtrā'zŭmän), 1878–1929, German chancellor (1923) and foreign minister (1923–29). Originally a spokesman for industrial interests, he devoted himself after 1923 to securing a respected place for Germany by conscientious fulfillment of its treaty obligations and by conciliation of its former enemies. He obtained the evacuation of the RUHR (1924) and later of the Rhineland; accepted the Dawes Plan (1924) and the Young Plan (1929) for reparations; was one of the architects of the LOCARNO PACT (1925); had Germany admitted into the League of Nations as a great power (1926); and signed the KELLOGG-BRIAND PACT (1928). Shared 1929 Nobel Peace Prize with Briand.

Streuvels, Stijn (stīn strû'vùls), pseud. of **Frank Lateur** lätûr'), 1871–, Flemish novelist and short-story writer; one of the chief artists in his language. His works (e.g., *Old Jan,* 1902) are realistic portrayals of everday life.

Streymoy, Faeroe Islands: see STROMO.

Strickland, William, 1787–1854, American architect of the classic revival. Worked in Philadelphia.

strike, concerted stoppage of work by a group of employees, the chief weapon of labor in industrial disputes. A suspension of work on the employer's part is called a lockout. Issues usually involved are employees' demands for higher wages, shorter hours, better working conditions, and union recognition. See PICKETING; GENERAL STRIKE; TAFT-HARTLEY LABOR ACT.

Strindberg, (Johan) August (strĭnd'bûrg, Swed. strĭnd'bĕr″yù), 1849–1912, Swedish dramatist, novelist, and short-story writer. Notable for its masterly use of language and for its innovations, his writing varies from naturalistic to mystical but is always individual. Wrote some 70 plays, *The Father* (1887) and *Julie* (or *Miss Julia* or *Countess Julia,* 1888) being particularly well known abroad. Much of his fiction concerns his unhappy life and three disastrous marriages (e.g., *Married,* 1884–85; *The Son of a Servant,* 1886–87, 1909; *The Inferno,* 1897).

stringed instruments, musical instruments whose tone is produced by vibrating strings. For those played with a bow, see VIOL and VIOLIN family. Those whose strings are plucked with the fingers or a plectrum include the HARP, the lute and mandolin, the guitar and members of its family, the psaltery and zither, and the lyre. Both the lute and mandolin have a pear-shaped body, a rounded back, a fretted neck (the lute's neck being sometimes longer than its body, sometimes shorter), and a variable number of strings. Both are of concert caliber—the lute being the chief European instrument of the Middle Ages and Renaissance. The guitar has a fretted neck, a flat back, sides which curve inward, and from four to seven strings or pairs of strings. It appeared in 12th-cent. Spain, and concert music has been written for it. Resembling the guitar in shape, but smaller and with very limited capabilities, is the ukulele, which has four strings. Another member of the guitar family, the banjo, has from five to nine strings. Its body consists of a hoop over which parchment is stretched, resembling a tambourine. The balalaika (associated with Russia) has a triangular body, a long fretted neck, and usually three strings. Various sizes of balalaikas are often used in ensemble. Two instruments related to the DULCIMER (except that their strings are plucked instead of struck) are the psaltery and the zither. Both have a sounding board over which strings are stretched (a variable number in the psaltery; from 30 to 45 in the zither). The zither has four or five melody strings, which are fretted; remaining strings furnish the accompaniment. The last of the plucked-stringed instruments is the lyre, usually shaped somewhat like a U, with a sound box at the base and a crossbar connecting the two arms. Strings (varying in number) are stretched between the crossbar and sound box. Instruments whose strings are struck include the dulcimer and some keyboard instruments such as the PIANO and clavichord. See *ill.*, p. 667.

Stritch, Samuel Alphonsus, 1887–, American Roman Catholic clergyman; bishop of Toledo (1921–30), archbishop of Milwaukee (1930–40), archbishop of Chicago (1940–); made cardinal 1946.

stroke: see APOPLEXY.

Stromboli, island, Italy: see LIPARI ISLANDS.

Stromo, Dan. *Strømø* (strû'mû″), Faeroese *Streymoy,* largest island (144 sq. mi.; pop. 7,865) of Faeroe Isls., Denmark. Thorshavn, cap. of the Faeroes, is here.

Strong, George Templeton, 1820–75, American diarist, a lawyer. His diary (4 vols., 1952) is a valuable record of New York life.

Strong, Theodore, 1790–1869, American mathematician, known for solving Cardan's irreducible case of cubic equation and for mathematical treatises.

Strongbow, Richard: see PEMBROKE, RICHARD DE CLARE, 2D EARL OF.

strontium (strŏn'shùm), soft, white, metallic element (symbol = Sr; see also ELEMENT, table), a metal of alkaline earths. The metal is prepared by electrolysis of the fused chloride. Compounds are used to add crimson color to fireworks; hydroxide is used to purify beet sugar. Isolated in 1808 by Sir Humphry Davy.

Stroudsburg, resort borough (pop. 6,361), E Pa., near Delaware Water Gap in Pocono Mts. region.

Strozzi (strôt'tsē), noble Florentine family which produced eminent soldiers, scholars, and men of letters. They usually opposed the Medici rule in Florence.

SMALL CAPITALS = cross references. Pronunciation key on inside end pages. Abbreviations: p. 2.

The celebrated Strozzi Palace, Florence, was begun by Filippo Strozzi (1426–91).

Struensee, Johann Friedrich (yō'hän frē'drĭkh shtroo'-ŭnzä, stroo'-), 1737–72, Danish statesman, b. Germany. As physician to Christian VII he gained complete mastery over the insane king and became the favorite of the young queen, Caroline Matilda. Made minister of state and a count (1771) he governed dictatorially and accomplished many reforms in favor of the lower classes (esp. the peasants). His enemies among the nobles terrorized the king into arresting him on the charge of adultery with the queen. He was executed.

Struma (stroo'mä), Gr. *Strymon*, river, 215 mi. long, rising S of Sofia, Bulgaria. Flows S into Greece and to the Aegean Sea.

Struthers, city (pop. 11,941), NE Ohio, on Mahoning R. and SE of Youngstown. Iron and steel mills.

Struve, Friedrich Georg Wilhelm von (frē'drĭkh gāôrk vĭl'hĕlm fŭn shtroo'vu), 1793–1864, German-Russian astronomer. Discovered many double stars, pioneered in measuring star parallax; developed noted Pulkovo Observatory. His son **Otto Wilhelm von Struve** (ô'tō), 1819–1905, succeeded him as director and made many discoveries, especially of double stars. **Otto Struve** (ô'tō stroo'vĕ), 1897–, son of Otto Wilhelm, came to U.S. 1921. Distinguished as professor of astrophysics (Univ. of Chicago) and director of Yerkes and McDonald observatories.

strychnine (strĭk'nĭn), alkaloid derived from seeds of a tree (*Strychnos nux vomica*) native to India. It has long been used to poison rats. In small doses it is sometimes used medicinally; it stimulates the central nervous system (esp. the spinal cord), the respiratory center, and the circulatory system.

Stuart or **Stewart,** royal family which ruled Scotland and England. Began as family of hereditary stewards of Scotland c.1160. Royal power remained in family after accession of ROBERT II in 1371. Marriage of JAMES IV of Scotland to Margaret Tudor, daughter of Henry VII of England, eventually made MARY QUEEN OF SCOTS claimant to English throne. This claim was recognized when her son, James VI of Scotland, became JAMES I of England in 1603. After PURITAN REVOLUTION and execution of Charles I, his son CHARLES II was restored to throne. After deposition of James II, crown passed to Mary II and William III. Anne, last Stuart to rule England, saw crowns of Scotland and England united by Act of Union of 1707. On Anne's death crown passed to George I of house of Hanover by Act of Settlement. Hanoverian claim was through a granddaughter of James I. Parliamentary rule of succession was adopted because claim to throne by James Edward STUART and his descendants was upheld by JACOBITES. After 1807 this claim ceased to be politically important.

Stuart or **Stewart, Alexander, duke of Albany,** 1454?–1485, son of James II of Scotland. Imprisoned by his brother, James III, who suspected him of plotting against throne, he escaped to England. Agreed with Edward IV to rule Scotland as England's vassal and returned to Scotland with English army. Later was reconciled with the nobles who controlled the government. His son, **John Stuart** or **Stewart, 4th duke of Albany,** 1481–1536, was regent (1515–24) for James V. Worked for the French interest in Scotland against English party and Margaret Tudor. After military failures, his regency was annulled.

Stuart or **Stewart, Arabella,** 1575–1615, cousin of James I of England. Secretly married William Seymour, heir to throne by will of Henry VIII. They were imprisoned and escaped. Recaptured (1611), she died insane in the Tower.

Stuart or **Stewart, Charles Edward:** see STUART OR STEWART, JAMES FRANCIS EDWARD.

Stuart or **Stewart, Esmé, 1st duke of Lennox,** 1542?–1583, cousin of James VI of Scotland (later James I of England). Reared in France, he was sent (1579) to Scotland to weaken Protestantism. Quickly became powerful, but was forced to return to France after the "raid of Ruthven" (1582) placed the king in control of Protestant lords. His son, **Ludovick Stuart** or **Stewart, 2d duke of Lennox** and **duke of Richmond,** 1574–1624, was recalled by James and remained influential.

Stuart or **Stewart, Frances Teresa, duchess of Richmond and Lennox,** 1648–1702, mistress of Charles II of England. King planned to divorce queen and marry "La Belle Stuart," but she eloped (1667) with duke of Richmond and Lennox. Later returned to court.

Stuart, Gilbert, 1755–1828, American portrait painter, the most eminent of his day, b. North Kingstown, R.I. Studied under Benjamin West. Though highly successful in London, he was kept in debt by his lavish mode of living. Returned c.1792 to America with plans of achieving solvency by painting the portrait of Washington and making replicas of it. Settled 1794 in Philadelphia, but moved 1805 to Boston. Painted three portraits of Washington from life. The so-called Vaughan Type (1795) shows head and shoulders; the original has vanished, but at least 15 replicas exist. The Lansdowne Type (1796), painted for marquess of Lansdowne, shows Washington standing (original in Pennsylvania Acad. of Fine Arts). The unfinished Athenaeum Head was acquired first by Boston Athenaeum and later by Mus. of Fine Arts, Boston; of this there are 75 replicas. Other famous sitters included Jefferson, Madison, Benjamin West, and Sir Joshua Reynolds.

Stuart or **Stewart, Henry:** see DARNLEY, HENRY STUART OR STEWART, LORD.

Stuart or **Stewart, Henry Benedict Maria:** see STUART OR STEWART, JAMES FRANCIS EDWARD.

Stuart or **Stewart, James, earl of Arran** (ăr'ŭn), d. 1596, Scottish nobleman. Became powerful (after 1579) at court of James VI (later James I of England). Imprisoned at "raid of Ruthven" (1582) that put king in hands of nobles, he later set out to crush his opponents. Was banished in 1586.

Stuart or **Stewart, James:** see MURRAY, JAMES STUART OR STEWART, 1ST EARL OF.

Stuart, James, 1713–88, English architect, archaeologist, and painter. Visited Athens in 1751 with Nicholas Revett. Their joint work, *Classical Antiquities of Athens* (first volume published 1762), vitally influenced the CLASSIC REVIVAL.

Stuart, J(ames) E(well) B(rown) (Jeb Stuart), 1833–64, Confederate cavalry commander. Noted for brilliant raids and ability to get information. His first raid greatly aided Lee in Seven Days battles. He covered Stonewall Jackson at second battle of Bull Run (Aug., 1862). Aided victory at battle of CHANCELLORSVILLE (1863). Fought his greatest cavalry battle at Brandy Station (June, 1863). Mortally wounded at Yellow Tavern (May 11, 1864).

Stuart or **Stewart, James Francis Edward,** 1688–1766, claimant to the English throne, son of JAMES II and Mary of Modena. Called the Old Pretender. Glorious Revolution (1688) was followed by Act of Settlement, excluding male STUART line from succession. Recognition of James as king by Louis XIV was minor cause of English involvement in War of the Spanish Succession. His hopes of succeeding Queen Anne were dashed by succession of George I in 1714. After rising of earl of Mar (1715), he was hailed as James VIII of Scotland and as James III of England by the JACOBITES. Their many abortive plots (1708–45) to restore him as king included rising of 1745, led by his son, **Charles Edward Stuart** or **Stewart,** 1720–88, known as Bonnie Prince Charlie and the Young Pretender. After defeat at Culloden Moor he escaped abroad. Expelled from France after Treaty of Aix-la-Chapelle, he died in Rome. He married Louise of Stoberg Gedern. Subject of much English and Scottish poetry. His brother, **Henry Benedict**

Maria Stuart or **Stewart**, known as **Cardinal York**, 1725–1807, was the last of the direct male Stuart line to claim the throne (as Henry IX). He was made a cardinal of the Catholic Church in 1747.

Stuart or **Stewart, John**, 4th duke of Albany: see STUART OR STEWART, ALEXANDER, DUKE OF ALBANY.

Stuart, John: see BUTE, JOHN STUART, 3D EARL OF.

Stuart or **Stewart, John**, 4th earl of Atholl (äth′ŭl), d. 1579, Scottish nobleman. Leader of Catholic nobles, he supported Mary Queen of Scots until the rise of Bothwell. After Mary's capture (1567), he was again friendly to her. Ousted Morton as regent in 1578.

Stuart, John McDouall, 1815–66, Scottish explorer in Australia. First to reach center of Australia (1860).

Stuart or **Stewart, Ludovick**, 2d duke of Lennox and duke of Richmond: see STUART OR STEWART, ESMÉ, 1ST DUKE OF LENNOX.

Stuart or **Stewart, Mary:** see MARY QUEEN OF SCOTS.

Stuart or **Stewart, Matthew:** see LENNOX, MATTHEW STUART OR STEWART, 4TH EARL OF.

Stuart or **Stewart, Robert**, 1st duke of Albany, d. 1420, regent of Scotland. Given control (1388) because of old age of his father, Robert II, he kept it during reign of his brother, Robert III. Ousted (1399) by David Stewart, he returned to power in 1402. James I, successor of Robert III, was a prisoner in England, and Albany ruled until his death.

Stuart, Australia: see ALICE SPRINGS.

Stubbs, William, 1825–1901, English historian. Major work *Constitutional History of England* (3 vols., 1874–78). Bishop of Chester (1884).

Stuhlweissenburg, Hungary: see SZEKESFEHERVAR.

Sture (stü′rŭ), noble Swedish family which played a leading role in the 15th–16th cent. **Sten Sture** (stān′), c.1440–1503, regent after 1470, defeated the Danes at Brunkeberg (1471) but recognized Sweden's personal union with Denmark in 1497. Founded Univ. of Uppsala. **Svante Sture** (svän′tŭ″), d. 1512, succeeded him as regent. His rule was one of continual warfare. His son and successor as regent, **Sten Sture**, c.1492–1520, asserted the superiority of state over Church by causing the deposition of his rival, Archbishop Gustav Trolle (1517), and refused his recognition to Christian II of Denmark as king of Sweden. War resulted, but Sture died in battle before Christian took Stockholm and had himself crowned.

sturgeon, large fish of fresh and salt water in Eurasia and North America. It is a primitive fish with cartilaginous skeleton. Largest (up to c.2,000 lb.) is beluga of Caspian and Black seas and Sea of Azov. Sturgeon roe is source of CAVIAR.

Sturgeon Bay, city (pop. 7,054), NE Wis., at head of Sturgeon Bay, inlet of Green Bay. Ship canal here cuts across DOOR PENINSULA to L. Michigan. Summer resort, shipping, and shipbuilding center.

Sturgis, Russell (stûr′jĭs), 1836–1909, American architect and writer, an authority on history of architecture and art.

Sturgis, city (pop. 7,786), S Mich., SE of Kalamazoo. Trade center with mfg. of wood products.

Stürgkh, Karl, Graf von (kärl′ gräf′ fŭn shtürk′), 1859–1916, premier of Austria (1911–16). Suspended parliament in World War I. Was assassinated by Friedrich ADLER.

Sturluson, Snorri: see SNORRI STURLUSON.

Sturm, Jacques Charles François (zhäk′ shärl′ fräswä′ stürm′), 1803–55, French mathematician. Originated Sturm's theorem for determination of the number of real roots of an equation (algebraic or numerical) within given limits. Wrote on optics, mechanics, mathematical analysis.

Sturm und Drang (shtoŏrm′ oŏnt dräng′) or **Storm and Stress**, term applied to the period (roughly 1767–87) of German literature in which youthful genius revolted against accepted standards. Influenced by Rousseau and Lessing, the period takes its name from Klinger's *Die Wirrwarr; oder, Sturm und Drang* (1776). Goethe's *Götz von Berlichingen* and *The Sor-*

rows of Werther and Schiller's *Robbers* are major expressions of the movement.

Sturt, Charles (stûrt), 1795–1869, English explorer and administrator in Australia. Explored river system of S Australia; discovered Darling R. in 1828. Colonial secretary (1849–51).

stuttering or **stammering** (dysphemia), inability to enunciate consonants without spasmodic repetition, generally attributed to psychological disorders. Stuttering is usually precipitated in childhood by sudden emotional shock or by the cumulative impact of a neurotic environment. It tends to cause feelings of inadequacy and morbid anxiety, thus intensifying the condition. Before a child realizes that he stutters, removal of stress plus a regime of relaxation and counseling may correct the condition. If personality deviations have already developed because of self-consciousness, intensive and prolonged psychiatric treatment may be needed.

Stuttgart (stŭt′gärt, Ger. shtoŏt′gärt), city (pop. 481,-845), cap. of Württemberg-Baden, SW Germany, on the Neckar; until 1945 cap. of all Württemberg. Lutheran episcopal see. Important communications point. Publishing center. Produces vehicles, machinery, precision instruments, chemicals, textiles. Chartered 13th cent. Expanded rapidly 19th–20th cent. Became famous after 1918 for its pioneering housing developments. Old central part of city was largely destroyed in World War II.

Stuttgart (stŭt′gärt), city (pop. 7,276), E Ark., NE of Pine Bluff. Trade center for farm area (esp. rice).

Stuyvesant, Peter (stī′vŭsŭnt), 1592–1672, Dutch director general of New Netherland (1647–64). Ruled autocratically. Conquered NEW SWEDEN in 1655. Surrendered New Netherland to English in 1664.

Stymphalian birds (stĭmfā′lēŭn), in Greek mythology, man-eating birds. HERCULES killed them as one of his 12 labors.

Styria (stĭ′rēŭ), Ger. *Steiermark*, province (6,326 sq. mi.; pop. 1,106,581), SE and central Austria; cap. Graz. Predominantly mountainous. Chief Austrian mining district (iron, lignite, magnesite), with metal industry. Has many mountain resorts. Originally part of Carinthia, Styria became a separate duchy 1180. It passed to dukes of Austria 1192; to Ottocar II of Bohemia 1260; to Rudolf I of Hapsburg 1276. S portion passed to Yugoslavia 1919.

Styx (stĭks), in Greek religion, river in the underworld (see HELL), which souls of the dead must cross on their trip from earth. There is a real Styx R. in N Peloponnesus.

Suárez, Francisco (soŏä′rĕz), 1548–1617, Spanish Jesuit theologian, last of the old scholastics. His political doctrine that the power of kings is properly derived from the body of men and not by divine right was significant, as was his distinction between natural law and international law (anticipating Grotius).

subconscious: see UNCONSCIOUS.

Subiaco (soŏbyä′kō), village, Latium, central Italy, in the Apennines. Out of community of St. Benedict of Nursia, who lived here c.497–529, grew a Benedictine abbey which rose to great wealth and power in the Middle Ages. St. Scholastica estab. here first monastic community for women.

sublimation, in chemistry, process in which solid changes directly to vapor without passing through liquid stage, then reverts to solid on sudden cooling. When iodine is heated it changes from a dark solid to a purplish vapor, then condenses to a solid on striking a cool surface.

sublimation, in psychology: see DEFENSE MECHANISM.

submarine, naval craft capable of operating under water, used in warfare to attack surface vessels, mainly with torpedoes. First practical one was a leather-covered rowboat built (c.1620) in England by C. J. Drebbel. In the American Revolution, David Bushnell tried to sink a warship with an underwater vessel (1776). Several used in the Civil War. The work of

J. P. Holland and Simon LAKE did much to advance the modern submarine, first used on a large scale by Germany in World War I. Germans and Japanese used them extensively in World War II. Antisubmarine tactics rely on spotting from the air or the surface, and radio devices for spotting were developed. Experiments with use of atomic energy in submarines seemed in 1953 to promise a new era.

Subotica (sōō″bô′tĭtsä), Ger. *Maria Theresiopel*, Hung. *Szabadka,* city (pop. 112,551), N Serbia, Yugoslavia; chief city of Vojvodina. Has meat-packing plants, flour mills, chemical and electrotechnical industries. Was part of Hungary until 1920.

subsidy, financial assistance granted by a government for the furtherance of an enterprise considered in the public good. For example, subsidies are granted to private business concerns under certain circumstances (e.g., to encourage shipping) and to farmers (to encourage growing of certain crops).

subtraction, one of four fundamental operations of arithmetic. Symbol for the operation is the minus sign (−). Result of subtracting one number from another is the difference; number subtracted is subtrahend; minuend is number from which subtrahend is subtracted. The inverse of addition, subtraction is process of finding what number added to subtrahend gives minuend. Only like quantities can be subtracted. Operation does not have properties of associativity and commutivity but does have distributivity, i.e., result of multiplying difference of two numbers by a third is same as result of multiplying each of first two numbers by third and subtracting these products.

subtreasury. Subtreasury system was finally estab. in 1846 with creation of INDEPENDENT TREASURY SYSTEM. Public funds were not to be deposited in any bank, but must be kept in coin in the Treasury or in subtreasuries or retained by public officers receiving them until paid out on proper authority, and no banknotes were to be received in payments to the government. After passage of General Appropriations Act, May 29, 1920, transfer was made of subtreasury functions to the Treasury, the mints and assay offices, and Federal reserve banks.

Succession Act: see SETTLEMENT, ACT OF.

succory: see CHICORY.

sucker, sluggish fresh-water fish related to carp, found in most of North America. Flesh is palatable but the fish is bony.

Suckert, Curzio: see MALAPARTE, CURZIO.

Suckling, Sir John, 1609–1642?, one of the CAVALIER POETS. Handsome, talented, he was a model courtier and royalist. Best known for "Ballad upon a Wedding" and for his lyrics, including "Constancy" and the song "Why so pale and wan, fond lover" from his play *Aglaura* (presented 1637).

Sucre, Antonio José de (äntō′nyō hōsā′ dā sōō′krā), 1795–1830, South American revolutionist, b. Venezuela. Was Bolivar's chief lieutenant in fight against Spain and victor at Ayacucho (1824), completing liberation of N South America. Later reluctant president of Bolivia and a chief figure in the Quito Conference for maintaining unity in the N independent countries, he was ambushed and killed by local patriots. A military genius but ineffective administrator

Sucre (sōō′krā), city (pop. 32,500), S central Bolivia, legal capital of Bolivia (*de facto* capital is La Paz). Founded as La Plata (1538), it has also been called Chuquisaca and Charcas: cap. of captaincy general of Charcas in colonial period. First revolt in wars of independence in South America broke out here (1809). Today it is a commercial and agr. center.

sucrose (sōō′krōs), commonest sugar, a white, crystalline solid. Yields caramel when heated above melting point. It is a carbohydrate with 12 carbon atoms, 22 hydrogen, 11 oxygen. Yields glucose and fructose on HYDROLYSIS; process called inversion and mixture is called invert sugar because it rotates plane of polarized light to left, while sucrose rotates it to

right. It is obtained from sugar cane, sugar beet, sugar maple.

Sudan (sōōdăn′), vaguely defined region, E Africa, S of the Sahara. Generally considered to include parts of French West Africa (including FRENCH SUDAN), N French Equatorial Africa, and N and central ANGLO-EGYPTIAN SUDAN. Comprises mainly desert and grassy plains.

Sudbury, city (pop. 42,410), S Ont., Canada, E of Sault Ste Marie. Center of important mining region.

Sudbury, town (pop. 2,596), E Mass., W of Boston. Howe or Red Horse tavern (built 1686; restored) was scene of Longfellow's *Tales of a Wayside Inn.*

Sudermann, Hermann (hĕr′män zōō′dürmän), 1857–1928, German dramatist and novelist. His most popular works include the play *Honor* (1889; Eng. trs., 1906, 1915); the novel *Dame Care* (1887; Eng. tr., 1891); the play *Heimat* (1893; Eng. tr., *Magda,* 1896); and the short stories *The Excursion to Tilsit* (1917; Eng. tr., 1930). Influenced by Ibsen and Nietzsche.

Sudetes (sōōdē′tēz), Czech *Sudety,* Ger. *Sudeten,* mountain system, extending c.170 mi. along N border of Czechoslovakia between Elbe and Oder rivers and rising to 5,259 ft. in the RIESENGEBIRGE range. Rich mineral deposits (e.g., coal, iron); mineral springs; resorts. Lumbering; glass, porcelain, and textile mfg. The term "Sudete Germans" designated all Germans in the regions of Czechoslovakia bordering on Germany. The Sudete German party (founded 1934), an offshoot of the German National Socialist party, was instrumental in the annexation of the Sudetenland to Germany after the MUNICH PACT (1938). District reverted to Czechoslovakia 1945; majority of Germans were expelled.

Sue, Eugène (ûzhĕn′ sü′), 1804–57, French novelist, author of *The Mysteries of Paris* (1842–43) and *The Wandering Jew* (1844–45), both widely translated.

Suetonius (Caius Suetonius Tranquillus) (swētō′nēus), fl. c.120, Roman biographer. His *De vita Caesarum* survives almost in full.

Suez (sōōĕz′), city (pop. 108,250), NE Egypt; port at S end of Suez Canal. In near-by oasis, the Springs of Moses, is a spring which Moses is supposed to have miraculously made sweet.

Suez Canal, waterway of Egypt extending from Port Said to Port Tewfik (near Suez) and connecting the Mediterranean with Gulf of Suez and thus with Red Sea. Canal is 107 mi. long, 42.5 ft. deep, and 197 ft. wide. There are no locks. As early as 20th or 19th cent. B.C. a canal was built to L. Timsah, then the N end of Red Sea. When Red Sea receded, the canal was extended by Xerxes I, but in 8th cent. A.D. it was closed and fell into disrepair. The modern canal was built 1859–69 by Ferdinand de Lesseps. Owned by Suez Canal Co., whose controlling interest has been held (since 1875) by Great Britain. Concession terminates 1968, when the canal reverts to the Egyptian government.

Suffolk, dukes and earls of: see also POLE, family.

Suffolk, Charles Brandon, 1st duke of (sü′fŭk), d. 1545. Married Mary of England, widow of Louis XII and sister of Henry VIII. Led troops in two invasions of France (1523, 1544) and in Pilgrimage of Grace (1536). He supported all of Henry's policies and achieved great power.

Suffolk, Henry Grey, duke of, d. 1554. Father of Lady Jane Grey, whom he tried to place on throne on death of Edward VI. Joined rebellion of Sir Thomas Wyatt, was convicted of treason, and executed.

Suffolk, Thomas Howard, 1st earl of: see HOWARD, family.

Suffolk (sü′fŭk), maritime county, E England, divided administratively into Suffolk East (871 sq. mi.; pop. 321,849) and Suffolk West (611 sq. mi.; pop. 120,-590). Low, undulating, mainly agr. region, it is one of England's chief grain producers. Ipswich and Bury St. Edmonds are chief towns.

Suffolk, city (pop. 12,339), SE Va., on Nansemond R.

and near Dismal Swamp; settled 1720. Peanut market and processing center with mfg. of machinery and boxes. Burned by British 1779; occupied by Union troops 1862; besieged by Confederates 1863.

Sufism (sōo'fizùm), mystical philosophy in Islam, arising in late 10th and early 11th cent. and gaining great strength particularly in Persia. Members of a semi-monastic order (Sufis) emphasized personal union of the soul with God. The great philosopher of the movement was Al-Gazel. Its chief importance was, however, its expression in symbolic Persian poetry (e.g., poets Ferid ed-Din Attar, Hafiz, Jami, Omar Khayyam).

sugar, compound of carbon, hydrogen, oxygen, a carbohydrate. There are several types of sugars—monosaccharides, the simplest, include glucose and fructose; disaccharides, as the name implies, are formed by two monosaccharides with loss of one molecule of water and include lactose, maltose, and sucrose; and trisaccharides, of which little is known. Letters d- and l- before name of sugar indicates position of certain hydroxyl group in molecule. The transformation and use of various sugars in body chemistry are essential to human life, and intravenous injection of sugar is much used to keep persons alive when they are unable to take nourishment.

sugar cane, tall perennial grass (*Saccharum officinarum*), somewhat like corn in appearance, widely cultivated in tropics and subtropics. Sugar (sucrose) is obtained from its stalks; by-products include molasses, rum, alcohol, livestock food, and wallboard. One planting may yield several harvests.

sugar of lead, lead acetate, a white, very poisonous, crystalline substance with sweet taste. Used as mordant in textile dyeing and as drier in paints.

Sui (swē), dynasty of China, which ruled from A.D. 581 to 618. Succeeded by T'ang dynasty.

Suidas (sū'ĭdùs), name of a Greek lexicon-encyclopedia, also applied to its compiler, who seems to have lived in the 10th cent. A.D.

suite, in music, a succession of short pieces, an instrumental form which developed from the 16th-cent. practice of playing in sequence dances of contrasting meter. Usually the dances were linked together by a common key. The best-known suites of the baroque period are those of J. S. Bach. Suites of the 19th cent. were often collections of pieces drawn from incidental music to a play or from ballet (e.g., Grieg's *Peer Gynt Suite;* Tchaikovsky's *Nutcracker Suite*).

Suiyuan (swā'yüän'), province (135,000 sq. mi.; pop. 2,000,000), N China, partly in Inner Mongolia; cap. Kweisui. Mainly an arid plateau crossed by Yellow R. Livestock raising and limited agr. (grains, ramie). Held 1937–45 by Japan.

Sukarno or **Soekarno** (both: sōokär'nō), 1902–, first president of Indonesia. Headed the original Indonesian republic (founded Aug., 1945), which comprised only a part of Indonesia. Became president of sovereign state of United States of Indonesia, created Dec., 1949, and of Republic of Indonesia, which replaced the federation, Aug., 1950.

Sukhum (sōokhōom') or **Sukhumi** (sōokhōo'mē), city (pop. 44,350), cap. of Abkhaz ASSR, Georgian SSR; a Black Sea port and subtropical resort with sulphur baths (since Roman times).

Sukkertoppen (sōo'kùrtô''pùn), district (pop. 1,831), SW Greenland. The chief settlement, Sukkertoppen (pop. 821), is a harbor N of Godthaab.

Sukkoth: see TABERNACLES, FEAST OF.

Suleiman (sōo'lĭmän'', –lā–, sōo'lämän'), Ottoman sultans; also spelled Soliman or Solyman. **Suleiman I,** 1494–1566, called the Magnificent in the West and the Lawgiver by Moslems, succeeded his father Selim I in 1520. He is also known (erroneously) as Suleiman II. Under his rule the Ottoman Empire reached the height of its glory. He conquered Belgrade (1521) and Rhodes (1522); crushed Hungary at MOHACS (1526); annexed most of Hungary 1541; undertook several successful

campaigns against Persia; conquered the Arabian coast lands. His vassal, BARBAROSSA, made the Turkish fleet the terror of the Mediterranean. His failures were hardly less important than his victories. His siege of Vienna (1529) and his attack on Malta (1565) were repulsed; he lost Tunis to Emperor Charles V (1535); his naval warfare against Spain and Venice was generally unsuccessful. Suleiman's alliance with France against Austria (1536) set the pattern for later Turkish foreign policy. His grand vizier Ibrahim had a large share in Suleiman's rule, but in 1536, for obscure reasons, he had Ibrahim strangled. A still blacker spot in his career was the murder (1553) of his own son Mustafa, instigated by his favorite wife, Roxelana, who thus secured the succession for her own son, Selim II. His government was, however, generally mild. He introduced important reforms and was a lavish patron of the arts and of literature. **Suleiman II,** 1642–91, reigned 1687–91. His whole reign was taken up with war on Austria.

sulfa drugs (sùl'fù), name for sulfanilamide, a synthetic, organic drug, and certain of its compounds and derivatives. They are believed to check growth and reproduction of many bacteria; used to treat variety of bacterial infections. Bactericidal properties of prontosil discovered 1932 by Domagk; active agent found to be sulfanilamide, whose therapeutic value was confirmed 1936.

Sulgrave Manor, Tudor house, Sulgrave village, Northamptonshire, England; home of George Washington's ancestors. Now a museum and shrine.

Sulitelma or **Sulitjelma** (both: sōolĕtyĕl'mä), mountain, 6,279 ft. high, N Norway, on Swedish border. Copper mines operated by a Swedish company.

Sulla, Lucius Cornelius (sù'lù), 138 B.C.–78 B.C., Roman general, leader of the conservative senatorial party. He and MARIUS both wanted the appointment as commander against Mithridates VI; Sulla got it by marching against Rome (88 B.C.). He conquered Mithridates, sacked Athens (86 B.C.), defeated Fimbria (a Roman general sent to Greece originally by Marius' party), and returned triumphantly to Rome. In the civil war that followed he defeated the Marians. He captured and massacred 8,000 prisoners, declared himself dictator (82 B.C.), and butchered all who had opposed him. Retired 79 B.C.

Sullivan, Anne, maiden name of MACY, ANNE S.

Sullivan, Sir Arthur (Seymour), 1842–1900, English composer. Although he wrote oratorios and serious operas, and although his songs (e.g., *The Lost Chord*) and hymns (e.g., *Onward, Christian Soldiers*) became very popular, he is best known for writing the music for the Gilbert and Sullivan operas (see GILBERT, SIR W(ILLIAM) S(CHWENK).

Sullivan, Harry Stack, 1892–1949, American psychiatrist. He believed psychoanalysis should be supplemented by a thorough study of the impact of cultural forces on the personality. As head of the William Alanson White Foundation (1934–43) and the Washington School of Psychiatry (1936–47), he brought this view to public and professional attention.

Sullivan, John, 1740–95, American Revolutionary general. Led punitive expedition against Iroquois in Chemung valley, N.Y. (1778); defeated John and Walter Butler.

Sullivan, John L(awrence), 1858–1918, American boxer. Won (1882) bare-knuckles heavyweight championship. Fighting with gloves under Queensberry rules for boxing, Sullivan was defeated (1892) by James J. Corbett. Sullivan retired (1896) from ring, still in possession of bare-knuckles crown.

Sullivan, Louis H(enry), 1856–1924, American architect, important in evolution of modern architecture in U.S. Associated with William Le Baron Jenney and Denkmar Adler. His designs, mainly in Chicago, expressed a new functional approach, exemplified by his famous Transportation Bldg. at World's Columbian Exposition (1893).

Sullivan, city (pop. 5,423), SW Ind., near Wabash R. and S of Terre Haute. Coal mining.

Sullivans Island: see MOULTRIE, FORT.

Sully, Maximilien de Béthune, duc de (mäksēmēlyē′ dü bätün′ dük′ dü sülē′), 1560–1641, French statesman, chief adviser to Henry IV. He was a Protestant. As superintendent of finances (1598–1611) he restored French prosperity by encouraging agr. and industry; built network of roads and canals; left a surplus in the treasury. He was the author of the Great Design, a plan for a confederation of all Christian nations, which he attributed to Henry IV.

Sully, Thomas (sŭ′lē), 1783–1872, American portrait painter, b. England. Influenced by Sir Thomas Lawrence. Flourished in Philadelphia, where he painted many eminent contemporaries.

Sully-Prudhomme, Armand (ärmä′ sülē′-prüdôm′), 1839–1907, French poet; one of the PARNASSIANS. Won 1901 Nobel Prize in Literature. His works include *Les Solitudes* (1869), *Les Vaines Tendresses* (1875), *La Justice* (1878), and *Le Bonheur* (1888).

sulphate, salt or ester of SULPHURIC ACID. Consists in general of a metal or radical united with sulphate radical (one sulphur, four oxygen atoms). Acid sulphates have hydrogen atom in addition. Generally metallic sulphates are water soluble; test for sulphate ion involves precipitation of insoluble barium sulphate. Lead sulphate is used in pigments; potassium sulphate in fertilizers and in medicine; sodium sulphate used to make sulphide and window glass.

sulphide, compound of sulphur and one other element or radical. Sulphides are salts of hydrosulphuric acid, a water solution of hydrogen sulphide. Hydrogen sulphide is colorless gas that smells like rotten eggs; used as test for metals. Tarnishing of silver results from formation of silver sulphide. Sulphides are important ores of metals. Carbon disulphide is an important organic solvent.

Sulphur. 1 Town (pop. 5,996), SW La., near Lake Charles. Oil discovered near by, 1924. **2** Resort city (pop. 4,389), S Okla., near Washita R. and Arbuckle Mts. Near by is Platte Natl. Park.

sulphur, nonmetallic element (symbol = S; see also ELEMENT, table). It shows ALLOTROPY, having two crystalline yellow forms and one amorphous, dark form. It is chemically active; widely and abundantly distributed in nature. As one of the elements in protoplasm it is a constituent of organic matter. FRASCH PROCESS is used to extract uncombined sulphur from deposits. It is used in making gunpowder, sulphur dioxide, sulphuric acid, pulp paper, rubber, matches, insecticides. Was known to the ancients and is the brimstone of the Bible.

sulphuric acid, colorless, heavy, oily, inorganic, strong acid. It is a compound of hydrogen, sulphur, and oxygen. Ionizes readily. Concentrated acid is sometimes called oil of vitriol; it is used as dehydrating agent and oxidizing agent. Sulphuric acid has two replaceable hydrogen atoms (is dibasic); forms normal and acid salts. It is a stable acid and one of most important chemicals in industry. For commercial use it is prepared chiefly by the contact process and the lead-chamber process. It is used in making dyes, drugs, explosives, fertilizers, lead storage batteries, and in metallurgical processes, petroleum refining. Its salts (see SULPHATE) are widely used.

Sulphur Springs, city (pop. 8,991), E Texas, WSW of Texarkana, in dairying and agr. region.

Sulu Archipelago (sŏō′lŏō), island group (1,086 sq. mi.; pop. 240,826), P.I., W of Mindanao, between Celebes and Sulu seas. Basilan is largest of several hundred volcanic islands and coral islets. Pearl fishing, cattle, agr. Populated mainly by Moros. Under Spanish control in 19th cent.; under U.S. control 1899–1940. Ceded to Philippines 1940.

sumac (sŏō′măk), name for shrubs and trees of a widely distributed genus *Rhus*. The large pinnate leaves turn bright red in fall; conical fruit clusters are usually deep red. Most botanists now place the poisonous forms in a separate genus, *Toxicodendron*. From Asiatic *Toxicodendron vernicifluum* (or *Rhus verniciflua*) is produced lacquer. Poison sumac *Toxicodendron vernix* (or *Rhus vernix*) grows in swamps and bears white fruits.

Sumatra (sŏōmä′trŭ), island (163,557 sq. mi.; pop. c.12,000,000), Indonesia, in Indian Ocean, S and W of Malay Peninsula and NW of Java. Volcanic Barisan Mts. form central ridge of long, narrow island, and much of interior is jungle. Has large oil and coal fields. Forest and agr. products include camphor, ebony, rattan, tea, coffee, rubber, and pepper. PALEMBANG is chief center. Sumatra was nucleus of Hindu kingdom of Sri Vijaya, which flourished in 8th cent. and controlled much of Indonesia and Malay Peninsula. By 14th cent. Sumatran supremacy had waned, and center of power shifted to Java. First European traders were the Portuguese. After 1596 the Dutch slowly gained control of all the native states including Achin (subjugated 1904).

Sumava: see BOHEMIAN FOREST.

Sumer (sŏō′mŭr) **and Sumerian civilization** (sŏōmēr′-ēŭn). A notable culture appeared in S Mesopotamia (Sumer) at least as early as the 5th millennium B.C. Sumerian city-states (e.g., Erech, Kish, Lagash, Ur) developed considerable power, based on flourishing agr. (with irrigation). Pottery and metalwork were made into fine arts, and the Sumerians began cuneiform writing. They rivaled the Semitic cities and ultimately were conquered by them (e.g., Akkad under Sargon). A Sumerian revival at Ur (c.2300) fell before the rise of Elam, and growth of Babylonia ended Sumerians as a nation.

Sumer Is Icumen In (sŏō′mŭr ĭs ēkŏō′mŭn ĭn) [Mid. Eng.,= summer has (literally: is) come in], English round, dating from the 13th or 14th cent. It is a CANON for four voices supported by a short, two-voice ground bass.

Summerfield, Arthur E(llsworth), 1899–, U.S. Postmaster General (1953–). President of automobile agency in Flint, Mich., since 1929. Republican national chairman in 1952.

Summerside, town (pop. 6,547), SW Prince Edward Isl., Canada, WNW of Charlottetown and on Bedeque Bay. Port and resort with fox farms.

Summit. 1 Village (pop. 8,957), NE Ill., near Chicago. Corn products. Limestone quarried near by. **2** Residential suburban city (pop. 17,929), NE N.J., in Watchung Mts. and W of Newark.

Summit Hill, resort borough (pop. 4,924), E Pa., SW of Mauch Chunk. Burning Mine here has been smoldering since 1859.

Sumner, Charles, 1811–74, U.S. Senator from Mass. (1851–74). Victim of assault by Rep. P. S. Brooks after notable antislavery speech on May 19–20, 1856. Sumner was a leader of radical RECONSTRUCTION program. Opposed Pres. Grant on annexation of Santo Domingo.

Sumner, James Batcheller, 1887–, American biochemist. Shared 1946 Nobel Prize for work on enzymes.

Sumner, William Graham, 1840–1910, American sociologist and economist, professor at Yale. In economics he advocated an extreme laissez-faire policy. As a sociologist he concluded that human folkways and customs were so entrenched as to make reform useless. He wrote *Folkways* (1907); his monumental 4-volume study *Science of Society,* with A. G. Keller, appeared in 1927.

Sumter, Thomas, 1734–1832, American partisan leader in Revolution. Harassed British in S.C. as leader of guerrilla band; called the Gamecock. Fort Sumter named for him.

Sumter, city (pop. 20,185), central S.C., ESE of Columbia; laid out 1800. Trade, processing, and shipping center of lumber, livestock and farm area with mfg. of furniture.

Sumter, Fort, fortification at mouth of harbor of

Charleston, S.C., scene of first clash of Civil War. When S.C. seceded (Dec. 20, 1860) it demanded all Federal property within the state, particularly Forts Moultrie and Sumter. Major Robert Anderson moved his U.S. army command from Fort Moultrie to stronger site of Fort Sumter. After refusals to surrender, Confederates opened fire (April 12, 1861) and bombarded fort for 34 hours. Anderson finally accepted terms. Civil War had begun. Fort Sumter was made a national monument in 1948.

Sun, river rising in NW Mont. near Great Divide and flowing c.130 mi. SE and E to Missouri R. at Great Falls. Sun R. project waters c.100,000 acres.

sun, STAR whose gravitational attraction maintains the bodies of the SOLAR SYSTEM in their orbits. Appears larger than other stars because of relative nearness to earth (mean distance is c.93,004,000 mi.). Life as we know it could not exist without heat and light from sun. Its light is ultimate source of energy stored in food and coal; its heat sets up air currents and is related to water cycle. Sun's diameter c.865,400 mi.; its mass c.332,000 times mass of earth; its volume c.1,300,000 times that of earth. Gaseous nature causes latitudinal variation in speed of rotation; period c.25 days at equator, c.35 days at poles. At least ⅔ of elements known on earth have been identified in sun's atmosphere. Above surface (PHOTOSPHERE) lie CHROMOSPHERE and CORONA. Vast and continual production of energy has been attributed chiefly to release of energy in a "carbon cycle" involving atomic disintegrations and transmutations and more recently to a reaction of proton upon proton (i.e., hydrogen nuclei interact to produce double-weight hydrogen atoms with release of energy). See also ECLIPSE; SUNSPOTS. See *ills.,* pp. 773, 927.

Sunapee (sŭ′nŭpē), town (pop. 1,108), SW N.H., NW of Concord and on L. Sunapee (9 mi. long, 3 mi. wide), a fishing and boating resort.

Sunbury, city (pop. 15,570), E Pa., on Susquehanna R. and N of Harrisburg; laid out 1772. Rail center with mfg. of textiles and clothing. Site of Indian village in early 18th cent.; mission estab. 1742; Fort Augusta built 1756.

Sunda Islands (sŭn′dŭ, soōn′dŭ), Indonesia, between South China Sea and Indian Ocean, comprising part of Malay Archipelago. Largest islands (Borneo, Sumatra, Java, and Celebes) are sometimes called the Greater Sundas. Between Java and Timor are the Lesser Sundas, including Bali, Lombok, and Flores.

Sunday, William Ashley (Billy Sunday), 1863–1935, American evangelist (after 1896), a baseball player who was converted to religious work.

Sunday: see SABBATH; WEEK.

Sunday school, institution for instruction in religion and morals, usually part of church organization. Idea developed by Robert Raikes in Gloucester, England, 1780. Plan was widely copied; by 1795 Sunday School Society (1785) had helped found over 1,000 schools. Sunday School Union (1803) provided lesson plans, spellers, catechisms, and other aids. The effect of the movement in spreading popular education in England is almost incalculable. In 1786 Francis Asbury estab. in Hanover co., Va. first Sunday school in present U.S. after Raikes's plan. American Sunday-School Union was founded 1824. Plan of uniform lessons was adopted (1872) in cooperation with British Sunday School Union. World Council of Christian Education (1947) has units in 55 countries.

Sunderland, county borough (pop. 181,515), Durham, England, at mouth of the Wear. Includes Bishopwearmouth and Monkwearmouth. Bede studied here at monastery founded in 674 and destroyed by the Danes. Shipbuilding and rail center and coal-shipping port, it also has varied industry.

sundial, instrument that indicates time of day by shadow of an object. Forerunners include poles, upright stones; pyramids and obelisks were used in ancient Egypt. Development of trigonometry permitted precise calculations for marking dials. Difference between solar time indicated by sundials and clock (mean) time is correlated by use of standard tables. Correction is made also for difference between local standard meridian and longitude of sundial.

sunfish, name for certain small perchlike fishes of family Centrarchidae, abundant in North American fresh waters, and also for a salt-water fish of family Molidae.

sunflower, annual or perennial plant of genus *Helianthus,* native to the New World. The composite flowers, usually with yellow rays, are up to a foot across. The common sunflower (*Helianthus annuus*) is grown throughout the world for its edible seeds, also used as poultry food and as source of oil. Tuber of the Jerusalem artichoke (*H. tuberosus*) is eaten as a vegetable.

Sung (soōng), dynasty of China, which ruled A.D. 960–1279. Empire at its height extended from Great Wall to Hainan. Its early period saw improvements in transport facilities and increased trade with India and Persia. Notable achievements in literature (novel, drama) and landscape painting. Overthrown by Mongols who estab. Yüan dynasty.

Sungari (soōng″gŭrē′), Chinese *Sunghwa Kiang,* largest river of Manchuria, c.1,150 mi. long, converges with Amur R. Important trade artery.

Sungkiang: see MANCHURIA.

Sunnites (soō′nīts) [from Arabic *Sunna* = tradition], majority group of Moslems, predominant in Arabia, Turkey, and Africa. See ISLAM.

Sunnyvale, residential city (pop. 9,829), W Calif., E of San Francisco. Ironworks, fruit canneries.

Sunset Crater National Monument: see NATIONAL PARKS AND MONUMENTS (table).

sunspots, dark spots visible on sun's surface and believed to be tornadolike solar storms. Average duration about two weeks. Periods of sunspot activity occur in 11-year cycles; correlated with disturbances on earth including magnetic storms and increased rainfall.

sunstroke or **heatstroke,** illness caused by exposure to excessive heat. Believed to result from disturbance of heat-regulating mechanism of body and to be aggravated by loss of sodium chloride through perspiration. Commonly attended by unconsciousness, labored breathing, rapid pulse, high temperature. Requires prompt treatment by a physician.

Sun Valley, resort, S central Idaho, N of Hailey and SW of Mt. Hyndman; built 1936. Winter sports.

Sun Yat-sen (soōn′ yät′-sĕn′), 1866–1925, Chinese revolutionary hero, b. near Canton, of Christian family. Received medical diploma in 1892. Thereafter he devoted himself to revolutionary work against Ch'ing dynasty. Developed political theory embodied in Three People's Principles (San Min Chu I), namely, nationalism, democracy, and guaranteed livelihood. After the revolution (1911) he was elected first president of Chinese republic (Dec., 1911) but resigned four months later in favor of Yüan Shih-kai. Withdrew from northern government and estab. power in S, organizing the KUOMINTANG. Elected president of unofficial government at Canton, 1921; agreed 1924 to work with Chinese Communists and accept Russian help. His tomb at Nanking is a national shrine. His widow is SOONG Ching-ling.

Suomenlinna (soō′ōmĕnlĭn′nä), Swed. *Sveaborg,* fortress, S Finland, at entrance to Helsinki harbor. Built 1749, it now covers seven small islands. Was known as Gibraltar of the North.

superheterodyne (syoō″pŭrhĕ′tŭrŭdīn), in radio receivers, commonest and most efficient circuit for selecting and amplifying radio frequency. Incoming signals mix with oscillator voltage, producing intermediate-voltage frequency equal to arithmetical difference between the two voltages.

Superior, city (pop. 35,325), NW Wis., on Superior Bay of W L. Superior, where St. Louis and Nemadji rivers enter; platted 1852. Radisson explored region 1661, sieur Duluth visited site 1679. Grew after 1880s discovery of iron ore in Gogebic range. Shares harbor with Duluth, Minn. Ships iron-ore and grain; mfg. of coal briquettes. A major consumer cooperative center.

Superior, Lake, largest of Great Lakes and largest fresh-water lake in world; 350 mi. long, 160 mi. wide, covers 31,820 sq. mi. Bounded by Minn., Ont., Wis., and Mich., it lies c.602 ft. above sea level with maximum depth of 1,290 ft. Connects with L. Huron by St. Marys R. Receives many rivers, e.g., Kaministikwia and Pigeon. Islands include Grand Isl. and Apostle group. Iron, copper, silver, and nickel in region. Cities on shores ship ore, grain, fish. Étienne Brulé possibly first white man to see lake; sieur Duluth visited it 1678–79.

Suppé, Franz von (fün zōō'pä), 1819–95, Austrian composer of operettas. His *Poet and Peasant* and *Light Cavalry* overtures are still popular.

suprarenal gland: see ADRENAL GLAND.

Supreme Court, United States, highest court of U.S., estab. by Article 3 of U.S. Constitution. Judicial power extends to all cases arising under the Constitution, laws, and treaties of U.S.; to cases concerning foreign diplomats and admiralty practice; to diversity cases (those between citizens of different states) and cases in which U.S. or a state is a party (Eleventh Amendment forbids Federal cognizance of cases brought against a state by a private party). Cases in which another court need not first consider the controversy are those in which diplomats or a state is a party; even here, it has been held, inferior courts may enjoy concomitant jurisdiction. In all other Federal cases Supreme Court exercises appellate jurisdiction, but subject to all limitations and regulations made by Congress. Members of court are appointed by the President with advice and consent of Senate. Size of Supreme Court is not prescribed by the Constitution and is set by statute. It began in 1789 with six members; since 1869 there have been nine members. Under Judiciary Law as amended in 1934 cases are usually brought to the court by appeal or by writ of certiorari. Court has basically a dual function. It must interpret and expand all congressional enactments brought before it in proper cases; it has power (superseding that of all other courts) to examine Federal and state statutes and executive actions to determine whether they conform to U.S. Constitution. Although in U.S. governmental system the Supreme Court potentially wields the highest power, the court has found many constitutional limitations on its powers and has voluntarily adopted others. History of the court reflects development of U.S. economy, alteration of political views, evolution of the Federal structure. John MARSHALL increased power of court. R. B. TANEY increased power of states by advancing concept of POLICE POWER. Most recent instance of hostility between court and various Presidents occurred under F. D. ROOSEVELT.

Surabaya or **Soerabaja** (both: sōōräbä'yä), city (pop. 341,675), on NE Java, Indonesia; industrial center. Its port is Tanjungperak (on Madura Strait), which ships sugar, tobacco, coffee, tea, rubber, and spices. Near by is Ujung, site of Indonesia's chief naval base.

Surakarta or **Soerakarta** (both: sōōräkär'tä), town (pop. 165,484), on central Java, Indonesia, on Solo R. Here is vast walled palace of sultan of Surakarta. European section has Dutch fort built 1779.

Surat (sōō'rùt), city (pop. 171,443), NW Bombay, India; port on Gulf of Cambay. Main center of European trade in 17th cent. Ships cotton goods.

surface, in geometry, boundary (curved or flat) between two volumes. It has no thickness but separates two regions in space. May be closed or finite, like a sphere, or of infinite extent, like a plane.

surface tension, property of liquids in which surface exposed tends to be reduced to smallest possible area. Attributed to cohesion between molecules of liquid; molecules at surface tend to be drawn toward center by other molecules; surface then appears to act like very thin membrane.

surgery, branch of MEDICINE concerned with diagnosis and treatment of conditions requiring operations. From prehistoric times date trephining (removal of circular pieces of skull), opening abscesses, and performing amputations. Greek physicians skilled in surgery include Hippocrates, Erasistratus, Herophilus. During the Middle Ages arose belief that surgery was demeaning and its practice fell into hands of barber-surgeons, often unskilled itinerants. However, before surgery began to achieve professional status in the 18th cent., there were a few notable surgeons, among them Guy de CHAULIAC and Ambroise PARÉ. Infections resulted in mortality rate so high that surgery was practiced chiefly in desperate cases until introduction of antiseptic methods by LISTER. The development of ANESTHESIA facilitated complex surgical feats. Surgery has benefited by evolution of instruments, X-ray techniques, fluoroscope, blood transfusion, and drugs including anticlotting agents, and sulfa drugs and antibiotic substances valuable in conquering infection.

Surinam (sōōrĭnäm'), name for Dutch GUIANA.

Surratt, Mary Eugenia (sùrăt'), 1820–65, alleged conspirator in assassination of Abraham Lincoln, hanged on July 7, 1865. Kept boardinghouse where J. W. BOOTH hatched unsuccessful plot to abduct Lincoln. It now seems certain she was not a party to assassination plans. Her hanging is generally considered a gross miscarriage of justice.

surrealism (sùrē'ŭlĭzŭm), literary and art movement, influenced by Freudianism and aiming to express the imagination as revealed in dreams. Founded 1924 in Paris by André Breton, with his *Manifeste du surréalisme,* but its ancestry is traceable to Baudelaire and Rimbaud. In literature it was confined almost exclusively to France, where Breton and Paul Eluard were its main exponents. In art it became internationally important in '20s and '30s and dominated the works of many artists using varying techniques; these included Salvador Dali, Yves Tanguy, Max Ernst, Marc Chagall, Giorgio de Chirico, Joan Miró, and Marcel Duchamp. Surrealism has also been used in films, notably by Jean Cocteau.

Surrey, Henry Howard, earl of, c.1517–1547, English poet, son of the duke of Norfolk. Beheaded for treason. A friend of Wyatt, he introduced blank verse into English.

Surrey, inland county (722 sq. mi.; pop. 1,601,555), S England; co. town Guildford. One of "Home Counties" around London, it is chiefly agr. with dairying and sheep raising. Towns include Croyden (airport), Wimbledon (tennis matches), Epsom (horse racing), and Kew (botanical gardens). King John signed Magna Carta at Runnymede in 1215.

Surtees, Robert Smith (sûr'tēz), 1803–64, English novelist, known for his stories of hunting life (e.g., *Jorrocks' Jaunts and Jollities,* 1838).

surveying, the science of finding the relative position of points on or near the earth's surface. Boundaries, areas, elevations, construction lines, geographical or artificial features are determined by measuring horizontal and vertical distances and angles and by computations based partly on geometry and trigonometry. Field work consists in obtaining data for delineation on maps, charts, and profiles or in fixing points from predetermined data. Methods of surveying include transit, plane-table, or photogrammetic surveying. The height of points in relation to a datum line (usually mean sea level) is measured by a leveling instrument consisting of a telescope fitted with a spirit level, usually on a tripod, and used with a leveling rod.

Susa (sū'zù), city, cap. of anc. Elam, SW of present Dizful, Iran. Destroyed by Assur-bani-pal, it was revived by ancient Persian kings, who built winter palaces there.

Susak, Yugoslavia: see FIUME.

Susanna [Gr. from Heb.,= lily], heroine of story told in Dan. 13, a chapter placed in the Apocrypha of AV, included in Western canon. Two elders try to seduce Susanna and are repulsed; they accuse her of misconduct, but she is exonerated by Daniel.

Susanville, city (pop. 5,338), NE Calif., in timber, dairy, and grain area. Lassen Volcanic Natl. Park and Honey L. are near.

suspension, in chemistry, mixture of finely divided solid and liquid or gas in which solid remains dispersed and suspended before settling out. Particles are larger than those of colloid. Mixture is not homogeneous like solution. Emulsions are mixtures of liquids, one suspended in another.

Susquehanna (sŭskwĭhă'nù), river, 450 mi. long, crossing N.Y. and Pa. coal region. Flows from Otsego L., N.Y., SE and SW to point near Pittston, Pa., where Lackawanna R. enters, thence SW joining West Branch. Juniata R. enters united stream above Harrisburg; river then flows S and SE into Md. and enters Chesapeake Bay at Havre de Grace. Commonly called North Branch above juncture with West Branch. U.S. flood control plan approved 1936.

Susquehanna Company or **Susquehannah Company,** land company formed in Conn. (1753) to develop Wyoming Valley in Pa.

Sussex, maritime county, S England, divided administratively into Sussex East (829 sq. mi.; pop. 618,083) and Sussex West (628 sq. mi.; pop. 318,661); co. town Lewes. South Downs cross county from E to W. It is almost entirely an agr. and pastoral region. William the Conqueror defeated Saxons at Hastings in 1066. Chichester is famous for its cathedral. Brighton and Eastbourne are noted as resorts.

Sussex, kingdom of, in England. Settled, according to tradition, in 477 by Saxons who defeated Celts. After 5th cent. it became subkingdom and later included modern Sussex, E Hampshire, and Isle of Wight. St. Wilfrid of York led (681–86) conversion of people. Conquered by Caedwalla of Wessex (685–88) and later by Offa of Mercia. Remained under Mercia from 771 until it submitted to Egbert of Wessex in 825. Thereafter it existed as an earldom.

Sutherlandshire (sŭ'dhùrlùndshĭr) or **Sutherland,** maritime county (2,028 sq. mi.; pop. 13,664), N Scotland; co. town Dornoch. Mountainous region with moors and forests, its poor soil and heavy rainfall make farming difficult. Sheep grazing is important. Deer, grouse, fishing attract sportsmen.

Sutlej (sŭt'lĕj), river, flowing c.900 mi. from SW Tibet through India and Pakistan to Indus R.

suttee, funeral practice of Hindus according to which the widow sacrificed herself on husband's pyre. Aim was to help her soul and his in world to come.

Sutter, John Augustus, 1803–80, American frontiersman, b. Baden, of Swiss parents. Original name was Johann August Suter. Built Sutter's Fort (see SACRAMENTO). After discovery of gold at Sutter's Mill, activities of gold-seekers ruined Sutter.

Sutter Creek, city (pop. 1,151), central Calif., ESE of Sacramento, in gold-mining area. Leland Stanford made his fortune here.

Suttner, Bertha (Kinsky), Baroness von (bĕr'tä, fŭn zōōt'nùr), 1843–1914, Austrian novelist and pacifist. Her novel *Lay Down Your Arms* (1889; Eng. tr., 1906) had immense influence on the pacifist movement. Was awarded 1905 Nobel Peace Prize.

Suva (sōō'vä), town (pop. 11,398; Greater Suva pop. 23,513), on Viti Levu; cap. and chief port of British colony of Fiji. Exports sugar and gold.

Suvarov, Aleksandr Vasilyevich (ŭlyĭksän'dùr vŭsē'lyùvĭch sōōvô'rùf), 1729–1800, Russian field marshal. He fought in the Russo-Turkish Wars and put down the Pugachev rebellion (1775) and the Kosciusko rebellion (1794). In the FRENCH REVOLUTIONARY WARS he defeated the French in N Italy (1798), crossed the St. Gotthard and, after the defeat of his colleague Korsakov at Zurich, led his ragged troops across the Alps to Lindau (late 1799). The Russian defeat in Switzerland was due largely to poor Austrian cooperation. Suvarov was idolized by his soldiers.

Suwanee (swô'nē), river rising in Okefenokee Swamp, SE Ga., and winding 250 mi. S through N Fla. to Gulf of Mexico. Name used in Stephen Foster's song *Old Folks at Home* or *Swanee River.*

Suzdal (sōōz'dŭl), city (1926 pop. 6,904), central European RSFSR, ENE of Moscow. An important city of VLADIMIR-Suzdal in 12th cent. and a religious center of NE Russia, it was destroyed by Tatars 1238 and annexed by Moscow 1451. Has kremlin with 13th-cent. monastery and cathedral.

Svalbard: see SPITSBERGEN.

Sveaborg, Finland: see SUOMENLINNA.

Svealand or **Svearike:** see SWEDEN.

Svedberg, Theodor (tä'ōdôr sväd'bĕryù), 1884–, Swedish chemist. Won 1926 Nobel Prize for fundamental research on colloid chemistry. Made studies of protein molecules and developed a centrifuge.

Svein, king of Denmark: see SWEYN.

Sverdlovsk (svyĭrdlôfsk'), city (pop. c.600,000), RSFSR, in E foothills of the central Urals. Leading industrial city of the Urals and a major machine-mfg. center of the USSR; W terminus of Trans-Siberian RR. It was founded 1722 as a fortress and originally named Ekaterinburg (until 1924). Its earliest ironworks were built 1725. Here in 1918 Emperor Nicholas II and his family were shot by the Bolsheviks.

Sverdrup, Johan (yōhän' svĕr'drōop), 1816–92, Norwegian statesman. He founded the party of the Left (1869) and fought for parliamentary government. In 1880 he submitted a resolution in the Storting which would have waived a royal veto. The struggle over the veto question continued till 1884, when the Conservative cabinet was impeached and Sverdrup became premier. He failed to satisfy the extremists in his party and resigned 1889.

Sverre (svĕ'rù), d. 1202, king of Norway (1177–1202); possibly a natural son of King Sigurd. His cause was adopted by the popular Birkebeiner party, who fought the Baglar (aristocratic and clerical party) until 1201. The Birkebeiner's victory led to the destruction of the nobles' power. Sverre prepared the way for absolute monarchy.

Sviatoslav (svyä'tùslŭf), 920–72, duke of Kiev (964–72); son of Igor and St. Olga. He overthrew the empire of the KHAZARS and brought Kievan Russia to the height of its power. His defeat by John I of Byzantium (971) forced him to evacuate Bulgaria.

Svir (svēr), river, NW European RSFSR, issuing from L. Onega and flowing 140 mi. W into L. Ladoga. Wholly navigable, it is part of MARIINSK SYSTEM.

Swabia (swä'bèù), Ger. *Schwaben,* region, SW Germany, comprising SW Bavaria, S Württemberg, Hohenzollern, and S Baden. It includes the BLACK FOREST, Swabian Jura range, and upper waters of the Danube and Neckar. Mainly agr. and forested, it is famous for its loveliness. Settled by Germanic Suevi and Alemanni during the great migrations, it was also known as Alamannia. Swabia, which then also comprised Alsace and E Switzerland, became a stem duchy of Germany in the 9th cent. and passed to the HOHENSTAUFEN dynasty 1079. After 1268 it broke up into smaller temporal and ecclesiastic lordships and free imperial cities, such as AUGSBURG and ULM. While the cities accepted the Reformation, the country remained largely Catholic. In 1801–3 Swabia was apportioned among Bavaria, Württemberg, and Baden. The **Swabian League** of 1488–1534 was an association of 26 cities and several ecclesiastic and temporal lords which sought to oppose the large territorial princes and supported the cause of imperial reform. It had a powerful army, a court, and a formal constitution, and it played a major role in the defeat of Franz von SICKINGEN and of the peasants in the PEASANTS' WAR. Its dissolution resulted from the split caused by the Reformation. There had been other Swabian leagues of somewhat lesser importance in earlier centuries.

Swahili (swähē'lē) [Arabic,= coast people], generic name for native population of coast of Kenya, Tanganyika, and Zanzibar, who are descendants of Bantu Negroes and Arab traders. **Swahili language,** a Bantu tongue, with large Arabic admixtures, is lingua franca of much of E Africa.

swallow, small migratory bird of both hemispheres. Including the martin there are c.100 species. Plumage is usually iridescent black or blue. Swallows are graceful in flight; they have long, narrow wings, forked or notched tails, and weak feet. Have short bills and wide mouths; they catch insects on the wing.

Swammerdam, Jan (yän' svä'mùrdäm), 1637–80, Dutch naturalist. Pioneered in use of microscope and was probably first to detect red corpuscles and valves of lymphatics.

swamp, area where the soil, saturated with water, is spongy and in places inundated. Moisture accumulates where normal drainage is prevented by flatness of land, impervious subsoil, or luxuriant vegetation. Types of swamp include the BOG; the fen, inundated lowland; the marsh, covered with water and treeless; the moorland, overlaid with peat and in N Europe characterized by heather.

Swampscott (swŏmp'skùt), coast-resort town (pop. 11,-580), E Mass., NE of Boston; settled 1629.

swan, large aquatic bird of both hemispheres, related to duck and goose. It has a long, graceful neck; its convoluted trachea makes possible its loud trumpeting call. Much used in poetry as a symbol of remote unworldly beauty, the swan is the subject of many legends, the most familiar being that the swan sings once in his life and then when he is dying (hence, "swan song"). In Germanic legend used by Wagner, the Swan Knight is the mysterious deliverer (Lohengrin). The swan was a chief symbol in Spanish *modernismo* poetry.

Swanee, river: see SUWANEE, river.

Swansea (swŏn'sē, –zē), village (pop. 8,072), S Ont., Canada, W residential suburb of Toronto.

Swansea (swŏn'zē), town (pop. 6,121), SE Mass., NW of Fall River. Textiles.

Swansea (swŏn'zē, –sē) or **Abertawe** (ăbùrtou'ē), county borough (pop. 160,832), Glamorganshire, Wales. Metallurgical center with sheet-metal mills and foundries. Has Royal Inst. of South Wales and Univ. Col. of Swansea. Heavily bombed 1941.

Swarthmore, residential borough (pop. 4,825), SE Pa., near Philadelphia. Seat of **Swarthmore College** (nonsectarian; coed.; opened 1869 by Friends). Pioneer in plan by which exceptional upperclassmen replace usual schedule by reading for honor, with comprehensive examinations. On campus is birthplace of Benjamin West.

Swat (svät), state (4,000 sq. mi.; pop. 569,000), Northwest Frontier Prov., W Pakistan. Ruler is called the wali.

Swatow (swä'tou'), Mandarin *Shan-t'ou,* city (pop. 214,-990), Kwangtung prov., China; port in Han R. delta on South China Sea. Opened 1860 to foreign trade. Sugar is chief export.

Swaziland (swä'zēlănd), British protectorate (6,704 sq. mi.; pop. 186,880), SE Africa; cap. Mbabane. Bordered on S, W, and N by South Africa. Mainly a high plateau. Chief export is cattle. Asbestos, tin, and gold are mined.

Sweden, Swed. *Sverige,* kingdom (173,423 sq. mi., incl. 14,937 sq. mi. covered by lakes; pop. 7,046,920), N Europe, in E part of Scandinavian peninsula; cap. Stockholm. Its W border, with Norway, is mountainous, rising to 6,965 ft. in the Kebnekaise. In the NE Sweden borders on Finland; in the E and S, on the Baltic Sea. The three main subdivisions are Gotaland or Gotarike (S), Svealand or Svearike (S center), and Norrland (occupying N two thirds, incl. LAPLAND). The chief Baltic islands are GOTLAND and OLAND. The largest cities (all coastal), such as Stockholm, Gote-

borg, and Malmo, are in the S half, as are the largest lakes—Vanern, Vattern, and Malaren. Less than 10% of Sweden is under cultivation, but the agr. districts are very prosperous (wheat growing, dairying). The chief resources are timber (covering more than half of Sweden), high-grade iron ore (esp. at Kiruna), and hydroelectric power, which has been used on a large scale in the absence of coal. Chief industries: lumber and lumber products (furniture, paper, matches); electrometallurgy (quality steels, machinery, cutlery, armaments); fishing; shipbuilding; glass mfg. (Orrefors ware). In practice, Sweden is a parliamentary democracy, with a bicameral RIKSDAG. The king enjoys wide powers but rarely uses them. Reigning king: Gustavus VI. Population is predominantly Lutheran. Sweden has an advanced social legislation and has pioneered in the cooperative movement. Its prosperity and harmonious solution of social economic problems have made it a widely admired, little imitated model. Except for Lapps and Finns in the N, most Swedes are descendants of Germanic tribes that were probably settled in Scandinavia by the neolithic period. By the 6th cent. A.D. the Svear, from whom the Swedes derive their name, had conquered their S neighbors, the Gotar (traditionally identified with the Goths). The early Swedes shared in the Viking raids and were known in Russia as VARANGIANS. Christianity, introduced c.829 by St. Ansgar, became fully estab. only in the 12th cent. by ERIC IX, who also conquered Finland. Sweden and Norway were united 1319 by MAGNUS VII; in 1397 Queen MARGARET estab. the KALMAR UNION of Denmark, Norway, and Sweden. The actual power, however, was held by regents (esp. those of the STURE family) in the 15th cent. After Christian II's STOCKHOLM massacre (1520), the Swedes rose against the Danes and chose as their king GUSTAVUS I, founder of the VASA dynasty. Under him and his successors ERIC XIV, CHARLES IX, GUSTAVUS II, CHRISTINA, CHARLES X, and CHARLES XI Sweden became a major European power, conquering LIVONIA, INGERMANLAND, KARELIA, the S provinces of Sweden (Danish till 1658), and POMERANIA. Its intervention in the THIRTY YEARS WAR was decisive, and its numerous wars against Poland and Denmark all proved its military superiority. Lutheranism was estab. by Gustavus I; Charles XI made the monarchy absolute. In the NORTHERN WAR (1700–21), which broke out on the accession of CHARLES XII, Sweden at first won its greatest victories, then was crushed by an overpowering coalition, headed by Russia. In the 18th cent. Sweden was torn in the factional strife between the "Hats" (anti-Russian nobles) and the "Caps" (who favored peaceful relations with Russia). GUSTAVUS III restored absolutism (1772) but was murdered. His despotic successor, GUSTAVUS IV, joined the coalition against Napoleon I (1803), lost Finland to Russia (1808), and was deposed by a liberal revolution. His successor, Charles XIII, adopted marshal Bernadotte (later CHARLES XIV) as heir. Sweden again made war on Napoleon in 1813–14 and was rewarded at the Congress of Vienna, which estab. a personal union of Sweden and NORWAY (dissolved 1905). Since 1815 Sweden has remained neutral in all wars. The 19th cent. was marked by industrial progress, liberalization of the government, and large-scale emigration (c.1,500,000) to the U.S. The 20th cent. saw the rise of the Social Democratic party and the introduction of cooperatives and social legislation. Sweden entered the UN 1946.

Swedenborg, Emanuel (swē'dùnbôrg, Swed., ämä'nüĕl" svä'dùnbôry"), 1688–1772, Swedish scientist, philosopher, and theologian, whose original name was Swedberg. Appointed (1716) assessor of Royal Col. of Mines, but in 1747 he resigned position, abandoned science, and turned wholly to religious study. He believed that Scriptures reveal law of correspondence—that every natural object is expression of a spiritual cause. There is one God; in Him is divine Trinity, not of persons but of essence. Several experiences of divine revelation convinced Swedenborg that he was direct instrument of God. He had no intention of founding a new sect, but after his death his followers organized Church of the NEW JERUSALEM.

Swedesboro, borough (pop. 2,459), SW N.J., SW of Camden. Swedes bought area from Indians 1641, built fort, planted settlement c.1670. Partly burned by British 1778. Trinity Church built 1784.

Swedish language, North Germanic language of Indo-European family. See LANGUAGE (table).

Sweet, Henry, 1845–1912, English philologist and phonetician. An authority on Anglo-Saxon and the history of the English language, he was also a pioneer in modern scientific phonetics.

sweet alyssum: see ALYSSUM.

sweet bay: see LAUREL; MAGNOLIA.

sweetbread, term given to certain parts of calf and lamb when prepared as food. They are principally the thymus gland (throat sweetbread) and the pancreas (stomach sweetbread). They are highly regarded in some regions and are believed to be rich in minerals and vitamins.

Sweet Briar College: see LYNCHBURG, Va.

sweetbrier, wild pink rose of Europe (*Rosa eglanteria* or *R. rubiginosa*), naturalized in U.S. Often called eglantine, a name also used for other roses and for a honeysuckle (*Lonicera periclymenum*).

sweet cicely (sĭs'ŭlē), European perennial herb (*Myrrhis odorata*), also called myrrh. It has fragrant foliage, white flowers, and licorice-flavored roots.

sweet clover, leguminous plant (*Melilotus*) with three leaflets and white or yellow flower clusters. It is valued for forage, cover crops, and hay.

sweet fern, small North American shrub (*Comptonia peregrina*), related to bayberry, with fragrant, fernlike foliage. It is also a name for a true fern.

sweet flag, perennial bog plant (*Acorus calamus*) of N Hemisphere, with leaves resembling those of the iris and a club-shaped yellow inflorescence. The rootstalk is used as a confection, a flavoring, and in perfumery.

sweet gum, deciduous tree (*Liquidambar styraciflua*) native from S New England to Mexico and Guatemala. The star-shaped leaves display vivid yellow to crimson autumn colors; the round fruits have hornlike projections. Its hard wood is valuable commercially. In southern part of range, it produces a fragrant balsam called American storax or copalm.

sweet marjoram (mär'jŭrùm), Old World aromatic downy herb (*Majorana hortensis*), grown for flavoring.

sweet pea, annual climbing legume (*Lathyrus odoratus*), cultivated as a cut flower. Its fragrant blooms range from white to deep red and purple.

sweet potato, tropical vinelike plant (*Ipomoea batatas*) widely grown for its edible tuberous roots. It is an important crop in the S U.S. Sweet potatoes are often, though incorrectly, called YAM.

Sweetwater, city (pop. 13,619), W Texas, W of Abilene; founded c.1876, moved to railroad 1881. Ships wool, mohair, livestock, and grains and processes dairy products and cotton. Has gypsum plant, oil refinery, and railroad shops. Near by are L. Trammel and L. Sweetwater reservoirs.

sweet William, biennial species (*Dianthus barbatus*) of pink. It has dense clusters of fragrant flowers usually white and shades of red. Wild sweet William is a kind of phlox.

Sweyn (swān), c.960–1014, king of Denmark (986–1014), son of Harold Bluetooth; also spelled Svein. He apostatized from Christianity and rebelled against his father, who was slain in battle. In alliance with Sweden, he defeated Olaf I of Norway at Svolder (1000) and partitioned Norway. Having exacted Danegeld from King ÆTHELRED on a previous occasion, he again invaded England in 1003–4 and in 1013, when the English accepted him as king. His son Canute succeeded him.

Swift, Jonathan, 1667–1745, English author, b. Dublin; greatest satirist in the English language; a clergyman, dean of St. Patrick's, Dublin, after 1713. As a young man he was secretary to Sir William Temple, wrote for him *The Battle of the Books* (1704; with *A Tale of a Tub*), and tutored Esther Johnson (the "Stella" of his *Journal to Stella*). Spent much time in London after 1708, taking part in literary and political life (as Tory propagandist). His friendship for Esther Vanhomrigh ("Vanessa") led to his poem *Cadenus and Vanessa*. Later works included two on the Irish question: *Drapier Letters* (1724) and the savage *A Modest Proposal* (1729). His most familiar and greatest work is *Gulliver's Travels* (1726), a brilliantly imaginative and bitter attack on humankind. Swift's last years were lost in insanity. He is generally considered one of the masters of English prose.

swift, bird related to hummingbird and superficially resembling swallow. It has long wings and flies rapidly, catching its insect food on the wing. Inhabits most of world, particularly the tropics. See *ill.*, p. 105.

Swift Current, city (pop. 7,458), SW Sask., Canada, on Swift Current Creek and W of Moose Jaw. Trade center for SW Sask. with grain elevators, lumber and coal yards, and oil refinery.

Swinburne, Algernon (Charles), 1837–1909, English poet, whose work represents a blending of classical theme with flamboyant romanticism. His life was disorderly. In 1878–79 he became very ill, but was restored to health and thereafter supervised by Theodore Watts-Dunton. He wrote more than 25 volumes of poetry, which showed almost too great technical ability in alliteration, assonance, internal rhyme, and intricate metrical pattern. This fault does not appear in such masterly poems as the choruses in *Atalanta in Calydon* (1865; a poetic drama; best-known chorus, "When the hounds of spring") and shorter pieces such as "The Garden of Proserpine," "The Triumph of Time," and "A Forsaken Garden." Two volumes, *A Song of Italy* (1867) and *Songs before Sunrise* (1871), show his enthusiasm for Mazzini's Italian nationalism. Three poetic dramas deal with Mary Queen of Scots—*Chastelard* (1865), *Bothwell* (1874), and *Mary Stuart* (1881); *Tristram of Lyonesse* (1882) is a rich retelling of a medieval legend. His literary criticism, though extravagant, helped to popularize older English dramatists.

swine, cloven-hoofed mammal of genus *Sus* and family Suidae, with a long snout, thick bristly hide, and heavy short-legged body. Domestic breeds are also known as hogs or pigs, although pigs is more correctly a term for the young animals. Wild hogs, found in Tenn., N.C., and elsewhere, are descendants of the European wild boar (*Sus scrofa*), introduced for hunting. Modern hog breeds are descended from this boar and a smaller Asiatic species. Swine are valued for meat (ham, bacon, pork), fat (lard), leather, and bristles. The Corn Belt of the Middle West is the chief hog-raising region in U.S.

swing music, a type of American popular music. An offshoot of jazz, it uses highly stylized arrangements rather than improvisation. Important names in swing music have been Benny Goodman, Artie Shaw, Glen Miller, and the brothers Tommy and Jimmy Dorsey.

Swiss Confederation: see SWITZERLAND.

Swiss Family Robinson: see WYSS, JOHANN DAVID.

Swiss Guards. Swiss mercenaries served in various European armies from the 15th cent. to 1874, when the Swiss constitution forbade service under foreign flags. Usually, Swiss contingents were furnished to the hiring powers under special treaties (called capitulations) with the Swiss diet or individual cantons. Swiss troops played a conspicuous role in France, where they furnished the royal palace guard, called "Hundred Swiss," and several regiments, including the regiment of Swiss Guards, which was part of the king's military household. On Aug. 10, 1792, when a mob invaded the Tuileries palace in Paris, the Swiss Guards resisted until Louis XVI sent orders to cease fighting; some 500 Swiss were massacred in the resulting confusion. The Lion of Lucerne, a monument by Thorvaldsen at Lucerne, commemorates the event. Swiss troops, abolished in 1792, were again used after the Bourbon restoration; many were massacred in the July Revolution of 1830, after which they were permanently abolished. The Swiss Guards of the Vatican, founded 1505 by Julius II, are not a military body but the pope's personal guard. Famed for their colorful Renaissance costumes, they are recruited from the Catholic cantons of Switzerland.

Swissvale, borough (pop. 16,488), SW Pa., on Monongahela R. and near Pittsburgh; settled c.1760. Mfg. of railroad equipment and glass products.

Swithin, Saint (swĭ′dhŭn), fl. 860, English bishop of Winchester. Folklore says that weather of his day (July 15) foretells weather for 40 days.

Switzerland (swĭ′tsûrlŭnd), Fr. *Suisse,* Ger. *Schweiz,* Ital. *Svizzera,* more properly **Swiss Confederation,** republic (15,944 sq. mi.; pop. 4,700,297), central Europe, between France, Germany, Austria, and Italy; cap. Bern. Largest cities: Zurich, Basel, Geneva, Bern. Between the ALPS, which cover more than half the country, and the JURA mts. (W), there is an agr. plateau, drained by the Aar R. and containing the L. of Zurich and the L. of Neuchâtel. Other large lakes are those of Geneva, Constance, Lucerne, and Lugano. The Rhine and Rhone have their sources in Switzerland. Numerous passes and tunnels (notably the SIMPLON and SAINT GOTTHARD) assure trans-Alpine communications. With few natural resources and a largely barren soil, Switzerland has achieved prosperity through technological skill and export mfg.— textiles, machinery, watch movements, processed foods (esp. cheese and chocolate), chemicals. Its beauty attracts a huge tourist trade. Politically, Switzerland consists of 22 cantons. Admitted into confederation 1291–1513: URI; SCHWYZ; UNTERWALDEN; LUCERNE; ZURICH; ZUG; GLARUS; BERN; FRIBOURG; SOLOTHURN; BASEL; SCHAFFHAUSEN; APPENZELL. Admitted as cantons 1803–15: AARGAU; THURGAU; SAINT GALL; TICINO; GRISONS; VALAIS; VAUD; GENEVA; NEUCHÂTEL. Three of these—Unterwalden, Basel, Appenzell—are divided into half-cantons. Constitution of 1874 assigns foreign relations and tariffs to federal government, leaving cantons sovereign in most other respects. The chief executive is the federal council, chosen by the federal assembly; its seven members rotate as presidents. Popular initiative and referendum have much reduced the importance of the assembly's two legislative chambers. German dialects are spoken by c.72% of population; French, by 20% (mostly in SW); Italian and Romansh by the rest (Ticino and Grisons). German, French, and Italian are the official languages of the confederation. Protestantism prevails in 11½ cantons and is the faith of 57% of the people. Conquered by Rome 58 B.C. (see HELVETIA; RHAETIA), the region fell to the Germanic Alemanni and Burgundii (5th cent. A.D.) and to the Franks (6th cent.). Split between SWABIA and Transjurane BURGUNDY (9th cent.), it was held for the most part by feudal families after the 11th cent. By the 13th cent. the counts of HAPSBURG and SAVOY had emerged as the chief lords. Hapsburg encroachments on local rights caused Uri, Schwyz, and Unterwalden to enter into a defensive alliance (1291), basis of the rapidly growing confederation. Victorious over the Austrians at Morgarten (1315), Sempach (1386), and Näfels (1388), the Swiss expelled the Hapsburgs; won virtual independence from Holy Roman Empire 1499; full independence 1648. Swiss Confederation until 1798 consisted of 13 cantons, which ruled their conquests (e.g., Vaud, Aargau, Ticino) as subject territories, and of several allies (e.g., Grisons, Valais, Geneva). Its military prestige reached its climax through victories over CHARLES THE BOLD of Burgundy and in the ITALIAN WARS, but the Swiss defeat

at Marignano (1515) resulted in a policy of neutrality. Swiss mercenaries continued to fight in foreign armies (see SWISS GUARDS). The Reformation split the loose confederation into two hostile halves and led to several civil wars. In the 17th–18th cent. the cantons were governed largely by patrician oligarchies. Democracy disappeared, but prosperity grew. Revolutionary outbreaks led to French occupation and the creation of the Helvetic Republic (1798), but in 1803 Napoleon's Act of Mediation somewhat restored the old confederation. In 1815 the old regime was substantially restored; Treaty of Paris guaranteed Switzerland's perpetual neutrality. In the 1830s the Radical party estab. democratic governments in most cantons, but Catholic opposition led to the SONDERBUND war (1847) and the transformation of Switzerland from a federation into a federal state (constitution of 1848). Switzerland joined the League of Nations, but its strict neutrality policy prevents its membership in the UN.

Swope, Herbert Bayard, 1882–, American journalist and public official. Executive editor of New York *World* (1920–29); consultant to U.S. Secretary of War (1942–46).

swordfish, food fish of warmer parts of Atlantic and Pacific oceans. It has an elongated, blade-shaped upper jaw; weighs up to 250–400 lb.

Swoyersville (swoi′ûrzvĭl), borough (pop. 7,795), NE Pa., N of Wilkes-Barre. Anthracite mining; mfg. of textiles and metal products.

Sybaris (sĭ′bŭrĭs), anc. Greek city in S Italy, on the Gulf of Taranto; founded 720 B.C. The voluptuousness of its people gave rise to the term *sybaritic.* Destroyed 510 B.C.

Sybel, Heinrich von (hīn′rĭkh fŭn zē′bŭl), 1817–95, German historian. Chief works *Founding of the German Empire by William I* (Eng. tr., 7 vols., 1890–98) and *Geschichte des ersten Kreuzzugs* (1841).

Sycamore, city (pop. 5,912), N Ill., W of Chicago; center of farm area. Metal products.

sycamore: see PLANE TREE.

Sydenham, Thomas (sĭ′dŭnŭm), 1624–89, English physician, a founder of modern clinical medicine and of epidemiology.

Sydney, Sir Philip: see SIDNEY, SIR PHILIP.

Sydney, city (pop. 95,925); metropolitan pop. 1,484,004), cap. of New South Wales, Australia, on S shore of Port JACKSON. Seat of Univ. of Sydney (1852), Natl. Art Gall. (1904), and Australian Mus. (1830). Produces textiles, automobiles, and chemicals. Founded 1788 as Australia's first penal settlement, Sydney became cap. of early colony of New South Wales. In World War II an Allied naval and air base was here.

Sydney, city (pop. 31,317) on NE coast of Cape Breton Isl., NE N.S., Canada, NE of Halifax. Center of coalmining and agr. area with steel mills, shipyards, and mfg. of wood, food, and metal products. Founded 1783. Cap. of Cape Breton prov. 1784–1820.

Sydney Harbour, Australia: see JACKSON, PORT.

Sydney Mines, town (pop. 8,410), on NE coast of Cape Breton Isl., N.S., Canada, NNW of Sydney. Coal-mining center.

Sylacauga (sĭlŭkô′gŭ), city (pop. 9,606), central Ala., SE of Birmingham. Processes cotton, lumber, marble (quarries near), dairy products.

Sylt (zĭlt), island (36 sq. mi.; pop. 26,346), N Germany, in North Sea off Schleswig-Holstein; one of North Frisian Isls. Seaside resort.

Sylva, Carmen: see ELIZABETH, queen of Rumania.

Sylvester II (sĭlvĕ′stŭr), d. 1003, pope (999–1003), a Frenchman. Under his original name, Gerbert, he was widely known for his learning and for ability shown in the school at Rheims. He taught Emperor Otto III, who brought about his election as pope. He proved able and energetic. Also Silvester.

symbiosis (sĭmbēō′sĭs), habitual living together of organisms of different species. Usually it refers to a relationship benefiting at least one participant and harming none. One example is relationship between NITROGEN-FIXING BACTERIA and leguminous plants.

symbol, sign representing something having an independent existence (i.e., standing for something else). Writing and use of numbers are both symbolic processes. Science employs many symbols for conciseness (e.g., chemical symbols). In art a symbol is generally distinguished from a likeness of a person or an object. Symbols have been used in religion from most ancient days and are now used in complex combinations (e.g., candle, incense, the figures of iconography). Patriotism also uses such symbols as the flag, and business uses symbols in trade-marks. Freud's studies in psychology make much of the use of symbols.

symbolists, in literature, school originating in France, late 19th cent. Designed to convey impressions by suggestion instead of direct statement, symbolism first appeared in poetry, later in drama (Maeterlinck), criticism (Remy de Gourmont), music (Debussy). Early symbolists (e.g., Verlaine, Malarmé, Rimbaud) were accused of decadent morbidity, partly for using imagination as a reality; their experiments led to free verse. Symbolist influence was very wide; it appears in development of the imagists and decadents, in work of T. S. Eliot, Proust, James Joyce, Gertrude Stein.

Symonds, John Addington (sĭm'ŭnz), 1840–93, English author of *The Renaissance in Italy* (7 vols., 1875–86), a classic of cultural history.

Symons, Arthur (sĭm'ŭnz), 1865–1945, English lyric poet and literary critic; leader of symbolists in England and interpreter of French poets.

sympathetic nervous system: see NERVOUS SYSTEM.

symphonic poem: see TONE POEM.

symphony, a SONATA for orchestra, developed from the 17th-cent. Italian operatic overture (called the *sinfonia,* of three sections in contrasting tempi). It is in the works of Haydn and Mozart that the classical symphony reached maturity. As further developed by Beethoven, Schubert, and later, Brahms, the symphony emerges as one of the highest forms of musical expression. The romantic symphony of the late 19th cent. (usually in four sections) emphasized emotional appeal before classical form. Some 20th-cent. composers have adhered to the classic form but use modern harmonic techniques, others apply the term *symphony* freely to compositions of all types.

Symplegades (sĭmplē'gǔdēz) [Gr.,= dashing together], in Greek mythology, two floating cliffs. After the ARGO passed between them without being crushed, they remained still, forming Black Sea entrance.

synagogue (sĭ'nŭgŏg) [from Gr.,= assembly], building where Jews gather for worship. As early as the days of Moses, the term was used to denote a gathering of Jews, usually for religious purposes. The synagogue assumed importance after the destruction of the first Temple; in the Middle Ages, it was the intellectual and social center of Jewish life. The services were simple; there was no officially appointed priest. Its use is now restricted almost purely to religious purposes. The oldest U.S. synagogue is at Newport, R.I. (1763).

syndicalism includes both a strategy of revolution and a plan for social reorganization. Syndicalists believe that the state, an instrument of oppression, should be abolished, and that the trade union is the essential unit of production and of government. Their doctrines were inspired by P. J. Proudhon and Georges SOREL. In the U.S., they formed the INDUSTRIAL WORKERS OF THE WORLD.

Synge, J(ohn) M(illington) (sĭng), 1871–1909, Irish poet and dramatist, notable for plays of Irish peasant life in rhythmic, expressive language of the people of W Ireland. A friend of W. B. Yeats and Lady Gregory, he helped to found the Abbey Theatre. Best known of his works are one-act plays, *In the Shadow of the Glen* (1903) and *Riders to the Sea* (1904); full-length comedies, *The Well of the Saints* (1905) and *The Playboy of the Western World* (1907); and unfinished tragedy, *Deirdre of the Sorrows.*

Synge, Richard Laurence Millington, 1914–, British biochemist. Shared 1952 Nobel Prize in Chemistry for discovery of partition chromatography, a new method for separating compounds in chemical analysis.

Synoptic Gospels (sĭnŏp'tĭk) [Gr. *synopsis* = view together], name given to the first three Gospels (Matthew, Mark, and Luke) as contrasted to John. They are similar to each other in that they are chiefly straight biographical narratives whereas John is primarily a philosophical essay on the mission of Jesus. The question of relationship between the three is called the Synoptic problem, the heart of the problem being why Matthew and Luke contain material that does not appear in Mark. Critics have proposed numerous answers.

synthesis, chemical reaction in which two or more substances combine to form another substance. In synthesis of a compound, definite quantities of each constituent are needed to form given quantity of compound.

syphilis (sĭ'fŭlĭs), contagious VENEREAL DISEASE caused by infection with a spirochete. Usually is acquired through sexual intercourse or through infection before birth. Initial sore (chancre) precedes second stage in which spirochetes spread through body and a Wassermann test is positive. In third stage, lesions (gummata) occur in various sites; if nervous system is affected, victim may have LOCOMOTOR ATAXIA or paresis (a brain disease). Syphilis is treated by use of penicillin or derivatives of arsenic, mercury, and bismuth. See *ill.,* p. 633.

Syracuse (sĭ'rŭkūs, –kūz), Italian *Siracusa,* city (pop. 43,-639), cap. of Syracuse prov., SE Sicily, Italy; port of the Ionian Sea. Founded by Greeks in 743 B.C., it became the leading city of ancient Sicily under the tyrant GELON, who defeated the Carthaginians (480 B.C.). Later it was a center of Greek culture under several celebrated tyrants (with periods of democratic government); among them were Hiero I, Dionysius the Elder, Dionysius the Younger, Dion of Syracuse, and Hiero II. Syracuse in 413 B.C. defeated a great Athenian force sent against it. Taking the side of Carthage in the Second Punic War, it was sacked by the Romans (212 B.C.) and declined.

Syracuse (sĭ'rŭkūs), city (pop. 220,583), central N.Y., at S end of Onondaga L., on the Barge Canal and SE of Rochester; settled 1805. Rail center; mfg. of typewriters, farm machinery, cooling equipment; metal, paper, wood, food, soap products. Saltmaking declined after Civil War, but Erie Canal (opened here 1819) and railroads stimulated industrial growth. Has Mus. of Fine Arts and Mills Rose Garden. Seat of **Syracuse University** (coed.; chartered as Genesee Col., at Lima, N.Y., 1849, moved to Syracuse 1869, rechartered 1870); has Goudy typographical laboratory and a natural science museum.

Syr Darya (sēr" där'yä), anc. *Jaxartes* or *Yaxartes,* river, c.1,300 mi. long, USSR. Formed in FERGANA VALLEY (Uzbek SSR) by junction of Naryn and Kara Darya rivers, flows through Tadzhik SSR and Kazakh SSR to Aral Sea. Unfit for navigation but used for irrigation. Trans-Caspian RR parallels the river's lower course.

Syria (sĭ'rēŭ), Arabic *Esh Sham,* republic (66,063 sq. mi.; pop. 3,006,028), SW Asia; cap. DAMASCUS. Bounded on W by the Mediterranean and Lebanon, S by Jordan, E by Iraq, and N by Turkey. Most of Syria is occupied by Syrian Desert, crossed by Euphrates R. In W are the Anti-Lebanon mts. and in SW the fertile HAURAN plain. Syria is mainly a pastoral and agr. country. Most of the people are of Arab origin and are Moslems; the DRUSES inhabit the S. Historically, the name Syria has comprised those lands of the Levant corresponding to modern Syria and Lebanon, most of Israel and Jordan, and parts of N Arabia. The area was probably under the HITTITES, 19th–13th cent. B.C. First great indigenous culture was PHOENICIAN CIVILIZATION, which flourished after 1250 B.C. Before it became part of Persian Empire, Syria suffered under invasions by Assyrians, Babylonians, and Egyptians. After its conquest by Alexander the Great (332–331 B.C.) Syria came under the rule of Seleucus I and his successors, the Seleucidae. Romans under Pompey conquered the region by 63 B.C. After division of Roman Empire, Syria was under Byzantine rule until it came under Arab influence in 7th cent. Syria was largely converted to Islam, but there still remained groups of Christians, who later gave aid to Crusaders. By end of 12th cent. the conqueror SALADIN was dominant. His rule was followed by that of the Mamelukes and by Mongol invasions. In early 16th cent. Ottoman Turks took over the area, which in early 19th cent. was held by Egyptians under IBRAHIM PASHA. After World War I France was given a mandate in 1920 over the Levant States (roughly present Syria and Lebanon). In 1926 Lebanon was made a separate state, but Syria remained a region split into separate territories until 1941, when republic of Syria was proclaimed. In World War II British and Free French forces invaded and occupied Syria in June, 1941. In 1944 France declared Syria completely independent. A member of Arab League, Syria joined in war against Israel (1948). A military regime was estab. 1949.

Syriac language, Aramaic language of Semitic family. See LANGUAGE (table).

syringa: see MOCK ORANGE. For the genus *Syringa,* see LILAC.

Syros (sī′rōs), Aegean island (33 sq. mi.; pop. 25,918), one of the Cyclades; cap. Hermopolis.

Syzran (sĭzrän′yù), city (pop. c.150,000), E European RSFSR; a port on the Volga. It is a rapidly expanding industrial and mining center (oil shale, asphalt, phosphorite).

Szatmarnemeti or **Szatmar:** see SATU-MARE.

Szechwan (sĕ′chwän, sŭ′chwän), province (120,000 sq. mi.; pop. 45,000,000), SW China; cap. Chengtu. Surrounded by mountains and crossed by Yangtze R. Extensive agr. (rice, sugar cane, tobacco); gold and iron mining. Tung oil and salt industries.

Szeged (sĕ′gĕd), formerly **Szegedin** (–ēn), city (pop. 136,752), S Hungary, on the Tisza. Agr. processing center. University was founded 1921.

Szekely (sā′kā), one of the three historic "nations" of TRANSYLVANIA.

Szekesfehervar (sā′kĕshfĕ″hârvär), Ger. *Stuhlweissenburg,* city (pop. 47,968), W central Hungary. Dates from Roman times. Hungarian kings were crowned here 1027–1527.

Szent-Gyorgyi, Albert von (äl′bĕrt fŭn sĕnt″-dyûr′dyĭ), 1893–, Hungarian biochemist. Won 1937 Nobel Prize in Physiology and Medicine for work on biological oxidation and on ascorbic acid.

Szigeti, Joseph (sēgĕ′tē), 1892–, Hungarian violinist. Made his American debut in 1925. He is known for playing unfamiliar works.

Szold, Henrietta (zōld), 1860–1945, American Jewish leader. Founder of the American women's organization Hadassah, president from 1912 to 1926. Translated many works from French, German, and Hebrew.

Szondi Test: see MENTAL TESTS.

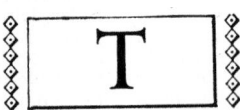

Ta, chemical symbol of the element TANTALUM.

Taaffe, Eduard, Graf von (ä′dōōärt gräf′ fŭn tä′fù), 1833–95, Austrian statesman of Irish descent. Premier 1868–69, 1879–93.

Taal, Lake (tä-äl′), 94 sq. mi., SW Luzon, P.I., S of Manila. Contains Volcano Isl. with Mt. Taal (active; 984 ft. high).

Tabard Inn (tă′bùrd), Southwark, London; traditional starting place of Canterbury pilgrims. Described in Prologue of Chaucer's *Canterbury Tales.*

Tabasco (täbä′skō), state (9,783 sq. mi.; pop. 351,106), SE Mexico, on Gulf of Campeche; cap. VILLAHERMOSA. State is predominantly a jungle plain broken by swamps, lagoons, and rivers, which provide practically the only means of communication. Cortés crossed region on march to Honduras (1524), and Montejo conquered it (1530). Tropical agr. is main occupation.

Tabernacle [Latin,= tent, hut], in Bible, the portable holy place of the Hebrews during their wanderings in the wilderness. It was considered in a peculiar sense the dwelling of God Himself, and the Ark of the Covenant was kept here. For description see Ex. 25–27; 30–31; 35–40. Term is applied also to a small receptacle, used in the Roman Catholic Church, in which the Host is reserved on the altar.

Tabernacles, Feast of, often called by its Hebrew name, Sukkoth (sŏŏkōth′) [Heb.,= booth], in anc.

Palestine a harvest festival, now observed by the taking of meals in lattice huts which commemorate the wanderings of the Jews. It begins on the 15th day of Tishri, the 7th month of the Jewish calendar, and lasts for 9 days.

Tabitha (tă′bĭthù), same as DORCAS.

tablature (tă′blùchōōr), in music, name for various systems of MUSICAL NOTATION used from the 15th to 17th cent. for keyboard and lute music. These systems used letters, numbers, or symbols to indicate the pitch and duration of a tone. Lute tablatures have lines representing the strings of the lute, with numbers or letters to indicate the position for stopping the strings. In general, tablatures tell the player what to do rather than what music to play. They are used today to notate music for guitar and ukulele. These have vertical lines representing the strings of the instrument, horizontal lines for the frets, and dots to show the position of the fingers.

Table Mountain, 3,549 ft. high, W Cape Prov., South Africa, overlooking Capetown and Table Bay (inlet of the Atlantic).

table tennis. Also called ping-pong, trade name of kind of table tennis. Played on table which should measure 9 ft. by 5 ft. and which should stand 2½ ft. above floor. Table tennis probably originated in 19th cent., first became popular in England.

taboo or **tabu** (both: tăbŏŏ′), prohibition of an action under pain of supernatural punishment. Name originated in Polynesia but its use is common among all primitive peoples.

Tabor, Horace Austin Warner (tā'bùr), 1830–99, American prospector, known as Silver Dollar Tabor. Made fortune mining silver from Matchless Mine at Leadville, Colo. Spent money lavishly and lost his fortune. His second wife **Elizabeth McCourt ("Baby Doe") Tabor**, 1862–1935, refused to give up faith in the mine, lived beside it in poverty, and died of exposure there.

Tabor, in Bible: see TABOR, MOUNT.

Tabor (tä'bôr), town (pop. 17,596), S Bohemia, Czechoslovakia. Founded (1420) by John ZIZKA and named after Mt. Tabor in Palestine, it became the stronghold of the TABORITES. Town hall (16th cent.) has collection of Hussite relics.

Tabor (tā'bùr), town (pop. 373), SE S.Dak., near Nebr. line SW of Yankton. HUTTERISCHE COMMUNITY settled here 1874.

Tabor, Mount, mountain of N Palestine. Here Barak assembled the army which defeated Sisera.

Taborites (tā'bùrīts), HUSSITES, called after their stronghold in Bohemia, Tabor. More radical than UTRAQUISTS, they rejected belief in the real presence of Christ in the Eucharist and swept away rites and forms. Under the leadership of John Zizka and Procopius the Great, they were for years triumphant in the Hussite Wars but, after refusing to accept the settlement of the Compactata (1434), were defeated by Catholics and Utraquists at Lipany. The Moravian Church is supposed to have continued Taborite movement.

Tabriz (täbrēz'), anc. *Tauris,* city (pop. 213,542), NW Iran, in Azerbaijan; second largest city of Iran. Has manufactures and handicrafts, notably rugmaking. Despite severe earthquakes, several old buildings (including the 15th-cent. Blue Mosque) survive. In c.1500 Iranians took the city from Turks, who subsequently recaptured it several times. Occupied by Russians 1827–28 and in World War I and World War II. In 1946 it was hq. of a short-lived regime set up by leftist Tudeh party and supported by Russians.

tabu: see TABOO.

Taché, Sir Étienne Paschal (ātyĕn' päskäl' tächä'), 1795–1865, Canadian statesman. Premier with J. A. Macdonald (1856–57, 1864–65).

Tacitus (tā'sĭtùs), A.D. c.55–c.117, Roman historian. His high moral tone and severe criticism of Rome are present in all three of his most notable surviving works—the *Germania* (an accurate account of the Germanic tribes), the *Histories* (of which 4 books and a fragment, covering Galba's reign and the beginning of Vespasian's, survive), and the *Annals* (of which 12 books, covering the reign of Tiberius and parts of the reigns of Claudius and Nero, survive). The style of these works is clean, polished, highly individualistic.

Tacloban (täklō'bän), town (pop. 45,421), NE Leyte, P.I. Port; ships rice and sugar. Captured by Japanese (1942) in World War II; retaken, Oct., 1944, and made temporary cap. of Philippines.

Tacna-Arica Controversy, 1883–1929, dispute between Chile and Peru which arose from provisions of the treaty ending war of Pacific (see PACIFIC, WAR OF THE). Victorious Chile was ceded S provinces of Peru (Tacna and Arica), with understanding that plebiscite would be held at end of 10 years to determine ownership. Plebiscite was not held, and Chile began to colonize area (1909). In 1922 the two countries agreed to arbitration by president of U.S. and accepted decision (1929) that Tacna be returned to Peru; that Chile retain Arica, construct free port for Peru with port and rail installations, transfer all state-owned real estate and buildings in Tacna to Peru, and pay indemnity of $6,000,000.

Tacoma (tùkō'mù), city (pop. 143,673), W Wash., on Commencement Bay of Puget Sound, near Mt. Rai-

nier; settled 1852. Important port, rail terminus, and industrial center. Produces lumber, flour, food and foundry products, and electrochemicals. Fur Market. Seat of College of Puget Sound (Methodist; coed.; 1888). In Point Defiance Park is reconstructed Fort Nisqually, historic trading post. Near by are an air force base and Fort Lewis.

Taconic Mountains (tùkŏ'nĭk), range of Appalachian Mts., extending c.150 mi. S from point in Vt. In Vt. range is W of Green Mts. and in N.Y. is E of Hudson R. Mt. Equinox (3,816 ft.), near Manchester, Vt., is highest point. Includes BERKSHIRE HILLS.

Tadoussac (tä'dōōsäk, Fr. tädōōsäk'), village (pop. 1,064), S Que., at the mouth of the Saguenay on the St. Lawrence; visited by Cartier 1535. An unsuccessful French colony was founded here (1600–1601), and a later fur-trading post was successful.

tadpole, larval, aquatic form of any amphibian animal from time of hatching to growth of adult organs.

Tadzhik Soviet Socialist Republic (täjĭk') or **Tadzhikistan** (tùjĭ'kĭstän''), constituent republic (c.55,000 sq. mi.; pop. c.1,455,000) of the USSR, in central Asia; cap. Stalinabad. Contains part of Pamir mts. (incl. STALIN PEAK); a high, arid plateau (SE); and FERGANA VALLEY (N). Amu Darya and Syr Darya rivers are used for irrigation. Chief products: cotton, rice, wheat, fruit, silk. Livestock raising. Mining (lead, zinc, silver, uranium, gold, coal). Tadzhiks (c.78% of pop.) are an Iranian people of Moslem faith. Most of Tadzhikistan was part of emirate of BUKHARA until the Russian Revolution of 1917. Became constituent republic 1929.

Tafilelt or **Tafilalet** (both: täfē'lĕlt), largest Saharan oasis, area c.530 sq. mi., of S French Morocco. Town of Sijilmassa (now in ruins) was Berber stronghold, 8th–9th cent. A.D. Ruling dynasty of Morocco, estab. 1649, originated here.

Taft, Lorado (lùrä'dō), 1860–1936, American sculptor, writer, and lecturer on art. Exerted a wide influence on young sculptors of the West.

Taft, William Howard, 1857–1930, 26th President of the United States (1909–13), Chief Justice of the Supreme Court (1921–30). First civil governor of Philippine Isls. (1901–4). As U.S. Secretary of War (1904–8) Taft was prominent in Latin American affairs. As President he continued Theodore Roosevelt's trust-busting policy; promoted "dollar diplomacy" in Latin America. However, his emphasis was more conservative than Roosevelt's. Critics quarreled with what they regarded as undue favoritism toward individual enterprisers; there was great dissatisfaction over Payne-Aldrich Tariff Act. Opposition to Taft led to disaffection of Republican progressives and to Taft's defeat in 1912 election. His son, **Robert A(lphonso) Taft,** 1889–, is U.S. Senator (1939–) from Ohio. Expert in financial affairs. Helped write TAFT-HARTLEY LABOR ACT. Several times candidate for Republican presidential nomination.

Taft-Hartley Labor Act, 1947, passed by U.S. Congress, also known as Labor-Management Relations Act. Sponsored by Sen. R. A. Taft and Rep. F. A. Hartley. Estab. control of labor disputes on a new basis. Enlarged the NATIONAL LABOR RELATIONS BOARD; empowered government to obtain 80-day injunction against any strike endangering national health or safety; prohibited jurisdictional strikes; retained most collective-bargaining provisions, adding provision for signing of affidavit that union officers are not Communists. Passed over Pres. Truman's veto, act has been target of much criticism.

Tagalog (tùgä'lùg, tägä'lŏg) or **Tagal** (tägäl'), dominant people of Luzon, Philippine Isls., second in population of the Philippine peoples. Tagalog is a Malayo-Polynesian language, made official in 1940.

Taganrog (tügùnrôk'), city (pop. 188,808), E European RSFSR; a port on a gulf of the Sea of Azov. Metallurgy; mfg. of machinery; fish canning. Founded 1698 as a fortress, it was later captured by the Turks but definitively passed to Russia 1774. Was Denikin's hq. in civil war (1919); twice occupied by Germans in World War II (1941, 1942–43). Birthplace of Anton Chekhov.

Taglioni, Filippo (tälyō'nē), 1777–1871, Italian ballet master and composer of ballets. Trained his daughter, **Maria Taglioni**, 1804–84, considered greatest dancer of her day. Was the idol of Paris when she appeared (1832) in his ballet, *La Sylphide*.

Tagore, Sir Rabindranath (rŭbĭn'drŭnät tŭgōr'), 1861–1941, Indian author, b. Calcutta. Briefly studied law in England (1877) and for a time managed his father's vast estates in Bengal. Joining the Indian nationalists, he wrote many propaganda poems and songs. Gradually he evolved his characteristic later manner, combining delicate descriptions of nature with religious and philosophical speculation. He wrote c.50 dramas, c.100 books of verse, and c.40 volumes of fiction and philosophical writings. His wide range of material and style made his appeal in India nearly universal. He wrote in Bengali but translated much of his work into English. In 1913 he won the Nobel Prize in Literature. The school he founded in 1901 at Santiniketan, Bengal, was expanded in 1922 into Visva-Bharati Univ.

tagua (tä'gwä), fruit of the ivory-nut palm (*Phytelephas macrocarpa*), commercially produced chiefly in Ecuador, Panama, Colombia, and N Peru. Fruit is a burr or pod containing up to 40 or more very hard nuts c.2 in. in diameter whose content is used as a substitute for ivory (known as vegetable ivory). It is shipped to the U.S. and Europe for making buttons and other small articles. When tested with a concentrated solution of sulphuric acid, tagua becomes reddish; true ivory is unaffected. Tagua is also known as coroza.

Tagus (tä'gŭs), Span. *Tajo,* Port. *Tejo,* river, 565–625 mi. long, rising in E Spain and flowing W and SW, along part of Spanish-Portuguese border and through Portugal, into the Atlantic at Lisbon. Usually considered longest river of Iberian Peninsula.

Taharka, Egyptian king: see TIRHAKAH.

Tahiti (tähē'tē), island (402 sq. mi.; pop. 24,820), S Pacific, in Windward group of SOCIETY ISLANDS; cap. PAPEETE, which is also cap. of French Oceania. Mountainous and scenic. Discovered 1767 by British, visited 1788 by the *Bounty.* French and English missionaries arrived in late 18th cent. Became French protectorate 1843, ceded to France 1880. GAUGUIN did his most famous paintings here.

Tahlequah (tä'lūkwô), city (pop. 4,750), NE Okla., SE of Tulsa. Settled by Cherokees 1839 and made their cap., it has museum with Indian relics.

Tahoe, Lake (tä'hō, tä'–), 21.6 mi. long, 12 mi. wide, on Calif.-Nev. line, between Sierra Nevada (W) and Carson Range, in beautiful summer-resort area.

Tahquamenon (tùkwä'mùnùn), river rising in E Upper Peninsula, N Mich., and flowing E and NE to Whitefish Bay of L. Superior. Noted for waterfalls, it was celebrated in Longfellow's *Hiawatha.*

Tai (tī), Chinese *Tai Shan,* sacred peak, 5,069 ft. high, W central Shantung prov., China.

Tai, lake, c.40 mi. long, 35 mi. wide, China, on Kiangsu-Chekiang border.

taille: see TALLAGE.

Taimyr Peninsula (tīmīr'), northernmost projection of Siberia, RSFSR, on the Kara and Laptev seas, terminating in Cape Chelyuskin; also spelled Taymyr. Tundra region. Inhabited by nomadic Nentsy (formerly called Samoyedes) and Dolgans, who subsist on reindeer raising, hunting, and fishing.

Tainan (tī'nän'), city (pop. 229,452), Formosa; port on Formosa Strait. Cap. of Formosa 1662–1885.

Taine, Hippolyte (tän, Fr. ēpôlēt' tēn'), 1828–93, French critic and historian. His deterministic theories, regarding man as the product of heredity and environment, formed the basis of the naturalistic school. Wrote *History of English Literature* (1864), *The Origins of Contemporary France* (6 vols., 1876–93).

Taipei or **Taipeh** (both: tī'pā), Jap. *Taihoku,* industrial city (pop. 326,407), cap. of Formosa, China. In 1949 it became seat of Nationalist government.

Taiping Rebellion (tī'pĭng'), 1850–65, revolt against Ch'ing dynasty of China. Led by Hung Hsiu-ch'üan, a visionary scholar, who tried to set up a new dynasty, the Taiping [great peace]. Nanking, captured 1853, became his capital. Serious threat to Ch'ing dynasty brought aid of Western powers; revolt was crushed by army led by Charles George Gordon.

Tait, Archibald Campbell, 1811–82, Anglican prelate. Succeeded Thomas Arnold as headmaster of Rugby (1842). He became dean of Carlisle (1849), bishop of London (1856), and archbishop of Canterbury (1869). Stoutly supported the Low Church cause.

Taiwan: see FORMOSA.

Taiyüan (tī'yüän'), city (pop. 251,566), cap. of Shansi prov., China; agr. and industrial center. Formerly called Yangkü.

Taj Mahal (täj' mùhŭl'), mausoleum, Agra, Uttar Pradesh, India. Considered to be greatest example of late style of Indian Moslem architecture. Built (1630–1648?) by Shah Jehan for his favorite wife, Mumtaz Mahal, and himself. The building, reflected in an oblong pool, is of white marble inlaid with semiprecious stones. Its bulbous dome tapers to a spire topped by a crescent, and a minaret rises from each corner of the platform on which the building stands. The royal couple lie in a vault beneath the illuminated tomb chamber.

Tajo, river: see TAGUS.

Taklamakan (tä"klämäkän'), sandy desert, c.125,000 sq. mi., Sinkiang prov., China. Rimmed by oases.

Takoma Park, town (pop. 13,341), W central Md., NE suburb of Washington, D.C.

Talbot, Richard: see TYRCONNEL, RICHARD TALBOT, DUKE AND EARL OF.

talc, very soft mineral with a greasy, soapy feel. It is a hydrous silicate of magnesium, usually with small amounts of nickel, iron, aluminum; ranges in color from white through shades of gray and green to red and brown. Of wide distribution, commonly associated with metamorphic rocks. Used in making paper, paints, cosmetics, soap, lubricants, linoleum, electrical insulation, and pottery.

Talca (täl'cä), city (pop. 42,994), S central Chile; founded 1692; today one of most important cities in central valley of Chile, in a wheat- and wine-producing area. Rebuilt after earthquake of 1928. Here Bernardo O'Higgins proclaimed Chile's independence (1818).

Talcahuano (tälkäwä'nō), city (pop. 38,605), S central Chile, port just N of Concepción. Has fishing industries, dry-dock facilities, metallurgical plants.

Talien, China: see DAIREN.

Taliesin or **Taliessin** (both: tălē'sĭn), 6th cent.?, Welsh bard, whose *Book of Taliesin* is one of great works of Welsh poetry.

Talitha cumi (tä'lĭthù kū'mĭ) [Aramaic,= maiden, arise], words spoken by Jesus to the daughter of the ruler of the synagogue as he raised her from the dead. Mark 5.41. Aramaic words left and translation given in all Continental vernacular versions of this Gospel.

Talladega (tălŭdē'gù), city (pop. 13,134), NE central Ala., E of Birmingham and in Blue Ridge foothills. Cotton and metal goods. Andrew Jackson defeated Creek Indians here, Nov., 1813. Seat of Talladega Col. (Negro; coed.; opened 1867).

tallage (tä'lĭj), feudal impost in medieval England. Important chiefly because king collected it from demesne lands, with which chartered towns were included. Instituted by Henry I to replace DANEGELD, it was imposed, usually over protest, until reign of Edward III. French *taille,* originally similar to tallage, was later part personal, part land tax.

Tallahassee (tălŭhă'sē), city (pop. 27,237), state cap., NW Fla., in hilly agr. area. Processes wood. De Soto arrived here 1539, and region was subsequently settled by Spanish. City founded 1824 as cap. of Fla. Territory. Ordinance of secession adopted here, 1861. Union capture resisted in Civil War. Seat of FLORIDA STATE UNIVERSITY and FLORIDA AGRICULTURAL AND MECHANICAL COLLEGE.

Tallapoosa (tălŭpoō'sŭ), river rising in Ga. and flowing 268 mi. S and W through Ala. to Coosa R., forming Alabama R. near Montgomery. Martin Dam forms Martin L.

Talleyrand or **Talleyrand-Périgord, Charles Maurice de** (tă'lĕrănd″, Fr. shärl′ mōrēs′ dü tälärä′, -pārēgôr′), 1754–1838, French statesman, of an anc. noble family. A childhood accident left him lame, and he was intended for the Church. Made bishop of Autun (1788) despite his notorious immorality, he was a deputy of the clergy in the States-General of 1789; sided with the revolutionists; was excommunicated by the pope (1791); fled to England, then to the U.S., after the fall of the monarchy; returned to France 1795; became foreign minister under the Directory (1797–99) and under Napoleon (1799–1807). Napoleon ignored his cautious advice, and although Talleyrand served on diplomatic missions after his resignation, he secretly worked in Austria's rather than Napoleon's interest. When the allies entered Paris (1814), Talleyrand persuaded them to restore the Bourbons and won mild peace terms (see PARIS, TREATY OF, 1814). As foreign minister of Louis XVIII, he scored his greatest diplomatic triumph at the Congress of VIENNA (1814–15), which his intervention saved from collapse. He resigned his ministry after the Treaty of Paris of 1815. Under Louis Philippe, he served as ambassador to London (1830–34). His excommunication was lifted 1802. Corrupt, cynical, witty, dissolute, Talleyrand was nevertheless above all a good European. In his seeming deviousness he pursued the steadfast aim of European peace and stability. He wrote memoirs (Eng. tr., 5 vols., 1891–92).

Tallien, Jean Lambert (zhä′ läbĕr′ tälyē′), 1767–1820, French revolutionist. As secretary of Commune of Paris and member of the Convention he took active part in September massacres of 1792 and in Reign of Terror. In 1794 he led in overthrow of Robespierre and in subsequent Thermidorian reaction. His wife, **Thérésa (Cabarrus) Tallien,** 1773–1835, of Spanish parentage, strongly influenced his policies; was nicknamed Notre Dame de Septembre and Notre Dame de Thermidor. A leading social figure, she originated neo-Greek fashions of Directoire period. She divorced Tallien 1805 and married the banker Caraman, later created prince de Chimay.

Tallinn (tä′lĭn), Ger. *Reval,* city (pop. c.168,000), cap. of Estonia; a major Baltic port on S coast of Gulf of Finland. Produces textiles, machinery, plastics, plywood, furniture. Founded 1219 by Waldemar II of Denmark; joined Hanseatic League 1285; was sold 1346 by Denmark to Livonian Knights; passed to Sweden 1561; was captured by Peter I of Russia 1710. Suffered heavy damage during German occupation (1941–44) in World War II. The picturesque lower town, dating from Hanseatic times, is surrounded by medieval walls.

Tallis or **Tallys, Thomas,** c.1510–1585, English organist and composer. He wrote madrigals, motets, and instrumental music, but is best known for his hymn tunes, services, and anthems.

tallow, solid fat extracted from tissues and fat deposits of animals. Pure form is white, odorless, tasteless. Used to make soap, candles, and butter substitutes; formerly was used as a lubricant.

tallow tree, popular name for trees of spurge family that yield vegetable tallow. Seed coverings of the Chinese tallow tree (*Sapium sebiferum*) yield a substance used to make candles and soap. Nuts of the tropical candlenut tree (*Aleurites moluccana*) produce a valuable oil and have been used as candles.

Tallulah (tŭloō′lŭ), village (pop. 7,758), NE La., W of

Vicksburg, Miss. Cotton raising, commercial fishing, and frog raising.

Tallys, Thomas: see TALLIS, THOMAS.

Talma, François Joseph (tälmä′), 1763–1826, French actor; greatest tragedian of his time. Made important reforms in costuming and technique.

Talmadge, Eugene, 1884–1946, governor of Ga. (1933–37, 1941–43). A leader of a "white supremacy" group largely made up of small farmers, he triumphed over the "liberal" group in Ga. and instituted reactionary, anti-intellectual measures. His mantle fell upon his son, **Herman Talmadge,** 1913–, who became governor in 1947.

Talmage, (Thomas) De Witt, 1832–1902, American Presbyterian clergyman. His dramatic preaching drew great audiences to the Brooklyn (N.Y.) Tabernacle.

Talmud (tăl′mŭd) [Aramaic from Heb.,= learning], compilation of the Oral Law of the Jews, with rabbinical commentaries, in contradistinction to the Scriptures or Written Laws; the accepted authority for orthodox Jews everywhere. Its two divisions are the Mishna or text of the Oral Law (in Hebrew) and the Gemara (in Aramaic), a sort of commentary upon the Mishna, which it supplements. The Mishna is divided into six orders (Sedarim) and comprises 63 tractates, only 36½ of which have a Gemara. The compilation of the present Mishna is practically the work of Judah I (ha-Nassi). Although the mission of the Gemara was to expound the text of the Mishna, it became a mass of information on a variety of subjects. The legal sections of the Gemara are known as the halakah; the poetical digressions, the haggada. Talmuds were produced in Palestine and in Babylon in the 5th and 6th cent. The Babylonian Talmud became the authoritative work. The term *Talmud* is sometimes used with reference to the Gemara alone.

talus (tā′lŭs), fragmentary mantle rock detached from cliffs by weathering (chiefly by frost action) and piled up at bases of mountain slopes.

tamale (tŭmä′lē), Mexican dish in which a thick dough of corn meal surrounds filling of meat, chilies, and seasonings; the whole, wrapped in cornhusks, is then steamed.

Tamalpais, Mount (tă′mŭlpīs″), 2,604 ft. high, W Calif., across the Golden Gate from San Francisco. Game preserve and resort.

Tamaqua (tŭmô′kwŭ), borough (pop. 11,508), E Pa., NE of Pottsville; settled 1799. Coal mining.

Tamar (tā′mär). **1** Daughter-in-law of Judah; widow of his eldest sons in succession. When Judah failed to keep his promise to give her in marriage to his third son, she tricked Judah himself into marriage. Gen. 38; Ruth 4.12; I Chron. 2.4. Thamar: Mat. 1.3. **2** Daughter of David, sister of Absalom. Victim of Amnon's passion. 2 Sam. 13.

tamarack: see LARCH.

tamarind (tă′mŭrĭnd), tropical, ornamental, leguminous tree (*Tamarindus indica*). Its fruit, a brown pod, contains a juicy acid pulp used in chutneys and curries, in medicine, and for preserving fish.

tamarisk (tă′mŭrĭsk), small ornamental tree or shrub of genus *Tamarix,* native to S Europe and Asia and cultivated in U.S. The slender branches are covered with small leaves and bear inconspicuous white or pink blossoms in spring or summer. Tamarisks thrive on seacoasts, even in salt-water spray.

Tamaulipas (tämoulē′päs), state (30,734 sq. mi.; pop. 716,029), NE Mexico, on Gulf of Mexico; cap. VICTORIA. Chief cities: MATAMOROS and TAMPICO. Central and W sections are mountainous; S and N have arable plains. Chief products: agr. produce, cattle and hides, asphalt and petroleum. In colonial days called Pánuco, then Nuevo Santander.

tambourine: see PERCUSSION INSTRUMENTS.

Tamerlane (tă′mŭrlān) or **Timur** (tĭmoōr′), c.1336–1405, Mongol conqueror, first of the TIMURIDS; also called Timur Leng [Timur the lame]. Claimed descent from Jenghiz Khan. From SAMARKAND, his capital, in what is now Russian Turkistan he invaded Persia, S Russia, India (where he took Delhi), and the Levant. In Asia Minor he defeated the Ottoman Turks at Angora (1402) and captured their sultan, Bajazet I. Though notorious for his deeds of cruelty, he was also capable of constructive action; he encouraged the arts and sciences and built vast public works. Christopher Marlowe's play *Tamburlaine* luridly recounts his conquests.

Tamil (tă'mĭl), language of Dravidian family. Grouped with Malayalam. See LANGUAGE (table).

Tammany (tă'mŭnē). The Tammany Society or Columbian Order of New York city, formed c.1786, is only survivor of several Tammany societies founded in various American cities after American Revolution; name was taken from an Indian chief. Its activities at first mostly social, ceremonial, and patriotic, the society became a leading political force, furthering reforms in behalf of the common man, though increasingly controlled by men of privileged classes. Tammany domination of New York city politics began in 1854, and Tammany bosses (e.g., W. M. TWEED, Richard CROKER) were a source of corrupt city politics for many years. Election of 1932 gave Tammany a telling defeat, and it did not regain its former strength in succeeding elections.

Tammerfors, Finland: see TAMPERE.

Tammuz (tă'mŭz"), in Babylonian religion, young god loved by Ishtar. She killed him, but restored him to life. His festival symbolized yearly death and rebirth of vegetation.

Tampa (tăm'pŭ), city (pop. 124,681), W. Fla., on fine harbor on Tampa Bay (bridged to Pinellas peninsula), at mouth of Hillsboro R. Chief cigar-mfg. center and phosphate-shipping port in U.S., it is also a major citrus-fruit (esp. grapefruit) canner and shipper. Has mfg. of wood products and shipyards and rail shops. Resort. Probably visited by Narváez in 1528 and by De Soto in 1539. Grew around U.S. Fort Brooke (1823). Taken by Federals in Civil War. City was military base during Spanish-American War; Theodore Roosevelt's Rough Riders trained here. Ybor City in Tampa is hq. of cigar industry and home of its Spanish and Cuban workers. Davis Isls. (artificial) here are residential.

Tampa Bay, inlet of Gulf of Mexico, c.25 mi. long and 7–12 mi. wide, W Fla. The double-necked bay is sheltered on extreme W by Pinellas peninsula, where is St. Petersburg. E neck dredged to Tampa.

Tampere (täm'pĕrä), Swed. *Tammerfors,* city (pop. 102,910), SW Finland. Its industries (textiles, footwear, iron and pulp mills) receive power from near-by rapids.

Tampico (tämpē'kō), city (pop. 82,475), Tamaulipas, NE Mexico, rivaling Veracruz as Mexico's most important seaport; founded c.1554 on Pánuco R. a few miles inland from Gulf of Mexico. With discovery of oil (c.1900) rapid expansion began. Until Mexico expropriated foreign-owned property (1938), about a third of landowners were American. Besides oil, other exports include cattle and hides, rubber, vanilla, fruits, coconuts, coffee.

Tamworth (tăm'wûrth), municipal borough (pop. 12,-889), Staffordshire, England. Burned (9th cent.) by Danes, town was rebuilt (10th cent.) by Æthelflæd. Church of St. Editha was built 8th cent.; rebuilt 1345. Tamworth hogs originally raised here.

Tamworth, resort town (pop. 1,025), E central N.H., NW of Ossipee, in lake and mountain region.

Tana (tä'nä) or **Tsana** (tsä'nä), lake, area c.1,400 sq. mi., NE Ethiopia; largest in Ethiopia. Its outlet is the Blue Nile.

tanager (tă'nŭjŭr), New World migratory perching bird, chiefly tropical. North American species include scarlet tanager; male is scarlet with black wings, tail, beak; female, olive green and yellow.

Tanagra (tă'nŭgrŭ), anc. town, E Boeotia, Greece. Spartans defeated Athenians here 457 B.C. Town is best known for **Tanagra figurines,** delicate statuettes made here in the Hellenistic period.

Tanaka, Giichi, Baron (gē-ē'chē tä'näkä), 1863–1929, Japanese general. Best known as alleged author of so-called Tanaka Memorial (1927) mapping Japan's plans for foreign conquest. Premier 1927–29.

Tananarive (tänänärēv'), city (pop. 171,000), cap. of Madagascar; mfg. and commercial center.

Tancred (Tancred of Lecce) (täng'krĭd; lĕ'chä), d. 1194, king of Sicily (1190–94); natural son of Roger of Apulia, grandson of Roger II of Sicily. Usurped Sicilian throne from his aunt, Empress CONSTANCE.

Tancred, d. 1112, Crusader; a relative of BOHEMOND I. Took part in capture of Antioch and Jerusalem. Regent of Antioch for Bohemond 1100–1103 and after 1108. Although Bohemond in 1108 submitted to Alexius I, Tancred refused to do the emperor homage.

Taney, Roger Brooke (tô'nē), 1777–1864, Chief Justice of U.S. Supreme Court (1836–64). As U.S. Attorney General (1831–33) and Secretary of State (1833–34), Taney aided Pres. Jackson in struggle with Bank of the United States. As Chief Justice, Taney outraged conservatives by his opinion in Charles River Bridge Case (1837). He felt that state's POLICE POWER entitled it to make reasonable regulatory laws even if they appeared to override provisions of U.S. Constitution. His support of slavery laws was most clearly expressed in DRED SCOTT CASE (1857).

Taneycomo, Lake (tä'nēkō'mō), c.25 mi. long, SW Mo., S of Springfield and near Ark. line. Formed by Forsyth Dam in White R. Resort in the Ozarks.

T'ang (täng) dynasty of China, which ruled 618–906, succeeding the Sui. Empire at its height included Korea and Turkistan. Its highest artistic achievements were in sculpture and poetry. Confucianism provided basis for reforming civil-service examinations. Dynasty's decline began 9th cent.; succeeded by the Sung after chaotic period of Five Dynasties.

Tanganyika (täng"gùnyē'kù), UN trust territory (343,-000 sq. mi.; pop. 7,412,327), E Africa, on Indian Ocean; cap. Dar-es-Salaam. Under British administration. Borders are formed partly by Victoria Nyanza, L. Tanganyika, and L. Nyasa. Comprises coastal lowlands and high central plateau rising to Mt. Kilimanjaro (19,565 ft.). Diamonds, gold, and tin are mined. Crops include sisal, cotton, tobacco, coffee, and peanuts. Most of the natives are Bantu. The coast, which had previously been ruled from Zanzibar, was explored in 16th cent. by the Portuguese. In 17th cent., when area came under Arab sultans of Muscat, there was much trade in ivory and slaves. Brought under German protection in 1885, the area was called German East Africa until 1920 when it became a British mandate under League of Nations. Became a UN trust territory in 1945.

Tanganyika, Lake, area 12,700 sq. mi., E central Africa, in Great Rift Valley, forming boundary between Belgian Congo and Tanganyika. It is c.450 mi. long and 15–50 mi. wide. About 4,700 ft. deep, it is the world's deepest fresh-water lake except for L. Baikal. Discovered 1858 by John Speke and Sir Richard Burton. Explored in 1870s by David Livingstone and Henry Stanley.

tangerine, small, thin-skinned variety of mandarin orange (*Citrus reticulata*) with a sweet, dry pulp. It is easily peeled. The tangelo is a hybrid, the result of crossing the tangerine and grapefruit.

Tangier (tănjēr'), international zone (147 sq. mi.; pop. c.151,000), NW Africa, on Strait of Gibraltar and bordered by Spanish Morocco. Zone is named for port city of Tangier, where most of the population lives. City consists of a walled Moorish town and modern garden suburb. Probably founded by the Phoenicians, Tangier was successively under the Romans, Portuguese, Arabs, Spaniards, English, and Moors. In 19th cent. it became a focus of the dispute among the European powers over MOROCCO. In accordance with convention of 1925 the area is governed by the consuls of major European powers and by a legislative assembly headed by a representative of sultan of Morocco.

Tangier (tănjēr'), town (pop. 915) on Tangier Isl., E Va., in Chesapeake Bay near Eastern Shore of Md.; island discovered by John Smith 1608, town settled in late 17th cent.

Tanglewood: see LENOX, Mass.

Tanis (tā'nĭs), anc. city, NE Egypt, cap. of XXI dynasty. Important in strategy and commerce until it was abandoned. The biblical Zoan.

Tanjore (tănjôr'), town (pop. 68,702), S Madras, India. Has noted 11th-cent. Dravidian temple. Long known for silks, carpets, and jewelry.

tank, military, armored vehicle with caterpillar traction, armed with weapons for offense in warfare, first used by the British on the Somme (1916) in World War I. Tanks were highly important in World War II, notably in the campaigns in N Africa.

Tannenberg (tä'nŭnbĕrk″), Pol. *Sztymbark*, village near Allenstein, former East Prussia; after 1945 in Polish-administered territory. In 1410 the Poles and Lithuanians under Ladislaus II defeated the Teutonic Knights between Tannenberg and near-by Grünwald, thus halting the order's eastward expansion. In World War I the Germans under Hindenburg and Ludendorff routed the Russian army under Samsonov at Tannenberg, taking over 100,000 prisoners (Aug. 26-30, 1914). Samsonov committed suicide. A second Russian army, under Rennenkampf (whose failure to come to Samsonov's aid has been much criticized), was defeated soon afterward in the battle of the MASURIAN LAKES.

Tannhäuser (tän'hoizŭr), 13th cent., German minnesinger at the court of the duke of Austria. According to a legend, he escaped from the Venusberg but was refused papal absolution until the miraculous budding of his staff indicated divine grace. The legend is used in Wagner's opera *Tannhäuser.*

tannin and **tannic acid,** astringent, water-soluble compounds found associated in many plants; terms are commonly used as synonyms. Used as tanning agent, in inks, as mordant in dyeing, and to clarify solutions. Syntans are synthesized tannins.

tanning, process of converting skins and hides into leather. Methods include vegetable tanning with tannin, used for heavy leathers; mineral tanning with chrome (commonly used for light leathers) or alum; methods employing artificial agents (syntans).

Tannu-Tuva, RSFSR: see TUVA AUTONOMOUS OBLAST.

tansy, strong-scented European perennial herb (*Tanacetum vulgare*), with fine-cut foliage and clustered yellow, buttonlike flowers. Naturalized in America, it was long used in cookery and for medicinal tea.

tantalum (tăn'tŭlŭm), rare, lustrous, silver-white metallic element (symbol = Ta; see also ELEMENT, table). Has great ductility and malleability, high resistance to acids and corrosion. Used in making laboratory apparatus and surgical instruments.

Tantalus (tăn'tŭlŭs), in Greek legend, a king. His father, Zeus, angered by his insolence, condemned him to Tartarus. There he suffered thirst and hunger in presence of water and fruit he could not reach.

Tantum ergo, hymn: see PANGE LINGUA.

Taoism (dou'ĭzŭm, tou'–), philosophical system of China, chiefly derived from the book *Tao-teh-king,* ascribed to LAO-TZE, elucidated by Chuang-Tze. Broadly the *Tao* is the path natural events take, with spontaneous creativity and regular alternation (e.g., day and night). Man to follow the *Tao* gives up all striving; his highest goal is to escape from the illusion of desire through mystical contemplation. Taoism, a fully developed religious system by the 5th cent. A.D., adopted many gods and developed monastic orders. Taoists later tended to stress alchemy and the search for the elixir of immortality. It offered more emotional outlet than the rival system, Confucianism.

Taormina (täōrmē'nä), town (pop. 4,293), E Sicily, Italy; a winter resort near Ionian Sea at foot of Mt. Etna. Has remains of large Greek theater.

Taos (tous), resort village (pop. 1,815; alt. c.7,000 ft.), N N.Mex., between Sangre de Cristo Mts. and Rio Grande. Founded in early 1600s by Spanish; long-time center of Spanish-Indian trade; hub of Pueblo revolt of 1680 and anti-American Indian revolt of 1847. In scenic region, Taos developed after 1898 as a colony for painters and writers, notably D. H. Lawrence. Has art groups, galleries, Harwood Foundation of Univ. of New Mexico, and Kit Carson's house. Near are adobe farm village with old mission and **Taos** Indian pueblo village (1948 pop. 921). Seat in early 1600s of San Gerónimo mission, destroyed in Pueblo revolt of 1680. Scene of 1847 revolt, in which Indians killed Gov. Charles Bent. Tanoan language. Grain, livestock raised. Corn and sundown ceremonial dances.

tapa cloth: see BARK CLOTH.

Tapajós (täpäzhôsh'), river formed at border of Mato Grosso, Pará, and Amazonas states, N Brazil, and flowing c.500 mi. NNE into Amazon R. at Santarém.

tapestry, heavy hand-woven fabric of plain weave, made by threading the design of weft threads into the warp with the fingers or a bobbin. The warp (linen or wool), entirely covered by the weft (wool, silk, or metal), is evident only as ribs. Each color is worked in separately, in blocks or patches; the slits between blocks are later sewn up. The name tapestry is sometimes given to materials woven on Jacquard looms and to types of carpets and upholstery stuffs. The so-called BAYEUX TAPESTRY is actually an embroidery. History of tapestry is continuous; true tapestries were woven in ancient Egypt, China, Greece, and pre-Columbian Peru. European wool tapestries from the 10th or 11th cent. are preserved, and beautiful examples from 14th to 17th cent. are treasured by museums and cathedrals. The first great French weaving was done, in wool, at Arras in the 14th cent. (hence the name, Arras, given to tapestry in use in England long before any was made there); other notable centers were Brussels, Paris (particularly after rise in 17th cent. of Gobelins works, still in operation), Beauvais, and Aubusson. France leads in weaving modern tapestries.

tapeworm, parasitic cestode flat worm. Some species spend one stage of life cycle in muscle tissue of certain mammals and fish; if tissue is eaten improperly cooked, worm may enter host from whose intestinal walls it absorbs food. Some grow many feet long.

tapioca (tăpēō'kù), starchy food obtained by heating the root of the bitter CASSAVA. Sold as flour, flakes, or pellets, it is used to thicken puddings and soups.

tapir (tā'pùr), nocturnal, herbivorous ungulate mammal (genus *Tapirus*) of Central and South America and SE Asia.

Tappan, Arthur (tă'pùn), 1786–1865, American abolitionist. First president of American Anti-Slavery Society; split with W. L. Garrison. His brother, **Lewis Tappan,** 1788–1873, was also an abolitionist.

Tappan (tăpăn'), village (1940 pop. 1,249), SE N.Y., SW of Nyack. De Wint mansion was Washington's hq. 1780, 1783. John André was tried and hanged here.

Tappan Zee: see HUDSON, river.

Tar, river rising in N N.C. and flowing 217 mi. SE to Pamlico Sound. Called the Pamlico below Washington, N.C.

Tara (tă'rù), village, Co. Meath, Ireland. Hill of Tara was until 6th cent. seat of Irish kings. Supposedly the Coronation Stone of the ancient high kings was here. There are ruins.

tar and pitch, viscous, black substances obtained from destructive distillation of coal, wood, petroleum, etc. Tar is more fluid than pitch. Most tar produced now is fractionated to give naphtha, creosote, and other crude products; pine wood tar is used in soap and medications. Pitch is used to make roofing paper, as lubricant, in varnishes.

Taranto (tä'räntō), Latin *Tarentum,* city (pop. 103,306),

Apulia, S Italy, on Gulf of Taranto, an arm of the Ionian Sea. Major naval base; agr., commercial, and fishing center. A flourishing town of Magna Graecia, it resisted Rome until 272 B.C. Was strongly fortified under kingdom of Naples. Restored cathedral dates from 11th cent.; Byzantine castle was restored 1480.

tarantula (tŭrăn′chŭlŭ, –tŭlŭ), wolf spider (*Lycosa tarantula*) of Italy. Name is also applied to some Asiatic spiders and various species of large, dark, hairy spiders (family Aviculariidae) of W Hemisphere. *Tarantula* is genus name of certain tailless whip scorpions.

Tarascan (tärä′skän), Indian people of Michoacán, Mexico. Stubbornly resisted Aztec and Spanish domination. Depend on agr. and fishing (in L. Pátzcuaro) for livelihood. Former cap. Tzintzuntzan.

Tarascon (täräskŏ′), town (pop. 4,919), Bouches-du-Rhône dept., SE France, on the Rhone. Was immortalized by Alphonse Daudet in his *Tartarin de Tarascon*. Its medieval castle was the residence of RENÉ of Anjou.

Tarawa: see GILBERT ISLANDS.

Tarbell, Ida M(inerva), 1857–1944, American author. One of the "muckrakers," who attacked evils in American business, she wrote a much-read *History of the Standard Oil Company* (2 vols., 1904). Also wrote books on Lincoln.

Tarbes (tärb), city (pop. 42,778), cap. of Hautes-Pyrénées dept., SW France, on Adour R. Has Romanesque cathedral (11th–13th cent.). Tourist center.

Tarboro (tär′bŭrŭ), town (pop. 8,120), E N.C., E of Rocky Mount and on Tar R. Farm center (tobacco, peanuts, corn) with cotton mills.

Tarde, Gabriel de (gäbrēĕl′ dŭ tärd′), 1843–1904, French sociologist and criminologist, known for his general social theory, distinguishing between inventive and imitative persons.

Tardieu, André (ädrā′ tärdyû′), 1876–1945, French statesman, a conservative and nationalist. Helped write Treaty of Versailles. Was premier in 1929–30 and in 1932. His insistence on safeguard of French security wrecked Disarmament Conference of 1932.

tare (târ), a VETCH. The tare of the Bible was probably darnel rye grass (*Lolium temulentum*).

Tarentum (tŭrĕn′tŭm), borough (pop. 9,540), SW Pa., on Allegheny R. and NE of Pittsburgh. Mfg. of metal, wood, and paper products; coal mining.

Targoviste (tŭr″gōvĕsh′tĕ), town (pop. 26,038), S central Rumania, in Walachia. Commercial center. Cap. of Walachia 1383–1698. Has remarkable 16th-cent. cathedral.

Targul-Mures (tûr′gōol-mōō′rĕsh) or **Targu-Mures** (tûr′gōo–), Hung. *Maros Vásárhely*, city (pop. 47,043), central Rumania, in Transylvania, on Mures R. Agr. processing; oil refinery. Old cultural center dating from 12th cent. Has Telekiana library (13th cent.), repository of valuable manuscripts; modern "cultural" palace, containing art gallery, ethnographic museum, library, and conservatory of music. Under Hungary 1940–45.

Targum (tär′gŭm) [Aramaic,= translation], Aramaic paraphrase of the Old Testament written when Aramaic replaced Hebrew among Jews of Palestine and Babylon.

Tarifa (tärē′fä), city (pop. 6,362), S Spain, in Andalusia, a fortified seaport on Strait of Gibraltar. Southernmost city of European mainland.

tariff: see CUSTOMS; FREE TRADE; PROTECTION.

Tariff Commission, United States, created (1916) by act of U.S. Congress. Consists of six members, who advise on tariff legislation. Since 1949 the commission has had further functions in administration of reciprocal trade agreements.

Tarik (tä′rĭk), fl. 711, Berber conqueror of Spain. Crossed 711 from Africa to Gibraltar (named for him, in Arabic, Jebel-al-Tarik, i.e., Tarik's mountain); defeated King RODERICK.

Tarim (därēm′), river, c.1,300 mi. long, Sinkiang prov., China. Terminates in marshes near Lob Nor.

Tarkington, (Newton) Booth, 1869–1946, American author and dramatist, b. Indianapolis. Realistic novels on Indiana include *The Gentleman from Indiana* (1899); *The Turmoil* (1915); *The Magnificent Ambersons* (1918); *The Midlander* (1923); *Alice Adams* (1921). His highly popular stories of boyhood include *Penrod* (1914) and *Seventeen* (1916). He dramatized his romance, *Monsieur Beaucaire* (1900), which was also a successful movie, as were other novels.

Tarn (tärn), department (2,232 sq. mi.; pop. 298,117), S France, in Languedoc; cap. Albi. The **Tarn** river, 233 mi. long, rises in the Cévennes and flows SW past Albi and Montauban into the Garonne.

Tarn-et-Garonne (–ä–gärôn′), department (1,440 sq. mi.; pop. 167,664), SW France, in Guienne and Languedoc; cap. Montauban.

Tarnopol (tärnô′pôl), Rus. *Ternopol*, city (1931 pop. 35,831), W Ukraine, on the Seret. Agr. center. Once an important fortress, it passed from Poland to Austria 1772; reverted to Poland 1919; was ceded to USSR 1945. Here in 1915 Russians resisted Austrians.

Tarnow, Pol. *Tarnów* (tär′nŏof), city (pop. 33,108), S Poland. Trade center. Noted for medieval architecture, particularly cathedral (c.1400). Was under Austrian rule 1772–1918.

taro (tä′rō, tâ′rō), name for several coarse, perennial herbs (genus *Colocasia*). The starchy rootstocks (baked, boiled, or made into poi) form a major food in many tropical and subtropical regions. The common taro (*Colocasia antiquorum*), probably native to SE Asia, has been introduced in tropical Africa and America. Dasheen (*C. esculenta*) has mealy flesh rich in carbohydrates and proteins; it is sometimes considered a variant of taro rather than a separate species. Because of their large ornamental leaves some taro plants are called elephant's-ear.

tarpan (tär′păn) or **Przhevalsky's horse** (pŭrzhĭväl′skēz), wild horse of central Asia, the only extant wild horse not descended from tame horses. Smaller than domestic horse, it is dun color with brown mane (short, erect) and tail, large head, bulging forehead. Breeds in captivity; seen in some zoological gardens. Name *Przhevalsky's horse* is in honor of Russian explorer.

Tarpeia (tärpē′yù), in Roman legend, woman who betrayed her city to Sabines for their gold bracelets. They killed her. **Tarpeian Rock** at Rome, from which criminals were thrown, bears her name.

tarpon (tär′pŏn), large herringlike marine game fish (genus *Tarpon*). Ranges from Long Island to Brazil and Africa; sometimes enters rivers. It has silvery scales and is 6–8 ft. long.

Tarpon Springs, city (pop. 4,323), W Fla., on Gulf coast NW of Tampa. Major sponge-fishing center. Greek religious festivals draw visitors.

Tarquin (tär′kwĭn), Latin *Tarquinius*, legendary Etruscan family ruling in early Rome. **Lucius Tarquinius Priscus** is said to have come to Rome on the advice of his prophetess wife, Tanaquil. There he was made king (616 B.C.). His son, **Lucius Tarquinius Superbus** (Tarquin the Proud), murdered his father-in-law, Servius Tullius, to get the throne. He ruled with despotism and cruelty. His son, **Sextus Tarquinius,** ravaged LUCRECE, wife of his kinsman, **Tarquinius Collatinus.** The Romans drove Tarquin the Proud from the throne (510 B.C.). Lars Porsena restored the family but only briefly (c.500? B.C.).

tarragon, tender perennial Old World herb (*Artemisia dracunculus*), related to wormwood. It is a flavoring for vinegars, salads, sauces, and soups.

Tarragona (tärägō′nä), city (pop. 33,708), cap. of Tarragona prov., NE Spain, in Catalonia; a Mediterranean port. Archiepiscopal see. Wine. Captured by Romans 218 B.C.; became cap. of Tarraconensis prov. Recovered from Moors 1089. Ruins include Roman and pre-Roman walls. There is a well-preserved Roman aqueduct. Romanesque-Gothic cathedral has one of finest cloisters (13th cent.) in Spain.

Tarrant (tä′rŭnt) or **Tarrant City,** city (pop. 7,571), N central Ala., near Birmingham. Foundry products.

Tarrytown, residential village (pop. 8,851), SE N.Y., on Hudson R. and N of New York city; settled 17th cent. by Dutch. Auto assembling. Near by is Marymount Col. (R.C.; for women; 1918).

Tarsus (tär'sŭs), city (pop. 33,822), S Turkey, on the Tarsus (anc. Cydnus); agr. center. Ancient Tarsus was cap. of Cilicia and a major city in Asia Minor. Birthplace of St. Paul.

tartan: see PLAID.

tartar (tär'tŭr) or **argol** (är'gŭl), impure acid potassium tartrate deposited as crust in vessels with fermented wine. CREAM OF TARTAR is purified form.

tartar emetic, white, crystalline, water-soluble salt. Used as emetic, expectorant, diaphoretic, and in dyeing and calico printing as a mordant.

Tartars: see TATARS.

Tartarus: see HELL.

Tartini, Giuseppe (tärtē'nē), 1692–1770, Italian violinist, the greatest master of his day. He altered the shape of the bow and revised bowing technique. He composed much violin music, including the G major sonata and the famous *Devil's Trill,* supposedly played to him by the devil in a dream.

Tartu (tär'tōō), Ger. and Swed. *Dorpat,* city (pop. c.71,-000), E Estonia. Its noted university (founded 1632 by Gustavus II of Sweden) makes it the cultural center of Estonia. Tartu was founded 1030 by a Kievan prince; fell to Livonian Knights 1224; joined Hanseatic League 14th cent.; was contested after 1561 among Russia, Sweden, and Poland; fell to Peter I of Russia 1704. It has an old castle and a 13th-cent. cathedral.

Tashkent (täshkĕnt', täsh–), city (pop. 585,005), cap. of Uzbek SSR, in Tashkent oasis, on Trans-Caspian RR. Largest and one of oldest cities of central Asia. Has large cotton-textile industry. Seat of Central Asian State Univ. and of other scientific and cultural institutions. Founded 7th cent., it passed from Arabic rule to shahs of Khorezm in 12th cent. A center on Samarkand-Peking trade route, it was conquered 13th cent. by Jenghiz Khan and 1361 by Tamerlane. As part of khanate of KOKAND it fell to Russia in 1865 and became cap. of Russian Turkistan. Has few historic relics. Tashkent oasis produces fruit, vegetables, cotton, silk.

Tasman, Abel Janszoon (täz'mŭn), 1603?–1659, Dutch navigator. Made trading and exploring voyages (c.1632 –1653) in Pacific and Indian oceans. Discovered Tasmania, New Zealand; sailed around Australia.

Tasmania (tăzmā'nēŭ), island, area c.24,450 sq. mi., S of SE Australia, between Indian Ocean and Tasman Sea and separated from Victoria by Bass Strait. Geologically a continuation of Australian continent. Mountainous and partly forested. Exports wool, canned fruit, and metals (copper, zinc, tin, lead, gold, and silver). Fauna includes the marsupials popularly known as the Tasmanian tiger and Tasmanian devil. The island was discovered 1642 by Tasman, who named it Van Diemen's Land. Visited 1777 by Capt. James Cook and brought under British control in 1803, when a penal colony was estab. here. **Tasmania** state (26,215 sq. mi.; pop. 257,117), with cap. at Hobart, is part of the Commonwealth of Australia. Attached to New South Wales until 1825, it joined the commonwealth as a state in 1901.

Tasman Sea, arm of the S Pacific, with SE Australia and Tasmania on W and New Zealand on E.

Tasso, Torquato (tōrkwä'tō täs'sō), 1544–95, Italian epic poet, b. Sorrento. Wrote *Jerusalem Delivered* (1575; Ital., *Gerusalemme liberata*), an epic rivaling Ariosto's *Orlando Furioso* in popularity. Tasso also wrote the pastoral drama *Aminta.*

taste, sense produced by stimulation of taste buds, which occur chiefly on tongue. Four fundamental tastes are—bitter, salt, sweet, acid.

Tatar Autonomous Soviet Socialist Republic (tä'tŭr), administrative division (26,100 sq. mi.; pop. 2,919,-423), E central European RSFSR, in middle Volga and lower Kama valleys; cap. KAZAN. Predominantly agr. Rich in timber. Population is 49% Turco-Tatar (Moslems) and 43% Russian.

Tatars (tä'tŭrz) or **Tartars** (tär'tŭrz), collective name applied to peoples that overran parts of Asia and Europe under Mongol leadership in 13th cent. The original Tatars probably came from E central Asia or central Siberia. After the wave of invasion receded eastward, the Tatars continued to dominate nearly all of Russia and Siberia. The Empire of the GOLDEN HORDE lasted until the late 15th cent., when it broke up into several independent khanates, which fell to the Ottoman Turks and Tsar Ivan IV. Nevertheless Siberia long continued to be known as Tartary and CRIMEA as Little Tartary. By the late 16th cent. the majority of the Tatars in Russia had reached a high degree of civilization, and only minorities (e.g., the Nogais) remained nomadic. The whole course of Russian history shows great Tatar influence. In 1939 there were c.4,300,000 Tatars in the USSR. They speak a Turkic language and are mainly Moslems. They predominate in Tatar ASSR, but the majority live dispersed in E European RSFSR and in W Siberia.

Tate, Allen, 1899–, American poet and critic. Helped found the magazine *Fugitive* to express Southern agrarian views. Taught at Princeton and other universities, held chair of poetry at Library of Congress (1943–44). Works include *Poems, 1922–1947* (1948) and essay *On the Limits of Poetry* (1948).

Tate, Nahum (nā'hŭm), 1652–1715, British poet, poet laureate after 1692. Collaborated with Dryden on second part of *Absalom and Achitophel* (1682).

Tate Gallery, Millbank, London, originally the National Gall. of British Art; opened 1897. Building and original collection were given by the sugar merchant and philanthropist Sir Henry Tate. Notable features are the Turner wing (gift of Sir Joseph Duveen), a gallery of works of John Singer Sargent, and four galleries of modern foreign art.

Tatler, journal: see SPECTATOR.

Tatra (tä'trŭ) or **Tatras,** Pol. and Slovak *Tatry,* highest mountain group of Carpathians, extending along Polish-Czechoslovak border. Stalin Peak (formerly Franz Joseph Spitze and Gerlachovka) rises to 8,737 ft. Has many mountaineering and winter sports resorts, notably Zakopane (Poland).

Tauber, Richard (tou'bŭr), 1892–1948, Austrian tenor. Although he was noted as an opera and lieder singer, he was best known for his work in operettas, particularly those of Lehar.

Tauler, Johannes (tou'lŭr), c.1300–1361, German mystic, a Dominican, disciple of Meister Eckhart. Associated with the popular mystical movement, the Friends of God, he was a notable preacher.

Taunton (tôn'tŭn), municipal borough (pop. 33,613), co. seat of Somerset, England; trade center. Lord Jeffreys held "Bloody Assizes" here in 1685.

Taunton (tän'tŭn, tôn–), city (pop. 40,109), SE Mass., on Taunton R.; area settled 1638. Textiles, silverware, stoves, machinery, and plastics.

Taupo, Lake (tou'pō), largest lake of New Zealand, area 238 sq. mi., on central North Isl.

Tauroggen or Taurage, Convention of: see YORCK VON WARTENBURG.

Taurus (tô'rŭs), mountain chain, S Turkey, extending parallel to Mediterranean coast of S Asia Minor. Its NE extension is called the Anti-Taurus. Rises to 12,251 ft. at Ala Dag. Chain is crossed, N of Tarsus, by CILICIAN GATES. Mineral deposits include chromium, copper, silver, and lignite.

Taurus (tô'rŭs) [Latin,= the bull], sign of ZODIAC.

tavern: see INN.

Tawas City (tô'wŭs), city (pop. 1,441), N Mich., on Tawas Bay, inlet of Saginaw Bay. Resort and commercial fishing center.

Tawney, R(ichard) H(enry) (tô'nē), 1880–, English economist, author of *Religion and the Rise of Capitalism* (1926).

taxation, regular levy to provide revenue for a government. Emergency levies and special fees (such as postage) are not taxes. Ease of collection is accounted a merit in a tax, and ability to pay is one test of the amount that an individual should contribute. See INCOME TAX; SINGLE TAX; POLL TAX.

Taxco (tä'skō), city (pop. 4,963), Guerrero, SW Mexico. Founded as silver-mining community (1529), it was also important stop between Mexico City and Acapulco in Spanish colonial trade with Philippines. Kept as an example of colonial town, it is a tourist center.

Tay (tā), largest river of Scotland, 118 mi. long. Rising in Argyllshire, it is called Fillan as far as Loch Dochart and then called Dochart as far as Loch Tay (14½ mi. long and 1 mi. wide). It enters North Sea through tidal Firth of Tay (25 mi. long). River has valuable salmon fisheries.

Taylor, Bayard, 1825–78, American journalist and author. Correspondent for New York *Tribune,* he traveled widely and wrote travel books, such as *Views Afoot* (1846). Verse in such volumes as *Poems of the Orient* (1854) is highly rhymed, singable, and exotic in content (as in "Bedouin Love Song"). His verse translation of Goethe's *Faust* is still read.

Taylor, Brook, 1685–1731, English mathematician. Known for Taylor's theorem (complex mathematical formula concerning functions), which forms basis of differential calculus; first exposition of principle of vanishing points; solution of problem of center of oscillation which led to mathematical expression of principles governing vibration of string.

Taylor, (Joseph) Deems, 1885–, American composer and music critic. His compositions include the orchestral suite *Through the Looking Glass* and the operas *The King's Henchman* (libretto by Edna St. Vincent Millay) and *Peter Ibbetson* (based on George Du Maurier's novel). Also a newspaper music critic and music consultant and commentator for radio.

Taylor, Edward, c.1645–1729, American poet and clergyman, long a Congregational minister at Westfield, Mass.

Taylor, Edward Thompson, 1793–1871, American Methodist missionary preacher, called Father Taylor. A sailor in youth, he began in 1830 his successful work as missionary in Seamen's Bethel, Boston. He appears as Father Mapple in Melville's *Moby Dick.*

Taylor, Francis Henry, 1903–, American museum director. Director of Worcester (Mass.) Art Mus. (1931–40) and of Metropolitan Mus., New York (1940–).

Taylor, Henry Osborn, 1856–1941, American scholar, author of the much-admired *The Medieval Mind* (1911).

Taylor, Jeremy, 1613–67, English bishop, theological and devotional writer. Chaplain to Archbishop Laud and chaplain in ordinary to Charles I, he received on the Restoration (1660) bishopric of Down and Connor in Ireland. In sermons he was master of fine metaphor and poetic imagination. Author of *Holy Living* (1650) and *Holy Dying* (1651).

Taylor, John, 1753–1824, American political philosopher. Known as "John Taylor of Caroline." Early formulator of STATES' RIGHTS doctrine. His greatest work is *An Inquiry into the Principles and Policy of the Government of the United States* (1814).

Taylor, John, 1808–87, American Mormon leader, b. England. In the U.S. he was made (1838) apostle and missionary. He succeeded Brigham Young as president of Mormon church.

Taylor, Tom, 1817–80, English dramatist, editor of *Punch* (1874–80). Wrote over 100 plays, notably *Our American Cousin* (1858) and *The Ticket of Leave Man* (1863).

Taylor, Zachary (ză'kûrē), 1784–1850, 12th President of the United States. Won nickname of "Old Rough and Ready" in army campaigns against Indians. Commanding U.S. troops in MEXICAN WAR, he won victories at Palo Alto, Resaca de la Palma, and Buena Vista. Elected President on Whig party ticket, he took

office in 1849. On his death Millard Fillmore became president. Taylor's son, **Richard (Dick) Taylor,** 1826–79, was a Confederate general. Fought in Shenandoah Valley and Seven Days battles. Commander in W La. (1862), later commander of Lower South.

Taylor. 1 Industrial borough (pop. 7,176), NE Pa., on Lackawanna R. and near Scranton. **2** City (pop. 9,071), central Texas, NNE of Austin. Center of agr. area with mattress factory; meat and poultry packing.

Taylorville, city (pop. 9,188), central Ill., SE of Springfield. Center of farm and coal area with mfg. of paper, feed, and tools.

Tb, chemical symbol of the element TERBIUM.

Tbilisi, Georgian SSR: see TIFLIS.

Tc, chemical symbol of the element TECHNETIUM.

Tch–. For Russian names not listed thus, see CH–; e.g., Tchekhoff, see CHEKHOV.

Tchaikovsky, Piotr Ilich (pyô'tùr ĭlyēch' chĭkôf'skē), 1840–93, Russian composer. He taught at the Moscow Conservatory until an annuity from a wealthy patroness, Mme von Meck (whom he knew only through letters), allowed him to devote himself to composition. His music, melodious and emotional, is perhaps today the most popular and most often played of all notable composers. Most successful are his orchestral works —his last three symphonies, including the Fifth Symphony and the Sixth, or Pathetique, Symphony; the fantasies *Romeo and Juliet* and *Francesca da Rimini;* the ballets *Swan Lake, The Sleeping Beauty,* and the *Nutcracker;* the Piano Concerto in B Flat Minor; the Violin Concerto in D; and the popular "1812" Overture. His operas include *Eugene Onegin* and *Pique Dame (The Queen of Spades),* both based on stories by Pushkin; of his many songs, perhaps *None But the Lonely Heart* is best known. He conducted at the opening concert in Carnegie Hall in 1891. Tschaikowsky is another spelling of the name.

Tchelitchew, Pavel (chĕlĭ'chĕf, Rus. pä'vĭl chĭlyē'chĭf), 1898–, Russian-American painter. His technique involves the juxtaposition of many objects in such a way that most of them are not apparent at first glance. Best-known work is *Hide and Seek* (Mus. of Modern Art, New York).

Te, chemical symbol of the element TELLURIUM.

tea, a tree or bush, its leaves, and the beverage made from them. The common tea plant (*Camellia sinensis* or *Thea sinensis*), an evergreen native to E Asia, grows to c.30 ft., but is usually pruned in cultivation to 3–5 ft. Leading producers are India, China, Ceylon, Indonesia, Japan, Formosa. Shrubs, propagated from seed, can be picked in three years and may yield for 50 years. Leaves are picked by hand during active growth periods and are then withered, rolled, and fired (or heated). For green tea, firing follows close upon picking; for black, leaves are fermented for c.24 hours; for oolong, intermediate in flavor and color, they are partly fermented. Most teas are classed under either the Chinese or the English system of nomenclature; some are named for the growing district. Flavor of tea is produced by volatile oils, the stimulating properties by caffeine, and the astringency by tannin. Tea is world's most widely used beverage other than water.

Teach, Edward: see BLACKBEARD.

teak (tēk), tall, deciduous tree (*Tectona grandis*), native to India, Burma, and Siam, with 10- to 20-inch rough-surfaced leaves. Teakwood, which darkens on exposure, is hard but easily worked; it is used for ship-building, agricultural implements, flooring.

Teaneck (tē'nĕk"), residential suburban township (pop. 33,772), NE N.J., E of Hackensack.

Teapot Dome, area near Casper, Wyo., set aside by Pres. Wilson in 1915 as naval oil reserve, transferred to Dept. of the Interior in 1921. In 1922 A. B. FALL, Secretary of the Interior, leased, without competitive bidding, the Teapot Dome fields and another field in Calif. Senate investigation under Sen. T. J. Walsh led to criminal prosecutions, bringing notoriety upon a number of prominent officials.

tear gas, gas (usually a compound of bromine), causing temporary blindness through excessive flow of tears. Used in warfare and mob dispersal.

Teasdale, Sara, 1884–1933, American lyric poet. Her *Collected Poems* appeared in 1937.

teasel (tē′zŭl), Old World thistlelike biennial plant with small lilac flower heads. The common teasel (*Dipsacus sylvestris*) is naturalized in North America. Fuller's teasel (*D. fullonum*) was long used to raise the nap on wool. Both species are grown for use in EVERLASTING bouquets.

Teche, Bayou (bī′ō tĕsh′, bī′ōō), S La., flows from E of Lafayette SE between Atchafalaya basin and Gulf of Mexico to Atchafalaya R. Navigable for over 100 mi. Setting for Longfellow's *Evangeline.*

technetium (tĕknē′shŭm), silvery metallic element (symbol = Tc; atomic no. = 43), similar to rhenium in properties. Existence reported in 1925 (then called masurium); radioactive isotopes produced 1937.

Tecumseh (tĭkŭm′sē), 1768?–1813, chief of the SHAWNEE INDIANS. Sought to unite Indian tribes against U.S. Plan failed with defeat of his brother Tenskwatawa, the SHAWNEE PROPHET, at Tippecanoe (1811). Aided British in War of 1812; killed at battle of the THAMES.

Tedder, Arthur William Tedder, 1st Baron, 1890–, British air chief marshal. Helped sweep Germans from Libya (1941–43). Deputy supreme commander and chief of allied air operations in W Europe (1944). Air chief of staff 1946–50.

Teddington, former urban district, now part of Twickenham, Middlesex, England, on the Thames. Port of London officially begins here.

Te Deum laudamus (tā dē′ŏom loudä′mōos [Latin,= we praise Thee, O God], anc. hymn of the Western Church, dating from the 4th or 5th cent. It is sung at morning prayer in Anglican churches and is the chief hymn of rejoicing of the Roman Catholic Church.

Tees, river rising in Cumberland, England, and flowing c.70 mi. E to the North Sea.

teeth, structures embedded in jaws of many vertebrates and serving chiefly to masticate food. In man a set of 20 deciduous teeth (also called milk teeth) begins to erupt at c.6 months; these are replaced by 32 permanent teeth erupting after sixth year. Each tooth is composed of dentine surrounding core of nerves and blood vessels; visible portion (crown) is coated with enamel; cement-coated roots are attached to jaw by membrane.

Tegucigalpa (tāgōō″sēgäl′pä), city (pop. 55,755 including Comayagüela, its twin city across river), S central Honduras, cap. and largest city of republic, in mountain valley. Founded late 16th cent., it was colonial mining center.

Teheran (tĕ″hūrän′) or **Tehran** (tĕrän′), city (pop. 989,-871), cap. of Iran, in N Iran, at foot of Elburz mts. and c.70 mi. S of Caspian Sea; commercial center. Trans-Iranian RR connects it with Persian Gulf and with Caspian Sea. University here was founded 1934. City is near ancient Rages and was itself a medieval town. Its rise dates from 1788, when Aga Mohamad Khan made it the capital. Modernized by Reza Shah Pahlevi, it has grown steadily in recent years. An important war conference was held here in 1943.

Teheran Conference, Nov. 28–Dec. 1, 1943, meeting of Pres. F. D. Roosevelt, Prime Minister Churchill, and Premier Stalin in World War II. Agreed on scope and timing of war against Germany and cooperation of UN for problems for peace. Protocol pledged respect for sovereignty and integrity of Iran.

Tehuantepec (tāwäntāpĕk′), town (pop. 6,731), Oaxaca, S Mexico, on wide bend of river not far from Gulf of Tehuantepec, an arm of Pacific. Town is on S end of Isthmus of Tehuantepec, a narrow strip of land between Gulf of Campeche and Gulf of Tehuantepec. Climate is hot and tropical; the population is largely Zapotec.

Teixeira, Pedro (pā′drō tā′shärù), d. 1640, Portuguese

explorer, one of the early voyagers on the Amazon (1637–38).

Tejo, river: see TAGUS.

Tekoa or **Tekoah** (both: tēkō′ù), anc. town, S of Bethlehem, at the extreme edge of cultivated lands and at the beginning of the wilderness of Tekoa. This wilderness was the home of Amos.

Tel-Aviv (tĕl″ùvēv′), city (pop. c.250,000), central Israel, on the Mediterranean; founded 1909. Largest city and financial center of Israel; a joint municipality with adjoining Jaffa (since 1949). Has textile mills and clothing factories. Cultural institutions include Herzliah Hebrew Col. and famed Habima theater. After World War II there was sporadic fighting between this all-Jewish city and Jaffa, then predominantly Arab. State of Israel was proclaimed here, May 14, 1948.

telegraph. Name now generally restricted to electric telegraph but used earlier for methods of signaling, by sound or sight, beyond the range of human voice. Method of electric signaling that has come into general use over most of world is based on invention by S. F. B. Morse; electric circuit is set up generally with only a single overhead wire and using earth as other conductor to complete the circuit. Signals are sent by making and breaking current in this circuit. Receiving instrument is actuated by an electromagnet; reception by sound, in which Morse code signals are received as audible clicks, has proved swift and reliable method. First permanently successful telegraphic cable crossing Atlantic Ocean was laid in 1866. J. B. Stearns introduced (1872) method of sending two messages over same wire at same time and Thomas A. Edison invented (1874) "quadruplex" method for sending four messages over same wire at same time. Later instruments include those for receiving messages in printed form (e.g., by teletypewriter), for transmitting messages in handwriting of sender (telautograph), for transmitting photographs and other pictures. For wireless telegraphy, see RADIO.

Teleki, Count Paul, Hung. *Teleki Pál* (tĕ′lĕkĭ päl′), 1879–1941, Hungarian statesman and scholar; a geographer and political writer. Premier 1920–21 and 1939–41. Signed Berlin Pact (1940; see AXIS) but committed suicide on eve of attack on Yugoslavia.

Tel-el-Amarna (tĕl″-ĕl-ämär′nä), locality, near the Nile, N of Asyut, Egypt. Here was Ikhnaton's capital, and here were found (1887–88) tablets with inscriptions of Amenhotep III and Ikhnaton. Also Tell-el-Amarna.

Telemachus (tĭlĕ′mùkùs), in Greek legend, son of PENELOPE and Odysseus. After Odysseus' return from Trojan War, Telemachus helped his father kill his mother's unwelcome suitors.

Telemark (tĕ′lùmärk), county of S Norway, between Hardanger plateau and the Skagerrak; cap. Skien. Famous for lake and mountain scenery, handicrafts (e.g., wood carving, silversmith work, weaving). Birthplace of skiing as a sport (late 19th cent.).

telepathy, word invented 1862 by F. W. H. Myers to indicate the communication of impressions from one living mind to another without recourse to physical (sensory) channels. Also known as thought or mind reading. See also PSYCHICAL RESEARCH.

telephone. Telephones now in general use developed from a device invented by Alexander Graham Bell (patented 1876 and 1877). It used an electric current of fluctuating intensity and frequency generated by mirroring the acoustic characteristics of sound waves. A diaphragm (thin iron plate) vibrated to sound waves just as does the human eardrum. These vibrations disturbed the magnetic field of a near-by bar magnet inducing an electric current in a thin copper wire wound about the magnet. The current, upon reaching a distant instrument, caused its diaphragm to vibrate by similarly fluctuating the near-by magnetic field. Bell's instrument was both transmitter and receiver; first major improvement made transmitter and receiver separate. Telephone lines used include open

telescope, optical instrument for viewing distant objects. Invention (1608) is attributed to Hans Lippershey; development for astronomical use to Galileo (1609). In refracting telescope, light is collected by lens set at far end of tube; image magnified by smaller lens (eyepiece). In reflecting telescope, light is gathered by mirror; image magnified by eyepiece. Refractors are preferred for detailed observation of nearer celestial bodies; reflectors, for viewing of more distant bodies. Practicable limit of refractors probably attained in 40-in. instrument at Yerkes Observatory. Reflectors larger than 200-in. Mt. Palomar telescope theoretically achievable. Visual telescopes have been adjusted for use with camera and spectroscope.

teletypewriter: see TYPEWRITER.

television, transmission of pictures and sound simultaneously by electrical impulses. Development of television followed discovery in 1873 of variation in electrical conductivity of selenium when exposed to light; selenium cells were used in early devices but really satisfactory results were obtained only after invention of electron tube (phototube). Progress toward television can be traced through demonstration of nature of electron by Sir J. J. Thomson in 1897, development of Einstein's theory of photoelectric effect (1905), Lee de Forest's three-element vacuum tube (1906), and E. H. Armstrong's regenerative circuit (1912). Decade of 1930–40 saw laboratory perfection of television equipment which began to be marketed at end of World War II. Integral part of television device is some method of "scanning" picture to be transmitted. In 1926 television using mechanical scanning disk was demonstrated in U.S. and England. Mechanical method was soon superseded by electronic scanning methods. Basic types of camera tubes include the Iconoscope invented by V. K. Zworykin and the Orthicon, a later development. The main steps in effecting television can be merely touched upon in a brief description of the process. The scene before the camera is focused by a lens on the plate or mosaic (the specially treated surface) of the electronic pick-up tube; differing light intensities of the scene cause photosensitive particles of mosaic to develop a charge (greatest where light is brightest). A beam of electrons sweeps over mosaic in a 525-line zigzag, 30 times each second; beam causes formation of current which passes through external circuit of camera tube and thence through various stages of amplification to be sent out on carrier wave. Minute parts of picture are transmitted in orderly sequence. In receiving set dissected images are reconstructed by changing electrical impulses back into light values; this is done in a cathode-ray tube where an electronic beam scans inner surface of tube at synchronized rate of 525 lines every 1/30 of a second. Several systems of color television have been developed but none had been adopted commercially by early 1953.

Tell, William, legendary Swiss hero. In best-known version of his story, Tell, a native of Bürglen in Uri, refused obeisance to Gessler, the Austrian bailiff, was forced in punishment to shoot an apple off his son's head, and shot Gessler in revenge from an ambush at Kussnacht, thus setting off the revolt which ousted the bailiffs on Jan. 1, 1308. Connected with the legend is the story of the RÜTLI OATH. Tell probably never existed, and the account is a distortion of the historic events of 1291 (see SWITZERLAND). Its best-known treatments are Schiller's drama (1804) and Rossini's opera (1829).

Tell (těl), Mediterranean coastal region, 50–120 mi. wide, of French North Africa. In E Algeria it includes the coastal Atlas ranges. Exports include cereals, wine, and olive oil.

Tell City, city (pop. 5,735), S Ind., on Ohio R. and W of Evansville; settled 1857 by Swiss. Wood products.

Tell-el-Amarna, Egypt: see TEL-EL-AMARNA.

Téllez, Gabriel: see TIRSO DE MOLINA.

tellurium (tĕlŏŏ′rēŭm), element with some metallic properties (symbol = Te; see also ELEMENT, table). Appears in white crystalline form and as black powder. Resembles sulphur in properties.

Telugu (tĕ′lùgōō), language of Dravidian family. See LANGUAGE (table).

Temesvar, Banat of: see BANAT.

Tempe (tĕm′pē′), city (pop. 7,684), S central Ariz., in SALT RIVER VALLEY, on the river; founded 1872.

Tempe (tĕm′pē), valley, NE Thessaly, Greece, between Mt. Olympus and Mt. Ossa. Crossed by Peneus R. Vale of Tempe was sacred to Apollo; ancient poets celebrated its beauty.

Tempelhof (tĕm′pùlhöf), district (pop. 119,825), S central Berlin, Germany, after 1945 in U.S. occupation sector. Workers' residential quarter. Has chief airfield of Berlin (terminal of American "air lift" 1948–49).

temperance movements, organized efforts to induce people to abstain from alcoholic beverages. Among the most powerful of the movements in U.S. were the Woman's Christian Temperance Union (founded 1874) and the Anti-Saloon League (1893). They influenced passage of many liquor laws, and secured Federal PROHIBITION (1919–33).

temperature, measurement of relative "hotness" or "coldness" of body, not a measurement of heat contained in that body. Water is used as basis for comparison; comparison is made by scale so designed that temperature can be given in degrees. There are several different scales; all have two fixed points—the melting point of ice and the boiling point of water. THERMOMETER is named for scale with which it is marked. On centigrade scale or Celsius scale freezing point of water is 0°C., boiling point, 100°C.; there are 100 equal degrees between these two. On Fahrenheit scale, the corresponding figures are 32°F. and 212°F., respectively, with 180 degrees between. One Fahrenheit degree is 5/9 of a centigrade degree. On the Kelvin (absolute) scale, the freezing point of water is 273°K., boiling point, 373°K.; this is used in formulae derived from gas laws. Zero point is absolute zero, point at which molecules have no heat energy. On Réaumur scale, freezing point of water is 0°R., boiling point 80°R. For changes between centigrade, Fahrenheit, and Réaumur scales, values can be found by working out the formula $\frac{F-32}{9} = \frac{C}{5} = \frac{R}{4}$. To convert from Kelvin scale, the formula is $C + 273° = K$ or $C = K - 273°$.

Templars: see KNIGHTS TEMPLARS.

Temple, Frederick, 1821–1902, Anglican prelate. Appointed (1858) headmaster of Rugby, he became bishop of Exeter (1869), of London (1885), and archbishop of Canterbury (1896). His son, **William Temple**, 1881–1944, was bishop of Manchester (1921–29), archbishop of York (after 1929), and archbishop of Canterbury (after 1942). He was first president (1908–24) of the Workers' Educational Association, and a leader in the movement to form a world council of churches.

Temple, Richard Grenville-Temple, Earl, 1711–79, English statesman. Opposed his brother, George Grenville, and supported his brother-in-law, William Pitt. Backed Pitt's war policy (1761), but later broke with him and was reconciled with Grenville.

Temple, Sir William, 1628–99, English statesman and author. Married Dorothy OSBORNE. Negotiated (1668) triple alliance with Netherlands and Sweden against France. As ambassador to The Hague arranged (1677) marriage of William of Orange to Princess Mary. Retired (1681) and wrote essays.

Temple, William: see TEMPLE, FREDERICK.

Temple, city (pop. 25,467), central Texas, SSW of Waco; founded 1881 by Santa Fe RR. Center of agr. area with railroad shops, it has textile, flour, and cottonseed oil mills and mfg. of mattresses, rock wool, and tools. Stonecutting. Has VA hospital. **Near** by is co-operative conservation project.

Temple, the, district of central London, England. Here are Inner and Middle Temple, belonging to INNS OF COURT. World War II bombing destroyed Temple Church and part of Inner Temple. Temple Bar was gate built c.1672 by Wren on the site of one of City of London's entrances.

Temple, Knights of the: see KNIGHTS TEMPLARS.

Temple University, at Philadelphia; nonsectarian, coed.; opened 1884 by R. H. Conwell, chartered 1888, became university 1907.

tempo, in music, the speed of a composition. A composer usually indicates tempo by a set of Italian terms, such as *presto* (very fast), *allegro* (fast), *andante* (moderate; literally "walking"), *adagio* (slow), and *largo* (very slow); *accelerando* and *ritardando* are used to indicate a momentary increase or decrease of tempo. Despite such indications, tempo remains a matter of the individual interpretation of the performer.

Temuco (tämoo'kō), city (pop. 37,375), S central Chile; founded 1881 at N limit of lake district. On near-by hill a treaty was signed (1881) ending last serious uprising of Araucanian Indians. German immigrants began colonization of S Chile here.

Ten, Council of, secret tribunal set up in Venice in 1310 to safeguard internal security. It soon became the supreme organ of the republic, dealing with foreign affairs and finances, but also remained a dreaded secret court from which there was no appeal. It actually was made up of the doge and 16 members, 10 of whom were elected, and was assisted by three inquisitors of state and by an efficient secret police.

Tenafly (těn'ŭflĭ), residential borough (pop. 9,651), NE N.J., near the Hudson and N of Englewood.

Tenasserim (těnă'sŭrĭm), division (31,588 sq. mi.; pop. 1,635,562), Lower Burma. Long disputed by Burma and Thailand, area came under British control after first Anglo-Burmese War (1824–26). Contains principal tin and tungsten mines of Burma.

Ten Commandments or **Decalogue** [Gr.,= ten words], in Bible, the cardinal summary of divine law, given by God to Moses on Mt. Sinai. Ex. 20.2–17; 31.18; 32.15–19; 34; Deut. 5.6–21; 9–10. They are of primary importance in the ethical systems of Judaism, Christianity, and Islam. There are two traditions concerning the division of the commandments; one survives in Roman Catholic and Lutheran churches, the other in Orthodox and most Protestant churches. Roman Catholics and Lutherans combine injunction to worship only one God and not to adore graven images in first commandment; others make them first two. Numbering continues different through commands: not to profane the name of the Lord; to keep the Sabbath holy; to honor one's parents; not to kill; not to give way to lust; not to steal; not to bear false witness. Catholics and Lutherans make prohibition on coveting a neighbor's wife (ninth commandment) separate from prohibition on coveting a neighbor's goods (tenth); others combine as the tenth.

Tenda or **Tende:** see BRIGUE AND TENDE.

Tenedos (tě'nŭdŏs), Aegean island (15 sq. mi.; pop. 1,765), Turkey, off NW Asia Minor. Modern name Bozca. Was station of Greek fleet in Trojan Wars and of Xerxes in 5th cent. B.C.

Tenerife: see CANARY ISLANDS.

Teniers, David (tŭnēr', těn'yŭrz, Flemish těnērs'), the elder, 1582–1649, Flemish painter. His little scenes of peasant life are sometimes confused with the brownish early work of his famous son, **David Teniers,** the younger, 1610–90, who in his mature period used silver tones and subtle color.

Tennent, Gilbert, 1703–64, American Presbyterian clergyman, a leader in GREAT AWAKENING, b. Ireland. As pastor (after 1726) at New Brunswick, N.J., and friend of Whitefield, he became evangelistic leader in E U.S. His father, **William Tennent,** 1673–1745, Presbyterian clergyman and educator, founded c.1726 at

Neshaminy, Pa., the famous Log College, predecessor of many schools along frontier. Here many revivalists were trained.

Tennessee, state (41,961 sq. mi.; pop. 3,291,718), S central U.S.; admitted 1796 as 16th state (slaveholding); cap. NASHVILLE. Other cities are MEMPHIS, CHATTANOOGA, KNOXVILLE. Bounded W by Mississippi R. E are GREAT SMOKY MOUNTAINS, CUMBERLAND PLATEAU; W Tenn. is broad rolling plain. Mfg. of textiles, chemicals, food products, wood and metal products, cement. Farming (cotton, corn, tobacco, livestock). Mining (pyrites, phosphate, zinc, barite, coal, clay, marble, limestone); lumbering. French claim to area lost by British victory in French and Indian Wars. First permanent settlement in Watauga valley 1769; WATAUGA ASSOCIATION formed 1772. JONESBORO, oldest town, founded 1779. Settlers in E Tenn. formed short-lived government (1784–88) under John Sevier (see FRANKLIN, STATE OF). Andrew Jackson was a state and national leader. State seceded 1861. Biggest Civil War battleground, next to Va. (see SHILOH, BATTLE OF; MURFREESBORO; CHATTANOOGA CAMPAIGN). KU KLUX KLAN estab. here 1865. Recently state has profited much from benefits of TENNESSEE VALLEY AUTHORITY. Atomic energy plant at OAK RIDGE.

Tennessee, river, main Ohio R. tributary, formed by junction of Holston and French Broad rivers near Knoxville, Tenn. Flows 650 mi. SW, W, and N through E Tenn., N Ala., W Tenn., and SW Ky. to the Ohio at Paducah. Receives Clinch, Little Tennessee, Hiwassee, Elk, and Duck rivers; has drainage basin of c.41,000 sq. mi. Much benefited by TENNESSEE VALLEY AUTHORITY. Important during Civil War.

Tennessee, University of, mainly at Knoxville; land-grant, state supported, coed.; chartered 1794, opened 1795, became Univ. of Tennessee 1879. Branches at Memphis and Martin.

Tennessee Valley Authority (TVA), independent corporate agency, created May 18, 1933, by U.S. Congress. Agency empowered to take over and operate installations at MUSCLE SHOALS, Ala., and to integrate development of entire Tennessee R. basin. Main offices in the region. TVA's most noteworthy feature is system of multipurpose dams and reservoirs which dominate the valley's economic life. Hydroelectric plants provide cheap power. A navigation channel from the Tennessee's mouth to Knoxville, Tenn., has greatly increased river traffic, chiefly in petroleum, grain, automobiles, and steel. Other TVA activities include conservation and development of natural resources, social and educational programs. In World War II, TVA supplied power to the atomic energy plant at Oak Ridge, Tenn. Although it has been bitterly criticized as being "socialistic," TVA has been declared constitutional, and its remarkable success has made it a model for similar river projects.

Tenniel, Sir John (těn'yŭl), 1820–1914, English caricaturist and illustrator. Perhaps best known for illustrations of Lewis Carroll's *Alice in Wonderland*. Did political cartoons for *Punch*, 1851–1901.

tennis, game played indoors or outdoors by two or four players on level, hard court. In singles play court measures 78 ft. by 27 ft.; in doubles 78 ft. by 36 ft. Probably descendant of court tennis, it was introduced (1873) as a new game by Walter C. Wingfield in Wales. First championship match was held (1887) at Wimbledon, England. In 1881 U.S. Lawn Tennis Association was formed.

Tennyson, Alfred Tennyson, 1st Baron, 1809–92, English poet; poet laureate after 1850. While at Cambridge he wrote *Poems, Chiefly Lyrical* (1830) and began his friendship with Arthur Henry Hallam. *Poems* (1832) was scathingly attacked, and Hallam's sudden death in 1833 overwhelmed him. But *Poems* (2 vols., 1842)—including revisions of earlier work and powerful new poems such as "Locksley Hall," "Ulysses," and "Break, Break, Break"—won him wide acclaim. *The Princess* (1847) was reissued with beautiful interspersed songs in 1850. *In Memoriam* (1850) is a series of elegies written after Hallam's death, some of Tennyson's best poetry. As laureate he wrote occasional poems such as *The Charge of the Light Brigade* (1855). Other works include the "monodrama" *Maud* (1855); *Idylls of the King* (1859; enlarged 1869, 1872); *Enoch Arden* (1864); and *Demeter and Other Poems* (1889), containing "Crossing the Bar." Master of lyric perfection, Tennyson is the representative poet of the Victorian period.

Tenochtitlán (tänōchtětlän'), anc. city, central Mexico, in valley of Mexico; cap. of the Aztec, founded on a marshy island c.1325. Spanish came to city in 1519, retreated in 1520, and Cortés took it after three-month siege (1521). Mexico city was built on its ruins.

Tenos or **Tinos** (both: tē'nôs), Aegean island (74 sq. mi.; pop. 11,380), Greece; one of the Cyclades. Wine, figs, wheat, silk, marble. Venetian colony after 1390; fell to Turks 1715.

tense [O.Fr., from Latin,= time], category of verb forms referring to the time of an action. Inflection of Latin and other languages has sets of personal verb forms that are themselves members of moods. English tenses are simple (*look, looked*) or compound (*have looked, am looking*). Some languages (e.g., Russian, Hebrew) in verb forms include aspect—the completeness or incompleteness of the action. English borrows from Greek some aspectlike terms (imperfect, perfect, pluperfect).

tent caterpillar, destructive larva of native American moth. Apple-tree tent caterpillar larvae live in broods of 150 or more in white silk tent woven in tree fork; they feed on leaves.

Ten Thousand Smokes, Valley of: see VALLEY OF TEN THOUSAND SMOKES.

Tenure of Office Act, in U.S. history, measure passed on March 2, 1867, by Congress over veto of Pres. Andrew JOHNSON which forbade the President to remove any Federal officeholder "appointed by and with the advice and consent of the Senate" without further Senate approval. It also provided for tenure of cabinet members throughout full term of President who had appointed them and for one month thereafter, subject to removal by Senate. With this measure radical Republicans hoped to assure tenure of Secretary of War E. M. STANTON and thus prevent any interference with military occupation of South in their RECONSTRUCTION plan. Johnson's alleged violation of act in dismissing Stanton was principal charge in impeachment proceedings against him. Act was in large part repealed in 1887; in 1926 Supreme Court declared it unconstitutional.

Ten Years War, 1868–78, struggle for Cuban independence from Spain. Cuban discontent with excessive taxation, trade restrictions, and virtual exclusion of Cubans from government grew until revolt started in 1868. A rebel republic was set up, and guerrilla warfare was bloody and costly. Seemingly without result, it actually foreshadowed Cuban war of independence (1895) and the Spanish-American War (1898). Spain deeply resented U.S. sympathy for Cuba in the Ten Years War, shown notably in trouble over the ship *Virginius.*

teosinte (tēusĭn'tē), tall, cornlike, broad-leaved, annual grass (*Euchlaena mexicana*), native to Central America and Mexico. It is grown for forage in S U.S. Perennial species is *E. perennis.*

Teotihuacán (tāōtēwäkän'), ruins of Toltec religious center (c.6th–11th cent. A.D.), central Mexico, c.30 mi. NE of Mexico city. Pyramids to the Sun, to the Moon, numerous smaller pyramids, and the Temple of QUETZACOATL still stand.

Tepic (tāpēk'), city (pop. 17,547), cap. of Nayarit, W Mexico, on Tepic R. in rich agr. region that produces grains, coffee, rice, and sugar.

teraphim (tě'rŭfĭm) [Heb., = idols], anc. household idols of the Jews, used for divination. Probably similar to the LARES AND PENATES of Rome.

terbium (tûr'bēŭm), rare metallic element (symbol = Tb; see also ELEMENT, table).

Ter Borch or **Terburg, Gerard** (gä'rärt tür bôrkh', türbûrkh'), 1617–81, one of Dutch Little Masters. Portrayed life and customs of wealthy burgher class. His celebrated group *The Peace of Münster* is in National Gall., London.

terebinth (tě'rŭbinth) or **turpentine tree,** small deciduous tree (*Pistacia terebinthus*), native to Mediterranean region. It yielded the earliest known form of turpentine.

Terek (tyě'rĭk), river, 367 mi. long, USSR, rising in glaciers of Caucasus near Mt. Kazbek and flowing through DARYAL gorge and past Dzaudzhikau into Caspian Sea. Its swampy delta is 60 mi. wide. Lower course is used for irrigation. Cossacks of Terek valley formed autonomous community under tsars.

Terence (Publius Terentius Afer) (tě'rŭns), b. c.185 or c.195 B.C., d. c.159 B.C., Roman writer of comedies. Six comedies survive—*Andria, Heautontimorumenos, Eunuchus, Phormio, Adelphi,* and *Hecyra.* All are adapted from the Greek plays of Menander and others. The writing is skillful, the humor broad, the characters realistic.

Teresa, Saint: see THERESA, SAINT.

Teresina (těrŭzē'nù), city (pop. 53,425), cap. of Piauí state, NE Brazil, on Parnaíba R. Name formerly spelled Therezina. Has cotton and sugar mills and trades in cattle, hides, and rice.

Tereus, Thracian king: see PHILOMELA.

Terman, Lewis Madison, 1877–, American psychologist, known for his application of intelligence tests to school children. His chief work is the Stanford Revision of the Binet-Simon Intelligence Tests.

Terminus [Latin,= boundary], in Roman religion, aspect of Jupiter as god of boundaries. Immobility of feast of boundaries forced peculiar system of counting days in extra years interpolated in the calendar.

termite (tûr'mīt), social insect of order Isoptera. Often called white ant but is not an ant (has no constriction at waist as ants have) and is more closely related to roaches. Termites are divided into soil dwellers and wood dwellers. Subterranean soil dwellers do most damage in U.S.; they attack only wood in contact with ground or close to it. See *ill.,* p. 469.

tern, bird of Old and New Worlds, smaller than the related gull. Some terns are called sea swallows because of long, pointed wings and graceful flight. Arctic tern migrates from arctic to antarctic.

Ternate (těrnä'tä), volcanic island (41 sq. mi.; pop. 130,022), E Indonesia, in Molucca Sea W of Halmahera. Became important Moslem center in 15th cent. Forts were built here in 1522 by the Portuguese and by the Dutch in 1607.

Terni (těr'nē), city (pop. 37,295), Umbria, central Italy. Mfg. center (arms, machinery, chemicals; iron and steel plants). Uses hydroelectric power.

Ternopol, Ukraine: see TARNOPOL.

Terpsichore: see MUSES.

terrapin (tě'rŭpĭn), edible fresh-water TURTLE.

Terre Haute (tě'rù hōt'), city (pop. 64,214), W Ind., on Wabash R. and WSW of Indianapolis; settled 1811. Commercial, banking center for farming, mining area. Mfg. of paint, coke by-products, metal products, brick, and tile. Birthplace of E. V. Debs, Theodore Dreiser. Seat of Rose Polytechnic Inst.

Terrell (tě'rŭl), city (pop. 11,544), N Texas, E of Dallas; settled c.1860, laid out 1872. Processes cotton, lumber, wheat, and milk.

terrier, any of a number of alert, lively dogs once bred chiefly for hunting foxes, badgers, rabbits, and rats, but now raised mostly for pets. Terriers are known for their intelligence and their courage which is all out of proportion to their rather small size. One of the best-known terriers is the Airedale, whose tan, wiry coat is marked with a black or dark grizzled saddle. It stands c.22 in. high at the shoulder and weighs 35–40 lb. Resembling the Airedale but smaller (18 in.

high; weighing c.27 lb.) are the Irish terrier, whose wiry coat is of solid color, usually red, red wheaten, or golden red; and the Welsh terrier (15 in. high; weighing c.20 lb.), a black and tan dog, sometimes marked with a saddle like the Airedale's. Fox terriers are of two kinds, the smooth and the wire-haired. Both stand at c.15½ in. at the shoulder, weigh c.18 lb., and are predominantly white marked with black and tan. There are three distinct breeds of schnauzers, the miniature (averaging 12 in. shoulder height), the standard (c.18 in. at shoulder), and the giant (c.24 in. at shoulder). All have wiry coats of pepper-and-salt mixture, solid black, or black and tan. The Scottish terrier or "Scottie" is easily known by its low-slung silhouette, short, strong legs, and rather broad muzzle. Its rough coat is usually black, gray, brindle, or wheaten. Resembling the Scottie in size and shape is the West Highland white terrier whose rather long coat is always white. The Sealyham is low-slung like the Scottie, its body length equal to its shoulder height (c.10½ in.). It weighs c.20 lb. and its wiry topcoat is white or white marked with lemon, tan, or liver. One of the smallest of this general type of dog is the Skye terrier, c.9 in. high at shoulder and weighing c.18 lb. Its body, including head and tail, is c.40 in. long. It is generally blue, gray, or fawn in color with black-tipped hairs c.5½ in. long which almost brush the floor and hang over the eyes. The Bedlington terrier is easily recognized because its head is shaped somewhat like that of a sheep. It is c.15 in. high, weighs c.24 lb., and is usually dark blue, liver, or sandy in color. The Manchester terrier, also known as the black-and-tan terrier, stands c.18 in. high at shoulder and weighs 16–20 lb. With its glossy black and tan coat, it resembles the much larger DOBERMAN PINSCHER. The bull terrier was originally bred for dog fighting in a pit. It is a strong, tenacious dog with a long even muzzle and heavy jaw muscles. The majority of bull terriers weigh over 35 lb. The coat is glossy and pure white, and the nose is black.

territory, in U.S. history, portion of national domain which is given limited self-government, usually in preparation for statehood. ORDINANCE OF 1787 furnished basis for organization of territorial governments. Following Louisiana Purchase U.S. Supreme Court decision gave Congress right to establish territorial governments and to admit territories to the Union. A territory may be admitted as a state after its officers petition Congress for an enabling act, establish a constitution, meet certain requirements set by Congress. Present territories of Hawaii, Puerto Rico, Alaska are supervised by Dept. of the Interior. Each has a nonvoting Congressional delegate.

Terror, Reign of: see REIGN OF TERROR.

Terry, Dame Ellen (Alicia), 1848–1928, English actress, of a prominent theatrical family. With Sir Henry Irving she formed (1878) an acting partnership which lasted over 20 years. Charming and graceful, she was unrivaled in Shaksperian roles.

Tertiary period (tûr′shēē″rē), name given in mid-18th cent. to first and main portion of Cenozoic era. Portion following Tertiary was called Quaternary. Geologists now tend to drop these divisions and to consider the Cenozoic era of one period only, called also Cenozoic. North American outlines were similar to the present, with marine submergence along both coasts and Mississippi valley. There was extensive mountain making in North America with reelevation of existing ranges; in Europe the formation of Alps, Pyrenees, Carpathians, and others; and in Asia, the Himalayas. Volcanic activity was almost continuous. At the beginning mammals replaced reptiles as dominant animals, and modern forms of life soon became numerous—these included modern types of birds, reptiles, amphibians, and invertebrates.

Tertullian (tûrtŭl′yŭn), c.150–c.230, Roman theologian, b. Carthage. He wrote many theological works. Some of his opinions departed from the main course of Christian thought, and the Montanists are sometimes called Tertullianists.

Teruel (těrwěl′), city (pop. 14,377), cap. of Teruel prov., E central Spain, in Aragon, on Guadalaviar R. Agr. trade center. Was almost totally destroyed in civil war of 1936–39, during which it changed hands three times; later rebuilt.

Teschen (tě′shŭn), city and former principality (c.850 sq. mi.), now divided between Czechoslovakia and Poland. As part of Silesia, principality was held by Austria 1526–1918. Has important coal basin. The Conference of Ambassadors (1920) divided disputed territory and city: W section (with coal basin) and W suburb (Český Těšín; pop. 9,986) went to Czechoslovakia; Poland received E section and main part of city (Cieszyn; pop. 16, 536). Poland seized W section Oct., 1938, but status quo as of 1920 was restored in 1945.

Tesla, Nikola (tě′slŭ), 1856–1943, American electrician and inventor, b. Croatia (then in Austria-Hungary). Came to U.S. in 1884. Pioneer in field of high-tension electricity, he made many inventions of great value to development of radio transmission, wireless communication, alternating-current transmission. He designed power system at Niagara.

Test Act, 1673, passed by British Parliament to exclude from office all who refused to take oaths of allegiance and supremacy, to receive communion according to Church of England, and to renounce belief in transubstantiation. Directed mainly against Catholics. Extended to members of Parliament (1678). Repealed at time of Catholic Emancipation.

testament: see NEW TESTAMENT; OLD TESTAMENT; WILL.

testis (tě′stĭs) or **testicle** (tě′stĭkŭl), one of two glands in male functioning in production of sperm and secretion of male hormone testosterone.

Tesuque (těsoō′kä), Indian pueblo village (1948 pop. 162), N central N.Mex., in Sangre de Cristo Mts., N of Santa Fe; present village settled c.1700. Tanoan language. Painting and pottery making. Annual San Diego feast.

tetanus (tě′tŭnŭs) or **lockjaw,** infectious disease caused by bacillus and marked by muscular spasms and difficulty in opening mouth. Fatalities resulting from effect of toxin on heart and breathing muscles are reduced by injection of antitoxin after a wound. Toxoid injections give immunity. See ill., p. 633.

Teterboro (tě′tŭr–), borough (pop. 28), NE N.J., E of Passaic. Freight airport here administered by Port of New York Authority. Called Bendix 1937–43.

Teton (tētŏn′), river, 60 mi. long, rising in W Wyo., in forks which join in SE Idaho. Flows N and W to Henrys Fork R. Early course is through Teton Basin (as Pierre's Hole a haunt of trappers).

Teton Range, branch of Rocky Mts., NW Wyo. and SE Idaho, just S of Yellowstone Natl. Park and W of Jackson L. and Snake R. Largely in Grand Teton Natl. Park (see NATIONAL PARKS AND MONUMENTS, table), and partly in Targhee Natl. Forest. Frequented by mountain men in first half of 19th cent. Topped by Grand Teton (13,766 ft.).

Tetrazzini, Luisa (tětrūzě′nē), 1871–1940, Italian coloratura soprano. She sang with the Manhattan Opera Co., 1908–10; with the Metropolitan Opera, New York, 1911–12. Was especially notable for her brilliant high tones and her range.

Tetuán (tātwän′), city (pop. 93,658), cap. of Spanish Morocco, near the Mediterranean; industrial center of protectorate. Its port is Río Martín. Founded in 14th cent., it was an early Corsair stronghold. Rebuilt 1492 by Jewish refugees from Portugal. Fell 1860 to Spaniards led by Leopoldo O'Donnell; permanently occupied by Spain 1915.

Tetzel, Johann (yō′hän tět′sěl), 1465–1519, German Dominican preacher. He promoted (1516) in Germany a campaign of indulgences and was plunged into a dispute with Martin Luther.

Teutoburg Forest, Ger. *Teutoburger Wald* (toi'tōbōōr"-gŭr vält'), hilly, forested range, Westphalia, NW Germany, largely in former state of Lippe. Monument near Detmold commemorates victory of ARMINIUS over VARUS (A.D. 9), when the Germans annihilated three Roman legions.

Teutones or **Teutons:** see GERMANS.

Teutonic Knights (tōōtŏ'nĭk, tū–) or **German Order,** German military religious order, founded 1090–91 in Holy Land and modeled on those of the Templars and Hospitalers. It rose into prominence when it undertook the conquest of pagan PRUSSIA (1226). Its domains on the Baltic were at first under nominal papal overlordship but in 1466 the knights lost territories to Poland and accepted Polish suzerainty. They were united with the LIVONIAN KNIGHTS 1237–1525. After virtually exterminating the native population, they resettled Prussia with German colonists. Their first seat was MARIENBURG, replaced after 1466 by KÖNIGSBERG. In 1525 Grand Master ALBERT of BRANDENBURG accepted Protestantism and changed the order's domain into the hereditary duchy of Prussia. The order continued in Catholic Germany till 1805; was later revived in Austria as an honorary body. Habit: white robe with black cross embroidered in gold.

Teutonic religion: see GERMANIC RELIGION.

Teviot (tē'vēut, tĕ'–), river, mainly in Roxburghshire, Scotland. Flows 40 mi. NE to the Tweed.

Tewfik Pasha (tū'fĭk), 1852–92, khedive of Egypt (1879–92). Succeeded his father, Ismail Pasha. Under British military pressure he gave up Egypt's claim to full sovereignty over the Sudan, which later came under joint Anglo-Egyptian control.

Tewkesbury (tūks'bŭrē), municipal borough (pop. 5,292), Gloucestershire, England. Site of one of richest and most renowned 12th-cent. Benedictine abbeys. Dramatic festivals are held, a survival of festival plays which began in the 17th cent.

Tewksbury, residential town (pop. 7,505), NE Mass., ESE of Lowell.

Texarkana (tĕx"särkă'nù), city (pop. in Texas, 24,753; in Ark., 15,875), on Texas-Ark. line, settled 1873. Rail center, it ships cotton, livestock, and dairy products. Mfg. of cotton, wood, and clay products, fertilizer, and feeds.

Texas, state (267,339 sq. mi.; pop. 7,711,194), SW U.S.; admitted 1845 as 28th state (slaveholding); cap. AUSTIN. Other cities are HOUSTON, DALLAS, SAN ANTONIO, FORT WORTH, EL PASO, CORPUS CHRISTI, GALVESTON. Bordered S by Gulf of Mexico, SW by the RIO GRANDE. Central Texas has rolling prairies; W are plains, hills; S is Rio Grande Valley; SE are Gulf plains. The Panhandle projects N. Cotton main crop; also livestock, winter wheat, oats, corn, rice, truck, pecans, grain sorghums. Mines petroleum, natural gas, sulphur, salt, clay products, limestone, magnesium, other minerals. Processing of minerals, metals, food, lumber; mfg. of paper, textiles, cement, leather goods, airplanes, ships. Spanish estab. first white settlement at YSLETA in 1681 or 1682. Several American filibustering expeditions were undertaken in early 19th cent. S. F. AUSTIN brought settlers in 1821. In the revolution for independence from Mexico fall of the ALAMO was redeemed by victory of Sam HOUSTON in battle of SAN JACINTO (1836). Texas was independent republic until its annexation to the U.S. (1845), which led to MEXICAN WAR. Joined Confederacy in 1861. Railroads expanded stockraising, increased settlement. Discovery of oil (esp. after 1901) hastened industrialization. Industrial output greatly increased by World War II.

Texas, Agricultural and Mechanical College of, at College Station; land-grant; state supported; for men; chartered 1871, opened 1876. Military plan. Has firemen's training school and radio station. Prairie View Agricultural and Mechanical Col. of Texas (Negro; land-grant; coed.; 1876) is branch.

Texas, University of, mainly at Austin; state supported, coed.; chartered 1881, opened 1883. Research bureaus include anthropology, bio-chemistry, zoology, and economic geology. Has several museums, institute of Latin American studies, observatory, and notable library. Owns rich oil lands. Texas Western Col. (formerly Texas Col. of Mines and Metallurgy; coed.; 1913) is El Paso branch.

Texas Christian University, at Forth Worth; coed.; opened 1873, chartered 1874 by Disciples of Christ. Called Add-Ran Col. or Add-Ran Christian Univ. until 1902; moved to Forth Worth 1910. Has Brite Col. of the Bible.

Texas City, city (pop. 16,620), S Texas, on Galveston Bay NW of Galveston. World War II brought expansion. It has tin smelter, chemical plants, and refineries. Recovered from disastrous fires, blasts from exploding ship (April 16, 1947).

Texas Rangers, mounted fighting force organized (1835) during Texas Revolution. In time of the republic they became estab. as guardians of Texas frontier, particularly against marauding Indians. Served in Mexican War, Civil War. Organized for first time on permanent basis in 1874, their heyday was the period of great cattle business, with its feuds, its outlaws and "rustlers." By act of Texas legislature in 1935, rangers were merged with state highway patrol.

Texas State College for Women: see DENTON.

Texas Technological College: see LUBBOCK.

Texas Western College: see TEXAS, UNIVERSITY OF.

Texcoco, Lake: see MEXICO, city; TENOCHTITLÁN.

Texel (tĕk'sŭl), island (64 sq. mi.; pop. 9,401), North Holland prov., NW Netherlands, in North Sea. Largest and southernmost of West Frisian Isls.

Texoma, Lake: see DENISON DAM.

textiles, all fabrics made by weaving, felting, knitting, braiding, or netting. They can be classified according to their component fibers as SILK, WOOL, LINEN, and COTTON, synthetics such as RAYON and NYLON, and some inorganic substances, such as cloth of gold, and glass and asbestos cloth. Fabrics are also classed as to structure according to the manner in which warp and weft cross each other in the loom (see WEAVING). Modern textile manufacture is mostly carried on in factories with power machinery, but many fine fabrics are still made by hand. Textile tools have been found among the earliest relics of human habitation. Exquisite fabrics have been made in many lands since antiquity; basic processes have not changed since about the 14th cent., though equipment and methods have altered.

Th, chemical symbol of the element THORIUM.

Thackeray, William Makepeace, 1811–63, English novelist, b. India. Went to England in 1817. Traveled on Continent in 1830 and then studied law. In 1836 he married and, having lost his patrimony, was forced to do literary hack work. Tragedy struck in 1841 when his wife became hopelessly insane. During the 1830s and '40s he did miscellaneous magazine writing, such as the satiric "Yellowplush Correspondence" in *Frazer's Magazine* in 1837–38, and wrote novels which appeared serially. In 1848 his satirical *Book of Snobs* and the novel *Vanity Fair,* his masterpiece, won him fame. This grew with the novels *Pendennis* (1850), *Henry Esmond* (1852), *The Newcomes* (1853–55), and *The Virginians* (1857–59). In 1851 and 1852–53 he lectured in England and in the U.S. on *English Humorists of the Eighteenth Century.* A satirical and disillusioned man, Thackeray wrote parodies of and satires against romantic sentiment, expressing the futility and vanity of human life.

Thaddaeus, apostle: see JUDE, SAINT.

Thailand (tī'lănd) or **Siam** (sīam'), kingdom (197,242 sq. mi.; pop. 17,324,291), SE Asia, between Burma and Indo-China, and extending S into Malay Peninsula; cap. Bangkok. The heart of the country is the central plain, where much rice is grown. The mountainous NW area has teak forests, while the peninsular section is mostly jungle, with tin, tungsten, and rubber production. Fisheries are important along the coast. The population, mostly Buddhist, includes Chinese, Malays, Annamese, Cambodians, Mons, and Negritos, as well as the dominant Thai or Siamese. In 11th cent., part of the country fell to the KHMER EMPIRE. History of modern Siam began when the Khmers were expelled in 13th cent. and a rising Thai dynasty made its capital at Ayuthia. Arrival of Portuguese traders and missionaries in 16th cent. marked the beginning of Siam's relations with the West. Her independence was threatened in 19th cent. by the British and the French, but the Siamese managed to remain free by bringing in Western advisers and by playing off British against French interests. Even so, Siam lost its claims to Cambodia, Laos, and other territories. The Chakkri dynasty (founded 1782 and still in power today) produced some able monarchs, including Mongkut (reigned 1851–68) and Chulalongkorn (reigned 1868–1910), who introduced economic and social reforms. Politically, however, Siam continued as an absolute monarchy until 1932, when a coup d'état forced Prajadhipok (reigned 1925–35) to grant a constitution. But the trend toward democratization was checked in 1938 by the rise of the militarist Gen. Luang Pibul Songgram (later known as Phibun Songgram) in the reign of Ananda (1935–46). He was ousted in 1944 but returned to power in 1947. Occupied by Japanese troops in Dec., 1941, Thailand was allied with Japan in World War II. Phumiphon succeeded to the throne in 1950.

Thaïs (thā′ĭs, tä′ēs), 4th cent. B.C., legendary Athenian courtesan, said to have been mistress of Alexander the Great and Ptolemy I.

Thaïs, 4th cent. A.D., legendary Alexandrian courtesan, supposed to have been converted to Christianity by St. Paphnutius or by Bessarion.

Thales (thā′lēz) c.636–c.546 B.C., Greek philosopher, called the first Greek philosopher. Thought water the origin of all things.

Thalia, one of the MUSES: also one of the GRACES.

thallium (thă′lēŭm), rare, soft, malleable, metallic element (symbol = Tl; see also ELEMENT, table). Salts are poisons. Metal is used in alloys with lead and other metals and in making optical glass.

Thames (tĕmz), principal river of England. Rising in Gloucestershire in four headstreams (the Thames or Isis, the Churn, the Coln, and the Leach), it bounds part of nine counties and flows through London to enter the North Sea at the Nore. Joined by canals (including Oxford, Thames, Severn, and Grand Junction), it is navigable by barges to Lechlade, Gloucestershire. Part near London Bridge is called the Pool. Port of London extends from London Bridge to Blackwall. Docks and tidal area are administered by Port of London Authority. River's total length is 210 mi.; its width at Gravesend is 2,700 ft. Up to London the Thames valley is mainly agr. and, in parts, very beautiful; much used for boating.

Thames (thāmz, tĕmz), tidal estuary, E Conn. Extends 15 mi. S from Norwich to Long Isl. Sound at New London, whose harbor it forms. Scene of annual Yale–Harvard rowing contests since 1878.

Thames, battle of the, Oct. 5, 1813, in War of 1812, fought near Chatham on Thames R. in S Ont., Canada, which rises NNW of Woodstock and flows 163 mi. SW to L. St. Clair, WSW of Chatham. American forces under Gen. W. H. Harrison defeated British army, reinforced by Indians under Tecumseh. Victory restored U.S. control in Northwest.

Thanet, Isle of (thă′nĭt), island forming NE part of Kent, England. There are many seaside resorts.

Thanksgiving Day, national holiday in U.S. commemorating harvest of Plymouth Colony in 1621, following a winter of great hardship. Colonists and neighboring Indians shared the first feast. First national celebration, proclaimed by George Washington, Nov. 26, 1789. Lincoln revived the custom in 1863.

Since 1941, according to a joint resolution of Congress, holiday falls on fourth Thursday in Nov. Customary turkey is reminder of four wild turkeys served at Pilgrims' first Thanksgiving.

Thasos (thā′sŏs), Aegean island (170 sq. mi.; pop. 13,829), Greece, off Macedonia. Olive oil, wine, timber, lead-zinc ores. In legend Thasus, son of Poseidon, led earliest colonists here. The ancient Phoenicians exploited island's famous gold mines. Parians colonized it 708 B.C. Later came under Persia and Athens. Held by Genoese and Venetians 14th–15th cent.

Thaxter, Celia (Laighton), 1835–94, American poet, known especially for *Drift-Weed* (1879). This and her prose *Among the Isles of Shoals* (1873) mirror life along her native N.H. coast.

Thayer, Abbott Handerson, 1849–1921, American painter, known for idealized figures of women.

Théâtre Français: see COMÉDIE FRANÇAISE.

Theatre Guild, organization formed in 1919 by members of the Washington Square Players, New York city. Financed largely by subscription. Has successfully presented works of such dramatists as Shaw, O'Neill, Molnar, and S. N. Behrman.

Thebes (thēbz), city of anc. Egypt, on the site occupied later by Karnak and Luxor. Magnificent ruins recall the rise of the XI dynasty, which made Thebes, the center of Amon worship, important (c.2160 B.C.). Thebes remained important for many centuries. It was sacked by Assyrians (661 B.C.) and Romans (29 B.C.). It is biblical No.

Thebes, anc. city of Boeotia, Greece. Prominent in Greek legends (see CADMUS, OEDIPUS, SEVEN AGAINST THEBES, EPIGONI). Jealous of Athens, Thebes favored the Persians in the Persian Wars, the Spartans in the Peloponnesian War. Afraid of Sparta later, Thebes joined the confederacy against Sparta, and, under Pelopidas, Thebans won independence (379 B.C.), guaranteed by the victory of Epaminondas at Leuctra (371 B.C.). Thebes joined Athens against Philip II of Macedon and shared in the defeat at Chaeronea (338 B.C.). A revolt against Alexander the Great brought destruction of the city (336 B.C.). The modern Thevai or Thivai occupies part of the site.

The Dalles (dălz), inland port city (pop. 7,676), N Oregon, on Columbia R. and E of Portland. Grew c.1852 around fort on mission (1838–47) site. Canal with locks (1908–15) by-passes river's rapids. Downstream, ships also use locks (1937) at Bonneville Dam. Processes and ships grain, fruit, wool, livestock, salmon, and lumber.

The Dells: see DELLS OF THE WISCONSIN.

Theiler, Max, 1899–, American research physician, b. South Africa. Won 1951 Nobel Prize in Physiology and Medicine for his work in developing the first effective vaccine (called 17-D) against yellow fever. Associated with Harvard (1922–29) and with Rockefeller Inst. for Medical Research (1930–).

theine: see CAFFEINE.

Theiss (tīs), Hung. *Tisza,* river, c.800 mi. long, rising in the Carpathians and flowing S across Hungary to join the Danube above Belgrade, Yugoslavia. Navigable in part.

Thematic Apperception Test: see MENTAL TESTS.

Themis (thē′mĭs), in Greek religion, a Titaness, goddess of law and order; daughter of Uranus and Gaea and mother by Zeus of the Horae and Fates.

Themistocles (thŭmy′stŭklēz), c.525–c.460 B.C., Athenian statesman. In the PERSIAN WARS he persuaded the Athenians to build a navy. Though he could not prevent the Persians from taking Athens, it was his strategy that triumphed in the naval victory at Salamis (480 B.C.) and his foresight that built the strength of Athens. Died in exile in Persia.

Theocritus (thēŏ′krĭtŭs), fl. c.270 B.C., Alexandrian Greek poet. The pastoral begins with him. His poetic form is finished, his characters realistic. His idyls— much imitated—show his sensitivity to nature.

Theodora (thēŭdô′rŭ) d. 548, Byzantine empress, wife

of JUSTINIAN I. She suppressed the *Nika* sedition (532; see BLUES AND GREENS) and determined many of her husband's religious policies. The account of her origins and early career as a circus and dancing girl in the *Secret History* of Procopius is probably spitefully colored.

Theodore, Russian rulers: see FEODOR.

Theodore of Mopsuestia (mŏp"sūēs'chù), c.350–428, Syrian theologian; friend of St. John Chrysostom. Wrote historical, rationalistic commentaries on the Bible. Some of his writings were influenced by monarchianism. Nestorius was his pupil.

Theodore of Studium, Saint, 759–826, Byzantine monastic reformer. His reforms at the monastery of Studium had a lasting effect on the Basilian monks. He opposed iconoclasm and was thrice exiled for stiff-necked opposition by three emperors, Constantine VI, Nicephorus I, and Leo V. Feast: Nov. 12.

Theodore Roosevelt National Memorial Park: see NATIONAL PARKS AND MONUMENTS (table).

Theodoric I (thēŏd'ŭrĭk) or **Thierry I** (tērē', tēĕr'ē), d. 534, Frankish king of Austrasia (511–34); son of Clovis I. Divided his brother Clodomer's kingdom of Orléans with his brothers Childebert I and Clotaire I. Subjugated Thuringians with Clotaire.

Theodoric the Great, c.454–526, king of the OSTROGOTHS (c.474–526). Under Emperor ZENO, he was made imperial master of soldiers (483) and consul (484) and was sent to Italy to fight ODOACER (488). He repeatedly defeated Odoacer, took Ravenna (493), had Odoacer murdered after accepting his surrender, and took the title "governor of the Romans." His rule in Italy was beneficent, and he respected Roman institutions. His last years were clouded by a quarrel with the pope over his Arianism and by his hasty execution of BOETHIUS and Symmachas. His tomb is one of Ravenna's finest monuments.

Theodosia, RSFSR: see FEODOSIYA.

Theodosian Code (thē"ùdō'shùn), Roman legal code issued by Theodosius II, emperor of the East (A.D. 438). Based on Gregorian and Hermogenian codes; used in making the *Corpus Juris Civilis.*

Theodosius, Roman emperors. **Theodosius I** (the Great), 346?–395, son of the general Theodosius, was chosen by Emperor Gratian to rule the East as co-Augustus (379). He made an advantageous peace with the Visigoths. When Gratian's legal successor in the West, Valentinian II, was deposed in 387 by Maximus (Gratian's assassin), Theodosius invaded Italy, slew the usurper, and restored Valentinian (388). He again entered Italy when Valentinian was strangled, presumably by order of ARBOGAST, who installed the puppet emperor Eugenius (392). Claiming the succession of the West, Theodosius defeated the pagan army of Eugenius and Arbogast in a two-day battle (394). His death, however, left the Roman Empire permanently divided. His sons Arcadius and Honorius succeeded him, respectively, in the East and West. Theodosius rooted out ARIANISM and called the First Council of CONSTANTINOPLE. When St. AMBROSE excommunicated him for the massacre of the rebellious citizens of Salonica (390), the emperor humbly did penance in Milan Cathedral. **Theodosius II,** 401–50, emperor of the East (408–50), summoned the Council of EPHESUS (431), upheld the Robber Synod (449; see EUTYCHES), and published the THEODOSIAN CODE (438). During his reign ATTILA invaded the empire and obtained heavy tribute.

Theognis (thēŏg'nĭs), fl. late 6th cent. B.C., Greek didactic poet of Megara. His elegies, often passionate in hate and love, counsel moderation and faithfulness.

Theophilus (thēŏ'fĭlùs), person addressed at beginning of Gospel according to St. Luke and the Acts of the Apostles. Luke 1.3; Acts 1.1.

Theophrastus (thē"ofrä'stùs), c.372–c.287 B.C., Greek philosopher, successor to Aristotle as head of the Peripatetic school. His *Characters,* sketches of various types, was imitated by later writers (e.g., La Bruyère).

theosophy (thēŏ'sùfē), any philosophical system starting with mystical belief in the pervading force of infinite divinity (God) in the universe, with evil the result of man's devotion to finite goals. The Neoplatonists and the Cabalists had theosophical systems, as did Jacob Boehme. More specifically, theosophy is the movement fostered by Helena Petrovna BLAVATSKY in the late 19th cent., based largely on Indian philosophy and stressing the latent spiritual power of man, refined by various transmigrations of the soul and enlightened by occult knowledge. Annie BESANT wrote much on theosophy.

The Pas (thù päz'), town (pop. 3,376), W Man., Canada, on the Saskatchewan and SSE of Flin Flon. Trade center for mining and fur-trapping region.

Thera (thēr'ù), volcanic island (31 sq. mi.; pop. 9,704), Greece, in Aegean Sea; one of the Cyclades. Wine, pumice stone. Prehistoric and classical remains have been excavated.

Theresa, Saint (Theresa of Jesus), Span. *Teresa de Ávila,* 1515–82, Spanish Carmelite nun, one of the chief women saints; originally named Teresa de Cepeda y Ahumada; of a well-to-do family. She founded (1562) a convent of Discalced Carmelites in Ávila and later many other convents. A friend of St. John of the Cross, she combined her talents with his to advance the Catholic Reform, bringing about a remarkable awakening of religious fervor—a movement that finally spread far beyond Spain. Her writings, in simple, earth-born language, are some of the greatest in mystical literature. Among them are her spiritual autobiography (written 1562–65), supplementary *Relations, The Way of Perfection, The Interior Castle, Foundations* (1573–82), *Exclamations of the Soul to God* (1569), and *Constitutions* (for the Discalced Carmelites). Also Teresa.

Theresa, Saint (Theresa of the Child Jesus), Fr. *Thérèse de Lisieux,* 1873–97, French Carmelite nun, one of the most beloved of Roman Catholic saints, called the Little Flower of Jesus; originally named Thérèse Martin. Her complete and shining goodness is reflected in her much-read spiritual autobiography. She taught the Little Way—sanctity through humble tasks. Her cryptic promise, "After my death I will let fall a shower of roses," is recalled by statues showing her with an armful of roses. Also Teresa.

Thermidor (Fr. tĕrmēdôr'), 11th month of French Revolutionary calendar. The coup d'état of 9 Thermidor (July 27, 1794) marked the downfall of ROBESPIERRE and the end of the Great Terror. The Thermidorian leaders (Barras, Cambacérès, Sieyès, Tallien) took reprisals against the Terrorists (though some had themselves taken part in the Terror); repealed the maximum-price laws; made a truce with the counterrevolutionists in the Vendée. The period of "Thermidorian reaction" ended with the establishment of the DIRECTORY (1795).

thermometer, instrument for measuring TEMPERATURE. Fahrenheit thermometer (developed by G. D. Fahrenheit) initiated mercury as heat-measuring medium; Réaumur thermometer (invented by R. A. F. de Réaumur) used alcohol. Centigrade or Celsius thermometer (invented by Anders Celsius) is most commonly used in laboratories. Clinical thermometer is small, uses mercury, and is marked with Fahrenheit or Centigrade scales. Maximum and minimum thermometers indicate highest and lowest temperatures during period of exposure. For low temperatures alcohol, ether, and toluol are used; for very high, there are special devices that work on principle of measurable change varying with temperature (e.g., electrical resistance).

Thermopolis (thùrmŏ'pùlĭs), town (pop. 2,870), N central Wyo., on Bighorn R. Resort with hot springs. Near by is Wind River Canyon.

Thermopylae (thùrmŏ'pĭlē), pass between Mt. Oeta and the swamps of the shore of the Malic Gulf, Greece. Here in 480 B.C. Leonidas and his Spartans and their allies fought against the Persians to the last man (see PERSIAN WARS). The Greeks long held back the Gauls under Brennus at this pass in 279 B.C., and the Romans defeated Antiochus III of Syria in 191 B.C.

thermostat, device for automatically regulating temperature. Is commonly connected to heating systems which it turns on or off, according to need, to maintain predetermined temperature. Principle of operation is based on expansion of metals, liquids, and gases when heated; movement of component substance as it takes expanded or contracted position actuates a control on a furnace, cooling system, or piece of machinery.

Thersander (thûrsăn′dûr), in Greek legend, son of POLYNICES. The Epigoni made him king of Thebes.

Theseus (thē′sūs, –sēus), in Greek mythology, hero of Athens; son of AEGEUS, king of Athens. He had many adventures, e.g., slaying of the bull of Marathon and the Minotaur of Crete (with Ariadne's help). He succeeded his father as king of Athens. After participating in expedition against the Amazons and in Calydonian hunt he married Phaedra, who caused death of his son, HIPPOLYTUS.

Thespis (thē′spĭs), fl. 534 B.C., in Greek tradition, the inventor of tragedy. He modified the dithyramb so as to introduce a second actor.

Thessalonians (thĕ″sŭlō′nēŭnz), epistles of New Testament, called 1 and 2 Thessalonians, written by St. Paul to church at Thessalonica. In 1 Thessalonians, Paul praises the church for the strength of its faith but corrects certain misconceptions that had arisen regarding the Second Coming of Christ. In 2 Thessalonians, Paul strongly condemns these false notions. Authenticity of apocalyptic passages (1.6–10 and 2.1–12) questioned by some critics.

Thessalonica, Thessalonike, or **Thessaloniki,** Greece: see SALONICA.

Thessaly (thĕ′sŭlē), region of N Greece. In ancient times the mountain-girt plains yielded grain, horses, and cattle. Jason, tyrant of Pherae, briefly united it with other cities, Larissa and Crannon (374 B.C.), but Thessaly fell to Philip II of Macedon in 344 B.C. A province in the late Roman Empire, it passed to the Venetians (1204), the Turks (1355), and modern Greece (1881).

Thetford, municipal borough (pop. 4,445), Norfolk, England. Here is Castle Hill, one of Great Britain's largest earthworks.

Thetford Mines, city (pop. 15,095), SE Que., Canada, S of Quebec. Asbestos-mining center.

Thetis (thē′tĭs), in Greek legend, a nereid; mother of Achilles. Because of a prophecy that her son would be greater than his father, Zeus and Poseidon, who loved her, gave her to a mortal, PELEUS.

thiamine: see VITAMINS.

Thiaucourt (tyōkōor′), village (1946 pop. 995), NE France, in Lorraine, NW of Nancy. Captured by American troops (Sept., 1918) in World War I; now site of Saint-Mihiel American cemetery.

Thibault, Jacques Anatole: see FRANCE, ANATOLE.

Thibodaux (tĭ′bŭdō), town (pop. 7,730) SE La., on Bayou Lafourche and SW of New Orleans, in oil and sugar area. Chief Justice White born near by.

Thief River Falls, city (pop. 6,926), NW Minn., at junction of Thief and Red Lake rivers. Farm trade center. Near-by tracts were used in Federal resettlement project for farm families.

Thierry I, Frankish king: see THEODORIC I.

Thierry, Augustin (ōgüstĕ′ tyĕrē′), 1795–1856, French historian. Chief work is Récits des temps mérovingiens (1870).

Thiers, Adolphe (ädôlf′ tyĕr′), 1797–1877, French statesman, journalist, and historian. In the opposition against Charles X he represented the middle-of-the-road Doctrinaires or bourgeois liberals. His journal Le National helped to bring about the JULY REVOLUTION of 1830. Under Louis Philippe he was minister

of the interior (1832–34) and twice premier (1836, 1840), then passed to the opposition. He was a leader of the right-wing liberals in the Second Republic and Second Empire; voted against declaring war on Prussia (1870); was chosen, during the FRANCO-PRUSSIAN WAR, chief executive of the provisional government. After negotiating the preliminary Peace of Versailles with Bismarck, he suppressed the COMMUNE OF PARIS of 1871 with ferocious severity and was named president of the republic. Though an Orleanist at heart, he sought to conciliate the republican minority in the national assembly and was forced to resign by the monarchists. MacMahon succeeded him. Thiers' historic works—History of the French Revolution (10 vols., 1823–27; Eng. tr., 5 vols., 1895); History of the Consulate and the Empire (20 vols., 1840–55; Eng. tr., 1845–62)—hail the French Revolution and Napoleon and reflect his somewhat shallow liberalism.

Thionville (työvēl′), Ger. Diedenhofen, town (pop. 15,-195), Moselle dept., NE France, in a rich iron-mining district. Scene of a Prussian victory over Bazaine (1870).

Third Republic: see FRANCE.

Thirteen Colonies, the, term used for colonies of British North America that joined in American Revolution and became the United States. They were New Hampshire, Massachusetts, Rhode Island, Connecticut, New York, New Jersey, Pennsylvania, Delaware, Maryland, Virginia, North Carolina, South Carolina, and Georgia.

Thirty-nine Articles: see CREED.

Thirty Tyrants, oligarchy organized at Athens after Sparta had won the Peloponnesian War (404 B.C.). Lysander was its leader. They were overthrown by Thrasybulus (403 B.C.).

Thirty Years War, 1618–48, general European war, fought mainly in Germany. There were many issues —territorial, dynastic, religious—and throughout the war there were shifting alliances and local peace treaties. The whole conflict can be understood only as the struggle of a number of German princes, backed by foreign powers such as France, Sweden, Denmark, and England, against the unity of the Holy Roman Empire and the house of Hapsburg, which then ruled Spain, the empire, Austria, Bohemia, Hungary, most of Italy, and the S Netherlands. The war began when the Protestant Bohemian nobles deposed King Ferdinand (later Emperor Ferdinand II) and elected FREDERICK THE WINTER KING in his stead. The imperialist forces under TILLY and the Catholic League under Duke MAXIMILIAN I of Bavaria defeated the Bohemians at the White Mt. (1620) and were victorious in the Palatinate over Mansfeld and Christian of Brunswick (1622–23), but the intervention of CHRISTIAN IV of Denmark on the "Protestant" side opened a new phase. Defeated by Tilly and WALLENSTEIN, the Danes by the Treaty of Lübeck withdrew from the war (1629). A new issue was brought up in 1629, when Ferdinand II attempted to enforce the Peace of AUGSBURG of 1555 and to confiscate lands that had been secularized after 1552. GUSTAVUS II of Sweden, backed by France, marched into Germany, defeated the imperials at Breitenfeld (1631), on the Lech (1632), and at Lützen (1632); though he was killed in his last victory, the Swedes continued in the war. The tide seemed to turn in 1634, when the imperials won the great victory of Nördlingen. A compromise peace was concluded among the German states at Prague (1635). To prevent an imperial victory and the expulsion of the Swedes, France now openly joined Sweden, and the war entered its last and bloodiest phase, spreading to the Low Countries, Italy, the Iberian Peninsula, and Scandinavia. BERNHARD OF SAXE-WEIMAR, the Swedes BANÉR, TORSTENSSON, and WRANGEL, and the French under Louis II de CONDÉ and TURENNE were, despite temporary setbacks, victorious. Peace negotiations began 1640 but the fighting continued until the Peace of WESTPHALIA (1648) and—in the case of France and Spain—until the Peace of the PYRENEES (1659). Germany was in ruins, depopulated and starving. The Holy Roman Empire became a hollow shell. The house of Austria began its decline. France emerged as the chief power of Europe.

Thisbe: see PYRAMUS AND THISBE.

thistle, spiny, usually weedy plant with showy flower heads (purple, rose, yellow, or white), and thistledown seeds. The Scotch thistle (*Onopordum acanthium*) is the emblem of Scotland. The blessed thistle or St.-Benedict's-thistle (*Cnicus benedictus*), an ancient heal-all, is sometimes grown in gardens. Other thistles are the bull thistle (*Cirsium lanceolatum*) and a pernicious weed, Canada thistle (*C. arvense*).

Thistlewood, Arthur, 1770–1820, English conspirator. Plotted to assassinate cabinet members. Government (warned of plan) discovered arsenal in Cato Street. He was executed. Plot is known as Cato Street Conspiracy.

Thököly or **Tököly, Emeric** (both: tû′kûē), Hung. *Thököly Imre,* 1665–1705, Hungarian nobleman. Commanded Hungarian uprising against Austrian rule; received French subsidies; persuaded Sultan Mohammed IV to undertake siege of VIENNA (1683). He later was interned near Constantinople.

Thomas, Saint, one of the Twelve Apostles, called Didymus [Gr.,= twin]. He doubted the Resurrection until he saw Jesus and touched His side. John 11.16; 14.5; 20.24–29; 21.2. Feast: Dec. 21. Among the pseudepigrapha are a Gospel and an Acts of Thomas.

Thomas, Albert (älbĕr′ tômä′), 1878–1932, French Socialist. Held cabinet positions in World War I; directed International Labor Office (1919–32).

Thomas, Ambroise (tômä′), 1811–96, French composer of numerous ballets and 20 operas, of which *Mignon, Le Caïd,* and *Hamlet* were the most successful.

Thomas, Augustus (tŏ′mŭs), 1857–1934, American dramatist. Highly popular plays include *Alabama* (1891), *The Witching Hour* (1907), *The Copperhead* (1918).

Thomas, Dylan (Marlais) (dĭ′lŭn), 1914–, British poet, b. Wales. His fresh, exuberant poems have caused him to be considered one of the most important of living poets. His *Collected Poems* appeared in 1952.

Thomas, George Henry, 1816–70, Union general in Civil War. In CHATTANOOGA CAMPAIGN his stand on Sept. 20, 1863, won him sobriquet Rock of Chickamauga. He commanded Army of the Cumberland, fought under Sherman in Atlanta campaign.

Thomas, M(artha) Carey, 1857–1935, American educator and feminist. In 1884 she organized Bryn Mawr, serving as dean until 1894 and then as president until 1922. She was president (1906–13) of Natl. Collegiate Equal Suffrage League.

Thomas, Norman M(attoon), 1884–, American Socialist leader. Often Socialist party candidate for President since 1928.

Thomas, Seth, 1785–1859, American clock manufacturer. Estab. 1812 at Plymouth Hollow (later Thomaston), Conn., factory enlarged by son **Seth Thomas,** 1816–88.

Thomas, Theodore, 1835–1905, American conductor, b. Germany; came to the U.S. 1845. He conducted his own orchestra (founded 1862) with which he toured the country; the New York Philharmonic, 1877–78 and after 1880; and the Chicago Orchestra, 1891–1905. He introduced major works of Brahms, Wagner, and Richard Strauss to American audiences and did much to create an interest in music.

Thomas à Becket, Saint, 1117–70, English martyr, archbishop of Canterbury. Of good family and well educated, he attracted the attention of Henry II, who made him chancellor (1155). Then, contrary to Thomas's wishes, he was made archbishop, after being ordained and consecrated (1162). King and archbishop were then opposed, particularly over the king's effort to gain jurisdiction over "criminous clerks"

(i.e., clergymen accused of crime). Thomas refused to accept the Constitutions of Clarendon (1164) and opposed the growing royal power. He fled to the Continent (1164). In 1170 a sort of peace was patched up, and Thomas returned to England. Meanwhile, Henry had had his son crowned by the archbishop of York. The bishops who took part in the ceremony were suspended by the pope. Feeling between king and archbishop grew high. Thomas was on Dec. 29, 1170, murdered in the cathedral by partisans of Henry, who may or may not have known of the plot to kill Thomas. In 1174 the king was forced to do penance at the tomb of St. Thomas in Canterbury, which became the greatest of English shrines. Feast: Dec. 29. Also Thomas Becket.

Thomas à Kempis, b. 1379 or 1380, d. 1471, German monk, b. Kempen, author or copyist of the devotional work, *The Following* (or *Imitation*) *of Christ,* possibly an adaptation of a work by Gerard GROOTE.

Thomas Aquinas, Saint (ŭkwī′nŭs), 1225–74, Italian philosopher, known as the Angelic Doctor; of the ruling family of Aquino, S Italy. A Dominican, he became the favorite pupil of Albertus Magnus at Paris and in 1248 went to Cologne with Albertus. He returned to Paris, where he was professor of theology. He opposed the Averroistic philosophy of Siger de Brabant successfully. He spent his last years at Naples. Called the Dumb Ox because he was slow and heavy, he was nevertheless the most brilliant of scholastic philosophers. His major work is the *Summa theologica* (1267–73), an incomplete but systematic exposition of theology on rational principles. Thomas, holding that theology and science cannot contradict each other since truth is indivisible, set out to reconcile Aristotelian philosophy and Christian belief. His synthesis of these is one of the greatest achievements of philosophy and the highest point of SCHOLASTICISM. He held to the distinction between form and matter—erased only in God himself. He argued that a thing that needs completion by another is in a state of potency. Everything is arranged in ascending order to God, who combines potency and act. To Thomas, evil is only the absence of good. Long misunderstood in the Church, he was finally accepted and his philosophy, Thomism, was declared official by Leo XIII (1879). This does not mean that all Catholics must subscribe to Thomistic doctrines, but they are held in respect by all Catholic believers. Neo-Thomism is a 20th-cent. school of thought both within and outside the Church, applying the principles of St. Thomas Aquinas to modern economic, social, and political problems. Prominent in the movement have been Jacques Maritain, Étienne Gilson, and Mortimer Adler. Feast: March 7.

Thomas Jefferson Memorial, monument, Washington, D.C., in East Potomac Park and on Tidal Basin; dedicated 1943. Building is of white marble in modified Pantheon form. Inside is a statue of Jefferson by Rudulph Evans.

Thomas More, Saint: see MORE, SIR THOMAS.

Thomaston (tŏ′mŭstŭn), city (pop. 6,580), W central Ga., W of Macon near Flint R. Textile center in agr. (cotton, peaches) and livestock area.

Thomasville. 1 City (pop. 14,424), SW Ga., near Fla. line and Ochlockonee R.; founded 1826. Processing center for agr. (cotton, fruit, vegetables, peanuts), livestock, and timber area. Winter resort in section of large estates and gardens. **2** City (pop. 11,154), central N.C., SE of Winston-Salem. Mfg. of furniture and textiles.

Thompson, Benjamin: see RUMFORD, BENJAMIN THOMPSON, COUNT.

Thompson, David, 1770–1857, Canadian geographer, fur trader, and explorer, b. England. Made important map of W Canada. Explored Columbia R. region.

Thompson, Denman, 1833–1911, American actor, author of rural drama *The Old Homestead* (1886).

Thompson, Ernest Seton: see SETON.

Thompson, Francis, 1859–1907, English Roman Catholic poet. Abandoning medicine, he lived in poverty, ill and an opium addict, until in 1888 Wilfrid and Alice Meynell took care of him. His poetry, in three slender volumes—*Poems* (1893), including "The Hound of Heaven"; *Sister Songs* (1895); and *New Poems* (1897)—reveals a deep religious sense, expressed in brilliant imagery and sonorous language.

Thompson, town (pop. 5,585), extreme NE Conn., at R.I. and Mass. lines. Has mfg. of textiles.

Thompson, river of S B.C., Canada, formed by junction of the North Thompson and South Thompson at Kamloops and flowing W and S to the Fraser at Lytton. Discovered 1808 by Simon Fraser.

Thompsonville, Conn.: see ENFIELD.

Thomsen, Vilhelm (vĭl′hĕlm tŏm′sĕn), 1842–1927, Danish philologist. Deciphered bilingual Turkish-Chinese inscription found on Orkhon R. in Mongolia.

Thomson, Sir George Paget: see THOMSON, SIR JOSEPH JOHN.

Thomson, James, 1700–1748, British poet, b. Scotland. Most notable work is blank-verse poem, *The Seasons* ("Winter," 1726; "Summer," 1727; "Spring," 1728; collected, with "Autumn," 1730). Also wrote plays, e.g., *Coriolanus* (produced 1749), and, with David Mallet, masque *Alfred* (1840), containing the famous ode, "Rule Britannia." His poetry, first to challenge 18th-cent. classicism, influenced later poets such as Gray and Cowper.

Thomson, James, 1834–82, British poet and essayist, who used the pseudonym B. V. (Bysshe Vanolis). Noted for darkly pessimistic poem *The City of Dreadful Night* (1880) and lyrics such as "Sunday up the River." Also wrote essays and much criticism.

Thomson, Joseph, 1858–95, Scottish explorer in Africa. Explored Great Rift Valley lakes (1879). Explored Sudan (1885), forestalling German designs on area by concluding treaties with natives for British. In 1890 he explored Zambezi R.

Thomson, Sir Joseph John, 1856–1940. English physicist. Won 1906 Nobel Prize for study of electrical conduction through gases; known also for discovery of electron, study of its mass and charge, development of mathematical theory of electricity and magnetism, and work in radioactivity. His son, **Sir George Paget Thomson,** 1892–, also a physicist, shared the 1937 Nobel Prize for discovery of diffraction phenomena in the electron.

Thomson, Virgil, 1896–, American music critic and composer. Among his works are the opera *Four Saints in Three Acts* (1928; libretto by Gertrude Stein) and film music, including *The Plough That Broke the Plains* (1936), *The River* (1937), and *Louisiana Story* (1948). Music critic for the New York *Herald Tribune* after 1940.

Thomson, William: see KELVIN, WILLIAM THOMSON, 1st BARON.

Thor (thôr), in Germanic religion, Norse god of thunder, hence of might and war; son of Odin. Armed with magical hammer that returned to him, belt of strength, and iron gloves, he warred on giants. His chariot wheels made the thunder. He was kind to humanity and protected marriage. His was chief cult among Norsemen. Identification with Jupiter resulted in translation of *Jove's Day* into *Thursday*.

Thoreau, Henry David (thô′rō, thŭrō′), 1817–62, American poet, naturalist, and essayist. A native of Concord, Mass., he was a transcendentalist and an intimate friend of Emerson. Wrote for the *Dial*. A strong individualist, he lived for two years in a cabin at Walden Pond; from this experience came his best-known and classic work, *Walden* (1854). Other works are *A Week on the Concord and Merrimack Rivers* (1849), *The Maine Woods* (1863), and *Cape Cod* (1865). He was a powerful social critic, and his essay "Civil Disobedience" inspired such men as Gandhi. More famous now than in his own time, he and his ideas have been widely influential.

Thorfinn Karlsefni (thôr′fĭn kärl′sĕvnē), fl. 1002–10, Icelandic leader of attempt to colonize North America. Sought VINLAND; returned to Greenland after three winters. There is disagreement on the dates of his expedition and sites visited.

thorium (thô′rēŭm), gray, metallic, radioactive element (symbol = Th; see also ELEMENT, table). Undergoes disintegration, final product is an isotope of lead. Present in number of minerals. Is a source of atomic energy; some salts are used in medicine.

Thorn, Poland: see TORUN.

Thorndike, Ashley H(orace), 1871–1933, American educator and scholar, professor of English at Columbia Univ. from 1906. Wrote distinguished studies on the drama (e.g., *Tragedy,* 1908; *Shakespeare's Theater,* 1916). A brother, **Edward L(ee) Thorndike,** 1874–1949, was an educator and psychologist at Teachers Col., Columbia (1899–1940). Made important contributions to educational psychology in methods to test and measure intelligence. Another brother, **Lynn Thorndike,** 1882–, became a historian, professor at Columbia after 1924. Known especially for studies on magic and early science.

Thorndike, Dame Sybil, 1882–, English actress. Won acclaim for her Shaksperian portrayals and in such plays as *Medea, Candida,* and *Saint Joan.*

Thornton, William, 1759–1828, American architect, b. Tortola, British Virgin Isls. Received his medical degree in Scotland and came to U.S. in 1787. Though untrained as an architect he submitted a plan for the Capitol at Washington which was accepted in 1793. E. S. Hallet and James Hoban were the original supervisors, but Thornton himself was in charge 1794–1802. Served as commissioner of patents from 1802 until his death.

Thorold, town (pop. 6,397), S Ont., Canada, on Welland Ship Canal and SE of St. Catharines. Paper, pulp, and lumber mills and abrasive works.

thorough bass: see FIGURED BASS.

Thorpe, James, 1888–1953, U.S. athlete. All-American left-halfback at Carlisle Indian School; led team to upset wins (1911–12) over Harvard, Army, and Univ. of Pennsylvania. Won (1912) Olympic pentathlon and decathlon, but was forced to surrender awards because he had played semi-professional baseball. Thorpe later played professional baseball, football.

Thorvaldsen or **Thorwaldsen, Albert Bertel** (tôr′väl-sŭn), 1770–1844, Danish sculptor, a leader of the neoclassicists. Worked mainly in Rome and Copenhagen. Designed the *Lion of Lucerne,* carved from the native rock at Lucerne by his pupils. Thorvaldsen Mus. in Copenhagen has a large collection of his work (originals and models).

Thoth (thŏth, tōt), moon-god and secretary god of anc. Egyptian religion. He supposedly possessed all secret wisdom. Equated with the Greek Hermes, he is intended by the name HERMES TRISMEGISTUS.

Thothmes, Egyptian kings: see THUTMOSE.

Thousand and One Nights or **Arabian Nights,** a series of stories in Arabic, strung together by the story of Scheherazade or Sheherazade, who kept her husband (a sultan) from killing her by telling these tales over 1,001 nights. Includes stories of Ali Baba and Aladdin. Many of the stories were derived from India, but the collection in its present form is probably native to Persia. First European translation was that by Antoine Galland into French (1704–17). English translations include E. W. Lane's expurgated edition (1840) and Richard Burton's unexpurgated edition (1885–88).

Thousand Islands, N N.Y. and S Ont., Canada, group of over 1,500 islands in the St. Lawrence at outlet of L. Ontario. Some belong to the U.S. and some to Canada. Many are privately owned. Popular summer resort. N.Y. and Ont. mainlands connected by international bridge and viaducts.

Thrace (thrās), region, SE Europe, occupying SE tip of the Balkan Peninsula and comprising NE Greece,

S Bulgaria, and Turkey in Europe. Chief cities are Istanbul (considered a separate entity), Adrianople, and Gallipoli. Region is largely agr. Early Thracians inhabited area extending W to the Adriatic; they were pushed E by the Illyrians (c.1300 B.C.) and by the Macedonians (5th cent. B.C.). Although Greek colonies were founded (e.g., at Byzantium), Thrace did not absorb Greek culture. Philip II of Macedon subdued (342 B.C.) S Thrace; Lysimachus ruled (after 323 B.C.) most of the region. Roman rule (after 1st cent. B.C.) greatly benefited Thrace. Since the barbarian invasions (3d cent.) it has remained a battleground. N Thrace passed (7th cent.) to Bulgarians. Ottoman Turks ruled the entire region after the fall of Constantinople (1453). After Bulgaria annexed (1885) Eastern Rumelia, term Thrace referred only to S part of region. After the BALKAN WARS (1912–13), Turkey held E Thrace and Bulgaria held W Thrace. In World War I Greece gained part of Bulgarian Thrace and most of E Thrace, but was later required (1923) to restore E Thrace to Turkey. In World War II, Bulgaria occupied (1941–44) Greek Thrace, but previous boundaries were restored.

Thrale, Hester Lynch, later **Madame Piozzi** (pēōz′ē, pēôt′tsē), 1741–1821, English friend of Dr. Johnson.

thrasher, bird of mockingbird and catbird family. Name probably refers to its habit of tail twitching. Brown thrasher of E U.S. (often miscalled brown thrush) is larger than a robin and reddish brown above with pale under parts streaked with brown. Other species found in W and SW U.S.

Thrasybulus (thrā″sĭbū′lŭs), d. c.389 B.C., Athenian leader. After Athens lost the Peloponnesian War, he got Theban help and came back from Phyle with other exiles to overthrow the Thirty Tyrants installed in Athens by Sparta (403 B.C.).

Three Emperors' League, informal alliance among Austria-Hungary, Germany, and Russia, announced officially 1872. Its aim was to insure peace among the three powers in case any of them became involved in war. Shaken by Russo-Turkish War (1877–78), it was eclipsed by German-Austrian alliance (1879), which later became the Triple Alliance.

Three Holy Children, the three Jews who were cast into the fiery furnace by Nebuchadnezzar and delivered by an angel. Their names are Shadrach, Meshach, and Abed-nego, in Babylonian; Azariah, Hananiah, and Mishael, in Hebrew; and Azarias, Ananias, and Misael, in Greek. Dan. 1.7; 3. The Song of the Three Holy Children, consisting of their prayers while in the furnace, is included in Western canon but is placed in the Apocrypha in AV.

Three Kingdoms, period of Chinese history from 220 to 265, following collapse of Han dynasty. So called because of division of China into three states: Wei, Shu, and Wu. The Wei became dominant and estab. TSIN dynasty.

Three Kings: see WISE MEN OF THE EAST.

Three Rivers, Que.: see TROIS RIVIÈRES.

Three Rivers, city (pop. 6,785), SW Mich., S of Kalamazoo, on St. Joseph R. at junction of Portage and Rocky rivers. Farm trade center with mfg. of metal products. Has Indian remains.

threshing, separation of seed or grain from plant stalks. The first known method, flail threshing, was striking the ear with a stick. The essential operation in Andrew Meikle's drum threshing machine, invented in 1784, is implicit in the thresher of today. The machines feed in the grain, which is threshed from the head, separated from the straw, and delivered, after cleaning, to a weigher. A combine is a machine that first reaps and then threshes. Tractors powered by gasoline or kerosene are commonly used to operate threshing equipment.

thrift: see SEA PINK.

thrips, minute, agile, black, yellowish, or reddish-brown sapsucking insect found on plants. Species include onion, pear, greenhouse, and grass thrips.

thrombosis (thrŏmbō′sĭs), formation of blood clot (thrombus) in heart or blood vessels. If circulation is blocked, instant death may follow. In coronary thrombosis, clot forms in a coronary artery supplying blood to the heart.

Throop, borough (pop. 5,861), NE Pa., on Lackawanna R. and NE of Scranton. Coal mining.

thrush (thrŭsh), bird of family (Turdidae) of c.700 species and subspecies of almost worldwide distribution and noted for their beautiful songs. Includes North American ROBIN and BLUEBIRD and the solitaire, hermit, and wood thrushes.

Thucydides (thūsĭ′dĭdēz), c.460–400 B.C., Greek historian of Athens, one of greatest ancient historians. His one work, history of Peloponnesian War to 411 B.C., is military record devoid of social and political references apart from war, noted for famous speeches, e.g., Pericles' funeral oration.

Thugs (thŭgz), former religious fraternity of robbers and murderers in India, also called Phansigars [stranglers]. Disguised as merchants or holy men, they waylaid wealthy travelers whom they killed as sacrifices to Hindu goddess Kali. Repressed 1829–36 by British, who executed some 300 of them.

Thule (thū′lē, thōō′lē), name the ancients gave to most northerly land of Europe, an island discovered c.310 B.C. by Pytheas and variously identified with modern lands. Phrase "Ultima Thule" figuratively denotes the most distant goal of human endeavor.

Thule (thōō′lē), settlement and colony district (pop. 322), NW Greenland. Founded 1910 by Knud Rasmussen. In 1952 an air base was being built here.

thulium (thū′lēŭm), metallic element of rare earths (symbol = Tm; see also ELEMENT, table).

Thun (tōōn), resort town (pop. 24,135), Bern canton, Switzerland, on Aar R. and L. of Thun, at foot of Bernese Alps.

thunderstorm, violent local atmospheric disturbance with lightning, thunder, heavy rain, often strong wind gusts, sometimes HAIL. Caused by instability; may result from sun's heating of moist air mass near surface on summer afternoon. Expansion-cooled rising air condenses, forming cumulus (turning to cumulonimbus) cloud, turbulent within. Amidst turbulence raindrops continually break up and reunite, building up electrical charges that produce lightning. (Discharge of lightning may take place within cloud, between two clouds, or between cloud and earth.) Storms are also caused by cooling of upper layers of air at night and by advance of wedge-shaped cold air mass against warm air, forcing it to rise.

Thurber, James, 1894–, American humorist. Many of his drawings and sketches appeared in *The New Yorker;* they are collected in such books as *The Seal in the Bedroom* (1932) and *The Thurber Album* (1952). With E. B. White he wrote the satire *Is Sex Necessary?* (1929); and with Elliott Nugent the comedy *The Male Animal* (1940).

Thurgau (tōōr′gou), canton (388 sq. mi.; pop. 149,360), NE Switzerland, on L. of Constance; cap. Frauenfeld. Fertile cultivated region, watered by Thur R. Was conquered in 1460 from the Hapsburgs by the Swiss cantons, which ruled it jointly until 1798. Became canton 1803. Population is mainly Protestant and German-speaking.

Thuringia (thyoōrĭn′jů), Ger. *Thüringen,* state (6,022 sq. mi.; pop. 2,927,497), central Germany; cap. Erfurt. It is crossed by the Thuringian Forest, a wooded range rising to 3,222 ft., and extends to the foot of the Harz mts. in the N. Fertile agr. land. Industries (textiles, optical and precision instruments, machinery, glass) are centered at Jena, Gotha, Gera Erfurt, Mühlhausen. Ancient Germanic tribe of Thuringians were conquered by the Franks in 6th–8th cent. and converted to Christianity by St. Boniface. Landgraves of Thuringia, whose seat was the Wartburg, became immediate princes of Holy Roman Empire in 11th cent., but after 1247 the succession was long contested; the major share eventually fell to the WETTIN dynasty of Saxony. The division of Wettin lands (1485) left most of Thuringia to the Ernestine branch, which split up into several duchies (see SAXE-ALTENBURG; SAXE-COBURG; SAXE-COBURG-GOTHA; SAXE-GOTHA; SAXE-MEININGEN; SAXE-WEIMAR; SAXE-WEIMAR-EISENACH). The Reformation was introduced in the 16th cent. The duchies joined the German Confederation (1815), the German Empire (1871), and, after the expulsion of the dukes in 1918, were united as the state of Thuringia under the Weimar Republic (1920). After World War II its territory was considerably increased by the addition of Prussian enclaves and the state came under Russian occupation. It joined the [East] German Democratic Republic in 1949.

Thursday: see WEEK.

Thurso (thûr'sō), burgh (pop. 3,203), Caithness, Scotland, most northerly burgh on Scottish mainland.

Thutmose (thŭt'mōz, tŭt'–), kings of anc. Egypt. Name also Thothmes. **Thutmose I,** fl. 1540 B.C., successor of Amenhotep I in XVIII dynasty. Subjugated peoples of the upper Nile and Syria. Had two sons, **Thutmose II** and **Thutmose III,** and a daughter, Hatshepsut (also wife of Thutmose III). Thutmose III seized the throne from his father (1501 B.C.), but it was Hatshepsut who ruled long as "king." After her death (c.1481 B.C.), Thutmose III defeated the Syrians and their allies at Megiddo (1479? B.C.) and made all Asia Minor tributary to Egypt. **Thutmose IV** was son and successor of Amenhotep II and reigned c.1420–c.1411 B.C

Thyestes (thī-ĕs'tēz), in Greek legend, son of PELOPS, brother of ATREUS, and father of AEGISTHUS.

thyme (tīm), aromatic herb or shrubby plant (*Thymus*) of the mint family. The common Old World thyme (*Thymus vulgaris*) is used for seasoning and yields an essential oil containing THYMOL. Creeping thyme or mother-of-thyme (*T. serpyllum*), a ground cover and rock garden plant, has small purple flowers.

thymol (thī'mōl), colorless, crystalline organic compound with thymelike odor. Used as antiseptic and in treatment of hookworm disease and trichinosis.

thymus gland (thī'mŭs), mass of lymphoid tissue found in many vertebrates. In man, it lies in chest cavity. Enlarges until puberty, then grows smaller. Function is uncertain; there is some evidence that its secretion helps to control growth.

thyroid gland (thī'roid), ductless gland in neck functioning in control of metabolism rate. Secretes thyroxin, an iodine compound, directly into blood. Enlargement of gland is known as goiter. Simple (endemic) goiter results from iodine deficiency; prevented or cured by adding iodine to diet. Exophthalmic goiter (Graves's disease) is caused by oversecretion of thyroxin. Thyroid insufficiency may result in myxedema in adult or in CRETINISM.

Ti, chemical symbol of the element TITANIUM.

Tia Juana, Mexico: see TIJUANA.

Tibbett, Lawrence, 1896–, American baritone. Made his debut at the Metropolitan Opera, New York, in 1923. Also appeared in several moving pictures.

Tiber (tī'bŭr), Ital. *Tevere,* Latin *Tiberis,* river, 251 mi. long, central Italy, rising in Tuscan Apennines and flowing S and SW through Rome into the Tyrrhenian.

Tiberias (tī-bēr'ēŭs), town (est. pop. 7,700), NE Israel, on Sea of Galilee. Built by Herod Antipas, it was named for Emperor Tiberius. Became a center for Jews after destruction of Jerusalem. Health resort with hot springs.

Tiberius (tī-bēr'ēŭs), 42 B.C.–A.D. 37, Roman emperor (A.D. 14–37); son of Tiberius Claudius Nero and Livia Drusilla. He was governor of Transalpine Gaul, aided his brother Drusus in Germany, and later campaigned in Germany and in Illyricum himself. He succeeded his stepfather Augustus and regularized state finances. For years Sejanus was his chief aid, but Tiberius in later years grew suspicious of everyone and even had Sejanus killed.

Tibet (tĭbĕt'), country (560,000 sq. mi.; pop. 3,000,000), central Asia; cap. Lhasa; autonomous province (since 1951) of China. Bordered on N and E by China proper and on S by India. One of highest regions of the world (average elevation c.15,000 ft.), it is mainly a vast plateau between Kunlun mts. (N) and Himalayas (S). Farming is possible only in valleys of Tsangpo (Brahmaputra), Indus, and Sutlej rivers. Chief mineral deposits are gold, iron pyrites, salt, soda, and borax. Tibet's religion is LAMAISM, derived from a form of Buddhism. Titular head of Tibetan government is the Dalai Lama, with the Panchen (or Tashi) Lama second in importance. After adopting Buddhism from India in 8th cent. Tibet practically isolated itself from the rest of the world. China conquered the area in 1720 and thereafter claimed suzerainty, but Tibet, encouraged by Britain, declared its independence in 1913. Chinese Communists invaded Tibet in 1950 and reduced it to its present status. Though supposedly still ruled by the Dalai Lama and the Panchen Lama (installed by the Chinese), Tibet is actually under a Chinese military commission.

Tibetan art shows the influence of India, China, and Persia. The Bon (pre-Buddhist) statues are Chinese in feeling. After the introduction of Buddhism from India (8th cent.), Tibetan artists copied the sculptures and paintings illustrating Buddhist teachings, giving a native interpretation to their work but failing to create a truly original art. In architecture the Chinese roof and the bulbous dome of India are much used. Tibetan painting, usually in tempera, appears most often in temple banners (tankas) made of cotton or silk and is characterized by crude colors (e.g., vermilion, vivid green, and blue). The rendering of the restricted subject matter (controlled by the lamas) has been so unvarying that examples of ancient art have sometimes been confused with those of the modern period. Tibetan craftsmen excel in all kinds of metalwork, ranging from the huge bronze statues, with their many heads and arms, to jewelry and intricate silver and gold receptacles for religious objects.

Tibetan language, Tibeto-Burman language of Indo-Chinese family. See LANGUAGE (table).

Tibullus (Albius Tibullus) (tĭbŭ'lŭs), c.55 B.C.–19 B.C., Roman poet. Master of the Latin love elegy.

Ticino (tēchē'nō), canton (1,086 sq. mi.; pop. 175,520), S Switzerland, on S slope of central Alps, bordering on Italy; cap. Bellinzona. Has pastures, vineyards; some agr. There are many resorts on Lake MAGGIORE and L. LUGANO. Population is largely Catholic and Italian-speaking. Region shared history of Lombardy until its conquest by the Swiss from Milan in 15th–16th cent. It was ruled as subject territory by Schwyz and Uri cantons until 1798; became a canton 1803. The **Ticino** river, 154 mi. long, rises in the Saint Gotthard and flows S through L. Maggiore into Italy, joining the Po below Padua. The river was the scene of Hannibal's victory over Scipio (218 B.C.).

tick, an arachnid, nearly identical with mite but larger than most species. It is parasitic, living on mammal or bird blood. Certain ticks spread diseases including tularemia and Rocky Mountain spotted fever, relapsing fever, and cattle fever.

Ticknor, George, 1791–1871, American author and teacher of languages. At Harvard after study abroad, he introduced thorough German methods. His *History of Spanish Literature* (1849) was notable.

tickseed: see COREOPSIS.

Ticonderoga (tī"kŏndŭrō'gù), resort village (pop. 3,517), NE N.Y., between Lakes George and Champlain; settled in 17th cent. Graphite mines supply local pencil industry. Site of battles in French and Indian Wars and American Revolution.

tidal theory, hypothesis of origin of solar system, formulated 1918 by James Jeans and later modified by Harold Jeffreys. Differs from PLANETESIMAL HYPOTHESIS chiefly in assuming tidal-wave crest was detached from sun by attraction of visiting star and separated into masses which then condensed to form planets.

tide, alternate rise and fall of waters in large bodies of water, caused by the gravitational effect of moon, sun, and, slightly, of other planets and stars. The moon's effective force is about 2¼ times that of the sun. Two high tides come at once: direct, on the side of the globe facing the moon; indirect, on the opposite side. The average interval between them is 12 hr. and 25 min. Irregularities from other factors cause (1) two high and two low water tides per lunar day, (2) one tidal cycle per lunar day, (3) two tidal cycles with marked disparities in height and duration. Tidal range is difference in level of successive high and low waters. Max. range (spring tide) occurs when earth, moon, and sun are in line; min. range (neap tide) occurs when sun and moon are at right angles. Tidal range also varies with coastal configuration and barometric pressure. Tidal ebb and flow cause tidal currents.

tidewater, in U.S. history, that part of the Atlantic coastal plain extending inland to the area reached by oceanic tides or to the fall line. Settled first, it became in the Southern colonies the region of large plantations and of important commercial towns. Tidewater aristocracy, allied with colonial officialdom, so completely dominated local government that frontier people were several times driven to insurrection. Eventually other areas triumphed.

Tieck, Ludwig (lōōt'vĭkh tēk'), 1773–1853, German romantic poet, dramatist, and novelist. Made notable translation of *Don Quixote* and with others completed Schlegel's translation of Shakspere. His works include the satirical comedy *Puss in Boots* (1797; Eng. tr., 1913) and *Tales from the Phantasus* (1812–16; Eng. tr., 1845).

Tien Shan (tyĕn' shän'), mountain system of central Asia, in Russian Turkestan and Sinkiang prov., China. Highest peaks are Pobeda Peak (24,406 ft.) and Khan Tengri (22,949 ft.).

Tientsin (tĭn"tsĭn', tĭn"sĭn'), city (pop. 1,686,543), Hopeh prov., China, at junction of Pai R. and Grand Canal; leading port of N China plain. It produces textiles, glass, leather goods, and processed foods. Seat of two universities. Occupied by British and French in mid-19th cent. After 1861 when it became a treaty port, concessions were made for foreign settlements. Occupied by foreign troops in Boxer Rebellion (1900). Held 1937–45 by the Japanese. Fell to Communists in 1949.

Tiepolo, (Giovanni Battista) (tyä'pōlō), 1696–1770, Venetian painter. Revived the grand manner of Venetian baroque. Won fame by his early frescoes in Labia Palace and the doge's palace in Venice. Worked in Würzburg and Madrid (after 1763), where he created frescoes for palaces. Also produced many oils. His style is marked by superb draughtsmanship and scintillating brushwork.

Tierra del Fuego (tyĕ'rä dĕl fwā'gō), archipelago, area c.18,500 sq. mi., off S South America, comprising one large and several small islands separated from mainland by Strait of Magellan. E part, an extension of Patagonia, belongs to Argentina (cap. Ushuaia); W part, a continuation of Andes, belongs to Chile (cap. MAGALLANES.) Sheep are raised, timber is exported, and there is some mining. Aborigines are called Fuegians.

Tiffany, Charles Lewis (tĭ'fŭnē), 1812–1902, American merchant, founder of Tiffany and Co., New York city. Introduced English standard of sterling silver, 1851. An art patron in later life. His son, **Louis Comfort Tiffany,** 1848–1943, was an artist and manufacturer of stained glass. In 1919 he endowed a foundation providing for study of art at his summer home at Oyster Bay, N.Y. Foundation was reorganized 1946 to provide for study and travel grants to art students.

Tiffin, city (pop. 18,952), N Ohio, on Sandusky R. and SE of Toledo; founded c.1820. Mfg. of glass and electrical products. Seat of Heidelberg Col. (Evangelical-Reformed; coed.; 1850).

Tiflis (tĭ'flĭs), Georgian *Tbilisi,* city (pop. 519,175), cap.

of Georgian SSR, on Kura R., hemmed in by spurs of Greater and Lesser Caucasus. Economic and cultural metropolis of Transcaucasia. Produces machinery, silk, cotton, tobacco, and wine. Has a university (founded 1918), polytechnic and medical schools, opera, and other cultural institutions. First mentioned 4th cent. A.D., it reached its greatest flowering in the 12th–13th cent. Its old section, with picturesque streets and bazaars, has hot sulphur springs. Most of city, however, is modern. Among many churches are Zion Cathedral (first built 7th cent.), St. David's (6th cent.), and Metskh Church (13th cent.; now a museum). Mt. David, a favorite excursion point, dominates the city.

Tifton, city (pop. 6,831), S central Ga., ESE of Albany. Tobacco market. Yarns, cottonseed oil.

tiger, Asiatic carnivorous mammal (*Panthera tigris* or *Felis tigris*) of cat family. It has no mane; coat is usually orange-yellow striped with black. Males are 8–10 ft. in total length and some weigh over 500 lb. Hunt mostly at night.

Tiglath-pileser (tĭ'glăth-pŭlē'zŭr), kings of anc. Assyria. **Tiglath-pileser I,** d. c.1102 B.C. He conquered much of Asia Minor. **Tiglath-pileser III,** d. 728 B.C., made himself master of rebellious Babylonia, of Syria, and of Media. He aided Ahaz, king of Judah.

Tigris (tī'grĭs), biblical *Hiddekil,* river, SW Asia, rising in E Turkey and flowing c.1,150 mi., mostly in Iraq, to join the EUPHRATES, with which it forms the SHATT EL ARAB. Ancient cities of Nineveh and Ctesiphon were on its banks. Navigable by small steamers upstream to Baghdad. Lower course is connected with the Euphrates by canals.

Tihwa, China: see URUMCHI.

Tijuana (tēhwä'nä), city (pop. 16,486), Lower California, NW Mexico; formerly Tia Juana. Popular resort with famous race tracks and gambling casinos at Agua Caliente.

Tilburg (tĭl'bûrg), municipality (pop. 114,312), North Brabant prov., S Netherlands. Mfg. center (textiles, dyes).

Tilbury (tĭl'bûrē), former urban district (1931 pop. 16,-825), now part of Thurrock, Essex, England, on Thames R. Tilbury Docks (part of Port of London) are terminus of passenger steamship lines.

Tilden, Samuel J(ones), 1814–86, American presidential candidate of the Democratic party in 1876. Governor of N.Y. (1875–76). It seems clear now that Tilden actually won 1876 election, but division of electoral commission along partisan lines gave victory to Republican R. B. Hayes.

Tilden, William Tatem, Jr. (Bill), 1893–, American tennis player. Won U.S. singles (1920–26, 1929), British singles (1920–21, 1930) championships, many other amateur titles. Won (1931, 1935) professional singles crown.

Tillamook (tĭ'lùmōōk), city (pop. 3,685), NW Oregon, at head of Tillamook Bay and W of Portland. Noted for cheese.

Till Eulenspiegel: see EULENSPIEGEL, TILL.

Tillman, Benjamin Ryan, 1847–1918, U.S. Senator from S.C. (1895–1918). Governor of S.C. (1890–94); helped to restrict Negro suffrage. As Senator he opposed Cleveland, generally supported Wilson.

Tillsonburg, town (pop. 5,330), S Ont., Canada, ENE of St. Thomas, in tobacco and fruit region.

Tilly, Johannes Tserklaes, count of (yōhä'nùs tsĕrkläs' tĭ'lē), 1559–1632, imperialist general in Thirty Years War, b. Brabant. Commanded army of the Catholic League in victories at WHITE MOUNTAIN (1620), Wimpfen and Höchst (1622), and LUTTER AM BARENBERGE (1626). Took over Wallenstein's command 1630. Stormed MAGDEBURG 1631 (but was not responsible for ensuing massacre). Was defeated by Gustavus II of Sweden at Breitenfeld (1631) and on the Lech, where he was mortally wounded.

Tilsit (tĭl'zĭt), city (1939 pop., 58,468), former East Prussia, a port on the Niemen; transferred to Russian administration 1945 and renamed Sovetsk. Produces leather, a well-known cheese, and lumber. By the Treaty of Tilsit of July 7, 1807, Napoleon I and Alexander I restored peace between France and Russia. Russia recognized the duchy of Warsaw and secretly promised its alliance against England. Two days later, in a second treaty, Napoleon forced Frederick William III of Prussia to cede all Prussian territory W of the Elbe to France and Prussian Poland to the duchy of Warsaw; to reduce his army to 42,000 men; to surrender his chief fortresses to French garrisons; and to join the Continental system.

Tilton, Theodore, 1835–1907, American journalist. He and his wife were parishioners of H. W. BEECHER, whom Tilton sued in 1874 for alleged adultery with Mrs. Tilton. Jury disagreed.

Timanthes (tĭmăn′thēz), c.400 B.C., Greek painter. His masterpiece was the *Sacrifice of Iphigenia.*

timber line, line beyond which trees do not grow. It depends on conditions affecting temperature—altitude, latitude, winds, exposure. Probably limited by an isotherm of 50°F. for warmest month.

Timbuktu (tĭm″bŭktōō′), town (pop. c.7,000), French Sudan, near the Niger; center of caravan trade on trans-Saharan road to Algeria and Morocco. Settled 1087, it flourished as a center of Moslem culture until late 16th cent. and was famous for its gold and slave market.

time, concept variously defined from philosophical, psychological, physical, and biological aspects. Distinction is usually made between experienced duration and time measured by movements of bodies through space. Methods of measuring time are based on some recurring phenomenon, usually on rotation of earth either in relation to sun (solar time) or star (sidereal time). Since solar days are unequal in length, modern time reckoning is based on mean solar day. Because sun's apparent course is westward, local time is 4 min. later for each degree of longitude westward. Standard time (estab. 1884) is based on mean solar day reckoned by Royal Observatory, Greenwich, England, whose longitude is accepted as 0°. Earth's circumference is divided into 24 time belts of 15° each. See also CALENDAR; CLOCK; DAYLIGHT-SAVING TIME; SPACE TIME; SUNDIAL.

time, in music: see TEMPO; RHYTHM; MUSICAL NOTATION.

Timgad (tĭm′găd), ruined city, Algeria, S of Constantine. Called the Pompeii of N Africa because of extensive ruins of a Roman city founded here by Trajan in A.D. 100.

Timiskaming, Lake (tĭmĭ′skŭmĭng), SW Que. and E Ont., Canada, an expansion of Ottawa R., 62 mi. long. Haileybury is on NW shore.

Timisoara (tēmēshwä′rä), Hung. *Temesvár,* city (pop. 111,987), W Rumania; chief city of the Banat (former BANAT OF TEMESVAR). Commercial and industrial center. Roman Catholic and Orthodox episcopal see. University (founded 1945). A Roman settlement, Timisoara was annexed to Hungary 1010; fell to the Turks 1552; was recaptured by Eugene of Savoy 1716; was transferred to Rumania 1920. Castle of John of Hunyadi is now a barracks.

Timmins, town (pop. 27,743), E Ont., Canada, on Mattagami R. and NNW of Sudbury. Trade center in rich Porcupine gold-mining district.

Timon (tī′mŭn), one of the seven deacons. Acts 6.5.

Timon of Athens, fl. after 450 B.C., Greek misanthrope, who supported Alcibiades, who, he thought, would ruin Athens. A play about him is attributed to Shakspere.

Timor (tē′môr), island, area 13,071 sq. mi., Indonesia, largest and easternmost of the Lesser Sundas. Long, narrow, and mountainous. Natives are of Malay and Papuan stock. Products include copra and sandalwood. The Portuguese settled here c.1520, the Dutch in 1613. Border between their territories was settled 1859 by treaty and made effective 1914. With creation of state of Indonesia (1949), Dutch Timor (5,765 sq. mi.; pop.

350,064), comprising W half of island, became Indonesian territory. Colony of Portuguese Timor (7,383 sq. mi.; pop. 438,350) comprises E half of island and territory of Oe-Cusse in Indonesian section; cap. Dili.

Timothy, Saint, d. c.100, early Christian, companion of St. Paul. Also called Timotheus. Two epistles bear his name. Acts 16.1–3; Rom. 16.21; 1 Cor. 4.17; 2 Cor. 1.1; Philip 2.19; 1 Thess. 3.2; 2 Thess. 1.1; Philemon 1; Heb. 13.23. Feast: Jan. 24.

Timothy, epistles of New Testament, called 1 and 2 Timothy, traditionally written by St. Paul to Timothy. In 1 Timothy Paul discusses public prayer and qualifications of the clergy. 2 Timothy is more a personal letter. Paul emphasizes courage and fidelity and speaks of his own impending death.

timothy, widely planted North American perennial hay grass (*Phleum pratense*), introduced from Europe. It is not suitable for permanent pasture since it will not survive continuous grazing.

timpani: see PERCUSSION INSTRUMENTS.

Timpanogos Cave National Monument: see NATIONAL PARKS AND MONUMENTS (table).

Timrod, Henry, 1828–67, American poet of the Old South and Civil War, b. S.C. Among his poems are "The Cotton Boll," "Carolina," and "Ethnogenesis," an ode.

Timurids (tĭmōō′rĭdz), dynasty founded by TAMERLANE (or Timur). At his death (1405) his empire extended from Euphrates R. to Jaxartes and Indus rivers. The western empire was quickly brought to an end by capture of Baghdad by the Turkoman horde (1410). But the eastern empire (E of Amu Darya R.) continued to flourish, with Samarkand and Herat as its great cultural centers. In mid-15th cent. the Timurid empire fell into anarchy; the Turkoman horde took much territory, while Uzbeks looted Samarkand. The last of the Timurids, BABER, was one of the petty princes who took over the rule.

tin, lustrous, silver-white, crystalline, metallic element (symbol = SN; see also ELEMENT, table). Below 18°C. tends to turn to gray powder; very soft, malleable, barely affected by moisture. Used to protect other metals, in alloys. Relatively active, forms stannous (valence = 2) and stannic (valence = 4) compounds. Compounds are used in dyeing, enamels, weighting silk, fireproofing, and medicine. Tin plate for tin cans is iron or steel with thin coating of tin. Tin rarely occurs uncombined in nature; ores are found in Bolivia, Indonesia, Malay Peninsula, Belgian Congo, Nigeria, Cornwall (England).

tinamou (tĭ′nŭmōō), South American game bird resembling partridge but more closely related to ostrich. Plumage is dark, usually barred; bill is slender, wings short.

Tinchebrai or **Tinchebray** (tēshbrā′), small town in Normandy, NW France, where Henry I of England defeated his brother Robert II of Normandy (1106).

Tindal or **Tindale, William:** see TYNDALE, WILLIAM.

Tinian: see MARIANAS ISLANDS.

Tinicum Island (tĭn′ĭkŭm), SE Pa., in Delaware R., SW of Philadelphia; separated from mainland by marshes. Cap. of New Sweden 1643–55.

Tinos: see TENOS.

Tintagel Head (tĭntăj′ŭl), cape, Cornwall, England. Ruined Tintagel Castle (Norman) is the reputed birthplace of King Arthur.

Tintern Abbey, ruins of an abbey, Monmouthshire, England. Subject of a poem by Wordsworth.

Tinto, Río: see RÍO TINTO.

Tintoretto (tĭntŭrĕ′tō, Ital. tēntōrĕt′tō), 1518–94, Venetian painter, one of the great masters of the Renaissance. Real name was Jacopo Robusti; called Il Tintoretto [little dyer] from his father's trade. His impressive paintings (esp. those of late period) are marked by dramatic lighting and broad impressionistic brushwork. Worked c.1564–c.1587 on the great cycle of paintings in Scuola di San Rocco (Venice), which includes the enormous *Crucifixion.* Reputedly the largest oil canvas in the world is his *Paradise* in the ducal palace at Venice.

Tippecanoe (tĭ″pŭkŭnoō′), river rising in the lake district of NE Ind. and flowing 200 mi. SW to Wabash R. above Lafayette. Gen. W. H. Harrison broke power of the Indians in battle of Tippecanoe, Nov. 7, 1811, on site of present village of Battle Ground.

Tipperary (tĭ″pŭrâ′rē), inland county (1,643 sq. mi.; pop. 136,014), S Ireland, in Munster; co. town Tipperary. Administratively divided into North Riding and South Riding. Mountains include Knockmealdowns and Galtees. Golden Vale is richest agr. land in Ireland; dairying is chief occupation. Some lead mining and slate quarrying.

Tippoo Sahib (tĭ′poō sä′hĭb), 1753–99, maharajah of Mysore, India (1782–99), son of HYDER ALI. Generally allied with French against British, whom he defeated 1782. His invasion of British-held Travancore resulted in his defeat by Cornwallis. Rejecting British demand to disarm, he was besieged and killed at Seringapatam.

Tipton, city (pop. 5,633), central Ind., W of Elwood, in agr. area. Mfg. of machinery.

Tiptonville, town (pop. 1,953), W Tenn., center of recreation area on Reelfoot L.

Tirana or **Tiranë** (tērä′nä, –nŭ), city (pop. 59,887), cap. of Albania, in central Albania. Was founded early 17th cent. by Turks; modern city was built after 1920, when it became the cap. Has fine mosques of the 17th and 18th cent.

tire. Rubber or synthetic rubber tires include solid tires used on some heavy trucks and pneumatic tires, first manufactured commercially for bicycles c.1889 by John Dunlop in Ireland. One form in common use has inner tube and outer casing built up of alternate plies of diagonal cords and sheets of rubber, topped with rubber padding, breaker strips, and tough thread added after side walls; molds for vulcanizing form tread pattern. Pneumatic tire requiring no inner tube has been developed.

Tiresias (tīrē′shŭs, –sēŭs), in Greek mythology, blind prophet of Thebes. Blinded either by Athena or by Hera, he was given in compensation prophetic powers. He is said to have foretold most of the great events of Greek mythology.

Tirhakah (tēr′ŭkŭ, tērhä′kŭ) or **Taharka** (tŭhär′kŭ), d. 663 B.C., king of anc. Egypt (688–663 B.C.), last of XXV dynasty, ruling from Tanis. He lost Lower Egypt to Esar-Haddon and later to Assur-bani-pal.

Tirol, Austria: see TYROL.

Tirpitz, Alfred von (äl′frät fŭn tĭr′pĭts), 1849–1930, German admiral; secretary of state for naval affairs 1897–1916. In World War I he began construction of submarines and advocated unrestricted warfare.

Tirso de Molina (tēr′sō dä mōlē′nä), pseud. of **Gabriel Téllez** (gäbrēĕl′ tĕl′yäth), 1571–1648, Spanish dramatist, an outstanding figure of the Golden Age, author of 300 to 400 plays.

Tisbury, Mass.: see VINEYARD HAVEN.

Tiselius, Arne (är′nŭ tēsä′lyŭs), 1902–, Swedish biochemist. Won 1948 Nobel Prize for developing new methods of separating and detecting colloids.

Tishomingo (tĭshŭmĭn′gō), city (pop. 2,325), S Okla., NW of Durant and on L. Texoma. Long chief city of Chickasaw Indians.

Tisquantum: see SQUANTO.

Tissaphernes (tĭ″sŭfûr′nēz), d. 395 B.C., Persian satrap (governor) in Asia Minor. Aided Artaxerxes II to defeat Cyrus the Younger at Cunaxa (401 B.C.) and pursued the Greeks who had supported Cyrus.

Tisza, Count Stephen, Hung. *Tisza István* (tĭ′sō ĭst′vän), 1861–1918, premier of Hungary (1903–5, 1913–17). A nationalist, he sought to make Hungary the dominant partner in Austro-Hungarian Monarchy; took repressive measure against Serbian and Rumanian minorities. In 1914 he at first opposed declaration of war against Serbia, but reversed himself when assured that no Serbian territory would be annexed. Was

murdered by soldiers who believed him chief instigator of war.

Tisza, river: see THEISS.

Titan, in Greek mythology, one of 12 male and female giants; children of Uranus and Gaea. They were Cronus, Iapetus, Hyperion, Oceanus, Coeus, Creus, Theia, Rhea, Mnemosyne, Phoebe, Tethys, and Themis. Led by Cronus, they deposed Uranus, and were themselves overthrown by their descendants, the Olympians, in the battle called TITANOMACHY.

Titanic, White Star liner sunk on night of April 14–15, 1912, after hitting iceberg in N Atlantic, with loss of 1,517 lives among some 2,000 passengers. Causes included excessive speed and insufficient, inefficiently manned lifeboats. Resulted in iceberg patrol and in stringent safety rules.

titanium (tītä′nēŭm), silver-white, lustrous, metallic element (symbol = Ti; see also ELEMENT, table). Adds hardness and tensile strength to steel alloys. It is active chemically; forms a number of compounds. Titanium tetrachloride is used in making smoke screens; titanium dioxide, as white pigment; other compounds are used as yellow pigments, mordants, electric-arc electrodes.

Titanomachy (tī″tŭnŏ′mŭkē), in Greek mythology, battle between Titans under Cronus and Olympian gods under Zeus, in Thessaly. After 10 years of battle Titans were overthrown when the Cyclopes forged thunderbolt for Zeus. Cronus then went to rule Isles of the Blessed, Atlas had to hold up the sky, and all the other Titans, except Prometheus and Oceanus, who had aided Zeus, were condemned to Tartarus.

Tithonus (tĭthŏ′nŭs), mythical handsome prince of Troy; father of Memnon by the goddess Eos. She won for him immortality but not eternal youth. When he was old, she changed him into a grasshopper.

Titian (tĭ′shŭn), 1477–1576, celebrated Venetian painter, whose real name was Tiziano Vecellio, b. Pieve di Cadore in the Dolomites. Influenced by Giovanni Bellini and Giorgione, he developed a sumptuous, coloristic style in the grand manner typical of the High Renaissance. Throughout his long career he was showered with honors. On his visit to Rome (1545–46) he did the famous portrait of Pope Paul III with his nephews (Naples); at this time he met Michelangelo. He was twice invited to Augsburg by Charles V, for whom he painted the *Trinity,* "La Gloria" (Prado). For Philip II Titian painted many religious works and a cycle of mythological paintings which included the *Rape of Europa* (Gardner Mus., Boston). Typifying the heightened emotional content of his final phase is his last work, the magnificent *Pietà* (Academy, Venice).

Titicaca, Lake (tētēkä′kä), area 3,205 sq. mi., divided between Bolivia and Peru. Largest fresh-water lake in South America and highest in world (c.12,500 ft. above sea level; max. depth c.900 ft.). From pre-Incan times it has been center of Indian life. In middle of lake is an island, the legendary birthplace of first Inca. Lake is drained by Desaguadero R.

titles of sovereignty, nobility, and honor. Highest-ranking title, emperor, was originally military. Assumed by Augustus Caesar and sovereigns of later Roman and Byzantine empires; conferred on Charlemagne 800; and assumed by Napoleon 1804. Queen Victoria proclaimed Empress of India 1877. Under Holy Roman Empire titles in descending order below emperor or king were *Herzog* (feminine *Herzogin*); *Pfalzgraf* (*Pfalzgräfin*), *Markgraf* (*Markgräfin*), and *Landgraf* (*Landgräfin*); *Graf* (*Gräfin*); *Baron* (*baronin*) and *Freiherr* (*Freiherrin*); and *Ritter*. Prefix *Reichs–* before these indicated holding direct from emperor. French titles in descending order are *duc* (*duchesse*); *prince* (*princesse*); *marquis* (*marquise*); *comte* (*comtesse*); *vicomte* (*vicomtesse*); *baron* (*baronne*); *seigneur* or *sire*; and *chevalier*. English titles are *prince* (*princess*); *duke* (*duchess*); *marquess* (*marchioness*); *earl* (*countess*); *viscount* (*viscountess*); *baron* (*baroness*); *baronet*; and knight (dame). In Italy titles of nobility are duca (duchessa); principe (principessa); marchese (marchesa); conte (contessa); visconte (viscontessa); barone (baronessa). Spanish titles are duque (duquesa); príncipe (principesa); marqués (marquesa); conde (condesa); visconde (viscondesa); and barón (baronesa).

Tito, Josip Broz (yô'sĕp brôz' tē'tô), 1892–, Yugoslav Communist leader, b. Croatia, whose original name was Josip Broz. A blacksmith's son, he turned to Communism in his poverty-stricken youth; was imprisoned by Yugoslav authorities; emerged in 1941 as a partisan leader against the Axis occupation forces in World War II. His successful raids immobilized large Axis forces in Yugoslavia, and by 1943 Tito controlled vast areas with an army of more than 200,-000. His rival, Gen. MIKHAILOVICH, soon clashed with Tito, who by 1944 had the full support of the USSR, England, and the U.S. and who was in full control of Yugoslavia at the war's end. After the electoral victory of his Communist-led National Liberation Front (the opposition abstained from voting), Marshal Tito had King Peter II deposed and became premier of the People's Republic of YUGOSLAVIA (1945). He ruled dictatorially. In 1948 the COMINFORM accused him of deviationism, but Tito held his own against Russian pressure. Yugoslav relations with the USSR and other Communist countries grew tense. Tito, while continuing with his Communist program at home, had to turn to the West in his foreign policy.

Titograd (tē'tôgräd), formerly **Podgorica** (pôd'gô"rĭtsä), town (pop. 12,206), cap. of Montenegro, Yugoslavia. Trade center.

Titus (tī'tŭs), A.D. c.40–81, Roman emperor (79–81), son of Vespasian and coruler after 71. It was Titus who destroyed Jerusalem. In Rome he was notable as a builder, completing the Colosseum and building a large bath. Succeeded by Domitian, who erected the **Arch of Titus.**

Titus, early Christian, a missionary and friend of St. Paul. An epistle bears his name. 2 Cor. 2.13; 7.6,7; 8.16–24; Gal. 2.3. Feast: Jan. 4.

Titus, epistle of New Testament, traditionally written by St. Paul to Titus. Like 1 Timothy, it gives points of regulation for governing the church.

Titusville, city (pop. 8,923), NW Pa., N of Oil City. Mfg. of machinery and tools. Near-by state park marks site of first successful oil well (1859) in U.S.

Tiumen, RSFSR: see TYUMEN.

Tiverton (tī'vŭrtŭn), town (pop. 5,659), SE R.I., SE of Providence. Farming, fishing, mfg. of textiles; resorts.

Tivoli (tē'vōlē), town (pop. 16,886), Latium, central Italy, NE of Rome. Famed for its beautiful site, villas, gardens (notably the VILLA D'ESTE) and for the falls of the Aniene R. Has ruins of Roman villas. Roman Temple of Vesta is now a church.

Tiw (tē'ōō), in Germanic religion, god of battle. Called Tyr by the Norse. He was a wrestler. Tiw's identification with Mars caused Latin Mars' day to be translated into Tiw's Day, now Tuesday.

Tiy (tē), queens of anc. Egypt. **Tiy,** fl. 1400 B.C., was influential in the reigns of her husband, Amenhotep III, and her son, Ikhnaton. Another **Tiy,** fl. 1167 B.C., led an unsuccessful conspiracy against her husband, Ramses III.

Tl, chemical symbol of the element THALLIUM.

Tlaxcala (tläskä'lä), state (1,555 sq. mi.; pop. 282,495), E central Mexico; cap. Tlaxcala (pop. 3,261). Smallest of Mexican states, it is almost surrounded by Puebla. Tlaxcaltec Indians fiercely resisted Cortés but, when defeated, were his valuable allies against Aztec.

Tlemcen (tlĕmsĕn'), city (pop. 50,272), NW Algeria, in the Tell. Flourished 13th–15th cent. as cap. of Moslem Berber dynasty. Known for its numerous splendid mosques and handicraft industries.

Tm, chemical symbol of the element THULIUM.

T.N.T. or **TNT:** see TRINITROTOLUENE.

toad, amphibian animal, more terrestrial than the related frog. It has dry, warty skin and often is dull

reddish or yellowish brown with gray median stripe and dark markings. Lives usually in moist, cool place. Horned toad is a LIZARD.

toadflax: see BUTTER-AND-EGGS.

toadstool: see MUSHROOM.

tobacco, plant (genus Nicotiana) and product manufactured from leaf. Use originated in W Hemisphere in pre-Columbian times, reached Spain and Portugal in mid-16th cent. and spread into Europe, Asia, Africa. Chief commercial species Nicotiana tabacum, native to America, is best grown from seed as annual in regions with mean temperature of c.40°F. Leaves are cured, fermented, and aged. U.S. produces annually c.1,400,000,000 lb. of which c.60% is grown in N.C. and Ky. See also CIGAR AND CIGARETTE.

Tobago: see TRINIDAD AND TOBAGO.

Tobit (tō'–) or **Tobias** (–bī'–), book of Old Testament, placed in Apocrypha in AV, included in Western canon. It tells of Tobit (Vulgate Tobias), a devout Jew in exile, and of his son Tobias. Sent on business to a distant city, the young Tobias and his dog are guided by the archangel Raphael in the form of a young man. They come to the house of a Jew whose daughter, Sara, is afflicted by a demon (Asmodeus). Tobias under the guidance of Raphael exorcises the demon and marries Sara. They return home where Tobias, with Raphael's help, cures his father's blindness. Tobias and his dog with the angel have been a favorite subject of Christian art.

Tobol (tŭbôl'), river, 1,042 mi. long, W Siberia, rising in Mugodzhar Hills, Kazakh SSR, and flowing NNE into RSFSR to join the Irtysh at Tobolsk.

Tobolsk (tŭbôlsk'), city (pop. 32,200), RSFSR, in W Siberia, on Irtysh and Tobol rivers. Market center for furs and fish. Shipyards, sawmills. Founded 1587 near former Tatar cap. of Sibir, it was administrative center of W Siberia until replaced by Omsk in 1824. Nicholas II and family were exiled here 1917–18. Birthplace of Mendelejeff.

Tobruk (tôbrŏŏk'), town (pop. 4,130), Cyrenaica, Libya, on the Mediterranean. A major supply port in World War II, it was taken Jan., 1941, by Australians. Later besieged by Rommel's forces for more than eight months until relieved Dec., 1941. In Rommel's second great offensive it fell June, 1942. Recaptured by the British late in 1942. See NORTH AFRICA, CAMPAIGNS IN.

Tocantins (tōkăntēnsh'), river, c.1,560 mi. long, rising in S central Goiás state, Brazil, and flowing N to Pará R., southern arm of the Amazon.

Toccoa (tŏ'kōŭ), city (pop. 6,781), NE Ga., in Appalachian foothills near Tugaloo R. Industrial center producing textile goods and machinery.

Tocqueville, Alexis de (älĕksēs' dü tôkvēl'), 1805–59, French liberal politician and writer. His Democracy in America (2 vols., 1835; Eng. tr., 4 vols., 1835–40, revised ed., 2 vols., 1945) is a classic.

Todhunter, Isaac, 1820–84, English mathematician, known for mathematics textbooks, work on equations and calculus, and research and writings on history of mathematics.

Todos os Santos Bay (tō'dŏŏs ŏŏs sän'tŏŏsh), inlet of the Atlantic, 25 mi. long and 20 mi. wide, Bahia, E Brazil. Discovered by Vespucci (1501).

toga (tō'gŭ), Roman garment worn in earliest days by both men and women of all classes, later by men alone. It ultimately became a roughly semicircular garment, c.7 ft. wide and three times the wearer's height in length, and was elaborately draped over the tunic. Status was indicated by color of the toga itself, or by a colored border or embroidery. It expressed the dignity of citizenship and was forbidden to foreigners, subjects, and exiles. It was the ceremonial state dress of patricians until the TUNIC came to be preferred.

Toggenburg (tô'gŭnbŏŏrk), district in St. Gall canton, E Switzerland. Cotton textiles; dairying (Toggenburg goats were developed here). Territory was purchased by abbot of St. Gall 1468. In 1712 quarrels between abbot and Protestant communities of Toggenburg led to **War of the Toggenburg,** between Catholic and Protestant cantons of Swiss Confederation. Protestants won; religious equality was estab.

Togliatti, Palmiro (pälmē′rō tōlyät′tē), 1893–, leader of Italian Communist party.

Togo, Heihachiro, Count (hä′hächĭrō′ tō′gō), 1847–1934, Japanese admiral, hero of Russo-Japanese War.

Togoland (tō′gōländ″) or **Togo** (tō′gō), former German protectorate (c.35,000 sq. mi.), W Africa, on Gulf of Guinea. Under German control from 1886 to 1914, when it was occupied by French and British troops. In 1922 the League of Nations divided it into two mandates—French Togoland (c.21,500 sq. mi.; pop. c.944,500) in E on the coast, with cap. at Lomé, and British Togoland (13,040 sq. mi.; pop. 378,666), in W and inland, and governed as part of Gold Coast. These became UN trust territories in 1946. Products include cattle, cacao, and cotton.

Tojo, Hideki (hēdä′kē tō′jō), 1884–1948, Japanese general. Rise to premiership in Oct., 1941 marked final triumph of military party which favored war with the Allies. Resigned July, 1944, after loss of Marianas. Executed as war criminal after the war.

Tokay (tōkā′), Hung. *Tokaj,* town (pop. 5,903), NE Hungary, on the Tisza. Famed for its wine, of which there are three types (dry, sweet, and Tokay Essence, made from unpressed grapes).

Tokelau (tōkŭlou′) or **Union Islands,** group of three atolls in S Pacific, c.300 mi. N of Western Samoa. Discovered 1765 by the British. Governed by New Zealand since 1926.

Tokio, Japan: see TOKYO.

Tokoly, Emeric: see THOKOLY, EMERIC.

Tokugawa (tō″kōōgä′wä), family that held the shogunate (see SHOGUN) and controlled Japan, 1603–1867. Founded by IEYASU. Under its system of centralized feudalism the family itself held only a quarter of the land but kept close watch on the daimyo, who ruled over separate domains. Its collapse was caused by a complex of internal and external pressures. Its overthrow restored power to the emperor.

Tokyo or **Tokio** (both: tō′kēō), city (pop. 6,275,190) cap. of Japan, in central Honshu; port on Tokyo Bay. Crossed by small Sumida R. Financial, industrial and cultural center; focal point of urban belt (including Yokohama). Founded 12th cent. as Yedo (or Edo), it rose after 1603 when it became the seat of Ieyasu, first Tokugawa shogun. After Meiji restoration (1868) city was renamed Tokyo and succeeded Kyoto as imperial cap. Earthquake of 1923 ruined nearly half the city. In World War II was first raided by U.S. bombers under Gen. James Doolittle, April, 1942. Later raids destroyed half the city, including most of its industrial plant. Chief academic institutions are Keio-Gijuku Univ. (1867), Tokyo Univ. (1869; formerly Tokyo Imperial Univ.), Waseda Univ. (1882), and Rikkyo or St. Paul's Univ. (1883).

Tolbukhin (tôlbōō′khĭn), formerly **Dobrich** (dô′brĭch), city (pop. 31,049), NE Bulgaria, in S Dobruja. Agr. trade center. Under Rumanian rule 1913–40 (Rumanian name was Bazargic). Renamed in 1949 in honor of Marshal Tolbukhin of USSR.

Toledo, Francisco de (fränthē′skō dä tōlā′dhō), d. 1584, Spanish viceroy of Peru (1569–81). Of one of noblest families in Spain, he had served with distinction there before going to Peru. His able administration marked the end of tumultuous period after Spanish Conquest. One blot on his career was the unjust execution of last Inca, Tupac Amaru.

Toledo (tŭlē′dō, Span. tōlā′dhō), city (pop. 27,427), cap. of Toledo prov., central Spain, in New Castile, on a granite hill surrounded on three sides by a gorge of the Tagus. Played important role in Spanish history and culture. It fell to Rome 193 B.C.; became an early archiepiscopal see, scene of several Church councils (see TOLEDO, COUNCILS OF), and cap. of Visigothic

Spain. Under Moorish rule (A.D. 712–1085) it was the cap. of an emirate (after 1031 an independent kingdom) and a center of Moorish, Spanish, and Jewish cultures. Its great prosperity was due to its steel industry (Toledan sword blades were famous throughout the world) and to its silk and wool mfg. After its conquest by Castile, Toledo became the chief royal residence but was superseded by Valladolid in the 15th cent. Its general aspect has changed little since EL GRECO painted his famous *View of Toledo,* but the alcazar (originally a Moorish structure) was heavily damaged (1936) in the Spanish civil war, when the Insurgents heroically resisted a two-month siege of the fortress. Among other landmarks are the Gothic cathedral (begun 1227), with paintings by El Greco, and the Church of Santo Tomé, with El Greco's *Burial of the Conde de Orgaz.*

Toledo (tŭlē′dō), city (pop. 303,616), NW Ohio on Maumee R. near its mouth on L. Erie; settled 1817 as Port Lawrence on site of Fort Industry (1794). A major Great Lakes' shipping point with shipbuilding, oil refining, and mfg. of automobiles, glass, and electrical equipment. Toledo War (1835–36) was Ohio-Mich. boundary dispute, settled by Congress awarding Toledo strip to Ohio. Growth stimulated by completion of canals and railroads, and by development of gas, oil, and coal resources. Toledo plan of labor conciliation (1946) has been adopted by other cities. Seat of Univ. of Toledo (coed.; 1875). City has art museum, zoological park, Catholic cathedral, and, near by, memorials on sites of Fort Meigs and battle of Fallen Timbers.

Toledo, Councils of, assemblies of the nation and Church in Spain from the 4th to the 16th cent. At one of them in 589 Visigothic King Recared abjured Arianism. The council of 1565–66 saw enunciation of many regulations later embodied in canon law.

Toller, Ernst (ĕrnst′ tô′lùr), 1893–1939, German dramatist. His plays, strong in social protest, include *Man and the Masses* (1920; Eng. tr., 1924) and *Hinkeman* (1924; Eng. tr., *Brokenbrow,* 1926). Died in New York by suicide.

Tolosa (tōlō′sä), town (pop. 10,114), N Spain, in Basque Provs.; former cap. of Guipúzcoa. Mfg. of paper, textiles, machinery. Old section has preserved medieval aspect.

Tolstoy, Leo (tŏl′stoi), Rus. *Lev Nikolayevich Tolstoi,* 1828–1910, Russian writer and religious philosopher, b. Yasnaya Polyana, the estate of his noble family. His youth was spent like that of other Russian nobles, in army service (campaigns in the Caucasus and the Crimean War) and in dissipated pleasure, but his soul-searching and desire for social reform were early expressed by his attempt to create a school for serfs in 1849 (he made another attempt in 1859). Early autobiographical works (*Childhood,* 1852; *Boyhood,* 1854; *Youth,* 1857) strengthened his position as a literary figure. Trips (1857, 1860) to the West led him to question the basis of modern civilization. After marriage (1862), he retired to Yasnaya Polyana, where he wrote *The Cossacks* (1863); *War and Peace* (1865–69), a prose epic of the Napoleonic Wars, considered by many the greatest novel ever written; *Anna Karenina* (1875–77), a moral tragedy against the background of St. Petersburg society; and lesser works. He underwent about 1876 a "conversion" to belief in Christian love, nonresistance to evil, and the simple faith of the peasants. He gathered many followers, and his cult of nonviolence and the simple life has many admirers in the world today. He attempted to give up all his property, broke with his wife, and died at the railroad station of Astapovo, where he was accompanied only by his daughter Alexandra. His later works in fiction include *The Death of Ivan Ilyich* (1884), *The Kreutzer Sonata* (1889), *Hadji Murad* (1896–1904), *Resurrection* (1889–1900), and the dramas *The Power of Darkness* (1886) and *The Living Corpse* (1911). Other works deal with religion, ethics, and moral aesthetics.

Toltec (tŏl′tĕk), anc. civilization of Mexico estab. sometime between the 6th and 8th cent. A.D. Toltec language was related to that of later Aztec civilization. Cap. was Tollán (modern Tule, Hidalgo); other centers at Teotihuacán and Cholula. Had fundamentals of earlier Olmec culture, advanced features such as metallurgy, massive pyramid construction, and astronomical knowledge. Civilization fell after the destruction of Tollán (c.1116?).

Toluca (tōlōō′kä), city (pop. 43,429), cap. of Mexico state, central Mexico. On SW border of central plateau, Toluca is high and cold. Settlement established by Hernán Cortés (1530). Agr. and cattle raising are important. Noted for its basket weaving. Volcano, Nevado de Toluca, is near by.

toluene (tŏl′ūēn), **methylbenzene** (mĕ″thĭlbĕn′zēn), or **toluol** (tŏl′ūōl), colorless, liquid hydrocarbon of BENZENE SERIES. Used as solvent and to make dyes and explosives (e.g., T.N.T.).

Tomar (tōōmär′), city (pop. 6,246), central Portugal, in Estremadura. Noted as center of the Knights Templars and, after their suppression in 14th cent., of the wealthy Military Order of Christ, whose great convent-castle overlooks the city from a hill.

tomato, tender perennial plant (*Lycopersicon esculentum*) of nightshade family, native to W South America and widely grown for its juicy, globular red or yellow fruits. In early days the tomato was known as the love apple. The vitamin-rich fruit is used in salads, soups, sauces, and as juice. There are many varieties, including small-fruited types. The currant tomato (*L. pimpinellifolium*) has red fruits of c.½ in. diameter. See *ill.*, p. 783.

Tombaugh, Clyde William (tŏm′bô), 1906–, American astronomer, discoverer (1930) of planet Pluto.

Tombigbee (tŏmbĭg′bē), river, 409 mi. long, rising in NE Miss. and flowing SSE into W Ala., then S to Alabama R. near Mobile, forming Mobile R.

Tombstone, city (pop. 910), SE Ariz., NNW of Bisbee. Laid out 1879 by Ed Schieffelin, who found silver here, 1877. Was large, rich, tough mining town till c.1900; lead, gold, silver still mined. Now a health resort; tourism is main industry.

Tomlinson, H(enry) M(ajor), 1873–, English novelist, author of sea stories (e.g., *Gallions Reach*, 1927). Other works include *The Sea and the Jungle* (1912).

Tomsk (tômsk), city (pop. 141,215), RSFSR, in W central Siberia, on Tom R. and on a spur of Trans-Siberian RR. Cultural center (university, founded 1888). Light mfg.; agr. processing. Founded 1604. Was the leading Siberian city in 19th cent.

Toms River, village (pop. 2,517), E N.J., on Toms R. near Barnegat Bay. Fishing center. Privateering port in Revolution, when burned by British.

Tom Thumb, 1838–83, American dwarf and entertainer, whose real name was Charles Sherwood Stratton. Named and made famous (after 1842) by P. T. Barnum. Appearing with his wife (also a Barnum dwarf) he was enormously popular until his retirement in 1882.

tonality, in music, the quality by which all tones of a composition are heard in relation to a central tone called the keynote or tonic. In music which has harmony, tonality is practically synonomous with *key*, a term used to indicate the SCALE from which the tonal material of a composition is derived. A composition in C major uses as its basic tonal material the tones from the C major scale; its harmony employs chords built on tones of that scale; and C is the keynote. Deliberate avoidance of a feeling of key is called ATONALITY.

Tonawanda (tŏnŭwŏn′dù), city (pop. 14,617), W N.Y., N of Buffalo and on Niagara R. at end of the Barge Canal; organized 1836. Canal-shipping and rail center. Chemicals and paper, metal, wood products.

Tone, (Theobald) Wolfe, 1763–98, Irish revolutionary. Intrigued for French aid in an Irish rebellion and fostered several abortive expeditions to Ireland. In 1798 rebellion he was defeated and captured by the English. Committed suicide.

tone, in music, a sound of definite pitch caused by the regularity of vibrations which produce it. Through EQUAL TEMPERAMENT, the octave is divided into 12 tones of equal intervals, an interval being the difference in PITCH between two tones. In a SCALE, a tone whose interval from the tone preceding it is approximately one-sixth that of the octave is called a whole tone or whole step (e.g., C-D, F sharp-G sharp, A-B); a tone whose interval from the tone preceding it is approximately one-twelfth that of the octave is called a half tone, half step, or semi-tone (e.g., C-C sharp, A sharp to B, or E-F).

tone poem or **symphonic poem**, type of orchestral composition created by Liszt. It discards classical form and favors poetic or other literary inspiration. Tone poems can "tell a story," as in those of Richard Strauss; state feelings of nationalism, as in those of Sibelius; or reflect impressions, as in those of Debussy.

Tonga (tŏng′gù), island group (250 sq. mi.; pop. 34,130), S Pacific. Most of the islands are coral; a few are volcanic. Discovered 1616–43 by the Dutch. Visited 1773 by Capt. James Cook, the group received English missionaries in 1797. Constitutional monarchy was estab. 1862; group became British protectorate, 1900. Its present ruler, Queen Salote, is last hereditary monarch of Polynesia.

Tongareva, island: see PENRHYN.

tonka bean (tŏng′kù), seed of the pod of a leguminous tree (*Dipteryx odorata*) of tropical South America. Used as a vanilla substitute and in perfume.

Tonkin (tŏn′kĭn), state (44,670 sq. mi.; pop. 9,851,200), N Indo-China, constituting part of VIET NAM; cap. Hanoi. Bounded on N by China, SW by Laos, S by Annam, and SE by Gulf of Tonkin. Consists mainly of highlands enclosing the Red R. delta. Crops include rice, corn, coffee, and tea. Tonkin has the only important coal fields of Indo-China. Population is mainly Annamese, with a large minority of Chinese. Area surrounding Tonkin was the original state of ANNAM (10th–16th cent.). The French first came in 1866 to open the Red R. to trade. After war with China (1882–85), which claimed sovereignty over Tonkin, the French established a protectorate over the area 1884–85, and Tonkin joined Union of Indo-China in 1887. After World War II it was the seat of the Vietminh revolt.

Tonle Sap (tŏn′lä säp′), lake, central Cambodia. At low water, it covers c.1,000 sq. mi.; in flood periods the area is more than tripled. Its outlet joins Mekong R. near Pnom Penh.

Tonsberg, Nor. **Tønsberg** (tûns′bĕr), city (pop. 11,883), SE Norway; a seaport on the Skagerrak near mouth of Oslo Fjord. Norway's oldest city. Major whaling base since 18th cent.

tonsils, lymphoid masses of tissue. Palatine tonsils lie in throat on either side of soft palate. Pharyngeal tonsils are commonly called adenoids.

Tonti or **Tonty, Henri de**, c.1650–1704, French explorer in present Canada and U.S., b. Italy. Lieutenant of LA SALLE.

Tonto National Monument: see NATIONAL PARKS AND MONUMENTS (table).

Tonty, Henri de: see TONTI, HENRI DE.

Tooele (tōō′lù), city (pop. 7,269), N central Utah, S of Great Salt L. Smelting and reduction of ores (silver, lead, copper). Elton Tunnel (built 1937–42) extends E to Bingham Canyon mines.

Toombs, Robert, 1810–85, American statesman, Confederate leader. U.S. Senator from Ga. (1853–61). Active in Ga. secession and organization of Confederacy. Commanded Ga. troops in Civil War. Active in post-war Ga. politics.

tooth: see TEETH.

topaz, widely distributed aluminum silicate mineral used as gem. Color varies, but is usually pale yellow. Occurs in certain igneous and metamorphic rocks.

Sources include Russia, Czechoslovakia, Norway, Sweden, Brazil, Mexico, and parts of U.S.

Topeka (tùpē'kù), city (pop. 78,791), state cap., NE Kansas, on Kansas R. and W of Kansas City. Laid out 1854 by Free State settlers as rail center on old Oregon Trail ferry site (1842). Short-lived Free State constitution was framed here 1855. Became state cap. when Kansas entered the Union in 1861. Trade and industrial center for rich agr. area, it has railway shops and offices, wholesale houses, and food-processing plants. Seat of Menninger Clinic for psychiatric research and Washburn Municipal Univ. of Topeka (coed.; 1865).

Tophet (tō'fĭt), place in vale of HINNOM. Associated with evil cults, hence became a name for hell. 2 Kings 23.10; Isa. 30.33; Jer. 7.31–33.

Toppenish (tŏ'pŭnĭsh), farm trade city (pop. 5,265), S Wash., S of Yakima. Processes food.

Torah (tō'rù), Hebrew name for the first five books of the Bible, the Law of Moses or the Pentateuch, supposed in Judaism to have been given to Moses on Mt. Sinai.

Tordesillas (tōr"dhāsē'lyäs), town (pop. 3,700), N central Spain, in Leon. Here in 1494 Spain and Portugal signed treaty dividing non-Christian world into two zones of influence. The treaty followed the papal bull of 1493 which had given the New World to Spain and Africa and India to Portugal, but it shifted the line of demarcation to the W, giving Portugal a claim to Brazil. Castle of Tordesillas was residence of Joanna of Castile 1516–55.

Torgau (tôr'gou), town (pop. 18,455), Saxony-Anhalt, E Germany, on the Elbe. Chemicals, glass, pottery, machinery. Torgau League of Protestant princes was founded here 1526. Frederick II of Prussia defeated Austrians near here 1760. U.S. and USSR troops made their first contact here April 27, 1945.

Torino, Italy: see TURIN.

tornado (tôrnā'dō), rotating storm, more violent and of shorter duration than hurricane and with lower barometric pressure at center. Dark funnel-shaped cloud, around axis of which winds blow spirally upward, extends toward earth, twists, rises, and falls, causing destruction. Diameter of tornado ranges from few feet to a mile; winds estimated at 200–300 mi. per hour. Occur chiefly in central U.S.

Torne (tôr'nù), Finnish *Tornio,* Swed. *Torne älv,* river, 250 mi. long, rising in N Sweden and flowing SW into Gulf of Bothnia at Tornio, Finland. Forms Swedish-Finnish frontier below its junction with the Muonio.

Torngat Mountains, N Labrador, northernmost range of Laurentian Plateau, extending 120 mi. N–S between Atlantic coast and Que. border.

Toronto (tùrŏn'tō), city (pop. 675,754), provincial cap., S Ont., Canada, on N shore of L. Ontario at mouth of Humber R. and NNW of Buffalo, N.Y. Second largest city in Canada, port of entry, and important commercial, financial, and industrial center with railroad shops, food processing, printing, and mfg. of machinery and other metal products. Here are Royal Ontario Mus., Ontario Mus. of Archaeology, Osgoode Hale Law School, Anglican and Roman Catholic cathedrals. Seat of Univ. of Toronto (nonsectarian; coed.; opened 1843 by Anglicans as King's Col.) with many affiliated colleges. French built Fort Rouillé here (1749); post destroyed (1759) and site occupied by British as Fort Toronto. After American Revolution it received many United Empire Loyalists. As York, it became cap. of Upper Canada in 1796. Twice taken by Americans in War of 1812. Renamed Toronto 1834, it became center of insurrection led by W. L. Mackenzie (1837). By the Act of Union (1840) cap. was moved to Kingston, but returned 1849.

Toronto, city (pop. 7,253), E Ohio, on Ohio R. and near Steubenville. Mfg. of steel and clay products and glass.

Toronto, University of: see TORONTO, Ont.

torpedo, in naval warfare, a self-propelled submarine projectile. The first effective torpedo, built in 1866 by an Englishman, Robert Whitehead, operated with compressed air. A typical modern torpedo is 21 in. in diameter and from 20 ft. to 24 ft. long. It may be driven by a steam or electric engine, or it may be jet-propelled.

Torquay (tôrkē'), municipal borough (pop. 53,216), Devonshire, England; seaside resort and yachting center. South Devon Technical Col. is here.

Torquemada, Juan de (hwän' dä tôrkämä'dhä), 1388–1468, Spanish cardinal; a Dominican monk. Upheld papal authority against conciliar theory at councils of Constance and Basel. His nephew, **Tomás de Torquemada** (tōmäs'), 1420–98, also a Dominican, was confessor to Ferdinand and Isabella, and in 1483 became inquisitor general of Castile and Aragon. The founder of the Spanish INQUISITION, he devised extremely harsh rules of procedure and enforced them rigorously. He also played a major part in the expulsion of the Jews (1492). His name became a by-word for cruelty.

Torrance, residential city (pop. 31,834), S Calif., S of Los Angeles; planned 1911. Oil wells and rail shops. Produces steel and metal products.

Torrence, (Frederic) Ridgely, 1875–1950, American poet and dramatist. Works include *Plays for a Negro Theater* (1917); *Hesperides* (1925) and *Poems* (1941).

Torrens, Lake, shallow salt lake, 120 mi. long, 40 mi. wide, S central South Australia.

Torreón (tōräōn'), city (pop. 75,796), Coahuila, N Mexico; metropolis of LAGUNA DISTRICT; estab. 1893. Grew rapidly. Has rubber factory, cotton and flour mills, brewery, foundries, and smelter.

Tôrres Vedras (tô'rĭsh vä'drùsh), town (pop. 4,762), W Portugal, in Estremadura. Important fortress and royal residence in Middle Ages. In the Peninsular War it was the key point of Wellington's line of defense.

Torrey, John, 1796–1873, American botanist and chemist. He was founder of the New York Academy of Sciences and of the Torrey Botanical Club and author of works on North American plants.

Torricelli, Evangelista (tôrĭchĕ'lē, Ital. ävänjālē'stä tōr-rēchĕl'lē), 1608–47, Italian physicist and mathematician. Invented mercurial BAROMETER and a microscope and improved the telescope.

torrid zone: see TROPICS.

Torrington, George Byng, Viscount, 1663–1733, British admiral. Was a commander in War of Spanish Succession. Drove off (1708) the fleet with which James Edward Stuart hoped to invade Great Britain.

Torrington, city (pop. 27,820), NW Conn., on Naugatuck R. and W of Hartford; settled c.1735. Metal (esp. brass) products center. Site of John Brown's birthplace is marked.

torsion (tôr'shùn). Force can be applied to solid body—e.g., metal rod, wire, or thread—in such a way as to turn or twist one part of it in plane parallel to adjoining part. Such stress is torsion. Since metal shafts used as rotating parts in machines must resist twisting of this kind, materials used in making them are tested to determine capacity to resist without breaking or becoming permanently deformed. **Torsion balance** is instrument one type of which is used for measuring small electric or magnetic forces and another type for measuring small weights, like the ordinary balance. Is based on fact that a wire or thread resists twisting with force proportional to stress. Torsion balance has wire or thread attached at one end so that force applied at free end tends to twist it out of shape; extent of twisting is a measure of the force.

Torstensson, Lennart (lĕ'närt tōr'stùnsōn), 1603–51, Swedish general in Thirty Years War. A brilliant artillery commander, he succeeded Baner as commander in chief (1641). Fought victoriously in Saxony, Bohemia, Moravia, and Silesia; overran Denmark (1643–44). His victory at Jankau (1645) laid Prague and Vienna open to Swedish attack.

tortoise (tôr'tùs), reptile of order Chelonia (or Testudinata), often called TURTLE. In U.S., tortoise usually is applied only to terrestrial forms.

Tortosa (tôrtō′sä), city (pop. 11,951), NE Spain, in Catalonia, on Ebro R. Founded as Roman colony. Held by Moors 8th cent.–1148. Has Gothic cathedral.

Tortugas: see DRY TORTUGAS.

Torun (tô′rōōnyù), Ger. *Thorn,* city (pop. 68,085), NW Poland, on the Vistula. Trade center. Founded 1231 as castle by Teutonic Knights. First Peace of Torun (1411) was short-lived settlement of struggle between Poland and Teutonic Knights; Second Peace of Torun (1466) gave Poland access to Baltic Sea and overlordship over domain of the knights. City passed to Prussia 1793, reverted to Poland 1919. Birthplace of Copernicus.

Tory, Geofroy (tôrē′), c.1480–1533, Parisian printer, artist, engraver, bookbinder. His *Book of Hours* (1525) introduced type design independent of the influence of handwriting. Also wrote *Champfleury* (1529).

Tory, English political party. Name first used for supporters of duke of York (later James II). After 1688 the Tories favored landed aristocracy and opposed rights of non-Anglicans and foreign entanglements. Reaching zenith under Queen Anne, with Robert HARLEY and Henry ST. JOHN as leaders, the party was discredited for Jacobite leanings under George I. WHIG party ruled for 50 years. Revived by younger William Pitt, Tories promoted idea of popular rule. Made reactionary again by French Revolution, Tories lost power after Reform Bill of 1832 and evolved into the CONSERVATIVE PARTY.

Toscana, Italy: see TUSCANY.

Toscanelli, Paolo dal Pozzo (päō′lō däl pôt′tsō tōskänĕl′lē), 1397–1482, Italian cosmographer and mathematician, a physician. It is said that his map of the world was used by Columbus on the 1492 voyage to America.

Toscanini, Arturo (tŏ″skŭnē′nē), 1867–, Italian conductor. He began his career as a cellist, until, substituting as conductor in Rio de Janeiro (1886), he was so successful that he was engaged for the rest of the season. In Italy he conducted the world première of Puccini's *La Bohème* (1896) and Italian premières of Wagner's *Götterdämmerung, Die Meistersinger,* and *Siegfried.* He later conducted at La Scala, Milan (where he was musical director) and at the Bayreuth and Salzburg Festivals. In the U.S. he conducted at the Metropolitan Opera, New York, 1908–14, and the New York Philharmonic, 1926–36. In 1937 the NBC Symphony was especially formed for him.

Tosti, Sir Francesco (Paolo) (fränchă′skō tô′stē), 1846–1916, Italian composer and teacher. Went to London 1875; knighted 1908. His *Serenade* and *Goodbye* are the best known of his many songs.

Tostig (tŏ′stĭg), d. 1066, earl of Northumbria. Northumbrians revolted (1055) against his severe rule and chose Morcar as their earl. Tostig and his ally, Harold III of Norway, were killed by Tostig's brother, Harold, at battle of Stamford Bridge.

totem (tō′tùm), in animistic religion, an object, usually animal, which a man regards with unusual respect, and to which he considers himself intimately related, as by kinship or descent. Clan totem, to which all members of clan consider themselves related in same way, is most common form. Member of clan totem bears totem name; must marry outside totem group (exogamy); believes himself to be descended from totem; and must not kill, eat, or touch totem animal, or call it by its true name. Totemism exists largely in Australia, Melanesia, and North America. No generally acceptable theory for origin of totemism exists.

Totila (tō′tĭlù) or **Baduila** (bädūī′lù), d. 552, last king of the Ostrogoths (541–52). Took Naples (543) and Rome (546) from the Byzantines, making himself master of central and S Italy. In 552 Justinian I sent an army under NARSES against him. Totila's defeat and death in battle restored temporary control over Italy to Byzantium.

Tottenham (tŏt′ùnùm), urban district (pop. 126,921), Middlesex, England; residential suburb of London.

toucan (tōōkăn′), perching bird of tropical America. It has an enormous bill, usually brightly colored. See *ill.,* p. 105.

touch, sense by which pressure against body is perceived. Stimulus is received in specialized nerve cells or end organs in skin or membranes.

touch-me-not: see IMPATIENS.

Toul (tōōl), city (pop. 8,971), Meurthe-et-Moselle dept., NE France, on the Moselle. Episcopal see 5th cent.–1801; free imperial city until annexation to France (1552). Was fortified by Vauban. Damaged in World War II.

Toulon (tōōlō′), city (pop. 116,141), Var dept., SE France; a Mediterranean port and chief French naval station. After its surrender to English by royalists (1793), Bonaparte won his first fame in its recapture. French fleet was scuttled here in Nov., 1942, to avoid capture by Germans. Toulon was heavily bombed as German submarine base (1944).

Toulouse (tōōlōōz′), city (pop. 225,854), cap. of Haute-Garonne dept., S France, on the Garonne; historic cap. of Languedoc. Commercial and cultural center. Archiepiscopal see. Has university (founded 1230). Dating from pre-Roman times, it was the cap. of the Visigoths A.D. 419–507; later became a county which, by the 12th cent., held overlordship over most of Languedoc. The court of the counts was the center of S French medieval culture. The crusades against the ALBIGENSES (13th cent.) laid the county waste. On the death of Count Raymond VII (1249) Toulouse passed to Alphonse, brother of King Louis IX, and in 1271 it was added to the royal domain. The famous annual poetic contests—Académie des Jeux Floraux—began c.1223 and are still held. Toulouse is rich in historic monuments (e.g., Romanesque basilica, with tomb of St. Thomas Aquinas; Gothic cathedral; 18th-cent. "old quarter").

Toulouse-Lautrec (Monfa), Henri de (tōōlōōz′ lōtrĕk′), 1864–1901, French artist, son of a wealthy nobleman. Prolific as a painter, poster artist, and illustrator, he is noted for his satiric studies of music halls, circuses, and low-life types of Paris. Grotesquely deformed since childhood, he led a life of debauchery in Paris.

Toungoo (toung′gōō′), town (pop. 23,223), SE Burma, on Rangoon-Mandalay railroad. Preceded Pegu as cap. of unified Burmese kingdom in 16th cent.

Touraine (tōōrān′, Fr. tōōrĕn′), region and former province, W central France, in Indre-et-Loire dept., drained by Loire R.; cap. Tours. The "garden of France," it is a fertile region of orchards and vineyards, famed for its many historic castles (e.g., Chinon and Amboise). Originally the county of Tours, it passed to the counts of Blois (10th cent.), then to Anjou (11th cent.) and to England (1152). It was retaken by Philip II in 1204 and incorporated into the royal domain.

Tourcoing (tōōrkwĕ′), city (pop. 73,772), Nord dept., N France. Textile center.

tourmaline (tōōr′mùlĭn, –lēn), complex borosilicate mineral used as gem. Occurs in three-, six-, and nine-sided crystals. Color varies with impurities—red and pink, blue, green, yellow, violet-red. Sources include Burma, Siberia, Brazil, U.S.

Tournai (tōōrnă′), Flemish *Doornik,* city (pop. 32,507), Hainaut prov., W Belgium, on the Scheldt. Textile center (wool, linen, carpets). Dates from Roman times. Has 11th-cent. cathedral; 17th-cent. cloth hall. Also spelled Tournay and Doornijk.

Tournefort, Joseph Pitton de (zhôzĕf′ pĕtō′ dù tōōrnfôr′), 1656–1708, French botanist. His system of classification, in vogue until superseded by that of Linnaeus, based plant genera on similarities in flower and fruit and classed plants as herbs, bushes, and trees.

Tours (tōōr, tōōrz), city (pop. 76,207), cap. of Indre-et-Loire dept., W central France, on the Loire; historic cap. of Touraine. Has wine, silk, and other industries. An old Gallo-Roman town, it grew after death (397?) of St. MARTIN, bishop of Tours (buried in Basilica of

St. Martin, built 1887–1924). Charles Martel defeated Saracens in great battle between Tours and Poitiers (732). Gregory of Tours (6th cent.) and Alcuin (9th cent.) made city a center of medieval learning. Louis XI died in near-by château of Plessis-lès-Tours. Tours was temporary French cap. 1870–71 and 1940. Despite damage suffered in World War II, it remains a handsome city and important tourist center. Birthplace of Balzac.

Toussaint L'Ouverture, François Dominique (fräswä′ dômēnēk′ tōōsĕ′ lōōvĕrtür′), c.1744–1803, Haitian Negro patriot and martyr. A self-educated slave, he led Negro rebellion, and because of his fast-moving campaigns became known as L'Ouverture [opening]. In 1793 when the British occupied Haiti's coastal cities and allied themselves with Spanish in E part of island, Toussaint forced their withdrawal. In 1801 he conquered Santo Domingo and governed whole island until Napoleon sent Gen. Leclerc in 1802. Haitian resistance was stubborn, and a peace treaty was drawn up, but Toussaint was treacherously seized and taken to France, where he died in prison.

Tower of London, anc. fortress and royal residence in London, on N bank of the Thames, covering c.13 acres. Now mainly an arsenal, it was for centuries the jail of illustrious prisoners. Enclosed by a dry moat, in center is White Tower (built c.1078). Other towers include Wakefield Tower, housing the crown jewels. Traitors' Gate and Bloody Tower have many historical associations. Many persons were beheaded here. Yeomen of the Guard ("Beefeaters"), in Tudor garb, still guard the Tower. N bastion was destroyed in World War II bombing.

towhee (tō′hē), North American bird of finch family. Red-eyed towhee (also called chewink and ground robin) is found E of Great Plains in U.S. and in parts of Canada; male has glossy back upper parts, chestnut brown sides, white breast and abdomen.

Townsend, Francis Everett (toun′zùnd), 1867–, American reformer, author of popular Townsend plan (1933). Plan proposed an old-age pension, to be financed by a 2% Federal sales tax.

Townshend, Charles Townshend, 2d Viscount (toun′zĕnd), 1674–1738, English statesman. Concluded Barrier Treaty (1709) guaranteeing Hanoverian Succession. As Whig secretary of state (1714–16) under George I he crushed Jacobite rising of 1715. Shared power with his brother-in-law, Robert WALPOLE, but opposed his foreign policy and retired (1730).

Townshend, Charles, 1725–67, English statesman. Chancellor of exchequer (1766–67), he undertook the hated levies known as the **Townshend Acts** (1767). Passed by English Parliament after repeal of Stamp Act, they imposed customs duties on imports of glass, lead, paints, paper, and tea. Resulting colonial unrest led to BOSTON MASSACRE and BOSTON TEA PARTY.

Townsville, town (pop. 34,109), Queensland, Australia; state's second port on inlet of Pacific Ocean; founded 1868. Exports include wool and sugar.

Towson (tou′sùn), town (1940 pop. 10,606), N Md., N of Baltimore; settled c.1750. Near by is new campus of Goucher Col. (nonsectarian; for women; opened 1888 by Methodists). Mfg. of tools and aircraft precision equipment.

Towton Field (tou′tùn), West Riding of Yorkshire, England. Forces of Edward IV defeated the Lancastrians here in 1461.

toxin (tŏk′sĭn), poison produced by certain organisms, especially bacteria. Presence of toxins in blood stream stimulates production of antitoxins tending to counteract poison. Use of toxin or toxin-antitoxin mixture to produce immunity to toxin-caused disease (e.g., diphtheria) has been largely replaced by injections of toxoids (toxins treated to destroy poisonous property but retain capacity to stimulate antitoxin formation).

toy. Over 100,000 different kinds are made; some known since prehistoric times.Toy industry was initiated during Middle Ages by distributors, chiefly of Sonneberg and Nuremberg in Germany, who obtained toys from home craftsmen. Large-scale manufacture dates from c.1850; leaders are U.S., Germany, Japan, and Czechoslovakia.

toy dogs. Many small dogs have been developed from the larger breeds for the sole purpose of being pets. One of the smallest of these is the Chihuahua, which weighs from 1 to 6 lb. It has a round skull, wide-set eyes, and large, erect ears, and varies in color from white, through shades of tan, to black. The Mexican hairless is about the size of a fox terrier. Its body is hairless except for fuzz on the top of its head, and its smooth skin may be any of several colors and is often mottled. Easily recognized by its flat nose and round, protruding eyes is the Pekingese (or Pekinese). Its coat is straight and silky and may be black, tan, fawn, brown, or white. The Pomeranian, resembling a miniature spitz dog, has a long-haired tail curling over its back. Its coat is especially abundant around the head and neck and may be black, brown, red, cream, blue, or white. The dog usually weighs less than 8 lb. The pug is distinguished by its short blunt muzzle and tightly curled tail. Its smooth short coat may be silver, fawn, or black. One variety of POODLE is a toy dog.

Toynbee, Arnold, 1852–83, English economic historian and reformer. His *Lectures on the Industrial Revolution of the 18th Century in England* (1884) is a pioneer work in economic history. Toynbee Hall, first social settlement, was named for him. His nephew, **Arnold J(oseph) Toynbee,** 1889– is an English historian. His *Study of History* (6 vols., 1934–39; incomplete) rejects deterministic philosophy and holds that course of history is ruled by psychic, not materialistic, forces. He maintains that the well-being of a civilization lies in its ability to respond successfully to human and environmental challenges. He was working on final volume in 1952.

Toyokuni (tōyō′kōōnē), 1769–1825, Japanese color-print artist, famous for portrayals of stage favorites in dramatic situations.

toyon: see CHRISTMASBERRY.

Trabzon, Turkey: see TREBIZOND.

trachea: see WINDPIPE.

trachoma (trŭkō′mù), chronic, contagious granular inflammation of lining of eyelid and eyeball, a form of conjunctivitis. Probably caused by a virus. Incidence is high in Egypt and Palestine and in parts of U.S. Unless healed in early stages, may result in blindness.

track and field athletics, athletic events, principally running, jumping, and throwing (as of a javelin). These events dominated early Olympic Games, were popular in Rome, but lapsed in early Middle Ages. Revived in England in 12th cent. In modern Olympic games track events include 100-, 200-, 400-, 800-, 1,500-, 5,000-, and 10,000 meter runs; the MARATHON RACE; 110- and 400-meter hurdle races; 400- and 1,600-meter relay; 3,000-meter steeplechase; 50,000-meter walk. Field events include broad jump, high jump, pole vault, shot-put, discus throw, javelin throw, hammer throw, and running hop-step-and-jump.

Tractarian movement: see OXFORD MOVEMENT.

tractor, machine, usually powered by gasoline, used primarily to draw agricultural implements, e.g., plow and harvester, and to furnish power for spraying, sawing, and other purposes. Main types are wheel type and crawler or caterpillar type, from which military tank is adapted.

Tracy, city (pop. 8,410), central Calif., SW of Stockton. Agr. shipping and processing center. Has a pumping plant of Central Valley project.

trade union: see UNION, LABOR.

Trafalgar, Cape (trùfăl′gùr), on SW coast of Spain, near NW shore of Strait of Gibraltar. In the **battle of Trafalgar,** Oct. 21, 1805, the British under Nelson defeated the French and Spanish fleets under Villeneuve, capturing 20 ships and losing none. Nelson's maneuvers were among the most brilliant in naval history. At the beginning of the battle his flagship, the

Victory, signaled the famous words: "England expects that every man will do his duty." Nelson was fatally wounded in the battle.

Trafalgar Square, in London, named for Nelson's victory; site of the Nelson column.

tragacanth (trăˈgŭkănth), gummy exudation from shrub *Astragalus gummifer* and related plants of E Europe and Asia. It is used as an emulsifying agent, in pills, hand lotions, medicinal lubricating jellies, and for sizing.

tragedy. Aristotle defined tragedy as imitation of a painful action (usually resulting in death) by a person of stature which by pity and fear purges these emotions. Modern tragedy may contain comic elements or subplots for contrast or relief of emotional intensity. Tragedy evolved from ancient Greek religious rites, but the tragedies of Aeschylus, Sophocles, and Euripides were literary rather than ritual. Tragedy in 17th-cent. France (esp. in plays of Racine and Corneille) held to the classical unities of time, place, action; this unity contrasts with such English tragedy as the plays of Shakspere. In recent times tragedy in traditional sense has declined. In Ibsen's work the tragedy is often in political and social problems. Some modern writers of tragedy are Chekhov, Strindberg, Synge, Eugene O'Neill, Maxwell Anderson.

Traherne, Thomas (trŭhûrnˈ), b. 1637 or 1639, d. 1674, English author, one of the metaphysical poets.

Trail, city (pop. 11,430), SE B.C., Canada, on Columbia R., just N of Wash. border. Metal-smelting center in mining region.

trailing arbutus or **Mayflower,** one of the best loved of American wild flowers, a creeping plant (*Epigaea repens*) with hairy evergreen leaves which often hide the sweetly fragrant, flesh-tinted flowers in early spring. Wild plants are difficult to establish in the garden, but nursery-grown plants (from cuttings or seeds) can be cultivated in acid soil and shade. In England, a hawthorn is called Mayflower; the strawberry tree and madroña of genus *Arbutus* are not related to trailing arbutus.

Trajan (trāˈjŭn), A.D. c.53–117, Roman emperor (A.D. 98–117), b. Spain; the adopted son and successor of Nerva. Brought Dacia under Roman control and conquered much of Parthia. Built much in Rome (including the Forum of Trajan). Succeeded by Hadrian.

Tralee (trŭlēˈ, trā–), urban district (pop. 9,990), county town of Co. Kerry, Ireland; seaport.

Trani (träˈnē), city (pop. 29,962), Apulia, S Italy; an Adriatic port. Famous for its wine. Flourished at times of Crusades. Its *ordinamenta maris* of 1063 were probably the first medieval maritime code. Has noted Romanesque cathedral.

Trans-Alai (trănsˈ-älīˈ), mountain range, central Asia; part of Pamir system. Extends c.125 mi. W from USSR-China border into USSR. Rises to Lenin Peak (23,382 ft. high).

Transandine Railway, between Mendoza, Argentina, and Los Andes, Chile (distance 156 mi.), traversing Uspallata Pass. Completed in 1910, road rises to c.10,500 ft. at tunnel on international boundary. Another Transandine Railway extending from Antofagasta (Chile) to Salta (Argentina) was completed in 1948.

Trans-Caspian Railroad, important rail link of Soviet central Asia; also known as Central Asiatic RR. Built 1880–1905, it begins at Krasnovodsk on Caspian Sea, passes Bukhara, Samarkand, and Tashkent, and ends at Chkalov. Connected with Turkistan-Siberia RR N of Tashkent.

transcendentalism, in philosophy, any system holding that there are modes of being beyond the reach of mundane experience. The term is generally associated with Kant, who felt that space, time, and categories of judgment were transcendent—above the evidence of the senses. In American literature, a movement in New England from 1836 to 1860 is called transcendentalism. The transcendentalists (Emerson, Thoreau, Margaret Fuller, Bronson Alcott, and others) were high-minded and idealistic, laying stress on individualism, self-reliance, and social reform. Their journal was the *Dial* (1840–44), and BROOK FARM stemmed from transcendentalism.

Transcona, town (pop. 6,752), SE Man., Canada, E of Winnipeg. Railroad and industrial center.

transference: see PSYCHOANALYSIS.

Transfiguration, the "shining" appearance of Jesus before Peter, James, and John. Mat. 17; Mark 9.

transformer, in electricity, device commonly used for increasing or decreasing voltage of an alternating current. Two separate insulated coils wound around iron core are used. Alternating current led through first (primary) coil induces similar current in other (secondary) coil of different voltage. If secondary coil has more turns than primary, voltage is "stepped up"; if secondary has less turns than primary the voltage is "stepped down." Since alternating current of high voltage is cheaper to transmit than low voltage, transformers are used first to step up voltage for transmission and then to step it down when lower voltage and higher amperage are required for ordinary needs.

transit, in astronomy, passage of one heavenly body across disk of another. Transit obscuring a disk is called an eclipse. Transits of MERCURY and VENUS occur if either of these planets passes between earth and sun when earth crosses intersection of ecliptic and the planet's orbit.

Trans-Jordan or **Transjordania:** see JORDAN.

Transkeian Territories (trănskīˈŭn, –kāˈŭn), division (16,554 sq. mi.; pop. 1,279,922), E Cape Prov., South Africa. Largely a native reservation.

transmutation of elements, conversion of one element into another. One of the quests of the alchemists was to turn other metals into gold by the philosopher's stone. Transmutation occurs during RADIOACTIVITY and bombardment of elements in the cyclotron. See *ill.,* p. 773.

Transpadane Republic: see CISALPINE REPUBLIC.

transpiration, in botany, the normal loss of water by evaporation through the pores (stomata) of a plant's leaves. Transpiration is usually correlated with the dryness of the air although closing of the stomata retards excessive loss of water to some extent. Wilting of a plant results when more water is lost than is absorbed by the roots. Many plants (e.g., cacti) have structural modifications to reduce transpiration.

Trans-Siberian Railroad, c.4,350 mi. long, linking European Russia with Pacific coast. Vladivostok is the terminus. A S branch crosses Manchuria and is known as Chinese Eastern Railway. Construction of railroad (1892–1905) opened up Siberia for colonization and economic exploitation.

transubstantiation: see EUCHARIST.

Transvaal (trănzvälˈ), province (110,450 sq. mi.; pop. 4,283,038), South Africa; cap. Pretoria. Bordered on S by Vaal R., the boundary with Orange Free State. Mainly in the veld, it has good ranching land and a relatively large European population. Wool, hides, and skins are exported, and grain and citrus fruit are grown. The area's wealth, however, lies in its vast mineral resources (esp. of the WITWATERSRAND), including gold, diamonds, coal, and platinum. Settled by the Boers (see TREK), who by 1837 had driven out the Matabele tribe and set up a strong Boer state under A. W. Pretorius. The new state was recognized by the British in 1852 and was named the South African Republic; its chief leader was S. J. P. KRUGER. Britain annexed it in 1877 but restored its independence in 1881. The discovery of gold (1886) led to an influx of British prospectors, whose difficulties with the Boer government were a major cause of the SOUTH AFRICAN WAR. With the Boer defeat, Transvaal was made a British crown colony (1902). It became self-governing in 1907 and joined the Union in 1910.

Transylvania (trănˈsĭlvāˈnyŭ), Ger. *Siebenbürgen,* Hung. *Erdély,* Rumanian *Transilvania* or *Ardeal,* historic province (24,009 sq. mi.; pop. 3,420,829), central Rumania. Chief cities: Cluj, Brasov, Sibiu. A high plateau (1,000–1,600 ft.), it rises in the E and S to the Carpathians. S part of Carpathians, known as Transylvanian Alps, reach 8,361 ft. in Negoiul. The region has agr., vineyards, pastures, orchards and is rich in natural resources (timber, lignite, methane, iron, manganese, lead, sulphur). It has metallurgical, chemical, and textile industries. The large Magyar and German-speaking minorities are mostly urban and largely Protestant. Part of ancient Dacia, Transylvania came, after many invasions, into possession of Hungary (11th cent.). With the Szekely (originally a Turkic tribe which arrived with or before the Magyars and adopted the Magyar language) and the "Saxons" (German colonists who settled in 12th cent.), the Magyars formed the three privileged "nations" of Transylvania. The Rumanians (called Vlachs or Walachs) began to arrive in the 13th cent. and formed the bulk of the peasant serfs. A voivode (royal governor) governed the seven counties of Transylvania for the Hungarian crown. After 1526 the voivode John Zapolya claimed the Hungarian throne as JOHN I against the later emperor FERDINAND I. In the subsequent tripartite partition of HUNGARY, Transylvania became a semi-independent principality, frequently changing allegiance between the emperors and the sultans. Notable among the princes of the 16th–17th cent. were the BATHORY family, Stephen BOCSKAY (who obtained recognition of freedom of worship from the emperor), Gabriel BETHLEN, Emeric THOKOLY, and the RAKOCZY family. In 1711 the princes' efforts to maintain independence from Austrian interference collapsed; Transylvania passed under direct Hapsburg rule. Under the Austro-Hungarian Monarchy (estab. 1867), full Hungarian control was restored, much to the detriment of the Rumanian peasants. Transylvania was seized by Rumania after World War I and was formally ceded by Hungary 1920. The Magyar magnates were expropriated, their vast estates redistributed among the peasants. In World War II many Transylvanian Germans fled to Germany before the arrival of the Russian armies.

Transylvania College: see LEXINGTON, Ky.

Transylvania Company, organized under leadership of Richard Henderson to exploit and colonize territory embraced by Ohio, Kentucky, and Cumberland rivers. Charter claims by Va. and N.C. voided company's land titles.

Trapani (trä'pänē), anc. *Drepanum,* city (pop. 52,661), W Sicily, Italy. A Carthaginian naval base, it fell to Rome after battle of Aegates (241 B.C.).

Trappists, Roman Catholic monks (Reformed CISTERCIANS or Cistercians of the Stricter Observance), whose name comes from La Trappe, France, where a monastic reform was begun c.1660. Trappists lead lives of strict seclusion, giving their hours to worship, labor, and study. There is no recreation, no meat is eaten, and silence is observed (except under unusual circumstances).

Trasimeno (träzēmā'nō), lake, area 50 sq. mi., Umbria, central Italy. Scene of Hannibal's great victory over Romans under Flaminius (217 B.C.).

Tras-os-Montes (trä'zōōzhmō"tĭsh), former province, NE Portugal, N of Douro R.; historic cap. Braganza Sheep raising. Vineyards in Douro valley. Region now is part of Trás-os-Montes-e-Alto-Douro prov. (4,569 sq. mi.; pop. 592,079; cap. Vila Real).

Travancore (trävŭnkôr'), former princely state, SW India, on Arabian Sea. Unified in 18th cent. by descendant of ancient Chera kings. Allied with the British in wars with Hyder Ali and Tippoo Sahib. Was known for progressive government and comparatively high rate of literacy. Merged 1949 with Cochin to form state of **Travancore-Cochin** (9,155 sq. mi.; pop. 9,265,-157), with cap. at Trivandrum. Cardamom, tea, and coffee plantations. Deposits of ilmenite and monazite.

Traverse, Lake (trä'vŭrs), c.30 mi. long, on Minn.-S.Dak. line, source of Bois de Sioux R. and a headstream of Red R.

Traverse City, city (pop. 16,974), N Mich., N. of Cadillac and at head of West Arm of Grand Traverse Bay; settled 1847. In cherry-growing area, has annual national cherry festival. Lakes attract tourists. Mfg. of metal and wood products.

Travis, William Barrett (trăv'ĭs), 1811–36, hero of Texas Revolution. Commanded forces at the Alamo.

treason, crime of endangering the security of the state by acts threatening the existence of the legal government (in monarchies attempts on the life of the monarch or heir) or the security of the armed forces (e.g., by aiding the enemy). Such acts were called high treason in the English Statute of Treasons (1350), petit treason being the murder of one's lawful superior. In the 19th cent. petit treason was abolished. Treason is defined in Article 3 of the U.S. Constitution as levying war against the U.S. or giving aid and comfort to its enemies.

Treasury, United States Department of the, executive department of Federal government, estab. by act of Congress in 1789 to collect taxes, take charge of Federal funds, and keep accounts. Functions of department have been considerably broadened, including affairs indirectly related to finance. See also BANK OF THE UNITED STATES; FEDERAL RESERVE SYSTEM; INDEPENDENT TREASURY SYSTEM; SUBTREASURY.

Treat, Robert, 1622?–1710, British governor of colony of Conn. (1683–87, 1689–98). Helped found Newark, N.J., in 1666.

treaty port, port opened to foreign trade by treaty, especially in China and Japan in 19th cent. After OPIUM WAR, treaty of Nanking (1842) opened five Chinese treaty ports, later increased to 69. In all, foreigners enjoyed EXTERRITORIALITY. Similar system in Japan followed 1854 expedition of Matthew Perry. End of exterritoriality saw disappearance of treaty ports—in Japan 1899, in China 1946.

Trebbia (trĕb'byä), river, 70 mi. long, N Italy, rising in Liguria and flowing NE into the Po. In 218 B.C. Hannibal won a major victory on the Trebbia near Piacenza.

Trebizond (trĕ'bĭzŏnd"), Turkish *Trabzon,* city (pop. 33,969), NE Turkey, in Turkish Armenia; a Black Sea port. Exports food products, tobacco. The ancient Trapezus, city was founded 8th cent. B.C. Conquered by Mithridates VI 1st cent. B.C.; incorporated into Roman Empire 1st cent. A.D. Again a prosperous port under Byzantine Empire, but reached zenith after establishment of empire of Trebizond. Under rule of Alexius III (1349–90), city was one of world's great trade centers, renowned for wealth and beauty. Declined under Turkish rule. Included 1920 in ephemeral independent state of Armenia. Large Greek population was deported 1923. The **empire of Trebizond,** 1204–1461, was one of the Greek successor states formed after the overthrow (1204) of the Byzantine Empire by the Crusaders. Founded by Alexius I (Comnenus), it remained separate when the Byzantine Empire was restored 1261. Despite periods of vassalage to the Turks and Mongols, the empire prospered economically because of its position on trade route to Middle East and Russia. In 1461, Trebizond, last refuge of Hellenistic civilization, was taken by Mohammed II.

Tree, Ellen: see KEAN, EDMUND.

Tree, Sir Herbert Beerbohm, 1853–1917, English actor-manager, originally named Beerbohm; half brother of Max Beerbohm. At Haymarket theater (1887–97) and at Her Majesty's Theatre (which he built in 1897) he produced and acted in Shakspere, Ibsen, Wilde, and Maeterlinck dramas.

tree, perennial plant with single trunk or stem branching some distance from the ground. Differences between trees and shrubs are often slight; there are some trees with more than one trunk and some shrubs with a single treelike stem. Generally trees are taller and have larger stems. Leaves of deciduous trees and shrubs are shed regularly at the end of the growing season. Leaves of both coniferous and broad-leaved evergreens are shed gradually, often over a period of several years. See also BARK; CAMBIUM; FOREST; LEAF; WOOD.

tree fern, any fern with a treelike trunk, chiefly native to tropics. They often resemble palms.

tree frog, small arboreal frog with adhesive disk on each digit. Common tree frog is also called tree toad. Spring peeper is a tree frog which inflates its throat sac to deliver its loud "peeping."

tree of heaven: see AILANTHUS.

tree surgery, practice of repairing cut or injured trees to preserve their appearance or prevent disease. Cavities are filled with cement or rubber; fresh wounds are often treated with shellac. Extensive repairs should be done by a qualified tree surgeon.

trefoil, name for several plants, chiefly legumes, with trifoliate leaves, e.g., clover, tick trefoil (*Desmodium*), bird's-foot trefoil (*Lotus corniculatus*), a forage plant and weed, and shrubby trefoil.

Treitschke, Heinrich von (hīn'rĭkh fŭn trīch'kù), 1834–96, German historian. Known for stirring and graphic works, notably *History of Germany in the Nineteenth Century* (Eng. tr., 7 vols., 1915–19).

trek (trĕk) [Dutch,= draft], South African term applied to an organized migration. In the Great Trek (1835–36), Boer farmers moved N from Cape of Good Hope to escape British domination.

Trelease, William (trĭlēs'), 1857–1945, American botanist. Director of the Missouri Botanical Garden from 1889 to 1912, he made a special study of genus *Agave*. His son, **Sam Farlow Trelease,** 1892–, a plant physiologist, became head of department of botany, Columbia Univ., in 1930. He has contributed especially to knowledge of photosynthesis, plant respiration, and selenium poisoning of grazing animals.

trench mouth (Vincent's stomatitis), inflammation of soft tissues of mouth. Causative agents believed to be two associated organisms, a bacillus and a spirochete, normally found in mouth. Predisposing factors include certain diseases, effects of certain drugs, vitamin deficiencies, allergies.

Trengganu: see MALAYA.

Trent, Ital. *Trento,* Latin *Tridentum,* city (pop. 37,290), cap. of Trentino-Alto Adige, N Italy, on Adige R. Was cap. of prince-bishopric of Trent from 12th cent, until its secularization and annexation to TYROL (1802). Italian in language and culture, it was awarded to Italy 1919. Was scene of Council of Trent (16th cent.). Landmarks include former episcopal residence, Romanesque cathedral, and statue of Dante.

Trent, third longest river of England. Flows 170 mi. from Staffordshire to join the Ouse W of Hull and form the Humber. Navigable for barges to Nottingham; connects with other streams by canal.

Trent, Council of, 1545–47, 1551–52, 1562–63, 19th ecumenical council of the Roman Catholic Church, chief instrument of the Catholic REFORM; called by PAUL III, after long delays; continued by Julius III and PIUS IV. It clarified Catholic doctrines and issued lucid definitions. The reform measure of the council touched all aspects of religious life and set the pattern for modern Catholicism. The work of the council was confirmed by a bull of Pius IV (*Benedictus Deus,* 1564) and issuance of the official *Catechism of the Council of Trent* (1566).

Trent Affair, incident in diplomatic relations of U.S. and Great Britain in Civil War. On Nov. 8, 1861, Capt. Charles Wilkes halted British ship *Trent,* removed Confederate commissioners J. M. MASON and John SLIDELL, and had them interned at Boston. Britain's sharp protest led U.S. Secretary of State W. H. Seward to send note disavowing action and to release men, thus averting trouble.

Trent Canal, waterways system, 240 mi. long, S Ont.,

Canada, connecting L. Ontario (from Trenton on Bay of Quinte) with L. Huron (at Georgian Bay). Comprises Trent R., Rice L., Otonabee R., Kawartha Lakes, artificial channels to L. Simcoe, L. Couchiching, and Severn R. Primarily for water power.

Trentino-Alto Adige (träntē'nō-äl'tō-ä'dējä), autonomous region (5,252 sq. mi.; pop. 669,029), N Italy, bordering on Switzerland and Austria; cap. Trent. Includes Tyrolean Alps S of Brenner Pass, part of DOLOMITES. Has forests, pastures, vineyards, orchards. Many resorts. Hydroelectric plants. Trento prov. (i.e., the Trentino) is predominantly Italian-speaking. BOLZANO prov. (i.e., the Alto Adige or Upper Adige valley) is largely German-speaking. History up to 1801 is that of bishoprics of TRENT and Bressanone; after 1801, that of S TYROL. Passing to Italy in 1919, it was called Venezia Tridentina until it was granted autonomy (1947), with special rights for German population.

Trento, Italy: see TRENT.

Trenton, town (pop. 10,085), S Ont., Canada, on Bay of Quinte at mouth of Trent R. and at S end of Trent Canal. Wool, paper, and flour mills, and mfg. of machinery and clothing.

Trenton. 1 Village (pop. 6,222), SE Mich., port on Detroit R. Farm trade center producing chemicals. 2 City (pop. 6,157), N Mo., N of Chillicothe. Farm shipping center with railroad shops and food-processing plants. Socialist experiment here 1897–1905. 3 City (pop. 128,009), state cap. (since 1790), W N.J., on Delaware R. (head of navigation) above Camden; settled by Friends 1679. Mfg. of wire rope, structural steel, pottery, rubber goods, airplane and auto equipment, steam turbines, and hardware. Monument (1893) commemorates Revolutionary battle of Dec. 20, 1776, when Washington crossed the Delaware to surprise and capture c.900 Hessians. Notable buildings include the capitol (1792); capitol annex (1931), with state library and museum; World War I memorial (1932); barracks (1758), now restored as museum; Bloomsbury Court (c.1719); Friends' meetinghouse (1739).

Tresca, Carlo (kär'lō trĕ'skä), c.1877–1943, Italian-American anti-Fascist leader and syndicalist, b. Italy, assassinated in New York city.

Tres Marías, Las (läs träs' märē'äs), archipelago, N Mexico, in the Pacific off coast of Nayarit. Islands produce maguey, salt, lumber. One island is used as federal penal colony.

Trevelyan, Sir George Otto, 1838–1928, English historian and politician. *Early History of Charles James Fox* (1880), *American Revolution* (4 vols., 1899–1907), and *George the Third and Charles Fox* (2 vols., 1912) were widely popular in U.S. He also wrote a biography of Lord Macaulay (1876). His son **George Macaulay Trevelyan,** 1876–, a "literary" rather than a "scientific" historian, is best known for *History of England* (1926).

Treves or **Trèves,** Germany: see TRIER.

Trevithick, Richard (trĕ'vĭthĭk), 1771–1833, English engineer. Inventor of a high-pressure steam engine (1800), a locomotive (1801); builder and developer of a steam-operated carriage (1803), steam engines for use in mines, and a steam threshing machine.

triangle, in mathematics, a plane figure bounded by three straight lines. Their points of intersection are called vertices; lines between vertices are called sides; altitude is perpendicular distance from base (any side) to opposite vertex. Area of triangle equals one half product of base and corresponding altitude. Median is line joining midpoint of side to opposite vertex. Triangles usually are classified according to size of angles as equilateral (all three angles equal), isosceles (two angles equal), scalene (all angles different), and right (having one right angle).

triangle, in music: see PERCUSSION INSTRUMENTS.

Trianon (trēänō'), two small châteaux in the park of Versailles, France. The Grand Trianon was built by J. H. Mansart in 1687; the Petit Trianon, favorite residence of Marie Antoinette, was finished by J. A. Gabriel in 1768. The **Treaty of Trianon,** 1920, was signed in the Grand Trianon after World War I by Hungary and the Allies (excluding U.S. and USSR). Reducing Hungary by one third and depriving it of access to the sea, it gave Transylvania, the E Banat, and other districts to Rumania; Slovakia and Ruthenia to Czechoslovakia; Croatia, Slavonia, and the W Banat to Yugoslavia; the BURGENLAND to Austria. Subsequent Hungarian efforts to secure revision of the treaty were supported by the 3,000,000 Magyars living in the ceded territories.

Triassic period (trīă'sĭk), first period of the Mesozoic era of geologic time. Throughout Triassic, E North America was elevated; there was prolonged erosion; at the end extensive faulting (Palisade disturbance). In the West were submergences (with emergence at end of period) and much volcanic activity. Reptiles were dominant in the sea and on land; numerous types of dinosaurs had developed. Conifers were the principal plant life. A new group, cycads (intermediate between tree ferns and palms), arose. See also GEOLOGY, table.

tribe, an aggregate of peoples sharing common descent, dialect, territory, culture. Intermarriage permitted except within proscribed relationships.

Tribonian (trĭbō'nēun), d. 545?, Roman jurist, who at command of Justinian I directed the compilation of the CORPUS JURIS CIVILIS.

Trichinopoly (trĭchĭnŏ'pŭlē), city (pop. 159,566), S Madras, India, on Cauvery R. Here is an enormous rock topped by a Dravidian temple. Was cap. of Chola kingdom, 15th–16th cent. Cotton mills.

trichinosis (trĭ"kĭnō'sĭs) or **trichiniasis** (trĭ"kĭnī'ŭsĭs), serious disease caused by *Trichinella spiralis,* a round worm. Parasite reproduces in intestine; young migrate to muscle and encyst. Caused in man by eating insufficiently cooked infected pork.

trident, in Greek legend, three-pronged fork borne by Poseidon. It probably represented a fishing spear, goad, and forked lightning, because he was god of the sea, of horses, and of forked lightning.

Tridentum: see TRENT, Italy.

Trier (trēr), city (pop. 74,709), Rhineland-Palatinate, W Germany, on the Moselle; also called Treves (trēvz) in English. Center of Moselle wine dist. Textile mfg.; steel industry. Founded by Augustus as Augusta Treverorum, it was a flourishing Roman city (pop. c.50,000) and a residence of the Western emperors from c.295 until its capture by the Franks (early 5th cent.). The archbishops of Trier later ruled considerable territory on both sides of the Rhine as princes and electors of the Holy Roman Empire. Under them Trier prospered and was the seat (1473–1797) of a university. Trier passed to France 1797; the archbishopric was secularized. In 1815 the Congress of Vienna gave the former archiepiscopal lands W of the Rhine (incl. Trier) to Prussia; the rest went to Nassau. Catholic episcopal see was estab. 1821. Trier suffered much destruction in World War II. Its Roman monuments (Porta Nigra, a well-preserved fortified gate; amphitheater; imperial baths) were preserved, but the Gothic Liebfrauenkirche (13th-cent. church), the Romanesque cathedral (partly dating from 4th cent.), and the baroque electoral palace all were heavily damaged. The cathedral contains the Holy Coat, supposedly the seamless coat of Jesus.

Trieste (trēēst', Ital. trēē'stä), Serbo-Croatian *Trst,* city (pop. 248,379); major seaport at head of the Adriatic. Has shipyards, ironworks, and oil refineries. A free commune from the 12th cent., it placed itself (1382) under the dukes of Austria, but kept its administrative autonomy until 18th cent. Became a free port in 1719, flourishing as outlet of Central Europe and the only Austrian port. Having retained Italian language and culture, it was a center of Italian irredentism until annexed to Italy in 1919. Landmarks include Cathedral of San Giusto (partly 6th cent.) and Miramar castle (built for Archduke Maximilian

of Austria). Trieste is now cap. of **Free Territory of Trieste,** free state (285 sq. mi.; pop. c.380,000) under protection of UN Security Council. It comprises the city and a coastal strip of NW ISTRIA, with Slovenian population. The Free Territory was created in 1947 by annexes to Italian peace treaty as a compromise between conflicting claims of Italy and Yugoslavia.

trifoliate orange, small ornamental spiny tree (*Poncirus trifoliata*) of China, with white flowers and aromatic orangelike fruits. Used as an understock for the orange to increase its hardiness.

Triglav (trē'gläv), highest peak (c.9,395 ft.) of Yugoslavia, in Julian Alps.

trigonometry, literally, the science of measuring a TRIANGLE, i.e., measuring its sides, angles, and particularly the ratios of certain pairs of sides. For all right angles having a given acute angle, ratio of a certain pair of sides (side opposite the given angle divided by hypotenuse) is same; hence value of this ratio is function solely of the given acute angle. Using various pairs of sides, six such ratios are obtainable and are called trigonometric functions of a given angle; they are the sine, cosine, tangent, cotangent, secant, and cosecant. Values of these have been tabulated for acute angles of all sizes. Thus, generally, if any three (independent) parts of a triangle are known, its altitude, area, length of all sides, and sizes of all angles, are computable. If all six functions are defined for angles of all sizes, they have certain properties which are periodic (values repeat previous value sequence of preceding interval of angle sizes) and thus indispensable in mathematical applications to study of physical phenomena such as light, sound, color, etc.

trillium or **wake-robin,** spring wild flower of genus *Trillium,* chiefly native to North America. Leaves, petals, and sepals are in threes, the single flower (white, pink, or purplish) is borne erect or nodding from the center of the whorl of leaves.

trilobite (trī'lūbīt), primitive arthropod having body divided into three sections (head, thorax, abdomen). Trilobites were the most numerous inhabitants of the Cambrian seas; they became extinct in Permian period.

Trincomalee (trĭng"kŭmŭlē'), town (pop. 29,146), NE Ceylon; port on Indian Ocean. In World War II it was chief British naval base in Far East after fall of Singapore.

Trinidad, city (pop. 12,204; alt. c.6,000 ft.), S Colo., E of Sangre de Cristo Mts. near N.Mex. line; settled 1859 on Santa Fe Trail. Shipping center for coalmining, dairying, and livestock region.

Trinidad and Tobago (trī'nĭdäd, tōbä'gō), crown colony (pop. 557,970), British West Indies; cap. PORT OF SPAIN. Trinidad (1,864 sq. mi.), lying just N of mouths of Orinoco R. in Venezuela, has natural asphalt lake (Pitch Lake). City of San Fernando is market center for petroleum. Discovered by Columbus in 1498, island did not attract Spanish colonists because of its lack of gold. Subsequently raided by Dutch, French, and English buccaneers. Spain finally ceded island to England (1802). Tobago (116 sq. mi.), just N of Trinidad, is a mountain ridge, densely forested with hardwoods.

trinitrotoluene (T.N.T., TNT) (trī'nī"trōtŏl'ūēn), explosive, yellow crystalline compound of carbon, hydrogen, and oxygen, prepared from toluene. It is stable and can be exploded only with a detonator. It is used alone and in mixtures.

Trinity, in Christianity, God considered as existing in three persons (Father, Son, and Holy Ghost). Definition of the doctrine came early and many of the first Church councils were concerned mainly with the problem (see CREED; NICAEA, COUNCIL OF; ARIANISM).

Trinity, river rising in N Texas through confluence of three forks and flowing c.510 mi. SSE to Trinity Bay, Galveston Bay arm. Several reservoirs upstream (esp. for Fort Worth and Dallas). Soil conservation and flood control projects include Benbrook, Lavon, Grapevine, and Garza–Little Dam reservoirs.

Trinity Bay, Atlantic inlet, 80 mi. long, SE N.F., Canada, between Avalon Peninsula and mainland. At Trinity, port on W shore, first permanent transatlantic cable was laid 1866.

Trinity College: see CAMBRIDGE UNIVERSITY; OXFORD UNIVERSITY.

Trinity College: see DUBLIN, Ireland.

Trinity College: see HARTFORD, Conn.; WASHINGTON, D.C.

Trinity Hall: see CAMBRIDGE UNIVERSITY.

Trinity Sunday, first Sunday after PENTECOST, observed as feast of the Trinity.

Trinity University: see SAN ANTONIO, Texas.

Triple Alliance, name of several European coalitions. That of **1668** was formed by England, Sweden, and Netherlands against Louis XIV of France and forced him to end the War of DEVOLUTION. That of **1717** (among England, France, and Netherlands) became in 1718 the QUADRUPLE ALLIANCE. For alliances of **1872,** see THREE EMPERORS' LEAGUE. For alliance of **1882,** see TRIPLE ALLIANCE AND TRIPLE ENTENTE.

Triple Alliance, War of the, 1865–70, fought by Paraguay under the dictator Francisco Solano López against alliance of Argentina, Brazil, and Uruguay. Defense of Paraguay against powerful odds was heroic, but end of war found Paraguay defeated, with land devastated and population reduced by half.

Triple Alliance and Triple Entente, two international combinations of states that dominated Europe's diplomatic history after 1882 until they came into armed conflict in WORLD WAR I. The secret Dual Alliance of Germany and Austria-Hungary, formed 1879, was joined in 1882 by Italy (incensed by the French occupation of Tunis) and thus became the Triple Alliance. Rumania joined the group 1883, but actually both Italian and Rumanian interests were opposed to Austria-Hungary's, and both states eventually entered World War I on the Allied side. A rapprochement between Russia and France began after 1890, when Germany declined to renew its reinsurance treaty with Russia. The Franco-Russian Dual Entente came into existence by gradual stages and was openly acknowledged in 1895. German commercial and colonial imperialism disquieted Great Britain, which composed its difference with France after 1898 and arrived at the Franco-British Entente Cordiale–an informal understanding. Russia's defeat in the Russo-Japanese War removed some of Britain's fears of Russian expansionism in Asia and made possible a Russo-British understanding (1907). The Triple Entente of France, England, and Russia, though not a formal alliance, proved effective at the outbreak of World War I.

Tripoli (trĭ′pů̇lē), anc. *Tripolis,* city (pop. 59,001), N Lebanon; port on the Mediterranean. Probably founded after 700 B.C., it was the cap. of a Phoenician federation. Flourished under Seleucids and Romans. Captured by Arabs in A.D. 638. Taken 1109 by Crusaders, sacked 1289 by sultan of Egypt. Terminus of an oil pipe line from Iraq, it has an oil refinery. Exports oil, silk, and citrus fruit.

Tripoli (trĭ′pů̇lē), anc. *Oea,* city (pop. 144,616), winter cap. of Libya, in Tripolitania; port on the Mediterranean. Exports include hides, dates, salt, sponges, and carpets. It was the site of a Tyrian colony (7th cent.? B.C.). Passed to Italy in 1911 and became cap. of Libya. It was a base of the Barbary corsairs, whom the U.S. fought in TRIPOLITAN WAR. An Axis base in World War II, it fell to the British in 1943.

Tripolitania (trĭ′pŭlĭtā′nēů̇), region, W Libya, along the Mediterranean coast. Colonized 7th cent. B.C. by the Phoenicians. Under Turkish rule from 1553 to 1912, when it was acquired by Italy. In World War II it fell to the British in 1943.

Tripolitan War, 1801–5, U.S. campaigns against the BARBARY STATES, after demands for more tribute than stipulated in treaties (1786–99) to halt piracy. Expeditions were sent by the U.S. against Tripoli in 1801, 1802, 1804, and a land expedition under William Eaton. A notable incident was the firing of the PHILADELPHIA (1804) by Stephen DECATUR, who later commanded a successful expedition against Algiers (1815; the Algerine War).

Triptolemus (trĭptŏ′lĭmù̇s), in Greek religion, one of chief figures of Eleusinian Mysteries. He was said to be inventor of the plow and of agriculture.

Trist, Nicholas Philip, 1800–1874, American diplomat. Conducted negotiations to end Mexican War. Ignoring recall, he negotiated Treaty of GUADALUPE HIDALGO.

Tristan: see TRISTRAM AND ISOLDE.

Tristan da Cunha (trĭ′stăn dä kōōn′yù), chief island (pop. 230) of an isolated volcanic group in the S Atlantic. Has an important meteorological and radio station. Discovered (1506) by Portuguese, it was annexed (1816) by Great Britain and became a dependency of St. Helena in 1938.

Tristan l'Hermite, Louis (lwē′ trĕstä′ lĕrmēt′), d. c.1477, provost of France under Charles VII and Louis XI. Reformed army; notorious for cruelty.

Tristram and Isolde (trĭ′strŭm, ĭsōl′dù̇), medieval romance, mainly Irish in origin. In it Tristram, sent to Ireland to bring Isolde back as the bride of King Mark of Cornwall, drinks a love potion with her. Their irresistible passion leads to the death of both. Thomas of Britain wrote an Anglo-Norman verse account (c.1185), and Gottfried von Strassburg wrote a German version (c.1210). Sir Thomas Malory combined the story with the Arthurian legend. Also Tristan, Tristran; Isolt, Iseult, Yseult.

Triton (trī′tŭn), in Greek myth, merman son of Poseidon. Later literature speaks of many Tritons. They rode over the sea on horses and blew conch shells.

Triumvirate (trīŭm′vĭrĭt), in anc. Rome, governing board of three men. Most important were the First Triumvirate (Julius CAESAR, POMPEY, and CRASSUS), formed in 60 B.C., and the Second Triumvirate (AUGUSTUS, ANTONY, and LEPIDUS), formed in 43 B.C.

Trivandrum (trĭvăn′drù̇m), city (pop. 128,365), cap. of Tranvancore-Cochin, India. Textile mfg.

trivium: see LIBERAL ARTS.

Trnava (tŭr′nävä), Hung. *Nagyszombat,* town (pop. 24,-226), SW Slovakia, Czechoslovakia. Agr. center. Religious center of medieval Slovakia; called the Slovak Rome for its many churches (incl. a notable Gothic cathedral). University founded here by Peter Pazmany (1635) was moved to Budapest 1777.

Trnovo (tûr′nōvō), town (pop. 16,182), N central Bulgaria. Was cap. of old Bulgaria under Ivan II (13th cent.). Fell to Turks 1393.

Troas (trō′ăs) or **the Troad** (trō′ăd), region about anc. Troy on NW coast of Asia Minor.

Trobriand Islands (trō′brēănd″), small volcanic group, off SE New Guinea and part of Territory of Papua. Site of Allied base in 1943.

Trogir (trō′gēr), small port and resort, Croatia, W Yugoslavia, on an Adriatic island W of Split. Contested between Hungary and Venice in Middle Ages; eventually kept by Venice until 1797. Has splendid 13th-cent. cathedral and several medieval and Renaissance castles.

Troilus and Cressida (trō′ĭlùs, troi′lùs, krĕ′sĭdù̇), medieval romance distantly related to a Greek legend. Troilus, a Trojan prince, loved Cressida, but she was faithless to him. Story first used by Benoît de Sainte-More, from whom Boccaccio drew. Chaucer and Shakspere followed in same tradition.

Trois Rivières (trōȯä″ rēvyĕr′) or **Three Rivers,** city (pop. 46,074), S Que., Canada, on St. Lawrence R. at mouth of St. Maurice R. and NE of Montreal; founded 1634 by Champlain. Pulp, paper, and cotton mills, grain elevators, and foundries. Was a major trading post and fortified port. First iron forges in Que. built here 1737.

Trojan War, in Greek mythology, war between Greeks and Trojans. It is the setting for the *Iliad* and background for the *Odyssey.* Strife began when PARIS eloped with HELEN, wife of Menelaus. Greeks under Agamemnon besieged Troy for 10 years. City was well fortified, and Greeks finally won only by a deceit. Pretending to depart, they left a wooden horse, which the Trojans, deaf to warnings of Cassandra and Laocoön, took into city as an offering to Athena. Warriors hidden in the horse opened the city gates to the Greek army, which sacked Troy. Among Greek heroes were Achilles, Patroclus, Odysseus, and Nestor. Trojan heroes, led by Hector, included Paris, Aeneas, Memnon, and Penthesilea. Some of the gods took sides in the war. Trojan War in reality (c.1200 B.C.) was probably over control of trade in the Dardanelles.

Trollhattan (trôl′hĕ″tän), Swed. *Trollhättan,* city (pop. 24,264), SW Sweden, on Gota R. and near Vanern L. River here falls 108 ft. in six falls and rapids; water power is used by Sweden's largest hydroelectric plant.

Trollope (trŏ′lŭp), English family of authors. **Frances (Milton) Trollope,** 1780–1863, wrote travel books and novels. A stay in the U.S. prompted her *Domestic Manners of the Americans* (1832). Wrote many novels. Her eldest son, **Thomas Adolphus Trollope,** 1810–92, was also a prolific writer of novels and historical works. Her youngest and most famous son, **Anthony Trollope,** 1815–82, was a novelist of note, remarkable for his ability to build up character by using commonplace scenes. Travel through S England gave him background for his imaginary county of Barset, in which are set the most popular of his novels, the *Barsetshire Chronicles,* including *The Warden* (1855), *Barchester Towers* (1857), *Framley Parsonage* (1861), and *The Last Chronicle of Barset* (1867). A later group of stories, including *The Eustace Diamonds* (1873), share a common reference to parliamentary background. Besides more than 50 novels, he wrote travel books and biographies and an autobiography (pub. posthumously).

trombone: see WIND INSTRUMENTS.

Tromp, Maarten Harpertszoon (märtŭn här′pŭrtsōn trômp′), 1597–1653, Dutch admiral. His victory (1639) over the Spanish fleet in the lee of the Downs marked the passing of Spanish sea power. In the first Dutch War he defeated the English off Dungeness (1652). Though he later had to withdraw from the Channel, he eventually broke the blockade of the Dutch coast. His son **Cornelis Tromp** (kôrnā′lĭs), 1629–91, served as admiral in second and third Dutch Wars.

Tromso (trŏm′zō), Nor. *Tromsø,* city (pop. 10,990), N Norway; a port and chief city of Arctic Norway. Exports fish, fish products, furs.

Trondheim (trôn′hām), city (pop. 57,128), central Norway; a fortified seaport on Trondheim Fjord; variant spellings are Drontheim, Trondhjem. Has hydroelectric plant and shipyards; exports fish, lumber, copper ore, wood pulp. Lutheran episcopal see. Founded 997 as Nidaros, it became political and religious cap. of medieval Norway, and was an archiepiscopal see from 1152 until forcible introduction of the Reformation (1537), when city was renamed Trondheim. Its historic role was reaffirmed when Haakon VII was crowned (1906) in its splendid Gothic cathedral (12th–13th cent.; ravaged by repeated fires but restored after 1869). As a major German naval base in World War II, city was severely bombed. **Trondheim Fjord** is an inlet of Norwegian Sea. Extending c.80 mi. inland, it is considered natural boundary between N and S Norway.

tropical medicine, branch of medicine concerned with diseases occurring most frequently in warmer climates. Causative organisms of certain diseases including malaria, yellow fever, amoebic dysentery, hookworm, dengue fever, and filariasis breed best in the warmth, humidity, and conditions of life in the tropics. Pioneer work accomplished in field by Latin-American scientists, notably at Univ. of Puerto Rico, and by several U.S. universities.

tropics. The Tropics of Cancer (23½°N) Capricorn (23½°S) delimit the tropical or torrid zone. Since this zone receives more of the direct rays of the sun than areas in other latitudes and since the angle at which the rays strike varies little, the average annual temperature is high and seasonal change of temperature is less than in other zones. Tropical climate types (determined by latitude, distance from oceans, elevation, prevailing winds) include tropical rain forest, savanna, steppe, desert, and highland.

tropism (trō′pĭzŭm), involuntary response of whole or part of organism involving orientation toward (positive tropism) or away from (negative tropism) external stimulus. Tropistic stimuli include heat, light, moisture, gravity, electricity, and chemical agents. Response to sun is heliotropism; to gravity, geotropism; to light, phototropism.

troposphere: see ATMOSPHERE.

Troppau (trôp′ou), Czech *Opava,* city (pop. 20,441), N Czechoslovakia; former cap. of Austrian Silesia. Textile mfg. The **Congress of Troppau,** 1820, was held under the provisions of the QUADRUPLE ALLIANCE to consider action against the liberal uprisings in the Two Sicilies and Spain. These problems were merely referred to later meetings (see LAIBACH, CONGRESS OF; VERONA, CONGRESS OF). However, at the behest of Alexander I (who personally represented Russia) a protocol was signed by Russia, Austria, and Prussia, asserting that any state where a revolutionary change of government took place was to be brought back, by force of arms if necessary, into the bosom of the HOLY ALLIANCE. England rejected the protocol; France adhered with reservations.

Trossachs (trŏ′säks, –sŭks), wooded valley, Perthshire, Scotland. Associated with Scott's works.

Trotsky, Leon (trŏt′skē), 1879–1940, Russian revolutionist. His original name was Lev Davidovich Bronstein. An early convert to Marxism, he was repeatedly exiled to Siberia; spent much of the years 1902–17 abroad as propagandist, agitator, and journalist; took a major part in Bolshevik October Revolution of 1917; became commissar for foreign affairs under Lenin. He negotiated the Treaty of BREST-LITOVSK (1918) and organized the victorious Red Army in the civil war of 1918–20. After Lenin's death (1924), Trotsky led the leftist opposition against STALIN but was expelled from the party (1927), exiled to Alma-Ata, and ordered to leave the USSR (1929). He found asylum in Turkey (until 1933), then in France (until 1935) and in Norway (until 1937). The Soviet government obtained his expulsion from Norway after Trotsky's name had been linked, perhaps somewhat fantastically, with vast plots against Stalin in the Moscow treason trials of the 1930s. Trotsky denied these charges and hurled countercharges at Stalin. He settled near Mexico city in 1937, founded the Fourth International, a minor but highly articulate group of intellectuals dedicated to the establishment of pure communism. In 1940, Trotsky was killed with an axe by Jacques van den Dreschd (an *alias;* his real identity remains mysterious), who previously had wormed himself into Trotsky's confidence. Trotsky wrote numerous political and polemical works, most of them available in English.

troubadour (trōō′bùdôr), medieval poet of S France whose songs were composed in *langue d'oc.* His counterpart in the *langue d'oïl* of N France was the TROUVÈRE. Troubadour poetry, essentially aristocratic, was characterized by metrical and poetic skill; its main theme was romantic love. Among troubadours were Peire Vidal, Bertrand de Born, Gaucelm Faidit, Peire Cardinal. Decline began in 13th cent.

Troubetzkoy, Paul, Prince (trōōbĕtskoi′, trōōbĕts′koi, Rus. trōōbyĭtskoi′), 1866–1938, Russian sculptor, b. Italy. Best known for portrait busts of famous contemporaries.

trout, game fish of salmon family, commercially valuable as food, found chiefly in clear, cold, fresh waters. Genera include *Salmo* (e.g., European sea trout), *Sal-*

velinus (e.g., brook trout and other chars), *Cristivomer* (e.g., lake trout).

trouvère (trōovâr'), medieval poet of N France whose songs were composed in *langue d'oïl* (see also TROUBADOUR). Their poetry, which flourished in the 12th–13th cent., includes the CHANSONS DE GESTE. Well-known trouvères were Le Châtelain de Coucy and ADAM DE LA HALLE.

Trowbridge, John Townsend, 1827–1916, American writer, best remembered for his poem "Darius Green and His Flying Machine" and for many stories for boys (e.g., *Cudjo's Cave,* 1864).

Troy, anc. city of Asia Minor, almost universally believed to have been on the mound, Hissarlik, in Asiatic Turkey (as identified by Heinrich Schliemann). The seventh of nine settlements excavated here is said to have been that of the TROJAN WAR. Called also Ilion and Ilium.

Troy. 1 City (pop. 8,555), SE Ala., on Conecuh R. and SE of Montgomery, in cotton, peanut, corn area. **2** City (pop. 72,311), E N.Y., on E bank of Hudson R. and NE of Albany; laid out 1786. Site included in Kiliaen Van Rensselaer's patroonship. Port and industrial center, known for shirts, collars; mfg. also of machinery, valves, brushes. Seat of RENSSELAER POLYTECHNIC INSTITUTE; Russell Sage Col. (nonsectarian; for women; opened 1916; stresses preparation for group living; Emma Willard School (nonsectarian; for girls; opened 1814 at Middlebury, Vt., moved to Troy 1821; renamed 1892 for its founder, Emma WILLARD; preceded first women's colleges as experiment in higher education). **3** City (pop. 10,661), W Ohio, on Great Miami R. and N of Dayton; settled c.1807. Mfg. of machinery, airplanes, and furniture.

Troyes (trōoä'), city (pop. 53,521), cap. of Aube dept., NE France, on the Seine; historic cap. of Champagne. Textile mfg. Its two annual fairs were the most important medieval fairs of W Europe until the 14th cent.; troy weight became an international standard. Has Gothic cathedral (13th–16th cent.) and Church of St. Urban (13th cent.); fine museum. The Champenoise school of sculpture flourished at Troyes in the Renaissance. In the **Treaty of Troyes,** 1420, among HENRY V of England, CHARLES VI of France, and PHILIP THE GOOD of Burgundy, France reached its lowest point in the Hundred Years War. The dauphin (later CHARLES VII) was disinherited; Henry was made regent of France, received Catherine of Valois in marriage, and was declared heir to Charles VI (who merely retained his royal title).

troy weight: see WEIGHTS AND MEASURES.

Truchas, peaks: see SANGRE DE CRISTO MOUNTAINS

Trucial Oman (trōo'shŭl ōmän'), region (6,000 sq. mi.; pop. c.40,000), E Arabia, occupying Persian Gulf coast from Qatar to Oman. Comprises seven constituent states bound to Great Britain by truce (1820) and agreement (1892). Formerly notorious for piracy, the area was called the Pirate Coast. Pearl-diving and fishing are chief activities.

Truckee (trŭ'kē), mountain resort (pop. 1,025), E Calif., on Truckee R. and SW of Reno, Nev. L. Tahoe is to S and Donner L. is just W.

Truckee, river rising in NE Calif. in L. Tahoe and flowing c.100 mi. N and E into W Nev. to Pyramid L. Has L. Tahoe Dam of NEWLANDS PROJECT.

truck farming, practice of growing one or a few kinds of crops of vegetables or certain fruits on a large scale at some distance from the market. Market gardening, though similar, is more intensive and diversified.

Trudeau, Edward Livingston (trōo'dō), 1848–1915, American physician, a pioneer in open-air treatment of tuberculosis at Saranac Lake, N.Y.

truffle (trŭ'fŭl), subterranean edible fungus, fleshy and globular (1–4 in. in diameter). Truffles are found in groups, often a foot below the ground's surface, close to roots of trees. They have not been successfully cultivated but are found in a number of European countries; they are usually hunted with dogs or hogs.

In Périgord, France, their collection is an important industry.

Trujillo (Ciudad Trujillo) (trōohē'yō; syōodhädh'), city (pop. 181,533), S Dominican Republic; cap., largest city, and chief port of republic. Founded as SANTO DOMINGO (1496), it was rebuilt after disastrous hurricane of 1930 and renamed for Trujillo Molina. Among surviving colonial edifices is oldest cathedral of the New World.

Trujillo, city (pop. 38,961), NW Peru; founded by Diego de Almagro (1534). An oasis in coastal desert of Peru, it is a thriving commercial center for irrigated area with growing of sugar cane. Near by are pre-Incan ruins of Chanchan.

Trujillo Molina, Rafael Leonidas (räfäĕl' läōnē'dhäs trōohē'yō mōlē'nä), 1891–, president of Dominican Republic (1930–38, 1942–50). By a military coup he ousted President Horacio Vásquez in 1930 and later was dictator even when not president. Became constantly embroiled with other Caribbean countries. Internally, his efficient, though corrupt, rule brought material progress to country. He was appointed ambassador-at-large to UN in 1952.

Truk (trŭk, trōok), island group (39 sq. mi.; pop. 9,510), W Pacific, in E Caroline Isls. Consists of c.55 volcanic islands surrounded by an atoll reef. Japanese naval base in World War II.

Truman, Harry S., 1884–, 32d President of the United States, b. Lamar, Mo. U.S. Senator from Mo. (1935–45); headed committee to investigate government expenditures in World War II. Served as Democratic Vice President of U.S. (1945); succeeded to presidency at death of F. D. Roosevelt. Attended POTSDAM CONFERENCE (July, 1945). Growing U.S.-USSR tension created problems. The "Truman Doctrine" of March, 1947, aimed at aiding Communist-threatened nations to curb spread of Soviet influence. EUROPEAN RECOVERY PROGRAM was brought forth. Fair Deal domestic program, including civil rights and price controls, was largely thwarted by Republican majority in 80th Congress. Handicapped in 1948 by a Southern bolt and disaffection under H. A. Wallace, Truman won reelection in a victory that was surprising to many. In 1949 he promoted NORTH ATLANTIC TREATY; failed to get TAFT-HARTLEY LABOR ACT repealed. Escaped assassination attempt in 1950. Embroiled in dispute with Gen. Douglas MACARTHUR (1951). Succeeded as President by Dwight D. Eisenhower in 1953.

Trumbull, John, 1750–1831, American poet and judge in Conn., a leader of Connecticut Wits. Wrote satires, *Progress of Dulness* (1772–73), *M'Fingal* (1775–82).

Trumbull, Jonathan (trŭm'bŭl), 1710–85, colonial governor of Conn. (1769–84). Aided patriot cause in American Revolution. His son, **Jonathan Trumbull,** 1740–1809, was also governor of Conn. (1797–1809). Another son, **John Trumbull,** 1756–1843, was a noted historical painter, who studied under Benjamin West in London. Much of his work is in Trumbull Gall. which he founded at Yale Univ. 1831. Several large paintings (e.g., *Signing of the Declaration of Independence*) are at the Capitol, Washington, D.C. He served for a time as secretary to John Jay.

Trumbull, town (pop. 8,641), SW Conn., adjoining N Bridgeport; settled c.1690.

trumpet: see WIND INSTRUMENTS.

trumpet creeper or **trumpet vine,** woody, climbing or shrubby plant of genus *Campsis,* with clusters of large trumpet-shaped scarlet or orange-red flowers.

Truro (trōo'rō), town (pop. 10,756), N N.S., Canada, near head of Cobequid Bay of Bay of Fundy. Railroad center with mfg. of clothing and machinery. First settled by Acadians as Cobequid.

Truro, resort town (pop. 661), SE Mass., on N Cape Cod. Site of Highland Light, one of most powerful on Atlantic Coast.

truss, in architecture and engineering, a supporting structure commonly composed of steel or wood beams, girders, or rods, used especially in roofs and bridges.

It is usually in the form of a triangle or series of triangles to insure greatest rigidity.

trust, in finance, business combination which controls the policy of a number of organizations; defined in antitrust legislation as being in restraint of trade. Term derives from use of legal trust form by many such organizations. Horizontal trust is combination of corporations which ordinarily would be in direct competition; vertical trust controls operations from procuring of materials to retailing of product. Trust is similar to cartel, but smaller in scope. Trusts grew rapidly in U.S. 1880–1905, although attacked as monopolies. Series of laws were passed to curb trusts (notably, Sherman Anti-Trust Act, 1890, and Clayton Anti-Trust Act, 1914).

trusteeship, territorial, system for control of territories not self-governing, administered by UN. Replacing MANDATES of League of Nations, and regulated by chapters 12 and 13 of UN Charter, it promotes welfare of people and prepares them for self government. Supervision is by Trusteeship Council, made up of UN members holding trust territories plus equal number of other members, and each territory is governed by a trusteeship agreement.

Truth, Sojourner, c.1797–1883, American abolitionist, a freed slave, originally named Isabella. Traveled throughout North preaching emancipation and woman's rights.

Truth or Consequences, health resort (pop. 4,563), SW N.Mex., on Rio Grande near Elephant Butte Dam. Formerly Hot Springs.

Tryon, Dwight William (trī′ŭn), 1849–1925, American landscape painter, influenced by Daubigny.

Tryon, William, 1725–88, British colonial governor of N.C. (1765–71). Rigorously suppressed REGULATOR MOVEMENT. Governor of N.Y. (1771–78). Led Tory raids in Conn.

Tsana, lake in Ethiopia: see TANA.

Tsaritsyn, RSFSR: see STALINGRAD.

Tsarskoye Selo, RSFSR: see PUSHKIN.

Tschaikowsky, Piotr Ilich: see TCHAIKOVSKY.

Tschermak-Seysenegg, Erich (ä′rĭkh chĕr′mäk-sī′zŭnĕk), 1871–, Austrian botanist, one of several scientists who simultaneously in 1900 confirmed Mendel's laws of heredity.

Tschudi, Aegidius or **Gilg** (ējĭ′dĕŭs chōō′dē, gĭlk′), 1505–72, Swiss historian, author of *Chronicon Helveticum,* which immortalized the William Tell legend.

tsetse fly (tsĕt′sē), African insect (*Glossina*) slightly larger than housefly. Sucks blood; certain species transmit African sleeping sickness.

Tsin (dzĭn) or **Chin** (chĭn), dynasty of China, which ruled 265–420, after period of Three Kingdoms. Saw continued growth of Buddhism. Chaos reigned in period between its fall and founding of Sui dynasty.

Tsinan (jē′nän′), city (pop. 574,781), cap. of Shantung prov., E China; textile mfg. Cheloo Univ.

Tsinghai or **Chinghai** (both: chĭng′hī′), province (250,-000 sq. mi.; pop. 1,200,000), NW China; cap. Sining. Bounded on SW by Tibet. Mainly a high plateau, it contains the lake KOKO NOR. Wool and hides are chief exports. The area came came under Chinese domination, c.1724. Also called Koko Nor.

Tsingtao (chĭng′dou′), city (pop. 787,722), E Shantung prov., China; port and naval base on Yellow Sea. Under German rule 1898–1914 as part of Kiaochow lease, it was held by Japanese 1914–22. After World War II it was U.S. naval base until 1949.

Tsugaru Strait (tsōōgä′rōō), channel between Honshu and Hokkaido, Japan.

Tsu Hsi: see TZ′U HSI.

Tsunetaka (tsōō′nätä′kä), fl. 13th cent., Japanese landscape painter. Changed his name to Tosa Tsunetaka, giving the name Tosa to a school of art.

Tsushima (tsōō′shēmä), Japanese island (271 sq. mi.; pop. 57,482), in Korea Strait. In Russo-Japanese War, Japan won decisive naval battle (May, 1905) fought near the island.

Tuamotu Islands (tōōämō′tōō) or **Low Archipelago,** coral group, area c.330 sq. mi., S Pacific; part of French Oceania. Comprises 80 atolls in 1,300-mi. chain. Includes the phosphate island Makatea. Discovered 1606 by the Spanish, annexed 1881 by France. Formerly called Paumotu.

Tuareg (twä′rĕg), Moslem Berber people, nomads of the Sahara. Among most highly civilized peoples of Africa. Tuareg men go veiled, while the women are unveiled. Descent and inheritance are through female line. Long resisted European domination.

tuba: see WIND INSTRUMENTS.

Tubal-cain (tū′bŭl-kän), in Bible, son of Lamech. The first worker of brass and iron. Gen. 4.22.

tube, vacuum, or **electron tube,** electronic device used as rectifier, amplifier, mixer, and detector of audio and radio frequencies and for electrical measurements. Also called thermionic valve, it is essentially a glass vacuum tube containing a negative electrode (cathode), which when heated releases electrons that flow to positive electrode (anode). When rays emitted by cathode are focused on metal plate in tube, X rays result. See also PHOTOELECTRIC CELL; *ill.,* p. 293.

tuber, enlarged underground plant stem, such as the edible part of the potato plant. Tubers contain stored food, usually starch. See *ill.,* p. 783.

tuberculosis, contagious, infectious disease of vertebrates caused by bacterium known as tubercle bacillus. Similar forms of the germ cause the disease in humans and cattle; cows are generally tested to prevent spread of infection through milk. As bacteria attack body tissues, small nodules (tubercles) form; from unhealed tubercles in lungs of victim of pulmonary form (also called consumption and phthisis), germs enter sputum, which may spread infection. Other forms of tuberculosis attack bones, intestines, skin, lymph nodes (a form early known as scrofula and King's evil). Mortality and spread are reduced by early detection by X-ray photographs and skin tests, use of vaccines, and of sulfa drugs and antibiotics. Treatment of pulmonary type includes also rest, fresh air, and proper diet. Many sanatoriums use regime introduced in U.S. at Saranac Lake, N.Y. by TRUDEAU.

tuberose, a tuberous-rooted tender plant (*Polianthes tuberosa*), native to Mexico but grown in gardens elsewhere. It has waxy white, fragrant flowers.

Tübingen (tü′bĭng-ŭn), city (pop. 37,278), S Württemberg, SW Germany, on the Neckar; cap. (after 1945) of Württemberg-Hohenzollern. Mfg. of textiles, machinery, precision instruments. Has famous university (founded 1477), where Melanchthon taught; theological faculty was famous in 19th cent. City center, which has retained medieval character, contains late-Gothic Church of St. George.

Tubman, Harriet, c.1820–1913, American abolitionist, an escaped slave. Freed over 300 slaves through Underground Railroad. In Civil War she was Union nurse, laundress, and spy.

Tubuai Islands (tōōbōō-ī′) or **Austral Islands,** volcanic group, S Pacific, S of Society Isls.; part of French Oceania. Tubuai, largest of the five islands, was discovered 1777 by Capt. James Cook and annexed 1880 by France. Coffee, arrowroot, and copra are produced.

Tuckahoe, N.Y.: see EASTCHESTER.

tuckahoe, name for two Indian foods known also as Indian bread. One is the rootstock (edible when cooked) of certain plants of the arum family. The other is a fungus (*Poria cocos*) found on roots of trees in the S U.S.

Tucson (tōō′sŏn″), city (pop. 45,454), SE Ariz., SE of Phoenix; settled by Spaniards in late 17th cent. In 1776 presidio was moved here; served as border post of New Spain, of Mexico, and, after Gadsden Purchase, of U.S. Was territorial cap. 1867–77. Longtime trade center for mines, ranches, irrigated farms and (since 1880) important rail center. Sunny winter and health resort, it has annual fiesta and rodeo in Feb. To S is Mission San Xavier del Bac (founded

1700 by Father Kino). Near-by desert (Saguaro Natl. Monument) contrasts with cool Santa Catalina Mts. Davis-Monthan Air Force Base is near. Seat of Univ. of Arizona (land-grant, state supported; coed.; chartered 1885, opened 1891); pueblo remains in vicinity have stimulated study of Indian archaeology here; has U.S. experiment stations (mining, botanical, agr.).

Tucumán (tōōkōōmän'), city (pop. 194,166), cap. of Tucumán prov., NW Argentina; founded 1565, moved to present site 1685; metropolis of large irrigated area. Lumbering also important. Seat of university and popular shrine of Our Lady of Mercy.

Tucumcari (tōō'kŭmkâ"rē), city (pop. 8,419), E N.Mex., E of Albuquerque, near Texas line. Railroad division point and trade center in grain, stock area. Conchas Dam and resort area are near.

Tudor, royal family that ruled England 1485–1603. Founder was Owen Tudor, d. 1461, of an old Welsh family. Married (1429?) Catherine of Valois, widow of Henry V. Lancastrian, he was killed in the Wars of the Roses. His grandson became HENRY VII after defeating (1485) Richard III at Bosworth Field, ending Wars of the Roses. Henry's marriage to daughter of Edward IV united Lancastrian and Yorkist claims to throne. His children were MARGARET TUDOR, MARY OF ENGLAND, and HENRY VIII. Henry VIII's children ruled as EDWARD VI, MARY I, and ELIZABETH. Attempt to place Lady Jane GREY on throne ended with her execution. House of Stuart succeeded Tudor dynasty on the death of Elizabeth in 1603.

Tudor style, English architecture and decoration of first half of 16th cent., during the reigns (1485–1558) of Henry VII, Henry VIII, Edward VI, and Mary I. The manor house, a characteristic building of the period, showed greater emphasis on privacy with the introduction of many small rooms, which decreased the former importance of the great hall. Rooms frequently were fitted with oak paneling, and walls and ceilings had rich plaster relief ornament, and articles of furniture (see *ill.,* p. 356) came into greater use. Typical exteriors showed use of brickwork combined with half-timber, high gables, bay windows, and numerous decorative chimneys.

Tuesday: see WEEK.

Tufts College: see MEDFORD, Mass.

Tu Fu (dōō' fōō', tōō'), 713?–770, Chinese poet of T'ang dynasty. His work reveals his sympathy with the common people and a delight in nature.

Tug Fork, river rising in S W.Va. and flowing 154 mi. NW along Ky.–W.Va. line, joining Levisa Fork to form Big Sandy R.

Tuileries (twē'lŭrēz, Fr. tüēlrē'), former palace in Paris. Planned by Catherine de' Medici and begun in 1564, it occupied part of present Tuileries gardens (laid out by Lenôtre) between Louvre and Place de la Concorde. Rarely a royal residence until French Revolution, when Louis XVI was forced to move (1789) his court here from Versailles, it served as chief residence of Napoleon I and his successors. During Commune of Paris of 1871 a mob burned it down.

Tula (tōō'lù), city (pop. 272,404), central European RSFSR, S of Moscow. Rail and mfg. center (machinery, arms). Flour mills, tanneries, sugar refineries. Founded 12th cent. Became a key fortress of grand duchy of Moscow in 16th cent. Withstood German siege (1941) in World War II. Its turreted, 16th-cent. kremlin occupies city center.

Tulane University of Louisiana (tōōlān'), at New Orleans; nonsectarian, private, for men and women; opened 1834, chartered 1835; received present name 1884. Famous medical school. Women's division is Newcomb Col. Tulane has Middle American Research Inst. (with Mayan library collection and museum).

Tulare (tùlâr'), city (pop. 12,445), S central Calif., SE of Fresno. Processes and ships dairy products, cotton, and fruit.

Tulare Lake, virtually dry lake, S central Calif., S of Hanford. Fed by Kings, Kaweah, and Kern rivers only in very wet seasons. Connected by slough to Buena Vista L. Before it was used for irrigation, it was c.50 mi. long and c.35 mi. wide.

tularemia (tōōlŭrē'mēū) or **rabbit fever,** infectious disease of small mammals (e.g., rabbits) and birds, caused by an aerobic bacillus and transmitted to man in handling, skinning, or eating diseased animals or by bites of ticks, fleas, and lice. Symptoms include ulcer at site of inoculation, regional inflammation of lymph nodes, headache, chills, fever, and vomiting. Streptomycin is often effective in treatment.

tulip, hardy, bulbous-rooted, spring-flowering Old World plant (*Tulipa*), long popular for the cup-shaped blossoms of various rich colors. Tulips were probably introduced into Europe from Turkey in 1554. In the 17th cent. the wild speculation in tulip bulbs in Holland was known as tulipomania. Holland is still an important center for their culture, although bulbs are grown commercially in other countries.

tulip tree, yellow poplar, or **whitewood,** handsome, deciduous tree (*Liriodendron tulipifera*) of magnolia family, native E of the Mississippi. It has yellow and orange tuliplike flowers. The wood is valued for interiors, cabinetmaking, etc.

Tull, Jethro, 1674–1741, English agriculturist and inventor. He influenced British agriculture through his writings and invented (c.1701) a machine drill.

Tullahoma (tŭlŭhō'mù), town (pop. 7,562), central Tenn., SE of Nashville. Industrial center in farm and timber area. Fell to Federals (July, 1863) before Chattanooga campaign.

Tully, Roman consul and philosopher: see CICERO.

Tulsa, city (pop. 182,740), NE Okla., on Arkansas R. E of junction with Cimarron R.; settled c.1860 by Indian exiles, founded as rail depot 1880. With its refineries and company hq., it is known as "oil cap. of world." Mfg. of metal products, aircraft, glass, furniture, and chemicals; commercial center of farm and mineral area. Seat of Univ. of Tulsa (coed.; 1894).

Tumacacori National Monument: see NATIONAL PARKS AND MONUMENTS (table).

tumblebug, name for dark, bronzed, or brightly colored beetles of various genera, e.g., *Scarabaeus, Canthon, Copris, Phanaeus*. They make balls of dung in each of which an egg is laid. See also SCARAB.

tumbleweed, any of several plants, especially abundant in prairie regions, that break from their roots, and, forming a dry tangle, roll before the wind scattering seeds. Common ones are the Russian thistle (*Salsola*), amaranth, and witch grass.

Tumwater, town (pop. 2,725), W Wash., S of Olympia. Sometimes considered end of Oregon Trail. First American settlement in Puget Sound area (1845).

tuna (tōō'nù) or **tunny** (tŭ'nē), largest game fish of mackerel family, swift and powerful. Warm-water tuna (*Thunnus*), also called bluefin and horse mackerel, travels in schools; average weight 60–200 lb. Tuna fisheries are important in Mediterranean, Atlantic, and Pacific waters; large quantities are canned, chiefly in U.S.

Tunbridge Wells, municipal borough (pop. 38,397), Kent, England. Also called Royal Tunbridge Wells. Became fashionable inland resort after chalybeate springs were discovered in 1606.

tung oil, China wood oil or nut oil, a product of the tropical tung tree. It is expressed from poisonous seeds in heart of fruit. It is widely used in paints and varnishes, in insulating compounds, in making linoleum and oilcloth. China is chief source but tung trees are grown also in S U.S.

tungsten: see WOLFRAM.

Tungting (dōōng'tǐng'), lake, N Hunan prov., China. In summer it receives overflow from the Yangtze and attains max. area of c.4,000 sq. mi.

tung tree: see TUNG OIL.

Tungus (tōōn-gōōz'), Siberian ethnic group, numbering c.40,000, called also Evenki. Closely related to the Manchus. Certain cultural traits indicate that some

Japanese may be descended from the Tungus. Tungusic languages, family including Manchu literary language, may be related to Mongolic and Turkic families. Sometimes classified as Ural-Altaic.

Tunguska (tŏon-gŏos'kù), three E tributaries of the Yenisei R., RSFSR, in E central Siberia. They are, from N to S: the **Lower Tunguska,** 1,587 mi. long; the **Stony** or **Middle Tunguska,** 975 mi. long; and the **Upper Tunguska,** as the lower course of the Angara R. is called. The Angara, which drains L. Baikal, flows 1,075 mi. from the lake into the Yenisei and receives the Ilim and Oka. The Tunguskas flow through a large unexploited coal basin.

tunic (tū'nĭk), probably the earliest shaped garment, at first merely two skins laced together. Later it was of cloth, seamed, and usually worn with sleeves and girded. The Roman tunic, first worn under the toga, eventually became a long outer garment.

Tunis (tū'nĭs), city (pop. 364,593), cap. of Tunisia; a port on Lake of Tunis. Access to the Mediterranean is by canal. Exports iron ore, phosphates, dates, olive oil, and carpets. A tourist center with a casbah, notable mosques, a Moslem university, and a museum. Near by are ruins of CARTHAGE. Tunis is of Phoenician origin. It became cap. of Tunis under the powerful Hafsid dynasty (13th–16th cent.) and a leading center for trade with Europe. Turkish and Spanish rule alternated in 16th cent. Turkey prevailed, but her governors in Tunis were virtually independent. Until the French occupation (1881) it flourished as a center of piracy and trade. Held by Axis troops from Nov., 1942, to May 7, 1943.

Tunisia (tūnē'zhù), protectorate (48,362 sq. mi.; pop. 3,230,952), N Africa; since 1946 an associated state of the French Union; cap. Tunis. Bounded on N and E by the Mediterranean, on W by Algeria, and on SE by Libya. Ports include Tunis and Bizerta. Atlas Mts. are in N; in S, below a great salt lake, stretches the Sahara. Typical oasis crops are raised, including dates, cereals, olives, and grapes. Phosphates are the leading export product. The coast, early settled by Phoenicians, passed to Carthage in 6th cent. B.C. As a Roman province (from 2d cent. B.C.) it became a rich wheat-growing region. Held by Vandals and Byzantines before it fell to Arabs in 7th cent. and was converted to Islam. Tunisia reached its greatest power under the Berber Hafsid dynasty (1228–1574). Held by Turkey after 1579, it became virtually independent under the Turkish governors (beys), and as one of the BARBARY STATES it became a pirate base. Heavy debts contracted by the beys led to French, British, and Italian economic intervention in 1869. France occupied the country in 1881 and despite Italy's opposition established a protectorate under a French resident general with the bey as titular ruler. After fall of France (1940) Tunisia remained loyal to Vichy regime and became the focus of the war in N Africa (see NORTH AFRICA, CAMPAIGNS IN). After the war a growing nationalist movement led to riots in 1952. France began instituting reforms (e.g., rural elections, first held in 1953) which would give greater autonomy to Tunisia.

Tunkers, another name for DUNKARDS.

Tunney, James Joseph (Gene), 1898–, American boxer. Won (1926) heavyweight championship from Jack Dempsey. Defeated Dempsey in return bout (1927) marked by the "long count" when Tunney was knocked down in seventh round. Retired undefeated (1928).

tunny: see TUNA.

Tupac Amaru (tŏo'päk ämä'rŏo), 1742?–1781, Indian leader in Peru, baptized José Gabriel Condorcanqui. Led rebellion in 1780; it was crushed; he was captured and brutally executed. Yet many reforms for which he fought were granted.

Tupelo (tŏo'pĭlō), city (pop. 11,527), NE Miss., NNW of Columbus; founded 1859. Processes and ships cotton, dairy, and fertilizer products. Near by are Tupelo

Natl. Battlefield Site marking fight between Gen. N. B. Forrest's Confederates and Union troops, July 14, 1864; and Ackia Battleground Natl. Monument, scene of victory of Chickasaw and English over Choctaw and French, May 26, 1736.

tupelo: see BLACK GUM.

Tupí Indians: see GUARANÍ INDIANS.

Tupper Lake, resort village (pop. 5,441), N N.Y., in the Adirondacks near Big Tupper L.

Tura, Cosmé or **Cosimo** (kōzmä' tŏo'rä, kō'zēmō), c.1430–1495, Italian painter of Ferrarese school. His work is usually realistic but often symbolic.

turbine (tûr'bĭn, tûr'bīn), engine which converts force of moving air, steam, or water into mechanical energy capable of doing work. Water turbines are of the impulse type (actuated by force of water falling into buckets) or reaction type (impact of expanding pressure and kinetic energy of flow turn wheel). Steam turbines employ jets of steam, directed into and through a series of curved vanes on a rotating wheel and through similar ones on a stationary wheel. Principle of the turbine is ancient; first practical use was c.1880. See *ill.,* p. 303.

turbot (tûr'bùt), large European flatfish, valued for food. In U.S. some flounders are inaccurately called turbots.

Turcoman: see TURKMEN SSR.

Turenne, Henri de la Tour d'Auvergne, vicomte de (ärĕ' dù lä tŏor' dōvĕr'nyù vēkôt' dù türĕn'), 1611–75, marshal of France; son of the duc de Bouillon. Brought up a Protestant, he became a Catholic late in life. In the last years of the Thirty Years War he led the French from victory to victory. He at first sided with the princes in the FRONDE but soon took command of the government forces and roundly defeated Condé at the Faubourg Saint-Antoine (1652) and in the battle of the Dunes (1658). He was killed in the third Dutch War after his victory at Sinzheim (1674). One of France's greatest military leaders, he is also celebrated for his courage, integrity, and serious disposition.

Turfan (tŏor'fän), depression, area c.5,000 sq. mi., N central Sinkiang prov., China; 300 ft. below sea level at its lowest point.

Turgenev, Ivan Sergeyevich (ēvän' sĭrgā'ùvĭch tŏorgä'nyĭf), 1818–83, Russian author. His novels deal mostly with social problems. *A Sportsman's Sketches* (1852), a collection of stories on peasant life, dealt a telling blow to serfdom. In 1850–61 appeared his great novels—*A Nest of Gentlefolk, Rudin,* and *Fathers and Sons.* This last, his masterpiece, alienated his more radical followers because of its merciless portrait of Bazarov, the young nihilist. He spent most of his later life abroad. His last long works were *Smoke* (1867) and *Virgin Soil* (1876).

Turgot, Anne Robert Jacques (än' rōbĕr' zhäk' türgō'), 1727–81, French economist and statesman. As intendant of Limoges (1761–74) and as controller general of finances (1774–76) he sought to put into practice his theories—strongly influenced by the PHYSIOCRATS—of free trade, scientific agr. methods, and tax reforms. He made himself numerous enemies, and his downfall (abetted by Marie Antoinette) prevented his carrying out drastic reforms. Turgot's writings (incl. articles in the *Encyclopédie*) reveal him as a major economic thinker of his century.

Turgutlu, Turkey: see KASSABA.

Turin (tŏo'rĭn, tyŏo'–, tyŏorĭn'), Ital. *Torino,* city (pop. 608,211), cap. of Piedmont, NW Italy, on the Po. Leads Italy in mfg. of autos, clothing, leather goods, vermouth. A Roman city, later a Lombard duchy, a Frankish march, and a free commune, it passed to Savoy c.1280; became cap. of Savoy after 1562; cap. of kingdom of Sardinia 1720–98, 1814–61; cap. of Italy, 1861–64. Suffered severe air raids in World War II. A fine example of city planning, most of modern Turin dates from 17th–19th cent. Notable buildings include royal palace and Renaissance cathedral (with shroud in which body of Jesus is said to have been wrapped). University was founded 1404.

Turkestan: see TURKISTAN.

Turkey, republic (296,185 sq. mi.; pop. 18,790,174), Asia Minor and SE Europe; cap. Ankara. Asiatic Turkey (97% of the whole) occupies Anatolian Peninsula (W tip of Asia), washed on N by the Black Sea, on W and S by the Mediterranean. Turkey in Europe, separated from Asiatic Turkey by the DARDANELLES, Sea of Marmara, and Bosporus, comprises E Thrace and is a rolling plain. Asiatic Turkey, a semi-arid plateau, is fringed by mountains, with fertile coastal strips. Half the total area consists of pastures; only 20% is arable. Istanbul, Smyrna, Trebizond, Sinope, and Mersin are chief ports; other important cities are Adrianople, Ankara, Bursa, Adana, Konya, Kayseri, Antioch. Mining (coal, copper, lignite, chrome) is chief industry. Country is one of world's leading exporters of chrome and meerschaum. Massacres and emigration of Armenians, Greeks, and Bulgarians (19th–20th cent.) have left Turkey with a largely Turkish-speaking population. For early history of Turkey, see OTTOMAN EMPIRE and EASTERN QUESTION. History of Turkey as a national state began after World War I. Treaty of SÈVRES (1920), reducing Ottoman Empire to insignificance, was accepted by Sultan Mohammed VI. Nationalist elements, led by Kemal ATATURK, defied sultan's authority. Kemal made a treaty with Russia, routed attacking Greeks and captured Smyrna, and deposed the sultan. Conference of LAUSANNE (1923) estab. present Turkish boundaries (except for Sanjak of Alexandretta, acquired 1939). Turkey was declared a republic (1923). Ataturk became president and, as virtual dictator, effected complete cultural transformation and Westernization—Islam ceased to be the state religion; Latin alphabet replaced Arabic script; women were emancipated. Kemal's economic policy, aimed at freedom from foreign capital, led to wide government controls and ownership of industry. Ismet Inonu, who succeeded Ataturk (1938), kept Turkey neutral in World War II until Jan., 1945, when Turkey joined the Allied side. Turkey joined the UN; received U.S. aid under the Truman Doctrine (1947); and entered North Atlantic Treaty (1951). Celal Bayar, opposition leader, succeeded Inonu in 1950 elections.

turkey, large game and poultry bird, allied to pheasant, native to North America. Plumage is chiefly greenish bronze and copper. Explorers in 16th cent. found turkeys domesticated in Central America and Mexico. American colonists ate wild turkey.

turkey buzzard: see VULTURE.

Turki (tŏŏr′kē) or **Turkic,** family of languages, to which Turkish belongs. See LANGUAGE (table).

Turkish, name given to several languages of Turkic family. See LANGUAGE (table).

Turkistan or **Turkestan** (both: tûrkĭstän′, –stän′), region, USSR, comprising Turkmen SSR, Uzbek SSR, Tadhzik SSR, Kirghiz SSR, and S Kazakh SSR. This region is sometimes called Western Turkistan or Russian Turkistan in distinction to Eastern Turkistan or Chinese Turkistan (now in Sinkiang prov., China). Nearly all the inhabitants speak Turkic languages. Historically Turkistan has been the bridge connecting the East and West and the route taken by many great conquerors and migrating peoples.

Turkistan-Siberia Railroad, abbreviated **Turk-Sib,** SW Asiatic USSR, links Trans-Siberian RR (junction Novosibirsk) with Trans-Caspian RR at Tashkent. Built 1926–30. Has great economic importance.

Turkmen Soviet Socialist Republic or **Turkmenistan** (tûrk″mĕnĭstän′), constituent republic (187,200 sq. mi.; pop. c.1,170,000) of the USSR, in central Asia, bordering in S on Afghanistan, Iran, and Caspian Sea; cap. Ashkabad. KARA KUM desert occupies 90% of area (camel and caracul sheep raising). Irrigated oases and Amu Darya and Murgab river valleys yield cotton, silk, wine, fruit. Fisheries in Caspian Sea. Mineral resources include petroleum, ozocerite, iodine, bromine, salts. The population is 72% Turkmen (also called Turcomans, Turkomans), a Turkic-speaking Moslem people. Inhabited part of Turkmenistan formed part of Margiana prov. of ancient Persia (see MERV). Under Arab rule 8th–9th cent. A.D., it then passed to KHOREZM; fell to the Mongols (13th cent.), the Uzbeks (15th cent.), and the Khans of KHIVA (c.1800); and was conquered by Russia 1869–95. Became constituent republic 1924. Many Turkmen live in Iran and Afghanistan.

Turkoman: see TURKMEN SSR.

Turks, term applied in its wider meaning to the Turkic-speaking peoples of Turkey, USSR, Chinese Turkistan, and E Iran (see LANGUAGE, table). Totaling c.25,000,000 and distributed from E Siberia to the Dardanelles, their only ties are religious (Islam is religion of almost all Turks) and linguistic. Original Turks probably lived in S Siberia and in Turkistan. They expanded S and W; estab. several empires in Asia. Seljuks and Osmanli or Ottoman Turks have been two groups prominent in W Asia and Europe. Seljuks appeared (10th cent.) in Iran. By victory (1071) over Byzantine emperor at Manzikert, they estab. empire and helped cause the Crusades. Seljuk empire fell apart in 12th cent.; successor states were overrun by Tatars. Osmanli Turks under Osman I estab. (14th cent.) huge Ottoman Empire. People of modern Turkey are called Osmanli Turks.

Turks and Caicos Islands (kī′kōs), islands (c.201 sq. mi.; pop. 8,929), British West Indies. Geographically SE continuation of Bahamas, but administered by Jamaica. Produce salt, sponges, fibers.

Turk-Sib: see TURKISTAN-SIBERIA RAILROAD.

Turku (tŏŏr′kŏŏ), Swedish *Åbo,* city (103,899), SW Finland; an ice-free Baltic port. Commercial and industrial center (shipyards, sawmills, textile mfg.). Was cap. of Finland until 1812; seat of Finnish national university (founded 1640) until its transfer to Helsinki (1828). Its present Swedish university was founded 1918, its Finnish university 1922. Called the "cradle of Finnish culture." Has 13th-cent. cathedral.

Turlock, city (pop. 6,235), central Calif., SE of Stockton. Center of an irrigation project using Tuolumne R. and producing truck, fruit, grain, dairy products.

turmeric (tûr′mŭrĭk), perennial herb (*Curcuma longa*), cultivated in the tropics for its rootstalk, which in the form of a powder is used as a condiment and dye. The plant has a spike of yellow flowers.

Turner, Frederick Jackson, 1861–1932, American historian. Known for brilliant studies of American frontier and of sectionalism. An address, "The Significance of the Frontier in American History," delivered 1893 before American Historical Association and reprinted in *The Frontier in American History* (1920), was pioneer work that opened new and important fields for historical study.

Turner, J(oseph) M(allord) W(illiam), 1775–1851, English landscape painter, a celebrated water-colorist. Received almost no general education but at 14 was a student at the Royal Acad. of Arts. Despite his early and continued success he lived the life of a recluse with his father, a London barber. In his early work he successfully imitated the classical landscape painters, notably Claude Lorrain. His later paintings (e.g., *Snow Storm*) became increasingly abstract and poetic. Turner's will left over 19,000 water colors, drawings, and oils to the nation. Most of these are in Natl. Gall. and Tate Gall., London.

Turner, Nat, 1800–1831, American Negro, leader of Southampton Insurrection of slaves in Va. (Aug., 1831). Uprising led to more stringent slave laws in South, end of manumission societies there.

Turners Falls, Mass.: see MONTAGUE.

turnip, hardy garden vegetable related to the cabbage and having edible tubers. Chief kinds are *Brassica rapa* with white tubers and rutabaga or Swedish turnip (*B.*

napobrassica) with yellow tubers. Both are used also for stock feed. See *ill.*, p. 783.

turnpike, road paid for partly or wholly by fees collected at tollgates. Hinged bar preventing passage through gate until toll was paid was original turnpike from which road took its name. First American turnpike road was a state enterprise (Va., 1785). Lancaster Turnpike in Pa. (1792) inaugurated era of turnpikes as private enterprises. Great period of American turnpikes was c.1800–c.1840.

Turnu-Severin (tŏŏr'nŏŏ-sĕvĕrēn'), city (pop. 31,296), SW Rumania, in Walachia, on the Danube below the Iron Gate. River port.

Turnverein (tŏŏrn'fŭrīn), society emphasizing gymnastic exercises as well as social and patriotic functions. Originated by F. L. Jahn, it was used to organize German resistance to Napoleon. The German government later disapproved of it as a possible source of liberal ideas.

turpentine (tûr'pŭntīn), resinous, semifluid substance from sapwood of conifers. Chemically it is a mixture of oil of turpentine and ROSIN. Used as solvent and drying agent in paints and varnishes; purest grade is used in medicine.

turpentine tree: see TEREBINTH.

Turpin, Richard, 1706–39, English robber, known as Dick Turpin. Achieved notoriety from short and brutal career of horse stealing and general crime.

turquoise (tûr'kwoiz, –koiz), hydrous phosphate of aluminum and copper used as gem. Rarely occurs in crystal form. Color varies from greenish gray to sky blue. Sources include Persia and SW U.S.

turtle, reptile of order Chelonia (or Testudinata). The name *tortoise* is often reserved for land forms, terrapin for edible fresh-water species. Turtles have strong, sharp, toothless jaws; body is encased in shell consisting usually of bony plates fused with ribs and vertebrae and overlaid with horny shields. Largest is marine leatherback turtle (c.1,000 lb.). Chief food form is marine green turtle. Tortoise shell is obtained from marine hawksbill turtle.

Turtle Creek, borough (pop. 12,363), SW Pa., ESE of Pittsburgh; settled c.1765. Coal mining; mfg. of cement blocks and electrical equipment.

turtledove, wild dove native to Europe and Asia. It has a plaintive song and affectionate ways.

Tuscaloosa (tŭskŭlŏŏ'sŭ), city (pop. 46,396), W central Ala., on Black Warrior R. and SW of Birmingham; settled after Creek revolt of 1813. State cap. 1826–46. Farm trade center; mfg. of paper, cotton goods, bricks, rubber tires; woodworking; oil refining. Coal mines. Univ. of ALABAMA near.

Tuscan order: see DORIC ORDER.

Tuscany (tŭ'skŭnē), Ital. *Toscana,* region (8,876 sq. mi., incl. ELBA; pop. 2,978,013), central Italy, along Tyrrhenian Sea; cap. FLORENCE. Other cities: Leghorn, Arrezzo, Lucca, Massa, Carrara, Pisa, Pistoia, Siena. Mostly hilly, fertile region, it produces wines, olive oil, cereals. Chief river is the Arno. The Apennines (E) and the Alpi Apuane (W) yield marble, iron, magnesium, quicksilver. Mfg. of machinery, textiles, glass. Site of ancient Etruria, region has many relics of ETRUSCAN CIVILIZATION. Conquered (3d cent. B.C.) by Romans, area later became a powerful Frankish march. Most cities became free communes in 11th–12th cent. Despite Guelph-Ghibelline strife, some (i.e., PISA, LUCCA, SIENA, Florence) developed into strong republics. Florence gained hegemony (14th–15th cent.). The MEDICI created (1569) grand duchy of Tuscany, which later passed (1737) to house of Hapsburg-Lorraine who remained in control (except for Napoleonic period) until union was voted (1860) with Sardinia. Tuscany was a center of art and learning during Renaissance; Tuscan language became literary language of Italy.

Tuscumbia (tŭskŭm'bēü), city (pop. 6,734), NW Ala., on Tennessee R. near Muscle Shoals. Cotton, rubber products; fertilizer. Birthplace of Helen Keller.

Tuskegee (tŭskē'gē), city (pop. 6,712), SE Ala., E of Montgomery, in cotton, corn, potato area. U.S. Negro veterans' hospital here. Seat of **Tuskegee Institute** (Negro; nonsectarian; coed.); chartered and opened 1881 as normal school, assumed present name 1937. College dept. added 1927. Has schools of agr. (with research dept. and extension service), education, home economics and commercial dietetics, mechanical industries, nurse training (with hospital). Until his death (1915), B. T. WASHINGTON was principal; succeeded by R. R. MOTON. G. W. CARVER taught here.

Tussaud, Marie (tŏŏsō'), 1760–1850, Swiss modeler in wax. While imprisoned during French Reign of Terror, Mme Tussaud modeled heads of famous persons, which were brought to her. Emigrated to London in 1802 and estab. her still-famous wax museum.

Tut-ankh-amen (tŏŏt'-ängk-ä'mŭn), fl. c.1355 B.C., king of anc. Egypt of the XVIII dynasty; son-in-law of Ikhnaton. Revised Ikhnaton's policy, returned to worship of Amon, and restored the capital to Thebes. His chief officer was Harmhab. Tut-ankh-amen's tomb, opened (1922) by Howard Carter and the earl of Carnarvon, yielded many treasures.

Tuticorin (tŏŏ"tĭkôrĭn'), city (75,614), S Madras, India; port on Bay of Bengal. Founded 1540 by the Portuguese, occupied 1658 by the Dutch, ceded to the British 1825. Exports cotton, coffee, and tea.

Tutuila (tŏŏtŏŏē'lä), island (40 sq. mi.; pop. 15,556), largest in American SAMOA. Harbor at PAGOPAGO. Rugged E area; fertile plain in SW. Ceded to U.S. 1900 and made naval station under Dept. of Navy. Land privately owned. Copra chief product.

Tuva or **Tuvinian Autonomous Oblast** (tŏŏ'vü, ō'bläst) Rus. tŏŏvä', ō'blüstyü), region (66,100 sq. mi.; pop. c.150,000), Asiatic RSFSR, between Mongolia (S) and Sayan Mts. (N); cap. Kizil. Agr., livestock raising. Natural resources include timber, gold, coal, salt, asbestos, copper. Tuvinians (c.75% of pop.) are a Turkic-speaking group. Formerly part of Chinese Empire (Uriankhai Territory), region became Russian protectorate 1912; was declared independent 1921 as Tannu-Tuva (after 1934, simply Tuva) People's Republic; incorporated into USSR 1944.

Tuxedo Park, residential village (1940 pop. 1,651), SE N.Y., in the Ramapos near N.J. line. After 1886, Pierre Lorillard developed it as exclusive, wealthy colony, noted for sports and social functions. Plans made in 1941 to introduce inexpensive homes. The tuxedo or "tux" (tailless dress coat) may have originated here.

Tuxtla (tŏŏs'tlä) or **Tuxtla Gutiérrez** (gŏŏtyē'räs), city (pop. 15,883), cap. of Chiapas state, S Mexico, in fertile Grijalva R. valley at foot of Chiapas highlands. Chief industry is a cigar factory.

Tuzigoot National Monument: see NATIONAL PARKS AND MONUMENTS (table).

TVA: see TENNESSEE VALLEY AUTHORITY.

Tver, RSFSR: see KALININ.

Twachtman, John Henry (twäkt'mŭn), 1853–1902, American landscape painter, influenced by the impressionists.

Twain, Mark, pseud. of **Samuel Langhorne Clemens,** 1835–1910, American humorist. After youth in Hannibal, Mo., he was a pilot on the Mississippi from 1857 until the Civil War and took his pen name from the leadsman's call ("mark twain" = two fathoms sounded). In Nev. in 1862, he wrote for Virginia City *Enterprise*. He first won fame in 1865 with his story "The Celebrated Jumping Frog of Calaveras County." A trip to the Holy Land led to his very popular *Innocents Abroad* (1869). After marriage in 1870 he settled in N.Y. and then Conn. Here he wrote his masterly re-creations of his boyhood, *The Adventures of Tom Sawyer* (1876) and *The Adventures of Huckleberry Finn* (1884); also other popular works including the travel book *A Tramp Abroad* (1879), *Life on the Mississippi* (1883), and two novels, *The Prince and the Pauper* (1880) and *A Connecticut Yankee in King*

Arthur's Court (1889). Plunged into debt in 1893 by unfortunate investments, he lectured his way around the world. Saddened by the deaths of two daughters and his wife, he wrote bitter pessimism into later work, such as *The Man That Corrupted Hadleyburg* (1899). Besides hearty reflections of his childhood and youth, humorous travel books, and mordant satire, he wrote the curious *Personal Recollections of Joan of Arc* (1896).

Tweed, William Marcy, 1823–78, American politician and Tammany leader. Controlled Democratic party nominations and patronage in New York city. Made great fortune chiefly from graft in city expenditures. **Tweed Ring,** consisting of Tweed and his henchmen, defrauded city at least to extent of $30,000,000 through padded and fictitious charges and through tax favors. Downfall came with publication in New York *Times* of evidence of wholesale graft; cartoons of Thomas NAST aroused public indignation. Tweed died in prison.

Tweed, river, 90 mi. long, mainly in SE Scotland, but also in England. Rises in Peeblesshire (often called Tweeddale) and enters North Sea at Berwick.

tweed, generally rough woolen fabric of a soft, flexible texture and with an unfinished surface. Genuine tweeds, such as Harris and Donegal, are especially durable and moisture resistant.

Tweeddale, county, Scotland: see PEEBLESSHIRE.

Tweed Ring: see TWEED, WILLIAM MARCY.

Tweedsmuir, John Buchan, 1st Baron: see BUCHAN.

Tweedsmuir Park (twēdz′myo͞or), provincial reserve, 5,400 sq. mi., W central B.C., Canada, W of Prince George; estab. 1936.

Twelfth Night, Jan. 5, vigil or eve of EPIPHANY, so called because it is 12th night from Christmas, counting Christmas as the first.

Twelve Apostles or **Twelve Disciples:** see APOSTLE.

Twelve Tables, early code of Roman law, drawn up according to tradition c.450 B.C.

Twenty-one Demands, ultimatum secretly presented in 1915 to China by Japan. Demands provided for Japanese control over German leasehold of Kiaochow, control over Manchuria and Mongolia, exploitation of China's main coal deposits, exclusion of other powers from further territorial concessions, and guidance of China's military and domestic affairs. Treaties signed 1915 extended Japan's lease of Liaotung and of Manchurian railroads and gave Kiaochow to Japan.

Twickenham (twĭk′ŭnŭm), municipal borough (pop. 105,645), Middlesex, England, on the Thames; residential suburb of London. Scene of Oxford-Cambridge Rugby football matches. Has varied mfg. Alexander Pope lived here and Horace Walpole had famous residence (Strawberry Hill) near by.

Twin Falls, city (pop. 17,600), S Idaho, in Snake R. valley; laid out 1903. Begun as center of private irrigation project, which now serves c.360,000 acres N and S of the Snake. Flow of S falls diverted for water power; N falls are c.125 ft. high. Processing and shipping center for agr., dairying, stock-raising area.

twins, two infants born of one pregnancy. Identical twins, always of same sex and counterparts in appearance, result from division of single fertilized egg. Fraternal twins, of two-egg origin (each egg separately fertilized), resemble each other no more than do any two offspring of same parents. In U.S. twins occur once in c.86 births; one fourth of sets are identical twins.

Two Harbors, city (pop. 4,400), NE Minn., on L. Superior and NE of Duluth. Resort with U.S. coast guard base.

Two Rivers, city (pop. 10,243), E Wis., at base of Door Peninsula on L. Michigan. Commercial fishing and mfg. of aluminum ware.

Two Sicilies, kingdom of the, the kingdoms of SICILY and of NAPLES, officially merged into a single kingdom under house of BOURBON-SICILY in 1816. United with Italy 1861. Kings of the Two Sicilies: FERDI-

NAND I; FRANCIS I; FERDINAND II; and FRANCIS II.

Tyburn (tī′bŭrn), underground river of London, England. It gave its name to famous gallows. After 1783 executions were held at Newgate prison.

Tyche (tī′kē) [Gr.,= chance], in Greek religion, personification of luck, corresponding to Roman Fortuna.

Tycho Brahe: see BRAHE, TYCHO.

Tydeus (tī′dēŭs), Greek legendary hero, brother of Meleager and one of the Seven against Thebes.

Tyler, John, 1790–1862, 10th President of the United States. Governor of Va. (1825–27) and U.S. Senator (1827–36); a moderate states' rights Democrat who resigned from Senate and joined WHIG PARTY out of dislike of FORCE BILL and Pres. Jackson's fiscal policies. On April 4, 1841, following death of W. H. Harrison, he became first Vice President to succeed to presidency. After he had vetoed Whig bank measures and his cabinet had resigned, Tyler became a President without a party. Nevertheless, his plan of annexation was accepted by Texas before he left office in 1845. Died before taking his seat in "permanent" Confederate Congress.

Tyler, Moses Coit, 1835–1900, American writer on intellectual history, teacher of both English (at Univ. of Mich.) and history (at Cornell). His fame rests chiefly upon *A History of American Literature, 1607–1765* (1878) and *The Literary History of the American Revolution* (1897).

Tyler, Royall, 1757–1826, American dramatist, remembered for Yankee comedy *The Contrast* (1787).

Tyler, Wat, d. 1381, English rebel. After Black Death of 1348–49 killed much of England's population, the Statute of Laborers (1351) was adopted, fixing rates of pay to prevent rises. These restrictions and the desire of the commoners of city for liberty finally flamed into rebellion when capital tax was increased. Of this movement in 1381 Tyler became leader. He seized Canterbury, then marched to London, burning prisons and public buildings. Richard II came to meet him and promised to abolish serfdom, feudal service, and market monopolies. At second meeting with the king, Tyler was killed by mayor of London. The promises were forgotten, the revolt put down with force.

Tyler, city (pop. 38,968), E Texas, ESE of Dallas; founded 1846. Center of agr. area with oil refineries and offices and railroad shops. Noted for roses.

Tylor, Sir Edward Burnett, 1832–1917, English anthropologist. His early contributions helped establish scope of anthropology. Author of *Primitive Culture* (1871; rev. ed., 1924) and other works.

Tyl Ulenspiegel: see EULENSPIEGEL, TILL.

Tyndale, Tindal, or **Tindale, William** (all: tĭn′dŭl), d. 1536, English reformer. A humanist, he determined to translate the New Testament, and, meeting opposition in England, he went to the Continent, where he met Luther and completed his New Testament, promptly banned by Cardinal Wolsey and the English bishops. Hunted, living in concealment, Tyndale went on translating the Scriptures and writing tracts (one against Henry VIII's divorce). He was seized at Antwerp in 1535, was condemned for heresy, and was put to death, still defending his own beliefs.

Tyndareus, king of Sparta and husband of LEDA.

Tyne (tīn), river of Northumberland, England. North Tyne (which rises 80 mi. from its mouth) joins South Tyne at Hexham and flows thence c.30 mi. to North Sea. Lower course is lined with docks, shipbuilding yards, and coal-mining and ironworking towns.

Tynemouth (tīn′mŭth, tĭn′–), county borough (pop. 66,544), Northumberland, England, on the Tyne. Includes Tynemouth, Cullercoats, Chirton, North Shields, and Preston. It is a shipbuilding center and a coal and fishing port.

type, for printing, was invented in China; movable type (made from molds of individual characters) was used in Korea before its independent invention in Europe, attributed to Johann GUTENBERG. The MAZARIN BIBLE, probably his work, is believed to have been first book printed in Europe from movable types (c.1456; at Mainz). Forms of letters were derived from handwriting of the time and place; originally "black letter" or "gothic" (now represented by "Old English" and "German" types), later "roman" and "italic." Nicolas JENSON developed roman type to the point where it became standard; italic was introduced by ALDUS MANUTIUS. "Modern" roman type faces emphasize contrast in weight of lines and have strong, level serifs; "old style" roman has less contrast and smaller, often sloping, serifs. The clean modern "sans-serif" faces (i.e., without serifs) are now much favored. Other famous type designers are GARAMOND, GRANJON, CASLON, BASKERVILLE, BODONI, DIDOT, GOUDY. For type set by machine, see LINOTYPE; MONOTYPE. See also TYPOGRAPHY.

type metal, alloy of lead with antimony, tin, and sometimes copper, extensively used for making various kinds of type. Since the alloy expands upon solidification, it takes a fine, clear impression of the mold in which it is hardening. Also used for metal parts of musical instruments and for ornaments.

typewriter. Early models were chiefly for the blind. Commercial machine with capitals only was invented 1867 by C. L. Sholes and associates and manufactured by firm of E. Remington. Shift-key model appeared 1878; electric typewriter c.1935. Teletypewriter, invented 1904, transmits typing over telephone or other electric circuit (in some cases this typing may be electrically transmuted into type). The use of typewritten copy for books through the offset process has led to the development of new typewriters that produce script closely resembling type and of many different typewriter letter faces. See *ill.,* p. 619.

typhoid fever, infectious disease caused by bacillus taken into body in food or water which has been contaminated by feces of a person having disease or of disease carrier. Attended by fever, prostration, rash. Bacteria lodge chiefly in small intestine. Recovery slow, relapse common. Vaccination gives immunity for two to three years. See *ill.,* p. 633.

typhus (tī'fŭs), infectious disease carried by body louse infected from biting diseased person. Causative organism believed to be a rickettsia. Mild type is known as Brill's disease.

typography (tīpŏ'grŭfē), in the graphic arts, is the selection and arrangement for PRINTING of type faces, sizes, spacing, and decorative material (e.g., rules, type ornaments). The first principle is legibility. Aim is to enhance the presentation of ideas by attractive appearance, wise use of emphasis and variety, and creation of appropriate atmosphere. Books, periodicals, and advertising have special requirements related to their particular purposes. Today's styles show historic influences, such as that of inscriptions on classical monuments, medieval calligraphy, the elegant books of the ESTIENNE family and of BASKERVILLE and BODONI, as well as the blatant circus poster and the modern German (BAUHAUS) influence. A notable contemporary typographer is Bruce ROGERS.

Tyr, Norse name of TIW.

Tyrannosaurus (tīră"nŏsŏ'rŭs, tĭ–), giant biped carnivorous dinosaur, c.45 ft. in length and 19 ft. tall. Probably the greatest land-dwelling flesh eater. Existed during late Cretaceous period; parts of skeletons have been found in Mont. and S.Dak.

tyrant, in anc. history, ruler exercising absolute authority without legal warrant. In Greek city-states they generally rose to power in the struggle between popular and noble (or wealthy) classes. Some of the better-known Greek tyrants were Periander of Corinth; Pisistratus, Hipparchus, and Hippias of Athens;

Gelon, Hiero I and Hiero II, Dionysius the Elder and Dionysius the Younger of Syracuse. Their reigns were frequently beneficial for the cities, but growth of democratic sentiment in Greece made the name tyrant unpleasant.

Tyrconnel, Richard Talbot, duke and earl of (tùrkŏ'-nùl), 1630–91, Irish royalist. Supporter of James II, he was (1687–88) commander in chief of forces in Ireland and lord deputy. Supplanted Protestants with Catholics in many key positions.

Tyrconnel, Rory O'Donnell, earl of, 1575–1608, Irish chieftain. Conspired with Spain to start a general uprising and was discovered. His flight marked end of political power of the tribal chieftains.

Tyrconnell, anc. kingdom (5th cent.–11th cent.) in NW Ireland in what is now Co. Donegal.

Tyre (tīr), Phoenician port, one of the great cities of the anc. world; modern Sur in Lebanon, S of Beirut. Built on an island perhaps as early as 2800 B.C., it was a great mercantile city with wide-flung colonies by 1100 B.C. Tyrians founded Carthage (9th cent. B.C.). Tyre was famous for its commerce and its purple Tyrian dye. Taken by Assyrians, Babylonians, and Persians, it survived. It recovered even from the siege and sack by Alexander the Great (333–332 B.C.), who built a mole that has since made the island a peninsula. Under the Romans after 64 B.C., it throve. Until it was destroyed by Moslems in A.D. 1291 it continued important.

Tyrol (tī'rùl, tīrōl'), Ger. *Tirol,* province (4,884 sq. mi.; pop. 426,499), W Austria, in the Alps; cap. Innsbruck. Economy is typically Alpine. Tourist trade yields large revenues. Conquered by Rome 15 B.C., later part of Frankish empire, Tyrol was divided into several fiefs under the Holy Roman Empire—the prince-bishoprics of TRENT and Bressanone (which passed to Austria in 1801, to Italy in 1919; see TRENTINO-ALTO ADIGE) and the county of Tyrol (to Austria 1363). Napoleon awarded Tyrol to Bavaria (1805–15) and suppressed the insurrection led by Andreas HOFER (1809).

Tyrone, Hugh O'Neill, 2d earl of (tīrōn'), 1547?–1616, Irish chieftain. Siding first with English, he later joined Irish chiefs and sought aid from Spain. After defeat (1601) he surrendered tribal authority. His final flight (1607) to Flanders with other nobles marked end of tribalism in Ireland.

Tyrone (tīrōn'), inland county (1,218 sq. mi.; pop. 132,-049), N. Ireland, in Ulster; cap. Omagh. This large, hilly county is pastoral and agr. Has mfg. of linens, woolen goods, and whisky.

Tyrone (tīrōn'), borough (pop. 8,214), central Pa., NE of Altoona; center of bituminous coal area.

Tyrrell, Joseph Burr (tī'rùl), 1858–, Canadian explorer and geologist. A member of Canadian Geological Survey, he explored in N and W Canada. His best-known feat was crossing BARREN GROUNDS in 1893 from L. Athabaska to Chesterfield Inlet.

Tyrrhenian Sea (tīrē'nēŭn), part of W Mediterranean, between W coast of Italy, N coast of Sicily, and E coast of Sardinia and Corsica.

Tyumen or **Tiumen** (both: tyōōmân'yù), city (pop. 75,-537), RSFSR, in W Siberia, on Tura R. and on Trans-Siberian RR. Sawmilling. Oldest Russian town in Siberia (founded 1586).

Tz'u Hsi or **Tsu Hsi** (both: tsū' shē'), 1834–1908, dowager empress of Ch'ing dynasty of China. As consort of Emperor Hsien Feng (d. 1861) she bore his successor T'ung Chih, after whose death (1875) she made her nephew KWANG Hsü emperor. Forced his abdication in 1898. As direct ruler she remained hostile toward the West and encouraged BOXER REBELLION.

U

U, chemical symbol of the element URANIUM.

Ubangi (ōōbäng'gē), river, c.660 mi. long, major tributary of the Congo in N and W central Africa. Name was used by press agent Roland Butler, for "show" Africans, not from this area.

Ucayali (ōōkäyä'lē), river, c.1,000 mi. long, E Peru, headwater of the Amazon, formed by confluence of Apurimac and Urubamba, flowing generally N to the Marañón.

Uccello, Paolo (pä'ōlō ōot-chĕl'lō), c.1396–1475, Florentine painter, a pioneer in linear perspective. Famous for series called *Battle of San Romano.*

Udaipur (ōōdīpōōr') or **Mewar** (māwär'), former princely state, NW India; part of Rajasthan since 1948.

Udine (ōō'dēnā), city (pop. 54,638), cap. of Friuli-Venezia Giulia, NE Italy. Held by patriarchs of Aquileia from 10th cent., it passed to Venice in 1420, to Austria in 1797 and 1814, and to Italy in 1866. It was hq. of Italian army in World War I until occupied by Austria, 1917–18.

Udmurt Autonomous Soviet Socialist Republic (ōōd-mōōrt'), administrative division (16,300 sq. mi.; pop. 1,220,007), E central European RSFSR, in highlands between Kama and Vyatka rivers; cap. Izhevsk. Predominantly agr. Udmurts, formerly called Votyaks, belong to Finno-Permian language group and form 52% of population; the rest are mainly Russians. Region was ruled by Golden Horde 13th–15th cent.

Ufa (ōōfä'), city (pop. 245,863), cap. of Bashkir ASSR, E European RSFSR; a port on Ufa and Belaya rivers. Mfg. of airplanes, mining machinery, textiles. Founded 1586, it has old cathedral and several educational and scientific institutions.

Uffizi (ōōfē'tsē), palace in Florence, Italy, built in 16th cent. by Vasari for Cosimo I de' Medici. Houses Italian National Library and **Uffizi Gallery,** one of world's richest art collections.

Uganda (ūgän'dù), British protectorate (93,981 sq. mi.; pop. 4,937,712), E central Africa, S of Anglo-Egyptian Sudan; cap. Entebbe. Largely a fertile plateau with well-forested hills, but also contains swampy lowlands and a desert region. Inhabited by the Bantu, who produce such export crops as cotton, coffee, and sugar. Arabs from Zanzibar tried to control the area in 19th cent. Among first Europeans to explore Uganda were John Speke (1862) and Henry Stanley (1875). In 1888 the native kingdom of Buganda was held by Arab traders and native Moslems, but in 1890 it was brought under the control of British East Africa Co. Britain estab. a protectorate over Buganda in 1894 and later added to it several adjacent regions.

Ugarit (ōōgùrēt'), anc. city, cap. of Ugarit kingdom, W Syria. On its site is the small Arab village of Ras Shamra near modern Latakia. Remains of ancient city (dating from 5th millennium B.C.) were discovered in 1931. Among the important finds are tablets from 14th cent. B.C. written in Ugaritic, which has been identified as a Semitic language, related to classical Hebrew.

Ugolino della Gherardesca (ōōgōlē'nō dĕl'lä gärärdä'skä), d. 1289, Italian nobleman, podestà [lord] of Pisa. Accused of treason, he was locked into a tower and left to starve to death with his sons and grandsons. Dante relates story in *Inferno.*

Ugrian (ū'grēùn, ōō'-) or **Ugric** (ū'grĭk, ōō'-), group of Finno-Ugric languages. See LANGUAGE (table).

Uhde, Fritz von (frĭts' fŭn ōō'dù), 1848–1911, German genre painter, best known for his popular pictures of scriptural subjects in modern costume and setting.

Uhland, Ludwig (lōōt'vĭkh ōō'länt), 1787–1862, German romantic poet. Among his ballads are *The Minstrel's Curse, The Good Comrade,* and *Taillefer.*

Uhrichsville (ū'rĭksvĭl), city (pop. 6,614), E Ohio, S of Canton. Mfg. of clay products.

Uigurs or **Uighurs** (wē'gōōrz), people of Asia, of Turkic stock. Settled along Orkhon R. in 7th cent.; founded several cities, notably Karakorum. Estab. an empire in Mongolia which lasted 745–856. Migrated to E Turkistan and estab. another empire which was conquered by the Mongols in 13th cent. Many present-day inhabitants of Sinkiang prov., China, speak the Uigur language.

Uinta Mountains (ūĭn'tù), range of Rocky Mts. in NE Utah and SW Wyo., rising to 13,498 ft. in Kings Peak. Includes High Uintas Primitive Area (243,957 acres; 1931).

Uist, North (ū'ĭst, ōō'ĭst), and **South Uist,** islands (total pop. 7,063) of the Outer Hebrides, off NW Scotland, in Inverness-shire. Benbecula and other islands lie between the two. Most of the inhabitants are crofters.

Ujiji (ōōjē'jē), town (pop. c.10,000), Tanganyika; port on L. Tanganyika. Henry Stanley found David Livingstone here on Nov. 10, 1871.

Uji-yamada (ōō'jē-yä'mädä), city (pop. 65,970), S Honshu, Japan, on Ise Bay. Important Shinto center; site of shrines of Ise.

Ujjain (ōōjĭn'), city (pop. 81,272), Madhya Bharat, India; Hindu pilgrimage center. On site of cap. of ancient Aryan kingdom of Avanti.

Ujpest, Hung. *Újpest* (ōō'ēpĕsht), city (pop. 76,001), N central Hungary. Industrial suburb of Budapest.

Ukiah (ūkī'ù), city (pop. 6,120), W Calif., NNW of San Francisco, in a fruit and hops area. Hot springs. Seat of an international latitude observatory.

Ukraine (ūkrän', ū'krän) or **Ukrainian Soviet Socialist Republic,** Rus. *Ukraina,* constituent republic (222,-600 sq. mi.; pop. c.40,800,000), of the USSR, in E Europe; cap. Kiev. It is also called Little Russia. Drained by the Southern Bug, DNIEPER, and DONETS rivers, it consists largely of fertile steppes, particularly in the S Ukraine, one of Europe's chief wheat-growing regions. In the NW are the PRIPET MARSHES; in the W rise the Carpathians. Odessa, Kherson, and Zhdanov are the main Black Sea ports. The central and E Ukraine has mighty industrial concentrations, based on iron from KRIVOI ROG, coal from DONETS BASIN. Chief industrial centers: KHARKOV; DNEPRO-PETROVSK; ZAPOROZHE. W Ukraine, with Lvov as chief center, has petroleum. Population is c.80% Ukrainian, an E Slavic group closely akin to the Great Russians. There are Polish, Russian, and Jewish minorities. For history before Mongol invasion (13th cent.), see RUSSIA and KIEV. Most of the Ukraine fell to LITHUANIA after the Mongol invasion of Russia and became part of the Polish-Lithuanian state; the Black Sea shore fell to the Tatars of CRIMEA. Polish oppression of the Ukrainian peasants and the union of the Ukrainian Church with Rome (1596; see RUTHENIA) led to rebellion of the virtually independent ZAPOROZHE COSSACKS under CHMIELNICKI (1648). In 1667, after long Polish-Russian warfare, the NE Ukraine (incl. Kiev) was ceded by Poland to Russia. Cossack autonomy was abolished by Peter I after the rebellion of MAZEPPA. Russian annexation of Crimean khanate (1783) and the Polish partitions of 1772, 1793, and 1795 gave all Ukraine to Russia except GALICIA (Austrian) and

SMALL CAPITALS = cross references. Pronunciation key on inside end pages. Abbreviations: p. 2.

Ruthenia (Hungarian). Ukrainian nationalists proclaimed their independence in 1918. The years 1918–20 saw a bloody four-cornered struggle among Ukrainian nationalists, Red Army, White Army of DENIKIN, and Poles—a struggle complicated by German, later by French intervention. The Soviets gained control over most of the Ukraine, which became one of the original constituent republics of the UNION OF SOVIET SOCIALIST REPUBLICS. E Galicia, N Bukovina, S Bessarabia, and Ruthenia were added 1939–45 as a result of World War II. In 1945 the Ukraine was admitted into the UN.

ukulele: see STRINGED INSTRUMENTS.

Uladislaus (ōō″lä′dĭslous), Hung. *Ulászló,* Hungarian kings. **Uladislaus I:** see LADISLAUS III, king of Poland. **Uladislaus II,** c.1456–1516, son of Casimir IV of Poland, was chosen king of Bohemia 1471, of Hungary 1490. He lost Moravia, Silesia, and Lusatia to MATTHIAS CORVINUS of Hungary in 1478. Both in Bohemia and Hungary his weakness was exploited by the great nobles for their own aggrandizement. In 1515 he made an important treaty with Emperor Maximilian I: his daughter Anna was betrothed to Maximilian's son Ferdinand (later Emperor Ferdinand I); his son Louis (later LOUIS II) was betrothed to Ferdinand's sister Mary. If Louis died childless (as he did) Hungary and Bohemia were to pass to the Hapsburgs.

Ulan Bator (ōōlän′ bä′tôr), city (pop. 70,000), cap. of Mongolian People's Republic; chief center of Outer Mongolia. Formerly called Urga.

Ulan-Ude (ōōlän″-ōōdĕ′), city (pop. c.150,000), cap. of Buryat-Mongol ASSR, Asiatic RSFSR, on Selenga R. and Trans-Siberian RR. It is a rapidly expanding transportation and mfg. center (locomotives, lumber, textiles, glass, agr. products). Founded 1666, it was first named Udinsk, later Verkhneudinsk (until c.1935). Population is 80% Russian, 20% Mongol.

ulcer (ŭl′sûr), open sore tending not to heal and usually occurring on skin or mucous membranes. Predisposing factors include injury, varicose veins, certain diseases, e.g., syphilis, leprosy, tuberculosis. Some ulcers develop into cancer.

Uleaborg, Finland: see OULU.

Ulenspiegel, Tyl: see EULENSPIEGEL, TILL.

Ulfilas (ŭl′fĭlùs), c.311–383, Gothic bishop, educated at Constantinople. An Arian, he converted many to Arianism. Translated Bible into Gothic.

Ulithi: see CAROLINE ISLANDS.

Ullswater, lake, 7½ mi. long and ¼ to ¾ mi. wide, on Cumberland-Westmorland co. border, England; second largest in the country. Beautiful Lake District scenery has inspired many writers.

Ulm (ōōlm), city (pop. 69,941), Württemberg-Baden, SW Germany; a port on the Danube, which becomes navigable here. Mfg. of metal products, beer, textiles. Politically and commercially it reached its zenith in 15th cent., but declined in religious wars and commercial revolution. Accepted Reformation c.1530. Free imperial city (incl. considerable territory N of the Danube) after 14th cent.; passed to Bavaria 1802, to Württemberg 1810. Over half the city was destroyed in World War II, but the Gothic minster (begun 1377) was spared. Birthplace of Albert Einstein.

Ulpian (ŭl′pēun), d. 228, Roman jurist. Much of the *Corpus Juris Civilis* is based on his writings.

Ulster, northernmost of historic four provinces of Ireland. Consists of nine counties. Antrim, Armagh, Down, Fermanagh, Londonderry, and Tyrone make up NORTHERN IRELAND (or Ulster). Cavan, Donegal, and Monaghan are in the Irish republic.

Ultima Thule: see THULE.

ultraviolet ray, invisible component of sun's radiation. It can be produced artificially by electrode arc lamps, including mercury arc lamps. Much of sun's ultraviolet radiation is lost before it reaches earth; it is unable to penetrate thick clothing, window glass, or air heavy with impurities. Wave lengths range from 4,000 to 400 angstrom units, lying between visible violet light and X rays. Vitamin D is produced when rays act on ergosterol in human skin. Ultraviolet radiation can be used to enrich certain foods with vitamin D and to destroy germs in air and tissues.

Ulyanov, Vladimir Ilyich: see LENIN.

Ulyanovsk (ōōlyä′nùfsk), city (pop. 102,106), RSFSR, on right bank of the middle Volga. River port; mfg. center (trucks, lathes, precision instruments, agr. processing). Founded 1648 as Simbirsk, it was renamed 1924 for Lenin, who was born here and whose real name was V. I. Ulyanov.

Ulysses, Latin name for ODYSSEUS.

Umanak (ōō′münäk), settlement (pop. 394) and colony district (pop. 1,477), W Greenland, on an inlet of Baffin Bay. Hunting and fishing base.

Umatilla (ümùtĭl′lù), river, NE Oregon, rising in Blue Mts. and flowing c.85 mi. W and NW to Columbia R. at Umatilla town. Used for irrigation.

Umbria (ŭm′brĕù, ōōm′brĕä), region (3,270 sq. mi.; pop. 722,544), central Italy; cap. Perugia. Mainly agr., but there are hydroelectric plants around Terni, which has mfg. Little is known of the ancient Umbrians, who were conquered by Rome in the 3d cent. B.C. In the Middle Ages Umbria was noted as the home of St. Francis of Assisi. The Umbrian school of painting (15th–16th cent.) included Pinturicchio and Perugino.

Umbrian (ŭm′brĕùn), language of Italic subfamily of Indo-European languages. See LANGUAGE (table).

umlaut (ōōm′lout), in linguistics, variation of vowels in inflection (e.g., man, men; mouse, mice). It is also called mutation. See also ABLAUT.

Umnak (ōōm′näk), island, 83 mi. long, off W Alaska, one of ALEUTIAN ISLANDS. Sheep herds, introduced 1923, were destroyed when U.S. base was estab. here in World War II; island restocked in 1944.

UN: see UNITED NATIONS.

Unaka Mountains (ū′nùkù), Appalachian range, forming part of N.C.–Tenn. line, NE of Great Smoky Mts.

Unalaska (ū″nùlä′skù), island, 30 mi. long, off W Alaska, one of ALEUTIAN ISLANDS. Discovered by Vitus Bering 1741. Russian fur center until Kodiak rose. Dutch Harbor on Amaknak island in bay.

Unamuno, Miguel de (mēgĕl′ dä ōōnämōō′nō), 1864–1936, Spanish philosopher, scholar, poet, novelist, of Basque descent. Notable is *The Tragic Sense of Life in Men and in Peoples* (1913), expressing his individualistic philosophy of faith only in faith itself.

Uncas (ŭng′kùs), c.1588–c.1683, chief of Mohegan Indians. Sought British support, expanded tribe. Constantly at war with Miantonomo, Narragansett chief; captured him in 1643, murdered him.

uncial: see PALEOGRAPHY.

Uncle Remus: see HARRIS, JOEL CHANDLER.

Uncle Sam, name used to designate U.S. government. Uncertain origin is sometimes credited to Samuel Wilson of Troy, N.Y., known as "Uncle Sam." Wilson inspected army supplies in War of 1812; U.S. stamped on supplies was jokingly referred to as "Uncle Sam" by workmen.

Uncompahgre (ŭn-kùmpä′grē), river rising in SW Colo. in San Juan Mts., S of Ouray, and flowing c.75 mi. NNW to Gunnison R., from which water is diverted by Gunnison Tunnel to Uncompahgre R.

Uncompahgre Peak: see SAN JUAN MOUNTAINS.

unconscious, in psychology, term generally used to mean that aspect of mental life which is apart from immediate consciousness and which is not subject to recall at will; also called the subconscious. With the work of Freud in PSYCHOANALYSIS, the concept became vital in explaining mental activity and neurosis. Freud saw the unconscious as a vast submerged part of the mind containing the motivating force of human behavior. To this concept Jung added an inherited unconscious, the collective experience of man in his total existence as a race. The concept of the unconscious is rejected or disregarded by some schools of psychology.

SMALL CAPITALS = cross references. Pronunciation key on inside end pages. Abbreviations: p. 2.

Underground Railroad, in U.S. history, secret system of helping fugitive slaves from South reach free states and Canada. Slaves were guided, mostly at night, over fixed routes by "conductors" from one "station" to another, often homes of abolitionists. "U.G." existed in every free state and by Civil War had delivered about 75,000 slaves to freedom.

Undset, Sigrid, 1882–1949, Norwegian novelist. Her great trilogy of medieval Norway, *Kristin Lavransdatter* (1920–22) was followed by the tetralogy *The Master of Hestviken* (1925–27). Her writing deepened in religious intensity after her conversion to Roman Catholicism in 1924. She was awarded the 1928 Nobel Prize in Literature.

undulant fever: see BRUCELLOSIS.

unemployment insurance, method of maintaining unemployed workers until they are reabsorbed into industry. Insurance may be compulsory or voluntary. First devised in late-19th-cent. Europe, such insurance schemes were gradually adopted by most countries, and in 1935 by the U.S. See SOCIAL SECURITY.

UNESCO: see UNITED NATIONS EDUCATIONAL, SCIENTIFIC, AND CULTURAL ORGANIZATION.

Ungava Bay (ŭng-gä'vŭ, –gä'vŭ), inlet, 200 mi. long, 160 mi. wide, extending S from Hudson Strait, N Que., Canada. **Ungava** region (239,780 sq. mi.), S of the bay, is a high plateau forming watershed between St. Lawrence R. and Hudson Bay. Formerly owned by Hudson's Bay Co., was made part of Northwest Territories 1869, became separate district 1895, added to Que. 1912. Boundary with Lab. estab. 1927. Rich in minerals and iron.

Ungvar, Ukraine: see UZHGOROD.

unicorn [Latin,= one horned], in fable, an equine beast of India with long horn jutting from middle of forehead. Usually pure white, animal has been used as a symbol of virginity. Hunting of the unicorn was a favorite tapestry subject in Middle Ages and Renaissance. Unicorn, representing Scottish arms, appears in royal arms of Great Britain. Biblical unicorn is probably a wild ox.

uniformism or **uniformitarianism,** in geology, the doctrine that past changes in the earth's crust were brought about by same causes as changes now taking place. Advanced in 1785 by James Hutton, it made little progress at first, because it was overshadowed by doctrine of CATASTROPHISM, and because it seemed contrary to religion and roused religious opposition. In 19th cent. it gained support largely through efforts of Sir Charles Lyell. More recent tendency is to try to synthesize the two theories.

Unimak (ōō'nĭmăk), volcanic island, 70 mi. long, off W Alaska, one of ALEUTIAN ISLANDS, nearest of chain to Alaska Peninsula.

Union. 1 Township (pop. 38,004), NE N.J., SW of Newark; settled from Conn. 1749. Mfg. of machinery, paint, metal and concrete products, chemicals. **2** City (pop. 9,730), N S.C., near Broad R. and NNW of Columbus; textile center in farm area.

Unión, La (lä'ōōnyōn'), city (pop. 6,757), SE Salvador, principal port of republic, on Gulf of Fonseca. Chief exports are coffee, hides, henequen, and Peruvian balsam.

Union, Act of. For the union of England and Scotland, see GREAT BRITAIN; for the union of Ireland with Great Britain, see IRELAND. For both, see UNITED KINGDOM OF GREAT BRITAIN AND IRELAND.

Union, Fort, important trading post of American Fur Co. Erected (1828) near confluence of Yellowstone and Missouri rivers. For almost 40 years it was most important post in U.S. fur country.

union, labor, organization of workers for the purpose of improving their economic status, particularly through COLLECTIVE BARGAINING with employers. Two main types are craft and INDUSTRIAL UNIONS; company unions are employer-controlled. Unions began to organize in the 19th cent. but have often been bitterly fought by employers. See CLOSED SHOP AND OPEN SHOP; LABOR; STRIKE; AMERICAN FEDERATION OF LABOR; CONGRESS OF INDUSTRIAL ORGANIZATIONS.

Union City. 1 City (pop. 3,572), E Ind., E of Muncie. Farm produce and automobile parts. Adjoins Union City, village (pop. 1,622), Ohio. **2** City (pop. 55,537), NE N.J., N of Hoboken. Mfg. of embroideries, silk, soap, lamps, and clothing. Holy Family Church has sponsored passion play, *Veronica's Veil,* each Lent since 1914. **3** City (pop. 7,665), W Tenn., near Ky. line. Farm trade center with mfg. of shoes, shirts, and dairy products.

Union College: see BARBOURVILLE, Ky.; LINCOLN, Nebr.; SCHENECTADY, N.Y.

Union Islands: see TOKELAU.

Union League Clubs, formed in North in Civil War (1863) to further soldier relief and recruit volunteers. In South after the war, the league developed into strong Republican political organization, controlled Negro vote. Clubs of New York, Philadelphia, and Washington survive as social organizations.

Union of South Africa: see SOUTH AFRICA, UNION OF.

Union of Soviet Socialist Republics (USSR), federal state (c.8,570,600 sq. mi.; pop. c.201,300,000), E Europe and N Asia; cap. Moscow. It is also known as Soviet Union or Soviet Russia. The world's largest state, it stretches from the Baltic Sea to the Pacific; from the Arctic Ocean to the Black and Caspian seas, the CAUCASUS, and the great mountain ranges of Central Asia (PAMIR, TIEN SHAN, and ALTAI). As of 1953, the USSR consists of 16 constituent republics, of which the RUSSIAN SOVIET FEDERATED SOCIALIST REPUBLIC (RSFSR) is the largest. The 15 others are: in W USSR—KARELO-FINNISH SSR, ESTONIA, LATVIA, LITHUANIA, BELORUSSIA, UKRAINE, MOLDAVIAN SSR; in Transcaucasia—GEORGIAN SSR, ARMENIAN SSR, AZERBAIJAN SSR; in Central Asia—KAZAKH SSR, TURKMEN SSR, UZBEK SSR, TADZHIK SSR, KIRGHIZ SSR. The European USSR (incl. Transcaucasia and Ural region, c.2,100,000 sq. mi.; pop. c.162,900,000) forms the major part of the East European Plain and is drained by the Dnieper, Don, Volga, and other mighty rivers. E of the URALS extend the Asiatic RSFSR (see SIBERIA) and the steppes, deserts, and peaks of Central Asia. Mt. ELBRUS is the highest peak of Europe; STALIN PEAK, of the USSR. Vegetation zones are the arctic tundra, the dense central forest belt, the fertile S steppes, and the subtropical Black Sea and Caspian littorals. The climate is generally continental and extreme. Aside from its immense forests and rich agr. areas, the USSR possesses in abundance virtually all of the natural resources necessary for its economy. Among them are the huge coal fields of the DONETS BASIN and KUZNETSK BASIN; iron, copper, and other ores in the Urals; and petroleum (esp. at BAKU). Only tin and rubber are scarce. Main exports: timber, furs, manganese, chromium. Among largest cities are Moscow, Leningrad, Kiev, Kharkov, Baku, Gorki. Chief ports: Odessa, Leningrad, Murmansk, Vladivostok. The first country to adopt the Communist system, the USSR was formed in 1922. (For earlier history, see RUSSIA; RUSSIAN REVOLUTION. See also COMMUNISM.) Under the 1936 constitution, the constituent republics and most of the Union's 140 ethnic groups are represented in the council of nationalities—i.e., one of the chambers of the supreme SOVIET or council of the USSR. (Russians, c.50% of total pop., predominate.) The other chamber, or council of the Union, represents the USSR at large. Below these two chambers, there is a complicated hierarchy of regional, municipal, and local soviets as well as of autonomous ethnic subdivisions. The two chambers elect a presidium (the chairman of which—as of 1953, Marshal Voroshilov—acts as president of the USSR) and the council of ministers. Since the Communist party is the sole legal party and holds all power, elections and legislative deliberations are largely academic. The "dictatorship of the proletariat" (with which the Communist party identifies itself) was introduced by V. I. LENIN. In order to revive the economy of war-torn Russia, Lenin in 1921 inaugurated the mildly capitalistic NEW ECONOMIC POLICY. After his death (1924), Joseph STALIN bested his rivals for power and soon consolidated his absolute dictatorship by "purging" other Bolshevik leaders such as TROTSKY, KAMENEV, ZINOVIEV, and RYKOV. The first FIVE-YEAR PLAN (begun 1928) and its successors transformed Russia into one of the world's most powerful industrial nations; "liquidated" the independent farmers (*kulaks*); made virtually all farmland into collective farms (*kolkhoz*) or state-owned farms (*sovkhoz*); developed the Urals, Siberia, and Central Asia; and extended education and social services to backward areas. These results were achieved at the price of all political freedom and with the help of mass deportations and forced labor. At the same time, there was an evident trend toward revived nationalism and a new conservatism. Persecution of religion relented in the 1940s, but the state took virtual control over the churches. The original liberal policy toward national minorities was replaced by increasing Russification. In its foreign policy, the USSR was faced from the beginning by a hostile and apprehensive world. Russia entered the League of Nations in 1934 and its diplomatic position improved. Whatever the motives of the Russo-German nonaggression pact of Aug., 1939, it permitted Germany to begin WORLD WAR II and allowed Russia to annex E Poland, the Baltic republics, N Bukovina, and Bessarabia (1939–40) and to attack FINLAND. In 1941 Germany attacked Russia without warning, and by 1943 Axis armies had reached STALINGRAD and the Caucasus. Russia fought back heroically, but its eventual victory was achieved only after staggering material and human losses. In the postwar years, the expansion of Soviet influence in Europe and Asia created mounting world tension and intensive rearmament both in the Soviet and the Western camps. Stalin's death (March, 1953) and the accession of Malenkov as premier were interpreted by optimists as marking the beginning of a more conciliatory policy abroad and an easing of totalitarianism inside the USSR.

Union Pacific Railroad, chartered 1862 as Union Pacific Railway Co. Construction began from Omaha W in 1865. On May 10, 1869, Union Pacific joined Central Pacific W of Ogden, Utah, thus connecting Missouri R. and Pacific Ocean by rail. Joining of roads was marked by driving of a golden spike. Construction involved tremendous profiteering (see CRÉDIT MOBILIER OF AMERICA). Reincorporated 1897 as Union Pacific Railroad Co., railroad expanded under E. H. Harriman. Later, Union Pacific acquired large holdings in Eastern railroads, gained control of Western motor-coach lines.

Union Theological Seminary, in Manhattan borough of New York city; interdenominational, coed.; opened 1836, chartered 1839 by Presbyterians. Reciprocal educational relationship with Columbia Univ. Since 1928. Includes school of sacred music (1928).

Uniontown, city (pop. 20,471), SW Pa., SSE of Pittsburgh; settled c.1767. Coal, coke, and metal products. Birthplace of Gen. G. C. Marshall. Near by is Fort Necessity Natl. Battlefield Site (see NECESSITY, FORT).

Union University: see SCHENECTADY, N.Y.

Unionville, Conn.: see FARMINGTON.

Unitarianism, religious belief based on conception of God in one person, in contrast to that of one God in three persons (Trinitarianism). It began in Reformation under such leaders as SERVETUS and SOCINUS. John Biddle estab. English Unitarianism, which was gradually welded into separate body. In America, it had its birth as early as 1785 when liberals withdrew from Congregational churches of New England and formed separate congregations. Its doctrines were stated in the ordination sermon (1819) of William Ellery Channing. American Unitarian Association

was formed 1825; a national conference was organized 1865. Congregational polity prevails. No particular profession of faith is required of ministers or members, and no creed has been adopted.

United Brethren in Christ: see EVANGELICAL UNITED BRETHREN CHURCH.

United Church of Canada, Protestant denomination formed (1925) by union of Methodist, Congregationalist, and most Presbyterian churches in Canada.

United Empire Loyalists, name applied to Canadian settlers who, loyal to British cause in American Revolution, migrated to Canada from the Thirteen Colonies. The greatest number left the colonies in 1783–84. Most went to Nova Scotia and Quebec, resulting in establishment of New Brunswick in 1784 and creation of Upper Canada in 1791.

United Fruit Company, incorporated in N.J. in 1899 by Andrew Preston and M. C. KEITH. Soon outstripped all competition in growing, transporting, and merchandising bananas; later handled other produce. Company has often played a deciding role in Caribbean politics.

United Irishmen or **United Irish Society,** Irish political organization. Founded in 1791 by Wolfe Tone, it spread rapidly. Suppressed (1794), it became secret revolutionary body and sought aid from France. After failure of 1798 rebellion, its leaders were executed or imprisoned.

United Kingdom of Great Britain and Ireland, political body composed of ENGLAND, SCOTLAND, and IRELAND. Created by Act of Union (1800), uniting politically GREAT BRITAIN and Ireland. After formation of Irish Free State (1922) the name **United Kingdom of Great Britain and Northern Ireland** was adopted by act of Parliament 1927. Abbreviation is U.K.

United Methodist Church or **United Methodists,** nonconformist community in England, a union (1907) of Methodist New Connection, United Methodist Free Churches, and Bible Christians. Merged (1932) with Wesleyan Methodists and Primitive Methodists.

United Mine Workers of America (U.M.W.), labor union formed 1890. John L. LEWIS became president of the union in 1920. Many goals have been won, including a health and welfare fund. It was expelled (1937) from the A.F. of L., withdrew (1942) from the C.I.O., was readmitted (1946) to the A.F. of L., and was again disaffiliated (1947).

United Nations, international organization estab. after World War II to replace LEAGUE OF NATIONS. Name first officially used on Jan. 1, 1942, when 26 states joined in declaration pledging to continue joint war effort and not to make peace separately. Moscow Declaration of Oct. 30, 1943, issued by U.S., Great Britain, China, and USSR, stated need for international body to replace League. At Dumbarton Oaks Conference (Sept.-Oct., 1944) same countries drafted proposals for UN charter. At Yalta Conference (Feb. 4–11, 1945) USSR, U.S., and Great Britain agreed on "veto" system of voting in Security Council and (joined later by China and France) decided to call a founding conference of all states that had declared war on Germany or Japan by March 1, 1945. This conference was held in San Francisco, April 25–June 26, 1945, with 51 members: Argentina, Australia, Belgium, Belorussia, Bolivia, Brazil, Canada, Chile, China, Colombia, Costa Rica, Cuba, Czechoslovakia, Denmark, Dominican Republic, Ecuador, Egypt, Ethiopia, France, Greece, Guatemala, Haiti, Honduras, India, Iran, Iraq, Lebanon, Liberia, Luxembourg, Mexico, Netherlands, New Zealand, Nicaragua, Norway, Panama, Paraguay, Peru, Philippine Isls., Poland, El Salvador, Saudi Arabia, Syria, Turkey, Ukraine, Union of South Africa, USSR, United Kingdom (Great Britain), U.S., Uruguay, Venezuela, and Yugoslavia. Other nations admitted (to Dec., 1952) were Afghanistan, Burma, Iceland, Indonesia, Israel, Pakistan, Sweden, Thailand, and Yemen. San Francisco Conference drafted a governing treaty, the UN

Charter, signed on June 26 and ratified by required number of states by Oct. 24 (UN Day). General Assembly first met in London, Jan. 10, 1946; Security Council two days later. It was decided to place UN nq. in E U.S. UN occupied its permanent hq. in New York city in summer of 1952, with first General Assembly in Sept., 1952.

Organization and Principles. The UN Charter comprises preamble and 19 chapters with 111 articles. Principal organs of UN, as specified in Charter, are General Assembly, Security Council, Economic and Social Council, Trusteeship Council, Internatl. Court of Justice, and Secretariat. Other agencies are Food and Agriculture Organization, Internatl. Bank for Reconstruction and Development, Internatl. Civil Aviation Organization, Internatl. Labor Organization, Internatl. Monetary Fund, Internatl. Refugee Organization, Internatl. Telecommunication Union, UN Educational, Scientific, and Cultural Organization, Universal Postal Union, and World Health Organization. A temporary agency was UN Relief and Rehabilitation Administration. Charter sets forth purposes of UN as maintenance of international peace and security, development of friendly relations between states, and achievement of cooperation in the solving of international economic, social, cultural, and humanitarian problems. All UN administrative functions are handled by Secretariat, with a secretary general as its head, and a staff recruited on a wide geographical basis. The only UN body in which all members are represented is General Assembly; it meets in regular annual session beginning third Monday in Sept., with special sessions if necessary. It is primarily a deliberative body dealing to a large degree with political, social, or economic questions. Security Council is an organ with power to enforce measures to preserve peace, and it functions continuously. It has 11 members. Five—China, France, Great Britain, U.S., and USSR—are permanent; six nonpermanent members are elected for two-year terms to represent W Europe, E Europe, Arab states, Far East, and Latin America. In voting, unanimity is required among "Big Five"; hence the veto. As guardian of world peace Security Council acts for entire UN. Under Charter it can deal with all dangers to world peace. Security Council makes its own evaluation of matters brought before it, and it may either make recommendations or itself take enforcement measures.

Disagreements among the "Big Five." The Security Council has never been able, because of the veto, to come to agreement, through its Military Staff Committee, on a military force to represent UN and to enforce its decisions. Nor has it been able to agree, through its Atomic Energy Commission, to control atomic weapons, or through its Commission on Conventional Armaments, to reduce armaments. Likewise admission of new members to UN has been blocked, and Chinese representation has been a source of contention. The Interim Committee (or "Little Assembly," estab. 1947) was born as an attempt to bypass Russian misuse of the veto, and is boycotted by USSR. But on the other hand, such regional security agreements as NORTH ATLANTIC TREATY, Act of Chapultepec, and Rio Treaty have been advances toward world peace. International problems settled include complaint (1946) of Syria and Lebanon that France and Great Britain were illegally occupying their territory; acute situation in Palestine in 1947–48; end of hostilities in Indonesia between Dutch and native governments; and checking of the fighting in Kashmir between India and Pakistan. In 1950, when N Korea attacked S Korea, the Security Council on June 25, with USSR absent, voted to give military assistance to S Korea, and by the end of the year 52 nations had given moral support to UN. Communist China later joined N Korea. From Dec., 1950, UN has made efforts to secure a cease-fire, but at end of 1952 there was little progress.

United Nations Atomic Energy Commission: see ATOMIC ENERGY.

United Nations Commission for the Investigation of War Crimes: see WAR CRIMES.

United Nations Commission on Conventional Armaments: see UNITED NATIONS.

United Nations Economic and Social Council: see ECONOMIC AND SOCIAL COUNCIL.

United Nations Educational, Scientific, and Cultural Organization (UNESCO), agency of UN, hq. in Paris, estab. 1945. Furthers world peace by removing social, religious, and racial tensions, encouraging interchange of ideas and achievements, and improving and expanding education.

United Nations General Assembly: see UNITED NATIONS.

United Nations Relief and Rehabilitation Administration (UNRRA), estab. 1943 to aid in areas freed from Axis. Spent some $4,000,000,000; repatriated 7,000,000 persons and cared for 1,000,000 others. Discontinued in Europe, June 30, 1947; in China, March 31, 1949. Work continued by FAO and IRO.

United Nations Security Council: see UNITED NATIONS.

United Nations Trusteeship Council: see TRUSTEESHIP, TERRITORIAL.

United Presbyterian Church, in Scotland, a union (1847) of United Secession Church with part of Relief Church; in 1900 United Church merged with Free Church to form United Free Church of Scotland; in 1929 this group merged with Church of Scotland. In the U.S., United Presbyterian Church of North America represents union (1858) of Associate Presbyterian Church with Associate Reformed Presbyterian Church.

United Provinces, India: see UTTAR PRADESH.

United Provinces, Low Countries: see NETHERLANDS.

United Service Organizations (USO), organization which supplied social, recreational, welfare, and spiritual facilities for armed services and, to a limited extent, for war production workers in World War II and for a few years thereafter. Organized 1941; had volunteer support. A new organization with same name came into existence in 1951.

United States, republic (3,022,387 sq. mi.; pop. 150,-697,361), North America; cap. Washington, D.C. Continental U.S. consists of 48 states: Alabama, Arizona, Arkansas, California, Colorado, Connecticut, Delaware, Florida, Georgia, Idaho, Illinois, Indiana, Iowa, Kansas, Kentucky, Louisiana, Maine, Maryland, Massachusetts, Michigan, Minnesota, Mississippi, Missouri, Montana, Nebraska, Nevada, New Hampshire, New Jersey, New Mexico, New York, North Carolina, North Dakota, Ohio, Oklahoma, Oregon, Pennsylvania, Rhode Island, South Carolina, South Dakota, Tennessee, Texas, Utah, Vermont, Virginia, Washington, West Virginia, Wisconsin, and Wyoming, plus District of Columbia. U.S. territories and possessions: Alaska, Puerto Rico, Virgin Isls. of the United States, Hawaiian Isls., Guam, American Samoa, Wake Isl., Midway, Canton Isl., Enderbury Isl., several other islands. Trusteeship under UN of Caroline, Marshall, Marianas (except Guam) island chains. Panama Canal Zone held under perpetual lease from Panama. U.S. bounded by Atlantic Ocean (E), Pacific Ocean (W), Canada (N), Mexico and Gulf of Mexico (S). Atlantic lowlands rise to Appalachian Mts.; S drainage area of Great Lakes is in N central U.S.; heart of the country drained by great Mississippi and Missouri river systems. Prairies rise to Great Plains (W) which are sheltered by Rocky Mts. Further W, beyond Great Basin (sinking to 280 ft. below sea level in Death Valley), are the Sierra Nevada (rising to 14,495 ft. in Mt. Whitney) and Coast Ranges rising from narrow Pacific lowlands. Pacific Northwest is drainage area of Columbia R. Colorado R. drains large area and is stream of the Grand Canyon. Natural resources, man power, highly developed transportation and communication facilities make U.S. world's leading industrial nation. Agr. products include all those of temperate zone as well as subtropical produce. Has practically all resources needed for self-sufficiency.

Government. The U.S. government is that of a Federal republic set up by CONSTITUTION OF THE UNITED STATES. Division of power is between Federal and state governments. Federal government has threefold division of powers into executive (President, Vice President, cabinet); legislative (Congress); judicial (Supreme Court, lesser courts).

From Colonies to World Power. Spain, England, and France were the chief nations to establish colonies in present U.S. St. Augustine, Fla., founded 1565 by Spanish, was first permanent settlement. French influence spread through Great Lakes and down Mississippi R. to colony of Louisiana. First permanent British settlement was at Jamestown, Va., in 1607. Plymouth Colony, in New England, was estab. in 1620 by Pilgrims. British position strengthened after victory in FRENCH AND INDIAN WARS. Increasing conflict between colonies and mother country led to AMERICAN REVOLUTION, resulting in independence of Thirteen Colonies. These colonies, become states, united under Articles of Confederation, which were soon discarded for the Constitution. George WASHINGTON was first President. Controversy over division of power between states and Federal government introduced perennial problem of STATES' RIGHTS and gave rise to first political parties (see FEDERALIST PARTY; DEMOCRATIC PARTY). The frontier became a great molding force in American life. Expansion W accelerated: LOUISIANA PURCHASE (1803) added much new territory. WAR OF 1812 quickened growth of nationalism. Radical doctrines of frontier democracy focused on figure of Andrew JACKSON. Texas was annexed 1845; Calif. and vast areas of W were acquired through MEXICAN WAR. Brewing dispute over sectionalism and the slavery question erupted into CIVIL WAR (1861–65) after Abraham LINCOLN became President. War and RECONSTRUCTION period that followed left the South broken and impoverished. Industrial development became driving force in U.S. after 1865; excesses of new capitalism aroused much opposition. Through SPANISH-AMERICAN WAR, U.S. emerged as first-rate power. Imperialism expanded as a vigorous foreign policy was pursued. General progress marked period up to World War I. Despite efforts of Woodrow WILSON for peace, U.S. entered war in 1917 on side of the Allies. Boom afterwards ended in depression which began in 1929 and which was countered by measures taken under presidency of F. D. ROOSEVELT. World War II brought greatly expanded economy and underscored position of U.S. in world affairs. Today, through participation in UN and aid to other nations, U.S. has generally realized its role as a leader in world community. Action in Europe and Asia shows change from isolationism of past to responsible world position.

List of Presidents. This list uses one of two methods of numbering Presidents. The other method counts Grover Cleveland's terms separately, thus changing numbers 24 through 33 to read 25 through 34. **1** George Washington, 1789–97; **2** John Adams, 1797–1801; **3** Thomas Jefferson, 1801–9; **4** James Madison, 1809–17; **5** James Monroe, 1817–25; **6** John Quincy Adams, 1825–29; **7** Andrew Jackson, 1829–37; **8** Martin Van Buren, 1837–41; **9** William Henry Harrison (died in office), 1841; **10** John Tyler, 1841–45; **11** James K. Polk, 1845–49; **12** Zachary Taylor (died in office), 1849–50; **13** Millard Fillmore, 1850–53; **14** Franklin Pierce, 1853–57; **15** James Buchanan, 1857–61; **16** Abraham Lincoln (assassinated), 1861–65; **17** Andrew Johnson, 1865–69; **18** Ulysses S. Grant, 1869–77; **19** Rutherford B. Hayes, 1877–81; **20** James A. Garfield (assassinated), 1881; **21** Chester A. Arthur, 1881–85; **22** Grover Cleveland, 1885–89, 1893–97; **23** Benjamin Harrison, 1889–93; **24** William

McKinley (assassinated), 1897–1901; **25** Theodore Roosevelt, 1901–9; **26** William Howard Taft, 1909–13; **27** Woodrow Wilson, 1913–21; **28** Warren G. Harding (died in office), 1921–23; **29** Calvin Coolidge, 1923–29; **30** Herbert C. Hoover, 1929–33; **31** Franklin D. Roosevelt (died in office), 1933–45; **32** Harry S. Truman, 1945–53; **33** Dwight D. Eisenhower, 1953–. For further information, see articles on the states, towns and cities, physical features, major Americans, significant events in American history.

United States Government Printing Office: see GOVERNMENT PRINTING OFFICE, UNITED STATES.

United States Military Academy, institution founded (1802) at WEST POINT, N.Y., to prepare young men to be officers of U.S. army. Popularly known as West Point or Army. Act of 1812 laid basis for broader establishment of academy, and Sylvanus Thayer, superintendent 1817–33, shaped the curriculum and organization anew. War Dept. took control in 1866. Course of instruction takes four years for the students (cadets; called plebes as freshmen), who then normally become second lieutenants. The students are chosen according to Congressional dist. (with eight from states at large) except for a number from actual service.

United States National Museum: see SMITHSONIAN INSTITUTION.

United States Naval Academy, institution at Annapolis, Md., for training officers of U.S. navy. In 1845 George BANCROFT founded Naval School at Annapolis. School was reorganized 1850–51 under present name. Moved during Civil War to Newport, R.I.; returned in 1865. Four-year course for students (midshipmen) includes practical work on cruises and normally leads to commission as ensign. Many students are drawn from the Navy and the Marine Corps, others by the President, Vice President, and members of both houses of Congress.

United States Naval Observatory, government astronomical observatory in Washington, D.C. It evolved from chart and instrument depot estab. 1830; naval observatory completed 1844; moved to present site 1893. Supervised by chief of naval operations. Functions include making astronomical observations, sending time signals, publishing (from 1894) *American Ephemeris and Nautical Guide.*

United States Supreme Court: see SUPREME COURT, UNITED STATES.

Unity, religious movement inc. as Unity School of Christianity, with hq. at Lee's Summit, Mo. Founded by Charles and Myrtle Fillmore as faith-healing cult, with affinities to both Christian Science and New Thought, it has acquired character of denomination with "centers" or churches, ordained ministry, and statement of faith (1921). In 1922 it withdrew from Internatl. New Thought Alliance.

Universalist Church of America, Protestant denomination based on belief in salvation for every soul through divine grace of Jesus Christ. In Gloucester, Mass., John MURRAY became pastor of first Universalist church in U.S. Convention in Philadelphia (1790) agreed on Congregational policy and articles of faith. Movement changed (c.1796–1852) from Calvinism to Unitarianism. Winchester Profession (1803) accepts universal fatherhood of God, spiritual authority of Christ, and final harmony with God.

universal language, invented language intended for auxiliary purposes. Expanding 19th-cent. horizons brought several such creations, but Esperanto (a simplified, regular language with Latin-type grammar and European vocabulary), devised by L. L. Zamenhof, is the only one even moderately successful.

Universal Military Training (UMT). Although U.S. has used SELECTIVE SERVICE to conscript men in times of war, it has never had a system of military training for all male citizens, unlike some countries. However, such a system was urged as part of preparedness program instituted after World War II as a means of insuring enough trained men if the need for them should suddenly arise. Question of UMT has aroused much controversy. Although Pres. Truman urged passage of a bill authorizing UMT, Congress compromised by passing a draft bill in 1948 which was extended in 1951.

Universal Postal Union, agency of UN, hq. Bern, Switzerland. Originally estab. 1875, under UN 1947. Members constitute unified postal territory with easy international exchange of mail. Nearly all nations and territories in world belong.

universe, in astronomy, whole cosmic system, consisting of our Milky Way system and the many extragalactic nebulae scattered through space at average distance apart of 2,000,000 light-years. Einstein's relativity theories postulated four-dimensional space-time background; his work on cosmology (1917), stimulus for studies by De Sitter and others, defined space as curved and unlimited but finite. From spectroscopic studies revealing displacement toward red end of certain lines of spectra of extragalactic nebulae (red shift), it appears that external galaxies are moving away from our galaxy at velocities roughly proportional to their distance from us. Although controversy exists, many scientists agree that universe is expanding and finite.

University City, suburban city (pop. 39,892), E Mo., W of St. Louis.

University College: see OXFORD UNIVERSITY.

University Heights, city (pop. 11,566), NE Ohio, E suburb of Cleveland. Here is John Carroll Univ. (Jesuit; for men; 1886).

University Park, city (pop. 22,275), N Texas, adjoining Dallas; settled 1914. Seat of SOUTHERN METHODIST UNIVERSITY.

UNRRA: see UNITED NATIONS RELIEF AND REHABILITATION ADMINISTRATION.

Unruh, Fritz von (frĭts' fŭn ŏŏn'rōō), 1885–, German author. His prose epic, *The Way of Sacrifice* (1916–18; Eng. tr., 1928), is a passionate denunciation of war. The novel *The End Is Not Yet* (Eng. tr., 1947) deals with the Nazi period, during which Unruh lived in exile in the U.S.

Untermeyer, Louis, 1885–, American poet and anthologist, known for *Modern American Poetry* (1919 and later eds.) and *Modern British Poetry* (1920 and later eds.). His own works include *Selected Poems and Parodies* (1935), prose works, and criticism.

Unterwalden (ŏŏn'tŭrväldŭn), canton, central Switzerland. Mountainous, forested, chiefly pastoral. Divided into half-cantons of Obwalden (190 sq. mi.; pop. 22,075; cap. Sarnen) and Nidwalden (106 sq. mi.; pop. 19,459; cap. Stans). In 1291 Unterwalden formed with Uri and Schwyz a league which became the Swiss Confederation (see SWITZERLAND). Population is German-speaking and Catholic.

untouchables: see CASTE.

Upanishads (ŏŏ'pănʹĭshădz), dialogues on metaphysics, written after the Vedas and in part a commentary on them; important in development of Vedanta.

upas tree (ūʹpŭs), East Indian tree (*Antiaris toxicaria*) of the mulberry family. The poisonous milky juice has been used for tipping arrows.

Updike, D(aniel) B(erkeley), 1860–1941, American printer, founder of the Merrymount Press at Boston; author of *Printing Types: Their History, Forms, and Use* (1922).

Upernivik (ōōpĕr'nùvĕk), settlement (pop. 321) and colony district (pop. 1,443), W Greenland, on small island in Baffin Bay. Sealing and whaling base.

Upjohn, Richard, 1802–78, American architect, b. England, important in the Gothic revival. Rebuilt Trinity Church, New York city.

Upland, city (pop. 9,203), S Calif., E of Los Angeles near San Antonio Peak. Packs citrus fruit.

Upolu (ōōpōʹlōō), volcanic island (430 sq. mi.; pop. 42,764), Western SAMOA, under New Zealand mandate. Apia is seat of government; Saluafata, on N

coast, is U.S. naval station. Vailima, home of Robert Louis Stevenson, is near Mt. Vaea.

Upper Austria, Ger. *Oberösterreich,* province (4,625 sq. mi.; pop. 1,107,562), N Austria, bordering on Czechoslovakia and Germany; cap. Linz. Agr. region, drained by the Danube. Includes much of the SALZKAMMERGUT. Was created a duchy 1156 and given to dukes of Austria.

Upper Palatinate: see PALATINATE.

Upper Volta (vŏl'tù), overseas territory (c.113,100 sq. mi.; pop. c.3,037,000), central French West Africa; cap. Ouagadougou. Mainly a wooded savanna land used for stock raising. Export crops include peanuts and sesame. Under French control since 1897.

Uppland (ŭp'länd), historic province of central Sweden; chief city Uppsala.

Uppsala (ŭp'sä"lä), city (pop. 63,072), E central Sweden. Archiepiscopal see since 1270 (now Lutheran). Seat of oldest Swedish university (founded 1477), one of the world's great centers of learning. University library has many invaluable manuscripts, e.g., the Codex argenteus of Ulfilas. The 13th-cent. cathedral contains the tombs of Gustavus I, Linnaeus, and Swedenborg.

Upsala College: see EAST ORANGE, N.J.

Upshur, Abel Parker (ŭp'shùr), 1790–1844, U.S. Secretary of State (1843–44). Aided annexation of Texas. Upshur was killed in the explosion on the USS *Princeton,* and his death high-lighted the possibility of many high officials being killed at once and stressed the need for a law setting presidential succession.

Ur, anc. Sumerian city of Mesopotamia, on the Euphrates; of unknown antiquity (it was flourishing by 3500 B.C.); identified in the Bible as the home of Abraham. It was captured (c.2800 B.C.) by Sargon, but later was again independent. Ur declined after the 6th cent. B.C. C. Leonard Woolley led in excavations of the city in the late 19th cent. Called Ur of the Chaldees.

Ural (yōō'rùl, Rus. ōōräl'), river, 1,574 mi. long, RSFSR and Kazakh SSR, part of conventional geographic border between Europe and Asia. Rising in S Urals, it flows S, then W, then S again, past Magnitogorsk, to Caspian Sea. Partly navigable.

Ural-Altaic (yōō'rùl-ältā'ĭk), designation of a hypothetical grouping of certain language families of Europe and Asia. Finno-Ugric and Samoyede form Uralian stock. While Turkic, Tungusic, and Mongolian, the so-called Altaic languages, resemble one another, there is no clear evidence of relationship among them and Uralian.

Urals or **Ural Mountains,** USSR, extending c.1,300 mi. N–S between Europe and Asia. Highest peak is Naroda (6,184 ft.). Densely forested (except in rocky N part), they also are rich in mineral resources (iron, manganese, nickel, chrome, copper, precious stones and metals, bauxite, asbestos, coal, oil). Huge industrial centers were created in 1930s at SVERDLOVSK, MAGNITOGORSK, Nizhni Tagil, Molotov, Chelyabinsk. During World War II entire industries were transferred to the Urals from the W USSR.

Urania (ūrā'nēù) [Gr.,= celestial], in Greek religion. 1 Muse of astronomy. See MUSES. 2 Aphrodite as goddess of heavens, patroness of heavenly love.

uranium (ūrā'nēùm), hard, silver-white, radioactive metallic element (symbol = U; see also ELEMENT, table). Isotopes include those with atomic weights of 235, 238, and 239. Uranium 238 is parent substance of disintegration series, in which radium occurs; final product is lead of atomic wt. 206. Uranium occurs in ores, especially in PITCHBLENDE and carnotite. See also ATOMIC ENERGY. See *ill.,* p. 773.

Uranus (ūrā'nùs, yōō'rùnùs) [Gr.,= sky, heaven], in Greek religion, sky-god, first ruler of universe; son of Gaea and father of Titans and Cyclopes. He was wounded and dethroned by Cronus. From his blood which fell on earth sprang the Erinyes and giants, from that which fell into the sea arose Aphrodite.

Uranus, in astronomy, PLANET seventh in distance from sun. Revolves about sun at mean distance of 1,782,700,000 mi. in period of c.84 years. Diameter c.30,878 mi. Rotation period c.10 hr. 45 min. Attended by five satellites (fifth reported 1948). Recognized as planet by Herschel 1781. See *ill.,* p. 927.

Urban II, c.1042–1099, pope (1088–99), a Frenchman. He furthered the reforms of Gregory VII and preached at Clermont the sermon launching the First Crusade.

Urban IV, d. 1264, pope (1261–64), a Frenchman. Opposed the Hohenstaufen by offering Sicilian throne to Charles of Anjou.

Urban V, 1310–70, pope (1362–70), b. Provence; a Benedictine learned in canon law. Tried with the help of Cardinal Albornoz to move the papacy to Rome (1367), but had to return to Avignon (1370).

Urban VI, 1318?–1389, pope (1378–89), a Neapolitan. Chosen as successor to Gregory XI, he proved violently unruly. The cardinals, claiming intimidation by the Roman mob, went to Anagni and elected ROBERT OF GENEVA, thus beginning the Great SCHISM. Urban is thought by many to have been insane.

Urbana (ûrbă′nù). **1** City (pop. 22,834), E central Ill., adjoining CHAMPAIGN, with which it is allied economically. Trade center in farm area. Seat of Univ. of ILLINOIS. Tablet in courthouse commemorates Lincoln speech against Kansas-Nebraska bill 1854. **2** City (pop. 9,335), W central Ohio, N of Springfield, in agr area. Mfg. of paper, metal products, and tools. Simon Kenton buried here.

Urbino (ōōrbē′nō), town (pop. 5,459), the Marches, central Italy. Flourished under Montefeltro family from 12th cent. and under dukes Della Rovere (1508–1626). Had noted school of painting (15th–17th cent.). Early Renaissance ducal palace is rich in works of art. Birthplace of Raphael.

Urdu (ōōr′dōō), language of Indic group of Indo-Iranian subfamily of Indo-European languages. See LANGUAGE (table).

Urey, Harold Clayton (yōō′rē), 1893–, American chemist. Won 1934 Nobel Prize for isolation of heavy hydrogen. Known also for work on atomic bomb, including methods of separating uranium isotopes and production of heavy water.

Urfa (ōōr′fä), anc. *Edessa,* city (pop. 37,456), S Turkey. An ancient center of Christianity, it fell 1144 to Moslems. Many Armenian Christians were massacred here in 19th cent.

Urfé, Honoré d' (ōnōrā′ dürfā′), 1567–1625, French author of *L'Astrée* (5 vols., 1607–10), the principal French pastoral novel.

Urga, Mongolia: see ULAN BATOR.

Urgench (ōōrgyĕnch′). **1** Ancient city of central Asia, on site of present Kunya-Urgench (pop. over 2,000), Turkmen SSR, in Khiva oasis. Once the cap. of KHOREZM, it was abandoned in 16th cent. when the Amu Darya, on which it was situated, changed its course. **2** City (pop. over 10,000), Uzbek SSR, in Khiva oasis. Cotton mfg. Known as Novy [new] Urgench till 1937.

Uri (ōō′rē), canton (415 sq. mi.; pop. 28,569), Switzerland; cap. Altdorf. Alpine region of glaciers and pastures; forests and meadows in Reuss R. valley. The scene of the TELL legend, Uri in 1291 formed with Schwyz and Unterwalden the league which became the nucleus of SWITZERLAND.

Uriah (ūrī′ù) [Heb.,= light of God], husband of Bathsheba. 2 Sam. 11. Urias: Mat. 1.6.

uric acid (yōō′rĭk), white, odorless, tasteless, weak crystalline organic acid, formed as a result of protein metabolism in humans and some other vertebrates. Occurs in small amount in human urine and blood. Pure acid is obtained from GUANO. Yields urea on decomposition.

Uriel (ū′rēul) [Heb.,= flame of God], name of an angel in the pseudepigrapha. He is introduced in Milton's *Paradise Lost* as the angel of the sun.

urine, in human and some other vertebrates, a fluid secreted by KIDNEYS, stored in BLADDER, and eliminated through urethra. Contains execretory products collected from tissues by circulating blood; consists of water (95%) and salts, urea, uric acid, pigments, and mucus.

Urmia (ōōr′mĕù, ōōrmĕä′), shallow salt lake, 90 mi. long, 30 mi. wide, NW Iran, in Azerbaijan; largest lake in Iran. Has no outlet.

Urquhart, Sir Thomas (ûr′kùrt), 1611–60, Scottish author, noted for his translation of three books of the *Gargantua* of Rabelais.

Urquiza, Justo José de (hōō′stō hōsä′ dā ōōrkē′zä), 1801–70, Argentine political leader. In control of Entre Ríos prov., he supported Rosas until 1851, when he led the revolt, successful at the battle of Monte Caseros (1853). He was then the ruler of Argentina, but was opposed by Buenos Aires prov. The battle at Pavón (1861) was indecisive, but Urquiza surrendered power to Mitre. He was assassinated.

Urraca (ōōrä′kä), d. 1126, Spanish queen of Castile and Leon (1109–26); daughter of Alfonso VI. Her second husband, Alfonso I of Aragon, seized her lands and repudiated her in 1114. Her son and successor, Alfonso VII, helped her to recover her kingdoms from his stepfather.

Ursins, Marie Anne de la Trémoille, princesse des (märē′ än′ dù lä trämwä′yù prēsĕs′ däz ürsē′), 1642–1722, French noblewoman. Arranged marriage of Philip V of Spain with María Luisa of Savoy. Held almost dictatorial powers at the Spanish court till the queen's death (1714).

Ursúa, Pedro de (pā′dhrō dā ōōrsōō′ä), c.1526–1561, Spanish conquistador and explorer in South America. A restless adventurer, he came to New Granada in 1545, was temporary governor of Bogotá, subjugated neighboring Indians, sought El Dorado, founded towns; joined viceroy of Peru in Panama and subdued *cimarrones* (escaped Negro slaves). He was murdered on expedition to Marañón when again seeking El Dorado.

Ursula, Saint, 4th cent.?, virgin martyr of Cologne. Legend says 11,000 virgins were her companions. Feast: Oct. 21.

Uruapan (ōōrwä′pän), city (pop. 20,583), Michoacán, W Mexico; founded 1540. In semitropical, mountainous agr. region, city has mfg. of gourd lacquerware by Tarascan Indians. Near by is volcano Paricutín.

Uruguaiana (ōō″rōōgwiä′nù), city (pop. 33,272), W Rio Grande do Sul state, S Brazil, on Uruguay R.; rail junction and cattle-raising center, with meat-processing plants.

Uruguay (ōōrōōgwī′), republic (72,152 sq. mi.; pop. 2,202,936), SE South America; cap. MONTEVIDEO. The Río de la Plata and the Uruguay R. separate Uruguay from Argentina, and Brazil lies to the N; the Atlantic is to E. The BANDA ORIENTAL, a rich alluvial plain, where most of Uruguay's population lives, produces wheat, wine, tobacco, and olives, but sheep and cattle raising on the grasslands in N is most important activity. The owners and the *gauchos* of the large *estancias* there played a major role in Uruguayan economy and political life. The Spanish and Portuguese contended for ownership of the region in the 17th and 18th cent. The Spanish were in control when the movement for independence began and Uruguay declared for independence with Argentina in 1810. In 1814, however, ARTIGAS broke with the military junta of Buenos Aires and the struggle for Uruguay's separate existence began. In 1820, the Brazilians occupied Montevideo. A group of patriots known as the Thirty-three Immortals declared Uruguay independent in 1825, and at the battle of Ituzaingo in 1827 Brazil was defeated. Immediately thereafter a fratricidal struggle ensued (1828–51) between two political parties known as Colorados [reds] and Blancos [whites]; this was mixed with the rising against Rosas in Argentina and resulted in a long siege of Montevideo. In 1864, Uruguay again became involved with her neighbors, Brazil and Paraguay (see TRIPLE ALLIANCE, WAR OF THE). Not until the 20th cent. was Uruguay free from revolutions and counterrevolutions and able to launch a program of social and material progress that has characterized its subsequent development. In 1952 a nine-man council was substituted for the presidency of Uruguay's democratic government.

Uruguay, river, c.1,000 mi. long, rising in S Brazil near Atlantic and flowing in arc W to Argentina, then SW and S to Río de la Plata. Principal cities on river are Salto and Paysandú (Uruguay) and Concepción del Uruguay (Argentina).

Urumchi (ōōrōōmchē'), Chinese *Tihwa,* commercial city (pop. 69,991), cap. of Sinkiang prov., NW China, in the Dzungaria.

Ushant (ŭ'shŭnt), Fr. *Ouessant,* island, 5 mi. long, NW France, in the Atlantic off tip of Brittany. Lord Howe defeated a French fleet here (1794).

Usher, James: see USSHER, JAMES.

Usk, river of Wales and England. Flows c.60 mi. from Caermarthenshire to the Severn estuary. Noted for its beauty and associations with King Arthur.

Uskudar, Turkey: see SCUTARI.

Uspallata Pass (ōōspäyä'tä), c.12,500 ft. high, over Andes between Mendoza, Argentina, and Santiago, Chile. Used by San Martín for conquest of Chile 1817; Christ of the Andes was built here 1904; Transandine Railway completed through Pass 1910; Mt. Aconcagua towers N and Tupungato S of Pass.

Ussher or **Usher, James,** 1581–1656, Irish churchman, chancellor of St. Patrick's Cathedral, Dublin, bishop of Meath (1621–25), archbishop of Armagh (after 1625). He was notable for his great learning. His chronology of biblical events was long accepted as authoritative.

USSR: see UNION OF SOVIET SOCIALIST REPUBLICS.

Usti nad Labem (ōōs'tyē näd lä'bĕm), Ger. *Aussig,* city (pop. 34,410), N Bohemia, Czechoslovakia, on the Elbe. Industrial center (chemicals, machinery, foodstuffs). Founded 13th cent., city has fine Gothic and Renaissance architecture.

Ust Urt (ōōst" ōōrt'), desert plateau, area c.62,000 sq. mi., Asiatic USSR, between Caspian and Aral seas. Sheep, goat, and camel raising.

usury: see INTEREST.

Utah, state (84,916 sq. mi.; pop. 688,862), W U.S.; admitted 1896 as 45th state; cap. SALT LAKE CITY. Other cities are PROVO, OGDEN. Has varied topography of mountains, plateaus, basins, valleys. Main rivers are the Colorado and the Green. Mining (copper, silver, gold, lead, coal, zinc). Sheep, cattle raising; agr. of wheat, potatoes, potatoes. Processes minerals, agr. products. MORMONS arrived 1847, led by Brigham YOUNG. Region passed to U.S. (1848) after Mexican War. Opposition between Mormons and U.S. government produced much trouble. Following repeated petitions, statehood was finally granted after Mormon church renounced polygamy. Present economic problems arise from Mormon distrust of industry, high freight rates, distance from markets.

Utah, University of, at Salt Lake City; state supported, coed.; opened 1850, chartered 1851 as Univ. of Deseret, closed 1851–67, renamed 1892.

Utah Lake, N central Utah. Fresh-water lake (23 mi. long, 8 mi. wide), which was part of prehistoric L. Bonneville. Drains via Jordan R. to Great Salt L. Much used for irrigation, its low waters in 1930s caused construction of Provo R. project.

Utah State Agricultural College, at Logan; land-grant support, coed.; opened 1890.

Utamaro (ōōtä'märō), 1753–1806, one of first Japanese color-print artists to be known in Europe. Noted for landscapes, pictures of insects, and portraits of women.

Ute Indians (ūt), North American tribe of Uto-Aztecan linguistic stock, occupying W Colo. and E Utah in the early 19th cent. They were then fierce nomadic horse-men, who sometimes raided the villages of the Pueblo Indians in Ariz. and N.Mex. There was some trouble with the whites, especially in 1879, but no full-fledged war. They live on reservations in Colo. and Utah. Also called Utah Indians.

uterus (ū'tŭrŭs), hollow muscular organ in which fetus develops. In human it is normally in pelvis; supported on neck (cervix) opening into vagina. Ova pass from ovaries into openings of near-by paired oviducts leading into uterus. Ovum fertilized in oviduct is implanted in uterine wall; unfertilized ovum is eliminated during MENSTRUATION.

Uther Pendragon: see ARTHURIAN LEGEND.

Utica (ū'tĭkŭ), anc. city, N of Carthage, supposedly founded by Phoenicians from Tyre (c.1100 B.C.). Joined Rome against Carthage in the Third Punic War. Was later capital of the Roman province of Africa. Finally destroyed by Arabs (A.D. c.700).

Utica, city (pop. 101,531), central N.Y., on Mohawk R. and the Barge Canal and NW of Albany, in rich dairying region. Permanent settlement began after Revolution. Opening of Erie Canal and railroads spurred industrial growth. Has large textile industry (sheets, pillowcases, knit goods), begun 1840s; mfg. also of firearms, machinery. Park system has facilities for summer, winter sports. Large Welsh pop. holds annual eisteddfod.

utilitarianism, philosophical movement centered upon the ethical idea that the criterion of morality is attaining the greatest happiness for the greatest number. Jeremy Bentham was its founder, and John Stuart Mill and Herbert Spencer developed the doctrines.

Uto-Aztecan (ū"tō-ăztĕ'kŭn), linguistic family of North America. See LANGUAGE (table).

Utopia [Gr.,= no place], title of book by Sir Thomas MORE (in Latin, 1516). Work pictures ideal state where all is ordered for best for mankind as whole, and evils such as poverty and misery do not exist. Book's popularity has given generic name to all concepts of ideal states created by social philosophers and visionaries. Among great early utopian works are Plato's *Republic* and St. Augustine's *City of God.* Among other famous utopias before 19th cent., besides More's, were Campanella's *The City of the Sun* (1623), Francis Bacon's *The New Atlantis* (1627), and James Harrington's *Oceana* (1656). French writers on utopian themes include SAINT-SIMON, Étienne CABET, Charles FOURIER, and P. J. PROUDHON; in England Robert OWEN was typical. Famous novels on utopian theme are Edward Bellamy's *Looking Backward* (1888), Samuel Butler's *Erewhon* (1872), and William Morris's *A Dream of John Ball* (1888) and *News from Nowhere* (1891). Satiric utopias are in Aristophanes' *The Birds,* Mandeville's *The Fable of the Bees,* and parts of Swift's *Gulliver's Travels.* Legends of actual ideal states have persisted in tales of ATLANTIS, FORTUNATE ISLES, and EL DORADO.

Utraquists (ū'trŭkwĭsts), moderate HUSSITES, opposed to the radical Taborites (led by Procopius the Great). Insisted on communion in both kinds (*sub utraque specie*) but did not vary much from Roman Catholic doctrines and were reunited with the Church by signing the Compactata. Later New Utraquists joined the Lutherans. They supported George of Podebrad. Called also Calixtines.

Utrecht (ū'trĕkt, Dutch ü'trĕkht), province (502 sq. mi.; pop. 549,566), central Netherlands, bounded by the Ijsselmeer in N. Agr. lowland. It shares the history of its cap., the municipality of **Utrecht** (pop. 183,251), on a branch of the Lower Rhine. Roman Catholic archiepiscopal see. University (founded 1636). Mfg. of machinery, textiles, food. St. Willibrord was first bishop of Utrecht. Later bishops ruled Utrecht and Overijssel as princes of Holy Roman Empire until 1527, when the bishop sold his territorial rights to Emperor Charles V. Utrecht joined in the rebellion against Spain. By the Union of Utrecht (1577) the seven provinces of the N NETHERLANDS drew together for their common defense. A picturesque old city, Utrecht has retained its 14th-cent. cathedral.

Utrecht, Peace of, ending War of the SPANISH SUCCESSION, consisted of several treaties signed at Utrecht (1713) and was complemented by Franco-Austrian treaties of Rastatt and Baden (1714). Chief clauses: PHILIP V was recognized as king of Spain. Spanish Netherlands, Milan, Naples, and Sardinia were transferred to Austria; Gibraltar and Minorca, to Britain; Sicily, to Savoy. France recognized house of Hanover on English throne. Philip V renounced right of succession to French throne. England and Netherlands won advantageous commercial clauses.

Utrillo, Maurice (mōrēs′ ütrēlō′), 1883–, French painter; son of the painter Suzanne Valadon. Best known for vivid paintings of streets and suburbs of Paris.

Uttar Pradesh (ŏŏtŭr prŭdäsh′), state (112,523 sq. mi.; pop. 63,254,118), N India; cap. Allahabad. Extends S from Himalayas into plains of Ganges and Jumna rivers. Chief crops are grains and sugar cane. Has five universities and many Hindu pilgrimage centers (notably Allahabad and Benares). Dominated 13th–18th cent. by Moslems. Under the Moguls the area roughly comprised Agra prov., which was annexed by the British in late 18th cent. and joined 1877 with historic region of Oudh to form what was later called United Provinces. Enlarged 1949 by inclusion of former princely states, renamed Uttar Pradesh 1950.

Uvalde (ūväl′dē), city (pop. 8,674), SW Texas, WSW of San Antonio. Center of ranching area, it ships cattle, mohair, pecans, honey, and asphalt. Home of J. N. Garner.

Uxbridge, town (pop. 7,007), S Mass., SE of Worcester; settled 1662. Woolens and worsteds.

Uxmal (ōŏshmäl′), ruined city, Yucatan, E Mexico, center of Maya New Empire; founded 987, abandoned 1441. Finest expression of Mayan architectural renaissance.

Uzbek Soviet Socialist Republic (ōŏz′bĕk, ōŏzbĕk′) or **Uzbekistan** (ōŏz″bĕkĭstän′), constituent republic (157,-300 sq. mi.; pop. c.6,000,000) of the USSR, in central Asia; cap. Tashkent. Drained by Amu Darya and Syr Darya rivers, it consists of the Kizil Kum desert (W) and fertile irrigated lands (E), notably the FERGANA VALLEY and the oases of KHIVA, TASHKENT, SAMARKAND, and BUKHARA. Chief products: cotton, rice, silk. Uzbeks (c.75% of pop.) are a Moslem, Turkic-speaking group of Persian culture. Ancient SOGDIANA, the region fell to the Arabs (8th cent. A.D.), to KHOREZM (12th cent.), and to the Mongols (13th cent.); was the center of Tamerlane's empire (14th cent.); fell to the Uzbeks, a remnant of the Golden Horde (16th cent.); and broke up into separate principalities (Khiva, Kokand, Bukhara). Conquered by Russia 1875–76, Uzbekistan became a constituent republic 1924.

Uzhgorod (ōŏzh′gŭrŭt), Czech *Užhorod*, Hung. *Ungvár*, city (pop. 35,250), W Ukraine; former cap. of RUTHENIA. Agr. center. Founded 13th cent. Ceded by Hungary to Czechoslovakia 1920; by Czechoslovakia to USSR 1945.

Uzza or **Uzzah** (ŭ′zŭ), man who met sudden death after touching the ark. 2 Sam. 6.3–8; 1 Chron. 13.7–11.

Uzziah (ŭzī′ŭ), d. c.735 B.C., king of Judah (c.775–c.735 B.C.). He was a strong leader, but his pride made him try to usurp the duties of the high priest. For this sacrilege he was smitten with leprosy. 2 Chron. 26. Called Azariah in 2 Kings 15. Ozias: Mat. 1.8,9.

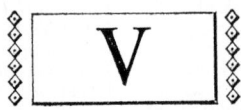

V, chemical symbol of the element VANADIUM.

Vaasa or **Vasa** (both: vä′sä), city (pop. 36,178), W Finland; a Baltic port on Gulf of Bothnia. Shipping center for timber. Mfg. of textiles, motors.

Vaca, Cabeza de: see CABEZA DE VACA, ÁLVAR NÚÑEZ.

Vaca de Castro, Cristóbal (krēstō′väl vä′kä dä kä′strō), fl. 1540–45, Spanish colonial administrator in Peru. Attempted to settle the Pizarro-Almagro feud, but was arrested by Núñez Vela and sent back to Spain, where he spent 12 years in prison before being cleared of charges.

vaccination, inoculation with vaccine to produce active IMMUNITY to disease. Introduced by Edward JENNER to immunize against smallpox. Vaccines usually are prepared from killed or weakened organisms causing specific disease or from their toxins.

vacuum, theoretically, space without matter in it. Perfect vacuum not yet obtained. Torricelli obtained nearly perfect one in mercury BAROMETER. Apparent "suction" caused by vacuum is measure of pressure of atmosphere tending to rush in and fill space; perfect vacuum exerts no pressure, for it contains no matter. There are a number of methods of producing vacuums and number of pumps for removing air from confined space; difficulty arises because matter is apparently composed of molecules in rapid motion and

for perfect vacuum all molecules must be removed. Vacuum is used in vacuum cleaner, vacuum tube, vacuum bottle, and barometer.

vacuum tube: see TUBE, VACUUM OR ELECTRON.

Vaduz (vädŏŏts′), town (pop. 2,041), cap. of principality of LIECHTENSTEIN.

Vagharshapat, Armenian SSR: see ECHMIADZIN.

Vailima (vīlē′mŭ), estate, home of R. L. Stevenson for five years, Upolu, Western Samoa. His tomb is atop near-by Mt. Vaea.

Valais (välā′), Ger. *Wallis,* canton (2,021 sq. mi.; pop. 158,227), S Switzerland, crossed by the upper Rhone valley, with the Bernese Alps to the N and the Valais Alps (part of Pennine Alps) to the S; cap. Sion. Has many peaks (e.g., Dufourspitze, Matterhorn) and famous resorts. Stock raising, agr., vineyards. Population is Catholic, French-speaking in Lower Valais (W), mostly German-speaking in Upper Valais (E). The bishop of Sion and the communes of Upper Valais, allies of the Swiss Confederation from the 15th cent., conquered Lower Valais from Savoy 1475 and ruled it as subject territory till 1797. Valais joined Helvetic Republic 1798; became independent republic 1802; was annexed to France 1810; became Swiss canton 1815.

Valcour Island (vălkŏŏr′), c.2 mi. long, NE N.Y., in L.

Champlain, near Plattsburg. On Oct. 11, 1776, American vessels under Benedict Arnold were routed by British.

Valdai Hills (vŭldī'), moraine region, NW European RSFSR. Extending in parallel ridges for c.300 mi. NE–SW, it rises to 1,053 ft. in Mt. Kámmenik.

Valdemar. For Danish rulers, see WALDEMAR.

Valdés, Armando Palacio: see PALACIO VALDÉS.

Valdés-Leal, Juan de (hwän' dä väldäs-lääl', 1622?–1690?, Spanish painter of Seville school. Excelled in painting gruesome subjects, such as *Two Cadavers in Their Worms.*

Valdez (văldēz'), town (pop. 554), S Alaska, on Prince William Sound. Ice-free harbor explored and named by Spanish, 1790. Created 1898 as debarkation point for Yukon gold fields. Center of gold-mining and fur-producing area. Seaplane base and coastal terminus of Richardson Highway to Fairbanks.

Valdivia, Pedro de (pä'dhrō dä välde'vyä), c.1500–1554, Spanish conquistador, conqueror of Chile. One of Pizarro's best officers in conquest of Peru, he was commissioned by Pizarro to subdue Chile (1540). Santiago was founded (1541) and other settlements made but colony did not prosper because of scarcity of gold and ferocity of Araucanian Indians. Made governor of Chile by viceroy of Peru (1549), Valdivia continued S, founding Concepción (1550) and Valdivia (1552). In revolt of Indians (1553), led by Lautaro, Valdivia and his men were massacred.

Valdivia, city (pop. 31,674), S central Chile, on the Pacific; founded 1552 by Valdivia, on Valdivia R. 11 mi. from its port, Corral. An active industrial city, it has tanneries, sugar refineries, shipyards, breweries, flour, lumber, and steel mills.

Val d'Or (väl dôr'), town (pop. 8,685), W Que., Canada, ESE of Rouyn. Mining center producing gold, copper, zinc, lead, and molybdenum.

Valdosta (văldŏ'stŭ), city (pop. 20,046), S Ga., near Fla. line, in lake region; founded 1860. Processes and ships cotton, pecans, vegetables, tobacco, and lumber. Has railroad shops. Seat of Valdosta State College (coed.; 1906), formerly Georgia State Womans Col.

Vale (väl), town (pop. 1,518), E Oregon, on Malheur R. near Idaho line. Has hot springs. Chief town in Vale irrigation project, estab. 1928 to supply c.32,000 acres (sugar beets, livestock, potatoes).

Valence (väläs'), city (pop. 34,249), cap of Drôme dept., SE France, on Rhone R. Silk mfg. Romanesque cathedral escaped damage in World War II.

valence (vā'lŭns), in chemistry, a number representing relative ability of one element to combine with another. Unit of comparison is ability of hydrogen to combine; i.e., number of hydrogen atoms an element combines with or displaces (in the case of those that do not combine with hydrogen) from a compound is valence of the element. Some elements have more than one valence but more have only one. Valence is explained by number and arrangement of electrons outside nucleus of atom. See *ill.,* p. 773.

Valencia, Guillermo (gēyĕr'mō välän'syä), 1873–1943, Colombian poet, author of austere, subtle lyrics, some of the best of the *modernismo* movement.

Valencia (vŭlĕn'shŭ, Sp. välän'thëä), region (8,998 sq. mi.; pop. 2,176,670), E Spain, on the Mediterranean. Its fertile, irrigated coastal plain, the "garden of Spain," produces oranges, grapes, rice, olives, and vegetables. It was an independent Moorish emirate (11th cent.); later passed to the Almoravides and Almohades; was conquered by Aragon 1238–52. Its status as one of the Spanish kingdoms was abolished in 18th cent. Its cap., **Valencia** (pop. 409,670), is a commercial and industrial center and has a busy port (Villanueva del Grao). Mfg. of silk, tobacco, colored tiles. Exports oranges, wine. University was founded c.1500. A Roman colony, it later flourished under the Moors; was ruled the CID 1094–99; rivaled Barcelona after its conquest by Aragon (1238). A picturesque city, it has a cathedral (13th–15th cent.),

a 16th-cent. citadel, Renaissance palace of justice, and Gothic silk exchange (*La Lonja*).

Valencia (välĕn'syä), city (pop. 85,243), N Venezuela; founded 1555 on L. Valencia (c.120 sq. mi., second largest lake in Venezuela). City has many industries to process products from surrounding agr. and cattle-raising region.

Valenciennes (vŭlĕn"sēĕnz', Fr. väläsyĕn'), town (pop. 37,716), Nord dept., N France, on Escaut R. Famous since 15th cent. for lace industry. Part of Hainaut, it passed to France 1678. Heavily damaged in World War II.

Valens (vā'lŭnz), c.328–78, East Roman emperor (364–78); brother of Valentinian I. Embraced Arianism; was defeated by Visigoths in great battle of Adrianople, in which he was slain. Theodosius I (the Great) succeeded him.

Valentine, Saint, d. c.270, Roman martyr priest. Possibly by association with a pagan festival, his feast, Feb. 14, is the day of lovers.

Valentinian (vā"lŭntĭ'nēŭn), West Roman emperors. **Valentinian I,** 321–75, reigned 364–75. His son **Valentinian II,** 371–92, reigned 375–92 (jointly with his brother Gratian until 383). Made THEODOSIUS I emperor of the East (378). Was expelled from Italy by MAXIMUS (387), restored by Theodosius (388). Died strangled, probably by order of ARBOGAST. **Valentinian III,** 419–55, reigned 425–55, first under the regency of his mother, Galla Placidia. His general AETIUS held the actual power from 433 to 454, when Valentinian murdered him. His reign saw the invasions of VANDALS and HUNS. He was murdered.

Valentino, Rudolph (vălŭntē'nō), 1895–1926, American film actor, whose real name was Rodolpho d'Antonguolla, b. Italy. In U.S. after 1913, he won fame in such films as *The Sheik* and *Blood and Sand.*

Valentinus, Basilius: see BASILIUS VALENTINUS.

Valera, Eamon de: see DE VALERA, EAMON.

Valerian (vŭlēr'ēŭn), d. after 260, Roman emperor (253–60). Made his son Gallienus coregent and undertook a campaign against Shapur I of Persia, who defeated and captured him (260).

Valerius Maximus (vŭlēr'ēŭs mǎk'sĭmŭs), 1st cent. B.C.–1st cent. A.D., Roman compiler of anecdotes.

Valéry, Paul (pôl' välārē'), 1871–1945, French poet, critic, and intellectual leader. His poems *La Jeune Parque* (1917) and *Le Cimetière marin* (1920; Eng. tr., *The Graveyard by the Sea,* 1932), considered his masterpiece, are as difficult as they are profound and had great influence on contemporary poetry. Valéry's keen intellect is revealed in his prose works—*An Evening with Mr. Teste* (1896; Eng. tr., 1925) and collections of essays, *Variétés* (5 vols., 1924–44; partial Eng. tr., 1927, 1928).

Valhalla or **Walhalla** (both: välhäl'ù) [Norse,= hall of the slain], in Norse mythology, Odin's home for slain heroes, brought there by Valkyries.

Valkyries (vălkēr'ēz) [Norse,= choosers of the slain], Ger. *Walküre,* in Germanic myth, Odin's daughters or attendants. They came to the battlefield, chose those who were to die, and bore them back to Valhalla. Chief among them was Brynhild.

Valla, Lorenzo (lōrän'tsō väl'lä), c.1407–1457, Italian humanist. Demonstration that the Donation of Constantine was a forgery was a pioneer work in textual criticism.

Valladolid (välyä-dhōlēdh'), city (pop. 111,253), cap. of Valladolid prov., N central Spain, in Leon. Grain market; mfg. of chemicals, textiles. Conquered from Moors in 10th cent.; replaced Toledo as chief residence of kings of Castile in 15th cent.; declined after Philip II made Madrid his cap. (1561). Landmarks include the late Renaissance cathedral, completed by Churriguera; the plateresque Colegio de San José; the 15th-cent. Colegio de San Gregorio; the homes of Cervantes and Columbus; the royal palace; and the baroque building housing the university (founded 1346).

Vallandigham, Clement Laird (vŭlăn′dĭghăm″, –găm″), 1820–71, American politician. U.S. Congressman from Ohio (1858–63). Court-martialed for speech sympathetic to South (1863). Most prominent of COPPERHEADS; commanded Sons of Liberty (see KNIGHTS OF THE GOLDEN CIRCLE).

Valle Inclán, Ramón del (väl′yä ēnklän′), 1866?–1936, Spanish novelist, author of four linked novels called "sonatas" (1902–5), in exquisite style.

Vallejo (vălā′hō), city (pop. 34,913), W Calif., port on San Pablo Bay at mouth of Napa R. Founded on property of Gen. M. G. Vallejo, it was nominal state cap. 1851–54. Flour and lumber milling, meat packing, and dairying. On Mare Isl. is U.S. navy yard, estab. 1854 by D. G. Farragut.

Valletta (vŭlĕ′tŭ), seaport (pop. 18,666), cap. of British colony of Malta. An old town with many relics of Knights Hospitalers or Knights of Malta, it has a 16th-cent. cathedral and a museum of antiquities. Severely bombed in World War II.

valley, the drainage basin of a river system or any elongated depression between elevations, usually formed by stream erosion. Shape of a river valley depends on age of stream and rate of erosion of river bed and valley sides. "Young" valleys have steep sides, and floor has narrow flood plain or no flood plain. Great river valleys have long been natural travel routes. The Tigris-Euphrates and Nile valleys were cradles of early civilization.

Valley City, city (pop. 6,851), SE N.Dak., on Sheyenne R. and W of Fargo. Processes flour, dairy products.

Valleyfield, city (pop. 22,414), Que., Canada, on L. St. Francis and SW of Montreal. Textile mills, distilling, and dairying.

Valley Forge, locality, SE Pa., on the Schuylkill NW of Philadelphia. Main camp of Continental army estab. here (Dec., 1777–June, 1778); troops suffered through severe winter. Site now state park.

Valley Junction, Iowa: see WEST DES MOINES.

Valley of Ten Thousand Smokes, area 72 sq. mi. in Katmai Natl. Monument, S Alaska. Punctured by thousands of small volcanoes created by eruption of Katmai volcano 1912.

Valley Stream, suburban village (pop. 26,854), SE N.Y., on SW Long Isl., SE of Jamaica.

Vallombrosa (väl-lōmbrō′zä), resort village, Tuscany, central Italy, SE of Florence, in Apennine forests. Has 11th-cent. Benedictine abbey.

Valmy (välmē′), village in the Argonne, NE France. On Sept. 20, 1792, the Prussians were stopped by French artillery at Valmy and, without further battle, began their retreat across the Rhine. The action gave France the initiative in the French Revolutionary Wars and thus was decisive.

Valois (välwä′), French dynasty, descended from CHARLES OF VALOIS, third son of Philip III. Succeeding the direct Capetians 1328, it ruled in direct line till 1498 (see PHILIP VI; JOHN II; CHARLES V; CHARLES VI; CHARLES VII; LOUIS XI; CHARLES VIII). Louis XII, of the collateral line of Valois-Orléans, reigned 1498–1515. He was succeeded by another collateral line—Valois-Angoulême (see FRANCIS I; HENRY II; FRANCIS II; CHARLES IX; HENRY III). The line failed 1589 and was succeeded by the BOURBON dynasty.

Valona (vŭlō′nù), Albanian *Vlonë, Vlona, Vlorë,* or *Vlora,* anc. *Aulon,* city (pop. 14,640), SW Albania; an Adriatic port on Bay of Valona. Trades in olive oil, bitumen, petroleum. Was important in Middle Ages. Albanian independence proclaimed here 1912.

Valparaiso (välpäräē′sō), city (pop. 182,689), central Chile, chief port of W South America and second largest city of Chile. Founded in 1536 by order of Almagro, it was not permanently established until 1544 by Valdivia. Today it is a flourishing industrial city and tourist resort, with near-by Viña del Mar.

Valparaiso (vălpûrā′zō), city (pop. 12,028), NW Ind., SE of Gary; settled 1834. Mfg. of metal products and paints. Seat of Valparaiso Univ.

Van. For names not listed thus, see second element; e.g., for Van Gogh, see GOGH, VINCENT VAN.

Van (vän), town (pop. 13,471), SE Turkey, near E shore of L. Van. Trade center of wheat-growing region. Was cap. of ancient Vannic kingdom of Ararat. Many of the so-called Vannic inscriptions relating to early Armenian history have been found here. **Lake Van,** area 1,453 sq. mi., is largest in Turkey. It is salty.

vanadium (vŭnā′dēùm), silver-gray, lustrous metallic element (symbol = V; see also ELEMENT, table). Its oxides are used in dyeing and ceramics, in making ink, and as catalysts; the element is used in alloys. Occurs in various minerals but not uncombined.

Vanbrugh, Sir John (văn′brù, vănbrōō′), 1664–1726, English dramatist and architect. Wrote coarse, witty comedies (e.g., *The Provoked Wife,* 1697). Designed Castle Howard (near York) and the palace at Blenheim Park.

Van Buren, Martin, 1782–1862, 8th President of the United States (1837–41). A principal figure in ALBANY REGENCY. As U.S. Secretary of State (1829–31) he was Pres. Jackson's close adviser. U.S. Vice President (1833–37); choice of Jackson as his successor. Panic of 1837 and subsequent hard times brought Van Buren much unpopularity. Wary of the existing banking system, he backed INDEPENDENT TREASURY SYSTEM. In 1840 campaign the Whigs unfairly painted Van Buren as man of great wealth who was out of sympathy with common man. FREE-SOIL PARTY presidential candidate in 1848.

Van Buren. 1 City (pop. 6,413), NW Ark., on Arkansas R. and near Fort Smith. Ships farm produce (chiefly strawberries). Mfg. of metal products. **2** Town (pop. 5,094), NE Maine, on St. John R. and N of Caribou. Trade center in lumbering and potato-growing area.

Vancouver, George (văn″kōō′vùr), 1758?–1798, English navigator and explorer. Commanded expedition (1791–94) to take over Nootka Sound territory assigned to England and to explore and survey NW coast of America.

Vancouver, city (pop. 344,833), SW B.C., Canada, on Burrard Inlet of the Strait of Georgia, opposite Vancouver Isl., just N of the Wash. line; settled before 1875. Largest city in W Canada and its chief Pacific port and major rail and air terminus, it has shipbuilding, fish canning, lumbering, and mfg. of steel products and furniture. Seat of Univ. of British Columbia (provincially supported; coed.; opened 1915). Stanley Park, one of many, has zoo and noted gardens.

Vancouver, city (pop. 41,664), SW Wash., on Columbia R. (bridged) opposite Portland, Oregon, and near Bonneville Dam. Founded 1825–26 by Hudson's Bay Co. as a fort. Oldest settlement in state; became an American possession 1846. Important port; ships grain and lumber. Mfg. of paper, textiles, aluminum products, and aircraft.

Vancouver Island, 13,049 sq. mi., SW B.C., Canada, largest island off W coast of North America. Separated from mainland by Queen Charlotte Sound and Strait of Georgia (E) and from NW Wash. by Juan de Fuca Strait (S). Heavily forested and mountainous with mining, lumbering, fishing, fruitgrowing, and canning. Largest cities are VICTORIA, NANAIMO, and PORT ALBERNI. Esquimalt is naval base. Visited by English and Spanish explorers in 16th and 17th cent. John Meares built fort on NOOTKA SOUND 1778. Circumnavigated 1792 by Capt. George Vancouver. Became crown colony 1846; united with mainland colony 1866.

Vandalia (vändā′lyù), city (pop. 5,471), S central Ill., on Kaskaskia R. and SSE of Springfield, in farm and oil area. Was second state cap 1820–39 (Lincoln and Douglas served in legislature here). Old capitol (1836) now state memorial. Was on National Road.

Vandals (văn′dùlz), anc. Germanic tribe. They invaded Gaul (406), then moved into Spain and, under GAISERIC, invaded Africa and captured (439) Carthage. They gained control over the Mediterranean but declined after Gaiseric's death (477). Carthage was captured (533) by Belisarius; Vandals soon ceased to exist as a nation. Arian Christians, they severely persecuted Orthodox Christianity. Their destructive reputation may be due to their sack of Rome (455).

Vandenberg, Arthur H(endrick), 1884–1951, U.S. Senator from Mich. (1928–51). Influential Republican leader; joined Democratic administration in bipartisan foreign policy. His nephew, **Hoyt S(anford) Vandenberg,** 1899–, is a general, chief of staff of U.S. Air Force after 1948.

Van der. For names beginning thus and not listed here, see following element; e.g., for Van der Goes, see GOES, HUGO VAN DER.

Vanderbilt, Cornelius, 1794–1877, American railroad magnate. Expanded shipping interests; known as Commodore Vanderbilt. In Civil War entered railroad field and by 1867 controlled New York Central RR. He extended railroad empire and amassed large fortune. Gave money to found Vanderbilt Univ. A son, **William Henry Vanderbilt,** 1821–85, succeeded his father as president of New York Central RR. His son, **Cornelius Vanderbilt,** 1843–99, helped found Cathedral of St. John the Divine in New York city. Another son of W. H. Vanderbilt, **George Washington Vanderbilt,** 1862–1914, donated land for Teachers Col., Columbia Univ.

Vanderbilt University, at Nashville, Tenn.; nonsectarian; coed.; chartered 1872 by Methodists, rechartered 1873, opened 1875 with grant from Cornelius Vanderbilt. Here are geology museum, social science research and training institute, and joint library with George Peabody and Scarritt colleges.

Van der Goes, Hugo: see GOES, HUGO VAN DER.

Vandergrift, borough (pop. 9,524), SW Pa., NE of Pittsburgh. Iron and steel works.

Vanderlyn, John (–lĭn), 1775?–1852, American portrait and historical painter, b. Kingston, N.Y. Studied in Paris under patronage of Aaron Burr. *Landing of Columbus* is in the Capitol, Washington, D.C.

Van der Waals, Johannes Diderik: see WAALS.

Van der Weyden, Roger: see WEYDEN.

Van de Velde or **Vandevelde** (vän″dŭvĕl′dù), Dutch family of artists. **Jan Van de Velde** (yän), 1593?–c.1641, was a wood engraver. His brother, the marine painter **Willem Van de Velde** (vĭ′lùm), c.1611–1693, was the father of **Willem Van de Velde,** 1633–1707, who is famous for his marine paintings, and **Adrian Van de Velde** (ä′drēän), 1636?–1672, the celebrated etcher and animal painter.

Van Doren, Carl (Clinton), 1885–1950, American editor and author. An editor of *The Cambridge History of American Literature* (1917–21), the *Nation* (1919–22), the *Century Magazine* (1922–25), and the *Literary Guild* (1926–34). Works include criticism (e.g., *The American Novel, 1789–1939,* 1940), history (e.g., *The Great Rehearsal,* 1948), and biography (e.g., of Swift, 1930, and of Benjamin Franklin, 1938). His brother, **Mark Van Doren,** 1894–, won a name as a poet and critic; long at Columbia. Works include critical studies (e.g., Dryden, 1920, and of Hawthorne, 1949), anthologies, novels, and several volumes of poetry (e.g., *Collected Poems, 1922–1938,* 1939).

Van Dorn, Earl, 1820–63, Confederate general. In 1862 he commanded in trans-Mississippi district; defeated at Pea Ridge, Ark. Commanded Army of the Mississippi until defeat at Corinth, Miss.; transferred to command of cavalry.

Van Dyck or **Vandyke, Sir Anthony** (both: văn dīk′), 1599–1641, Flemish portrait and religious painter, b. Antwerp. Studied under Rubens. In 1620 he was summoned to England by James I, whose portrait he painted. During his five years in Italy he studied the works of the great Venetians and painted the portraits of the Genoese nobility. Returning in 1627 to Antwerp, he soon rivaled Rubens in popularity. There he painted a series of religious pictures, including the

Crucifixion (cathedral, Mechlin). After 1632 he lived mainly in England as court painter to Charles I and painted over 350 portraits (partly executed by assistants). His masterly *Deposition* was done on a visit to Antwerp. He also produced a fine series of etched portraits called the *Iconography.*

van Dyke, Henry, 1852–1933, American clergyman, educator, and author, best known for his Christmas story *The Other Wise Man* (1896).

Vane, Sir Henry, 1589–1655, English courtier. Influential under James I and Charles I, he lost power after he had testified against Strafford. His son, **Sir Henry Vane,** 1613–62, was perhaps the ablest administrator of the Puritan Revolution. While he was governor of Massachusetts (1636), Harvard Col. was founded. Sat in Short and Long Parliaments. Negotiated Solemn League and Covenant with Scotland. Held office under Oliver Cromwell. Executed for treason by Restoration government.

Vanern, Swed. **Vänern** (vě′nŭrn), lake, area 2,141 sq. mi., SW Sweden, fed by Klar R. and drained by the Gota into the Kattegat. Largest lake in Sweden.

Van Fleet, James A(lward), 1892–, American general, commander of UN forces in Korea (1951–53). Led 8th Infantry Regt., commanded 90th Div. in World War II. Led military mission to Greece (1948–50).

Van Gogh, Vincent: see GOGH, VINCENT VAN.

vanilla, tropical American climbing orchid (genus *Vanilla*) cultivated for the fruits which yield the flavoring vanilla. The fruit is a seed pod called a "bean." Vanilla is also produced synthetically.

van Loon, Hendrik Willem (văn lōn′), 1882–1944, American author and journalist, b. Netherlands; in the U.S. after 1903. Later a newspaper correspondent in Russia and in Belgium. Popular works include histories such as *The Story of Mankind* (1921); *Van Loon's Geography* (1932); and *Simón Bolívar* (1943).

Vannes (vän), city (pop. 23,510), cap. of Morbihan dept., NW France, in Brittany. Surrounding region is rich in megalithic monuments. Inner city has 13th-cent. ramparts.

Vanport, former town, NW Oregon, just N of Portland and on Columbia R. opposite Vancouver, Wash. Built 1942–43 to house World War II shipyard workers (pop. 42,000). Low-cost housing project (pop. c.18,-500) after 1945. Destroyed May 30, 1948, by flood.

Van Rensselaer, Stephen, 1764–1839, American statesman and soldier, called the Patroon. Lieutenant governor of N.Y. (1795–1801). Led state militia in War of 1812. Founded school at Troy, N.Y., in 1824, which became Rensselaer Polytechnic Inst.

van't Hoff, Jacobus Hendricus (yäkō′bùs hĕndrē′kùs vänt hôf′), 1852–1911, Dutch physical chemist. Won 1901 Nobel Prize for work in chemical dynamics and osmotic electrical conductivity. His studies in molecular structure laid foundation of steriochemistry.

Vanua Levu: see FIJI.

Van Vechten, Carl (văn vĕk′tùn), 1880–, American critic, novelist, and photographer. His works include criticism, sophisticated novels (e.g., *Nigger Heaven,* 1926), and an autobiography (1932).

Van Wert, city (pop. 10,364), NW Ohio, NW of Lima; settled 1835. Trade and mfg. center in farm area.

Van Zeeland, Paul (pōl′ vän zä′länt), 1893–, Belgian economist and statesman; a leader of the Catholic party. As premier (1935–37) he instituted legislation similar to the American New Deal, suppressed the fascist Rexists, adopted neutrality policy. He later championed international economic cooperation; became foreign minister 1949.

vaporization, change of liquid or solid to gas or vapor. Term *gas* is commonly used to describe substance that appears in that form under standard conditions; and *vapor* for substance that is ordinarily liquid or solid. When change is from solid to vapor, it is SUBLIMATION. Vaporization is explained by kinetic molecular theory of matter; when heat is applied to substance at boiling point, molecules move faster and become farther apart until vaporization is complete. Quantity of heat needed to cause vaporization varies for each substance. Heat needed to change one gram water to steam at its boiling point, i.e., heat of vaporization, is c.540 calories. Liquids change to vapors by EVAPORATION at any temperature when surface is exposed in unconfined space.

Var (vär), department (2,325 sq. mi.; pop. 370,688), SE France, in Provence; cap. Draguignan.

Varanger Fjord (väräng'ùr fyōr"), inlet of Arctic Ocean, 60 mi. long, NE Norway, near Russian border. S shore has iron mines.

Varangians (vùràn'jēùnz), Scandinavian merchant-warriors who penetrated RUSSIA in 9th cent. Their leader Rurik, according to tradition, estab. himself at Novgorod 862, thus founding Russian state. They gradually merged with the Slavs. From Russia, they raided Volga region and Byzantine Empire. Varangians also served as mercenaries under Byzantine emperors.

Vardar (vär'där), river, c.230 mi. long, rising in S Yugoslavia and flowing W and S through Yugoslav and Greek Macedonia into Aegean Sea near Salonica.

Vardon, Harry, 1870–1939, British golfer. Won British Open (1896, 1898–99, 1903, 1911, 1914), U.S. Open (1900) championships, total of more than 60 important golf tournaments.

Varenius, Bernardus (vùrē'nēùs), or **Bernhard Varen** (vä'run), 1622–50, Dutch geographer. Attempted to define geography as a science. His *Geographia generalis* (1650) was standard for a century.

Varennes (värĕn'), village, Meuse dept., NE France. Here Louis XVI and his family were arrested on their attempted flight (1791).

Varèse, Edgar (värēs'), 1885–, French-American composer. Often uses extreme registers of orchestral instruments or new instruments of electrically produced tone to produce a harshly dissonant effect. Among his works are *Hyperprism* (1923) for wind instruments and percussion; *Ionisation* (1931), for percussion; and *Espace* (1937), a symphony with chorus.

Vargas, Getulio (Dornelles) (zhùtōō'lyō dôrnĕ'lĭsh vär'gùsh), 1883–, president of Brazil (1930–45; 1951–). Governor of his native state, Rio Grande do Sul (1928–30), he ran for president and, when defeated, led a successful revolt, becoming provisional president and later president. His social and industrial programs for improvement in Brazil were offset by his autocratic rule by decree. Several revolts (most serious that in São Paulo, 1932) were put down, but he was deposed in 1945 by Eurico Dutra and group of army officers. Re-elected to presidency 1951.

Vargas Zapata y Luján Ponce de León, Diego de (dyä'gō dä vär'gäs thäpä'tä ē lōōhän' pōn'thä dä lāōn'), c.1643–1704, Spanish governor and captain general of N.Mex. (1691–97, 1703–4). Resettled N.Mex. for Spanish after Pueblo revolt of 1680.

variable star, star that changes in brightness and often in other characteristics (e.g., color, temperature, atmosphere, apparent diameter). Classifications differ but variable stars are often grouped as temporary stars (novae and supernovae), or Cepheid, long-period, eclipsing, or irregular variables. Novae change from faintness to spectacular brightness; then fade; some recur. Usually reach absolute magnitude of −5 or −6; those reaching greater magnitudes of −14 to −15 called supernovae. Cepheid variables, believed to be pulsating stars, alternately expanding and contracting, are giant yellow stars with periods up to c.50 days. Cycles of long-period variables (red giant and supergiant stars), range from 50 days to two years. Eclipsing variables are double stars that eclipse each other as they revolve around common center. Irregular variables include other variable stars.

varicose vein, chronically enlarged vein. Congestion results from weakness of valves in veins. Commonest in legs and thighs and about rectum (see HEMORRHOIDS).

Varmland, Swed. *Värmland* (vĕrm'länt), historic province, W central Sweden, N of Vanern lake; cap. Karlstad. Agr.; iron mining and processing; wood products.

Varna, Bulgaria: see STALIN, Bulgaria.

varnish, solution of gum or resin in oil (oil varnish) or in volatile solvent (spirit varnish) which, on drying, forms hard, usually glossy, film. Shellac is solution of lac in alcohol; enamel is varnish with added pigments; lacquer is either cellulose derivative dissolved in volatile solvent or a natural varnish made in Orient from juice of trees.

Varro, Marcus Terentius, 116 B.C.–27? B.C., Roman man of letters. Most erudite man of his times, he wrote c.120 volumes in all fields of learning. Of his many works only one—*De re rustica libri III* (three books on farming)—remains intact. Six books out of 25 remain of *De lingua latina* (on the Latin language).

Varus, Publius Quintilius (vâ'rùs), d. A.D. 9, Roman general defeated by the Germans under Arminius in the Teutoburg Forest. He committed suicide. It is said that later Augustus would cry in his sleep, "Varus, Varus, bring me back my legions!"

Vasa (vä'zù), royal dynasty of Sweden (1523–1654) and of Poland (1587–1668), founded by GUSTAVUS I. Senior line turned Catholic with SIGISMUND III, who was deposed in Sweden, and continued in Poland with Ladislaus IV and JOHN II. It was chronically at war with the Protestant Swedish line (CHARLES IX; GUSTAVUS II; CHRISTINA). Swedish Vasas were succeeded by ZWEIBRÜCKEN dynasty (1654), OLDENBURG dynasty (1751), and Bernadotte dynasty (1818).

Vasa, Finland: see VAASA.

Vasari, Giorgio (jōr'jō väzä'rē), 1511–74, Italian artist. Best known for his *Lives of the Painters,* a series of entertaining if frequently inaccurate biographies of Italian artists. His most famous architectural work is the Uffizi. Also did murals in the Vatican and in Florence cathedral.

Vasco da Gama: see GAMA, VASCO DA.

Vasconcelos, José (hōsā' väskōnsä'lōs), 1882–, Mexican educator and writer. Headed National Univ. of Mexico (1920–24); minister of education (1920–25); forced into exile by his successful opponent for the presidency, Plutarco E. Calles. Worked vigorously to raise literacy rate in Mexico.

Vashti (väsh'tī), queen whom Ahasuerus deposed for disobedience. Esther 1.

Vasily III (vùsē'lyē), 1479–1533, grand duke of Moscow (1503–33). He rounded out the conquests of his father, Ivan III, annexing Pskov, Ryazan, and Smolensk. Father of Ivan the Terrible.

Vassar, Matthew (vă'sùr), 1792–1868, American philanthropist. He built his fortune with a brewery at Poughkeepsie, N.Y., and founded (1861) what is now VASSAR COLLEGE, giving it more than $800,000.

Vassar College, at Arlington, adjoining Poughkeepsie, N.Y.; nonsectarian, for women; chartered 1861 by Matthew Vassar, opened 1865 as Vassar Female Col., renamed 1867. Pioneered in music, physical education; had first department of euthenics; conducts summer institute of euthenics. Known for work in experimental drama. Its first woman president, Sarah G. Blanding, took office in 1946.

Vasteras, Swed. *Västerås* (vĕs"tùrōs'), city (pop. 59,-990), E central Sweden, on Malaren L. Electrical industry. Important diets convened here, notably the Vasteras Recess (1527), when the church was taken over by the state and Lutheranized.

Vastergotland, Swed. *Västergötland* (vĕ'stùryût"länd), historic province of S central Sweden, now divided between Skaraborg and Alvsborg counties.

Vatican (vă'tĭkùn), at Rome, residence of the pope, who is according to the LATERAN TREATY (1929) ruler of **Vatican City** (108.7 acres, pop. c.1,000). It has SAINT PETER'S CHURCH, the Vatican proper (pontifical palaces), basilicas and churches, the BELVEDERE. CASTEL GANDOLFO belongs to the Vatican. It is the heart of the Roman Catholic Church and is entirely churchly. The Papal Court (Curia Romana), administered by cardinals (see CARDINAL), has an austere splendor, defended by the SWISS GUARDS. There are museums of some importance and beautiful chapels, including the SISTINE CHAPEL. The **Vatican Library** (founded 15th cent.) is the oldest public library in the world. Has c.50,000 manuscripts and some 400,000 printed books (many very rare). See also PAPACY; ROMAN CATHOLIC CHURCH.

Vatican Council, 1869–70, 20th ecumenical council of the Roman Catholic Church. Convened when the seizure of the Papal States by Italy was imminent, it had to be prorogued by Pius IX when Italian soldiers took Rome. It was primarily important for the enunciation of the doctrine that the pope when speaking *ex cathedra* on matters of faith and morals cannot be wrong (papal infallibility).

Vatnajökull (vät′näyû′kōōl), large ice field, area 3,200 sq. mi., SE Iceland. Rises to a peak 6,952 ft. high, which is surrounded by Oraefajökull glacier.

Vattel, Emerich de (dù vätĕl′), 1714–67, Swiss philosopher and jurist. Set forth principle of a natural law superior to artificial legislation.

Vattern, Swed. *Vättern* (vĕ′tùrn), lake, area 733 sq. mi., S Sweden, draining to Baltic Sea through Motala R. Crossed by Gota Canal. Jonkoping is on its shores.

Vauban, Sébastien le Prestre, marquis de (vōbă′), 1633–1707, French military engineer, famous for fortifications of French cities and treatise on fortification; marshal of France.

Vaucluse (vōklüz′), department (1,381 sq. mi.; pop. 249,838), SE France; cap. Avignon. Includes former Comtat Venaissin and principality of Orange. Named for the village of **Vaucluse** (officially, Fontaine-de-Vaucluse), made famous by Petrarch, who lived here.

Vaucouleurs (vōkōōlûr′), town (pop. 2,452), Meuse dept., NE France, on Meuse R. Here Joan of Arc persuaded Robert de Baudricourt, governor of the town, of her mission (winter 1428–29).

Vaud (vō), Ger. *Waadt,* canton (1,239 sq. mi.; pop. 376,707), SW Switzerland, between L. of Geneva, Jura mts., and Bernese Alps; cap. Lausanne. Agr., vineyards. Many resorts. Population is largely French-speaking and Protestant. Vaud was conquered by Bern from Savoy in 1536. Its rebellion (1798) against Bernese rule led to French intervention in Switzerland and creation of Helvetic Republic. Became a canton of Swiss Confederation 1803.

vaudeville (vô′dùvĭl, vōd′vĭl), originally a light song, derived from *Vau,* or *Vaux, de Vire,* songs attributed to Olivier Basselin. American vaudeville was a stage entertainment consisting of unrelated sketches, humorous skits, songs, dances, and acrobatic and magic acts. Popular c.1880–c.1932. Attempts have been made to revive it (as in New York in the '50s), and many moving picture houses have "stage shows."

Vaudois, French name of WALDENSES.

Vaudreuil de Cavagnal, Pierre François de Rigaud, marquis de (vōdrû′yù dù kävänyäl′), 1698–1765, last French governor of Canada. After his surrender of Canada to British (1760), he was charged with maladministration, tried in France, and acquitted.

Vaugelas, Claude Favre de (klōd′ fä′vrù dù vōzhùlä′), 1585–1650, French grammarian. He set up, in *Remarques sur la langue française* (1647), usage of cultured people as standard for correct French.

Vaughan, Henry (vôn), 1621–95, British metaphysical poet, b. Wales. Poems (as in *Poems,* 1646; *Olor Iscanus,* 1651; *Silex Scintillans,* 1650; *Thalia Rediviva,* 1678) include secular as well as religious verse (e.g., "I saw Eternity the other night").

Vaughan, Herbert, 1832–1903, English Roman Catholic clergyman, an Oblate Father; archbishop of Westminster (1892–1903); made cardinal 1893.

Vaughan Williams, Ralph, 1872–, English composer, notable for use of English folk elements in music. Among his compositions are six symphonies, including the well-known *London Symphony* (1914; revised

1920), the *Fantasia on a Theme by Thomas Tallis* (1910), operas, choral music, concertos, and songs. Of his many stage works, his ballet *Job* (1930) is perhaps best known.

Vauxhall (vŏks′hôl′), district of Lambeth metropolitan borough, London, England. Named for former Vauxhall Gardens or New Spring Gardens, a fashionable pleasure resort c.1660–1859.

Vavilov, Nikolai Ivanovich (nyĭkûlī′ ēvä′nùvĭch vŭvē′-lùf), 1887–, Russian botanist. Reported to have died in a Soviet concentration camp c.1943. His wheat studies indicated Ethiopia and Afghanistan to be birthplaces of agriculture and civilization. He opposed Lysenko's theory of heredity.

Veblen, Thorstein (thôr′stīn vĕ′blùn), 1857–1929, American social scientist. In analyzing the psychological bases of social institutions, he helped found institutional economics. His analyses of the price system, the business cycle, and the role of the technician have had great influence. His works include *The Theory of the Leisure Class* (1899) and *The Theory of Business Enterprise* (1904).

Vecchietta, Il: see LORENZO DI PIETRO.

Veda (vā′dù, vē′–), scriptures of Hinduism, including the oldest, the *Rig-Veda,* containing some 1,000 hymns; the *Sama-Veda,* a rearrangement of hymns from the *Rig-Veda;* the *Yajur-Veda,* including prose formulas. The much later *Atharva-Veda* includes spells and incantations. Immediate inspiration of the Vedas may have been the Aryan conquest of India. Indra was the warlike national god of the Vedas, which are classics of Sanskrit literature. The *Brahmanas* and *Upanishads* later augmented the Vedas.

Vedanta (vĭdän′tù), certain of the UPANISHADS, written after Vedas; also group name for six related philosophic systems interpreting them. The aim of all these philosophies is the extinction of suffering through YOGA. The three stages leading to ultimate knowledge are faith, understanding, and realization. The systems, one builded upon another (from 550 B.C.), include Nyaya, Vaisesika, Samkhya, the Mimamsa, and the Vedanta. Vedanta as a system was founded by Badarayana (fl. sometime between 500 B.C. and A.D. 200) and has a pantheistic doctrine of Brahma (the all-one), known only by intuition; there are varying schools.

Vedder, Elihu (ĕ′lĭhū), 1836–1923, American painter and illustrator, perhaps best known for illustrations for *The Rubaiyat.* Murals in Library of Congress.

veery or **Wilson's thrush,** American woodland thrush. It is reddish brown above with lightly spotted buff and white under parts. Has a delicate song.

Vega, Garcilaso de la: see GARCILASO DE LA VEGA.

Vega Carpio, Lope de: see LOPE DE VEGA CARPIO.

vegetable ivory: see TAGUA.

vegetable marrow, long, slender pumpkin variety, with yellow or green skin, especially popular in Europe.

Veglia, Yugoslavia: see KRK.

Vehmgericht (fām′gùrĭkht), **Vehme** (fā′mù), or **vehmic court** (fā′mĭk), unofficial secret criminal tribunal in Middle Ages. Such courts (first estab. in Westphalia to curb lawlessness in era of weak governments), worked through secrecy and terrorism, doing much good but finally becoming menace. As central powers grew stronger in 16th cent., organizations ceased. Also Fehmgericht, Femgericht.

vein, vessel carrying blood from tissues to heart in CIRCULATION OF THE BLOOD. Most veins have valves preventing backward flow of blood. See *ill.,* p. 595.

Veit, Philipp (fē′lĭp fīt′), 1793–1877, German historical painter, one of the Nazarenes in Rome.

Velasco, José María (hōsā′ märē′ä välä′skō), 1840–1912, Mexican landscape painter; teacher of Diego Rivera. His study of anatomy, botany, and geology enabled him to paint with scientific detail.

Velasco, Luis de (lwēs′ dä välä′skō), d. 1564, Spanish administrator, second viceroy of New Spain (1550–64). An energetic, honest humanitarian, he did much to improve lot of Indians; sent out numerous exploring expeditions. Univ. of Mexico was founded (1553) during his administration. His son, **Luis de Velasco,** 1534–1617, was viceroy of New Spain (1590–95; 1607–11) and of Peru (1595–1604). Continued work of his father in Mexico by aiding Indians and extending conquests. Similar achievements marked his administration in Peru. Was later president of Council of the Indies and was granted title marqués de Salinas.

Velasco (vŭlă′skō), town (pop. 2,260), S Texas, on Brazos R. opposite Freeport. Texans defeated Mexican garrison here 1832; treaty ending Texas Revolution signed here 1836. Revived by Freeport Boom.

Velázquez, Diego de (dēā′gō dā vălăth′kăth), c.1460–1524?, Spanish conquistador, first governor of Cuba. Sailed with Christopher Columbus on second voyage to Hispaniola (1493) and was sent out by Diego Columbus to command expedition to conquer Cuba (1511). Completing conquest by 1514, he continued colonization and established himself as governor of island (he was later named *adelantado* by king of Spain). It was he who commissioned Hernán Cortés to conquer Mexico (1519). Later he sent Pánfilo de Narváez in an unsuccessful attempt to bring Cortés to obedience.

Velázquez, Diego Rodríguez de Silva y, 1599–1660, celebrated painter of the Spanish school, b. Seville; son of a lawyer of Portuguese descent. Studied with Francisco de Herrera and Francisco Pacheco. Moving to Madrid (1622) he became court painter to Philip IV, a post he held for the rest of his life. The famous *Borrachos* [the topers] (Prado) was done in his early period at court. On his first visit to Italy (1629–31) he painted the *Forge of Vulcan* and two landscapes of the Villa Medici gardens. To his second period (1631–49) belong the famous equestrian portraits of the king and the condé de Olivares, the *Surrender of Breda* (all: Prado), and the portrait of Philip IV (Frick Coll., New York). His superb portrait of Pope Innocent X was done on his second visit to Italy (1649–51). Outstanding works of his last period include the series of dwarfs and buffoons of the court, the portrait of the Infanta Margarita, and *Maids of Honor.*

veld or **veldt** (both: vĕlt) [Dutch,= field], term applied to grassy, undulating plateaus of South Africa and Southern Rhodesia. Elevation ranges from 500 to 6,000 ft. Used mainly for stockraising.

Velde, Van de: see VAN DE VELDE.

Vélez de Guevara, Luis (vā′lăth dā gāvä′rä), 1579?–1644, Spanish author of picaresque novel, *El diablo cojuelo* (1641), many plays.

Vellore (vŭlôr′), city (pop. 71,502), E central Madras, India, on Palar R. Was strategic military base during 18th-cent. struggle between French and English for dominance in India.

Velsen (vĕl′sŭn), municipality (pop. 41,329), North Holland prov., W Netherlands, near mouth of North Sea Canal. Center of steel industry.

velvetweed, tall annual plant of genus *Abutilon,* also called Indian mallow. It has velvety leaves and yellow flowers. A weed in the U.S., it is grown in its native Asia as "Chinese jute" for fiber.

Venaissin (vŭnĕsĕ′) or **Comtat Venaissin** (kōtä′), district in Vaucluse dept., SE France, in Provence, around Avignon; cap. Carpentras. Was acquired by popes 1274; annexed to France 1791.

Venantius Fortunatus, Latin poet: see FORTUNATUS.

Vendée (vädä′), department (2,709 sq. mi.; pop. 393,-787), W France, on Atlantic coast, in Poitou; cap. La Roche-sur-Yon. In 1793 the devoutly Catholic peasants of the Vendée united with the local nobility in a formidable insurrection against the French revolutionary government. Under such leaders as Cathelineau, Charrette de la Contrie, and La Rochejaquelein, the Vendeans fought ably and heroically and soon controlled most of NW France save Nantes, but they suffered severe defeats in 1794. After Robespierre's overthrow, they concluded an advantageous peace with the central government (1795), but warfare recommenced in 1796. The royalist émigrés and the English, who had instigated the new revolt, abandoned the Vendeans to their fate after Gen. Hoche's victory over an émigré landing party at Quiberon. Hoche's moderation helped to pacify the region in 1796.

Vendémiaire (vädämyĕr′), first month of French Revolutionary Calendar. On 13 Vendémiaire, Year IV (Oct. 5, 1795), Napoleon Bonaparte leaped into fame by putting down an insurrection, at Paris, against the establishment of the Directory. His use of artillery he described as a "whiff of grapeshot."

Vendôme, César, duc de (säzär′ dük′ dü vädōm′), 1594–1665, French general; natural son of Henry IV and Gabrielle d'Estrées. Was imprisoned (1626–30) for conspiring against Richelieu. Fought on government side in the Fronde, taking Bordeaux (1653) and defeating Spanish fleet at Barcelona (1655). His grandson, **Louis Joseph, duc de Vendôme** (lwē′ zhôzĕf′), 1654–1712, marshal of France, fought in War of Spanish Succession. He defeated his cousin, Eugene of Savoy, at Cassano (1705); was sent to Flanders (1706), where he was successful against Eugene and Marlborough until defeated at Oudenarde (1708); expelled allies from Spain (1710).

Vendôme (vädōm′), town (pop. 7,907), Loir-et-Cher dept., N central France. Was cap. of a county (duchy from 1515), which as part of the Bourbon lands was united with royal domain in 1589.

venereal disease (vŭnēr′ēŭl), infectious disease acquired usually through sexual relationships. Includes SYPHILIS and GONORRHEA. Creates problem of institutional care of victims and support of dependents. Publicity campaign (1937) resulted in legislation requiring syphilis test before marriage and during pregnancy and in spreading knowledge of how to obtain treatment. See also SOCIAL HYGIENE.

Venetia (vŭnē′shŭ), Ital. *Veneto,* region (7,098 sq. mi.; pop. 3,566,136), NE Italy, between the Alps (N) and the Po R. and Adriatic Sea (S); cap. VENICE. Other cities include PADUA, VERONA, Vicenza. Fertile Venetian plain and Alpine foothills produce grain, grapes, fruit. Sericulture. Named for the ancient Veneti, who came under Roman rule 2d cent. B.C., Venetia suffered heavily in the barbarian invasions. After the 10th cent. the mainland towns developed into free communes, but by the 15th cent. most of present Venetia had been absorbed by the powerful republic of Venice, whose subsequent history it shared. Venetia passed to Austria 1797; to the Napoleonic kingdom of Italy 1805; to Austria 1814 (as part of Lombardo-Venetian kingdom); to Italy 1866. After World War II, Udine prov. was detached to become part of FRIULI-VENEZIA GIULIA.

Venezia, Italy: see VENICE.

Venezia Giulia (vänä′tsyä jōō′lyä), former administrative region, NE Italy, on the Adriatic, formed after World War I from territories ceded by Austria (E FRIULI, Trieste, ISTRIA, part of CARNIOLA). FIUME was added 1921. Inland population is mostly Slovenian. After World War II most of region was ceded to Yugoslavia and the Free Territory of TRIESTE. The rest was merged with Udine prov. to form new Italian region of FRIULI-VENEZIA GIULIA.

Veneziano, Domenico: see DOMENICO VENEZIANO.

Venezia Tridentina: see TRENTINO-ALTO ADIGE.

Venezuela (vĕnŭzwä′lù), republic (352,141 sq. mi.; pop. 4,985,716, not counting some 100,000 Indians not included in the census), N South America; cap. CARACAS. Faces on the Caribbean in the N and has four geographic areas. The coastal lowlands are rich with petroleum around L. Maracaibo, and oil is the chief export of the country. Off the coast lie the islands of Trinidad (British) and Margarita (Venezuelan). The ORINOCO basin has vast plains, the *llanos,* which support the cattle industry of Venezuela. The GUIANA

EGYPTIAN CHARIOT

ASSYRIAN CHARIOT

GREEK CHARIOT

CAMBODIAN CHARIOT

NORSE SLEDGE

HORSE LITTER

CHAISE OR SHAY

SEDAN CHAIR

GEORGE WASHINGTON'S COACH

BAROUCHE

SPRING VICTORIA

BROUGHAM

SURREY

FULL-TOP CABRIOLET

LANDAU

HANSOM CAB

GIG

JINRIKISHA

HIGHLANDS are mostly unknown and unexplored. The mountains in the W (a continuation of the Andes) have most of the population. Coffee is grown on the cool slopes, cacao in the foothills. Chief cities of the country besides Caracas are MARACAIBO, Coro, Puerto Cabello, Cumaná, BARQUISIMETO, and VALENCIA. Columbus discovered the mouth of the Orinoco in 1498, and settlements were estab. on the coast in the early 16th cent., but conquest of the interior was accomplished by German adventurers (notably Nicolás Federmann). Associated with New Granada, Venezuela was much raided by buccaneers. Francisco de MIRANDA began (1810) the war for independence from Spain, which was successful only under the leadership of Bolívar, who made it part of Greater Colombia. In 1830 José Antonio Páez led a successful separatist movement, and Venezuela became a republic largely dominated since by *caudillos* (José T. Monagas, 1847–68; Antonio Guzmán Blanco, 1870–88; Cipriano Castro, 1901–8; Juan Vicente Gómez, 1908–35). The Spanish Conquest left a heritage of conflict between great landholders (often absentee) and propertyless workers which still goes on. A new constitution in 1947 provided for election of the president, but disorders continue.

Venezuela Boundary Dispute, diplomatic controversy arising over the limits of territory Venezuela inherited from Spain and Great Britain acquired in Guiana from the Dutch. Discovery of gold in the disputed region sharpened the issue. Great Britain refused to arbitrate the matter, and Venezuela in 1887 broke off diplomatic relations. The U.S., intervening under the Monroe Doctrine, was rebuffed by Britain, and Pres. Cleveland sent a message to Congress (1895), denouncing the British refusal to arbitrate. Difficulties in S Africa made the British conciliatory. An American Commission was appointed and in 1899 made an award generally favorable to Britain.

Venezuela Claims. In 1902, because of the internal chaotic conditions and longstanding public and private debts, Great Britain, Germany, and Italy sent a joint naval expedition against Venezuela to secure redress for their nationals. Theodore Roosevelt took no action, and refused to act as arbiter. The resentment of Spanish-American nations over the violation of sovereignty resulted in the DRAGO DOCTRINE. The claims were adjusted by mixed commissions in 1903.

Venice (vĕ′nĭs), Ital. *Venezia,* city (pop. 170,830; with suburbs, 264,027), cap. of Venetia, NE Italy, built on 118 islets within a lagoon in the Gulf of Venice (N end of Adriatic Sea). It is linked with the mainland by rail and highway bridges. On near-by islands are Murano (glass mfg.), the Lido (beach resort); Porto Marghera, the new port, is on the mainland. Famed for its splendid palaces and churches, its hundreds of canals and bridges, it is a major tourist resort and has a unique wealth of art treasures. Its narrow lanes and arched bridges allow only pedestrian traffic; all other traffic is by water. Settled by refugees from barbarian invaders (5th cent.), Venice became in 697 a republican city-state headed by an elected doge [duke]. Rising to a major maritime power, it conquered (10th–15th cent.) most of DALMATIA, all VENETIA, CYPRUS, CRETE, and other Greek islands and ruled the Mediterranean as "queen of the seas." Its government early passed to a patrician oligarchy; after 1310 the Council of TEN controlled the state. Decline set in in the late 15th cent. By 1715 Venice had lost most of its Greek possessions to Turkey. In 1797 the republic fell without a blow to Bonaparte, who gave it to Austria. An anti-Austrian insurrection (1848–49) was put down, but in 1866 Venice and Venetia were united with Italy. Much of Venetian architecture shows Byzantine influences; later architecture is a graceful baroque (e.g., churches of San Giorgio Maggiore and Santa Maria della Salute). At the city's center are St. Mark's Square and the Piazzetta, with SAINT MARK'S CHURCH (see of the patriarch of

Venice) and the Gothic doges' palace, joined by the BRIDGE OF SIGHS to the former prisons. The Grand Canal, chief traffic artery, is spanned by the RIALTO bridge. The churches and palaces of Venice contain treasures of Venetian painting, which reached its zenith with TITIAN, TINTORETTO, and Paolo VERONESE.

Venice (vĕ′nĭs), city (pop. 6,226), SW Ill., on the Mississippi opposite St. Louis. Steel mills.

Venizelos, Eleutherios (ĕlĕfthâ′rēôs vĕnēzĕ′lôs), 1864–1936, Greek statesman, b. Crete, leader of republican liberals. Six times premier (1910–15, 1915, 1917–20, 1924, 1928–32, 1933), he secured union of Crete with Greece (1913); led Greece victoriously through Balkan Wars (1912–13); set up a provisional pro-Allied government at Salonica (1915); led Greece into World War I after King Constantine's abdication (1917); secured establishment of Greek republic (1924); organized armed uprisings in Crete and elsewhere in unsuccessful attempt to prevent restoration of monarchy (1935). Died in exile.

Venlo (vĕn′lō), municipality (pop. 26,822), Limburg prov., SE Netherlands, on Maas (Meuse) R. and near German border. Industrial center (lumber, chemicals, electric bulbs, optical instruments).

ventilation, process of supplying fresh air to an enclosed space and removing undesirable odors, gases, and smoke. Proper ventilation requires circulation of air within the space, and maintenance of temperature and humidity that allows adequate evaporation of perspiration from skin. Injurious effects in badly ventilated room are largely the result of interference with heat-regulating mechanism of body; formerly it was thought that ill effects were caused solely by increase in carbon dioxide and decrease in oxygen. Creation of currents depends upon fact that warm air, being lighter than cold air, tends to rise, thus creating an area of low pressure into which cooler air flows. When heating systems are in use care must be taken to avoid overheating and extreme lowering of humidity. If a fuel-burning device is used in an enclosed space a supply of fresh air must be provided since the burning fuel exhausts the oxygen and forms poisonous carbon monoxide. Mechanical devices are used where simple ventilating methods are inadequate. Air conditioning systems are independent of outdoor atmospheric conditions and can therefore maintain indoor air at most healthful temperature and humidity.

Ventnor (vĕnt′nŭr) health resort, on Isle of Wight, England. Has tuberculosis sanatoriums.

Ventnor or **Ventnor City,** resort city (pop. 8,158), SE N.J., on Absecon Beach SW of Atlantic City.

Ventspils (vĕnts′pēls), Ger. *Windau,* city (pop. 15,671), NW Latvia; an icefree port on Baltic Sea. City grew around 13th-cent. castle of Livonian Knights.

Ventura (vĕntōō′rû), city (pop. 16,534), S Calif., on Pacific coast and NW of Los Angeles, in farm and oil area. Here is restored mission of San Buenaventura (city's official name) founded 1782.

Venus, in Roman religion, goddess of vegetation, later identified with Greek APHRODITE. In imperial times she was worshiped as Venus Genetrix, mother of Aeneas; Venus Felix, bringer of good fortune; Venus Victrix, bringer of victory; and Venus Verticordia, protector of feminine chastity. Famous statues of her are *Venus of Milo* or *Melos* (Louvre) and *Venus of Medici* or *Medicean Aphrodite* (Uffizi).

Venus, in astronomy, PLANET second in distance from sun. Revolves about sun at mean distance of 67,200,-000 mi. in c.225 days. Diameter c.7,575 mi. Rotation period not known because planet is masked by layers of clouds or vapor. Appears as brilliant star in evening or morning sky. Displays phases similar to moon's. Transits across sun's disk occur in June or December. Has no known satellite. See *ill.,* p. 927.

Venus's-flytrap, insectivorous perennial plant (*Dionaea muscipula*), native to moist, acid places in the Carolinas. Its leaves, hinged at the midrib, close when touched. Insects trapped between the halves of the leaves are digested.

Veracruz (vārākrōōs'), state (27,759 sq. mi.; pop. 2,057,-175), E Mexico; cap. JALAPA. Stretching c.430 mi. along Gulf of Mexico, it rises from tropical coastal plain to temperate valleys and highlands of Sierra Madre Oriental. From tropical forests come dyewoods and hardwoods, chicle, rubber; from semitropical and temperate zones, cattle, sugar cane, cacao, coffee, vanilla, tobacco, cotton, fruits. Minerals are largely unexploited. Coast discovered by Grijalva (1518); became state 1824. Important cities are VERACRUZ, ORIZABA, CÓRDOBA.

Veracruz, city (pop. 71,720), Veracruz, E Mexico, on Gulf of Mexico E of Mexico city, rivaling Tampico as republic's chief port. Cortés landed 1519 near site later chosen for present city (1599). Has played an important part throughout Mexico's history and is today center of important oil region. Was last stronghold of Spanish in the revolution; was attacked by French in 1838, and Santa Anna won reputation for defense; taken by Winfield Scott in 1847, by Spanish, French, and British in 1861. Landing of U.S. forces in 1914 caused an international incident.

verbena, tender perennial, often shrubby, plant of genus *Verbena,* chiefly native to America. The variously colored showy flowers in broad clusters are grown as annuals in northern gardens. Verbenas are often called vervain. The fragrant lemon verbena (*Lippia citriodora*) is unrelated.

Verboeckhoven, Eugène Joseph (vùrbōōk-hō'vùn), 1798–1881, Belgian animal painter.

Vercingetorix (vûr″sĭnjĕ'tûrĭks), d. 46 B.C., leader of the Gauls in a revolt against Rome put down by Julius Caesar, who besieged and took the fort of Alesia (52 B.C.). After gracing Caesar's triumph, Vercingetorix was put to death.

Verde (vĕr'dē), river, central Ariz., rising N of Prescott, flowing c.190 mi. S to Salt R. above Phoenix. Contains Bartlett Dam (see SALT RIVER VALLEY).

Verde, Cape (vûrd), westernmost extremity of Africa, on coast of Senegal.

Verdi, Giuseppe (jōōzĕp'pē vār'dē), 1813–1901, Italian composer. A master of dramatic composition, he is known for his operas, including *Rigoletto* (1851), *Il Trovatore* and *La Traviata* (both 1853), *Un ballo in maschera* (1859); *La forza del destino* (1862), and *Aïda* (1871). Three of his operas are based on plays of Shakspere—*Macbeth* (1847), and the two masterpieces of his old age, *Otello* (1887) and *Falstaff* (1893). His *Requiem* and *Stabat Mater* are also well known. Verdi is the outstanding figure of 19th-cent. Italian opera.

verdict, official decision of a JURY on questions of fact laid before it by a judge. A general verdict is one of "guilty" or "not guilty." A special verdict answers specific question or questions and leaves decision to judge. The judge in no criminal case may modify the verdict of "not guilty."

verdigris (vûr'dùgrēs), greenish basic acetate of copper or mixture of copper acetates, formed on surface of copper plates which have been treated with acid. Poisonous; sometimes used as green pigment, mordant in dyeing, in medicine.

Verdun, city (pop. 77,391), S Que., Canada, on S shore of Montreal Isl., S suburb of Montreal.

Verdun (vĕrdŭn', Fr. vĕrdü'), town (pop. 12,948), Meuse dept., NE France, on the Meuse. Annexed to France 1552, it became after 1871 a key fortress and was in 1916 the scene of the longest and bloodiest battle of World War I. Of 2,000,000 men engaged, 1,000,000 were killed. Douaumont and Vaux, two outer fortresses, were taken by the Germans, but Verdun itself, under Marshal Pétain and Gen. Nivelle, repulsed all assaults. "They shall not pass" was the rallying phrase of the French. The city and battlefields, with huge military cemeteries, are a national sanctuary.

Verdun, Treaty of, 843, partition of Frankish empire among three sons of Emperor Louis I. Louis the German received E portion (Germany); Charles II, the W (France); Emperor Lothair I, the center (LOTHARINGIA, Burgundy, Provence, Italy).

Vereeniging (vùrā'nĭging), city (pop. 40,490), S Transvaal, South Africa, on Vaal R. Treaty ending South African War was signed here (1902). Steel center in largest coal-mining region of South Africa.

Vérendrye, Pierre Gaultier de Varennes, sieur de la (pyĕr' gōtyā' dù värĕn' syûr dù lä vārädrē'), 1685–1749, explorer in N Great Plains of W Canada and U.S. Estab. fur-trading posts.

Verendrye National Monument: see NATIONAL PARKS AND MONUMENTS (table).

Verga, Giovanni (jōvän'nē vĕr'gä), 1840–1922, Italian realistic novelist, b. Sicily. Outstanding works include *Cavalleria rusticana* (1880), *The House by the Medlar Tree* (1881), *Mastro-don Gesualdo* (1889).

Vergennes, Charles Gravier, comte de (shärl' grävyä' kōt' dù vĕrzhĕn'), 1717–87, French foreign minister under Louis XVI. Supported American Revolution—secretly at first, officially after signing alliance of 1778 with Benjamin Franklin.

Vergennes (vùrjĕnz'), city (pop. 1,736), W Vt., S of Burlington, near L. Champlain. Trade center of dairy region. Macdonough's fleet built here in War of 1812.

Vergil or **Virgil** (Publius Vergilius Maro) (both: vûr'jĭl), 70 B.C.–19 B.C., Roman poet, b. near Mantua. The son of a farmer, he received a good education and finally went (after 41 B.C.) to Rome and joined the circle patronized by Maecenas and Augustus. His *Eclogues,* or *Bucolics* (37 B.C.), after the Greek Theocritus, idealize rural life, while his *Georgics* (30 B.C.), also in praise of rural life, were more didactic and realistic. He devoted his remaining years to the AENEID, a national epic and a literary masterpiece, which owes much to Homer. Illness prevented its revision, and he would have burned the manuscript but for Augustus. Vergil is the dominant figure in Latin literature.

Verhaeren, Émile (āmĕl' vārärĕn', vùrhä'rùn), 1855–1916, Belgian poet. His feverishly imaginative style has affinities with symbolism. His themes are primarily social and humanitarian, as in *Les Villes tentaculaires* [grasping cities] (1895) and his great war poems, *Les Ailes rouges de la guerre* [red wings of war] (1917).

Veria, Macedonia, Greece: see VEROIA.

Verkhoyansk (vyĕrkhŭyänsk'), town (pop. over 500), N Yakut ASSR, RSFSR, in N Siberia. Fur-trading post. Lies in coldest part of the earth (lowest temperature recorded, −92°F.). The **Verkhoyansk Range,** a mountain chain between the Lena and Aldan rivers, rises to 8,000 ft. It has coal, silver, lead, and zinc deposits.

Verlaine, Paul (pôl' vĕrlĕn'), 1844–96, French poet, first of the SYMBOLISTS. His attempt at killing his friend RIMBAUD earned him two years' imprisonment. Though this sobering experience led Verlaine back to the Catholic faith and good resolutions (evidenced in *Sagesse,* 1881), his later years were spent in abject drunkenness. Aside from *Sagesse* his best-known collections of verse include *Romances sans paroles* (1874), *Jadis et Naguère* (1884), and *Parallèlement* (1889). At its best, his musical verse is extremely evocative and moving.

Vermeer, Jan or **Johannes** (vùrmēr', Du. yän' vùr-mār', yōhä'nùs), 1632–75, one of the great Dutch painters, b. Delft. Also known as Vermeer of Delft and as Jan or Johannes van der Meer. Excelled in painting subtle gradations of light. His intimate interiors, often with the solitary figure of a woman, are painted with almost mirror-like naturalism. A slow worker, he produced less than 40 paintings. Among most famous works is *Young Woman with a Water Jug* (Metropolitan Mus.).

Vermigli, Pietro Martire (pyä'trō märtē'rä vĕrmē'lyē), 1500–1562, Italian Protestant reformer, known as Peter Martyr. An honored Augustinian scholar and

preacher, he became a Protestant and fled from persecution to Switzerland and, at the invitation of Archbishop Cranmer, to England, where he taught at Oxford (1547–53), later at Strasbourg and Zurich.

Vermilion, iron range in Minnesota: see MESABI.

vermilion, vivid red pigment, lasting and durable. It is
red sulphide of mercury. Used in paints to protect iron
and steel. Imitation vermilion is prepared from red
lead or basic red chromate.

Vermillion, city (pop. 5,337), extreme SE S.Dak., E of
Yankton and on Vermillion R. Farm trade center.
Seat of Univ. of South Dakota (state supported; coed;
chartered 1862, opened 1882).

Vermont, state (9,609 sq. mi.; pop. 377,747), NE U.S.;
admitted 1791 as 14th state (free); cap. MONTPELIER.
Other cities are BURLINGTON, RUTLAND, BARRE, BRAT-
TLEBORO. Bordered E by Connecticut R., partly W by
L. Champlain. Mountain ranges run N–S, most prominent being GREEN MOUNTAINS (center of state), TA-
CONIC MOUNTAINS (SW). Dairy farming is chief occupation; corn, oats, potatoes, apples, maple syrup
other agr. products. Mining (granite, lime, talc, slate,
asbestos). Mfg. of machinery, cut stone, wood products, paper, textiles. A summer and winter resort area.
Champlain was first white man to enter area (1609).
Region was object of conflicting N.H. and N.Y. claims
after 1740. GREEN MOUNTAIN BOYS, under Ethan AL-
LEN, resisted N.Y. authority. Vt. declared its independence 1777. Settlement was rapid. SAINT ALBANS
was scene of Confederate raid in Civil War (1864).
State has been dominated by Republican party since
party's rise in 19th cent.

**Vermont, University of, and State Agricultural Col-
lege:** see BURLINGTON.

vermouth (vŭrmŏŏth'), blended, fortified white wine,
flavored with aromatic substances. It is used as an
appetizer and in cocktails. Italian vermouth is sweeter
and darker than French.

Vernadsky, Vladimir Ivanovich (vlŭdyē'mĭr ēvä'nŭvĭch
vĕrnät'skē), 1863–1945, Russian scientist. He introduced method of determining age of rocks and minerals based on measurable rate of radioactivity. Contributed to knowledge of mineralogy, geochemistry,
and isomorphism of chemical elements.

Vernal (vûr'nŭl), city (pop. 2,845), NE Utah, near
Dinosaur Natl. Monument.

Verne, Jules (vûrn; zhül' vĕrn'), 1828–1905, French
novelist, father of modern science fiction. Author of
From the Earth to the Moon (1865), *Twenty Thousand Leagues under the Sea* (1870), and *The Tour of
the World in Eighty Days* (1873).

Vernet (vĕrnā'), French family of artists. **Claude Joseph
Vernet,** 1714–89, marine painter, studied with his fa-
ther, Antoine Vernet, a decorative artist. His son
Antoine Charles Horace Vernet, 1758–1835, called
Carle Vernet, was a popular lithographer and painter
of hunt scenes. Antoine's son **Émile Jean Horace
Vernet,** 1789–1863, was one of most popular military
painters of 19th cent.

Vernon, city (pop. 7,822), S B.C., Canada, SE of
Kamloops. Fruitgrowing center with processing plants,
woodworking, and mfg. of cement.

Vernon. 1 See ROCKVILLE, Conn. **2** City (pop. 12,651),
N Texas, near Pease R. and NW of Wichita Falls;
founded 1880 on Dodge City cattle trail. Highway
and processing center for agr. and oil area, it has meat
packing and cotton and cottonseed processing.

Vero Beach (vē'rō), resort city (pop. 4,746), E Fla., on
Indian R. and NE of L. Okeechobee. McKee Jungle
Gardens (opened 1931) are near.

Veroia or **Veria** (both: vĕ'rēä), town, Macedonia,
Greece, W of Salonica. Anciently called Berea or
Beroea. Paul preached here. Acts 17.10.

Verona (vŭrō'nŭ, Ital. vārō'nä), city (pop. 84,862), Venetia, N Italy, on Adige R. and Brenner road. A commercial and strategic center since Roman times, it
became a free commune in the 11th cent. Verona led
a league of towns which merged with the LOMBARD

LEAGUE in its struggle against the Hohenstaufen emperors, but in 1226 the Ghibelline EZZELINO DA RO-
MANO took control, and the Ghibelline Della Scala
family became lords of Verona in 1277. The story
of Romeo and Juliet recalls the Guelph-Ghibelline
strife of the time. Verona reached its greatest power
under Can Francesco della SCALA, but it fell to Milan 1387 and to Venice 1405. Under Austrian rule
(1797–1805, 1814–66) Verona was the chief fortress
of N Italy. At the end of World War II the Germans
blew up Verona's early Roman stone bridge and the
famous pinnacled Ponte Scaligero (built 1354). The
Romanesque cathedral suffered bomb damage, but
many other monuments survive—the huge Roman
amphitheater, the 12th-cent. city hall; the Gothic
Scaligeri tombs, the 14th-cent. castle; and the Renaissance Loggia del Consiglio. Birthplace of Paolo
Veronese. The **Congress of Verona,** 1822, last meeting held under the provisions of the QUADRUPLE AL-
LIANCE of 1814, gave France a mandate for suppressing the revolution against Ferdinand VII of
Spain. England protested the decision.

Verona, borough (pop. 10,921), NE N.J., near Montclair. Metal products.

Veronese, Paolo (pä'ōlō vārōnā'zä), 1528–88, celebrated Italian painter of the Venetian school, b. Verona. Real name was Paolo Caliari. In Venice after
1553, he executed many important works for the
ducal palace and the Church of San Sebastiano. His
decorative genius is revealed in all his works, including the many religious feast scenes (e.g., *Supper at
Emmaus,* Louvre). The well-known *Rape of Europa*
is now in the ducal palace. His use of cool, clear
color harmonies anticipated the 18th-cent. style (esp.
of Tiepolo).

veronica, plant: see SPEEDWELL.

Verrazano, Giovanni da (vĕr"rätsä'nō), c.1480–1527?,
Italian navigator and explorer, in service of France.
Explored North American coast (1524).

Verrocchio, Andrea del (ändrā'ä dĕl vĕr-rôk'kyō),
1435–88, Florentine sculptor and painter of the early
Renaissance. Studied under Donatello and later taught
Leonardo da Vinci. Did the famous equestrian statue
of Bartolomeo Colleoni in Venice.

Versailles (vûrsālz', vûrsī', Fr. vĕrsī'), city (pop. 63,-
114), cap. of Seine-et-Oise dept., N France, SW of
Paris. It grew around the palace built for Louis XIV
by Louis Le Vau and J. H. Mansart. Charles Le Brun
was the chief decorator; Lenôtre laid out the park
and gardens, with their magnificent fountains, reservoirs, and sculptures. Construction began 1661; Louis
XIV moved his court to Versailles 1682, but many
later additions were made, notably the Grand and
Petit TRIANON palaces. The cost and labor involved
were staggering, but Versailles became the world's
most famous palace and remains the crowning glory
of the classic age of France. The French Revolution forced Louis XVI to move to the Tuileries in
Paris (1790). Louis Philippe made Versailles a national monument and museum.

Versailles, Treaty of, name of several treaties signed
at palace of Versailles. For treaty of **1783,** see PARIS,
TREATY OF, 1783. In preliminary treaty of **1871,** end-
ing FRANCO-PRUSSIAN WAR and ratified by Treaty of
Frankfort, France ceded most of Alsace and part of
Lorraine to Germany and agreed to pay $1,000,000,-
000 as indemnity. Treaty of **1919,** between Allies of
World War I (except Russia) and Germany, embodied
the result of the Paris Peace Conference of 1918–19.
The "Big Four" in the negotiations were Pres. Wilson
(U.S.), Clemenceau (France), Lloyd George (Britain),
and Orlando (Italy). Wilson had to sacrifice his
FOURTEEN POINTS but obtained inclusion of covenant
of LEAGUE OF NATIONS in treaty. Germany, not represented in negotiations, accepted treaty after futile
protests. It accepted burden of REPARATIONS payments; restored Alsace and Lorraine to France; ceded
Prussian Poland and most of West Prussia to Poland.

Treaty provided for plebiscites in Upper SILESIA, N SCHLESWIG, EUPEN, and Malmédy; placed SAAR TERRITORY under French administration; placed German colonies under League of Nations MANDATES; made Danzig a free city; limited German army and armaments; provided for Allied occupation and subsequent demilitarization of RHINELAND. The U.S. Senate refused to ratify the treaty. Hitler unilaterally abrogated most of its terms after 1935.

vers libre: see FREE VERSE.

vertebral column: see SPINAL COLUMN.

vertebrate (vûr′tŭbrāt″), any animal having a spinal column. Subphylum Vertebrata (Craniata) is divided into classes including fish, amphibians, reptiles, birds, mammals. Vertebrates have internal skeleton of bone and cartilage or cartilage alone, spinal cord, brain enclosed in cranium, heart with two, three, or four chambers, and a maximum of four limbs (variously modified). Phylum Chordata comprises Vertebrata and three subphyla of primitive marine forms having gelatinous rod or notochord but no true spinal column.

vervain: see VERBENA.

Verviers (vĕrvyä′), town (pop. 40,422), Liége prov., E Belgium. Metal goods, textiles.

Vervins, Treaty of (vĕrvĕ′), 1598, between France and Spain; signed at Vervins, Aisne dept., N France. Spain withdrew support from Catholic League; Wars of Religion thus ended with victory of Henry IV.

Very, Jones, 1813–80, American poet; friend of Thoreau and of Emerson, who helped him edit his mystical *Essays and Poems* (1839).

Vesalius, Andreas (vĭsā′lēŭs), 1514–64, Flemish anatomist whose discoveries overthrew many doctrines of Galen. While professor at Univ. of Padua he produced *De humani corporis fabrica* (1543), illustrated work on human anatomy based on dissections.

Vespasian (vĕspā′zhŭn), A.D. 9–A.D. 79, Roman emperor (A.D. 69–A.D. 79), founder of the Flavian dynasty; proclaimed emperor by the soldiers. The warfare he waged against Jewish rebels was completed by his son TITUS. Vespasian built the Colosseum.

Vespucci, Amerigo (ämārĕ′gō väspoōt′chē), 1454–1512, Italian navigator. Discovered and explored mouths of the Amazon (1499), sailed along N shore of South America. Evolved system for computing nearly exact longitude. His acceptance of South America as a new continent greatly altered cosmography. Name America was used to honor him.

Vesta, in Roman religion, goddess of hearth and home, identified with Greek HESTIA. Her temple in Rome had undying fire tended by VESTAL virgins.

vestal, in Roman religion, priestess of Vesta. The six vestals in temple at Rome were daughters of best families, dedicated to Vesta in childhood and trained in obedience and chastity, though they could marry after 30 years. Their duties included preparation of sacrifices and tending of sacred fire. Their influence was great. Penalty for breaking of vows was burial alive after public funeral.

Vesteralen Islands, Norway: see LOFOTEN.

Vestmannaeyjar, Iceland: see WESTMAN ISLANDS.

Vestris, Lucia Elizabeth (Bartolozzi) (vĕ′strĭs), 1797–1856, English actress and manager; first woman lessee of a theater. Produced (after 1831) extravaganzas and Shaksperian comedies.

Vesuvius (vŭsoō′vēŭs), Ital. *Vesuvio,* only active volcano on European mainland, S Italy, near E shore of Bay of Naples. Height of main cone varies (now 3,891 ft.). Fertile lower slopes have famous Lachryma Christi vineyards. Funicular railway reaches almost to crater rim. Seismological observatory at 1,995 ft. Most famous eruption was that of A.D. 79, which destroyed Pompeii and Herculaneum.

vetch, weak-stemmed leguminous plant of genus *Vicia,* chiefly annual. Common or spring vetch or tare (*Vicia sativa*) is a purple-flowered climber grown in Europe and U.S. for fodder and green manure. Blue-flowered hairy or winter vetch (*V. villosa*) is also widely grown.

Certain vetches sometimes become pests in grainfields.

Veterans of Foreign Wars, organization created in 1899 at Columbus, Ohio, by veterans of Spanish-American War. Later admitted veterans who saw action in subsequent wars and U.S. military expeditions. Organization has large membership; takes firm stand on various political issues.

veterinary medicine, diagnosis and treatment of diseases and injuries of animals. The importance of the horse early led to special care; horseshoers (farriers) were sought when medical care was needed. A pioneer school of veterinary medicine was established in Lyon, France, in 1761; in the U.S. the first schools opened about the time of the Civil War. Veterinary experiments with animals, e.g., with vaccination, have contributed to medical science.

veto (Latin,= I forbid), action of a chief executive in some governments in withholding approval of laws passed by the legislature. In the U.S., the President's veto power is given in Article 1, Section 7, of the Constitution; it can be overridden by a two-thirds vote of Congress. Also, the casting of a negative vote by one of the five permanent members of the Security Council of the UN is called, unofficially, veto.

Vevey (vŭvā′), resort (pop. 14,182), Vaud canton, Switzerland, on L. of Geneva.

viaduct, series of bridges or arches over a valley or low ground to carry a highway or railroad. Constructed of wood, iron, steel, stone, or concrete (usually reinforced with steel bars). A concrete and steel elevated viaduct is the Pulaski Skyway, 3 mi. long, between Jersey City and Newark, N.J.

Viardot-Garcia, Pauline (vyärdō′-gärsēä′), 1821–1910, mezzo-soprano, b. Paris; pupil of her father, Manuel GARCÍA. Her range was three and one-half octaves.

Viareggio (vēärĕd′jō), city (pop. 30,384), Tuscany, central Italy; a bathing resort and fishing port on Tyrrhenian Sea.

Viborg (vē′bôr), city (pop. 21,522), N central Jutland, Denmark. Mfg. of tobacco, beer, textiles, machinery. Religious center in pagan times. Restored cathedral was founded 1130.

Viborg, RSFSR: see VYBORG.

vibration, in physics, oscillatory motion, e.g., motion of swinging pendulum or of prongs of a struck tuning fork. SOUND is transmitted in waves and vibration is longitudinal. Light waves have transverse vibration. Heat may be defined as energy of continuous vibratory movement of molecules. See also BROWNIAN MOVEMENT.

viburnum, ornamental shrub or small tree of genus *Viburnum* of wide distribution. Viburnums have showy flat-topped clusters of white flowers (the snowballs have sterile flowers in rounded clusters) in spring followed by berrylike fruits, often edible. Well known species are the HOBBLEBUSH, HIGH-BUSH CRANBERRY.

Vicente, Gil (Port. zhēl′ vēsĕnt′; Span. hēl′ vēcĕn′tä), 1470?–1536?, Portuguese dramatist, who wrote both in Spanish and Portuguese, one of the chief figures of the Renaissance and shaper of the drama in both countries.

Vicenza (vēchĕn′tsä), city (pop. 48,279), Venetia, NE Italy. Birthplace of Andrea PALLADIO. Basilica, Loggia del Capitano, Teatro Olimpico, Rotonda, and Chiericati Palace, all built by Palladio, inspired Georgian style in England and Colonial style in U.S.

Vichy (vĭ′shē, Fr. vēshē′), town (pop. 29,128), Allier dept., central France, on Allier R. Its hot mineral springs make it world's best-known spa for liver and stomach disorders. Bottled Vichy water is exported. Vichy was the seat (1940–44) of the **Vichy government** of France during World War II. Estab. by Marshal PÉTAIN, it effectively controlled only the part of France not occupied by the Germans and the parts of the French overseas empire not held by the "Free French" forces of Gen. de GAULLE. Operating as a CORPORATIVE STATE under its constitution of 1940, the Vichy government became a German tool

Vicksburg in the hands of Pierre LAVAL and Jean François DARLAN. After the Allied invasion of N Africa (Nov., 1942), Hitler occupied all France. The Vichy government continued a shadow existence, fled to Germany in 1944, and broke up in 1945.

Vicksburg, city (pop. 27,948), W Miss., on Mississippi R. at mouth of Yazoo R. and W of Jackson. Important river port; commercial, processing, and shipping center for cotton, timber, and livestock area. Laid out 1819 on site of early 18th cent. French fort and Spanish Fort Nogales (1791). U.S. took possession 1798. In Civil War it was objective of Grant's VICKSBURG CAMPAIGN. River traffic aided by U.S. Mississippi River Commission (hq. here). Has U.S. Waterways Experiment Station, Vicksburg Natl. Military Park, and national cemetery.

Vicksburg campaign, Nov., 1862–July, 1863, of Civil War. Undertaken by U. S. Grant to control all of Mississippi R. and so split Confederacy. South still held Vicksburg and 200 mi. of river. In late 1862 Grant and W. T. Sherman converged on city from N and E, but were repulsed. After several attempts from N, Grant reached city from S in May, 1863; failing to storm it, he laid siege. After six weeks of resistance Vicksburg fell on July 4. Consequent fall of Port Hudson put entire river in Union hands.

Vico, Giovanni Battista (vē′kō), 1668–1744, Italian philosopher and jurist. Attempted to apply scientific method to study of history. Developed cyclical theory of civilization—three periods of society (theocracy, aristocracy, democracy), each containing seeds of its own dissolution. Long unappreciated, Vico has had great influence on such historians as Michelet, such writers as James Joyce.

Vicq-d'Azyr, Félix (fālēks′ vēk″-däzēr′), 1748–94, French comparative anatomist and physician. Noted for research on nervous system and muscles.

Victor Emmanuel, Italian kings. **Victor Emmanuel I,** 1759–1824, king of Sardinia (1802–21), was forced to abdicate by uprising against his reactionary rule. **Victor Emmanuel II,** 1820–78, succeeded his father Charles Albert as king of Sardinia 1849; led in wars of RISORGIMENTO, aided by CAVOUR; became king of united Italy 1861; ruled as a liberal constitutional monarch. **Victor Emmanuel III,** 1869–1947, son of Humbert I, succeeded as king of Italy 1900; appointed MUSSOLINI 1922; assumed titles emperor of Ethiopia 1936 and king of Albania 1939 (both titles renounced 1943); dismissed Mussolini and made armistice with Allies of World War II (1943); abdicated 1946.

Victoria, 1819–1901, queen of England (1837–1901) and empress of India (1876–1901). Her accession ended connection between English and Hanoverian thrones. Lord Melbourne, her first prime minister, became her friend and adviser. She was married to her cousin, Prince ALBERT of Saxe-Coburg, whom she loved very deeply. Marriages of their nine children led to alliances of English royal house with Russia, Germany, Greece, Denmark, and Rumania. Their interests in foreign affairs led to friction with Lord Palmerston. Supported Crimean War. Her emergence from seclusion after three years of grief for Albert's death was due to Benjamin DISRAELI, who, with William GLADSTONE, dominated latter part of her reign. Disraeli secured title of empress of India for her 1876. Diamond jubilee (1897) proved her great popularity. Her last years saw the South African War 1899–1902. Her reign, the longest in English history, saw rise of industrial civilization, accompanied by humanitarianism at home and aggressive imperialism abroad. The term "Victorian era" attests the queen's personification of her times.

Victoria, Guadalupe: see GUADALUPE VICTORIA.

Victoria, Tomás Luis de (tōmäs′ lwēs′ dā vēktō′ryä), c.1540–1611, Spanish composer of sacred music. He wrote motets (e.g., *O quam gloriosum* and *O vos omnes*), Masses, settings of hymns, and Passion music. His greatest work was the *Officium defunctorum.*

Victoria, state (87,884 sq. mi.; pop. 2,055,252), SE Australia; cap. Melbourne. Most densely populated and smallest state (except Tasmania) of Australia. Climate is temperate; Australian Alps are snow-covered, May–Nov. Produces wool, wheat, and dairy products. Settlements were estab. at Portland Bay in 1834 and on site of Melbourne in 1835. Originally a part of the colony of New South Wales, it became a separate colony in 1851. Joined the commonwealth as a state in 1901.

Victoria, Brazil: see VITÓRIA.

Victoria, city (pop. 51,331), provincial cap., SW B.C., Canada, on SE tip of Vancouver Isl. Largest city, major port, and commercial center of island. Industries include fish canning, lumbering, and paper milling. Deep-sea fishing fleet. Residential and tourist city with fine scenery, mild climate, and beautiful parks. Founded 1843 as Fort Camosun (later Fort Victoria); laid out 1851–52 as Victoria. Became cap. of crown colony 1859. Here are Dominion Astrophysical Observatory and Victoria Col. (affiliated with Univ. of British Columbia).

Victoria (vēktō′ryä), city (pop. 19,513), cap. of Tamaulipas, NE Mexico; founded (1750) at foot of Sierra Madre Oriental. Principal products: sugar cane and citrus fruits. Also called Ciudad Victoria.

Victoria, city (pop. 16,126), S Texas, near Guadalupe R. and SE of San Antonio; founded 1824. Early Mexican town attracted U.S. settlers and German immigrants. Remains German in architecture and spirit. Center of oil and agr. area, it processes oil, chemicals, cotton, and food; railroad shops. Air fields estab. near by in World War II.

Victoria, Lake: see VICTORIA NYANZA.

Victoria and Albert Museum, in South Kensington, London, opened 1857 as South Kensington Mus. Housed in present building since 1901 and controlled by Board of Education. Has fine examples of decorative and applied arts as well as a noted collection of paintings and sculptures and the collections of the India Mus., which it absorbed.

Victoria Falls, in upper Zambezi R., on border of Southern Rhodesia and Northern Rhodesia; 1 mi. wide, 420 ft. high. Discovered 1855 by David Livingstone, who named them for Queen Victoria.

Victoria Island, 320 mi. long, 170–370 mi. wide, SW Franklin dist., Northwest Territories, Canada, in Arctic Ocean, one of largest islands in ARCTIC ARCHIPELAGO. On SE coast is Cambridge Bay, U.S.-Canadian weather station and trading post. Discovered by Thomas Simpson 1836–39.

Victoria Land, Antarctic region, S of New Zealand. Series of snow-covered mountains with high interior plateau; bounded E by Ross Sea, W by Wilkes Land. Discovered 1841 by Sir J. C. Ross; formerly called South Victoria Land.

Victorian style, in architecture, an eclectic fashion based on revivals of older styles. Private dwellings were supposedly based on Gothic style and public buildings on Greco-Roman models, but the basic design was lost in the mass of cluttered detail and overuse of turrets, bays, towers, and other excrescences.

Victoria Nyanza (nēän′zù, nī–), lake, area 26,828 sq. mi., E central Africa, bordered by Uganda, Tanganyika, and Kenya. Of the fresh-water lakes of the world, only L. Superior is larger. It is 250 mi. long, 150 mi. wide, with an altitude of c.3,725 ft. Usually considered the chief source of the Nile, which (as the Victoria Nile) issues from it over Ripon Falls. Steamer service links the lake-shore towns. Discovered 1858 by John Speke and explored 1875 by Henry Stanley.

Victoriaville, town (pop. 13,124), SE Que., Canada, on Nicolet R. and N of Sherbrooke, in farm region. Mfg. of furniture and clothing.

Victory of Samothrace: see NIKE.

vicuña (vĭkū′nù), South American wild mammal (*Lama*) of camel family. Wool is woven into fine cloth.

Vidal, Peire (pēr′ vēdäl′), fl. 1180–1206, Provençal

troubadour. Among his patrons was Richard I of England. His love poems are notable for strong personal feeling and simple style.

Vidalia (vĭdāl'yů), city (pop. 5,819), SE Ga., W of Savannah, in farm area.

Vidocq, Eugène François (ûzhĕn' frăswä' vēdôk'), 1775–1857, noted French detective, who, after a career of crime, joined (1809) the Paris *Sûreté*.

Vienna (vēē'nů), Ger. *Wien*, city (469 sq. mi.; pop. 1,760,784), cap. of Austria and of Lower Austria, on the Danube. It is coextensive with Vienna prov. Archiepiscopal see; seat of a university (founded 1365); cultural and commercial center. Varied mfg. The Roman Vindobona, it became the seat of the dukes of Austria (12th cent.) and imperial residence (15th cent.). It repulsed a Turkish siege in 1529. In the Turkish siege of 1683, the city heroically defended itself under the leadership of Starhemberg but was on the verge of starvation when it was saved by John III of Poland. In the 18th, 19th, and early 20th cent. Vienna reached its height as a center of art and science, notably of music (Mozart, Haydn, Beethoven, Schubert, Brahms, and others) and of medicine and psychiatry (Wagner-Jauregg, Freud). Its importance declined after World War I. Among the chief landmarks of Vienna are St. Stephen's cathedral (12th cent.); the Hofburg (imperial residence), Karlskirche, Schönbrunn palace, and Belvedere palace (all 18th cent., by Fischer von Erlach); the Prater (a park); the classic parliament building; and the opera and Burgtheater (in Renaissance style). Vienna was heavily damaged in World War II; its former Jewish population (c.115,000) was virtually wiped out by the Nazis. Captured by the Russian army in April, 1945, it was jointly occupied by Russian, U.S., British, and French troops. The WIENER WALD is near by.

Vienna (vēē'nů), city (pop. 6,020), NW W.Va., near Parkersburg. Mfg. of glass, silk, vitrolite.

Vienna, Congress of, Sept., 1814–June, 1815, general political conference called to complement TREATY OF PARIS of 1814 in a general settlement of European affairs after the first abdication of NAPOLEON I. Among chief figures were the host, Emperor Francis I of Austria, and Metternich, chief Austrian negotiator; Alexander I of Russia; Frederick William III and K. A. von Hardenberg (Prussia); Castlereagh (Britain); and Talleyrand (France). There were hundreds of secondary representatives and agents, but no plenary session ever took place. The main work was carried on in committees and was dominated by the Big Three (Big Four, after Talleyrand secured equal status for France). The congress was the occasion for brilliant social activities, but despite the famous saying of the prince de LIGNE, work as well as dancing was done. Among the many thorny problems were those of Poland and Saxony, where Russian and Prussian interests clashed with those of Austria, France, and England. War seemed imminent when these last three powers concluded a defensive alliance (Jan., 1815), but Talleyrand's brilliant intervention, aided by Castlereagh, made the principle of legitimacy paramount and secured a compromise on which the European balance of power was based. The Final Act of the congress (June 9, 1815) was hurriedly drawn up after Napoleon's landing in France. The GERMAN CONFEDERATION was estab. For other territorial changes, see articles on countries, notably PRUSSIA; POLAND; SAXONY; NORWAY; NETHERLANDS; ITALY.

Vienne (vyĕn), department (2,720 sq. mi.; pop. 313,-932), W central France, in Poitou; cap. Poitiers. It is crossed by the Vienne R., 230 mi. long, a tributary of the Loire.

Vienne, city (pop. 19,958), Isère dept., SE France, on the Rhone. Textile mfg. Was a major city of Roman Gaul; an early archiepiscopal see (suppressed 1790); seat of several kings of Burgundy (5th–9th cent.) and of counts of Vienne (see DAUPHINÉ); scene of an

ecumenical council of the Roman Catholic Church (1311–12; resulted in suppression of Knights Templars by Pope Clement V). Has well-preserved Roman remains.

Vierge, Daniel (Urrabieta) (dänyĕl' vyĕr'hä), 1851–1904, Spanish illustrator, a master of pen-and-ink drawing. Worked mainly in Paris.

Vierwaldstättersee, Switzerland: see LUCERNE.

Viète or Vieta, François (fräswä' vyĕt', vyätä'), 1540–1603, French mathematician. A founder of modern algebra, he introduced letters as algebraic symbols and correlated algebra, geometry, and trigonometry.

Viet Nam (vēĕt' näm'), state (c.127,300 sq. mi.; pop. 22,600,000), E Indo-China; formed by the union of TONKIN, ANNAM, and COCHIN CHINA; cap. Saigon. At end of World War II, the Viet Minh party (a coalition of nationalist and Communist groups) resisted the return of French rule and set up a republic, headed by Ho CHI-MINH, with the capital at Hanoi. French objection to the inclusion of Cochin China in the new state and denial of full sovereignty led to a guerrilla war, which began Dec., 1946. In 1949 the French set up a rival Viet Nam regime, installing Bao Dai (former emperor of Annam) as ruler. A treaty granting Viet Nam independence within the French Union was ratified in 1950, and Bao Dai's government was promptly recognized by the U.S. and Great Britain, but not by the USSR and its allies, which recognized the Ho regime. The war between Viet Minh troops and French Union forces, which for seven years had been restricted to Viet Nam, spread into the neighboring state of Laos in 1953.

Vieuxtemps, Henri (vyûtä'), 1820–81, Belgian composer and violinist. A famous concert violinist, he wrote six concertos and other works, many of which are part of the standard violin repertoire.

Vigée-Lebrun, Élisabeth (ālēzäbĕt' vēzhä'-lùbrü'), 1755–1842, French painter, noted for her portraits of Marie Antoinette and of Mme de Staël.

Vigeland, Adolf Gustav (vē'gůlän), 1869–1943, Norwegian sculptor. Executed c.100 figures for decorating Frogner Park, Oslo.

vigilantes (vĭjĭlän'tēz), members of a vigilance committee. Such committees were formed in U.S. frontier communities to suppress lawlessness and disorder before a regularly constituted government could be created or have real force. Most famous were those formed in San Francisco in 1851 and 1856 to bring order to the Barbary Coast. Extreme penalty imposed by vigilantes was LYNCHING. Measures taken by them were at best extralegal. The name has sometimes been used by later groups illegally imposing force on others.

Vignemale (vēnyůmäl'), mountain, 10,821 ft. high, S France; highest in French Pyrenees.

Vignola, Giacomo da (jä'kōmō dä vēnyō'lä), 1507–73, Italian architect, one of initiators of baroque design. Real name was Giacomo Barozzi or Barocchio. Succeeded Michelangelo as architect of St. Peter's, for which he designed the lateral domes. In 1568 he designed sumptuous interior of Church of the Gesù (Rome). Universally known for treatise (based on Vitruvius) on five orders of architecture.

Vigny, Alfred, comte de (älfrĕd kŏt' dù vēnyē'), 1797–1863, French author. Primarily a poet-philosopher, he expressed his noble stoicism in *Poèmes antiques et modernes* (1826) and *Destinées* (1864) and the semi-autobiographical prose sketches, *Servitude et grandeur militaires* (1835). His best-known novel is *Cinq-Mars* (1826); his best-known play, *Chatterton* (1835).

Vigo (vē'gō), city (pop. 44,188), NW Spain, in Galicia. An active Atlantic port, it has a large fishing fleet. Canning industry.

Viipuri, Finnish name of VYBORG, RSFSR.

Vikings (vī'kĭngz), Scandinavian warriors whose raids of coasts of Europe and British Isles gave period 8th–10th cent. name of the Viking Age. Causes of raids are obscure, but overpopulation was one of them. Scandinavians at that time were best shipbuilders and sailors in the world. Viking religion, Germanic paganism whose legends form Old Norse Literature, was replaced by Christianity at end of age. Vikings were known as VARANGIANS in Russia; as NORSEMEN or Danes elsewhere.

Villa, Francisco (fränsē'skō vē'yä), 1877?–1923, Mexican revolutionist, whose vigorous fighting in revolution of 1910 was largely responsible for triumph of Madero. When in 1913 Huerta overthrew Madero, Villa opposed him and later opposed Carranza; he gained control of N Mexico and with Zapata briefly occupied Mexico city (Dec., 1914,–Jan., 1915). Piqued after Pres. Wilson recognized Carranza, Villa turned his wrath on U.S. citizens in Mexico and on U.S. border towns. A U.S. expedition under Pershing went then into Chihuahua (March, 1916–Feb., 1917) but was fruitless. Villa was assassinated in 1923.

Villa d'Este (vēl'lä dē'stä), famous villa near Tivoli, Italy, built 1550 for Cardinal Ippolito II d'Este. Its beautiful Renaissance garden has a Bernini fountain. Another Villa d'Este was built 16th cent. on W shore of L. Como; now a hotel.

Villa Doria Pamphili (vēl'lä dô'ryä päm'fēlē), Roman villa, built in 17th cent. for Camillo Pamphili, nephew of Pope Innocent X. Designed by Algardi.

Villafranca di Verona (vēl''läfräng'kä dē vārō'nä), town (pop. 4,986), Venetia, NE Italy. Here in 1859 France and Austria concluded a preliminary peace after the battle of Solferino (see RISORGIMENTO). Austria ceded Lombardy, which was added to Sardinia. Tuscany, Parma, and Modena, where revolutions had broken out, were to be restored to their rulers. Sardinia, which was not represented at the negotiations, repudiated some of the clauses and in 1860 annexed the central Italian states.

Villahermosa (vē''yäërmō'sä), city (pop. 25,114), cap. of Tabasco, SE Mexico; founded in late 16th cent., well inland on Grijalva R. Makes rum, hats, soap, candles, cigars, bricks and tile, and is distributing center.

Villa-Lobos, Heitor (ā'tôr vē'lä-lō'bôs), 1884?–, Brazilian composer. Inspired by Brazilian folk and popular music, he wrote a series of pieces which he called *Chôros*. Other compositions include symphonies, operas, concertos, chamber music, and many songs.

Villani, Giovanni (jōvän'nē vēl-lä'nē), c.1275–1348, Italian historian of Florence. His history in 12 books is an early monument of Italian prose, and helped fix Tuscan language as standard of Italy.

Villanova, village, SE Pa., near Philadelphia. Seat of Villanova Col. (R.C., for men; 1843).

Villard, Henry (vīlärd'), 1835–1900, American journalist and financier, b. Germany. Original name Hilgard Villard. In the U.S. after 1853, he was a distinguished reporter through the Civil War, became interested in promoting railroads, gained controlling interest in Northern Pacific RR (1881), was forced into bankruptcy by difficulties of building (1883), regained control (1889). Also founded predecessor of General Electric Co. He bought control of the New York *Evening Post* (1881). He married a daughter of William Lloyd Garrison. Their son, **Oswald Garrison Villard**, 1872–1949, inherited and edited (until 1918) the *Evening Post* and made its weekly, the *Nation,* an outstanding liberal journal (which he owned until 1932). A militant pacifist and a friend of Germany.

Villari, Pasquale (päskwä'lā vēl'lärē), 1827–1917, Italian historian, author of notable biographies of Savonarola (1859–61) and Machiavelli (1877–82).

Villarrica (vē''yärē'kä), city (pop. 27,687), SE Paraguay; commercial center and shipping point for cattle, fruits, tobacco, and mate.

Villars, Claude, duc de (klōd' dük dù vēlär'), 1653–1734, marshal of France. In War of the Spanish Succession he won victories at Friedlingen (1702), Höchstädt (1703), and Denain (1714); was defeated at Malplaquet (1709); negotiated Treaty of Rastatt (1714). Wrote memoirs.

Villehardouin (vēlärdwē'), French noble family that ruled Peloponnesus 1210–78. **Geoffroi de Villehardouin** (zhôfrōöä'), c.1160–c.1212, marshal of Champagne, was a leader in Fourth Crusade, which he related in his *De la conqueste de Constantinople* (first pub. 1585), an early masterpiece of French historical writing. He received a rich fief in Thrace. His nephew **Geoffroi I de Villehardouin**, d. 1218, conquered the Peloponnesus in 1205; ruled (1210–18) principality of Achaia as fief under Latin Empire. It prospered under his son **Geoffroi II de Villehardouin**, d. 1246, an excellent administrator. Another son, **Guillaume or William de Villehardouin** (gēyōm'), d. 1278, prince of Achaia (1246–78), waged war against Emperor Michael VIII (who had restored the Byzantine Empire in 1261) in alliance with his son-in-law, Charles I of Naples.

villein (vĭl'lŭn) [O. Fr.,= village dweller], under MANORIAL SYSTEM, one who was personally free, though holding land that was not. He was distinguished from freeholder by services and duties owed to a lord. Term villeinage thus denoted half-free status. It began to disappear in England in 14th cent., due partly to substitution of money payments for work service, partly to growth of towns, which broke down local systems. See also SERF.

Ville Lasalle, Que.: see LASALLE.

Villèle, Jean Baptiste Séraphin Joseph, comte de (zhä' bätēst' säräfē' zhôzēf' kõt' dù vēlēl'), 1773–1854, French premier (1822–28); an ultraroyalist. Among other extreme reactionary measures, he enacted a plan to indemnify the émigrés out of public savings. Dissolved chamber of deputies 1827. Defeated in new elections, he resigned.

Villeneuve, Pierre de (pyēr' dù vēlnûv'), 1763–1806, French admiral. Defeated at TRAFALGAR (1805), he committed suicide.

Ville Platte (vēl' plăt'), town (pop. 6,633), S central La., WNW of Baton Rouge. Trade and processing center for cotton, rice, lumber, and oil area.

Villeroi, François, duc de (fräswä' dük' dù vēlrwä'), 1644–1730, marshal of France; a favorite of Louis XIV. Incompetent, he was repeatedly defeated, notably at Ramillies in 1706.

Villeurbanne (vēlürbän'), city (pop. 80,193), Rhône dept., E France; an industrial suburb of Lyons. Metallurgy; rayon and chemical plants.

Villiers, George: see BUCKINGHAM, GEORGE VILLIERS, DUKE OF.

Villiers, George William Frederick: see CLARENDON, GEORGE WILLIAM FREDERICK VILLIERS, 4TH EARL OF.

Villiers de l'Isle-Adam, Auguste, comte de (ōgüst' kõt' dù vēyä' dù lēl'-ädä'), 1838–89, French author, a master of the tale of fantasy and horror. Among his works are the novel *L'Ève future* (1886) and the short stories collected in *Contes cruels* (1883).

Villon, François (fräswä' vēyō'), b. 1431, d. after 1463, French poet. He associated with criminal gangs, was several times imprisoned for homicide and robbery, and in 1463 was sentenced to hang. His appeal resulted in commutation to 10 years' exile. One of the greatest medieval poets, Villon strikes a strongly personal, modern note. His chief works are the *Lais* or *Little Testament* (written 1456) and the *Testament* (1461)—both in the form of facetious bequests to his family, friends, and, especially, enemies. Interspersed in the *Testament* are such famous poems as "Ballade des dames du temps jadis" (with the refrain, "But where are the snows of yester-year?"). Later poems include the "Ballad of the Hanged." In turn mocking, ribald, and movingly pious, Villon's work always reflects his preoccupation with death and decay. There are several more or less successful English translations.

Vilna (vĭl'nù), Lithuanian *Vilnius*, Pol. *Wilno*, city (1931 pop. 196,345), cap. of Lithuania. Mfg. of agr. machinery, processed foods, lumber, electric equipment. University was founded 1578. The cap. of Lithuania from 1323, it passed to Russia 1795; was occupied by German troops in World War I; was assigned to Lithuania at the Paris Peace Conference, but was seized by Polish troops in 1920 and annexed by Poland after a plebiscite of doubtful validity (1922). The USSR occupied Vilna (along with E Poland) in 1939 but soon afterward transferred it to Lithuania. The interim Lithuanian cap., 1920–39, was Kaunas. During German occupation (1941–44) in World War II, Vilna's large Jewish population was virtually exterminated.

Vilyui (vĭlyōō'ē), river, 1,512 mi. long, RSFSR, in Siberia; a western tributary of the Lena. Platinum and gold are found along its banks.

Vimeiro (vēmā'rō), village of central Portugal, NNW of Lisbon, where Wellington defeated the French under Junot (1808).

Viña del Mar (vē'nyä dĕl mär') [Span.,= vineyard by the sea], port (pop. 98,156), central Chile. Practically a suburb of Valparaiso, it is one of most popular resorts in South America. Its industries include sugar and oil refineries, cloth and yarn mills, dyeing and printing plants.

Vincennes (vĭnsĕnz', Fr. vēsĕn'), town (pop. 48,851), Seine dept., N France; a W suburb of Paris. Has huge castle (once a royal residence) and dungeon (state prison in 17th–18th cent.). Forest of Vincennes is near by.

Vincennes (vĭnsĕnz'), city (pop. 18,831), SW Ind., on Wabash R. (here forms Ill. line) and S of Terre Haute. French mission estab. here 1702, fortified 1730, occupied by British 1763. Captured in American Revolution by G. R. Clark 1779. Cap. of Indiana territory 1800–1813 (W. H. Harrison then lived here). River port and rail center in agr., coal, and oil area. Mfg. of glass, metal, food, and paper products. Has memorial to G. R. Clark.

Vincent, John Heyl, 1832–1920, American Methodist bishop. His work in improving teaching methods in Sunday schools had widespread results. With Lewis Miller he organized (1874) at Chautauqua, N.Y., a Sunday-school teachers' institute, out of which grew Chautauqua movement. He became bishop in 1888. His son, **George Edgar Vincent,** 1864–1941, aided his father and was president (1907–15) of the Chautauqua Inst. As head (1917–29) of Rockefeller Foundation, he greatly expanded its activities, especially in medical aid and research.

Vincent de Paul, Saint, 1576–1660, French priest. Having himself suffered enslavement by Tunisian pirates, he later worked to better the conditions of the galley slaves. He then zealously began organized charity in France, initiated the foundling hospital, and founded an order of secular priests, the Congregation of the Mission (Lazarists or Vincentians), for rural work (1629) and the SISTERS OF CHARITY for city work. St. Francis of Sales made him director of the Order of the Visitation. Feast: July 19.

Vincent Ferrer, Saint (fĕr'ür), 1350?–1419, Spanish Dominican preacher. Traveled over Europe, urging sinners to repent, converting many. Feast: April 5.

Vincent of Beauvais (bōvā'), c.1190–c.1264, French Dominican friar. Wrote three of four parts of the *Speculum majus,* a Latin encyclopedia that summarized 13th-cent. knowledge.

Vinci, Leonardo da: see LEONARDO DA VINCI.

vine, any climbing or trailing plant; the grape is often called the "vine."

vinegar, sour liquid, mainly acetic acid and water, produced by action of bacteria on solutions of ethyl alcohol derived from previous yeast FERMENTATION; varieties vary in color and flavor according to the alcoholic liquor (cider, wine, solution of barley malt, etc.) from which the vinegar is made. Used as condiment, preservative, household remedy, and in cookery. Vinegar has been known since antiquity as a natural byproduct of wine.

Vineland, borough (pop. 8,155), S N.J., N of Millville. Agr. market center (poultry, fruit); clothing, fireworks,

machinery. Seat of state school for sub-normal children (noted for research work).

Vineyard Haven, resort village (pop. 1,864) in Tisbury town (pop. 1,930) on N Martha's Vineyard, with harbor on Vineyard Sound, SE Mass.

Vinita (vĭnē'tù), city (pop. 5,518), NE Okla., NE of Tulsa, center of agr. and livestock area. Near by is Grand River Dam.

Vinland or **Wineland,** section of North America discovered by LEIF ERICSSON in 11th cent. A.D. Later sought by THORFINN KARLSEFNI. Southern coast of New England generally accepted as disputed site.

Vinnitsa (vē'nyĭtsŭ), city (pop. 92,868), W Ukraine, on the Southern Bug; an agr. center of Podolia. Population was 40% Jewish until German occupation (1941–43) in World War II.

Vinogradoff, Sir Paul (vĭnŭgrä'dùf), 1854–1925, English historian. Works include *Villainage in England* (1892), *English Society in the Eleventh Century* (1908), and *Outlines of Historical Jurisprudence* (2 vols., 1920–23).

Vinson, Fred(erick) M(oore), 1890–, Chief Justice of U.S. Supreme Court (1946–).

viol (vī'ùl), family of stringed instruments played with a bow, developed in the 15th cent. and popular until supplanted by the VIOLIN family. Despite a general resemblance, there are many differences between the two families. Viols have a flat rather than a rounded back; deep ribs; shoulders that slope into the neck (usually fretted); from five to eight strings; and a soft, delicate tone. The sizes and range (treble, tenor, bass) of members of the viol family correspond somewhat to those of the violin family. Many viols, regardless of size, are played usually resting on the knees—hence the term *viola da gamba* [knee viol]. In a limited sense, the viola da gamba refers to the bass (not double bass) member of the family, a six-stringed instrument similar to the cello in range. Another type of viol was the viola da braccio [arm viol]. An important arm viol is the viola d'amore. Held like a violin, it has from five to seven strings and an unfretted neck; it is distinguished by its set of sympathetic strings (strings not themselves directly played upon but stretched behind the bowed strings and tuned to vibrate sympathetically with them).

viola, flower: see VIOLET.

viola, musical instrument: see VIOLIN, family.

viola da gamba and **viola d'amore:** see VIOL.

violet, low, perennial flowering plant of genus *Viola.* Many violets are spring-blooming North American wild flowers. Florists' violets are chiefly varieties of the sweet or English violet (*Viola odorata*). Garden violets, known as violas or tufted pansies, are hybrids or varieties of *V. cornuta.* The PANSY and johnny-jump-up are derived from *V. tricolor.* Many violets bear, besides their typical flowers, capsulelike flowers which never open but produce seed after self-fertilization. The African violet is not related.

violin, family of stringed musical instruments played with a bow; chief members are the violin (the terms "first" and "second" violin refer merely to the part that a violin plays in an ensemble), the viola, the violoncello (usually simply called the cello), and the double bass. These four form the string section of the usual symphony orchestra, the first three being also used in string quartets. All except the double bass are important solo instruments. Collectively these instruments have great capabilities and a wide range (the distance between the lowest note on the double bass and the highest possible note on the violin is over six octaves). A variety of effects may be produced by different bowing techniques. Members of the violin family resemble each other in having a slightly convex front and back, an unfretted neck, and four strings—with the exception of the double bass, which more closely resembles the VIOL family. Each member has its own characteristic tone, the violin ranging from the sentimental to the brilliant; the viola (resembling a large violin) more reserved, but warm; the cello (about twice the size of the violin), known for its rich color; and the double bass, deep and serious. Both the violin and viola are played held more or less horizontally with the body of the instrument supported by the shoulder and held firm by the chin; the cello and double bass are played vertically, resting on the floor. The peak of violinmaking was reached in the 16th and 17th cent. by such master craftsmen as the Amati, Guarneri, and Stradivari families of Cremona. See *ill.*, p. 667.

Viollet-le-Duc, Eugène Emmanuel (vyôlā′-lù-dük′), 1814–79, French architect, foremost exponent of Gothic revival in France. Famous for restorations of Notre Dame and the Sainte-Chapelle in Paris and cathedrals of Amien and of Laon. Author of standard works on medieval architecture.

violoncello: see VIOLIN, family.

viper, any of several poisonous snakes including true vipers (*Vipera*) of Europe, Asia, Africa and the pit vipers of America and Asia. ADDER is a true viper; pit vipers (pit on each side of head) include RATTLESNAKE, COPPERHEAD, WATER MOCCASIN, BUSHMASTER.

Virchow, Rudolf (rōō′dôlf fir′khō), 1821–1902, German pathologist, a founder of cellular pathology. Eminent also as anthropologist and in politics.

vireo (vī′rēō), small, migratory bird of New World. Some species nest in U.S., but majority are tropical. Most vireos are greenish above with white or yellow under parts. They are chiefly insectivorous. Some are fine singers. See *ill.*, p. 105.

Virgil, Roman poet: see VERGIL.

virginal, musical instrument: see PIANO.

Virginia, in Roman legend, daughter of a centurion. Her father stabbed her to save her from lust of Appius Claudius Crassus, a decemvir, and this precipitated downfall of the decemvirs.

Virginia, state (39,899 sq. mi.; pop. 3,318,680), E U.S.; first of the Thirteen Colonies; cap. RICHMOND. Other cities are NORFOLK, ROANOKE, PORTSMOUTH. HAMPTON ROADS is major port of entry, center of shipbuilding and shipping. The TIDEWATER region extends W from the Atlantic to the piedmont. Between the BLUE RIDGE and the Appalachian plateau farther W lies Valley of Virginia (including valley of the SHENANDOAH). Major rivers are the Potomac (part of Md. line), Rappahannock, York, and James. Farming (corn, tobacco, hay, wheat, peanuts, apples, livestock, dairying); fishing. Coal mining. Mfg. of tobacco products, wood products, textiles, chemicals, food products. JAMESTOWN was first permanent English settlement in America (1607). Early hardships lessened as new settlers arrived and as agr. was estab. House of burgesses, first representative assembly in New World, convened 1619. Became royal colony in 1624. Economic dissatisfaction of small farmers expressed in BACON'S REBELLION (1676). OHIO COMPANY grant (1749) led to further development. Va. was active in colonial opposition to British before American Revolution. Of first 12 Presidents, seven were Virginians. Joined Confederacy in 1861; chief battleground of Civil War. Counties W of the Appalachians opposed secession; this section admitted to Union as W.Va. in 1863. Industrial growth was hastened afterwards; industry boomed in both World Wars. Harry F. Byrd has been most influential political figure in state's Democratic organization since mid-1920s.

Virginia, city (pop. 12,486), NE Minn., NNW of Duluth and on Mesabi iron range; settled before 1883. Resort area and trade center with mines and foundries. Rebuilt after fires 1893, 1900.

Virginia, Confederate name for ironclad *Merrimac.* See MONITOR AND MERRIMAC.

Virginia, University of, at Charlottesville; state supported, mainly for men; chartered 1819, opened 1825. Thomas Jefferson, the first rector, planned original buildings and organization and curriculum. Had first elective system in a university. Consolidated with Mary Washington Col. (at Fredericksburg; for women; 1908) in 1944.

Virginia Beach, Atlantic resort town (pop. 5,390), SE Va., E of Norfolk. Has seafood industry. Near by are Fort Story and Cape Henry.

Virginia bluebell: see VIRGINIA COWSLIP.

Virginia City. 1 Town (pop. 323), SW Mont., SE of Butte. Founded when gold was discovered (1863) in Alder Gulch. Territorial cap. 1865–74. **2** Uninc. town (1940 pop. 952), W Nev., SE of Reno. Founded 1859, when rich gold and silver deposits, notably COMSTOCK LODE, were discovered near by. In 1880 population was c.11,000. Town is now tourist center.

Virginia Company, created in 1606 by British royal charter to estab. two colonies in America between lat. 34° N and lat. 45° N.

Virginia cowslip or **Virginia bluebell,** beautiful spring wild flower (*Mertensia virginica*), native from N.Y. to Tenn. It has nodding, blue bell–shaped flowers.

Virginia creeper, native woody vine (*Parthenocissus quinquefolia*), much used as a wall covering. It has black berries and five-fingered leaves, red in autumn. It is often called woodbine.

Virginia Military Institute: see LEXINGTON.

Virginia Mountains, W Nev., W of Pyramid L. between Astor Pass and Carson R. Here are Pyramid Range (N) and Washoe Mts. or Virginia Range (S), with Mt. Davidson (7,870 ft.), site of COMSTOCK LODE.

Virginia Polytechnic Institute: see BLACKSBURG.

Virginia Resolutions: see KENTUCKY AND VIRGINIA RESOLUTIONS.

Virgin Islands, group of c.100 small islands, West Indies, E of Puerto Rico; discovered by Columbus (1493). The **Virgin Islands of the United States** (132 sq. mi.; pop. 26,665), territory, formerly part of Danish West Indies, purchased 1917 for $25,000,000; cap. CHARLOTTE AMALIE (St. Thomas). Other cities are Christiansted and Frederiksted, on St. Croix. Although 68 islands compose group, only three are of importance. St. Croix (23 mi. long) is mountainous and uncultivated but has many good harbors; St. Thomas (12 mi. long) has flat terrain and is dominated by agr. (sugar cane mainly); St. John (9 mi. long) is also agricultural. Real importance of these islands is their strategic location at juncture of Caribbean and Atlantic. **British Virgin Islands** (67 sq. mi.; pop. 6,505), c.30 in number, form a presidency of the Leeward Islands colony; cap. Road Town. The principal islands are Tortola (12 mi. long), Anegada (10 mi. long), Virgin Gorda (10 mi. long). Acquired by Great Britain in 1666. Crops include sea-island cotton and tobacco; there is some grazing.

Virginius, filibustering ship, fraudulently flying American flag and carrying arms to Cubans in Ten Years War. Captured by Spanish off Cuba, Oct. 31, 1873. Captain and 52 of the crew and passengers were executed. Incident almost caused war between U.S. and Spain, but Hamilton Fish negotiated settlement. Spain paid U.S. $80,000.

Virgin Mary: see MARY.

Virgo (vûr′gō) [Latin, = the virgin], sixth sign of ZODIAC.

Viriatus (vērēā′tùs), d. 139 B.C., leader of the Lusitani (see LUSITANIA). He headed a successful rebellion against Roman rule, inflicted defeats on Roman armies, and maintained an independent state until some of his followers were bribed to kill him.

Virtanen or **Wirtanen, Artturi Ilmari** (both: ärt′tōōrē ïl′märē vir′tänen), 1895–, Finnish biochemist. Won 1945 Nobel Prize for work on use of nitrogen by plants.

virus (vī′rùs), name for a submicroscopic infectious agent capable of causing disease in plants and animals. Viruses are generally considered to be filtrable, i.e., they can pass through porcelain filters having pores so fine that bacteria cannot pass through them. In general, viruses can be described as parasites incapable of growth except in the presence of living cells. An attack of some virus diseases makes the victim immune to further attacks of the same disease. Virus diseases include poliomyelitis, rabies, smallpox and chickenpox, yellow fever, mumps, measles, and probably the common cold. Mosaic diseases in plants are attributed to viruses.

Visalia (vīsā′lyù), city (pop. 11,749), S central Calif., SE of Fresno; founded 1852. Processing center for farms and dairies of San Joaquin Valley.

Visayan Islands (vīsī′ùn) or **Bisayas** (bēsä′yäs), island group, in Visayan Sea, central P.I., including Samar, Leyte, Negros, Panay, Bohol, Cebu, Masbate, and others.

Visby, Sweden: see WISBY.

Vischer, Peter (fĭ′shùr), the elder, c.1455–1529, German sculptor, foremost bronze founder in Germany. Assisted by his five sons in his Nuremberg workshop. Masterpiece is richly ornamented bronze canopy over the reliquary of St. Sebald at Nuremberg.

Visconti (vēskōn′tē), Italian Ghibelline family which ruled Milan from 13th cent. to 1447 (first as lords, later as imperial vicars and dukes, from 1395 as hereditary dukes). They gradually acquired all Lombardy and neighboring districts. **Gian Galeazzo Visconti** (jän′ gäläät′tsō), 1351?–1402, bought his investiture as hereditary duke from Emperor Wenceslaus (1395) and defeated Emperor Rupert, who sought to restore imperial rule over Italy (1401). Seeking to set up an Italian kingdom, Gian Galeazzo embarked on a systematic program of conquest, in which he was assisted by the best condottieri of his time and by his own diplomatic skill, but he died of the plague while preparing an attack on Florence, his stoutest enemy. He reformed and centralized the government, promoted art and industry, and allied his house with France by marrying Isabella, daughter of King John II; his daughter Valentina married Louis d'Orléans. (It was through Valentina that Louis XII of France derived his claim to Milan.) He was succeeded by his sons **Giovanni Maria Visconti** (jōvän′nē), 1389–1412, a dissolute and cruel ruler, who was assassinated, and **Filippo Maria Visconti** (fēlēp′pō), 1392–1447, who used both force and diplomacy to restore the duchy from the chaos into which it had fallen after Gian Galeazzo's death. He warred with Venice and Florence. His daughter and sole heir, Bianca Maria, married Francesco I SFORZA, who became duke after the fall of the short-lived Ambrosian Republic (1447–50), set up after Filippo Maria's death.

viscose process (vĭs′kōs), method for preparing RAYON from cellulose. Sheets of cellulose prepared either from wood pulp or cotton linters are treated with sodium hydroxide, then carbon disulphide; product is cellulose xanthate. When this is mixed with dilute sodium hydroxide, viscose is produced. Yarn is made from this by forcing the viscose through spinneret into acid solution.

Viscount Melville Sound, arm of the Arctic Ocean, 250 mi. long, 100 mi. wide, W Franklin dist., Northwest territories, Canada. Navigable only under favorable weather conditions. W part discovered by Sir Robert McClure 1850–53.

Viseu (vēzā′ōō), city (pop. 13,499), cap. of Beira Alta prov., N central Portugal. Grain and fruit trade; textile mfg. Founded by Romans; captured from Moors 1058. Has 12th-cent. cathedral and notable museum.

Vishinsky or **Vyshinsky, Andrei Y(anuarievich)** (ŭndrä′ yŭnōōär′yĭvĭch vĭshēn′skē), 1883–, Russian jurist and diplomat. Chief prosecutor at Moscow treason trials of 1936–38; deputy foreign minister 1941–49; foreign minister 1949–53; deputy foreign minister and permanent representative of USSR at UN 1953–. Wrote *The Law of the Soviet State* (Eng. tr., 1948).

Vishnu: see HINDUISM.

Visigoths or **West Goths,** division of the Goths, one of the chief groups of the GERMANS. Separated from the OSTROGOTHS early in 4th cent. A.D., they began to penetrate the Danubian provinces of the East Roman Empire. ULFILAS began their conversion to Arianism.

In 376, under pressure of the Hunnic invasion, the Visigoths under their chief Fritigern fled into Roman territory. Their troubles with the Roman officials led to a punitive expedition by Emperor Valens, whom they utterly routed at Adrianople (378). Rome ceded certain provinces for their occupation (382), but in 395 ALARIC I, proclaimed king of the Visigoths, began his conquests which took the Visigoths across Italy (sack of Rome, 410) and, under King ATAULF, into S Gaul and N Spain (412). They increased their Spanish possessions at the expense of the Vandals and pushed N to the Loire. Visigothic power reached its height under EURIC, but in 507 ALARIC II was defeated by the Franks and lost nearly all his lands N of the Pyrenees. The history of the Visigoths became essentially that of SPAIN. They accepted Catholicism and merged with the Hispano-Roman population. After the death of RECESWINTH (672) Visigothic Spain fell into virtual anarchy. The last king, RODERICK, was defeated in 711 by TARIK, leader of the Moors.

vision, sense by which objects and colors are perceived. Depends on sensitivity of retina of EYE to light; rays pass through cornea and lens, by which they are bent and focused on retina. Shape of lens can be changed by accommodation so that both near and far objects are brought into focus. Layer of retina closest to choroid (or chorioid) is pigment layer, in which visual purple (rhodopsin) is believed to be made. Visual purple affects ability of eye to adapt to light and dark; it is decomposed in light; vitamin A is needed for its regeneration. Next layer has nerve cells known as rods and cones; this area is light sensitive. Nerve impulses from rods and cones are transmitted to cerebrum of brain through optic nerve. Image formed on retina is inverted because light rays cross; mental image is right side up. Retina has central depression (where only cones are present) which is area of most acute vision. Cones are believed to be concerned with vision in bright light; rods, in darkness. Color perception is considered function of cones; no completely satisfactory theory is known. Young-Helmholtz theory is based on assumption that there are three fundamental color sensations (red, green, violet) and three groups of cones in retina, each sensitive to one color. White is produced by combination of all three, black by lack of stimulation. Hering's theory suggests existence of three photochemical substances producing six primary sensations. Man has binocular vision; separate images formed by each eye are fused to give one impression. Since each eye forms its own image from a slightly different angle, depth, distance, and solidity are appreciated.

Vistula (vĭs′chŏolù), Pol. *Wisła,* Ger. *Weichsel,* chief river of Poland, 667 mi. long, rising in the Carpathians and flowing N past Cracow, Warsaw, and Torun into the Baltic at Danzig. Navigable for nearly entire length. Connected by canals with Oder, Dnieper, and Niemen rivers.

visual education, term denoting use of nonverbal materials to enrich learning experiences. It applies particularly to pictures and other materials appealing to the eye, but sound is also used, and the term *audiovisual* applies to combined program. Use of nonverbal materials—restricted largely to schools in U.S.—now includes all the developments of photographic industries, radio, sound recordings, and television.

visual purple: see VISION.

vitamins, group of substances essential for growth and maintenance of normal body structure and function. Well-balanced diet usually provides minimum requirements. Vitamins are often grouped as those soluble in fat (vitamins A, D, E, K) and those soluble in water (B complex and C). **Vitamin A** helps keep skin and mucous membranes healthy, is needed for normal growth of young, prevents certain eye diseases. Early symptom of deficiency is night blindness. High intake postpones senility in laboratory animals. It is a derivative of carotinoid pigments of plants and can be made synthetically on a commercial scale. Rich sources are milk and its products, fish-liver oils, dark green and yellow vegetables. About 12 water-soluble factors are grouped as **vitamin B complex.** Thiamine (thiamine hydrochloride, vitamin B₁ or B) is concerned with maintenance of normal appetite, good digestion, and carbohydrate metabolism; is essential to normal growth of young. It helps to maintain health of nervous system; prevents BERIBERI. Good sources are yeast, whole grains and their products, eggs, some meats, dried legumes. Riboflavin (vitamin B₂, vitamin G, or lactoflavin) is present in respiratory enzymes and is believed to be concerned with oxidation in body cells. Lack of the vitamin in humans results in skin lesions and damage to conjunctiva and cornea of eye. Sources include green leaf vegetables, milk, eggs, liver, and whole-grain products. Niacin (nicotinic acid) prevents PELLAGRA and a diet deficient in niacin results in disturbances of digestive and nervous systems. Vitamin B₁₂ discovered in liver is believed to be effective against various kinds of anemia. A number of other substances in B complex have not yet been investigated fully. These include pyridoxine, pantothenic acid, para-aminobenzoic acid, biotin, choline, folic acid, inositol. **Vitamin C** (ascorbic acid) prevents SCURVY. Symptoms of insufficiency include tenderness and bleeding of gums, loosening of teeth, soreness of joints, weakness, fatigue, and weakening of walls of capillaries. Little can be stored in body, thus daily intake is important. Good sources are citrus fruits, tomatoes, and raw cabbage. Vitamin C is easily destroyed in cooking. **Vitamin D** plays essential role in use of calcium and phosphorus by body and prevents RICKETS. Especially important during growth, pregnancy, lactation. Present in fish-liver oils and liver. Sometimes is added to milk by irradiation with ultraviolet light. Exposure to sunlight causes irradiation of cholesterol in skin and produces much of human requirement. Certain chemical compounds have **vitamin E** activity; essential to reproduction in some animals; value in humans is not known. It is especially abundant in wheat-germ oil and lettuce. **Vitamin K** is concerned with normal clotting of blood and functioning of the liver. **Vitamin P** is believed to function with vitamin C in preventing permeability of capillary walls.

Vitebsk (vē'těpsk, vě'tyǐpsk), city (pop. 167,424), NE Belorussia, on the W Dvina. Textile and machinery mfg. Passed to Lithuania 14th cent., to Russia 1772. Population was c.45% Jewish until German occupation (1941–44).

Vitellius, Aulus (ô'lŭs vĭtĕ'lēŭs), A.D. 15–A.D. 69, Roman emperor (A.D. 69). Succeeded Galba, triumphed over Otho, but was defeated and murdered by Vespasian.

Viterbo (vētĕr'bō), city (pop. 21,281), Latium, central Italy. A residence of 13th-cent. popes, it has a picturesque medieval quarter with many fine palaces, fountains, and a Romanesque cathedral. Damaged in World War II.

Viti Levu: see FIJI.

Vitim (vētyĕm'), river, 1,132 mi. long, RSFSR, in SE Siberia. Rises in gold-rich Vitim Plateau and flows S, then NE, then N into the Lena.

Vitória (vētō'rēŭ), formerly **Victoria,** city (pop. 51,329), cap. of Espírito Santo, E Brazil, port on the Atlantic; founded in mid-16th cent. Ships quantities of coffee and iron ore.

Vitoria (vētō'rēä), city (pop. 44,341), cap. of Álava prov., N Spain, in Basque Provs. Mfg. center (machinery, sugar, paper). Has Gothic cathedral. Here in 1813 Wellington won a decisive battle against the French under Joseph Bonaparte and Jourdan.

vitriol. For oil of vitriol, see SULPHURIC ACID; for green vitriol, see COPPERAS. See also BLUE VITRIOL and WHITE VITRIOL.

Vitruvius (Marcus Vitruvius Pollio) (vĭtrōō'vēŭs), 1st cent. A.D., Roman writer on architecture. His *De architectura* was much used by Renaissance architects in the classical revival.

Vittorino da Feltre (vēt-tōrē'nō dä fěl'trä), 1378–1446, Italian humanist and teacher. At his school in Mantua he taught the marchese's children, together with many poor children, treating them all equally. His methods and his emphasis were novel.

Vittorio Veneto (vēt-tō'ryō vānā'tō), town (pop. 12,034), Venetia, NE Italy. Scene of decisive Italian victory over Austrians, which led to surrender of Austria-Hungary (Oct.–Nov., 1918).

Vivaldi, Antonio (vēväl'dē), c.1675–1743, Italian composer, known chiefly for his instrumental music. He standardized the three-movement form of the *concerto grosso*. Bach made organ transcriptions of four of Vivaldi's concertos.

Vivarini (vēvärē'nē), Italian family of painters. **Antonio Vivarini,** b. c.1415, d. between 1476 and 1484, had a workshop in Murano. His brother, **Bartolomeo Vivarini,** c.1432–c.1499, was one of first to paint in oils in Venice. Antonio's son, **Alvise Vivarini** (älvē'zä), c.1446–c.1503, was a religious painter.

Vives, Juan Luis (hwän' lwēs' vē'väs), 1492–1540, Spanish humanist philosopher. Opposed the conventions of scholasticism; argued for inductive reasoning and experiment.

Vizagapatam (vĭ"zùgùpù'tùm), town (pop. 70,243), NE Madras, India; port on Bay of Bengal. Shipyards.

Vizcaíno, Sebastián (sävästyän' vēthkäē'nō), fl. 1602, Spanish explorer. Explored Calif. coast; discovered and named Monterey bay.

Vizcaya, Spain: see BASQUE PROVINCES.

Vlachs: see WALACHIA.

Vladikavkaz, RSFSR: see DZAUDZHIKAU.

Vladimir I or **Saint Vladimir** (vlă'dĭmēr, Rus. vlŭdyē'mĭr), d. 1015, first Christian duke of Kiev (980–1015); son of Sviatoslav. Was baptized 988 or 989. Fostered friendly relations with Byzantium.

Vladimir, city (pop. 66,761), central European RSFSR, ENE of Moscow. Textile, machinery, and plastics mfg. It became (c.1150) the cap. of the grand duchy of Vladimir-Suzdal, the chief Russian principality after the breakup of the Kievan state. After its destruction by the Mongols in 1238 the dukes of Moscow emerged as leading Russian princes; they acquired Vladimir in 1364, took the title grand dukes, and long continued to be crowned at Vladimir. Among its historic buildings are the Uspenski and Demetrius cathedrals (12th cent.) and the Golden Gate, a city gate erected 1164. The Vladimir-Suzdal style of Russian architecture was a fusion of the Romanesque and Byzantine styles.

Vladimir-Volynski (–vŭlĭn'skē), Pol. *Włodzimierz,* city (1931 pop. 24,581), W Ukraine. Became c.988 the cap. of duchy of Vladimir or Lodomeria, founded by Vladimir I of Kiev. Originally dependent on Kiev, it included, for some time, all of VOLHYNIA; was united with duchy of GALICH 1188; passed to Russia 1795; reverted to Poland 1921; was ceded to USSR 1945.

Vladislav, kings of Bohemia: see LADISLAUS V and ULADISLAUS II, kings of Hungary.

Vladivostok (vlă"dĭvō'stŏk, –vùstŏk'), city (pop. c.300,-000), cap. of Maritime Territory, RSFSR, in Far Eastern Siberia, on a peninsula in an inlet of Sea of Japan. Chief Russian Pacific port (kept ice free in winter); terminus of Trans-Siberian RR; fishing and whaling base. Has shipyards, airplane plants, canneries, lumber mills. Several scientific institutions. Settled 1860 by Russians, it grew after completion of Trans-Siberian RR (1905) and developed as a naval base after Russian loss of Port Arthur to Japan (1905). A major supply depot in World War I, Vladivostok was occupied by Allies (incl. Americans) 1918–20; Japanese occupation troops stayed on till 1922.

Vlaminck, Maurice de (vlämĕk'), 1876–, French painter. Best known for landscapes of later period, but some of best work was done in early fauvist phase.

Vlissingen, Netherlands: see FLUSHING.

Vlona, Vionë, Vlora, or **Vlorë,** Albania: see VALONA.

Vltava, river of Czechoslovakia: see MOLDAU.

vocational training, designed to advance a person's general proficiency, especially in relation to his present or future occupation. Prior to Industrial Revolution APPRENTICESHIP system and home were the sources of training. Manual training developed in Scandinavia c.1866 and became popular in U.S. after 1880. While not originally vocational in aim, it evolved into industrial training. Courses in clerical work also started early. Pioneer private trade schools in U.S. were COOPER UNION (1859) and PRATT INSTITUTE (1887), and HAMPTON INSTITUTE (1868) and TUSKEGEE INSTITUTE (1881) for Negroes. The agricultural high school (1888) of Univ. of Minnesota was first regular public vocational high school. Public schools often work closely with industries and trades in establishing curriculums, in guidance programs, and in setting up cooperative training techniques. Theorists in vocational training state its aims as being both cultural and technical. This viewpoint is shown in academic requirements of public vocational schools and in work of continuation schools.

vocative: see CASE.

vodka (vŏd′kŭ), national spirituous drink of Russia, also popular elsewhere in Europe. Best vodka is distilled from rye and barley malt; maize and potatoes are also used. May be over 90% alcohol.

voice, grammatical category according to which an action is referred to as done by the subject (active) or to the subject (passive). In Latin, voice, like mood and tense, is a category of INFLECTION.

Voisin, La, French poisoner: see POISON AFFAIR.

Vojvodina or **Voivodina** (both: voi″vōdē′nä), autonomous province (8,683 sq. mi.; pop. 1,661,632), N Serbia, Yugoslavia; cap. Novi Sad. Drained by Danube, Theiss, and Sava rivers, it is an extremely fertile region (grain, fruit, grapes, vegetables, cattle). Conquered from Hungary by Turkey in 16th cent., it reverted to Hungary 1699, passed to Yugoslavia after World War I. It includes the W Banat of Temesvar. Population includes Serbs, Croats, Magyars, Rumanians, Slovaks.

volcano, term used for aperture in earth's crust from which gas and rock (molten and solid) are discharged and also for a conical mountain built up by erupted material. Often there is a cavity, or crater, at the summit. Eruptions range from the quiet type (Hawaiian) to the violently explosive (Mont Pelée and Krakatoa). The explosive force, which may blow a whole mountain to bits, results from accumulation of superheated steam and other gases held back by a plug of hardened lava in the vent. Torrents of rain often accompany this type of eruption.

Volcano Islands, island group (11 sq. mi.; pop. 1,154), W Pacific. Iwo JIMA is chief island. Annexed 1887 by Japan. Governed by U.S. after World War II. Sulphur is mined.

Volga (vŏl′gŭ), river, 2,290 mi. long, European RSFSR; largest river of Europe. Rising in the Valdai Hills and winding E past Gorki to Kazan, then S past Kuibyshev and Stalingrad, it forms a wide delta at Astrakhan near its mouth on the Caspian Sea. Chief tributaries: Kama and Oka. Volga basin comprises one third of European USSR. Linked by the Mariinsk system with the Baltic Sea and the Baltic-White Sea Canal, by the Moscow Canal with Moscow, and by the Volga-Don Canal (completed 1952) with the Don, its carries c.30% of total river freight of USSR and is navigable late April to late Nov. from Shcherbakov and early March to mid-Dec. at Astrakhan. There are numerous dams and hydroelectric stations along the upper Volga, notably at SHCHERBAKOV; its waters are used to irrigate the vast steppes of the lower Volga region. The "Mother Volga" of Russian folklore, it has always played an immensely important part in the life of the Russian people and was the lifeline of Russian colonization in the E.

Volhynia (vŏlĭ′nyŭ), Pol. *Wolyn,* Rus. *Volyn,* historic region, NW Ukraine, one of oldest Slavic settlements. After the breakup of the duchy of Galich-Vladimir (see GALICH; VLADIMIR-VOLYNSKI) in the 14th cent., Volhynia was disputed between Poland and Lithuania. The Polish-Lithuanian Union of Lublin (1569) made Volhynia into a quasi-autonomous Polish province. It passed to Russia in the Polish partitions of 1793 and 1795. Its W section (incl. LUTSK) was again under Polish rule 1921–39; its cession to USSR was confirmed 1945.

Vollard, Ambroise, (äbrŏŏäz′ vôlär′), 1867–1939, French art dealer and publisher. Noted for early recognition and sponsorship of such artists as Van Gogh, Cézanne, and Roualt. Published fine editions illustrated with original prints by many of the modern masters, notably Picasso.

volleyball, outdoor or indoor game played on level court. Upright net, top of which is 8 ft. high, divides court (60 ft. long and 30 ft. wide) in half. Volleyball was originated (1895) by William C. Morgan at Holyoke, Mass.

Vologda (vô′lŭgdŭ), city (pop. 95,194), N European RSFSR, on Vologda R. Rail junction; dairy center. Founded 1147. Ruled at first by Novgorod, it became the cap. of a principality (1397); fell to Moscow 1481. Old kremlin has 18th-cent. episcopal palace (now museum). Cathedral of St. Sophia dates from 16th cent.; Spasso-Priluki monastery from 1371.

Volos (vô′lôs), city (pop. 51,134), E Greece, in SE Thessaly, on Gulf of Volos or Pagasaean Gulf, an inlet of Aegean Sea. Mfg. and trading center (textiles, tobacco, agr. produce). Damaged in World War II.

Volscians (vŏl′shŭnz) or **Volsci** (vŏl′sī), people of anc. Italy, SE of the Alban Hills. With the Samnites they opposed Rome. Story of CORIOLANUS reflects fierceness of their attacks. In the 4th cent. B.C., they were conquered and Romanized.

Volsinii (vŏlsī′nēī), anc. Etruscan city, probably on the site of Orvieto. Sacked by Romans (280 B.C.), it was refounded near L. Bolsena.

Volstead Act, 1919, Federal prohibition act providing for enforcement of Eighteenth Amendment.

Volsungasaga (vŏl′sōŏng-gùsä′gù), [Icelandic,= saga of the Volsungs], Icelandic prose saga founded, apparently, on earlier poetic materials (kin to German NIBELUNGENLIED) and probably assembled in the 12th or 13th cent. Its heroine, Gudrun, accomplishes the ruin of the Volsungs, who are led by Sigurd. Brynhild (see BRUNHILD) is Sigurd's beloved, whom he betrays. Elements of this saga were used by Wagner in his operas based on the Nibelungenlied.

volt [for A. Volta], unit of electromotive force (emf); both emf and difference in potential are measured in volts. Instrument for measuring emf is a type of GALVANOMETER. International volt is emf that produces current of one AMPERE when acting on conductor with resistance of one OHM.

Volta, Alessandro, Conte (älēssän′drō kōn′tä vōl′tä), 1745–1827, Italian physicist. He invented the electrophorus, a device for producing electric charge by induction and **Volta's** (or **voltaic**) pile: a stack of metal disks (of two different metals, e.g., copper and zinc, arranged alternately). Disks of cloth or paper moistened with an electrolyte are placed between disks. Each set of two disks corresponds to a voltaic cell and the whole to an electric battery. **Voltaic cell** is an electric cell consisting of two dissimilar metal plates suspended, without touching each other, in a solution of an acid or a salt. The VOLT is named for Volta.

voltaic cell: see VOLTA, ALESSANDRO.

Voltaire, François Marie Arouet de (fräswä′ märē′ ärwä′ dù vôltēr′), 1694–1778, French philosopher and author, whose original name was Arouet. He was the leading figure of 18th-cent. ENLIGHTENMENT. Two imprisonments in the Bastille (1717, 1726) and his visit to England (1726–29) taught him hatred of arbitrary absolutism and admiration of English liberalism. His tempestuous friendship with Frederick II of Prussia, to whose court he came in 1749, ended with Voltaire's flight from Berlin (1753) but was later resumed from a safe distance. Having won a large fortune through speculation, Voltaire bought himself an estate, first at Geneva, then at near-by Ferney (1758). His trip to Paris (1778) and the triumphal acclaim he received there were too much for him, and he died. Voltaire's work is immense (rev. and enl. ed., 52 vols., 1883). Among his many tragedies, in the classic style, *Zaïre* (1732) is probably the best. His *Letters concerning the English Nation* (in Eng., 1732; in Fr., 1733) exerted a profound influence. His great historical works—*Siècle de Louis XIV* (1751) and *Essai sur l'histoire générale et sur les mœurs et l'esprit des nations* (7 vols., 1756)—show a new approach to history, with the chief emphasis on cultural and economic developments. Most widely read today are his short "philosophical novels," notably *Candide* (1759) an unsurpassed masterpiece of flippant satire. His philosophy was rationalist to the point of shallowness; his religious outlook was deistic ("If God did not exist, He would have to be invented") and aggressively tolerant (*Écrasez l'infâme!*—Crush the infamous one! —was his slogan against religious fanaticism). In his political and social views, he inclined toward conservatism; the French Revolution, often blamed on him, would have horrified him. Voltaire was a propagandist in several *causes célèbres* involving victims of religious and political persecution. His correspondence was tremendous and fully reveals the glitter and polish of his style.

Volta's (voltaic) pile: see VOLTA, ALESSANDRO.

Volterra, Daniele da (dänyā'lā dä vōltĕr'rä), 1509–66, Italian painter and sculptor; pupil of Michelangelo. Real name was Ricciarelli. Famous for his *Descent from the Cross* in Church of Trinità dei Monti, Rome.

Volterra, town (pop. 11,704), Tuscany, central Italy. A powerful Etruscan town in antiquity. Has well-preserved Etruscan and medieval walls; 10th-cent. cathedral; oldest town hall in Tuscany. Medieval fortress (14th–15th cent.) is now a prison.

voltmeter: see GALVANOMETER.

Volturno (vōltōōr'nō), river, 109 mi. long, S Italy, flowing from Apennines past Capua into Tyrrhenian Sea. Scene of Garibaldi's victory over Bourbon army (1860) and of a crossing by U.S. troops, after heavy fighting (Oct., 1943).

volume, measure of solid content. Units of measurement are either the cube of a linear unit (e.g., cubic inches or cubic centimeters) or units of dry and liquid measure (e.g., bushel and gallon, and in metric system, the liter). Formulas for some common solids (B = area of base; h = height; r = radius; l = length; w = width):

Solid	Volume	Solid	Volume
cube	1^3	right rectangular	
prism	Bh	parallelepiped	lwh
pyramid	$\frac{1}{3}Bh$	right circular cylinder	$\pi r^2 h$
sphere	$\frac{4}{3}\pi r^3$	right circular cone	$\frac{1}{3}\pi r^2 h$

Volunteers of America, religious and philanthropic body founded (1896) by Gen. Ballington Booth and his wife, Maud Ballington Booth (see BOOTH, family). The volunteers aim to act as auxiliary to churches; converts are urged to join church of their preference. They also conduct services, missions, and Sunday schools, and foster many welfare activities, notably the Volunteer Prison League, founded (1896) by Mrs. Booth.

Von. For German names beginning thus, see proper name; e.g., for Von Bismarck, see BISMARCK.

Vondel, Joost van den (vôn'dŭl), 1587–1679, Dutch poet and dramatist. His many works include translations, polemical and religious poetry, and over 30 dramas. His most famous play, *Lucifer* (1654), may have been known to Milton.

voodooism, name for beliefs and practices attributed to Negroes of West Indies (esp. Haiti) and S U.S. Rites are linked with serpent worship and in extreme cases with human sacrifice and cannibalistic ceremonies. Ritual is reminiscent of magical observances practiced by many peoples.

Voragine, Jacobus de: see JACOBUS DE VORAGINE.

Vorarlberg (fōr"ärl'bĕrk), westernmost province (1,004 sq. mi.; pop. 193,715) of Austria, in the Alps; cap. Bregenz (on L. of Constance). Dairying; textile and embroidery mfg. Many resorts (esp. for winter sports). Acquired piecemeal by the Hapsburgs in 14th–16th cent., it was administered as a crownland by Tyrol 1523–1918.

Voronezh (vŏrô'nĕsh), city (pop. 326,836), S central European RSFSR, on Voronezh R. near its confluence with the Don. Industrial center (synthetic rubber, locomotives, aircraft, machinery, processed foods). University; medical, agr., and engineering schools. City was largely destroyed in World War II, when a German advance was stopped here (1942–43).

Voronoff, Serge (sĕrzh' vôrônôf'), 1866–1951, French surgeon. He transplanted animal (chiefly monkey) glands in treating thyroid deficiency in children and for rejuvenation in old age.

Voroshilov, Kliment Yefremovich (vŭrŭshĕ'lŭf), 1881–, Russian field marshal. Won fame as Red Army commander in civil war. Commissar for defense 1925–40. Commanded defense of Leningrad in World War II. Became chairman of the presidium of the supreme council of the USSR (i.e., president of USSR) in 1953, after Stalin's death.

Voroshilov, city (pop. 70,628), S Maritime Territory, RSFSR, in Far Eastern Siberia. Junction of Trans-Siberian RR and Chinese Eastern RR.

Voroshilovgrad (–gräd"), city (pop. 213,007), SE Ukraine, in Donets Basin; named Lugansk till c.1935. Produces locomotives, steel pipes, and machinery. German-held (1941–43) in World War II.

vortex (vôr'tĕks), mass of fluid (liquid or gas) whose particles have rotary motion. In theory, vortex motion is considered in a frictionless fluid where motion would be continuous and could be neither created nor destroyed. Since no frictionless fluid exists, a continuous supply of energy is needed to maintain vortex motion.

vorticism (vôr'tĭsĭzŭm), short-lived 20th-cent. school of art related to cubism but stressing rhythmic movement. Chief exponent was Gaudier-Brzeska, but movement was strongest in England.

Vos, Cornelis de (kôrnā'lĭs dù vōs'), 1585–1651, Flemish painter of the school of Rubens.

Vosges (vōzh), department (2,279 sq. mi.; pop. 342,315), E France, in Lorraine; cap. Épinal. Borders in E on **Vosges** mountain range, which extends N from Belfort for c.120 mi. Pastures; pine forests; vineyards on E slope (in Alsace). Resorts (notably Plombières). Highest point: Ballon de Guebwiller (4,672 ft.).

Vouet, Simon (sēmō vwä'), 1590–1649, French portrait and decorative painter in service of Louis XIII.

Vouvray (vōōvrā'), town (pop. 1,567), Indre-et-Loire dept., N central France, on Loire R. near Tours. Famous white and rosé wines.

Vrchlicky, Jaroslav (yä'rôsläf vŭrkh'lĭtskē), 1853–1912, Czech writer, whose real name was Emil Bohuslav Frida. By many translations and his own writings he immensely forwarded modern Czech literature.

Vries, Hugo de (hü'gō dù vrēs'), 1848–1935, Dutch botanist. His studies of evolution led to his rediscovery (reported in 1900) of Mendel's laws of heredity and to his development of the theory of mutation.

Vulcan, Roman fire-god, same as Greek HEPHAESTUS.

vulcanization (vŭl"kŭnŭzā'shŭn), treatment of rubber to give it certain qualities, e.g., strength, elasticity, and resistance to solvents, and to render it unaffected by moderate heat and cold. It is usually accomplished by process invented by Charles Goodyear in 1839. Rubber and sulphur are mixed (as a rule with an organic accelerator) and usually placed in molds and subjected to heat and pressure. Cold vulcanization process (treating rubber with a bath or vapors of a sulphur compound) was developed by Alexander Parkes in 1846. For most ordinary purposes natural rubbers as well as many synthetics are vulcanized.

Vulgate (vŭl′gāt) [Latin *Vulgata editio* = common edition], most ancient extant version of the whole Bible; the official, Latin version of the Roman Catholic Church. Made by St. Jerome to replace the Old Latin version (the Itala). Old Testament is a translation of the Hebrew Masoretic text; New Testament is a careful revision of the Old Latin text. Jerome translated Tobias, Judith, and the additions to Daniel of the deuterocanonical books of the Old Testament; the rest are still in the Old Latin text. In 1546 the council of Trent made the Vulgate the official version of the Church; in 1592 the official text with no variants was promulgated by Clement VIII. The order of books is accepted as Western canon. All subsequent editions published with the Church's imprimatur represent this Clementine edition. In 20th cent., the Benedictines,

deputed by the Holy See, began a thorough revision of the Vulgate.

vulture (vŭl′chŭr), bird of prey of temperate and tropical regions. It eats chiefly carrion. Old World vultures are similar to hawks. New World vultures are of another family which includes CONDOR, turkey buzzard, and black vulture.

Vyatka, RSFSR: see KIROV.

Vyborg (vē′bôrg), Finnish *Viipuri,* Swed. *Viborg,* city (pop. 56,687), NW European RSFSR, NW of Leningrad, near Finnish border; a Baltic port on Gulf of Finland. Chartered 1403, it was ceded by Sweden to Russia 1721; inc. with Finland (then under Russian sovereignty) 1812. It remained Finnish until 1940, when it was ceded to USSR. Though recaptured by Finnish forces in World War II, it was finally awarded to USSR in 1947.

Vyshinsky, Andrei Yanuarievich: see VISHINSKY.

Vytautas, grand duke of Lithuania: see WITOWT.

W, chemical symbol of the element WOLFRAM.

Waadt, Switzerland: see VAUD.

Waal (väl), main arm of Rhine R., central Netherlands. Branches off the Rhine near German border and flows W to join the Meuse near Gorinchem. Joined rivers form the upper Merwede.

Waals, Johannes Diderik van der (yōhä′nùs dē′dùrĭk vän dùr väls′), 1837–1923, Dutch physicist. Won 1910 Nobel Prize for evolving an equation expressing equilibrium of states of matter for homogeneous substances when pressure, volume, and temperature are stated in terms of critical constants for each substance.

Wabash, (wô′băsh″), city (pop. 10,621), NE Ind., on Wabash R. and WSW of Fort Wayne; settled 1835. Trade center of agr. area with mfg. of electronic equipment and furniture.

Wabash, river rising in W central Ohio near Ind. line and flowing 475 mi. SW across Ind. to the Ohio. Forms Ind.-Ill. line below Terre Haute.

WAC (Women's Army Corps), created in 1942 in World War II to enlist women for noncombatant duty in the army. Directed by Oveta Culp Hobby until 1945. Congressional bill of 1948 estab. Women's Auxiliary Corps within regular army.

Wace (wās, wäs), c.1100–1174, Norman-French poet, author of a British chronicle, *Roman de Brut.*

Wachusett Reservoir (wôchoō′sĭt), central Mass., near Clinton; built 1897–1905. Receives some water from QUABBIN RESERVOIR; supplies Boston area.

Waco (wā′kō), city (pop. 84,706), E central Texas, on Brazos R. below mouth of Bosque R.; laid out 1849. Market of rich cotton area and rail, air, highway trading and shipping center, it has mfg. of tires, cloth, clothing, glass, and drugs. Near by is L. Waco on Bosque R. Here are BAYLOR UNIVERSITY and a VA hospital.

Wade, Benjamin Franklin, 1800–1878, U.S. Senator from Ohio (1851–69). Advocate of radical Reconstruction; co-author of Wade-Davis Bill, vetoed by Pres. Lincoln in favor of more lenient program.

Wadham College: see OXFORD UNIVERSITY.

Wadsworth, city (pop. 7,966), N Ohio, SW of Akron. Mfg. of matches, valves, and iron products.

Wafd (wŏft), Egyptian political party, founded 1919 by ZAGHLUL PASHA. It aimed to free Egypt from British influence and to bring about social and economic reforms. Between 1924 and 1952 the Wafd dominated the parliament, which was opposed and dissolved several times by King Fuad I and his successor, Farouk I. After 1927 the party's leader was NAHAS PASHA. Opponents have accused the Wafd of being committed less to principles than to personalities and even of being implicated in assassinations. Dissolved in early 1953 by Gen. Naguib, who assumed control of the government in Sept., 1952.

wages, payment, in goods, services, or money, for work done. Wages reckoned in money are called nominal wages; real wages are revealed by the amount of goods that the money will buy. Theories of wages have been proposed by David Ricardo and Karl Marx.

Wages and Hours Act, also called the Fair Labor Standards Act, is intended to establish min. living standards for workers in interstate commerce and to abolish oppressive child labor. Passed in 1938, it was amended in 1950 so as to provide for a 40-hr. week and a min. hourly wage of 75 cents.

Wagner, Cosima: see WAGNER, RICHARD.

Wagner, Honus (wăg′nùr), 1874–, American baseball infielder. Fine fielding shortstop with Pittsburgh Pirates. Had lifetime batting average of .329, led Natl. League in batting eight times (1900, 1903–4, 1906–9, 1911), made 3,430 base hits.

Wagner, Richard (väg′nùr), 1813–1883, German composer of operas. A difficult, violent person, he made enemies easily, attracting as friends chiefly other defiers of convention such as Franz Liszt and Friedrich Nietzsche. Many consider him the greatest operatic genius of all time. He used a continuous flow of melody instead of the sharply differentiated recitative and aria and called his operas music dramas to signify their fusion of text and music. His librettos, which he wrote himself, were drawn chiefly from the vast store of Germanic legend and literature. His works include

W

Rienzi (1840); *Der fliegende Holländer* (The Flying Dutchman, 1843); *Tannhäuser* (1843–45); *Lohengrin* (1846–48); his great tetralogy, *Der Ring des Nibelungen*, comprising *Das Rheingold* (1853–54), *Die Walküre* (1854–56), *Siegfried* (completed 1871), and *Die Götterdämmerung* (completed 1874); *Tristan und Isolde* (1857–59); *Die Meistersinger von Nürnberg* (1862–67), his only comic opera; and his final work, *Parsifal* (1877–82). After moving to Bayreuth in 1872, he built a theater adequate for a proper performance of his works. His second wife, **Cosima Wagner**, 1837–1930, daughter of Franz Liszt and the Comtesse d'Agoult, was wife (1857–69) of Hans von Bülow. She was married to Wagner in 1870. She continued the Bayreuth festivals after his death. Their son, **Siegfried Wagner**, 1869–1930, was known as a conductor.

Wagner, Robert F(erdinand) (wăg'nùr), 1877–1953, U.S. Senator from N.Y. (1927–49), b. Germany. A leader in directing New Deal legislation (e.g., act establishing NATIONAL LABOR RELATIONS BOARD).

Wagner-Jauregg, Julius (yōō'lyŏōs väg'nùr-you'rĕk), 1857–1940, Austrian neurologist. A pioneer of fever therapy, he treated paresis by inoculation with organisms causing malaria; for this work he won 1927 Nobel Prize in Physiology and Medicine.

Wagram (vä'gräm), town (pop. 3,917), Lower Austria, NE of Vienna, in the Marshfield; officially called Deutsch-Wagram. Here on July 5–6, 1809, Napoleon I won a brilliant victory over Austria.

Wahabi (wähä'bē), Puritanical reform movement in Islam, begun by Mohammed ibn Abd al-Wahab (1703?–1787). Rejects veneration of saints, ostentatious rites, luxurious living. The Saud tribe adopted the religion and managed to gain control of most of Arabia. Ottoman rulers were unable to stamp out the troublesome Wahabi movement, which finally triumphed in Saudi Arabia as the official religion.

Wahiawa (wä'hēuwä'), city (pop. 8,369), Oahu, T.H., NW of Honolulu, in pineapple district.

Wahlstatt, Silesia: see LIEGNITZ.

wahoo: see BURNING BUSH.

Wahpeton (wô'pĭtùn), city (pop. 5,125), SE N.Dak., on Red R. Dairy center with U.S. Indian school.

Waialeale (wī'ä"lää'lä), peak, 5,080 ft. high, central Kauai, T.H. Contains Waimea Canyon. Average yearly rainfall on summit, 476 in. Shares, with Cherrapunji, India, record of having world's heaviest rainfall.

Waianae Range (wī'ùnī'), SW Oahu, T.H. Rises to 4,030 ft. in Mt. Kaala, highest point on island.

Waikiki (wī'kēkē'), bathing beach, Honolulu, T.H. Site of Fort De Russy.

Wailuku (wīlōō'kōō), city (pop. 7,424), N Maui, T.H. Island's largest town and tourist center.

Wainwright, Jonathan M(ayhew), 1883–, American general. In World War II he led fight in Philippine Isls. which ended in surrender of Bataan and Corregidor. Prisoner of war 1942–45.

Waite, Morrison Remick (wāt), 1816–88, Chief Justice of U.S. Supreme Court (1874–88).

waits, in England, band of itinerant musicians who celebrate Christmas by the nocturnal open-air singing of carols or other seasonable music. Waits were originally watchmen, who blew a horn or sang a tune to mark the hours or change of guard. The custom survives especially in rural communities.

Wakamatsu (wäkä'mätsōō), city (pop. 78,694), N Kyushu, Japan, on Sea of Japan; chief coal-loading port of Japan.

Wakayama (wäkä'yämù), city (pop. 171,800), S Honshu, Japan, on Inland Sea. Railroad and mfg. center. Site of castle (16th cent.) of Hideyoshi.

Wakefield, Edward Gibbon, 1796–1862, British statesman. His views on colonial affairs led to establishment (1836) of South Australian colony. His New Zealand Land Co. (1839) colonized that country.

Wakefield, county borough (pop. 60,380), cap. of West Riding of Yorkshire, England. A center of cloth in-

dustry since 14th cent., it also has varied mfg. An important farm center. Richard, duke of York, was slain in battle here in 1460. Towneley miracle plays originated here.

Wakefield, town (pop. 19,633), NE Mass., N of Boston; settled 1639. Shoes, dies, and knit goods.

Wakefield, family estate of George Washington, E Va., near Potomac R. and E of Fredericksburg. John Washington settled here 1665. Original buildings burned; period buildings reconstructed. Made national monument 1930.

Wake Forest, town (pop. 3,704), E central N.C., NNE of Raleigh. Seat of Wake Forest Col. (Baptist; mainly for men; 1833).

Wake Island, atoll and three islets, central Pacific, between Hawaii and Guam. Discovered 1796 by British. Claimed 1900 by U.S. and made a U.S. naval reservation 1934. Became Pan-American air base 1935. Appropriations made 1939 for naval air base and submarine base. Attacked by Japanese on Dec. 7, 1941; fell Dec. 23, after heroic defense by small marine garrison. Japan surrendered it Sept., 1945.

wake-robin: see TRILLIUM.

Waksman, Selman Abraham (wäks'mùn), 1888–, American microbiologist, b. Russia. Won 1952 Nobel Prize in Physiology and Medicine for his work as codiscoverer of the antibiotic substance streptomycin and for its value in treating tuberculosis.

Walachia or **Wallachia** (both: wälä'kĕù, wù–), historic division (29,575 sq. mi.; pop. 6,707,271), S Rumania, in the lower Danubian plain; chief city Bucharest. Largely agr., it has rich oil fields at Ploesti. It consists of two historic provinces—Muntenia or Greater Walachia (E) and Oltenia or Lesser Walachia (W). Part of Roman Dacia, it was overrun by many invaders. The native Rumanians (called Vlachs or Walachs by their Slavic neighbors) estab. a principality c.1290. Its later history paralleled that of its sister principality, Moldavia, with which it was united in 1859 (see MOLDAVIA).

Walcheren (väl'khùrùn), island, area 80 sq. mi., Zeeland prov., SW Netherlands, in North Sea at entrance to Scheldt estuary. Chief cities: Middleburg, Flushing. Its capture by British commandos in World War II opened up port of Antwerp for Allied use (Nov. 1, 1944).

Wald, Lillian D., 1867–1940, American social worker and pioneer in public health nursing. The visiting nurse service she founded in 1893 became the nucleus of the Henry St. Settlement in New York city.

Waldeck (väl'dĕk), former principality (433 sq. mi.; 1910 pop. 61,707), W Germany; cap. Arolsen. Agr., forests. A county from c.1200, Waldeck was united with PYRMONT and raised to a principality in the 17th cent. Waldeck-Pyrmont was incorporated with Prussia in 1922, Pyrmont becoming part of Hanover prov. and Waldeck of Hesse-Nassau prov.

Waldeck-Rousseau, René (rùnä' väldĕk'-rōōsō'), 1846–1904, French premier (1899–1902). Secured presidential pardon for Capt. Dreyfus. Initiated anticlerical legislation but opposed extreme measures.

Waldemar (väl'dùmär), Dan. *Valdemar,* kings of Denmark. **Waldemar I** (the Great), 1131–82, became king 1157, after defeating two rivals. Helped Henry the Lion and Albert the Bear in subjugating the Wends; codified Danish law; gained territory in Norway. His second son, **Waldemar II**, 1170–1241, reigned 1202–41. Extended Danish control over Estonia but was forced to relinquish control over Schwerin after his defeat at Bornhöved (1227). **Waldemar IV** (Valdemar Atterdag), c.1320–1375, reigned 1340–75. At his accession, he found Denmark dismembered by foreign rulers, but by 1361 he had succeeded in reuniting his kingdom. He conquered Skane, in violation of a treaty with the Swedish king; obtained temporary possession of Gotland through his victory over Hanseatic League (1362), but was later defeated by the Hanseatic towns and forced to accept the Treaty of STRALSUND (1370).

His daughter MARGARET was to unite Denmark, Norway, and Sweden.

Walden Pond: See CONCORD, Mass.

Waldenses (wôlděn'sēz), Fr. *Vaudois,* Protestant sect, arising from the Poor Men of Lyons, organized by Peter Waldo (d. 1217), a lay preacher, who laid great stress on poverty. Adopted unorthodox views and were condemned by Pope Lucius III in 1184. Persisted in Dauphiné until the persecution of 1487 and continued in Piedmont. Met with German and Swiss Protestants in 1532. In 1655 the French and Charles Emmanuel II of Savoy campaigned against them. When the Edict of Nantes was revoked (1686) Henri Arnaud led the Waldenses to Switzerland, later led them back. Assured of toleration after the French Revolution, they were granted full rights by Charles Albert of Savoy in 1848.

Waldseemüller, Martin (vält'zämü''lùr), 1470?–1522?, German cosmographer. The first cartographer to call the New World *America* (1507).

Waldstein, Albrecht von: see WALLENSTEIN.

Wales, Welsh *Cymru* (kōōm'rē), region (8,012 sq. mi.; pop. 2,956,986, with border co. of Monmouth, included administratively in Wales), W Great Britain, a peninsula W of England. Politically united with England since 1536. Counties of Wales proper are (in the N) Anglesey, Caernarvonshire, Denbighshire, Flintshire, Merionethshire, and Montgomeryshire and (in the S) Cardiganshire, Radnorshire, Brecknockshire, Pembrokeshire, Caermarthenshire, and Glamorganshire. Peninsula (130 mi. long N–S; 37–92 mi. wide) is bounded by Irish Sea (N), St. Georges Channel (W), and Bristol Channel (S), and is deeply indented by Cardigan Bay. Wales is almost entirely occupied by Cambrian Mts., rising to 3,560 ft. in Mt. Snowdon. Rivers include Clwyd, Conway, Teifi, Dovey, Mawddoch, Dee, Severn, and Wye. Region has kept its distinctive culture. Half population speaks Welsh in addition to English, and c.100,000 speak only Welsh. Central Highlands and N counties are pastoral, agr., and thinly populated. Modern wealth of Wales is in great coalfields and industry in S, which has cities of Cardiff, Swansea, Rhondda, and Merthyr Tydfil. Roman impress upon Wales was light, and Anglo-Saxon conquest of E England little affected Welsh. There were fierce border wars as kingdoms of heptarchy grew; King Offa supposedly built Offa's Dyke to mark boundary between Mercia and Wales. Welsh poetry, music, and learning (see EISTEDDFOD) flourished despite continued invasion. William I recognized power of Welsh (see WELSH MARCHES) who resisted through 200 years of guerrilla warfare. Conquest of Wales was completed (1282) by Edward I, who originated English custom of making eldest son of the king prince of Wales. In 15th cent. Owen Glendower led a revolt, and Owen Tudor (whose grandson Henry VII became first Tudor Monarch) was involved in Wars of the Roses. Act of Union (1536) abolished all law at variance with that of British and estab. English as legal language. Reformation came slowly to Wales. Later many turned to CALVINISTIC METHODIST CHURCH. This bolstered Welsh Nationalism, one of world's most successful nonpolitical nationalistic movements. Industrial Revolution exploited mineral wealth. Resulting shift of population promoted emigration (esp. to U.S.). In late 19th cent. S Wales became chief coal-exporting region of world. In late 1920s and '30s Wales suffered heavily from economic decline. Industrial boom of World War II and government's control of mines improved situation. The Univ. of Wales (founded 1893) has four constituent colleges—Aberystwyth (1872), Cardiff (1883), Bangor (1884), and Swansea (1920).

Walewska, Countess Maria (märē'ä välěf'skä), 1789–1817, Polish noblewoman. Napoleon met her at Warsaw in 1807 and made her his mistress. She bore him a son, **Comte Alexandre Walewski,** 1810–68, who served as a diplomat under Napoleon III (foreign minister, 1855–60) and played an important part in the reforms of the "Liberal Empire."

Walhalla, in Germanic mythology: see VALHALLA.

Walhalla (wŏlhă'lù), city (pop. 1,463), NE N.Dak., near Canadian line and on Pembina R. Resort center for Pembina Mts.

Walker, James J(ohn), 1881–1946, mayor of New York city (1925–32). Immensely popular with voters, he resigned after investigation led by Samuel Seabury disclosed extensive municipal corruption.

Walker, Robert John, 1801–69, American statesman. Name sometimes given as Robert James. U.S. Senator from Miss. (1835–45); advocate of American expansion. U.S. Secretary of the Treasury (1845–49); one of ablest in history of department. Walker Tariff of 1846 helped build up Anglo-American commerce. Governor of Kansas in 1857.

Walker, William, 1824–60, American FILIBUSTER in Nicaragua. "Colonized" Nicaragua in 1855 at request of government at León; capturing Granada, he was "elected" president of Nicaragua, July, 1856. Administration of U.S. Pres. Franklin Pierce vacillated between recognition of his government and probability of antagonizing Great Britain. Surrendered to U.S. navy in May, 1857. Shot by firing squad in Honduras after final attempt to conquer Central America.

Walker Lake, 24 mi. long, W Nev., part of anc. L. Lahontan. Fed by Walker R., but has no outlet.

walking stick or **stick insect,** name for certain leaf insects with long, slender twiglike bodies.

Walküre, German name for VALKYRIES.

Wallace, Alfred Russel, 1823–1913, English naturalist. Independently of Charles Darwin he evolved a theory of EVOLUTION. He pioneered in the modern study of animal geography and postulated an imaginary line (Wallace's line) as the dividing line between Asiatic and Australian fauna in the Malay Archipelago.

Wallace, Henry, 1836–1916, American agr. leader. With his son Henry Cantwell Wallace he founded (1895) newspaper which later was called *Wallace's Farmer;* it became leading agr. journal of country. **Henry Cantwell Wallace,** 1866–1924, was U.S. Secretary of Agriculture (1921–24). His son, **Henry A(gard) Wallace,** 1888–, was U.S. Secretary of Agriculture (1933–41), Vice President of U.S. (1941–45), and U.S. Secretary of Commerce (1945–46). PROGRESSIVE PARTY presidential candidate 1948.

Wallace, Lew(is), 1827–1905, American soldier, diplomat, and novelist, best remembered for highly popular novel *Ben-Hur: a Tale of the Christ* (1880).

Wallace, Sir Richard, 1818–90, English art collector; natural son of marquess of Hertford. His father's collection was given to the government by Lady Wallace. The Wallace Collection, noted for 18th-cent. art, was opened 1900 in Hertford House, London.

Wallace, Sir William, c.1272–1306, Scottish hero in struggle against Edward I. Chief source for his life is poem attributed to Blind Harry. After burning Lanark, he organized an army and routed (1297) English at Stirling. Acted briefly as guardian of realm for John de Baliol. Later captured and executed for treason.

Wallace, city (pop. 3,140), N Idaho, near Mont. line. Trade center in Coeur d'Alene Mts.

Wallaceburg, town (pop. 7,688), S Ont., Canada, on Sydenham R. and NNW of Chatham. Sugar refining, flour milling, and lumbering.

Wallace Collection: see WALLACE, SIR RICHARD.

Wallach, Otto (ô'tō vä'läkh), 1847–1931, German chemist. Won 1910 Nobel Prize for pioneer work on alicyclic compounds; worked also on azotic compounds.

Wallachia, Rumania: see WALACHIA.

Wallack, James William (wŏ'lùk), c.1795–1864, Anglo-American actor and manager. Leading actor (1812–32) at Drury Lane. In U.S. after 1852. His son, **Lester Wallack,** 1820–88, became manager of Wallack's Theater in 1861.

Wallas, Graham, 1858–1932, English political scientist

and sociologist, member of Fabian Society. Noted for psychological analyses of politics.

Walla Walla (wŏ'lŭ wŏ'lŭ), city (pop. 24,102), SE Wash., on Walla Walla R., near Oregon line; settled c.1859 on site of mission of Marcus WHITMAN. Center for rich farm and lumber area with fruit canneries and lumber mills. Seat of Whitman Col. (nonsectarian; coed.; chartered 1859, opened 1866 as Congregationalist seminary, became college 1883). Near by are Walla Walla Col., Fort Walla Walla (estab. 1857; now VA hospital), Whitman Natl. Monument.

Wallenstein or **Waldstein, Albrecht von** (Ger. äl'brěkht fŭn vä'lŭnshtīn, vält'shtīn), 1583–1634, imperialist generalissimo in THIRTY YEARS WAR. For his victories, Emperor Ferdinand II created him duke of Friedland (1625) and of Mecklenburg (1627). After his failure to take Stralsund (1628), his enemies secured his dismissal (1630), but he was recalled in 1632. Defeated by the Swedes at Lützen (1632), he began secret peace negotiations, was accused of treason, and was murdered, probably on the emperor's instigation, by a group of conspirators including his lieutenants Piccolomini and Gallas. He is the subject of a dramatic trilogy by Schiller.

Waller, Edmund, 1606–87, English poet. Banished for plot in behalf of Charles I, he lived in France in exile for years. His first poem, "To a King on His Return," appeared in *Rex Redux* (1633). His popular *Poems* (1645 and later eds.) contained courtly lyrics such as "Go, Lovely Rose" and "On a Girdle."

wallflower, Old World biennial or perennial (*Cheiranthus cheiri*) with fragrant, stocklike flowers in shades of red, brown, and yellow; often cultivated in America. It is also called gillyflower. The orange-flowered Siberian wallflower (*Erysimum asperum*) is found wild and cultivated in North America.

Wallingford, borough (pop. 11,994) in Wallingford town (pop. 16,976), S Conn., NNE of New Haven. Mfg. of silverware (since 1835), metal goods, and plastics. Choate School for boys (1896) is here.

Wallington, borough (pop. 8,910), NE N.J., SE of Passaic. Machinery, steel tubing, and plastics.

Wallis, John (wŏ'lĭs), 1616–1703, English mathematician. He systematized use of formulas, introduced use of symbol ∞ for infinity, studied quadrature of curves.

Wallis, Switzerland: see VALAIS.

Wallis and Futuna Islands (wŏ'lĭs, fōōtōō'nä), French protectorate (c.75 sq. mi.; pop. 6,770), S Pacific, 250 mi. W of Samoa. Comprises Wallis and Hoorn Isls.

Walloons (wŭlōōnz', wŏ–), the French-speaking people of Belgium, in contrast to the Flemings of the N provinces. More specifically, Walloon is the French dialect spoken in the Liége region. The movement for reviving Walloon literature centered in Liége in the 19th cent. Rivalry between Walloons and Flemings has long been a critical political issue in Belgium. In America, the Dutch indiscriminately called all Huguenot refugees Walloons.

Wallowa Lake (wŭlou'ù), NE Oregon, at foot of Wallowa Mts. Resort; used for irrigation. Drained by Wallowa R. of the Snake system.

Wall Street, narrow street in lower Manhattan, New York city, extending E from Broadway to the East River. Center of one of world's great financial districts. By extension, "Wall St." designates American financial interests.

Walmer (wŏl'mùr), former urban district, now part of Deal, Kent, England. Walmer Castle is official residence of lord warden of the CINQUE PORTS.

walnut, name for several deciduous trees of genus *Juglans,* valued for wood and nuts. Nuts of the Persian or English walnut (*Juglans regia*), which thrives in Calif., are eaten both plain and in confectionery. Nuts of the black walnut (*J. nigra*), native to E U.S., are used for flavoring. The wood is highly valued for furniture. For the white walnut, see BUTTERNUT.

Walnut Canyon National Monument: see NATIONAL PARKS AND MONUMENTS (table).

Walpi (wăl'pē), picturesque Hopi Indian pueblo (pop. c.150), NE Ariz., on mesa NE of Winslow; founded c.1700. Holds Antelope rites (even years), Hopi snake dance (odd years) in Aug. Many of its people have moved to Polacca village, at foot of mesa.

Walpole, Sir Hugh (Seymour), 1884–1941, British novelist, b. New Zealand; author of many popular novels, including *The Cathedral* (1922) and the historical series begun with *Rogue Herries* (1930).

Walpole, Robert, 1st **earl of Orford,** 1676–1745, English statesman. His successful handling of financial wreckage after SOUTH SEA BUBBLE led to his dominance in political life 1721–42. His influence with Caroline of Anspach, wife of George II, led to his becoming in effect first prime minister in English history. In domestic affairs he encouraged trade while reducing land tax to mollify the Tory gentry. In foreign affairs he favored friendship with France; avoidance of war. After War of Jenkins's Ear, leading to War of the Austrian Succession, military reverses forced him to resign in 1742. His son, **Horace** or **Horatio Walpole,** 4th **earl of Orford,** 1717–97, was an author. In 1747 he settled at Twickenham and estab. his Strawberry Hill press. A friend of Thomas Gray, he printed Gray's *Odes* as his first production. His own letters and reminiscences illuminate Georgian England, and his "terror" novel, *The Castle of Otranto* (1764), spurred the Gothic cultural revival.

Walpole, town (pop. 9,109), E Mass., SW of Boston. Machinery, building supplies, and textiles.

walrus (wŏl'rùs, wôl'–), gregarious aquatic mammal (*Odobenus*) of arctic waters, related to seal. There are two similar species, the Atlantic and the Pacific walruses. Adult males reach length of 10–12 ft. and a weight of over a ton. Tusks in male range from 14 to 16 in. long; smaller in female. Formerly walrus was commercial source of walrus ivory (from tusks), leather, and oil.

Walsall (wôl'sôl), county borough (pop. 114,514), Staffordshire, England. Has coal and iron mining, leather-tanning, and varied mfg.

Walsenburg (wôl'sùnbûrg), city (pop. 5,596), S Colo., S of Pueblo, in grain, livestock, coal region.

Walsh, Thomas J(ames), 1859–1933, American statesman, U.S. Senator from Mont. (1913–33). Adviser and supporter of Pres. Wilson. Led investigation of TEAPOT DOME scandal.

Walsingham, village, Norfolk, England. Site of Walsingham Abbey, great shrine of medieval England.

Walter, Bruno, 1876–, German-American conductor, whose name was originally Bruno Walter Schlesinger. He conducted in Germany and Austria until the Nazis forced him to leave. In the U.S. he has conducted the NBC Symphony and at the Metropolitan Opera, and in 1941 he became annual guest conductor of the New York Philharmonic.

Walter, Hubert, d. 1205, English archbishop and statesman. Made archbishop of Canterbury and justiciar (1193), he was virtual ruler of England during absences of Richard I. Made important administrative and tax reforms.

Walter, Thomas Ustick, 1804–87, American architect of the classic revival. As government architect (1851–65) he designed extensions for the CAPITOL at Washington. Works in Philadelphia included main building of Girard Col. and Biddle country home.

Walter of Henley or **Walter de Henley,** 13th cent. English writer on agriculture. His *Husbandry* was for 200 years the authority in England on rural economy.

Walter the Penniless, d. 1096, French Crusader. Setting out in advance of the main army of the First Crusade, his followers plundered the Belgrade area and were set upon by the Bulgarians. They joined with the forces of Peter the Hermit at Constantinople but were routed by the Seljuks in Asia Minor.

Waltham (wôl'thăm), city (pop. 47,187), E Mass., on Charles R. and W of Boston; settled 1634. Metal goods, precision instruments, machinery. Had Waltham Watch Co., 1854–1950. Seat of Brandeis Univ. (1948), first Jewish-sponsored nonsectarian institution of higher education in U.S.

Waltham Holy Cross (wôl'tùm, wôl'thùm) or **Waltham Abbey,** urban district (pop. 8,197), Essex, England. Abbey, built in 1030 to contain miraculous cross found in Somerset, was enlarged by King Harold (who is probably buried here). Nearby are great gunpowder factories. **Waltham Cross,** 1 mi. west, is site of an Eleanor Cross.

Walthamstow (–stō), municipal borough (pop. 121,069), Essex, England; industrial suburb of London.

Walther von der Vogelweide (väl'tùr fùn dĕr fō'gùlvī'dù), c.1170–c.1230, Austrian minnesinger. Considered the finest German lyric poet of the Middle Ages, he wrote love lyrics, religious poems, and *Sprüche* [sayings].

Walton, Ernest Thomas Sinton, 1903–, British physicist, b. Ireland. Shared 1951 Nobel Prize for pioneer work on transmutation of atomic nuclei by means of atomic particles accelerated artificially and used as projectiles.

Walton, Izaak, 1593–1683, English author of *The Compleat Angler; or, The Contemplative Man's Recreation* (1653), a masterpiece on fishing and thought.

Walton, William (Turner), 1902–, English composer. Among his compositions are his *Façade* suite, a musical setting of poems by Edith Sitwell; *Portsmouth Point* (1925) and *Belshazzar's Feast* (1931) for orchestra; a symphony (1935); a viola concerto (1929); a violin concerto (1936–39); and musical scores for the films *Henry V* (1945) and *Hamlet* (1947).

waltz, dance in moderate triple time evolved in 18th cent. from German *Landler.* Viennese waltz made famous by Johann Strauss, father and son. Came to U.S. via England in early 19th cent.

Wanamaker, John (wŏ'nùmākùr), 1838–1922, American merchant, founder of large department stores in Philadelphia and New York city.

Wanaque (wŏ'nùkē), borough (pop. 4,222), NE N.J., NW of Paterson. Wanaque Reservoir is largest in N.J.

Wanchüan, China: see CHANGKIAKOW.

Wandering Jew, legendary Jew who mocked Jesus when He was carrying the Cross and so was doomed to live a wandering life until the Last Judgment.

Wang Ching-wei (wäng' jĭng'-wä'), 1885–1944, Chinese statesman. Originally leader of left wing of Kuomintang but frequently changed sides between 1927 and 1937. Broke with the Nationalists 1938. Headed Japanese puppet government at Nanking (1939–44).

Wang Wei (wäng' wä'), 699–759, Chinese poet and painter. His quatrains delicately portray quiet scenes like those in his few extant paintings.

Wapakoneta (wŏpùkùnĕ'tù), city (pop. 5,797), W Ohio, S of Lima. Mfg. of machinery and toys.

wapiti (wŏ'pĭtē), member of deer family of genus *Cervus.* It is also called elk in America, but is not closely related to elk. Once abundant, it was exterminated in E U.S., is protected in parts of the West.

Wappers, Gustave, Baron (güstäv' väpĕrs', vä'pùrs), 1803–74, Belgian historical and genre painter.

Wapping (wŏp'ĭng), riverside district of Stepney, London, England, near the Tower; a dock section. N terminus of Thames Tunnel to Rotherhithe.

Warbeck, Perkin, 1474?–1499, pretender to English throne. Persuaded by Yorkist adherents that he was son of Edward IV, he proclaimed himself Richard IV in 1497. Captured by forces of Henry VII, he admitted the plot and was hanged.

warbler, name in New World for birds of wood warbler family, small, migratory, insectivorous birds, usually brightly colored and mediocre singers. Old World warblers belong to another family; they are generally fine songsters with dull plumage.

Warburg, Otto Heinrich (ô'tō hīn'rĭkh vär'bōŏrk), 1883–, German physiologist. Won 1931 Nobel Prize in Physiology and Medicine for work on respiratory enzyme.

war crimes. In World War II Allied powers determined to punish Axis war criminals. Crimes were to include aggressive warfare and atrocities in any civilian group (notably extermination of a people or genocide). UN Commission for the Investigation of War Crimes was estab. to compile and classify lists of suspects. In Aug., 1945, U.S., USSR, and Great Britain adopted statute for trying Nazi leaders. Trials held in Nuremberg, Nov., 1945. After voluminous evidence, those sentenced to death in 1946 included Goering, Ribbentrop, and Streicher; Schacht and von Papen were acquitted. Likewise 28 war criminals were tried by 11-nation tribunal in Tokyo (1946–47). Many were also tried in civil courts for crimes committed in war.

Ward, Artemas (är'tĭmùs), 1727–1800, American general in American Revolution. Head of Mass. troops; commanded at siege of Boston (1775), directed fortification of Dorchester Heights.

Ward, Artemus (är'tùmùs), pseud. of Charles Farrar Browne, 1834–67, American humorist, a reporter for the Cleveland *Plain Dealer.* His column, "Artemus Ward's Sayings," with shrewd observations, misspelled words, and quaint turns of speech, was popular.

Ward, Mrs. Humphry, 1851–1920, English novelist; granddaughter of Thomas Arnold. Wrote many sober novels (e.g., *Robert Elsmere,* 1888).

Ward, John Quincy Adams, 1830–1910, American sculptor of portrait statues and monuments. Several of his works are in Central Park, New York city.

Ward, Lester Frank, 1841–1913, American sociologist, developed theory of planned progress called telesis, whereby man through education and development of intellect could direct social evolution. Noted for his *Dynamic Sociology* (1883).

Ward, Nathaniel, 1578–1652, British clergyman, a Puritan minister in Agawam (Ipswich), Mass. (1634–36). There he helped compile Body of Liberties (1641). *The Simple Cobler of Aggawam* (1647) is a lively, crotchety book, arguing for a new theory of constitutional government for England and against women's fashions and religious toleration.

Ward, William George, 1812–82, English Roman Catholic apologist, associated with Newman in the OXFORD MOVEMENT. Ordained an Anglican clergyman, he lost his university degrees after writing *The Ideal of a Christian Church* (1844) and shortly became a Catholic.

ward: see GUARDIAN AND WARD.

war debts, obligations to U.S. incurred by foreign nations in World War I. When U.S. entered war in 1917, allies had little foreign exchange. Credits were extended to them in and after war, in 1922 set at about $3,350,000,000. Payments made, mostly from German reparations, until 1931, when Pres. Hoover proposed moratorium. Lausanne Pact of 1932 reduced reparations in hope U.S. would release claims, but it did not. After 1932 all nations defaulted except Finland and Hungary. For international obligations of World War II, see LEND-LEASE.

War Department, United States, organized (1789) under U.S. Constitution as an executive department of Federal government to administer the military establishment. Reconstituted in 1947 as Dept. of the Army within U.S. Dept of Defense (see DEFENSE, UNITED STATES DEPARTMENT OF).

Ware, Henry, 1764–1845, American clergyman, a founder of Unitarianism in U.S. Opposition to his appointment as Hollis professor of divinity at Harvard (1805) hastened split of the Unitarians from Congregationalists. His son, **Henry Ware,** 1794–1843, pastor and teacher, was editor (1819–22) of first Unitarian organ, *Christian Disciple,* and a leader in development of denomination.

Ware, town (pop. 7,517), with Ware village (pop. 6,217), central Mass., W of Worcester. Textiles.

Wareham (wâr'hăm", wâ'rùm), resort town (pop. 7,569), SE Mass., on inlet of Buzzards Bay. Ships cranberries and shellfish.

Warfield, David, 1866–1951, American actor. Associated with David Belasco who first sponsored him (in *The Auctioneer,* 1901). His acting was memorable in such plays as *The Return of Peter Grimm* (1911).

Warming, Johannes Eugenius Bülow (yōhä'nŭs ûōōgā'nēōōs bü'lou vär'mĭng), 1841–1924, Danish botanist, a founder of the science of plant ecology.

Warm Springs, historic watering place, W Ga., NE of Columbus, famous for studying and treating aftereffects of poliomyelitis. Healthful properties of water known since Indian times. In 1927 F. D. Roosevelt founded Georgia Warm Springs Foundation, to which he donated his large farm here, to help fellow-sufferers from poliomyelitis. He died here at the "Little White House" (now a national shrine), 1945. Near by is Warm Springs city (pop. 557).

Warner, Charles Dudley, 1829–1900, American editor, Contributed to Hartford *Courant* and *Harper's Magazine* travel articles. Edited the "American Men of Letters" series and the "Library of the World's Best Literature." Collaborated with Mark Twain on a novel, *The Gilded Age* (1873).

Warner, Glenn Scobey (Pop Warner), 1871–, American football coach. Three of his Univ. of Pittsburgh football teams were unbeaten (1915–17); at Stanford (1924–32) he produced three Rose Bowl teams.

Warner, Olin Levi, 1844–96, American sculptor of portrait busts and statues. His *Diana,* an ideal figure, is in Metropolitan Mus.

Warner, Seth, 1743–84, hero of American Revolution. One of leaders of Green Mountain Boys. Captured Crown Point in 1775. Shared with John Stark the victory at Bennington in 1777.

Warner Robins, town (pop. 7,986), central Ga., S of Macon. Also called Wellston.

War of 1812, name given to war between U.S. and Great Britain, 1812–15. Partly occasioned by a desire for neutral shipping rights by Americans in a period of strain in Franco-British relations. Practice of IMPRESSMENT of British sailors from American ships was added cause of trouble. EMBARGO ACT OF 1807 and its successors proved ineffective against British and French measures. Actual outbreak of hostilities, however, stemmed from desire of frontiersmen for free land, which could only be obtained at expense of the Indians and the British. The "war hawks" in Congress overrode the moderates; war was declared June 18, 1812. American navy won victories in 1812 that balanced defeat of land forces; in 1813 most American ships were either captured or bottled up in harbor for duration of the war. U.S. victories in a war that brought few decisive military gains for either side were won by Oliver PERRY on L. Erie (Sept. 1813); by W. H. Harrison at Detroit and in battle of the Thames (Oct., 1813); by Thomas MACDONOUGH on L. Champlain (Sept., 1814); and in halting of the British at Fort McHenry (Sept., 1814) after they had taken Washington. Treaty of GHENT ended war on Dec. 24, 1814. Final action occurred after signing of the treaty, when Andrew Jackson decisively defeated the British at New Orleans on Jan. 8, 1815. War quickened growth of American nationalism, opened West for expansion; country embarked on a period of political isolation from Europe.

War Production Board (WPB), estab. (1942) by executive order in World War II to direct war production and the procurement of materials. WPB assigned priorities to deliveries of scarce materials, prohibited nonessential industrial activities. Abolished in 1945.

War Relocation Authority: see RELOCATION CENTER.

Warren, Earl, 1891–, American political leader, governor of Calif. (1943–). Unsuccessful Republican vice presidential nominee in 1948.

Warren, Gouverneur Kemble (gŭvŭrnēr'), 1830–82, American army engineer, Union general in Civil War. Distinguished himself in Seven Days battles; at Gettysburg, where he saved the Round Tops; and in Wilderness campaign. Removed from command by Gen. Philip H. Sheridan in 1865, he was later exonerated.

Warren, Mercy Otis, 1728–1814, American author of propaganda for the patriot cause in the American Revolution and of the first history of that war (1805), b. Mass.; sister of James Otis.

Warren, Robert Penn, 1905–, American writer. When a student at Vanderbilt he contributed to *Fugitive* magazine. Later he was a Southern literary leader. His poetry is much admired. Novels include *Night Rider* (1939), *At Heaven's Gate* (1943), *All the King's Men* (1946), and *World Enough and Time* (1950). Distinguished short stories are collected in *Circus in the Attic and Other Stories* (1948).

Warren, Whitney, 1864–1943, American architect. Joined C. D. Wetmore in a firm known for designing of Grand Central Terminal (1913) and New York hotels (e.g., Ritz-Carlton, Biltmore).

Warren. 1 City (pop. 49,856), NE Ohio, NW of Youngstown; settled 1799. Trade and industrial center in farm area with steel mills and mfg. of metal products, machinery, and electrical apparatus. **2** Borough (pop. 14,849), NW Pa., ESE of Erie; laid out c.1795. Oil refining and mfg. of furniture and metal products. **3** Town (pop. 8,513), E R.I., N of Bristol and on Narragansett Bay arm. Shellfishing; textiles.

Warrensburg, city (pop. 6,857), W Mo., ESE of Kansas City, in agr. area with coal, sandstone, and clay deposits. Clothing mfg. and meat packing.

Warrenton. 1 City (pop. 1,584), E Mo., WNW of St. Louis. Daniel Boone lived here and was at first buried near by. **2** Town (pop. 1,797), N Va., NNW of Fredericksburg; settled 18th cent. Center of horse breeding and racing and fox hunting.

Warrington, village (pop. 13,570), NW Fla., on Pensacola Bay near Pensacola.

Warroad, resort village (pop. 1,276) NW Minn., on L. of the Woods near Canadian line.

Warsaw (wôr'sô), Pol. *Warszawa,* city (1939 pop. c.1,289,000; 1950 pop. c.650,000), cap. of Poland, on the Vistula. Right-bank section of city is called Praga. Commercial and industrial center (chemicals, automobiles, textiles, food products). Archiepiscopal see; seat of a university (founded 1818) and of many cultural institutions. Became cap. of Masovia 15th cent.; replaced Cracow as cap. of Poland 1595. Passed to Prussia 1795; was cap. of duchy of Warsaw (see POLAND) 1807–13. Congress of Vienna (1814–15) created kingdom of Poland, under rule of Russian emperors, with Warsaw as cap. Warsaw led the anti-Russian insurrection of 1830, but had to capitulate 1831. In World War II, 87% of Warsaw proper was destroyed. It fell to the Germans after stubborn resistance (Sept. 27, 1939). The Jewish ghetto (1942 pop. c.500,000) was walled in by the Germans and, after it offered armed resistance, was obliterated after a heavy battle. (Only c.200 Jews were left by 1945.) In Aug.–Oct., 1944, c.250,000 Polish underground fighters lost their lives battling the Germans in Warsaw, while the Russian army, across the Vistula, stood by inactive. The Russians took Warsaw in Jan., 1945. Little was left of the lavish palaces of the great nobility, the churches, and public buildings that had made Warsaw one of Europe's finest cities.

Warsaw. 1 City (pop. 6,625), NE Ind., SE of South Bend. Resort center in lake region. Mfg. of automotive and aircraft products. **2** City (pop. 936), central Mo., on Osage R., at W end of L. of the Ozarks. Fishing and hunting resort.

Warta (vär'tä), Ger. *Warthe,* river, 492 mi. long, Poland and Polish-administered Germany, rising near Cracow and flowing NW past Czestochowa and Poznan into the Oder at Küstrin.

Wartburg (värt'bŏŏrk), castle near Eisenach, Thuringia, central Germany. Built c.1070; later enlarged; renovated 19th cent. Was seat of medieval landgraves of Thuringia. Luther, brought to Wartburg for his safety by the elector of Saxony (1521), completed translation of New Testament here.

Warton, Joseph, 1722–1800, English author of romantic nature poetry and a work on Pope (1756–82), attacking 18th-cent. classicism. His brother, **Thomas Warton,** 1728–90, wrote competent poetry and by his *History of English Poetry* (1774–81) awakened interest in medieval culture. Made poet laureate in 1785.

Warwick, Guy de Beauchamp, earl of (bē'chŭm, wŏ'rĭk), d. 1315, English nobleman. Foremost opponent of Piers Gaveston, whose banishment and later death he procured. His grandson, **Thomas de Beauchamp, earl of Warwick,** d. 1401, was one of lords appellant (1387) who accused courtiers of Richard II of treason and curbed king's power. Imprisoned (1397) for treason, he was released on accession of Henry IV. His son, **Richard de Beauchamp, earl of Warwick,** 1382–1439, was famed as a chivalric knight. Made pilgrimage to Holy Land 1408–10. Served Henry IV and Henry V and was (1429–37) tutor and guardian of Henry VI. His daughter married Richard Neville.

Warwick, Richard Neville, earl of: see NEVILLE, family.

Warwick, Thomas de Beauchamp, earl of: see WARWICK, GUY DE BEAUCHAMP, EARL OF.

Warwick, England: see WARWICKSHIRE.

Warwick, city (pop. 43,028), central R.I., S of Providence; settled 1642 by Samuel GORTON. Mfg. of textiles (since 1794). Has several resort villages. Birthplace of Nathanael Greene. Warwick village nearly destroyed in King Philip's War 1676. Gaspee Point was scene of burning of *Gaspée* 1772.

Warwickshire (wŏ'rĭkshĭr) or **Warwick,** inland county (983 sq. mi.; pop. 1,860,874), central England. Largely pastoral and agr., it also has great industrial centers of Birmingham and Coventry. There are deposits of coal, iron ore, limestone, and fireclay. Rugby is site of famous school. There are remains of abbeys and Kenilworth Castle. County is rich in literary associations. Stratford-on-Avon was Shakspere's birthplace. County town is **Warwick,** municipal borough (pop. 15,350), on the Upper Avon. Castle, begun by Æthelflæd, contains Warwick Vase, antiquities, and art works. St. Mary's Church (partly 12th cent.) has Beauchamp Chapel.

Wasatch Range (wô'sǎch), part of Rocky Mts., extending from Idaho S to central Utah, and rising to 12,008 ft. in Mt. Timpanogos. Most of Utah's important cities are just W.

Wash, the, inlet of North Sea, 20 mi. long and 15 mi. wide, between Lincolnshire and Norfolk, England. Mostly shallow with low, marshy shores; sandbanks impede navigation.

Washburne, Elihu Benjamin, 1816–87, U.S. Representative from Ill. (1853–69), minister to France (1869–77).

Washburn Municipal University: see TOPEKA, Kansas.

Washington, Booker T(aliaferro), c.1858–1915, American Negro educator. Principal of Tuskegee Inst. after 1881, he lectured widely, urged industrial training to produce real efficiency and independence for the Negro. *Up from Slavery* (1901) is his autobiography.

Washington, George, 1732–99, first President of the United States (1789–97), commander in chief of Continental Army in American Revolution, called the Father of His Country, b. Va. First gained public notice late in 1753 by carrying a message of warning from governor of Va. to the French moving into the Ohio country. Defeated at Fort Necessity (1754), he later was an aide to Edward Braddock and commanded Va. militia defending the frontier. Married, settled at Mt. Vernon, he served in Va. house of burgesses (1759–74) and in Continental Congress (1774–75). Named, on June 15, 1775, commander in chief of Continental forces. Forced British evacuation of Boston on March 17, 1776. Defeated in attempt to defend New York city (see LONG ISLAND, BATTLE OF) and at Philadelphia (see BRANDYWINE, BATTLE OF; GERMANTOWN). Victories at Trenton and Princeton followed heroic crossing of the Delaware on Christmas night, 1776. Spent desperate winter of 1777–78 at VALLEY FORGE. Subsequent patriot victories preceded surrender of Cornwallis to Washington on Oct. 19, 1781. Washington presided over Federal Constitutional Convention (1787). Unanimously chosen first President. His efforts to remain aloof from partisan struggles were unsuccessful; he approved of Alexander Hamilton's financial measures, consistently supported conservative policies. His second administration was Federalist, bitterly criticized by Jeffersonians. Weary with political life, Washington refused a third term. His *Farewell Address* (Sept. 17, 1796) contained famous warning against "entangling alliances" with foreign powers. His figure has bulked large in American literature and American legend (e.g., legend of the cherry tree made up by "Parson" WEEMS). His wife, **Martha Washington,** 1731–1802, wealthy widow of Daniel Parke Custis when she married Washington in 1759, was noted for her great common sense, her charm, and her graciousness.

Washington, state (68,192 sq. mi.; pop. 2,378,963), NW U.S., in Pacific Northwest; admitted 1889 as 42d state; cap. OLYMPIA. Other cities are SEATTLE, TACOMA, SPOKANE. Bounded W by Pacific Ocean. Cascade Range runs N–S, divides semi-arid plains of E from Puget Sound area and Olympic Peninsula in W. COLUMBIA R. drains both regions. Chief industries are agr. (esp. fruits, wheat, fishing, lumbering; also diversified mfg. Mining (coal, silver, gold, zinc). Early history centered around fur trade. Became territory in 1853. Advent of railroads boosted lumbering and fishing industries, increased population. Shipbuilding and maritime trades grew, and labor troubles, particularly violent in the days of the I.W.W., gave Wash. a reputation as a radical state. Fruit growing and various types of agr. in 20th cent. brought new wealth, and the "Inland Empire" about Spokane grew more important. Industries developed, and Seattle was one of the great industrial centers of World War II. Continuing development of power and irrigation on the Columbia (e.g., BONNEVILLE DAM; GRAND COULEE DAM) presaged much wider development.

Washington, cap. (pop. 802,178) of the U.S., coextensive (since 1895, when GEORGETOWN became part of Washington) with DISTRICT OF COLUMBIA, on Potomac R. and SW of Baltimore. Argument as to the site (whether in North or South) was settled (1790) by compromise. Land was donated by Md. and Va. George Washington selected exact spot for "Federal City." Building of WHITE HOUSE began 1792, of CAPITOL 1793. Congress first met here in 1800. Jefferson was first President inaugurated here. British captured and sacked city in 1814. Not until 20th cent. did city cease to be unkempt village and assume urban aspect. Designed by Pierre L'ENFANT, laid out by Andrew ELLICOTT, it is a gridiron arrangement of streets cut by diagonal avenues radiating from Capitol and White House. Many parks, monuments, historic sites of city and its environs are in Natl. Capital Parks system. Parks in city include Potomac (has Tidal Basin with Japanese cherry trees), Rock Creek, Anacostia, and Natl. Zoological. Important buildings include LIBRARY OF CONGRESS, Folger Shakespeare Memorial Library, National Archives Building, Supreme Court Building, NATIONAL GALLERY OF ART, and Walter Reed General Hospital. Well-known monuments are WASHINGTON MONUMENT, LINCOLN MEMORIAL, and THOMAS JEFFERSON MEMORIAL. Outside Washington across the Potomac ARLINGTON NATIONAL CEMETERY, MOUNT VERNON, and the Pentagon. Cathedral of St. Peter and St. Paul (Protestant Episcopal; known as National Cathedral or Washington Cathedral) is on Mt. St. Alban. City is seat of CATHOLIC UNIVERSITY OF AMERICA, Georgetown Univ., GEORGE WASHINGTON UNIVERSITY, HOWARD UNIVERSITY, SMITHSONIAN INSTITUTION, BROOKINGS INSTITUTION, CARNEGIE INSTITUTION OF WASHINGTON, American Univ. (coed.; chartered 1893, opened 1914), Trinity Col. (R.C.; for women; 1897), and National War Col. Many Federal agencies, bureaus, and installations are in suburban Md. and Va.

Washington. 1 Town (pop. 344), SW Ark., near Red R.; settled c.1824. One of state's oldest towns. State cap. 1863–65. **2** Town (pop. 2,227), W Conn., NE of New Milford, in hilly resort and agr. area. The green is typical of English 17th-cent. commons. **3** City (pop. 10,987), SW Ind., E of Vincennes; settled 1805. Trade center with railroad shops and wood products. **4** City (pop. 5,902), SE Iowa, SSW of Iowa City. Trade center of agr. area with mfg. of pearl buttons and calendars. **5** City (pop. 6,850), E Mo., on the Missouri and W of St. Louis. Agr. trade center, with mfg. of shoes, clothing, and pipes. **6** City (pop. 9,698), E N.C., at head of Pamlico (Tar) estuary; founded before 1776. Shipping center for farming, fishing, and timber area. **7** City (pop. 26,280), SW Pa., SW of Pittsburgh; settled 1769. Mfg. of glass, metal, and fiber products; coal mining. David Bradford House (1787) was hq. in Whisky Rebellion. Seat of Washington and Jefferson Col. (for men; Washington Col. united with Jefferson Col. 1865). **8** Village, S central Texas, on Brazos R. and NW of Houston. Saw declaration of Texas independence from Mexico, March 2, 1836.

Washington, Mount, 6,288 ft. high, N N.H., in Presidential Range of White Mts.; highest peak in New England. Bare summit has hotel and meteorological station (estab. 1932) and offers view of several states and Canada. Ascended 1642 by Darby Field. Bridle path built 1840, road 1861, cog railway 1869.

Washington, State College of: see PULLMAN, Wash.

Washington, Treaty of, May, 1871, concluded between U.S. and Great Britain in Washington, D.C. Included provisions for arbitration of ALABAMA CLAIMS, SAN JUAN BOUNDARY DISPUTE.

Washington, University of, at Seattle; state supported, coed.; opened 1861. Has forest-products and oceanographic laboratories, large wind tunnel, and the Pacific Northwest historical collection.

Washington and Jefferson College: see WASHINGTON, Pa.

Washington and Lee University, at Lexington, Va.; nonsectarian, for men; opened 1749 by Presbyterians, had several names before receiving present title in 1871. R. E. Lee was president 1865–70. His tomb is here.

Washington Conference: see NAVAL CONFERENCES.

Washington Court House, city (pop. 10,560), SW central Ohio, SW of Columbus, in agr. area; founded c.1810. Mfg. of auto and airplane parts.

Washington Island, atoll, area c.3 sq. mi., central Pacific; part of Gilbert and Ellice Isls. colony. Discovered 1798 by the American trader Edmund Fanning, annexed 1889 by British.

Washington Monument, hollow shaft, 555 ft. 5⅛ in. high, in Washington, D.C., on the Mall. Design of Robert Mills was accepted 1836. Site was granted 1848 by Congress, but no appropriations were made until 1876. Finally completed 1884 and opened to the public four years later.

Washington University, at St. Louis, Mo.; nonsectarian, coed.; chartered 1853, opened 1856. Its Henry Shaw School of Botany works with Missouri Botanical Garden. Institute of radiology has cyclotron.

Washita (wŏ'shĭtô), river, rising in Texas Panhandle, at Okla. line, and flowing c.450 mi. SE across Okla. to L. Texoma near Tishomingo. Custer defeated Cheyenne at battle of Washita on its banks 1868.

Washoe Mountains: see VIRGINIA MOUNTAINS.

wasp, insect of order Hymenoptera. There are several wasp families. Vespidae family includes both social forms (e.g., yellow jackets, hornets, and other paper wasps) and solitary forms (e.g., potter wasp). Usually there are three castes in social forms: queens, workers, and males or drones. White-faced hornet makes papery nest of many layers of cells. A dark brown to black wasp of genus *Polistes* makes open paper nest of single layer of cells.

wassail (wŏ'sŭl), anc. drinking salutation in England,

meaning "be whole" or "have health." By association, it came to mean the liquor in which healths are drunk, and it also implied revelries and drinking songs as the original meaning faded.

Wassermann, Jakob (yä'kôp vä'sŭrmän), 1873–1934, Austrian novelist, b. Bavaria. Among his best-known works are *Caspar Hauser* (1908; Eng. tr., 1928); *Das Gänsemännchen* (1915; Eng. tr., *The Goose Man*); *Christian Wahnschaffe* (1918; Eng. tr., *The World's Illusion*), usually considered his best; and *Der Fall Maurizius* (1928; Eng. tr., *The Maurizius Case*).

Wassermann test (wŏ'sŭrmŭn), test of blood or spinal fluid used in diagnosis of syphilis. Devised 1906 by German bacteriologist **August von Wassermann** (ou'gŏost fŭn vä'sŭrmän), 1866–1925.

Wastwater (wŏst'–), lake, 3 mi. long and ½ mi. wide, Cumberland, England, in Lake District; deepest lake in England (258 ft. max.).

Watauga (wŏtô'gŭ), river, rising in W N.C. in Blue Ridge and flowing c.75 mi. NW to Holston R. NE of Jonesboro, Tenn. Has Sycamore Shoals Monument at ELIZABETHTON, Tenn., and Watauga Dam.

Watauga Association, government (1772–75) formed by settlers along Watauga R. in present E Tenn.

watch, small portable timepiece. Probably watches were first made c.1500. Stem replaced the key for winding in late 19th cent. In modern machine-made watch the hairspring controls swing of balance wheel, which in turn regulates rate of escapement of energy through train of toothed wheels that derive their motor power from mainspring. Parts are held by pivots that rest on bearings, preferably made of jewels at points subject to wear.

Watch Hill, R.I.: see WESTERLEY.

Watchung Mountains or **Orange Mountains,** two long low ridges of volcanic origin, N central N.J., curving SW from SW of Paterson to N of Somerville.

water, when pure, is odorless, tasteless, transparent liquid, colorless in small amounts, but showing bluish tinge in large quantities. At 4°C. (temperature of maximum density) one cubic centimeter of water weighs one gram. When cooled to 0°C. (32°F.), it changes to colorless crystalline solid (ice); this is less dense than liquid at 4°C. Water expands in freezing. When heated to boiling point (100°C., 212°F.), it vaporizes to steam. Evaporates at ordinary temperatures. Pure water is poor electrical conductor. It is a compound of hydrogen (two atoms) and oxygen (one atom), its chemical formula being H_2O; composition by weight is one part of hydrogen to eight of oxygen. Water reacts with some active metals and metallic oxides to form bases; forms acids with some other oxides. HYDRATE is a salt having its molecule linked with definite number of water molecules. Efflorescence is loss of this water on exposure to air at ordinary temperatures. Deliquescent substances absorb water from air. Water is one of best solvents. MINERAL WATER has great variety and quantity of minerals; salt water has minerals in addition to large amount of sodium chloride. Temporary hardness of water occurs when bicarbonates of calcium or magnesium are present; permanent, when sulphates or chlorides of these are there. Temporary hardness can be eliminated by boiling or by adding lime; permanent, by adding such substances as sodium carbonate or sodium hydroxide, which form precipitates with materials causing hardness. Water covers about 70% of earth's surface; land is constantly being worn down, carried away, and redeposited by its action. Rain and humidity, as well as presence of large bodies of water, are important factors in climate. Water is necessary for life; it forms greater part of animal and plant protoplasm, is present in plant sap and animal blood and is essential to PHOTOSYNTHESIS. Water supply must be pure. Processes of purification of a city water supply include coagulation (usually by adding an aluminum salt or ferric iron which cause clumping and settling out of high percentage of bacteria), filtration (water passes through layers of fine sand), and disinfection (usually with chlorine). Water power is of great economic importance. Heavy water (deuterium oxide) molecule consists of two atoms of heavy hydrogen and one of oxygen.

water bug, commonly refers to the giant water bug, water strider, water boatman, back swimmer, and water scorpion of order Hemiptera (see BUG). Term is also used for Croton bug and some aquatic beetles.

Waterbury, industrial city (pop. 104,477), W Conn., on Naugatuck R. and SW of Hartford. Its brass industry began in mid-18th cent. Clocks and watches and silverware are made.

water cress, hardy perennial European herb (*Rorippa nasturtium-aquaticum* or *Nasturtium officinale*) naturalized in North America, found in or around water. The pungent leaves are used as a garnish and in salads.

Wateree (wôtûrē'), river rising in W N.C. and flowing 295 mi. SE past Camden, S.C., joining Congaree R. to form Santee R. SE of Columbia. Called the Catawba in early course.

waterfall, sudden drop in a stream passing over harder rock to softer, more easily eroded, rock. In time, the waterfall (by undercutting and erosion) will move upstream, become lower, then become a series of rapids, and finally disappear. See FALL LINE.

Waterford (wô'tûrfûrd), maritime county (710 sq. mi.; pop. 76,108), S Ireland, in Munster. Largely a hilly area, Waterford has much farming land. Dairying and hog raising are important; fishing and quarrying are also carried on. County town is **Waterford,** county borough (pop. 28,269), on Suir R. at head of Waterford Harbour. An outlet for produce of S. Ireland. Famous Waterford glass was made in 18th cent. Saw much early fighting. Has Protestant and Catholic cathedrals.

Waterford, residential town (pop. 9,100), SE Conn., on Long Isl. Sound W of New London; settled c.1653.

water gas, colorless gas which burns with very hot, light bluish flame. It is a mixture of carbon monoxide and hydrogen, with small amounts of other gases; is almost completely combustible. Used in industry in preparing hydrogen, as fuel in steelmaking, and when enriched as an illuminant.

water glass or **soluble glass,** colorless, transparent substance, usually sodium silicate, ordinarily a solid but usually marketed in water solution. It is used as a cement for glass, pottery, etc.; for fireproofing and waterproofing; for fixing pigments. It serves as preservative for eggs since it fills up pores of shell and prevents entrance of air.

water hemlock: see HEMLOCK.

water hyacinth, perennial aquatic plant (*Eichhornia crassipes*). It has round floating leaves and blue-violet flowers borne on fleshy stalks. Plants hinder navigation in waterways in Fla. and Calif.

water lily, showy-flowered aquatic plant of genus *Nymphaea* with large beautiful blossoms of various colors, often fragrant, and rounded floating leaves. Tender water lilies, prized for garden pools, are tropical species, but some hardy kinds are native, e.g., *Nymphaea odorata*. There are both day- and night-blooming types.

Waterloo, Belgium: see WATERLOO CAMPAIGN.

Waterloo, town (pop. 11,991), S Ont., Canada, NW suburb of Kitchener. Distilling center with flour mills and mfg. of shoes and clothing.

Waterloo, city (pop. 65,198), NE Iowa, on Cedar R.; settled 1845. Trade and industrial center for farm and livestock area, it has railroad shops, meat packing plants, mfg. of agr. machinery. Annual Dairy Cattle Congress, National Belgian Horse Show.

Waterloo campaign, June, 1815, last action of Napoleonic Wars, fought in S Belgium. NAPOLEON I, faced with European coalition, hoped to defeat British and Prussians before dealing with Austrians and Russians. Defeated Blücher at Ligny (June 16); de-

tached Grouchy to pursue him; went to assist Ney in fight against Wellington at Quatre Bras. Wellington withdrew to position S of Waterloo; waited attack. Napoleon attacked June 18. English resisted successfully and were joined by Blücher, who had eluded the French. French were routed. Napoleon abdicated June 22.

watermelon, tender, annual trailing vine (*Citrullus vulgaris*) and its large, juicy, round or ovoid fruit, greenskinned and pink-fleshed. Native to Africa, it now is extensively grown in the S U.S. (esp. in Texas and Ga.). The citron melon is a variety with firm white flesh used like citron for preserving.

water moccasin or **cottonmouth,** highly venomous pit viper of S U.S. swamps and bayous. It often climbs tree branches. Mothers give direct birth to the young.

water polo, swimming sport played in pool measuring not more than 20 ft. wide, not less than 19 ft. long. An event of Olympic games since 1900.

watershed, elevation or divide separating catchment area or drainage basin of one river system from another. Rocky Mts. and Andes form watershed between westward-flowing and eastward-flowing streams. Term is also used synonymously with drainage basin.

Waters of Merom (mē'-): see BAHR EL-HULEH.

Waterton-Glacier International Peace Park, S Alta. and N Mont., created 1932 by Canadian Parliament and U.S. Congress. Consists of Waterton Lakes Natl. Park in Canada and Glacier Natl. Park in U.S.

Waterton Lakes National Park, 204 sq. mi., SW Alta., Canada, SW of Lethbridge at Mont. border. It is the Canadian part of Waterton-Glacier Internatl. Peace Park, created 1932 by acts of Canadian Parliament and U.S. Congress.

Watertown. 1 Town (pop. 10,699), W Conn., on Naugatuck R. and NW of Waterbury. Mfg. of textile and metal goods. Has Taft School for boys (1890). **2** Town (pop. 37,329), E Mass., on Charles R. and W of Boston; settled 1630. Footwear, textiles, and electrical supplies. Has U.S. arsenal (1816). Seat of PERKINS INSTITUTION and MASSACHUSETTS SCHOOL FOR THE BLIND. **3** City (pop. 34,350), N N.Y., on Black R. (water power) and N of Syracuse; settled c.1800. Trade center for rich dairy area and gateway to Thousand Isl. resort region. Mfg. of air brakes and paper products. **4** City (pop. 12,699), NE S.Dak., NNW of Sioux Falls and on Big Sioux R.; laid out 1878. Shipping and trade center for resort and agr. area, it has food processing. **5** City (pop. 12,417), SE Wis., NE of Madison and at falls of Rock R., in farm and dairy area; settled c.1836. Mfg. of shoes; goose market. Was home of Carl Schurz 1855–57. Octagon House (c.1849) near by is museum.

Waterville, city (pop. 18,287), S Maine, at Kennebec R. falls above Augusta; settled 1754. Rail and agr. trade center, with textile and paper mills. Colby Col. (for men and women; 1813) is here.

Watervliet (wô"tûrvlēt'), city (pop. 15,197), E N.Y., on Hudson R. (bridged) opposite Troy. Steel castings, abrasives, chemicals. Ann Lee headed first American community of Shakers here 1776.

Waterways, village, N Alta., Canada, on Clearwater R. and near Fort McMurray. River boat service to Wood Buffalo Natl. Park.

Watkins, Franklin (Chenault), 1894–, American painter, noted as a colorist in postimpressionist style.

Watkins Glen, resort village (pop. 3,052), W central N.Y., in Finger Lakes region at S end of Seneca L. Adjoining is Watkins Glen State Park, with 2-mi. gorge, mineral springs, waterfalls.

Watling Street (wŏt'lĭng), important anc. road in England, built by the Romans. Ran over 100 mi. NW from London, through St. Albans, to Wroxeter in Shropshire. Used throughout Middle Ages, parts of road are still in perfect condition.

Watson, J(ohn) B(roadus), 1878–, American psychologist. Director of the Johns Hopkins psychological laboratory and founder of school of psychology known as BEHAVIORISM, which describes behavior solely in terms of physiological response to stimuli. He accepted only three responses as unconditioned or unlearned—fear, love, and rage.

Watson, Sir William, 1858–1935, English traditional, romantic poet. Wrote *Wordsworth's Grave* (1890) and elegy for Tennyson, *Lachrymae Musarum* (1892).

Watson-Gordon, Sir John: see GORDON, SIR JOHN WATSON-.

Watson Lake, village, SE Yukon, Canada. Here are Royal Canadian Mounted Police post, airfield, and radio and weather station.

Watsonville, city (pop. 11,572), W Calif., near Monterey Bay. Shipping and processing center (esp. for lettuce, apples). Beach and mountain resorts are near.

Watt, James, 1736–1819, Scottish inventor of new type steam engine patented 1769. Unit of power, the watt, was named after him.

watt [for James Watt], unit of electrical power, the power necessary to maintain a current of one ampere under a pressure of one volt. Electrical power (number of watts) of a circuit is number of volts multiplied by number of amperes; is measured by a wattmeter. Kilowatt equals 1,000 watts; electric power is usually sold by kilowatt hours (kilowatts × hours).

Watteau, Antoine (wätō', wŏ'tō, Fr. ätwän' vätō'), 1684–1721, French painter of Flemish origin, b. Valenciennes, an outstanding colorist. Celebrated for lyric quality of his gay and sensuous scenes of open-air festivities (e.g., *Embarkation for Cythera*, Louvre).

wattle: see ACACIA.

Watts, George Frederic, 1817–1904, English painter. Used glowing color and soft contours in his popular allegorical paintings. His sculptures include many monuments. Married to Ellen Terry 1864–77.

Watts, Isaac, 1674–1748, English dissenting clergyman and hymn writer. Only a few of his several hundred hymns survive today, but they are among the finest examples of English metrical hymnody. Those beginning "When I survey the wondrous cross," "Joy to the World," and "Our God, our help in ages past," appeared in his *Psalms of David Imitated in the Language of the New Testament* (1719). *Divine Songs for Children* (1715) contains the famous "How doth the little busy bee."

Watts-Dunton, (Walter) Theodore, 1832–1914, English poet, novelist, and critic. Wrote much, but is remembered best as friend of Rossetti and especially of Swinburne.

Watt's Dyke: see OFFA'S DYKE.

Waugh, Evelyn (ēv'lǐn wô'), 1903–, English novelist, author of brilliant satires (e.g., *Decline and Fall*, 1928; *Vile Bodies*, 1930; *A Handful of Dust*, 1934) as well as more serious works (e.g., *Brideshead Revisited*, 1945; *Men at Arms*, 1952).

Waukegan (wôkē'gùn), residential and industrial city (pop. 38,946), NE Ill., on L. Michigan and N of Chicago. Settled 1835 as Little Fort near old French stockade, on site of Indian village. Air, rail, and lake shipping center. Mfg. of metal products, chemicals, and asbestos products.

Waukesha (wô'kǐshô), city (pop. 21,233), SE Wis., on Fox R. and W of Milwaukee; settled 1834. Health resort with bottled waters and metal products.

Waupun (wôpŭn'), city (pop. 6,725), central Wis., SW of Fond du Lac and on Rock R., in farm and dairy area. Machinery and shoes.

Wausau (wô'sô), city (pop. 30,414), central Wis., on Wisconsin R. and NW of Green Bay, in dairy area; settled 1839. Wood and paper products. Winter sports at near-by Rib Mt.

Wauwatosa (wôwùtō'sù), industrial city (pop. 33,324), SE Wis., near Milwaukee; settled 1835. Metal, leather, and wood products.

wave, in physics, disturbance advancing through a medium that is set in vibration as wave moves along. If particles of transmitting medium move up and down, waves are called transverse, e.g., water and

LIGHT waves; if particles vibrate in line with wave direction, waves are longitudinal, i.e., SOUND waves. Wave length is distance from any point on one wave to corresponding point on next. Frequency is number of crests that pass given point in a second. See also RADIATION.

Wavell, Archibald P(ercival) Wavell, 1st Earl (wā'vùl), 1883–1950, British field marshal. As World War II commander in chief of Middle East (1939–41) he defeated (1940) the Italians in Cyrenaica. Viceroy and governor general of India 1943–47.

Waverley, village, Surrey, England. Has remains of 12th-cent. abbey. Swift lived at "Moor Park," estate of Sir William Temple.

Waverly. 1 City (pop. 5,124), NE Iowa, on Cedar R. above Waterloo. Processes farm and dairy produce. **2** Village (pop. 6,037), S N.Y., at Pa. line, on Chemung R. and SE of Elmira.

Waves (Women Appointed for Voluntary Emergency Service), created 1942 in World War II to release male naval personnel for sea duty. Served in clerical and other jobs. Directed by M. H. McAfee 1942–46. Women's Armed Service Integration Act of 1948 authorized enlistment of women in regular navy.

wax, name for substance secreted by glands on abdomen of bee (beeswax) and for various similar substances. Waxes are usually mixtures containing esters of fatty acids and certain alcohols (other than glycerol) and other alcohols and sometimes hydrocarbons. They are harder and less greasy than fats. Carnauba wax is obtained from a PALM; LANOLIN from wool; SPERMACETI from whales. Mineral waxes include ozocerite and paraffin.

Waxahachie (wŏk"sǐhă'chē), city (pop. 11,204), N Texas, S of Dallas; founded 1847. Market and processing center in rich blackland agr. area with mfg. of garments and textiles.

waxwing, perching bird of N Hemisphere of Old and New Worlds. Waxwings are crested and have sleek, brownish-gray plumage with dashes of red like sealing wax on the wings. Cedar waxwing breeds throughout most of Canada and U.S.

Waycross, city (pop. 18,899), SE Ga., SW of Savannah and just N of Okefenokee Swamp; settled 1818. Tobacco market and shipping center. Has railroad shops and mfg. of wood products.

wayfaring tree: see HOBBLEBUSH.

Wayne, Anthony, 1745–96, patriot general in American Revolution. Most famous achievement was capture of Stony Point, N.Y. (1779). Decisively defeated Indians at Fallen Timbers, Ohio (1794); negotiated treaty 1795. Known as "mad Anthony."

Wayne, village (pop. 9,409), SE Mich., on River Rouge branch and SW of Dearborn. Mfg. of aircraft and auto parts.

Waynesboro. 1 Borough (pop. 10,334), S Pa., near Md. line, SW of Harrisburg; settled 1798. Resort with fruit growing and mfg. of machinery, metal goods. **2** City (pop. 12,357), central Va., SE of Staunton, near S entrance to Skyline Drive; settled 1700. Trade and mfg. (rayon, furniture, wood products). Near here Union forces defeated Confederates, March, 1865.

Waynesburg, borough (pop. 5,514), SW Pa., SSW of Pittsburgh, in coal, dairy, and livestock area. Seat of Waynesburg Col.

Waynesville, resort town (pop. 5,295), W N.C., WSW of Asheville. Mfg. of shoes, rubber and wood products. Near Great Smoky Mts. Natl. Park and L. Junaluska (with Methodist assembly).

Wayne University: see DETROIT, Mich.

Wayzata (wīzē'tù), city (pop. 1,791), E Minn., W suburb of Minneapolis. Resort on L. Minnetonka.

Waziristan (wùzēr'ĭstän"), mountainous region, North-West Frontier Prov., W Pakistan. Inhabited by warlike Pathan tribes.

Weald, the (wēld), area between North and South Downs, England, forming part of Sussex, Surrey, and Kent Counties. Now largely an agr. district.

weasel (wē'zŭl), small, carnivorous animal (*Mustela*) of Europe, Asia, North America; related to stoat. The fur is various shades of brown above and white below; in winter, weasels living in regions of snow usually become all white, except for the dark tail, and are then called ermine.

weather, atmospheric state at given place and time regarding temperature, barometric pressure, WIND, HUMIDITY, CLOUD formation, and precipitation. METEOROLOGY ancient; greatly developed today with rapid communication from remote areas. In U.S. weather service (estab. 1870) later became Weather Bureau which now includes over 200 main stations. Bureau prepares daily country-wide map showing weather elements at each station by symbols and figures (ISOBARS show areas of high or low pressure, fronts demark warm-air from cold-air masses, shading reflects precipitation); prepares upper-air charts. Predictions born of experience, since factors controlling weather not fully understood.

Weatherford, city (pop. 8,093), N Texas, W of Fort Worth. Center of rich fruit and truck area, it processes cottonseed and peanut oil, and has mfg. of oil equipment and clothing.

weathering, decomposition of rock near the earth's surface by atmospheric agencies. Involves mechanical processes, e.g., expansion and contraction resulting from sudden temperature changes, impact of running water; and chemical processes, e.g., oxidation, carbonization, loss of chemical elements by solution in water. Results of weathering include formation of soil and preparation of materials for erosion.

weather map: see WEATHER.

Weaver, James Baird, 1833–1912, American political leader. U.S. Representative from Iowa (1879–81, 1885–89). A free silver advocate, he was POPULIST PARTY presidential candidate 1892.

weaver bird, member of Old World family of birds (Ploceidae) which build intricately woven nests. The birds resemble the finch family and are sometimes called weaver finches.

weaving, art of forming a fabric by interlacing at right angles two or more sets of yarn or other material. One of the most ancient of the fundamental arts, weaving grew up independently in different parts of the world. In the 18th cent., spinning and weaving inventions virtually ended the era of domestic craftsmanship and began the huge organized industry of today; some fine fabrics, however, are still woven by hand. First step in weaving is to stretch the strong warp (longitudinal) yarns. The weft, woof, or filling crosses the warp, binding it at either side to form the selvage. After warp is stretched, three essential steps are: shedding, or raising alternate warp yarns or sets of yarns to receive the weft; picking, or inserting the weft; battening, or pressing home the weft to make the fabric compact. These operations were done by the hands before development of the LOOM. Fundamental weaves, of which all others are variations, are the plain, twill, and satin. Figure weaves are made by causing warp and weft to intersect in varied groups.

Webb, Beatrice (Potter), 1858–1943, English socialist economist, wife of **Sidney (James) Webb,** 1858–1947. The Webbs worked together in the Fabian Society, helped build the British Labour party, and wrote numerous works on socialist history and theory.

Webb, James Watson, 1802–84, American journalist and diplomat. Edited *Morning Courier and New York Enquirer.* Estab. express service by horse to hasten news, sent schooners to sea for incoming news. Minister to Brazil 1861–69.

Webb, Mary (Meredith), 1881–1927, English novelist, known for somber novels of rural Shropshire (e.g., *Precious Bane,* 1924).

Webb, Philip Speakman, 1830–1915, English architect, who influenced revival of Queen Anne and Georgian styles. Was a member of William Morris's famous decorating firm.

Webb, Sidney James: see WEBB, BEATRICE POTTER.

Webb City, city (pop. 6,919), SW Mo., near Joplin, in agr. area. Apparel and dairy products.

Weber, Carl Maria (Friedrich Ernst) von (vā'bŭr), 1786–1826, German composer and pianist. He composed such romantic operas as *Der Freischütz* (1821), *Euryanthe* (1823), and *Oberon* (1826). His instrumental works include the popular *Invitation to the Dance* (1819).

Weber, Ernst Heinrich, 1795–1878, German physiologist. Noted for research on touch and sensation and on inhibitory power of vagus nerve. With his brother **Wilhelm Eduard Weber** (vĭl'hĕlm ā'dōōärt), 1804–91, a physicist, he wrote a book on wave motion (1825) and made studies of acoustics. Wilhelm also contributed to knowledge of terrestrial magnetism and electrical measurements and devised an electromagnetic telegraph.

Weber, Joseph (wĕ'bŭr), 1867–1942, American comedian, partner of Lew Fields. In chin whiskers, loud check clothes, and low crown derbies, they long delighted audiences (1875–1904 and after 1912) with dialect jokes, slapstick, and burlesque.

Weber, Max (mäks' vā'bŭr), 1864–1920, German sociologist. Sought to develop a methodology for social science. He opposed Marxism and stressed the plurality of causes. In his *Protestant Ethic and the Spirit of Capitalism* (1920; Eng. tr., 1930) he developed his thesis of the intimate connection between the ascetic character of Calvinism and the rise of capitalist institutions.

Weber, Max (wĕ'bŭr), 1881–, American painter, b. Russia. Painted abstractions in early period, but later works tended toward naturalism.

Weber, Wilhelm Eduard: see WEBER, ERNST HEINRICH.

Weber (wĕ'bŭr), river rising in N central Utah in Uinta Mts. and flowing NW to join Ogden R. at Ogden. Combined stream enters Great Salt L. Dammed for irrigation. Some water diverted to Provo R. project.

Webern, Anton von (vā'bŭrn), 1883–1945, Austrian composer; pupil of Arnold Schönberg and devoted adherent to his 12-tone technique (see ATONALITY). Webern's music is even less accepted by the public than Schönberg's. His compositions are characterized by unusual combinations of instruments, a broken melodic line (two successive notes are rarely played by the same instrument), and extreme brevity (often a movement of a symphony, quartet, or sonata is less than two minutes in length). Most of his works are for small orchestral groups or piano.

Webster, Daniel, 1782–1852, American statesman, lawyer, and orator. Won fame as lawyer in DARTMOUTH COLLEGE CASE and in McCULLOCH VS. MARYLAND. Delivered eloquent public orations. U.S. Congressman (1813–17, 1823–27). A leading political figure as U.S. Senator from Mass. (1827–41); defended Union in 1830 debate with R. Y. HAYNE. WHIG PARTY leader. U.S. Secretary of State (1841–43); signed WEBSTER-ASHBURTON TREATY. Again U.S. Senator 1845–50; cherishing preservation of the Union above his own popularity, he backed COMPROMISE OF 1850 in a notable speech. Served again as U.S. Secretary of State 1850–52.

Webster, John, 1580?–1625?, English dramatist, author of two tragedies, *The White Devil* (1612) and *The Duchess of Malfi* (c.1614). Collaborated on many plays, especially with Dekker.

Webster, Noah, 1758–1843, American scholar, a lexicographer, b. Conn. Fired with the desire to standardize American grammar and spelling, he wrote *Grammatical Institute of the English Language* (1783–85), of which the first part, often revised, became the "blue-backed speller" dominant in American schooling for generations. His later *Compendious Dictionary* (1806) preceded his *American Dictionary of the English Language* (1828); this in many revised editions to the present day made the name Webster a

SMALL CAPITALS = cross references. Pronunciation key on inside end pages. Abbreviations: p. 2.

household word meaning standard dictionary. He hoped by his work to improve morals and patriotism as well as language and he backed many causes (including his vigorous campaign for a copyright law). He argued for a centralized government at the time of the Articles of Confederation, particularly in his *Sketches of American Policy* (1785), and later as a newspaper editor supported Washington's administration. The influence of his work through a long life is incalculable.

Webster, town (pop. 13,194), including Webster village (pop. 12,160), S Mass., SSW of Worcester; settled c.1713. Woolens, shoes, optical goods.

Webster-Ashburton Treaty, concluded in 1842 by U.S., represented by Secretary of State Daniel Webster, and Great Britain, represented by Commissioner A. B. Ashburton. Settled disputed boundaries of NE U.S.; gave U.S. over 7,000 sq. mi. of disputed area, including Aroostook Valley; opened St. Johns R. to free navigation by both countries. Also fixed U.S.-Canada border in Great Lakes region. Treaty served as precedent in peaceful settlements of subsequent Anglo-American disputes.

Webster City, city (pop. 7,611), central Iowa, on Boone R. and E of Fort Dodge. Mfg. of metal goods and dairy products.

Webster Groves, city (pop. 23,390), E Mo., just W of St. Louis; settled 1854. Petroleum products. Seat of Webster Col. (corporate college of St. Louis Univ.; for women).

Webster Springs, town (pop. 1,313), central W.Va., on Elk R.; official name Addison. Health resort and sports center.

Weddell Sea, embayment of S Atlantic, Antarctica, SSE of South America. Discovered 1823 by James Weddell.

Wedekind, Frank (vā′dŭkĭnt), 1864–1918, German dramatist. He anticipated expressionism in his dramas *The Awakening of Spring* (1891), *Earth Spirit* (1895), and *Pandora's Box* (1903). The heroine of those, Lulu, symbolizes woman as an instinctual, amoral being. Alban Berg based *Lulu* on Wedekind's dramas.

wedge, piece of wood or metal thick at one end and sloping to thin edge at other, an application of the inclined plane. Used to separate two bodies or one part of a body from an adjoining part (e.g., in splitting wood). Ax, chisel, knife, nail, and carpenter's plane are forms of wedges. See *ill.,* p. 619.

Wedgwood, Josiah, 1730–95, celebrated English potter, descendant of a family of Staffordshire potters. In 1769 he opened his works at Etruria (a village he built for his workmen) near Stoke-upon-Trent. Here he transformed pottery making into a major industry. Invented jasper ware, best known in delicate blue with white Greek figures embossed on it. Also made cream-colored earthenware ("queen's ware"), vases of black composition ("Egyptian ware"), veined ware in imitation of granite, and an unglazed semiporcelain.

Wednesday: see WEEK.

Weed, Thurlow (thûr′lō), 1797–1882, American journalist and political leader. Newspaper editor in New York state. A power in Whig party. Guided political career of W. H. Seward. Personally genial but utterly unscrupulous politically, Weed headed a formidable state machine.

weed, name for any wild plant especially for an undesired plant growing in cultivated ground. Weeds may crowd out desired crops by appropriating space, sunlight, moisture, and soil nutrients. Methods of control include cultivation of the soil, crop rotation, and chemicals, e.g., 2,4-*D* (dichlorophenoxyacetic acid).

Weehawken (wē′hô″kŭn), township (pop. 14,830), NE N.J., on Hudson R. (Lincoln Tunnel) and N of Hoboken. Scene of Burr-Hamilton duel 1804.

week, period of time shorter than month, commonly seven days. Seven-day week believed to have originated in W Asia in ancient times as planetary week based on concept of influence of planets, then erroneously believed to be sun, moon, Mars, Mercury, Jupiter, Venus,

Saturn. Use of planetary names, derived from names of deities, remained even after Constantine made Christian week beginning on Sunday official. In most languages the forms are translations from Latin or corresponding names of divinities. Latin names and translations, English equivalents (largely from names of Germanic deities) and derivations follow: *dies solis* [sun's day], Sunday; *dies lunae* [moon's day], Monday [moon-day]; *dies Martis* [Mars' day], Tuesday [Tiw's day]; *dies Mercurii* [Mercury's day] Wednesday [Woden's day]; *dies Jovis* [Jove's or Jupiter's day] Thursday [Thor's day]; *dies Veneris* [Venus's day], Friday [Frigg's day]; *dies Saturni,* Saturday [both: Saturn's day].

Weeks, Sinclair, 1893–, U.S. Secretary of Commerce (1953–). A Mass. industrialist. U.S. Senator (interim appointment) 1944.

Weems, Mason L(ocke), 1759–1825, American author, an ordained Anglican minister, called Parson Weems. An enterprising book salesman, he wrote popular works but is remembered almost solely for his baseless story of the boy George Washington chopping down a cherry tree and confessing to his father, saying, "I cannot tell a lie." This appeared in the fifth edition of his biography of Washington.

weevil, name for certain snout beetles of curculio family. Some damage stored grains, others (e.g., cotton boll weevil) attack plants.

Wei, China: see TSIN, dynasty.

weigela (wījĕ′lù or **weigelia** (wījĕ′lyù), ornamental Asiatic shrub of genus *Weigela* widely cultivated for the funnel-shaped white, pink, or red blossoms in spring or summer.

weight, molecular: see MOLECULAR WEIGHT.

weight lifting. Popular sport in Europe for many centuries. An event in Olympic games since 1896.

weights and measures. Crude measurements of length, capacity, and weight probably date from prehistoric times. Early units were based on body measurements and plant seeds. High degree of standardization achieved by Roman Empire became diversified after its fall. Chief modern systems are American and British system and METRIC SYSTEM (see WEIGHTS AND MEASURES, table, for conversion table and common units). American and British system employs two sets of weights: avoirdupois (used in general commerce); troy (for precious metals). Avoirdupois weight is based on 16-ounce pound; troy weight (basis of apothecary weight) based on 12-ounce pound. U.S. Congress has constitutional right to fix standards; most legislation, except for customs and internal revenue purposes, has been permissive. Sets of official weights and measures were sent to the states in 1856, but legislation and enforcement are largely state prerogatives. Federal government permitted use of metric system (1866) and established a conversion table based on the pound and the yard; since 1893, yard in U.S. has been derived from international prototype meter and the pound from the prototype kilogram (both kept at International Bureau of Weights and Measures near Paris; copies are deposited with participating governments). In U.S. copies are kept by government bureau established to correlate standards (see STANDARDS, NATIONAL BUREAU OF).

Weihaiwei (wā′hī′wā) or **Weihai,** commercial city (pop. 175,000), NE Shantung prov., China; port on Yellow Sea. City and surrounding area (285 sq. mi.) was leased 1898–1920 to Great Britain. Naval base was developed by the British.

Weill, Kurt (vīl), 1900–1950, German-American composer. He wrote satirical operas, such as *Der Protagonist* (1926) and *Die Dreigroschenoper* (1928; based on *The Beggar's Opera*). Upon coming to the U.S. in 1935, he began writing musical comedies. Among these are *Knickerbocker Holiday* (1938), containing *September Song; Lady in the Dark* (1941); and *One Touch of Venus* (1943), containing *Speak Low.* His last works include a musical version of *Street Scene*

WEIGHTS AND MEASURES COMMONLY USED

American and British System	*Metric System*	*Conversion Table*
LINEAR MEASURE	**LINEAR MEASURE**	**LINEAR MEASURE**
12 inches = 1 foot 3 feet = 1 yard 5½ yards = 1 rod 220 yards = 1 furlong 5,280 feet = 1 mile 6 feet = 1 fathom 6,080 feet = 1 nautical mile	10 millimeters = 1 centimeter 10 centimeters = 1 decimeter 10 decimeters = 1 meter 10 meters = 1 dekameter 1,000 meters = 1 kilometer	1 inch = 2.54 centimeters 0.393700 inches = 1 centimeter 1 mile = 1.609344 kilometers 0.62137 miles = 1 kilometer
SQUARE MEASURE	**SQUARE MEASURE**	**SQUARE MEASURE**
144 square inches = 1 square foot 9 square feet = 1 square yard 30¼ square yards = 1 square rod 160 square rods = 1 acre 4,840 square yards = 1 acre 640 acres = 1 square mile	100 square millimeters = 1 square centimeter 100 square centimeters = 1 square decimeter 10,000 square centimeters = 1 square meter 100 square meters = 1 are 100 ares = 1 hectare 10,000 ares = 1 square kilometer	1 square inch = 6.4516 square centimeters 0.15500 square inches = 1 square centimeter 1 hectare = 2.471 acres 1 square mile = 2.58999 square kilometers 0.3861 square miles = 1 square kilometer
CUBIC MEASURE	**CUBIC MEASURE**	**CUBIC MEASURE**
1,728 cubic inches = 1 cubic foot 27 cubic feet = 1 cubic yard	1,000 cubic millimeters = 1 cubic centimeter 1,000 cubic centimeters = 1 cubic decimeter 1,000 cubic decimeters = 1 cubic meter	1 cubic inch = 16.3871 cubic centimeters 0.061024 cubic inches = 1 cubic centimeter 1 cubic yard = 0.76455 cubic meters 1.30795 cubic yards = 1 cubic meter
LIQUID MEASURE	**LIQUID MEASURE**	**LIQUID MEASURE**
16 ounces = 1 (U.S.) pint 20 ounces = 1 imperial (British) pint 2 cups = 1 pint 2 pints = 1 quart 4 quarts = 1 gallon 1.2 U.S. gallons = 1 imperial (British) gallon	10 milliliters = 1 centiliter 100 centiliters = 1 liter 1,000 liters = 1 kiloliter	1 ounce = 0.46871 centiliters 0.33815 ounces = 1 centiliter 1 (U.S.) liquid quart = 0.9463 liters 1.0567 liters = 1 (U.S.) liquid quart 1 (U.S.) gallon = .0037853 kiloliters 264.17 (U.S.) gallons = 1 kiloliter
WEIGHTS: AVOIRDUPOIS	**WEIGHTS**	**WEIGHTS**
16 drams = 1 ounce 16 ounces = 1 pound 112 pounds = 1 long hundredweight 2,000 pounds = 1 short ton 2,240 pounds = 1 long ton	10 milligrams = 1 centigram 10 centigrams = 1 decigram 10 decigrams = 1 gram 100 centigrams = 1 gram 10 grams = 1 dekagram 10 dekagrams = 1 hectogram 10 hectograms = 1 kilogram 1,000 grams = 1 kilogram 1,000 kilograms = 1 ton	1 ounce (avoirdupois) = 28.3495 grams 0.035274 ounces (avoirdupois) = 1 gram 1 pound (avoirdupois) = 0.453592 kilograms 2.20462 pounds (avoirdupois) = 1 kilogram 1 (short) ton = 0.90718 (metric) tons 1.10231 (short) tons = 1 (metric) ton 1 pound (avoirdupois) = 1.21528 pounds (troy) 0.82286 pounds (avoirdupois) = 1 pound (troy)

WEIGHTS: TROY AND APOTHECARY

480 grains = 1 ounce
12 ounces = 1 pound

(1947) and *Lost in the Stars* (1949), based on Alan Paton's novel, *Cry, the Beloved Country.*

Weimar (vī'mär), city (pop. 66,659), Thuringia, central Germany, on Ilm R. Has varied mfg. but is chiefly known as cultural center. Became cap. of duchy (later grand duchy) of SAXE-WEIMAR in 16th cent.; was cap. of Thuringia 1920–47. It was the residence of Lucas Cranach the elder (16th cent.); J. S. Bach (1708–17); Wieland, Goethe, Herder, Schiller (late 18th–early 19th cent.); Liszt (1848–59). In 1920 Weimar was the scene of the German national assembly that created the Weimar Republic (see GERMANY). The Nazis estab., in 1933, a notorious concentration camp at Buchenwald, a few miles NW of Weimar. Among Weimar's landmarks are the parish church (altarpiece by Cranach); grand ducal palace and crypt (with graves of Goethe and Schiller); theater (long directed by Goethe); residences of Goethe, Schiller, and Liszt; near-by ducal castle of Tiefurt. Weimar is the seat of the Goethe, Schiller, and Nietzsche archives.

Weinberger, Jaromir (yä'rômĕr vīn'bĕrgĕr), 1896–, Czech composer. His most popular works are the polka and fugue from the opera *Schwanda, the Bagpipe Player* (1927) and his orchestral *Variations and Fugue on Under the Spreading Chestnut Tree* (1939).

Weir, Robert Walter, 1803–89, American portrait and historical painter. His son, **John Ferguson Weir,** 1841–1926, was a painter and sculptor, who was director of School of Fine Arts, Yale, 1869–1913. Another son, **J(ulian) Alden Weir,** 1852–1919, was one of earliest American impressionist painters.

Weirton, city (pop. 24,005), NW W.Va., in N Panhandle, on Ohio R. and N of Wheeling. Mfg. of steel and chemicals. Coal and clay mining. Absorbed neighboring towns, including Hollidays Cove, 1947.

Weiser (wē'zùr), city (pop. 3,961), W Idaho, N of Payette, at confluence of Weiser and Snake rivers. Terminus of North and South Panoramic Highway.

Weismann, August (ou'gŏŏst vī'män), 1834–1914, German biologist. He originated the germ-plasm theory of HEREDITY; his doctrine stressed unbroken continuity of germ plasm and nonheritability of acquired characters.

Weisshorn (vīs'hôrn"), peak, 14,792 ft. high, Valais canton, Switzerland, in Pennine Alps.

Weizmann, Chaim (khīm' vītsmän), 1874–1952, scientist and Zionist leader, first president of Israel, b. Russia. Became British citizen in 1910, and in World War I created a synthetic acetone needed by Great Britain for the manufacture of explosives. He helped procure the famous declaration of Arthur James BALFOUR. After 1920 he became the leader of Zionism.

Welch, William Henry, 1850–1934, American pathologist. Noted in research and as medical historian. Associated with the Johns Hopkins Univ. from 1884.

Welch, city (pop. 6,603), S W.Va., on Tug Fork R., NW of Bluefield. Coal mining and lumber milling.

Weld, Theodore Dwight, 1803–95, American abolitionist. Recruited converts for abolitionist cause, trained agents for American Anti-Slavery Society, directed national campaign for sending antislavery petitions to Congress.

welding, the joining of separate pieces of same kind of metal. Modern methods include: use of electric arc, thermite process, OXYACETYLENE TORCH, oxyhydrogen blowpipe, and atomic hydrogen flame.

Welfs: see GUELPHS.

Welhaven, Johan Sebastian (vĕl'hävùn), 1807–73, Norwegian poet and critic, upholder of the classic style and opposed to Wergeland.

well, cylindrical hole in the ground through which oil or water is brought to surface. Shallow wells are usually dug or driven; deep wells are drilled. Driven wells are made by pounding into the earth a casing with sharp edges at bottom and holes near casing end to admit water. Bored wells are made by percussion or rotary drills.

Welland, city (pop. 15,382), S Ont., Canada, on Welland Ship Canal and W of Buffalo, N.Y. Port and trade center in fruitgrowing region with cotton, steel, and cordage mills.

Welland Ship Canal, S Ont., Canada, between L. Ontario (at Port Weller) and L. Erie (at Port Colborne), bypassing the Niagara Falls. Built 1914–32 to replace canal opened 1833. It is 27.6 mi. long, with eight locks overcoming 326 ft. difference in level between the two lakes.

Welles, Gideon (wĕlz), 1802–78, U.S. Secretary of the Navy (1861–69). Built powerful Union navy of Civil War; stood by Lincoln and Johnson in Reconstruction struggle. His diary is of immense value to the historian.

Welles, Orson, 1915–, American stage, film, and radio actor, director, and producer. Productions include *Julius Caesar* in modern dress, film *Citizen Kane,* and an alarmingly realistic radio version (1938) of H. G. Wells's *War of the Worlds.*

Welles, Sumner, 1892–, U.S. Undersecretary of State 1937–43). An authority on Latin America.

Wellesley, Richard Colley Wellesley, Marquess (wĕlz'lē), 1760–1842, British governor general of India (1797–1805). Extended British influence there, wiped out French power, and, aided by his brother (later duke of WELLINGTON), checked power of native rulers. Was foreign secretary (1810–12) and lord lieutenant of Ireland (1821–28, 1833–34).

Wellesley, suburban town (pop. 20,549), E Mass., WSW of Boston; settled 1660. **Wellesley College** (nonsectarian; for women; chartered 1870 and 1873, opened 1875). First to have scientific laboratories in woman's college. Has noted department of hygiene and physical education (graduate). Faculty noted for constructive influence in social movements.

Wellfleet, resort town (pop. 1,123), SE Mass., on N Cape Cod, SSE of Provincetown.

Wellington, Arthur Wellesley, 1st duke of, 1769–1852, British soldier and statesman. In India (1796–1805), he assisted his brother, Richard Wellesley, by defeating Tippoo Sahib and the Mahratta chiefs. Commander (1809–13) in the PENINSULAR WAR, he drove French from Spain. In the WATERLOO CAMPAIGN he defeated Napoleon I. Prime minister 1828–30, he secured passage of Catholic Emancipation (which he had previously opposed). Was made (1842) commander in chief for life.

Wellington, city (pop. 123,771; metropolitan pop. 173,-520), cap. of New Zealand, at S tip of North Isl., on Cook Strait; founded 1840. Succeeded Auckland as dominion's capital, 1865. Here are governor general's residence, Houses of Parliament, National Art Gall. (1936), and Dominion Mus. (1936) with Maori art collection.

Wellington, city (pop. 7,747), S Kansas, S of Wichita, in wheat area on Chisholm Trail. Oil fields near.

Wells, Henry, 1805–78, American pioneer expressman. Associated in business with W. G. FARGO.

Wells, H(erbert) G(eorge), 1866–1946, English novelist. Clothed scientific speculation and social reform in fiction, as in *The Time Machine* (1895), *The Invisible Man* (1897), *The War of the Worlds* (1898), *Kipps* (1905), *Tono Bungay* (1909), *The History of Mr. Polly* (1910), and *The World of William Clissold* (1926). His *Outline of History* (1920) was overwhelmingly popular.

Wells, Horace, 1815–48, American dentist, first to use laughing gas as anesthetic in dentistry (1844).

Wells, municipal borough (pop. 5,835), Somerset, England, SW of Bath. Near by is Wookey Hole, subterranean caverns where remains of prehistoric men were found. Cathedral of Bath and Wells (12th–13th cent.) is one of England's most magnificent.

Wells, town (pop. 2,321), SW Maine, on the coast SW of Portland; settled c.1640. Includes resorts of Wells Beach and Ogunquit (1940 pop. 615), which has artists' colony and summer playhouse.

SMALL CAPITALS = cross references. Pronunciation key on inside end pages. Abbreviations: p. 2.

Wellsburg, city (pop. 5,787), NW W.Va., in N Panhandle, on Ohio R. and NNE of Wheeling. Mfg. of paper products, glass, and cement.

Wells College: see AURORA, N.Y.

Wellston. 1 See WARNER ROBINS, Ga. **2** Town (pop. 9,396), E Mo., W suburb of St. Louis. **3** City (pop. 5,691), S Ohio, NE of Portsmouth. Mfg. of machinery and clothing.

Wellsville. 1 Village (pop. 6,402), W N.Y., on Genesee R. and SE of Buffalo. Oil-refining center. **2** City (pop. 7,854), NE Ohio, on Ohio R. and N of Steubenville. Clay products center.

Welsh language, Brythonic language of Celtic subfamily of Indo-European languages. See LANGUAGE (table).

Welsh Marches, lands in Wales along English border. After Norman Conquest, William I estab. border earldoms to protect his English kingdom. Encouraged his barons to conquer other Welsh earldoms. Abolished by Act of Union (1536).

Welsh terrier: see TERRIER.

Welty, Eudora, 1909–, American author of short stories (as in *Curtain of Green,* 1941; *Golden Apples,* 1949) and notable novel, *Delta Wedding* (1946), about Miss. life. Her delicate, involved style and approach make all her work notable.

Wembley, municipal borough (pop. 131,369), Middlesex, England. British Empire Exhibition was held here 1924–25. Olympic Games were held (1948) in stadium which accommodates 100,000. Has metal casting and mfg. of electrical goods and chemicals.

Wenatchee (wĭnă′chē), city (pop. 13,072), central Wash., on Columbia R. below mouth of Wenatchee R.; founded 1888. Trade center of apple-growing area. Aluminum plant. Wheat, lumber, and dairy products. Wenatchee L., 5 mi. long, is NW.

Wenceslaus, Saint (wĕn′sŭslŭs), Czech *Vaclav,* d. 936?, duke of Bohemia, reared a Christian by his grandmother. He promoted Christianity, made peace with Henry I of Germany, and was killed by his brother Boleslav. Patron saint of Bohemia. The "good King Wenceslaus" of the English Christmas carol. Feast: Sept. 28.

Wenceslaus, 1361–1419, emperor (never crowned) and German king (1378–1400); as Wencelaus IV, king of Bohemia (1378–1419). He was elector of Brandenburg from 1373 until he succeeded his father, Emperor Charles IV, in 1378. His main interest was in Bohemia, and his clashes with the German nobles led in 1400 to his deposition as German king and the election of Emperor RUPERT. Wenceslaus never accepted his deposition but in 1411 agreed to the election of his brother SIGISMUND as emperor. In Bohemia, Wenceslaus was popular with the commons but quarreled with the nobles and clergy, notably with the archbishop of Prague, whose vicar general, St. John of Nepomuk, he had killed in one of his recurrent fits of rage. His decree of Kutna Hora (1409) gave the Czechs preponderance in the Univ. of Prague and made possible the election of John Huss as its rector. He continued to support Huss secretly even after the interdict was laid on Prague (1412), but the rise of the TABORITES cooled his feelings toward the reformers. When several councilors appointed by him were thrown out of the window (first Defenestration of Prague, 1419), Wenceslaus had a fit and died. His vile temper and drunken habits, though much stressed by historians, were shared by many of his contemporaries.

Wenceslaus, kings of Bohemia. **Wenceslaus I,** d. 1253, son of Ottocar I, reigned 1230–53. Called German settlers into Bohemian and Moravian cities, which received liberal charters. Repulsed Mongol invasion 1241. His grandson **Wenceslaus II,** 1271–1305, son of Ottocar II, reigned 1278–83. After a turbulent regency during which he was imprisoned, he began his personal rule with the execution of his mother's lover, Zavis of Falckenstein (1290). In 1291 he accepted the offer of the duchy of Cracow; in 1300 he was crowned king of all Poland; in 1301 he accepted the crown of Hungary for his son (later Wenceslaus III); in 1304 he repulsed the invasion of Albert I of Germany, who had demanded that Wenceslaus give up Poland and Hungary. **Wenceslaus III,** c.1289–1306, who succeeded him, was unable to assert his authority in Hungary, which he renounced in 1305. He was assassinated while preparing to invade Poland, the succession to which he claimed. The last of the Premysl dynasty, he was succeeded by his brother-in-law, John of Luxemburg. **Wenceslaus IV:** see WENCESLAUS, emperor.

Wenden, Latvia: see CESIS.

Wends (wĕndz), in medieval usage, name of all Slavs in Germany E of the Elbe; in modern usage, the small group of Slavic-speaking inhabitants of LUSATIA, E Germany. Charlemagne's conquest of the Wends (8th cent.) had no lasting effect. A crusade against the pagan Wends was launched in 1147 under HENRY THE LION and ALBERT THE BEAR; it failed, but in the following years these two princes, aided by Waldemar I of Denmark, carried out a systematic campaign of conquest. By the end of the 12th cent. nearly all Germany had been Germanized and Christianized. The term *Sorbs* (cognate with Serbs) is sometimes used interchangeably with Wends; specifically, the Sorbs were one of the Wendish nations, settled between the Elbe and Saale rivers.

Wentworth, Benning, 1696–1770, colonial governor of N.H. (1741–65). Precipitated trouble with his NEW HAMPSHIRE GRANTS. His nephew, **Sir John Wentworth,** 1737–1820, succeeded him as governor of N.H., but was forced to flee on outbreak of American Revolution because of his Loyalist sympathies.

Wentworth, Thomas: see STRAFFORD, THOMAS WENTWORTH, 1ST EARL OF.

Werfel, Franz (fränts′ vĕr′fŭl), 1890–1945, Austrian author, b. Prague. His philosophy of the brotherhood of man and his mysticism were expressed in verse, drama, and epic novels. He is best known in the U.S. for the novels *The Forty Days of Musa Dagh* (1933) and *The Song of Bernadette* (1941). Died in U.S.

Wergeland, Henrik (vĕr′gülän), 1808–45, Norwegian poet, novelist, and patriot. An ardent, tempestuous romanticist, he worked zealously for liberty, international cooperation, social improvement, the admission of Jews to Norway. His poetry (some in verse dramas) was aimed at liberating all humanity.

Werner, Alfred (äl′frät vĕr′nür), 1866–1919, Swiss chemist. Won 1913 Nobel Prize for research on the linking up of atoms in the molecule, important to development of study of isomerism.

Wertenbaker, Thomas Jefferson (wûr′tŭnbākùr), 1879–, American historian, authority on colonial history of Va. Author of *Virginia under the Stuarts* (1914), *Patrician and Plebeian in Virginia* (1916), and *Planters of Virginia* (1922).

Weser (vā′zür), river, c.300 mi. long, NW Germany, formed by junction of Fulda and Werra rivers and flowing N past Bremen into North Sea. Entirely navigable; linked by canals with Rhine, Ems, and Elbe rivers.

Weslaco (wĕs′līkō), city (pop. 7,514), S Texas, WNW of Brownsville. Processing and shipping center of vegetable and citrus fruit area, has mfg. of fertilizer and boxes.

Wesley, John, 1703–91, English evangelical preacher, founder of METHODISM. Ordained a priest in the Church of England, at Oxford he led a group gathered round his brother Charles, derisively called Methodists for their methodical habits of study and religious duties. In 1735 the Wesleys accompanied James Oglethorpe to Ga. On May 24, 1738, at a religious meeting in London, Wesley experienced an assurance of salvation through faith in Christ alone. This conviction formed the basis of his message to the world. In his lifelong evangelistic work, he is said to have preached some 40,000 sermons and to have traveled some 250,000 mi., mostly on horseback. Persuaded by George WHITEFIELD, he did open-air or field preaching. About 1740 he repudiated Calvinism, his act causing a religious break with Whitefield. In 1784 he estab. legal status of Methodist societies, and, though he had not thought to form a separate church, he made plans for the societies to go on after his death. His brother, **Charles Wesley,** 1707–88, was also a priest of the Church of England and a Methodist evangelical preacher. He wrote some 6,500 hymns, among them *Hark! the Herald Angels Sing* and *Jesus, Lover of My Soul.*

Wesleyan College: see MACON, Ga.

Wesleyan Methodist Church, branch of Methodism founded in England by followers of John Wesley. At Conference of 1791 they engaged "to follow strictly the plan" he had left to them when he died.

Wesleyan University: see MIDDLETOWN, Conn.

Wessex (wĕ'sĭks), Anglo-Saxon kingdom in England. Possibly settled by Saxons as early as 494. Until end of 8th cent. it was overshadowed successively by Kent, Northumbria, and Mercia. With reign of Alfred (1871–99?), Wessex's history becomes that of England. In Thomas Hardy's novels Wessex is used to mean mainly Dorsetshire.

West, Benjamin, 1738–1820, American historical painter in England, b. Springfield, Pa. Worked as a portrait painter in Philadelphia and New York before going to Europe in 1760. After studying in Italy he settled in London. A founder of the Royal Acad. His many oils, done on a grand scale, show skill in composition.

West, Thomas: see DE LA WARR, THOMAS WEST, BARON.

West Allis, city (pop. 42,959), SE Wis., industrial and residential suburb of Milwaukee. Mfg. of machinery and industrial gases.

West Baden Springs (bā'dŭn), village (pop. 1,047), S Ind., on Lost R. and SSW of Bedford. Long a noted mineral-springs resort. Here is West Baden Col., a branch of LOYOLA UNIVERSITY (Chicago).

West Bend, city (pop. 6,849), E Wis., NW of Milwaukee and on Milwaukee R. Aluminum ware.

Westboro or **Westborough,** town (pop. 7,378), E central Mass., E of Worcester. Birthplace of Eli Whitney. Abrasives and shoes.

Westbrook, city (pop. 12,284), SW Maine, W suburb of Portland. Mfg. of textiles, paper, machinery.

Westbury, village (pop. 7,112), on W Long Isl., SE N.Y., E of Mineola. Holds auto races.

West Chester, borough (pop. 15,168), SE Pa., W of Philadelphia; laid out 1786. Farm trade center with mfg. of metal products and canned goods. Battle of Brandywine fought in area 1777.

West Columbia, city (pop. 2,100), S Texas, near Brazos R. and SSW of Houston; founded 1826. Center, with East Columbia, of S. F. Austin's plantations. Briefly cap. of Texas Republic 1836.

Westcott, Edward Noyes, 1846–98, American writer, a banker, known for his one novel, *David Harum* (1898).

West Covina (kōvē'nù), city (pop. 8,361), S Calif., E of Los Angeles, in farm area.

West Des Moines (dù moin'), city (pop. 5,615), S central Iowa, suburb of Des Moines; called Valley Junction before 1938.

Westerly, town (pop. 12,380), including Westerly village (pop. 8,415), SW R.I., between Pawcatuck R. (bridged) and Block Isl. Sound. Mfg. of textiles, machinery, furniture. Includes Watch Hill resort, site of lighthouse, coast guard station.

Westermarck, Edward Alexander (vĕ'stûrmärk), 1862–1939, Finnish anthropologist, authority on history of morals and marriage. Wrote *The History of Human Marriage* (1891; 5th ed., 3 vols., 1921) and other works.

Western Australia, state (975,920 sq. mi.; pop. 502,-

731), Australia, comprising a third of the continent; cap. Perth. Largest Australian state, but only SW corner is fertile and substantially settled. Most of the state is occupied by state-owned gold fields and a vast central desert. Climate is tropical in NW, temperate in SW. Products include wool, wine, wheat, fruit, and hardwood. Chief port is Fremantle. First visited by the Dutch (1616). Penal colony was estab. 1826 at Albany and first free settlement in 1829 in Perth-Fremantle area. Governed by New South Wales until 1831. Became a state 1901.

Western canon consists of books of the Bible that were accepted as official by the Western Church at the time St. Jerome edited the Bible (VULGATE). See OLD TESTAMENT.

Western College: see OXFORD, Ohio.

Western Dvina, river: see DVINA.

Western Empire: see HOLY ROMAN EMPIRE; ROME.

Western Islands: see HEBRIDES.

Western Ontario, University of: see LONDON, Ont.

Western Reserve, tract of land in NE Ohio from Pa. line to W of Sandusky, on S shore of L. Erie. Reserved by Conn. for its own settlers when it ceded its western lands in 1786 (see NORTHWEST TERRITORY). Conn. gave land as "fire lands" to its citizens who were burned out in Revolution 1792. Connecticut Land Co. bought remaining land 1795; area taken into Northwest Territory 1800.

Western Reserve University, at Cleveland; nonsectarian, for men and women; chartered and opened 1826, moved to Cleveland 1882, became university 1884. Includes two coordinate colleges—Adelbert (for men; the old Western Reserve Col.) and Flora Stone Mather (for women; 1888). Cleveland Col. is downtown center.

Western Samoa, Territory of: see SAMOA.

Westerville, village (pop. 4,112), central Ohio, NE of Columbus. Seat of Otterbein Col. (United Brethren; coed.; 1847).

Westfalen, Germany: see WESTPHALIA.

Westfield. 1 City (pop. 20,962), SW Mass., on Westfield R. and W of Springfield; settled c.1660. Metal, paper products; machinery. **2** Residential town (pop. 21,243), NE N.J., SW of Newark; settled before 1700.

West Flanders, province (1,249 sq. mi.; pop. 1,002,-904), NW Belgium; cap. Bruges. Agr., stock raising, dairying. Fishing on North Sea coast. Textile mfg. (notably at Courtrai, Ypres). Population is mainly Flemish-speaking. For history, see FLANDERS.

West Florida Controversy, boundary dispute between U.S. and Spain. Developed when Great Britain ceded Fla. back to Spain after American Revolution. Treaty concluded in 1795 fixed northern boundary of W Fla. at lat. 31° N. Louisiana Purchase (1803) increased dispute. Seizure in 1810 of land between Mississippi and East Pearl rivers and, in 1813, of land between East Pearl and Perdido rivers left land in American hands.

West Frankfort, city (pop. 11,384), S Ill., NNE of Cairo. Center of coal-mining area.

West Goths: see VISIGOTHS.

West Ham, county borough (pop. 170,987), Essex, England; industrial suburb of London.

Westhampton Beach, fashionable resort village (pop. 1,087), on E Long Isl., SE N.Y., on Moriches Bay.

West Hartford, town (pop. 44,402), central Conn., suburb of Hartford; settled 1679. Mfg. of metal goods. Seat of American School for the Deaf (1817).

West Haven, town (pop. 32,010), S Conn., suburb of New Haven. Mfg. of metal goods, tires, and textiles.

West Indies, archipelago, between North and South America, curving c.2,500 mi. from Florida to NE Venezuela and separating the Caribbean from the Atlantic. Sometimes called Antilles (ăntĭ'lēz), it is divided into three main sections: BAHAMA ISLANDS; Greater Antilles (CUBA, JAMAICA, HISPANIOLA, PUERTO RICO); Lesser Antilles (LEEWARD ISLANDS, WINDWARD ISLANDS, TRINIDAD AND TOBAGO, BARBADOS, Dutch and Venezuelan islands). VIRGIN ISLANDS are considered as part of both Greater and Lesser Antilles. But for Hispaniola (HAITI and DOMINICAN REPUBLIC) and Cuba, islands are dependencies. British West Indies: Bahamas, Jamaica, British Leeward Isls., British Windward Isls. Trinidad and Tobago, Barbados, and British Virgin Isls. Dutch West Indies: CURAÇAO, Aruba, St. Eustatius, part of SAINT MARTIN. French West Indies: GUADELOUPE and MARTINIQUE. American dependencies: Puerto Rico and Virgin Isls. (U.S.). MARGARITA belongs to Venezuela. Many of islands were discovered by Columbus (1492) and first permanent white settlement was made on Hispaniola (1496). See *maps*, pp. 703, 933.

Westinghouse, George, 1846–1914, American inventor and manufacturer. Invented reversible railway frog, air brake, and signal devices; was influential in introducing alternating current in U.S.

West Lafayette (lă″fēĕt′), city (pop. 11,873), W Ind., on Wabash R. opposite Lafayette. Business and industrial center.

West Long Branch, borough (pop. 2,739), E N.J., near Long Branch. "Shadow Lawn" here was Pres. Wilson's summer White House.

West Lothian (lō′dhēŭn), formerly **Linlithgow** (lĭnlĭth′gō), county (120 sq. mi.; pop. 88,576), S Scotland, on Firth of Forth; co. town Linlithgow. There is much dairy farming, but county is more important for its mineral wealth.

Westman Islands, Icelandic *Vestmannaeyjar,* group of 14 small islands, c.8 mi. off SW Iceland. Heimaey, the largest, has chief town (Vestmannaeyjar, pop. 3,548). Abounds in waterfowl. When Iceland was first colonized, a group of Irish slaves fled to these islands. In 1627 Algerian pirates raided islands and carried c.400 people into slavery.

Westmeath (wĕstmēth′, wĕst′mēdh), inland county (681 sq. mi.; pop. 54,949), central Ireland, in Leinster; co. town Mullingar. Mostly level and fertile with many lakes and bogs. Dairy farming and cattle raising are chief occupations. Some mfg. of textiles and flour milling. Athlone is largest town.

West Memphis, cotton and lumber city (pop. 9,112), NE Ark., across the Mississippi (bridged near by) from Memphis, Tenn.

West Mifflin, borough (pop. 17,985), W Pa., SE of Pittsburgh, in industrial region.

West Milwaukee (mĭlwô′kē), village (pop. 5,429), SE Wis., near Milwaukee. Steel castings.

Westminster (wĕst′mĭnstŭr), city, metropolitan borough (pop. 98,895) of W London, England. Here are WESTMINSTER ABBEY, Houses of Parliament (WESTMINSTER PALACE), BUCKINGHAM PALACE, SAINT JAMES'S PALACE, and DOWNING STREET. Westminster Cathedral is senior archiepiscopal see of Catholic Church in England and Wales. Westminster School, founded in 14th cent., is a leading public school.

Westminster. 1 City (pop. 6,140), N Md., NW of Baltimore, in farm area. Mfg. of clothing and shoes. Was Union supply base during Gettysburg campaign. **2** Town (pop. 1,400), SE Vt., on Connecticut R. and S of Bellow Falls. "Westminster Massacre" occurred March 13, 1775, when N.Y. officials tried forcibly to hold a Cumberland co. (N.Y.) court session. Here, Jan. 15, 1777, Vt. was declared an independent state (called New Conn.).

Westminster, Statute of, 1931, an act of Parliament by which the British Commonwealth of Nations was declared to be a free association of autonomous dominions and the United Kingdom, bound only by common allegiance to the crown. Gave legal force to work of IMPERIAL CONFERENCE.

Westminster, Statutes of, legislative promulgations made by Edward I of England in Parliament at Westminster. Westminster I (1275) constitutes a code of law. Westminster II (1285) is similar. Had a clause which radically altered English landholding. Westminster III (1290) dealt with land tenure.

Westminster Abbey, in London, a national shrine and one of England's finest Gothic buildings; scene of coronation of all English kings since William I. It is the burial place of many kings and of distinguished citizens; Poets' Corner in S transept contains tombs of great English poets. Cruciform in plan, it shows French influence by the height of its nave (loftiest in England) and in strongly emphasized flying buttresses. First of several churches on the site is said to have been built in 616. Name comes from fact that church of a Benedictine monastery was here. Present church was built mainly between the 13th and 15th cent. The Lady Chapel, dedicated to Henry VII and famous for its fan vaulting, was finished in early 16th cent. The two W towers were built 1722–40 by Wren and Hawksmoor.

Westminster College: see FULTON, MO.

Westminster Conference, 1866–67, held in London to settle the plan for Canadian confederation.

Westminster Confession: see CREED.

Westminster Palace or **Houses of Parliament,** in London. Present structure was built 1840–60, following fire of 1834. Original palace buildings were built by Edward the Confessor. Served as royal abode until 16th cent. when they became assembly place for House of Commons and House of Lords. Great Hall was built at end of 11th cent. Westminster Hall, long the meeting place of highest English court of law, was scene of many historical events. Seriously damaged in World War II.

West Monroe, city (pop. 10,302), NE La., on Ouachita R. opposite Monroe, in farm and livestock area. Processes lumber and cotton.

Westmorland, Ralph Neville, 1st earl of: see NEVILLE, family.

Westmorland (wĕst′mûrlŭnd), county (789 sq. mi.; pop. 67,383), N England; co. town Appleby. Largely mountainous, it is most sparsely populated county in England. Much of county is in the LAKE DISTRICT. Dairy farming and cattle raising are chief occupations. Wordsworth and other poets are associated with the Lake District.

Westmount, city (pop. 25,222), S Que., Canada, on Montreal Isl., W residential suburb of Montreal.

West New York, town (pop. 37,683), NE N.J., on Hudson R. and N of Weehawken; settled 1790. Mfg. of radio parts, embroideries, clothing, leather goods.

Weston, town (pop. 8,677), S Ont., Canada, NW of Toronto. Mfg. of motors, bicycles, and stoves.

Weston. 1 Residential town (pop. 5,026), E Mass., W of Boston. **2** Town (pop. 8,945), central W.Va., on West Fork R. and SSW of Clarksburg. Glassmaking.

West Orange, residential town (pop. 28,605), NE N.J., NW of Newark. Edison estab. laboratories and home here 1887. Mfg. of electrical equipment.

West Palm Beach, city (pop. 43,162), SE Fla., on L. Worth (lagoon) opposite Palm Beach (connected by bridges). Resort and rail center, it has mfg. of airconditioning equipment and prefabricated buildings. Developed 1893 by H. M. Flagler. Seat of Norton Gall. and School of Art (1941). Canal to L. Okeechobee.

Westphalia (wĕstfā′lyŭ), Ger. *Westfalen,* region, NW Germany. Level in the N, hilly in the S, it has agr. districts as well as heaths and moors. In the W, it forms part of the industrial RUHR dist. and the great Westphalian coal basin. Bielefeld has important textile mfg. Westphalia was the W part of the first duchy of SAXONY, which broke up in 1180. Most of the territory passed under the rule of ecclesiastic princes (bishops of Münster, Osnabrück, Minden, Padernborn; archbishops of Cologne) and of minor temporal lords (counts of Lippe, Ravensberg, Mark). The towns prospered as members of the Hanseatic League. Brandenburg-Prussia acquired Ravensberg, Mark, and Minden in 17th cent. In 1807 Napoleon created the kingdom of Westphalia, consisting of parts of Westphalia and of adjacent territories (notably Hesse-

Kassel) for his brother Jérôme Bonaparte. The Congress of Vienna gave most of Westphalia to Prussia (1815), of which it became a province (7,806 sq. mi.; 1939 pop. 5,209,401; cap. Münster). After World War II the province became part of the state of NORTH RHINE-WESTPHALIA.

Westphalia, Peace of, 1648, general European settlement ending THIRTY YEARS WAR. Negotiations had begun 1644 at two concurrent conferences, at Münster and Osnabrück, and resulted in two treaties which together formed the peace settlement. Through the French and Swedish "satisfactions," the power of the house of Hapsburg was lessened and the HOLY ROMAN EMPIRE became a mere loose confederation of sovereign states. France obtained most of Alsace and several border fortresses. Sweden received W Pomerania and the bishoprics of Bremen and Verden. Switzerland and the United Provs. of the Netherlands obtained full independence. France, which emerged as dominant power, continued warfare with Spain until the Peace of the PYRENEES (1659).

West Pittston, residential borough (pop. 7,230), NE Pa., on Susquehanna R. and near Wilkes-Barre. Fort Jenkins built near here 1772.

West Point, city (pop. 6,432), NE Miss., NW of Columbus. Processes cottonseed oil, cheese, lumber.

West Point, U.S. military reservation, SE N.Y., on W bank of the Hudson and S of Newburg. Seat of UNITED STATES MILITARY ACADEMY since 1802. Site of Revolutionary forts guarding the Hudson. Constitution Isl., E anchorage of a chain across the river to prevent ascent of British ships in Revolution, is in reservation. Benedict Arnold's plan to surrender (1780) West Point to British was disclosed by capture of Major John André.

Westport. 1 Residential town (pop. 11,667), SW Conn., on Long Isl. Sound E of Norwalk; settled 1645-50. Has writers' and artists' colony and a summer theater. **2** See KANSAS CITY, Mo.

West Prussia, Ger. *Westpreussen,* former province of Prussia; chief city Danzig. It was formed after the Congress of Vienna from previously Polish Pomerelia (see POMERANIA) and from part of the original duchy of PRUSSIA. The Treaty of Versailles (1919) gave most of West Prussia to Poland (see POLISH CORRIDOR) and made Danzig a free city. Reannexed by Germany in 1939, the whole area was placed under Polish administration in 1945.

West Quoddy Head, promontory on Atlantic coast, SE Maine, SE of Lubec; easternmost point of U.S.

West Reading, borough (pop. 5,072), SE Pa., on Schuylkill R. and near Reading. Textiles, paper.

West Riding: see YORKSHIRE, England.

West River or **Si-kiang** (shē'jyäng'), chief river of S China, 1,250 mi. long, in Yunnan, Kwangsi, and Kwantung provs.

West Roman Empire: see ROME.

West Springfield, town (pop. 20,438), SW Mass., on Westfield and Connecticut rivers opposite Springfield; settled c.1660. Machinery, paper, chemicals.

West Virginia, state (24,282 sq. mi.; pop. 2,005,552), E central U.S.; admitted 1863 as 35th state; cap. CHARLESTON. Other cities are HUNTINGTON, PARKERSBURG, WHEELING, MOUNDSVILLE. Irregularly shaped, with one panhandle in E, another in NW. Some agr. of grains and fruit, raising of livestock. Leads in production of bituminous coal. Mfg. of iron and steel products, chemicals, glass, wood products. Settlement began c.1730; defeat of the French and the Indians speeded colonization. Although a part of Va., political and economic differences created friction. W part broke away from Va. in Civil War, joined Union, was admitted as new state. Industrial expansion began in late 19th cent., was furthered by two World Wars.

West Virginia University: see MORGANTOWN.

West Warwick, town (pop. 19,096), central R.I., SSW of Providence. Has textile mfg.

Westwego (wĕstwē'gō), town (pop. 8,328), SE La., near New Orleans. Processes seafood and chemicals.

West York, borough (pop. 5,756), SE Pa., near York. Mfg. of machinery, pottery, and hosiery.

Wethersfield, residential town (pop. 12,533), central Conn., on Connecticut R. adjoining S Hartford; settled 1633-34. One of oldest Conn. towns.

Wettin (vĕ'tēn), German dynasty, named for a castle near Halle, Germany. Margraves of Meissen from c.1100, they acquired most of SAXONY and THURINGIA; became ELECTORS 1425; split into two main lines 1485. The Ernestine (senior) line lost Saxony and electoral title to the Albertine line (1547); its Thuringian possessions split into several duchies, which were ruled by separate branches till 1918. From one of the Ernestine branches—Saxe-Coburg-Gotha—are descended the ruling houses of Great Britain (through Prince ALBERT) and Belgium (through LEOPOLD I) and former rulers of Bulgaria (through Tsar FERDINAND) and Portugal (through FERDINAND II). The Albertine line ruled Saxony 1547-1918 (in personal union with POLAND, 1697-1764).

Wewoka (wēwō'kù), city (pop. 6,747), central Okla., SE of Oklahoma City, in oil and agr. section.

Wexford (wĕks'fúrd), maritime county (910 sq. mi.; pop. 91,855), SE Ireland, in Leinster. Low, fertile land, it rises in W to Mt. Leinster (2,610 ft.). Agr. is the chief occupation; fishing is of some importance. County town is **Wexford,** urban district (pop. 12,296), on Wexford Harbour. Site of 12th-cent. abbey, old Bull Ring, and Church of St. Patrick. English landed here 1169.

Weyburn, city (pop. 7,148), SE Sask., Canada, SE of Regina. Trade center for agr. area.

Weyden, Roger van der (văn' dùr wī'dùn, Flemish vän dùr vī'dùn), c.1400-1464, Flemish artist, known also as Roger de la Pasture, successor to the Van Eycks as head of Flemish school of painting. Worked mainly in Brussels. Though his work resembles that of the Eycks in clarity and luminous glazed color, it is distinctive in its severity and dramatic power. A favorite theme is *Descent from the Cross.*

Weygand, Maxime (mäksēm' vägä'), 1867-, French general, b. Belgium. Was chief of staff to Marshal Foch in World War I; directed defense of Warsaw against Red Army (1920); replaced Gen. Gamelin as supreme Allied commander in 1940 but could not avert French rout by Germans. He served in the Vichy government as war minister, delegate general to French Africa, and governor of Algeria; was arrested by the Germans in 1942. After his liberation (1945) he was exonerated of the charge of collaboration with Germany.

Weyler y Nicolau, Valeriano (väläryä'nō wā'lĕr ē nēkōlä'ōō), 1839-1930, Spanish general; created marquis of Tenerife. Fought in Cuba in Ten Years War and in Spain against the Carlists (1875-76). In 1896 he replaced Martínez de Campos in Cuba, but his cruel methods against the rebels led to a protest by the U.S. and his recall (1897). He later was several times minister of war.

Weymouth (wā'mùth), town (pop. 32,690), E Mass., on the coast SE of Boston; settled 1622. Shoes, tools, machinery, and paper boxes.

Weymouth and Melcombe Regis (wā'mùth, mĕl'kùm rē'jĭs), municipal borough (pop. 37,097), Dorsetshire, England; a seaport and watering place.

whale, aquatic mammal of order Cetacea. Its skin is almost hairless and a layer of fat or blubber lies beneath it; the forelimbs are swimming flippers; hind limbs are absent; horizontal, fluked tail is chief means of locomotion. Most species can remain under water 5-15 min.; condensation of moist air exhaled on emerging causes "spouting." Two major groups: whalebone or baleen whales, e.g., right whale, gray whale, rorqual; toothed whales, including sperm whale (source of sperm oil and ambergris), dolphin, and porpoise.

---

whale oil, oil extracted from blubber and other parts of whales. Formerly used as illuminant, it is now used in soap making, as leather dressing, and as a lubricant.

Whales, Bay of: see ROSS SEA.

whaling. Large-scale whaling was first organized at Spitsbergen at beginning of 17th cent., largely by the Dutch. By middle of 17th cent. whaling from land was estab. in America. Later, New Bedford, Mass., became world's greatest whaling port until decline of industry (c.1850). Modern whaling began c.1856 with invention of a harpoon containing an explosive head. International whaling commission restricts whaling to a few months of year, determines size of legal catch. See WHALE; WHALE OIL.

Whampoa (hwămpō'ù), town, S Kwangtung prov., China, on an island in Canton R.; outer port for Canton. Shipbuilding. Military and naval academies.

Whangpoo or **Hwangpoo** (both: hwäng'pōō'), river, c.60 mi. long, S Kiangsu prov., China; flows past Shanghai to the Yangtze. Major navigation channel.

Wharton, Edith (Jones), 1862–1937, American novelist. Her works range widely, but she is best known for studies of high society in somewhat the manner of Henry James (e.g., *The House of Mirth*, 1905; *The Age of Innocence*, 1920; connected short novels in *Old New York*, 4 vols., 1924) and for one starkly tragic short novel of New England, *Ethan Frome* (1911). Also wrote short stories, travel books, literary criticism.

wheat, plant of genus *Triticum* of grass family. A major food and commodity on the world grain market, it was probably the first grain domesticated. Wheat has long been the white man's chief source of bread. There are varieties adapted to growing as winter wheat (fall planted) or as spring wheat. Flour from hard-kernel wheat is used to make fine cakes and bread; the hardest flour, from durum wheat, is used in making macaroni, while soft-wheat varieties provide flour for piecrust and biscuits. Wheat is used as livestock feed and in making whisky and beer. Leading wheat producers are U.S., China, USSR, India, Canada, Argentina, and Australia. See *ill.,* p. 783.

wheat fly, any of several insects harmful to wheat (e.g., HESSIAN FLY, wheat gallfly, wheat midge).

Wheatley, Henry Benjamin (hwēt'lē), 1838–1917, English bibliographer and antiquarian, a founder of the Early English Text Society and of the Index Society. He edited Pepys's diary (10 vols., 1893–99).

Wheatley, Phillis, 1753?–1784, American Negro poet. Bought as a slave by Boston merchant John Wheatley, she learned to write and produced graceful poems.

Wheaton, residential city (pop. 11,638), NE Ill., W of Chicago, in farm area; settled in 1830s. Seat of **Wheaton College** (coed.; c.1854).

Wheaton College: see NORTON, Mass.

Wheatstone, Sir Charles (hwēt'stōn), 1802–75, English physicist and inventor. He was coinventor of an electric telegraph (patented 1837), inventor of an automatic transmitter and electric recording apparatus. Is credited with invention of concertina. Known also for research on light, sound, electricity; popularized (but did not invent) the **Wheatstone bridge,** a specially devised electric circuit for accurate measurement of electrical resistance.

wheel. Came into use during Bronze Age in Old World as potter's wheel and as solid wood disks for vehicles. Spoked wheel was introduced c.1800 B.C. **Wheel and axle** classed in physics as simple machine related to lever. Relatively small effort applied to wheel overcomes resistance acting on axle; mechanical advantage is indicated by ratio of wheel radius to that of axle radius. Crank or handle may replace wheel part. Applications include windmill, doorknob, clockwork, and waterwheel. See *ill.,* p. 619.

Wheeler, Burton K(endall), 1882–, U.S. Senator from Mont. (1923–47). New Deal backer who became a leading isolationist.

Wheeler, Joseph, 1836–1906, Confederate general. Commanded cavalry in many battles. In Chattanooga campaign he destroyed Rosecrans's supplies and covered Confederate retreat. Operated against Sherman in Atlanta campaign.

Wheeler Field, U.S. army air base, Oahu, T.H., near S edge of Schofield Barracks; estab. 1922. Bombed by Japanese, Dec. 7, 1941.

Wheeler National Monument: see NATIONAL PARKS AND MONUMENTS (table).

Wheeling, city (pop. 58,891), NW W.Va., in N Panhandle, on Ohio R. and SW of Pittsburgh; settled 1769. Third largest city in state and commercial and industrial center of rich coal and gas area, it has mfg. of iron, steel, metal products, and chinaware; railroad shops. One of last skirmishes of the Revolution fought here 1782 at Fort Henry (1774; originally Fort Fincastle). Pro-Unionist center in Civil War. Site of Wheeling Conventions 1861–62. First cap. of W.Va. (1863–70, and again 1875–85).

Wheelock, Eleazar or **Eleazer** (ĕlēā'zùr hwē'lŏk), 1711–79, American clergyman, founder of DARTMOUTH COLLEGE (1770) and its first president. His son, **John Wheelock,** 1754–1817, was also president of Dartmouth (1779–1815).

Wheelwright, John, c.1592–1679, American Puritan clergyman, b. England. Founded Exeter, N.H., 1638.

Wheelwright, William, 1798–1873, American pioneer in South American railroad building and steam navigation of the Pacific.

Whig, English political party. Name was probably derived from *whiggamor* [cattle driver], used in 17th cent. for Scottish dissenters. Party upheld power of Parliament against the crown, and was supported by landed gentry and trade as against aristocratic TORY group. The Glorious Revolution (1688) began long period of Whig control. Dominating figure until his fall (1742) was Sir Robert WALPOLE, who gave party political power and shaped modern British cabinet government. Party, mercantilist in policy, followed democratic theories of John Locke. Accession of George III (1760) brought Tory control. Whigs took on middle-class character after French Revolution and became identified with movement which culminated in Reform Bill of 1832. Thereafter the Whigs became the LIBERAL PARTY.

Whig party, one of the dominant political parties of U.S. in second quarter of 19th cent. Groups that composed it arose in 1824. NATIONAL REPUBLICAN PARTY, created by Andrew Jackson's enemies, grew stronger after his 1828 triumph. Other opposition parties sprang up; opposition was correlated by Henry Clay in 1832 election. In 1836 Daniel Webster was one of several Whig presidential candidates. Clay and Webster were party's great leaders, but neither could lead it to victory, partly because of sectionalism within the party, partly because of power held by N.Y. "bosses," Thurlow WEED and W. H. Seward. Whigs succeeded with W. H. HARRISON in 1840, but inauguration of John TYLER brought trouble. In 1848 several Whig delegates bolted and joined FREE-SOIL PARTY. Though party won 1848 election, a bitter internal struggle developed between antislavery and proslavery elements. Marked failure in 1852 election brought quick end to party; remnants went to other parties in a new alignment.

Whipple, Abraham, 1733–1819, American Revolutionary naval officer. Led raid on GASPEE in 1772. Captured eight ships of British Jamaica fleet (1779).

Whipple, George Hoyt, 1878–, American pathologist. Shared 1934 Nobel Prize in Physiology and Medicine for his independent research on use of liver in treatment of pernicious anemia.

whippoorwill (hwĭ"pùrwĭl', hwĭ'pùrwĭl"), North American nocturnal bird of goatsucker family. Plumage is a mixture of brown, black, and gray above; abdomen is lighter and speckled. Weird song is monotonous repetition of its name.

whisky, spirituous liquor distilled from fermented mash of grains, usually rye, barley, oats, wheat, or corn. Inferior grades are made from potatoes or beets. Scotch whisky takes its characteristic dry, rather smoky flavor from malt cured over peat fires; the somewhat similar Irish whisky is fuller and sweeter in taste; no peat is used in the curing. American whiskies (U.S. and Canada), classed as rye and Bourbon (a corn whisky), are higher in color and flavor than Scotch and Irish.

Whisky Rebellion, 1794, insurrection in Pa. counties W of the Alleghenies, caused by Alexander Hamilton's excise tax of 1791. Settlers, who made whisky extensively, considered tax discriminatory. Troops were called out to quell rioting. Federal government's power to enforce its laws had been proved, but frontiersmen's hatred of Federalists had political consequences.

Whisky Ring, in U.S. history, conspiracy which defrauded Federal government of liquor taxes. Soon after Civil War these taxes were raised very high. Large distillers bribed government officials to retain the tax proceeds. U.S. Secretary of the Treasury B. H. Bristow struck suddenly in 1875 and arrested persons and seized distilleries involved. Over $3,000,000 in taxes were recovered; 110 persons were convicted.

Whistler, James (Abbott) McNeill, 1834–1903, American painter and etcher, b. Lowell, Mass. In 1855 he went to Paris and successfully exhibited his *Little White Girl* (1863). Moved to London, where he became famous for his eccentricities and stinging wit long before he was recognized as an artist. His famous lawsuit against Ruskin was an example of his efforts to publicize his art. Deeply influenced as a painter by Velásquez and the Japanese print artists, he created a highly personal style marked by great subtlety. Excelled also as an etcher, producing c.400 superb plates. One of the best Whistler collections is in Freer Gall. of Art, Washington, D.C., which also contains the Peacock Room (originally decorated for the Leyland home in London). His famous portrait of his mother is in the Louvre. Wrote brilliant essays and aphorisms, e.g., *The Gentle Art of Making Enemies.*

Whitby, town (pop. 7,267), S Ont., Canada, ENE of Toronto and on L. Ontario. Tanning, lumbering, mfg. of leather goods and hardware.

Whitby, urban district (pop. 11,668), North Riding of Yorkshire, England. Seaport and resort. Site of abbey (founded 657) in which poet Cædmon lived. Capt. Cook's ship *Resolution* was built here. **Synod of Whitby** was called by King Oswy of Northumbria in 664 to choose between usages of Celtic and Roman churches, primarily in determining Easter. Oswy decided for Roman usages and so determined that English church would be in main stream of European Christianity.

White, Andrew Dickson, 1832–1918, American educator and diplomat. First president of Cornell Univ. (1867–85). One of first educators to use free-elective system. Minister to Germany (1879–81) and to Russia (1892–94).

White, Edward Douglass, 1845–1921, Chief Justice of U.S. Supreme Court (1910–21).

White, E(lwyn) B(rooks), 1899–, American writer, notable for pure grace of style and humor in many contributions to the *New Yorker* magazine as well as humorous books (e.g., *Is Sex Necessary?,* 1929, with James Thurber) and juveniles (e.g., *Stuart Little,* 1945; *Charlotte's Web,* 1952). Also author of pleasantly humorous verse.

White, Gilbert, 1720–93, English naturalist. While serving as curate at Selborne and near-by parishes (from 1751), he recorded observations of nature in letters, on which he based *The Natural History and Antiquities of Selborne* (1789; often reprinted).

White, Pearl, 1889–1938, American film actress. Starred in such weekly serials as *The Perils of Pauline.* Always in danger, she was always rescued.

White, Peregrine, 1620–1704, American pioneer. He was first English child born in New England.

White, Stanford, 1853–1906, American architect, a partner of C. F. McKim and W. R. Mead. His individual works, which include Washington Arch and Century club (both in New York city), show his interest in sculptured Renaissance ornament. He was murdered by Harry K. Thaw, whose trial became a national sensation.

White, Walter (Francis), 1893–, American Negro leader, secretary of National Association for the Advancement of Colored People (1931–).

White, William, 1748–1836, American Episcopal bishop of Pa. (after 1786). He helped organize Protestant Episcopal Church in the U.S., drafted constitution, and aided in American revision of Book of Common Prayer.

White, William Alanson, 1870–1937, American psychiatrist. Superintendent of St. Elizabeth's Hospital, Washington, D.C., 1903–37. An early Freudian, he experimented with new psychiatric methods. His supporters estab. the William Alanson White Foundation (1934) which fostered the influential Washington School of Psychiatry (1936).

White, William Allen, 1868–1944, American editor and author. After 1895 owner and editor of Emporia, Kansas, *Gazette,* he was the influential exponent of "grass-roots" Republican liberal views. Wrote short stories, novels, biographies of Wilson and Coolidge, and politico-historical studies.

Whiteboys, members of small, illegal bands of Irish peasants organized c.1761 to resist demands of tax collectors, landlords. On raids they wore white disguises. Suppressed within 10 years, movement hastened establishment of Irish Parliament (1782).

white corpuscle, small protoplasmic body of which large numbers exist in blood and lymph. In humans main types are lymphocytes, of uncertain function; monocytes, functioning in repair of tissues and engulfing microorganisms not attacked by leucocytes; and leucocytes (55% to 75% of total), subdivided into three types (neutrophiles, eosinophiles or acidophiles, and basophiles). Leucocytes capable of destroying microorganisms, which they engulf by amoeboid movement, are called phagocytes. See *ill.,* p. 633.

Whiteface: see ADIRONDACK MOUNTAINS.

Whitefield, George (hwĭt'fēld), 1714–70, English evangelistic preacher, leader of Calvinistic Methodists. At Oxford he joined the Methodist group led by John and Charles WESLEY. Like the Wesleys, he was ordained in the Church of England. He made seven tours in America, where he drew great throngs and was influential in the GREAT AWAKENING. He adopted (c.1741) Calvinistic views (esp. predestination) and, breaking with the Wesleys, became leader of the Calvinistic Methodists, strong in Wales.

whitefish, fresh-water food fish of N Hemisphere, related to trout and salmon. Largest U.S. species is common or lake whitefish of Great Lakes region.

Whitefish Bay, village (pop. 14,665), SE Wis., N suburb of Milwaukee.

White Hall, city (pop. 3,082), W central Ill., N of Alton. Has Lorado Taft memorial to Annie Louise Keller, heroic teacher.

Whitehall. 1 Resort city (pop. 1,819), S Mich., N of Muskegon, on White L. near L. Michigan. Holds Swedish midsummer festival. **2** Borough (pop. 7,342), SW Pa., S of Pittsburgh.

Whitehall, street in London, running from Charing Cross to Parliament St. Has government offices and Cenotaph (war memorial). Was site of palace of the archbishops of York, in which Henry VIII and Cromwell died and outside which Charles I was executed.

Whitehead, Alfred North, 1861–1947, British philosopher and mathematician; grad. Trinity Col., Cambridge, long a teacher of mathematics at Univ. of London, then professor of philosophy at Harvard (1924–37). Wrote *Principia Mathematica* (with Bertrand Russell; 3 vols., 1910–13) and other mathematical works. His books on philosophy set forth an idealism (philosophy of organism), in which God is viewed as the principle of union in a universe where interrelated organisms adjust to the environment.

White Hill, battle of the: see WHITE MOUNTAIN.

White Horse, city (pop. 2,594), S Yukon, Canada, at head of navigation of Lewes R. On Alaska Highway at terminus of White Pass and Yukon RR. Steamer connection with Dawson June–Oct. Center of mining, hunting, and trapping region. Hq. of Royal Canadian Mounted Police for S Yukon. Has airport and radio and meteorological stations. Supply point in Klondike gold rush. Center of World War II Canol oil project (closed 1945).

White Horse, Vale of the, Berkshire, England. Has many associations with King Alfred, whose victory at Ashdown is commemorated by the White Horse on White Horse Hill at Uffington. Formed by cutting away turf to expose white chalk beneath, its crude outline (over 350 ft. long) is visible for miles.

White House, executive mansion of U.S. Presidents, on S side of Pennsylvania Ave., Washington, D.C., facing Lafayette Square. Made of Va. freestone, it is simple and stately in design. Main entrance is on N front. Main building (4 stories high) is c.170 ft. long by 85 ft. wide. E and W terraces, executive office (1902), E wing (1942), and air-raid shelter (1942) have been added. Complete rebuilding of interior structure was authorized 1949 and completed 1952. Colonnade at E end is public entrance. East Room (40 ft. by 82 ft.) is scene of most large receptions, elliptical Blue Room of official receptions. Has Red and Green rooms. Oldest public building in Washington (cornerstone laid 1792), it was designed by James Hoban and is on site chosen by George Washington. John Adams was first president to live here (1800). Restored after British burned it (1814) in War of 1812. Walls were then painted white, but "White House" did not become official name until Theodore Roosevelt's administration. Attractive grounds (c.18 acres) planned by A. J. Downing.

White Huns, people of obscure origin, possibly of Tibetan or Turkish stock and apparently unrelated to the Huns. Conquered Transoxania and Khurasan before A.D. 425. Subjugated Persia 483–513 but were defeated by Khosru I. Briefly held Gupta empire in India in 6th cent. Some remained in India.

white lead, heavy, white, amorphous basic lead carbonate, very poisonous (see LEAD POISONING). One of the oldest known pigments, it is widely used in paints (as a pigment and base) and in making putty and certain pottery.

white metal: see ANTIFRICTION METAL; BABBITT METAL.

White Mountain or **White Hill,** Czech *Bílá Hora,* hill near Prague, Bohemia, Czechoslovakia. Here in 1620, Czech Protestants under Frederick the Winter King were routed by imperials under Tilly. Battle ended Bohemian independence for three centuries and was first major engagement of Thirty Years War.

White Mountains, N N.H., a granitic part of Appalachian system, rising to 6,288 ft. in Mt. WASHINGTON of PRESIDENTIAL RANGE and to 5,249 ft. in Mt. Lafayette of FRANCONIA MOUNTAINS. CRAWFORD NOTCH separates these two main groups. Some 1,200 sq. mi. of this area is in White Mt. Natl. Forest. Noted for scenic beauty, White Mts. have long been a popular resort area.

White Nile, Arabic *Bahr-el-Abiad,* river, 600 mi. long, in Anglo-Egyptian Sudan. Joins the Blue Nile at Khartoum to form the NILE.

White Pass, 2,888 ft. high, in Coast Range, on Alaska-B.C., Canada, border and NE of Skagway. Summit of White Pass and Yukon RR (built 1898–1900). Pass traversed 1897 by Klondike-bound prospectors as alternate route to CHILKOOT PASS.

white-pine blister rust: see BLISTER RUST.

White Plains, residential city (pop. 43,466), SE N.Y.,

NE of New York city; settled late 17th cent. Plumbing and heating equipment, wire, dairy foods, textiles. Provincial congress met here, ratified Declaration of Independence 1776. Battle of White Plains (1776) followed Washington's retreat from Manhattan. Elijah Miller House (1738) was his hq.

White River. 1 Partly navigable, rising in NW Ark. and flowing 690 mi. N into Mo., then SE through Ark. to Mississippi R. above Arkansas City. North Fork has Norfolk Dam; Bull Shoals Dam is in N Ark. **2** Rising in two forks near Muncie, E central Ind., and flowing SW to unite NE of Petersburg before entering Wabash R. **3** Rising in NW Nebr. and flowing 507 mi. N and E through Badlands of S.Dak. to Missouri R. near Chamberlain.

White River Junction, Vt.: see HARTFORD.

White Russia: see BELORUSSIA.

White Sands National Monument: see NATIONAL PARKS AND MONUMENTS (table).

White Sea, inlet of Barents Sea, N European USSR; 365 mi. long, area 36,680 sq. mi., max. depth 1,115 ft. Receives Northern Dvina and Onega rivers. Chief port is Archangel. Connected by canal system with the Baltic at Leningrad. Though frozen Nov.-May (except in center), it is important for lumber exports, fisheries, and sealing.

White Settlement, residential town (pop. 10,827), N Texas, W suburb of Fort Worth. Formerly Liberator Village or Liberator.

white slave traffic: see PROSTITUTION.

white snakeroot, North American woodland perennial (*Eupatorium rugosum*), with clusters of white flowers. Leaves contain tremetol, a cause of milk fever.

White Sulphur Springs, town (pop. 2,643), SE W.Va., E of Lewisburg near Va. border. Health resort with mineral springs. Representatives of Axis nations confined here early in World War II.

white vitriol (vĭt′rēul), transparent, crystalline, hydrated zinc sulphate. Used as mordant, in making varnishes, as hide preservative, as disinfectant.

whitewash, preparation for whitening walls of cellars, stables, and various outside structures. Soluble in water, the mixture may contain quicklime, flour, glue, and whiting, often with molasses or soap added.

Whitewater, city (pop. 5,101), SE Wis., SE of Madison, in dairy and farm area. Hardware.

whitewood: see TULIP TREE.

Whiting, city (pop. 9,669), NW Ind., on L. Michigan SE of Chicago. Oil refining; chemicals.

whiting, a white powdery substance, pure calcium carbonate. Used as pigment and metal polish. Mixed with linseed oil it forms putty; with water is whitewash.

Whitinsville, Mass.: see NORTHBRIDGE.

Whitlock, Brand, 1869–1934, American author of realistic novels, a book on Belgium, and a biography of Lafayette (1929), U.S. minister and ambassador to Belgium (1913–22). A lawyer, he was also reform mayor of Toledo (1905–13).

Whitman, Marcus, 1802–47, American pioneer and missionary in Oregon country. Founded mission at Waiilatpu in 1836 (now national monument, estab. 1940, near present Walla Walla, Wash.). Following return E, he accompanied "great emigration" of 1843 over Oregon Trail. Killed in Indian massacre.

Whitman, Sarah Helen (Power), 1803–78, American poet, a widow for a time engaged to Poe.

Whitman, Walt(er), 1819–92, American poet. In early life on Long Isl., he was a country schoolteacher, a compositor, and an editor. He wrote for several papers and edited (1846–47) Brooklyn *Daily Eagle.* Spent three months in New Orleans, returned to edit (1848–49) Brooklyn *Freeman.* His *Leaves of Grass* first appeared in 1855 and was praised by Emerson. A larger edition (1856)—criticized for daring content and free-verse technique—showed him a mystic, a pantheist, and a lover of all humanity. Successive enlarged editions (final, 1892) mirrored his growth as thinker and poet. He served as unofficial nurse in

Civil War, of which he wrote both in prose and in poetry; some of his best poems are included in *Drum-Taps* (1865) and *Sequel to Drum-Taps* (1866)—e.g., "When Lilacs Last in the Dooryard Bloom'd" and "O Captain! My Captain!" He worked for the government until partially paralyzed in 1873, and lived thereafter from writing and lectures, in Camden, N.J., from 1884. Chief prose works are *Democratic Vistas* (1871) and *Specimen Days and Collect* (1882–83). He was one of America's greatest poets, and profoundly influenced both poetic form and content, particularly abroad. His major themes were love, death, nationalism and democracy, and the beauty and significance of the human body. His is the chief poetic voice of American democracy. Called "the good gray poet."

Whitman, town (pop. 8,413), SE Mass., SSE of Boston. Shoes. Toll House (1709) is restored.

Whitman College: see WALLA WALLA, Wash.

Whitman National Monument: see NATIONAL PARKS AND MONUMENTS (table).

Whitney, Eli, 1765–1825, American inventor of the cotton gin (1793). Invention made others wealthy, but not Whitney. He later manufactured first muskets to have standardized, interchangeable parts.

Whitney, Mount, E Calif., highest peak (14,495 ft.) in U.S. proper, in the Sierra Nevada at E edge of Sequoia Natl. Park. Connected by scenic highway with Death Valley (SE), lowest area in U.S.

Whitney Museum of American Art, in New York city, founded and inc. 1930 by Gertrude Vanderbilt Whitney. Most of its collection (oils, water colors, sculptures) was bought from living artists.

Whitsunday: see PENTECOST.

Whittier, John Greenleaf, 1807–92, American Quaker poet and reformer, b. Mass. He was a vigorous and politically powerful abolitionist editor and writer, especially from 1833 to 1840. In his first books, *Legends of New-England* (1831) and poem *Moll Pitcher* (1832), he was a pioneer in regional writing. His poetry was first collected in 1838. Later volumes were *Songs of Labor* (1850) and a series depicting New England, including famous *Snow-bound* (1866) and *Maud Muller* (1867). His "Barbara Frietchie," "The Barefoot Boy," "Skipper Ireson's Ride," and "Laus Deo" are among the poems, chiefly of New England life, which won him tremendous popularity in his day. Of nearly 100 hymns the best known is *Dear Lord and Father of Mankind.*

Whittier, city (pop. 29,265), S Calif., ESE of Los Angeles; founded 1887. Center of citrus fruit, dairy, and oil area with mfg. of metal products. Seat of Whittier Col. (coed.; 1888).

Whittington, Richard, d. 1423, thrice mayor of London. Contrary to the legend of Dick Whittington and his cat, he was the son of a knight. He first made his fortune as a mercer and supplied large loans to Henry IV and Henry V.

Whittredge, Worthington, 1820–1910, American landscape painter, identified with Hudson River school.

whooping cough (pertussis), infectious disease caused by a bacterium and characterized by series of coughs followed by effort to draw in breath resulting in a "whoop." Common in young children; very serious in infants. Vaccine is used to lessen severity and to immunize children.

Whymper, Edward (hwǐm'pùr), 1840–1911, English mountain climber. First to climb Matterhorn (1865).

Wichita (wǐ'chǐtô), city (pop. 168,279), S Kansas, at junction of Arkansas and Little Arkansas rivers. A Wichita Indian village (1863–65) and a trading post (1864) were estab. here, and city was founded 1868 on Chisholm Trail. Grew as cow town and rail hub after 1872. State's largest city, it has flour mills, meat-packing plants, stockyards, grain elevators, oil refineries, and airplane factories. Seat of Municipal Univ. of Wichita (coed.; 1892).

Wichita Falls, city (pop. 68,042), N Texas, on Wichita R. and NW of Fort Worth; settled in 1870s. Grew with advent of railroad 1882. Boomed c.1918 with discovery of oil. Center of oil, wheat, and cattle region with refineries, foundries, and mfg. of machinery, flour, chemicals, and glass. Kemp and Diversion lakes formed by impounded Wichita R.

Wichita Mountains, low granite range in SW Okla., c.60 mi. long, 25 mi. wide, up to 2,464 ft. high.

Wick, burgh (pop. 7,161), co. town of Caithness, Scotland; a hq. of herring fishing.

Wickenburg, town (pop. 1,736), central Ariz., NW of Phoenix. Founded as mining town after gold strike of 1863. Center now for near-by dude ranches.

Wickersham, George W(oodward), 1858–1936, American government official. Head (1929–31) of Natl. Commission on Law Observance and Law Enforcement (usually called the Wickersham Commission), which concluded that the means for enforcing criminal law in U.S. were inadequate.

Wickford, R.I.: see NORTH KINGSTOWN.

Wickham, William of: see WILLIAM OF WYKEHAM.

Wickliffe, John: see WYCLIF, JOHN.

Wickliffe (wǐ'klǐf). **1** Town (pop. 1,019), SW Ky., at confluence of Ohio and Mississippi rivers and WSW of Paducah. Buried Indian city which has yielded much material is near by. **2** City (pop. 5,002), NE Ohio, near Cleveland. Oil refining.

Wicklow (wǐ'klō), maritime county (782 sq. mi.; pop. 60,451), E Ireland, in Leinster; co. town Wicklow. Wicklow Mts. and foothills occupy most of county, which is chiefly devoted to cattle grazing. Area is popular with tourists.

Wiclif, John: see WYCLIF, JOHN.

Widsith (wǐd'sǐth), 7th-cent. Anglo-Saxon poem describing repertory and travels of Germanic minstrel.

Widukind (wǐ'dōōkǐnd) or **Wittekind** (wǐ'tùkǐnd), 8th cent., leader of the Saxons against Charlemagne. After bloody warfare over their refusal to accept baptism, Saxons were subdued when Widukind accepted baptism (785).

Wieland, Christoph Martin (vē'länt), 1733–1813, German poet. Spent later part of his life at court of Weimar. His powerful, largely satirical romances exerted much influence on German literature. Among them were *Musarion* (1768), *Die Abderiten* (1774; Eng. tr., *The Republic of Fools*), and his masterpiece, *Oberon* (1780; basis of Weber's opera).

Wieland, Heinrich, 1877–, German chemist. Won 1927 Nobel Prize for study of acids in bile.

Wien, Wilhelm (vĭl'hĕlm vēn'), 1864–1928, German physicist. Won 1911 Nobel Prize for studies on laws of heat radiation; also worked on hydrodynamics, X rays, radiation of light.

Wiener Wald (vē'nùr vält') [Ger.,= Vienna forest], low forested range, Lower Austria, W of Vienna. Its loveliness has made it a popular excursion area.

Wieniawski, Henri (vyĕnyäf'skē), 1835–80, Polish virtuoso violinist and composer. He wrote two violin concertos and some salon pieces.

Wiesbaden (vēs'bä"dùn), city (pop. 218,255), cap. of Hesse, on the Rhine and at foot of the Taunus. Famous spa, with saline springs known since antiquity. Trade center for Rhine wines. Mfg. of metal goods, chemicals, plastics, textiles. Was cap. of duchy of Nassau 1816–66; belonged to Prussia 1866–1945. The fine city was half destroyed in World War II.

wig, shortened form of periwig, an arrangement of artificial hair (human or animal) worn to conceal baldness, as a disguise, or as part of a costume, either theatrical, ceremonial, or merely fashionable. Wigs were used by the ancient Egyptians, Greeks, and Romans, and by fashionable Europeans from the middle of the 16th cent. into the 18th. They survive in England as part of the official dress of certain officials, barristers, and bishops.

Wigan (wĭg'ùn), county borough (pop. 84,546), Lancashire, England. Has cotton factories, engineering and machinery plants, and near-by coal mines.

Wiggin, Kate Douglas (Smith), 1856–1923, American author of children's books, such as *The Birds' Christmas Carol* (1887), *Rebecca of Sunnybrook Farm* (1903), and *Mother Carey's Chickens* (1911).

Wigglesworth, Michael, 1631–1705, American didactic poet, a Puritan clergyman, b. England, known for his *Day of Doom* (1662?), Calvinist theology in verse.

Wight, Isle of (wīt), island (147 sq. mi.; pop. 95,594), off Hampshire, S England. Mild climate and picturesque scenery make it a resort. Sheep raising and dairy farming are chief occupations. Conquered by Romans A.D. 43, it was hq. of Danes at end of 10th cent. Separate administrative county since 1888. Queen Victoria's seaside home, Osborne House, is near the famous yachting center, Cowes.

Wigman, Mary, 1886–, German dancer. Her theory (that dance movement must evolve from emotion) and her angular style greatly influenced modern dance.

Wigtownshire (wig'tŭnshĭr) or **Wigtown** (wig'tŭn), county (487 sq. mi.; pop. 31,625), SW Scotland, part of Galloway; co. town Wigtown. Includes peninsula, Rhinns of Galloway. Agr. is almost only industry; sheep, cattle, and pigs are raised.

Wilberforce, William, 1759–1833, British statesman and humanitarian. Friend of the younger Pitt. Secured passage of bill abolishing slave trade (1807). Worked for universal abolition of slavery. His son, **Samuel Wilberforce**, 1805–73, was bishop of Oxford (after 1845), of Winchester (after 1869). Was influential in restoring ecclesiastical authority to English church conventions.

Wilberforce University, at Wilberforce, Ohio, near Xenia; Negro, partly state supported, coed.; chartered and opened 1856 by Methodists. Bought by African Methodist Episcopal Church 1863, it absorbed Union Seminary. Named for William Wilberforce.

Wilcox, Ella Wheeler, 1855–1919, American writer of popular verse (e.g., "Laugh, and the world laughs with you"), collected in *Poems of Passion* (1883) and *Poems of Pleasure* (1888).

wild carrot or **Queen Anne's lace**, annual or biennial plant (*Daucus carota*) from which the CARROT was derived. Native to Eurasia, it is widely naturalized in North America. It has feathery foliage, a lacy flower cluster, and woody roots.

Wilde, Oscar (Fingall O'Flahertie Wills), 1854–1900, British author, b. Dublin. A conspicuous exponent of "art for art's sake" aestheticism, he wrote highly melodic poems; a novel, *The Picture of Dorian Gray* (1891); witty drawing-room comedies (e.g., *Lady Windermere's Fan*, 1892; *The Importance of Being Earnest*, 1895); and fairy tales. Convicted on morals charges, he was imprisoned (1895–97). *De Profundis* (1905) was his apologia.

Wildenbruch, Ernst von (vil'dŭnbrookh), 1845–1909, German author. His verse, novels, and historical dramas (e.g., *Heinrich und Heinrichs Geschlecht*, 1895) were much admired in the days of William II.

Wilder, Thornton (Niven) (wil'dŭr), 1897–, American novelist and playwright. Of his novels perhaps *The Cabala* (1926), *The Bridge of San Luis Rey* (1927), and *The Woman of Andros* (1930) won most acclaim. His plays *Our Town* (1938) and *The Skin of Our Teeth* (1942) won popular and critical success.

Wilderness campaign, May-June, 1864, of Civil War. Attempt by U. S. Grant to clear wild woodland W of Fredericksburg before trying to destroy Army of Northern Virginia under R. E. Lee. But Lee attacked first, forcing Grant to counterattack in series of bloody battles, especially at Spotsylvania Courthouse (May 8–19, 1864). Assaulting a strongly entrenched enemy at Cold Harbor, June 3, 1864, Grant was repulsed with horrible slaughter. Grant then withdrew, having lost about 60,000 men in the campaign, and moved against Petersburg.

Wilderness Road, route taken by American pioneers of Old Southwest, running down the Valley of Virginia to Fort Watauga (now in E Tenn.). From there in 1775 Daniel Boone blazed the trail further, through Cumberland Gap, into Ky. Road became a principal avenue of migration W. Impassable and deserted for much of 19th cent., it has been a section of U.S. 25, the Dixie Highway, since 1926.

wildlife refuge, animal haven or sanctuary providing suitable environment and protection from hunters. Before conservation movement, wildlife population was reduced alarmingly and some birds had become extinct. Causes of such depletion included drainage of swamps, destruction of forests, drought, and slaughter of animals for hides, feathers, food, and sport. National and state conservation commissions resulted from 1908 conference on natural resources. National Park Service (estab. 1916) prohibited hunting in parks under its administration. Protective legislation for birds included a U.S.–Canadian treaty (1918) protecting migratory birds; Norbeck-Andresen Migratory-Bird Conservation Act (1929) providing for a system of refuges; an act (1934) requiring purchase of a stamp by hunters of migratory birds, funds to be used for developing refuges; U.S.–Mexico migratory bird treaty (1937). Inter-American Convention on Nature Protection and Wildlife Preservation (1940) was evidence of progress in international conservation movements. By 1947 there were 291 Federal refuges in U.S. and territories; these are administered by Fish and Wildlife Service of Dept. of Interior; Service was estab. 1940 by consolidation of Bureau of Biological Survey and Bureau of Fisheries. National Audubon Society maintains numerous refuges. National parks and forests and lands controlled by Soil Conservation Service of Dept. of Agriculture also afford protection to wildlife.

wild rice, tall, aquatic grass (*Zizania aquatica*) of N U.S. and its grain, one of the chief foods of certain Indian tribes, especially in Great Lakes regions. The seed is now harvested for epicurean markets. The plants provide shelter and food for fish and waterfowl. Other names are Indian rice and Canada rice.

Wildwood, resort city (pop. 5,475), S N.J., on island off Cape May.

Wiley, Harvey Washington, 1844–1930, American chemist. He was largely responsible for enactment of Food and Drugs Act of 1906.

Wilhelm. For German rulers thus named, see WILLIAM.

Wilhelmina (vĭl″hĕlmē′nä), 1880–, queen of the Netherlands (1890–1948); daughter of William III. Married (1901) to Prince Henry of Mecklenburg-Schwerin (d. 1934). Fled to England after German invasion of Netherlands (1940); returned 1945; abdicated in favor of her daughter Juliana 1948. Her strength of character and wise leadership earned her much popularity.

Wilhelmina, Mount, c.15,600 ft. high, on W central New Guinea; highest peak of Orange Range.

Wilhelmshaven (vĭl″hĕlms-hä′fŭn), city (pop. 100,926), Lower Saxony, NW Germany, NW of Bremen and on an inlet of the North Sea. Founded 1869. Was chief German naval base on North Sea until 1945. Heavily damaged in World War II. Naval installations were dismantled by Allies.

Wilkes, Charles, 1798–1877, American naval officer and explorer. In command of government exploring expedition, he circled globe (1838–42) with group of scientists. They did research in S Pacific, explored Antarctic, Fiji, Pacific Northwest. In Civil War he precipitated TRENT AFFAIR.

Wilkes, John, 1727–97, English political leader. Angered George III by criticism of speech from throne. Twice imprisoned. Often elected to Parliament but denied his seat through king's influence. Organized party for parliamentary reform and protection of civil rights; championed cause of American colonists. Became a symbol of opposition to tyranny.

Wilkes-Barre (wilks'-bă″rē), city (pop. 76,826), E Pa., on Susquehanna R. and SW of Scranton; settled 1769. Coal mining and mfg. of textiles, clothing, and food products. Named for John Wilkes and Isaac Barré, defenders of colonies before Parliament. Burned 1778 and 1784 by British and Indians.

Wilkes Land, part of Antarctica, bordering Indian Ocean. Named for Charles Wilkes, leader of U.S. expedition 1838–42.

Wilkins, Sir (George) Hubert, 1888–, British explorer, b. Australia. Led several polar expeditions. A pioneer explorer by air. Headed arctic submarine expedition (1931).

Wilkins, Mary Eleanor: see FREEMAN, MARY E. WILKINS.

Wilkinsburg, residential borough (pop. 31,418), SW Pa., near Pittsburgh; settled c.1800.

Wilkinson, James, 1757–1825, American general. Fought in American Revolution. A key figure in conspiracy to split off SW U.S. as a separate nation allied with Spain. Ranking army officer after 1796. Involved in plans of Aaron BURR in Southwest; testified against Burr at trial, narrowly escaped indictment himself.

Wilkinson, Jemima (jŭmī'mù), 1752–1819, American religious leader, founder (c.1790) of colony of "Jerusalem" near present Penn Yan, N.Y.

will, in law, document expressing the wishes of a person concerning disposition of his property after his death. Ordinarily it must be in writing, subscribed by the person (the testator) and by at least two witnesses. In very special circumstances, an oral will is recognized in law. The testator must be of sound mind and not unduly influenced by an interested party. The usual phrase of the testator is "my last will and testament."

will, in philosophy and psychology, that inner force by which a person undertakes conscious, purposeful action. Some philosophies deny the existence of the will, others define it variously—one usual view being that on intuitive grounds the will must simply be accepted as the function that is the motive power of a personality, another that the will is the net result of interacting elements. It is not commonly discussed by present-day psychologists on the ground that such discussion is unscientific.

Willamette (wĭlă'mĭt), river, c.300 mi. long, rising in several streams in Cascade Range, W Oregon, and flowing N, past Eugene, Salem, Portland, to Columbia R. NW of Portland. Navigable to Eugene. River valley (settled in 1830s; most populous part of state) supports agr. (esp. fruit growing), food processing, lumbering. U.S. flood control, navigation, power project, begun 1938, includes Fern Ridge Dam (1941) in Long Tom R. and Cottage Grove Dam (1942) in Coast Fork.

Willamette University: see SALEM, Oregon.

Willard, Emma (Hart), 1787–1870, American educator, pioneer in women's education. After submitting her *Plan for Improving Female Education,* she came in 1818 by invitation of the governor to N.Y. state to open her school. She was head (1821–38) of TROY (N.Y.) Female Seminary, later renamed in her honor.

Willard, Frances (Elizabeth), 1839–98, American temperance leader and reformer. Helped organize (1874) the Woman's Christian Temperance Union, whose second president she was, 1879–98.

Willemstad (vĭ'lümstät), city (pop. 40,000), cap. of Curaçao colony, Dutch West Indies, on Curaçao isl. Important as commercial center of colony and free port, it is also transshipping point for oil sent from Maracaibo, Venezuela.

William, emperors of Germany and kings of Prussia. **William I,** 1797–1888, became regent for his insane brother, Frederick William IV, in 1858 and succeeded him as king of Prussia in 1861. His reign was dominated by BISMARCK, whom he appointed chancellor in 1862. He took personal command in the Franco-Prussian War, at the conclusion of which he was proclaimed emperor of GERMANY in the Hall of Mirrors at Versailles (Jan. 18, 1871). Bismarck continued to guide the destinies of Prussia and Germany, with the emperor little more than a symbol of the reborn

unity of Germany. He was succeeded by his son Frederick III (d. 1888) and his grandson **William II,** 1859–1941, who was also a grandson of Queen Victoria of England. His overbearing character soon clashed with Bismarck, whom he dismissed in 1890. His ambitious naval, colonial, and commercial program antagonized Britain and drove it into the Entente Cordiale with France. His failure to renew the reinsurance treaty with Russia (1890) and his encouragement of Austria's Balkan policy contributed to the formation of the Triple Entente (see TRIPLE ALLIANCE AND TRIPLE ENTENTE). His intensive armament and his diplomacy (or lack of diplomacy) was in part responsible for the outbreak of World War I. His abdication having been declared a prerequisite for peace negotiation by Pres. Wilson, revolts broke out in Germany late in 1918. William fled to Holland (Nov. 10) and abdicated soon afterward. He retired to Doorn; the Dutch government refused to extradite him for trial as a promoter of the war. After the death of Empress Augusta Victoria he married the widowed princess Hermine of Schönaich-Carolath (1922). He wrote memoirs.

William, king of Albania: see WILLIAM, PRINCE OF WIED.

William, kings of England. **William I** or **William the Conqueror,** 1027?–1087, king 1066–87, was illegitimate son of Robert I, duke of Normandy. While visiting England in 1051, he was probably named by his cousin Edward the Confessor as successor to the throne. In 1064 he released HAROLD, who had been shipwrecked on French coast, after extracting his promise to support duke's claims to English throne. Hearing of Harold's coronation, William invaded England, defeated (1066) and slew Harold at battle of Hastings, and was crowned king. Built castles and garrisoned them, put down rebellions, and ravaged great sections of land. Substituted foreign prelates for many English bishops and estab. separate ecclesiastical courts. After 1075 he dealt frequently with continental quarrels, fighting with his son ROBERT II. In 1085–86 he had made a survey of England (see DOMESDAY BOOK). He estab. precedent that loyalty to king is superior to loyalty to any subordinate lord. He was one of greatest English monarchs and pivotal figures in European history. See also NORMAN CONQUEST. His son, **William II** or **William Rufus,** d. 1100, king 1087–1100, extracted enormous moneys from his subjects on flimsiest pretexts and terrified clergy by his sales of churches and church lands. He occupied Normandy when his brother, Robert II, was on crusade. Gained control of Scottish throne (1097). **William III,** 1650–1702, king of England, Scotland, and Ireland 1689–1702, was son of William II of Orange. Made peace with England in DUTCH WARS. Married Mary, Protestant daughter of JAMES II. Formed coalition with Sweden, Austria, and Spain, which began (1688) War of Grand Alliance against Louis XIV. Unable to persuade James II to abandon Louis, he turned to English opposition. After secret negotiations, William came to England, allowed James to escape to France, and accepted throne of England jointly (with his wife as MARY II). This Glorious Revolution saw no bloodshed and forced William to accept BILL OF RIGHTS (1689) and Act of SETTLEMENT (1701). In Ireland he continued ruthless policy of confiscating land and giving it to English courtiers, soldiers, and adventurers. He was constantly involved in continental wars until Louis XIV recognized him as king in 1697. Wars caused unpopular taxes; Bank of England was chartered 1694; and policy of permanent national debt was begun. William of necessity chose men of Whig persuasion, and so started system of responsible ministry. His popularity diminished with death of his wife and War of Spanish Succession. **William IV,** 1765–1837, king 1830–37, was third son of George III. Agreed to passage of Reform Bill of 1832, but political leadership was left to duke of Wellington, Earl

Grey, Melbourne, and Sir Robert Peel. His niece Victoria succeeded him.

William, kings of the Netherlands and grand dukes of Luxembourg. **William I,** 1772–1843, was the son of William V of Orange, last stadholder of the Netherlands. In 1815 the Congress of Vienna made him king of the Netherlands (incl. modern Belgium) and awarded him Luxembourg in exchange for his family holdings in Germany, which he ceded to Prussia. His reactionary rule and anti-Catholic measures led to rebellion in BELGIUM, which proclaimed its independence. Anglo-French intervention eventually compelled William to withdraw his troops from Belgium. He abdicated in 1840 in favor of his son **William II,** 1792–1849, who granted a constitutional reform in 1848. His son and successor, **William III,** 1817–90, ruled as a constitutional monarch. His daughter Wilhelmina succeeded him in the Netherlands.

William, king of Scotland: see WILLIAM THE LION.

William, kings of Sicily. **William I** (the Bad), 1120–66, reigned 1154–66; son of Roger II. A wise lawgiver, despite his nickname. His son **William II** (the Good), c.1153–1189, reigned 1166–89. Sided with Lombard League against Emperor Frederick I; took Durazzo and Salonica in attempt to conquer Byzantine Empire but was defeated by Isaac II. He willed Sicily to his aunt, Empress Constance, but was succeeded by his cousin, Tancred of Lecce.

William or **Frederick William,** 1882–1951, crown prince of Prussia and Germany; son of William II. In command of attack on Verdun (1916), he ruthlessly sent thousands to certain death. Fled to Netherlands 1918 but was allowed to return to Germany 1923. Later supported Hitler regime.

William, princes of Orange. **William I:** see WILLIAM THE SILENT. **William II,** 1626–50, son of Frederick Henry, was stadholder of the Netherlands 1647–50. **William III:** see WILLIAM III, king of England.

William, prince of Wied (vēt), 1876–, king of Albania (1914); of a noble family originating in the Holy Roman Empire. Elected king 1914. Unable to impose his authority, he was forced to abdicate by Essad Pasha soon after outbreak of World War II.

William, count of Holland, 1227?–1256, German king (1254–56), previously rival king (1247–54) to CONRAD IV. His rule was purely nominal.

William, Fort: see FORT WILLIAM.

William and Mary, College of, mainly at Williamsburg, Va., with departments at Richmond and Norfolk; state supported, coed.; opened 1694 as second colonial college, became university 1779. Closed when occupied by Revolutionary troops (1781), in Civil War, and 1881–88 because of lack of funds. Phi Beta Kappa founded here 1776. Elective system (1799; suggested by Jefferson), and honor system introduced here. Main building (oldest U.S. college building, 1697) has been restored.

William of Champeaux (shămpō', shăpō'), d. 1121, French scholastic philosopher. An extreme realist, he was loser in famous dispute with Abelard.

William of Occam or **Ockham** (both: ŏ'kŭm), d. c.1349, English scholastic philosopher, a Franciscan. Embroiled in a general quarrel with Pope John XXII, he was imprisoned in Avignon but fled to the protection of Emperor Louis IV and supported him by attacking the temporal power of the papacy. Rejecting the doctrines of St. Thomas Aquinas, he argued that reality exists solely in individual things and universals are merely abstract signs. This view led him to exclude questions such as the existence of God from intellectual knowledge, referring them to faith alone.

William of Orange: see WILLIAM THE SILENT; WILLIAM II, prince of Orange; WILLIAM III, king of England.

William of Tyre, b. c.1130, d. before 1185, historian, archbishop of Tyre; author of a notable history of the Crusades.

William of Wykeham or **William of Wickham** (both:

wĭ'kŭm), 1324–1404, English churchman. Made bishop of Winchester and lord chancellor in 1367. Mediocre statesman, his lasting importance is as founder of New Col., Oxford (1379), and of Winchester Col. (1394), one of greatest English public schools.

William Rufus: see WILLIAM II, king of England.

Williams, Bill: see WILLIAMS, WILLIAM SHERLEY.

Williams, Eleazer (ĕlēā'zŭr), c.1787–1858, American Protestant Episcopal missionary among Indians. Thought by a few to be the Lost Dauphin.

Williams, Frankwood Earl, 1883–1936, American psychiatrist and psychoanalyst, a leader of the international mental hygiene movement. He helped estab. World War I psychiatric work, was on the National Committee for Mental Hygiene (1917–31), and edited *Mental Hygiene* (1917–32).

Williams, Ralph Vaughan: see VAUGHAN WILLIAMS.

Williams, Robert R., 1886–, American chemist. Isolated and synthesized thiamine (vitamin B_1); worked in alipathic and rubber chemistry.

Williams, Roger, c.1603–1683, clergyman, advocate of religious freedom, founder of R.I., b. England. Banished from Mass., he founded Providence, R.I., in 1636. Trusted friend of Indians.

Williams, Tennessee, 1914–, American dramatist, b. Miss., author of *The Glass Menagerie* (1945), *A Streetcar Named Desire* (1947), *Summer and Smoke* (1949), and *The Rose Tattoo* (1951). Original name Thomas Lanier Williams.

Williams, Theodore Samuel (Ted), 1914–, American baseball player. With Boston Red Sox, he led American League in batting 1941, 1942, 1947, 1948.

Williams, William (of Pantycelin), 1717–91, Welsh poet, a clergyman. Wrote romantic lyrics and hymns (e.g., *Guide Me, O Thou Great Jehovah*).

Williams, William Carlos, 1883–, American poet, a physician. From imagist style of early poems he went to free verse notable for use of ordinary speech, fluid lines, and stark realism. His long poem on a N.J. city, *Paterson,* began to appear in 1946; the fourth book appeared in 1951. Also wrote essays, novels, stories.

Williams, William Sherley (Old Bill Williams), 1787–1849, American trader and trapper. One of the most colorful of MOUNTAIN MEN. Guided disastrous expedition of J. C. Frémont in 1848.

Williams, tourist town (pop. 2,152), N central Ariz., W of Flagstaff. A gateway to Grand Canyon.

Williamsburg, historic city (pop. 6,735), SE Va., SE of Richmond; settled 1632 as Middle Plantation, name changed 1699. Temporary cap. after burning of Jamestown in Bacon's Rebellion (1676; see BACON, NATHANIEL); made cap. 1699. Scene of important conventions in movement for colonies' independence. City declined after cap. was moved to Richmond 1779. Rearguard action fought here in PENINSULAR CAMPAIGN of Civil War. Restoration of city to colonial aspect began 1927; city now included in Colonial National Historic Park. Major points of interest are old capitol, governor's palace, Raleigh Tavern, courthouse, Bruton Parish Church. Annual Garden Week. State general assembly meets in old capitol once each session. Seat of Col. of WILLIAM AND MARY.

Williams College: see WILLIAMSTOWN, Mass.

William Smith College: see Geneva, N.Y.

Williamson, city (pop. 8,624), SW W.Va., on Tug Fork at Ky. line. Trade center for coal region.

Williamsport, city (pop. 45,047), N central Pa., on West Branch of Susquehanna R. and N of Harrisburg; settled 1772. Tourist and trade center for agr. and mining region with mfg. of machinery and metal, wire, and wood products. Scene of Indian massacres in colonial days.

Williamstown, town (pop. 6,194), including Williamstown village (pop. 5,015), extreme NW Mass., in the Berkshires, on Hoosic R. and W of North Adams. Seat of Williams Col. (nonsectarian; for men); chartered 1785, opened as free school 1791, became college 1793, named for Ephraim Williams; has oldest

U.S. observatory (1838). First American mission was outgrowth of "haystack prayer meeting" here (1806).

William Tell: see TELL, WILLIAM.

William the Conqueror: see WILLIAM I, king of England.

William the Lion, 1143–1214, king of Scotland (1165–1214). Alliance he made (1168) with Louis VII started long friendship between France and Scotland. His capture by Henry II of England (whose rebelling sons he aided) forced him to sign (1174) treaty making Scotland a feudal possession of England. Later bought annulment of treaty from Richard I.

William the Silent or **William of Orange** (William I, prince of Orange), 1533–84, chief leader in the Dutch struggle for independence. Born in Germany, a prince of the house of NASSAU, he served the Spanish court, which appointed him stadholder of Holland (1555). He supported the GUEUX against Spanish encroachments (1566) and after Alba's arrival in the Netherlands openly took up arms against Spain; became a Calvinist (1573); and was the uncrowned ruler of the United Provs. after they declared Philip II of Spain deposed (1581). He was assassinated by a Catholic fanatic while the struggle against Spain was still in a critical stage.

Willimantic, city (pop. 13,586) in Windham (wĭn'dŭm) town (pop. 15,884), E Conn., ESE of Hartford. Known as the Thread City (cotton spinning since 1822), it has mfg. of yarns, textiles, and metal goods.

Willis, N(athaniel) P(arker), 1806–67, American journalist. Founded and edited several magazines. His own contributions were gathered in volumes such as *Pencillings by the Way* (1835). Also wrote plays.

Willis, Thomas, 1621–75, English physician and anatomist, authority on brain and nervous system.

Williston, city (pop. 7,378), NW N.Dak., on the Missouri. Trade center for irrigated agr. area with rail shops, stockyards, creamery, and grain elevator. Development of Williston Basin oil field was brisk in early 1950s.

Willkie, Wendell L(ewis), 1892–1944, American industrialist and political leader, Republican candidate for the presidency in 1940. President of Commonwealth and Southern Corp. (1933–40). Led fight (1942–44) to liberalize Republican party, mainly attacking isolationism.

Willmar, city (pop. 9,410), central Minn., W of Minneapolis. Resort, trade, and rail center with dairy, wood, and metal products.

will-o'-the-wisp, pale flickering light seen over marshland at night. It may result from spontaneous ignition of gases or may be a form of phosphorescence.

Willoughby, city (pop. 5,602), NE Ohio, on Chagrin R. near L. Erie and NE of Cleveland. Mfg. of auto parts and rubber products.

Willoughby, Lake, 5 mi. long, NE Vt., N of St. Johnsbury, in high wooded resort area.

willow, deciduous tree and shrub of widely distributed genus *Salix* with long narrow leaves. Male and female flowers are borne in catkins on separate plants. The pussy willow (*Salix discolor*) of NE U.S. and Canada, and the weeping willow (*S. babylonica*) native to Eurasia, are two decorative species. The wood is used for boxes and artificial limbs; twigs for basketry and wickerwork. Willow twigs and the bushes that bear them are often called osiers.

willow-pattern ware, blue-and-white chinaware which originated in Staffordshire, England, c.1780. Thomas Minton developed the design after a Chinese legend about the elopement of a rich mandarin's daughter. The scene, set in a garden with a willow tree and a bridge, tells the story of the lovers who make their escape by being changed into birds.

Willow Run, residential and industrial suburb, SE Mich., ENE of Ypsilanti. Machinery made in huge Willow Run plant which produced bombers in World War II. Univ. of Michigan has aeronautical research center at airport here.

Wills, Helen (Newington), 1906–, American tennis player. U.S. singles champion 1923–25, 1927–29, 1931. Married F. S. Moody, 1929.

Willstätter, Richard (rĭkh'ärt vĭl'shtĕtŭr), 1872–1942, German chemist. Won 1915 Nobel Prize for work on chlorophyll and red, blue, and violet plant pigments.

Wilmerding (wĭl'mŭrdĭng), borough (pop. 5,325), SW Pa., ESE of Pittsburgh. Railroad equipment.

Wilmette (wĭlmĕt'), residential village (pop. 18,162), NE Ill., N suburb of Chicago. Has Bahaist Temple (see BAHAISM).

Wilmington. 1 City (pop. 110,356), NE Del., on Delaware R. at influx of Brandywine Creek and Christina R. Commercial and industrial center of state; deepwater port. Has shipyards, rail shops, and mfg. of chemicals (near by), leather, and iron, steel, cork, and rubber products. Swedes built Fort Christina here, 1638; later held by Dutch, then British; William Penn took possession in 1682. Powder mill estab. here 1802 was first of many Du Pont enterprises for which Wilmington is hq. Here are Old Swedes Church (1698), Rodney Square (civic center), Delaware Acad. of Medicine, and Wilmington Art Center. **2** Town (pop. 7,039), NE Mass., NNW of Boston. **3** City (pop. 45,-043), SE N.C., port with harbor on Cape Fear R. c.30 mi. from mouth; founded 1730. Rail and mfg. (textiles, phosphates, lumber) center. Cornwallis's hq. 1781. Important port for Confederate blockade-runners until Fort FISHER fell, Jan. 15, 1865. Has national cemetery. **4** City (pop. 7,387), SW Ohio, NE of Cincinnati. Trade center for agr. area with mfg. of metal products and electrical goods.

Wilmot Proviso, 1846, amendment to a bill put before U.S. House of Representatives. Bill provided appropriation of $2,000,000 to enable Pres. Polk to negotiate a treaty with Mexico in settlement of the boundary question. Amendment stipulated that none of the territory acquired in Mexican War should be open to slavery. Amended bill passed the House but was purposely ignored by the Senate. Wilmot Proviso created great bitterness and helped crystallize North-South conflict.

Wilno, Lithuania: see VILNA.

Wilson, Charles E(dward), 1886–, American government official and industrialist. President of General Electric Co. (1940–42, 1944–50). Executive vice chairman of War Production Board (1942–44). Directed Office of Defense Mobilization (1950–52).

Wilson, Charles E(rwin), 1890–, U.S. Secretary of Defense (1953–). President of General Motors Corp. (1941–52).

Wilson, Charles Thomson Rees, 1869–, British physicist. Shared 1927 Nobel Prize. He developed a method for studying the activity of ionized particles by means of the **Wilson cloud chamber.** This device contains air or other gas cleansed and saturated with water vapor. Vapor condenses on atoms or subatomic particles made to pass through chamber, making their paths visible as water droplets.

Wilson, Edmund, 1895–, American critic. Works include literary criticism (e.g., *Axel's Castle,* 1931; *The Wound and the Bow,* 1941; *The Shores of Light,* 1952) and social criticism (e.g., *To the Finland Station,* 1940), plays, poems, a novel, and stories (as in *Memoirs of Hecate County,* 1946).

Wilson, Ernest Henry, 1876–1930, Anglo-American horticulturist, b. England. Assistant director (1919–27) and keeper (from 1927) of Arnold Arboretum, Harvard Univ. He introduced the regal lily and other oriental plants into Western gardens.

Wilson, Harry Leon, 1867–1939, American humorist, author of mild satires such as the novels *Ruggles of Red Gap* (1915) and *Merton of the Movies* (1922).

Wilson, James, 1742–98, American jurist, signer of Declaration of Independence, b. Scotland. Incorporated into U.S. Constitution the principle that sovereignty resides in the people. He was Associate Justice of U.S. Supreme Court (1789–98).

SMALL CAPITALS = cross references. Pronunciation key on inside end pages. Abbreviations: p. 2.

Wilson, John: see NORTH, CHRISTOPHER.

Wilson, William Lyne, 1843–1900, American legislator. U.S. Representative from W.Va. (1883–95). Tariff bill he introduced in 1894 substantially reduced many rates; altered in Senate by A. P. GORMAN, it passed over Pres. Cleveland's veto.

Wilson, (Thomas) Woodrow, 1856–1924, 27th President of the United States (1913–21). President of Princeton Univ. (1902–10). Governor of N.J. (1911–13). As President of U.S. (Democrat) he inaugurated a series of reforms called the "New Freedom." In foreign affairs relations with Mexico were particularly difficult, but outbreak of World War I overshadowed other problems. During first term, Wilson sought to maintain an impartial neutrality; following reelection, he attempted to mediate between warring nations, but without success. German submarine warfare brought about U.S. declaration of war in 1917. Wilson viewed war as necessary to make world "safe for democracy." He outlined FOURTEEN POINTS necessary for peace settlement. At Paris Peace Conference he worked for a new world society governed by "self-determination of peoples," but in resulting treaty (see VERSAILLES, TREATY OF) he secured little except covenant establishing LEAGUE OF NATIONS. H. C. Lodge led Republican opposition in Congress to the League. Wilson, while seeking popular support on a speaking tour, suffered a breakdown on Sept. 26, 1919. Never entirely recovering, he detached himself from politics for remainder of his term. His addresses are considered among the finest produced by an American.

Wilson. 1 Town (pop. 23,010), E N.C., E of Raleigh. Tobacco market with textile and fertilizer plants. **2** Borough (pop. 8,159), E Pa., W of Easton. Foundries; mfg. of textiles.

Wilson, Mount. 1 See SAN GABRIEL MOUNTAINS, Calif. **2** Peak, 14,250 ft. high, SW Colo., highest point in San Miguel Mts. of the Rockies.

Wilson cloud chamber: see WILSON, CHARLES T. R.

Wilson College: see CHAMBERSBURG, Pa.

Wilson-Gorman Tariff Act: see WILSON, WILLIAM LYNE; GORMAN, ARTHUR PUE.

Wilton, municipal borough (pop. 2,857), Wiltshire, England. Ancient cap. of Wessex and scene of a battle (871) between Alfred and the Danes. Carpets have been made here for centuries.

Wiltshire (wĭlt'shĭr, –shùr) or **Wilts,** county (1,345 sq. mi.; pop. 387,379), S England; co. town Salisbury. Salisbury Plain and Marlborough Downs cover more than half of county. Stonehenge, Avebury, and Silbury Hill have monuments of early British. Salisbury has famous cathedral. Mainly pastoral and agr., there is sheep grazing and dairy farming. Has mfg. of textiles, metal products, and pottery.

Wimbledon, municipal borough (pop. 58,158), Surrey, England, suburb of London. Tennis hq. of England, international matches are held here.

Winchendon (wĭn'chùndùn), town (pop. 6,585), N Mass., NW of Fitchburg. Wood and paper products.

Winchester (wĭn'chĭstùr), municipal borough (pop. 25,710), co. town of Hampshire, England. Was cap. of Wessex and center of art and learning. Malory mistakenly identified town with Camelot. Has had great ecclesiastical influence. Cathedral, founded 1079 and reflecting many architectural periods, is largest Gothic church in Europe. **Winchester College** (1382) is one of great English public schools.

Winchester. 1 See WINSTED, Conn. **2** City (pop. 5,467), E Ind., E of Muncie. Ships grain and livestock. Mfg. of glass products. **3** City (pop. 9,226), N central Ky., E of Lexington. Tobacco and livestock center. Henry Clay made first and last Ky. speeches here. **4** Town (pop. 15,509), E Mass., N of Boston; settled 1640. Leather mfg. center. **5** City (pop. 13,841), N Va., in Shenandoah Valley, WNW of Washington, D.C.; settled 1744. Center of agr. area; holds annual Apple Blossom Festival. Mfg. of textiles, hosiery, and rubber goods. George Washington began career as sur-

veyor here. In Civil War city changed hands many times; many engagements fought near by.

Winchester College: see WINCHESTER, England.

Winchilsea, Anne Finch, countess of, 1661–1720, English poet, noted for attention to nature.

Winckelmann, Johann Joachim (yō′hän yōä′khĭm vĭng′kŭlmän), 1717–68, German classical archaeologist and historian of ancient art, who greatly promoted classic revival of late 18th and early 19th cent.

Winckler, Hugo (hōō′gō vĭng′klùr), 1863–1913, German Orientalist. He discovered cuneiform tablets in Hittite (1906–7).

Wind (wĭnd), river rising in W Wyo. in Wind River Range and flowing c.110 mi. SE to join Popo Agie R. in forming Bighorn R. at Riverton.

wind, air flow paralleling earth's surface. Wind vane points direction it blows from (or compass point that gives name to the wind). Robinson cup anemometer (with metal cups set on arms revolving about a vertical rod) electrically records wind velocity, as measured on U.S. Weather Bureau's adaptation of Beaufort scale. Winds from 0 to 75 (or more) mi. per hour on a 0 to 12 scale, categorized as calm, light air, breeze (slight, gentle, moderate, fresh, strong), gale (moderate, fresh, strong, whole), storm, or hurricane. Earth's winds either vary day to day or blow mostly from one direction throughout year or season, reflecting general atmospheric circulation of wind systems blowing from several high-pressure belts to adjacent low-pressure belts: e.g., the trade winds, prevailing westerlies, and polar easterlies. Earth's rotation deflects winds according to Ferrel's law.

Windau, Latvia: see VENTSPILS.

Windaus, Adolf (ä′dôlf vĭn′dous), 1876–, German chemist. Won 1928 Nobel Prize for research on sterols (higher solid alcohols) especially in relation to vitamins; discovered and synthesized vitamin D_3.

Windber (wĭnd′bùr), borough (pop. 8,010), SW Pa., SE of Johnstown. Coal mining; mfg. of bricks.

Wind Cave National Park: see NATIONAL PARKS AND MONUMENTS (table).

Windermere wĭn′dùrmēr), largest lake in England, near Scafell, between Lancashire and Westmorland. It is 10½ mi. long, 210 ft. deep, and c.1 mi. wide. Windermere and Ambleside are near-by towns.

windflower: see ANEMONE.

Windham, Conn.: see WILLIMANTIC.

wind instruments, any instrument whose tone is produced by a vibrating column of air. In the ORGAN the wind supply is mechanically produced. Other instruments are blown by the performer and are divided into two groups—the wood winds and the brass winds or brasses. The wood winds include the flute family (flute, piccolo, flageolet, and recorder), the oboe family (oboe, English horn, bassoon, and contrabassoon), and the clarinet family. Brasses include the French horn, the trombone, the trumpet and cornet, and the tuba. The material (metal or wood) and the shape (straight or wound) are less important than the length of the pipe (which affects the pitch) and the mouthpiece (which affects the timbre). Kinds of mouthpieces are the mouth-hole (as in the flute and piccolo); the reed, a thin strip of wood, cane, or metal which vibrates as air is forced over it—a single reed distinguishing the clarinet family and a double reed distinguishing the oboe family; the funnel-shaped mouthpiece (the French horn); and the cup-shaped mouthpiece (the trombone, trumpet, and tuba). From earliest times, fingers were used on side holes (in the piccolo, flageolet, and recorder) to shorten or lengthen the air column temporarily; in the 18th and 19th cent. various mechanical devices such as slides (in the trombone) and crooks and valves (in the French horn, trumpet, and tuba) were developed. The wind passage of an instrument is called its bore and may either be cylindrical (as in the flute, clarinet, trumpet, and trombone) or conical (as in the oboe, French horn, and tuba); the flared edge of a wind instrument is called the bell. The principal modern flute is a transverse flute; it is held horizontally, and the player blows across the mouth-hole (the same is true of the piccolo). It replaced the less expressive recorder, which, like the flageolet, is held vertically and has a whistle-shaped mouthpiece. The oboe (sometimes called hautboy), the English horn (the alto of the oboe family, known by its pear-shaped bell), the bassoon (bass of the oboe family; called *fagotto* in Italian because of its resemblance to a bundle of sticks), and the larger, deeper-toned contrabassoon are distinguished by their expressive, melancholy tone. There are many kinds of clarinets (e.g., bass clarinet, A clarinet, E flat clarinet) and horns (e.g., E, E flat, and D) used in military bands, but the B flat clarinet and F horn are the ones in standard orchestra use today. Although its single reed makes it a member of the clarinet family, the saxophone is a hybrid instrument, having a conical bore (like an oboe) and being made of metal (like the brasses). The tuba, larger than the trumpet and therefore lower pitched, is often confused with other instruments that play the low brass parts in orchestra and band, such as the helicon (sousaphone), euphonium, *Flügelhorn*, barytone, saxhorn, Wagner tuba. See *ill.*, p. 667.

Windischgrätz or **Windisch-Grätz, Alfred, Fürst zu** (fürst′ tsoo vĭn′dishgrĕts′), 1787–1862, Austrian field marshal. In Revolution of 1848 he bombarded Prague and Vienna into submission and helped Schwarzenberg in installing Francis Joseph on throne.

windmill, apparatus harnessing wind power for various uses, e.g., pumping water, grinding grain, driving sawmills. Known in Europe from 12th cent. Dutch type consists of tower topped with revolving canvas sails on frames. In U.S. type, steel tower bears wheel with metal vanes.

windpipe or **trachea** (trā′kēu), main air passage of respiratory tract of vertebrates. It is a membranous and cartilaginous tube c.4½ in. long, lying in front of esophagus. Extends from larynx and divides into two bronchi. See *ill.*, p. 595.

Wind River Range (wĭnd), W Wyo., part of Rocky Mts. and Continental Divide, running SE c.120 mi. Includes Gannett Peak (13,785 ft.), highest point in Wyo., and several others over 13,000 ft.; several historic passes: e.g., SOUTH PASS, Washakie (11,610 ft.), Indian (12,130 ft.), Green River (12,222 ft.), and Togwotee (9,658 ft.).

Windsor (wĭn′zŭr), family name of royal house of Great Britain. The name Wettin, family name of Albert of Saxe-Coburg-Gotha, consort of Queen Victoria, was changed to Windsor by George V in 1917.

Windsor, Edward, duke of: see EDWARD VIII, king of England.

Windsor, Wallis Warfield, duchess of, 1894–, American-born English duchess. She was twice divorced. Her friendship with EDWARD VIII of England led to his abdication. After her marriage to him as duke of Windsor (1937) special letters patent denied her a share in his royal rank.

Windsor. 1 Town (pop. 3,439), W central N.S., Canada, NW of Halifax and on Avon R. Trade and shipping center in quarrying region. Has mfg. of furniture, fertilizer, and clothing. Founded 1703 by French as Piziquid. Acadians were expelled after town fell to British 1750. Seat of King's Col., first Canadian university by royal charter 1802. **2** City (pop. 120,049), S Ont., Canada, on Detroit R. opposite Detroit, Mich. (connected by bridge, tunnel, ferries). Mfg. of steel, machinery, and chemicals. Suburbs of East Windsor, Sandwich, and Walkerville merged with Windsor 1935.

Windsor or **New Windsor,** municipal borough (pop. 23,181), Berkshire, England, on the Thames. Had many inns in Elizabethan times. Nell Gwyn and Jane Seymour lived here. **Windsor Castle,** chief residence of English rulers since William the Conqueror, was rebuilt by successive sovereigns. St. George's Chapel, one of England's most splendid churches, is scene of investiture of Knights of the Garter. Many English kings are buried in its vaults.

Windsor. 1 Town (pop. 11,833), N Conn., on Connecticut R. just above Hartford, in agr. (tobacco, truck) area. Settled 1633 for Plymouth Colony, it was first English settlement in Conn. Has Loomis School for boys. **2** Town (pop. 3,467), SE Vt., on Connecticut R. and N of Bellows Falls. Convention (July, 1777) that organized Vt. as a state under that name and first Vt. legislature (1778) met here.

Windsor Castle: see WINDSOR, Berkshire, England.

Windsor Locks, town (pop. 5,221), N Conn., on Connecticut R. above Windsor. Mfg. developed after canal was built (1829) around rapids here.

Windward Islands, S group of Lesser Antilles in West Indies, curving generally S from Leeward Isls. toward NE Venezuela. Consist of French MARTINIQUE and **British Windward Islands** colony (821 sq. mi.; pop. 251,771). British islands comprise colonies of DOMINICA, SAINT LUCIA, SAINT VINCENT, and GRENADA. The Grenadines, an archipelago of tiny islands strung out between St. Vincent and Grenada, are divided administratively between them. Although discovered by Columbus, Windward Isls. were not colonized by Spanish. English and French colonization in 17th cent. brought long struggle for dominance, part of world-wide Anglo-French conflict. Present ownership confirmed by Congress of Vienna 1815.

wine, alcoholic beverage made by fermentation of the juice of the grape. Wines are distinguished by color, flavor, bouquet or aroma, and alcoholic content, and classified as natural or fortified, sweet or dry, still or sparkling. Differences between wines depend on variety of grape, climate, the location and soil of vineyards, treatment of grapes before and during wine making. For red wines the entire crushed grape is used; for white, the juice only. Grape pulp or must (juice) is fermented through action of wine yeasts (*Saccharomyces ellipsoideus*) existing on skins of grapes (additional yeast is sometimes introduced); the new wine then undergoes chemical processes including oxidation, precipitation of proteids, and formation of esters, which create bouquet. After repeated clarification and maturing in casks for months or years, the wine is ready for bottling. Light wines (e.g., claret, sauterne) contain from 7% to 15% alcohol; fortified, or brandied, wines (e.g., SHERRY, PORT) contain added alcohol; their strength varies from 16% to 35%. Natural effervescent wines (CHAMPAGNE is best known) retain some carbon dioxide. France is the world's leading wine-producing area, both for quantity and quality; best known are the wines of Bordeaux and Burgundy (both red and white), the Loire and Rhone valleys, Alsace, and the Jura mts. Fine German wines, mainly light, dry white wines, come from the Rhine districts, the Moselle valley, Baden, Bavaria. Italy makes quantities of wine, much of it of ordinary quality; however, Chianti, Lachryma Christi, Capri, and Falerno varieties are esteemed, and Sicily makes Marsala, usually fortified. The U.S. produces some excellent wines; California, the leading region, makes European-type wines from grapes of the Old World species, *Vitis vinifera;* Eastern wines, mostly from New York state and Ohio, are made from such native grapes as the Concord and the Catawba. The term *wine* is also applied to beverages made from plants other than the grape (e.g., dandelion wine, elderberry wine).

Wineland: see VINLAND.

Winfield, city (pop. 10,264), S Kansas, SSE of Wichita; laid out 1870. Rail and trade center in agr., livestock, and oil area. Seat of Southwestern Col. (Methodist; coed.; opened 1886.

Wingate, Orde Charles (ôrd), 1903–44, British general. In World War II, he ousted Italians from Ethiopia (1941); led raiders into Burma (1943). Killed in an airplane accident.

wings, FLIGHT organs of BIRD, BAT, INSECT. Birds' wings

are feathered and vary in size and shape, and in the number of primaries and secondaries (principal flight feathers). Among insects, a basis for classification is the number, kind, and vein-marking of wings. See *ills.*, pp. 105, 469.

Winkelried, Arnold von (är'nôlt fün vĭng'kŭlrēt), d. 1386, Swiss hero. According to legend, upheld by some historians, after the Swiss had failed to break through Austrian ranks in battle of Sempach, Winkelried of Unterwalden sacrificed himself to make an opening in the enemy ranks through which his compatriots rushed to victory.

Winnebago Indians (wĭnĭbä'gō), North American tribe of Siouan linguistic stock, in E Wis. in the 17th cent. Now on reservations in Nebr. and Wis.

Winnebago, Lake, c.30 mi. long, 5–10 mi. wide, E Wis.; largest in state. Fox R. enters at Oshkosh, leaves at Menasha; Fond du Lac is at S end.

Winnetka (wĭnĕt'kù), residential village (pop. 12,105), NE Ill., N suburb of Chicago, on L. Michigan. Pharmaceuticals.

Winnfield, town (pop. 5,629), N central La., NNW of Alexandria. Timber region with salt mines and limestone quarries. Birthplace of Huey Long.

Winnipeg, city (pop. 235,710), provincial cap., SE Man., Canada, on Red R. at mouth of Assiniboine R., S of L. Winnipeg. Largest city and center of the Prairie Provs. One of world's largest wheat markets with railroad yards and shops, stockyards, and meat-packing plants. Seat of Univ. of Manitoba (provincially supported; coed.; 1877). Fort Rouge built here 1738 by Vérendrye. Hudson's Bay Co. and North West Co. contested area. Fort Garry (formerly Fort Gibraltar) was important in Red R. traffic and settlement grew up around it; inc. as Winnipeg 1873. Grew rapidly after arrival of railroad 1881.

Winnipeg, river, W Ont. and SE Man., Canada, issuing from N end of Lake of the Woods and flowing 200 mi. generally NW to L. Winnipeg.

Winnipeg, Lake, 9,398 sq. mi., 240 mi. long and 55 mi. wide, S central Man., Canada, N of Winnipeg. Receives the Red, Winnipeg, and Saskatchewan rivers and drains NE by the Nelson to Hudson Bay. A remnant of glacial L. Agassiz. Lake discovered 1733 by Vérendrye. Lumbering and fishing.

Winnipegosis, Lake, 2,086 sq. mi., 125 mi. long and 25 mi. wide, W Man., Canada, W of L. Winnipeg. Drains SE into L. Manitoba, thence into L. Winnipeg.

Winnipesaukee, Lake (wĭ"nĭpùsô'kē), 25 mi. long and 12 mi. wide, E central N.H.; largest lake in state. Girded by irregular hilly wooded shores; drains into Merrimack R. through short Winnipesaukee R. Lake region is popular summer resort.

Winona (wĭnō'nù, wī–), city (pop. 25,031), SE Minn., on the Mississippi and SE of St. Paul; settled 1851 as trade and lumber center, grew with river traffic. Food products, bricks, and patent medicines. Limestone quarrying. Seat of Col. of St. Teresa.

Winooski (wĭnoo'skē), city (pop. 6,734), NW Vt., on Winooski R. near Burlington. Textiles, wood and metal products. Seat of St. Michael's Col.

Winooski, river, c.90 mi. long, rising in NE Vt. and swinging SW, then NW to L. Champlain between Burlington and Winooski. Because floods devastated its valley in 1927, three flood-control dams were built, 1933–37, in its tributaries.

Winslow, Edward, 1595–1655, one of founders of Plymouth Colony in New England, b. England. Held administrative offices in colony. His son, **Josiah Winslow,** c.1629–1680, was governor of Plymouth Colony (1673–80).

Winslow, city (pop. 6,518), E central Ariz., near Little Colorado R., ESE of Flagstaff, in livestock area. To W is Meteor Crater, depression c.1 mi. in diameter and 600 ft. deep.

Winstanley, Gerrard: see DIGGERS.

Winsted, city (pop. 8,781) in Winchester (wĭn'chě"stùr) town (pop. 10,535; settled c.1750), NW Conn., in

Litchfield Hills and N of Torrington. Mfg. of clocks (since 1807), clothing, and precision metal goods.

Winston-Salem (wĭn'stùn-sā'lùm), city (pop. 87,811), central N.C., W of Greensboro, in piedmont; Salem founded 1766 by Moravians, Winston founded 1850; united 1913. Port of entry and tobacco center, it has textile, hosiery, and furniture industries. Seat of Salem Col.

winterberry, name for two shrubby deciduous species of the holly genus, *Ilex.* The Virginia winterberry or black alder (*Ilex verticillata*), found in E U.S. and the Middle West, has bright red berries (sometimes yellow) which remain on the branches into winter. The smooth winterberry (*I. laevigata*), a similar shrub, has orange-red berries.

wintergreen, creeping, evergreen plant (*Gaultheria procumbens*) of E North America woods, with glossy, oval leaves, small, waxy white flowers, and red berry-like, edible fruits. The leaves are a source of wintergreen oil. Also called checkerberry, teaberry.

Winter Haven, city (pop. 8,605), central Fla., E of Tampa. Processes and ships citrus fruit. Boating resort with c.100 lakes in a 5–mi. radius.

Winter Park, residential and resort city (pop. 8,250), central Fla., N of Orlando. Seat of ROLLINS COLLEGE.

Winterset, city (pop. 3,570), SW Iowa, SW of Des Moines. Near by is original Delicious apple tree, planted 1872.

Winterthur (vĭn'tùrtoor"), city (pop. 66,971), Zurich canton, N Switzerland. Industrial center (locomotives, machinery, textiles). Has an outstanding art gallery.

Winthrop, John, 1588–1649, governor of Mass. Bay colony, b. England. Helped shape theocratic policy of colony; opposed Anne Hutchinson. His son, **John Winthrop,** 1606–76, b. England, founded New London, Conn., in 1646 and was governor of Conn. (1657, 1659–76). His son, **John Winthrop,** 1638–1707, commonly called Fitz-John Winthrop, was also governor of Conn. (1698–1707).

Winthrop, residential and resort town (pop. 19,496), E Mass., on peninsula NE of Boston; settled 1635.

Winthrop College: see ROCK HILL, S.C.

Winton, borough (pop. 6,280), NE Pa., NE of Scranton. Anthracite mines and silk mills.

wire, metal thread or rod, usually flexible. Uses include conduction of electricity, manufacture of fences, mesh, springs, and parts of various scientific instruments. For sizing, wires are arranged in series of decreasing diameter and numbered; number is known as gauge. U.S. standards are American or Brown & Sharpe wire gauge and, for steel, special steel wire gauge. Wire has been used since before 2000 B.C. Manufactured since 13th cent. by drawing metal through successively smaller holes to desired size.

wireworm, larva of elater or click beetle. Most wireworms are hard and brown. They destroy the roots, stems, seeds of many grasses, grains, and vegetables.

Wirt, William (wûrt), 1772–1834, American author and lawyer. Wrote sketches in style of Joseph Addison. Won fame as Aaron Burr's prosecutor (1807). U.S. Attorney General (1817–29).

Wirtanen, Artturi Ilmari: see VIRTANEN.

Wisby (wĭz'bē), Swed. *Visby,* city (pop. 14,770), cap. of GOTLAND co. and isl., Sweden; a Baltic port. Lutheran episcopal see. Tourist resort. As an early member of the HANSEATIC LEAGUE, medieval Visby grew into a prosperous republic, commercial center of N Europe. The ruins of 10 fine churches and the restored cathedral bear witness to its former glory. Gotland was conquered by the Swedes 1280 and by the Danes 1361–62; though restored to the Hanseatic League in 1370, it declined and became a pirate stronghold. It fell to Denmark 1570, to Sweden 1645.

Wisconsin, state (56,154 sq. mi.; pop. 3,434,575), N central U.S.; admitted 1848 as 30th state (free); cap. MADISON. Other cities are MILWAUKEE, RACINE, KENOSHA. Bordered N by L. Superior, E by L. Michigan, W by Mississippi and St. Croix rivers. Surface is broken by many glacial lakes. Major industries are farming (dairying, livestock, grains, fruits, potatoes), mfg. (dairy products, motor vehicles and parts, paper, beer), and lumbering. Region was in French hands, then fell to British. Became part of Northwest Territory in 1787; effective U.S. control began after War of 1812. Lead mines brought rush of settlers in 1820s. Made separate territory in 1836. European immigration (esp. German) was extensive. GRANGER MOVEMENT was popular in period of economic stress. Trend toward liberalism gave birth to "Wisconsin idea" under R. M. LA FOLLETTE, continued afterward.

Wisconsin, river rising in NE Wis. at Mich. line and flowing c.430 mi. generally SW to the Mississippi near Prairie du Chien. At PORTAGE it is connected by short canal with Fox R. and thus with L. Michigan. Has DELLS OF THE WISCONSIN.

Wisconsin, University of, at Madison, land-grant and state supported, coed.; chartered 1848, opened 1849. Includes Washburn Observatory, libraries of state historical society, and state academy of science, arts, and letters. Long noted for graduate and research work, scientific equipment, service to state. Experimental Col. (1927–32) made influential findings (see MEIKLEJOHN, ALEXANDER).

Wisconsin Dells, city (pop. 1,957), central Wis., on Wisconsin R. and NW of Portage. Gateway to unusual rock formations in The Dells along river.

Wisconsin Rapids, city (pop. 13,496), central Wis., on Wisconsin R. and SE of Eau Claire; formed 1900 by joining of Grand Rapids and Centralia, name changed 1920. Cranberries and paper products.

Wisdom, book of Old Testament, placed in the Apocrypha in AV, included in Western canon. Traditionally named the Wisdom of Solomon. Book contains exhortations to seek wisdom, passages on immortality, and a history of God's care of the Jews. It is an example of Wisdom literature, the critical term for Jewish philosophical writings of the pre-Christian era. Old Testament books also of this type are Job, Proverbs, Ecclesiastes, and Ecclesiasticus.

Wisdom of Jesus the Son of Sirach (sī'rŭk): see ECCLESIASTICUS.

Wise, Isaac Mayer, 1819–1900, American reform rabbi and scholar, notable as the founder (1875) of Hebrew Union College.

Wise, John, 1652–1725, American Congregational clergyman; pastor (after 1680) at Ipswich, Mass. Through preaching and writing he opposed plan of Increase and Cotton Mather to put individual churches under jurisdiction of associations of ministers and expounded democratic principles.

Wise, Stephen (Samuel), 1874–1949, American reform rabbi, b. Budapest; founder (1907) of the Free Synagogue in New York city; a leader of Zionism and reformed Judaism.

Wise, Thomas James, 1859–1937, English bibliographer and book collector. He also printed privately nearly 300 works of English authors (some exposed as forgeries by John Carter and Graham Pollard).

Wiseman, Nicholas Patrick Stephen, 1802–65, English Roman Catholic clergyman, b. Seville, of Irish-English parentage. Made archbishop of Westminster and cardinal in 1850. Aided by Manning and Newman. One of his many books was the novel *Fabiola* (1854).

Wise Men of the East, Magi, or **Three Kings,** men who, bringing gifts of gold, frankincense, and myrrh, came to adore the baby Jesus. Mat. 2. They had followed the STAR OF BETHLEHEM. According to Christian tradition there were three of them, they were kings, and their names were Caspar or Gaspar, Melchior, and Balthazar. Feast of EPIPHANY commemorates them.

Wishart, George, 1513?–1546, martyred Scottish reformer. Most eventful result of his preaching was conversion of John Knox. Charged with heresy by Cardinal BEATON, he was burned at St. Andrews.

Wishaw, Scotland: see MOTHERWELL AND WISHAW.

Wismar (vĭs'mär), city (pop. 42,018), Mecklenburg, N Germany, on the Baltic Sea. Fishing port. Has shipyards, machinery mfg. Was a leading city of Hanseatic League. Passed to Sweden 1648, to Mecklenburg-Schwerin 1803. Retained some fine medieval architecture until World War II.

Wissman, Hermann von (fŭn vĭs'män), 1853–1905, German explorer in Africa. Explored Kasai R. system, Belgian Congo (1883–85). Founded Moshi on slopes of Mt. Kilimanjaro.

Wistar, Caspar (wĭs'tŭr), 1761–1818, American physician, author of first American anatomy text. Genus *Wistaria* named in his honor.

wistaria or **wisteria,** leguminous, woody twining vines of genus *Wistaria,* highly esteemed for the beautiful pendent clusters of spring flowers (similar to sweet pea blossoms) in lilac, pink, or white. Wistaria is usually grown over porches or arbors.

Wistar Institute of Anatomy and Biology, in Philadelphia, estab. 1892. Research institute; museum.

Wister, Owen, 1860–1938, American author, best known for *The Virginian* (1902), a novel of Wyoming.

wisteria: see WISTARIA.

witchcraft, practice of sorcery or magic. When Christian Church came into power in the Western world, it banned pagan religion and magic, but belief in witchcraft persisted among people and clergy. By 14th cent., witchcraft had become a complex system, and religious persecution of supposed witches was common. From 1450 to 1650 thousands of so-called witches were executed. Even scientific interest was suspect. An accusation of witchcraft became an easy means to destroy an enemy. American colonies shared in fanaticism, and Salem was the center of a famous "witch hunt" in 1692. Last execution for witchcraft was in Scotland in 1722.

witch hazel, North American deciduous shrub or small tree (*Hamamelis virginiana*), bearing bright yellow flowers in late fall or winter. An astringent is obtained from the leaves and bark.

witenagemot (wĭ"tûnûgĭmōt') [Old Eng.,= meeting of counselors], a session of counselors (the witan) of a king in Anglo-Saxon England. Composed of aristocrats, it was dependent upon appointments of king or his immediate predecessor. Its assent was sought by king in important matters. Probably had power (esp. in Wessex) to elect king.

Wither, George (wĭ'dhŭr), 1588–1667, English poet. For his satires, *Abuses Stript and Whipt* (1613), he was imprisoned. Later wrote pastorals, which included several well-known lyrics.

Witherspoon, John, 1723–94, Scottish-American Presbyterian clergyman, signer of Declaration of Independence, b. Scotland. President (1768–94) of College of New Jersey (now Princeton Univ.).

witness: see EVIDENCE.

Witowt (vĭ'tôft), Lithuanian *Vytautas,* 1350–1430, grand duke of Lithuania. His first cousin, Ladislaus II of Poland, was obliged to recognize him as grand duke in 1392 but remained Witowt's overlord. Lithuania under Witowt reached its greatest extent—from Baltic Sea to Black Sea—and its greatest cultural flowering.

Witt, Jan de (yän' dĭ wĭt', Dutch dù vĭt'), 1625–72, Dutch republican leader. In control of state affairs as grand pensionary (1653–72), he ended first Dutch War with England (1654; see DUTCH WARS); led Netherlands to victory in Second Dutch War; abolished stadholderat in order to end power of house of Orange; negotiated TRIPLE ALLIANCE of 1668 against Louis XIV. In Third Dutch War he unsuccessfully sued for peace and resigned when popular feeling suddenly turned in favor of WILLIAM III of Orange (1672). He was killed by a mob while he visited his brother, **Cornelius de Witt,** 1623–72, a naval officer who was in prison on a charge of plotting against William. Cornelius was also slain.

Witte, Count Sergei Yulyevich (sĭrgā' yōō'lyĭvĭch vĭ'tù), 1849–1915, Russian statesman. In charge of communications, finance, commerce, and industry after 1892, he built up Russian industries with foreign loans; had Trans-Siberian RR constructed. He negotiated the Treaty of PORTSMOUTH (1905); was briefly premier after 1905 revolution.

Wittekind, Saxon leader: see WIDUKIND.

Wittelsbach (vĭ'tŭlsbäkh), Bavarian dynasty. Received duchy of Bavaria 1180; Rhenish Palatinate 1214. Emperor LOUIS IV, a Wittelsbach, divided family lands between two main lines (1329). For the Palatinate line and its ramifications, see PALATINATE. The Bavarian line, which ruled Bavaria proper, gained great power and an electoral vote under Duke MAXIMILIAN I, Catholic leader in the Thirty Years War. Its failure in 1777 brought the Palatinate line on the Bavarian throne. In 1799 all family lands were reunited under a single ruler, who in 1806 became king of a much-enlarged BAVARIA. The dynasty was deposed 1918.

Wittenberg (vĭ'tŭnbĕrk), city (pop. 41,304), Saxony-Anhalt, E Germany, on the Elbe. Railroad and mfg. center. It was the seat (1273–1422) of the Ascanian dukes of Saxe-Wittenberg (see SAXONY); passed (1423) to margraves of Meissen (after 1425, electors of Saxony). Univ. of Wittenberg, founded 1502, became the cradle of the Lutheran Reformation. In 1517 Luther nailed his 95 theses to the door of the Schlosskirche [castle church]; in 1520 he burned the papal bull against him in the market place; in 1534 the first complete Lutheran Bible was printed here. Wittenberg fell to Emperor Charles V in 1547. By the Capitulation of Wittenberg (1547) the electoral dignity, along with the duchy of Saxony, passed from the Ernestine to the Albertine branch of the WETTIN dynasty. With the Saxon cap. thus transferred to Dresden, Wittenberg declined. Its university was absorbed by that of Halle in 1817. Landmarks include Schlosskirche (with Luther's tomb) and Luther's house (now a museum).

Wittenberg College: see SPRINGFIELD, Ohio.

Witwatersrand (wĭtwô'tŭrzränd") [Afrikaans,= white water ridge] or **the Rand,** region, Transvaal, South Africa. Extending c.150 mi. E-W, it includes a gold-bearing reef which produces c.33% of the world's gold. Almost entirely urban, its chief center is Johannesburg. Surface gold was discovered 1884; main reef was reached 1889 at depth of 581 ft.

Wladimir I, duke of Kiev: see VLADIMIR I.

Wladislaw, Wladyslav, and **Wladislas.** For Polish kings thus named, see LADISLAUS.

Wlodzimierz, Ukraine: see VLADIMIR-VOLYNSKI.

Woburn (wō'bŭrn), city (pop. 20,492), NE Mass., NNW of Boston; settled 1640. Animal extracts.

Wodehouse, P(elham) G(renville) (wŏŏd'hous), 1881–, English humorist, author of many novels and stories notable for hilarious caricature of English types.

Woden (wō'dŭn), chief Germanic god, called by the Norse Odin and by Wagner Wotan. His cult was important mainly in Germany and England. In Icelandic literature, he is all-wise head of Asgard and VALHALLA, patron of poetry, but second in rank to his son THOR. Frigg is his consort. Woden of southerly Germans was god of battle. Identified with Mercury because of his wisdom and magic; hence Latin *Mercury's Day* became *Woden's Day* or *Wednesday.*

Woffington, Margaret, 1714?–1760, English actress. Popular (1737–57) in such roles as Ophelia, Sir Harry Wildair in Farquhar's *Constant Couple,* and Cordelia in *King Lear.* Of Peg Woffington's many affairs, her most notorious was with Garrick.

Wöhler, Friedrich (frē'rĭkh vū'lŭr), 1800–1882, German chemist. His synthesis of urea (1828) was the first synthesis of an organic compound and marked a new era in organic chemistry. He devised a new method for isolating aluminum and by this method isolated also beryllium and yttrium.

Wolf, Friedrich August (frē'drĭkh ou'gŏŏst vôlf'), 1759–1824, German classical scholar and philologist. He was in a sense founder of modern philology. His

Prolegomena ad Homerum (1795) suggested that the Homeric works were of composite authorship and by its methods pointed the way to higher criticism of the Bible in 19th cent.

Wolf, Hugo, 1860–1903, Austrian composer; one of the greatest writers of German lied. His more than 300 lieder include settings of poems by Goethe.

Wolf, Max (mäks' vôlf'), 1863–1932, German astronomer, introducer (1891) of astronomical photography which facilitated discovery of minor planets.

Wolf, river rising in NE Wis. and flowing c.220 mi. S to Fox R. above Oshkosh.

wolf, carnivorous mammal (*Canis*) of dog family, resembling German shepherd dog. Once found over much of N Hemisphere but now exterminated in most settled areas. Commonly runs in packs whose strength, speed, and numbers cause great destruction of wild and domestic animals. European gray wolf (*Canis lupus*) formerly was common in N regions; the larger North American gray wolf (also called timber wolf or lobo) is classed by some as a subspecies, by others as a separate species.

Wolfe, Humbert, 1885–1940, English poet and critic. His fragile verse appears in such volumes as *Kensington Gardens* (1924) and *Requiem* (1927). He also wrote satires, e.g., *Lampoons* (1925), and critical biographies of Tennyson and George Moore.

Wolfe, James, 1727–59, British soldier. Second in command to Jeffrey Amherst in French and Indian War. Commanded expedition against Quebec. Wolfe forced open battle with the French under MONTCALM on the Plains of Abraham, won a victory that was decisive in giving New France to England. Both he and Montcalm were mortally wounded.

Wolfe, Thomas (Clayton), 1900–1938, American novelist, b. Asheville, N.C. His minutely realistic but lyric *Look Homeward, Angel* (1929), *Of Time and the River* (1935), *The Web and the Rock* (1939), and *You Can't Go Home Again* (1940), are drawn from his own experiences.

Wolfeboro, resort town (pop. 2,581), E N.H., on SE L. Winnipesaukee. The Friends estab. American Seminar for European refugees here in 1940.

Wolfenbüttel (vôl'fŭnbü"tŭl), town (pop. 33,968), Lower Saxony, W central Germany, on Oker R. Was residence of dukes of Brunswick-Wolfenbüttel (see BRUNSWICK) till 1753. Famous ducal library, where Leibniz and G. E. Lessing were librarians, has c.3,000 incunabula, c.7,000 manuscripts. Has ducal palace (15th–18th cent.), many 17th-cent. houses.

Wolff, Caspar Friedrich (käs'pär frē'drĭkh vôlf'), 1733–94, German biologist, a founder of observational embryology.

Wolff, Elisabeth (Bekker) (vôlf), 1738–1804, Dutch novelist. Collaborated with Agatha Deken (dä'kŭn) (1741–1804) in sentimental epistolary novels.

Wolf-Ferrari, Ermanno (ärmän'nō vôlf'-fär-rä'rē), 1876–1948, German-Italian composer. Best known of his operas are *The Secret of Suzanne* (1909) and *The Jewels of the Madonna* (1911), his one serious opera.

wolfhound: see HOUND.

wolfram (wŏŏl'frŭm), white, very hard, metallic element (symbol = W; see also ELEMENT, table); also called tungsten. It is ductile and wires made of it have very high tensile strength. Because it has a high melting point and since less electricity is needed in operation (than for carbon, for example) it is used for electric-lamp filaments. Its alloys are important in industry because of their hardness and strength. Element occurs in ores (not free) in Asia, Europe, South America, and U.S.

Wolfram von Eschenbach (vôl'främ fŭn ĕ'shŭnbäkh), c.1170–c.1220, German epic poet and minnesinger. His only complete work is the epic *Parzival,* notable for its lyric passages, humor, and profundity of conception (see PARSIFAL); this ranks him among the greatest medieval poets.

Wolfville, town (pop. 2,313), N N.S., Canada, on SW

shore of Minas Bay of Bay of Fundy. Site of Acadia Univ. (Baptist; coed.; 1839).

Wollstonecraft, Mary (wŏol'stŭnkräft), 1759–97, English writer and feminist. Her *Vindication of the Rights of Woman* (1792) was first great feminist document. Had an affair with Gilbert Imlay. Married William Godwin (1797); their daughter was Mary Wollstonecraft Shelley.

Wolsey, Thomas (wŏol'zē), 1472?–1530, English statesman and prelate, lord chancellor (1515–29), archbishop of York (1514–30), cardinal of Roman Church. Rose rapidly, gaining high favor with Henry VIII. By 1514 he virtually controlled English domestic and foreign policy. By his treaty with France, England held balance of power between France and Hapsburgs. Made cardinal (1515), he twice failed to attain papacy. Wolsey built several palaces (e.g., Hampton Court) and his court rivaled the king's in pomp. His enemies used Henry's divorce from KATHARINE OF ARAGON as a means for his ruin. Presided at Katharine's trial. Lost all honors except his archbishopric. Arrested for treason, he died en route to London. Wolsey was largely responsible for England's emergence as first-rate power in 16th cent.

Wolverhampton (wŏol'vŭrhăm"tŭn), county borough (pop. 162,669), Staffordshire, England. One of chief centers of Black Country, it has great factories.

wolverine, carnivorous mammal (*Gulo*), largest of weasel family, found in N parts of N Hemisphere. Long, brown fur is valued for lining parkas.

Woman's Christian Temperance Union, organization founded 1874 to press for restriction of use of alcohol and harmful drugs and abolition of prostitution. Frances Willard was its second president.

Woman's Medical College of Pennsylvania: see PHILADELPHIA.

woman suffrage. Right of U.S. women to vote was first proposed at convention of 1848, Seneca Falls, N.Y. Early leaders in U.S. were Susan B. ANTHONY, Elizabeth Cady STANTON, Lucretia MOTT, Lucy STONE, and GRIMKÉ sisters; later were Anna Howard SHAW and Carrie Chapman CATT. Suffrage groups formed in 1869—united in 1890 as National American Woman Suffrage Association—worked through state and Federal agencies for vote by amendment to Constitution. Campaign finally resulted in Nineteenth Amendment (1920). Movement in England began in 1851. Early propaganda was John Stuart Mill's *Subjection of Women* (1869). Emmeline PANKHURST and a large group waged a militant campaign. In 1928 voting rights were equalized for men and women. In Europe, Finland and Norway first granted suffrage, France in 1945, Belgium in 1946. Six Latin American nations have granted suffrage since 1934, Philippines in 1937, and Japan in 1945.

Women's Army Corps: see WAC.

women's clubs, important phase of American town life in latter part of 19th cent. One of earliest was Sorosis (1868) in New York city. In 1890 General Federation of Women's Clubs was organized. Aim of early clubs was social and cultural; they have become increasingly active in social welfare, international concern; have effected many reforms.

Wood, Edward Frederick Lindley: see HALIFAX, EDWARD FREDERICK LINDLEY WOOD, 1ST EARL OF.

Wood, Grant, 1892–1942, American painter, b. Anamosa, Iowa. Known for deliberately stylized paintings of Middle Western life. Won national recognition in 1933 with his *American Gothic*.

Wood, John, 1705?–1754, English architect. Called Wood of BATH because of his extensive work in planning that city.

Wood, Leonard, 1860–1927, American general and administrator. Commanded ROUGH RIDERS in Spanish-American War. Governor general of the Philippines (1921–27); followed harsh, unpopular policy.

wood, botanically, the elements of the secondary xylem comprising the bulk of the stem in shrubs and trees

and produced by the CAMBIUM. Wood or xylem consists of cells with firm thickened walls and serves both for mechanical support and conduction of SAP. Cells in the central part (heartwood) of a tree trunk become nonfunctional as growth produces a new xylem tissue. The outer sapwood still functions for conduction. Wood is comparatively resistant to decay and to many chemicals. Proper seasoning after cutting reduces weight, prevents warping, often increases strength. Although supplanted in many uses by other natural and synthetic materials, wood is extensively used for fuel, construction, furniture, and paper manufacture. Distillation yields charcoal, methyl alcohol, tar, acetate of lime, wood gas.

wood alcohol: see METHYL ALCOHOL.

Woodberry, George Edward, 1855–1930, American poet and critic; long a professor at Columbia Univ. (1891–1904). He wrote many chiseled sonnets, and biographies of Poe and Hawthorne.

woodbine: see VIRGINIA CREEPER.

Woodbridge, Frederick James Eugene, 1867–1940, American philosopher, b. Canada. Long a professor and dean at Columbia Univ., he was author of many philosophical works (e.g., *An Essay on Nature*, 1940).

Woodbridge, township (pop. 35,758), NE N.J., N of Perth Amboy; settled 1665 from Mass. Mfg. of ceramics, bricks, and chemicals.

Wood Buffalo National Park, 17,300 sq. mi., in NE Alta. and S Mackenzie Dist., Canada, W of L. Athabaska and E of Athabaska and Slave rivers. This vast, unfenced area is largest game preserve in North America.

Woodbury, Levi, 1789–1851, American cabinet officer and jurist. U.S. Secretary of the Navy (1831–34); Secretary of the Treasury (1834–41). Associate Justice of U.S. Supreme Court (1846–51).

Woodbury, city (pop. 10,391), SW N.J., S of Camden; settled 1683. Farm trade center. Here are Cooper House, where Cornwallis stopped 1777; Lawrence House (1765); and Friends' meetinghouse.

woodchuck or **ground hog,** a North American rodent of MARMOT family, chiefly herbivorous. It is c.14 in. long and has thick, brownish fur. Old superstition holds that it leaves burrow on Candlemas Day, Feb. 2, returning to it for six weeks if it sees its shadow.

woodcock, nocturnal game bird of snipe family. It has brown and black plumage, large eyes, long bill. American woodcock, called whistling, wood, and mud snipe, is larger than European woodcock.

Woodhull, Victoria (Claflin), 1838–1927, American lecturer and journalist, a noted eccentric; proprietor, with her sister Tennessee Claflin, of *Woodhull and Claflin's Weekly* (1870). People's party nominee for President (1872).

Woodlake, city (pop. 2,525), S central Calif., SE of Fresno. Sequoia Natl. Park is near.

Woodland, city (pop. 9,386), N central Calif., NW of Sacramento. Processes meat, sugar, beets, truck, and fruit. Seat of Woodland Clinic Hospital.

wood louse, name for various small isopod crustaceans. Includes terrestrial forms, e.g., *Oniscus, Porcellio, Armadillidium* (pill bug), and marine forms.

woodpecker, widely distributed climbing bird. Bird bores into trees with chisellike bill; extracts insects with sticky, barbed tongue. Spiny tail aids in climbing. Tattoo on tree trunk is characteristic call. Male usually has red or orange head patches. North American forms include the downy (c.6½ in. long), hairy c.9½ in. long), and pileated (c.17 in. long) woodpeckers; the redheaded and three-toed woodpeckers; and the FLICKER and SAPSUCKER. See *ill.*, p. 105.

Wood-Ridge, borough (pop. 6,283), NE N.J., E of Passaic. Mfg. of airplane motors.

Wood River, city (pop. 10,190), SW Ill., on the Mississippi above East St. Louis; founded 1907. Oil refinery, tannery, and planing mill.

Woodruff, Lorande Loss, 1879–1947, American biologist, authority on protozoa. He was known as a teacher (at Yale Univ. from 1907), author, and editor.

Woods Hole, Mass.: see FALMOUTH.

Woodstock, city (pop. 15,544), S Ont., Canada, WSW of Toronto, in stock-raising region. Mfg. of furniture, pianos, organs, and hardware.

Woodstock, municipal borough (pop. 1,713), Oxfordshire, England. Site of castle in which the Black Prince was born and Elizabeth imprisoned. Scene of Scott's novel *Woodstock.*

Woodstock. 1 City (pop. 7,192), NE Ill., NW of Chicago. Mfg. of metal products. **2** Summer-resort village (pop. 2,271), SE N.Y., in Catskills foothills. Artists' colony founded 1902. Has Art Students League summer school. **3** Town (pop. 2,613), E Vt., W of White River Junction. Winter and summer resort with noted village green and fine old houses. **4** Town (pop. 1,816), N Va., SW of Winchester in Shenandoah Valley. Courthouse dates from 1791. Observation tower on near-by Massanuten Mt. views seven horseshoe bends of Shenandoah R.

Woodsworth, James Shaver, 1874–1942, Canadian politician and reformer. Entered Canadian House of Commons in 1921. Regarded as founder of CoOPERATIVE COMMONWEALTH FEDERATION.

Woodville, Elizabeth, c.1437–1492, queen consort of EDWARD IV of England. Her secret marriage to Edward (1464) angered Richard Neville, earl of Warwick, who drove Edward from England and restored Henry VI. Edward recaptured throne. On his death (1483) Elizabeth claimed throne for her son, Edward V. Richard, duke of Gloucester, usurped throne as Richard III, had her sons killed, and declared void Elizabeth's marriage to Edward IV. Her daughter was queen of Henry VII.

Woodward, Robert Simpson (wŏŏd'wùrd), 1849–1924, American scientist and educator. Contributed to mechanics, astronomy, geodesy. President of Carnegie Institution (1905–20).

Woodward, city (pop. 5,915), NW Okla., on North Canadian R. Trade and processing center for wheat and cattle area. Mfg. of dairy products, brooms.

wood wind instruments: see WIND INSTRUMENTS.

Wool, John Ellis, 1784–1869, American general. Brevetted major general for services in Mexican War, especially at Buena Vista.

wool, fiber from the fleece of domestic sheep. Wool is warm (its fibers do not conduct heat and its crimp permits it to enmesh air), elastic, crease resistant, absorbent, strong (one fourth stronger than cotton), and especially adaptable to felting (see FELT). Unless specially treated, it will shrink when soaked. No known wild animals bear wool; the fleece of the sheep has developed under domestication. Wool is classed as to fineness, length, and crimp of staple, and according to the age of the animal. Sheep are sheared with clippers. After removal of dirt and LANOLIN by various means, wool may be bleached and dyed (as raw stock, yarn, or in the piece), may be oiled to withstand processing, and is often blended. Woolen goods are those woven from carded short-staple fibers adapted to fulling and napping; worsted fabrics (e.g., whipcord, gabardine) have a hard, smooth texture and were formerly made only from long-staple wool; spinning methods have now been developed to use short-staple wool. Industrially, such other animal fibers as those of the camel, Angora goat, and vicuña are classed as wool. In the U.S., the term *wool* may be applied only to fabrics of new wool; *reprocessed wool* is recovered from unused articles and waste, *reused wool* from used articles.

Woolf, Virginia, 1882–1941, English novelist and essayist; daughter of Sir Leslie Stephen; wife of Leonard Woolf, with whom she estab. the Hogarth Press. Early novels (e.g., *The Voyage Out,* 1915; *Night and Day,* 1919) were traditional in form; later used stream-of-consciousness method (e.g., *Mrs. Dalloway,* 1925; *To the Lighthouse,* 1927; *The Waves,* 1931), while some (e.g., *Orlando,* 1928) were highly experimental.

All are notable for subtle characterization and fluid style. Her polished and distinguished essays are collected in several volumes (e.g., *The Common Reader,* 1925). *A Room of One's Own* (1929) is feminist. She drowned herself.

Woollcott, Alexander, 1887–1943, American literary and dramatic critic, noted also for his colorful personality. Exerted great influence on popular taste, especially through a radio program (1929–40). Wrote many short pieces—reviews, popular tales, essays.

Woolley, Mary Emma, 1863–1947, American educator. She was president of Mt. Holyoke Col. (1901–37).

Woolman, John, 1720–72, American Quaker leader. Recorded a minister 1743, he traveled throughout the colonies. An ardent humanitarian, he was among first to oppose slavery. Of his works the best known is his immortal *Journal* (1774).

Woolner, Thomas (wŏŏl'nùr), 1825–92, English pre-Raphaelite sculptor and poet, best known for portrait busts of famous contemporaries.

Woolson, Constance Fenimore, 1840–94, American writer; grandniece of James Fenimore Cooper. Wrote regional stories and novels of the Old Northwest and the South.

Woolwich (wŏŏl'ĭj, –ĭch), metropolitan borough (pop. 147,824) of SE London, on Thames R. Site of Royal Military Academy (1741), Royal Arsenal, and related institutions. Suffered heavy bombing 1940.

Woolworth, Frank Winfield, 1852–1919, American merchant, founder of dime-store chain.

Woonsocket (wŏŏnsŏ'kĭt), city (pop. 50,211), N R.I., at Mass. line on Blackstone R.; settled before 1675. Mfg. of textiles (since c.1814), metal, paper, and rubber products.

Wooster (wŏŏ'stùr), city (pop. 14,005), N central Ohio, SW of Akron; settled 1807. Oil and gas wells and mfg. of rubber products and motor vehicles. Seat of **College of Wooster** (Presbyterian; coed.; opened 1870).

Worcester, Dean Conant (wŏŏ'stùr), 1866–1924, American zoologist and authority on Philippines; secretary of the interior (1901–13) of Philippines.

Worcester, Thomas Percy, earl of: see PERCY, family.

Worcester, England: see WORCESTERSHIRE.

Worcester, city (pop. 203,486), central Mass., on Blackstone R. (canalized 1828) and W of Boston; first settled 1668, permanently settled 1713. Second largest Mass. city; rail and industrial center; metal products, electrical supplies, paper, textiles, abrasives. Courthouse besieged in Shays's Rebellion 1786. Annual music festival since 1858. Seat of Worcester Polytechnic Inst. (for men; 1865); Col. of the Holy Cross (Jesuit; for men; 1843); Clark Univ. (nonsectarian; coed.; chartered 1887, opened 1889 by J. G. Clark), with a pioneer graduate school and notable school of geography.

Worcester College: see OXFORD UNIVERSITY.

Worcestershire (wŏŏ'stùrshĭr, –shùr) or **Worcester,** county (700 sq. mi.; pop. 522,974), W central England. Mostly hilly, it has famous orchards and much sheep pasturage. Avon valley is called Vale of Evesham. Has rich iron and coal deposits in N part. Population has increased in recent years. County town is **Worcester,** county borough (pop. 59,700), on the Severn. In the cathedral are held, alternately with Hereford and Gloucester, Festivals of the Three Choirs. Last city to yield to Parliament in 1646, it was scene of Cromwell's final victory 1651. Porcelain, gloves, "Worcestershire" sauce, and metal goods are made.

Wordsworth, William, 1770–1850, English romantic poet; educ. at Cambridge. In France c.1791, he was influenced by Rousseau and the French Revolution. Returning to England, he published in 1793 *An Evening Walk* and *Descriptive Sketches.* With his sister Dorothy he moved to Dorsetshire, where he began friendship with Coleridge and with him wrote *Lyrical Ballads* (1798)—including "Tintern Abbey"—an effort to use in poetry "the real language of men." In 1799 Wordsworth and Dorothy moved to the Lake

District, where they lived thereafter. He married Mary Hutchinson in 1802. In 1805 he completed *The Prelude* (not pub. until much later). In 1807 appeared *Poems in Two Volumes,* including his "Ode to Duty," "Ode: Intimations of Immortality," and several famous sonnets. His creative powers diminished, but some notable later poems were *The Excursion* (1814), "Laodamia" (1815), and "Yarrow Revisited" (1835). In 1843 he succeeded Southey as poet laureate. Influenced by his life in the Lake District, Wordsworth was the greatest of English poets of nature. His attempts to show the beauty of the commonplace were often ridiculed, but his work, with its exalted air, simple language, and sheer beauty is recognized as among the world's finest poetry. Some of his shorter poems, such as the "Lucy" series, "The Solitary Reaper," "Daffodils," "The Rainbow," and the sonnet "The World Is Too Much with Us" are familiar to most English-speaking readers. His sister and devoted companion, **Dorothy Wordsworth,** 1771–1855, is known chiefly for beautifully written journals. Another brother, **Christopher Wordsworth,** 1774–1846, was an English clergyman, educator, and writer, master of Trinity Col., Cambridge (1820–41). Most noted work is *Ecclesiastical Biography* (6 vols., 1810). One of his sons, **Charles Wordsworth,** 1806–92, became bishop of St. Andrews, Dunkeld, and Dunblane, Scotland. He worked for reuniting of churches of Scotland and England. Another son, **Christopher Wordsworth,** 1807–85, became (1869) bishop of Lincoln.

work, in physics, action of some force upon some object in which friction or other resistance is overcome. Work, the product of MOTION and FORCE, is expressed in terms of distance and force, e.g., when a 10-lb. object is lifted 5 ft., work done is said to be 50 foot-pounds. ENERGY is capacity to do work. POWER involves time element and is rate at which work is done. Work unit measurements include ERG, JOULE, foot-pound, gram-centimeter. Efficiency of a machine, i.e., ratio between amount of apparent work done and amount put into it, is always less than one.

Workman, Fanny (Bullock), 1850–1925, American mountain climber. With her husband, William Hunter Workman (1847–1937), she explored and mapped Himalayan glaciers, achieved several first ascents of more than 20,000 ft. Estab. world mountaineering record for women in 1906.

Work Projects Administration (WPA), 1935–43, estab. by executive order of Pres. F. D. Roosevelt as Works Progress Administration, redesignated in 1939. Undertook extensive building and improvement program to provide work for unemployed; also included Federal Art Project (noted for decorating public buildings with murals), Federal Writers Project (produced a valuable series of U.S. guidebooks), Federal Theatre Project (introduced fresh ideas), and National Youth Administration (to 1939).

Works Progress Administration: see WORK PROJECTS ADMINISTRATION.

World Bank: see INTERNATIONAL BANK FOR RECONSTRUCTION AND DEVELOPMENT.

World Council of Churches, formally constituted by representatives from 150 Protestant and Orthodox denominations of some 44 countries, assembled at Amsterdam in 1948. Constitution provides for a permanent organization representing constituent churches. Council has no legislative power, but it gives opportunity for cooperation in matters of common concern. Hq. are at Geneva, Switzerland.

World Court, popular name for the Permanent Court of International Justice at The Hague, 1921–45; organized under the League of Nations. The court rendered judgment in international disputes voluntarily submitted to it. The U.S. did not join, but there was always a U.S. judge. Superseded by International Court of Justice.

World Health Organization (WHO), agency of UN, estab. 1948, hq. Geneva. Goal is "attainment by all peoples of the highest level of health." WHO operates by regional bodies, and has done notable work in checking cholera, malaria, and tuberculosis.

world's fair: see EXPOSITION.

World War I, 1914–18. The immediate cause of conflict was the assassination (June 28, 1914) of Archduke Francis Ferdinand of Austria-Hungary at Sarajevo by a Serbian nationalist. Hostilities began slowly, but by the end of summer, 1914, the Allies (i.e., England, France, Russia, Belgium, Serbia, Montenegro, and Japan) were involved in a general conflict with the Central Powers (i.e., Germany, Austria-Hungary, and the Ottoman Empire). On the Western Front, Germany occupied Belgium and advanced on Paris. After the first battle of the Marne and the first battle of Ypres, there was a military stalemate and grueling trench warfare for three years. On the Eastern Front, the Germans under Hindenburg, Ludendorff, and Mackensen defeated (Aug.–Sept., 1914) the Russians at Tannenberg and the Masurian Lakes. Russian counterattack failed (1916) and Russian Revolution eliminated Russia as a useful ally. Bulgaria joined (Oct., 1915) the Central Powers; Serbia and Montenegro fell by end of 1915. Allied Gallipoli campaign (1915) against Turkey was a failure. Italy joined (May, 1915) the Allies, but Italian fighting was indecisive until rout at Caporetto (1917), which was not offset until the Italian victory of Vittorio Veneto in 1918. The year 1916 saw little real change in Western Front, despite huge casualties in battles of Verdun and the Somme offensive. Portugal and Rumania joined the Allies in 1916; Greece, involved by the Salonica campaigns, declared war on the Central Powers in 1917. U.S. neutrality had been imperiled (1915) by sinking of the *Lusitania.* German fleet had been bottled up since indecisive battle of Jutland. Germany had announced (1916) decision to begin unrestricted submarine warfare. U.S. broke off relations; declared war (April 6, 1917) on Germany. American Expeditionary Force under Gen. Pershing landed in France, but did not participate in any important action until Château-Thierry battle (June, 1918). T. E. Lawrence stirred Arab revolt against Turkey; Baghdad and Jerusalem fell in 1917. Unified Allied command, under Foch, was created in April, 1918. Central Powers signed (March, 1918) Treaty of Brest-Litovsk with Russia. Germans were stopped just short of Paris in second battle of the Marne; Allied counterattack was successful. Bulgaria, Turkey, and Austria-Hungary surrendered. After revolt broke out in Germany, an armistice was signed (Nov. 11, 1918) at Compiègne. War and resulting peace treaties of Versailles, Saint-Germain, Trianon, Neuilly, and Sèvres radically changed face of Europe. Warfare itself had been revolutionized. Suffering caused by war (conservative estimate of losses is 10,000,000 dead and 20,000,000 wounded) brought on a general revulsion; led many to put their trust in newly-formed League of Nations.

World War II, 1939–45. Chief political events leading to World War II were the aggressive policies of the principal AXIS powers—Germany, Italy, Japan—culminating in the German seizure of Bohemia and Moravia (March, 1939). The W powers—Britain and France—after crowning their "appeasement policy" with the MUNICH PACT (1938), began to rearm and extended guarantees to other possible victims of aggression, notably to Poland. While Hitler demanded the return of DANZIG and the POLISH CORRIDOR, the USSR concluded a nonaggression pact with Germany (Aug., 1939). Hitler thus was left free to break off negotiations and attack POLAND (Sept. 1). England (joined by nearly all members of British Commonwealth) and France declared war on Germany. German lightning tactics (*Blitzkrieg*) won a quick victory in Poland. In the W, the British and French spent an inactive winter behind the MAGINOT LINE. In

April, 1940, Germany invaded and occupied Denmark and Norway; in May, it overran the Low Countries, broke into France, swept to the Channel ports, and cut off the Allies, who were evacuated from DUNKIRK. Italy entered the war June 10. On June 22 FRANCE surrendered. England, under Churchill's leadership, fought on alone and in the "battle of Britain" resisted the German attempt to bomb it into submission. Land operations continued in N Africa, where Italy attacked the British, and in the Balkans, where Italy attacked GREECE (Oct., 1940) and where Germany, Hungary, and Bulgaria invaded YUGOSLAVIA (April, 1941). The first round appeared to be won by the Axis, and on June 22, 1941, Hitler launched the invasion of the USSR. Meanwhile, the U.S. was gradually drawn closer to the war. Congress voted LEND-LEASE aid to England (1941) and, to protect its shipping, the U.S. occupied Iceland and Greenland. Japanese aggression in Indo-China and Thailand led to extreme tension. On Dec. 7, 1941, Japan attacked Pearl Harbor, the Philippine Isls., and Malaya. The U.S., followed by most of the Allies (except USSR), declared war on Japan. Germany and its allies (except Finland) declared war on the U.S. By 1942, Japan had conquered the Philippines, many other Pacific islands, and all SE Asia; in Russia the Axis forces had reached Stalingrad and the Caucasus; in Africa, Gen. Rommel seemed about to take Cairo; in naval warfare, German submarines threatened to wipe out Allied shipping. At this dark hour the Allies rallied and in a series of victories turned the tide. In N Africa, Montgomery's victory at Alamein (Oct., 1942), followed by the U.S. landing in Algeria, resulted in total victory over the Axis forces, the Allied conquest of Sicily and S Italy, and Italy's surrender (Sept., 1943). In the Pacific, the U.S. won the naval battles of Coral Sea and Midway, landed at Guadalcanal (1942), and under the leadership of Gen. Douglas MacArthur and Admirals Halsey and Nimitz began the "island-hopping" strategy which by 1945 had won back the Philippines, and brought a striking force to Japan's doorstep at Iwo Jima and Okinawa. In Russia, the victory of Stalingrad (1943) was followed by the mighty Russian drive which by 1944 brought Russian armies deep into Poland and Hungary and drove the Axis forces out of the Balkans. The "battle of the Atlantic" ended with the virtual extermination of German submarines. In central Italy, the Allies met stubborn German resistance and slow, grueling warfare set in (see CASSINO; ANZIO), but on June 6, 1944, the Allies under the command of Gen. Eisenhower landed in NORMANDY, and in Aug. a second Allied force landed in S France. By late 1944, France and Belgium were liberated; the war was carried into the Netherlands and Germany. Allied air power was annihilating Germany's industrial centers. In April, 1945, German resistance collapsed; on May 7, Germany surrendered unconditionally. In Aug., the U.S. dropped the first atomic bombs on Hiroshima and Nagasaki; Russia declared war on Japan and invaded Manchuria. Japan announced its surrender Aug. 14 (signed Sept. 2, 1945). The fighting was over. The world's material and human losses were incalculable. Bombing of cities and German attempts at GENOCIDE (esp. of Jews) had killed millions of civilians. Entire nations were close to starving. Never had war been more destructive, and yet the world was unable to reach true peace. Peace treaties were signed (1947) with Italy, Rumania, Bulgaria, Hungary, and FINLAND (whose war with the USSR was in a manner separate from the general conflict). However, mounting tension between the U.S. and the USSR—which emerged from the war as the two chief powers—prevented agreement on general peace treaties with Germany, Austria, and Japan (as of May, 1953). The chief positive result of the war was the formation of the UNITED NATIONS.
worm, name for several phyla of elongated, soft-bodied

invertebrates. These include segmented worms (Annelida or Annulata), e.g., EARTHWORM; flat worms (Platyhelminthes), e.g., TAPEWORM, FLUKE, other parasites; round or thread worms (Nemathelminthes), including agricultural pests and parasites causing diseases, e.g., hookworm, filariasis, trichinosis.
Worms (wûrmz, Ger. vôrms), city (pop. 51,857), Rhineland-Palatinate, W Germany, on the Rhine. Varied mfg.; export center for Rhine wines. Fell to Romans 14 B.C.; was an early episcopal see and cap. of first kingdom of Burgundy (5th cent.). Bishops ruled some territory as princes of Holy Roman Empire till 1803; city itself became (1150) the first free imperial city. Annexed to France 1797, it passed to Hesse-Darmstadt 1815 and to Rhineland-Palatinate after World War II, in which it was more than half destroyed. Among damaged buildings are the Romanesque basilica and the Romanesque-Gothic synagogue (founded 1034; destroyed by Nazis 1938). Worms was the scene of important historic events. The Synod of Worms (1076) declared Pope Gregory VII deposed. The **Concordat of Worms,** 1122, was an agreement between Pope Calixtus II and Emperor Henry V to end the struggle over INVESTITURE. The emperor conceded to the pope the right to invest bishops and abbots but reserved the right to veto elections of prelates to whom he objected. The **Diet of Worms,** 1521, was called by Emperor Charles V and among other matters took up the doctrines spread by Martin LUTHER. Luther arrived under a safe-conduct April 16; refused to yield ground in lengthy arguments with theologians; was ordered to leave the city April 26. The diet widened the gap between Roman Church and Reformed beliefs.
wormwood, perennial herb (*Artemisia absinthium*) with silvery gray leaves and tiny yellow composite flower heads. It is native to the Old World but also grown elsewhere. Wormwood oil has been used medicinally and as an insect repellent, and is the source of the bitter principle in ABSINTHE. Other artemisia species are also called wormwood.
worsted: see WOOL.
Worth, Charles Frederick, 1825–95, Parisian dress designer, b. England. For over a generation after the 1850s he was the leading arbiter of women's styles.
Worth, William Jenkins, 1794–1849, American general. A superior battle leader who fought under Zachary Taylor in northern campaign of Mexican War and, later, received surrender of Mexico city. Fort Worth, Texas, named for him.
Worthington, city (pop. 7,923), SW Minn., near Iowa line, in lake region. Farm trade center.
Wotan, Richard Wagner's name for WODEN.
Wouwerman, Philips (fē'lĭps vou'vûrmän), 1619–68, Dutch painter of Haarlem, best known for his spirited scenes of battles and hunts.
Wovoka, Indian messianic leader. See GHOST DANCE.
WPA: see WORK PROJECTS ADMINISTRATION.
WPB: see WAR PRODUCTION BOARD.
Wrangel or **Wrangell, Baron Ferdinand Petrovich von** (both: räng'gŭl; Rus. vrän'gĭl), 1794–1870, Russian naval officer, arctic explorer, and administrator. Commanded Russian naval arctic expedition (1820–23). Governor of Russian colonies in Alaska (1829–34); opposed sale to U.S.
Wrangel, Karl Gustaf (vrän'gĕl), 1613–76, Swedish field marshal. With Turenne, he overran Bavaria at end of Thirty Years War (1646). Commanded land and naval forces in Polish wars. Invaded Denmark 1657–58. Was created a count 1651.
Wrangel, Baron Piotr Nikolayevich (räng'gŭl; Rus. vrän'gĭl), 1878–1928, Russian general. Succeeded (1920) Denikin in command of White Army. After initial successes, he was forced back into the Crimea by the Reds and had to evacuate his forces to Constantinople.
Wrangel Island or **Wrangell Island** (both: räng'gŭl), island 75 mi. long, 45 mi. wide, off Khabarovsk Terri-

tory, RSFSR (NE Siberia), in Chukchi Sea (on edge of Arctic Ocean). Has government arctic station and trading post. Although barren, is breeding ground for arctic animals. Discovered 1867 by Thomas Long, American whaling-ship captain. Russians landed 1911, claimed it 1924, and estab. colony 1926.

Wrangell, Baron Ferdinand Petrovich von: see WRANGEL, BARON FERDINAND PETROVICH VON.

Wrangell Island (răng'gŭl), 30 mi. long, 5–14 mi. wide, off SE Alaska, in Alexander Archipelago. Occupied 1834 by Russians. Wrangell town (pop. 1,263) on N coast, grew out of Russian fort. U.S. military post 1867–77; later became outfitting point for miners. Lumbering, fishing, fur farming now carried on. Wrangell Inst., U.S. vocational school for natives, is near.

Wrangell Mountains, S Alaska, extending c.100 mi. SE from Copper R. to Yukon border, where St. Elias Mts. begin. Have Mt. Sanford (16,208 ft.), Mt. Blackburn (16,140 ft.), Mt. Wrangell (14,005 ft.).

Wrath, Cape, northwestern extremity of Scotland.

wreck, in law, goods washed ashore as distinguished from goods lost at sea, i.e., FLOTSAM, JETSAM, AND LIGAN. In English law the goods, unless claimed by the owner within a year and a day, became the king's property. In the U.S. (where wreck includes goods lost on lakes or rivers), laws vary; if the owner does not claim wreck promptly, title may go to the finder or to the state.

Wren, Sir Christopher, 1632–1723, outstanding English architect, whose works are notable for dignity and elegance. Also known in his time as a mathematician. Drew plans, never executed, for reconstruction of London after great fire of 1666. Of the 52 London churches he built (1670–1711), the greatest is SAINT PAUL'S CATHEDRAL. Among many secular works are Chelsea Hospital, parts of Greenwich Hospital, the garden façade of Hampton Court Palace, and the buildings of the Temple, London.

wren, small singing bird of both hemispheres, especially numerous in tropical America. Plumage is usually brown or reddish above and white, gray, or buff below. Bill is long; tail usually upturned. Destroys insects.

Wrentham (rĕn'thŭm), town (pop. 5,341), SE Mass., SW of Boston. Former home of Helen Keller and Anne Sullivan Macy is now workers' rest home.

Wrexham (rĕk'sŭm), municipal borough (pop. 30,962), Denbighshire, Wales; a livestock market. Seat of Catholic bishopric of Menevia, which includes all of Wales except Glamorganshire.

Wright, Sir Almroth Edward, 1861–1947, British pathologist, pioneer in vaccine therapy and antityphoid inoculation.

Wright, Elizur (ĭlī'zŭr), 1804–85, American actuary and antislavery leader. His actuarial work and his work in furthering laws governing insurance practices earned him the title "father of life insurance."

Wright, Frances, 1795–1852, British-American reformer. Her *Views of Society and Manners in America* (1821) enthusiastically recounted her travels (1818–20) in the U.S., where, impressed by the Rappite colonies and Robert Dale Owen's colony, she later (1825) founded NASHOBA. After its failure she lectured and, with Owen, edited the *Free Enquirer*. Her marriage (1831) to W. P. Darusmont (or D'Arusmont) was dissolved 1835.

Wright, Frank Lloyd, 1869–, American architect, b. Richland Center, Wis. He developed his so-called prairie style in Oak Park, Ill., in the series of homes he built with low horizontal proportions and strongly projecting eaves. From the beginning he practiced radical innovation both in structure and aesthetics. He pioneered in the integration of machine methods and materials into a true architectural expression and was the first to produce open planning in houses, in a break from the traditional closed volume. Among his notable works are the Imperial Hotel (1916–20), Tokyo, Japan, which survived the 1923 earthquake,

and his own home "Taliesin" (1911) at Spring Green, Wis. "Taliesin West" is near Phoenix, Ariz.

Wright, Henry, 1878?–1936, American architect and community planner. Wrote *Rehousing Urban America* (1935), an outstanding technical work.

Wright, Horatio Gouverneur, 1820–99, Union general in Civil War. Captured Fla. coastal towns in 1862. Commanded 6th Corps in Wilderness campaign (1864). At Petersburg (1865) his men were first to break through Confederate lines.

Wright, Orville, 1871–1948, and **Wilbur Wright,** 1867–1912, American airplane inventors, brothers. Their interest in flying aroused by Lilienthal's glider flights of 1890s, they made early aircraft in Dayton, Ohio, bicycle repair shop. Encouraged and advised by Octave Chanute, they improved the glider. Orville designed engine for it. First controlled and sustained power-driven airplane flight made at Kitty Hawk, N.C., Dec. 17, 1903.

Wright, Richard, 1908–, American Negro author, noted especially for a powerful novel, *Native Son* (1940), and for autobiographical *Black Boy* (1945).

Wright, Russel, 1905–, American industrial designer, who popularized functional forms in furniture and chinaware.

Wright, Wilbur: see WRIGHT, ORVILLE.

Wrightstown, borough (pop. 1,199), central N.J., SE of Trenton. U.S. Fort Dix is here.

Wriothesley, English noble family: see SOUTHAMPTON, THOMAS WRIOTHESLEY, 1ST EARL OF.

writ, in law, order issued in the name of the sovereign or the state in connection with a judicial or administrative proceeding, usually compelling a person to report at a fixed time with proof of compliance or reason for disobedience. The principle of "no writ, no right" was somewhat overcome in England by development of equity. Notable survivals of writs are habeas corpus and mandamus.

Wroclaw, Lower Silesia: see BRESLAU.

wrought iron: see IRON.

Wuchang (wŏō'chäng'), city (pop. 204,634), cap. of Hopeh prov., China; port at junction of Yangtze and Han rivers, opposite Hanyang and Hankow. Seat of two universities.

Wuhsien, China: see SOOCHOW.

Wundt, Wilhelm Max (vĭl'hĕlm mäks vŏont'), 1832–1920, German physiologist and psychologist. He founded the first experimental psychology laboratory, Leipzig, 1878, and also the science of folk psychology.

Wupatki National Monument: see NATIONAL PARKS AND MONUMENTS (table).

Wu P'ei-fu (wŏō' pā'-fŏō'), 1873–1939, Chinese general. Leader of Peking government after Yüan Shih-kai's death (1916), he fought with other war lords, notably Chang Tso-lin, for control of N China. Defeated 1927 by Chiang Kai-shek.

Wupper (vŏō'pŭr), river, c.65 mi. long, NW Germany, a W tributary of the Rhine. Its middle course, with WUPPERTAL, REMSCHEID, and SOLINGEN, is of major industrial importance.

Wuppertal (vŏō'pŭrtäl), city (pop. 362,125), North Rhine–Westphalia, NW Germany, on the Wupper, adjoining Solingen and Remscheid. Was formed 1929 by merger of Barmen, Elberfeld, and several lesser towns. Major industrial center, producing textiles, iron, steel, dyes, pharmaceuticals. City was half destroyed in World War II.

Württemberg (wûr'tŭmbûrg", Ger. vür'tŭmbĕrk"), former German state (7,532 sq. mi.; 1939 pop. 2,896,-920), SW Germany; cap. Stuttgart. Drained by the Neckar and the upper Danube, it is a hilly, agr. region, famous for its lovely landscape. It includes the Swabian Jura (S) and part of the Black Forest (W). The county of Württemberg emerged from the ruins of the old duchies of Swabia and Franconia and became a duchy in 1495. In 1801–10, Württemberg doubled its territory by acquiring the numerous small ecclesiastic and temporal fiefs of the region and the former free imperial cities of Ulm, Hall, Gmünd, Esslingen, and others. In 1806, it was made a kingdom by Napoleon I, against whom it turned in 1813. It sided with Austria in the Austro-Prussian War of 1866 but joined the German Empire 1871. The monarchy was abolished 1918, and in 1919 Württemberg joined the Weimar Republic. After World War II the state was partitioned between WÜRTTEMBERG-BADEN and WÜRTTEMBERG-HOHENZOLLERN.

Württemberg-Baden (–bä′dùn), German state (6,062 sq. mi.; pop. 3,884,462), SW Germany; cap. Stuttgart. Formed 1945 in U.S. occupation zone from N parts of former states of BADEN and WÜRTTEMBERG (incl. Ulm, Mannheim, Karlsruhe, Heidelberg). Joined Federal Republic of [West] Germany 1949.

Württemberg-Hohenzollern (–hō″ùntsô′lùrn), German state (4,018 sq. mi.; pop. 1,240,999), SW Germany; cap. Tübingen. Formed 1946 in French occupation zone from S WÜRTTEMBERG, former HOHENZOLLERN prov., and LINDAU dist. (i.e., most of SWABIA). Joined Federal Republic of [West] Germany 1949.

Wurtz, Charles Adolphe (shärl′ ädôlf′ vürts′), 1817–84, French chemist. He discovered methyl and ethyl amines, glycol, and aldol condensation; developed method of synthesizing hydrocarbons by treating alkyl halides with sodium (Wurtz reaction), adapted by Rudolf Fittig to preparation of mixed aliphatic and aromatic hydrocarbons.

Würzburg (wûrts′bûrg, Ger. vürts′bŏŏrk), city (pop. 78,195), cap. of Lower Franconia, NW Bavaria, on the Main, in a region of vineyards. Mfg. of machine tools, chemicals, textiles. Became episcopal see 741. Its prince-bishops ruled a large part of FRANCONIA until 1802. They founded Würzburg univ. (1582) and made the city one of Europe's most splendid residences in the baroque and rococo periods. The episcopal residence (1720–44), Romanesque cathedral (11th–13th cent.), and numerous other famous buildings were destroyed in World War II.

Wusih (wōō′shē′), city (pop. 273,346), cap. of South Kiangsu, China, on Grand Canal. Textile center.

Wyandotte (wī′ùndŏt), industrial city (pop. 36,846), SE Mich., on Detroit R. and S of Detroit. Salt deposits here basis of large chemical industry. Also mfg. of metal and rubber products. Bessemer steel first commercially produced here 1864.

Wyandotte Cave, S Ind., just N of Ohio R. and W of New Albany. Limestone cave (one of largest in North America) with miles of passages on five levels and notable chambers.

Wyant, Alexander Helwig (wī′ùnt), 1836–92, American landscape painter, influenced by Inness. Best known for scenes in the Adirondacks and Catskills.

Wyatt, Sir Thomas, 1503?–1542, English poet. Wrote first sonnets in English and varied lyrics, introducing genuinely personal quality into English Renaissance love poetry. His son, **Sir Thomas Wyatt,** d. 1554, was famous conspirator. Rebelled when Mary I announced plan to marry Philip II of Spain. Temporarily successful, he was checked at London. Surrendered and was hanged.

Wycherley, William (wī′chùrlē), 1640?–1716, English Restoration dramatist. In such plays as *Love in a Wood* (produced 1671), *The Country Wife* (1675), and *The Plain Dealer* (produced 1676), he added a note of realism and robust, coarse satire to the witty artificiality of Restoration comedy.

Wyclif, Wycliffe, Wickliffe, or **Wiclif, John** (all: wī′-klĭf), c.1328–1384, English religious reformer; educ. at Oxford. He boldly asserted that Christ is man's only overlord; that the clergy should own no property; that the Scriptures are the supreme authority; that many Church doctrines (notably transubstantiation) were false. His teachings were spread by his "poor priests" (see LOLLARDRY) and influenced John Huss. He brought about the first translation of the BIBLE into English. Condemned as a heretic in 1380 and 1382, he was not molested.

Wye, river of Wales and England. Flows 130 mi. from Plinlimmon mt., Wales, to the Severn estuary. Noted for its beautiful valley, especially part forming Gloucestershire-Monmouthshire border.

Wyeth, Nathaniel Jarvis, 1802–56, American explorer and trader in Far West. Founded Fort Hall 1834.

Wykeham, William of: see WILLIAM OF WYKEHAM.

Wylie, Elinor (Hoyt), 1885–1928, American poet and novelist. Although she is best known for the exquisite lyricism and subtle irony of her poems (as in *Nets to Catch the Wind,* 1921; *Trivial Breath,* 1928; *Angels and Earthly Creatures,* sonnets, 1929), her four extraordinary novels (*Jennifer Lorn,* 1923; *The Venetian Glass Nephew,* 1925; *The Orphan Angel,* 1926; *Mr. Hodge and Mr. Hazard,* 1928) have won admirers. Her third husband was William Rose Benét.

Wyoming, state (97,914 sq. mi.; pop. 290,529), W U.S.; admitted 1890 as 44th state; cap. CHEYENNE. Other cities are CASPER, LARAMIE. Vast upland crossed by mountain ranges, with river basins and rolling plains. Continental Divide traverses state from NW corner to S central border. E of Divide are Bighorn Mts. and Absaroka Range, W is Teton Range. In NW is Yellowstone Natl. Park. Mountain snows feed many rivers, including the Snake, Yellowstone, and Green. Farming (livestock, horses, grains). Deposits of coal, petroleum, natural gas. Oil refining, beet sugar processing, mfg. on small scale. Popular health resort. Early development linked with fur trade, westward migration. Fur-trading posts were estab. at Fort Laramie and Fort Bridger. Indian wars of 1860s and 1870s failed to stem tide of immigration. Open ranges attracted cattle raisers; cattle rustling and feuds between cattlemen and sheepmen marked late 19th cent. Oil boom began in 1910. Reclamation and conservation have aided state's development.

Wyoming. 1 City (pop. 5,582), SW Ohio, N suburb of Cincinnati. **2** Borough (pop. 4,511), NE Pa., on Susquehanna R. and near Wilkes-Barre. Monument commemorates massacre (1778) of Conn. settlers in Wyoming Valley during Revolution.

Wyoming, University of: see LARAMIE.

Wyoming Valley, NE Pa., on N branch of Susquehanna R.; rich anthracite region. Scene of contest between Conn. and Pa. over conflicting land claims. Conn. settlement after 1754 resulted in Pennamite Wars. Settlers were massacred by John BUTLER in 1778. Land quarrel decided in favor of Pa.; trouble was gradually solved after 1799.

Wyspianski, Stanislaus (vĭspyä′nyùskē), 1869–1907, Polish dramatist. His symbolic dramas include *The Wedding* (1901), *November Night* (1904), and *Meleager* (Eng. tr., 1933).

Wyss, Johann David (yō′hän dä′vĕt vĕs′), 1743–1818, Swiss author of *The Swiss Family Robinson* (1813), A juvenile classic, it is the story of a shipwrecked family, in the vein of Defoe's *Robinson Crusoe.*

Wythe, George (wĭth), 1726–1806, American jurist, signer of Declaration of Independence. One of the greatest of early U.S. lawyers.

Wytheville (wĭth′vĭl), town (pop. 5,513), SW Va., SW of Roanoke. Trade and mfg. center of agr. area.

X

Xanthippe (zăntĭ′pē), 5th cent. B.C., wife of Socrates, said in legend to be a shrew. Also Xantippe.

Xauen (hou′än), town (pop. 14,476), Spanish Morocco. Moslem holy city, founded 15th cent. by Moors expelled from Granada, and long closed to non-Moslems. Known for its crafts.

Xavier, Saint Francis: see FRANCIS XAVIER, SAINT.

Xavier University: see NEW ORLEANS, La.

Xe, chemical symbol of the element XENON.

Xenia (zē′nēù), city (pop. 12,877), SW Ohio, SE of Dayton; laid out 1803. Trade center for agr. area with mfg. of rope, twine, furniture, and shoes. NE is WILBERFORCE UNIVERSITY.

xenon (zē′nŏn), rare, chemically inert, gaseous element (symbol = Xe; see also ELEMENT, table). It is heavy, colorless, and odorless and is present in minute quantities in the earth's atmosphere.

Xenophon (zĕ′nùfŏn), c.430–c.355 B.C., Greek historian, an Athenian. Well-to-do young disciple of Socrates, he joined the Greek force (the Ten Thousand) that supported CYRUS THE YOUNGER of Persia. They fought well at disastrous battle of Cunaxa (401 B.C.) and were left to fight their way back. Xenophon was chosen a leader. He tells the story of this retreat in the most celebrated of his works, the *Anabasis.* Later fought for Sparta against Athens and Thebes at Coronea (394), and the Athenians banished him. Also wrote *Hellenica* and *Memorabilia.* His memoirs on Socrates are invaluable.

Xerxes I (the Great) (zûrk′sēz), d. 465 B.C., king of Persia (485–465 B.C.), son of DARIUS I. After subduing Egypt, he invaded Greece in PERSIAN WARS by building a bridge of boats over the Hellespont. He was victorious at Thermopylae and pillaged Athens, but his fleet was destroyed at Salamis (480 B.C.). He retired to Asia, leaving army under Mardonius, who was defeated at Plataea (479). Xerxes was murdered by one of his soldiers. The Bible has his name as Ahasuerus. He was succeeded by Artaxerxes I.

Ximenes. For Spaniards thus named, see JIMÉNEZ.

Xingu (zĭng″gŏŏ′), river, c.1,200 mi. long, rising in Mato Grosso, Brazil, and flowing N across Pará state into Amazon R. at head of Amazon delta.

Xochimilco (sōchēmēl′kō), city (pop. 14,370), central Mexico. A suburb of Mexico city, it is famous for its canals lined with poplars and flowers. Rafts which Indians had covered with soil and floated on a shallow lake became islands which continue to supply city with vegetables and flowers. Boating on canals is popular diversion.

X ray, Roentgen ray, or **Röntgen ray** (both: rĕnt′gĭn, rŭnt′gĭn, rŭnt′yĭn), invisible radiation of short wave length, discovered 1895 by Roentgen. Commonly produced in tubes called X-ray tubes (see TUBE, VACUUM) in which are sealed two electrodes (the anode and the cathode). When electric current of high voltage is applied, streams of electrons (cathode rays) flow from cathode, pass through tube, and strike plate of wolfram or platinum where X rays are given off. Penetrating ability is increased by high degree of exhaustion of gas from tube and by high voltage. Although X rays can destroy living tissue and cause severe burns, they are of inestimable value in radiotherapy, fluoroscopy, and in making pictures (radiographs) used in diagnosis. Other uses include study of crystals, examination of jewels, and paintings.

xylene (zī′lēn) or **xylol** (–lōl), colorless oily liquid mixture of three benzene hydrocarbons showing isomerism. It is widely used as a solvent.

xylophone (zī′lùfōn) [Gr.,= wood sound], musical instrument having graduated wooden (or sometimes metal) slabs which are struck by the player with small mallets. When tubular resonators are attached to the bars, instrument is called a marimba.

XYZ Affair, name usually given to an incident (1797–98) in Franco-American diplomatic relations. Three-man mission of John Marshall, Elbridge Gerry, and C. C. Pinckney, sent to France to resolve Franco-American difficulties, ran into trouble. Indirect suggestions of loans and bribes to France came through Mme de Villette, a friend of Talleyrand. Negotiations were carried on through her with X (Jean Conrad Hottinguer), Y (a Mr. Bellamy, an American banker in Hamburg), and Z (Lucien Hauteval, like Hottinguer, a Swiss). Proposal that Americans pay Talleyrand £50,000 created uproar in U.S. Mission broke up. Convention of Mortefontaine (Sept. 30, 1800) settled arguments.

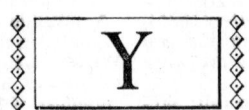

Y

Y, chemical symbol of the element YTTRIUM.

Y-. For Dutch names beginning thus, see IJ-.

Yablonovy Range (yä′blùnùvē), mountain chain, RSFSR, in SE Siberia. Part of watershed between the Arctic and the Pacific, it extends NE from Mongolian border to Olekma R. Rises to 5,280 ft.

Yadkin, river: see PEE DEE, river.

Yahata, Japan: see YAWATA.

Yahweh: see JAHVE.

yak, mammal (genus *Bos* or *Poephagus*) of Tibet and other parts of central Asia. It is larger than most domestic cattle, has curved horns, short legs, high shoulders, and long hair hanging from flanks, legs, and tail. Domesticated yak is a source of meat and

SMALL CAPITALS = cross references. Pronunciation key on inside end pages. Abbreviations: p. 2.

1080

milk; it is useful also as a saddle and pack animal.

Yakima (yă'kŭmô), city (pop. 38,486), S central Wash., SE of Seattle; settled near here 1861, moved here 1885. Trade center of area yielding vegetables, fruit, sugar beets, grain, and livestock. Canneries, packing plants, flour and lumber mills. City is on the **Yakima**, river rising in Cascade Range and flowing 203 mi. SE to Columbia R. near Kennewick. Supports irrigation and hydroelectric project, begun 1906.

Yakut Autonomous Soviet Socialist Republic (yŭkōōt'), (1,182,500 sq. mi.; pop. c.450,000), RSFSR, in NE Siberia, between Arctic Ocean and Stanovoi Range. Rich natural resources (forests, minerals) are little exploited because of poor transportation. Exports include furs, gold, mammoth ivory. Relatively warm in summer, climate reaches the extreme of cold at VERKHOYANSK in winter. Yakuts, of Turkic linguistic family, comprise 80% of population. The cap., **Yakutsk** (pop. 52,888), is a port on the Lena R.

Yale, Elihu, 1649–1721, English merchant, b. Boston. Built fortune by private trade in East. Yale Univ. named for him for his financial support.

Yale University, at New Haven, Conn. Chartered 1701, opened 1702 as Collegiate School of Connecticut at Killingworth (now Clinton), moved 1707 to Saybrook (now Old Saybrook), 1716 to New Haven. Name changed 1718 to Yale Col. to honor Elihu YALE, a benefactor. School was sternly Puritan in early years, when such men as EZRA STILES and the elder Timothy DWIGHT were presidents. Special schools were estab.—medicine (1813), divinity (1822), law (1824), Sheffield Scientific School (1861), and fine arts (1869; the first in any U.S. university). Under the younger Timothy DWIGHT as president, name changed to Yale Univ. (1887). It is now nonsectarian. Core is still Yale Col., reorganized 1933 into resident-college system. Women are admitted to graduate and special schools. Yale includes allied Inst. of Human Relations (founded 1929); Peabody Mus. of Natural History; Yale Univ. Press (estab. 1908); art gallery (1832); library, with several notable collections; and observatory (1879), with a branch (Yale-Columbia Southern Station) at Univ. of Witwatersrand, Union of South Africa. Yale-in-China (Ya-li) in Changsha (1902) was much damaged by Japanese in World War II. Yale has traditional sports rivalry with Harvard (boat race since 1852, football game since 1875).

Yalta (yôl'tŭ, Rus. yäl'tŭ), city (pop. 78,838), S Crimea, RSFSR; a major health resort on the subtropical Black Sea coast. The former imperial palace of LIVADIYA is near by. Here was held the historic **Yalta Conference,** Feb. 4–11, 1945, attended by F. D. Roosevelt, Joseph Stalin, and Winston Churchill, at the end of World War II. Complete text of agreements was published only in 1947. Among chief decisions were: (1) Regarding Germany, renewal of policy of unconditional surrender; four-power occupation of Germany (with France as fourth power). (2) A founding conference of the UNITED NATIONS was to be held in San Francisco; "veto" system of voting was agreed upon for projected Security Council. (3) USSR secretly agreed to enter war against Japan within three months after Germany's surrender and was promised S Sakhalin, Kurile Isls., restoration of Port Arthur and Dairen to status as of 1904 (see LIAOTUNG), and joint Chinese-Soviet administration of Manchurian railroads. These last decisions were later protested by China as an infringement of its sovereignty and were much criticized in the U.S.

Yalu (yä'lōō'), river, on Manchuria-Korea border, rising in Changpai mts. and flowing c.500 mi. SW to Bay of Korea near Antung. Frozen Nov.–March.

yam, tropical twining plant of genus *Dioscorea* and its edible starchy, tuberous roots. The roots can be baked, boiled, ground into flour, or fed to livestock. In the S U.S. the SWEET POTATO is often called yam. The decorative cinnamon vine is *Dioscorea batatas*.

Yamagata, Aritomo, Prince (ärē'tōmō yämä'gätä), 1838–1922, Japanese soldier and statesman, chief founder of modern Japanese army. Studied military science in France and Germany. Twice prime minister, but more important as genro (elder statesman).

Yamaguchi (yämä'gōōchē), commercial city (pop. 97,975), SW Honshu, Japan. Was great castle city from 14th to 16th cent. Site of mission estab. 1550 by St. Francis Xavier.

Yamashita, Tomoyuki (tōmō'yōōkē yämäsh'tä), 1885–1946, Japanese general. Surrendered in Philippines to Gen. MacArthur (Sept. 2, 1945). Convicted as war criminal, he appealed in vain to U.S. Supreme Court; hanged.

Yamaska (yŭmä'skŭ), river of S Que., Canada, rising near Vt. border and flowing 110 mi. NW and N to St. Lawrence R. at L. St. Peter.

Yancey, William Lowndes, 1814–63, American leader of SECESSION. Congressman from Ala. (1844–46). Wrote Alabama Platform (1848), demanding protection of slavery in territories by Congress. An extreme "fire-eater," he was foremost in the secession movement.

Yangchow or **Yang-chou** (both: yäng'jō'), commercial city (pop. 127,104), cap. of North Kiangsu, China, on Grand Canal. Called Yangiu when Marco Polo was its honorary governor. Formerly called Kiangtu.

Yangku, China: see TAIYÜAN.

Yangtze (yäng'dzŭ'), longest river of China, c.3,430 mi. long. Rises in SW Tsinghai prov., flows past Chungking, Hankow, and Nanking to East China Sea near Shanghai. A major trade artery of central China; navigable for 1,000 mi. by ocean liners. Disastrous floods are rare.

Yankee, term used by Americans generally to refer to native of New England and by non-Americans in reference to any American. Word is probably from Knickerbocker Dutch. Wide usage in American Revolution overcame insulting connotation. In Civil War applied generally to Northerners. Shortened form *Yank* became popular in World War I.

Yankee Doodle, song beginning, "Yankee .Doodle went to town, A-riding on a pony," which was especially popular with American troops during the American Revolution and is still included in various song collections. Origin of title, tune, and words is uncertain. It seems probable that the song was first used by the British in derision of the colonial soldiers, and that it was later adopted by the Americans as their favorite marching song.

Yankton, city (pop. 7,709), SE S.Dak., on the Missouri near James R. mouth and SSW of Sioux Falls; settled 1858. Dakota territorial cap. 1861–83. Rail and shipping center in grain and livestock area. Seat of Yankton Col. (coed.; 1881).

Yannina, Greece: see IOANNINA.

Yap (yăp), island group (39 sq. mi.; pop. 2,744), W Pacific, in W Caroline Isls. Consists of 14 islands surrounded by coral reef. Site of cable and radio stations. Japanese had air base here in World War II. Micronesian natives use stone money (large disks of aragonite).

Yaphank, village on E central Long Isl., SE N.Y., NE of Patchogue. Camp Upton was U.S. army induction center in both World Wars.

Yaqui Indians (yä'kē), people of Sonora, Mexico, stubbornly resistant to white conquest. Language is of Uto-Aztecan stock; engage in agr. and weaving.

Yarkand (yärkänd'), town (pop. 60,000), SW Sinkiang prov., China, on Yarkand R. and in oasis at edge of Taklamakan desert. Trade center.

Yarmouth, city (pop. 8,106), SW N.S., Canada, on the Atlantic at entrance to Bay of Fundy. Port, industrial and fishing center and summer resort. Visited by Champlain 1604. Received settlers from Yarmouth, Mass., 1759. Great shipbuilding center in days of wooden sailing ships.

Yarmouth, officially **Great Yarmouth,** county borough

X
Y
Z

(pop. 51,105), Norfolk, England; resort and important fishing center. Church of St. Nicholas (12th cent.) is largest parish church in England. Borough figures in Dickens's *David Copperfield*.

Yarmouth. 1 Town (pop. 2,669), SW Maine, NNE of Portland. Includes resort and fishing village of Yarmouth (pop. 2,189) on Casco Bay. **2** Resort town (pop. 3,297), SE Mass., on Cape Cod E of Barnstable.

Yaroslavl (yŭrŭslä′vŭl), city (pop. 298,065), N central European RSFSR, on the Upper Volga. River port and mfg. center (autos, synthetic rubber, asbestos, machinery, textiles). Founded 1024; cap. of a principality after 1218; annexed by Moscow 1463. Was seat of English trading station, where first modern Russian ships were built (1564–65). Has 12th-cent. monastery; several fine 17th-cent. churches; oldest theater in Russia (founded 1747).

Yarrow or **Yarrow Water**, stream of Scotland. Rises near point where counties of Peebles, Selkirk, and Dumfries meet and flows to Ettrick Water, Selkirkshire. Valley is celebrated for its beauty.

yarrow, strong-scented Eurasian perennial. Common yarrow (*Achillea millefolium*), called also milfoil, has long been naturalized in North America. It has a flat-topped cluster of white, pink, or red composite flowers and fine, carrotlike leaves.

Yasnaya Polyana (yäs′nĭŭ pŭlyä′nŭ), village near Tula, RSFSR. Here was the estate of Leo Tolstoy.

Yawata (yä″wä′tä) or **Yahata**, city (pop. 167,829), N Kyushu, Japan; island's main industrial center.

yawl, small fore-and-aft rigged sailing ship similar to the cutter, but with added mizzenmast.

Yaxartes, river: see SYR DARYA.

Yazoo (yă′zōō), river formed in W central Miss. by junction of Tallahatchie and Yalobusha rivers. Flows 189 mi. SW to Mississippi R. at Vicksburg.

Yazoo City, city (pop. 9,746), W central Miss., on Yazoo R. Trades, processes cotton.

Yazoo land claims. Ga. legislature of 1796 offered to restore purchase price of land holdings in Yazoo R. region; holdings had been secured through bribery by act of 1795 legislature. Large numbers of investors declined to accept payment and pressed their land claims. Terms of 1802 Ga.–U.S. cession agreement provided that Yazooists might receive 5,000,000 acres or the money received from their sale, an arrangement they rejected. In 1810 the U.S. Supreme Court held land claims to be valid, and speculators later received over $4,000,000 from Congress.

Yb, chemical symbol of the element YTTERBIUM.

Yeadon (yē′dŭn), borough (pop. 11,068), SE Pa., W suburb of Philadelphia.

year: see CALENDAR.

Yeardley, Sir George (yärd′lē), c.1587–1627, British colonial governor of Va. (1618–21, 1626–27). Convened first representative assembly in New World.

yeast, name given to certain microscopic fungi and to commercial preparations of yeast cells or of yeast mixed with a starchy material. True yeasts are unicellular and reproduce chiefly by budding. As chief agents in alcoholic FERMENTATION, yeasts are essential to the making of beer, wine, and industrial alcohol. In breadmaking, yeast acts upon carbohydrates to form carbon dioxide and alcohol, which are driven off in baking; escape of carbon dioxide causes the bread to rise. See *ill.*, p. 633.

Yeats, William Butler (yāts), 1865–1939, Irish poet and dramatist, b. Dublin; considered by many the greatest 20th-cent. poet to write in English. He was attracted by the occult and was concerned with Rosicrucianism and theosophy as well as old Irish legend and Irish patriotism (encouraged by his long-lasting love of Maud Gonne). Long poems in *The Wanderings of Oisin* (1889) were followed by notable poetic dramas—*The Countess Cathleen; Cathleen Ni Houlihan* (1902); *The Land of Heart's Desire* (1904); *Deirdre* (1907)—and Yeats was a towering figure in the Abbey Theatre. The rich symbolism of his lyrics and his

narrative poems (e.g., in *The Green Helmet and Other Poems,* 1910; *The Wild Swans at Coole,* 1917) is partly explained by his mystical work in prose, *A Vision* (1926). Clear music unites with cloudy symbolism in his popular collected poems. Awarded 1923 Nobel Prize in Literature.

Yedo, Japan: see TOKYO.

Yehoash: see BLOOMGARDEN, SOLOMON.

Yellow Book, English illustrated quarterly periodical in book form, published in London 1894–97. Enlivened by drawings of Aubrey Beardsley, it put literary emphasis on the bizarre and "art for art's sake." Contributors included Oscar Wilde, Max Beerbohm, Richard Le Gallienne, and W. B. Yeats.

yellow fever, infectious disease caused by virus. In critical stage it is characterized by black vomit. Survivors generally are immune; immunization vaccine exists. In 1900 a commission headed by Walter Reed proved in Havana that the disease is transmitted by bite of mosquito. W. C. Gorgas demonstrated in Panama Canal Zone that disease can be eradicated through mosquito control.

Yellowhead Pass, 3,711 ft. high, in Rocky Mts. on Alta.–B.C., Canada, border.

yellow jacket: see WASP.

Yellowknife, town (pop. 2,724), S Mackenzie dist., Northwest Territories, Canada, on N shore of Great Slave L. at mouth of Yellowknife R. Founded 1935 after discovery of gold and silver. Largest town in Territories, trade and transportation center with airport, radio and meteorological stations, and Royal Canadian Mounted Police post.

Yellow River, Chinese *Hwang Ho* or *Huang Ho,* river, c.2,900 mi. long, second longest in China. Rises in Tsinghai prov. and flows to Gulf of Chihli of Yellow Sea. Called "China's Sorrow" because of catastrophic floods.

Yellow Sea, Chinese *Hwang Hai,* arm of the Pacific, between China and Korea.

Yellow Springs, village (pop. 2,896), SW Ohio, S of Springfield. Here is ANTIOCH COLLEGE.

Yellowstone, river, 671 mi. long, rising in NW Wyo. in the Absaroka Range and flowing N into Yellowstone Natl. Park, where it flows through Yellowstone L. (alt. c.7,731 ft.; area 139 sq. mi.), forms great falls, and traverses deep canyon. Enters Mont. and flows NE to the Missouri near old Fort Union, just within N.Dak. Bighorn and Powder rivers among tributaries. Used for irrigation since late 1860s, it has many private developments; public projects at Miles City and Billings; and several U.S. projects in Yellowstone sub-basin division of MISSOURI RIVER BASIN PROJECT.

Yellowstone National Park: see NATIONAL PARKS AND MONUMENTS (table).

yellowwood, ornamental leguminous tree (*Cladrastis LUTEA*), native to SE U.S., with panicles of fragrant white flowers. The wood yields a yellow dye.

Yemen (yĕ′mŭn), kingdom (75,000 sq. mi.; pop. c.4,500,000) SW Arabia, on Red Sea; cap. Sana (pop. 28,000). Bounded on N by Saudi Arabia, S by Aden protectorate, and E by Rub al Khali desert. Mountainous except for narrow coastal strip. Coffee, grains, and fruits are raised. Hodeida and Mocha are chief ports. Early historical records indicate an active trade between Yemen and Somali coast of Africa. Later (8th–4th cent.? B.C.) Yemen may have belonged to SHEBA. The Himyaritic dynasty, founded in 1st cent. B.C., adopted Judaism in 4th cent. A.D. Yemen fell to Ethiopians in 525 and to Persians in 570. With acceptance of Islam in A.D. 628, the history of Yemen became that of all Arabia. In 10th cent. a new power arose in Yemen, the Zeidi sect of Islam. The king of Yemen is also the IMAM of the Zeidi line. Zeidi rule was contested by Turkish occupation from 16th–17th cent. and again from 1849 until end of World War I. In 1934 Yemen was briefly conquered by Saudi Arabia, but the occupation was soon ended and the present frontier established. Yemen is a member of the Arab League and in 1947 joined the UN. In 1949–50 most of the Jewish population was evacuated to Israel.

Yenan, China: see SHENSI.

Yenisei or **Enisei** (both: yěnĭsā', Rus. yěnyĭsyä'), river, 2,364 mi. long, RSFSR, in central Siberia, rising in E Sayan Mts. and flowing generally N past Krasnoyarsk, Yeniseisk, and Igarka into the Kara Sea. Precipitous in its upper course, it is c.4 mi. wide in its lower section. A canal system links it with the Ob. Navigable for part of the year, it carries lumber, grain, and construction materials.

Yentai, China: see CHEFOO.

yeoman, class in English society. Generally means landowning farmers below the gentry. Under feudal system yeoman had service obligations. Agrarian and Industrial revolutions of 18th cent. took away his land. Workingman without master, he was thought to strengthen English society. Class supplied patriot armies of American Revolution. In military and naval use the term signifies rank or function.

Yeomen of the Guard, bodyguard, now ceremonial in function, of sovereign of England. When originated by Henry VII in 1485, their duties as defenders of king's person were very real. Until 1743 they accompanied king in battle. Sometimes called Beefeaters, they still wear 15th-cent. uniforms.

Yerba Buena Island (yâr'bŭ bwä'nù), 300 acres, W Calif., in San Francisco Bay; midpoint of SAN FRANCISCO–OAKLAND BAY BRIDGE.

yerba mate: see MATE.

Yermak or **Ermak** (yěrmäk'), d. 1584 or 1585, Russian Cossack leader and conqueror of Siberia. With his small armed band, advancing in river boats, he conquered (1582) the Tatar khanate of SIBIR and turned it over to Tsar Ivan IV.

Yersin, Alexandre (älĕksä'drù yĕrsĕ'), 1863–1943, French bacteriologist. Discovered PLAGUE bacillus and prepared serum to combat it. Worked on diphtheria antitoxin. Served with Pasteur Inst.

Yesenin or **Esenin, Sergei Aleksandrovich** (sĭrgā' ŭlyĭksän'drùvĭch yĭsyä'nĭn), 1895–1925, Russian poet. His lyrics were very popular in the early years of the revolution. Also wrote *Pugachev* (1922), a tragedy in verse. He repudiated the revolution when it turned into dictatorship. In 1922 he married Isadora Duncan but they were soon separated. Died by suicide.

Yevpatoriya, RSFSR: see EUPATORIA.

yew, handsome evergreen tree or shrub of genus *Taxus* with dark green leaves and red berrylike fruits. Since antiquity it has been associated with death and funeral rites. Ground hemlock or Canada yew of Canada and NE U.S. is *Taxus canadensis*.

Yezd (yĕzd), city (pop. 60,066), central Iran; founded c.5th cent. Has large Zoroastrian colony. Produces hand-woven carpets and textiles.

Yezo, Japan: see HOKKAIDO.

Yggdrasill (ĭg'drùsĭl), in Norse legend, great tree of the world. At its top was an eagle, at bottom a serpent; a squirrel ran between to arouse strife.

Yiddish [Ger. *jüdisch* = Jewish], language spoken by the Jews of Eastern Europe. Descended from the German of the Middle Ages, with many Hebrew words, it has absorbed expressions from whatever country the Jews reside in. The Hebrew characters are used. Hebrew being the language of the learned Jews, Yiddish was long scorned as a medium for authors, and literature in Yiddish did not begin to flourish until the middle of the 19th cent. The father of modern Yiddish literature is MENDELE MOCHER SFORIM. He was followed by the humorist Sholom ALEICHEM and the mystic I. L. PERETZ. Yiddish journalism owes its fullest development to the immigrant Jews in the U.S., where Abraham CAHAN founded the Jewish *Daily Forward* in 1897. Yiddish drama was born when Goldfadden, the playwright, founded a theater in Odessa in 1878. Ansky (author of *The*

Dybbuk) and Singer (author of *Yoshe Kalb*) wrote notable plays in Yiddish.

Yin, dynasty of China: see SHANG.

Yoakum (yō'kùm), city (pop. 5,231), S Texas, N of Victoria. In tomato growing area, it processes leather, food, and wood products.

yoga (yō'gù) [Sanskrit,= union], mystical system developed in Hinduism, intended primarily to liberate the individual from the illusory world of sense perception. Liberation is difficult and may take several lifetimes. The yogi who believes in pantheism seeks union with the universal soul; the yogi who is atheistic seeks absolute isolation from all other souls and perfect self-knowledge. The ultimate state sought is one of perfect illumination. Yogis use physical disciplines to attain it—purgation, cleanliness, concentration, exercises.

Yoho National Park (yō'hō), 507 sq. mi., SE B.C., Canada, in Rocky Mts. at Alta. border; estab. 1886. Adjoins Banff and Kootenay national parks.

Yokohama (yō"kähä'mä), industrial city (pop. 814,-379), central Honshu, Japan; major foreign-trade port on Tokyo Bay. Chief export is silk. Has steel mills, shipyards, oil refineries, and chemical and automobile plants. Visited 1854 by Commodore Perry; opened 1859 to foreign trade. Extensively rebuilt after destruction by 1923 earthquake. Heavily bombed in 1945 during World War II.

Yokosuka (yōkō'sōōkä), city (pop. 252,923), central Honshu, Japan, on Tokyo Bay; major naval base.

Yom Kippur: see ATONEMENT, DAY OF.

Yonkers, residential city (pop. 152,798), SE N.Y., on E bank of Hudson R. and N of Bronx borough of New York city. Mfg. of carpets, elevators, cables, clothing; sugar refining. Site included in land grant made 1646 by Dutch West India Co. to Adriaen Van der Donck. Frederick Philipse built a manor hall of PHILIPSE MANOR here. Seat of BOYCE THOMPSON INSTITUTE FOR PLANT RESEARCH.

Yonne (yôn), department (2,881 sq. mi.; pop. 266,014), N central France, named for a tributary of the Seine; cap. Auxerre.

Yorck von Wartenburg or **York von Wartenburg, Johann David Ludwig, Graf** (yō'hän dä'vĭt lōōt'vĭkh gräf' yôrk' fŭn vär'tùnbōörk), 1759–1830, Prussian field marshal. Commanded Prussian auxiliary corps in Napoleon's campaign of 1812 against Russia. In Dec., 1812, he concluded, on his own responsibility, the Convention of Tauroggen (now Taurage, Lithuania) with the Russians, by which Prussian troops withdrew from the fighting. His action prepared Prussia's declaration of war on Napoleon (1813).

Yoritomo (Yoritomo Minamoto) (yōrē'tōmō mēnä'mōtō), 1147?–1199, Japanese warrior and dictator. Led his clan (Minamoto) to victory over rival Taira clan, 1185. Named SHOGUN 1192 by emperor and became actual ruler of Japan. Estab. system of centralized feudalism.

York, Alvin (Cullum), 1887–, American soldier. In World War I, Sgt. York was hero of an engagement in the Argonne Forest (Oct. 8, 1918).

York, Cardinal: see STUART, HENRY BENEDICT MARIA CLEMENT.

York, Edmund of Langley, duke of, 1341–1402, fifth son of Edward III. Served on various continental expeditions. Regent while Richard II was abroad, he halfheartedly opposed landing of Henry IV in 1399 and then supported him. Royal house of York dates from his creation (1385) as duke of York. His son, **Edward, duke of York,** 1373?–1415, served under Richard II, but finally supported Henry IV. Joined unsuccessful plot to kill Henry IV. Imprisoned (1405), he was later released and served the king.

York, Frederick Augustus, duke of, 1763–1827, second son of George III of England. Commanded (1793 –95, 1799) unsuccessful English forces in Flanders. Influential in reforming army abuses.

York, Richard, duke of, 1411–60, English nobleman.

Became heir to throne 1447. Struggled unsuccessfully against MARGARET OF ANJOU, whose son's birth (1453) displaced York as heir. Protector during insanity of Henry VI, he resorted to force after king's recovery and thus began Wars of the ROSES. Claimed throne (1460) but was slain in battle of Wakefield. His son seized throne as Edward IV in 1461.

York, Ont.: see TORONTO.

York, England: see YORKSHIRE.

York. 1 Town (pop. 3,256), SW Maine, on the coast NE of Kittery; settled 1624. Stone jail (1653) is historical museum. York is said to have been site of first sawmill (c.1624) and first pile drawbridge (pre-Revolutionary; rebuilt 1933) in U.S. Includes York Harbor and York Beach resorts. **2** City (pop. 6,178), SE Nebr., in prairie region W of Lincoln; agr. trade center. Mfg. of metal castings, bricks, and dairy products. **3** City (pop. 59,953), SE Pa., SSE of Harrisburg; laid out 1741. Farm trade center in Pa. Dutch region with mfg. of machinery, metal products, and cement. Meeting place of Continental Congress 1777–78; occupied by Confederates 1863.

York, Cape, promontory, NW Greenland, in N Baffin Bay, W of Melville Bay. In 1896–97 R. E. Peary discovered noted meteorites here.

York, house of, royal house of England, dating from creation of Edmund of Langley as duke of York in 1385. Claims of his grandson, Richard, duke of York, to the throne against Henry VI, head of the house of LANCASTER, resulted in Wars of the ROSES. Royal members were EDWARD IV, EDWARD V, and RICHARD III. Houses of York and Lancaster were united by marriage of Henry VII (first of Tudor kings) to Elizabeth, daughter of Edward IV.

Yorke Peninsula, South Australia, between Spencer Gulf and Gulf St. Vincent.

Yorker Brethren: see RIVER BRETHREN.

York Factory, fur-trading post, N Man., Canada, at mouth of Hayes R. on Hudson Bay. Fur-trading posts here (first built in late 17th cent.) fought for by England and France. Present post (built 1788–90) is warehouse of Hudson's Bay Co.

Yorkshire (yôrk'shïr), **York,** or **Yorks,** county (6,081 sq. mi.; pop. 4,516,362), N England. Divided into three administrative sections: East Riding, cap. Beverley; North Riding, cap. Northallerton; West Riding, cap. Wakefield. Largest English county, it borders on North Sea and extends almost to Irish Sea. Pennine Chain in W rises to 2,600 ft.; E part has fertile Yorkshire plain. West Riding, with rich coal deposits, is part of great industrial area. Hull is one of England's chief ports. There is also much stock raising and agr. Dissolution of over 100 religious institutions by Henry VIII was resisted (1536) in the Pilgrimage of Grace. There are many historic and religious remains. Has many literary associations (e.g., with Cædmon, Laurence Sterne, and the Brontë sisters). County town, **York,** county borough (pop. 105,336), is not included in any of the three ridings. As Eboracum, it was chief station of British province of Roman Empire. Constantine was proclaimed emperor here. A bishop of York is mentioned in 314, and first archbishop was consecrated in 7th cent. Ecclesiastical center of N England, it is second only to Canterbury in Church of England. Was one of most famous European centers of education in 8th cent.; St. Peter's School is one of England's oldest. Cathedral of St. Peter (York Minster) dates from Saxon and Norman period. Other noteworthy buildings include York Castle and palace of archbishops of York. There is varied mfg.

Yorkton, city (pop. 7,074), SE Sask., Canada, on Yorkton R. and NE of Regina. Rail center in E Sask.

Yorktown, historic town (pop. 384), SE Va., on York R. near Chesapeake Bay; settled 1631. Town included in Colonial Natl. Historical Park. YORKTOWN CAMPAIGN brought Revolution to a close. Town besieged and taken by Federals in PENINSULAR CAMPAIGN of Civil War (April–May, 1862). Places of interest are

customhouse (c.1706), Grace Church (1697), Moore House (terms of Cornwallis's surrender negotiated here), Yorktown Monument.

Yorktown campaign, 1781, closing military operations of American Revolution. After CAROLINA CAMPAIGN Cornwallis retreated into Va., fortified Yorktown, and waited for reinforcements. In August a French fleet under Adm. De Grasse blockaded Chesapeake Bay. By September Washington, aided by French troops under Rochambeau, broke through outer defenses. Cornwallis surrendered Oct. 19, 1781.

York von Wartenburg: see YORCK VON WARTENBURG.

Yosemite National Park: see NATIONAL PARKS AND MONUMENTS (table).

Yoshida, Shigeru (shēgā'rōō yō'shēdä), 1878–, Japanese statesman. Premier 1946–47, 1948–. Under his leadership conservative parties were merged into single Democratic Liberal party, 1948. Signed Japanese peace treaty at San Francisco (1951).

Yoshihito (yōshē'hētō), 1879–1926, emperor of Japan (1912–26). Under reign name of Taisho he succeeded his father, Mutsuhito. Became insane; his son Hirohito was made regent in 1921.

Youghal (yôl), urban district (pop. 4,809), Co. Cork, Ireland. Sir Walter Ralegh, mayor 1588–89, traditionally planted first potato in Ireland here.

Youghiogheny (yŏkūgā'nē), river rising in Alleghenies near W.Va.–Md. line and flowing c.135 mi. N and NW into Pa. to Monongahela R. at McKeesport.

Young, Art(hur), 1866–1943, American cartoonist, noted for his lively satire and whimsical humor.

Young, Brigham, 1801–77, American leader of Church of Jesus Christ of Latter-Day Saints; perhaps the greatest molder of Mormonism. He led a group to Mormon community at Kirtland, Ohio, became prominent after the persecutions in Mo., and was a leader in the move to Nauvoo, Ill. After Joseph Smith's assassination (1844) he became the dominant figure, led migration West in 1846–47, and directed settlement at Salt Lake City. There he was the guiding figure in building the cooperative theocracy, which prospered greatly. Young headed the church and after creation of U.S. provisional government was territorial governor. In trouble between U.S. and Mormons that led to the military expedition of 1857–58 he avoided an open break with U.S. government. Though he is popularly best known for championing polygamy (he seems to have been married in all to 27 wives), he was actually a stern moralist as well as a brilliant leader. His grandson **Mahonri (Mackintosh) Young** (mühŏn'rē), 1877–, is a well-known sculptor.

Young, Denton T. (Cy), 1867–, American baseball pitcher. Won more major-league games (511) than any other pitcher; pitched three no-hitters.

Young, Edward, 1683–1765, English poet and dramatist, known best for *The Complaint; or, Night Thoughts on Life, Death, and Immortality* (1742–44), a somber blank-verse poem of the "graveyard school."

Young, Mahonri Mackintosh: see YOUNG, BRIGHAM.

Young, Owen D., 1874–, American corporation official, promoter of **Young Plan,** program for settlement of German REPARATIONS debts after World War I. Adopted by Allied powers in 1930 to supersede DAWES PLAN. Defined German obligations, reduced payments. German depression and Hitler's rise to power made plan inoperative.

Young, Thomas, 1773–1829, English physicist and physician. An authority on VISION and optics he stated the Young-Helmholtz theory of color vision, studied structure of eye, and described astigmatism. He revived the wave theory of LIGHT. He established **Young's modulus,** a number representing (in pounds per square inch or dynes per square centimeter) the ratio of stress to strain for a wire or bar of a given substance.

Younger, Cole (Thomas Coleman Younger), 1844–1916, American desperado. One of band of Jesse

JAMES. With two of his brothers, James and Robert, he was captured at Northfield, Minn., in 1876.

Young-Helmholtz theory: see VISION.

Younghusband, Sir Francis (Edward), 1863–1942, British explorer. After exploring Mongolia (1887) he was sent to Tibet. Forced treaty on Dalai Lama (1904) which opened Tibet to Western trade.

Young Men's Christian Association (Y.M.C.A.), organization seeking to improve conditions and opportunities of young men, founded (1844) in London; U.S. movement begun 1851. Housing facilities, summer camps, and recreational programs are provided; Bible study is emphasized.

Young Plan: see YOUNG, OWEN D.

Young Pretender: see STUART, CHARLES EDWARD.

Young's modulus: see YOUNG, THOMAS.

Youngstown, city (pop. 168,330), NE Ohio, on Mahoning R. near Pa. line; founded 1797. Easy access to coal and iron made Youngstown one of country's largest iron and steel centers. Has mfg. of metal products, rubber tires, and furniture.

Young Turks: see OTTOMAN EMPIRE.

Young Women's Christian Association (Y.W.C.A.), organization designed to promote welfare of women and girls. Founded independently in mid-19th cent. in Britain and U.S., it is now world-wide in scope, the international organization dating from 1894. The most recent U.S. body was formed in 1906.

Ypres (ē′prù), Flemish *Ieper,* town (pop. 17,073), West Flanders prov., NW Belgium, near French frontier. During Middle Ages, Ypres was a powerful center of the cloth industry, rivaling Ghent and Bruges. Lacking a maritime outlet, it declined in 16th cent. A battleground for centuries, it was center of one of most hotly contested theaters of World War I. In first battle of Ypres (Oct.–Nov., 1914) British and Belgians stopped German thrust toward the Channel ports. In second battle (April–May, 1915) Allied offensive was halted when Germans used poison gas. Third battle (July–Nov., 1917) saw British sacrifice c.400,000 men to push their line 5 mi. E. German assault of April, 1918, failed, and in early Oct., 1918, British began here their victorious march E. Thoroughly devastated, city was rebuilt (e.g., 13th-cent. Gothic cathedral and cloth hall). Outside city walls there are c.40 military cemeteries.

Ypsilanti (ēpsēlän′tē), prominent Greek family of PHANARIOTS. **Constantine Ypsilanti,** 1760–1816, became hospodar of Moldavia (1799) and Walachia (1802) but was deposed by the sultan in 1806 because of his pro-Russian sympathies. He entered Russian service, as did his sons, **Alexander Ypsilanti,** 1792–1828, and **Demetrios Ypsilanti,** 1793–1832. Both played important parts in the Greek War of Independence. Alexander headed the secret patriotic society, Hetairia Philike. In 1821, with Russian support, he raised a revolt at Jassy and proclaimed the independence of Greece. The Greeks in Moldavia and Walachia rallied to him, but the Rumanian population, weary of Phanariot rule, rose against the Greeks and helped the Turks defeat them. Alexander fled to Austria, where he was imprisoned till 1827. Though it failed, the uprising in Moldavia made possible the Greek insurrection in the Peloponnesus, where Demetrios Ypsilanti distinguished himself as a commander against Ibrahim Pasha.

Ypsilanti (ĭpsĭlän′tē), city (pop. 18,302), SE Mich., on Huron R. and E of Ann Arbor; settled 1823 on sites of Indian village and French trading post (1809–c.1819). Industrial, commercial, and farm trade center with mfg. of metal products. Seat of Michigan State Normal Col. and Cleary Col.

Ysaÿe, Eugène (ēzäē′), 1858–1931, Belgian violinist, conductor, and teacher; one of the greatest violinists of his time. He made his American debut in 1894; conducted the Cincinnati Symphony, 1918–20.

Yser (ēzĕr′), river, 48 mi. long, in French and Belgian Flanders, entering North Sea at Nieuport. In World War I the German drive toward Calais was stopped here after heavy fighting (late 1914).

Yseult (ēsûlt′): see TRISTRAM AND ISOLDE.

Ysleta, (īslē′tù), uninc. town (pop. 4,782), W Texas, on Rio Grande just below El Paso. Oldest settlement in Texas, founded near mission estab. (1681–82) after Pueblo revolt.

Yssel, Netherlands: see IJSSEL.

ytterbium (ĭtûr′bēŭm), rare metallic element of rare earths (symbol = Yb; see also ELEMENT, table), found with other elements of the group in various minerals, especially gadolinite.

yttrium (ĭ′trēŭm), rare metallic element of rare earths (symbol = Y; see also ELEMENT, table), found in gadolinite and certain other minerals.

Yüan (yüän′), dynasty of China, which ruled 1260–1368; part of great empire conquered by MONGOLS. Its founder, KUBLAI KHAN, dealt final blow to Sung dynasty in 1279. Early Yüan period saw development of postal system, improvement of roads and canals, and increase in overland trade with the West. Traditional system of civil service examinations suspended until 1315. The drama (with music) notable in period. Succeeded by Ming dynasty.

Yüan Shih-kai (yüän′ shē-kī′), 1859–1916, president of China (1912–16). As high official under Ch'ing dynasty he supported dowager empress Tz'u Hsi against Emperor Kwang Hsü while helping to overthrow the dynasty. Succeeded Sun Yat-sen as president of republic, 1912. Crushed opposition to his dictatorial rule by dissolving parliament, 1914. Declared himself emperor in 1915 but died before enthronement.

Yuba City (yōō′bù), town (pop. 7,861), N central Calif., N of Sacramento. Boomed in gold-rush days, like Marysville across Feather R. Processes fruits (esp. peaches), vegetables, and dairy products.

Yucatan (yōōkütän′), Span. *Yucatán,* peninsula, area c.70,000 sq. mi., mostly in SE Mexico, separating the Caribbean from the Gulf of Mexico. Comprises states of Yucatan and Campeche, territory of Quintana Roo, British Honduras, and part of Petén, Guatemala. For the most part, peninsula is low, limestone tableland, with tropical dry and rainy seasons, though cold winds blow from N in winter. Agricultural products include henequen (see SISAL HEMP), tobacco, maize, sugar cane, cotton, coffee. From the forests of Petén, SW Campeche, and British Honduras come logwood, mahogany, dyewood, vanilla. Peninsula had been for centuries seat of MAYA civilization when first white men arrived. Of these men, Cortés in 1519 rescued sole survivor who acted as his interpreter on the epic march across peninsula to Honduras in 1524–25. Before Cortés, Fernández de Córdoba had skirted coast (1517) and Grijalva had explored it (1518). Francisco de Montejo began conquest of the Mayas in 1527, and it was finally completed by his son of the same name (1546).

Yucatan, state (14,868 sq. mi.; pop. 515,256), SE Mexico, occupying most of N half of Yucatan peninsula; cap. MÉRIDA. Became state when Mexico won independence (1821) but seceded (1839–43). Principal product is henequen (see SISAL HEMP).

yucca (yŭk′ù), stiff-leaved stemless or treelike plant native to North and Central America and the West Indies. Yuccas produce a large stalk of white or purplish blossoms pollinated by the yucca moth. The Joshua tree (*Yucca brevifolia*) is a picturesque treelike species of desert regions, the Spanish bayonet (*Y. aloifolia*) is another treelike form, and the Spanish dagger (*Y. gloriosa*) is stemless or has a short trunk.

Yucca House National Monument: see NATIONAL PARKS AND MONUMENTS (table).

Yugoslavia (yōō″gōslä′vēù, –s¹ä′vēù), Serbo-Croatian *Jugoslavija,* federal republic (99,079 sq. mi.; pop. 15,-751,953), SE Europe, largely in the Balkan Peninsula; cap. Belgrade. It is mostly mountainous, with Julian Alps and KARST in NW and Dinaric Alps running parallel to Adriatic coast (see DALMATIA). TRIGLAV is highest peak. Drained by the Danube and its tributaries, the country is largely agr. There are rich mineral resources (coal, copper, iron, mercury, lead, zinc, bauxite). The Yugoslav [i.e., South Slav] people consists of four groups—Serbs (43%), Croats (34%), Slovenes (7%), Macedonians (7%)—the remainder being Magyars, Italians, and other minorities. As of 1931, 49% of Yugoslavs were Greek Orthodox, 37% Roman Catholic (Croats and Slovenes), 11% Moslem. For history before 1918 and for other geographic data, see articles on the six constituent people's republics estab. under constitution of 1946: SERBIA; CROATIA; SLOVENIA; BOSNIA AND HERCEGOVINA; MACEDONIA; MONTENEGRO. These six regions were included in the "Kingdom of the Serbs, Croats, and Slovenes," proclaimed in 1918 at the end of World War I, with King PETER I of Serbia at its head. Its name was changed to Yugoslavia 1929. Among its internal problems was the opposition between the ruling Serbian element and the Croatian nationalists, who demanded autonomy. King ALEXANDER exercised dictatorship 1929–31 and continued to rule with a firm hand under the parliamentary constitution of 1931. Violence culminated in 1934 in his assassination. Yugoslavia clashed with Italy over FIUME question (settled 1924) and had tense relations with Hungary and Bulgaria, which claimed parts of N Yugoslavia and Macedonia. Yugoslavia joined the LITTLE ENTENTE but in 1939 it drew closer to the Axis powers. The pro-Axis government was overthrown by a military coup d'état in March, 1941, but on April 6 German, Hungarian, Italian, and Bulgarian forces struck against Yugoslavia. King PETER II fled abroad; Serbia and Croatia became puppet states; the rest was partitioned among the aggressors. However, partisan troops under Gen. MIKHAILOVICH and Marshal TITO effectively battled the occupying forces. Civil war between the two rival leaders began 1943; the Communist Tito won out. In 1944 Russian and Allied forces joined with Tito in driving out the Germans. Tito became premier in 1945, deposed the king, and transformed Yugoslavia into a Communist state. The peace treaty with Italy (1947) gave Yugoslavia most of VENEZIA GIULIA. The imprisonment of Archbishop Stepinac of Zagreb led to a break with the Vatican (1946). More serious was Tito's break with the Russian-dominated COMINFORM (1948) and the resulting strain with Yugoslavia's neighbors.

Yukawa, Hideki (hē′dĕkē yōōkä′wä), 1907–, Japanese physicist. Won 1949 Nobel Prize for predicting existence of MESON.

Yukon (yōō′kŏn), territory (205,346 sq. mi.; with water surface 207,076 sq. mi.; pop. 9,096), NW Canada; cap. DAWSON. WHITE HORSE is the only other city, with settlements on the river banks. The N Arctic country is generally uninhabited. The Rockies are E and the Coast Range W, with Mt. LOGAN in the SW corner. The Mackenzie R. (N and E) and the Yukon R. systems drain many snow-fed lakes. Mining (gold,

silver, copper, lead, coal), fur trapping, and fishing are important. Air transport supplemented by one railroad, Alaska Highway, and summer river transport. Explored in 1840s by Robert Campbell. Posts were soon estab. The search for gold resulted in the famous KLONDIKE gold rush of 1890s, brought over 30,000 adventurers into region. Unorganized part of Northwest Territories until 1895, it was given separate administration in 1898. Rejected plan of union with B.C. 1937. Governed by a controller appointed by the dominion government, with a popularly-elected council of three members. It elects one member to the dominion Parliament. Controversial Canol oil project, started by U.S. in World War II and abandoned 1945, gained over 100 mi. of needed highway for Yukon.

Yukon, river of Yukon and Alaska, formed by Lewes R. (upper Yukon) and Pelly R. at Fort Selkirk. Flows W and N to Dawson, NW to Fort Yukon, Alaska, then SW and N to Bering Sea through several channels. With headstreams is c.2,000 mi. long, one of longest rivers in North America. White horse on Lewes R. is head of navigation. Was major route to Klondike gold fields in 1890s. Lower reaches explored 1836–37, 1843 by Russians; upper reaches by Robert Campbell 1843.

Yule: see CHRISTMAS.

Yuma, city (pop. 9,145), extreme SW Ariz., on Colorado R. at mouth of Gila R., in warm, dry area. European settlement came after Fort Yuma was built on W bank (1850). River port and gold-boom town after 1858. Rail and trade center now of Yuma project, reclaimed desert served by ALL-AMERICAN CANAL system; cotton, alfalfa, citrus, truck are raised.

Yuman, linguistic stock of North American Indians. See LANGUAGE (table).

yungas (yōōng′gäs), region of lowland valleys in E piedmont of Andes, extending from Peru-Bolivia border SE into central Bolivia. Assumed economic importance in 20th cent. as major source of rubber and quinine before development of Far Eastern sources.

Yunnan (yün′nän′), province (160,000 sq. mi.; pop. 10,000,000), SW China; cap. Kunming. Bounded on W by Burma. Mainly a high plateau, drained by many rivers, notably the Salween, Mekong, and Yangtze. China's leading tin producer, Yunnan is rich in varied mineral resources. In Second Chino-Japanese War it was major center of Chinese resistance.

Yuste, San Jerónimo de (sän härō′nēmō dā yōō′stä), former monastery, in Cacéres prov., W Spain, where Emperor Charles V retired (1556) and died (1558).

Yvetot (ēvtō′), town (pop. 5,789), Seine-Inférieure dept., N France, in Normandy. The lords of Yvetot held their tiny seigniory free of duties to any other lord and wore the title king 14th–16th cent., an early instance of French individualism immortalized in Béranger's song Le Roi d'Yvetot (Eng. tr. by Thackeray).

Z

Zaandam (zän"däm'), municipality (pop. 41,698), North Holland prov., Netherlands. Lumber center. Famous for its many windmills. Peter I of Russia stayed at Zaandam 1697 to learn shipbuilding, which at the time flourished there.

Zabrze, Upper Silesia: see HINDENBURG.

Zacatecas (säkätä'käs), state (28,125 sq. mi.; pop. 664,-394), N central Mexico; cap. Zacatecas (pop. 21,846). Semiarid plains are good grazing land, and cattle raising is a major occupation. Mining is of greatest importance, however, with copper, iron, zinc, lead, gold, silver, mercury, bismuth, antimony, and salt, all mined in the mountains of the Sierra Madre Occidental. It was important in wars and revolutions of Mexico. Zacatecas and Fresnillo are chief cities.

Zacchaeus or **Zaccheus** (both: zăkē'ŭs), publican who climbed a tree to see Jesus. Luke 19.1–10.

Zachariah (ză"kŭrī'ŭ). **1** Died c.749 B.C., king of Israel for six months. Murdered by Shallum. 2 Kings 14.29; 15.8–12. **2** See ZECHARIAH **2.**

Zacharias (zăkŭrī'ŭs) or **Zachary** (ză'kŭrē), **Saint,** pope (741–52), a Calabrian Greek. Strengthened power of the Holy See. Opposed the Lombards and was friendly with Frankish Pepin the Short. Feast: March 22.

Zacharias or **Zachary. 1** Father of John the Baptist. Luke 1.5–80. He and Elizabeth, his wife, are saints of the Roman Catholic Church. Their feast: Nov. 5. **2** For martyred prophet, see ZECHARIAH **2. 3** For book of Old Testament, see ZECHARIAH.

Zadar, Yugoslavia: see ZARA.

Zagazig (zägäzēg'), town (pop. 82,912), N Egypt, in Nile delta; cotton-ginning center. Near by are ruins of ancient Bubastis.

Zaghlul Pasha, Saad (säd' zäglōōl'), c.1850–1927, Egyptian nationalist leader, founder of WAFD party.

Zagorsk (zŭgôrsk'), city (1926 pop. 21,563), RSFSR, NNE of Moscow. Toy mfg. Known as Sergievski Posad before 1917 and as Sergiev until c.1930, it is the site of the Troitsko-Sergievskaya Lavra, one of the most famous Russian monasteries (founded 1340; now a museum). Lavra contains Troitski Cathedral (1427); Uspenski Cathedral (16th cent.; with tomb of Boris Godunov); many treasures of liturgical art.

Zagreb (zä'grĕb), Ger. *Agram,* city (pop. 290,417), cap. of Croatia, NW Yugoslavia, on the Sava. Has diversified mfg. See of two archbishops—Roman Catholic and Orthodox. University (founded 1669). Unlike most of Croatia, Zagreb escaped Turkish domination in the 16th–17th cent. A fine modern city, it has its historic center in the old Kaptol dist., with the Catholic cathedral (begun 1093) and archiepiscopal palace (18th cent.).

Zagros (zä'grōs), mountain range, W Iran, rising to c.15,000 ft. Its parallel ridges are separated by deep, fertile valleys. Formed boundary between Assyria and Media in ancient times.

Zaharias, Mildred Babe Didrikson: see DIDRIKSON.

Zaharoff, Sir Basil (Basileios Zacharias) (ză'hŭrŏf), 1850–1936, international financier and munitions manufacturer, b. Turkey; often called Mystery Man of Europe. Generally considered greatest armament salesman of all time (notably for British firm of Vickers-Armstrong), he played an important though unofficial role in world affairs, especially in World War I. Was knighted by George V.

Zähringen (tsä'rĭngŭn), noble German family. Held extensive fiefs in Baden and W Switzerland until 1218, when main line died out with Duke Berthold V. His domains passed largely to the related Kyburg and Hapsburg families. A younger branch continued in N Baden. It split (16th cent.) into branches of Baden-Baden and Baden-Durlach, reunited 1771, and ruled grand duchy of Baden 1806–1918.

zaibatsu (zī'bätsōō) [Jap.,= money clique], great family trusts of modern Japan. Leading zaibatsu are Mitsui, Mitsubishi, Sumitomo, and Yasuda. Dominated Japanese economy after Meiji restoration (1868), winning privileged position through financial aid to new imperial government. Vitally influenced chief political parties. Their breakup was an announced aim of Allied occupation after World War II.

Zaïmis, Alexander (zä'ēmēs), 1855–1936, Greek statesman. Six times premier between 1897 and 1928; high commissioner in Crete 1906–11; president of Greece 1929–35. In World War I he advocated "armed neutrality" but did not interfere with Allied landing at Salonica and made way for VENIZELOS on King Constantine's abdication. His presidency was marked by struggles between royalists and republicans (culminating in Venizelist uprising of 1935) and ended with restoration of King George II. Zaïmis died in exile at Vienna. He was famous for his cautious inscrutability.

Zama (zä'mù), anc. town, N coast of Africa, in present Algeria. Scipio Africanus Major defeated Hannibal at or near Zama (202 B.C.), but there were several towns named Zama.

Zambezi (zămbē'zē), river, c.1,600 mi. long, in S central and SE Africa. Rises in Northern Rhodesia, flows generally E (forming boundary between Northern Rhodesia and Southern Rhodesia), enters Mozambique, and empties into Mozambique Channel of Indian Ocean. Broken by VICTORIA FALLS.

Zamboanga (säm"bōäng'gä), city (pop. 103,317), SW Mindanao, P.I. Includes Basilan isl. Exports copra, coconuts, timber, and rubber. Japanese stronghold in World War II until taken by U.S. forces, March, 1945.

Zamojski or **Zamoyski, Jan** (yän' zämoi'skē), 1541–1605, Polish chancellor under Stephen Bathory and Sigismund III. An admirer of the constitutional principles of republican Rome, he used his tremendous influence to restrict the royal power and made POLAND into a royal republic. Held military commands under Bathory.

Zamora (thämō'rä), city (pop. 29,036), cap. of Zamora prov., NW Spain, in Leon, on Duero R. Has Romanesque cathedral, medieval fortifications.

Zamosc, Pol. *Zamość* (zä'môshch), town (pop. 20,899), SE Poland. Founded 1579 by Jan Zamojski, who also estab. a university here, it was reconstructed 1937 according to original plans.

Zampieri, Domenico: see DOMENICHINO.

Zanesville, city (pop. 40,517), E central Ohio, E of Columbus and at junction of Muskingum R. and Licking R.; platted 1799. Trade and industrial center with mfg. of glass, tile, pottery, and electrical apparatus. State cap. 1810–12. Has art institute.

Zangwill, Israel, 1864–1926, English Jewish author of *The Melting Pot* (1914); a Zionist.

Zante (zăn'tē), Gr. *Zakynthos,* island (157 sq. mi.; pop. 41,154), Greece, in Ionian Sea, one of IONIAN ISLANDS; cap. Zante (pop. 11,315). Produces fruit, wine, olive oil, wheat. Sheep and goat raising; fishing.

Zanzibar (zăn'zĭbär), British protectorate (1,020 sq. mi.; pop. 264,236), off the coast of Tanganyika, E Africa. Comprises two islands of coral origin, Zanzibar (640 sq. mi.; pop. 148,000) and PEMBA. Protectorate is world's leading producer of cloves. In early Moslem era, rival Arab and Persian sultanates were

SMALL CAPITALS = cross references. Pronunciation key on inside end pages. Abbreviations: p. 2.

1087

estab. here. In 1503 the Portuguese gained control and used Zanzibar as base for territorial gains in E Africa. In 1652 the islands fell to Oman (or Muscat) Arabs, who pushed deep into Africa in their quest for slaves, gold, and ivory. Declared independent of Oman in 1856, Zanzibar became a British protectorate in 1890. Britain satisfied Germany's claim to the islands by ceding Helgoland. Zanzibar city (pop. 45,275), cap. of protectorate, is on Zanzibar island.

Zapata, Emiliano (ämēlyä'nō säpä'tä), c.1879–1919, Mexican revolutionist, b. Morelos, of almost pure Indian blood. With army of Indians recruited from plantations and villages he led the revolution in S after 1910 and occupied Mexico city three times in 1914–15 (once with Villa). Considered a bandit by opponents, he was a savior and hero to Indians, who embraced his agrarian movement, called *zapatismo*. He was treacherously killed by emissary of Carranza.

Zapolya (zä'pôlyō), noble Hungarian family. **Stephen Zapolya,** d. 1499, palatine of Hungary (1492–99), successfully fought the Turks and, after conquering Austria for King Matthias Corvinus, was appointed its governor (1485). For his son, **John Zapolya,** and his grandson **John Sigismund Zapolya,** see JOHN I and JOHN II, kings of Hungary.

Zaporozhe (zäpŭrô'zhē), city (pop. 289,188), S Ukraine, on the Dnieper. Industrial center (steel mills, coking and machinery plants, aluminum and magnesium works). Site of DNEPROGES dam. Suffered heavily in World War II. Khortitsa isl. in the river here was hq. of **Zaporozhe Cossacks** (16th–18th cent.; see COSSACKS). When they settled here, S Ukraine nominally belonged to Polish-Lithuanian kingdom, but they were allowed self-government in exchange for defending border. Polish encroachments and persecution of Greek Orthodox faith resulted in Cossack uprising (1648) and transfer of their allegiance to Russia (1654). Russia got left bank of the Dnieper and Kiev from Poland (1667). Cossack privileges were curtailed after MAZEPPA rebellion; abolished 1775.

Zapotec (sä'pŭtĕk), Indian people of Mexico, primarily S Oaxaca and Isthmus of Tehuantepec. Zapotec languages are a separate linguistic family. Early Zapotec were sedentary agriculturists, city-dwellers. Highly developed civilization flourished at Monte Albán possibly more than 2,000 years ago. Their great religious center was Mitla. Had strong cultural affinity with the Maya of Old Empire and, particularly after c.1300, with the Toltec.

Zara (zä'rù), Serbo-Croatian *Zadar,* city (pop. 14,847), Croatia, NW Yugoslavia, in Dalmatia; an Adriatic port. Roman Catholic archiepiscopal see. Dating from Roman times, it fell to Venice in 1000. Zara having been seized by the Hungarians, the doge Enrico Dandolo of Venice persuaded the leaders of the Fourth Crusade to reconquer the city for Venice. The Crusaders took and sacked the city (1202), thus calling on themselves papal condemnation. Passing from Venice to Austria in 1797, Zara was the cap. of Austrian Dalmatia 1815–1918; passed to Italy 1919; to Yugoslavia 1945 (confirmed by treaty, 1947). Has several medieval churches.

Zaragoza, Spain: see SARAGOSSA.

Zarathustra: see ZOROASTER.

Zealand (zē'lùnd), Dan. *Sjælland,* Ger. *Seeland,* largest island (2,709 sq. mi.; pop. 1,482,978) of Denmark, between Kattegat and Baltic Sea, separated from Sweden by the Oresund. Chief cities: Copenhagen, Roskilde, Elsinore, Agr., dairying, fishing.

Zealots (zē'lùts), Jewish faction (c.37 B.C.–A.D. 70), created primarily to resist idolatrous practices. In A.D. c.6 a Roman attempt to take a census touched off a revolt of the Zealots. A period of sporadic violence ended with Roman destruction of Jerusalem (A.D. 70). The Zealots then disappeared as the Jews were dispersed from Palestine.

Zebadiah (zĕ"bŭdī'ŭ), ally of David. 1 Chron. 12.7.

Zebedee (zĕ'bùdē), father of St. James the Greater

and St. John. Mat. 4.21; 20.20; 27.56; Mark 15.40.

zebra, African animal of horse genus, *Equus.* Its form is like that of a small horse with slender legs and small hoofs. Stripes vary with species in color (black, white, brown), width, and pattern. Zebra is an example of protective coloration. It is threatened with extinction.

zebu (zē'bū), domestic cattle (*Bos indicus*) of parts of E Asia, India, Africa. It is usually fawn, gray, black, or bay and is recognizable by the large fatty lump (sometimes two lumps) over the withers. Introduced into U.S. in mid-19th cent. and again in early 20th cent., it has interbred with cattle in Gulf states.

Zebulun (zĕ'bŭlùn, zēbū'lùn), son of Jacob and ancestor of one of the 12 tribes of Israel. Tribe settled in N Palestine. Gen. 30.20; 46.14; Num. 26.26; Deut. 33.19,20; Joshua 19.10; Judges 5.14,18. Zabulon: Mat. 4.13,15; Rev. 7.8.

Zechariah (zĕ'kŭrī'ŭ). **1** Prophet and author of the book of Zechariah. **2** Prophet who was stoned to death for denouncing idolatry. 2 Chron. 24.15–22. In Mat. 23.35 and Luke 11.51 it is apparently this Zechariah (NT Zacharias) to whom Jesus referred. Zacharias, Zachariah, and Zachary are forms of Zechariah.

Zechariah or **Zacharias** (zä"kŭrī'ùs), book of Old Testament. The prophet urged restoration of the Temple. Book contains: visions of a Messianic kingdom; a sermon on the observance of the Law; prophecies regarding the redemption of Jerusalem.

Zedekiah (zĕ"dùkī'ù), d. after 586 B.C., last king of Judah (c.595–586 B.C.). A puppet of Nebuchadnezzar, he made an alliance with Egypt despite warnings of JEREMIAH. Nebuchadnezzar's armies came to Palestine and destroyed Judah. Zedekiah was carried into captivity with his people. 2 Kings 24.17–25.7; 1 Chron. 3.15; 2 Chron. 36.10–13; Jer. 38; 39; 52.

Zeebrugge (zā'brü"gù), outer port of Bruges, West Flanders prov., Belgium, on North Sea; part of Bruges commune. Was developed c.1900 to replace silted-up port of Bruges, with which it is linked by a 9-mi. canal. Was a German submarine base in World War I until April, 1918, when British blocked harbor entrance by sinking three cruisers.

Zeeland, Paul van: see VAN ZEELAND, PAUL.

Zeeland (zē'lùnd, Dutch zā'länt), province (651 sq. mi.; pop. 260,800), SW Netherlands; cap. Middelburg. Includes WALCHEREN, N and S BEVELAND, and other islands at mouth of Scheldt estuary on North Sea. Much of the land is below sea level, protected by dikes. Agr., dairying, fishing. Was part of HOLLAND from 10th cent. Later became separate county but continued to be ruled by counts of Holland. Joined Union of Utrecht 1579.

Zeeman, Pieter (pē'tùr zā'män), 1865–1943, Dutch physicist. Shared 1902 Nobel Prize. Discovered **Zeeman effect,** produced on spectrum of a beam of light as a result of its passage through magnetic field; each spectrum line is split into two or more lines.

Zeiss, Carl (zīs, Ger. kärl' tsīs'), 1816–88, German manufacturer of optical instruments. In 1846 he founded at Jena a factory that achieved world fame after Zeiss became partner (1866) of Ernst Abbe.

Zelaya, José Santos (hōsā' sän'tōs sälä'yä), 1853–1919, president of Nicaragua (1894–1909). He developed the country materially but drained its resources for his own profit. He seized MOSQUITO COAST from British (1894); attempted to reestab. CENTRAL AMERICAN FEDERATION with himself as head. Foreign opposition to his dictatorship led to Washington Conference of 1907 and establishment of Central American Court of Justice. U.S. cruisers aided rebel forces in his overthrow.

Zell am See (tsĕl' äm zā'), mountain resort (pop. 6,320), Salzburg, W central Austria, on the Zellersee.

Zelotes (zĕlō'tēz) [Gr.,= zealot], name of St. Simon. See also ZEALOTS.

zemstvo (zĕmst'vō), Russian local assembly which functioned as a body of provincial self-government (1864 –1917). Each county (after 1870, also each town) elected a zemstvo, which in turn elected a provincial assembly and executive council. Although the electoral system favored the landowners, the zemstvos were strongholds of liberalism and accomplished much progress in education and public health.

Zen Buddhism, Buddhist sect in Japan. Originated in India as Dhyana school founded by semilegendary Boddhidarma (fl. 516–534?). Later entered China as Chan school. Adopted in Japan in 14th cent. where its rigid discipline and utter scorn for metaphysical subtleties won special support of the samurai.

Zend: see ZOROASTRIANISM.

Zenger, John Peter (zĕng'ŭr), 1697–1746, American journalist, b. Germany. His acquittal in libel trial helped further freedom of press in America.

Zeno (zē'nō), d. 491, Roman emperor of the East (474–91). During his reign concessions were made to GAISERIC in Africa and to ODOACER in Italy. He freed the East from the raids of the Ostrogoths by encouraging THEODORIC THE GREAT to invade Italy (488).

Zenobia (zĭnō'bēŭ), d. after A.D. 272, queen of PALMYRA. After the murder of her husband, Septimius Odenathus, she ruled for her son, increasing the extent and power of Palmyra. Her ambition brought conflict with Rome. Aurelian took Palmyra (272) and carried the proud, beautiful queen as captive to grace his triumph in Rome. She later lived on a Roman pension.

Zeno of Citium (zē'nō, sĭ'shēŭm), c.336–c.264 B.C., Greek philosopher, founder of STOICISM (a name derived from Zeno's teaching in the Painted Porch at Athens [Stoa Poecile]).

Zeno of Elea (ē'lēŭ), c.490–c.430 B.C., Greek philosopher of the Eleatic school; follower of Parmenides.

Zenta, Yugoslavia: see SENTA.

Zephaniah (zĕ"fŭnī'ŭ) or **Sophonias** (sōfōnī'ŭs), book of Old Testament, named for prophet contemporary with Jeremiah. Book denounces Judah for its idolatry and wealth; ends with a prediction of salvation and the return from captivity of a remnant of Israel.

Zephyr, Greek personification of westerly winds. He had mythical role of gentle peacemaker.

Zeppelin, Ferdinand, Graf von (zĕ'pŭlĭn), 1838–1917, German army officer. Invented and built first rigid AIRSHIP in 1900.

Zermatt (tsĕrmät'), Alpine resort, Valais canton, Switzerland, facing the Matterhorn.

zero, digit that signifies nothing; symbol = 0. Its introduction was inestimably important in development of practical number system. Arabs probably obtained it from Hindus and passed it on to Europe in latter part of Middle Ages. Zero is used to indicate the position on a scale of integers between +1 and −1; it is used in this sense on centigrade and Fahrenheit temperature scales. Absolute zero is the theoretically lowest possible temperature; i.e., temperature at which no heat is present. Zero added to or subtracted from any number leaves the number unchanged; any number multiplied by zero gives zero; zero multiplied by or divided by any number (other than zero) is zero; there is no number which is the value of a number divided by zero.

Zeromski, Stephen (zhĕrôm'skē), 1864–1925, Polish author. Wrote *Ashes* (1904; Eng. tr., 1928), a novel of the Napoleonic period; *Faithful River* (1912), a story of the 1863 uprising.

Zerubbabel (zĕrŭb'ŭbŭl), fl. 520 B.C., prince of the house of David, governor of Jerusalem. Under the encouragement of Haggai and Zechariah, he led in the rebuilding of the Temple. Ezra 2.2; 3.2,8; Hag. 1–2; Zech. 4.9,10. Zorobabel: Mat. 1.12,13; Luke 3.27.

Zetkin, Klara (klä'rä tsĕt'kēn), 1857–1933, German Communist leader; member of the Reichstag 1919–32.

Zetland, Scotland: see SHETLAND.

Zeus (zoōs), in Greek religion, supreme god; son of Cronus and Rhea and husband of his sister Hera. In the battle called Titanomachy Zeus led successful revolt against Cronus. Then he and his brothers divided up the universe, Poseidon getting the sea, Hades the underworld, and Zeus heaven and earth. Many local goddesses, mortal women, and nymphs, as well as Hera, bore him children; among his children were Aphrodite, Artemis, Hermes, Apollo, and Athena (she sprang from his brow). The name Zeus means "sky." As weather-god he had attributes of thunder and lightning, with which he exercised authority, and rain, with which he made earth fertile. He was father-god, the symbol of power and law, who enforced morals and punished those who defied him. He ruled in patriarchal majesty in his court on Mt. Olympus. Romans equated him with Jupiter or Jove.

Zeuxis (zūk'sĭs), fl. 5th cent. B.C., Greek painter. Helped develop technique of light and shadow.

Zhdanov, Andrei Aleksandrovich (ŭndrā' ŭlyĭksän'drŭvĭch zhdä'nôf), 1896–1948, Russian Communist leader; member of Politburo 1939–48. Held rank of general in World War II. Delivered important party pronouncements in post-war period (notably against cosmopolitanism in art, 1946). Organized Cominform (1947).

Zhdanov, city (pop. 222,427), SE Ukraine; a port on the Sea of Azov. Steel, machinery, and chemical mfg. Called Mariupol until 1948.

Zhitomir (zhĭtô'mēr), city (pop. 95,090), Ukraine, in Volhynia. Communications, lumber, and grain center. During German occupation (1941–43) in World War II its Jewish population (40% of total) was virtually exterminated.

Zhukov, Georgi Konstantinovich (gēôr'gē kŭnstûntyĕ'nŭvĭch zhōō'kôf), 1896?–, Russian field marshal in World War II. Took prominent part in battle of Stalingrad, relief of Leningrad, capture of Berlin. Became deputy defense minister 1953.

Zhukovsky, Vasily Andreyevich (vūsē'lyē ŭndrā'ŭvĭch zhōōkôf'skē), 1783–1852, Russian poet. Author of fine lyrics and odes. Translated English, French, and German poets.

Zia (zē'ŭ), Indian pueblo village (1948 pop. 269), central N.Mex. NW of Albuquerque. Keresan language. Grain and chili growing; pottery making. Mission of Nuestra Señora de la Asunción was built 1692. Annual fiesta.

Ziegfeld, Florenz (flô'rŭnz zēg'fĕld), 1869–1932, American theatrical producer. Productions included his annual *Ziegfeld Follies* (an elaborate revue), *Sally,* and *Show Boat.*

Zieten, Hans Joachim von (häns' yōä'khĭm fŭn tsē'tŭn), 1699–1786, Prussian general of cavalry under Frederick II.

Ziklag (zĭ'klăg), place of anc. Palestine, probably S of Beersheba. David lived here while hiding from Saul.

Zillebeke (zĭ'lŭbā"kŭ), village (pop. 1,644), West Flanders prov., NW Belgium, near Ypres. Scene of severe fighting in World War I.

Zilpah (zĭl'pŭ), Leah's maid, mother of two of Jacob's sons, Gad and Asher. Gen. 30.9–13.

Zimbabwe (zĭmbäb'wä) [Bantu,= stone houses], ruined city, Southern Rhodesia. Discovered 1871 by white explorers. Identified by some with the biblical Ophir. Ruins include a massive wall, a "temple," and a citadel.

Zimri (zĭm'rī), d. c.885 B.C., king of Israel for seven days. He murdered Elah for the throne but was deposed by Omri. Zimri set fire to the palace, destroying himself with it. I Kings 16.8–19.

Zin, wilderness through which the Hebrews wandered, probably S of the Dead Sea.

zinc, silvery, bluish-white, metallic element (symbol = Zn; see also ELEMENT, table). Brittle and crystalline at ordinary temperatures, it can be rolled into sheets when heated to 110°–150° C. It forms a number of compounds. Metal is used in alloys. Iron is galvanized by dipping it into molten zinc or coating it by electroplating. Zinc is often used for negative plates in electric cells. Zinc ores are widely and abundantly distributed.

zinc white, a white powder, zinc oxide. It is used as a paint pigment; in medicinal ointments; as filler in rubber goods, linoleum, oilcloth, etc.; in making white rubber goods and white glass.

zinnia, coarse, annual flowering plant of genus *Zinnia,* chiefly native to Mexico. Called also youth-and-old-age, it is popular in gardens and for cutting for its variety of flower forms of vivid and pastel colors.

Zinoviev, Grigori Evseyevich (grĭgô′rē yĭfsyā′ŭvĭch zēnô′vēēf), 1883–1936, Russian Communist leader. Member of Politburo from 1918; president of the Comintern from 1919. After Lenin's death he at first cooperated with Stalin, but in 1925 he joined with TROTSKY in opposition. He was expelled from the party in 1927; though readmitted in 1928, he lost his influence. Implicated in the murder of Kirov, he was publicly tried in 1936, confessed himself guilty of all charges, and was executed. The **Zinoviev letter,** published 1924 by several English newspapers, purported to be a letter of secret instructions for a Communist uprising in England. Though later proved a forgery, it helped defeat the Labour party in 1924.

Zinsser, Hans (zĭn′sûr), 1878–1940, American bacteriologist, authority on typhus. Author of *Rats, Lice, and History* (1935) and medical texts.

Zinzendorf, Nikolaus Ludwig, Graf von (zĭn′ zùndôrf; Ger. tsĭn′tsùndôrf), 1700–1760, bishop of refounded Moravian Church. He estab. (1722) Moravian colony called Herrnhut on his estate in Saxony and was forced into exile. Traveled widely in behalf of church, of which he became bishop in 1737. In America (1741–43) he was responsible for many Moravian settlements in E Pa.

Zion (zī′ŭn) or **Sion** (sī′ŭn), part of Jerusalem, defined in Bible as City of David. 2 Sam. 5.7. Tradition names SW hill of city as Zion. Name is symbolic of Jerusalem, of the Promised land, of the Messianic hope of Israel (hence the term *Zionism*), and, among Christians, of heaven and the hoped-for realm of religion on earth.

Zion, city (pop. 8,950), extreme NE Ill., on L. Michigan and N of Chicago. Founded 1901 by J. A. DOWIE of Christian Catholic Apostolic Church; had theocratic government until 1935. Annual Passion Play. Mfg. of lace and food products.

Zionism, movement for reconstituting a Jewish nation, largely theoretical until Theodor HERZL called the first World Zionist Congress (Basel, 1897), which set up Zionist organizations in countries with large Jewish populations. Among great leaders as the movement gained strength were Max Nordau and Chaim Weizmann. The aspiration for Palestine grew promising with the 1917 Balfour Declaration (see BALFOUR, ARTHUR JAMES), which promised to help establish a home for the Jewish people there; in 1923 Great Britain was given a mandate of Palestine. Jewish colonization vastly increased (see PALESTINE for the period up to 1945), but then the British restricted immigration. After World War II, the suffering of the European Jews demanded the opening of a refuge. The majority of the Zionists reluctantly accepted the United Nations plan to partition Palestine (see ISRAEL). After the Jewish state was proclaimed (May 14, 1948), the World Zionist Congress was separated from the Israeli government.

Zionites: see CHRISTIAN CATHOLIC APOSTOLIC CHURCH IN ZION.

Zion National Park and **Zion National Monument:** see NATIONAL PARKS AND MONUMENTS (table).

Zipporah (zĭ′pùrù), daughter of Jethro and wife of Moses. Ex. 2.16–22; 4.18–26; 18.1–6.

zirconium (zûrkō′nēŭm), metallic element (symbol = Zr; see also ELEMENT, table). It appears as a black, amorphous powder or a gray crystalline solid. The oxide, resistant to extreme heat, is used for laboratory utensils. Metal is used in alloys; when added to steel it acts as a purifying agent, removing deleterious substances.

Zistersdorf (tsĭs′dùrsdôrf″), town (pop. 3,044), Lower Austria, NNE of Vienna. Has large oil field (developed mainly in World War II). Much equipment was removed by Russian authorities after 1945.

Zita (zē′tù), 1892–, empress of Austria, queen of Hungary (1916–18); consort of Charles I; daughter of Duke Robert of Parma. Was blamed for Charles's secret correspondence with her brother, SIXTUS OF BOURBON-PARMA, and his later attempts to regain the Hungarian throne. Brought up her family in Belgium; lived in U.S. and Canada 1940–49. Her son, Archduke Otto, became Hapsburg pretender.

zither: see STRINGED INSTRUMENTS.

Zizka, John (zĭs′kù), Czech *Jan Žižka,* d. 1424, Czech soldier. Took command of Hussite forces 1420 (see HUSSITE WARS). Though totally blind after 1421, he gained brilliant victories over the Catholics. Originally belonging to the radical TABORITES, he founded (1423) the more moderate "Union" but continued to oppose the Utraquist wing of Hussites. A bold military genius, he anticipated modern tank warfare by his use of artillery on armored wagons.

Zlatoust (zlŭtùōōst′), city (pop. 99,272), RSFSR, in S Urals. Metallurgical center.

Zlin (zlēn), city (pop. 45,737), Moravia, Czechoslovakia; renamed Gottwaldov after 1948. The center of the Czech shoe industry (now nationalized), it was developed as a model company town by the Bata family of shoe manufacturers.

Zn, chemical symbol of the element ZINC.

Zoar (zō′ùr), the one of the Cities of the Plain (see SODOM) to escape destruction. Lot and his daughters took refuge there. Also called Bela.

Zoar (zôr, zō′ùr), village (pop. c.200), E central Ohio, on the Tuscarawas river, near New Philadelphia. Formed by a group of Separatists who fled Germany in 1817, under J. M. Bimeler. A communistic system was established, and the commune flourished until after Bimeler's death. The communistic mode of life was abandoned in 1898.

zodiac (zō′dĕăk), in astronomy, imaginary zone in sky, extending c.8° on each side of ECLIPTIC. Stars in zone are arranged in 12 constellations, each with a corresponding sign. In order eastward from vernal EQUINOX (point from which positions are calculated), these are:

Aries (Ram) ♈	Libra (Balance) ♎
Taurus (Bull) ♉	Scorpio (Scorpion) ♏
Gemini (Twins) ♊	Sagittarius (Archer) ♐
Cancer (Crab) ♋	Capricornus (Goat) ♑
Leo (Lion) ♌	Aquarius (Water-Bearer) ♒
Virgo (Virgin) ♍	Pisces (Fishes) ♓

First six lie north of celestial equator; others, south. Because of PRECESSION OF THE EQUINOXES, in 2,000 years each sign has moved 30° and now is in constellation W of the one to which it corresponds in theory.

Zoë (zō′ē), d. 1050, Byzantine empress, daughter of Constantine VIII. Ruled jointly with her first husband, Romanus III (murdered 1034); her second husband, Michael IV (who presumably helped her murder Romanus and who, though 30 years her junior, died 1041); Michael's nephew, Michael V (who had her briefly exiled in 1042 but whom she deposed and had blinded soon afterward); and, after 1042, with her third husband, Constantine IX, and her sister, Theodora (both succeeded in surviving her). The threesome rule was remarkable for its corruption and vice even by Byzantine standards. In 1042 began the final schism between East and West (see LEO IX, pope).

Zog (zôg), 1895–, king of Albania; originally Ahmed Zogu. Premier 1922–24; dictator after 1925; proclaimed himself king 1928. In exchange for Italian loans, he gave Italy ever-increasing rights over Albania. In April, 1939, Italian troops occupied Albania and Zog fled abroad. He had married the Hungarian countess Geraldine Apponyi in 1938.

SMALL CAPITALS = cross references. Pronunciation key on inside end pages. Abbreviations: p. 2.

Zola, Émile (ämēl' zōlä'), 1840–1902, French novelist, leading exponent of naturalism. He wrote "scientific" novels in which characters are controlled by heredity and environment, as in his 20-vol. series *Les Rougon-Macquart* (1871–93), including *L'Assommoir* (1877; Eng. tr., *The Dram-Shop*), *Nana* (1880), and *Germinal* (1885). Anticlerical and an ardent social reformer, he took a strong stand in the DREYFUS AFFAIR with *J'accuse* (1898). Prosecuted for libel, he escaped to England.

Zollverein (tsôl'fŭrīn) [Ger.,= customs union], customs union among states of 19th-cent. Germany; a major step toward German political union. Began 1818 with abolition of internal tariff barriers in Prussia; grew under Prussian leadership, absorbing other regional tariff unions; reorganized 1867 with its own constitution and parliament. Its regulations were taken over by German Empire 1871. Last to join imperial customs area were the Hanseatic cities Hamburg and Bremen (1888).

zone, in geography, an area with a certain physical unity distinguishing it from other areas. Parmenides (5th cent. B.C.) probably first divided the earth into five climatic zones—a torrid or tropical zone, two temperate zones, and two frigid or arctic zones—a classification still in use. Some modern geographers have used other bases for zoning.

zoological garden, public or private park where living animals and birds are exhibited and studied. Menageries and aviaries of China, Egypt, and Rome were famous in ancient times. Medieval rulers had private menageries, some of which later formed nucleus of public exhibits. Nearly all large cities now have zoological reserves.

zoology, branch of BIOLOGY concerned with study of animal life. Early classification systems included Aristotle's; most systems were based on external resemblances or similarity of environment. Binomial nomenclature system, commonly attributed to Linnaeus and to which John Ray earlier contributed, designates each plant or animal by two Latin names indicating genus and species. Scope of zoology was expanded by study of embryology, internal morphology and physiology, and by use of microscope and experimental method. Modern zoology has been marked by progress especially in genetics, cytology, physiology, and biochemistry.

Zorach, William (zōr'äk), 1887–, American sculptor, b. Lithuania. His *Spirit of the Dance,* a characteristic kneeling figure (cast in aluminum), is in Radio City Music Hall, New York city.

Zorn, Anders (Leonhard) (än'dùrs lā'ōōnärd sôrn'), 1860–1920, Swedish painter and etcher. Worked in London, Paris, and Mora, Sweden. Excelled in figure painting and portraits.

Zoroaster (zō'rōä'stùr), Gr. *Zarathushtra* or *Zarathustra,* 660?–583? B.C. (some say c.570?–c.500 B.C.), Persian religious leader, founder of **Zoroastrianism,** which has *Zend Avesta* as its scripture. Originally this was apparently a reformed type of Persian nature worship, but dualism was strong. Ahura Mazdah (also Ormazd) headed the gods of goodness (Amesha Spentas) and Ahriman (also Angra Mainyu) headed the gods of evil (daevas). War between these forces is the motive power of the universe, in which good will finally triumph. Much attention was given to purification rites. The religion triumphed under the Achaemenidae, but was disrupted under Alexander the Great's conquest; revived under the Sassanidae. Gave rise to Mithraism. Ghebers in Iran and Parsis in India keep Zoroastrianism alive.

Zorrilla y Moral, José (hōsā' thōrē'lyä ē mōräl'), 1817–93, Spanish romantic dramatist, author of *Don Juan Tenorio* (1844).

Zr, chemical symbol of the element ZIRCONIUM.

Zrinyi (zrĭn'yē), noble Hungarian family of Croatian origin. **Nicholas Zrinyi,** 1508–66, was appointed ban (viceroy) of Croatia by Ferdinand I (1542). Defended Szigetvar against the army of Suleiman I; was killed while attempting a sortie. His great-grandson, **Nicolas Zrinyi,** 1616–64, ban of Croatia (1647–64), campaigned successfully against the Turks. A distinguished poet, he wrote an epic on the defense of Szigetvar by his ancestor, lyric poems, and prose on political subjects. He was one of the first to use Hungarian as a literary language. His brother, **Peter Zrinyi,** 1621–71, became ban of Croatia 1665. He conspired, with French help, against Emperor Leopold I, but the plot was ill organized and he was executed. His daughter Helen (d. 1703) married Francis I Rakoczy and Emeric Thokoly.

Zsigmondy, Richard (rĭkh'ärt shĭg'mōn"dē), 1865–1929, Austrian chemist. Won 1925 Nobel Prize for work on colloids and development of ultramicroscope.

Zug (tsōōk), canton (93 sq. mi.; pop. 42,268), central Switzerland. Has Alpine economy (meadows, forests, pastures). German-speaking. Passed to Hapsburgs 1273; joined Swiss Confederation 1352 (confirmed 1364). Member of SONDERBUND 1845–47. Its cap., **Zug** (pop. 14,601), on the L. of Zug, preserves much Gothic architecture. Machinery mfg.

Zugspitze (tsōōk'shpĭ"tsù), mountain, 9,721 ft. high, in Bavarian Alps and on Bavarian-Austrian border; highest peak of Bavaria and of Germany. A rack-and-pinion railroad reaches the summit from Garmisch-Partenkirchen.

Zuider Zee (zī'dùr zē', Dutch zoi'dùr zā'), former shallow inlet of North Sea, c.80 mi. long, N and central Netherlands. Once a lake, it was joined to the sea by a great flood in the 13th cent. It is now divided by the Ijsselmeer dam into the IJSSELMEER (S) and the Waddenzee (N).

Zuloaga, Ignacio (ēgnä'thyō thōōlōä'gä), 1870–1945, Spanish painter. Lived mainly in Paris after 1889, but painted Spanish subjects (e.g., Basque peasants and bull fighters).

Zululand (zōō'lōōländ"), district (10,427 sq. mi.; pop. 398,940), NE Natal, South Africa, on Indian Ocean. Comprises mostly tribal reservations. Annexed by Great Britain in 1887, it became part of Natal in 1897. Inhabited mainly by the **Zulu,** who belong to S branch of the Bantu-speaking peoples. The MATABELE are a Zulu offshoot. Among the Zulu, marriage may be polygamous and is contracted by gifts of cattle to the bride's family. The Zulu ordinarily do not live in villages but in fenced compounds (kraals). In 1830s they waged war against the Boer settlers who came on the Great Trek. Were finally subdued in 1879 by the British.

Zumárraga, Juan de (hwän' dä thōōmä'rägä), 1468–1584, Spanish churchman, first bishop of Mexico, a Franciscan. Going to Mexico in 1528, he did much to improve conditions in New Spain; founded College of Santa Cruz of Tlaltelolco for education of Indians; and helped bring printing to New World.

Zuni (zōō'nē), Indian pueblo village (pop. 2,563), W N.Mex., S of Gallup. Inhabitants are chiefly Pueblo Indians of distinct linguistic family (Zuni). Irrigated land is farmed. Noted for basketry, pottery, turquoise jewelry, weaving, and dances. Annual Shalako feast to Zuni gods. Original seven Zuni villages (usually identified with mythical Seven Cities of Cibola) attacked 1540 by Coronado. Evacuated in Pueblo revolt of 1680. Present pueblo built c.1695 on one of old sites.

Zurbarán, Francisco de (fränthē'skō dä thōōrbärän'), 1598–1662, Spanish painter of school of Seville. Noted for vigorous realism and fine use of subdued color (esp. in his scenes of monastic life).

Zurich (zōō'rĭk), Ger. *Zürich* (tsü'rĭkh), canton (668 sq. mi.; pop. 772,617), N Switzerland, in the Alpine foothills. Has agr., meadows, forests. Population, German-speaking and largely Protestant, is mainly engaged in industry and commerce. Industrial centers include WINTERTHUR and **Zurich** city (pop. 386,485), the cantonal cap. and largest Swiss city, on the Limmat R. and the L. of Zurich. Produces textiles, machinery, radios, chemicals. Printing and publishing. Commercial, financial, and cultural center. Has university (founded as academy 1523) and world-famous Federal Inst. of Technology (1854). Became free imperial city 1218; joined Swiss Confederation 1351; acquired considerable rural districts. Its corporative guild constitution, lasting till 1798, gave its government a patrician character. ZWINGLI made Zurich the starting point of the Swiss Reformation (16th cent.). The city is a fine blend of modern and historic structures, notably the Romanesque Gross-Münster and the Romanesque-Gothic Fraumünster churches and the 17th-cent. city hall. The **Lake of Zurich,** c.25 mi. long and c.2 mi. wide, is noted for peaceful scenery. The Limmat drains it into the Aar.

Zweibrücken (tsvī″brü′kûn), Fr. *Deux-Ponts*, city (pop. 25,725), Rhineland-Palatinate, W Germany, in the Rhenish PALATINATE. Metal, leather, textile mfg. Was 80% destroyed in World War II. It was the seat after 1410 of a branch of the WITTELSBACH dynasty—the counts, later dukes, palatine of Zweibrücken. Through Charles X of Sweden, nephew of Duke Palatine John II, this branch ascended the Swedish throne 1654 and held it till 1741. Zweibrücken was annexed to France 1797–1814. In 1799, however, the deprived ruler inherited all Wittelsbach lands; in 1806 he became king of Bavaria as Maximilian I.

Zweig, Arnold (är′nôlt tsvīkh′), 1887–, Austrian novelist. Best known for his great war novel *The Case of Sergeant Grischa* (1927).

Zweig, Stefan (shtĕ′fän), 1881–1942, Austrian author. Best known for his biographies, notably of Marie Antoinette (1932) and Mary Stuart (1935). A refugee from Nazi persecution, he died by suicide in Brazil.

Zwickau (tsvī′kou), city (pop. 122,862), Saxony, E Germany, in an important coal-mining region. Major industrial center (textiles, machinery, automobiles, chemicals, mining equipment, pianos, paper). Free imperial city 1290–1323. Center of Anabaptist movement of Thomas Münzer 1520–23. Repeatedly plundered in Thirty Years War. Birthplace of Robert Schumann.

Zwicky, Fritz (tsvĭ′kē), 1898–, Swiss-American astrophysicist, authority on novae and supernovae. Known also for work on jet propulsion, cosmic rays, and behavior of slow electrons and ions in gases.

Zwingli, Huldreich or **Ulrich** (tsvĭng′lē), 1484–1531, Swiss Protestant reformer. A learned humanist and a priest, he became convinced that religion should be derived directly from the Bible. At Zurich he initiated Protestant practices; his *Architeles* (1522) and 67 theses (1523) set forth his doctrines. He opposed rituals, use of images and pictures in churches, clerical celibacy, the papacy, and monasticism and strongly favored individual responsibility for belief. The civil authorities of Zurich backed him, and he became a Protestant leader in S Germany as well as in much of Switzerland. His doctrine of the Lord's Supper (that it is merely a commemorative feast) differed from that of Luther, and at the Marburg Colloquy (1529) the two men (together with Oecolampadius and Melanchthon) failed to agree. Zwingli was killed at Kappel and his forces were defeated in a war between the Protestant and Catholic cantons of Switzerland. His teachings lost out to Calvinism, which is partly based on Zwinglian doctrine.

Zwolle (zwô′lù), municipality (pop. 47,462), cap. of Overijssel prov., N central Netherlands. Mfg. of chemicals, clothing, and metal goods. Gothic Church of St. Michael (15th cent.) is notable. Thomas à Kempis lived at 14th-cent. monastery near by.

Zworykin, Vladimir Kosma (zwô′rĭkĭn), 1889–, American physicist. Developed Iconoscope (electric eye) used in television and Kinescope, cathode-ray tube of television receiver.

NOTES

The purpose of the pronunciation symbols is to give at least one serviceable way in which the word in question may be pronounced when used by careful speakers of English.

In this work a pronunciation is ordinarily indicated for words printed in boldface when this pronunciation is not obvious to the English-speaking reader. Of two or more words or names in succession spelled and pronounced alike, a pronunciation is frequently indicated for the first occurrence only.

For names of localities in English-speaking areas the local pronunciation is preferred, provided it is acceptable to careful speakers.

For foreign words and names the speaker of English desires to use a pronunciation that will be acceptable to other speakers of English (unless he is speaking in a foreign language). In many cases (e.g., Paris) there is a traditional pronunciation that resembles little the current native pronunciation, and attempts to introduce into English conversation an approximation of the native form (something like pärē′) are regarded as an affectation. It is customary with foreign names that have no conventional English form to pronounce them with English sounds approximating the foreign ones. Such an approximation is indicated in this work, whenever there is no established usage to follow.

Actual good foreign-language pronunciations can be acquired only through imitation and study. Nevertheless, Englishmen and Americans have for many years made a practice of imitating roughly five French sounds: ã, ẽ, õ, ũ, and ü. A speaker of English can attain ã by saying äng without the closure at the back of the mouth necessary to make ng, breathing through nose and mouth as well; ẽ is similarly like the beginning of äng, õ like that of ŏng, and ũ like that of ûng. To approximate ü say o͞o with vigor, then, keeping the lips rounded, change the sound quickly to ē.

For Latin words the venerable English tradition is followed [e.g., Caesar (sē′zᵘr)], except where some other pronunciation is well established, as in ecclesiastical names [e.g., Salve Regina (säl′vä räjē′nú)]. The so-called classical pronunciation, which approximates the pronunciation Caesar used [e.g., Caesar (kī′sär)], is not given, as being not usual in English conversation.

ā	fate (fāt), fail (fāl), vacation (vākā′shún)
â	care (kâr), Mary (mâ′rē)
ă	bat (băt), add (ăd), marry (mă′rē)
ä	father (fä′dhùr), marble (mär′ᴅul)
ã	French tant (tã), Rouen (ro͞oã′), and similar sounds in some other languages
b	back (băk), cab (kăb)
ch	chap (chăp)
d	dock (dŏk), cod (kŏd)
dh	father (fä′dhùr), then (dhĕn). Compare with th.
ē	even (ē′vún), clearing (klēr′ĭng), obvious (ŏb′vēús)
ĕ	end (ĕnd), met (mĕt), merry (mĕ′rē)
ẽ	French vin (vẽ), bien (byẽ), and similar sounds in some other languages
f	fat (făt), Philip (fĭ′lĭp)
g	get (gĕt), tag (tăg)
h	hat (hăt). See also ch, dh, kh, sh, th, zh, and hw
hw	where (hwâr), what (hwŏt)
ī	fine (fīn), buyer (bī′ur)
ĭ	pin (pĭn), pit (pĭt), spirit (spĭ′rĭt), fated (fā′tĭd)
j	jam (jăm), edge (ĕj), ginger (jĭn′jùr)
k	cook (ko͝ok), tackle (tă′kùl)
kh	loch (lŏkh), German Aachen (ä′khùn), Licht (lĭkht), and similar sounds in some other languages
l	peal (pēl), pull (po͝ol)
m	hammer (hă′mùr)
n	dinner (dĭ′nùr)
ng	singing (sĭng′ĭng), finger (fĭng′gùr), sang (săng), sank (săngk)
ō	hope (hōp), potato (pútā′tō)
ô	orbit (ôr′bĭt), fall (fôl)
ŏ	hot (hŏt), toddy (tŏ′dē), borrow (bŏ′rō)
õ	French dont (dõ), chanson (shäsõ′), and similar sounds in some other languages
oi	boil (boil), royal (roi′úl)
o͞o	boot (bo͞ot), lose (lo͞oz)
o͝o	foot (fo͝ot), purely (pyo͝or′lē), manipulate (múnĭ′pyo͝olāt)
ou	scout (skout), crowd (kroud)

p	pipe (pīp), happy (hă′pē)
r	road (rōd), appeared (úpērd′), carpenter (kär′púntùr)
s	saw (sô), case (kās)
sh	shall (shăl), nation (nā′shún)
t	tight (tīt), rating (rā′tĭng)
th	thin (thĭn), myth (mĭth). Compare with dh.
ū	fume (fūm), euphemism (ū′fūmĭzm)
û	curl (kûrl), Hamburg (hăm′bûrg), French œuvre (û′vrù), peu (pû), German schön (shûn), Goethe (gû′tù), and similar sounds in some other languages
ŭ	butter (bŭ′tùr), suds (sŭdz), hurry (hŭ′rē)
ù	affair (ùfâr′), sofa (sō′fù), contravene (kŏntrùvēn′), monopoly (mùnŏ′pùlē), suburban (sùbûr′bùn), callous (kă′lùs), rather (ră′dhùr)
ü	French Cluny (klünē′), German Lübeck (lü′bĕk), and similar sounds in some other languages
ũ	French Melun (mùlũ′), Chambrun (shäbrũ′), and similar sounds in some other languages
v	vest (vĕst), trivial (trĭ′vēul)
w	wax (wăks)
y	you (yo͞o), bunion (bŭ′nyùn)
z	zipper (zĭ′pùr), ease (ēz), treads (trĕdz)
zh	pleasure (plĕ′zhùr), rouge (ro͞ozh)
′	main accent, written after accented vowel or syllable: Nebraska (nùbră′skù), James Buchanan (jāmz′ būkă′nùn)
″	secondary accent: Mississippi (mĭ″sùsĭ′pē)
—	dash, replacing obvious portion of pronunciation: hegemony (hĭjĕ′mùnē, hē—, hĕ′jùmō″nē, hĕ′gù—)
-	hyphen, to prevent ambiguity: Erlanger (ûr′lăng-ùr), dishearten dĭs-här′tùn)

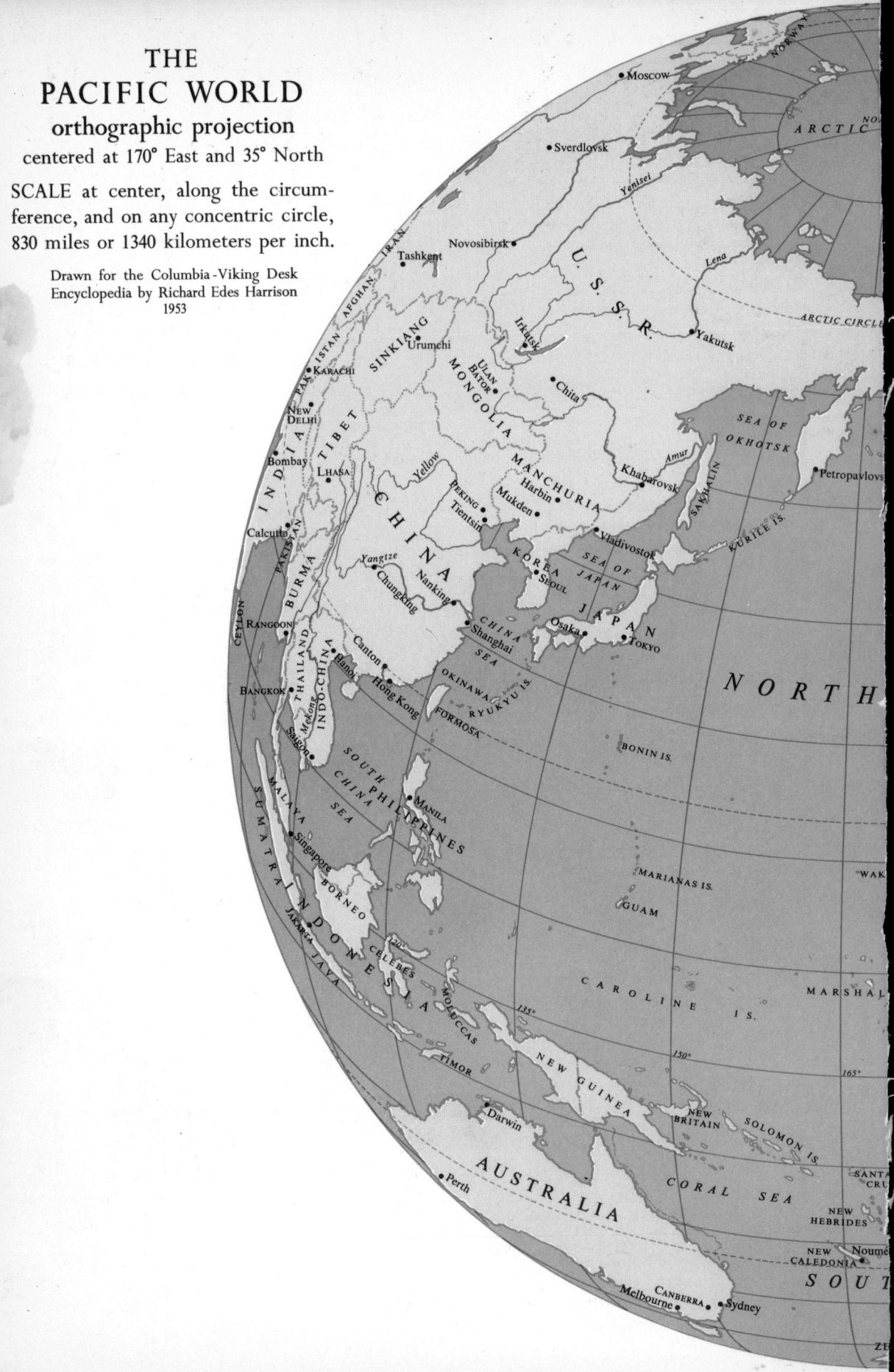

THE
PACIFIC WORLD
orthographic projection
centered at 170° East and 35° North

SCALE at center, along the circumference, and on any concentric circle,
830 miles or 1340 kilometers per inch.

Drawn for the Columbia-Viking Desk
Encyclopedia by Richard Edes Harrison
1953